KOMPASS

Company Information Register

KOMPASS PUBLISHERS
St. James House
150 London Road
East Grinstead
West Sussex
RH19 1ES
England

Telephone: (0800) 0185 882
Fax: (01342) 327940
Marketing: (01342) 778560

e-mail: kompasseditorial@kompass.co.uk
Internet: www.kompass.co.uk

The 51st Edition of Kompass

Supported by

ISSN 1353-1069
ISBN (this volume) 978-0-86268-529-4
ISBN (set) 978-0-86268-531-7

Kompass (UK) Limited. Registered in England Number 7819067. Registered Office: 1 Swan Wood Park, Gun Hill, Horam, East Sussex TN21 0LL
Printed in the UK by CPI William Clowes Ltd, Beccles, NR34 7TL

Preface

KOMPASS Company Information Register 2

Welcome to this, the 51st annual edition of UK Kompass Register. The Kompass range includes three volumes containing the following information:

Volume 1 Products & Services	Details of over 57,000 different products and services offered by British industrial companies.
Volume 2 Company Information	Corporate information on over 37,000 leading companies in British Industry, including financial information taken from the last three years filed accounts, on over 17,000 companies.
Volume 3 Industrial Trade Names	Details of over 9,000 companies and 42,000 registered trade names.

Kompass is as accurate and up to date as any annual publication ever can be. We endeavour to check each entry every year, either by personal visit, by mail or by telephone. We are, of course, reliant on each company giving us the most up to date information available.

Our general editorial policy on inclusion of companies for Volumes I-II is as follows:

(i) They should be industrial or industrial service companies.

(ii) They should be trading nationally.

Generally we do not cover companies outside these parameters, such as consumer goods companies or companies offering a 'business' service rather than an industrial service. Naturally, there may be the odd exception to this, such as where a company has been included for the sake of completeness of coverage of all subsidiaries in a group.

Therefore, what Kompass provides is the most in-depth, up to date and accurate information on British industry available in any directory. Our classification system of over 57,000 products is quite unique for depth of information. Our company information section gives more corporate details than will be found in any other directory.

The company information volume lists companies alphabetically broken down by towns within counties. The towns appearing in this volume are all designated POST TOWNS as identified by the Post Office. NON-POST TOWNS are cross referred to their nearest post town. Sections for Northern Ireland, Scotland and Wales are shown separately and, for these sections, companies are listed alphabetically by company name with their county details shown alongside.

We are confident that whether you use Kompass for purchasing, marketing, research, selling or simply for reference, you will find it offers you tremendous assistance and exceptional value for money.

Kompass Worldwide

TRUSTED COMPANY INFORMATION FROM AROUND THE WORLD

The Kompass International series provides an unrivalled range of business directories and CD-Roms for over 60 countries worldwide.

The range uses the classification system unique to Kompass and familiar to users of the UK products. It allows you to select companies by business types at a level of detail to suit you. A typical company profile includes:

- Detailed product information
- Executive names
- Contact details – Address, Telephone, Fax and Email
- Number of employees
- Turnover.

This information can assist you with the following activities:

- To help you do business internationally whether starting up or expanding
- To research overseas competitors
- To start or develop your export markets
- To source from overseas
- To assist on trade missions.

Kompass International editions are available for the following countries in either directory or CD format:

COUNTRY	EDITION AVAILABLE IN
Algeria	Book & Online
Armenia	Online
Australia	Online
Austria	Online
Azerbaijan	CD & Book & Online
Belarus	Online
Belgium	Online
Bulgaria	Book & Online
Canada	Online
Chile	Online
China	Book & Online
Croatia	Online
Czech Republic	CD & Online
Denmark	Online
Egypt	Online
Estonia	Online
Finland	Online
France	CD & Online
Germany	Online
Greece	Online
Hong Kong	Online

COUNTRY	EDITION AVAILABLE IN
Hungary	Online
India	CD & Book & Online
Iran	Online
Ireland	Online
Israel	Online
Italy	CD & Online
Japan	Online
Kazakhstan	Online
Kyrgyzstan	Online
Korea, Rep (S. Korea)	Online
Latvia	Online
Lebanon	CD & Online
Lithuania	Online
Luxembourg	Online
Malaysia	Online
Mexico	Online
Moldova	CD & Online
Monaco	Book & Online
Morocco	CD & Book & Online
Netherlands	Online
New Zealand	Online

COUNTRY	EDITION AVAILABLE IN
Norway	Online
Poland	CD & Online
Portugal	Online
Romania	Online
Russian Federation	Online
San Marino	Online
Serbia & Montenegro	Online
Singapore	Online
Slovakia	Online
Slovenia	Online
South Africa	Online
Spain	CD & Online
Sri Lanka	Book & Online
Sweden	Online
Switzerland	Online
Taiwan	Online
Thailand	Online
Turkey	Online
UAE	Book & Online
Ukraine	CD & Online
USA	Online

Contents

KOMPASS
Company Information Register 2

How to use Volume 1

KOMPASS Company Information **Register** **2**

PRODUCTS & SERVICES

Step 1

Turn to alphabetical product index to find unique 7 figure product reference No. 33.95.0.12

Step 2

Locate table (first 5 digits) 33-95.0

Step 3

The final 2 digits of reference indicate the column in the product grid in which symbols pinpoint your potential suppliers.

Step 4

Supplier Companies
Identify the companies and their telecommunication details. For further information on these companies turn to Volume II, Company Information.

33-95.0 Abrasive tools

1 Grindstones
2 Millstones
3 Lapping stones and wheels
4 Honing stones, oilstones, whetstones
7 Grinding wheels
8 Grinding wheel segments
10 Grinding discs
11 Grinding points
12 Grinding tools, emery cloth, cylindrical or spirally wound, for bevelling
15 Cutting-off wheels
16 Cutting discs, metal and abrasive material
19 Flap wheels, abrasive
20 Flap discs, abrasive
22 Cones, abrasive
23 Abrasive discs

	post code	☎	page	E	I	1	2	3	4	5	6	7	8
3M Abrasive Systems, Bracknell	RG12 8HT	01344 858974	70			●		●	●		●	●	
3M United Kingdom P.L.C, Bracknell	RG12 8HT	01344 858000	70			●		●					
A & M Fastener & Engineering Supplies, Redditch	B98 0DH	01527 520770	1784			●		●			●		
A T A Grinding Processes Ltd, Sheffield	S9 3FG	0114 244 0066	1838	●									
Abacon Ltd, Sheffield	S4 7QQ	0114 256 2266	1838			●		●	●		●	●	
Addison Saws Ltd, Dudley	DY2 0UW	01384 456333	1243										
Ahlstrom (FiberComposites Division), Edinburgh	EH11 4DH	0131 458 2000	2059			●							
Ahlstrom FiberComposite (a division of Dexter Speciality Materials Ltd), Duns	TD11 3JW	01890 818303	2059			●							
Alansons Industrial Supplies, Bristol	BS4 5JJ	0117 971 1364	6			●		●			●		
Alpha Finishing Supplies Ltd, Colchester	CO1 1BN	01206 760500	415			●							
Anglo Abrasives Ltd, Bellshill	ML4 3LR	01698 741020	2044			○							
Anglo Abrasives Ltd, Manchester	M17 1HP	0161 872 1777	775			○							
Anglo Abrasives Ltd, New Milton	BH25 6TG	01425 612532	528			○							
Anglo Abrasives Ltd, Nuneaton	CV11 6RZ	024 7638 7621	1729			○							
Anglo Abrasives Ltd, Sheffield	S9 3WZ	0114 244 9126	1839			○							
Antron Engineers Supplies, Horsham	RH12 1DQ	01403 275222	1672			●							

How to use Volume 2

COMPANY INFORMATION

- Companies arranged alphabetically by town, within county *(West Midlands, Birmingham)*
- Basic Company Details
- Names of Directors, Senior Executives and Managers
- Names of holding companies where applicable
- Annual Turnover and Company Registration No.; No. of Employees; Size of Sales Force; Product Range
- Nature of Business
- Principal Customers/Markets
- Name of Agent
- Registered Office
- Sales Office
- Branches
- Agents
- Group Details
- Other Information
- Quality Assessment awarded
- Financial Information

A.B. SMITH ELECTRONICS LTD
(Head Office)

ABS
ELECTRONICS

1 Kings Buildings, Kings Street, Birmingham B10 6JA
Tel: 0121-666 0303 **Fax:** 0121-666 3030
Telex: 123456
E-mail: abs@dial.pipex.com
Web Address: http://www.absmith.com.uk
Sales Contact: E.G. Smith (Sales Manager)
Purchase Contact: S. Brownsword (Production Manager)
Bank: Barclays, Colmore Row, Birmingham
Directors: A.B. Smith (MD), C.D. Smith (Sales), E.F. Smith (Fin)
Executives: G.H. Jones, I.J. Brown (Tech)
Directors: A. Hayes (Acct Mgr), P. Tilbury (Sales Mgr)
Ultimate Holding Company: A.B. Smith Inc (USA)
Immediate Holding Company: A.B. Smith (UK) Ltd
Co. Reg. No: 0098765 **Incorporation:** 1958 **VAT No:** 123 4567 89;
Turnover: £75-£125M; **Employees:** 150 (Estab) 1,500 (Group); **Size of Sales Force:** 50; **Product Groups:** 37, 38
Nature of Business: Manufacture of electronic assembly equipment; precision turned components for electronic and electrical industries
Principal Customers/Markets: F.L. Electrical Industries, Manchester
Agents for Products: J. Langen, A.G. France, electrical wiring
Registered Office: 2 Kings Buildings, Kings Street, Birmingham B10 6JB
Sales Office: 10 Queens Road, Birmingham; 123 East Street, New York
Branches: 20 Sheep Street, Coventry
Agents (Overseas): Worldwide, details on request
Agents for Companies: J.Langen A.G.
Subsidiary Companies: Wires (UK) Ltd
Associate Companies: Green Electrical Ltd
Trade Associations: BEAMA
Quality Assessment: BS5750 Part 2 QAS 34/51
Manufacture of electronic assemblies sub assemblies and component assemblies.

Date of accounts	**Mar 03**	**Mar 02**	**Mar 01**
Turnover	13,103	15,356	16.864
Profit before Tax	1,205	1,504	1,427
Fixed Assets	1,821	2,202	2,717
Current Assets	8,799	7,563	5,586
Current Liabilities	5,790	4,736	3,454
Share Capital	110	110	110
Working Capital	3,010	2,827	2,133
ROCE%	24.9	29.9	29.4
ROT%	9.2	9.8	8.5

This map lists all the Postcode areas used in KOMPASS REGISTER and shows the area to which they refer

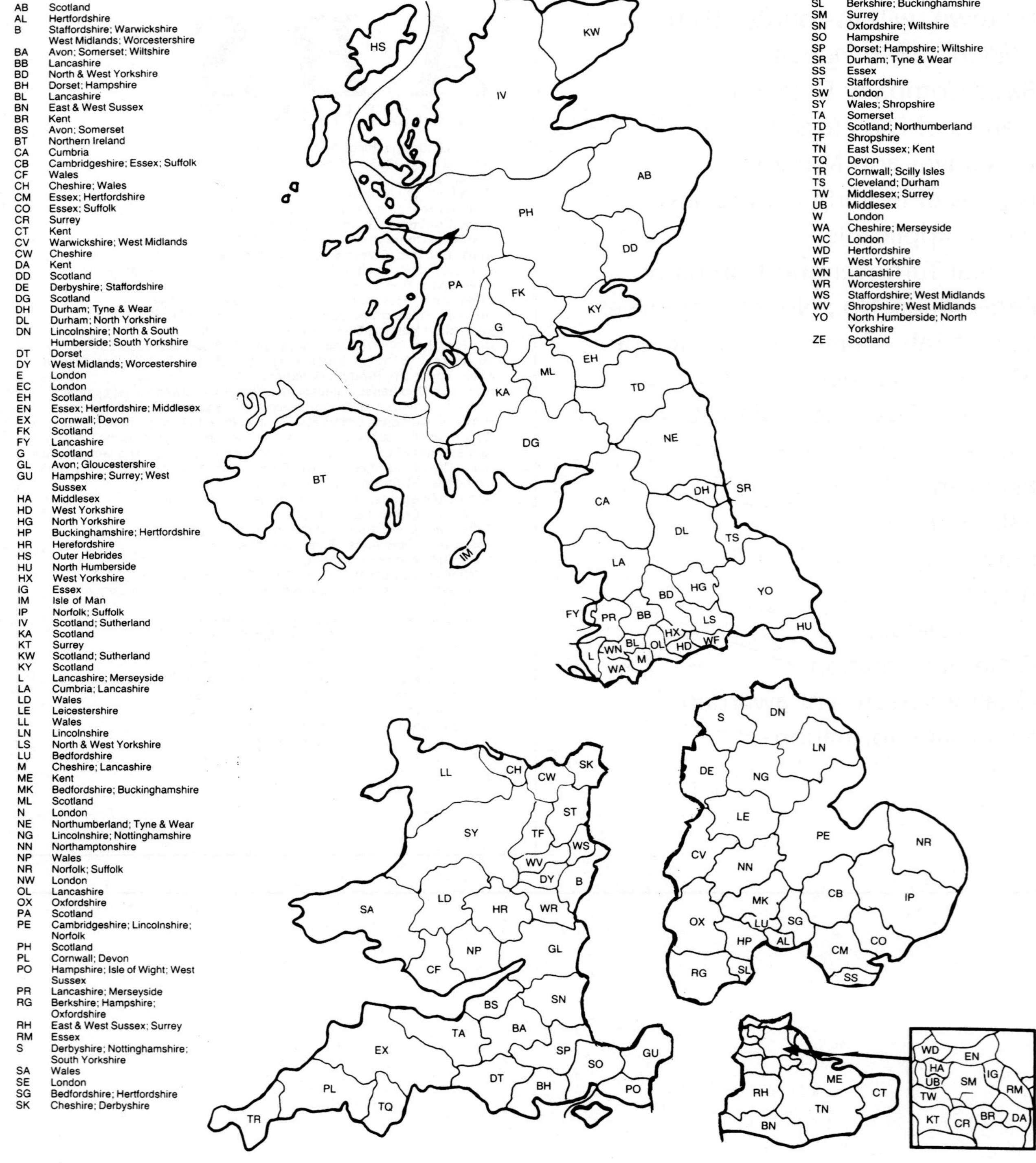

AB	Scotland
AL	Hertfordshire
B	Staffordshire; Warwickshire West Midlands; Worcestershire
BA	Avon; Somerset; Wiltshire
BB	Lancashire
BD	North & West Yorkshire
BH	Dorset; Hampshire
BL	Lancashire
BN	East & West Sussex
BR	Kent
BS	Avon; Somerset
BT	Northern Ireland
CA	Cumbria
CB	Cambridgeshire; Essex; Suffolk
CF	Wales
CH	Cheshire; Wales
CM	Essex; Hertfordshire
CO	Essex; Suffolk
CR	Surrey
CT	Kent
CV	Warwickshire; West Midlands
CW	Cheshire
DA	Kent
DD	Scotland
DE	Derbyshire; Staffordshire
DG	Scotland
DH	Durham; Tyne & Wear
DL	Durham; North Yorkshire
DN	Lincolnshire; North & South Humberside; South Yorkshire
DT	Dorset
DY	West Midlands; Worcestershire
E	London
EC	London
EH	Scotland
EN	Essex; Hertfordshire; Middlesex
EX	Cornwall; Devon
FK	Scotland
FY	Lancashire
G	Scotland
GL	Avon; Gloucestershire
GU	Hampshire; Surrey; West Sussex
HA	Middlesex
HD	West Yorkshire
HG	North Yorkshire
HP	Buckinghamshire; Hertfordshire
HR	Herefordshire
HS	Outer Hebrides
HU	North Humberside
HX	West Yorkshire
IG	Essex
IM	Isle of Man
IP	Norfolk; Suffolk
IV	Scotland; Sutherland
KA	Scotland
KT	Surrey
KW	Scotland; Sutherland
KY	Scotland
L	Lancashire; Merseyside
LA	Cumbria; Lancashire
LD	Wales
LE	Leicestershire
LL	Wales
LN	Lincolnshire
LS	North & West Yorkshire
LU	Bedfordshire
M	Cheshire; Lancashire
ME	Kent
MK	Bedfordshire; Buckinghamshire
ML	Scotland
N	London
NE	Northumberland; Tyne & Wear
NG	Lincolnshire; Nottinghamshire
NN	Northamptonshire
NP	Wales
NR	Norfolk; Suffolk
NW	London
OL	Lancashire
OX	Oxfordshire
PA	Scotland
PE	Cambridgeshire; Lincolnshire; Norfolk
PH	Scotland
PL	Cornwall; Devon
PO	Hampshire; Isle of Wight; West Sussex
PR	Lancashire; Merseyside
RG	Berkshire; Hampshire; Oxfordshire
RH	East & West Sussex; Surrey
RM	Essex
S	Derbyshire; Nottinghamshire; South Yorkshire
SA	Wales
SE	London
SG	Bedfordshire; Hertfordshire
SK	Cheshire; Derbyshire
SL	Berkshire; Buckinghamshire
SM	Surrey
SN	Oxfordshire; Wiltshire
SO	Hampshire
SP	Dorset; Hampshire; Wiltshire
SR	Durham; Tyne & Wear
SS	Essex
ST	Staffordshire
SW	London
SY	Wales; Shropshire
TA	Somerset
TD	Scotland; Northumberland
TF	Shropshire
TN	East Sussex; Kent
TQ	Devon
TR	Cornwall; Scilly Isles
TS	Cleveland; Durham
TW	Middlesex; Surrey
UB	Middlesex
W	London
WA	Cheshire; Merseyside
WC	London
WD	Hertfordshire
WF	West Yorkshire
WN	Lancashire
WR	Worcestershire
WS	Staffordshire; West Midlands
WV	Shropshire; West Midlands
YO	North Humberside; North Yorkshire
ZE	Scotland

The Chartered Institute of Marketing

Anne Godfrey
Chief Executive
CIM

Founded in 1911, The Chartered Institute of Marketing (CIM) is the largest international body for marketing. The organisation exists to further the interests of marketers and the marketing profession, with a focus on responsible business. CIM is a champion of best practice and sets out the professional standards and competencies which will deliver value to marketers' businesses.

Moor Hall, Cookham
Maidenhead, Berkshire, SL6 9QH
Tel: 01628 427500 Fax: 01628 427499
Email: marketing@cim.co.uk
http://www.cim.co.uk

The Chartered Institute of Marketing

CIM aims to be a lifelong career partner to professional marketers and is the only body able to award Chartered Marketer status. We place Continuing Professional Development (CPD) the heart of all we do, whether through qualifications and awards, training programmes or the delivery of industry insight and research initiatives. Some 30% of the total CIM membership community is now based outside the UK, and part of our role in a fast evolving landscape is to ensure that the networking and business development opportunities for marketers internationally are supported as effectively and comprehensively as they are in the UK.

Lifelong learning
We offer a wide range of marketing and sales qualifications, such as the Introductory Certificate in Marketing, the Chartered Postgraduate Diploma in Marketing and the Intensive Diploma in Strategic Sales Practice. Alongside qualifications, we run an extensive suite of training programmes ranging from one-day workshops to intensive residential courses, as well as bespoke in-company learning and development programmes. We believe that lifelong learning is an essential component both of personal career growth, and wider business success. Learning is not something that stops the day we sign up to a new job; it's something we do all our lives, and CIM is committed to furthering this principle. Keeping abreast of technological changes in business is one of the strongest challenges facing professionals today, and responding to this we have recently introduced a raft of digital courses focusing on areas such as mobile marketing and social networking.

Marketing unlocks growth
By placing customers at the heart of business, companies can anticipate, fulfil and exceed customer needs and wants. Effective marketing triggers innovation, provides products and services that have demand in the marketplace, identifies and fills gaps in that marketplace, and contributes to economic growth. Marketing is not just about communications; communications are merely the visible end of a long and integrated process. We work with government bodies, captains of industry and industry bodies in order to bring the value of marketing to wider attention and to support its place in the building of economies. CIM believes that businesses do not exist in a vacuum, and that an important part of best practice is to recognise, and commit to, social and environmental responsibilities.

Contributing knowledge and expertise
CIM augments its courses and qualifications with a knowledge bank of original research initiatives, thought leadership papers as well as national and regional events with leading speakers from business and academia. Many of our recent initiatives – such as the Social Media Benchmark and the Marketing Confidence Monitor – have also attracted wide participation from the marketing community, as well as significant media attention and coverage. We are also proud to recognise the very best in marketing practice through CIM's Marketing Excellence Awards, attracting hundreds of entries from across industry and from organisations of all sizes.

More information
Visit www.cim.co.uk for up-to-date information to find out how CIM can support marketers, sales professionals and organisations seeking to put best practice and customers at the heart of their business.

The Chartered Institute of Library and Information Professionals

Annie Mauger
Chief Executive
CILIP: the Chartered Institute of Library and Information Professionals

7 Ridgmount Street
London WC1E 7AE

Tel: +44 (0)20 7255 0500
Textphone: +44 (0)20 7255 0505
Fax: +44 (0)20 7255 0501
Email: info@cilip.org.uk
Web: www.cilip.org.uk

Chartered Institute of Library and Information Professionals

Information is your organisation's most important asset. To manage it properly you need skilled and qualified information professionals. The Chartered Institute of Library & Information Professionals supports our members - knowledge managers, information specialists and librarians – helping them develop the skills and knowledge they need to excel.

You'll find information professionals in all aspects of working life - the health service, financial services, small and medium sized enterprises, research and development, charities and pharmaceutical companies.

Wherever they work, they all share the same goal - managing their organisation's information assets as efficiently as possible. They use the latest technology to keep their colleagues informed about new developments that might affect their business. They hunt out hard-to-find information. They manage corporate intranets. They contribute to their organisation's knowledge management capability.

They are an essential part of revenue earning capability in business and efficient delivery of services in the public sector.

As the leading professional body for librarians, information specialists and knowledge managers we speak out on behalf of the profession to the media, government and decision makers. Our vision is a fair and economically prosperous society that is underpinned by literacy, access to information and the transfer of knowledge. We advocate the value of library and information services, and the difference that skilled and knowledgeable staff make to organisations, communities and society.

We award internationally recognised qualifications which are objective and respected guarantees of competence and quality. We offer three levels of qualification, providing opportunities for everyone employed in the library and information sector to demonstrate their skills, learning and value.

With a qualified library and information professional, or one working towards qualification, employers are assured that the people who manage their information assets are receiving the best possible professional support.

Organisations can join CILIP so staff will stay informed, benefit from networking, access free resources and take advantage of discounts. Your staff can stay fully up to date about information developments that affect their work and your business. Go to **www.cilip.org.uk/organisationmembership** for more details.

CILIP is committed to a strong knowledge economy, and we recognise that *Kompass* is an indispensable tool for thousands of information professionals in all sectors. Its comprehensiveness and flexibility makes it suitable for a myriad of information applications - in procurement, market research, competitor analysis and more. We're very pleased to be able to endorse this latest edition.

Source of Information

The 1985 Companies Act laid down the requirement that private companies must submit accounts within ten months of the end of its accounting period and other companies a seven months' time allowance:–

	PLC	Private Limited
Directors Report and Accounts	7 months after financial year end	10 months after financial year end

	Both PLC and Private
Annual Return	42 days after AGM
Change of Director	Within 14 days
Mortgage Register	21 days after creation of new mortgage
Increase in share capital	15 days after Company passes resolution

The 1981 Act created for the first time, size categories of companies into small, medium and large. This was designed to reduce the legal disclosure requirements for the SMALL company. Since November 1986, a SMALL company does not have to provide a profit and loss account or directors' report. A company is classed as a small or medium size if it meets two or more of the following criteria:–

	Small	Medium
Turnover not above	£2.8M	£11.2M
Gross assets not above	£1.4M	£5.6M
Average number of employees not above	50	250

This is the main reason why N/A (not available) is shown against turnover and profit before tax in some of the entries in this volume.

Every effort has been made to include information filed at Companies House during 2008.

The financial data shown in this volume of Kompass has been extracted from the official records held at Companies House.

KOMPASS HAS NOT ALLOWED THE ORIGINAL FINANCIAL DATA EXTRACTED FROM THE FILES AT COMPANIES HOUSE TO BE CHANGED IN ANY WAY WHATSOEVER.

Further COMPANY INFORMATION is obtainable from:–

COMPANIES HOUSE at
21 Bloomsbury Street,
London WC1B 3XD.

Crown Way,
Maindy,
Cardiff CF14 3UZ.

4th Floor, Edinburgh Quay 2,
139 Fountainbridge,
Edinburgh EH3 9FF.

The COMPANY INFORMATION held at Companies House is in accordance with the legal requirements for companies to disclose information about their activities. The 1985 Companies Act provides the foundations for UK Company Law even though an amending Act has been passed in 1989.

Amongst the Company Law disclosure foundations are:–

(a) Public and private Companies are required to lodge a copy of their annual accounts and Annual Return with the Registrar of Companies for public record.

(b) The minimum content of the accounts to be disclosed is defined.

Glossary and Explanation of terms

KOMPASS Company Information Register 2

The Company Name
This is the registered name of the company.

Address
This is supplied by the company and is the normal trading address, telephone and fax number.

Registered Office
This is the Registered Office Address at Companies House. Where this is not provided separately, the trading address and registered office are one and the same.

Company Registered Number
This is the correct Company Registered Number at Companies House. Numbers without any alphabetical prefixes are ordinary English and Welsh companies. The list of alphabetical prefixes is as follows:

AC Assurance Companies.
FC Overseas Companies which appear to have a place of business in England or Wales.
LP Limited Partnerships.
ZC Companies incorporated under other than Companies Acts.
IP Industrial & Provident Societies.
RC Incorporated by Royal Charter or letters patent.
SC Ordinary Scottish Companies.
SA Scottish Assurance Companies.
SF Scottish Overseas Companies which appear to have a place of business in Scotland.
SL Scottish Limited Partnerships.
SZ Scottish Companies incorporated under other than Companies Acts.
SP Scottish Industrial & Provident Societies.
SR Scottish Incorporated by Royal Charter or letters patent.
NI Ordinary Northern Ireland Companies.

Incorporation
This is the year of incorporation of the company.

Financial Information
This is taken from the last three years of accounts available at Companies House. A number of companies delay filing their accounts and this is reflected in some entries. The information has been extracted by Equifax specialists and brought into line with the 1981 Companies Act format. This makes for ease of comparison between different years and across companies' accounts. Where a company has filed less than three years accounts the maximum number of years available have been shown.

Units of Account
The figures are expressed in thousands of pounds sterling (£000s) unless there is a note to the contrary. All three years of accounts will have the same monetary unit.

Consolidated Accounts
Consolidated accounts are generally submitted where a company owns 50% or more of another company and has included that subsidiary's results with its own.

Date of Accounts
Up to three years' accounts information is displayed. For each year the accounts date is the end date for the period covered by the accounts, the number of months covered by the accounts is also shown and whether the accounts are consolidated or not.

Accounting Requirements
Every limited company must have an accounting reference period the first of which may not be later than 18 months after incorporation. Private companies must file their accounts with the Registrar of Companies within ten months of their accounting reference period and public companies within seven months.

Modified Accounts
Modified Accounts may be submitted by private companies meeting any two of three:
(a) Turnover less than £5.75 million;
(b) Balance sheet total less than £2.5 million;
(c) Less than 250 Employees.

Turnover
Turnover represents the amount of sales for the accounting period.

Profit before Tax
The Pre-Tax Profit figure shows the amount of profit before tax for the same period. Where companies have submitted Modified Accounts a N/A message will appear in the Turnover & Profit fields.

Fixed Assets
The value of the assets not intended for resale.

Current Assets
Assets of a company that are reasonably expected to be realised in cash, or sold, or consumed during the normal operating cycle of the business.

Current Liabilities
The total amount owed which falls due within one year.

Share Capital
The nominal value of the Issued Share Capital of the company.

Working Capital
Working Capital is calculated by deducting Current Liabilities from Current Assets.

Ratio of Capital Employment (ROCE %)
Profits as a percentage of capital employed. A missing figure(s) means that no percentage can be calculated for that year(s).

Ratio of Turnover (ROT %)
Profits as a percentage of turnover. A missing figure(s) means that no percentage can be calculated for that year(s).

Rounding of Figures
In preparing the data we have followed a consistent set of rules. Rounding of figures is undertaken as follows: 0.5 to 0.9 is rounded up to 1, and 0.1 to 0.4 is round down to 0. This practice will introduce a margin of error in figures derived from the accounts, especially calculation of ratios. Users should allow for this when comparing figures.

Treatment of Banks, Insurance Companies, etc.
Certain companies follow different conventions in their filed accounts reflecting the nature of their business. Companies which do not have a conventional profit and loss account have not had their accounts displayed. To do so would be misleading. Companies in this category include: banks and insurance companies.

Guarantee Companies
Companies limited by guarantee are generally formed charitable, social or other non trading purposes. They are required to file accounts but as they do not have a conventional profit and loss and balance sheet they have not had their accounts displayed.

Symbols
The following symbols have been used:

Minus sign before a figure denotes a negative amount.

N/A indicates that the data is not available often because modified accounts have been filed.

Nil will be shown where the company has indicated in its accounts that there is a nil figure against that item.

Main Industrial Groups

01 Live animals
02 Agricultural, horticultural and floricultural products
07 Agricultural and animal services
08 Forestry
09 Fish and other marine and freshwater products
11 Coal and peat
12 Ores
13 Crude oil (petroleum) and natural gases
14 Quarried stone
16 Rough precious stones
17 Minerals, non-metallic
18 Electricity, gas and water
20 Food and tobacco
21 Beverages
22 Leathers, skins, furs and their products. Travel goods. Footwear
23 Textiles
24 Clothing and textile products
25 Wood and cork products
26 Furniture
27 Cellulose, paper, board and their products
28 Printing and publishing
29 Rubber and synthetic rubber products
30 Plastic products
31 Acids, alkalis, chemical base materials, alcohols, petroleum products, pharmaceuticals, resins
32 Agricultural chemicals, insecticides. Detergents, soaps, perfumes, cosmetics, waxes and polishes. Dyes, colourants, paints and inks. Adhesives, sealants, starch, gelatine, explosives and other chemicals
33 Non-metallic mineral products
34 Basic metal products
35 Metal constructions for the building industry. Metal tanks, containers, cables, ropes, wires and fabrics. Wire goods. Filters and strainers. Chains, screws, bolts, nuts and rivets. Fasteners and springs. Metal turned articles. Bearings, pulleys, couplings
36 Metal pipes, tubes, hoses, taps, valves, cocks, packings and gaskets. Metal sanitary and household articles. Knives, scissors, shears and blades. Hand tools. Ironmongery and hardware. Arms and weapons
37 Electrical, electronic and nuclear equipment
38 Measuring and testing equipment. Optical, photographic and cinematographic equipment. Medical, surgical, dental and veterinary equipment
39 Means of transport. Transport infrastructure equipment
40 Turbines, engines, steam machines, pumps, pneumatic and hydraulic equipment, boilers, ovens, kilns, furnaces and burners. Heating, ventilation, air conditioning (HVAC), cleaning, catering, cooking and refrigeration equipment. Fire-fighting, protection and safety equipment
41 Agricultural and forestry machinery and equipment. Food, drink and tobacco industry machinery and equipment
42 Plant, machinery and equipment for chemicals, rubber, plastic, refuse and water. Packaging machinery and equipment
43 Textile, clothing, leather and shoemaking machinery and equipment
44 Pulp, paper and board making machinery and equipment. Printing and office machinery and equipment. Electronic data processing (EDP) equipment
45 Machinery and equipment for mining, quarrying and stoneworking, oil and gas extraction, cement, clay, ceramics and glass industries machinery and equipment. Road making, building, offshore and underwater machinery and equipment. Mechanical handling machinery and equipment. Industrial robots
46 Plant, machinery and equipment for metalworking
47 Plant, machinery and equipment for wood and cork. Machinery and equipment for the precious stone, optical and watchmaking industries. Assembly plant, machinery and equipment
48 Forging, stamping, hot pressing, surface treatment and machining contractors. Mechanical construction and assembly contractors. Industrial packaging contractors. Mould, foundry core and pattern making contractors. Reconditioning, repair and maintenance services. After sales services.
49 Watches, clocks and jewellery. Costume jewellery. Smokers' requisites. Models for trade. Souvenirs and religious articles. Wigs and brushes. Advertising and display articles. Games, toys and musical instruments. Vending machines. Office requisites. Sports and camping equipment
51 Civil and marine engineering contractors
52 Building industry
54 Environmental services
61 Importers and exporters, general. General traders and commodity merchants. Department and chain stores
62 Wholesalers and distributors, importers and exporters of consumer goods: animals, agricultural products, plants, food, drink and tobacco
63 Wholesalers and distributors, importers and exporters of consumer goods: textiles, clothing, household articles, domestic furniture, toiletries, cosmetics and pharmaceuticals
64 Wholesalers and distributors, importers and exporters of consumer goods: publications, stationery and office requisites
65 Wholesalers, distributors, importers and exporters of consumer goods: cameras, watches, clocks, precious stones, jewellery, costume jewellery, giftware, leisure and sports goods, musical instruments, coins, philately, antiques
66 Wholesalers and distributors, importers and exporters of industrial and commercial products: base materials and their products. Prefabricated buildings, heating, ventilation, air conditioning (HVAC) and sanitary equipment
67 Wholesalers, distributors, importers and exporters of industrial and commercial products: machinery and equipment, hospital and medical equipment, electrical and electronic products, telecommunication equipment, computers, office machinery, commercial furniture and military equipment
68 Wholesalers, distributors, importers and exporters: means of transport and related spare parts and accessories
69 Hospitality and tourism, hotels, motels, catering services. Conference centres.
71 Transport infrastructure administration
72 Land transportation
74 Sea and inland waterway transportation
75 Air transportation
76 Supplementary transport services
77 Warehousing and storage services
79 Postal services, telecommunications, radio and television
80 Administrative, personnel and property services
81 Commercial services
82 Financial and insurance services
83 Hire and rental services
84 Technical offices and engineering consultancies, architects
85 Research and testing
86 Education and training
87 International and national organisations. Public administration
88 Medical care, social services
89 Leisure and entertainment industry

Index to Localities

KOMPASS Company Information Register 2

This index lists all towns contained within Kompass and provides cross reference information for districts not listed in their own right. E.g. entries for Ash Vale, Hampshire will be found under Aldershot, Hampshire

Barnehurst, see Bexleyheath, Kent
Barnet, Hertfordshire
Barnetby, South Humberside
Barnham, see Thetford, Norfolk
Barnoldswick, Lancashire
Barnsley, South Yorkshire
Barnstaple, Devon
Barnstone, see Nottingham, Nottinghamshire
Barnwood, see Gloucester, Gloucestershire
Barrhead, see Glasgow, Lanarkshire
Barrington, see Cambridge, Cambridgeshire
Barrow Gurney, see Bristol, Avon
Barrow upon Soar, see Loughborough, Leicestershire
Barrow-in-Furness, Cumbria
Barrow-on-Trent, see Derby, Derbyshire
Barrow-upon-Humber, South Humberside
Barrowford, see Nelson, Lancashire
Barry, South Glamorgan
Barton, see Nottingham, Nottinghamshire
Barton-le-Clay, see Bedford, Bedfordshire
Barton-upon-Humber, South Humberside
Barwell, see Leicester, Leicestershire
Basildon, Essex
Basingstoke, Hampshire
Baslow, see Bakewell, Derbyshire
Bath, Avon
Bathgate, West Lothian
Batley, West Yorkshire
Battle, East Sussex
Bawtry, see Doncaster, South Yorkshire
Baxterley, see Atherstone, Warwickshire
Beaconsfield, Buckinghamshire
Beaminster, Dorset
Bearsden, see Glasgow, Lanarkshire
Bearsted, see Maidstone, Kent
Beaulieu, see Brockenhurst, Hampshire
Beauly, Inverness-Shire
Beaumaris, Gwynedd
Beaworthy, Devon
Bebington, see Wirral, Merseyside
Beccles, Suffolk
Beckenham, Kent
Beckermet, Cumbria
Bedale, North Yorkshire
Beddgelert, see Caernarfon, Gwynedd
Bedfont, see Feltham, Middlesex
Bedford, Bedfordshire
Bedhampton, see Havant, Hampshire
Bedlington, Northumberland
Bedwas, see Newport, Gwent
Bedworth, Warwickshire
Beeston, see Nottingham, Nottinghamshire
Beith, Ayrshire
Belfast, Antrim
Belford, Northumberland
Bellaghy, see Magherafelt, Londonderry
Bellingham, see Hexham, Northumberland
Bellshill, Lanarkshire
Belmont, see Durham, Durham
Belmont, see Sutton, Surrey
Belper, Derbyshire
Belton, see Doncaster, South Yorkshire
Belvedere, Kent
Bembridge, Isle of Wight
Benenden, see Cranbrook, Kent
Benfleet, Essex
Benington, see Stevenage, Hertfordshire
Benson, see Wallingford, Oxfordshire
Bentham, see Lancaster, Lancashire
Bentley, see Doncaster, South Yorkshire
Berkeley, Gloucestershire
Berkhamsted, Hertfordshire
Berriedale, Caithness
Berwick-upon-Tweed, Northumberland
Bessbrook, see Newry, Down
Bestwood Village, see Nottingham, Nottinghamshire
Betchworth, Surrey
Bethersden, see Ashford, Kent
Bethesda, see Bangor, Gwynedd
Betws-y-Coed, Gwynedd
Beverley, North Humberside
Bewdley, Worcestershire
Bexhill-on-Sea, East Sussex
Bexley, Kent
Bexleyheath, Kent
Bibury, see Cirencester, Gloucestershire
Bicester, Oxfordshire
Biddulph, see Stoke-on-Trent, Staffordshire
Bideford, Devon
Bidford-on-Avon, see Alcester, Warwickshire
Biggar, Lanarkshire
Biggin Hill, see Westerham, Kent
Biggleswade, Bedfordshire
Billericay, Essex
Billesdon, see Leicester, Leicestershire
Billinge, see Wigan, Lancashire
Billingham, Cleveland
Billinghay, see Lincoln, Lincolnshire
Billingshurst, West Sussex
Billington, see Clitheroe, Lancashire
Bilston, West Midlands
Binbrook, see Market Rasen, Lincolnshire
Bingham, see Nottingham, Nottinghamshire
Bingley, West Yorkshire
Birchington, Kent
Birdlip, see Gloucester, Gloucestershire
Birkenhead, Merseyside
Birmingham, West Midlands
Birstall, see Batley, West Yorkshire
Birtley, see Chester le Street, Durham
Bishop Auckland, Durham
Bishop Sutton, see Bristol, Avon
Bishop's Stortford, Hertfordshire
Bishopbriggs, see Glasgow, Lanarkshire
Bishops Castle, Shropshire
Bishops Cleeve, see Cheltenham, Gloucestershire
Bishops Waltham, see Southampton, Hampshire
Bishopton, Renfrewshire
Bispham, see Ormskirk, Lancashire
Bisterne, see Ringwood, Hampshire
Bitton, see Bristol, Avon
Bixter, see Shetland, Shetland Islands
Blaby, see Leicester, Leicestershire
Blackburn, Lancashire
Blackburn, see Bathgate, West Lothian
Blackford, see Auchterarder, Perthshire
Blackmore, see Ingatestone, Essex
Blacko, see Nelson, Lancashire
Blackpool, Lancashire
Blackshiels, see Pathhead, Midlothian
Blackwood, Gwent
Blaenau Ffestiniog, Gwynedd
Blaenavon, see Pontypool, Gwent
Blagdon, see Bristol, Avon
Blaina, see Abertillery, Gwent
Blair-Atholl, see Pitlochry, Perthshire
Blairgowrie, Perthshire
Blakeney, Gloucestershire
Blandford Forum, Dorset
Blanefield, see Glasgow, Lanarkshire
Blantyre, see Glasgow, Lanarkshire
Blaydon-on-Tyne, Tyne and Wear
Bledlow, see Princes Risborough, Buckinghamshire
Bletchingley, see Redhill, Surrey
Bletchley, see Milton Keynes, Buckinghamshire
Blickling, see Norwich, Norfolk
Blidworth, see Mansfield, Nottinghamshire
Bloxwich, see Walsall, West Midlands
Blyth, Northumberland
Blythe Bridge, see Stoke-on-Trent, Staffordshire
Bo'ness, West Lothian
Boat of Garten, Inverness-Shire
Bodmin, Cornwall
Bodorgan, Gwynedd
Bognor Regis, West Sussex
Boldon Colliery, Tyne and Wear
Bollington, see Macclesfield, Cheshire
Bolsover, see Chesterfield, Derbyshire
Bolton, Lancashire
Bolton Abbey, see Skipton, North Yorkshire
Bolton-upon-Dearne, see Rotherham, South Yorkshire
Bonar Bridge, see Ardgay, Sutherland
Boncath, Dyfed
Bonnybridge, Stirlingshire
Bonnyrigg, Midlothian
Bookham, see Leatherhead, Surrey
Bootle, Merseyside
Bootle Station, see Millom, Cumbria
Bordon, Hampshire
Borehamwood, Hertfordshire
Borough Green, see Sevenoaks, Kent
Boroughbridge, see York, North Yorkshire
Borrowash, see Derby, Derbyshire
Borth, Dyfed
Borth-y-Gest, see Porthmadog, Gwynedd
Boscastle, Cornwall
Boscombe, see Bournemouth, Dorset
Bosham, see Chichester, West Sussex
Boston, Lincolnshire
Boston Spa, see Wetherby, West Yorkshire
Bothel, see Carlisle, Cumbria
Bothwell, see Glasgow, Lanarkshire
Botley, see Oxford, Oxfordshire
Bottesford, see Nottingham, Nottinghamshire
Bourne, Lincolnshire
Bourne End, Buckinghamshire
Bournemouth, Dorset
Bourton-on-the-Water, see Cheltenham, Gloucestershire
Bovey Tracey, see Newton Abbot, Devon
Bovingdon, see Hemel Hempstead, Hertfordshire
Bow Street, Dyfed
Bowmore, Isle of Islay
Box, see Corsham, Wiltshire
Brackley, Northamptonshire
Bracknell, Berkshire
Bradfield, see Reading, Berkshire
Bradford, West Yorkshire
Bradford-on-Avon, Wiltshire
Brading, see Sandown, Isle of Wight
Bradley Stoke, see Bristol, Avon
Bradmore, see Nottingham, Nottinghamshire
Bradwell, see Hope Valley, Derbyshire
Brae, see Shetland, Shetland Islands
Braemar, see Ballater, Aberdeenshire
Brailsford, see Ashbourne, Derbyshire
Braintree, Essex
Bramcote, Beeston, see Nottingham, Nottinghamshire
Bramhall, see Stockport, Cheshire
Bramhope, see Leeds, West Yorkshire
Bramley, see Guildford, Surrey
Brampton, Cumbria
Brampton, see Huntingdon, Cambridgeshire
Brandon, Suffolk
Brandon, see Durham, Durham
Branksome, see Poole, Dorset
Bransgore, see Christchurch, Dorset
Brassington, see Matlock, Derbyshire
Braunton, Devon
Breanish, see Isle of Lewis, Isle of Lewis
Brechin, Angus
Brecon, Powys
Bredbury, see Stockport, Cheshire
Breedon-on-the-Hill, see Derby, Derbyshire
Breighton, see Selby, North Yorkshire
Brent Knoll, see Highbridge, Somerset
Brentford, Middlesex
Brentwood, Essex
Brewood, see Stafford, Staffordshire
Bricket Wood, see St. Albans, Hertfordshire
Bridge, see Canterbury, Kent
Bridge of Allan, see Stirling, Stirlingshire
Bridge of Don, see Aberdeen, Aberdeenshire
Bridge of Orchy, Argyll
Bridge of Weir, Renfrewshire
Bridgend, Mid Glamorgan
Bridgend, Isle of Islay
Bridgnorth, Shropshire
Bridgwater, Somerset
Bridlington, North Humberside
Bridport, Dorset
Brierfield, see Nelson, Lancashire
Brierley Hill, West Midlands
Brigg, South Humberside
Brighouse, West Yorkshire
Brightlingsea, see Colchester, Essex
Brighton, East Sussex
Brigstock, see Kettering, Northamptonshire
Bristol, Avon
Briton Ferry, see Neath, West Glamorgan
Brixham, Devon
Broadford, see Isle of Skye, Isle of Skye
Broadstairs, Kent
Broadstone, Dorset
Broadway, Worcestershire
Brockenhurst, Hampshire
Brocton, see Stafford, Staffordshire
Brodick, Isle of Arran
Bromborough, see Wirral, Merseyside
Bromham, see Bedford, Bedfordshire
Bromley, Kent

Brookwood, see Woking, Surrey
Brora, Sutherland
Broseley, Shropshire
Brough, North Humberside
Broughton, see Brigg, South Humberside
Broughton, see Stockbridge, Hampshire
Broughton Astley, see Leicester, Leicestershire
Broughton-in-Furness, Cumbria
Brownhills, see Walsall, West Midlands
Broxbourne, Hertfordshire
Broxburn, West Lothian
Bruichladdich, Isle of Islay
Bruton, Somerset
Bryher, Isles of Scilly
Brynmawr, see Ebbw Vale, Gwent
Brynmenyn, see Bridgend, Mid Glamorgan
Brynsiencyn, see Llanfairpwllgwyngyll, Gwynedd
Brynteg, Gwynedd
Buchlyvie, see Stirling, Stirlingshire
Buckfastleigh, Devon
Buckhaven, see Leven, Fife
Buckhurst Hill, Essex
Buckie, Banffshire
Buckingham, Buckinghamshire
Buckley, Clwyd
Bucklow Hill, see Knutsford, Cheshire
Bucknell, Shropshire
Bucksburn, see Aberdeen, Aberdeenshire
Bude, Cornwall
Budleigh Salterton, Devon
Bugle, see St. Austell, Cornwall
Builth Wells, Powys
Bulford, see Salisbury, Wiltshire
Bulkington, see Bedworth, Warwickshire
Bulwell, see Nottingham, Nottinghamshire
Bunchrew, see Inverness, Inverness-Shire
Bunessan, see Isle of Mull, Isle of Mull
Bungay, Suffolk
Bunny, see Nottingham, Nottinghamshire
Buntingford, Hertfordshire
Burbage, see Hinckley, Leicestershire
Bures, Suffolk
Burford, Oxfordshire
Burgess Hill, West Sussex
Burgh Le Marsh, see Skegness, Lincolnshire
Burley, see Ringwood, Hampshire
Burley in Wharfedale, see Ilkley, West Yorkshire
Burnham, see Slough, Berkshire
Burnham Market, see King's Lynn, Norfolk
Burnham-on-Crouch, Essex
Burnham-on-Sea, Somerset
Burnley, Lancashire
Burntisland, Fife
Burntwood, Staffordshire
Burrington, see Bristol, Avon
Burry Port, Dyfed
Burscough, see Ormskirk, Lancashire
Burslem, see Stoke-on-Trent, Staffordshire
Burstwick, see Hull, North Humberside
Burton Joyce, see Nottingham, Nottinghamshire
Burton Latimer, see Kettering, Northamptonshire
Burton Overy, see Leicester, Leicestershire
Burton-on-Trent, Staffordshire
Burwash, see Etchingham, East Sussex
Bury, Lancashire
Bury St. Edmunds, Suffolk
Bushey, see Watford, Hertfordshire
Bushmills, Antrim
Buxton, Derbyshire
Buxworth, see High Peak, Derbyshire
Bwlch-y-Cibau, see Llanfyllin, Powys
Byfleet, see West Byfleet, Surrey
Bylchau, see Denbigh, Clwyd
Cadishead, see Manchester, Lancashire
Cadnam, see Southampton, Hampshire
Caergwrle, see Wrexham, Clwyd
Caerleon, see Newport, Gwent
Caernarfon, Gwynedd
Caerphilly, Mid Glamorgan
Caersws, Powys
Caerwys, see Mold, Clwyd
Cairndow, Argyll
Cairnryan, see Stranraer, Wigtownshire
Caister-on-Sea, see Great Yarmouth, Norfolk
Caistor, see Market Rasen, Lincolnshire
Calderbridge, see Seascale, Cumbria
Caldicot, Gwent
Caledon, Tyrone
Callander, Perthshire
Callington, Cornwall
Calne, Wiltshire
Calstock, Cornwall
Calver, see Hope Valley, Derbyshire
Calverhall, see Whitchurch, Shropshire
Calverton, see Nottingham, Nottinghamshire
Calvine, see Pitlochry, Perthshire
Camberley, Surrey
Camborne, Cornwall
Cambridge, Cambridgeshire
Camelford, Cornwall
Campbeltown, Argyll
Canford Cliffs, see Poole, Dorset
Cannock, Staffordshire
Canonbie, Dumfriesshire
Canterbury, Kent
Canvey Island, Essex
Capel, see Dorking, Surrey
Capel Curig, see Betws-y-Coed, Gwynedd
Car Colston, see Nottingham, Nottinghamshire
Carbost, see Isle of Skye, Isle of Skye
Cardenden, see Lochgelly, Fife
Cardiff, South Glamorgan
Cardigan, Dyfed
Cardington, see Bedford, Bedfordshire
Cardross, see Dumbarton, Dunbartonshire
Carfin, see Motherwell, Lanarkshire
Carlisle, Cumbria
Carlton, see Nottingham, Nottinghamshire
Carluke, Lanarkshire
Carmarthen, Dyfed
Carnforth, Lancashire
Carnlough, see Ballymena, Antrim
Carnoustie, Angus
Carnwath, see Lanark, Lanarkshire
Carrbridge, Inverness-Shire
Carrickfergus, Antrim
Carron, see Aberlour, Banffshire
Carrville, see Durham, Durham
Carshalton, Surrey
Carterton, Oxfordshire
Cassington, see Witney, Oxfordshire
Castle Ashby, see Northampton, Northamptonshire
Castle Bromwich, see Birmingham, West Midlands
Castle Cary, Somerset
Castle Donington, see Derby, Derbyshire
Castle Douglas, Kirkcudbrightshire
Castle Eden, Durham
Castle Gresley, see Swadlincote, Derbyshire
Castlebay, Isle of Barra
Castledawson, see Magherafelt, Londonderry
Castlederg, Tyrone
Castleford, West Yorkshire
Castletown, Isle of Man
Castlewellan, Down
Caterham, Surrey
Catrine, see Mauchline, Ayrshire
Catterick Garrison, North Yorkshire
Caversham, see Reading, Berkshire
Cawston, see Norwich, Norfolk
Caythorpe, see Nottingham, Nottinghamshire
Cefn-y-Bedd, see Wrexham, Clwyd
Cemaes Bay, Gwynedd
Cerrigydrudion, see Corwen, Clwyd
Chadderton, see Oldham, Lancashire
Chadlington, see Chipping Norton, Oxfordshire
Chadwell Heath, see Romford, Essex
Chagford, see Newton Abbot, Devon
Chalfont St. Giles, Buckinghamshire
Chalfont St. Peter, see Gerrards Cross, Buckinghamshire
Chapel-en-le-Frith, see High Peak, Derbyshire
Chapeltown, see Sheffield, South Yorkshire
Chard, Somerset
Charing, see Ashford, Kent
Charlbury, see Chipping Norton, Oxfordshire
Charmouth, see Bridport, Dorset
Chatham, Kent
Chathill, Northumberland
Chatteris, Cambridgeshire
Cheadle, see Stoke-on-Trent, Staffordshire
Cheadle, Cheshire
Cheadle Hulme, see Cheadle, Cheshire
Cheam, see Sutton, Surrey
Cheddar, Somerset
Chelmsford, Essex
Chelsfield, see Orpington, Kent
Cheltenham, Gloucestershire
Chelwood Gate, see Haywards Heath, West Sussex
Chepstow, Gwent
Chertsey, Surrey
Chesham, Buckinghamshire
Cheshunt, see Waltham Cross, Hertfordshire
Chessington, Surrey
Chester, Cheshire
Chester le Street, Durham
Chesterfield, Derbyshire
Chew Magna, see Bristol, Avon
Chew Stoke, see Bristol, Avon
Chewton Mendip, Somerset
Chichester, West Sussex
Chiddingfold, see Godalming, Surrey
Chiddingstone, see Edenbridge, Kent
Chidham, see Chichester, West Sussex
Chigwell, Essex
Chilcompton, Somerset
Chilham, see Canterbury, Kent
Chilton, see Aylesbury, Buckinghamshire
Chilwell, Beeston, see Nottingham, Nottinghamshire
Chinnor, Oxfordshire
Chippenham, Wiltshire
Chipperfield, see Kings Langley, Hertfordshire
Chipping Campden, Gloucestershire
Chipping Norton, Oxfordshire
Chipping Sodbury, see Bristol, Avon
Chipstead, see Coulsdon, Surrey
Chirbury, see Montgomery, Powys
Chirk, see Wrexham, Clwyd
Chislehurst, Kent
Chobham, see Woking, Surrey
Choppington, Northumberland
Chorley, Lancashire
Chorleywood, see Rickmansworth, Hertfordshire
Chorlton, see Crewe, Cheshire
Christchurch, Dorset
Chudleigh, see Newton Abbot, Devon
Chulmleigh, Devon
Church, see Accrington, Lancashire
Church Crookham, see Fleet, Hampshire
Church Stretton, Shropshire
Churchdown, see Gloucester, Gloucestershire
Churchill, see Winscombe, Avon
Churchill, see Chipping Norton, Oxfordshire
Chwilog, see Pwllheli, Gwynedd
Cinderford, Gloucestershire
Cirencester, Gloucestershire
Clackmannan, Clackmannanshire
Clacton-on-Sea, Essex
Clanfield, see Bampton, Oxfordshire
Clanfield, see Waterlooville, Hampshire
Clapham, see Lancaster, Lancashire
Clapton in Gordano, see Bristol, Avon
Clarbeston Road, Dyfed
Clare, see Sudbury, Suffolk
Claverham, see Bristol, Avon
Clay Cross, see Chesterfield, Derbyshire
Claygate, see Esher, Surrey
Clayton Le Moors, see Accrington, Lancashire
Cleadon, see Sunderland, Tyne and Wear
Cleator, Cumbria
Cleator Moor, Cumbria
Cleckheaton, West Yorkshire
Cleethorpes, South Humberside
Cleeve, see Bristol, Avon
Cleland, see Motherwell, Lanarkshire
Cleobury Mortimer, see Kidderminster, Worcestershire
Clevedon, Avon
Clifton, see Bristol, Avon
Clifton-on-Teme, see Worcester, Worcestershire
Cliftonville, see Margate, Kent
Clitheroe, Lancashire
Clogher, Tyrone
Clun, see Craven Arms, Shropshire
Clutton, see Bristol, Avon
Clydach, see Swansea, West Glamorgan
Clydebank, Dunbartonshire
Clynder, see Helensburgh, Dunbartonshire
Clynderwen, Dyfed
Coalpit Heath, see Bristol, Avon
Coalville, Leicestershire

Greasby, see Wirral, Merseyside
Great Ayton, see Middlesbrough, Cleveland
Great Barrow, see Chester, Cheshire
Great Brickhill, see Milton Keynes, Buckinghamshire
Great Glen, see Leicester, Leicestershire
Great Harwood, see Blackburn, Lancashire
Great Missenden, Buckinghamshire
Great Salkeld, see Penrith, Cumbria
Great Shelford, see Cambridge, Cambridgeshire
Great Staughton, St. Neots, see Huntingdon, Cambridgeshire
Great Warley, see Brentwood, Essex
Great Wyrley, see Walsall, West Midlands
Great Yarmouth, Norfolk
Greatham, see Billingham, Cleveland
Greenfield, see Oldham, Lancashire
Greenford, Middlesex
Greenhithe, Kent
Greenlaw, see Duns, Berwickshire
Greenock, Renfrewshire
Greetland, see Halifax, West Yorkshire
Gresham, see Norwich, Norfolk
Gretna, Dumfriesshire
Gribun, see Isle of Mull, Isle of Mull
Griffithstown, see Pontypool, Gwent
Grimsby, South Humberside
Grimston, see York, North Yorkshire
Grindleton, see Clitheroe, Lancashire
Groby, see Leicester, Leicestershire
Groes, see Denbigh, Clwyd
Gronant, see Prestatyn, Clwyd
Gruline, see Isle of Mull, Isle of Mull
Guardbridge, see St. Andrews, Fife
Guernsey, Channel Islands
Guildford, Surrey
Guisborough, Cleveland
Guiseley, see Leeds, West Yorkshire
Gullane, East Lothian
Gunnislake, Cornwall
Gunthorpe, see Nottingham, Nottinghamshire
Gurney Slade, Somerset
Gwaelod-y-Garth, see Cardiff, South Glamorgan
Habrough, see Immingham, South Humberside
Hackbridge, see Wallington, Surrey
Haddenham, see Ely, Cambridgeshire
Haddenham, see Aylesbury, Buckinghamshire
Haddington, East Lothian
Hadfield, see Glossop, Derbyshire
Hadleigh, see Ipswich, Suffolk
Hadleigh, see Benfleet, Essex
Hagley, see Stourbridge, West Midlands
Haigh, see Wigan, Lancashire
Hailsham, East Sussex
Hale, see Altrincham, Cheshire
Halebarns, see Altrincham, Cheshire
Halesfield, see Telford, Shropshire
Halesowen, West Midlands
Halesworth, Suffolk
Halifax, West Yorkshire
Halkirk, Caithness
Hallatrow, see Bristol, Avon
Hallen, see Bristol, Avon
Halstead, Essex
Halton, see Runcorn, Cheshire
Haltwhistle, Northumberland
Ham, see Deal, Kent
Hambledon, see Waterlooville, Hampshire
Hambrook, see Bristol, Avon
Hamilton, Lanarkshire
Hampton, Middlesex
Hampton Hill, see Hampton, Middlesex
Hampton-in-Arden, see Solihull, West Midlands
Handcross, see Haywards Heath, West Sussex
Handforth, see Wilmslow, Cheshire
Hanham, see Bristol, Avon
Hanley, see Stoke-on-Trent, Staffordshire
Hanley Castle, see Worcester, Worcestershire
Hannington, see Northampton, Northamptonshire
Harborough Magna, see Rugby, Warwickshire
Harbury, see Leamington Spa, Warwickshire
Harefield, see Uxbridge, Middlesex
Harlech, Gwynedd
Harleston, Norfolk
Harlow, Essex
Harlton, see Cambridge, Cambridgeshire
Harold Wood, see Romford, Essex
Harpenden, Hertfordshire
Harray, see Orkney, Orkney
Harrietsham, see Maidstone, Kent
Harris, Isle of Harris
Harrogate, North Yorkshire
Harrold, see Bedford, Bedfordshire
Harrow, Middlesex
Harrow Weald, see Harrow, Middlesex
Harswell, see York, North Yorkshire
Hartfield, East Sussex
Harthill, see Shotts, Lanarkshire
Hartlepool, Cleveland
Hartley, see Longfield, Kent
Hartley Wintney, see Hook, Hampshire
Harwell, see Didcot, Oxfordshire
Harwich, Essex
Harwood, see Bolton, Lancashire
Haslemere, Surrey
Haslingden, see Rossendale, Lancashire
Hassocks, West Sussex
Hastings, East Sussex
Haswell, see Durham, Durham
Hatch End, see Pinner, Middlesex
Hatfield, Hertfordshire
Hatherleigh, see Okehampton, Devon
Hatton, see Derby, Derbyshire
Hatton, see Peterhead, Aberdeenshire
Havant, Hampshire
Haverfordwest, Dyfed
Haverhill, Suffolk
Hawarden, see Deeside, Clwyd
Hawes, North Yorkshire
Hawick, Roxburghshire
Hawkhurst, see Cranbrook, Kent
Hawksworth, see Nottingham, Nottinghamshire
Haworth, see Keighley, West Yorkshire
Hawthorn, see Corsham, Wiltshire
Haxey, see Doncaster, South Yorkshire
Haxey Junction, see Doncaster, South Yorkshire
Hay-on-Wye, see Hereford, Herefordshire
Haydock, see St. Helens, Merseyside
Hayes, Middlesex
Hayes, see Bromley, Kent
Hayfield, see High Peak, Derbyshire
Hayle, Cornwall
Hayling Island, Hampshire
Haynes, see Bedford, Bedfordshire
Haywards Heath, West Sussex
Hazel Grove, see Stockport, Cheshire
Hazlemere, see High Wycombe, Buckinghamshire
Heacham, see King's Lynn, Norfolk
Headcorn, see Ashford, Kent
Headingley, see Leeds, West Yorkshire
Headington, see Oxford, Oxfordshire
Headley, see Bordon, Hampshire
Headley, see Thatcham, Berkshire
Heage, see Belper, Derbyshire
Heald Green, see Cheadle, Cheshire
Heanor, Derbyshire
Heather, see Coalville, Leicestershire
Heathfield, East Sussex
Heathrow, see Hounslow, Middlesex
Hebburn, Tyne and Wear
Hebden Bridge, West Yorkshire
Heckmondwike, West Yorkshire
Hedge End, see Southampton, Hampshire
Hednesford, see Cannock, Staffordshire
Heighington, see Darlington, Durham
Helensburgh, Dunbartonshire
Helmsdale, Sutherland
Helmsley, see York, North Yorkshire
Helperby, see York, North Yorkshire
Helsby, see Warrington, Cheshire
Helston, Cornwall
Hemel Hempstead, Hertfordshire
Hemingford Grey, see Huntingdon, Cambridgeshire
Hempnall, see Norwich, Norfolk
Henfield, West Sussex
Hengoed, Mid Glamorgan
Henley-in-Arden, see Solihull, West Midlands
Henley-on-Thames, Oxfordshire
Henlow, Bedfordshire
Hensingham, see Whitehaven, Cumbria
Hereford, Herefordshire
Heriot, Midlothian
Herne Bay, Kent
Hertford, Hertfordshire
Hesketh Bank, see Preston, Lancashire
Heslington, see York, North Yorkshire
Hessle, North Humberside
Hest Bank, see Lancaster, Lancashire
Heswall, see Wirral, Merseyside
Hetton-le-Hole, see Houghton le Spring, Tyne and Wear
Hewish, see Weston-super-Mare, Avon
Hewish, see Crewkerne, Somerset
Hexham, Northumberland
Heywood, Lancashire
High Bentham, see Lancaster, Lancashire
High Lane, see Stockport, Cheshire
High Littleton, see Bristol, Avon
High Peak, Derbyshire
High Wycombe, Buckinghamshire
Higham Ferrers, see Rushden, Northamptonshire
Highbridge, Somerset
Highworth, see Swindon, Wiltshire
Hildenborough, see Tonbridge, Kent
Hildersham, see Cambridge, Cambridgeshire
Hillingdon, see Uxbridge, Middlesex
Hillsborough, Down
Hillswick, see Shetland, Shetland Islands
Hilton, see Huntingdon, Cambridgeshire
Hilton, see Derby, Derbyshire
Hinckley, Leicestershire
Hindhead, Surrey
Hindley, see Wigan, Lancashire
Hingham, see Norwich, Norfolk
Hinton St. George, Somerset
Histon, see Cambridge, Cambridgeshire
Hitchin, Hertfordshire
Hoarwithy, see Hereford, Herefordshire
Hockley, Essex
Hockliffe, see Leighton Buzzard, Bedfordshire
Hoddesdon, Hertfordshire
Hoddlesden, see Darwen, Lancashire
Hognaston, see Ashbourne, Derbyshire
Holbeach, see Spalding, Lincolnshire
Holcombe, see Bury, Lancashire
Hollingworth, see Hyde, Cheshire
Holme-on-Spalding-Moor, see York, North Yorkshire
Holmer Green, see High Wycombe, Buckinghamshire
Holmes Chapel, see Crewe, Cheshire
Holmfirth, see Huddersfield, West Yorkshire
Holmrook, Cumbria
Holmwood, see Dorking, Surrey
Holsworthy, Devon
Holt, see Trowbridge, Wiltshire
Holt, Norfolk
Holyhead, Gwynedd
Holywell, Clwyd
Holywood, Down
Honiton, Devon
Honley, see Huddersfield, West Yorkshire
Hoobrook, see Kidderminster, Worcestershire
Hooe, see Battle, East Sussex
Hook, Hampshire
Hooton, see Ellesmere Port, Merseyside
Hope Valley, Derbyshire
Hopeman, see Elgin, Morayshire
Horam, see Heathfield, East Sussex
Horbury, see Wakefield, West Yorkshire
Horden, see Peterlee, Durham
Horley, Surrey
Horncastle, Lincolnshire
Hornchurch, Essex
Horndean, see Waterlooville, Hampshire
Horndon-on-the-Hill, see Stanford-le-Hope, Essex
Horning, see Norwich, Norfolk
Hornsea, North Humberside
Horrabridge, see Yelverton, Devon
Horsforth, see Leeds, West Yorkshire
Horsham, West Sussex
Horsley, see Stroud, Gloucestershire
Horsley Woodhouse, see Ilkeston, Derbyshire
Horspath, see Oxford, Oxfordshire
Horton, see Bristol, Avon
Horwich, see Bolton, Lancashire
Houghton, see Huntingdon, Cambridgeshire
Houghton le Spring, Tyne and Wear
Houghton Regis, see Dunstable, Bedfordshire

Penwortham, see Preston, Lancashire
Penysarn, Gwynedd
Penzance, Cornwall
Perranporth, Cornwall
Pershore, Worcestershire
Perth, Perthshire
Peterborough, Cambridgeshire
Peterculter, Aberdeenshire
Peterhead, Aberdeenshire
Peterlee, Durham
Petersfield, Hampshire
Petts Wood, see Orpington, Kent
Petworth, West Sussex
Pevensey, East Sussex
Pevensey Bay, see Pevensey, East Sussex
Pewsey, Wiltshire
Philleigh, see Truro, Cornwall
Pickering, North Yorkshire
Pill, see Bristol, Avon
Pilning, see Bristol, Avon
Pilton, see Shepton Mallet, Somerset
Pinner, Middlesex
Pinxton, see Nottingham, Nottinghamshire
Pitlochry, Perthshire
Pitmedden, see Ellon, Aberdeenshire
Pitsea, see Basildon, Essex
Pittenweem, see Anstruther, Fife
Plaistow, see Billingshurst, West Sussex
Plaxtol, see Sevenoaks, Kent
Plean, see Stirling, Stirlingshire
Plockton, Ross-Shire
Plumtree, see Nottingham, Nottinghamshire
Plungar, see Nottingham, Nottinghamshire
Plymouth, Devon
Plympton, see Plymouth, Devon
Plymstock, see Plymouth, Devon
Pocklington, see York, North Yorkshire
Polegate, East Sussex
Pontardawe, see Swansea, West Glamorgan
Pontarddulais, see Swansea, West Glamorgan
Pontefract, West Yorkshire
Ponteland, see Newcastle upon Tyne, Tyne and Wear
Ponthir, see Newport, Gwent
Ponthirwaun, see Cardigan, Dyfed
Pontllanfraith, see Blackwood, Gwent
Pontwelly, see Llandysul, Dyfed
Pontyclun, Mid Glamorgan
Pontypool, Gwent
Pontypridd, Mid Glamorgan
Pool-in-Wharfedale, see Otley, West Yorkshire
Poole, Dorset
Poolewe, see Achnasheen, Ross-Shire
Poringland, see Norwich, Norfolk
Porlock, see Minehead, Somerset
Port Askaig, Isle of Islay
Port Charlotte, Isle of Islay
Port Clarence, see Middlesbrough, Cleveland
Port Ellen, Isle of Islay
Port Erin, Isle of Man
Port Glasgow, Renfrewshire
Port Isaac, Cornwall
Port Logan, see Stranraer, Wigtownshire
Port St. Mary, Isle of Man
Port Sunlight, see Wirral, Merseyside
Port Talbot, West Glamorgan
Port William, see Newton Stewart, Wigtownshire
Portadown, see Craigavon, Armagh
Portbury, see Bristol, Avon
Portglenone, see Ballymena, Antrim
Porth, Mid Glamorgan
Porthcawl, Mid Glamorgan
Porthleven, see Helston, Cornwall
Porthmadog, Gwynedd
Portishead, see Bristol, Avon
Portknockie, see Buckie, Banffshire
Portland, Dorset
Portlethen, see Aberdeen, Aberdeenshire
Portnahaven, Isle of Islay
Portnalong, Carbost, see Isle of Skye, Isle of Skye
Portree, Isle of Skye
Portrush, Antrim
Portslade, see Brighton, East Sussex
Portsmouth, Hampshire
Portsoy, see Banff, Banffshire
Portstewart, Londonderry
Potters Bar, Hertfordshire
Potton, see Sandy, Bedfordshire
Poulton-le-Fylde, Lancashire
Powick, see Worcester, Worcestershire
Poynton, see Stockport, Cheshire
Prenton, Merseyside
Prescot, Merseyside
Prestatyn, Clwyd
Prestbury, see Macclesfield, Cheshire
Presteigne, Powys
Preston, Lancashire
Prestonpans, East Lothian
Prestwich, see Manchester, Lancashire
Prestwick, Ayrshire
Prestwood, see Great Missenden, Buckinghamshire
Princes Risborough, Buckinghamshire
Princetown, see Yelverton, Devon
Prudhoe, Northumberland
Pucklechurch, see Bristol, Avon
Pudsey, West Yorkshire
Pulborough, West Sussex
Purfleet, Essex
Purley, Surrey
Pwllheli, Gwynedd
Pyle, see Bridgend, Mid Glamorgan
Queenborough, Kent
Queensferry, see Deeside, Clwyd
Radcliffe, see Manchester, Lancashire
Radcliffe-on-Trent, see Nottingham, Nottinghamshire
Radlett, Hertfordshire
Radstock, see Bath, Avon
Radyr, see Cardiff, South Glamorgan
Raglan, see Usk, Gwent
Rainford, see St. Helens, Merseyside
Rainham, Essex
Rainham, see Gillingham, Kent
Rainhill, see Prescot, Merseyside
Ramsbottom, see Bury, Lancashire
Ramsbury, see Marlborough, Wiltshire
Ramsey, see Huntingdon, Cambridgeshire
Ramsey, Isle of Man
Ramsgate, Kent
Randalstown, Antrim
Rannoch, see Pitlochry, Perthshire
Ranskill, see Retford, Nottinghamshire
Rathfriland, see Newry, Down
Raunds, see Wellingborough, Northamptonshire
Ravenglass, Cumbria
Ravenshead, see Nottingham, Nottinghamshire
Ravensthorpe, see Dewsbury, West Yorkshire
Rawdon, see Leeds, West Yorkshire
Rawtenstall, see Rossendale, Lancashire
Rayleigh, Essex
Reading, Berkshire
Redbourn, see St. Albans, Hertfordshire
Redcar, Cleveland
Reddish, see Stockport, Cheshire
Redditch, Worcestershire
Redhill, see Bristol, Avon
Redhill, Surrey
Redhill, see Hereford, Herefordshire
Redlynch, see Salisbury, Wiltshire
Redmarley, see Gloucester, Gloucestershire
Redmile, see Nottingham, Nottinghamshire
Redruth, Cornwall
Reedham, see Norwich, Norfolk
Reepham, see Norwich, Norfolk
Reigate, Surrey
Renfrew, Renfrewshire
Renton, see Dumbarton, Dunbartonshire
Repton, see Derby, Derbyshire
Reston, see Eyemouth, Berwickshire
Retford, Nottinghamshire
Rhayader, Powys
Rhos on Sea, see Colwyn Bay, Clwyd
Rhosgoch, Gwynedd
Rhosgoch, see Builth Wells, Powys
Rhosneigr, Gwynedd
Rhyl, Clwyd
Rhymney, see Tredegar, Gwent
Richmond, Surrey
Richmond, North Yorkshire
Rickmansworth, Hertfordshire
Riddings, see Alfreton, Derbyshire
Riding Mill, Northumberland
Ringmer, see Lewes, East Sussex
Ringwood, Hampshire
Ripley, see Woking, Surrey
Ripley, Derbyshire
Ripon, North Yorkshire
Ripponden, see Sowerby Bridge, West Yorkshire
Risca, see Newport, Gwent
Rishton, see Blackburn, Lancashire
Risley, see Warrington, Cheshire
Roade, see Northampton, Northamptonshire
Robertsbridge, East Sussex
Rocester, see Uttoxeter, Staffordshire
Rochdale, Lancashire
Rochester, Kent
Rochford, Essex
Rockbourne, see Fordingbridge, Hampshire
Rode, Somerset
Rodley, see Leeds, West Yorkshire
Rogart, Sutherland
Rogate, see Petersfield, Hampshire
Romford, Essex
Romiley, see Stockport, Cheshire
Romney Marsh, Kent
Romsey, Hampshire
Ropley, see Alresford, Hampshire
Rosewell, Midlothian
Roslin, Midlothian
Ross-on-Wye, Herefordshire
Rossendale, Lancashire
Rossett, see Wrexham, Clwyd
Rosyth, see Dunfermline, Fife
Rothbury, see Morpeth, Northumberland
Rotherfield, see Crowborough, East Sussex
Rotherham, South Yorkshire
Rothes, see Aberlour, Banffshire
Rothesay, Isle of Bute
Rothienorman, see Inverurie, Aberdeenshire
Rothley, see Leicester, Leicestershire
Rothwell, see Kettering, Northamptonshire
Rothwell, see Leeds, West Yorkshire
Rothwell, see Market Rasen, Lincolnshire
Rottingdean, see Brighton, East Sussex
Rowland's Castle, Hampshire
Rowlands Gill, Tyne and Wear
Rowley Regis, West Midlands
Roxwell, see Chelmsford, Essex
Roy Bridge, Inverness-Shire
Royston, Hertfordshire
Royton, see Oldham, Lancashire
Ruardean, Gloucestershire
Rubery, Rednal, see Birmingham, West Midlands
Ruddington, see Nottingham, Nottinghamshire
Rudgeway, see Bristol, Avon
Rudgwick, see Horsham, West Sussex
Rugby, Warwickshire
Rugeley, Staffordshire
Ruislip, Middlesex
Runcorn, Cheshire
Rushden, Northamptonshire
Rustington, see Littlehampton, West Sussex
Rutherglen, see Glasgow, Lanarkshire
Ruthin, Clwyd
Ryde, Isle of Wight
Rye, East Sussex
Ryton, Tyne and Wear
Ryton on Dunsmore, see Coventry, West Midlands
Sabden, see Clitheroe, Lancashire
Sacriston, see Durham, Durham
Saffron Walden, Essex
Saintfield, see Ballynahinch, Down
Salcombe, Devon
Sale, Cheshire
Salford, Lancashire
Salford Priors, see Evesham, Worcestershire
Salisbury, Wiltshire
Saltash, Cornwall
Saltburn-by-the-Sea, Cleveland
Saltcoats, Ayrshire
Saltdean, see Brighton, East Sussex
Salterforth, see Barnoldswick, Lancashire
Saltford, see Bristol, Avon
Saltney, see Chester, Cheshire
Sanday, see Orkney, Orkney
Sandbach, Cheshire
Sandbank, see Dunoon, Argyll
Sandford, see Winscombe, Avon
Sandhurst, see Cranbrook, Kent
Sandhurst, Berkshire
Sandiacre, see Nottingham, Nottinghamshire
Sandness, see Shetland, Shetland Islands
Sandon, see Chelmsford, Essex
Sandon, see Stafford, Staffordshire
Sandown, Isle of Wight

Wareham, Dorset
Wargrave, see Reading, Berkshire
Warkworth, see Morpeth, Northumberland
Warley, West Midlands
Warlingham, Surrey
Warminster, Wiltshire
Warmley, see Bristol, Avon
Warnham, see Horsham, West Sussex
Warrenpoint, see Newry, Down
Warrington, Cheshire
Warsash, see Southampton, Hampshire
Warsop, see Mansfield, Nottinghamshire
Warter, see York, North Yorkshire
Warwick, Warwickshire
Washington, Tyne and Wear
Washington, see Pulborough, West Sussex
Watchet, Somerset
Waterfoot, see Rossendale, Lancashire
Waterlooville, Hampshire
Waterrow, see Taunton, Somerset
Watford, Hertfordshire
Wath-upon-Dearne, see Rotherham, South Yorkshire
Watlington, Oxfordshire
Watton, see Thetford, Norfolk
Watton at Stone, see Hertford, Hertfordshire
Waunfawr, see Caernarfon, Gwynedd
Wavendon, see Milton Keynes, Buckinghamshire
Wedmore, Somerset
Wednesbury, West Midlands
Weedon, see Northampton, Northamptonshire
Wellesbourne, see Warwick, Warwickshire
Welling, Kent
Wellingborough, Northamptonshire
Wellington, see Telford, Shropshire
Wellington, see Hereford, Herefordshire
Wellington, Somerset
Wells, Somerset
Wells-next-the-Sea, Norfolk
Welshpool, Powys
Welton, see Brough, North Humberside
Welwyn, Hertfordshire
Welwyn Garden City, Hertfordshire
Wem, see Shrewsbury, Shropshire
Wembley, Middlesex
Wemyss Bay, Renfrewshire
Wendover, see Aylesbury, Buckinghamshire
Wenvoe, see Cardiff, South Glamorgan
West Bridgford, see Nottingham, Nottinghamshire
West Bromwich, West Midlands
West Byfleet, Surrey
West Calder, West Lothian
West Chiltington, see Pulborough, West Sussex
West Clandon, see Guildford, Surrey
West Dereham, see King's Lynn, Norfolk
West Drayton, Middlesex
West End, see Southampton, Hampshire
West Harptree, see Bristol, Avon
West Horndon, see Brentwood, Essex
West Kilbride, Ayrshire
West Kirby, see Wirral, Merseyside
West Linton, Peeblesshire
West Malling, Kent
West Molesey, Surrey
West Moors, see Ferndown, Dorset
West Wickham, Kent
Westbury, Wiltshire
Westbury-on-Severn, Gloucestershire
Westbury-on-Trym, see Bristol, Avon
Westcliff-on-Sea, Essex
Westerham, Kent
Westgate-on-Sea, Kent
Westhill, Aberdeenshire
Westhoughton, see Bolton, Lancashire
Weston-on-the-Green, see Bicester, Oxfordshire
Weston-super-Mare, Avon
Westray, see Orkney, Orkney
Westwood, see Nottingham, Nottinghamshire
Westwoodside, see Doncaster, South Yorkshire
Wetherby, West Yorkshire
Weybridge, Surrey
Weymouth, Dorset
Whaley Bridge, see Stockport, Cheshire
Whalley, see Clitheroe, Lancashire
Whatton, see Nottingham, Nottinghamshire
Wheathampstead, see St. Albans, Hertfordshire
Wheatley, see Oxford, Oxfordshire
Whetstone, see Leicester, Leicestershire
Whickham, see Newcastle upon Tyne, Tyne and Wear
Whimple, see Exeter, Devon
Whitburn, see Bathgate, West Lothian
Whitburn, see Sunderland, Tyne and Wear
Whitby, North Yorkshire
Whitchurch, Shropshire
Whitchurch, Hampshire
Whitchurch, see Bristol, Avon
Whitchurch on Thames, see Reading, Berkshire
Whitecairns, see Aberdeen, Aberdeenshire
Whitefield, see Manchester, Lancashire
Whitehaven, Cumbria
Whitehead, see Carrickfergus, Antrim
Whithorn, see Newton Stewart, Wigtownshire
Whitland, Dyfed
Whitley Bay, Tyne and Wear
Whitley Bridge, see Goole, North Humberside
Whitminster, see Gloucester, Gloucestershire
Whitstable, Kent
Whittlesey, see Peterborough, Cambridgeshire
Whittlesford, see Cambridge, Cambridgeshire
Whitton, see Twickenham, Middlesex
Whitwell, see Ventnor, Isle of Wight
Whyteleafe, Surrey
Wick, see Bristol, Avon
Wick, Caithness
Wickford, Essex
Wickham, see Fareham, Hampshire
Wickham Bishops, see Witham, Essex
Wickham Market, see Woodbridge, Suffolk
Widecombe-in-the-Moor, see Newton Abbot, Devon
Wideopen, see Newcastle upon Tyne, Tyne and Wear
Widnes, Cheshire
Wigan, Lancashire
Wigston, Leicestershire
Wigton, Cumbria
Wigtown, see Newton Stewart, Wigtownshire
Willenhall, West Midlands
Willerby, see Hull, North Humberside
Willingham, see Cambridge, Cambridgeshire
Willington, see Crook, Durham
Williton, see Taunton, Somerset
Willsbridge, see Bristol, Avon
Wilmslow, Cheshire
Wilnecote, see Tamworth, Staffordshire
Wilton, see Marlborough, Wiltshire
Wilton, see Redcar, Cleveland
Wimblington, see March, Cambridgeshire
Wimborne, Dorset
Wincanton, Somerset
Winchburgh, see Broxburn, West Lothian
Winchcombe, see Cheltenham, Gloucestershire
Winchelsea, East Sussex
Winchester, Hampshire
Windermere, Cumbria
Windlesham, Surrey
Windsor, Berkshire
Windygates, see Leven, Fife
Winford, see Bristol, Avon
Wingate, Durham
Wingham, see Canterbury, Kent
Winkleigh, Devon
Winnersh, see Wokingham, Berkshire
Winscombe, Avon
Winsford, Cheshire
Winslow, see Buckingham, Buckinghamshire
Winterbourne, see Bristol, Avon
Winterbourne Down, see Bristol, Avon
Wirksworth, see Matlock, Derbyshire
Wirral, Merseyside
Wisbech, Cambridgeshire
Wishaw, Lanarkshire
Witham, Essex
Withernsea, North Humberside
Witney, Oxfordshire
Wiveliscombe, see Taunton, Somerset
Wivelsfield Green, see Haywards Heath, West Sussex
Wivenhoe, see Colchester, Essex
Woburn, see Milton Keynes, Buckinghamshire
Woburn Sands, see Milton Keynes, Buckinghamshire
Woking, Surrey
Wokingham, Berkshire
Woldingham, see Caterham, Surrey
Wollaston, see Wellingborough, Northamptonshire
Wolsingham, see Bishop Auckland, Durham
Wolston, see Coventry, West Midlands
Wolverhampton, West Midlands
Wolverton, see Milton Keynes, Buckinghamshire
Wombwell, see Barnsley, South Yorkshire
Wonersh, see Guildford, Surrey
Wooburn Green, see High Wycombe, Buckinghamshire
Woodborough, see Nottingham, Nottinghamshire
Woodbridge, Suffolk
Woodford, see Stockport, Cheshire
Woodford Green, Essex
Woodhall Spa, Lincolnshire
Woodhouse, see Sheffield, South Yorkshire
Woodhouse Mill, see Sheffield, South Yorkshire
Woodlesford, see Leeds, West Yorkshire
Woodley, see Reading, Berkshire
Woodstock, Oxfordshire
Woolacombe, Devon
Wooler, Northumberland
Woolmer Green, see Knebworth, Hertfordshire
Woolton, see Liverpool, Merseyside
Wootton, see Ulceby, South Humberside
Wootton Bassett, see Swindon, Wiltshire
Worcester, Worcestershire
Worcester Park, Surrey
Workington, Cumbria
Worksop, Nottinghamshire
Worle, see Weston-super-Mare, Avon
Wormley, see Godalming, Surrey
Worplesden, see Guildford, Surrey
Worrall, see Sheffield, South Yorkshire
Worsley, see Manchester, Lancashire
Worsthorne, see Burnley, Lancashire
Worston, Yealmpton, see Plymouth, Devon
Worthing, West Sussex
Wortley, see Sheffield, South Yorkshire
Wotton-under-Edge, Gloucestershire
Wragby, see Market Rasen, Lincolnshire
Wraysbury, see Staines, Middlesex
Wrentham, see Beccles, Suffolk
Wrexham, Clwyd
Wrington, see Bristol, Avon
Writtle, see Chelmsford, Essex
Wroot, see Doncaster, South Yorkshire
Wrotham, see Sevenoaks, Kent
Wroxham, see Norwich, Norfolk
Wylam, Northumberland
Wymondham, Norfolk
Wysall, see Nottingham, Nottinghamshire
Wythall, see Birmingham, West Midlands
Wythenshawe, see Manchester, Lancashire
Y Felinheli, Gwynedd
Yalding, see Maidstone, Kent
Yarm, Cleveland
Yarmouth, Isle of Wight
Yate, see Bristol, Avon
Yateley, Hampshire
Yatton, see Bristol, Avon
Yaxley, see Peterborough, Cambridgeshire
Yeadon, see Leeds, West Yorkshire
Yealmpton, see Plymouth, Devon
Yelverton, Devon
Yeovil, Somerset
York, North Yorkshire
Youlthorpe, see York, North Yorkshire
Ystalyfera, see Swansea, West Glamorgan
Ystrad Meurig, Dyfed
Ystrad Mynach, see Hengoed, Mid Glamorgan
Ystradgynlais, see Swansea, West Glamorgan
Ythanbank, see Ellon, Aberdeenshire

ALPHABETICAL INDEX OF COMPANIES

This index gives the names and locations of all companies listed in Kompass, together with the page number on which the information on that company appears. If the location is known you need not consult this index, simply turn to the appropriate county and town using the headlines at the top of each page. Under the appropriate town you will find companies listed in alphabetical sequence.

1,2,3,..

A

B

C

D

E

F

H

I

K

L

M

N

O

P

Q

R

S

T

U

V

W

X

Y

Z

AVON

Banwell

Mark Compton
Towerhead Farm Towerhead, Banwell, BS29 6PQ
Tel: 01934-822183
Directors: M. Compton (Prop)
Date established: 1994 **No.of Employees:** 1 - 10 **Product Groups:** 41

Dataroll Ltd
Knightcott Industrial Estate, Banwell, BS29 6JN
Tel: 01934-823253 **Fax:** 01934-822990
E-mail: mail@dataroll.co.uk
Website: http://www.dataroll.co.uk
Directors: V. Griffiths (Dir)
Immediate Holding Company: DATAROLL LIMITED
Registration no: 04011324 **VAT No.:** GB 130 7726 84
Date established: 2000 **Turnover:** Up to £250,000
No.of Employees: 1 - 10 **Product Groups:** 23, 29, 30, 31, 35, 39, 43, 44, 48, 63, 66

Date of Accounts	Sep 11	Sep 10	Sep 09
Working Capital	27	11	-9
Fixed Assets	4	N/A	1
Current Assets	73	69	47

Doug Taylor Metal Finishing
Unit 10 Knightcott Indl-Est, Banwell, BS29 6JN
Tel: 01934-820454 **Fax:** 01934- 824058
E-mail: doug-taylor@btconnect.com
Website: http://www.dougtaylor.co.uk
Directors: D. Taylor (Prop)
Date established: 1980 **No.of Employees:** 1 - 10 **Product Groups:** 46, 48

Wessex Test Equipment Ltd
Unit 11 Knightcott Industrial Estate, Banwell, BS29 6JN
Tel: 01934-824000 **Fax:** 01934-820532
E-mail: sales@wessextestequipment.co.uk
Website: http://www.wessextestequipment.co.uk
Directors: J. Mackenzie (Dir)
Ultimate Holding Company: NORTHEND (HOLDINGS) LIMITED
Immediate Holding Company: WESSEX TEST EQUIPMENT LIMITED
Registration no: 06827398 **Date established:** 2009
Turnover: £250,000 - £500,000 **No.of Employees:** 1 - 10
Product Groups: 38, 42, 67

Date of Accounts	Mar 11	Feb 10
Working Capital	-38	N/A
Fixed Assets	93	N/A
Current Assets	437	N/A

Bath

Avery Knight & Bowlers Engineering Ltd
34 James Street West, Bath, BA1 2BT
Tel: 01225-425894 **Fax:** 01225-445753
E-mail: sales@averyknight.co.uk
Website: http://www.averyknight.co.uk
Managers: S. Page (Sales Prom Mgr)
Ultimate Holding Company: BOWLERS ENGINEERING SUPPLIES LIMITED
Immediate Holding Company: AVERY KNIGHT & BOWLERS ENGINEERING LIMITED
Registration no: 01069468 **Date established:** 1972
Turnover: £500,000 - £1m **No.of Employees:** 11 - 20
Product Groups: 34, 35, 36, 38, 39, 42, 43, 49, 66

Date of Accounts	Dec 11	Dec 10	Dec 09
Working Capital	195	223	225
Fixed Assets	5	6	8
Current Assets	306	326	311

B M T Defence Services
210 Lower Bristol Road, Bath, BA2 3DQ
Tel: 01225-473555 **Fax:** 01225- 339665
E-mail: info@bmtdsl.co.uk
Website: http://www.bmt-defence.com
Directors: G. Turner (Co Sec)
Ultimate Holding Company: BMT GROUP LIMITED
Immediate Holding Company: BMT MARINE PROJECTS LIMITED
Registration no: 03100016 **Date established:** 1995
Turnover: £500,000 - £1m **No.of Employees:** 101 - 250
Product Groups: 84

Date of Accounts	Sep 11	Sep 10	Sep 09
Sales Turnover	946	13m	9m
Pre Tax Profit/Loss	403	4m	2m
Working Capital	238	4m	1m
Fixed Assets	5	5	6
Current Assets	280	6m	7m
Current Liabilities	15	1m	4m

B S A Bath
91 Mount Road Southdown, Bath, BA2 1LL
Tel: 01225-313088 **Fax:** 01225-303341
E-mail: len@bsabath.co.uk
Website: http://www.bsabath.co.uk
Directors: L. Gunstone (MD)
Immediate Holding Company: B.S.A. (BATH) LTD
Registration no: 04768453 **Date established:** 2003
Turnover: Up to £250,000 **No.of Employees:** 1 - 10 **Product Groups:** 37, 40, 67

Date of Accounts	Aug 11	Aug 10	Aug 09
Working Capital	-25	-17	-20
Fixed Assets	13	17	20
Current Assets	29	35	37

Buro Happold Consulting Engineers Ltd
Camden Mill Lower Bristol Road, Bath, BA2 3DQ
Tel: 01225-320600 **Fax:** 01225-320601
E-mail: enquiries@burohappold.com
Website: http://www.burohappold.com
Bank(s): National Westminster Bank Plc
Directors: D. Wookey (Fin), G. Thompson (MD), F. Berredjem (Pers)
Managers: R. Davies (Mktg Serv Mgr), M. Williamson (Fin Mgr)
Ultimate Holding Company: HAPPOLD LLP
Immediate Holding Company: BURO HAPPOLD CONSULTING ENGINEERS LIMITED
Registration no: 02005673 **VAT No.:** GB 639 4230 34
Date established: 1986 **Turnover:** £10m - £20m
No.of Employees: 251 - 500 **Product Groups:** 84

Date of Accounts	Apr 11	Apr 10	Apr 09
Sales Turnover	12m	12m	17m
Pre Tax Profit/Loss	202	307	158
Working Capital	1m	2m	1m
Fixed Assets	190	131	153
Current Assets	10m	8m	8m
Current Liabilities	3m	3m	2m

Candlelight Table Mats
11 Combe Park, Bath, BA1 3NP
Tel: 01225-470129
E-mail: richardcook1@hotmail.com
Directors: R. Cook (Prop)
Turnover: Up to £250,000 **No.of Employees:** 1 - 10 **Product Groups:** 24, 25, 27, 30, 33, 67

Carillion plc
Green Park Road, Bath, BA1 1XH
Tel: 01225-428441 **Fax:** 01225-422577
E-mail: paul.reynolds@carillionplc.com
Website: http://www.carillionplc.com
Bank(s): Lloyds TSB Bank plc
Directors: P. Reynolds (MD)
Immediate Holding Company: CARILLION PLC
Registration no: 03782379 **VAT No.:** GB 222 8311 95
Date established: 1999 **Turnover:** £50m - £75m
No.of Employees: 51 - 100 **Product Groups:** 52

Date of Accounts	Dec 11	Dec 10	Dec 09
Sales Turnover	4153m	4237m	4504m
Pre Tax Profit/Loss	143m	168m	148m
Working Capital	-188m	-284m	-413m
Fixed Assets	2030m	1658m	1722m
Current Assets	1669m	1494m	1348m
Current Liabilities	1083m	1119m	1120m

Circuits Manufacture
2 Wansdyke Business Centre Oldfield Lane, Bath, BA2 3LY
Tel: 01225-758250 **Fax:** 01225- 758251
Directors: D. Watson (Prop)
Immediate Holding Company: CIRCUIT MANUFACTURE LTD
Registration no: 04909250 **Date established:** 2003
No.of Employees: 11 - 20 **Product Groups:** 36, 37

Cost-A-Call Ltd
De Montalt WD Summer Lane Combe Down, Bath, BA2 7EU
Tel: 01225-835799 **Fax:** 01225-835998
E-mail: charles@kentel.co.uk
Website: http://www.gophones.co.uk
Directors: C. Kent (MD)
Immediate Holding Company: COST-A-CALL LIMITED
Registration no: 01568990 **Date established:** 1981
Turnover: Up to £250,000 **No.of Employees:** 1 - 10 **Product Groups:** 37

Date of Accounts	Sep 11	Sep 10	Sep 09
Working Capital	-10	-5	3
Fixed Assets	2	3	2
Current Assets	51	54	61
Current Liabilities	N/A	53	N/A

Dispatchit Couriers
11 Cheltenham Street, Bath, BA2 3EX
Tel: 01225-444443 **Fax:** 01225-461123
E-mail: dispatchit@btconnect.com
Website: http://www.dispatchit.com
Directors: D. Scaramanga (Prop)
Immediate Holding Company: PARKERS PRIVATE HIRE LIMITED
Registration no: 04206549 **Date established:** 2011
Turnover: Up to £250,000 **No.of Employees:** 1 - 10 **Product Groups:** 79

Date of Accounts	Apr 08	Apr 07	Apr 06
Sales Turnover	192	N/A	N/A
Pre Tax Profit/Loss	21	N/A	N/A
Working Capital	46	31	19
Fixed Assets	8	6	6
Current Assets	62	50	66
Current Liabilities	16	18	47

Drainage Castings - S J C Ltd
Unit 14 Brassmill Enterprise Centre, Bath, BA1 3JN
Tel: 01225-448003 **Fax:** 01225-448033
Website: http://www.drainagecastings-sjc.co.uk
Directors: L. Cook (Fin), S. Cook (MD)
Immediate Holding Company: DRAINAGE CASTINGS SJC LIMITED
Registration no: 04596605 **Date established:** 2002
Turnover: £250,000 - £500,000 **No.of Employees:** 1 - 10
Product Groups: 30, 34, 35, 36, 83

Date of Accounts	Mar 11	Mar 10	Mar 09
Sales Turnover	N/A	349	376
Pre Tax Profit/Loss	N/A	43	48
Working Capital	-16	-3	4
Fixed Assets	35	36	38
Current Assets	56	63	73
Current Liabilities	N/A	17	14

Eco Technical Services Ltd
2 Bailbrook Court Bailbrook Lane Bath, Bath, BA1 7AB
Tel: 01225-852395 **Fax:** 01225-852066
E-mail: ken@ecotechnical.co.uk
Website: http://www.ecotechnical.com
Directors: K. Kohut (MD)
Immediate Holding Company: ECO TECHNICAL SERVICES LTD
Registration no: 03410048 **Date established:** 1997
No.of Employees: 1 - 10 **Product Groups:** 39

Date of Accounts	Dec 11	Dec 10	Dec 09
Working Capital	-73	-41	-31
Fixed Assets	93	57	32
Current Assets	39	138	53

Endeavour International Ltd
Unit 13 The Maltings Industrial Estate Brassmill Lane, Bath, BA1 3JL
Tel: 01225-446770 **Fax:** 01225-446775
E-mail: sales@endeavourinternational.co.uk
Website: http://www.endeavourinternational.ltd.uk
Bank(s): Barclays, Bristol
Directors: S. Turtle (Dir)
Ultimate Holding Company: E I HOLDINGS LIMITED
Immediate Holding Company: ENDEAVOUR INTERNATIONAL LTD
Registration no: 01947295 **VAT No.:** GB 520 4621 88
Date established: 1985 **Turnover:** £1m - £2m **No.of Employees:** 11 - 20
Product Groups: 36, 46

Date of Accounts	Mar 12	Mar 11	Mar 10
Working Capital	836	879	770
Fixed Assets	7	8	11
Current Assets	1m	1m	1m

ERIKS Industrial Services Limited (Bath Electro Mechanical)
Electro Mechanical Service Centre Brassmill Lane Trading Estate, Bath, BA1 3JF
Tel: 01225-426258 **Fax:** 01225-445372
E-mail: bath.repair@eriks.co.uk
Website: http://www.eriks.co.uk
Managers: S. Lewis (Ops Mgr), A. Thompson (Sales Admin)
Registration no: 03142338 **Turnover:** £250m - £500m
No.of Employees: 21 - 50 **Product Groups:** 35

Eureka Software Ltd
Overleigh House Southstoke Road, Bath, BA2 5SJ
Tel: 01225-840022 **Fax:** 07876-867230
E-mail: sales@eurekasoftware.co.uk
Website: http://www.eurekasoftware.co.uk
Directors: G. Evans (Sales), S. Newman (Mkt Research), D. Evans (Sales)
Registration no: 04371195 **Date established:** 1902
Turnover: £500,000 - £1m **No.of Employees:** 1 - 10 **Product Groups:** 44

Date of Accounts	Feb 06
Working Capital	14
Fixed Assets	3
Current Assets	36
Current Liabilities	22

Future Publishing Ltd
30 Monmouth Street, Bath, BA1 2BW
Tel: 01225-442244 **Fax:** 01225-446019
E-mail: mark.wood@futurenet.com
Website: http://www.futurenet.com
Directors: M. Millar (Dir), J. Caple (Adv), M. Wood (Grp Chief Exec), J. Bowman (Fin)
Managers: R. Dark (Purch Mgr)
Ultimate Holding Company: FUTURE PLC
Immediate Holding Company: FUTURE PUBLISHING HOLDINGS LIMITED
Registration no: 03430449 **Date established:** 1997
Turnover: £125m - £250m **No.of Employees:** 501 - 1000
Product Groups: 28

Date of Accounts	Sep 11	Sep 10	Sep 09
Pre Tax Profit/Loss	103	104	133
Working Capital	-11m	-11m	-11m
Current Assets	3m	3m	3m

Helphire
Pinesgate Lower Bristol Road, Bath, BA2 3DP
Tel: 01225-321000 **Fax:** 01225-321100
E-mail: sales@helphire.co.uk
Website: http://www.helphire.co.uk
Directors: M. Simmonds (Dir), N. Tilley (Dir)
Ultimate Holding Company: HELPHIRE GROUP PLC.
Immediate Holding Company: HELPHIRE FINANCE LIMITED
Registration no: 03069954 **Date established:** 1995
Turnover: £50m - £75m **No.of Employees:** 501 - 1000
Product Groups: 72

Date of Accounts	Sep 08	Jun 11	Jun 10
Sales Turnover	7m	235m	304m
Pre Tax Profit/Loss	22m	-34m	392
Working Capital	114m	-26m	72m
Fixed Assets	90m	89m	137m
Current Assets	178m	126m	202m
Current Liabilities	14m	25m	47m

Huggett Automation & Control
Twerton Mill Lower Bristol Road, Bath, BA2 1EW
Tel: 01225-426271 **Fax:** 01225-448154
E-mail: mail@huggettelectrical.co.uk
Website: http://www.huggettelectrical.co.uk
Bank(s): National Westminster
Managers: S. Corradi (Chief Mgr)
Immediate Holding Company: HUGGETT ELECTRICAL LIMITED
Registration no: 00840290 **VAT No.:** GB 137 7869 20
Date established: 1965 **Turnover:** £1m - £2m **No.of Employees:** 11 - 20
Product Groups: 37

Date of Accounts	Mar 08	Mar 07	Mar 06
Working Capital	-476	-618	-598
Fixed Assets	954	954	956
Current Assets	342	476	254

Hurley Engine Services Ltd
7 The Maltings Industrial Estate Brassmill Lane, Bath, BA1 3JL
Tel: 01225-336812 **Fax:** 01225-442477
E-mail: info@hurleyengines.co.uk
Website: http://www.hurleyengines.co.uk
Directors: P. Hurley (Fin)
Immediate Holding Company: HURLEY ENGINE SERVICES LIMITED
Registration no: 01897892 **VAT No.:** GB 138 8997 00
Date established: 1985 **Turnover:** £1m - £2m **No.of Employees:** 11 - 20
Product Groups: 48

Date of Accounts	Apr 11	Apr 10	Apr 09
Working Capital	48	3	37
Fixed Assets	44	56	73
Current Assets	252	213	211

I P L Information Processing Ltd
Eveleigh House Grove Street, Bath, BA1 5LR
Tel: 01225-475000 **Fax:** 01225-444400
E-mail: sean.davey@ipl.com
Website: http://www.ipl.com
Bank(s): National Westminster Bank Plc
Managers: S. Davey
Ultimate Holding Company: IPL GROUP LIMITED
Immediate Holding Company: IPL SOFTWARE PRODUCTS LTD.
Registration no: 02897354 **VAT No.:** GB 601 2931 83
Date established: 1994 **Turnover:** Up to £250,000
No.of Employees: 251 - 500 **Product Groups:** 44

Date of Accounts	Sep 11	Sep 10	Sep 09
Sales Turnover	62	132	187
Pre Tax Profit/Loss	63	138	238
Working Capital	606	555	430
Current Assets	618	568	462
Current Liabilities	12	13	32

Impact Plants
37 Eastbourne Avenue, Bath, BA1 6EN
Tel: 01225-447962 **Fax:** 01225-447962
E-mail: enquiries@impactplants.co.uk
Website: http://www.impactplants.co.uk
Directors: C. Greenway (Fin), J. Ingham (Dir)
Immediate Holding Company: BATH SPECIALIST GARDENS LIMITED
Registration no: 02288599 **Date established:** 1988
Turnover: Up to £250,000 **No.of Employees:** 1 - 10 **Product Groups:** 02, 29, 30, 35, 62

Date of Accounts	Sep 11	Sep 10	Sep 09
Working Capital	5	3	1
Current Assets	19	6	3

Information Technology Infrastructure Ltd
12 Pierrepont Street, Bath, BA1 1LA
Tel: 01225-313549 **Fax:** 01225-448620
E-mail: enquiries@itiltd.co.uk
Website: http://www.itiltd.co.uk
Directors: M. Groves (MD)
Immediate Holding Company: INFORMATION TECHNOLOGY INFRASTRUCTURE LIMITED
Registration no: 04002956 **Date established:** 2000
Turnover: Up to £250,000 **No.of Employees:** 1 - 10 **Product Groups:** 44

Date of Accounts	Mar 12	Mar 11	Mar 10
Working Capital	23	35	19
Fixed Assets	14	8	6
Current Assets	84	97	67

Ironart Of Bath
Upper Lambridge Street, Bath, BA1 6RY
Tel: 01225-311273
Website: http://www.ironart.co.uk
Directors: A. Thearle (Dir)
Date established: 1970 **No.of Employees:** 1 - 10 **Product Groups:** 26, 35

Kelston Forge
5 Bath Road Kelston, Bath, BA1 9AQ
Tel: 01225-319046 **Fax:** 01225-319046
Directors: J. Holder (Prop), J. Holder (Prop)
Date established: 1976 **No.of Employees:** 1 - 10 **Product Groups:** 26, 35

Keynsham Welding
Unit 6a Timsbury Industrial Estate Hayeswood Road, Timsbury, Bath, BA2 0HQ
Tel: 0117-986 7971 **Fax:** 0117-986 7971
E-mail: info@keynshamwelding.co.uk
Website: http://www.keynshamwelding.co.uk
Directors: R. Pope (Prop)
Date established: 1982 **No.of Employees:** 1 - 10 **Product Groups:** 26, 35

Lambeth Comutators
Brassmill Lane Trading Estate, Bath, BA1 3JF
Tel: 01225-426250 **Fax:** 01225-445372
E-mail: stuart.lewis@eriks.co.uk
Website: http://www.eriks.co.uk
Managers: S. Lewis (Mgr)
Ultimate Holding Company: WYKO LTD
Registration no: 00161905 **Turnover:** £500,000 - £1m
No.of Employees: 1 - 10 **Product Groups:** 37

Lucas & Weston Ltd
3 Gay Street, Bath, BA1 2PH
Tel: 01225-460777 **Fax:** 01225-329812
E-mail: ask@lucasweston.com
Website: http://www.lucasweston.com
Directors: J. Weston (Dir)
Immediate Holding Company: LUCAS & WESTON LIMITED
Registration no: 05113980 **Date established:** 2004
No.of Employees: 1 - 10 **Product Groups:** 80

Date of Accounts	Mar 12	Mar 11	Mar 10
Working Capital	-18	10	-2
Fixed Assets	18	9	2
Current Assets	21	74	15

Milsom Industrial Designs Ltd
11 Kelso Place Upper Bristol Road, Bath, BA1 3AU
Tel: 01225-444809 **Fax:** 01225-444787
E-mail: info@milsom.uk.com
Website: http://www.milsom.uk.com
Directors: R. Horgan (Comm), D. Sharp (Dir), K. Crawford (Co Sec)
Ultimate Holding Company: GP STRATEGIES CORP (USA)
Immediate Holding Company: MILSOM INDUSTRIAL DESIGNS LIMITED
Registration no: 02083473 **Date established:** 1986 **Turnover:** £5m - £10m
No.of Employees: 21 - 50 **Product Groups:** 44, 84, 87

Date of Accounts	Dec 11	Dec 10	Dec 09
Sales Turnover	7m	7m	352
Pre Tax Profit/Loss	463	764	730
Working Capital	2m	1m	748
Fixed Assets	91	90	104
Current Assets	2m	2m	1m
Current Liabilities	355	461	514

N E Old Ironwork
Timsbury Industrial Estate Hayeswood Road, Timsbury, Bath, BA2 0HQ
Tel: 01761-472773 **Fax:** 01761-472773
Directors: R. Hawtin (Prop)
Immediate Holding Company: N E OLD IRONWORK LIMITED
Registration no: 05935453 **Date established:** 2006
No.of Employees: 1 - 10 **Product Groups:** 26, 35

Date of Accounts	Sep 11	Sep 10	Sep 09
Working Capital	-3	4	39
Fixed Assets	15	18	23
Current Assets	68	81	81

P C P Micro Products Ltd
18 St Peters Terrace, Bath, BA2 3BT
Tel: 01225-480888 **Fax:** 01225-483232
E-mail: info@electrocoin.net
Website: http://www.pcpmicro.co.uk
Managers: K. Weir (Admin Off)
Immediate Holding Company: P.C.P. MICRO PRODUCTS (DEV) LIMITED
Registration no: 02798448 **Date established:** 1993
Turnover: Up to £250,000 **No.of Employees:** 1 - 10 **Product Groups:** 44

Date of Accounts	Jun 11	Jun 10	Jun 09
Working Capital	229	237	252
Fixed Assets	102	104	105
Current Assets	239	249	262

Parragon Books Ltd
4 Queen Street, Bath, BA1 1HE
Tel: 01225-478888 **Fax:** 01225-443681
E-mail: ukinfo@parragon.com
Website: http://www.parragon.com
Bank(s): Barclays
Directors: D. Monk (Tech Serv), P. Taylor (Dir), S. Staunton (Co Sec)
Managers: I. Tyer, S. Bailey, C. Williams (Personnel)
Ultimate Holding Company: D.C. THOMSON & COMPANY. LIMITED
Immediate Holding Company: PARRAGON BOOKS LIMITED
Registration no: 02252808 **VAT No.:** GB 520 0885 74
Date established: 1988 **Turnover:** £50m - £75m
No.of Employees: 101 - 250 **Product Groups:** 28

Date of Accounts	Mar 11	Mar 10	Mar 09
Sales Turnover	57m	59m	63m
Pre Tax Profit/Loss	2m	143	-445
Working Capital	32m	37m	36m
Fixed Assets	246	337	466
Current Assets	48m	50m	61m
Current Liabilities	9m	7m	6m

Roger J Perry
Heather Farm Lansdown Lane, Bath, BA1 4NA
Tel: 01225-421531 **Fax:** 01225-445974
Directors: R. Perry (Prop)
Date established: 1980 **No.of Employees:** 1 - 10 **Product Groups:** 41

Phil Weeks Factors
151 Locksbrook Road, Bath, BA1 3EU
Tel: 01225-312177 **Fax:** 01225-333304
E-mail: weldingmachines@tiscali.co.uk
Website: http://www.philweeksweldingmachines.co.uk
Directors: P. Weeks (Prop)
Date established: 1993 **No.of Employees:** 1 - 10 **Product Groups:** 46

Polamco Ltd
Weston Lock Retail Lower Bristol Road, Bath, BA2 1EP
Tel: 01225-322500 **Fax:** 01225-425940
E-mail: sales@polamco.co.uk
Website: http://www.polamco.co.uk
Bank(s): Lloyds TSB
Directors: D. Payne (Fin)
Managers: B. Wilson (Purch Mgr), M. Wheeler (Sales Prom Mgr), T. Roberts (Tech Serv Mgr)
Immediate Holding Company: POLAMCO LIMITED
Registration no: 01784597 **VAT No.:** GB 398 8626 74
Date established: 1984 **Turnover:** £5m - £10m
No.of Employees: 51 - 100 **Product Groups:** 27, 30, 37, 39, 47

Date of Accounts	May 11	May 10	May 09
Sales Turnover	10m	8m	8m
Pre Tax Profit/Loss	330	458	534
Working Capital	2m	2m	2m
Fixed Assets	2m	1m	1m
Current Assets	4m	3m	3m
Current Liabilities	461	532	494

Portals Bathford Ltd
Bathford Paper Mill Bathford, Bath, BA1 7QG
Tel: 01225-859903 **Fax:** 01225-852128
E-mail: laura.redmanthomas@uk.delarue.com
Website: http://www.uk.delarue.com
Directors: M. Bryant (MD), R. Gardiner (MD), C. Driscoll (Co Sec)
Managers: M. Brian (Chief Mgr), L. Redman-Thomas (Chief Mgr)
Ultimate Holding Company: De La Rue plc
Immediate Holding Company: PORTALS (BATHFORD) LIMITED
Registration no: 00120528 **VAT No.:** GB 238 9404 40
Date established: 1912 **Turnover:** £10m - £20m
No.of Employees: 101 - 250 **Product Groups:** 27

Date of Accounts	Mar 08	Mar 07
Working Capital	150	150
Current Assets	150	150
Total Share Capital	90	90

Practical Metalwork
73 Rush Hill, Bath, BA2 2QT
Tel: 01225-318818 **Fax:** 01225-318818
E-mail: paul@practicalmetalwork.co.uk
Website: http://www.practicalmetalwork.co.uk
Directors: P. Vowles (Prop)
Date established: 2002 **No.of Employees:** 1 - 10 **Product Groups:** 35

professional hypnosis and hypnotherapy in bath
38 Gay Street 29 Brock Street, Bath, BA1 2NT
Tel: 01225-580557
E-mail: daniel@bathhypnotherapist.co.uk
Website: http://bathhypnotherapist.co.uk
Directors: D. Nuttall (Dir)
Date established: 2005 **Turnover:** Up to £250,000
No.of Employees: 1 - 10 **Product Groups:** 88

Radan
Limpley Mill Limpley Stoke, Bath, BA2 7FJ
Tel: 01225-721330 **Fax:** 01225-721333
E-mail: sales@uk.radan.com
Website: http://www.radan.com
Bank(s): National Westminster Bank Plc
Directors: C. Aston (Chief Op Offcr), C. Cooper (Dir), J. Lee (Fin), K. O'Conner (Dir), R. Franks (Dir), R. Billett (Non Exec)
Ultimate Holding Company: Velocity Holdings Ltd
Immediate Holding Company: Planit Holdings Ltd
Registration no: 01282479 **VAT No.:** GB 140 4813 00
Date established: 1976 **Turnover:** £1m - £2m **No.of Employees:** 21 - 50
Product Groups: 44

Redlaw
51 Newbridge Road, Bath, BA1 3HF
Tel: 01225-310309 **Fax:** 01225-423422
Directors: C. Batten (Dir)
Immediate Holding Company: BARCOL-AIR (UK) LTD
Date established: 1991 **No.of Employees:** 1 - 10 **Product Groups:** 40, 66

Date of Accounts	Dec 11	Dec 10	Dec 09
Working Capital	241	192	352
Fixed Assets	6	7	2
Current Assets	337	466	667

Reed Employment Ltd
Third Floor Upper Borough Court Upper Borough Walls, Bath, BA1 1RG
Tel: 01225-421314
Website: http://www.reed.co.uk
Ultimate Holding Company: REED GLOBAL LTD (MALTA)
Immediate Holding Company: REED EMPLOYMENT LIMITED
Registration no: 00669854 **Date established:** 1960
No.of Employees: 1 - 10 **Product Groups:** 80

Date of Accounts	Jun 11	Jun 10	Dec 07
Sales Turnover	618	450	287m
Pre Tax Profit/Loss	-2m	310	8m
Working Capital	23m	28m	28m
Fixed Assets	31	36	5m
Current Assets	28m	30m	74m
Current Liabilities	37	29	21m

Rotork plc

Brassmill Lane, Bath, BA1 3JQ
Tel: 01225-733200 **Fax:** 01225-333467
E-mail: information@rotork.com
Website: http://www.rotork.com
Bank(s): Barclays
Directors: R. Lockwood (Ch), A. Spurr (Chief Op Offcr), C. Elvira (Sales & Mktg)
Managers: P. France, P. Wood (I.T. Exec)
Immediate Holding Company: Rotork P.L.C.
Registration no: 00608345 **VAT No.:** GB 137 4855 46
Date established: 1958 **Turnover:** £250m - £500m
No.of Employees: 1001 - 1500 **Product Groups:** 35, 36, 37, 38, 39, 40

Date of Accounts	Dec 11	Dec 10	Dec 09
Sales Turnover	112m	96m	88m
Pre Tax Profit/Loss	47m	36m	28m
Working Capital	19m	18m	20m
Fixed Assets	18m	15m	14m
Current Assets	109m	84m	61m
Current Liabilities	46m	14m	7m

Schulte & Loughborough Electro Systems Ltd

32 Prospect Place Camden Road, Bath, BA1 5JD
Tel: 01225-330242 **Fax:** 01225-448848
E-mail: info@sl-electro.co.uk
Website: http://www.sl-electro.co.uk
Managers: B. Cullum (Ops Mgr)
Immediate Holding Company: SCHULTE AND LOUGHBOROUGH ELECTRO SYSTEMS LIMITED
Registration no: 01931138 **Date established:** 1985
No.of Employees: 1 - 10 **Product Groups:** 36, 40

Date of Accounts	Dec 11	Dec 10	Sep 09
Working Capital	222	192	144
Fixed Assets	4	2	5
Current Assets	371	360	416

Stone Vineyard

23 Dorset Street, Bath, BA2 3RA
Tel: 01225-789974 **Fax:** 01225-345043
E-mail: kirsty@stonevineyard.co.uk
Website: http://www.stonevineyard.co.uk
Directors: K. Whittle (Ptnr)
Turnover: Up to £250,000 **No.of Employees:** 1 - 10 **Product Groups:** 49, 64

Steve Vick International Ltd

Pines Way, Bath, BA2 3ET
Tel: 01225-480488 **Fax:** 01225-480484
E-mail: info@stevevick.com
Website: http://www.stevevick.com
Bank(s): HSBC Bank plc
Directors: A. Day (Fin), S. Vick (MD)
Immediate Holding Company: STEVE VICK INTERNATIONAL LIMITED
Registration no: 01564477 **VAT No.:** GB 543 4915 39
Date established: 1981 **Turnover:** £2m - £5m **No.of Employees:** 21 - 50
Product Groups: 45, 52, 54

Date of Accounts	Jun 11	Jun 10	Jun 09
Working Capital	921	690	636
Fixed Assets	155	206	152
Current Assets	2m	2m	2m

Wessexwater Ltd

Operations Centre Claverton Down Road, Claverton Down, Bath, BA2 7WW
Tel: 01225-526000 **Fax:** 01225-528000
E-mail: customer.services@wessexwater.co.uk
Website: http://www.wessexwater.co.uk
Directors: M. Watts (Fin), A. Phillips (Co Sec), C. Skelett (Grp Chief Exec)
Managers: J. Craddock (Buyer), M. Smith (Mktg Serv Mgr), M. Nicholson (Personnel), G. Hunt
Ultimate Holding Company: YTL CORPORATION BERHAD (MALAYSIA)
Immediate Holding Company: WESSEX WATER SERVICES LIMITED
Registration no: 02366648 **VAT No.:** 567 7800 03 **Date established:** 1989
Turnover: £250m - £500m **No.of Employees:** 1501 & over
Product Groups: 18

Date of Accounts	Jun 12	Jun 11	Jun 10
Sales Turnover	475m	451m	437m
Pre Tax Profit/Loss	134m	151m	156m
Working Capital	104m	-61m	6m
Fixed Assets	2084m	2018m	2003m
Current Assets	344m	148m	195m
Current Liabilities	133m	138m	84m

Woodcott Signs

16 Holcombe Lane, Bathampton,, Bath, BA2 6UL
Tel: 07775-503401
E-mail: rob@woodcott.net
Website: http://www.woodcott.net
Directors: A. George (Ptnr), R. Eyley (Ptnr)
Registration no: 04956287 **Date established:** 2003
Turnover: Up to £250,000 **No.of Employees:** 1 - 10 **Product Groups:** 49

Bristol

A C Services Southern Ltd

Unit 12-13 Dean Court Great Western Business Park Yate, Bristol, BS37 5NJ
Tel: 01454-322222 **Fax:** 01454-850232
E-mail: service@acservicessouthern.co.uk
Website: http://www.acservicessouthern.co.uk
Directors: H. Hagger (Dir)
Immediate Holding Company: AC SERVICES (SOUTHERN) LIMITED
Registration no: 04054837 **Date established:** 2000
No.of Employees: 1 - 10 **Product Groups:** 20, 40, 41

Date of Accounts	Sep 11	Sep 10	Sep 09
Working Capital	85	33	53
Fixed Assets	29	31	33
Current Assets	192	146	168

ADT Fire & Security plc

180 Aztec West Almondsbury, Bristol, BS32 4TU
Tel: 0800-542 3108 **Fax:** 01454-843484
Website: http://www.adt.co.uk
Directors: B. Mumford (Sales & Mktg), H. Jones (Fin), J. Nixon (Grp Chief Exec)
Managers: P. O'Meara (Chief Mgr)
Ultimate Holding Company: TYCO INTERNATIONAL LIMITED (SWITZERLAND)
Immediate Holding Company: ADT FIRE AND SECURITY PLC
Registration no: 01161045 **Date established:** 1974
No.of Employees: 21 - 50 **Product Groups:** 37, 38, 40, 47, 52, 81

Date of Accounts	Sep 11	Sep 08	Sep 09
Sales Turnover	363m	414m	384m
Pre Tax Profit/Loss	18m	4m	10m
Working Capital	450m	618m	561m
Fixed Assets	120m	193m	171m
Current Assets	710m	765m	722m
Current Liabilities	81m	57m	42m

A L D Automotive Ltd

Oakwood Park Lodge Causeway, Bristol, BS16 3JA
Tel: 0117-908 2000 **Fax:** 0117-908 9000
E-mail: david.yates@aldautomotive.com
Website: http://www.aldautomotive.co.uk
Directors: D. Yates (Mkt Research), D. Barer (Tech Serv), T. Laver (Fin)
Managers: N. Fletcher, J. Monk (Personnel)
Ultimate Holding Company: SOCIETE GENERALE
Immediate Holding Company: ALD AUTOMOTIVE LIMITED
Registration no: 00987418 **Date established:** 1970
Turnover: £125m - £250m **No.of Employees:** 251 - 500
Product Groups: 82

Date of Accounts	Dec 11	Dec 10	Dec 09
Sales Turnover	219m	175m	153m
Pre Tax Profit/Loss	17m	14m	7m
Working Capital	-120m	-114m	-53m
Fixed Assets	561m	391m	258m
Current Assets	227m	206m	183m
Current Liabilities	34m	30m	35m

A O N Hewitt

25 Marsh House Marsh Street, Bristol, BS1 4AQ
Tel: 0117-929 4001 **Fax:** 0117-925 0188
E-mail: richard.cox@ars.aon.co.uk
Website: http://www.aon.com
Bank(s): National Westminster Bank Plc
Managers: R. Cox (Bldg Mgr)
Ultimate Holding Company: AON CORPORATION INC (USA)
Immediate Holding Company: A1 VENTURES LIMITED
Registration no: 04578543 **VAT No.:** GB 508 9239 26
Date established: 2002 **Turnover:** £10m - £20m
No.of Employees: 51 - 100 **Product Groups:** 82

A P Burt & Sons Ltd

Severn Paper Mill Portishead, Bristol, BS20 7DJ
Tel: 01275-842454 **Fax:** 01275-849613
E-mail: sales@apburt.co.uk
Website: http://www.apburt.co.uk
Bank(s): National Westminster Bank Plc
Directors: J. Nicholls (MD)
Ultimate Holding Company: CLONDALKIN GROUP HOLDINGS BV (NETHERLANDS)
Immediate Holding Company: A.P. BURT & SONS, LIMITED
Registration no: 00282209 **VAT No.:** GB 137 4314 80
Date established: 1933 **Turnover:** £5m - £10m
No.of Employees: 51 - 100 **Product Groups:** 27, 30

Date of Accounts	Dec 11	Dec 10	Dec 09
Sales Turnover	7m	7m	7m
Pre Tax Profit/Loss	409	534	530
Working Capital	2m	2m	2m
Fixed Assets	2m	2m	2m
Current Assets	3m	4m	4m
Current Liabilities	601	659	657

Aaron Metal & Plastic Supplies Ltd

Unit 7-8 Barnack Trading Centre Novers Hill, Bedminster, Bristol, BS3 5QE
Tel: 0117-923 1988 **Fax:** 0117-923 1469
E-mail: info@aaronmetals.co.uk
Directors: J. Bowker (Dir)
Immediate Holding Company: AARON METAL & PLASTIC SUPPLIES LIMITED
Registration no: 02313648 **Date established:** 1988
Turnover: £250,000 - £500,000 **No.of Employees:** 1 - 10
Product Groups: 23, 24, 27, 28, 29, 30, 31, 34, 35, 36, 37, 39, 40, 42, 44, 46, 48, 49, 66, 67, 84

Date of Accounts	Sep 11	Sep 10	Sep 09
Working Capital	34	28	9
Fixed Assets	100	101	103
Current Assets	146	140	120

Abbey Products Ltd

6 Avon Gorge Industrial Estate Portview Road, Bristol, BS11 9LQ
Tel: 0117-938 1666 **Fax:** 0117-316 7024
E-mail: sales@abbeyproducts.co.uk
Website: http://www.abbeyproducts.co.uk
Managers: J. Gamam (Prod Eng)
Immediate Holding Company: ABBEY PRODUCTS LIMITED
Registration no: 02875980 **Date established:** 1993 **Turnover:** £1m - £2m
No.of Employees: 1 - 10 **Product Groups:** 25

Date of Accounts	Mar 12	Mar 11	Mar 10
Working Capital	100	185	193
Fixed Assets	1	1	1
Current Assets	139	207	235

Ace Systems Ltd

Unit 3 Rose Green Road, Bristol, BS5 7UW
Tel: 0117-952 0624 **Fax:** 0117-935 4255
E-mail: sales@acesystems.ltd.uk
Website: http://www.acesystems.ltd.uk
Bank(s): Barclays
Directors: S. Sperrings (Dir)
Immediate Holding Company: ACE SYSTEMS LIMITED
Registration no: 01657471 **Date established:** 1982 **Turnover:** £1m - £2m
No.of Employees: 11 - 20 **Product Groups:** 26, 52, 80

Date of Accounts	Sep 11	Sep 10	Sep 09
Working Capital	84	-17	-154
Fixed Assets	91	68	166
Current Assets	509	323	193

Action Products Ltd

270 North Road Yate, Bristol, BS37 7LQ
Tel: 01454-228702 **Fax:** 01454-228703
E-mail: info@action-products.co.uk
Website: http://www.action-products.co.uk
Directors: I. Mogridge (Dir)
Immediate Holding Company: ACTION PRODUCTS LIMITED
Registration no: 02791518 **Date established:** 1993
No.of Employees: 1 - 10 **Product Groups:** 32

Date of Accounts	Feb 11	Feb 10	Feb 08
Working Capital	-113	-113	-103
Fixed Assets	38	40	45
Current Assets	4	3	6

Activ-Air Automation Ltd

Unit 8 Birchills Trading Estate Emery Road, Bristol, BS4 5PF
Tel: 0117-977 7616 **Fax:** 0117-977 7664
E-mail: sales@activ-air.co.uk
Website: http://www.activ-air.co.uk
Managers: T. Cawley (District Mgr)
Immediate Holding Company: ACTIV-AIR AUTOMATION LIMITED
Registration no: 01512387 **Date established:** 1980
No.of Employees: 1 - 10 **Product Groups:** 36, 40, 67

Date of Accounts	Mar 11	Mar 10	Mar 09
Working Capital	185	160	133
Fixed Assets	766	732	743
Current Assets	1m	791	620

Adjust Procurment Solutions Ltd

5 Briar Close Nailsea, Bristol, BS48 1QG
Tel: 01275-790737 **Fax:** 08701-352725
E-mail: info@adjustps.com
Website: http://www.adjustps.com
Directors: R. Hatton (MD)
Immediate Holding Company: ADJUST PROCUREMENT SOLUTIONS LIMITED
Registration no: 04992026 **Date established:** 2003
No.of Employees: 1 - 10 **Product Groups:** 61

Date of Accounts	Dec 10	Dec 08	Dec 07
Working Capital	11	21	15
Fixed Assets	1	2	2
Current Assets	21	28	21

Advanced Commercial Kitchens Ltd

Advance Enterprise House Farrington Fields Trading Estate, Farrington Gurney, Bristol, BS39 6UU
Tel: 01761-453666 **Fax:** 01761-452343
E-mail: info@ack-wokcookers.com
Website: http://www.ack-wokcookers.com
Directors: C. Wong (MD)
Immediate Holding Company: ADVANCED COMMERCIAL KITCHENS LIMITED
Registration no: 02426685 **Date established:** 1989
Turnover: £75m - £125m **No.of Employees:** 1 - 10 **Product Groups:** 20, 40, 41

Date of Accounts	Apr 11	Apr 10	Apr 09
Working Capital	-13	-96	-1
Fixed Assets	20	21	6
Current Assets	110	83	198

Advanced Engineering

Farrington Fields Trading Estate Farrington Gurney, Bristol, BS39 6UU
Tel: 01761-451202 **Fax:** 01761-452343
E-mail: clive@wokcooker.fsnet.co.uk
Directors: Y. Wong (Prop)
Immediate Holding Company: MAILGREEN LIMITED
Registration no: 02237482 **Date established:** 2009
Turnover: £75m - £125m **No.of Employees:** 1 - 10 **Product Groups:** 20, 40, 41

Date of Accounts	Oct 11	Oct 10	Apr 10
Sales Turnover	101m	39m	76m
Pre Tax Profit/Loss	347	265	390
Working Capital	4m	4m	3m
Fixed Assets	2m	2m	2m
Current Assets	16m	13m	12m
Current Liabilities	2m	791	1m

Ainscough Crane Hire Ltd

Burcott Road, Bristol, BS11 8AB
Tel: 0117-982 8334 **Fax:** 0117-923 5769
E-mail: bristol@ainscough.co.uk
Website: http://www.ainscough.co.uk
Directors: M. Ainscough (MD), N. Partridge (Fin)
Ultimate Holding Company: BRADLEY HALL HOLDINGS LIMITED
Immediate Holding Company: AINSCOUGH CRANE HIRE LTD
Registration no: 03245223 **Date established:** 1996 **Turnover:** £2m - £5m
No.of Employees: 21 - 50 **Product Groups:** 45, 83

Date of Accounts	May 11	May 10	May 09
Sales Turnover	98m	110m	129m
Pre Tax Profit/Loss	11m	19m	30m
Working Capital	16m	72m	48m
Fixed Assets	152m	150m	149m
Current Assets	24m	81m	60m
Current Liabilities	8m	8m	10m

Aktion Automotive Ltd

Unit 18 Garonor Way Royal Portbury Dock, Portbury, Bristol, BS20 7XE
Tel: 029-2046 4668 **Fax:** 029-2046 4669
E-mail: parts@rollopowersolutions.co.uk
Website: http://www.rolluk.com
Directors: S. Jones (Fin)
Managers: P. Taylor (Chief Mgr), T. Coulson (Parts Mgr)
Registration no: 05000872 **Date established:** 2003
Turnover: £250,000 - £500,000 **No.of Employees:** 21 - 50
Product Groups: 40, 66, 67

Alansons Industrial Supplies

7 Flowers Hill, Bristol, BS4 5JJ
Tel: 0117-971 1364 **Fax:** 08707-773272
E-mail: sales@alansonsuk.com
Website: http://www.alansonsuk.com
Directors: A. Nunn (Ptnr)
Managers: A. Nunn (Mktg Serv Mgr), A. Nunn (Purch Mgr), D. Nunn (Accounts), R. Nunn (Sales Prom Mgr)
Immediate Holding Company: GEKKO INDUSTRIES LIMITED
Date established: 2011 **Turnover:** £1m - £2m **No.of Employees:** 1 - 10
Product Groups: 23, 27, 29, 30, 31, 32, 41, 42

Alder King

15 Pembroke Road Clifton, Bristol, BS8 3BA
Tel: 0117-317 1000 **Fax:** 0117-317 1001
E-mail: martyn.jones@alder-king.co.uk
Website: http://www.alderking.com

see next page

Alder King - Cont'd

Directors: G. Watson (Ptnr), A. Maynard (Dir), P. Barefoot (Dir)
Managers: M. Jones (Mgr)
Immediate Holding Company: ALDER KING LLP
Registration no: OC306796 **Date established:** 2004
Turnover: £10m - £20m **No.of Employees:** 51 - 100 **Product Groups:** 80

Alfia Services Ltd

Unit 4 Fiston Centre, Kingswood, Bristol, BS15 4GQ
Tel: 0117-918 1000 **Fax:** 0117-947 5533
E-mail: sales@alfia.co.uk
Website: http://www.alfia.co.uk
Bank(s): Barclays
Directors: C. Cook (Prop), C. Cook (MD), B. Ginnever (Dir), A. Burke (Fin), I. Elliott (Chief Op Offcr)
Managers: M. Sugg (Purch Mgr), R. Beard (Research & Deve), R. Johnson, P. Mawer, P. Gillespie (Sales Prom Mgr), A. Summers, M. Fugg (Purch Mgr)
Registration no: 02276171 **VAT No.:** GB 501 8048 80
Date established: 1988 **Turnover:** £2m - £5m **No.of Employees:** 51 - 100
Product Groups: 35, 39, 40, 44, 49, 80, 84

Allianz Legal Protection

Redwood House Brotherswood Court Great Park Road, Bradley Stoke, Bristol, BS32 4QW
Tel: 08702-434340 **Fax:** 01454-455601
E-mail: phil.ruse@allianz.co.uk
Website: http://www.allianz-ni.co.uk
Directors: C. Johnson (Fin)
Managers: P. Ruse (Mgr), G. Gould (Personnel)
Ultimate Holding Company: KHAZANAH NASIONAL BERHAD (MALAYSIA)
Immediate Holding Company: THE JOYNES PIKE GROUP LIMITED
Date established: 1988 **No.of Employees:** 101 - 250 **Product Groups:** 80, 82

Date of Accounts	Dec 10	Dec 09	Dec 08
Working Capital	1	1	1
Current Assets	1	1	1

Altaroute Ltd

10 North Road Yate, Bristol, BS37 7PA
Tel: 01454-311475 **Fax:** 01454-273065
E-mail: info@altaroute.com
Website: http://www.altaroute.com
Directors: J. Hobbs (Fin)
Immediate Holding Company: ALTAROUTE LIMITED
Registration no: 01381677 **VAT No.:** GB 302 7803 85
Date established: 1978 **No.of Employees:** 11 - 20 **Product Groups:** 37, 39

Date of Accounts	Nov 11	Nov 10	Nov 09
Working Capital	606	649	650
Fixed Assets	1m	1m	1m
Current Assets	817	851	952

Alto Digital

Liberty House South Liberty Lane, Bristol, BS3 2ST
Tel: 0117-902 1155 **Fax:** 0117-966 2606
E-mail: sales@victoriacopiers.com
Website: http://www.altodigital.com
Directors: A. Gardiner (Reg Sales), R. Walker (Reg Sales)
Immediate Holding Company: COURT CONSTRUCTION (BRISTOL) LIMITED
Registration no: 03152375 **Date established:** 1996
No.of Employees: 1 - 10 **Product Groups:** 27, 29, 30, 32, 37, 38, 41, 44, 48, 49, 67, 83

Date of Accounts	Mar 11	Mar 10	Mar 09
Working Capital	344	344	340
Fixed Assets	30	30	35
Current Assets	898	851	894

Amcor Flexibles

Winterbourne Road Bradley Stoke, Bristol, BS34 8PT
Tel: 0117-987 2000 **Fax:** 0117-987 2002
E-mail: keith.owen@amcor.com
Website: http://www.amcor.com
Bank(s): HSBC
Directors: K. Owen (Dir)
Ultimate Holding Company: REXAM PLC, LONDON
Registration no: 02456291 **Date established:** 1989
Turnover: £20m - £50m **No.of Employees:** 251 - 500
Product Groups: 30, 31

Amcore Central Services

83 Tower Road North, Bristol, BS30 8XP
Tel: 0117-975 3200 **Fax:** 0117-975 3311
Website: http://www.amcore.com
Directors: A. Derrick (Tech Serv), T. Kilbride (Fin)
Immediate Holding Company: AMCOR UK
Registration no: 04406435 **Date established:** 2002
No.of Employees: 101 - 250 **Product Groups:** 27, 30

Anglo Welsh Waterway Holidays

2 The Hide Market West Street, St Philips, Bristol, BS2 0BH
Tel: 0117-304 1122 **Fax:** 0117-304 1133
E-mail: bookings@anglowelsh.co.uk
Website: http://www.anglowelsh.co.uk
Directors: S. Thomson (Ch), R. Lawrence (Dir), R. Lawrence (MD), D. Page (Co Sec), M. Hill (Fin)
Managers: S. Clarke (Mgr)
Immediate Holding Company: ANGLO WELSH LIMITED
Registration no: 04062985 **Date established:** 2000
No.of Employees: 11 - 20 **Product Groups:** 39

Date of Accounts	Oct 10	Oct 09	Oct 08
Working Capital	255	273	149
Fixed Assets	696	586	497
Current Assets	862	853	570
Current Liabilities	N/A	N/A	8

Anglox

182 Sturminster Road, Bristol, BS14 8AR
Tel: 01275-837577
E-mail: bill@knight-writer.co.uk
Website: http://www.knight-writer.co.uk
Directors: B. Knight (Prop), B. Knight (Snr Part)
Date established: 2001 **No.of Employees:** 1 - 10 **Product Groups:** 81

Annex Interconnect Ltd

Unit 56 Waverley Road, Yate, Bristol, BS37 5QR
Tel: 01454-326600 **Fax:** 01454-326622
E-mail: kevin@annex-interconnect.co.uk
Website: http://www.annex-interconnect.co.uk
Directors: B. Edwards (Sales)
Managers: A. Anderson (Mgr)
Ultimate Holding Company: ANNEX PROPERTIES LIMITED
Immediate Holding Company: ANNEX (INTERCONNECT) LIMITED
Registration no: 04285328 **VAT No.:** GB 543 3901 55
Date established: 2001 **No.of Employees:** 11 - 20 **Product Groups:** 37

Date of Accounts	Jul 11	Jul 10	Jul 09
Working Capital	-154	-114	-64
Fixed Assets	N/A	14	18
Current Assets	4	88	213

Anstee & Ware Ltd

St Georges Trading Estate St Andrews Road, Avonmouth, Bristol, BS11 9HS
Tel: 0117-982 0081 **Fax:** 0117-982 3501
E-mail: enquiries@ansteeware.co.uk
Website: http://www.ansteeware.co.uk
Bank(s): Barclays
Directors: W. Anstee (Ch), M. Trigg (Fin)
Managers: D. Rausi, B. Hicks (Purch Mgr), R. Stephens (Tech Serv Mgr)
Ultimate Holding Company: A W HOLDING COMPANY LIMITED
Immediate Holding Company: ANSTEE & WARE LIMITED
Registration no: 00477097 **VAT No.:** GB 137 4072 78
Date established: 1950 **Turnover:** £10m - £20m
No.of Employees: 51 - 100 **Product Groups:** 37, 39, 48, 84

Date of Accounts	Dec 11	Dec 10	Dec 09
Sales Turnover	19m	16m	15m
Pre Tax Profit/Loss	842	713	183
Working Capital	2m	1m	911
Fixed Assets	1m	1m	1m
Current Assets	8m	6m	6m
Current Liabilities	4m	3m	4m

Antalis Mcnaughton Ltd

Gateway House Cribbs Causeway Centre, Bristol, BS10 7TT
Tel: 08706-073102 **Fax:** 0117-948 8286
E-mail: west@antalis-mcnaughton.co.uk
Website: http://www.antalis-mcnaughton.co.uk
Managers: D. Morrish (Ops Mgr)
Ultimate Holding Company: EXOR SPA (ITALY)
Immediate Holding Company: ANTALIS MCNAUGHTON LIMITED
Registration no: 01088345 **Date established:** 1972 **Turnover:** £5m - £10m
No.of Employees: 21 - 50 **Product Groups:** 44

Date of Accounts	Dec 11	Dec 10	Dec 09
Sales Turnover	451m	393m	256m
Pre Tax Profit/Loss	-1m	-6m	-11m
Working Capital	40m	44m	-21m
Fixed Assets	525	8m	37m
Current Assets	140m	161m	121m
Current Liabilities	14m	11m	43m

Antifriction Components Ltd

Unit 8-9 The Commercial Centre Days Road, St Philips, Bristol, BS2 0QS
Tel: 0117-955 6678 **Fax:** 0117-955 1287
E-mail: sales@afc-uk.com
Website: http://www.afc-uk.com
Directors: N. Davies (Dir)
Ultimate Holding Company: KOWLOON INVESTMENTS LIMITED (MAURITIUS)
Immediate Holding Company: ANTI-FRICTION COMPONENTS LIMITED
Registration no: 01275175 **Date established:** 1976
Turnover: £10m - £20m **No.of Employees:** 11 - 20 **Product Groups:** 35, 66

Date of Accounts	Sep 11	Sep 10	Sep 09
Sales Turnover	12m	11m	9m
Pre Tax Profit/Loss	427	231	93
Working Capital	592	357	275
Fixed Assets	206	17	28
Current Assets	4m	4m	3m
Current Liabilities	1m	1m	1m

Apex Fluid Engineering Ltd

4 Morley Road Staple Hill, Bristol, BS16 4QT
Tel: 0117-907 7555 **Fax:** 0117-907 7556
E-mail: enquiries@apexpumps.com
Website: http://www.apexpumps.com
Bank(s): Bank of Scotland
Directors: N. Sole (MD)
Immediate Holding Company: APEX FLUID ENGINEERING LIMITED
Registration no: 02189688 **Date established:** 1987 **Turnover:** £2m - £5m
No.of Employees: 21 - 50 **Product Groups:** 40

Date of Accounts	Jan 12	Jan 11	Jan 10
Working Capital	579	625	568
Fixed Assets	226	200	282
Current Assets	865	876	844
Current Liabilities	N/A	N/A	59

Arbil Ltd

Foundry Lane, Bristol, BS5 7XH
Tel: 0117-965 3143 **Fax:** 0117-965 8607
E-mail: info@arbil.co.uk
Website: http://www.arbil.com
Managers: D. Vale
Ultimate Holding Company: BILLS GROUP LIMITED
Immediate Holding Company: ARBIL LIMITED
Registration no: 01406906 **VAT No.:** GB 333 1004 21
Date established: 1978 **No.of Employees:** 1 - 10 **Product Groups:** 83

Date of Accounts	Dec 11	Dec 10	Dec 09
Sales Turnover	8m	7m	7m
Pre Tax Profit/Loss	373	118	1
Working Capital	1m	1m	1m
Fixed Assets	251	200	184
Current Assets	3m	2m	3m
Current Liabilities	345	205	163

Arco Ltd

PO Box 6, Bristol, BS11 8YA
Tel: 0117-982 3751 **Fax:** 0117-923 5574
E-mail: avonmouth.branch@arco.co.uk
Website: http://www.arco.co.uk
Managers: T. Legge (District Mgr)
Immediate Holding Company: ARCO LIMITED
Registration no: 00133804 **Date established:** 2014
No.of Employees: 11 - 20 **Product Groups:** 24, 29, 30, 40

Date of Accounts	Jun 11	Jun 10	Jun 09
Sales Turnover	229m	216m	214m
Pre Tax Profit/Loss	8m	6m	260
Working Capital	32m	27m	29m
Fixed Assets	19m	21m	23m
Current Assets	82m	67m	62m
Current Liabilities	12m	13m	8m

Arno GB

Victorian House Coronation Road, Southville, Bristol, BS3 1AA
Tel: 0117-953 6500 **Fax:** 0117-953 2125
E-mail: guypalmer@arno-online.co.uk
Website: http://www.arno-online.com
Bank(s): National Westminster Bank Plc
Managers: A. Rowsell, D. Neilson (Admin Off)
Ultimate Holding Company: ARNO GMBH (GERMANY)
Immediate Holding Company: ARNO GB LIMITED
Registration no: 01385669 **VAT No.:** GB 138 2274 70
Date established: 1978 **Turnover:** £5m - £10m **No.of Employees:** 21 - 50
Product Groups: 49, 81, 87

Date of Accounts	Dec 11	Dec 10	Dec 09
Sales Turnover	10m	6m	4m
Pre Tax Profit/Loss	1m	472	-1m
Working Capital	1m	922	349
Fixed Assets	2m	2m	2m
Current Assets	4m	3m	2m
Current Liabilities	2m	547	336

Arnolfini

16 Narrow Quay, Bristol, BS1 4QA
Tel: 0117-917 2300 **Fax:** 0117-917 2303
E-mail: boxoffice@arnolfini.org.uk
Website: http://www.arnolfini.org.uk
Directors: T. Trevor (Dir)
Managers: L. Evans (Fin Mgr), L. Yockney (Sales Admin), V. Wooley, G. Evans, R. Webster (Mktg Serv Mgr)
Ultimate Holding Company: ARNOLFINI GALLERY LIMITED
Immediate Holding Company: ARNOLFINI TRADING LIMITED
Registration no: 02142916 **Date established:** 1987
Turnover: Up to £250,000 **No.of Employees:** 21 - 50 **Product Groups:** 69, 81

Date of Accounts	Mar 11	Mar 10	Mar 09
Sales Turnover	128	44	67
Pre Tax Profit/Loss	56	26	-0
Working Capital	-51	-74	-90
Fixed Assets	59	68	78
Current Assets	81	64	49
Current Liabilities	11	25	5

Arup

63 St Thomas Street, Bristol, BS1 6JZ
Tel: 0117-976 5432 **Fax:** 0117-976 5433
E-mail: roy.cowap@arup.com
Website: http://www.arup.com
Directors: P. Wood (Dir)
Immediate Holding Company: ARUP GROUP LTD
Registration no: SC062237 **Turnover:** £250m - £500m
No.of Employees: 51 - 100 **Product Groups:** 44

Ashworth

Unit 9 Oak Lane Fishponds Trading Estate, Bristol, BS5 7UY
Tel: 0117-961 7000 **Fax:** 0117-961 7001
E-mail: steve.lang@sgbd.co.uk
Website: http://www.sgps.co.uk
Bank(s): Lloyds TSB Bank plc
Managers: S. Lang (Mgr)
Ultimate Holding Company: SAINT GOBIAN
Turnover: £2m - £5m **No.of Employees:** 21 - 50 **Product Groups:** 34, 35, 36

Aspect Film & Video

St Georges Court 1 St Georges Road, Bristol, BS1 5UG
Tel: 0117-930 4613 **Fax:** 0117-930 4830
E-mail: tellmemore@aspectfilmandvideo.co.uk
Website: http://www.aspectfilmandvideo.co.uk
Directors: A. Etheridge (MD)
Immediate Holding Company: CONVEX SOLUTIONS LTD
Registration no: 05727812 **Date established:** 2003
No.of Employees: 11 - 20 **Product Groups:** 81, 89

Assystem UK Ltd

1 The Brooms Emersons Green, Bristol, BS16 7FD
Tel: 0117-987 4000 **Fax:** 0117-987 4040
E-mail: mailbox@assystemuk.com
Website: http://www.assystemuk.com
Bank(s): Lloyds TSB Bank plc
Directors: D. Bradley (Dir), D. Caunce (Co Sec)
Managers: A. Clulow (Personnel), N. Henley (Fin Mgr)
Ultimate Holding Company: ASSYSTEM SA (FRANCE)
Immediate Holding Company: INBIS TECHNOLOGY LIMITED
Registration no: 00710001 **VAT No.:** GB 508 8221 50
Date established: 1961 **No.of Employees:** 101 - 250 **Product Groups:** 35, 36, 37, 38, 39, 44, 46, 47, 48, 52, 67, 68, 76, 80, 81, 83, 84, 85

Atkins Consultants Limited

The Hub 500 Park Avenue, Aztec West, Bristol, BS32 4RZ
Tel: 01454-662000 **Fax:** 01454-663333
E-mail: info@atkinsglobal.co.uk
Website: http://www.atkinsglobal.com
Directors: A. Brook (Dir), M. Williams (MD)
Managers: M. Wood (I.T. Exec)
Immediate Holding Company: W.S. Atkins Ltd
Registration no: 00755613 **VAT No.:** GB 209 8612 53
Date established: 1999 **No.of Employees:** 21 - 50 **Product Groups:** 84

Aurora Bearing Co UK

94a High Street Portishead, Bristol, BS20 6AJ
Tel: 01275-818918 **Fax:** 01275-818828
E-mail: peter@rotaprecision.com
Website: http://www.rotaprecision.com
Directors: P. Lench (MD)
Registration no: 02793478 **Date established:** 1993
Turnover: £250,000 - £500,000 **No.of Employees:** 1 - 10
Product Groups: 35

Date of Accounts	Nov 10	Nov 09	Nov 08
Working Capital	7	14	19
Fixed Assets	1	1	1
Current Assets	90	118	83

Avdon Bristol Ltd

Unit 1 Longbrook Trading Estate Ashton Vale Road, Bristol, BS3 2HT
Tel: 0117-953 3300 **Fax:** 0117-966 4948
E-mail: delaney@avdon.co.uk
Website: http://www.avdon.co.uk
Bank(s): National Westminster

Directors: R. Delaney (MD), R. Page (Fab)
Managers: T. Evans (Sales Prom Mgr)
Immediate Holding Company: AVDON BRISTOL LIMITED
Registration no: 02981259 **VAT No.:** GB 650 5079 47
Date established: 1994 **Turnover:** £2m - £5m **No.of Employees:** 21 - 50
Product Groups: 30, 35

Date of Accounts	Sep 11	Sep 10	Sep 09
Working Capital	515	567	608
Fixed Assets	24	22	23
Current Assets	733	871	852

Averys

4 High Street Nailsea, Bristol, BS48 1BT
Tel: 08451-283797 **Fax:** 01275-811101
E-mail: johnavery@averys.com
Website: http://www.averys.com
Directors: J. Avery (MD)
Managers: E. Roberts (Buyer)
Ultimate Holding Company: DIRECT WINES HOLDINGS LIMITED
Immediate Holding Company: AVERYS OF BRISTOL LIMITED
Registration no: 00376920 **Date established:** 1942
Turnover: £10m - £20m **No.of Employees:** 21 - 50 **Product Groups:** 62

Date of Accounts	Jun 08	Jun 09	Jul 10
Sales Turnover	19m	15m	18m
Pre Tax Profit/Loss	-4m	-49	862
Working Capital	-2m	-2m	-1m
Fixed Assets	354	203	135
Current Assets	4m	4m	7m
Current Liabilities	2m	3m	5m

Avon Barrier Co. Ltd

191-195 South Liberty Lane, Bristol, BS3 2TN
Tel: 0117-953 5252 **Fax:** 0117-953 5373
E-mail: sales@avon-barrier.co.uk
Website: http://www.avon-barrier.co.uk
Bank(s): Lloyds TSB Bank plc
Directors: P. Jeffrey (Dir)
Managers: N. Venner (Comptroller), M. Sorowar (Purch Mgr), J. Smallwood
Immediate Holding Company: AVON BARRIER COMPANY LIMITED
Registration no: 02297622 **Date established:** 1988
No.of Employees: 21 - 50 **Product Groups:** 35, 36, 37, 39, 40, 45, 49, 51, 68, 83

Date of Accounts	Mar 11	Mar 10	Mar 09
Working Capital	874	769	906
Fixed Assets	290	260	241
Current Assets	3m	2m	2m

Avon Catering Equipment

Birds Farm Winford, Bristol, BS40 8DW
Tel: 01275-475283 **Fax:** 01275-475283
Website: http://www.avoncateringequipment.co.uk
Directors: T. Gauld (Prop)
Registration no: 05923778 **Date established:** 2006
No.of Employees: 1 - 10 **Product Groups:** 20, 40, 41

Avon Dies Manufacturing Ltd

5-6 Bonville Road, Bristol, BS4 5NZ
Tel: 0117-977 1872 **Fax:** 0117-972 3703
E-mail: michael.hill@foliobristol.co.uk
Website: http://www.avon-dies.com
Directors: A. Bird (Fin), M. Hill (Dir), S. Fearley (Dir), S. Fearnley (Dir)
Managers: J. Lang
Immediate Holding Company: FOLIO (BRISTOL) LIMITED
Registration no: 04708149 **Date established:** 1983
No.of Employees: 1 - 10 **Product Groups:** 28, 44

Date of Accounts	Apr 09	Apr 08	Apr 07
Working Capital	-77	-51	-72
Fixed Assets	109	136	181
Current Assets	146	202	139

Avon Group Manufacturing Ltd

30 Vale Lane, Bristol, BS3 5RU
Tel: 0117-904 3355 **Fax:** 0117-904 3366
E-mail: sales@avon-group.co.uk
Website: http://www.avon-group.co.uk
Bank(s): Barclays Bank
Directors: M. Rushin (Dir), A. Patel (Fin)
Managers: L. Duncan, F. Humphries (Purch Mgr)
Ultimate Holding Company: AVON GROUP MANUFACTURING (HOLDINGS) LIMITED
Immediate Holding Company: AVON GROUP MANUFACTURING LIMITED
Registration no: 01562118 **VAT No.:** 302 8059 85 **Date established:** 1981
Turnover: £2m - £5m **No.of Employees:** 21 - 50 **Product Groups:** 29

Date of Accounts	Mar 12	Mar 11	Mar 10
Sales Turnover	4m	3m	3m
Pre Tax Profit/Loss	26	10	7
Working Capital	465	49	-37
Fixed Assets	656	444	502
Current Assets	3m	2m	1m
Current Liabilities	946	847	625

Avon Industrial Doors Ltd

Armstrong Way Yate, Bristol, BS37 5NG
Tel: 01454-273110 **Fax:** 01454-323224
E-mail: sales@avondoors.co.uk
Website: http://www.avondoors.co.uk
Directors: S. Bezer (Fin), D. Reid (MD)
Immediate Holding Company: AVON INDUSTRIAL DOORS LIMITED
Registration no: 02121712 **Date established:** 1987 **Turnover:** £1m - £2m
No.of Employees: 1 - 10 **Product Groups:** 35, 36, 39, 48

Date of Accounts	Sep 11	Sep 10	Sep 09
Working Capital	-37	-36	-5
Fixed Assets	89	92	115
Current Assets	486	502	506
Current Liabilities	N/A	6	2

Avon Spraying Centre

S B I Centre Memorial Road, Bristol, BS15 3JY
Tel: 0117-961 5910
E-mail: avonspraying@msn.co.uk
Website: http://www.avonspraying.co.uk
Directors: D. Scrase (Prop), R. Scrase (Prop)
Date established: 1987 **No.of Employees:** 1 - 10 **Product Groups:** 46, 48

Date of Accounts	Feb 08	Feb 07
Working Capital	-60	-67
Fixed Assets	61	69
Current Assets	47	48
Current Liabilities	106	115

Avon Stainless Fasteners Ltd

Unit 10 Riverside Business Park St Annes Road, St Annes Park, Bristol, BS4 4ED
Tel: 0117-972 8560 **Fax:** 0117-972 8570
E-mail: sales@avonstainlessfasteners.co.uk
Website: http://www.avonstainlessfasteners.co.uk
Directors: F. Canfield (MD)
Immediate Holding Company: AVON STAINLESS FASTENERS LIMITED
Registration no: 06525926 **Date established:** 2008
Turnover: Up to £250,000 **No.of Employees:** 1 - 10 **Product Groups:** 22, 23, 25, 29, 30, 35, 36, 66

Date of Accounts	Mar 12	Mar 11	Mar 10
Working Capital	118	82	4
Fixed Assets	129	115	121
Current Assets	326	317	243

Avonmouth Paint & Supplies

6 Gloucester Road Avonmouth, Bristol, BS11 9AA
Tel: 0117-982 2718 **Fax:** 0117-982 2718
E-mail: pat.capaldi@blueyonder.co.uk
Website: http://www.paintandsupplies.co.uk
Directors: P. Capaldi (Prop)
Managers: B. Marshall (Mgr)
No.of Employees: 1 - 10 **Product Groups:** 31, 32

B M I Solutions Ltd

5 Dragon Court Crofts End Road, Bristol, BS5 7XX
Tel: 0117-951 7517 **Fax:** 0117-952 5363
E-mail: sales@b-m-i.co.uk
Website: http://www.bmisolutions.co.uk
Directors: W. Orchid (MD), Z. Manning (Fin), B. Manning (MD), J. Orchid (Dir)
Immediate Holding Company: BMI LIMITED
Registration no: 03135674 **Date established:** 1995
Turnover: Up to £250,000 **No.of Employees:** 1 - 10 **Product Groups:** 67, 81

Date of Accounts	Dec 07	Dec 06	Dec 05
Sales Turnover	127	97	89
Pre Tax Profit/Loss	34	26	25
Working Capital	26	18	22
Fixed Assets	20	N/A	N/A
Current Assets	44	34	33
Current Liabilities	18	16	11
ROCE% (Return on Capital Employed)	74.4	139.5	110.7
ROT% (Return on Turnover)	26.3	26.6	27.5

Bailey Of Bristol

South Liberty Lane, Bristol, BS3 2SS
Tel: 0117-966 5967 **Fax:** 0117-963 6554
E-mail: sales@bailey-caravans.co.uk
Website: http://www.bailey-caravans.co.uk
Bank(s): Barclays
Directors: S. Howard (Sales & Mktg), N. Howard (MD), C. Harvey (Fin), J. Tanner (Comm)
Ultimate Holding Company: KEENWORK LIMITED
Immediate Holding Company: BAILEY CARAVANS LIMITED
Registration no: 00354363 **VAT No.:** GB 496 6968 60
Date established: 1939 **Turnover:** £75m - £125m
No.of Employees: 251 - 500 **Product Groups:** 39

Date of Accounts	Dec 11	Dec 10	Dec 09
Sales Turnover	90m	98m	75m
Pre Tax Profit/Loss	3m	5m	4m
Working Capital	12m	8m	6m
Fixed Assets	4m	4m	3m
Current Assets	23m	23m	20m
Current Liabilities	4m	3m	3m

Baldor UK

Mint Motion Centre Unit 6 Bristol Distribution Park Hawkley Drive, Bradley Stoke, Bristol, BS32 0BF
Tel: 01454-850000 **Fax:** 01454-859002
E-mail: sales.uk@baldor.com
Website: http://www.baldor.com
Managers: T. Fuge (Ops Mgr)
Ultimate Holding Company: ABB LTD (SWITZERLAND)
Immediate Holding Company: BALDOR UK LIMITED
Registration no: 02188833 **Date established:** 1987
Turnover: £10m - £20m **No.of Employees:** 51 - 100 **Product Groups:** 25, 29, 30, 33, 34, 35, 37, 38, 39, 43, 44, 45, 46, 48, 66, 67, 84

Date of Accounts	Dec 11	Dec 10	Dec 09
Sales Turnover	17m	16m	10m
Pre Tax Profit/Loss	-140	1m	-249
Working Capital	6m	6m	5m
Fixed Assets	2m	2m	2m
Current Assets	9m	7m	5m
Current Liabilities	495	591	293

The Bambach Saddle Seat

13 Glanville Drive Hinton Blewett, Bristol, BS39 5GF
Tel: 01761-452525 **Fax:** 01761-452525
Directors: H. Gray (Ptnr)
No.of Employees: 1 - 10 **Product Groups:** 38

J.V. Barrett & Co. Ltd (Barrettine Industrial)

Barrettine Works St. Ivel Way, Warmley, Bristol, BS30 8TY
Tel: 0117-960 0060 **Fax:** 0117-935 2437
E-mail: sales@barrettine.co.uk
Website: http://www.barrettine.co.uk
Directors: S. Bailey (MD), A. Greer (Sales)
Ultimate Holding Company: J.V. Barrett & Co. Ltd
Registration no: 01675749 **Turnover:** £10m - £20m
No.of Employees: 21 - 50 **Product Groups:** 31, 32, 66

Date of Accounts	Dec 07	Dec 06	Dec 05
Sales Turnover	13355	12523	12221
Pre Tax Profit/Loss	337	280	197
Working Capital	985	882	693
Fixed Assets	2102	2087	2046
Current Assets	3786	3368	3480
Current Liabilities	2801	2486	2787
Total Share Capital	194	194	194
ROCE% (Return on Capital Employed)	10.9	9.4	7.2
ROT% (Return on Turnover)	2.5	2.2	1.6

Bart Spices Ltd

York Road Bedminster, Bristol, BS3 4AD
Tel: 0117-977 3474 **Fax:** 0117-972 0216
E-mail: edwardshaw@bartspices.com
Website: http://www.bartspices.com
Bank(s): National Westminster Bank Plc
Managers: K. Crossley, F. Campbell, C. Bond, D. Collard, A. Hallett
Ultimate Holding Company: BART SPICES GROUP HOLDINGS LIMITED
Immediate Holding Company: THE BART INGREDIENTS CO. LTD
Registration no: 04937130 **VAT No.:** GB 678 9351 72
Date established: 2003 **Turnover:** £10m - £20m
No.of Employees: 101 - 250 **Product Groups:** 20, 62

Date of Accounts	Mar 11	Mar 10	Mar 09
Sales Turnover	15m	16m	N/A
Pre Tax Profit/Loss	4m	3m	360
Working Capital	3m	3m	392
Fixed Assets	2m	2m	3m
Current Assets	6m	6m	4m
Current Liabilities	868	1m	1m

Barton Fabrication Ltd

Harbour Road Trading Estate Portishead, Bristol, BS20 7BL
Tel: 01275-845901 **Fax:** 01275-849462
E-mail: sales@bartonfabs.co.uk
Website: http://www.bartonfabs.co.uk
Bank(s): National Westminster
Directors: S. Chadwick (Co Sec)
Immediate Holding Company: BARTON FABRICATIONS LIMITED
Registration no: 02118065 **VAT No.:** GB 357 8284 13
Date established: 1987 **Turnover:** £1m - £2m **No.of Employees:** 11 - 20
Product Groups: 48

Date of Accounts	Oct 11	Oct 10	Oct 09
Working Capital	519	430	382
Fixed Assets	302	296	309
Current Assets	1m	567	656

Barton Willmore Partnership

101 Victoria Street, Bristol, BS1 6PU
Tel: 0117-929 9677 **Fax:** 0117-929 4569
E-mail: ian.mellor@bartonwillmore.co.uk
Website: http://www.bartonwillmore.co.uk
Directors: I. Mellor (Snr Part)
Managers: A. Bevan (Tech Serv Mgr)
Immediate Holding Company: SPORTING RESULTS LTD
Registration no: 02131349 **VAT No.:** GB 512 6340 81
Date established: 2006 **Turnover:** £5m - £10m **No.of Employees:** 21 - 50
Product Groups: 84

Date of Accounts	Mar 11	Mar 10	Mar 09
Pre Tax Profit/Loss	1m	775	N/A
Working Capital	2m	71	71
Fixed Assets	3	3	N/A
Current Assets	2m	71	71

Batt Cables plc

1 Liberty Industrial Park South Liberty Lane, Bristol, BS3 2SU
Tel: 0117-966 6333 **Fax:** 0117-953 3602
E-mail: mark.cooper@batt.co.uk
Website: http://www.batt.co.uk
Managers: A. Kline (District Mgr)
Immediate Holding Company: BATT CABLES PLC
Registration no: 01353688 **Date established:** 1978
No.of Employees: 11 - 20 **Product Groups:** 30, 35, 36, 37, 38, 44, 66, 67

Date of Accounts	Mar 12	Mar 11	Mar 10
Sales Turnover	106m	98m	84m
Pre Tax Profit/Loss	8m	9m	5m
Working Capital	41m	36m	31m
Fixed Assets	8m	9m	8m
Current Assets	69m	60m	54m
Current Liabilities	3m	3m	2m

Battrick Clark Solicitors

151 Whiteladies Road Cliftons, Bristol, BS8 2RA
Tel: 0117-973 1391 **Fax:** 0117-973 5782
E-mail: info@battrickclark.co.uk
Website: http://www.battrickclark.co.uk
Directors: H. Battrick (MD)
Immediate Holding Company: BATTRICK CLARK SOLICITORS LTD
Registration no: 04589331 **Date established:** 2002
No.of Employees: 11 - 20 **Product Groups:** 80

Date of Accounts	Apr 12	Apr 11	Apr 10
Working Capital	88	23	37
Fixed Assets	13	14	13
Current Assets	347	258	288

Beachcroft LLP

Portwall Place Portwall Lane, Bristol, BS1 6NA
Tel: 0117-918 2000 **Fax:** 0117-918 2100
E-mail: mbothamley@bwlaw.co.uk
Website: http://www.dacbeachcroft.com
Managers: T. Cherry, S. Young (Personnel), P. Bolster (Comptroller), N. Attree (Tech Serv Mgr), D. Appleton (Sales Admin), L. Blytham (Mktg Serv Mgr)
Immediate Holding Company: BEACHCROFT CLAIMS LIMITED
Registration no: 07720271 **Date established:** 2011 **Turnover:** £1m - £2m
No.of Employees: 251 - 500 **Product Groups:** 80

Bell Tools

84-86 Filton Road Horfield, Bristol, BS7 0PD
Tel: 0117-969 0288 **Fax:** 0117-969 6662
Website: http://www.belltoolsbristol.co.uk
Directors: A. Bell (MD)
Date established: 1995 **No.of Employees:** 1 - 10 **Product Groups:** 37

Benson Bros Bristol Ltd

110 Princess Victoria Street Clifton, Bristol, BS8 4DB
Tel: 0117-946 6255 **Fax:** 0117-9466 332
E-mail: info@bensonbros.co.uk
Website: http://www.bensonbros.co.uk
Bank(s): HSBC Bank plc
Directors: D. Schofield (Fin), J. Benson (Dir), P. Wright (MD)
Immediate Holding Company: Benson Bros (Bristol) Ltd
Registration no: 00356470 **VAT No.:** GB 137 4963 43
Date established: 1939 **Turnover:** £5m - £10m **No.of Employees:** 21 - 50
Product Groups: 51

Date of Accounts	Aug 07	Aug 06
Sales Turnover	7892	6972
Pre Tax Profit/Loss	498	328
Working Capital	6684	6450
Fixed Assets	1410	1041
Current Assets	7798	7568
Current Liabilities	1114	1118
Total Share Capital	240	240
ROCE% (Return on Capital Employed)	6.2	4.4
ROT% (Return on Turnover)	6.3	4.7

Beyond The Bean
Unit 6 Cala Trading Estate, Bristol, BS3 2HA
Tel: 0117-953 3522 **Fax:** 0117-953 3422
E-mail: sales@beyondthebean.com
Website: http://www.beyondthebean.com
Managers: T. Osborn (Chief Mgr)
Immediate Holding Company: BEYOND THE BEAN LIMITED
Registration no: 03342222 **Date established:** 1997 **Turnover:** £2m - £5m
No.of Employees: 11 - 20 **Product Groups:** 20, 62

Date of Accounts	Sep 11	Sep 10	Sep 09
Working Capital	741	680	554
Fixed Assets	62	80	186
Current Assets	3m	2m	2m

BIE Magnum
Unit 2 Oak Lane, Fishponds, Bristol, BS5 7UY
Tel: 0117-965 1234 **Fax:** 0117-965 4123
E-mail: sales@biemagnum.com
Website: http://www.biemagnum.com
Bank(s): Barclays
Directors: N. Bath (Ptnr)
Managers: J. Dring (Sales Prom Mgr)
Turnover: £500,000 - £1m **No.of Employees:** 11 - 20
Product Groups: 28, 32, 44, 46, 48, 49

Billington Structures Ltd
456 Badminton Road Yate, Bristol, BS37 5HY
Tel: 01454-318181 **Fax:** 01454-318231
E-mail: postroom@billington-modern.co.uk
Website: http://www.billington-structures.co.uk
Directors: T. Taylor (Fin), S. Fareham (MD), P. Hart (Fin)
Managers: C. Houghton (Mktg Serv Mgr), G. Hawley (I.T. Exec), D. Kemplay (Personnel), C. Evans (Chief Buyer), B. King (Sales & Mktg Mg), A. Bickerstaff (Tech Serv Mgr), D. Kempley (Personnel)
Ultimate Holding Company: BILLINGTON HOLDINGS PLC
Immediate Holding Company: BILLINGTON STRUCTURES LIMITED
Registration no: 01567759 **Date established:** 1981
Turnover: Up to £250,000 **No.of Employees:** 51 - 100
Product Groups: 34, 35

Date of Accounts	Dec 11	Dec 10	Dec 09
Sales Turnover	48m	39m	56m
Pre Tax Profit/Loss	-3m	184	4m
Working Capital	3m	5m	5m
Fixed Assets	1m	1m	1m
Current Assets	14m	14m	18m
Current Liabilities	1m	954	2m

Bissa Waste Services Ltd
Hydro Estate St Andrews Road, Avonmouth, Bristol, BS11 9HW
Tel: 0117-982 8476 **Fax:** 0117-938 1695
E-mail: marketing@biffa.co.uk
Website: http://www.bissa.co.uk
Managers: M. Dwyer (Mgr)
Registration no: 00946107 **No.of Employees:** 11 - 20
Product Groups: 32, 54

Blackwell's
87 Park Street, Bristol, BS1 5PW
Tel: 0117-927 6602 **Fax:** 0117-925 1854
E-mail: info@blackwells.co.uk
Website: http://www.blackwells.co.uk
Managers: L. Stainer (Chief Mgr)
Immediate Holding Company: BLACKWELL LIMITED
Registration no: 02762961 **Date established:** 1992
Turnover: £20m - £50m **No.of Employees:** 1 - 10 **Product Groups:** 61

Blue Arrow Personnel Services Ltd
Apex Court Woodlands, Bradley Stoke, Bristol, BS32 4JT
Tel: 01454-620755 **Fax:** 0117-925 0231
E-mail: info@bluearrow.co.uk
Website: http://www.bluearrow.co.uk
Directors: T. Barber (MD), S. Mcbride (MD), M. Adams (MD)
Managers: R. Waldron (District Mgr), A. Carrigan (Mgr), L. Raymond (Mgr)
Immediate Holding Company: SALES SERVICES LTD
Registration no: 00641659 **Turnover:** £500,000 - £1m
No.of Employees: 1 - 10 **Product Groups:** 80

Bob Martin UK Ltd
Wemberham Lane Yatton, Bristol, BS49 4BS
Tel: 01934-831000 **Fax:** 01934-831050
E-mail: sales@bobmartin.co.uk
Website: http://www.bobmartin.co.uk
Bank(s): Barclays, Southport
Directors: A. Ford (Dir), B. Martin (Ch), J. Powell (MD), W. Steele (Dir), R. Buchanan (Co Sec), R. Buchanan (Dir)
Managers: J. Rosswell
Immediate Holding Company: BOB MARTIN (UK) LIMITED
Registration no: 04380953 **VAT No.:** GB 609 3620 40
Date established: 2002 **Turnover:** £20m - £50m
No.of Employees: 101 - 250 **Product Groups:** 32, 49, 62

Date of Accounts	Dec 09	Mar 09	Mar 08
Sales Turnover	28m	30m	26m
Pre Tax Profit/Loss	1m	-539	166
Working Capital	-485	-1m	-54
Fixed Assets	5m	5m	4m
Current Assets	12m	10m	8m
Current Liabilities	8m	6m	5m

Bob Ritchie Ltd
12 Catley Grove Long Ashton, Bristol, BS41 9NH
Tel: 01275-394209
E-mail: bob@bobritchieltd.co.uk
Website: http://www.bobritchieltd.co.uk
Directors: R. Ritchie (MD), M. Ritchie (Fin)
Immediate Holding Company: BOB RITCHIE LIMITED
Registration no: 03873045 **Date established:** 1999
No.of Employees: 1 - 10 **Product Groups:** 46

Date of Accounts	Jan 11	Jan 10	Jan 09
Working Capital	428	393	426
Fixed Assets	8	2	6
Current Assets	482	439	494

Bolton Gate Services
Unit 9 Short Way Thornbury, Bristol, BS35 3UT
Tel: 01454-413300 **Fax:** 01454-413377
Managers: G. Humphrey (Reg Mgr)
No.of Employees: 11 - 20 **Product Groups:** 35

Borsatec Ltd
Unit 1 Simmonds Buildings Bristol Road, Hambrook, Bristol, BS16 1RY
Tel: 0117-957 4949 **Fax:** 0117-957 4964
E-mail: borsatec@borsatec.com
Website: http://www.borsatec.com
Directors: J. Muorane (Ch), S. Wiltshire (Dir), J. Prendergrat (MD), G. Wilson (Sales), G. Moran (Sales), G. Morlan (Dir), E. Scolard (Fin), A. Reddick (Procurement)
Managers: J. Prease (Admin Off), A. Fletcher (Sales Prom Mgr), P. Garner (Mgr)
Registration no: 00200061 **No.of Employees:** 1 - 10 **Product Groups:** 37, 40

Bourne Steel
2 Brook Office Park Folly Brook Road, Emersons Green, Bristol, BS16 7ZU
Tel: 0117-956 7766 **Fax:** 0117-957 9933
Website: http://www.bournesteel.co.uk
Managers: G. Cole (Mgr)
No.of Employees: 11 - 20 **Product Groups:** 35

Boxes & Packaging
Douglas House Wood Road, Kingswood, Bristol, BS15 8RA
Tel: 0117-960 0776 **Fax:** 0117-960 4676
E-mail: sales@bristol.co.uk
Website: http://www.boxesandpackaging.co.uk
Bank(s): National Westminster Bank Plc
Directors: A. Clarke (MD)
Managers: M. Dorney (Chief Acct)
Ultimate Holding Company: BOXES AND PACKAGING (UK) LIMITED
Immediate Holding Company: BOXES AND PACKAGING LIMITED
Registration no: 05291434 **VAT No.:** GB 139 1628 60
Date established: 2004 **Turnover:** £5m - £10m **No.of Employees:** 21 - 50
Product Groups: 27

Braby Ltd
Cumberland House Marsh Road, Bristol, BS3 2NA
Tel: 0117-934 1300 **Fax:** 0117-923 1445
E-mail: jlee@braby.co.uk
Website: http://www.braby.co.uk
Directors: J. Lee (Dir)
Managers: I. Pring (Comptroller)
Ultimate Holding Company: BRABY HOLDINGS LIMITED
Immediate Holding Company: MOUNTAIN IN VIEW LTD
Registration no: 02595645 **VAT No.:** GB 593 5733 05
Date established: 2009 **Turnover:** £2m - £5m **No.of Employees:** 21 - 50
Product Groups: 48

Date of Accounts	Mar 11	Mar 10	Mar 09
Working Capital	-1	-0	-1
Fixed Assets	1	1	1
Current Assets	23	19	22

Bray & Slaughter Ltd
Parson Street, Bristol, BS3 5RD
Tel: 0117-963 3103 **Fax:** 0117-963 2546
E-mail: enq@brayandslaughterltd.co.uk
Website: http://www.brayandslaughterltd.co.uk
Bank(s): National Westminster Bank Plc
Directors: S. Webber (Co Sec)
Immediate Holding Company: BRAY AND SLAUGHTER LIMITED
Registration no: 00286527 **VAT No.:** GB 137 4329 67
Date established: 1934 **Turnover:** £10m - £20m
No.of Employees: 51 - 100 **Product Groups:** 52

Date of Accounts	Mar 11	Mar 10	Mar 09
Sales Turnover	14m	10m	11m
Pre Tax Profit/Loss	320	276	676
Working Capital	975	707	783
Fixed Assets	975	1m	916
Current Assets	4m	4m	3m
Current Liabilities	N/A	1m	875

Bremskerl(UK)Ltd
4B Ashmead Industrial Estate
Ashmead Road
Keynsham, Bristol, BS31 1TU
Tel: 0117-946 1600
E-mail: matthew.hemmings@bremskerl.com
Website: http://www.bremskerl.de
Directors: R. Gramatke (Dir)
Managers: .. Gramatke (Tech Serv Mgr), D. Whitmarsh (Sales Prom Mgr), J. Parkin (Accounts)
Ultimate Holding Company: Bremskerl Reibbelagwerke Emmerling & CO KG (Ger)
Immediate Holding Company: BREMSKERL (UK) LIMITED
Registration no: 02191297 **Date established:** 1987
Turnover: £20m - £50m **No.of Employees:** 1 - 10 **Product Groups:** 29, 30, 33, 34, 35, 39, 43, 45, 46, 68, 84

Date of Accounts	Mar 11	Mar 10	Mar 09
Working Capital	559	409	317
Fixed Assets	11	9	14
Current Assets	1m	717	625

Bribex
10 North Road Yate, Bristol, BS37 7PA
Tel: 01454-310150 **Fax:** 01454-310191
E-mail: info@bribex.com
Website: http://www.bribex.com
Directors: J. Hobbs (Dir)
Ultimate Holding Company: FINDLAY ASSOCIATES LIMITED
Immediate Holding Company: BRIBEX LIMITED
Registration no: 00780876 **VAT No.:** GB 137 4732 62
Date established: 1963 **Turnover:** £1m - £2m **No.of Employees:** 11 - 20
Product Groups: 23, 28, 30, 37, 39

Date of Accounts	May 08	Nov 11	Nov 10
Working Capital	-4	158	162
Fixed Assets	675	721	673
Current Assets	597	392	325

Brissco Ltd
Cater Road Bishops Worth, Bristol, BS13 7TX
Tel: 0117-311 3777 **Fax:** 0117-311 6777
E-mail: mandyf@brissco.co.uk
Website: http://www.brissco.com
Bank(s): Barclays
Directors: C. Page (Fin), R. Dooley (Jt MD), C. Ellis (Jt MD)
Managers: M. Freak (Sales Admin), M. Freake (Sales Prom Mgr)
Immediate Holding Company: BRISSCO (EQUIPMENT) LIMITED
Registration no: 00455916 **Date established:** 1948 **Turnover:** £1m - £2m
No.of Employees: 11 - 20 **Product Groups:** 39, 40, 45, 49

Date of Accounts	Dec 09	Dec 08	Dec 07
Working Capital	370	417	500
Fixed Assets	467	542	601
Current Assets	478	478	647

Bristlewand Ltd
48 Ashton Vale Road, Bristol, BS3 2HQ
Tel: 0117-963 6141 **Fax:** 0117-963 1954
E-mail: reception@kennygroup.co.uk
Website: http://www.kennygroup.co.uk
Bank(s): National Westminster Bank Plc
Directors: R. Hunt (Comm)
Managers: H. Hough, E. Newton
Immediate Holding Company: BRISTLEWAND LIMITED
Registration no: 01437269 **Date established:** 1979
Turnover: £10m - £20m **No.of Employees:** 21 - 50 **Product Groups:** 51, 52, 72, 83

Date of Accounts	Mar 11	Mar 10	Mar 09
Sales Turnover	10m	8m	8m
Pre Tax Profit/Loss	-73	118	5
Working Capital	547	683	680
Fixed Assets	1m	1m	1m
Current Assets	3m	3m	2m
Current Liabilities	526	438	521

Bristol & Avon Transport & Skip Hire Ltd
Holesmouth Avonmouth, Bristol, BS11 9BP
Tel: 0117-982 9561 **Fax:** 0117-938 2739
E-mail: liamkirwan@bristolandavontransport.co.uk
Website: http://www.bristolandavontransport.co.uk
Directors: L. Kirwan (Fin), C. Berkley (Fin)
Managers: C. Berkely
Immediate Holding Company: BRISTOL & AVON TRANSPORT & RECYCLING LTD
Registration no: 02830141 **Date established:** 1993
No.of Employees: 21 - 50 **Product Groups:** 32, 34, 37, 39, 40, 42, 44, 52, 54, 84

Date of Accounts	Dec 11	Dec 10	Dec 09
Working Capital	354	443	375
Fixed Assets	71	118	225
Current Assets	2m	2m	2m

Bristol Batteries Ltd
3 St Philips Trade Centre Albert Road, St Philips, Bristol, BS2 0YB
Tel: 0117-955 0535 **Fax:** 0117-935 1791
E-mail: sales@bristolbatteries.com
Website: http://www.bristolbatteries.com
Bank(s): National Westminster Bank Plc
Managers: S. Coles (District Mgr)
Immediate Holding Company: BRISTOL BATTERIES LIMITED
Registration no: 01066031 **VAT No.:** GB 138 6316 60
Date established: 1972 **Turnover:** £2m - £5m **No.of Employees:** 21 - 50
Product Groups: 37, 39, 67, 68

Date of Accounts	Aug 11	Aug 10	Aug 09
Working Capital	594	426	361
Fixed Assets	226	231	205
Current Assets	2m	2m	1m

Bristol Cameras
47 High Street, Bristol, BS1 2AZ
Tel: 0117-914 0089 **Fax:** 0117-914 0090
E-mail: l.flynn@bristolcameras.co.uk
Website: http://www.bristolcameras.co.uk
Directors: L. Flynn (Prop)
Immediate Holding Company: BRISTOL CAMERAS LIMITED
Registration no: 05266139 **Date established:** 2004 **Turnover:** £2m - £5m
No.of Employees: 1 - 10 **Product Groups:** 38

Date of Accounts	Mar 11	Mar 10	Mar 09
Working Capital	-90	-93	-110
Fixed Assets	110	115	122
Current Assets	105	168	173
Current Liabilities	28	49	N/A

Bristol Car & Van Hire Ltd
290-294 Southmead Road Westbury-on-Trym, Bristol, BS10 5EN
Tel: 0117-959 3333 **Fax:** 0117-959 1999
E-mail: info@bristolcar-vanhire.co.uk
Website: http://www.bristolcar-vanhire.co.uk
Directors: P. Partlett (MD)
Ultimate Holding Company: BRISTOL CAR & VAN HIRE (HOLDINGS) LIMITED
Immediate Holding Company: BRISTOL CAR & VAN HIRE LIMITED
Registration no: 02918887 **VAT No.:** GB 650 4122 77
Date established: 1994 **No.of Employees:** 1 - 10 **Product Groups:** 72

Date of Accounts	Mar 11	Mar 10	Mar 09
Working Capital	480	429	237
Fixed Assets	582	593	627
Current Assets	761	752	726

Bristol Cars
Concorde Road Patchway, Bristol, BS34 5TB
Tel: 0117-979 9444 **Fax:** 0117-923 6356
E-mail: sales@bristolcars.co.uk
Website: http://www.bristolcars.co.uk
Bank(s): Barclays
Directors: A. Silverton (Dir), S. Lovesy (Dir), T. Crook (MD)
Managers: T. Silverton (Gen Contact)
Immediate Holding Company: BRISTOL CARS LIMITED
Registration no: 00427126 **Date established:** 1947
No.of Employees: 21 - 50 **Product Groups:** 39, 68

Bristol Chinese Pain Relief Acupuncture
39 Cotham Hill, Bristol, BS6 6JY
Tel: 0117-974 1199 **Fax:** 0117-923 7266
E-mail: hanzhentong@hotmail.com
Website: http://www.backachetherapy.co.uk
Managers: Z. Han (Mgr)
Immediate Holding Company: THE NATURAL HEALTH CLINIC LIMITED
Registration no: 07199952 **Date established:** 2007
Turnover: Up to £250,000 **No.of Employees:** 1 - 10 **Product Groups:** 38, 88

Bristol Decorative Surfaces
Unit 2-3 New Gatton Road, Bristol, BS2 9SH
Tel: 0117-954 2120 **Fax:** 0117-954 1993
Directors: J. Phillips (Fin)
Immediate Holding Company: BRISTOL DECORATIVE SURFACES LIMITED
Registration no: 04199661 **Date established:** 2001 **Turnover:** £2m - £5m
No.of Employees: 11 - 20 **Product Groups:** 30, 33, 52

Bristol Fire
Covert End Westleigh Court Westleigh Close, Yate, Bristol, BS37 4PR
Tel: 01458-315779 **Fax:** 01454-273312
E-mail: j.meese@bristolfire.co.uk
Website: http://www.bristolfire.com
Directors: J. Meese (Prop)
Date established: 1990 **No.of Employees:** 11 - 20 **Product Groups:** 38, 42

Bristol Fluid System Technologies Ltd
Fourth Way Avonmouth Way Avonmouth, Bristol, BS11 8DL
Tel: 0117-982 1107 **Fax:** 0117-982 6436
E-mail: info@bristol.swagelok.com
Website: http://www.swagelok.com/bristol
Directors: S. Cooke (MD)
Immediate Holding Company: BRISTOL 2010 LIMITED
Registration no: 03365495 **Date established:** 1997
No.of Employees: 11 - 20 **Product Groups:** 29, 30, 31, 33, 34, 35, 36, 37, 38, 39, 40, 41, 45, 46, 48, 49, 66, 67, 68

Date of Accounts	Dec 11	Dec 10	Dec 09
Working Capital	1m	1m	1m
Fixed Assets	N/A	N/A	157
Current Assets	1m	2m	1m

Bristol Forklifts Ltd
Grove Industrial Estate Gloucester Road, Patchway, Bristol, BS34 5BB
Tel: 0117-969 4141 **Fax:** 0117-969 1211
E-mail: info@bristolforklifts.co.uk
Website: http://www.bristolforklifts.co.uk
Directors: I. Mounce (Dir), J. Bronson (Dir)
Immediate Holding Company: BRISTOL FORKLIFTS LTD.
Registration no: 04413507 **Date established:** 2002
No.of Employees: 21 - 50 **Product Groups:** 45, 48, 67, 71, 83, 86

Date of Accounts	Apr 12	Apr 11	Apr 10
Working Capital	-19	-134	-178
Fixed Assets	715	765	637
Current Assets	459	445	489

The Bristol Kitchen Company
14 Redcross Street St Judes, Bristol, BS2 0BA
Tel: 0117-914 0340
E-mail: info@thebristolkitchencompany.co.uk
Website: http://www.thebristolkitchencompany.co.uk
Directors: H. Purse (Prop)
Date established: 2008 **Turnover:** £250,000 - £500,000
No.of Employees: 1 - 10 **Product Groups:** 26

Bristol Metal Spraying & Protective Coatings Ltd
Payne's Shipyard Coronation Road, Bristol, BS3 1RP
Tel: 0117-966 2206 **Fax:** 0117-966 1158
E-mail: sales@bmspc.co.uk
Website: http://www.bmspc.co.uk
Bank(s): HSBC
Directors: G. Payne (MD)
Ultimate Holding Company: BARRIE PAYNE GROUP LIMITED(THE)
Immediate Holding Company: BRISTOL METAL SPRAYING AND PROTECTIVE COATINGS LIMITED
Registration no: 00314475 **VAT No.:** GB 137 4469 51
Date established: 1936 **Turnover:** £1m - £2m **No.of Employees:** 21 - 50
Product Groups: 48

Date of Accounts	Jun 11	Jun 10	Jun 09
Working Capital	562	521	486
Fixed Assets	322	334	317
Current Assets	832	716	692

Bristol Office Machines
Petherton Road, Bristol, BS14 9BZ
Tel: 01275-890140 **Fax:** 01275-890111
E-mail: info@bom.co.uk
Website: http://www.bom.co.uk
Bank(s): HSBC Bank plc
Directors: N. Morgan (MD), T. Drohan (Chief Op Offcr)
Managers: G. Wignall (Sales Prom Mgr)
Immediate Holding Company: BRISTOL OFFICE MACHINES LIMITED
Registration no: 05836256 **VAT No.:** GB 416 8624 41
Date established: 2006 **Turnover:** £5m - £10m
No.of Employees: 51 - 100 **Product Groups:** 38, 44, 67, 85

Bristol Port Company
St Andrews House St Andrews Road, Avonmouth, Bristol, BS11 9DQ
Tel: 0117-982 0000 **Fax:** 0117-982 0698
E-mail: kieron.flower@bristolport.co.uk
Website: http://www.bristolport.co.uk
Directors: R. Harvey (Fin), P. Kearon (Mkt Research), K. Flower (Dir), D. Morris (Pers), T. Nicholson (Tech Serv), P. Kearon (Mkt Research)
Managers: P. Taylor (Purch Mgr)
Ultimate Holding Company: First Corporate Shipping
Registration no: 02641767 **Date established:** 2004
Turnover: Up to £250,000 **No.of Employees:** 251 - 500
Product Groups: 71

Bristol Product Coating Ltd
The Mill Bath Road Swineford, Bitton, Bristol, BS30 6LW
Tel: 0117-932 3647 **Fax:** 0117-932 6183
E-mail: sales@bpcltd.fsnet.co.uk
Directors: M. Hendy (MD), T. Hendy (Fin)
Immediate Holding Company: BRISTOL PRODUCT COATING LIMITED
Registration no: 00988567 **VAT No.:** GB 138 7272 49
Date established: 1970 **Turnover:** Up to £250,000
No.of Employees: 1 - 10 **Product Groups:** 40, 48

Date of Accounts	Feb 12	Feb 11	Feb 10
Sales Turnover	217	208	181
Pre Tax Profit/Loss	16	3	-0
Working Capital	2	8	30
Fixed Assets	11	13	18
Current Assets	85	67	66
Current Liabilities	40	38	12

Bristol Rope & Twine Co.
80 Feeder Road, Bristol, BS2 0TQ
Tel: 0117-977 7033 **Fax:** 0117-971 7621
E-mail: bristolrope@ukonline.co.uk
Website: http://www.bristolrope.com
Directors: G. Clements (Ptnr)
Date established: 1959 **Turnover:** £500,000 - £1m
No.of Employees: 1 - 10 **Product Groups:** 23, 35, 40, 42, 63

Bristol Steel Stockholders Ltd
Unit 13-14 Avonbridge Trading Estate Atlantic Road, Bristol, BS11 9QD
Tel: 0117-982 8131 **Fax:** 0117-982 8137
E-mail: robert@ellissteelgroup.co.uk
Website: http://www.ellissteelgroup.co.uk
Directors: R. Ellis (MD), H. Brown (MD), I. Walters (Co Sec)
Managers: L. Gillham (Tech Serv Mgr)
Ultimate Holding Company: ELLIS STEEL HOLDINGS LIMITED
Immediate Holding Company: BRISTOL STEEL STOCKHOLDERS LIMITED
Registration no: 01280791 **VAT No.:** GB 438 5150 49
Date established: 1976 **Turnover:** £2m - £5m **No.of Employees:** 21 - 50
Product Groups: 46

Date of Accounts	Dec 11	Dec 10	Dec 09
Sales Turnover	6m	5m	4m
Pre Tax Profit/Loss	142	299	14
Working Capital	2m	3m	2m
Fixed Assets	334	315	434
Current Assets	5m	4m	3m
Current Liabilities	224	338	138

Bristol Storage Equipment
Cambridge House Waterloo Street, St Philips, Bristol, BS2 0PH
Tel: 0117-955 5211 **Fax:** 0117-955 6194
E-mail: janet.ives@dexionsw.co.uk
Website: http://www.dexionsw.com
Directors: J. Ives (Fin)
Ultimate Holding Company: 04718114
Immediate Holding Company: BRISTOL STORAGE EQUIPMENT LIMITED
Registration no: 01033862 **Date established:** 1971 **Turnover:** £1m - £2m
No.of Employees: 1 - 10 **Product Groups:** 07, 25, 26, 33, 35, 39, 40, 41, 45, 52, 66, 67, 72, 85

Date of Accounts	Dec 09	Dec 08	Dec 07
Working Capital	8	-1	-8
Fixed Assets	15	31	40
Current Assets	116	217	160

Bristol Uniforms Ltd
Wathen Street Staple Hill, Bristol, BS16 5LL
Tel: 0117-956 3101 **Fax:** 0117-956 5927
E-mail: enquiries@bristoluniforms.com
Website: http://www.bristol.uniforms.com
Bank(s): Barclays
Directors: A. Ring (Fin), R. Startin (Dir)
Managers: A. Luckett (Tech Serv Mgr), A. Williams, M. England (Purch Mgr)
Ultimate Holding Company: B T Q LIMITED
Immediate Holding Company: BRISTOL UNIFORMS LIMITED
Registration no: 00708126 **VAT No.:** GB 139 1582 58
Date established: 1961 **Turnover:** £10m - £20m
No.of Employees: 101 - 250 **Product Groups:** 24

Date of Accounts	Dec 11	Dec 10	Dec 09
Sales Turnover	13m	19m	13m
Pre Tax Profit/Loss	932	1m	1m
Working Capital	5m	4m	7m
Fixed Assets	9m	8m	1m
Current Assets	8m	9m	16m
Current Liabilities	723	1m	587

Bristol Wash Tub Rentals
3 Main Road Mangotsfield, Bristol, BS16 9NH
Tel: 0117-937 4726
Managers: F. Merchant (Mgr)
No.of Employees: 1 - 10 **Product Groups:** 43

Bristol Water plc
PO Box 218, Bristol, BS99 7AU
Tel: 0117-966 5881 **Fax:** 0117-963 4576
E-mail: customer.services@bristolwater.co.uk
Website: http://www.bristolwater.co.uk
Bank(s): National Westminster Bank Plc
Directors: S. Robson (Co Sec), M. Anglada Gali (Fin), L. Garcia (Grp Chief Exec)
Managers: J. Saunders (Mktg Serv Mgr), L. Tanner (Buyer), A. Barnstable (Tech Serv Mgr), B. Edwards (Personnel)
Ultimate Holding Company: SOCIEDAD GENERAL DE AGUAS DE BARCELONA SA
Immediate Holding Company: BRISTOL WATER PLC
Registration no: 02662226 **Date established:** 1991
Turnover: £75m - £125m **No.of Employees:** 251 - 500
Product Groups: 18

Date of Accounts	Mar 12	Mar 11	Mar 10
Sales Turnover	108m	101m	100m
Pre Tax Profit/Loss	11m	8m	23m
Working Capital	42m	75m	20m
Fixed Assets	342m	317m	326m
Current Assets	101m	103m	51m
Current Liabilities	24m	19m	23m

Trevor Brodrick
White Chimneys Paulton Road, Hallatrow, Bristol, BS39 6EG
Tel: 01761-452409 **Fax:** 01761-453435
E-mail: trevor@tbws.co.uk
Website: http://www.tbws.co.uk
Directors: T. Brodrick (Prop)
Date established: 1980 **No.of Employees:** 1 - 10 **Product Groups:** 46

Bronev Lifts Ltd
9 Redcatch Road, Bristol, BS4 2EP
Tel: 0117-977 0076 **Fax:** 0117-971 7556
E-mail: enq@bronev.co.uk
Website: http://www.bronev.co.uk
Directors: S. Neville (Dir), P. Broom (Fin)
Immediate Holding Company: BRONEV LIFTS LIMITED
Registration no: 04553067 **Date established:** 2002
No.of Employees: 11 - 20 **Product Groups:** 35, 39, 45

Date of Accounts	Dec 10	Dec 09	Dec 08
Working Capital	-12	-9	-5
Fixed Assets	27	35	20
Current Assets	79	80	72

Broughton & Co Bristol Ltd (t/a Busicom Business Machines)
4 Axis Hawkfield Way, Hawkfield Business Park, Bristol, BS14 0BY
Tel: 0117-964 1300 **Fax:** 0117-964 1003
E-mail: broughtons1bristol@btinternet.com
Website: http://www.busicom.com
Directors: J. Broughton (Fin)
Immediate Holding Company: BROUGHTON & CO. (BRISTOL) LIMITED
Registration no: 00488398 **Date established:** 1950
No.of Employees: 1 - 10 **Product Groups:** 44, 67

Date of Accounts	Jan 12	Jan 11	Jan 10
Working Capital	662	758	900
Fixed Assets	15	18	24
Current Assets	734	842	974

Brown Rutter Ltd
Salisbury Street Barton Hill, Bristol, BS5 9UD
Tel: 0117-955 0781 **Fax:** 0117-941 3685
E-mail: sales@brownrutter.com
Website: http://www.brownrutter.com
Directors: B. Brown (I.T. Dir), G. Brown (Dir)
Immediate Holding Company: BROWN-RUTTER LIMITED
Registration no: 01153501 **Date established:** 1973
Turnover: Up to £250,000 **No.of Employees:** 1 - 10 **Product Groups:** 30

Date of Accounts	Jan 11	Jan 10	Jan 09
Sales Turnover	121	96	119
Pre Tax Profit/Loss	1	-22	-8
Working Capital	5	2	22
Fixed Assets	8	10	12
Current Assets	40	41	56
Current Liabilities	25	16	16

Brunel Ford
175 Muller Road Horfield, Bristol, BS7 9RB
Tel: 0117-908 9999 **Fax:** 0117-908 9299
E-mail: neil.scull@fordretail.uk.com
Website: http://www.brunelford.co.uk
Managers: N. Scull (Mgr), R. Robertson (Chief Mgr)
Immediate Holding Company: QUARTIC CO. LTD
Registration no: 02796252 **No.of Employees:** 21 - 50 **Product Groups:** 68

Brunel Promotions Ltd
Hope Road, Bristol, BS3 3NZ
Tel: 0117-963 6161 **Fax:** 0117-966 4235
E-mail: trade@bruneltradeservices.co.uk
Website: http://www.brunelpromotions.co.uk
Bank(s): National Westminster Bank Plc
Directors: S. Cole (Tech Serv), S. Tugman (Prop), D. Gardiner (Chief Op Offcr)
Managers: M. Home (Comptroller)
Ultimate Holding Company: BRUNEL HOLDINGS (BRISTOL) LIMITED
Immediate Holding Company: BRUNEL HOLDINGS (BRISTOL) LIMITED
Registration no: 05515092 **Date established:** 2005 **Turnover:** £5m - £10m
No.of Employees: 21 - 50 **Product Groups:** 27, 28, 49

Date of Accounts	Dec 11	Dec 10	Dec 09
Sales Turnover	6m	6m	5m
Pre Tax Profit/Loss	335	1m	74
Working Capital	2m	3m	1m
Fixed Assets	873	649	417
Current Assets	4m	4m	4m
Current Liabilities	715	594	539

Buck & Hickman Ltd
126 Albert Road St Philips, Bristol, BS2 0YA
Tel: 0117-916 8660 **Fax:** 0117-957 9799
E-mail: bristol@buckandhickman.com
Website: http://www.buckandhickman.com
Managers: D. Slade (District Mgr)
Ultimate Holding Company: TRAVIS PERKINS PLC
Immediate Holding Company: BOSTON (2011) LIMITED
Registration no: 06028304 **Date established:** 2006
Turnover: £75m - £125m **No.of Employees:** 11 - 20 **Product Groups:** 24, 29, 30, 33, 36, 37, 41, 46

Date of Accounts	Dec 10	Mar 10	Mar 09
Working Capital	6m	6m	6m
Current Assets	27m	27m	27m

Budd Communiactions
Unit 3 Willcock House Southway Drive, Bristol, BS30 5LW
Tel: 0117-932 1060
E-mail: mike@budds.co.uk
Website: http://www.budd.co.uk
Directors: B. Barclay (Fin), M. Budds (Dir)
Immediate Holding Company: INTER-GROUP COMMUNICATIONS LTD
Registration no: 04162389 **Date established:** 2001
No.of Employees: 11 - 20 **Product Groups:** 37, 67

Builder Center Ltd
2 London Road Warmley, Bristol, BS30 5JB
Tel: 0117-967 0702 **Fax:** 0117-967 5719
E-mail: tony.belston@wolseley.co.uk
Website: http://www.buildcenter.co.uk
Bank(s): Natwest
Directors: T. Belston (Sales)
Managers: T. Belsten (Mgr)
Ultimate Holding Company: Wolseley plc
Immediate Holding Company: BUILD CENTER LIMITED
Registration no: 00462397 **VAT No.:** GB 362 0233 93
Date established: 1948 **Turnover:** Over £1,000m
No.of Employees: 11 - 20 **Product Groups:** 25, 66

Building Design Patnership
7 Hill Street, Bristol, BS1 5RW
Tel: 0117-929 9861 **Fax:** 0117-922 5280
E-mail: bristol@bdp.co.uk
Website: http://www.bdp.com
Managers: P. Winter (I.T. Exec), L. Chandler (Sales Admin)
Ultimate Holding Company: BDP HOLDINGS LTD
Immediate Holding Company: WHICHELOE MACFARLANE PARTNERSHIP LTD
Registration no: 03228395 **Turnover:** £5m - £10m
No.of Employees: 51 - 100 **Product Groups:** 80, 84

Bunzl Vending Services Ltd
Unit 2 The Commercial Centre Days Road, St Philips, Bristol, BS2 0QS
Tel: 0117-955 8844 **Fax:** 0117-955 9781
E-mail: lynda.forrester@bunzlvend.com
Website: http://www.bunzlvend.com
Managers: L. Forrester (District Mgr)
Immediate Holding Company: BUNZL VENDING SERVICES LIMITED
Registration no: 02605313 **VAT No.:** GB 581 7059 24
Date established: 1991 **Turnover:** £20m - £50m **No.of Employees:** 1 - 10
Product Groups: 49

Burden Ltd
5 The Cobden Centre Folly Brook Road, Emersons Green, Bristol, BS16 7FQ
Tel: 08706-006068 **Fax:** 0117-301 4400
E-mail: j-burden@burdens.co.uk
Website: http://www.burdens.co.uk

see next page

***Burden Ltd** - Cont'd*
Bank(s): National Westminster
Directors: C. Briginshaw (Sales & Mktg), J. Burden (Grp Chief Exec), J. Dooham (Fin), L. Doran (Pers)
Managers: I. Thomas (Purch Mgr), T. Brice (Tech Serv Mgr)
Ultimate Holding Company: W.T. BURDEN LIMITED
Immediate Holding Company: BURDENS LTD.
Registration no: 03593372 **VAT No.:** GB 681 9578 79
Date established: 1998 **Turnover:** £250m - £500m
No.of Employees: 21 - 50 **Product Groups:** 66

Date of Accounts	Jun 11	Jun 10	Jun 09
Sales Turnover	289m	269m	280m
Pre Tax Profit/Loss	5m	4m	3m
Working Capital	4m	4m	867
Fixed Assets	27m	28m	28m
Current Assets	123m	105m	94m
Current Liabilities	8m	4m	5m

Burges Salmon LLP
1 Glass Wharf, Bristol, BS2 0ZX
Tel: 0117-939 2000 **Fax:** 0117-902 4400
E-mail: email@burges-salmon.com
Website: http://www.burges-salmon.com
Directors: A. Barr (Snr Part)
Managers: J. Fountaine, S. Whitwham, R. Rex, S. Russell
Ultimate Holding Company: BURGES SALMON LLP
Immediate Holding Company: TEMPLE TRUSTEES LIMITED
Registration no: 02682277 **Date established:** 1992
Turnover: £50m - £75m **No.of Employees:** 501 - 1000
Product Groups: 80

Date of Accounts	Apr 11	Apr 10	Apr 09
Working Capital	17	17	18
Current Assets	199	66	105

Business Environment Group
Westpoint 78 Queens Road, Clifton, Bristol, BS8 1QU
Tel: 0117-907 5555 **Fax:** 0117-921 1594
E-mail: info@beoffices.com
Website: http://www.beoffices.com
Managers: L. Raschka (Mgr)
Immediate Holding Company: SERECCO LTD
Registration no: 00501655 **VAT No.:** GB 139 3336 63
Date established: 2004 **Turnover:** £250,000 - £500,000
No.of Employees: 1 - 10 **Product Groups:** 80

Date of Accounts	Mar 11	Mar 10	Mar 09
Working Capital	-6	N/A	N/A
Fixed Assets	2	N/A	N/A
Current Assets	1	9	7

Business West
Leigh Court Business Centre Pill Road, Abbots Leigh, Bristol, BS8 3RA
Tel: 01275-373373 **Fax:** 01793-645151
E-mail: info@businesswest.co.uk
Website: http://www.businesswest.co.uk
Directors: J. Greenwood (Fin)
Managers: M. Martin (Commun Mgr), A. Crombleholme (Personnel), S. Osipiuk (Tech Serv Mgr)
Immediate Holding Company: GREAT WESTERN ENTERPRISE (HOLDINGS) LIMITED
Registration no: 02021993 **Date established:** 1986 **Turnover:** £5m - £10m
No.of Employees: 101 - 250 **Product Groups:** 80, 81

Date of Accounts	Mar 11	Mar 10	Mar 09
Pre Tax Profit/Loss	119	215	115
Working Capital	348	329	115
Fixed Assets	4m	4m	4m
Current Assets	348	329	166

C & F Millier & Co.
272 Southmead Road Westbury-on-trym, Bristol, BS10 5EW
Tel: 0117-950 5252 **Fax:** 0117-950 8969
E-mail: sales@cfmillier.co.uk
Website: http://www.cfmillier.co.uk
Bank(s): Barclays
Directors: A. Stuckes (MD), A. Stuckes (MD), C. Morton (Ch)
Managers: G. Archer
Ultimate Holding Company: MILLIER HOLDINGS LIMITED
Immediate Holding Company: C & F MILLIER LIMITED
Registration no: 00724656 **VAT No.:** GB 609 7964 92
Date established: 1962 **No.of Employees:** 21 - 50 **Product Groups:** 30, 35, 39, 48

Date of Accounts	Dec 11	Dec 10	Dec 09
Working Capital	1m	1m	1m
Fixed Assets	542	353	406
Current Assets	2m	2m	2m

C L Electrical Controls Ltd
Unit 1 Kendleshire Farm Down Road Winterbourne, Winterbourne Down, Bristol, BS36 1AU
Tel: 01454-250555 **Fax:** 01454-250540
E-mail: enquiries@clelectricalcontrols.co.uk
Website: http://www.clelectricalcontrols.co.uk
Bank(s): Barclays P.L.C., Bristol
Directors: S. Newman (MD)
Immediate Holding Company: C.L. ELECTRICAL CONTROLS LIMITED
Registration no: 05263920 **VAT No.:** GB 302 6281 94
Date established: 2004 **Turnover:** £500,000 - £1m
No.of Employees: 11 - 20 **Product Groups:** 35, 37, 39, 40, 45

Date of Accounts	Jun 11	Jun 10	Jun 09
Working Capital	-100	-117	-19
Fixed Assets	38	38	43
Current Assets	245	233	452

C M S Engineering Services Ltd
Unit 10 Satellite Business Park Blackswarth Road, Bristol, BS5 8GU
Tel: 0117-941 2596 **Fax:** 0117-955 3200
E-mail: cmsengineering@btconnect.com
Website: http://www.cms-engineering.com
Directors: G. Barry (Dir)
Immediate Holding Company: CMS ENGINEERING SERVICES LTD
Registration no: 04715513 **Date established:** 2003
No.of Employees: 1 - 10 **Product Groups:** 42, 45

Date of Accounts	Mar 11	Mar 10	Mar 09
Working Capital	72	132	180
Fixed Assets	42	40	28
Current Assets	127	207	267

Cabot Engineering Ltd
3 Camwal Road Chapel Street, Bristol, BS2 0UZ
Tel: 0117-971 7044 **Fax:** 0117-977 5366
Bank(s): HSBC Bank plc
Directors: A. Wild (MD), A. Wild (Dir)
Managers: M. Jones (Chief Acct), P. Watkins (Buyer)
Immediate Holding Company: CABOT ENGINEERING LIMITED
Registration no: 02982866 **VAT No.:** GB 650 4933 40
Date established: 1994 **Turnover:** £500,000 - £1m
No.of Employees: 11 - 20 **Product Groups:** 35, 48

Date of Accounts	Jan 11	Jan 10	Jan 09
Working Capital	-12	29	136
Fixed Assets	16	18	22
Current Assets	255	247	349

Camb Machine Knives International
Unit 6 The Alpha Centre Armstrong Way, Great Western Business Pk, Yate, Bristol, BS37 5NG
Tel: 01454-322178 **Fax:** 01454-321172
E-mail: sales@camb-knives.co.uk
Website: http://www.camb-knives.co.uk
Directors: J. Milner (Ptnr), Milner (Ptnr)
VAT No.: GB 422 9947 29 **Date established:** 1989 **Turnover:** £1m - £2m
Product Groups: 36, 41, 42, 43, 44, 45, 46, 47, 48

Cameron Balloons
St Johns Street, Bristol, BS3 4NH
Tel: 0117-963 7216 **Fax:** 0117-966 1168
E-mail: anoble@cameronballoons.co.uk
Website: http://www.cameronballoons.co.uk
Directors: D. Cameron (MD), N. Purvis (Sales), A. Noble (Co Sec)
Managers: S. Tatford (Buyer), N. Pervis (Mgr), A. Noble (Mktg Serv Mgr), J. Reed (Mgr)
Ultimate Holding Company: CAMERON HOLDINGS LIMITED
Immediate Holding Company: CAMERON BALLOONS LIMITED
Registration no: 01006715 **VAT No.:** GB 137 4986 31
Date established: 1971 **Turnover:** £250,000 - £500,000
No.of Employees: 1 - 10 **Product Groups:** 39

Date of Accounts	Jan 11	Jan 10	Jan 09
Working Capital	564	461	265
Fixed Assets	211	229	150
Current Assets	2m	2m	2m

Cannon Textiles Care
37 Whitehouse Street, Bristol, BS3 4AY
Tel: 0117-953 7536 **Fax:** 0117-953 2188
E-mail: info@ocs.co.uk
Website: http://www.ocs.co.uk
Managers: J. Tuck (District Mgr)
Registration no: 00186246 **Turnover:** £500,000 - £1m
No.of Employees: 21 - 50 **Product Groups:** 23, 83

Car Paint Warehouse Ltd
17 & 18 Bonville Business Centre Bonville Road, Bristol, BS4 5QR
Tel: 0117-300 9058 **Fax:** 0117-300 9681
E-mail: sales@carpaintwarehouse.co.uk
Website: http://www.carpaintwarehouse.co.uk
Directors: J. Morgan (Dir)
Immediate Holding Company: CAR PAINT WAREHOUSE LIMITED
Registration no: 04082523 **Date established:** 2000
No.of Employees: 1 - 10 **Product Groups:** 32

Date of Accounts	Aug 11	Aug 10	Aug 09
Working Capital	204	117	155
Fixed Assets	440	416	24
Current Assets	442	325	306

Cartridge World Ltd
184 Wells Road Totterdown, Bristol, BS4 2AL
Tel: 0117-971 9305 **Fax:** 0117-971 9306
Website: http://www.cartridgeworld.org
Directors: A. Hawkins (Dir)
Immediate Holding Company: CARTRIDGE WORLD LIMITED
Registration no: 04124067 **Date established:** 2000 **Turnover:** £5m - £10m
No.of Employees: 1 - 10 **Product Groups:** 28, 30, 44

Date of Accounts	Dec 10	Dec 09	Dec 08
Sales Turnover	7m	8m	7m
Pre Tax Profit/Loss	164	210	122
Working Capital	967	878	662
Fixed Assets	455	524	603
Current Assets	7m	6m	4m
Current Liabilities	1m	2m	1m

Catalogue Consultancy
19 Fernbank Road, Bristol, BS6 6QA
Tel: 0117-944 5226 **Fax:** 0117-944 5227
E-mail: mw@protocolpr.co.uk
Website: http://www.catalogueconsultancy.com
Directors: M. Wilson (Dir), A. Wilson (Fin)
Immediate Holding Company: DIRECT COMMERCE LTD
Registration no: 04829979 **Date established:** 2003
Turnover: Up to £250,000 **No.of Employees:** 1 - 10 **Product Groups:** 61

Date of Accounts	Apr 11	Apr 10	Apr 09
Working Capital	15	19	94
Fixed Assets	1	N/A	5
Current Assets	33	37	126

Cementation Skanska Ltd
400 Woodlands Court Bradley Stoke, Bristol, BS32 4LB
Tel: 01454-453200 **Fax:** 01454-453215
E-mail: mark.bradshaw@skanska.co.uk
Website: http://www.skanska.co.uk/piling-foundations
Directors: C. Foley (Chief Op Offcr)
Managers: M. Bradshaw (Mgr)
Ultimate Holding Company: SKANSKA AB (SWEDEN)
Immediate Holding Company: CEMENTATION SKANSKA LIMITED
Registration no: 00937574 **Date established:** 1968
No.of Employees: 1 - 10 **Product Groups:** 45, 51, 52, 84

Date of Accounts	Dec 10	Dec 09	Dec 08
Sales Turnover	39m	48m	85m
Pre Tax Profit/Loss	-2m	88	4m
Working Capital	2m	3m	2m
Fixed Assets	11m	11m	12m
Current Assets	15m	17m	23m
Current Liabilities	5m	7m	10m

Cemex Floors
London Road Wick, Bristol, BS30 5SJ
Tel: 0117-937 3740 **Fax:** 01865-842303
E-mail: barrie.march@cemex.co.uk
Website: http://www.cemex.com
Bank(s): National Westminster
Managers: B. March (Comm)
Immediate Holding Company: R M C GROUP P.L.C.
Registration no: 00302263 **VAT No.:** GB 222 8284 72
Turnover: Up to £250,000 **No.of Employees:** 21 - 50 **Product Groups:** 33

Chaplin Fabrications
Iron Masters Cotswold Road, Bristol, BS3 4NS
Tel: 0117-963 8800 **Fax:** 0117- 9638800
Directors: J. Chaplin (Prop)
Date established: 2003 **No.of Employees:** 1 - 10 **Product Groups:** 26, 35

Charles Church Severn Valley
Churchward House Churchward Road, Yate, Bristol, BS37 5NN
Tel: 01454-333800 **Fax:** 01454-327123
Website: http://www.charleschurch.com
Directors: C. Haley (MD)
Managers: N. Reed (Mktg Serv Mgr), A. Jones (Comptroller), D. Cummings (Buyer)
Ultimate Holding Company: BEAZER HOMES P.L.C.
Immediate Holding Company: BEAZER GROUP
Registration no: 00161750 **VAT No.:** GB 464 6311 49
Date established: 2001 **Turnover:** £10m - £20m
No.of Employees: 21 - 50 **Product Groups:** 87

Cibo Ristorante
289 Gloucester Road Bishopston, Bristol, BS7 8NY
Tel: 0117-942 9475 **Fax:** 0117-9429 483
E-mail: dino@cibo.co.uk
Website: http://www.ciboristorante.co.uk
Directors: D. Caidominici (Dir)
Immediate Holding Company: FOODCO NI LTD
Registration no: NI018146 **Date established:** 1984
Turnover: Up to £250,000 **No.of Employees:** 1 - 10 **Product Groups:** 20, 62

City Engineering Bristol Ltd
7 Maggs Lane Fishponds, Bristol, BS5 7EP
Tel: 0117-965 4314 **Fax:** 0117-958 3552
E-mail: sales@cityengineering.com
Website: http://www.cityengineering.com
Bank(s): National Westminster
Directors: S. Woodbury (MD), R. Davies (Ch), J. Davies (Fin)
Managers: R. Ashby (Sales & Mktg Mg)
Ultimate Holding Company: CITY ENGINEERING (HOLDINGS) LIMITED
Immediate Holding Company: CITY ENGINEERING (BRISTOL) LIMITED
Registration no: 05277160 **VAT No.:** GB 137 6819 40
Date established: 2004 **Turnover:** £2m - £5m **No.of Employees:** 21 - 50
Product Groups: 35, 36, 45, 48

Date of Accounts	Oct 11	Oct 10	Oct 09
Sales Turnover	5m	3m	N/A
Pre Tax Profit/Loss	694	197	N/A
Working Capital	775	574	553
Fixed Assets	1m	594	594
Current Assets	2m	1m	879
Current Liabilities	281	135	N/A

Clarke Willmott LLP
1 Georges Square, Bristol, BS1 6BA
Tel: 08452-091000 **Fax:** 0117-917 7025
E-mail: info@clarkewillmott.com
Website: http://www.clarkewillmott.com
Bank(s): National Westminster
Directors: S. Rossor (Grp Chief Exec)
Managers: J. Moore (Personnel), B. Bruce (Fin Mgr), I. Hepburn (Tech Serv Mgr), S. Jones (Mktg Serv Mgr)
Immediate Holding Company: CLARKE WILLMOTT LIMITED
Registration no: 04502077 **VAT No.:** GB 129 9130 60
Date established: 2002 **Turnover:** £10m - £20m
No.of Employees: 251 - 500 **Product Groups:** 80

Claverham
Bishops Road Claverham, Bristol, BS49 4NF
Tel: 01934-835224 **Fax:** 01934-835337
E-mail: reception@claverham.com
Website: http://www.claverham.com
Directors: R. Buxton (Pers)
Managers: G. Wallace (Develop Mgr), K. Thomas, R. Packham (Fin Mgr)
Ultimate Holding Company: UNITED TECHNOLOGIES CORP INC (USA)
Immediate Holding Company: CLAVERHAM HOLDINGS LIMITED
Registration no: 00839154 **Date established:** 1965
Turnover: £20m - £50m **No.of Employees:** 101 - 250
Product Groups: 35, 36, 38, 40, 42, 67, 81

Date of Accounts	Nov 11	Nov 10	Nov 09
Working Capital	2m	2m	2m
Fixed Assets	2	2	2
Current Assets	16m	16m	16m

Clear Design
1 Gas Ferry Road, Bristol, BS1 6UN
Tel: 0117-930 0222
E-mail: info@cleardesignuk.com
Website: http://www.cleardesignuk.com
Directors: D. Jones (Dir)
Immediate Holding Company: CLEAR DESIGN UK LIMITED
Registration no: 04597034 **Date established:** 2002
Turnover: Up to £250,000 **No.of Employees:** 1 - 10 **Product Groups:** 44, 79

Date of Accounts	Nov 11	Nov 10	Nov 09
Working Capital	28	87	86
Fixed Assets	2	3	4
Current Assets	28	87	117

Clerical Medical Investment Group Ltd
10 Canons Way, Bristol, BS1 5LF
Tel: 0117-929 0290 **Fax:** 01275-552667
E-mail: info@clericalmedical.co.uk
Website: http://www.clericalmedical.co.uk
Bank(s): National Westminster
Directors: M. Christophers (Dir), T. Leonard (Fin)
Ultimate Holding Company: LLOYDS BANKING GROUP PLC
Immediate Holding Company: CLERICAL MEDICAL INVESTMENT GROUP LIMITED
Registration no: 03196171 **Date established:** 1996
Turnover: Over £1,000m **No.of Employees:** 1501 & over
Product Groups: 82

Date of Accounts	Dec 11	Dec 10	Dec 09
Pre Tax Profit/Loss	7m	-136m	-324m
Fixed Assets	17960m	28549m	28347m
Current Assets	8903m	325m	1384m
Current Liabilities	24400m	128m	27156m

Clip Display

Church Road Wick, Bristol, BS30 5RD
Tel: 0117-937 2636 **Fax:** 0117-937 3172
E-mail: info@clipdisplay.com
Website: http://www.clipdisplay.com
Directors: G. Barrett (MD)
Managers: I. Fletcher (Tech Serv Mgr), P. Runacres (Sales & Mktg Mg), S. Eliott, J. Fern (Cust Serv Mgr)
Ultimate Holding Company: CLIP INTERNATIONAL LIMITED
Immediate Holding Company: CLIP LIMITED
Registration no: 00933144 **Date established:** 1968 **Turnover:** £5m - £10m
No.of Employees: 21 - 50 **Product Groups:** 26, 81

Date of Accounts	Dec 11	Dec 10	Dec 09
Sales Turnover	5m	6m	6m
Pre Tax Profit/Loss	265	383	-386
Working Capital	136	27	-147
Fixed Assets	3m	2m	3m
Current Assets	2m	2m	1m
Current Liabilities	768	1m	846

Colliers International UK plc

Floor 7 Broad Quay House Broad Quay, Bristol, BS1 4DJ
Tel: 01285-852852 **Fax:** 01285-852888
E-mail: tim.davies@colliers.com
Website: http://www.colliers.com
Managers: T. Davies (Sales Admin)
Immediate Holding Company: COLLIERS INTERNATIONAL UK PLC
Registration no: 04195561 **Date established:** 2001 **Turnover:** £5m - £10m
No.of Employees: 21 - 50 **Product Groups:** 52, 80, 82, 84

Date of Accounts	Dec 10	Dec 09	Dec 08
Sales Turnover	66m	58m	78m
Pre Tax Profit/Loss	-8m	-40m	-11m
Working Capital	11m	14m	-65
Fixed Assets	39m	40m	67m
Current Assets	23m	24m	35m
Current Liabilities	10m	9m	13m

T A Collinson

41 Dark Lane Backwell, Bristol, BS48 3NT
Tel: 01275-462626
Directors: T. Collinson (Prop)
Date established: 1992 **No.of Employees:** 1 - 10 **Product Groups:** 35

Conference Connections

Unit 1 Pegasus Park Gipsy Patch Lane, Patchway, Bristol, BS34 6QD
Tel: 08701-203891 **Fax:** 0870-120 3890
E-mail: selina.morgan@conference-connections.co.uk
Website: http://www.conference-connections.co.uk
Directors: S. Morgan (Dir)
Immediate Holding Company: CONFERENCE CONNECTIONS LIMITED
Registration no: 04294832 **Date established:** 2001
No.of Employees: 11 - 20 **Product Groups:** 69, 79, 81

Date of Accounts	Dec 11	Dec 10	Dec 09
Working Capital	-0	-0	-0
Current Assets	-0	1	1
Current Liabilities	N/A	1	1

Connexion Technology Ltd

3 Glentworth Road Clifton, Bristol, BS8 4TB
Tel: 0117-907 0480 **Fax:** 0117-927 7693
E-mail: dave@connexiontechnology.co.uk
Website: http://www.connexiontechnology.co.uk
Directors: D. Cooley (Dir), D. Cooley (MD)
Immediate Holding Company: CONNEXION TECHNOLOGY LTD
Registration no: 03712590 **Date established:** 1999
Turnover: Up to £250,000 **No.of Employees:** 1 - 10 **Product Groups:** 30, 31

Date of Accounts	May 08	May 07	May 06
Sales Turnover	N/A	93	N/A
Pre Tax Profit/Loss	N/A	11	N/A
Working Capital	16	23	24
Fixed Assets	1	N/A	N/A
Current Assets	39	35	47
Current Liabilities	22	13	23
ROCE% (Return on Capital Employed)		46.9	
ROT% (Return on Turnover)		11.6	

Constellation Europe Ltd

Whitchurch Lane Whitchurch, Bristol, BS14 0JZ
Tel: 01483-690000 **Fax:** 01275-836726
E-mail: snezana.saleta@cbrands.eu.com
Website: http://www.cbrands.com
Bank(s): Barclays
Directors: J. Mills (Dep Pres)
Managers: L. Williams (Security), S. Saleta (Sales Admin)
Immediate Holding Company: MATTHEW CLARK AND SONS LIMITED
Registration no: 00137407 **VAT No.:** GB 524 7076 48
Date established: 2011 **Turnover:** £500m - £1,000m
No.of Employees: 101 - 250 **Product Groups:** 62

Date of Accounts	Feb 08
Sales Turnover	629500
Pre Tax Profit/Loss	1300
Working Capital	53340
Fixed Assets	62970
Current Assets	432040
Current Liabilities	378700
Total Share Capital	2870
ROCE% (Return on Capital Employed)	1.1

Corus

Badminton Road Trading Estate Yate, Bristol, BS37 5JU
Tel: 01454-315314 **Fax:** 01454-326946
E-mail: info@corusgroup.com
Website: http://www.corus-servicecentres.com
Directors: I. Beveradge (Ch)
Managers: M. Eldridge (Chief Mgr), P. McArther (Chief Mgr)
Immediate Holding Company: CORUS GROUP LIMITED
Registration no: 03811373 **Date established:** 1999
Turnover: £20m - £50m **No.of Employees:** 11 - 20 **Product Groups:** 66

Cotswold Spring Water

Dodington Spring Codrington, Chipping Sodbury, Bristol, BS37 6RX
Tel: 01454-312403 **Fax:** 01454-273378
E-mail: sales@cotswold-spring.co.uk
Website: http://www.cotswold-spring.co.uk
Directors: J. Marshall (Co Sec)
Managers: C. Marshall (Ops Mgr)
Immediate Holding Company: COOLERS 4 U LIMITED
Registration no: 06294350 **Date established:** 2007 **Turnover:** £1m - £2m
No.of Employees: 11 - 20 **Product Groups:** 21

Cotswold Treatment P P Ltd

Abadan House Gloucester Road, Thornbury, Bristol, BS35 3TU
Tel: 01454-417199 **Fax:** 01454-201252
E-mail: sales@cotswoldtreatments.co.uk
Website: http://www.cotswoldtreatments.co.uk
Directors: P. Hawkins (Dir)
Immediate Holding Company: COMPLETE FLOORING SOLUTIONS MP LIMITED
Registration no: 06868784 **Date established:** 2009
Turnover: £500,000 - £1m **No.of Employees:** 1 - 10 **Product Groups:** 32

Cowlin Construction

Stratton House Cater Road, Bristol, BS13 7UH
Tel: 0117-983 2000 **Fax:** 0117-987 7758
E-mail: info@cowlin.co.uk
Website: http://www.cowlin.co.uk
Bank(s): HSBC Bank plc
Directors: D. Stockham (MD)
Ultimate Holding Company: BALFOUR BEATTY PLC
Immediate Holding Company: BRISCARD PROPERTY INVESTMENTS LIMITED
Registration no: 03078617 **Date established:** 1995
Turnover: £125m - £250m **No.of Employees:** 21 - 50
Product Groups: 51, 52, 80

Date of Accounts	Sep 11	Sep 10	Sep 09
Pre Tax Profit/Loss	-109	-106	-92
Working Capital	14	31	34
Fixed Assets	2m	2m	2m
Current Assets	21	36	44
Current Liabilities	7	5	5

CPC Packaging Ltd

Knapp's Lane Fishponds Trading Estate, St. George, Bristol, BS5 7UN
Tel: 0117-951 6751 **Fax:** 0117-935 4038
E-mail: info@groupecpc.co.uk
Website: http://www.groupecpc.com
Bank(s): National Westminster Bank Plc
Directors: C. Dew (MD), P. Cook (Dir)
Managers: J. Bryan (Sales Prom Mgr)
Ultimate Holding Company: The Berkshire Printing Group Ltd
Registration no: 02286578 **Turnover:** £2m - £5m
No.of Employees: 51 - 100 **Product Groups:** 27, 28

Crescent Universal Tungsten Ltd

Unit 8 Avon Business Park Lodge Causeway, Bristol, BS16 3JP
Tel: 0117-965 5605 **Fax:** 0117-958 4390
Directors: J. Brookbank (MD)
Managers: J. Brookbank (Mgr)
Date established: 1995 **No.of Employees:** 1 - 10 **Product Groups:** 46, 48

Cross Engineering Services Ltd

218 South Liberty Lane, Bristol, BS3 2TY
Tel: 0117-963 8643 **Fax:** 0117-963 8643
Directors: C. Cross (MD)
Immediate Holding Company: CROSS ENGINEERING SERVICES LIMITED
Registration no: 04589081 **Date established:** 2002
Turnover: £250,000 - £500,000 **No.of Employees:** 1 - 10
Product Groups: 35

Date of Accounts	Mar 11	Mar 10	Mar 09
Sales Turnover	269	326	325
Pre Tax Profit/Loss	49	90	75
Working Capital	11	32	25
Fixed Assets	8	12	16
Current Assets	152	152	136
Current Liabilities	131	45	30

Crown Conveyors UK Ltd

Wood Road Industrial Centre Kingswood, Bristol, BS15 8NN
Tel: 0117-967 1370 **Fax:** 0117-935 3194
E-mail: mail@crownconveyors.com
Website: http://www.crownconveyors.com
Directors: A. Hinton (MD), N. Lintern (Fin), T. Hinton (MD)
Managers: T. Hawker (Mktg Serv Mgr)
Immediate Holding Company: CROWN CONVEYORS (UK) LIMITED
Registration no: 04960433 **VAT No.:** GB 328 3987 19
Date established: 2003 **Turnover:** £1m - £2m **No.of Employees:** 11 - 20
Product Groups: 41

Cube Epos Ltd

2 Montpelier Central Station Road, Montpelier, Bristol, BS6 5EE
Tel: 0117-970 5000 **Fax:** 0117-970 5050
E-mail: jeff@qube-epos.co.uk
Website: http://www.bcgcomputers.co.uk
Directors: J. Davis (MD)
Immediate Holding Company: QUBE EPOS LIMITED
Registration no: 04467406 **Date established:** 2002
Turnover: £250,000 - £500,000 **No.of Employees:** 1 - 10
Product Groups: 44, 67

Date of Accounts	Apr 12	Apr 11	Apr 10
Sales Turnover	N/A	N/A	290
Pre Tax Profit/Loss	N/A	N/A	1
Working Capital	4	-15	-26
Fixed Assets	31	22	29
Current Assets	53	59	44
Current Liabilities	N/A	N/A	47

Cypherseal Ltd

Qtac House, Kingsfield Lane Longwell Green, Bristol, BS30 6DL
Tel: 0117-947 4762
E-mail: nick.shaw@cypherseal.com
Website: http://www.cypherseal.com
Directors: N. Shaw (Grp Chief Exec)
Registration no: 05915595 **Date established:** 2008
Turnover: Up to £250,000 **No.of Employees:** 1 - 10 **Product Groups:** 44

D A S Legal Expenses Insurance Co. Ltd

D A S House Quay Side Temple Back, Bristol, BS1 6NH
Tel: 0117-934 2000 **Fax:** 0117-934 2109
E-mail: s_skull@das.co.uk
Website: http://www.das.co.uk
Directors: P. Asplin (Grp Chief Exec)
Managers: K. Dursley, C. O'Sullivan, P. Gibson, P. Jacobs, J. Boichot (Personnel)
Ultimate Holding Company: MUNICH RUCKVERSICHERUNGS GESELLSCHAFT AG
Immediate Holding Company: D A S LEGAL EXPENSES INSURANCE COMPANY LIMITED
Registration no: 00103274 **Date established:** 2009
Turnover: £10m - £20m **No.of Employees:** 251 - 500 **Product Groups:** 82

Date of Accounts	Dec 11	Dec 10	Dec 09
Pre Tax Profit/Loss	6m	-2m	-16m
Fixed Assets	156m	167m	156m
Current Assets	123m	89m	83m
Current Liabilities	11m	7m	9m

D C S Associates

50 High Street Kingswood, Bristol, BS15 4AJ
Tel: 0117-960 3242 **Fax:** 0117-960 3282
E-mail: jason@dcsassociates.co.uk
Website: http://www.dcsassociates.co.uk
Directors: J. Nicholas (Prop), K. Rayford (Ptnr)
Immediate Holding Company: I.C.G. LTD.
Registration no: 06344212 **Date established:** 2006
No.of Employees: 1 - 10 **Product Groups:** 35

Daktronics UK Ltd

Unit B1 Ashville Park Short Way, Thornbury, Bristol, BS35 3UU
Tel: 01454-413606 **Fax:** 01454-415139
E-mail: uksales@daktronics.com
Website: http://www.daktronics.com
Bank(s): National Westminster Bank Plc
Directors: P. Halliwell (Dir)
Immediate Holding Company: DAKTRONICS UK LIMITED
Registration no: 04515209 **VAT No.:** GB 321 9361 73
Date established: 2002 **Turnover:** £5m - £10m **No.of Employees:** 11 - 20
Product Groups: 37, 39, 40, 49

Date of Accounts	Apr 12	Apr 11	Apr 10
Sales Turnover	6m	3m	3m
Pre Tax Profit/Loss	255	-111	37
Working Capital	-14	-246	-183
Fixed Assets	43	70	104
Current Assets	2m	2m	1m
Current Liabilities	331	1m	563

Dantec Dynamics Ltd UK

Garanor Way Portbury, Bristol, BS20 7XE
Tel: 01275-375333 **Fax:** 01275-375336
E-mail: uk@dantecdynamics.com
Website: http://www.dantecdynamics.com
Bank(s): Lloyds TSB Bank plc
Directors: G. Hassail (Sales)
Managers: S. Kristiansen (Comptroller), P. Walker (Mgr)
Immediate Holding Company: DANTEC DYNAMICS LIMITED
Registration no: 01730643 **Date established:** 1983 **Turnover:** £2m - £5m
No.of Employees: 11 - 20 **Product Groups:** 37, 38, 85

Date of Accounts	Dec 11	Dec 10	Dec 09
Working Capital	-44	408	759
Fixed Assets	N/A	N/A	1
Current Assets	1m	1m	3m

The Database Group Holdings Ltd

Colston Tower Colston Avenue, Bristol, BS1 4UH
Tel: 0117-918 3500 **Fax:** 0117-918 3501
E-mail: info@databasegroup.co.uk
Website: http://www.databasegroup.co.uk
Directors: A. Watson (Dir)
Ultimate Holding Company: ALCO HOLDINGS LTD (BVI)
Immediate Holding Company: THE DATABASE GROUP (HOLDINGS) LIMITED
Registration no: 02779559 **Date established:** 1993 **Turnover:** £2m - £5m
No.of Employees: 1 - 10 **Product Groups:** 44, 81

Date of Accounts	Jun 11	Jun 10	Jun 09
Working Capital	70	70	70
Fixed Assets	322	322	322
Current Assets	70	70	70

Davies Turner & Co. Ltd

Western Freight Terminal Fifth Way, Bristol, BS11 8DT
Tel: 0117-982 8341 **Fax:** 0117-982 6253
E-mail: rogerlucy@daviesturner.co.uk
Website: http://www.daviesturner.co.uk
Bank(s): National Westminster Bank Plc
Directors: R. Lucy (Dir)
Ultimate Holding Company: DAVIES TURNER HOLDINGS PLC
Immediate Holding Company: DAVIES TURNER & CO. LIMITED
Registration no: 04345197 **VAT No.:** GB 235 6746 45
Date established: 2001 **Turnover:** £250,000 - £500,000
No.of Employees: 51 - 100 **Product Groups:** 72, 74, 76, 79

Date of Accounts	Mar 12	Mar 11	Mar 10
Sales Turnover	97m	100m	84m
Pre Tax Profit/Loss	2m	2m	1m
Working Capital	3m	8m	7m
Fixed Assets	2m	1m	2m
Current Assets	20m	24m	22m
Current Liabilities	3m	4m	3m

Deloitte LLP

3 Rivergate, Bristol, BS1 6GD
Tel: 0117-921 1622 **Fax:** 0117-929 2801
E-mail: dwoulfe@deloitte.co.uk
Website: http://www.deloitte.co.uk
Managers: D. Woulfe
Ultimate Holding Company: TREVILLE LIMITED (CHANNEL ISLANDS)
Immediate Holding Company: DELOITTE LLP
Registration no: OC303675 **Date established:** 2003
No.of Employees: 251 - 500 **Product Groups:** 44, 80, 81, 82, 86

Date of Accounts	May 12	May 11	May 10
Sales Turnover	2329m	2098m	1953m
Pre Tax Profit/Loss	560m	510m	543m
Working Capital	221m	263m	365m
Fixed Assets	233m	242m	251m
Current Assets	713m	623m	623m
Current Liabilities	330m	300m	239m

Denholm Barwil

Avonmouth Dock, Bristol, BS11 9DN
Tel: 0117-980 2710 **Fax:** 0117-982 1265
E-mail: enquiries@denholm-group.co.uk
Website: http://www.denholm-group.co.uk
Bank(s): Bank of Scotland
Directors: G. Tranter (MD), G. Hanson (Co Sec)
Ultimate Holding Company: J. & J. DENHOLM LIMITED
Immediate Holding Company: DENHOLM WILHELMSEN LIMITED
Registration no: SC032785 **VAT No.:** GB 369 2644 20
Date established: 1958 **Turnover:** £5m - £10m
No.of Employees: 101 - 250 **Product Groups:** 71, 72, 74, 75, 76, 77, 82

Date of Accounts	Dec 11	Dec 10	Dec 09
Sales Turnover	7m	8m	9m
Pre Tax Profit/Loss	283	372	406

see next page

***Denholm Barwil** - Cont'd*

Working Capital	72	-6	-176
Fixed Assets	312	399	613
Current Assets	6m	7m	5m
Current Liabilities	1m	2m	2m

Denholm Global Logistics Ltd

1 First Way Avonmouth, Bristol, BS11 9EF
Tel: 0117-982 5313 **Fax:** 0117-982 5885
Website: http://www.dgluk.com
Managers: T. Hewitt (Sales Admin)
Ultimate Holding Company: J. & J. DENHOLM LIMITED
Immediate Holding Company: DENHOLM GLOBAL LOGISTICS LIMITED
Registration no: 02922837 **Date established:** 1994
Turnover: £20m - £50m **No.of Employees:** 1 - 10 **Product Groups:** 72, 74

Date of Accounts	Dec 11	Dec 10	Dec 09
Sales Turnover	72m	62m	43m
Pre Tax Profit/Loss	572	378	576
Working Capital	3m	3m	1m
Fixed Assets	3m	2m	2m
Current Assets	9m	9m	7m
Current Liabilities	2m	2m	2m

Dexion

Waterloo Street St Philips, Bristol, BS2 0PH
Tel: 0117-955 5211 **Fax:** 0117-955 6194
E-mail: andyburns@dexionsw.com
Website: http://www.dexionsw.com
Directors: A. Burns (Sales)
Managers: D. Ives (Mgr)
Immediate Holding Company: Westcountry Storage Equipment Ltd
Registration no: 06013228 **Date established:** 2006
No.of Employees: 1 - 10 **Product Groups:** 35, 42, 45

Direct Mail Systems

Unit G Malago Vale Industrial Estate St Johns Lane, Bristol, BS3 5BQ
Tel: 0117-934 1600 **Fax:** 0117-934 9601
E-mail: info@directmailsystems.co.uk
Website: http://www.directmailsystems.co.uk
Bank(s): HSBC
Directors: A. Rayner (MD)
Immediate Holding Company: DIRECT MAIL SYSTEMS LIMITED
Registration no: 06891078 **VAT No.:** GB 103 7493 84
Date established: 2009 **Turnover:** £500,000 - £1m
No.of Employees: 11 - 20 **Product Groups:** 81

Date of Accounts	Apr 11	Apr 10
Working Capital	1	1
Current Assets	1	1

Docscan Service Point

23 Cater Road, Bristol, BS13 7TW
Tel: 0117-935 9808 **Fax:** 0117-935 9828
E-mail: docscan@servicepointuk.com
Website: http://www.docscan.co.uk
Bank(s): Barclays
Managers: D. Nicholas (Mgr)
Registration no: 01093958 **VAT No.:** GB 682 3568 09
Turnover: £500,000 - £1m **No.of Employees:** 21 - 50
Product Groups: 44, 81

Dok Tek Systems Ltd

D7d Woodland Way, Bristol, BS15 1QH
Tel: 0117-914 5510 **Fax:** 0117-914 5103
E-mail: sales.doktek@ukf.net
Website: http://www.dok-tek.co.uk
Directors: A. Beary (Fin), M. Lake (MD)
Immediate Holding Company: DOK-TEK SYSTEMS LTD
Registration no: 03109202 **Date established:** 1995
Turnover: Up to £250,000 **No.of Employees:** 1 - 10 **Product Groups:** 37, 39, 40, 45

Date of Accounts	Oct 11	Oct 10	Oct 09
Working Capital	144	118	122
Fixed Assets	7	8	9
Current Assets	183	142	141

Door Services

Unit 1a Severnside Trading Estate, Avonmouth, Bristol, BS11 9YQ
Tel: 0117-982 7030 **Fax:** 0117-938 1711
E-mail: rupert@doorservices.co.uk
Website: http://www.doorservices.co.uk
Managers: R. Riley (Mgr)
Immediate Holding Company: DOOR SERVICES (BRISTOL) LIMITED
Registration no: 02638425 **VAT No.:** GB 567 7118 12
Date established: 1991 **Turnover:** £500,000 - £1m
No.of Employees: 1 - 10 **Product Groups:** 35, 48, 52

Date of Accounts	Jul 11	Jul 10	Jul 09
Working Capital	195	187	204
Fixed Assets	67	67	62
Current Assets	315	310	317

Dorothea Restorations Ltd

Barton Hill Trading Estate Herapath Street, Bristol, BS5 9RD
Tel: 0117-941 5010 **Fax:** 0117-955 9661
E-mail: peter@dorothearestorations.com
Website: http://www.dorothearestorations.com
Bank(s): HSBC Bank plc
Directors: P. Meehan (Dir)
Ultimate Holding Company: F. & E.V. LINFORD LIMITED
Immediate Holding Company: DOROTHEA RESTORATIONS LIMITED
Registration no: 01874820 **VAT No.:** GB 419 5566 26
Date established: 1984 **Turnover:** £1m - £2m **No.of Employees:** 21 - 50
Product Groups: 33, 35, 81

Date of Accounts	Sep 10	Sep 09	Sep 08
Sales Turnover	3m	3m	3m
Pre Tax Profit/Loss	26	-155	22
Working Capital	-210	-266	-150
Fixed Assets	413	450	488
Current Assets	1m	1m	1m
Current Liabilities	266	253	249

Dragon Ceramex

5 Nomis Park Congresbury, Bristol, BS49 5HB
Tel: 01934-833409 **Fax:** 01934-833409
Directors: O. Bulley (MD)
Managers: S. Bulley (Mgr)
No.of Employees: 1 - 10 **Product Groups:** 45, 85, 86

Drain Center Ltd (a division of Wolseley UK)

St Andrews Road Avonmouth, Bristol, BS11 9HS
Tel: 0117-916 2700 **Fax:** 0117-982 6820
E-mail: paul.lyons@wolseley.co.uk
Website: http://www.draincenter.co.uk
Managers: L. Richard (District Mgr)
Ultimate Holding Company: WOLSELEY PLC (JERSEY)
Immediate Holding Company: DRAIN CENTER LIMITED
Registration no: 00424702 **Date established:** 1946
No.of Employees: 1 - 10 **Product Groups:** 30, 36, 39, 40, 42, 48, 66

D T Z

Rivergate House 70 Redcliff Street, Bristol, BS1 6AL
Tel: 0117-910 6640 **Fax:** 0117-923 9521
E-mail: info@merseyway.com
Website: http://www.dtz.com
Directors: T. Davis (Dir)
Immediate Holding Company: DTZ MCCOMBE PIERCE LLP
Registration no: NC000516 **Date established:** 2009 **Turnover:** £2m - £5m
No.of Employees: 21 - 50 **Product Groups:** 54, 80, 84

Date of Accounts	Apr 12	Apr 11	Apr 10
Working Capital	544	613	968
Fixed Assets	68	105	156
Current Assets	1m	1m	3m

Durbin Metal Industries Ltd

Unit 0 Lawrence Drive, Yate, Bristol, BS37 5PG
Tel: 01454-322668 **Fax:** 01454-317415
E-mail: mail@durbinmetals.co.uk
Website: http://www.durbinmetals.co.uk
Directors: M. Greenaway (MD)
Managers: M. Corrish, S. Jones (Sales Admin), M. Li (Fin Mgr)
Ultimate Holding Company: HENLEY MANAGEMENT COMPANY (USA)
Immediate Holding Company: DURBIN METAL INDUSTRIES LIMITED
Registration no: 01631973 **Date established:** 1982 **Turnover:** £5m - £10m
No.of Employees: 51 - 100 **Product Groups:** 66

Date of Accounts	Dec 11	Dec 10	Dec 09
Sales Turnover	11m	11m	9m
Pre Tax Profit/Loss	-16	102	-239
Working Capital	390	376	233
Fixed Assets	82	109	175
Current Assets	3m	4m	3m
Current Liabilities	161	149	125

Dycem Ltd

Unit 2-4 Ashley Trading Estate Ashley Parade, Bristol, BS2 9BB
Tel: 0117-955 9921 **Fax:** 0117-954 1194
E-mail: mark.dalziel@dycem.com
Website: http://www.dycem.com
Bank(s): Bank of Scotland
Directors: M. Dalziel (MD)
Managers: D. Richardson, K. Pearce (Tech Serv Mgr)
Immediate Holding Company: DYCEM LIMITED
Registration no: 03239439 **VAT No.:** 127 8248 47 **Date established:** 1996
Turnover: £1m - £2m **No.of Employees:** 21 - 50 **Product Groups:** 30

Date of Accounts	Dec 11	Dec 10	Dec 09
Working Capital	1m	989	989
Fixed Assets	625	639	613
Current Assets	2m	2m	2m

Eatec Ltd

3 Armstrong Court Armstrong Way, Yate, Bristol, BS37 5NG
Tel: 01454-332240 **Fax:** 01454-332249
E-mail: enquiries@eatec.co.uk
Website: http://www.eatec.co.uk
Directors: B. Williams (Fin)
Immediate Holding Company: EATEC LIMITED
Registration no: 03895439 **Date established:** 1999
Turnover: £500,000 - £1m **No.of Employees:** 1 - 10 **Product Groups:** 38, 44, 54, 80, 84, 85

Date of Accounts	Jul 11	Jul 10	Jul 09
Working Capital	-70	116	350
Current Assets	248	178	389

Ebtrade Ltd

Albion Dockside Works, Bristol, BS1 6UT
Tel: 0117-927 9204 **Fax:** 0117-929 8193
E-mail: enquiries@seetru.com
Website: http://www.seetru.com
Directors: O. Varga (MD), A. Varga (Dir)
Managers: D. Coleman (Sales Prom Mgr), P. Vennables (Sales Admin), A. Belcher (Purch Mgr), M. Johnson (Prod Mgr), D. Leech (Sales Prom Mgr)
Immediate Holding Company: BPC ON TRACK LIMITED
Registration no: 00530613 **Date established:** 1983
Turnover: £500,000 - £1m **No.of Employees:** 1 - 10 **Product Groups:** 33, 35, 36

Date of Accounts	Jun 11	Jun 10	Jun 09
Working Capital	-65	-166	-114
Current Assets	27	184	174

Elite Cables & Components Ltd

5 Smiths Forge North End Road, Yatton, Bristol, BS49 4AU
Tel: 01934-876661 **Fax:** 01934-876646
E-mail: sales@elitecables.co.uk
Website: http://www.elitecables.co.uk
Directors: G. Miner (MD)
Immediate Holding Company: ELITE CABLES AND COMPONENTS LIMITED
Registration no: 03821687 **VAT No.:** GB 140 5079 94
Date established: 1999 **Turnover:** £2m - £5m **No.of Employees:** 1 - 10
Product Groups: 30, 35, 37, 46

Date of Accounts	Nov 11	Nov 10	Nov 09
Working Capital	125	126	124
Fixed Assets	19	19	21
Current Assets	261	229	191

Eriks UK (Bristol Service Centre)

Unit 110 Longmead Road, Emersons Green, Bristol, BS16 7FG
Tel: 0117-957 2458 **Fax:** 0117-955 6364
E-mail: bristol@eriks.co.uk
Website: http://www.eriks.co.uk
Managers: N. Smyth (District Mgr)
Immediate Holding Company: WYKO HOLDINGS LTD
Registration no: 00917112 **Date established:** 2001
Turnover: £250m - £500m **No.of Employees:** 1 - 10 **Product Groups:** 35

Ernest S Till South West & Company Ltd

2 Gloucester Road North, Bristol, BS7 0SF
Tel: 0117-914 5400 **Fax:** 0117-914 5404
E-mail: info@estillsouthwest.co.uk
Website: http://www.estillsouthwest.co.uk
Bank(s): National Westminster Bank Plc
Directors: N. Turpin (MD)
Immediate Holding Company: ERNEST S. TILL (SOUTH WEST) & CO. LIMITED
Registration no: 02716386 **VAT No.:** GB 609 3647 27
Date established: 1992 **Turnover:** £2m - £5m **No.of Employees:** 11 - 20
Product Groups: 52

Eurobrick Systems Limited

Unit 7 Wilverley Trading Estate Bath Road, Brislington, Bristol, BS4 5NL
Tel: 0117-971 7117 **Fax:** 0117-971 7217
E-mail: info@eurobrick.co.uk
Website: http://www.eurobrick.co.uk
Product Groups: 25, 29, 30, 33, 35, 37, 39, 45, 48, 52, 66, 84

Date of Accounts	Dec 09	Dec 08	Dec 07
Working Capital	438	328	236
Fixed Assets	2	5	8
Current Assets	567	502	391

Eurocarb Products Ltd

Unit 1 Point 4 Second Way, Bristol, BS11 8DF
Tel: 0117-982 0333 **Fax:** 0117-982 9808
E-mail: info@eurocarb.com
Website: http://www.eurocarb.com
Directors: G. Pears (Co Sec)
Ultimate Holding Company: HAYLEYS LTD (SRI LANKA)
Immediate Holding Company: EUROCARB PRODUCTS LIMITED
Registration no: 02040658 **VAT No.:** GB 425 1714 74
Date established: 1986 **Turnover:** £2m - £5m **No.of Employees:** 1 - 10
Product Groups: 33

Date of Accounts	Mar 12	Mar 11	Mar 10
Sales Turnover	4m	3m	3m
Pre Tax Profit/Loss	172	161	131
Working Capital	850	830	809
Fixed Assets	66	59	29
Current Assets	1m	1m	1m
Current Liabilities	118	97	85

Europa Worldwide Services

Europa House Unit 3 Severnside Trading Estate St Andrews Road, Avonmouth, Bristol, BS11 9AG
Tel: 0117-982 1000 **Fax:** 0117-923 5741
E-mail: bristol@europa-worldwide.co.uk
Website: http://www.europa-worldwide.co.uk
Directors: R. Rampat (Fin), V. Woodfall (I.T. Dir)
Managers: G. Dunmow (Chief Mgr)
Immediate Holding Company: EUROPA FREIGHT CORP
Registration no: 01223028 **Turnover:** £2m - £5m
No.of Employees: 1 - 10 **Product Groups:** 76

European Friction Industries Ltd

6-7 Bonville Road, Bristol, BS4 5NZ
Tel: 0117-977 7859 **Fax:** 0117-971 0573
E-mail: sales@efiltd.co.uk
Website: http://www.efiltd.co.uk
Bank(s): Barclays
Directors: T. Prideaux (Fin)
Managers: J. Hallet (Mktg Serv Mgr), N. Drummond (Tech Serv Mgr)
Ultimate Holding Company: FREEMAN AUTOMOTIVE (UK) LTD
Immediate Holding Company: EUROPEAN FRICTION INDUSTRIES LIMITED
Registration no: 02002865 **VAT No.:** GB 449 2130 57
Date established: 1986 **Turnover:** £10m - £20m
No.of Employees: 11 - 20 **Product Groups:** 33, 35, 39

Date of Accounts	Oct 11	Oct 10	Oct 09
Sales Turnover	10m	9m	8m
Pre Tax Profit/Loss	1m	1m	391
Working Capital	4m	4m	3m
Fixed Assets	970	1m	1m
Current Assets	6m	5m	4m
Current Liabilities	600	576	513

Excel Steel Stock

Harbour Road Trading Estate Portishead, Bristol, BS20 7AT
Tel: 01275-847997 **Fax:** 01275-849855
Bank(s): HSBC Bank plc
Managers: C. Morse (Chief Mgr)
Immediate Holding Company: DYFED STEELS LTD
VAT No.: GB 302 6636 83 **Turnover:** £1m - £2m **No.of Employees:** 11 - 20
Product Groups: 66

Expeditors International UK Ltd

Unit R1c Rockingham Gate Cabot Park Poplar Way West, Bristol, BS11 0YW
Tel: 0117-980 2780 **Fax:** 0117-982 5778
E-mail: mairead.drennan@expeditors.co.uk
Website: http://www.expeditors.com
Directors: M. Drennan (MD)
Ultimate Holding Company: EXPEDITORS INTERNATIONAL OF WASHINGTON INC (USA)
Immediate Holding Company: EXPEDITORS INTERNATIONAL (UK) LIMITED
Registration no: 01872622 **Date established:** 1984
No.of Employees: 21 - 50 **Product Groups:** 76

Date of Accounts	Dec 11	Dec 10	Dec 09
Sales Turnover	108m	94m	72m
Pre Tax Profit/Loss	7m	5m	7m
Working Capital	7m	11m	9m
Fixed Assets	59m	46m	40m
Current Assets	37m	40m	29m
Current Liabilities	2m	2m	1m

Fabtech Ltd

Awkley Lane Olveston, Bristol, BS35 4EW
Tel: 01454-615919 **Fax:** 01454-615919
E-mail: steve-fabtech@msn.com
Immediate Holding Company: FABTECH LIMITED
Registration no: 05884627 **Date established:** 2006
No.of Employees: 1 - 10 **Product Groups:** 30, 35, 36, 37, 39, 40, 41, 48, 49, 52, 66

Date of Accounts	Jul 11	Jul 10	Jul 09
Working Capital	-54	-39	-25
Fixed Assets	19	13	16
Current Assets	10	22	34

K J Farrow
Unit 6-8 Dixon Business Centre Dixon Road, Bristol, BS4 5QW
Tel: 0117-972 3584 **Fax:** 0117-972 3584
Directors: K. Farrow (Prop)
Immediate Holding Company: FILE CENTRE (BRISTOL) LIMITED
Registration no: 02991891 **Date established:** 2006
No.of Employees: 1 - 10 **Product Groups:** 46, 48

Fastfix
Circuit 32 Easton Road, Bristol, BS5 0DB
Tel: 0117-955 1616 **Fax:** 0117-955 1818
E-mail: info@fastfix.co.uk
Website: http://www.fastfix.co.uk
Directors: A. Burridge (Prop)
Date established: 1999 **No.of Employees:** 1 - 10 **Product Groups:** 37

Find Bristol Business
30 Queen Charlotte Street, Bristol, BS1 4HJ
Tel: 0117-929 1630 **Fax:** 08704-601256
E-mail: info@findbristolbusiness.co.uk
Website: http://www.findbristolbusiness.co.uk
Directors: R. Grave (Ptnr)
Managers: R. Graves (Mktg Serv Mgr)
Immediate Holding Company: WORLD PROFESSIONAL BILLIARDS AND SNOOKER ASSOCIATI
Registration no: 06777133 **Date established:** 2008
No.of Employees: 1 - 10 **Product Groups:** 80

Fine Images
6 Oaksey Grove Nailsea, Bristol, BS48 2TP
Tel: 01275-790418
E-mail: info@fineimages.co.uk
Website: http://www.fineimages.co.uk
Directors: G. Balsam (MD)
Turnover: Up to £250,000 **No.of Employees:** 1 - 10 **Product Groups:** 28, 38, 64, 81

Fine Line
The Old Quarry Clevedon Road, Failand, Bristol, BS8 3TU
Tel: 01275-395000 **Fax:** 01275-395001
E-mail: contact@fineline.uk.com
Website: http://www.fineline.uk.com
Directors: D. Wring (Prop)
Immediate Holding Company: FINELINE LIMITED
Registration no: 06435595 **Date established:** 2007
Turnover: Over £1,000m **No.of Employees:** 1 - 10 **Product Groups:** 52, 85

Finecal Distributors
Temple Trading Estate Cole Road, Bristol, BS2 0UG
Tel: 0117-971 1111 **Fax:** 0117-972 4449
E-mail: simon.gough@finecal.co.uk
Website: http://www.finecal.co.uk
Directors: S. Gough (MD)
Immediate Holding Company: FINECAL DISTRIBUTORS LIMITED
Registration no: 05061286 **Date established:** 2004
No.of Employees: 21 - 50 **Product Groups:** 27, 30, 32

Fire Line Services
29 Cleeve Wood Road, Bristol, BS16 2SH
Tel: 0800-169 2326 **Fax:** 0117-956 0037
E-mail: info@firelineservices.co.uk
Website: http://www.firelineservices.co.uk
Directors: S. Harris (Prop)
Date established: 2001 **No.of Employees:** 1 - 10 **Product Groups:** 38, 42

First Group plc
Enterprise House Easton Road, Bristol, BS5 0DZ
Tel: 0117-955 8211 **Fax:** 0117-955 1248
E-mail: amelia.price@firstgroup.com
Website: http://www.firstgroup.com
Directors: A. Price (Fin)
Ultimate Holding Company: FIRSTGROUP PLC
Immediate Holding Company: FIRST SOMERSET & AVON LIMITED
Registration no: 00025088 **Date established:** 1987
Turnover: £20m - £50m **No.of Employees:** 1001 - 1500
Product Groups: 72

Date of Accounts	Mar 08	Mar 09	Mar 10
Sales Turnover	46m	47m	47m
Pre Tax Profit/Loss	-993	3m	6m
Working Capital	-37m	-34m	-30m
Fixed Assets	31m	30m	30m
Current Assets	5m	6m	8m
Current Liabilities	7m	8m	11m

1st Response
37 Cottrell Road, Bristol, BS5 6TJ
Tel: 0117-951 8339 **Fax:** 0117-951 8339
E-mail: stresponse@hotmail.com
Website: http://www.blockeddrains.biz/
Directors: R. Mccarthy (Prop)
Date established: 1996 **No.of Employees:** 1 - 10 **Product Groups:** 36, 52

S H Fiske Ltd
Unit 2 The Coachworks Kingsfield Lane, Longwell Green, Bristol, BS30 6DL
Tel: 0117-960 4136 **Fax:** 0117-960 0187
E-mail: sales@sh-fiske.com
Website: http://www.sh-fiske.com
Managers: N. Thompson (Chief Mgr)
Immediate Holding Company: S.H. FISKE LIMITED
Registration no: 01394957 **Date established:** 1978 **Turnover:** £1m - £2m
No.of Employees: 11 - 20 **Product Groups:** 27, 28, 49, 85

Date of Accounts	Mar 12	Mar 11	Mar 10
Working Capital	358	332	268
Fixed Assets	242	278	325
Current Assets	512	474	452

Flexo Springs Ltd
Hill Street Kingswood, Bristol, BS15 4HB
Tel: 0117-967 3313 **Fax:** 0117-935 2597
E-mail: sales@flexosprings.com
Website: http://www.flexosprings.com
Directors: M. Fawcett (MD)
Ultimate Holding Company: THIRLWALL FAWCETT GROUP OF COMPANIES LTD.
Immediate Holding Company: FLEXO SPRINGS LIMITED
Registration no: 00228767 **VAT No.:** GB 137 6648 41
Date established: 2028 **Turnover:** £250,000 - £500,000
No.of Employees: 11 - 20 **Product Groups:** 02, 20, 21, 26, 29, 34, 35, 36, 38, 39, 40, 43, 48, 49, 66, 68, 85

Date of Accounts	Mar 12	Mar 11	Mar 10
Working Capital	381	402	388
Fixed Assets	149	108	107
Current Assets	492	541	539

Fowlers Of Bristol (Engineers) Ltd
25a Bath Buildings, Bristol, BS6 5PT
Tel: 0117-942 2563 **Fax:** 0117-942 4770
E-mail: sales@fowlers-eng.com
Website: http://www.fowlers-eng.com
Bank(s): National Westminster Bank Plc
Directors: G. White (Dir), S. Dobbins (Fin), J. Witherten (Fin)
Immediate Holding Company: FOWLER'S OF BRISTOL (ENGINEERS) LIMITED
Registration no: 00705126 **Date established:** 1961 **Turnover:** £1m - £2m
No.of Employees: 21 - 50 **Product Groups:** 30, 35, 46, 48, 49

Date of Accounts	Mar 12	Mar 11	Mar 10
Sales Turnover	N/A	N/A	1m
Pre Tax Profit/Loss	N/A	N/A	48
Working Capital	755	654	591
Fixed Assets	262	295	269
Current Assets	1m	1m	802
Current Liabilities	361	N/A	118

Franchiseexpo
3Rd Floor Colston Tower Colston Street, Bristol, BS1 4UX
Tel: 0117-930 4927
E-mail: dan.wall@prysmgroup.co.uk
Website: http://www.franchiseexpo.co.uk
Directors: S. Chicken (Dir), C. Chicken (MD)
Registration no: 06220856 **Date established:** 2007
No.of Employees: 1 - 10 **Product Groups:** 80

Fridge Trader
Unit 15 16 Pucklechurch Trading Estate, Pucklechurch, Bristol, BS16 9QH
Tel: 0117-937 4883 **Fax:** 0117- 9373316
E-mail: marcushowarth@dawsongroup.co.uk
Website: http://www.thefridgetrader.co.uk
Managers: M. Hawarth (Sales Prom Mgr)
No.of Employees: 21 - 50 **Product Groups:** 40, 67

Fulton
Broomhill Road, Bristol, BS4 4TU
Tel: 0117-972332 **Fax:** 01535-274734
Website: http://www.fulton.com
Managers: M. Nield (Mgr)
Immediate Holding Company: FULTON LIMITED
Registration no: 04450049 **Date established:** 2002
No.of Employees: 51 - 100 **Product Groups:** 40

Fulton Boiler Works Ltd
210 Broomhill Road, Bristol, BS4 4TU
Tel: 0117-977 2563 **Fax:** 0117-972 3358
E-mail: paul.richards@fulton.com
Website: http://www.fulton.com
Directors: J. Ashby (Dir), G. Stephens (Fin), G. Bareham (Sales & Mktg), P. Richards (MD)
Managers: P. Knight (Intern Sales En), C. Rahn (Tech Serv Mgr), A. Walker (Accounts), F. Tucker (Prod Mgr)
Immediate Holding Company: FULTON LIMITED
Registration no: 04450049 **Date established:** 2002 **Turnover:** £2m - £5m
No.of Employees: 21 - 50 **Product Groups:** 40

G C C Innova Ltd
Trym Lodge 1 Henbury Road, Westbury-On-Trym, Bristol, BS9 3HQ
Tel: 0117-310 1316 **Fax:** 0117-310 1317
E-mail: sales@gccinnova.co.uk
Website: http://www.gccinnova.co.uk
Managers: M. Lindop
Registration no: 02709564 **Turnover:** £2m - £5m
No.of Employees: 1 - 10 **Product Groups:** 44, 80

Date of Accounts	Dec 07	Dec 06	Dec 05
Working Capital	-138	-222	-42
Fixed Assets	69	70	48
Current Assets	480	488	448
Current Liabilities	619	710	490
Total Share Capital	29	29	29

G V A Grimley Ltd
University Gate Park Row, Bristol, BS1 5UB
Tel: 08709-008990 **Fax:** 0117-926 0607
Website: http://www.gvagrimley.co.uk
Directors: M. Corbett (MD)
Managers: L. Cooper (Mgr)
Ultimate Holding Company: GVA GRIMLEY HOLDINGS LIMITED
Immediate Holding Company: GVA GRIMLEY LIMITED
Registration no: 06382509 **Date established:** 2007
Turnover: £10m - £20m **No.of Employees:** 21 - 50 **Product Groups:** 52, 80, 82, 84

Date of Accounts	Apr 11	Apr 10	Apr 09
Sales Turnover	115m	112m	118m
Pre Tax Profit/Loss	574	4m	3m
Working Capital	9m	11m	7m
Fixed Assets	113m	114m	117m
Current Assets	42m	42m	35m
Current Liabilities	22m	22m	16m

G W S Media Ltd
30 Queen Charlotte Street, Bristol, BS1 4HJ
Tel: 0117-972 4835 **Fax:** 0870-460 1256
E-mail: enquiries@gwsmedia.com
Website: http://www.gwsmedia.com
Directors: R. Graves (Dir)
Immediate Holding Company: GWS MEDIA LIMITED
Registration no: 06183284 **Date established:** 2007
No.of Employees: 11 - 20 **Product Groups:** 44

Date of Accounts	Mar 11	Mar 10	Mar 09
Working Capital	-87	-87	-82
Fixed Assets	66	69	65
Current Assets	46	29	28

Gawler Tapes & Plastics Ltd
Unit 7 Easter Court Woodward Avenue, Yate, Bristol, BS37 5YS
Tel: 01454-324265 **Fax:** 01454-315158
E-mail: phil@gawlertapes.co.uk
Website: http://www.gawlertapes.co.uk
Directors: P. Bray (MD)
Immediate Holding Company: GAWLER TAPES AND PLASTICS LIMITED
Registration no: 02291725 **VAT No.:** GB 398 8079 77
Date established: 1988 **Turnover:** £1m - £2m **No.of Employees:** 1 - 10
Product Groups: 23, 27, 30, 31, 32, 42, 44, 49, 66, 68

Date of Accounts	Dec 11	Dec 10	Dec 09
Working Capital	486	425	356
Fixed Assets	22	27	26
Current Assets	874	762	768

Golding Timber & Board Merchants Ltd
Unit C Moravian Road, Bristol, BS15 8NF
Tel: 0117-960 6813 **Fax:** 0117-961 8678
E-mail: sales@goldingtimber.co.uk
Website: http://www.goldingtimberbristol.co.uk
Directors: C. Daw (MD), S. Bull (Fin)
Immediate Holding Company: GOLDING TIMBER AND BOARD MERCHANTS LIMITED
Registration no: 01776752 **Date established:** 1983
No.of Employees: 1 - 10 **Product Groups:** 36, 38, 41, 45, 47, 48, 52, 61, 66, 67, 74, 76, 80, 84, 85, 87

Date of Accounts	May 11	May 10	May 09
Working Capital	504	403	376
Fixed Assets	13	17	39
Current Assets	788	684	632

Graham
Unit 3 Feeder Road, Bristol, BS2 0SB
Tel: 0117-971 2205 **Fax:** 0117-971 2834
E-mail: scottyounger@graham-group.co.uk
Website: http://www.graham-group.com
Managers: S. Younger (Mgr)
Immediate Holding Company: DAVID GRAHAM VEHICLE REPAIRS LTD
Registration no: SC254141 **No.of Employees:** 11 - 20
Product Groups: 66

Grant Contractors Ltd
The Old Mill Works Station Lane, Bristol, BS7 9NB
Tel: 0117-30 9400 **Fax:** 0117-951 5155
E-mail: grantcontractors@aol.com
Website: http://www.grantcontractors.co.uk
Directors: M. Grant (MD), N. Grant (MD)
Immediate Holding Company: Groundbreaker Contracting Ltd
Registration no: 03880035 **Date established:** 1999
No.of Employees: 1 - 10 **Product Groups:** 31, 51, 84

Date of Accounts	Mar 06	Mar 05
Working Capital	-246	-127
Fixed Assets	N/A	1
Current Assets	28	93
Current Liabilities	274	220

Green Goose Tooling Co.
Unit 2-4 River Mead Dean Road, Yate, Bristol, BS37 5NH
Tel: 01454-312948 **Fax:** 01454-313704
Directors: S. Dunn (Prop)
Registration no: 02267400 **VAT No.:** GB 302 7880 67
Turnover: Up to £250,000 **No.of Employees:** 1 - 10 **Product Groups:** 46, 48

Grontmij Ltd
41 Corn Street, Bristol, BS1 1HS
Tel: 0117-927 8850 **Fax:** 0117-927 8888
E-mail: charles.williams@grontmij.co.uk
Website: http://www.grontmij.co.uk
Directors: C. Williams (MD)
Ultimate Holding Company: GRONTMIJ NV (NETHERLANDS)
Immediate Holding Company: GRONTMIJ LIMITED
Registration no: 02888385 **VAT No.:** GB 418 0640 71
Date established: 1994 **Turnover:** £1m - £2m **No.of Employees:** 51 - 100
Product Groups: 84

Date of Accounts	Dec 11	Dec 10	Dec 09
Sales Turnover	50m	41m	49m
Pre Tax Profit/Loss	-5m	-2m	730
Working Capital	6m	1m	3m
Fixed Assets	1m	2m	2m
Current Assets	12m	13m	10m
Current Liabilities	3m	3m	4m

Grooms House Turnery
Grooms House Stanshawes Court, Yate, Bristol, BS37 4DZ
Tel: 01454-325525 **Fax:** 01454-325525
E-mail: info@grooms-house-turnery.co.uk
Directors: P. Ridley (Prop)
VAT No.: GB 357 9933 94 **No.of Employees:** 1 - 10 **Product Groups:** 25

H R P Ltd
Unit 100 Quadrant Industrial Estate Ash Ridge Road, Bradley Stoke, Bristol, BS32 4QA
Tel: 01454-456430 **Fax:** 01454-456431
E-mail: bristol@hrpltd.co.uk
Website: http://www.hrponline.co.uk
Managers: M. Read (Mgr)
Ultimate Holding Company: HRP HOLDINGS LIMITED
Immediate Holding Company: HRP LIMITED
Registration no: 00832237 **Date established:** 1964
Turnover: £50m - £75m **No.of Employees:** 1 - 10 **Product Groups:** 40, 66

Date of Accounts	Dec 11	Dec 10	Dec 09
Sales Turnover	55m	52m	46m
Pre Tax Profit/Loss	1m	1m	651
Working Capital	8m	7m	6m
Fixed Assets	2m	2m	3m
Current Assets	22m	22m	17m
Current Liabilities	3m	4m	3m

H-Te Western Automation
4 Cala Trading Estate Ashton Vale Road, Bristol, BS3 2HA
Tel: 0117-966 5925 **Fax:** 0117-966 1940
E-mail: sales@htecontrols.co.uk
Website: http://www.htecontrols.co.uk
Managers: N. Sandier (Mgr)
Immediate Holding Company: U.K. ELECTRIC LTD
Registration no: 00775728 **Turnover:** £50m - £75m
No.of Employees: 1 - 10 **Product Groups:** 37

Habia Cable Ltd
Unit 10 Short Way Thornbury, Bristol, BS35 3UT
Tel: 01454-412522 **Fax:** 01454-416121
E-mail: info.uk@habia.com
Website: http://www.habia.com
Directors: M. Hall (Fin)
Managers: J. Clements (Fin Mgr), S. Yates (Mktg Serv Mgr)
Ultimate Holding Company: BEIJER ALMA AB (SWEDEN)
Immediate Holding Company: HABIA CABLE LIMITED
Registration no: 01285451 **VAT No.:** GB 113 3041 35
Date established: 1976 **Turnover:** £5m - £10m **No.of Employees:** 1 - 10
Product Groups: 35, 36, 37, 39, 40

Date of Accounts	Dec 11	Dec 10	Dec 09
Sales Turnover	6m	6m	6m
Pre Tax Profit/Loss	132	132	127
Working Capital	832	739	636
Fixed Assets	10	11	15
Current Assets	2m	2m	1m
Current Liabilities	350	266	408

Hager Ltd
135 Aztec West Almondsbury, Bristol, BS32 4UB
Tel: 01454-616245 **Fax:** 01454-617172
Website: http://www.hager.co.uk
Managers: A. Neal (Mgr)
Immediate Holding Company: HAGER LIMITED
Registration no: 01551990 **Date established:** 1981
No.of Employees: 11 - 20 **Product Groups:** 36, 40

Alner Hamblin Electronics Ltd
3 Boultons Road, Bristol, BS15 1RU
Tel: 0117-961 4239 **Fax:** 0117-961 4239
E-mail: david@globalnet.co.uk
Website: http://www.alnerhamblin.com
Directors: D. Alner (MD)
Immediate Holding Company: ALNER HAMBLIN ELECTRONICS LIMITED
Registration no: 02128700 **Date established:** 1987
Turnover: Up to £250,000 **No.of Employees:** 11 - 20 **Product Groups:** 28, 37, 84

Date of Accounts	Oct 11	Oct 10	Oct 09
Working Capital	574	520	499
Fixed Assets	50	41	53
Current Assets	657	570	528

F C Hammonds
13-17 Dove Lane Newfoundland Road, Bristol, BS2 9HS
Tel: 0117-955 1377 **Fax:** 0117-987 2377
E-mail: sales@fchammonds.co.uk
Website: http://www.fchammonds.co.uk
Directors: P. Hammonds (Prop)
VAT No.: GB 137 8593 30 **Date established:** 1921
Turnover: £250,000 - £500,000 **No.of Employees:** 1 - 10
Product Groups: 48

P.J. Hare Ltd
Havyatt Road Wrington, Bristol, BS40 5NL
Tel: 01934-862608 **Fax:** 01934-863126
E-mail: sales@harepress.co.uk
Website: http://www.harepress.co.uk
Bank(s): National Westminster Bank Plc
Directors: M. Hare (Tech Serv), K. Baston (MD)
Registration no: 00465757 **Date established:** 1947
No.of Employees: 21 - 50 **Product Groups:** 46, 47

Date of Accounts	Mar 12	Mar 11	Mar 10
Working Capital	1m	856	759
Fixed Assets	431	369	365
Current Assets	2m	1m	990

Roger Harle Engine Services
17 Upper Stone Close Frampton Cotterell, Bristol, BS36 2LB
Tel: 07788-798066
E-mail: roger.harle@gmail.com
Website: http://www.whitemetalbearings.co.uk
Directors: R. Harle (Prop)
No.of Employees: 1 - 10 **Product Groups:** 35, 48, 66

Harris & Co.
Farrs Lane, Bristol, BS1 4PZ
Tel: 0117-927 7434 **Fax:** 0117-925 2354
E-mail: info@harrisand.co.uk
Website: http://www.harrisand.co.uk
Directors: A. Lowe (Ptnr)
Immediate Holding Company: KIND OFFICE LIMITED
Registration no: 06480997 **VAT No.:** GB 137 6651 52
Date established: 2008 **Turnover:** £500,000 - £1m
No.of Employees: 1 - 10 **Product Groups:** 27

Harris Brothers Contract Furnishings Ltd
Avondale House 0 Woodland Way, Bristol, BS15 1PA
Tel: 0117-908 5151 **Fax:** 0117-908 5147
E-mail: info@harris-brothers.co.uk
Website: http://www.harris-brothers.co.uk
Directors: D. Harris (MD)
Immediate Holding Company: HARRIS BROTHERS (CONTRACTS) LIMITED
Registration no: 04017877 **Date established:** 2000 **Turnover:** £1m - £2m
No.of Employees: 11 - 20 **Product Groups:** 26, 49, 52, 67, 84, 89

Date of Accounts	Jun 09	Jun 08	Jun 07
Sales Turnover	1m	2m	2m
Pre Tax Profit/Loss	-369	15	1
Working Capital	-390	5	19
Fixed Assets	50	63	65
Current Assets	136	526	533
Current Liabilities	247	102	169

Hartnell Taylor Cook LLP
18 Canynge Road, Bristol, BS8 3JX
Tel: 0117-923 9234 **Fax:** 0117-923 9237
E-mail: alasdair.mcleod@htc.uk.com
Website: http://www.htc.uk.com
Bank(s): National Westminster Bank Plc
Directors: A. McLeod (Fin), A. Mcleod (Co Sec), C. Killen (Mkt Research)
Managers: L. Clark, C. Northam (Sales Admin)
Immediate Holding Company: HARTNELL LIMITED
Registration no: 02070119 **Date established:** 1986 **Turnover:** £2m - £5m
No.of Employees: 51 - 100 **Product Groups:** 80

Hay Group
3 Hubbard Wing Leigh Court Business Centre Pill Road, Abbots Leigh, Bristol, BS8 3RJ
Tel: 01275-813600 **Fax:** 01275-813601
E-mail: val_ball@haygroup.com
Website: http://www.haygroup.com
Managers: V. Ball (Sales Admin)
Registration no: 05681964 **Date established:** 2006
Turnover: £20m - £50m **No.of Employees:** 1 - 10 **Product Groups:** 80

Hayes Parsons Ltd
St Lawrence House 29-31 Broad Street, Bristol, BS1 2HF
Tel: 0117-929 9381 **Fax:** 0117-926 5644
E-mail: enquiries@hayesparsons.co.uk
Website: http://www.hayesparsons.co.uk
Bank(s): T.S.B.
Directors: J. Woollam (MD)
Immediate Holding Company: HAYES PARSONS LIMITED
Registration no: 00816448 **Date established:** 1964 **Turnover:** £1m - £2m
No.of Employees: 21 - 50 **Product Groups:** 82

Date of Accounts	Dec 11	Dec 10	Dec 09
Working Capital	67	-124	-128
Fixed Assets	26	32	97
Current Assets	926	953	1m

Headstart Training Solutions
PO Box 1184, Bristol, BS36 1WU
Tel: 01454-772751
E-mail: info@hstrainingsolutions.co.uk
Website: http://www.hstrainingsolutions.co.uk
Directors: A. Wilson (Dir)
Immediate Holding Company: WINTERBOURNE MEDIEVAL BARN TRUST
Date established: 2003 **No.of Employees:** 1 - 10 **Product Groups:** 86

Date of Accounts	Jun 11	Jun 10	Jun 09
Sales Turnover	N/A	N/A	9
Pre Tax Profit/Loss	N/A	N/A	2
Working Capital	6	-1	5
Fixed Assets	3	3	1
Current Assets	9	5	5
Current Liabilities	3	5	N/A

Heli-Tec International
24 Bonville Road, Bristol, BS4 5QH
Tel: 0117-977 6645 **Fax:** 0117-972 4992
Website: http://www.dowson.com
Managers: P. Campho (Mgr)
Immediate Holding Company: WRIGHT GAMLINGAY LTD
Registration no: 00709486 **Date established:** 1993
Turnover: £250,000 - £500,000 **No.of Employees:** 1 - 10
Product Groups: 38, 43

Walter Hill Plant Ltd
Maze Street, Bristol, BS5 9TQ
Tel: 0117-955 5151 **Fax:** 0117-941 3685
Directors: J. Hill (Fin)
Immediate Holding Company: WALTER HILL (PLANT) LIMITED
Registration no: 02276667 **VAT No.:** GB 664 3053 44
Date established: 1988 **Turnover:** Up to £250,000
No.of Employees: 1 - 10 **Product Groups:** 67

Date of Accounts	Jun 11	Jun 10	Jun 08
Working Capital	-54	-49	-38
Current Assets	8	5	6

Hilti GT Britain Ltd
1 The Commercial Centre Days Road, St Philips, Bristol, BS2 0QS
Tel: 0800-886100 **Fax:** 0800-886200
Website: http://www.hilti.co.uk
Managers: N. Hopton (Mgr)
Ultimate Holding Company: HILTI AG (LIECHTENSTEIN)
Immediate Holding Company: HILTI (GT.BRITAIN) LIMITED
Registration no: 00479786 **Date established:** 1950
Turnover: £75m - £125m **No.of Employees:** 1 - 10 **Product Groups:** 35, 37, 48

Holroyds
P.O.Box 121, Bristol, BS31 9AD
Tel: 01225-873000 **Fax:** 01225-873834
E-mail: enquiry@holroyds.org
Website: http://www.holroyds.org
Directors: S. Holroyd (Prop)
Managers: D. Nash (Purch Mgr)
VAT No.: GB 771 8438 02 **Date established:** 1984
Turnover: £250,000 - £500,000 **No.of Employees:** 1 - 10
Product Groups: 40, 41, 42, 67

Horizon Mechanical Services International Ltd
Unit 1 Willment Way, Bristol, BS11 8DJ
Tel: 0117-982 1415 **Fax:** 0117-982 0630
E-mail: sales@horizon-int.com
Website: http://www.horizon-int.co.uk
Directors: D. Wilson (Fin), D. Wilson (MD)
Immediate Holding Company: HORIZON MECHANICAL SERVICES (INTERNATIONAL) LIMITED
Registration no: 01278897 **VAT No.:** GB 140 4483 92
Date established: 1976 **No.of Employees:** 1 - 10 **Product Groups:** 36, 40, 42, 52, 54

Date of Accounts	Jan 12	Jan 11	Jan 10
Working Capital	91	98	79
Fixed Assets	61	44	53
Current Assets	134	152	107

Robert Horne Ltd
16-17 Bonville Road, Bristol, BS4 5QF
Tel: 0117-972 5888 **Fax:** 0117-972 5899
E-mail: rh.bristol@roberthorne.co.uk
Website: http://www.roberthorne.co.uk
Managers: A. Delaney (District Mgr)
Registration no: 00584756 **Date established:** 1950
No.of Employees: 1 - 10 **Product Groups:** 66

Horstmann Group Ltd
Roman Farm Road, Bristol, BS4 1UP
Tel: 0117-978 8700 **Fax:** 0117-987 8701
E-mail: reception@horstmann.co.uk
Website: http://www.horstmann.co.uk
Bank(s): HSBC
Directors: L. Woolner (MD), C. Wilcox (Co Sec), A. Dudley (Fin)
Managers: A. Parson, P. Hemmings (Sales Prom Mgr), A. Tooney (Personnel), J. Wilfred (Mktg Serv Mgr)
Ultimate Holding Company: SECURE METERS LTD (INDIA)
Immediate Holding Company: SECURE CONTROLS (UK) LIMITED
Registration no: 00457553 **VAT No.:** 448 6132 39 **Date established:** 1948
Turnover: £10m - £20m **No.of Employees:** 101 - 250
Product Groups: 37, 38, 49

Date of Accounts	Mar 12	Mar 11	Mar 10
Sales Turnover	11m	12m	10m
Pre Tax Profit/Loss	-2m	-716	-717
Working Capital	-4	169	-987
Fixed Assets	2m	2m	1m
Current Assets	5m	6m	4m
Current Liabilities	2m	2m	2m

Horwood Homeware Ltd
Avonmouth Way, Bristol, BS11 9HX
Tel: 0117-940 0000 **Fax:** 0117-940 1100
E-mail: sales@horwood.co.uk
Website: http://www.stellarcookware.co.uk
Bank(s): Bank of Scotland
Directors: J. Horwood (Sales), N. Rosati (Purch), N. Hardman (Fin)
Managers: H. McPherson (Tech Serv Mgr), J. Robinson (Mktg Serv Mgr)
Ultimate Holding Company: SILAMPOS UK LIMITED
Immediate Holding Company: HORWOOD HOMEWARES LIMITED
Registration no: 00308589 **VAT No.:** GB 137 7432 59
Date established: 1935 **Turnover:** £10m - £20m
No.of Employees: 21 - 50 **Product Groups:** 36

Date of Accounts	Dec 11	Dec 10	Dec 09
Sales Turnover	18m	19m	19m
Pre Tax Profit/Loss	3m	3m	3m
Working Capital	5m	6m	5m
Fixed Assets	2m	2m	1m
Current Assets	28m	25m	23m
Current Liabilities	2m	2m	2m

Hotelscene
17 Portland Square, Bristol, BS2 8SJ
Tel: 0117-916 6300 **Fax:** 0844-826 4423
E-mail: chris.needham@hotelscene.co.uk
Website: http://www.hotelscene.co.uk
Directors: C. Needham (Dir)
Managers: T. Whitney (Sales Prom)
Ultimate Holding Company: HOTELSCENE GROUP LIMITED
Immediate Holding Company: HOTELSCENE LIMITED
Registration no: 01535923 **Date established:** 1980 **Turnover:** £5m - £10m
No.of Employees: 51 - 100 **Product Groups:** 69

Date of Accounts	Mar 11	Mar 10	Mar 09
Sales Turnover	5m	5m	6m
Pre Tax Profit/Loss	1m	847	660
Working Capital	1m	544	454
Fixed Assets	269	266	339
Current Assets	4m	7m	6m
Current Liabilities	1m	1m	1m

M A Howard Associates
190 Bedminster Down Road, Bristol, BS13 7AF
Tel: 0117-949 6749 **Fax:** 0117-949 6749
E-mail: mahowardassociates@wwwmail.co.uk
Directors: M. Howard (Prop)
Date established: 1989 **No.of Employees:** 1 - 10 **Product Groups:** 35

Hudson Engineering Nailsea Ltd
Unit 34-35 Nailsea Trading Estate Southfield Road, Nailsea, Bristol, BS48 1JE
Tel: 01275-857335 **Fax:** 01275-810587
E-mail: hudson.eng@btconnect.com
Website: http://www.nylaplas.co.uk
Directors: C. Cheetham (MD)
Immediate Holding Company: HUDSON ENGINEERING (NAILSEA) LIMITED
Registration no: 01562912 **VAT No.:** GB 357 8589 88
Date established: 1981 **Turnover:** £250,000 - £500,000
No.of Employees: 1 - 10 **Product Groups:** 48

Date of Accounts	Dec 11	Dec 10	Dec 09
Working Capital	155	109	69
Fixed Assets	41	43	48
Current Assets	235	151	84

John Hudson The Photographer
8 Chelmer Grove Keynsham, Bristol, BS31 1QA
Tel: 0117-986 4811
E-mail: summer_studios@hotmail.com
Directors: J. Hudson (Prop)
Turnover: Up to £250,000 **No.of Employees:** 1 - 10 **Product Groups:** 38, 44, 80, 81

Hyder Consulting
The Pithay, Bristol, BS1 2NL
Tel: 0117-372 1200 **Fax:** 0117-988 1661
E-mail: roz.calvert@hyderconsulting.com
Website: http://www.hyderconsulting.com
Directors: J. Langdon (Dir)
Managers: T. Wyatt (Tech Serv Mgr), R. Addison (Develop Mgr)
Ultimate Holding Company: HYDER P.L.C.
Immediate Holding Company: HYDER CONSULTING PLC
Registration no: 04052317 **Date established:** 1988
No.of Employees: 51 - 100 **Product Groups:** 54, 84

Hygiene Warehouse
Unit 6 Ashmead Park, Keynsham, Bristol, BS31 1SU
Tel: 0117-946 1960 **Fax:** 0117-946 1959
E-mail: sales@hygienewarehouse.co.uk
Website: http://www.hygienewarehouse.co.uk
Managers: L. Kidner (Mktg Serv Mgr)
Immediate Holding Company: THE INGRAM GROUP
Registration no: 02469888 **No.of Employees:** 1 - 10 **Product Groups:** 27

I E S
1 Portview Road, Bristol, BS11 9LS
Tel: 08452-267125 **Fax:** 0117-938 0900
E-mail: info@iese.co.uk
Website: http://www.iese.co.uk
Managers: A. Coombes (Mgr)
Immediate Holding Company: I E S GROUP LTD
Registration no: 04221955 **VAT No.:** GB 567 6081 14
Date established: 2001 **Turnover:** £2m - £5m **No.of Employees:** 1 - 10
Product Groups: 25, 47, 48, 61, 66, 72, 76, 77, 80, 85

I S G

Parklands Hambrook Lane, Stoke Gifford, Bristol, BS34 8QU
Tel: 0117-923 6500 **Fax:** 0117-923 6555
E-mail: colin.forrest@isgplc.com
Website: http://www.isgplc.com
Bank(s): Lloyds TSB Bank plc
Directors: C. Forrest (Grp Chief Exec), J. Youds (Pers), M. Bird (Fin)
Managers: A. Hill (Personnel), R. Earey (Tech Serv Mgr), N. Regan (I.T. Exec), D. Fitzpatrick (Purch Mgr), B. Lancastle (Mktg Serv Mgr), A. Taylor (Sales & Mktg Mg), A. Kelford (Purch Mgr)
Ultimate Holding Company: ISG UK RETAIL LIMITED
Immediate Holding Company: PEARCE LIMITED
Registration no: 02152862 **Date established:** 1987
No.of Employees: 251 - 500 **Product Groups:** 52, 84

Identify Engraving Systems Ltd

2 Windmill Farm Business Centre Bartley Street, Bristol, BS3 4DB
Tel: 0117-953 0800 **Fax:** 0117-953 0900
E-mail: stephen@indentify.co.uk
Website: http://www.identify.co.uk
Directors: S. Jater (Dir)
Immediate Holding Company: IDENTIFY ENGRAVING SYSTEMS LIMITED
Registration no: 03267194 **Date established:** 1996
No.of Employees: 1 - 10 **Product Groups:** 27, 28, 29, 32, 33, 35, 36, 42, 44, 45, 46, 47, 48, 49

Date of Accounts	Mar 08	Mar 07	Mar 06
Working Capital	43	43	22
Fixed Assets	73	98	78
Current Assets	738	596	588
Current Liabilities	695	553	565
Total Share Capital	30	30	30

Imperial Civil Inforcement Solutions

7 Hill Street, Bristol, BS1 5PU
Tel: 0117-925 1700 **Fax:** 0117-925 2515
E-mail: sales@imperial.co.uk
Website: http://www.imperial.co.uk
Directors: A. Bijster (MD)
Managers: M. Bubb
Ultimate Holding Company: IMPERIAL BUSINESS SYSTEMS LIMITED
Immediate Holding Company: IMPERIAL BUSINESS SYSTEMS LIMITED
Registration no: 02281405 **Date established:** 1988 **Turnover:** £5m - £10m
No.of Employees: 21 - 50 **Product Groups:** 84

Date of Accounts	Oct 11	Oct 10	Oct 09
Sales Turnover	7m	8m	6m
Pre Tax Profit/Loss	812	726	393
Working Capital	1m	513	-134
Fixed Assets	2m	2m	3m
Current Assets	4m	3m	2m
Current Liabilities	2m	2m	2m

Imperial Tobacco Group PLC (Incorporating W.D. & H.O. Wills, John Player & Sons and Ogdens)

PO Box 244 Upton Road, Bristol, BS99 7UJ
Tel: 0117-963 6636 **Fax:** 0117-966 7405
E-mail: itg@uk.imptob.com
Website: http://www.imperial-tobacco.com
Bank(s): National Westminster Bank Plc
Directors: R. Dyrbus (Fin), D. Cresswell (Fab), M. Phillips (Co Sec)
Managers: T. Williams, G. Blashill, G. Davis, F. Rogerson, G. Good, K. Hill, J. Hayes, P. Holmes, J. Smithson, K. Brown, P. Green, J. Jones, A. Cooper, J. Thompson, M. Coleman, C. Hazel (Purch Mgr)
Ultimate Holding Company: Imperial Tobacco Group PLC
Immediate Holding Company: Imperial Tobacco Holdings Ltd
Registration no: 03236483 **VAT No.:** GB 238 5789 14
Turnover: Over £1,000m **No.of Employees:** 1501 & over
Product Groups: 20, 49, 61

Date of Accounts	Sep 09	Sep 08	Sep 07
Sales Turnover	4870m	4733m	4808m
Pre Tax Profit/Loss	147m	292m	406m
Working Capital	-12758m	-12015m	-2410m
Fixed Assets	15717m	15168m	3835m
Current Assets	1724m	1207m	3287m
Current Liabilities	948m	913m	657m

Independent Welding Services Ltd

Unit 2 15 Douglas Road Kingswood, Bristol, BS15 8NH
Tel: 0117-935 2540 **Fax:** 0117-935 2627
E-mail: info@indeweld.co.uk
Website: http://www.indeweld.co.uk
Directors: G. Rendall (Dir)
Immediate Holding Company: INDEPENDENT WELDING SERVICES LIMITED
Registration no: 01905241 **Date established:** 1985
Turnover: £250,000 - £500,000 **No.of Employees:** 1 - 10
Product Groups: 24, 30, 33, 34, 35, 36, 37, 38, 40, 42, 46, 48, 67, 83, 84

Date of Accounts	Jun 11	Jun 10	Jun 09
Working Capital	-89	-66	-30
Fixed Assets	211	186	346
Current Assets	100	84	82

inkstinx

744 Bishport Avenue, Bristol, BS13 9EJ
Tel: 0117 -3042396
E-mail: sales@inkstinx.co.uk
Website: http://www.inkstinx.co.uk
Managers: K. Bale (Sales Prom Mgr)
Date established: 2009 **Turnover:** **No.of Employees:** 1 - 10
Product Groups: 44

Installation By Design

Unit D Upper Littleton Mill Chew Road, Winford, Bristol, BS40 8HJ
Tel: 01275-331771 **Fax:** 01275-331771
Directors: P. Parson (Dir)
Immediate Holding Company: WINFORD ROAD GARAGES LIMITED
Registration no: 02435306 **Date established:** 1967
Turnover: Up to £250,000 **No.of Employees:** 1 - 10 **Product Groups:** 35, 42, 45

Date of Accounts	Dec 11	Dec 10	Dec 09
Sales Turnover	N/A	609	636
Pre Tax Profit/Loss	N/A	16	45
Working Capital	233	183	262
Fixed Assets	21	56	50
Current Assets	336	274	386
Current Liabilities	N/A	42	67

Isis Diamond Drilling

31 Bradley Road Patchway, Bristol, BS34 5LF
Tel: 0117-907 7265 **Fax:** 0117- 9077265
E-mail: info@isisdiamonddrilling.co.uk
Website: http://www.isisdiamonddrilling.co.uk
Directors: I. Smitham (Prop)
Date established: 2001 **No.of Employees:** 1 - 10 **Product Groups:** 37, 45, 51

J B P Associates Ltd

The White House 6 Whiteladies Road, Bristol, BS8 1PD
Tel: 0117-907 3400 **Fax:** 0117-907 3417
E-mail: jennifer@jbp.co.uk
Website: http://www.jbp.co.uk
Bank(s): Barclays, Bristol
Directors: J. Bryant Pearson (Ch)
Managers: A. Bonham (Chief Acct)
Ultimate Holding Company: JBP (HOLDINGS) LIMITED
Immediate Holding Company: JBP ASSOCIATES LIMITED
Registration no: 02970219 **VAT No.:** GB 397 4380 09
Date established: 1994 **Turnover:** £1m - £2m **No.of Employees:** 21 - 50
Product Groups: 81

Date of Accounts	May 11	May 10	May 09
Working Capital	347	206	252
Fixed Assets	122	145	13
Current Assets	664	532	442

J & G Fencing Ltd

Unit 25 Brookgate South Liberty Lane, Bristol, BS3 2UQ
Tel: 0117-923 1001 **Fax:** 0117-953 2400
E-mail: john@jgfencing.com
Website: http://www.jgfencing.com
Directors: J. Gwyther (Dir)
Immediate Holding Company: J & G FENCING LIMITED
Registration no: 04502579 **Date established:** 2002 **Turnover:** £2m - £5m
No.of Employees: 11 - 20 **Product Groups:** 25, 26, 27, 30, 33, 34, 35, 36, 37, 39, 40, 41, 45, 49, 52, 66, 68, 83

Date of Accounts	Aug 11	Aug 10	Aug 09
Sales Turnover	N/A	3m	3m
Pre Tax Profit/Loss	N/A	163	157
Working Capital	44	64	116
Fixed Assets	223	96	31
Current Assets	1m	868	800
Current Liabilities	N/A	134	106

Alec Jarrett Ltd

High Street Oldland Common, Bristol, BS30 9TN
Tel: 0117-932 2725 **Fax:** 0117-932 3553
E-mail: stuartjarrett@alec-jarrett.co.uk
Website: http://www.alecjarrett.co.uk
Directors: S. Jarrett (Fin), R. Jarrett (MD)
Managers: S. Jarrett, A. Dillamore (Comptroller)
Ultimate Holding Company: ALEC JARRETT LIMITED
Registration no: 00723594 **VAT No.:** GB 137 7099 43
Date established: 1962 **Turnover:** £20m - £50m
No.of Employees: 51 - 100 **Product Groups:** 20, 62

Date of Accounts	Jan 09	Jan 10	Jan 11
Sales Turnover	N/A	34m	41m
Pre Tax Profit/Loss	251	256	258
Working Capital	4m	4m	4m
Fixed Assets	1m	1m	1m
Current Assets	6m	7m	8m
Current Liabilities	2m	2m	3m

Jencan Ltd

Unit 5 Badminton Road Trading Estate Yate, Bristol, BS37 5NS
Tel: 01454-321171 **Fax:** 01454-320897
E-mail: sales@jencan.com
Website: http://www.jencan.com
Directors: N. Cann (Dir), J. Cann (Co Sec)
Immediate Holding Company: JENCAN LIMITED
Registration no: 02902978 **VAT No.:** GB 639 4456 08
Date established: 1994 **Turnover:** £500,000 - £1m
No.of Employees: 1 - 10 **Product Groups:** 30, 35, 36, 39, 46, 66

Date of Accounts	Mar 12	Mar 11	Mar 10
Working Capital	270	254	211
Fixed Assets	67	4	6
Current Assets	486	476	404

Jewson Ltd

Station Incline Yatton, Bristol, BS49 4AG
Tel: 01934-838293 **Fax:** 01934-876956
E-mail: d.harvey@jewson.co.uk
Website: http://www.jewson.co.uk
Managers: S. Harvey (District Mgr)
Ultimate Holding Company: Saint-Gobain Ltd
Immediate Holding Company: JEWSON LIMITED
Registration no: 00348407 **VAT No.:** GB 394 1212 63
Date established: 1939 **Turnover:** £250,000 - £500,000
No.of Employees: 1 - 10 **Product Groups:** 66

Jewson Ltd

Unit L Stover Trading Estate Millbrook Road, Yate, Bristol, BS37 5PB
Tel: 01454-324378 **Fax:** 01454-324317
Website: http://www.jewson.co.uk
Managers: D. Jones (District Mgr)
Ultimate Holding Company: COMPAGNIE DE SAINT GOBAIN (FRANCE)
Immediate Holding Company: JEWSON LIMITED
Registration no: 00348407 **Date established:** 1939
No.of Employees: 1 - 10 **Product Groups:** 66

Date of Accounts	Dec 11	Dec 10	Dec 09
Sales Turnover	1606m	1547m	1485m
Pre Tax Profit/Loss	18m	100m	45m
Working Capital	-345m	-250m	-349m
Fixed Assets	496m	387m	461m
Current Assets	657m	1005m	1320m
Current Liabilities	66m	120m	64m

C W Jones Flooring Ltd

10 Vale Lane Bed Minister, Bristol, BS3 5RU
Tel: 0117-966 1454 **Fax:** 0117-963 9733
E-mail: info@jonesflooring.co.uk
Website: http://www.jonesflooring.co.uk
Bank(s): Barclays
Directors: J. Jones (Fin)
Ultimate Holding Company: FALLWAY LIMITED
Immediate Holding Company: C.W.JONES (FLOORINGS) LIMITED
Registration no: 00694925 **VAT No.:** GB 138 0460 83
Date established: 1961 **Turnover:** £2m - £5m **No.of Employees:** 11 - 20
Product Groups: 63

Date of Accounts	Feb 12	Feb 11	Feb 10
Sales Turnover	2m	3m	3m
Pre Tax Profit/Loss	49	32	21
Working Capital	71	15	-19
Fixed Assets	76	97	108
Current Assets	668	715	618
Current Liabilities	471	143	489

Jordans Ltd

21 St Thomas Street, Bristol, BS1 6JS
Tel: 0117-923 0600 **Fax:** 0117-923 0063
E-mail: customersupport@jordans.co.uk
Website: http://www.jordans.co.uk
Managers: J. Shackleton (Sales Admin)
Ultimate Holding Company: WEST OF ENGLAND TRUST LIMITED(THE)
Immediate Holding Company: JORDANS LIMITED
Registration no: 00865285 **Date established:** 1965
Turnover: £10m - £20m **No.of Employees:** 101 - 250
Product Groups: 28, 35, 44, 49, 81

Date of Accounts	Mar 11	Mar 10	Mar 09
Sales Turnover	10m	10m	14m
Pre Tax Profit/Loss	1m	2m	-299
Working Capital	924	2m	873
Fixed Assets	439	572	891
Current Assets	3m	4m	5m
Current Liabilities	1m	2m	2m

JR Packaging Supplies

Worthy Road Chittening Industrial Estate, Avonmouth, Bristol, BS11 9EA
Tel: 0117-982 8583 **Fax:** 0117-938 0060
E-mail: sales@jrpack.co.uk
Website: http://www.jrpack.co.uk
Product Groups: 21, 30, 33, 35, 38, 48, 49, 66

K F C Fine Artist Art Ltd

39 Fairway, Bristol, BS4 5DF
Tel: 0117-972 3938 **Fax:** 0117-972 1938
E-mail: tim@brightenyourwalls.fsbusiness.co.uk
Website: http://www.brghtenyourwalls.co.uk
Directors: T. Nash (Dir)
Immediate Holding Company: BRIGHTEN YOUR WALLS LIMITED
Registration no: 05551209 **Date established:** 2005
No.of Employees: 1 - 10 **Product Groups:** 26, 63, 64, 65, 69, 84

K M Engineering Ltd

Unit 7b Parnall Road Trading Estate
Parnall Road
Fishponds, Bristol, BS16 3JQ
Tel: 0117-965 9336 **Fax:** 0117-958 3673
E-mail: enquiries@km-engineering.co.uk
Website: http://www.km-engineering.co.uk
Directors: W. Nicholson (Fin), S. Coggins (Dir)
Immediate Holding Company: K.M. ENGINEERING LIMITED
Registration no: 04259021 **VAT No.:** GB 303 2170 20
Date established: 2001 **Turnover:** £500,000 - £1m
No.of Employees: 11 - 20 **Product Groups:** 48

Date of Accounts	Dec 11	Dec 10	Dec 09
Working Capital	-85	34	36
Fixed Assets	299	211	249
Current Assets	454	447	474

Kenton Technical Products Ltd

25-26 Barnack Trading Centre Novers Hill, Bedminster, Bristol, BS3 5QE
Tel: 0117-963 4579 **Fax:** 0117-963 4501
E-mail: holes@kentons.biz
Website: http://www.kentons.biz
Directors: F. Milton (Fin)
Ultimate Holding Company: KENTON MANUFACTURING LIMITED
Immediate Holding Company: KENTON TECHNICAL PRODUCTS LIMITED
Registration no: 02021034 **Date established:** 1986
Turnover: £500,000 - £1m **No.of Employees:** 1 - 10 **Product Groups:** 35, 48

Date of Accounts	Aug 11	Aug 10	Aug 09
Working Capital	229	234	198
Fixed Assets	167	169	171
Current Assets	437	466	399

Keynsham Powder Coatings

Unit 11a Broadmead Lane, Keynsham, Bristol, BS31 1ST
Tel: 0117-986 8323 **Fax:** 0117-986 8323
E-mail: info@keynsham-powder-coatings.co.uk
Website: http://www.keynsham-powder-coatings.co.uk
Directors: P. Slade (Prop)
Date established: 1992 **No.of Employees:** 1 - 10 **Product Groups:** 46, 48

Keyplan Engineering Ltd

Fishponds Road Fishponds, Bristol, BS16 3UA
Tel: 0117-965 9461 **Fax:** 0117-958 3683
E-mail: s.underwood@keyplaneng.co.uk
Website: http://www.keyplaneng.co.uk
Bank(s): Midland, Weston-Super-Mare
Directors: R. Isles (Dir), S. Underwood (MD), S. Underwood (MD)
Ultimate Holding Company: KEYPLAN SERVICES LIMITED
Immediate Holding Company: KEYPLAN ENGINEERING LIMITED
Registration no: 02064696 **VAT No.:** GB 449 1945 17
Date established: 1986 **Turnover:** £5m - £10m **No.of Employees:** 21 - 50
Product Groups: 52

Date of Accounts	Mar 12	Mar 11	Mar 10
Sales Turnover	N/A	N/A	5m
Pre Tax Profit/Loss	N/A	N/A	736
Working Capital	1m	829	493
Current Assets	3m	2m	2m
Current Liabilities	N/A	N/A	1m

Keystone Castor Co.

Unit 19 Avon Business Park Lodge Causeway, Bristol, BS16 3JP
Tel: 0117-965 7777 **Fax:** 0117-965 2177
E-mail: bristol@keystonecastors.com
Website: http://www.keystonecastors.com
Managers: H. Tanner (Mgr)
Ultimate Holding Company: KEYSTONE WOOD LTD
Registration no: 00541197 **VAT No.:** GB 559 0340 41
Date established: 1999 **No.of Employees:** 1 - 10 **Product Groups:** 29, 39, 66

Kier Western

The Old Mill Chapel Lane, Warmley, Bristol, BS15 4WW
Tel: 0117-961 8000 **Fax:** 0117-961 8628
E-mail: info.bristol@keir.co.uk
Website: http://www.kier.co.uk
Directors: P. Young (MD)
Managers: N. Connelly (I.T. Exec), T. Westwood (Sales & Mktg Mg), S. Riddles (Personnel)
Ultimate Holding Company: KIER GROUP PLC
Immediate Holding Company: KIER MORTIMER LTD
Registration no: 00546145 **Turnover:** £10m - £20m
No.of Employees: 101 - 250 **Product Groups:** 51

King Lifting Ltd

King Road Avenue Avonmouth, Bristol, BS11 9HF
Tel: 0117-982 1121 **Fax:** 0117-923 5762
E-mail: sales@kinglifting.co.uk
Website: http://www.kinglifting.co.uk
Directors: R. King (MD)
Immediate Holding Company: KING LIFTING LIMITED
Registration no: 01607970 **Date established:** 1982
No.of Employees: 51 - 100 **Product Groups:** 45, 48, 67, 72, 83, 84

Date of Accounts	Jan 12	Jan 11	Jan 10
Sales Turnover	15m	14m	11m
Pre Tax Profit/Loss	165	-290	-1m
Working Capital	-4m	-3m	-2m
Fixed Assets	13m	12m	13m
Current Assets	3m	4m	3m
Current Liabilities	3m	3m	2m

R G D King Ltd

Pennywell House Pennywell Road, Bristol, BS5 0TX
Tel: 0117-941 4500 **Fax:** 0117-941 4678
E-mail: admin@rgdking.co.uk
Website: http://www.rgdking.co.uk
Managers: P. Mogg (Chief Mgr)
Immediate Holding Company: R.G.D. KING LIMITED
Registration no: 00662752 **VAT No.:** 137 9464 36 **Date established:** 1960
Turnover: £1m - £2m **No.of Employees:** 1 - 10 **Product Groups:** 52

Date of Accounts	Dec 11	Dec 10	Dec 09
Working Capital	285	267	854
Fixed Assets	2m	2m	1m
Current Assets	1m	1m	2m

Kingsway Gears Limited

Unit 50 Moravian Business Park Hanham Road, Bristol, BS15 8PX
Tel: 0117-961 3168 **Fax:** 0117-960 4718
E-mail: sales@kingswaygears.co.uk
Website: http://www.kingswaygears.co.uk
Directors: K. Norman (Fin), B. Davis (MD)
Immediate Holding Company: KINGSWAY GEARS LIMITED
Registration no: 06243056 **VAT No.:** GB 140 4661 94
Date established: 2007 **Turnover:** £500,000 - £1m
No.of Employees: 1 - 10 **Product Groups:** 25, 30, 35, 36, 39, 48

Date of Accounts	Jun 11	Jun 10	Jun 09
Working Capital	-145	-225	-229
Fixed Assets	107	126	151
Current Assets	100	86	80

Kingswood Canvas Ltd

Unit 8-9 Douglas Road Industrial Park Douglas Road Kingswood, Bristol, BS15 8PD
Tel: 0117-960 1281 **Fax:** 0117-935 2632
E-mail: kingswoodcanvas@btconnect.com
Website: http://www.kingswoodcanvas.co.uk
Directors: A. Eyers (Fin), G. Eyers (MD)
Immediate Holding Company: KINGSWOOD CANVAS LIMITED
Registration no: 01404541 **VAT No.:** GB 318 7571 37
Date established: 1978 **Turnover:** £500,000 - £1m
No.of Employees: 1 - 10 **Product Groups:** 23, 24, 49

Date of Accounts	Jan 11	Jan 10	Jan 07
Working Capital	281	284	239
Fixed Assets	55	41	51
Current Assets	326	312	285

Kinneir Dufort Design Ltd

5 Host Street, Bristol, BS1 5BU
Tel: 0117-901 4000 **Fax:** 0117-901 4001
E-mail: info@kinneirdufort.com
Website: http://www.kinneirdufort.com
Bank(s): Lloyds TSB Bank plc
Managers: F. Clasby (Mktg Serv Mgr), M. Norris (Chief Acct), M. Hall (Mktg Serv Mgr)
Ultimate Holding Company: KINNEIR DUFORT LIMITED
Immediate Holding Company: KINNEIR DUFORT DESIGN LIMITED
Registration no: 01311968 **Date established:** 1977
Turnover: £500,000 - £1m **No.of Employees:** 51 - 100
Product Groups: 44, 84, 85

Date of Accounts	Dec 11	Dec 10	Dec 09
Working Capital	1m	811	2m
Fixed Assets	296	175	154
Current Assets	2m	1m	3m

Kleeneze Sealtech Ltd

Ansteys Road Hanham, Bristol, BS15 3SS
Tel: 0117-958 2450 **Fax:** 0117-960 0141
E-mail: sales@ksl.uk.com
Website: http://www.ksltd.com
Bank(s): Bank of Scotland
Directors: A. Bruhn (Co Sec), D. Love (Comm), D. Kullen (Ch)
Ultimate Holding Company: KULLEN GMBH & CO KG (GERMANY)
Immediate Holding Company: KLEENEZE - KOTI LIMITED
Registration no: 02506478 **Date established:** 1990 **Turnover:** £5m - £10m
No.of Employees: 21 - 50 **Product Groups:** 29, 30, 32, 33, 35, 36, 37, 39, 40, 41, 43, 44, 45, 49

Date of Accounts	Mar 11	Mar 10	Mar 09
Pre Tax Profit/Loss	250	12	213
Working Capital	2m	1m	2m
Fixed Assets	70	87	100
Current Assets	2m	2m	2m
Current Liabilities	460	447	280

Kool-Car Air Conditioning Ltd

Lays Farm Trading Estate Charlton Road, Keynsham, Bristol, BS31 2SE
Tel: 0117-986 5000
E-mail: marie@kool-car.co.uk
Website: http://www.kool-car.co.uk
Directors: M. Ricketts (Dir)
Immediate Holding Company: Kool-Car Air-Conditioning Ltd
Registration no: 05697672 **Date established:** 2006
No.of Employees: 1 - 10 **Product Groups:** 40, 66

KPMG UK Ltd

100 Temple Street, Bristol, BS1 6AG
Tel: 0117-905 4000 **Fax:** 0117-946 4001
Website: http://www.kpmg.co.uk
Directors: R. Boot (Ptnr)
Ultimate Holding Company: KPMG EUROPE LLP
Immediate Holding Company: KPMG UK LIMITED
Registration no: 03580549 **Date established:** 1998
Turnover: £250,000 - £500,000 **No.of Employees:** 251 - 500
Product Groups: 80

Date of Accounts	Sep 11	Sep 10	Sep 09
Sales Turnover	698m	632m	624m
Pre Tax Profit/Loss	655	593	584
Working Capital	1m	847	419
Current Assets	23m	21m	25m
Current Liabilities	22m	20m	20m

Kuehne & Nagel UK Ltd (Branch)

Unit 0-1 Hazelmere Trading Estate Third Way, Avonmouth, Bristol, BS11 9YE
Tel: 0117-982 7101 **Fax:** 0117-982 4606
E-mail: robert.jones@kuehne-nagel.com
Website: http://www.kuehne-nagel.com
Managers: R. Jones (District Mgr), T. Nel
Ultimate Holding Company: KUEHNE & NAGEL INTERNATIONAL AG (SWITZERLAND)
Immediate Holding Company: KUEHNE + NAGEL (UK) LIMITED
Registration no: 01463105 **VAT No.:** GB 584 6403 22
Date established: 1979 **Turnover:** £2m - £5m **No.of Employees:** 21 - 50
Product Groups: 75, 76

L G C Executive Search

148 Westbury Road Westbury-on-Trym, Bristol, BS9 3AL
Tel: 0117-904 6504 **Fax:** 0117-904 6504
E-mail: les@lgcexecsearch.com
Website: http://www.lgcexecsearch.com
Directors: L. Collisson (Prop)
Date established: 1997 **Turnover:** £250,000 - £500,000
No.of Employees: 1 - 10 **Product Groups:** 80

Lafarge Aggregates Ltd

Marsh Lane Easton-in-Gordano, Bristol, BS20 0NF
Tel: 0800-373636 **Fax:** 01275-377700
Website: http://www.lafargeplasterboard.com
Bank(s): Barclays
Directors: R. Mould (Sales), K. Hehir (Sales & Mktg), C. Ellwood (Fin), B. Slatton (MD)
Managers: M. Crump (Chief Acct), C. Wilson (Mktg Serv Mgr)
Ultimate Holding Company: LAFARGE SA (FRANCE)
Immediate Holding Company: LAFARGE AGGREGATES LIMITED
Registration no: 00297905 **VAT No.:** GB 479 6787 60
Date established: 1935 **Turnover:** £75m - £125m
No.of Employees: 251 - 500 **Product Groups:** 33

Lifting Logic

Ashmead Business Centre Ashmead Road, Keynsham, Bristol, BS31 1SX
Tel: 0117-937 6790 **Fax:** 0117-937 6799
E-mail: sales@sparrowcrane.co.uk
Website: http://www.liftinglogic.com
Managers: T. Williams (Mgr)
Immediate Holding Company: WICKEYPOINT LIMITED
Registration no: 05239795 **Date established:** 1996
No.of Employees: 1 - 10 **Product Groups:** 35, 39, 45

Date of Accounts	Apr 12	Apr 11	Apr 10
Working Capital	12	8	6
Current Assets	25	16	15

Lindab Ltd

7 Clothier Road Brislington Trading Estate, Brislington, Bristol, BS4 5PS
Tel: 0117-972 9800 **Fax:** 0117-972 9801
E-mail: brislington.sales@lindab.co.uk
Website: http://www.lindab.com
Managers: S. Bird (Mgr)
Registration no: 01641399 **Date established:** 2006
No.of Employees: 1 - 10 **Product Groups:** 37, 40, 48

Lindab Ltd

16 Eldon Way, Bristol, BS4 3QQ
Tel: 0117-977 1345 **Fax:** 0117-971 3123
E-mail: bristol.south@lindab.co.uk
Website: http://www.lindab.co.uk
Bank(s): National Westminster Bank Plc
Managers: S. Bird (District Mgr)
Ultimate Holding Company: LINDAB INTERNATIONAL AB (SWEDEN)
Immediate Holding Company: LINDAB LIMITED
Registration no: 01641399 **VAT No.:** GB 589 7030 00
Date established: 1982 **Turnover:** £10m - £20m
No.of Employees: 11 - 20 **Product Groups:** 23, 32, 35, 36

Date of Accounts	Dec 11	Dec 10	Dec 09
Sales Turnover	51m	47m	49m
Pre Tax Profit/Loss	1m	-204	354
Working Capital	16m	-3m	-4m
Fixed Assets	16m	20m	22m
Current Assets	22m	20m	23m
Current Liabilities	1m	980	775

Line Bridge Ltd

340 Bristol Business Park, Bristol, BS16 1EJ
Tel: 0117-372 9741 **Fax:** 0117-931 9721
Website: http://www.bowneglobal.com
Managers: A. Doggett (Tech Serv Mgr), I. Wood (Sales Admin)
Ultimate Holding Company: BATH STREET INVESTMENTS LTD.
Immediate Holding Company: LINEBRIDGE LIMITED
Registration no: SC314309 **Date established:** 2007
No.of Employees: 21 - 50 **Product Groups:** 28, 37, 52, 79

Date of Accounts	Jan 08	Jun 11	Jun 10
Working Capital	N/A	-226	-226
Fixed Assets	6m	3m	7m

Locate Display Fixtures

Unit 4 Sheene Court Industrial Estate Sheene Road, Bristol, BS3 4EG
Tel: 0117-953 3600 **Fax:** 0117-966 3332
Website: http://www.displayfixings.net
Directors: J. Sulzmann (Prop)
Immediate Holding Company: GOLFPLAN MARKETING LIMITED
Registration no: 03525578 **Date established:** 1998
No.of Employees: 21 - 50 **Product Groups:** 26, 37, 49, 67

Date of Accounts	Dec 10	Dec 09	Dec 08
Working Capital	N/A	63	63
Current Assets	N/A	67	67

Lorne Stewart plc (Electrical Small Works Department)

Second Floor 1 Broad Walk, Bristol, BS4 2RA
Tel: 0117-972 3172 **Fax:** 0117-972 3102
E-mail: gary.worrall@lornestewart.co.uk
Website: http://www.lornestewart.com
Managers: G. Worrall (Mgr)
Ultimate Holding Company: LAFFAYETTE HOLDINGS LIMITED (JERSEY)
Immediate Holding Company: LORNE STEWART PLC
Registration no: 01348218 **VAT No.:** GB 225 7789 29
Date established: 1978 **No.of Employees:** 51 - 100 **Product Groups:** 52

Date of Accounts	Dec 11	Dec 10	Dec 09
Sales Turnover	162m	173m	183m
Pre Tax Profit/Loss	8m	6m	6m
Working Capital	15m	14m	9m
Fixed Assets	3m	3m	4m
Current Assets	62m	62m	60m
Current Liabilities	23m	19m	21m

Lusso Interiors

Unit 20 Marsh Lane Industrial Estate Marsh Lane, Easton-In-Gordano, Bristol, BS20 0NH
Tel: 01275-372293 **Fax:** 01275-371217
E-mail: andrewbailey@lussointerior.com
Website: http://www.lussointerior.com
Directors: A. Bailey (Dir), L. Bailey (Fin)
Immediate Holding Company: LUSSO INTERIORS LIMITED
Registration no: 04612486 **Date established:** 2002
No.of Employees: 1 - 10 **Product Groups:** 24, 25, 26, 30, 33, 35, 36, 37, 40, 45, 47, 48, 52, 66, 67, 84

Date of Accounts	Dec 11	Dec 10	Dec 09
Working Capital	950	843	843
Fixed Assets	90	91	91
Current Assets	1m	1m	1m

M D C Auto Electrical

139 Hampstead Road, Bristol, BS4 3HR
Tel: 0117-949 7754 **Fax:** 0117-949 7754
E-mail: mark@mdcautoelectrical.co.uk
Website: http://www.mdcautoelectrical.co.uk
Directors: M. Collins (Prop)
No.of Employees: 1 - 10 **Product Groups:** 37, 39, 67

M J M Woodworking Machinery

Unit 7 Marsh Lane Trading Estate Marsh Lane, Easton-In-Gordano, Bristol, BS20 0NH
Tel: 01275-371922 **Fax:** 01275-371922
E-mail: mjmwoodmachines@aol.com
Website: http://www.mjmwoodmachines.com
Directors: M. Martin (Prop)
Date established: 2002 **No.of Employees:** 1 - 10 **Product Groups:** 46

M J N Colston Ltd Staveley Engineering Services

Eden House Eastgate Office Centre Eastgate Road, Bristol, BS5 6XY
Tel: 0117-301 3000 **Fax:** 0117- 3013001
E-mail: klloyd@mkjncolston.co.uk
Website: http://www.mjncolston.co.uk
Bank(s): National Westminster
Directors: S. Elford (Fin), J. March (Reg), A. Salway (Dir), P. Churchard (MD)
Managers: D. Fews (Sales Prom Mgr)
Ultimate Holding Company: STAVELEY ENGINEERING SERVICES GROUP LIMITED
Immediate Holding Company: MJN COLSTON LIMITED
Registration no: 05211561 **VAT No.:** GB 239 3550 53
Date established: 2004 **Turnover:** £50m - £75m
No.of Employees: 51 - 100 **Product Groups:** 52, 54

Date of Accounts	May 11	May 10	May 09
Sales Turnover	96m	114m	51m
Pre Tax Profit/Loss	2m	1m	686
Working Capital	4m	2m	2m
Fixed Assets	10m	10m	10m
Current Assets	37m	30m	17m
Current Liabilities	3m	3m	1m

M P S I Systems Ltd

19B Osprey Court Hawkfield Business Park, Whitchurch, Bristol, BS14 0BB
Tel: 0117-964 5132 **Fax:** 0117-964 5163
E-mail: info@mpsisys.co.uk
Website: http://www.mpsisys.com
Directors: L. Wells (Fin), R. Harper (Ch)
Managers: A. Hay (Sales Prom Mgr), A. Renshaw (Chief Mgr)
Ultimate Holding Company: MPSI Systems Inc. (USA)
Registration no: 01458176 **VAT No.:** GB 340 6064 86
Date established: 1979 **Turnover:** Up to £250,000
No.of Employees: 1 - 10 **Product Groups:** 44

Date of Accounts	Dec 08
Sales Turnover	359
Pre Tax Profit/Loss	-120
Working Capital	113
Fixed Assets	4
Current Assets	143
Current Liabilities	30
Total Share Capital	4062
ROCE% (Return on Capital Employed)	-102.3

Mail Handling International Ltd

77-79 Feeder Road, Bristol, BS2 0TQ
Tel: 0117-977 6655 **Fax:** 0117-977 9966
E-mail: sales@mh-international.co.uk
Website: http://www.mh-international.com
Managers: P. Brown
Immediate Holding Company: MAIL HANDLING INTERNATIONAL LIMITED
Registration no: 03241562 **Date established:** 1996
Turnover: £10m - £20m **No.of Employees:** 11 - 20 **Product Groups:** 81

Date of Accounts	Mar 09	Sep 11	Sep 10
Sales Turnover	N/A	18m	N/A
Pre Tax Profit/Loss	N/A	465	N/A

Working Capital	347	301	259
Fixed Assets	56	2m	1m
Current Assets	2m	4m	3m
Current Liabilities	N/A	899	N/A

Makro Self Service Wholesalers Ltd

Cribbs Causeway Industrial Estate Lysander Road, Westbury-On-Trym, Bristol, BS10 7TZ
Tel: 08444-457445
Website: http://www.makro.co.uk
Managers: D. Bown (Mgr)
Ultimate Holding Company: METRO AG (GERMANY)
Immediate Holding Company: MAKRO SELF SERVICE WHOLESALERS LIMITED
Registration no: 00973269 **Date established:** 1970
No.of Employees: 101 - 250 **Product Groups:** 36, 40

Date of Accounts	Dec 11	Dec 10	Dec 09
Sales Turnover	766m	797m	868m
Pre Tax Profit/Loss	-62m	-20m	-45m
Working Capital	-132m	-58m	-163m
Fixed Assets	101m	101m	92m
Current Assets	105m	165m	152m
Current Liabilities	20m	16m	89m

Manor Scrap Ltd

59-61 Feeder Road, Bristol, BS2 0SH
Tel: 0117-965 8834 **Fax:** 0117-971 2626
E-mail: manorscrap@aol.com
Website: http://www.manorscrap.com
Directors: J. Newland (Fin), P. Newland (MD)
No.of Employees: 11 - 20 **Product Groups:** 34, 42, 46, 51, 83

Manufacturing Techniques Corporation UK Ltd

Units 5-6 North Avon Business Centre Dean Road, Yate, Bristol, BS37 5NH
Tel: 01454-318491 **Fax:** 01454-318575
Directors: K. Williams (Fin)
Immediate Holding Company: MANUFACTURING TECHNIQUES CORPORATION (U.K.) LIMITED
Registration no: 02238152 **Date established:** 1988
No.of Employees: 1 - 10 **Product Groups:** 45

Date of Accounts	Aug 11	Aug 10	Aug 09
Working Capital	86	90	97
Current Assets	121	139	133

Maplin Electronics Ltd

Unit 2b Brislington Retail Park Bath Road, Brislington, Bristol, BS4 5NG
Tel: 08432-277381
E-mail: customercare@maplin.co.uk
Website: http://www.maplin.co.uk
Ultimate Holding Company: MONTAGU PRIVATE EQUITY LLP
Immediate Holding Company: MAPLIN ELECTRONICS LIMITED
Registration no: 01264385 **Date established:** 1976
Turnover: £125m - £250m **No.of Employees:** 1 - 10 **Product Groups:** 37, 61

Date of Accounts	Dec 11	Dec 08	Dec 09
Sales Turnover	205m	204m	204m
Pre Tax Profit/Loss	25m	32m	35m
Working Capital	118m	49m	75m
Fixed Assets	27m	28m	28m
Current Assets	207m	108m	142m
Current Liabilities	78m	51m	59m

Marigold Industrial Ltd

B2 Vantage Office Park Old Gloucester Road, Hambrook, Bristol, BS16 1GW
Tel: 08450-753355 **Fax:** 0845-075 3356
E-mail: sales@marigold-industrial.com
Website: http://www.marigold-industrial.com
Bank(s): Barclays
Managers: M. Credicott (Chief Mgr)
Ultimate Holding Company: COMASEC INTERNATIONAL SAS (FRANCE)
Immediate Holding Company: MARIGOLD INDUSTRIAL LIMITED
Registration no: 00971595 **Date established:** 1970
Turnover: £10m - £20m **No.of Employees:** 11 - 20 **Product Groups:** 24, 29

Date of Accounts	Dec 11	Dec 10	Dec 09
Sales Turnover	12m	13m	10m
Pre Tax Profit/Loss	280	-297	-204
Working Capital	2m	1m	2m
Fixed Assets	71	93	85
Current Assets	3m	4m	3m
Current Liabilities	1m	2m	1m

Matki plc

Churchward Road Yate, Bristol, BS37 5PL
Tel: 01454-322888 **Fax:** 01454-315284
E-mail: helpline@matki.co.uk
Website: http://www.matki.co.uk
Bank(s): Nat West
Directors: F. Cunild (MD), M. Bruce (Co Sec)
Immediate Holding Company: MATKI PUBLIC LIMITED COMPANY
Registration no: 01010424 **Date established:** 1971
Turnover: £10m - £20m **No.of Employees:** 101 - 250 **Product Groups:** 30

Date of Accounts	Dec 11	Dec 10	Dec 09
Sales Turnover	12m	13m	14m
Pre Tax Profit/Loss	155	-262	-1m
Working Capital	7m	7m	7m
Fixed Assets	6m	6m	6m
Current Assets	8m	8m	8m
Current Liabilities	628	682	825

Matrix Composite Materials Company Ltd

Unit E Paintworks, Arnos Vale, Bristol, BS4 3EH
Tel: 0117-971 5145 **Fax:** 0117-977 8388
E-mail: sales@mcmc-uk.com
Website: http://www.mcmc-uk.com
Directors: S. Deas (Dir), S. Darby (Fin)
Immediate Holding Company: MATRIX COMPOSITE MATERIALS COMPANY LIMITED
Registration no: 03448185 **VAT No.:** GB 701 0372 95
Date established: 1997 **Turnover:** £500,000 - £1m
No.of Employees: 1 - 10 **Product Groups:** 30

Date of Accounts	Dec 11	Dec 10	Dec 09
Working Capital	166	198	127
Fixed Assets	12	15	10
Current Assets	367	331	310

Maurice Lay Distributors Ltd

Fourth Way, Bristol, BS11 8DW
Tel: 0117-938 1900 **Fax:** 0117-938 2446
E-mail: sales@mlay.co.uk
Website: http://www.mlay.co.uk
Directors: D. Lay (Sales), G. Perry (Co Sec), M. Lay (MD), M. Bracknell (Co Sec)
Managers: M. Raven (Tech Serv Mgr), P. Stevens (Purch Mgr)
Immediate Holding Company: MAURICE LAY DISTRIBUTORS LIMITED
Registration no: 02070141 **VAT No.:** GB 298 6522 07
Date established: 1986 **Turnover:** £10m - £20m
No.of Employees: 51 - 100 **Product Groups:** 40

Date of Accounts	Dec 11	Dec 10	Dec 09
Sales Turnover	20m	19m	20m
Pre Tax Profit/Loss	1m	918	350
Working Capital	1m	861	561
Fixed Assets	3m	3m	4m
Current Assets	6m	5m	5m
Current Liabilities	2m	2m	2m

Maypole Marketing

Lower Bristol Road Clutton, Bristol, BS39 5PA
Tel: 01761-452240 **Fax:** 01761-452275
Directors: P. Williams (Prop)
Date established: 1989 **No.of Employees:** 1 - 10 **Product Groups:** 46, 48

Mccann Erickson Ltd

Communications House 125 Redcliff Street, Bristol, BS1 6HU
Tel: 0117-921 1764 **Fax:** 0117-949 3395
E-mail: info@corixa.co.uk
Website: http://www.corixa.co.uk
Bank(s): Lloyds TSB Bank plc
Directors: A. Marsden (Co Sec), F. Bradshaw (MD)
Ultimate Holding Company: INTERPUBLIC GROUP OF COMPANIES INC (USA)
Immediate Holding Company: CORIXA COMMUNICATIONS LIMITED
Registration no: 02857649 **VAT No.:** GB 466 2488 18
Date established: 1993 **Turnover:** £10m - £20m
No.of Employees: 21 - 50 **Product Groups:** 81

Date of Accounts	Dec 10	Dec 09	Dec 08
Working Capital	355	355	355
Current Assets	476	476	476

MCM Special Products Ltd

Unit 7-8 Century Park Chittening Industrial Estate, Avonmouth, Bristol, BS11 0YD
Tel: 0117-982 2224 **Fax:** 0117-982 2434
E-mail: sales@mcmproducts.com
Website: http://www.mcmproducts.com
Directors: A. Timbrell (Dir)
Registration no: 05006176 **No.of Employees:** 1 - 10 **Product Groups:** 35, 45, 67

Melhuish & Bateman Ltd

3-5 Flowers Hill Close, Bristol, BS4 5LF
Tel: 0117-971 2136 **Fax:** 0117-971 7388
E-mail: sales@melhuishandbateman.co.uk
Website: http://www.melhuishandbateman.co.uk
Directors: C. Salter (Fin), P. Salter (MD), S. Salter (Dir)
Registration no: 01234833 **VAT No.:** GB 140 2069 15
Date established: 1975 **Turnover:** £1m - £2m **No.of Employees:** 1 - 10
Product Groups: 48

Date of Accounts	Nov 07	Nov 06	Nov 05
Working Capital	227	243	159
Fixed Assets	288	110	106
Current Assets	830	680	454
Current Liabilities	603	438	295

Merlett Plastics UK Ltd

Unit 2 Waverley Road Beeches Industrial Estate, Yate, Bristol, BS37 5QT
Tel: 01454-329888 **Fax:** 01454-324499
E-mail: pvchose@merlett.com
Website: http://www.merlett.com
Bank(s): Barclays
Directors: A. Gibbons (MD)
Immediate Holding Company: MERLETT PLASTICS (U.K.) LIMITED
Registration no: 01507767 **VAT No.:** GB 336 7729 26
Date established: 1980 **Turnover:** £5m - £10m **No.of Employees:** 21 - 50
Product Groups: 29, 30, 36, 37

Date of Accounts	Dec 11	Dec 10	Dec 09
Working Capital	782	568	423
Fixed Assets	32	30	60
Current Assets	3m	3m	3m

Metal Contract Management Ltd

Unit 7-8 Century Park Chittening Industrial Estate, Chittening, Bristol, BS11 0YD
Tel: 0117-982 2224 **Fax:** 0117-982 7600
E-mail: sales@mcmmetals.com
Website: http://www.mcmmetals.com
Directors: S. Heard (Fin), S. Bradley (MD)
Immediate Holding Company: METAL CONTRACT MANAGEMENT LIMITED
Registration no: 03659298 **Date established:** 1998 **Turnover:** £1m - £2m
No.of Employees: 21 - 50 **Product Groups:** 30, 31, 34, 35, 36, 48

Date of Accounts	Mar 11	Mar 10	Mar 09
Sales Turnover	N/A	N/A	8m
Pre Tax Profit/Loss	N/A	N/A	136
Working Capital	-21	154	174
Fixed Assets	107	101	125
Current Assets	3m	3m	2m
Current Liabilities	801	N/A	141

MFS Stone Surfaces Ltd

Verona House Filwood Road, Fishpond, Bristol, BS16 3RY
Tel: 0117-965 6565 **Fax:** 0117-965 6573
E-mail: maryford@marbleflooring.co.uk
Website: http://www.marbleflooring.co.uk
Bank(s): Barclays
Directors: P. Zannetti (MD), D. Zannetti (Dir)
Managers: M. Ford (Personnel)
Immediate Holding Company: Zanetti & Bailey
Registration no: 00718205 **VAT No.:** GB 567 7563 88
Turnover: £1m - £2m **No.of Employees:** 51 - 100 **Product Groups:** 33

Date of Accounts	Mar 10	Mar 09	Mar 08
Working Capital	611	513	395
Fixed Assets	199	234	309
Current Assets	1m	1m	2m

Midas Electronics

4 Northwood Road Pilning, Bristol, BS35 4HF
Tel: 01454-632967 **Fax:** 01454-633832
E-mail: chrisgray@midaselectronics.co.uk
Website: http://www.midaselectronics.co.uk
Directors: C. Gray (Dir)
Immediate Holding Company: MIDAS ELECTRONICS LIMITED
Registration no: 02987939 **Date established:** 1994
No.of Employees: 1 - 10 **Product Groups:** 38

Date of Accounts	Nov 11	Nov 10	Nov 09
Working Capital	2	-0	-1
Fixed Assets	5	5	7
Current Assets	15	5	14

Minuteman Press Ltd

15 Nelson Parade, Bristol, BS3 4HY
Tel: 0117-966 5566 **Fax:** 0117-966 5511
E-mail: info@minutemanbristol.com
Website: http://www.minutemanbristol.com
Directors: P. Wise (MD)
Immediate Holding Company: MMP BRISTOL LTD
Registration no: 05872035 **Date established:** 2006
Turnover: Up to £250,000 **No.of Employees:** 1 - 10 **Product Groups:** 28

Date of Accounts	Jul 09	Jul 08	Mar 11
Sales Turnover	181	146	302
Pre Tax Profit/Loss	4	-0	2
Working Capital	11	19	-7
Fixed Assets	33	35	22
Current Assets	31	28	48
Current Liabilities	3	4	32

Mirage Mortgages

55 Queen Square, Bristol, BS1 4LH
Tel: 0117-945 8790 **Fax:** 0117-9458788
E-mail: enquiries@miragemortgages.co.uk
Website: http://www.miragemortgages.co.uk
Directors: I. Macdonald (Dir), I. Macdonald (Ptnr)
Ultimate Holding Company: BLADON STUDIOS LTD
Immediate Holding Company: PURPLE HAZE PRODUCTIONS LIMITED
Registration no: 03825877 **Date established:** 1999
No.of Employees: 1 - 10 **Product Groups:** 82

Mobile Storage Sales Ltd

Unit 4 Oak Lane Fishponds Trading Estate, Bristol, BS5 7UY
Tel: 0117-965 5665 **Fax:** 0117-965 5664
E-mail: adrian.harvey@hotmail.com
Website: http://mssbristol.co.uk
Directors: A. Harvey (MD)
Immediate Holding Company: MOBILE STORAGE SALES LIMITED
Registration no: 02622193 **Date established:** 1991
No.of Employees: 1 - 10 **Product Groups:** 35, 42, 45

Date of Accounts	Jul 11	Jul 10	Jul 09
Working Capital	97	142	187
Fixed Assets	296	288	290
Current Assets	199	218	315

Modern Baking Systems Bristol Ltd

26 Clothier Road, Bristol, BS4 5PS
Tel: 0117-977 9494 **Fax:** 0117-971 9926
Website: http://www.modernbaking.co.uk
Directors: A. Smith (MD), B. Smith (Fin)
Immediate Holding Company: MODERN BAKING SYSTEMS (BRISTOL) LIMITED
Registration no: 01813319 **Date established:** 1984
No.of Employees: 1 - 10 **Product Groups:** 20, 40, 41

Date of Accounts	Jun 11	Jun 10	Jun 09
Working Capital	12	-30	-40
Fixed Assets	690	696	678
Current Assets	117	175	127

Mott Macdonald Ltd

Prince House 43-51 Prince Street, Bristol, BS1 4PS
Tel: 0117-906 9500 **Fax:** 0117-922 1924
E-mail: bristol@mottmac.com
Website: http://www.mottmac.co.uk
Directors: M. Shields (Dir)
Ultimate Holding Company: MOTT MACDONALD GROUP LIMITED
Immediate Holding Company: MOTT MACDONALD LIMITED
Registration no: 01243967 **Date established:** 1976
No.of Employees: 21 - 50 **Product Groups:** 54, 84

Date of Accounts	Dec 11	Dec 10	Dec 09
Sales Turnover	531m	573m	610m
Pre Tax Profit/Loss	13m	25m	21m
Working Capital	288m	302m	299m
Fixed Assets	19m	19m	19m
Current Assets	498m	505m	502m
Current Liabilities	124m	120m	131m

Multicom Products Ltd

33 Victoria Street, Bristol, BS1 6AS
Tel: 0117-908 1250 **Fax:** 0117-908 1394
E-mail: info@multicom.co.uk
Website: http://www.multicom.co.uk
Bank(s): Barclays P.L.C., Corn St, Bris
Directors: J. Howell (Co Sec), R. Howell (Ch)
Managers: A. Abby (Tech Serv Mgr), C. Warden (Fin Mgr), K. Newbury (Personnel)
Immediate Holding Company: MULTICOM PRODUCTS LIMITED
Registration no: 02447353 **VAT No.:** GB 650 5285 44
Date established: 1989 **Turnover:** £2m - £5m **No.of Employees:** 51 - 100
Product Groups: 44

Date of Accounts	Jun 11	Jun 10	Jun 09
Sales Turnover	N/A	N/A	3m
Pre Tax Profit/Loss	N/A	N/A	465
Working Capital	514	470	385
Fixed Assets	609	568	455
Current Assets	1m	1m	1m
Current Liabilities	N/A	N/A	605

Murco Petroleum Ltd

Oakley Green Westerleigh, Bristol, BS37 8QE
Tel: 0117-957 4086 **Fax:** 0117-956 3353
E-mail: bristol@cplpetroleum.co.uk
Website: http://www.cplpetroleum.co.uk
Bank(s): National Westminster Bank Plc
Managers: B. Young (Mgr), P. Dury (Mgr), P. Joy (Chief Mgr)
Ultimate Holding Company: CPL Industries Holdings Ltd
Immediate Holding Company: MURCO PETROLEUM LIMITED
Registration no: 00677691 **VAT No.:** GB 721 5764 39
Date established: 1960 **No.of Employees:** 11 - 20 **Product Groups:** 66

Mwuk Ltd (t/a Alexandra)

Midland Way Thornbury, Bristol, BS35 2NT
Tel: 0845-1552288 **Fax:** 020-7515 0077
E-mail: sales@primawear.com
Website: http://www.alexandra.co.uk
Bank(s): Barclays
Directors: N. Acaster (Mkt Research), P. Rosser (Co Sec), N. Atkinson (MD), I. Fountain (Sales)
Managers: C. Ellermen (Purch Mgr), R. Thompson (Personnel), G. Ford (Sales & Mktg Mg)
Ultimate Holding Company: 00229018
Immediate Holding Company: PCW REALISATIONS LIMITED
Registration no: 03864167 **VAT No.:** GB 744 3597 10
Date established: 1999 **Turnover:** £2m - £5m
No.of Employees: 101 - 250 **Product Groups:** 22, 23, 24

Date of Accounts	Jan 08
Sales Turnover	6091
Pre Tax Profit/Loss	473
Working Capital	2194
Fixed Assets	833
Current Assets	4837
Current Liabilities	2643
Total Share Capital	403
ROCE% (Return on Capital Employed)	15.6

Needham Haddrell

8 Hide Market West Street, St Philips, Bristol, BS2 0BH
Tel: 08454-818952 **Fax:** 0117-971 6744
E-mail: jonathan.haddrell@needhamhaddrell.com
Website: http://www.needhamhaddrell.com
Directors: J. Haddrell (Dir)
Immediate Holding Company: NEEDHAM HADDRELL LTD
Registration no: 03733925 **Date established:** 1999
No.of Employees: 1 - 10 **Product Groups:** 80

Neptune Plating Ltd

Barton Manor Trading Estate, Bristol, BS2 0RL
Tel: 0117-955 2041 **Fax:** 0117-935 0805
E-mail: neptune@eicgroup.co.uk
Website: http://www.eicgroup.co.uk
Bank(s): Barclays
Directors: C. Thomson (MD), J. Tolliday (Dir), M. Alcott (Chief Op Offcr)
Managers: R. Tuplin (Works Gen Mgr)
Immediate Holding Company: E.I.C. Group Ltd
Registration no: 01129450 **VAT No.:** GB 138 4212 82
Date established: 1973 **Turnover:** £1m - £2m **No.of Employees:** 11 - 20
Product Groups: 48

Date of Accounts	Mar 08	Mar 07	Mar 06
Working Capital	410	601	498
Fixed Assets	269	424	470
Current Assets	1629	1634	1420
Current Liabilities	1219	1033	923
Total Share Capital	10	10	10

New Work Trust Company Ltd

Station Road Workshops Station Road, Kingswood, Bristol, BS15 4PJ
Tel: 0117-957 5577 **Fax:** 0117-956 8776
E-mail: g.lewis@newworktrust.co.uk
Website: http://www.newworktrust.co.uk
Managers: G. Lovell (Chief Mgr)
Immediate Holding Company: NEW WORK TRUST COMPANY LIMITED
Registration no: 01585927 **VAT No.:** GB 357 5224 46
Date established: 1981 **Turnover:** £500,000 - £1m
No.of Employees: 1 - 10 **Product Groups:** 80

Date of Accounts	Dec 11	Dec 10	Dec 09
Sales Turnover	574	556	613
Pre Tax Profit/Loss	-5	1	3
Working Capital	47	81	104
Fixed Assets	5	2	3
Current Assets	233	283	302
Current Liabilities	105	114	111

Nisbets plc

Fourth Way, Bristol, BS11 8DW
Tel: 08451-405555 **Fax:** 08451-435555
E-mail: sales@nisbets.co.uk
Website: http://www.nisbets.co.uk
Directors: R. Cromwell (Mkt Research), J. Pritchard (Fin)
Managers: T. Cursons, E. McAnn (Tech Serv Mgr), S. Aylmer
Immediate Holding Company: NISBETS PLC
Registration no: 01693112 **Date established:** 1983
Turnover: £125m - £250m **No.of Employees:** 251 - 500
Product Groups: 40, 67

Date of Accounts	Dec 11	Dec 10	Dec 09
Sales Turnover	161m	148m	131m
Pre Tax Profit/Loss	26m	23m	21m
Working Capital	53m	35m	28m
Fixed Assets	26m	27m	27m
Current Assets	74m	52m	46m
Current Liabilities	12m	10m	11m

Nomensa Ltd

13 Queen Square, Bristol, BS1 4NT
Tel: 0117-929 7333 **Fax:** 0117-929 7543
E-mail: info@nomensa.com
Website: http://www.nomensa.com
Directors: S. Lincoln (MD)
Immediate Holding Company: NOMENSA LTD
Registration no: 04214477 **Date established:** 2001
No.of Employees: 21 - 50 **Product Groups:** 44

Date of Accounts	Dec 11	Dec 10	Dec 09
Working Capital	322	265	243
Fixed Assets	13	11	16
Current Assets	525	380	403

Nova Aluminium

11 Lawfords Gate, Bristol, BS2 0DY
Tel: 0117-955 6463 **Fax:** 0117-955 6472
E-mail: sales@nova-aluminium.com
Website: http://www.nova-aluminium.com
Directors: P. Harvie (Dir), P. Vickery (Dir), P. Harvey (Dir)
Immediate Holding Company: METALCRAFT (BRISTOL) LIMITED
Registration no: 00879262 **Date established:** 1966
No.of Employees: 21 - 50 **Product Groups:** 34, 35, 48, 66

Date of Accounts	Dec 11	Dec 10	Dec 09
Working Capital	2	2	2
Current Assets	2	2	2

Oasis Systems

31 Quarry Road Kingswood, Bristol, BS15 8PA
Tel: 0117-960 3882
E-mail: info@oasis-systems.co.uk
Website: http://www.oasis-systems.co.uk
Directors: M. Hayward (Ptnr)
No.of Employees: 1 - 10 **Product Groups:** 44, 67

Ocrobotics Ltd

Unit 5 Abbey Wood Business Park Emma Chris Way, Filton, Bristol, BS34 7JU
Tel: 0117-314 4700 **Fax:** 0117-314 4799
E-mail: contactus@ocrobotics.com
Website: http://www.ocrobotics.com
Directors: R. Buckingham (MD)
No.of Employees: 11 - 20 **Product Groups:** 84

Octavius Hunt Ltd

Dove Lane Redfield, Bristol, BS5 9NQ
Tel: 0117-955 5304 **Fax:** 0117-955 7875
E-mail: info@octavius-hunt.co.uk
Website: http://www.octavius-hunt.co.uk
Bank(s): National Westminster Bank Plc
Directors: A. Cox (MD), D. Connors (Fin), K. Healey (Dir)
Immediate Holding Company: OCTAVIUS HUNT LIMITED
Registration no: 03555496 **VAT No.:** GB 709 8223 24
Date established: 1998 **Turnover:** £2m - £5m **No.of Employees:** 21 - 50
Product Groups: 32, 38

Date of Accounts	Jun 11	Jun 10	Jun 09
Working Capital	1m	1m	706
Fixed Assets	413	314	273
Current Assets	2m	1m	859

Office24 Ltd

18a Heath Road Nailsea, Bristol, BS48 1AD
Tel: 0117-911 9190 **Fax:** 0117-911 9191
E-mail: info@office24.co.uk
Website: http://www.office24.co.uk
Directors: E. Pinnells (Dir)
Registration no: 05449671 **No.of Employees:** 1 - 10 **Product Groups:** 37

Date of Accounts	Dec 07	Dec 06	Dec 05
Working Capital	-43	-2	N/A
Current Assets	20	43	6
Current Liabilities	63	45	6
Total Share Capital	5	5	5

On The Spot Signs

19 Hollway Road, Bristol, BS14 8PY
Tel: 01275-833775 **Fax:** 01275-545286
E-mail: graham@onthespotsigns.com
Website: http://www.onthespotsigns.com
Directors: G. Potts (Prop)
Immediate Holding Company: ON THE SPOT SIGNS LIMITED
Registration no: 04017783 **Date established:** 2000
No.of Employees: 1 - 10 **Product Groups:** 39, 40, 49

Online Coating Ltd

Unit 406 Central Park Petherton Road, Bristol, BS14 9BZ
Tel: 01275-540058 **Fax:** 01275-540059
E-mail: mikebaxter@blueyonder.co.uk
Website: http://www.onlinecoating.co.uk
Directors: P. Baxter (Dir), A. Baxter (Dir), M. Baxter (Dir)
Immediate Holding Company: M A P Holdings Ltd
Registration no: 02506691 **VAT No.:** GB 567 4092 19
Date established: 1990 **Turnover:** £500,000 - £1m
No.of Employees: 21 - 50 **Product Groups:** 48

Date of Accounts	Jul 10	Jul 09	Jul 08
Working Capital	96	206	326
Fixed Assets	86	98	118
Current Assets	285	322	522
Current Liabilities	N/A	58	N/A

Open Connections

4 Buckingham Court Beaufort Office Park Woodlands, Bradley Stoke, Bristol, BS32 4NF
Tel: 01454-889966 **Fax:** 01454-889000
E-mail: sales@openc.co.uk
Website: http://www.openc.co.uk
Bank(s): The Royal Bank Of Scotland, Bristol
Directors: S. King (Sales)
Immediate Holding Company: ZETA HOLDINGS LTD
Registration no: 00200512 **VAT No.:** GB 449 1417 42
Turnover: £2m - £5m **No.of Employees:** 21 - 50 **Product Groups:** 44

Optimal Industrial Automation Ltd

8 Goodrich Close Yate, Bristol, BS37 5YT
Tel: 01454-333222 **Fax:** 01454-322240
E-mail: enquiries@optimal-ltd.co.uk
Website: http://www.optimal-ltd.co.uk
Directors: M. Gadsby (MD), R. Esain (Dir)
Managers: N. Batton (Chief Mgr)
Immediate Holding Company: OPTIMAL INDUSTRIAL AUTOMATION LIMITED
Registration no: 02482877 **Date established:** 1990 **Turnover:** £2m - £5m
No.of Employees: 21 - 50 **Product Groups:** 37, 38, 44, 46, 49, 67, 84

Date of Accounts	Mar 11	Mar 10	Mar 09
Working Capital	369	352	432
Current Assets	508	637	637
Current Liabilities	N/A	8	135

Orange Holdings UK Ltd

St James' Court Great Park Road, Bradley Stoke, Bristol, BS32 4QJ
Tel: 01454-624600 **Fax:** 01454-618501
Website: http://www.ocfl.net
Directors: C. Caldwell (Co Sec), J. Pontal (Grp Chief Exec)
Managers: D. Le Brat, G. Howe
Ultimate Holding Company: FRANCE TELECOM SA {FRANCE}
Immediate Holding Company: ORANGE HOLDINGS (UK) LIMITED
Registration no: 02412603 **Date established:** 1989
No.of Employees: 1501 & over **Product Groups:** 37

Date of Accounts	Dec 10	Dec 09	Dec 08
Pre Tax Profit/Loss	28m	-8m	-12m
Working Capital	83m	74m	1897m
Current Assets	104m	228m	1897m
Current Liabilities	21m	N/A	N/A

Orbitals New Media

25, Victoria Street, Bristol, BS1 6AA
Tel: 0117-911 7818 **Fax:** 01291-627673
E-mail: info@orbitals.net
Website: http://www.orbitals.net
Directors: A. Booth (Dir)
Managers: M. Power (Accounts)
Date established: 2006 **No.of Employees:** 1 - 10 **Product Groups:** 44

Orchard Installations

24 Orchard Boulevard Oldland Common, Bristol, BS30 9PT
Tel: 07798-727385 **Fax:** 0117-949 1822
Directors: J. Kiely (Prop)
Date established: 1989 **No.of Employees:** 1 - 10 **Product Groups:** 35, 39, 45

Osborne Clarke

2 Temple Back East Temple Quay, Bristol, BS1 6EG
Tel: 0117-917 3000 **Fax:** 0117-917 3005
E-mail: enquiries@osborneclarke.com
Website: http://www.osborneclarke.com
Bank(s): National Westminster
Directors: S. Beswick (Snr Part)
Managers: D. Shufflebotham (Personnel), M. Smith (Fin Mgr)
Immediate Holding Company: OSBORNE CLARKE LIMITED
Registration no: 02040669 **Date established:** 1986
Turnover: £50m - £75m **No.of Employees:** 251 - 500 **Product Groups:** 80

Osmond Hartley & Son Ltd

57 Wholesale Fruit Centre Albert CR, Bristol, BS2 0YU
Tel: 0117-977 7312 **Fax:** 0117-977 7312
Managers: S. Jones (Mgr)
Ultimate Holding Company: MEESDEN PROPERTIES LTD (ISLE OF MAN)
Immediate Holding Company: OSMOND HARTLEY & SON LIMITED
Registration no: 02263304 **Date established:** 1988
No.of Employees: 1 - 10 **Product Groups:** 38, 42

Date of Accounts	Jun 09	Jun 08
Working Capital	451	451
Current Assets	451	451

Osprey Shipping Ltd

Gordano Road Royal Portbury Dock, Portbury, Bristol, BS20 7XQ
Tel: 01275-374636 **Fax:** 01275-373250
E-mail: nigel.fletcher@ospreyltd.com
Website: http://www.ospreyltd.com
Directors: N. Fletcher (MD)
Ultimate Holding Company: OSPREY MARITIME LIMITED
Immediate Holding Company: OSPREY SHIPPING LIMITED
Registration no: 01440983 **VAT No.:** GB 682 0612 47
Date established: 1979 **No.of Employees:** 1 - 10 **Product Groups:** 39, 74

Date of Accounts	Mar 12	Mar 11	Mar 10
Sales Turnover	11m	10m	26m
Pre Tax Profit/Loss	1m	1m	7m
Working Capital	1m	9m	4m
Fixed Assets	3m	4m	7m
Current Assets	4m	11m	8m
Current Liabilities	833	419	686

Overland Transport Services Ltd

152 Sundridge Park Yate, Bristol, BS37 4DX
Tel: 01454-311900 **Fax:** 01454-311900
E-mail: jerry@overlandtransport.co.uk
Website: http://www.overlandtransport.co.uk
Directors: J. Coster (Prop)
No.of Employees: 1 - 10 **Product Groups:** 79

Oxford Neckties

Oxford Houseunit 6, Bristol, BS15 9GE
Tel: 0871-9960323 **Fax:** 0871-9960502
E-mail: sales@ehomeshopper.biz
Website: http://www.ehomeshopper.biz
Date established: 2005 **Turnover:** £250,000 - £500,000
No.of Employees: 1 - 10 **Product Groups:** 23, 24

P J C Services

14 Corfe Crescent Keynsham, Bristol, BS31 1AQ
Tel: 0117-949 9399 **Fax:** 0117-949 9399
Directors: P. Cockram (Prop)
Date established: 1992 **No.of Employees:** 1 - 10 **Product Groups:** 35, 39, 45

P L H Tools

137 High Street Hanham, Bristol, BS15 3QY
Tel: 0117-961 3954 **Fax:** 0117-961 3954
E-mail: plhtools@lhending.freeserve.co.uk
Website: http://www.plhtools.co.uk
Directors: L. Hendin (Ptnr)
Date established: 2001 **No.of Employees:** 1 - 10 **Product Groups:** 37

P Thorne & Son Ltd

11 West Street St Philips, Bristol, BS2 0DF
Tel: 0117-954 7430 **Fax:** 0117-955 2262
E-mail: enquiries@thorne-securitygroup.co.uk
Website: http://www.thorne-security.com
Directors: D. Thorne (Jt MD), T. Thorne (MD), S. Thorne (Co Sec), A. Thorne (Jt MD)
Immediate Holding Company: Thorne Holdings Ltd
Registration no: 00892423 **VAT No.:** GB 140 0602 33
Date established: 1966 **Turnover:** £2m - £5m **No.of Employees:** 1 - 10
Product Groups: 26, 33, 35, 36

Date of Accounts	Jul 08	Jul 07	Jul 06
Working Capital	-31	11	83
Fixed Assets	65	84	74
Current Assets	166	230	237
Current Liabilities	198	219	154
Total Share Capital	1	1	1

P3 Medical Ltd

Unit 1 Newbridge Close, Bristol, BS4 4AX
Tel: 0117-972 8888 **Fax:** 0117-972 4863
E-mail: hallj@p3-medical.com
Website: http://www.p3medical.com
Managers: J. Hall (Sales Admin), E. Hurley
Ultimate Holding Company: JARDINES (U.K.) LIMITED
Immediate Holding Company: P3 MEDICAL LIMITED
Registration no: 01072913 **Date established:** 1972 **Turnover:** £5m - £10m
No.of Employees: 21 - 50 **Product Groups:** 30, 38, 42

Date of Accounts	Oct 11	Oct 10	Oct 09
Sales Turnover	5m	5m	6m
Pre Tax Profit/Loss	354	-250	-391
Working Capital	1m	2m	2m
Fixed Assets	1m	378	951
Current Assets	2m	2m	2m
Current Liabilities	398	302	239

P V R Direct Ltd
Olympia House 196 Broomhill Road, Bristol, BS4 5RG
Tel: 0117-977 0184 **Fax:** 0117-935 2399
E-mail: sales@pvrdirect.co.uk
Website: http://www.pvrdirect.co.uk
Managers: S. Taylor (Mgr)
Immediate Holding Company: PVR DIRECT LIMITED
Registration no: 04125497 **Date established:** 2000 **Turnover:** £1m - £2m
No.of Employees: 1 - 10 **Product Groups:** 67

Date of Accounts	Jan 12	Jan 11	Jan 10
Working Capital	369	145	66
Fixed Assets	56	51	60
Current Assets	684	484	404

Pack 2 Pack UK Ltd
Avonmouth Way West, Bristol, BS11 9HD
Tel: 0117-982 3584 **Fax:** 0117-923 5396
E-mail: sales.avo@uk.pack2pack.com
Website: http://www.pack2pack.com
Bank(s): National Westminster Bank Plc
Directors: C. Scapens (MD)
Ultimate Holding Company: PACK2PACK COOP NL (NETHERLANDS)
Immediate Holding Company: PACK2PACK UK LTD
Registration no: 05961878 **VAT No.:** GB 696 2876 69
Date established: 2006 **Turnover:** £5m - £10m **No.of Employees:** 21 - 50
Product Groups: 35

Date of Accounts	Dec 10	Dec 09	Dec 08
Sales Turnover	5m	6m	8m
Pre Tax Profit/Loss	499	-1m	-6m
Working Capital	1m	5m	2m
Fixed Assets	2m	2m	2m
Current Assets	2m	6m	3m
Current Liabilities	343	223	384

Pamela Neave
18 St Augustines Parade, Bristol, BS1 4UL
Tel: 0117-921 1831 **Fax:** 0117-925 1019
E-mail: pamela.neave@pamela-neave.co.uk
Website: http://www.pamela-neave.co.uk
Bank(s): National Westminster Bank Plc
Directors: P. Neave (MD), L. Garrett (Co Sec)
Immediate Holding Company: Neave Employment Ltd
Registration no: 01097389 **Date established:** 1973 **Turnover:** £1m - £2m
No.of Employees: 21 - 50 **Product Groups:** 80, 86

Panacea Selection Ltd
Dyrham Lodge 16 Clifton Park, Bristol, BS8 3BY
Tel: 0117-973 8090 **Fax:** 0117-973 4422
E-mail: martynklax@panacea-selection.co.uk
Website: http://www.panacea-selection.co.uk
Directors: M. Lax (MD)
Immediate Holding Company: PANACEA SELECTION LIMITED
Registration no: 04386743 **Date established:** 2002
Turnover: £500,000 - £1m **No.of Employees:** 1 - 10 **Product Groups:** 80

Date of Accounts	Mar 11	Mar 10	Mar 09
Working Capital	-87	-39	-148
Fixed Assets	4	7	2
Current Assets	44	63	20

Parglas Ltd
Barton Manor, Bristol, BS2 0RP
Tel: 0117-955 2325 **Fax:** 0117-941 1806
E-mail: parglas@btclick.com
Website: http://www.parglas.com
Bank(s): HSBC, Bristol
Directors: D. Elston (MD)
Immediate Holding Company: PARGLAS LIMITED
Registration no: 00614427 **VAT No.:** GB 138 3777 39
Date established: 1958 **Turnover:** £500,000 - £1m
No.of Employees: 11 - 20 **Product Groups:** 30

Date of Accounts	Dec 11	Dec 10	Dec 09
Working Capital	147	81	40
Fixed Assets	391	413	309
Current Assets	499	397	537

Parker Merchanting Ltd (Depot)
Unit 1-3 Garonor Way Portbury, Bristol, BS20 7XE
Tel: 08451-202454 **Fax:** 01275-375050
E-mail: info.parker@hagemeyer.co.uk
Managers: L. Paterson (Mgr)
Ultimate Holding Company: RAY INVESTMENT SARL (LUXEMBOURG)
Immediate Holding Company: PARKER MERCHANTING LIMITED
Registration no: 00224779 **VAT No.:** GB 614 2136 80
Date established: 2027 **Turnover:** £75m - £125m
No.of Employees: 1 - 10 **Product Groups:** 22, 23, 24, 29, 30, 33, 37, 39, 40, 45, 63, 66, 68

Date of Accounts	Dec 10	Dec 09	Dec 08
Working Capital	51	51	51
Current Assets	51	51	51

Parts Center
Unit C Tamar Road, Bristol, BS2 0TX
Tel: 0117-972 1376 **Fax:** 0117-977 6399
E-mail: nrs-bristol@climatecentre.co.uk
Website: http://www.climatecentre.co.uk
Directors: M. Henderson (Sales), R. Lock (MD)
Managers: M. Elliott (Mgr), S. Bailey (Mgr)
Ultimate Holding Company: Wolseley Group Holdings Ltd
Immediate Holding Company: Wolseley Investments Ltd
Registration no: 01195768 **VAT No.:** GB 363 3279 48
Turnover: £10m - £20m **No.of Employees:** 1 - 10 **Product Groups:** 40

Paton Hawksley Education Ltd
Unit 17 Ashmead Business Centre Ashmead Road, Keynsham, Bristol, BS31 1SX
Tel: 0117-986 2364 **Fax:** 0117-986 8285
E-mail: info@patonhawksley.co.uk
Website: http://www.patonhawksley.co.uk
Directors: R. Hawksley (MD), L. Turner (Fin)
Immediate Holding Company: PATON HAWKSLEY EDUCATION LIMITED
Registration no: 00642455 **VAT No.:** GB 138 9460 38
Date established: 1959 **Turnover:** Up to £250,000
No.of Employees: 1 - 10 **Product Groups:** 28, 38

Date of Accounts	Mar 11	Mar 10	Mar 09
Sales Turnover	N/A	N/A	209
Pre Tax Profit/Loss	N/A	N/A	104
Working Capital	209	202	185
Fixed Assets	12	8	9
Current Assets	307	272	220
Current Liabilities	N/A	N/A	36

Paul O'Brien Solar Installations SW Ltd
Unit 6 Ashton Trading Estate Brookgate, Bristol, BS16 1NR
Tel: 0117-952 2522 **Fax:** 0117-952 3027
E-mail: info@pobsolar.co.uk
Website: http://www.pobsolar.co.uk
Directors: P. O'brien (Dir)
Immediate Holding Company: PAUL O'BRIEN SOLAR INSTALLATIONS (SW) LIMITED
Registration no: 07529600 **Date established:** 2011
No.of Employees: 21 - 50 **Product Groups:** 14, 23, 24, 29, 30, 31, 32, 33, 34, 35, 36, 39, 40, 48, 49, 52, 66, 67, 83, 84, 86

Pegasus Fork Truck Services Ltd
3-4 Quarry Farm Row of Ashes Lane, Redhill, Bristol, BS40 5TU
Tel: 01934-863781 **Fax:** 01934-863782
E-mail: annmarieworthy@yahoo.co.uk
Website: http://www.pegasusfts.co.uk
Directors: A. Worthy (Fin), K. Worthy (MD), K. Worthy (Sales)
Immediate Holding Company: PEGASUS FORK TRUCK SERVICES LTD.
Registration no: 03472168 **Date established:** 1997
Turnover: Up to £250,000 **No.of Employees:** 1 - 10 **Product Groups:** 35, 39, 45

Date of Accounts	Nov 11	Nov 10	Nov 09
Working Capital	-45	-45	-49
Fixed Assets	55	64	74
Current Assets	44	37	34

Permagard Products Ltd
Worthy Road Chittening Industrial Estate, Bristol, BS11 0YB
Tel: 0117-938 1596 **Fax:** 0117-938 1584
E-mail: sales@permagard.co.uk
Website: http://www.permagard.co.uk
Product Groups: 25, 30, 32, 38, 52

Date of Accounts	May 08	May 07	May 06
Working Capital	-160	-145	-133
Fixed Assets	219	224	230
Current Assets	220	289	300
Current Liabilities	380	434	433

Perrigo Carpentry Design & Build
3 Cloud Hill Enterprises Temple Cloud, Bristol, BS39 5BX
Tel: 01761-451530
E-mail: info@perrigocarpentry.co.uk
Website: http://www.perrigocarpentry.co.uk
Product Groups: 26, 30, 52, 67

Peter Cox Ltd
Unit 6 Avonbank Industrial Centre West Town Road, Bristol, BS11 9DE
Tel: 0117-938 7130 **Fax:** 0117-938 7137
E-mail: bristol@petercox.com
Website: http://www.petercox.com
Managers: M. Greenwood (District Mgr)
Ultimate Holding Company: GERALDTON SERVICES INC (USA)
Immediate Holding Company: PETER COX LIMITED
Registration no: 02438126 **Date established:** 1989
No.of Employees: 1 - 10 **Product Groups:** 07, 32, 52, 66

Date of Accounts	Dec 11	Dec 10	Dec 09
Sales Turnover	15m	15m	14m
Pre Tax Profit/Loss	645	282	-350
Working Capital	3m	3m	2m
Fixed Assets	459	542	643
Current Assets	6m	5m	4m
Current Liabilities	2m	2m	961

Phineas Products Ltd
Hebron House Sion Road, Bristol, BS3 3BD
Tel: 08458-386333 **Fax:** 0845-838 1613
E-mail: sales@phineasproducts.com
Website: http://www.phineasproducts.com
Directors: D. Wright (MD)
Ultimate Holding Company: NEW WAVE PROJECTS LIMITED
Immediate Holding Company: PHINEAS PRODUCTS LIMITED
Registration no: 01814992 **VAT No.:** GB 395 9639 78
Date established: 1984 **Turnover:** £500,000 - £1m
No.of Employees: 1 - 10 **Product Groups:** 22, 30, 49

Date of Accounts	Mar 12	Mar 11	Mar 10
Working Capital	499	443	440
Fixed Assets	408	185	157
Current Assets	1m	734	639

Phoenix Corporate Ltd
Unit 1 Chapel Mill Chapel Lane, Warmley, Bristol, BS15 4NG
Tel: 0117-935 2244 **Fax:** 0117-935 2299
E-mail: enquiries@phoenixcorporate.co.uk
Website: http://www.phoenixcorporate.co.uk
Directors: N. Paling (Dir)
Immediate Holding Company: PHOENIX CORPORATE LIMITED
Registration no: 02827784 **Date established:** 1993
No.of Employees: 1 - 10 **Product Groups:** 83, 89

Date of Accounts	Jun 12	Jun 11	Jun 10
Working Capital	36	-29	-27
Fixed Assets	239	249	259
Current Assets	74	65	86

Phoenix Surveying Equipment Ltd
Unit 4 Armstrong Court Armstrong Way, Yate, Bristol, BS37 5NG
Tel: 01454-312560 **Fax:** 01454-273118
E-mail: sales@phoenixse.com
Website: http://www.phoenixse.com
Bank(s): Lloyds TSB
Directors: M. Purchase (Sales)
Managers: L. Masey (Chief Acct)
Ultimate Holding Company: BRANDON HIRE GROUP HOLDINGS LIMITED
Immediate Holding Company: PHOENIX SURVEYING EQUIPMENT LIMITED
Registration no: 01336159 **VAT No.:** GB 302 6074 02
Date established: 1977 **Turnover:** £2m - £5m **No.of Employees:** 21 - 50
Product Groups: 48

Date of Accounts	Dec 11	Dec 10	Dec 09
Sales Turnover	5m	N/A	N/A
Pre Tax Profit/Loss	800	N/A	N/A
Working Capital	-508	-667	-891
Fixed Assets	2m	1m	2m
Current Assets	2m	2m	1m
Current Liabilities	490	N/A	N/A

Pipe & Climate Centre
Unit 2 Bonville Trading Estate, Bristol, BS4 5SE
Tel: 0117-977 0733 **Fax:** 01225-777370
E-mail: karen.palmer@wolseley.co.uk
Website: http://www.wolsley.co.uk
Managers: K. Palmer (District Mgr)
Ultimate Holding Company: BRITISH FITTINGS GROUP PLC
Immediate Holding Company: PROFIT FOCUS (UK) LIMITED
Registration no: 03244411 **Date established:** 1996
No.of Employees: 11 - 20 **Product Groups:** 30, 36

Date of Accounts	Jun 11	Jun 10	Jun 09
Sales Turnover	87m	96m	96m
Pre Tax Profit/Loss	-2m	5m	5m
Working Capital	-2m	1m	4m
Fixed Assets	36m	34m	26m
Current Assets	34m	33m	45m
Current Liabilities	9m	7m	9m

Pitman
Long Acre Farm Doddington Lane, Chipping Sodbury, Bristol, BS37 6SD
Tel: 01454-318131
Directors: I. Pitman (Prop)
Date established: 1998 **No.of Employees:** 1 - 10 **Product Groups:** 35

Planglow Ltd
Quorum House Bond Street South, Bristol, BS1 3AE
Tel: 0117-317 8600 **Fax:** 0117-317 8639
E-mail: contactus@planglow.com
Website: http://www.planglow.com
Directors: J. Scott (MD)
Immediate Holding Company: PLANGLOW LIMITED
Registration no: 01975062 **Date established:** 1986 **Turnover:** £2m - £5m
No.of Employees: 21 - 50 **Product Groups:** 27, 28, 49, 64, 66, 67, 69, 81

Date of Accounts	Mar 12	Mar 11	Mar 10
Working Capital	866	839	674
Fixed Assets	25	19	49
Current Assets	1m	1m	1m

Plant Speed Ltd
Unit 1 River Fields Estate Central Avenue, Hallen, Bristol, BS10 7ES
Tel: 0117-982 1309 **Fax:** 0117-982 8981
E-mail: info@plantspeed.com
Website: http://www.plantspeed.com
Directors: P. Lomas (MD)
Immediate Holding Company: PLANT SPEED LIMITED
Registration no: 04692060 **Date established:** 2003
No.of Employees: 1 - 10 **Product Groups:** 36, 37, 39, 45, 72, 74, 81, 84

Date of Accounts	Mar 12	Mar 11	Mar 10
Working Capital	759	467	272
Fixed Assets	963	1m	1m
Current Assets	1m	1m	906

Polystrop Ltd
Unit 7 Bridge Road Kingswood, Bristol, BS15 4FW
Tel: 0117-970 1196 **Fax:** 0117-970 1205
E-mail: info@polystrop.co.uk
Website: http://www.polystrop.co.uk
Directors: C. Porter (MD)
Immediate Holding Company: POLYSTROP LIMITED
Registration no: 01323404 **Date established:** 1977
No.of Employees: 11 - 20 **Product Groups:** 35, 39, 45

Date of Accounts	Jul 11	Jul 10	Jul 09
Working Capital	-10	-7	24
Fixed Assets	46	42	41
Current Assets	673	596	508

Portman Travel Ltd
Mariner House 62 Prince Street, Bristol, BS1 4QD
Tel: 01932-797100 **Fax:** 01932-797101
E-mail: sales@portmantravel.com
Website: http://www.portmantravel.com
Managers: L. Cains (District Mgr)
Ultimate Holding Company: Portman Group Holdings Ltd
Immediate Holding Company: Macrocom (371) Ltd
Registration no: 00620104 **Date established:** 1990
Turnover: Up to £250,000 **No.of Employees:** 1 - 10 **Product Groups:** 69

Fred R Powell & Son Ltd
Avonside Road, Bristol, BS2 0TS
Tel: 0117-971 7971 **Fax:** 0117-971 9864
E-mail: sales@fredpowell.co.uk
Website: http://www.fredpowell.co.uk
Bank(s): Lloyds TSB Bank plc
Directors: C. Air (Fin), R. Ellis (Dir)
Immediate Holding Company: FRED R. POWELL & SON LIMITED
Registration no: 00375606 **VAT No.:** GB 137 8751 38
Date established: 1942 **Turnover:** £1m - £2m **No.of Employees:** 11 - 20
Product Groups: 35, 66

Date of Accounts	Dec 11	Sep 10	Sep 09
Working Capital	281	312	284
Fixed Assets	N/A	36	55
Current Assets	281	494	448

Power Fixings Bristol
Crompton House 240 Broomhill Road, Bristol, BS4 5RG
Tel: 0117-977 8999 **Fax:** 0117-977 8998
E-mail: sales@powerfixings.co.uk
Directors: P. James (Snr Part)
Registration no: 05372751 **Date established:** 2005
No.of Employees: 11 - 20 **Product Groups:** 35

Power Tools Plus
131 Gloucester Road Bishopston, Bristol, BS7 8AX
Tel: 0117-949 9700 **Fax:** 0117-914 7758
Website: http://www.powertoolsplus.co.uk
Directors: C. Evans (Ptnr)
No.of Employees: 1 - 10 **Product Groups:** 37

Powersystems UK Ltd
Unit 1 Badminton Road Trading Estate, Yate, Bristol, BS37 5GG
Tel: 01454-318000 **Fax:** 01454-318111
E-mail: sales@powersystemsuk.com
Website: http://www.powersystemsuk.com

see next page

Powersystems UK Ltd - Cont'd

Directors: S. Wilsmore (MD)
Managers: R. Berry (Chief Acct)
Immediate Holding Company: POWERSYSTEMS UK LTD
Registration no: 01534161 **VAT No.:** GB 140 6467 80
Date established: 1980 **Turnover:** £10m - £20m
No.of Employees: 21 - 50 **Product Groups:** 52

Date of Accounts	Dec 11	Dec 10	Dec 09
Sales Turnover	15m	16m	18m
Pre Tax Profit/Loss	1m	1m	1m
Working Capital	4m	3m	2m
Fixed Assets	1m	958	1m
Current Assets	9m	8m	7m
Current Liabilities	2m	2m	4m

Precision Dippings Marketing Ltd

Unit J Lawrence Drive, Yate, Bristol, BS37 5PG
Tel: 01454-318004 **Fax:** 01454-319961
E-mail: sales@precisiondippings.co.uk
Website: http://www.precisiondippings.co.uk
Bank(s): Bank of Scotland
Directors: D. King (Dir)
Immediate Holding Company: PRECISION DIPPINGS MARKETING LIMITED
Registration no: 01631071 **VAT No.:** GB 357 9844 93
Date established: 1982 **Turnover:** £500,000 - £1m
No.of Employees: 11 - 20 **Product Groups:** 24, 29, 63

Date of Accounts	Sep 11	Sep 10	Sep 09
Working Capital	304	282	249
Fixed Assets	37	43	60
Current Assets	377	360	315

P E S

Parkway House Hambrook Lane, Stoke Gifford, Bristol, BS34 8QB
Tel: 08454-509110 **Fax:** 0117-923 6120
E-mail: andy@plainenglishguide.co.uk
Website: http://www.pesconsulting.co.uk
Directors: D. Curtis (Co Sec), I. Rumels (MD), R. Pomphrett (Dir)
Immediate Holding Company: PREMIER EMPLOYER SOLUTIONS LTD
Registration no: 04316451 **Date established:** 2001
Turnover: £500,000 - £1m **No.of Employees:** 11 - 20
Product Groups: 80, 82

Premier Mobiles

89 High Street Hanham, Bristol, BS15 3QG
Tel: 0117-947 7377 **Fax:** 0117-935 2773
E-mail: info@premiermobileshop.co.uk
Website: http://www.premiermobileshop.co.uk
Managers: R. Peters (Mgr)
Immediate Holding Company: INDEPENDENT MOBILES LTD
Date established: 2003 **Turnover:** Up to £250,000
No.of Employees: 1 - 10 **Product Groups:** 22, 37

Protag Retail Security

Unit 3 Short Way, Thornbury, Bristol, BS35 3UT
Tel: 01454-418500 **Fax:** 01454-413708
E-mail: m.strange@protagsecurity.co.uk
Website: http://www.protagsecurity.co.uk
Managers: M. Strange (Prod Mgr)
Ultimate Holding Company: PERMASIGN LIMITED
Immediate Holding Company: PROTAG RETAIL SECURITY LIMITED
Registration no: 04049844 **Date established:** 2000 **Turnover:** £1m - £2m
No.of Employees: 1 - 10 **Product Groups:** 37, 40, 81

Protechnic

Unit 1 West End Trading Estate Netherton Wood Lane, Nailsea, Bristol, BS48 4DG
Tel: 01275-811312 **Fax:** 01275-835560
E-mail: sales@protechnic.com
Website: http://www.protechnic.com
Bank(s): HSBC Bank plc
Directors: K. Judson (MD)
Immediate Holding Company: PROTECHNIC LIMITED
Registration no: 02925732 **Date established:** 1994 **Turnover:** £1m - £2m
No.of Employees: 21 - 50 **Product Groups:** 22, 27, 29, 30, 35, 38, 49

Date of Accounts	Oct 11	Oct 10	Oct 09
Sales Turnover	N/A	N/A	1m
Pre Tax Profit/Loss	N/A	N/A	67
Working Capital	376	369	349
Fixed Assets	134	123	128
Current Assets	601	541	551
Current Liabilities	N/A	N/A	99

Provincial Rubber

Unit 6 Riverside Business Park St Annes Road, St Annes Park, Bristol, BS4 4ED
Tel: 0117-954 1117 **Fax:** 0117-955 9695
E-mail: info@provincialrubber.co.uk
Website: http://www.provincialrubber.co.uk
Directors: B. Caragher (MD)
Immediate Holding Company: PROVINCIAL RUBBER AGENCIES LIMITED
Registration no: 00269381 **Date established:** 1932
Turnover: £500,000 - £1m **No.of Employees:** 11 - 20 **Product Groups:** 22, 23, 24, 25, 27, 29, 30, 31, 32, 33, 35, 36, 37, 38, 39, 40, 41, 42, 45, 46, 47, 48, 49, 66, 68, 85

Date of Accounts	Mar 11	Mar 10	Mar 09
Working Capital	204	160	166
Fixed Assets	19	19	14
Current Assets	405	293	443

Pulse Roll Label Products Ltd

Unit U Lawrence Drive, Yate, Bristol, BS37 5PG
Tel: 01454-272433 **Fax:** 01454-272434
E-mail: info@pulserl.com
Website: http://www.pulserl.com
Directors: G. Seward (MD)
Immediate Holding Company: PULSE ROLL LABEL PRODUCTS LIMITED
Registration no: 04225530 **Date established:** 2001
Turnover: £500,000 - £1m **No.of Employees:** 21 - 50
Product Groups: 32, 66

Date of Accounts	Mar 11	Mar 10	Mar 09
Working Capital	552	342	181
Fixed Assets	87	73	90
Current Assets	1m	1m	732
Current Liabilities	N/A	254	N/A

Puma Marking & Packaging Ltd

Littleton Mill Chew Road, Winford, Bristol, BS40 8HJ
Tel: 01275-332576 **Fax:** 01275-333626
Directors: S. Gough (MD), S. Gough (Co Sec)
Immediate Holding Company: HARLECH OUTDOOR LIMITED
Registration no: 01391352 **VAT No.:** GB 302 7581 77
Date established: 2003 **Turnover:** £500,000 - £1m
No.of Employees: 1 - 10 **Product Groups:** 48

Date of Accounts	Dec 07
Working Capital	-22
Fixed Assets	3
Current Assets	161
Current Liabilities	183

Q T A C Solutions Ltd

Apex House Kingsfield Lane, Longwell Green, Bristol, BS30 6DL
Tel: 0117-935 3500 **Fax:** 0117-935 3545
E-mail: info@qtac.co.uk
Website: http://www.qtac.co.uk
Directors: A. Rowson (Dir), M. Smith (Dir), K. House (Fin)
Immediate Holding Company: QTAC SOLUTIONS LIMITED
Registration no: 02942085 **Date established:** 1994
Turnover: Up to £250,000 **No.of Employees:** 21 - 50 **Product Groups:** 44

Date of Accounts	Jun 11	Jun 10	Jun 09
Working Capital	42	-8	35
Fixed Assets	64	90	355
Current Assets	256	167	260

Quay Marinas Ltd

Portishead Quay Marina The Docks, Portishead, Bristol, BS20 7DF
Tel: 01275-841941 **Fax:** 01275-841189
E-mail: ayates@quaymarinas.com
Website: http://www.quaymarinas.com
Directors: A. Yates (Dir), P. Rye (Co Sec)
Ultimate Holding Company: QUAY MARINAS HOLDINGS LIMITED
Immediate Holding Company: QUAY MARINAS LIMITED
Registration no: 01094247 **Date established:** 1973 **Turnover:** £5m - £10m
No.of Employees: 1 - 10 **Product Groups:** 71, 80, 84

Date of Accounts	Mar 12	Mar 11	Mar 10
Sales Turnover	6m	6m	6m
Pre Tax Profit/Loss	328	254	324
Working Capital	-284	-236	-213
Fixed Assets	7m	7m	8m
Current Assets	4m	4m	4m
Current Liabilities	4m	4m	4m

Quitmann Furniture (t/a Old Mill Oak Furniture Ltd)

Unit 1 Avonmouth Way West, Bristol, BS11 9EX
Tel: 0117-982 2004 **Fax:** 0117-982 2009
E-mail: info@quitmannfurniture.co.uk
Website: http://www.quitmannfurniture.co.uk
Directors: J. Newey (MD)
Registration no: 05700148 **VAT No.:** GB 783 2155 25
Date established: 1884 **Turnover:** £2m - £5m **No.of Employees:** 21 - 50
Product Groups: 61

R H Freight Services Ltd

2 Glentworth Court Lime Kiln Close Stoke Gifford, Bristol, BS34 8SR
Tel: 0117-933 4455 **Fax:** 0117-933 4466
E-mail: bristol@rhgroup.com
Website: http://www.rhfreight.com
Managers: S. Thomas (District Mgr)
Ultimate Holding Company: 01876845
Immediate Holding Company: RH FREIGHT SERVICES LIMITED
Registration no: 01336260 **Date established:** 1977 **Turnover:** £1m - £2m
No.of Employees: 11 - 20 **Product Groups:** 72, 74, 84

R H Windows Ltd

Unit 5 Farrington Fields Trading Estate, Farrington Gurney, Bristol, BS39 6UU
Tel: 01761-452171 **Fax:** 01761-453342
E-mail: info@rhwindowsltd.co.uk
Website: http://www.rhwindowsltd.co.uk
Directors: A. Nash (MD)
Immediate Holding Company: R.H. WINDOWS LIMITED
Registration no: 01606669 **VAT No.:** GB 302 8138 89
Date established: 1982 **Turnover:** £500,000 - £1m
No.of Employees: 11 - 20 **Product Groups:** 48, 52

Date of Accounts	Mar 12	Mar 11	Mar 10
Working Capital	16	38	63
Fixed Assets	327	323	346
Current Assets	196	228	249

R & P Access

2 Weetwood Road Congresbury, Bristol, BS49 5BN
Tel: 01934-834435
E-mail: enquiries@rp-access.co.uk
Website: http://www.rp-access.co.uk
Directors: R. Wyatt (Dir)
Immediate Holding Company: R & P ACCESS LIMITED
Registration no: 05001510 **Date established:** 2003
Turnover: Up to £250,000 **No.of Employees:** 1 - 10 **Product Groups:** 23, 35, 67

Date of Accounts	Dec 06	Mar 11	Mar 10
Sales Turnover	N/A	N/A	147
Pre Tax Profit/Loss	N/A	N/A	37
Working Capital	N/A	101	87
Fixed Assets	N/A	7	6
Current Assets	N/A	145	114
Current Liabilities	N/A	N/A	18

Radio Detection

Western Drive, Bristol, BS14 0AZ
Tel: 0117-976 7776 **Fax:** 0117-976 7775
E-mail: info@radiodetection.spx.com
Website: http://www.radiodetection.com
Bank(s): Bank of Scotland
Directors: L. Williams (Fin), R. Holmes (Prop), N. Gibbs (Pers)
Managers: P. Standen (Purch Mgr), J. Tott, R. White (Sales Prom Mgr), A. Farley (Tech Serv Mgr)
Ultimate Holding Company: SPX CORPORATION INC (USA)
Immediate Holding Company: RADIODETECTION LIMITED
Registration no: 01334448 **Date established:** 1977
Turnover: £20m - £50m **No.of Employees:** 101 - 250
Product Groups: 37, 38, 39, 40, 42, 44, 48, 52, 67, 81, 84, 85

Date of Accounts	Dec 11	Dec 10	Dec 09
Sales Turnover	35m	30m	26m
Pre Tax Profit/Loss	10m	8m	5m
Working Capital	41m	33m	25m
Fixed Assets	3m	3m	4m
Current Assets	50m	41m	32m
Current Liabilities	4m	4m	3m

Ravenscourt Engineering Ltd

Millbrook Road Yate, Bristol, BS37 5PB
Tel: 01454-316361 **Fax:** 01454-324114
E-mail: office@ravenscourtengineering.co.uk
Website: http://www.ravenscourtengineering.co.uk
Directors: A. Olver (Fin), H. Smart (Dir)
Immediate Holding Company: RAVENSCOURT ENGINEERING LIMITED
Registration no: 02225089 **VAT No.:** GB 496 6125 13
Date established: 1988 **Turnover:** £1m - £2m **No.of Employees:** 21 - 50
Product Groups: 48

Date of Accounts	Mar 12	Mar 11	Mar 10
Sales Turnover	N/A	2m	N/A
Pre Tax Profit/Loss	N/A	95	N/A
Working Capital	231	-69	-131
Fixed Assets	938	993	994
Current Assets	1m	342	368
Current Liabilities	N/A	77	N/A

Redland House Clinic

30 Queen Charlotte Street, Bristol, BS1 4HJ
Tel: 0117-942 0200 **Fax:** 0117-924 1663
E-mail: info@thehouseclinics.co.uk
Website: http://www.thehouseclinics.co.uk
Directors: J. Cook (Prop)
Date established: 1987 **No.of Employees:** 11 - 20 **Product Groups:** 88

Reed Accountancy Personnel Ltd

Prudential Building Wine Street, Bristol, BS1 2PH
Tel: 0117-921 5429 **Fax:** 0117-923 0631
E-mail: rapbristol@reed.co.uk
Website: http://www.reed.co.uk
Managers: S. Walker
Immediate Holding Company: POSITIVECAUSES LTD
Registration no: 00973629 **Date established:** 2009
Turnover: £125m - £250m **No.of Employees:** 1 - 10 **Product Groups:** 80

Reliance Security Services Ltd

Almondsbury Business Centre Woodlands, Bradley Stoke, Bristol, BS32 4QH
Tel: 01454-617179 **Fax:** 01454-616438
E-mail: info@reliancesecurity.co.uk
Website: http://www.reliancesecurity.co.uk
Directors: A. Topp (Div)
Managers: G. Muir (Chief Mgr)
Ultimate Holding Company: RELIANCE CORPORATION LIMITED
Immediate Holding Company: RELIANCE PROPERTY HOLDINGS LIMITED
Registration no: 01033997 **VAT No.:** 640 8335 71 **Date established:** 1971
Turnover: Over £1,000m **No.of Employees:** 11 - 20 **Product Groups:** 81

Rencol Components Ltd (Ray Engineering Co Ltd)

Unit 2 Avonbridge Trading Estate Atlantic Road, Bristol, BS11 9QD
Tel: 0117-916 0090 **Fax:** 0117-950 4550
E-mail: sales@rencol.com
Website: http://www.rencol.com
Bank(s): Bank of Scotland, Bristol
Directors: T. Swash (Sales)
Immediate Holding Company: RENCOL COMPONENTS LIMITED
Registration no: 07043676 **VAT No.:** GB 692 0758 12
Date established: 2009 **Turnover:** £2m - £5m **No.of Employees:** 11 - 20
Product Groups: 24, 29, 30, 33, 35, 36, 37, 39, 42, 46, 47, 48, 49, 66

Date of Accounts	Dec 11	Dec 10
Working Capital	130	-41
Fixed Assets	45	60
Current Assets	1m	942

R H C Lifting Ltd

Unit 6 Easter Court Woodward Avenue, Yate, Bristol, BS37 5YS
Tel: 01454-332270 **Fax:** 01454-317999
E-mail: sales@rhclifting.co.uk
Website: http://www.rhclifting.co.uk
Directors: T. Morgan (MD)
Immediate Holding Company: RHC LIFTING LIMITED
Registration no: 04156878 **Date established:** 2001
No.of Employees: 11 - 20 **Product Groups:** 35, 39, 45

Date of Accounts	Mar 11	Mar 10	Mar 09
Working Capital	-48	-66	-9
Fixed Assets	247	299	113
Current Assets	761	792	1m

Righton Ltd

Unit 7-10 Waverley Road Beeches Industrial Estate, Yate, Bristol, BS37 5FF
Tel: 01454-318601 **Fax:** 01454-273392
E-mail: mike.vince@righton.co.uk
Website: http://www.righton.co.uk
Bank(s): Bank of Scotland
Directors: M. Vincent (Dir)
Ultimate Holding Company: HENLEY MANAGEMENT COMPANY (USA)
Immediate Holding Company: RIGHTON LIMITED
Registration no: 00143411 **VAT No.:** GB 687 9071 99
Date established: 2016 **Turnover:** £20m - £50m
No.of Employees: 11 - 20 **Product Groups:** 30, 66

Date of Accounts	Dec 11	Dec 10	Dec 09
Sales Turnover	71m	74m	50m
Pre Tax Profit/Loss	943	1m	-632
Working Capital	11m	7m	6m
Fixed Assets	1m	2m	2m
Current Assets	31m	30m	27m
Current Liabilities	2m	4m	2m

Rio Tinto Consultants Ltd

Castlemead Lower Castle Street, Bristol, BS99 7YR
Tel: 0117-927 6407 **Fax:** 0117-927 3317
Website: http://www.riotinto.com
Directors: D. Totten (Fin), R. Dowding (Co Sec)
Immediate Holding Company: ESTIA LIMITED
Registration no: 01739682 **Date established:** 2001 **Turnover:** £5m - £10m
No.of Employees: 51 - 100 **Product Groups:** 54

Robbin Engineering

Nelson Court Nelson Road, Bristol, BS16 5EY
Tel: 0117-956 8143
Website: http://www.robbin.co.uk

Directors: I. French (Comm)
Immediate Holding Company: BRIGHTWORKS MEDIA LIMITED
Registration no: 02740369 **Date established:** 2010
No.of Employees: 1 - 10 **Product Groups:** 35, 52, 84

Rollo Power Solutions Ltd

Unit 18 Garonor Way Royal Portbury Dock, Portbury, Bristol, BS20 7XE
Tel: 01275-377800 **Fax:** 0113-272 0499
E-mail: info@rollouk.com
Website: http://www.rollopowersolutions.co.uk
Bank(s): Barclays
Managers: S. Taylor
Ultimate Holding Company: PON HOLDINGS BV (NETHERLANDS)
Immediate Holding Company: ROLLO UK LTD
Registration no: 01343019 **VAT No.:** GB 391 3015 73
Date established: 1977 **Turnover:** £5m - £10m **No.of Employees:** 11 - 20
Product Groups: 37

Date of Accounts	Dec 08	Dec 07
Sales Turnover	6112	6648
Pre Tax Profit/Loss	-78	-394
Working Capital	749	-222
Fixed Assets	162	150
Current Assets	1893	1996
Current Liabilities	1144	2218
Total Share Capital	1200	200
ROCE% (Return on Capital Employed)	-8.6	545.7
ROT% (Return on Turnover)	-1.3	-5.9

Rota Precision Ltd

94a High Street Portishead, Bristol, BS20 6AJ
Tel: 01275-818918 **Fax:** 01275-818828
E-mail: sales@rotaprecision.com
Website: http://www.rotaprecision.com
Directors: P. Lench (MD)
Immediate Holding Company: ROTA PRECISION LIMITED
Registration no: 02793478 **VAT No.:** GB 650 4972 30
Date established: 1993 **No.of Employees:** 1 - 10 **Product Groups:** 35

Date of Accounts	Nov 11	Nov 10	Nov 09
Working Capital	11	7	14
Fixed Assets	1	1	1
Current Assets	81	90	118

Royal Bank Of Scotland Group plc

PO Box 886, Bristol, BS99 5LJ
Tel: 0117-940 4040 **Fax:** 0117-940 4222
Website: http://www.rbs.co.uk
Bank(s): Royal Bank of Scotland
Directors: D. Edmonds (Dir)
Managers: R. Reeves (Property Mgr)
Date established: 1993 **Turnover:** £20m - £50m
No.of Employees: 1501 & over **Product Groups:** 82

Royal Oak Garage

8 Pennywell Road, Bristol, BS5 0TJ
Tel: 0117-955 6866 **Fax:** 0117- 9542346
E-mail: royaloak@engineer.com
Directors: P. Kington (Prop)
Registration no: 01219876 **No.of Employees:** 1 - 10 **Product Groups:** 39

Rudrumholdings

33-35 High Street Shirehampton, Bristol, BS11 0DX
Tel: 0117-982 6781 **Fax:** 0117-937 9037
E-mail: enquiries@rudrumholdings.co.uk
Website: http://www.rudrumholdings.co.uk
Directors: R. Whitehouse (MD), D. Phillips (Dir)
Managers: I. Thornell
Ultimate Holding Company: RUDRUM (HOLDINGS) LIMITED
Immediate Holding Company: EVANS & REID (SOLID FUELS DISTRIBUTION) LIMITED
Registration no: 02161335 **Date established:** 1987
Turnover: £10m - £20m **No.of Employees:** 11 - 20 **Product Groups:** 11, 66

Date of Accounts	Jun 11	Jun 10	Jun 09
Sales Turnover	14m	11m	15m
Pre Tax Profit/Loss	41	59	92
Working Capital	671	641	592
Fixed Assets	N/A	1	6
Current Assets	5m	5m	4m
Current Liabilities	26	38	64

Runway Engineering Ltd

Dean Road Great Western Business Park, Yate, Bristol, BS37 5NQ
Tel: 01454-316404 **Fax:** 01454-325926
E-mail: info@runwayeng.co.uk
Website: http://www.runwayeng.co.uk
Bank(s): National Westminster
Directors: P. Woonton (MD)
Immediate Holding Company: RUNWAY ENGINEERING LIMITED
Registration no: 01609144 **VAT No.:** GB 357 8900 17
Date established: 1982 **Turnover:** £1m - £2m **No.of Employees:** 11 - 20
Product Groups: 48

Date of Accounts	Mar 11	Mar 10	Mar 09
Working Capital	256	119	82
Fixed Assets	350	379	357
Current Assets	502	475	235

S C A Packaging

Brook Road Speedwell, Bristol, BS5 7TE
Tel: 0117-951 7415 **Fax:** 0117-935 4260
E-mail: chris.courtney@sca.com
Website: http://www.scaindustrial.com
Bank(s): Lloyds TSB Bank plc
Managers: P. Gilbert
VAT No.: GB 138 5431 65 **Turnover:** £2m - £5m **No.of Employees:** 11 - 20
Product Groups: 27, 45, 76

S & J Roofing Ltd

Apex House Kingsfield Lane, Longwell Green, Bristol, BS30 6DL
Tel: 0117-960 4161 **Fax:** 0117-935 2084
E-mail: enquiries@sjroofing.co.uk
Website: http://www.sjroofing.co.uk
Directors: J. Saunders (MD)
Ultimate Holding Company: S. & J. HOLDINGS LIMITED
Immediate Holding Company: S. & J. HOLDINGS LIMITED
Registration no: 00979886 **Date established:** 1970 **Turnover:** £1m - £2m
No.of Employees: 1 - 10 **Product Groups:** 52

Date of Accounts	Apr 11	Apr 10	Apr 09
Working Capital	69	84	185
Fixed Assets	17	22	28
Current Assets	109	102	240

S M Gauge Co. Ltd

308-312 Lodge Causeway, Bristol, BS16 3RD
Tel: 0117-965 4615 **Fax:** 0117-958 3660
E-mail: sales@pressuregauge.co.uk
Website: http://www.pressuregauge.co.uk
Directors: T. Sheppard (MD)
Immediate Holding Company: SM GAUGE COMPANY LIMITED
Registration no: 04673783 **VAT No.:** GB 357 8962 92
Date established: 2003 **No.of Employees:** 11 - 20 **Product Groups:** 38, 67, 85

Date of Accounts	Jul 11	Jul 10	Jul 09
Working Capital	-151	-249	-218
Fixed Assets	642	751	282
Current Assets	540	394	483
Current Liabilities	429	N/A	462

S & T Electroplate

15-16 The Alpha Centre Armstrong Way, Yate, Bristol, BS37 5NG
Tel: 01454-313162 **Fax:** 01454-321875
E-mail: mail@chromebysandt.com
Website: http://www.stchrome.co.uk
Directors: K. Saleh (Prop)
Immediate Holding Company: S & T ELECTRO-PLATE LIMITED
Registration no: 05477570 **VAT No.:** GB 543 4073 61
Date established: 2005 **Turnover:** £500,000 - £1m
No.of Employees: 11 - 20 **Product Groups:** 48

S T Micro Electronics Ltd

1000 Aztec West Almondsbury, Bristol, BS32 4SQ
Tel: 01454-616616 **Fax:** 01454-617910
E-mail: postmaster@st.com
Website: http://www.st.com
Bank(s): National Westminster Bank Plc
Directors: P. Morris (Pers)
Managers: G. Collins (Tech Serv Mgr), P. Mcelwee
Ultimate Holding Company: ST MICROELECTRONICS NV (FRANCE)
Immediate Holding Company: STMICROELECTRONICS (BRISTOL) PENSION TRUST LTD
Registration no: 01522768 **Date established:** 1980
No.of Employees: 101 - 250 **Product Groups:** 37, 38, 39, 40, 44, 49

Saint-Gobain Ltd

Unit 16 Concorde Road Patchway, Bristol, BS34 5TB
Tel: 0117-938 1700 **Fax:** 0117-915 7982
E-mail: alan.holcombe@rencol.co.uk
Website: http://www.saint-gobain.com
Directors: A. Holcombe (MD), J. Penn (MD), S. Wood (Fin)
Managers: A. Bancalri, C. Roberts (Personnel)
Ultimate Holding Company: COMPAGNIE DE SAINT GOBAIN (FRANCE)
Immediate Holding Company: SAINT-GOBAIN LIMITED
Registration no: 03291592 **VAT No.:** GB 609 4946 12
Date established: 1996 **No.of Employees:** 51 - 100 **Product Groups:** 37, 48

Date of Accounts	Dec 11	Dec 10	Dec 09
Sales Turnover	13m	8m	6m
Pre Tax Profit/Loss	-92m	44m	50m
Working Capital	-128m	72m	24m
Fixed Assets	2049m	1943m	1946m
Current Assets	482m	487m	315m
Current Liabilities	4m	3m	25m

Sally Walker Language Centre

43 St Nicholas Street, Bristol, BS1 1TP
Tel: 0117-929 1594 **Fax:** 0117-929 0633
E-mail: translations@sallywalker.co.uk
Website: http://www.sallywalker.co.uk
Directors: S. Walker (Prop)
Immediate Holding Company: SALLY WALKER LIMITED
Registration no: 01409375 **VAT No.:** GB 302 9029 89
Date established: 1979 **No.of Employees:** 1 - 10 **Product Groups:** 28, 80

Date of Accounts	May 11	May 10	May 09
Working Capital	-15	-4	1
Fixed Assets	6	6	6
Current Assets	134	131	159

Saunders & Weeks (Bristol) Ltd

265-267 Church Road Redfield, Bristol, BS5 9HU
Tel: 0117-955 7142 **Fax:** 0117-955 6064
E-mail: sales@saundersweeks.co.uk
Website: http://www.saundersweeks.co.uk
Directors: R. Smale (MD)
Immediate Holding Company: SAUNDERS & WEEKS (BRISTOL) LIMITED
Registration no: 01105582 **VAT No.:** GB 138 7170 57
Date established: 1973 **Turnover:** £250,000 - £500,000
No.of Employees: 1 - 10 **Product Groups:** 38, 39, 49

Date of Accounts	Mar 12	Mar 11	Mar 10
Working Capital	71	63	56
Fixed Assets	3	12	4
Current Assets	103	102	92

Scottys Gates Ltd

27 Dixon Road Brislington, Bristol, BS4 5QW
Tel: 0117-977 8865 **Fax:** 0117-907 4698
E-mail: scottysgates@yahoo.co.uk
Website: http://www.scottysgates.co.uk
Directors: L. Scott (Fin), S. Scott (MD)
Immediate Holding Company: SCOTTYS GATES LIMITED
Registration no: 04194991 **Date established:** 2001
No.of Employees: 21 - 50 **Product Groups:** 26, 35

Date of Accounts	Apr 12	Apr 11	Apr 10
Working Capital	56	24	24
Fixed Assets	50	64	70
Current Assets	320	386	352

Severn Sales

1 Lodge Road, Bristol, BS15 1LD
Tel: 0117-960 8858 **Fax:** 0870-777 6071
E-mail: info@severnsaleslabequip.com
Website: http://www.severnsaleslabequip.com
Directors: A. Biggs (Ptnr)
VAT No.: GB 140 1820 18 **Turnover:** £500,000 - £1m
No.of Employees: 1 - 10 **Product Groups:** 38, 40, 42

Severnside Fabrics Ltd

Gordon Road Whitehall, Bristol, BS5 7DR
Tel: 0117-951 0412 **Fax:** 0117-935 4165
E-mail: sales@severnsidefabrics.co.uk
Website: http://www.severnsidefabrics.co.uk
Bank(s): Barclays
Directors: G. White (Sales)
Ultimate Holding Company: ANDREW INDUSTRIES LIMITED
Immediate Holding Company: SEVERNSIDE FABRICS LIMITED
Registration no: 01093949 **VAT No.:** GB 138 938 820
Date established: 1973 **Turnover:** £2m - £5m **No.of Employees:** 11 - 20
Product Groups: 23

Date of Accounts	Mar 11	Mar 10	Mar 09
Working Capital	2m	2m	2m
Fixed Assets	201	161	169
Current Assets	3m	2m	2m

Severnside Recycling

Avon Mill Lane Keynsham, Bristol, BS31 2UG
Tel: 0117-986 9077 **Fax:** 0117-986 9049
E-mail: nick.hannah@severnside.com
Website: http://www.severnside.com
Bank(s): National Westminster
Directors: J. Malone (Sales), P. McGuinness (MD), T. Price (Mkt Research)
Managers: M. Howes (Mgr)
Ultimate Holding Company: LINE BUSINESS SERVICES LIMITED
Immediate Holding Company: SOVISION LIMITED
Registration no: 00489560 **VAT No.:** 479 5202 22 **Date established:** 2000
Turnover: £20m - £50m **No.of Employees:** 21 - 50 **Product Groups:** 66

Sew Personal Ltd

7 The Dingle Yate, Bristol, BS37 7GA
Tel: 01454-313166
E-mail: info@sewpersonal.biz
Website: http://www.sewpersonal.co.uk
Directors: D. Miller (Dir), H. Miller (Dir)
Immediate Holding Company: SEW PERSONAL LIMITED
Registration no: 05574883 **Date established:** 2005
Turnover: Up to £250,000 **No.of Employees:** 1 - 10 **Product Groups:** 23, 24, 49, 63

Date of Accounts	Sep 08	Sep 07	Sep 06
Working Capital	-21	-8	-6
Fixed Assets	26	8	5
Current Assets	5	4	2

Shiner Ltd

22 Church Road Lawrence Hill, Bristol, BS5 9JB
Tel: 0117-955 7432 **Fax:** 0117-955 4686
E-mail: admin@shiner.co.uk
Website: http://www.shiner.co.uk
Bank(s): Barclays
Directors: C. Allen (Dir), C. Allen (MD), M. Allen (MD)
Managers: C. Allen (Sales Prom Mgr), N. Rodgers (Chief Acct)
Immediate Holding Company: SHINER LIMITED
Registration no: 00315108 **VAT No.:** GB 137 5548 50
Date established: 1936 **Turnover:** £2m - £5m **No.of Employees:** 21 - 50
Product Groups: 52, 66

Date of Accounts	Apr 11	Apr 10	Apr 09
Sales Turnover	N/A	N/A	4m
Pre Tax Profit/Loss	N/A	N/A	809
Working Capital	5m	5m	4m
Fixed Assets	2m	2m	2m
Current Assets	6m	5m	5m
Current Liabilities	N/A	N/A	469

Shoreheat Ltd

2 Smyth Road, Bristol, BS3 2BX
Tel: 0117-966 9501 **Fax:** 0117-963 6824
Managers: S. Bird (Mgr)
Ultimate Holding Company: PROGRESS GROUP LIMITED
Immediate Holding Company: SHOREHEAT LIMITED
Registration no: 01566154 **VAT No.:** GB 484 6088 12
Date established: 1981 **Turnover:** Up to £250,000
No.of Employees: 1 - 10 **Product Groups:** 36, 38, 40

Date of Accounts	Dec 10	Dec 09	Dec 08
Sales Turnover	17m	13m	14m
Pre Tax Profit/Loss	540	327	393
Working Capital	2m	2m	2m
Fixed Assets	461	505	481
Current Assets	6m	6m	5m
Current Liabilities	480	388	504

Signconex Ltd

Peartree Industrial Estate Bath Road, Langford, Bristol, BS40 5DJ
Tel: 0161-764 9500 **Fax:** 0161-764 9600
E-mail: info@signconex.co.uk
Website: http://www.signconex.co.uk
Bank(s): T.S.B., The Rock, Bury
Directors: A. Moore (MD)
Immediate Holding Company: SIGNCONEX LIMITED
Registration no: 01005017 **VAT No.:** GB 147 6421 62
Date established: 1971 **Turnover:** £1m - £2m **No.of Employees:** 11 - 20
Product Groups: 49

Date of Accounts	Dec 11	Dec 10	Jun 10
Working Capital	241	166	187
Fixed Assets	220	248	251
Current Assets	450	318	358

Signet Signs Ltd

45 West Town Road Backwell, Bristol, BS48 3HG
Tel: 01275-463601 **Fax:** 01275-462990
E-mail: mail@signetsigns.co.uk
Website: http://www.signetsigns.co.uk
Directors: S. Rawlings (Co Sec), M. Rawlings (MD)
Immediate Holding Company: SIGNET SIGNS LIMITED
Registration no: 01352965 **VAT No.:** GB 302 6627 84
Date established: 1978 **Turnover:** £500,000 - £1m
No.of Employees: 1 - 10 **Product Groups:** 30, 49

Date of Accounts	May 12	May 11	May 10
Working Capital	-41	-44	-35
Fixed Assets	68	80	92
Current Assets	38	37	79

Signscape Systems Ltd

Bath Road Langford, Bristol, BS40 5DJ
Tel: 01934-852888 **Fax:** 01934-852816
E-mail: hamish@signscape.co.uk
Website: http://www.sign-making-supplies.co.uk
Bank(s): Lloyds TSB Bank plc
Managers: H. Patterson (Mgr)
Immediate Holding Company: SIGNSCAPE SYSTEMS LTD
Registration no: 05763360 **VAT No.:** GB 520 4453 83
Date established: 2006 **No.of Employees:** 11 - 20 **Product Groups:** 35, 37, 39, 49, 64, 68

see next page

Signscape Systems Ltd - Cont'd

Date of Accounts	Dec 11	Dec 10	Dec 09
Working Capital	19	-23	-28
Fixed Assets	941	618	646
Current Assets	255	247	233

Sil Inc UK
17 Carmarthen Close Yate, Bristol, BS37 7RR
Tel: 01454-325944
E-mail: info@sil-inc.co.uk
Website: http://www.sil-inc.co.uk
Managers: C. Goodchild (Sales Prom Mgr)
No.of Employees: 1 - 10 **Product Groups:** 37, 38, 67

Thomas Silvey Ltd
111-119 Newfoundland Road, Bristol, BS2 9LU
Tel: 0117-955 5251 **Fax:** 0117-955 1436
E-mail: david.hatherell@silvey.co.uk
Website: http://www.slivey.co.uk
Bank(s): Lloyds TSB Bank plc
Managers: D. Hatherell (Mgr)
Registration no: 00360922 **VAT No.:** GB 358 1209 56
Date established: 1870 **Turnover:** £20m - £50m
No.of Employees: 11 - 20 **Product Groups:** 30, 31, 32, 35, 38, 66, 68, 77

Date of Accounts	Jun 08	Jun 07	Jun 06
Sales Turnover	42570	38260	36280
Pre Tax Profit/Loss	-380	-560	-240
Working Capital	-570	-220	310
Fixed Assets	1800	1890	1910
Current Assets	5310	5170	6080
Current Liabilities	5880	5390	5770
Total Share Capital	20	20	20
ROCE% (Return on Capital Employed)	-30.9	-33.5	-10.8
ROT% (Return on Turnover)	-0.9	-1.5	-0.7

Simply Health
James Tudor House 90 Victoria Street, Bristol, BS1 6DF
Tel: 0117-929 5529 **Fax:** 0117-929 5539
E-mail: info@bcwa.co.uk
Website: http://www.simplyhealth.co.uk
Directors: J. Holden (Co Sec)
Managers: M. Wilson (I.T. Exec), S. Jones (Personnel), J. Wilson (Mgr), H. Hughes (Sales & Mktg Mg)
Registration no: 03819304 **No.of Employees:** 251 - 500
Product Groups: 88

SKF Economos U.K. Ltd South West Region Branch
Unit 20 Avonbank Industrial Estate West Town Rd, Bristol, BS11 9DE
Tel: 0117-982 5729 **Fax:** 0117-982 5730
E-mail: bristol@economos.com
Website: http://www.economos.co.uk
Directors: P. Chambers (MD), R. Kumra (MD)
Registration no: 02414449 **Turnover:** £2m - £5m
No.of Employees: 1 - 10 **Product Groups:** 29, 30, 33, 40, 42, 48

Skyvent Systems Ltd
Unit C Malago Vale Trading Estate St Johns Lane, Bristol, BS3 5BQ
Tel: 0117-966 9522 **Fax:** 0117-963 9523
E-mail: skyvent@gmail.com
Website: http://www.skyvent.co.uk
Directors: T. Allan (MD)
Immediate Holding Company: SKYVENT SYSTEMS LTD.
Registration no: 03871776 **Date established:** 1999
No.of Employees: 1 - 10 **Product Groups:** 40, 66

Date of Accounts	Mar 12	Mar 11	Mar 10
Working Capital	92	82	81
Fixed Assets	133	146	160
Current Assets	129	129	161

Sleepyheads Mail Order Ltd
336 Gloucester Road Horfield, Bristol, BS7 8TJ
Tel: 0117-944 4595 **Fax:** 0117-944 4597
E-mail: sales@sleepyheadsmailorder.co.uk
Website: http://www.sleepyheadsmailorder.co.uk
Directors: R. Hynam (Dir), C. Hynam (Dir)
Immediate Holding Company: SLEEPYHEADS MAIL ORDER LIMITED
Registration no: 04939975 **Date established:** 2003
No.of Employees: 1 - 10 **Product Groups:** 24, 26

Date of Accounts	Oct 07	Oct 06	Oct 05
Working Capital	6	6	-41
Fixed Assets	N/A	N/A	2
Current Assets	49	51	57
Current Liabilities	43	45	98
Total Share Capital	50	50	N/A

Smith & Williamson Corporate Finance
Portwall Place Portwall Lane, Bristol, BS1 6NA
Tel: 0117-376 2000 **Fax:** 0117-376 2001
E-mail: info@smith.williamson.co.uk
Website: http://www.smith.williamson.co.uk
Directors: M. Lea (Snr Part)
Immediate Holding Company: SMITH TRUSTEE COMPANY LIMITED(THE)
Registration no: 00451388 **Date established:** 1948
No.of Employees: 101 - 250 **Product Groups:** 80

Smiths Metal Centres Ltd
Unit 10 Unicorn Business Centre
Whitby Road
St. Annes, Bristol, BS4 4EX
Tel: 0117-971 2800 **Fax:** 0117-971 6300
E-mail: bristol@smithmetal.com
Website: http://www.smithmetal.com
Managers: R. Jones (Mgr)
Ultimate Holding Company: HENLEY MANAGEMENT COMPANY (USA)
Immediate Holding Company: SMITHS METAL CENTRES LIMITED
Registration no: 03485838 **Date established:** 1997
No.of Employees: 1 - 10 **Product Groups:** 34

Date of Accounts	Dec 11	May 10	May 09
Sales Turnover	45m	46m	49m
Pre Tax Profit/Loss	2m	830	629
Working Capital	7m	12m	13m
Fixed Assets	1m	1m	2m
Current Assets	28m	23m	21m
Current Liabilities	4m	2m	2m

Solution M H E
Unit 118b Burcott Road, Bristol, BS11 8AB
Tel: 0117-938 2012 **Fax:** 0117-982 5481
E-mail: info@solutionmhe.com
Website: http://www.solutionmhe.com
Managers: E. Palmer
Immediate Holding Company: SOLUTION M.H.E. LIMITED
Registration no: 04081750 **Date established:** 2000
No.of Employees: 11 - 20 **Product Groups:** 45, 48, 67, 71, 83, 86

Date of Accounts	Jun 11	Jun 10	Jun 09
Working Capital	166	64	65
Fixed Assets	397	441	452
Current Assets	387	364	373

Somerglaze Windows Ltd
20a Stonewell Drive Congresbury, Bristol, BS49 5DW
Tel: 01934-830479 **Fax:** 01934-838557
E-mail: info@somerglazewindows.co.uk
Website: http://www.somerglazewindows.co.uk
Directors: G. Hembrow (Dir)
Immediate Holding Company: SOMERGLAZE WINDOWS LTD
Registration no: 06698467 **Date established:** 2008
Turnover: Up to £250,000 **No.of Employees:** 1 - 10 **Product Groups:** 30

Date of Accounts	Mar 12	Mar 11	Mar 10
Working Capital	-29	-52	-55
Fixed Assets	56	58	57
Current Assets	18	8	6

South West Fasteners Ltd
Unit 7-9 306 Industrial Estate 242-244 Broomhill Road, Bristol, BS4 5RG
Tel: 0117-972 3242 **Fax:** 0117-971 7555
E-mail: southwestfasteners@dial.pipex.com
Website: http://www.southwestfasteners.com
Directors: S. Curtis (MD)
Immediate Holding Company: SOUTH WEST FASTENERS LIMITED
Registration no: 03803835 **VAT No.:** GB 358 1204 66
Date established: 1999 **Turnover:** £2m - £5m **No.of Employees:** 1 - 10
Product Groups: 35, 66

Date of Accounts	Sep 11	Sep 10	Sep 09
Working Capital	951	1m	1m
Fixed Assets	67	71	78
Current Assets	1m	1m	1m

South Western Equipment Catering Services
Southlands Farm Cockers Hill, Compton Dando, Bristol, BS39 4JX
Tel: 01761-490167 **Fax:** 01761-490167
E-mail: loisswecs@btconnect.com
Directors: L. Turner (Prop)
No.of Employees: 1 - 10 **Product Groups:** 20, 40, 41

South Western Tools Ltd
26 New Station Road, Bristol, BS16 3RU
Tel: 0117-965 9596 **Fax:** 0117-965 9566
E-mail: peter@wire-eroding.com
Website: http://www.wire-eroding.com
Directors: S. Barrett (Fin), P. Barrett (MD)
Immediate Holding Company: SOUTH WESTERN TOOLS LIMITED
Registration no: 00568290 **Date established:** 1956
No.of Employees: 1 - 10 **Product Groups:** 46

Date of Accounts	Jun 11	Jun 10	Jun 09
Working Capital	112	118	113
Fixed Assets	168	181	165
Current Assets	164	155	154

Southern PVC Systems Ltd
1 Carrick Busines Centre Bonville Road, Bristol, BS4 5NZ
Tel: 0117-971 0359 **Fax:** 0117-972 0998
E-mail: sales@diypvcwindows.co.uk
Website: http://www.diypvcwindows.co.uk
Directors: L. Coles (Fin), R. Coles (MD)
Immediate Holding Company: SOUTHERN P.V.C. SYSTEMS LIMITED
Registration no: 01704971 **Date established:** 1983
Turnover: £250,000 - £500,000 **No.of Employees:** 1 - 10
Product Groups: 36, 52

Date of Accounts	Mar 11	Mar 10	Mar 09
Working Capital	13	23	29
Fixed Assets	6	5	5
Current Assets	42	45	47

Spandex plc
1600 Park Avenue Almondsbury, Bristol, BS32 4UA
Tel: 01454-616444 **Fax:** 01454-616777
E-mail: info@spandex.com
Website: http://www.spandex.co.uk
Bank(s): Lloyds
Managers: K. Mcgeown (Sales Prom Mgr)
Immediate Holding Company: SPANDEX LIMITED
Registration no: 01266024 **VAT No.:** GB 140 3855 86
Date established: 1976 **Turnover:** £20m - £50m
No.of Employees: 51 - 100 **Product Groups:** 35, 39

Date of Accounts	Apr 11	Apr 10	Apr 09
Sales Turnover	27m	25m	25m
Pre Tax Profit/Loss	9m	2m	-1m
Working Capital	21m	10m	7m
Fixed Assets	16m	26m	27m
Current Assets	28m	18m	17m
Current Liabilities	768	890	1m

Speedy Lifting Ltd
Avonmouth Way West, Bristol, BS11 9HD
Tel: 0117-982 0777 **Fax:** 0117-982 0660
Website: http://www.speedyhire.com
Managers: A. Coles (Mgr), A. Ross (Mgr)
Immediate Holding Company: SPEEDY LIFTING LIMITED
Registration no: 04529136 **Date established:** 2002
No.of Employees: 1 - 10 **Product Groups:** 35, 39, 45

Stancold plc (Coldroom Manufacturing).
Portview Road, Bristol, BS11 9LQ
Tel: 0117-316 7000 **Fax:** 0117-316 7001
E-mail: sales@stancold.co.uk
Website: http://www.stancold.co.uk
Bank(s): National Westminster Bank Plc
Directors: M. O'Neill (Fin)
Managers: M. Kendrick (Mktg Serv Mgr), Z. Hicks (Mktg Serv Mgr), A. Pelc (Personnel)
Ultimate Holding Company: GILCREST GROUP LIMITED
Immediate Holding Company: STANCOLD PLC
Registration no: 00425982 **Date established:** 1946 **Turnover:** £5m - £10m
No.of Employees: 21 - 50 **Product Groups:** 38, 40, 48

Date of Accounts	Jun 11	Jun 10	Jun 09
Sales Turnover	5m	5m	7m
Pre Tax Profit/Loss	26	111	123
Working Capital	107	136	62
Fixed Assets	150	86	64
Current Assets	2m	3m	2m
Current Liabilities	397	383	347

Starline
Hope Road, Bristol, BS3 3NZ
Tel: 0117-300 2213 **Fax:** 01253-307149
E-mail: sales@starlinesales.co.uk
Website: http://www.starlinesales.co.uk
Bank(s): HSBC
Directors: S. Tugman (MD), D. Gardiner (Chief Op Offcr)
Managers: M. Holmes (Fin Mgr), S. Coles (Prod Mgr)
Ultimate Holding Company: BRUNEL HOLDINGS (BRISTOL) LIMITED
Immediate Holding Company: STARLINE (HOLDINGS) LIMITED
Registration no: 00519632 **VAT No.:** GB 153 5103 01
Date established: 1953 **Turnover:** £5m - £10m **No.of Employees:** 21 - 50
Product Groups: 49

Date of Accounts	Sep 11	Sep 10	Sep 09
Working Capital	366	626	764
Fixed Assets	2m	2m	2m
Current Assets	385	647	792

The Stocking Shop Ltd
1 Chantry Road Thornbury Thornbury, Bristol, BS35 1ER
Tel: 07771-822972
E-mail: sales@the-stocking-shop.com
Website: http://the-stocking-shop.com
Directors: C. McCluskey (MD)
Registration no: 05370766 **Date established:** 2005
Turnover: Up to £250,000 **No.of Employees:** 11 - 20 **Product Groups:** 24, 63

Date of Accounts	Feb 07	Feb 06
Working Capital	-2	N/A
Current Assets	-2	1
Current Liabilities	N/A	1

Stripe Consulting Ltd
1 Whiteladies Gate, Bristol, BS8 2PH
Tel: 0117-974 5179 **Fax:** 01278-457299
E-mail: mark@stripeconsulting.com
Website: http://www.stripeconsulting.com
Directors: M. Dale (MD)
Immediate Holding Company: STRIPE CONSULTING LIMITED
Registration no: 05225880 **VAT No.:** GB 709 6159 17
Date established: 2004 **Turnover:** Up to £250,000
No.of Employees: 1 - 10 **Product Groups:** 84

Date of Accounts	Sep 11	Sep 10	Sep 09
Working Capital	23	42	16
Fixed Assets	7	4	5
Current Assets	127	149	90

Structural Services
13 Fairfield Road Montpelier, Bristol, BS6 5JN
Tel: 0800-163779 **Fax:** 01834- 813058
Directors: G. James (Dir)
No.of Employees: 1 - 10 **Product Groups:** 35

Stute Foods Ltd
Stute House Sunderland Place, Bristol, BS8 1EG
Tel: 0117-923 8823 **Fax:** 0117-946 6446
E-mail: laurence.hybs@stute-foods.com
Website: http://www.stute-foods.com
Directors: L. Hybs (MD), S. Hybs (Fin)
Immediate Holding Company: STUTE FOODS LIMITED
Registration no: 00958378 **Date established:** 1969 **Turnover:** £5m - £10m
No.of Employees: 1 - 10 **Product Groups:** 01, 20, 62

Date of Accounts	Dec 11	Dec 10	Dec 09
Working Capital	591	561	556
Fixed Assets	239	267	269
Current Assets	1m	1m	1m

Sulzer Pump
Banyard Road Portbury, Bristol, BS20 7XH
Tel: 01275-374240 **Fax:** 01275-371044
E-mail: chris.powles@sulzer.com
Website: http://www.sulzerpump.com
Managers: C. Powles (Chief Mgr)
Ultimate Holding Company: A-GAS (ORB) LIMITED
Immediate Holding Company: A-GAS (UK) LIMITED
Registration no: 02991666 **Date established:** 1992 **Turnover:** £2m - £5m
No.of Employees: 11 - 20 **Product Groups:** 40

Sun Chemical Ltd (UK Liquid Inks)
Highway Station Road Yate, Bristol, BS37 7AA
Tel: 01454-318850 **Fax:** 01454-325907
E-mail: brian.corcoran@sunchemical.com
Website: http://www.suneurope.com
Managers: B. Corcoran (Site Co-ord), M. Bush (Tech Serv Mgr), M. Chapman (Personnel)
Ultimate Holding Company: DAINIPPON INK & CHEMICALS INC (JAPAN)
Immediate Holding Company: SUN CHEMICAL LIMITED
Registration no: 02647054 **Date established:** 1991
Turnover: £75m - £125m **No.of Employees:** 51 - 100
Product Groups: 28, 30, 32, 38

Date of Accounts	Dec 11	Dec 10	Dec 09
Sales Turnover	277m	282m	271m
Pre Tax Profit/Loss	2m	6m	-23m
Working Capital	17m	20m	27m
Fixed Assets	59m	62m	65m
Current Assets	100m	98m	104m
Current Liabilities	11m	13m	12m

Sureway Express Transport Ltd
Unit 12 I O Centre Moorend Farm Avenue, Bristol, BS11 0QL
Tel: 0117-982 1020 **Fax:** 0117-982 1021
E-mail: info@surewaytransport.co.uk
Website: http://www.surewaytransport.co.uk
Directors: R. Lloyd (Dir), C. Howell (Fin)
Managers: N. Richards (Develop Mgr)
Immediate Holding Company: SUREWAY EXPRESS TRANSPORT LIMITED
Registration no: 04498410 **Date established:** 2002
No.of Employees: 21 - 50 **Product Groups:** 77

Date of Accounts	Aug 11	Aug 10	Aug 09
Working Capital	-360	-297	-210
Fixed Assets	2m	2m	2m
Current Assets	455	570	493

Swift Computing
1 & 2 The Sanctuary Eden Office Park, Pill, Bristol, BS20 0DD
Tel: 01275-376180 **Fax:** 01275-376 181
E-mail: info@swift-computing.com
Website: http://www.swift-computing.com
Directors: J. Rossetti (MD)
Immediate Holding Company: SWIFT COMPUTING LIMITED
Registration no: 02009394 **Date established:** 1986 **Turnover:** £1m - £2m
No.of Employees: 51 - 100 **Product Groups:** 44

Date of Accounts	Apr 10	Apr 09	Apr 08
Sales Turnover	N/A	1m	1m
Pre Tax Profit/Loss	N/A	468	-664
Working Capital	566	373	76
Fixed Assets	681	541	115
Current Assets	2m	1m	825
Current Liabilities	N/A	363	268

Andrew Sykes Hire Ltd (Regional Centre)
Unit 7 Severnside Trading Estate, St Andrews Road, Bristol, BS11 8AG
Tel: 0117-982 7677 **Fax:** 0117-982 0755
E-mail: depot.bri@andrews-sykes.com
Website: http://www.andrews-sykes.com
Directors: C. Brickley (Prop)
Immediate Holding Company: ANDREW SYKES GROUP
Registration no: 02985657 **VAT No.:** GB 100 4295 24
Turnover: £10m - £20m **No.of Employees:** 1 - 10 **Product Groups:** 83

T L C Electrical Distributors
2 Camwal Road, Bristol, BS2 0UZ
Tel: 0117-977 9656
E-mail: enquiries@tlc-direct.co.uk
Website: http://www.tlc-direct.co.uk
Managers: R. Pullman (Mgr)
No.of Employees: 21 - 50 **Product Groups:** 36, 40

T M Ventham Practice
184 Kellaway Avenue, Bristol, BS6 7YL
Tel: 0117-942 1199 **Fax:** 0117-924 0561
E-mail: mail@tmventham.com
Website: http://www.tmventham.com
Managers: D. Ventham (Mgr)
Date established: 1992 **No.of Employees:** 1 - 10 **Product Groups:** 35

Tacklestore Ltd
Unit 23 Atlantic Road, Bristol, BS11 9QD
Tel: 0117-938 1600
E-mail: sales@tacklestore.net
Website: http://www.tacklestore.net
Directors: M. Hughes (Dir)
Immediate Holding Company: TACKLESTORE LIMITED
Registration no: 04464608 **Date established:** 2002
No.of Employees: 11 - 20 **Product Groups:** 45

Date of Accounts	Jun 11	Jun 10	Jun 09
Working Capital	167	19	17
Fixed Assets	50	59	78
Current Assets	1m	1m	1m

Talbot Owen Tools & Fasteners Ltd
Stoke View Road, Bristol, BS16 3AE
Tel: 0117-965 4221 **Fax:** 0117-965 1846
E-mail: helen@talbot-owen.co.uk
Website: http://www.talbot-owen.co.uk
Bank(s): Lloyds TSB Bank plc
Managers: H. Harding (Mgr)
Ultimate Holding Company: CLIFFORD - DAVIS LIMITED
Immediate Holding Company: TALBOT-OWEN LIMITED
Registration no: 01192725 **Date established:** 1974
No.of Employees: 11 - 20 **Product Groups:** 67

Date of Accounts	Jan 12	Jan 11	Jan 10
Working Capital	148	137	127
Fixed Assets	252	259	251
Current Assets	288	278	239

Tangy Retail Giftware
284-288 Stapleton Road, Bristol, BS5 0NW
Tel: 0117-951 2202
E-mail: sales@tangygifts.co.uk
Website: http://www.tangygifts.co.uk
Directors: S. Marwah (MD)
No.of Employees: 1 - 10 **Product Groups:** 38, 49

Tappelectric Ltd
2 Dragon Court Crofts End Road, Bristol, BS5 7XX
Tel: 0117-951 8274 **Fax:** 0117-951 3751
E-mail: info@tappelectric.co.uk
Website: http://www.tappelectric.co.uk
Bank(s): Barclays
Directors: L. Woodward (Dir), S. Legge (Tech Serv), T. Shaul (MD), B. Shaul (Co Sec)
Immediate Holding Company: TAPPELECTRIC LIMITED
Registration no: 00541088 **VAT No.:** GB 138 2864 49
Date established: 1954 **Turnover:** £250,000 - £500,000
No.of Employees: 11 - 20 **Product Groups:** 52

Date of Accounts	Feb 10	Feb 09	Feb 08
Sales Turnover	360	752	738
Pre Tax Profit/Loss	-61	-10	25
Working Capital	148	195	197
Fixed Assets	86	90	97
Current Assets	232	282	370
Current Liabilities	25	77	95

Tarmac Southern Ltd
Durnford Quarry Longwood Lane, Long Ashton, Bristol, BS41 9DW
Tel: 01275-392471 **Fax:** 01275-392205
Website: http://www.tarmacltd.co.uk
Managers: P. Oneil (Mgr), R. Tyler (Mgr)
Ultimate Holding Company: Anglo American plc
Immediate Holding Company: TARMAC SOUTHERN LIMITED
Registration no: 00415260 **Date established:** 1946
No.of Employees: 21 - 50 **Product Groups:** 31, 33, 52, 66

Tarmac Ltd
Stancombe Lane Flax Bourton, Bristol, BS48 3QD
Tel: 01275-464441 **Fax:** 01275-463767
E-mail: martin.riley@tarmac.co.uk
Website: http://www.tarmac.co.uk
Directors: M. Riley (Dir)
Managers: M. Jones (Mgr)
Immediate Holding Company: TARMAC TOPMIX LIMITED
Registration no: 03132032 **Date established:** 1995 **Turnover:** £5m - £10m
No.of Employees: 1 - 10 **Product Groups:** 14, 31, 33

Taylor Maxwell & Co. Ltd
The Promenade, Bristol, BS8 3NW
Tel: 0117-973 7888 **Fax:** 0117-946 6039
E-mail: info@taylormaxwell.co.uk
Website: http://www.taylormaxwell.co.uk
Bank(s): Lloyd TSB
Directors: M. Sawyer (MD), M. Phillips (Fin), A. Downes (Chief Op Offcr)
Managers: S. Diamond (Sec)
Ultimate Holding Company: TAYLOR MAXWELL GROUP LIMITED
Immediate Holding Company: TAYLOR,MAXWELL & CO.LIMITED
Registration no: 00476749 **VAT No.:** GB 433 7113 75
Date established: 1950 **Turnover:** £50m - £75m
No.of Employees: 11 - 20 **Product Groups:** 66

Date of Accounts	Mar 12	Mar 11	Mar 10
Sales Turnover	52m	49m	39m
Pre Tax Profit/Loss	1m	768	346
Working Capital	7m	9m	8m
Fixed Assets	189	165	221
Current Assets	17m	19m	16m
Current Liabilities	2m	2m	1m

Team Partners Ltd
16 Whitehouse Street, Bristol, BS3 4AY
Tel: 08456-013323 **Fax:** 0845-644 5423
E-mail: enquiries@teampartners.co.uk
Website: http://www.teampartners.co.uk
Directors: S. Sermon (MD)
Immediate Holding Company: TEAM PARTNERS LIMITED
Registration no: 03772227 **VAT No.:** GB 800 6797 31
Date established: 1999 **No.of Employees:** 1 - 10 **Product Groups:** 44, 79, 80, 86

Date of Accounts	May 11	May 10	May 09
Working Capital	6	-7	-3
Current Assets	19	23	30

Teffont Business Systems Ltd
Unit 9 Falcon's Gate Dean Road, Yate, Bristol, BS37 5NH
Tel: 0800-018 6222 **Fax:** 01454-321686
E-mail: sales@teffont.co.uk
Website: http://www.teffont.co.uk
Bank(s): Lloyds TSB
Directors: I. Hodgson (Dir)
Ultimate Holding Company: TRANSCRIBE COPIER SYSTEMS LIMITED
Immediate Holding Company: TEFFONT BUSINESS SYSTEMS LIMITED
Registration no: 01389527 **Date established:** 1978
Turnover: £500,000 - £1m **No.of Employees:** 11 - 20
Product Groups: 44, 64

Date of Accounts	Mar 10	Mar 09	Mar 08
Sales Turnover	987	960	1m
Pre Tax Profit/Loss	59	32	132
Working Capital	552	507	424
Fixed Assets	11	23	35
Current Assets	918	865	845
Current Liabilities	301	282	335

Thermo Logistics
21-23 Emery Road, Bristol, BS4 5PF
Tel: 0117-971 7001 **Fax:** 0117-971 7113
E-mail: info@thermologistics.co.uk
Website: http://www.thermologistics.co.uk
Directors: J. Stokes (Ptnr)
Immediate Holding Company: K R F METALS LIMITED
Registration no: 04607263 **VAT No.:** GB 609 6084 30
Date established: 2011 **Turnover:** Up to £250,000
No.of Employees: 1 - 10 **Product Groups:** 40, 41

Date of Accounts	Oct 11	Oct 10	Oct 09
Working Capital	-137	-149	-205
Fixed Assets	531	611	701
Current Assets	275	305	222

Thruput
Studio House 5 Flowers Hill, Bristol, BS4 5JJ
Tel: 0117-330 5980 **Fax:** 0117-330 5980
Directors: L. Holder (Dir)
No.of Employees: 11 - 20 **Product Groups:** 37, 38, 44

Thyssen Krupp Materails (UK) Ltd
Aztec Centre 1st Floor Aztec West, Almondsbury, Bristol, BS32 4TD
Tel: 0117-953 3100 **Fax:** 0117-953 2418
E-mail: plastics.tkmuk@thyssenkrupp.com
Website: http://www.thyssen.co.uk
Directors: M. May (Dir)
Managers: R. Marshall (District Mgr)
Immediate Holding Company: Thyssen AG
Registration no: 00645702 **Date established:** 1978 **Turnover:** £5m - £10m
No.of Employees: 1 - 10 **Product Groups:** 34, 35, 36, 48, 66

Tidy Software Ltd
14 Rockwell Avenue, Bristol, BS11 0UF
Tel: 0117-982 4445
E-mail: gerard.harris@tidysoftware.co.uk
Website: http://www.tidy.co.uk
Directors: G. Harris (MD)
Immediate Holding Company: TIDY SOFTWARE LIMITED
Registration no: 03451657 **Date established:** 1997
Turnover: Up to £250,000 **No.of Employees:** 1 - 10 **Product Groups:** 44

Date of Accounts	Oct 11	Oct 10	Oct 09
Working Capital	-3	-10	-1
Fixed Assets	1	2	2
Current Assets	10	13	18

Tildenet Ltd (Agricultural Division)
Hartcliffe Way, Bristol, BS3 5RJ
Tel: 0117-966 9684 **Fax:** 0117-923 1251
E-mail: enquiries@tildenet.co.uk
Website: http://www.tildenet.com
Bank(s): Barclays
Directors: A. Downey (MD), B. Downey (MD), P. James (Fin), S. Palmer (Dir)
Managers: N. Hammond (Sales Prom Mgr), P. Morgan (Transport)
Registration no: 01284227 **VAT No.:** GB 140 523 60
Date established: 1976 **Turnover:** £2m - £5m **No.of Employees:** 21 - 50
Product Groups: 23, 30, 35

Timberwise (UK) Ltd
Suite 38 179 Whiteladies Road, Clifton, Bristol, BS8 2AG
Tel: 0800-2888660 **Fax:** 029-2076 1004
E-mail: bristol@timberwise.co.uk
Website: http://www.timberwise.co.uk
Registration no: 03230356 **Product Groups:** 07, 32, 52

Titan Ladders Ltd
Mendip Road Yatton, Bristol, BS49 4ET
Tel: 01934-832161 **Fax:** 01934-876180
E-mail: sales@titanladders.co.uk
Website: http://www.titanladders.co.uk
Bank(s): National Westminster Bank Plc
Directors: B. Candy (Sales)
Immediate Holding Company: TITAN LADDERS HOLDINGS LIMITED
Registration no: 00881103 **VAT No.:** GB 130 4992 78
Date established: 1966 **Turnover:** £5m - £10m **No.of Employees:** 11 - 20
Product Groups: 25, 30, 35

Date of Accounts	Dec 11	Dec 10	Dec 09
Sales Turnover	5m	5m	6m
Pre Tax Profit/Loss	12	-82	-201
Working Capital	2m	2m	2m
Fixed Assets	2m	2m	2m
Current Assets	3m	3m	3m
Current Liabilities	105	117	218

Titus Pumps Ltd
3 Chiphouse Road, Bristol, BS15 4TR
Tel: 0117-940 6293 **Fax:** 08707- 877472
E-mail: sales@tituspumps.co.uk
Website: http://www.tituspumps.co.uk
Directors: D. Gray (Fin)
Immediate Holding Company: TITUS PUMPS LIMITED
Registration no: 03069586 **VAT No.:** GB 639 6967 70
Date established: 1995 **Turnover:** £250,000 - £500,000
No.of Employees: 1 - 10 **Product Groups:** 30, 40

Date of Accounts	Jun 11	Jun 10	Jun 09
Working Capital	-2	-0	7
Fixed Assets	N/A	1	1
Current Assets	6	5	11

Tocris Cookson Ltd
Unit 5b I O Centre, Bristol, BS11 0QL
Tel: 0117-916 3333 **Fax:** 0117-916 3344
E-mail: customerservice@tocris.co.uk
Website: http://www.tocris.com
Bank(s): HSBC
Directors: L. Ede (MD)
Managers: A. Sheehan (Sales & Mktg Mg), A. Birnie (Fin Mgr)
Ultimate Holding Company: TOCRIS HOLDINGS LIMITED
Immediate Holding Company: TOCRIS COOKSON LIMITED
Registration no: 02869577 **VAT No.:** GB 415 5144 76
Date established: 1993 **Turnover:** £5m - £10m
No.of Employees: 51 - 100 **Product Groups:** 63

Date of Accounts	Dec 10	Dec 09	Dec 08
Sales Turnover	10m	9m	7m
Pre Tax Profit/Loss	7m	6m	4m
Working Capital	7m	5m	4m
Fixed Assets	778	801	797
Current Assets	9m	8m	7m
Current Liabilities	1m	2m	500

Topcoat Metal Finishing Ltd
1 Kelston Road, Bristol, BS10 5EP
Tel: 0117-914 1173 **Fax:** 0117-949 6494
E-mail: enquiries@strencotools.co.uk
Directors: J. Ridding (Dir), S. Ridding (Dir)
Immediate Holding Company: TOPCOAT METAL FINISHINGS LIMITED
Registration no: 03269167 **Date established:** 1996
No.of Employees: 1 - 10 **Product Groups:** 46, 48

Date of Accounts	Dec 09	Dec 08	Mar 12
Working Capital	59	47	73
Fixed Assets	1	2	1
Current Assets	65	59	80
Current Liabilities	7	N/A	6

Trac Structural Ltd
23 Belvoir Road, Bristol, BS6 5DQ
Tel: 0117-924 0224 **Fax:** 0117-924 8574
E-mail: info@trac.demon.co.uk
Website: http://www.trac-structural.co.uk
Directors: S. Chen (Fin)
Immediate Holding Company: TRAC STRUCTURAL LIMITED
Registration no: 03576517 **Date established:** 1998
No.of Employees: 1 - 10 **Product Groups:** 30, 33, 35, 37, 48, 51, 52, 66, 84, 85

Date of Accounts	Jun 11	Jun 10	Jun 09
Working Capital	28	37	133
Fixed Assets	27	36	34
Current Assets	108	109	191

Translations Chamber UK
45 Hampden Close Yate, Bristol, BS37 5UP
Tel: 01454-854693 **Fax:** 01454-854693
E-mail: transchamber@blueyonder.co.uk
Website: http://www.transchamber.co.uk
Directors: A. Dawson (Prop)
Date established: 2004 **Turnover:** Up to £250,000
No.of Employees: 1 - 10 **Product Groups:** 80

Transportation & Recovery Systems
Foundry Lane, Bristol, BS5 7UE
Tel: 0117-952 5900 **Fax:** 0117-952 5911
E-mail: info@trstrucks.com
Website: http://www.trstrucks.com
Directors: H. Oliver (MD)
Immediate Holding Company: TRANSPORTATION AND RECOVERY SYSTEMS LIMITED
Registration no: 04975196 **Date established:** 2003
No.of Employees: 1 - 10 **Product Groups:** 39, 40, 68

Date of Accounts	Sep 11	Sep 10	Sep 09
Working Capital	-49	-64	-64
Fixed Assets	12	19	25
Current Assets	N/A	22	112

True North GB Ltd
Trym Lodge 1 Henbury Road, Westbury-on-Trym, Bristol, BS9 3HQ
Tel: 08451-305500 **Fax:** 08704-001059
E-mail: info@truenorthgb.com
Website: http://www.truenorthgb.com
Directors: C. Halward (MD)
Immediate Holding Company: TRUE NORTH (G.B.) LIMITED
Registration no: 04208062 **Date established:** 2001
No.of Employees: 1 - 10 **Product Groups:** 86

Date of Accounts	Apr 11	Apr 10	Apr 09
Working Capital	26	15	13
Current Assets	123	74	46

Tuckers & Cabot
5 Portbury Saw Mills Industrial Estate Marsh Lane, Easton-in-Gordano, Bristol, BS20 0NH
Tel: 01275-371532 **Fax:** 01275-371533
Directors: I. Blake (Prop)
Date established: 1999 **No.of Employees:** 1 - 10 **Product Groups:** 35

Tumi
Unit 2 Ashmead Business Park Ashmead Road, Keynsham, Bristol, BS31 1SX
Tel: 0117-986 9216 **Fax:** 01225-444870
E-mail: info@tumicrafts.com
Website: http://www.tumiwholesale.com
Directors: L. Davies (Fin)
Managers: D. Treasure (Mgr)
Ultimate Holding Company: TUMI (CRAFTS) LIMITED
Immediate Holding Company: TUMI (MUSIC) LIMITED
Registration no: 02470948 **Date established:** 1990
Turnover: Up to £250,000 **No.of Employees:** 1 - 10 **Product Groups:** 28

Date of Accounts	Aug 11	Aug 10	Aug 09
Working Capital	-122	-133	-133
Fixed Assets	1	2	1
Current Assets	92	128	132

Unicorn Office Products
10-16 York Street St Werburghs, Bristol, BS2 9XT
Tel: 0117-907 6662 **Fax:** 0117-907 6663
E-mail: sales@unicornonline.net
Website: http://www.unicornonline.net
Directors: R. Green (Prop)
Immediate Holding Company: UNICORN OFFICE PRODUCTS LIMITED
Registration no: 03150065 **Date established:** 1996 **Turnover:** £1m - £2m
No.of Employees: 11 - 20 **Product Groups:** 27

Date of Accounts	Jan 12	Jan 11	Jan 10
Working Capital	83	62	26
Fixed Assets	169	175	167
Current Assets	330	336	220

Universal Components
Universal House Pennywell Road, Bristol, BS5 0ER
Tel: 0117-955 9091 **Fax:** 0117-955 6091
E-mail: info@universal-aluminium.co.uk
Website: http://www.universal-aluminium.co.uk
Bank(s): National Westminster
Directors: P. Cawley (MD), C. Hadjisavvas (Fin)
Managers: S. Lewis (Purch Mgr), L. Luxgon (Personnel), T. Moult (Sales Prom Mgr)
Ultimate Holding Company: MUSKITA ALUMINIUM INDUSTRIES LTD (CYPRUS)
Immediate Holding Company: UNIVERSAL COMPONENTS LIMITED
Registration no: 01532208 **VAT No.:** GB 303 2425 13
Date established: 1980 **Turnover:** £5m - £10m
No.of Employees: 51 - 100 **Product Groups:** 34, 37, 49

Date of Accounts	Dec 11	Dec 10	Dec 09
Sales Turnover	6m	6m	6m
Pre Tax Profit/Loss	-764	-468	-518
Working Capital	-75	451	994
Fixed Assets	3m	3m	3m
Current Assets	3m	3m	3m
Current Liabilities	199	207	168

University Of The West Of England
Frenchay Campus Coldharbour Lane, Bristol, BS16 1QY
Tel: 0117-328 5678 **Fax:** 01225-824235
Website: http://www.uwe.ac.uk
Directors: I. Apperley (Pers)
Managers: V. Millward (Mgr)
Immediate Holding Company: WEST OF ENGLAND SPORT TRUST
Registration no: 05794916 **Date established:** 2006 **Turnover:** £1m - £2m
No.of Employees: 1501 & over **Product Groups:** 28, 80, 84, 85

Date of Accounts	Mar 12	Mar 11	Mar 10
Sales Turnover	858	933	1m
Pre Tax Profit/Loss	132	-200	-130
Working Capital	360	240	440
Current Assets	430	479	612
Current Liabilities	18	42	19

Victorian Greenhouse NClosure
Long Paddock Peppershells Lane, Compton Dando, Bristol, BS39 4LL
Tel: 0845-0091237 **Fax:** 0871-6615701
E-mail: info@victoriangreenhouse.co.uk
Website: http://www.victoriangreenhouse.co.uk
Registration no: 06356981 **Product Groups:** 25, 30, 33, 35

Vitcas Ltd Refractories
8 Bonville Road, Bristol, BS4 5NZ
Tel: 0117-911 7895 **Fax:** 0117-971 1152
E-mail: info@vitcas.com
Website: http://www.vitcas.com
Managers: M. Meller (Admin Off)
Immediate Holding Company: VITCAS LTD
Registration no: 06497991 **VAT No.:** GB 567 5316 18
Date established: 2008 **Turnover:** £250,000 - £500,000
No.of Employees: 1 - 10 **Product Groups:** 32, 33

Date of Accounts	Apr 11	Apr 10	Apr 09
Sales Turnover	N/A	403	227
Pre Tax Profit/Loss	N/A	-5	-8
Working Capital	-45	-31	-7
Fixed Assets	57	42	27
Current Assets	198	151	89
Current Liabilities	N/A	41	24

Ward & Company Letters Ltd
Unit 18 Maze Street Barton Hill Trading Estate, Bristol, BS5 9TE
Tel: 0117-955 3385 **Fax:** 0117- 9557518
E-mail: info@ward-signs.co.uk
Website: http://www.ward-signs.co.uk
Directors: G. Hickling (Jt MD), A. Ward (Jt MD), A. Ward (Dir), G. Hickley (Dir)
Managers: J. Pachowsky (I.T. Exec)
Immediate Holding Company: WARD & CO. (LETTERS) LTD
Registration no: 00603289 **VAT No.:** 138 8668 19 **Date established:** 1958
Turnover: £250,000 - £500,000 **No.of Employees:** 1 - 10
Product Groups: 30, 35, 36, 37, 49

Date of Accounts	Jul 08	Jul 07	Jul 06
Working Capital	5	-1	-16
Fixed Assets	1	1	9
Current Assets	9	13	N/A
Current Liabilities	4	14	16

Thomas Ware & Sons Ltd
Coronation Road Southville, Bristol, BS3 1RN
Tel: 0117-966 4021 **Fax:** 0117-966 3885
E-mail: thomas.ware@btconnect.com
Website: http://www.thomasware.co.uk
Directors: P. Walley (Fin), A. Brearley (Dir)
Immediate Holding Company: THOMAS WARE & SONS LIMITED
Registration no: 00031652 **Date established:** 1990 **Turnover:** £2m - £5m
No.of Employees: 51 - 100 **Product Groups:** 22, 63

Date of Accounts	Dec 11	Dec 10	Dec 09
Sales Turnover	N/A	3m	3m
Pre Tax Profit/Loss	N/A	-141	-118
Working Capital	2m	3m	3m
Fixed Assets	716	747	794
Current Assets	3m	3m	3m
Current Liabilities	N/A	67	103

Waste Compaction Equipment Ltd
Unit 3-4 Soaphouse Industrial Estate Howard Street, Bristol, BS5 7AZ
Tel: 0117-955 6682 **Fax:** 0117-935 0185
E-mail: sales@wceltd.co.uk
Website: http://www.wceltd.co.uk
Directors: J. Laurence (Fin), J. Laurence (Dir & Buyer), R. Laurence (MD)
Immediate Holding Company: SOAPHOUSE ESTATE LIMITED
Registration no: 03708664 **VAT No.:** GB 138 4774 40
Date established: 1999 **Turnover:** £1m - £2m **No.of Employees:** 1 - 10
Product Groups: 42, 54

Date of Accounts	Mar 08	Mar 07	Mar 06
Working Capital	-201	-197	-141
Fixed Assets	311	326	346
Current Assets	24	102	90
Current Liabilities	225	298	231

Waste Handling Solutions Ltd
Unit 5 Crown Industrial Estate Crown Road, Warmley, Bristol, BS30 8JJ
Tel: 01454-228899 **Fax:** 01454-228805
E-mail: info@waste-handling-solutions.com
Website: http://www.waste-handling-solutions.com
Directors: E. Smith (Sales), P. Brown (MD)
Immediate Holding Company: WASTE HANDLING SOLUTIONS LIMITED
Registration no: 04171142 **Date established:** 2001
No.of Employees: 11 - 20 **Product Groups:** 41, 42, 43, 45, 48, 54, 67, 83

Date of Accounts	Mar 11	Mar 10	Mar 09
Working Capital	154	239	216
Fixed Assets	430	97	80
Current Assets	720	507	484

Watts Tyre & Rubber Co. Ltd
301 Dean Road, Bristol, BS11 8AT
Tel: 0117-982 4896 **Fax:** 0117-982 4896
Managers: R. Ray (Mgr)
No.of Employees: 1 - 10 **Product Groups:** 29, 68

Weatherproof Wall Coatings
Henroost Barn Old Gloucester Road, Winterbourne, Bristol, BS36 1RZ
Tel: 01454-777780 **Fax:** 01454-250917
Directors: P. Kelly (Prop)
Date established: 1998 **No.of Employees:** 1 - 10 **Product Groups:** 46, 48

Welding Products
4 Dean Court Great Western Business Park, Yate, Bristol, BS37 5NJ
Tel: 01454-312029 **Fax:** 01454-881088
E-mail: iestyngwyn@blueyonder.co.uk
Directors: I. Phillips (Prop)
Date established: 1983 **No.of Employees:** 1 - 10 **Product Groups:** 46

Weldmec Ltd
Unit 6a Marsh Lane Industrial Estate Marsh Lane, Easton-In-Gordano, Bristol, BS20 0NH
Tel: 01275-813840 **Fax:** 01275-813842
E-mail: barry.scaplehorn@gmail.com
Website: http://www.weldmecconstruction.co.uk
Directors: B. Scaplehorn (Dir)
No.of Employees: 11 - 20 **Product Groups:** 35, 40, 52, 84

Wessex Welding & Industrial Supplies Ltd
Unit 10 Brunel Court Dean Road, Yate, Bristol, BS37 5PD
Tel: 01454-311033 **Fax:** 01454-321871
E-mail: keith.larkin@boc.com
Website: http://www.leengate.com
Managers: K. Larkin (Mgr)
Ultimate Holding Company: BOC GROUP P.L.C.
Immediate Holding Company: LEENGATE WELDING GROUP LTD
Registration no: 03883456 **Turnover:** £500,000 - £1m
No.of Employees: 1 - 10 **Product Groups:** 24, 30, 33, 34, 35, 36, 37, 38, 40, 46, 48, 63, 66, 67, 83, 84

Date of Accounts	Dec 07	Dec 06	Sep 05
Sales Turnover	835	912	715
Pre Tax Profit/Loss	-16	-3	-31
Working Capital	-168	-155	-163
Fixed Assets	11	14	18
Current Assets	232	200	280
Current Liabilities	400	356	443
ROCE% (Return on Capital Employed)	10.0	2.0	21.1
ROT% (Return on Turnover)	-1.9	-0.3	-4.3

West Country Welding Supplies Ltd
4 Ashmead Business Centre Ashmead Road, Keynsham, Bristol, BS31 1SX
Tel: 0117-986 6006 **Fax:** 0117-986 1892
E-mail: sales@westcoweld.co.uk
Website: http://www.westcoweld.co.uk
Directors: G. Johnson (Fin), C. Elliott (MD)
Immediate Holding Company: WEST COUNTRY WELDING SUPPLIES LIMITED
Registration no: 03183375 **Date established:** 1996
No.of Employees: 11 - 20 **Product Groups:** 46

Date of Accounts	Sep 11	Sep 10	Sep 09
Working Capital	756	738	841
Fixed Assets	49	33	30
Current Assets	1m	1m	1m

West Technology Systems Ltd
Armstrong Way Great Western Business Park Yate, Bristol, BS37 5NG
Tel: 01454-329898 **Fax:** 01454-325154
E-mail: sales@west-technology.co.uk
Website: http://www.west-technology.co.uk
Directors: I. Harris (MD)
Immediate Holding Company: WEST TECHNOLOGY SYSTEMS LIMITED
Registration no: 02823838 **Date established:** 1993
No.of Employees: 11 - 20 **Product Groups:** 29, 30, 33, 35, 36, 37, 38, 40, 42, 45, 66, 67, 83, 84

Date of Accounts	Sep 11	Sep 10	Sep 09
Working Capital	144	-101	-177
Fixed Assets	368	352	374
Current Assets	772	918	699

Western Computer Group Ltd
Unit 4 Victoria House, Bristol, BS1 6PW
Tel: 0117-922 5661 **Fax:** 0117-922 6504
E-mail: bristol@western.co.uk
Website: http://www.western.co.uk
Bank(s): Lloyds TSB Bank plc
Directors: A. Dobson (Tech Serv), K. Courtman (MD), L. Ford (Sales)
Managers: P. Mills
Immediate Holding Company: WESTERN COMPUTER GROUP LIMITED
Registration no: 01850885 **VAT No.:** GB 329 0146 74
Date established: 1984 **Turnover:** £10m - £20m
No.of Employees: 11 - 20 **Product Groups:** 44, 67

Date of Accounts	Jan 09	Jan 11	Jan 10
Sales Turnover	8m	10m	8m
Pre Tax Profit/Loss	211	258	205
Working Capital	552	832	665
Fixed Assets	200	200	195
Current Assets	1m	2m	2m
Current Liabilities	407	478	423

Western Power Steering
Hanham Business Park Memorial Road, Bristol, BS15 3JE
Tel: 0117-960 2906 **Fax:** 0117-960 2910
E-mail: enquiries@westernpowersteering.co.uk
Website: http://www.westernpowersteering.co.uk
Directors: G. Brunwin (Prop)
No.of Employees: 1 - 10 **Product Groups:** 39, 40, 67, 68

Wheale Thomas Hodgins plc
Berkeley Square House 13 Berkeley Square, Bristol, BS8 1HB
Tel: 0117-927 2311 **Fax:** 0117-927 2315
E-mail: admin@wth.co.uk
Website: http://www.wth.co.uk
Bank(s): Lloyds TSB
Directors: A. Hodgins (Co Sec)
Managers: C. O'Regan (Sales Admin)
Ultimate Holding Company: PEOPLECARE (EUROPE) LIMITED
Immediate Holding Company: WHEALE THOMAS HODGINS PLC
Registration no: 02470369 **Date established:** 1990 **Turnover:** £1m - £2m
No.of Employees: 11 - 20 **Product Groups:** 80

Date of Accounts	Jun 11	Jun 10	Jun 09
Sales Turnover	1m	1m	1m
Pre Tax Profit/Loss	44	-43	-98
Working Capital	115	82	153
Fixed Assets	31	39	7
Current Assets	357	398	378
Current Liabilities	212	235	168

Wheelchair & Equipment Loan
83 Tower Road North, Bristol, BS30 8XP
Tel: 0117-301 2606 **Fax:** 0117-301 2615
Website: http://www.redcross.org.uk
Managers: J. Simon
Immediate Holding Company: ELECTRABUILD LIMITED
Registration no: 06854198 **Date established:** 2010
No.of Employees: 1 - 10 **Product Groups:** 38, 67

Date of Accounts	Dec 11	Dec 10	Dec 09
Working Capital	54	66	26
Fixed Assets	6	9	11
Current Assets	131	130	52

Whites Material Handling Ltd
10-12 Dixon Road, Bristol, BS4 5QW
Tel: 0117-972 0006 **Fax:** 0117-972 3296
E-mail: sales@whitesmh.co.uk
Website: http://www.whitesmh.co.uk
Bank(s): Bank of Scotland
Directors: L. Sinclair (Fin), P. White (MD)
Ultimate Holding Company: F & B PROFILES (HOLDINGS) LIMITED
Immediate Holding Company: WHITES MATERIAL HANDLING LIMITED
Registration no: 01248229 **VAT No.:** GB 609 5442 35
Date established: 1976 **Turnover:** £5m - £10m **No.of Employees:** 21 - 50
Product Groups: 45

Date of Accounts	Mar 12	Mar 11	Mar 10
Sales Turnover	6m	4m	2m
Pre Tax Profit/Loss	121	219	135
Working Capital	2m	2m	2m
Fixed Assets	317	117	81
Current Assets	4m	4m	3m
Current Liabilities	273	172	147

Alan Williams & Co Bristol Ltd
4 Bonville Business Centre Dixon Road, Bristol, BS4 5QQ
Tel: 0117-971 7606 **Fax:** 0117-971 7366
E-mail: bristol@alanwilliams.co.uk
Website: http://www.alanwilliams.co.uk
Directors: A. Williams (MD)
Immediate Holding Company: ALAN WILLIAMS AND CO (BRISTOL) LIMITED
Registration no: 02035320 **Date established:** 1986
No.of Employees: 1 - 10 **Product Groups:** 39, 40, 48, 52

Date of Accounts	Apr 11	Apr 10	Apr 09
Working Capital	-2	-2	-2
Fixed Assets	2	2	3
Current Assets	469	366	413

Wilts & Cloud Electrical Wholesalers
Unit 3 Jacob Street, Bristol, BS2 0HG
Tel: 0117-925 4300 **Fax:** 0117-925 8303
E-mail: bristol@wilts.co.uk
Website: http://www.wilts.co.uk

Managers: R. Lowther (Mgr)
Immediate Holding Company: WILTS WHOLESALE ELECTRICAL COMPANY,LIMITED
Registration no: 00679117 **VAT No.:** GB 422 9006 79
Date established: 1960 **Turnover:** £500m - £1,000m
No.of Employees: 1 - 10 **Product Groups:** 37

Wrapex Ltd
Unit 6 Lodge Causeway, Bristol, BS16 3JB
Tel: 0117-965 7000 **Fax:** 0117-935 3212
E-mail: graham@wrapex.co.uk
Website: http://www.wrapex.co.uk
Bank(s): HSBC
Directors: G. New (Dir)
Immediate Holding Company: WRAPEX LIMITED
Registration no: 02981251 **VAT No.:** 639 6106 25 **Date established:** 1994
No.of Employees: 21 - 50 **Product Groups:** 34

Date of Accounts	Sep 11	Sep 10	Sep 09
Working Capital	-146	-266	183
Fixed Assets	550	687	678
Current Assets	2m	2m	1m

Wright Minimix
2 St Ivel Way, Bristol, BS30 8TY
Tel: 0117-958 2090 **Fax:** 0117-967 1673
E-mail: sales@wrightminimix.co.uk
Website: http://www.wrightminimix.co.uk
Directors: L. Wright (Prop)
Managers: G. Ogdon (Comm)
Immediate Holding Company: WRIGHT MINIMIX LIMITED
Registration no: 03772583 **Date established:** 1999 **Turnover:** £1m - £2m
No.of Employees: 21 - 50 **Product Groups:** 33, 40, 45, 52, 83

Date of Accounts	Jun 11	Jun 10	Jun 09
Working Capital	229	22	-136
Fixed Assets	1m	856	926
Current Assets	2m	2m	2m

WTB Geotechnics
Earl Russell Way Lawrence Hill, Bristol, BS5 0WT
Tel: 0845-6005505 **Fax:** 0845-6092525
E-mail: geotechnics@wtbgroup.com
Website: http://www.geotechnics-uk.com
Managers: T. Martin (Works Gen Mgr)
Registration no: 04420255 **Date established:** 1998
No.of Employees: 1 - 10 **Product Groups:** 23, 35

Wyman Dillon
Silverhill Rudgeway, Bristol, BS35 3NS
Tel: 01454-200000 **Fax:** 01454-200002
E-mail: mail@wymandillon.co.uk
Website: http://www.wymandillon.co.uk
Bank(s): Lloyds
Directors: A. Douglas (MD), L. Dare (Dir)
Immediate Holding Company: WYMAN DILLON LIMITED
Registration no: 01266200 **Date established:** 1976 **Turnover:** £1m - £2m
No.of Employees: 21 - 50 **Product Groups:** 81

Date of Accounts	May 11	May 10	May 09
Working Capital	93	86	110
Fixed Assets	75	90	119
Current Assets	376	232	278
Current Liabilities	164	N/A	N/A

Xena Batteries Ltd
Morialta The Inner Down, Old Down, Bristol, BS32 4PR
Tel: 01454-414135 **Fax:** 01454-419385
E-mail: xenabatteries@tiscali.co.uk
Website: http://www.xenoenergy.com
Directors: P. Trott (Fin), H. Trott (MD)
Immediate Holding Company: XENA BATTERIES LIMITED
Registration no: 04408574 **VAT No.:** GB 793 5159 92
Date established: 2002 **Turnover:** Up to £250,000
No.of Employees: 1 - 10 **Product Groups:** 37, 67

Date of Accounts	Apr 11	Apr 09	Apr 08
Working Capital	-3	-15	2
Fixed Assets	4	8	1
Current Assets	24	13	42

Zephyr Services
Dorlea Cameley Road, Temple Cloud, Bristol, BS39 5AF
Tel: 01761-453888
Directors: R. Fisher (Ptnr)
Date established: 1989 **No.of Employees:** 1 - 10 **Product Groups:** 20, 40, 41

Zuken
1500 Aztec West Almondsbury, Bristol, BS32 4RF
Tel: 01454-207800 **Fax:** 01454-207803
E-mail: info@zuken.co.uk
Website: http://www.zuken.com
Bank(s): Barclays
Directors: G. Lipski (Sales)
Managers: M. Williams (Tech Serv Mgr), B. Evans (Personnel), M. Sandham (Comptroller), M. Knight (Mktg Serv Mgr), C. Brown (Sales Prom Mgr)
Ultimate Holding Company: ZUKEN INC (JAPAN)
Immediate Holding Company: ZUKEN UK LIMITED
Registration no: 01477257 **Date established:** 1980 **Turnover:** £2m - £5m
No.of Employees: 51 - 100 **Product Groups:** 44, 84

Date of Accounts	Mar 11	Mar 10	Mar 09
Sales Turnover	4m	3m	3m
Pre Tax Profit/Loss	15	-319	-64
Working Capital	-585	-582	-188
Fixed Assets	31	88	88
Current Assets	3m	2m	2m
Current Liabilities	2m	1m	1m

Clevedon

4d Lighting Ltd
Unit 5b Yeo Bank Business Park Kenn Road, Kenn, Clevedon, BS21 6UW
Tel: 01275-349383 **Fax:** 08700-100185
Website: http://www.4dlighting.co.uk
Directors: D. Summers (Co Sec), S. Sutcliffe (MD)
Immediate Holding Company: 4D LIGHTING LIMITED
Registration no: 04675355 **Date established:** 2003
No.of Employees: 1 - 10 **Product Groups:** 37, 67

Date of Accounts	Oct 11	Oct 10	Mar 10
Working Capital	14	34	-29
Fixed Assets	36	20	33
Current Assets	253	259	116

B P L Services
Unit 31-32 Hither Green, Clevedon, BS21 6XU
Tel: 01275-878339 **Fax:** 01275-343752
Website: http://www.bplservices.com
Directors: C. Smyth (Dir)
Date established: 1997 **No.of Employees:** 1 - 10 **Product Groups:** 46, 48

Britannia Windows
Kimberley Road, Clevedon, BS21 6QJ
Tel: 01275-878153 **Fax:** 01275-343134
E-mail: info@britanniawindows.co.uk
Website: http://www.britanniawindows.co.uk
Bank(s): Lloyds TSB Bank plc
Directors: H. Rushton (MD)
Managers: S. Threasher (Ops Mgr), S. Harris
Immediate Holding Company: BRITANNIA WINDOWS (UK) LIMITED
Registration no: 01641907 **VAT No.:** GB 303 2173 14
Date established: 1982 **Turnover:** £500,000 - £1m
No.of Employees: 21 - 50 **Product Groups:** 30

Date of Accounts	Sep 11	Sep 10	Sep 09
Working Capital	450	278	144
Fixed Assets	3m	3m	4m
Current Assets	2m	2m	1m

C B C Design
12 Jubilee Place, Clevedon, BS21 5EA
Tel: 07768-206649 **Fax:** 01275-878362
E-mail: cbcdesign@o2.co.uk
Website: http://www.cbcdesign.co.uk
Directors: A. Fidler (Prop)
No.of Employees: 1 - 10 **Product Groups:** 37, 38, 63

Create Flavours Ltd
11 Windmill Business Park Windmill Road, Kenn, Clevedon, BS21 6SR
Tel: 01275-349300 **Fax:** 01275-349800
E-mail: enquiries@createflavours.com
Website: http://www.createflavours.com
Directors: J. Jones (Dir), A. Matthews (Fin)
Immediate Holding Company: CREATE FLAVOURS LIMITED
Registration no: 04540927 **Date established:** 2002
Turnover: £10m - £20m **No.of Employees:** 1 - 10 **Product Groups:** 20

Date of Accounts	Aug 11	Aug 10	Aug 09
Working Capital	553	281	82
Fixed Assets	69	78	62
Current Assets	757	511	273

Dart Services
12a Hill Road, Clevedon, BS21 7NZ
Tel: 01275-799777 **Fax:** 01275-799778
E-mail: admin@dart-services.co.uk
Website: http://www.dartbusinesssolutions.co.uk
Directors: B. Ford (MD), M. Ford (Fin)
Immediate Holding Company: DART ACCOUNTANCY & SOFTWARE LIMITED
Registration no: 03687002 **Date established:** 1998
No.of Employees: 1 - 10 **Product Groups:** 44

Gordano Ltd
Unit 1 Yeo Bank Business Park Kenn Road, Kenn, Clevedon, BS21 6UW
Tel: 01275-345100 **Fax:** 01275-345132
E-mail: sales@gordano.com
Website: http://www.gordano.com
Directors: L. Kirman (Chief Op Offcr)
Immediate Holding Company: GORDANO LIMITED
Registration no: 04754464 **Date established:** 2003
No.of Employees: 11 - 20 **Product Groups:** 44, 67

Date of Accounts	Dec 11	Dec 10	Dec 09
Working Capital	96	224	285
Fixed Assets	268	173	1
Current Assets	356	535	707

Interwest Ltd
Unit 1 Kimberley Road, Clevedon, BS21 6QJ
Tel: 01275-870600 **Fax:** 01275-340305
E-mail: admin@interwestltd.co.uk
Website: http://www.interwestltd.co.uk
Directors: H. Harris (Fin)
Managers: J. Bessant
Immediate Holding Company: INTERWEST LIMITED
Registration no: 01798294 **VAT No.:** GB 397 4240 25
Date established: 1984 **Turnover:** £250,000 - £500,000
No.of Employees: 11 - 20 **Product Groups:** 35

Date of Accounts	May 11	May 10	Mar 10
Working Capital	377	436	436
Fixed Assets	60	13	13
Current Assets	771	649	649
Current Liabilities	354	N/A	N/A

Labcaire Systems Ltd
175 Kenn Road, Clevedon, BS21 6LH
Tel: 01275-793000 **Fax:** 01275-341313
E-mail: simonk@labcaire.co.uk
Website: http://www.labcaire.co.uk
Bank(s): HSBC, 30 High St, Weston Super Mare, BS23 1SE
Directors: G. Oliver (Tech Serv), G. Keare (MD)
Managers: D. Pomeroy (Mktg Serv Mgr)
Ultimate Holding Company: Misonix Inc (U.S.A.)
Registration no: 02683459 **Date established:** 1992 **Turnover:** £5m - £10m
No.of Employees: 51 - 100 **Product Groups:** 26, 30, 35, 38, 40, 42, 52, 67, 83, 84, 85

Date of Accounts	Jun 09	Jun 08	Jun 07
Sales Turnover	9m	7m	6m
Pre Tax Profit/Loss	-190	-340	592
Working Capital	-648	-406	-56
Fixed Assets	1m	1m	1m
Current Assets	5m	5m	4m
Current Liabilities	2m	2m	1m

P R Forklifts
Lift 4 Lessunit 5a Tweed Road, Clevedon, BS21 6RR
Tel: 01275-874333 **Fax:** 01275-876173
E-mail: paul@prforklifts.com
Website: http://www.prforklifts.com
Directors: P. Jarvis (Ptnr), P. Jarvis (Sales)
Immediate Holding Company: PR FORKLIFTS LIMITED
Registration no: 06531049 **Date established:** 2008
No.of Employees: 11 - 20 **Product Groups:** 35, 39, 45

Date of Accounts	Oct 04	Apr 08	Apr 07
Sales Turnover	3m	3m	2m
Pre Tax Profit/Loss	43	-104	-509
Working Capital	-518	-542	-750
Fixed Assets	5m	2m	2m
Current Assets	1m	807	688
Current Liabilities	252	201	230

Pipeline Products Ltd
Unit 15 Five C Business Centre Concorde Drive, Clevedon, BS21 6UH
Tel: 01275-873103 **Fax:** 01275-873801
E-mail: info@pipelineproducts.ltd.uk
Website: http://www.pipelineproducts.ltd.uk
Directors: R. Anderson (MD), J. Evans (Fin)
Ultimate Holding Company: PIPELINE PRODUCTS HOLDINGS LTD
Immediate Holding Company: PIPELINE PRODUCTS LIMITED
Registration no: 01805228 **Date established:** 1984
No.of Employees: 1 - 10 **Product Groups:** 36

Date of Accounts	Dec 11	Dec 10	Dec 09
Working Capital	757	530	178
Fixed Assets	43	42	344
Current Assets	1m	1m	837

The Resource Group P.L.C.
Clevedon Hall Victoria Road, Clevedon, BS21 7RQ
Tel: 01275-344344 **Fax:** 01275-344101
E-mail: response@trgworld.com
Website: http://www.trgworld.com
Directors: C. Hollanby (Ch & MD), P. Hollanby (MD), M. Chagla (Fin)
Managers: D. Jones (Sales Prom Mgr), K. Kirby (Mktg Serv Mgr), S. Pullar (I.T. Exec), L. Mctaggart
Registration no: 01570098 **Turnover:** £5m - £10m
No.of Employees: 51 - 100 **Product Groups:** 37, 79, 84

S K F UK Ltd
Strode Road, Clevedon, BS21 6QQ
Tel: 01275-876021 **Fax:** 01275-878480
E-mail: mail@ampep.co.uk
Website: http://www.sks.co.uk
Bank(s): Societe Generale, Valance
Managers: F. Vonelek (Site Co-ord)
Ultimate Holding Company: AKTIEBOLAGET SKF (SWEDEN)
Immediate Holding Company: SKF (U.K) LIMITED
Registration no: 00107367 **VAT No.:** GB 223 6367 72
Date established: 2010 **No.of Employees:** 101 - 250 **Product Groups:** 39

Date of Accounts	Dec 11	Dec 10	Dec 09
Sales Turnover	251m	203m	182m
Pre Tax Profit/Loss	54m	35m	21m
Working Capital	83m	64m	76m
Fixed Assets	19m	20m	18m
Current Assets	120m	97m	107m
Current Liabilities	19m	16m	16m

Sewing Unit Developments
22a Griffin Road, Clevedon, BS21 6HH
Tel: 01275-878509 **Fax:** 01275-340897
E-mail: info@sewingunitdevelopments.co.uk
Website: http://www.sewingunitdevelopments.co.uk
Directors: L. Owen (Ptnr)
Immediate Holding Company: HARRIS'S SPORTS LIMITED
Date established: 1986 **No.of Employees:** 1 - 10 **Product Groups:** 43

Date of Accounts	Jul 11	Jul 10	Jul 09
Working Capital	-71	-53	-33
Fixed Assets	8	11	7
Current Assets	115	144	141

Technical Inspection Services UK Ltd
11 Somerset Road, Clevedon, BS21 6DP
Tel: 01275-871130 **Fax:** 01275-875917
E-mail: services@tis-uk.co.uk
Website: http://www.tis-uk.co.uk
Directors: K. Stockham (MD)
Immediate Holding Company: TECHNICAL INSPECTION SERVICES (U.K.) LIMITED
Registration no: 01583998 **Date established:** 1981
Turnover: £500,000 - £1m **No.of Employees:** 1 - 10 **Product Groups:** 85

Date of Accounts	Mar 12	Mar 11	Mar 10
Sales Turnover	982	302	1m
Pre Tax Profit/Loss	225	46	293
Working Capital	156	39	208
Fixed Assets	209	209	70
Current Assets	213	85	287
Current Liabilities	38	10	67

Thule Ltd
Five C Business Centre Concorde Drive, Clevedon, BS21 6UH
Tel: 01275-340404 **Fax:** 01275-340686
E-mail: info@thule.co.uk
Website: http://www.thule.co.uk
Bank(s): Handels
Managers: P. Barker (Chief Mgr)
Ultimate Holding Company: THULE INVESTMENTS AB (SWEDEN)
Immediate Holding Company: THULE LIMITED
Registration no: 02476936 **VAT No.:** 567 3625 15 **Date established:** 1990
Turnover: £5m - £10m **No.of Employees:** 11 - 20 **Product Groups:** 39, 68

Date of Accounts	Dec 10	Dec 09	Dec 07
Working Capital	1m	1m	1m
Current Assets	1m	1m	1m

Triangle Lift Services Ltd
8 Windmill Business Park Windmill Road, Kenn, Clevedon, BS21 6SR
Tel: 01275-344050 **Fax:** 01275-344051
E-mail: service@trianglelifts.co.uk
Website: http://www.trianglelifts.co.uk
Directors: R. Hooper (MD), S. Hooper (Fin)
Immediate Holding Company: TRIANGLE LIFT SERVICES LIMITED
Registration no: 03262929 **Date established:** 1996
No.of Employees: 21 - 50 **Product Groups:** 35, 39, 45

Date of Accounts	Nov 11	Nov 10	Nov 09
Working Capital	642	594	528
Fixed Assets	146	112	135
Current Assets	2m	1m	1m

Willcocks Engineering Avon Ltd

Pizey Avenue, Clevedon, BS21 7TS
Tel: 01275-873035 **Fax:** 01275-870209
E-mail: willcocksavon@btconnect.com
Website: http://www.willcocksengineering.co.uk
Bank(s): National Westminster
Directors: G. Woollard (MD)
Immediate Holding Company: WILLCOCKS ENGINEERING (AVON) LIMITED
Registration no: 01255864 **VAT No.:** GB 140 3291 09
Date established: 1976 **Turnover:** £500,000 - £1m
No.of Employees: 11 - 20 **Product Groups:** 48, 84

Date of Accounts	Mar 11	Mar 10	Mar 09
Working Capital	163	123	119
Fixed Assets	46	43	51
Current Assets	280	177	242

Radstock

A P Sales

Unit 19 Midsomer Enterprise Park Radstock Road, Midsomer Norton, Radstock, BA3 2BB
Tel: 01761-411773 **Fax:** 01761-411761
E-mail: dave@apsales.entadsl.com
Website: http://www.apsales.ltd.uk
Directors: D. Pritchard (Dir)
Immediate Holding Company: A.P. SALES LIMITED
Registration no: 04440839 **Date established:** 2002
Turnover: £250,000 - £500,000 **No.of Employees:** 1 - 10
Product Groups: 40, 45, 48, 67

Date of Accounts	Apr 11	Apr 10	Apr 09
Working Capital	13	-8	79
Fixed Assets	8	9	12
Current Assets	67	65	79

Air Cargo Express (incorporating Sea Cargo Express & A J Williams Shipping)

Fourth Avenue Westfield Industrial Estate, Midsomer Norton, Radstock, BA3 4XE
Tel: 01761-410185 **Fax:** 01761-410868
E-mail: aircargouk@googlemail.com
Website: http://www.aircargoexpress.co.uk
Directors: I. Ottway (Dir)
No.of Employees: 1 - 10 **Product Groups:** 76, 79

Avon Steel Co. Ltd

Unit 18 Midsomer Enterprise Park Radstock Road, Midsomer Norton, Radstock, BA3 2BB
Tel: 01761-416721 **Fax:** 01761-412870
E-mail: sales@avonsteel.co.uk
Website: http://www.avonsteel.co.uk
Bank(s): Bank of Scotland
Directors: S. Parson (MD)
Immediate Holding Company: AVON STEEL COMPANY LIMITED
Registration no: 01346397 **VAT No.:** GB 318 7572 35
Date established: 1977 **Turnover:** £5m - £10m **No.of Employees:** 21 - 50
Product Groups: 66

Date of Accounts	Dec 11	Dec 10	Dec 09
Sales Turnover	9m	9m	8m
Pre Tax Profit/Loss	-71	47	-159
Working Capital	474	547	489
Fixed Assets	335	315	350
Current Assets	3m	3m	2m
Current Liabilities	157	143	73

Beechcraft Ltd

First Avenue Westfield Industrial Estate, Midsomer Norton, Radstock, BA3 4BS
Tel: 01761-416642 **Fax:** 01761-419267
E-mail: dhbeech@aol.com
Website: http://www.beechcraft-ltd.com
Directors: P. Quennell (Fin), D. Beech (Grp Chief Exec)
Managers: P. Oxley (Purch Mgr)
Immediate Holding Company: BEECHCRAFT LIMITED
Registration no: 01023029 **Date established:** 1971 **Turnover:** £2m - £5m
No.of Employees: 51 - 100 **Product Groups:** 30

Date of Accounts	Mar 12	Mar 11	Mar 10
Working Capital	307	245	182
Fixed Assets	119	127	107
Current Assets	712	664	476

BOCM Pauls Ltd

Mill Road, Radstock, BA3 5TT
Tel: 01761-438055 **Fax:** 01275-373828
E-mail: info@bocmpauls.co.uk
Website: http://www.bocmpauls.co.uk
Managers: A. Sandsfield, D. Purse (Ops Mgr), J. Foulger (Fin Mgr), N. Sudds (Personnel)
Ultimate Holding Company: AGRICOLA GROUP LIMITED
Immediate Holding Company: BOCM PAULS LTD
Registration no: 00062904 **Date established:** 1999
Turnover: £500m - £1,000m **No.of Employees:** 21 - 50
Product Groups: 20

Date of Accounts	Dec 10	Dec 09	Dec 08
Sales Turnover	425m	401m	473m
Pre Tax Profit/Loss	11m	4m	762
Working Capital	75m	61m	65m
Fixed Assets	70m	67m	65m
Current Assets	149m	130m	147m
Current Liabilities	8m	6m	6m

C A M Tyre & Welding Co. Ltd

Frome Road, Radstock, BA3 3PY
Tel: 01761-434226 **Fax:** 01761-435541
E-mail: enquiries@camequipment.co.uk
Website: http://www.camequipment.co.uk
Directors: N. Corp (Dir)
Ultimate Holding Company: MALTARCH LIMITED
Immediate Holding Company: CAM TYRE AND WELDING COMPANY LIMITED
Registration no: 01165230 **VAT No.:** GB 140 1246 24
Date established: 1974 **Turnover:** £500,000 - £1m
No.of Employees: 11 - 20 **Product Groups:** 39, 45, 68

Date of Accounts	Aug 11	Aug 10	Aug 09
Working Capital	83	42	-19
Fixed Assets	54	45	57
Current Assets	211	171	186

C F H Total Document Management Ltd (Continu-Forms Ltd)

St Peter S Park Wells Road Radstock, Radstock, BA3 3UP
Tel: 01761-416311 **Fax:** 01761-409700
E-mail: sales@cfh.com
Website: http://www.cfh.com
Bank(s): National Westminster Bank Plc
Directors: B. McFedries (Tech Serv), J. Helps (Fin), C. Clarke (Pers), P. Clarke (Sales), D. Broadway (MD), J. Marsh (Comm)
Ultimate Holding Company: CFH TOTAL DOCUMENT MANAGEMENT LTD
Immediate Holding Company: CFH TOTAL DOCUMENT MANAGEMENT LTD
Registration no: 01716891 **VAT No.:** GB 398 7084 89
Date established: 1983 **Turnover:** £20m - £50m
No.of Employees: 101 - 250 **Product Groups:** 27, 28, 80, 81

Date of Accounts	Mar 12	Mar 11	Mar 10
Sales Turnover	25m	28m	26m
Pre Tax Profit/Loss	582	538	117
Working Capital	20	34	199
Fixed Assets	6m	5m	5m
Current Assets	5m	6m	6m
Current Liabilities	3m	3m	3m

Code A Weld Holdings Ltd

2nd Avenue Westfield Trading Estate Charlton Lane, Midsomer Norton, Radstock, BA3 4BE
Tel: 01761-410410 **Fax:** 01761-418388
E-mail: info@codeaweld.com
Website: http://www.codeaweld.com
Bank(s): Lloyds TSB Bank plc
Directors: D. Millington (MD)
Managers: A. Gould (Sales Prom Mgr)
Immediate Holding Company: CODE A WELD HOLDINGS LIMITED
Registration no: 04217426 **Date established:** 2001
Turnover: Up to £250,000 **No.of Employees:** 11 - 20 **Product Groups:** 85

Date of Accounts	Mar 11	Mar 10	Mar 09
Working Capital	-20	-1	-50
Fixed Assets	83	92	124
Current Assets	316	271	295

Coltraco Ltd

Chewton Fields Farm Ston Easton, Radstock, BA3 4BX
Tel: 01761-241601 **Fax:** 01761-241685
E-mail: ghchunter@coltraco.co.uk
Website: http://www.coltraco.co.uk
Directors: E. Hunter (Tech Serv), G. Hunter (Dir)
Managers: L. Jones (Export Sales Mg), D. Crookenden (Sales Prom Mgr), E. Freebody (Purch Mgr)
Immediate Holding Company: COLTRACO LIMITED
Registration no: 02955021 **Date established:** 1994
No.of Employees: 11 - 20 **Product Groups:** 37, 38, 40, 45, 49

Date of Accounts	Dec 07	Dec 06	Dec 05
Working Capital	-1	-32	-33
Fixed Assets	1	2	2
Current Assets	46	28	16
Current Liabilities	47	60	49

Delkor UK Ltd

Unit C First Avenue, Midsomer Norton, Radstock, BA3 4BS
Tel: 01761-417079 **Fax:** 01761-414435
Website: http://www.delkorglobal.co.uk
Bank(s): Barclays
Managers: S. Hull, R. Talkal (Sales Prom Mgr)
Ultimate Holding Company: IST INDUSTRIAL (PTY) LTD (SOUTH AFRICA)
Immediate Holding Company: DELKOR LIMITED
Registration no: 01327392 **VAT No.:** GB 242 1791 76
Date established: 1977 **Turnover:** £2m - £5m **No.of Employees:** 11 - 20
Product Groups: 42, 54

Date of Accounts	Dec 04	Dec 03	Dec 02
Sales Turnover	3m	4m	3m
Pre Tax Profit/Loss	80	-44	-362
Working Capital	-151	-248	-204
Fixed Assets	523	525	508
Current Assets	1m	1m	2m
Current Liabilities	324	188	90

Dickies Workwear

Second Avenue Westfield Trading Estate, Midsomer Norton, Radstock, BA3 4BH
Tel: 01761-419419 **Fax:** 01761-414825
E-mail: eurosales@dickies.com
Website: http://www.dickiesworkwear.com
Bank(s): HSBC Bank plc
Directors: C. Ford (Fin), M. Morton (Sales & Mktg), M. Strange (MD)
Managers: S. Cooper, J. Clay, K. Ehrlich, N. Silivestros, S. Longden (Export Sales Mg)
Ultimate Holding Company: Williamson-Dickie Manufacturing Co. (USA)
Immediate Holding Company: Williamson Dickie-Manufacturing (UK) Ltd
Registration no: 01757853 **VAT No.:** GB 543 3724 51
Date established: 1983 **Turnover:** £20m - £50m
No.of Employees: 101 - 250 **Product Groups:** 22, 24, 29, 31, 40

Date of Accounts	Dec 11	Dec 10	Dec 09
Sales Turnover	54m	45m	36m
Pre Tax Profit/Loss	2m	1m	1m
Working Capital	13m	13m	16m
Fixed Assets	6m	5m	4m
Current Assets	26m	26m	24m
Current Liabilities	3m	5m	2m

Facade Hoists Ltd

Acl House Coombend, Radstock, BA3 3AS
Tel: 01761-434929 **Fax:** 01761-432271
E-mail: info@facadehoists.co.uk
Website: http://www.facadehoists.co.uk
Directors: G. Wilson (Dir), L. Wilson (Fin)
Immediate Holding Company: FACADE HOISTS LIMITED
Registration no: 06096464 **Date established:** 2007
Turnover: £500,000 - £1m **No.of Employees:** 21 - 50
Product Groups: 35, 39, 45

Date of Accounts	Jun 12	Jun 11	Jun 10
Working Capital	465	452	306
Fixed Assets	55	60	36
Current Assets	571	596	449

Flowco Ltd

Unit 27 Midsomer Enterprise Park Radstock Road, Midsomer Norton, Radstock, BA3 2BB
Tel: 01761-411440 **Fax:** 01761-411449
E-mail: steve@flowcoltd.co.ukflowcoltd.co.uk
Website: http://www.flowco.ltd.uk
Directors: S. Alsop (MD)
Immediate Holding Company: FLOWCO LIMITED
Registration no: 02891839 **Date established:** 1994
No.of Employees: 11 - 20 **Product Groups:** 36, 37, 38

Date of Accounts	Jun 11	Jun 10	Jun 09
Working Capital	176	182	133
Fixed Assets	180	62	60
Current Assets	471	344	299

G W E Business West

Unit 22 Midsomer Enterprise Park Radstock Road, Midsomer Norton, Radstock, BA3 2BB
Tel: 01761-411800 **Fax:** 01761-411431
E-mail: info.wansdyke@businesswest.co.uk
Website: http://www.businesswest.co.uk
Managers: R. Gilbertson
Immediate Holding Company: JOHN BRAITHWAITE FOODS LIMITED
Date established: 1993 **Turnover:** £250,000 - £500,000
No.of Employees: 1 - 10 **Product Groups:** 69

Date of Accounts	Mar 12	Mar 11	Mar 10
Working Capital	925	869	774
Fixed Assets	179	182	184
Current Assets	1m	1m	956

The Green Consultancy

Unit D Second Avenue Westfield Industrial Estate, Midsomer Norton, Radstock, BA3 4BH
Tel: 08450-176300 **Fax:** 0845-017 6277
E-mail: manager@greenconsultancy.com
Website: http://www.greenconsultancy.com
Directors: J. Treble (MD)
Immediate Holding Company: THE GREEN CONSULTANCY LIMITED
Registration no: 05129033 **VAT No.:** GB 200 2924 21
Date established: 2004 **Turnover:** £250,000 - £500,000
No.of Employees: 1 - 10 **Product Groups:** 54, 80, 84

Date of Accounts	Oct 11	Oct 10	Oct 09
Working Capital	16	38	43
Fixed Assets	15	18	23
Current Assets	177	127	122

H C L Fasteners Ltd

Unit 4 First Avenue Midsomer Norton, Radstock, BA3 4BS
Tel: 01761-417714 **Fax:** 01761-417710
E-mail: sales@hcl-clamping.co.uk
Website: http://www.hclfasteners.co.uk
Directors: D. Coles (MD)
Immediate Holding Company: HCL FASTENERS LIMITED
Registration no: 02860032 **VAT No.:** GB 639 3894 86
Date established: 1993 **Turnover:** £1m - £2m **No.of Employees:** 1 - 10
Product Groups: 30, 36, 46

Date of Accounts	Dec 11	Dec 10	Dec 09
Working Capital	577	503	523
Fixed Assets	387	489	535
Current Assets	720	713	604

H Z Sound Systems

Combe House Giddy Lane, Stoke St Michael, Radstock, BA3 5HN
Tel: 01749-840102 **Fax:** 01749-840887
E-mail: tech@hzsoundsystems.com
Website: http://www.hzsoundsystems.com
Directors: L. Roch (Dir)
Registration no: 01979936 **Date established:** 1986
Turnover: £500,000 - £1m **No.of Employees:** 1 - 10 **Product Groups:** 37

Ian Hobbs Technical Services Ltd

Unit 40a Charlton Lane Midsomer Norton, Radstock, BA3 4BD
Tel: 01761-414356 **Fax:** 01761-414778
E-mail: info@ianhobbs.com
Website: http://www.ianhobbs.com
Bank(s): National Westminster Bank Plc
Directors: I. Hobbs (MD)
Managers: L. Hobbs (Develop Mgr), D. Bradley (Chief Acct)
Immediate Holding Company: IAN HOBBS TECHNICAL SERVICES LIMITED
Registration no: 02830447 **VAT No.:** GB 399 0768 88
Date established: 1993 **Turnover:** £2m - £5m **No.of Employees:** 11 - 20
Product Groups: 40, 52, 66

Date of Accounts	Jun 11	Jun 10	Jun 09
Working Capital	-140	-130	-65
Fixed Assets	1m	1m	1m
Current Assets	449	436	342

Jewson Ltd

Unit 1 St Peters Park Cobblers Way, Radstock, BA3 3BX
Tel: 01761-413531 **Fax:** 01761-413514
Website: http://www.jewson.co.uk
Directors: P. Hindle (MD)
Managers: S. Desborough (District Mgr)
Ultimate Holding Company: COMPAGNIE DE SAINT GOBAIN (FRANCE)
Immediate Holding Company: JEWSON LIMITED
Registration no: 00348407 **VAT No.:** GB 497 7184 83
Date established: 1939 **Turnover:** £2m - £5m **No.of Employees:** 1 - 10
Product Groups: 66

Date of Accounts	Dec 11	Dec 10	Dec 09
Sales Turnover	1606m	1547m	1485m
Pre Tax Profit/Loss	18m	100m	45m
Working Capital	-345m	-250m	-349m
Fixed Assets	496m	387m	461m
Current Assets	657m	1005m	1320m
Current Liabilities	66m	120m	64m

K M Steel Fabrications Ltd

Unit 17 & Unit 71 Haydon Industrial Estate, Radstock, BA3 3RD
Tel: 01761-435646 **Fax:** 01761-437899
Directors: J. Steel (Fin), K. Steel (MD)
Immediate Holding Company: K.M. STEEL FABRICATIONS LIMITED
Registration no: 03448459 **Date established:** 1997
No.of Employees: 1 - 10 **Product Groups:** 26, 35

Date of Accounts	Sep 11	Sep 10	Sep 09
Working Capital	419	454	374
Fixed Assets	86	94	105
Current Assets	577	641	517

M M A Architectural Systems Ltd

Broadway House Second Avenue Westfield Industrial Estate, Midsomer Norton, Radstock, BA3 4BH
Tel: 01761-419427 **Fax:** 08451-300136
E-mail: sales@jakob.co.uk
Website: http://www.jakob.co.uk
Directors: J. Errington (Dir)
Immediate Holding Company: MMA ARCHITECTURAL SYSTEMS LIMITED
Registration no: 06342130 **Date established:** 2007
No.of Employees: 1 - 10 **Product Groups:** 23, 34, 35, 41

Date of Accounts	Mar 12	Mar 11	Mar 10
Working Capital	110	109	116
Fixed Assets	224	249	135
Current Assets	376	278	268
Current Liabilities	N/A	N/A	56

Machines 4 Food Ltd

Unit 40 Second Avenue Westfield Industrial Estate, Midsomer Norton, Radstock, BA3 4BH
Tel: 01761-410345 **Fax:** 01761-410332
E-mail: sales@machines4food.co.uk
Website: http://www.machines4food.co.uk
Directors: R. Davies (Dir)
Immediate Holding Company: MACHINES 4 FOOD LTD
Registration no: 04702598 **Date established:** 2003
No.of Employees: 1 - 10 **Product Groups:** 20, 40, 41

Date of Accounts	May 11	May 10	May 09
Working Capital	138	145	71
Fixed Assets	28	29	35
Current Assets	377	343	293

Mendip Engineering Ltd

Mendip House Pows Orchard, Midsomer Norton, Radstock, BA3 2HY
Tel: 01761-413698 **Fax:** 01761-416172
E-mail: office@mendipengineering.co.uk
Website: http://www.mendipengineering.co.uk
Bank(s): National Westminster
Directors: I. Friend (Dir)
Immediate Holding Company: MENDIP ENGINEERING LIMITED
Registration no: 02578177 **VAT No.:** GB 543 5184 47
Date established: 1991 **Turnover:** Up to £250,000
No.of Employees: 11 - 20 **Product Groups:** 84

Date of Accounts	Mar 11	Mar 10	Mar 09
Working Capital	-25	-4	6
Fixed Assets	13	16	19
Current Assets	135	114	123

MJM Data Recovery Ltd

The Somerset Barn The Old Redhouse Farm, Stratton-on-the-Fosse, Radstock, BA3 4QE
Tel: 01761-402686 **Fax:** 01462-483648
E-mail: mjm@mjm.co.uk
Website: http://www.mjm.co.uk
Directors: M. Montgomery (Prop)
Registration no: 03762435 **Turnover:** Up to £250,000
No.of Employees: 1 - 10 **Product Groups:** 44

Optima Ltd

Mill Road, Radstock, BA3 5TX
Tel: 01761-433461 **Fax:** 01761-433919
E-mail: marketing@optima-group.co.uk
Website: http://www.optimasystems.com
Bank(s): Barclays, London
Directors: N. Westray (MD)
Managers: J. Durham (Purch Mgr)
Immediate Holding Company: OPTIMA+ LIMITED
Registration no: 05131078 **VAT No.:** GB 137 6328 59
Date established: 2004 **Turnover:** £5m - £10m
No.of Employees: 51 - 100 **Product Groups:** 26, 35, 36, 40, 48, 52

Date of Accounts	Dec 10	Dec 09	Dec 07
Working Capital	1	1	1
Current Assets	1	1	1

P H Gates & Fabrications

Unit H4 Second Avenue Westfield Industrial Estate, Midsomer Norton, Radstock, BA3 4BH
Tel: 01761-411322
E-mail: hicks540@aol.com
Website: http://www.phgates.co.uk
Directors: P. Hickling (Prop)
Date established: 1997 **No.of Employees:** 1 - 10 **Product Groups:** 26, 35

Perfectools

Coombend, Radstock, BA3 3AS
Tel: 01761-432299 **Fax:** 01761-435575
E-mail: sales@perfectools.co.uk
Website: http://www.perfecttools.co.uk
Directors: G. Wallen (Prop)
Date established: 1955 **Turnover:** £250,000 - £500,000
No.of Employees: 1 - 10 **Product Groups:** 30, 42

Rainbow Woodchips

Higher Whitnell Farm Binegar, Radstock, BA3 4UJ
Tel: 01749-841728 **Fax:** 01749-841728
E-mail: enquiries@rainbowwoodchips.com
Website: http://www.rainbowwoodchips.com
Directors: R. Croaker (Dir)
Immediate Holding Company: RAINBOW DECORATIVE PRODUCTS LTD.
Registration no: 05512091 **Date established:** 2005
Turnover: Up to £250,000 **No.of Employees:** 1 - 10 **Product Groups:** 25

Date of Accounts	Mar 10	Mar 09	Mar 08
Working Capital	-33	-23	-30
Fixed Assets	1	1	2
Current Assets	15	8	9

Software Radio Technology

Wireless House First Avenue, Midsomer Norton, Radstock, BA3 4BS
Tel: 01761-409500 **Fax:** 01761-410093
E-mail: enquiries@softwarerad.com
Website: http://www.softwarerad.com
Directors: R. Hurd (Fin), S. Tucker (Grp Chief Exec)
Managers: C. Hunt (Tech Serv Mgr), G. Evans, M. Clarke (Sales & Mktg Mg), A. Morris (Develop Mgr)
Ultimate Holding Company: SOFTWARE RADIO TECHNOLOGY PLC
Immediate Holding Company: SOFTWARE RADIO TECHNOLOGY PLC
Registration no: 05459678 **Date established:** 2005 **Turnover:** £1m - £2m
No.of Employees: 21 - 50 **Product Groups:** 37

Date of Accounts	Mar 12	Mar 11	Mar 10
Sales Turnover	6m	9m	4m
Pre Tax Profit/Loss	175	2m	-386
Working Capital	4m	5m	784
Fixed Assets	4m	2m	2m
Current Assets	6m	7m	2m
Current Liabilities	269	400	954

Strainstall UK Ltd

Unit 1 Charlton Lane Midsomer Norton, Radstock, BA3 4BE
Tel: 01761-414939 **Fax:** 01761-416655
E-mail: info@strainstallbath.co.uk
Website: http://www.strainstallmonitoring.com
Bank(s): HSBC Bank plc
Directors: A. Owens (I.T. Dir), J. Tyler (Co Sec), K. Lucas (Fin)
Managers: D. Lishmund (Sales Admin), J. Evans, H. Cornish (Mktg Serv Mgr)
Ultimate Holding Company: JAMES FISHER AND SONS PUBLIC LIMITED COMPANY
Immediate Holding Company: STRAINSTALL UK LIMITED
Registration no: 04042929 **Date established:** 2000
Turnover: £10m - £20m **No.of Employees:** 21 - 50 **Product Groups:** 37, 38, 39, 44, 45, 84, 85

Date of Accounts	Dec 11	Dec 10	Dec 09
Sales Turnover	11m	7m	8m
Pre Tax Profit/Loss	2m	659	1m
Working Capital	1m	1m	1m
Fixed Assets	336	302	372
Current Assets	5m	4m	3m
Current Liabilities	1m	1m	1m

Tarmac National Contracting Ltd

Leigh Upon Mendip, Radstock, BA3 5QG
Tel: 01373-812300 **Fax:** 01373-813442
E-mail: info@tarmac.co.uk
Website: http://www.tarmac.co.uk
Bank(s): Barclays
Managers: N. Holpin (Chief Mgr)
Immediate Holding Company: ANGLO AMERICAN PLC GROUP
Registration no: 00453791 **VAT No.:** GB 532 3679 43
Date established: 1996 **Turnover:** £20m - £50m
No.of Employees: 21 - 50 **Product Groups:** 31

Triton Welding Ltd

Mill Road Radstock, Radstock, BA3 5TX
Tel: 01761-433945 **Fax:** 01761-437414
E-mail: enquiries@tritonwelding.co.uk
Bank(s): Lloyds
Directors: D. Robinson (MD), S. Burrell (Co Sec)
Immediate Holding Company: SPRINGFIELD ROAD SURFACING CO. LIMITED
Registration no: 04680990 **VAT No.:** GB 139 9938 05
Date established: 2003 **Turnover:** £1m - £2m **No.of Employees:** 11 - 20
Product Groups: 48

Date of Accounts	Mar 11	Mar 10	Mar 09
Working Capital	144	167	181
Fixed Assets	N/A	1	N/A
Current Assets	328	336	325

John Wainwright & Co. Ltd

Wainwrights Moonshill Quarry Mendip Road, Stoke St Michael, Radstock, BA3 5JU
Tel: 01749-840274 **Fax:** 01749-841003
E-mail: info@wainwright.co.uk
Website: http://www.wainwright.co.uk
Bank(s): National Westminster Bank Plc
Directors: J. Snow (Co Sec), B. Rexworthy (Fin), P. Barkwill (MD)
Managers: J. Sargant
Immediate Holding Company: JOHN WAINWRIGHT & CO. LIMITED
Registration no: 00073151 **VAT No.:** GB 130 4336 15
Date established: 2002 **Turnover:** £10m - £20m
No.of Employees: 51 - 100 **Product Groups:** 14

Date of Accounts	Mar 11	Mar 10	Mar 09
Sales Turnover	16m	15m	18m
Pre Tax Profit/Loss	1m	1m	1m
Working Capital	6m	6m	5m
Fixed Assets	9m	8m	8m
Current Assets	10m	9m	8m
Current Liabilities	2m	2m	1m

Welton Bibby & Baron

Station Road Midsomer Norton, Radstock, BA3 2BE
Tel: 01761-416523 **Fax:** 01761-413862
E-mail: enquiries@welton.co.uk
Website: http://www.welton.co.uk
Bank(s): Lloyds TSB plc
Directors: M. Ross (Dir), N. Tomkins (Sales & Mktg), R. Brooksbank (Co Sec)
Managers: Y. Walton (Personnel), Y. Walton (Personnel), G. Foster (Tech Serv Mgr), C. Postalethwaite (I.T. Exec), R. Maidment (Comptroller)
Ultimate Holding Company: PAPIER-METTLER INTERNATIONAL GMBH (GERMANY)
Immediate Holding Company: WELTON BIBBY AND BARON LIMITED
Registration no: 04946078 **VAT No.:** GB 268 9911 02
Date established: 2003 **Turnover:** £20m - £50m
No.of Employees: 251 - 500 **Product Groups:** 27, 84

Date of Accounts	Dec 11	Dec 10	Dec 09
Sales Turnover	45m	41m	24m
Pre Tax Profit/Loss	3m	2m	1m
Working Capital	662	-159	-408
Fixed Assets	18m	10m	10m
Current Assets	14m	13m	10m
Current Liabilities	4m	3m	3m

Weston Super Mare

Avon Electro Plating Services Ltd

2 Crown Works Oldmixon Crescent, Weston Super Mare, BS24 9AX
Tel: 01934-631277 **Fax:** 01934-631277
E-mail: sales@avonelectroplating.co.uk
Website: http://www.avonelectroplating.co.uk
Directors: M. Raymond (MD), K. Clark (Fin)
Immediate Holding Company: AVON ELECTRO-PLATING SERVICES LIMITED
Registration no: 01265523 **VAT No.:** GB 131 5756 79
Date established: 1976 **Turnover:** Up to £250,000
No.of Employees: 1 - 10 **Product Groups:** 48

Date of Accounts	Jul 11	Jul 10	Jul 09
Working Capital	35	27	38
Fixed Assets	13	17	23
Current Assets	61	46	68
Current Liabilities	23	N/A	14

Bristol Oilskin & Overall Co. Ltd

Fox House Searle Crescent, Weston Super Mare, BS23 3YX
Tel: 01934-414142 **Fax:** 01934-618472
E-mail: contact@foxwear.co.uk
Website: http://www.foxwear.co.uk
Bank(s): Barclays
Directors: L. Fox (Fin), M. Fox (MD)
Ultimate Holding Company: BRISTOL OILSKIN & OVERALL PROPERTY LIMITED
Immediate Holding Company: BRISTOL OILSKIN & OVERALL COMPANY LIMITED
Registration no: 00445868 **VAT No.:** GB 137 6793 32
Date established: 1947 **Turnover:** £1m - £2m **No.of Employees:** 21 - 50
Product Groups: 24

Date of Accounts	Aug 11	Aug 10	Aug 09
Working Capital	75	137	141
Fixed Assets	20	27	24
Current Assets	285	456	454
Current Liabilities	57	84	72

Cartridge World Ltd

4 Waterloo Street, Weston Super Mare, BS23 1LG
Tel: 01934-419991 **Fax:** 01934-631112
Website: http://www.cartridgeworld.org
Managers: G. Whittacre (Mgr)
Registration no: 04124067 **Date established:** 2000 **Turnover:** £5m - £10m
No.of Employees: 1 - 10 **Product Groups:** 28, 30, 44, 64

Champion Process Ltd

2 Brimbleworth Lane St Georges, Weston Super Mare, BS22 7XS
Tel: 01934-511818 **Fax:** 01934-512019
E-mail: championprocess@o2.co.uk
Directors: H. Champion (MD)
Immediate Holding Company: CHAMPION PROCESS LIMITED
Registration no: 07039277 **Date established:** 2009
No.of Employees: 11 - 20 **Product Groups:** 46, 48

Date of Accounts	Jun 11	Feb 10
Working Capital	29	11
Fixed Assets	23	24
Current Assets	245	223
Current Liabilities	185	193

Clark Components Co. Ltd

Microclutch Devs Ltd Unit 8 Kiln Park, Searle Crescent, Weston Super Mare, BS23 3XP
Tel: 01934-415606 **Fax:** 01934-636658
E-mail: info@microclutch.com
Website: http://www.clarkcomponents.co.uk
Directors: T. Hanmer (MD)
Immediate Holding Company: Clark Components Company Ltd
Registration no: 03491398 **Turnover:** £500,000 - £1m
No.of Employees: 1 - 10 **Product Groups:** 35, 37, 38

Cooper Lighting & Safety Ltd

Unit 5 Sunnyside Road North, Weston Super Mare, BS23 3PZ
Tel: 01934-622139 **Fax:** 08701-161044
Website: http://www.cooper-ls.com
Directors: M. Millens (Dir), T. Helz (Co Sec)
Ultimate Holding Company: COOPER INDUSTRIES LTD (BERMUDA)
Immediate Holding Company: COOPER LIGHTING AND SAFETY LIMITED
Registration no: 03012749 **Date established:** 1995
No.of Employees: 1 - 10 **Product Groups:** 37, 67

Date of Accounts	Dec 11	Dec 10	Dec 09
Sales Turnover	72m	67m	69m
Pre Tax Profit/Loss	68	-3m	344
Working Capital	34m	35m	37m
Fixed Assets	7m	6m	7m
Current Assets	60m	58m	55m
Current Liabilities	4m	3m	3m

Cropley Glass Houses Ltd

11 Elmhyrst Road, Weston Super Mare, BS23 2SJ
Tel: 01934-636742 **Fax:** 01934-642954
E-mail: sue@cropleyglasshouses.co.uk
Website: http://www.cropleyglasshomes.co.uk
Directors: J. Cropley (MD)
Immediate Holding Company: CROPLEY GLASSHOUSES LIMITED
Registration no: 04082588 **Date established:** 2000
No.of Employees: 1 - 10 **Product Groups:** 26, 35

Date of Accounts	Dec 10	Dec 09	Dec 08
Working Capital	-29	4	-33
Fixed Assets	65	58	72
Current Assets	51	270	59

Davan Caravans Ltd

Shepherds Way Willow Close, St Georges, Weston Super Mare, BS22 7XF
Tel: 01934-510606 **Fax:** 01934-516025
E-mail: info@davan.co.uk
Website: http://www.davan.co.uk
Directors: G. Davies (MD)
Managers: J. Carter (Mgr), M. Gollicker, R. Burton
Immediate Holding Company: DAVAN CARAVANS LIMITED
Registration no: 00593600 **VAT No.:** GB 130 3213 36
Date established: 1957 **Turnover:** £5m - £10m **No.of Employees:** 21 - 50
Product Groups: 39

Date of Accounts	Dec 11	Dec 10	Dec 09
Sales Turnover	8m	8m	8m
Pre Tax Profit/Loss	-156	54	207
Working Capital	413	576	62
Fixed Assets	1m	1m	876
Current Assets	3m	3m	3m
Current Liabilities	215	710	1m

Eagle Peak Consulting

35 Badgers Way, Weston Super Mare, BS24 7ED
Tel: 08452-304191
E-mail: neilodoherty@eaglepeakconsulting.co.uk
Website: http://www.eaglepeakconsulting.co.uk
Directors: N. O'doherty (Dir)
Immediate Holding Company: EAGLEPEAK CONSULTING LTD
Registration no: 05799537 **Date established:** 2006
Turnover: Up to £250,000 **No.of Employees:** 1 - 10 **Product Groups:** 85

see next page

Eagle Peak Consulting - Cont'd

Date of Accounts	Apr 11	Apr 10	Apr 09
Sales Turnover	61	5	35
Pre Tax Profit/Loss	45	2	14
Working Capital	-1	-1	-3
Fixed Assets	2	N/A	N/A
Current Assets	11	3	1
Current Liabilities	10	1	3

Exodus Market Research & Strategic Planning

Brent House Farm Edingworth Road, Edingworth, Weston Super Mare, BS24 0JA
Tel: 01934-751009 **Fax:** 01934-750176
E-mail: mail@exodusresearch.com
Website: http://www.exodusresearch.com
Directors: R. Page (Dir), R. Ventour Page (Fin)
Immediate Holding Company: EXODUS MARKET RESEARCH & STRATEGIC PLANNING LTD
Registration no: 04439787 **Date established:** 2002
Turnover: Up to £250,000 **No.of Employees:** 1 - 10 **Product Groups:** 81

Date of Accounts	Jun 11	Jun 10	Jun 09
Working Capital	8	-54	-27
Fixed Assets	77	55	56
Current Assets	62	11	24

Fairweigh Scales

26 Greenacre, Weston Super Mare, BS22 9SL
Tel: 01934-413076 **Fax:** 01934-413076
E-mail: fairweighscale@aol.com
Directors: B. Ashford (Prop)
No.of Employees: 1 - 10 **Product Groups:** 38, 42

Fastback UK

Presentation House Oldmixon Crescent, Weston Super Mare, BS24 9AX
Tel: 0500-360333 **Fax:** 01934-412 588
E-mail: service@fastback-uk.com
Website: http://www.fastback-uk.com
Directors: B. Monks (Dir)
Registration no: SC279432 **Turnover:** Up to £250,000
No.of Employees: 11 - 20 **Product Groups:** 52

Feature Fireplaces

1-2 Warne Park Warne Road, Weston Super Mare, BS23 3TP
Tel: 01934-628142 **Fax:** 01934-645625
E-mail: info@feature-fireplaces.co.uk
Website: http://www.feature-fireplaces.co.uk
Directors: R. Atkin (Prop)
Registration no: 05428270 **No.of Employees:** 1 - 10 **Product Groups:** 33

Fussell's Rubber Co. Ltd

2 Brimbleworth Lane St Georges, Weston Super Mare, BS22 7XS
Tel: 01934-513473 **Fax:** 01934-521529
Directors: H. Champion (MD), H. Hitchcock (MD)
Immediate Holding Company: Fussell's Rubber Company,Limited
Registration no: 00201475 **VAT No.:** GB 130 1487 09
Turnover: £500,000 - £1m **No.of Employees:** 1 - 10 **Product Groups:** 22, 29

Date of Accounts	Jun 08
Working Capital	4890
Fixed Assets	154
Current Assets	4990
Current Liabilities	100
Total Share Capital	6

Gilda Cane & Cushions Ltd

Gilda Buildings Winterstoke Road, Weston Super Mare, BS23 3YS
Tel: 01934-635260 **Fax:** 01934-642339
E-mail: info@gildacaneandcushions.co.uk
Website: http://www.gildacushions.co.uk
Directors: S. Penny (Fin), G. Bute (Dir)
Immediate Holding Company: GILDA LIMITED
Registration no: 04592731 **Date established:** 2002
No.of Employees: 1 - 10 **Product Groups:** 24, 26

Date of Accounts	Dec 11	Dec 10	Dec 09
Working Capital	-67	-70	-78
Fixed Assets	104	106	109
Current Assets	121	110	105

Grand Pier Ltd

Marine Parade, Weston Super Mare, BS23 1AL
Tel: 01934-620238 **Fax:** 01934-626135
E-mail: michelle.michael@agmholdings.com
Website: http://www.grandpier.co.uk
Directors: M. Michael (Co Sec)
Ultimate Holding Company: AGM HOLDINGS PLC
Immediate Holding Company: GRAND PIER LIMITED
Registration no: 00152507 **Date established:** 2019 **Turnover:** £2m - £5m
No.of Employees: 51 - 100 **Product Groups:** 89

Date of Accounts	Dec 07	Mar 11	Mar 10
Sales Turnover	N/A	3m	14
Pre Tax Profit/Loss	365	1m	11m
Working Capital	2m	-11m	4m
Fixed Assets	814	32m	16m
Current Assets	2m	1m	7m
Current Liabilities	173	392	123

Hazelton's Ltd

Batch Industrial Estate Rectory Way, Lympsham, Weston Super Mare, BS24 0ES
Tel: 01934-751007 **Fax:** 01934-751006
E-mail: hazeltonsales@aol.com
Website: http://www.hazeltonslimited.com
Directors: K. Hazelton (Prop), K. Hazelton (Dir)
Managers: G. Weston (Ops Mgr)
Immediate Holding Company: HAZELTON'S LIMITED
Registration no: 05386422 **Date established:** 2005
No.of Employees: 1 - 10 **Product Groups:** 52

Date of Accounts	May 09	May 08	May 07
Working Capital	-228	-243	-223
Fixed Assets	251	257	269
Current Assets	127	231	321

I Dance

Purn House Farm Purn Way, Bleadon, Weston Super Mare, BS24 0QE
Tel: 01934-813686 **Fax:** 01934-815521
Website: http://www.iandanceservices.com
Directors: I. Dance (Ptnr), B. Dance (Ptnr)
Date established: 1989 **No.of Employees:** 1 - 10 **Product Groups:** 20, 40, 41

Date of Accounts	Jun 11	Jun 10
Working Capital	-40	-62
Fixed Assets	85	86
Current Assets	64	37

Jewson Ltd

Winterstoke Road, Weston Super Mare, BS23 3YF
Tel: 01934-628121 **Fax:** 01934-631038
E-mail: mike.frost@jewson.co.uk
Website: http://www.jewson.co.uk
Bank(s): Barclays
Managers: M. Frost (District Mgr)
Ultimate Holding Company: COMPAGNIE DE SAINT GOBAIN (FRANCE)
Immediate Holding Company: JEWSON LIMITED
Registration no: 00348407 **VAT No.:** GB 394 1212 63
Date established: 1939 **Turnover:** £500m - £1,000m
No.of Employees: 11 - 20 **Product Groups:** 25, 66

Date of Accounts	Dec 11	Dec 10	Dec 09
Sales Turnover	1606m	1547m	1485m
Pre Tax Profit/Loss	18m	100m	45m
Working Capital	-345m	-250m	-349m
Fixed Assets	496m	387m	461m
Current Assets	657m	1005m	1320m
Current Liabilities	66m	120m	64m

K G Diecasting Weston Ltd

Tudor Centre 264 Milton Road, Weston Super Mare, BS22 8EN
Tel: 01934-412665 **Fax:** 01934-412886
E-mail: kgdiecasting@btclick.com
Directors: K. Glimstead (MD)
Immediate Holding Company: K.G. DIECASTING (WESTON) LIMITED
Registration no: 01143805 **VAT No.:** GB 131 2284 12
Date established: 1973 **Turnover:** £250,000 - £500,000
No.of Employees: 1 - 10 **Product Groups:** 34

Date of Accounts	Jan 12	Jan 11	Jan 10
Working Capital	25	7	6
Fixed Assets	49	43	52
Current Assets	61	38	25

K P R Engineering M E Ltd

Unit 6-7 Mendip Business Park Hewish, Weston Super Mare, BS24 6RU
Tel: 01934-835098 **Fax:** 01934-876265
E-mail: info@kpr-engineering.com
Website: http://www.kpr-engineering.com
Directors: B. Gilbert (Dir)
Immediate Holding Company: KPR ENGINEERING (M & E) LTD
Registration no: 06434180 **VAT No.:** GB 358 1344 50
Date established: 2007 **Turnover:** £1m - £2m **No.of Employees:** 1 - 10
Product Groups: 37, 38, 40, 44, 45, 52, 84

Date of Accounts	Nov 11	Nov 10	Nov 09
Working Capital	8	-36	28
Fixed Assets	4	5	3
Current Assets	56	116	95

K & S Fire Protection Ltd

Unit 1 Manor Farm Collum Lane, Kewstoke, Weston Super Mare, BS22 9JL
Tel: 01934-519594 **Fax:** 01934-519594
E-mail: kandsfireltd@btconnect.com
Directors: K. Sprake (Dir), G. Sprake (Fin)
Immediate Holding Company: K & S FIRE PROTECTION LIMITED
Registration no: 04352124 **Date established:** 2002
No.of Employees: 1 - 10 **Product Groups:** 38, 42

Date of Accounts	Mar 11	Mar 10	Mar 09
Working Capital	-9	-4	1
Fixed Assets	43	44	45
Current Assets	35	36	36

M C T Reman Ltd

Winterstoke Road, Weston Super Mare, BS24 9AT
Tel: 01934-428000 **Fax:** 01934-428001
E-mail: gearboxes@gearboxes.com
Website: http://www.gearboxes.com
Directors: R. Atkinson (Dir)
Immediate Holding Company: MCT REMAN LIMITED
Registration no: 06849861 **Date established:** 2009 **Turnover:** £2m - £5m
No.of Employees: 1 - 10 **Product Groups:** 39, 48

Date of Accounts	Apr 11	Apr 10	Apr 12
Sales Turnover	8m	7m	7m
Pre Tax Profit/Loss	496	562	283
Working Capital	643	644	639
Fixed Assets	172	102	226
Current Assets	2m	3m	2m
Current Liabilities	789	1m	845

Marble Mosaic Co. Ltd

Winterstoke Road, Weston Super Mare, BS23 3YE
Tel: 01934-419941 **Fax:** 01934-625479
E-mail: sales@marble-mosaic.co.uk
Website: http://www.marble-mosaic.co.uk
Directors: B. Maddalena (Fin)
Ultimate Holding Company: THE MARBLE MOSAIC COMPANY (HOLDINGS) LIMITED
Immediate Holding Company: MARBLE MOSAIC COMPANY LIMITED(THE)
Registration no: 00187988 **VAT No.:** GB 567 6071 17
Date established: 2023 **Turnover:** £5m - £10m
No.of Employees: 51 - 100 **Product Groups:** 33

Date of Accounts	Mar 11	Mar 10	Mar 09
Sales Turnover	N/A	6m	8m
Pre Tax Profit/Loss	N/A	-70	100
Working Capital	694	944	989
Current Assets	1m	2m	3m
Current Liabilities	N/A	66	232

Micro Clutch Developments Ltd

Unit 8-9 Kiln Park Searle Crescent, Weston Super Mare, BS23 3XP
Tel: 01934-415606 **Fax:** 01934-636658
E-mail: info@microclutch.com
Website: http://www.microclutch.com
Directors: E. Darling (Dir)
Immediate Holding Company: MICRO CLUTCH DEVELOPMENTS LIMITED
Registration no: 01383365 **VAT No.:** GB 319 4783 31
Date established: 1978 **Turnover:** £2m - £5m **No.of Employees:** 1 - 10
Product Groups: 35, 36, 37

Date of Accounts	Aug 11	Aug 10	Aug 09
Working Capital	2m	1m	1m
Fixed Assets	148	140	122
Current Assets	2m	2m	2m

Moor Fabs

Unit 34 B W Estates Oldmixon CR, Weston Super Mare, BS24 9BA
Tel: 01934-614080
E-mail: info@moorfabs.co.uk
Website: http://www.moorfabs.co.uk
Directors: M. King (Sales)
Immediate Holding Company: MOOR FABRICATIONS (PLASTICS) LIMITED
Registration no: 05145161 **Date established:** 2004
No.of Employees: 1 - 10 **Product Groups:** 40, 42, 48

Date of Accounts	Jun 12	Jun 11	Jun 10
Working Capital	170	215	152
Fixed Assets	6	6	4
Current Assets	295	406	327

Murodigital

Oldmixon Crescent, Weston Super Mare, BS24 9AY
Tel: 01934-636393 **Fax:** 01934-641194
E-mail: sales@muro.co.uk
Website: http://www.muro.co.uk
Managers: A. Brook, M. Winterton (Comptroller)
Immediate Holding Company: LITHO SUPPLIES P.L.C.
Registration no: 02456232 **Date established:** 1975
No.of Employees: 21 - 50 **Product Groups:** 44

Nickel Electro Ltd

Oldmixon Cresent, Weston Super Mare, BS24 9BL
Tel: 01934-626691 **Fax:** 01934-630300
E-mail: adrian@nickel-electro.co.uk
Website: http://www.nickel-electro.co.uk
Bank(s): HSBC Bank plc
Directors: M. Dickson (MD)
Managers: C. Dickson, G. Lee (Purch Mgr), R. Andrews (Personnel), T. Gardner (Chief Acct)
Immediate Holding Company: NICKEL-ELECTRO LIMITED
Registration no: 00370743 **VAT No.:** GB 130 2668 00
Date established: 1941 **No.of Employees:** 21 - 50 **Product Groups:** 20, 37, 42, 67

Date of Accounts	Dec 11	Dec 10	Dec 09
Working Capital	553	564	647
Fixed Assets	223	258	285
Current Assets	1m	1m	1m

Nuts & Bolts

Unit 10 Longton Industrial Estate, Weston Super Mare, BS23 3YB
Tel: 01934-416765 **Fax:** 01934-418704
E-mail: enquiries@nuts-and-bolts.co.uk
Website: http://www.fixingsupplies.co.uk
Directors: C. Hart (Dir)
VAT No.: GB 567 3418 20 **Turnover:** £500,000 - £1m
No.of Employees: 1 - 10 **Product Groups:** 66

Orchids For You

25-27 Meadow Street, Weston Super Mare, BS23 1QQ
Tel: 07951-393363 **Fax:** 01934-623627
E-mail: sales@orchidsforyou.co.uk
Website: http://www.orchidsforyou.co.uk
Directors: K. Everard (Ptnr)
Turnover: Up to £250,000 **No.of Employees:** 1 - 10 **Product Groups:** 02

P T S

Unit 30 Lynx Crescent, Weston Super Mare, BS24 9BP
Tel: 01934-641794 **Fax:** 01934-644255
E-mail: sales@tdcsystems.co.uk
Managers: E. Chir (Admin Off)
Ultimate Holding Company: TRAVIS PERKINS PLC
Immediate Holding Company: P.T.S. PLUMBING TRADE SUPPLIES LIMITED
Registration no: 01851210 **Date established:** 1984
No.of Employees: 1 - 10 **Product Groups:** 26, 38, 40

Date of Accounts	Dec 10	Mar 10	Mar 09
Working Capital	1m	1m	1m
Current Assets	1m	1m	1m

P W Engineering

100 Kewstoke Road Kewstoke, Weston Super Mare, BS22 9YL
Tel: 01934-621769
Directors: A. Lyne (Ptnr)
Immediate Holding Company: EC PAY LIMITED
Date established: 2010 **No.of Employees:** 1 - 10 **Product Groups:** 35

Pro Wash

47 Milton Hill, Weston Super Mare, BS22 9RE
Tel: 01934-418177 **Fax:** 01934-643580
E-mail: prowash@btconnect.com
Directors: R. Priest (Prop)
Date established: 1989 **No.of Employees:** 1 - 10 **Product Groups:** 20, 40, 41

Professional Mobile Valet Service

31 Brimbleworth Lane St Georges, Weston Super Mare, BS22 7XS
Tel: 0781-115 8953
E-mail: woodpecker1972@hotmail.com
Website: http://www.freewebs.com/professionalmobilevaletservice
Directors: G. Wood (Prop)
Turnover: Up to £250,000 **No.of Employees:** 1 - 10 **Product Groups:** 32, 39, 68

Quick's Of Weston

North Street, Weston Super Mare, BS23 1QF
Tel: 01934-629045 **Fax:** 01934-629045
Website: http://www.quicksweston.co.uk
Directors: M. Jordan (Ptnr)
Turnover: Up to £250,000 **No.of Employees:** 1 - 10 **Product Groups:** 20, 40, 41

Ringway Specialist Services Ltd

Winterstoke Road Springfield Road, V, Weston Super Mare, BS24 9BQ
Tel: 01934-421400 **Fax:** 01934-421401
E-mail: info@ringway.co.uk
Website: http://www.ringway.co.uk
Bank(s): National Westminster

Directors: P. Girod (Dir), R. Gregg (MD), S. Lysionek (Co Sec)
Managers: C. Kittridge (Sales Prom Mgr)
Immediate Holding Company: Ringway Group Ltd
Registration no: 02884116 **VAT No.:** GB 321 9318 74
Turnover: £5m - £10m **No.of Employees:** 51 - 100 **Product Groups:** 26, 35, 37, 39, 45

Date of Accounts	Dec 07	Dec 06	Dec 05
Sales Turnover	47481	54541	28097
Pre Tax Profit/Loss	-1669	-2015	913
Working Capital	-3275	-2611	85
Fixed Assets	2511	3534	1737
Current Assets	33978	13423	4180
Current Liabilities	37253	16034	4095
Total Share Capital	5	5	5
ROCE% (Return on Capital Employed)	218.5	-218.3	50.1
ROT% (Return on Turnover)	-3.5	-3.7	3.2

RM Signs & Textiles

85 Meadow Street, Weston Super Mare, BS23 1QL
Tel: 01934-64488 **Fax:** 01934-641272
E-mail: enquiries@rmsigns.biz
Website: http://www.t-shirtsprinters.co.uk
Managers: R. Hill (Mgr)
No.of Employees: 1 - 10 **Product Groups:** 24, 28

Safe Digging Ltd

Unit 6 Manor Farm Collum Lane, Kewstoke, Weston Super Mare, BS22 9JL
Tel: 08455-007867 **Fax:** 0845-500 7868
E-mail: info@safedigging.com
Website: http://www.safedigging.com
Directors: S. Thomas (Dir)
Immediate Holding Company: SAFEDIGGING LIMITED
Registration no: 04654010 **Date established:** 2003
No.of Employees: 1 - 10 **Product Groups:** 52, 54

Date of Accounts	Mar 11	Mar 10	Mar 09
Sales Turnover	140	154	308
Pre Tax Profit/Loss	9	6	-26
Working Capital	-32	-46	-59
Fixed Assets	30	36	43
Current Assets	17	38	25
Current Liabilities	13	28	15

Safelab Systems Ltd

Unit 29 Lynx Crescent, Weston Super Mare, BS24 9DJ
Tel: 01934-421340 **Fax:** 0870-240 2274
E-mail: r.guess@safelab.co.uk
Website: http://www.safelab.co.uk
Bank(s): Barclays Bank Plc
Directors: R. Guess (MD)
Immediate Holding Company: SAFELAB SYSTEMS LIMITED
Registration no: 05336826 **VAT No.:** GB 416 7600 60
Date established: 2005 **Turnover:** £2m - £5m **No.of Employees:** 21 - 50
Product Groups: 26, 36, 38, 42, 67, 85

Date of Accounts	Feb 12	Feb 11	Feb 10
Working Capital	533	209	-7
Fixed Assets	67	79	65
Current Assets	1m	774	714
Current Liabilities	N/A	N/A	306

Scale Models Weston

The Wheel House 10 Alfred Street, Weston Super Mare, BS23 1PU
Tel: 01934-413462 **Fax:** 01934-643301
E-mail: workshop@scalemodelsweston.co.uk
Website: http://www.scalemodelsweston.co.uk
Directors: K. Goodfrey (Dir)
Turnover: £250,000 - £500,000 **No.of Employees:** 1 - 10
Product Groups: 49, 64, 84

UK Installations

Unit 10 Weston Business Park The Airport, Locking, Weston Super Mare, BS24 8RA
Tel: 0783-628 1877 **Fax:** 01278-785959
Website: http://www.uk-installations.co.uk
Directors: S. Biggs (Prop)
Immediate Holding Company: ARSHAD & SONS (UK) LIMITED
Date established: 2009 **No.of Employees:** 1 - 10 **Product Groups:** 35, 39, 45

West Coast Sales

24 Lynx Cresent Western Industrial Estate, Weston Super Mare, BS24 9DJ
Tel: 01934-641422 **Fax:** 01934-641416
Directors: A. Heeney (Dir)
No.of Employees: 1 - 10 **Product Groups:** 37

Date of Accounts	Oct 06	Oct 05
Working Capital	2	-2
Fixed Assets	6	7
Current Assets	30	39
Current Liabilities	28	42

Westwood Tankers

B W Estates Oldmixon CR, Weston Super Mare, BS24 9BA
Tel: 01934-629945 **Fax:** 01934-629945
Directors: B. Watmough (Prop)
Date established: 1994 **No.of Employees:** 1 - 10 **Product Groups:** 35

Winscombe

Brinsea Products Ltd

Station Road Sandford, Winscombe, BS25 5RA
Tel: 01934-823039 **Fax:** 01934-820250
E-mail: info@brinsea.co.uk
Website: http://www.brinsea.co.uk
Directors: F. Pearce (Co Sec), I. Pearce (MD)
Immediate Holding Company: BRINSEA PRODUCTS LIMITED
Registration no: 01279698 **Date established:** 1976
No.of Employees: 21 - 50 **Product Groups:** 41

Date of Accounts	Oct 11	Oct 10	Oct 09
Working Capital	303	311	294
Fixed Assets	401	432	378
Current Assets	583	1m	710

Thatchers Cider Company Ltd

Myrtle Farm Station Road, Sandford, Winscombe, BS25 5RA
Tel: 01934-822862 **Fax:** 01934-822313
E-mail: info@thatcherscider.co.uk
Website: http://www.thatcherscider.co.uk
Directors: C. Milton (Sales & Mktg), M. Thatcher (MD)
Managers: A. Meeks, M. Hannam (Tech Serv Mgr), M. Jelbert (Fin Mgr)
Ultimate Holding Company: THATCHERS HOLDINGS LIMITED
Immediate Holding Company: THATCHERS CIDER COMPANY LIMITED
Registration no: 00550634 **Date established:** 1955
Turnover: £20m - £50m **No.of Employees:** 51 - 100 **Product Groups:** 21

Date of Accounts	Aug 11	Aug 10	Aug 09
Sales Turnover	31m	23m	18m
Pre Tax Profit/Loss	4m	3m	2m
Working Capital	2m	1m	5m
Fixed Assets	6m	4m	3m
Current Assets	13m	9m	9m
Current Liabilities	4m	2m	2m

BEDFORDSHIRE

Arlesey

Heatherside Sheet Metal Ltd
Old Oak Close Industrial Estate Old Oak Close, Arlesey, SG15 6XD
Tel: 01462-731575 **Fax:** 01462-731575
E-mail: heatherside@btconnect.com
Directors: L. Hay (Dir)
Immediate Holding Company: HEATHERSIDE SHEET METAL LIMITED
Registration no: 04689114 **Date established:** 2003
Turnover: Up to £250,000 **No.of Employees:** 1 - 10 **Product Groups:** 48

Date of Accounts	May 11	May 10	May 09
Working Capital	61	61	80
Fixed Assets	23	2	2
Current Assets	313	229	142

Vehicle & General Polishers & Platers Ltd
4a Portland Industrial Estate Hitchin Road, Arlesey, SG15 6SG
Tel: 01462-835847 **Fax:** 01462-835079
E-mail: vehicleandgeneral@btopenworld.com
Website: http://www.vehicleandgeneralelectroplaters.co.uk
Directors: C. Weddell (MD)
Immediate Holding Company: VEHICLE AND GENERAL POLISHERS AND PLATERS LIMITED
Registration no: 02571192 **Date established:** 1991
No.of Employees: 11 - 20 **Product Groups:** 46, 48

Date of Accounts	Mar 11	Mar 10	Mar 09
Working Capital	-10	-28	-52
Fixed Assets	10	28	44
Current Assets	133	112	143

Bedford

A & A Cellar Services
8 Alexia Court Cambridge Road Industrial Estate Aston Road, Bedford, MK42 0LW
Tel: 01234-262183 **Fax:** 01234-341258
E-mail: alan.nicholson@capss.co.uk
Website: http://www.capss.co.uk
Directors: V. Nicholson (Fin), A. Nicholson (MD)
Immediate Holding Company: A & A CELLAR SERVICES LIMITED
Registration no: 05393235 **Date established:** 2005
No.of Employees: 1 - 10 **Product Groups:** 20, 40, 41

Date of Accounts	Mar 12	Mar 11	Mar 10
Working Capital	-4	1	-2
Fixed Assets	N/A	1	1
Current Assets	22	25	12

A S K Europe plc
Trent House University Way Cranfield Technology Park, Cranfield, Bedford, MK43 0AN
Tel: 01234-757575 **Fax:** 01234-757576
E-mail: mail@askeurope.com
Website: http://www.askeurope.com
Directors: H. Terry (Chief Op Offcr)
Managers: N. Masters (Comptroller)
Immediate Holding Company: ASK EUROPE PLC
Registration no: 02989543 **Date established:** 1994 **Turnover:** £2m - £5m
No.of Employees: 21 - 50 **Product Groups:** 80, 86

Date of Accounts	Dec 11	Dec 10	Dec 09
Sales Turnover	3m	3m	3m
Pre Tax Profit/Loss	74	196	58
Working Capital	477	476	518
Fixed Assets	38	116	139
Current Assets	1m	1m	1m
Current Liabilities	524	457	308

Acorn Woodworking
58 Barford Road Blunham, Bedford, MK44 3ND
Tel: 01767-641444 **Fax:** 01767-641444
E-mail: j.claughton@acorn-woodworking.co.uk
Website: http://www.acorn-woodworking.co.uk
Directors: J. Claughton (Prop)
Immediate Holding Company: BOSTOCK RESOURCING SERVICES LIMITED
Date established: 2010 **No.of Employees:** 1 - 10 **Product Groups:** 46

Aetna UK Ltd
Highfield Road Oakley, Bedford, MK43 7TA
Tel: 01234-825050 **Fax:** 01234-827070
E-mail: sales@aetnagroup.com
Website: http://www.aetnagroup.com
Managers: C. Barker (Chief Mgr)
Immediate Holding Company: AETNA (UK) LIMITED
Registration no: 02522111 **Date established:** 1990 **Turnover:** £2m - £5m
No.of Employees: 11 - 20 **Product Groups:** 67

Date of Accounts	Dec 11	Dec 10	Dec 09
Sales Turnover	N/A	4m	3m
Pre Tax Profit/Loss	N/A	138	-98
Working Capital	368	292	131
Fixed Assets	28	36	74
Current Assets	2m	1m	1m
Current Liabilities	N/A	378	336

Air Equipment
5 Kings Road Flitwick, Bedford, MK45 1ED
Tel: 01525-723700 **Fax:** 01525-723737
E-mail: info@air-equipment.co.uk
Website: http://www.air-equipment.co.uk
Bank(s): Barclays
Directors: A. Yandall (MD), L. Garratt (Co Sec)
Immediate Holding Company: METERPARK LIMITED
Registration no: 03407569 **Date established:** 1997 **Turnover:** £1m - £2m
No.of Employees: 11 - 20 **Product Groups:** 40

Date of Accounts	Sep 11	Sep 10	Sep 09
Working Capital	304	274	230
Fixed Assets	124	111	121
Current Assets	811	625	428

Ampthill Metal Company Ltd
Station Road Industrial Estate Ampthill, Bedford, MK45 2QY
Tel: 01525-403388 **Fax:** 01525-404908
E-mail: info@ampthillmetal.co.uk
Website: http://www.ampthillmetal.co.uk
Bank(s): Barclays, Bedford
Managers: C. Thomas (Comptroller), M. Leech (Comm), S. Clarkson (Mgr)
Ultimate Holding Company: ONE FIFTY ONE PUBLIC LIMITED COMPANY
Immediate Holding Company: AMPTHILL METAL COMPANY LIMITED
Registration no: 01407513 **VAT No.:** GB 322 4657 71
Date established: 1979 **Turnover:** £20m - £50m
No.of Employees: 21 - 50 **Product Groups:** 54, 66

Date of Accounts	Dec 11	Dec 10	Dec 09
Sales Turnover	24m	20m	13m
Pre Tax Profit/Loss	6m	4m	2m
Working Capital	9m	1m	-611
Fixed Assets	3m	5m	3m
Current Assets	17m	13m	8m
Current Liabilities	6m	7m	6m

Anglian Fasteners Ltd
20-21 Shuttleworth Road Elm Farm Industrial Estate, Bedford, MK41 0EP
Tel: 01234-345641 **Fax:** 01234-358241
E-mail: info@anglianfasteners.co.uk
Website: http://www.anglianfasteners.co.uk
Bank(s): Barclays
Managers: K. Dodson, D. Dodd (Mgr)
Immediate Holding Company: ANGLIAN FASTENERS LIMITED
Registration no: 00963304 **VAT No.:** GB 196 2071 54
Date established: 1969 **Turnover:** £2m - £5m **No.of Employees:** 21 - 50
Product Groups: 30, 35, 37

Date of Accounts	Dec 11	Dec 10	Dec 09
Working Capital	360	328	350
Fixed Assets	776	783	794
Current Assets	934	792	751

Ark H Handling Ltd
Unit 1 Wilstead Industrial Park Kenneth Way, Wilstead, Bedford, MK45 3PD
Tel: 01234-742777 **Fax:** 01234-742999
E-mail: sales@ark-h.co.uk
Website: http://www.ark-h.co.uk
Directors: F. Strong (Dir), K. Phillips (Fin), M. Scantlin (Sales & Mktg), P. Dennis (Co Sec)
Managers: M. Coates (Tech Serv Mgr), M. Simkins (Personnel)
Immediate Holding Company: ARK-H HANDLING LIMITED
Registration no: 02518086 **Date established:** 1990
Turnover: £10m - £20m **No.of Employees:** 51 - 100 **Product Groups:** 49, 80, 81

Date of Accounts	Dec 11	Dec 10	Dec 09
Sales Turnover	10m	9m	6m
Pre Tax Profit/Loss	139	150	75
Working Capital	606	620	435
Fixed Assets	1m	1m	2m
Current Assets	4m	3m	2m
Current Liabilities	2m	777	411

Armfibre Ltd
Unit 7 Wilstead Industrial Park, Kenneth Way, Wilstead, Bedford, MK45 3PD
Tel: 01234-741444 **Fax:** 01234-742095
Website: http://www.productionglassfibre.co.uk
Bank(s): Royal Bank of Scotland
Managers: M. Albone (Purch Mgr), G. Brown (Sales Prom Mgr)
Immediate Holding Company: Armfibre Holdings Ltd
Registration no: 00944283 **VAT No.:** GB 491 2487 29
Date established: 1974 **Turnover:** £5m - £10m **No.of Employees:** 200
Product Groups: 30

Date of Accounts	May 09	May 08	Mar 07
Working Capital	634	391	-13
Fixed Assets	298	208	60
Current Assets	976	916	1m

Arqadia Ltd
2 Wolseley Road Wolburn Road Industrial Estate, Kempston, Bedford, MK42 7AD
Tel: 01234-857488 **Fax:** 01234-840190
E-mail: michael.brown@arqadia.co.uk
Website: http://www.arqadia.co.uk
Bank(s): Barclays
Directors: M. Brown (MD), R. Goodson (Fin)
Managers: T. Masters
Ultimate Holding Company: BERKSHIRE HATHAWAY INC (USA)
Immediate Holding Company: ARQADIA LIMITED
Registration no: 01196875 **VAT No.:** GB 678 8641 68
Date established: 1975 **Turnover:** £10m - £20m
No.of Employees: 51 - 100 **Product Groups:** 25, 27, 36

Date of Accounts	Dec 07	Dec 08	Jan 10
Sales Turnover	16m	16m	16m
Pre Tax Profit/Loss	2m	2m	1m
Working Capital	-958	773	668
Fixed Assets	6m	6m	6m
Current Assets	6m	8m	9m
Current Liabilities	4m	4m	4m

Arrow Supply Co. Ltd
Fastener House 7- 9 Sunbeam Rd, Kempston, Bedford, MK42 7BZ
Tel: 01234-840404 (01234) 305450 (Tools) **Fax:** 01234-840374
E-mail: information@arrow-supply.co.uk
Website: http://www.arrow-supply.co.uk
Bank(s): Barclays
Directors: G. Swain (MD), R. Emery (Sales), T. Emery (Co Sec)
Registration no: 01622553 **VAT No.:** GB 365 9908 01
Date established: 1982 **Turnover:** £2m - £5m **No.of Employees:** 21 - 50
Product Groups: 25, 29, 30, 33, 35, 36, 37, 38, 39, 40, 41, 42, 43, 45, 46, 48, 49, 66, 67, 83

Date of Accounts	Mar 06	Mar 05
Working Capital	153	202
Fixed Assets	141	152
Current Assets	851	929
Current Liabilities	698	727

Assessco
30 Grovebury Court Wooton, Wootton, Bedford, MK43 9HZ
Tel: 07703-180299
E-mail: info@assessco.co.uk
Website: http://www.assessco.co.uk
Directors: A. Omerod (Prop)
Date established: 2000 **No.of Employees:** 1 - 10 **Product Groups:** 84

Atlas Converting
Wolseley Road Kempston, Bedford, MK42 7XT
Tel: 01234-852553 **Fax:** 01234-851151
E-mail: alan.johnson@bobstgroup.com
Website: http://www.atlasconverting.com
Directors: A. Johnson (MD)
Managers: S. Braycotton (Sales Prom Mgr), E. Mossop (Personnel), S. Yallop (Personnel), T. Walker, R. Astell (Mktg Serv Mgr), T. Meagan (Fin Mgr), P. Green (Purch Mgr), M. Savin (Tech Serv Mgr), M. Savin (I.T. Exec), D. Lewis (Purch Mgr), R. Aspell (Mktg Serv Mgr)
Ultimate Holding Company: ATLAS CONVERTING (UK HOLDINGS) LIMITED
Immediate Holding Company: ATLAS CONVERTING EQUIPMENT LIMITED
Registration no: 01276725 **Date established:** 1976
Turnover: £20m - £50m **No.of Employees:** 51 - 100 **Product Groups:** 42, 44, 46, 48, 67

Date of Accounts	Dec 11	Dec 10	Dec 09
Sales Turnover	36m	23m	23m
Pre Tax Profit/Loss	1m	7m	-4m

Working Capital	10m	10m	1m
Fixed Assets	227	76	3m
Current Assets	19m	22m	27m
Current Liabilities	8m	8m	4m

Auto Crash Repairs

Lorita House Brunel Road, Bedford, MK41 9TG
Tel: 01234-266881 **Fax:** 01234-351601
E-mail: acrbedford@btconnect.com
Website: http://www.acrbedford.co.uk
Directors: L. Coladangelo (Prop)
Managers: D. Holyoake, A. Talats (Tech Serv Mgr)
Turnover: £1m - £2m **No.of Employees:** 21 - 50 **Product Groups:** 39

Autoglass Ltd

1 Priory Business Park Cardington, Bedford, MK44 3US
Tel: 01234-273636 **Fax:** 01234-831100
E-mail: ronald.lubner@autoglass.co.uk
Website: http://www.autoglass.co.uk
Bank(s): National Westminster Bank Plc
Directors: R. Lubner (Dir), N. Atherton (Fin)
Managers: M. Pearson (Property Mgr)
Ultimate Holding Company: SA D'LETEREN NV (BELGIUM)
Immediate Holding Company: BELRON UK LIMITED
Registration no: 00494648 **Date established:** 1951
Turnover: £125m - £250m **No.of Employees:** 101 - 250
Product Groups: 39

Date of Accounts	Dec 11	Dec 10	Dec 09
Sales Turnover	241m	248m	204m
Pre Tax Profit/Loss	6m	8m	-4m
Working Capital	3m	4m	16m
Fixed Assets	17m	31m	16m
Current Assets	48m	56m	46m
Current Liabilities	19m	25m	19m

Axo Shredders Ltd

Unit 11 Kenneth Way Wilstead, Bedford, MK45 3PD
Tel: 01234-742400 **Fax:** 01234-742401
E-mail: uk@axo.cc
Website: http://www.axo.cc
Directors: G. Corrigan (Dir)
Date established: 2000 **Turnover:** £10m - £20m **No.of Employees:** 1 - 10
Product Groups: 42

B B A K Control Panels Ltd

Unit 2 Hudson Road, Elm Farm Industrial Estate, Bedford, MK41 0LZ
Tel: 01234-355339 **Fax:** 01234-352215
E-mail: info@bbak.co.uk
Website: http://www.bbak.co.uk
Directors: C. Bond (MD)
Immediate Holding Company: B B A K CONTROL PANELS LIMITED
Registration no: 03574473 **Date established:** 1998
No.of Employees: 11 - 20 **Product Groups:** 37, 46, 48

Date of Accounts	Oct 11	Oct 10	Oct 09
Working Capital	-65	-117	-102
Fixed Assets	56	62	85
Current Assets	274	100	83

B H R Group

The Fluid Engineering Centre Wharley End, Cranfield, Bedford, MK43 0AJ
Tel: 01234-750422 **Fax:** 01234-750074
E-mail: contactus@bhrgroup.co.uk
Website: http://www.bhrgroup.com
Bank(s): National Westminster Bank Plc
Directors: J. Muir (Fin), R. Chand (MD)
Managers: A. Colburn (Buyer), K. Page (Tech Serv Mgr), M. Harris (Admin Off), S. Harrison (Sales & Mktg Mg)
Ultimate Holding Company: BHR GROUP LIMITED
Immediate Holding Company: BHR GROUP LIMITED
Registration no: 02420351 **VAT No.:** GB 536 4271 46
Date established: 1989 **Turnover:** £2m - £5m **No.of Employees:** 51 - 100
Product Groups: 32, 38, 40, 41, 42, 44, 45, 46, 48, 51, 54, 80, 82, 84, 85, 86

Date of Accounts	Dec 09	Dec 08	Dec 07
Sales Turnover	4m	N/A	N/A
Pre Tax Profit/Loss	171	-251	181
Working Capital	-602	-750	-437
Fixed Assets	3m	3m	3m
Current Assets	2m	2m	2m
Current Liabilities	2m	2m	1m

B L M Group UK Ltd

Unit 4 Ampthill Business Park, Ampthill, Bedford, MK45 2QW
Tel: 01525-402555 **Fax:** 01525-402312
E-mail: sales@blmgroup.uk.com
Website: http://www.blmgroup.uk.com
Directors: P. Lake (MD)
Immediate Holding Company: BLM GROUP UK LTD
Registration no: 03301614 **Date established:** 1997 **Turnover:** £5m - £10m
No.of Employees: 1 - 10 **Product Groups:** 46

Date of Accounts	Dec 11	Dec 10	Dec 09
Sales Turnover	8m	6m	3m
Pre Tax Profit/Loss	37	14	6
Working Capital	68	137	236
Fixed Assets	48	51	52
Current Assets	6m	4m	3m
Current Liabilities	1m	510	272

B W Aluminium Ltd

Unit B3 Arc Progress Beckerings Park, Lidlington, Bedford, MK43 0RD
Tel: 01525-288191 **Fax:** 01952-462261
E-mail: sales@bwaluminium.co.uk
Website: http://www.bwcplastics.co.uk
Directors: G. Barker (MD)
Ultimate Holding Company: B.W.C. GROUP LIMITED
Immediate Holding Company: B.W. ALUMINIUM LIMITED
Registration no: 03753580 **Date established:** 1999
No.of Employees: 1 - 10 **Product Groups:** 30, 34, 42, 48

Date of Accounts	Jun 11	Jun 10	Jun 09
Working Capital	748	645	555
Fixed Assets	144	149	103
Current Assets	2m	1m	1m

Banner Fluid Power Ltd

Shuttleworth Road Goldington, Bedford, MK41 0EA
Tel: 01234-215407 **Fax:** 01234-272461
E-mail: sales@banner-uk.com
Website: http://www.swagingmachines.com
Directors: M. Holdaway (Grp Chief Exec), D. Holdway (Co Sec)
Managers: M. Holdway (Sales Admin)
Immediate Holding Company: Banner Fluid Power Ltd
Registration no: 04438985 **Date established:** 2002
Turnover: £250,000 - £500,000 **No.of Employees:** 1 - 10
Product Groups: 29, 36, 40, 46

Date of Accounts	Mar 07	Mar 06	Mar 05
Working Capital	58	67	37
Fixed Assets	3	3	4
Current Assets	104	144	114

Barkers International Communications Ltd

Barker House Barkers Lane, Bedford, MK41 9TR
Tel: 01234-327772 **Fax:** 01234-325526
E-mail: info@barkersinternational.com
Website: http://www.barkersinternational.com
Bank(s): Barclays
Directors: L. Rutter (Fin)
Immediate Holding Company: BARKERS INTERNATIONAL COMMUNICATIONS LIMITED
Registration no: 00826661 **VAT No.:** GB 197 0127 57
Date established: 1964 **Turnover:** £2m - £5m **No.of Employees:** 11 - 20
Product Groups: 44

Date of Accounts	Oct 11	Oct 10	Oct 09
Working Capital	-347	-393	-177
Fixed Assets	1m	1m	1m
Current Assets	260	434	283

Bawa Engineering Ltd

Units 4 & 5 Fenlake Industrial Estate Fenlake Road, Bedford, MK42 0ET
Tel: 01234-215906 **Fax:** 01234-327858
Directors: A. Bahel (MD)
Immediate Holding Company: BAWA ENGINEERING LIMITED
Registration no: 01486521 **Date established:** 1980
Turnover: £250,000 - £500,000 **No.of Employees:** 1 - 10
Product Groups: 85

Date of Accounts	Mar 11	Mar 10	Mar 09
Working Capital	-71	-76	-64
Fixed Assets	499	501	503
Current Assets	89	101	69

Beaumont TM Ltd

2-4 Lyall Court Flitwick Industrial Estate, Flitwick, Bedford, MK45 1UQ
Tel: 01525-722500 **Fax:** 01525-718902
E-mail: info@beaumonttm.co.uk
Website: http://www.beaumonttm.co.uk
Directors: B. Ward (Co Sec), S. Barnes (MD)
Managers: R. Henman (Ops Mgr), E. Summerfield
Immediate Holding Company: BEAUMONT HOUSE LIMITED
Registration no: 03461072 **VAT No.:** GB 333 9400 70
Date established: 1997 **Turnover:** £2m - £5m **No.of Employees:** 21 - 50
Product Groups: 26, 30, 40

Date of Accounts	Dec 11	Dec 10	Dec 09
Working Capital	-170	-169	-148
Fixed Assets	186	186	186
Current Assets	15	25	23

Bedford Fixings

1a Dean Street, Bedford, MK40 3EQ
Tel: 01525-360747 **Fax:** 01234-217414
E-mail: sales@bedfordfixings.co.uk
Directors: A. Denny (Ptnr)
VAT No.: GB 290 8087 37 **Turnover:** £1m - £2m **No.of Employees:** 1 - 10
Product Groups: 37, 66

Binney & Smith Europe Ltd

Bedford Heights Brickhill Drive, Bedford, MK41 7PH
Tel: 01234-266702 **Fax:** 01234-342110
E-mail: vyoung@binneysmith.com
Website: http://www.crayola.com
Bank(s): HSBC Bank plc
Directors: V. Young (Co Sec), P. Blackett (Fin)
Ultimate Holding Company: HALLMARK CARDS INC (USA)
Immediate Holding Company: BINNEY & SMITH (EUROPE) LIMITED
Registration no: 00143803 **VAT No.:** GB 196 2103 67
Date established: 2016 **Turnover:** £20m - £50m
No.of Employees: 11 - 20 **Product Groups:** 32, 49, 64, 65

Date of Accounts	Dec 11	Dec 10	Dec 09
Sales Turnover	21m	21m	16m
Pre Tax Profit/Loss	1m	3m	-2m
Working Capital	2m	2m	-711
Fixed Assets	1m	883	11
Current Assets	10m	9m	6m
Current Liabilities	2m	1m	1m

Bocol Services (a division of Norse Precision Castings Ltd)

276-280 Ampthill Road, Bedford, MK42 9QJ
Tel: 01234-350907 **Fax:** 01234-210573
E-mail: sales@bocol.co.uk
Website: http://www.bocol.co.uk
Directors: C. Steed (Prop)
Ultimate Holding Company: NORSE PRECISION CASTINGS LTD
Turnover: Up to £250,000 **No.of Employees:** 1 - 10 **Product Groups:** 48

The Body Shop International plc

12 Silver Street, Bedford, MK40 1SU
Tel: 01234-341126 **Fax:** 01234-210104
Website: http://www.thebodyshop.co.uk
Managers: K. Mctabish (Mgr)
Immediate Holding Company: THE BODY SHOP INTERNATIONAL PLC
Registration no: 01284170 **Date established:** 1976
Turnover: £250m - £500m **No.of Employees:** 1 - 10 **Product Groups:** 32, 63

Date of Accounts	Dec 11	Dec 08	Jan 10
Sales Turnover	421m	290m	321m
Pre Tax Profit/Loss	49m	26m	35m
Working Capital	84m	14m	56m
Fixed Assets	214m	236m	224m
Current Assets	170m	146m	125m
Current Liabilities	49m	96m	42m

Boxclever

Technology House 239 Ampthill Road, Bedford, MK42 9QQ
Tel: 01234-355233 **Fax:** 01234-226090
E-mail: enquiries@boxclever.co.uk
Website: http://www.boxclever.co.uk
Bank(s): Barclays
Directors: D. Cowan (Grp Chief Exec), D. Cowan (MD), J. Meadows (Chief Op Offcr), J. Weight (Dir), S. Norman (Comm), Z. Mohammed (Co Sec)
Ultimate Holding Company: BXC UK LIMITED
Immediate Holding Company: BOX CLEVER LIMITED
Registration no: 04140077 **Date established:** 2001
Turnover: £125m - £250m **No.of Employees:** 51 - 100
Product Groups: 83

Date of Accounts	Dec 11	Dec 09	Dec 08
Working Capital	-13	-13	-13

Brice Baker Systems Ltd

Rookery Road Wyboston, Bedford, MK44 3AX
Tel: 01480-216618 **Fax:** 01480-406226
E-mail: info@bricebaker.co.uk
Website: http://www.bricebaker.co.uk
Bank(s): Trustee Savings Bank
Directors: I. Gorozhakin (Dir), R. Juffs (MD), I. Corozhankin (Dir), A. Gurney (Dir)
Managers: C. Juffs (Admin Off)
Ultimate Holding Company: BRICE-BAKER FINANCE LIMITED
Immediate Holding Company: BRICE-BAKER HOLDINGS LIMITED
Registration no: 00976440 **VAT No.:** GB 198 9423 02
Date established: 1970 **Turnover:** £2m - £5m **No.of Employees:** 21 - 50
Product Groups: 35, 41

Date of Accounts	Dec 09	Dec 08	Dec 07
Pre Tax Profit/Loss	173	80	N/A
Working Capital	5m	678	875
Fixed Assets	1m	1m	1m
Current Assets	5m	939	915
Current Liabilities	82	254	N/A

Brite Consulting Ltd

19 Pavenham Road Oakley, Bedford, MK43 7SY
Tel: 01234-828777 **Fax:** 01234- 828788
E-mail: info@briteconsulting.co.uk
Website: http://www.briteconsulting.co.uk
Directors: P. North (MD), R. Westgate (Fin)
Immediate Holding Company: BRITE CONSULTING LIMITED
Registration no: 04528118 **VAT No.:** GB 801 6733 51
Date established: 2002 **No.of Employees:** 1 - 10 **Product Groups:** 44, 80

Date of Accounts	Sep 11	Sep 10	Sep 09
Working Capital	35	21	4
Fixed Assets	2	1	N/A
Current Assets	61	43	44

Briton EMS Ltd

4 Shuttleworth Road Elms Industrial Estate Elm Farm Industrial Estate, Bedford, MK41 0EP
Tel: 01234-266300 **Fax:** 01234-266488
E-mail: info@britonems.co.uk
Website: http://www.britonems.co.uk
Bank(s): National Westminster Bank Plc
Directors: A. Abri (Dir)
Immediate Holding Company: BRITON EMS LIMITED
Registration no: 02039377 **VAT No.:** GB 455 9275 13
Date established: 1986 **Turnover:** £5m - £10m
No.of Employees: 51 - 100 **Product Groups:** 37

Date of Accounts	Nov 11	Nov 10	Nov 09
Sales Turnover	9m	7m	6m
Pre Tax Profit/Loss	925	657	228
Working Capital	2m	1m	1m
Fixed Assets	484	466	581
Current Assets	5m	3m	3m
Current Liabilities	2m	989	715

Builder Center Ltd

Windsor Road, Bedford, MK42 9SU
Tel: 01234-272292 **Fax:** 01234-365395
E-mail: peter.abbott@wolseley.co.uk
Website: http://www.buildercenter.co.uk
Bank(s): National Westminster Bank Plc
Directors: P. Abbot (MD)
Managers: P. Abbott (District Mgr)
Ultimate Holding Company: Wolseley plc
Immediate Holding Company: BUILD CENTER LIMITED
Registration no: 00462397 **Date established:** 1948 **Turnover:** £2m - £5m
No.of Employees: 21 - 50 **Product Groups:** 25

C Hughes

89 Station Road Home, Flitwick, Bedford, MK45 1LA
Tel: 01525-717270 **Fax:** 01525-717270
E-mail: clive.hughes@o2.co.uk
Directors: C. Hughes (Prop)
Turnover: Up to £250,000 **No.of Employees:** 1 - 10 **Product Groups:** 35, 52

Capita Business Services Ltd

Unit 3 Franklin Court Stannard Way Priory Business Park, Bedford, MK44 3JZ
Tel: 01234-838080 **Fax:** 01234-838091
E-mail: info@capita.co.uk
Website: http://www.capita.co.uk
Directors: D. Turnpenny (Fin), P. Pindar (Dir)
Managers: D. Feehan
Ultimate Holding Company: CAPITA PLC
Immediate Holding Company: CAPITA BUSINESS SERVICES LTD
Registration no: 02299747 **VAT No.:** GB 674 7727 87
Date established: 1988 **No.of Employees:** 251 - 500 **Product Groups:** 44, 84

Date of Accounts	Dec 11	Dec 10	Dec 09
Sales Turnover	885m	941m	1017m
Pre Tax Profit/Loss	215m	203m	226m
Working Capital	190m	146m	-374m
Fixed Assets	525m	504m	661m
Current Assets	531m	609m	311m
Current Liabilities	246m	281m	302m

Castlework Contractors

98 College Street Kempston, Bedford, MK42 8LU
Tel: 01234-217941 **Fax:** 01234-357232
E-mail: info@castlework.co.uk
Website: http://www.castlework.co.uk
Bank(s): Co-operative
Directors: D. Reynolds (MD)
Immediate Holding Company: CASTLEWORK CONTRACTORS LIMITED
Registration no: 01620585 **VAT No.:** GB 365 9698 83
Date established: 1982 **Turnover:** £500,000 - £1m
No.of Employees: 11 - 20 **Product Groups:** 32

Date of Accounts	Feb 08	Feb 11	Feb 10
Working Capital	225	-48	73
Fixed Assets	74	74	85
Current Assets	536	125	263

Central Industrial Automation
4 Singer Court Woburn Road Industrial Estate Woburn Road Industrial Estate, Kempston, Bedford, MK42 7AW
Tel: 01234-853396
Directors: D. Bicknell (Prop)
Immediate Holding Company: CENTRAL INDUSTRIAL AUTOMATION LTD.
Registration no: 03365105 **Date established:** 1997
No.of Employees: 1 - 10 **Product Groups:** 38, 40, 47

Chaggar Engineering G S C N C Sheetmetal Work
Murdock Road Manton Industrial Estate, Bedford, MK41 7PE
Tel: 01234-360557 **Fax:** 08712-422493
E-mail: pchagger@orange.net
Directors: P. Chaggar (Dir), P. Chaggar (Prop)
Immediate Holding Company: CHAGGAR ENGINEERING LIMITED
Registration no: 07567432 **VAT No.:** GB 335 0153 94
Date established: 2011 **Turnover:** £500,000 - £1m
No.of Employees: 1 - 10 **Product Groups:** 48

Challenge Europe Ltd
Shuttleworth Road Elm Farm Industrial Estate, Bedford, MK41 0EP
Tel: 01234-346242 **Fax:** 01234-327349
E-mail: sales@challenge-indfast.co.uk
Website: http://www.challenge-indfast.co.uk
Directors: K. Moorecroft (MD), P. Wild (Co Sec)
Immediate Holding Company: CHALLENGE (EUROPE) LIMITED
Registration no: 04715830 **VAT No.:** GB 196 8691 91
Date established: 2003 **Turnover:** £1m - £2m **No.of Employees:** 1 - 10
Product Groups: 30, 35

Date of Accounts	Mar 11	Mar 10	Mar 09
Working Capital	236	186	143
Fixed Assets	38	22	7
Current Assets	340	295	244

S J Clarke Company Ltd
Unit D Firs Farm West End, Stagsden, Bedford, MK43 8TB
Tel: 01234-346513 **Fax:** 01234-364047
E-mail: sales@sjclarke.co.uk
Website: http://www.sjclarke.co.uk
Bank(s): Midland P.L.C., Uxbridge
Directors: G. Kidd (Co Sec), R. Willcox (MD), A. Stennet (MD), S. Ludbrook (Dir)
Immediate Holding Company: S.J. CLARKE LTD
Registration no: 00732687 **VAT No.:** GB 213 4167 00
Date established: 1962 **No.of Employees:** 11 - 20 **Product Groups:** 23, 52

Clements Engineering St Neots Ltd
120 Airfield Industrial Park Little Staughton, Bedford, MK44 2BN
Tel: 01234-378814 **Fax:** 01234-376779
E-mail: sales@clementsmarine.co.uk
Website: http://www.clementsmarine.co.uk
Bank(s): Barclays
Directors: M. Kerrigon (Dir), P. Williams (MD), P. Williams (Fin)
Managers: M. Major (Sales Prom Mgr)
Immediate Holding Company: CLEMENTS ENGINEERING (ST. NEOTS) LIMITED
Registration no: 01588949 **VAT No.:** GB 361 9004 69
Date established: 1981 **Turnover:** £1m - £2m **No.of Employees:** 21 - 50
Product Groups: 39

Date of Accounts	Sep 11	Sep 10	Sep 09
Working Capital	86	63	38
Fixed Assets	325	358	387
Current Assets	811	786	718
Current Liabilities	130	247	234

Collins Walker UK Ltd (Dept Kom)
78 College Street Kempston, Bedford, MK42 8LU
Tel: 01234-340044 **Fax:** 01234-340065
E-mail: enquiries@collins-walker.co.uk
Website: http://www.collins-walker.co.uk
Directors: C. Goddard (Dir)
Immediate Holding Company: COLLINS WALKER INTERNATIONAL LTD
Registration no: 07717184 **Date established:** 2011
Turnover: £250,000 - £500,000 **No.of Employees:** 1 - 10
Product Groups: 40

Date of Accounts	Mar 08	Mar 07	Mar 06
Working Capital	-39	-91	-75
Fixed Assets	8	10	11
Current Assets	18	26	48
Current Liabilities	57	117	123

Control Transducers Ltd
25 Kimbolton Road, Bedford, MK40 2NY
Tel: 01234-217704 **Fax:** 01234-217083
E-mail: ray.mather@controlt.co.uk
Website: http://www.controlt.co.uk
Directors: A. Mather (Fin), R. Mather (MD)
Immediate Holding Company: CONTROL TRANSDUCERS LIMITED
Registration no: 03020885 **VAT No.:** GB 650 7109 54
Date established: 1995 **Turnover:** £500,000 - £1m
No.of Employees: 1 - 10 **Product Groups:** 37, 38

Date of Accounts	Sep 11	Sep 10	Sep 09
Working Capital	11	27	35
Fixed Assets	11	2	3
Current Assets	80	100	77

Cranfield Electrical Ltd
2 Adams Close Kempston, Bedford, MK42 7JE
Tel: 01234-853044 **Fax:** 01234-853054
E-mail: sales@cranfieldelectrical.com
Website: http://www.cranfieldelectrical.com
Bank(s): National Westminster Bank Plc
Directors: R. Samels (MD)
Immediate Holding Company: CRANFIELD ELECTRICAL LIMITED
Registration no: 00638868 **VAT No.:** GB 196 2237 46
Date established: 1959 **Turnover:** £500,000 - £1m
No.of Employees: 11 - 20 **Product Groups:** 37

Date of Accounts	Sep 11	Sep 10	Sep 09
Working Capital	752	718	937
Fixed Assets	363	471	281
Current Assets	802	785	998

Cranfield School Of Management
Cranfield, Bedford, MK43 0AL
Tel: 01234-751122 **Fax:** 01234-751806
E-mail: j.clarke@cranfield.ac.uk
Website: http://www.cranfield.ac.uk
Bank(s): National Westminster Bank Plc
Managers: A. Burch
Immediate Holding Company: BOB FRY PHOTOGRAPHY LIMITED
Registration no: 04625656 **Date established:** 2002
Turnover: £10m - £20m **No.of Employees:** 251 - 500 **Product Groups:** 86

Date of Accounts	Mar 12	Mar 11	Mar 10
Working Capital	-5	-8	-9
Fixed Assets	6	8	9
Current Assets	12	10	10

Creative Graphics International Ltd
6-8 Singer Way Woburn Road Industrial Estate, Kempston, Bedford, MK42 7AN
Tel: 01234-846000 **Fax:** 01789-414160
E-mail: steven.perry@cgi-visual.com
Website: http://www.cgi-visual.com
Directors: S. Perry (MD)
Managers: E. Nicholson-clinch (Personnel), N. Henstone (Sales Prom Mgr), P. Adamson (Fin Mgr)
Immediate Holding Company: CREATIVE GRAPHICS INTERNATIONAL LIMITED
Registration no: 02858212 **Date established:** 1993
Turnover: £10m - £20m **No.of Employees:** 21 - 50 **Product Groups:** 27, 28, 30, 49

Date of Accounts	Nov 11	Nov 10	Nov 09
Sales Turnover	11m	11m	9m
Pre Tax Profit/Loss	848	915	-520
Working Capital	1m	800	507
Fixed Assets	3m	4m	4m
Current Assets	4m	4m	4m
Current Liabilities	1m	2m	2m

Cromwell Industrial Supplies Ltd
Unit 11 Manton Centre Manton Lane, Manton Industrial Estate, Bedford, MK41 7PX
Tel: 01234-716470 **Fax:** 01234-211214
E-mail: bedford@cromwell.co.uk
Website: http://www.cromwell.co.uk
Bank(s): Lloyds TSB Bank plc
Managers: B. Smith (Mgr), D. Barrell (Sales Prom Mgr)
Immediate Holding Company: CROMWELL TOOLS LTD
Registration no: 00986161 **VAT No.:** GB 115 5713 87
Turnover: £1m - £2m **No.of Employees:** 21 - 50 **Product Groups:** 27, 32, 66, 67

C T M Systems Ltd
78 Arkwright Road Industrial Estate Arkwright Road, Bedford, MK42 0LQ
Tel: 01234-355700 **Fax:** 01234-351155
E-mail: sales@ctm-systems.co.uk
Website: http://www.ctm-systems.co.uk
Managers: D. Ellmers (Mgr)
Immediate Holding Company: CTM SYSTEMS LIMITED
Registration no: 02719932 **VAT No.:** GB 608 4388 26
Date established: 1992 **Turnover:** £2m - £5m **No.of Employees:** 11 - 20
Product Groups: 41

Date of Accounts	Aug 11	Aug 10	Aug 09
Working Capital	324	224	88
Fixed Assets	51	61	80
Current Assets	973	980	634

D M S Computer Recruitment
1 Union Street, Bedford, MK40 2SF
Tel: 01234-214571 **Fax:** 01234-349696
E-mail: cv@dmsitjobs.co.uk
Website: http://www.dmsitjobs.co.uk
Directors: A. Marin (Prop)
Registration no: 02134908 **Date established:** 1977
Turnover: £250,000 - £500,000 **No.of Employees:** 1 - 10
Product Groups: 44, 80, 86

Danfoss Randall
Ampthill Road, Bedford, MK42 9ER
Tel: 08451-217400 **Fax:** 08451-217515
E-mail: gordon_macpherson@danfoss.com
Website: http://www.danfoss-randall.co.uk
Bank(s): HSBC Bank plc
Directors: G. Macpherson (MD)
Managers: P. Bing (Tech Serv Mgr), C. Isles (Personnel), T. Flecknell (Purch Mgr), B. Neilson (Mktg Serv Mgr), G. Smith (Sales Prom Mgr)
Ultimate Holding Company: DANFOSS AS (DENMARK)
Immediate Holding Company: DANFOSS RANDALL LIMITED
Registration no: 02579403 **Date established:** 1991
Turnover: £20m - £50m **No.of Employees:** 101 - 250
Product Groups: 35, 36, 38, 49, 52

Date of Accounts	Dec 11	Dec 10	Dec 09
Sales Turnover	35m	35m	33m
Pre Tax Profit/Loss	1m	2m	5m
Working Capital	9m	13m	12m
Fixed Assets	1m	2m	2m
Current Assets	19m	23m	20m
Current Liabilities	3m	4m	3m

Delkim Ltd
PO Box 270, Bedford, MK43 7DZ
Tel: 01234-721116 **Fax:** 01234-721116
E-mail: office@delkim.co.uk
Website: http://www.delkim.co.uk
Directors: D. Romang (MD), C. Romang (Fin)
Immediate Holding Company: DELKIM LIMITED
Registration no: 02662128 **Date established:** 1991
No.of Employees: 1 - 10 **Product Groups:** 49

Date of Accounts	Dec 11	Dec 10	Dec 09
Working Capital	2m	2m	2m
Fixed Assets	N/A	98	101
Current Assets	3m	3m	2m

Drive Lines
45 Murdock Road Manton Industrial Estate, Bedford, MK41 7PQ
Tel: 01234-360689 **Fax:** 01234-345673
E-mail: sales@drivelines.co.uk
Website: http://www.drivelines.co.uk
Managers: I. Carr (Mgr)
Immediate Holding Company: DRIVE LINES TECHNOLOGIES LIMITED
Registration no: 02695331 **Date established:** 1992
No.of Employees: 1 - 10 **Product Groups:** 35, 36, 39, 43, 45, 46, 66, 68, 84

Date of Accounts	Feb 12	Feb 11	Feb 10
Working Capital	198	126	94
Fixed Assets	7	10	1
Current Assets	473	405	258

E J Watts Pipeworks Ltd
Barton Industrial Estate Faldo Road, Barton-Le-Clay, Bedford, MK45 4RJ
Tel: 01582-881601 **Fax:** 01582-881075
E-mail: enquiries@ejwatts.co.uk
Website: http://www.ejwatts.co.uk
Directors: P. Taverner (Dir)
Managers: M. Willis (Sales Admin), B. Brimmell
Immediate Holding Company: E. J. WATTS PIPEWORKS LIMITED
Registration no: 00556626 **VAT No.:** GB 197 6243 25
Date established: 1955 **Turnover:** £1m - £2m **No.of Employees:** 21 - 50
Product Groups: 34, 39, 46, 48, 84, 85

Date of Accounts	Sep 11	Sep 10	Sep 09
Working Capital	81	383	543
Fixed Assets	233	209	145
Current Assets	1m	879	872

Electronic Reading Systems Ltd
14 Wolseley Business Park Kempston, Bedford, MK42 7PW
Tel: 01234-855300 **Fax:** 01234-855446
E-mail: sales@ersltd.co.uk
Website: http://www.ers-online.co.uk
Bank(s): Lloyds TSB Bank plc
Directors: S. Ball (Dir)
Immediate Holding Company: ELECTRONIC READING SYSTEMS LIMITED
Registration no: 02233595 **VAT No.:** GB 491 1807 42
Date established: 1988 **Turnover:** £1m - £2m **No.of Employees:** 11 - 20
Product Groups: 28, 44, 67

Date of Accounts	Jul 09	Jul 08	Jul 07
Working Capital	178	162	154
Fixed Assets	52	76	72
Current Assets	548	395	486

Europa Plant Services Ltd
Unit 1 Blackburn Hall Compound Milton Road, Thurleigh, Bedford, MK44 2DG
Tel: 01234-772377 **Fax:** 01234-771116
E-mail: sales@europaplant.com
Website: http://www.europaplant.com
Directors: I. Ettrick (MD), N. Ettrick (Fin)
Immediate Holding Company: EUROPA PLANT SERVICES LIMITED
Registration no: 01401328 **Date established:** 1978
No.of Employees: 1 - 10 **Product Groups:** 40, 67

Date of Accounts	Nov 11	Nov 10	Nov 09
Working Capital	307	132	5
Fixed Assets	170	183	197
Current Assets	844	861	977

European Metals Recycling Ltd
Cauldwell Walk, Bedford, MK42 9DT
Tel: 01234-272572 **Fax:** 01234-271891
E-mail: info@emrltd.com
Website: http://www.emrltd.com
Bank(s): National Westminster Bank Plc
Directors: P. Shepherd (Prop)
Immediate Holding Company: EUROPEAN METAL RECYCLING LIMITED
Registration no: 02954623 **VAT No.:** GB 322 4860 74
Date established: 1994 **Turnover:** £5m - £10m **No.of Employees:** 11 - 20
Product Groups: 66

Date of Accounts	Dec 11	Dec 10	Dec 09
Sales Turnover	3032m	2431m	1843m
Pre Tax Profit/Loss	116m	155m	91m
Working Capital	414m	371m	167m
Fixed Assets	518m	483m	480m
Current Assets	1027m	717m	557m
Current Liabilities	124m	118m	185m

F & P Wholesale
Chantry Road Kempston, Bedford, MK42 7SU
Tel: 01234-845600 **Fax:** 01234-840379
E-mail: bedford@fpwholesale.co.uk
Website: http://www.fpwholesale.co.uk
Managers: S. Simms (District Mgr)
Immediate Holding Company: MANNESMANN
Registration no: 00704322 **Date established:** 1968
No.of Employees: 21 - 50 **Product Groups:** 30, 36, 40

Fords Packaging Systems Ltd
Ronald Close Kempston, Bedford, MK42 7SH
Tel: 01234-846600 **Fax:** 01234-841820
E-mail: geoff.brim@fords-packsys.co.uk
Website: http://www.fords-packsys.co.uk
Bank(s): Lloyds TSB Bank plc
Directors: G. Brim (Fin)
Ultimate Holding Company: FORDS PACKAGING SYSTEMS LIMITED
Immediate Holding Company: ALUMINIUM CAPPING SERVICES LIMITED
Registration no: 02633380 **VAT No.:** GB 706 0035 83
Date established: 1991 **Turnover:** £5m - £10m **No.of Employees:** 21 - 50
Product Groups: 42

Date of Accounts	Jul 09	Jul 08	Jun 11
Working Capital	231	215	N/A
Fixed Assets	27	34	N/A
Current Assets	476	388	N/A

Freelance Fork Lift Co.
Unit 60 The Airfield Little Staughton, Bedford, MK44 2BN
Tel: 01234-376639 **Fax:** 01234-376130
E-mail: peilow@btinternet.com
Directors: H. Peilow (Snr Part)
Date established: 1985 **No.of Employees:** 1 - 10 **Product Groups:** 35, 39, 45

Fuji Film Digital Camera Support Line
13 St Martins Business Centre St Martins Way, Bedford, MK42 0LF
Tel: 08445-532322 **Fax:** 01234-360294
Website: http://www.fujifilm.co.uk
Managers: C. Leeds (Mgr)
Ultimate Holding Company: FUJIFILM HOLDINGS CORPORATION (JAPAN)
Immediate Holding Company: FUJIFILM UK LIMITED
Registration no: 01264514 **Date established:** 1976
Turnover: £125m - £250m **No.of Employees:** 1 - 10 **Product Groups:** 37, 38, 65

Date of Accounts	Mar 11	Mar 10	Mar 09
Sales Turnover	249m	217m	220m
Pre Tax Profit/Loss	6m	5m	6m
Working Capital	62m	54m	49m
Fixed Assets	3m	3m	2m
Current Assets	110m	90m	83m
Current Liabilities	10m	9m	6m

G T Markyate Ltd
4 Pulloxhill Business Park Greenfield Road, Pulloxhill, Bedford, MK45 5EU
Tel: 01525-718585 **Fax:** 01525-715440
E-mail: sales@gtengineering.co.uk
Website: http://gtengineering.co.uk
Directors: B. Thorne (MD), S. Thorne (Fin)
Registration no: 01333906 **No.of Employees:** 1 - 10 **Product Groups:** 34, 35, 46, 48, 68, 84, 85

Date of Accounts	Dec 07	Dec 06	Dec 05
Sales Turnover	N/A	N/A	487
Pre Tax Profit/Loss	N/A	N/A	99
Working Capital	133	86	80
Fixed Assets	311	317	296
Current Assets	249	183	160
Current Liabilities	116	97	80
Total Share Capital	1	1	1
ROCE% (Return on Capital Employed)			26.2
ROT% (Return on Turnover)			20.3

Galup Ltd
48 Elmsdale Road Wootton, Bedford, MK43 9JN
Tel: 01234-768805 **Fax:** 01234-767532
E-mail: sales@galupltd.co.uk
Website: http://www.galupltd.co.uk
Managers: P. Gulliver (Mgr)
Immediate Holding Company: GALUP LIMITED
Registration no: 02990648 **Date established:** 1994
Turnover: £500,000 - £1m **No.of Employees:** 1 - 10 **Product Groups:** 36

Date of Accounts	Dec 11	Dec 10	Dec 09
Working Capital	148	141	105
Fixed Assets	43	14	16
Current Assets	277	141	105

H R P Ltd
Manton Centre Manton Lane, Manton Industrial Estate, Bedford, MK41 7PX
Tel: 01234-272702 **Fax:** 01234-273424
E-mail: bedford@hrpltd.co.uk
Website: http://www.hrponline.co.uk
Managers: T. Kimmings
Ultimate Holding Company: HRP HOLDINGS LIMITED
Immediate Holding Company: HRP LIMITED
Registration no: 00832237 **Date established:** 1964
Turnover: £50m - £75m **No.of Employees:** 1 - 10 **Product Groups:** 40, 66

Date of Accounts	Dec 11	Dec 10	Dec 09
Sales Turnover	55m	52m	46m
Pre Tax Profit/Loss	1m	1m	651
Working Capital	8m	7m	6m
Fixed Assets	2m	2m	3m
Current Assets	22m	22m	17m
Current Liabilities	3m	4m	3m

Hace Technical Services
15 St Cuthberts Street, Bedford, MK40 3JB
Tel: 01234-272772 **Fax:** 01234-218239
E-mail: hace_consulting@hotmail.com
Directors: P. Carruthers (MD)
Immediate Holding Company: HACE TECHNICAL SERVICES LTD
Registration no: 04324340 **Date established:** 2001
No.of Employees: 1 - 10 **Product Groups:** 35

Hackfield Leasing Ltd
121 High Street Cranfield, Bedford, MK43 0BS
Tel: 01234-756152 **Fax:** 01234-750850
E-mail: debbie.thorne@hackfield.com
Website: http://www.hackfield.com
Directors: R. Holton (MD)
Managers: D. Thorne (Admin Off)
Registration no: 01367746 **Date established:** 1978 **Turnover:** £1m - £2m
No.of Employees: 1 - 10 **Product Groups:** 72, 80, 82

Date of Accounts	Mar 11	Mar 10	Mar 09
Working Capital	-318	-369	-490
Fixed Assets	1m	2m	2m
Current Assets	435	397	427

H C L Safety Ltd (a part of the Latchways Group)
Unit 20 106a Bedford Road Wootton, Bedford, MK43 9JB
Tel: 01234-830900 **Fax:** 01234-830999
E-mail: bedford@hclsafety.com
Website: http://www.hclsafety.com
Managers: G. Davis (District Mgr)
Ultimate Holding Company: LATCHWAYS PLC
Immediate Holding Company: HCL-SAFETY LIMITED
Registration no: 02691137 **Date established:** 1992
No.of Employees: 1 - 10 **Product Groups:** 37, 40, 67, 86

Date of Accounts	Mar 11	Mar 10	Mar 09
Sales Turnover	9m	8m	10m
Pre Tax Profit/Loss	971	1m	1m
Working Capital	2m	2m	1m
Fixed Assets	251	311	360
Current Assets	3m	3m	3m
Current Liabilities	1m	783	640

I D G T E
Bedford Heights Brickhill Drive, Bedford, MK41 7PH
Tel: 01234-214340 **Fax:** 01234-355493
E-mail: enquiries@idgte.org
Website: http://www.idgte.org
Managers: M. Raine
Immediate Holding Company: THE INSTITUTION OF DIESEL AND GAS TURBINE ENGINEERS
Registration no: 07244044 **VAT No.:** GB 728 4960 02
Date established: 2010 **Turnover:** Up to £250,000
No.of Employees: 1 - 10 **Product Groups:** 87

Date of Accounts	Jun 11
Sales Turnover	76
Pre Tax Profit/Loss	-3
Working Capital	40
Fixed Assets	1
Current Assets	41
Current Liabilities	1

I T Works
51 Water End Road Maulden, Bedford, MK45 2BD
Tel: 01525-862266 **Fax:** 01525-862166
E-mail: j.upton@itworks-uk.com
Website: http://www.itworks-uk.com
Directors: S. Finch (Ptnr)
Immediate Holding Company: IT WORKS-UK.COM LIMITED
Registration no: 03323272 **Date established:** 1997
Turnover: Up to £250,000 **No.of Employees:** 1 - 10 **Product Groups:** 34, 44, 49, 67, 69, 80, 86

Date of Accounts	Feb 08	Feb 11	Feb 10
Sales Turnover	N/A	60	85
Pre Tax Profit/Loss	N/A	-6	-29
Working Capital	14	-3	-22
Fixed Assets	21	4	7
Current Assets	47	14	14
Current Liabilities	N/A	N/A	24

Igranic Control Systems Ltd
Murdoch Road, Bedford, MK41 7PT
Tel: 01234-267242 **Fax:** 01234-219061
E-mail: info@igranic.com
Website: http://www.igranic.com
Bank(s): National Westminster Bank Plc
Directors: M. Fenn (MD), P. Whitbread (Sales), A. Seabrook (Fin)
Managers: K. Lee (Tech Serv Mgr)
Ultimate Holding Company: THE IGRANIC GROUP LIMITED
Immediate Holding Company: IGRANIC CONTROL SYSTEMS LIMITED
Registration no: 02087915 **VAT No.:** GB 491 2514 52
Date established: 1987 **Turnover:** £2m - £5m **No.of Employees:** 51 - 100
Product Groups: 37, 38, 45, 67

Date of Accounts	Mar 11	Mar 10	Mar 09
Sales Turnover	4m	6m	6m
Pre Tax Profit/Loss	147	106	151
Working Capital	987	843	772
Fixed Assets	74	62	81
Current Assets	2m	3m	3m
Current Liabilities	510	1m	1m

Industrial Calibrations Ltd
1 Sunbeam Road Kempston, Bedford, MK42 7BZ
Tel: 01234-857171 **Fax:** 01234-840371
E-mail: sales@industrialcalibration.com
Website: http://www.industrialcalibration.com
Bank(s): HSBC
Directors: C. Beech (MD)
Immediate Holding Company: INDUSTRIAL CALIBRATION LIMITED
Registration no: 02257654 **VAT No.:** GB 335 3325 76
Date established: 1988 **Turnover:** £500,000 - £1m
No.of Employees: 11 - 20 **Product Groups:** 38

Date of Accounts	May 11	May 10	May 09
Working Capital	147	132	101
Fixed Assets	84	89	94
Current Assets	260	284	286

Interfoam Ltd
15-16 Ronald Close Woburn Road Industrial Estate, Kempston, Bedford, MK42 7SH
Tel: 01234-855355 **Fax:** 01234-855665
E-mail: sales@interfoam.co.uk
Website: http://www.interfoam.co.uk
Bank(s): Barclays
Directors: L. Fregapane (Fin), N. Read (Sales), C. Fregapane (MD)
Managers: C. Shirley (Personnel), R. Fregapane (Prod Mgr)
Immediate Holding Company: INTERFOAM LIMITED
Registration no: 02737780 **Date established:** 1992 **Turnover:** £2m - £5m
No.of Employees: 51 - 100 **Product Groups:** 26, 29, 30, 31

Date of Accounts	Dec 11	Dec 10	Dec 09
Sales Turnover	N/A	N/A	4m
Pre Tax Profit/Loss	N/A	N/A	27
Working Capital	1m	1m	1m
Fixed Assets	550	606	457
Current Assets	3m	2m	2m
Current Liabilities	N/A	N/A	143

Irvine Whitlock Ltd
Priory Business Park Stannard Way, Bedford, MK44 3JW
Tel: 01234-832300 **Fax:** 01234-832400
E-mail: paul.dewick@iwltd.co.uk
Website: http://www.irvine-whitlock.co.uk
Directors: P. Dewick (MD)
Managers: K. Beattie (Comptroller), A. Moore (Chief Buyer)
Ultimate Holding Company: HEIDELBERG CEMENT AG (GERMANY)
Immediate Holding Company: IRVINE-WHITLOCK LIMITED
Registration no: 00870262 **Date established:** 1966 **Turnover:** £5m - £10m
No.of Employees: 251 - 500 **Product Groups:** 51, 52, 84

Date of Accounts	Dec 11	Dec 10	Dec 09
Sales Turnover	24m	27m	32m
Pre Tax Profit/Loss	-668	744	401
Working Capital	5m	15m	14m
Fixed Assets	2m	2m	2m
Current Assets	10m	17m	18m
Current Liabilities	506	403	1m

J P D T Trading
Maulden Road Industrial Estate Commerce Way, Flitwick, Bedford, MK45 5BP
Tel: 01525-716422 **Fax:** 01525-719889
Website: http://www.jpdt-engines.co.uk
Directors: P. Canavan (Ptnr)
Immediate Holding Company: STUDER LIMITED
Registration no: 05510529 **Date established:** 2005
No.of Employees: 1 - 10 **Product Groups:** 35, 36, 39

JBT FoodTech (formerly FMC FoodTech)
Wolseley Road Woburn Road Industrial Estate, Kempston, Bedford, MK42 7EF
Tel: 01234-841177 **Fax:** 01234-841400
E-mail: diane.kemp@jbtc.com
Website: http://www.jbtfoodtech.com
Managers: R. Pitcher, B. Jackson
Immediate Holding Company: John Bean Technologies
Registration no: 06512478 **VAT No.:** GB 927 2376 11
Date established: 1931 **Turnover:** £10m - £20m
No.of Employees: 21 - 50 **Product Groups:** 20, 36, 39, 40, 41, 42, 47, 48, 52, 66, 67, 84

Kaltenbach Ltd
6 Brunel Road, Bedford, MK41 9TG
Tel: 01234-213201 **Fax:** 01234-351226
E-mail: sales@kaltenbach.co.uk
Website: http://www.kaltenbach.co.uk
Bank(s): Barclays
Directors: D. Mills (Co Sec)
Managers: B. Rooney
Ultimate Holding Company: DIETER KALTENBACH VERWALTUNGS GMBH
Immediate Holding Company: KALTENBACH LIMITED
Registration no: 01089420 **VAT No.:** GB 196 8509 09
Date established: 1973 **Turnover:** £2m - £5m **No.of Employees:** 21 - 50
Product Groups: 36, 46, 67

Date of Accounts	Dec 11	Dec 10	Dec 09
Sales Turnover	N/A	N/A	3m
Pre Tax Profit/Loss	N/A	N/A	9
Working Capital	1m	1m	1m
Fixed Assets	356	369	390
Current Assets	2m	2m	2m
Current Liabilities	N/A	N/A	347

Kemppi UK Ltd
Martti Kemppi Building Priory Business Park, Bedford, MK44 3WH
Tel: 08456-444201 **Fax:** 08456-444202
E-mail: sales.uk@kemppi.com
Website: http://www.kemppi.com
Directors: M. Pixley (MD)
Ultimate Holding Company: KEMPPI OY (FINLAND)
Immediate Holding Company: KEMPPI (U.K.) LIMITED
Registration no: 00916454 **VAT No.:** GB 322 5494 68
Date established: 1967 **Turnover:** £2m - £5m **No.of Employees:** 11 - 20
Product Groups: 46

Date of Accounts	Dec 11	Dec 10	Dec 09
Working Capital	-1	-550	-467
Fixed Assets	902	935	1m
Current Assets	1m	2m	1m

Lenze UK Ltd
Lenze Limited Caxton Road Elm Farm, Elm Farm Industrial Estate, Bedford, MK41 0HT
Tel: 01234-321200 **Fax:** 01234-261815
E-mail: sales@lenze.co.uk
Website: http://www.lenze.co.uk
Bank(s): HSBC, Bedford
Directors: D. Foster (MD), D. Foster (Jt MD), H. Hylden (Jt MD), S. Cherry (Co Sec), S. Hylden (Jt MD)
Managers: G. Spear (Mktg Serv Mgr)
Ultimate Holding Company: LENZE AG (GERMANY)
Immediate Holding Company: LENZE U.K. LIMITED
Registration no: 03697815 **Date established:** 1999
Turnover: £10m - £20m **No.of Employees:** 101 - 250
Product Groups: 35, 37, 38, 45

Date of Accounts	Apr 10	Apr 09	Apr 08
Pre Tax Profit/Loss	-1	-1	-1
Working Capital	-5m	N/A	N/A
Fixed Assets	13m	13m	13m
Current Assets	2	2	2
Current Liabilities	5m	5m	5m

Graham Lloyd Bedford Ltd
Ampthill Road, Bedford, MK42 9JN
Tel: 01234-267810 **Fax:** 01234-212942
E-mail: graham@grahamlloyd.co.uk
Website: http://www.grahamlloyd.co.uk
Bank(s): National Westminster Bank Plc
Directors: G. Inskip (MD)
Immediate Holding Company: GRAHAM LLOYD (BEDFORD) LIMITED
Registration no: 01911018 **VAT No.:** GB 426 5759 26
Date established: 1985 **Turnover:** £2m - £5m **No.of Employees:** 21 - 50
Product Groups: 48

Date of Accounts	Jun 12	Jun 11	Jun 10
Working Capital	-4	49	59
Fixed Assets	405	394	402
Current Assets	120	148	182

Gordon Low Products Ltd
Rookery Road Wyboston, Bedford, MK44 3UG
Tel: 01480-405433 **Fax:** 01480-405434
E-mail: info@gordonlowproducts.co.uk
Website: http://www.gordonlowproducts.co.uk
Bank(s): Barclays
Directors: R. Low (MD)
Immediate Holding Company: GORDON LOW PRODUCTS LIMITED
Registration no: 01544486 **Date established:** 1981 **Turnover:** £2m - £5m
No.of Employees: 11 - 20 **Product Groups:** 29, 30

Date of Accounts	Dec 11	Dec 10	Dec 09
Working Capital	1m	1m	1m
Fixed Assets	46	49	65
Current Assets	2m	1m	1m

Luton Steels Ltd
Wharley Farm College Road, Cranfield, Bedford, MK43 0AH
Tel: 01234-750003 **Fax:** 01234-750084
E-mail: sales@lutonsteels.com
Website: http://www.lutonsteels.com
Managers: M. Challis (Projects)
Immediate Holding Company: LUTON STEELS LIMITED
Registration no: 03539175 **VAT No.:** GB 418 9966 93
Date established: 1998 **Turnover:** £1m - £2m **No.of Employees:** 1 - 10
Product Groups: 48, 66

Date of Accounts	Mar 11	Mar 10	Mar 09
Working Capital	-38	-44	-53
Fixed Assets	46	52	60
Current Assets	85	132	55

M & D H Insurance Services Ltd
Sandland Court The Pilgrim Centre Brickhill Drive, Bedford, MK41 7PZ
Tel: 01234-352230 **Fax:** 01234-352330
E-mail: info@mdh-insurance.co.uk
Website: http://www.mdh-insurance.co.uk
Directors: D. Hames (Fin), R. Hames (MD)
Immediate Holding Company: M & D H INSURANCE SERVICES LTD
Registration no: 04567536 **Date established:** 2002 **Turnover:** £1m - £2m
No.of Employees: 21 - 50 **Product Groups:** 14, 23, 25, 27, 28, 29, 30, 31, 32, 33, 34, 35, 36, 38, 39, 40, 44, 45, 48, 51, 52, 54, 66, 67, 69, 72, 75, 80, 81, 82, 83, 84, 85, 86, 87, 89

Date of Accounts	Dec 11	Dec 10	Dec 09
Sales Turnover	N/A	N/A	2m
Pre Tax Profit/Loss	N/A	N/A	169
Working Capital	63	97	-12
Fixed Assets	83	70	74
Current Assets	807	812	584
Current Liabilities	N/A	N/A	145

M & M International UK Ltd
12 Railton Road Kempston, Bedford, MK42 7PW
Tel: 01234-855888 **Fax:** 01234-856999
E-mail: sales@mmint.co.uk
Website: http://www.mmint.co.uk
Directors: M. Taylor (Fin), D. Norford (Dir)
Immediate Holding Company: M & M INTERNATIONAL (U.K.) LIMITED
Registration no: 02547501 **Date established:** 1990 **Turnover:** £1m - £2m
No.of Employees: 1 - 10 **Product Groups:** 36, 37, 40

Date of Accounts	Dec 11	Dec 10	Dec 09
Working Capital	313	282	226
Fixed Assets	19	22	26
Current Assets	438	477	348

M S Engineering
PO Box 255, Bedford, MK41 9BH
Tel: 01234-772255 **Fax:** 01234-772266
E-mail: info@msengineering.co.uk
Website: http://www.msengineering.co.uk
Directors: M. Scott (Prop)
Turnover: Up to £250,000 **No.of Employees:** 11 - 20 **Product Groups:** 39

M S Y S Inc
4a Goldington Road, Bedford, MK40 3NF
Tel: 01234-213715 **Fax:** 01234-213736
E-mail: info@msysinc.com
Website: http://www.msysinc.com
Directors: V. Mandadi (MD), V. Naini (Fin)
Immediate Holding Company: MSYS UK LTD
Registration no: 04092738 **Date established:** 2000
No.of Employees: 11 - 20 **Product Groups:** 81

Date of Accounts	Dec 11	Dec 10	Dec 09
Working Capital	-95	-72	-90
Fixed Assets	3	4	4
Current Assets	32	43	57

Marshall Bedford
Woburn Road Kempston, Bedford, MK42 7QN
Tel: 01234-856161 **Fax:** 01234-857801
E-mail: peugeotbedford@marshallweb.co.uk
Website: http://www.marshallweb.co.uk
Managers: S. Pattern (Mgr)
Registration no: 00312159 **VAT No.:** GB 684 0225 42
Turnover: £500,000 - £1m **No.of Employees:** 21 - 50 **Product Groups:** 68

Mastergrave Bedford Ltd
65 Murdock Road Manton Industrial Estate, Bedford, MK41 7PL
Tel: 01234-218226 **Fax:** 01234-269899
E-mail: info@mastergrave.co.uk
Website: http://www.mastergrave.co.uk
Bank(s): Lloyds TSB Bank plc
Directors: G. Luddington (MD), A. Luddington (Fin)
Immediate Holding Company: MASTERGRAVE (BEDFORD) LTD.
Registration no: 01977681 **VAT No.:** GB 440 7927 43
Date established: 1986 **Turnover:** £1m - £2m **No.of Employees:** 11 - 20
Product Groups: 27, 28, 30, 33, 35, 36, 38, 42, 44, 45, 46, 47, 48, 49, 64, 65, 81

Date of Accounts	Apr 11	Apr 10	Apr 09
Working Capital	325	272	227
Fixed Assets	66	67	71
Current Assets	528	485	445

Melrose Packaging Ltd
6 Lyon Close Woburn Road Industrial Estate, Kempston, Bedford, MK42 7SB
Tel: 01234-841144 **Fax:** 01234-841166
E-mail: steve@melrosepackaging.co.uk
Website: http://www.melrosepackaging.co.uk
Directors: S. Jarman (Prop)
Registration no: 01573606 **VAT No.:** 640 1587 55
No.of Employees: 1 - 10 **Product Groups:** 30

Mobile Freezer Rentals Ltd
Greensbury Farm Thurleigh Road, Bolnhurst, Bedford, MK44 2ET
Tel: 01234-376999 **Fax:** 01234-376060
E-mail: sales@refrigerationrentals.co.uk
Website: http://www.mobilefreezerrentals.com
Bank(s): National Westminster
Directors: H. Sadler (Co Sec), J. Sadler (Dir)
Immediate Holding Company: MOBILE FREEZER RENTALS LIMITED
Registration no: 02234321 **VAT No.:** 608 6588 08 **Date established:** 1988
Turnover: £500,000 - £1m **No.of Employees:** 21 - 50 **Product Groups:** 72

Date of Accounts	Apr 12	Apr 11	Apr 10
Working Capital	-327	-422	-421
Fixed Assets	1m	1m	2m
Current Assets	218	427	326

Mount Design Ltd
12a Stuart Road Kempston, Bedford, MK42 8HS
Tel: 01234-841148 **Fax:** 01234-840014
E-mail: dan@mountdesign.co.uk
Website: http://www.mountdesign.com
Directors: D. Rout (MD)
Immediate Holding Company: MOUNT DESIGN LIMITED
Registration no: 00927163 **VAT No.:** GB 608 5134 52
Date established: 1968 **Turnover:** £500,000 - £1m
No.of Employees: 1 - 10 **Product Groups:** 86

Date of Accounts	Jan 12	Jan 11	Jan 10
Working Capital	-31	-54	-54
Fixed Assets	22	29	34
Current Assets	45	42	37

Multequip
84-90 College Street Kempston, Bedford, MK42 8LU
Tel: 01234-340461 **Fax:** 01234-340461
E-mail: asf@thxuk.com
Website: http://www.toolhirexpress.co.uk
Directors: S. Fryer (Ptnr), A. Friar (Prop)
Immediate Holding Company: MULTEQUIP LLP
Registration no: OC354484 **Date established:** 2010
Turnover: £500,000 - £1m **No.of Employees:** 1 - 10 **Product Groups:** 37, 48, 51, 83

Date of Accounts	Apr 11
Working Capital	305
Fixed Assets	216
Current Assets	432

N B Services Ltd
8 Leyside Bromham, Bedford, MK43 8NF
Tel: 01234-828900 **Fax:** 01234-308972
Directors: N. Buckle (MD), M. Mckenzie (Dir)
Immediate Holding Company: N.B. SERVICES OLNEY LIMITED
Registration no: 01482422 **Date established:** 1980
Turnover: Up to £250,000 **No.of Employees:** 1 - 10 **Product Groups:** 40, 42

Date of Accounts	Mar 12	Mar 11	Mar 10
Sales Turnover	N/A	23	31
Pre Tax Profit/Loss	N/A	1	3
Working Capital	22	23	21
Fixed Assets	1	3	4
Current Assets	26	27	27
Current Liabilities	N/A	3	4

N D A Engineering Equipment Ltd
24 Singer Way Woburn Road Industrial Estate, Kempston, Bedford, MK42 7AE
Tel: 01234-855030 **Fax:** 01234-840779
E-mail: sales@nda-eng.co.uk
Website: http://www.nda-eng.co.uk
Directors: A. Austin (Sales)
Immediate Holding Company: N.D.A. ENGINEERING EQUIPMENT LIMITED
Registration no: 01368156 **Date established:** 1978
Turnover: Up to £250,000 **No.of Employees:** 1 - 10 **Product Groups:** 23, 25, 30, 33

Date of Accounts	Oct 11	Oct 10	Oct 09
Working Capital	80	58	50
Fixed Assets	3	1	1
Current Assets	154	121	98

N E A Engineering Ltd
113 Murdock Road Manton Industrial Estate, Bedford, MK41 7PE
Tel: 01234-349863 **Fax:** 01234-272676
Website: http://www.nea-engineering.co.uk
Directors: M. Arena (MD), L. Arena (Fin)
Immediate Holding Company: NEA ENGINEERING LIMITED
Registration no: 03447422 **Date established:** 1997
No.of Employees: 1 - 10 **Product Groups:** 20, 40, 41

Date of Accounts	Oct 11	Oct 10	Oct 09
Working Capital	298	164	218
Fixed Assets	7	8	9
Current Assets	725	428	608

N J Metrology
PO Box 413, Bedford, MK41 8WE
Tel: 0783-120 7506 **Fax:** 01234-266474
E-mail: sales@njmetrology.com
Website: http://www.njmetrology.com
Directors: N. Marriott (Dir)
No.of Employees: 1 - 10 **Product Groups:** 38, 85

National Federation Of Enterprise Agencies Ltd
Unit 12 Stephenson Court Fraser Road Priory Business Park, Bedford, MK44 3WJ
Tel: 01234-831623 **Fax:** 01234-831625
E-mail: g.derbyshire@nfea.com
Website: http://www.nfea.com
Directors: G. Derbyshire (Grp Chief Exec)
Immediate Holding Company: BOX & CHARNOCK LIMITED
Registration no: 02785742 **VAT No.:** GB 614 3167 64
Date established: 1977 **Turnover:** Up to £250,000
No.of Employees: 1 - 10 **Product Groups:** 80

Newnorth Print Ltd
College Street Kempston, Bedford, MK42 8NA
Tel: 01234-341111 **Fax:** 01234-271112
E-mail: reception@newnorth.co.uk
Website: http://www.newnorth.co.uk
Bank(s): Natwest
Directors: A. Kampta (Sales), K. Burgess (MD), M. Seamarks (Fin)
Ultimate Holding Company: INTROVIEW LIMITED
Immediate Holding Company: NEWNORTH PRINT LTD.
Registration no: 01005393 **VAT No.:** GB 196 6665 05
Date established: 1971 **Turnover:** £5m - £10m
No.of Employees: 51 - 100 **Product Groups:** 28, 81

Date of Accounts	Oct 11	Oct 10	Oct 09
Sales Turnover	9m	8m	8m
Pre Tax Profit/Loss	354	307	350
Working Capital	983	897	1m
Fixed Assets	3m	3m	3m
Current Assets	3m	3m	3m
Current Liabilities	297	285	222

Newtech Ltd
Unit 3 Stoke Mill Mill Road, Sharnbrook, Bedford, MK44 1NP
Tel: 01234-783680 **Fax:** 01234-782093
E-mail: sales@newtech-ltd.co.uk
Website: http://www.newtech-ltd.co.uk
Directors: S. Rawlinson (MD)
Managers: P. Waters (Sales Prom Mgr), K. Tucker (Chief Acct)
Ultimate Holding Company: HORBERG & CO FORVALTING AB (SWEDEN)
Immediate Holding Company: NAVIGATOR PROPERTY LIMITED
Registration no: 00416089 **Date established:** 2011
No.of Employees: 11 - 20 **Product Groups:** 20, 40, 41

Nissan Technical Centre Europe Ltd
Cranfield Technology Park Moulsoe Road, Cranfield, Bedford, MK43 0DB
Tel: 01234-755555 **Fax:** 01234-755799
E-mail: kunio.nakaguro@ntc-europe.co.uk
Website: http://www.nissan-europe.com
Directors: K. Nakaguro (MD), J. Thompson (Co Sec)
Managers: S. Lowdon (Purch Mgr), C. Nelson (Tech Serv Mgr)
Ultimate Holding Company: NISSAN MOTOR CO LTD (JAPAN)
Immediate Holding Company: NISSAN PROPERTY (UK)
Registration no: 02228415 **Date established:** 1988
No.of Employees: 501 - 1000 **Product Groups:** 85

Date of Accounts	Dec 07	Dec 06	Dec 05
Sales Turnover	N/A	N/A	98m
Pre Tax Profit/Loss	N/A	N/A	19m
Working Capital	29m	29m	19m
Fixed Assets	N/A	N/A	30m
Current Assets	48m	48m	51m
Current Liabilities	N/A	N/A	16m

Norinco UK Ltd
The Sharman Law Building 1 Harpur Street, Bedford, MK40 1PF
Tel: 01234-348219 **Fax:** 01234-349497
E-mail: sales@norinco-uk.com
Website: http://www.norinco-uk.com
Directors: B. Turbat (Dir), L. Clavier (MD)
Ultimate Holding Company: EAST JORDAN EUROPE HOLDINGS SAS (USA)
Immediate Holding Company: S.A. France
Registration no: 00640135 **Date established:** 1959 **Turnover:** £2m - £5m
No.of Employees: 1 - 10 **Product Groups:** 33, 34, 35

Date of Accounts	Dec 09	Dec 08	Dec 07
Working Capital	962	1m	624
Fixed Assets	N/A	8	16
Current Assets	1m	2m	1m

Norse Precision Castings Ltd
276-280 Ampthill Road, Bedford, MK42 9QJ
Tel: 01234-217091 **Fax:** 01234-210573
E-mail: info@norsecastings.com
Website: http://www.norsecastings.com
Directors: H. Dickinson (MD)
Immediate Holding Company: NORSE PRECISION CASTINGS LIMITED
Registration no: 01331795 **Date established:** 1977 **Turnover:** £1m - £2m
No.of Employees: 1 - 10 **Product Groups:** 30, 31, 34, 39, 48

Date of Accounts	Mar 08	Sep 11	Sep 10
Working Capital	-46	150	-249
Fixed Assets	43	312	331
Current Assets	420	523	542

Orion Air Conditioning & Refrigeration
1 Denton Drive Marston Moretaine, Bedford, MK43 0NA
Tel: 08455-677080 **Fax:** 01234-765580
E-mail: info@orionair.co.uk
Website: http://www.orionairsales.co.uk
Directors: S. Handley (Dir)
Immediate Holding Company: ORION AIR CONDITIONING & REFRIGERATION LIMITED
Registration no: 05500693 **Date established:** 2005
Turnover: Up to £250,000 **No.of Employees:** 1 - 10 **Product Groups:** 38, 40

P S H A
14 St Cuthberts Street, Bedford, MK40 3JU
Tel: 0800-389 4433 **Fax:** 01234-218174
E-mail: secretariat@phsa.org.uk
Website: http://www.phsa.org.uk
Bank(s): HSBC
Directors: M. Gilbert (Co Sec), M. Gilbert (Grp Chief Exec)
Immediate Holding Company: ENGAGE MUTUAL HEALTH
Registration no: 00515058 **Date established:** 1953 **Turnover:** £2m - £5m
No.of Employees: 11 - 20 **Product Groups:** 82

P S J Fabrication Ltd
Murdoch Road, Bedford, MK41 7PT
Tel: 01234-268484 **Fax:** 01234-268487
E-mail: info@igranic.com
Website: http://www.igranic.com
Bank(s): National Westminster Bank Plc
Directors: A. Seabrook (Dir)
Ultimate Holding Company: THE IGRANIC GROUP LIMITED
Immediate Holding Company: PSJ FABRICATIONS LTD
Registration no: 01205595 **VAT No.:** GB 491 2514 52
Date established: 1975 **Turnover:** £500,000 - £1m
No.of Employees: 11 - 20 **Product Groups:** 22, 26, 30, 34, 35, 36, 37, 40, 46, 48, 84

Date of Accounts	Mar 11	Mar 10	Mar 09
Sales Turnover	997	1m	1m
Pre Tax Profit/Loss	-134	-60	22
Working Capital	203	315	350
Fixed Assets	74	100	107
Current Assets	565	697	751
Current Liabilities	59	119	137

Paragon Electronic Components plc
Wolseley Road Kempston, Bedford, MK42 7UP
Tel: 01234-840101 **Fax:** 01234-840707
E-mail: enquiries@paragon-plc.com
Website: http://www.paragon-plc.com
Bank(s): Barclays, Bedford
Directors: J. Mayes (MD), M. Stuart (MD), P. Keane (Tech Serv)
Managers: G. Smith (Sales Prom Mgr), M. Shiers (Personnel), M. Dilks (Purch Mgr), S. Dabson (Chief Acct)
Ultimate Holding Company: PARAGON ELECTRONICS LIMITED
Immediate Holding Company: PARAGON ELECTRONIC COMPONENTS PLC
Registration no: 02590508 **VAT No.:** GB 608 7791 06
Date established: 1991 **Turnover:** £10m - £20m
No.of Employees: 51 - 100 **Product Groups:** 30, 33, 35, 37, 45, 67, 84

Date of Accounts	Sep 11	Sep 10	Sep 09
Sales Turnover	16m	15m	15m
Pre Tax Profit/Loss	99	150	285
Working Capital	2m	2m	3m
Fixed Assets	365	350	230
Current Assets	7m	6m	6m
Current Liabilities	537	489	509

H M & J M Parrott
49 St Michaels Road, Bedford, MK40 2LZ
Tel: 01234-354790 **Fax:** 01234-354790
Directors: H. Parrott (Ptnr)
Date established: 1987 **No.of Employees:** 1 - 10 **Product Groups:** 26, 35

Paxton Computers Ltd
15 Kingsway, Bedford, MK42 9EZ
Tel: 01234-216666 **Fax:** 01234-212705
E-mail: info@paxsoft.co.uk
Website: http://www.paxsoft.co.uk
Directors: G. Jones (MD)
Immediate Holding Company: PAXTON COMPUTERS LIMITED
Registration no: 01424228 **VAT No.:** GB 440 7366 57
Date established: 1979 **Turnover:** £500,000 - £1m
No.of Employees: 1 - 10 **Product Groups:** 44

Date of Accounts	Jun 12	Jun 11	Jun 10
Working Capital	209	194	132
Fixed Assets	258	267	272
Current Assets	233	233	158

Pembury Fencing

Tythe Farm Staploe Road, Wyboston, Bedford, MK44 3AT
Tel: 01480-474400 **Fax:** 01480-471100
E-mail: sales@pemburygroup.co.uk
Website: http://www.pemburyfencing.co.uk
Directors: C. Glanvill (MD)
Immediate Holding Company: PEMBURY FENCING LIMITED
Registration no: 02318119 **Date established:** 1988
No.of Employees: 1 - 10 **Product Groups:** 35

Date of Accounts	Dec 11	Dec 10	Dec 09
Working Capital	6	83	61
Fixed Assets	59	74	87
Current Assets	633	461	551

Pipeline Center

Badgers Rise Ridgmont, Bedford, MK43 0YL
Tel: 01525-262000 **Fax:** 01525-262020
Website: http://www.pipecenter.co.uk
No.of Employees: 21 - 50 **Product Groups:** 36, 40, 80

Prestige Glazing Services

2 Shuttleworth Road Elm Farm Industrial Estate, Bedford, MK41 0EP
Tel: 01234-213526 **Fax:** 01234-219063
E-mail: info@prestigeglazingservices.com
Website: http://www.prestigeglazingservices.com
Bank(s): Barclays
Directors: D. Zubrot (Dir), S. Zubrot (Co Sec)
Immediate Holding Company: PRESTIGE GLAZING SERVICES LTD.
Registration no: 03102014 **VAT No.:** GB 667 3155 18
Date established: 1995 **Turnover:** £1m - £2m **No.of Employees:** 11 - 20
Product Groups: 30

Date of Accounts	Oct 11	Oct 10	Oct 09
Working Capital	75	54	126
Fixed Assets	29	36	45
Current Assets	572	477	640

Prices Patent Candles Ltd

16 Hudson Road Elm Farm Industrial Estate, Bedford, MK41 0LZ
Tel: 01234-264500 **Fax:** 01234-264561
E-mail: sales@prices-candles.co.uk
Website: http://www.prices-candles.co.uk
Bank(s): Bank of Scotland
Managers: P. Pettit, L. Standen (Sales Prom Mgr), B. Stewart (Tech Serv Mgr)
Immediate Holding Company: PRICE'S PATENT CANDLES LIMITED
Registration no: 04130027 **VAT No.:** GB 602 8173 63
Date established: 2000 **Turnover:** £10m - £20m
No.of Employees: 11 - 20 **Product Groups:** 32

Date of Accounts	Dec 11	Dec 10	Dec 09
Working Capital	938	1m	2m
Fixed Assets	341	365	454
Current Assets	2m	2m	5m

R B UK Ltd

Element House Napier Road, Elm Farm Industrial Estate, Bedford, MK41 0QS
Tel: 01234-272717 **Fax:** 01234-270202
E-mail: janice.thorn@rbuk.co.uk
Website: http://www.rbuk.co.uk
Managers: J. Thorn (Fin Mgr)
Ultimate Holding Company: BAYLIS ENTERPRISES LIMITED
Immediate Holding Company: RB UK LIMITED
Registration no: 01730290 **VAT No.:** GB 396 7372 92
Date established: 1983 **Turnover:** £2m - £5m **No.of Employees:** 21 - 50
Product Groups: 26

Date of Accounts	Dec 11	Dec 10	Dec 09
Working Capital	1m	2m	1m
Fixed Assets	512	650	770
Current Assets	2m	2m	3m
Current Liabilities	N/A	1	N/A

R S Mechanical Repairs

Redgate Farm Scald End Mill Road, Thurleigh, Bedford, MK44 2DP
Tel: 01234-771884 **Fax:** 01234-771884
Directors: R. Skinner (Prop)
Immediate Holding Company: MARTINE HORWOOD LIMITED
Date established: 2010 **No.of Employees:** 1 - 10 **Product Groups:** 41

Ringspann UK Ltd

3 Napier Road Elm Farm Industrial Estate, Bedford, MK41 0QS
Tel: 01234-342511 **Fax:** 01234-217322
E-mail: info@ringspann.co.uk
Website: http://www.ringspann.co.uk
Bank(s): Barclays, 111 High St
Managers: P. Woolmer (Chief Mgr)
Ultimate Holding Company: RINGSPANN GMBH (GERMANY)
Immediate Holding Company: RINGSPANN (U.K.) LIMITED
Registration no: 00979775 **Date established:** 1970 **Turnover:** £1m - £2m
No.of Employees: 11 - 20 **Product Groups:** 29, 30, 31, 32, 35, 36, 37, 38, 39, 40, 43, 44, 45, 46, 47, 66, 67

Date of Accounts	Dec 11	Dec 10	Dec 09
Working Capital	1m	1m	1m
Fixed Assets	107	100	109
Current Assets	2m	1m	2m

Rotatrim

8 Caxton Park Caxton Road, Elm Farm Industrial Estate, Bedford, MK41 0TY
Tel: 01234-224545 **Fax:** 01234-224540
E-mail: uksales@rotatrim.co.uk
Website: http://www.rotatrim.co.uk
Bank(s): Royal Bank of Scotland, London SW1
Directors: L. Ogborne (Dir), L. Ogbourne (Co Sec)
Ultimate Holding Company: ROTATRIM INTERNATIONAL LIMITED
Immediate Holding Company: ROTATRIM LIMITED
Registration no: 00627340 **VAT No.:** GB 222 2419 09
Date established: 1959 **Turnover:** £1m - £2m **No.of Employees:** 11 - 20
Product Groups: 38, 44, 49

Date of Accounts	May 09	May 08	Nov 11
Working Capital	509	481	707
Fixed Assets	91	93	64
Current Assets	670	753	1m

S D C Builders Ltd

Limegrove House Caxton Road, Elm Farm Industrial Estate, Bedford, MK41 0QQ
Tel: 01234-363155 **Fax:** 01234-266385
E-mail: marketing@sdc.co.uk
Website: http://www.sdcbuilders.co.uk
Bank(s): Barclays
Directors: G. Wykes (Dir), M. Lowndes (Fin)
Managers: M. Clifford (Tech Serv Mgr), O. Ebsworth
Ultimate Holding Company: S D C (HOLDINGS) LIMITED
Immediate Holding Company: S.D.C. BUILDERS LIMITED
Registration no: 01251716 **Date established:** 1976
Turnover: £75m - £125m **No.of Employees:** 101 - 250
Product Groups: 51, 52, 84

Date of Accounts	Sep 11	Sep 10	Sep 09
Sales Turnover	97m	121m	87m
Pre Tax Profit/Loss	513	379	533
Working Capital	2m	2m	1m
Fixed Assets	2m	2m	2m
Current Assets	30m	32m	32m
Current Liabilities	3m	5m	829

S M I

7 Gipping Close, Bedford, MK41 7XY
Tel: 01234-266255 **Fax:** 01234-266255
E-mail: grawatts@aol.com
Website: http://www.smi.com.sa
Managers: G. Watts (Mgr)
Date established: 1982 **No.of Employees:** 501 - 1000
Product Groups: 34, 35, 40, 48, 66

S M S Electrical Services Ltd

1 Cartmel Priory, Bedford, MK41 0WE
Tel: 01234-294271
E-mail: info@sms.uk.com
Website: http://www.sms.uk.com
Directors: S. Roberts (MD)
Immediate Holding Company: SMS ELECTRICAL SERVICES LIMITED
Registration no: 05301659 **Date established:** 2004
Turnover: £250,000 - £500,000 **No.of Employees:** 1 - 10
Product Groups: 84

Date of Accounts	May 12	May 11	May 10
Working Capital	1	19	41
Fixed Assets	N/A	N/A	3
Current Assets	44	60	67

S T G Ltd

Unit 14 Stephenson Court Fraser Road, Bedford, MK44 3WJ
Tel: 01234-213339 **Fax:** 01234-212224
E-mail: info@stgtransport.com
Website: http://www.stgtransport.com
Bank(s): Nat West
Directors: M. Cave (Dir)
Ultimate Holding Company: STG (HOLDINGS) LTD
Immediate Holding Company: S.T.G. LTD
Registration no: 02969424 **VAT No.:** GB 650 6234 56
Date established: 1994 **Turnover:** £2m - £5m **No.of Employees:** 11 - 20
Product Groups: 72

Date of Accounts	Dec 11	Dec 10	Dec 09
Working Capital	77	119	165
Fixed Assets	N/A	56	16
Current Assets	83	354	212

Sampson International Machine Tools

Keeley Lane Wootton, Bedford, MK43 9HS
Tel: 01234-851200 **Fax:** 01234- 851123
E-mail: sales@sampsonmachinetools.com
Website: http://www.sampsonmachinetools.com
Directors: B. Sampson (Prop)
Date established: 2001 **No.of Employees:** 1 - 10 **Product Groups:** 46

Shillingford & Morgan Scaffolding

63 Ruffs Furze Oakley, Bedford, MK43 7RT
Tel: 01234-826574 **Fax:** 01234-826574
E-mail: tamsin.morgan@btopenworld.com
Managers: T. Morgans (Mgr)
Turnover: Up to £250,000 **No.of Employees:** 1 - 10 **Product Groups:** 35, 52, 83

Shiner Plant Hire Ltd

Lower East End Farm Marston Hill, Marston Moretaine, Bedford, MK43 0QJ
Tel: 01234-750047 **Fax:** 01234-750341
E-mail: enquiries@diggersforhire.co.uk
Website: http://www.diggersforhire.co.uk
Directors: R. Shiner (MD)
Ultimate Holding Company: AGAMEMNON ESTATES LTD
Immediate Holding Company: SHINER PLANT HIRE LIMITED
Registration no: 04428997 **Date established:** 2002
No.of Employees: 1 - 10 **Product Groups:** 67, 83

Date of Accounts	May 12	May 11	May 10
Working Capital	173	117	-38
Fixed Assets	320	393	439
Current Assets	247	278	170

Simflex Grilles & Closures Ltd

9 Woburn Street Ampthill, Bedford, MK45 2HP
Tel: 01525-841100 **Fax:** 01525-405561
E-mail: carl@simflex.co.uk
Website: http://www.simflex.co.uk
Directors: C. Fraser (Dir), S. Smith (Co Sec)
Immediate Holding Company: SIMFLEX GRILLES AND CLOSURES LIMITED
Registration no: 02347541 **Date established:** 1989
No.of Employees: 1 - 10 **Product Groups:** 26, 35

Date of Accounts	Sep 11	Sep 10	Sep 09
Working Capital	843	606	576
Fixed Assets	56	29	51
Current Assets	2m	882	981

Harvey Smith Luton Ltd

Unit Cacb Barton Industrial Estate Faldo Road, Barton-Le-Clay, Bedford, MK45 4RJ
Tel: 01582-885100 **Fax:** 01582-885109
E-mail: sales@harveysmithluton.co.uk
Website: http://www.harveysmithluton.co.uk
Directors: R. Clennett (MD)
Immediate Holding Company: HARVEY SMITH (LUTON) LIMITED
Registration no: 00662363 **VAT No.:** GB 197 7400 30
Date established: 1960 **Turnover:** £500,000 - £1m
No.of Employees: 1 - 10 **Product Groups:** 48

Date of Accounts	Dec 11	Dec 10	Dec 09
Pre Tax Profit/Loss	N/A	-123	N/A
Working Capital	-578	-546	-427
Fixed Assets	25	26	31
Current Assets	175	142	144
Current Liabilities	632	N/A	N/A

Smith Pack Ltd

Arkwright Indl-Est Arkwright Road, Bedford, MK42 0LE
Tel: 01234-340096 **Fax:** 01234-325063
E-mail: martincanty@smithpack.co.uk
Website: http://www.smithpack.co.uk
Directors: M. Canty (Dir), S. Knowles (Co Sec)
Managers: E. Garner (Chief Mgr)
Ultimate Holding Company: WSPH LIMITED
Immediate Holding Company: SMITHPACK LIMITED
Registration no: 01850712 **Date established:** 1984 **Turnover:** £2m - £5m
No.of Employees: 1 - 10 **Product Groups:** 27, 85

Date of Accounts	Apr 11	Apr 10	Apr 09
Sales Turnover	7m	7m	7m
Pre Tax Profit/Loss	105	73	-400
Working Capital	226	66	-187
Fixed Assets	431	528	752
Current Assets	2m	2m	2m
Current Liabilities	872	1m	1m

Soft Shock Ltd

PO Box 650, Bedford, MK40 4YG
Tel: 01234-325177 **Fax:** 01234-354559
E-mail: info@softshock.co.uk
Website: http://www.softshock.co.uk
Directors: T. Burton (Dir)
Immediate Holding Company: SOFTSHOCK LIMITED
Registration no: 04025120 **VAT No.:** GB 746 2827 12
Date established: 2000 **Turnover:** Up to £250,000
No.of Employees: 1 - 10 **Product Groups:** 29

Date of Accounts	Jul 11	Jul 10	Jul 09
Working Capital	-9	N/A	5
Fixed Assets	1	2	1
Current Assets	38	34	44
Current Liabilities	42	N/A	N/A

Stafford Bridge Doors Ltd

Bedford Road Pavenham, Bedford, MK43 7PS
Tel: 01234-826316 **Fax:** 01234-826319
E-mail: sales@sbdoors.com
Website: http://www.sbdoors.com
Directors: A. Purcell (Fin), J. Mcgill (MD)
Ultimate Holding Company: SURELOCK MCGILL LIMITED
Immediate Holding Company: STAFFORD BRIDGE DOORS LIMITED
Registration no: 03884200 **Date established:** 1999 **Turnover:** £2m - £5m
No.of Employees: 21 - 50 **Product Groups:** 26, 35

Date of Accounts	Mar 11	Mar 10	Mar 09
Sales Turnover	3m	3m	3m
Pre Tax Profit/Loss	-137	226	122
Working Capital	384	542	367
Fixed Assets	232	204	243
Current Assets	2m	2m	1m
Current Liabilities	216	286	149

Stieber Clutch

Twiflex Building Ampthill Road, Bedford, MK42 9RD
Tel: 01234-355499 **Fax:** 01234-214264
E-mail: graham.whiffin@wichita.co.uk
Website: http://www.stieber.de
Managers: G. Whiffin, L. Moss (Maint), M. Shawland (Ops Mgr), O. Anderson (Sales & Mktg Mg), V. Hughes (Systems Mgr)
Ultimate Holding Company: ALTRA INDUSTRIAL MOTION INC (USA)
Registration no: 03897701 **Date established:** 1999 **Turnover:** £5m - £10m
No.of Employees: 1 - 10 **Product Groups:** 35, 41, 43, 46

Supplements For Pets Ltd

50 Oakley Road Bromham, Bedford, MK43 8HZ
Tel: 01234-826584
E-mail: info@supplementsforpets.co.uk
Website: http://www.supplementsforpets.co.uk
Directors: P. Clark (MD)
Registration no: 06567735 **Date established:** 2008
Turnover: Up to £250,000 **No.of Employees:** 1 - 10 **Product Groups:** 20, 49

Sven Saunas Ltd

25-27 Sergeants Way, Bedford, MK41 0EH
Tel: 01234-356666 **Fax:** 01234-355887
E-mail: info@sven-saunas.co.uk
Website: http://www.sven-saunas.co.uk
Directors: A. Davis (MD)
Immediate Holding Company: SVEN SAUNAS LIMITED
Registration no: 03297357 **Date established:** 1996
No.of Employees: 1 - 10 **Product Groups:** 66

Date of Accounts	Dec 11	Dec 10	Dec 09
Working Capital	563	445	314
Fixed Assets	75	63	82
Current Assets	657	712	414

Switch & Sence

50a Bunyan Road Kempston, Bedford, MK42 8HL
Tel: 01234-854321
E-mail: pete@switchandsence.co.uk
Website: http://www.switchandsence.co.uk
Directors: P. Beddall (MD)
Immediate Holding Company: KEMPSTON SURVEYS LTD
Date established: 2005 **Turnover:** Up to £250,000
No.of Employees: 1 - 10 **Product Groups:** 38, 40

Date of Accounts	Mar 12	Mar 11	Mar 10
Working Capital	N/A	-3	-9
Fixed Assets	26	32	29
Current Assets	91	74	60

T T UK Ltd

10 Windsor Road, Bedford, MK42 9SU
Tel: 01234-342566 **Fax:** 01234-352184
E-mail: sales@tt-uk.com
Website: http://www.tt-uk.com
Bank(s): Lloyds TSB
Directors: S. Wells (Co Sec), D. Toms (Dir)
Managers: S. Buckle (Buyer)
Ultimate Holding Company: wolfgang schmidt e.k (germany)
Immediate Holding Company: T T UK LIMITED
Registration no: 01676000 **VAT No.:** GB 382 1505 67
Date established: 1982 **Turnover:** £5m - £10m **No.of Employees:** 21 - 50
Product Groups: 36, 37, 40, 45

Date of Accounts	Dec 11	Dec 10	Dec 09
Sales Turnover	6m	7m	10m
Pre Tax Profit/Loss	12	190	336

see next page

T T UK Ltd - Cont'd

Working Capital	2m	2m	2m
Fixed Assets	137	157	192
Current Assets	3m	3m	3m
Current Liabilities	996	381	986

Telephone Engineers Local
26 Mitre Close, Bedford, MK41 0SS
Tel: 08444-145156
E-mail: info@telecomengineers.co.uk
Website: http://www.telecomengineers.co.uk
Directors: D. Bolton (Ptnr)
Date established: 2003 **No.of Employees:** 1 - 10 **Product Groups:** 52

Terinex Ltd
Hammond Road Elm Farm Industrial Estate, Bedford, MK41 0ND
Tel: 01234-364411 **Fax:** 01234-271486
E-mail: paul@terinex.co.uk
Website: http://www.terinex.co.uk
Bank(s): HSBC Bank plc
Directors: P. Cain (Co Sec), P. Wightman (Dir)
Managers: K. Green (Mktg Serv Mgr), G. Trott, D. Simpson (Sales Prom Mgr)
Ultimate Holding Company: OWEN GREENINGS & MUMFORD (HOLDINGS) LIMITED
Immediate Holding Company: TERINEX LIMITED
Registration no: 04937132 **Date established:** 2003
Turnover: £10m - £20m **No.of Employees:** 51 - 100 **Product Groups:** 27, 30

Date of Accounts	May 11	May 10	May 09
Sales Turnover	10m	8m	7m
Pre Tax Profit/Loss	1m	857	794
Working Capital	2m	2m	2m
Fixed Assets	745	706	679
Current Assets	4m	3m	3m
Current Liabilities	564	663	394

Transam Rubber & Extrusions Ltd
Barton Industrial Estate Faldo Road Barton-Le-Clay, Bedford, MK45 4RP
Tel: 01582-883883 **Fax:** 01582-883138
E-mail: sales@transamltd.co.uk
Website: http://www.transamltd.co.uk
Directors: R. Brazier (MD)
Immediate Holding Company: TRANSAM RUBBER AND EXTRUSIONS LIMITED
Registration no: 02560410 **Date established:** 1990
Turnover: £250,000 - £500,000 **No.of Employees:** 1 - 10
Product Groups: 26, 29, 30, 31, 36, 37, 39, 40, 42, 48, 49, 66, 67, 68

Date of Accounts	Jul 11	Jul 10	Jul 09
Working Capital	-30	-25	-25
Fixed Assets	156	137	102
Current Assets	228	178	134

Trist Draper Hydraulics
Unit 16 Murdock Road, Manton Industrial Estate, Bedford, MK41 7PD
Tel: 01234-212661 **Fax:** 01234-270421
E-mail: s@tristdraper.co.uk
Website: http://www.tristdraper.co.uk
Managers: S. Kumar (District Mgr)
Registration no: 15993634 **Turnover:** £500,000 - £1m
No.of Employees: 1 - 10 **Product Groups:** 29, 30, 36, 66

Turbo Machinery Services
Unit 4a Aston Road Cambridge Road Industrial Estate, Bedford, MK42 0LJ
Tel: 01234-272177 **Fax:** 01234-272188
E-mail: jimsmith@tms-uk.net
Website: http://www.tms-uk.net
Directors: J. Smith (MD)
Registration no: 04165137 **Date established:** 2001
No.of Employees: 1 - 10 **Product Groups:** 31, 33, 37, 38, 40, 48, 86

Date of Accounts	Feb 08	Feb 07	Feb 06
Working Capital	282	237	82
Fixed Assets	82	55	71
Current Assets	428	400	283
Current Liabilities	146	163	200
Total Share Capital	2	2	2

Twiflex Ltd
Ampthill Road, Bedford, MK42 9RD
Tel: 01234-350311 **Fax:** 01234-350317
E-mail: info@twiflex.co.uk
Website: http://www.twiflex.co.uk
Bank(s): National Westminster Bank Plc
Managers: O. Anderson (Sales & Mktg Mg), P. Turvey (Comptroller), R. Playford (Comptroller), L. Moss (Tech Serv Mgr), V. Hughes (Personnel), M. Shotland (Buyer)
Ultimate Holding Company: ALTRA HOLDINGS INC (USA)
Immediate Holding Company: WICHITA COMPANY LIMITED
Registration no: 03897701 **VAT No.:** GB 738 0712 34
Date established: 1999 **Turnover:** £5m - £10m
No.of Employees: 51 - 100 **Product Groups:** 35, 38, 39, 43, 44, 45, 46

Date of Accounts	Dec 11	Dec 10	Dec 09
Sales Turnover	N/A	N/A	7m
Pre Tax Profit/Loss	176	323	904
Working Capital	5m	5m	5m
Current Assets	5m	5m	5m
Current Liabilities	N/A	90	N/A

Unipower Solutions Ltd
Bluebells 32 Croyland Drive, Elstow, Bedford, MK42 9GH
Tel: 020-3286 9069 **Fax:** 0845-500 1921
E-mail: steve@unipower-ltd.com
Website: http://www.unipower-ltd.com
Registration no: 06835597 **Product Groups:** 37, 67, 83

L W Vass Holdings Ltd
Station Road Ampthill, Bedford, MK45 2RB
Tel: 01525-403255 **Fax:** 01525-404194
E-mail: sales@vass.co.uk
Website: http://www.vass.co.uk
Bank(s): Royal Bank Of Scotland
Directors: T. Demaine (MD), T. Demaine (MD)
Ultimate Holding Company: L W VASS HOLDINGS LIMITED
Immediate Holding Company: L W VASS HOLDINGS LIMITED
Registration no: 03229386 **VAT No.:** GB 196 6684 01
Date established: 1996 **Turnover:** £2m - £5m **No.of Employees:** 11 - 20
Product Groups: 29, 40, 68

Date of Accounts	Jul 11	Jul 10	Jul 09
Working Capital	-31	-96	-161
Fixed Assets	599	599	599
Current Assets	18	4	4

Waggett Bradford
Redhouse Farm Riseley Road, Bletsoe, Bedford, MK44 1QU
Tel: 01234-708736 **Fax:** 01234-708736
Directors: L. Matthews (Prop)
Date established: 1977 **No.of Employees:** 1 - 10 **Product Groups:** 35

Watson & Brookman Engineers Ltd
Chawston Crossroads Chawston, Bedford, MK44 3BL
Tel: 01480-212064 **Fax:** 01480-403773
E-mail: sales@watsonbrookman.com
Website: http://www.watsonbrookman.co.uk
Directors: C. Brookman (Ptnr)
Immediate Holding Company: WATSON & BROOKMAN (ENGINEERS) LIMITED
Registration no: 01400647 **Date established:** 1978
No.of Employees: 11 - 20 **Product Groups:** 41

Date of Accounts	Dec 11	Dec 10	Dec 09
Working Capital	544	480	609
Fixed Assets	460	493	308
Current Assets	664	682	772

Wells & Young's Brewing Co.
Havelock Street, Bedford, MK40 4LU
Tel: 01234-272766 **Fax:** 01234-279000
E-mail: info@wellsandyoungs.co.uk
Website: http://www.wellsandyoungs.co.uk
Bank(s): HSBC Bank plc
Directors: N. Mcnally (MD)
Ultimate Holding Company: CHARLES WELLS,LIMITED
Immediate Holding Company: WELLS & YOUNG'S BREWING COMPANY LIMITED
Registration no: 05720806 **VAT No.:** GB 365 9596 91
Date established: 2006 **Turnover:** £125m - £250m
No.of Employees: 251 - 500 **Product Groups:** 21, 62

Date of Accounts	Sep 08	Sep 09	Sep 10
Sales Turnover	210m	212m	213m
Pre Tax Profit/Loss	-3m	-2m	6m
Working Capital	-413	5m	9m
Fixed Assets	97m	87m	85m
Current Assets	47m	47m	52m
Current Liabilities	29m	28m	31m

Wilson Peacock Estate Agents
58 St Loyes Street, Bedford, MK40 1HD
Tel: 01234-350812 **Fax:** 01234-341797
E-mail: bedford@wilsonpeacock.co.uk
Website: http://www.wilsonpeacock.co.uk
Managers: D. Garafalo (District Mgr)
Immediate Holding Company: TAYLORS ESTATE AGENTS LTD
Registration no: 02596967 **Date established:** 1991
No.of Employees: 11 - 20 **Product Groups:** 80, 82

Yeoman Upholstery plc
Enterprise Way Flitwick, Bedford, MK45 5BS
Tel: 01525-713771 **Fax:** 01525-717877
E-mail: info@yeomanupholstery.co.uk
Website: http://www.yeomanupholstery.co.uk
Bank(s): Barclays
Directors: N. West (Dir), P. Rainbow (Sales)
Immediate Holding Company: YEOMAN UPHOLSTERY PLC
Registration no: 00953973 **Date established:** 1969 **Turnover:** £2m - £5m
No.of Employees: 21 - 50 **Product Groups:** 26

Date of Accounts	Apr 11	Apr 10	Apr 09
Sales Turnover	2m	2m	2m
Pre Tax Profit/Loss	-106	2	-200
Working Capital	306	360	359
Fixed Assets	63	79	36
Current Assets	718	781	736
Current Liabilities	143	130	88

Zoedale plc
Stannard Way Priory Business Park, Bedford, MK44 3WG
Tel: 01234-832832 **Fax:** 01234-832800
E-mail: enquiries@zoedale.co.uk
Website: http://www.zoedale.co.uk
Bank(s): National Westminster Bank Plc
Managers: A. Jakeman (Chief Mgr)
Immediate Holding Company: ZOEDALE PLC
Registration no: 01245868 **Date established:** 1976 **Turnover:** £2m - £5m
No.of Employees: 11 - 20 **Product Groups:** 30, 33, 36, 38, 39, 40

Date of Accounts	Aug 11	Aug 10	Aug 09
Sales Turnover	2m	2m	2m
Pre Tax Profit/Loss	120	181	41
Working Capital	499	529	437
Fixed Assets	515	472	495
Current Assets	811	789	670
Current Liabilities	130	121	95

Biggleswade

2Digital Limited
29A Market Square, Biggleswade, SG18 8A
Tel: 0845-056 2885 **Fax:** 01767-262497
E-mail: mike@2digital.co.uk
Website: http://www.2digital.co.uk
Directors: M. Okeefe (Prop), M. O'Keefe (Prop)
Registration no: 05161505 **Turnover:** Up to £250,000
No.of Employees: 1 - 10 **Product Groups:** 44, 79

A M G Systems Ltd
3 Omega Centre Stratton Business Park London Road, Biggleswade, SG18 8QB
Tel: 01767-600777 **Fax:** 01767-600077
E-mail: sales@amgsystems.com
Website: http://www.amgsystems.co.uk
Directors: A. Hayes (Dir)
Immediate Holding Company: AMG SYSTEMS LIMITED
Registration no: 02838846 **VAT No.:** 563 5694 10 **Date established:** 1993
Turnover: £2m - £5m **No.of Employees:** 11 - 20 **Product Groups:** 37, 40

Date of Accounts	Dec 11	Dec 10	Dec 09
Working Capital	1m	1m	2m
Fixed Assets	528	450	34
Current Assets	2m	2m	3m

Advance Security Screening Ltd
Unit 8 The Acorn Centre Chestnut Avenue, Biggleswade, SG18 0RA
Tel: 01296-623587 **Fax:** 01296-623962
E-mail: info@advancesecurityscreening.co.uk
Website: http://www.advancesecurityscreening.co.uk
Directors: A. Nurse (MD)
Immediate Holding Company: ADVANCE SECURITY SCREENING LIMITED
Registration no: 03404533 **Date established:** 1997
Turnover: Up to £250,000 **No.of Employees:** 1 - 10 **Product Groups:** 35, 36

Date of Accounts	Sep 11	Sep 10	Sep 09
Working Capital	-121	-163	-180
Fixed Assets	111	127	147
Current Assets	87	41	19

Anglia Handling Services Ltd
Unit 3 Montgomery Way, Biggleswade, SG18 8QB
Tel: 01767-312125 **Fax:** 01767-601375
E-mail: sales@angliahandling.co.uk
Website: http://www.angliahandling.co.uk
Bank(s): National Westminster Bank Plc
Directors: M. Burgess (Dir)
Immediate Holding Company: ANGLIA HANDLING SERVICES LIMITED
Registration no: 01545263 **VAT No.:** GB 335 2809 59
Date established: 1981 **Turnover:** £1m - £2m **No.of Employees:** 11 - 20
Product Groups: 22, 23, 26, 29, 30, 35, 36, 37, 39, 40, 41, 44, 45, 48, 52, 66, 67, 84

Date of Accounts	Mar 11	Mar 10	Mar 09
Working Capital	304	276	286
Fixed Assets	23	16	35
Current Assets	479	461	492

Blow Moulding Machinery Ltd BD Repairs
44 Ivel Gardens, Biggleswade, SG18 0AN
Tel: 01767-318910 **Fax:** 01767-600097
E-mail: blowmachines@tiscali.com
Website: http://www.blowmachine.com
Directors: B. Dilley (MD)
Immediate Holding Company: BLOW MOULDING MACHINERY LIMITED
Registration no: 03121601 **Date established:** 1995
No.of Employees: 1 - 10 **Product Groups:** 42

Date of Accounts	Mar 12	Mar 11	Mar 10
Working Capital	4	36	48
Fixed Assets	1	1	1
Current Assets	21	56	68

Endoline Machinery Ltd
Stratton Business Park London Road, Biggleswade, SG18 8QB
Tel: 01767-316422 **Fax:** 01767-318033
E-mail: info@endoline.co.uk
Website: http://www.endoline.co.uk
Bank(s): Barclays, Welwyn Garden City
Directors: A. Yates (MD)
Immediate Holding Company: ENDOLINE MACHINERY LIMITED
Registration no: 01563793 **VAT No.:** GB 563 5736 20
Date established: 1981 **Turnover:** £2m - £5m **No.of Employees:** 21 - 50
Product Groups: 42

Date of Accounts	May 11	May 10	May 09
Working Capital	412	173	-161
Fixed Assets	898	991	1m
Current Assets	2m	1m	950

Godber Engineering
4 Riverside Court, Biggleswade, SG18 0AE
Tel: 01767-631616 **Fax:** 01767-631616
Directors: D. Cox (Prop)
Immediate Holding Company: A.P. SPECIALIST DOORS & JOINERY LIMITED
Registration no: 04444081 **Date established:** 2002
No.of Employees: 1 - 10 **Product Groups:** 35

Illig UK Ltd
Stratton Business Park London Road, Biggleswade, SG18 8QB
Tel: 01767-310555 **Fax:** 01767-318888
E-mail: sales@illig.co.uk
Website: http://www.illig.co.uk
Bank(s): HSBC
Directors: G. Brooks (Dir)
Immediate Holding Company: ILLIG UK LIMITED
Registration no: 01704106 **Date established:** 1983 **Turnover:** £2m - £5m
No.of Employees: 11 - 20 **Product Groups:** 42

Date of Accounts	Dec 11	Dec 10	Dec 09
Working Capital	566	315	246
Fixed Assets	727	751	740
Current Assets	890	530	538

Jantec Electronic Services Ltd
23 Eldon Way, Biggleswade, SG18 8NH
Tel: 01767-313838 **Fax:** 01767-315080
E-mail: admin@jantecelectronic.co.uk
Website: http://www.jantecelectronic.co.uk
Bank(s): Barclays, Hemel Hempstead
Directors: M. Berridge (MD)
Ultimate Holding Company: AWS GROUP HOLDINGS LTD
Immediate Holding Company: JANTEC ELECTRONIC SERVICES LIMITED
Registration no: 01535793 **Date established:** 1980
No.of Employees: 11 - 20 **Product Groups:** 37, 48

Date of Accounts	Jun 11	Jun 10	Jun 09
Sales Turnover	735	679	627
Pre Tax Profit/Loss	103	60	40
Working Capital	961	879	827
Fixed Assets	4	8	13
Current Assets	1m	1m	917
Current Liabilities	69	72	55

Jewers Doors Ltd
Unit 1 Stratton Business Park Normandy Lane, Biggleswade, SG18 8QB
Tel: 01767-317090 **Fax:** 01767-312305
E-mail: postroom@jewersdoors.co.uk
Website: http://www.jewersdoors.co.uk
Directors: J. Domagala (Fab), P. Jewers (Fin), C. Jewers (MD), C. Jewers (MD)
Managers: G. Noon (Buyer), D. Primett (Tech Serv Mgr), D. Hancock (Mktg Serv Mgr)
Immediate Holding Company: JEWERS DOORS LIMITED
Registration no: 01837182 **Date established:** 1984 **Turnover:** £5m - £10m
No.of Employees: 21 - 50 **Product Groups:** 35

Date of Accounts	Sep 11	Sep 10	Sep 09
Sales Turnover	7m	13m	11m
Pre Tax Profit/Loss	1m	2m	1m
Working Capital	5m	4m	3m
Fixed Assets	829	871	887
Current Assets	7m	8m	7m
Current Liabilities	650	1m	1m

Jordans Riveta Co. Ltd
Holme Mills Langford Road, Biggleswade, SG18 9JY
Tel: 01767-318222 **Fax:** 01767-600695
E-mail: info@ryvita.com
Website: http://www.jordanscereal.com
Bank(s): Lloyds, London
Directors: W. Jordan (Dir), R. Schofield (Co Sec)
Managers: D. Jehan (Tech Serv Mgr)
Ultimate Holding Company: WITTINGTON INVESTMENTS LIMITED
Immediate Holding Company: W.JORDAN (CEREALS) LIMITED
Registration no: 01545794 **VAT No.:** GB 186 0475 47
Date established: 1981 **Turnover:** £20m - £50m
No.of Employees: 251 - 500 **Product Groups:** 20, 62

Date of Accounts	Sep 10	Sep 08	Sep 09
Sales Turnover	N/A	35m	N/A
Pre Tax Profit/Loss	N/A	2m	N/A
Working Capital	22m	22m	22m
Fixed Assets	5	5	5
Current Assets	22m	22m	22m

Kramp UK Ltd
Stratton Business Park, Biggleswade, SG18 8QB
Tel: 01767-602600 **Fax:** 01767-602620
E-mail: info.agri.uk@kramp.com
Website: http://www.kramp.com
Bank(s): HSBC, Stevenage
Directors: S. Callahan (Fin)
Managers: M. McKendrick (Tech Serv Mgr), J. Thompson (Sales & Mktg Mg)
Ultimate Holding Company: KRAMP GROEP BV (NETHERLANDS)
Immediate Holding Company: KRAMP U.K. LTD.
Registration no: 01139130 **Date established:** 1973
Turnover: £10m - £20m **No.of Employees:** 51 - 100 **Product Groups:** 07

Date of Accounts	Dec 11	Dec 10	Dec 09
Sales Turnover	19m	17m	16m
Pre Tax Profit/Loss	497	901	482
Working Capital	7m	7m	6m
Fixed Assets	298	183	237
Current Assets	10m	8m	7m
Current Liabilities	813	443	446

Lemin & Co Product Finishers
Unit 4 Albone Way, Biggleswade, SG18 8BN
Tel: 01767-600120 **Fax:** 01767-600121
E-mail: enquiries@lemin.co.uk
Website: http://www.lemin.co.uk
Bank(s): Lloyds
Directors: J. Scott (Dir)
Immediate Holding Company: LEMIN & CO (PRODUCT FINISHERS) LTD
Registration no: 01318507 **VAT No.:** GB 215 1814 93
Turnover: £1m - £2m **No.of Employees:** 11 - 20 **Product Groups:** 32, 48

Date of Accounts	Mar 08	Mar 07	Mar 06
Working Capital	74	138	106
Fixed Assets	81	12	20
Current Assets	210	263	281
Current Liabilities	137	125	175

Liebherr-Great Britain Ltd
Normandy Lane Stratton Business Park, Biggleswade, SG18 8QB
Tel: 01767-602100 **Fax:** 01767-602110
E-mail: info.lgb@liebherr.com
Website: http://www.liebherr.com/lh/
Bank(s): Barclays
Directors: B. Field (MD), D. Milne (Dir), S. Heidmaar (Fin)
Managers: C. Davies (Mgr), S. Onyon (I.T. Exec)
Ultimate Holding Company: LIEBHERR - INTERNATIONAL AG (SWITZERLAND
Immediate Holding Company: Liebherr Int AG
Registration no: 00677497 **VAT No.:** GB 229 7293 34
Date established: 1960 **Turnover:** £125m - £250m
No.of Employees: 21 - 50 **Product Groups:** 39, 45

Miller Pattison Ltd
9 Albone Way, Biggleswade, SG18 8BN
Tel: 01767-314444 **Fax:** 01767-317601
E-mail: biggleswade@miller-patterson.co.uk
Website: http://www.miller-pattison.co.uk
Directors: M. Dyson (MD), W. Hinchelle-Word (Dir)
Managers: V. Keys (Personnel), J. Orchiston (Accounts), S. Strong (Est), A. Harner (District Mgr), S. Strong (District Mgr)
Immediate Holding Company: MILLER PATTISON LIMITED
Registration no: 07340972 **VAT No.:** GB 170 0904 93
Date established: 2010 **Turnover:** Up to £250,000
No.of Employees: 1 - 10 **Product Groups:** 27, 33, 52

Mountstar Metal Corporation Ltd
Rail Works Railway Sidings, Biggleswade, SG18 8BD
Tel: 01767-319600 **Fax:** 01767-317764
E-mail: mmc@mountstar.com
Website: http://www.mountstar.com
Directors: N. Stinson (Co Sec), R. Holt (Fab), P. Sheppard (Dir)
Managers: S. Bucknell (I.T. Exec)
Ultimate Holding Company: Preussag AG
Immediate Holding Company: European Metal Recycling Ltd
Registration no: 00941219 **VAT No.:** GB 229 4838 33
Turnover: £250m - £500m **No.of Employees:** 21 - 50
Product Groups: 30, 34, 66

F D O'Dell & Sons Ltd
Cow Close Langford Road Langford Road, Biggleswade, SG18 9JT
Tel: 01767-313113 **Fax:** 01767-313113
Directors: T. Allan (Dir)
Immediate Holding Company: F.D. O DELL & SONS LIMITED
Registration no: 00531127 **VAT No.:** GB 197 4046 37
Date established: 1954 **Turnover:** £250,000 - £500,000
No.of Employees: 1 - 10 **Product Groups:** 66, 83

Date of Accounts	Dec 11	Dec 10	Dec 09
Working Capital	652	626	532
Fixed Assets	1m	1m	1m
Current Assets	761	786	669

Smiths Metal Centres Ltd Part of (Smith Metal Centres)
Straton Business Park London Road, Biggleswade, SG18 8QB
Tel: 01767-604704 **Fax:** 01767-315 340
E-mail: info@smithmetal.com
Website: http://www.smithmetal.com
Managers: J. Rox (Mgr)
Ultimate Holding Company: HENLEY MANAGEMENT COMPANY (USA)
Immediate Holding Company: SMITHS METAL CENTRES LIMITED
Registration no: 03485838 **Date established:** 1997
Turnover: £20m - £50m **No.of Employees:** 101 - 250
Product Groups: 34, 66

Date of Accounts	Dec 11	May 10	May 09
Sales Turnover	45m	46m	49m
Pre Tax Profit/Loss	2m	830	629
Working Capital	7m	12m	13m
Fixed Assets	1m	1m	2m
Current Assets	28m	23m	21m
Current Liabilities	4m	2m	2m

Solutions Four
24 Brunel Drive, Biggleswade, SG18 8BH
Tel: 01767-687 646 **Fax:** 020-3009 3444
E-mail: info@solutionsfour.co.uk
Website: http://www.solutionsfour.co.uk/
Directors: A. Rose (Snr Part), S. Mackie (MD)
Immediate Holding Company: INTELLIGENT TAX SOLUTIONS LLP
Registration no: 04531003 **Date established:** 2009
Turnover: Up to £250,000 **No.of Employees:** 1 - 10 **Product Groups:** 44

Spectrum Acoustic Consultants Ltd
27-29 High Street, Biggleswade, SG18 0JE
Tel: 01767-318871 **Fax:** 01767-317704
E-mail: enquiries@spectrumacoustic.com
Website: http://www.spectrumacoustic.com
Bank(s): National Westminster
Managers: M. Smith (Mktg Serv Mgr)
Immediate Holding Company: SPECTRUM ACOUSTIC CONSULTANTS LIMITED
Registration no: 02378475 **VAT No.:** GB 476 0741 35
Date established: 1989 **Turnover:** £1m - £2m **No.of Employees:** 11 - 20
Product Groups: 54

Date of Accounts	Sep 11	Sep 10	Sep 09
Sales Turnover	1m	1m	1m
Pre Tax Profit/Loss	-8	5	41
Working Capital	435	473	486
Fixed Assets	121	91	90
Current Assets	516	528	555
Current Liabilities	73	50	65

Stratton Technologies Ltd
PO Box 82, Biggleswade, SG18 8ZN
Tel: 0870-7606528 **Fax:** 0870-0116275
E-mail: sales@strattontechnologies.co.uk
Website: http://www.strattontechnologies.co.uk
Directors: C. Brady (MD)
Immediate Holding Company: STRATTON TECHNOLOGIES LIMITED
Registration no: 04802890 **Date established:** 2003
Turnover: Up to £250,000 **No.of Employees:** 1 - 10 **Product Groups:** 28, 33, 37, 52, 84, 85

Date of Accounts	Jun 08	Jun 07	Jun 06
Working Capital	42	38	27
Fixed Assets	1	N/A	N/A
Current Assets	118	102	63
Current Liabilities	77	65	35
Total Share Capital	1	1	1

Summit Solder Products (a division of Mountstar Metal Corporation Ltd)
Rail Works Railway Sidings, Biggleswade, SG18 8BD
Tel: 01767-318999 **Fax:** 01767-318912
E-mail: chris.burton@summitsolder.com
Website: http://www.emrltd.com
Managers: C. Burton (Mgr)
Immediate Holding Company: AMALGAMATED METAL CORP P.L.C.
Registration no: 00941219 **VAT No.:** GB 229 4838 33
Turnover: £2m - £5m **No.of Employees:** 1 - 10 **Product Groups:** 32, 34

Travis Perkins plc
67 Shortmead Street, Biggleswade, SG18 0BB
Tel: 01767-313020 **Fax:** 01767-601774
E-mail: david.johnson@travisperkins.co.uk
Website: http://www.travisperkins.co.uk
Managers: D. Johnson (District Mgr)
Immediate Holding Company: TRAVIS PERKINS PLC
Registration no: 00824821 **Date established:** 1964
No.of Employees: 11 - 20 **Product Groups:** 66

Date of Accounts	Dec 11	Dec 10	Dec 09
Sales Turnover	4779m	3153m	2931m
Pre Tax Profit/Loss	270m	197m	213m
Working Capital	133m	159m	248m
Fixed Assets	2771m	2749m	2108m
Current Assets	1421m	1329m	1035m
Current Liabilities	473m	412m	109m

21st Century Radiators
Ickwell Bury The Green, Ickwell, Biggleswade, SG18 9EF
Tel: 01767-627500 **Fax:** 01767-627503
E-mail: info@21stcenturyradiators.com
Website: http://www.21stcenturyradiators.com
Directors: M. Guest (MD)
Immediate Holding Company: 21ST CENTURY RADIATOR COMPANY LIMITED
Registration no: 03361492 **Date established:** 1997
No.of Employees: 1 - 10 **Product Groups:** 36, 38, 40

Date of Accounts	Jul 11	Jul 10	Jul 09
Working Capital	61	-3	-28
Fixed Assets	31	36	44
Current Assets	233	184	160

Dunstable

Access Electrical Services Ltd
Admiral Place High Street North, Dunstable, LU6 1LW
Tel: 01582-697711 **Fax:** 01582-667347
E-mail: sales@access-electrical.co.uk
Website: http://www.access-electrical.co.uk
Directors: M. Cooper (MD)
Immediate Holding Company: ACCESS ELECTRICAL (SERVICES) LIMITED
Registration no: 01084120 **Date established:** 1972
Turnover: £500,000 - £1m **No.of Employees:** 1 - 10 **Product Groups:** 37

Date of Accounts	Apr 12	Apr 11	Apr 10
Working Capital	454	439	452
Fixed Assets	13	12	12
Current Assets	618	603	637

Aquator Watercoolers Ltd
Unit 8 Packhorse Place Industrial Estate Watling Street, Kensworth, Dunstable, LU6 3QL
Tel: 01582-842828 **Fax:** 01582-842727
Directors: M. Bottrill (Dir)
Registration no: 04318003 **No.of Employees:** 1 - 10 **Product Groups:** 40, 42, 67

Barwest Fabrications Ltd
Lodge Farm Long Lane, Toddington, Dunstable, LU5 6HN
Tel: 01525-876777 **Fax:** 01525-876888
E-mail: phil.barwest@btinternet.com
Website: http://www.barwestfabrications.co.uk
Directors: P. Muncaster (MD)
Date established: 1996 **No.of Employees:** 21 - 50 **Product Groups:** 35

Bespoke Software Solutions Ltd
74 Northfields, Dunstable, LU5 5AL
Tel: 07859-796713
E-mail: enquiries@bespoke-software-solutions.co.uk
Website: http://www.bespoke-software-solutions.co.uk
Directors: T. Broderick (Fin), N. Broderick (Dir)
Registration no: 05792499 **Date established:** 2006
No.of Employees: 1 - 10 **Product Groups:** 79

Cedar Ceramics Wall & Floor Tiling (Dunstable)
Englands Lane, Dunstable, LU5 4HT
Tel: 01323-505696
E-mail: enquires@cedarceramicstiling.co.uk
Website: http://www.cedarceramicstiling.co.uk
Directors: R. Mabbott (Prop)
No.of Employees: 1 - 10 **Product Groups:** 14, 33, 49, 66

D B Dental
Unit 2 Apex Business Centre Boscombe Road, Dunstable, LU5 4SB
Tel: 01582-672778
Website: http://www.dbdental.co.uk
Directors: D. Bennett (MD)
No.of Employees: 1 - 10 **Product Groups:** 26, 38, 40, 88

Dunstable Waste Group Ltd
Townsend Farm Industrial Estate Blackburn Road, Houghton Regis, Dunstable, LU5 5DD
Tel: 01582-476600 **Fax:** 01582-664117
E-mail: mark.jones@greenstar.co.uk
Website: http://www.greenstar.co.uk
Directors: R. Levick (MD)
Managers: J. Halesay (Mgr), M. Jones (Site Co-ord), W. Basham (Sales Prom Mgr)
Ultimate Holding Company: GREENSTAR HOLDINGS LTD
Immediate Holding Company: FFR SERVICES (SOUTHERN) LTD
Registration no: 02018703 **Date established:** 2010 **Turnover:** £2m - £5m
No.of Employees: 21 - 50 **Product Groups:** 54, 81

Date of Accounts	Mar 11	Mar 10	Mar 09
Sales Turnover	5m	6m	5m
Pre Tax Profit/Loss	-328	79	47
Working Capital	981	-533	-460
Fixed Assets	8	2m	2m
Current Assets	1m	1m	697
Current Liabilities	6	726	332

E F D International Inc
Unit 14 Apex Business Centre Boscombe Road, Dunstable, LU5 4SB
Tel: 01582-666334 **Fax:** 01582-664227
E-mail: sales@efd-inc.com
Website: http://www.efd.co.uk
Directors: T. O'Connell (Co Sec)
Managers: S. Auger (Ops Mgr)
Immediate Holding Company: EFD INTERNATIONAL INC.
Registration no: FC014622 **Date established:** 1988 **Turnover:** £2m - £5m
No.of Employees: 11 - 20 **Product Groups:** 32, 42, 61, 66, 67, 76, 83, 85

Eaton Valve Products Limited
32 The Nurseries Eaton Bray, Dunstable, LU6 2AX
Tel: 01525-229170 **Fax:** 01525-229425
E-mail: sales@eaton-valves.co.uk
Website: http://www.eaton-valves.co.uk
Directors: N. Cavanagh (Dir), J. Cavanagh (Co Sec)
Registration no: 04104244 **VAT No.:** GB 755 5421 24
Date established: 2000 **Turnover:** £250,000 - £500,000
No.of Employees: 1 - 10 **Product Groups:** 36, 40

Frimatec UK Ltd
5 Townsend Centre Blackburn Road Townsend Industrial Estate, Houghton Regis, Dunstable, LU5 5BQ
Tel: 01582-471600 **Fax:** 01582-472050
E-mail: info@frimatecuk.com
Website: http://www.frimatec-isocab.com
Directors: A. Strange (MD)
Immediate Holding Company: FRIMATEC U.K. LIMITED
Registration no: 01959738 **VAT No.:** GB 433 0149 89
Date established: 1985 **Turnover:** £2m - £5m **No.of Employees:** 1 - 10
Product Groups: 38, 40, 41, 42, 48, 52

see next page

***Frimatec UK Ltd** - Cont'd*

Date of Accounts	Sep 11	Sep 10	Sep 09
Working Capital	2	20	37
Fixed Assets	101	166	172
Current Assets	688	734	517
Current Liabilities	N/A	N/A	352

G T Drawing Services Ltd

61a High Street South, Dunstable, LU6 3SF
Tel: 01582-502883 **Fax:** 01582-572201
E-mail: diane.gomersal@gtdrawings.com
Website: http://www.gtdrawings.com
Directors: A. Gomersal (MD)
Immediate Holding Company: G.T. DRAWING SERVICES LIMITED
Registration no: 01384204 **VAT No.:** GB 322 5545 77
Date established: 1978 **Turnover:** £500,000 - £1m
No.of Employees: 1 - 10 **Product Groups:** 44, 80, 81, 85

Date of Accounts	Apr 12	Apr 11	Apr 10
Working Capital	49	52	66
Fixed Assets	3	4	6
Current Assets	52	62	72

G T I Corporation Ltd

Portland House Mayer Way, Houghton Regis, Dunstable, LU5 5BF
Tel: 01582-477589 **Fax:** 01582-477811
E-mail: enquiries@gtiltd.com
Website: http://www.gtiltd.com
Directors: G. Nye (Fin), K. Stibbards (MD), S. Fountain (Sales)
Immediate Holding Company: GTI CORPORATION LIMITED
Registration no: 02871867 **Date established:** 1993 **Turnover:** £2m - £5m
No.of Employees: 21 - 50 **Product Groups:** 46

Date of Accounts	Mar 12	Mar 11	Mar 10
Sales Turnover	3m	3m	N/A
Pre Tax Profit/Loss	130	70	N/A
Working Capital	156	181	107
Fixed Assets	503	574	434
Current Assets	1m	1m	1m
Current Liabilities	559	727	N/A

Halfen Ltd

Unit 2 Humphrys Road Woodside Estate, Dunstable, LU5 4TP
Tel: 01582-470300 **Fax:** 08705-316304
E-mail: info@halfen.co.uk
Website: http://www.halfen.co.uk
Bank(s): Barclays
Directors: B. Davis (MD), P. Riches (MD), J. Mindenhall (I.T. Dir)
Managers: D. Locker (Fin Mgr)
Ultimate Holding Company: CRH PUBLIC LIMITED COMPANY
Immediate Holding Company: HALFEN LIMITED
Registration no: 02455626 **VAT No.:** GB 678 1922 87
Date established: 1989 **Turnover:** £5m - £10m **No.of Employees:** 21 - 50
Product Groups: 34, 35

Date of Accounts	Dec 11	Dec 10	Dec 09
Sales Turnover	6m	7m	9m
Pre Tax Profit/Loss	709	-145	-387
Working Capital	6m	5m	5m
Fixed Assets	551	706	994
Current Assets	7m	6m	6m
Current Liabilities	690	609	795

Hardall International Ltd

Fairway Works Southfields Road, Dunstable, LU6 3EP
Tel: 01582-500860 **Fax:** 01582-690975
E-mail: abishop@hardalluk.com
Website: http://www.hardall.co.uk
Bank(s): HSBC Bank plc
Directors: A. Bishop (MD), J. Ledwidge (Sales), J. Brummage (Co Sec)
Managers: G. Hammond (Tech Serv Mgr), J. Jones (Purch Mgr)
Ultimate Holding Company: HARDALL HOLDINGS LIMITED
Immediate Holding Company: HARDALL INTERNATIONAL LIMITED
Registration no: 02174882 **VAT No.:** GB 478 0415 36
Date established: 1987 **Turnover:** £2m - £5m **No.of Employees:** 21 - 50
Product Groups: 42

Date of Accounts	Dec 11	Dec 10	Dec 09
Working Capital	2m	3m	-592
Fixed Assets	1m	312	3m
Current Assets	3m	3m	482

Hartwell Automotive Group Ltd

77-87 London Road, Dunstable, LU6 3DT
Tel: 08443-241780 **Fax:** 01582-443521
E-mail: graham.betts@hartwellford.co.uk
Website: http://www.hartwell.co.uk
Directors: C. Lathwell (Fin)
Managers: G. Betts (Mgr)
Ultimate Holding Company: FAIRVIEW ANSTALT (LIECHTENSTEIN)
Immediate Holding Company: HARTWELL AUTOMOTIVE GROUP LIMITED
Registration no: 00158447 **Date established:** 2019
Turnover: £20m - £50m **No.of Employees:** 101 - 250
Product Groups: 39, 68, 72

Date of Accounts	Nov 11	Nov 10	Nov 09
Sales Turnover	253m	268m	165m
Pre Tax Profit/Loss	5m	5m	2m
Working Capital	37m	34m	27m
Fixed Assets	6m	6m	9m
Current Assets	71m	78m	62m
Current Liabilities	26m	35m	26m

Jewson Ltd

Beale Street, Dunstable, LU6 1LZ
Tel: 01582-603111 **Fax:** 01582-609654
Website: http://www.jewson.co.uk
Managers: J. Anderson (District Mgr)
Ultimate Holding Company: COMPAGNIE DE SAINT GOBAIN (FRANCE)
Immediate Holding Company: JEWSON LIMITED
Registration no: 00348407 **Date established:** 1939
Turnover: £500m - £1,000m **No.of Employees:** 1 - 10
Product Groups: 66

Date of Accounts	Dec 11	Dec 10	Dec 09
Sales Turnover	1606m	1547m	1485m
Pre Tax Profit/Loss	18m	100m	45m
Working Capital	-345m	-250m	-349m
Fixed Assets	496m	387m	461m
Current Assets	657m	1005m	1320m
Current Liabilities	66m	120m	64m

K A S Paper Systems Ltd

Brewers Hill Road, Dunstable, LU6 1AD
Tel: 01582-662211 **Fax:** 01582-664222
E-mail: mail@kaspapersystems.com
Website: http://www.kaspapersystems.com
Bank(s): HSBC, Dunstable
Directors: A. Hampstead (Tech Serv), S. Hampstead (MD)
Immediate Holding Company: KAS PAPER SYSTEMS LIMITED
Registration no: 00520281 **VAT No.:** GB 216 2219 96
Date established: 1953 **Turnover:** £2m - £5m **No.of Employees:** 21 - 50
Product Groups: 44

Date of Accounts	Jan 12	Jan 11	Jan 10
Pre Tax Profit/Loss	N/A	N/A	505
Working Capital	569	502	413
Fixed Assets	2m	2m	2m
Current Assets	1m	1m	1m
Current Liabilities	424	N/A	488

Kenco Techniques Ltd

Unit D Kensworth Industrial Estate Common Road, Kensworth, Dunstable, LU6 2PN
Tel: 01582-873010 **Fax:** 01582-873020
E-mail: ray@kenco-techniques.co.uk
Website: http://www.kenco-techniques.co.uk
Bank(s): HSBC
Directors: R. Rockley (Dir)
Immediate Holding Company: KENCO TECHNIQUES LIMITED
Registration no: 02354647 **VAT No.:** GB 197 6840 07
Date established: 1989 **No.of Employees:** 11 - 20 **Product Groups:** 34, 48

Date of Accounts	Jul 11	Jul 10	Jul 09
Working Capital	359	224	182
Fixed Assets	422	301	330
Current Assets	718	500	424

Keygrove International

15 Houghton Road, Dunstable, LU5 5AA
Tel: 01582-605575 **Fax:** 01582-478240
E-mail: info@keygrovemarketing.co.uk
Website: http://www.keygrovemarketing.co.uk
Directors: J. Tree (Fin)
Immediate Holding Company: KEYGROVE INTERNATIONAL LIMITED
Registration no: 02686903 **VAT No.:** GB 486 0818 19
Date established: 1992 **Turnover:** £250,000 - £500,000
No.of Employees: 1 - 10 **Product Groups:** 40

Date of Accounts	Mar 12	Mar 11	Mar 10
Working Capital	27	76	161
Current Assets	74	141	238

Luton Fabrications Ltd

Unit 21a Icknield Way Farm Tring Road, Dunstable, LU6 2JX
Tel: 01582-663330 **Fax:** 01582-662333
Website: http://www.lutonfabricationsltd.com
Directors: A. Wright (Fin), V. Wright (MD)
Immediate Holding Company: LUTON FABRICATIONS LIMITED
Registration no: 01516755 **Date established:** 1980
Turnover: Up to £250,000 **No.of Employees:** 1 - 10 **Product Groups:** 48

Date of Accounts	Sep 11	Sep 10	Sep 09
Sales Turnover	151	166	93
Pre Tax Profit/Loss	3	4	-5
Working Capital	15	32	48
Fixed Assets	3	4	5
Current Assets	53	65	70
Current Liabilities	20	5	8

Manor Fabrications

Sewell, Dunstable, LU6 1RP
Tel: 01582-671682 **Fax:** 01582-671681
Directors: G. Philip (Prop)
Date established: 2006 **No.of Employees:** 1 - 10 **Product Groups:** 35

March Designs & Measurements

11 Alfred Street, Dunstable, LU5 4HZ
Tel: 01582-600016 **Fax:** 01582-600016
E-mail: enquiries@marchdesigns.com
Website: http://www.marchdesigns.com
Directors: J. Marjaram (Prop)
VAT No.: GB 382 3886 19 **Turnover:** Up to £250,000
No.of Employees: 1 - 10 **Product Groups:** 38, 67, 84

Marshall Thermo King Ltd

Houghton Regis Trading Centre Houghton Regis, Dunstable, LU5 5QH
Tel: 01582-867778 **Fax:** 01582-866648
E-mail: houghtonregis@marshallthermoking.co.uk
Website: http://www.marshallfleetsolutions.co.uk
Bank(s): Barclays
Managers: C. Newbold (Mgr)
Ultimate Holding Company: MARSHALL OF CAMBRIDGE (HOLDINGS) LIMITED
Immediate Holding Company: MARSHALL THERMO KING LIMITED
Registration no: 00759572 **VAT No.:** GB 213 2090 19
Date established: 1963 **Turnover:** £500,000 - £1m
No.of Employees: 11 - 20 **Product Groups:** 52

Date of Accounts	Dec 10	Dec 09	Dec 08
Sales Turnover	18m	16m	21m
Pre Tax Profit/Loss	-2m	-852	-662
Working Capital	70	1m	1m
Fixed Assets	551	619	922
Current Assets	6m	4m	7m
Current Liabilities	1m	2m	4m

MEC Medical Ltd

Ivenhoe Business Centre Blackburn Road, Dunstable, LU5 5BQ
Tel: 01582-661885 **Fax:** 01582-602527
E-mail: sales@mecmedical.com
Website: http://www.mecmedical.com
Directors: J. Rayner (Dir)
Managers: D. Watson (Mgr), G. Ivory (Sales Prom Mgr), N. Powers (Sales Prom Mgr)
Registration no: 05095440 **VAT No.:** GB 836 0922 27
Date established: 1975 **No.of Employees:** 1 - 10 **Product Groups:** 29, 33, 38, 40, 67

Date of Accounts	Sep 11	Sep 10	Sep 09
Working Capital	488	363	285
Fixed Assets	35	51	65
Current Assets	641	602	502

Meggitt Control Systems

Unit 19 Eyncourt Road, Woodside Estate, Dunstable, LU5 4TS
Tel: 01582-473600 **Fax:** 01442-230035
E-mail: alanclark@meggitt.com
Website: http://www.meggit.com
Directors: A. Trayner (Dir)
Managers: S. Prichard (Buyer), R. Lancaster (Chief Mgr), M. Lee (Fin Mgr)
Ultimate Holding Company: MEGGITT P.L.C.
Immediate Holding Company: A.T.A. (ENGINEERING PROCESSES)
Registration no: 00629814 **VAT No.:** GB 348 8101 48
Date established: 1963 **Turnover:** £20m - £50m **No.of Employees:** 1 - 10
Product Groups: 36

Moto Hospitality Ltd

PO Box 218, Dunstable, LU5 6QG
Tel: 01525-873933 **Fax:** 01525-878325
E-mail: tim.moss@moto-way.co.uk
Website: http://www.moto-way.co.uk
Directors: C. Rogers (Mkt Research), G. Latcham (Tech Serv), R. Prynn (Fin), T. Moss (Grp Chief Exec), H. Budd (Pers)
Managers: A. Neill (Purch Mgr)
Ultimate Holding Company: MOTO INTERNATIONAL PARENT LIMITED (BERMUDA)
Immediate Holding Company: MOTO HOSPITALITY LIMITED
Registration no: 00734299 **Date established:** 1962
Turnover: £500m - £1,000m **No.of Employees:** 251 - 500
Product Groups: 61

Date of Accounts	Dec 09	Dec 10	Dec 11
Sales Turnover	830m	848m	864m
Pre Tax Profit/Loss	-70m	-64m	-48m
Working Capital	-676m	-710m	-760m
Fixed Assets	565m	535m	671m
Current Assets	54m	73m	68m
Current Liabilities	29m	30m	24m

O A G Worldwide

Church Street, Dunstable, LU5 4HB
Tel: 01582-600111 **Fax:** 01582-695230
E-mail: les.higgins@oag.com
Website: http://www.oag.com
Directors: S. Bray (Jt MD), B. Young (I.T. Dir), D. Alexander (MD), L. Higgins (Ch), M. Edis (Co Sec), N. Salter (Sales)
Immediate Holding Company: NORMAN K. (DUNSTABLE) LIMITED
Registration no: 00181427 **Date established:** 2010
Turnover: £50m - £75m **No.of Employees:** 101 - 250
Product Groups: 28, 80, 84, 86

Date of Accounts	Dec 06	Dec 05
Sales Turnover	20593	20884
Pre Tax Profit/Loss	-10452	-5796
Working Capital	-8223	-3058
Fixed Assets	1104	5718
Current Assets	4283	6686
Current Liabilities	12506	9744
ROCE% (Return on Capital Employed)	146.8	-217.9
ROT% (Return on Turnover)	-50.8	-27.8

Palagan Ltd

Tavistock Street, Dunstable, LU6 1NE
Tel: 01582-600234 **Fax:** 01582-601636
E-mail: sales@palagan.co.uk
Website: http://www.palagan.co.uk
Directors: S. Barton (MD)
Managers: J. Carter (Mktg Serv Mgr), C. Myhre (Tech Serv Mgr), B. Green (Fin Mgr)
Ultimate Holding Company: PLASTICS CAPITAL TRADING LIMITED
Immediate Holding Company: PALAGAN LIMITED
Registration no: 01221384 **Date established:** 1975
Turnover: £10m - £20m **No.of Employees:** 21 - 50 **Product Groups:** 30

Date of Accounts	Oct 07	Mar 11	Mar 10
Sales Turnover	N/A	11m	9m
Pre Tax Profit/Loss	821	482	249
Working Capital	2m	4m	3m
Fixed Assets	715	255	317
Current Assets	5m	6m	5m
Current Liabilities	2m	653	297

Polestar UK Print Ltd

Unit 1 Apex Business Centre Boscombe Road, Dunstable, LU5 4SB
Tel: 01582-678900 **Fax:** 01582-678901
E-mail: marie.baldwin@polestar-group.com
Website: http://www.polestar-group.com
Bank(s): Lloyds
Directors: I. Webster (Tech Serv), S. Jones (Pers), J. Povey (Mkt Research), P. Johnson (Fin)
Managers: M. Baldwin (Sales Admin), J. Kenyon (Purch Mgr)
Ultimate Holding Company: INK ACQUISITIONS LTD (CAYMAN IS)
Immediate Holding Company: POLESTAR UK PRINT LIMITED
Registration no: 05674948 **VAT No.:** GB 545 3588 21
Date established: 2006 **Turnover:** £125m - £250m
No.of Employees: 21 - 50 **Product Groups:** 28, 81

Date of Accounts	Sep 11	Sep 10	Sep 09
Sales Turnover	233m	262m	276m
Pre Tax Profit/Loss	-71m	-23m	-38m
Working Capital	-19m	-6m	-38m
Fixed Assets	118m	149m	206m
Current Assets	43m	79m	52m
Current Liabilities	24m	36m	23m

Renault Truck UK Ltd

Houghton Hall Business Park Polz Avenue, Houghton Regis, Dunstable, LU5 5FT
Tel: 01582-471122 **Fax:** 01582-479456
E-mail: laurent.farman@renault-trucks.com
Website: http://www.renault-trucks.co.uk
Directors: R. Alins (Fin), M. Martinez (MD)
Managers: J. Twitchen (Buyer), P. Randall (Sales & Mktg Mg), B. Dawson (Personnel), L. Hildenbrand (Comptroller), J. Nicholls (Tech Serv Mgr)
Ultimate Holding Company: AB VOLVO (SWEDEN)
Immediate Holding Company: RENAULT TRUCK COMMERCIALS LIMITED
Registration no: 00290604 **Date established:** 1934
Turnover: £75m - £125m **No.of Employees:** 101 - 250
Product Groups: 39, 72, 85

Date of Accounts	Dec 11	Dec 10	Dec 09
Sales Turnover	90m	69m	47m
Pre Tax Profit/Loss	-333	-2m	-3m
Working Capital	10m	-3m	-2m
Fixed Assets	6m	6m	6m
Current Assets	37m	24m	21m
Current Liabilities	8m	5m	5m

S C A Hygiene Products UK Ltd
Southfields Road, Dunstable, LU6 3EJ
Tel: 01582-677400 **Fax:** 01582-677502
E-mail: customers.servicesafh@sca.com
Website: http://www.sca-hygiene.co.uk
Directors: P. Bailey (Fin), J. Thorburn (Pers)
Managers: B. Dwason (I.T. Exec)
Ultimate Holding Company: SVENSKA CELLULOSA AB (SWEDEN)
Immediate Holding Company: SCA HYGIENE PRODUCTS UK LIMITED
Registration no: 03226403 **Date established:** 1996
Turnover: £500m - £1,000m **No.of Employees:** 101 - 250
Product Groups: 27

Date of Accounts	Dec 11	Dec 10	Dec 09
Sales Turnover	535m	571m	572m
Pre Tax Profit/Loss	26m	19m	25m
Working Capital	165m	154m	163m
Fixed Assets	162m	164m	170m
Current Assets	299m	302m	301m
Current Liabilities	64m	65m	65m

Satco
Satco House Unit 2 Aragon Park, Dunstable, LU5 5GN
Tel: 01582-608070
E-mail: info@satcoplastics.com
Website: http://www.satcoplastics.com
Managers: H. Karawalli (Comptroller)
Immediate Holding Company: SATCO PLASTICS LIMITED
Registration no: 05603745 **Date established:** 2005
No.of Employees: 21 - 50 **Product Groups:** 30, 35, 48, 63

Date of Accounts	Mar 12	Mar 11	Mar 10
Working Capital	-112	-85	-267
Fixed Assets	4m	3m	3m
Current Assets	2m	2m	1m

Sedgewall Communications Group Ltd
Unit 19 Apex Business Centre, Dunstable, LU5 4SB
Tel: 01582-475555 **Fax:** 01582-475553
E-mail: robert@sedgewall.co.uk
Website: http://www.sedgewall.com
Bank(s): Lloyds TSB Bank plc
Directors: S. Green (MD)
Managers: R. Gillespie (Fin Mgr), A. Smith (Sales Admin), D. Griffith (Ops Mgr)
Immediate Holding Company: FULCRUM HEADSETS LIMITED
Registration no: 03994636 **VAT No.:** GB 596 1467 02
Date established: 2000 **Turnover:** £2m - £5m **No.of Employees:** 11 - 20
Product Groups: 37, 39, 40

Sekisui Alveo Ag
Queens Chambers Eleanors Cross, Dunstable, LU6 1SU
Tel: 01582-600456 **Fax:** 01582-600567
E-mail: info.gb@sekisuialveo.com
Website: http://www.sekisuialveo.com
Managers: C. Vowles (Mgr)
Ultimate Holding Company: Sekisui Chemical Ltd
Immediate Holding Company: SEKISUI ALVEO AG
Registration no: FC024376 **VAT No.:** GB 402 3642 95
Date established: 2003 **Turnover:** £50m - £75m **No.of Employees:** 1 - 10
Product Groups: 30

Silkmead Tubular Ltd
Unit 3 Southfields Road, Dunstable, LU6 3EJ
Tel: 01582-609988 **Fax:** 01582-609930
E-mail: simonb@silkmead.co.uk
Website: http://www.silkmead.co.uk
Bank(s): Barclays, Business Centre, St. Albans
Directors: S. Boba (MD)
Managers: M. James
Immediate Holding Company: SILKMEAD TUBULAR LIMITED
Registration no: 00868860 **VAT No.:** GB 197 2254 40
Date established: 1966 **Turnover:** £1m - £2m **No.of Employees:** 21 - 50
Product Groups: 46, 48

Date of Accounts	Dec 11	Dec 10	Dec 09
Working Capital	-132	-117	-133
Fixed Assets	688	713	754
Current Assets	377	381	339
Current Liabilities	96	N/A	N/A

Square Deals T V Rentals
13-13a West Street, Dunstable, LU6 1SL
Tel: 01582-603037
Website: http://www.azrental.co.uk
Directors: G. Strange (Ptnr), G. Strange (Ptnr)
Immediate Holding Company: SQUARE DEALS LTD
Registration no: 05172431 **Date established:** 1980
No.of Employees: 1 - 10 **Product Groups:** 36, 40

C D Stone Dunstable Ltd
Fairway Works Southfields Road, Dunstable, LU6 3EP
Tel: 01582-605353 **Fax:** 01582-660103
E-mail: patrick@cdstone.co.uk
Website: http://www.cdstone.co.uk
Bank(s): Barclays
Directors: H. Gordon (MD), J. Gordon (MD), N. Stone (MD)
Immediate Holding Company: C. D. STONE (HOLDINGS) LIMITED
Registration no: 00542726 **Date established:** 1955 **Turnover:** £1m - £2m
No.of Employees: 21 - 50 **Product Groups:** 52

Date of Accounts	Apr 11	Apr 10	Apr 09
Working Capital	201	199	206
Fixed Assets	118	118	118
Current Assets	230	229	236

Strictly Flooring
20 Park Lane Eaton Bray, Dunstable, LU6 2BB
Tel: 01525-220833 **Fax:** 01525-220833
E-mail: daren@strictlyflooring.co.uk
Website: http://www.strictlyflooring.co.uk
Directors: D. Cant (Grp Chief Exec), J. Barnby (Grp Chief Exec)
Date established: 2008 **No.of Employees:** 1 - 10 **Product Groups:** 23

Swift Metal Fabrications
Unit 6-7 Townsend Centre Blackburn Road, Houghton Regis, Dunstable, LU5 5BQ
Tel: 01582-607677
E-mail: info@swiftmetalfab.com
Website: http://www.swiftmetalfab.com
Directors: N. Hing (MD)
Immediate Holding Company: SWIFT METAL FABRICATIONS LIMITED
Registration no: 02341023 **Date established:** 1989
No.of Employees: 11 - 20 **Product Groups:** 34, 44, 84

Date of Accounts	Mar 11	Mar 10	Mar 09
Working Capital	-16	43	83
Fixed Assets	25	33	43
Current Assets	304	149	281

T O M R A Systems
Unit 13 Apex Business Centre, Dunstable, LU5 4SB
Tel: 01582-666739
E-mail: info@tomra.com
Website: http://www.tomra.com
Directors: S. Ford (Dir), J. Giaever (Co Sec)
Immediate Holding Company: TOMRA SYSTEMS LIMITED
Registration no: 05814294 **Date established:** 2006 **Turnover:** £1m - £2m
No.of Employees: 11 - 20 **Product Groups:** 42, 45, 49

Date of Accounts	Dec 11	Dec 10	Dec 09
Sales Turnover	2m	2m	2m
Pre Tax Profit/Loss	291	194	-12
Working Capital	-2m	-2m	-2m
Fixed Assets	7	14	22
Current Assets	631	325	535
Current Liabilities	154	212	308

Tool & Fastener Solutions Ltd
Unit 7 Packhorse Industrial Estate
Watling Street
Kensworth, Dunstable, LU6 3QL
Tel: 01582-842157 **Fax:** 0844-736 9651
E-mail: sales@tfsolutions.co.uk
Website: http://www.tfsolutions.co.uk
Product Groups: 35

Torex Retail Holdings Ltd
The XN Centre Houghton Hall Park, Houghton Regis, Dunstable, LU5 5YG
Tel: 01582-869600 **Fax:** 01582-869601
E-mail: info@torex.com
Website: http://www.torex.com
Bank(s): Co-operative Bank
Managers: J. Pead, S. Rowley
Immediate Holding Company: MICROS SYSTEMS UK LIMITED
Registration no: 06273940 **VAT No.:** GB 354 6097 40
Date established: 2007 **Turnover:** £10m - £20m
No.of Employees: 101 - 250 **Product Groups:** 44

Date of Accounts	Jun 11	Jun 10	Jun 09
Sales Turnover	136m	161m	205m
Pre Tax Profit/Loss	-8m	-9m	70m
Working Capital	4m	-6m	-5m
Fixed Assets	105m	121m	142m
Current Assets	54m	48m	75m
Current Liabilities	40m	43m	66m

Wardown Engineering Ltd
Townsend Farm Road Townsend Industrial Estate, Houghton Regis, Dunstable, LU5 5BA
Tel: 01582-471919 **Fax:** 01582-471993
E-mail: sales@wardown.com
Website: http://www.wardown.com
Bank(s): National Westminster Bank Plc
Directors: M. Jabri (MD), P. Baldwin (Fin)
Managers: L. Davies (Sales Admin)
Immediate Holding Company: WARDOWN ENGINEERING LIMITED
Registration no: 00946568 **VAT No.:** GB 197 2375 28
Date established: 1969 **Turnover:** £2m - £5m **No.of Employees:** 21 - 50
Product Groups: 30, 33, 34, 35, 36, 46, 48

Date of Accounts	May 11	May 10	May 09
Working Capital	1m	880	1m
Fixed Assets	374	320	354
Current Assets	1m	1m	2m

Flitwick

Prolou Ltd
Unit 11, Pilgrims Close, Flitwick, MK45 1UL
Tel: 01525-715786 **Fax:** 01525-715717
E-mail: tracey@prolou.co.uk
Website: http://www.prolou.com
Directors: T. Belger (Co Sec)
Registration no: 892979052 **Date established:** 2006 **Turnover:** £1m - £2m
No.of Employees: 11 - 20 **Product Groups:** 63

Date of Accounts	Dec 07
Working Capital	-9
Fixed Assets	1
Current Assets	2
Current Liabilities	11

Henlow

Colin Hill Bar & Catering Supplies
Peckworth House Bedford Road Lower Stondon, Henlow, SG16 6EE
Tel: 08448-261700 **Fax:** 08448-261706
E-mail: info@colinhill.co.uk
Website: http://www.colinhill.co.uk
Directors: L. Hill (Dir)
Immediate Holding Company: COLIN HILL BAR & CATERING SUPPLIES LTD
Registration no: 03739228 **Date established:** 1999 **Turnover:** £2m - £5m
No.of Employees: 1 - 10 **Product Groups:** 30, 40, 48, 61, 67, 83

Date of Accounts	Aug 09	Aug 08	May 11
Working Capital	-67	-29	-12
Fixed Assets	43	34	60
Current Assets	148	188	193

Emerald Precision Ltd
4 Henlow Industrial Estate, Henlow, SG16 6DS
Tel: 01462-817203 **Fax:** 01462-817268
E-mail: sales@emerald-engineering.co.uk
Website: http://www.emerald-engineering.co.uk
Directors: A. Balk (MD)
Immediate Holding Company: EMERALD PRECISION LIMITED
Registration no: 06996898 **VAT No.:** GB 981 5409 01
Date established: 2009 **Turnover:** £500,000 - £1m
No.of Employees: 1 - 10 **Product Groups:** 30, 35, 48, 66, 84

Date of Accounts	Jul 11	Jul 10
Working Capital	-101	-70
Fixed Assets	168	171
Current Assets	96	76

P H Engineering Services Ltd
Unit F Oldfield Farm, Henlow, SG16 6EJ
Tel: 01462-811133
Directors: P. Hooper (MD)
Immediate Holding Company: P.H.ENGINEERING SERVICES LIMITED
Registration no: 05405071 **Date established:** 2005
No.of Employees: 1 - 10 **Product Groups:** 35, 45, 48

Date of Accounts	Mar 12	Mar 11	Mar 10
Working Capital	419	319	238
Fixed Assets	30	24	27
Current Assets	517	424	319

Schlegel UK
25 Henlow Industrial Estate, Henlow, SG16 6DS
Tel: 01462-815500 **Fax:** 01462-814781
E-mail: ian.pawson@schlegel.com
Website: http://www.schlegel.com
Bank(s): Lloyds TSB
Directors: I. Pawson (MD)
Managers: D. Warrick (Purch Mgr), G. Lethbridge (Sales & Mktg Mg), D. Dear (Personnel), L. Wicks
Immediate Holding Company: UNIPOLY
Registration no: 01157470 **VAT No.:** GB 242 3380 87
Date established: 1974 **Turnover:** £10m - £20m
No.of Employees: 51 - 100 **Product Groups:** 30, 36

Date of Accounts	Dec 06
Working Capital	323
Current Assets	323
Total Share Capital	323

Leighton Buzzard

1st-Packaging
K7 Cherry Court Way, Leighton Buzzard, LU7 4UH
Tel: 01525-382580 **Fax:** 01525-851465
E-mail: sales@1st-packaging.co.uk
Website: http://www.1st-packaging.co.uk
Product Groups: 27, 30, 31, 48, 66, 84

AI Solutions
PO Box 5025, Leighton Buzzard, LU7 1ZN
Tel: 01525-850080 **Fax:** 01525-851539
E-mail: david.marlowe@aisolutions.co.uk
Website: http://www.aisolutions.co.uk
Directors: D. Marlowe (MD)
Immediate Holding Company: AI SOLUTIONS LIMITED
Registration no: 03009721 **Date established:** 1995
Turnover: £500,000 - £1m **No.of Employees:** 1 - 10 **Product Groups:** 84, 86

Date of Accounts	Dec 11	Dec 10	Dec 09
Working Capital	49	71	100
Fixed Assets	9	12	17
Current Assets	49	263	315

Air Chill Refrigeration
Unit 15 81 Leighton Road Stanbridge, Leighton Buzzard, LU7 9HW
Tel: 01525-211350 **Fax:** 01525- 211470
E-mail: steve.botten@airchill.co.uk
Website: http://www.airchill.co.uk
Directors: S. Botton (MD)
Immediate Holding Company: EFR CONTRACTS LTD
Registration no: 02963235 **Turnover:** £250,000 - £500,000
No.of Employees: 1 - 10 **Product Groups:** 40, 42, 80

Date of Accounts	Mar 06
Working Capital	-53
Fixed Assets	16
Current Assets	212
Current Liabilities	265

Autobox Machinery Ltd
Unit 15 Youngs Industrial Estate Stanbridge Road, Leighton Buzzard, LU7 4QB
Tel: 01525-379359 **Fax:** 01525-382353
E-mail: b.tabor@autobox.co.uk
Website: http://www.autobox.co.uk
Bank(s): Trustee Savings Bank
Directors: B. Tabor (MD)
Immediate Holding Company: AUTOBOX MACHINERY LTD
Registration no: 06763206 **Date established:** 2008 **Turnover:** £1m - £2m
No.of Employees: 11 - 20 **Product Groups:** 23, 27, 30, 32, 42, 44

Date of Accounts	Dec 11	Dec 10	Dec 09
Working Capital	138	112	160
Fixed Assets	224	187	70
Current Assets	560	593	401

B K Engineering Ltd
Kingswood Works Heath and Reach, Leighton Buzzard, LU7 0AZ
Tel: 01525-237411 **Fax:** 01525-237827
E-mail: sales@bkengineering.com
Website: http://www.bkengineering.com
Bank(s): Barclays, Aylesbury
Directors: D. Cook (MD), V. Bellanti (Fin)
Ultimate Holding Company: KEELEX 302 LIMITED
Immediate Holding Company: BK ENGINEERING LIMITED
Registration no: 05172156 **VAT No.:** GB 198 1633 31
Date established: 2004 **Turnover:** £2m - £5m **No.of Employees:** 11 - 20
Product Groups: 32, 46

Date of Accounts	Dec 10	Dec 09	Dec 08
Working Capital	-83	28	115
Fixed Assets	416	497	565
Current Assets	443	598	704
Current Liabilities	208	N/A	319

B & Z
O2 Cherrycourt Way, Leighton Buzzard, LU7 4UH
Tel: 01525-373018 **Fax:** 01525-851439
E-mail: enquiries@bandz.co.uk
Website: http://www.b-and-z.co.uk

see next page

B & Z - Cont'd
Directors: N. Brown (Ptnr)
Ultimate Holding Company: LODANS HOLDING AG (SWITZERLAND)
Immediate Holding Company: LINDAL HOLDINGS PLC
Registration no: 01683463 **VAT No.:** GB 196 4281 33
Date established: 1982 **Turnover:** £250,000 - £500,000
No.of Employees: 1 - 10 **Product Groups:** 48

Balguard Engineering Ltd

Unit 8 Cherrycourt Way, Leighton Buzzard, LU7 4UH
Tel: 01525-373673 **Fax:** 01525-850287
E-mail: steve.l@balguard.co.uk
Website: http://www.balguard.co.uk
Bank(s): Barclays
Directors: S. Levkouskis (Dir), S. Levkouskis (Co Sec)
Managers: K. Guyatt (Sales Prom Mgr), N. Garnett (Fin Mgr), T. Grey (Purch Mgr)
Immediate Holding Company: BALGUARD ENGINEERING LIMITED
Registration no: 01345009 **VAT No.:** GB 301 7884 65
Date established: 1977 **Turnover:** £1m - £2m **No.of Employees:** 21 - 50
Product Groups: 34, 35

Date of Accounts	Dec 08	Dec 07	Jun 11
Working Capital	930	688	993
Fixed Assets	313	359	176
Current Assets	1m	2m	2m

Barbrak Ltd

5 Eden Court Eden Way, Leighton Buzzard, LU7 4FY
Tel: 01525-376605 **Fax:** 01525-370505
E-mail: rob@frictionmarketing.co.uk
Website: http://www.frictionmarketing.co.uk
Bank(s): HSBC Bank plc
Directors: C. Pratt (Sales), M. Nowell (MD), R. Holden (MD)
Managers: C. Murphy (Sales Admin), S. Kavanagh (Shipping Mgr)
Immediate Holding Company: PRIORY RECORDS LIMITED
Registration no: 01003503 **VAT No.:** GB 120 9074 01
Date established: 1997 **Turnover:** £2m - £5m **No.of Employees:** 11 - 20
Product Groups: 34

Bedford Shelving Ltd

8 Greaves Way Industrial Estate Stanbridge Road, Leighton Buzzard, LU7 4UB
Tel: 01525-852121 **Fax:** 01525-851666
E-mail: sales@bedfordshelf.com
Website: http://www.bedfordshelf.co.uk
Directors: P. Mills (Co Sec), R. Soar (Ch)
Managers: D. Duckworth (I.T. Exec), V. Short (Cust Serv Mgr), S. Heath (Buyer), L. Clapham (Admin Off)
Immediate Holding Company: Soar Engineering Ltd
Registration no: 06696455 **VAT No.:** GB 294 4848 11
Turnover: £1m - £2m **No.of Employees:** 1 - 10 **Product Groups:** 26, 35, 36

Beltech Specialist Machinery Belting Ltd

Unit 25 Acacia Close Cherrycourt Way, Leighton Buzzard, LU7 4QE
Tel: 01525-851155 **Fax:** 01525-851156
E-mail: v.yeoman@beltechsmb.co.uk
Website: http://www.beltechsmb.co.uk
Directors: V. Yeoman (MD)
Immediate Holding Company: BELTECH SPECIALIST MACHINERY BELTING LIMITED
Registration no: 03124107 **VAT No.:** GB 640 1426 79
Date established: 1995 **Turnover:** £250,000 - £500,000
No.of Employees: 1 - 10 **Product Groups:** 45

Date of Accounts	Dec 11	Dec 10	Dec 09
Working Capital	-1	-4	-5
Fixed Assets	5	4	5
Current Assets	28	35	25

Boss Fork Truck Training Ltd

Grovebury Road, Leighton Buzzard, LU7 4SR
Tel: 01525-383128 **Fax:** 01525-854143
E-mail: info@the-resources-group.com
Website: http://www.the-resources-group.com
Directors: L. Cave (MD), M. Hetterley (Fin)
Immediate Holding Company: BOSS FORK TRUCK TRAINING LIMITED
Registration no: 03478533 **Date established:** 1997
No.of Employees: 1 - 10 **Product Groups:** 45, 67, 86

Date of Accounts	Dec 10	Dec 09	Dec 08
Working Capital	242	-9	124
Fixed Assets	4	217	65
Current Assets	305	49	176

Bramley Engineering (Lifting Gear) Ltd

Pages Industrial Park 22 Eden Way, Leighton Buzzard, LU7 4TZ
Tel: 01525-375225 **Fax:** 01525-850593
E-mail: enquiries@bramleyengineering.co.uk
Website: http://www.bramleyengineering.co.uk
Directors: J. Andrewes (MD), J. Bramley (MD)
Registration no: 01555522 **VAT No.:** GB 322 4869 56
Date established: 1981 **Turnover:** £500,000 - £1m
No.of Employees: 1 - 10 **Product Groups:** 45, 46

Date of Accounts	Apr 09	Apr 08	Apr 07
Sales Turnover	N/A	N/A	777
Pre Tax Profit/Loss	N/A	N/A	77
Working Capital	289	235	130
Fixed Assets	11	17	19
Current Assets	477	399	373
Current Liabilities	N/A	N/A	76

Bray Plastics Ltd

Cherrycourt Way Stanbridge Road, Leighton Buzzard, LU7 4UH
Tel: 01525-219100 **Fax:** 01525-852202
E-mail: bray@brayimaging.co.uk
Website: http://www.brayplastics.co.uk
Directors: G. Bray (MD), K. Cooke (Grp Chief Exec)
Managers: A. Doyle (Sales Admin)
Product Groups: 28, 30, 31, 42, 48, 66, 68, 84

Date of Accounts	Dec 11	Dec 10	Dec 09
Working Capital	88	55	36
Fixed Assets	37	43	49
Current Assets	153	148	161

Brown's Agricultural Machinery Company Ltd

Grovebury Road, Leighton Buzzard, LU7 4UX
Tel: 01525-375157 **Fax:** 01525-385222
E-mail: john.bam@btconnect.com
Website: http://www.brownsagricultural.co.uk
Bank(s): Giro Bank
Directors: J. Brown (MD)
Managers: K. Perry (Tech Serv Mgr), P. Doe
Ultimate Holding Company: GEORGE BROWN'S IMPLEMENTS (HOLDINGS) LIMITED
Immediate Holding Company: BROWN'S AGRICULTURAL MACHINERY COMPANY LIMITED
Registration no: 00720517 **VAT No.:** GB 196 2999 93
Date established: 1962 **Turnover:** £2m - £5m **No.of Employees:** 11 - 20
Product Groups: 40, 41, 44, 45, 67

Date of Accounts	Dec 11	Dec 10	Dec 09
Sales Turnover	3m	3m	3m
Pre Tax Profit/Loss	115	47	36
Working Capital	493	413	362
Fixed Assets	104	81	97
Current Assets	840	825	660
Current Liabilities	228	309	159

Calex Electronics Ltd

Unit 7 Pages Industrial Park Eden Way, Leighton Buzzard, LU7 4TZ
Tel: 01525-373178 **Fax:** 01525-851319
E-mail: mail@calex.co.uk
Website: http://www.calex.co.uk
Bank(s): HSBC Bank plc
Directors: G. Fuller (MD)
Immediate Holding Company: CALEX ELECTRONICS LIMITED
Registration no: 03737294 **Date established:** 1999 **Turnover:** £2m - £5m
No.of Employees: 11 - 20 **Product Groups:** 37

Date of Accounts	Mar 12	Mar 11	Mar 10
Working Capital	463	339	262
Fixed Assets	59	47	43
Current Assets	598	437	341

Cavalier Packaging Services

Unit 1 Pages Industrial Park Eden Way, Leighton Buzzard, LU7 4TZ
Tel: 01525-383636 **Fax:** 01525-370461
E-mail: sales@cavalier-services.co.uk
Website: http://www.cavalierservices.co.uk
Bank(s): Barclays
Directors: D. Nicholas (Prop)
Managers: N. Tallett (Fin Mgr)
Date established: 1980 **Turnover:** £1m - £2m **No.of Employees:** 11 - 20
Product Groups: 31, 44, 48, 76

Chassis Developments Ltd

Grovebury Road, Leighton Buzzard, LU7 4SL
Tel: 01525-374151 **Fax:** 01525-370127
E-mail: sales@chasissdevelopments.com
Website: http://www.chassisdevelopments.co.uk
Bank(s): Barclays, Luton
Directors: D. Brian (Jt MD), F. Berchett (Jt MD), F. Burchett (Jt MD), D. Burchett (Fin)
Managers: C. Young ()
Ultimate Holding Company: BEDFORDSHIRE S.V.E. LTD.
Immediate Holding Company: CHASSIS DEVELOPMENTS LIMITED
Registration no: 00640622 **Date established:** 1959 **Turnover:** £2m - £5m
No.of Employees: 51 - 100 **Product Groups:** 39

Date of Accounts	Mar 10	Mar 09	Mar 08
Sales Turnover	N/A	5m	5m
Pre Tax Profit/Loss	N/A	16	56
Working Capital	210	601	619
Fixed Assets	383	430	411
Current Assets	2m	2m	2m
Current Liabilities	N/A	567	563

Cooper Plastics Machinery

Unit 12 Harmill Industrial Estate Grovebury Road, Leighton Buzzard, LU7 4FF
Tel: 01525-850610 **Fax:** 01525-218008
E-mail: cooperplastics@btclick.com
Website: http://www.cooperplastics.co.uk
Directors: S. Cooper (Prop)
VAT No.: GB 491 1957 23 **Date established:** 2000
Turnover: Up to £250,000 **No.of Employees:** 1 - 10 **Product Groups:** 67

Crafted Handrails

14 Dingle Dell, Leighton Buzzard, LU7 3JL
Tel: 01525-375393 **Fax:** 01525-375393
Website: http://www.craftedhandrails.co.uk
Directors: A. West (Prop)
Immediate Holding Company: CRAFTED HANDRAILS LIMITED
Registration no: 04744090 **Date established:** 2003
No.of Employees: 1 - 10 **Product Groups:** 26, 35

Date of Accounts	Mar 11	Mar 10	Mar 09
Working Capital	-10	-16	9
Fixed Assets	11	22	21
Current Assets	89	83	169

Cramar Contracts

8 Clipstone Brook Industrial Estate Cherrycourt Way, Leighton Buzzard, LU7 4GP
Tel: 01525-850957 **Fax:** 01525-851347
E-mail: info@cramarcontracts.co.uk
Website: http://www.cramarcontracts.co.uk
Directors: D. Power (MD), J. Power (Fin)
Immediate Holding Company: CRAMAR CONTRACTS LIMITED
Registration no: 02597631 **VAT No.:** GB 366 9180 19
Date established: 1991 **Turnover:** £500,000 - £1m
No.of Employees: 1 - 10 **Product Groups:** 25, 26

Date of Accounts	Apr 12	Apr 11	Apr 10
Working Capital	31	23	-2
Fixed Assets	2	4	6
Current Assets	147	131	70

Cravenmount Ltd

Water Lane, Leighton Buzzard, LU7 1FA
Tel: 01525-378104 **Fax:** 01525-383630
E-mail: sales@cravenmount.com
Website: http://www.cravenmount.com
Directors: B. Doggett (MD)
Immediate Holding Company: CRAVENMOUNT LIMITED
Registration no: 01770155 **Date established:** 1983
Turnover: £500,000 - £1m **No.of Employees:** 1 - 10 **Product Groups:** 24

Date of Accounts	Nov 11	Nov 10	Nov 09
Working Capital	118	110	156
Fixed Assets	12	15	6
Current Assets	291	258	301

Data Harvest Group Ltd

1 Eden Court Eden Way, Leighton Buzzard, LU7 4FY
Tel: 01525-373666 **Fax:** 01525-851638
E-mail: sales@data-harvest.co.uk
Website: http://www.data-harvest.co.uk
Directors: K. Bak (Dir), M. Armstrong (Fin), B. Higginbotham (Sales)
Managers: R. Nelson
Immediate Holding Company: DATA HARVEST GROUP LIMITED
Registration no: 01933090 **Date established:** 1985
Turnover: £500,000 - £1m **No.of Employees:** 21 - 50
Product Groups: 28, 38, 44

Date of Accounts	Jun 11	Jun 10	Jun 09
Working Capital	834	874	792
Fixed Assets	255	253	248
Current Assets	1m	1m	1m

Direct Adhesives Ltd

Unit 15 Chartmoor Road, Leighton Buzzard, LU7 4WG
Tel: 01525-381111 **Fax:** 01525-381115
E-mail: simon.walker@directsportswear.com
Website: http://www.directnationaladhesives.co.uk
Bank(s): National Westminster Bank Plc
Directors: S. Irvine (Co Sec), S. Walker (MD)
Immediate Holding Company: DIRECT ADHESIVES LIMITED
Registration no: 03144443 **VAT No.:** GB 663 4038 41
Date established: 1996 **Turnover:** £1m - £2m **No.of Employees:** 11 - 20
Product Groups: 32

Date of Accounts	Mar 12	Mar 11	Mar 10
Working Capital	817	596	435
Fixed Assets	74	80	99
Current Assets	2m	2m	2m

Ele International

Chartmoor Road, Leighton Buzzard, LU7 4WG
Tel: 01525-249200 **Fax:** 01525-249249
E-mail: giovanni.simoni@eleint.co.uk
Website: http://www.ele.com
Bank(s): Barclays
Directors: M. Heeley (Fin), P. Stanford (Fin), G. Simoni (MD)
Managers: M. Rose (Personnel), M. Walsh, D. Papworth, R. Shah (Mktg Serv Mgr), P. Deane (Tech Serv Mgr)
Ultimate Holding Company: PENNON P.L.C.
Immediate Holding Company: VIRIDOR LTD
Registration no: 02307609 **VAT No.:** GB 490 3373 45
Date established: 1961 **Turnover:** £10m - £20m
No.of Employees: 21 - 50 **Product Groups:** 67

Date of Accounts	Dec 07	Dec 06	Dec 05
Working Capital	-5675	-5675	-5675
Fixed Assets	5730	5730	5730
Current Assets	55	55	55
Current Liabilities	5730	5730	5730
Total Share Capital	2000	2000	2000

Encapsulite

Chartwell Business Park Chartmoor Road, Leighton Buzzard, LU7 4WG
Tel: 01525-376974 **Fax:** 01525-850306
E-mail: simon@encapsulite.co.uk
Website: http://www.encapsulite.co.uk
Bank(s): Natwest, Milton Keynes
Directors: S. Waumsley (MD)
Ultimate Holding Company: ENCAPSULITE INTERNATIONAL LIMITED
Immediate Holding Company: ENCAPSULITE PROJECTS LIMITED
Registration no: 06457053 **VAT No.:** GB 196 8596 85
Date established: 2007 **Turnover:** £1m - £2m **No.of Employees:** 11 - 20
Product Groups: 37, 40

Date of Accounts	Sep 11	Sep 10	Sep 09
Working Capital	186	174	143
Current Assets	212	220	208

Engineering Solution Ltd

Unit 4 Commerce Way, Leighton Buzzard, LU7 4RW
Tel: 01525-373800 **Fax:** 01525-374468
E-mail: sales@cirris.co.uk
Website: http://www.overmould.com
Directors: D. Morris (MD), C. Morris (Co Sec)
Ultimate Holding Company: Cirris Systems Corporation
Immediate Holding Company: ENGINEERING SOLUTION LIMITED
Registration no: 04753739 **Date established:** 2003 **Turnover:** £5m - £10m
No.of Employees: 1 - 10 **Product Groups:** 38

Date of Accounts	May 11	May 10	May 09
Working Capital	201	174	145
Fixed Assets	31	12	22
Current Assets	299	199	164

Freed Veneers Ltd

Unit 4 Eden Court Eden Way, Leighton Buzzard, LU7 4FY
Tel: 01525-217777 **Fax:** 01525-217858
E-mail: sales@veneeruk.com
Website: http://www.veneeruk.com
Directors: B. Freed (Fin), L. Freed (MD)
Immediate Holding Company: FREED (VENEERS) LIMITED
Registration no: 03917796 **Date established:** 2000
Turnover: £500,000 - £1m **No.of Employees:** 1 - 10 **Product Groups:** 08, 25, 26, 39, 63, 66, 67, 87

Date of Accounts	Mar 12	Mar 11	Mar 10
Working Capital	15	-4	-77
Fixed Assets	3	5	8
Current Assets	499	667	630

Fyne Packaging Ltd

PO Box 443, Leighton Buzzard, LU7 4WG
Tel: 01525-852246 **Fax:** 01525-376010
E-mail: carol@fyne-packaging.co.uk
Website: http://www.fyne-packaging.co.uk
Directors: C. Mclafferty (MD)
Immediate Holding Company: FYNE PACKAGING LIMITED
Registration no: 02810677 **Date established:** 1993
Turnover: £250,000 - £500,000 **No.of Employees:** 11 - 20
Product Groups: 27

Date of Accounts	Nov 11	Nov 10	Nov 09
Working Capital	-8	-9	-7
Fixed Assets	19	31	24
Current Assets	138	123	116

G P E Scientific Ltd

5 Greaves Way Industrial Estate Stanbridge Road, Leighton Buzzard, LU7 4UB
Tel: 01525-382277 **Fax:** 01525-382263
E-mail: sales@gpelimited.co.uk
Website: http://www.gpelimited.co.uk

Directors: K. Doyle (Sales)
Ultimate Holding Company: HADENCASTLE LIMITED
Immediate Holding Company: GPE SCIENTIFIC LIMITED
Registration no: 00715866 **VAT No.:** GB 207 7024 87
Date established: 1962 **Turnover:** £250,000 - £500,000
No.of Employees: 1 - 10 **Product Groups:** 33, 48

Date of Accounts	Oct 11	Oct 10	Oct 09
Working Capital	382	282	193
Fixed Assets	75	52	35
Current Assets	665	640	462

G W Ceramics

80 North Street, Leighton Buzzard, LU7 1ES
Tel: 01525-381736 **Fax:** 01525-377702
Directors: G. Wood (Prop)
Date established: 1995 **No.of Employees:** 1 - 10 **Product Groups:** 38, 67

Richard Grant Mouldings Ltd

Unit K4 & K5 Cherrycourt Way, Leighton Buzzard, LU7 4UH
Tel: 01525-853888 **Fax:** 01525-383229
E-mail: sales@rgmouldings.com
Website: http://www.rearguards.co.uk
Bank(s): Lloyds TSB
Directors: K. Dumbleton (Dir)
Managers: D. Foster (Chief Acct)
Immediate Holding Company: RICHARD GRANT MOULDINGS LIMITED
Registration no: 02739399 **VAT No.:** GB 600 6353 83
Date established: 1992 **Turnover:** £2m - £5m **No.of Employees:** 11 - 20
Product Groups: 30

Date of Accounts	Dec 11	Dec 10	Dec 09
Working Capital	79	280	293
Fixed Assets	275	156	125
Current Assets	760	1m	1m

Grundfos Pumps Ltd

Grovebury Road, Leighton Buzzard, LU7 4TL
Tel: 01525-850000 **Fax:** 01525-850011
E-mail: ukindustry@grundfos.com
Website: http://www.grundfos.com
Bank(s): Barclays, London
Directors: D. Cooper (Reg MD), J. Matthews (Co Sec)
Ultimate Holding Company: POUL DUE JENSENS FOUNDATION (DENMARK)
Immediate Holding Company: GRUNDFOS PUMPS LIMITED
Registration no: 00805960 **Date established:** 1964
Turnover: £75m - £125m **No.of Employees:** 101 - 250
Product Groups: 39, 40, 45

Date of Accounts	Dec 11	Dec 10	Dec 09
Sales Turnover	97m	92m	86m
Pre Tax Profit/Loss	12m	14m	10m
Working Capital	8m	8m	6m
Fixed Assets	6m	8m	9m
Current Assets	26m	28m	25m
Current Liabilities	12m	13m	12m

Handtmann Ltd

Unit 9 Chartmoor Road, Leighton Buzzard, LU7 4WG
Tel: 01525-244440 **Fax:** 01525-244469
E-mail: enquiries@handtmann.co.uk
Website: http://www.handtmann.co.uk
Bank(s): Barclays
Directors: M. Garrod (MD)
Managers: T. Brett (Chief Acct)
Immediate Holding Company: HANDTMANN LIMITED
Registration no: 01969491 **VAT No.:** GB 433 0425 91
Date established: 1985 **Turnover:** £2m - £5m **No.of Employees:** 11 - 20
Product Groups: 36, 38, 41, 84

Date of Accounts	Dec 11	Dec 10	Dec 09
Sales Turnover	9m	9m	7m
Pre Tax Profit/Loss	2m	1m	1m
Working Capital	3m	3m	2m
Fixed Assets	464	224	407
Current Assets	5m	4m	4m
Current Liabilities	922	695	521

Hanna Instruments Ltd

Unit 28 Pages Industrial Estate, Leighton Buzzard, LU7 4AD
Tel: 01525-850855 **Fax:** 01525-853668
E-mail: sales@hannainst.co.uk
Website: http://www.hannainst.co.uk
Bank(s): Bank of Scotland
Directors: N. Lammond (MD), N. Lamond (MD)
Immediate Holding Company: HANNA INSTRUMENTS LIMITED
Registration no: 02166999 **Date established:** 1987 **Turnover:** £5m - £10m
No.of Employees: 11 - 20 **Product Groups:** 38

Date of Accounts	Dec 11	Dec 10	Dec 09
Working Capital	1m	1m	1m
Fixed Assets	321	304	251
Current Assets	3m	3m	4m

Hone-All Precision Limited

Unit 4 Cherrycourt Way, Leighton Buzzard, LU7 4UH
Tel: 0845-5555 111 **Fax:** 0845-5555 222
E-mail: sales@hone-all.co.uk
Website: http://www.hone-all.co.uk
Bank(s): HSBC Bank plc
Directors: A. Rodney (Dir), C. Rodney (MD)
Managers: T. Barchard (Sales Prom Mgr), R. Hills (Works Gen Mgr), L. Gosling, W. Wilson
Registration no: 02982075 **VAT No.:** GB 640 0250 95
Date established: 1994 **Turnover:** £1m - £2m **No.of Employees:** 21 - 50
Product Groups: 35, 46, 48

Date of Accounts	Oct 11	Oct 10	Oct 09
Working Capital	167	-81	-177
Fixed Assets	1m	2m	2m
Current Assets	684	549	403

Jewson Ltd

Leighton Road, Leighton Buzzard, LU7 1LA
Tel: 01525-373486 **Fax:** 01525-385381
E-mail: jamie.lingard@jewson.co.uk
Website: http://www.jewson.co.uk
Bank(s): HSBC Bank plc
Managers: J. Lingard (District Mgr)
Ultimate Holding Company: COMPAGNIE DE SAINT GOBAIN (FRANCE)
Immediate Holding Company: JEWSON LIMITED
Registration no: 00348407 **VAT No.:** GB 394 1212 63
Date established: 1939 **Turnover:** Up to £250,000
No.of Employees: 11 - 20 **Product Groups:** 66

Date of Accounts	Dec 11	Dec 10	Dec 09
Sales Turnover	1606m	1547m	1485m
Pre Tax Profit/Loss	18m	100m	45m
Working Capital	-345m	-250m	-349m
Fixed Assets	496m	387m	461m
Current Assets	657m	1005m	1320m
Current Liabilities	66m	120m	64m

K N P Finishing Ltd

Unit 10 Commerce Way, Leighton Buzzard, LU7 4RW
Tel: 01525-850478 **Fax:** 01525-850479
E-mail: andykendall@btconnect.com
Directors: A. Kendall (MD)
Immediate Holding Company: KNP FINISHING LIMITED
Registration no: 01760307 **VAT No.:** GB 563 4386 26
Date established: 1983 **Turnover:** £250,000 - £500,000
No.of Employees: 1 - 10 **Product Groups:** 28, 48

Date of Accounts	Mar 11	Mar 10	Mar 09
Sales Turnover	N/A	N/A	437
Pre Tax Profit/Loss	N/A	N/A	32
Working Capital	88	76	62
Fixed Assets	16	8	15
Current Assets	174	135	123
Current Liabilities	N/A	N/A	37

Lancer Sideloaders Ltd

Chartmoor Road, Leighton Buzzard, LU7 4WG
Tel: 01525-378000 **Fax:** 01525-377400
E-mail: r.george@bulmor.com
Website: http://www.lancertrucks.com
Directors: R. George (Fin), R. George (MD), S. Abbott (Fin)
Immediate Holding Company: BULMOR LANCER LTD
Registration no: 04119507 **Date established:** 2000 **Turnover:** £2m - £5m
No.of Employees: 1 - 10 **Product Groups:** 35, 39, 45

Date of Accounts	Dec 10	Dec 09	Dec 08
Sales Turnover	4m	3m	7m
Pre Tax Profit/Loss	9	-537	89
Working Capital	-708	-697	-161
Fixed Assets	378	297	309
Current Assets	1m	2m	3m
Current Liabilities	187	219	104

Leighton Buzzard Bowling Club

Grovebury Road, Leighton Buzzard, LU7 4SW
Tel: 01525-372033
E-mail: info@thesecure-store.com
Website: http://www.thesecure-store.com
Managers: D. Mitchell (Mgr)
Immediate Holding Company: LEIGHTON BUZZARD BOWLING CLUB LIMITED
Registration no: 07372080 **Date established:** 2010
No.of Employees: 1 - 10 **Product Groups:** 72, 77

Leighton Buzzard Observer & Citizen

17 Bridge Street, Leighton Buzzard, LU7 1AH
Tel: 01525-858400 **Fax:** 01525-850043
E-mail: news@lbobserver.co.uk
Website: http://www.leightonbuzzardtoday.co.uk
Managers: J. Francis (Mgr)
Turnover: £50m - £75m **No.of Employees:** 1 - 10 **Product Groups:** 28

M M Fork Truck Services

Greenhill Farm Dunstable Road, Tilsworth, Leighton Buzzard, LU7 9PU
Tel: 01525-210605 **Fax:** 01525-384864
Website: http://www.mmforktrucks.co.uk
Managers: B. Jeffcoate (Mgr)
Ultimate Holding Company: NEW LEISURE (MK) LIMITED
Immediate Holding Company: MAPLE GROVE MANAGEMENT COMPANY LIMITED
Registration no: 01950396 **Date established:** 2011
No.of Employees: 1 - 10 **Product Groups:** 35, 39, 45

Date of Accounts	Feb 08	Feb 11	Feb 10
Working Capital	-186	-247	-235
Fixed Assets	659	629	648
Current Assets	242	207	248

Mini Clipper Logistics

Clipper House Billington Road, Leighton Buzzard, LU7 4AJ
Tel: 01525-244700 **Fax:** 01525-851445
E-mail: davel@miniclipper.co.uk
Website: http://www.miniclipper.co.uk
Bank(s): Barclays.
Directors: A. Hickmott (Fin), D. Lightfoot (Dir), P. Masters (MD)
Managers: J. Masters (Sales Prom Mgr), A. Hickmott (Chief Acct)
Immediate Holding Company: MINI CLIPPER LIMITED
Registration no: 02112488 **VAT No.:** GB 476 0277 34
Date established: 1987 **Turnover:** £5m - £10m **No.of Employees:** 21 - 50
Product Groups: 72, 76

Date of Accounts	May 11	May 10	May 09
Sales Turnover	8m	7m	7m
Pre Tax Profit/Loss	284	-95	24
Working Capital	-207	-251	-120
Fixed Assets	988	999	772
Current Assets	2m	2m	2m
Current Liabilities	1m	234	268

Monier Ltd

Vandyke Works Miletree Road, Heath And Reach, Leighton Buzzard, LU7 9LA
Tel: 01525-244000
Website: http://www.monier.com
Managers: C. Scott (Plant)
Immediate Holding Company: MONIER LIMITED
Registration no: 00407552 **Date established:** 1946
No.of Employees: 51 - 100 **Product Groups:** 14, 24, 33, 37, 40, 66

Mont Blanc Industry UK Ltd

Unit 21 Pages Industrial Park Eden Way, Leighton Buzzard, LU7 4TZ
Tel: 01525-850800 **Fax:** 01525-850808
E-mail: mike.holmes@montblancuk.co.uk
Website: http://www.montblancuk.co.uk
Bank(s): HSBC
Directors: M. Holmes (MD), R. Lynn (Fin)
Managers: A. Miller (Sales Prom Mgr), W. Ranpy
Ultimate Holding Company: MONT BLANC GROUP AB (SWEDEN)
Immediate Holding Company: MONT BLANC INDUSTRI UK LIMITED
Registration no: 00158830 **VAT No.:** GB 551 0506 81
Date established: 2019 **Turnover:** £5m - £10m **No.of Employees:** 21 - 50
Product Groups: 39

Date of Accounts	Dec 11	Dec 10	Dec 09
Sales Turnover	7m	7m	6m
Pre Tax Profit/Loss	-343	-463	-214
Working Capital	-96	227	659
Fixed Assets	81	101	132
Current Assets	2m	2m	2m
Current Liabilities	356	365	304

Multiple Press Ltd

Unit D Chiltern Trading Estate Grovebury Road, Leighton Buzzard, LU7 4TU
Tel: 01525-380800 **Fax:** 01525-380802
E-mail: jane@multiplepress.co.uk
Website: http://www.multiplepress.co.uk
Bank(s): Barclays
Directors: J. Filmer (MD), J. Filmer (Dir)
Immediate Holding Company: MULTIPLE PRESS LIMITED
Registration no: 01176365 **VAT No.:** GB 198 7540 08
Date established: 1974 **No.of Employees:** 11 - 20 **Product Groups:** 28

Date of Accounts	Jul 11	Jul 10	Jul 09
Working Capital	67	-1	-49
Fixed Assets	196	253	320
Current Assets	295	351	331

NGR Ltd (N G R Ltd)

190B Heath Road, Leighton Buzzard, LU7 3AT
Tel: 07713-508 619 **Fax:** 01525-378185
E-mail: info@cagefabricator.com
Website: http://www.cagefabricator.com
Registration no: 03954469 **Product Groups:** 34, 35, 51

Nlightn Multimedia Ltd

Leck House 4 Lake Street, Leighton Buzzard, LU7 1TQ
Tel: 01525-218054 **Fax:** 01525-370041
E-mail: info@nlightn.co.uk
Website: http://www.nlightn.co.uk
Directors: K. Partner (MD), W. Keeley (Fin)
Managers: N. Dixon (Sales Prom Mgr)
Registration no: 03674714 **Date established:** 1998
No.of Employees: 1 - 10 **Product Groups:** 44, 89

Date of Accounts	Mar 08	Mar 07	Mar 06
Working Capital	-45	-15	-21
Fixed Assets	1	4	5
Current Assets	12	27	24
Current Liabilities	57	42	45

Osprey Ltd

Unit 12a Pages Industrial Park Eden Way, Leighton Buzzard, LU7 4TZ
Tel: 01525-851505 **Fax:** 01525-851501
E-mail: denise@osprey.co.uk
Website: http://www.osprey-plastics.co.uk
Managers: A. Weston
Ultimate Holding Company: PANDIONIDAE LIMITED
Immediate Holding Company: OSPREY LIMITED
Registration no: 00628763 **VAT No.:** 167 1201 87 **Date established:** 1959
Turnover: £500,000 - £1m **No.of Employees:** 1 - 10 **Product Groups:** 30, 39, 66

Date of Accounts	May 11	May 10	May 09
Pre Tax Profit/Loss	212	365	326
Working Capital	3m	3m	3m
Fixed Assets	909	761	579
Current Assets	4m	3m	3m
Current Liabilities	249	273	224

Payne & Starnes UK Ltd

Unit 6 Leighton Industrial Park Billington Road, Leighton Buzzard, LU7 4AJ
Tel: 01525-371661 **Fax:** 01525-851492
E-mail: paystar@btconnect.co.uk
Directors: T. Payne (Dir)
Immediate Holding Company: PAYNE AND STARNES (U.K.) LIMITED
Registration no: 01104877 **VAT No.:** GB 225 2141 09
Date established: 1973 **Turnover:** £250,000 - £500,000
No.of Employees: 1 - 10 **Product Groups:** 61, 66

Date of Accounts	Dec 11	Dec 10	Dec 09
Working Capital	80	80	73
Fixed Assets	1	1	2
Current Assets	194	188	175

Photon Beard Ltd

Unit K3 Cherrycourt Way, Leighton Buzzard, LU7 4UH
Tel: 01525-850911 **Fax:** 01525-850922
E-mail: peter@photonbeard.com
Website: http://www.photonbeard.com
Directors: P. Daffarn (Dir)
Immediate Holding Company: PHOTON BEARD LIMITED
Registration no: 02322251 **VAT No.:** GB 547 7411 28
Date established: 1988 **No.of Employees:** 1 - 10 **Product Groups:** 23, 30, 33, 35, 36, 37, 38, 39, 45, 52, 65, 67, 84, 89

Date of Accounts	Sep 11	Sep 10	Sep 09
Working Capital	57	171	193
Fixed Assets	94	103	111
Current Assets	433	458	527

Pledge Office Chairs Ltd

Millstream Works Mill Road, Leighton Buzzard, LU7 1BA
Tel: 01525-376181 **Fax:** 01525-382392
E-mail: sales@pledgechairs.co.uk
Website: http://www.pledgechairs.com
Bank(s): National Westminster Bank Plc
Directors: M. Mugford (I.T. Dir), C. Ioannou (Fin)
Managers: B. Pledger (Sales Admin)
Immediate Holding Company: PLEDGE OFFICE CHAIRS LIMITED
Registration no: 00979183 **Date established:** 1970 **Turnover:** £5m - £10m
No.of Employees: 101 - 250 **Product Groups:** 26

Date of Accounts	May 11	May 10	May 09
Sales Turnover	8m	10m	9m
Pre Tax Profit/Loss	-406	-89	-408
Working Capital	5m	5m	5m
Fixed Assets	6m	6m	6m
Current Assets	6m	6m	6m
Current Liabilities	403	430	397

Polyformes Ltd

Cherrycourt Way, Leighton Buzzard, LU7 4UH
Tel: 01525-852444 **Fax:** 01525-850484
E-mail: info@polyformes.co.uk
Website: http://www.polyformes.co.uk

see next page

Polyformes Ltd - Cont'd
Directors: R. Belger (MD)
Managers: T. Bryans (Mgr), C. Tarling (Comptroller)
Ultimate Holding Company: LODANS HOLDING AG (SWITZERLAND)
Immediate Holding Company: POLYFORMES LIMITED
Registration no: 01296564 **Date established:** 1977 **Turnover:** £5m - £10m
No.of Employees: 51 - 100 **Product Groups:** 29, 30

Date of Accounts	Dec 11	Dec 10	Dec 09
Sales Turnover	8m	7m	6m
Pre Tax Profit/Loss	405	228	-84
Working Capital	93	-54	-426
Fixed Assets	2m	2m	2m
Current Assets	3m	3m	2m
Current Liabilities	565	340	314

Power Drive Drum Co. Ltd
Unit M1 Cherrycourt Way, Leighton Buzzard, LU7 4UH
Tel: 01525-370292 **Fax:** 01525-852126
E-mail: info@mypowerdrive.com
Website: http://www.mypowerdrive.com
Directors: K. Dowzell (MD)
Immediate Holding Company: POWER DRIVE DRUM CO. LIMITED (THE)
Registration no: 01021469 **VAT No.:** GB 214 5867 58
Date established: 1971 **Turnover:** £1m - £2m **No.of Employees:** 1 - 10
Product Groups: 35, 37

Date of Accounts	May 11	May 10	May 09
Working Capital	105	110	129
Fixed Assets	127	130	132
Current Assets	153	153	179

Purity Productions Ltd
Glebe Close Farm Cublington Road, Wing, Leighton Buzzard, LU7 0LB
Tel: 01296-682555
E-mail: info@purityproductions.co.uk
Website: http://www.purityproductions.co.uk
Directors: R. Quinn (MD)
Immediate Holding Company: PURITY PRODUCTIONS LIMITED
Registration no: 06416093 **Date established:** 2007
Turnover: £250,000 - £500,000 **No.of Employees:** 1 - 10
Product Groups: 89

Date of Accounts	Mar 12	Mar 11	Mar 10
Working Capital	190	111	17
Fixed Assets	11	7	N/A
Current Assets	373	361	152

Robebo Ltd
17 Bossard Court, Leighton Buzzard, LU7 1DF
Tel: 01525-850407 **Fax:** 01525-850488
E-mail: sales@robebo.co.uk
Website: http://www.robebo.co.uk
Directors: B. Bourne (MD)
Registration no: 04359009 **Date established:** 2002
No.of Employees: 1 - 10 **Product Groups:** 37, 44, 89

Sidetrack Solutions
Clarence Road, Leighton Buzzard, LU7 3EJ
Tel: 08453-010363
E-mail: sales@sidetracksolutions.co.uk
Website: http://www.sidetracksolutions.co.uk
Managers: J. Crosland (Sales Prom Mgr)
Date established: 2009 **Turnover:** **No.of Employees:** 1 - 10
Product Groups: 44, 79

Skylight Solutions
1 Quarry Court Pitstone Green Business Park Quarry Road, Pitstone, Leighton Buzzard, LU7 9GW
Tel: 01296-662221 **Fax:** 01296-662066
E-mail: info@skylightsolutions.co.uk
Website: http://www.skylightsolutions.co.uk
Directors: R. Culley (Prop)
Immediate Holding Company: SKYLIGHT SOLUTIONS LIMITED
Registration no: 04110170 **Date established:** 2000
No.of Employees: 1 - 10 **Product Groups:** 26, 35

Date of Accounts	Dec 11	Dec 10	Dec 09
Working Capital	148	253	216
Fixed Assets	107	147	145
Current Assets	400	524	391

Steel Fast
Stanbridge Road Great Billington, Leighton Buzzard, LU7 9JH
Tel: 01525-851603 **Fax:** 01525-851836
Directors: S. Albiston (Ptnr)
Immediate Holding Company: B.S. TRAILER SERVICES LIMITED
Registration no: 03400340 **VAT No.:** GB 449 3919 08
Date established: 1997 **Turnover:** £500,000 - £1m
No.of Employees: 1 - 10 **Product Groups:** 66, 77

Date of Accounts	Jan 12	Jan 11	Jan 10
Working Capital	-632	-646	-785
Fixed Assets	3m	3m	3m
Current Assets	621	625	488

Steel Protection Consultancy
7a High Street Mews High Street, Leighton Buzzard, LU7 1EA
Tel: 01525-852500 **Fax:** 01525-852502
E-mail: david.deacon@steel-protection.co.uk
Website: http://www.steel-protection.co.uk
Directors: D. Deacon (Dir)
Immediate Holding Company: THE STEEL PROTECTION CONSULTANCY LTD
Registration no: 02955425 **Date established:** 1937
Turnover: £20m - £50m **No.of Employees:** 1 - 10 **Product Groups:** 46, 48

Date of Accounts	Dec 06	Dec 05
Working Capital	-41	-41
Fixed Assets	139	139
Current Assets	60	69
Current Liabilities	100	110
Total Share Capital	1	1

Track & Rally Performance Driveshafts
Cherrycourt Way, Leighton Buzzard, LU7 4UH
Tel: 0845-5555111 **Fax:** 0845-5555222
E-mail: info@trackandrally.co.uk
Website: http://www.trackandrally.co.uk
Directors: R. Tyler (MD)
Date established: 2006 **No.of Employees:** 1 - 10 **Product Groups:** 48

Ultra Vision International Ltd
Commerce Way, Leighton Buzzard, LU7 4RW
Tel: 01525-381112 **Fax:** 01525-370091
E-mail: info@ultravision.co.uk
Website: http://www.ultravisiongroup.com
Bank(s): HSBC
Directors: J. Clamp (Dir)
Managers: S. Saleem, A. Smith, P. Andrews (Fin Mgr), L. Jaffrey
Ultimate Holding Company: CONTACT LENS PRECISION LABORATORIES LIMITED
Immediate Holding Company: ULTRAVISION INTERNATIONAL LIMITED
Registration no: 01408851 **VAT No.:** GB 322 5509 81
Date established: 1979 **Turnover:** £5m - £10m
No.of Employees: 51 - 100 **Product Groups:** 38

Date of Accounts	Sep 11	Sep 10	Sep 09
Working Capital	3m	2m	2m
Fixed Assets	107	230	249
Current Assets	3m	3m	3m

Walker Magnetics Ltd (t/a Lift Hold and Separate Ltd)
Lift Hold & Separate Ltd Units 4 Firbank Way, Leighton Buzzard, LU7 4YJ
Tel: 01525-372714 **Fax:** 01525-375852
E-mail: sales@lhs.uk.com
Website: http://www.lhs.uk.com
Directors: C. MacKenzie (Dir), A. Budman (Sales), A. Badman (Fin), C. McKenzie (Sales)
Immediate Holding Company: WALKER MAGNETICS LTD
Registration no: 06527289 **Date established:** 2008 **Turnover:** £1m - £2m
No.of Employees: 1 - 10 **Product Groups:** 29, 37, 39, 45, 46

Luton

A Cars Express Despatch Ltd
Unit 14 Langley Terrace Industrial Park Latimer Road, Luton, LU1 3XQ
Tel: 01582-731900 **Fax:** 08702-330612
E-mail: acars@acars.co.uk
Website: http://www.acars.co.uk
Bank(s): Lloyds TSB Bank plc
Managers: K. Wright (Mgr)
Immediate Holding Company: A. CARS (EXPRESS DESPATCH) LIMITED
Registration no: 01635506 **VAT No.:** GB 336 9473 25
Date established: 1982 **Turnover:** £1m - £2m **No.of Employees:** 11 - 20
Product Groups: 72, 79

Date of Accounts	Sep 11	Sep 10	Sep 09
Working Capital	-103	-97	-125
Fixed Assets	254	255	256
Current Assets	57	30	34

A M A Plastics
Unit 1 Moreton Park Industrial Estate Moreton Road South, Luton, LU2 0TL
Tel: 01582-734630 **Fax:** 01582-419260
Website: http://www.amaplastics.co.uk/
Bank(s): Lloyds TSB Bank plc
Directors: D. Mitchell (Dir), G. Atkinson (Dir), R. Atkinson (Dir)
Managers: Atkinson ()
Registration no: 03709854 **Date established:** 1982 **Turnover:** £2m - £5m
No.of Employees: 11 - 20 **Product Groups:** 30, 33, 48

Date of Accounts	Jan 08	Jan 07	Jan 06
Working Capital	-7	-1	5
Fixed Assets	10	14	N/A
Current Assets	113	136	153
Current Liabilities	120	136	148

A M Philpot Hard Chrome Ltd
Unit D Cradock Road Industrial Estate, Luton, LU4 0JF
Tel: 01582-571234 **Fax:** 01582-584924
E-mail: sales@amphardchrome.co.uk
Website: http://www.amphardchrome.co.uk
Directors: S. Philpot (Fin)
Immediate Holding Company: A.M.PHILPOT(HARD CHROME)LIMITED
Registration no: 00697388 **Date established:** 1961
Turnover: Up to £250,000 **No.of Employees:** 11 - 20 **Product Groups:** 31, 32, 34, 35, 39, 40, 43, 46, 48, 68

Date of Accounts	Jun 11	Jun 10	Jun 09
Working Capital	152	85	18
Fixed Assets	116	92	103
Current Assets	334	222	201

Abacus Direct Marketing & Computer Services
Abacus House Dudley Street, Luton, LU2 0NS
Tel: 01582-702702 **Fax:** 01582-702703
E-mail: enquiries@abacusuk.com
Website: http://www.abacusuk.org
Bank(s): HSBC Bank plc
Directors: M. Davies (MD), R. Murphy (MD)
Registration no: 02657378 **Turnover:** £1m - £2m
No.of Employees: 21 - 50 **Product Groups:** 44

Accent Office Interiors
21-25 Kingsway, Luton, LU4 8EQ
Tel: 08456-595911 **Fax:** 08456-595922
E-mail: interiors@accentoffice.co.uk
Website: http://www.accentoffice.co.uk
Directors: R. Hibbert (Ptnr)
Date established: 2002 **No.of Employees:** 1 - 10 **Product Groups:** 26, 35, 52, 67

Action Circuits UK Ltd
Unit 5 Sovereign Park Laporte Way, Luton, LU4 8EL
Tel: 01582-412323 **Fax:** 01582-412424
E-mail: info@actioncircuits.com
Website: http://www.actionpalletstorage.co.uk
Bank(s): HSBC Bank plc
Directors: D. Lane (MD), M. Harvey (Comm)
Managers: B. Szpala (Comptroller)
Immediate Holding Company: ACTION CIRCUITS (U.K.) LIMITED
Registration no: 02096524 **VAT No.:** GB 449 4871 05
Date established: 1987 **Turnover:** £1m - £2m **No.of Employees:** 21 - 50
Product Groups: 44

Date of Accounts	Apr 11	Apr 10	Apr 09
Working Capital	486	531	394
Fixed Assets	305	133	186
Current Assets	947	819	719

Anachem Ltd
20 Charles Street, Luton, LU2 0EB
Tel: 01582-456666 **Fax:** 01582-483332
E-mail: sales@anachem.co.uk
Website: http://www.anachem.co.uk
Directors: J. Hunt (Fin), I. Henderson (MD), I. Henderson (Fin), G. Cerroni (Sales), S. West (Fin), S. West (Co Sec)
Managers: S. Wheeler (Mktg Serv Mgr), C. Stevens (Personnel), K. Smart (Sales Prom Mgr)
Ultimate Holding Company: METTLER TOLEDO INTERNATIONAL INC (USA)
Immediate Holding Company: ANACHEM LIMITED
Registration no: 00974301 **VAT No.:** GB 196 2842 29
Date established: 1970 **Turnover:** £10m - £20m **No.of Employees:** 1 - 10
Product Groups: 38, 42, 44, 67

Date of Accounts	Mar 11	Mar 10	Sep 09
Sales Turnover	4m	1m	N/A
Pre Tax Profit/Loss	5	-634	N/A
Working Capital	173	49	N/A
Fixed Assets	68	84	N/A
Current Assets	2m	2m	N/A
Current Liabilities	684	666	N/A

Anixter Ltd
Unit 10 Sundon Business Park 6 Dencora Way, Luton, LU3 3HP
Tel: 01582-491748 **Fax:** 01582-491280
E-mail: luton.adesco@infast.com
Website: http://www.anixter.co.uk
Managers: D. Bartrick (Warehouse Mgr)
Ultimate Holding Company: ANIXTER INTERNATIONAL INC (USA)
Immediate Holding Company: ANIXTER LIMITED
Registration no: 00248952 **Date established:** 1930
No.of Employees: 1 - 10 **Product Groups:** 30

Date of Accounts	Dec 10	Dec 11	Jan 09
Sales Turnover	319m	355m	366m
Pre Tax Profit/Loss	1m	5m	19m
Working Capital	23m	39m	23m
Fixed Assets	10m	10m	16m
Current Assets	163m	178m	227m
Current Liabilities	11m	12m	14m

Anritsu Ltd
200 Capability Green, Luton, LU1 3LU
Tel: 01582-433200 **Fax:** 01438-740202
E-mail: sales@anritsu.co.uk
Website: http://www.anritsu.com
Directors: P. Chalfant (MD)
Ultimate Holding Company: ANRITSU CORP (JAPAN)
Immediate Holding Company: ANRITSU INDUSTRIAL SOLUTIONS EUROPE LTD
Registration no: 05310391 **VAT No.:** GB 600 4838 69
Date established: 2004 **Turnover:** £500,000 - £1m
No.of Employees: 101 - 250 **Product Groups:** 37, 38, 44, 67, 85

Date of Accounts	Mar 12	Mar 11	Mar 10
Sales Turnover	548	426	416
Pre Tax Profit/Loss	20	75	184
Working Capital	541	526	475
Fixed Assets	8	3	2
Current Assets	650	604	678
Current Liabilities	12	33	60

Arriva The Shires & Essex Ltd
487 Dunstable Road, Luton, LU4 8DS
Tel: 01582-587000 **Fax:** 01582-587000
E-mail: heathwilliams@arriva-shires.com
Website: http://www.arriva.co.uk
Directors: H. Williams (MD)
Immediate Holding Company: THE BUS STOP CANTEEN LTD
Registration no: 02116519 **Date established:** 2012
Turnover: £50m - £75m **No.of Employees:** 1 - 10 **Product Groups:** 72

Astrazeneca
600 Capability Green, Luton, LU1 3LU
Tel: 01582-836000 **Fax:** 01582-835800
Website: http://www.astrazeneca.com
No.of Employees: 251 - 500 **Product Groups:** 31

Audio Mouldings Ltd
Unit 4 Langley Terrace Industrial Park Latimer Road, Luton, LU1 3XQ
Tel: 01582-424606 **Fax:** 01582-459891
E-mail: audiomouldings@aol.com
Website: http://www.audiomouldings.com
Directors: T. Eade (MD), P. Forsyth (Fin)
Immediate Holding Company: AUDIO MOULDINGS LIMITED
Registration no: 01015211 **VAT No.:** GB 196 7006 40
Date established: 1971 **Turnover:** £500,000 - £1m
No.of Employees: 1 - 10 **Product Groups:** 37

Date of Accounts	Jun 11	Jun 10	Jun 09
Working Capital	931	846	724
Fixed Assets	349	358	372
Current Assets	1m	948	843

B M S Products
22 Cosgrove Way, Luton, LU1 1XL
Tel: 01582-758444 **Fax:** 01582-758555
E-mail: info@bms-europe.co.uk
Website: http://www.greenkeeper.co.uk
Directors: J. Buckholt (MD)
Immediate Holding Company: BMS EUROPE LIMITED
Registration no: 05056317 **VAT No.:** GB 716 6674 12
Date established: 2004 **Turnover:** £250,000 - £500,000
No.of Employees: 11 - 20 **Product Groups:** 25, 36, 41, 49

Chas A Blatchford & Sons Ltd
Artificial Limbs Centre Lewesy Road, Luton, LU4 0EP
Tel: 01582-492250 **Fax:** 01582-560992
E-mail: bposluton@blatchford.co.uk
Website: http://www.blatchford.co.uk
Directors: T. Hauxwell (Fin)
Managers: A. Reid (Mgr)
No.of Employees: 11 - 20 **Product Groups:** 38, 67

Border Engineering Ltd
2 Moreton Park Moreton Road South, Luton, LU2 0TL
Tel: 01582-415933 **Fax:** 01582-485155
E-mail: sales@borderengineering.co.uk
Website: http://www.borderengineering.co.uk
Bank(s): HSBC

Directors: A. Gerrard (Dir), J. Mills (Fin)
Immediate Holding Company: BORDER ENGINEERING LIMITED
Registration no: 02128248 **VAT No.:** GB 479 1267 14
Date established: 1987 **Turnover:** £2m - £5m **No.of Employees:** 11 - 20
Product Groups: 48

Date of Accounts	Oct 11	Oct 10	Oct 09
Working Capital	165	96	94
Fixed Assets	66	78	91
Current Assets	400	253	209

Bransted
Regent Court Laporte Way, Luton, LU4 8SB
Tel: 01582-811658 **Fax:** 01727-842841
E-mail: information@select.co.uk
Website: http://www.select.co.uk
Directors: J. King (Co Sec), D. Martyn (MD), B. Wilkinson (Grp Chief Exec), T. Martin (Ch & MD)
Managers: S. Campion (I.T. Exec)
Ultimate Holding Company: RANDSTAD HOLDING NV (NETHERLANDS)
Immediate Holding Company: RANDSTAD UK HOLDING LIMITED
Registration no: 01753882 **Date established:** 1983
Turnover: £75m - £125m **No.of Employees:** 11 - 20 **Product Groups:** 80

Date of Accounts	Dec 09	Dec 08	Dec 07
Sales Turnover	29m	61m	78m
Pre Tax Profit/Loss	193	-3m	309
Working Capital	28m	26m	27m
Fixed Assets	4m	6m	6m
Current Assets	31m	40m	37m
Current Liabilities	2m	4m	6m

British Homeopathic Association
29 Park Street West, Luton, LU1 3BE
Tel: 01582-408675 **Fax:** 01582-723032
E-mail: info@britishhomeopathic.org
Website: http://www.britishhomeopathic.org
Directors: C. Sumner (Grp Chief Exec)
Immediate Holding Company: BRITISH HOMEOPATHIC ASSOCIATION
Registration no: 00102915 **Date established:** 2009
Turnover: Up to £250,000 **No.of Employees:** 1 - 10 **Product Groups:** 31, 88

Date of Accounts	Aug 11	Aug 10	Aug 09
Sales Turnover	127	395	258
Pre Tax Profit/Loss	-127	110	-134
Working Capital	105	200	213
Fixed Assets	985	1m	866
Current Assets	139	225	237
Current Liabilities	34	25	24

Bruderer UK Ltd
Cradock Industrial Estate Cradock Road, Luton, LU4 0JF
Tel: 01582-560300 **Fax:** 01582-570611
E-mail: mail@bruderer.co.uk
Website: http://www.bruderer.co.uk
Directors: J. Piercy (MD)
Immediate Holding Company: BRUDERER UK LIMITED
Registration no: 00938338 **Date established:** 1968 **Turnover:** £2m - £5m
No.of Employees: 1 - 10 **Product Groups:** 46

Date of Accounts	Dec 11	Dec 10	Dec 09
Sales Turnover	3m	2m	2m
Pre Tax Profit/Loss	8	12	23
Working Capital	233	236	215
Fixed Assets	666	665	690
Current Assets	2m	1m	999
Current Liabilities	1m	742	223

C O B Engineering
Midland Road, Luton, LU2 0HR
Tel: 01582-736721 **Fax:** 01582-402497
E-mail: info@cobengineering.co.uk
Website: http://www.cobengineering.co.uk
Directors: D. Sharpe (MD), D. Sharp (Dir)
Immediate Holding Company: COB INVESTMENTS LTD
Registration no: 05411580 **Date established:** 2005
Turnover: £500,000 - £1m **No.of Employees:** 21 - 50 **Product Groups:** 46

Date of Accounts	Jul 09	Jul 08	Jul 07
Working Capital	-173	-231	-216
Fixed Assets	360	360	360
Current Assets	N/A	N/A	1

C P D
Cradock Road Unit 11-12, Luton, LU4 0JF
Tel: 01582-594222 **Fax:** 01582-595222
E-mail: info@cpd.co.uk
Website: http://www.cpd.co.uk
Managers: D. Reed (Mgr)
Ultimate Holding Company: SIG PLC
Immediate Holding Company: SIG TRADING LTD
Registration no: 01540271 **Date established:** 1978
No.of Employees: 11 - 20 **Product Groups:** 26, 38, 48, 52, 64, 84

Cardale Garage Doors
Unit 6 Dalroad Industrial Estate Dallow Road, Luton, LU1 1SP
Tel: 01582-722262
E-mail: enquiries@cardale.co.uk
Website: http://www.cardale.com
Directors: S. Hobbs (Prop)
No.of Employees: 51 - 100 **Product Groups:** 26, 35

Chamber Business Ltd
Business Competitiveness Centre Kimpton Road, Luton, LU2 0SX
Tel: 01582-522448 **Fax:** 01582-522450
E-mail: justin.richardson@chamber-business.com
Website: http://www.chamber-business.com
Directors: J. Richardson (Fin)
Ultimate Holding Company: INTERBUSINESS GROUP LIMITED
Immediate Holding Company: CHAMBER OF COMMERCE (BEDFORDSHIRE) LTD
Registration no: 05398859 **Date established:** 2005
Turnover: £500,000 - £1m **No.of Employees:** 11 - 20
Product Groups: 80, 81

Date of Accounts	Mar 12	Mar 11	Mar 10
Working Capital	N/A	1	1
Current Assets	N/A	1	1

Chiltern Batteries
44 Camford Way, Luton, LU3 3AN
Tel: 01582-597358 **Fax:** 01582-491964
Directors: G. Mapp (Dir)
Registration no: 00405765 **VAT No.:** GB 196 4935 12
Date established: 1986 **No.of Employees:** 1 - 10 **Product Groups:** 37, 68

Chiltern Casting Co
Cradock Road, Luton, LU4 0JF
Tel: 01582-490102 **Fax:** 01582- 561644
Directors: D. Oliver (Ptnr), P. Davies (Ptnr)
VAT No.: GB 354 0775 52 **Date established:** 1981
Turnover: £500,000 - £1m **No.of Employees:** 1 - 10 **Product Groups:** 34

Colour Bond
97 Stoneygate Road, Luton, LU4 9TL
Tel: 01582-560381 **Fax:** 01582-599982
Website: http://www.colourbond.co.uk
Directors: W. Harper (Prop)
Date established: 1993 **No.of Employees:** 1 - 10 **Product Groups:** 46, 48

Critical Research Ltd
Critical House Alma Street, Luton, LU1 2PL
Tel: 01582-480588 **Fax:** 01582-485015
E-mail: ro.marriott@critical.co.uk
Website: http://www.critical.co.uk
Bank(s): Barclays
Directors: S. Connis (Research), D. Krushner (Tech Serv)
Managers: R. Marriott
Ultimate Holding Company: CRITICAL RESEARCH LIMITED
Immediate Holding Company: CRITICAL REVIEWS LIMITED
Registration no: 02615248 **VAT No.:** GB 600 9496 76
Date established: 1991 **Turnover:** £1m - £2m **No.of Employees:** 21 - 50
Product Groups: 81

Date of Accounts	Dec 11	Dec 09	Dec 08
Working Capital	7	7	459
Fixed Assets	N/A	N/A	36
Current Assets	7	14	568
Current Liabilities	N/A	7	N/A

Custom Enclosures Ltd
Concorde House Concorde Street, Luton, LU2 0JD
Tel: 01582-480425 **Fax:** 01582-414372
E-mail: custom.enclosures@btconnect.com
Directors: R. Coleman (Dir), N. Dale (Dir)
Managers: T. Nolan (I.T. Exec), N. Dale (Prod Mgr), S. Kiff (Sales Admin)
Immediate Holding Company: CUSTOM ENCLOSURES LIMITED
Registration no: 01387764 **VAT No.:** GB 382 4949 16
Date established: 1978 **Turnover:** £500,000 - £1m
No.of Employees: 1 - 10 **Product Groups:** 42, 67

Date of Accounts	Sep 11	Sep 10	Sep 09
Working Capital	662	857	833
Fixed Assets	8	9	11
Current Assets	804	1m	1m

Cutter Grinding Services
22b Guildford Street, Luton, LU1 2NR
Tel: 01582-735626 **Fax:** 01582-404164
E-mail: john@cgsmanufacturers.co.uk
Website: http://www.dgsmanufacturing.sagehost.co.uk
Directors: J. Malia (Prop)
Turnover: Up to £250,000 **No.of Employees:** 1 - 10 **Product Groups:** 46

D & K Wiring Services Ltd
Unit 1 Urban Hive Luton Enterprise Park Sundon Park Road, Luton, LU3 3GU
Tel: 01582-492033 **Fax:** 01582-565944
E-mail: whayward@dkwiring.co.uk
Website: http://www.dkwiring.co.uk
Bank(s): National Westminster Bank Plc
Directors: K. Smith (MD)
Immediate Holding Company: D & K WIRING SERVICES LIMITED
Registration no: 01936500 **Date established:** 1985 **Turnover:** £1m - £2m
No.of Employees: 21 - 50 **Product Groups:** 37

Date of Accounts	Aug 11	Aug 10	Aug 09
Working Capital	262	243	261
Fixed Assets	314	342	375
Current Assets	517	424	362

Deritend
Shoolbred Works Cumberland Street, Luton, LU1 3BP
Tel: 01582-729301 **Fax:** 01582-729977
E-mail: luton@deritend.co.uk
Website: http://www.deritend.co.uk
Managers: M. Smith
Ultimate Holding Company: VINCI (FRANCE)
Immediate Holding Company: LEE BEESLEY DERITEND P.L.C.
Registration no: 04140677 **No.of Employees:** 21 - 50
Product Groups: 35, 37, 38, 39, 40, 46, 48, 52, 66, 67, 68, 85

Deta Electrical Co. Ltd
Kingsway House Laporte Way, Luton, LU4 8RJ
Tel: 01582-544544 **Fax:** 01582-544501
E-mail: sales@detaelectrical.co.uk
Website: http://www.detaelectrical.co.uk
Bank(s): National Westminster
Directors: J. Lane (Fin), G. Barnett (MD)
Managers: J. Alderman (Personnel), K. Smith (Sales Prom Mgr), J. Peters, M. Salmons (Tech Serv Mgr)
Ultimate Holding Company: NEWBURY INVESTMENTS BV (NETHERLANDS)
Immediate Holding Company: DETA ELECTRICAL COMPANY LIMITED
Registration no: 00612799 **VAT No.:** GB 694 2016 34
Date established: 1958 **Turnover:** £20m - £50m
No.of Employees: 51 - 100 **Product Groups:** 37, 40

Date of Accounts	Dec 11	Dec 10	Dec 09
Sales Turnover	22m	22m	17m
Pre Tax Profit/Loss	1m	705	84
Working Capital	6m	7m	5m
Fixed Assets	240	295	324
Current Assets	15m	14m	11m
Current Liabilities	3m	3m	2m

Diversey Ltd
4 Finway Dallow Road, Luton, LU1 1TR
Tel: 01582-702100 **Fax:** 01582- 702171
E-mail: vince.sullivan@diversey.com
Website: http://www.diversey.com
Bank(s): National Westminster Bank Plc
Directors: L. Brown (Pers)
Managers: V. Sullivan (Fin Mgr), T. King (Comptroller), L. Osborne, C. Stubbs
Ultimate Holding Company: SEALED AIR CORP (USA)
Immediate Holding Company: DIVERSEY UK SERVICES LIMITED
Registration no: 00530187 **VAT No.:** GB 354 0975 44
Date established: 1954 **Turnover:** £10m - £20m
No.of Employees: 51 - 100 **Product Groups:** 40, 42

Date of Accounts	Dec 11	Dec 10	Dec 09
Sales Turnover	20m	17m	15m
Pre Tax Profit/Loss	3m	3m	639
Working Capital	13m	10m	7m
Fixed Assets	798	1m	1m
Current Assets	16m	13m	11m
Current Liabilities	611	1m	771

Dockguard Ltd
1 Burr Street, Luton, LU2 0HN
Tel: 08452-778800
E-mail: sales@dockguard.com
Website: http://www.dockguard.com
Directors: T. Tancred (MD)
Immediate Holding Company: DOCKGUARD LIMITED
Registration no: 03702914 **Date established:** 1999
No.of Employees: 1 - 10 **Product Groups:** 29, 39

Date of Accounts	Jan 11	Jan 10	Jan 09
Working Capital	-159	-153	96
Current Assets	379	525	786
Current Liabilities	284	N/A	N/A

Drilltech Diamond Drilling UK Llp
Diamond House Dencora Way, Luton, LU3 3HP
Tel: 01582-564455 **Fax:** 01582-847016
E-mail: info@drilltec.co.uk
Website: http://www.drilltech.co.uk
Directors: A. Bourn (Prop)
Immediate Holding Company: DRILLTEC DIAMOND DRILLING UK LLP
Registration no: OC343817 **Date established:** 2009
Turnover: £500,000 - £1m **No.of Employees:** 1 - 10 **Product Groups:** 36, 45, 49, 51

Date of Accounts	Aug 11	Aug 10	Aug 09
Working Capital	-197	-77	-33
Current Assets	128	11	23

E C Smith & Sons Ltd
Unit H-J Kingsway Industrial Estate Kingsway, Luton, LU1 1LP
Tel: 01582-729721 **Fax:** 01582-458893
E-mail: enquiries@ecsmith.com
Website: http://www.ecsmith.com
Directors: R. Cannon (Fin), S. Smith (MD)
Immediate Holding Company: E.C. SMITH & SONS (MARINE FACTORS) LIMITED
Registration no: 01101047 **VAT No.:** GB 432 9280 52
Date established: 1973 **Turnover:** £2m - £5m **No.of Employees:** 11 - 20
Product Groups: 23, 26, 29, 31, 32, 34, 35, 37, 39, 40, 45, 49, 68, 74, 80, 85

Date of Accounts	Oct 11	Oct 10	Oct 09
Working Capital	489	540	624
Fixed Assets	30	43	62
Current Assets	879	1m	1m
Current Liabilities	N/A	95	33

E K A Fabrications
Unit 12 Park Avenue Industrial Estate Sundon Park Road, Luton, LU3 3BP
Tel: 01582-560082 **Fax:** 01582-560087
Directors: J. Bright (Ptnr)
Date established: 1995 **No.of Employees:** 1 - 10 **Product Groups:** 35

Easirent Ltd
Unit B3 110 Butterfield Great Marlings, Luton, LU2 8DL
Tel: 08458-458585 **Fax:** 01462-675577
E-mail: sales@easirentonline.co.uk
Website: http://www.easirentonline.co.uk
Directors: H. Umradia (Dir)
Immediate Holding Company: EASIRENT LIMITED
Registration no: 03547250 **Date established:** 1998 **Turnover:** £1m - £2m
No.of Employees: 1 - 10 **Product Groups:** 37, 38, 44, 67, 81, 83, 84

Date of Accounts	Apr 12	Apr 11	Apr 10
Working Capital	-108	-113	-116
Current Assets	19	24	4
Current Liabilities	117	N/A	N/A

Electrolux Laundry Systems
99 Oakley Road, Luton, LU4 9GE
Tel: 01582-578900 **Fax:** 08700-604113
E-mail: els.info@electrolux.co.uk
Website: http://www.electrolux.co.uk
Directors: C. Garbutt (MD)
Managers: D. Beesley (Mgr), A. Sutcliffe (Mktg Serv Mgr)
Immediate Holding Company: ELECTROLUX GROUP
Registration no: 00637383 **VAT No.:** GB 196 2439 21
No.of Employees: 1 - 10 **Product Groups:** 40

Electroversal Ltd
Unit 2 North Luton Industrial Estate Sedgewick Road, Luton, LU4 9DT
Tel: 01582-582023 **Fax:** 01582-582087
E-mail: sales@electroversal.com
Website: http://www.electroversal.com
Bank(s): Barclays
Directors: G. Wade (Dir), K. Joyce (Ch), J. Keith (Co Sec)
Ultimate Holding Company: CALYX GROUP LIMITED
Immediate Holding Company: ELECTROVERSAL LIMITED
Registration no: 01443701 **VAT No.:** GB 336 8621 41
Date established: 1979 **Turnover:** £2m - £5m **No.of Employees:** 21 - 50
Product Groups: 48

Date of Accounts	Sep 11	Sep 10	Sep 09
Working Capital	685	626	575
Fixed Assets	49	54	63
Current Assets	864	849	799

Eurolines UK Ltd
4 Cardiff Road, Luton, LU1 1PP
Tel: 01582-404311 **Fax:** 01582-400694
E-mail: welcome@eurolines.co.uk
Website: http://www.eurolines.co.uk
Managers: P. Heyward (Comptroller)
Ultimate Holding Company: NATIONAL EXPRESS GROUP PLC
Immediate Holding Company: EUROLINES (U.K.) LIMITED
Registration no: 01991069 **Date established:** 1986
Turnover: £10m - £20m **No.of Employees:** 11 - 20 **Product Groups:** 72

Date of Accounts	Dec 11	Dec 10	Dec 09
Sales Turnover	10m	9m	8m
Pre Tax Profit/Loss	1m	1m	846
Working Capital	1m	5m	1m
Fixed Assets	8	5	14
Current Assets	4m	8m	6m
Current Liabilities	728	725	382

Europa Components
Europa House Airport Way, Luton, LU2 9NH
Tel: 01582-692440 **Fax:** 01582-692450
E-mail: sales@europacomponents.com
Website: http://www.europacomponents.com
Managers: T. Holder (Tech Serv Mgr), A. Jageffar (Mgr), D. Sherridan (Comptroller)
Immediate Holding Company: VERUTH HOLDINGS LTD
Registration no: 02646133 **Date established:** 1991 **Turnover:** £2m - £5m
No.of Employees: 11 - 20 **Product Groups:** 35, 37

Russell Eves Electrical Ltd
Unit 7 Hitchin Road Indl-Est Oxen Road, Luton, LU2 0DX
Tel: 01582-732766 **Fax:** 01582-726147
E-mail: evesrussell@aol.com
Directors: M. Eves (MD)
Managers: S. Osborn (Contracts Mgr), S. Osbourne (Contracts Mgr)
Immediate Holding Company: RUSSELL EVES ELECTRICAL LIMITED
Registration no: 01294067 **VAT No.:** 290 8169 35 **Date established:** 1977
Turnover: £250,000 - £500,000 **No.of Employees:** 1 - 10
Product Groups: 84

Date of Accounts	Jan 08	Jan 07	Jan 06
Working Capital	18	17	6
Fixed Assets	19	17	22
Current Assets	110	130	130

G K N Aerospace
Percival Way London Luton Airport, Luton, LU2 9PQ
Tel: 01582-731441 **Fax:** 01582-423456
E-mail: gkn@ts.aero.gknplc.com
Website: http://www.gkntransparencysystems.com
Bank(s): Bank of Scotland
Directors: M. Bryceson (Pres)
Managers: D. Armstrong (Sales Prom Mgr), S. Tenent (Personnel), K. Layland (I.T. Exec), J. Chiappe (Fin Mgr), I. Hubbard (Sales Prom Mgr), C. Spokes (Purch Mgr), J. White (Personnel), J. Chiappe (Chief Acct)
Ultimate Holding Company: GKN PLC
Immediate Holding Company: GKN WESTLAND AEROSPACE HOLDINGS LTD
Registration no: 02829302 **Date established:** 1993
Turnover: £20m - £50m **No.of Employees:** 251 - 500 **Product Groups:** 39

Date of Accounts	Dec 07
Sales Turnover	25036
Working Capital	43540
Current Assets	43540
Total Share Capital	24000

G & S Kitchens & Tiles
36 Kimpton Road, Luton, LU2 0SX
Tel: 01582-729828 **Fax:** 01582-415081
E-mail: sales@gands.uk.com
Website: http://www.gands.uk.com
Product Groups: 25, 26, 30, 31, 32, 33, 35, 36, 37, 40, 42, 45, 47, 49, 52, 63, 66, 67, 84

Gibbs & Dandy
P O Box 17, Luton, LU1 1YB
Tel: 01582-798798 **Fax:** 01582-451211
E-mail: luton@gibbsanddandy.com
Website: http://www.gibbsanddandy.com
Bank(s): Barclays
Directors: A. Sharma (Fin), W. Naylor (MD)
Managers: D. Carter (Comm), G. Hodges (Personnel), K. Forder (District Mgr), D. Browne (Mktg Serv Mgr), A. Bass (Tech Serv Mgr)
Immediate Holding Company: TIMBER FORCE UK LIMITED
Registration no: 04021174 **VAT No.:** GB 196 2442 45
Date established: 2000 **Turnover:** £50m - £75m
No.of Employees: 51 - 100 **Product Groups:** 25, 33, 36, 40, 52, 66

Stephen Glover & Co. Ltd
2-8 Laporte Way, Luton, LU4 8RJ
Tel: 01922-611311 **Fax:** 01922-721824
Directors: S. Westbrook (Fin), J. Nixon (MD), N. Palmer (Dir)
Managers: A. Littlehales (Mgr), R. Cleverdon (Nat Sales Mgr)
Ultimate Holding Company: FP004869
Immediate Holding Company: STEPHEN GLOVER & CO LIMITED
Registration no: 00756939 **VAT No.:** GB 100 3488 18
Date established: 1963 **Turnover:** £500,000 - £1m
No.of Employees: 1 - 10 **Product Groups:** 30, 35, 36, 37

Date of Accounts	Dec 07	Mar 07	Mar 06
Sales Turnover	852	N/A	N/A
Pre Tax Profit/Loss	412	N/A	N/A
Working Capital	2304	1900	1764
Fixed Assets	N/A	113	111
Current Assets	2304	1994	1943
Current Liabilities	N/A	94	179
Total Share Capital	7	7	7
ROT% (Return on Turnover)	48.4		

H Schreiber Ltd
Unit 8 Stadium Industrial Estate Cradock Road, Luton, LU4 0JF
Tel: 01582-575727 **Fax:** 01582-575733
E-mail: laraine@techscrew.com
Directors: S. O'Neill (MD)
Ultimate Holding Company: TECH HOLDINGS LIMITED
Immediate Holding Company: H. SCHREIBER LIMITED
Registration no: 01325691 **Date established:** 1977 **Turnover:** £1m - £2m
No.of Employees: 1 - 10 **Product Groups:** 61

Date of Accounts	Feb 12	Feb 11	Feb 10
Working Capital	211	195	201
Fixed Assets	149	149	144
Current Assets	2m	2m	1m

Hayward Tyler Ltd
1 Kimpton Road, Luton, LU1 3LD
Tel: 01582-731144 **Fax:** 01582-393400
E-mail: info@haywardtyler.com
Website: http://www.haywardtyler.com
Bank(s): Bank of Scotland
Directors: E. Lloyd-Baker (Grp Chief Exec), E. Coeshall (Co Sec), D. Boughey (MD)
Ultimate Holding Company: SPECIALIST ENERGY GROUP PLC (ISLE OF MAN)
Immediate Holding Company: HAYWARD TYLER GROUP LIMITED
Registration no: 03232768 **VAT No.:** GB 196 6205 39
Date established: 1996 **Turnover:** £20m - £50m
No.of Employees: 101 - 250 **Product Groups:** 37, 40, 45

Date of Accounts	Dec 11	Dec 10	Dec 09
Sales Turnover	32m	39m	37m
Pre Tax Profit/Loss	1m	4m	512
Working Capital	9m	8m	5m
Fixed Assets	3m	3m	3m
Current Assets	25m	26m	25m
Current Liabilities	4m	5m	11m

Herald & Post Newspapers Ltd
39 Upper George Street, Luton, LU1 2RD
Tel: 01582-700600 **Fax:** 01582-700640
E-mail: paul.gibson@jpress.co.uk
Website: http://www.lutontoday.co.uk
Directors: C. Harris (Fin), P. Gibson (MD), S. Clark (Dir)
Managers: G. Rush (Prod Mgr), L. Philpott (Sales Prom Mgr), I. Hughes (Mgr)
Ultimate Holding Company: Johnson Press Edinburgh
Immediate Holding Company: Johnston Press P.L.C.
Registration no: 01021920 **VAT No.:** GB 551 0827 61
Turnover: £5m - £10m **No.of Employees:** 21 - 50 **Product Groups:** 28

Idcardit
524a Hitchin Road, Luton, LU2 7UE
Tel: 07941-150329
E-mail: info@idcardit.co.uk
Website: http://www.idcardit.co.uk
Directors: J. Norris (Dir)
No.of Employees: 1 - 10 **Product Groups:** 30, 44

Instalec Electrical Engineers & Contractors Ltd
2 Greenwood Court Ramridge Road, Luton, LU2 0TN
Tel: 01582-402455 **Fax:** 01582-402466
E-mail: enquiries@1ainstalec.co.uk
Website: http://www.1ainstalec.co.uk
Directors: C. Cazin (Fin), P. Jones (MD)
Ultimate Holding Company: BROOKMEAD HOLDINGS LIMITED
Immediate Holding Company: 1A INSTALEC LIMITED
Registration no: 04054944 **Date established:** 2000
Turnover: Up to £250,000 **No.of Employees:** 1 - 10 **Product Groups:** 37, 38, 52, 85

Date of Accounts	Sep 11	Sep 10	Sep 09
Working Capital	55	-11	-6
Fixed Assets	10	14	17
Current Assets	181	80	68

Iron Mountain Ltd
3 The Borough Indl-Est Leagrave Road, Luton, LU3 1RJ
Tel: 0800-270270 **Fax:** 0870-241 3346
Website: http://www.ironmountain.co.uk
Managers: P. Lyons
Immediate Holding Company: IRON MOUNTAIN LIMITED
Registration no: 02236749 **Date established:** 1988 **Turnover:** £5m - £10m
No.of Employees: 1 - 10 **Product Groups:** 42, 44, 67

Date of Accounts	Apr 11	Apr 10	Apr 09
Working Capital	-274	-245	-239
Fixed Assets	128	109	113
Current Assets	14	48	133

Islebest Ltd
187 Camford Way, Luton, LU3 3AN
Tel: 01582-492949 **Fax:** 01582-493411
E-mail: sales@islebest.co.uk
Website: http://www.islebest.co.uk
Directors: P. Burchmore (Dir)
Managers: P. Jones (Works Gen Mgr)
Immediate Holding Company: ISLEBEST LIMITED
Registration no: 02599082 **Date established:** 1991 **Turnover:** £2m - £5m
No.of Employees: 21 - 50 **Product Groups:** 33, 34, 35, 36, 37, 39, 40, 42, 46, 48, 49, 51, 84, 85

Date of Accounts	Apr 12	Apr 11	Apr 10
Working Capital	-68	-180	-203
Fixed Assets	2m	2m	2m
Current Assets	646	646	459

J J Electronics Ltd
3a Telmere Industrial Estate Albert Road, Luton, LU1 3QF
Tel: 01582-391156 **Fax:** 01582-391896
E-mail: sales@jjelectronics.net
Website: http://www.jjelectronics.net
Directors: M. Hall (Dir)
Immediate Holding Company: J J ELECTRONICS LIMITED
Registration no: 01559319 **Date established:** 1981
Turnover: £250,000 - £500,000 **No.of Employees:** 1 - 10
Product Groups: 37, 84

Date of Accounts	Aug 11	Aug 10	Aug 09
Working Capital	-3	-6	12
Fixed Assets	1	7	10
Current Assets	56	57	58

Jaltek Systems
Unit 13 Sundon Business Park Dencora Way, Luton, LU3 3HP
Tel: 01582-578170 **Fax:** 01582-578171
E-mail: pravins@jaltek.com
Website: http://www.jaltek.com
Directors: R. Sood (Fin), S. Pittom (Sales), P. Sood (Ch)
Managers: D. Waller (Buyer), R. Cannon (Mats Contrlr)
Immediate Holding Company: JALTEK SYSTEMS LIMITED
Registration no: 02312905 **Date established:** 1988 **Turnover:** £5m - £10m
No.of Employees: 51 - 100 **Product Groups:** 37, 44, 45, 46, 47, 48, 49, 52, 84, 85

Date of Accounts	Jul 10	Jul 09	Jul 08
Sales Turnover	9m	10m	8m
Pre Tax Profit/Loss	-1m	34	1m
Working Capital	-391	399	2m
Fixed Assets	4m	4m	2m
Current Assets	3m	4m	5m
Current Liabilities	1m	2m	506

James R Harris
2a Oxford Road, Luton, LU1 3AX
Tel: 01582-458844 **Fax:** 01582- 459362
Directors: J. Harris (Prop)
Date established: 1987 **No.of Employees:** 1 - 10 **Product Groups:** 35

K Addams Roofing Contractors Ltd
ARC House Sundon Road, Chalton, Luton, LU4 9UA
Tel: 01525-877740 **Fax:** 01525-877118
E-mail: k.addams@btinternet.com
Website: http://www.k-addamsroofing.com
Directors: K. Addams (Dir)
Immediate Holding Company: K ADDAMS ROOFING CONTRACTORS LIMITED
Registration no: 04606947 **Date established:** 2002
No.of Employees: 1 - 10 **Product Groups:** 14, 23, 24, 29, 30, 31, 32, 33, 35, 48, 52, 66

Date of Accounts	Dec 11	Dec 10	Dec 09
Sales Turnover	N/A	N/A	103
Pre Tax Profit/Loss	N/A	N/A	-14
Working Capital	26	29	-20
Fixed Assets	19	25	33
Current Assets	49	75	15
Current Liabilities	14	29	19

Kango Service Centre
308 Biscot Road, Luton, LU3 1AZ
Tel: 01582-411025 **Fax:** 01582-736875
E-mail: sales@magnitotoolhire.co.uk
Website: http://www.magnitotoolhire.co.uk
Directors: D. Santos (Prop)
Date established: 1993 **No.of Employees:** 1 - 10 **Product Groups:** 37

Kensal Ltd
Kensal House President Way, Luton, LU2 9NR
Tel: 01582-425777 **Fax:** 01582-425776
E-mail: sales@kensal.com
Website: http://www.kensal.com
Bank(s): Lloyds TSB
Directors: A. Southwood (MD), J. Southwood (Fin)
Immediate Holding Company: KENSAL LIMITED
Registration no: 07569075 **Date established:** 2011 **Turnover:** £2m - £5m
No.of Employees: 21 - 50 **Product Groups:** 45

Date of Accounts	Dec 09	Dec 08	Dec 07
Working Capital	439	342	218
Fixed Assets	11	N/A	N/A
Current Assets	1m	1m	725

Kombimatec Machines Ltd
Unit 10-11 Kingfisher Trading Estate Camford Way, Luton, LU3 3AN
Tel: 01582-562218 **Fax:** 01582-564468
E-mail: derek.parsons@gtikombi.co.uk
Website: http://www.kombimatec.com
Directors: D. Parsons (Dir)
Immediate Holding Company: KOMBIMATEC MACHINES LTD
Registration no: 01849846 **Date established:** 1984 **Turnover:** £1m - £2m
No.of Employees: 11 - 20 **Product Groups:** 42, 46

Date of Accounts	Sep 11	Sep 10	Sep 09
Working Capital	29	55	109
Fixed Assets	6	9	7
Current Assets	147	213	289

Kudos Security Services Ltd
Surety House Kingsway Industrial Estate Kingsway, Luton, LU1 1LP
Tel: 01582-452278 **Fax:** 01582-720505
E-mail: info@reliancesecurity.co.uk
Website: http://www.reliancesecurity.co.uk
Managers: J. Fountain (Fin Mgr), S. Burrell (Mgr), S. Burrell (Chief Mgr), T. Banks, V. Donnelly (Personnel)
Immediate Holding Company: RELIANCE SECURITY SERVICES LIMITED
Registration no: 01146486 **Date established:** 1973
Turnover: £250m - £500m **No.of Employees:** 251 - 500
Product Groups: 81

L P Signs
82 Toddington Road, Luton, LU4 9DY
Tel: 01582-492051 **Fax:** 01582-508198
E-mail: peternormington@btclick.com
Directors: P. Normington (Prop)
Date established: 1997 **Turnover:** Up to £250,000
No.of Employees: 1 - 10 **Product Groups:** 30, 49, 64, 66, 67, 81

L T H Electronics Ltd
Eltelec Works Chaul End Lane, Luton, LU4 8EZ
Tel: 01582-593693 **Fax:** 01582-598036
E-mail: sales@lth.co.uk
Website: http://www.lth.co.uk
Bank(s): National Westminster
Directors: N. Adams (MD), R. Mills (Fin), S. Wotton (Sales)
Ultimate Holding Company: MARKELL LUTON LIMITED
Immediate Holding Company: L.T.H.ELECTRONICS LIMITED
Registration no: 00908792 **VAT No.:** GB 196 4446 27
Date established: 1967 **Turnover:** £1m - £2m **No.of Employees:** 11 - 20
Product Groups: 38, 41

Date of Accounts	Jun 11	Jun 10	Jun 09
Sales Turnover	2m	1m	1m
Pre Tax Profit/Loss	76	80	39
Working Capital	615	644	574
Fixed Assets	255	267	264
Current Assets	948	882	804
Current Liabilities	60	105	23

Lea Boxes Ltd
38 Camford Way, Luton, LU3 3AN
Tel: 01582-505561 **Fax:** 01582-490352
E-mail: info@leaboxes.co.uk
Website: http://www.leaboxes.co.uk
Managers: M. Ball
Immediate Holding Company: LEA BOXES LIMITED
Registration no: 00132129 **VAT No.:** GB 196 6418 22
Date established: 2013 **Turnover:** £500,000 - £1m
No.of Employees: 1 - 10 **Product Groups:** 27

Date of Accounts	Jun 12	Jun 11	Jun 10
Working Capital	55	52	57
Fixed Assets	69	80	80
Current Assets	358	388	282

Long Range Europe
29 Tythe Road, Luton, LU4 9JH
Tel: 01582-582880 **Fax:** 020-8311 0081
E-mail: sales@long-range.co.uk
Website: http://www.longrange.co.uk
Directors: R. Adeyemi (Fin)
Managers: D. Johnson (Mktg Serv Mgr), W. Thompson (Mgr)
Immediate Holding Company: LONG-RANGE EUROPE LIMITED
Registration no: 04318211 **Date established:** 2001
No.of Employees: 1 - 10 **Product Groups:** 61

Date of Accounts	Nov 11	Nov 10	Nov 09
Working Capital	-2	3	7
Fixed Assets	N/A	N/A	1
Current Assets	46	36	6

Luton Hire Centre

11 Sundon Park Parade, Luton, LU3 3BH
Tel: 01582-573694 **Fax:** 01582-565680
E-mail: info@lutonhirecentre.com
Website: http://www.lutonhirecentre.com
Directors: G. Hammond (Prop)
Date established: 1983 **No.of Employees:** 1 - 10 **Product Groups:** 36, 37, 40, 67, 83

M P M Engineering Services Ltd

Unit 2 192 Camford Way, Luton, LU3 3AN
Tel: 01582-582811 **Fax:** 01582-491865
E-mail: enquiries@mpm-eng.co.uk
Website: http://www.mpm-eng.co.uk
Directors: T. Cater (Co Sec)
Immediate Holding Company: M.P.M. ENGINEERING SERVICES LIMITED
Registration no: 02215585 **Date established:** 1988
Turnover: Up to £250,000 **No.of Employees:** 1 - 10 **Product Groups:** 26, 36

Date of Accounts	Apr 11	Apr 10	Apr 09
Working Capital	-0	56	53
Fixed Assets	60	77	20
Current Assets	129	216	173

M 3 Associates Ltd

Conquest House 248 Toddington Road, Luton, LU4 9DZ
Tel: 01582-866800 **Fax:** 01582-866446
E-mail: enquiries@m3associates.co.uk
Website: http://www.m3associates.co.uk
Directors: J. Motture (Dir)
Ultimate Holding Company: BLUE CHERRY INVESTMENTS LIMITED
Immediate Holding Company: M3 ASSOCIATES LIMITED
Registration no: 03167831 **Date established:** 1996
No.of Employees: 1 - 10 **Product Groups:** 54

Date of Accounts	Mar 12	Mar 11	Mar 10
Working Capital	61	48	31
Fixed Assets	12	15	22
Current Assets	113	100	76

Magnetic Component Engineering UK Ltd

1 Union Street, Luton, LU1 3AN
Tel: 01582-735226 **Fax:** 01582-734226
E-mail: eurosales@mceproducts.com
Website: http://www.mceproducts.com
Directors: D. Nanji (Dir)
Immediate Holding Company: MAGNETIC COMPONENT ENGINEERING (UK) LTD.
Registration no: 02965581 **VAT No.:** GB 640 1120 06
Date established: 1994 **Turnover:** Up to £250,000
No.of Employees: 1 - 10 **Product Groups:** 29, 34, 37

Date of Accounts	Sep 11	Sep 10	Sep 09
Working Capital	115	78	87
Fixed Assets	1	1	N/A
Current Assets	157	100	99

Maplin Electronics Ltd

50-52 The Arndale Shopping Centre, Luton, LU1 2TE
Tel: 08432-277319 **Fax:** 01582-486333
E-mail: customercare@maplin.co.uk
Website: http://www.maplin.co.uk
Ultimate Holding Company: MONTAGU PRIVATE EQUITY LLP
Immediate Holding Company: MAPLIN ELECTRONICS LIMITED
Registration no: 01264385 **Date established:** 1976
Turnover: £125m - £250m **No.of Employees:** 1 - 10 **Product Groups:** 37, 61

Date of Accounts	Dec 11	Dec 08	Dec 09
Sales Turnover	205m	204m	204m
Pre Tax Profit/Loss	25m	32m	35m
Working Capital	118m	49m	75m
Fixed Assets	27m	28m	28m
Current Assets	207m	108m	142m
Current Liabilities	78m	51m	59m

Markell Luton Ltd

Unit M Cradock Road, Luton, LU4 0JF
Tel: 01582-572582 **Fax:** 01582-594703
E-mail: tom@markell-luton.co.uk
Website: http://www.markell-luton.co.uk
Directors: T. Thorn (Dir)
Immediate Holding Company: MARKELL LUTON LIMITED
Registration no: 00848542 **Date established:** 1965
Turnover: £250,000 - £500,000 **No.of Employees:** 1 - 10
Product Groups: 46, 48

Date of Accounts	Jun 11	Jun 10	Jun 09
Sales Turnover	369	288	362
Pre Tax Profit/Loss	112	-48	84
Working Capital	878	765	786
Fixed Assets	483	540	597
Current Assets	983	850	879
Current Liabilities	76	49	55

Markell Luton Ltd

Eltelec Works Chaul End Lane, Luton, LU4 8EZ
Tel: 01582-593693
Website: http://www.lth.co.uk
Registration no: 00848542 **Date established:** 1965
Turnover: £250,000 - £500,000 **No.of Employees:** 1 - 10
Product Groups: 38, 48, 67

Measurement Technology Ltd

920 Butterfield Great Marlings, Luton, LU2 8DL
Tel: 01582-723633 **Fax:** 01582-422283
E-mail: enquiry@mtl-inst.com
Website: http://www.mtl-inst.com
Bank(s): Barclays
Directors: S. Botterill (Pers), I. Thompson (Fin), L. Wilkins (Co Sec), J. Malins (Dir)
Managers: B. Ashton (Purch Mgr), D. Foster (Mktg Serv Mgr), L. Morgan (Tech Serv Mgr)
Ultimate Holding Company: THE MTL INSTRUMENTS GROUP LIMITED
Immediate Holding Company: MEASUREMENT TECHNOLOGY LIMITED
Registration no: 01012778 **VAT No.:** GB 449 3430 40
Date established: 1971 **Turnover:** £20m - £50m
No.of Employees: 251 - 500 **Product Groups:** 37, 38, 44, 67

Date of Accounts	Dec 11	Dec 10	Dec 09
Sales Turnover	53m	41m	38m
Pre Tax Profit/Loss	14m	5m	6m
Working Capital	34m	21m	16m
Fixed Assets	4m	6m	7m
Current Assets	41m	33m	39m
Current Liabilities	1m	2m	1m

Mitie Lyndhurst Services Ltd

30 North Luton Industrial Estate Sedgewick Road, Luton, LU4 9DT
Tel: 01582-579545 **Fax:** 01582-491615
Website: http://www.mitie.co.uk
Bank(s): Lloyds, Leighton Buzzard
Directors: S. Cook (Fin), T. Howell (Dir), R. McGregor Smith (Fin)
Managers: C. Kallmeier (Personnel)
Ultimate Holding Company: MITIE GROUP PLC
Immediate Holding Company: MITIE LANDSCAPES LIMITED
Registration no: 01383623 **VAT No.:** GB 322 4048 96
Date established: 1978 **Turnover:** £10m - £20m
No.of Employees: 251 - 500 **Product Groups:** 07, 52

Date of Accounts	Mar 12	Mar 11	Mar 10
Sales Turnover	20m	21m	19m
Pre Tax Profit/Loss	3m	4m	2m
Working Capital	3m	4m	2m
Fixed Assets	3m	3m	3m
Current Assets	8m	8m	7m
Current Liabilities	3m	3m	2m

Monarch Airlines

London Luton Airport, Luton, LU2 9LX
Tel: 01582-424211 **Fax:** 01582-398323
E-mail: sales@flymonarch.com
Website: http://www.flymonarch.com
Bank(s): Barclays
Directors: G. Atkinson (Co Sec), N. Adam (Dir)
Managers: D. Websdale, L. Diffey
Ultimate Holding Company: AMERALD INVESTMENTS NV (NETHERLAND ANTILLES)
Immediate Holding Company: MONARCH AIRCRAFT ENGINEERING LIMITED
Registration no: 00902230 **Date established:** 1967
Turnover: £50m - £75m **No.of Employees:** 501 - 1000
Product Groups: 39, 75

Date of Accounts	Oct 11	Oct 10	Oct 09
Sales Turnover	75m	68m	84m
Pre Tax Profit/Loss	4m	2m	2m
Working Capital	-16m	-7m	10m
Fixed Assets	26m	10m	12m
Current Assets	11m	6m	23m
Current Liabilities	9m	4m	5m

Moog Fernau Ltd

Unit C Airport Executive Park President Way, Luton, LU2 9NY
Tel: 01582-483111 **Fax:** 01582-484404
E-mail: reception@moogfernau.com
Website: http://www.moogfernau.com
Bank(s): Lloyds
Directors: A. Bennett (Fin), P. Revell (MD)
Ultimate Holding Company: MOOG INCORPORATED (USA)
Immediate Holding Company: MOOG FERNAU LIMITED
Registration no: 00989895 **VAT No.:** GB 540 0022 19
Date established: 1970 **Turnover:** £10m - £20m
No.of Employees: 51 - 100 **Product Groups:** 37, 38, 39, 40

Date of Accounts	Nov 08	Sep 11	Sep 10
Sales Turnover	16m	18m	14m
Pre Tax Profit/Loss	3m	3m	3m
Working Capital	6m	14m	12m
Fixed Assets	467	572	458
Current Assets	9m	21m	15m
Current Liabilities	3m	2m	2m

Morris Gordon Engineering

Unit 1 New Mill End Farm, Chiltern Green Road, Luton, LU1 3TS
Tel: 01582-460002 **Fax:** 01582-460038
E-mail: sales@morrisgordon.co.uk
Website: http://www.morrisgordonengineering.co.uk
Directors: C. Cleevely (MD)
Registration no: 02096026 **VAT No.:** GB 467 2017 51
No.of Employees: 1 - 10 **Product Groups:** 67

Multishape Metal Craft Ltd

120 Camford Way, Luton, LU3 3AN
Tel: 01582-581133 **Fax:** 01582-581158
E-mail: info@multishape.co.uk
Website: http://www.multishape.co.uk
Bank(s): National Westminster Bank Plc
Managers: P. Quarman (Sales Admin)
Immediate Holding Company: MULTISHAPE METALCRAFT LIMITED
Registration no: 02992159 **VAT No.:** GB 640 0730 81
Date established: 1994 **Turnover:** £1m - £2m **No.of Employees:** 11 - 20
Product Groups: 48

Date of Accounts	Apr 12	Apr 11	Apr 10
Working Capital	59	27	-18
Fixed Assets	136	177	219
Current Assets	156	152	194

Multispark Erosion Ltd

145 Camford Way, Luton, LU3 3AN
Tel: 01582-502015 **Fax:** 01582-507836
E-mail: sales@multispark.co.uk
Website: http://www.multispark.co.uk
Directors: S. Perkins (Co Sec)
Immediate Holding Company: MULTISPARK EROSION LIMITED
Registration no: 00844863 **Date established:** 1965 **Turnover:** £1m - £2m
No.of Employees: 1 - 10 **Product Groups:** 48

Date of Accounts	Apr 11	Apr 10	Apr 09
Sales Turnover	N/A	N/A	1m
Pre Tax Profit/Loss	N/A	N/A	212
Working Capital	335	159	46
Fixed Assets	480	527	607
Current Assets	562	477	486
Current Liabilities	N/A	N/A	155

T & E Neville Ltd

Neville House 301 Marsh Road, Luton, LU3 2RZ
Tel: 01582-573496 **Fax:** 01582-490216
E-mail: enquiries@nevilleconstruction.co.uk
Website: http://www.nevilleconstruction.co.uk
Bank(s): Barclays, Luton
Directors: I. Trumper (Dir)
Managers: L. Harlow (Tech Serv Mgr), T. Perrett (Personnel)
Ultimate Holding Company: NEVILLE TRUST LIMITED
Immediate Holding Company: T. & E. NEVILLE LIMITED
Registration no: 00359855 **VAT No.:** GB 283 7887 96
Date established: 1940 **Turnover:** £5m - £10m
No.of Employees: 101 - 250 **Product Groups:** 52, 84

Date of Accounts	Mar 11	Mar 10	Mar 09
Sales Turnover	9m	9m	10m
Pre Tax Profit/Loss	-435	-289	165
Working Capital	862	1m	1m
Fixed Assets	267	331	385
Current Assets	3m	3m	3m
Current Liabilities	1m	2m	1m

A T Oliver & Sons Ltd

Wandon End Works Wandon End, Luton, LU2 8NY
Tel: 01582-727111 **Fax:** 01582-729763
E-mail: ajso@atoliver.co.uk
Website: http://www.atoliver.co.uk
Directors: A. Oliver (MD), N. Milward (Co Sec)
Ultimate Holding Company: ATO HOLDINGS LIMITED
Immediate Holding Company: A.T. OLIVER & SONS LIMITED
Registration no: 05301498 **Date established:** 2004
Turnover: £10m - £20m **No.of Employees:** 21 - 50 **Product Groups:** 07

Date of Accounts	Sep 11	Sep 10	Sep 09
Sales Turnover	N/A	N/A	19m
Pre Tax Profit/Loss	N/A	N/A	331
Working Capital	389	340	836
Fixed Assets	N/A	N/A	453
Current Assets	848	789	5m
Current Liabilities	N/A	N/A	267

Olney Headwear Ltd

106 Old Bedford Road, Luton, LU2 7PD
Tel: 01582-731512 **Fax:** 01582-729066
E-mail: info@olney-headwear.co.uk
Website: http://www.olney-headwear.co.uk
Directors: A. Olney (MD), D. Olney (Fin)
Immediate Holding Company: OLNEY HEADWEAR LIMITED
Registration no: 00215440 **VAT No.:** GB 196 2081 51
Date established: 2026 **Turnover:** £1m - £2m **No.of Employees:** 11 - 20
Product Groups: 24

Date of Accounts	Oct 11	Oct 10	Oct 09
Working Capital	669	666	658
Fixed Assets	409	441	430
Current Assets	1m	1m	1m

Olympic Blinds Ltd

Unit 11 Bilton Court Bilton Way, Luton, LU1 1LX
Tel: 01582-737878 **Fax:** 01582-402182
E-mail: joew@olympicblinds.co.uk
Website: http://www.olympicblinds.co.uk
Directors: J. Walker (MD)
Immediate Holding Company: OLYMPIC BLINDS LIMITED
Registration no: 05633019 **Date established:** 2005 **Turnover:** £1m - £2m
No.of Employees: 11 - 20 **Product Groups:** 24, 35, 39

Date of Accounts	Dec 09	Dec 08	Dec 07
Working Capital	-141	-122	-193
Fixed Assets	67	85	290
Current Assets	181	247	250

Online Distribution Ltd

The Business Centre 1 Finway, Luton, LU1 1TR
Tel: 0844-4823004 **Fax:** 0844-4823005
E-mail: sales@watford.co.uk
Website: http://www.savastore.co.uk
Directors: M. Raqeeb (Fin), S. Jessa (Dir)
Immediate Holding Company: Digital Pos Ltd
Registration no: 06083590 **VAT No.:** GB 198 3523 28
Date established: 2006 **Turnover:** £20m - £50m
No.of Employees: 51 - 100 **Product Groups:** 44

Optikinetics Ltd

38 Cromwell Road, Luton, LU3 1DN
Tel: 01582-411413 **Fax:** 01582-400613
E-mail: phil@optikinetics.com
Website: http://www.optikinetics.com
Bank(s): Natwest
Directors: P. Brunker (I.T. Dir)
Immediate Holding Company: OPTIKINETICS LIMITED
Registration no: 00995561 **VAT No.:** GB 197 0669 21
Date established: 1970 **Turnover:** £2m - £5m **No.of Employees:** 11 - 20
Product Groups: 35, 37, 38

Date of Accounts	Nov 11	Nov 10	Nov 09
Working Capital	271	338	95
Fixed Assets	8	5	179
Current Assets	758	883	862

P M C

43-45 Crawley Green Road, Luton, LU2 0AA
Tel: 01582-405694
E-mail: admin@promonitor.co.uk
Website: http://www.pmc-speakers.com
Directors: J. Thomas (MD), I. Downs (Sales), K. Tonge (Mkt Research)
Managers: J. Robinson (Comptroller)
Immediate Holding Company: THE PROFESSIONAL MONITOR COMPANY LIMITED
Registration no: 03328009 **Date established:** 1997
No.of Employees: 21 - 50 **Product Groups:** 37

Date of Accounts	Dec 11	Dec 10	Dec 09
Working Capital	324	316	358
Fixed Assets	163	117	132
Current Assets	1m	969	1m

Peverel Property Management

Marlborough House Wigmore Place, Luton, LU2 9EX
Tel: 01582-393700 **Fax:** 01582-393701
E-mail: customercare@ompropertymanagement.co.uk
Website: http://www.ompropertymanagement.co.uk
Directors: P. Rayden (Grp Chief Exec), M. Gaston (Dir)
Immediate Holding Company: IMPACT COURT LIMITED
Registration no: 02231168 **Date established:** 2003 **Turnover:** £5m - £10m
No.of Employees: 1 - 10 **Product Groups:** 80

Date of Accounts	Sep 11	Sep 10	Sep 09
Sales Turnover	N/A	39	N/A
Pre Tax Profit/Loss	N/A	6	N/A
Working Capital	N/A	3	2
Current Assets	N/A	5	2
Current Liabilities	N/A	2	N/A

PIC Wire & Cable
Coverdale 73 lea Meadows, Luton, LU4 9JP
Tel: 01582-650263
E-mail: nmorgan@picwire.com
Website: http://www.picwire.com
Managers: N. Morgan (Chief Mgr)
Turnover: £20m - £50m **No.of Employees:** 21 - 50 **Product Groups:** 37

Pirtek Ltd
7 Scott Road, Luton, LU3 3BF
Tel: 01582-597050 **Fax:** 01582-597696
E-mail: luton@pirtekcentre.co.uk
Website: http://www.pirtekuk.com
Managers: N. Dixon (Mgr)
Date established: 2001 **No.of Employees:** 1 - 10 **Product Groups:** 40, 41, 67

Precision Car Leather Dye
6 Manor Farm, Luton, LU4 9LA
Tel: 01582-499777
E-mail: steve@carleatherdye.co.uk
Website: http://www.carleatherdye.co.uk
Directors: S. Lewis (Prop)
No.of Employees: 1 - 10 **Product Groups:** 39, 40, 68

Prolateral Consulting Ltd
Unit B2 Bramingham Business Park Enterprise Way, Luton, LU3 4BU
Tel: 08450-763760 **Fax:** 08450-763761
E-mail: info@prolateral.com
Website: http://www.prolateral.com
Directors: I. Chilvers (MD)
Immediate Holding Company: PROLATERAL CONSULTING LIMITED
Registration no: 04676923 **Date established:** 2003
Turnover: £250,000 - £500,000 **No.of Employees:** 1 - 10
Product Groups: 44

Date of Accounts	Jun 11	Jun 10	Jun 09
Working Capital	-0	-0	-2
Fixed Assets	1	1	2
Current Assets	75	55	43

Protronix E M S Ltd
3-15 Cross Street, Luton, LU2 0DP
Tel: 01582-418490 **Fax:** 01582-486588
E-mail: info@protronix.co.uk
Website: http://www.protronix.co.uk
Bank(s): Lloyds TSB Bank plc
Directors: J. Clark (Prop)
Immediate Holding Company: PROTRONIX EMS LIMITED
Registration no: 05835002 **VAT No.:** GB 433 0498 64
Date established: 2006 **Turnover:** Up to £250,000
No.of Employees: 11 - 20 **Product Groups:** 32, 37, 38, 44, 45, 84

Date of Accounts	Mar 12	Mar 11	Mar 10
Working Capital	6	-3	6
Fixed Assets	13	14	17
Current Assets	59	40	32

Randall Ribbons
12 Frederick Street, Luton, LU2 7QS
Tel: 01582-721301 **Fax:** 01582-720060
E-mail: sales@randallribbons.co.uk
Website: http://www.randallribbons.co.uk
Managers: J. Streeter (Mgr)
Immediate Holding Company: KEN PEIRSON & SON LTD
VAT No.: 197 3426 32 **Turnover:** £250,000 - £500,000
No.of Employees: 1 - 10 **Product Groups:** 23, 24, 35

Reco-Prop UK Ltd
Unit 4 New Town Trading Estate Chase Street, Luton, LU1 3QZ
Tel: 01582-412110 **Fax:** 01582-480432
E-mail: info@reco-prop.com
Website: http://www.reco-prop.com
Directors: J. Mcphail (Dir)
Immediate Holding Company: RECO PROP (U.K.) LIMITED
Registration no: 01731674 **Date established:** 1983
Turnover: £250,000 - £500,000 **No.of Employees:** 1 - 10
Product Groups: 29, 35, 39, 68

Date of Accounts	Jun 11	Jun 10	Jun 09
Working Capital	4	14	16
Fixed Assets	6	8	10
Current Assets	58	62	64

Redline Group Ltd
26-34 Liverpool Road, Luton, LU1 1RS
Tel: 01582-450054 **Fax:** 01582-878855
E-mail: cv@redlineplc.com
Website: http://www.ta-marcom.com
Directors: A. Walker (Dir), R. Davies (Co Sec), N. Livingstone (Develop), M. Crapper (Dir), M. Crapper (MD)
Immediate Holding Company: TECHNICAL PUBLICITY LIMITED
Registration no: 02384040 **Date established:** 1989 **Turnover:** £2m - £5m
No.of Employees: 21 - 50 **Product Groups:** 80

Date of Accounts	Mar 11	Mar 10	Mar 09
Working Capital	-29	5	48
Fixed Assets	31	6	12
Current Assets	153	84	103

Reliant Machinery Ltd
Unit L Cradock Road, Luton, LU4 0JF
Tel: 01582-584999 **Fax:** 01582-581117
E-mail: sales@reliant-machinery.co.uk
Website: http://www.reliant-machinery.com
Managers: A. Khan (Chief Mgr), N. Weisfeld (Sales Prom Mgr), T. Page (Sales Prom Mgr)
Immediate Holding Company: Reliant Group Ltd
Registration no: 04319620 **VAT No.:** GB 663 2349 34
Turnover: £2m - £5m **No.of Employees:** 1 - 10 **Product Groups:** 43

Rexam Beverage Can UK Ltd
100 Capability Green, Luton, LU1 3LG
Tel: 01582-408999 **Fax:** 01582-726065
E-mail: tomas.sjolin@rexam.com
Website: http://www.rexam.com
Bank(s): HSBC
Directors: J. Gorton (Fin), T. Sjolin (Dir)
Managers: C. Ormand (Personnel), R. Downes (Purch Mgr)
Ultimate Holding Company: REXAM PLC
Immediate Holding Company: REXAM BEVERAGE CAN UK LTD
Registration no: 00197480 **VAT No.:** GB 540 3138 82
Date established: 2024 **Turnover:** £125m - £250m
No.of Employees: 101 - 250 **Product Groups:** 30, 31, 35

Date of Accounts	Dec 11	Dec 10	Dec 09
Sales Turnover	197m	184m	155m
Pre Tax Profit/Loss	4m	5m	10m
Working Capital	109m	106m	104m
Fixed Assets	36m	36m	35m
Current Assets	219m	220m	217m
Current Liabilities	13m	12m	12m

Robinson Metalwork Ltd
51 Camford Way, Luton, LU3 3AN
Tel: 01582-573866 **Fax:** 01582-490385
E-mail: simon@robinsonmetalwork.co.uk
Website: http://www.robinsonmetalwork.co.uk
Bank(s): HSBC
Directors: S. Robinson (MD)
Immediate Holding Company: ROBINSON METALWORK LIMITED
Registration no: 00713244 **VAT No.:** GB 197 8958 71
Date established: 1962 **Turnover:** £1m - £2m **No.of Employees:** 11 - 20
Product Groups: 34, 35, 36, 39, 40, 46, 48, 49, 51, 66, 68, 84

Date of Accounts	Apr 11	Apr 10	Apr 09
Working Capital	-85	N/A	19
Fixed Assets	8	20	29
Current Assets	171	310	182

Round Green Luton Ltd
Progress Way, Luton, LU4 9TR
Tel: 01582-503808 **Fax:** 01582-503898
E-mail: barryie@roundgreenluton.co.uk
Website: http://www.roundgreenluton.co.uk
Directors: K. Bleming (Dir)
Immediate Holding Company: ROUND GREEN (LUTON) LTD
Registration no: 06822452 **VAT No.:** GB 382 3905 41
Date established: 2009 **Turnover:** £250,000 - £500,000
No.of Employees: 1 - 10 **Product Groups:** 48

Date of Accounts	Mar 12	Mar 11	Mar 10
Working Capital	145	108	36
Fixed Assets	8	11	2
Current Assets	304	185	309

Runex Ltd
14 Bilton Way, Luton, LU1 1UU
Tel: 01582-512222 **Fax:** 01582-512223
E-mail: england@runex.com
Website: http://www.runex.com
Directors: F. Nilsson (Co Sec), P. Nillson (Ch)
Ultimate Holding Company: RUNEX AB (SWEDEN)
Immediate Holding Company: RUNEX LIMITED
Registration no: 02298571 **Date established:** 1988
No.of Employees: 1 - 10 **Product Groups:** 20, 35, 36, 40, 41

Date of Accounts	Dec 11	Dec 10	Dec 09
Working Capital	198	184	119
Fixed Assets	121	150	173
Current Assets	524	452	339
Current Liabilities	N/A	9	N/A

S D E
Unit 3 250 Toddington Road, Luton, LU4 9DZ
Tel: 01582-599055 **Fax:** 01582-492395
E-mail: keith@sde-civils.co.uk
Website: http://www.sde-civils.co.uk
Directors: L. Robinson (Fin), K. Moore (MD)
No.of Employees: 1 - 10 **Product Groups:** 30, 66, 84

S K S Spindle Service Centre
8 Dencora Way Sundon Business Park, Luton, LU3 3HP
Tel: 01582-494674 **Fax:** 01582-494301
E-mail: tom.gray@sks.com
Website: http://www.sks.co.uk
Managers: T. Gray (Mgr)
Immediate Holding Company: 8 UK LIMITED
Registration no: 00107367 **VAT No.:** GB 563 7782 03
Date established: 2008 **Turnover:** £1m - £2m **No.of Employees:** 1 - 10
Product Groups: 37, 46

Saffron Tools & Equipment
12 Saffron Close, Luton, LU2 7GF
Tel: 01582-722212 **Fax:** 01582-736006
E-mail: saffrontools@hotmail.com
Directors: D. Kelly (Prop)
Date established: 2004 **No.of Employees:** 1 - 10 **Product Groups:** 37

Serck Controls Ltd
1 Dencora Way, Luton, LU3 3HP
Tel: 01582-509900 **Fax:** 01582-509901
E-mail: acarrington@serck-controls.co.uk
Website: http://www.serck-controls.co.uk
Managers: A. Carrington (Eng Serv Mgr)
Ultimate Holding Company: SCADA GROUP PTY LTD
Immediate Holding Company: SERCK CONTROLS LIMITED
Registration no: 04353634 **Date established:** 2002 **Turnover:** £5m - £10m
No.of Employees: 11 - 20 **Product Groups:** 37, 38, 44

Date of Accounts	Dec 11	Dec 10	Jun 09
Sales Turnover	16m	20m	12m
Pre Tax Profit/Loss	5m	5m	2m
Working Capital	5m	4m	3m
Fixed Assets	2m	2m	2m
Current Assets	11m	8m	6m
Current Liabilities	4m	3m	3m

Silicon Fabrication Services Ltd
Unit E Bramingham Business Park Enterprise Way, Luton, LU3 4BU
Tel: 01582-503357 **Fax:** 01582-412277
E-mail: sales@sfs-ltd.co.uk
Website: http://www.sfs-ltd.co.uk
Directors: D. Sargent (Dir), D. Sargent (MD), J. Soanes (Dir)
Ultimate Holding Company: THE SFS MANUFACTURING GROUP LIMITED
Immediate Holding Company: SILICONE FABRICATION SERVICES LIMITED
Registration no: 03358653 **VAT No.:** GB 690 4610 36
Date established: 1997 **Turnover:** Up to £250,000
No.of Employees: 1 - 10 **Product Groups:** 29

Simorg Ltd
Unit C Abbeygate Business Centre Hitchin Road, Luton, LU2 0ER
Tel: 01582-484785 **Fax:** 01582-484157
E-mail: simorglimited@btinetmet.com
Website: http://www.simorglimited.co.uk
Directors: D. Gordon (Co Sec)
Immediate Holding Company: SIMORG LIMITED
Registration no: 02573452 **VAT No.:** GB 540 3711 78
Date established: 1991 **Turnover:** £250,000 - £500,000
No.of Employees: 1 - 10 **Product Groups:** 26, 35, 39

Date of Accounts	Feb 11	Feb 10	Feb 09
Working Capital	-8	-0	10
Fixed Assets	81	80	35
Current Assets	53	77	111

S K F Machine Tool Sales UK
Unit 8 Sundon Business Park Dencora Way, Luton, LU3 3HP
Tel: 01582-574858 **Fax:** 01582-494301
E-mail: skfmtsuk@sks.com
Website: http://www.skf.co.uk
Managers: B. Archer (Sales Prom Mgr)
Immediate Holding Company: 8 UK LIMITED
Registration no: 00107367 **Date established:** 2008
No.of Employees: 1 - 10 **Product Groups:** 35, 46

Smiths Medical International Ltd
Bramingham Business Park Enterprise Way, Luton, LU3 4BU
Tel: 01582-430000 **Fax:** 01582-430001
E-mail: pneupac@smiths-medical.com
Website: http://www.smiths-medical.co.uk
Bank(s): Barclays
Directors: P. Flack (Dir)
Managers: J. Ben (Site Co-ord)
Ultimate Holding Company: SMITHS GROUP PLC
Immediate Holding Company: SMITHS MEDICAL INTERNATIONAL LIMITED
Registration no: 00362847 **VAT No.:** 196 7928 91 **Date established:** 1940
No.of Employees: 51 - 100 **Product Groups:** 38, 40

Date of Accounts	Jul 12	Jul 11	Jul 10
Sales Turnover	235m	233m	273m
Pre Tax Profit/Loss	20m	16m	44m
Working Capital	56m	52m	72m
Fixed Assets	29m	33m	41m
Current Assets	101m	95m	123m
Current Liabilities	6m	6m	7m

Solutions Photographic
Manor Road Caddington, Luton, LU1 4ED
Tel: 01582-725065
E-mail: rod@solphoto.co.uk
Website: http://rod-wynne-powell.blogspot.com
Directors: R. Wynne-Powell (Prop)
VAT No.: 449 3789 92 **Date established:** 1988 **Turnover:** Up to £250,000
No.of Employees: 1 - 10 **Product Groups:** 81

Sos Direct Ltd
Unit 1-3 Sovereign Park Laporte Way, Luton, LU4 8EL
Tel: 01582-408650 **Fax:** 01582-395979
E-mail: sales@sosdirectmail.com
Website: http://www.sosdirectmail.com
Directors: J. Smirthwaite (MD)
Registration no: 00635617 **Turnover:** £2m - £5m
No.of Employees: 21 - 50 **Product Groups:** 30, 44, 61, 76, 79, 80, 81

Studio Music
Cadence House Eaton Green Road, Luton, LU2 9LD
Tel: 01582-432139 **Fax:** 01582-731989
E-mail: sales@studio-music.co.uk
Website: http://www.studio-music.co.uk
Directors: P. Williams (MD), S. Kitchen (Prop)
Registration no: 06177545 **VAT No.:** 227 6454 53
Turnover: £250,000 - £500,000 **No.of Employees:** 1 - 10
Product Groups: 28

Ted UK
Unit 24 Titan Court Laporte Way, Luton, LU4 8EF
Tel: 01582-488888 **Fax:** 01582-488877
E-mail: mark.morley@tedav.com
Website: http://www.tedav.com
Directors: M. Morely (Tech Serv), M. Morley (MD)
Managers: A. Prior (Fin Mgr)
No.of Employees: 21 - 50 **Product Groups:** 30, 32, 37

Telefonica O2 UK Limited
Correspondence Department PO Box 202, Houghton Regis, Luton, LU6 9AG
Tel: 0880-90200 **Fax:** 01753-565010
Website: http://www.o2.co.uk
Directors: M. Key (Grp Chief Exec)
Registration no: 04330394 **Product Groups:** 37

Date of Accounts	Dec 07	Dec 06	Jan 06
Sales Turnover	N/A	7498m	6124m
Pre Tax Profit/Loss	2303m	681000	182000
Working Capital	-7659m	179000	-63000
Fixed Assets	19262m	12666m	11644m
Current Assets	1117m	2905m	2043m
Current Liabilities	8776m	2726m	2106m
Total Share Capital	12000	12000	12000
ROCE% (Return on Capital Employed)	19.8	5.3	1.6
ROT% (Return on Turnover)		9.1	3.0

Restmor Ltd
226-248 Toddington Road, Luton, LU4 9DZ
Tel: 01582-807488 **Fax:** 01582-807489
E-mail: sales@restmor.co.uk
Website: http://www.restmor.co.uk
Bank(s): Nat West, North Audley St, London, W1A 4UQ
Directors: D. Phillips (Dir), G. Tyler (Dir), R. Ragbir (Fin)
Immediate Holding Company: RESTMOR LIMITED
Registration no: 06876331 **VAT No.:** GB 233 2973 66
Date established: 2009 **Turnover:** £5m - £10m **No.of Employees:** 11 - 20
Product Groups: 63

Date of Accounts	Apr 11	Apr 10
Working Capital	467	269
Fixed Assets	63	75
Current Assets	1m	1m

Theobald Sewing Machines Ltd
71-73 Wellington Street, Luton, LU1 5AA
Tel: 01582-724644 **Fax:** 01582-417867
E-mail: lunadeplata@onetel.net.uk
Website: http://www.theobaldsewingmachines.co.uk
Directors: R. Theobald (MD)
Immediate Holding Company: THEOBALD SEWING MACHINES LIMITED
Registration no: 00651455 **VAT No.:** GB 197 3353 33
Date established: 1960 **Turnover:** Up to £250,000
No.of Employees: 1 - 10 **Product Groups:** 43, 61

Date of Accounts	Apr 12	Apr 11	Apr 10
Sales Turnover	114	96	98
Pre Tax Profit/Loss	13	10	5
Working Capital	11	55	61
Fixed Assets	140	85	72
Current Assets	53	91	89
Current Liabilities	39	35	25

Thermal Economics Ltd
8 Cardiff Road, Luton, LU1 1PP
Tel: 01582-450814 **Fax:** 01582-429305
E-mail: info@thermal-economics.co.uk
Website: http://www.thermal-economics.co.uk
Directors: H. Brown (MD)
Immediate Holding Company: THERMAL ECONOMICS LIMITED
Registration no: 01665995 **Date established:** 1982 **Turnover:** £5m - £10m
No.of Employees: 1 - 10 **Product Groups:** 33

Date of Accounts	Oct 11	Oct 10	Oct 09
Sales Turnover	N/A	N/A	6m
Pre Tax Profit/Loss	N/A	N/A	939
Working Capital	1m	998	1m
Fixed Assets	431	439	449
Current Assets	2m	2m	2m
Current Liabilities	N/A	N/A	542

Trumpf Ltd
Unit A President Way, Luton, LU2 9NL
Tel: 08444-820188 **Fax:** 01582-399250
E-mail: sales@uk.trumpf.com
Website: http://www.uk.trumpf.com
Bank(s): Lloyds TSB Bank plc
Directors: S. Binns (Co Sec)
Managers: C. Vyse (Sales Prom Mgr)
Ultimate Holding Company: TRUMPF GMBH & CO (GERMANY)
Immediate Holding Company: TRUMPF LIMITED
Registration no: 01160907 **Date established:** 1974
Turnover: £20m - £50m **No.of Employees:** 51 - 100 **Product Groups:** 37, 38, 44, 46, 48

Date of Accounts	Jun 12	Jun 11	Jun 10
Sales Turnover	43m	34m	25m
Pre Tax Profit/Loss	650	-1	359
Working Capital	3m	2m	-1m
Fixed Assets	370	276	193
Current Assets	14m	10m	8m
Current Liabilities	3m	4m	3m

Ultra Contract Services (a division of Home Counties Conveyers Ltd)
Camford Way, Luton, LU3 3AN
Tel: 01582-490000 **Fax:** 01582-597038
E-mail: mail@ultracs.co.uk
Website: http://www.ultracs.co.uk
Directors: D. Whitley (MD), L. Read (Fin)
Managers: A. Lomax (Eng), J. Peter (Ops Mgr), A. Mark (Admin Off)
Immediate Holding Company: ULTRA CONTRACT SERVICES LIMITED
Registration no: 05083881 **VAT No.:** GB 540 0279 79
Date established: 2004 **Turnover:** £500,000 - £1m
No.of Employees: 1 - 10 **Product Groups:** 26, 30, 35, 36, 40, 45, 48, 49

Date of Accounts	Mar 10	Mar 09	Mar 08
Working Capital	94	193	208
Fixed Assets	7	10	14
Current Assets	106	213	251

Varley Pumps Ltd
1 Kimpton Road, Luton, LU1 3LD
Tel: 01582-731144 **Fax:** 01582-402563
E-mail: sales@varleypumps.com
Website: http://www.varleypumps.com
Directors: K. Jackson (Chief Op Offcr), K. Greenwell (Dir & Gen Mgr)
Managers: B. Jangra (Mgr)
Ultimate Holding Company: Hayward Tyler Group Ltd
Registration no: 03467902 **Turnover:** £1m - £2m
No.of Employees: 11 - 20 **Product Groups:** 39, 40, 46

Date of Accounts	Dec 09	Dec 08	Dec 07
Sales Turnover	1m	2m	1m
Pre Tax Profit/Loss	196	373	175
Working Capital	802	603	249
Fixed Assets	48	45	27
Current Assets	1m	1m	2m
Current Liabilities	40	136	352

Verto Ltd
Unit 14 Britannia Estate Leagrave Road, Luton, LU3 1RJ
Tel: 01582-410969 **Fax:** 01582-482557
E-mail: paul.verto@virgin.net
Directors: C. Morgan (Fin), P. Holmes (Dir)
Immediate Holding Company: VERTO LIMITED
Registration no: 02130972 **VAT No.:** GB 467 2771 17
Date established: 1987 **Turnover:** £500,000 - £1m
No.of Employees: 1 - 10 **Product Groups:** 33

Date of Accounts	Jun 09	Jun 08	Jun 07
Working Capital	76	120	125
Fixed Assets	5	6	4
Current Assets	127	210	228

Warden Plastics Luton Ltd
Unit 31 Sundon Business Park Dencora Way, Luton, LU3 3HP
Tel: 01582-573030 **Fax:** 01582-508751
E-mail: admin@wardenplastics.co.uk
Website: http://www.wardenplastics.co.uk
Bank(s): Lloyds TSB
Directors: M. Barrett (MD)
Managers: D. Piper (Comptroller), M. Bellingham, D. House (Tech Serv Mgr)
Immediate Holding Company: WARDEN PLASTICS LIMITED
Registration no: 00585969 **VAT No.:** GB 196 5027 42
Date established: 1957 **Turnover:** £1m - £2m **No.of Employees:** 21 - 50
Product Groups: 30

Date of Accounts	Jun 11	Jun 10	Jun 09
Sales Turnover	N/A	2m	N/A
Pre Tax Profit/Loss	N/A	90	N/A

Working Capital	-4	-47	-105
Fixed Assets	605	511	574
Current Assets	627	585	492
Current Liabilities	N/A	262	N/A

Wasp Supplies Ltd
Unit 1 Ribocon Way Progress Park, Luton, LU4 9UR
Tel: 01582-566560 **Fax:** 01582-566056
E-mail: sales@waspsupplies.co.uk
Website: http://www.waspsupplies.co.uk
Directors: L. Spratley (Fin), A. Chapman (Sales)
Immediate Holding Company: WASP SUPPLIES LIMITED
Registration no: 04964188 **Date established:** 2003
Turnover: £250,000 - £500,000 **No.of Employees:** 1 - 10
Product Groups: 46

Date of Accounts	Dec 11	Dec 10	Dec 09
Working Capital	91	52	60
Fixed Assets	6	14	16
Current Assets	229	151	142

Whitehill Spindle Tools Ltd
2 Bolton Road, Luton, LU1 3HR
Tel: 01582-736881 **Fax:** 01582-488987
E-mail: sales@whitehill-tools.com
Website: http://www.whitehill-tools.com
Directors: D. Hudson (MD)
Ultimate Holding Company: PORTASA LIMITED
Immediate Holding Company: WHITEHILL SPINDLE TOOLS LIMITED
Registration no: 00346217 **VAT No.:** GB 301 8879 53
Date established: 1938 **Turnover:** £500,000 - £1m
No.of Employees: 1 - 10 **Product Groups:** 36

Date of Accounts	Apr 12	Apr 11	Apr 10
Working Capital	356	344	79
Fixed Assets	508	593	739
Current Assets	589	545	414

Wiper Supply Services Ltd
41 Sedgewick Road, Luton, LU4 9DT
Tel: 0844-209 2620 **Fax:** 0844-209 2621
E-mail: sales@wipersupply.com
Website: http://www.wipersupply.com
Bank(s): National Westminster
Directors: P. Samuels (MD), A. Farleigh (Grp Chief Exec)
Registration no: 02817463 **VAT No.:** GB 626 7811 24
Date established: 1993 **No.of Employees:** 21 - 50 **Product Groups:** 23, 24, 27, 30, 32, 36, 42, 46, 63, 68

Date of Accounts	Apr 12	Apr 11	Apr 10
Working Capital	1m	1m	1m
Fixed Assets	144	168	199
Current Assets	2m	2m	2m

Xfurth Ltd
Unit 4 Firbank Industrial Estate Dallow Road, Luton, LU1 1TW
Tel: 01582-436000 **Fax:** 01582-455955
E-mail: sales@xfurth.com
Website: http://www.xfurth.com
Directors: C. Coles (MD), R. Prater (Co Sec)
Immediate Holding Company: XFURTH LTD.
Registration no: 04388978 **Date established:** 2002
No.of Employees: 1 - 10 **Product Groups:** 30, 37, 42, 46, 48, 67

Date of Accounts	Aug 11	Aug 10	Aug 09
Working Capital	118	117	107
Fixed Assets	14	16	21
Current Assets	215	182	163

Xixin Ltd
Bilton Way, Luton, LU1 1UU
Tel: 01582-400340 **Fax:** 01582-481498
E-mail: sales@xixin.co.uk
Website: http://www.xixin.co.uk
Bank(s): Lloyds TSB
Directors: B. Almey (MD)
Managers: K. Fulcher (Sales Prom Mgr), K. Fulcher (Sales Admin), K. Collins (Sales Prom Mgr)
Immediate Holding Company: XIXIN LIMITED
Registration no: 01804104 **VAT No.:** GB 433 0037 03
Date established: 1984 **Turnover:** £1m - £2m **No.of Employees:** 11 - 20
Product Groups: 37

Date of Accounts	Dec 10	Dec 09	Dec 08
Working Capital	-78	14	14
Fixed Assets	31	33	36
Current Assets	173	307	234

Sandy

A Harvey & Co. Ltd
2 Stockton End Sunderland Road, Sandy, SG19 1SB
Tel: 01767-684666 **Fax:** 01767-683111
E-mail: sales@harveywire.co.uk
Website: http://www.harveywire.co.uk
Bank(s): Barclays
Directors: I. Parker (MD)
Immediate Holding Company: A. HARVEY & CO. (THE WIREWORKERS) LIMITED
Registration no: 00226896 **VAT No.:** GB 232 6464 73
Date established: 2027 **Turnover:** £500,000 - £1m
No.of Employees: 21 - 50 **Product Groups:** 35, 36, 49

Date of Accounts	Dec 09	Dec 08	Aug 11
Working Capital	220	222	253
Fixed Assets	291	308	156
Current Assets	284	281	425

Activ Web Design
88 Sandy Road Potton, Sandy, SG19 2QQ
Tel: 01767-260063
E-mail: cecilia.holden@activwebdesign.com
Website: http://www.activwebdesign.com
Directors: C. Holden (Prop)
Date established: 2008 **No.of Employees:** 1 - 10 **Product Groups:** 44

Barber Insys
5 Swan Lane, Sandy, SG19 1NE
Tel: 01767-692692 **Fax:** 01767-691831
E-mail: info@barber-insys.co.uk
Website: http://www.barber-insys.co.uk
Directors: A. Barber (Ptnr)
Date established: 2000 **No.of Employees:** 1 - 10 **Product Groups:** 86

Boyton B R J System Buildings Ltd
1 Tyne Road, Sandy, SG19 1SA
Tel: 01767-692572 **Fax:** 01767-691268
E-mail: paul@boyton-brj.co.uk
Website: http://www.boyton-brg.co.uk
Bank(s): National Westminster Bank Plc
Directors: P. Joyce (Dir)
Ultimate Holding Company: BRJ HOLDINGS LIMITED
Immediate Holding Company: BOYTON - BRJ SYSTEM BUILDINGS LIMITED
Registration no: SC056056 **VAT No.:** GB 382 1875 34
Date established: 1974 **Turnover:** £1m - £2m **No.of Employees:** 11 - 20
Product Groups: 35

Date of Accounts	Jun 11	Jun 10	Jun 09
Working Capital	642	881	1m
Fixed Assets	98	115	49
Current Assets	1m	2m	2m

Bulldog Steel Fabrication Ltd
Grange Nurseries The Green, Beeston, Sandy, SG19 1PG
Tel: 01767-681627 **Fax:** 08712-260008
E-mail: bulldogsteel@btconnect.com
Website: http://www.bulldogsteelfabrications.net
Directors: T. Dennis (Prop)
No.of Employees: 1 - 10 **Product Groups:** 35

Business To Business Associates Ltd
3a Market Square, Sandy, SG19 1HT
Tel: 08458-380284 **Fax:** 01767-681750
E-mail: enquiries@b-b-a.co.uk
Website: http://www.b-b-a.co.uk
Directors: J. Miller (MD)
Immediate Holding Company: BUSINESS TO BUSINESS ASSOCIATES LIMITED
Registration no: 03198320 **Date established:** 1996
Turnover: Up to £250,000 **No.of Employees:** 1 - 10 **Product Groups:** 80, 81

Date of Accounts	Jul 11	Jul 10	Jul 09
Sales Turnover	N/A	61	70
Pre Tax Profit/Loss	N/A	17	31
Working Capital	31	-64	-84
Fixed Assets	2	1	4
Current Assets	36	18	30
Current Liabilities	N/A	43	55

Camlit Precision Engineering Ltd
Sand Road Indl-Est Sand Road, Great Gransden, Sandy, SG19 3AH
Tel: 01767-677263 **Fax:** 01767-677720
Directors: C. Harrison (MD), J. Harrison (Fin)
Managers: J. Harrison (Sales Prom Mgr)
Immediate Holding Company: CAMLIT PRECISION ENGINEERING LIMITED
Registration no: 04223777 **Date established:** 2001
Turnover: Up to £250,000 **No.of Employees:** 1 - 10 **Product Groups:** 48

Date of Accounts	May 11	May 09	May 08
Working Capital	-16	-37	-35
Fixed Assets	52	68	76
Current Assets	44	29	31

D C Norris & Co. Ltd
Sand House Sand Road, Great Gransden, Sandy, SG19 3AH
Tel: 01767-677515 **Fax:** 01767-677956
E-mail: mail@dcnorris.co.uk
Website: http://www.dcnorris.co.uk
Bank(s): Barclays
Directors: A. Best (Co Sec), D. Norris (MD)
Managers: A. Norris (Mktg Serv Mgr), I. Jones (Chief Mgr)
Immediate Holding Company: D C NORRIS & COMPANY LTD.
Registration no: 01131910 **VAT No.:** GB 197 0528 39
Date established: 1973 **Turnover:** £5m - £10m
No.of Employees: 51 - 100 **Product Groups:** 40, 41, 42, 45

Date of Accounts	Aug 11	Aug 10	Aug 09
Sales Turnover	9m	5m	4m
Pre Tax Profit/Loss	638	221	12
Working Capital	923	407	34
Fixed Assets	2m	2m	2m
Current Assets	2m	3m	2m
Current Liabilities	415	976	358

D W Mouldings Ltd
58 Sunderland Road, Sandy, SG19 1QY
Tel: 01767-683400 **Fax:** 01767-692296
E-mail: mouldings@dwmouldings.co.uk
Website: http://www.dwmouldings.co.uk
Bank(s): HSBC Bank plc
Directors: M. Howard (Dir)
Immediate Holding Company: D.W.MOULDINGS LIMITED
Registration no: 00786399 **Date established:** 1964 **Turnover:** £1m - £2m
No.of Employees: 11 - 20 **Product Groups:** 25, 61

Date of Accounts	Aug 11	Aug 10	Aug 09
Working Capital	2m	2m	2m
Fixed Assets	387	371	206
Current Assets	2m	2m	2m

F S T (a division of Midshires.Net Ltd)
5 Tyne Road, Sandy, SG19 1SA
Tel: 01767-680332 **Fax:** 01767-682888
E-mail: flexibleswitch@btconnect.com
Website: http://www.flexible-switch.co.uk
Directors: S. Johnston (MD)
Immediate Holding Company: MIDSHIRES.NET LTD
Registration no: 02290022 **Date established:** 2000
Turnover: £500,000 - £1m **No.of Employees:** 1 - 10 **Product Groups:** 37

Date of Accounts	Jun 11	Jun 10	Jun 09
Working Capital	-8	-8	-9
Fixed Assets	14	14	14
Current Assets	7	7	5

First Response Fire Protection Ltd
1 Arran Close, Sandy, SG19 1QN
Tel: 01767-690997 **Fax:** 01767-690997
Website: http://www.1stresponcefireprotectionltd.com
Directors: R. Gaylor (Prop), R. Gaylor (MD), W. Gaylor (Fin)
Immediate Holding Company: FIRST RESPONSE FIRE PROTECTION AND ELECTRICAL LIMITED
Registration no: 04736107 **Date established:** 2003
No.of Employees: 1 - 10 **Product Groups:** 38, 42

G P S Developments Ltd
14 Darlington Close, Sandy, SG19 1RW
Tel: 01767-681560 **Fax:** 01767-691685
E-mail: sales@gpsdevelopments.co.uk
Website: http://www.gpsdevelopments.co.uk
Directors: S. Steward (MD), P. Steward (Fin)
Managers: G. Purbrick (Prod Mgr)
Immediate Holding Company: G.P.S. DEVELOPMENTS LIMITED
Registration no: 01539785 **Date established:** 1981
Turnover: £250,000 - £500,000 **No.of Employees:** 1 - 10
Product Groups: 27, 37

Date of Accounts	May 08	May 07	May 06
Working Capital	24	14	20
Fixed Assets	6	7	8
Current Assets	70	57	66

GeeJay Chemicals Ltd
1 Beamish Close, Sandy, SG19 1SD
Tel: 01767-682774 **Fax:** 01767-699697
E-mail: sales@geejaychemicals.co.uk
Website: http://www.geejaychemicals.co.uk
Directors: G. Covington (MD)
Immediate Holding Company: GEEJAY CHEMICALS LIMITED
Registration no: 01659760 **VAT No.:** GB 382 1340 73
Date established: 1982 **Turnover:** £500,000 - £1m
No.of Employees: 1 - 10 **Product Groups:** 14, 17, 31, 32, 42, 76

Date of Accounts	Oct 11	Oct 10	Oct 09
Working Capital	858	691	593
Fixed Assets	1m	1m	1m
Current Assets	1m	805	676

Gy-Roll Ltd
Caxton Road Great Gransden, Sandy, SG19 3AW
Tel: 01767-677377 **Fax:** 01767-677900
E-mail: info@gy-roll.com
Website: http://www.gy-roll.com
Directors: A. Best (Fin)
Immediate Holding Company: GY-ROLL LIMITED
Registration no: 01171668 **VAT No.:** GB 301 5234 17
Date established: 1974 **Turnover:** Up to £250,000
No.of Employees: 1 - 10 **Product Groups:** 46

Integra I C T Ltd
1 Gateshead Close, Sandy, SG19 1RS
Tel: 01767-692792 **Fax:** 01767-692992
E-mail: info@integra-ict.co.uk
Website: http://www.integra-ict.co.uk
Bank(s): HSBC
Directors: P. Ruggiero (MD), P. Ruggiero (MD)
Managers: D. Ager (Fin Mgr), D. Carter (Tech Serv Mgr)
Immediate Holding Company: INTEGRA ICT LIMITED
Registration no: 03658073 **Date established:** 1998 **Turnover:** £2m - £5m
No.of Employees: 21 - 50 **Product Groups:** 37, 44, 79, 81, 84

Date of Accounts	Oct 11	Oct 10	Oct 09
Working Capital	36	-8	-26
Fixed Assets	137	122	135
Current Assets	1m	959	945

Ionic Engineering Ltd
5 Gosforth Close, Sandy, SG19 1RB
Tel: 01767-684000 **Fax:** 01767-684009
E-mail: info@ionic-engineering.co.uk
Website: http://www.ionic-engineering.co.uk
Bank(s): Barclays
Directors: J. Lane (Fin)
Immediate Holding Company: IONIC ENGINEERING LIMITED
Registration no: 02254117 **VAT No.:** GB 491 1825 40
Date established: 1988 **Turnover:** £1m - £2m **No.of Employees:** 11 - 20
Product Groups: 48

Date of Accounts	Dec 11	Dec 10	Dec 09
Working Capital	221	174	173
Fixed Assets	827	833	659
Current Assets	531	425	349
Current Liabilities	N/A	45	N/A

K M G Systems Ltd
Station Road Gamlingay, Sandy, SG19 3HE
Tel: 01767-650760 **Fax:** 01767-651622
E-mail: admin@kmgsystems.com
Website: http://www.kmgsystems.com
Directors: H. Weatherley (Fin), J. Richards (Pers), K. Maddocks (MD)
Managers: P. Clarke (Chief Buyer)
Immediate Holding Company: KMG SYSTEMS LIMITED
Registration no: 01357835 **VAT No.:** GB 335 1716 71
Date established: 1978 **Turnover:** £5m - £10m
No.of Employees: 51 - 100 **Product Groups:** 22

Date of Accounts	Apr 11	Apr 10	Apr 09
Sales Turnover	10m	9m	765
Pre Tax Profit/Loss	297	183	-962
Working Capital	2m	2m	2m
Fixed Assets	2m	2m	2m
Current Assets	6m	5m	5m
Current Liabilities	3m	2m	1m

Kier Group plc
Tempsford Hall, Sandy, SG19 2BD
Tel: 01767-640111 **Fax:** 01767-641711
E-mail: ian.gordon@kier.co.uk
Website: http://www.kier.co.uk
Directors: D. Mattar (Fin), I. Gordon (Chief Op Offcr)
Managers: J. Dodds (Officer), N. Chidgey (Chief Acct)
Ultimate Holding Company: 02708030
Immediate Holding Company: KIER FLEET SERVICES LIMITED
Registration no: 02127113 **VAT No.:** GB 632 3104 86
Date established: 1987 **Turnover:** £5m - £10m **No.of Employees:** 1 - 10
Product Groups: 80

Date of Accounts	Jun 10	Jun 09	Jun 08
Sales Turnover	N/A	787	513
Pre Tax Profit/Loss	-1m	-407	595
Working Capital	-8m	-7m	-7m
Current Assets	14m	13m	11m
Current Liabilities	5m	N/A	380

Kopak Walker
7 Ivel View, Sandy, SG19 1AU
Tel: 01767-689853
E-mail: s.jacobs@kopak-walker.co.uk
Website: http://www.kopak-walker.co.uk
Managers: S. Jacobs (Mgr)
No.of Employees: 11 - 20 **Product Groups:** 29, 63, 66

Kypol Electroplating Ltd
55 Gosforth Close, Sandy, SG19 1RB
Tel: 01767-682424 **Fax:** 01767-681180
E-mail: kypol@globalnet.co.uk
Website: http://www.kypol.co.uk
Directors: R. Kapoor (MD)
Immediate Holding Company: KYPOL ELECTROPLATING LIMITED
Registration no: 02686217 **Date established:** 1992
No.of Employees: 1 - 10 **Product Groups:** 48

Date of Accounts	Mar 12	Mar 11	Mar 10
Working Capital	22	-2	-18
Fixed Assets	18	16	19
Current Assets	121	97	77

Laser-Tech
Church Farm High Street, Eyeworth, Sandy, SG19 2HH
Tel: 01767-631800 **Fax:** 01767-631801
E-mail: sales@laser-tech.uk.com
Website: http://www.laser-tech.org.uk
Directors: T. Collins (Prop)
Immediate Holding Company: A.P. SPECIALIST DOORS & JOINERY LIMITED
Date established: 2002 **No.of Employees:** 1 - 10 **Product Groups:** 37, 38, 42, 43, 44, 46, 48, 84, 85

Date of Accounts	May 11	May 10	May 09
Working Capital	86	46	74
Fixed Assets	15	20	26
Current Assets	138	89	111

Harry Major Machine UK Ltd (a division of Harry Major Machine and Tool Michigan USA)
3 Gosforth Close, Sandy, SG19 1RB
Tel: 01767-689500 **Fax:** 01767-691398
E-mail: sales@hmm-uk.com
Website: http://www.hmm-uk.com
Bank(s): The Royal Bank of Scotland
Directors: M. Gillespie (MD)
Ultimate Holding Company: HARRY MAJOR MACHINE & TOOL COMPANY INC (USA)
Immediate Holding Company: HARRY MAJOR MACHINE-UK LIMITED
Registration no: 01461718 **VAT No.:** GB 335 0182 87
Date established: 1979 **Turnover:** £2m - £5m **No.of Employees:** 21 - 50
Product Groups: 45

Date of Accounts	Dec 11	Dec 10	Dec 09
Working Capital	313	100	76
Fixed Assets	40	49	44
Current Assets	842	552	452

Morite Winding Co. Ltd
Unit 10c Sand Road Industrial Estate Great Gransden, Sandy, SG19 3AH
Tel: 01767-677811 **Fax:** 01767-677812
E-mail: sales@morite.co.uk
Website: http://www.morite.co.uk
Bank(s): HSBC
Directors: B. Matheron (MD)
Managers: G. Armstrong (Chief Mgr)
Immediate Holding Company: MORITE WINDING CO. LIMITED
Registration no: 01114388 **VAT No.:** GB 215 1643 94
Date established: 1973 **Turnover:** £500,000 - £1m
No.of Employees: 11 - 20 **Product Groups:** 37

Date of Accounts	Mar 08	Mar 07	Mar 06
Sales Turnover	835	894	698
Pre Tax Profit/Loss	38	61	12
Working Capital	151	133	63
Fixed Assets	49	59	69
Current Assets	431	502	352
Current Liabilities	280	369	289
Total Share Capital	12	12	12
ROCE% (Return on Capital Employed)	19.0	31.6	9.3
ROT% (Return on Turnover)	4.6	6.8	1.8

Pinewood Structures Ltd
1 Station Road Gamlingay, Sandy, SG19 3HA
Tel: 01767-651218 **Fax:** 01767-651928
E-mail: geoff.arnold@pinewood-structures.co.uk
Website: http://www.pinewoodstructures.co.uk
Bank(s): Barclays
Directors: A. Vallely (Co Sec), G. Arnold (MD), S. Boness (Sales)
Managers: A. Davies (Transport), M. Spavins (Personnel)
Ultimate Holding Company: PXP HOLDINGS LIMITED
Immediate Holding Company: PINEWOOD STRUCTURES LIMITED
Registration no: 01560406 **VAT No.:** GB 335 3358 61
Date established: 1981 **Turnover:** £10m - £20m
No.of Employees: 101 - 250 **Product Groups:** 52

Date of Accounts	Dec 09	Dec 08	Dec 07
Sales Turnover	14m	N/A	25m
Pre Tax Profit/Loss	308	1m	2m
Working Capital	6m	6m	5m
Fixed Assets	179	253	347
Current Assets	9m	9m	10m
Current Liabilities	951	769	894

Rush Industrial Sales
126 Station Road Tempsford, Sandy, SG19 2AY
Tel: 01767-640779 **Fax:** 01767-640617
E-mail: sales@rushind.com
Website: http://www.rushind.com
Directors: A. Quinn (Prop)
VAT No.: GB 440 8584 42 **Date established:** 1986
Turnover: £250,000 - £500,000 **No.of Employees:** 1 - 10
Product Groups: 37, 40

T H S P
16a Market Square, Sandy, SG19 1HU
Tel: 08456-122144 **Fax:** 01767-683883
E-mail: enquiries@thsp.co.uk
Website: http://www.thsp.co.uk
Directors: J. Phoday (MD)
Immediate Holding Company: THE HEALTH & SAFETY PEOPLE LIMITED
Registration no: 02730817 **Date established:** 1992
No.of Employees: 21 - 50 **Product Groups:** 40, 84, 86

Date of Accounts	Mar 12	Mar 11	Mar 10
Working Capital	688	767	848
Fixed Assets	226	226	206
Current Assets	2m	2m	2m

Verto Data
33 Brickhill road, Sandy, SG19 1JH
Tel: 01767-683925 **Fax:** 07031-151701
E-mail: sales@vertodata.net
Website: http://www.vertodata.net
Directors: N. Sheppard (MD), N. Sheppard (Dir)
Date established: 2008 **Turnover:** Up to £250,000
No.of Employees: 1 - 10 **Product Groups:** 79

Wedge Engineering Ltd
16 Darlington Close, Sandy, SG19 1RW
Tel: 01767-683527 **Fax:** 01767-683529
E-mail: wedgeeng@live.com
Directors: P. Hodge (MD), L. Norman (Fin)
Immediate Holding Company: WEDGE ENGINEERING LIMITED
Registration no: 04285837 **Date established:** 2001
Turnover: £500,000 - £1m **No.of Employees:** 1 - 10 **Product Groups:** 35, 48

Date of Accounts	Sep 11	Sep 10	Sep 09
Working Capital	-125	-110	-86
Fixed Assets	268	281	298
Current Assets	105	92	134

Wentworth Laboratories Ltd
1 Gosforth Close, Sandy, SG19 1RB
Tel: 01767-681221 **Fax:** 01767-691951
E-mail: info@wentworthlabs.com
Website: http://www.wentworthlabs.com
Bank(s): Barclays
Managers: J. Hope (Chief Mgr)
Immediate Holding Company: WENTWORTH LABORATORIES LIMITED
Registration no: 01309949 **VAT No.:** GB 301 5429 02
Date established: 1977 **Turnover:** £2m - £5m **No.of Employees:** 11 - 20
Product Groups: 47

Date of Accounts	Dec 10	Dec 09	Dec 08
Working Capital	-27	-540	-512
Fixed Assets	328	374	413
Current Assets	1m	946	1m

Wrights Dowson Ltd
Green End Gamlingay, Sandy, SG19 3LA
Tel: 01767-650294 **Fax:** 01767-651149
E-mail: post@dowsongroup.com
Website: http://www.dowsongroup.com
Bank(s): Barclays
Directors: N. Wright (Dir)
Ultimate Holding Company: WRIGHTS TRADING LIMITED
Immediate Holding Company: WRIGHTS (GAMLINGAY) LIMITED
Registration no: 00709486 **VAT No.:** GB 335 1351 85
Date established: 1961 **Turnover:** £1m - £2m **No.of Employees:** 11 - 20
Product Groups: 45, 67

Date of Accounts	Jun 11	Jun 10	Jun 09
Working Capital	543	356	355
Fixed Assets	30	33	54
Current Assets	2m	1m	2m

York House Meat Products Ltd
Shannon Place Potton, Sandy, SG19 2YH
Tel: 01767-260114 **Fax:** 01767-262165
E-mail: trm@yorkhousemeatproducts.com
Website: http://www.yorkhousefoods.com
Directors: I. Affleck (MD), T. Michelson (Fin)
Managers: D. Hunt (Buyer)
Ultimate Holding Company: YORK HOUSE FOODS LIMITED
Immediate Holding Company: YORK HOUSE (MEAT PRODUCTS) LIMITED
Registration no: 00992229 **Date established:** 1970
Turnover: £10m - £20m **No.of Employees:** 51 - 100 **Product Groups:** 20

Date of Accounts	Dec 11	Dec 10	Dec 09
Sales Turnover	21m	19m	17m
Pre Tax Profit/Loss	2m	1m	736
Working Capital	3m	3m	2m
Fixed Assets	1m	1m	1m
Current Assets	9m	7m	6m
Current Liabilities	1m	1m	794

Shefford

A.F.A.C Ltd
Unit 2A/2 St. Francis Way, Shefford Industrial Park, Shefford, SG17 5DZ
Tel: 01462-811767 **Fax:** 01462-811944
E-mail: lee@afac.co.uk
Website: http://www.afac.co.uk
Registration no: 02499444 **Turnover:** Up to £250,000
No.of Employees: 1 - 10 **Product Groups:** 29, 30, 35

Date of Accounts	Mar 08	Mar 07	Mar 06
Working Capital	32	15	21
Fixed Assets	2	3	3
Current Assets	82	47	61
Current Liabilities	50	32	41

A & M Welding & Fabrication
Chapel Road Meppershall, Shefford, SG17 5NG
Tel: 01462-851409 **Fax:** 01462-851409
Directors: M. Mcreynolds (Ptnr)
No.of Employees: 1 - 10 **Product Groups:** 35

C P L Petroleum
139 Clifton Road, Shefford, SG17 5AG
Tel: 01462-811201 **Fax:** 01462-816488
E-mail: corporate@cplindustries.co.uk
Website: http://www.cplpetroleum.co.uk
Directors: C. Dawson (MD)
Ultimate Holding Company: CPL INDUSTRIES HOLDINGS LIMITED
Immediate Holding Company: CPL PETROLEUM LIMITED
Registration no: 03003860 **Date established:** 1994
No.of Employees: 1 - 10 **Product Groups:** 66

Date of Accounts	Mar 12	Mar 11	Mar 10
Pre Tax Profit/Loss	N/A	878	904
Working Capital	31	30m	30m
Fixed Assets	26	26m	26m
Current Assets	57	56m	56m
Current Liabilities	26	246	253

Elwen Eos Ltd

PO Box 261, Shefford, SG17 5PW
Tel: 01462-814708 **Fax:** 01462-814708
E-mail: elweneos@aol.com
Website: http://www.elweneos.co.uk
Directors: J. Richards (Co Sec), P. Richards (Dir)
Immediate Holding Company: ELWEN EOS LIMITED
Registration no: 02088442 **VAT No.:** GB 456 0177 52
Date established: 1987 **Turnover:** Up to £250,000
No.of Employees: 1 - 10 **Product Groups:** 38, 84

Date of Accounts	Apr 11	Apr 10	Apr 09
Sales Turnover	N/A	6	14
Pre Tax Profit/Loss	N/A	-0	-0
Working Capital	-0	-0	-0
Fixed Assets	N/A	1	1
Current Assets	9	5	7
Current Liabilities	N/A	1	1

H Squared Electronics Ltd

Conifer House Old Bridge Way, Shefford, SG17 5HQ
Tel: 01462-815115 **Fax:** 01462-815187
E-mail: sales@h-squared.co.uk
Website: http://www.h-squared.co.uk
Bank(s): Barclays
Directors: G. Hughes (Sales), R. Marriott (MD), T. Champion (Comm), W. Marriott (Fin)
Managers: M. Headington (Tech Serv Mgr)
Ultimate Holding Company: GLADPOWER LIMITED
Immediate Holding Company: H. SQUARED ELECTRONICS LIMITED
Registration no: 01448627 **VAT No.:** GB 322 5740 72
Date established: 1979 **Turnover:** £5m - £10m **No.of Employees:** 21 - 50
Product Groups: 37, 67

Date of Accounts	Mar 12	Mar 11	Mar 10
Sales Turnover	10m	10m	N/A
Pre Tax Profit/Loss	840	869	N/A
Working Capital	3m	3m	2m
Fixed Assets	190	101	133
Current Assets	5m	4m	4m
Current Liabilities	657	707	N/A

J J & B Engineering

Highlands Farm Gravenhurst Road, Campton, Shefford, SG17 5NZ
Tel: 01462-813301 **Fax:** 01462-811240
E-mail: sales@construction-equipment.co.uk
Website: http://www.loaderhire.com
Directors: R. Hanlon (Ptnr)
Date established: 1977 **No.of Employees:** 21 - 50 **Product Groups:** 42, 45

L Squared Laser

6b St Francis Way, Shefford, SG17 5DZ
Tel: 01462-816623 **Fax:** 01462-817427
E-mail: info@lasermarked.com
Website: http://www.lasermarked.com
Managers: M. Knott (Mgr)
No.of Employees: 1 - 10 **Product Groups:** 44, 46

London Electronics Ltd

Warren Court Chicksands, Shefford, SG17 5QB
Tel: 01462-850967 **Fax:** 01462-850968
E-mail: support@london-electronics.com
Website: http://www.london-electronics.com
Directors: G. Laming (Sales), J. Dauncey (Co Sec), J. Lees (MD)
Registration no: 02722503 **VAT No.:** GB 573 2929 17
Date established: 1992 **Turnover:** £1m - £2m **No.of Employees:** 21 - 50
Product Groups: 37, 38, 44, 45, 49, 67

Date of Accounts	Dec 09	Dec 08	Dec 07
Working Capital	162	239	224
Fixed Assets	203	124	144
Current Assets	310	376	354

Millenium Sheet Metal & Fabrication

2 Rectory Road Campton, Shefford, SG17 5PF
Tel: 01462-811100 **Fax:** 01462- 811100
Directors: K. Hobbs (Prop)
Immediate Holding Company: MILLENIUM SHEETMETAL & FABRICATION LIMITED
Registration no: 05566667 **Date established:** 2005
No.of Employees: 21 - 50 **Product Groups:** 35

Pippin Products

41 Church Street Clifton, Shefford, SG17 5ET
Tel: 01462-811485 **Fax:** 01462-851618
E-mail: janeparry@tiscali.co.uk
Directors: J. Parry (Prop)
VAT No.: GB 563 4053 53 **Date established:** 1990
No.of Employees: 1 - 10 **Product Groups:** 28

Time Medical & Scientific Network

127 High Street Meppershall, Shefford, SG17 5LZ
Tel: 01462-813943 **Fax:** 01462-422042
E-mail: timemedical.network@btconnect.com
Website: http://www.timemedical.co.uk
Directors: P. Trivedi (MD)
Managers: T. Hills (Mgr)
No.of Employees: 1 - 10 **Product Groups:** 67

BERKSHIRE

Ascot

Apex Marine Consultants
Silwood Mews 15 Silwood Road, Sunninghill, Ascot, SL5 0PY
Tel: 01344-625727 **Fax:** 07092-345670
E-mail: enquiries@apexmarine.com
Website: http://www.apexmarine.com
Directors: F. Gaffney (MD)
Registration no: 4569002 **Date established:** 2002
Turnover: Up to £250,000 **No.of Employees:** 1 - 10 **Product Groups:** 38, 67, 74, 82, 84

Date of Accounts	Oct 07	Oct 06	Oct 05
Working Capital	55	-2	13
Fixed Assets	3	3	1
Current Assets	82	39	22
Current Liabilities	28	41	9

Ascot Tool Hire
The Forge Fernbank Road, Ascot, SL5 8ED
Tel: 01344-884318 **Fax:** 01344-886845
E-mail: info@toolhireascot.co.uk
Website: http://www.toolhireascot.co.uk
Directors: A. Durham (Prop)
No.of Employees: 1 - 10 **Product Groups:** 41, 54, 74, 83

Bar Billiards Ltd
Winkfield Road, Ascot, SL5 7EX
Tel: 01344-626244 **Fax:** 01344-625415
E-mail: info@bar-billiards.co.uk
Website: http://www.bar-billiards.co.uk
Bank(s): Barclays Bank PLC, 17 High St, Ascot
Directors: P. Slattery (Ch), R. Gipps (MD), Slattery (MD), H. Slattery (Co Sec)
Managers: K. Hussey (Sales Prom Mgr), D. Brisley (Chief Mgr), G. Townsend (I.T. Exec)
Immediate Holding Company: BAR BILLIARDS LIMITED
Registration no: 01746037 **VAT No.:** GB 207 5720 77
Date established: 1983 **Turnover:** £1m - £2m **No.of Employees:** 21 - 50
Product Groups: 49, 83

Date of Accounts	Mar 10	Mar 09	Oct 07
Working Capital	234	289	93
Fixed Assets	679	786	520
Current Assets	1m	1m	585

Ben - Motor & Allied Trades Benevolent Fund
Lynwood Rise Road, Ascot, SL5 0AJ
Tel: 01344-620191 **Fax:** 01344-622042
E-mail: david.main@ben.org.uk
Website: http://www.ben.org.uk
Bank(s): Barclays High Street
Directors: B. Cottrell (Fin), D. Main (Grp Chief Exec)
Immediate Holding Company: BEN-MOTOR AND ALLIED TRADES BENEVOLENT FUND
Registration no: 02163894 **VAT No.:** GB 635 8379 04
Date established: 1987 **Turnover:** £10m - £20m
No.of Employees: 101 - 250 **Product Groups:** 80

Date of Accounts	Mar 11	Mar 10	Mar 09
Sales Turnover	15m	12m	12m
Pre Tax Profit/Loss	4m	396	-2m
Working Capital	2m	1m	369
Fixed Assets	16m	14m	13m
Current Assets	3m	2m	1m
Current Liabilities	155	145	N/A

Chancellors
31 High Street, Ascot, SL5 7HG
Tel: 01344-627101 **Fax:** 01344-875422
E-mail: paul.bosanko@chancellors.co.uk
Website: http://www.chancellors.co.uk
Directors: I. Simpson (Dir)
Managers: H. Williams (Mgr), M. George (Mgr), M. Forren (Mgr), P. Bosanko (Mgr)
Immediate Holding Company: CHANCELLORS ASSOCIATES LIMITED
Registration no: 05856303 **VAT No.:** 666 2484 10 **Date established:** 2006
No.of Employees: 1 - 10 **Product Groups:** 80

Chartered Institute of Building
Englemere Kings Ride, Ascot, SL5 7TB
Tel: 01344-630700 **Fax:** 01344-630777
E-mail: reception@ciob.org.uk
Website: http://www.ciob.org.uk
Directors: C. Blythe (Grp Chief Exec)
Managers: J. Cox (I.T. Exec)
No.of Employees: 51 - 100 **Product Groups:** 87

CMI Healthcare Services Ltd
5 Rise Road Sunningdale, Ascot, SL5 0BH
Tel: 01344-621378 **Fax:** 01344-872204
E-mail: sales@cmihealthcare.co.uk
Website: http://www.cmihealthcare.co.uk
Managers: N. Cengiz (Sales Prom Mgr)
Registration no: 02656509 **Date established:** 1980 **Turnover:** £2m - £5m
No.of Employees: 21 - 50 **Product Groups:** 38, 40, 41, 42, 67, 88

Connect Two Promotions Ltd
Kingswick House Kingswick Drive, Ascot, SL5 7BH
Tel: 01344-292370 **Fax:** 01344-626176
E-mail: info@connecttwo.co.uk
Website: http://www.connecttwo.co.uk
Directors: E. Walker (Dir)
Registration no: 06468237 **Date established:** 2006
Turnover: Up to £250,000 **No.of Employees:** 1 - 10 **Product Groups:** 49

Diamond Detectors
Element Six House Kings Ride Park, Ascot, SL5 8BP
Tel: 01344-638200 **Fax:** 01344-638236
E-mail: c.hultner@e6.com
Website: http://www.e6.com
Directors: C. Thompson (Dir)
Ultimate Holding Company: DE BEERS SA (LUXEMBOURG)
Immediate Holding Company: DIAMOND DETECTORS LIMITED
Registration no: 06097934 **Date established:** 2007
Turnover: £250,000 - £500,000 **No.of Employees:** 1 - 10
Product Groups: 33, 36, 49

Date of Accounts	Dec 11	Dec 10	Dec 09
Sales Turnover	N/A	491	375
Pre Tax Profit/Loss	N/A	-403	-423
Working Capital	246	799	1m
Fixed Assets	130	312	383
Current Assets	360	941	2m
Current Liabilities	N/A	61	475

Executive Security Solutions Ltd
Unit 6 Kings Ride Park, Ascot, SL5 8BL
Tel: 01344-319403 **Fax:** 01344-319404
E-mail: mail@essukltd.co.uk
Website: http://www.executivesecurity.com
Directors: M. Middleton (Dir)
Immediate Holding Company: EXECUTIVE SECURITY SOLUTIONS LIMITED
Registration no: 05538981 **Date established:** 2005
Turnover: £250,000 - £500,000 **No.of Employees:** 1 - 10
Product Groups: 36, 38, 81

Date of Accounts	Aug 11	Aug 10
Working Capital	8	5
Fixed Assets	2	1
Current Assets	13	9
Current Liabilities	4	2

Key Equipment Finance
Ashurst Manor Church Lane, Ascot, SL5 7DD
Tel: 01344-627470 **Fax:** 01344-621894
E-mail: philip.venner@key.com
Website: http://www.kefonline.co.uk
Directors: J. Reynolds (MD)
Managers: P. Nolan, C. Coombs (Admin Off), R. Sandhu (Tech Serv Mgr), S. Good
Ultimate Holding Company: KEYCORP INVESTMENTS PTY LTD (AUSTRALIA)
Immediate Holding Company: KEY EQUIPMENT FINANCE LIMITED
Registration no: 03031539 **VAT No.:** GB 636 1366 42
Date established: 1995 **Turnover:** £20m - £50m
No.of Employees: 21 - 50 **Product Groups:** 82

Date of Accounts	Dec 11	Dec 10	Dec 09
Sales Turnover	26m	27m	22m
Pre Tax Profit/Loss	-2m	3m	-2m
Working Capital	44m	56m	60m
Fixed Assets	15m	9m	10m
Current Assets	101m	101m	110m
Current Liabilities	3m	4m	6m

Mechon Ltd
Index House St Georges Lane, Ascot, SL5 7ET
Tel: 020-8892 9352 **Fax:** 08707-622175
E-mail: sales@mechon.co.uk
Website: http://www.mechon.co.uk
Directors: S. Taylor (Dir), H. Prinsloo (Fin)
Immediate Holding Company: MECHON LIMITED
Registration no: 05028349 **Date established:** 2004
Turnover: Up to £250,000 **No.of Employees:** 1 - 10 **Product Groups:** 40

Date of Accounts	Apr 11	Apr 10	Apr 09
Sales Turnover	680	N/A	N/A
Pre Tax Profit/Loss	32	N/A	N/A
Working Capital	9	33	34
Fixed Assets	4	5	3
Current Assets	170	89	74
Current Liabilities	56	30	N/A

National School Of Government
Sunningdale Park Larch Avenue, Ascot, SL5 0QE
Tel: 01344-634272 **Fax:** 01344-634233
E-mail: rod.clark@nationalschool.gsi.gov.uk
Website: http://www.nationalschool.gov.uk
Directors: R. Clark (Grp Chief Exec)
Managers: A. Hall, D. Lane (Personnel), M. Timmis (Fin Mgr), B. Alston
Ultimate Holding Company: THE CABINET OFFICE
Date established: 1970 **Turnover:** £20m - £50m
No.of Employees: 101 - 250 **Product Groups:** 86

Okanargon Ltd
Kingswick House Kingswick Drive, Ascot, SL5 7BH
Tel: 01344-292200 **Fax:** 01344-626176
E-mail: info@businesscentre-berkshire.co.uk
Website: http://www.businesscentre-berkshire.co.uk
Directors: T. Wynn Williams (Dir)
Immediate Holding Company: OKANARGON LIMITED
Registration no: 01181741 **VAT No.:** GB 604 2828 58
Date established: 1974 **Turnover:** £250,000 - £500,000
No.of Employees: 1 - 10 **Product Groups:** 80

Date of Accounts	Aug 10	Aug 09	Aug 08
Working Capital	-555	-481	-468
Fixed Assets	2m	2m	2m
Current Assets	233	73	73

Polysius Ltd
The Brackens London Road, Ascot, SL5 8BE
Tel: 01344-884161 **Fax:** 01344-886438
E-mail: martyn.crump@thyssenkrupp.com
Website: http://www.thyssenkrupp.com
Managers: M. Crump (Chief Mgr)
Ultimate Holding Company: THYSSEN KRUPP AG (GERMANY)
Immediate Holding Company: POLYSIUS LIMITED
Registration no: 00442739 **Date established:** 1947 **Turnover:** £1m - £2m
No.of Employees: 1 - 10 **Product Groups:** 40, 42, 45

Date of Accounts	Sep 11	Sep 10	Sep 09
Sales Turnover	1m	2m	2m
Pre Tax Profit/Loss	14	280	252
Working Capital	1m	1m	1m
Fixed Assets	2m	2m	2m
Current Assets	1m	2m	2m
Current Liabilities	162	218	178

S D T Ltd
Unit 4 Silwood Business Centre Buckhurst Road, Ascot, SL5 7PW
Tel: 01344-870062 **Fax:** 01344-874025
E-mail: info@sdt.co.uk
Website: http://www.sdt.co.uk
Directors: A. Wayman (MD)
Immediate Holding Company: SDT LTD
Registration no: 02938419 **Date established:** 1994 **Turnover:** £2m - £5m
No.of Employees: 1 - 10 **Product Groups:** 44

Date of Accounts	Dec 11	Dec 09	Dec 08
Working Capital	8	39	35
Fixed Assets	13	30	46
Current Assets	117	148	122

Steel Construction Institute
Silwood Park Buckhurst Road, Ascot, SL5 7QN
Tel: 01344-636525 **Fax:** 01344-622944
E-mail: reception@steel-sci.com
Website: http://www.steel-sci.com
Bank(s): Lloyds TSB Bank plc
Managers: L. Chamberlain (Mgr)
Immediate Holding Company: STEEL CONSTRUCTION INSTITUTE(THE)
Registration no: 01916698 **VAT No.:** GB 407 7668 31
Date established: 1985 **Turnover:** £2m - £5m **No.of Employees:** 21 - 50
Product Groups: 84, 85, 86, 87

Date of Accounts	Mar 11	Mar 10	Mar 09
Sales Turnover	3m	4m	4m
Pre Tax Profit/Loss	32	200	292

Working Capital	1m	2m	2m
Fixed Assets	247	255	302
Current Assets	3m	3m	3m
Current Liabilities	2m	1m	2m

T K Water Systems Ltd

Gibbs House Kennel Ride, Ascot, SL5 7NT
Tel: 01344-893337 **Fax:** 01344-887899
E-mail: anthony.sanders@skw.co.uk
Website: http://www.skw.co.uk
Directors: A. Sanders (Fin)
Immediate Holding Company: T K WATER SYSTEMS LIMITED
Registration no: 03764093 **Date established:** 1999
Turnover: Up to £250,000 **No.of Employees:** 1 - 10 **Product Groups:** 36, 67

Date of Accounts	Apr 11	Apr 10	Apr 09
Working Capital	-59	-54	-92
Fixed Assets	240	258	269
Current Assets	17	-54	33

Tecbridge Ltd

5 New Road, Ascot, SL5 8QB
Tel: 020-7993 6503
E-mail: sales@tecbridgecircuits.co.uk
Website: http://www.tecbridgecircuits.co.uk
Registration no: 03056332 **Product Groups:** 37, 44, 67, 84

Thorp Modelmakers Ltd

High Street Sunningdale, Ascot, SL5 0NG
Tel: 01344-876776 **Fax:** 01344-876583
E-mail: info@atomltd.com
Website: http://www.atomltd.com
Bank(s): Lloyds TSB Bank plc
Managers: A. Saunders (Mgr)
Ultimate Holding Company: A.T.O.M. LIMITED
Immediate Holding Company: THORP MODELMAKERS LIMITED
Registration no: 00876442 **Date established:** 1966
Turnover: £500,000 - £1m **No.of Employees:** 21 - 50 **Product Groups:** 49

Date of Accounts	Oct 08
Working Capital	-96
Fixed Assets	23
Current Assets	86

Bracknell

3 M

3m Centre Cain Road, Bracknell, RG12 1HT
Tel: 01344-858000 **Fax:** 01344-858278
E-mail: abrasives.uk@mmm.com
Website: http://www.3m.co.uk
Directors: J. Mcsheffrey (MD), J. Skinner (Pers)
Ultimate Holding Company: 3M COMPANY (USA)
Immediate Holding Company: 3M UK HOLDINGS LIMITED
Registration no: 00241888 **Date established:** 2029
No.of Employees: 251 - 500 **Product Groups:** 33, 40

Date of Accounts	Dec 11	Dec 10	Dec 09
Pre Tax Profit/Loss	-5m	-4m	-56m
Working Capital	-321m	-318m	-302m
Fixed Assets	359m	328m	316m
Current Assets	26m	30m	32m
Current Liabilities	433	433	485

Afton Chemical

London Road, Bracknell, RG12 2UW
Tel: 01344-304141 **Fax:** 01344-420666
E-mail: barrie.horsted@aftonchemical.com
Website: http://www.aftonchemical.com
Bank(s): Lloyds TSB Bank plc
Managers: B. Horsted (Sales Admin)
Ultimate Holding Company: NEWMARKET CORP (USA)
Immediate Holding Company: AFTON CHEMICAL LIMITED
Registration no: 01213092 **VAT No.:** GB 200 6037 28
Date established: 1975 **Turnover:** £250m - £500m
No.of Employees: 101 - 250 **Product Groups:** 32

Date of Accounts	Dec 11	Dec 10	Dec 09
Sales Turnover	483m	411m	377m
Pre Tax Profit/Loss	41m	46m	18m
Working Capital	101m	104m	74m
Fixed Assets	23m	4m	2m
Current Assets	164m	140m	156m
Current Liabilities	15m	19m	6m

Air Tube Carrier Systems

79 Turnberry, Bracknell, RG12 8ZH
Tel: 01344-423659 **Fax:** 01344-423659
Directors: W. Donovan (Prop)
Ultimate Holding Company: SUMETZBERGER (AUSTRIA)
Turnover: £1m - £2m **No.of Employees:** 1 - 10 **Product Groups:** 45

Arto Chemicals Ltd

Arto House London Road, Binfield, Bracknell, RG42 4BU
Tel: 01344-860737 **Fax:** 01344-860820
E-mail: sales@artochemicals.com
Website: http://www.artochemicals.com
Directors: A. Miklos (Dir), S. Miklos (MD)
Managers: S. Weit, C. Snook (Fin Mgr)
Immediate Holding Company: ARTO CHEMICALS LIMITED
Registration no: 01068577 **VAT No.:** GB 208 4219 81
Date established: 1972 **Turnover:** £10m - £20m **No.of Employees:** 1 - 10
Product Groups: 29, 30, 31, 32, 66

Date of Accounts	Sep 11	Sep 10	Sep 09
Sales Turnover	18m	16m	15m
Pre Tax Profit/Loss	407	468	518
Working Capital	7m	6m	6m
Fixed Assets	928	952	992
Current Assets	9m	9m	8m
Current Liabilities	698	615	556

Atmel UK Ltd

2 The Braccans London Road, Bracknell, RG12 2XH
Tel: 01344-390060 **Fax:** 01344-390070
E-mail: sales@atmel.com
Website: http://www.atmel.com
Directors: S. Macrae (Sales), S. Mcrae (Sales)
Ultimate Holding Company: ATMEL CORPORATION (USA)
Immediate Holding Company: ATMEL U.K., LIMITED
Registration no: 02337754 **Date established:** 1989 **Turnover:** £1m - £2m
No.of Employees: 11 - 20 **Product Groups:** 37

Date of Accounts	Dec 11	Dec 10	Dec 09
Sales Turnover	2m	2m	2m
Pre Tax Profit/Loss	662	575	2m
Working Capital	-17m	596	7m
Fixed Assets	18m	N/A	N/A
Current Assets	3m	2m	8m
Current Liabilities	211	205	179

Attunity UK Ltd

Venture House 2 Arlington Square Downshire Way, Bracknell, RG12 1WA
Tel: 01344-742805 **Fax:** 0118-975 3005
Website: http://www.attunity.co.uk
Managers: R. Giles (Fin Mgr)
Ultimate Holding Company: ATTUNITY LIMITED (ISRAEL)
Immediate Holding Company: ATTUNITY (UK) LIMITED
Registration no: 00572054 **Date established:** 1956
Turnover: £500,000 - £1m **No.of Employees:** 1 - 10 **Product Groups:** 44

Date of Accounts	Dec 11	Dec 10	Dec 09
Sales Turnover	574	866	660
Pre Tax Profit/Loss	9	18	16
Working Capital	447	438	426
Fixed Assets	8	N/A	N/A
Current Assets	662	731	629
Current Liabilities	212	283	203

Avnet Technology Solutions

Unit 5 Sterling Centre, Bracknell, RG12 2PW
Tel: 01344-662000 **Fax:** 01793-784653
E-mail: sales@eizo.co.uk
Website: http://www.avnet.com
Bank(s): Barclays
Directors: M. Gower (MD), O. Reichl (Dir), J. Li (Co Sec), S. Rayat (Dir)
Managers: C. Woodley (Sales Prom Mgr)
Ultimate Holding Company: AVNET INC (USA)
Immediate Holding Company: AVNET TECHNOLOGY SOLUTIONS LIMITED
Registration no: 03538262 **Date established:** 1998
Turnover: £10m - £20m **No.of Employees:** 101 - 250 **Product Groups:** 44

Date of Accounts	Jun 07	Jun 08	Jun 09
Sales Turnover	146m	185m	207m
Pre Tax Profit/Loss	223	-24m	-7m
Working Capital	2m	-20m	-26m
Fixed Assets	2m	22m	47m
Current Assets	33m	68m	36m
Current Liabilities	4m	5m	5m

Barco Ltd

Atrium Court The Ring, Bracknell, RG12 1BW
Tel: 01344-393090 **Fax:** 0118-926 7716
E-mail: info@barco.com
Website: http://www.barco.com
Bank(s): Lloyds TSB Bank plc
Directors: S. Turtle (Sales)
Managers: M. Banton
Ultimate Holding Company: BARCO NV (BELGIUM)
Immediate Holding Company: BARCO LIMITED
Registration no: 04039048 **Date established:** 2000 **Turnover:** £2m - £5m
No.of Employees: 21 - 50 **Product Groups:** 37, 38, 44

Date of Accounts	Dec 11	Dec 10	Dec 09
Sales Turnover	3m	2m	3m
Pre Tax Profit/Loss	-41	61	441
Working Capital	1m	-283	-322
Fixed Assets	4m	5m	5m
Current Assets	1m	525	475
Current Liabilities	306	261	214

Berkshire Hiab Services

5 Kenilworth Avenue, Bracknell, RG12 2JJ
Tel: 01344-307143 **Fax:** 01344-429593
E-mail: admin@berkshirehiab.co.uk
Website: http://www.ukhiabhire.co.uk
Directors: D. Everest (Prop)
Immediate Holding Company: BERKSHIRE HIAB SERVICES LIMITED
Registration no: 04767528 **Date established:** 2003
No.of Employees: 1 - 10 **Product Groups:** 72

B M W UK Ltd

Ellesfield Avenue, Bracknell, RG12 8TA
Tel: 01344-426565 **Fax:** 01344-480203
E-mail: customer.service@bmw.co.uk
Website: http://www.bmw.co.uk
Directors: C. Brownridge (Mkt Research), T. Abbott (MD)
Managers: M. Todd (Comptroller), S. Newton (Tech Serv Mgr)
Ultimate Holding Company: BAYERISCHE MOTOREN WERKE AG (GERMANY)
Immediate Holding Company: BMW (GB) LIMITED
Registration no: 02907080 **VAT No.:** GB 584 4519 13
Date established: 1994 **Turnover:** Over £1,000m
No.of Employees: 251 - 500 **Product Groups:** 39

Boehringer Ingelheim Ltd

Ellesfield Avenue, Bracknell, RG12 8YS
Tel: 01344-424600 **Fax:** 01344-741444
E-mail: vetmedica.uk@boehringer-ingelheim.com
Website: http://www.boehringer-ingelheim.com
Bank(s): Barclays
Directors: G. Tanser (Pers), U. Weiler (MD)
Ultimate Holding Company: C H BOEHRINGER SOHN (GERMANY)
Immediate Holding Company: BOEHRINGER INGELHEIM LIMITED
Registration no: 00711858 **Date established:** 1962
Turnover: £250m - £500m **No.of Employees:** 501 - 1000
Product Groups: 31, 63

Date of Accounts	Dec 11	Dec 10	Dec 09
Sales Turnover	348m	339m	304m
Pre Tax Profit/Loss	20m	13m	19m
Working Capital	44m	50m	42m
Fixed Assets	19m	24m	31m
Current Assets	163m	124m	127m
Current Liabilities	42m	18m	20m

Cadence Design Systems Ltd

Bag Shot Road, Bracknell, RG12 0PH
Tel: 01344-360333 **Fax:** 01506-595959
Website: http://www.cadence.com
Directors: C. Adams (MD), C. Pahljina (Co Sec), C. Thomas (Pers), S. Redmond (MD)
Managers: S. Penfold (Purch Mgr), C. Thomas
Ultimate Holding Company: Cadence Design Systems Inc.
Immediate Holding Company: CADENCE DESIGN SYSTEMS LIMITED
Registration no: 02457888 **Date established:** 1990
Turnover: £20m - £50m **No.of Employees:** 101 - 250
Product Groups: 44, 84

Date of Accounts	Jan 10	Jan 09	Dec 07
Sales Turnover	25m	28m	31m
Pre Tax Profit/Loss	820	3m	-5m
Working Capital	4m	9m	8m
Fixed Assets	901	1m	1m
Current Assets	25m	42m	29m
Current Liabilities	4m	7m	7m

Campbell Birch Ltd

Broadway, Bracknell, RG12 1AG
Tel: 01344-424117 **Fax:** 01344-360534
E-mail: info@campbellbirch.com
Website: http://www.campbellbirch.com
Directors: B. Birch (Ptnr)
Immediate Holding Company: CAMPBELL BIRCH LIMITED
Registration no: 04082138 **VAT No.:** GB 362 6439 43
Date established: 2000 **Turnover:** £500,000 - £1m
No.of Employees: 1 - 10 **Product Groups:** 80

Date of Accounts	Jul 12	Jul 11	Jul 10
Working Capital	-72	-76	-80
Fixed Assets	30	33	37
Current Assets	N/A	N/A	2

Cognos Ltd

Westerly Point Market Street, Bracknell, RG12 1QB
Tel: 01344-486668 **Fax:** 01344-485124
E-mail: uk.marketing@cognos.com
Website: http://www.cognos.com
Bank(s): Barclays
Directors: A. Voogt (Dep Pres), R. Herd (Co Sec)
Ultimate Holding Company: INTERNATIONAL BUSINESS MACHINES CORP (USA)
Immediate Holding Company: Cognos Europe Ltd
Registration no: 04625339 **Date established:** 2002
Turnover: £20m - £50m **No.of Employees:** 101 - 250 **Product Groups:** 44

Date of Accounts	Dec 09	Dec 08	Feb 08
Sales Turnover	N/A	45m	51m
Pre Tax Profit/Loss	-933	-1m	5m
Working Capital	36m	30m	24m
Fixed Assets	2m	13m	16m
Current Assets	36m	69m	62m
Current Liabilities	N/A	25m	25m

Cogswell & Harrison

Heathcliffe Parkers Lane, Maidens Green, Bracknell, RG42 6LE
Tel: 01344-885091 **Fax:** 01344-890906
E-mail: alancrewe@hotmail.co.uk
Website: http://www.thegunmaker.co.uk
Directors: A. Crewe (Prop)
Immediate Holding Company: COGSWELL & HARRISON LIMITED
Registration no: 02819542 **Date established:** 1993
No.of Employees: 1 - 10 **Product Groups:** 36, 39, 40

Date of Accounts	Dec 11	Dec 10	Sep 03
Current Assets	N/A	N/A	1

Corporate Gifts Online Ltd

Ryehurst Barn Ryehurst Lane, Binfield, Bracknell, RG42 5QZ
Tel: 01344-860861 **Fax:** 08707-770536
E-mail: sales@corporate-gifts.co.uk
Website: http://www.corporate-gifts.co.uk
Directors: A. Reeves (Fin), S. Haskell (Dir)
Immediate Holding Company: CORPORATE GIFTS ONLINE LIMITED
Registration no: 04800644 **Date established:** 2003
Turnover: Up to £250,000 **No.of Employees:** 11 - 20 **Product Groups:** 22, 23, 24, 25, 28, 30, 33, 37, 49, 65, 81

Date of Accounts	May 11	May 10	May 09
Sales Turnover	N/A	N/A	169
Pre Tax Profit/Loss	N/A	N/A	3
Working Capital	4	5	1
Fixed Assets	N/A	N/A	3
Current Assets	28	38	25
Current Liabilities	N/A	N/A	12

Dell Inc

Technology House Dell Campus Cain Road, Bracknell, RG12 1BF
Tel: 01344-860456 **Fax:** 01344-372767
Website: http://www.dell.com/ukc
Directors: P. Gallagher (Fin), W. Rodrigues (Dir)
Managers: J. Davidson (Personnel)
Ultimate Holding Company: DELL INC (USA)
Immediate Holding Company: DELL CORPORATION LIMITED
Registration no: 02081369 **Date established:** 1986
Turnover: £20m - £50m **No.of Employees:** 501 - 1000
Product Groups: 44

Date of Accounts	Jan 09	Jan 10	Jan 11
Sales Turnover	98m	206m	197m
Pre Tax Profit/Loss	4m	4m	4m
Working Capital	103m	118m	139m
Fixed Assets	39m	30m	26m
Current Assets	225m	233m	289m
Current Liabilities	37m	48m	79m

Epicor Software UK Ltd

1 The Arena Downshire Way, Bracknell, RG12 1PU
Tel: 01344-468468 **Fax:** 01344-468010
E-mail: jbrims@epicor.com
Website: http://www.epicor.com
Directors: J. Brims (Fin)
Ultimate Holding Company: EPICOR SOFTWARE CORP (USA)
Immediate Holding Company: EPICOR SOFTWARE (UK) LIMITED
Registration no: 02338274 **Date established:** 1989
Turnover: £10m - £20m **No.of Employees:** 101 - 250 **Product Groups:** 44

Date of Accounts	Dec 10	Dec 09	Dec 08
Sales Turnover	15m	17m	17m
Pre Tax Profit/Loss	89	888	821
Working Capital	6m	6m	5m
Fixed Assets	746	685	796
Current Assets	14m	14m	13m
Current Liabilities	6m	6m	6m

Exel
Ocean House The Ring, Bracknell, RG12 1AN
Tel: 01344-302000 **Fax:** 01344-710037
E-mail: aaron.brown@fahlgren.com
Website: http://www.exel.com
Directors: J. Allan (Grp Chief Exec), J. Coghlan (Fin), A. Parris (Fin)
Managers: R. Stringer, C. Stephens
Ultimate Holding Company: DEUTSCHE POST AG (GERMANY)
Registration no: 00073975 **Date established:** 2002
Turnover: £500m - £1,000m **No.of Employees:** 101 - 250
Product Groups: 61, 80

Date of Accounts	Dec 09	Dec 08	Dec 07
Pre Tax Profit/Loss	337m	-29m	147m
Working Capital	-588m	-217m	-421m
Fixed Assets	1156m	652m	910m
Current Assets	679m	826m	905m
Current Liabilities	24m	12m	28m

First Bus
Coldborough House Market Street, Bracknell, RG12 1JA
Tel: 01344-782222 **Fax:** 01344-868332
E-mail: simon.goff@firstgroup.com
Website: http://www.firstgroup.com
Managers: S. Goff (Ops Mgr)
Immediate Holding Company: FIRST GROUP
Registration no: 01966624 **Turnover:** £2m - £5m
No.of Employees: 101 - 250 **Product Groups:** 72

G & M Technology
2 Eddington Road, Bracknell, RG12 8GF
Tel: 01344-456965 **Fax:** 01344-456965
E-mail: gm.technology@ntlworld.com
Directors: G. Pearce (Prop)
Immediate Holding Company: G & M TECHNOLOGY LIMITED
Registration no: 02765227 **Date established:** 1992
No.of Employees: 1 - 10 **Product Groups:** 32, 68

Hay Tech Engineering
12 Market Street, Bracknell, RG12 1JG
Tel: 01344-861208 **Fax:** 01344-867979
E-mail: wood.c@btconnect.com
Website: http://www.hay-tech.co.uk
Directors: C. Wood (Ptnr)
Immediate Holding Company: HAY-TECH PRECISION ENGINEERING LIMITED
Registration no: 07158388 **Date established:** 2010
Turnover: £250,000 - £500,000 **No.of Employees:** 1 - 10
Product Groups: 46, 48

Date of Accounts	Mar 12	Feb 11
Working Capital	-317	-311
Fixed Assets	420	452
Current Assets	145	186

Hewlett Packard Ltd
Cain Road, Bracknell, RG12 1HN
Tel: 01344-360000 **Fax:** 01344-363344
E-mail: info@jobshp.com
Website: http://www.hp.com
Bank(s): Barclays
Directors: J. Ormrod (Dir)
Managers: W. Heath (Mktg Serv Mgr)
Ultimate Holding Company: HEWLETT-PACKARD COMPANY (USA)
Immediate Holding Company: HEWLETT - PACKARD LIMITED
Registration no: 00690597 **Date established:** 1961
Turnover: Over £1,000m **No.of Employees:** 1501 & over
Product Groups: 44

Date of Accounts	Oct 11	Oct 10	Oct 09
Sales Turnover	2834m	2935m	2954m
Pre Tax Profit/Loss	193m	170m	250m
Working Capital	268m	184m	206m
Fixed Assets	632m	719m	767m
Current Assets	1847m	1615m	1568m
Current Liabilities	552m	560m	467m

Hire It Limited
Magnum House Cookham Road, Bracknell, RG12 1RB
Tel: 01344-456600 **Fax:** 01344-401344
E-mail: info@hamilton.co.uk
Website: http://www.hamilton.co.uk
Bank(s): Lloyds TSB Bank plc
Directors: M. O'Conner (Sales & Mktg), P. Surrey (Fin), S. Lakey (MD)
Managers: A. Cook (Mgr)
Ultimate Holding Company: Brewton Ltd
Immediate Holding Company: Advance Technical Systems Ltd
Registration no: 02749984 **Turnover:** £1m - £2m
No.of Employees: 51 - 100 **Product Groups:** 38, 44

Date of Accounts	May 08	May 07	May 06
Working Capital	-455	-484	-130
Fixed Assets	1747	1730	1729
Current Assets	173	81	711
Current Liabilities	628	565	841

Hydro Systems Europe Ltd
Unit 3 Sterling Centre, Bracknell, RG12 2PW
Tel: 01344-488880 **Fax:** 01344-488879
E-mail: svogel@hydronovaeurope.com
Website: http://www.hydrosystemseurope.com
Directors: S. Vogel (Co Sec), L. Ship (Chief Op Offcr)
Managers: S. Darraugh, G. Pratt, A. Blaire-davies (Mktg Serv Mgr)
Ultimate Holding Company: DOVER CORPORATION (U.S.A.)
Immediate Holding Company: HYDRO SYSTEMS EUROPE LTD
Registration no: 03297546 **Date established:** 1996
Turnover: £10m - £20m **No.of Employees:** 21 - 50 **Product Groups:** 38, 42

Date of Accounts	Dec 11	Dec 10	Dec 09
Sales Turnover	10m	9m	8m
Pre Tax Profit/Loss	2m	2m	2m
Working Capital	11m	10m	9m
Fixed Assets	452	154	163
Current Assets	12m	11m	10m
Current Liabilities	683	750	502

I H S Global
Willoughby Road, Bracknell, RG12 8FB
Tel: 01344-328000 **Fax:** 01344-424971
E-mail: customer.support@ihs.com
Website: http://www.uk.ihs.com
Bank(s): Midland
Directors: F. Mullins (Co Sec), J. Coldicott (Mkt Research)
Managers: V. Masson (Buyer), E. Twining (Personnel)
Ultimate Holding Company: IHS INC (USA)
Immediate Holding Company: IHS GLOBAL LIMITED
Registration no: 00788737 **VAT No.:** GB 207 8513 67
Date established: 1964 **Turnover:** £125m - £250m
No.of Employees: 101 - 250 **Product Groups:** 28

Date of Accounts	Nov 11	Nov 10	Nov 09
Sales Turnover	197m	159m	118m
Pre Tax Profit/Loss	22m	19m	6m
Working Capital	-137m	-162m	-53m
Fixed Assets	428m	404m	251m
Current Assets	200m	128m	161m
Current Liabilities	90m	71m	54m

I N G Car Lease
Pheonix House Cookham Road, Bracknell, RG12 1RR
Tel: 08448-716810 **Fax:** 01344-300401
E-mail: info@ingcarlease.co.uk
Website: http://www.ingcarlease.co.uk
Directors: I. Tilerook (MD), R. Pridmore (Fin), R. Pridmore (Fin)
Managers: K. Pinner (Tech Serv Mgr), L. Mitchell (Personnel)
Ultimate Holding Company: I N G GROEP NV (NETHERLANDS)
Immediate Holding Company: ALPHABET (UK) FLEET MANAGEMENT LIMITED
Registration no: SC084727 **Date established:** 1983
Turnover: £125m - £250m **No.of Employees:** 51 - 100
Product Groups: 82

Date of Accounts	Dec 11	Dec 10	Dec 09
Sales Turnover	159m	157m	163m
Pre Tax Profit/Loss	23m	11m	7m
Working Capital	-125m	-77m	-85m
Fixed Assets	359m	337m	328m
Current Assets	110m	100m	72m
Current Liabilities	233m	170m	47m

Imation UK Ltd
Century Court Millennium Way, Bracknell, RG12 2XT
Tel: 01344-402000
E-mail: jbeckett@imation.com
Website: http://www.imation.co.uk
Directors: J. Beckett (Dir)
Ultimate Holding Company: IMATION CORP (USA)
Immediate Holding Company: IMATION UK LIMITED
Registration no: 03193263 **Date established:** 1996 **Turnover:** £2m - £5m
No.of Employees: 11 - 20 **Product Groups:** 37, 44

Initial
The Columbia Centre Station Road, Bracknell, RG12 1LP
Tel: 01344-300444 **Fax:** 01344-360928
E-mail: adam.councell@initial-catering.co.uk
Website: http://www.initial-catering.co.uk
Directors: Y. Alireza (Dir), J. Reid (Co Sec), P. Daly (MD), A. Councell (Fin)
Immediate Holding Company: INITIAL MEDICAL SERVICES LIMITED
Registration no: 03174140 **Date established:** 1996 **Turnover:** £1m - £2m
No.of Employees: 51 - 100 **Product Groups:** 69

iQlink Ltd
Abbey House Grenville Place, Bracknell, RG12 1BP
Tel: 01344-667363
E-mail: marketing@iqlink.co.uk
Website: http://www.iqlink.co.uk
Managers: J. Anstee (Admin Off)
Immediate Holding Company: IQLINK LTD
Registration no: 05249782 **Date established:** 2004
No.of Employees: 1 - 10 **Product Groups:** 44

Date of Accounts	Nov 11	Nov 10	Nov 09
Working Capital	-20	35	56
Fixed Assets	N/A	6	9
Current Assets	147	179	271

Kognitio Ltd
3a Waterside Park Cookham Road, Bracknell, RG12 1RB
Tel: 01344-300770 **Fax:** 01344-301424
E-mail: info@kognitio.com
Website: http://www.kognitio.com
Bank(s): National Westminster
Directors: G. Squire (Ch)
Ultimate Holding Company: KOGNITIO HOLDINGS LIMITED
Immediate Holding Company: KOGNITIO LIMITED
Registration no: 02127833 **VAT No.:** GB 494 2448 21
Date established: 1987 **Turnover:** £5m - £10m **No.of Employees:** 21 - 50
Product Groups: 44

Date of Accounts	Mar 11	Mar 10	Mar 09
Sales Turnover	7m	8m	9m
Pre Tax Profit/Loss	-1m	-692	-721
Working Capital	-5m	-4m	-4m
Fixed Assets	210	589	2m
Current Assets	7m	3m	3m
Current Liabilities	1m	2m	2m

L-3 Communications Security & Detection Systems
Astro House Brants Bridge, Bracknell, RG12 9BG
Tel: 01344-477900 **Fax:** 01344-477901
E-mail: melanie.dormand@l-3com.com
Website: http://www.l-3com.com
Bank(s): Barclays
Managers: M. Dormand (Mktg Serv Mgr)
Registration no: 00683910 **VAT No.:** GB 385 8380 08
Turnover: £10m - £20m **No.of Employees:** 51 - 100 **Product Groups:** 35, 36, 37, 40

Marketpoint Europe Ltd
Unit 6 The Western Centre Western Road, Bracknell, RG12 1RW
Tel: 01344-350250 **Fax:** 01344-488045
E-mail: sales@mktpoint.com
Website: http://www.mktpoint.com
Bank(s): Royal Of Scotland
Directors: P. Gillett (MD)
Managers: J. Pegden (Fin Mgr), S. St Quinton, J. Franklin (Tech Serv Mgr)
Immediate Holding Company: MARKETPOINT (EUROPE) LIMITED
Registration no: 02787052 **Date established:** 1993
Turnover: £500,000 - £1m **No.of Employees:** 11 - 20
Product Groups: 81, 82

Date of Accounts	Dec 09	Jun 11	Apr 09
Working Capital	367	264	365
Fixed Assets	18	10	28
Current Assets	658	495	597

Maximizer Software Ltd
Apex House London Road London Road, Bracknell, RG12 2XH
Tel: 08455-559955 **Fax:** 01344-766901
E-mail: info@max.co.uk
Website: http://www.max.co.uk
Directors: M. Richardson (MD)
Managers: M. Carter, K. Dewar (Fin Mgr)
Ultimate Holding Company: MSI ACQUISITION CORPORATION (CANADA)
Immediate Holding Company: MAXIMIZER SOFTWARE LIMITED
Registration no: 01896712 **Date established:** 1985 **Turnover:** £2m - £5m
No.of Employees: 21 - 50 **Product Groups:** 44, 80, 86

Date of Accounts	Nov 11	Nov 10	Nov 09
Sales Turnover	2m	2m	2m
Pre Tax Profit/Loss	19	-84	11
Working Capital	-17	-15	165
Fixed Assets	41	54	62
Current Assets	554	585	861
Current Liabilities	532	557	648

Micron Europe Ltd
Lavenir Opladen Way, Bracknell, RG12 0PH
Tel: 01344-383400 **Fax:** 01344-750710
E-mail: sgamble@micron.com
Website: http://www.micron.com
Managers: S. Gamble (Admin Off)
Ultimate Holding Company: MICRON TECHNOLOGY INC (USA)
Immediate Holding Company: MICRON EUROPE LIMITED
Registration no: 02341071 **VAT No.:** GB 544 3978 14
Date established: 1989 **Turnover:** £500m - £1,000m
No.of Employees: 1 - 10 **Product Groups:** 37

Date of Accounts	Aug 07	Aug 06
Sales Turnover	705790	828760
Pre Tax Profit/Loss	20950	16990
Working Capital	113100	130100
Fixed Assets	11010	6090
Current Assets	268870	213030
Current Liabilities	155770	82930
Total Share Capital	780	780
ROCE% (Return on Capital Employed)	16.9	12.5
ROT% (Return on Turnover)	3.0	2.1

John Nike Leisuresport Ltd
Jubilee House John Nike Way,, Bracknell, RG12 8TN
Tel: 01344-789555 **Fax:** 01344-789 556
E-mail: ski-bracknello@nikegroup.co.uk
Website: http://jnll.co.uk
Bank(s): National Westminster Bank Plc
Directors: J. Nike (Ch), L. Nike (Dir), L. Stafford (Co Sec)
Immediate Holding Company: Nike Land Securities Ltd
Registration no: 01792420 **VAT No.:** GB 363 2226 74
Date established: 1984 **Turnover:** £2m - £5m
No.of Employees: 501 - 1000 **Product Groups:** 69, 89

Date of Accounts	Apr 10	Apr 09	Apr 08
Sales Turnover	5m	N/A	N/A
Pre Tax Profit/Loss	-335	N/A	N/A
Working Capital	-1m	-1m	-402
Fixed Assets	1m	1m	1m
Current Assets	702	652	800
Current Liabilities	411	N/A	N/A

Onyx Software
6 Tamar House Brants Bridge, Bracknell, RG12 9BQ
Tel: 01344-322000 **Fax:** 01344-489035
E-mail: sales@onyx.com
Website: http://www.onyx.com
Directors: N. Burton (MD)
Managers: B. McKenna (Mktg Serv Mgr)
Immediate Holding Company: ONYX SOFTWARE LIMITED
Registration no: 03051102 **Date established:** 1995
Turnover: Up to £250,000 **No.of Employees:** 51 - 100
Product Groups: 44

Date of Accounts	Apr 11	Apr 10	Apr 09
Sales Turnover	N/A	54	49
Pre Tax Profit/Loss	N/A	38	25
Working Capital	-4	2	-0
Fixed Assets	N/A	N/A	1
Current Assets	N/A	11	7
Current Liabilities	N/A	10	7

Packaging Team Ltd
Venture House Arlington Square Downshire Way, Bracknell, RG12 1WA
Tel: 08450-941791
E-mail: enquiries@packagingteam.com
Website: http://www.packagingteam.com
Managers: M. White (Consultant)
Immediate Holding Company: PACKAGING TEAM LIMITED
Registration no: 05813310 **Date established:** 2006
Turnover: Up to £250,000 **No.of Employees:** 1 - 10 **Product Groups:** 44

Date of Accounts	May 11	May 09	May 08
Working Capital	43	62	52
Fixed Assets	24	39	5
Current Assets	65	140	97

Promat UK Ltd
Sterling Centre, Bracknell, RG12 2TD
Tel: 01344-381300 **Fax:** 01344-381301
E-mail: salesuk@promat.co.uk
Website: http://www.promat.co.uk
Directors: E. Spillemaeckers (Sales), J. Stevenson (MD), N. Stopford (Co Sec)
Ultimate Holding Company: ETEX GROUP SA (BELGIUM)
Immediate Holding Company: PROMAT UK LIMITED
Registration no: 01785071 **Date established:** 1984
Turnover: £20m - £50m **No.of Employees:** 51 - 100 **Product Groups:** 32, 33

Date of Accounts	Dec 11	Dec 10	Dec 09
Sales Turnover	27m	29m	34m
Pre Tax Profit/Loss	2m	3m	3m
Working Capital	9m	8m	6m
Fixed Assets	5m	5m	5m
Current Assets	12m	12m	12m
Current Liabilities	647	2m	300

Protec I T
Venture House Downshire Way, Bracknell, RG12 1WA
Tel: 01344-876123 **Fax:** 01344-668 200
E-mail: info@protecit.co.uk
Website: http://www.protecit.co.uk

Directors: L. Hostein (Prop)
Immediate Holding Company: PROTEC IT SOLUTIONS LTD
Registration no: 04647018 **Date established:** 2003
Turnover: Up to £250,000 **No.of Employees:** 1 - 10 **Product Groups:** 44

Date of Accounts	Jan 12	Jan 11	Jan 10
Working Capital	32	44	31
Fixed Assets	6	8	11
Current Assets	73	74	60

R I W Ltd
Arc House Terrace Road South, Binfield, Bracknell, RG42 4PZ
Tel: 01344-397788 **Fax:** 01344-862010
E-mail: enquiries@riw.co.uk
Website: http://www.riw.co.uk
Bank(s): Lloyds TSB Bank plc
Directors: M. Walker (MD)
Ultimate Holding Company: ALFA TECHNICAL INDUSTRIES LIMITED
Immediate Holding Company: R.I.W. LIMITED
Registration no: 00177476 **Date established:** 2021 **Turnover:** £2m - £5m
No.of Employees: 11 - 20 **Product Groups:** 29, 31, 32, 33, 34, 52, 66

Date of Accounts	Dec 11	Dec 10	Dec 09
Sales Turnover	N/A	N/A	5m
Pre Tax Profit/Loss	N/A	N/A	901
Working Capital	4m	4m	4m
Fixed Assets	46	26	28
Current Assets	4m	5m	5m
Current Liabilities	N/A	N/A	600

Redwood Technologies Ltd
The Redwood Building Broad Lane, Bracknell, RG12 9GU
Tel: 01344-304344 **Fax:** 01344-304345
E-mail: pmt@redwoodtech.com
Website: http://www.redwoodtech.com
Bank(s): Barclays
Directors: P. Taylor (Co Sec)
Immediate Holding Company: REDWOOD TECHNOLOGIES LIMITED
Registration no: 02817863 **VAT No.:** 592 0064 53 **Date established:** 1993
Turnover: £2m - £5m **No.of Employees:** 21 - 50 **Product Groups:** 37, 44

Date of Accounts	Dec 11	Dec 10	Dec 09
Sales Turnover	5m	5m	3m
Pre Tax Profit/Loss	121	51	52
Working Capital	2m	1m	1m
Fixed Assets	43	59	63
Current Assets	2m	2m	2m
Current Liabilities	792	687	820

Reed Accountancy Personnel Ltd
15 High Street, Bracknell, RG12 1DL
Tel: 01344-869286 **Fax:** 01344-860752
E-mail: rapbracknell@reed.co.uk
Website: http://www.reed.co.uk
Managers: S. Perring (Mgr)
Immediate Holding Company: REED PERSONNEL SERVICES LTD
Registration no: 00973629 **Turnover:** £250m - £500m
No.of Employees: 1 - 10 **Product Groups:** 80

Reed Employment Ltd
1a Crossway, Bracknell, RG12 1BG
Tel: 01344-486777 **Fax:** 01344-860162
Website: http://www.reed.co.uk
Managers: D. Spencer Webb (Mgr)
Ultimate Holding Company: REED GLOBAL LTD (MALTA)
Immediate Holding Company: REED EMPLOYMENT LIMITED
Registration no: 00669854 **Date established:** 1960
Turnover: £500m - £1,000m **No.of Employees:** 1 - 10
Product Groups: 80

Date of Accounts	Jun 11	Jun 10	Dec 07
Sales Turnover	618	450	287m
Pre Tax Profit/Loss	-2m	310	8m
Working Capital	23m	28m	28m
Fixed Assets	31	36	5m
Current Assets	28m	30m	74m
Current Liabilities	37	29	21m

Thomas Ross Ltd
St Marks Road Binfield, Bracknell, RG42 4TR
Tel: 01344-862686 **Fax:** 01344-862575
E-mail: sales@thomasross.co.uk
Website: http://www.thomasross.co.uk
Directors: L. Nutbrown (MD)
Ultimate Holding Company: NUTBROWN GROUP LIMITED
Immediate Holding Company: THOMAS ROSS LIMITED
Registration no: 01939844 **VAT No.:** GB 216 3344 88
Date established: 1985 **Turnover:** £2m - £5m **No.of Employees:** 1 - 10
Product Groups: 28, 49

Date of Accounts	Dec 11	Dec 10	Dec 09
Working Capital	260	279	309
Fixed Assets	1	2	3
Current Assets	396	413	431
Current Liabilities	N/A	14	N/A

Scootermart Mobility Centres Ltd
69 Broadway, Bracknell, RG12 1BB
Tel: 01344-867755 **Fax:** 01344-867755
Directors: C. Webb (Dir)
Ultimate Holding Company: SUSSEX RESEARCH LTD
Immediate Holding Company: THE MOBILITY GROUP LTD
Registration no: 03885227 **Turnover:** Up to £250,000
No.of Employees: 1 - 10 **Product Groups:** 35, 39, 45

Date of Accounts	Sep 06	Dec 05
Sales Turnover	N/A	165
Pre Tax Profit/Loss	N/A	-89
Working Capital	-93	-89
Current Assets	33	37
Current Liabilities	126	126
ROCE% (Return on Capital Employed)		100.1
ROT% (Return on Turnover)		-54.0

Solar Turbines Europe S A
O T V House Wokingham Road, Bracknell, RG42 1NG
Tel: 01344-782920 **Fax:** 01344-782930
E-mail: crook_richard_p@solarturbines.com
Website: http://www.solarturbines.com
Managers: R. Mundy (Reg Mgr), R. Crook
No.of Employees: 1 - 10 **Product Groups:** 35, 36, 39

Synergix
Unit B Cookham Road, Bracknell, RG12 1RB
Tel: 01344-312770 **Fax:** 01344-409227
E-mail: info@synergix.co.uk
Website: http://www.synergix.co.uk
Bank(s): HSBC
Directors: P. Fenton (MD), T. Churcher (Ch)
Managers: A. Ayres (Sales Prom Mgr)
Immediate Holding Company: KOGNITIO HOLDINGS LIMITED
Registration no: 02156884 **VAT No.:** 664 5838 95 **Date established:** 2002
Turnover: £2m - £5m **No.of Employees:** 11 - 20 **Product Groups:** 44

Syngenta Agra Chemicals
Jealotts Hill Warfield, Bracknell, RG42 6EY
Tel: 01344-424701 **Fax:** 01344-455629
E-mail: info@syngenta.com
Website: http://www.syngenta.com
Directors: S. Nicholson (Co Sec)
Immediate Holding Company: SYNJENTA INC
No.of Employees: 501 - 1000 **Product Groups:** 85

Tabaq Software Limited
Building A Trinity Court, Wokingham Road, Bracknell, RG42 1PL
Tel: 01344-668400 **Fax:** 01344-668200
E-mail: sales@tabaqsoftware.com
Website: http://www.tabaqsoftware.com
Managers: A. Noori (Mktg Serv Mgr)
Registration no: 06039350 **Date established:** 2007
Turnover: £250,000 - £500,000 **No.of Employees:** 1 - 10
Product Groups: 44

Techtronics Network Systems
Western Peninsula Western Road, Bracknell, RG12 1RF
Tel: 01344-767000 **Fax:** 01344-767001
Website: http://www.tek.com
Managers: D. Neville (Mgr)
No.of Employees: 21 - 50 **Product Groups:** 38

Tektronix UK Holdings Ltd (Head Office UK)
Western Peninsula Western Road, Bracknell, RG12 1RF
Tel: 01344-392000 **Fax:** 01344-392001
E-mail: info@tektronix.com
Website: http://www.tek.com
Bank(s): National Westminster Bank Plc
Directors: D. Stone (Legal)
Immediate Holding Company: TEKTRONIX U.K. HOLDINGS LIMITED
Registration no: 03378342 **VAT No.:** GB 669 4160 08
Date established: 1997 **Turnover:** £2m - £5m **No.of Employees:** 21 - 50
Product Groups: 37

Date of Accounts	Dec 11	Dec 10	Dec 09
Pre Tax Profit/Loss	51	5m	-18m
Working Capital	28m	28m	23m
Fixed Assets	3m	3m	3m
Current Assets	29m	29m	23m

Teradyne Ltd
The Western Centre Western Road, Bracknell, RG12 1RW
Tel: 01344-426899 **Fax:** 01344- 725884
E-mail: info@teradyne.com
Website: http://www.teradyne.com
Bank(s): Boston
Directors: M. Hart (Dir)
Ultimate Holding Company: TERADYNE INC (USA)
Immediate Holding Company: TERADYNE LIMITED
Registration no: 00920424 **Date established:** 1967 **Turnover:** £5m - £10m
No.of Employees: 51 - 100 **Product Groups:** 38

Towry Ltd
Towry House Western Road, Bracknell, RG12 1TL
Tel: 01344-828000 **Fax:** 01202-475652
E-mail: paul.wright@towrylaw.com
Website: http://www.towry.com
Bank(s): Barclays, London
Directors: P. Wright (Fin)
Managers: A. Fisher
Ultimate Holding Company: TOWRY HOLDINGS LIMITED
Immediate Holding Company: TOWRY LAW LIMITED
Registration no: 01000324 **VAT No.:** GB 302 2071 28
Date established: 1971 **Turnover:** £20m - £50m
No.of Employees: 101 - 250 **Product Groups:** 80

Date of Accounts	Dec 11	Dec 10	Dec 09
Sales Turnover	74m	63m	44m
Pre Tax Profit/Loss	2m	2m	1m
Working Capital	9m	9m	7m
Fixed Assets	4m	6m	2m
Current Assets	21m	19m	14m
Current Liabilities	9m	9m	7m

Waitrose
Doncastle Road Southern Industrial Area, Bracknell, RG12 8YA
Tel: 01344-424680 **Fax:** 0800-188888
E-mail: mark_price@waitrose.co.uk
Website: http://www.waitrose.com
Directors: M. Price (MD)
Ultimate Holding Company: JOHN LEWIS PARTNERSHIP PLC
Immediate Holding Company: WAITROSE LIMITED
Registration no: 00099405 **Date established:** 2008
Turnover: Over £1,000m **No.of Employees:** 1501 & over
Product Groups: 61

Date of Accounts	Jan 09	Jan 10	Jan 11
Sales Turnover	4156m	4317m	4700m
Pre Tax Profit/Loss	129m	154m	151m
Working Capital	-847m	-837m	-923m
Fixed Assets	1800m	1911m	2123m
Current Assets	273m	304m	341m
Current Liabilities	108m	115m	107m

Crowthorne

Access Controlled Solutions Ltd
Pine Drive Lower Wokingham Road, Crowthorne, RG45 6BX
Tel: 01344-771569
E-mail: sales@acsltd.eu
Website: http://www.acsltd.eu
Directors: A. Halfe (MD)
Immediate Holding Company: ACCESS CONTROLLED SOLUTIONS LTD
Registration no: 06037605 **Date established:** 2006
Turnover: Up to £250,000 **No.of Employees:** 1 - 10 **Product Groups:** 35, 36

Date of Accounts	Dec 10	Dec 09	Dec 08
Sales Turnover	212	N/A	N/A
Pre Tax Profit/Loss	-29	N/A	N/A
Working Capital	-77	-61	-41
Fixed Assets	22	37	36
Current Assets	33	54	17
Current Liabilities	48	N/A	45

Churchill Controls Ltd
30 Wellington Business Park Dukes Ride, Crowthorne, RG45 6LS
Tel: 01344-750233 **Fax:** 0118-989 2007
E-mail: sales@churchill-controls.co.uk
Website: http://www.churchill-controls.co.uk
Managers: P. Masters (Chief Mgr)
Immediate Holding Company: CHURCHILL CONTROLS LIMITED
Registration no: 01166152 **VAT No.:** GB 200 3873 07
Date established: 1974 **Turnover:** £1m - £2m **No.of Employees:** 1 - 10
Product Groups: 37

Date of Accounts	Mar 11	Mar 10	Mar 09
Working Capital	745	629	512
Fixed Assets	N/A	1	4
Current Assets	843	714	700

Data Systems Computers Ltd
Unit 21 Wellington Business Park Dukes Ride, Crowthorne, RG45 6LS
Tel: 01344-755000 **Fax:** 01344-779256
E-mail: sales@datasystemsltd.co.uk
Website: http://www.datasystemsltd.co.uk
Bank(s): Lloyds TSB Bank plc
Directors: J. Waters (MD)
Immediate Holding Company: DATA SYSTEMS (COMPUTERS) LIMITED
Registration no: 02179329 **Date established:** 1987 **Turnover:** £2m - £5m
No.of Employees: 11 - 20 **Product Groups:** 37, 44

Date of Accounts	Mar 12	Mar 11	Mar 10
Working Capital	285	130	65
Fixed Assets	104	55	53
Current Assets	1m	801	1m

G T S Flexible Materials Ltd
G T S House 3 Wellington Business Park, Crowthorne, RG45 6LS
Tel: 01344-762376 **Fax:** 01344-761615
E-mail: sales@gts-flexible.co.uk
Website: http://www.gts-flexible.co.uk
Directors: B. O'leary (Fin)
Immediate Holding Company: G T S FLEXIBLE MATERIALS LIMITED
Registration no: 01336286 **VAT No.:** GB 292 6749 15
Date established: 1977 **Turnover:** £10m - £20m **No.of Employees:** 1 - 10
Product Groups: 30

Date of Accounts	Nov 11	Nov 10	Nov 09
Sales Turnover	12m	8m	5m
Pre Tax Profit/Loss	3m	2m	450
Working Capital	7m	4m	3m
Fixed Assets	764	828	885
Current Assets	8m	6m	4m
Current Liabilities	973	843	258

Interface Force Measurements Ltd
Ground Floor Unit 19 Wellington Business Park Dukes Ride, Crowthorne, RG45 6LS
Tel: 01344-776666 **Fax:** 01344-774765
E-mail: admin@interface.uk.com
Website: http://www.interface.co.uk
Directors: N. Johnstone (MD)
Immediate Holding Company: INTERFACE FORCE MEASUREMENTS LIMITED
Registration no: 03000521 **Date established:** 1994
Turnover: £500,000 - £1m **No.of Employees:** 1 - 10 **Product Groups:** 37, 38, 44

Date of Accounts	Sep 11	Sep 10	Sep 09
Sales Turnover	691	701	634
Pre Tax Profit/Loss	34	-1	-0
Working Capital	384	387	415
Fixed Assets	59	45	32
Current Assets	516	438	519
Current Liabilities	32	N/A	N/A

Maypole Engineering Solutions
Unit G7 Crowthorne Business Estate Old Wokingham Road, Crowthorne, RG45 6AW
Tel: 01344-750650
E-mail: solutions@maypole-engineering.com
Website: http://www.maypole-engineering.com
Directors: J. Macswan (Fin), S. Macswan (MD)
Immediate Holding Company: MAYPOLE ENGINEERING SOLUTIONS LTD
Registration no: 04918046 **Date established:** 2003
No.of Employees: 1 - 10 **Product Groups:** 35, 39, 45

Date of Accounts	Oct 11	Oct 10	Oct 09
Working Capital	332	404	459
Fixed Assets	22	28	16
Current Assets	557	693	582

New Information Paradigms Ltd
Manhattan House 140 High Street, Crowthorne, RG45 7AY
Tel: 01344-753700 **Fax:** 01344-772510
E-mail: sales@nipltd.com
Website: http://www.nipltd.com
Directors: P. Hattersley (Fin)
Immediate Holding Company: NEW INFORMATION PARADIGMS LIMITED
Registration no: 02329007 **VAT No.:** GB 529 0840 42
Date established: 1988 **Turnover:** £1m - £2m **No.of Employees:** 1 - 10
Product Groups: 44

Date of Accounts	Sep 11	Sep 10	Sep 09
Working Capital	-45	-22	50
Fixed Assets	73	78	81
Current Assets	73	76	141

Paris Hose & Ducting Ltd
Unit 22 Wellington Business Park Dukes Ride, Crowthorne, RG45 6LS
Tel: 01344-758600 **Fax:** 01344-758610
E-mail: sales@parishose.co.uk
Website: http://www.parishose.com
Bank(s): HSBC,29 High Street, Camberley
Directors: M. White (MD), S. Curling (Co Sec)
Ultimate Holding Company: SPECIALIST DUCTING SUPPLIES LIMITED
Immediate Holding Company: PARIS HOSE & DUCTING LIMITED
Registration no: 02010194 **VAT No.:** GB 413 7690 51
Date established: 1986 **Turnover:** £1m - £2m **No.of Employees:** 11 - 20
Product Groups: 23, 29, 30, 36, 40, 45

see next page

Paris Hose & Ducting Ltd - Cont'd

Date of Accounts	May 11	May 10	May 09
Working Capital	389	283	409
Fixed Assets	12	21	25
Current Assets	662	505	608

Target Four Ltd
Manhattan House High Street, Crowthorne, RG45 7AY
Tel: 01344-762721
E-mail: helpdesk@targetfour.com
Website: http://www.targetfour.com
Managers: C. Hands (Projects)
Immediate Holding Company: TARGETFOUR LIMITED
Registration no: 02030315 **Date established:** 1986 **Turnover:** £1m - £2m
No.of Employees: 1 - 10 **Product Groups:** 44, 81

Date of Accounts	Oct 11	Oct 10	Oct 09
Working Capital	76	203	218
Fixed Assets	3	2	3
Current Assets	115	249	276

Hungerford

Andover Norton International Ltd
3 Old Farm Buildings Standen Manor Estate, Hungerford, RG17 0RB
Tel: 01488-686816 **Fax:** 01488-686826
E-mail: office@andover-norton.co.uk
Website: http://www.andover-norton.co.uk
Directors: N. Hopkins (Dir), P. Albutt (Fin)
Immediate Holding Company: ANDOVER NORTON INTERNATIONAL LIMITED
Registration no: 03020586 **VAT No.:** GB 619 9337 05
Date established: 1995 **Turnover:** Up to £250,000
No.of Employees: 1 - 10 **Product Groups:** 39, 40

Date of Accounts	Mar 12	Mar 11	Mar 10
Working Capital	270	177	93
Fixed Assets	24	21	20
Current Assets	925	850	818

Cablelines Pronet Ltd
1 Tealgate Charnham Park, Hungerford, RG17 0YT
Tel: 01488-689689 **Fax:** 01488-681515
E-mail: tim@pronet.co.uk
Website: http://www.cablelines.com
Bank(s): Barclays
Directors: P. Pearson (Dir), T. Coomer (Fin), P. Pearson (MD)
Managers: P. Rigby (Mgr)
Ultimate Holding Company: A & GP (GROUP) LIMITED
Immediate Holding Company: CABLELINES PRONET LIMITED
Registration no: 01693318 **Date established:** 1983
Turnover: £10m - £20m **No.of Employees:** 21 - 50 **Product Groups:** 37, 44

Date of Accounts	Feb 08	Feb 11	Feb 10
Working Capital	204	59	173
Current Assets	204	73	173

Chr. Hansen (UK) Ltd
2 Tealgate, Hungerford, RG17 0YT
Tel: 01488-689800 **Fax:** 01488-685436
E-mail: techservice-gb@chr-hansen.com
Website: http://www.chr-hansen.com
Directors: M. Hurley (MD)
Managers: M. Oaten (Quality Control)
Immediate Holding Company: Christian Hansen Holding A.S.
Registration no: 00145472 **Turnover:** £5m - £10m
No.of Employees: 21 - 50 **Product Groups:** 20, 32

Date of Accounts	Aug 08	Aug 07	Aug 06
Sales Turnover	13m	14m	14m
Pre Tax Profit/Loss	280	78	-169
Working Capital	-61	-348	-482
Fixed Assets	2m	2m	2m
Current Assets	3m	3m	3m
Current Liabilities	698	574	579

Martin Collins Enterprises Ltd
Cuckoo Copse Lambourn Woodlands, Hungerford, RG17 7TJ
Tel: 01488-71100 **Fax:** 01488-73177
E-mail: martin@mceltd.com
Website: http://www.mceltd.com
Directors: M. Collins (Dir)
Managers: E. Doughty (Sales Prom Mgr)
Ultimate Holding Company: MARTIN COLLINS ENTERPRISES (HOLDINGS) LIMITED
Immediate Holding Company: MARTIN COLLINS ENTERPRISES LIMITED
Registration no: 03659431 **Date established:** 1998
No.of Employees: 11 - 20 **Product Groups:** 49

Date of Accounts	Jul 10	Jul 09	Jul 08
Pre Tax Profit/Loss	N/A	N/A	-42
Working Capital	1m	1m	1m
Fixed Assets	172	205	254
Current Assets	3m	3m	3m
Current Liabilities	N/A	N/A	416

Combe Products
4 Wantage Road Eddington, Hungerford, RG17 0HA
Tel: 01488-684364 **Fax:** 01488-686425
E-mail: sales@combeproducts.com
Website: http://www.combeproducts.com
Directors: R. Chicken (Prop)
No.of Employees: 1 - 10 **Product Groups:** 37, 44, 52, 67

Components Electronic & Lighting Ltd
93 Chilton Way, Hungerford, RG17 0JF
Tel: 01488-684625 **Fax:** 01488-683184
E-mail: celclive@btconnect.com
Directors: C. Ealding (Dir), C. Ealding (MD)
Registration no: 03468373 **Turnover:** Up to £250,000
No.of Employees: 1 - 10 **Product Groups:** 30, 37

Compressor Products International Ltd
Unit 5 Smitham Bridge Road, Hungerford, RG17 0QP
Tel: 01488-684585 **Fax:** 01488-684001
E-mail: sales@compressor-products.com
Website: http://www.compressor-products.com
Bank(s): Lloyds TSB Bank plc
Managers: J. Nayler (Chief Mgr), V. Clarke (Buyer), M. Gundy
Ultimate Holding Company: ENPRO INDUSTRIES INC (USA)
Immediate Holding Company: COMPRESSOR PRODUCTS INTERNATIONAL LIMITED
Registration no: 01794754 **Date established:** 1984
Turnover: £10m - £20m **No.of Employees:** 51 - 100 **Product Groups:** 36, 39, 40, 45, 68

Date of Accounts	Dec 11	Dec 10	Dec 09
Sales Turnover	14m	13m	10m
Pre Tax Profit/Loss	3m	3m	-869
Working Capital	4m	3m	937
Fixed Assets	10m	10m	10m
Current Assets	8m	7m	6m
Current Liabilities	2m	928	885

Doves Farm Foods Ltd
Salisbury Road, Hungerford, RG17 0RF
Tel: 01488-684880 **Fax:** 01488-685235
E-mail: mail@dovesfarm.co.uk
Website: http://www.dovesfarm.co.uk
Bank(s): Barclays
Managers: C. Marriage
Immediate Holding Company: DOVES FARM FOODS LIMITED
Registration no: 02301391 **Date established:** 1988
Turnover: £10m - £20m **No.of Employees:** 51 - 100 **Product Groups:** 20, 41

Date of Accounts	Jun 12	Jun 11	Jun 10
Sales Turnover	13m	12m	11m
Pre Tax Profit/Loss	1m	1m	1m
Working Capital	4m	4m	4m
Fixed Assets	4m	3m	2m
Current Assets	5m	6m	5m
Current Liabilities	634	658	647

Dunedin Sports & Promotions
3 Chantry Mead, Hungerford, RG17 0HT
Tel: 01488-680622 **Fax:** 01488-683849
E-mail: dune@hung123.fsnet.co.uk
Directors: D. Clayton (Prop)
Date established: 1994 **No.of Employees:** 1 - 10 **Product Groups:** 24

Forest Companies Ltd
Unit 5 Northfield Farm, Great Shefford, Hungerford, RG17 7DQ
Tel: 01488-649120 **Fax:** 01488-649121
E-mail: sales@forestcompanies.com
Website: http://www.forestcompanies.com
Managers: K. Tym (Sales Admin)
Immediate Holding Company: FOREST COMPANIES LIMITED
Registration no: 04323316 **Date established:** 2001 **Turnover:** £1m - £2m
No.of Employees: 1 - 10 **Product Groups:** 27

Date of Accounts	Mar 11	Mar 10	Mar 09
Working Capital	538	383	502
Fixed Assets	109	106	17
Current Assets	2m	2m	1m

Gates Systems Ltd
Unit B Aerial Business Park, Lambourn Woodlands, Hungerford, RG17 7RZ
Tel: 01488-674750 **Fax:** 0800-328 8298
E-mail: info@gates.uk.com
Website: http://www.gates.uk.com
Directors: K. Witt (MD)
Immediate Holding Company: GATES SYSTEMS LIMITED
Registration no: 03305247 **Date established:** 1997 **Turnover:** £2m - £5m
No.of Employees: 1 - 10 **Product Groups:** 26, 35

Date of Accounts	Dec 11	Dec 10	Dec 09
Sales Turnover	4m	4m	N/A
Pre Tax Profit/Loss	662	579	N/A
Working Capital	2m	2m	1m
Fixed Assets	48	27	14
Current Assets	2m	2m	2m
Current Liabilities	217	197	N/A

Hyper Tec Ltd
2 Swangate, Hungerford, RG17 0YX
Tel: 08448-792282 **Fax:** 01488-686845
E-mail: info@hypertec.co.uk
Website: http://www.hypertec.co.uk
Directors: K. Groves (Co Sec), G. Ward (Sales), S. Smart (I.T. Dir), V. Roberts (Mkt Research), L. Denness (MD), L. Denness (MD)
Immediate Holding Company: HYPERTEC LIMITED
Registration no: 03258927 **VAT No.:** GB 642 2573 49
Date established: 1996 **Turnover:** £10m - £20m
No.of Employees: 21 - 50 **Product Groups:** 44

Date of Accounts	Jun 11	Jun 10	Jun 09
Sales Turnover	12m	11m	10m
Pre Tax Profit/Loss	422	82	329
Working Capital	1m	1m	2m
Fixed Assets	59	40	54
Current Assets	3m	3m	3m
Current Liabilities	622	544	624

Jacquet Weston Engineering
Tower Works Membury Airfield Industrial Estate, Lambourn Woodlands, Hungerford, RG17 7TJ
Tel: 01488-674400 **Fax:** 01488-674405
E-mail: info@jweltd.com
Website: http://www.jweltd.com
Bank(s): National Westminster Bank Plc
Directors: J. Lear (Fin), N. Weston (MD), T. Lear (Fin)
Immediate Holding Company: RHYMNEY ENGINEERING LIMITED
Registration no: 02083809 **VAT No.:** GB 757 2490 08
Date established: 1986 **Turnover:** £1m - £2m **No.of Employees:** 11 - 20
Product Groups: 38, 48

Kennet Plastics Ltd (t/a Tupak)
Unit A Aerial Business Park Lambourn Woodlands, Hungerford, RG17 7RZ
Tel: 01488-72070 **Fax:** 01488-71122
E-mail: kennetplastics@hotmail.com
Website: http://www.kennet-pack.co.uk
Directors: A. Hamilton (MD)
Immediate Holding Company: KENNET PLASTICS LIMITED
Registration no: 00880125 **VAT No.:** GB 207 7217 76
Date established: 1966 **Turnover:** £500,000 - £1m
No.of Employees: 1 - 10 **Product Groups:** 27

Date of Accounts	Sep 11	Sep 10	Sep 09
Working Capital	38	45	30
Fixed Assets	68	67	77
Current Assets	280	269	233

Pavigres UK Ltd
Unit E Aerial Business Park Lambourn Woodlands, Hungerford, RG17 7RZ
Tel: 01488-674500 **Fax:** 01488-674505
Website: http://www.pavigres.com
Managers: R. Milsom (Mgr)
Immediate Holding Company: PAVIGRES UK LIMITED
Registration no: 02569135 **Date established:** 1990 **Turnover:** £2m - £5m
No.of Employees: 1 - 10 **Product Groups:** 33

Date of Accounts	Dec 11	Dec 10	Dec 07
Working Capital	20	16	17
Fixed Assets	N/A	N/A	1
Current Assets	95	221	603

Pixie Developments Ltd
2 New Mills Industrial Estate Post Office Road, Inkpen, Hungerford, RG17 9PU
Tel: 01488-669184 **Fax:** 01488-669185
E-mail: info@pixiedevelopments.co.uk
Website: http://www.pixiedevelopments.co.uk
Directors: M. Player (MD)
Immediate Holding Company: PIXIE DEVELOPMENTS LIMITED
Registration no: 01340744 **VAT No.:** GB 302 2874 87
Date established: 1977 **Turnover:** £250,000 - £500,000
No.of Employees: 1 - 10 **Product Groups:** 30

Date of Accounts	Jul 11	Jul 10	Jul 09
Working Capital	71	56	53
Fixed Assets	257	254	249
Current Assets	178	151	114

Primac
Post Office Road Inkpen, Hungerford, RG17 9PU
Tel: 01488-668008 **Fax:** 01488-668883
E-mail: fred@primac.ltd.uk
Directors: I. Prismall (MD), V. Prismall (Fin)
Immediate Holding Company: PRIMAC LIMITED
Registration no: 01989995 **Date established:** 1986
Turnover: Up to £250,000 **No.of Employees:** 1 - 10 **Product Groups:** 26

Date of Accounts	Mar 11	Mar 10	Mar 09
Working Capital	-20	-9	-9
Fixed Assets	11	12	19
Current Assets	37	43	36

Safeguard Electronic Systems Ltd (t/a Thermatek)
Unit 5A Station Yard Station Road, Hungerford, RG17 0DY
Tel: 01488-684888 **Fax:** 01488-682686
E-mail: sales@thermatek.co.uk
Website: http://www.thermatek.co.uk
Directors: D. Lawrence (Dir)
Managers: D. Lawrence (Mgr)
Immediate Holding Company: SAFEGUARD ELECTRONIC SYSTEMS LIMITED
Registration no: 02119660 **VAT No.:** GB 569 9957 45
Date established: 1987 **Turnover:** £250,000 - £500,000
No.of Employees: 1 - 10 **Product Groups:** 37, 40, 42, 48

Date of Accounts	May 11	May 10	May 09
Working Capital	67	39	53
Fixed Assets	4	4	5
Current Assets	188	124	104
Current Liabilities	6	4	4

Saxon Industries
Everland Road, Hungerford, RG17 0DX
Tel: 01488-689400 **Fax:** 01488-684317
E-mail: info@saxon-brands.com
Website: http://www.saxon-brands.com
Bank(s): National Westminster, Liverpool
Directors: M. Rawings (Fin), T. Redfern (Fin)
Managers: V. Smith (Sales Prom Mgr), R. Sherwood (Purch Mgr), L. Sheridan, N. Matthews (Tech Serv Mgr)
Immediate Holding Company: H. YOUNG HOLDINGS P.L.C.
Registration no: 00706712 **VAT No.:** GB 578 4195 93
Date established: 1979 **Turnover:** £1m - £2m **No.of Employees:** 21 - 50
Product Groups: 36, 39, 41, 45, 68

Southern Sailplanes
Membury Airfield Industrial Estate Lambourn Woodlands, Hungerford, RG17 7TJ
Tel: 01488-71774 **Fax:** 01488-72482
E-mail: wendy@southernsailplanes.com
Website: http://southernsailplanes.com
Directors: S. Jones (Ptnr), J. Jones (Fin)
Immediate Holding Company: SOUTHERN SAILPLANES LIMITED
Registration no: 01778101 **Date established:** 1983
Turnover: Up to £250,000 **No.of Employees:** 1 - 10 **Product Groups:** 39

Speedwell Automation Ltd
The Lodge East Shefford, Great Shefford, Hungerford, RG17 7EF
Tel: 01488-648119
E-mail: sales@speedgates.co.uk
Website: http://www.speedgates.co.uk
Directors: P. Croysdill (Fin), A. Croysdill (MD)
Ultimate Holding Company: B S POVEY 1 LIMITED
Immediate Holding Company: SPEEDWELL AUTOMATION LTD
Registration no: 03226885 **Date established:** 1996
Turnover: Up to £250,000 **No.of Employees:** 1 - 10 **Product Groups:** 25, 35, 36, 49, 66

Date of Accounts	Mar 11	Mar 10	Mar 09
Working Capital	-8	-28	-25
Fixed Assets	15	6	13
Current Assets	39	19	21

Triteq Ltd
Unit 1 The Innovation Centre Station Road, Hungerford, RG17 0DY
Tel: 01488-684554 **Fax:** 01488-685335
E-mail: info@triteq.com
Website: http://www.triteq.com
Directors: S. Lane (Dir), S. Leach (Pers)
Managers: V. Monger (Purch Mgr), A. Hobbs (Mktg Serv Mgr), S. Grindell (Chief Acct)
Immediate Holding Company: TRITEQ LIMITED
Registration no: 02757740 **Date established:** 1992
No.of Employees: 21 - 50 **Product Groups:** 37, 84, 85

Date of Accounts	Mar 11	Mar 10	Mar 09
Working Capital	8	84	111
Fixed Assets	132	49	11
Current Assets	859	820	481

Tynemount
Unit 5 Northfield Farm Great Shefford, Hungerford, RG17 7DQ
Tel: 01488-648865 **Fax:** 01488-648816
E-mail: sales@tynemount.com
Website: http://www.tynemount.com
Directors: J. Kilczynski (Prop)
Immediate Holding Company: TYNEMOUNT LIMITED
Registration no: 01226791 **VAT No.:** GB 329 9414 30
Date established: 1975 **No.of Employees:** 1 - 10 **Product Groups:** 37

Date of Accounts	Jun 11	Jun 10	Jun 09
Working Capital	376	364	393
Fixed Assets	N/A	N/A	3
Current Assets	435	438	480

Ups Systems plc
Herongate, Hungerford, RG17 0YU
Tel: 01488-680500 **Fax:** 01488-686315
E-mail: sales@upssystems.co.uk
Website: http://www.upssystems.co.uk
Directors: K. Sperrey (Chief Op Offcr), S. Benger (Sales)
Managers: R. Foggitt (Mktg Serv Mgr), T. Chicken (Tech Serv Mgr), C. Neild (Fin Mgr)
Immediate Holding Company: U.P.S SYSTEMS PLC
Registration no: 02784286 **Date established:** 1993 **Turnover:** £2m - £5m
No.of Employees: 21 - 50 **Product Groups:** 37

Date of Accounts	Jun 11	Jun 10	Jun 09
Sales Turnover	5m	5m	5m
Pre Tax Profit/Loss	-96	97	265
Working Capital	224	345	689
Fixed Assets	3	4	N/A
Current Assets	1m	1m	2m
Current Liabilities	699	620	797

Westfield Distribution Ltd
Unit 2 Station Yard Station Road, Hungerford, RG17 0DY
Tel: 01488-685183 **Fax:** 01488-685430
E-mail: sales@westfield.co.uk
Website: http://www.westfield.co.uk
Directors: S. Chappell (MD)
Immediate Holding Company: WESTFIELD DISTRIBUTION LIMITED
Registration no: 02102267 **Date established:** 1987 **Turnover:** £2m - £5m
No.of Employees: 1 - 10 **Product Groups:** 30, 35, 36

Date of Accounts	Oct 11	Oct 10	Oct 09
Working Capital	129	96	85
Fixed Assets	10	12	16
Current Assets	219	162	138

Maidenhead

A B Machine Control Services Ltd
49 Forlease Road, Maidenhead, SL6 1RX
Tel: 01628-639991 **Fax:** 01628-639991
Website: http://www.abfoodmachinery.co.uk
Directors: A. Bhogal (Dir)
Immediate Holding Company: AB MACHINE CONTROL SERVICES LIMITED
Registration no: 06036762 **Date established:** 2006
No.of Employees: 1 - 10 **Product Groups:** 20, 40, 41

Date of Accounts	Jan 12	Jan 11	Jan 10
Sales Turnover	7	9	19
Pre Tax Profit/Loss	-3	-7	-1
Working Capital	2	N/A	-0
Fixed Assets	12	12	14
Current Assets	2	2	2
Current Liabilities	N/A	1	1

A L P Electrical Ltd
70 St Marks Road, Maidenhead, SL6 6DW
Tel: 01628-633998 **Fax:** 01628-760981
E-mail: alp.electrical@btinternet.com
Website: http://www.alpelectrical.co.uk
Directors: A. Pattinson (MD), V. Purchese (Co Sec)
Immediate Holding Company: A.L.P. ELECTRICAL (MAIDENHEAD) LIMITED
Registration no: 01096513 **VAT No.:** GB 208 7901 57
Date established: 1973 **Turnover:** £1m - £2m **No.of Employees:** 1 - 10
Product Groups: 37, 44, 52

Date of Accounts	Nov 11	Nov 10	Nov 09
Sales Turnover	2m	1m	1m
Pre Tax Profit/Loss	3	56	-189
Working Capital	62	58	-11
Fixed Assets	58	50	63
Current Assets	542	379	339
Current Liabilities	94	98	74

Abbott Laboratories Ltd
Abbot House Vanwall Business Park, Maidenhead, SL6 4XE
Tel: 0800-973246 **Fax:** 01628-644305
Website: http://www.abbott.com
Bank(s): National Westminster Bank Plc
Directors: J. Ranking (Dir)
Managers: L. Annereau (Cust Serv Mgr), T. Trevor (Sales Prom Mgr), A. Bufton (Mktg Serv Mgr)
Ultimate Holding Company: ABBOTT LABORATORIES (USA)
Immediate Holding Company: ABBOTT LABORATORIES LIMITED
Registration no: 00329102 **Date established:** 1937
Turnover: £500m - £1,000m **No.of Employees:** 251 - 500
Product Groups: 31, 37

Date of Accounts	Dec 11	Dec 10	Nov 09
Sales Turnover	536m	539m	471m
Pre Tax Profit/Loss	18m	-31m	36m
Working Capital	161m	155m	222m
Fixed Assets	94m	88m	94m
Current Assets	248m	222m	293m
Current Liabilities	46m	33m	31m

Acorn Cutters
Unit 13 Rawcliffe House, Maidenhead, SL6 1AP
Tel: 01628-781401 **Fax:** 01628-75051
Managers: C. Hing (Mgr)
Registration no: 03045658 **Date established:** 1995
No.of Employees: 1 - 10 **Product Groups:** 46

Adelante Software Ltd
Unit 22 Grove Park Industrial Estate Waltham Road, White Waltham, Maidenhead, SL6 3LW
Tel: 01628-820500 **Fax:** 01628-820509
E-mail: darrellb@adelante.co.uk
Website: http://www.adelante.co.uk
Directors: D. Bluck (MD), E. Williamson (Dir)
Managers: D. Bluck (Chief Acct)
Immediate Holding Company: ADELANTE SOFTWARE LTD
Registration no: 04450760 **Date established:** 2002 **Turnover:** £1m - £2m
No.of Employees: 11 - 20 **Product Groups:** 44

Date of Accounts	Apr 08	Apr 07	Apr 06
Working Capital	35	4	-15
Fixed Assets	25	18	14
Current Assets	260	165	190
Current Liabilities	225	161	205

Aker Subsea Ltd
Unit 12 Clivemont Road, Cordwallis Industrial Estate, Maidenhead, SL6 7BZ
Tel: 01628-506560 **Fax:** 01628-506501
E-mail: info@kvaerner.com
Website: http://www.akerkvaerner.com
Directors: J. Cardno (Purch), P. Helsing (MD)
Managers: M. Taulois (Sales & Mktg Mg), A. Warpole (Admin Off)
Ultimate Holding Company: Kvaerner A/S (Norway)
Immediate Holding Company: Kvaerner Oilfield Products Group Ltd
Registration no: 04977339 **VAT No.:** GB 495 4446 09
Turnover: £50m - £75m **No.of Employees:** 21 - 50 **Product Groups:** 38

Date of Accounts	Dec 09	Dec 08	Dec 07
Sales Turnover	239m	228m	200m
Pre Tax Profit/Loss	26m	13m	6m
Working Capital	29m	-11m	11m
Fixed Assets	20m	55m	30m
Current Assets	115m	153m	89m
Current Liabilities	29m	57m	6m

Allied Bakeries Ltd
Vanwell Road, Maidenhead, SL6 4UF
Tel: 01628-764300 **Fax:** 01628-764390
E-mail: mark.fairweather@alliedbakeries.co.uk
Website: http://www.alliedbakeries.co.uk
Directors: M. Fairweather (Grp Chief Exec), W. Hudson (Fin)
Ultimate Holding Company: WITTINGTON INVESTMENTS LIMITED
Immediate Holding Company: ALLIED BAKERIES LIMITED
Registration no: 00214377 **Date established:** 2026
Turnover: £250m - £500m **No.of Employees:** 101 - 250
Product Groups: 62

Date of Accounts	Sep 10	Sep 11	Sep 08
Working Capital	10	10	10
Current Assets	10	10	10

Alsigns Surelite Ltd (Self Luminous)
Unit 7a First Floor Waldeck House Waldeck Road, Maidenhead, SL6 8BR
Tel: 01628-636992 **Fax:** 01780-479032
Website: http://www.surelite.co.uk
Directors: B. Chapman (MD)
Immediate Holding Company: ALSIGNS [BEST-SURELITE] SELF-POWERED LIMITED
Registration no: 02120660 **Date established:** 1987
Turnover: Up to £250,000 **No.of Employees:** 1 - 10 **Product Groups:** 33, 37, 61

Alternative Minds Limited
Unit 25 Cookham Road, Maidenhead, SL6 7EF
Tel: 020-8123 6968 **Fax:** 0871-4290088
E-mail: contactus@alternativeminds.com
Website: http://www.alternativeminds.com
Directors: J. Hurst (Dir)
Registration no: 05168709 **Turnover:** £250,000 - £500,000
No.of Employees: 11 - 20 **Product Groups:** 80

And Design
39 Derment Drive, Maidenhead, SL6 6LE
Tel: 07747-782816
E-mail: ant@and-design.co.uk
Website: http://www.and-design.co.uk
Directors: A. Noyce (Design)
Registration no: 03407876 **Turnover:** Up to £250,000
No.of Employees: 1 - 10 **Product Groups:** 44

Asset Lifecycle Management
Mga House Ray Mill Road East, Maidenhead, SL6 8ST
Tel: 01628-626018 **Fax:** 01628-626079
Directors: J. Evans (Dir), J. Holder (Fin), J. Mcgovern (Dir), J. McGovern (MD)
Ultimate Holding Company: SAMSON LIMITED
Immediate Holding Company: ASSET LIFECYCLE MANAGEMENT LIMITED
Registration no: 04594291 **Date established:** 2002
No.of Employees: 1 - 10 **Product Groups:** 80, 81

Date of Accounts	Jul 07	Jul 06
Working Capital	-157	-146
Fixed Assets	N/A	28
Current Assets	10	1
Current Liabilities	166	147
Total Share Capital	25	25

Aventis Pasteur M S D Ltd
Mallards Reach Bridge Avenue, Maidenhead, SL6 1QP
Tel: 01628-785281 **Fax:** 01628-671722
E-mail: enquiries@aventispasteur.com
Website: http://www.sanofi-aventis.com
Directors: C. Sunshine (Co Sec), R. Stubbins (MD), A. Meyer (Pers)
Immediate Holding Company: SANOFI PASTEUR MSD LIMITED
Registration no: 01227497 **VAT No.:** GB 247 9665 11
Date established: 1975 **Turnover:** £125m - £250m
No.of Employees: 1 - 10 **Product Groups:** 63

Date of Accounts	Dec 07	Dec 06	Dec 05
Sales Turnover	127180	133610	140720
Pre Tax Profit/Loss	-4110	8460	21100
Working Capital	3870	6730	14880
Fixed Assets	350	430	390
Current Assets	44140	54430	43100
Current Liabilities	40270	47700	28220
Total Share Capital	300	300	300
ROCE% (Return on Capital Employed)	-97.4	118.2	138.2
ROT% (Return on Turnover)	-3.2	6.3	15.0

Barr Rosin Ltd
48 Bell Street, Maidenhead, SL6 1BR
Tel: 01628-641700 **Fax:** 01628-776118
E-mail: steve@barr-rosin.co.uk
Website: http://www.barr-rosin.com
Bank(s): Barclays, 93 Baker St, W1
Directors: S. Harrison (Fin)
Ultimate Holding Company: GEA AG
Immediate Holding Company: GEA BARR-ROSIN LIMITED
Registration no: 00636280 **VAT No.:** GB 277 8743 01
Date established: 1959 **Turnover:** £5m - £10m **No.of Employees:** 11 - 20
Product Groups: 40, 41, 42, 45

Date of Accounts	Dec 11	Dec 10	Dec 09
Sales Turnover	11m	8m	14m
Pre Tax Profit/Loss	503	388	338
Working Capital	2m	3m	3m
Fixed Assets	626	554	578
Current Assets	6m	8m	8m
Current Liabilities	2m	3m	1m

Benz Oldco
The Mews Guards Club Road, Maidenhead, SL6 8DN
Tel: 0845-170 0123 **Fax:** 0845-390 0123
E-mail: sales@khbenz.co.uk
Website: http://www.khbenz.co.uk
Directors: C. Benz (Fin)
Immediate Holding Company: BENZ LIMITED
Registration no: 02419916 **Date established:** 1989
Turnover: £250,000 - £500,000 **No.of Employees:** 1 - 10
Product Groups: 47

Date of Accounts	Dec 11	Dec 10	Dec 09
Working Capital	27	16	23
Fixed Assets	9	12	2
Current Assets	44	24	31

B F S International
20 Bray Road, Maidenhead, SL6 1UE
Tel: 01628-671458 **Fax:** 01628-784337
E-mail: sales@bfs-international.co.uk
Website: http://www.bfs-international.co.uk
Directors: B. Shepherd (Prop)
Turnover: £500,000 - £1m **No.of Employees:** 1 - 10 **Product Groups:** 36, 40, 42, 61, 67, 68

Britannia 2000 Ltd
Unit 5-9 Cedar Court Grove Park Industrial Estate Waltham Road, White Waltham, Maidenhead, SL6 3LW
Tel: 01628-829356 **Fax:** 01628-824316
E-mail: info@britannia2000.co.uk
Website: http://www.britannia2000.co.uk
Bank(s): Lloyds
Directors: H. Tomes (Fin), W. Jones (MD)
Managers: A. Davies (Sales & Mktg Mg)
Immediate Holding Company: BRITANNIA 2000 LIMITED
Registration no: 03371602 **VAT No.:** 697 500 408 **Date established:** 1997
Turnover: £500,000 - £1m **No.of Employees:** 11 - 20
Product Groups: 37, 40

Date of Accounts	Apr 11	Apr 10	Apr 09
Working Capital	545	392	295
Fixed Assets	80	33	31
Current Assets	785	899	1m

C Brewer & Sons
Reform Road, Maidenhead, SL6 8DA
Tel: 01628-672616 **Fax:** 01628-776182
E-mail: decorating@brewers.co.uk
Website: http://www.brewers.co.uk
Managers: M. Perry (District Mgr)
Immediate Holding Company: ULTRAQUICK LIMITED
Registration no: 00203852 **Date established:** 1985
Turnover: £10m - £20m **No.of Employees:** 21 - 50 **Product Groups:** 27, 30, 32

Date of Accounts	Dec 11	Dec 10	Dec 09
Working Capital	-397	-347	-142
Fixed Assets	615	620	499
Current Assets	103	68	60

Chartered Institute Of Marketing
Moor Hall Cookham, Maidenhead, SL6 9QH
Tel: 01628-427500 **Fax:** 01628-427499
E-mail: reception@cim.co.uk
Website: http://www.cim.co.uk
Bank(s): Royal Bank of Scotland, Cavendish Square, London W1
Directors: S. Mahoney (Fin)
Managers: T. Blount (Personnel), J. Sutton, R. Jones (Mktg Serv Mgr)
Ultimate Holding Company: THE CHARTERED INSTITUTE OF MARKETING
Immediate Holding Company: MARKETING FOUNDATION(THE)
Registration no: 01423105 **Date established:** 1979
Turnover: £10m - £20m **No.of Employees:** 101 - 250
Product Groups: 80, 81, 86, 87

Date of Accounts	Jun 10	Jun 09	Jun 08
Pre Tax Profit/Loss	-0	N/A	-2

Cincom Systems UK Ltd
1 Grenfell Road, Maidenhead, SL6 1HN
Tel: 01628-542300 **Fax:** 01625-533223
E-mail: uking@cincom.com
Website: http://www.cincom.com
Bank(s): Barclays, Slough
Directors: U. King (Fin), T. King (Fin)
Managers: B. Craig (Tech Serv Mgr), G. Pinkhardt
Ultimate Holding Company: CINCOM SYSTEMS INC (USA)
Immediate Holding Company: CINCOM SYSTEMS (UK) LIMITED
Registration no: 01666547 **VAT No.:** GB 370 2208 87
Date established: 1982 **Turnover:** £10m - £20m
No.of Employees: 51 - 100 **Product Groups:** 44

Date of Accounts	Sep 11	Sep 10	Sep 09
Sales Turnover	11m	11m	11m
Pre Tax Profit/Loss	218	770	769
Working Capital	8m	8m	8m
Fixed Assets	320	358	353
Current Assets	13m	14m	13m
Current Liabilities	4m	6m	5m

Cliveden House Hotel
Taplow, Maidenhead, SL6 0JF
Tel: 01628-668561 **Fax:** 01628-661837
E-mail: reservations@clivedenhouse.co.uk
Website: http://www.clivedenhouse.co.uk
Managers: N. Gamble (Chief Mgr), T. Solarz
Registration no: 04583951 **No.of Employees:** 51 - 100
Product Groups: 69

Conference Contacts Ltd
16 College Avenue, Maidenhead, SL6 6AX
Tel: 01628-773300 **Fax:** 01628-621033
E-mail: enquiries@conferencecontacts.co.uk
Website: http://www.conferencecontacts.co.uk
Managers: D. Ellis
Immediate Holding Company: CONFERENCE CONTACTS LIMITED
Registration no: 02118204 **Date established:** 1987 **Turnover:** £1m - £2m
No.of Employees: 1 - 10 **Product Groups:** 89

Date of Accounts	Apr 11	Apr 10	Apr 09
Sales Turnover	N/A	1m	901
Pre Tax Profit/Loss	N/A	40	-11
Working Capital	113	159	130
Fixed Assets	8	24	19
Current Assets	784	513	412
Current Liabilities	N/A	86	28

D B Marine
Cookham Bridge Cookham On Thames, Cookham, Maidenhead, SL6 9SN
Tel: 01628-526032 **Fax:** 01628-520564
E-mail: sales@dbmarine.co.uk
Website: http://www.dbmarine.co.uk
Directors: N. Jankovic (Fin)
Immediate Holding Company: D B MARINE LIMITED
Registration no: 05308456 **VAT No.:** GB 302 0600 37
Date established: 2004 **Turnover:** £500,000 - £1m
No.of Employees: 1 - 10 **Product Groups:** 40, 68

Date of Accounts	Dec 11	Dec 10	Dec 09
Working Capital	8	6	4
Current Assets	19	7	14

Digital Space
Stroud Farm Road Holyport, Maidenhead, SL6 2LJ
Tel: 01628-636513
E-mail: info@digitalspace-uk.com
Website: http://www.digitalspace-uk.com
Directors: A. Edwards (Prop)
Turnover: Up to £250,000 **No.of Employees:** 1 - 10 **Product Groups:** 35, 49, 81

A R Fabb Bros Ltd
29-31 Risborough Road, Maidenhead, SL6 7BJ
Tel: 01628-623533 **Fax:** 01628-622705
E-mail: info@fabb.co.uk
Website: http://www.fabb.co.uk
Directors: A. Quick (Jt MD), E. Quick (Jt MD)
Immediate Holding Company: A.R.Fabb Bros.Limited
Registration no: 00370523 **VAT No.:** GB 207 8789 26
Date established: 1941 **Turnover:** £250,000 - £500,000
No.of Employees: 1 - 10 **Product Groups:** 49

Force Components 89 Ltd
Maple Court Grove Park Industrial Estate Waltham Road, White Waltham, Maidenhead, SL6 3LW
Tel: 07768-723239 **Fax:** 01628-825530
E-mail: sales@force89.co.uk
Website: http://www.force89.co.uk
Directors: N. Hopkins (MD)
Registration no: 01738932 **VAT No.:** GB 532 1576 63
Turnover: £2m - £5m **No.of Employees:** 1 - 10 **Product Groups:** 37, 44

Formscan Limited
Park House, Kidwells Park Drive,, Maidenhead, SL6 8AQ
Tel: 0844-561 7276 **Fax:** 07006-082546
E-mail: info@formscan.com
Website: http://www.formscan.com
Directors: A. Discipio (Dir), C. Haden (MD), J. Cramer (Grp Chief Exec), M. Roche (Dir)
Managers: A. Freer (Fin Mgr)
Ultimate Holding Company: ANACOMP INC (USA)
Immediate Holding Company: Anacomp Holdings Ltd
Registration no: 03587758 **Date established:** 2001
Turnover: Over £1,000m **No.of Employees:** 21 - 50 **Product Groups:** 44

Date of Accounts	Sep 07
Sales Turnover	11030
Pre Tax Profit/Loss	-2010
Working Capital	-1250
Fixed Assets	430
Current Assets	9800
Current Liabilities	11050
ROCE% (Return on Capital Employed)	245.1

Hamilton Design Ltd
Netherclift Nurseries Green Lane, Littlewick Green, Maidenhead, SL6 3RH
Tel: 01628-826747
E-mail: info@hamilton-design.co.uk
Website: http://www.hamilton-design.co.uk
Directors: C. Hamilton (Co Sec), R. Hamilton (MD)
Immediate Holding Company: T.W. HAMILTON DESIGN LIMITED
Registration no: 01410194 **VAT No.:** GB 321 3327 06
Date established: 1979 **No.of Employees:** 1 - 10 **Product Groups:** 41, 67

Date of Accounts	Mar 12	Mar 11	Mar 10
Working Capital	248	305	328
Fixed Assets	7	4	4
Current Assets	289	352	398

Hamptons International
11-13 Queen Street, Maidenhead, SL6 1NB
Tel: 01628-622131 **Fax:** 01628-785446
E-mail: maidenhead@hamptons-int.com
Website: http://www.hamptons.co.uk
Managers: C. Butler (Mgr)
Registration no: 02036215 **No.of Employees:** 11 - 20 **Product Groups:** 80

Hanson Building Products
Hanson House 14 Castle Hill, Maidenhead, SL6 4JJ
Tel: 01628-774100 **Fax:** 020-7235 3455
E-mail: enquiries@hanson.com
Website: http://www.hanson.com
Bank(s): Lloyds TSB Bank plc
Directors: C. Mayo (Pers)
Managers: P. O'shea
Ultimate Holding Company: HEIDELBERG CEMENT AG (GERMANY)
Immediate Holding Company: HANSON BUILDING PRODUCTS (2003) LIMITED
Registration no: 02448833 **Date established:** 1989
Turnover: Over £1,000m **No.of Employees:** 51 - 100 **Product Groups:** 61, 87

Date of Accounts	Dec 11	Dec 10	Dec 09
Sales Turnover	N/A	N/A	50
Pre Tax Profit/Loss	N/A	234	5m
Working Capital	1326m	1326m	1326m
Fixed Assets	189m	189m	189m
Current Assets	1718m	1718m	1718m

Hitachi Europe Ltd
Whitebrook Park Lower Cookham Road, Maidenhead, SL6 8XY
Tel: 01628-585000 **Fax:** 01628-778322
E-mail: dave.gilbert@hitachi-eu.com
Website: http://www.hitachi-eu.com
Bank(s): National Westminster Bank Plc
Directors: A. Tolan (Co Sec), H. Ariyasu (MD), M. Yotsu (MD)
Managers: V. Pitt (Mktg Serv Mgr), D. Hancock (Buyer)
Ultimate Holding Company: HITACHI LTD (JAPAN)
Immediate Holding Company: HITACHI EUROPE LIMITED
Registration no: 02210686 **VAT No.:** GB 603 9214 64
Date established: 1988 **Turnover:** £250m - £500m
No.of Employees: 251 - 500 **Product Groups:** 37, 44

Date of Accounts	Mar 11	Mar 10	Mar 09
Sales Turnover	290m	574m	480m
Pre Tax Profit/Loss	5m	2m	-11m
Working Capital	-980	-9m	-12m
Fixed Assets	87m	91m	97m
Current Assets	297m	255m	511m
Current Liabilities	26m	25m	22m

Hooke Ventilation Services
Hans House Cordwallis Street, Maidenhead, SL6 7BE
Tel: 01628-672244 **Fax:** 01628-784436
Directors: R. Baker (Ptnr)
Immediate Holding Company: IEC WINE SERVICES LIMITED
Registration no: 00988751 **Date established:** 2006
Turnover: £20m - £50m **No.of Employees:** 1 - 10 **Product Groups:** 37, 40, 48

Instrument Plastics Ltd
33-37 Kings Grove Industrial Estate Kings Grove, Maidenhead, SL6 4DP
Tel: 01628-770018 **Fax:** 01628-773299
E-mail: tim@instrumentplastics.co.uk
Website: http://www.instrumentplastics.co.uk
Directors: T. Butterly (MD)
Managers: R. Fishmistr (Sales Prom Mgr), D. Hawkins (Fin Mgr)
Immediate Holding Company: INSTRUMENT PLASTICS LIMITED
Registration no: 02180804 **Date established:** 1987 **Turnover:** £1m - £2m
No.of Employees: 11 - 20 **Product Groups:** 38

Date of Accounts	Nov 11	Nov 10	Nov 09
Working Capital	629	565	636
Fixed Assets	273	382	289
Current Assets	799	780	881

Jet Lube UK Ltd
Reform Road, Maidenhead, SL6 8BY
Tel: 01628-631913 **Fax:** 01628-773138
E-mail: uksales@jetlube.com
Website: http://www.jet-lube.co.uk
Bank(s): Barclays, High Street.
Managers: G. Boots (Chief Mgr)
Ultimate Holding Company: CAPITAL SOUTHWEST CORPORATION (USA)
Immediate Holding Company: JET-LUBE (UK) LIMITED
Registration no: 00739489 **Date established:** 1962 **Turnover:** £2m - £5m
No.of Employees: 11 - 20 **Product Groups:** 31, 32, 66

Date of Accounts	Mar 11	Mar 10	Mar 09
Sales Turnover	4m	3m	4m
Pre Tax Profit/Loss	536	606	744
Working Capital	3m	2m	2m
Fixed Assets	358	339	338
Current Assets	3m	3m	2m
Current Liabilities	218	202	193

Jetnexus Solutions Ltd
Grove Park Industrial Estate Waltham Road, White Waltham, Maidenhead, SL6 3LW
Tel: 08703-825050
E-mail: info@jetnexus.com
Website: http://www.jetnexus.com
Managers: E. Hawkins (Mktg Serv Mgr)
Immediate Holding Company: JETNEXUS SOLUTIONS LTD
Registration no: 04514991 **Date established:** 2002
No.of Employees: 1 - 10 **Product Groups:** 44

Date of Accounts	Mar 12	Mar 11	Mar 10
Working Capital	66	94	-2
Fixed Assets	89	88	17
Current Assets	451	720	621

Johnson & Johnson Ltd
Foundation Park Roxborough Way, Maidenhead, SL6 3UG
Tel: 01628-822222 **Fax:** 01628-821222
Website: http://www.jnj.com
Bank(s): Barclays
Ultimate Holding Company: JOHNSON & JOHNSON (USA)
Immediate Holding Company: JOHNSON & JOHNSON LIMITED
Registration no: 02175750 **VAT No.:** GB 349 1430 58
Date established: 1987 **Turnover:** £20m - £50m
No.of Employees: 501 - 1000 **Product Groups:** 20, 24, 30, 31, 32, 40, 62

Date of Accounts	Dec 08	Jan 10	Jan 11
Sales Turnover	73m	60m	45m
Pre Tax Profit/Loss	18m	6m	7m
Working Capital	-9m	-4m	22m
Fixed Assets	22m	22m	2m
Current Assets	180m	160m	171m
Current Liabilities	46m	12m	8m

Kenlowe Accessories & Co. Ltd
Burchetts Green, Maidenhead, SL6 6QU
Tel: 01628-823303 **Fax:** 01628-823451
E-mail: sales@kenlowe.com
Website: http://www.kenlowe.com
Directors: P. Lowe (MD), C. Lowe (Fin)
Immediate Holding Company: KENLOWE ACCESSORIES AND COMPANY LIMITED
Registration no: 00685680 **VAT No.:** GB 442 3084 75
Date established: 1961 **Turnover:** £500,000 - £1m
No.of Employees: 1 - 10 **Product Groups:** 38, 39, 40, 68

Date of Accounts	Dec 10	Dec 09	Dec 08
Working Capital	119	119	119
Current Assets	119	119	119

Kepner Tregoe Ltd
Moorbridge Court Moorbridge Road, Maidenhead, SL6 8LT
Tel: 01628-778776 **Fax:** 01753-854929
E-mail: info@kepner-tregoe.com
Website: http://www.kepner-tregoe.com
Directors: S. Wheeler (Fin)
Ultimate Holding Company: KEPNER TREGOE INC (USA)
Immediate Holding Company: KEPNER-TREGOE LIMITED
Registration no: 00887737 **Date established:** 1966 **Turnover:** £2m - £5m
No.of Employees: 11 - 20 **Product Groups:** 80, 86

Date of Accounts	Dec 11	Dec 10	Dec 09
Working Capital	-1m	-630	-262
Fixed Assets	31	33	47
Current Assets	400	927	819

Label-Form Ltd
Reform Road, Maidenhead, SL6 8BY
Tel: 01628-782082 **Fax:** 01628-770879
E-mail: sales@label-form.co.uk
Website: http://www.label-form.co.uk
Directors: D. Millett (MD)
Managers: S. Serls (Sales Prom Mgr), S. Oliver (Prod Mgr)
Ultimate Holding Company: A&B HIGH HOLDINGS LIMITED
Immediate Holding Company: LABEL-FORM LIMITED
Registration no: 00815002 **VAT No.:** GB 208 2368 74
Date established: 1964 **Turnover:** £2m - £5m **No.of Employees:** 1 - 10
Product Groups: 27, 28, 30

Date of Accounts	Dec 11	Dec 10	Dec 09
Working Capital	230	81	265
Fixed Assets	154	638	670
Current Assets	570	473	536
Current Liabilities	N/A	4	N/A

Link Mediapack Ltd
Link House Gardner Road, Maidenhead, SL6 7TU
Tel: 01628-776528 **Fax:** 01628-777097
E-mail: kevin@linkindustrial.co.uk
Website: http://www.linkmediapac.com
Directors: K. French (MD)
Managers: D. Dunster (Ops Mgr)
Immediate Holding Company: Link Mediapac Ltd
Registration no: 03527277 **No.of Employees:** 1 - 10 **Product Groups:** 48, 76

Date of Accounts	Apr 08
Working Capital	327
Fixed Assets	70
Current Assets	471
Current Liabilities	144

M A S T International Group Ltd
Hermitage House Bath Road, Taplow, Maidenhead, SL6 0AR
Tel: 01628-784062 **Fax:** 01628-773061
E-mail: earmstrong@mast.co.uk
Website: http://www.mast.co.uk
Bank(s): National Westminster
Directors: S. Kennedy (MD), E. Armstrong (Co Sec)
Immediate Holding Company: MAST INTERNATIONAL GROUP LIMITED
Registration no: 02993949 **VAT No.:** GB 604 1179 74
Date established: 1994 **Turnover:** £1m - £2m **No.of Employees:** 11 - 20
Product Groups: 69, 81, 86

Date of Accounts	Dec 11	Dec 10	Dec 09
Sales Turnover	2m	2m	2m
Pre Tax Profit/Loss	5	9	10
Working Capital	-76	-79	-42
Fixed Assets	228	226	186
Current Assets	261	311	271
Current Liabilities	89	265	202

Mcgraw-Hill International UK Ltd
Mcgraw-Hill House Shoppenhangers Road, Maidenhead, SL6 2QL
Tel: 01628-502500 **Fax:** 01628-770224
E-mail: john_donovan@mcgraw-hill.com
Website: http://www.mcgraw-hill.co.uk
Bank(s): National Westminster Bank Plc
Directors: J. Donovan (Dir), P. Samson (Fin), R. Brotherton (Pers)
Ultimate Holding Company: MCGRAW-HILL COMPANIES INC (USA)
Immediate Holding Company: MCGRAW-HILL INTERNATIONAL (U.K.) LIMITED
Registration no: 00064070 **Date established:** 1989
Turnover: £125m - £250m **No.of Employees:** 101 - 250
Product Groups: 28, 64

Date of Accounts	Dec 11	Dec 10	Dec 09
Sales Turnover	145m	150m	224m
Pre Tax Profit/Loss	28m	248m	27m
Working Capital	13m	21m	47m
Fixed Assets	35m	38m	34m
Current Assets	88m	78m	125m
Current Liabilities	39m	36m	68m

Maidenhead Plating
3 Martin Road, Maidenhead, SL6 7DE
Tel: 01628-783747 **Fax:** 01628-778717
Directors: S. Hodges (Ptnr)
Date established: 1990 **No.of Employees:** 1 - 10 **Product Groups:** 46, 48

Maplin Electronics Ltd
Unit 3 Maidenhead Retail Park, Maidenhead, SL6 1AA
Tel: 01628-776473
E-mail: maidenhead@maplin.co.uk
Website: http://www.maplin.co.uk
Managers: P. Vince
Ultimate Holding Company: MONTAGU PRIVATE EQUITY LLP
Immediate Holding Company: MAPLIN ELECTRONICS LIMITED
Registration no: 01264385 **Date established:** 1976
Turnover: £125m - £250m **No.of Employees:** 1 - 10 **Product Groups:** 37, 61

Date of Accounts	Dec 11	Dec 08	Dec 09
Sales Turnover	205m	204m	204m
Pre Tax Profit/Loss	25m	32m	35m
Working Capital	118m	49m	75m
Fixed Assets	27m	28m	28m
Current Assets	207m	108m	142m
Current Liabilities	78m	51m	59m

Mattel
Vanwall Road, Maidenhead, SL6 4UB
Tel: 01628-500000 **Fax:** 01628-500075
Website: http://www.mattel.com
Directors: S. Tung (Co Sec), D. Geddes (Sales)
Ultimate Holding Company: MATTEL INC.
Immediate Holding Company: MATTEL TYCO UK LIMITED
Registration no: 03482893 **Date established:** 1997 **Turnover:** £5m - £10m
No.of Employees: 101 - 250 **Product Groups:** 65

Date of Accounts	Dec 11	Dec 10	Dec 09
Sales Turnover	7m	5m	2m
Pre Tax Profit/Loss	140	-55	317
Working Capital	-4m	-5m	-5m
Current Assets	747	747	747
Current Liabilities	35	N/A	N/A

Melitta System Service
Unit 21 Grove Park Industrial Estate Waltham Road, White Waltham, Maidenhead, SL6 3LW
Tel: 01628-829888 **Fax:** 01628-825111
E-mail: paul@mssuk.co.uk
Website: http://www.melittasystemservice.co.uk
Bank(s): National Westminster
Directors: P. Hobkins (MD), P. Hopkins (MD), J. Hopkins (Fin)
Immediate Holding Company: PROJECT SUPPORT SERVICES (PSS) LTD
Registration no: 05410256 **VAT No.:** GB 540 2974 51
Date established: 2005 **Turnover:** £1m - £2m **No.of Employees:** 11 - 20
Product Groups: 27, 40

Memco Ltd
Clyde House Reform Road, Maidenhead, SL6 8BY
Tel: 01628-540100 **Fax:** 01628-621947
E-mail: sales@memco.co.uk
Website: http://www.memco.co.uk
Managers: A. Harbidge
Ultimate Holding Company: HALMA PUBLIC LIMITED COMPANY
Immediate Holding Company: MEMCO LIMITED
Registration no: 01006657 **Date established:** 1971
Turnover: £20m - £50m **No.of Employees:** 51 - 100 **Product Groups:** 40

Date of Accounts	Mar 08	Mar 09	Apr 10
Sales Turnover	20m	22m	20m
Pre Tax Profit/Loss	2m	3m	2m
Working Capital	-283	-327	-39
Fixed Assets	2m	2m	2m
Current Assets	9m	8m	9m
Current Liabilities	898	868	921

Middlehurst Ltd
99 Boyn Valley Road, Maidenhead, SL6 4EA
Tel: 01628-628044 **Fax:** 01628-773143
E-mail: office@middlehurstlimited.com
Website: http://www.middlehurstlimited.com
Bank(s): Barclays
Directors: A. Anderson (Sales), A. Twelftree (MD), T. Anderson (Sales)
Managers: I. Walker (Purch Mgr)
Immediate Holding Company: MIDDLEHURST LIMITED
Registration no: 00515075 **VAT No.:** GB 207 8454 57
Date established: 1953 **Turnover:** £1m - £2m **No.of Employees:** 21 - 50
Product Groups: 45, 49

Date of Accounts	Dec 11	Dec 10	Dec 09
Working Capital	1m	1m	1m
Fixed Assets	282	318	366
Current Assets	1m	1m	1m

National Newspaper Safe Home Ordering Protection Scheme
22-24 King Street, Maidenhead, SL6 1EF
Tel: 01628-641930 **Fax:** 01628-637112
E-mail: satkins@shops-uk.org.uk
Website: http://www.shops-uk.org.uk
Managers: S. Atkins (Mgr)
Ultimate Holding Company: NEWSPAPER PUBLISHERS ASSOCIATION LIMITED (THE)
Immediate Holding Company: THE NATIONAL NEWSPAPERS' MAIL ORDER PROTECTION SCHEME LIMITED
Registration no: 05704184 **Date established:** 2006
Turnover: £500,000 - £1m **No.of Employees:** 1 - 10 **Product Groups:** 82

Nortel Networks UK Ltd
Maidenhead Office Park Westacott Way, Littlewick Green, Maidenhead, SL6 3QH
Tel: 01628-432000 **Fax:** 01628-432810
E-mail: enquiries@nortelnetworks.com
Website: http://www.nortel.com
Directors: N. Elbaz (Co Sec), S. Rolston (Dir)
Ultimate Holding Company: NORTEL NETWORKS CORP (CANADA)
Immediate Holding Company: NORTEL NETWORKS UK LIMITED
Registration no: 03937799 **Date established:** 2000
Turnover: £500m - £1,000m **No.of Employees:** 1501 & over
Product Groups: 37, 38, 44

Date of Accounts	Dec 07	Dec 06	Dec 05
Sales Turnover	665m	713m	495m
Pre Tax Profit/Loss	25m	57m	106m
Working Capital	500m	870m	825m
Fixed Assets	767m	476m	507m
Current Assets	837m	1192m	1204m
Current Liabilities	163m	132m	177m

Orthofix Ltd
Burney Court Cordwallis Park Clivemont Road, Maidenhead, SL6 7BU
Tel: 01628-594500 **Fax:** 01628-789400
E-mail: enquiries@orthofix.com
Website: http://www.orthofix.com
Bank(s): National Westminster Bank Plc
Managers: S. Howe (Tech Serv Mgr), S. Walker (Fin Mgr), M. Hastings (Fin Mgr)
Ultimate Holding Company: ORTHOFIX INTERNATIONAL NV (NETHERLANDS ANTILLES)
Immediate Holding Company: ORTHOFIX LIMITED
Registration no: 02853159 **VAT No.:** GB 636 0678 28
Date established: 1993 **Turnover:** £5m - £10m **No.of Employees:** 11 - 20
Product Groups: 29, 30, 38

Date of Accounts	Dec 11	Dec 10	Dec 09
Sales Turnover	4m	7m	11m
Pre Tax Profit/Loss	-716	1m	-1m
Working Capital	954	2m	308
Fixed Assets	161m	161m	161m
Current Assets	18m	17m	5m
Current Liabilities	673	674	776

Pacific Scientific
Howarth Road, Maidenhead, SL6 1AP
Tel: 01628-682200 **Fax:** 01628-682250
E-mail: howard.faulks@meggitt.com
Website: http://www.pacscieurope.com
Directors: D. Tunley (Fin)
Managers: H. Faulks
No.of Employees: 11 - 20 **Product Groups:** 38, 42

Passages International Inc Ltd
P.O. Box 3313, Maidenhead, SL6 8HN
Tel: 01628-633730
E-mail: passages@tiscali.co.uk
Website: http://www.earthandern.co.uk
Directors: D. Crouch (Fin), R. Crouch (MD)
Immediate Holding Company: PASSAGES INTERNATIONAL INC LIMITED
Registration no: 05073597 **Date established:** 2004
Turnover: Up to £250,000 **No.of Employees:** 1 - 10 **Product Groups:** 49

Date of Accounts	Mar 10	Mar 09	Mar 06
Working Capital	-26	-33	-20
Fixed Assets	N/A	N/A	2
Current Assets	21	12	9

Plannja Ltd
69 High Street, Maidenhead, SL6 1JX
Tel: 01628-637313 **Fax:** 01628-674940
E-mail: enquire@plannja.co.uk
Website: http://www.plannja.co.uk
Directors: B. Runesson (MD), J. Johansson (Dir)
Immediate Holding Company: GRACE PERSONNEL LIMITED
Registration no: 01034562 **Date established:** 1999
Turnover: £500,000 - £1m **No.of Employees:** 1 - 10 **Product Groups:** 35

Date of Accounts	Jul 11	Jul 10	Jul 09
Working Capital	141	99	343
Fixed Assets	22	22	28
Current Assets	434	320	598

Plastor Containers Ltd
Smithfield Road, Maidenhead, SL6 3NP
Tel: 01628-829800 **Fax:** 01628-822366
E-mail: sales@plastor.co.uk
Website: http://www.plastor.co.uk
Directors: J. Yates (Dir)
Immediate Holding Company: PLASTOR LIMITED
Registration no: 04401139 **VAT No.:** GB 578 3727 91
Date established: 2002 **No.of Employees:** 1 - 10 **Product Groups:** 30

Date of Accounts	Mar 11	Mar 10	Mar 09
Working Capital	243	191	146
Fixed Assets	101	96	87
Current Assets	458	390	294

Prelude Engineering & Design Ltd
Unit 6 Grove Park Industrial Estate Waltham Road, White Waltham, Maidenhead, SL6 3LW
Tel: 01628-829600 **Fax:** 01628-823663
Directors: K. Gill (Fin), R. Webill (MD)
Immediate Holding Company: PRELUDE ENGINEERING LIMITED
Registration no: 03113338 **Date established:** 1995
No.of Employees: 1 - 10 **Product Groups:** 38, 42

Date of Accounts	Oct 07	Oct 06	Oct 05
Working Capital	391	342	674
Fixed Assets	34	44	58
Current Assets	1m	1m	2m

Pythagoras Communications Ltd
Ashwood House Grove Business Park Waltham Road, White Waltham, Maidenhead, SL6 3LW
Tel: 01628-519000 **Fax:** 01628-519 019
E-mail: sales@pythagoras.co.uk
Website: http://www.pythagoras.co.uk
Directors: J. Stone (MD), J. Langdon (Develop)
Immediate Holding Company: PYTHAGORAS COMMUNICATIONS LIMITED
Registration no: 03000842 **Date established:** 1994
Turnover: £10m - £20m **No.of Employees:** 21 - 50 **Product Groups:** 44

Date of Accounts	Mar 11	Mar 10	Mar 09
Working Capital	-151	-81	-359
Fixed Assets	898	998	1m
Current Assets	1m	2m	2m

Rank Group plc
Stafferton Way, Maidenhead, SL6 1AY
Tel: 01628-504000 **Fax:** 01628-504429
E-mail: susan.waldock@rank.com
Website: http://www.rank.com
Directors: D. Boden (MD), S. Waldock (Dir), S. Waldock (Pers), F. Bingham (Co Sec)
Managers: J. Abarham (Sales Prom Mgr), J. Carter (Admin Off)
Ultimate Holding Company: HONG LEONG COMPANY (MALAYSIA) BERHAD
Immediate Holding Company: RANK GROUP GAMING DIVISION LIMITED
Registration no: 03213743 **Date established:** 1996
Turnover: £20m - £50m **No.of Employees:** 101 - 250 **Product Groups:** 89

Reed Accountancy Personnel Ltd
103 High Street, Maidenhead, SL6 1JX
Tel: 01628-672932 **Fax:** 01628-625590
E-mail: sales@reed.co.uk
Website: http://www.reed.co.uk
Managers: P. Sheppard (Mgr), R. Blood (District Mgr), D. Patel (Mgr)
Immediate Holding Company: Reed Personnel Services Ltd
Registration no: 00973629 **Turnover:** £125m - £250m
No.of Employees: 1 - 10 **Product Groups:** 80

Riverside Decking Co.
3 Old Kiln Cottages Malders Lane, Maidenhead, SL6 6NJ
Tel: 07958-963768
E-mail: mklewis19@yahoo.com
Website: http://www.riversidedeckingcompany.co.uk
Directors: M. Lewis (Prop)
No.of Employees: 1 - 10 **Product Groups:** 25

Sally Hair & Beauty Supplies Ltd
28 Nicholsons Walk, Maidenhead, SL6 1LB
Tel: 01628-777456
Website: http://www.sallybeauty.com
Managers: J. Ashmin (Mgr), L. Hainestock (Mgr)
Ultimate Holding Company: Sally UK Holdings Ltd
Immediate Holding Company: SALLY SALON SERVICES LIMITED
Registration no: 01060763 **Date established:** 1972
No.of Employees: 1 - 10 **Product Groups:** 30, 36, 40

Schneider Electric
Braywick House East Windsor Road, Maidenhead, SL6 1DN
Tel: 01628-741050 **Fax:** 01628-741 101
E-mail: chris.trinder@schneider-electric.com
Website: http://www.schneider-electric.com
Bank(s): National Westminster Bank Plc
Managers: C. Lang (Mktg Serv Mgr)
Immediate Holding Company: INVENSYS P.L.C.
Registration no: 01407228 **VAT No.:** GB 764 1239 13
Turnover: £75m - £125m **No.of Employees:** 51 - 100 **Product Groups:** 40

Sehlbach & Whiting Ltd
Exclusive House Oldfield Road, Maidenhead, SL6 1TA
Tel: 01628-591600 **Fax:** 01628-770761
E-mail: sales@sehlbach.co.uk
Website: http://www.sehlbach.co.uk
Directors: P. Pandya (Fin), P. Tandya (Fin), P. Ripley (Sales)
Ultimate Holding Company: SEHLBACH & WHITING HOLDINGS LIMITED
Immediate Holding Company: SEHLBACH & WHITING LIMITED
Registration no: 00180727 **VAT No.:** GB 207 9582 43
Date established: 2022 **No.of Employees:** 21 - 50 **Product Groups:** 22, 23, 35

Date of Accounts	Dec 11	Dec 10	Dec 09
Working Capital	3m	3m	3m
Fixed Assets	146	145	153
Current Assets	4m	4m	4m

Seiko UK Ltd
S C House Vanwall Road, Maidenhead, SL6 4UW
Tel: 01628-770988 **Fax:** 01628-770655
E-mail: service@seiko.co.uk
Website: http://www.seiko.co.uk
Directors: H. Ouchi (MD)
Ultimate Holding Company: SEIKO HOLDINGS CORPORATION (JAPAN)
Immediate Holding Company: SEIKO U.K. LIMITED
Registration no: 01032911 **VAT No.:** 538 0925 33 **Date established:** 1971
Turnover: £50m - £75m **No.of Employees:** 251 - 500
Product Groups: 49, 65

Date of Accounts	Mar 12	Mar 11	Mar 10
Sales Turnover	65m	65m	73m
Pre Tax Profit/Loss	3m	3m	-263
Working Capital	17m	17m	22m
Fixed Assets	16m	20m	15m
Current Assets	33m	37m	44m
Current Liabilities	4m	6m	3m

Sequent Ltd
Four Gables 62 Lower Cookham Road, Maidenhead, SL6 8JZ
Tel: 01628-628190 **Fax:** 01628-623336
E-mail: seq1989@aol.com
Website: http://www.sequentcars.co.uk
Directors: J. Roberts (MD)
Immediate Holding Company: SEQUENT LIMITED
Registration no: 02361852 **VAT No.:** GB 527 2598 25
Date established: 1989 **Turnover:** £2m - £5m **No.of Employees:** 1 - 10
Product Groups: 68, 82

Date of Accounts	Mar 11	Mar 10	Mar 09
Working Capital	101	111	1
Current Assets	239	256	136

Severnside Recycling
Mill Lane Taplow, Maidenhead, SL6 0AF
Tel: 01628-636703 **Fax:** 01628-771432
E-mail: enquiries@severnside-paper.co.uk
Website: http://www.severnside.com
Bank(s): National Westminster
Directors: P. McGuinness (MD), J. Malone (Sales), E. Jeffery (Dir)
Managers: B. Collins (Mgr)
Ultimate Holding Company: David S. Smith P.L.C.
Immediate Holding Company: DS Smith plc
Registration no: 01377658 **VAT No.:** GB 479 5202 22
Turnover: £20m - £50m **No.of Employees:** 51 - 100 **Product Groups:** 66

Sita UK Ltd
13-35 Grenfell Road, Maidenhead, SL6 1ES
Tel: 01628-513100 **Fax:** 01628-513101
E-mail: info@sita.co.uk
Website: http://www.sita.co.uk
Bank(s): National Westminster
Directors: M. Thompson (Co Sec), C. Chapron (Fin)
Managers: J. Wheeler, N. Jones, D. Ward (Sales Admin)
Ultimate Holding Company: GDF SUEZ SA (FRANCE)
Immediate Holding Company: SITA SOUTH GLOUCESTERSHIRE LIMITED
Registration no: 03962228 **VAT No.:** GB 492 9907 89
Date established: 2000 **Turnover:** £20m - £50m
No.of Employees: 251 - 500 **Product Groups:** 54

Date of Accounts	Dec 11	Dec 10	Dec 09
Sales Turnover	20m	20m	15m
Pre Tax Profit/Loss	5m	4m	2m
Working Capital	12m	8m	6m
Current Assets	13m	10m	9m
Current Liabilities	2m	1m	968

Southern Bearings Ltd
Unit 16 Waldeck House Waldeck Road, Maidenhead, SL6 8BR
Tel: 01628-674123 **Fax:** 01628-776502
E-mail: info@southernbearings.co.uk
Website: http://www.southernbearings.co.uk
Directors: C. May (MD)
Immediate Holding Company: SOUTHERN BEARINGS LIMITED
Registration no: 01507618 **Date established:** 1980
Turnover: £500,000 - £1m **No.of Employees:** 1 - 10 **Product Groups:** 35

Date of Accounts	Dec 11	Dec 10	Dec 09
Working Capital	73	101	93
Fixed Assets	7	3	11
Current Assets	159	199	188
Current Liabilities	32	20	20

Stiefel Laboratories (UK) Ltd
Eurasia Headquarters Concorde Road, Maidenhead, SL6 4BY
Tel: 01628-612000 **Fax:** 01628-810021
E-mail: general@stiefel.co.uk
Website: http://www.stiefel.com
Bank(s): Barclays Bank
Directors: G. McGlynn (Dep Pres), M. Hughes (MD)
Immediate Holding Company: Stiefel Laboratories Inc. (USA)
Registration no: 00831160 **VAT No.:** GB 491 9517 11
Date established: 1964 **Turnover:** £10m - £20m
No.of Employees: 51 - 100 **Product Groups:** 31, 63

Sybase UK Ltd
Sybase Court Crown Lane, Maidenhead, SL6 8QZ
Tel: 01628-597100 **Fax:** 01628-597000
E-mail: ukinfo@sybase.com
Website: http://www.sybase.com
Bank(s): Barclays
Directors: J. Hillman (Fin)
Managers: B. Coyne (Personnel), L. Hill (Mktg Serv Mgr), J. Ehlers (Sales Admin), K. Mahmood (Sales Prom Mgr), D. Steward (Tech Serv Mgr), G. West (Sales Prom Mgr)
Ultimate Holding Company: S.A.P. AG (GERMANY)
Immediate Holding Company: SYBASE (UK) LIMITED
Registration no: 02175260 **VAT No.:** GB 530 2883 61
Date established: 1987 **Turnover:** £20m - £50m
No.of Employees: 101 - 250 **Product Groups:** 44, 79

Date of Accounts	Dec 11	Dec 10	Dec 09
Sales Turnover	37m	39m	35m
Pre Tax Profit/Loss	3m	3m	-3m
Working Capital	7m	5m	2m
Fixed Assets	3m	3m	3m
Current Assets	16m	15m	11m
Current Liabilities	6m	10m	8m

Synergy B S S Ltd
Grove House Waltham Road, White Waltham, Maidenhead, SL6 3TN
Tel: 01628-828777 **Fax:** 01628-823789
E-mail: info@synergy-bss.co.uk
Website: http://www.synergy-bss.co.uk
Directors: S. Little (Dir)
Managers: P. Cownley (Tech Serv Mgr)
Immediate Holding Company: BLUE RIDGE NUMERICS LIMITED
Registration no: 03417565 **Date established:** 1997
Turnover: £500,000 - £1m **No.of Employees:** 21 - 50 **Product Groups:** 84

T P A Studio Ltd
Broadway, Maidenhead, SL6 1LU
Tel: 01628-412388 **Fax:** 01628-412390
E-mail: enquiries@tparch.co.uk
Website: http://www.tparch.co.uk
Directors: P. Thomas (Dir)
Immediate Holding Company: TPA STUDIO LIMITED
Registration no: 05295000 **Date established:** 2004
No.of Employees: 1 - 10 **Product Groups:** 07, 84

Date of Accounts	Mar 11	Mar 10	Mar 09
Working Capital	354	371	312
Fixed Assets	4	5	11
Current Assets	890	499	466

Television Systems Ltd
Vanwall Road, Maidenhead, SL6 4UB
Tel: 01628-676200 **Fax:** 01628-676299
E-mail: sales@tsl.co.uk
Website: http://www.tsl.co.uk
Bank(s): National Westminster Bank Plc
Directors: D. Phillips (MD), R. Bentley (Fin)
Managers: T. Williams (Ops Mgr), H. Cahill
Immediate Holding Company: TELEVISION SYSTEMS LIMITED
Registration no: 02041722 **VAT No.:** GB 442 4712 67
Date established: 1986 **Turnover:** £20m - £50m
No.of Employees: 51 - 100 **Product Groups:** 37

Date of Accounts	Jun 11	Jun 10	Jun 09
Sales Turnover	23m	25m	21m
Pre Tax Profit/Loss	178	806	721
Working Capital	4m	4m	4m
Fixed Assets	2m	400	450
Current Assets	13m	9m	6m
Current Liabilities	6m	3m	2m

Thames Forge Ltd
Fullers Yard Sheephouse Road, Maidenhead, SL6 8HA
Tel: 01628-622423 **Fax:** 01628-622423
Directors: D. Allen (Co Sec), K. Cartland (MD)
Immediate Holding Company: THAMES FORGE LIMITED
Registration no: 00765944 **Date established:** 1963
No.of Employees: 1 - 10 **Product Groups:** 26, 35

Date of Accounts	Aug 11	Aug 10	Aug 09
Working Capital	67	48	24
Fixed Assets	N/A	6	10
Current Assets	161	139	79

Thames Marine Bray Ltd
Monkey Island Lane Bray, Maidenhead, SL6 2EB
Tel: 01628-773472 **Fax:** 01628-778183
Directors: D. Bailey (Fin), T. Bailey (Sales)
Immediate Holding Company: THAMES MARINE (BRAY) LIMITED
Registration no: 02199929 **Date established:** 1987
No.of Employees: 1 - 10 **Product Groups:** 35, 36, 39

Date of Accounts	Apr 11	Apr 10	Apr 09
Working Capital	6	17	20
Fixed Assets	4	1	2
Current Assets	42	62	48

Thames Van & Truck
Waldeck House Waldeck Road, Maidenhead, SL6 8BR
Tel: 01628-770331 **Fax:** 01628-621012
E-mail: sales@thamesvanhire-sales.co.uk
Website: http://www.thamesvanhire-sales.co.uk
Directors: P. Lazenby (Prop)
Immediate Holding Company: IVORY TOWER CARDS LIMITED
Registration no: 03965154 **VAT No.:** GB 442 5904 53
Date established: 2000 **Turnover:** £250,000 - £500,000
No.of Employees: 1 - 10 **Product Groups:** 68, 72

Date of Accounts	Mar 11	Mar 10	Mar 09
Sales Turnover	140	N/A	N/A
Working Capital	68	84	94
Fixed Assets	2	4	5
Current Assets	97	140	147

Tibco Software Ltd
Braywick Gate Braywick Road, Maidenhead, SL6 1DA
Tel: 01628-786800 **Fax:** 01628-786874
E-mail: bsmith@tibco.com
Website: http://www.tibco.com
Directors: D. Smith (Sales & Mktg)
Managers: B. Smith, S. Ismail, L. McCloskey (Personnel)
Ultimate Holding Company: TIBCO SOFTWARE INC (USA)
Immediate Holding Company: TIBCO SOFTWARE LIMITED
Registration no: 03875990 **VAT No.:** GB 245 3229 73
Date established: 1999 **Turnover:** £10m - £20m
No.of Employees: 51 - 100 **Product Groups:** 44

Date of Accounts	Nov 11	Nov 10	Nov 09
Pre Tax Profit/Loss	7m	6m	7m
Working Capital	82m	73m	66m
Fixed Assets	32m	32m	32m
Current Assets	90m	77m	71m
Current Liabilities	5m	2m	3m

Travis Perkins plc
Baltic Wharf Boyn Valley Road, Maidenhead, SL6 4EE
Tel: 01628-770577 **Fax:** 01628-625919
Website: http://www.travisperkins.co.uk
Managers: T. Stevens (District Mgr)
Immediate Holding Company: TRAVIS PERKINS PLC
Registration no: 00824821 **VAT No.:** GB 408 5567 37
Date established: 1964 **Turnover:** £5m - £10m
No.of Employees: 51 - 100 **Product Groups:** 66

Date of Accounts	Dec 11	Dec 10	Dec 09
Sales Turnover	4779m	3153m	2931m
Pre Tax Profit/Loss	270m	197m	213m
Working Capital	133m	159m	248m
Fixed Assets	2771m	2749m	2108m
Current Assets	1421m	1329m	1035m
Current Liabilities	473m	412m	109m

Universal Crop Protection Ltd
Park House Maidenhead Road Cookham, Maidenhead, SL6 9DS
Tel: 01628-526083 **Fax:** 01628-810457
E-mail: enquiries@unicrop.com
Website: http://www.unicrop.com
Directors: P. Stainton (MD)
Ultimate Holding Company: UNICROP HOLDINGS LIMITED
Immediate Holding Company: UNIVERSAL CROP PROTECTION LIMITED
Registration no: 02463894 **VAT No.:** GB 207 8091 67
Date established: 1990 **Turnover:** £1m - £2m **No.of Employees:** 1 - 10
Product Groups: 31, 32

Date of Accounts	Oct 11	Oct 10	Oct 09
Working Capital	416	404	391
Fixed Assets	2	13	24
Current Assets	933	841	1m

Wye Valley Services Ltd
Unit 11 Woodlands Business Park Woodlands Park Avenue, Maidenhead, SL6 3UA
Tel: 01628-828285 **Fax:** 01628-820085
E-mail: sales@wyevalleyservices.co.uk
Website: http://www.wyevalleyservices.co.uk
Directors: M. Palethorpe (MD)
Immediate Holding Company: WYE VALLEY SERVICES LIMITED
Registration no: 04620746 **Date established:** 2002
No.of Employees: 1 - 10 **Product Groups:** 35, 48

Date of Accounts	Dec 11	Dec 10	Dec 09
Working Capital	39	-37	-16
Fixed Assets	110	142	53
Current Assets	209	225	204

Wyeth Laboratories
Huntercombe Lane South Taplow, Maidenhead, SL6 0PH
Tel: 01628-604377 **Fax:** 01628-666368
Website: http://www.wyeth.co.uk
Directors: B. Holdgate (Dir), C. Hubball (Dir), G. Michael (Fin)
Managers: D. Hood (Mgr)
Ultimate Holding Company: PFIZER INC (USA)
Immediate Holding Company: American Home Products Holdings (U.K.) Ltd
Registration no: 00132018 **Date established:** 1978
Turnover: £50m - £75m **No.of Employees:** 1501 & over
Product Groups: 20, 32

Wyre Repairs Ltd
Unit J Boyn Valley Industrial Estate Boyn Valley Road, Maidenhead, SL6 4EJ
Tel: 01628-671312 **Fax:** 01628-674691
E-mail: info@wyrerepairs.co.uk
Website: http://www.wyrerepairs.co.uk
Directors: V. Lightfoot (Fin), P. Edmunds (MD)
Immediate Holding Company: WYRE REPAIRS LIMITED
Registration no: 01961598 **Date established:** 1985
Turnover: £500,000 - £1m **No.of Employees:** 1 - 10 **Product Groups:** 48

Date of Accounts	Apr 12	Apr 11	Apr 10
Sales Turnover	596	643	620
Pre Tax Profit/Loss	25	46	27
Working Capital	260	258	240
Fixed Assets	6	7	10
Current Assets	366	355	367
Current Liabilities	51	58	30

Zinsser Analytic
The Quadrant Howarth Road, Maidenhead, SL6 1AP
Tel: 01628-773202 **Fax:** 01628-672199
E-mail: t.wells@zinsser-analytic.com
Website: http://www.zinsser-analytic.com
Directors: T. Wells (MD), R. Huggett (Tech Serv), W. Zinsser (MD)
Managers: F. Truluck (Sales & Mktg Mg)
Immediate Holding Company: ZINSSER ANALYTIC (UK) LIMITED
Registration no: 01670459 **VAT No.:** GB 385 5005 49
Date established: 1982 **No.of Employees:** 1 - 10 **Product Groups:** 31, 33, 38, 40, 42

Date of Accounts	Dec 10	Dec 09	Dec 08
Working Capital	415	528	701
Fixed Assets	34	50	50
Current Assets	532	672	1m

Newbury

Acedes Gear Tools Ltd
2-4 Fleming Road, Newbury, RG14 2DE
Tel: 01635-524252 **Fax:** 01635-521085
E-mail: sales@acedes.co.uk
Website: http://www.acedes.co.uk
Bank(s): National Westminster Bank Plc
Directors: T. Coleman (MD)
Managers: B. Emms (Tech Serv Mgr)
Registration no: 03450354 **VAT No.:** GB 362 9713 34
Date established: 1984 **Turnover:** £2m - £5m **No.of Employees:** 21 - 50
Product Groups: 36, 46

All Aboard Marine Services
Greenham Lock Cottage Ampere Road, Newbury, RG14 5SN
Tel: 01635-37606
E-mail: p.hutley@aquamarine.co.uk
Website: http://www.aamarine.co.uk
Directors: P. Hutley (Prop)
No.of Employees: 1 - 10 **Product Groups:** 35, 36, 39

Alrad Instruments
Turnpike Industrial Estate Turnpike Road, Newbury, RG14 2NS
Tel: 01635-30345 **Fax:** 01635-32630
E-mail: sales@alrad.co.uk
Website: http://www.alrad.co.uk
Directors: G. Alderton (Dir)
Ultimate Holding Company: ALCHEM HOLDINGS LTD
Registration no: 02438982 **VAT No.:** GB 537 7030 47
Turnover: £1m - £2m **No.of Employees:** 1 - 10 **Product Groups:** 37, 38

Date of Accounts	Dec 08	Dec 07	Dec 06
Sales Turnover	1270	1279	1274
Pre Tax Profit/Loss	1	12	2
Working Capital	32	47	50
Fixed Assets	64	50	37
Current Assets	201	289	279
Current Liabilities	169	242	230
ROCE% (Return on Capital Employed)	0.5	11.9	1.8
ROT% (Return on Turnover)	0.0	0.9	0.1

Armstrong Commercial Laundry Systems
Ampere Road, Newbury, RG14 2AE
Tel: 01635-33881 **Fax:** 01635-32434
E-mail: enquiries@armstrong-laundry.co.uk
Website: http://www.armstrong-laundry.co.uk
Bank(s): Lloyds TSB Bank plc
Directors: T. Lowes (Dir)
Managers: K. Yewer, C. Weyer, R. Newton (Serv Mgr)
Immediate Holding Company: ARMSTRONG FRANCE HOLDINGS LIMITED
Registration no: 07872478 **VAT No.:** GB 491 6456 20
Date established: 2011 **Turnover:** £5m - £10m **No.of Employees:** 21 - 50
Product Groups: 40, 42, 48

B C M S Ltd
Plantagenet House 16b Kingsclere Park, Kingsclere, Newbury, RG20 4SW
Tel: 01635-299616 **Fax:** 01635-299502
E-mail: brian.ribbettes@bcmscorporate.com
Website: http://www.bcmscorporate.com
Bank(s): HSBC Bank plc
Directors: B. Ribbettes (Ch), D. Rebbettes (Dir)
Immediate Holding Company: BCMS CORPORATE LIMITED
Registration no: 02932734 **Date established:** 1994
Turnover: £10m - £20m **No.of Employees:** 101 - 250
Product Groups: 80, 81

Date of Accounts	Jul 11	Jul 10	Jul 09
Working Capital	-163	-149	-2
Fixed Assets	N/A	10	N/A
Current Assets	15	13	28

Baxter Healthcare Ltd
Wallingford Road Compton, Newbury, RG20 7QW
Tel: 01635-206000 **Fax:** 01635-206115
E-mail: enquiries@baxter.com
Website: http://www.baxter.com
Directors: G. Braham (Fin)
Managers: G. May (I.T. Exec), A. Squirell (Buyer), N. Scott ()
Ultimate Holding Company: BAXTER INTERNATIONAL INC (USA)
Immediate Holding Company: BAXTER HEALTHCARE LIMITED
Registration no: 00461365 **VAT No.:** GB 103 2224 39
Date established: 1948 **Turnover:** £125m - £250m
No.of Employees: 1 - 10 **Product Groups:** 61

Date of Accounts	Dec 11	Dec 10	Dec 09
Sales Turnover	154m	138m	127m
Pre Tax Profit/Loss	13m	15m	8m
Working Capital	-33m	-34m	-51m
Fixed Assets	94m	92m	90m
Current Assets	93m	86m	103m
Current Liabilities	12m	13m	16m

Benoil Services Ltd
Kennet Building Trade Street, Woolton Hill, Newbury, RG20 9UJ
Tel: 01635-253412 **Fax:** 01635-253899
E-mail: sales@benoil.com
Website: http://www.benoil.com
Directors: R. Bentham (Dir)
Ultimate Holding Company: SECOIL LIMITED
Immediate Holding Company: BENOIL SERVICES LIMITED
Registration no: 01946620 **VAT No.:** GB 438 1177 49
Date established: 1985 **Turnover:** £250,000 - £500,000
No.of Employees: 1 - 10 **Product Groups:** 29, 30, 36, 42, 48, 66, 67

Date of Accounts	Sep 11	Sep 10	Sep 09
Working Capital	380	243	326
Fixed Assets	3	1	N/A
Current Assets	512	343	403

Bunzl Cleaning & Hygiene Supplies
Bone Lane, Newbury, RG14 5SH
Tel: 01635-528550 **Fax:** 01635-528822
E-mail: newbury@bunzlchs.co.uk
Website: http://www.bunzlchs.com
Bank(s): National Westminster Bank Plc

Managers: K. Hyslop (District Mgr)
Ultimate Holding Company: BUNZL PUBLIC LIMITED COMPANY
Immediate Holding Company: NMP CONSTRUCTION (NEWBURY) LTD.
Registration no: 03888254 **VAT No.:** GB 138 8181 47
Date established: 2004 **Turnover:** £2m - £5m **No.of Employees:** 11 - 20
Product Groups: 63

Date of Accounts	Dec 11	Dec 10	Dec 09
Working Capital	253	233	390
Fixed Assets	1	1	1
Current Assets	529	508	741

C Y Finishes Ltd

4 Arnhem Road, Newbury, RG14 5RU
Tel: 01635-43860 **Fax:** 01635-38547
E-mail: sales@cyfinishes.com
Website: http://www.cyfinishes.co.uk
Bank(s): Barclays
Directors: I. Passey (MD), G. Passey (Fin)
Ultimate Holding Company: IPERA COATINGS LIMITED
Immediate Holding Company: C. Y. FINISHES LIMITED
Registration no: 01712515 **VAT No.:** GB 362 7432 52
Date established: 1983 **Turnover:** £1m - £2m **No.of Employees:** 11 - 20
Product Groups: 48

Date of Accounts	Apr 11	Apr 10	Apr 09
Working Capital	414	365	332
Fixed Assets	11	28	31
Current Assets	692	720	550

Cabletime Ltd

64 Greenham Road, Newbury, RG14 7HX
Tel: 01635-35111 **Fax:** 01635-35913
E-mail: info@cabletime.com
Website: http://www.cabletime.com
Bank(s): HSBC Bank plc
Directors: K. Watts (Tech Serv)
Ultimate Holding Company: CABLETIME HOLDINGS LIMITED
Immediate Holding Company: CABLETIME LIMITED
Registration no: 03830974 **VAT No.:** GB 614 7032 67
Date established: 1999 **Turnover:** £2m - £5m **No.of Employees:** 11 - 20
Product Groups: 37

Date of Accounts	Sep 11	Sep 10	Sep 09
Working Capital	1m	1m	1m
Fixed Assets	7	20	41
Current Assets	2m	1m	2m

CCV Telecom

Unit A 46 Brummell Road, Newbury, RG14 1TL
Tel: 0800-5677568 **Fax:** 01635-47123
E-mail: jonathan@ccvtelecom.co.uk
Website: http://www.ccvtelecom.co.uk
Directors: J. Smith (Dir)
Immediate Holding Company: CCV Telecom Ltd
Registration no: 05973535 **Date established:** 2006
Turnover: Up to £250,000 **No.of Employees:** 1 - 10 **Product Groups:** 37

Close Invoice Finance Ltd

25 Bartholomew Street, Newbury, RG14 5LL
Tel: 01590-674790 **Fax:** 01202-849447
E-mail: wharney@closeinvoice.co.uk
Website: http://www.closeinvoice.co.uk
Directors: P. Flynn (Sales & Mktg), W. Harney (Dir), D. Thompson (MD), M. Webster (Fin)
Managers: N. Long (Sec), P. Fylnn (Mktg Serv Mgr), B. Warwick (I.T. Exec)
Ultimate Holding Company: CLOSE BROTHERS GROUP PLC
Immediate Holding Company: CLOSE INVOICE FINANCE LIMITED
Registration no: 00935949 **VAT No.:** GB 398 9250 88
Date established: 1968 **Turnover:** £20m - £50m **No.of Employees:** 1 - 10
Product Groups: 82

Date of Accounts	Jul 11	Jul 10	Jul 09
Sales Turnover	34m	29m	29m
Pre Tax Profit/Loss	13m	7m	4m
Working Capital	-2m	-445	19m
Fixed Assets	5m	5m	3m
Current Assets	599m	504m	290m
Current Liabilities	5m	4m	3m

Cognito Ltd

Benham Valence Speen, Newbury, RG20 8LU
Tel: 01635-508200 **Fax:** 01635-550783
E-mail: info@cognitomobile.com
Website: http://www.cognito.co.uk
Directors: S. Alderson (MD), C. Rolfe (Fin)
Managers: M. Cross (Sales Prom Mgr), M. Slaughter (Tech Serv Mgr), V. Faulkner (Personnel)
Immediate Holding Company: COGNITO LIMITED
Registration no: 02723032 **Date established:** 1992
Turnover: £10m - £20m **No.of Employees:** 101 - 250 **Product Groups:** 37

Date of Accounts	Sep 11	Sep 10	Sep 09
Sales Turnover	10m	9m	10m
Pre Tax Profit/Loss	1m	1m	1m
Working Capital	4m	3m	3m
Fixed Assets	1m	1m	1m
Current Assets	7m	5m	5m
Current Liabilities	3m	2m	2m

Cottage Stoves

Scouses Corner Old Burghclere, Newbury, RG20 9LL
Tel: 01635-278768
Directors: C. Thompson (Prop)
No.of Employees: 1 - 10 **Product Groups:** 40

Craigs Electrical Co.

203 Kersey Crescent Speen, Newbury, RG14 1SW
Tel: 07876-550331 **Fax:** 01635-820308
E-mail: craig@youhirewewire.co.uk
Directors: C. Preston (Prop)
No.of Employees: 1 - 10 **Product Groups:** 37, 38, 52, 67, 84

D D C (U K) Ltd

Mill Reef House 9-14 Cheap Street, Newbury, RG14 5DD
Tel: 01635-811140 **Fax:** 01635-32264
E-mail: northfield@ddc-web.com
Website: http://www.ddc-web.com
Directors: G. Mullan (Dir)
Managers: J. Northfield (Sales Prom Mgr)
Ultimate Holding Company: ILC INDUSTRIES INC (USA)
Immediate Holding Company: Data Device Corporation (USA)
Registration no: 01829528 **VAT No.:** GB 363 1306 81
Date established: 1984 **Turnover:** £1m - £2m **No.of Employees:** 1 - 10
Product Groups: 37

Date of Accounts	Dec 08	Dec 07	Dec 06
Working Capital	1105	720	551
Fixed Assets	8	7	11
Current Assets	1960	1529	1058
Current Liabilities	855	809	507
Total Share Capital	50	50	50

Dinks Ltd

PO Box 149, Newbury, RG20 9DR
Tel: 01635-278556 **Fax:** 01635-278709
E-mail: info@dinksltd.co.uk
Website: http://www.dinksltd.co.uk
Managers: E. Jones (Sales Admin)
Immediate Holding Company: DINKS LIMITED
Registration no: 02338212 **Date established:** 1989
No.of Employees: 1 - 10 **Product Groups:** 22, 24, 48, 49

Date of Accounts	Jul 11	Jul 10	Jul 09
Working Capital	243	256	318
Current Assets	410	316	377

Du Pre plc

Unit 3-4 The Vo-Tec Centre Hambridge Lane, Newbury, RG14 5TN
Tel: 01635-555555 **Fax:** 01635-555533
E-mail: info@dupre.co.uk
Website: http://www.dupre.co.uk
Bank(s): Lloyds TSB Bank plc
Directors: K. Millar (Fin), K. Hollanby (Gen Sec), P. Du Pre (Ch), R. Jones (Sales)
Managers: D. Du Pre (Tech Serv Mgr), J. Kent (Purch Mgr)
Immediate Holding Company: DU PRE PLC
Registration no: 01520800 **Date established:** 1980 **Turnover:** £5m - £10m
No.of Employees: 51 - 100 **Product Groups:** 37, 38, 44

Date of Accounts	Mar 12	Mar 11	Mar 10
Sales Turnover	6m	6m	6m
Pre Tax Profit/Loss	118	256	156
Working Capital	1m	1m	1m
Fixed Assets	74	87	93
Current Assets	3m	2m	3m
Current Liabilities	1m	810	1m

Ebm-Papst

The Barn Sheepdown, East Ilsley, Newbury, RG20 7ND
Tel: 0870-7665170 **Fax:** 0870-7665180
E-mail: gareth.jones@uk.ebmpapst.com
Website: http://www.ebmpapst.co.uk
Directors: G. Jones (MD), M. Maliphant (Chief Op Offcr), I. Gibb (Fin), I. McLeod (Eng Serv)
Managers: C. Smith (Transport)
Ultimate Holding Company: Elektrobau Mulfingen GmbH & Co.
Immediate Holding Company: Papst Motoren GmbH & KG (Germany)
Registration no: 01206852 **Date established:** 2004
Turnover: £10m - £20m **No.of Employees:** 1 - 10 **Product Groups:** 37, 40

Edwards & Co.

376 London Road, Newbury, RG14 2QH
Tel: 01635-552629
E-mail: davidedwards2009@hotmail.co.uk
Website: http://www.edwardsproperty.co.uk
Directors: D. Edwards (Prop)
Immediate Holding Company: EDWARDS & COMPANY (PROPERTY) LTD
Registration no: 03580996 **Date established:** 1970
No.of Employees: 1 - 10 **Product Groups:** 46, 48

Environmental Equipments Ltd

12 Queen Eleanor House Kings Clere, Kingsclere, Newbury, RG20 4SW
Tel: 01635-298502 **Fax:** 01635-296499
E-mail: info@e-equipments.com
Website: http://www.e-equipment.com
Managers: B. Kalra
Immediate Holding Company: ENVIRONMENTAL EQUIPMENTS LIMITED
Registration no: 00760878 **VAT No.:** GB 199 0579 10
Date established: 1963 **Turnover:** £1m - £2m **No.of Employees:** 1 - 10
Product Groups: 37, 38, 39, 85

Date of Accounts	Mar 11	Mar 10	Mar 09
Working Capital	-91	54	309
Fixed Assets	N/A	2	5
Current Assets	35	97	457

F T Component Services

Unit 12 Bone Lane, Newbury, RG14 5SH
Tel: 01635-528267 **Fax:** 01635-523496
E-mail: info@forkliftparts.co.uk
Website: http://www.forkliftparts.co.uk
Managers: P. Kay (Mgr)
No.of Employees: 1 - 10 **Product Groups:** 45, 66, 67

The First Financial Consultancy Ltd

33-34 Cheap Street, Newbury, RG14 5DB
Tel: 01635-35071 **Fax:** 01635-529933
E-mail: tony@thefirstfinancial.co.uk
Website: http://www.thefirstfinancial.co.uk
Directors: A. Davies (MD)
Immediate Holding Company: THE FIRST FINANCIAL CONSULTANCY LIMITED
Registration no: 03503976 **Date established:** 1998
Turnover: £250,000 - £500,000 **No.of Employees:** 1 - 10
Product Groups: 80

Date of Accounts	Feb 12	Feb 11	Feb 10
Working Capital	13	14	15
Current Assets	27	26	30

G K B Electronics Ltd

Unit 9 Orchard Business Park Newbury Road, Kingsclere, Newbury, RG20 4SY
Tel: 08704-036508 **Fax:** 08704-036509
E-mail: chrisoleary@gkbltd.co.uk
Website: http://www.gkbltd.co.uk
Directors: C. O'leary (MD), S. Poole (Fin)
Immediate Holding Company: GKB ELECTRONICS LIMITED
Registration no: 04102987 **Date established:** 2000
Turnover: £500,000 - £1m **No.of Employees:** 1 - 10 **Product Groups:** 37

Date of Accounts	Oct 09	Oct 08	Oct 11
Working Capital	91	94	66
Fixed Assets	107	108	106
Current Assets	130	108	195

Gandlake Computer Services Ltd

Gandlake House London Road, Newbury, RG14 1LA
Tel: 01635-34547
E-mail: john.gandley@gandlake.com
Website: http://www.gandlake.com
Directors: J. Gandley (MD), J. Gandley (Prop)
Managers: A. Bennett (Mktg Serv Mgr)
Immediate Holding Company: GANDLAKE LIMITED
Registration no: 04667925 **Date established:** 2003 **Turnover:** £2m - £5m
No.of Employees: 51 - 100 **Product Groups:** 44

Date of Accounts	Mar 10	Mar 09	Mar 08
Sales Turnover	4m	4m	5m
Pre Tax Profit/Loss	687	-19	930
Working Capital	601	157	250
Fixed Assets	11m	11m	11m
Current Assets	2m	1m	1m
Current Liabilities	1m	856	807

Gilson Engineering Newbury Ltd

3 Sandleford Farm Sandleford, Newtown, Newbury, RG20 9BB
Tel: 01635-41924 **Fax:** 01635-42286
E-mail: info@gilsoneng.co.uk
Website: http://www.gilsoneng.co.uk
Directors: S. Johnson (Dir)
Ultimate Holding Company: GILSON HOLDINGS LIMITED
Immediate Holding Company: GILSON ENGINEERING (NEWBURY) LIMITED
Registration no: 01055619 **VAT No.:** GB 757 2819 95
Date established: 1972 **Turnover:** £500,000 - £1m
No.of Employees: 11 - 20 **Product Groups:** 29, 30, 35, 36, 39, 40, 45, 46, 48, 67, 68, 85

Date of Accounts	May 11	May 10	May 09
Working Capital	431	-301	-319
Fixed Assets	42	936	919
Current Assets	719	333	282

Gowrings Mobility Ltd

Bone Lane, Newbury, RG14 5UE
Tel: 08456-088020 **Fax:** 01635-529400
E-mail: info@gowringsmobility.co.uk
Website: http://www.gowringsmobility.co.uk
Bank(s): Bank of Scotland
Directors: J. Seward (MD), N. Moggs (Co Sec)
Immediate Holding Company: GOWRINGS MOBILITY LIMITED
Registration no: 02910640 **VAT No.:** GB 614 9455 29
Date established: 1994 **Turnover:** £10m - £20m
No.of Employees: 101 - 250 **Product Groups:** 39

Date of Accounts	Mar 08	Mar 07	Mar 06
Sales Turnover	18517	13711	12346
Pre Tax Profit/Loss	209	243	150
Working Capital	-255	-365	-599
Fixed Assets	813	678	696
Current Assets	4927	3588	2751
Current Liabilities	5182	3953	3350
Total Share Capital	100	100	100
ROCE% (Return on Capital Employed)	37.4	77.6	153.9
ROT% (Return on Turnover)	1.1	1.8	1.2

Harris Roofing Supplies

20 Hambridge Road, Newbury, RG14 5XA
Tel: 01635-521210 **Fax:** 01635-45243
E-mail: bmnewbury@harris-roofing.co.uk
Website: http://www.harrisroofingltd.co.uk
Managers: T. Irvine (District Mgr)
Registration no: 05393314 **Turnover:** £1m - £2m
No.of Employees: 1 - 10 **Product Groups:** 66

Date of Accounts	Mar 08	Mar 07	Mar 06
Working Capital	-2	-21	-28
Fixed Assets	N/A	4	7
Current Assets	N/A	386	374
Current Liabilities	2	407	402

Highfield Human Solutions Ltd

1 London Road, Newbury, RG14 1JL
Tel: 01635-33923 **Fax:** 01635-38837
E-mail: admin@highfielduk.co.uk
Website: http://www.highfielduk.co.uk
Directors: R. Weston (Fin)
Immediate Holding Company: HIGHFIELD HUMAN SOLUTIONS LIMITED
Registration no: 04155442 **Date established:** 2001
No.of Employees: 1 - 10 **Product Groups:** 80

Date of Accounts	Dec 07	Jun 11	Jun 10
Working Capital	22	-104	-119
Fixed Assets	271	217	255
Current Assets	381	89	110

Hitachi Capital Vehicle Solutions Ltd

Kiln House Kiln Road, Newbury, RG14 2NU
Tel: 01635-589500 **Fax:** 01635-589750
E-mail: simon.oliphant@hitachi-capital.co.jp
Website: http://www.hitachicaptialvehiclesolutions.co.uk
Bank(s): HSBC, Hayes
Directors: S. Oliphant (Grp Chief Exec)
Managers: J. Worraker, N. Haywood (Personnel), P. Peace (Sales Prom Mgr), T. Griffiths, R. Harty (Mktg Serv Mgr)
Ultimate Holding Company: HITACHI LTD (JAPAN)
Immediate Holding Company: HITACHI CAPITAL VEHICLE SOLUTIONS LTD
Registration no: 01413993 **VAT No.:** GB 450 3774 55
Date established: 1979 **Turnover:** £125m - £250m
No.of Employees: 101 - 250 **Product Groups:** 72, 80, 82

Date of Accounts	Mar 12	Mar 11	Mar 10
Sales Turnover	161m	134m	109m
Pre Tax Profit/Loss	14m	11m	11m
Working Capital	-20m	-28m	-19m
Fixed Assets	369m	324m	263m
Current Assets	34m	35m	24m
Current Liabilities	38m	35m	33m

Hotlizard Ltd

18 London Road, Newbury, RG14 1JX
Tel: 01635-527900 **Fax:** 01635-527955
E-mail: info@hotlizard.net
Website: http://www.hotlizard.net
Directors: R. Cowling (Co Sec), R. Cowling (Dir)
Managers: J. Knight (Ops Mgr)
Immediate Holding Company: HOTLIZARD LIMITED
Registration no: 03811966 **Date established:** 1999
Turnover: £500,000 - £1m **No.of Employees:** 11 - 20 **Product Groups:** 44

see next page

Hotlizard Ltd - *Cont'd*

Date of Accounts	Nov 09	Nov 08	Sep 11
Sales Turnover	753	N/A	783
Pre Tax Profit/Loss	-1m	N/A	-450
Working Capital	-50	-182	-20
Fixed Assets	73	318	42
Current Assets	667	555	325
Current Liabilities	642	N/A	257

Infodata Systems Ltd

Mill Reef House 9-14 Cheap Street, Newbury, RG14 5DD
Tel: 01635-32741 **Fax:** 01635- 523330
E-mail: mbowman@infodata.uk.com
Website: http://www.infodata.uk.com
Directors: M. Bowman (Dir)
Immediate Holding Company: INFODATA SYSTEMS LIMITED
Registration no: 01534826 **VAT No.:** GB 330 0468 02
Date established: 1980 **Turnover:** £500,000 - £1m
No.of Employees: 1 - 10 **Product Groups:** 44, 80, 81

Date of Accounts	Dec 11	Dec 10	Dec 09
Working Capital	562	528	394
Fixed Assets	16	25	16
Current Assets	655	1m	1m

Intermail plc

Canal View Road, Newbury, RG14 5XF
Tel: 01635-565000 **Fax:** 01635-41678
E-mail: sales@intermail.co.uk
Website: http://www.intermail.co.uk
Bank(s): National Westminster Bank Plc
Directors: E. Martin (MD)
Managers: D. Champion (Tech Serv Mgr), K. Weston (Comm), J. Whiting
Immediate Holding Company: INTERMAIL PUBLIC LIMITED COMPANY
Registration no: 03244323 **VAT No.:** GB 228 2691 55
Date established: 1996 **Turnover:** £2m - £5m **No.of Employees:** 51 - 100
Product Groups: 44, 80, 81

Date of Accounts	Dec 11	Jun 10	Jun 09
Sales Turnover	3m	3m	3m
Pre Tax Profit/Loss	-376	-78	49
Working Capital	-44	85	141
Fixed Assets	74	337	345
Current Assets	612	677	939
Current Liabilities	490	225	393

J T L Systems Ltd

Unit 41 Kingfisher Court, Newbury, RG14 5SJ
Tel: 01635-263646 **Fax:** 01635-263647
E-mail: info@jtl.co.uk
Website: http://www.jtl.co.uk
Bank(s): Barclays, Newbury
Directors: J. Harkness (MD)
Immediate Holding Company: JTL SYSTEMS LIMITED
Registration no: 01927833 **VAT No.:** GB 363 3885 29
Date established: 1985 **Turnover:** £2m - £5m **No.of Employees:** 11 - 20
Product Groups: 38, 47

Date of Accounts	May 11	May 10	May 09
Working Capital	758	642	392
Fixed Assets	69	84	68
Current Assets	1m	1m	663
Current Liabilities	212	N/A	N/A

Jewson Ltd

Hambridge Road, Newbury, RG14 5EA
Tel: 01635-44146 **Fax:** 01635-49914
E-mail: coventry@jewson.co.uk
Website: http://www.jewson.co.uk
Directors: P. Hindle (MD)
Managers: G. Warren (District Mgr)
Ultimate Holding Company: COMPAGNIE DE SAINT GOBAIN (FRANCE)
Immediate Holding Company: JEWSON LIMITED
Registration no: 00348407 **VAT No.:** GB 394 1212 63
Date established: 1939 **Turnover:** £2m - £5m **No.of Employees:** 21 - 50
Product Groups: 63, 66

Date of Accounts	Dec 11	Dec 10	Dec 09
Sales Turnover	1606m	1547m	1485m
Pre Tax Profit/Loss	18m	100m	45m
Working Capital	-345m	-250m	-349m
Fixed Assets	496m	387m	461m
Current Assets	657m	1005m	1320m
Current Liabilities	66m	120m	64m

Keen World Marketing Ltd

1 Northbrook Street, Newbury, RG14 1DJ
Tel: 01635-34600 **Fax:** 01635-33360
E-mail: info@keen-newport.com
Website: http://www.keen-newport.com
Directors: G. Keen (Fin), O. Keen (MD)
Immediate Holding Company: KEEN (WORLD MARKETING) LIMITED
Registration no: 00906221 **VAT No.:** GB 222 7064 91
Date established: 1967 **Turnover:** £2m - £5m **No.of Employees:** 1 - 10
Product Groups: 32, 49

Date of Accounts	Dec 11	Dec 10	Dec 09
Working Capital	863	723	582
Fixed Assets	7	9	11
Current Assets	1m	1m	1m

Kosnic UK Ltd

Unit D Kennet Side, Newbury, RG14 5PX
Tel: 08458-386851
E-mail: admin@kosnic.com
Website: http://www.kosnic.com
Directors: Y. Hu (Dir)
Ultimate Holding Company: CONSORT (HOLDINGS) LIMITED
Immediate Holding Company: KOSNIC (U.K.) LIMITED
Registration no: 04380474 **Date established:** 2002
No.of Employees: 21 - 50 **Product Groups:** 37, 67

Date of Accounts	Mar 11	Mar 10	Mar 09
Working Capital	711	323	164
Fixed Assets	6	5	6
Current Assets	2m	1m	516

M E C Signs Ltd

Unit 8&9 Waterside Court Bone Lane, Newbury, RG14 5SH
Tel: 01635-41745 **Fax:** 01635-31923
E-mail: sales@mecsigns.co.uk
Website: http://www.mecsigns.co.uk
Directors: D. Kiggin (Fin)
Immediate Holding Company: M.E.C. SIGNS LIMITED
Registration no: 00733335 **VAT No.:** GB 390 9398 07
Date established: 1962 **No.of Employees:** 1 - 10 **Product Groups:** 30, 48, 49, 66

Date of Accounts	Apr 11	Apr 10	Apr 09
Working Capital	119	193	202
Fixed Assets	12	15	17
Current Assets	122	222	222

Macklin Controls UK

Raceview Businesss Centre Hambridge Road, Newbury, RG14 5SA
Tel: 01635-40122 **Fax:** 01635-231170
E-mail: sales@macklincontrols.co.uk
Website: http://www.macklincontrols.co.uk
Directors: S. Highnett (Prop)
Immediate Holding Company: TELEPATHIX LIMITED
Registration no: 06531190 **Date established:** 2007
No.of Employees: 1 - 10 **Product Groups:** 30, 36, 37, 38, 39, 40, 44, 48, 49, 65, 67, 68

Date of Accounts	Apr 11
Working Capital	-16
Fixed Assets	15
Current Assets	29

Measurement Systems Ltd

16 Kingfisher Court, Newbury, RG14 5SJ
Tel: 01635-576800 **Fax:** 01635-31023
E-mail: info@measys.com
Website: http://www.measurementsystems.co.uk
Directors: C. Waddell (Chief Op Offcr)
Immediate Holding Company: MEASUREMENT SYSTEMS TRUSTEE COMPANY LIMITED
Registration no: 02725710 **VAT No.:** GB 338 5150 57
Date established: 1992 **Turnover:** £2m - £5m **No.of Employees:** 1 - 10
Product Groups: 44

Metal Improvement Company LLC (a subsidiary of Curtiss-Wright Corporation)

European Corporate Office Hambridge Lane, Newbury, RG14 5TU
Tel: 01635-279621 **Fax:** 01635-279629
E-mail: eurosales@metalimprovement.co.uk
Website: http://www.metalimprovement.co.uk
Bank(s): HSBC Bank plc
Directors: P. O'Hara (Dep Pres)
Managers: L. Robinson (Mktg Serv Mgr), B. Hayes (Reg Sales Mgr)
Ultimate Holding Company: Curtiss-Wright Corporation
Registration no: FC006968 **VAT No.:** GB 126 7764 47
Date established: 1949 **No.of Employees:** 251 - 500 **Product Groups:** 30, 32, 48, 52, 67

Micro Focus Ltd

The Lawn 22-30 Old Bath Road, Newbury, RG14 1QN
Tel: 01635-565200 **Fax:** 0118-924 1401
E-mail: enquiries@microfocus.com
Website: http://www.microfocus.com
Directors: J. Smithard (Co Sec), M. Baker (Tech Serv), D. Valentine (Sales), P. Rogers (Pers)
Managers: D. Dundas, K. Racey (Fin Mgr), D. Tucker (Mktg Serv Mgr), M. Cox (Buyer)
Ultimate Holding Company: MICRO FOCUS INTERNATIONAL PLC
Immediate Holding Company: BORLAND (UK) LIMITED
Registration no: 01694442 **VAT No.:** GB 362 9748 15
Date established: 1983 **Turnover:** £500,000 - £1m
No.of Employees: 101 - 250 **Product Groups:** 44, 67, 80

Date of Accounts	Dec 08	Apr 12	Apr 11
Sales Turnover	6m	22	855
Pre Tax Profit/Loss	-1m	1	22
Working Capital	2m	2m	2m
Fixed Assets	444	N/A	14
Current Assets	10m	3m	3m
Current Liabilities	1m	106	63

National Instrument UK Corp Ltd

Measurement House Newbury Business Park London Road, Newbury, RG14 2PS
Tel: 01635-34189 **Fax:** 01635-523154
E-mail: info.uk@ni.com
Website: http://www.ni.com
Directors: A. Gokhele (MD), J. Truchard (MD)
Immediate Holding Company: NATIONAL INSTRUMENTS CORPORATION (UK) LIMITED
Registration no: 02999356 **VAT No.:** GB 493 5987 79
Date established: 1994 **Turnover:** £5m - £10m **No.of Employees:** 1 - 10
Product Groups: 44, 84

Newbury Fork Truck Centre Ltd

Unit 12 Bone Lane, Newbury, RG14 5SH
Tel: 01635-41635 **Fax:** 01635-35388
E-mail: admin@nftcltd.com
Website: http://www.nftcltd.com
Directors: D. Hawkins (MD), K. Hawkins (Fin)
Ultimate Holding Company: D. & R. FORK TRUCK HIRE LIMITED
Immediate Holding Company: NEWBURY FORK TRUCK CENTRE LIMITED
Registration no: 01303222 **Date established:** 1977 **Turnover:** £2m - £5m
No.of Employees: 1 - 10 **Product Groups:** 35, 39, 45

Date of Accounts	Mar 11	Mar 10	Mar 09
Working Capital	268	250	188
Fixed Assets	82	106	120
Current Assets	585	559	500

Newbury Reclaim

7 St Marys Road, Newbury, RG14 1ES
Tel: 01635-37183
E-mail: paul339@btinternet.com
Website: http://www.newburyreclaim.com
Directors: S. Paul (Prop)
No.of Employees: 1 - 10 **Product Groups:** 34, 54, 66, 68

Oakes Bros Ltd

Ridgeway Works Ball Pit Road, East Ilsley, Newbury, RG20 7DJ
Tel: 01635-281222 **Fax:** 01635-281200
E-mail: edmundl@oakesbros.co.uk
Website: http://www.oakesbros.co.uk
Directors: E. Lindley (MD)
Ultimate Holding Company: ARMOX TRUST (NEVIS)
Immediate Holding Company: OAKES BROS. LIMITED
Registration no: 00395809 **Date established:** 1945
Turnover: £10m - £20m **No.of Employees:** 21 - 50 **Product Groups:** 41

Date of Accounts	Dec 11	Dec 10	Dec 09
Sales Turnover	22m	22m	23m
Pre Tax Profit/Loss	381	232	262
Working Capital	2m	3m	3m
Fixed Assets	539	559	600
Current Assets	7m	5m	7m
Current Liabilities	3m	1m	1m

Ocme UK Ltd

Unit 1-2 King John House Kingsclere Park, Kingsclere, Newbury, RG20 4SW
Tel: 01635-298171 **Fax:** 01635-297936
E-mail: sales@ocme.co.uk
Website: http://www.ocme.it
Directors: E. Gatteschi (MD), C. Gatteschi (Co Sec)
Ultimate Holding Company: OCME SRL (ITALY)
Immediate Holding Company: OCME U.K. LIMITED
Registration no: 01530263 **Date established:** 1980 **Turnover:** £5m - £10m
No.of Employees: 1 - 10 **Product Groups:** 41, 42, 45, 84

Date of Accounts	Dec 11	Dec 10	Dec 09
Sales Turnover	9m	7m	6m
Pre Tax Profit/Loss	50	-11	41
Working Capital	379	345	375
Fixed Assets	459	575	548
Current Assets	8m	2m	4m
Current Liabilities	2m	182	2m

Opal Telecom

24 Kingfisher Court Hambridge Road, Newbury, RG14 5SJ
Tel: 01635-573300 **Fax:** 01635-573329
Website: http://www.opal.co.uk
Directors: N. Callaghan (MD), R. Sharpe (MD)
Managers: D. Toy (Mgr), Z. Shepherd (Mktg Serv Mgr)
No.of Employees: 1 - 10 **Product Groups:** 37, 44, 79

Opperman Mastergear Ltd

Hambridge Lane, Newbury, RG14 5TS
Tel: 01635-811500 **Fax:** 01635-811501
E-mail: sales@opperman-mastergear.co.uk
Website: http://www.opperman-mastergear.co.uk
Managers: K. Rush (Sales Prom Mgr)
Ultimate Holding Company: REGAL-BELOIT CORPORATION (USA)
Immediate Holding Company: OPPERMAN MASTERGEAR LIMITED
Registration no: 02618553 **Date established:** 1991 **Turnover:** £2m - £5m
No.of Employees: 1 - 10 **Product Groups:** 35, 37, 39

Date of Accounts	Dec 11	Dec 10	Dec 09
Sales Turnover	4m	4m	4m
Pre Tax Profit/Loss	-435	-464	-325
Working Capital	2m	2m	3m
Fixed Assets	1m	1m	1m
Current Assets	3m	3m	3m
Current Liabilities	258	157	139

P A Testing Ltd

Bow House 3 Brookway, Newbury, RG14 5RY
Tel: 07920-221 422 **Fax:** 01635-48600
E-mail: info@pa-testing.co.uk
Website: http://www.pa-testing.co.uk
Directors: M. Robertshaw (Dir)
Registration no: 07560904 **Date established:** 2008
Turnover: Up to £250,000 **No.of Employees:** 1 - 10 **Product Groups:** 85

P C Cox Ltd Moulding Division

Turnpike Industrial Estate Turnpike Road, Newbury, RG14 2LR
Tel: 01635-264500 **Fax:** 01635-264555
E-mail: sales@pccox.co.uk
Website: http://www.pccox.co.uk
Bank(s): Barclays Bank Plc
Directors: F. Lumb (MD), I. Newberry (Mkt Research), P. Crawford (Fin)
Managers: L. Foster (Purch Mgr), J. Hannah (Personnel), I. Lyford (Tech Serv Mgr)
Ultimate Holding Company: PC COX GROUP LTD.
Immediate Holding Company: P C COX LIMITED
Registration no: 03338184 **VAT No.:** GB 642 2851 47
Date established: 1997 **Turnover:** £10m - £20m
No.of Employees: 101 - 250 **Product Groups:** 30, 31

Date of Accounts	Dec 11	Dec 10	Dec 09
Sales Turnover	14m	14m	12m
Pre Tax Profit/Loss	2m	1m	3m
Working Capital	3m	2m	641
Fixed Assets	6m	6m	6m
Current Assets	5m	5m	4m
Current Liabilities	903	1m	1m

P F X Services

Fridays Andover Road, Highclere, Newbury, RG20 9PF
Tel: 01635-253394
E-mail: info@pfxservices.co.uk
Website: http://www.pfxservices.co.uk
Directors: D. Steggall (Prop)
No.of Employees: 1 - 10 **Product Groups:** 44, 48, 67

Powersolve Electronics Ltd

8a Arnhem Road, Newbury, RG14 5RU
Tel: 01635-521858 **Fax:** 01635-523771
E-mail: sales@powersolve.co.uk
Website: http://www.powersolve.co.uk
Bank(s): Lloyds TSB
Directors: N. Clark (Co Sec), P. Clark (MD)
Managers: K. Smith
Immediate Holding Company: POWERSOLVE ELECTRONICS LIMITED
Registration no: 02136010 **VAT No.:** GB 450 4224 85
Date established: 1987 **Turnover:** £5m - £10m **No.of Employees:** 11 - 20
Product Groups: 37

Date of Accounts	Dec 11	Dec 10	Dec 09
Sales Turnover	8m	8m	7m
Pre Tax Profit/Loss	2m	2m	2m
Working Capital	2m	2m	1m
Fixed Assets	725	736	753
Current Assets	3m	4m	3m
Current Liabilities	443	639	655

Precision Tools

Unit 40 Kingfisher Court, Newbury, RG14 5SJ
Tel: 01635-31977 **Fax:** 01635- 528865
E-mail: enquiries@precisiontoolsnewbury.co.uk
Website: http://www.precisiontoolsnewbury.co.uk
Directors: K. Horn (Dir)
Immediate Holding Company: PRECISION TOOLS LIMITED
Registration no: 07589184 **Date established:** 2011
Turnover: £500,000 - £1m **No.of Employees:** 11 - 20
Product Groups: 33, 36, 37, 39, 40, 45, 46, 47, 66, 67

Date of Accounts	Jun 12
Working Capital	-240
Fixed Assets	256

Current Assets			692

Quantel Ltd

31 Turnpike Road, Newbury, RG14 2NX
Tel: 01635-48222 **Fax:** 01635- 815815
E-mail: john.claridge@quantel.com
Website: http://www.quantel.com
Bank(s): HSBC Bank plc
Directors: I. Cooper (Fin), M. Mulligan (Sales)
Managers: J. Claridge (Sales Admin), M. Jeffrey, S. Owen
Ultimate Holding Company: QUANTEL HOLDINGS LIMITED
Immediate Holding Company: QUANTEL LIMITED
Registration no: 01130271 **VAT No.:** GB 312 9165 74
Date established: 1973 **Turnover:** £20m - £50m
No.of Employees: 101 - 250 **Product Groups:** 37, 44

Date of Accounts	Sep 11	Sep 10	Sep 09
Sales Turnover	45m	39m	35m
Pre Tax Profit/Loss	5m	1m	19m
Working Capital	22m	3m	-5m
Fixed Assets	2m	860	785
Current Assets	43m	23m	14m
Current Liabilities	8m	9m	8m

R C S Energy Management (Control Systems Division)

R M S House Kennet Side, Newbury, RG14 5PX
Tel: 01635-231600 **Fax:** 01635-231699
E-mail: enquiries@rcsenergymanagement.co.uk
Website: http://www.rcsenergymanagement.co.uk
Directors: A. Beckett (Dir), L. Croft (Dir)
Ultimate Holding Company: LINDE AG
Registration no: 06803398 **VAT No.:** GB 768 3051 16
No.of Employees: 11 - 20 **Product Groups:** 38

Radamec Control Systems Ltd

Euro House Abex Road, Newbury, RG14 5EY
Tel: 01635-40528 **Fax:** 01635-47453
E-mail: sales@radamec-controls.co.uk
Website: http://www.radamec-controls.co.uk
Directors: T. Leech (MD)
Ultimate Holding Company: WEGMANN & CO UNTERNEHMENS - HOLDINGS KG (GERMANY)
Immediate Holding Company: RADAMEC CONTROL SYSTEMS LIMITED
Registration no: 02071196 **VAT No.:** GB 450 3000 15
Date established: 1986 **Turnover:** £1m - £2m **No.of Employees:** 1 - 10
Product Groups: 38, 39

Date of Accounts	Dec 11	Dec 10	Dec 09
Working Capital	421	354	511
Fixed Assets	26	19	17
Current Assets	556	569	618

Rayner Diesel Services

2 Sterling Industrial Estate Kings Road, Newbury, RG14 5RQ
Tel: 01635-46323 **Fax:** 01635-35205
E-mail: info@raynerdiesel.co.uk
Website: http://www.raynerdiesel.co.uk
Directors: K. Haynes (Dir)
Immediate Holding Company: RAYNER DIESEL SERVICES LIMITED
Registration no: 04646813 **Date established:** 2003
No.of Employees: 1 - 10 **Product Groups:** 35, 36, 39

Date of Accounts	Jan 11	Jan 10	Jan 09
Working Capital	-47	-45	-46
Fixed Assets	48	47	47
Current Assets	52	48	43

Brian Reece Scientific Ltd

12 West Mills, Newbury, RG14 5HG
Tel: 01635-32827 **Fax:** 01635-34542
E-mail: brian@brsl.co.uk
Website: http://www.brsl.co.uk
Directors: L. Reece (Fin), B. Reece (Dir)
Immediate Holding Company: BRIAN REECE SCIENTIFIC LIMITED
Registration no: 02368823 **VAT No.:** GB 362 6998 07
Date established: 1989 **Turnover:** £500,000 - £1m
No.of Employees: 1 - 10 **Product Groups:** 37, 44

Date of Accounts	May 12	May 11	May 10
Working Capital	28	72	109
Fixed Assets	71	75	80
Current Assets	49	116	138

Reed Specialist Ltd

28 Northbrook Street, Newbury, RG14 1DJ
Tel: 01635-529199 **Fax:** 01635-529091
E-mail: newbury@reedglobal.com
Website: http://www.reed.co.uk
Managers: J. Sharpe (Mgr)
Registration no: 00669854 **Date established:** 1993
Turnover: £75m - £125m **No.of Employees:** 1 - 10 **Product Groups:** 80

Resource Plus

Festival House 39 Oxford Street, Newbury, RG14 1JG
Tel: 01635-387530
E-mail: bita.newman@resourceplus.co.uk
Website: http://www.resourceplus.co.uk
Directors: B. Newman (Dir)
Registration no: 6224832 **Date established:** 2008
No.of Employees: 1 - 10 **Product Groups:** 80

Roplan Ltd

Prince Henry House Kingsclere Park, Kingsclere, Newbury, RG20 4SW
Tel: 01635-299091 **Fax:** 01635-298505
E-mail: info@roplan.com
Website: http://www.roplan.com
Bank(s): Lloyds TSB Bank plc
Directors: O. Sparen (Fin), S. Chadwick (MD)
Ultimate Holding Company: ROPLAN INTERNATIONAL AB (SWEDEN)
Immediate Holding Company: ROPLAN LIMITED
Registration no: 02155002 **VAT No.:** GB 491 4295 28
Date established: 1987 **No.of Employees:** 21 - 50 **Product Groups:** 30, 33, 39

Date of Accounts	Dec 11	Dec 10	Dec 09
Working Capital	705	1m	1m
Fixed Assets	245	272	302
Current Assets	2m	2m	2m

Rose Corrosion Services Ltd

1 The Galloway Centre Hambridge Lane, Newbury, RG14 5TL
Tel: 01635-552225 **Fax:** 01635-568690
E-mail: rcsl@rosecorrosionservices.co.uk
Website: http://www.rosecorrosionservices.co.uk
Directors: D. Marston (Fin)
Immediate Holding Company: ROSE CORROSION SERVICES LTD.
Registration no: 02480648 **VAT No.:** GB 537 7244 28
Date established: 1990 **Turnover:** £2m - £5m **No.of Employees:** 1 - 10
Product Groups: 37, 38, 67, 84, 85

Date of Accounts	Sep 11	Sep 10	Sep 09
Working Capital	584	541	474
Fixed Assets	6	8	12
Current Assets	875	1m	671
Current Liabilities	55	N/A	N/A

Schleifring Systems Ltd

Abex Road, Newbury, RG14 5EY
Tel: 01635-232900 **Fax:** 01635-38334
E-mail: dfinnegan@schleifring.co.uk
Website: http://www.schleifring.com
Bank(s): National Westminster
Directors: L. Parson (Fin), D. Finnegan (MD)
Managers: A. Meredith (Sales Prom Mgr)
Ultimate Holding Company: WEGMANN & CO UNTERNEHMENS - HOLDINGS KG (GERMANY)
Immediate Holding Company: SCHLEIFRING SYSTEMS LIMITED
Registration no: 01800218 **Date established:** 1984 **Turnover:** £5m - £10m
No.of Employees: 51 - 100 **Product Groups:** 35, 37, 45, 46

Date of Accounts	Dec 11	Dec 10	Dec 09
Sales Turnover	6m	6m	5m
Pre Tax Profit/Loss	287	471	638
Working Capital	1m	1m	1m
Fixed Assets	2m	1m	2m
Current Assets	3m	3m	3m
Current Liabilities	623	743	755

Sharpstuff Event & Business Development

Steadman House, High Street East Ilsley, Newbury, RG20 7LF
Tel: 01635-280654
E-mail: info@sharpstuff.biz
Website: http://www.sharpstuff.co.uk/Contact.asp
Directors: A. Sharp (Grp Chief Exec)
Registration no: SC254353 **Date established:** 1997
Turnover: Up to £250,000 **No.of Employees:** 1 - 10 **Product Groups:** 80

Solving Ltd

Wessex House Oxford Road, Newbury, RG14 1PA
Tel: 01635-814488 **Fax:** 01635-814480
E-mail: sales@solving.co.uk
Website: http://www.solving.co.uk
Directors: J. Cownley (MD)
Registration no: 03532532 **Date established:** 1991 **Turnover:** £5m - £10m
No.of Employees: 1 - 10 **Product Groups:** 39, 45, 49

Date of Accounts	Dec 08	Dec 07	Dec 06
Sales Turnover	401	564	870
Pre Tax Profit/Loss	-1	7	11
Working Capital	38	38	33
Fixed Assets	1	2	1
Current Assets	141	286	433
Current Liabilities	103	248	400
Total Share Capital	20	20	20
ROCE% (Return on Capital Employed)	-1.3	16.8	31.4
ROT% (Return on Turnover)	-0.1	1.2	1.2

Southern Maintenance Solutions Ltd

Unit 35a Kingfisher Court, Newbury, RG14 5SJ
Tel: 01635-33363 **Fax:** 01635-580383
E-mail: info@smsmaintenance.com
Website: http://www.southernmaintenancesolutions.com
Directors: M. Lund (Dir)
Immediate Holding Company: SOUTHERN MAINTENANCE SOLUTIONS LTD
Registration no: 05767534 **Date established:** 2006
No.of Employees: 11 - 20 **Product Groups:** 40, 84

Stearn Electric Company Ltd

Votec House Hambridge Lane, Newbury, RG14 5TN
Tel: 01635-556600 **Fax:** 01543-253581
Website: http://www.stearn.co.uk
Managers: D. Edwards (Property Mgr), P. Toomes (Chief Mgr)
Ultimate Holding Company: NEWBURY INVESTMENTS BV (NETHERLANDS)
Immediate Holding Company: STEARN ELECTRIC COMPANY LIMITED
Registration no: 00201097 **Date established:** 1924
Turnover: £75m - £125m **No.of Employees:** 21 - 50 **Product Groups:** 36, 40

Stryker UK Ltd

Stryker House Hambridge Road, Newbury, RG14 5AW
Tel: 01635-262400 **Fax:** 01635-580300
E-mail: laurence.hipkin@emea.strykercorp.com
Website: http://www.stryker.co.uk
Bank(s): Barclays
Directors: T. McKinney (Fin)
Managers: L. Hipkin (Chief Mgr)
Ultimate Holding Company: STRYKER CORPORATION (USA)
Immediate Holding Company: STRYKER UK LIMITED
Registration no: 03669454 **VAT No.:** GB 537 6882 01
Date established: 1998 **Turnover:** £125m - £250m
No.of Employees: 101 - 250 **Product Groups:** 38

Date of Accounts	Dec 10	Dec 09	Dec 08
Sales Turnover	177m	173m	168m
Pre Tax Profit/Loss	11m	12m	6m
Working Capital	31m	36m	26m
Fixed Assets	29m	18m	18m
Current Assets	85m	80m	78m
Current Liabilities	18m	17m	17m

T W Electronics Newbury

Beacon House Winchester Road, Burghclere, Newbury, RG20 9JZ
Tel: 01635-278678 **Fax:** 01635-278266
E-mail: sales@twelectronics.co.uk
Website: http://www.twelectronics.co.uk
Directors: O. Teece (MD)
Immediate Holding Company: T.W. ELECTRONICS (NEWBURY) LIMITED
Registration no: 01496877 **Date established:** 1980 **Turnover:** £2m - £5m
No.of Employees: 11 - 20 **Product Groups:** 37

Date of Accounts	Sep 11	Sep 10	Sep 09
Working Capital	843	792	726
Fixed Assets	160	106	118

Current Assets	2m	2m	943

Touchstone Nav Ltd

Beacon House Harts Lane, Burghclere, Newbury, RG20 9JZ
Tel: 020-8328 9818
E-mail: natasha.elliott@cenium.co.uk
Website: http://www.cenium.co.uk
Directors: P. Lingham (MD), S. Dawood (MD), P. Lingham (Prop)
Managers: N. Elliott
Ultimate Holding Company: TOUCHSTONE GROUP PLC
Immediate Holding Company: VEDBAEK LIMITED
Registration no: 06858712 **Date established:** 2009
No.of Employees: 21 - 50 **Product Groups:** 44

Date of Accounts	Mar 11	Mar 10
Sales Turnover	3m	1m
Pre Tax Profit/Loss	32	61
Working Capital	-157	-229
Fixed Assets	263	303
Current Assets	919	459
Current Liabilities	638	262

Vacational Studies

Pepys Oak Tydehams, Newbury, RG14 6JT
Tel: 01635-523333 **Fax:** 01635-523999
E-mail: vacstuds@vacstuds.com
Website: http://www.vacstuds.com
Directors: I. Mucklejohn (MD)
Registration no: 01147578 **VAT No.:** GB 200 3313 45
Date established: 1973 **Turnover:** £250,000 - £500,000
No.of Employees: 1 - 10 **Product Groups:** 86

Visual Security Group (K9 Guards)

1 Coxeter Road, Newbury, RG14 1SJ
Tel: 01635-842665 **Fax:** 01635-827292
E-mail: info@visualsecuritygroup.co.uk
Website: http://www.visualsecuritygroup.co.uk
Directors: M. Harper (Prop)
Date established: 2003 **No.of Employees:** 1 - 10 **Product Groups:** 81

Vodafone Retail Ltd

Vodafone House The Connection, Newbury, RG14 2FN
Tel: 01635-33251 **Fax:** 01635-45713
E-mail: info@vodafone.co.uk
Website: http://www.vodafone.co.uk
Directors: R. Martin (Fin)
Ultimate Holding Company: VODAFONE GROUP PUBLIC LIMITED COMPANY
Immediate Holding Company: VODAFONE RETAIL LIMITED
Registration no: 01759785 **VAT No.:** GB 569 9523 77
Date established: 1983 **No.of Employees:** 1 - 10 **Product Groups:** 37, 44

Date of Accounts	Mar 11	Mar 10
Working Capital	138m	138m
Current Assets	138m	138m

Zussman Bear

66 Kiln Road, Newbury, RG14 2LS
Tel: 01635-231199 **Fax:** 01635-37529
E-mail: robertshepperd@zussmanbear.com
Website: http://www.zussmanbear.com
Directors: R. Shepperd (Ptnr)
Immediate Holding Company: ENGINEERING DESIGN CONSULTANCY LIMITED
Registration no: 06588605 **Date established:** 2008
No.of Employees: 1 - 10 **Product Groups:** 35

Reading

A Better Service Ltd

The Homestead Park Lane, Charvil, Reading, RG10 9TR
Tel: 0118-934 0104 **Fax:** 0118-934 4380
E-mail: gary@abetterserviceuk.co.uk
Website: http://www.abetterserviceuk.co.uk
Directors: G. Bicknell (Dir)
Immediate Holding Company: A BETTER SERVICE LTD
Registration no: 03186899 **Date established:** 1996
No.of Employees: 21 - 50 **Product Groups:** 30, 35, 39, 52, 54

Date of Accounts	Apr 11	Apr 10	Apr 09
Working Capital	94	58	150
Fixed Assets	760	1m	986
Current Assets	650	750	718

A I T Partnership Group Ltd

1 Southern Court South Street, Reading, RG1 4QS
Tel: 08450-177017 **Fax:** 08450-177019
E-mail: customer.services@ait-pg.co.uk
Website: http://www.ait-pg.co.uk
Directors: S. Bailey (MD)
Immediate Holding Company: AIT PARTNERSHIP GROUP LIMITED
Registration no: 04499201 **Date established:** 2002
No.of Employees: 21 - 50 **Product Groups:** 37

Date of Accounts	Mar 12	Mar 11	Mar 10
Working Capital	114	34	-91
Fixed Assets	1m	1m	1m
Current Assets	1m	983	743

A W E

Aldermaston, Reading, RG7 4PR
Tel: 0118-981 4111 **Fax:** 0118-982 1452
E-mail: andrew.jupp@awe.co.uk
Website: http://www.awe.co.uk
Directors: A. Jupp (MD)
Ultimate Holding Company: AWE MANAGEMENT LIMITED
Immediate Holding Company: AWE PLC
Registration no: 02763902 **Date established:** 1992
Turnover: £500m - £1,000m **No.of Employees:** 1501 & over
Product Groups: 80

Date of Accounts	Dec 11	Dec 10	Dec 09
Sales Turnover	753m	788m	783m
Pre Tax Profit/Loss	1m	447	6m
Working Capital	415m	339m	525m
Fixed Assets	1	1	1
Current Assets	521m	435m	633m
Current Liabilities	61m	57m	61m

Able Instruments & Controls Ltd (Level Division)

Danehill Lower Earley, Reading, RG6 4UT
Tel: 0118-931 1188 **Fax:** 0118-931 2161
E-mail: analytical@able.co.uk
Website: http://www.able.co.uk
Bank(s): Barclays, Enfield
Directors: S. Shortall (Fin)
Managers: A. Page (Mktg Serv Mgr), R. Sygrove (Mktg Serv Mgr)
Ultimate Holding Company: HALWELL TRADING LIMITED
Immediate Holding Company: ABLE INSTRUMENTS AND CONTROLS LIMITED
Registration no: 01851002 **VAT No.:** GB 417 2481 61
Date established: 1984 **Turnover:** £5m - £10m **No.of Employees:** 21 - 50
Product Groups: 37, 38

Date of Accounts	Dec 10	Dec 09	Dec 08
Sales Turnover	7m	8m	9m
Pre Tax Profit/Loss	492	1m	1m
Working Capital	1m	901	2m
Fixed Assets	1m	2m	1m
Current Assets	4m	5m	5m
Current Liabilities	1m	959	1m

Access Garage Doors

Unit 4 Gresham Way Industrial Estate Gresham Way, Tilehurst, Reading, RG30 6AW
Tel: 0118-963 9805 **Fax:** 0118-938 2025
E-mail: watford@accessgaragedoors.com
Website: http://www.accessgaragedoors.com
Managers: P. Flannigan (Mgr)
Immediate Holding Company: SOPER GROVE PROPERTIES LIMITED
Registration no: 05135562 **Date established:** 2004
No.of Employees: 1 - 10 **Product Groups:** 25, 30, 35

Date of Accounts	Apr 08	Apr 07	Apr 06
Working Capital	1m	219	1m
Fixed Assets	100	100	N/A
Current Assets	2m	1m	1m

Ace Testing Ltd

103 Underwood Road, Reading, RG30 3PA
Tel: 0118-962 3451
E-mail: enquiries@acetesting.co.uk
Website: http://www.acetesting.co.uk
Directors: G. Rogers (Dir)
Immediate Holding Company: ACE TESTING LTD
Registration no: 06968469 **Date established:** 2009
No.of Employees: 1 - 10 **Product Groups:** 38, 85

Date of Accounts	Sep 11	Sep 10
Working Capital	28	23
Fixed Assets	6	6
Current Assets	52	66

Active Load Ltd

28 Folly Green Woodcote, Reading, RG8 0ND
Tel: 01491-680123 **Fax:** 01491-680397
E-mail: info@activeload.co.uk
Website: http://www.activeload.co.uk
Directors: L. Hewitt (Fin), S. Hewitt (MD)
Immediate Holding Company: ACTIVE LOAD LTD
Registration no: 04361671 **VAT No.:** GB 760 1924 41
Date established: 2002 **Turnover:** £250,000 - £500,000
No.of Employees: 1 - 10 **Product Groups:** 37, 38, 67, 84

Date of Accounts	Dec 11	Dec 10	Dec 09
Sales Turnover	302	306	311
Pre Tax Profit/Loss	89	76	65
Working Capital	41	20	N/A
Fixed Assets	6	6	14
Current Assets	113	85	87
Current Liabilities	21	45	21

Adphos UK

8 Fowler Close Earley, Reading, RG6 7SS
Tel: 0118-986 1928
E-mail: info@adphos.co.uk
Website: http://www.adphos.com
Directors: D. Pelling (MD)
Immediate Holding Company: ADVANCED PHOTONICS TECHNOLOGIES UK LIMITED
Registration no: 04401501 **Date established:** 2002
No.of Employees: 1 - 10 **Product Groups:** 40

Date of Accounts	Dec 10	Dec 09	Dec 08
Working Capital	-86	-24	32
Fixed Assets	1	2	3
Current Assets	18	35	129

Advanced Maintenance

Unit 2 Chiltern Enterprise Centre Station Road, Theale, Reading, RG7 4AA
Tel: 0118-930 3738 **Fax:** 0118-930 3741
E-mail: info@advancedmaintenance.co.uk
Website: http://www.advancedmaintenance.co.uk
Managers: D. Jones (Mgr)
Immediate Holding Company: ADVANCED MAINTENANCE UK LIMITED
Registration no: 03568457 **Date established:** 1998
No.of Employees: 11 - 20 **Product Groups:** 40, 48, 52

Date of Accounts	May 11	May 10	May 09
Working Capital	495	272	147
Fixed Assets	143	129	87
Current Assets	915	693	349

Aerotech

Unit -3 Jupiter House Calleva Park, Aldermaston, Reading, RG7 8NN
Tel: 0118-940 9400 **Fax:** 0118-940 9401
E-mail: sales@aerotech.com
Website: http://www.aerotech.com
Directors: C. Jollisse (MD)
Managers: S. Botos (Mktg Serv Mgr), H. Strong (Comptroller)
Ultimate Holding Company: AEROTECH INC (USA)
Immediate Holding Company: AEROTECH, LIMITED
Registration no: 01548414 **Date established:** 1981 **Turnover:** £5m - £10m
No.of Employees: 1 - 10 **Product Groups:** 35, 37, 38, 39, 40, 45, 48, 49, 67, 68, 83

Date of Accounts	Jun 11	Jun 10	Jun 09
Working Capital	2m	1m	1m
Fixed Assets	13	16	1
Current Assets	2m	2m	1m

Agil Chemicals Products

Hercules 2 Calleva Park, Aldermaston, Reading, RG7 8DN
Tel: 0118-981 3333 **Fax:** 0118-981 0909
E-mail: david@kiotechagil.com
Website: http://www.kiotechagil.com
Directors: M. Rogers (Comm), P. Powell (Tech Sales), M. Hyden (Dir)
Managers: D. Bullen (Mgr)
Ultimate Holding Company: LAWRENCE P.L.C.
Registration no: 02544987 **VAT No.:** GB 523 9367 33
Date established: 1990 **Turnover:** £5m - £10m **No.of Employees:** 1 - 10
Product Groups: 20

Airdale Aerospace

2 School Lane Wargrave, Reading, RG10 8AA
Tel: 01628-488411 **Fax:** 01628-484646
E-mail: guy@airdaleuk.com
Website: http://www.airdaleuk.com
Managers: G. Dinsdale (Mgr)
VAT No.: GB 385 8742 00 **No.of Employees:** 1 - 10 **Product Groups:** 38, 39

All In One Security Products

6 Gaskells End Tokers Green, Reading, RG4 9EW
Tel: 0118-972 4077 **Fax:** 0118-972 3905
E-mail: sales@all-in-one.co.uk
Website: http://www.all-in-one.co.uk
Directors: J. Oakley (MD), E. Oakley (Fin)
Immediate Holding Company: ALL IN ONE SECURITY PRODUCTS LIMITED
Registration no: 05302860 **Date established:** 2004
Turnover: Up to £250,000 **No.of Employees:** 1 - 10 **Product Groups:** 26, 35

Date of Accounts	Dec 11	Dec 10	Dec 09
Working Capital	-7	-6	6
Fixed Assets	21	24	27
Current Assets	51	40	55

Applied Measurements Ltd

3 Mercury House Calleva Park, Aldermaston, Reading, RG7 8PN
Tel: 0118-981 7339 **Fax:** 0118-981 9121
E-mail: info@appmeas.co.uk
Website: http://www.appmeas.co.uk
Directors: R. Davies (Fin)
Ultimate Holding Company: APPLIED MEASUREMENTS (HOLDINGS) LIMITED
Immediate Holding Company: APPLIED MEASUREMENTS LIMITED
Registration no: 02583968 **VAT No.:** GB 569 8531 84
Date established: 1991 **Turnover:** £1m - £2m **No.of Employees:** 1 - 10
Product Groups: 37, 38, 48, 67, 84

Date of Accounts	Mar 12	Mar 11	Mar 10
Working Capital	326	202	182
Fixed Assets	23	24	33
Current Assets	654	405	377

Arc Tooling Technology UK Ltd

23 Jesse Terrace, Reading, RG1 7RS
Tel: 0118-937 1224 **Fax:** 0118-937 1224
E-mail: ola.hellgren@arctooling.com
Website: http://www.arctooling.com
Directors: O. Hellgren (MD)
Immediate Holding Company: ARC TOOLING TECHNOLOGY (UK) LIMITED
Registration no: 06630287 **Date established:** 2008
No.of Employees: 101 - 250 **Product Groups:** 30, 48

Date of Accounts	Oct 11	Oct 10	Oct 09
Sales Turnover	N/A	N/A	170
Pre Tax Profit/Loss	N/A	N/A	-25
Working Capital	107	-4	-26
Fixed Assets	6	6	2
Current Assets	349	189	48
Current Liabilities	N/A	N/A	44

Arm A-V Services

57 St Johns Road Caversham, Reading, RG4 5AL
Tel: 0118-948 2559
E-mail: mekka@lentil.org
Directors: R. Mekka (Prop)
No.of Employees: 1 - 10 **Product Groups:** 28, 37, 48

Aspentech Ltd

C1 Reading International Business Park Basingstoke Road, Reading, RG2 6DT
Tel: 0118-922 6400 **Fax:** 0118-922 6401
E-mail: info@aspentech.com
Website: http://www.aspentech.com
Ultimate Holding Company: ASPEN TECHNOLOGY INC (USA)
Immediate Holding Company: ASPENTECH LTD.
Registration no: 01703614 **Date established:** 1983
Turnover: £10m - £20m **No.of Employees:** 1 - 10 **Product Groups:** 44, 84

Date of Accounts	Jun 11	Jun 10	Jun 09
Sales Turnover	17m	19m	17m
Pre Tax Profit/Loss	-10	-508	389
Working Capital	6m	6m	6m
Fixed Assets	84	138	163
Current Assets	15m	16m	19m
Current Liabilities	3m	6m	5m

Assa Abloy Hospitality Ltd

Unit 21 Stadium Way Tilehurst, Reading, RG30 6BX
Tel: 0118-945 2200 **Fax:** 0118-945 1375
E-mail: uk@vcegroup.com
Website: http://www.vingcardelsafe.com
Directors: H. Witt (MD), M. Windall (Fin)
Managers: M. Roberts (Eng Serv Mgr), N. Parr (Sales & Mktg Mg)
Ultimate Holding Company: ASSA ABLOY AB (PUBL) (SWEDEN)
Immediate Holding Company: UNIQEY LIMITED
Registration no: 01591345 **Date established:** 1981 **Turnover:** £5m - £10m
No.of Employees: 21 - 50 **Product Groups:** 26, 33, 36, 39, 41, 66

Date of Accounts	Dec 10	Dec 09	Dec 08
Sales Turnover	8m	8m	10m
Pre Tax Profit/Loss	1m	863	2m
Working Capital	9m	8m	7m
Fixed Assets	33	19	27
Current Assets	11m	10m	10m
Current Liabilities	2m	1m	1m

Audicom Pendax Ltd

57 Sutton Park Avenue Earley, Reading, RG6 1AZ
Tel: 0118-966 8383 **Fax:** 0118-966 8895
E-mail: support@aupx.com
Website: http://www.aupx.com
Directors: R. Baldwin (MD)
Ultimate Holding Company: ERIK FRISELL AB (SWEDEN)
Immediate Holding Company: AUDICOMPENDAX LIMITED
Registration no: 01716114 **VAT No.:** GB 393 7773 96
Date established: 1983 **Turnover:** £1m - £2m **No.of Employees:** 11 - 20
Product Groups: 26, 28

Date of Accounts	Dec 11	Dec 10	Dec 09
Sales Turnover	510	1m	1m
Pre Tax Profit/Loss	-343	-122	-336
Working Capital	-362	-54	15
Fixed Assets	6	21	75
Current Assets	473	562	548
Current Liabilities	105	139	126

Azure Hygiene Ltd

14 Chalgrove Way Emmer Green, Reading, RG4 8SJ
Tel: 0118-962 6564
E-mail: info@azurehygiene.co.uk
Website: http://www.azurehygiene.co.uk
Directors: K. Lambden (Dir)
Immediate Holding Company: AZURE HYGIENE LTD
Registration no: 07853605 **Date established:** 2011
No.of Employees: 1 - 10 **Product Groups:** 32, 63, 65

B K I Europe Ltd

Theale Technology Centre Station Road Theale, Reading, RG7 4AA
Tel: 08709-904242 **Fax:** 0870-990 4243
E-mail: peterst@bkideas.co.uk
Website: http://www.bkideas.co.uk
Bank(s): Lloyds TSB Bank plc
Managers: P. Styles
Immediate Holding Company: STANDEX GROUP
Registration no: 00094496 **VAT No.:** GB 157 3981 32
No.of Employees: 11 - 20 **Product Groups:** 36, 40, 41, 63

Baltec UK Ltd

Danehill Lower Earley, Reading, RG6 4UT
Tel: 0118-931 1191 **Fax:** 0118-931 1103
E-mail: design@baltecuk.com
Website: http://www.baltecuk.com
Managers: D. Abbott (Chief Mgr)
Ultimate Holding Company: FEINTOOL INTERNATIONAL HOLDING AG (SWITZERLAND)
Immediate Holding Company: BALTEC (U.K.) LIMITED
Registration no: 02078457 **VAT No.:** GB 450 3142 92
Date established: 1986 **Turnover:** £1m - £2m **No.of Employees:** 1 - 10
Product Groups: 34, 36, 37, 38, 40, 45, 46, 48, 84

Date of Accounts	Sep 11	Sep 10	Sep 09
Sales Turnover	N/A	N/A	1m
Pre Tax Profit/Loss	N/A	N/A	-93
Working Capital	102	50	259
Fixed Assets	430	433	415
Current Assets	557	453	512
Current Liabilities	N/A	N/A	184

Barton Willmore LLP

Beansheaf Farm House Bourne Close, Calcot, Reading, RG31 7BW
Tel: 0118-943 0000 **Fax:** 0118-943 0001
E-mail: duncan.west@bartonwillmore.co.uk
Website: http://www.bartonwillmore.co.uk
Directors: S. Toole (Snr Part)
Managers: A. Bevan (Tech Serv Mgr), D. West (Sales Admin), M. West-taylor, J. Montgomery (Mktg Serv Mgr)
Immediate Holding Company: BARTON WILLMORE HOLDINGS LIMITED
Registration no: 02131349 **VAT No.:** GB 512 6340 81
Date established: 1987 **No.of Employees:** 51 - 100 **Product Groups:** 84

Date of Accounts	Mar 11	Mar 10	Mar 09
Pre Tax Profit/Loss	1m	775	N/A
Working Capital	2m	71	71
Fixed Assets	3	3	N/A
Current Assets	2m	71	71

Beech Hill Electronics

Beechcroft Beech Hill Road, Beech Hill, Reading, RG7 2AU
Tel: 0118-988 4622
E-mail: info@beech-hill.co.uk
Website: http://www.beech-hill.co.uk
Directors: P. Simpson (Ptnr)
Date established: 1992 **No.of Employees:** 1 - 10 **Product Groups:** 37, 44, 67, 84

Bentham Instruments Ltd

2 Boulton Road, Reading, RG2 0NH
Tel: 0118-975 1355 **Fax:** 0118-931 2971
E-mail: info@bentham.co.uk
Website: http://www.bentham.co.uk
Directors: M. Clark (Sales)
Immediate Holding Company: BENTHAM INSTRUMENTS LIMITED
Registration no: 01197391 **VAT No.:** GB 200 5418 21
Date established: 1975 **Turnover:** £1m - £2m **No.of Employees:** 11 - 20
Product Groups: 38

Date of Accounts	May 11	May 10	May 09
Working Capital	2m	2m	2m
Fixed Assets	291	293	280
Current Assets	2m	2m	2m

Berkshire Metals Ltd

10-12 Armour Road Tilehurst, Reading, RG31 6HS
Tel: 0118-942 9476 **Fax:** 0118-942 4800
Directors: A. Pankhurst (MD), M. Pankhurst (Fin)
Immediate Holding Company: BERKSHIRE METALS LIMITED
Registration no: 04424178 **Date established:** 2002
Turnover: £500,000 - £1m **No.of Employees:** 1 - 10 **Product Groups:** 34, 66

Date of Accounts	Mar 12	Mar 11	Mar 10
Working Capital	66	41	43
Fixed Assets	5	7	5
Current Assets	125	99	85

Blandy & Blandy

1 Friar Street, Reading, RG1 1DA
Tel: 0118-951 6800 **Fax:** 0118-958 3032
E-mail: law@blandy.co.uk
Website: http://www.blandy.co.uk
Bank(s): Lloyds TSB Bank plc

Directors: P. Darcy (Snr Part)
Managers: J. Moore, M. Moppett (Sales Admin), F. Baxter (Personnel), N. Burrows, A. Ewbank (Mktg Serv Mgr)
Immediate Holding Company: BLANDY & BLANDY LLP
Registration no: OC348096 **Date established:** 2009
Turnover: £5m - £10m **No.of Employees:** 51 - 100 **Product Groups:** 80

Date of Accounts	Jun 11	Jun 10	Jun 09
Sales Turnover	6m	6m	6m
Pre Tax Profit/Loss	2m	2m	2m
Working Capital	3m	2m	2m
Fixed Assets	67	82	130
Current Assets	3m	3m	3m
Current Liabilities	490	592	572

Blue Nine Marine
Willow Marina Willow Lane, Wargrave, Reading, RG10 8LH
Tel: 0118-940 6482 **Fax:** 0118-940 6483
E-mail: bluenine@marine7957.fsnet.co.uk
Website: http://www.blueninemarine.co.uk
Directors: E. Smillie (Ptnr)
Date established: 2003 **No.of Employees:** 1 - 10 **Product Groups:** 35, 36, 39

Bombardier Transportation Ltd
Letcombe Street, Reading, RG1 1LZ
Tel: 0118-953 8100 **Fax:** 0118-953 8009
E-mail: allan.morgan@uk.transport.bombardier.com
Website: http://www.bombardier.com
Managers: A. Morgan
Ultimate Holding Company: BOMBARDIER INC (CANADA)
Immediate Holding Company: BOMBARDIER TRANSPORTATION (SIGNAL MANAGEMENT) UK LTD
Registration no: 00653221 **Date established:** 1960
Turnover: £75m - £125m **No.of Employees:** 1 - 10 **Product Groups:** 37, 39

Date of Accounts	Dec 05
Current Assets	19520
Current Liabilities	19520
Total Share Capital	31530

Boult Wade Tennant
34 Bridge Street, Reading, RG1 2LU
Tel: 0118-956 5900 **Fax:** 0118-950 0442
E-mail: boult@boult.com
Website: http://www.boult.com
Directors: R. Cross (Snr Part)
Managers: D. Gillman (Tech Serv Mgr), T. Kelly (Sales Admin), J. Mannion (Personnel), N. Chandler (Mktg Serv Mgr)
Registration no: OC331852 **Date established:** 2007
No.of Employees: 21 - 50 **Product Groups:** 44, 80, 87

Bowak Ltd
Unit 5 Sterling Way, Reading, RG30 6HW
Tel: 0118-941 5511 **Fax:** 0118-945 1961
E-mail: info@bowak.co.uk
Website: http://www.bowak.co.uk
Directors: R. Lennard (MD)
Immediate Holding Company: BOWAK LIMITED
Registration no: 01002841 **Date established:** 1971 **Turnover:** £1m - £2m
No.of Employees: 11 - 20 **Product Groups:** 63

Date of Accounts	Sep 11	Sep 10	Sep 09
Working Capital	337	279	209
Fixed Assets	95	71	93
Current Assets	610	570	509

Braemac Ltd
Richfield House Thames Court 2 Richfield Avenue, Reading, RG1 8EQ
Tel: 0118-958 4447
Website: http://www.braemac.com.au
Directors: M. Radovanovic (MD)
Registration no: 03488704 **Date established:** 1998
No.of Employees: 1 - 10 **Product Groups:** 37, 44, 67

Breach Bros Bronze Restoration
44 Norton Road Woodley, Reading, RG5 4AJ
Tel: 0118-944 1403 **Fax:** 0118-944 0018
E-mail: jbreach@hotmail.com
Directors: J. Breach (Prop)
Date established: 1967 **No.of Employees:** 1 - 10 **Product Groups:** 26, 35

Bunzl Lockhart Catering Equipment
Lockhart House Brunel Road, Theale, Reading, RG7 4XE
Tel: 0118-930 3900 **Fax:** 0118-930 3931
E-mail: lockhart.marketing@bunzl.co.uk
Website: http://www.bunzlce.com
Bank(s): National Westminster Bank Plc
Directors: P. Hussey (Co Sec)
Managers: K. Mills, B. Tearall (Comm), R. Swift (Mktg Serv Mgr), M. Caswell (Personnel)
Ultimate Holding Company: BUNZL PUBLIC LIMITED COMPANY
Immediate Holding Company: LOCKHART CATERING EQUIPMENT LIMITED
Registration no: 00970892 **VAT No.:** GB 561 2290 61
Date established: 1970 **Turnover:** £50m - £75m
No.of Employees: 101 - 250 **Product Groups:** 33, 36

Date of Accounts	Dec 11	Dec 10	Dec 09
Pre Tax Profit/Loss	20m	15	18m
Working Capital	-50m	-52m	-35m
Fixed Assets	73m	73m	56m
Current Assets	62m	62m	51m
Current Liabilities	138	137	139

Business Furniture Online Ltd
16A Upton Road Tilehurst, Reading, RG30 4BJ
Tel: 0118-941 1144
E-mail: enquiries@businessfurnitureonline.co.uk
Website: http://www.businessfurnitureonline.co.uk
Directors: D. Jackson (Dir), A. Mackay (Fin)
Immediate Holding Company: BUSINESS FURNITURE ONLINE LIMITED
Registration no: 05922542 **Date established:** 2006
No.of Employees: 1 - 10 **Product Groups:** 26, 67

Date of Accounts	Mar 12	Mar 11	Mar 10
Working Capital	21	12	8
Fixed Assets	1	1	1
Current Assets	55	49	31

C F B T Education Trust
60 Queens Road, Reading, RG1 4BS
Tel: 0118-902 1000 **Fax:** 0118-902 1434
Website: http://www.cfbt.com
Bank(s): Lloyds TSB Bank plc
Directors: A. Terry (Pers), N. Mcintosh (Grp Chief Exec), R. Birkett (Fin)
Managers: H. Isham (Personnel), A. Scott (Tech Serv Mgr), P. Binns (Sales Prom Mgr), K. Borrar (Mktg Serv Mgr)
Ultimate Holding Company: CFBT EDUCATION TRUST
Immediate Holding Company: CFBT ADVICE AND GUIDANCE LIMITED
Registration no: 03370728 **VAT No.:** GB 614 8679 12
Date established: 1997 **Turnover:** £10m - £20m
No.of Employees: 101 - 250 **Product Groups:** 86, 87

Date of Accounts	Mar 11	Mar 10	Mar 09
Sales Turnover	17m	21m	22m
Pre Tax Profit/Loss	13m	-8m	-6m
Working Capital	266	282	450
Fixed Assets	5m	163	10m
Current Assets	2m	3m	4m
Current Liabilities	1m	3m	3m

C G E Ltd
The Chapel The Slade, Bucklebury, Reading, RG7 6TE
Tel: 01635-866021 **Fax:** 01635-871572
E-mail: cgeglobes@aol.com
Website: http://www.cgeglobes.co.uk
Directors: H. Cairns (Jt MD), C. Cairns (Fin), C. Cairns (Jt MD)
Immediate Holding Company: CGE LIMITED
Registration no: NI603546 **Date established:** 2010
Turnover: £250,000 - £500,000 **No.of Employees:** 1 - 10
Product Groups: 28, 38

Capture Ltd
The Old Coach House 14 High Street, Goring, Reading, RG8 9AR
Tel: 01491-873011 **Fax:** 01491-875558
E-mail: info@capture.co.uk
Website: http://www.capture.co.uk
Directors: A. Enock (Dir)
Immediate Holding Company: CAPTURE LIMITED
Registration no: 03669825 **Date established:** 1998
Turnover: £500,000 - £1m **No.of Employees:** 11 - 20 **Product Groups:** 44

Date of Accounts	Dec 11	Dec 10	Dec 09
Working Capital	100	58	-12
Fixed Assets	516	90	132
Current Assets	229	213	140

Carters Ltd
99-113 Caversham Road, Reading, RG1 8AR
Tel: 0118-959 9022 **Fax:** 0118-950 0618
E-mail: info@carterandsonltd.co.uk
Website: http://carters360.com
Bank(s): HSBC Bank plc
Directors: S. Carter (Dir)
Immediate Holding Company: CARTERS LTD
Registration no: SC328589 **Date established:** 2007 **Turnover:** £1m - £2m
No.of Employees: 11 - 20 **Product Groups:** 24, 63, 83

Cassell Welding Ltd
30-32 Lemart Close Tilehurst, Reading, RG30 4UE
Tel: 0118-942 5810 **Fax:** 0118-945 2454
E-mail: info@cassellwelding.com
Directors: B. Dales (Co Sec), J. Cassell (Dir)
Immediate Holding Company: CASSELL WELDING LTD
Registration no: 04226349 **Date established:** 2001
No.of Employees: 1 - 10 **Product Groups:** 46

Date of Accounts	Jul 11	Jul 09	Jul 08
Working Capital	52	37	44
Fixed Assets	22	25	31
Current Assets	96	110	111

Chantesse
25 Orchard Estate Twyford, Reading, RG10 9JY
Tel: 0118-970 6846 **Fax:** 08701-383878
E-mail: sally@chantesse.com
Website: http://www.chantesse.com
Directors: S. Roese (Prop)
No.of Employees: 1 - 10 **Product Groups:** 22, 24, 33, 49

Chemtech International Ltd
1a High Street Theale, Reading, RG7 5AH
Tel: 0118-986 1222 **Fax:** 0118-986 0028
E-mail: info@chemtechinternational.com
Website: http://www.chemtechinternational.com
Bank(s): HSBC, Guildford & Barclays, Reading
Directors: N. Smales (MD)
Ultimate Holding Company: TMCI HOLDINGS LTD (GUERNSEY)
Immediate Holding Company: CHEMTECH INTERNATIONAL LIMITED
Registration no: 02628540 **VAT No.:** GB 614 6131 70
Date established: 1991 **Turnover:** £1m - £2m **No.of Employees:** 11 - 20
Product Groups: 20, 32, 40, 41, 42, 67, 84

Date of Accounts	Dec 11	Dec 10	Dec 09
Sales Turnover	2m	N/A	N/A
Pre Tax Profit/Loss	130	N/A	N/A
Working Capital	918	660	700
Fixed Assets	2	18	28
Current Assets	1m	1m	1m
Current Liabilities	75	N/A	N/A

Chepherenrepairs.Com
21 Radnor Road Earley, Reading, RG6 7NP
Tel: 0118-935 2873
E-mail: repairs@chephrenrepairs.com
Website: http://www.chephrenrepairs.com
Directors: J. Bowler (Prop)
Immediate Holding Company: GLYCOMIX LTD
Date established: 2007 **No.of Employees:** 1 - 10 **Product Groups:** 44, 48, 67, 79

Date of Accounts	Sep 11	Sep 10
Working Capital	58	30
Fixed Assets	10	7
Current Assets	76	36

Chiltern Agricultural Services
Blackhorse Checkendon, Reading, RG8 0TE
Tel: 01491-682456
E-mail: richard_textor@yahoo.co.uk
Directors: R. Textor (Prop)
Turnover: £250,000 - £500,000 **No.of Employees:** 1 - 10
Product Groups: 07, 29, 40, 41, 48, 67

Chubb Fire & Security Limited
Unit 6, Worton Grange Industrial Estate Worton Drive, Reading, RG2 0SB
Tel: 0844-8791820 **Fax:** 0118-931 2551
E-mail: info@chubb.co.uk
Website: http://www.chubb.co.uk
Directors: N. Savill (Dir)
Managers: M. Fox (Comm)
Immediate Holding Company: Chubb Group Security Ltd
Registration no: 00524469 **VAT No.:** GB 198 9556 80
Date established: 1987 **No.of Employees:** 1 - 10 **Product Groups:** 81

Cistermiser Ltd
1 Woodley Park Estate 59-69 Reading Road, Woodley, Reading, RG5 3AN
Tel: 0118-969 1611 **Fax:** 0118-944 1426
E-mail: sales@cistermiser.co.uk
Website: http://www.cistermiser.co.uk
Bank(s): Bank of Scotland
Directors: G. Gestetner (MD), S. Johnson (Fin)
Managers: N. Peters (Mktg Serv Mgr), S. Dell (Mgr), B. Blincowe (Sales Prom Mgr)
Ultimate Holding Company: DAVIDSON HOLDINGS LIMITED
Immediate Holding Company: CISTERMISER LIMITED
Registration no: 01455630 **VAT No.:** 834842121 **Date established:** 1979
Turnover: £2m - £5m **No.of Employees:** 21 - 50 **Product Groups:** 30, 32, 33, 36, 66

Date of Accounts	Apr 11	Apr 10	Apr 09
Sales Turnover	N/A	3m	4m
Pre Tax Profit/Loss	N/A	315	780
Working Capital	3m	2m	2m
Fixed Assets	290	266	304
Current Assets	4m	3m	3m
Current Liabilities	N/A	348	477

Claridge Onestop Engineering Ltd
11 Bolton Road, Reading, RG2 0NH
Tel: 0118-986 0114 **Fax:** 0118-931 3842
E-mail: sales@springsandwireforms.co.uk
Website: http://www.claridgeone-stop.co.uk
Bank(s): Lloyds
Directors: M. Hamilton (Dir)
Registration no: 01030699 **Date established:** 1971 **Turnover:** £2m - £5m
No.of Employees: 11 - 20 **Product Groups:** 35, 48

Communications Solutions UK Ltd
5 Woodside Business Park Whitley Wood Lane, Reading, RG2 8LW
Tel: 0118-920 9420
E-mail: julie.watling@com-solutions.co.uk
Website: http://www.com-solutions.co.uk
Directors: J. Watling (MD)
Immediate Holding Company: COMMUNICATIONS SOLUTIONS UK LIMITED
Registration no: 03913465 **Date established:** 2000
No.of Employees: 1 - 10 **Product Groups:** 37, 67

Date of Accounts	Feb 12	Feb 11	Feb 10
Working Capital	327	252	263
Fixed Assets	3	1	2
Current Assets	500	339	376

Computer Task Group UK Ltd
11 Beacontree Plaza Gillette Way, Reading, RG2 0BS
Tel: 0118-975 0877 **Fax:** 0118-931 0249
E-mail: info.uk@ctg.com
Website: http://www.ctg.com
Managers: P. Ruffles (Fin Mgr)
Ultimate Holding Company: COMPUTER TASK GROUP INC (USA)
Immediate Holding Company: COMPUTER TASK GROUP (UK) LIMITED
Registration no: 01262284 **Date established:** 1976 **Turnover:** £5m - £10m
No.of Employees: 21 - 50 **Product Groups:** 44, 84

Date of Accounts	Dec 11	Dec 10	Dec 09
Sales Turnover	2m	2m	3m
Pre Tax Profit/Loss	-415	-656	-535
Working Capital	111	516	1m
Fixed Assets	26	36	46
Current Assets	796	1m	2m
Current Liabilities	214	234	297

Concept Aluminium Ltd
Mapledurham, Reading, RG4 7UP
Tel: 0118-972 2290 **Fax:** 0118-972 2320
E-mail: paul@conceptaluminium.co.uk
Website: http://www.conceptaluminium.co.uk
Directors: P. Butler (Dir)
Immediate Holding Company: CONCEPT ALUMINIUM LIMITED
Registration no: 06100955 **Date established:** 2007
No.of Employees: 1 - 10 **Product Groups:** 35, 48

Date of Accounts	Mar 11	Mar 10	Mar 09
Working Capital	-173	-75	-62
Fixed Assets	8	9	11
Current Assets	97	120	64

Cox & Wyman Ltd
Cardiff Road, Reading, RG1 8EX
Tel: 0118-953 0500 **Fax:** 0118-950 7222
E-mail: swieliczko@cpi-group.co.uk
Website: http://www.cpi-group.co.uk
Managers: C. Taylor (Tech Serv Mgr), S. Wieliczko (Mgr)
Ultimate Holding Company: CAMERON FRANCE HOLDING SAS (FRANCE)
Immediate Holding Company: CPI COX & WYMAN LTD
Registration no: 03705748 **Date established:** 1999
Turnover: £10m - £20m **No.of Employees:** 51 - 100 **Product Groups:** 28

Date of Accounts	Mar 11	Mar 10	Mar 09
Sales Turnover	18m	15m	15m
Pre Tax Profit/Loss	2m	1m	1m
Working Capital	5m	7m	7m
Fixed Assets	3m	3m	3m
Current Assets	9m	13m	11m
Current Liabilities	1m	946	451

Cromwell Metalworkers Ltd
31 Milford Road, Reading, RG1 8LG
Tel: 0118-958 6818 **Fax:** 0118-958 6826
Directors: J. Cromwell (Co Sec)
Immediate Holding Company: CROMWELL (METALWORKERS) LIMITED
Registration no: 03401725 **Date established:** 1997
Turnover: £250,000 - £500,000 **No.of Employees:** 1 - 10
Product Groups: 26, 35

see next page

Cromwell Metalworkers Ltd - Cont'd

Date of Accounts	Jul 07	Jul 06
Working Capital	20	41
Fixed Assets	5	4
Current Assets	103	113
Current Liabilities	84	72

Custom Control Sensors International

Apollo House Calleva Park, Aldermaston, Reading, RG7 8TN
Tel: 0118-982 0702 **Fax:** 0118-982 1825
E-mail: pswitch@ccsdualsnap.co.uk
Website: http://www.ccsdualsnap.com
Managers: W. Wainwright (Mgr)
Immediate Holding Company: CUSTOM CONTROL SENSORS INTERNATIONAL
Registration no: FC015163 **Date established:** 1989 **Turnover:** £1m - £2m
No.of Employees: 1 - 10 **Product Groups:** 37, 40

D A C O Scientific Ltd

Vulcan House Calleva Industrial Park, Aldermaston, Reading, RG7 8PB
Tel: 0118-981 7311 **Fax:** 0118-981 9963
E-mail: admin@daco.co.uk
Website: http://www.daco.co.uk
Bank(s): National Westminster Bank Plc
Directors: R. Engel (MD)
Immediate Holding Company: DACO SCIENTIFIC LIMITED
Registration no: 02151964 **VAT No.:** GB 200 9279 86
Date established: 1987 **Turnover:** £1m - £2m **No.of Employees:** 21 - 50
Product Groups: 37, 38, 39, 85

Date of Accounts	Sep 11	Sep 10	Sep 09
Working Capital	2m	1m	980
Fixed Assets	144	145	142
Current Assets	4m	2m	2m

D & S Agricultural

Meadowcroft Lambs Lane, Spencers Wood, Reading, RG7 1JB
Tel: 0118-988 3157 **Fax:** 0118-988 3120
E-mail: simon@dsargic.co.uk
Website: http://www.dsagric.co.uk
Directors: S. Peterson (Prop)
Immediate Holding Company: D & S AGRICULTURAL ENGINEERS LIMITED
Registration no: 05941109 **Date established:** 2006
No.of Employees: 1 - 10 **Product Groups:** 41

Date of Accounts	Oct 11	Oct 10	Oct 09
Working Capital	108	99	22
Fixed Assets	110	109	120
Current Assets	442	383	222

Dannah Materials Handling Equipment

43 Walmer Road Woodley, Reading, RG5 4PN
Tel: 0118-969 7386 **Fax:** 0118-961 8903
E-mail: info@dannahstorage.co.uk
Website: http://www.dannahstorage.co.uk
Directors: L. Shaw (Prop)
Date established: 1987 **No.of Employees:** 1 - 10 **Product Groups:** 35, 39, 45

Dawson Marketing

Unit 5 Worton Drive Imperial Way, Reading, RG2 0TG
Tel: 01628-628777 **Fax:** 01628-789634
E-mail: ibale@dawson-marketing.co.uk
Website: http://www.dawsonmarketing.co.uk
Directors: D. Louther (Dir)
Managers: I. Bale (Chief Mgr)
Registration no: 06882361 **Turnover:** £2m - £5m
No.of Employees: 11 - 20 **Product Groups:** 81

Dicoll Data

Unit G1 Lambs Farm Business Park Basingstoke Road, Swallowfield, Reading, RG7 1PQ
Tel: 0118-988 6817 **Fax:** 0118-988 5918
E-mail: sales@dicoll.co.uk
Website: http://www.dicolldata.co.uk
Directors: M. Vandevelde (Prop)
Immediate Holding Company: DICOLL LIMITED
Registration no: 04346835 **Date established:** 2002
No.of Employees: 1 - 10 **Product Groups:** 38, 44

Date of Accounts	Feb 12	Feb 11	Feb 10
Working Capital	85	63	15
Fixed Assets	76	80	92
Current Assets	694	660	727

Direct Wines Ltd

New Aquitaine House Exeter Way, Theale, Reading, RG7 4PL
Tel: 0118-903 0903 **Fax:** 0118-903 0130
E-mail: winesupply@directwines.co.uk
Website: http://www.laithwaites.co.uk
Bank(s): Barclays
Directors: M. Wayne (Pers), S. Mcmurtrie (MD), A. Humpries (Fin)
Ultimate Holding Company: DIRECT WINES HOLDINGS LIMITED
Immediate Holding Company: DIRECT WINES LIMITED
Registration no: 01095091 **Date established:** 1973
Turnover: £125m - £250m **No.of Employees:** 251 - 500
Product Groups: 62, 82

Date of Accounts	Jun 08	Jun 09	Jul 10
Sales Turnover	338m	235m	217m
Pre Tax Profit/Loss	-4m	12m	11m
Working Capital	-7m	-9m	-12m
Fixed Assets	42m	72m	74m
Current Assets	55m	38m	32m
Current Liabilities	2m	21m	18m

Drain & Able

124 Grovelands Road, Reading, RG30 2PD
Tel: 0118-957 6244 **Fax:** 0118-956 7416
E-mail: info@drainandable.co.uk
Website: http://www.drainandable.co.uk
Directors: K. Andrews (Prop)
Immediate Holding Company: DRAIN & ABLE LTD
Registration no: 06686632 **Date established:** 2008
No.of Employees: 1 - 10 **Product Groups:** 35, 48, 54

E D C International Ltd

Brook House 14 Station Road Pangbourne, Reading, RG8 7AN
Tel: 0118-984 2040 **Fax:** 0118-984 5300
E-mail: j.major@edcpumps.com
Website: http://www.edcpumps.com
Managers: J. Major (Comm)
Ultimate Holding Company: CELBAR GMBH (GERMANY)
Immediate Holding Company: E.D.C. INTERNATIONAL LIMITED
Registration no: 01862342 **Date established:** 1984 **Turnover:** £2m - £5m
No.of Employees: 21 - 50 **Product Groups:** 40, 67

Date of Accounts	Dec 11	Dec 10	Dec 09
Working Capital	2m	2m	1m
Fixed Assets	71	46	49
Current Assets	2m	2m	2m

Electro Mechanical Systems (EMS) Ltd (EMS)

Eros House Calleva Industrial Pk, Aldermaston, Reading, RG7 8LN
Tel: 0118-981 7391 **Fax:** 0118-981 7613
E-mail: sgoulding@emsltd.com
Website: http://www.ems-limited.co.uk
Bank(s): Lloyds TSB Bank plc
Directors: M. Seedall (Fab), S. Goulding (Sales & Mktg), M. Seedall (MD)
Registration no: 01902502 **VAT No.:** GB 363 3799 22
Turnover: £5m - £10m **No.of Employees:** 99 **Product Groups:** 35, 37, 38, 39, 45, 49, 67, 68

Date of Accounts	Aug 11	Aug 10	Aug 09
Sales Turnover	13m	12m	10m
Pre Tax Profit/Loss	1m	1m	1m
Working Capital	2m	783	3m
Fixed Assets	772	746	764
Current Assets	4m	4m	5m
Current Liabilities	812	2m	1m

Emerson Climate Technologies Ltd

Unit 17 Theale Lakes Business Park, Sulhamstead, Reading, RG7 4GB
Tel: 0118-983 8000 **Fax:** 0118-983 8001
E-mail: uk.sales@emerson.com
Website: http://www.emersonclimate.eu
Directors: R. Kebby (Sales)
Ultimate Holding Company: EMERSON ELECTRIC CO INC (USA)
Immediate Holding Company: EMERSON CLIMATE TECHNOLOGIES LIMITED
Registration no: 01741737 **Date established:** 1983
Turnover: £20m - £50m **No.of Employees:** 1 - 10 **Product Groups:** 40, 52

Date of Accounts	Sep 11	Sep 10	Sep 09
Sales Turnover	956	975	1m
Pre Tax Profit/Loss	400	351	559
Working Capital	22m	21m	22m
Fixed Assets	7	10	16
Current Assets	22m	21m	23m
Current Liabilities	383	244	637

Esmerk

County House 3rd Floor 17 Friar Street, Reading, RG1 1DB
Tel: 0118-956 5820 **Fax:** 0118-956 5850
E-mail: response@esmerk.com
Website: http://www.esmerk.com
Bank(s): National Westminster Bank Plc
Directors: R. Bigg (Co Sec), D. Cox (MD)
Managers: S. Adams
Ultimate Holding Company: SAMONA CORPORATION (FINLAND)
Immediate Holding Company: ESMERK LIMITED
Registration no: 01518344 **VAT No.:** GB 344 8794 15
Date established: 1980 **Turnover:** £1m - £2m **No.of Employees:** 51 - 100
Product Groups: 80

Date of Accounts	Dec 11	Dec 10	Dec 09
Sales Turnover	2m	2m	2m
Pre Tax Profit/Loss	277	257	304
Working Capital	380	128	35
Fixed Assets	94	123	25
Current Assets	981	636	548
Current Liabilities	600	494	509

European Lighting Group Ltd

6a Portman Road, Reading, RG30 1EA
Tel: 0118-955 3240
Directors: M. Beckett (Fin)
Immediate Holding Company: PIERLITE 2005 LIMITED
Registration no: 05075256 **Date established:** 2004 **Turnover:** £1m - £2m
No.of Employees: 1 - 10 **Product Groups:** 37, 67

Date of Accounts	Jun 10	Jun 09	Jun 08
Sales Turnover	1m	2m	1m
Pre Tax Profit/Loss	-946	-1m	-1m
Working Capital	-5m	-4m	-2m
Fixed Assets	477	493	506
Current Assets	530	658	1m
Current Liabilities	2m	2m	2m

Executive Communications Centres

252-256 Kings Road, Reading, RG1 4HP
Tel: 0118-956 6660 **Fax:** 0118-956 6415
Website: http://www.execentres.co.uk
Bank(s): Barclays
Directors: C. Christofi (Fin)
Managers: S. Fiddy (Mgr)
Immediate Holding Company: LEADING REHAB LIMITED
Registration no: 06770266 **Date established:** 2006
Turnover: Up to £250,000 **No.of Employees:** 11 - 20 **Product Groups:** 80

Date of Accounts	Dec 11	Dec 10	Dec 09
Working Capital	-35	-8	-0
Fixed Assets	1	1	N/A
Current Assets	5	6	1

Expro Group

Davidson House The Forbury, Reading, RG1 3EU
Tel: 0118-959 1341 **Fax:** 0118-958 9000
E-mail: enquiries@exprogroup.com
Website: http://www.exprogroup.com
Bank(s): Bank of Scotland
Directors: A. Geddes (Pers), J. Vernet (Fin)
Managers: C. Woodsburn, M. Ogdan, K. Drumond (Sales & Mktg Mg)
Ultimate Holding Company: UMBRELLASTREAM LIMITED PARTNERSHIP (GUERNSEY)
Immediate Holding Company: EXPRO LION 2 LIMITED
Registration no: 07049428 **VAT No.:** GB 340 4870 69
Date established: 2009 **Turnover:** £75m - £125m
No.of Employees: 21 - 50 **Product Groups:** 13, 51

Date of Accounts	Apr 08	Apr 07	Apr 06
Working Capital	2	4	3
Fixed Assets	1	1	3
Current Assets	3	24	35
Current Liabilities	2	20	32

F P-I M S Southern Ltd

4 Saturn House Calleva Park, Aldermaston, Reading, RG7 8HA
Tel: 0118-982 0988 **Fax:** 0118-982 0924
E-mail: info@ims-franking.co.uk
Website: http://www.ims-franking.co.uk
Directors: J. Lafferty (MD)
Ultimate Holding Company: SNAIL MAIL LIMITED
Immediate Holding Company: FP-IMS (SOUTHERN) LIMITED
Registration no: 03085443 **Date established:** 1995
No.of Employees: 1 - 10 **Product Groups:** 27, 30, 44, 67

Date of Accounts	Jul 11	Jul 10	Jul 09
Working Capital	114	23	112
Fixed Assets	254	307	227
Current Assets	579	456	592

Farm Energy & Control Services Ltd

Unit 4 Wyvols Court Farm Basingstoke Road, Swallowfield, Reading, RG7 1WY
Tel: 0118-988 9093 **Fax:** 0118-931 4432
E-mail: hugh@farmex.co.uk
Website: http://www.farmex.com
Directors: N. Bird (MD)
Immediate Holding Company: FARM ENERGY AND CONTROL SERVICES LIMITED
Registration no: 01493072 **VAT No.:** GB 314 5753 65
Date established: 1980 **Turnover:** £500,000 - £1m
No.of Employees: 1 - 10 **Product Groups:** 38, 49

Date of Accounts	Mar 12	Mar 11	Mar 10
Working Capital	148	100	118
Fixed Assets	20	27	35
Current Assets	261	171	196

FFS Brands Ltd

Unit 1 Headley Park 9 Headley Road East, Woodley, Reading, RG5 4SQ
Tel: 0118-944 1100 **Fax:** 0118-944 1080
E-mail: sales@fast-food-systems.co.uk
Website: http://www.fast-food-systems.co.uk
Bank(s): Lloyds TSB Bank plc
Directors: J. Howard (Sales), A. Withers (MD)
Registration no: 01027727 **VAT No.:** GB 205 9964 41
Date established: 1971 **Turnover:** £5m - £10m **No.of Employees:** 21 - 50
Product Groups: 40, 49, 67, 69, 84

Date of Accounts	Oct 09	Oct 08	Oct 07
Working Capital	-365	-699	-289
Fixed Assets	1m	1m	1m
Current Assets	4	N/A	N/A

Firma Nicand Plastic Products Ltd

Unit D Headley Road East Woodley, Reading, RG5 4SA
Tel: 0118-969 6939 **Fax:** 0118-944 1625
E-mail: kiran@firmanicand.com
Website: http://www.firmanicand.com
Directors: K. Sodhi (Dir), T. Norris (Dir), R. Sodhi (MD)
Immediate Holding Company: FIRMA NICAND PLASTIC PRODUCTS LIMITED
Registration no: 00850082 **VAT No.:** GB 207 9345 55
Date established: 1965 **Turnover:** Up to £250,000
No.of Employees: 1 - 10 **Product Groups:** 30

Date of Accounts	Jul 08	Jul 07	Jul 06
Working Capital	145	124	135
Fixed Assets	92	108	90
Current Assets	364	304	290
Current Liabilities	219	180	156
Total Share Capital	7	7	7

Flowtech Fluid Handling Ltd

8 Gresham Way Industrial Estate Gresham Way, Tilehurst, Reading, RG30 6AW
Tel: 0118-941 3121 **Fax:** 0118-943 1221
E-mail: info@flowtechfh.com
Website: http://www.flowtech.com
Bank(s): HSBC, Broad St
Directors: G. Peacock (MD)
Immediate Holding Company: FLOWTECH FLUID HANDLING LIMITED
Registration no: 01263898 **VAT No.:** GB 200 8197 93
Date established: 1976 **Turnover:** £1m - £2m **No.of Employees:** 11 - 20
Product Groups: 31, 41, 42

Date of Accounts	Apr 11	Apr 10	Apr 09
Working Capital	416	412	404
Fixed Assets	6	13	32
Current Assets	578	600	626

Force Logic UK Ltd

Brookside Business Centre Church Road, Swallowfield, Reading, RG7 1TH
Tel: 0118-988 8807
E-mail: info@force-logic.co.uk
Website: http://www.force-logic.co.uk
Directors: T. Williams (Dir)
Immediate Holding Company: FORCE LOGIC UK LTD
Registration no: 06603297 **Date established:** 2008
No.of Employees: 1 - 10 **Product Groups:** 37, 38, 85

Date of Accounts	Jun 12	Jun 11	Jun 10
Working Capital	41	9	-3
Fixed Assets	11	14	16
Current Assets	114	73	35

Foster Wheeler Energy Ltd

Shinfield Park Shinfield, Reading, RG2 9FW
Tel: 0118-913 1234 **Fax:** 0118-913 2333
E-mail: stephen_culshaw@fwc.com
Website: http://www.fwc.com
Bank(s): Barclays, 9 Gracechurch St, London EC3V 0BB
Directors: M. Beaumont (Dir), M. Davies (Co Sec)
Managers: A. Chong
Ultimate Holding Company: FOSTER WHEELER LTD (BERMUDA)
Immediate Holding Company: FOSTER WHEELER (PROCESS PLANTS) LIMITED
Registration no: 01184855 **VAT No.:** GB 314 5050 02
Date established: 1974 **Turnover:** £250m - £500m
No.of Employees: 1501 & over **Product Groups:** 84

Date of Accounts	Dec 11	Dec 10	Dec 09
Sales Turnover	221m	279m	490m
Pre Tax Profit/Loss	18m	-17m	49m
Working Capital	122m	128m	140m
Fixed Assets	13m	15m	20m
Current Assets	253m	260m	348m
Current Liabilities	68m	71m	98m

Foxconn Emea

Unit 5 Saturn House Calleva Park, Aldermaston, Reading, RG7 8HA
Tel: 0118-982 1472 **Fax:** 0118-982 1343
Website: http://www.foxconn.com
Directors: W. Neen (Dir)
No.of Employees: 1 - 10 **Product Groups:** 37, 67

Fusion Workshop

200 Brook Drive Green Park, Reading, RG2 6UB
Tel: 0118-949 7557
E-mail: chris.short@fusionworkshop.com
Website: http://www.fusionworkshop.com
Directors: C. Short (Grp Chief Exec), M. Topham (Grp Chief Exec)
Managers: M. Kampf (Consultant)
Immediate Holding Company: FUSION WORKSHOP LIMITED
Registration no: 03749987 **Date established:** 1999
Turnover: £250,000 - £500,000 **No.of Employees:** 11 - 20
Product Groups: 44, 79, 80

G B R Technology Ltd

6 Jupiter House Calleva Park, Aldermaston, Reading, RG7 8NN
Tel: 0118-982 0567 **Fax:** 0118-982 0590
E-mail: info@gbrtech.co.uk
Website: http://www.gbrtech.co.uk
Directors: P. Morris (MD)
Immediate Holding Company: GBR TECHNOLOGY LIMITED
Registration no: 01921190 **VAT No.:** GB 592 0282 43
Date established: 1985 **Turnover:** £1m - £2m **No.of Employees:** 1 - 10
Product Groups: 31, 32

Date of Accounts	Jun 11	Jun 10	Jun 09
Sales Turnover	N/A	N/A	1m
Pre Tax Profit/Loss	N/A	N/A	14
Working Capital	491	408	361
Fixed Assets	23	24	27
Current Assets	757	589	488
Current Liabilities	N/A	N/A	45

G D Technik

24 High Street Twyford, Reading, RG10 9AG
Tel: 0118-934 2277 **Fax:** 0118-934 2896
E-mail: info@gd-technik.com
Website: http://www.gd-technik.com
Bank(s): National Westminster Bank Plc
Directors: P. Hargreaves (Fin)
Immediate Holding Company: G D TECHNIK LIMITED
Registration no: 02406535 **Date established:** 1989 **Turnover:** £2m - £5m
No.of Employees: 21 - 50 **Product Groups:** 37, 44

Date of Accounts	Mar 11	Mar 10	Mar 09
Working Capital	-100	-133	-131
Fixed Assets	304	312	319
Current Assets	81	87	319

G T O Engineering Ltd

Scarlett Farm Scarlett Lane Hare Hatch, Kiln Green, Reading, RG10 9XE
Tel: 0118-940 1101
Website: http://www.gtoengineering.com
Directors: M. Lyon (MD)
Immediate Holding Company: GTO ENGINEERING LIMITED
Registration no: 05003180 **Date established:** 2003
No.of Employees: 11 - 20 **Product Groups:** 39, 40

Date of Accounts	Dec 11	Dec 10	Dec 09
Working Capital	-16	-134	-173
Fixed Assets	212	223	318
Current Assets	281	243	139

John Gatward Packaging Ltd

118 Severn Way Tilehurst, Reading, RG30 4HJ
Tel: 0118-942 5851 **Fax:** 0870-051 0342
E-mail: john@gatpack.prestel.co.uk
Website: http://www.gatpack.co.uk
Directors: J. Gatward (MD)
Immediate Holding Company: JOHN GATWARD PACKAGING LIMITED
Registration no: 04774988 **Date established:** 2003
Turnover: £250,000 - £500,000 **No.of Employees:** 1 - 10
Product Groups: 23, 42, 43, 45

Date of Accounts	May 12	May 11	May 10
Working Capital	307	258	203
Fixed Assets	4	4	5
Current Assets	391	359	319
Current Liabilities	57	59	N/A

Gemini Technology Ltd

Unit 5 Wellington Industrial Estate Basingstoke Road, Spencers Wood, Reading, RG7 1AW
Tel: 0118-988 8260 **Fax:** 0118-988 5637
E-mail: tonybates@gemini-tech.demon.co.uk
Website: http://www.geminitechnologyltd.com
Directors: T. Bates (MD)
Immediate Holding Company: GEMINI TECHNOLOGY (READING) LIMITED
Registration no: 02933564 **Date established:** 1994
Turnover: £50m - £75m **No.of Employees:** 1 - 10 **Product Groups:** 37, 84

Date of Accounts	May 11	May 10	May 09
Sales Turnover	N/A	N/A	718
Pre Tax Profit/Loss	N/A	N/A	126
Working Capital	2	7	77
Fixed Assets	327	346	357
Current Assets	91	123	224
Current Liabilities	N/A	72	75

John George & Sons Ltd

2-4 Deacon Way Tilehurst, Reading, RG30 6AZ
Tel: 0118-941 1234 **Fax:** 0118-945 1059
E-mail: reading@johngeorge.co.uk
Website: http://www.johngeorge.co.uk
Bank(s): Barclays
Directors: B. Lambert (MD), M. Lambert (Dir)
Ultimate Holding Company: DEACON HOLDINGS LIMITED
Immediate Holding Company: JOHN GEORGE & SONS LIMITED
Registration no: 01573582 **VAT No.:** GB 200 4881 03
Date established: 1981 **Turnover:** £5m - £10m **No.of Employees:** 21 - 50
Product Groups: 35, 66

Date of Accounts	Dec 11	Dec 10	Dec 09
Sales Turnover	8m	8m	7m
Pre Tax Profit/Loss	185	199	298
Working Capital	2m	1m	1m
Fixed Assets	236	211	177
Current Assets	3m	2m	2m
Current Liabilities	537	661	209

Gift Time Ltd

Jade House 25-27 Farnham Drive Caversham, Reading, RG4 6NY
Tel: 0118-947 1405 **Fax:** 0118-947 1605
E-mail: david@gtltd.eu
Website: http://www.gift-time-products.co.uk
Directors: D. Weiss (MD)
Immediate Holding Company: GIFT TIME LIMITED
Registration no: 04386522 **VAT No.:** GB 614 5337 55
Date established: 2002 **Turnover:** Up to £250,000
No.of Employees: 1 - 10 **Product Groups:** 49, 65

Date of Accounts	Mar 12	Mar 11	Mar 10
Working Capital	-139	-97	-81
Current Assets	240	246	244

Gillette UK Ltd

452 Basingstoke Road, Reading, RG2 0QE
Tel: 0118-987 5222 **Fax:** 0118-986 3144
Website: http://www.gillette.com
Bank(s): National Westminster Bank Plc
Directors: K. Powell (Dir)
Managers: N. Ryder (Sales Prom Mgr)
Ultimate Holding Company: Procter & Gamble Holdings UK Ltd
Immediate Holding Company: Gillette Industries Ltd
Registration no: 00254912 **Date established:** 2002
Turnover: £500,000 - £1m **No.of Employees:** 251 - 500
Product Groups: 30, 32, 85

Campbell Gordon

50 Queens Road, Reading, RG1 4HU
Tel: 0118-959 7555 **Fax:** 0118-959 7550
E-mail: info@campbellgordon.co.uk
Website: http://www.campbellgordon.co.uk
Directors: L. Campbell (Fin), I. Campbell (Snr Part)
Immediate Holding Company: CAMPBELL GORDON
Registration no: 04637950 **Date established:** 2003
Turnover: £500,000 - £1m **No.of Employees:** 1 - 10 **Product Groups:** 80

Graham

Cradock Road, Reading, RG2 0JT
Tel: 0118-987 5321 **Fax:** 0118-986 3814
E-mail: chris.thomas@jewson.co.uk
Website: http://www.graham-group.co.uk
Managers: C. Thomas (Chief Mgr)
Registration no: 00066738 **No.of Employees:** 51 - 100
Product Groups: 66

Greenwood Electronic Components Ltd

Ferndale Court 6 West End Road, Mortimer Common, Reading, RG7 3SY
Tel: 0118-933 3788 **Fax:** 0118-933 3878
E-mail: sales@greenwood-electronics.co.uk
Website: http://www.greenwood-electronics.co.uk
Managers: S. Janison (Sales Prom Mgr)
Immediate Holding Company: GREENWOOD ELECTRONIC COMPONENTS LIMITED
Registration no: 02616969 **VAT No.:** GB 569 9228 80
Date established: 1991 **Turnover:** £2m - £5m **No.of Employees:** 1 - 10
Product Groups: 37, 46

Date of Accounts	Jun 11	Jun 10	Jun 09
Working Capital	104	135	177
Fixed Assets	1	N/A	N/A
Current Assets	200	221	303
Current Liabilities	54	N/A	N/A

Alan Hadley Ltd

Station Road Theale, Reading, RG7 4AJ
Tel: 0118-932 3444 **Fax:** 0118-930 6508
E-mail: waste@hadleys.co.uk
Website: http://www.hadleys.co.uk
Bank(s): National Westminster Bank Plc
Directors: T. Harper (MD)
Managers: A. Gardiner (Tech Serv Mgr)
Ultimate Holding Company: CLAUDE FENTON (HOLDINGS) LIMITED
Immediate Holding Company: ALAN HADLEY LIMITED
Registration no: 00277871 **Date established:** 1933 **Turnover:** £5m - £10m
No.of Employees: 21 - 50 **Product Groups:** 14, 51, 54, 83

Date of Accounts	Sep 11	Sep 10	Sep 09
Sales Turnover	4m	5m	8m
Pre Tax Profit/Loss	23	-640	-2m
Working Capital	-1m	-1m	-1m
Fixed Assets	527	844	2m
Current Assets	703	1m	2m
Current Liabilities	271	621	1m

Heath Lambert Group

175 Kings Road, Reading, RG1 4EY
Tel: 0118-959 7951 **Fax:** 0118-950 8545
E-mail: info@heathlambert.com
Website: http://www.keyconnect.co.uk
Directors: D. Herring (Ch)
Ultimate Holding Company: HLG HOLDINGS LIMITED
Immediate Holding Company: HEATH LAMBERT GROUP LIMITED
Registration no: 05347036 **Date established:** 2005
Turnover: £125m - £250m **No.of Employees:** 51 - 100
Product Groups: 80, 82

Henley Marketing Services Ltd

Tavistock Industrial Estate Ruscombe Lane, Ruscombe, Reading, RG10 9NQ
Tel: 0118-924 1800 **Fax:** 0118-934 1335
E-mail: sally@henleymarketing.com
Website: http://www.henleymarketing.com
Bank(s): Barclays, Reading
Directors: D. Amor (MD), S. Why (MD)
Managers: D. Killoran (I.T. Exec)
Immediate Holding Company: HENLEY MARKETING SERVICES LIMITED
Registration no: 01468525 **Date established:** 1979 **Turnover:** £5m - £10m
No.of Employees: 11 - 20 **Product Groups:** 44, 81

Date of Accounts	Dec 08	Dec 07	Dec 06
Working Capital	-88	14	19
Fixed Assets	14	24	35
Current Assets	279	414	368

Hills Rubber Co. Ltd

85 Bedford Road, Reading, RG1 7EZ
Tel: 0118-958 0535 **Fax:** 0118-950 3083
E-mail: hillsrubber@hotmail.com
Website: http://www.hillsrubber.co.uk
Directors: S. Coughlin (Dir)
Immediate Holding Company: HILL'S RUBBER COMPANY,LIMITED
Registration no: 00063593 **VAT No.:** GB 199 1184 28
Date established: 1999 **Turnover:** £250,000 - £500,000
No.of Employees: 1 - 10 **Product Groups:** 02, 22, 23, 24, 25, 26, 27, 28, 29, 30, 31, 32, 33, 35, 36, 37, 38, 39, 40, 41, 42, 43, 44, 46, 48, 49, 52, 61, 63, 64, 65, 66, 67, 81, 84, 85

Date of Accounts	Jan 11	Jan 10	Jan 09
Working Capital	5	15	7
Fixed Assets	19	9	10
Current Assets	60	68	69

Holt Broadcast Services Ltd

Unit 13 Nimrod Industrial Estate Nimrod Way, Reading, RG2 0EB
Tel: 0118-931 0770 **Fax:** 0118-931 0696
E-mail: info@holtbroadcast.co.uk
Website: http://www.holtbroadcast.co.uk
Bank(s): Yorkshire Bank PLC
Managers: C. Hunter (Sales Admin)
Immediate Holding Company: HOLT BROADCAST SERVICES LIMITED
Registration no: 05252786 **VAT No.:** GB 614 9043 52
Date established: 2004 **Turnover:** £1m - £2m **No.of Employees:** 11 - 20
Product Groups: 37, 48

Date of Accounts	Mar 12	Mar 11	Mar 10
Working Capital	595	669	515
Fixed Assets	75	102	207
Current Assets	972	1m	914

Horsleys Ltd

PO Box 119, Reading, RG7 5NQ
Tel: 0118-971 3223 **Fax:** 0118-971 3225
E-mail: info@horsleys.com
Website: http://www.horsleys.com
Directors: E. Feltham (Co Sec), G. Horsley (MD)
Immediate Holding Company: HORSLEYS LIMITED
Registration no: 02209265 **VAT No.:** GB 491 5493 19
Date established: 1987 **Turnover:** £500,000 - £1m
No.of Employees: 1 - 10 **Product Groups:** 39, 41

Date of Accounts	Jun 11	Jun 10	Jun 09
Working Capital	13	11	1
Fixed Assets	7	8	10
Current Assets	157	165	178

Hydromech Manufacturing (Incorporating Brimpex-Eccles)

Unit 41 Youngs Industrial Estate, Aldermaston, Reading, RG7 4PW
Tel: 0118-981 7787 **Fax:** 0118-981 0181
Website: http://www.hydromech.co.uk
Directors: R. Philpotts (Prop)
Turnover: Up to £250,000 **No.of Employees:** 1 - 10 **Product Groups:** 45

Hytec Electronics Ltd

5 Craddock Road, Reading, RG2 0JT
Tel: 0118-975 7770 **Fax:** 0118-975 7566
E-mail: sales@hytec-electronics.co.uk
Website: http://www.hytec-electronics.co.uk
Bank(s): National Westminster Bank Plc
Directors: R. Tatham (MD)
Immediate Holding Company: HYTEC ELECTRONICS LIMITED
Registration no: 01246940 **Date established:** 1976 **Turnover:** £1m - £2m
No.of Employees: 11 - 20 **Product Groups:** 37, 38, 44

Date of Accounts	Sep 11	Sep 10	Sep 09
Working Capital	694	620	417
Fixed Assets	174	205	169
Current Assets	932	869	929

I N I Environmental Services Ltd

77 Westwood Glen Tilehurst, Reading, RG31 5NW
Tel: 0118-942 7314 **Fax:** 0118-942 7313
E-mail: inienviro@aol.com
Directors: J. Woodward (Fin), J. Woodward (Co Sec), I. Woodward (Chief Op Offcr)
Immediate Holding Company: INI ENVIRONMENTAL SERVICES LIMITED
Registration no: 02411612 **Date established:** 1989
Turnover: Up to £250,000 **No.of Employees:** 1 - 10 **Product Groups:** 54, 67

Date of Accounts	Aug 10	Aug 09	Aug 07
Working Capital	-10	-5	-4
Fixed Assets	14	6	5
Current Assets	12	16	19

Impact Handling

Atlantic House Imperial Way, Reading, RG2 0TD
Tel: 0118-903 6018
E-mail: sales@impact-handling.com
Website: http://www.impact-handling.com
Managers: A. Deklerk (Develop Mgr)
Immediate Holding Company: IMPACT BUSINESS GROUP LTD
Registration no: 07081523 **Date established:** 2009
Turnover: Up to £250,000 **No.of Employees:** 1 - 10 **Product Groups:** 45, 67, 86

Date of Accounts	Nov 11	Nov 10
Working Capital	1	1
Current Assets	1	1

Infotec UK Ltd

1650 Arlington Business Park Theale, Reading, RG7 4SA
Tel: 0118-928 4900 **Fax:** 0118-928 4901
Website: http://www.ukinfotec.co.uk
Directors: P. McKenna (MD), N. Downing (Dir), P. Williams (Grp Chief Exec)
Immediate Holding Company: INFOTEC UK LIMITED
Registration no: 02199112 **Date established:** 1987
Turnover: £20m - £50m **No.of Employees:** 251 - 500
Product Groups: 44, 67

Installation Technology

Unit 13 Headley Park Area 10, Woodley, Reading, RG5 4SW
Tel: 0118-969 9777 **Fax:** 0118-969 8282
E-mail: info@installationtechnology.com
Website: http://www.installationtechnology.com
Bank(s): Bank of Scotland
Directors: B. Gough (Dir)
Managers: K. Roberts (Projects)
Ultimate Holding Company: TECHOLD LIMITED
Immediate Holding Company: INSTALLATION TECHNOLOGY LIMITED
Registration no: SC147188 **VAT No.:** GB 603 8593 37
Date established: 1993 **Turnover:** £2m - £5m **No.of Employees:** 11 - 20
Product Groups: 37, 44

see next page

***Installation Technology** - Cont'd*

Date of Accounts	Sep 11	Sep 10	Sep 09
Working Capital	277	-94	-32
Fixed Assets	306	494	520
Current Assets	2m	787	905

Integralis Ltd
Theale House Brunel Road, Theale, Reading, RG7 4AQ
Tel: 0118-930 6060 **Fax:** 0118-930 2143
E-mail: info@integralis.com
Website: http://www.integralis.com
Bank(s): Barclays
Directors: R. Woudberg (Co Sec)
Ultimate Holding Company: NTT COMMUNICATIONS CORP (JAPAN)
Immediate Holding Company: INTEGRALIS LIMITED
Registration no: 03403334 **Date established:** 1997
Turnover: £50m - £75m **No.of Employees:** 101 - 250
Product Groups: 44, 80

Date of Accounts	Dec 11	Dec 10	Dec 09
Sales Turnover	68m	69m	61m
Pre Tax Profit/Loss	-321	1m	-1m
Working Capital	9m	10m	9m
Fixed Assets	3m	3m	2m
Current Assets	43m	49m	40m
Current Liabilities	22m	28m	23m

Interserve plc
Interserve House Ruscombe Park, Ruscombe, Reading, RG10 9JU
Tel: 0118-932 0123 **Fax:** 0118-932 0206
E-mail: info@interserve.com
Website: http://www.interserve.com
Bank(s): Royal Bank of Scotland, HSBC
Directors: A. Ringrose (Grp Chief Exec), T. Hayward (Fin), T. Bradbury (Co Sec)
Managers: E. Clarke (Personnel)
Ultimate Holding Company: INTERSERVE PLC
Immediate Holding Company: INTERSERVE HOLDINGS LIMITED
Registration no: 00252221 **VAT No.:** GB 527 1285 46
Date established: 1930 **Turnover:** Over £1,000m
No.of Employees: 51 - 100 **Product Groups:** 51, 52, 83, 84

Date of Accounts	Dec 11	Dec 10	Dec 09
Pre Tax Profit/Loss	16m	17m	3m
Working Capital	26m	2m	-15m
Fixed Assets	34m	34m	31m
Current Assets	29m	2m	22m

Isotron Ltd
Unit 2 Marcus Close Tilehurst, Reading, RG30 4EA
Tel: 0118-942 1061 **Fax:** 0118-943 1262
E-mail: info@isotron.com
Website: http://www.isotron.com
Managers: D. Newell (Mgr)
Ultimate Holding Company: SYNERGY HEALTH PLC
Immediate Holding Company: ISOTRON LIMITED
Registration no: 04828896 **Date established:** 2003
No.of Employees: 1 - 10 **Product Groups:** 84

J Brant Reclamation Ltd
Lakeside Farm Within Lakeside Garden Centre Brimpton Common Road, Brimpton Common, Reading, RG7 4RT
Tel: 0118-981 3882 **Fax:** 0118-981 9700
E-mail: juliebrant@hotmail.co.uk
Website: http://www.jbrant.co.uk
Directors: J. Brant (Prop)
Immediate Holding Company: J BRANT RECLAMATION LIMITED
Registration no: 03381646 **Date established:** 1997
Turnover: £500,000 - £1m **No.of Employees:** 1 - 10 **Product Groups:** 33, 51

Date of Accounts	Jun 11	Jun 10	Jun 09
Working Capital	22	25	25
Fixed Assets	8	2	3
Current Assets	152	122	85

J C Engineering
17-19 Loverock Road, Reading, RG30 1DZ
Tel: 0118-958 1926 **Fax:** 0118-950 4018
E-mail: ashley.churchill@btinternet.com
Website: http://www.jceng.co.uk
Directors: D. Churchill (Prop)
Date established: 1966 **Turnover:** £500,000 - £1m
No.of Employees: 1 - 10 **Product Groups:** 48

J V S Protective Clothing
216 Hyde End Road Spencers Wood, Reading, RG7 1DG
Tel: 0118-988 5686 **Fax:** 0118-988 5686
E-mail: info@jvsprocloth.co.uk
Website: http://www.jvsprocloth.co.uk
Directors: J. Vennell (Prop)
No.of Employees: 1 - 10 **Product Groups:** 22, 24, 40, 49

Jaguar Epresso Systems
Unit 1 Albury Close, Reading, RG30 1BD
Tel: 0118-959 9204 **Fax:** 0118-959 9205
E-mail: sales@jaguarespresso.co.uk
Website: http://www.jaguarespresso.co.uk
Managers: J. Russell (Mgr)
Immediate Holding Company: JAMES & ALAN RUSSELL
Date established: 2001 **Turnover:** £1m - £2m **No.of Employees:** 11 - 20
Product Groups: 40

Jamesway Ltd
Orchard Nursery Orchard Road, Hurst, Reading, RG10 0SD
Tel: 0118-932 0775 **Fax:** 0118-932 0705
E-mail: sales@jamesautomation.co.uk
Website: http://www.jamesautomation.co.uk
Directors: P. James (MD)
Registration no: 05145140 **Date established:** 2004
No.of Employees: 1 - 10 **Product Groups:** 26, 35

Date of Accounts	Nov 07	Nov 06	Nov 05
Working Capital	-5	10	10
Fixed Assets	48	55	52
Current Assets	128	131	78
Current Liabilities	134	122	68

Jaymar Engineering
Headley Road East Woodley, Reading, RG5 4SZ
Tel: 0118-944 8899 **Fax:** 0118-944 9883
E-mail: steve-heath@btconnect.com
Directors: S. Heath (Prop)
Immediate Holding Company: LANTEC SECURITY LIMITED
Registration no: 01078701 **Date established:** 2009
Turnover: Up to £250,000 **No.of Employees:** 1 - 10 **Product Groups:** 85

Date of Accounts	Jun 11	Jun 10
Working Capital	26	22
Fixed Assets	5	3
Current Assets	149	72
Current Liabilities	37	N/A

Jekyll Electronic Technology Ltd
Unit 3 Zephyr House Calleva Park, Aldermaston, Reading, RG7 8JN
Tel: 0118-981 7321 **Fax:** 0118-981 4743
E-mail: mail@jekyll-electronic.co.uk
Website: http://www.jekyll-electronic.co.uk
Directors: I. Robinson (MD)
Managers: N. Lundy (Tech Serv Mgr)
Ultimate Holding Company: The Imc Group Ltd
Immediate Holding Company: Lamerholm Holdings Ltd
Registration no: 01554249 **VAT No.:** GB 342 9628 39
Date established: 1991 **Turnover:** £1m - £2m **No.of Employees:** 1 - 10
Product Groups: 37, 44, 67

Jewson Ltd
468 Basingstoke Road, Reading, RG2 0QQ
Tel: 0118-986 1992 **Fax:** 0118-975 0395
Website: http://www.jewson.co.uk
Managers: D. Gibbs (Mgr)
Ultimate Holding Company: COMPAGNIE DE SAINT GOBAIN (FRANCE)
Immediate Holding Company: JEWSON LIMITED
Registration no: 00348407 **VAT No.:** GB 497 7184 83
Date established: 1939 **Turnover:** £2m - £5m **No.of Employees:** 1 - 10
Product Groups: 66

Date of Accounts	Dec 11	Dec 10	Dec 09
Sales Turnover	1606m	1547m	1485m
Pre Tax Profit/Loss	18m	100m	45m
Working Capital	-345m	-250m	-349m
Fixed Assets	496m	387m	461m
Current Assets	657m	1005m	1320m
Current Liabilities	66m	120m	64m

Johnstone's Paints Ltd
3 Mayfield Trade Centre Acre Road, Reading, RG2 0RJ
Tel: 0118-987 5266 **Fax:** 0118-975 0281
Website: http://www.johnstonespaint.com
Managers: G. Trehan (Mgr)
Ultimate Holding Company: P P G INDUSTRIES INC (USA)
Immediate Holding Company: JOHNSTONE'S PAINTS LIMITED
Registration no: 00513910 **Date established:** 1952
No.of Employees: 1 - 10 **Product Groups:** 61

Date of Accounts	Dec 11	Dec 10	Dec 09
Working Capital	41m	41m	41m
Fixed Assets	1m	1m	1m
Current Assets	42m	42m	42m
Current Liabilities	N/A	9	9

Just Tiles Ltd
88 Headley Road Woodley, Reading, RG5 4JE
Tel: 0118-969 7774 **Fax:** 0118-944 1235
E-mail: enquiries@justtiles.co.uk
Website: http://www.justtiles.co.uk
Directors: A. Packham (Dir), G. Elson (Fin)
Immediate Holding Company: JUST TILES LIMITED
Registration no: 01055466 **Date established:** 1972
Turnover: £250,000 - £500,000 **No.of Employees:** 11 - 20
Product Groups: 33, 66

Date of Accounts	Jun 11	Jun 10	Jun 09
Working Capital	197	179	208
Fixed Assets	74	80	103
Current Assets	428	383	420

K A P Welding Services Ltd
Thurley Farm Lambwood Hill, Grazeley, Reading, RG7 1JN
Tel: 0118-988 5615
E-mail: info@kapwelding.co.uk
Website: http://www.kapwelding.co.uk
Directors: P. Ayres (MD)
Immediate Holding Company: K.A.P. WELDING SERVICES LTD
Registration no: 04493253 **Date established:** 2002
No.of Employees: 11 - 20 **Product Groups:** 35, 48

Date of Accounts	Sep 11	Sep 10	Sep 09
Working Capital	5	39	38
Fixed Assets	37	39	104
Current Assets	572	367	213

K E C Ltd
Unit 5 Orpheus House Calleva Park, Aldermaston, Reading, RG7 8TA
Tel: 0118-981 1571 **Fax:** 0118-981 1570
E-mail: sales@kec.co.uk
Website: http://www.kec.co.uk
Directors: C. Watson (MD)
Immediate Holding Company: KEC LIMITED
Registration no: 01287711 **VAT No.:** GB 641 7443 43
Date established: 1976 **Turnover:** £500,000 - £1m
No.of Employees: 1 - 10 **Product Groups:** 37, 38

Date of Accounts	Sep 11	Sep 10	Sep 09
Working Capital	79	81	76
Fixed Assets	26	20	19
Current Assets	276	256	272

Keithley Instruments Ltd
2 Commerce Park Brunel Road, Theale, Reading, RG7 4AB
Tel: 0118-929 7500 **Fax:** 0118-929 7519
E-mail: info@keithley.co.uk
Website: http://www.keithley.com
Directors: J. Keithley (MD)
Managers: I. Ramsey (Mgr)
Ultimate Holding Company: KEITHLEY INSTRUMENTS INC (USA)
Immediate Holding Company: KEITHLEY INSTRUMENTS LIMITED
Registration no: 00918130 **VAT No.:** GB 199 3995 78
Date established: 1967 **Turnover:** £1m - £2m **No.of Employees:** 1 - 10
Product Groups: 38

Date of Accounts	Sep 10	Sep 09	Sep 08
Sales Turnover	2m	2m	2m
Pre Tax Profit/Loss	13	-512	-15
Working Capital	100	85	69
Fixed Assets	N/A	N/A	26
Current Assets	354	398	411
Current Liabilities	193	200	169

Keraflo Ltd
Unit 1 Woodley Park Estate 59-69 Reading Road, Woodley, Reading, RG5 3AN
Tel: 0118-921 9920 **Fax:** 0118-921 9921
E-mail: info@keraflo.co.uk
Website: http://www.keraflo.co.uk
Directors: S. Johnson (Fin)
Ultimate Holding Company: DAVIDSON HOLDINGS LIMITED
Immediate Holding Company: KERAFLO LIMITED
Registration no: 01774986 **VAT No.:** GB 348 9364 11
Date established: 1983 **Turnover:** £500,000 - £1m
No.of Employees: 21 - 50 **Product Groups:** 36, 40

Date of Accounts	Apr 11	Apr 10	Apr 09
Sales Turnover	N/A	1m	1m
Pre Tax Profit/Loss	N/A	361	372
Working Capital	1m	988	752
Fixed Assets	20	13	4
Current Assets	2m	2m	1m
Current Liabilities	N/A	206	214

Key Electronic Components
4 Kitwood Drive Lower Earley, Reading, RG6 3TA
Tel: 0118-935 1546 **Fax:** 0118-966 0294
E-mail: sales@keyelectronic.com
Website: http://www.keyelectronic.com
Directors: M. Brackenberry (Ptnr), M. Brackenberry (MD), M. Brackenbury (Fin), H. Brackenberry (Ptnr), H. Brackenbury (MD)
Immediate Holding Company: KEY ELECTRONIC COMPONENTS LIMITED
Registration no: 04456220 **VAT No.:** GB 569 8945 57
Date established: 2002 **Turnover:** Up to £250,000
No.of Employees: 1 - 10 **Product Groups:** 37, 40

Date of Accounts	May 11	May 10	May 09
Working Capital	-0	2	-1
Fixed Assets	1	1	2
Current Assets	19	22	21

Kover It
Care of Ladds Garden Village Bath Road, Hare Hatch, Reading, RG10 9SW
Tel: 0118-940 6095 **Fax:** 08719-895598
E-mail: sales@kover-it.co.uk
Website: http://www.kover-it.co.uk
Directors: D. Beecham (Prop)
Immediate Holding Company: L.A.D.D. LIMITED
Registration no: 01089020 **Date established:** 1972
No.of Employees: 1 - 10 **Product Groups:** 24, 35, 63

Date of Accounts	Dec 11	Dec 10	Dec 09
Working Capital	-113	-84	-89
Fixed Assets	373	383	402
Current Assets	18	40	44

Kreaser
215 Wykeham Road, Reading, RG6 1PL
Tel: 0118-967 6825
E-mail: info@kreaser.co.uk
Website: http://www.kreaser.co.uk
Product Groups: 23, 24, 63

Lamport Gilbert Ltd
3 Darwin Close, Reading, RG2 0TB
Tel: 0118-931 0013 **Fax:** 0118-916 9250
E-mail: arobbins@lamport.co.uk
Website: http://www.lamportgilbert.co.uk
Bank(s): The Royal Bank of Scotland
Directors: S. Morris (Fin), C. Day (Sales), A. Robbins (Comm)
Managers: J. Evans (Tech Serv Mgr), S. Prosser (Personnel)
Ultimate Holding Company: BRICKELL HOLDINGS LIMITED
Immediate Holding Company: LAMPORT GILBERT LIMITED
Registration no: 03278552 **Date established:** 1996 **Turnover:** £2m - £5m
No.of Employees: 21 - 50 **Product Groups:** 28

Date of Accounts	Jun 11	Jun 10	Jun 09
Sales Turnover	4m	3m	4m
Pre Tax Profit/Loss	-224	-113	-39
Working Capital	-610	-490	-75
Fixed Assets	1m	896	1m
Current Assets	636	739	1m
Current Liabilities	157	108	86

Le Carousel Ipf Ltd
35 Easter Park Benyon Road, Silchester, Reading, RG7 2PQ
Tel: 0118-970 0228 **Fax:** 0118-970 1944
E-mail: info@lecarouselipf.co.uk
Website: http://www.lecarouselipf.co.uk
Directors: S. Mitchell (Dir)
Immediate Holding Company: LE CAROUSEL IPF LTD.
Registration no: 06917294 **Date established:** 2009
No.of Employees: 1 - 10 **Product Groups:** 48

Date of Accounts	Aug 11
Working Capital	16
Fixed Assets	12
Current Assets	58

Light Speed Business Solutions Ltd
Unit 4a Woodley Park Estate 59-69 Reading Road, Woodley, Reading, RG5 3AW
Tel: 0118-927 2777 **Fax:** 0118-927 2888
E-mail: info@lightsol.co.uk
Website: http://www.lightsol.co.uk
Directors: A. Guice (MD), A. Forward (Dir)
Immediate Holding Company: LIGHTSPEED BUSINESS SOLUTIONS LIMITED
Registration no: 03760270 **Date established:** 1999
Turnover: £500,000 - £1m **No.of Employees:** 11 - 20
Product Groups: 44, 81

Date of Accounts	Mar 12	Mar 11	Mar 10
Working Capital	46	29	19
Fixed Assets	32	31	37
Current Assets	156	162	140

Lighting Services Inc
252-256 Kings Road, Reading, RG1 4HP
Tel: 0118-953 3753 **Fax:** 0118-956 6415
Managers: M. Roberts (Sales Prom Mgr), J. Brown (Mgr)
Immediate Holding Company: LEADING REHAB LIMITED
Date established: 2006 **No.of Employees:** 1 - 10 **Product Groups:** 37, 67

Date of Accounts	Dec 11	Dec 10	Dec 09
Working Capital	-35	-8	-0
Fixed Assets	1	1	N/A
Current Assets	5	6	1

M D 3 D Ltd
4 Reading Road Pangbourne, Reading, RG8 7LY
Tel: 01491-671800 **Fax:** 01491-672173
E-mail: sales@md3d.uk.com
Website: http://www.md3d.uk.com
Directors: M. Davies (MD)
Immediate Holding Company: MD3D LTD
Registration no: 05327633 **Date established:** 2005
Turnover: Up to £250,000 **No.of Employees:** 1 - 10 **Product Groups:** 38

Date of Accounts	Jan 12	Jan 11	Jan 10
Working Capital	17	14	18
Fixed Assets	1	2	1
Current Assets	39	74	163

M M A Insurance plc
2 Norman Place, Reading, RG1 8DA
Tel: 0118-955 2222 **Fax:** 0118-955 2211
E-mail: info@mma-insurance.com
Website: http://www.mma-insurance.com
Bank(s): HSBC
Directors: S. Whittaker (Fin), D. Plummer (Comm), G. Fearn (MD)
Managers: M. Flower (Personnel), B. Wallace (Sales Admin)
Ultimate Holding Company: LE MANS CONSEIL (FRANCE)
Immediate Holding Company: MMA INSURANCE PLC
Registration no: 00613259 **Date established:** 1958
Turnover: £75m - £125m **No.of Employees:** 251 - 500
Product Groups: 82

Date of Accounts	Dec 11	Dec 10	Dec 09
Pre Tax Profit/Loss	7m	1m	-14m
Working Capital	79m	N/A	N/A
Fixed Assets	313m	305m	294m
Current Assets	92m	118m	142m
Current Liabilities	13m	6m	14m

M & R Airflow Ltd
11 St James Close Pangbourne, Reading, RG8 7AP
Tel: 0118-984 5111 **Fax:** 0118-984 5111
E-mail: richard@mrairflow.com
Website: http://www.mrairflow.com
Directors: J. Short (Fin), R. Elbro (MD)
Immediate Holding Company: M & R AIRFLOW LIMITED
Registration no: 04592115 **Date established:** 2002 **Turnover:** £1m - £2m
No.of Employees: 1 - 10 **Product Groups:** 37, 40, 48

Date of Accounts	Nov 11	Nov 10	Nov 09
Sales Turnover	1m	593	1m
Pre Tax Profit/Loss	280	64	457
Working Capital	190	135	318
Fixed Assets	27	26	32
Current Assets	372	223	639
Current Liabilities	125	50	175

Mabey Holdings Ltd
Floral Mile Twyford, Hare Hatch, Reading, RG10 9SQ
Tel: 0118-940 3921 **Fax:** 0118-940 3941
E-mail: sales@mabey.co.uk
Website: http://www.mabey.co.uk
Directors: S. Precious (Dir)
Ultimate Holding Company: MABEY HOLDINGS LIMITED
Immediate Holding Company: MABEY ENGINEERING (HOLDINGS) LIMITED
Registration no: 01560295 **VAT No.:** GB 419 4576 28
Date established: 1981 **Turnover:** £75m - £125m
No.of Employees: 1 - 10 **Product Groups:** 35, 51

Date of Accounts	Sep 11	Sep 10	Sep 09
Pre Tax Profit/Loss	12m	-1m	-865
Working Capital	6m	-35m	-26m
Fixed Assets	184m	65m	58m
Current Assets	6m	1m	4m
Current Liabilities	134	N/A	N/A

Materion Brush Ltd
Unit 4 Ely Road Theale Commercial Estate, Theale, Reading, RG7 4BQ
Tel: 0118-930 3733 **Fax:** 0118-920 3635
E-mail: guy.shapland@materion.com
Website: http://www.materion.com
Directors: R. Trate (Dir), G. Shapland (MD), B. Ballinger (Dir)
Managers: A. Whitaker (Sales Eng)
Ultimate Holding Company: MATERION CORPORATION INC (USA)
Immediate Holding Company: MATERION BRUSH INC
Registration no: 00731182 **VAT No.:** GB 198 9769 63
Date established: 1962 **Turnover:** £500,000 - £1m **No.of Employees:** 10
Product Groups: 12, 31, 34, 35, 37, 66

Date of Accounts	Dec 11	Dec 10	Dec 09
Sales Turnover	514	583	2m
Pre Tax Profit/Loss	-252	-123	18
Working Capital	566	809	877
Fixed Assets	34	44	98
Current Assets	660	1m	1m
Current Liabilities	89	200	224

Maxim Integrated Products Ltd
Unit 3 Technology Centre, Station Road, Reading, RG7 4XX
Tel: 0118-900 6300
E-mail: sales@maxim-ic.com
Website: http://www.maxim-ic.com
Directors: J. Sanchez (MD)
Registration no: 01873931 **No.of Employees:** 1 - 10 **Product Groups:** 36, 37

Maxtag UK Ltd
8 Suttons Business Park Earley, Reading, RG6 1AZ
Tel: 0118-935 6180 **Fax:** 0118-935 6181
E-mail: enquiries@maxtag.com
Website: http://www.maxtag.com
Directors: G. Gordon (MD)
Immediate Holding Company: MAXTAG (UK) LIMITED
Registration no: 03314657 **Date established:** 1997
No.of Employees: 11 - 20 **Product Groups:** 36, 40, 42, 67

Date of Accounts	Dec 11	Dec 10	Dec 09
Working Capital	515	540	544
Fixed Assets	34	31	59
Current Assets	799	789	898

Medical Solutions UK
11 Reading Road Woodley, Reading, RG5 3DA
Tel: 0118-961 8204 **Fax:** 0118-962 8795
E-mail: info@itmd.co.uk
Directors: R. Platt (Dir)
Turnover: £500,000 - £1m **No.of Employees:** 1 - 10 **Product Groups:** 24, 63, 64

MetalPaper Ltd
Unit 3B Pincents Kiln Industrial Park Pincents Lane, Calcot, Reading, RG31 7SD
Tel: 0118-930 6040 **Fax:** 0118-932 3184
E-mail: sales@metalpaper.co.uk
Website: http://www.metalpaper.co.uk
Directors: S. Livesey (MD)
Ultimate Holding Company: FOIL RIBBON & IMPACT PRINTING GROUP LIMITED
Immediate Holding Company: METALPAPER LIMITED
Registration no: 06011479 **Date established:** 2006
Turnover: Up to £250,000 **No.of Employees:** 1 - 10 **Product Groups:** 27

Date of Accounts	Mar 12	Mar 11	Mar 10
Sales Turnover	N/A	602	379
Pre Tax Profit/Loss	N/A	-0	-44
Working Capital	59	9	25
Fixed Assets	156	168	185
Current Assets	249	225	270
Current Liabilities	N/A	138	138

Michael Aubery Ltd
1 Maiden Lane Centre Lower Earley, Reading, RG6 3HD
Tel: 0118-962 9666 **Fax:** 0118-962 7999
E-mail: john.staves@mapl.co.uk
Website: http://www.mapl.co.uk
Directors: J. Staves (MD)
Immediate Holding Company: MICHAEL AUBREY PARTNERSHIP LIMITED
Registration no: 03002348 **Date established:** 1994
Turnover: £500,000 - £1m **No.of Employees:** 1 - 10 **Product Groups:** 80, 85

Date of Accounts	Dec 11	Dec 10	Dec 09
Working Capital	60	-1	-11
Fixed Assets	16	19	23
Current Assets	186	59	30

Microsoft Ltd
Microsoft Campus, Reading, RG6 1WG
Tel: 08448-002400 **Fax:** 08706-010700
E-mail: gordonfr@microsoft.com
Website: http://www.microsoft.com
Directors: G. Frazer (MD), M. Bishop (Mkt Research)
Ultimate Holding Company: MICRO-SOFT CORPORATION (USA)
Immediate Holding Company: MICROSOFT LIMITED
Registration no: 01624297 **VAT No.:** GB 370 1411 95
Date established: 1982 **Turnover:** £500m - £1,000m
No.of Employees: 1501 & over **Product Groups:** 44

Date of Accounts	Jun 11	Jun 08	Jul 09
Sales Turnover	663m	591m	640m
Pre Tax Profit/Loss	67m	79m	86m
Working Capital	178m	164m	128m
Fixed Assets	11m	17m	17m
Current Assets	310m	285m	257m
Current Liabilities	121m	110m	115m

Minco UK Ltd
The White House Goring, Reading, RG8 9DD
Tel: 020-8133 3916 **Fax:** 01453-764008
E-mail: sales@minco.org
Website: http://www.minco.org
Directors: M. Danks (Dir)
Immediate Holding Company: MINCO UK LIMITED
Registration no: 03135911 **Date established:** 1995
Turnover: £250,000 - £500,000 **No.of Employees:** 1 - 10
Product Groups: 32, 66, 67

Date of Accounts	Dec 10	Dec 09	Dec 08
Sales Turnover	N/A	N/A	453
Pre Tax Profit/Loss	N/A	N/A	32
Working Capital	49	25	6
Fixed Assets	2	2	N/A
Current Assets	70	77	155
Current Liabilities	N/A	N/A	96

Moog Components
Unit 30 Suttons Park Avenue Earley, Reading, RG6 1AW
Tel: 0118-966 6044 **Fax:** 0118-966 6524
E-mail: david.norman@idmelectronics.co.uk
Website: http://www.moog.com
Bank(s): National Westminster Bank Plc
Directors: D. Norman (MD)
Ultimate Holding Company: MOOG INCORPORATED (USA)
Immediate Holding Company: MOOG COMPONENTS GROUP LIMITED
Registration no: 00586505 **VAT No.:** GB 199 2968 84
Date established: 1957 **Turnover:** £10m - £20m
No.of Employees: 51 - 100 **Product Groups:** 37

Date of Accounts	Sep 08	Oct 09	Oct 10
Sales Turnover	8m	11m	17m
Pre Tax Profit/Loss	867	789	3m
Working Capital	3m	3m	6m
Fixed Assets	630	567	690
Current Assets	5m	6m	9m
Current Liabilities	1m	1m	2m

MW Trading UK Ltd
South Suite The Old Bakery Hyde End Lane, Brimpton, Reading, RG7 4RH
Tel: 0118-971 4574
Website: http://www.mwsecurity.org.uk
Managers: R. Reef (Chief Mgr)
Ultimate Holding Company: Active Capital Ab (Sweden)
Registration no: 04026190 **Date established:** 2000 **Turnover:** £1m - £2m
No.of Employees: 1 - 10 **Product Groups:** 36, 38, 49

Nabishi UK
16c Upton Road Tilehurst, Reading, RG30 4BJ
Tel: 0118-943 3311 **Fax:** 0118-943 3366
E-mail: sales@nabishi.com
Website: http://www.nabishi.com
Directors: J. Choudhrui (Prop)
Immediate Holding Company: NABISHI LIMITED
Registration no: 03286640 **Date established:** 1996
No.of Employees: 11 - 20 **Product Groups:** 37, 38

Nash & Co.
14 Bridge Street Caversham, Reading, RG4 8AA
Tel: 0118-947 2295 **Fax:** 0118-947 7010
E-mail: paulthejewel@aol.com
Website: http://www.philipbaker.co.uk
Directors: P. Ranson (Dir)
Immediate Holding Company: NASH & CO (CAVERSHAM) LIMITED
Registration no: 05230618 **Date established:** 2004
Turnover: £250,000 - £500,000 **No.of Employees:** 1 - 10
Product Groups: 28, 34, 48

Date of Accounts	Feb 12	Feb 11	Feb 10
Working Capital	-36	-36	-16
Fixed Assets	36	37	16
Current Assets	64	62	53

Nationwide Fire Protection Associates
Southcote Mill Southcote Farm Lane, Reading, RG30 3DZ
Tel: 0118-951 1799 **Fax:** 0118-951 1799
Directors: J. Farrell (Prop)
Date established: 1982 **No.of Employees:** 1 - 10 **Product Groups:** 38, 42

N C I
2 Nelsons Lane Hurst, Reading, RG10 0RR
Tel: 0118-934 5316 **Fax:** 0118-934 2010
E-mail: info@nciservices.co.uk
Website: http://www.nci-services.com
Directors: K. Hughes (Ptnr)
Turnover: £500,000 - £1m **No.of Employees:** 1 - 10 **Product Groups:** 48

Nec Technologies UK Ltd
Imperium Imperial Way, Reading, RG2 0TD
Tel: 0118-925 7190 **Fax:** 0118-925 7191
E-mail: webmaster@nectech.co.uk
Website: http://www.nectech.co.uk
Bank(s): HSBC Bank plc
Directors: D. Sutherland (Fin), K. Nishidai (Dir), L. Poisson (Dir), T. Claridge (Co Sec), Y. Matsuo (MD)
Managers: I. Crane (Mgr)
Immediate Holding Company: N.E.C. Corporation (UK)
Registration no: 04072718 **VAT No.:** 451 7739 31 **Date established:** 2000
Turnover: £10m - £20m **No.of Employees:** 101 - 250 **Product Groups:** 37

Date of Accounts	Mar 10	Mar 09	Mar 08
Sales Turnover	7m	15m	16m
Pre Tax Profit/Loss	619	830	301
Working Capital	12m	11m	11m
Fixed Assets	408	1m	967
Current Assets	14m	15m	14m
Current Liabilities	3m	3m	2m

Need A Cake
Unit 4c Woodley Park Estate 59-69 Reading Road, Woodley, Reading, RG5 3AW
Tel: 0118-969 0221 **Fax:** 0118-969 4228
E-mail: info@need-a-cake.co.uk
Website: http://www.need-a-cake.co.uk
Directors: R. Brown (Prop)
No.of Employees: 1 - 10 **Product Groups:** 20, 41, 62

Newfold Ltd
Bridgewater Close, Reading, RG30 1NS
Tel: 0118-957 3074
E-mail: sales@newfold.com
Website: http://www.newfold.co.uk
Directors: P. Hensley (Dir)
Immediate Holding Company: NEWFOLD LIMITED
Registration no: 02721680 **Date established:** 1992
Turnover: £500,000 - £1m **No.of Employees:** 11 - 20
Product Groups: 26, 48, 67

Date of Accounts	Dec 11	Dec 10	Dec 09
Working Capital	15	7	11
Fixed Assets	67	79	42
Current Assets	318	253	214

Octagon Toyota Reading
Rose Kiln Lane, Reading, RG2 0LJ
Tel: 0118-975 1300 **Fax:** 0118-931 4295
E-mail: keith.barnard@octagon.toyota.co.uk
Website: http://www.toyota.co.uk/octagon-reading
Managers: K. Barnard (District Mgr), P. Jessup (Comptroller)
No.of Employees: 21 - 50 **Product Groups:** 68

The Open Group Ltd
Apex Plaza Forbury Road, Reading, RG1 1AX
Tel: 0118-950 8311 **Fax:** 0118-950 0110
E-mail: info@opengroup.org
Website: http://www3.opengroup.org
Directors: A. Brown (Dir)
Ultimate Holding Company: CUNNINGHAM LINDSEY GROUP LTD (CAYMAN ISLANDS)
Immediate Holding Company: LINDSEY MORDEN ACQUISITIONS
Registration no: 05770685 **Date established:** 1998 **Turnover:** £1m - £2m
No.of Employees: 21 - 50 **Product Groups:** 44

Date of Accounts	Dec 11	Dec 10	Dec 09
Sales Turnover	110m	109m	105m
Pre Tax Profit/Loss	8m	10m	8m
Working Capital	27m	25m	18m
Fixed Assets	13m	14m	14m
Current Assets	51m	48m	40m
Current Liabilities	17m	19m	18m

Opti-Cal Survey Equipment Ltd
Unit 3 Orpheus House Calleva Park, Aldermaston, Reading, RG7 8TA
Tel: 0118-982 0500 **Fax:** 0118-982 0509
E-mail: sales@surveyequipment.com
Website: http://www.surveyequipment.com
Directors: S. Palin (Fin), J. Warner (Dir)
Managers: S. Lafferty (Mgr)
Immediate Holding Company: OPTI-CAL SURVEY EQUIPMENT LIMITED
Registration no: 06246981 **Date established:** 2007
No.of Employees: 21 - 50 **Product Groups:** 38, 48, 83, 85

Date of Accounts	Aug 11	Aug 10	Aug 09
Working Capital	422	477	132
Fixed Assets	1m	1m	1m
Current Assets	2m	2m	1m

Optus Services Ltd
21 Corsham Road Calcot, Reading, RG31 7ZH
Tel: 0118-967 9126 **Fax:** 0118-375 0506
E-mail: info@optusservices.com
Website: http://www.optusservices.com

see next page

Optus Services Ltd - Cont'd

Directors: A. Mealing (Dir)
Immediate Holding Company: OPTUS SERVICES LIMITED
Registration no: 04508109 **Date established:** 2002
Turnover: Up to £250,000 **No.of Employees:** 1 - 10 **Product Groups:** 44, 67

Date of Accounts	Aug 12	Aug 11	Aug 10
Working Capital	N/A	N/A	26
Current Assets	44	36	52

Oracle

Oracle Parkway, Reading, RG6 1RA
Tel: 0118-924 0000 **Fax:** 0118-924 3000
E-mail: sales@uk.oracle.com
Website: http://www.oracle.com
Directors: D. Hudson (Dir), C. James (Co Sec)
Managers: R. Bellis (Purch Mgr), N. Barley (Mktg Serv Mgr)
Ultimate Holding Company: ORACLE CORPORATION (USA)
Immediate Holding Company: ORACLE CORPORATION UK LIMITED
Registration no: 01782505 **Date established:** 1984
Turnover: £250m - £500m **No.of Employees:** 1501 & over
Product Groups: 44

Date of Accounts	May 11	May 10	May 09
Sales Turnover	653m	455m	439m
Pre Tax Profit/Loss	-20m	8m	14m
Working Capital	-132m	-143m	7m
Fixed Assets	257m	277m	106m
Current Assets	367m	482m	496m
Current Liabilities	166m	137m	111m

Oracle Storage Systems

PO Box 2391 Tilehurst, Reading, RG31 5ZQ
Tel: 0118-941 1786 **Fax:** 0118-941 5100
E-mail: sales@oraclestorage.co.uk
Website: http://www.oraclestorage.co.uk
Directors: S. Taylor (Prop)
Managers: C. Taylor (Purch Mgr), S. Taylor (Accounts)
Immediate Holding Company: ORACLE STORAGE SYSTEMS LIMITED
Registration no: 06134715 **Date established:** 2007
Turnover: Up to £250,000 **No.of Employees:** 1 - 10 **Product Groups:** 26

Oriental Commodities

Unit 3 The Portman Centre 37-45 Loverock Road, Reading, RG30 1DZ
Tel: 0118-959 1988 **Fax:** 0118-959 1888
E-mail: orientcomuk@yahoo.co.uk
Website: http://www.o-c-l.com
Directors: D. Bhatti (Fin)
Managers: S. Hewett (Sales Prom Mgr)
Immediate Holding Company: MIRACLE TAXIS LIMITED
Registration no: 02904722 **VAT No.:** GB 570 0670 60
Date established: 1993 **Turnover:** £500,000 - £1m
No.of Employees: 1 - 10 **Product Groups:** 32

Outbound Marketing Services Ltd

Waterloo House Riseley Business Park, Riseley, Reading, RG7 1NW
Tel: 0118-988 8801 **Fax:** 0845-634 4071
E-mail: info@out-bound.co.uk
Website: http://www.out-bound.co.uk
Directors: M. Fawler (Develop), P. Ash (Jt MD), S. Mcgillivray (Jt MD)
Managers: J. Crummy (Sales Admin)
Immediate Holding Company: OUTBOUND MARKETING SERVICES LIMITED
Registration no: 05234821 **Date established:** 2004
No.of Employees: 1 - 10 **Product Groups:** 81

P H Marine

Willow Marina Willow Lane, Wargrave, Reading, RG10 8LH
Tel: 0118-940 4419 **Fax:** 0118-940 4890
E-mail: peter@phmarine.co.uk
Website: http://www.phmarine.co.uk
Directors: P. Humphreys (Prop)
Date established: 1979 **No.of Employees:** 1 - 10 **Product Groups:** 35, 36, 39

P S I Ltd

Glade House Loves Wood, Mortimer Common, Reading, RG7 2JX
Tel: 0118-933 3331 **Fax:** 0118-933 3579
E-mail: royhillyard@promosource.co.uk
Website: http://www.promosource.co.uk
Directors: R. Hillyard (MD)
Immediate Holding Company: PSI LIMITED
Registration no: 07007498 **Date established:** 2009
No.of Employees: 1 - 10 **Product Groups:** 22, 23, 24, 25, 27, 28, 29, 30, 33, 35, 40, 43, 44, 49, 61, 63, 65, 77, 80, 81, 82, 89

Date of Accounts	Dec 07	Dec 06	Dec 05
Working Capital	-2	-1	-22
Fixed Assets	2	2	2
Current Assets	90	92	42
Current Liabilities	92	93	64

Pacer Components plc

Unit 4 Horseshoe Park Pangbourne, Reading, RG8 7JW
Tel: 0118-984 5280 **Fax:** 0118-984 5425
E-mail: graham_rothon@pacer.co.uk
Website: http://www.pacer.co.uk
Bank(s): Barclays, Newbury
Directors: J. Davies (Fin), G. Rothon (MD)
Managers: S. Sendall (Sales Prom Mgr), W. Walker (Mktg Serv Mgr), C. English (Chief Acct), P. Kennedy
Ultimate Holding Company: PACER TECHNOLOGIES LIMITED
Immediate Holding Company: PACER COMPONENTS LIMITED
Registration no: 02448361 **VAT No.:** GB 537 5764 12
Date established: 1989 **Turnover:** £10m - £20m
No.of Employees: 21 - 50 **Product Groups:** 37

Date of Accounts	Mar 12	Mar 11	Mar 10
Sales Turnover	19m	19m	17m
Pre Tax Profit/Loss	295	267	64
Working Capital	5m	5m	4m
Fixed Assets	234	254	390
Current Assets	9m	8m	6m
Current Liabilities	2m	350	176

Pathtrace plc

45 Boulton Road, Reading, RG2 0NH
Tel: 0118-975 6084 **Fax:** 0118-975 6143
E-mail: enquiry@pathtrace.com
Website: http://www.pathtrace.com
Directors: B. Pryce (Dir), J. Lee (Fin), B. Steatham (MD), D. Boucher (Develop)
Managers: S. Lee, R. Lobato, S. Sivitter
Immediate Holding Company: PATHTRACE LIMITED
Registration no: 02485210 **Date established:** 1990 **Turnover:** £1m - £2m
No.of Employees: 21 - 50 **Product Groups:** 44

Patol Ltd

Rectory Road Padworth Common, Reading, RG7 4JD
Tel: 0118-970 1701 **Fax:** 0118-970 1458
E-mail: info@patol.co.uk
Website: http://www.patol.co.uk
Bank(s): Lloyds TSB
Directors: B. Jenkins (MD)
Managers: H. Thompson (Fin Mgr)
Immediate Holding Company: PATOL LTD.
Registration no: 01341651 **VAT No.:** GB 533 3873 41
Date established: 1977 **Turnover:** £1m - £2m **No.of Employees:** 21 - 50
Product Groups: 38, 40, 52

Date of Accounts	Mar 11	Mar 10	Mar 09
Sales Turnover	1m	N/A	N/A
Pre Tax Profit/Loss	148	N/A	N/A
Working Capital	89	15	36
Fixed Assets	531	530	494
Current Assets	586	466	395
Current Liabilities	151	N/A	N/A

Pepsico

1600 Arlington Business Park Theale, Reading, RG7 4SA
Tel: 0118-930 6666 **Fax:** 0118-930 3152
Website: http://www.pepsicola.com
Managers: M. Glenn
Ultimate Holding Company: PEPSICO INC (USA)
Immediate Holding Company: GATORADE LIMITED
Registration no: 02658670 **Date established:** 1991
Turnover: £500,000 - £1m **No.of Employees:** 501 - 1000
Product Groups: 20

Date of Accounts	Dec 11	Dec 08	Dec 09
Sales Turnover	N/A	3m	857
Pre Tax Profit/Loss	299	3m	722
Working Capital	4	36m	45m
Fixed Assets	N/A	16m	N/A
Current Assets	4	39m	47m
Current Liabilities	N/A	3m	2m

Perma Contracts Ltd

45 Park View Drive South Charvil, Reading, RG10 9QX
Tel: 0118-934 3953 **Fax:** 0118-901 7707
E-mail: info@permacontracts.co.uk
Website: http://www.permacontracts.co.uk
Directors: H. Morgan (MD)
Immediate Holding Company: PERMA CONTRACTS LTD
Registration no: 06255547 **Date established:** 2007
No.of Employees: 1 - 10 **Product Groups:** 25, 35, 49

Date of Accounts	Mar 11	Mar 10	Mar 09
Working Capital	-13	-6	-10
Fixed Assets	5	11	15
Current Assets	11	32	45

David Peterson Ltd (David Peterson Clocks Ltd)

Jade House 25-27 Farnham Drive Caversham, Reading, RG4 6NY
Tel: 0118-947 1405 **Fax:** 0118-947 1605
E-mail: sales@dpclocks.co.uk
Website: http://www.dpclocks.co.uk
Directors: D. Weiss (Fin)
Immediate Holding Company: DAVID PETERSON LIMITED
Registration no: 03363126 **VAT No.:** GB 642 0261 78
Date established: 1997 **Turnover:** Up to £250,000
No.of Employees: 1 - 10 **Product Groups:** 49

Date of Accounts	Mar 12	Mar 11	Mar 10
Working Capital	-45	-47	-58
Fixed Assets	14	19	24
Current Assets	73	62	57

Phytron UK Ltd

17 Kingsway Caversham, Reading, RG4 6RA
Tel: 0118-946 2132 **Fax:** 0118-947 3059
E-mail: info@phytron.co.uk
Website: http://www.phytron.co.uk
Directors: C. Huntington (MD)
Immediate Holding Company: PHYTRON UK LIMITED
Registration no: 06483231 **Date established:** 2008
Turnover: £250,000 - £500,000 **No.of Employees:** 1 - 10
Product Groups: 37

Date of Accounts	Mar 11	Mar 10	Mar 09
Working Capital	-17	-33	-41
Fixed Assets	N/A	N/A	1
Current Assets	104	52	89

Pitmans Ltd

47 Castle Street, Reading, RG1 7SR
Tel: 0118-958 0224 **Fax:** 0118-958 5097
E-mail: info@pitmans.com
Website: http://www.pitmans.com
Bank(s): National Westminster
Directors: C. Barber (Mkt Research), J. Hargrave (Fin), S. Brooker (Dir), W. Somerville (Pers)
Managers: J. Hunt (Sales Admin)
Immediate Holding Company: PITMANS TRUSTEES LIMITED
Registration no: 02952373 **Date established:** 1994 **Turnover:** £1m - £2m
No.of Employees: 101 - 250 **Product Groups:** 80

Date of Accounts	Apr 11	Apr 10	Apr 09
Working Capital	326	-50	-67
Fixed Assets	53	60	68
Current Assets	1m	732	345

Pittsburgh Corning UK Ltd

63 Milford Road, Reading, RG1 8LG
Tel: 0118-950 0655 **Fax:** 0118-950 9019
E-mail: paul.jones@pcenet.com
Website: http://www.foamglass.co.uk
Bank(s): Barclays, Reading
Managers: C. Lindsay (District Mgr)
Ultimate Holding Company: PITTSBURGH CORNING EUROPE SA (BELGIUM)
Immediate Holding Company: PITTSBURGH CORNING(UNITED KINGDOM)LIMITED
Registration no: 00947101 **VAT No.:** GB 238 4376 44
Date established: 1969 **Turnover:** £2m - £5m **No.of Employees:** 11 - 20
Product Groups: 33

Date of Accounts	Dec 11	Dec 10	Dec 09
Sales Turnover	4m	5m	5m
Pre Tax Profit/Loss	360	593	553
Working Capital	3m	3m	2m
Fixed Assets	68	71	72
Current Assets	3m	3m	3m
Current Liabilities	337	238	309

Planit Software Ltd

45 Boulton Road, Reading, RG2 0NH
Tel: 01233-506100 **Fax:** 01233-502200
E-mail: reception@planit.com
Website: http://www.planit.com
Managers: R. Lobato (Mgr)
Ultimate Holding Company: VELOCITY HOLDINGS LIMITED
Immediate Holding Company: PLANIT SOFTWARE LIMITED
Registration no: 02093062 **Date established:** 1987 **Turnover:** £5m - £10m
No.of Employees: 11 - 20 **Product Groups:** 44

Date of Accounts	Apr 11	Apr 10	Apr 09
Sales Turnover	15m	13m	11m
Pre Tax Profit/Loss	4m	2m	5m
Working Capital	15m	12m	9m
Fixed Assets	1m	1m	2m
Current Assets	29m	24m	21m
Current Liabilities	5m	5m	5m

PolyPlus Packaging Ltd

Unit 1 & 2 Headley Park East, Woodley, Reading, RG5 4SA
Tel: 0118-944 2888 **Fax:** 0118-944 8141
E-mail: sales@polypluspackaging.co.uk
Website: http://www.polypluspackaging.co.uk
Directors: P. Browne (MD), M. Browne (Fin)
Immediate Holding Company: POLYPLUS PACKAGING LIMITED
Registration no: 02555933 **Date established:** 1990 **Turnover:** £1m - £2m
No.of Employees: 1 - 10 **Product Groups:** 30

Date of Accounts	Dec 11	Dec 10	Dec 09
Working Capital	399	243	123
Fixed Assets	89	105	131
Current Assets	846	726	516

Porsche Cars Great Britain Ltd

Pincents Kiln Calcot, Reading, RG31 7SE
Tel: 0118-930 3666 **Fax:** 0118-925 2704
E-mail: info@porschereading.co.uk
Website: http://www.porsche.co.uk
Bank(s): Barclays
Directors: C. Craft (MD)
Managers: I. Moulson (Tech Serv Mgr), N. Lambourne (Personnel)
Ultimate Holding Company: DR ING H C F PORSCHE A G (GERMANY)
Immediate Holding Company: PORSCHE CARS GREAT BRITAIN LIMITED
Registration no: 00861097 **VAT No.:** GB 222 2412 22
Date established: 1965 **Turnover:** £125m - £250m
No.of Employees: 101 - 250 **Product Groups:** 39, 68

Date of Accounts	Dec 11	Dec 10	Jul 10
Sales Turnover	365m	150m	338m
Pre Tax Profit/Loss	24m	4m	8m
Working Capital	27m	17m	13m
Fixed Assets	45m	37m	38m
Current Assets	114m	81m	106m
Current Liabilities	64m	47m	74m

Porsche Centre

Bath Road Calcot, Reading, RG31 7SG
Tel: 0118-930 3911 **Fax:** 0118-925 2898
E-mail: info@porsche.co.uk
Website: http://www.porsche.co.uk
Directors: G. Turrill (Dir)
Managers: S. Layne, D. Hunt, I. Moulson (Tech Serv Mgr), S. Butler (Comm)
Ultimate Holding Company: DR ING H C F PORSCHE A G (GERMANY)
Immediate Holding Company: PORSCHE RETAIL GROUP LIMITED
Registration no: 00220221 **Date established:** 2027
Turnover: £50m - £75m **No.of Employees:** 251 - 500 **Product Groups:** 68

Date of Accounts	Dec 11	Dec 10	Jul 10
Sales Turnover	161m	72m	168m
Pre Tax Profit/Loss	794	1m	4m
Working Capital	6m	13m	12m
Fixed Assets	2m	2m	2m
Current Assets	24m	30m	30m
Current Liabilities	8m	14m	11m

J Pratley & Sons Ltd

Pingemead Farm Pingewood, Reading, RG30 3UR
Tel: 0118-975 7500 **Fax:** 0118-975 6787
E-mail: sales@j.pratleysons.co.uk
Website: http://www.j.pratleysons.co.uk
Directors: M. Pratley (Fin), L. Pratley (Co Sec)
Immediate Holding Company: J. PRATLEY & SONS LIMITED
Registration no: 03768203 **VAT No.:** GB 537 4948 07
Date established: 1999 **Turnover:** £500,000 - £1m
No.of Employees: 11 - 20 **Product Groups:** 34, 48

Date of Accounts	May 11	May 10	May 09
Working Capital	155	101	233
Fixed Assets	40	45	45
Current Assets	423	389	574

Precision Machine Engraving

Unit11 Robert Cort Industrial Estate, Britten Road, Reading, RG2 0AU
Tel: 0118-986 4858 **Fax:** 0118-975 3415
E-mail: sales@pme-engraving.com
Website: http://www.pme-engraving.com
Registration no: 05334335 **Turnover:** Up to £250,000
No.of Employees: 1 - 10 **Product Groups:** 46, 48

Premier

PO Box 2663, Reading, RG2 0EG
Tel: 0118-987 2894 **Fax:** 0118-987 2894
E-mail: sales@rombouts.co.uk
Website: http://www.rombouts.co.uk
Directors: A. Aziz (Prop)
Ultimate Holding Company: TOMKINS P.L.C.
Immediate Holding Company: RHM/TOMKINS
Registration no: 05160050 **VAT No.:** GB 208 0096 91
Turnover: £5m - £10m **No.of Employees:** 1 - 10 **Product Groups:** 20, 62

Press To Print

6 Beacontree Plaza Gillette Way, Reading, RG2 0BS
Tel: 0118-931 0210 **Fax:** 0118-931 0220
E-mail: reading@presstoprint.co.uk
Website: http://www.presstoprint.co.uk

Directors: M. Poore (Chief Op Offcr)
Ultimate Holding Company: WATERDECREE LIMITED
Immediate Holding Company: PRESS TO PRINT LTD
Registration no: 01592765 **VAT No.:** GB 642 3005 81
Date established: 1981 **Turnover:** £5m - £10m **No.of Employees:** 1 - 10
Product Groups: 28

Date of Accounts	Jan 11	Jan 10	Jan 09
Working Capital	-241	-263	-379
Fixed Assets	324	359	456
Current Assets	417	363	572
Current Liabilities	N/A	125	236

J R Pridham Services Ltd

B2 Acre Business Park Acre Road, Reading, RG2 0SA
Tel: 0118-975 0326 **Fax:** 0118-975 0378
E-mail: enquiries@jrpservices.com
Website: http://www.jrpservices.com
Directors: S. Pridham (Co Sec), I. Procko (Sales & Mktg)
Managers: S. Drake (Personnel), K. Vallins (Tech Serv Mgr)
Immediate Holding Company: J.R. PRIDHAM SERVICES LIMITED
Registration no: 03716794 **Date established:** 1999 **Turnover:** £2m - £5m
No.of Employees: 51 - 100 **Product Groups:** 39

Date of Accounts	Mar 12	Mar 11	Mar 10
Working Capital	137	8	1
Fixed Assets	88	76	125
Current Assets	1m	1m	1m
Current Liabilities	331	195	N/A

Primarc Marketing

121 Loverock Road, Reading, RG30 1DZ
Tel: 0118-959 6777 **Fax:** 020-8900 2232
E-mail: ianmajor@primarc.co.uk
Website: http://www.primarc.co.uk
Directors: I. Major (Ch), I. Major (Prop), J. Edwards (Sales)
Managers: P. Vince, C. Anderson
Ultimate Holding Company: A.C. LIGHTING (HOLDINGS) LIMITED
Immediate Holding Company: PRIMARC (MARKETING) LIMITED
Registration no: 01070672 **VAT No.:** GB 199 4058 18
Date established: 1972 **Turnover:** £1m - £2m **No.of Employees:** 1 - 10
Product Groups: 37

Date of Accounts	Mar 09	Mar 08	Jan 11
Working Capital	513	327	518
Fixed Assets	4	299	2
Current Assets	901	890	653

Promac Solutions Ltd

Unit 5 Youngs Industrial Estate Paices Hill, Aldermaston, Reading, RG7 4PW
Tel: 0118-981 7337 **Fax:** 0118-981 1213
E-mail: grant.linton@firetecsolutions.com
Website: http://www.promac-solutions.co.uk
Directors: G. Linton (Dir), S. Long (Co Sec)
Immediate Holding Company: PROMAC SOLUTIONS LIMITED
Registration no: 05836391 **Date established:** 2006
Turnover: £10m - £20m **No.of Employees:** 1 - 10 **Product Groups:** 45

Date of Accounts	Dec 11	Dec 10	Dec 09
Sales Turnover	16m	11m	N/A
Pre Tax Profit/Loss	696	241	N/A
Working Capital	435	214	-23
Fixed Assets	92	88	81
Current Assets	3m	1m	883
Current Liabilities	340	156	N/A

Purdy Gates

1 Wards Farm Greenmore, Woodcote, Reading, RG8 0RB
Tel: 01491-681181 **Fax:** 01491-682933
E-mail: purdy.gates@btopenworld.co.uk
Website: http://www.purdygates.co.uk
Directors: J. Purdy (MD)
Immediate Holding Company: PURDY GATES LIMITED
Registration no: 06373008 **Date established:** 2007
Turnover: £500,000 - £1m **No.of Employees:** 1 - 10 **Product Groups:** 26, 35

Date of Accounts	Jun 11	Jun 10	Jun 09
Sales Turnover	670	630	644
Pre Tax Profit/Loss	120	124	166
Working Capital	-188	-219	-264
Fixed Assets	439	423	425
Current Assets	182	174	256
Current Liabilities	138	151	269

Quick Circuits Ltd

1 Loverock Road, Reading, RG30 1DZ
Tel: 0118-950 8921 **Fax:** 0118-956 8237
E-mail: info@quick-circuits.com
Website: http://www.quick-circuits.com
Directors: M. Prater (Fin), C. Withers (MD), A. Baxter (I.T. Dir)
Managers: A. Longmate (Sales Prom Mgr)
Immediate Holding Company: QUICK CIRCUITS LIMITED
Registration no: 01203058 **VAT No.:** GB 200 5582 08
Date established: 1975 **Turnover:** £2m - £5m **No.of Employees:** 51 - 100
Product Groups: 37, 84

Date of Accounts	Mar 12	Mar 11	Mar 10
Working Capital	103	50	-13
Fixed Assets	240	228	163
Current Assets	648	804	735

Raven Research Ltd

Westminster House Bath Road, Padworth, Reading, RG7 5HR
Tel: 0118-971 4540 **Fax:** 0118-971 4120
E-mail: info@raven-research.com
Website: http://www.raven-research.com
Bank(s): Barclays
Directors: A. Why (Dir), C. Radley (MD)
Ultimate Holding Company: RAVEN ELECTRONICS GROUP LIMITED
Immediate Holding Company: RAVEN RESEARCH LIMITED
Registration no: 02085417 **Date established:** 1986
Turnover: Up to £250,000 **No.of Employees:** 11 - 20 **Product Groups:** 35, 85

Date of Accounts	Jun 11	Jun 10	Jun 09
Working Capital	361	153	258
Fixed Assets	10	16	22
Current Assets	361	450	427

Ray Hudson Ltd

39 Suttons Business Park Sutton Park Avenue, Earley, Reading, RG6 1AZ
Tel: 08451-246066 **Fax:** 01491-413180
E-mail: ray@rhldirect.com
Website: http://www.rhldirect.com
Directors: R. Hudson (MD)
Immediate Holding Company: RAY HUDSON LIMITED
Registration no: 03046542 **Date established:** 1995
Turnover: £500,000 - £1m **No.of Employees:** 1 - 10 **Product Groups:** 40, 66

Date of Accounts	Jun 10	Jun 09	Jun 08
Sales Turnover	555	N/A	N/A
Working Capital	14	21	39
Fixed Assets	84	106	154
Current Assets	320	368	282
Current Liabilities	187	N/A	N/A

Reading Extinguisher Services

139b Caversham Road, Reading, RG1 8AU
Tel: 0118-950 0635 **Fax:** 0118-959 1167
E-mail: sales@extinguishers.co.uk
Website: http://www.extinguishers.co.uk
Directors: S. Flint (Dir)
Date established: 1985 **No.of Employees:** 11 - 20 **Product Groups:** 38, 42

Reading Scientific Services Ltd

PO Box 234, Reading, RG6 6LA
Tel: 0118-986 8541 **Fax:** 0118-986 8932
E-mail: enquiries@rssl.com
Website: http://www.rssl.com
Directors: T. Gale (Fin)
Ultimate Holding Company: KRAFT FOODS INC (USA)
Immediate Holding Company: READING SCIENTIFIC SERVICES LIMITED
Registration no: 00741326 **Date established:** 1962 **Turnover:** £5m - £10m
No.of Employees: 251 - 500 **Product Groups:** 85

Date of Accounts	Dec 11	Dec 10	Dec 09
Sales Turnover	10m	9m	9m
Pre Tax Profit/Loss	209	795	214
Working Capital	-724	3m	2m
Fixed Assets	10m	6m	6m
Current Assets	8m	7m	6m
Current Liabilities	3m	2m	2m

Rechner UK Ltd

Unit 6 The Old Mill 61 Reading Road, Pangbourne, Reading, RG8 7HY
Tel: 0118-976 6450 **Fax:** 0118-976 6451
E-mail: i.frais@rechner-sensors.co.uk
Website: http://www.rechner-sensors.co.uk
Directors: I. Frais (Dir)
Immediate Holding Company: RECHNER (UK) LIMITED
Registration no: 04003611 **Date established:** 2000
No.of Employees: 1 - 10 **Product Groups:** 37, 38, 84

Date of Accounts	Dec 11	Dec 10	Dec 09
Working Capital	-173	-212	-254
Fixed Assets	3	5	2
Current Assets	171	387	118

Reed Employment Ltd

66-68 St Marys Butts, Reading, RG1 2LG
Tel: 0118-957 3464 **Fax:** 0118-952 0000
E-mail: danyelle.tovey@reedglobal.com
Website: http://www.reed.co.uk
Managers: D. Tovey (Mgr)
Ultimate Holding Company: REED GLOBAL LTD (MALTA)
Immediate Holding Company: REED EMPLOYMENT LIMITED
Registration no: 00669854 **Date established:** 1960
Turnover: £500m - £1,000m **No.of Employees:** 11 - 20
Product Groups: 80

Date of Accounts	Jun 11	Jun 10	Dec 07
Sales Turnover	618	450	287m
Pre Tax Profit/Loss	-2m	310	8m
Working Capital	23m	28m	28m
Fixed Assets	31	36	5m
Current Assets	28m	30m	74m
Current Liabilities	37	29	21m

Reflex Ltd

1 Bennet Road, Reading, RG2 0QX
Tel: 0118-931 3611 **Fax:** 0118-931 4439
E-mail: info@reflex.co.uk
Website: http://www.reflex.co.uk
Bank(s): Bank of Scotland
Directors: R. Dreesden (MD), W. Jepps (Fin)
Ultimate Holding Company: REFLEX AUDIO VISUAL LIMITED
Immediate Holding Company: REFLEX LIMITED
Registration no: 03131814 **Date established:** 1995
Turnover: £10m - £20m **No.of Employees:** 21 - 50 **Product Groups:** 37, 38, 44, 83

Date of Accounts	Dec 11	Dec 10	Dec 09
Sales Turnover	12m	9m	10m
Pre Tax Profit/Loss	502	254	418
Working Capital	3m	3m	3m
Fixed Assets	51	61	57
Current Assets	6m	5m	4m
Current Liabilities	2m	2m	2m

Repair & Calibration Laboratories

1 Weighbridge Row Cardiff Road, Reading, RG1 8LX
Tel: 0118-958 9393 **Fax:** 0118-959 2189
E-mail: info@rcl-uk.com
Website: http://www.rcl-uk.com
Bank(s): Lloyds TSB
Directors: J. Lee (Prop)
Immediate Holding Company: REPAIR & CALIBRATION LABORATORIES LTD
Registration no: 02007369 **VAT No.:** GB 642 1042 85
Turnover: £500,000 - £1m **No.of Employees:** 11 - 20 **Product Groups:** 85

Reynard Health Supplies REYNARD MANAGEMENT SERVICES

Smallmead Gate Pingewood, Reading, RG30 3UR
Tel: 08452-637335 **Fax:** 0845-263 7336
E-mail: international@reynardhealth.com
Website: http://www.reynardhealth.com
Directors: C. Voller (Dir)
Immediate Holding Company: DELTIC COSRATE LIMITED
Registration no: 06504132 **Date established:** 2009
No.of Employees: 1 - 10 **Product Groups:** 24, 38, 67, 74

Date of Accounts	Mar 12	Mar 11	Mar 10
Pre Tax Profit/Loss	N/A	N/A	227
Working Capital	98	139	200
Current Assets	100	139	200

Robojet Ltd

49 Gosbrook Road Caversham, Reading, RG4 8BT
Tel: 0118-947 9900 **Fax:** 0118-946 1110
E-mail: sales@robojet.co.uk
Website: http://www.robojet.co.uk
Directors: J. Worsfold (MD)
Immediate Holding Company: ROBOJET LIMITED
Registration no: 04532701 **VAT No.:** 803 5186 47 **Date established:** 2002
Turnover: £250,000 - £500,000 **No.of Employees:** 1 - 10
Product Groups: 40, 45

Date of Accounts	Sep 11	Sep 10	Sep 09
Sales Turnover	440	442	530
Pre Tax Profit/Loss	10	-6	18
Working Capital	65	68	73
Fixed Assets	7	7	5
Current Assets	98	123	155
Current Liabilities	9	13	78

S G I

Oracle Parkway, Reading, RG6 1RA
Tel: 0118-912 7500 **Fax:** 0118-912 7505
Website: http://www.sgi.com
Directors: T. Robinson (MD)
Ultimate Holding Company: ORACLE CORPORATION (USA)
Immediate Holding Company: ORACLE CORPORATION UK HOLDINGS LIMITED
Registration no: 04828923 **Date established:** 2005
Turnover: £250,000 - £500,000 **No.of Employees:** 51 - 100
Product Groups: 44

S N S Building Products

Ikon House 3 Arkwright Road, Reading, RG2 0LU
Tel: 0118-987 3344
E-mail: sales@snsbp.co.uk
Website: http://www.snsbp.co.uk
Directors: M. Brown (MD)
Immediate Holding Company: REDLANDS CONSTRUCTION LTD
Registration no: 05869026 **Date established:** 2006
Turnover: £250,000 - £500,000 **No.of Employees:** 11 - 20
Product Groups: 35, 66

Date of Accounts	Jun 11	Jun 10	Jun 09
Working Capital	-0	-0	N/A
Current Assets	16	85	23
Current Liabilities	N/A	30	N/A

S P P Pumps

Theale Cross Pincents Kiln, Calcot, Reading, RG31 7SP
Tel: 0118-932 3123 **Fax:** 0161-932 3302
E-mail: enquiries@spppumps.com
Website: http://www.spppumps.com
Bank(s): Lloyds TSB Bank plc
Managers: M. Fussey
Ultimate Holding Company: KIRLOSKAR BROTHERS LIMITED (INDIA)
Immediate Holding Company: SPP PUMPS LIMITED
Registration no: 04839607 **Date established:** 2003
Turnover: £50m - £75m **No.of Employees:** 251 - 500
Product Groups: 40, 42, 45

Date of Accounts	Dec 11	Dec 10	Dec 09
Sales Turnover	69m	55m	59m
Pre Tax Profit/Loss	5m	4m	3m
Working Capital	9m	7m	6m
Fixed Assets	5m	4m	4m
Current Assets	33m	27m	27m
Current Liabilities	10m	10m	10m

S T R UK Ltd

10 Portman Road, Reading, RG30 1EA
Tel: 0118-939 8700 **Fax:** 0118-939 8701
E-mail: enquiries@struk.co.uk
Website: http://www.struk.co.uk
Bank(s): HSBC Bank plc
Managers: I. Saunderson, C. Biswell (Fin Mgr), D. Shoeman (Tech Serv Mgr)
Ultimate Holding Company: SPECIALISED TECHNOLOGY RESOURCES INC (USA)
Immediate Holding Company: STRATEGIC VALUE PARTNERS (UK) LLP
Registration no: OC306906 **VAT No.:** GB 117 6404 83
Date established: 2004 **Turnover:** £10m - £20m
No.of Employees: 21 - 50 **Product Groups:** 32, 66, 85

Date of Accounts	Dec 11	Dec 10	Dec 09
Sales Turnover	13m	16m	15m
Pre Tax Profit/Loss	8m	9m	8m
Working Capital	6m	8m	7m
Fixed Assets	48	188	332
Current Assets	8m	10m	10m
Current Liabilities	2m	2m	3m

Sagetech

Danesforde Pamber Road, Silchester, Reading, RG7 2NU
Tel: 0118-970 1950 **Fax:** 0118-970 0921
E-mail: info@sagetech.co.uk
Website: http://www.sagetech.co.uk
Directors: N. Bunker (Fin), K. Bunker (MD)
Immediate Holding Company: SAGETECH INDUSTRIES LIMITED
Registration no: 04464610 **Date established:** 2002
No.of Employees: 1 - 10 **Product Groups:** 36, 37, 47, 67

Date of Accounts	Sep 09	Sep 08	Sep 07
Working Capital	19	32	19
Fixed Assets	2	2	2
Current Assets	88	157	107

Sales Recruitment Network

New Stocks Farm 1a Paices Hill, Aldermaston, Reading, RG7 4PG
Tel: 0118-971 2422 **Fax:** 0118-971 2461
E-mail: thames.valley@tsrn.co.uk
Website: http://www.tsrn.co.uk
Managers: T. Darnell (Mgr)
Immediate Holding Company: PROSPER RECRUITMENT UK LTD
Registration no: 03469365 **Date established:** 2009
No.of Employees: 1 - 10 **Product Groups:** 80

Satec Service Ltd

The Street Englefield, Reading, RG7 5ES
Tel: 0118-964 9006 **Fax:** 0118-964 0074
E-mail: info@satec.co.uk
Website: http://www.satec.co.uk

see next page

Satec Service Ltd - Cont'd

Directors: G. Davies (Dir)
Immediate Holding Company: SATEC SERVICE LIMITED
Registration no: 07903824 **VAT No.:** GB 422 0592 85
Date established: 2012 **Turnover:** £10m - £20m **No.of Employees:** 1 - 10
Product Groups: 18, 40, 42, 51, 84

Date of Accounts	Dec 10	Dec 09	Dec 08
Working Capital	868	845	656
Fixed Assets	362	356	411
Current Assets	2m	1m	2m

Secret Silver International

19 Bromley Walk, Tilehurst, Reading, RG30 4LR
Tel: 0118-954 0791
E-mail: info@secretsilverinternational.com
Website: http://www.secretsilverinternational.com
Directors: B. Ahmad (Dir), A. Ahmad (Dir)
Date established: 2009 **No.of Employees:** 1 - 10 **Product Groups:** 36, 37, 61, 67

Selectronix Ltd

Unit 5-6 Minerva House Calleva Park, Aldermaston, Reading, RG7 8NE
Tel: 0118-981 7387 **Fax:** 0118-981 7608
E-mail: sales@selectronix.co.uk
Website: http://www.selectronix.co.uk
Directors: G. Reading (MD), L. White (Fin)
Immediate Holding Company: SELECTRONIX LIMITED
Registration no: 01459422 **Date established:** 1979 **Turnover:** £1m - £2m
No.of Employees: 1 - 10 **Product Groups:** 30, 35, 37, 38, 44, 67

Date of Accounts	Dec 10	Dec 09	Dec 08
Working Capital	-144	-189	-165
Fixed Assets	370	375	379
Current Assets	441	333	405

Self Adhesive Supplies

7-9 The Portman Centre, Reading, RG30 1DZ
Tel: 0118-957 5111 **Fax:** 0118-948 1089
E-mail: info@selfadhesive.co.uk
Website: http://www.selfadhesive.co.uk
Bank(s): Lloyds TSB Bank plc
Directors: R. Howard (Fin)
Managers: F. Hughes
Ultimate Holding Company: BLACKFRIARS CORP (USA)
Immediate Holding Company: SELF-ADHESIVE SUPPLIES LIMITED
Registration no: 01080385 **VAT No.:** GB 563 3494 28
Date established: 1972 **No.of Employees:** 11 - 20 **Product Groups:** 27, 30, 32

Date of Accounts	Dec 10	Dec 09	Oct 07
Working Capital	1	161	46
Fixed Assets	N/A	N/A	142
Current Assets	1	161	863

Selway Packaging

Unit 3 Paddock Road Industrial Estate Caversham, Reading, RG4 5BY
Tel: 0118-946 2333 **Fax:** 0118-946 2313
E-mail: malcolmselway@selway.co.uk
Website: http://www.selway.co.uk
Directors: M. Selway (Prop)
Date established: 1981 **No.of Employees:** 1 - 10 **Product Groups:** 38, 42

Sequoia Technology Ltd

Basingstoke Road Spencers Wood, Reading, RG7 1PW
Tel: 0118-976 9000 **Fax:** 0118-976 9070
E-mail: sales@sequoia.co.uk
Website: http://www.sequoia.co.uk
Bank(s): National Westminster
Directors: N. Lidington (MD)
Managers: R. Wardle (Fin Mgr), A. Graham (Quality Control), Z. Danelian (Product)
Immediate Holding Company: SEQUOIA TECHNOLOGY GROUP LTD
Registration no: 04004881 **VAT No.:** GB 614 5653 45
Date established: 2000 **Turnover:** £5m - £10m **No.of Employees:** 21 - 50
Product Groups: 37, 44

Date of Accounts	Dec 07	Mar 11	Mar 10
Sales Turnover	8m	N/A	N/A
Pre Tax Profit/Loss	316	N/A	N/A
Working Capital	149	174	237
Fixed Assets	544	864	801
Current Assets	2m	2m	1m
Current Liabilities	174	N/A	N/A

Shoreheat Ltd

4b Woodside Business Park Whitley Wood Lane, Reading, RG2 8LW
Tel: 0118-931 3595 **Fax:** 0118-975 0512
Managers: A. Cusden (District Mgr)
Ultimate Holding Company: PROGRESS GROUP LIMITED
Immediate Holding Company: SHOREHEAT LIMITED
Registration no: 01566154 **Date established:** 1981 **Turnover:** £5m - £10m
No.of Employees: 1 - 10 **Product Groups:** 36, 38, 40

Date of Accounts	Dec 10	Dec 09	Dec 08
Sales Turnover	17m	13m	14m
Pre Tax Profit/Loss	540	327	393
Working Capital	2m	2m	2m
Fixed Assets	461	505	481
Current Assets	6m	6m	5m
Current Liabilities	480	388	504

Simac Masic & TSS

2-12 Whitchurch Road Pangbourne, Reading, RG8 7BP
Tel: 0118-983 3347 **Fax:** 0118-983 1440
E-mail: keith-hill@btconnect.com
Website: http://www.simac-masic.com
Directors: K. Hill (MD)
Registration no: 02705357 **Date established:** 1992
Turnover: £250,000 - £500,000 **No.of Employees:** 1 - 10
Product Groups: 38, 44

Smet Ltd

Unit 19 The Markham Centre Station Road, Theale, Reading, RG7 4PE
Tel: 0118-930 2113 **Fax:** 0118-930 2206
E-mail: info@custompsudesign.com
Website: http://www.custompsudesign.com
Directors: R. Batchelor (Fab), J. Craig (Dir), J. Craig (Admin), R. Aston (Dir)
Managers: R. Aston
Immediate Holding Company: SMET LIMITED
Registration no: 06760677 **VAT No.:** GB 491 4645 27
Date established: 2008 **Turnover:** £500,000 - £1m
No.of Employees: 1 - 10 **Product Groups:** 37

Date of Accounts	Apr 11	Apr 10
Working Capital	26	26
Current Assets	98	113

Softbrands

The Waterfront 300 Thames Valley Park Drive, Reading, RG6 1PT
Tel: 08452-236050 **Fax:** 0118-935 8811
E-mail: michael.knight@softbrands.com
Website: http://www.softbrands.com/hospitality
Directors: M. Knight (MD), G. Ellis (Ch), G. Robinson (MD)
Managers: J. Hammonds (Sales Prom Mgr), S. Alexander (Mktg Serv Mgr), A. Handcock (I.T. Exec), S. Stroud (Purch Mgr)
Ultimate Holding Company: WESTBURY STREET LIMITED
Immediate Holding Company: BENUGO LIMITED
Registration no: 02579692 **Date established:** 1998
No.of Employees: 11 - 20 **Product Groups:** 44, 79, 80

Date of Accounts	Dec 10	Dec 08	Dec 07
Sales Turnover	N/A	N/A	90
Pre Tax Profit/Loss	N/A	-3	454
Working Capital	28	28	31
Current Assets	28	601	605
Current Liabilities	N/A	145	145

Softel Ltd

7 Horseshoe Park Pangbourne, Reading, RG8 7JW
Tel: 0118-984 2151 **Fax:** 0118-984 3939
E-mail: sales@softel.co.uk
Website: http://www.softel.co.uk
Directors: D. Berry (Co Sec)
Immediate Holding Company: SOFTEL LIMITED
Registration no: 01726537 **VAT No.:** GB 641 6314 59
Date established: 1983 **Turnover:** £2m - £5m **No.of Employees:** 21 - 50
Product Groups: 37, 44

Date of Accounts	Jun 12	Jun 11	Jun 10
Sales Turnover	3m	3m	3m
Pre Tax Profit/Loss	649	269	6
Working Capital	2m	1m	1m
Fixed Assets	40	72	109
Current Assets	2m	2m	2m
Current Liabilities	589	477	476

Southern Stoves

Gravelly Bridge Farm Grazeley Green Road, Grazeley, Reading, RG7 1LG
Tel: 0118-988 7459 **Fax:** 0118-988 7459
E-mail: southern.stoves@btinternet.com
Website: http://www.southernstoves.com
Directors: C. Farr (Prop)
Immediate Holding Company: TROLLEY MEDIA LTD
Registration no: 06995993 **Date established:** 2005
No.of Employees: 1 - 10 **Product Groups:** 40

Spanish & Portuguese At Fultons

The Chase Behoes Lane, Woodcote, Reading, RG8 0PP
Tel: 01491-680042 **Fax:** 01491-680085
E-mail: mike@mikefulton.co.uk
Website: http://www.mikefulton.co.uk
Directors: M. Fulton (Snr Part)
VAT No.: GB 314 5273 79 **Date established:** 1970
No.of Employees: 1 - 10 **Product Groups:** 80

Spirited Events

41 Granby Gardens, Reading, RG1 5RT
Tel: 0118-966 5939
E-mail: info@spirited-events.com
Website: http://www.spirited-events.com
Directors: M. Smith (Prop)
No.of Employees: 1 - 10 **Product Groups:** 24, 81, 83, 89

Stontronics Ltd

Unit 2-4 Chancery Gate Business Centre Cradock Road, Reading, RG2 0AH
Tel: 0118-931 1199 **Fax:** 0118-931 1145
E-mail: info@stontronics.co.uk
Website: http://www.stontronics.co.uk
Bank(s): National Westminster Bank Plc
Directors: T. Branston (Fin)
Managers: S. Dunn (Sales Prom Mgr)
Immediate Holding Company: STONTRONICS LIMITED
Registration no: 02270716 **VAT No.:** GB 491 1521 60
Date established: 1988 **Turnover:** £2m - £5m **No.of Employees:** 21 - 50
Product Groups: 37, 44

Date of Accounts	Sep 11	Sep 10	Sep 09
Working Capital	372	363	213
Fixed Assets	1m	1m	1m
Current Assets	2m	2m	2m

Strayfield Ltd

Unit 10-11 Ely Road, Theale, Reading, RG7 4BQ
Tel: 0118-932 7760 **Fax:** 0118-930 5634
E-mail: info@strayfield.co.uk
Website: http://www.strayfield.co.uk
Bank(s): HSBC, Wokingham
Directors: R. Monger (MD)
Immediate Holding Company: STRAYFIELD LIMITED
Registration no: 05585424 **VAT No.:** GB 199 6000 39
Date established: 2005 **Turnover:** £5m - £10m **No.of Employees:** 11 - 20
Product Groups: 40, 41, 42, 43, 44

Date of Accounts	Mar 11	Mar 10	Mar 09
Working Capital	1m	853	662
Fixed Assets	30	54	100
Current Assets	1m	2m	1m

Street Furnishing Ltd

Festival House Mumberry Hill, Wargrave, Reading, RG10 8EE
Tel: 0118-940 4717 **Fax:** 0118-940 3216
E-mail: mail@streetfurnishings.co.uk
Website: http://www.streetfurnishings.co.uk
Directors: T. Bendall (MD)
Immediate Holding Company: STREET FURNISHINGS LTD
Registration no: 03817080 **VAT No.:** GB 529 9871 83
Date established: 1999 **Turnover:** £1m - £2m **No.of Employees:** 1 - 10
Product Groups: 30, 33, 35, 37, 39

Date of Accounts	Aug 11	Aug 10	Aug 09
Working Capital	104	114	149
Current Assets	276	270	319

Surrey & Berkshire Media Ltd

8 Tessa Road, Reading, RG1 8NS
Tel: 0118-918 3000 **Fax:** 0118-950 3592
E-mail: editorial@reading-epost.co.uk
Website: http://www.getreading.co.uk
Managers: A. Murrill, S. Westwood (Personnel), K. Flannery (Mktg Serv Mgr)
Ultimate Holding Company: TRINITY MIRROR PLC
Immediate Holding Company: SURREY & BERKSHIRE MEDIA LIMITED
Registration no: 07146286 **Date established:** 2010
Turnover: £10m - £20m **No.of Employees:** 21 - 50 **Product Groups:** 28

Swerve

Office 15, 62 Portman Road, Reading, RG30 1EA
Tel: 0118-958 1634
E-mail: contact@swerve.co.uk
Website: http://www.swerve.co.uk
Managers: Q. K (Mktg Serv Mgr)
Registration no: 05322044 **Date established:** 1999
No.of Employees: 1 - 10 **Product Groups:** 63

Synopsys Northern Europe Ltd

100 Brook Drive, Reading, RG2 6UJ
Tel: 0118-931 3822 **Fax:** 0118-975 0081
E-mail: admin@synopsys.com
Website: http://www.synopsys.com
Bank(s): Barclays
Directors: C. Watchorn (Dir)
Ultimate Holding Company: SYNOPSYS INC (USA)
Immediate Holding Company: SYNOPSYS (NORTHERN EUROPE) LIMITED
Registration no: 02642054 **VAT No.:** GB 537 5053 45
Date established: 1991 **Turnover:** £10m - £20m
No.of Employees: 51 - 100 **Product Groups:** 44

Date of Accounts	Oct 09	Oct 10	Oct 11
Sales Turnover	11m	11m	12m
Pre Tax Profit/Loss	804	555	603
Working Capital	3m	2m	2m
Fixed Assets	604	375	172
Current Assets	4m	4m	4m
Current Liabilities	N/A	2m	2m

T E Electronics Ltd

The Jackdaw The Devil's Highway, Mortimer, Reading, RG7 2AD
Tel: 0118-933 2533 **Fax:** 0118-933 1224
E-mail: sales@teelectronics.co.uk
Website: http://www.teelectronics.co.uk
Directors: R. Owen (MD)
Immediate Holding Company: T.E. ELECTRONICS LIMITED
Registration no: 01203232 **VAT No.:** GB 212 8875 56
Date established: 1975 **Turnover:** Up to £250,000
No.of Employees: 1 - 10 **Product Groups:** 37, 44, 67

Date of Accounts	Mar 11	Mar 10	Mar 09
Sales Turnover	39	3	25
Pre Tax Profit/Loss	12	-8	-7
Working Capital	N/A	-13	-5
Fixed Assets	N/A	1	1
Current Assets	18	2	12
Current Liabilities	4	2	2

Tascom International Ltd

1 Mars House Calleva Park, Aldermaston, Reading, RG7 8LA
Tel: 0118-982 0400
E-mail: alan@tascom.co.uk
Website: http://www.tascom.co.uk
Directors: A. Gornall (MD)
Ultimate Holding Company: HIFI CINEMA LIMITED
Immediate Holding Company: TASCOM (INTERNATIONAL) LIMITED
Registration no: 05891512 **Date established:** 2006
Turnover: £500,000 - £1m **No.of Employees:** 1 - 10 **Product Groups:** 37

Date of Accounts	Dec 11	Dec 10	Dec 09
Working Capital	2	27	6
Current Assets	12	35	11

Teamco International Ltd

2 Old Bath Road Charvil, Reading, RG10 9QR
Tel: 0118-969 4104 **Fax:** 0118-969 4103
E-mail: sales@valves.org.uk
Website: http://www.valves.org.uk
Directors: M. Zubairy (MD)
Immediate Holding Company: TEAMCO INTERNATIONAL LIMITED
Registration no: 02323892 **VAT No.:** GB 527 1780 41
Date established: 1988 **Turnover:** Up to £250,000
No.of Employees: 1 - 10 **Product Groups:** 36, 40, 66

Date of Accounts	Dec 11	Dec 10	Dec 09
Sales Turnover	112	131	64
Pre Tax Profit/Loss	-7	23	-6
Working Capital	34	41	18
Current Assets	74	90	38
Current Liabilities	25	29	N/A

Tecfacs Ltd

PO Box 2967, Reading, RG1 9PW
Tel: 0118-977 6645 **Fax:** 0118-989 4461
E-mail: frank@tecfacs.com
Website: http://www.tecfacs.com
Directors: F. Carstairs (Fin)
Immediate Holding Company: TECFACS LIMITED
Registration no: 02214727 **VAT No.:** 491 4575 22 **Date established:** 1988
Turnover: £1m - £2m **No.of Employees:** 1 - 10 **Product Groups:** 44

Date of Accounts	May 11	May 10	May 09
Working Capital	-245	-198	-191
Fixed Assets	226	292	339
Current Assets	417	280	313

Tempatron Controls

5 Darwin Close, Reading, RG2 0TB
Tel: 0118-931 4062 **Fax:** 0118-931 0175
E-mail: info@tempatron.co.uk
Website: http://www.tempatron.co.uk
Directors: P. Neundegg (MD), P. Neudegg (Dir), B. McVitty (Fin)
Managers: C. Toogood (I.T. Exec), P. Bowers (Sales Prom Mgr), S. Rathgay (Sales Prom Mgr)
Immediate Holding Company: GOODBURN PLASTICS LIMITED
Registration no: 06243013 **VAT No.:** GB 198 9155 01
Date established: 2007 **Turnover:** £1m - £2m **No.of Employees:** 1 - 10
Product Groups: 37, 38

Date of Accounts	Mar 10	Mar 09	Mar 08
Working Capital	87	90	437
Fixed Assets	174	221	78
Current Assets	657	559	1m

TF Groundworks

291 Northumberland Ave, reading, RG2 7QE
Tel: 0118-987 4039
E-mail: info@tfgroundworks.co.uk
Website: http://www.tfgroundworks.co.uk

Directors: T. Farrelly (Prop)
Date established: 2009 **Turnover:** Up to £250,000
No.of Employees: 1 - 10 **Product Groups:** 07, 84

Thames Metal Crafts

James Farm Grazeley Green, Reading, RG7 1NB
Tel: 0118-983 4505 **Fax:** 0118-983 4505
E-mail: thamesmetalcraft@aol.com
Website: http://www.thamesmetalcrafts.co.uk
Directors: R. Hoskins (Prop)
Ultimate Holding Company: NASHLINE HOLDINGS LIMITED
Immediate Holding Company: NAGRO (FRAMES) LIMITED
Registration no: 00989255 **Date established:** 1970
Turnover: £500,000 - £1m **No.of Employees:** 1 - 10 **Product Groups:** 26, 35

Date of Accounts	Aug 11	Aug 10	Aug 09
Working Capital	99	169	128
Fixed Assets	21	18	24
Current Assets	201	298	279

The Hunter Fan Company Ltd

Castle End Business Park Ruscombe, Reading, RG10 9XQ
Tel: 0845-0940296 **Fax:** 0845-0940297
E-mail: plloyd@hunterfan.co.uk
Website: http://www.hunterfan.co.uk
Directors: P. Lloyd (Prop)
Managers: N. Cligg (Mgr)
Registration no: 05644334 **No.of Employees:** 1 - 10 **Product Groups:** 40, 66

The Water Quality Centre

Spencer House Manor Farm Road, Reading, RG2 0JN
Tel: 020-3577 8523 **Fax:** 0118-923 6373
E-mail: matthew.angel@thameswater.co.uk
Website: http://www.materialtesting.co.uk
Managers: A. Maddox
Turnover: £5m - £10m **No.of Employees:** 1 - 10 **Product Groups:** 38, 42, 85

Theale Fireplaces Reading Ltd

A4 Bath Road Sulhamstead, Reading, RG7 5HJ
Tel: 0118-930 2232 **Fax:** 0118-932 3344
E-mail: mail@theale-fireplaces.co.uk
Website: http://www.theale-fireplaces.co.uk
Directors: J. Woosnam (MD)
Immediate Holding Company: THEALE FIREPLACES (READING) LIMITED
Registration no: 02427017 **VAT No.:** GB 537 5124 48
Date established: 1989 **Turnover:** £250,000 - £500,000
No.of Employees: 1 - 10 **Product Groups:** 25, 33, 35

Date of Accounts	Apr 11	Apr 10	Apr 09
Working Capital	49	41	91
Fixed Assets	46	28	11
Current Assets	206	162	145
Current Liabilities	18	N/A	N/A

Therma Group

Green Lane Burghfield Bridge, Reading, RG30 3XN
Tel: 0118-950 0606 **Fax:** 0118-956 0039
E-mail: sales@thermagroup.com
Website: http://www.thermagroup.com
Directors: T. Brumwell (MD), T. Dann (Dir)
Registration no: 03474141 **Turnover:** £500,000 - £1m
No.of Employees: 21 - 50 **Product Groups:** 35, 36, 38, 39, 40, 48, 52, 61, 66, 67, 84, 87

Date of Accounts	Nov 09	Nov 08	Nov 07
Working Capital	275	146	172
Fixed Assets	145	125	142
Current Assets	322	423	313

Thermo Scientific

Grange Lane Beenham, Reading, RG7 5PR
Tel: 0118-971 2121 **Fax:** 0118-971 2835
E-mail: admin@thermormp.co.uk
Website: http://www.thermoscientific.com
Bank(s): Barclays
Directors: D. Kaczorowski (Dir)
Managers: J. Landreath (Personnel), M. Pottinger (Mktg Serv Mgr), E. Outlaw (Personnel), D. Mckay (Fin Mgr)
Immediate Holding Company: THERMO ELECTRON GROUP
Registration no: 02144110 **VAT No.:** GB 479 4202 27
Date established: 1953 **Turnover:** £1m - £2m **No.of Employees:** 11 - 20
Product Groups: 37, 38, 45

Thomas Turner Gunmaker

208 Gosbrook Road Caversham, Reading, RG4 8BL
Tel: 0118-948 1699 **Fax:** 0118-946 1678
Website: http://www.ttgm.freeserve.co.uk
Managers: P. Barford (Mgr)
Date established: 1984 **No.of Employees:** 1 - 10 **Product Groups:** 36, 39, 40

Twofold Ltd

77 Milford Road, Reading, RG1 8LG
Tel: 0118-951 9800 **Fax:** 0118-951 9899
E-mail: info@twofold.co.uk
Website: http://www.twofold.co.uk
Bank(s): Barclays
Directors: P. Rooke (Co Sec), P. Charnick (Dir)
Immediate Holding Company: TWOFOLD LIMITED
Registration no: 04043149 **Date established:** 2000 **Turnover:** £2m - £5m
No.of Employees: 21 - 50 **Product Groups:** 42, 43, 44, 46, 49, 81

Date of Accounts	Aug 11	Aug 10	Aug 09
Sales Turnover	N/A	N/A	4m
Pre Tax Profit/Loss	N/A	N/A	246
Working Capital	159	43	155
Fixed Assets	757	800	519
Current Assets	2m	2m	2m
Current Liabilities	N/A	N/A	1m

U T I Worldwide UK Ltd (Head Office)

Hyperion Way Rose Kiln Lane, Reading, RG2 0JS
Tel: 0118-986 9595 **Fax:** 0118-987 6074
Website: http://www.go2uti.com
Bank(s): Barclays
Directors: K. Sichau (Fin), S. Hallisey (Prop), B. Kearney (MD)
Ultimate Holding Company: UTI WORLDWIDE INC (BRITISH VIRGIN ISLANDS)
Immediate Holding Company: UTI WORLDWIDE (UK) LIMITED
Registration no: 02402322 **VAT No.:** GB 641 9441 37
Date established: 1989 **Turnover:** £75m - £125m
No.of Employees: 21 - 50 **Product Groups:** 76

Date of Accounts	Jan 12	Jan 11	Jan 10
Sales Turnover	135m	95m	75m
Pre Tax Profit/Loss	-816	-3m	-3m
Working Capital	-972	-325	-1m
Fixed Assets	878	849	2m
Current Assets	15m	20m	16m
Current Liabilities	5m	4m	3m

UK Equipment Ltd

48 Suttons Park Avenue Earley, Reading, RG6 1AZ
Tel: 0118-966 9121 **Fax:** 0118-966 4369
Website: http://www.hofmann.co.uk
Bank(s): National Westminster Bank Plc
Directors: B. O'sullivan (Dir), C. Pleasf (Sales), C. Behan (MD), A. Cumming (I.T. Dir)
Managers: B. O' Sullivan (Chief Mgr)
Immediate Holding Company: SNAP-ON EQUIPMENT LIMITED
Registration no: 04312415 **Date established:** 2001 **Turnover:** £2m - £5m
No.of Employees: 21 - 50 **Product Groups:** 38, 39

United Alloys

20D Horseshoe Park Pangbourne, Reading, RG8 7JW
Tel: 0118-976 7140 **Fax:** 0118-976 7141
E-mail: dheath@united-alloys.com
Website: http://www.united-alloys.com
Product Groups: 34, 36, 66

Valentine Equipment Ltd

4 Trafford Road, Reading, RG1 8JS
Tel: 0118-957 1344 **Fax:** 0118-939 4236
E-mail: info@valentinefryers.com
Website: http://www.valentinefryers.com
Directors: B. Witherall (MD)
Immediate Holding Company: VALENTINE EQUIPMENT LIMITED
Registration no: 00589763 **VAT No.:** GB 199 4678 85
Date established: 1957 **Turnover:** £2m - £5m **No.of Employees:** 1 - 10
Product Groups: 40

Date of Accounts	Oct 11	Oct 10	Oct 09
Working Capital	3m	3m	3m
Fixed Assets	371	388	399
Current Assets	3m	3m	3m

Walker Outboard Services

The Boatyard Mill Green, Caversham, Reading, RG4 8EX
Tel: 0118-947 8641 **Fax:** 0118-948 4779
E-mail: info@walkeroutboards.co.uk
Website: http://www.walkeroutboards.co.uk
Directors: D. Walker (Prop)
Date established: 1986 **No.of Employees:** 1 - 10 **Product Groups:** 35, 36, 39

Warner Land Surveys

Beaumont House 59 High Street, Theale, Reading, RG7 5AL
Tel: 0118-930 3314 **Fax:** 0118-930 1859
E-mail: petef@warnerlandsurveys.com
Website: http://www.warnerlandsurveys.com
Directors: M. Green (Co Sec), P. Field (MD)
Managers: G. Allwork (Tech Serv Mgr)
Ultimate Holding Company: WARNER LAND SURVEYS HOLDINGS LIMITED
Immediate Holding Company: WARNER LAND SURVEYS LIMITED
Registration no: 02945461 **Date established:** 1994
No.of Employees: 21 - 50 **Product Groups:** 38, 39, 48, 51, 80, 84, 85, 86

Date of Accounts	Jul 11	Jul 10	Jul 09
Working Capital	812	822	755
Fixed Assets	139	169	252
Current Assets	1m	1m	1m

Westronics Ltd

11-12 Marcus Close Tilehurst, Reading, RG30 4EA
Tel: 0118-942 6726 **Fax:** 0118-945 1481
E-mail: sales@westronics.co.uk
Website: http://www.westronics.co.uk
Bank(s): Barclays
Directors: G. Miller (Dir), R. Miller (Fin)
Managers: A. Miller (Mktg Serv Mgr), M. Hoskins (Chief Mgr)
Immediate Holding Company: WESTRONICS LIMITED
Registration no: 00962442 **Date established:** 1969
Turnover: £500,000 - £1m **No.of Employees:** 21 - 50
Product Groups: 38, 40, 47, 67

Date of Accounts	Apr 12	Apr 11	Apr 10
Working Capital	2m	1m	2m
Fixed Assets	618	664	681
Current Assets	3m	3m	3m

White Knight Laundry Services Ltd

72 George Street Caversham, Reading, RG4 8DW
Tel: 0118-946 2233 **Fax:** 0118-946 1152
E-mail: info@white-knight.co.uk
Website: http://www.white-knight.co.uk
Directors: J. Woolcock (Fin), P. Tomlins (Co Sec), R. Adams (MD)
Managers: P. Jeeves (Purch Mgr), N. Thomson (Tech Serv Mgr), A. Coombs (Personnel)
Ultimate Holding Company: H.TOMLINS,LIMITED
Immediate Holding Company: WHITE KNIGHT LAUNDRY SERVICES LTD.
Registration no: 00836274 **Date established:** 1965 **Turnover:** £5m - £10m
No.of Employees: 251 - 500 **Product Groups:** 23

Date of Accounts	Dec 11	Dec 10	Dec 09
Sales Turnover	9m	10m	10m
Pre Tax Profit/Loss	-848	4	27
Working Capital	428	390	371
Fixed Assets	6m	6m	6m
Current Assets	2m	2m	2m
Current Liabilities	655	960	963

Winkworth Machinery Ltd

Willow Tree Works Swallowfield Street, Swallowfield, Reading, RG7 1QX
Tel: 0118-988 3551 **Fax:** 0118-988 4031
E-mail: info@mixer.co.uk
Website: http://www.mixer.co.uk
Bank(s): National Westminster, Staines
Directors: G. Jamieson (MD), C. Winkworth (Fin)
Ultimate Holding Company: WINKWORTH MIXERS LIMITED
Immediate Holding Company: WINKWORTH MACHINERY LIMITED
Registration no: 02852052 **VAT No.:** GB 208 4965 46
Date established: 1993 **Turnover:** £2m - £5m **No.of Employees:** 21 - 50
Product Groups: 40, 41, 42

Date of Accounts	May 11	May 10	May 09
Working Capital	1m	559	487
Fixed Assets	203	242	228
Current Assets	3m	2m	2m

Wyse Technology UK Ltd

1 The Pavilions Ruscombe Business Park, Ruscombe, Reading, RG10 9NN
Tel: 0118-934 2200 **Fax:** 0118-934 0749
E-mail: sales@wyse.com
Website: http://www.uk.wyse.com
Bank(s): Barclays
Directors: M. Jordan (Dep Pres), S. Brown (MD), A. Gee (Sales), M. Alexandrian Adams (Dir)
Managers: D. Angwin (Mgr), M. Jordan (Chief Mgr)
Ultimate Holding Company: CHANNEL OVERSEAS CORPORATION LTD (TAIWAN)
Immediate Holding Company: WYSE TECHNOLOGY (UK) LIMITED
Registration no: 01945769 **Date established:** 1985 **Turnover:** £2m - £5m
No.of Employees: 11 - 20 **Product Groups:** 26, 37, 44

Date of Accounts	Mar 11	Mar 10	Mar 09
Sales Turnover	3m	3m	2m
Pre Tax Profit/Loss	79	142	112
Working Capital	568	553	428
Fixed Assets	5	5	5
Current Assets	1m	1m	1m
Current Liabilities	419	374	310

XP Power

Horseshoe Park Pangbourne, Reading, RG8 7JW
Tel: 0118-984 5515 **Fax:** 0118-984 3423
E-mail: eusales@xppower.com
Website: http://www.xppower.com
Bank(s): Bank of Scotland
Directors: R. Bartlett (Dir), S. Head (Sales & Mktg), J. Peters (Ch), S. Robinson (MD), G. Bocock (Tech Serv), E. Swann (Sales), D. Penny (Dir), S. Elliott (Dir), M. Brabham (Dir), S. Willis (Dir)
Ultimate Holding Company: XP Power Plc
Registration no: 02297983 **VAT No.:** GB 491 7131 43
Date established: 1989 **Turnover:** £50m - £75m
No.of Employees: 101 - 250 **Product Groups:** 37, 40, 44

Date of Accounts	Dec 06	Dec 05
Sales Turnover	78700	69500
Pre Tax Profit/Loss	8000	7700
Working Capital	11100	-1900
Fixed Assets	36600	33600
Current Assets	32600	30100
Current Liabilities	21500	32000
Total Share Capital	200	200
ROCE% (Return on Capital Employed)	16.8	24.3
ROT% (Return on Turnover)	10.2	11.1

Sandhurst

E Braude London Ltd (Head Office)

Liberta House 17 Scotland Hill, Sandhurst, GU47 8JR
Tel: 01252-876123 **Fax:** 01252-875281
E-mail: admin@braude.co.uk
Website: http://www.braude.co.uk
Directors: D. Snoxhill (MD)
Immediate Holding Company: E. BRAUDE (LONDON) LIMITED
Registration no: 00585474 **Date established:** 1957
No.of Employees: 11 - 20 **Product Groups:** 30, 35, 37, 38, 40, 46, 66, 67

Date of Accounts	Oct 11	Oct 10	Oct 09
Working Capital	981	1m	537
Fixed Assets	77	79	789
Current Assets	1m	1m	630

Cove Industrial Enterprises

Paint Shop 2 Vulcan Close, Sandhurst, GU47 9DD
Tel: 01252-873092 **Fax:** 01252-873092
Website: http://www.cove-industries.co.uk
Managers: C. Newman (Mgr)
Date established: 1996 **No.of Employees:** 1 - 10 **Product Groups:** 46, 48

Andy Crane Transport Ltd

9 Vulcan Way, Sandhurst, GU47 9DB
Tel: 01252-878989 **Fax:** 01252-890404
E-mail: andy@andycrane.com
Website: http://www.andycrane.com
Directors: A. Morrison Crane (MD)
Immediate Holding Company: ANDY CRANE TRANSPORT LIMITED
Registration no: 03536021 **Date established:** 1998
No.of Employees: 11 - 20 **Product Groups:** 77

Date of Accounts	Jun 11	Jun 10	Jun 09
Working Capital	169	72	156
Fixed Assets	623	538	628
Current Assets	644	577	588

Distributed Micro Technology Ltd

265 College Town, Sandhurst, GU47 0QA
Tel: 01276-33391 **Fax:** 01276-36703
E-mail: info@dmtl.co.uk
Website: http://www.dmtl.co.uk
Directors: P. Leahy (Dir)
Immediate Holding Company: DISTRIBUTED MICRO TECHNOLOGY LIMITED
Registration no: 02091386 **Date established:** 1987 **Turnover:** £2m - £5m
No.of Employees: 1 - 10 **Product Groups:** 37, 67

Date of Accounts	Dec 11	Dec 10	Dec 09
Working Capital	753	649	416
Fixed Assets	31	30	30
Current Assets	1m	1m	1m

Electronworks Ltd

PO Box 1212, Sandhurst, GU47 7DY
Tel: 08712-317645
E-mail: simon.bramble@electronworks.co.uk
Website: http://www.electronworks.co.uk

see next page

Electronworks Ltd - Cont'd

Directors: S. Bramble (Prop)
Immediate Holding Company: ELECTRONWORKS LIMITED
Registration no: 06577659 **Date established:** 2008
Turnover: Up to £250,000 **No.of Employees:** 1 - 10 **Product Groups:** 84

Date of Accounts	Jul 11	Jul 10	Jul 09
Working Capital	-2	-2	-1
Current Assets	N/A	N/A	1
Current Liabilities	2	N/A	N/A

Freight Products UK Ltd

Unit 1 Vulcan Way, Sandhurst, GU47 9DB
Tel: 01926-641222 **Fax:** 01926-641783
E-mail: sales@freightproducts.co.uk
Website: http://www.freightproducts.co.uk
Bank(s): Yorkshire Bank PLC
Directors: T. Sanders (MD)
Managers: N. Brooks (Tech Serv Mgr), E. Manchester (Admin Off), A. Rose (Fin Mgr)
Ultimate Holding Company: SANDHURST AUTOPRINT LIMITED
Immediate Holding Company: FREIGHT PRODUCTS (U.K.) LIMITED
Registration no: 05056816 **Date established:** 2004 **Turnover:** £1m - £2m
No.of Employees: 21 - 50 **Product Groups:** 23, 30, 38, 39

Date of Accounts	Jul 11	Jul 10	Jul 09
Sales Turnover	2m	1m	1m
Pre Tax Profit/Loss	222	145	95
Working Capital	345	177	189
Fixed Assets	71	97	127
Current Assets	957	592	568
Current Liabilities	113	85	60

N F I UK Ltd

259 York Town Road College Town, Sandhurst, GU47 0RT
Tel: 01276-600200 **Fax:** 01276-600161
E-mail: info@nfi.uk.com
Website: http://www.nfi.uk.com
Directors: I. Storrie (MD)
Immediate Holding Company: NFI UK LIMITED
Registration no: 07977322 **VAT No.:** GB 592 0520 53
Date established: 2012 **Turnover:** £1m - £2m **No.of Employees:** 1 - 10
Product Groups: 36, 37, 38, 44, 45, 51, 52, 68, 84

Date of Accounts	Jun 11	Jun 10	Jun 09
Working Capital	1m	1m	2m
Fixed Assets	7	9	12
Current Assets	1m	1m	2m

R K Components

Unit 14 Lakeside Business Park Swan Lane, Sandhurst, GU47 9DN
Tel: 020-8884 1366 **Fax:** 020-8884 3881
E-mail: info@rkcomponents.com
Website: http://www.rkcomponents.com
Directors: S. Khatri (Prop)
Immediate Holding Company: R K COMPONENTS LIMITED
Registration no: 07018371 **Date established:** 2009
Turnover: £250,000 - £500,000 **No.of Employees:** 1 - 10
Product Groups: 35, 48

Date of Accounts	Sep 11	Sep 10
Working Capital	30	19
Fixed Assets	9	12
Current Assets	80	58
Current Liabilities	N/A	33

Uhlmann UK Ltd

6 Lakeside Business Park Swan Lane, Sandhurst, GU47 9DN
Tel: 01252-743120
E-mail: info@uhlmann.co.uk
Website: http://www.uhlmann.de
Managers: T. Maskell (Sales Admin)
Immediate Holding Company: UHLMANN U.K. LIMITED
Registration no: 03744923 **Date established:** 1999
No.of Employees: 1 - 10 **Product Groups:** 38, 42

Date of Accounts	Mar 12	Mar 11	Mar 10
Working Capital	822	499	534
Fixed Assets	46	59	61
Current Assets	1m	604	710

Slough

5 Fifteen Ltd

180 Bedford Avenue, Slough, SL1 4RA
Tel: 01753-440515 **Fax:** 01753-440550
E-mail: info@5fifteen.com
Website: http://www.5fifteen.com
Bank(s): National Westminster
Directors: P. McKinley (Sales), R. Fenwick (Fin)
Managers: D. Bakster (Sales Prom Mgr), D. Baxter (Sales Prom Mgr), E. Adam (Cust Serv Mgr)
Registration no: 03820158 **Date established:** 2000 **Turnover:** £1m - £2m
No.of Employees: 11 - 20 **Product Groups:** 44

Date of Accounts	Jul 07	Jul 06	Jul 05
Sales Turnover	1571	1325	1779
Pre Tax Profit/Loss	77	10	110
Working Capital	195	161	-551
Fixed Assets	346	234	123
Current Assets	682	558	672
Current Liabilities	487	397	1223
Total Share Capital	307	307	307
ROCE% (Return on Capital Employed)	14.2	2.6	-25.6
ROT% (Return on Turnover)	4.9	0.8	6.2

A & O Systems & Services

Prescott Road Colnbrook, Slough, SL3 0AE
Tel: 08706-068800 **Fax:** 08706- 068801
Website: http://www.aogroup.co.uk
Bank(s): Bank of Scotland
Directors: L. Frenzel (Dir), C. Banforth (Fin), A. Davison (Sales & Mktg)
Managers: L. Johnson (Tech Serv Mgr), S. Fox (Personnel), H. Vogelhuber (Purch Mgr)
Ultimate Holding Company: A & O MANAGEMENT SARL (LUXEMBURG)
Immediate Holding Company: A&O SYSTEMS + SERVICES UK LIMITED
Registration no: 00827981 **Date established:** 1964
Turnover: £20m - £50m **No.of Employees:** 251 - 500
Product Groups: 26, 28, 37, 44

Date of Accounts	Dec 09	Dec 08	Dec 07
Sales Turnover	39m	45m	65m
Pre Tax Profit/Loss	404	133	2m
Working Capital	5m	6m	10m
Fixed Assets	439	811	683
Current Assets	11m	12m	19m
Current Liabilities	4m	4m	7m

A T I Advanced Technologies International Ltd

893 Plymouth Road, Slough, SL1 4LP
Tel: 020-8283 3000 **Fax:** 0845-885 5222
E-mail: info@ati-uk.com
Website: http://www.ati-uk.com
Bank(s): National Westminster Bank Plc
Directors: P. Owles (MD)
Ultimate Holding Company: RENTAL RESEARCH LIMITED
Immediate Holding Company: EASY TREAT & CLEAN LIMITED
Registration no: 04931223 **VAT No.:** GB 584 5101 43
Date established: 2003 **Turnover:** £10m - £20m
No.of Employees: 11 - 20 **Product Groups:** 44

Acer UK Ltd

Acer House Poyle Road, Colnbrook, Slough, SL3 0QX
Tel: 01753-699200 **Fax:** 01753-699201
E-mail: sales@acer-euro.com
Website: http://www.acer.co.uk
Bank(s): National Westminster Bank Plc
Directors: G. Pierot (MD), P. Dobbin (Co Sec)
Managers: S. Levitt
Ultimate Holding Company: Acer Inc
Immediate Holding Company: Acer European Holdings
Registration no: 02252821 **VAT No.:** GB 494 0753 26
Turnover: £250m - £500m **No.of Employees:** 21 - 50
Product Groups: 37, 44, 81

Airport Freight Services Ltd

21 Willow Road Colnbrook, Slough, SL3 0BS
Tel: 01753-685335 **Fax:** 01753-684925
E-mail: michael@airport.co.uk
Website: http://www.airport.co.uk
Directors: M. Wong (MD)
Immediate Holding Company: AIRPORT SERVICES LIMITED
Registration no: 01651045 **Date established:** 1982 **Turnover:** £2m - £5m
No.of Employees: 11 - 20 **Product Groups:** 76

Date of Accounts	Jun 11	Jun 10	Jun 09
Sales Turnover	N/A	N/A	3m
Pre Tax Profit/Loss	N/A	N/A	209
Working Capital	274	257	162
Fixed Assets	9	19	26
Current Assets	617	584	405
Current Liabilities	N/A	N/A	60

Akzonobel

Wexham Road, Slough, SL2 5DS
Tel: 01753-550000 **Fax:** 01753-578218
E-mail: richard.stuckes@akzonobel.com
Website: http://www.dulux.com
Bank(s): Lloyds TSB Bank plc
Directors: K. Bright (Dir), A. Kukla (Dir), M. McLean (Co Sec), J. Webb (Dir), R. Stuckes (MD), D. Loose (Dir), D. Hamill (Grp Chief Exec)
Immediate Holding Company: I C I P.L.C.
No.of Employees: 501 - 1000 **Product Groups:** 32

Date of Accounts	Dec 07	Dec 06
Sales Turnover	4900m	4850m
Pre Tax Profit/Loss	360000	390000
Working Capital	310000	N/A
Fixed Assets	2120m	1920m
Current Assets	2300m	2370m
Current Liabilities	1990m	2370m
Total Share Capital	1210m	1190m
ROCE% (Return on Capital Employed)	14.8	20.3
ROT% (Return on Turnover)	7.3	8.0

Andrews Sykes Hire Ltd

761-762 Henley Road, Slough, SL1 4JW
Tel: 01753-820622 **Fax:** 01753-520595
Website: http://www.andrews-sykes.com
Managers: J. Wheatley (Mgr)
Immediate Holding Company: ANDREWS SYKES HIRE LIMITED
Registration no: 02985657 **VAT No.:** GB 100 4295 24
Date established: 1994 **Turnover:** £5m - £10m **No.of Employees:** 21 - 50
Product Groups: 40

Date of Accounts	Dec 11	Dec 10	Dec 09
Sales Turnover	35m	36m	34m
Pre Tax Profit/Loss	10m	10m	8m
Working Capital	8m	6m	2m
Fixed Assets	7m	7m	9m
Current Assets	33m	35m	35m
Current Liabilities	7m	7m	5m

Apex Commercial Refrigeration & Aircon

Eton House 4 Waterside Drive, Langley, Slough, SL3 6EZ
Tel: 01689-892510 **Fax:** 0870-998 5000
E-mail: apexrefrigeration@apexonline.co.uk
Website: http://www.carrieraircon.co.uk
Managers: M. Bickle (Mgr)
Immediate Holding Company: SPE FIRE LIMITED
Registration no: 02044550 **Date established:** 2005 **Turnover:** £1m - £2m
No.of Employees: 11 - 20 **Product Groups:** 37, 38, 40, 41, 42, 44, 48, 52, 66, 67, 83, 84, 85

Date of Accounts	Dec 07	Dec 06	Dec 05
Sales Turnover	1515	N/A	N/A
Pre Tax Profit/Loss	-170	N/A	N/A
Working Capital	-67	105	357
Fixed Assets	N/A	N/A	49
Current Assets	N/A	442	924
Current Liabilities	67	337	567
Total Share Capital	1	1	1
ROT% (Return on Turnover)	-11.2		

Apex Fasteners Ltd

494 Ipswich Road, Slough, SL1 4EP
Tel: 01753-525334 **Fax:** 01753-534863
E-mail: vixta83@yahoo.co.uk
Website: http://www.yahoo.co.uk
Directors: D. Sherwin (MD)
Immediate Holding Company: APEX FASTENERS LIMITED
Registration no: 02156432 **VAT No.:** GB 491 8629 05
Date established: 1987 **Turnover:** £250,000 - £500,000
No.of Employees: 1 - 10 **Product Groups:** 30, 35, 36, 38, 39, 40, 42, 45, 46, 49, 63, 66

Date of Accounts	Dec 11	Dec 10	Dec 09
Working Capital	71	79	70
Fixed Assets	12	14	8
Current Assets	130	128	112
Current Liabilities	1	N/A	N/A

Arben Sheet Metal Ltd

204 Bedford Avenue Slough Trading Estate, Slough, SL1 4RY
Tel: 01753-531066 **Fax:** 01753-694724
E-mail: arben@globalnet.co.uk
Directors: B. Duncan (MD)
Managers: S. Burtenshaw (Eng Serv Mgr)
Immediate Holding Company: ARBEN PRECISION SHEET METAL LIMITED
Registration no: 06435297 **VAT No.:** GB 207 5907 61
Date established: 2007 **Turnover:** £1m - £2m **No.of Employees:** 1 - 10
Product Groups: 48

Date of Accounts	Mar 11	Mar 10	Mar 09
Working Capital	93	125	105
Fixed Assets	74	79	100
Current Assets	338	328	402

Ark Wrought Ironwork & Gate Automation Ltd

34 Wild Green North, Slough, SL3 8NU
Tel: 01753-717861 **Fax:** 01753-670965
Directors: Y. Keates (Fin), A. Keates (MD)
Immediate Holding Company: ARK WROUGHT-IRONWORK LTD
Registration no: 04927908 **Date established:** 2003
No.of Employees: 1 - 10 **Product Groups:** 26, 35

Date of Accounts	Oct 11	Oct 10	Oct 09
Working Capital	16	29	26
Fixed Assets	19	15	19
Current Assets	55	86	73

Arrow Embroidery Services

Unit 7 Business Village Wexham Road, Slough, SL2 5HF
Tel: 01753-533503 **Fax:** 01753-523603
E-mail: sales@arrow-embroidery.co.uk
Website: http://www.arrow-embroidery.co.uk
Directors: R. Verdi (MD)
Immediate Holding Company: ARROW EMBROIDERY LIMITED
Registration no: 07245492 **Date established:** 2010
No.of Employees: 1 - 10 **Product Groups:** 23, 24, 63

Date of Accounts	Jul 11
Working Capital	-20
Fixed Assets	87
Current Assets	61

Ascot Metal Finishers Ltd

6 David Road Colnbrook, Slough, SL3 0DG
Tel: 01753-682416 **Fax:** 01753-680493
E-mail: info@ascotfinishers.co.uk
Website: http://www.ascotfinishers.co.uk
Bank(s): Lloyds TSB Bank plc
Directors: T. Bourke (MD)
Ultimate Holding Company: ASCOT POLYMER COATING LIMITED
Immediate Holding Company: ASCOT METAL FINISHERS LIMITED
Registration no: 03216529 **VAT No.:** GB 674 1162 42
Date established: 1996 **Turnover:** £1m - £2m **No.of Employees:** 21 - 50
Product Groups: 48

Date of Accounts	Sep 11	Sep 10	Sep 09
Working Capital	286	204	111
Fixed Assets	53	36	19
Current Assets	754	768	546

Association Of International & Courier Express Service

Unit 1 Riverside Cargo Centre Mathisen Way, Colnbrook, Slough, SL3 0HF
Tel: 01753-680550 **Fax:** 01753-681710
E-mail: info@aices.org
Website: http://www.aices.org
Managers: C. Cox
Immediate Holding Company: ASSOCIATION OF INTERNATIONAL COURIER & EXPRESS SERVICES
Registration no: 01634113 **VAT No.:** GB 226 2874 57
Date established: 1982 **Turnover:** Up to £250,000
No.of Employees: 1 - 10 **Product Groups:** 72, 79

Date of Accounts	Dec 11	Dec 10	Dec 09
Sales Turnover	150	142	153
Pre Tax Profit/Loss	10	-2	-16
Working Capital	166	156	158
Fixed Assets	2	2	2
Current Assets	180	168	173
Current Liabilities	4	4	4

Astro Med Inc

Astro Med House 11 Progress Business Centre Whittle Parkway, Slough, SL1 6DQ
Tel: 01628-668836 **Fax:** 01628-664994
E-mail: astromeduk@astromed.com
Website: http://www.astromed.com
Directors: A. Ondis (Ch)
Managers: D. Stillingfleet (Ops Mgr)
Immediate Holding Company: ASTRO-MED INC.
Registration no: FC014557 **Date established:** 1988
Turnover: £50m - £75m **No.of Employees:** 1 - 10 **Product Groups:** 38, 44

Auriema Ltd

661 Ajax Avenue, Slough, SL1 4BG
Tel: 01753-573603 **Fax:** 01753-577146
E-mail: sales@auriema.com
Website: http://www.auriema.com
Directors: C. Newman (Dir)
Immediate Holding Company: AURIEMA LTD
Registration no: 04766312 **Date established:** 2003
Turnover: £500,000 - £1m **No.of Employees:** 1 - 10 **Product Groups:** 36

Date of Accounts	May 11	May 10	May 09
Sales Turnover	N/A	N/A	187
Pre Tax Profit/Loss	N/A	N/A	15
Working Capital	92	79	80
Fixed Assets	2	2	2
Current Assets	111	98	107
Current Liabilities	N/A	N/A	10

Avenue Office Supplies The Avenue Group
3 David Road Colnbrook, Slough, SL3 0TW
Tel: 01753-687687 **Fax:** 01753-681681
E-mail: admin@avenue-group.co.uk
Website: http://www.avenue-group.co.uk
Directors: B. Pike (MD), D. Clarke (Dir), D. Clarke (MD)
Managers: P. Howe (Sales Admin)
Immediate Holding Company: AVENUE OFFICE SUPPLIES LIMITED
Registration no: 03167352 **VAT No.:** 666 2150 39 **Date established:** 1996
Turnover: £500,000 - £1m **No.of Employees:** 1 - 10 **Product Groups:** 27, 64

Date of Accounts	Nov 10	Nov 09	Nov 08
Working Capital	81	79	84
Current Assets	114	98	105

Avenue Tools Ltd
3 David Road Colnbrook, Slough, SL3 0TW
Tel: 01753-685921 **Fax:** 01753-685922
E-mail: avenue@avenue-group.co.uk
Website: http://www.avenue-group.co.uk
Bank(s): Barclays, Heathrow
Directors: D. Clarke (MD)
Immediate Holding Company: AVENUE TOOLS LIMITED
Registration no: 00727765 **VAT No.:** GB 207 8965 32
Date established: 1962 **Turnover:** £2m - £5m **No.of Employees:** 11 - 20
Product Groups: 66, 67

Date of Accounts	Jul 12	Jul 11	Jul 10
Working Capital	257	264	191
Fixed Assets	27	20	20
Current Assets	600	774	573

B C D Audio
5 Bristol Way Stoke Gardens, Slough, SL1 3QE
Tel: 01753-579524 **Fax:** 01753-577981
Website: http://www.bcd-audio.com
Directors: L. Law (Fin)
Immediate Holding Company: STOKE GARDENS MANAGEMENT LIMITED
Registration no: 02707964 **Date established:** 1987
No.of Employees: 1 - 10 **Product Groups:** 37, 39

B R T Bearings Ltd
83 Whitby Road, Slough, SL1 3DR
Tel: 01753-526851
E-mail: slough@brt-bearings.com
Website: http://www.brt-bearings.com
Directors: P. Clarke (MD)
Immediate Holding Company: B.R.T. BEARINGS (MERCIA) LTD
Registration no: 02084268 **Date established:** 1986
No.of Employees: 1 - 10 **Product Groups:** 35, 41

B T Rolatruc Ltd
705-707 Stirling Road, Slough, SL1 4SY
Tel: 01753-530551 **Fax:** 01753-570885
Website: http://www.toyota-industries.se
Bank(s): Barclays
Directors: A. Prior (Co Sec), T. Pier (Fin)
Managers: C. Andy (I.T. Exec), D. Seymore (Accounts), H. Armstrong (Personnel)
Immediate Holding Company: BT Rolatruc Ltd
Registration no: 07543309 **VAT No.:** GB 669 2842 89
Date established: 1961 **Turnover:** £5m - £10m
No.of Employees: 501 - 1000 **Product Groups:** 67

Bruce Bishop & Sons Ltd
Lake Avenue, Slough, SL1 3BZ
Tel: 01753-525206 **Fax:** 01753-532801
Directors: M. Bishop (MD), N. Bishop (Co Sec)
Immediate Holding Company: BRUCE BISHOP & SONS LIMITED
Registration no: 00739618 **VAT No.:** GB 208 3485 65
Date established: 1962 **No.of Employees:** 11 - 20 **Product Groups:** 66

Date of Accounts	Jun 10	Jun 09	Jun 08
Working Capital	-350	-482	-235
Fixed Assets	306	374	461
Current Assets	1m	1m	1m

Bishop Sports & Leisure Ltd
Bishops House Crown Lane, Farnham Royal, Slough, SL2 3SF
Tel: 01753-648666 **Fax:** 01753-648989
E-mail: sales@bishopsport.co.uk
Website: http://www.bishopsport.co.uk
Bank(s): National Westminster Bank Plc
Directors: C. Halcomb (Dir)
Managers: E. Newell (Sales Prom Mgr), K. Tanna
Ultimate Holding Company: BISHOPS HOLDINGS LIMITED
Immediate Holding Company: BISHOP SPORTS & LEISURE LIMITED
Registration no: 00842463 **VAT No.:** GB 207 9874 30
Date established: 1965 **Turnover:** £2m - £5m **No.of Employees:** 21 - 50
Product Groups: 22, 24, 26, 35, 49, 64

Date of Accounts	Oct 11	Oct 10	Oct 09
Sales Turnover	3m	4m	4m
Pre Tax Profit/Loss	341	349	467
Working Capital	1m	2m	2m
Fixed Assets	2m	3m	2m
Current Assets	2m	2m	3m
Current Liabilities	707	563	410

Black & Decker Ltd
210 Bath Road, Slough, SL1 3YD
Tel: 01753-511234 **Fax:** 01753-551155
E-mail: gavin.johnson@blackanddecker.co.uk
Website: http://www.bmjpower.com
Directors: M. Whitthread (Pers), G. Johnston (Fin)
Managers: J. Cowley (Chief Mgr), P. Garget (Purch Mgr)
Ultimate Holding Company: STANLEY BLACK & DECKER CORPORATION (USA)
Immediate Holding Company: BLACK & DECKER
Registration no: 00291547 **VAT No.:** GB 207 9108 71
Date established: 1934 **Turnover:** £20m - £50m
No.of Employees: 501 - 1000 **Product Groups:** 36, 37, 46, 47

Date of Accounts	Dec 10	Dec 09	Dec 08
Sales Turnover	23m	79m	100m
Pre Tax Profit/Loss	-3m	-19m	-10m
Working Capital	61m	131m	152m
Fixed Assets	296m	297m	299m
Current Assets	121m	198m	269m
Current Liabilities	2m	9m	8m

Bridgelock Engineering & Marketing Ltd
137 Slough Road Datchet, Slough, SL3 9AE
Tel: 01753-549373 **Fax:** 01753-580269
E-mail: sales@bridgelock.com
Website: http://www.bridgelock.com
Directors: M. Donnelly (MD)
Immediate Holding Company: BRIDGELOCK ENGINEERING & MARKETING LIMITED
Registration no: 01774413 **Date established:** 1983
Turnover: Up to £250,000 **No.of Employees:** 1 - 10 **Product Groups:** 22, 27, 28, 30, 36, 40, 42, 44, 49

Date of Accounts	Jul 11	Jul 10	Jul 09
Working Capital	9	8	4
Fixed Assets	1	1	2
Current Assets	50	26	49

Bob Burge Ltd
Unit 18 Trident Industrial Estate Blackthorne Road, Colnbrook, Slough, SL3 0AX
Tel: 01753-689688 **Fax:** 01753-681563
E-mail: info@bob-burge.co.uk
Website: http://www.bobburge.co.uk
Directors: P. Velounias (Dir)
Immediate Holding Company: BOB BURGE LIMITED
Registration no: 00843091 **VAT No.:** GB 232 1650 04
Date established: 1965 **Turnover:** £250,000 - £500,000
No.of Employees: 1 - 10 **Product Groups:** 75, 76

Date of Accounts	Mar 12	Mar 11	Mar 10
Working Capital	277	383	364
Fixed Assets	47	63	49
Current Assets	388	546	551

C H Robinson
8-9 Blackthorne Cresent Colnbrook, Slough, SL3 0QR
Tel: 01753-683288 **Fax:** 01753-681917
E-mail: phil.collins@chreurope.com
Website: http://www.walkerfreight.com
Directors: W. Feys (Co Sec)
Managers: C. Lifford (Tech Serv Mgr), M. Dell, P. Collins (District Mgr), J. Gillyland
Ultimate Holding Company: C H ROBINSON INCORPORATED (USA)
Immediate Holding Company: C.H. ROBINSON WORLDWIDE (UK) LIMITED
Registration no: 01383545 **VAT No.:** 225 4332 89 **Date established:** 1978
Turnover: £10m - £20m **No.of Employees:** 21 - 50 **Product Groups:** 76

Date of Accounts	Dec 11	Dec 10	Dec 09
Sales Turnover	8m	17m	14m
Pre Tax Profit/Loss	-35	560	21
Working Capital	1m	1m	876
Fixed Assets	50	58	140
Current Assets	3m	5m	5m
Current Liabilities	330	511	173

C I T International Freight Ltd
Unit 5 Mckay Trading Estate Blackthorne Road, Colnbrook, Slough, SL3 0AH
Tel: 01753-521484 **Fax:** 01753-693886
E-mail: sales@citint.com
Website: http://www.citint.com
Directors: K. Namihas (Fin)
Managers: J. Emmett (Ops Mgr)
Immediate Holding Company: CIT INTERNATIONAL FREIGHT LIMITED
Registration no: 01451141 **Date established:** 1979
No.of Employees: 1 - 10 **Product Groups:** 76

Date of Accounts	Jan 12	Jan 11	Jan 10
Working Capital	46	44	26
Fixed Assets	59	63	63
Current Assets	453	472	449

C M C Consulting Ltd
2 Progress Business Centre Whittle Parkway, Slough, SL1 6DQ
Tel: 01628-600870 **Fax:** 01628-660688
E-mail: slough@cmcconsulting.co.uk
Website: http://www.cmcconsulting.co.uk
Directors: R. Sussum (Dir)
Immediate Holding Company: C M C CONSULTING LIMITED
Registration no: 02894587 **Date established:** 1994 **Turnover:** £5m - £10m
No.of Employees: 1 - 10 **Product Groups:** 37, 44, 79, 80, 84

Date of Accounts	Mar 11	Mar 10	Mar 09
Sales Turnover	N/A	N/A	6m
Pre Tax Profit/Loss	N/A	N/A	284
Working Capital	-130	-168	56
Fixed Assets	612	616	642
Current Assets	821	698	874
Current Liabilities	N/A	N/A	657

C M F Slough Ltd
661 Ajax Avenue, Slough, SL1 4BG
Tel: 01753-551500 **Fax:** 01753-693163
E-mail: cmf@paintco.co.uk
Website: http://www.paintco.co.uk
Directors: C. Newman (Dir)
Immediate Holding Company: C.M.F. (SLOUGH) LIMITED
Registration no: 03134610 **Date established:** 1995
Turnover: £500,000 - £1m **No.of Employees:** 11 - 20
Product Groups: 48, 52

Date of Accounts	Dec 11	Dec 10	Dec 09
Working Capital	105	99	109
Fixed Assets	19	22	27
Current Assets	185	161	157

Cadmean Ltd
38 Lawn Close Datchet, Slough, SL3 9JZ
Tel: 01753-547744 **Fax:** 01753-547744
Website: http://www.cadmean.co.uk
Directors: C. Adams (MD)
Immediate Holding Company: CADMEAN LIMITED
Registration no: 02702626 **Date established:** 1992
No.of Employees: 1 - 10 **Product Groups:** 38, 42

Date of Accounts	Mar 12	Mar 11	Mar 10
Working Capital	28	30	30
Fixed Assets	N/A	N/A	1
Current Assets	31	36	37

Carclo Technical Plastics
103 Buckingham Avenue, Slough, SL1 4PF
Tel: 01753-575011 **Fax:** 01753-811359
E-mail: optics@carclo-optics.com
Website: http://www.carclo-plc.com
Bank(s): Lloyds TSB Bank plc
Directors: D. Sumner (MD)
Managers: J. Marzetti (Cust Serv Mgr)
Ultimate Holding Company: QUADRAMATIC PLC
Immediate Holding Company: CARCLO PLC
Registration no: 00315171 **VAT No.:** GB 697 9082 65
Date established: 1936 **Turnover:** £10m - £20m
No.of Employees: 11 - 20 **Product Groups:** 22, 28, 30

Channel Dynamics
Bay 10 Banbury Avenue, Slough, SL1 4LH
Tel: 08706-070540 **Fax:** 08706-070541
E-mail: sales@channeldynamics.net
Website: http://www.channeldynamics.net
Directors: B. Wood (Fin), W. Wood (MD)
Immediate Holding Company: CHANNEL DYNAMICS DISTRIBUTION LIMITED
Registration no: 03489345 **Date established:** 1998 **Turnover:** £2m - £5m
No.of Employees: 1 - 10 **Product Groups:** 44

Date of Accounts	Mar 11	Mar 10	Mar 09
Working Capital	75	48	1
Fixed Assets	123	146	165
Current Assets	2m	3m	3m

Chiltern Airfreight
Wraysbury House Poyle Road, Colnbrook, Slough, SL3 0AY
Tel: 01753-680535 **Fax:** 01753-681094
E-mail: office@chilternairfreight.co.uk
Website: http://www.chilternairfreight.co.uk
Managers: M. Hughes (Mgr)
Immediate Holding Company: CHILTERN AIR FREIGHT LIMITED
Registration no: 01671724 **VAT No.:** GB 349 0754 37
Date established: 1982 **Turnover:** Up to £250,000
No.of Employees: 1 - 10 **Product Groups:** 39, 75, 76, 82

Date of Accounts	Feb 11	Feb 10	Feb 09
Working Capital	11	3	9
Fixed Assets	8	8	11
Current Assets	142	107	123

Comxo
18 Horton Road Datchet, Slough, SL3 9ER
Tel: 01753-710430 **Fax:** 01753-710419
E-mail: andrew.try@comxo.com
Website: http://www.comxo.com
Directors: S. Swan (Fin), A. Try (Dir), A. Try (MD)
Immediate Holding Company: COMXO LIMITED
Registration no: 03727666 **Date established:** 1999 **Turnover:** £2m - £5m
No.of Employees: 51 - 100 **Product Groups:** 37, 44, 79, 80

Date of Accounts	Mar 11	Mar 10	Mar 09
Sales Turnover	2m	2m	2m
Pre Tax Profit/Loss	203	207	-65
Working Capital	233	50	-193
Fixed Assets	147	127	129
Current Assets	664	443	363
Current Liabilities	245	189	320

Concrete Cutters Ltd
18 David Road Colnbrook, Slough, SL3 0DG
Tel: 01753-688280 **Fax:** 01753-684537
E-mail: info@concut.co.uk
Website: http://www.concut.com
Bank(s): HSBC Bank plc
Directors: P. Denyer (Dir), K. Play (MD), K. Clay (Dir)
Immediate Holding Company: CONCRETE CUTTERS LIMITED
Registration no: 07520707 **VAT No.:** GB 188 0377 35
Date established: 2011 **Turnover:** £1m - £2m **No.of Employees:** 11 - 20
Product Groups: 51

Date of Accounts	Jun 08	Jun 07	Jun 06
Working Capital	-416	372	265
Fixed Assets	1577	415	427
Current Assets	1369	998	1197
Current Liabilities	1785	626	931
Total Share Capital	2	2	3

Corporate Health Ltd
30 Bradford Road, Slough, SL1 4PG
Tel: 01753-781600 **Fax:** 01753-517889
E-mail: customer.services@corporatehealth.co.uk
Website: http://www.corporatehealth.co.uk
Bank(s): Barclays
Directors: B. Edwards (MD), D. Upton (Fin), A. Wilkinson (Sales & Mktg)
Ultimate Holding Company: CORPORATE HEALTH LIMITED
Immediate Holding Company: CORPORATE HEALTH SUPPLIES LIMITED
Registration no: 02633412 **Date established:** 1991
Turnover: Up to £250,000 **No.of Employees:** 21 - 50 **Product Groups:** 54, 80, 84, 86, 88

Date of Accounts	Mar 11	Mar 10	Mar 09
Sales Turnover	97	85	72
Working Capital	9	9	9
Fixed Assets	1	1	1
Current Assets	46	37	23
Current Liabilities	30	23	11

Corus
Colndale Road Colnbrook, Slough, SL3 0HL
Tel: 01753-683131 **Fax:** 01753-684372
E-mail: james.larner@corusgroup.com
Website: http://www.corusgroup.com
Bank(s): National Westminster Bank Plc
Managers: J. Larner (Chief Mgr), J. Raistrick (Chief Mgr)
Ultimate Holding Company: British Steel P.L.C.
Immediate Holding Company: CORUS GROUP LIMITED
Registration no: 03811373 **Date established:** 1999
Turnover: £20m - £50m **No.of Employees:** 51 - 100 **Product Groups:** 66

John Crane UK Ltd
Buckingham House 361-366 Buckingham Avenue, Slough, SL1 4LU
Tel: 01753-224000 **Fax:** 01753-224153
E-mail: libby.thompson@johncrane.co.uk
Website: http://www.johncrane.co.uk
Managers: L. Thompson
Ultimate Holding Company: SMITHS GROUP PLC
Immediate Holding Company: JOHN CRANE UK LIMITED
Registration no: 00192121 **Date established:** 2023
Turnover: £75m - £125m **No.of Employees:** 101 - 250
Product Groups: 36, 39

Date of Accounts	Jul 11	Jul 10	Jul 09
Sales Turnover	80m	74m	68m
Pre Tax Profit/Loss	15m	17m	4m

see next page

***John Crane UK Ltd** - Cont'd*

Working Capital	77m	62m	49m
Fixed Assets	18m	22m	24m
Current Assets	106m	92m	74m
Current Liabilities	9m	9m	10m

Croft Brothers UK Ltd
755 Deal Avenue, Slough, SL1 4SH
Tel: 01753-539462 **Fax:** 01753-571843
E-mail: info@croftbrothers.co.uk
Website: http://www.croftbrothers.co.uk
Directors: G. Vancuylenberg (MD)
Immediate Holding Company: CROFT BROTHERS U.K. LIMITED
Registration no: 02605120 **Date established:** 1991
Turnover: £10m - £20m **No.of Employees:** 1 - 10 **Product Groups:** 39, 40, 68

Date of Accounts	Oct 11	Oct 10	Oct 09
Working Capital	-32	-23	9
Fixed Assets	33	8	8
Current Assets	275	242	260

Croft Television Ltd
Croft House 17 Progress Business Centre Whittle Parkway, Slough, SL1 6DQ
Tel: 01628-668735 **Fax:** 01628-668791
E-mail: info@croft-tv.com
Website: http://www.croft-tv.com
Directors: N. Devonshire (MD)
Immediate Holding Company: CROFT TELEVISION LIMITED
Registration no: 02204673 **Date established:** 1987
Turnover: Up to £250,000 **No.of Employees:** 1 - 10 **Product Groups:** 44, 81, 89

Date of Accounts	May 12	May 11	May 10
Sales Turnover	N/A	N/A	170
Pre Tax Profit/Loss	N/A	N/A	-9
Working Capital	58	42	27
Fixed Assets	22	24	15
Current Assets	93	66	40
Current Liabilities	N/A	N/A	13

Crossflight Ltd
Crossflight House Unit B1 Skyway 14 Calder Way, Colnbrook, Slough, SL3 0BQ
Tel: 01753-776060 **Fax:** 0870-224 0103
E-mail: enquiries@crossflight.com
Website: http://www.crossflight.com
Bank(s): Duncan Lawrie Ltd
Directors: R. Stoughton (MD), K. Stoughton (Sales)
Managers: N. Rattanpal (Personnel), G. Dawson (Tech Serv Mgr)
Immediate Holding Company: CROSSFLIGHT LIMITED
Registration no: 02111027 **Date established:** 1987
Turnover: £10m - £20m **No.of Employees:** 101 - 250
Product Groups: 76, 79, 81

Date of Accounts	Mar 12	Mar 11	Mar 10
Sales Turnover	14m	12m	11m
Pre Tax Profit/Loss	913	552	202
Working Capital	1m	966	538
Fixed Assets	194	47	72
Current Assets	3m	3m	3m
Current Liabilities	766	679	617

D P S Industrial Finishers Ltd
C P K House Colndale Road, Colnbrook, Slough, SL3 0HQ
Tel: 01753-684666 **Fax:** 01753-685272
E-mail: sales@dpsindustrialfinishers.co.uk
Website: http://www.dpsindustrialfinishers.co.uk
Directors: D. Balu (Dir)
Immediate Holding Company: DPS INDUSTRIAL FINISHERS LIMITED
Registration no: 06703145 **Date established:** 2008
Turnover: £250,000 - £500,000 **No.of Employees:** 1 - 10
Product Groups: 48

Date of Accounts	Sep 11	Sep 10	Sep 09
Working Capital	96	89	58
Fixed Assets	4	6	7
Current Assets	239	179	154

Diskel Ltd
212-214 Farnham Road, Slough, SL1 4XE
Tel: 01753-821091 **Fax:** 01753-512438
E-mail: ash@diskel.co.uk
Website: http://www.diskel.co.uk
Bank(s): HSBC Bank plc
Directors: A. Chani (Dir)
Ultimate Holding Company: DISKEL CONSULTING (UK) LIMITED
Immediate Holding Company: DISKEL LIMITED
Registration no: 01342805 **VAT No.:** GB 302 1355 19
Date established: 1977 **Turnover:** £500,000 - £1m
No.of Employees: 11 - 20 **Product Groups:** 44

Date of Accounts	Dec 11	Dec 10	Dec 09
Working Capital	186	136	134
Current Assets	612	402	399
Current Liabilities	264	230	N/A

Douwe Egberts UK
225 Bath Road, Slough, SL1 3UQ
Tel: 08452-711818 **Fax:** 0845-271 1819
E-mail: info@douwe.com
Website: http://www.douwe.com
Immediate Holding Company: DOUWE EGBERTS COFFEE SYSTEMS LIMITED
Registration no: 01435632 **Date established:** 1979
Turnover: £20m - £50m **No.of Employees:** 51 - 100 **Product Groups:** 20, 40, 49, 62, 67, 86

Date of Accounts	Jun 09	Jun 08	Jun 07
Sales Turnover	15m	15m	16m
Pre Tax Profit/Loss	6m	-2m	-1m
Working Capital	-700	-8m	-27m
Fixed Assets	11m	20m	38m
Current Assets	3m	4m	6m
Current Liabilities	868	2m	2m

Duco International Ltd
4 Eastbourne Road, Slough, SL1 4SF
Tel: 01753-522274 **Fax:** 01753-691952
E-mail: info@duco.co.uk
Website: http://www.duco.co.uk
Bank(s): Bank of Scotland
Directors: A. Taubet (MD), D. Healey (Dir), D. Healy (MD), D. Wolters (Dir), J. Connell (Co Sec)
Immediate Holding Company: DUCO INTERNATIONAL LIMITED
Registration no: 03471699 **VAT No.:** GB 727 2081 46
Date established: 1997 **Turnover:** £10m - £20m
No.of Employees: 51 - 100 **Product Groups:** 44

Date of Accounts	Dec 07	Dec 06	Dec 05
Sales Turnover	16316	16517	16376
Pre Tax Profit/Loss	760	-108	148
Working Capital	5692	3219	2834
Fixed Assets	9581	10834	12132
Current Assets	9049	6358	5969
Current Liabilities	3357	3139	3135
Total Share Capital	1	1	1
ROCE% (Return on Capital Employed)	5.0	-0.8	1.0
ROT% (Return on Turnover)	4.7	-0.7	0.9

Eaton Electric Sales Ltd (a division of Eaton Group)
221 Dover Road, Slough, SL1 4RF
Tel: 01753-608700 **Fax:** 01753-608995
E-mail: razahussain@eaton.com
Website: http://www.eaton.com/powerquality
Bank(s): Lloyds TSB Bank plc
Directors: G. Patridge (Fin)
Managers: A. Scattergood (Tech Serv Mgr), L. Phillips (Buyer), M. Derbyshire (Mgr), A. Delamotta (Mktg Serv Mgr), S. Brown (Personnel)
Ultimate Holding Company: EATON CORPORATION (USA)
Immediate Holding Company: EATON ELECTRIC SALES LIMITED
Registration no: 03170565 **VAT No.:** 242 3380 87 **Date established:** 1996
Turnover: £1m - £2m **No.of Employees:** 21 - 50 **Product Groups:** 37, 44

Date of Accounts	Dec 10	Dec 09	Dec 08
Sales Turnover	14m	13m	12m
Pre Tax Profit/Loss	-2m	-2m	138
Working Capital	3m	-1m	397
Fixed Assets	960	5m	5m
Current Assets	8m	8m	7m
Current Liabilities	2m	1m	778

Elesta
PO Box 3418, Slough, SL1 0BR
Tel: 01628-664441 **Fax:** 01628-664441
E-mail: info@elesta.co.uk
Website: http://www.elesta.co.uk
Managers: M. Morrison (Mktg Serv Mgr)
Registration no: HRB 181 **Date established:** 1952
No.of Employees: 1 - 10 **Product Groups:** 37, 52

Emerson Process Management
158 Edinburgh Avenue, Slough, SL1 4UE
Tel: 01753-756600 **Fax:** 01753-823589
E-mail: sales@solartron.com
Website: http://www.emersonprocess.co.uk
Directors: J. Rowley (Fin), C. Rooke (MD)
Managers: A. Roper (Personnel), D. Good (Personnel), A. Juddery (Comptroller), D. Eyley, T. Green (Purch Mgr), P. Glenister
Ultimate Holding Company: ROXBORO GROUP P.L.C.
Immediate Holding Company: EMERSON PROCESS MANAGEMENT LIMITED
Registration no: 00671801 **Date established:** 1960
Turnover: £20m - £50m **No.of Employees:** 251 - 500
Product Groups: 37, 38

Date of Accounts	Sep 08
Sales Turnover	30700
Pre Tax Profit/Loss	-420
Working Capital	5550
Fixed Assets	6370
Current Assets	11940
Current Liabilities	6390
Total Share Capital	18120
ROCE% (Return on Capital Employed)	-3.5

Enodis Group Enodis UK Food Service
Unit 5e Langley Business Centre Station Road, Langley, Slough, SL3 8DS
Tel: 020-7304 6000 **Fax:** 01753-485901
E-mail: thomas.doerr@manitowoc.com
Website: http://www.enodis.com
Directors: M. Jones (Dir)
Ultimate Holding Company: THE MANITOWOC CO INC(USA)
Immediate Holding Company: ENODIS GROUP LIMITED
Registration no: 04330202 **Date established:** 2001 **Turnover:** £2m - £5m
No.of Employees: 21 - 50 **Product Groups:** 40

Date of Accounts	Dec 11	Dec 10	Dec 09
Sales Turnover	N/A	3m	2m
Pre Tax Profit/Loss	-12m	-10m	-477m
Working Capital	-728m	-717m	-710m
Fixed Assets	781m	781m	783m
Current Assets	574m	573m	968m
Current Liabilities	2m	2m	2m

Envirogreen Special Waste Services Ltd
Regus House 268 Bath Road, Slough, SL1 4DX
Tel: 01753-537362 **Fax:** 01753-537314
E-mail: info@envirogreen.co.uk
Website: http://www.envirogreen.co.uk
Directors: N. Stewart (Dir), D. McAleenan (MD)
Managers: D. Banbury (Mgr)
Immediate Holding Company: GLOBAL MEDICAL CONSULTANCY LIMITED
Registration no: 02343006 **Date established:** 2006
Turnover: £500,000 - £1m **No.of Employees:** 1 - 10 **Product Groups:** 42, 54

Eurolink Corporation Ltd
11 Rosken Grove Farnham Royal, Slough, SL2 3DZ
Tel: 01753-642500 **Fax:** 01753-642999
E-mail: info@eurolinkcorp.com
Website: http://www.eurolinkcorp.com
Directors: S. Chaudhry (MD)
Immediate Holding Company: EUROLINK CORPORATION LIMITED
Registration no: 02527336 **Date established:** 1990 **Turnover:** £2m - £5m
No.of Employees: 1 - 10 **Product Groups:** 20, 62

Date of Accounts	Feb 08	Feb 11	Feb 10
Working Capital	122	236	200
Fixed Assets	30	10	21
Current Assets	192	378	442

Executive-Chauffeur.Com
Lambert Avenue, Slough, SL3 7EB
Tel: 08451-307065 **Fax:** 08451-307066
E-mail: info@executive-chauffeur.com
Website: http://www.executive-chauffeur.com
Directors: T. Thanjal (Prop)
No.of Employees: 1 - 10 **Product Groups:** 72

Expertex Exterior Wall Coatings
179 Tamar Way Langley, Slough, SL3 8SZ
Tel: 01753-596256
E-mail: coatings@expertex.co.uk
Website: http://www.expertex.co.uk
Product Groups: 31, 32, 33, 66

Express Fire Protection Ltd
45 Furnival Avenue, Slough, SL2 1DH
Tel: 01753-821111 **Fax:** 01753-820100
E-mail: sales@express-fire.co.uk
Website: http://www.express-fire.co.uk
Directors: R. Ray (Prop)
Immediate Holding Company: EXPRESS FIRE PROTECTION LIMITED
Registration no: 06656069 **Date established:** 2008
No.of Employees: 1 - 10 **Product Groups:** 38, 42

Date of Accounts	Jul 11	Jul 10	Jul 09
Working Capital	14	-1	-16
Fixed Assets	19	24	30
Current Assets	44	51	19

Ferring Pharmaceuticals Ltd
The Courtyard Waterside Drive, Langley, Slough, SL3 6EZ
Tel: 01753-214800 **Fax:** 020-8893 1577
E-mail: contact@ferring.co.uk
Website: http://www.ferring.co.uk
Directors: P. Wilden (Fin)
Managers: B. Reuzala (Chief Mgr), S. Paige (I.T. Exec), R. Knight (Sales Admin)
Ultimate Holding Company: INSULA LTD (BVI)
Immediate Holding Company: FERRING LABORATORIES LIMITED
Registration no: 01508287 **VAT No.:** GB 224 1069 02
Date established: 1980 **Turnover:** £50m - £75m
No.of Employees: 101 - 250 **Product Groups:** 63

Date of Accounts	Dec 09	Dec 08	Dec 07
Sales Turnover	55m	52m	54m
Pre Tax Profit/Loss	2m	1m	3m
Working Capital	8m	9m	7m
Fixed Assets	1m	1m	3m
Current Assets	17m	16m	15m
Current Liabilities	2m	3m	3m

Finning UK Ltd
688-689 Stirling Road, Slough, SL1 4ST
Tel: 01753-497300 **Fax:** 01753-497333
E-mail: mbarnes@finning.co.uk
Website: http://www.finning.co.uk
Bank(s): National Westminster Bank Plc
Managers: M. Barnes (Chief Mgr)
Ultimate Holding Company: FINNING INTERNATIONAL INC (CANADA)
Immediate Holding Company: FINNING (UK) LTD.
Registration no: 00367090 **Date established:** 1941
Turnover: £125m - £250m **No.of Employees:** 51 - 100
Product Groups: 45

Date of Accounts	Dec 11	Dec 10	Dec 09
Sales Turnover	522m	413m	334m
Pre Tax Profit/Loss	31m	10m	8m
Working Capital	98m	79m	49m
Fixed Assets	71m	81m	77m
Current Assets	236m	207m	170m
Current Liabilities	70m	38m	34m

Forsteel Ltd
18 St Johns Road, Slough, SL2 5EY
Tel: 01753-517322 **Fax:** 01753-517832
E-mail: lsimm42778@aol.com
Directors: L. Simmonds (MD), M. Wilson (Sales)
Immediate Holding Company: FORSTEEL LIMITED
Registration no: 02349937 **VAT No.:** GB 529 9462 03
Date established: 1989 **Turnover:** £1m - £2m **No.of Employees:** 1 - 10
Product Groups: 77

Date of Accounts	Apr 11	Apr 10	Apr 09
Working Capital	104	112	98
Fixed Assets	2	3	3
Current Assets	426	417	345

G A C Logistics UK Ltd
Unit 1 Argonaut Park Galleymead Road, Colnbrook, Slough, SL3 0EN
Tel: 01753-671671 **Fax:** 01753-684682
E-mail: lhr.uk-lo@gac.com
Website: http://www.gac.com
Directors: P. Cole (MD)
Managers: P. De Souza (Chief Mgr)
Ultimate Holding Company: GULF AGENCY COMPANY LIMITED (LEICHTENSTEIN)
Immediate Holding Company: GAC LOGISTICS (UK) LIMITED
Registration no: 01025125 **Date established:** 1971
Turnover: £10m - £20m **No.of Employees:** 21 - 50 **Product Groups:** 76

Date of Accounts	Dec 11	Dec 10	Dec 09
Sales Turnover	36m	35m	27m
Pre Tax Profit/Loss	-1m	-542	-37
Working Capital	-924	299	670
Fixed Assets	342	308	333
Current Assets	7m	8m	5m
Current Liabilities	967	793	645

G B A Engineering & Construction Ltd
Burnham House 93 High Street, Burnham, Slough, SL1 7JZ
Tel: 01628-610100 **Fax:** 01628-610170
E-mail: sales@gba.com
Website: http://www.gba.com
Directors: P. Watts (MD)
Immediate Holding Company: GBA ENGINEERING AND CONSTRUCTION LIMITED
Registration no: 03452488 **Date established:** 1997 **Turnover:** £1m - £2m
No.of Employees: 1 - 10 **Product Groups:** 40, 67

Date of Accounts	Jun 11	Jun 10	Jun 09
Working Capital	1m	1m	1m
Fixed Assets	18	57	81
Current Assets	3m	3m	2m
Current Liabilities	N/A	N/A	142

GB Beverages
3 Drake Avenue, Slough, SL3 7JR
Tel: 08706-094652 **Fax:** 01753-584545
Website: http://www.gbbeverages.co.uk
Directors: S. Dhillon (Dir)
No.of Employees: 1 - 10 **Product Groups:** 20, 21, 62

Date of Accounts	Sep 07	Sep 06	Sep 05
Sales Turnover	N/A	8585	1196
Pre Tax Profit/Loss	N/A	61	-13
Working Capital	-35	46	-7
Fixed Assets	4	3	5
Current Assets	130	788	151
Current Liabilities	166	742	159
ROCE% (Return on Capital Employed)		122.6	470.5
ROT% (Return on Turnover)		0.7	-1.1

G C H Test & Computer Services Ltd

G C H House Progress Business Centre 5 Whittle Parkway, Slough, SL1 6DQ
Tel: 01628-559980 **Fax:** 01628-559990
E-mail: sales@gch-services.com
Website: http://www.gch-services.com
Directors: N. Collier (Dir)
Immediate Holding Company: G.C.H. TEST & COMPUTER SERVICES LIMITED
Registration no: 02810696 **VAT No.:** GB 626 8547 10
Date established: 1993 **Turnover:** £1m - £2m **No.of Employees:** 1 - 10
Product Groups: 44

Date of Accounts	Mar 12	Mar 11	Mar 10
Working Capital	40	-7	-29
Fixed Assets	2	11	32
Current Assets	532	574	1m

GE Healthcare

Coolidge House 352 Buckingham Avenue, Slough, SL1 4ER
Tel: 01753-874000 **Fax:** 01753-874578
E-mail: info@gehealthcare.com
Website: http://www.gehealthcare.com
Bank(s): Barclays
Directors: M. Blick (Jt MD), K. Blight (Jt MD)
Ultimate Holding Company: General Electric Co. (USA)
Immediate Holding Company: General Electric (USA)
Registration no: 01002610 **VAT No.:** GB 578 4387 84
Turnover: £75m - £125m **No.of Employees:** 101 - 250
Product Groups: 37

Gibbs & Dandy

462 Bath Road, Slough, SL1 6BQ
Tel: 01628-600743 **Fax:** 01628-604572
E-mail: slough@gibbsanddandy.com
Website: http://www.gibbsanddandy.co.uk
Directors: H. Jones (Co Sec), R. Dandy (Dir)
Immediate Holding Company: TIMBER FORCE UK LIMITED
Registration no: 04021174 **VAT No.:** GB 196 2442 45
Date established: 2000 **Turnover:** £50m - £75m
No.of Employees: 21 - 50 **Product Groups:** 66

Glaxo Smithkline plc (Consumer Healthcare International)

11 Stoke Poges Lane, Slough, SL1 3NW
Tel: 01753-533433 **Fax:** 01753-502000
Website: http://www.gsk.com
Bank(s): HSBC
Directors: J. Garnier (Grp Chief Exec)
Immediate Holding Company: GLAXOSMITHKLINE PLC
Registration no: 03888792 **VAT No.:** GB 493 9256 01
Date established: 1999 **Turnover:** £500m - £1,000m
No.of Employees: 101 - 250 **Product Groups:** 20

Date of Accounts	Dec 11	Dec 10	Dec 09
Sales Turnover	27387m	28392m	28368m
Pre Tax Profit/Loss	7698m	4505m	7891m
Working Capital	1157m	3242m	5452m
Fixed Assets	24913m	26194m	25292m
Current Assets	16167m	16036m	17570m
Current Liabilities	12243m	10362m	10041m

Grace Construction Ltd

58- Ipswich Road, Slough, SL1 4EQ
Tel: 01753-790000 **Fax:** 01753-691623
E-mail: graham.moorfield@grace.com
Website: http://www.gracec-onstruction.co.uk
Bank(s): Barclays
Directors: D. Boer (Fin), D. Michaels (Fin)
Managers: K. Christian (Personnel), K. Chriatian (Personnel), G. Mckeown (I.T. Exec), G. Moorfield (Sales Prom Mgr), S. Macwan (Tech Serv Mgr), J. Staines (Purch Mgr)
Ultimate Holding Company: W R GRACE & COMPANY (USA)
Immediate Holding Company: SERVICISED LIMITED
Registration no: 01046441 **VAT No.:** GB 705 7450 42
Date established: 1972 **Turnover:** £50m - £75m
No.of Employees: 51 - 100 **Product Groups:** 29, 30, 31, 32, 40

Group Seb Ltd

11-49 Station Road Langley, Slough, SL3 8DR
Tel: 01753-713000 **Fax:** 01753-583938
E-mail: groupseb@groupseb.co.uk
Website: http://www.groupseb.co.uk
Bank(s): Lloyds TSB
Directors: M. Hughan (Dir), A. Shepherd (Dir), B. Daley (Fin), G. Prior (Dir)
Ultimate Holding Company: SEB SA (FRANCE)
Immediate Holding Company: TEFAL U.K. LIMITED
Registration no: 01051980 **Date established:** 1972
Turnover: £50m - £75m **No.of Employees:** 51 - 100 **Product Groups:** 40

Date of Accounts	Dec 07	Dec 05	Dec 04
Working Capital	N/A	7m	7m
Current Assets	N/A	7m	7m

H M Plant

964 Weston Road Slough Trading Estate, Slough, SL1 4HR
Tel: 01753-213900 **Fax:** 01753-213901
E-mail: info@hmplant.ltd.uk
Website: http://www.hmplant.ltd.uk
Managers: G. Donaldson (Mgr)
Ultimate Holding Company: HITACHI LTD (JAPAN)
Immediate Holding Company: HM PLANT LIMITED
Registration no: 01082975 **Date established:** 1972
No.of Employees: 1 - 10 **Product Groups:** 45

Date of Accounts	Dec 07	Mar 11	Mar 10
Sales Turnover	139m	83m	84m
Pre Tax Profit/Loss	8m	4m	2m
Working Capital	711	7m	4m
Fixed Assets	4m	4m	4m
Current Assets	47m	36m	38m
Current Liabilities	6m	4m	3m

Hane Instruments Ltd

691 Stirling Road, Slough, SL1 4ST
Tel: 01753-528884 **Fax:** 01753-823301
E-mail: info@haneinstruments.co.uk
Website: http://www.haneinstruments.co.uk
Directors: T. Dovey (Fin), P. Cahill (Sales)
Ultimate Holding Company: HANE (2003) LIMITED
Immediate Holding Company: HANE INSTRUMENTS LIMITED
Registration no: 01145684 **VAT No.:** GB 223 7888 39
Date established: 1973 **Turnover:** £2m - £5m **No.of Employees:** 11 - 20
Product Groups: 48

Date of Accounts	Mar 12	Mar 11	Mar 10
Working Capital	152	178	237
Fixed Assets	94	113	130
Current Assets	1m	983	916

Hanovia Ltd

780 Buckingham Avenue, Slough, SL1 4LA
Tel: 01753-515300 **Fax:** 01753-534277
E-mail: sales@hanovia.com
Website: http://www.hanovia.com
Bank(s): Lloyds TSB Bank plc
Managers: J. Cole
Ultimate Holding Company: HALMA PUBLIC LIMITED COMPANY
Immediate Holding Company: HANOVIA LIMITED
Registration no: 01473077 **VAT No.:** GB 537 8250 28
Date established: 1980 **Turnover:** £10m - £20m
No.of Employees: 51 - 100 **Product Groups:** 37, 38, 42

Date of Accounts	Mar 12	Mar 09	Apr 10
Sales Turnover	10m	9m	8m
Pre Tax Profit/Loss	1m	1m	1m
Working Capital	891	774	1m
Fixed Assets	1m	898	793
Current Assets	3m	3m	3m
Current Liabilities	206	354	475

Hellmann Worldwide Logistics Ltd

Hellmann House Colnbrook By Pass, Colnbrook, Slough, SL3 0EL
Tel: 01753-688500 **Fax:** 01753-684771
E-mail: jmclean@gb.hellmann.net
Website: http://www.hellmann.co.uk
Managers: J. Mclean (District Mgr)
Ultimate Holding Company: HELLMANN WORLDWIDE LOGISTICS GMBH (GERMANY)
Immediate Holding Company: HELLMANN WORLDWIDE LOGISTICS LIMITED
Registration no: 01108485 **Date established:** 1973
Turnover: £500,000 - £1m **No.of Employees:** 21 - 50 **Product Groups:** 76

Date of Accounts	Dec 11	Dec 10	Dec 09
Sales Turnover	54m	54m	62m
Pre Tax Profit/Loss	-4m	-3m	-5m
Working Capital	8m	6m	1m
Fixed Assets	514	407	2m
Current Assets	23m	23m	20m
Current Liabilities	4m	5m	9m

Hitachi Data Systems

Sefton Park Bells Hill, Stoke Poges, Slough, SL2 4HD
Tel: 01753-618000 **Fax:** 01753-618444
E-mail: enquiries@hds.co.uk
Website: http://www.eu.hds.com
Directors: P. Robinson (Mkt Research), T. Trower (Co Sec), M. Coombs (Dir), D. Manual (Pers)
Ultimate Holding Company: HITACHI LTD (JAPAN)
Immediate Holding Company: HITACHI DATA SYSTEMS LIMITED
Registration no: 02332239 **Date established:** 1989
Turnover: £500m - £1,000m **No.of Employees:** 251 - 500
Product Groups: 44

Date of Accounts	Mar 12	Mar 11	Mar 10
Sales Turnover	675m	604m	554m
Pre Tax Profit/Loss	10m	7m	8m
Working Capital	279m	77m	77m
Fixed Assets	3m	2m	5m
Current Assets	431m	265m	205m
Current Liabilities	58m	60m	61m

Honda Finance Europe

470 London Road, Slough, SL3 8QY
Tel: 08708-508856 **Fax:** 01753-590000
E-mail: philip.ross@honda-eu.com
Website: http://www.honda.co.uk
Directors: I. Howells (Co Sec)
Managers: T. Saxon (Fin Mgr), R. Weller (Mktg Serv Mgr), M. Harris (Purch Mgr), G. Jackson (Tech Serv Mgr), P. Ross (Chief Mgr)
Ultimate Holding Company: HONDA MOTOR CO LTD (JAPAN)
Immediate Holding Company: HONDA FINANCE EUROPE PLC
Registration no: 03289418 **Date established:** 1996
Turnover: £20m - £50m **No.of Employees:** 51 - 100 **Product Groups:** 41, 68

Date of Accounts	Mar 12	Mar 11	Mar 10
Sales Turnover	48m	52m	52m
Pre Tax Profit/Loss	23m	25m	20m
Working Capital	-87m	245m	-138m
Fixed Assets	277m	247m	255m
Current Assets	320m	347m	319m
Current Liabilities	275m	1m	223m

Hygiene Group Ltd

901 Yeovil Road, Slough, SL1 4JG
Tel: 01753-820991 **Fax:** 01753-578189
E-mail: sales@hygiene.co.uk
Website: http://www.hygiene.co.uk
Directors: R. Awoniyi (Fin)
Managers: H. Millership (Personnel), R. Cannell (Mktg Serv Mgr)
Immediate Holding Company: HYGIENE GROUP LIMITED
Registration no: 01905230 **Date established:** 1985
Turnover: £10m - £20m **No.of Employees:** 1 - 10 **Product Groups:** 41, 48, 52

Date of Accounts	May 11	May 10	May 09
Sales Turnover	15m	17m	18m
Pre Tax Profit/Loss	356	306	441
Working Capital	1m	1m	1m
Fixed Assets	263	459	561
Current Assets	5m	4m	5m
Current Liabilities	3m	2m	3m

Icore International

220 Bedford Avenue, Slough, SL1 4RY
Tel: 01753-696549 **Fax:** 01753-896601
E-mail: greg.burland@zodiacaerospace.com
Website: http://www.icore.co.uk
Bank(s): National Westminster Bank Plc
Directors: G. Burland (Dir), C. Bigare (Comm), P. Shorrocks (Pers)
Managers: C. Shintala, M. Shepherd (Purch Mgr)
Ultimate Holding Company: ZODIAC SA (FRANCE)
Immediate Holding Company: ICORE INTERNATIONAL LIMITED
Registration no: 00874618 **VAT No.:** GB 823 8401 77
Date established: 1966 **Turnover:** £20m - £50m
No.of Employees: 101 - 250 **Product Groups:** 30, 36, 37, 39

Date of Accounts	Aug 11	Aug 10	Aug 09
Sales Turnover	21m	21m	23m
Pre Tax Profit/Loss	2m	2m	3m
Working Capital	3m	3m	4m
Fixed Assets	7m	7m	7m
Current Assets	7m	6m	7m
Current Liabilities	942	1m	2m

Ikon Office Solutions Ltd

160 Edinburgh Avenue, Slough, SL1 4UE
Tel: 01753-771000 **Fax:** 01753-696045
Website: http://www.ikon.co.uk
Directors: P. Keyhogan (Ch)
Ultimate Holding Company: RICOH COMPANY LIMITED (JAPAN)
Immediate Holding Company: RICOH UK LIMITED
Registration no: 01271033 **VAT No.:** GB 303 8244 84
Date established: 1976 **No.of Employees:** 101 - 250 **Product Groups:** 64, 67

In Time Movements Ltd

Unit D Horton Trading Estate Stanwell Road, Horton, Slough, SL3 9PF
Tel: 01753-685223 **Fax:** 01753-683639
E-mail: info@intimemovements.co.uk
Website: http://www.intimemovements.co.uk
Directors: S. Lewis (MD)
Immediate Holding Company: IN TIME MOVEMENTS LIMITED
Registration no: 03889134 **Date established:** 1999
No.of Employees: 11 - 20 **Product Groups:** 74

Date of Accounts	Mar 12	Mar 11	Mar 10
Working Capital	51	35	-23
Fixed Assets	137	157	211
Current Assets	200	187	212

Industrial Design Consultancy Ltd

13 Portland Business Centre Manor House Lane, Datchet, Slough, SL3 9EG
Tel: 01753-547610 **Fax:** 01753-549224
E-mail: contact@idc.uk.com
Website: http://www.idc.uk.com
Directors: J. Eaton (Fin), S. Knowles (MD)
Managers: E. Armstrong
Immediate Holding Company: INDUSTRIAL DESIGN CONSULTANCY LIMITED
Registration no: 02006035 **VAT No.:** GB 208 5617 64
Date established: 1986 **No.of Employees:** 21 - 50 **Product Groups:** 85

Date of Accounts	Mar 12	Mar 11	Mar 10
Working Capital	330	268	604
Fixed Assets	82	110	94
Current Assets	526	924	814

Intergrated Mechanical Service Supplies Ltd

47 Cobblers Close Farnham Royal, Slough, SL2 3DT
Tel: 01753-647449 **Fax:** 01753-647449
E-mail: info@imss.uk.com
Website: http://www.imss.uk.com
Directors: A. Golding (MD)
Registration no: 05164792 **Date established:** 2004
Turnover: Up to £250,000 **No.of Employees:** 1 - 10 **Product Groups:** 32, 40, 66, 67

Ireland FX

Malindi House 14 Lambert Avenue, Slough, SL3 7EB
Tel: 028-9099 8578 **Fax:** 028-9099 8570
E-mail: info@irelandfx.com
Website: http://www.irelandfx.com
Managers: T. Thanjal (Accounts)
Registration no: 05155041 **Date established:** 2006
Turnover: Up to £250,000 **No.of Employees:** 1 - 10 **Product Groups:** 82

Iris

Riding Court Road Datchet, Slough, SL3 9JT
Tel: 01753-212200 **Fax:** 01753-212299
E-mail: contactus@iris.co.uk
Website: http://www.iris.co.uk
Managers: P. Robinson
Ultimate Holding Company: SOFTWARE (CAYMAN) LP (CAYMAN ISLANDS)
Immediate Holding Company: TRANSACTION TECHNOLOGY TRUSTEES LIMITED
Registration no: 04293973 **Date established:** 2001
No.of Employees: 101 - 250 **Product Groups:** 44

Date of Accounts	Apr 11	Apr 10	Apr 09
Current Assets	N/A	2	1m
Current Liabilities	N/A	2	1m

Jarshire Ltd (Waste Management Division)

2-4 Bristol Way Stoke Gardens, Slough, SL1 3QE
Tel: 01753-825122 **Fax:** 01753-694653
E-mail: sales@jarshire.co.uk
Website: http://www.jarshire.co.uk
Directors: D. Jobson (Dir), P. Jobson (Sales)
Immediate Holding Company: JARSHIRE LIMITED
Registration no: 01451249 **Date established:** 1979 **Turnover:** £1m - £2m
No.of Employees: 1 - 10 **Product Groups:** 42

Date of Accounts	Sep 11	Sep 10	Sep 09
Sales Turnover	2m	1m	1m
Pre Tax Profit/Loss	111	-23	75
Working Capital	11	18	103
Fixed Assets	179	182	190
Current Assets	733	611	519
Current Liabilities	228	95	48

Jetstream Logistics Ltd

Unit 12 Coln Industrial Estate Old Bath Road, Colnbrook, Slough, SL3 0NJ
Tel: 01895-430303 **Fax:** 01895-421010
E-mail: fionah@jsluk.com
Website: http://www.jsl.uk.com
Directors: F. Hancox (MD)
Immediate Holding Company: JETSTREAM LOGISTICS LIMITED
Registration no: 04512514 **Date established:** 2002
No.of Employees: 1 - 10 **Product Groups:** 79

see next page

***Jetstream Logistics Ltd** - Cont'd*

Date of Accounts	Sep 11	Sep 10	Sep 09
Working Capital	60	98	98
Fixed Assets	577	594	620
Current Assets	208	230	236

Keyzone Computer Products Ltd

89 Park Street, Slough, SL1 1PX
Tel: 01753-695090 **Fax:** 020-8903 1486
E-mail: sales@keyzone.com
Website: http://www.keyzone.com
Directors: H. Nathwani (MD)
Immediate Holding Company: KEYZONE COMPUTER PRODUCTS LIMITED
Registration no: 01687201 **VAT No.:** GB 379 6290 02
Date established: 1982 **Turnover:** £500,000 - £1m
No.of Employees: 11 - 20 **Product Groups:** 44

Date of Accounts	Dec 11	Dec 10	Dec 09
Working Capital	201	247	303
Fixed Assets	23	25	24
Current Assets	678	722	813

Kidde Graviner Ltd (Head Office)

Mathisen Way Colnbrook, Slough, SL3 0HB
Tel: 01753-689848 **Fax:** 01753-685126
E-mail: kidde.graviner@kiddegraviner.co.uk
Website: http://www.kiddegraviner.co.uk
Bank(s): Barclays
Directors: M. Tomlin (Fin)
Managers: J. Mackrell (Tech Serv Mgr), P. Maxwell (Personnel), P. Wheeler, S. Hill (Mktg Serv Mgr)
Ultimate Holding Company: UNITED TECHNOLOGIES CORP INC (USA)
Immediate Holding Company: KIDDE GRAVINER LIMITED
Registration no: 04622277 **VAT No.:** GB 439 4758 08
Date established: 2002 **Turnover:** £20m - £50m
No.of Employees: 101 - 250 **Product Groups:** 39, 40

Date of Accounts	Dec 11	Dec 10	Dec 09
Sales Turnover	28m	26m	27m
Pre Tax Profit/Loss	4m	2m	555
Working Capital	13m	7m	2m
Fixed Assets	65m	70m	76m
Current Assets	57m	51m	47m
Current Liabilities	1m	1m	2m

L J S Enamellers Ltd

Rear of B & K Garages Datchet Road, Horton, Slough, SL3 9PS
Tel: 01753-686291 **Fax:** 01753-686291
E-mail: larrysanders60@aol.com
Directors: L. Sanders (Dir)
Immediate Holding Company: L.J.S. ENAMELLERS LIMITED
Registration no: 07911226 **VAT No.:** GB 636 1928 26
Date established: 2012 **Turnover:** £250,000 - £500,000
No.of Employees: 1 - 10 **Product Groups:** 32, 48

Laboratory Facilities Ltd

24 Britwell Road Burnham, Slough, SL1 8AG
Tel: 01628-604149 **Fax:** 01628-667920
E-mail: ataka@laboratoryfacilities.com
Website: http://www.laboratoryfacilities.co.uk
Directors: D. Holmes (MD)
Immediate Holding Company: LABORATORY FACILITIES LIMITED
Registration no: 00383558 **VAT No.:** GB 207 7995 28
Date established: 1943 **Turnover:** £2m - £5m **No.of Employees:** 11 - 20
Product Groups: 48

Date of Accounts	Mar 11	Mar 10	Mar 09
Working Capital	759	716	739
Fixed Assets	48	57	65
Current Assets	972	1m	940

Leaseplan UK Ltd

165 Bath Road, Slough, SL1 4AA
Tel: 01753-802000 **Fax:** 01753-802010
E-mail: david.brennan@leaseplan.co.uk
Website: http://www.leaseplan.co.uk
Bank(s): Lloyds TSB Bank plc
Directors: M. Dyer (Sales), I. Gibson (Tech Serv), D. Stickland (Fin), D. Brennan (Dir), M. Andrews (Mkt Research)
Managers: S. West, S. Moss (Personnel)
Immediate Holding Company: LEASEPLAN UK LIMITED
Registration no: 01397939 **VAT No.:** GB 442 5587 39
Date established: 1978 **Turnover:** £500m - £1,000m
No.of Employees: 501 - 1000 **Product Groups:** 72, 80

Date of Accounts	Dec 11	Dec 10	Dec 09
Sales Turnover	769m	734m	767m
Pre Tax Profit/Loss	35m	24m	65m
Working Capital	-545m	-496m	-432m
Fixed Assets	1397m	1204m	1071m
Current Assets	135m	126m	206m
Current Liabilities	605m	84m	105m

Lego UK Ltd

33 Bath Road, Slough, SL1 3UF
Tel: 01753-495000 **Fax:** 01753-495100
E-mail: sales@lego.com
Website: http://www.lego.com
Directors: M. Popp (Co Sec)
Ultimate Holding Company: KIRKBI AS (DENMARK)
Immediate Holding Company: LEGO COMPANY LIMITED
Registration no: 00368236 **Date established:** 1941
Turnover: £75m - £125m **No.of Employees:** 101 - 250
Product Groups: 49

Date of Accounts	Dec 11	Dec 10	Dec 09
Sales Turnover	148m	121m	87m
Pre Tax Profit/Loss	4m	3m	981
Working Capital	10m	8m	6m
Fixed Assets	2m	1m	490
Current Assets	79m	82m	43m
Current Liabilities	22m	16m	12m

Lift Services UK Ltd

53 Huntercombe Lane North, Slough, SL1 6DX
Tel: 01628-660808 **Fax:** 01628-660477
Directors: V. Ellis (MD)
Immediate Holding Company: LIFT SERVICES (UK) LTD
Registration no: 04129656 **Date established:** 2000
No.of Employees: 1 - 10 **Product Groups:** 35, 39, 45

Date of Accounts	Dec 11	Dec 10	Dec 09
Working Capital	276	276	314
Fixed Assets	3	4	6
Current Assets	358	344	390

Logicalis UK Ltd

110 Buckingham Avenue, Slough, SL1 4PF
Tel: 01753-777200 **Fax:** 01753-777203
E-mail: info@uk.logicalis.com
Website: http://www.logicalis.com
Bank(s): Barclays, Reading
Directors: T. Kelly (MD), S. Ellis (MD), M. Rogers (Fin), M. Tyne (Fin), C. Miller (Sales)
Managers: G. Hogg (Transport), S. Bliss (Personnel), R. Anson
Ultimate Holding Company: DATATEC LTD (BRITISH VIRGIN ISLANDS)
Immediate Holding Company: LOGICALIS UK LIMITED
Registration no: 03732397 **Date established:** 1999 **Turnover:** £2m - £5m
No.of Employees: 101 - 250 **Product Groups:** 44

Date of Accounts	Feb 08	Feb 11	Feb 10
Sales Turnover	77m	187m	78m
Pre Tax Profit/Loss	2m	2m	4m
Working Capital	6m	33m	-676
Fixed Assets	4m	29m	22m
Current Assets	31m	70m	78m
Current Liabilities	13m	2m	37m

Lonza Biologics plc

224-230 Bath Road, Slough, SL1 4DX
Tel: 01753-777000 **Fax:** 01753-777001
E-mail: gerard.kennedy@lonza.com
Website: http://www.lonza.com
Directors: G. Kennedy (Co Sec)
Ultimate Holding Company: LONZA GROUP AG (SWITZERLAND)
Immediate Holding Company: LONZA BIOLOGICS PLC
Registration no: 02742471 **Date established:** 1992
Turnover: £75m - £125m **No.of Employees:** 501 - 1000
Product Groups: 32, 84

Date of Accounts	Dec 11	Dec 10	Dec 09
Sales Turnover	82m	75m	67m
Pre Tax Profit/Loss	7m	6m	6m
Working Capital	10m	12m	17m
Fixed Assets	41m	36m	34m
Current Assets	22m	22m	26m
Current Liabilities	6m	5m	4m

Manitowoc Food Service UK (A Manitowoc Company)

5 E Langley Business Centre Station Road, Langley, Slough, SL3 8DS
Tel: 01753-485900 **Fax:** 01753-485901
E-mail: john.rourke@manitowoc.com
Website: http://www.manitowocssuk.com
Bank(s): National Westminster Bank Plc
Directors: C. Abdy (Mkt Research), C. Cammoile (Fin), J. Rourke (MD)
Managers: D. Smith (Purch Mgr), P. Briggs (Chief Mgr), R. Adam (Sales Prom Mgr), R. Brundish (I.T. Exec)
Immediate Holding Company: Enodis plc
Registration no: 02656967 **VAT No.:** GB 243 1885 61
Turnover: £10m - £20m **No.of Employees:** 21 - 50 **Product Groups:** 38, 40, 67

Manrose Manufacturing Ltd

1 Albion Close, Slough, SL2 5DT
Tel: 01753-691399 **Fax:** 01753-692294
E-mail: sales@manrose.co.uk
Website: http://www.manrose.co.uk
Bank(s): Barclays
Directors: S. Diamond (Co Sec), C. Gibbs (Fab)
Managers: P. Watton (Comptroller), B. Botell, L. Rutter (Chief Mgr)
Ultimate Holding Company: VOLUTION GROUP LIMITED
Immediate Holding Company: MANROSE MANUFACTURING LIMITED
Registration no: 02197755 **VAT No.:** GB 532 1922 70
Date established: 1987 **Turnover:** £20m - £50m
No.of Employees: 101 - 250 **Product Groups:** 40

Date of Accounts	Jul 11	Jul 10	Jul 09
Sales Turnover	25m	21m	16m
Pre Tax Profit/Loss	5m	4m	2m
Working Capital	10m	6m	3m
Fixed Assets	934	971	1m
Current Assets	16m	12m	6m
Current Liabilities	2m	2m	1m

Maplin Electronics Ltd

216-218 Farnham Road, Slough, SL1 4XE
Tel: 01753-551419 **Fax:** 01753-694393
Website: http://www.maplin.co.uk
Ultimate Holding Company: MONTAGU PRIVATE EQUITY LLP
Immediate Holding Company: MAPLIN ELECTRONICS LIMITED
Registration no: 01264385 **Date established:** 1976
Turnover: £125m - £250m **No.of Employees:** 1 - 10 **Product Groups:** 37, 61

Date of Accounts	Dec 07	Dec 08	Dec 09
Sales Turnover	180m	204m	204m
Pre Tax Profit/Loss	24m	32m	35m
Working Capital	28m	49m	75m
Fixed Assets	26m	28m	28m
Current Assets	78m	108m	142m
Current Liabilities	44m	51m	59m

Mars UK Chocolate

Dundee Road, Slough, SL1 4JX
Tel: 01753-550055 **Fax:** 01753-550111
Website: http://www.mars.com
Bank(s): National Westminster
Directors: B. Parkin (Pers), D. Teasdale (Dir)
Managers: B. Parkin
Ultimate Holding Company: MARS INC (USA)
Immediate Holding Company: MARS CHOCOLATE UK LIMITED
Registration no: 06649982 **Date established:** 2008
No.of Employees: 251 - 500 **Product Groups:** 20

Date of Accounts	Dec 11	Dec 08	Jan 10
Sales Turnover	789m	185m	730m
Pre Tax Profit/Loss	100m	24m	138m
Working Capital	212m	-46m	72m
Fixed Assets	94m	111m	82m
Current Assets	465m	213m	305m
Current Liabilities	137m	141m	147m

Mealbox Ltd

235 Farnham Road, Slough, SL2 1DE
Tel: 01753-554391
E-mail: enq@mealbox.com
Website: http://www.mealbox.com
Directors: T. Mczinnes (MD), K. Maughan (I.T. Dir)
Managers: L. Joyce (Personnel)
Immediate Holding Company: MEALBOX LIMITED
Registration no: 04093098 **Date established:** 2000
No.of Employees: 1 - 10 **Product Groups:** 79, 81

Date of Accounts	Oct 11	Oct 10	Oct 09
Working Capital	-255	-84	N/A
Fixed Assets	165	94	N/A
Current Assets	39	45	N/A

Meiko UK Ltd

393 Edinburgh Avenue, Slough, SL1 4UF
Tel: 01753-215120 **Fax:** 01753-215159
E-mail: meikouk@meiko-uk.co.uk
Website: http://www.meiko-uk.co.uk
Directors: W. Downing (MD), L. Gallop (Pers), B. Downey (MD), P. Nimo (Sales)
Managers: L. Gallop (Personnel), P. Barry (Fin Mgr), P. Barrry (Fin Mgr)
Ultimate Holding Company: OSKAR UND ROSEL MEIER-STIFFUNG FOUNDATION (GERMANY)
Immediate Holding Company: MEIKO UK LIMITED
Registration no: 02846559 **Date established:** 1993
Turnover: £10m - £20m **No.of Employees:** 51 - 100 **Product Groups:** 40

Date of Accounts	Dec 11	Dec 10	Dec 09
Sales Turnover	15m	12m	11m
Pre Tax Profit/Loss	-43	92	414
Working Capital	742	836	695
Fixed Assets	617	504	625
Current Assets	7m	6m	5m
Current Liabilities	1m	1m	916

Mig Antig Workshops

21 Business Village Wexham Road, Slough, SL2 5HF
Tel: 01753-529961 **Fax:** 01753-529961
Directors: U. Tenuta (Prop)
Date established: 2001 **No.of Employees:** 1 - 10 **Product Groups:** 35

Moorwood Vulcan Enodis UK Food Service

5 E Langley Business Centre Station Road, Langley, Slough, SL3 8DS
Tel: 01753-485900 **Fax:** 01753-485901
E-mail: info@enodis.com
Website: http://www.moorwoodvulcan.co.uk
Ultimate Holding Company: Enodis plc
Immediate Holding Company: Enodis plc
Registration no: 02656967 **Turnover:** £10m - £20m
No.of Employees: 501 - 1000 **Product Groups:** 40, 67

N Tec Solutions Ltd

18 Business Village Wexham Road, Slough, SL2 5HF
Tel: 01753-528321 **Fax:** 01753-691250
E-mail: mail@ntecsolutions.com
Website: http://www.ntecsolutions.com
Directors: L. Williams (Fin), N. Williams (MD)
Immediate Holding Company: N TEC SOLUTIONS LIMITED
Registration no: 04115718 **VAT No.:** GB 538 0336 52
Date established: 2000 **Turnover:** £1m - £2m **No.of Employees:** 1 - 10
Product Groups: 40, 46

Date of Accounts	Mar 11	Mar 10	Mar 09
Working Capital	67	45	121
Fixed Assets	N/A	6	11
Current Assets	183	155	303

Nationwide Coatings UK Ltd

Canal Wharf Station Road, Langley, Slough, SL3 6EG
Tel: 01753-671612 **Fax:** 01753-671613
E-mail: sales@nationwidecoatings.co.uk
Website: http://www.nationwidecoatings.co.uk
Directors: R. Florey (MD)
Immediate Holding Company: NATIONWIDE COATINGS (UK) LTD
Registration no: 03538382 **Date established:** 1998
Turnover: Up to £250,000 **No.of Employees:** 1 - 10 **Product Groups:** 48

Date of Accounts	Dec 11	Dec 10	Dec 09
Working Capital	28	15	11
Fixed Assets	10	11	14
Current Assets	83	79	84

O K I (Europe) Ltd

550 Dundee Road, Slough, SL1 4LE
Tel: 01753-819819 **Fax:** 01753-819899
E-mail: ukenquiries@okieurope.co.uk
Website: http://www.oki.co.uk
Directors: A. Montgomery (Dir)
Managers: C. Cheug (I.T. Exec), A. Bell (Mktg Serv Mgr)
Ultimate Holding Company: Oki Electric Industry Co., Ltd
Immediate Holding Company: Oki Europe Ltd
Registration no: 02203086 **VAT No.:** GB 481 0119 75
Date established: 1984 **Turnover:** £250m - £500m
No.of Employees: 1 - 10 **Product Groups:** 44

Date of Accounts	Mar 08
Sales Turnover	439920
Pre Tax Profit/Loss	14120
Working Capital	48110
Fixed Assets	10340
Current Assets	251520
Current Liabilities	203410
Total Share Capital	33000
ROCE% (Return on Capital Employed)	24.2

The Oak Centre

2 Hawtrey Close, Slough, SL1 1TB
Tel: 01753-674322 **Fax:** 01753-674323
Directors: A. Chanin (Fin)
Immediate Holding Company: VOIP AND DATA SOLUTIONS LTD
Registration no: 06508427 **Date established:** 2008
No.of Employees: 1 - 10 **Product Groups:** 35, 39, 45

Oki Systems UK Ltd

550 Dundee Road, Slough, SL1 4LE
Tel: 01753-819819 **Fax:** 01753-819899
E-mail: ukenquiries@okieurope.co.uk
Website: http://www.okieurope.co.uk
Bank(s): HSBC Bank plc
Directors: G. Lowes (Mkt Research), P. Skinner (Fin), P. Scrase (MD)
Managers: K. White (Personnel), I. Younger (Tech Serv Mgr)
Ultimate Holding Company: OKI ELECTRIC INDUSTRY CO., LTD.
Immediate Holding Company: OKI SYSTEMS (UK) LIMITED
Registration no: 01341777 **Date established:** 1977
Turnover: £20m - £50m **No.of Employees:** 21 - 50 **Product Groups:** 44

Date of Accounts	Mar 11	Mar 10	Mar 09
Sales Turnover	40m	55m	50m
Pre Tax Profit/Loss	808	3m	2m

Working Capital	8m	8m	5m
Fixed Assets	989	1m	1m
Current Assets	18m	22m	14m
Current Liabilities	2m	1m	2m

1 & 1 Internet Ltd

10-14 Bath Road, Slough, SL1 3SA
Tel: 08443-351211 **Fax:** 0845-076 2205
E-mail: info@1and1.co.uk
Website: http://www.1and1.co.uk
Managers: A. Hamell
Ultimate Holding Company: UNITED INTERNET AG (GERMANY)
Immediate Holding Company: 1&1 INTERNET LIMITED
Registration no: 03953678 **Date established:** 2000
Turnover: £20m - £50m **No.of Employees:** 1 - 10 **Product Groups:** 44

Date of Accounts	Dec 11	Dec 10	Dec 09
Sales Turnover	37m	34m	30m
Pre Tax Profit/Loss	5m	9m	9m
Working Capital	135	509	1m
Fixed Assets	7	27	60
Current Assets	13m	16m	14m
Current Liabilities	13m	12m	11m

Orange Business Services

217 Bath Road, Slough, SL1 4AA
Tel: 020-8321 4000 **Fax:** 020-8321 4040
E-mail: richard.ellison@orange.com
Website: http://www.orange-business.com
Bank(s): HSBC Bank plc
Directors: R. Ellison (Prop)
Ultimate Holding Company: FRANCE TELECOM SA (FRANCE)
Immediate Holding Company: ORANGE BUSINESS HOLDINGS UK LIMITED
Registration no: 03051335 **VAT No.:** GB 578 1760 06
Date established: 1995 **Turnover:** £125m - £250m
No.of Employees: 501 - 1000 **Product Groups:** 37, 44, 52, 80

Date of Accounts	Dec 11	Dec 10	Dec 09
Sales Turnover	127m	137m	132m
Pre Tax Profit/Loss	-4m	61	-27m
Working Capital	24m	23m	33m
Fixed Assets	29m	33m	35m
Current Assets	57m	51m	74m
Current Liabilities	17m	9m	8m

Osram Ltd

PO Box 17, Slough, SL3 6EZ
Tel: 01744-812221 **Fax:** 01753-484222
E-mail: rune.narki@osram.co.uk
Website: http://www.osram.co.uk
Bank(s): HSBC Bank plc
Directors: M. Eber (Fin), R. Narki (MD)
Managers: S. Stark (Sales Prom Mgr), T. Rice (Tech Serv Mgr), L. Dryden (Mktg Serv Mgr), S. May (Personnel)
Ultimate Holding Company: SIEMENS AG (GERMANY)
Immediate Holding Company: OSRAM LIMITED
Registration no: 01961715 **VAT No.:** GB 495 1500 44
Date established: 1985 **Turnover:** Up to £250,000
No.of Employees: 101 - 250 **Product Groups:** 37, 67

Date of Accounts	Sep 11	Sep 10	Sep 09
Sales Turnover	58	56m	65m
Pre Tax Profit/Loss	5	4m	2m
Working Capital	9	9m	6m
Fixed Assets	1	1m	2m
Current Assets	16	14m	12m
Current Liabilities	6	4m	5m

P B E Marking Systems Ltd

717 Banbury Avenue, Slough, SL1 4LR
Tel: 01753-536536 **Fax:** 01753-692204
E-mail: sales@pbemarking.com
Website: http://www.pbemarking.com
Bank(s): National Westminster Bank Plc
Directors: K. Long (MD), P. Webb (Co Sec)
Ultimate Holding Company: DUBUIT INTERNATIONAL SARL (FRANCE)
Immediate Holding Company: PBE MARKING SYSTEMS LIMITED
Registration no: 03994846 **Date established:** 2000
Turnover: £500,000 - £1m **No.of Employees:** 11 - 20
Product Groups: 42, 43, 44

Date of Accounts	Dec 11	Dec 10	Dec 09
Sales Turnover	727	892	936
Pre Tax Profit/Loss	-4	-299	127
Working Capital	-391	-226	-81
Fixed Assets	18	19	38
Current Assets	220	300	374
Current Liabilities	29	64	77

P H Jackson & Son Building Ltd

Freestone Yard Park Street, Colnbrook, Slough, SL3 0HT
Tel: 01753-682480 **Fax:** 01753-681929
E-mail: info@phjlifts.co.uk
Directors: K. Jackson (MD), G. Fletcher (Fin)
Immediate Holding Company: P.H. JACKSON & SON (BUILDING) LIMITED
Registration no: 01194592 **Date established:** 1974
No.of Employees: 1 - 10 **Product Groups:** 35, 39, 45

Date of Accounts	Nov 11	Nov 10	Nov 09
Working Capital	51	133	189
Fixed Assets	31	19	27
Current Assets	202	338	320

P M G Worldwide Ltd

Argonaut House Galleymead Road, Colnbrook, Slough, SL3 0EN
Tel: 01753-687898 **Fax:** 01753-687838
E-mail: office@pmgw.co.uk
Website: http://www.pmgw.co.uk
Directors: A. O'Neill (MD)
Managers: C. O'Neill (Purch Mgr)
Ultimate Holding Company: SKYCLIFF HOLDINGS LIMITED
Immediate Holding Company: PMG WORLDWIDE LIMITED
Registration no: 02832402 **Date established:** 1993 **Turnover:** £2m - £5m
No.of Employees: 1 - 10 **Product Groups:** 74, 75, 76

Date of Accounts	Dec 11	Dec 10	Dec 09
Working Capital	114	77	38
Fixed Assets	25	34	11
Current Assets	581	617	492

Pentax UK Ltd

Pentax House Heron Drive, Slough, SL3 8PN
Tel: 01753-792792 **Fax:** 01753-792794
E-mail: info@accounts.pentax.co.uk
Website: http://www.pentax.co.uk
Bank(s): National Westminster
Directors: D. Moore (MD)
Managers: D. Wetherall (Tech Serv Mgr), H. Saeed, S. Castleton (Personnel)
Ultimate Holding Company: HOYA CORPORATION (JAPAN)
Immediate Holding Company: PENTAX U.K. LIMITED
Registration no: 01436524 **VAT No.:** GB 225 3252 92
Date established: 1979 **Turnover:** £5m - £10m
No.of Employees: 51 - 100 **Product Groups:** 29, 38, 40

Date of Accounts	Mar 12	Mar 11	Mar 10
Sales Turnover	9m	10m	23m
Pre Tax Profit/Loss	857	1m	2m
Working Capital	8m	8m	8m
Fixed Assets	413	394	506
Current Assets	13m	11m	14m
Current Liabilities	3m	2m	3m

Pioneer GB Ltd

Pioneer House Hollybush Hill, Stoke Poges, Slough, SL2 4QP
Tel: 01753-789789 **Fax:** 01753-789539
E-mail: executive@pgb.pioneer.co.uk
Website: http://www.pioneer.co.uk
Bank(s): National Westminster
Directors: P. Carpenter (MD), A. Wilkinson (Co Sec)
Managers: D. Hay, M. O'Marney, D. Ryan (Personnel), H. Johnson-cash (Mktg Serv Mgr)
Ultimate Holding Company: PIONEER CORP (JAPAN)
Immediate Holding Company: PIONEER GB LIMITED
Registration no: 00512829 **VAT No.:** GB 232 9458 53
Date established: 1952 **Turnover:** £20m - £50m
No.of Employees: 51 - 100 **Product Groups:** 37

Date of Accounts	Mar 11	Mar 10	Mar 09
Sales Turnover	24m	35m	60m
Pre Tax Profit/Loss	-1m	4m	1m
Working Capital	33m	13m	15m
Fixed Assets	6m	28m	23m
Current Assets	45m	42m	30m
Current Liabilities	6m	9m	11m

Pipe & Climate Centre

838-840 Yeovil Road, Slough, SL1 4JG
Tel: 01753-843550 **Fax:** 0118-941 4080
E-mail: eamonn.phelan@wolseley.co.uk
Website: http://www.pipescenter.co.uk
Managers: E. Phelan (District Mgr), E. Phelan (Mgr), R. Towser (District Mgr), G. Leahy (Sales Admin)
Immediate Holding Company: PROFIT FOCUS (UK) LIMITED
Registration no: 03244411 **Date established:** 1996
Turnover: £20m - £50m **No.of Employees:** 21 - 50 **Product Groups:** 66

Product Marking Solutions

86 Langley Road, Slough, SL3 7TB
Tel: 01753-675655 **Fax:** 01753-670089
E-mail: sales@productmarking.co.uk
Website: http://www.productmarking.co.uk
Directors: H. Sandhu (Dir)
Immediate Holding Company: PRODUCT MARKING SOLUTIONS LTD
Registration no: 06273808 **Date established:** 2007
No.of Employees: 1 - 10 **Product Groups:** 28, 32, 37, 42, 44

Date of Accounts	Nov 11	Nov 10	Nov 09
Working Capital	11	14	-20
Fixed Assets	N/A	N/A	20
Current Assets	21	111	52
Current Liabilities	11	N/A	N/A

Reckitt Benckiser plc

103-105 Bath Road, Slough, SL1 3UH
Tel: 01753-217800 **Fax:** 01753-217899
E-mail: sales@rb.com
Website: http://www.reckittbenckiser.com
Bank(s): National Westminster
Directors: M. Dawar (Dir)
Managers: L. Doherty (Comptroller)
Ultimate Holding Company: RECKITT BENCKISER GROUP PLC
Immediate Holding Company: RECKITT BENCKISER PLC
Registration no: 00527217 **Date established:** 1953
No.of Employees: 1001 - 1500 **Product Groups:** 63

Date of Accounts	Dec 11	Dec 10	Dec 09
Pre Tax Profit/Loss	-41m	30m	51m
Working Capital	471m	733m	2853m
Fixed Assets	10149m	9669m	4160m
Current Assets	2512m	3383m	7287m

Reed Accountancy

164 High Street, Slough, SL1 1JP
Tel: 01753-576677 **Fax:** 01753-694267
E-mail: rapslough@reed.co.uk
Website: http://www.reedglobal.com
Managers: J. Brown (Mgr)
Immediate Holding Company: REED PERSONNEL SERVICES LTD
Registration no: 00973629 **Date established:** 1961
Turnover: £125m - £250m **No.of Employees:** 1 - 10 **Product Groups:** 80

Richardsons R F P D Ltd

226 Berwick Avenue, Slough, SL1 4QT
Tel: 01753-733010 **Fax:** 01753-733012
E-mail: mevans@richardsonrftd.com
Website: http://www.richardsonrfpd.com
Bank(s): National Westminster
Directors: M. Evans (MD)
Immediate Holding Company: RICHARDSON RFPD UK LIMITED
Registration no: 07457506 **VAT No.:** GB 364 4105 70
Date established: 2010 **Turnover:** £20m - £50m
No.of Employees: 11 - 20 **Product Groups:** 37

Date of Accounts	Dec 11
Sales Turnover	5m
Pre Tax Profit/Loss	-4
Working Capital	-468
Fixed Assets	448
Current Assets	1m
Current Liabilities	175

Ross Consular Services Ltd

Beech Court 29 Summers Road, Burnham, Slough, SL1 7EP
Tel: 01628-666001 **Fax:** 01628-666511
E-mail: visa@rossconsular.com
Website: http://www.rossconsular.com
Directors: C. Newsome (MD)
Immediate Holding Company: ROSS CONSULAR SERVICES LIMITED
Registration no: 01209002 **VAT No.:** GB 209 3812 70
Date established: 1975 **Turnover:** £1m - £2m **No.of Employees:** 1 - 10
Product Groups: 80

Date of Accounts	Apr 11	Apr 10	Apr 09
Working Capital	141	78	87
Fixed Assets	329	331	343
Current Assets	329	252	265

S D V UK Ltd

Unit 5 Lakeside Industrial Estate Colnbrook By Pass, Colnbrook, Slough, SL3 0EE
Tel: 01753-683161 **Fax:** 01753-681624
Website: http://www.sdv.com
Directors: E. Kimber (MD), D. Oliver (Fin), A. Wood (Dir), C. Payne (Dir)
Managers: R. Kendall (Chief Mgr), M. Makwana (I.T. Exec)
Ultimate Holding Company: BOLLORE SA (FRANCE)
Immediate Holding Company: SDV (UK) LIMITED
Registration no: 02131120 **VAT No.:** GB 432 3813 73
Date established: 1987 **No.of Employees:** 51 - 100 **Product Groups:** 75

Date of Accounts	Dec 10	Dec 09	Dec 08
Sales Turnover	N/A	N/A	159
Pre Tax Profit/Loss	52	-594	181
Working Capital	884	926	-4m
Fixed Assets	N/A	N/A	39m
Current Assets	1m	1m	489
Current Liabilities	24	94	807

S E S Entertainment Services Ltd

Riding Court Road Datchet, Slough, SL3 9JU
Tel: 01753-585050 **Fax:** 01753-585059
E-mail: sales@site-electrics.co.uk
Website: http://www.site-electrics.co.uk
Directors: M. Cooper (MD)
Immediate Holding Company: S E S (ENTERTAINMENT SERVICES) LIMITED
Registration no: 03026495 **Date established:** 1995
No.of Employees: 11 - 20 **Product Groups:** 36, 40

Date of Accounts	Mar 11	Mar 10	Mar 09
Sales Turnover	N/A	1m	N/A
Pre Tax Profit/Loss	N/A	223	N/A
Working Capital	182	139	115
Fixed Assets	53	37	30
Current Assets	807	449	348
Current Liabilities	N/A	69	N/A

S P Surface Finishes Ltd

502 Ipswich Road, Slough, SL1 4EP
Tel: 01753-578728 **Fax:** 01753-578730
E-mail: joel@spsurfacefinishers.co.uk
Website: http://www.spsurfacefinishers.co.uk
Bank(s): National Westminster Bank Plc
Directors: J. Bacchus (Dir)
Registration no: 01483805 **VAT No.:** GB 342 6683 46
Turnover: £2m - £5m **No.of Employees:** 11 - 20 **Product Groups:** 48

S S E D Ltd

242 Trelawney Avenue Langley, Slough, SL3 7UD
Tel: 0845-0039566 **Fax:** 01753-542727
E-mail: sales@hunters-wholesalers.co.uk
Website: http://www.gx-security.com
Directors: H. Narula (MD), S. Narula (Dir)
Registration no: 04864055 **Turnover:** £250,000 - £500,000
No.of Employees: 1 - 10 **Product Groups:** 37

Sapphire Tooling Ltd

5-7 Colndale Road Colnbrook, Slough, SL3 0HQ
Tel: 01753-770004 **Fax:** 01753-770005
E-mail: info@sapphire-tooling.ltd.uk
Website: http://www.sapphire-tooling.ltd.uk
Directors: J. Gauld (Dir)
Immediate Holding Company: SAPPHIRE TOOLING LIMITED
Registration no: 02716301 **Date established:** 1992
No.of Employees: 1 - 10 **Product Groups:** 46

Date of Accounts	Feb 12	Feb 11	Feb 10
Working Capital	627	552	465
Current Assets	670	599	511

Sara Lee Household & Body Care UK Ltd

225 Bath Road, Slough, SL1 4AU
Tel: 01753-523971 **Fax:** 01753-570340
E-mail: nicolaas.vanholstein@saralee.com
Website: http://www.saralee.com
Bank(s): Lloyds TSB Bank plc
Directors: J. Stam (Dir), A. Van Bilsen (MD), J. Baker (Dir), N. Van Holstein (Dir)
Ultimate Holding Company: FP000361
Immediate Holding Company: SARA LEE UK FINANCE LIMITED
Registration no: 00300959 **VAT No.:** GB 207 6773 51
Date established: 1935 **Turnover:** £125m - £250m
No.of Employees: 251 - 500 **Product Groups:** 32

Date of Accounts	Jun 08	Jun 07
Pre Tax Profit/Loss	29080	31730
Working Capital	383490	554550
Fixed Assets	N/A	2860
Current Assets	500620	564150
Current Liabilities	117130	9600
Total Share Capital	3530	3530
ROCE% (Return on Capital Employed)	7.6	5.7

Sciaky Electric Welding Machines Ltd

212 Bedford Avenue, Slough, SL1 4RH
Tel: 01753-525551 **Fax:** 01753-821416
E-mail: info@sciaky.co.uk
Website: http://www.sciaky.co.uk
Bank(s): HSBC
Directors: L. Kunzig Iv (Dir), Z. Kunzig (Fin)
Immediate Holding Company: SCIAKY ELECTRIC WELDING MACHINES LIMITED
Registration no: 00285021 **VAT No.:** 208 0332 08 **Date established:** 1934
No.of Employees: 11 - 20 **Product Groups:** 35, 46, 67

Date of Accounts	Mar 12	Mar 11	Mar 10
Working Capital	-180	-172	-100
Fixed Assets	58	73	80
Current Assets	284	267	483

Self Powered Safety Products Ltd
907 Yeovil Road, Slough, SL1 4JG
Tel: 01753-554241 **Fax:** 01753-557110
Directors: D. Boyd (MD)
Immediate Holding Company: SELF POWERED SAFETY PRODUCTS LIMITED
Registration no: 05605813 **Date established:** 2005
No.of Employees: 1 - 10 **Product Groups:** 37, 67

Date of Accounts	Dec 11	Dec 10	Dec 09
Working Capital	37	47	39
Fixed Assets	15	18	18
Current Assets	103	110	151
Current Liabilities	N/A	32	26

Servier Laboratories Ltd
Wexham Springs Framewood Road, Wexham, Slough, SL3 6PJ
Tel: 01753-662744 **Fax:** 01753-663456
Website: http://www.servierlaboratories.com
Directors: K. Shankland (Dir)
Ultimate Holding Company: SERVIER SA (FRANCE)
Immediate Holding Company: SERVIER LABORATORIES LIMITED
Registration no: 00783023 **Date established:** 1963
Turnover: £20m - £50m **No.of Employees:** 101 - 250 **Product Groups:** 31

Date of Accounts	Sep 11	Sep 10	Sep 09
Sales Turnover	23m	23m	25m
Pre Tax Profit/Loss	155	2m	-4m
Working Capital	-579	649	3m
Fixed Assets	2m	2m	2m
Current Assets	14m	16m	18m
Current Liabilities	3m	3m	5m

Servis Heat Treatment Co. Ltd
258b Ipswich Road Trading Estate, Slough, SL1 4EP
Tel: 01753-521823 **Fax:** 01753-531094
E-mail: sales@servisheattreatment.co.uk
Website: http://www.servisheattreatment.co.uk
Directors: R. Randev (Fin), S. Randev (MD)
Immediate Holding Company: SERVIS HEAT TREATMENT CO.LIMITED
Registration no: 00616179 **Date established:** 1958
Turnover: £250,000 - £500,000 **No.of Employees:** 1 - 10
Product Groups: 34, 35, 37, 46, 48, 84

Date of Accounts	Dec 11	Dec 10	Dec 09
Working Capital	-84	-56	-2
Fixed Assets	142	123	114
Current Assets	118	140	93
Current Liabilities	76	N/A	N/A

Shoreheat Ltd
99 Whitby Road, Slough, SL1 3DR
Tel: 01753-536552 **Fax:** 01753-530116
Managers: P. Knight (Mgr)
Ultimate Holding Company: PROGRESS GROUP LIMITED
Immediate Holding Company: SHOREHEAT LIMITED
Registration no: 01566154 **VAT No.:** GB 484 6088 12
Date established: 1981 **Turnover:** £5m - £10m **No.of Employees:** 1 - 10
Product Groups: 36, 38, 40

Date of Accounts	Dec 11	Dec 10	Dec 09
Sales Turnover	14m	17m	13m
Pre Tax Profit/Loss	28	540	327
Working Capital	2m	2m	2m
Fixed Assets	560	461	505
Current Assets	6m	6m	6m
Current Liabilities	247	480	388

Simplex Westpile Limited
Unit 5 Lidstone Court Uxbridge Road, George Green, Slough, SL3 6AG
Tel: 01753-215350 **Fax:** 01753-534653
E-mail: estimating@westpile.co.uk
Website: http://www.simplexwestpile.co.uk
Bank(s): The Royal Bank of Scotland
Directors: J. Vyse (Dir), M. Webster (Co Sec), P. Webster (MD)
Ultimate Holding Company: Tilbury Douglas PLC
Immediate Holding Company: Bachy Soletanche Holdings (Europe) Ltd
Registration no: 04995370 **Date established:** 1924
Turnover: £10m - £20m **No.of Employees:** 21 - 50 **Product Groups:** 33, 34, 51, 52, 66

Slough International Freight & Packing Ltd
820 Yeovil Road, Slough, SL1 4JA
Tel: 01753-691011 **Fax:** 01753-825669
E-mail: sloughinter@btconnect.com
Website: http://www.btinternet.com
Directors: M. Matthews (Co Sec)
Immediate Holding Company: SLOUGH INTERNATIONAL FREIGHT AND PACKING LIMITED
Registration no: 01627411 **Date established:** 1982
Turnover: £500,000 - £1m **No.of Employees:** 11 - 20 **Product Groups:** 76

Date of Accounts	Jul 11	Jul 10	Jul 09
Working Capital	167	141	190
Fixed Assets	321	236	289
Current Assets	442	374	369

Slough Plastic Coatings
2-4 David Road Colnbrook, Slough, SL3 0DG
Tel: 01753-683907 **Fax:** 01753-682571
E-mail: sloughplastic@btconnect.com
Website: http://www.sloughpowdercoating.co.uk
Directors: M. Badyal (Ptnr)
VAT No.: GB 530 1489 70 **Date established:** 1981
Turnover: Up to £250,000 **No.of Employees:** 11 - 20 **Product Groups:** 48

Slough & South Berks Express
256 Ipswich Road, Slough, SL1 4EP
Tel: 01753-825111 **Fax:** 01753-692254
E-mail: sales@sloughexpress.co.uk
Website: http://www.maidenhead-advertiser.co.uk
Directors: R. Codd (MD)
Managers: J. Daffern (Personnel), S. Sullivan (Publicity), S. Keogh (Publicity)
Immediate Holding Company: Berkshire Regional Newspapers
Registration no: 06483209 **Date established:** 2008
Turnover: Up to £250,000 **No.of Employees:** 1 - 10 **Product Groups:** 28

source1securityservices Ltd
21 Duvall Court Merton Road, slough, SL1 1QA
Tel: 0845-474 8754 **Fax:** 01753-523803
E-mail: s1ss@live.co.uk
Website: http://www.source1securityservices.co.uk
Directors: A. Ali (Co Sec), S. Ghalib (Dir)
Registration no: 06442690 **Date established:** 2007
No.of Employees: 1 - 10 **Product Groups:** 81

Date of Accounts	Dec 08
Working Capital	-1
Current Liabilities	1

Southern Express
135b Edinburgh Avenue, Slough, SL1 4SW
Tel: 01753-820022 **Fax:** 01753-691276
E-mail: traffic@southernexpress.co.uk
Website: http://www.southernexpress.co.uk
Directors: J. Levin (Dir)
Immediate Holding Company: SOUTHERN EXPRESS DISTRIBUTION LTD
Registration no: 07671803 **Date established:** 2011 **Turnover:** £2m - £5m
No.of Employees: 11 - 20 **Product Groups:** 77

Sovrin Plastics Ltd
Stirling Road, Slough, SL1 4ST
Tel: 01753-825155 **Fax:** 01753-654923
E-mail: solutions@sovrin.com
Website: http://www.sovrin.com
Bank(s): Lloyds/TSB
Directors: A. Rankin (Chief Op Offcr), P. Joiner (MD)
Managers: J. Joiner (Tech Serv Mgr), P. Wigmore (Develop Mgr), A. Hughes (Personnel)
Immediate Holding Company: SOVRIN PLASTICS LIMITED
Registration no: 00958135 **VAT No.:** GB 208 1206 08
Date established: 1969 **Turnover:** £5m - £10m
No.of Employees: 101 - 250 **Product Groups:** 30, 66

Date of Accounts	Dec 11	Dec 10	Dec 09
Sales Turnover	9m	9m	11m
Pre Tax Profit/Loss	-134	236	1m
Working Capital	7m	7m	7m
Fixed Assets	1m	1m	1m
Current Assets	8m	8m	9m
Current Liabilities	520	793	1m

Space Station Self Storage
149 St Paul's Avenue, Slough, SL2 5EN
Tel: 01753-439022 **Fax:** 01753-707909
E-mail: info@space-station.co.uk
Website: http://www.space-station.co.uk
Managers: L. Tweed (Comptroller), K. Prince (Chief Mgr), L. Tweed (Sales Prom Mgr)
Immediate Holding Company: . A SPACE STATION PLC
Registration no: 01693618 **Date established:** 1983
Turnover: £500,000 - £1m **No.of Employees:** 11 - 20
Product Groups: 26, 77

Date of Accounts	Dec 11	Dec 10	Dec 09
Sales Turnover	4m	3m	3m
Pre Tax Profit/Loss	585	1m	882
Working Capital	-2m	-2m	-2m
Fixed Assets	12m	12m	11m
Current Assets	685	1m	615
Current Liabilities	2m	2m	2m

Stop Choc Ltd
Banbury Avenue, Slough, SL1 4LR
Tel: 01753-533223 **Fax:** 01753-693724
E-mail: sales@stop-choc.co.uk
Website: http://www.stop-choc.co.uk
Directors: M. Raszpla (Co Sec)
Ultimate Holding Company: TOTAL SAFETY INC (USA)
Immediate Holding Company: STOP-CHOC LIMITED
Registration no: 01286216 **Date established:** 1976
Turnover: £10m - £20m **No.of Employees:** 101 - 250
Product Groups: 23, 24, 26, 29, 30, 32, 35, 37, 38, 39, 40, 42, 44, 46, 48, 54, 66

Date of Accounts	Dec 11	Dec 10	Dec 09
Sales Turnover	15m	13m	15m
Pre Tax Profit/Loss	4m	3m	4m
Working Capital	33m	30m	28m
Fixed Assets	277	214	225
Current Assets	36m	32m	30m
Current Liabilities	1m	745	942

Taylor Made Machinery Ltd
Canal Estate Station Road, Langley, Slough, SL3 6EG
Tel: 07974-917079 **Fax:** 01753-591441
E-mail: sales@tmm-uk.com
Website: http://www.tmm-uk.com
Directors: A. Taylor (MD), A. Taylor (Prop)
Immediate Holding Company: TAYLOR MADE MACHINERY LIMITED
Registration no: 03863131 **Date established:** 1999
Turnover: £500,000 - £1m **No.of Employees:** 1 - 10 **Product Groups:** 67

Date of Accounts	Mar 10	Mar 09	Mar 08
Working Capital	-6	-8	-11
Fixed Assets	7	9	12
Current Assets	92	79	102

Technical Mouldings Ltd
500 Ipswich Road Trading Estate, Slough, SL1 4EP
Tel: 01753-521675 **Fax:** 01753-535005
Website: http://www.technical-mouldings.co.uk
Directors: A. Palmer (MD), G. Whitton (MD)
No.of Employees: 11 - 20 **Product Groups:** 30, 31, 38, 42, 43, 44, 48, 84

Technical Web Services
PO Box 3101 Datchet, Slough, SL3 9ZS
Tel: 08453-497665
E-mail: sales@technicalwebservices.com
Website: http://www.TechnicalWebServices.com
Directors: P. Findlay (Prop)
Turnover: Up to £250,000 **No.of Employees:** 1 - 10 **Product Groups:** 44

Thames Valley Chamber Of Commerce & Industry (Area Office)
467 Malton Avenue, Slough, SL1 4QU
Tel: 01753-870500 **Fax:** 01753-870501
E-mail: customerservices@tvchamber.co.uk
Website: http://www.tvchamber.co.uk
Directors: P. Briggs (Grp Chief Exec)
Immediate Holding Company: THAMES VALLEY CHAMBER OF COMMERCE AND INDUSTRY
Registration no: 00473106 **Date established:** 1949 **Turnover:** £2m - £5m
No.of Employees: 21 - 50 **Product Groups:** 87

Date of Accounts	Dec 11	Dec 10	Dec 09
Working Capital	1m	1m	1m
Fixed Assets	31	14	22
Current Assets	1m	1m	1m

W N Thomas & Sons Ltd
Stoke Gardens, Slough, SL1 3QA
Tel: 01753-524575 **Fax:** 01753-694765
E-mail: info@thomasmetalrecycling.co.uk
Website: http://www.thomasmetalrecycling.co.uk
Bank(s): National Westminster
Directors: J. Thomas (MD)
Immediate Holding Company: W.N. THOMAS & SONS LIMITED
Registration no: 00429205 **VAT No.:** GB 207 8040 84
Date established: 1947 **Turnover:** £2m - £5m **No.of Employees:** 11 - 20
Product Groups: 66

Date of Accounts	Mar 12	Mar 11	Mar 10
Working Capital	928	864	840
Fixed Assets	1m	1m	1m
Current Assets	1m	2m	2m

Thorn Security International
205-206 Bedford Avenue, Slough, SL1 4RY
Tel: 01753-702442 **Fax:** 01753-702365
Website: http://www.tycoint.com
No.of Employees: 21 - 50 **Product Groups:** 37, 40, 84

Tools-Paint Avenue Coatings
David Road Colnbrook, Slough, SL3 0TW
Tel: 01753-684084
E-mail: tools@avenue-group.co.uk
Website: http://www.tools-paint.com
Directors: D. Clarke (MD)
Managers: M. Wagstaff
No.of Employees: 21 - 50 **Product Groups:** 32, 35, 40, 42, 49, 63, 67

Transoft Ltd (Part of the Computer Software P.L.C.)
Unit 5j Langley Business Centre Station Road, Langley, Slough, SL3 8DS
Tel: 01753-778000 **Fax:** 01753-773050
E-mail: support@blackboxit.com
Website: http://www.transoft.com
Bank(s): National Westminster Bank Plc
Directors: O. Shaw (MD)
Managers: H. Farrell (Mktg Serv Mgr)
Ultimate Holding Company: PERENNIAL BIDCO A GUERNSEY LIMITED (GUERNSEY)
Immediate Holding Company: TRANSOFT GROUP LIMITED
Registration no: 01974716 **VAT No.:** GB 442 3809 57
Date established: 1986 **Turnover:** £5m - £10m **No.of Employees:** 11 - 20
Product Groups: 44

Date of Accounts	Apr 11	Apr 10	Apr 09
Pre Tax Profit/Loss	-29	116	721
Working Capital	895	895	-651
Fixed Assets	870	899	928
Current Assets	895	895	750

U T I Worldwide Ltd
Skyway 14 Calder Way, Colnbrook, Slough, SL3 0BQ
Tel: 01753-681212 **Fax:** 01753-764450
E-mail: creynolds@go2uti.com
Website: http://www.go2uti.com
Directors: R. McKenna (MD), S. Hallissey (Fin), D. Hugh (Mkt Research), C. Reynolds (Div), K. Sichau (Fin)
Managers: M. Brown (I.T. Exec), T. Delaney (I.T. Exec)
Ultimate Holding Company: UTI WORLDWIDE INC (BRITISH VIRGIN ISLANDS)
Immediate Holding Company: UTI WORLDWIDE (UK) LIMITED
Registration no: 02402322 **VAT No.:** GB 223 0259 08
Date established: 1989 **No.of Employees:** 51 - 100 **Product Groups:** 76

Date of Accounts	Mar 08	Mar 07	Mar 06
Working Capital	-83	-100	-124
Fixed Assets	6	3	6
Current Assets	78	73	57
Current Liabilities	161	173	181

Universal Locks Ltd T/A Universal Security Group
894 Plymouth Road Slough Trading Estate, Slough, SL1 4LP
Tel: 01753-696630 **Fax:** 01753-696374
E-mail: info@universalsecurity.co.uk
Website: http://www.universalsecurity.co.uk
Directors: A. Hogger (Dir)
Immediate Holding Company: UNIVERSAL LOCKS LIMITED
Registration no: 02224035 **Date established:** 1988 **Turnover:** £1m - £2m
No.of Employees: 11 - 20 **Product Groups:** 35, 36, 37, 40, 84

Date of Accounts	Oct 11	Oct 10	Oct 09
Working Capital	-26	-6	-1
Fixed Assets	107	105	107
Current Assets	602	498	424

Valentine Tools Ltd
770 Buckingham Avenue Slough Trading Estate, Slough, SL1 4NL
Tel: 01753-696 000 **Fax:** 01753-696 966
E-mail: sales@valentinetools.co.uk
Website: http://www.valentinetools.co.uk
Directors: M. Peachey (MD), M. Peachy (Prop)
Managers: C. Slattery (Mgr)
Registration no: 01044538 **VAT No.:** 222 5120 20 **Date established:** 1972
Turnover: £1m - £2m **No.of Employees:** 1 - 10 **Product Groups:** 66

Date of Accounts	Apr 08	Apr 07	Apr 06
Sales Turnover	N/A	N/A	1614
Pre Tax Profit/Loss	N/A	N/A	63
Working Capital	421	426	356
Fixed Assets	21	2	3
Current Assets	710	727	641
Current Liabilities	289	301	285
Total Share Capital	1	1	1
ROCE% (Return on Capital Employed)			17.6
ROT% (Return on Turnover)			3.9

Varatio Holdings plc
752-753 Deal Avenue, Slough, SL1 4SH
Tel: 01753-526655 **Fax:** 01753-693779
E-mail: alan.clinch@varatiouk.co.uk
Website: http://www.varatio.com
Bank(s): National Westminster Bank Plc

Directors: A. Clinch (Dir)
Immediate Holding Company: VARATIO HOLDINGS LIMITED
Registration no: 02670968 **Date established:** 1991 **Turnover:** £2m - £5m
No.of Employees: 51 - 100 **Product Groups:** 25, 35, 36, 39, 45, 48

Date of Accounts	Mar 11	Mar 10	Mar 09
Sales Turnover	4m	2m	3m
Pre Tax Profit/Loss	180	-301	-444
Working Capital	399	159	377
Fixed Assets	683	757	872
Current Assets	2m	1m	1m
Current Liabilities	819	513	524

Water Flow

12-16 David Road Colnbrook, Slough, SL3 0DG
Tel: 01753-810999 **Fax:** 01753-681442
E-mail: sales@waterflow.co.uk
Website: http://www.waterflow.co.uk
Bank(s): Bank of Scotland
Directors: N. Reilly (Sales)
Registration no: 00858432 **VAT No.:** GB 844 2823 24
Date established: 1965 **Turnover:** £10m - £20m
No.of Employees: 101 - 250 **Product Groups:** 37, 45, 47, 51, 52, 54

Westcon UK Ltd

210 Bath Road, Slough, SL1 3XE
Tel: 01753-797800 **Fax:** 01753-797801
E-mail: simon.minett@westcon.com
Website: http://www.westcon.co.uk
Bank(s): Barclays, Reading
Directors: R. Hodgetts (Fin), T. Brooks (Sales)
Managers: D. Claric (Tech Serv Mgr), S. Minett, D. Bain (Personnel), R. McLoud (Mktg Serv Mgr)
Ultimate Holding Company: DATATEC LTD (BRITISH VIRGIN ISLANDS)
Immediate Holding Company: WESTCON (UK) LIMITED
Registration no: 03668409 **Date established:** 1998 **Turnover:** £5m - £10m
No.of Employees: 21 - 50 **Product Groups:** 44

Date of Accounts	Feb 08	Feb 07
Sales Turnover	N/A	31810
Pre Tax Profit/Loss	-30	30
Working Capital	3360	3220
Current Assets	3360	6200
Current Liabilities	N/A	2980
Total Share Capital	60	60
ROCE% (Return on Capital Employed)		0.9
ROT% (Return on Turnover)		0.1

Whalin Logistics

Unit 5 Polygon Business Centre Blackthorne Road, Colnbrook, Slough, SL3 0QT
Tel: 01753-689299 **Fax:** 01753-689270
E-mail: info@whalinlogistics.com
Website: http://www.whalinlogistics.com
Directors: R. Whyte (Dir)
Immediate Holding Company: WHALIN LOGISTICS LIMITED
Registration no: 04520770 **Date established:** 2002
No.of Employees: 1 - 10 **Product Groups:** 72, 75, 76, 84

Date of Accounts	Aug 10	Aug 09	Aug 08
Working Capital	11	24	30
Fixed Assets	11	4	6
Current Assets	94	91	134

Wheelabrator Group

107-109 Whitby Road, Slough, SL1 3DR
Tel: 01753-572400 **Fax:** 01753-215662
E-mail: sales@wheelabratorgroup.co.uk
Website: http://www.wheelabratorgroup.com
Bank(s): H S B C
Managers: T. Grammauro (Chief Mgr)
Ultimate Holding Company: VIVENDI SA
Immediate Holding Company: U S FILTER
Registration no: 00366903 **VAT No.:** GB 561 0079 67
Turnover: £10m - £20m **No.of Employees:** 21 - 50 **Product Groups:** 33, 39, 40, 45, 46

Wilson & Scott Highways Ltd

Colndale Road Colnbrook, Slough, SL3 0HQ
Tel: 01753-671600 **Fax:** 01753-671611
E-mail: sales@wilsonandscott.co.uk
Website: http://www.wilsonandscott.co.uk
Bank(s): Barclays
Directors: S. Scott (Dir & Buyer), R. Meadows (Ch & MD)
Ultimate Holding Company: R.S.CLARE & CO.,LIMITED
Immediate Holding Company: WILSON & SCOTT (HIGHWAYS) LIMITED
Registration no: 00505380 **VAT No.:** GB 211 6690 84
Date established: 1952 **Turnover:** £1m - £2m **No.of Employees:** 21 - 50
Product Groups: 30

Date of Accounts	Dec 11	Dec 10	Dec 09
Sales Turnover	9m	6m	7m
Pre Tax Profit/Loss	486	-46	435
Working Capital	667	677	758
Fixed Assets	1m	887	879
Current Assets	2m	2m	2m
Current Liabilities	789	230	399

Thatcham

A F G Electronics

Fairlight House Goose Hill, Headley, Thatcham, RG19 8AU
Tel: 01635-268496 **Fax:** 01635-268020
E-mail: gibbjim@btinternet.com
Directors: J. Gibb (Prop)
Date established: 1984 **Turnover:** Up to £250,000
No.of Employees: 1 - 10 **Product Groups:** 37, 38

Ashtead Plant Hire Co.Ltd

Thatcham Depot (114) 20 Station Road, Thatcham, RG19 4PR
Tel: 01635-864222 **Fax:** 01635-873442
E-mail: enquiries@apollo-plant.co.uk
Website: http://www.aplant.com
Bank(s): Lloyds TSB Bank plc
Directors: S. Daywell (MD)
Managers: E. Webb (Mgr), S. Ruddiman (Mgr)
Immediate Holding Company: Ashtead Group PLC
Registration no: 00044569 **VAT No.:** GB 219 5687 37
No.of Employees: 11 - 20 **Product Groups:** 72, 83

Basingstoke Packaging Ltd

Terence House 24 London Road, Thatcham, RG18 4LQ
Tel: 01635-863783 **Fax:** 01635-861675
E-mail: sales@basingstokepackaging.co.uk
Website: http://www.basingstokepackaging.co.uk
Directors: V. Dodridge (Fin), R. Dodridge (MD)
Immediate Holding Company: BASINGSTOKE PACKAGING LIMITED
Registration no: 01440661 **VAT No.:** GB 314 3491 79
Date established: 1979 **Turnover:** £500,000 - £1m
No.of Employees: 1 - 10 **Product Groups:** 25, 45, 76

Date of Accounts	Jun 11	Jun 10	Jun 09
Working Capital	30	47	64
Fixed Assets	624	623	627
Current Assets	114	110	87

Before N After

New Greenham Park Greenham, Thatcham, RG19 6HN
Tel: 01635-32068
E-mail: chris@before-n-after.co.uk
Website: http://www.before-n-after.co.uk
Directors: C. Parkinson (Prop)
Immediate Holding Company: BLADE ELECTRONICS LIMITED
Registration no: 06247739 **Date established:** 2006
No.of Employees: 1 - 10 **Product Groups:** 46, 48

Berkshire Opthalmic Laboratories Ltd

Unit 6 Pipers Court Berkshire Drive, Thatcham, RG19 4ER
Tel: 01635-865050
E-mail: dennis@berkslabs.com
Website: http://www.berkslabs.com
Directors: D. Curcher (MD), W. Curcher (MD)
Ultimate Holding Company: BOL HOLDINGS LIMITED
Immediate Holding Company: BERKSHIRE OPHTHALMIC LABORATORIES LIMITED
Registration no: 00503358 **Date established:** 1952
No.of Employees: 21 - 50 **Product Groups:** 37, 38, 65

Date of Accounts	Dec 11	Dec 10	Dec 09
Working Capital	169	270	234
Fixed Assets	223	223	278
Current Assets	831	881	829

Biffa Waste Services Ltd

Pound Lane Depot, Thatcham, RG19 3TG
Tel: 01635-863394 **Fax:** 01635-874967
Website: http://www.biffa.co.uk
Managers: M. Sturgeon (Mgr)
Ultimate Holding Company: Wasteinvestments LLP
Immediate Holding Company: BIFFA WASTE SERVICES LIMITED
Registration no: 00946107 **Date established:** 1969
No.of Employees: 51 - 100 **Product Groups:** 32, 54

Business Cards on the Web

Helfenburg House, Main Street New Greenham Park, Newbury, Thatcham, RG19 6HN
Tel: 01635-522447 **Fax:** 01635-522449
E-mail: sales@businesscardsontheweb.co.uk
Website: http://www.businesscardsontheweb.co.uk
Directors: P. Hurza (Ptnr), R. Hill (Ptnr)
Turnover: £250,000 - £500,000 **No.of Employees:** 1 - 10
Product Groups: 28, 80

Castle Print & Design

Helfenburg House New Greenham Park, Greenham, Thatcham, RG19 6HN
Tel: 01635-522447 **Fax:** 01635-522449
E-mail: ron@castleprint.co.uk
Website: http://www.castleprint.co.uk
Directors: R. Hill (MD), R. Hill (Ptnr)
Date established: 1992 **No.of Employees:** 1 - 10 **Product Groups:** 28, 80

Crescent Lighting Ltd

8 Rivermead Pipers Lane, Thatcham, RG19 4EP
Tel: 01635-878888 **Fax:** 01635-873888
E-mail: sales@crescent.co.uk
Website: http://www.crescent.co.uk
Directors: M. Morrison (MD), N. Berchtold (Co Sec)
Immediate Holding Company: CRESCENT LIGHTING LIMITED
Registration no: 03642724 **Date established:** 1998 **Turnover:** £2m - £5m
No.of Employees: 11 - 20 **Product Groups:** 37, 38

Date of Accounts	Dec 11	Dec 10	Dec 09
Sales Turnover	N/A	N/A	3m
Pre Tax Profit/Loss	N/A	N/A	41
Working Capital	572	768	766
Fixed Assets	10	13	31
Current Assets	832	1m	1m
Current Liabilities	N/A	N/A	181

Dancap Electronics Ltd

24 Trent Crescent, Thatcham, RG18 3DN
Tel: 01635-866394 **Fax:** 01635-869589
E-mail: dancap@btinternet.com
Website: http://www.dancap.co.uk
Directors: P. West (Dir), C. West (Co Sec)
Registration no: 02650175 **Turnover:** £2m - £5m
No.of Employees: 1 - 10 **Product Groups:** 37, 38, 46, 47, 48, 67

Ergo Computer Accessories Ltd

5 Pipers Industrial Estate Pipers Lane, Thatcham, RG19 4NA
Tel: 01635-877979 **Fax:** 01635-877676
E-mail: sales@ergo-consumables.co.uk
Website: http://www.ergo-consumables.co.uk
Directors: K. Miles (MD), S. Bartlett (Co Sec)
Immediate Holding Company: ERGO COMPUTER ACCESSORIES LIMITED
Registration no: 01843409 **Date established:** 1984
Turnover: £250,000 - £500,000 **No.of Employees:** 1 - 10
Product Groups: 44, 67

Date of Accounts	Mar 11	Mar 10	Mar 09
Working Capital	11	1	-17
Fixed Assets	3	4	5
Current Assets	61	70	68

Fast Lane Training Ltd

The Oaks Water Lane Greenham, Thatcham, RG19 8SH
Tel: 01672-564481
E-mail: info@fastlanetraining.co.uk
Website: http://www.fastlaneresults.co.uk
Directors: Q. Dunstan (MD), H. Dunstan (Fin)
Immediate Holding Company: FAST LANE RESULTS LTD
Registration no: 04818239 **Date established:** 2003
Turnover: Up to £250,000 **No.of Employees:** 1 - 10 **Product Groups:** 86

Date of Accounts	Dec 11	Dec 10	Dec 09
Working Capital	-3	-2	-7
Fixed Assets	4	2	8
Current Assets	42	34	25

Filter Solutions Limited

5 Pipers Court, Berkshire Drive,, Thatcham, RG19 4ER
Tel: 01635-870250 **Fax:** 01635-867942
E-mail: office@filtersolutions.eu.com
Website: http://www.filtersolutions.eu.com
Directors: T. Hamilton (Dir)
Immediate Holding Company: Filter Solutions Ltd
Registration no: 04737997 **No.of Employees:** 1 - 10 **Product Groups:** 38, 42

Date of Accounts	Jun 08	Jun 07	Jun 06
Working Capital	35	5	-4
Fixed Assets	20	12	3
Current Assets	144	64	37
Current Liabilities	109	59	41

Frontier Agriculture Ltd

Red Shute Hill Industrial Estate Red Shute Hill, Hermitage, Thatcham, RG18 9QL
Tel: 01635-204100 **Fax:** 01635-201417
E-mail: info@frontierag.co.uk
Website: http://www.frontierag.co.uk
Managers: A. Wright
Immediate Holding Company: FRONTIER AGRICULTURE LIMITED
Registration no: 05288567 **Date established:** 2004
Turnover: £125m - £250m **No.of Employees:** 11 - 20 **Product Groups:** 62

Date of Accounts	Jun 11	Jun 10	Jun 09
Sales Turnover	1402m	981m	1154m
Pre Tax Profit/Loss	39m	24m	30m
Working Capital	100m	77m	59m
Fixed Assets	29m	24m	26m
Current Assets	357m	217m	201m
Current Liabilities	32m	16m	23m

Green Gate Mechanical Services

8 Pinewood Crescent Hermitage, Thatcham, RG18 9WL
Tel: 01635-201649 **Fax:** 01635-201649
E-mail: office@greengatemechanical.co.uk
Website: http://www.greengatemechanical.co.uk
Directors: R. Warren (Dir)
Immediate Holding Company: GREEN GATE MECHANICAL SERVICES LTD
Registration no: 06812227 **Date established:** 2009
Turnover: £500,000 - £1m **No.of Employees:** 1 - 10 **Product Groups:** 37, 38, 40

Ibis Packaging Solutions Ltd

10 Colthrop Business Park Colthrop Lane, Thatcham, RG19 4NB
Tel: 01639-890609
E-mail: accounts@ibispackaging.co.uk
Website: http://www.ibispackaging.co.uk
Directors: P. Atkin (MD)
Immediate Holding Company: IBIS PACKAGING SOLUTIONS LIMITED
Registration no: 05867131 **Date established:** 2006
No.of Employees: 1 - 10 **Product Groups:** 27, 30, 42, 67

Date of Accounts	Dec 11	Dec 10	Dec 09
Working Capital	-304	-512	-663
Fixed Assets	656	665	701
Current Assets	1m	1m	1m

Ion Systems Ltd

Venture West New Greenham Park, Greenham, Thatcham, RG19 6HX
Tel: 01635-500350 **Fax:** 01635-500351
E-mail: support@ion-systems.net
Website: http://www.ion-systems.net
Directors: P. Dean (MD)
Managers: V. Ho (Fin Mgr), M. Finlay (Purch Mgr), M. Sheperia (Sales Prom Mgr)
Ultimate Holding Company: SPEED-TRAP HOLDINGS LIMITED
Immediate Holding Company: ION SYSTEMS LIMITED
Registration no: 02029294 **Date established:** 1986
Turnover: Up to £250,000 **No.of Employees:** 1 - 10 **Product Groups:** 44

Date of Accounts	Jun 91	Jun 90	Jun 89
Sales Turnover	473	452	368
Pre Tax Profit/Loss	-32	23	-3
Fixed Assets	61	52	44
Current Assets	135	86	138

L P A Channel Electric

Bath Road, Thatcham, RG18 3ST
Tel: 01635-864866 **Fax:** 01635-869178
E-mail: enquiries@lpa-channel.com
Website: http://www.lpa-channel.com
Bank(s): National Westminster
Directors: C. Antysz (Sales)
Managers: C. Clough (Mgr)
Ultimate Holding Company: LPA GROUP PLC
Immediate Holding Company: CHANNEL ELECTRIC EQUIPMENT LIMITED
Registration no: 00919987 **VAT No.:** GB 198 9412 07
Date established: 1967 **Turnover:** £2m - £5m **No.of Employees:** 11 - 20
Product Groups: 37

Date of Accounts	Sep 11	Sep 10	Sep 09
Sales Turnover	4m	4m	4m
Pre Tax Profit/Loss	389	276	798
Working Capital	3m	3m	3m
Fixed Assets	133	134	130
Current Assets	4m	4m	4m
Current Liabilities	260	193	209

Lex Harvey Ltd

Colthrop Lane, Thatcham, RG19 4NH
Tel: 01635-865590
Website: http://www.lex-harvey.co.uk
Managers: M. Kidby (Mgr)
No.of Employees: 1 - 10 **Product Groups:** 35, 39, 45

Nitto UK Ltd
Unit2 Berkshire Business Centre Berkshire Drive, Thatcham, RG19 4EW
Tel: 01635-872172 **Fax:** 01635-872332
E-mail: nitto_uk@nittoeur.com
Website: http://www.nittoeurope.com
Managers: C. Spoor (Sales Prom Mgr), S. Strijckmans (Fin Mgr), L. Catheline (Fin Mgr)
Ultimate Holding Company: NITTO DENKO CORP (JAPAN)
Immediate Holding Company: Nitto Belgium N.V.
Registration no: 01858291 **Date established:** 1984
Turnover: £500,000 - £1m **No.of Employees:** 1 - 10 **Product Groups:** 27, 29, 30, 32, 37, 40

Date of Accounts	Mar 10	Mar 09	Mar 08
Sales Turnover	566	604	683
Pre Tax Profit/Loss	60	82	74
Working Capital	169	226	190
Fixed Assets	2	6	7
Current Assets	237	313	297
Current Liabilities	68	57	82

Norma UK Ltd
Unit 33 New Greenham Park Weber Road Greenham, Thatcham, RG19 6HW
Tel: 01635-521880 **Fax:** 01635-57403
E-mail: mike.lawrence@normagroup.com
Website: http://www.normagroup.com
Bank(s): Lloyds, Stourbridge
Directors: M. Lawrence (MD)
Managers: H. Eden (Tech Serv Mgr), C. Sykes (Personnel), D. Whittle (Mktg Serv Mgr), A. Rostron, C. Gilbert (Comptroller)
Ultimate Holding Company: NORMA GROUP HOLDING GMBH (GERMANY)
Immediate Holding Company: NORMA PRODUCTS LIMITED
Registration no: 06322617 **VAT No.:** GB 589 2654 84
Date established: 2007 **Turnover:** £1m - £2m
No.of Employees: 101 - 250 **Product Groups:** 35, 36, 46, 66

Precision Peripherals Ltd
Unit 2 Home Farm Industrial Estate, Yattendon, Thatcham, RG18 0XT
Tel: 01792-794773 **Fax:** 01635-206846
E-mail: crichards@printerpeople.demon.co.uk
Website: http://www.ppltd.net
Directors: C. Richards (Prop)
Immediate Holding Company: PRECISION PERIPHERALS LIMITED
Registration no: 01609626 **VAT No.:** GB 314 9561 54
Date established: 1982 **Turnover:** £1m - £2m **No.of Employees:** 21 - 50
Product Groups: 44

Date of Accounts	Mar 12	Mar 11	Mar 10
Working Capital	91	88	114
Fixed Assets	102	111	78
Current Assets	715	884	879

Service Metals South
Red Shute Hill Hermitage, Thatcham, RG18 9QX
Tel: 01635-201811 **Fax:** 01635-201894
E-mail: chris@smsouth.co.uk
Website: http://www.servicemetals.co.uk
Bank(s): National Westminster Bank Plc
Directors: C. Mitchell (Dir)
Immediate Holding Company: SERVICE METALS (SOUTH) LTD
Registration no: 02107615 **Turnover:** £2m - £5m
No.of Employees: 11 - 20 **Product Groups:** 66

H.J. Skelton & Co. Ltd
9 The Broadway, Thatcham, RG19 3JA
Tel: 01635-865256 **Fax:** 01635-865710
E-mail: js@hjskelton.com
Website: http://www.hjskelton.co.uk
Directors: J. Smith (Dir)
Ultimate Holding Company: N
Registration no: 00118102 **VAT No.:** GB 244 1126 02
Date established: 1883 **Turnover:** £500,000 - £1m
No.of Employees: 1 - 10 **Product Groups:** 34, 39

Date of Accounts	Nov 11	Nov 10	Nov 09
Working Capital	64	62	74
Fixed Assets	2	1	2
Current Assets	172	149	156

Southworth Handling Ltd
3 Berkshire Business Centre Berkshire Drive, Thatcham, RG19 4EW
Tel: 01635-874404 **Fax:** 01635-874027
E-mail: sales@southworth.co.uk
Website: http://www.southworth.co.uk
Directors: P. Brook (MD)
Ultimate Holding Company: RNM HANDLING LIMITED
Immediate Holding Company: SOUTHWORTH HANDLING LIMITED
Registration no: 02331460 **VAT No.:** GB 533 3953 43
Date established: 1988 **Turnover:** £500,000 - £1m
No.of Employees: 1 - 10 **Product Groups:** 45

Date of Accounts	Mar 12	Mar 11	Mar 10
Working Capital	224	228	229
Fixed Assets	12	2	1
Current Assets	295	305	291

Sportsmark Group Ltd
Unit 4 Clerewater Place Lower Way, Thatcham, RG19 3RF
Tel: 01635-867537 **Fax:** 01483-487919
E-mail: info@sportsmark.net
Website: http://www.sportsmark.net
Directors: M. Pocklington (MD)
Immediate Holding Company: SPORTSMARK GROUP LIMITED
Registration no: 00763911 **Date established:** 1963
Turnover: £500,000 - £1m **No.of Employees:** 1 - 10 **Product Groups:** 27, 30, 32, 45, 49, 51

Date of Accounts	May 11	May 10	May 09
Working Capital	16	38	33
Fixed Assets	4	5	8
Current Assets	76	144	103

T D G Logistics Ltd (Factory) UK Central Office
Bath Road Colthrop, Thatcham, RG19 4NQ
Tel: 01635-866366 **Fax:** 01635-874165
Website: http://www.sca.com
Directors: A. Pearson (Dir & Gen Mgr)
Managers: L. Quarry (Depot Mgr), P. Fitzsimmons (Chief Mgr), P. Chinnery (Depot Mgr)
Immediate Holding Company: TDG LOGISTICS LIMITED
Registration no: 03642760 **Date established:** 1998
No.of Employees: 21 - 50 **Product Groups:** 27

Windsor

Bray Film Studios
Down Place Water Oakley, Windsor, SL4 5UG
Tel: 01628-622111 **Fax:** 01628-770381
Website: http://www.brayfilmstudios.com
Managers: N. Partridge (Mgr)
Immediate Holding Company: ANDERBURR STUDIOS LIMITED
Registration no: 01285786 **Date established:** 1976
No.of Employees: 11 - 20 **Product Groups:** 89

Burleigh Marine Systems Ltd
5 Kimber Close, Windsor, SL4 4BJ
Tel: 01753-861943 **Fax:** 01753-861943
E-mail: ackroyd@burleighmarine.co.uk
Website: http://www.burleighmarine.co.uk
Directors: J. Bernson (MD), N. Chelton (MD)
Registration no: 03137607 **Date established:** 1995
Turnover: Up to £250,000 **No.of Employees:** 1 - 10 **Product Groups:** 39

Callsure Business Telephone & Fax Numbers
36 Duncroft, Windsor, SL4 4HH
Tel: 01753-624121
E-mail: sales@callsure07050.co.uk
Website: http://www.callsure07050.co.uk
Directors: J. Webb (Prop)
No.of Employees: 1 - 10 **Product Groups:** 37, 67, 79, 80

Centrica plc
Millstream Maidenhead Road, Windsor, SL4 5GD
Tel: 01753-494000 **Fax:** 01753-494001
Website: http://www.centrica.co.uk
Directors: R. Carr (Prop), R. Gardner (Dir)
Ultimate Holding Company: CENTRICA PLC
Immediate Holding Company: CENTRICA PLC
Registration no: 03033654 **Date established:** 1995
Turnover: Over £1,000m **No.of Employees:** 1501 & over
Product Groups: 11, 31, 80, 86, 89

Date of Accounts	Dec 11	Dec 10	Dec 09
Sales Turnover	22824m	22423m	21963m
Pre Tax Profit/Loss	1268m	2809m	996m
Working Capital	-674m	738m	808m
Fixed Assets	13973m	13269m	12472m
Current Assets	5596m	6006m	6970m
Current Liabilities	5282m	4128m	5292m

Enforce-logic Ltd
PO Box 3828, Windsor, SL4 5YN
Tel: 08456-805087
E-mail: customerservices@enforce-logic.co.uk
Website: http://www.enforce-logic.co.uk
Directors: M. Waite (Dir)
Immediate Holding Company: ENFORCE-LOGIC LIMITED
Registration no: 05565408 **Date established:** 2005
Turnover: Up to £250,000 **No.of Employees:** 1 - 10 **Product Groups:** 22, 36, 39

Date of Accounts	Sep 11	Sep 10	Sep 09
Working Capital	15	6	2
Current Assets	39	31	25

The Eton T-Shirt Company
60 High Street Eton, Windsor, SL4 6AA
Tel: 01753-731509 **Fax:** 01753-731503
E-mail: info@etontshirt.co.uk
Website: http://www.etontshirt.co.uk
Directors: J. Butler (Prop)
No.of Employees: 1 - 10 **Product Groups:** 24, 30, 35, 49, 63

Etoncastle Gunsmiths
103 High Street Eton, Windsor, SL4 6AF
Tel: 01753-800009
Website: http://www.etonguns.co.uk
Directors: E. Waddleton (MD), N. Beaton (Fin)
Immediate Holding Company: LEATHERGOODS & LUGGAGE REPAIRS LTD
Registration no: 02278565 **Date established:** 1988
No.of Employees: 1 - 10 **Product Groups:** 36, 39, 40

Date of Accounts	Mar 11	Mar 10	Jan 08
Working Capital	-6	35	22
Fixed Assets	35	38	40
Current Assets	10	78	83

Gusto Caribbean
267 St Leonards Road, Windsor, SL4 3DR
Tel: 01753-830060 **Fax:** 01753-830774
E-mail: mikelamprill@gustocaribbean.com
Website: http://www.gustocaribbean.com
Directors: M. Lamprill (Dir)
No.of Employees: 1 - 10 **Product Groups:** 80

H F C Bank (Head Office)
North Street Winkfield, Windsor, SL4 4TD
Tel: 01344-890000 **Fax:** 01344-892667
Website: http://www.hfcbank.co.uk
Directors: F. Forman (Dir)
Ultimate Holding Company: HSBC HOLDINGS PLC
Immediate Holding Company: HFC BANK LIMITED
Registration no: 01117305 **Date established:** 1973
Turnover: £125m - £250m **No.of Employees:** 1 - 10 **Product Groups:** 82

Date of Accounts	Dec 10	Dec 09	Dec 08
Pre Tax Profit/Loss	8m	-102m	-87m
Fixed Assets	104m	56m	123m
Current Assets	1178m	1802m	2272m
Current Liabilities	830m	1400m	1720m

Hovis
Hovis Court 69 Alma Road, Windsor, SL4 3HD
Tel: 08707-288888 **Fax:** 01753-791739
Website: http://www.premierfoods.co.uk
Bank(s): Barclays, London
Directors: M. Warnick (MD), T. Phillips (Fin)
Ultimate Holding Company: PREMIER FOODS PLC
Immediate Holding Company: RHM FOODBRANDS+ LTD
Registration no: 00241018 **VAT No.:** GB 527 2079 49
Turnover: £250m - £500m **No.of Employees:** 101 - 250
Product Groups: 62

Date of Accounts	Dec 07
Working Capital	32880
Current Assets	32880
Total Share Capital	32880

Itp International Travel Partnership
14 High Street, Windsor, SL4 1LD
Tel: 01753-832033 **Fax:** 01753-868197
E-mail: virginia@itptravel.net
Website: http://www.itptravel.net
Managers: V. Palla (Chief Mgr)
Ultimate Holding Company: HICKORY S A (SWITZERLAND)
Immediate Holding Company: ITP - INTERNATIONAL TRAVEL PARTNERSHIP LIMITED
Registration no: 02024270 **VAT No.:** GB 454 4274 46
Date established: 1986 **No.of Employees:** 1 - 10 **Product Groups:** 69, 80, 82

Date of Accounts	Dec 11	Dec 10	Dec 09
Working Capital	142	127	115
Fixed Assets	2	4	7
Current Assets	158	146	132

Gerald Judd Ltd
Providence House 2 River Street, Windsor, SL4 1QT
Tel: 01753-833666 **Fax:** 01753-833130
E-mail: geraldjudd@btconnect.com
Directors: C. Judd (MD)
Immediate Holding Company: GERALD JUDD LIMITED
Registration no: 00319959 **Date established:** 1936
Turnover: £500,000 - £1m **No.of Employees:** 1 - 10 **Product Groups:** 80

Date of Accounts	Apr 12	Apr 11	Apr 10
Working Capital	316	200	3m
Fixed Assets	4m	4m	1m
Current Assets	469	401	3m

Keeler Ltd
Clewer Green Works Clewer Hill Road, Windsor, SL4 4AA
Tel: 01753-857177 **Fax:** 01753-830247
E-mail: info@keeler.co.uk
Website: http://www.keeler.co.uk
Bank(s): Barclays, Birmingham
Directors: J. Woffinden (Pers), J. Wilson (Fin)
Managers: K. Watson (Sales & Mktg Mg), D. Knight (Tech Serv Mgr)
Ultimate Holding Company: HALMA PUBLIC LIMITED COMPANY
Immediate Holding Company: KEELER LIMITED
Registration no: 00408759 **VAT No.:** GB 349 0761 40
Date established: 1946 **Turnover:** £10m - £20m
No.of Employees: 101 - 250 **Product Groups:** 33, 37, 38

Date of Accounts	Mar 12	Mar 09	Apr 10
Sales Turnover	17m	16m	15m
Pre Tax Profit/Loss	4m	3m	3m
Working Capital	9m	9m	9m
Fixed Assets	3m	2m	3m
Current Assets	11m	11m	11m
Current Liabilities	734	531	498

New & Lingwood Ltd
118 High Street Eton, Windsor, SL4 6AN
Tel: 01753-866286 **Fax:** 01753-861892
E-mail: info@newandlingwood.com
Website: http://www.newandlingwood.com
Directors: B. Cohen (Co Sec)
Managers: N. Fugal (Mgr)
Ultimate Holding Company: PILLAR HOLDINGS LTD (JERSEY)
Immediate Holding Company: NEW AND LINGWOOD LIMITED
Registration no: 00143620 **Date established:** 2016
Turnover: Up to £250,000 **No.of Employees:** 1 - 10 **Product Groups:** 24

Date of Accounts	Jan 09	Jan 10	Jan 11
Sales Turnover	3m	3m	3m
Pre Tax Profit/Loss	27	119	274
Working Capital	628	562	581
Fixed Assets	86	71	55
Current Assets	1m	1m	1m
Current Liabilities	320	475	436

Oxford Filtration Ltd
Unit 15 Bridgewater Way, Windsor, SL4 1RD
Tel: 01628-440906 **Fax:** 01628-476667
E-mail: mark@oxfordfiltration.com
Website: http://www.oxfordfiltration.com
Directors: M. Jackson (MD), S. Jackson Cook (Fin)
Immediate Holding Company: OXFORD FILTRATION LIMITED
Registration no: 04058606 **Date established:** 2000
Turnover: £250,000 - £500,000 **No.of Employees:** 1 - 10
Product Groups: 38, 42

Date of Accounts	Aug 10	Aug 09	Aug 08
Sales Turnover	N/A	353	N/A
Pre Tax Profit/Loss	N/A	22	N/A
Working Capital	142	128	115
Fixed Assets	4	6	7
Current Assets	195	223	194
Current Liabilities	N/A	17	N/A

Park Street People Ltd
12 Park Street, Windsor, SL4 1LU
Tel: 01753-830706 **Fax:** 01753-831298
E-mail: windsor@parkstreetpeople.com
Website: http://www.parkstreetpeople.com
Directors: L. Vittozzi (MD), S. Brett (Co Sec)
Immediate Holding Company: PARK STREET PEOPLE LIMITED
Registration no: 02336356 **VAT No.:** GB 491 8853 00
Date established: 1989 **Turnover:** £250,000 - £500,000
No.of Employees: 11 - 20 **Product Groups:** 80

Date of Accounts	Apr 11	Apr 10	Apr 09
Working Capital	251	130	61
Fixed Assets	63	111	164
Current Assets	423	283	247

Pitney Bowes Software Ltd
Minton Place Victoria Street, Windsor, SL4 1EG
Tel: 01753-848200 **Fax:** 01753-621140
E-mail: gary.roberts@mapinfo.com
Website: http://www.pb.com
Bank(s): National Westminster

Directors: G. Willsher (Co Sec)
Managers: G. Roberts
Ultimate Holding Company: PITNEY BOWES INCORPORATED (USA)
Immediate Holding Company: PITNEY BOWES SOFTWARE LIMITED
Registration no: 03038694 **VAT No.:** GB 314 7335 73
Date established: 1995 **Turnover:** £20m - £50m
No.of Employees: 101 - 250 **Product Groups:** 44

Date of Accounts	Dec 11	Dec 10	Dec 09
Sales Turnover	28m	29m	32m
Pre Tax Profit/Loss	821	995	3m
Working Capital	13m	13m	12m
Fixed Assets	2m	2m	2m
Current Assets	33m	32m	30m
Current Liabilities	10m	10m	10m

Positive Image
25 Victoria Street, Windsor, SL4 1HE
Tel: 01753-842248 **Fax:** 01753-830878
E-mail: stuart.mclean@positiveimage.co.uk
Website: http://www.positiveimage.co.uk
Directors: S. McLean (Dir)
Immediate Holding Company: POSITIVE IMAGE LIMITED
Registration no: 01656771 **VAT No.:** GB 237 8572 30
Date established: 1982 **Turnover:** £500,000 - £1m
No.of Employees: 1 - 10 **Product Groups:** 28, 81, 86

Date of Accounts	Sep 11	Sep 10	Sep 09
Working Capital	292	185	69
Fixed Assets	49	35	34
Current Assets	515	356	130

Premier Bartleet Ltd
Mountbatten House Unit 5 Fairacres Industrial Estate, Windsor, SL4 4LE
Tel: 01753-754850 **Fax:** 01753-754851
E-mail: info@prembar.com
Website: http://www.prembar.com
Directors: R. Valentine (MD), C. Valentine (Fin)
Immediate Holding Company: PREMIER BARTLEET LIMITED
Registration no: 03642354 **VAT No.:** GB 578 4043 19
Date established: 1998 **No.of Employees:** 1 - 10 **Product Groups:** 41, 42

Date of Accounts	Mar 12	Feb 11	Feb 10
Working Capital	668	581	628
Fixed Assets	3	3	2
Current Assets	1m	1m	742

Shelfguard Systems
89 St Leonards Road, Windsor, SL4 3BZ
Tel: 01753-867257 **Fax:** 01753-830024
E-mail: info@shelfguard-systems.co.uk
Website: http://www.shelfguard-systems.co.uk
Directors: R. Just (MD)
No.of Employees: 1 - 10 **Product Groups:** 44, 48, 67

Silgan White Cap UK Ltd
1 Thames Side, Windsor, SL4 1QN
Tel: 01753-832828 **Fax:** 01753-620825
Website: http://www.amcor.com
Managers: D. Harding (Sales & Mktg Mg)
Ultimate Holding Company: SILGAN HOLDINGS INC (UNITED STATES OF AMERICA)
Immediate Holding Company: SILGAN WHITE CAP UK LIMITED
Registration no: 02416087 **Date established:** 1989 **Turnover:** £2m - £5m
No.of Employees: 1 - 10 **Product Groups:** 20, 40, 41

Date of Accounts	Dec 10	Dec 09	Dec 08
Sales Turnover	5m	5m	5m
Pre Tax Profit/Loss	538	-54	-677
Working Capital	612	75	129
Current Assets	2m	1m	1m
Current Liabilities	434	401	444

Spraytech Paint Services Ltd
Danleebar Farm Crouch Lane Winkfield, Windsor, SL4 4RZ
Tel: 01344-890091 **Fax:** 01344-883830
E-mail: info@spraytechltd.com
Website: http://www.spraytechltd.com
Directors: P. Munden (Dir)
Immediate Holding Company: SPRAYTECH PAINT SERVICES LTD
Registration no: 05497735 **Date established:** 2005
No.of Employees: 1 - 10 **Product Groups:** 46, 48

Date of Accounts	Oct 11	Oct 10	Oct 09
Working Capital	21	27	29
Fixed Assets	23	29	18
Current Assets	66	43	61

Standard Rubber Grommets Ltd
33 Victor Road, Windsor, SL4 3JS
Tel: 01753-852345 **Fax:** 01753-852345
E-mail: sales@standardrubber.co.uk
Website: http://www.standardrubbergrommets.biz
Directors: J. Elliot (Co Sec), J. Thomson (MD)
Immediate Holding Company: STANDARD RUBBER GROMMETS LTD
Registration no: 01894320 **Date established:** 1985
Turnover: Up to £250,000 **No.of Employees:** 1 - 10 **Product Groups:** 29

Date of Accounts	Oct 11	Oct 10	Oct 09
Working Capital	-8	-4	3
Current Assets	12	17	26

Super Hanger Manufacturing Co. Ltd
100 Vale Road, Windsor, SL4 5JL
Tel: 01753-622500 **Fax:** 01753-662770
E-mail: sales@super-hanger.co.uk
Website: http://www.super-hanger.co.uk
Directors: J. Thind (Dir), S. Thind (Fin)
Immediate Holding Company: SUPER HANGER MANUFACTURING COMPANY LIMITED
Registration no: 01567008 **VAT No.:** 302 2824 05 **Date established:** 1981
Turnover: £500,000 - £1m **No.of Employees:** 1 - 10 **Product Groups:** 32, 35

Date of Accounts	Apr 11	Apr 10	Apr 09
Working Capital	71	33	-9
Fixed Assets	4	5	5
Current Assets	160	161	130

Swallow Spray UK Ltd
Vansittart Estate, Windsor, SL4 1SE
Tel: 01753-866211 **Fax:** 01753-832324
Directors: B. Wall (MD)
Immediate Holding Company: SWALLOW SPRAY (UK) LIMITED
Registration no: 05744557 **Date established:** 2006
Turnover: £250,000 - £500,000 **No.of Employees:** 1 - 10
Product Groups: 46, 48

Date of Accounts	Mar 11	Mar 09	Mar 08
Sales Turnover	N/A	40	N/A
Pre Tax Profit/Loss	N/A	7	N/A
Working Capital	-10	-9	N/A
Fixed Assets	11	14	N/A
Current Assets	73	41	N/A
Current Liabilities	N/A	4	N/A

Valet Magic
Unit 2 Homelands North Street, Winkfield, Windsor, SL4 4SY
Tel: 01344-891891 **Fax:** 01753-680395
E-mail: info@valetmagic.com
Website: http://www.valetmagic.com
Directors: R. Orlando (Prop)
Registration no: 07370303 **No.of Employees:** 1 - 10 **Product Groups:** 32, 39, 68

Waymatic Ltd
15 Bridgewater Way, Windsor, SL4 1RD
Tel: 01753-869218 **Fax:** 01753-830519
E-mail: waymatic@btconnect.com
Directors: N. Hamilton (Dir), T. Kirby (MD), N. Hamilton (MD)
Managers: P. Jones (Sales & Mktg Mg)
Immediate Holding Company: WAYMATIC LIMITED
Registration no: 01720592 **Date established:** 1983
Turnover: Up to £250,000 **No.of Employees:** 1 - 10 **Product Groups:** 38

Date of Accounts	Mar 11	Mar 10	Mar 09
Working Capital	135	117	116
Fixed Assets	4	5	5
Current Assets	147	161	186

Wysetech Ltd
42 The arches Alma Road, Windsor, SL4 1QZ
Tel: 01753-855619 **Fax:** 05601-257438
E-mail: info@wysetech.co.uk
Website: http://www.wysetech.co.uk
Directors: D. Ford Young (Prop)
Immediate Holding Company: WYSETECH LTD
Registration no: 05084366 **Date established:** 2004
No.of Employees: 1 - 10 **Product Groups:** 41

Date of Accounts	Dec 11	Dec 10	Dec 09
Working Capital	37	22	18
Fixed Assets	4	4	5
Current Assets	177	131	140

Yellowfoot Experience Ltd
Yellowfoot Lodge Pococks Lane, Eton, Windsor, SL4 6HW
Tel: 01753-533070 **Fax:** 01753-533010
E-mail: why-its-different@yellowfoot.com
Website: http://www.yellowfoot.com
Directors: T. Tom (Dir)
No.of Employees: 1 - 10 **Product Groups:** 89

Wokingham

A1 Loo Hire Ltd
Silver Birches Highland Avenue, Wokingham, RG41 4SP
Tel: 0118-989 4652 **Fax:** 0118-979 4328
E-mail: info@a1groupcomp.co.uk
Website: http://www.a1loohire.info
Directors: S. Pike (Dir)
Immediate Holding Company: A1 LOO HIRE LIMITED
Registration no: 05333973 **Date established:** 2005
No.of Employees: 1 - 10 **Product Groups:** 30, 35, 36, 40

Advanced Crystal Technology
3 The Business Centre Molly Millars Lane, Wokingham, RG41 2EY
Tel: 0118-979 1238 **Fax:** 0118-979 1283
E-mail: info@actcrystals.com
Website: http://www.act.co.uk
Directors: C. Read (Fin), S. Sydes (MD), W. Axten (Sales)
Managers: E. Senescall (Transport), L. Hudson (Applic Eng), M. Jordan (Sales Prom Mgr)
Ultimate Holding Company: ACAL P.L.C.
Immediate Holding Company: Acal plc
Registration no: 01904334 **Date established:** 1984
Turnover: £20m - £50m **No.of Employees:** 21 - 50 **Product Groups:** 33, 37, 38, 42

Advanced Technology Machines Ltd
4 Molly Millars Bridge, Wokingham, RG41 2WY
Tel: 0118-977 0099 **Fax:** 0118-989 2288
E-mail: sales@atmmt.com
Website: http://www.atmmt.com
Directors: D. Clarke (MD), V. Wilton (Co Sec)
Immediate Holding Company: READYPOWER RENTALS LIMITED
Registration no: 02681963 **Date established:** 1999
Turnover: £10m - £20m **No.of Employees:** 1 - 10 **Product Groups:** 46

Agilent Technologies UK Ltd
Unit 610 Wharfedale Road Winnersh, Wokingham, RG41 5TP
Tel: 07002-445368 **Fax:** 07004-444555
E-mail: yvonne_mackie@agilent.com
Website: http://www.agilent.co.uk
Managers: P. Cousans (Mgr)
Ultimate Holding Company: AGILENT TECHNOLOGIES INC (USA)
Immediate Holding Company: AGILENT TECHNOLOGIES UK LIMITED
Registration no: 03809903 **Date established:** 1999
Turnover: £125m - £250m **No.of Employees:** 51 - 100
Product Groups: 37, 42, 44, 67, 80

Date of Accounts	Oct 11	Oct 10	Oct 09
Sales Turnover	206m	120m	155m
Pre Tax Profit/Loss	10m	7m	2m
Working Capital	112m	107m	117m
Fixed Assets	43m	15m	16m
Current Assets	158m	136m	136m
Current Liabilities	20m	14m	15m

All Gear Services 1990 Ltd
Unit 5b Hogwood Farm Sheerlands Road, Finchampstead, Wokingham, RG40 4QY
Tel: 0118-973 0053 **Fax:** 0118-973 4722
E-mail: steve@allgears.com
Website: http://www.allgears.com
Directors: S. Cooper (Dir)
Immediate Holding Company: ALL GEAR SERVICES (1990) LIMITED
Registration no: 04670339 **VAT No.:** GB 529 2061 56
Date established: 2003 **Turnover:** £500,000 - £1m
No.of Employees: 1 - 10 **Product Groups:** 46, 48, 67

Date of Accounts	Sep 11	Sep 10	Sep 09
Working Capital	-52	-19	-27
Fixed Assets	101	122	150
Current Assets	115	128	110

B D S Computer
1 Rookery Court Weller Drive, Finchampstead, Wokingham, RG40 4QZ
Tel: 0118-973 7000 **Fax:** 0118-973 7070
E-mail: brian@bds.co.uk
Website: http://www.bds.co.uk
Managers: B. Andrews (Mgr)
Registration no: 04875903 **VAT No.:** GB 450 3463 72
Date established: 1986 **Turnover:** £5m - £10m **No.of Employees:** 1 - 10
Product Groups: 44, 67

Date of Accounts	Mar 12	Mar 11	Mar 10
Working Capital	254	220	157
Fixed Assets	1	1	1
Current Assets	366	387	306

Bang & Olufsen
Unit 110 Wharfedale Road, Winnersh, Wokingham, RG41 5RB
Tel: 0118-969 2288 **Fax:** 0118-969 3388
E-mail: marlow@bang-olufsen.co.uk
Website: http://www.bang-olufsen.co.uk
Directors: L. Flyvhom (MD)
Managers: J. Romme (Fin Mgr), J. Smith, S. Hussain (Mktg Serv Mgr)
Ultimate Holding Company: BANG AND OLUFSEN AS (DENMARK)
Immediate Holding Company: BANG & OLUFSEN U.K. LIMITED
Registration no: 00157371 **Date established:** 2019
Turnover: £20m - £50m **No.of Employees:** 21 - 50 **Product Groups:** 37

Date of Accounts	May 11	May 10	May 09
Sales Turnover	24m	27m	31m
Pre Tax Profit/Loss	812	1m	1m
Working Capital	4m	5m	5m
Fixed Assets	438	429	485
Current Assets	9m	10m	13m
Current Liabilities	810	1m	1m

Banking Automation Ltd
Unit 510 Eskdale Road Winnersh, Wokingham, RG41 5TU
Tel: 0118-969 2224 **Fax:** 0118-944 1191
E-mail: davidtew@bankingautomation.co.uk
Website: http://www.bankingautomation.co.uk
Directors: D. Tew (MD), A. Jeffers (Fin)
Managers: R. Guest (Sales & Mktg Mg), L. Walters (Fin Mgr)
Immediate Holding Company: BANKING AUTOMATION LIMITED
Registration no: 01811448 **Date established:** 1984 **Turnover:** £2m - £5m
No.of Employees: 21 - 50 **Product Groups:** 44

Date of Accounts	Dec 11	Dec 10	Dec 09
Sales Turnover	6m	4m	5m
Pre Tax Profit/Loss	805	-82	395
Working Capital	3m	2m	2m
Fixed Assets	132	38	55
Current Assets	3m	2m	3m
Current Liabilities	418	138	347

Barbaran for all occassions
194a Reading Road, Wokingham, RG41 1LH
Tel: 0118-977 2331
E-mail: info@barbaran.co.uk
Website: http://www.barbaran.co.uk
Directors: B. Campbell (Prop)
Immediate Holding Company: LIBERTY HOME CARE PARTNERSHIP LIMITED
Date established: 2011 **No.of Employees:** 1 - 10 **Product Groups:** 22, 23, 24, 63

Bascomb & Drew Developments Ltd
Keephatch Farmhouse Clover Close, Wokingham, RG40 5PU
Tel: 0118-989 0700 **Fax:** 0118-989 0111
E-mail: enquiries@bascombdrew.com
Website: http://www.bascombdrew.com
Directors: W. Griffith (MD)
Immediate Holding Company: BASCOMB & DREW DEVELOPMENTS LTD.
Registration no: 04645147 **Date established:** 2003 **Turnover:** £1m - £2m
No.of Employees: 1 - 10 **Product Groups:** 52, 84

Benning Power UK Ltd
Oakley House Hogwood Lane Finchampstead, Wokingham, RG40 4QW
Tel: 0118-973 1506 **Fax:** 0118-973 1508
E-mail: info@benninguk.com
Website: http://www.benninguk.com
Bank(s): HSBC Bank plc
Managers: E. Roberts (Cust Serv Mgr)
Ultimate Holding Company: BENNING ELEKTROTECHNIK UND ELEKTRONIK GMBH & CO KG (GER
Immediate Holding Company: BENNING POWER ELECTRONICS (UK) LIMITED
Registration no: 04270344 **Date established:** 2001 **Turnover:** £2m - £5m
No.of Employees: 11 - 20 **Product Groups:** 37

Date of Accounts	Dec 11	Dec 10	Dec 09
Sales Turnover	2m	2m	2m
Pre Tax Profit/Loss	20	124	398
Working Capital	941	893	789
Fixed Assets	350	378	358
Current Assets	1m	1m	888
Current Liabilities	455	309	80

Borer Data Systems Ltd
Crown House Toutley Industrial Estate Toutley Road, Wokingham, RG41 1QN
Tel: 0118-979 1137 **Fax:** 0118-977 3526
E-mail: reception@borer.co.uk
Website: http://www.borer.co.uk
Directors: B. Chapman (MD)
Immediate Holding Company: BORER DATA SYSTEMS LIMITED
Registration no: 01207085 **VAT No.:** GB 200 6599 83
Date established: 1975 **Turnover:** £1m - £2m **No.of Employees:** 1 - 10
Product Groups: 36, 37, 40, 44, 49, 81

Date of Accounts	Dec 11	Dec 10	Dec 09
Working Capital	854	815	1m
Fixed Assets	12	20	26
Current Assets	938	887	1m

Broag Ltd
Remeha House Molly Millars Lane, Wokingham, RG41 2QP
Tel: 0118-978 3434 **Fax:** 0118-978 6977
E-mail: brian@broag-remeha.com
Website: http://www.uk.remeha.com
Directors: B. Price (MD), J. Zwiers (Fin)
Managers: M. Gibbs (Chief Acct), M. McCallum
Ultimate Holding Company: REMEHA BV (NETHERLANDS)
Immediate Holding Company: BROAG LIMITED
Registration no: 00403664 **VAT No.:** GB 218 1342 90
Date established: 1946 **Turnover:** £20m - £50m
No.of Employees: 21 - 50 **Product Groups:** 40

Date of Accounts	Dec 11	Dec 10	Dec 09
Sales Turnover	33m	47m	47m
Pre Tax Profit/Loss	9m	5m	5m
Working Capital	8m	14m	11m
Fixed Assets	764	871	734
Current Assets	17m	21m	17m
Current Liabilities	7m	5m	4m

Cantley House Hotel
Milton Road, Wokingham, RG40 5QG
Tel: 0118-978 9912 **Fax:** 0118-977 4294
E-mail: sales@cantleyhotel.co.uk
Website: http://www.cantleyhotel.co.uk
Bank(s): Barclays
Directors: M. Monk (MD), J. Carey (Co Sec)
Managers: N. Smith, C. Gallacher (Personnel), J. Cary (Chief Mgr)
Registration no: 01327998 **VAT No.:** GB 314 8549 49
Turnover: £1m - £2m **No.of Employees:** 21 - 50 **Product Groups:** 69, 81

Christie Digital Systems
200 Ashville Way, Wokingham, RG41 2PL
Tel: 0118-977 8000 **Fax:** 0118-977 8100
E-mail: sales-europe@christiedigital.com
Website: http://www.christiedigital.com
Directors: B. Eckett (Mkt Research)
Managers: R. Grosier (Fin Mgr), K. Brennan (Sales Admin), D. Miller, B. Eckett (Mktg Serv Mgr), R. Assi (Tech Serv Mgr)
No.of Employees: 21 - 50 **Product Groups:** 37, 38

Cole and Swallow Materials Limited
Fishponds Close, Wokingham, RG41 2QA
Tel: 0118-989 6000 **Fax:** 0118-989 6001
E-mail: info@coleandswallow.com
Website: http://www.coleandswallow.com
Bank(s): Bank of Scotland
Ultimate Holding Company: AR Brown McFarlane & Company Limited
Registration no: 01871458 **VAT No.:** GB 363 3349 53
Date established: 1985 **Turnover:** £2m - £5m **No.of Employees:** 21 - 50
Product Groups: 34, 35, 36, 37, 38, 40, 44

Date of Accounts	Dec 11	Dec 10	Dec 09
Sales Turnover	3m	2m	2m
Pre Tax Profit/Loss	302	-164	118
Working Capital	1m	955	1m
Fixed Assets	225	92	128
Current Assets	2m	1m	2m
Current Liabilities	N/A	152	133

Cox Wokingham Plastics Ltd
Fishponds Road, Wokingham, RG41 2QH
Tel: 0118-977 4861 **Fax:** 0118-977 1708
E-mail: sales@cwpl.net
Website: http://www.cwpl.net
Bank(s): Barclays
Directors: P. Parrick (Fin), C. Dodridge (Sales)
Managers: S. Wilkin, M. Bennett (Projects), L. Burnham (Sales Off Mgr), R. Dawe (Projects)
Immediate Holding Company: COX WOKINGHAM PLASTICS LIMITED
Registration no: 02959737 **VAT No.:** GB 537 1909 32
Date established: 1994 **Turnover:** £5m - £10m **No.of Employees:** 21 - 50
Product Groups: 30, 37, 42, 44, 46, 48, 68

Date of Accounts	Sep 11	Sep 10	Sep 09
Working Capital	558	283	-92
Fixed Assets	583	448	572
Current Assets	2m	1m	657

Emulex Ltd
Trinity Court Molly Millars Lane, Wokingham, RG41 2PY
Tel: 0118-977 2929 **Fax:** 0118-977 3237
E-mail: info@emulex.com
Website: http://www.emulex.com
Bank(s): Barclays
Directors: M. Rockenbach (Fin), A. Sharpe (Sales), J. Phippen (Mkt Research)
Managers: J. Dowsett (Sales Admin)
Immediate Holding Company: EMULEX CORPORATION
Registration no: FC021316 **VAT No.:** GB 362 9375 28
Date established: 1998 **Turnover:** £125m - £250m
No.of Employees: 11 - 20 **Product Groups:** 44

Ensilica
The Barn Waterloo Road, Wokingham, RG40 3BY
Tel: 0118-321 7310 **Fax:** 0118-979 8160
E-mail: info@ensilica.com
Website: http://www.ensilica.com
Directors: I. Lankshear (MD)
Immediate Holding Company: ENSILICA LIMITED
Registration no: 04220106 **Date established:** 2001
No.of Employees: 21 - 50 **Product Groups:** 84

Date of Accounts	May 11	May 10	May 09
Working Capital	428	353	283
Fixed Assets	24	13	13
Current Assets	608	485	445

Michael C Fina Ltd
Fina House Unit 7, The Business Centre, Molly Millars Lane, Wokingham, RG41 2QZ
Tel: 0118-936 7450 **Fax:** 0118-936 7401
E-mail: sales@mcfinaworldwide.com
Website: http://www.longservice.com
Directors: J. Haskell (MD), S. Sheldon (Chief Op Offcr)
Managers: P. Baker (I.T. Exec)
No.of Employees: 11 - 20 **Product Groups:** 22, 23, 24, 25, 28, 30, 33, 37, 49, 65, 81

Fireout Fire Equipment
6 Andrew Close, Wokingham, RG40 2HY
Tel: 0118-978 5010 **Fax:** 0118-989 1276
E-mail: fireout@ntlworld.com
Directors: J. Hawthorne (Co Sec), F. Clark (Prop)
Immediate Holding Company: FERNGLEBE LIMITED
Registration no: 01395422 **Date established:** 1978
No.of Employees: 1 - 10 **Product Groups:** 38, 42

Date of Accounts	Dec 11	Dec 10	Dec 09
Working Capital	14	14	14
Current Assets	28	33	32

Future Tech S C I Ltd
Eastheath House Eastheath Avenue, Wokingham, RG41 2PR
Tel: 08459-000127 **Fax:** 0118-979 5480
E-mail: info@future-tech.co.uk
Website: http://www.future-tech.co.uk
Managers: J. Wilman (Sales & Mktg Mg), M. Conway (Admin Off)
Immediate Holding Company: FUTURE-TECH S.C.I. LIMITED
Registration no: 02567648 **Date established:** 1990
No.of Employees: 11 - 20 **Product Groups:** 37, 40, 44, 52, 67

Date of Accounts	Nov 11	Nov 10	Nov 09
Working Capital	662	559	450
Fixed Assets	62	48	43
Current Assets	2m	2m	2m

Hydro-Lek
Falcon Business Park Ivanhoe Road Hogwood Industrial Estate, Finchampstead, Wokingham, RG40 4QQ
Tel: 0118-973 6903 **Fax:** 0118-973 6915
E-mail: enquiries@hydro-lek.com
Website: http://www.hydro-lek.com
Directors: M. Smith (Fin), C. Lokuciewski (MD)
Immediate Holding Company: HYDRO-LEK LIMITED
Registration no: 03106318 **Date established:** 1995 **Turnover:** £1m - £2m
No.of Employees: 11 - 20 **Product Groups:** 35, 36, 39

Date of Accounts	Sep 11	Sep 10	Sep 09
Working Capital	565	495	412
Fixed Assets	666	688	713
Current Assets	946	819	637

Irvin Brothers Ltd
Fishponds Road, Wokingham, RG41 2QX
Tel: 0118-978 1499 **Fax:** 0118-977 1530
E-mail: paul@padblocks.com
Website: http://www.padblocks.com
Directors: P. Hadden-Wight (Dir)
Immediate Holding Company: IRVIN BROS. (FLEET WORKS) LIMITED
Registration no: 00770190 **VAT No.:** GB 199 1180 36
Date established: 1963 **Turnover:** £500,000 - £1m
No.of Employees: 1 - 10 **Product Groups:** 27, 49

Date of Accounts	Apr 11	Apr 10	Apr 09
Working Capital	160	143	184
Fixed Assets	451	466	477
Current Assets	278	259	307

Jewson Ltd
1 Barkham Road, Wokingham, RG41 2XS
Tel: 0118-978 2058 **Fax:** 0118-977 3853
Website: http://www.jewson.co.uk
Managers: I. Hutchings (District Mgr)
Ultimate Holding Company: COMPAGNIE DE SAINT GOBAIN (FRANCE)
Immediate Holding Company: JEWSON LIMITED
Registration no: 00348407 **VAT No.:** GB 497 7184 33
Date established: 1939 **Turnover:** £500m - £1,000m
No.of Employees: 1 - 10 **Product Groups:** 66

Date of Accounts	Dec 11	Dec 10	Dec 09
Sales Turnover	1606m	1547m	1485m
Pre Tax Profit/Loss	18m	100m	45m
Working Capital	-345m	-250m	-349m
Fixed Assets	496m	387m	461m
Current Assets	657m	1005m	1320m
Current Liabilities	66m	120m	64m

K L A Tencor Ltd
Rosa House 19 Mulberry Business Park Fishponds Road, Wokingham, RG41 2GY
Tel: 0118-936 5700 **Fax:** 0118-936 5701
E-mail: paul.boudre@kla-tencor.com
Website: http://www.kla-tencor.com
Bank(s): Barclays
Directors: P. Boudre (Dir)
Managers: A. Wright (Fin Mgr)
Ultimate Holding Company: KLA TENCOR CORP (USA)
Immediate Holding Company: KLA-TENCOR LIMITED
Registration no: 01560324 **VAT No.:** GB 377 6183 15
Date established: 1981 **Turnover:** £10m - £20m
No.of Employees: 51 - 100 **Product Groups:** 37, 38

Date of Accounts	Jun 11	Jun 10	Jun 09
Sales Turnover	43m	36m	33m
Pre Tax Profit/Loss	2m	-734	3m
Working Capital	17m	16m	17m
Fixed Assets	2m	2m	2m
Current Assets	21m	21m	21m
Current Liabilities	1m	2m	2m

Kronos Systems Ltd
Kronos House 2 Carey Road, Wokingham, RG40 2NP
Tel: 0118-978 9784 **Fax:** 0118-978 2214
E-mail: ukinfo@kronos.com
Website: http://www.kronos.co.uk
Directors: D. Ghysles (Fin), T. Bisley (MD)
Managers: D. Brettenny (Tech Serv Mgr)
Ultimate Holding Company: KRONOS INC (USA)
Immediate Holding Company: KRONOS SYSTEMS LIMITED
Registration no: 02528089 **Date established:** 1990
Turnover: £10m - £20m **No.of Employees:** 51 - 100 **Product Groups:** 44, 49, 65, 83

Date of Accounts	Sep 11	Sep 10	Sep 09
Sales Turnover	14m	15m	16m
Pre Tax Profit/Loss	336	329	441
Working Capital	-2m	4m	4m
Fixed Assets	7m	69	93
Current Assets	5m	11m	12m
Current Liabilities	7m	6m	6m

Lee Spring Ltd
Latimer Road, Wokingham, RG41 2WA
Tel: 0118-978 1800 **Fax:** 0118-977 4832
E-mail: sales@leespring.co.uk
Website: http://www.leespring.co.uk
Bank(s): National Westminster Bank Plc
Directors: A. Mangels (Ch), B. Kemper (Dir), M. Johnston (MD), T. Scheinman (Dir)
Ultimate Holding Company: UTILITIES & INDUSTRIES MANAGEMENT CORP (USA)
Immediate Holding Company: Lee Spring Co.
Registration no: 01355982 **VAT No.:** GB 438 2251 58
Date established: 1978 **Turnover:** £2m - £5m **No.of Employees:** 11 - 20
Product Groups: 35, 66

Date of Accounts	Dec 09	Dec 08	Dec 07
Sales Turnover	N/A	2m	2m
Pre Tax Profit/Loss	N/A	281	298
Working Capital	688	771	765
Fixed Assets	16	21	27
Current Assets	833	982	937
Current Liabilities	N/A	57	72

Lodge Dental Laboratory
Unit 10 Station Industrial Estate Oxford Road, Wokingham, RG41 2YQ
Tel: 0118-989 0202 **Fax:** 0118-989 2009
E-mail: info@lodgedentallab.com
Directors: D. Turner (MD)
Immediate Holding Company: LODGE DENTAL LABORATORY LIMITED
Registration no: 04186110 **Date established:** 2001
No.of Employees: 1 - 10 **Product Groups:** 38, 67, 88

Date of Accounts	Mar 11	Mar 10	Mar 09
Working Capital	276	273	263
Fixed Assets	49	66	81
Current Assets	407	401	421

Duncan Lynch Precision Tools Ltd
Unit E Weller Drive Finchampstead, Wokingham, RG40 4QZ
Tel: 0118-973 4845 **Fax:** 0118-973 0381
E-mail: sales@duncan-lynch.co.uk
Website: http://www.duncan-lynch.co.uk
Bank(s): HSBC, Crowthorne
Directors: A. Lynch (Fin), A. Lynch (MD)
Immediate Holding Company: DUNCAN-LYNCH PRECISION TOOLS LIMITED
Registration no: 00694677 **VAT No.:** GB 199 0147 39
Date established: 1961 **Turnover:** £2m - £5m **No.of Employees:** 11 - 20
Product Groups: 35, 38, 46, 47, 48

Date of Accounts	Jun 11	Jun 10	Jun 09
Working Capital	-96	-26	41
Fixed Assets	1m	866	901
Current Assets	971	762	619

M B Technology
Benfieldside Milton Road, Wokingham, RG40 1DD
Tel: 0118-977 6039 **Fax:** 0118-978 9386
Directors: P. Baller (Prop)
No.of Employees: 1 - 10 **Product Groups:** 37, 38, 47, 67

Maxim Integrated Products UK Ltd
612 Reading Road Winnersh, Wokingham, RG41 5HE
Tel: 0118-900 6300 **Fax:** 0118-900 6400
E-mail: sales@maxim-ic.com
Website: http://www.maxim-ic.com
Directors: C. Brown (MD), G. Walls (Sales)
Managers: G. Bergman (I.T. Exec), B. Williams (Purch Mgr)
Ultimate Holding Company: MAXIM INTEGRATED PRODUCTS INC (USA)
Immediate Holding Company: MAXIM INTEGRATED PRODUCTS UK LIMITED
Registration no: 01873931 **Date established:** 1984
No.of Employees: 1 - 10 **Product Groups:** 37

maxon motor uk ltd
Hogwood Lane Finchampstead, Wokingham, RG40 4QW
Tel: 0118-973 3337 **Fax:** 0118-973 7472
E-mail: salesuk@maxonmotor.com
Website: http://www.maxonmotor.co.uk
Directors: W. Mason (Sales), P. Wellman (Purch)
Managers: K. Ellenden, K. Whittaker
Immediate Holding Company: MAXON MOTOR UK LTD
Registration no: 03745727 **Date established:** 1999 **Turnover:** £5m - £10m
No.of Employees: 11 - 20 **Product Groups:** 35, 37, 38, 39

Date of Accounts	Dec 11	Dec 10	Dec 09
Sales Turnover	11m	10m	7m
Pre Tax Profit/Loss	2m	2m	1m
Working Capital	3m	2m	2m
Fixed Assets	710	788	815
Current Assets	4m	4m	3m
Current Liabilities	767	568	387

Metrum Information Storage Ltd
Barkham Ride Finchampstead, Wokingham, RG40 4EU
Tel: 0118-973 3000 **Fax:** 0118-973 4363
E-mail: enquiries@metrum.co.uk
Website: http://www.metrum.co.uk
Directors: C. Beeton (MD)
Immediate Holding Company: METRUM INFORMATION STORAGE LIMITED
Registration no: 02648290 **VAT No.:** GB 584 4081 28
Date established: 1991 **Turnover:** £1m - £2m **No.of Employees:** 1 - 10
Product Groups: 27, 37, 38

Date of Accounts	Dec 11	Dec 10	Dec 09
Working Capital	-236	-202	-190
Fixed Assets	400	457	472
Current Assets	669	650	657

Mitime Office Refurbishment & Design
12 Tanglewood Finchampstead, Wokingham, RG40 3PR
Tel: 0118-932 8235
E-mail: info@mitimedesign.co.uk
Website: http://www.mitimedesign.co.uk
Directors: S. Crossman (Dir)
Turnover: Up to £250,000 **No.of Employees:** 1 - 10 **Product Groups:** 23, 26, 30, 52, 66

MODCOMP Ltd (Modular Computer Services Inc)
12a Oaklands Business Centre Oaklands Park, Wokingham, RG41 2FD
Tel: 0118-989 3843 **Fax:** 0118-989 3847
E-mail: kevin.magee@modcomp.co.uk
Website: http://www.modcomp.co.uk
Bank(s): Barclays
Directors: K. Magee (MD)
Ultimate Holding Company: CSP Inc
Immediate Holding Company: Modcomp Inc
Registration no: 03853020 **VAT No.:** GB 212 7456 81
Turnover: £2m - £5m **No.of Employees:** 11 - 20 **Product Groups:** 44

Date of Accounts	Sep 11	Sep 10	Sep 09
Sales Turnover	1m	N/A	N/A
Pre Tax Profit/Loss	59	N/A	N/A
Working Capital	2m	2m	2m
Fixed Assets	6m	6m	6m
Current Assets	2m	2m	3m
Current Liabilities	136	N/A	N/A

Morpho Cards UK Ltd

250 Wharfedale Road Winnersh, Wokingham, RG41 5TP
Tel: 0118-377 6000 **Fax:** 0118-377 6001
E-mail: info-uk@morpho.com
Website: http://www.morpho.com
Bank(s): Barclays
Directors: P. Alexander (Co Sec), S. Stewart (MD)
Ultimate Holding Company: SAFRAN SA (FRANCE)
Immediate Holding Company: MORPHO CARDS UK LIMITED
Registration no: 02586027 **VAT No.:** GB 538 1643 38
Date established: 1991 **Turnover:** £10m - £20m
No.of Employees: 11 - 20 **Product Groups:** 28, 37, 40

Date of Accounts	Dec 11	Dec 10	Dec 09
Sales Turnover	16m	15m	17m
Pre Tax Profit/Loss	470	250	806
Working Capital	2m	2m	2m
Fixed Assets	68	76	91
Current Assets	4m	4m	7m
Current Liabilities	881	698	1m

Ovenu

Unit 3 Station Industrial Estate Oxford Road, Wokingham, RG41 2YQ
Tel: 0800-975 6976 **Fax:** 0118-973 1876
E-mail: rik.ovenu@btconnect.com
Website: http://www.ovenu.co.uk
Directors: R. Hellewell (MD)
No.of Employees: 1 - 10 **Product Groups:** 32, 44, 52

Overland Storage Europe Ltd

Overland House 3 Ashville Way, Wokingham, RG41 2PL
Tel: 0118-989 8000 **Fax:** 0118-989 1897
E-mail: sales@overlandstorage.com
Website: http://www.overlandstorage.com
Bank(s): National Westminster Bank Plc
Directors: S. Rayner (Dir)
Managers: I. Sharpe (Tech Serv Mgr)
Ultimate Holding Company: OVERLAND STORAGE INC (USA)
Immediate Holding Company: OVERLAND STORAGE (EUROPE) LTD.
Registration no: 02760631 **Date established:** 1992 **Turnover:** £5m - £10m
No.of Employees: 21 - 50 **Product Groups:** 44

Date of Accounts	Jun 08	Jun 09	Jun 10
Sales Turnover	8m	8m	6m
Pre Tax Profit/Loss	119	307	109
Working Capital	952	1m	1m
Fixed Assets	50	91	39
Current Assets	3m	3m	3m
Current Liabilities	597	589	566

PACK Innovation Ltd

Unit 12, Sunfield Business Park New Mill Road, WOKINGHAM, RG40 4QT
Tel: 05603-449162 **Fax:** 05603-449163
E-mail: info@packinnovation.com
Website: http://www.packinnovation.com
Managers: E. Jones (Sales Prom Mgr)
Date established: 2010 **Turnover:** **No.of Employees:** 1 - 10
Product Groups: 20, 27, 30, 32, 41, 42, 48, 62

Padblocks Ltd

Fishponds Road, Wokingham, RG41 2QX
Tel: 0118-978 1499 **Fax:** 0118-977 1530
E-mail: info@padblocks.com
Website: http://www.padblocks.com
Directors: J. Hadden-Wight (MD)
Immediate Holding Company: Irvin Bros. (Fleet Works) Ltd
Registration no: 01346608 **VAT No.:** GB 199 1180 36
Date established: 1904 **Turnover:** £250,000 - £500,000
No.of Employees: 1 - 10 **Product Groups:** 27, 44

Precise Fastenings & Supplies Ltd

Ivanhoe Road Hogwood Lane Industrial Set Finchampstead, Wokingham, RG40 4QQ
Tel: 0118-932 8832 **Fax:** 0118-932 8519
E-mail: precisefastenings@fixings.fsworld.co.uk
Website: http://www.express-cleaning-supplies.co.uk
Directors: A. Williams (Dir)
Immediate Holding Company: PRECISE FASTENINGS & SUPPLIES LIMITED
Registration no: 02147950 **VAT No.:** GB 442 6755 39
Date established: 1987 **Turnover:** £500,000 - £1m
No.of Employees: 1 - 10 **Product Groups:** 30, 32, 33, 35, 36, 37, 40, 66

Date of Accounts	Jun 11	Jun 10	Jun 09
Working Capital	111	134	126
Fixed Assets	1	4	7
Current Assets	177	205	182

Printronix UK Ltd

Unit 3 Millars Brook Molly Millars Lane, Wokingham, RG41 2AD
Tel: 0118-977 1000 **Fax:** 01344-360967
Website: http://www.printronix.com
Directors: M. Bruens (MD)
Ultimate Holding Company: VECTOR CAPITAL
Immediate Holding Company: PRINTRONIX UK LIMITED
Registration no: 03777091 **VAT No.:** GB 636 1063 60
Date established: 1999 **Turnover:** £5m - £10m **No.of Employees:** 1 - 10
Product Groups: 44

Date of Accounts	Mar 11	Mar 10	Mar 09
Working Capital	398	401	390
Fixed Assets	23	32	26
Current Assets	532	579	472

Prisym ld

Tech House Oaklands Business Centre Oaklands Park, Wokingham, RG41 2FD
Tel: 0118-936 4400 **Fax:** 0118-936 4499
E-mail: info@prisymid.com
Website: http://www.prisymid.com
Directors: B. Cooper (Fin), L. Darby (Co Sec), M. Daw (Prop)
Managers: H. Purchase (Mktg Serv Mgr), C. Jones
Immediate Holding Company: PRISYMID LIMITED
Registration no: 05004963 **Date established:** 2003 **Turnover:** £2m - £5m
No.of Employees: 21 - 50 **Product Groups:** 27, 28, 30, 37, 38, 42, 43, 44, 48, 49, 64, 67, 76, 81

Date of Accounts	Mar 12	Mar 11	Mar 10
Sales Turnover	6m	4m	3m
Pre Tax Profit/Loss	444	314	306
Working Capital	892	593	496
Fixed Assets	763	765	640
Current Assets	3m	2m	2m
Current Liabilities	1m	522	618

Quin Systems Ltd

Oaklands Business Centre Oaklands Park, Wokingham, RG41 2FD
Tel: 0118-977 1077 **Fax:** 0118-977 6728
E-mail: info@quin.co.uk
Website: http://www.quin.co.uk
Bank(s): HSBC Bank plc
Directors: M. Webb (MD)
Ultimate Holding Company: SILVER FREEZE LIMITED
Immediate Holding Company: QUIN SYSTEMS LIMITED
Registration no: 01782394 **VAT No.:** GB 362 9813 30
Date established: 1984 **Turnover:** £2m - £5m **No.of Employees:** 21 - 50
Product Groups: 37, 38, 44, 45, 84

Date of Accounts	Mar 11	Mar 10	Mar 09
Working Capital	835	752	880
Fixed Assets	12	33	36
Current Assets	1m	1m	1m

Radyne

Molly Millars Lane, Wokingham, RG41 2PX
Tel: 0118-978 3033 **Fax:** 0118-977 1729
E-mail: info@radyne.co.uk
Website: http://www.radyne.co.uk
Directors: D. Oxbrough (Dir), P. Robinson (Co Sec)
Managers: J. Beasham (Purch Mgr), P. Pell (I.T. Exec), S. Baskerville (Chief Mgr)
Immediate Holding Company: LINKLAN LIMITED
Registration no: 06398079 **Date established:** 1999
No.of Employees: 51 - 100 **Product Groups:** 40, 42, 46

Rapid Hire Centres Ltd

34 Oxford Road, Wokingham, RG41 2XZ
Tel: 0118-977 6217 **Fax:** 0118-977 6218
E-mail: kaydmoss@hotmail.com
Directors: K. Moss (MD)
Immediate Holding Company: RAPID HIRE CENTRES (UK) LIMITED
Registration no: 07459118 **Date established:** 2010
Turnover: £250,000 - £500,000 **No.of Employees:** 1 - 10
Product Groups: 45, 46, 83

Date of Accounts	Feb 12
Sales Turnover	179
Pre Tax Profit/Loss	35
Working Capital	13
Fixed Assets	124
Current Assets	29
Current Liabilities	16

Recital Corporation Ltd

Seymour House The Courtyard Denmark Street, Wokingham, RG40 2AZ
Tel: 0118-978 3888
E-mail: sales@recitalsoftware.com
Website: http://www.recitalsoftware.com
Directors: B. Mavin (Co Sec), C. Mavin (Dir)
Immediate Holding Company: RECITAL CORPORATION LIMITED
Registration no: 02232282 **Date established:** 1988 **Turnover:** £5m - £10m
No.of Employees: 1 - 10 **Product Groups:** 44, 81

Date of Accounts	Dec 11	Dec 10	Dec 09
Working Capital	-3m	-3m	-2m
Fixed Assets	24	24	23
Current Assets	540	529	524

Rodnic Ltd

Unit 3 Metro Centre Toutley Road, Wokingham, RG41 1QW
Tel: 0118-977 2199 **Fax:** 0118-977 3005
E-mail: info@rodnic.co.uk
Website: http://www.rodnic.co.uk
Directors: S. Rodger (Dir), S. Rodger (Co Sec)
Immediate Holding Company: RODNIC LTD
Registration no: 07238795 **Date established:** 2010
Turnover: £500,000 - £1m **No.of Employees:** 1 - 10 **Product Groups:** 35, 52

Date of Accounts	Apr 11
Working Capital	6
Current Assets	12

Safe Albums UK Ltd

16 Falcon Business Park Hogwood Lane Industrial Estate, Finchampstead, Wokingham, RG40 4QQ
Tel: 0118-932 8976 **Fax:** 0118-932 8612
E-mail: info@safealbums.co.uk
Website: http://www.safealbums.co.uk
Managers: J. Carter (Sales Prom Mgr)
Immediate Holding Company: SAFE ALBUMS (U.K.) LIMITED
Registration no: 01543445 **VAT No.:** GB 314 7423 76
Date established: 1981 **Turnover:** £2m - £5m **No.of Employees:** 1 - 10
Product Groups: 22, 28

Date of Accounts	Jun 12	Jun 11	Jun 10
Working Capital	423	412	355
Fixed Assets	7	8	11
Current Assets	616	794	651

Schaffner Ltd

Ashville Way Molly Millers Lane, Wokingham, RG41 2PL
Tel: 0118-977 0070 **Fax:** 0118-979 2969
E-mail: paul.dixon@schaffner.com
Website: http://www.schaffner.com
Directors: P. Dixon (Dir), I. Lachowicz (Co Sec), P. Dixon (MD)
Managers: M. De Brion (Sales Prom Mgr), F. Gantert
Ultimate Holding Company: SCHAFFNER HOLDING AG (SWITZERLAND)
Immediate Holding Company: SCHAFFNER LIMITED
Registration no: 01817704 **VAT No.:** GB 363 1086 69
Date established: 1984 **Turnover:** £2m - £5m **No.of Employees:** 1 - 10
Product Groups: 37, 38, 85

Date of Accounts	Sep 10	Sep 09	Sep 08
Sales Turnover	N/A	4m	4m
Pre Tax Profit/Loss	N/A	87	-60
Working Capital	-0	-209	-323
Fixed Assets	2	6	12
Current Assets	1m	2m	2m
Current Liabilities	N/A	209	553

Shilcock Education Advisory Service Ltd (SEAS)

44 Mercury Avenue, WOKINGHAM, RG41 3GA
Tel: 0118-962 9576 **Fax:** 0118-962 9021
E-mail: jill@seasuk.com
Website: http://www.seasuk.com
Directors: J. Shilcock (MD)
Immediate Holding Company: SHILCOCK EDUCATION ADVISORY SERVICE LIMITED
Registration no: 05007336 **Date established:** 2004
Turnover: Up to £250,000 **No.of Employees:** 1 - 10 **Product Groups:** 86

Date of Accounts	Mar 11	Mar 10	Mar 08
Working Capital	-50	-48	-44
Fixed Assets	N/A	N/A	1
Current Assets	N/A	1	1

Simpson Springs & Pressings Ltd

Unit 1 Latimer Road Industrial Estate, Latimer Road, Wokingham, RG41 2YD
Tel: 0118-978 6573 **Fax:** 0118-989 4434
E-mail: simpson.springs@btinternet.com
Website: http://www.simpsonsprings.co.uk
Bank(s): Lloyds TSB Bank plc
Directors: D. Simpson (MD)
Managers: J. Goring (Sales Prom Mgr), J. Liddiard (Accounts)
Registration no: 01493544 **VAT No.:** GB 314 5584 62
Turnover: £500,000 - £1m **No.of Employees:** 21 - 50
Product Groups: 34, 35, 36, 38, 39, 40, 43, 48, 49, 66, 68, 85

Date of Accounts	Apr 11	Apr 10	Apr 09
Working Capital	287	284	253
Fixed Assets	23	17	33
Current Assets	470	470	449

Snacktime plc

West Forest Gate Wellington Road, Wokingham, RG40 2AQ
Tel: 0118-977 3344 **Fax:** 01789-766161
E-mail: sales@snacktime.com
Website: http://www.snacktime.com
Directors: J. Brand (Co Sec)
Managers: B. Jenkins, S. Rutter, A. Rike (Personnel), H. Taylor (Mktg Serv Mgr)
Ultimate Holding Company: SNACKTIME PLC
Immediate Holding Company: SNACKTIME UK LIMITED
Registration no: 04284338 **Date established:** 2001 **Turnover:** £2m - £5m
No.of Employees: 1 - 10 **Product Groups:** 49

Date of Accounts	Mar 11	Mar 10	Mar 09
Sales Turnover	4m	7m	7m
Pre Tax Profit/Loss	-1m	-558	202
Working Capital	-5m	-3m	-2m
Fixed Assets	7m	5m	5m
Current Assets	1m	6m	3m
Current Liabilities	134	1m	146

Symbol Technologies Ltd

Symbol Place Wharfedale Road, Winnersh, Wokingham, RG41 5TP
Tel: 0118-945 7529 **Fax:** 0118-945 7500
Website: http://www.motorola.com
Bank(s): Barclays
Directors: G. Hobbs (Dir), J. Pears (Sales & Mktg), S. Hughes (Co Sec)
Managers: J. Coon (Sales Prom Mgr)
Immediate Holding Company: Symbol Technologies UK Ltd
Registration no: 01096253 **Turnover:** £20m - £50m
No.of Employees: 101 - 250 **Product Groups:** 37, 44, 67

Date of Accounts	Dec 07	Dec 06	Dec 05
Sales Turnover	51513	42523	56814
Pre Tax Profit/Loss	3000	1340	2046
Working Capital	31292	29484	26447
Fixed Assets	128	975	1569
Current Assets	53473	39229	34603
Current Liabilities	22180	9745	8157
Total Share Capital	1028	1028	1028
ROCE% (Return on Capital Employed)	9.5	4.4	7.3
ROT% (Return on Turnover)	5.8	3.2	3.6

Target Fastenings Ltd

Unit 5-6 Pinecopse Industrial Estate Nine Mile Ride, Wokingham, RG40 3ND
Tel: 01344-777189 **Fax:** 01344-779038
E-mail: sales@targetfastenings.com
Website: http://www.targetfastenings.com
Directors: W. Winson (Fin)
Ultimate Holding Company: TARGET GROUP HOLDINGS LIMITED
Immediate Holding Company: TARGET FASTENINGS LIMITED
Registration no: 02009921 **VAT No.:** GB 689 0446 93
Date established: 1986 **Turnover:** £1m - £2m **No.of Employees:** 1 - 10
Product Groups: 35, 66, 84

Date of Accounts	Jun 12	Jun 11	Jun 10
Working Capital	149	135	160
Fixed Assets	5	2	3
Current Assets	221	285	347

Technical Elevator Services Ltd

Unit 6 Forest Court Oaklands Park, Wokingham, RG41 2FD
Tel: 0118-979 8880 **Fax:** 0115-979 7278
E-mail: sales@tesmail.co.uk
Website: http://www.tes-elevators.com
Directors: P. Strickland (MD)
Immediate Holding Company: TECHNICAL ELEVATOR SERVICES LIMITED
Registration no: 03970053 **Date established:** 2000
No.of Employees: 11 - 20 **Product Groups:** 35, 39, 45

Date of Accounts	Apr 11	Apr 10	Apr 09
Working Capital	-136	402	-21
Fixed Assets	40	47	57
Current Assets	1m	939	595

Temperature Technology Ltd

Kestrel Buildings Ivanhoe Road Hogwood Industrial Estate, Finchampstead, Wokingham, RG40 4QQ
Tel: 0118-973 0739 **Fax:** 0118-973 7222
E-mail: sales@temperaturetechnology.com
Website: http://www.temperaturetechnology.com
Managers: B. Stone
Immediate Holding Company: TEMPERATURE TECHNOLOGY LIMITED
Registration no: 03546705 **VAT No.:** GB 781 3281 27
Date established: 1998 **Turnover:** £1m - £2m **No.of Employees:** 1 - 10
Product Groups: 36, 37, 38

Date of Accounts	Sep 11	Sep 10	Sep 09
Working Capital	1m	911	870
Fixed Assets	3	9	17
Current Assets	2m	1m	1m

Terra Mould

Barkham Grange Barkham Street, Barkham, Wokingham, RG40 4PJ
Tel: 0118-976 1040 **Fax:** 0118-976 1040
Directors: S. Armstrong (Prop), S. Armstrong (MD)
Immediate Holding Company: RAH INVESTMENTS LIMITED
Registration no: 00844370 **Date established:** 1988
No.of Employees: 1 - 10 **Product Groups:** 30, 31, 33, 44, 48

Date of Accounts	Jun 11	Jun 10	Jun 09
Working Capital	50	46	50
Fixed Assets	999	408	402
Current Assets	105	89	89

Trident Engineering Ltd

2 King Street Lane Winnersh, Wokingham, RG41 5AS
Tel: 0118-978 6444 **Fax:** 0118-977 6345
E-mail: n-oldland@tridenteng.co.uk
Website: http://www.tridenteng.co.uk
Directors: N. Oldland (Sales), G. Oldland (Fin)
Immediate Holding Company: TRIDENT ENGINEERING LIMITED
Registration no: 00926893 **Date established:** 1968 **Turnover:** £2m - £5m
No.of Employees: 1 - 10 **Product Groups:** 37, 38, 40

Date of Accounts	Dec 11	Dec 10	Dec 09
Working Capital	196	275	201
Fixed Assets	931	922	943
Current Assets	688	798	825
Current Liabilities	N/A	N/A	122

Turbo Tools & Engineering

Unit 10 Marino Way Finchampstead, Wokingham, RG40 4RF
Tel: 0118-973 4900
Directors: A. Lynch (Prop)
Immediate Holding Company: Duncan-Lynch Precision Tools Ltd
Registration no: 05969846 **Date established:** 2006
No.of Employees: 1 - 10 **Product Groups:** 35, 84

Ventura Corporation

Unit 1 Chancerygate Business Centre Molly Millars Lane, Wokingham, RG41 2RF
Tel: 0118-977 2032 **Fax:** 0118-989 1490
E-mail: info@venturacorporation.co.uk
Website: http://www.venturacorporation.co.uk
Directors: A. Parsons (MD)
Immediate Holding Company: VENTURA CORPORATION LIMITED
Registration no: 01936846 **Date established:** 1985 **Turnover:** £5m - £10m
No.of Employees: 1 - 10 **Product Groups:** 49, 63

Date of Accounts	Mar 12	Mar 11	Mar 10
Sales Turnover	9m	7m	6m
Pre Tax Profit/Loss	606	94	-474
Working Capital	2m	2m	1m
Fixed Assets	82	27	46
Current Assets	3m	4m	4m
Current Liabilities	334	305	74

Vernalis plc

Oakdene Court 613 Reading Road, Winnersh, Wokingham, RG41 5UA
Tel: 0118-977 3133 **Fax:** 0118-989 9300
E-mail: admin@vernalis.com
Website: http://www.vernalis.com
Directors: E. Goldstien (Grp Chief Exec), C. Hampson (Ch)
Immediate Holding Company: VERNALIS PLC
Registration no: 02304992 **Date established:** 1988
Turnover: £10m - £20m **No.of Employees:** 11 - 20 **Product Groups:** 85

Date of Accounts	Dec 11	Dec 10	Dec 09
Sales Turnover	12m	14m	13m
Pre Tax Profit/Loss	-11m	-22m	-14m
Working Capital	27m	32m	26m
Fixed Assets	4m	6m	16m
Current Assets	32m	38m	33m
Current Liabilities	6m	5m	7m

Vysionics

Unit 3 Fishponds Close, Wokingham, RG41 2QA
Tel: 0118-979 2077 **Fax:** 0118-977 4734
E-mail: kevin.chevis@vysionics.com
Website: http://www.vysionics.com
Bank(s): Bank of Scotland, The Mound, Edinburgh
Managers: K. Chevis
Ultimate Holding Company: VYSIONICS ITS LIMITED
Immediate Holding Company: COMPUTER RECOGNITION SYSTEMS LIMITED
Registration no: 01558786 **VAT No.:** GB 314 8208 75
Date established: 1981 **Turnover:** £1m - £2m **No.of Employees:** 11 - 20
Product Groups: 38, 39, 44

Date of Accounts	Dec 11	Dec 10	Sep 09
Sales Turnover	N/A	2m	N/A
Pre Tax Profit/Loss	N/A	-274	N/A
Working Capital	511	511	2m
Fixed Assets	N/A	N/A	65
Current Assets	511	511	4m

BUCKINGHAMSHIRE

Incorporating **Milton Keynes**

Amersham

Atomisation Ltd
3 Chancellors Penn Street, Amersham, HP7 0QN
Tel: 01494-717138 **Fax:** 01494-717138
E-mail: atomisationltd@aol.com
Directors: G. Bilbey (MD)
Immediate Holding Company: ATOMISATION LIMITED
Registration no: 04880129 **Date established:** 2003
No.of Employees: 1 - 10 **Product Groups:** 38, 42

Date of Accounts	Mar 12	Mar 11	Mar 10
Working Capital	6	-1	-1
Fixed Assets	1	1	1
Current Assets	20	19	14

Frederick Beesley
132 White Lion Road, Amersham, HP7 9NQ
Tel: 01494-762370 **Fax:** 01494-765396
E-mail: sales@frederickbeesley.org
Website: http://www.frederickbeesley.org
Directors: B. Buller (Dir)
Immediate Holding Company: CHUBBS LIMITED
Registration no: 00588782 **Date established:** 1957
No.of Employees: 1 - 10 **Product Groups:** 36, 39, 40

Date of Accounts	Jan 12	Jan 11	Jan 09
Working Capital	63	87	132
Fixed Assets	1	1	1
Current Assets	143	149	162
Current Liabilities	50	N/A	N/A

British Vehicle Rental & Leasing Association
River Lodge Badminton Court Church Street, Amersham, HP7 0DD
Tel: 01494-434747 **Fax:** 01494-434499
E-mail: info@bvrla.co.uk
Website: http://www.bvrla.co.uk
Bank(s): Barclays
Managers: J. Lewis
Ultimate Holding Company: BRITISH VEHICLE RENTAL AND LEASING ASSOCIATION LIMITED
Immediate Holding Company: BRITISH VEHICLE RENTAL AND LEASING ASSOCIATION LIMITED
Registration no: 00924401 **VAT No.:** GB 208 7159 58
Date established: 1967 **Turnover:** £1m - £2m **No.of Employees:** 11 - 20
Product Groups: 87

Date of Accounts	Dec 11	Dec 10	Dec 09
Sales Turnover	1m	1m	1m
Pre Tax Profit/Loss	162	136	79
Working Capital	2m	2m	2m
Fixed Assets	372	372	378
Current Assets	2m	2m	2m
Current Liabilities	369	355	254

Foodnet Ltd
The Old Grammar School 3-7 Market Square, Amersham, HP7 0DF
Tel: 01494-434600 **Fax:** 01494-434435
E-mail: info@foodnet.ltd.uk
Website: http://www.foodnet.ltd.uk
Directors: R. Owen (MD), R. Owen (Dir)
Managers: S. Castle
Ultimate Holding Company: FOODNET HOLDINGS LIMITED
Immediate Holding Company: FOODNET LIMITED
Registration no: 02509681 **VAT No.:** GB 568 7861 74
Date established: 1990 **Turnover:** £20m - £50m **No.of Employees:** 1 - 10
Product Groups: 61

Date of Accounts	Apr 11	Apr 10	Apr 09
Sales Turnover	20m	17m	19m
Pre Tax Profit/Loss	125	315	-23
Working Capital	1m	1m	1m
Fixed Assets	42	41	48
Current Assets	5m	4m	4m
Current Liabilities	486	390	807

G E Healthcare
Amersham Place, Amersham, HP7 9NA
Tel: 01494-544000 **Fax:** 01494-542266
Website: http://www.amersham.com
Bank(s): Deutsche Bank, Citi Bank, Chase Manhattan Bank
Directors: J. Dineen (Grp Chief Exec)
Ultimate Holding Company: GENERAL ELECTRIC COMPANY (USA)
Immediate Holding Company: GE HEALTHCARE UK LIMITED
Registration no: 03337033 **VAT No.:** GB 669 3188 88
Date established: 1997 **Turnover:** £50m - £75m
No.of Employees: 1501 & over **Product Groups:** 32, 37, 66

Date of Accounts	Dec 11	Dec 10	Dec 09
Sales Turnover	61m	124m	106m
Pre Tax Profit/Loss	-49m	-967	11m
Working Capital	-38m	-33m	-32m
Fixed Assets	1638m	13m	9m
Current Assets	25m	22m	56m
Current Liabilities	13m	11m	13m

Kavo Dental Ltd
Corinium Industrial Estate Raans Road, Amersham, HP6 6JL
Tel: 01494-733000 **Fax:** 01494-431168
E-mail: sales@kavo.com
Website: http://www.kavo.com
Managers: S. Tipping (Mktg Serv Mgr)
Ultimate Holding Company: DANAHER CORPORATION (DELAWARE U.S.A)
Immediate Holding Company: KAVO DENTAL LIMITED
Registration no: 00969297 **VAT No.:** GB 207 5366 69
Date established: 1969 **Turnover:** £5m - £10m **No.of Employees:** 21 - 50
Product Groups: 38, 67

Date of Accounts	Dec 11	Dec 10	Dec 09
Sales Turnover	9m	14m	18m
Pre Tax Profit/Loss	226	722	708
Working Capital	8m	8m	7m
Fixed Assets	759	793	839
Current Assets	9m	9m	8m
Current Liabilities	680	537	719

Misbourne Valley Fixings
Willowbank London Road East, Amersham, HP7 9DT
Tel: 01494-764264 **Fax:** 01494-764264
Directors: B. Ringham (Prop)
Date established: 1992 **No.of Employees:** 1 - 10 **Product Groups:** 35

Purcon Consultants Ltd
Prospect House Repton Place, Amersham, HP7 9LP
Tel: 01494-737300 **Fax:** 01494-737333
E-mail: aenglish@purcon.com
Website: http://www.purcon.com
Directors: T. English (Dir)
Ultimate Holding Company: OXINIA LIMITED
Immediate Holding Company: KINGSFIELD RECRUITMENT LIMITED
Registration no: 01384214 **Date established:** 1978 **Turnover:** £5m - £10m
No.of Employees: 21 - 50 **Product Groups:** 80

Date of Accounts	Dec 10	Dec 09	Dec 08
Sales Turnover	8m	9m	15m
Pre Tax Profit/Loss	-463	-520	202
Working Capital	407	846	1m
Fixed Assets	32	65	237
Current Assets	2m	3m	3m
Current Liabilities	2m	1m	2m

Redefining Financial Solutions Ltd
9 Hardwicke Gardens, Amersham, HP6 6AH
Tel: 01494-431739
E-mail: barry.scott@redefiningfinancialsolutions.com
Website: http://www.redefiningfinancialsolutions.com
Directors: B. Scott (MD)
Registration no: 04734467 **Date established:** 2003
No.of Employees: 1 - 10 **Product Groups:** 80, 86

Roset UK Ltd
Overcroft House Badminton Court Church Street, Amersham, HP7 0DD
Tel: 01494-545910 **Fax:** 01494-545911
E-mail: info@ligne-roset.co.uk
Website: http://www.ligne-roset.co.uk
Managers: B. Allard
Ultimate Holding Company: ROSET SA (FRANCE)
Immediate Holding Company: ROSET (UK) LIMITED
Registration no: 01483337 **Date established:** 1980 **Turnover:** £5m - £10m
No.of Employees: 1 - 10 **Product Groups:** 23, 24, 26, 36, 48, 52, 61, 63, 65, 84

Date of Accounts	Sep 11	Sep 10	Sep 09
Sales Turnover	6m	7m	6m
Pre Tax Profit/Loss	-181	92	3
Working Capital	44	192	120
Fixed Assets	98	100	111
Current Assets	2m	2m	2m
Current Liabilities	325	473	210

Saleplane Ltd
1 The Willows Chesham Bois, Amersham, HP6 5NT
Tel: 0870-143 0430 **Fax:** 0870-143 0431
E-mail: aftermail@saleplane.com
Website: http://www.saleplane.com
Directors: M. Hart (Dir)
Immediate Holding Company: VORTALUS LIMITED
Registration no: 04735462 **Date established:** 2003
No.of Employees: 1 - 10 **Product Groups:** 44

Date of Accounts	Apr 11	Apr 09	Apr 08
Sales Turnover	N/A	N/A	21
Pre Tax Profit/Loss	N/A	N/A	-4
Working Capital	-39	-33	-32
Current Assets	3	5	8

Securon Amersham Ltd
Winchmore Hill, Amersham, HP7 0NZ
Tel: 01494-434455 **Fax:** 01494-726499
E-mail: adamsvictor@securon.co.uk
Website: http://www.securon.co.uk
Directors: V. Adams (Sales & Mktg)
Ultimate Holding Company: SECURON MANUFACTURING LIMITED
Immediate Holding Company: SECURON (AMERSHAM) LIMITED
Registration no: 00427013 **Date established:** 1947 **Turnover:** £2m - £5m
No.of Employees: 51 - 100 **Product Groups:** 39, 40, 68

Date of Accounts	Dec 11	Dec 10	Dec 09
Sales Turnover	2m	2m	2m
Pre Tax Profit/Loss	313	287	215
Working Capital	3m	3m	3m
Fixed Assets	343	273	218
Current Assets	4m	3m	3m
Current Liabilities	253	202	265

Aylesbury

Aalco
1 Premus Coldharbour Way, Aylesbury, HP19 8AP
Tel: 01296-461700 **Fax:** 01753-512227
E-mail: enquiries@aalco.co.uk
Website: http://www.aalco.co.uk
Bank(s): National Westminster Bank Plc
Managers: A. Hathaway (Sales Prom Mgr)
Ultimate Holding Company: UK STEELSTOCK LTD
Immediate Holding Company: AMARI METALS LTD
Registration no: 03551533 **Date established:** 1995
Turnover: £125m - £250m **No.of Employees:** 21 - 50
Product Groups: 34, 35, 36, 66

Accelerated Learning Systems Ltd
50 Aylesbury Road Aston Clinton, Aylesbury, HP22 5AH
Tel: 01296-631177 **Fax:** 01296-631074
E-mail: info@acceleratedlearning.com
Website: http://www.acceleratedlearning.com
Directors: C. Rose (Dir)
Immediate Holding Company: ACCELERATED LEARNING SYSTEMS LIMITED
Registration no: 01265110 **VAT No.:** GB 434 5193 55
Date established: 1976 **Turnover:** £1m - £2m **No.of Employees:** 1 - 10
Product Groups: 28

Date of Accounts	Jun 11	Jun 10	Jun 09
Working Capital	1	6	17
Fixed Assets	5	11	16
Current Assets	115	93	96

Acco UK Ltd
Oxford House Oxford Road, Aylesbury, HP21 8SZ
Tel: 01296-397444 **Fax:** 01296-392303
E-mail: peter.munk@acco.com
Website: http://www.acco.co.uk
Bank(s): HSBC Bank plc
Directors: R. Guest (Fin), S. Wells (Pers)
Managers: C. Framey, N. Hurlbatt (Develop Mgr)
Ultimate Holding Company: ACCO BRANDS CORP (USA)
Immediate Holding Company: ACCO UK LIMITED
Registration no: 00197754 **VAT No.:** GB 232 4189 79
Date established: 2024 **Turnover:** £75m - £125m
No.of Employees: 101 - 250 **Product Groups:** 28, 35, 49

Date of Accounts	Dec 11	Dec 10	Dec 09
Sales Turnover	80m	80m	73m
Pre Tax Profit/Loss	-2m	5m	4m

see next page

Acco UK Ltd - Cont'd

Working Capital	2m	-6m	-8m
Fixed Assets	53m	51m	52m
Current Assets	60m	59m	52m
Current Liabilities	7m	8m	7m

Aditech Ltd

Unit 7 Midshires Smeaton Close, Aylesbury, HP19 8HL
Tel: 01296-398085 **Fax:** 01296-337755
E-mail: sales@aditech.co.uk
Website: http://www.aditech.co.uk
Directors: P. Stanborough (Fin), P. Stanborough (MD)
Immediate Holding Company: ADITECH LIMITED
Registration no: 03106466 **Date established:** 1995
Turnover: £500,000 - £1m **No.of Employees:** 1 - 10 **Product Groups:** 36, 37, 44, 67

Date of Accounts	Sep 11	Sep 10	Sep 09
Working Capital	41	13	6
Fixed Assets	1	1	2
Current Assets	91	66	37

Airstar UK

13 Meadow View Drakes Drive, Long Crendon, Aylesbury, HP18 9EQ
Tel: 01844-203640 **Fax:** 01844-203649
E-mail: info@airstar-light.com
Website: http://www.airstar.co.uk
Directors: D. Gaine (MD)
Registration no: 02688475 **Date established:** 1992
No.of Employees: 1 - 10 **Product Groups:** 37, 39, 84

Apem Components Ltd

Drakes Drive Long Crendon, Aylesbury, HP18 9BA
Tel: 01844-202400 **Fax:** 01844-202500
E-mail: sales@apem.co.uk
Website: http://www.apem.co.uk
Bank(s): Lloyds
Directors: T. West (MD)
Ultimate Holding Company: IHM TECHNOLOGIES SAS (FRANCE)
Immediate Holding Company: APEM COMPONENTS LIMITED
Registration no: 01730676 **Date established:** 1983
Turnover: £10m - £20m **No.of Employees:** 51 - 100 **Product Groups:** 37

Date of Accounts	Dec 11	Dec 10	Dec 09
Sales Turnover	16m	16m	13m
Pre Tax Profit/Loss	3m	3m	2m
Working Capital	5m	4m	3m
Fixed Assets	2m	2m	2m
Current Assets	8m	8m	7m
Current Liabilities	839	875	512

Argosy

Unit 6-7 Ridgeway Drakes Drive, Long Crendon, Aylesbury, HP18 9BF
Tel: 01844-203627 **Fax:** 01844-202025
E-mail: sales@argosycable.com
Website: http://www.argosycable.com
Bank(s): National Westminster Bank Plc
Directors: R. Clark (Sales), K. Eckardt (Fin), M. Purnell (Dir)
Immediate Holding Company: ARGOSY COMPONENTS LIMITED
Registration no: 01839563 **Date established:** 1984 **Turnover:** £2m - £5m
No.of Employees: 11 - 20 **Product Groups:** 37, 44

Date of Accounts	Aug 11	Aug 10	Aug 09
Working Capital	528	648	728
Fixed Assets	438	347	358
Current Assets	2m	2m	1m

Askeys The Silver Spoon Company

Stocklake, Aylesbury, HP20 1DS
Tel: 01296-310200 **Fax:** 01296-434893
E-mail: info@askeys.co.uk
Website: http://www.askeys.co.uk
Bank(s): Bank of Scotland
Directors: B. Howes (Fin), M. Carr (MD)
Registration no: 00315158 **VAT No.:** GB 630 8728 35
Turnover: £10m - £20m **No.of Employees:** 101 - 250 **Product Groups:** 20

Aura Tools

Unit 3 Meadow View Long Crendon, Aylesbury, HP18 9EQ
Tel: 01844-202229
E-mail: auratools@hotmail.co.uk
Directors: G. Kingston (Prop)
Date established: 1994 **No.of Employees:** 1 - 10 **Product Groups:** 36

Aylesbury Automation Ltd

Unit 2 Farmbrough Close Stocklake Industrial Park, Aylesbury, HP20 1DQ
Tel: 01296-314300 **Fax:** 01296-482424
E-mail: enquiry@aylesbury-automation.co.uk
Website: http://www.aylesbury-automation.co.uk
Bank(s): Barclays
Directors: D. Manby (Dir)
Managers: D. O'shea (Comptroller)
Immediate Holding Company: AYLESBURY AUTOMATION LIMITED
Registration no: 04046524 **VAT No.:** 768 4542 89 **Date established:** 2000
Turnover: £2m - £5m **No.of Employees:** 21 - 50 **Product Groups:** 37

Date of Accounts	Dec 11	Dec 10	Dec 09
Sales Turnover	3m	2m	2m
Pre Tax Profit/Loss	69	20	N/A
Working Capital	240	199	179
Fixed Assets	43	7	10
Current Assets	3m	2m	448
Current Liabilities	2m	1m	136

Aylesbury Vale Chamber Of Commerce & Industry (Area Office)

Wing House Britannia Street, Aylesbury, HP20 1QS
Tel: 01296-434392 **Fax:** 01296-415405
E-mail: aylesbury@thamesvalleychamber.co.uk
Website: http://www.thamesvalleychamber.co.uk
Directors: P. Briggs (Dir)
Immediate Holding Company: MAPP LIMITED
Registration no: 02192094 **VAT No.:** GB 208 0947 68
Date established: 1987 **Turnover:** £2m - £5m **No.of Employees:** 1 - 10
Product Groups: 87

B L V Licht- Und Vakuumtechnik GmbH

Units 25-26 Rabans Close Rabans Lane Industrial A, Aylesbury, HP19 3RS
Tel: 01296-399334 **Fax:** 01296-393422
E-mail: sales@blv.co.uk
Website: http://www.blv.co.uk
Directors: D. Nausser (Fin)
Immediate Holding Company: BLV LICHT- UND VAKUUMTECHNIK GMBH
Registration no: FC016253 **Date established:** 1991
Turnover: £20m - £50m **No.of Employees:** 101 - 250
Product Groups: 37, 66

Bearing Traders Ltd

39 Edison Road Rabans Lane Industrial Area, Aylesbury, HP19 8TE
Tel: 01296-432537 **Fax:** 01296-426057
E-mail: aysales@bearingstraders.com
Website: http://www.bearingtraders.com
Managers: S. Gill (District Mgr)
Immediate Holding Company: BEARING TRADERS LIMITED
Registration no: 01994643 **VAT No.:** GB 285 1967 19
Date established: 1986 **Turnover:** £2m - £5m **No.of Employees:** 1 - 10
Product Groups: 30, 35, 39

Date of Accounts	Apr 11	Apr 10	Apr 09
Sales Turnover	N/A	N/A	4m
Pre Tax Profit/Loss	N/A	N/A	60
Working Capital	-10	-52	-61
Fixed Assets	91	111	115
Current Assets	1m	911	965
Current Liabilities	N/A	N/A	525

Bio Seekers Ltd

7 Notley Farm Chearsley Road, Long Crendon, Aylesbury, HP18 9ER
Tel: 01844-201745 **Fax:** 01844-201963
E-mail: bioseekers@aol.com
Website: http://www.bioseekers.co.uk
Directors: H. McKeand (MD)
Immediate Holding Company: BIO SEEKERS LIMITED
Registration no: 01546205 **VAT No.:** GB 349 3509 35
Date established: 1981 **No.of Employees:** 1 - 10 **Product Groups:** 31, 42

Date of Accounts	Feb 11	Feb 10	Feb 09
Working Capital	44	48	43
Fixed Assets	2	2	3
Current Assets	66	67	55

Boxes & Packaging Oxford Ltd

Unit 3 Long Crendon Industria Estate Drakes Drive, Long Crendon, Aylesbury, HP18 9BA
Tel: 01844-202188 **Fax:** 01844-202198
E-mail: oxford@boxesandpackaging.co.uk
Website: http://www.boxesandpackaging.co.uk
Directors: T. Quantrill (MD)
Managers: M. Gateley (Purch Mgr), S. Atkins (Fin Mgr)
Ultimate Holding Company: LOGSON LIMITED
Immediate Holding Company: BOXES AND PACKAGING (OXFORD) LIMITED
Registration no: 05562642 **Date established:** 2005 **Turnover:** £2m - £5m
No.of Employees: 21 - 50 **Product Groups:** 27

Date of Accounts	Dec 11	Dec 10	Dec 09
Working Capital	58	-59	43
Fixed Assets	358	395	410
Current Assets	1m	1m	1m
Current Liabilities	630	542	N/A

British American Tobacco plc

Oxford Road, Aylesbury, HP21 8SZ
Tel: 01296-335000 **Fax:** 01296-335999
E-mail: info@aylesford-newsprint.co.uk
Website: http://www.bat.com
Directors: R. Chamber (Fin)
Ultimate Holding Company: BRITISH AMERICAN TOBACCO P.L.C.
Immediate Holding Company: BRITISH AMERICAN TOBACCO P.L.C.
Registration no: 03407696 **Date established:** 1997
Turnover: £50m - £75m **No.of Employees:** 1 - 10 **Product Groups:** 20, 41, 62

Date of Accounts	Dec 11	Dec 10	Dec 09
Sales Turnover	15399m	14883m	14208m
Pre Tax Profit/Loss	4931m	4388m	4080m
Working Capital	648m	1012m	1190m
Fixed Assets	18624m	19203m	18508m
Current Assets	8495m	8657m	8106m
Current Liabilities	7179m	976m	6266m

C Brewer & Sons

1 Kempson Close Gatehouse Industrial Area, Aylesbury, HP19 8UQ
Tel: 01296-420136 **Fax:** 01296-394223
E-mail: aylesbury@brewers.co.uk
Website: http://www.brewers.co.uk
Managers: A. Newitt (Mgr)
Immediate Holding Company: C.BREWER & SONS LIMITED
Registration no: 00203852 **VAT No.:** GB 194 1565 70
Date established: 1925 **No.of Employees:** 1 - 10 **Product Groups:** 27, 30, 32

The Care Shop

3 Millennium Point Broadfields, Aylesbury, HP19 8TQ
Tel: 01296-394044 **Fax:** 01296-482729
E-mail: pam.fenner@bunzl.co.uk
Website: http://www.valecare.co.uk
Directors: B. Hatton (Dir), D. Molyneaux (Fin), J. Waller (Prop)
Managers: P. Fenner (Sales Admin)
No.of Employees: 11 - 20 **Product Groups:** 38, 67

Chambers Engineering Ltd

Warmstone Works Warmstone Lane, Waddesdon, Aylesbury, HP18 0NF
Tel: 01296-651380 **Fax:** 01296-651063
E-mail: tchambers@btconnect.com
Website: http://www.chambersengineering.co.uk
Directors: T. Chambers (MD)
Immediate Holding Company: CHAMBERS ENGINEERING LIMITED
Registration no: 02726611 **Date established:** 1992
Turnover: £500,000 - £1m **No.of Employees:** 11 - 20
Product Groups: 25, 39, 68

Date of Accounts	Jun 12	Jun 11	Jun 10
Sales Turnover	N/A	957	1m
Pre Tax Profit/Loss	N/A	16	23
Working Capital	135	153	155
Fixed Assets	60	56	75
Current Assets	290	306	373
Current Liabilities	46	18	21

Clynol Ltd

Oxford House Oxford Road, Aylesbury, HP21 8SZ
Tel: 01296-314100 **Fax:** 01296-433587
Website: http://www.clynol.com
Directors: P. Belcher (Sales), R. Ferneyhough (Co Sec)
Ultimate Holding Company: FORTUNE BRANDS INC (USA)
Immediate Holding Company: ACCO COMPANY LIMITED
Registration no: 01825834 **VAT No.:** GB 410 9724 68
Date established: 1969 **Turnover:** £5m - £10m **No.of Employees:** 1 - 10
Product Groups: 32

Date of Accounts	Dec 03	Dec 02	Dec 01
Pre Tax Profit/Loss	-70	-20	N/A
Working Capital	100m	100m	110m
Current Assets	110m	110m	110m

Com Development Europe Ltd

Triangle Business Park Quilters Way, Stoke Mandeville, Aylesbury, HP22 5SX
Tel: 01296-616400 **Fax:** 01296-616500
E-mail: info@comdev.co.uk
Website: http://www.comdev.co.uk
Bank(s): Royal Bank of Canada
Directors: C. D'cruze (Fin), G. Calhoun (Co Sec), J. Stuart (MD)
Managers: M. Freudmann (Tech Serv Mgr), S. Stamper (Personnel), L. Shepherd
Ultimate Holding Company: COM DEV INTERNATIONAL LTD(CANADA)
Immediate Holding Company: COM DEV EUROPE LIMITED
Registration no: 01863723 **VAT No.:** GB 434 5040 80
Date established: 1984 **Turnover:** £5m - £10m
No.of Employees: 51 - 100 **Product Groups:** 37

Date of Accounts	Oct 10	Oct 09	Oct 08
Sales Turnover	8m	6m	2m
Pre Tax Profit/Loss	-4m	1m	-3m
Working Capital	-1m	-817	857
Fixed Assets	1m	2m	2m
Current Assets	3m	3m	2m
Current Liabilities	3m	3m	986

Concept Tile Design Ltd

Unit 30 Wornal Park Menmarsh Road, Worminghall, Aylesbury, HP18 9JX
Tel: 01844-338882 **Fax:** 01844-219810
E-mail: nicky@concepttiledesign.co.uk
Website: http://www.concepttiledesign.co.uk
Directors: N. Crawford (MD), R. Koomen (Co Sec)
Ultimate Holding Company: 04115888
Immediate Holding Company: CONCEPT TILE DESIGN LIMITED
Registration no: 03041751 **Date established:** 1995
No.of Employees: 1 - 10 **Product Groups:** 33, 35

Construction Specialties UK Ltd

1010 Westcott Venture Park Westcott, Aylesbury, HP18 0XB
Tel: 01296-652800 **Fax:** 01296-652888
E-mail: info@c-sgroup.co.uk
Website: http://www.c-sgroup.co.uk
Directors: W. Duckham (MD)
Managers: D. Choules (Sales & Mktg Mg), A. English, M. Price (Tech Serv Mgr), A. Cousins, P. Clifford (Purch Mgr)
Ultimate Holding Company: EMEH INC (USA)
Immediate Holding Company: CONSTRUCTION SPECIALTIES (U.K.) LIMITED
Registration no: 01204719 **VAT No.:** GB 538 1876 15
Date established: 1975 **Turnover:** £5m - £10m
No.of Employees: 51 - 100 **Product Groups:** 23, 35

Date of Accounts	Dec 11	Dec 10	Dec 09
Sales Turnover	6m	7m	8m
Pre Tax Profit/Loss	561	910	1m
Working Capital	2m	2m	2m
Fixed Assets	178	150	190
Current Assets	3m	3m	3m
Current Liabilities	309	360	518

Danielson Ltd

29 Stocklake Industrial Estate Pembroke Road, Aylesbury, HP20 1DB
Tel: 01296-319000 **Fax:** 01296-392141
E-mail: sales@danielson.co.uk
Website: http://www.danielsoneurope.com
Bank(s): Svenska Handelsbanken - 3-5 Newgate St, EC1A 7DA
Directors: D. Phelan (MD)
Managers: K. Stewart (Buyer), G. Stiles (Fin Mgr), A. Birch (Prod Mgr), B. Phelan
Ultimate Holding Company: NYLOPLAST NV (NETHERLANDS)
Immediate Holding Company: DANIELSON (UK) LIMITED
Registration no: 04976568 **VAT No.:** GB 490 8971 00
Date established: 2003 **Turnover:** £2m - £5m **No.of Employees:** 51 - 100
Product Groups: 30, 37, 44, 49

Date of Accounts	Dec 11	Dec 10	Dec 09
Sales Turnover	5m	4m	3m
Pre Tax Profit/Loss	553	122	-268
Working Capital	664	828	779
Fixed Assets	481	480	572
Current Assets	2m	2m	1m
Current Liabilities	696	427	164

Data Imaging & Archiving

38 The Firs Brill, Aylesbury, HP18 9RY
Tel: 01844-238253 **Fax:** 01844-238253
E-mail: sales@imagingandarchiving.co.uk
Website: http://www.imagingandarchiving.co.uk
Directors: N. Strathdee (Dir)
Date established: 2001 **Turnover:** £500,000 - £1m
No.of Employees: 1 - 10 **Product Groups:** 44, 72, 80

Demag Hamilton Guarantee Ltd

Accent House, Triangle Business Park Wendover Road, Stoke Mandeville, Aylesbury, HP22 5BL
Tel: 01296-95 00 **Fax:** 01296-739501
E-mail: salesuk@dpg.com
Website: http://www.dpg.com
Bank(s): Barclays, Banbury
Directors: R. Herrington (Fin), N. Flowers (MD)
Managers: A. Gell (I.T. Exec)
Ultimate Holding Company: Mannesmann A G Dusseldorf (Germany)
Immediate Holding Company: Demag Hamilton Guarantee Ltd
Registration no: 01185700 **VAT No.:** GB 228 0324 90
Date established: 2001 **Turnover:** £20m - £50m
No.of Employees: 21 - 50 **Product Groups:** 42

Date of Accounts	Dec 09	Dec 08	Sep 07
Working Capital	8	N/A	N/A
Fixed Assets	26	N/A	N/A
Current Assets	100	N/A	N/A

Denka Service Ltd
Edgcott House Edgcott, Aylesbury, HP18 0QW
Tel: 01296-770576 **Fax:** 01296-770423
E-mail: bc@copsey-comms.com
Website: http://www.denka.co.uk
Directors: B. Copsey (MD), A. Marlin (Co Sec)
Immediate Holding Company: ASP FREQUENCY MANAGEMENT LIMITED
Registration no: 03322660 **Date established:** 1989
No.of Employees: 1 - 10 **Product Groups:** 35, 39, 45

Date of Accounts	Jul 11	Jul 10	Jul 09
Working Capital	N/A	-17	-5
Current Assets	N/A	4	12

E T A Circuit Breakers Ltd
Unit 6 Telford Close, Aylesbury, HP19 8DG
Tel: 01296-420336 **Fax:** 01296-488497
E-mail: info@e-t-a.co.uk
Website: http://www.e-t-a.com
Bank(s): Lloyds TSB Bank plc
Directors: J. Adams (Ch), R. Honour (Co Sec), S. Linnett (Gen Sec), C. Poensgen (Dir), I. Steininger (MD)
Managers: A. Pipe (Sales Prom Mgr)
Ultimate Holding Company: FP013129
Immediate Holding Company: E-T-A CIRCUIT BREAKERS LTD
Registration no: 01276004 **VAT No.:** GB 195 9896 74
Date established: 1976 **Turnover:** £2m - £5m **No.of Employees:** 21 - 50
Product Groups: 37, 38, 67

Date of Accounts	Dec 11	Dec 10	Dec 09
Sales Turnover	5m	5m	N/A
Pre Tax Profit/Loss	699	491	N/A
Working Capital	3m	2m	2m
Fixed Assets	2m	2m	2m
Current Assets	4m	3m	3m
Current Liabilities	661	456	N/A

Ecopure Waters
9 Alexander House Thame Road, Haddenham, Aylesbury, HP17 8BZ
Tel: 01844-290088 **Fax:** 01844-292969
E-mail: sales@ecopurewaters.com
Website: http://www.ecopurewaters.com
Directors: A. Whitehorn (Fin), P. Proctor (MD)
Managers: K. Cripps (Develop Mgr)
Immediate Holding Company: CLASSIC CRYSTAL LIMITED
Registration no: 02806173 **Date established:** 1993
Turnover: £500,000 - £1m **No.of Employees:** 11 - 20 **Product Groups:** 67

Edmundson Electrical Ltd
Unit 1 Westpoint, Aylesbury, HP19 8YZ
Tel: 01296-486251 **Fax:** 01296-423374
E-mail: aylesbury.218@eel.co.uk
Website: http://www.edmundson-electrical.co.uk/
Managers: E. Coleman (District Mgr)
Ultimate Holding Company: BLACKFRIARS CORP (USA)
Immediate Holding Company: EDMUNDSON ELECTRICAL LIMITED
Registration no: 02667012 **Date established:** 1991 **Turnover:** £1m - £2m
No.of Employees: 1 - 10 **Product Groups:** 33, 35, 40, 67

Date of Accounts	Dec 11	Dec 10	Dec 09
Sales Turnover	1023m	852m	788m
Pre Tax Profit/Loss	57m	53m	45m
Working Capital	256m	225m	184m
Fixed Assets	17m	3m	4m
Current Assets	439m	358m	298m
Current Liabilities	59m	38m	37m

Electrochemical Supplies Ltd
1 Aylesbury Business Centre Chamberlain Road, Aylesbury, HP19 8DY
Tel: 01296-428011 **Fax:** 01296-392375
E-mail: info@echemsupplies.co.uk
Website: http://www.electrochemicalsupplies.co.uk
Directors: R. Doody (Dir)
Immediate Holding Company: ELECTROCHEMICAL SUPPLIES LTD.
Registration no: 02932272 **VAT No.:** GB 630 7307 64
Date established: 1994 **Turnover:** £500,000 - £1m
No.of Employees: 1 - 10 **Product Groups:** 46

Date of Accounts	Jul 11	Jul 10	Jul 09
Working Capital	55	28	87
Current Assets	131	135	219

Everfresh Natural Foods
Gatehouse Close Gatehouse Industrial Area, Aylesbury, HP19 8DE
Tel: 01296-425333 **Fax:** 01296-422545
E-mail: sunnyvale@btconnect.com
Website: http://www.sunnyvaleorganic.com
Bank(s): Barclays
Directors: T. Russell (MD)
Immediate Holding Company: FULFILMENT MATTERS LIMITED
Registration no: 05642383 **VAT No.:** GB 427 7233 48
Date established: 2009 **Turnover:** £2m - £5m **No.of Employees:** 11 - 20
Product Groups: 62

Date of Accounts	Dec 11	Dec 10
Working Capital	32	30
Current Assets	68	57
Current Liabilities	20	N/A

Everything Electrical
Unit 20 Bridgegate Business Park Gatehouse Way, Gatehouse Industrial Area, Aylesbury, HP19 8XN
Tel: 01296-393039 **Fax:** 01296-394833
E-mail: sales@everythingelectrical.uk.com
Website: http://www.everythingelectrical.uk.com
Directors: M. Crockett (Prop)
Immediate Holding Company: EVERYTHING ELECTRICAL (AYLESBURY) LIMITED
Registration no: 03950608 **Date established:** 2000
No.of Employees: 1 - 10 **Product Groups:** 36, 40

Date of Accounts	Mar 11	Mar 10	Mar 09
Working Capital	80	71	61
Fixed Assets	1	1	N/A
Current Assets	166	119	106

F E P Hydraulics
Unit 1 March Place Gatehouse Way Gatehouse Industrial Area, Aylesbury, HP19 8UG
Tel: 01296-484934 **Fax:** 01296-436368
E-mail: sales@fephydraulics.co.uk
Website: http://www.fephydraulics.co.uk
Directors: J. Harman (Prop)
Immediate Holding Company: FEP HYDRAULICS AND PNEUMATICS LTD
Registration no: 03276929 **Date established:** 1996
Turnover: Up to £250,000 **No.of Employees:** 1 - 10 **Product Groups:** 23, 29, 30, 31, 32, 33, 34, 35, 36, 37, 38, 39, 40, 41, 42, 43, 44, 45, 46, 47, 48, 51, 61, 63, 66, 67, 68, 74, 83, 84, 85

Date of Accounts	Mar 11	Mar 10	Mar 09
Sales Turnover	177	192	244
Pre Tax Profit/Loss	10	7	5
Working Capital	N/A	-1	-3
Fixed Assets	N/A	1	4
Current Assets	97	105	115
Current Liabilities	35	36	30

Facilities System Building Services Ltd
9 Station Road Stoke Mandeville, Aylesbury, HP22 5UL
Tel: 01491-575438 **Fax:** 07000-373775
E-mail: facilities@firealarms.gb.com
Website: http://www.firealarms.gb.com
Directors: S. Carder (Dir)
Immediate Holding Company: FACILITIES SYSTEM BUILDING SERVICES LIMITED
Registration no: 03859725 **Date established:** 1999
No.of Employees: 1 - 10 **Product Groups:** 37, 40, 67

Date of Accounts	Mar 12	Mar 11	Mar 10
Working Capital	34	7	31
Fixed Assets	7	6	6
Current Assets	410	311	293

Filling & Capping Machines Ltd
Marsh Hill Centre Marsh, Aylesbury, HP17 8ST
Tel: 01296-615383 **Fax:** 01296-615383
E-mail: info@fillingandcapping.com
Website: http://www.fillingandcapping.com
Directors: B. Potiphar (Sales)
Managers: J. Richardson (Eng)
Registration no: 05478869 **Date established:** 1973
Turnover: £250,000 - £500,000 **No.of Employees:** 1 - 10
Product Groups: 20

Date of Accounts	Mar 08	Mar 07	Mar 06
Working Capital	31	15	15
Current Assets	76	15	18
Current Liabilities	45	N/A	2

Flowline Steel Fabricators
Unit 421 Westcott Venture Park Westcott, Aylesbury, HP18 0XB
Tel: 01296-651770 **Fax:** 01296-651006
E-mail: enquiries@flowline.uk.com
Website: http://www.flowline.uk.com
Directors: P. Stiegeler (Dir), J. Stiegeler (Fin)
Immediate Holding Company: ASHENDON LIMITED
Registration no: 06399500 **Date established:** 1997
Turnover: Up to £250,000 **No.of Employees:** 1 - 10 **Product Groups:** 35

Date of Accounts	Jul 11	Jul 10	Jul 09
Working Capital	228	225	260
Fixed Assets	3	4	6
Current Assets	418	443	317

Gartec Ltd
6 Midshires Business Park Smeaton Close, Aylesbury, HP19 8HL
Tel: 01296-397100 **Fax:** 01296-397600
E-mail: sales@gartec.com
Website: http://www.gartec.com
Directors: R. Smith (Co Sec), C. Falk (Sales)
Immediate Holding Company: GARTEC LTD.
Registration no: 02898632 **Date established:** 1994 **Turnover:** £5m - £10m
No.of Employees: 21 - 50 **Product Groups:** 45, 67, 81

Date of Accounts	Apr 12	Apr 11	Apr 10
Sales Turnover	8m	8m	8m
Pre Tax Profit/Loss	721	840	1m
Working Capital	2m	2m	2m
Fixed Assets	835	821	847
Current Assets	3m	4m	3m
Current Liabilities	1m	1m	1m

Gate-A-Matic
Verna House 9 Bicester Road, Aylesbury, HP19 9AG
Tel: 01296-489911 **Fax:** 01296-431533
Website: http://www.vernahouse.com
Directors: M. Coplin (Prop)
No.of Employees: 1 - 10 **Product Groups:** 35, 79, 80, 83

Good Thinking
9 Fort End Haddenham, Aylesbury, HP17 8EJ
Tel: 01844-291803
E-mail: info@goodthinking.co.uk
Directors: D. Watkins (Prop)
Immediate Holding Company: DAVE WATKINS LIMITED
Registration no: 05587361 **Date established:** 2005
Turnover: Up to £250,000 **No.of Employees:** 1 - 10 **Product Groups:** 38, 48

H M X Corporate Communication Ltd
The Stable Block The Firs High Street, Whitchurch, Aylesbury, HP22 4SJ
Tel: 01296-642070
E-mail: info@hmx.cc
Website: http://www.hmx.cc
Managers: A. Harrison (Mktg Serv Mgr)
Immediate Holding Company: HMX CORPORATE COMMUNICATION LIMITED
Registration no: 05368349 **Date established:** 2005
Turnover: £500,000 - £1m **No.of Employees:** 1 - 10 **Product Groups:** 89

Date of Accounts	Jul 11	Jul 10	Jul 09
Working Capital	217	12	-27
Fixed Assets	205	242	294
Current Assets	607	178	69

Hi-Pro Pressure Products Ltd
Unit 10 Bessemer Crescent, Rabans Lane Industrial Area, Aylesbury, HP19 8TF
Tel: 01296-431804 **Fax:** 01296-431845
E-mail: contactus@hi-pro.co.uk
Website: http://www.hi-pro.co.uk
Managers: D. Burton (Sales Prom Mgr)
Immediate Holding Company: HI-PRO PRESSURE PRODUCTS LTD
Registration no: 03636790 **Date established:** 1998
Turnover: £500,000 - £1m **No.of Employees:** 1 - 10 **Product Groups:** 36, 38, 40, 46, 85

Date of Accounts	Dec 11	Dec 10	Dec 09
Working Capital	-34	-96	-63
Fixed Assets	7	9	3
Current Assets	103	74	88

Holm Engineering Ltd
Unit 29 Wornal Park Menmarsh Road, Worminghall, Aylesbury, HP18 9PH
Tel: 01844-338690 **Fax:** 01844-338680
E-mail: holmengineering@talktalk.net
Website: http://www.holmengineering.co.uk
Registration no: 05948427 **Turnover:** £250,000 - £500,000
No.of Employees: 1 - 10 **Product Groups:** 40, 45, 46, 48

Hubdean Contracting Ltd
Unit 3 Wornal Park Menmarsh Road, Worminghall, Aylesbury, HP18 9PH
Tel: 01844-338833 **Fax:** 01844-338844
E-mail: taniasanders@hubdean.co.uk
Website: http://www.hubdean.co.uk
Directors: T. Sanders (Ptnr)
Managers: N. Chadbone (Tech Serv Mgr)
Immediate Holding Company: HUBDEAN CONTRACTING LTD
Registration no: 05739257 **Date established:** 2006
Turnover: £500,000 - £1m **No.of Employees:** 21 - 50
Product Groups: 80, 85

Date of Accounts	Mar 12	Mar 11	Mar 10
Working Capital	120	115	139
Fixed Assets	12	16	26
Current Assets	354	407	292

Ian Webb Engineering Services
38 Willis Road Haddenham, Aylesbury, HP17 8HF
Tel: 01844-291540
No.of Employees: 1 - 10 **Product Groups:** 37, 38

J B Systems Ltd
Unit 13 Bridgegate Business Park Gatehouse Way, Aylesbury, HP19 8DB
Tel: 01296-489967 **Fax:** 01296-393515
E-mail: info@jbsystems.co.uk
Website: http://www.jbsystems.co.uk
Directors: P. Jackson (Dir)
Immediate Holding Company: J B SYSTEMS LIMITED
Registration no: 05609610 **Date established:** 2005 **Turnover:** £1m - £2m
No.of Employees: 1 - 10 **Product Groups:** 30, 37, 38

Date of Accounts	Jun 11	Jun 10	Jun 09
Working Capital	722	432	329
Fixed Assets	46	57	53
Current Assets	1m	826	706

J Dewalleg Ltd
Unit 1 Anglo Business Park Smeaton Close, Aylesbury, HP19 8UP
Tel: 01296-394 555 **Fax:** 01296-422 219
E-mail: whaley@jdwltd.com
Website: http://www.jdwltd.com
Bank(s): HSBC, 1 Cornmarket
Directors: A. Richardson (Works), J. Whaley (MD), T. Alsop (Sales & Mktg), A. Whaley (MD)
Managers: S. Ellis (Sales Prom Mgr), S. Roberts (Accounts), J. May (Sec)
Immediate Holding Company: Watson & Ewen Ltd
Registration no: 01270092 **VAT No.:** GB 290 6401 67
Turnover: £1m - £2m **No.of Employees:** 11 - 20 **Product Groups:** 23

Date of Accounts	Feb 08	Feb 07	Feb 06
Working Capital	-309	-225	-196
Fixed Assets	173	123	139
Current Assets	549	410	480
Current Liabilities	858	635	676

Jacobs Industrial Services U.K. Limited
Lincoln Place Green End, Aylesbury, HP20 2TU
Tel: 01296-737 000 **Fax:** 01296-737 007
Website: http://www.jacobs.com
Bank(s): HSBC Bank plc
Directors: S. Brice (MD), W. Markley (Dir)
Managers: G. Jones (Chief Acct)
Ultimate Holding Company: E.ON AG (GERMANY)
Immediate Holding Company: Jacobs Engineering U.K. Ltd
Registration no: 02527622 **VAT No.:** GB 555 4822 27
Date established: 1987 **Turnover:** Over £1,000m
No.of Employees: 21 - 50 **Product Groups:** 35, 48

Kee Process Ltd
College Road Aston Clinton, Aylesbury, HP22 5EZ
Tel: 01296-634500 **Fax:** 01296-634501
E-mail: sales@keeprocess.com
Website: http://www.klargester.co.uk
Bank(s): Lloyds TSB Bank plc
Directors: S. Nathwani (Co Sec), L. Smith (MD)
Managers: R. Billyard (Fin Mgr), M. Bourne, M. Welsh
Immediate Holding Company: KEE PROCESS LIMITED
Registration no: 00543552 **VAT No.:** GB 537 3114 61
Date established: 1955 **Turnover:** £5m - £10m
No.of Employees: 51 - 100 **Product Groups:** 42, 54, 67

Date of Accounts	Dec 11	Dec 10	Dec 09
Sales Turnover	7m	7m	6m
Pre Tax Profit/Loss	268	768	165
Working Capital	2m	2m	2m
Fixed Assets	2m	2m	1m
Current Assets	4m	5m	3m
Current Liabilities	1m	985	728

Klargester Environmental Ltd
College Road North Aston Clinton, Aylesbury, HP22 5EW
Tel: 01296-633000 **Fax:** 01296-633001
E-mail: david.anderson@klargester.com
Website: http://www.klargester.com
Directors: D. Anderson (Fin)
Managers: N. Baldwin (Tech Serv Mgr), A. Callaway
Ultimate Holding Company: KINGSPAN GROUP PUBLIC LIMITED COMPANY
Immediate Holding Company: ENVIRONMENTAL TREATMENT SYSTEMS LIMITED
VAT No.: GB 434 2708 63 **Date established:** 1999
No.of Employees: 101 - 250 **Product Groups:** 30, 42

Date of Accounts	Dec 11	Dec 10	Dec 09
Sales Turnover	N/A	26m	29m
Pre Tax Profit/Loss	N/A	2m	3m
Working Capital	N/A	-2m	-4m
Fixed Assets	N/A	8m	9m
Current Assets	N/A	26m	24m
Current Liabilities	N/A	3m	3m

L M S Printing
Unit 2-3 Duck Farm Court Station Way West, Aylesbury, HP20 2SQ
Tel: 01296-420409
E-mail: lisa@lmsprinting.co.uk
Website: http://www.lmsprinting.co.uk
Directors: L. Smith (Prop)
Immediate Holding Company: SAVAGE ANGLING LIMITED
Date established: 2011 **Turnover:** Up to £250,000
No.of Employees: 1 - 10 **Product Groups:** 28

Little Heath Gates
Westwinds Woodham, Aylesbury, HP18 0QH
Tel: 01296-770126 **Fax:** 01296-770866
Directors: M. Messer (Prop)
Date established: 1979 **No.of Employees:** 1 - 10 **Product Groups:** 26, 35

M C D Virtak Ltd
13 Rabans Close Rabans Lane Industrial Area, Aylesbury, HP19 8RS
Tel: 01296-484877 **Fax:** 01296-393122
E-mail: john.mckenzie@btconnect.com
Website: http://www.x-stat.co.uk
Directors: A. Frank (Co Sec), J. Mckenzie (MD)
Immediate Holding Company: MCD VIRTAK LIMITED
Registration no: 05641309 **VAT No.:** GB 229 7350 48
Date established: 2005 **Turnover:** £1m - £2m **No.of Employees:** 1 - 10
Product Groups: 30, 37, 38, 42, 43

Date of Accounts	Mar 11	Mar 10	Mar 09
Working Capital	22	45	46
Fixed Assets	25	30	35
Current Assets	50	89	102

Mccormick Europe Ltd
Haddenham Business Park Pegasus Way, Haddenham, Aylesbury, HP17 8LB
Tel: 01844-292930 **Fax:** 01844-294294
E-mail: lawrence.kurzius@mccormick.co.uk
Website: http://www.mccormick.com
Bank(s): Royal Bank of Scotland
Directors: D. Steele (Fin), M. Swift (Dir)
Ultimate Holding Company: MCCORMICK & CO INC (USA)
Immediate Holding Company: MCCORMICK EUROPE LIMITED
Registration no: 03120427 **Date established:** 1995
Turnover: £125m - £250m **No.of Employees:** 251 - 500
Product Groups: 20, 41

Date of Accounts	Nov 11	Nov 10	Nov 09
Pre Tax Profit/Loss	-9m	46m	-7m
Working Capital	-77m	-68m	-80m
Fixed Assets	284m	284m	249m
Current Assets	4m	30m	11m

Nylon Colours Ltd
Chamberlain Rd, Aylesbury, HP19 8DY
Tel: 01296-433754 **Fax:** 01296-392285
E-mail: sales@nyloncolours.co.uk
Bank(s): HSBC
Directors: S. Rennie (Dir), R. Clark (Dir)
Ultimate Holding Company: Nylon Colours Holdings Ltd
Registration no: 03704160 **VAT No.:** GB 537 2252 54
Date established: 1990 **Turnover:** £1m - £2m **No.of Employees:** 11 - 20
Product Groups: 30, 31, 32, 48

Date of Accounts	Mar 09	Mar 10	Mar 11
Working Capital	19	25	29
Fixed Assets	13	11	9
Current Assets	301	382	336

E H Oakley & Co. Ltd
43 Edison Road Rabans Lane Industrial Area, Aylesbury, HP19 8TE
Tel: 01296-393133 **Fax:** 01296-397070
E-mail: sales@oakleyweigh.co.uk
Website: http://www.oakleyweigh.co.uk
Directors: D. Oakley (Dir), G. Oakley (Fin)
Immediate Holding Company: E.H.OAKLEY AND COMPANY LIMITED
Registration no: 00602377 **VAT No.:** GB 194 8209 33
Date established: 1958 **Turnover:** £500,000 - £1m
No.of Employees: 1 - 10 **Product Groups:** 27, 30, 38, 39, 41, 42, 44, 83

Date of Accounts	Mar 12	Mar 11	Mar 10
Working Capital	93	108	90
Fixed Assets	43	42	51
Current Assets	174	190	188

Omnikote Ltd
Chamberlain Road, Aylesbury, HP19 8DY
Tel: 01296-483266 **Fax:** 01296-392285
E-mail: sales@omnikote.co.uk
Website: http://www.omnikote.co.uk
Bank(s): HSBC
Directors: L. White (Co Sec), S. Rennie (MD), I. Dmytrenko (Fab)
Managers: P. George (Sales Prom Mgr)
Registration no: 03704991 **VAT No.:** GB 348 5686 09
Date established: 1981 **Turnover:** £1m - £2m **No.of Employees:** 21 - 50
Product Groups: 35, 36, 48

Date of Accounts	Mar 09	Mar 10	Mar 11
Working Capital	136	123	241
Fixed Assets	127	107	93
Current Assets	455	450	612

Perfect Pipework Ltd
49 Rabans Close Rabans Lane Industrial Area, Aylesbury, HP19 8RS
Tel: 01296-399330 **Fax:** 01296-487029
E-mail: sally@perfectpipework.co.uk
Website: http://www.perfectpipework.co.uk
Directors: S. Rowles (Fin)
Immediate Holding Company: PERFECT PIPEWORK LIMITED
Registration no: 02518129 **VAT No.:** GB 596 3928 79
Date established: 1990 **Turnover:** £1m - £2m **No.of Employees:** 1 - 10
Product Groups: 66

Date of Accounts	Jul 11	Jul 10	Jul 09
Working Capital	38	31	40
Fixed Assets	13	13	8
Current Assets	400	227	309

Perrys
Griffin Lane Industrial Estate Griffin Lane, Aylesbury, HP19 8BY
Tel: 01296-426162 **Fax:** 01296-745276
E-mail: normanholmes@perrys.co.uk
Website: http://www.perrys.co.uk
Managers: J. Daily (Mgr), T. Salma (Comm), M. Still (Sales & Mktg Mg)
Ultimate Holding Company: PERRYS GROUP LIMITED
Immediate Holding Company: PERRYS MOTOR SALES LIMITED
Registration no: 00972286 **VAT No.:** GB 685 8159 80
Date established: 1970 **Turnover:** £10m - £20m
No.of Employees: 51 - 100 **Product Groups:** 39

Plating Equipment Ltd
Unit 2 Pembroke Road Stocklake Industrial Estate, Aylesbury, HP20 1DB
Tel: 01296-431666 **Fax:** 01296-425956
E-mail: cedric@platingequipment.co.uk
Website: http://www.platingequipment.co.uk
Directors: A. Manders (Fin), C. Clifford (MD)
Immediate Holding Company: PLATING EQUIPMENT LIMITED
Registration no: 03991456 **Date established:** 2000
No.of Employees: 1 - 10 **Product Groups:** 46, 48

Date of Accounts	May 11	May 10	May 09
Working Capital	82	49	29
Fixed Assets	7	3	4
Current Assets	164	119	50

Possum
8 Farmbrough Close, Aylesbury, HP20 1DQ
Tel: 01296-461000 **Fax:** 01296-394349
E-mail: sales@possum.co.uk
Website: http://www.possum.co.uk
Bank(s): Barclays
Directors: D. Scott (Fin), P. Robinson (MD)
Managers: J. Wakely (Mktg Serv Mgr), J. Reed (Personnel), D. Jones (Tech Serv Mgr), D. Crockford (Sales Prom Mgr), M. Byrnes (Purch Mgr)
Ultimate Holding Company: EAMONT HOLDINGS LIMITED
Immediate Holding Company: POSSUM LIMITED
Registration no: 00711047 **Date established:** 1961 **Turnover:** £2m - £5m
No.of Employees: 51 - 100 **Product Groups:** 37, 38

Date of Accounts	Mar 11	Mar 10	Mar 09
Sales Turnover	5m	5m	6m
Pre Tax Profit/Loss	300	377	497
Working Capital	3m	3m	2m
Fixed Assets	2m	867	2m
Current Assets	4m	5m	3m
Current Liabilities	634	1m	1m

Precision Moulds & Tools Service Ltd
Triangle Business Park Quilters Way, Stoke Mandeville, Aylesbury, HP22 5BL
Tel: 01296-616300 **Fax:** 01296-616339
E-mail: sales@precisionmoulds.co.uk
Website: http://www.precisionmoulds.co.uk
Directors: M. Rush (Dir)
Date established: 2000 **No.of Employees:** 21 - 50 **Product Groups:** 36

Protech Spray Finishing
2 Crendon Way Long Crendon, Aylesbury, HP18 9BD
Tel: 01844-202515 **Fax:** 01844-202516
Directors: B. Amos (Ptnr)
Date established: 1997 **No.of Employees:** 1 - 10 **Product Groups:** 46, 48

Quality Electro Depositors Ltd
Unit 2 Gatehouse Close Gatehouse Industrial Area, Aylesbury, HP19 8DE
Tel: 01296-426214 **Fax:** 01296-487787
E-mail: wise.wise.owls@aol.com
Directors: J. Wise (MD)
Immediate Holding Company: QUALITY ELECTRO DEPOSITORS LIMITED
Registration no: 04406839 **Date established:** 2002 **Turnover:** £2m - £5m
No.of Employees: 1 - 10 **Product Groups:** 32, 37, 44, 46, 47, 48

Date of Accounts	Mar 11	Mar 10	Mar 09
Working Capital	12	7	1
Current Assets	28	29	17

R B Punching Services Ltd
The New Forge
College Road North
Aston Clinton, Aylesbury, HP22 5EZ
Tel: 01296-630262 **Fax:** 01296-630485
E-mail: sales@rbpunching.co.uk
Website: http://www.rbpunching.co.uk
Directors: R. Biggs (MD), C. Biggs (Dir)
Immediate Holding Company: R B PUNCHING SERVICES LIMITED
Registration no: 01581408 **VAT No.:** GB 385 5192 24
Date established: 1981 **Turnover:** £500,000 - £1m
No.of Employees: 1 - 10 **Product Groups:** 46, 48

Date of Accounts	Jan 12	Jan 11	Jan 10
Working Capital	491	532	564
Fixed Assets	458	470	342
Current Assets	575	651	663

R F S UK Ltd
9 Haddenham Business Park Thame Road, Haddenham, Aylesbury, HP17 8LJ
Tel: 01844-294900 **Fax:** 01844-294944
E-mail: sales@rfsworld.com
Website: http://www.rfsworld.com
Bank(s): HSBC Bank plc
Directors: J. Lloyd (Fin)
Managers: J. Lewis
Immediate Holding Company: R.F.S. (UK) LIMITED
Registration no: 02497031 **Date established:** 1990 **Turnover:** £5m - £10m
No.of Employees: 21 - 50 **Product Groups:** 37

Date of Accounts	Dec 11	Dec 10	Dec 09
Sales Turnover	10m	16m	N/A
Pre Tax Profit/Loss	638	995	-234
Working Capital	2m	1m	414
Fixed Assets	48	85	132
Current Assets	4m	6m	5m
Current Liabilities	772	1m	420

Rankin Brothers & Sons
Unit 3c Drakes Farm Drakes Drive, Long Crendon, Aylesbury, HP18 9BA
Tel: 01844-203100 **Fax:** 01844-203101
E-mail: sales@rankincork.co.uk
Website: http://www.rankincork.co.uk
Directors: J. Rankin (Sales)
Immediate Holding Company: RANKINS PARTNERS LIMITED
Registration no: 00387782 **VAT No.:** GB 235 9538 37
Date established: 1944 **Turnover:** £5m - £10m **No.of Employees:** 1 - 10
Product Groups: 25, 30, 36, 38, 39, 42, 61, 65

Date of Accounts	Apr 11	Apr 10	Apr 09
Sales Turnover	6m	6m	6m
Pre Tax Profit/Loss	321	193	-135
Working Capital	2m	1m	1m
Fixed Assets	1m	1m	1m
Current Assets	2m	2m	2m
Current Liabilities	486	264	287

Roblin Engineering
41-42 Rabans Close Rabans Lane Industrial Area, Aylesbury, HP19 8RS
Tel: 01296-423099 **Fax:** 01296-423099
E-mail: colin@roblinengineering.co.uk
Website: http://www.bucksbeams.co.uk
Directors: C. West (Prop)
Immediate Holding Company: ROBLIN & SON LIMITED
Registration no: 01905821 **Date established:** 1985
Turnover: Up to £250,000 **No.of Employees:** 1 - 10 **Product Groups:** 67

Date of Accounts	Dec 10	Dec 09	Dec 08
Working Capital	13	20	26
Current Assets	51	68	84

Rose Enclosures (a division of Phoenix Mecano Co.)
26 Faraday Road Rabans Lane Industrial Area, Aylesbury, HP19 8RY
Tel: 01296-611660 **Fax:** 01296-398866
E-mail: info@phoenix-mecano.co.uk
Website: http://www.phoenix-mecano.co.uk
Directors: P. Burnham (Fin)
Ultimate Holding Company: PHOENIX MECANO AG (SWITZERLAND)
Immediate Holding Company: PHOENIX MECANO AG
Registration no: 01325614 **Turnover:** £2m - £5m
No.of Employees: 1 - 10 **Product Groups:** 30, 35, 37, 47

Rose & Krieger (a Phoenix Mecano Company)
26 Faraday Road Rabans Lane Industrial Area, Aylesbury, HP19 8RY
Tel: 01296-611660 **Fax:** 01296-399339
E-mail: paul.burnham@phoenix-mecano.com
Website: http://www.rk-online.com
Directors: P. Burnham (Fin)
Ultimate Holding Company: PHOENIX MECANO AG
Registration no: 01325614 **Turnover:** £1m - £2m
No.of Employees: 1 - 10 **Product Groups:** 34, 35, 36, 37, 38, 40, 46, 47, 67

S Com Group Ltd
Buckingham House Buckingham Street, Aylesbury, HP20 2YD
Tel: 01296-311411 **Fax:** 01296-480688
E-mail: response@scom.com
Website: http://www.scom.com
Bank(s): Lloyds TSB Bank plc
Directors: N. Dettmar (MD)
Ultimate Holding Company: IMPELLAM GROUP PLC
Immediate Holding Company: S.COM GROUP LTD
Registration no: 02209742 **VAT No.:** GB 611 4330 92
Date established: 1988 **Turnover:** £75m - £125m
No.of Employees: 21 - 50 **Product Groups:** 80

Date of Accounts	Dec 10	Dec 09	Dec 08
Sales Turnover	74m	74m	54m
Pre Tax Profit/Loss	1m	667	211
Working Capital	6m	5m	3m
Fixed Assets	2m	3m	4m
Current Assets	15m	16m	17m
Current Liabilities	5m	5m	7m

Salzer UK Ltd
44 Edison Road Rabans Lane Industrial Area, Aylesbury, HP19 8TE
Tel: 01296-399992 **Fax:** 01296-392229
E-mail: info@salzeruk.co.uk
Website: http://www.salzer.co.uk
Managers: M. Higgins (Sales Admin)
Immediate Holding Company: SALZER U.K. LIMITED
Registration no: 02677783 **VAT No.:** GB 596 2064 19
Date established: 1992 **No.of Employees:** 1 - 10 **Product Groups:** 37

Date of Accounts	Dec 10	Dec 09	Dec 08
Working Capital	201	153	161
Fixed Assets	4	10	22
Current Assets	500	338	352

Schwarzkopf Ltd
Oxford House Oxford Road, Aylesbury, HP21 8SZ
Tel: 01296-314000 **Fax:** 01296-398012
Website: http://www.schwarzkopf.co.uk
Bank(s): National Westminster
Directors: L. Husbands (MD)
Ultimate Holding Company: HENKEL KG & A
Immediate Holding Company: SHWARZKOPF GMBH
Registration no: 00692772 **VAT No.:** GB 410 9724 68
Turnover: £20m - £50m **No.of Employees:** 51 - 100 **Product Groups:** 32, 63

Date of Accounts	Dec 06	Dec 05	Dec 04
Total Share Capital	4300	4300	4300

Scot Urquhart
Unit 12 Triangle Business Park Quilters Way, Stoke Mandeville, Aylesbury, HP22 5BL
Tel: 01296-613000 **Fax:** 01296-614000
E-mail: scoturquhart@btconnect.com
Website: http://www.scoturquhart.com
Directors: J. Dolans (Ptnr)
Turnover: £250,000 - £500,000 **No.of Employees:** 1 - 10
Product Groups: 37, 46

Signs Express Ltd
Unit 16 Anglo Business Park, Aylesbury, HP19 8UP
Tel: 01296-339998 **Fax:** 01296-331118
E-mail: info@signsexpress.co.uk
Website: http://www.signsexpress.co.uk
Directors: P. Harris (MD)
Immediate Holding Company: SIGNS EXPRESS LIMITED
Registration no: 02375913 **Date established:** 1989
No.of Employees: 1 - 10 **Product Groups:** 28, 40

Date of Accounts	May 11	May 10	May 09
Working Capital	2m	1m	988
Fixed Assets	112	87	105
Current Assets	2m	2m	1m

Signum Sign Studio
19 Anglo Business Park Smeaton Close, Aylesbury, HP19 8UP
Tel: 01296-489099
E-mail: welcome@signumsign.co.uk
Website: http://www.signumsign.co.uk

Directors: T. Pukalski (Ptnr)
Immediate Holding Company: ANTENNA DESIGN & SUPPLY LIMITED
Date established: 1999 **Turnover:** **No.of Employees:** 1 - 10
Product Groups: 27, 30, 49, 84

Simtech Simulation Techniques
Unit 70 Westcott Venture Park Westcott, Aylesbury, HP18 0XB
Tel: 01296-655787 **Fax:** 01296-651729
E-mail: info@simtech-simulation.com
Website: http://www.simtech-simulation.com
Directors: B. Hutton (MD), B. Hutton (Fin)
Immediate Holding Company: SIMTECH SIMULATION TECHNIQUES LIMITED
Registration no: 01161004 **VAT No.:** 195 5677 09 **Date established:** 1974
Turnover: £250,000 - £500,000 **No.of Employees:** 1 - 10
Product Groups: 44

Date of Accounts	Feb 11	Feb 10	Feb 09
Working Capital	-5	-12	-18
Fixed Assets	4	5	5
Current Assets	20	13	12

Sterling Thermal Technology Ltd
Brunel Road Rabans Lane Industrial Area, Aylesbury, HP19 8TD
Tel: 01296-487171 **Fax:** 01296-436805
E-mail: mail@sterlingtt.com
Website: http://www.sterlingthermaltech.com
Bank(s): Barclays
Directors: D. Blunn (Fin), N. Wilson (Sales), P. Michaluk (MD), S. Saganowski (Fin)
Managers: A. Gardner (Tech Serv Mgr), P. Spinks (Buyer)
Ultimate Holding Company: CALEDONIA INVESTMENTS PLC
Immediate Holding Company: STERLING THERMAL TECHNOLOGY LIMITED
Registration no: 01335179 **VAT No.:** GB 410 7083 90
Date established: 1977 **Turnover:** £10m - £20m
No.of Employees: 101 - 250 **Product Groups:** 36, 40, 42

Date of Accounts	Mar 12	Mar 11	Mar 10
Sales Turnover	15m	10m	10m
Pre Tax Profit/Loss	1m	1m	2m
Working Capital	4m	4m	3m
Fixed Assets	2m	908	996
Current Assets	7m	6m	5m
Current Liabilities	1m	2m	1m

Sterling Ultra Precision Ltd
13 Bessemer Crescent Rabans Lane Industrial Area, Aylesbury, HP19 8TF
Tel: 01296-487075 **Fax:** 01296-437005
E-mail: peterchilcott@sterlingint.com
Website: http://www.sterlingint.com
Directors: B. Davies (Grp Chief Exec), B. Davies (Prop)
Managers: G. Ross-Munro (Sales Admin), P. Chilcott (Export Sales Mg), F. Achkouti (Purch Mgr)
Immediate Holding Company: STERLING ULTRA PRECISION LIMITED
Registration no: 04477203 **Date established:** 2002
No.of Employees: 1 - 10 **Product Groups:** 47

Sunalex Ltd
The Wesleyan Chapel 185b Aylesbury Road, Bierton, Aylesbury, HP22 5DW
Tel: 01296-395400 **Fax:** 01296-393413
E-mail: info@sunalex.co.uk
Website: http://www.sunalex.co.uk
Bank(s): HSBC
Directors: A. Pratt (MD), J. Shepherd (Dir), A. Pratt (Fin)
Managers: H. Fearnley (Sales Admin)
Immediate Holding Company: Serious Brands Ltd
Registration no: 02485587 **VAT No.:** GB 537 2962 23
Date established: 2007 **Turnover:** £1m - £2m **No.of Employees:** 11 - 20
Product Groups: 29, 39

Techspan Systems Ltd
Techspan House Griffin Lane, Aylesbury, HP19 8BP
Tel: 01296-673000 **Fax:** 01296-673002
E-mail: enquiries@techspan.co.uk
Website: http://www.techspan.co.uk
Bank(s): Barclays
Directors: L. Martin (Fin), B. Greene (MD), D. Smith (Comm), J. Smith (Tech Serv)
Managers: C. Justice, S. Dolan
Ultimate Holding Company: HILL & SMITH HOLDINGS PLC
Immediate Holding Company: TECHSPAN SYSTEMS LIMITED
Registration no: 05419940 **VAT No.:** GB 649 7263 94
Date established: 2005 **Turnover:** £2m - £5m **No.of Employees:** 21 - 50
Product Groups: 37

Thame Engineering Co. Ltd
Field End Thame Road, Long Crendon, Aylesbury, HP18 9EJ
Tel: 01844-208050 **Fax:** 01844-201699
E-mail: sales@thame-eng.com
Website: http://www.thame-eng.com
Bank(s): Lloyds TSB
Directors: P. Mason (Dir), M. Day (Fin)
Managers: G. Barnet (Sales Prom Mgr)
Immediate Holding Company: THAME ENGINEERING CO LIMITED
Registration no: 02149520 **VAT No.:** GB 462 2561 58
Date established: 1987 **Turnover:** £2m - £5m **No.of Employees:** 21 - 50
Product Groups: 46, 48

Date of Accounts	Apr 12	Apr 11	Apr 10
Sales Turnover	N/A	N/A	2m
Pre Tax Profit/Loss	N/A	N/A	224
Working Capital	718	461	419
Fixed Assets	627	389	351
Current Assets	2m	1m	950
Current Liabilities	N/A	N/A	309

The Micha Design Co.
Unit 1 Bridgegate Business Park Gatehouse Industrial Area, Aylesbury, HP19 8XN
Tel: 01296-436161 **Fax:** 01296-420292
E-mail: info@micha.co.uk
Website: http://www.micha.co.uk
Bank(s): Barclays
Directors: L. Hytten (Prop)
Immediate Holding Company: MICHA DESIGN COMPANY LIMITED(THE)
Registration no: 02072488 **VAT No.:** GB 385 7734 04
Date established: 1986 **Turnover:** £500,000 - £1m
No.of Employees: 11 - 20 **Product Groups:** 67, 84

Date of Accounts	Dec 11	Dec 10	Dec 09
Working Capital	222	242	173
Fixed Assets	138	110	118
Current Assets	390	327	373

Thomas Bugden & Co. Ltd
Unit 4 Stocklake Industrial Estate Pembroke Road, Aylesbury, HP20 1DB
Tel: 01296-482030 **Fax:** 01296-487098
E-mail: thomasbugden@btconnect.com
Website: http://www.thomasbugden.co.uk
Directors: T. Child (Fin), D. Child (MD)
Managers: J. Peel (Accounts)
Immediate Holding Company: THOMAS BUGDEN & CO.LIMITED
Registration no: 00377199 **Date established:** 1942
No.of Employees: 1 - 10 **Product Groups:** 29

Date of Accounts	Nov 11	Nov 10	Nov 09
Working Capital	32	56	68
Fixed Assets	1	2	2
Current Assets	48	65	92

Timber Tooling Southern
97 Tring Road Wendover, Aylesbury, HP22 6NY
Tel: 01296-624843
E-mail: sales@timbertooling.com
Directors: K. Cuthbert (Fin), R. Chapman (Prop)
Immediate Holding Company: TIMBER TOOLING SOUTHERN LTD
Registration no: 04745318 **Date established:** 2003
No.of Employees: 1 - 10 **Product Groups:** 46, 48

Transaction International
Units 2b Drakes Drive Long Crendon, Aylesbury, HP18 9BA
Tel: 01844-204200 **Fax:** 01844-204210
E-mail: mail@transactioninternational.co.uk
Website: http://www.transactioninternational.co.uk
Directors: A. Johnstone (Dir)
Immediate Holding Company: TRANSACTION INTERNATIONAL LIMITED
Registration no: 02044498 **Date established:** 1986 **Turnover:** £2m - £5m
No.of Employees: 21 - 50 **Product Groups:** 77

Date of Accounts	Dec 11	Dec 10	Dec 09
Sales Turnover	N/A	3m	2m
Pre Tax Profit/Loss	N/A	39	6
Working Capital	-126	-57	-6
Fixed Assets	416	348	248
Current Assets	602	527	575
Current Liabilities	N/A	81	357

Uni Vite Healthcare
50 Aylesbury Road Aston Clinton, Aylesbury, HP22 5AH
Tel: 01296-630900 **Fax:** 01296-631074
E-mail: enquiries@acceleratedlearning.com
Website: http://www.acceleratedlearning.com
Directors: J. Downs (MD)
Immediate Holding Company: UNI-VITE HEALTHCARE LIMITED
Registration no: 03857627 **Date established:** 1999
Turnover: £250,000 - £500,000 **No.of Employees:** 1 - 10
Product Groups: 61

Date of Accounts	Jun 11	Jun 10	Jun 09
Working Capital	106	155	147
Fixed Assets	20	33	3
Current Assets	124	196	181

Unite Automation
17 Langdon Avenue, Aylesbury, HP21 9UL
Tel: 01296-423643
E-mail: david.kaye@uniteautomation.co.uk
Website: http://www.uniteautomation.co.uk
Directors: D. Kaye (Prop)
No.of Employees: 1 - 10 **Product Groups:** 37, 45, 84

The Woodwork Dust Control Company Ltd
Wotton Road Brill, Aylesbury, HP18 9UB
Tel: 01844-238833 **Fax:** 01844-238899
E-mail: enquiries@woodworkdustcontrol.co.uk
Website: http://www.woodworkdustcontrol.co.uk
Directors: D. Bruton (Dir), R. Preedy (Co Sec)
Immediate Holding Company: THE WOODWORK DUST CONTROL COMPANY LIMITED
Registration no: 02584429 **VAT No.:** GB 596 0271 24
Date established: 1991 **Turnover:** £500,000 - £1m
No.of Employees: 1 - 10 **Product Groups:** 40

Date of Accounts	Feb 12	Feb 11	Feb 10
Working Capital	65	18	32
Fixed Assets	21	23	26
Current Assets	131	101	98

Beaconsfield

Duplex Corporate Communications
55 Station Road, Beaconsfield, HP9 1QL
Tel: 08452-600781 **Fax:** 08452-600782
E-mail: sales@duplexcomms.co.uk
Website: http://www.ect-av.com
Managers: J. Begbie (Nat Sales Mgr), J. Bigbie (Mgr)
Ultimate Holding Company: LEXHAM HOLDINGS LIMITED (JERSEY)
Immediate Holding Company: NORTHCLIFF LIMITED
Registration no: 02942890 **Date established:** 1986
Turnover: Up to £250,000 **No.of Employees:** 1 - 10 **Product Groups:** 37

Date of Accounts	Jan 08
Working Capital	16
Fixed Assets	1
Current Assets	81
Current Liabilities	65

Gulfex Medical Supplies Ltd
7 Burgess Wood Road South, Beaconsfield, HP9 1EU
Tel: 01494-675353 **Fax:** 01494-675399
Directors: J. Stanbury (MD), I. Stanbury (Fin)
Immediate Holding Company: GULFEX MEDICAL SUPPLIES LIMITED
Registration no: 02812818 **VAT No.:** GB 603 8448 44
Date established: 1993 **Turnover:** Up to £250,000
No.of Employees: 1 - 10 **Product Groups:** 26, 30, 37, 38, 63, 66, 67

Date of Accounts	Dec 10	Dec 09	Dec 08
Sales Turnover	24	40	26
Pre Tax Profit/Loss	-19	6	-4
Working Capital	-15	3	9
Fixed Assets	4	1	1
Current Assets	6	14	11

Perkin Elmer
Chalfont Road Seer Green, Beaconsfield, HP9 2FX
Tel: 01494-874515 **Fax:** 01494-679331
E-mail: sandra.ward@perkinelmer.com
Website: http://www.perkinelmer.com
Bank(s): HSBC Bank plc
Directors: S. Ward (Fin)
Managers: L. Paladini
Ultimate Holding Company: PERKIN-ELMER INC (USA)
Immediate Holding Company: PERKINELMER LIMITED
Registration no: 03758366 **VAT No.:** GB 199 1481 22
Date established: 1999 **Turnover:** £10m - £20m
No.of Employees: 51 - 100 **Product Groups:** 28

Date of Accounts	Dec 08	Jan 10	Jan 11
Sales Turnover	14m	13m	15m
Pre Tax Profit/Loss	2m	1m	1m
Working Capital	29m	30m	32m
Fixed Assets	964	1m	2m
Current Assets	33m	33m	34m
Current Liabilities	3m	2m	2m

Bourne End

Causeway Technologies
Comino House Furlong Road, Bourne End, SL8 5AQ
Tel: 01628-552000 **Fax:** 01923-679288
E-mail: marketing@causeway.com
Website: http://www.causeway.com
Bank(s): Lloyds TSB Bank plc
Directors: B. Blake (Sales), F. Buchanan (Pers), G. O'Broin (Co Sec), J. Atkinson (Sales), M. Howell (Fin), L. Roberts (Tech Serv)
Managers: P. Brown, C. Davies (Mktg Serv Mgr)
Ultimate Holding Company: BRE TRUST
Immediate Holding Company: THE CAUSEWAY FOUNDATION
Registration no: 07461101 **Date established:** 2010 **Turnover:** £1m - £2m
No.of Employees: 51 - 100 **Product Groups:** 44

Date of Accounts	Dec 08	Dec 07	Dec 06
Sales Turnover	14853	10712	3888
Pre Tax Profit/Loss	2662	1513	-1347
Working Capital	5198	3600	963
Fixed Assets	3830	3942	834
Current Assets	13504	9794	3564
Current Liabilities	8306	6194	2601
Total Share Capital	11	11	11
ROCE% (Return on Capital Employed)	29.5	20.1	-75.0
ROT% (Return on Turnover)	17.9	14.1	-34.6

Chives
Station Road, Bourne End, SL8 5QA
Tel: 01628-533454 **Fax:** 01628-533454
E-mail: chives@technicalwebservices.com
Website: http://www.chivescatering.co.uk
Managers: P. Bridge (Mgr)
Immediate Holding Company: WE LOVE BROWNIES LIMITED
Date established: 2012 **No.of Employees:** 1 - 10 **Product Groups:** 20, 69

E C U Castings
Claytons Meadow, Bourne End, SL8 5DQ
Tel: 01628-524672 **Fax:** 01628-850914
E-mail: robinecu@aol.com
Website: http://www.ecucastings.co.uk
Directors: R. Blandy (Prop)
Registration no: 01555038 **Date established:** 1981
Turnover: Up to £250,000 **No.of Employees:** 1 - 10 **Product Groups:** 34, 35, 48

Maidenhead Machine Tool Co. Ltd
PO Box 833, Bourne End, SL8 5YR
Tel: 01628-526345 **Fax:** 01628-810732
E-mail: r.j.laverick@mmt1.com
Website: http://www.mmt1.com
Directors: J. Laverick (Dir), R. Laverick (MD)
Immediate Holding Company: MAIDENHEAD MACHINE TOOL CO.LIMITED
Registration no: 00946720 **Date established:** 1969
Turnover: Up to £250,000 **No.of Employees:** 1 - 10 **Product Groups:** 67

Date of Accounts	May 08	May 07	May 06
Sales Turnover	32	77	21
Pre Tax Profit/Loss	6	-11	-2
Working Capital	-170	-176	-165
Fixed Assets	1	1	1
Current Assets	29	41	54
Current Liabilities	199	217	219
Total Share Capital	10	10	10
ROCE% (Return on Capital Employed)	-3.4	6.4	1.1
ROT% (Return on Turnover)	17.5	-14.6	-8.8

Pacet Manufacturing Ltd
Wyebridge House Cores End Road, Bourne End, SL8 5HH
Tel: 01628-526754 **Fax:** 01628-810080
E-mail: sales@pacet.co.uk
Website: http://www.pacet.co.uk
Directors: E. Jack (Mkt Research)
Immediate Holding Company: PACET MANUFACTURING LIMITED
Registration no: 02634613 **VAT No.:** GB 578 1196 09
Date established: 1991 **Turnover:** Up to £250,000
No.of Employees: 1 - 10 **Product Groups:** 40

Date of Accounts	Nov 11	Nov 10	Nov 09
Sales Turnover	N/A	236	287
Pre Tax Profit/Loss	N/A	12	-18
Working Capital	-10	53	38
Fixed Assets	264	266	266
Current Assets	157	172	147
Current Liabilities	N/A	8	6

Psion Teklogix Ltd
Unit J Bourne End Business Park Cores End Road, Bourne End, SL8 5AS
Tel: 01628-648800 **Fax:** 01628-648810
E-mail: info@psion.com
Website: http://www.psion.com
Bank(s): Bank of Scotland
Directors: J. Mcmeeking (MD), P. Sherriff (Fin), A. Donn (Sales)
Managers: A. Pearce (Comptroller), H. Moule (Mktg Serv Mgr), D. Dye, G. Kelly (Personnel)

see next page

Psion Teklogix Ltd - Cont'd

Ultimate Holding Company: PSION PLC
Immediate Holding Company: PSION SHARED SERVICES LTD
Registration no: 01739564 **VAT No.:** GB 393 8220 35
Date established: 1983 **Turnover:** £2m - £5m **No.of Employees:** 21 - 50
Product Groups: 44

Date of Accounts	Dec 10	Dec 09	Dec 08
Sales Turnover	3m	N/A	N/A
Pre Tax Profit/Loss	217	N/A	N/A
Working Capital	1m	1m	N/A
Fixed Assets	100	50	50
Current Assets	4m	1m	3m
Current Liabilities	193	N/A	N/A

Renesas Electronic Europe Ltd
2 Dukes Meadow Millboard Road, Bourne End, SL8 5FH
Tel: 01628-585100
Website: http://www.renesas.com
Directors: J. Gorrie (Co Sec)
Managers: R. Green
Immediate Holding Company: RENESAS ELECTRONICS EUROPE LIMITED
Registration no: 04586709 **Date established:** 2002
Turnover: £250m - £500m **No.of Employees:** 101 - 250
Product Groups: 37, 67

Shanks Group plc
Astor House Station Road, Bourne End, SL8 5YP
Tel: 0800-028287 **Fax:** 01628-524114
E-mail: customerservices@shanks.co.uk
Website: http://www.shanks.co.uk
Bank(s): Royal Bank of Scotland
Directors: A. Auer (Dir), F. Welham (Fin), I. Goodfellow (MD), M. Averill (Grp Chief Exec)
Registration no: SC077438 **VAT No.:** GB 259 5477 13
Turnover: £500m - £1,000m **No.of Employees:** 1501 & over
Product Groups: 34, 54

Date of Accounts	Mar 08	Mar 07	Mar 06
Sales Turnover	563700	508500	442500
Pre Tax Profit/Loss	41300	46100	30300
Working Capital	11200	-6300	24700
Fixed Assets	726600	561800	466000
Current Assets	215100	169600	167100
Current Liabilities	203900	175900	142400
Total Share Capital	23700	23500	23500
ROCE% (Return on Capital Employed)	5.6	8.3	6.2
ROT% (Return on Turnover)	7.3	9.1	6.8

Technibond Ltd
Millboard Road, Bourne End, SL8 5XD
Tel: 01628-642800 **Fax:** 01628-642801
E-mail: sales@technibond.co.uk
Website: http://www.technibond.co.uk
Bank(s): HSBC, Oxford
Directors: S. Williams (Sales), M. Harrison (Sales), M. Summers (MD), P. Hunt (Fin)
Immediate Holding Company: TECHNIBOND LIMITED
Registration no: 01593212 **VAT No.:** GB 349 1208 59
Date established: 1981 **Turnover:** £5m - £10m **No.of Employees:** 21 - 50
Product Groups: 27, 66, 68

Date of Accounts	Dec 11	Dec 10	Dec 09
Working Capital	310	288	247
Fixed Assets	47	41	48
Current Assets	1m	1m	1m

D J Webster Ltd
Unit 2 Jackson Industrial Park Wessex Road, Bourne End, SL8 5DT
Tel: 01628-529724 **Fax:** 01628-529594
E-mail: sales@webstermachinery.co.uk
Website: http://www.webstermachinery.co.uk
Directors: D. Webster (Fin)
Managers: P. Webster (Chief Mgr)
Immediate Holding Company: D.J. WEBSTER LIMITED
Registration no: 01301882 **Date established:** 1977
Turnover: £500,000 - £1m **No.of Employees:** 1 - 10 **Product Groups:** 46, 48

Date of Accounts	Feb 08	Feb 11	Feb 10
Sales Turnover	1m	589	378
Pre Tax Profit/Loss	145	50	-26
Working Capital	872	744	741
Fixed Assets	1m	1m	1m
Current Assets	1m	921	891
Current Liabilities	113	31	22

Wessex & Co.
1 Eghams Court Boston Drive, Bourne End, SL8 5YS
Tel: 01628-522771 **Fax:** 01628-523090
E-mail: hugo@wessex-co.co.uk
Website: http://www.wessex-co.co.uk
Directors: S. Shellabear (Co Sec), H. Shellabear (MD)
Immediate Holding Company: SHELLWIN PLC
Registration no: 00820576 **VAT No.:** GB 342 6116 81
Date established: 1964 **Turnover:** £500,000 - £1m
No.of Employees: 1 - 10 **Product Groups:** 80, 82

Date of Accounts	Dec 11	Dec 10	Dec 09
Sales Turnover	887	886	980
Pre Tax Profit/Loss	441	405	458
Working Capital	58	35	305
Fixed Assets	8m	8m	8m
Current Assets	770	803	1m
Current Liabilities	448	467	440

Buckingham

4 D Storage Solutions Ltd
16 Kestrel Way, Buckingham, MK18 7HJ
Tel: 01280-823399
E-mail: enquiries@4dstoragesolutions.co.uk
Website: http://www.4dstoragesolutions.co.uk
Directors: C. Taylor (Dir)
Immediate Holding Company: 4D STORAGE SOLUTIONS LTD
Registration no: 06714564 **Date established:** 2008
Turnover: Up to £250,000 **No.of Employees:** 1 - 10 **Product Groups:** 26, 35, 86

Date of Accounts	Oct 11	Oct 10	Oct 09
Working Capital	-9	-9	-5
Fixed Assets	2	2	2
Current Assets	31	10	12

Automec Equipment & Parts Ltd
36 Ballmoor Buckingham Industrial Estate, Buckingham, MK18 1RQ
Tel: 01280-822818 **Fax:** 01280-823140
E-mail: info@automec.co.uk
Website: http://www.automec.co.uk
Directors: J. Smith (Dir)
Immediate Holding Company: AUTOMEC EQUIPMENT & PARTS LIMITED
Registration no: 01333857 **VAT No.:** GB 301 8349 82
Date established: 1977 **Turnover:** £500,000 - £1m
No.of Employees: 1 - 10 **Product Groups:** 68

Date of Accounts	Dec 11	Dec 10	Dec 09
Working Capital	181	152	149
Fixed Assets	12	16	21
Current Assets	331	292	278

B C Q
Unit 1 Osier Way, Buckingham, MK18 1TB
Tel: 01280-824000 **Fax:** 01280-822333
E-mail: info@bcqgroup.com
Website: http://www.bcqgroup.com
Bank(s): Royal Bank of Scotland
Directors: R. Knowles (Dir), N. Tangi (Sales), H. Knowles (Co Sec), B. Curryer (Dir), T. Spence (MD)
Managers: B. Currier (I.T. Exec)
Ultimate Holding Company: BCQ (HOLDINGS) LIMITED
Immediate Holding Company: BUCKINGHAM COLOUR GROUP LIMITED
Registration no: 01285920 **VAT No.:** GB 476 0963 17
Date established: 1976 **Turnover:** £2m - £5m **No.of Employees:** 51 - 100
Product Groups: 28

Date of Accounts	Mar 12	Mar 11	Mar 10
Working Capital	340	340	340
Current Assets	340	340	340

Brookside Engineering
Brookside Farm Great Horwood Road, Winslow, Buckingham, MK18 3LY
Tel: 01296-715059 **Fax:** 01296-712362
Website: http://www.ic24.net
Directors: D. Spooner (Prop)
Date established: 1995 **No.of Employees:** 1 - 10 **Product Groups:** 26, 35

Geo Brown Implements Ltd
Gawcott Road, Buckingham, MK18 1DR
Tel: 01280-812035 **Fax:** 01280-821115
E-mail: scowley@browns.gb.com
Website: http://www.browns.gb.com
Managers: Cowley (District Mgr)
Immediate Holding Company: RING ROAD GARAGE LIMITED
Registration no: 02095240 **Date established:** 1987
No.of Employees: 1 - 10 **Product Groups:** 41

Date of Accounts	Jul 11	Jul 10	Jul 09
Working Capital	2m	2m	2m
Fixed Assets	595	509	523
Current Assets	2m	2m	2m

C T P Wipac Ltd
London Road, Buckingham, MK18 1BH
Tel: 01280-822800 **Fax:** 01280-822802
E-mail: info@wipac.com
Website: http://www.wipac.com
Bank(s): Lloyds TSB Bank plc
Directors: N. Sibley (MD), S. Dollmann (Sales), M. White (Fin), M. Ross (Fin), S. Beck (Pers)
Managers: T. Lockwood (Personnel), R. Marshall (Tech Serv Mgr), D. Bates (Mktg Serv Mgr)
Ultimate Holding Company: CARCLO PLC
Immediate Holding Company: WIPAC LIMITED
Registration no: 00958139 **VAT No.:** GB 362 0233 93
Date established: 1969 **Turnover:** £20m - £50m
No.of Employees: 101 - 250 **Product Groups:** 37, 39, 42

Date of Accounts	Mar 11	Mar 10	Mar 09
Sales Turnover	26m	24m	25m
Pre Tax Profit/Loss	563	2m	2m
Working Capital	3m	900	1m
Fixed Assets	8m	6m	5m
Current Assets	13m	13m	10m
Current Liabilities	903	2m	2m

Crystal Lighting Ltd a division of Crystal Lighting Ltd
Priory Mill House Leckhampstead Road, Akeley, Buckingham, MK18 5HG
Tel: 01280-860154 **Fax:** 01280-860546
E-mail: sales@crystal-lighting-centre.com
Website: http://www.crystal-lighting-centre.com
Directors: J. Norman (MD)
Immediate Holding Company: CRYSTAL LIGHTING LIMITED
Registration no: 05379705 **Date established:** 2005
No.of Employees: 1 - 10 **Product Groups:** 37

Date of Accounts	Mar 10	Mar 09	Mar 08
Working Capital	-5	-7	-9
Fixed Assets	1	3	4
Current Assets	43	49	48

D & A Agricultural Engineers Ltd
Stonelands Main Street Gawcott, Buckingham, MK18 4HZ
Tel: 01280-822334 **Fax:** 01280-822334
Directors: A. Jenkinson (Dir)
Immediate Holding Company: D & A AGRICULTURAL ENGINEERS LTD
Registration no: 07916388 **Date established:** 2012
No.of Employees: 1 - 10 **Product Groups:** 41

Durotan Ltd
20 West Street, Buckingham, MK18 1HE
Tel: 01280-814048 **Fax:** 01280-817842
E-mail: sales@durotan.ltd.uk
Website: http://www.durotan.ltd.uk
Directors: L. Hanrahan (MD)
Ultimate Holding Company: DUROTAN LIMITED
Immediate Holding Company: DUROTAN CONTRACTS LIMITED
Registration no: 02799729 **Date established:** 1993 **Turnover:** £2m - £5m
No.of Employees: 1 - 10 **Product Groups:** 51, 52, 54

Date of Accounts	Sep 11	Sep 10	Sep 09
Working Capital	30	-36	248
Current Assets	5m	2m	2m

Flowering Plants Ltd
Unit 12 Homeground, Buckingham Industrial Estate, Buckingham, MK18 1UH
Tel: 01280-813764 **Fax:** 01280-823735
E-mail: mail@fpl-irrigation.com
Website: http://www.fpl-irrigation.com
Directors: F. Richardson (MD)
Immediate Holding Company: FLOWERING PLANTS LIMITED
Registration no: 01103601 **VAT No.:** GB 121 3344 22
Date established: 1973 **Turnover:** £500,000 - £1m
No.of Employees: 1 - 10 **Product Groups:** 41, 51

Date of Accounts	Nov 11	Nov 10	Nov 09
Working Capital	-18	-41	-54
Fixed Assets	2	2	1
Current Assets	223	134	135

Gemelli Childcare Vouchers Ltd
Gemelli House Shalstone, Buckingham, MK18 5DZ
Tel: 01280-851113
E-mail: enquiries@gemellicv.co.uk
Website: http://www.gemellichildcarevouchers.co.uk
Directors: H. Start (MD)
Immediate Holding Company: GEMELLI SOLUTIONS LTD.
Registration no: 06292426 **Date established:** 2007
Turnover: Up to £250,000 **No.of Employees:** 1 - 10 **Product Groups:** 80

Date of Accounts	Jul 11	Jul 10	Jul 09
Working Capital	25	-13	-17
Fixed Assets	6	4	5
Current Assets	191	97	61

Hartridge Ltd
The Hartridge Building Network 421 Radclive Road, Gawcott, Buckingham, MK18 4FD
Tel: 01280-825600 **Fax:** 01280-825601
E-mail: sales@hartridge.com
Website: http://www.hartridge.com
Bank(s): Barclays
Directors: G. Herring (MD)
Ultimate Holding Company: RADCLIVE HOLDINGS LIMITED
Immediate Holding Company: HARTRIDGE LIMITED
Registration no: 05048767 **Date established:** 2004
Turnover: £10m - £20m **No.of Employees:** 51 - 100 **Product Groups:** 38, 39, 67

Date of Accounts	Dec 11	Dec 10	Dec 09
Sales Turnover	12m	11m	10m
Pre Tax Profit/Loss	2m	1m	935
Working Capital	3m	2m	2m
Fixed Assets	243	246	268
Current Assets	6m	5m	5m
Current Liabilities	652	2m	631

J D Profile Ltd
30 Balmer Cut Buckingham Industrial Estate, Buckingham, MK18 1UL
Tel: 01280-822693 **Fax:** 01280-824003
E-mail: info@jdprofile.co.uk
Website: http://www.jdprofile.co.uk
Directors: D. Sheridan (Ptnr)
Immediate Holding Company: JD PROFILE LIMITED
Registration no: 07220116 **Date established:** 2010
Turnover: Up to £250,000 **No.of Employees:** 1 - 10 **Product Groups:** 30

Date of Accounts	Apr 12	Apr 11
Working Capital	-3	-5
Fixed Assets	4	5
Current Assets	30	33

Litre Meter Ltd
Hart Hill Barn Granborough Road, North Marston, Buckingham, MK18 3RZ
Tel: 01296-670200 **Fax:** 01296-670999
E-mail: sales@litremeter.com
Website: http://www.litremeter.com
Bank(s): Barclays, Market Square
Directors: C. Wemyss (Eng Serv)
Immediate Holding Company: LITRE METER LIMITED
Registration no: 01216862 **VAT No.:** GB 410 7160 01
Date established: 1975 **Turnover:** £1m - £2m **No.of Employees:** 11 - 20
Product Groups: 38

Date of Accounts	Dec 11	Dec 10	Jan 10
Sales Turnover	2m	N/A	N/A
Pre Tax Profit/Loss	108	N/A	N/A
Working Capital	374	-195	-33
Fixed Assets	1m	141	171
Current Assets	648	380	397
Current Liabilities	178	N/A	N/A

Microcopy Systems Ltd
32 Balmer Cut Buckingham Industrial Estate, Buckingham, MK18 1UL
Tel: 01280-822795 **Fax:** 01280-822795
E-mail: lee@microcopysystems.co.uk
Website: http://www.microcopysystems.co.uk
Directors: L. Stevens (MD)
Immediate Holding Company: MICROCOPY SERVICES LIMITED
Registration no: 02480074 **VAT No.:** GB 797 7803 76
Date established: 1990 **No.of Employees:** 11 - 20 **Product Groups:** 26, 38, 44, 64, 65, 67, 80, 81, 84, 86

Date of Accounts	Jun 11	Jun 10	Jun 09
Working Capital	224	231	223
Fixed Assets	370	370	271
Current Assets	414	372	353

Pace Components Ltd
15 Little Balmer Buckingham Industrial Estate, Buckingham, MK18 1TF
Tel: 01280-822733 **Fax:** 01280-823839
E-mail: sales@pacecomponents.co.uk
Website: http://www.pacecomponents.co.uk
Bank(s): Lloyds TSB Bank plc
Directors: A. Sturgess (Dir), C. Sturgess (Fin)
Immediate Holding Company: PACE COMPONENTS LIMITED
Registration no: 02423335 **VAT No.:** GB 536 3668 24
Date established: 1989 **No.of Employees:** 11 - 20 **Product Groups:** 37

Date of Accounts	Sep 11	Sep 10	Sep 09
Working Capital	243	231	215
Fixed Assets	132	161	197
Current Assets	398	395	299

Paragon Tool Hire Ltd
Wharf House Yard Stratford Road, Buckingham, MK18 1TD
Tel: 01280-822282 **Fax:** 01280-816697
E-mail: info@paragontoolhire.com
Website: http://www.paragontoolhire.com

Directors: S. Griffiths (Dir)
Immediate Holding Company: PARAGON TOOL HIRE LIMITED
Registration no: 02811523 **Date established:** 1993
Turnover: £250,000 - £500,000 **No.of Employees:** 1 - 10
Product Groups: 35, 37, 41, 45, 83

Date of Accounts	Dec 11	Dec 10	Dec 09
Working Capital	11	2	8
Fixed Assets	145	145	130
Current Assets	100	97	95

Paramount Electronics

4 Little Balmer Buckingham Industrial Estate, Buckingham, MK18 1TF
Tel: 01280-817877 **Fax:** 01280-814140
E-mail: purchasing@paramountelectronics.co.uk
Website: http://www.paramountelectronics.co.uk/amosweb
Bank(s): Barclays
Directors: C. Reeves (Dir)
Registration no: 02356906 **VAT No.:** GB 490 9820 16
Turnover: £250,000 - £500,000 **No.of Employees:** 11 - 20
Product Groups: 37, 48, 84

Pulse Training Solutions PTS Ltd

Rutland House 22 Chandos Road, Buckingham, MK18 1AH
Tel: 07776-007733 **Fax:** 01280-812340
E-mail: info@pulsetrainingsolutions.co.uk
Website: http://www.pulsetrainingsolutions.co.uk
Directors: L. Johnson (Fin), P. Turner (MD)
Immediate Holding Company: PULSE TRAINING SOLUTIONS (PTS) LIMITED
Registration no: 05153652 **VAT No.:** GB 314 1937 75
Date established: 2004 **Turnover:** Up to £250,000
No.of Employees: 1 - 10 **Product Groups:** 28, 38

Date of Accounts	Aug 11	Aug 10	Aug 09
Working Capital	25	1	42
Fixed Assets	3	4	3
Current Assets	103	82	117

Surrey Handling Supllies

Radclive Road Gawcott, Buckingham, MK18 4AA
Tel: 0800-619 0800 **Fax:** 01280-821744
E-mail: sales@surreyhandling.com
Directors: W. Dunn (Ptnr)
No.of Employees: 1 - 10 **Product Groups:** 45

Utranazz

Utranazz House Tingewick Road Industrial Park, Buckingham, MK18 1SU
Tel: 01280-820770 **Fax:** 01280-823500
E-mail: info@utranazz.com
Website: http://www.utranazz.com
Directors: T. Evans (Prop)
Managers: S. Wiseman (Mktg Serv Mgr)
Ultimate Holding Company: UTRANAZZ HOLDINGS LIMITED
Immediate Holding Company: UTRANAZZ LIMITED
Registration no: 05708024 **Date established:** 2006
No.of Employees: 11 - 20 **Product Groups:** 33, 36, 39, 40, 41, 42, 45, 48, 51, 61, 66, 67, 83

Date of Accounts	Dec 11	Dec 10	Dec 09
Working Capital	271	220	222
Current Assets	315	326	314

Vetoquinol Ltd

Vetoquinol House Great Slade, Buckingham Industrial Estate, Buckingham, MK18 1PA
Tel: 01280-814500 **Fax:** 01280-825462
E-mail: office@vetoquinol.co.uk
Website: http://www.vetoquinol.co.uk
Managers: G. Macniven (Chief Acct), M. Marshall (Ops Mgr)
Ultimate Holding Company: SOPARFIN SA
Immediate Holding Company: VETOQUINOL UK LIMITED
Registration no: 01578434 **Date established:** 1981
Turnover: £10m - £20m **No.of Employees:** 21 - 50 **Product Groups:** 07, 63

Date of Accounts	Dec 11	Dec 10	Dec 09
Sales Turnover	16m	18m	17m
Pre Tax Profit/Loss	3m	4m	4m
Working Capital	3m	3m	3m
Fixed Assets	238	365	612
Current Assets	8m	8m	7m
Current Liabilities	2m	3m	2m

Vitalograph UK Ltd

Vitalograph Business Park Maids Moreton, Buckingham, MK18 1SW
Tel: 01280-827110 **Fax:** 01280-823302
E-mail: sales@vitalograph.co.uk
Website: http://www.vitalograph.co.uk
Bank(s): Barclays
Directors: M. Garbe (Co Sec)
Managers: K. Moore (Comptroller), A. Christou (Mktg Serv Mgr), B. Bemister (Sales Prom Mgr)
Immediate Holding Company: VITALOGRAPH (UK) LIMITED
Registration no: 01955895 **VAT No.:** GB 120 6257 08
Date established: 1985 **Turnover:** £10m - £20m
No.of Employees: 21 - 50 **Product Groups:** 38

Date of Accounts	Dec 11	Dec 10	Dec 09
Sales Turnover	12m	10m	11m
Pre Tax Profit/Loss	653	-585	-92
Working Capital	2m	153	724
Fixed Assets	3m	2m	2m
Current Assets	11m	2m	3m
Current Liabilities	8m	1m	2m

World Tents

Redfield Buckingham Road, Winslow, Buckingham, MK18 3LZ
Tel: 01296-714555 **Fax:** 01296-714555
E-mail: info@worldtents.co.uk
Website: http://www.worldtents.co.uk
Directors: D. Field (Prop)
Immediate Holding Company: WORLD TENTS LIMITED
Registration no: 05869986 **Date established:** 2006
No.of Employees: 1 - 10 **Product Groups:** 24, 49

Date of Accounts	Jun 11	Jun 10	Jun 08
Working Capital	15	12	5
Current Assets	22	25	17

Zeitlauf

Little Balmer Buckingham Industrial Estate, Buckingham, MK18 1TF
Tel: 01280-824516 **Fax:** 01280-824517
E-mail: chris.robinson@zeitlauf.co.uk
Website: http://www.zeitlauf.co.uk
Directors: C. Robinson (MD)
Registration no: 07135023 **Date established:** 2005
Turnover: Up to £250,000 **No.of Employees:** 1 - 10 **Product Groups:** 35, 39

Chalfont St Giles

Castle Glass

The Shire Centre Model Farm Estate Gorelands Lane, Chalfont St Giles, HP8 4AB
Tel: 01494-873399 **Fax:** 01494-873020
E-mail: sales@castleglasscompany.co.uk
Website: http://www.castleglasscompany.co.uk
Directors: G. Castle (Prop)
Immediate Holding Company: CHILTERN OPEN-AIR MUSEUM LIMITED
Registration no: 01279396 **Date established:** 1976
Turnover: £500,000 - £1m **No.of Employees:** 1 - 10 **Product Groups:** 33, 35, 52, 66

Date of Accounts	Mar 11	Mar 10	Mar 09
Sales Turnover	356	355	774
Pre Tax Profit/Loss	-44	-69	395
Working Capital	436	498	561
Fixed Assets	369	374	380
Current Assets	479	550	594
Current Liabilities	43	52	33

Power Systems International Ltd

High Street, Chalfont St Giles, HP8 4QH
Tel: 01494-871544 **Fax:** 01494-873118
E-mail: info@powersystemsinternational.com
Website: http://www.powersystemsinternational.com
Directors: B. Wallace (MD)
Immediate Holding Company: POWER SYSTEMS INTERNATIONAL LIMITED
Registration no: 02239652 **VAT No.:** GB 527 2465 44
Date established: 1988 **No.of Employees:** 1 - 10 **Product Groups:** 37

Date of Accounts	Mar 12	Mar 11	Mar 10
Working Capital	182	179	170
Fixed Assets	11	12	10
Current Assets	416	318	336

Chesham

3 Way Displays Ltd

3 Orchard House Industrial Estate Amersham Road, Chesham, HP5 1NE
Tel: 01494-773553 **Fax:** 01494-771030
E-mail: sales@3waydisplays.com
Website: http://www.3waydisplays.com
Directors: M. Stroud (MD)
Immediate Holding Company: 3-WAY DISPLAYS LIMITED
Registration no: 03995268 **Date established:** 2000
No.of Employees: 21 - 50 **Product Groups:** 26, 30, 49, 67, 81

Date of Accounts	Oct 11	Oct 10	Oct 09
Working Capital	-139	-137	-107
Fixed Assets	200	21	36
Current Assets	360	519	334

Agricultural Central Trading

90 The Broadway, Chesham, HP5 1EG
Tel: 01494-784931 **Fax:** 01494-791553
E-mail: sales@actionfarm.co.uk
Website: http://www.actionfarm.co.uk
Directors: H. Fellows (Fin)
Managers: S. Stevens (Personnel)
Immediate Holding Company: AGRICULTURAL CENTRAL TRADING LIMITED
Registration no: 00713606 **Date established:** 1962
Turnover: £75m - £125m **No.of Employees:** 21 - 50 **Product Groups:** 61

Date of Accounts	Jun 12	Jun 11	Jun 10
Sales Turnover	115m	108m	86m
Pre Tax Profit/Loss	883	1m	1m
Working Capital	11m	10m	9m
Fixed Assets	1m	1m	1m
Current Assets	26m	27m	20m
Current Liabilities	2m	2m	2m

C P M Moulds Solutions Ltd

Pattison House Addison Road, Chesham, HP5 2BD
Tel: 01494-782131 **Fax:** 01494-778542
E-mail: precision@chesham-moulds.co.uk
Website: http://www.chesham-moulds.co.uk
Directors: R. Maidment (MD)
Immediate Holding Company: CPM MOULD SOLUTIONS LIMITED
Registration no: 05089007 **Date established:** 2004 **Turnover:** £1m - £2m
No.of Employees: 1 - 10 **Product Groups:** 46, 48

Date of Accounts	Mar 11	Mar 10	Mar 09
Working Capital	-50	-56	-48
Fixed Assets	1	2	4
Current Assets	222	137	89

Craft Data

92 Broad Street, Chesham, HP5 3ED
Tel: 01494-778235 **Fax:** 01494-773645
E-mail: sales@craftdata.co.uk
Website: http://www.craftdata.co.uk
Directors: P. Cooper (MD), P. Cooper (Fin), F. Tagg (MD), P. Cooper (Co Sec)
Managers: D. Tagg (Sales Prom Mgr), P. Tagg (Mktg Serv Mgr)
Immediate Holding Company: CRAFT DATA LIMITED
Registration no: 01673387 **Date established:** 1982
Turnover: £500,000 - £1m **No.of Employees:** 1 - 10 **Product Groups:** 37, 44

Date of Accounts	Dec 08	Dec 07	Dec 06
Sales Turnover	646	865	834
Pre Tax Profit/Loss	-46	10	-31
Working Capital	57	122	70
Fixed Assets	33	39	47
Current Assets	201	292	305
Current Liabilities	144	170	235
Total Share Capital	5	5	5
ROCE% (Return on Capital Employed)	-50.6	6.5	-26.7
ROT% (Return on Turnover)	-7.1	1.2	-3.7

Draycast Foundries Ltd

Bellingdon Road, Chesham, HP5 2NR
Tel: 01494-786077 **Fax:** 01494-791337
E-mail: steve@draycast.co.uk
Website: http://www.draycast.co.uk
Bank(s): Lloyds TSB
Directors: P. Nagle (MD), S. Nagle (MD)
Immediate Holding Company: DRAYCAST FOUNDRIES LIMITED
Registration no: 00817931 **VAT No.:** GB 207 6414 79
Date established: 1964 **No.of Employees:** 21 - 50 **Product Groups:** 34

Date of Accounts	Jul 11	Jul 10	Jul 09
Working Capital	173	88	153
Fixed Assets	663	691	723
Current Assets	832	794	771

W Durston Ltd

Progress House Hospital Hill, Chesham, HP5 1PJ
Tel: 01494-793244 **Fax:** 01494-792966
Website: http://www.durston.com
Directors: S. Durston (Fin)
Immediate Holding Company: W. DURSTON LIMITED
Registration no: 01161686 **Date established:** 1974
No.of Employees: 21 - 50 **Product Groups:** 46

Date of Accounts	Apr 08	Apr 07	Apr 06
Working Capital	-1	28	35
Fixed Assets	294	317	338
Current Assets	178	185	193
Current Liabilities	180	157	157
Total Share Capital	1	1	1

Flo-Dyne Controls UK Ltd Flow Dyne, Flowdyne, Flowdine, Flow_dyne, Flow-dyne, Flodyne, Flodine, Flo_dyne

Asheridge Business Centre Asheridge Road, Chesham, HP5 2PT
Tel: 01494-770088 **Fax:** 01494-770099
E-mail: sales@flo-dyne.net
Website: http://www.flo-dyne.net
Directors: M. Higginbotham (MD)
Immediate Holding Company: FLO-DYNE LIMITED
Registration no: 04745863 **VAT No.:** GB 814 2117 68
Date established: 2003 **Turnover:** £1m - £2m **No.of Employees:** 1 - 10
Product Groups: 35, 36, 39, 40, 45, 54

Date of Accounts	Apr 09	Apr 08	Apr 07
Working Capital	-125	34	66
Fixed Assets	217	64	25
Current Assets	742	852	829

Flying Service Engineering Sales Ltd

5 Springfield Road, Chesham, HP5 1PP
Tel: 01494-786666 **Fax:** 01494-791813
E-mail: fsee@talk21.com
Bank(s): Barclays
Directors: R. Burn (Mkt Research), R. Burne (MD), R. Burne (MD)
Immediate Holding Company: FLYING SERVICE ENGINEERING (SALES) LIMITED
Registration no: 00877142 **VAT No.:** GB 702 6661 62
Date established: 1966 **Turnover:** £5m - £10m **No.of Employees:** 21 - 50
Product Groups: 39

Date of Accounts	Oct 11	Oct 10	Oct 09
Working Capital	822	750	2m
Fixed Assets	68	71	259
Current Assets	825	753	2m

Guest Gear Services

Higham Mead, Chesham, HP5 2AH
Tel: 01494-794667 **Fax:** 01494-794668
E-mail: guestgears@yahoo.com
Website: http://www.guestgearservices.co.uk
Directors: N. Guest (Ptnr)
Immediate Holding Company: ENGLAND BROTHERS LIMITED
Registration no: 04883102 **VAT No.:** GB 579 4858 65
Date established: 1993 **Turnover:** Up to £250,000
No.of Employees: 1 - 10 **Product Groups:** 35

Date of Accounts	May 08	May 07	Sep 10
Working Capital	216	188	104
Fixed Assets	204	235	148
Current Assets	500	273	213

G W S Ironworks

31 Broadlands Avenue, Chesham, HP5 1AJ
Tel: 01494-783041
E-mail: chris1sheppard@yahoo.co.uk
Directors: G. Sheppard (Prop)
No.of Employees: 1 - 10 **Product Groups:** 26, 35

H M F Fixings Co.

Buckingham House Mineral Lane, Chesham, HP5 1NL
Tel: 01494-783173 **Fax:** 01494- 771500
E-mail: b.pilling@hmf-fsnet.co.uk
Directors: H. Davies (Prop)
Immediate Holding Company: THE BRITISH DENTAL TRADE ASSOCIATION LIMITED
Registration no: 03488299 **VAT No.:** GB 532 1440 88
Date established: 1997 **Turnover:** £1m - £2m **No.of Employees:** 1 - 10
Product Groups: 66

Date of Accounts	Dec 11	Dec 10	Dec 09
Sales Turnover	2m	2m	2m
Pre Tax Profit/Loss	-80	-161	-38
Working Capital	628	688	745
Fixed Assets	419	426	493
Current Assets	1m	1m	1m
Current Liabilities	500	493	223

Hypa Colour Ltd

Unit E-F Chiltern Commerce Centre Asheridge Road, Chesham, HP5 2PY
Tel: 01494-776965 **Fax:** 01494- 783806
E-mail: grant@hypacolour.com
Website: http://www.hypacolour.com
Directors: G. Horton (MD), P. Cannon (Fin)
Immediate Holding Company: HYPA COLOUR LIMITED
Registration no: 03290934 **Date established:** 1996
Turnover: £500,000 - £1m **No.of Employees:** 1 - 10 **Product Groups:** 28

Date of Accounts	Feb 08	Feb 10	Feb 09
Working Capital	56	-41	10
Fixed Assets	83	70	58
Current Assets	259	167	181

I D F Ltd
Moor Road, Chesham, HP5 1TE
Tel: 01494-791250 **Fax:** 01494-792618
E-mail: idfltd@aol.com
Website: http://www.idfsheetmetal.co.uk
Directors: I. Fletcher (MD)
Immediate Holding Company: I.D.F. LIMITED
Registration no: 02744383 **Date established:** 1992
No.of Employees: 1 - 10 **Product Groups:** 34, 35, 36, 37, 46, 48, 66

Date of Accounts	Jul 11	Jul 10	Jul 09
Working Capital	291	241	137
Fixed Assets	48	89	101
Current Assets	480	586	399

Jacarem Ltd
78 Asheridge Road, Chesham, HP5 2PY
Tel: 01494-791336 **Fax:** 01494-792336
E-mail: sales@jacarem.co.uk
Website: http://www.jacarem.co.uk
Directors: T. Reeve (Dir)
Immediate Holding Company: JACAREM LIMITED
Registration no: 02118154 **Date established:** 1987
Turnover: £500,000 - £1m **No.of Employees:** 11 - 20
Product Groups: 37, 38, 44, 67, 84

Date of Accounts	Aug 11	Aug 10	Aug 09
Working Capital	254	222	175
Fixed Assets	14	13	11
Current Assets	503	339	294

Kilrock Products Ltd
1b Alma Road Industrial Estate, Chesham, HP5 3HB
Tel: 01494-793900 **Fax:** 01494-793400
E-mail: sales@kilrock.co.uk
Website: http://www.kilrock.co.uk
Bank(s): Lloyds TSB Bank plc
Directors: R. Davis (MD)
Immediate Holding Company: KILROCK PRODUCTS LTD
Registration no: 02989166 **VAT No.:** GB 630 8156 54
Date established: 1994 **Turnover:** £1m - £2m **No.of Employees:** 11 - 20
Product Groups: 32

Date of Accounts	Mar 11	Mar 10	Mar 09
Working Capital	629	426	418
Fixed Assets	778	611	642
Current Assets	863	624	627

Lamps & Tubes Illuminations Ltd
Unit 1 Springfield Road, Chesham, HP5 1PW
Tel: 01494-783541 **Fax:** 01494-773972
E-mail: mike.taylor@ltilluminations.co.uk
Website: http://www.ltilluminations.co.uk
Directors: M. Taylor (MD)
Immediate Holding Company: LAMPS & TUBES ILLUMINATIONS LIMITED
Registration no: 04202245 **VAT No.:** GB 630 7741 48
Date established: 2001 **Turnover:** Up to £250,000
No.of Employees: 1 - 10 **Product Groups:** 37, 84

Date of Accounts	Jan 12	Jan 11	Jan 10
Working Capital	95	115	181
Fixed Assets	26	53	67
Current Assets	312	304	400

Mcminn Hardware Wholesalers
Latimer Road, Chesham, HP5 1QJ
Tel: 01494-786241 **Fax:** 01494-786864
E-mail: liam.hyland@decco.co.uk
Website: http://www.decco.co.uk
Bank(s): Nat West
Managers: L. Hyland (Mgr), T. Hall
Immediate Holding Company: DECCO LTD
Registration no: 00417021 **VAT No.:** GB 431 2745 75
Date established: 1976 **Turnover:** £125m - £250m
No.of Employees: 51 - 100 **Product Groups:** 63, 66

P C Xperts
118 Bois Moor Road, Chesham, HP5 1SS
Tel: 01494-785672
E-mail: info@pc-xperts.co.uk
Website: http://www.pc-xperts.co.uk
Directors: G. Smith (Prop)
Turnover: Up to £250,000 **No.of Employees:** 1 - 10 **Product Groups:** 37, 44, 48, 80, 84

Pentagon Protection plc
Solar House Amersham Road, Chesham, HP5 1NG
Tel: 01494-793333 **Fax:** 01494-794123
E-mail: enquiries@pentagonprotection.com
Website: http://www.pentagonprotection.com
Managers: S. Howard (Sales Admin)
Immediate Holding Company: PENTAGON PROTECTION PLC
Registration no: 04488281 **Date established:** 2002 **Turnover:** £2m - £5m
No.of Employees: 1 - 10 **Product Groups:** 30, 33, 35, 49, 52, 66

Date of Accounts	Sep 11	Sep 10	Sep 09
Sales Turnover	3m	2m	3m
Pre Tax Profit/Loss	-318	2	-1m
Working Capital	-189	84	620
Fixed Assets	453	367	405
Current Assets	876	732	1m
Current Liabilities	760	213	373

Rayner Opticians
Lowndes House The Bury Church Street, Chesham, HP5 1DJ
Tel: 01494-797400 **Fax:** 01494-797419
Website: http://www.rayneropticians.co.uk
Directors: J. Baxter (Co Sec), M. Bennett (Comm), R. Dickson (MD)
Ultimate Holding Company: RAYNER & KEELER LIMITED
Immediate Holding Company: LANCASTER & THORPE LIMITED
Registration no: 00249257 **Date established:** 1930
Turnover: £20m - £50m **No.of Employees:** 21 - 50 **Product Groups:** 61

Date of Accounts	Dec 11	Dec 10	Dec 09
Sales Turnover	49m	49m	47m
Pre Tax Profit/Loss	7m	6m	6m
Working Capital	15m	13m	10m
Fixed Assets	13m	12m	12m
Current Assets	21m	18m	15m
Current Liabilities	3m	2m	3m

R Russell
45 Townsend Road, Chesham, HP5 2AA
Tel: 01494-782837 **Fax:** 01494-791598
E-mail: info@r-russellbrush.co.uk
Website: http://www.russellbrush.co.uk
Directors: R. Russell (Ptnr)
VAT No.: GB 209 3934 56 **Turnover:** £250,000 - £500,000
No.of Employees: 1 - 10 **Product Groups:** 49, 63

Silverson Machines Ltd
Waterside, Chesham, HP5 1PQ
Tel: 01494-786331 **Fax:** 01494-791452
E-mail: sales@silverson.co.uk
Website: http://www.silverson.com
Directors: H. Rothman (MD)
Managers: M. Smith (Mktg Serv Mgr), R. McLellan (Buyer), S. Horler (Tech Serv Mgr)
Ultimate Holding Company: SILNAT HOLDINGS LIMITED
Immediate Holding Company: SILVERSON MACHINES LIMITED
Registration no: 00415969 **Date established:** 1946
Turnover: £10m - £20m **No.of Employees:** 51 - 100 **Product Groups:** 41, 84

Date of Accounts	Jun 11	Jun 10	Jun 09
Sales Turnover	11m	9m	9m
Pre Tax Profit/Loss	3m	1m	2m
Working Capital	5m	4m	1m
Fixed Assets	1m	1m	1m
Current Assets	10m	8m	8m
Current Liabilities	1m	594	561

T G W Services
2 Cogdells Close Chartridge, Chesham, HP5 2TR
Tel: 01494-837701 **Fax:** 01494-837970
Website: http://www.tgwservices.co.uk
Directors: T. Woodward (Prop)
Date established: 1970 **No.of Employees:** 1 - 10 **Product Groups:** 38, 42

TACK International
Tack House Latimer Park, Chesham, HP5 1TR
Tel: 01494-766 611 **Fax:** 01494-766622
E-mail: info@tack.co.uk
Website: http://www.tack.co.uk
Bank(s): National Westminster, Victoria Street SW1
Directors: I. Cowie (Co Sec), R. Barham (Grp Chief Exec)
Managers: K. Morfett (Maint), L. Gulliver (Mktg Serv Mgr)
Ultimate Holding Company: TACK Industries Ltd, London SW1
Registration no: 02936840 **Date established:** 1994 **Turnover:** £2m - £5m
No.of Employees: 21 - 50 **Product Groups:** 81, 86

Turtle & Pearce Ltd
9 Higham Road, Chesham, HP5 2AF
Tel: 01494-783938 **Fax:** 01494-791241
E-mail: sales@flagmakers.co.uk
Website: http://www.flags-turtle.co.uk
Directors: C. Deegan (Dir), P. Tripp (MD)
Registration no: 00220376 **VAT No.:** 235 7941 42 **Date established:** 2009
Turnover: £1m - £2m **No.of Employees:** 1 - 10 **Product Groups:** 23, 49

Date of Accounts	Dec 07	Dec 06	Dec 05
Working Capital	260	292	225
Fixed Assets	65	71	96
Current Assets	530	535	536
Current Liabilities	270	243	311
Total Share Capital	6	6	6

George Tutill Ltd
9 Higham Road, Chesham, HP5 2AF
Tel: 01494-783938 **Fax:** 01494-791241
E-mail: chris@flagmakers.co.uk
Website: http://www.flags-tutill.co.uk
Directors: A. Tripp (Dir), C. Deegan (Co Sec), C. Deegan (MD), P. Tripp (MD)
Managers: A. Garland (Sales Prom Mgr)
Immediate Holding Company: GEORGE TUTILL,LIMITED
Registration no: 00369605 **VAT No.:** GB 744 0294 43
Date established: 1941 **Turnover:** £1m - £2m **No.of Employees:** 11 - 20
Product Groups: 49, 83

Date of Accounts	Dec 10	Dec 09	Dec 08
Working Capital	3	3	3
Current Assets	3	3	3

Gerrards Cross

Activity Chest (Tulip Toys & Gifts Ltd)
17 Market Place Chalfont St Peter, Gerrards Cross, SL9 9EA
Tel: 01753-892828 **Fax:** 01753-892828
E-mail: sales@activitychest.com
Website: http://www.activitychest.com
Directors: L. Royal (Dir)
Registration no: 04667468 **No.of Employees:** 1 - 10 **Product Groups:** 61, 65

Chiltern I T Parts
Anamax House Oxford Road, Gerrards Cross, SL9 7BB
Tel: 01753-890088 **Fax:** 01753-891916
E-mail: graham@chilternit.com
Website: http://www.chilternit.com
Bank(s): National Westminster, Chalfont St. Peter
Directors: G. Nye (Ch)
Immediate Holding Company: UNITEK HOLDINGS LTD
Registration no: 01217170 **VAT No.:** 531 2452 82
No.of Employees: 21 - 50 **Product Groups:** 38, 44

Eka Ltd
Valkyrie House 38 Packhorse Road, Gerrards Cross, SL9 8EB
Tel: 01753-889818 **Fax:** 01753-880004
Website: http://www.ekalimited.com
Directors: M. Dixon (Dir)
Ultimate Holding Company: OXLEY FORSTER HOLDINGS LIMITED
Immediate Holding Company: EKA LIMITED
Registration no: 01402687 **Date established:** 1978
Turnover: £20m - £50m **No.of Employees:** 11 - 20 **Product Groups:** 40, 45

Date of Accounts	Jun 11	Jun 10	Jun 09
Sales Turnover	37m	40m	25m
Pre Tax Profit/Loss	7m	9m	4m
Working Capital	14m	11m	5m
Fixed Assets	258	344	499
Current Assets	19m	18m	11m
Current Liabilities	2m	3m	2m

Lee Products Ltd
3 High Street Chalfont St Peter, Gerrards Cross, SL9 9QE
Tel: 01753-886664 **Fax:** 01753-889588
E-mail: sales@leeproducts.co.uk
Website: http://www.leeproducts.co.uk
Directors: P. Roberts (Sales), W. Lee (Grp Chief Exec)
Managers: M. Stott (Chief Mgr), I. Flint (Comptroller)
Immediate Holding Company: LEE PRODUCTS LIMITED
Registration no: FC008627 **VAT No.:** GB 228 2148 74
Date established: 1975 **Turnover:** £10m - £20m **No.of Employees:** 1 - 10
Product Groups: 30, 36, 39, 40, 42

Date of Accounts	Oct 11	Oct 10	Oct 09
Sales Turnover	12m	10m	9m
Pre Tax Profit/Loss	2m	2m	2m
Working Capital	8m	7m	7m
Fixed Assets	78	48	66
Current Assets	9m	8m	8m
Current Liabilities	400	304	282

R W S Group plc
Europa House Chiltern Park Chiltern Hill, Chalfont St. Peter, Gerrards Cross, SL9 9FG
Tel: 01753-480200 **Fax:** 01753-480280
E-mail: rwstrans@rws.com
Website: http://www.rws.com
Bank(s): Barclays
Directors: M. Mccarthy (Fin)
Managers: G. Terrill (Mktg Serv Mgr), A. Ramsey (Personnel)
Ultimate Holding Company: RWS HOLDINGS PLC
Immediate Holding Company: RWS GROUP LIMITED
Registration no: 01575193 **Date established:** 1981 **Turnover:** £2m - £5m
No.of Employees: 251 - 500 **Product Groups:** 80, 81

Date of Accounts	Sep 11	Sep 10	Sep 09
Sales Turnover	4m	4m	4m
Pre Tax Profit/Loss	6m	7m	9m
Working Capital	9m	9m	9m
Fixed Assets	6m	6m	6m
Current Assets	9m	10m	10m
Current Liabilities	385	256	308

Regalzone LLP
Dukes Valley Windsor Road, Gerrards Cross, SL9 8SR
Tel: 01753-662666 **Fax:** 01753-664463
E-mail: info@regalzone.com
Website: http://www.regalzone.com
Directors: P. Preston (Ptnr), P. Blewett (Fin)
Immediate Holding Company: REGALZONE LLP
Registration no: OC301279 **Date established:** 2002
No.of Employees: 1 - 10 **Product Groups:** 26, 30, 33, 40, 62, 63, 66, 67

Date of Accounts	Jan 11	Jan 10	Jan 09
Working Capital	-409	-402	-424
Fixed Assets	410	417	451
Current Assets	329	307	338
Current Liabilities	107	N/A	58

The Services Sound & Vision Corporation
Chalfont Grove Narcot Lane, Chalfont St Peter, Gerrards Cross, SL9 8TN
Tel: 01494-874461 **Fax:** 01494-872982
E-mail: info@ssvc.com
Website: http://www.ssvc.com
Bank(s): HSBC Bank plc
Directors: D. Hamilton (Fin)
Immediate Holding Company: SERVICES SOUND AND VISION CORPORATION(THE)
Registration no: 00407270 **Date established:** 1946
Turnover: £20m - £50m **No.of Employees:** 251 - 500
Product Groups: 79, 84, 86, 89

Date of Accounts	Mar 11	Mar 10	Mar 09
Sales Turnover	39m	38m	38m
Pre Tax Profit/Loss	4m	4m	-15m
Working Capital	6m	3m	4m
Fixed Assets	19m	18m	13m
Current Assets	10m	12m	12m
Current Liabilities	3m	5m	5m

Truck Protect
44 The Uplands, Gerrards Cross, SL9 7JG
Tel: 07768-812994
Directors: R. Fowler (Prop)
No.of Employees: 1 - 10 **Product Groups:** 37, 39

Uniq plc
1 Chalfont Park, Gerrards Cross, SL9 0UN
Tel: 01753-276000 **Fax:** 01753-276071
E-mail: philip.stockill@abagri.com
Website: http://www.uniq.com
Directors: M. Beer (Fin), G. Summerfield (Grp Chief Exec), G. Eaton (Grp Chief Exec)
Immediate Holding Company: UNIQ PLC
Registration no: 03912506 **Date established:** 2000
Turnover: £250m - £500m **No.of Employees:** 1 - 10 **Product Groups:** 62

Date of Accounts	Dec 10	Dec 09	Dec 08
Sales Turnover	312m	287m	797m
Pre Tax Profit/Loss	-11m	-19m	-55m
Working Capital	4m	-3m	-19m
Fixed Assets	125m	223m	315m
Current Assets	58m	165m	222m
Current Liabilities	31m	142m	137m

Uxbridge Engineering Co. Ltd
2 Dukes Kiln Drive, Gerrards Cross, SL9 7HD
Tel: 01753-889511 **Fax:** 01753-880118
E-mail: enquiries@uxbridge-eng.demon.co.uk
Directors: G. Orrow (MD)
Immediate Holding Company: UXBRIDGE ENGINEERING CO. LIMITED
Registration no: 01248858 **Date established:** 1976
Turnover: £250,000 - £500,000 **No.of Employees:** 1 - 10
Product Groups: 32, 35, 39, 40, 42, 44, 48, 52, 66, 84

Date of Accounts	Apr 11	Apr 10	Apr 09
Working Capital	208	222	284
Fixed Assets	33	18	22
Current Assets	273	269	352

Veolia Enviromental Services Ltd
Oxford Road, Gerrards Cross, SL9 8TE
Tel: 01753-880579 **Fax:** 01753-891709
Website: http://www.veolia.co.uk
Managers: N. Revell (Depot Mgr)
Ultimate Holding Company: JCM HOLDINGS LTD
Immediate Holding Company: JCM GROUP LTD
Registration no: 03743461 **Turnover:** £20m - £50m
No.of Employees: 11 - 20 **Product Groups:** 39, 42, 54

Great Missenden

Andrew McLaren
The Chiltern Hospital, Great Missenden, HP16 0EN
Tel: 01494-890890 **Fax:** 01494-890250
E-mail: mclaren@bucksendocrine.com
Website: http://www.bucksendocrine.com
Directors: A. McLaren (Ch), T. Hart (Co Sec)
Date established: 2004 **No.of Employees:** 1 - 10 **Product Groups:** 88

Ashact Consulting Ltd (a division of Hyder Consulting)
Bridge House Station Approach, Great Missenden, HP16 9AZ
Tel: 01494-891100 **Fax:** 01494-890320
E-mail: info@ashactconsulting.com
Website: http://www.ashactconsulting.com
Directors: R. Barnard (Dir)
Ultimate Holding Company: HYDER CONSULTING PLC
Immediate Holding Company: ASHACT LIMITED
Registration no: 03860676 **VAT No.:** GB 727 2509 34
Date established: 1999 **Turnover:** £250,000 - £500,000
No.of Employees: 1 - 10 **Product Groups:** 54

Date of Accounts	Mar 12	Mar 11	Mar 10
Working Capital	N/A	N/A	72
Current Assets	N/A	N/A	72

Chiltern Services Ltd
Chiltern Road Ballinger, Great Missenden, HP16 9LH
Tel: 01494-837268 **Fax:** 01494-837718
Directors: R. Edwards (Dir)
Immediate Holding Company: CHILTERN SERVICES LIMITED
Registration no: 02144807 **Date established:** 1987
Turnover: Up to £250,000 **No.of Employees:** 1 - 10 **Product Groups:** 35, 36, 39

Date of Accounts	Dec 11	Dec 10	Dec 09
Sales Turnover	N/A	N/A	79
Working Capital	3	3	6
Fixed Assets	16	20	14
Current Assets	30	25	29
Current Liabilities	21	19	21

Cocredo
Missenden Abbey, Great Missenden, HP16 0BD
Tel: 01494-790600 **Fax:** 01494-790696
E-mail: helpdesk@cocredo.com
Website: http://www.cocredo.com
Directors: D. Hancocks (Dir)
Immediate Holding Company: COCREDO LIMITED
Registration no: 05319965 **Date established:** 2004
No.of Employees: 1 - 10 **Product Groups:** 80

Date of Accounts	Jan 12	Jan 11	Jan 10
Working Capital	10	-10	19
Fixed Assets	8	22	21
Current Assets	77	41	83

Roger Hance Sporting Guns
Orchard Corner Rignall Road, Great Missenden, HP16 9AN
Tel: 01494-864708 **Fax:** 01494-864708
E-mail: roger.hance@btinternet.com
Directors: R. Hance (Prop)
Date established: 1985 **No.of Employees:** 1 - 10 **Product Groups:** 36, 39, 40

Jewson Ltd
Chesham Road Hyde End, Great Missenden, HP16 0RD
Tel: 01494-864223 **Fax:** 01494-868792
Website: http://www.jewson.co.uk
Directors: P. Hindle (MD)
Managers: C. Holman (District Mgr)
Ultimate Holding Company: COMPAGNIE DE SAINT GOBAIN (FRANCE)
Immediate Holding Company: JEWSON LIMITED
Registration no: 00348407 **VAT No.:** GB 394 1212 63
Date established: 1939 **Turnover:** £2m - £5m **No.of Employees:** 1 - 10
Product Groups: 66

Date of Accounts	Dec 11	Dec 10	Dec 09
Sales Turnover	1606m	1547m	1485m
Pre Tax Profit/Loss	18m	100m	45m
Working Capital	-345m	-250m	-349m
Fixed Assets	496m	387m	461m
Current Assets	657m	1005m	1320m
Current Liabilities	66m	120m	64m

Organic Concentrates Ltd
Hotley Bottom Hotley Bottom Lane, Prestwood, Great Missenden, HP16 9PL
Tel: 01494-866768 **Fax:** 01494-867653
E-mail: organic6x@btconnect.com
Website: http://www.6-x.co.uk
Directors: C. Green (MD)
Registration no: 00744214 **VAT No.:** GB 207 6851 57
Date established: 1999 **Turnover:** £500,000 - £1m
No.of Employees: 1 - 10 **Product Groups:** 66

Date of Accounts	Aug 07	Aug 06
Working Capital	6	3
Fixed Assets	2	3
Current Assets	11	11
Current Liabilities	5	9
Total Share Capital	1	1

High Wycombe

3663
Buckingham Court Kingsmead Business Park, London Road, High Wycombe, HP11 1JU
Tel: 0370-3663 251
E-mail: advice_centre@3663.co.uk
Website: http://www.3663.co.uk
Product Groups: 20, 22, 24, 27, 30, 32, 33, 35, 36, 37, 38, 40, 41, 42, 44, 45, 62, 63, 64, 66, 67, 69, 87

Active Electronics plc
Albion House Gordon Road, High Wycombe, HP13 6ET
Tel: 01494-441414 **Fax:** 01494-524674
E-mail: pool@active-electronics.co.uk
Website: http://www.activeelectronic.co.uk
Bank(s): Lloyds TSB Bank plc
Directors: G. Cooper (Sales), G. Ireland (MD), P. Jones (Ch)
Managers: C. Homewood, C. Homewood (Buyer), N. Peach (Comptroller)
Immediate Holding Company: ACTIVE ELECTRONICS PLC
Registration no: 01531348 **VAT No.:** GB 342 8601 64
Date established: 1980 **Turnover:** £10m - £20m
No.of Employees: 21 - 50 **Product Groups:** 37, 38

Date of Accounts	Dec 07	Dec 06
Sales Turnover	13585	13305
Pre Tax Profit/Loss	275	247
Working Capital	3621	3493
Fixed Assets	159	124
Current Assets	5831	5443
Current Liabilities	2210	1950
Total Share Capital	50	50
ROCE% (Return on Capital Employed)	7.3	6.8
ROT% (Return on Turnover)	2.0	1.9

Adcal Labels Ltd
Jayem Works Gomm Road, High Wycombe, HP13 7DJ
Tel: 01494-530761 **Fax:** 01494-461651
E-mail: sales@adcal-labels.co.uk
Website: http://www.adcal-labels.co.uk
Bank(s): HSBC, Gerrards Cross
Directors: M. O'connor (MD), P. Mitchell (Fin)
Ultimate Holding Company: ADCAL HOLDINGS LIMITED
Immediate Holding Company: ADCAL LABELS LIMITED
Registration no: 01302244 **Date established:** 1977 **Turnover:** £1m - £2m
No.of Employees: 11 - 20 **Product Groups:** 27, 28

Date of Accounts	Apr 11	Apr 10	Apr 09
Working Capital	465	453	478
Fixed Assets	226	222	246
Current Assets	691	645	751

Airflow Developments Ltd
Aidelle House Lancaster Road Cressex Business Park, High Wycombe, HP12 3QP
Tel: 01494-525252 **Fax:** 01494-461073
E-mail: jkelly@airflow.co.uk
Website: http://www.airflow.com
Directors: G. Mueller (Fin)
Managers: J. Kelly (Mktg Serv Mgr), S. Headdey (Comptroller)
Immediate Holding Company: AIRFLOW DEVELOPMENTS LIMITED
Registration no: 00550374 **Date established:** 1955
Turnover: £10m - £20m **No.of Employees:** 51 - 100 **Product Groups:** 14

Date of Accounts	Dec 11	Dec 10	Dec 09
Sales Turnover	12m	11m	9m
Pre Tax Profit/Loss	701	607	218
Working Capital	5m	4m	4m
Fixed Assets	561	662	788
Current Assets	6m	5m	5m
Current Liabilities	634	572	576

Alba Precision Tooling
Unit 9 West Yard Industrial Estate Slough Lane, Saunderton, High Wycombe, HP14 4HN
Tel: 01494-563529 **Fax:** 01494-563529
Directors: B. Kitching (Prop)
Registration no: 02838403 **Date established:** 1993
Turnover: Up to £250,000 **No.of Employees:** 1 - 10 **Product Groups:** 36

Alrog Engineering Ltd
Unit 3 Halifax Road Cressex Business Park, High Wycombe, HP12 3SN
Tel: 01494-437031 **Fax:** 01494-528104
E-mail: alrog-engineering@btconnect.com
Website: http://www.cellar.worldonline.co.uk
Directors: R. Butler (Dir), P. Butler (Fin)
Immediate Holding Company: ALROG ENGINEERING LIMITED
Registration no: 01312096 **Date established:** 1977
No.of Employees: 1 - 10 **Product Groups:** 48

Date of Accounts	May 12	May 11	May 10
Working Capital	95	97	52
Fixed Assets	36	41	48
Current Assets	158	186	123

Archer Technicoat Ltd (Head Office)
Unit E Sands Industrial Estate Progress Road, Sands Industrial Estate, High Wycombe, HP12 4JD
Tel: 01494-462101 **Fax:** 01494-463049
E-mail: info@cvd.co.uk
Website: http://www.cvd.co.uk
Directors: C. Prentice (Tech Serv)
Immediate Holding Company: ARCHER TECHNICOAT LIMITED
Registration no: 01835470 **VAT No.:** GB 604 2439 69
Date established: 1984 **Turnover:** £500,000 - £1m
No.of Employees: 1 - 10 **Product Groups:** 40, 46

Date of Accounts	Jun 11	Jun 10	Jun 09
Working Capital	329	298	201
Fixed Assets	28	6	17
Current Assets	414	394	224

Ashmond Electronics Ltd
8 Gadwey House Leigh Street, High Wycombe, HP11 2QU
Tel: 01494-440925 **Fax:** 01494-446795
Website: http://www.ashmond.demon.co.uk
Directors: A. Arnold (MD)
Immediate Holding Company: ASHMOND ELECTRONICS LIMITED
Registration no: 01213709 **Date established:** 1975
Turnover: £500,000 - £1m **No.of Employees:** 1 - 10 **Product Groups:** 38

Date of Accounts	Dec 11	Dec 10	Dec 09
Working Capital	-62	-87	-84
Fixed Assets	133	140	146
Current Assets	47	30	60

Audio Ltd
Audio House Progress Road, Sands Industrial Estate, High Wycombe, HP12 4JD
Tel: 01494-511711 **Fax:** 01494-539600
E-mail: info@audioltd.com
Website: http://www.audioltd.com
Bank(s): National Westminster Bank Plc
Directors: K. Patel (Fin), L. Stone (I.T. Dir)
Immediate Holding Company: AUDIO LIMITED
Registration no: 00439619 **VAT No.:** GB 227 3638 38
Date established: 1947 **Turnover:** £1m - £2m **No.of Employees:** 11 - 20
Product Groups: 37

Date of Accounts	Mar 11	Mar 10	Mar 09
Working Capital	903	927	743
Fixed Assets	323	314	337
Current Assets	1m	1m	850

B F Components Solutions Ltd
209 Main Road Naphill, High Wycombe, HP14 4SE
Tel: 01494-565151 **Fax:** 01494-562077
E-mail: sales@bfcsltd.com
Website: http://www.bfcsltd.com
Bank(s): National Westminster Bank Plc
Directors: K. Pond (MD), G. Pond (Fin)
Ultimate Holding Company: BFC GROUP LIMITED
Immediate Holding Company: BF CS LIMITED
Registration no: 04018559 **Date established:** 2000 **Turnover:** £2m - £5m
No.of Employees: 21 - 50 **Product Groups:** 30, 35, 67

Date of Accounts	Oct 11	Oct 10	Oct 09
Working Capital	1m	918	821
Fixed Assets	63	57	78
Current Assets	2m	2m	1m

B M S Group
Oakridge House Wellington Road, Cressex Business Park, High Wycombe, HP12 3PR
Tel: 01494-557340 **Fax:** 01494-557310
E-mail: info@bmsservicedoffices.co.uk
Website: http://www.bmsservicedoffices.co.uk
Directors: D. Bradbury (Ptnr)
Immediate Holding Company: HAZLEMERE HOLDINGS LIMITED
Registration no: 04341544 **Date established:** 2003
No.of Employees: 1 - 10 **Product Groups:** 20, 48, 49, 61, 62, 65, 83

Date of Accounts	Jan 12	Jan 11	Jan 10
Sales Turnover	9m	9m	8m
Pre Tax Profit/Loss	588	-155	244
Working Capital	928	616	822
Fixed Assets	2m	2m	2m
Current Assets	3m	2m	2m
Current Liabilities	954	434	667

B M Trada Certification Ltd
Stocking Lane Hughenden Valley, High Wycombe, HP14 4ND
Tel: 01494-569700 **Fax:** 01494-565487
E-mail: enquiries@bmtrada.com
Website: http://www.bmtrada.com
Directors: C. Gill (Grp Chief Exec), D. Webb (Fin)
Managers: J. Owen (Sales & Mktg Mg), M. Withers, A. Endres (Tech Serv Mgr), M. Brooks (Personnel)
Ultimate Holding Company: BM TRADA GROUP LIMITED
Immediate Holding Company: TRADA CERTIFICATION LIMITED
Registration no: 03121112 **VAT No.:** GB 479 5222 16
Date established: 1995 **Turnover:** £5m - £10m **No.of Employees:** 21 - 50
Product Groups: 51, 80, 85

Balform Ltd
Unit 28 Soho Mills Industrial Estate Wooburn Green, High Wycombe, HP10 0PF
Tel: 01628-528021 **Fax:** 01628-810213
E-mail: enquiries@balform.co.uk
Website: http://www.balform.co.uk
Directors: B. Brian (Dir), B. Lovelock (MD), S. Butler (Dir), M. Young (Dir)
Immediate Holding Company: BALFORM LIMITED
Registration no: 01385214 **Date established:** 1978 **Turnover:** £5m - £10m
No.of Employees: 21 - 50 **Product Groups:** 30, 39, 44, 46, 48

Date of Accounts	Dec 11	Dec 10	Dec 09
Sales Turnover	N/A	4m	3m
Pre Tax Profit/Loss	N/A	66	3
Working Capital	-148	226	73
Fixed Assets	775	613	517
Current Assets	1m	2m	1m
Current Liabilities	N/A	797	745

Banfield Refrigeration Supplies Ltd
6 Wycombe Industrial Mall West End Street, High Wycombe, HP11 2QY
Tel: 01494-473330 **Fax:** 01494-473057
E-mail: sales@banfield-refrigeration.com
Website: http://www.banfield-refrigeration.com
Directors: M. Banfield (MD)
Immediate Holding Company: BANFIELD REFRIGERATION SUPPLIES LIMITED
Registration no: 01598632 **Date established:** 1981
No.of Employees: 1 - 10 **Product Groups:** 38, 40, 66

Date of Accounts	Dec 11	Dec 10	Dec 09
Working Capital	91	104	105
Fixed Assets	26	12	16
Current Assets	110	122	127

Bearing Traders Ltd
18-20 Desborough Street, High Wycombe, HP11 2LY
Tel: 01494-441301 **Fax:** 01494-438085
E-mail: garyhughes@bearingtraders.com
Website: http://www.bearingtraders.com
Directors: G. Hughes (MD), A. Hughes (Co Sec)
Immediate Holding Company: BEARING TRADERS LIMITED
Registration no: 01994643 **VAT No.:** GB 442 4178 61
Date established: 1986 **Turnover:** £2m - £5m **No.of Employees:** 1 - 10
Product Groups: 35, 36

Date of Accounts	Apr 11	Apr 10	Apr 09
Sales Turnover	N/A	N/A	4m
Pre Tax Profit/Loss	N/A	N/A	60
Working Capital	-10	-52	-61
Fixed Assets	91	111	115
Current Assets	1m	911	965
Current Liabilities	N/A	N/A	525

E Becker Ltd
2 Hazlemere View Hazlemere, High Wycombe, HP15 7BY
Tel: 01494-713777 **Fax:** 01494-713888
E-mail: brian.white@onmedica.com
Managers: B. White (Mgr)
Registration no: 00462934 **Turnover:** £500,000 - £1m
No.of Employees: 1 - 10 **Product Groups:** 23, 27, 32, 34, 64, 66

Date of Accounts	Mar 07	Mar 06
Working Capital	73	69
Fixed Assets	6	6
Current Assets	188	210
Current Liabilities	115	141
Total Share Capital	52	32

Beckman Coulter UK Ltd
Oakley Court Kingsmead Business Park Frederick Place, High Wycombe, HP11 1JU
Tel: 01494-441181 **Fax:** 01494-447558
E-mail: sakhtar@beckmancoulter.com
Website: http://www.beckmancoulter.com
Bank(s): National Westminster
Directors: S. Akhtar (MD)
Managers: L. Annereau (Mktg Serv Mgr)
Ultimate Holding Company: BECKMAN COULTER INC (USA)
Immediate Holding Company: BECKMAN HOLDINGS LIMITED
Registration no: 02303634 **Date established:** 1988
Turnover: £50m - £75m **No.of Employees:** 101 - 250
Product Groups: 38, 42

Date of Accounts	Dec 11	Dec 10	Dec 09
Pre Tax Profit/Loss	1	1m	1m
Working Capital	N/A	-1	-1
Fixed Assets	7m	7m	7m

Beta Valve Systems Ltd
Parkhouse Business Centre Desborough Park Road, High Wycombe, HP12 3DJ
Tel: 01494-459511 **Fax:** 01494-461136
E-mail: ian@betavalve.com
Website: http://www.betavalve.com
Directors: I. Sparrowhawk (MD), A. Allen (Fin)
Immediate Holding Company: BETA VALVE SYSTEMS LTD
Registration no: 01740537 **VAT No.:** GB 385 5884 92
Date established: 1983 **Turnover:** £1m - £2m **No.of Employees:** 1 - 10
Product Groups: 36, 38

Date of Accounts	Jul 11	Jul 10	Jul 09
Working Capital	229	175	142
Fixed Assets	25	35	4
Current Assets	680	634	491

Biffa Waste Services Ltd
High Wycombe Service Centre Kingsmill London Road, High Wycombe, HP11 1LH
Tel: 0800-601601 **Fax:** 01494- 528440
E-mail: customerservices@biffa.co.uk
Website: http://www.biffa.co.uk
Directors: I. Wakelin (MD)
Immediate Holding Company: BIFFA WASTE SERVICES LIMITED
Registration no: 00946107 **Date established:** 1969
Turnover: £250m - £500m **No.of Employees:** 1501 & over
Product Groups: 54, 72, 83

Date of Accounts	Mar 08	Mar 09	Apr 10
Sales Turnover	555m	574m	492m
Pre Tax Profit/Loss	23m	50m	30m
Working Capital	229m	271m	293m
Fixed Assets	371m	360m	378m
Current Assets	409m	534m	609m
Current Liabilities	50m	100m	115m

Biffa Waste Services Ltd
Coronation Road Cressex Business Park, High Wycombe, HP12 3TZ
Tel: 01494-521221 **Fax:** 01934-416222
E-mail: marketing@biffa.co.uk
Website: http://www.biffa.co.uk
Directors: I. Wakelin (Grp Chief Exec)
Managers: D. Kirkbride (Mgr), T. Derby (Sales & Mktg Mg), C. Meaker (Cr Control)
Immediate Holding Company: BIFFA WASTE SERVICES LIMITED
Registration no: 00946107 **Date established:** 1969 **Turnover:** £2m - £5m
No.of Employees: 251 - 500 **Product Groups:** 32, 54

Biffa Waste Servicesdo Not Use
Accuray House Coronation Road, Cressex Business Park, High Wycombe, HP12 3TZ
Tel: 01494-521221 **Fax:** 01934-416222
E-mail: info@biffa.co.uk
Website: http://www.biffa.co.uk
Directors: K. Woodward (Co Sec)
Managers: C. Meaker, T. Derby (Sales & Mktg Mg)
Ultimate Holding Company: WASTEINVESTMENTS LLP
Immediate Holding Company: BIFFA WASTE LIMITED
Registration no: 04084432 **Date established:** 2000
No.of Employees: 101 - 250 **Product Groups:** 32, 54

Date of Accounts	Mar 08	Mar 09	Apr 10
Sales Turnover	555m	574m	492m
Pre Tax Profit/Loss	23m	50m	30m
Working Capital	229m	271m	293m
Fixed Assets	371m	360m	378m
Current Assets	409m	534m	609m
Current Liabilities	50m	100m	115m

M E C Bird Associates
Horsleys Green, High Wycombe, HP14 3UX
Tel: 01494-482348 **Fax:** 01494-482931
E-mail: mecbird@medbird.com
Directors: M. Bird (Prop), A. Bird (Fin)
Immediate Holding Company: MEC BIRD ASSOCIATES LIMITED
Registration no: 04668516 **VAT No.:** GB 194 8433 28
Date established: 2003 **Turnover:** Up to £250,000
No.of Employees: 1 - 10 **Product Groups:** 84

Brophy Die Casting
15 Soho Mills Wooburn Green, High Wycombe, HP10 0PF
Tel: 01628-525068 **Fax:** 01628-525129
E-mail: michael.brophy@brophycastings.co.uk
Website: http://www.brophycastings.co.uk
Directors: M. Brophy (Ptnr)
Turnover: £250,000 - £500,000 **No.of Employees:** 1 - 10
Product Groups: 34, 66

Bucks Tackle
11 Ford Street, High Wycombe, HP11 1RU
Tel: 01494-437035 **Fax:** 01494-463132
Directors: S. Safri (Prop)
Date established: 1985 **No.of Employees:** 1 - 10 **Product Groups:** 36, 39, 40

C E S Hire Ltd
Binders Industrial Estate Cryers Hill Road, Cryers Hill, High Wycombe, HP15 6LJ
Tel: 01494-715472 **Fax:** 01494-712683
E-mail: info@ces-hire.com
Website: http://www.ces-hire.com
Directors: N. Rogers (Prop)
Immediate Holding Company: C.E.S. - HIRE LIMITED
Registration no: 01679280 **Date established:** 1982
No.of Employees: 1 - 10 **Product Groups:** 45, 66, 67, 83, 87

Date of Accounts	Mar 12	Mar 11	Mar 10
Working Capital	-5	-25	-36
Fixed Assets	111	98	114
Current Assets	104	76	73

C R D M Ltd Centre for Rapid Design and Manufacture
Unit D Lane End Road, High Wycombe, HP12 4HH
Tel: 01494-479680 **Fax:** 08450-514901
E-mail: marketing@crdm.co.uk
Website: http://www.crdm.co.uk
Bank(s): Barclays Bank PLC
Directors: A. Katkoria (Fin), B. Asherton (Sales), M. James (Ch)
Ultimate Holding Company: SCORCH SYSTEMS LIMITED
Immediate Holding Company: CRDM LIMITED
Registration no: 04929721 **VAT No.:** GB 527 2474 43
Date established: 2003 **Turnover:** £2m - £5m **No.of Employees:** 21 - 50
Product Groups: 28, 30, 34, 42, 48, 49, 66, 84, 85

Date of Accounts	Jul 11	Jul 10	Jul 09
Sales Turnover	N/A	N/A	3m
Pre Tax Profit/Loss	N/A	N/A	-462
Working Capital	307	406	-1m
Fixed Assets	399	400	450
Current Assets	1m	1m	637
Current Liabilities	N/A	N/A	2m

Cabcon A division of Young Electronics Group
Coronation Road Cressex Business Park, High Wycombe, HP12 3TA
Tel: 01494-753802 **Fax:** 01494-753803
E-mail: sales@cabcon.co.uk
Website: http://www.cabcon.co.uk
Bank(s): Barclays
Managers: D. Nicholson (Mgr)
Ultimate Holding Company: RALPH PETERS & SONS LIMITED
Immediate Holding Company: FRUTINA LIMITED
Registration no: 02926739 **Date established:** 1994 **Turnover:** £2m - £5m
No.of Employees: 21 - 50 **Product Groups:** 37, 44

Date of Accounts	Dec 11	Dec 10	Dec 09
Sales Turnover	8m	7m	6m
Pre Tax Profit/Loss	531	116	127
Working Capital	-489	-280	-273
Fixed Assets	5m	2m	2m
Current Assets	3m	1m	1m
Current Liabilities	2m	1m	1m

Cablelink Cables & Cabling
Lisle Road, High Wycombe, HP13 5SH
Tel: 01494-444036 **Fax:** 01494-525224
E-mail: sales@cablelink.co.uk
Website: http://www.cablelink.co.uk
Managers: E. Drofiak (Mgr)
Immediate Holding Company: SMEATON HANSCOMB & CO.,LIMITED
Registration no: 02777559 **VAT No.:** GB 578 5157 96
Date established: 1931 **Turnover:** £1m - £2m **No.of Employees:** 1 - 10
Product Groups: 37, 44

Date of Accounts	Sep 11	Sep 10	Sep 09
Working Capital	-10	17	14
Fixed Assets	602	602	802
Current Assets	53	78	68

Case Communication
Norths Estate Old Oxford Road, Piddington, High Wycombe, HP14 3BE
Tel: 01494-880240 **Fax:** 01494-833741
E-mail: sales@casecomms.com
Website: http://www.casecomms.com
Directors: A. Saoulis (Prop)
Immediate Holding Company: CASE COMMUNICATIONS LIMITED
Registration no: 03913540 **Date established:** 2000
Turnover: Up to £250,000 **No.of Employees:** 1 - 10 **Product Groups:** 44

Date of Accounts	Mar 11	Mar 10	Mar 09
Sales Turnover	199	238	497
Pre Tax Profit/Loss	-0	1	4
Working Capital	47	43	41
Fixed Assets	4	7	4
Current Assets	168	99	104
Current Liabilities	15	8	20

Catac Products Ltd
Unit 3-5 Chiltern Trading Estate Earl Howe Road, Holmer Green, High Wycombe, HP15 6QT
Tel: 08453-707040 **Fax:** 0870-620 7041
E-mail: sales@catacproducts.com
Website: http://www.catac.co.uk
Managers: L. Spaven (Mgr)
Immediate Holding Company: CATAC PRODUCTS UK LIMITED
Registration no: 05955321 **VAT No.:** GB 301 5748 83
Date established: 2006 **No.of Employees:** 1 - 10 **Product Groups:** 35, 49, 62

Chefskit.Com
3 Soho Studios Town Lane, Wooburn Green, High Wycombe, HP10 0PF
Tel: 01628-523352 **Fax:** 01628-530797
E-mail: tony@chefskit.com
Website: http://www.chefskit.com
Managers: T. Lee (Mgr)
No.of Employees: 1 - 10 **Product Groups:** 24, 33, 63

Chiltern International Fire Ltd
Stocking Lane Hughenden Valley, High Wycombe, HP14 4ND
Tel: 01494-569800 **Fax:** 01494-565487
E-mail: enquiries@chilternfire.co.uk
Website: http://www.chilternfire.co.uk
Directors: D. Webb (Fin)
Managers: J. Float (Personnel), A. Endress (Tech Serv Mgr)
Ultimate Holding Company: BM TRADA GROUP LIMITED
Immediate Holding Company: CHILTERN INTERNATIONAL FIRE LIMITED
Registration no: 03125010 **Date established:** 1995 **Turnover:** £2m - £5m
No.of Employees: 21 - 50 **Product Groups:** 85

Date of Accounts	Dec 11	Dec 10	Dec 09
Sales Turnover	4m	4m	3m
Pre Tax Profit/Loss	-600	397	322
Working Capital	196	820	420
Fixed Assets	339	330	383
Current Assets	802	1m	1m
Current Liabilities	526	558	527

CJ Associates Training
Park View 34 Copperfields, High Wycombe, HP12 4AN
Tel: 0845-371 0953 **Fax:** 0845-371 0954
E-mail: info@cjgroup.co.uk
Website: http://www.cjgroup.co.uk
Registration no: 04715779 **No.of Employees:** 1 - 10 **Product Groups:** 69, 86

Date of Accounts	Mar 10	Mar 09	Mar 08
Working Capital	31	6	11
Fixed Assets	9	14	7
Current Assets	110	99	89

Clarity Copiers
Capital House Park House Business Centre Desborough Park Road, High Wycombe, HP12 3DJ
Tel: 01494-448622 **Fax:** 01494-464765
E-mail: terry.h@claritycopiershw.co.uk
Website: http://www.claritycopiershw.co.uk
Directors: N. Campbell (Sales), T. Hunt (MD)
Immediate Holding Company: PENTACOR LIMITED
Registration no: 02034210 **Date established:** 1986 **Turnover:** £1m - £2m
No.of Employees: 11 - 20 **Product Groups:** 27, 32, 38, 44, 48, 64, 67, 80, 83, 86

Colourdrive Ltd
88 St Margarets Grove Great Kingshill, High Wycombe, HP15 6HP
Tel: 01494-717775 **Fax:** 01494-717775
E-mail: info@colourdrive.co.uk
Website: http://www.colourdrive.co.uk
Directors: G. Page (MD)
Immediate Holding Company: SANDSTONE SOFTWARE EUROPE LIMITED
Registration no: 05165957 **Date established:** 2004
No.of Employees: 1 - 10 **Product Groups:** 28, 44

Date of Accounts	Jun 11	Jun 10	Jun 09
Working Capital	-18	-16	-13
Fixed Assets	N/A	1	2
Current Assets	N/A	1	1

Constant Air Systems Ltd
Hillbottom Road Sands Industrial Estate, High Wycombe, HP12 4HJ
Tel: 01494-469529 **Fax:** 01494-469549
E-mail: admin@constantair.co.uk
Website: http://www.constantair.co.uk
Bank(s): National Westminster Bank Plc
Directors: R. Roberts (Grp Chief Exec)
Immediate Holding Company: CONSTANT AIR SYSTEMS LIMITED
Registration no: 00836280 **VAT No.:** GB 285 2546 38
Date established: 1965 **Turnover:** £5m - £10m
No.of Employees: 51 - 100 **Product Groups:** 52, 66, 84

Date of Accounts	Jan 10	Jan 09	Jan 08
Sales Turnover	10m	18m	17m
Pre Tax Profit/Loss	-332	1m	1m
Working Capital	4m	3m	2m
Fixed Assets	307	993	919
Current Assets	6m	6m	5m
Current Liabilities	361	1m	771

Conway Security Products Ltd
Seymour House Copyground Lane, High Wycombe, HP12 3HE
Tel: 01494-461373 **Fax:** 01494-531685
E-mail: sales@conway-cctv.co.uk
Website: http://www.conway-cctv.co.uk
Directors: C. Newman (Co Sec)
Immediate Holding Company: CONWAY SECURITY PRODUCTS LIMITED
Registration no: 02044953 **Date established:** 1986 **Turnover:** £2m - £5m
No.of Employees: 11 - 20 **Product Groups:** 37

Date of Accounts	Oct 11	Oct 10	Oct 09
Sales Turnover	1m	N/A	N/A
Pre Tax Profit/Loss	33	N/A	N/A
Working Capital	22	87	160
Fixed Assets	1m	1m	641
Current Assets	444	437	513
Current Liabilities	81	N/A	N/A

Coopers Engineering Ltd
Lane End Road Sands Industrial Estate, High Wycombe, HP12 4HG
Tel: 01494-450767 **Fax:** 01494-465450
E-mail: coopereng@aol.com
Website: http://www.jeffark.co.uk
Directors: R. Cooper (MD), S. Cooper (Fin)
Managers: P. Tilbury (Works Gen Mgr), S. Cooper (Personnel)
Immediate Holding Company: COOPERS ENGINEERING LIMITED
Registration no: 03686057 **VAT No.:** GB 669 0125 30
Date established: 1998 **Turnover:** £250,000 - £500,000
No.of Employees: 1 - 10 **Product Groups:** 48

Date of Accounts	Mar 10	Mar 09	Mar 08
Working Capital	-19	16	9
Fixed Assets	17	21	27
Current Assets	59	87	135

Culligan UK Ltd
Culligan House Unit 3 The Gateway Centre Coronation Road, Cressex Business Park, High Wycombe, HP12 3SU
Tel: 01494-441286 **Fax:** 01494-523833
E-mail: commercial@culligan.co.uk
Website: http://www.culligan.co.uk
Bank(s): HSBC Bank plc

Managers: M. Savill (Chief Mgr)
Immediate Holding Company: CULLIGAN (UK) LIMITED
Registration no: 05229188 **VAT No.:** GB 208 7584 43
Date established: 2004 **Turnover:** £500,000 - £1m
No.of Employees: 11 - 20 **Product Groups:** 38, 42

Date of Accounts	Dec 11	Dec 10	Dec 09
Sales Turnover	2m	786	N/A
Pre Tax Profit/Loss	6	762	1m
Working Capital	6m	6m	9m
Fixed Assets	31	8	12m
Current Assets	6m	6m	9m
Current Liabilities	174	156	113

D M S-Diemould
4a Anglo Office Park Lincoln Road Cressex Business Park, High Wycombe, HP12 3RH
Tel: 01494-523811 **Fax:** 01494-452898
E-mail: david.odlin@dms-diemould.co.uk
Website: http://www.dms-diemould.co.uk
Managers: A. Stubberfield (Sales Admin)
Ultimate Holding Company: WYSE GROUP LIMITED
Immediate Holding Company: WYSE (HOLDINGS) LIMITED
Registration no: 00728469 **VAT No.:** GB 645 2294 35
Date established: 2006 **Turnover:** £1m - £2m **No.of Employees:** 1 - 10
Product Groups: 46, 48

Date of Accounts	Mar 11	Mar 09	Mar 08
Sales Turnover	6m	N/A	N/A
Pre Tax Profit/Loss	362	N/A	N/A
Working Capital	360	N/A	N/A
Fixed Assets	2	N/A	N/A
Current Assets	2m	N/A	N/A
Current Liabilities	1m	N/A	N/A

Dawn Fire Ltd
26 Wooburn Industrial Park Wooburn Green, High Wycombe, HP10 0PF
Tel: 01628-526531 **Fax:** 01628-526634
E-mail: sales@dawnfire.co.uk
Website: http://www.dawnfire.co.uk
Directors: R. Bryant (Dir)
Immediate Holding Company: DAWN FIRE LIMITED
Registration no: 03665223 **Date established:** 1998
Turnover: Up to £250,000 **No.of Employees:** 1 - 10 **Product Groups:** 48, 67

Date of Accounts	Nov 11	Nov 10	Nov 09
Working Capital	91	74	49
Fixed Assets	207	232	150
Current Assets	142	124	92

Desboro Jig Builders
Chiltern Works Oakridge Road, High Wycombe, HP11 2PA
Tel: 01494-539534 **Fax:** 01494-499495
Directors: J. Vockings (Prop)
Immediate Holding Company: SEAWARDS OF HIGH WYCOMBE LIMITED
Registration no: 02597034 **Date established:** 1991
No.of Employees: 11 - 20 **Product Groups:** 46, 48

Date of Accounts	May 12	May 11	May 10
Working Capital	907	903	853
Fixed Assets	5	6	8
Current Assets	974	1m	980

Doig Spring
Unit 1 Fairview Estate Beech Road, High Wycombe, HP11 1RY
Tel: 01494-556700 **Fax:** 01494-511002
E-mail: enquiries@springs.co.uk
Website: http://www.doigspring.com
Bank(s): Barclays
Directors: A. Turner (Prop), T. Coade (MD)
Managers: S. Davison (Sales Prom Mgr)
Registration no: 00508900 **VAT No.:** GB 207 7221 85
Turnover: £2m - £5m **No.of Employees:** 21 - 50 **Product Groups:** 35, 38, 39, 40, 44, 48, 49, 66, 68

K Downs
143 Amersham Road, High Wycombe, HP13 5AD
Tel: 01494-436216 **Fax:** 01494-473003
E-mail: downspools@tiscali.co.uk
Website: http://downspools.co.uk
Directors: K. Downs (Prop)
No.of Employees: 1 - 10 **Product Groups:** 30, 32, 33, 40

Dwyer Instruments Ltd
Unit 16 The Wye Estate, High Wycombe, HP11 1LH
Tel: 01494-461707 **Fax:** 01494-465102
E-mail: sales@dwyer-inst.co.uk
Website: http://www.dwyer-inst.co.uk
Managers: D. Lindsay (Sales Admin)
Immediate Holding Company: DWYER INSTRUMENTS.LTD.
Registration no: FC015527 **Date established:** 1990 **Turnover:** £2m - £5m
No.of Employees: 1 - 10 **Product Groups:** 33, 38

Date of Accounts	Dec 09	Dec 08	Dec 07
Sales Turnover	2m	2m	3m
Pre Tax Profit/Loss	419	511	746
Working Capital	1m	932	1m
Fixed Assets	8	11	12
Current Assets	1m	1m	2m
Current Liabilities	73	87	170

E F I Marketing
17 Woodland Close, High Wycombe, HP12 4HB
Tel: 01494-462611
E-mail: contact@efi-marketing.co.uk
Website: http://www.efi-marketing.co.uk
Directors: D. Hayday (Prop)
Immediate Holding Company: ACUMEN SOCIAL ENTERPRISES LIMITED
Date established: 2010 **Turnover:** Up to £250,000
No.of Employees: 1 - 10 **Product Groups:** 81

E H C Teknik UK Ltd
5 Berber Business Centre Kitchener Road, High Wycombe, HP11 2TD
Tel: 01494-445503 **Fax:** 01494-442242
E-mail: sales@ehcteknik.co.uk
Website: http://www.ehcteknik.co.uk
Directors: K. Ohrankammen (Fin)
Immediate Holding Company: EHC TEKNIK (UK) LIMITED
Registration no: 02498531 **Date established:** 1990
No.of Employees: 1 - 10 **Product Groups:** 38, 42

Date of Accounts	Dec 11	Dec 10	Dec 09
Working Capital	1	-2	-4
Fixed Assets	1	4	5
Current Assets	58	94	98

E V Exports (Southern) Ltd
Wooburn Industrial Park Wooburn Green, High Wycombe, HP10 0PE
Tel: 01628-850044 **Fax:** 01628-850044
Directors: A. Peskin (MD), L. Peskin (Dir & Co Sec)
Immediate Holding Company: E. V. EXPORTS (SOUTHERN) LIMITED
Registration no: 00823553 **VAT No.:** GB 442 3826 57
Date established: 1964 **Turnover:** £20m - £50m **No.of Employees:** 1 - 10
Product Groups: 25

Date of Accounts	Dec 07	Dec 06
Sales Turnover	N/A	444
Pre Tax Profit/Loss	N/A	-139
Working Capital	-320	-225
Fixed Assets	199	199
Current Assets	241	183
Current Liabilities	561	408
Total Share Capital	90	90
ROCE% (Return on Capital Employed)		523.9
ROT% (Return on Turnover)		-31.3

Eldridge Electrical Ltd
Binders Industrial Estate Cryers Hill Road, Cryers Hill, High Wycombe, HP15 6LJ
Tel: 01494-715956 **Fax:** 01494-716176
E-mail: info@eldridgeelectricalltd.co.uk
Website: http://www.eldridgeelectricalltd.co.uk
Bank(s): HSBC Bank plc
Directors: J. Prentice (MD)
Immediate Holding Company: ELDRIDGE ELECTRICAL LIMITED
Registration no: 01658531 **VAT No.:** GB 285 1666 33
Date established: 1982 **Turnover:** £500,000 - £1m
No.of Employees: 11 - 20 **Product Groups:** 52

Date of Accounts	Jul 11	Jul 10	Jul 09
Working Capital	11	31	44
Fixed Assets	66	60	21
Current Assets	127	157	169

Envirotec Ltd
Desborough Park Road, High Wycombe, HP12 3BX
Tel: 01494-525342 **Fax:** 01494-440889
E-mail: sales.info@envirotec.co.uk
Website: http://www.envirotec.co.uk
Bank(s): Bank of Scotland
Directors: D. Wild (Comm), D. O'Donnell (Co Sec), F. Robertson (Sales), S. Brown (Chief Op Offcr), C. Lister (MD)
Ultimate Holding Company: CROSSCO (820) LIMITED
Immediate Holding Company: ENVIROTEC LIMITED
Registration no: 01504862 **VAT No.:** 697 9128 867 **Date established:** 1980
Turnover: £5m - £10m **No.of Employees:** 21 - 50 **Product Groups:** 40

Date of Accounts	Feb 08	Feb 11	Feb 10
Sales Turnover	7m	5m	5m
Pre Tax Profit/Loss	1m	1m	676
Working Capital	2m	2m	2m
Fixed Assets	2m	2m	2m
Current Assets	3m	4m	3m
Current Liabilities	475	898	694

John Ewans Design
Capital House Westbourne Street, High Wycombe, HP11 2PZ
Tel: 01494-473441 **Fax:** 01494-473442
E-mail: design@john-ewans-design.co.uk
Website: http://www.john-ewans-design.co.uk
Directors: J. Ewans (Prop)
Immediate Holding Company: CONCEPT CORPORATE INTERIORS PLC
Registration no: 03296879 **VAT No.:** GB 411 0109 30
Date established: 1994 **Turnover:** £1m - £2m **No.of Employees:** 1 - 10
Product Groups: 81, 85

Date of Accounts	Jan 11	Jan 10	Jan 09
Working Capital	102	108	158
Fixed Assets	N/A	1	4
Current Assets	154	144	188

Fabine Investments Ltd
Unit 3 Pilot Trading Estate West Wycombe Road, High Wycombe, HP12 3AH
Tel: 01494-462749 **Fax:** 01494-522325
E-mail: pilot@pilotgroup.co.uk
Website: http://www.pilotgroup.co.uk
Directors: S. Norris (Fin), A. Keates (MD)
Immediate Holding Company: PILOT INTERNATIONAL LOGISTICS LIMITED
Registration no: 01310085 **VAT No.:** GB 479 5105 20
Date established: 1977 **No.of Employees:** 1 - 10 **Product Groups:** 77, 84

Date of Accounts	Sep 11	Sep 10	Sep 09
Working Capital	-29	-1	-6
Fixed Assets	15	12	12
Current Assets	67	82	83

First Move Direct Marketing
4 Fairview Estate Beech Road, High Wycombe, HP11 1RY
Tel: 01494-539300 **Fax:** 01494-444350
E-mail: clientservices@firstmove.co.uk
Website: http://www.firstmove.co.uk
Directors: D. Amor (MD), T. Russell (Co Sec)
Immediate Holding Company: FIRST MOVE MARKETING SERVICES LIMITED
Registration no: 02455144 **Date established:** 1989 **Turnover:** £2m - £5m
No.of Employees: 21 - 50 **Product Groups:** 44, 79, 81

Date of Accounts	Dec 11	Dec 10	Dec 09
Working Capital	157	82	72
Fixed Assets	177	194	190
Current Assets	1m	1m	1m

Flare Services Ltd
59 Mill End Road, High Wycombe, HP12 4JN
Tel: 01494-473737 **Fax:** 01494-473730
E-mail: info@flareservicesltd.co.uk
Website: http://www.flareservicesltd.co.uk
Directors: N. Stead (MD)
Immediate Holding Company: FLARE (SERVICES) LIMITED
Registration no: 01482519 **Date established:** 1980
No.of Employees: 11 - 20 **Product Groups:** 35, 36, 39

Date of Accounts	Mar 12	Mar 11	Mar 10
Working Capital	-93	91	123
Fixed Assets	518	248	258
Current Assets	274	448	460

Foam Engineers Ltd
Dashwood Avenue, High Wycombe, HP12 3EA
Tel: 01494-448855 **Fax:** 01494-461841
E-mail: jwiles@foamengineers.co.uk
Website: http://www.foamengineers.co.uk
Bank(s): Barclays
Directors: J. Wiles (MD), A. Short (Fin)
Managers: F. Henry
Immediate Holding Company: FOAM ENGINEERS LIMITED
Registration no: 00864353 **Date established:** 1965 **Turnover:** £2m - £5m
No.of Employees: 21 - 50 **Product Groups:** 29, 30, 31, 49

Date of Accounts	Jun 12	Jun 11	Jun 10
Working Capital	57	-189	-288
Fixed Assets	2m	2m	2m
Current Assets	857	810	847

H Pickles & Son
Lincoln Road Cressex Business Park, High Wycombe, HP12 3RQ
Tel: 01494-520613 **Fax:** 01494-465373
E-mail: sales@scsaws.co.uk
Website: http://www.scsaws.co.uk
Directors: H. Styles (MD)
Immediate Holding Company: H. PICKLES & SON (SAWS) LIMITED
Registration no: 00648511 **VAT No.:** GB 207 5994 40
Date established: 1960 **Turnover:** £500,000 - £1m
No.of Employees: 1 - 10 **Product Groups:** 37, 41

Date of Accounts	Dec 11	Dec 10	Dec 09
Working Capital	1	1	1
Current Assets	1	1	1

Hempstead & Johnson Ltd
Oakridge Road, High Wycombe, HP11 2PF
Tel: 01494-444971 **Fax:** 01494-531152
E-mail: dlander@hempsteadandjohnson.co.uk
Bank(s): Lloyds
Directors: D. Lander (Works)
Managers: A. Cochran (Prod Mgr), B. Candish
Ultimate Holding Company: NICOL & ANDREW GROUP LIMITED
Immediate Holding Company: HEMPSTEAD & JOHNSON LIMITED
Registration no: 00746512 **Date established:** 1963
Turnover: £500,000 - £1m **No.of Employees:** 11 - 20 **Product Groups:** 46

Date of Accounts	Mar 11	Mar 10	Mar 09
Sales Turnover	1m	844	1m
Pre Tax Profit/Loss	-60	-109	-196
Working Capital	-157	-122	-43
Fixed Assets	683	675	680
Current Assets	469	361	483
Current Liabilities	90	73	95

Mike Henson Presentations Ltd
18 Portway Drive, High Wycombe, HP12 4AU
Tel: 01494-438904 **Fax:** 01494-448154
Website: http://www.mikehenson.com
Directors: M. Henson (MD), S. Henson (Fin)
Immediate Holding Company: MH-P INTERNET LIMITED
Registration no: 02243793 **Date established:** 1988
No.of Employees: 1 - 10 **Product Groups:** 89

Date of Accounts	Aug 11	Aug 10	Aug 09
Working Capital	1	4	2
Fixed Assets	17	18	17
Current Assets	12	16	14

Hot A V Ltd
6 Barnes Wallis Court Wellington Road, Cressex Business Park, High Wycombe, HP12 3PS
Tel: 08451-306161 **Fax:** 08451-306262
E-mail: info@hotav.uk.com
Website: http://www.hotav.uk.com
Directors: D. Savage (MD)
Immediate Holding Company: DYLAN 123 LIMITED
Registration no: 04454797 **Date established:** 2002
No.of Employees: 11 - 20 **Product Groups:** 37, 61, 83

Date of Accounts	Dec 09	Dec 08	Dec 07
Working Capital	-433	-424	-365
Fixed Assets	162	152	283
Current Assets	227	248	359

Hyundai Motor UK Ltd
728 London Road, High Wycombe, HP11 1HE
Tel: 01494-428600 **Fax:** 01494-428699
E-mail: fleet.sales@hyundai-car.co.uk
Website: http://www.hyundai-car.co.uk
Bank(s): Barclays, Bristol
Directors: T. Whitehorn (MD), R. Pope (Fin), R. Cadman (Fin), G. Pigounakis (Sales), G. Pigounakis (Sales), A. Cullis (Mkt Research), K. Lothian (Ptnr), J. Campbell (Mkt Research)
Managers: H. Phillips (Tech Serv Mgr), J. Burr
Ultimate Holding Company: HYUNDAI MOTOR CO (SOUTH KOREA)
Immediate Holding Company: HYUNDAI MOTOR UK LIMITED
Registration no: 05446560 **VAT No.:** GB 632 1819 55
Date established: 2005 **Turnover:** £500m - £1,000m
No.of Employees: 51 - 100 **Product Groups:** 68

Date of Accounts	Dec 11	Dec 10	Dec 09
Sales Turnover	606m	576m	459m
Pre Tax Profit/Loss	4m	11m	8m
Working Capital	51m	45m	1m
Fixed Assets	9m	9m	8m
Current Assets	281m	291m	217m
Current Liabilities	100m	82m	30m

I Q L Ltd
Stirling Road Cressex Business Park, High Wycombe, HP12 3ST
Tel: 01494-463636 **Fax:** 01494-439639
E-mail: sales@iqllimited.co.uk
Website: http://www.iqllimited.co.uk
Bank(s): Lloyds TSB Bank plc
Directors: M. Skyrme (MD), M. Sykrme (Co Sec)
Immediate Holding Company: I.Q.L. LIMITED
Registration no: 01709279 **VAT No.:** GB 226 2857 57
Date established: 1983 **No.of Employees:** 11 - 20 **Product Groups:** 48

Date of Accounts	Mar 11	Mar 10	Mar 09
Working Capital	298	356	370
Fixed Assets	175	202	223
Current Assets	1m	1m	1m

Imagineers Ltd
Unit 6 Fryers Works Abercromby Avenue, High Wycombe, HP12 3BW
Tel: 01494-473861 **Fax:** 01494-473863
E-mail: info@imagineersltd.co.uk
Website: http://www.imagineersltd.co.uk
Directors: D. Cooper (Dir)
Immediate Holding Company: IMAGINEERS LIMITED
Registration no: 01917492 **VAT No.:** GB 578 1098 09
Date established: 1985 **Turnover:** £500,000 - £1m
No.of Employees: 1 - 10 **Product Groups:** 30, 49

see next page

Imagineers Ltd - Cont'd

Date of Accounts	Dec 11	Dec 10	Dec 09
Sales Turnover	861	732	695
Pre Tax Profit/Loss	179	115	84
Working Capital	84	47	63
Fixed Assets	34	39	46
Current Assets	251	221	253
Current Liabilities	66	79	61

Instron

Coronation Road Cressex Business Park, High Wycombe, HP12 3SY
Tel: 01494-464646 **Fax:** 01494-456454
E-mail: adam_baxter@instron.com
Website: http://www.instron.com
Bank(s): HSBC Bank plc
Directors: A. Baxter (MD), J. Robinson (Fin)
Ultimate Holding Company: LABVANTAGE SOLUTIONS INC (USA)
Immediate Holding Company: LABVANTAGE SOLUTIONS LIMITED
Registration no: 03333308 **VAT No.:** GB 321 2554 00
Date established: 1997 **Turnover:** £5m - £10m
No.of Employees: 251 - 500 **Product Groups:** 38, 39, 42, 46, 65, 67, 83, 84

Date of Accounts	Dec 08	Dec 07	Mar 11
Sales Turnover	N/A	N/A	7m
Pre Tax Profit/Loss	N/A	N/A	363
Working Capital	325	-228	1m
Fixed Assets	16	22	13
Current Assets	3m	2m	10m
Current Liabilities	N/A	N/A	2m

Ion Information Technologies Ltd

Buckingham House Desborough Road, High Wycombe, HP11 2PR
Tel: 01494-512490 **Fax:** 01494-512491
E-mail: chander@ionit.co.uk
Website: http://www.ionit.com
Directors: Y. Vasdev (MD)
Managers: S. Granshaw (Personnel)
Immediate Holding Company: ION INFORMATION TECHNOLOGIES LIMITED
Registration no: 03137721 **Date established:** 1995
Turnover: £500,000 - £1m **No.of Employees:** 21 - 50 **Product Groups:** 44

Date of Accounts	May 11	May 10	May 09
Working Capital	148	198	257
Fixed Assets	129	104	10
Current Assets	305	330	455

Isotemp Heating & Ventilating Ltd

Loudwater Mill Station Road, Loudwater, High Wycombe, HP10 9UD
Tel: 01494-534364 **Fax:** 01494-461716
Website: http://www.isotemp-hv.co.uk
Bank(s): HSBC
Directors: S. Holmes (Co Sec), T. Grace (Dir)
Immediate Holding Company: ISOTEMP(HEATING & VENTILATING)LIMITED
Registration no: 00750351 **VAT No.:** GB 207 7347 63
Date established: 1963 **Turnover:** £2m - £5m **No.of Employees:** 11 - 20
Product Groups: 48

Date of Accounts	Mar 12	Mar 11	Mar 10
Working Capital	193	220	340
Fixed Assets	31	32	47
Current Assets	411	385	560

Jarvis Engineering Ltd

Oakridge Road, High Wycombe, HP11 2PA
Tel: 01494-530123 **Fax:** 01494-472864
E-mail: jarvis.engineering@virgin.net
Website: http://www.jarvisengineering.org.uk
Bank(s): Barclays
Directors: J. Smith (Fin)
Immediate Holding Company: JARVIS ENGINEERING LIMITED
Registration no: 00392349 **VAT No.:** GB 207 5525 75
Date established: 1945 **Turnover:** £500,000 - £1m
No.of Employees: 11 - 20 **Product Groups:** 22, 23, 29, 30, 33, 35, 45, 48

Date of Accounts	Oct 11	Oct 10	Oct 09
Working Capital	724	833	870
Fixed Assets	721	619	632
Current Assets	790	914	932

Jarvis Hotels Ltd

Castle House 71-75 Desborough Road, High Wycombe, HP11 2PR
Tel: 01494-473800 **Fax:** 01494-471666
E-mail: steve.hebborn@jarvis.co.uk
Website: http://www.ramadajarvis.co.uk
Bank(s): Natwest
Directors: D. Beveridge (Co Sec), S. Hebborn (Fin), S. Hebborn (Grp Chief Exec)
Managers: C. Russell (Mktg Serv Mgr)
Ultimate Holding Company: KAYTERM LIMITED
Immediate Holding Company: JARVIS HOTELS LTD.
Registration no: 02486634 **Date established:** 1990
Turnover: £75m - £125m **No.of Employees:** 1501 & over
Product Groups: 69

Date of Accounts	Mar 07	Mar 08	Mar 09
Sales Turnover	129m	130m	130m
Pre Tax Profit/Loss	65m	5m	-4m
Working Capital	4m	-7m	-3m
Fixed Assets	188m	201m	192m
Current Assets	41m	31m	37m
Current Liabilities	15m	16m	23m

Kestrel Building Services Ltd

George Street, High Wycombe, HP11 2RZ
Tel: 01494-472 545 **Fax:** 01494-472540
E-mail: info@kestreloffice.com
Website: http://www.kestreloffice.com
Directors: G. Gregory (MD)
Registration no: 01711809 **VAT No.:** GB 385 5512 32
Date established: 1998 **Turnover:** £1m - £2m **No.of Employees:** 1 - 10
Product Groups: 26, 52

Date of Accounts	Dec 07	Dec 06	Dec 05
Working Capital	24	38	45
Fixed Assets	13	9	12
Current Assets	130	66	102
Current Liabilities	106	28	57
Total Share Capital	5	5	5

Kingsmead Testing Services

1 Champan Lane Flackwell Heath, High Wycombe, HP10 9NZ
Tel: 01628-850650 **Fax:** 01628-522135
E-mail: info@pattestnow.co.uk
Website: http://www.pattestnow.co.uk
Directors: G. Arbones (Dir), G. Foster (Co Sec)
Immediate Holding Company: KINGSMEAD TESTING SERVICES LIMITED
Registration no: 06070388 **Date established:** 2007
No.of Employees: 1 - 10 **Product Groups:** 38, 85

Date of Accounts	Mar 11	Mar 10	Mar 09
Working Capital	1	1	-1
Fixed Assets	1	1	2
Current Assets	23	25	18

Kurt Mueller UK Ltd

Chapel Lane, High Wycombe, HP12 4BJ
Tel: 01494-524211 **Fax:** 01494-474886
E-mail: ukm@kurtmueller.com
Website: http://www.kurtmueller.com
Bank(s): Barclays
Directors: G. Haynes (Dir)
Managers: J. Welfare
Ultimate Holding Company: DR KURT MULLER KG (GERMANY)
Immediate Holding Company: KURT MUELLER (U.K.) LIMITED
Registration no: 00477895 **VAT No.:** GB 290 5338 53
Date established: 1950 **Turnover:** £1m - £2m **No.of Employees:** 21 - 50
Product Groups: 37

Date of Accounts	Sep 11	Sep 10	Sep 09
Working Capital	92	176	161
Fixed Assets	134	142	199
Current Assets	379	345	261

Labco

Brow Works Copyground Lane, High Wycombe, HP12 3HE
Tel: 01494-459741 **Fax:** 01494-465101
E-mail: sales@labco.co.uk
Website: http://www.labco.co.uk
Bank(s): Lloyds TSB Bank plc
Directors: D. Ashton (MD)
Immediate Holding Company: LABCO LIMITED
Registration no: 00962789 **VAT No.:** GB 208 7292 56
Date established: 1969 **No.of Employees:** 11 - 20 **Product Groups:** 33

Date of Accounts	Dec 11	Dec 10	Dec 09
Working Capital	605	421	260
Fixed Assets	41	41	41
Current Assets	918	720	451

Legno Tech Company Ltd

12 Stephenson Close, High Wycombe, HP13 5SY
Tel: 01494-528413 **Fax:** 01494-437786
Website: http://www.legnotech.co.uk
Directors: A. Parr (Dir)
Immediate Holding Company: LEGNO-TECH COMPANY LIMITED
Registration no: 02104080 **Date established:** 1987
No.of Employees: 1 - 10 **Product Groups:** 46

Date of Accounts	Mar 11	Feb 08	Feb 10
Working Capital	-39	18	12
Fixed Assets	2	18	6
Current Assets	59	140	123

Lindab

3b Hill Court Hillbottom Road, Sands Industrial Estate, High Wycombe, HP12 4ED
Tel: 01494-463490 **Fax:** 01494-471507
E-mail: fran.buxton@lindab.co.uk
Website: http://www.lindab.co.uk
Managers: F. Buxton (Mgr)
Registration no: 01641399 **Date established:** 1985
No.of Employees: 1 - 10 **Product Groups:** 37, 40, 48

Date of Accounts	Dec 11	Dec 10	Dec 09
Sales Turnover	51m	47m	49m
Pre Tax Profit/Loss	1m	-204	354
Working Capital	16m	-3m	-4m
Fixed Assets	16m	20m	22m
Current Assets	22m	20m	23m
Current Liabilities	1m	980	775

Link Hamson Ltd

6 York Way Lancaster Road, Cressex Business Park, High Wycombe, HP12 3PY
Tel: 01494-439786 **Fax:** 01494-526222
E-mail: sales@linkhamson.com
Website: http://www.linkhamson.com
Directors: G. Pennington (Dir)
Immediate Holding Company: LINK HAMSON LIMITED
Registration no: 02668260 **VAT No.:** GB 578 1963 89
Date established: 1991 **Turnover:** £250,000 - £500,000
No.of Employees: 1 - 10 **Product Groups:** 27, 28, 30, 34, 38, 47

Date of Accounts	Dec 11	Dec 10	Dec 09
Sales Turnover	459	414	365
Pre Tax Profit/Loss	26	14	12
Working Capital	229	207	276
Fixed Assets	1	2	7
Current Assets	295	243	322
Current Liabilities	42	23	28

Isaac Lord Ltd

185 Desborough Road, High Wycombe, HP11 2QN
Tel: 01494-835200 **Fax:** 01494-461376
E-mail: info@isaaclord.co.uk
Website: http://www.isaaclord.co.uk
Directors: R. Lancaster (Dir)
Managers: J. Stroud (Sales Prom Mgr), R. Cubbage (Personnel)
Ultimate Holding Company: JAMBEROO LIMITED
Immediate Holding Company: ISAAC LORD LIMITED
Registration no: 00455743 **Date established:** 1948 **Turnover:** £5m - £10m
No.of Employees: 21 - 50 **Product Groups:** 61, 66

Date of Accounts	Jun 11	Jun 10	Jun 09
Sales Turnover	6m	N/A	6m
Pre Tax Profit/Loss	214	N/A	171
Working Capital	1m	979	1m
Fixed Assets	2m	2m	2m
Current Assets	2m	2m	2m
Current Liabilities	274	N/A	218

M H P Industries Ltd (M.H.P.)

Coronation Road Cressex Business Park, High Wycombe, HP12 3RP
Tel: 01494-461561 **Fax:** 01494-462319
E-mail: mark@mhp-uk.com
Website: http://www.mhp-uk.com
Directors: M. Hipgrave (Snr Part)
Managers: G. Hipgrave (Fin Mgr)
Ultimate Holding Company: FLEDGE CHOICE LIMITED
Immediate Holding Company: M H P INDUSTRIES LIMITED
Registration no: 03535761 **Date established:** 1998 **Turnover:** £1m - £2m
No.of Employees: 21 - 50 **Product Groups:** 26, 30, 31, 34, 36, 42, 48, 49, 67, 81

Date of Accounts	Sep 11	Sep 10	Sep 09
Working Capital	-144	-151	-213
Fixed Assets	197	250	287
Current Assets	360	328	257

M K Fire Ltd

Unit 59-69 Queens Road, High Wycombe, HP13 6AH
Tel: 01494-769769 **Fax:** 01494-465378
E-mail: info@mkfire.co.uk
Website: http://www.mkfire.co.uk
Directors: M. Lunn (Dir)
Ultimate Holding Company: EOI FIRE SARL (LUXEMBOURG)
Immediate Holding Company: M K FIRE LIMITED
Registration no: 02134933 **Date established:** 1987
Turnover: Up to £250,000 **No.of Employees:** 11 - 20 **Product Groups:** 37, 38, 40, 52, 67, 68, 84

Date of Accounts	Dec 11	Dec 10	Dec 09
Sales Turnover	81	81	N/A
Pre Tax Profit/Loss	-105	-0	-1
Working Capital	908	985	985
Current Assets	1m	987	1m
Current Liabilities	105	N/A	1

M W H Europe Ltd

Terriers House 201 Amersham Road, High Wycombe, HP13 5AJ
Tel: 01494-526240 **Fax:** 01494-522074
E-mail: webinfo@mwhglobal.com
Website: http://www.mwhglobal.com
Bank(s): Barclays
Directors: V. Hall Sturt (Co Sec), J. Butts (Reg MD)
Managers: R. George
Ultimate Holding Company: MWH GLOBAL INC (USA)
Immediate Holding Company: MWH EUROPE LIMITED
Registration no: 02438136 **VAT No.:** GB 492 0040 75
Date established: 1989 **Turnover:** £125m - £250m
No.of Employees: 101 - 250 **Product Groups:** 18, 51, 80, 84

Date of Accounts	Dec 11	Dec 10	Dec 09
Sales Turnover	153m	144m	157m
Pre Tax Profit/Loss	6m	8m	-1m
Working Capital	33m	39m	25m
Fixed Assets	8m	9m	11m
Current Assets	73m	70m	59m
Current Liabilities	14m	19m	28m

Mcgill Signs

Highfield View Park Lane, Stokenchurch, High Wycombe, HP14 3TQ
Tel: 01494-482288 **Fax:** 01494-483152
E-mail: mcgillsign@aol.com
Website: http://www.mcgillsigns.co.uk
Directors: P. Mcgill (Prop)
Registration no: 02511556 **No.of Employees:** 1 - 10 **Product Groups:** 49, 89

Machine Tool Spraying Service

4 Dean Way Holmer Green, High Wycombe, HP15 6TR
Tel: 01494-712781 **Fax:** 01494- 712781
Directors: N. Barret (Prop)
Registration no: 04140170 **Date established:** 2001
Turnover: Up to £250,000 **No.of Employees:** 1 - 10 **Product Groups:** 46, 48

Maddison Commercial Ltd

Unit A2 Knaves Beech Industrial Estate Knaves Beech Way, Loudwater, High Wycombe, HP10 9QY
Tel: 01628-810000 **Fax:** 01628-810999
E-mail: sales@worldofenvelopes.com
Website: http://www.worldofenvelopes.com
Directors: J. Brown (MD)
Managers: S. Garrison (Sales & Mktg Mg), A. Maderm (Buyer), M. Begalova
No.of Employees: 21 - 50 **Product Groups:** 27, 28, 30, 32, 64

Maindec Computer Engineering Ltd

Maindec House Holtspur Lane, Wooburn Green, High Wycombe, HP10 0AB
Tel: 01628-810977 **Fax:** 01628-810733
E-mail: roger.timms@maindec.co.uk
Website: http://www.maindec.co.uk
Bank(s): Barclays
Directors: R. Timms (MD), P. Darraugh (Fin)
Managers: S. Freegaurd (Purch Mgr), J. Clay (Mktg Serv Mgr), S. Mullerworth (Personnel), R. Watson (Tech Serv Mgr)
Immediate Holding Company: MAINDEC COMPUTER SOLUTIONS LIMITED
Registration no: 01421913 **VAT No.:** GB 333 2952 66
Date established: 1979 **Turnover:** £10m - £20m
No.of Employees: 51 - 100 **Product Groups:** 44

Date of Accounts	Mar 12	Mar 11	Mar 10
Sales Turnover	13m	12m	11m
Pre Tax Profit/Loss	492	636	569
Working Capital	3m	2m	1m
Fixed Assets	1m	1m	2m
Current Assets	9m	8m	6m
Current Liabilities	5m	5m	4m

Maxim Live Ltd

London Road Loudwater, High Wycombe, HP10 9UB
Tel: 01494-463464 **Fax:** 01494-444330
E-mail: info@maximlive.co.uk
Website: http://www.maximlive.co.uk
Bank(s): HSBC
Directors: D. Wright (Prop)
Immediate Holding Company: MAXIM LIVE LIMITED
Registration no: 02927938 **Date established:** 1994 **Turnover:** £2m - £5m
No.of Employees: 11 - 20 **Product Groups:** 26, 30, 35, 49, 52, 69, 81, 83

Date of Accounts	Apr 11	Apr 10	Apr 09
Working Capital	-25	-55	-65
Fixed Assets	53	88	119
Current Assets	478	515	532

Maymac Co.

4 Norths Estate Old Oxford Road Piddington, High Wycombe, HP14 3BE
Tel: 01494-881881 **Fax:** 01494-881376

Directors: M. Macready (Prop)
Immediate Holding Company: WEST WYCOMBE MOTORS LIMITED
Registration no: 01588347 **Date established:** 1981
No.of Employees: 1 - 10 **Product Groups:** 38, 42

Date of Accounts	Dec 11	Dec 10	Dec 09
Working Capital	578	522	410
Fixed Assets	9	250	390
Current Assets	626	604	499

Mediplus Ltd

Unit 7 The Gateway Centre Coronation Road, Cressex Business Park, High Wycombe, HP12 3SU
Tel: 01494-551200 **Fax:** 01494-536333
E-mail: help@mediplus.co.uk
Website: http://www.mediplus.co.uk
Bank(s): Barclays
Directors: E. Gray (MD), J. Urie (Dir), R. Urie (Dir)
Ultimate Holding Company: BWT AG (AUSTRIA)
Immediate Holding Company: MEDIPLUS LIMITED
Registration no: 02051641 **VAT No.:** GB 442 4760 56
Date established: 1986 **Turnover:** £2m - £5m **No.of Employees:** 21 - 50
Product Groups: 30

Date of Accounts	Sep 11	Sep 10	Sep 09
Working Capital	563	434	322
Fixed Assets	141	199	192
Current Assets	2m	1m	1m

Melford Electronics Ltd

14 Blenheim Road Cresses Business Park, Cressex Business Park, High Wycombe, HP12 3RS
Tel: 01494-638069 **Fax:** 01494-463358
E-mail: info@melford-elec.co.uk
Website: http://www.melford-elec.co.uk
Directors: J. Bowden (Fin)
Immediate Holding Company: MELFORD ELECTRONICS LIMITED
Registration no: 00968851 **Date established:** 1969 **Turnover:** £1m - £2m
No.of Employees: 11 - 20 **Product Groups:** 37

Date of Accounts	Mar 12	Mar 11	Mar 10
Working Capital	670	688	654
Fixed Assets	64	74	85
Current Assets	2m	2m	2m

Metalkraft Ltd

Unit B Loudwater Mill Station Road, Loudwater, High Wycombe, HP10 9TY
Tel: 01494-523959 **Fax:** 01494-523959
E-mail: info@metalkraft.co.uk
Website: http://www.metalkraft.co.uk
Directors: T. Taylor (MD)
Immediate Holding Company: METALKRAFT LTD
Registration no: 05696296 **Date established:** 2006
Turnover: £500,000 - £1m **No.of Employees:** 1 - 10 **Product Groups:** 26, 35

Date of Accounts	Mar 11	Mar 10	Mar 09
Sales Turnover	N/A	N/A	627
Pre Tax Profit/Loss	N/A	N/A	44
Working Capital	7	25	22
Fixed Assets	9	12	14
Current Assets	306	201	177
Current Liabilities	N/A	N/A	64

Micro Rent plc

Unit 6 The Gateway Centre Coronation Road, Cressex Business Park, High Wycombe, HP12 3SU
Tel: 01494-768768 **Fax:** 01494-768700
E-mail: info@microrent.co.uk
Website: http://www.microrent.co.uk
Directors: P. Lambert (MD)
Immediate Holding Company: MICRORENT LTD
Registration no: 01719015 **Date established:** 1983 **Turnover:** £1m - £2m
No.of Employees: 11 - 20 **Product Groups:** 44

Date of Accounts	Dec 10	Dec 09	Dec 08
Sales Turnover	N/A	1m	1m
Pre Tax Profit/Loss	N/A	56	61
Working Capital	30	84	24
Fixed Assets	776	560	604
Current Assets	454	493	459
Current Liabilities	N/A	230	232

Micronics Ltd

Knaves Beech Business Centre Davies Way, Loudwater, High Wycombe, HP10 9QR
Tel: 01628-810456 **Fax:** 01628-531540
E-mail: sales@micronicsltd.co.uk
Website: http://www.micronicsflowmeters.com
Directors: M. Farnon (MD)
Immediate Holding Company: MICRONICS LIMITED
Registration no: 01289680 **Date established:** 1976 **Turnover:** £1m - £2m
No.of Employees: 11 - 20 **Product Groups:** 38

Date of Accounts	Nov 11	Nov 10	Nov 09
Working Capital	416	236	188
Fixed Assets	156	186	268
Current Assets	801	646	548

Microtech Electronics Ltd

Lancaster Road Cressex Business Park, High Wycombe, HP12 3QA
Tel: 01494-464764 **Fax:** 01494-464760
E-mail: sales@mtick.co.uk
Website: http://www.mtick.co.uk
Directors: L. Mitchell (Fin), S. Thomson (MD)
Managers: G. Piggin (Purch Mgr), G. Harvey (Tech Serv Mgr)
Ultimate Holding Company: MICROTECH ELECTRONICS MANAGEMENT LTD
Immediate Holding Company: MICROTECH ELECTRONICS LIMITED
Registration no: 01188738 **Date established:** 1974 **Turnover:** £1m - £2m
No.of Employees: 21 - 50 **Product Groups:** 84

Date of Accounts	Jul 11	Jul 10	Jul 09
Working Capital	318	278	199
Fixed Assets	183	195	229
Current Assets	1m	1m	1m

Minatol Ltd

K Progress Road Sands Industrial Estate, High Wycombe, HP12 4HW
Tel: 01494-523771 **Fax:** 01494-535526
E-mail: sales@minatol.co.uk
Website: http://www.minatol.co.uk
Directors: R. Abel (Dir)
Ultimate Holding Company: MINATOL LIMITED
Immediate Holding Company: LYNDALE INDUSTRIAL SUPPLIES LIMITED
Registration no: 00879812 **VAT No.:** GB 302 2595 91
Date established: 1966 **Turnover:** £1m - £2m **No.of Employees:** 1 - 10
Product Groups: 63, 66

Date of Accounts	Apr 11	Apr 10	Apr 09
Working Capital	416	416	416
Current Assets	416	416	416

Molins Tobacco Machinery Ltd

Haw Lane Saunderton, High Wycombe, HP14 4JE
Tel: 01844-343211 **Fax:** 01844-342410
E-mail: enquiries@molins.co.uk
Website: http://www.molins.co.uk
Directors: D. Cowen (MD), D. Hunter (MD), S. Boyce (Sales & Mktg)
Managers: D. Denton, G. Copeman (I.T. Exec), M. Phipps (Purch Mgr), V. Chivers (Sales Prom Mgr)
Immediate Holding Company: MOLINS TOBACCO MACHINERY LIMITED
Registration no: 01430235 **VAT No.:** 358 4557 18 **Date established:** 1979
Turnover: £125m - £250m **No.of Employees:** 251 - 500
Product Groups: 41

Monitran Ltd

Monitor House
33 Hazlemere Road
Penn, High Wycombe, HP10 8AD
Tel: 01494-816569 **Fax:** 01494-812256
E-mail: info@monitran.co.uk
Website: http://www.monitran.com
Bank(s): HSBC
Directors: R. Pickard (Dir), A. Anthony (MD), D. Lion (Prop)
Managers: S. Toyne (Mktg Serv Mgr), L. Goodall (Purch Mgr), K. Alger (Mktg Serv Mgr)
Immediate Holding Company: MONITRAN LIMITED
Registration no: 02054040 **Date established:** 1986
No.of Employees: 21 - 50 **Product Groups:** 37, 38

Date of Accounts	Feb 08	Feb 11	Feb 10
Working Capital	42	216	88
Fixed Assets	86	55	65
Current Assets	476	751	616
Current Liabilities	90	N/A	N/A

Multipond Ltd

20 St Johns Road Penn, High Wycombe, HP10 8HW
Tel: 01494-816644 **Fax:** 01494-816206
E-mail: info@multipond.co.uk
Website: http://www.multipond.com
Directors: G. Tandy (MD), R. Barton (Fin)
Ultimate Holding Company: ATOMA VERWALTUNGS GMBH & CO (GERMANY)
Immediate Holding Company: MULTIPOND LIMITED
Registration no: 02655742 **Date established:** 1991 **Turnover:** £2m - £5m
No.of Employees: 11 - 20 **Product Groups:** 38

Date of Accounts	Dec 11	Dec 10	Dec 09
Working Capital	148	-150	-245
Fixed Assets	94	135	90
Current Assets	2m	4m	1m

100% IT Recruitment Ltd

27 London Road, High Wycombe, HP11 1BJ
Tel: 0844-8794523 **Fax:** 0844-8794524
E-mail: info@100itrecruitment.co.uk
Website: http://www.100itrecruitment.co.uk
Directors: C. Gerald (Prop), C. Gerrard (Dir)
Registration no: 05069396 **Date established:** 1978 **Turnover:** £1m - £2m
No.of Employees: 1 - 10 **Product Groups:** 80

Date of Accounts	Mar 08	Mar 07	Mar 06
Working Capital	23	46	29
Fixed Assets	5	6	5
Current Assets	70	94	58
Current Liabilities	47	48	29

Oxford Instruments Analytical Ltd (Head Office - Microanalysis Group)

Halifax Road Cressex Business Park, High Wycombe, HP12 3SE
Tel: 01494-442255 **Fax:** 01494-524129
E-mail: dan.varnam@oxinst.com
Website: http://www.oxford-instruments.com
Directors: D. Scott (Sales), B. Hutchings (Fin)
Ultimate Holding Company: OXFORD INSTRUMENTS PLC
Immediate Holding Company: OXFORD INSTRUMENTS INDUSTRIAL PRODUCTS LIMITED
Registration no: 01044063 **VAT No.:** GB 596 1170 25
Date established: 1972 **Turnover:** £20m - £50m
No.of Employees: 101 - 250 **Product Groups:** 38

Date of Accounts	Mar 11	Mar 10	Mar 09
Sales Turnover	34m	37m	48m
Pre Tax Profit/Loss	3m	1m	85
Working Capital	17m	3m	3m
Fixed Assets	1m	5m	6m
Current Assets	20m	14m	16m
Current Liabilities	3m	3m	4m

Panache Fire Services Ltd

2 Wycombe Industrial Mall West End Street, High Wycombe, HP11 2QY
Tel: 01494-474787 **Fax:** 01494-474788
E-mail: sales@panachefire.co.uk
Website: http://www.panachefire.co.uk
Directors: T. Blaney (MD)
Immediate Holding Company: FIREPROTECTION4ALL LIMITED
Registration no: 03829463 **Date established:** 1999
No.of Employees: 1 - 10 **Product Groups:** 40, 52

Date of Accounts	Aug 11	Aug 10
Working Capital	39	-26
Current Assets	51	N/A

Pandect Instrument Laboratories Ltd

Wellington Road Cressex Business Park, High Wycombe, HP12 3PX
Tel: 01494-526301 **Fax:** 01494-464503
E-mail: rodney.pope@pandect.co.uk
Website: http://www.pandect.co.uk
Bank(s): Barclays, High St, High Wycombe
Directors: R. Pope (MD), J. Scott (Fin)
Managers: R. Stewart (Purch Mgr), B. Wilkins (Ops Mgr)
Immediate Holding Company: PANDECT INSTRUMENT LABORATORIES LIMITED
Registration no: 00533303 **VAT No.:** GB 385 8606 08
Date established: 1954 **Turnover:** £500,000 - £1m
No.of Employees: 21 - 50 **Product Groups:** 38, 39, 48, 67

Date of Accounts	Mar 11	Mar 10	Mar 09
Sales Turnover	881	N/A	N/A
Pre Tax Profit/Loss	8	N/A	N/A
Working Capital	338	657	679
Fixed Assets	700	431	449
Current Assets	487	847	939
Current Liabilities	102	N/A	N/A

Pandect Precision Components Ltd

Wellington Road Cressex Business Park, High Wycombe, HP12 3PX
Tel: 01494-526303 **Fax:** 01494-465557
E-mail: enquiries@pandect.demon.co.uk
Website: http://www.pandect.co.uk
Bank(s): Barclays
Directors: B. Wilkins (Dir), M. Ward (Sales), R. Pope (MD), J. Scott (Co Sec)
Managers: B. Wilkins (Comm), R. Stewart (Purch Mgr), M. Nixon (Mgr)
Immediate Holding Company: PANDECT PRECISION COMPONENTS LIMITED
Registration no: 00806716 **VAT No.:** 385 8604 12 **Date established:** 1964
Turnover: £1m - £2m **No.of Employees:** 21 - 50 **Product Groups:** 37, 38, 39, 49

Date of Accounts	Mar 08	Mar 07	Mar 06
Working Capital	669	596	616
Fixed Assets	83	85	81
Current Assets	1219	1153	1075
Current Liabilities	551	557	460
Total Share Capital	40	40	40

Portaprompt Ltd

Spearmast Industrial Park Lane End Road, High Wycombe, HP12 4JQ
Tel: 01494-450414 **Fax:** 01494-437591
E-mail: info@portaprompt.co.uk
Website: http://www.portaprompt.co.uk
Bank(s): National Westminster Bank Plc
Directors: H. Kingsbury (MD)
Immediate Holding Company: PORTAPROMPT LIMITED
Registration no: 01278694 **VAT No.:** GB 301 9540 87
Date established: 1976 **Turnover:** £500,000 - £1m
No.of Employees: 11 - 20 **Product Groups:** 37

Date of Accounts	Apr 11	Apr 10	Apr 09
Sales Turnover	966	826	865
Pre Tax Profit/Loss	169	85	100
Working Capital	101	26	61
Fixed Assets	59	44	38
Current Assets	282	229	207
Current Liabilities	102	126	65

Premier Filtration

26 St Birinus Flackwell Heath, High Wycombe, HP10 9DJ
Tel: 01628-527704 **Fax:** 01628-520502
E-mail: info@premierfiltration.com
Website: http://www.premierfiltration.com
Directors: C. Smith (Prop)
No.of Employees: 1 - 10 **Product Groups:** 27, 33, 34, 35, 40, 41, 42

Premier Plating

Lancaster Road Cressex Business Park, High Wycombe, HP12 3PY
Tel: 01494-450574 **Fax:** 01494-473726
E-mail: gregmurray@premier-plating.co.uk
Website: http://www.premier-plating.co.uk
Directors: D. Pocock (Dir), G. Murray (MD)
Managers: G. Murray (Purch Mgr), E. King (Purch Mgr)
Ultimate Holding Company: CATHEDRAL HOMES (U.K.) LIMITED
Immediate Holding Company: CATHEDRAL HOMES (SOUTH BUCKS) LTD
Registration no: 01642929 **VAT No.:** GB 349 1750 40
Date established: 2008 **Turnover:** £250,000 - £500,000
No.of Employees: 1 - 10 **Product Groups:** 48

Date of Accounts	Dec 11	Dec 10	Dec 09
Working Capital	-49	-49	-49
Current Assets	1	3	2

Presletta Graphics

66 Kitchener Road, High Wycombe, HP11 2SN
Tel: 01494-526285
E-mail: roy@presletta.com
Website: http://www.presletta.com
Directors: R. Smith (Prop)
Ultimate Holding Company: PRESLETTA GRAPHICS
Date established: 1966 **Turnover:** Up to £250,000
No.of Employees: 1 - 10 **Product Groups:** 44

Procter Media Ltd

Burleighfield House London Road, Loudwater, High Wycombe, HP10 9RF
Tel: 01494-755700 **Fax:** 01494-755717
E-mail: info@proctergroup.co.uk
Website: http://www.proctergroup.co.uk
Managers: L. Barsi
Immediate Holding Company: PROCTER MEDIA LIMITED
Registration no: 02865127 **Date established:** 1993
No.of Employees: 1 - 10 **Product Groups:** 81

Date of Accounts	Jun 11	Jun 10	Jun 09
Sales Turnover	901	494	705
Pre Tax Profit/Loss	-59	33	83
Working Capital	69	124	107
Fixed Assets	8	N/A	N/A
Current Assets	239	240	356
Current Liabilities	74	74	98

R O Metal Fabrication

Unit 14 Soho Mills, Wooburn Green, High Wycombe, HP10 0PS
Tel: 01628-529563
Website: http://www.millwrighteng.btinternet.co.uk
Managers: J. Thomas
Immediate Holding Company: MILLWRIGHT FABRICATIONS LTD
Registration no: 01739876 **No.of Employees:** 1 - 10 **Product Groups:** 42, 45

R P Towing

Unit 1d Abercromby Avenue, High Wycombe, HP12 3BW
Tel: 01494-528233 **Fax:** 01494-638802
E-mail: rp.towing@ntlworld.com
Directors: J. Poulton (Ptnr)
VAT No.: GB 669 4552 88 **Turnover:** Up to £250,000
No.of Employees: 1 - 10 **Product Groups:** 39, 68

Rank Hovis

The Lord Rank Centre Lincoln Road, High Wycombe, HP12 3QS
Tel: 0870-7281111 **Fax:** 0870-7281728
E-mail: customer.questionnaires@premierfoods.co.uk
Website: http://www.rankhovis.co.uk
Bank(s): Barclays

see next page

Rank Hovis - Cont'd

Directors: J. Clarke (Dir), J. Tanner (Sales & Mktg)
Ultimate Holding Company: Premier Foods plc
Immediate Holding Company: RHM Foodbrands+ Ltd
Registration no: 00062065 **VAT No.:** GB 697 9173 62
Date established: 1875 **Turnover:** £250m - £500m
No.of Employees: 501 - 1000 **Product Groups:** 41

Date of Accounts	Dec 07
Working Capital	144480
Fixed Assets	2520
Current Assets	145180
Current Liabilities	700
Total Share Capital	145000

Rant H G

Oakmead Works Desborough Street, High Wycombe, HP11 2LX
Tel: 01494-539113 **Fax:** 01494-539114
E-mail: alex.rant@hgrant-brushmakers.co.uk
Website: http://www.hgrant-brushmakers.co.uk
Bank(s): HSBC Bank plc
Directors: A. Rant (MD)
Immediate Holding Company: H.G. RANT LTD
Registration no: 05201043 **Date established:** 2004
Turnover: £250,000 - £500,000 **No.of Employees:** 11 - 20
Product Groups: 33, 35, 38, 39, 49, 63, 66

Date of Accounts	Dec 11	Dec 10	Dec 09
Working Capital	60	36	21
Fixed Assets	103	112	124
Current Assets	129	130	110

Redi Fire Ltd

59-63 Queens Road, High Wycombe, HP13 6AH
Tel: 01527-542369
Directors: M. Lunn (MD), L. Ross (Fin), B. Ross (MD)
Immediate Holding Company: REDI-FIRE LIMITED
Registration no: 01412328 **Date established:** 1979
Turnover: Up to £250,000 **No.of Employees:** 21 - 50 **Product Groups:** 38, 42

Date of Accounts	Mar 08	Mar 07	Mar 06
Working Capital	14	47	8
Fixed Assets	2	2	20
Current Assets	24	65	27
Current Liabilities	10	18	19

Resinex UK Ltd

11 Valley Business Centre Gordon Road, High Wycombe, HP13 6EQ
Tel: 01494-459881 **Fax:** 01494-795334
E-mail: info@resinex.co.uk
Website: http://www.resinex.co.uk
Bank(s): Lloyds TSB Bank plc
Directors: M. Marsh (MD), D. Gleeson (Fin)
Managers: Z. Patel (Tech Serv Mgr), K. Grewal (Sales Off Mgr)
Ultimate Holding Company: RAVAGO SA (LUXEMBOURG)
Immediate Holding Company: RESINEX UK LTD
Registration no: 01953217 **Date established:** 1985
Turnover: £50m - £75m **No.of Employees:** 21 - 50 **Product Groups:** 30, 31

Date of Accounts	Dec 11	Dec 10	Dec 09
Sales Turnover	64m	55m	43m
Pre Tax Profit/Loss	1m	4m	3m
Working Capital	2m	1m	4m
Fixed Assets	269	244	219
Current Assets	3m	3m	7m
Current Liabilities	599	1m	771

Sano Tools

Unit 4a Fryers Works Abercromby Avenue, High Wycombe, HP12 3BW
Tel: 01494-437949 **Fax:** 01494-471815
E-mail: office@sanotools.com
Website: http://www.chilterntooling.co.uk
Directors: W. Page (Prop)
Ultimate Holding Company: NICOL & ANDREW GROUP LIMITED
Immediate Holding Company: HEMPSTEAD & JOHNSON LIMITED
Date established: 1963 **Turnover:** Up to £250,000
No.of Employees: 1 - 10 **Product Groups:** 46, 66

Date of Accounts	Mar 11	Mar 10	Mar 09
Sales Turnover	1m	844	1m
Pre Tax Profit/Loss	-60	-109	-196
Working Capital	-157	-122	-43
Fixed Assets	683	675	680
Current Assets	469	361	483
Current Liabilities	90	73	95

Sebo UK Ltd

1 The Merlin Centre Lancaster Road, Cressex Business Park, High Wycombe, HP12 3QL
Tel: 01494-465533 **Fax:** 01494-461044
E-mail: info@sebo.co.uk
Website: http://www.sebo.co.uk
Directors: A. Binks (MD), J. Binks (MD)
Immediate Holding Company: SEBO (U.K.) LIMITED
Registration no: 01504408 **Date established:** 1980
Turnover: £10m - £20m **No.of Employees:** 11 - 20 **Product Groups:** 40

Date of Accounts	Dec 11	Dec 10	Dec 09
Sales Turnover	10m	11m	11m
Pre Tax Profit/Loss	645	-180	-589
Working Capital	2m	2m	2m
Fixed Assets	103	130	146
Current Assets	3m	3m	4m
Current Liabilities	796	727	2m

Select Moulds Ltd

Merlin House
Lancaster Road
Cressex Business Park, High Wycombe, HP12 3PY
Tel: 01494-459551 **Fax:** 01494-461533
E-mail: simon.collins@selectmoulds.co.uk
Website: http://www.selectmoulds.co.uk
Bank(s): Natwest
Directors: S. Collins (Dir), S. Barlow (Dir)
Managers: S. Collins (Sales Prom Mgr), A. Morgan (Fin Mgr)
Immediate Holding Company: Interplex Inc.
Registration no: 02527576 **VAT No.:** GB 538 0212 70
Date established: 1990 **Turnover:** £1m - £2m **No.of Employees:** 11 - 20
Product Groups: 30, 31, 42, 46, 48

Date of Accounts	Dec 11	Dec 10	Dec 09
Working Capital	-49	-49	-49
Current Assets	1	3	2

Seymour Taylor

57 London Road, High Wycombe, HP11 1BS
Tel: 01494-552100 **Fax:** 01494-61157
E-mail: enquiries@stca.co.uk
Website: http://www.stca.co.uk
Directors: S. Turner (MD)
Immediate Holding Company: SEYMOUR TAYLOR LIMITED
Registration no: 02982099 **VAT No.:** GB 207 9953 34
Date established: 1994 **Turnover:** £1m - £2m **No.of Employees:** 21 - 50
Product Groups: 80, 82

Sidney Cubbage Heating & Ventilating Ltd

Harrem House Ogilvie Road, High Wycombe, HP12 3DS
Tel: 01494-523661 **Fax:** 01494-462707
E-mail: d.smith@sidneycubbage.com
Website: http://www.sidneycubbage.com
Bank(s): Lloyds TSB Bank plc
Directors: C. Williams (Co Sec), D. Smith (Dir)
Ultimate Holding Company: SPAD HOLDINGS LIMITED
Immediate Holding Company: SIDNEY CUBBAGE (HEATING AND VENTILATING) LIMITED
Registration no: 01719631 **VAT No.:** GB 385 6296 07
Date established: 1983 **Turnover:** £2m - £5m **No.of Employees:** 21 - 50
Product Groups: 35, 36, 40, 42, 45, 48

Date of Accounts	May 12	May 11	May 10
Working Capital	236	44	132
Fixed Assets	85	82	57
Current Assets	1m	693	743

Slush Puppie Ltd

Coronation Road Cressex Business Park, High Wycombe, HP12 3TA
Tel: 020-8578 5785 **Fax:** 020-8575 3611
E-mail: info@slushpuppie.co.uk
Website: http://www.slushpuppie.co.uk
Directors: A. Lynskey (Fab), A. Lynskey (Fab), S. Rose (Dir)
Ultimate Holding Company: RALPH PETERS & SONS LIMITED
Immediate Holding Company: SLUSH PUPPIE LIMITED
Registration no: 00396263 **Date established:** 1945 **Turnover:** £5m - £10m
No.of Employees: 51 - 100 **Product Groups:** 40

Date of Accounts	Dec 11	Dec 10	Dec 09
Sales Turnover	8m	7m	6m
Pre Tax Profit/Loss	671	103	127
Working Capital	-586	-469	-440
Fixed Assets	5m	3m	3m
Current Assets	3m	1m	1m
Current Liabilities	2m	1m	1m

Smashing Supplies Ltd

42 The Basepoint Centre Lincoln Road, Cressex Business Park, High Wycombe, HP12 3RL
Tel: 01494-614524 **Fax:** 01494-614524
E-mail: debbiemash@aol.com
Directors: D. Mash (MD), J. Pawelczyk (Fin)
Immediate Holding Company: SMASHING SUPPLIES LIMITED
Registration no: 04849414 **Date established:** 2003
No.of Employees: 1 - 10 **Product Groups:** 20, 40, 41

Date of Accounts	Mar 11	Mar 10	Mar 09
Working Capital	-5	-8	-16
Fixed Assets	5	6	7
Current Assets	164	150	169

Smeaton Hanscomb & Co. Ltd

Lisle Road Hughenden Avenue, High Wycombe, HP13 5SQ
Tel: 01494-521051 **Fax:** 01494-461176
E-mail: sales@smeathans.plus.com
Website: http://www.smeathans.plus.com
Directors: W. Geddes (Prop)
Immediate Holding Company: SMEATON HANSCOMB & CO.,LIMITED
Registration no: 00256460 **Date established:** 1931
Turnover: £250,000 - £500,000 **No.of Employees:** 1 - 10
Product Groups: 36, 47

Date of Accounts	Sep 11	Sep 10	Sep 09
Working Capital	-10	17	14
Fixed Assets	602	602	802
Current Assets	53	78	68

Alan Spargo Ltd

Coronation Road Cressex Business Park, High Wycombe, HP12 3TA
Tel: 01494-529808 **Fax:** 01494-464077
E-mail: info@alanspargoltd.com
Website: http://www.alanspargoltd.com
Bank(s): National Westminster Bank Plc
Directors: R. Wainwright (Sales)
Managers: S. Highgate (Purch Mgr), S. Baker
Ultimate Holding Company: RALPH PETERS & SONS LIMITED
Immediate Holding Company: ALAN SPARGO LIMITED
Registration no: 01212214 **VAT No.:** GB 209 3971 50
Date established: 1975 **Turnover:** £2m - £5m **No.of Employees:** 21 - 50
Product Groups: 46

Date of Accounts	May 11	May 10	May 09
Working Capital	755	695	961
Fixed Assets	569	591	664
Current Assets	1m	1m	1m

Sparkle Bright Bath Restorers

38 Highwood Avenue, High Wycombe, HP12 4LS
Tel: 01494-462651 **Fax:** 01494-462651
E-mail: teresaprice67@virginmedia.com
Directors: G. Price (Prop)
Date established: 2002 **No.of Employees:** 1 - 10 **Product Groups:** 46, 48

Speck Pumps UK Ltd

11-12 Wycombe Industrial Mall West End Street, High Wycombe, HP11 2QY
Tel: 01494-523203 **Fax:** 01494-441542
E-mail: info@speck.co.uk
Website: http://www.speck.co.uk
Directors: O. Zinnecker (MD), E. Wurst (Fin)
Ultimate Holding Company: Speck Kolbenpumpfabrik Otto Speck GmbH & Co KG.
Immediate Holding Company: SPECK PUMPS (UK) LIMITED
Registration no: 01824324 **VAT No.:** GB 417 1332 83
Date established: 1984 **Turnover:** £1m - £2m **No.of Employees:** 1 - 10
Product Groups: 38, 39, 40, 45, 46, 67

Date of Accounts	Dec 11	Dec 10	Dec 09
Working Capital	452	424	380
Fixed Assets	150	137	157
Current Assets	856	794	725

Spectrum Hose Ltd

Unit 5 Desborough Industrial Park Desborough Park Road, High Wycombe, HP12 3BG
Tel: 01494-524332 **Fax:** 01494-464667
E-mail: sales@spectrum-hose.co.uk
Website: http://www.spectrum-hose.co.uk
Directors: P. Rutter (MD)
Immediate Holding Company: SPECTRUM HOSE LIMITED
Registration no: 01609052 **VAT No.:** GB 349 1344 51
Date established: 1982 **Turnover:** £1m - £2m **No.of Employees:** 1 - 10
Product Groups: 29, 30

Date of Accounts	Apr 12	Apr 11	Apr 10
Working Capital	235	267	227
Fixed Assets	437	441	458
Current Assets	418	442	493

Spira UK Ltd

Unit 38 Wooburn Industrial Park Wooburn Green, High Wycombe, HP10 0PF
Tel: 01628-529122 **Fax:** 01628-850219
E-mail: karen@spira-uk.co.uk
Website: http://www.ducting-online.co.uk
Directors: H. Gareppo (MD)
Immediate Holding Company: SPIRA U.K. LIMITED
Registration no: 02415049 **Date established:** 1989
No.of Employees: 1 - 10 **Product Groups:** 37, 40, 48

Date of Accounts	Nov 11	Nov 10	Nov 09
Working Capital	168	172	171
Fixed Assets	27	29	7
Current Assets	350	306	255

Sprayblast Engineering

2 Fairfield Works West Wycombe Road, High Wycombe, HP11 2LR
Tel: 01494-530854 **Fax:** 01494-465589
Directors: S. Ward (MD)
Date established: 1997 **No.of Employees:** 1 - 10 **Product Groups:** 46, 48

Staytite

Coronation Road Cressex Business Park, High Wycombe, HP12 3RP
Tel: 01494-462322 **Fax:** 01494-464747
E-mail: fasteners@staytite.com
Website: http://www.staytite.com
Directors: R. Black (Co Sec)
Managers: P. Nash (Ops Mgr)
Ultimate Holding Company: STAYTITE (HOLDINGS) LIMITED
Immediate Holding Company: STAYTITE LIMITED
Registration no: 01373472 **Date established:** 1978
No.of Employees: 11 - 20 **Product Groups:** 30, 34, 35, 36, 38, 39, 43, 45, 46, 49, 66

Date of Accounts	Dec 10	Dec 09	Dec 08
Working Capital	999	1m	992
Fixed Assets	30	26	26
Current Assets	2m	2m	2m

T P Technology plc

2-4 Copyground Lane, High Wycombe, HP12 3HE
Tel: 01494-535576 **Fax:** 01494-464175
E-mail: sales@tarn-pure.com
Website: http://www.tarn-pure.com
Managers: I. Bateman
Immediate Holding Company: T P TECHNOLOGY LIMITED
Registration no: 02307683 **Date established:** 1988
Turnover: £500,000 - £1m **No.of Employees:** 1 - 10 **Product Groups:** 36, 42

Date of Accounts	Mar 10	Mar 09	Mar 08
Sales Turnover	588	531	519
Pre Tax Profit/Loss	-87	-134	-96
Working Capital	17	35	5
Fixed Assets	329	307	169
Current Assets	242	279	208
Current Liabilities	97	69	63

Tapworks

Unit 1 Mill Road Stokenchurch, High Wycombe, HP14 3TP
Tel: 01494-480621 **Fax:** 01494-484396
E-mail: info@tapworks.co.uk
Website: http://www.tapworks.co.uk
Managers: B. Benson (Sales Prom Mgr)
Ultimate Holding Company: BERKSHIRE HATHAWAY INC (USA)
Immediate Holding Company: MARMON GROUP LIMITED(THE)
Registration no: 02135940 **Date established:** 1923 **Turnover:** £2m - £5m
No.of Employees: 21 - 50 **Product Groups:** 38, 42

Taylor Wimpey UK Ltd

Gate House Turnpike Road, High Wycombe, HP12 3NR
Tel: 01494-558323 **Fax:** 01494-885663
E-mail: russell.brittain@taylorwimpey.com
Website: http://www.taylorwimpey.co.uk
Bank(s): National Westminster Bank Plc
Directors: K. Belsham (Sales & Mktg)
Managers: R. Brittain (Personnel), R. Mangold
Ultimate Holding Company: TAYLOR WIMPEY PLC
Immediate Holding Company: TAYLOR WIMPEY UK LIMITED
Registration no: 01392762 **Date established:** 1978
Turnover: Over £1,000m **No.of Employees:** 51 - 100 **Product Groups:** 52

Date of Accounts	Dec 11	Dec 10	Dec 09
Sales Turnover	1749m	1712m	1680m
Pre Tax Profit/Loss	94m	51m	-111m
Working Capital	1068m	1042m	622m
Fixed Assets	117m	109m	107m
Current Assets	4003m	3070m	3159m
Current Liabilities	134m	132m	141m

Techland Group Ltd

Techland House Knaves Beech Business Centre, Loudwater, High Wycombe, HP10 9YJ
Tel: 01628-852000 **Fax:** 01628-643800
E-mail: sales@techland.co.uk
Website: http://www.techland.co.uk
Bank(s): Lloyds
Directors: A. Patel (MD)
Immediate Holding Company: TECHLAND GROUP LIMITED
Registration no: 06382820 **Date established:** 2007 **Turnover:** £2m - £5m
No.of Employees: 11 - 20 **Product Groups:** 44

Date of Accounts	Dec 10	Dec 09	Dec 08
Fixed Assets	554	554	347

Teleflex Medical

Stirling Road Cressex Business Park, High Wycombe, HP12 3ST
Tel: 01494-532761 **Fax:** 01494-524650
E-mail: dclarke@teleflexmedical.com
Website: http://www.teleflexmedical.com
Managers: D. Clark (Mgr)
Ultimate Holding Company: TELEFLEX INC (USA)
Immediate Holding Company: WATERCARE UTILITIES LIMITED
Registration no: 01482052 **Date established:** 2004 **Turnover:** £5m - £10m
No.of Employees: 1 - 10 **Product Groups:** 63

Date of Accounts	Mar 11	Mar 10	Mar 09
Working Capital	298	356	370
Fixed Assets	175	202	223
Current Assets	1m	1m	1m

Tellabs

Abbey Place 24-28 Easton Street, High Wycombe, HP11 1NT
Tel: 0871-574 7000 **Fax:** 0871-5747151
E-mail: prnews@tellabs.com
Website: http://www.tellabs.com
Directors: C. Wade (Dir), S. McCaffery (Dir)
Immediate Holding Company: Tellabs Inc (USA)
Registration no: 01405720 **Date established:** 1975 **Turnover:** £5m - £10m
No.of Employees: 51 - 100 **Product Groups:** 37

Tetra Pak Processing UK Ltd

Swan House Peregrine Business Park Gomm Road, High Wycombe, HP13 7DL
Tel: 08704-426400 **Fax:** 08704-426401
E-mail: fred.griemsmann@tetrapak.com
Website: http://www.tetrapakprocessinguk.co.uk
Directors: F. Griemsmann (MD), I. Chambers (Fin)
Managers: J. Szpack (Personnel), A. Stack (Mktg Serv Mgr), S. Jones
Ultimate Holding Company: TETRA LAVAL HOLDINGS BV (NETHERLANDS)
Immediate Holding Company: TETRA PAK PROCESSING UK LIMITED
Registration no: 04259617 **Date established:** 2001
Turnover: £10m - £20m **No.of Employees:** 21 - 50 **Product Groups:** 20, 40, 41

Date of Accounts	Dec 11	Dec 10	Dec 09
Sales Turnover	19m	19m	33m
Pre Tax Profit/Loss	319	-279	-39
Working Capital	-6m	-7m	-4m
Fixed Assets	159	1m	103
Current Assets	7m	7m	13m
Current Liabilities	4m	3m	3m

3663 Ltd

Buckingham Court London Road, High Wycombe, HP11 1JU
Tel: 01494-555900 **Fax:** 0370-3663 199
E-mail: info@3663.co.uk
Website: http://www.3663.co.uk
Bank(s): HSBC Bank plc
Directors: A. Selley (MD), A. Selly (MD), F. Barnes (Ch), P. Weir (Fin)
Managers: C. Colesells (I.T. Exec), C. Jones (Fin Mgr), E. Williamson (Depot Mgr), M. Dickinson (Sales Prom Mgr), N. Wildbore (Purch Mgr), V. Colesell (I.T. Exec), S. Winpenny (Personnel)
Ultimate Holding Company: Bid Foodservice (Europe) Ltd
Immediate Holding Company: Bidvest UK Ltd
Registration no: 03834103 **VAT No.:** GB 306 5573 62
Date established: 2000 **No.of Employees:** 501 - 1000
Product Groups: 62, 80, 85

Trada Technology

Chiltern House Stocking Lane, Hughenden Valley, High Wycombe, HP14 4ND
Tel: 01494-569600 **Fax:** 01494-565487
E-mail: information@trada.co.uk
Website: http://www.trada.co.uk
Bank(s): Lloyds
Directors: D. Webb (Grp Chief Exec)
Managers: A. Endres (Tech Serv Mgr)
Ultimate Holding Company: BM TRADA GROUP LIMITED
Immediate Holding Company: TRADA TECHNOLOGY LIMITED
Registration no: 02561166 **Date established:** 1990 **Turnover:** £2m - £5m
No.of Employees: 101 - 250 **Product Groups:** 80, 84, 85, 86, 87

Date of Accounts	Dec 11	Dec 10	Dec 09
Sales Turnover	4m	4m	4m
Pre Tax Profit/Loss	61	99	53
Working Capital	1m	967	787
Fixed Assets	66	131	234
Current Assets	2m	1m	1m
Current Liabilities	450	461	383

Unitemp Ltd

14 Treadaway Business Centre Treadaway Hill, Loudwater, High Wycombe, HP10 9RS
Tel: 01628-850611 **Fax:** 01628-850608
E-mail: info@unitemp.co.uk
Website: http://www.unitemp.co.uk
Directors: A. Karolak (Co Sec)
Immediate Holding Company: UNITEMP LIMITED
Registration no: 01785856 **VAT No.:** GB 374 4296 30
Date established: 1984 **Turnover:** £1m - £2m **No.of Employees:** 1 - 10
Product Groups: 38, 85

Date of Accounts	Jun 11	Jun 10	Jun 09
Working Capital	80	46	69
Fixed Assets	11	15	17
Current Assets	337	176	210

Universal Air Tool Company Ltd

Unit 8 Lane End Industrial Park, Lane End, High Wycombe, HP14 3BY
Tel: 01494-883300 **Fax:** 01494-883237
E-mail: sales@universal.co.uk
Website: http://www.universal.co.uk
Directors: C. Moppett (MD)
Immediate Holding Company: UNIVERSAL AIR TOOL COMPANY LIMITED
Registration no: 01122438 **Date established:** 1973
Turnover: £500,000 - £1m **No.of Employees:** 1 - 10 **Product Groups:** 37, 40, 67

Date of Accounts	Dec 11	Dec 10	Dec 09
Working Capital	578	599	559
Fixed Assets	389	317	338
Current Assets	1m	1m	1m

Universal Catering Equipment

15 Altona Road Loudwater, High Wycombe, HP10 9RW
Tel: 07973-322260 **Fax:** 01494-452538
E-mail: zoran_universal_catering@hotmail.com
Directors: Z. Zaharijevic (Prop)
Date established: 1994 **No.of Employees:** 1 - 10 **Product Groups:** 20, 40, 41

V & G Agricultural Services

West Wycombe, High Wycombe, HP14 3BA
Tel: 01494-882621 **Fax:** 01494-882545
E-mail: mick.vowles@btinternet.com
Website: http://www.vandgagricultural.co.uk
Directors: M. Vowles (Ptnr)
Immediate Holding Company: H&L CONSTRUCTION SOLUTIONS LIMITED
Registration no: 00730437 **Date established:** 2010
No.of Employees: 1 - 10 **Product Groups:** 41

Date of Accounts	Mar 11
Working Capital	-1
Current Assets	49

Verco Office Furniture Ltd

Chapel Lane, High Wycombe, HP12 4BG
Tel: 01494-448000 **Fax:** 01494-464216
E-mail: sales@verco.co.uk
Website: http://www.verco.co.uk
Bank(s): Barclays
Directors: C. Riley (Sales & Mktg), J. Roberts (Fin), D. Vere (MD)
Managers: P. Lewis (Tech Serv Mgr), S. Toye (Personnel), J. Elmer (Purch Mgr)
Ultimate Holding Company: WILLIAM VERE (HOLDINGS) LIMITED
Immediate Holding Company: VERCO OFFICE FURNITURE LIMITED
Registration no: 00396797 **VAT No.:** GB 207 8153 71
Date established: 1945 **Turnover:** £10m - £20m
No.of Employees: 101 - 250 **Product Groups:** 26

Date of Accounts	Dec 11	Dec 10	Dec 09
Sales Turnover	11m	10m	10m
Pre Tax Profit/Loss	-165	-957	-2m
Working Capital	4m	4m	5m
Fixed Assets	8m	8m	9m
Current Assets	6m	5m	6m
Current Liabilities	685	474	336

Verus Instruments Ltd

Clare House Pinewood Road, High Wycombe, HP12 4DA
Tel: 01494-558206 **Fax:** 01494-558383
E-mail: john@palletlink.co.uk
Website: http://verus.co.uk
Directors: I. Harvey (Fin), J. Harvey (MD)
Immediate Holding Company: VERUS INSTRUMENTS LIMITED
Registration no: 01876023 **Date established:** 1985
No.of Employees: 1 - 10 **Product Groups:** 38

Date of Accounts	Jul 11	Jul 10	Jul 09
Working Capital	4	6	4
Current Assets	8	11	10

Volkmann UK Ltd

Unit 50 Cressex Enterprise Centre Lincoln Road, High Wycombe, HP12 3RL
Tel: 01494-512228 **Fax:** 01494-512228
E-mail: mw@volkmann-vacuum.com
Website: http://www.volkmann.info
Directors: M. Walker (MD)
Registration no: 04175423 **Date established:** 2001
Turnover: £250,000 - £500,000 **No.of Employees:** 1 - 10
Product Groups: 42, 45

Walter Group Holdings

Walters House 12 The Merlin Centre Lancaster Road, Cressex Business Park, High Wycombe, HP12 3TB
Tel: 01494-453700 **Fax:** 01494-461107
E-mail: info@waltersmicro.co.uk
Website: http://www.waltergroup.co.uk
Bank(s): Barclays
Directors: C. Walters (Purch)
Managers: D. Leeser (Sales Admin), M. Newell, S. Michaels (Fin Mgr)
Immediate Holding Company: WALTERS MICROSYSTEMS LIMITED
Registration no: 01193939 **Date established:** 1974
Turnover: £10m - £20m **No.of Employees:** 51 - 100 **Product Groups:** 81, 84

A J Way & Co. Ltd

Sunters End Hillbottom Road, Sands Industrial Estate, High Wycombe, HP12 4HS
Tel: 01494-471821 **Fax:** 01494-450597
E-mail: sales@ajway.co.uk
Website: http://www.ajway.co.uk
Directors: B. Wharton (MD), E. Maslen (Co Sec)
Managers: B. Douglas
Ultimate Holding Company: KIRTON HOLDINGS LIMITED
Immediate Holding Company: A.J. WAY & CO. LIMITED
Registration no: 02088914 **Date established:** 1987 **Turnover:** £2m - £5m
No.of Employees: 51 - 100 **Product Groups:** 26

Date of Accounts	Dec 11	Dec 10	Mar 10
Sales Turnover	3m	2m	N/A
Pre Tax Profit/Loss	2	15	N/A
Working Capital	685	654	685
Fixed Assets	101	130	100
Current Assets	974	1m	1m
Current Liabilities	116	124	N/A

George Wimpey South Yorkshire Ltd

Gate House Turnpike Road, High Wycombe, HP12 3NR
Tel: 01494-558 323 **Fax:** 01709-560484
E-mail: customerservices@taylorwimpey.com
Website: http://www.georgewimpey.co.uk
Directors: T. McGuire (MD), N. Hastie (Co Sec)
Managers: A. Colles (I.T. Exec), J. Armstrong (Purch Mgr), M. Jones (Sales & Mktg Mg)
Immediate Holding Company: Taylor Wimpey UK Ltd
Registration no: 00911591 **Turnover:** £20m - £50m
No.of Employees: 21 - 50 **Product Groups:** 80

Date of Accounts	Dec 07	Dec 06	Dec 05
Working Capital	8070	8070	8070
Current Assets	8070	8070	8070
Total Share Capital	8000	8000	8000

Wood Waste Control Engineering Ltd

Units 2-3 Soho Mill Wooburn Green, High Wycombe, HP10 0PF
Tel: 01628-525290 **Fax:** 01628-810218
E-mail: info@w-w-c.co.uk
Website: http://www.w-w-c.co.uk
Bank(s): National Westminster Bank Plc
Directors: H. Gareppo (Co Sec), R. Gareppo (MD), L. Gareppo (Dir)
Managers: A. Carter (Mgr)
Registration no: 01694495 **Turnover:** £1m - £2m
No.of Employees: 11 - 20 **Product Groups:** 23, 29, 30, 34, 35, 36, 39, 40, 41, 42, 44, 46, 47, 52, 54, 66

Date of Accounts	Feb 12	Feb 11	Feb 10
Working Capital	299	196	257
Fixed Assets	180	155	131
Current Assets	410	426	369

Wooster & Williams Ltd

8 Jubilee Road, High Wycombe, HP11 2PG
Tel: 01494-525372 **Fax:** 01494-463469
Managers: P. Paice (Sales Admin)
Immediate Holding Company: WOOSTER & WILLIAMS LIMITED
Registration no: 04004637 **Date established:** 2000
Turnover: £500,000 - £1m **No.of Employees:** 1 - 10 **Product Groups:** 25

Date of Accounts	Mar 11	Mar 10	Mar 09
Working Capital	4	-0	21
Fixed Assets	N/A	4	8
Current Assets	96	86	132

Wycombe Panels Ltd

Coronation Road Cressex Business Park, High Wycombe, HP12 3RP
Tel: 01494-530473 **Fax:** 01494-461815
E-mail: jseymour@wycombepanels.co.uk
Website: http://www.wycombepanels.co.uk
Bank(s): HSBC
Directors: J. Seymour (Dir), J. Appleton (Co Sec)
Managers: J. Elliott (Tech Serv Mgr)
Ultimate Holding Company: FLEDGE CHOICE LIMITED
Immediate Holding Company: WYCOMBE PANELS LIMITED
Registration no: 02096817 **VAT No.:** GB 321 5400 12
Date established: 1987 **Turnover:** £1m - £2m **No.of Employees:** 21 - 50
Product Groups: 25

Date of Accounts	Dec 11	Dec 10	Dec 09
Sales Turnover	2m	2m	2m
Pre Tax Profit/Loss	-9	61	-37
Working Capital	962	1m	1m
Fixed Assets	789	982	1m
Current Assets	2m	2m	2m
Current Liabilities	286	112	86

WyseGroup Ltd

Lancaster Road Cressex Business Park, High Wycombe, HP12 3QP
Tel: 01494-560900 **Fax:** 01494-560889
E-mail: info@wysepower.com
Website: http://www.wysepower.com
Directors: M. Curran (MD), M. Law (Fin)
Immediate Holding Company: Bovis Construction Ltd & Tarmac Construction Ltd
Registration no: 05665971 **Date established:** 1998
No.of Employees: 1 - 10 **Product Groups:** 52

Young Electronics Ltd a division of H. Young Holdings plc

Crown House Coronation Road, Cressex Business Park, High Wycombe, HP12 3TA
Tel: 01494-753500 **Fax:** 01494-753501
E-mail: sales@youngelectronics.com
Website: http://www.youngelectronics.com
Bank(s): National Westminster Bank Plc
Directors: T. Janes (Grp Chief Exec)
Ultimate Holding Company: RALPH PETERS & SONS LIMITED
Immediate Holding Company: FRUTINA LIMITED
Registration no: 02926739 **Date established:** 1994
Turnover: £50m - £75m **No.of Employees:** 51 - 100 **Product Groups:** 37

Date of Accounts	Dec 11	Dec 10	Dec 09
Sales Turnover	8m	7m	6m
Pre Tax Profit/Loss	531	116	127
Working Capital	-489	-280	-273
Fixed Assets	5m	2m	2m
Current Assets	3m	1m	1m
Current Liabilities	2m	1m	1m

Zingaro Designs Ltd

19 Hazlemere Road Penn, High Wycombe, HP10 8AD
Tel: 01494-812783 **Fax:** 01494-814369
E-mail: david@zingarodesigns.co.uk
Website: http://www.zingarodesigns.co.uk
Directors: D. Knight (MD)
Immediate Holding Company: ZINGARO DESIGNS LIMITED
Registration no: 01489198 **VAT No.:** GB 225 5360 79
Date established: 1980 **No.of Employees:** 1 - 10 **Product Groups:** 38, 52, 84

Date of Accounts	Dec 11	Dec 10	Dec 09
Working Capital	190	195	185
Fixed Assets	1	3	N/A
Current Assets	317	350	285

Zygology Ltd

2 Barnes Wallis Court Wellington Rd, High Wycombe, HP12 3PS
Tel: 0845-812 1220 **Fax:** 0845-812 1221
E-mail: sales@zygology.com
Website: http://www.zygology.com
Bank(s): National Westminster Bank Plc
Directors: D. Harford (Fin), R. Harford (MD)
Managers: R. Avery (Sales Prom Mgr), A. Varnham (Sales Off Mgr)
Registration no: 06025984 **VAT No.:** GB 302 0135 38
Date established: 1977 **Turnover:** £2m - £5m **No.of Employees:** 11 - 20
Product Groups: 30, 35, 36, 37, 40, 46, 66, 67

Date of Accounts	Aug 11	Aug 10	Aug 09
Sales Turnover	3m	N/A	N/A
Pre Tax Profit/Loss	197	N/A	N/A
Working Capital	564	398	262
Fixed Assets	N/A	15	17
Current Assets	564	1m	903

Iver

Avid Technology Europe Ltd
Pinewood Studios Pinewood Road, Iver, SL0 0NH
Tel: 01753-655999 **Fax:** 01753-654999
E-mail: info@avid.com
Website: http://www.avid.com
Directors: A. Terry (Fin)
Managers: C. Melluzzi (Mktg Serv Mgr), A. Feldaman (Personnel), S. Bains (Tech Serv Mgr), T. Cordiner
Ultimate Holding Company: AVID TECHNOLOGY INC (USA)
Immediate Holding Company: AVID TECHNOLOGY EUROPE LIMITED
Registration no: 02670844 **Date established:** 1991
Turnover: £20m - £50m **No.of Employees:** 101 - 250
Product Groups: 37, 38

Date of Accounts	Dec 11	Dec 10	Dec 09
Sales Turnover	28m	27m	32m
Pre Tax Profit/Loss	2m	-8m	3m
Working Capital	4m	16m	10m
Fixed Assets	7m	8m	22m
Current Assets	26m	20m	18m
Current Liabilities	3m	3m	5m

The Bionic Group Ltd
Pinewood Studios Pinewood Road, Iver, SL0 0NH
Tel: 01753-653456 **Fax:** 01753-654507
E-mail: andrew@thebionicgroup.com
Website: http://www.thebionicgroup.com
Directors: A. Eio (Dir)
Ultimate Holding Company: RAGDOLL LIMITED
Immediate Holding Company: THE BIONIC GROUP LIMITED
Registration no: 05466755 **Date established:** 2005
Turnover: £20m - £50m **No.of Employees:** 1 - 10 **Product Groups:** 80

Date of Accounts	Dec 11	Dec 10	Dec 09
Working Capital	300	200	8
Fixed Assets	198	219	245
Current Assets	752	891	457

Cameo Bathrooms
5 High Street, Iver, SL0 9ND
Tel: 01753-655255 **Fax:** 01753-655322
E-mail: colin@cameobathrooms.co.uk
Website: http://www.cameobathrooms.co.uk
Directors: C. Plumridge (Prop)
Date established: 1990 **Turnover:** Up to £250,000
No.of Employees: 1 - 10 **Product Groups:** 66

The CNC Factory Ltd
Pinewood Studios Pinewood Road, Iver Heath, Iver, SL0 0NH
Tel: 01753-656975
E-mail: info@thecncfactory.com
Website: http://www.thecncfactory.com
Registration no: 06605242 **No.of Employees:** 1 - 10 **Product Groups:** 30, 48

Cummins UK
Unit 1b Union Gate The Ridgeway Trading Estate, Iver, SL0 9HX
Tel: 01753-232000 **Fax:** 01753-232020
Website: http://www.cummins.com
Managers: D. Coppard, M. Dunk (Mktg Serv Mgr)
No.of Employees: 21 - 50 **Product Groups:** 40, 47, 68

Exemplar
Unit 4 Thorney Business Park Thorney Lane North, Iver, SL0 9HF
Tel: 08456-770033 **Fax:** 01753-654621
E-mail: emma@exemplar-uk.com
Website: http://www.exemplar-uk.com
Directors: E. Christie (Ptnr)
Immediate Holding Company: EXEMPLAR UK LIMITED LIABILITY PARTNERSHIP
Registration no: OC302726 **Date established:** 2002
Turnover: £250,000 - £500,000 **No.of Employees:** 1 - 10
Product Groups: 44, 48, 89

Fagioli Ltd
The Ridgeway, Iver, SL0 9JE
Tel: 01753-659000 **Fax:** 01753-655998
E-mail: info@fagioli.com
Website: http://www.fagioli.com
Bank(s): National Westminster Bank Plc
Directors: E. Fontana (Fin), F. Belli (MD)
Managers: M. Haynes (Sales Prom Mgr), J. Flatt (Buyer)
Ultimate Holding Company: FAGIOLI SPA (ITALY)
Immediate Holding Company: FAGIOLI LIMITED
Registration no: 02532236 **VAT No.:** GB 452 9133 51
Date established: 1990 **Turnover:** £5m - £10m **No.of Employees:** 21 - 50
Product Groups: 39, 40, 45, 51, 52, 67, 72, 76, 80

Date of Accounts	Dec 11	Dec 10	Dec 09
Sales Turnover	5m	7m	8m
Pre Tax Profit/Loss	602	1m	2m
Working Capital	2m	3m	-382
Fixed Assets	3m	3m	6m
Current Assets	3m	4m	3m
Current Liabilities	159	597	476

High Line Yachting Ltd
Mansion Lane, Iver, SL0 9RG
Tel: 01753-651496 **Fax:** 01753-630095
E-mail: sales@high-line.co.uk
Website: http://www.high-line.co.uk
Directors: D. Bolson (MD), P. Hope (Dir)
Managers: J. Milne (I.T. Exec), S. Carline (Eng Serv Mgr)
Registration no: 01015338 **Date established:** 1971
Turnover: £500,000 - £1m **No.of Employees:** 1 - 10 **Product Groups:** 84

Date of Accounts	Oct 09	Oct 08	Oct 07
Sales Turnover	N/A	654	677
Pre Tax Profit/Loss	N/A	88	93
Working Capital	356	392	362
Fixed Assets	178	188	205
Current Assets	645	671	612
Current Liabilities	N/A	269	236

K B R Fabrications
Unit 28 Bangor Park Farm Bangors Park Bangors Road South, Iver, SL0 0AZ
Tel: 01753-654429 **Fax:** 01753-654429
E-mail: info@kbrfabrications.co.uk
Website: http://www.kbrfabrications.co.uk
Directors: K. Brazier (Dir)
Date established: 2003 **No.of Employees:** 1 - 10 **Product Groups:** 35

Living Props Ltd
Seven Hills Road, Iver, SL0 0PA
Tel: 01895-835100 **Fax:** 01895-835757
E-mail: info@livingprops.co.uk
Website: http://www.livingprops.co.uk
Directors: B. Maslin (Dir)
Immediate Holding Company: LIVING PROPS LIMITED
Registration no: 02633318 **Date established:** 1991 **Turnover:** £2m - £5m
No.of Employees: 11 - 20 **Product Groups:** 62, 83

Date of Accounts	Sep 11	Sep 10	Sep 09
Working Capital	-1	-23	-4
Fixed Assets	844	773	868
Current Assets	178	147	142

Relay Technical Transport
5 The Ridgeway, Iver, SL0 9HX
Tel: 01753-652457 **Fax:** 01753-652377
E-mail: jschulein@relayeurope.co.uk
Website: http://www.relayeurope.co.uk
Bank(s): Barclays
Directors: J. Schulein (Ch), H. Reid (Dir)
Managers: D. Rangecroft (Sales & Mktg Mg), J. Crooks (Transport)
Ultimate Holding Company: RELAY HOLDINGS (UK) LIMITED
Immediate Holding Company: RELAY TECHNICAL TRANSPORT LTD.
Registration no: 01314775 **Date established:** 1977 **Turnover:** £5m - £10m
No.of Employees: 101 - 250 **Product Groups:** 44, 52

Date of Accounts	Mar 12	Mar 11	Mar 10
Sales Turnover	9m	7m	7m
Pre Tax Profit/Loss	327	10	-322
Working Capital	1m	1m	1m
Fixed Assets	785	554	571
Current Assets	3m	2m	2m
Current Liabilities	615	635	574

S E C Industrial Battery Co. Ltd
Thorney Weir House Thorney Mill Road, Iver, SL0 9AQ
Tel: 01895-431543 **Fax:** 01895-431880
E-mail: brian.harper@secbattery.com
Website: http://www.secbattery.com
Directors: B. Harper (MD)
Ultimate Holding Company: SOLAR ENERGY CENTRE EC (BAHRAIN)
Immediate Holding Company: S E C INDUSTRIAL BATTERY COMPANY LIMITED
Registration no: 01190247 **VAT No.:** GB 438 4449 27
Date established: 1974 **Turnover:** Up to £250,000
No.of Employees: 1 - 10 **Product Groups:** 37

Date of Accounts	Jan 11	Jan 10	Jan 09
Sales Turnover	N/A	191	476
Pre Tax Profit/Loss	N/A	61	48
Working Capital	697	573	525
Fixed Assets	12	14	2
Current Assets	2m	631	759
Current Liabilities	N/A	32	46

Marlow

Allergan Ltd
1st Floor Marlow International The Parkway, Marlow, SL7 1YL
Tel: 01628-494444 **Fax:** 01494-473593
Website: http://www.allergan.com
Bank(s): Citibank International plc
Directors: J. Mazzo (Pres), M. Donohoe (Pres)
Ultimate Holding Company: ALLERGAN INC (USA)
Immediate Holding Company: ALLERGAN LIMITED
Registration no: 01049760 **VAT No.:** GB 727 3255 34
Date established: 1972 **Turnover:** £75m - £125m
No.of Employees: 251 - 500 **Product Groups:** 63

Date of Accounts	Dec 10	Dec 09	Dec 08
Sales Turnover	92m	80m	64m
Pre Tax Profit/Loss	6m	5m	2m
Working Capital	29m	25m	19m
Fixed Assets	7m	8m	9m
Current Assets	63m	54m	35m
Current Liabilities	18m	16m	13m

Alpha Anodising UK Ltd
54 Marlow Bottom, Marlow, SL7 3ND
Tel: 01494-535504 **Fax:** 01628-475949
E-mail: sales@alphaanodising.demon.co.uk
Website: http://www.alphaanodising.demon.co.uk
Bank(s): Barclays
Directors: F. Taylor (MD), J. Neal (Fin)
Immediate Holding Company: ALPHA ANODISING UK LIMITED
Registration no: 06775293 **VAT No.:** GB 208 6575 49
Date established: 2008 **Turnover:** £1m - £2m **No.of Employees:** 11 - 20
Product Groups: 23, 28, 48

Date of Accounts	Dec 10	Dec 09
Working Capital	147	124
Fixed Assets	89	50
Current Assets	465	292

Atom Recruitment Ltd
Willowbank House Station Road, Marlow, SL7 1NX
Tel: 01628-488144 **Fax:** 01628-894333
E-mail: lroger@atomrecruitment.com
Website: http://www.atomrecruitment.com
Directors: L. Rogers (Dir), L. Roger (Dir)
Immediate Holding Company: ATOM RECRUITMENT LIMITED
Registration no: 05027366 **Date established:** 2004
Turnover: Up to £250,000 **No.of Employees:** 1 - 10 **Product Groups:** 80, 81

Date of Accounts	Mar 12	Mar 11	Mar 10
Sales Turnover	N/A	205	158
Pre Tax Profit/Loss	N/A	139	106
Working Capital	-34	-25	-25
Fixed Assets	1	N/A	1
Current Assets	5	13	18
Current Liabilities	N/A	38	43

Cobham Antenna Systems
Fourth Avenue Cobham Centre, Marlow, SL7 1TF
Tel: 01628-472072 **Fax:** 01628-482255
E-mail: info@cobham.com
Website: http://www.cobham.com
Bank(s): Barclays
Directors: S. Morgan (Fin)
Managers: R. Evans (Buyer), M. Allen (Tech Serv Mgr), A. Josey (Comptroller)
Ultimate Holding Company: COBHAM PLC
Immediate Holding Company: CHELTON(HOLDINGS)LIMITED
Registration no: 00430582 **Date established:** 1947
Turnover: Up to £250,000 **No.of Employees:** 251 - 500
Product Groups: 37, 39

Date of Accounts	Dec 10	Dec 09	May 08
Sales Turnover	N/A	N/A	175
Pre Tax Profit/Loss	N/A	N/A	13m
Working Capital	921	921	921
Current Assets	921	921	921

Computers In Personnel Ltd
Abbey House 28-30 Chapel Street, Marlow, SL7 1DD
Tel: 01628-814000 **Fax:** 08703-662346
E-mail: pwatsham@ciphr.com
Website: http://www.computersinpersonnelhr.com
Bank(s): HSBC, Reading
Directors: C. Berry (Fin), P. Watsham (Ch)
Managers: P. Halls (Mgr), J. Green (Chief Acct), J. Haldon (Sales Admin)
Ultimate Holding Company: C1PHR (HOLDINGS) LIMITED
Immediate Holding Company: COMPUTERS IN PERSONNEL LIMITED
Registration no: 01960907 **VAT No.:** GB 363 4997 13
Date established: 1985 **Turnover:** £2m - £5m **No.of Employees:** 51 - 100
Product Groups: 44, 67, 80, 81

Date of Accounts	Dec 11	Dec 10	Dec 09
Sales Turnover	4m	4m	4m
Pre Tax Profit/Loss	-25	-49	53
Working Capital	-2m	-2m	-1m
Fixed Assets	2m	2m	1m
Current Assets	1m	1m	1m
Current Liabilities	3m	2m	2m

Concept Profiles
Bencombe Farm Marlow Bottom, Marlow, SL7 3LT
Tel: 01628-481642 **Fax:** 01628-481645
E-mail: info@conceptprofiles.co.uk
Website: http://www.conceptprofiles.co.uk
Directors: A. Houlder (Prop), C. Houlder (Fin)
Immediate Holding Company: CONCEPT PROFILES LIMITED
Registration no: 07081848 **Date established:** 2009
No.of Employees: 1 - 10 **Product Groups:** 46

Cooper Antennas
Thames Industrial Estate Fieldhouse Lane, Marlow, SL7 1TB
Tel: 01628-482360 **Fax:** 01628-478045
E-mail: sales@cooperantennas.com
Website: http://www.cooperantennas.com
Directors: I. Cooper (Fin)
Managers: T. Bojarzin (Eng)
Immediate Holding Company: Cooper Antennas Ltd
Registration no: 05559533 **Date established:** 2005
No.of Employees: 1 - 10 **Product Groups:** 36, 37, 39, 68

Date of Accounts	Sep 08	Sep 07	Sep 06
Working Capital	408	169	21
Fixed Assets	63	65	28
Current Assets	505	246	37
Current Liabilities	97	77	15

Corporate Project Solutions Ltd
Regal House 4 Station Road, Marlow, SL7 1NZ
Tel: 01628-895600 **Fax:** 01628-895601
E-mail: solutions@cps.co.uk
Website: http://www.cps.co.uk
Directors: I. Lloyd (Dir)
Managers: A. Rutland, N. Gorham (Sales Admin)
Immediate Holding Company: CORPORATE PROJECT SOLUTIONS LIMITED
Registration no: 03014568 **Date established:** 1995 **Turnover:** £2m - £5m
No.of Employees: 21 - 50 **Product Groups:** 44, 80

Date of Accounts	Mar 11	Mar 10	Mar 09
Sales Turnover	5m	4m	4m
Pre Tax Profit/Loss	707	673	304
Working Capital	1m	883	806
Fixed Assets	92	102	134
Current Assets	2m	2m	2m
Current Liabilities	743	762	744

Emerson Network Power Ltd
Fourth Avenue Globe Park, Marlow, SL7 1YG
Tel: 01628-403200 **Fax:** 01628-403203
E-mail: kevin.harris@emerson.com
Website: http://www.emersonnetworkpower.com
Bank(s): Bank of America NA & Barclays Bank PLC
Directors: K. Harris (MD), T. Moss (Fin)
Managers: M. Foreman (Personnel)
Ultimate Holding Company: EMERSON ELECTRIC CO INC (USA)
Immediate Holding Company: EMERSON NETWORK POWER LIMITED
Registration no: 03222196 **VAT No.:** GB 195 6527 23
Date established: 1996 **Turnover:** £20m - £50m
No.of Employees: 21 - 50 **Product Groups:** 37, 44

Date of Accounts	Sep 11	Sep 10	Sep 09
Sales Turnover	42m	36m	44m
Pre Tax Profit/Loss	2m	703	3m
Working Capital	-1m	-3m	7m
Fixed Assets	5m	5m	4m
Current Assets	12m	10m	16m
Current Liabilities	3m	3m	2m

Espar Ltd
Harleyford Marina Henley Road, Marlow, SL7 2DX
Tel: 01628-471368 **Fax:** 01628-474819
E-mail: sales@espar.co.uk
Website: http://www.espar.co.uk
Directors: J. Brasier (Dir)
Ultimate Holding Company: ESPAR HOLDINGS LTD
Immediate Holding Company: ESPAR LIMITED
Registration no: 04162059 **Date established:** 2001
No.of Employees: 11 - 20 **Product Groups:** 39, 40, 84

Date of Accounts	Mar 12	Mar 11	Mar 10
Working Capital	268	289	149
Fixed Assets	24	27	32

Current Assets	641	725	480

Foundocean Ltd
Liston Exchange Liston Court High Street, Marlow, SL7 1ER
Tel: 01628-567000 **Fax:** 01628-788604
E-mail: info@foundocean.com
Website: http://www.foundocean.com
Directors: M. Hardy (Tech Serv), J. Bell (MD)
Managers: T. Wallace (Sales Admin), A. Venn
Immediate Holding Company: FOUNDOCEAN LIMITED
Registration no: SC159257 **VAT No.:** GB 446 6213 51
Date established: 1995 **Turnover:** £2m - £5m **No.of Employees:** 21 - 50
Product Groups: 51, 52

Date of Accounts	Dec 11	Dec 10	Dec 09
Working Capital	115	-340	-380
Fixed Assets	5m	4m	3m
Current Assets	5m	4m	2m

Kell Systems Ltd
Regency House Mere Park Dedmere Road, Marlow, SL7 1FJ
Tel: 01628-474757 **Fax:** 01628-478857
E-mail: info@kellsystems.co.uk
Website: http://www.kellsystems.co.uk
Directors: S. Jones (Mkt Research)
Managers: N. Dickison (Mgr), N. Dickinson (Mgr)
Immediate Holding Company: KELL SYSTEMS LTD
Registration no: 04790504 **Date established:** 2003 **Turnover:** £2m - £5m
No.of Employees: 1 - 10 **Product Groups:** 44

Laurent Perrier UK Ltd
66-68 Chapel Street, Marlow, SL7 1DE
Tel: 01628-475404 **Fax:** 01628-471891
E-mail: michael.hesketh@laurent-perrier.co.uk
Website: http://www.laurent-perrier.com
Bank(s): Banque Nationale De Paris
Directors: M. Hesketh (MD), S. Brandwood (Sales)
Managers: D. Brennan (Mktg Serv Mgr), R. Smith (Comptroller)
Ultimate Holding Company: VVE LAURENT - PERRIER & CO (FRANCE)
Immediate Holding Company: LAURENT-PERRIER (UK) LIMITED
Registration no: 01383260 **VAT No.:** GB 385 7613 16
Date established: 1978 **Turnover:** £20m - £50m
No.of Employees: 21 - 50 **Product Groups:** 21, 62

Date of Accounts	Mar 12	Mar 11	Mar 10
Sales Turnover	29m	23m	19m
Pre Tax Profit/Loss	357	-137	38
Working Capital	4m	4m	4m
Fixed Assets	134	24	29
Current Assets	8m	8m	7m
Current Liabilities	716	793	683

Petzold & Co.
PO Box 3775, Marlow, SL7 2UW
Tel: 01628-552700 **Fax:** 01628-552707
E-mail: n.petzold@petzold.co.uk
Website: http://www.petzold.co.uk
Directors: N. Petzold (Prop)
No.of Employees: 1 - 10 **Product Groups:** 38, 42

Protim Solignum (t/a Osmose)
Thames Indl-Est Fieldhouse Lane, Marlow, SL7 1LS
Tel: 01628-486644 **Fax:** 01628-476757
E-mail: info@osmose.co.uk
Website: http://www.ofmose.co.uk
Bank(s): National Westminster Bank Plc
Directors: S. Jepson (Comm), I. McConnell (Grp Chief Exec), M. Kolaszynski (Chief Op Offcr)
Managers: G. Ewbank (Chief Mgr), A. Hodge (Mktg Serv Mgr)
Ultimate Holding Company: OSMOSE INC (USA)
Immediate Holding Company: PROTIM SOLIGNUM LIMITED
Registration no: 03037845 **Date established:** 1995
Turnover: £10m - £20m **No.of Employees:** 21 - 50 **Product Groups:** 31, 32

Date of Accounts	Dec 10	Dec 09	Dec 08
Sales Turnover	16m	15m	17m
Pre Tax Profit/Loss	-169	-2m	-162
Working Capital	7m	6m	7m
Fixed Assets	4m	5m	6m
Current Assets	9m	8m	9m
Current Liabilities	1m	903	1m

Pulsar Developments Ltd
Spracklen House Dukes Place, Marlow, SL7 2QH
Tel: 01628-474324 **Fax:** 01628-474325
E-mail: brian.murphy@pulsardevelopments.com
Website: http://www.pulsardev.com
Directors: B. Murphy (MD), M. Goode (Fin)
Immediate Holding Company: PULSAR DEVELOPMENTS LIMITED
Registration no: 01227046 **VAT No.:** GB 209 4967 36
Date established: 1975 **Turnover:** £500,000 - £1m
No.of Employees: 1 - 10 **Product Groups:** 37, 40

Date of Accounts	Oct 11	Oct 10	Oct 09
Working Capital	350	293	356
Fixed Assets	N/A	50	N/A
Current Assets	391	329	383

Six Degrees Ltd
Old Trinity Church Trinity Road, Marlow, SL7 3AN
Tel: 01628-480280 **Fax:** 01628-480281
E-mail: mail@sixdegreespr.com
Website: http://www.sixdegreespr.com
Bank(s): HSBC, Wokingham
Directors: J. Janson (Dir)
Immediate Holding Company: SIX DEGREES LIMITED
Registration no: 03047692 **Date established:** 1995 **Turnover:** £1m - £2m
No.of Employees: 11 - 20 **Product Groups:** 81

Date of Accounts	Dec 11	Dec 10	Dec 09
Working Capital	275	122	104
Fixed Assets	6	9	12
Current Assets	540	265	230

Stevend Engineering
Fieldhouse Lane, Marlow, SL7 1LW
Tel: 01628-472374 **Fax:** 01628-475050
E-mail: engineering@stevend.co.uk
Website: http://www.stevend.co.uk
Directors: R. Legg (MD)
Immediate Holding Company: STEVEND LIMITED
Registration no: 01110312 **Date established:** 2002
Turnover: £500,000 - £1m **No.of Employees:** 1 - 10 **Product Groups:** 34, 35

Date of Accounts	Aug 11	Aug 10	Aug 09
Working Capital	922	914	903
Fixed Assets	164	167	170
Current Assets	1m	996	981

Symrise Ltd
Thames Industrial Estate Fieldhouse Lane, Marlow, SL7 1TB
Tel: 01628-472051 **Fax:** 01628-646016
E-mail: markus.sattler@symrise.com
Website: http://www.symrise.com
Directors: M. Sattler (Dir), R. Fairhead (Fin)
Ultimate Holding Company: SYMRISE AG (GERMANY)
Immediate Holding Company: SYMRISE LIMITED
Registration no: 00868875 **Date established:** 1966
Turnover: £50m - £75m **No.of Employees:** 51 - 100 **Product Groups:** 20, 31, 32

Date of Accounts	Dec 11	Dec 10	Dec 09
Sales Turnover	51m	50m	44m
Pre Tax Profit/Loss	5m	3m	1m
Working Capital	8m	5m	-1m
Fixed Assets	3m	4m	6m
Current Assets	12m	12m	11m
Current Liabilities	2m	2m	2m

T N T Post
Unit 1 Globeside Business Park Fieldhouse Lane, Marlow, SL7 1HY
Tel: 01628-816889 **Fax:** 01628-816600
E-mail: info@tntpost.co.uk
Website: http://www.tntpost.co.uk
Bank(s): HSBC Bank plc
Directors: A. Goddard (Sales), J. Szwec (Tech Serv), M. Parmar (Fin)
Managers: N. Wells, M. Cooper (Personnel), M. Darvall, T. McCall (Buyer)
Ultimate Holding Company: LCMB LIMITED
Immediate Holding Company: LIFECYCLE MARKETING (MOTHER & BABY) LIMITED
Registration no: 02556692 **VAT No.:** GB 538 1493 31
Date established: 1990 **Turnover:** £2m - £5m
No.of Employees: 101 - 250 **Product Groups:** 81

Date of Accounts	Dec 11	Dec 10	Dec 09
Sales Turnover	N/A	3m	3m
Pre Tax Profit/Loss	N/A	2	-108
Working Capital	19	-218	-249
Fixed Assets	58	17	51
Current Assets	820	741	864
Current Liabilities	N/A	370	192

T V P Ltd
Unit 5 First Avenue, Marlow, SL7 1YA
Tel: 01628-473121 **Fax:** 01628-477563
E-mail: john@tvp.ltd.uk
Website: http://www.mailinghousebucks.co.uk
Bank(s): Lloyds TSB Bank plc
Directors: J. Atherton (MD)
Immediate Holding Company: T V P LIMITED
Registration no: 02348503 **VAT No.:** GB 417 4784 33
Date established: 1989 **Turnover:** £500,000 - £1m
No.of Employees: 11 - 20 **Product Groups:** 81

Date of Accounts	Dec 11	Dec 10	Dec 09
Sales Turnover	762	709	706
Pre Tax Profit/Loss	23	44	34
Working Capital	128	124	133
Fixed Assets	20	26	26
Current Assets	210	208	207
Current Liabilities	38	48	39

Volvo Car UK Ltd
Globe Park, Marlow, SL7 1YQ
Tel: 01628-477977 **Fax:** 01628-476173
E-mail: custcare@volvocars.co.uk
Website: http://www.volvocars.com
Bank(s): Barclays
Directors: P. Rask (Dir), C. Munn (Fin)
Managers: G. Williams, J. Leaver (Personnel), P. Lucas (Tech Serv Mgr)
Ultimate Holding Company: FORD MOTOR COMPANY (USA)
Immediate Holding Company: VOLVO CAR UK LIMITED
Registration no: 02281044 **Date established:** 1988
Turnover: £500m - £1,000m **No.of Employees:** 101 - 250
Product Groups: 68

Date of Accounts	Dec 11	Dec 10	Dec 09
Sales Turnover	674m	737m	610m
Pre Tax Profit/Loss	2m	5m	6m
Working Capital	32m	31m	37m
Fixed Assets	1m	9m	1m
Current Assets	171m	147m	145m
Current Liabilities	88m	78m	85m

Wimpy Restaurants Group Ltd
64 High Street, Marlow, SL7 1AH
Tel: 01628-483501 **Fax:** 01628-474025
E-mail: info@wimpy.uk.com
Website: http://www.wimpy.uk.com
Directors: M. D Ascencao (Prop)
Ultimate Holding Company: FAMOUS BRANDS LTD (SOUTH AFRICA)
Immediate Holding Company: WIMPY RESTAURANTS GROUP LIMITED
Registration no: 02458406 **VAT No.:** GB 524 2522 76
Date established: 1990 **Turnover:** £10m - £20m **No.of Employees:** 1 - 10
Product Groups: 69

Date of Accounts	Feb 08	Feb 11	Feb 10
Sales Turnover	N/A	8m	10m
Pre Tax Profit/Loss	1	1m	-221
Working Capital	-4m	9m	8m
Fixed Assets	13m	644	638
Current Assets	1m	11m	10m
Current Liabilities	10	658	310

Milton Keynes

A B I
9 Park Farm Cranfield Road, Wavendon, Milton Keynes, MK17 8AS
Tel: 01908-281418 **Fax:** 01908-281418
Directors: I. Craen (Ptnr)
Date established: 1995 **No.of Employees:** 1 - 10 **Product Groups:** 46, 48

A C Automation (Agents For Koberlein Gmbh)
Hartland Avenue Tattenhoe, Milton Keynes, MK4 3DN
Tel: 01908-501796 **Fax:** 01908-501796
E-mail: a.child@ac-automation.co.uk
Website: http://www.ac-automation.co.uk
Directors: A. Child (Prop)
No.of Employees: 1 - 10 **Product Groups:** 45, 46

A H Electrical Services Ltd
21 Manshead Court Galley Hill, Stony Stratford, Milton Keynes, MK11 1NR
Tel: 01908-569754 **Fax:** 01908-569754
E-mail: alanholland2005@yahoo.com
Directors: A. Holland (Prop)
Immediate Holding Company: A. H. ELECTRICAL SERVICES LIMITED
Registration no: 01984399 **Date established:** 1986
Turnover: Up to £250,000 **No.of Employees:** 1 - 10 **Product Groups:** 44

Date of Accounts	Mar 11	Mar 10	Mar 09
Working Capital	16	-8	-4
Fixed Assets	1	1	3
Current Assets	43	12	N/A
Current Liabilities	27	20	N/A

Action Storage Systems
6 Fitzhamon Court Wolverton Mill, Milton Keynes, MK12 6LB
Tel: 01908-525700 **Fax:** 01908-321650
E-mail: sales@action-storage.co.uk
Website: http://www.action-storage.co.uk
Bank(s): Allied Irish
Directors: T. Brialey (MD)
Immediate Holding Company: ACTION STORAGE SYSTEMS LTD
Registration no: 02005856 **VAT No.:** GB 443 7586 25
Date established: 1986 **Turnover:** £1m - £2m **No.of Employees:** 11 - 20
Product Groups: 26, 30, 35, 36, 39, 40, 44, 45, 46, 47, 49, 66, 67, 72, 77, 84, 85

Date of Accounts	Mar 12	Mar 11	Mar 10
Working Capital	1m	1m	938
Fixed Assets	166	160	196
Current Assets	2m	2m	1m

Adam Equipment Co. Ltd
Bond Avenue Bletchley, Milton Keynes, MK1 1SW
Tel: 01908-274545 **Fax:** 01908-641339
E-mail: info@adamequipment.com
Website: http://www.adamequipment.com
Bank(s): The Royal Bank of Scotland
Directors: J. Storey (MD)
Managers: S. Jackson (Sales Prom Mgr)
Immediate Holding Company: ADAM EQUIPMENT CO. LIMITED
Registration no: 01309669 **VAT No.:** GB 301 8065 96
Date established: 1977 **Turnover:** £10m - £20m
No.of Employees: 21 - 50 **Product Groups:** 38, 44, 48, 67, 83

Date of Accounts	Mar 11	Mar 10	Mar 09
Working Capital	1m	1m	997
Fixed Assets	2m	2m	2m
Current Assets	2m	2m	2m

Adhesive Dispensing Ltd
Willow House 20 Craigmore Avenue, Bletchley, Milton Keynes, MK3 6HD
Tel: 01908-639075 **Fax:** 08456-520059
E-mail: sales@adhesivedispensing.net
Website: http://www.adhesivedispensing.net
Managers: N. Hammond (Sales Prom Mgr)
Immediate Holding Company: ADHESIVE DISPENSING LIMITED
Registration no: 06048283 **Date established:** 2007
No.of Employees: 1 - 10 **Product Groups:** 30, 35, 37, 38, 40, 42, 45

Date of Accounts	Jan 12	Jan 11	Jan 09
Working Capital	19	-4	-8
Fixed Assets	6	4	1
Current Assets	57	26	27
Current Liabilities	N/A	N/A	5

Advanced Plastic Technology Ltd
44 Potters Lane Kiln Farm, Milton Keynes, MK11 3HQ
Tel: 01908-305710 **Fax:** 01908-305729
E-mail: sales@apt123.co.uk
Website: http://www.apt123.co.uk
Registration no: 02629314 **Turnover:** £500,000 - £1m
No.of Employees: 11 - 20 **Product Groups:** 26, 30, 33, 48, 66, 67, 68, 84

Date of Accounts	Apr 11	Apr 10	Apr 09
Working Capital	357	333	295
Fixed Assets	53	104	152
Current Assets	641	684	658

Alanod Ltd
Chippenham Drive Kingston, Milton Keynes, MK10 0AN
Tel: 01908-282044 **Fax:** 01908-282033
E-mail: goldbyr@alanod.co.uk
Website: http://www.alanod.co.uk
Bank(s): Barclays
Directors: L. Earl (MD)
Managers: C. Alcock (Tech Serv Mgr), V. Smith, Y. Downing (Sales Prom Mgr)
Ultimate Holding Company: ALANOD ALUMINIUM VEREDLUNG GMBH & CO (GERMANY)
Immediate Holding Company: ALANOD LIMITED
Registration no: 00592752 **Date established:** 1957
Turnover: £10m - £20m **No.of Employees:** 21 - 50 **Product Groups:** 34, 48

Date of Accounts	Dec 11	Dec 10	Dec 09
Sales Turnover	14m	14m	35m
Pre Tax Profit/Loss	689	516	-2m
Working Capital	6m	6m	6m
Fixed Assets	3m	3m	4m
Current Assets	8m	8m	8m
Current Liabilities	301	362	875

Alimex P I A
6 Fingle Drive Stonebridge, Milton Keynes, MK13 0AB
Tel: 01908-224240 **Fax:** 01908-224241
E-mail: info@alimex.uk.com
Website: http://www.alimex.uk.com
Managers: C. Watts
Ultimate Holding Company: AMBERHEART LTD
Immediate Holding Company: THRIFTYLIFT LIMITED
Registration no: 05568268 **Date established:** 1991
No.of Employees: 11 - 20 **Product Groups:** 34, 66

see next page

Alimex P I A - Cont'd

Date of Accounts	Dec 07	Sep 06
Working Capital	-969	62
Fixed Assets	160	113
Current Assets	1277	1587
Current Liabilities	2246	1525
Total Share Capital	10	10

Amelec Instruments

Unit 5 Cochran Close Crownhill, Milton Keynes, MK8 0AJ
Tel: 01908-567003 **Fax:** 01908-566735
E-mail: sales@amelec-uk.com
Website: http://www.amelec-uk.com
Bank(s): Barclays, St. Albans
Managers: D. Mundye (Eng Serv Mgr)
Immediate Holding Company: AMELEC INSTRUMENTS LTD
Registration no: 01199015 **VAT No.:** GB 234 7153 73
Turnover: £1m - £2m **No.of Employees:** 11 - 20 **Product Groups:** 37, 38

Date of Accounts	Dec 06	Dec 05
Working Capital	14	30
Fixed Assets	25	20
Current Assets	208	190
Current Liabilities	194	160

H Arnott

38 Bowyers Mews Neath Hill, Milton Keynes, MK14 6HP
Tel: 01908-675706
Directors: H. Arnott (Prop)
Date established: 1994 **No.of Employees:** 1 - 10 **Product Groups:** 35

Aster Interim Solutions Ltd

1 The Lane Mursley, Milton Keynes, MK17 0RY
Tel: 01296-720281
E-mail: enquiries@aster-training.co.uk
Website: http://www.aster-interim.co.uk
Directors: L. Wilson (Fin)
Immediate Holding Company: ASTER INTERIM SOLUTIONS LIMITED
Registration no: 04705537 **Date established:** 2003
No.of Employees: 11 - 20 **Product Groups:** 80

Date of Accounts	Mar 11	Mar 10	Mar 07
Working Capital	83	94	71
Fixed Assets	13	17	2
Current Assets	106	134	99

Axe & Status Machinery Ltd

2 Holdom Avenue Bletchley, Milton Keynes, MK1 1QU
Tel: 01908-647707 **Fax:** 01908-648087
E-mail: info@axestatus.com
Website: http://www.axestatus.com
Directors: S. Thomas (MD), K. Thomas (Fin)
Immediate Holding Company: AXE & STATUS MACHINERY LIMITED
Registration no: 05036242 **Date established:** 2004 **Turnover:** £1m - £2m
No.of Employees: 11 - 20 **Product Groups:** 46

Date of Accounts	Mar 12	Mar 11	Mar 10
Working Capital	274	200	359
Fixed Assets	49	59	41
Current Assets	2m	667	1m

B S H

Grand Union House Wolverton, Milton Keynes, MK12 5PT
Tel: 01908-328300 **Fax:** 01908-328440
E-mail: admin@neff.co.uk
Website: http://www.boschappliances.co.uk
Bank(s): HSBC Bank plc
Directors: R. Meier (MD), E. Hanneck (MD)
Managers: M. Jarrett (Sales & Mktg Mg), S. Sundarajan (I.T. Exec)
Ultimate Holding Company: BSH BOSCH UND SIEMENS HAUSERGATE GMBH (GERMANY)
Immediate Holding Company: BSH HOME APPLIANCES LIMITED
Registration no: 01844007 **VAT No.:** GB 531 0425 95
Date established: 1984 **Turnover:** £250m - £500m
No.of Employees: 101 - 250 **Product Groups:** 40

Date of Accounts	Dec 10	Dec 09	Dec 08
Sales Turnover	477m	459m	483m
Pre Tax Profit/Loss	28m	31m	38m
Working Capital	47m	36m	41m
Fixed Assets	10m	10m	11m
Current Assets	125m	92m	92m
Current Liabilities	15m	21m	19m

Basell Polyolefins UK Ltd

Bramley Road Bletchley, Milton Keynes, MK1 1LZ
Tel: 01908-360000 **Fax:** 01908-360036
Website: http://www.lyondellbasell.com
Bank(s): The Royal Bank of Scotland
Managers: M. Chaplin (Mgr)
Ultimate Holding Company: BASELL INTERNATIONAL SARL (NETHERLANDS)
Immediate Holding Company: BASELL POLYOLEFINS UK LIMITED
Registration no: 02811230 **VAT No.:** GB 444 0255 77
Date established: 1993 **Turnover:** £20m - £50m
No.of Employees: 51 - 100 **Product Groups:** 30, 31, 32, 42

Date of Accounts	Dec 11	Dec 10	Dec 09
Sales Turnover	280m	225m	217m
Pre Tax Profit/Loss	10m	10m	5m
Working Capital	62m	131m	121m
Fixed Assets	96m	20m	22m
Current Assets	93m	159m	148m
Current Liabilities	4m	4m	7m

Beardow Adams Ltd

30-32 Blundells Road Bradville, Milton Keynes, MK13 7HF
Tel: 01908-574000 **Fax:** 01908-574060
E-mail: info@beardowadams.com
Website: http://www.beardowadams.com
Directors: M. Rowland (Fin), N. Beardow (Export)
Managers: M. Lineham (Purch Mgr), S. Burley
Immediate Holding Company: BEARDOW AND ADAMS (ADHESIVES) LIMITED
Registration no: 01269127 **Date established:** 1976
Turnover: £50m - £75m **No.of Employees:** 51 - 100 **Product Groups:** 32, 42

Date of Accounts	Dec 11	Dec 10	Dec 09
Sales Turnover	58m	50m	42m
Pre Tax Profit/Loss	4m	3m	3m
Working Capital	5m	3m	1m
Fixed Assets	8m	7m	7m
Current Assets	16m	13m	12m
Current Liabilities	1m	867	1m

Bell System Telephones Ltd

Presley Way Crownhill, Milton Keynes, MK8 0ET
Tel: 01908-261106 **Fax:** 01908-261116
E-mail: sales@bellsystem.co.uk
Website: http://www.bellsystem.co.uk
Bank(s): National Westminster Bank Plc
Directors: D. Hanss (Ch), R. Jenkins (Sales & Mktg)
Managers: R. Cobb (Purch Mgr), P. Kelly (Tech Serv Mgr)
Immediate Holding Company: BELL SYSTEM (TELEPHONES) LIMITED
Registration no: 01008031 **VAT No.:** GB 229 1697 40
Date established: 1971 **Turnover:** £2m - £5m **No.of Employees:** 21 - 50
Product Groups: 40

Date of Accounts	Mar 12	Mar 11	Mar 10
Sales Turnover	N/A	N/A	2m
Pre Tax Profit/Loss	N/A	N/A	-46
Working Capital	1m	1m	1m
Fixed Assets	493	508	525
Current Assets	2m	1m	1m
Current Liabilities	N/A	N/A	106

Betterbox Communications Ltd

43 Burners Lane South Kiln Farm, Milton Keynes, MK11 3HA
Tel: 01908-560200 **Fax:** 01908-565533
E-mail: info@betterbox.co.uk
Website: http://www.betterbox.co.uk
Bank(s): Barclays, Milton Keynes
Directors: B. Baioes (Fin)
Immediate Holding Company: BETTER BOX COMMUNICATIONS LIMITED
Registration no: 02321771 **Date established:** 1988 **Turnover:** £2m - £5m
No.of Employees: 11 - 20 **Product Groups:** 52

Date of Accounts	Mar 11	Mar 10	Mar 09
Working Capital	203	105	259
Fixed Assets	45	69	62
Current Assets	682	687	691

BFI Optilas Ltd

Unit 2 Mill Square Featherstone Road, Wolverton Mill, Milton Keynes, MK12 5ZY
Tel: 01908-326326 **Fax:** 01908-221110
E-mail: andy.sumpter@bfioptilas.com
Website: http://www.bfioptilas.co.uk
Bank(s): Barclays
Directors: P. Gruson (Dir), D. Brown (Fin), A. Sumpter (MD), P. Sumpter (MD)
Managers: D. Brown (Comptroller), A. Bourne (Mktg Serv Mgr), S. Grey (Sales Prom Mgr), M. Banks (Purch Mgr)
Ultimate Holding Company: ACAL PLC
Immediate Holding Company: BFI OPTILAS LTD
Registration no: 01974765 **VAT No.:** 420 8783 50 **Date established:** 1986
Turnover: £5m - £10m **No.of Employees:** 21 - 50 **Product Groups:** 37

Biffa Waste Services Ltd

Chesney Wold Bleak Hall, Milton Keynes, MK6 1NE
Tel: 0800-601601 **Fax:** 01908- 692663
E-mail: chris.thornton@biffa.co.uk
Website: http://www.biffa.co.uk
Managers: C. Thornton (Mgr)
Immediate Holding Company: BIFFA WASTE SERVICES LIMITED
Registration no: 00946107 **Date established:** 1969
No.of Employees: 11 - 20 **Product Groups:** 32, 54

Date of Accounts	Mar 08	Mar 09	Apr 10
Sales Turnover	555m	574m	492m
Pre Tax Profit/Loss	23m	50m	30m
Working Capital	229m	271m	293m
Fixed Assets	371m	360m	378m
Current Assets	409m	534m	609m
Current Liabilities	50m	100m	115m

Billows Protocol Ltd

11 Bridgeturn Avenue Old Wolverton, Milton Keynes, MK12 5QL
Tel: 01908-315539 **Fax:** 01908-311795
E-mail: colin@billowsprotocol.com
Website: http://www.billowsprotocol.com
Bank(s): Lloyds
Directors: C. Billows (Jt MD), C. Billows (MD), S. Buckley (Fin)
Managers: S. Buckley (Sales Admin), T. Cousins (Sales Prom Mgr)
Immediate Holding Company: BILLOWS PROTOCOL LIMITED
Registration no: 01073563 **VAT No.:** GB 119 5016 85
Date established: 1972 **Turnover:** £2m - £5m **No.of Employees:** 11 - 20
Product Groups: 44, 87

Date of Accounts	Apr 10	Apr 09	Apr 08
Working Capital	131	307	474
Fixed Assets	1	4	11
Current Assets	316	512	718

Bishton Plant

11a Gold Street Hanslope, Milton Keynes, MK19 7LU
Tel: 01908-511225 **Fax:** 01908-511225
E-mail: lynnbishton@aol.com
Immediate Holding Company: S BISHTON PLANT & CONTRACTING LIMITED
Registration no: 04823453 **Date established:** 2003
No.of Employees: 1 - 10 **Product Groups:** 07, 51, 80, 84

Date of Accounts	Jul 10	Jul 09	Jul 08
Working Capital	-8	-132	-8
Fixed Assets	33	50	62
Current Assets	118	170	19

Bizerba (UK) Ltd

2-4 Erica Road Stacey Bushes Industrial Estate, Milton Keynes, MK12 6HS
Tel: 01908-682740 **Fax:** 01908-682777
E-mail: info@bizerba.co.uk
Website: http://www.bizerba.com
Bank(s): HSBC Bank plc
Directors: M. Harsch (Dir), M. Glenister (Co Sec), M. Harris (MD)
Managers: S. Heuitson (Sales Prom Mgr), T. Dillon
Ultimate Holding Company: FP007480
Immediate Holding Company: BIZERBA (U.K.) LIMITED
Registration no: 01718524 **VAT No.:** GB 348 7928 01
Date established: 1983 **Turnover:** £10m - £20m
No.of Employees: 51 - 100 **Product Groups:** 27, 28, 38, 41, 42, 45, 48

Date of Accounts	Dec 09	Dec 08	Dec 07
Sales Turnover	11m	9m	8m
Pre Tax Profit/Loss	588	-257	226
Working Capital	4m	4m	5m
Fixed Assets	630	474	77
Current Assets	6m	5m	6m
Current Liabilities	1m	799	749

Blanewood Andrews Computing plc

5 Grove Ash Dawson Road, Bletchley, Milton Keynes, MK1 1XL
Tel: 01908-368001 **Fax:** 01908-641034
E-mail: enquiries@blue-alligator.co.uk
Website: http://www.bacuk.com
Bank(s): Lloyds TSB Bank plc
Directors: A. Blane (Fin), J. Thorn (Sales), N. Leckie (Tech Serv)
Immediate Holding Company: BLUE ALLIGATOR COMPANY LIMITED
Registration no: 01763829 **VAT No.:** GB 461 0038 89
Date established: 1983 **Turnover:** £2m - £5m **No.of Employees:** 11 - 20
Product Groups: 28, 44

Date of Accounts	Apr 11	Apr 10	Apr 09
Working Capital	80	128	138
Fixed Assets	4	5	9
Current Assets	179	222	211

Blickle Castors & Wheels Ltd

30 Vincent Avenue Crownhill, Milton Keynes, MK8 0AB
Tel: 01908-560904 **Fax:** 01908-260510
E-mail: sales@blickle.co.uk
Website: http://www.blickle.co.uk
Directors: J. Austin (MD), R. Blickle (Dir), R. Blickle (MD), A. Austin (Co Sec)
Managers: F. Williams (Comm), D. Jones, D. Jones (Chief Mgr)
Immediate Holding Company: BLICKLE CASTORS & WHEELS LTD
Registration no: 02635215 **VAT No.:** GB 443 8390 37
Date established: 1991 **No.of Employees:** 1 - 10 **Product Groups:** 29, 30, 35, 36, 39, 45

Date of Accounts	Dec 11	Dec 10	Dec 09
Working Capital	559	511	444
Fixed Assets	53	71	63
Current Assets	877	838	636

Brauer Ltd

Mount Farm Dawson Road, Bletchley, Milton Keynes, MK1 1JP
Tel: 01908-374022 **Fax:** 01908-641628
E-mail: sales@brauer.co.uk
Website: http://www.brauer.co.uk
Bank(s): National Westminster Bank Plc
Directors: A. Taylor (MD), I. Windmill (Co Sec)
Managers: G. Main (Tech Serv Mgr), B. Grimditch (Sales Prom Mgr)
Ultimate Holding Company: ADROIT HOLDINGS LTD
Immediate Holding Company: BRAUER LIMITED
Registration no: 05980295 **Date established:** 2006 **Turnover:** £2m - £5m
No.of Employees: 21 - 50 **Product Groups:** 36, 39, 40

Date of Accounts	Jun 11	Jun 10	Jun 09
Sales Turnover	N/A	N/A	4m
Pre Tax Profit/Loss	N/A	N/A	76
Working Capital	168	114	225
Fixed Assets	54	34	N/A
Current Assets	1m	866	1m
Current Liabilities	N/A	N/A	674

British Felt Company

14 Drakes Mews Crownhill, Milton Keynes, MK8 0ER
Tel: 01908-263304 **Fax:** 01908-263305
E-mail: sales@britishfelt.co.uk
Website: http://www.britishfelt.co.uk
Directors: N. Arpino (Sales), G. Stewart (MD)
Ultimate Holding Company: WORLDWIDE WOOL FELTS LIMITED
Registration no: 02516179 **VAT No.:** GB 225 4337 79
Date established: 1990 **Turnover:** £1m - £2m **No.of Employees:** 1 - 10
Product Groups: 22, 23, 24, 25, 27, 29, 30, 32, 37, 39, 40, 42, 43, 49, 63, 66, 68

Date of Accounts	Oct 11	Oct 10	Oct 09
Working Capital	621	700	798
Fixed Assets	147	89	72
Current Assets	746	800	875

Broadways Stampings Ltd

Second Avenue Bletchley, Milton Keynes, MK1 1DT
Tel: 01908-647703 **Fax:** 01908-649279
E-mail: broadways@broadwaysstampings.co.uk
Website: http://www.broadwaysstampings.co.uk
Bank(s): Barclays
Directors: B. Ridgway (Tech Serv), G. Williams (Ch), J. Williams (Fab), E. Williams (Admin)
Managers: L. Tee
Immediate Holding Company: BROADWAYS STAMPINGS LIMITED
Registration no: 01311589 **Date established:** 1977
Turnover: £10m - £20m **No.of Employees:** 101 - 250
Product Groups: 35, 46, 48

Date of Accounts	Apr 11	Apr 10	Apr 09
Sales Turnover	12m	8m	8m
Pre Tax Profit/Loss	477	47	502
Working Capital	2m	1m	1m
Fixed Assets	3m	3m	3m
Current Assets	5m	3m	2m
Current Liabilities	868	454	477

C Brewers & Sons

81 Aston Drive Bradwell Abbey, Milton Keynes, MK13 9HF
Tel: 01908-316719 **Fax:** 01908-311423
E-mail: enquiries@brewers.co.uk
Website: http://www.brewers.co.uk
Managers: F. Eager (Mgr)
Immediate Holding Company: C.Brewer & Sons Ltd
Registration no: 00203852 **Turnover:** £250,000 - £500,000
No.of Employees: 1 - 10 **Product Groups:** 32, 66

C V T Ltd

4-6 Carters Lane Kiln Farm, Milton Keynes, MK11 3ER
Tel: 01908-563267 **Fax:** 01908-563854
E-mail: sales@cvt.ltd.uk
Website: http://www.cvt.ltd.uk
Directors: R. Davies (MD), S. Stelzer (Co Sec)
Managers: P. Cousins (Purch Mgr)
Immediate Holding Company: CVT LIMITED
Registration no: 02670152 **VAT No.:** GB 878 6068 66
Date established: 1991 **Turnover:** £2m - £5m **No.of Employees:** 21 - 50
Product Groups: 38, 40

Date of Accounts	Dec 11	Mar 11	Mar 10
Sales Turnover	N/A	N/A	3m
Pre Tax Profit/Loss	N/A	N/A	287
Working Capital	294	133	370
Fixed Assets	449	95	118
Current Assets	1m	1m	1m
Current Liabilities	N/A	N/A	187

Caljan Rite Hite Ltd
Clifford House 37-39 Simpson Road, Bletchley, Milton Keynes, MK1 1BA
Tel: 01908-648900 **Fax:** 01908-645564
E-mail: info@caljanritehite.co.uk
Website: http://www.caljanritehite.co.uk
Bank(s): Lloyds TSB
Directors: M. Baugh (Chief Op Offcr)
Managers: G. Sanderson (Chief Acct), J. Lauchery (Purch Mgr), R. Lumb (Software Mgr)
Ultimate Holding Company: RITE-HITE HOLDING CORPORATION (USA)
Immediate Holding Company: CALJAN RITE-HITE LIMITED
Registration no: 03223165 **VAT No.:** GB 476 1929 12
Date established: 1996 **Turnover:** £1m - £2m **No.of Employees:** 11 - 20
Product Groups: 37, 38, 39, 45

Date of Accounts	Dec 11	Dec 10	Dec 09
Working Capital	-668	268	411
Fixed Assets	1m	13	25
Current Assets	2m	1m	561

Capital Motorcycle Training
137 Stamford Avenue Springfield, Milton Keynes, MK6 3LG
Tel: 01908-559006 **Fax:** 01280-814654
Website: http://www.capital-mct.co.uk
Directors: S. Ashworth (Dir)
Date established: 1999 **No.of Employees:** 1 - 10 **Product Groups:** 38, 42

CD Bramall Motor Group Ltd
Cranfield Road Wavendon, Milton Keynes, MK17 8LQ
Tel: 01908-585123 **Fax:** 01908-281253
Website: http://www.cdbramall.com
Directors: A. Farmer (Dir), D. Breeze (Dir), G. Hobson (Dir), G. Findlay (Dir), I. Button (Dir), J. Ross (Dir), R. Edwards (Dir)
Managers: T. Farmer (Mgr)
Ultimate Holding Company: Pendragon plc
Immediate Holding Company: C D BRAMALL MOTOR GROUP LIMITED
Registration no: 02800465 **Date established:** 1993
Turnover: £125m - £250m **No.of Employees:** 1 - 10 **Product Groups:** 68

Cerulean
Rockingham Drive Linford Wood, Milton Keynes, MK14 6LY
Tel: 01908-233833 **Fax:** 01908-235333
E-mail: info@cerulean.com
Website: http://www.cerulean.com
Directors: A. Lancaster (Fin), S. Frankham (MD)
Managers: V. Diamond, D. Collins (Tech Serv Mgr), P. Glenn (Mktg Serv Mgr)
Immediate Holding Company: IMPACT COMMUNICATIONS LIMITED
Registration no: 05292432 **Date established:** 2004
Turnover: £500,000 - £1m **No.of Employees:** 11 - 20
Product Groups: 67, 85

Date of Accounts	Mar 11	Mar 10	Mar 09
Working Capital	-82	20	1
Fixed Assets	337	238	262
Current Assets	271	402	241

Charter-Kontron Ltd
Unit 18 Avant Business Centre Bletchley, Milton Keynes, MK1 1DT
Tel: 01908-646070 **Fax:** 01908-646030
E-mail: info@charter-kontron.co.uk
Website: http://www.charter-kontron.co.uk
Directors: S. Pearce (Co Sec)
Ultimate Holding Company: NEKTOP LTD (ISRAEL)
Immediate Holding Company: CHARTER-KONTRON LIMITED
Registration no: 03698371 **Date established:** 1999
Turnover: £500,000 - £1m **No.of Employees:** 11 - 20 **Product Groups:** 38

Date of Accounts	Dec 11	Dec 10	Dec 09
Sales Turnover	N/A	946	N/A
Pre Tax Profit/Loss	N/A	-23	N/A
Working Capital	477	-472	-448
Current Assets	1m	664	825
Current Liabilities	N/A	55	N/A

CIS Contracts
Dane Road Bletchley, Milton Keynes, MK1 1JQ
Tel: 01908-371333 **Fax:** 01908-370888
E-mail: ciscontractsmk@btinternet.com
Website: http://www.ciscontracts.com
Directors: G. Dilleigh (Snr Part)
No.of Employees: 1 - 10 **Product Groups:** 37, 39, 49, 51, 52

City Print Milton Keynes Ltd
17 Denbigh Hall Industrial Estate Denbigh Hall, Bletchley, Milton Keynes, MK3 7QT
Tel: 01908-377085 **Fax:** 01908-649335
E-mail: sales@cityprint.net
Website: http://www.cityprint.net
Directors: D. Vaughan (Dir), N. Vaughan (Dir), L. Power (Dir)
Immediate Holding Company: CITY PRINT (MILTON KEYNES) LIMITED
Registration no: 01160914 **Date established:** 1974 **Turnover:** £1m - £2m
No.of Employees: 21 - 50 **Product Groups:** 27, 28, 81

Date of Accounts	Mar 12	Mar 11	Mar 10
Working Capital	-187	-189	-143
Fixed Assets	431	427	472
Current Assets	410	484	402

Clifford Packaging Ltd
Bradbourne Drive Tilbrook, Milton Keynes, MK7 8AQ
Tel: 01908-270429 **Fax:** 01908-270429
E-mail: enquiries@cliffordpackaging.com
Website: http://www.cliffordpackaging.com
Bank(s): Barclays, Uxbridge
Directors: K. Cook (Sales), A. Leishman (Dir), G. Naughton (Dir)
Managers: J. Cranston (I.T. Exec)
Immediate Holding Company: CLIFFORD PACKAGING HOLDINGS LIMITED
Registration no: 01502927 **Date established:** 1980
Turnover: £10m - £20m **No.of Employees:** 11 - 20 **Product Groups:** 27

Date of Accounts	Jan 11	Jan 10	Jan 09
Sales Turnover	13m	12m	N/A
Pre Tax Profit/Loss	502	648	772
Working Capital	833	298	51
Fixed Assets	3m	4m	5m
Current Assets	4m	4m	5m
Current Liabilities	613	476	519

Cobham MAL Ltd
Featherstone Road Wolverton Mill, Milton Keynes, MK12 5EW
Tel: 01908-574200 **Fax:** 01908-574300
E-mail: malcolm.morgan@cobham.com
Website: http://www.cobham.com
Directors: K. Oddey (MD)
Managers: A. Blount (Mktg Serv Mgr), C. Reece (Sales Prom Mgr), D. Seymour (I.T. Exec), D. Seymour (Tech Serv Mgr), G. Lundgren, J. Oliver (Mktg Serv Mgr), P. Hancock (Purch Mgr), J. Tarvet (Personnel), F. Owen (Personnel)
Ultimate Holding Company: COBHAM PLC
Immediate Holding Company: COBHAM MAL LTD
Registration no: 08042203 **Date established:** 2012
Turnover: £10m - £20m **No.of Employees:** 51 - 100 **Product Groups:** 37, 39, 40

Date of Accounts	Dec 10	Dec 09
Sales Turnover	8m	11m
Pre Tax Profit/Loss	71	-117
Working Capital	-6m	-6m
Fixed Assets	7m	7m
Current Assets	6m	6m
Current Liabilities	493	367

Coca Cola Enterprises Ltd
7 Delaware Drive Tongwell, Milton Keynes, MK15 8HD
Tel: 01908-210828 **Fax:** 01908-216182
Website: http://www.coca-cola.com
Directors: M. Agates (MD), W. Davis (Fin)
Managers: S. Westall (Buyer)
Ultimate Holding Company: COCA-COLA ENTERPRISES INC (USA)
Immediate Holding Company: COCA-COLA ENTERPRISES LIMITED
Registration no: 00027173 **Date established:** 1988
No.of Employees: 251 - 500 **Product Groups:** 38, 42

Date of Accounts	Dec 11	Dec 10	Dec 09
Sales Turnover	1765m	1668m	1620m
Pre Tax Profit/Loss	256m	255m	239m
Working Capital	82m	170m	150m
Fixed Assets	457m	476m	434m
Current Assets	586m	613m	510m
Current Liabilities	245m	251m	228m

Computamation Services Ltd
9a Lower Way Great Brickhill, Milton Keynes, MK17 9AG
Tel: 07968-536068 **Fax:** 01525-850459
E-mail: john@computamation.co.uk
Website: http://www.computamation.co.uk
Directors: J. Wallace (MD)
Immediate Holding Company: COMPUTAMATION SERVICES LIMITED
Registration no: 03573715 **Date established:** 1998
Turnover: Up to £250,000 **No.of Employees:** 1 - 10 **Product Groups:** 44

Date of Accounts	Jun 11	Jun 09	Jun 08
Sales Turnover	N/A	N/A	162
Pre Tax Profit/Loss	N/A	N/A	54
Working Capital	15	7	1
Fixed Assets	22	13	16
Current Assets	53	40	52
Current Liabilities	34	N/A	19

Cooper Armer I T
Unit 2c Fernfield Farm Whaddon Road, Little Horwood, Milton Keynes, MK17 0PR
Tel: 01908-503018 **Fax:** 01908-503811
E-mail: info@caidata.co.uk
Website: http://www.caidata.co.uk
Directors: D. Armer (Dir)
Immediate Holding Company: MEDIATEX LIMITED
Registration no: 02148555 **VAT No.:** GB 479 3510 21
Date established: 2008 **Turnover:** £250,000 - £500,000
No.of Employees: 1 - 10 **Product Groups:** 44

Date of Accounts	Mar 11	Mar 10	Mar 09
Working Capital	9	N/A	3
Fixed Assets	1	N/A	N/A
Current Assets	28	10	11

Coplan Ltd
Michigan Drive Tongwell, Milton Keynes, MK15 8HQ
Tel: 01908-500000 **Fax:** 01908-500050
E-mail: sales@coplanlimited.com
Website: http://www.coplanltd.com
Directors: K. Brook (Dir), R. Brook (Co Sec)
Immediate Holding Company: COPLAN LIMITED
Registration no: 02107680 **Date established:** 1987 **Turnover:** £1m - £2m
No.of Employees: 1 - 10 **Product Groups:** 22, 24, 25, 26, 29, 30, 34, 35, 36, 37, 39, 40, 46, 49, 61, 66, 67, 68, 76

Date of Accounts	Oct 07	Oct 06	Oct 05
Working Capital	415	290	250
Fixed Assets	124	224	214
Current Assets	556	454	375
Current Liabilities	141	165	125
Total Share Capital	10	10	N/A

Cotels Management Ltd
Simply Apartments 500 Avebury Boulevard, Milton Keynes, MK9 2BE
Tel: 01908-802853 **Fax:** 01908-802864
E-mail: info@cotels.co.uk
Website: http://www.cotels.co.uk
Managers: M. Gomez (Mktg Serv Mgr)
Registration no: 06798288 **Date established:** 1997
No.of Employees: 1 - 10 **Product Groups:** 69

Crest Freight Forwarding Ltd
76 High Street Stony Stratford, Milton Keynes, MK11 1AH
Tel: 01908-307655 **Fax:** 01908-307656
E-mail: sales@crestfreight.co.uk
Website: http://www.crestfreight.co.uk
Directors: T. Hudson (MD)
Immediate Holding Company: CREST FREIGHT FORWARDING LIMITED
Registration no: 01794198 **Date established:** 1984
Turnover: £250,000 - £500,000 **No.of Employees:** 1 - 10
Product Groups: 76

Date of Accounts	Dec 11	Dec 10	Dec 09
Sales Turnover	283	200	325
Pre Tax Profit/Loss	20	N/A	12
Working Capital	19	15	15
Fixed Assets	1	N/A	N/A
Current Assets	49	47	53
Current Liabilities	11	12	17

Robert Cupitt Ltd
Joplin Court Crownhill, Milton Keynes, MK8 0JP
Tel: 01908-563063 **Fax:** 01908-562910
E-mail: sales@robertcupitt.co.uk
Website: http://www.robertcupitt.co.uk
Directors: G. Brandon (MD)
Immediate Holding Company: ROBERT CUPITT LIMITED
Registration no: 00540847 **VAT No.:** GB 194 2525 53
Date established: 1954 **Turnover:** £250,000 - £500,000
No.of Employees: 1 - 10 **Product Groups:** 35, 39, 45, 46, 47, 66, 68, 84

Date of Accounts	Nov 11	Nov 10	Nov 09
Working Capital	79	70	84
Fixed Assets	23	27	21
Current Assets	386	316	251

Custom Foams Ltd a division of Kay-Metzeler Ltd
2-17 Deans Road Old Wolverton, Milton Keynes, MK12 5NA
Tel: 01908-312331 **Fax:** 01908-220715
E-mail: vivien.gebbie@vcfuk.com
Website: http://www.customfoams.co.uk
Bank(s): Lloyds TSB Bank plc
Directors: M. Stirzaker (Fin)
Managers: V. Gebbie (Sales Admin), G. Cockram
Ultimate Holding Company: BRITISH VITA
Immediate Holding Company: CUSTOM FOAMS LIMITED
Registration no: 07825229 **VAT No.:** GB 257 5023 64
Date established: 2011 **Turnover:** £2m - £5m **No.of Employees:** 21 - 50
Product Groups: 29, 30, 31, 40, 42

D M G UK Ltd
Regus Regus House, Atterbury, Milton Keynes, MK10 9RG
Tel: 01582-570661 **Fax:** 01582-593700
E-mail: richard.watkins@gildemeister.com
Website: http://www.gildmeister.com
Bank(s): National Westminster Bank Plc
Directors: R. Watkins (MD), R. Kapitza (Mkt Research)
Managers: D. Taylor (Sales Off Mgr), J. Turner (Comptroller)
Ultimate Holding Company: GILDEMEISTER AKTIENGESELLSCHAFT (GERMANY)
Immediate Holding Company: UK UPSOLAR CO., LTD
Registration no: 01030108 **VAT No.:** GB 197 2021 63
Date established: 2011 **Turnover:** £10m - £20m
No.of Employees: 21 - 50 **Product Groups:** 46

Date of Accounts	Dec 11	Dec 10	Dec 09
Sales Turnover	17m	18m	17m
Pre Tax Profit/Loss	1m	919	866
Working Capital	4m	5m	3m
Fixed Assets	103	106	407
Current Assets	12m	8m	10m
Current Liabilities	5m	3m	4m

D R S Data Services Ltd
1 Danbury Court Linford Wood, Milton Keynes, MK14 6LR
Tel: 01908-666088 **Fax:** 01908-607668
E-mail: enquiries@drs.co.uk
Website: http://www.drs.co.uk
Bank(s): Barclays
Directors: A. Limb (Dir), M. Pebburt (Fin)
Managers: L. Noel, P. Jones
Ultimate Holding Company: DRS DATA AND RESEARCH SERVICES PUBLIC LIMITED COMPANY
Immediate Holding Company: DRS DATA SERVICES LIMITED
Registration no: 05568337 **Date established:** 2005
Turnover: £10m - £20m **No.of Employees:** 101 - 250 **Product Groups:** 44

Date of Accounts	Dec 11	Dec 10	Dec 09
Sales Turnover	16m	17m	15m
Pre Tax Profit/Loss	880	1m	-2m
Working Capital	3m	3m	2m
Fixed Assets	799	1m	2m
Current Assets	8m	7m	5m
Current Liabilities	3m	4m	2m

D W Group Ltd
Unit 7 Peverel Drive Bletchley, Milton Keynes, MK1 1NL
Tel: 01908-642323 **Fax:** 01908-640164
E-mail: sales@photopages.com
Website: http://www.photopages.com
Directors: P. Leigh (Dir)
Managers: T. Banks (Chief Acct)
Immediate Holding Company: D.W. GROUP LIMITED
Registration no: 02118127 **VAT No.:** GB 335 0982 55
Date established: 1987 **Turnover:** £500,000 - £1m
No.of Employees: 1 - 10 **Product Groups:** 30, 38

Date of Accounts	Dec 11	Dec 10	Dec 09
Working Capital	65	82	112
Fixed Assets	28	43	47
Current Assets	149	158	159
Current Liabilities	39	43	32

Dainippon Screen UK Ltd
Michigan Drive Tongwell, Milton Keynes, MK15 8HT
Tel: 01908-848500 **Fax:** 01908-848501
E-mail: forsdike@screen.co.uk
Website: http://www.screeneurope.com
Bank(s): National Westminster Bank Plc
Directors: B. Filler (MD), D. Pardy (Co Sec)
Managers: B. Burke (Sales Prom Mgr)
Ultimate Holding Company: DAINIPPON SCREEN MANUFACTURING CO LTD (JAPAN)
Immediate Holding Company: DAINIPPON SCREEN (U.K.) LIMITED
Registration no: 01171592 **Date established:** 1974
Turnover: £10m - £20m **No.of Employees:** 51 - 100 **Product Groups:** 44

Date of Accounts	Mar 11	Mar 10	Mar 09
Sales Turnover	15m	10m	15m
Pre Tax Profit/Loss	-314	-409	142
Working Capital	10m	10m	10m
Fixed Assets	1m	2m	2m
Current Assets	16m	14m	16m
Current Liabilities	2m	418	831

Dancing Bear
23 Horsefair Green Stony Stratford, Milton Keynes, MK11 1JP
Tel: 01908-307532 **Fax:** 01908- 561472
E-mail: joss@dancingbear.co.uk
Website: http://www.dancingbear.co.uk
Directors: J. Sanglier (Prop)
Date established: 2000 **No.of Employees:** 1 - 10 **Product Groups:** 81

Dawson Construction Plant Ltd
Chesney Wold Bleak Hall, Milton Keynes, MK6 1NE
Tel: 01908-240300 **Fax:** 01908-240222
E-mail: daveb@dcpuk.com
Website: http://www.dcpuk.com

see next page

***Dawson Construction Plant Ltd** - Cont'd*

Bank(s): HSBC, 22 West Street, Dunstaple
Directors: D. Brown (MD), J. King (Fin)
Managers: D. Day (Buyer), P. Childs (Chief Acct), T. Cliffe (Mktg Serv Mgr)
Immediate Holding Company: DAWSON CONSTRUCTION PLANT LIMITED
Registration no: 01057078 **VAT No.:** GB 196 2220 63
Date established: 1972 **Turnover:** £5m - £10m **No.of Employees:** 21 - 50
Product Groups: 34, 36, 45, 51

Date of Accounts	Apr 11	Apr 10	Apr 09
Sales Turnover	7m	6m	7m
Pre Tax Profit/Loss	-251	-258	342
Working Capital	2m	783	1m
Fixed Assets	5m	6m	5m
Current Assets	4m	4m	4m
Current Liabilities	140	633	495

Donaldson's Gunsmiths

10-12 Wharfside Bletchley, Milton Keynes, MK2 2AZ
Tel: 01908-377144
E-mail: sales@donaldson-guns.co.uk
Website: http://www.donaldson-guns.co.uk
Directors: C. Donaldson (Prop)
No.of Employees: 1 - 10 **Product Groups:** 36, 39, 40

Dynamic Air Ltd

26 Peverel Drive Granby, Bletchley, Milton Keynes, MK1 1QZ
Tel: 01908-622344 **Fax:** 01908-646633
E-mail: sales@dynamicair.com
Website: http://www.dynamicair.com
Directors: M. Williams (MD)
Ultimate Holding Company: DYNAMIC AIR INC (USA)
Immediate Holding Company: DYNAMIC AIR LIMITED
Registration no: 01706117 **VAT No.:** GB 382 2586 36
Date established: 1983 **Turnover:** £2m - £5m **No.of Employees:** 1 - 10
Product Groups: 32, 38, 41, 42, 45

Date of Accounts	Sep 11	Sep 10	Sep 09
Working Capital	313	153	53
Fixed Assets	2m	2m	2m
Current Assets	722	709	734

Dyson Diecastings (Alumasc Precision Ltd)

Second Avenue Bletchley, Milton Keynes, MK1 1EA
Tel: 01908-279200 **Fax:** 01908-279201
E-mail: leswhite@alumascprecision.co.uk
Website: http://www.alumascprecision.co.uk
Bank(s): Barclays
Directors: J. Robinson (Fin), L. White (MD)
Managers: G. Smith (Comm), M. Rigby (Prod Mgr)
Ultimate Holding Company: THE ALUMASC GROUP PLC
Immediate Holding Company: DYSON DIECASTINGS LIMITED
Registration no: 00158312 **VAT No.:** GB 395 9417 96
Date established: 1919 **Turnover:** £5m - £10m
No.of Employees: 51 - 100 **Product Groups:** 34

Elite Welding & Fabrications

Manor Farm Bullington End, Hanslope, Milton Keynes, MK19 7BQ
Tel: 01908-511660 **Fax:** 01908-370538
Directors: A. D'alanno (Prop)
Date established: 1984 **No.of Employees:** 1 - 10 **Product Groups:** 35

Elumatec UK Ltd

2 Europa Business Park Maidstone Road, Kingston, Milton Keynes, MK10 0BD
Tel: 01908-580800 **Fax:** 01908-580825
E-mail: sales@elumatec.co.uk
Website: http://www.elumatec.com
Directors: P. Heavey (MD)
Ultimate Holding Company: ELUMATEC GMBH & CO KG (GERMANY)
Immediate Holding Company: ELUMATEC UNITED KINGDOM LIMITED
Registration no: 02661167 **VAT No.:** GB 600 5535 82
Date established: 1991 **Turnover:** £5m - £10m **No.of Employees:** 1 - 10
Product Groups: 48, 67

Date of Accounts	Dec 11	Dec 10	Dec 09
Working Capital	143	-85	247
Fixed Assets	2m	807	289
Current Assets	1m	937	742

Engel Workwear

Carters Yard 23 Carters Lane Kiln Farm, Milton Keynes, MK11 3HL
Tel: 01908-561560 **Fax:** 01908-563805
E-mail: sales@f-engel.co.uk
Website: http://www.f-engel.co.uk
Directors: M. Hvass (Chief Op Offcr)
Immediate Holding Company: WORKWEAR TRADE CENTRE LIMITED
Registration no: 06943487 **Date established:** 2009
No.of Employees: 1 - 10 **Product Groups:** 24, 63

Date of Accounts	Sep 10
Working Capital	14
Current Assets	60

Ethos Europe UK Ltd

2 Bringewood Forge Blakelands, Milton Keynes, MK14 5FJ
Tel: 01908-216466 **Fax:** 01908-216467
E-mail: info@e2-ethos.com
Website: http://www.e2-ethos.com
Directors: B. Loines (MD)
Immediate Holding Company: RESPONSE FURNITURE SYSTEMS LIMITED
Registration no: 03174019 **Date established:** 1996
No.of Employees: 1 - 10 **Product Groups:** 26, 30, 33, 36, 84

Date of Accounts	Dec 07	Dec 06	Dec 05
Working Capital	-99	-78	-83
Fixed Assets	29	40	23
Current Assets	311	350	444
Current Liabilities	411	428	527

Euronetwork Ltd

1 Horwood Court Bilton Road, Bletchley, Milton Keynes, MK1 1RD
Tel: 01908-371909 **Fax:** 01908-378239
E-mail: info@euronetwork.co.uk
Website: http://www.euronetwork.co.uk
Directors: D. Smith (Prop)
Immediate Holding Company: EURONETWORK LIMITED
Registration no: 02420251 **Date established:** 1989 **Turnover:** £5m - £10m
No.of Employees: 1 - 10 **Product Groups:** 37, 44

Date of Accounts	Sep 11	Sep 10	Sep 09
Working Capital	49	47	32
Fixed Assets	40	30	39
Current Assets	251	234	166

Fastbolt Distributors UK Ltd

Sherbourne Drive Tilbrook, Milton Keynes, MK7 8AW
Tel: 01908-650100 **Fax:** 01908-650101
E-mail: sales@fastbolt.com
Website: http://www.fastbolt.com
Directors: A. True (Tech Serv), R. Brunger (Fin)
Managers: S. Clarke (Sales Prom Mgr)
Immediate Holding Company: FASTBOLT DISTRIBUTORS (UK) LIMITED
Registration no: 01660120 **VAT No.:** GB 382 1828 43
Date established: 1982 **No.of Employees:** 21 - 50 **Product Groups:** 35, 66

Date of Accounts	Dec 11	Dec 10	Dec 09
Working Capital	1m	799	525
Fixed Assets	2m	2m	2m
Current Assets	4m	4m	2m

Filtrona plc

201-249 Avebury Boulevard, Milton Keynes, MK9 1AU
Tel: 01908-359100 **Fax:** 01908-359120
E-mail: enquiries@filtrona.com
Website: http://www.filtrona.com
Bank(s): National Westminster Bank Plc
Directors: C. Day (Grp Chief Exec), A. Tidy (Pers), M. Wrigley (Tech Serv)
Managers: J. Speed, M. Gregory
Ultimate Holding Company: FILTRONA PLC
Immediate Holding Company: FILTRONA INTERNATIONAL LIMITED
Registration no: 01172804 **VAT No.:** GB 243 2909 68
Date established: 1974 **Turnover:** £250m - £500m
No.of Employees: 21 - 50 **Product Groups:** 49

Date of Accounts	Dec 11	Dec 10	Dec 09
Pre Tax Profit/Loss	26m	12m	30m
Working Capital	5m	10m	7m
Fixed Assets	172m	136m	151m
Current Assets	14m	16m	10m
Current Liabilities	7m	4m	2m

Firstlight Products Ltd

22 Erica Road Stacey Bushes, Milton Keynes, MK12 6HS
Tel: 01908-310221 **Fax:** 01908-310229
E-mail: gerald@firstlight-products.co.uk
Website: http://www.firstlight-products.co.uk
Directors: G. Furst (MD), S. Furst (Dir)
Managers: A. Barnett, J. Indge (Warehouse Mgr), M. Ryding
Immediate Holding Company: FIRSTLIGHT PRODUCTS LIMITED
Registration no: 01513210 **Date established:** 1980 **Turnover:** £2m - £5m
No.of Employees: 11 - 20 **Product Groups:** 37

Date of Accounts	Mar 11	Mar 10	Mar 09
Working Capital	1m	2m	2m
Fixed Assets	149	96	112
Current Assets	2m	2m	2m

Fisher & Paykel

Central Milton Keynes,, Milton Keynes, MK9 3EP
Tel: 0845-066 2200 **Fax:** 0845-3312360
Website: http://www.fisherpaykel.co.uk
Managers: H. Kuling, R. Bowe (Chief Mgr), S. Richardson (Serv Mgr)
Ultimate Holding Company: FISHER & PAYKEL APPLIANCES HOLDINGS LTD (NEW ZEALAND)
Registration no: 03957638 **Date established:** 2000
Turnover: £10m - £20m **No.of Employees:** 1 - 10 **Product Groups:** 40, 63

Fitafloor

64 Aylesbury Street Bletchley, Milton Keynes, MK2 2BA
Tel: 01908-888374 **Fax:** 01908-888128
E-mail: fitafloor@gmail.com
Website: http://www.fitafloor.co.uk
Directors: S. Barbieri (Dir)
No.of Employees: 1 - 10 **Product Groups:** 23, 25, 30, 66

Flexlink Systems Ltd

2 Tanners Drive Blakelands, Milton Keynes, MK14 5BN
Tel: 01908-327200 **Fax:** 01908-327201
E-mail: info.uk@flexlink.com
Website: http://www.flexlink.com
Directors: L. Cosford (Fin), S. Pinney (MD)
Managers: A. Woodward, D. Holiday (Sales Prom Mgr), D. Evans (Tech Serv Mgr)
Ultimate Holding Company: FLEXLINK HOLDINGS AB (SWEDEN)
Immediate Holding Company: FLEXLINK SYSTEMS LIMITED
Registration no: 01832229 **Date established:** 1984 **Turnover:** £2m - £5m
No.of Employees: 21 - 50 **Product Groups:** 30, 37, 41, 44, 45

Date of Accounts	Dec 11	Dec 10	Dec 09
Sales Turnover	5m	5m	5m
Pre Tax Profit/Loss	291	8	252
Working Capital	3m	3m	3m
Fixed Assets	75	113	135
Current Assets	5m	3m	4m
Current Liabilities	1m	512	595

Franklite Factory Shop

Snowdon Drive Winterhill, Milton Keynes, MK6 1AP
Tel: 01908-443090 **Fax:** 01908-691939
E-mail: info@franklite.ltd.uk
Website: http://www.franklite.net
Bank(s): National Westminster
Managers: C. Batt (Mgr)
Immediate Holding Company: FRANKLITE LTD
Registration no: 01057592 **Turnover:** £5m - £10m
No.of Employees: 21 - 50 **Product Groups:** 37

Fujipoly Europe Ltd

Unit 8 Third Avenue, Bletchley, Milton Keynes, MK1 1DR
Tel: 01908-277800 **Fax:** 01908-379916
E-mail: rob.humberstone@fujipolyeurope.co.uk
Website: http://www.fujipoly.com
Directors: F. Moto (MD)
Immediate Holding Company: FUJIPOLY EUROPE LIMITED
Registration no: 03645507 **Date established:** 1998
No.of Employees: 1 - 10 **Product Groups:** 37

Date of Accounts	Dec 11	Dec 10	Dec 09
Working Capital	556	274	60
Fixed Assets	82	36	41
Current Assets	924	573	380

Gaggenau UK Ltd

Grand Union House Old Wolverton Road, Wolverton, Milton Keynes, MK12 5PT
Tel: 01908-328360 **Fax:** 01908-328370
E-mail: info@gaggenau.com
Website: http://www.gaggenau.com
Directors: A. Roden (Sales), J. Pillay (Mkt Research)
Managers: M. Steinle, Watts (Personnel)
Immediate Holding Company: SAI LOGISTICS LIMITED
Registration no: 06455595 **Date established:** 2007
No.of Employees: 101 - 250 **Product Groups:** 40, 63, 66

Date of Accounts	Mar 11	Mar 10	Mar 09
Working Capital	40	53	18
Fixed Assets	146	78	95
Current Assets	1m	854	504

George Wimpey South Midlands

551 Avebury Boulevard, Milton Keynes, MK9 3DR
Tel: 01908-544800 **Fax:** 01908-544888
Website: http://www.georgewimpy.com
Directors: P. Carr (Dir), P. Gurr (MD)
Managers: K. Hanfon (Mktg Serv Mgr), S. Wright (Fin Mgr)
Immediate Holding Company: GEORGE WIMPEY SOUTH MIDLANDS LIMITED
Registration no: 00780367 **Date established:** 1963
Turnover: Over £1,000m **No.of Employees:** 51 - 100 **Product Groups:** 80

Date of Accounts	Dec 07	Dec 06	Dec 05
Working Capital	12000	12000	12000
Current Assets	12000	12000	12000
Total Share Capital	12000	12000	12000

Graphic West Packaging Machinery Ltd

77 Alston Drive Bradwell Abbey, Milton Keynes, MK13 9HG
Tel: 01908-319000 **Fax:** 01908-319999
E-mail: plewis@box-pro.co.uk
Website: http://www.box-pro.co.uk
Directors: P. Lewis (Fin)
Immediate Holding Company: GRAPHIC WEST PACKAGING MACHINERY LIMITED
Registration no: 03925957 **Date established:** 2000
No.of Employees: 11 - 20 **Product Groups:** 38, 42

Date of Accounts	Dec 11	Dec 10	Dec 09
Working Capital	356	487	478
Fixed Assets	121	37	60
Current Assets	586	648	585

Hallmark Construction

20 Burners Lane Kiln Farm, Milton Keynes, MK11 3HB
Tel: 01908-566555 **Fax:** 01908-566527
E-mail: sales@hallmarkconstruction.co.uk
Website: http://www.hallmarkconstructionuk.co.uk
Directors: T. Knight (Fin), S. Knight (Dir)
Immediate Holding Company: HALLMARK CONSTRUCTION (UK) LIMITED
Registration no: 03614575 **Date established:** 1998
No.of Employees: 1 - 10 **Product Groups:** 14, 34, 41, 42, 45, 51, 52, 67, 83, 84

Date of Accounts	Aug 11	Aug 10	Aug 09
Working Capital	-59	-90	-107
Fixed Assets	66	80	91
Current Assets	53	104	102

Hamilton

122 Severn Way Bletchley, Milton Keynes, MK3 7QB
Tel: 01908-641381 **Fax:** 01908-643565
E-mail: dave-hamiltonhfms@fsnet.com
Directors: V. Hamilton (Ptnr)
Date established: 1997 **No.of Employees:** 1 - 10 **Product Groups:** 20, 40, 41

Harland Simon plc

Bond Avenue Bletchley, Milton Keynes, MK1 1TJ
Tel: 01908-276700 **Fax:** 01908-276701
E-mail: sales@harlandsimon.com
Website: http://www.harlandsimon.com
Bank(s): National Westminster
Directors: R. Watson (Sales), K. Smith (Fin), R. Ashman (Dir)
Managers: R. Warren (Purch Mgr), J. Axon (Mktg Serv Mgr), P. Holoway (Tech Serv Mgr)
Immediate Holding Company: HARLAND SIMON PUBLIC LIMITED COMPANY
Registration no: 02733439 **VAT No.:** GB 608 4903 36
Date established: 1992 **Turnover:** £5m - £10m
No.of Employees: 51 - 100 **Product Groups:** 38, 44

Date of Accounts	Sep 11	Sep 10	Sep 09
Sales Turnover	6m	7m	5m
Pre Tax Profit/Loss	-239	16	113
Working Capital	53	247	30
Fixed Assets	470	508	723
Current Assets	2m	3m	1m
Current Liabilities	2m	2m	1m

G Hatton

49 Potters Lane Kiln Farm, Milton Keynes, MK11 3HQ
Tel: 01908-307607 **Fax:** 01908-635185
E-mail: enquiries@hattonfabs.co.uk
Directors: G. Hatton (Prop)
Immediate Holding Company: G HATTON FABRICATIONS LIMITED
Registration no: 04671986 **Date established:** 2003
No.of Employees: 1 - 10 **Product Groups:** 35

Date of Accounts	Feb 12	Feb 11	Feb 10
Working Capital	25	36	41
Fixed Assets	23	26	20
Current Assets	95	104	101

Hirose Electric Europe Bv

First Floor St Andrews House, Caldecotte Lake Business Park, Milton Keynes, MK7 8LE
Tel: 01908-369060 **Fax:** 01908-369078
E-mail: info@hiroseeurope.eu
Website: http://www.hiroseeurope.com
Directors: M. Sugino (Dir), Y. Narita (MD)
Ultimate Holding Company: HIROSE ELECTRIC COMPANY LTD (JAPAN)
Immediate Holding Company: Hirose Electric Co. Ltd (Japan)
Registration no: FC029550 **VAT No.:** GB 491 9130 35
Date established: 1988 **Turnover:** £2m - £5m **No.of Employees:** 1 - 10
Product Groups: 37, 47

Date of Accounts	Mar 08	Mar 07	Mar 06
Sales Turnover	2116	2443	2314
Pre Tax Profit/Loss	396	419	234

Working Capital	7863	7590	7264
Fixed Assets	4	5	40
Current Assets	8321	8102	7702
Current Liabilities	458	512	438
Total Share Capital	100	100	100
ROCE% (Return on Capital Employed)	5.0	5.5	3.2
ROT% (Return on Turnover)	18.7	17.1	10.1

Holophane Europe Ltd
Bond Avenue Bletchley, Milton Keynes, MK1 1JG
Tel: 01908-649292 **Fax:** 01908-367618
E-mail: amcrury@holophane.co.uk
Website: http://www.holophane.co.uk
Directors: A. McRury (MD), S. Carter (Co Sec), S. Childs (Fin), S. Lee (Sales), S. Carter (MD)
Managers: D. Barnwell (Mktg Serv Mgr)
Ultimate Holding Company: ACUITY BRANDS INC (USA)
Immediate Holding Company: HOLOPHANE EUROPE LIMITED
Registration no: 00843054 **VAT No.:** GB 119 1294 77
Date established: 1965 **Turnover:** £10m - £20m
No.of Employees: 101 - 250 **Product Groups:** 33, 35, 37, 39, 67, 84

Date of Accounts	Aug 09	Aug 08	Aug 07
Sales Turnover	17m	19m	18m
Pre Tax Profit/Loss	2m	3m	2m
Working Capital	7m	6m	11m
Fixed Assets	1m	1m	1m
Current Assets	10m	10m	14m
Current Liabilities	1m	2m	2m

Hydrafeed Ltd
Talgarth House Bond Avenue, Bletchley, Milton Keynes, MK1 1JD
Tel: 01908-376630 **Fax:** 01908-647843
E-mail: info@hydrafeed.co.uk
Website: http://www.hydrafeed.co.uk
Bank(s): Lloyds TSB Bank plc
Directors: M. Page (Chief Op Offcr), R. Passow (Dir), S. Southwood (MD)
Managers: D. Wells (Sales Admin)
Immediate Holding Company: HYDRAFEED LIMITED
Registration no: 02521773 **VAT No.:** GB 608 4691 25
Date established: 1990 **Turnover:** £1m - £2m **No.of Employees:** 21 - 50
Product Groups: 45, 46, 67

Date of Accounts	Jun 11	Jun 10	Jun 09
Working Capital	856	665	768
Fixed Assets	446	466	426
Current Assets	1m	921	965

I D Machinery Ltd
78 Alston Drive Bradwell Abbey, Milton Keynes, MK13 9HG
Tel: 01908-321778 **Fax:** 01908-322707
E-mail: sales@idmachinery.com
Website: http://www.idmachinery.com
Bank(s): National Westminster Bank Plc
Directors: J. Brasier (Sales)
Immediate Holding Company: I. D. MACHINERY LIMITED
Registration no: 01213480 **VAT No.:** GB 311 4388 85
Date established: 1975 **Turnover:** £2m - £5m **No.of Employees:** 11 - 20
Product Groups: 42, 44

Date of Accounts	Dec 11	Dec 10	Dec 09
Working Capital	3	52	79
Fixed Assets	100	119	109
Current Assets	1m	1m	1m

I P C
56 Western Drive Hanslope, Milton Keynes, MK19 7LE
Tel: 01908-511622
E-mail: alan.redman@ipcuk.com
Website: http://www.ipcuk.com
Directors: A. Redman (Dir)
No.of Employees: 1 - 10 **Product Groups:** 37, 40, 48

Inform Marketing Ltd
Gervaise House 35 Aylesbury Street, Bletchley, Milton Keynes, MK2 2BQ
Tel: 01908-370150 **Fax:** 01908-368610
E-mail: pca@inform-mk.co.uk
Website: http://www.inform-mk.co.uk
Directors: P. Ager (MD), H. Ager (Fin)
Immediate Holding Company: INFORM MARKETING LIMITED
Registration no: 02756893 **Date established:** 1992
No.of Employees: 1 - 10 **Product Groups:** 81

Date of Accounts	Mar 10	Mar 09	Mar 08
Working Capital	15	35	19
Fixed Assets	N/A	1	5
Current Assets	41	64	69

Interpower Components Ltd
10 Kelvin Drive Knowlhill, Milton Keynes, MK5 8NH
Tel: 01908-295300 **Fax:** 01908-295301
E-mail: infoeurope@interpower.com
Website: http://www.interpower.com
Managers: P. Bosson
Ultimate Holding Company: PANEL COMPONENTS CORPORATION (USA)
Immediate Holding Company: INTERPOWER COMPONENTS LIMITED
Registration no: 02682925 **Date established:** 1992 **Turnover:** £1m - £2m
No.of Employees: 1 - 10 **Product Groups:** 30, 37, 67

Date of Accounts	Sep 11	Sep 10	Sep 09
Working Capital	305	218	264
Fixed Assets	2m	2m	2m
Current Assets	366	289	299

Intervet UK Ltd
Walton Manor Walton, Milton Keynes, MK7 7AJ
Tel: 0370-060 3380 **Fax:** 01908-664778
E-mail: info@intervet.com
Website: http://www.intervet.co.uk
Bank(s): Barclays, Cambridge
Directors: S. Koehler (Dir), M. Van Heumen (Co Sec)
Ultimate Holding Company: MERCK & CO INC (USA)
Immediate Holding Company: INTERVET UK LIMITED
Registration no: 00946942 **Date established:** 1969
Turnover: £75m - £125m **No.of Employees:** 101 - 250
Product Groups: 63

Date of Accounts	Dec 10	Dec 09	Dec 08
Sales Turnover	106m	95m	85m
Pre Tax Profit/Loss	4m	740	2m
Working Capital	15m	10m	8m
Fixed Assets	47m	48m	49m
Current Assets	39m	42m	39m
Current Liabilities	10m	8m	7m

Intrinsys Ltd
Denbigh Road Bletchley, Milton Keynes, MK1 1DB
Tel: 01908-278606 **Fax:** 01908-278601
E-mail: info@intrinsys.co.uk
Website: http://www.intrinsys.co.uk
Directors: R. Duckworth (Co Sec)
Managers: N. Corner (Chief Mgr), S. Coleman (Accounts)
Registration no: 04286171 **Date established:** 2001
No.of Employees: 1 - 10 **Product Groups:** 44

J P Homw Brew
3a Ground Floor The Agora Shopping Centre Church Street Church Street, Wolverton, Milton Keynes, MK12 5LG
Tel: 01908-223328
E-mail: info@jphomebrew.co.uk
Website: http://www.homebrew-kits.co.uk
Directors: K. Hill (Prop)
Immediate Holding Company: LANDLORDS ADVICE CENTRE LIMITED
Date established: 2010 **No.of Employees:** 1 - 10 **Product Groups:** 20, 40, 41

Jewson Ltd
25 Dickens Road Old Wolverton, Milton Keynes, MK12 5QF
Tel: 01908-316171 **Fax:** 01908-222097
E-mail: keith.meakins@jewson.co.uk
Website: http://www.jewson.co.uk
Directors: P. Hindle (MD)
Managers: K. Meakins (District Mgr)
Ultimate Holding Company: COMPAGNIE DE SAINT GOBAIN (FRANCE)
Immediate Holding Company: JEWSON LIMITED
Registration no: 00348407 **VAT No.:** GB 394 1212 63
Date established: 1939 **Turnover:** £2m - £5m **No.of Employees:** 21 - 50
Product Groups: 66

Date of Accounts	Dec 11	Dec 10	Dec 09
Sales Turnover	1606m	1547m	1485m
Pre Tax Profit/Loss	18m	100m	45m
Working Capital	-345m	-250m	-349m
Fixed Assets	496m	387m	461m
Current Assets	657m	1005m	1320m
Current Liabilities	66m	120m	64m

Jokab Safety UK Ltd
Ground Floor Unit G Old Stratford Business Park, Old Stratford, Milton Keynes, MK19 6FG
Tel: 01908-261595 **Fax:** 01908-267100
E-mail: info@jokabsafety.com
Website: http://www.jokabsafety.com
Directors: N. Harvey (MD)
Ultimate Holding Company: ABB LTD (SWITZERLAND)
Immediate Holding Company: JOKAB SAFETY (UK) LIMITED
Registration no: 02638814 **Date established:** 1991
Turnover: £500,000 - £1m **No.of Employees:** 1 - 10 **Product Groups:** 35, 37, 38, 39, 40, 45, 84

Date of Accounts	Dec 10	Dec 09	Dec 08
Working Capital	11	-223	-151
Fixed Assets	N/A	2	2
Current Assets	72	94	136

Jungheinrich UK Ltd
Sherbourne House Sherbourne Drive, Tilbrook, Milton Keynes, MK7 8HX
Tel: 01908-363100 **Fax:** 020-8561 9733
E-mail: info@jungheinrich.co.uk
Website: http://www.jungheinrich.co.uk
Managers: C. McDougalls (Sales Prom Mgr), H. Herbert-Schultz
Ultimate Holding Company: JUNGHEINRICH BETEILIGUNGS GMBH (GERMANY)
Immediate Holding Company: JUNGHEINRICH UK HOLDINGS LIMITED
Registration no: 04294074 **Date established:** 2001
No.of Employees: 51 - 100 **Product Groups:** 35, 39, 45

Date of Accounts	Dec 11	Dec 10	Dec 09
Pre Tax Profit/Loss	-94	-71	-85
Working Capital	-6m	-6m	-6m
Fixed Assets	1m	1m	1m
Current Assets	N/A	N/A	1
Current Liabilities	8	7	17

K International
14 Davy Avenue Knowlhill, Milton Keynes, MK5 8PL
Tel: 01908-325400 **Fax:** 01908-670170
E-mail: info@k-international.co.uk
Website: http://www.kinternational.co.uk
Bank(s): Yorkshire Bank PLC
Directors: M. Brooks (MD), R. Venturi (Dir)
Managers: D. Brookes (Tech Serv Mgr), S. Kubiak
Immediate Holding Company: K INTERNATIONAL PLC
Registration no: 02722328 **VAT No.:** GB 600 4138 00
Date established: 1992 **Turnover:** £2m - £5m **No.of Employees:** 21 - 50
Product Groups: 80

Date of Accounts	Aug 11	Aug 10	Aug 09
Sales Turnover	3m	3m	3m
Pre Tax Profit/Loss	69	549	122
Working Capital	204	296	200
Fixed Assets	1m	1m	1m
Current Assets	770	1m	761
Current Liabilities	226	418	141

K V Ltd
Lunar House Crownhill, Milton Keynes, MK8 0HB
Tel: 01908-561515 **Fax:** 01908-561227
E-mail: rae.andrews@kvautomation.co.uk
Website: http://www.kvautomation.co.uk
Bank(s): National Westminster Bank Plc
Directors: N. Jones (Tech Serv), A. Cersell (MD), A. Hough (Export), C. Hothersall (I.T. Dir), F. Mills (Mkt Research), G. Weiss (Ch), N. Copley (Tech Serv), P. Mathews (Fin)
Managers: J. Osborn (Sales Off Mgr), L. Cayless (Comm), J. Askham (Personnel), F. Mills (Mktg Serv Mgr), G. Mason (Buyer), N. Winterbottom (), J. Askham
Ultimate Holding Company: Parker Hannifin (Holdings) Ltd
Immediate Holding Company: KV LIMITED
Registration no: 00971359 **VAT No.:** GB 196 7928 91
Date established: 1970 **Turnover:** £20m - £50m
No.of Employees: 101 - 250 **Product Groups:** 30, 36, 37, 38, 39, 40, 45, 46, 48

Date of Accounts	Apr 07
Sales Turnover	17429
Pre Tax Profit/Loss	1883

Working Capital	4626
Fixed Assets	1824
Current Assets	10685
Current Liabilities	6059
ROCE% (Return on Capital Employed)	29.2

Kemco Fabrications Ltd
Dane Road Bletchley, Milton Keynes, MK1 1JQ
Tel: 01908-375451 **Fax:** 01908-375044
E-mail: b.sullivan@kemco-aegis.com
Website: http://www.kemcoenv.com
Directors: P. Eversden (MD)
Managers: G. Eversden (I.T. Exec), B. Sullivan (Mgr)
Immediate Holding Company: OIL POLLUTION SERVICES LIMITED
Registration no: 00973592 **VAT No.:** GB 119 9600 56
Date established: 1970 **Turnover:** £1m - £2m **No.of Employees:** 11 - 20
Product Groups: 48

Date of Accounts	Jan 09	Apr 08	Apr 07
Working Capital	-20	-114	-0
Fixed Assets	38	9	19
Current Assets	306	253	401

Kennametal Extrude Hone Ltd
1 Sovereign Business Park Joplin Court, Crownhill, Milton Keynes, MK8 0JP
Tel: 01908-263636 **Fax:** 01908-262141
E-mail: sean.trengove@kennametal.com
Website: http://www.extrudehone.com
Directors: A. Godwin (Co Sec), S. Trengove (MD)
Ultimate Holding Company: KENNAMETAL INC (USA)
Immediate Holding Company: KENNAMETAL EXTRUDE HONE LIMITED
Registration no: 01763015 **Date established:** 1983 **Turnover:** £2m - £5m
No.of Employees: 1 - 10 **Product Groups:** 36, 37, 46

Date of Accounts	Jun 11	Jun 10	Jun 09
Sales Turnover	4m	2m	4m
Pre Tax Profit/Loss	346	104	-4
Working Capital	880	430	265
Fixed Assets	113	340	409
Current Assets	1m	799	567
Current Liabilities	352	180	162

Kit Scuba
PO Box 5700 Middleton, Milton Keynes, MK10 9WY
Tel: 0845-6443955
E-mail: sales@kitscuba.co.uk
Website: http://www.kitscuba.co.uk
Product Groups: 24, 40, 49, 74

Kluthe
314 Midsummer Boulevard, Milton Keynes, MK9 2UB
Tel: 01908-440120 **Fax:** 01908-440121
E-mail: info@kluthe.co.uk
Website: http://www.kluthe.co.uk
Managers: B. Warner (Chief Mgr), B. Warner (Mgr), T. Randall (Sales Admin)
Ultimate Holding Company: KLUTHE GMBH (GERMANY)
Immediate Holding Company: KLUTHE UK LTD
Registration no: 04149004 **Date established:** 2001
No.of Employees: 1 - 10 **Product Groups:** 31, 32, 66

Date of Accounts	Dec 10	Dec 09	Dec 08
Working Capital	311	-267	-384
Fixed Assets	67	119	157
Current Assets	846	654	584
Current Liabilities	N/A	N/A	644

Konica Minolta Business Solutions UK Ltd
Rooksley Park Precedent Drive, Rooksley, Milton Keynes, MK13 8HF
Tel: 01908-200400 **Fax:** 01268-644344
E-mail: info@konicaminolta.co.uk
Website: http://www.konicaminolta.co.uk
Bank(s): National Westminster Bank Plc
Directors: Y. Kobayashi (Dir)
Ultimate Holding Company: KONICA MINOLTA HOLDINGS INC (JAPAN)
Immediate Holding Company: KONICA MINOLTA BUSINESS SOLUTIONS (UK) LIMITED
Registration no: 01132885 **Date established:** 1973
Turnover: £75m - £125m **No.of Employees:** 21 - 50 **Product Groups:** 28, 32, 44, 49, 67, 80, 83

Date of Accounts	Mar 12	Mar 11	Mar 10
Sales Turnover	166m	159m	153m
Pre Tax Profit/Loss	11m	3m	2m
Working Capital	11m	7m	4m
Fixed Assets	5m	5m	6m
Current Assets	59m	53m	52m
Current Liabilities	21m	18m	13m

Korg UK Ltd
9 Newmarket Court Kingston, Milton Keynes, MK10 0AU
Tel: 01908-857100 **Fax:** 01908-857199
E-mail: john@korg.co.uk
Website: http://www.korg.co.uk
Directors: R. Castle (Dir), R. Castle (MD), I. Dixson (Fin)
Managers: P. Boondock (I.T. Exec), S. Williamson (Sales Prom Mgr), A. Scally (Mktg Serv Mgr)
Immediate Holding Company: KORG (UK) LIMITED
Registration no: 02355914 **Date established:** 1989
Turnover: £10m - £20m **No.of Employees:** 21 - 50 **Product Groups:** 65

Date of Accounts	Mar 10	Mar 09	Mar 08
Sales Turnover	13m	12m	12m
Pre Tax Profit/Loss	485	1m	710
Working Capital	5m	5m	4m
Fixed Assets	244	241	284
Current Assets	7m	8m	6m
Current Liabilities	888	1m	970

Koyo UK Ltd
Whitehall Avenue Kingston, Milton Keynes, MK10 0AX
Tel: 01908-289300 **Fax:** 01908-289333
E-mail: info@koyo.co.uk
Website: http://www.koyo.co.uk
Bank(s): HSBC Bank plc
Directors: C. Mayes (MD)
Managers: C. Pierson (Chief Mgr)
Ultimate Holding Company: JTEKT CORPORATION (JAPAN)
Immediate Holding Company: KOYO(U.K.)LIMITED
Registration no: 01047234 **Date established:** 1972
Turnover: £20m - £50m **No.of Employees:** 21 - 50 **Product Groups:** 30, 35, 39, 45

Date of Accounts	Dec 10	Dec 09	Dec 08
Sales Turnover	24m	20m	27m
Pre Tax Profit/Loss	750	251	65

see next page

Koyo UK Ltd - Cont'd

Working Capital	5m	5m	5m
Fixed Assets	3m	3m	3m
Current Assets	11m	9m	10m
Current Liabilities	353	225	222

Kuehne & Nagel Ltd

Kuehne & Nagel House Sunrise Parkway, Linford Wood, Milton Keynes, MK14 6BW
Tel: 01908-255000 **Fax:** 01908-255200
E-mail: robert.layton@kuehne-nagel.com
Website: http://www.kuehneandnagel.com
Bank(s): Barclays
Directors: G. Lindfield (MD)
Ultimate Holding Company: KUEHNE & NAGEL INTERNATIONAL AG (SWITZERLAND)
Immediate Holding Company: KUEHNE + NAGEL LIMITED
Registration no: 01722216 **Date established:** 1983
Turnover: £500m - £1,000m **No.of Employees:** 101 - 250
Product Groups: 84

Date of Accounts	Dec 11	Dec 10	Dec 09
Sales Turnover	958m	948m	833m
Pre Tax Profit/Loss	22m	27m	15m
Working Capital	20m	18m	16m
Fixed Assets	17m	12m	18m
Current Assets	175m	177m	148m
Current Liabilities	68m	73m	74m

Leica Camera Ltd

Davy Avenue Knowlhill, Milton Keynes, MK5 8LB
Tel: 01908-256400 **Fax:** 01908-609992
E-mail: dgailliez@leica-camera.co.uk
Website: http://www.leica-camera.co.uk
Bank(s): HSBC
Directors: D. Gailliez (Fin), D. Bell (MD)
Managers: D. Gailliez (Accounts), P. Melder (Sales Prom)
Immediate Holding Company: LEICA CAMERA LIMITED
Registration no: 02308025 **VAT No.:** GB 536 5451 39
Date established: 1988 **Turnover:** £5m - £10m **No.of Employees:** 11 - 20
Product Groups: 38

Date of Accounts	Mar 08	Mar 07	Mar 06
Sales Turnover	8m	8m	6m
Pre Tax Profit/Loss	307	266	20
Working Capital	2m	1m	1m
Fixed Assets	39	30	20
Current Assets	3m	3m	2m
Current Liabilities	1m	2m	1m

Leica Microsystems

Davy Avenue Knowlhill, Milton Keynes, MK5 8LB
Tel: 01908-246246 **Fax:** 01908-609992
E-mail: ukinfo@leica-microsystems.com
Website: http://www.leica-microsystems.co.uk
Directors: D. Edwards (Fin)
Managers: L. Howard (Mktg Serv Mgr), H. Sidhu (Personnel), R. Jenkins (Tech Serv Mgr)
Ultimate Holding Company: DANAHER CORPORATION (DELAWARE U.S.A)
Immediate Holding Company: LEICA MICROSYSTEMS (UK) LIMITED
Registration no: 00476611 **Date established:** 1949
Turnover: £50m - £75m **No.of Employees:** 51 - 100 **Product Groups:** 28

Date of Accounts	Dec 11	Dec 10	Dec 09
Sales Turnover	55m	51m	47m
Pre Tax Profit/Loss	4m	6m	5m
Working Capital	26m	22m	17m
Fixed Assets	3m	3m	766
Current Assets	35m	30m	24m
Current Liabilities	3m	3m	4m

Liftek Forktruck Hire Ltd

Unit 19c Tavistock House Tavistock Street, Bletchley, Milton Keynes, MK2 2PG
Tel: 07768-681662 **Fax:** 01908-585738
E-mail: steveswg@aol.com
Website: http://www.forktruckhire.net
Directors: S. Gifford (MD)
Immediate Holding Company: TOTAL MOVEMENT SERVICES (MK) LIMITED
Registration no: 06154293 **Date established:** 2007
No.of Employees: 1 - 10 **Product Groups:** 35, 39, 45

Lista UK Ltd

14 Warren Yard Wolverton Mill, Milton Keynes, MK12 5NW
Tel: 01908-222333 **Fax:** 01908-222433
E-mail: info.uk@lista.com
Website: http://www.lista.com
Managers: A. Byrne (Chief Mgr)
Ultimate Holding Company: ALID HOLDING AG (SWITZERLAND)
Immediate Holding Company: LISTA (UK) LIMITED
Registration no: 02530951 **VAT No.:** GB 536 6733 24
Date established: 1990 **Turnover:** £1m - £2m **No.of Employees:** 1 - 10
Product Groups: 26, 36, 45

Date of Accounts	Dec 11	Dec 10	Dec 09
Working Capital	-163	-204	-57
Fixed Assets	18	20	21
Current Assets	299	96	83

Lohmann Technologies

25 Kelvin Drive Knowlhill, Milton Keynes, MK5 8NH
Tel: 01296-337888 **Fax:** 01296-337772
E-mail: info@lohmann-tapes.co.uk
Website: http://www.lohmann-tapes.co.uk
Bank(s): Barclays
Directors: R. Churchill (MD)
Managers: L. Mackay (Comptroller)
Ultimate Holding Company: LOHMANN GMBH & CO. KG
Registration no: 02715934 **VAT No.:** GB 608 4404 54
Date established: 1989 **Turnover:** £2m - £5m **No.of Employees:** 21 - 50
Product Groups: 27, 30

Lyco Direct Ltd

10a Clarke Road Bletchley, Milton Keynes, MK1 1ZR
Tel: 08433-177820 **Fax:** 01908-643674
E-mail: sales@lyco.co.uk
Website: http://www.lyco.co.uk
Directors: J. Barnett (Co Sec), G. O'Donnell (Dir)
Managers: R. Tenzer (Chief Acct), M. Stafiere (Tech Serv Mgr)
Immediate Holding Company: LYCO DIRECT LIMITED
Registration no: 02923542 **Date established:** 1994
No.of Employees: 21 - 50 **Product Groups:** 33, 37, 67

Date of Accounts	Dec 11	Dec 10	Dec 09
Working Capital	143	54	-151
Fixed Assets	112	156	193
Current Assets	1m	894	921

M H A Macintyre Hudson

201 Silbury Boulevard, Milton Keynes, MK9 1LZ
Tel: 01908-662255 **Fax:** 01908-678247
E-mail: patrick.byrne@macintyrehudson.co.uk
Website: http://www.macintyrehudson.co.uk
Directors: V. Horton (Fin), P. Byrne (Ptnr)
Managers: A. Weston, P. King (Tech Serv Mgr)
Ultimate Holding Company: MH CAPITAL LLP
Immediate Holding Company: MACINTYRE HUDSON HOLDINGS LIMITED
Registration no: 03717255 **Date established:** 1999
Turnover: £500,000 - £1m **No.of Employees:** 21 - 50 **Product Groups:** 80

Date of Accounts	Mar 11	Mar 10	Mar 09
Sales Turnover	741	776	3m
Pre Tax Profit/Loss	429	435	314
Working Capital	3m	2m	3m
Fixed Assets	5m	4m	4m
Current Assets	4m	4m	6m
Current Liabilities	707	838	1m

Magne Tek

20 Drakes Mews Crownhill, Milton Keynes, MK8 0ER
Tel: 01908-261427 **Fax:** 01908-261674
E-mail: eurosales@magnetek.com
Website: http://www.magnetek.com
Managers: B. Preston (Chief Mgr)
Date established: 2004 **No.of Employees:** 1 - 10 **Product Groups:** 35, 39, 45

Makita UK Ltd

Vermont Place Michigan Drive, Tongwell, Milton Keynes, MK15 8JD
Tel: 01908-211678 **Fax:** 01908-211400
E-mail: info@makitauk.com
Website: http://www.makitauk.com
Bank(s): Barclays
Directors: S. Okada (MD)
Managers: C. Cookman (Comptroller)
Ultimate Holding Company: MAKITA CORPORATION (JAPAN)
Immediate Holding Company: MAKITA (UK) LIMITED
Registration no: 01086698 **Date established:** 1972
Turnover: £75m - £125m **No.of Employees:** 101 - 250
Product Groups: 36, 37

Date of Accounts	Mar 11	Mar 10	Mar 09
Sales Turnover	100m	87m	100m
Pre Tax Profit/Loss	6m	5m	-7m
Working Capital	37m	33m	29m
Fixed Assets	911	937	1m
Current Assets	69m	52m	67m
Current Liabilities	9m	9m	24m

Marshall Amplifications plc

Denbigh Road Bletchley, Milton Keynes, MK1 1DQ
Tel: 01908-375411 **Fax:** 01908-376118
E-mail: contactus@marshallamps.com
Website: http://www.marshallamps.com
Bank(s): Barclays
Directors: G. Young (Dir), V. Marshall (Co Sec), D. Cole (Fin)
Managers: S. Greenwood (Mktg Serv Mgr), S. Garrett, J. McKenna (Personnel), G. Lovelock (Tech Serv Mgr), T. McLean
Immediate Holding Company: MARSHALL AMPLIFICATION PLC
Registration no: 00805676 **VAT No.:** GB 120 4891 91
Date established: 1964 **Turnover:** £20m - £50m
No.of Employees: 101 - 250 **Product Groups:** 37

Date of Accounts	Dec 11	Dec 10	Dec 09
Sales Turnover	21m	23m	25m
Pre Tax Profit/Loss	-962	217	-412
Working Capital	17m	18m	17m
Fixed Assets	3m	4m	4m
Current Assets	19m	19m	18m
Current Liabilities	702	962	771

Massa Solutions Ltd

41 Alston Drive, Milton Keynes, BUCKINGHAMSHIRE
Tel: 01908-318844 **Fax:** 01908-318833
E-mail: mark.barber@itm.uk.com
Website: http://www.itm.uk.com
Directors: N. Murray (Dir)
Managers: J. Worsley (Develop Mgr)
Immediate Holding Company: ARQ Communications
Registration no: 04939463 **VAT No.:** GB 461 0852 63
Turnover: £1m - £2m **No.of Employees:** 11 - 20 **Product Groups:** 33, 37, 44, 45, 52, 67, 84, 85

Masterford Ltd

Unit B Lyon Road Bletchley, Milton Keynes, MK1 1EX
Tel: 01908-373106 **Fax:** 01908-377181
E-mail: john-forder@btconnect.com
Website: http://www.masterford.co.uk
Directors: J. Forder (MD)
Immediate Holding Company: MASTERFORD LIMITED
Registration no: 01084355 **Date established:** 1972
Turnover: £500,000 - £1m **No.of Employees:** 1 - 10 **Product Groups:** 34, 35, 38, 46, 48, 66

Date of Accounts	Jan 12	Jan 11	Jan 10
Working Capital	192	133	179
Fixed Assets	316	360	344
Current Assets	294	234	276

Materials Handling Systems UK

5-7 Victory Court Third Avenue, Bletchley, Milton Keynes, MK1 1EW
Tel: 01908-630690 **Fax:** 01908-630691
E-mail: mhsshirley@tiscali.co.uk
Directors: G. Rolls (Prop)
Date established: 1993 **No.of Employees:** 1 - 10 **Product Groups:** 35, 39, 45

Mechline Developments Ltd

15 Carters Lane Kiln Farm, Milton Keynes, MK11 3ER
Tel: 01908-261511 **Fax:** 01908-261522
E-mail: info@mechline.com
Website: http://www.mechline.com
Directors: D. Graves (Co Sec), P. Sage Passant (MD)
Managers: A. Farrell (Tech Serv Mgr), L. McCarthy (Sales & Mktg Mg)
Immediate Holding Company: MECHLINE DEVELOPMENTS LIMITED
Registration no: 02632823 **Date established:** 1991 **Turnover:** £1m - £2m
No.of Employees: 21 - 50 **Product Groups:** 29, 30, 33, 36, 37, 39, 40, 66, 67

Date of Accounts	Jul 11	Jul 10	Jul 09
Working Capital	1m	1m	921
Fixed Assets	381	331	348
Current Assets	3m	2m	2m

Megamat UK Ltd

29 Shenley Pavilions Chalkdell Drive, Shenley Wood, Milton Keynes, MK5 6LB
Tel: 01908-522322 **Fax:** 01908-522300
E-mail: sales@megamat.co.uk
Website: http://www.megamat.co.uk
Directors: D. Newman (MD)
Registration no: 03505521 **Date established:** 1998
Turnover: £500,000 - £1m **No.of Employees:** 1 - 10 **Product Groups:** 35, 42, 45

Date of Accounts	Dec 07	Dec 06	Dec 05
Sales Turnover	1016	1011	1317
Pre Tax Profit/Loss	-102	92	93
Working Capital	-510	-435	-503
Current Assets	405	707	746
Current Liabilities	915	1142	1249
Total Share Capital	1	1	1
ROCE% (Return on Capital Employed)	20.0	-21.1	-18.5
ROT% (Return on Turnover)	-10.0	9.1	7.1

Mercedes Benz UK Ltd

Delaware Drive Tongwell, Milton Keynes, MK15 8BA
Tel: 01908-245000 **Fax:** 01908-245472
Website: http://www.mercedes-benz.co.uk
Bank(s): National Westminster Bank Plc
Directors: W. Steffen (Dir)
Managers: A. Williamson (Comptroller)
Ultimate Holding Company: DAIMLER AKTIENGESELLSCHAFT (GERMANY)
Immediate Holding Company: MERCEDES-BENZ UK LIMITED
Registration no: 02448457 **Date established:** 1989
Turnover: Over £1,000m **No.of Employees:** 1001 - 1500
Product Groups: 36, 38, 39, 40, 68

Date of Accounts	Dec 11	Dec 10	Dec 09
Sales Turnover	2890m	2549m	1973m
Pre Tax Profit/Loss	54m	104m	67m
Working Capital	189m	146m	137m
Fixed Assets	358m	346m	359m
Current Assets	1050m	849m	755m
Current Liabilities	724m	595m	519m

Merchants Ltd (Telephone Marketing)

500 Avebury Boulevard, Milton Keynes, MK9 2BE
Tel: 01908-232323 **Fax:** 01908-242444
E-mail: sales@merchants.co.uk
Website: http://www.dimensiondata.co.uk
Directors: J. Patel (Co Sec), M. Dove (Dir), R. Taylor (Grp Chief Exec)
Managers: C. Batten (I.T. Exec), L. Crawford (Sales Prom Mgr), L. Werton (Chief Mgr), T. Barfield (Mktg Serv Mgr)
Ultimate Holding Company: THE MERCHANTS GROUP LIMITED
Immediate Holding Company: MERCHANTS HOLDINGS LIMITED
Registration no: 02674305 **VAT No.:** GB 650 7067 44
Date established: 1991 **Turnover:** £2m - £5m **No.of Employees:** 1 - 10
Product Groups: 81

Date of Accounts	Sep 09	Sep 08
Working Capital	10	10
Fixed Assets	10	10
Current Assets	10	10

Metals Express Ltd

9 Burners Lane Kiln Farm, Milton Keynes, MK11 3HA
Tel: 01908-262288 **Fax:** 01908-263388
E-mail: bob@metalsexpress.co.uk
Website: http://www.metalsexpress.co.uk
Directors: S. Mccorkindale (Fin)
Immediate Holding Company: METALS EXPRESS LIMITED
Registration no: 02721093 **Date established:** 1992
No.of Employees: 1 - 10 **Product Groups:** 34, 66

Date of Accounts	Sep 11	Sep 10	Sep 09
Working Capital	118	108	132
Fixed Assets	22	29	30
Current Assets	738	758	577

Metaltex UK Ltd

Brunleys Kiln Farm, Milton Keynes, MK11 3HR
Tel: 01908-262062 **Fax:** 01908-262162
E-mail: info@metaltex.co.uk
Website: http://www.metaltex.co.uk
Bank(s): Lloyds & National Westminster
Directors: J. Newbound (Dir), J. Burns (Co Sec)
Ultimate Holding Company: METALTEX HOLDINGS SA (SWITZERLAND)
Immediate Holding Company: METALTEX (UK) LTD.
Registration no: 00464129 **VAT No.:** GB 229 1927 49
Date established: 1949 **Turnover:** £2m - £5m **No.of Employees:** 21 - 50
Product Groups: 26, 30, 36, 63

Date of Accounts	Dec 11	Dec 10	Dec 09
Working Capital	291	439	576
Fixed Assets	2m	2m	2m
Current Assets	1m	2m	1m

Microwave Service Centre

6a London Road Stony Stratford, Milton Keynes, MK11 1JN
Tel: 01908-568745 **Fax:** 01908-568745
E-mail: msc@utdsl.com
Directors: C. Gavan (Prop)
No.of Employees: 1 - 10 **Product Groups:** 36, 40

Milton Keynes Citizen (a division of Johnson press)

Napier House Auckland Park, Bletchley, Milton Keynes, MK1 1BU
Tel: 01908-371133 **Fax:** 01908-371112
E-mail: john.francis@jpress.co.uk
Website: http://www.miltonkeynes.co.uk
Directors: S. Howard (MD)
Immediate Holding Company: MILTON KEYNES CITY FOOTBALL CLUB LIMITED
Registration no: 06236826 **Date established:** 2007
No.of Employees: 51 - 100 **Product Groups:** 28

Milton Keynes Metals Ltd
Ridge Hill Farm Little Horwood Road, Nash, Milton Keynes, MK17 0EH
Tel: 01296-713631 **Fax:** 01296-714155
E-mail: sales@mkmetals.co.uk
Website: http://www.mkmetals.co.uk
Directors: J. Wilson (Fin), V. Wilson (MD)
Immediate Holding Company: MILTON KEYNES METALS LTD
Registration no: 01401716 **VAT No.:** GB 608 6829 12
Date established: 1978 **Turnover:** £250,000 - £500,000
No.of Employees: 1 - 10 **Product Groups:** 23, 34, 35, 36, 37, 38, 39, 48, 49, 52, 61, 66, 67, 77, 84, 87

Date of Accounts	Oct 11	Oct 10	Oct 09
Working Capital	28	17	29
Current Assets	41	40	53

Milton Keynes & North Bucks Chamber Of Commerce
Silbury Court Silbury Boulevard, Milton Keynes, MK9 2AF
Tel: 01908-259000 **Fax:** 01908-246799
E-mail: enquiries@mk-chamber.co.uk
Website: http://www.mk-chamber.co.uk
Directors: C. Fox (Grp Chief Exec)
Immediate Holding Company: MILTON KEYNES ECONOMY AND LEARNING PARTNERSHIP LIMITED
Registration no: 03865566 **Date established:** 1999
Turnover: £10m - £20m **No.of Employees:** 1 - 10 **Product Groups:** 87

Date of Accounts	Mar 11	Mar 10	Mar 09
Sales Turnover	779	2m	1m
Pre Tax Profit/Loss	9	7	12
Working Capital	57	49	41
Fixed Assets	2	N/A	N/A
Current Assets	582	705	511
Current Liabilities	524	654	449

Milton Keynes Pressings Ltd
43a Barton Road Bletchley, Milton Keynes, MK2 3EF
Tel: 01908-271940 **Fax:** 01908-648906
E-mail: info@mkp.co.uk
Website: http://www.mkp.co.uk
Directors: M. Read (MD), A. Saunders (Fin), L. Deller (Chief Op Offcr)
Managers: S. Graves (Personnel), D. McGee (Sales Prom Mgr)
Immediate Holding Company: MILTON KEYNES PRESSINGS LIMITED
Registration no: 02428322 **VAT No.:** GB 536 4380 41
Date established: 1989 **Turnover:** £10m - £20m
No.of Employees: 101 - 250 **Product Groups:** 46, 48

Date of Accounts	Oct 11	Oct 10	Oct 09
Sales Turnover	17m	14m	11m
Pre Tax Profit/Loss	474	73	-1m
Working Capital	740	447	285
Fixed Assets	1m	787	1m
Current Assets	5m	4m	4m
Current Liabilities	2m	2m	2m

Mirka UK Ltd
Saxon House Shirwell Crescent, Furzton, Milton Keynes, MK4 1GA
Tel: 01908-375533 **Fax:** 01908-376611
E-mail: sales.uk@mirka.com
Website: http://www.mirka.com
Bank(s): Meriter bank ,London
Directors: C. Daycock (MD), P. Sandford (Co Sec), T. Nordstrom (Sales & Mktg)
Ultimate Holding Company: KWH GROUP LTD (FINLAND)
Immediate Holding Company: MIRKA (UK) LTD
Registration no: 01414812 **VAT No.:** GB 322 4937 65
Date established: 1979 **Turnover:** £2m - £5m **No.of Employees:** 11 - 20
Product Groups: 33

Date of Accounts	Dec 11	Dec 10	Dec 09
Working Capital	386	448	620
Fixed Assets	256	60	42
Current Assets	3m	3m	2m

Molins plc
Rockingham Drive Lindford Wood East, Linford Wood, Milton Keynes, MK14 6LY
Tel: 01908-246870 **Fax:** 01908-234224
E-mail: molins.ho@molins.com
Website: http://www.molins.com
Directors: R. Hunter (Grp Chief Exec)
Immediate Holding Company: MOLINS PUBLIC LIMITED COMPANY
Registration no: 00124855 **VAT No.:** GB 358 4557 18
Date established: 2012 **Turnover:** £75m - £125m
No.of Employees: 1 - 10 **Product Groups:** 41, 42, 44

Date of Accounts	Dec 11	Dec 10	Dec 09
Sales Turnover	90m	86m	84m
Pre Tax Profit/Loss	10m	4m	2m
Working Capital	23m	24m	23m
Fixed Assets	30m	36m	28m
Current Assets	49m	45m	46m
Current Liabilities	21m	16m	17m

Morgana Systems Ltd
Davy Avenue Knowlhill, Milton Keynes, MK5 8HJ
Tel: 01908-608888 **Fax:** 01908-692399
E-mail: info@morgana.co.uk
Website: http://www.morgana.co.uk
Bank(s): National Westminster
Managers: D. Arnold (Purch Mgr), R. Strain (Tech Serv Mgr)
Ultimate Holding Company: MORGANA HOLDINGS LIMITED
Immediate Holding Company: MORGANA SYSTEMS LIMITED
Registration no: 01335508 **VAT No.:** GB 301 7464 87
Date established: 1977 **Turnover:** £10m - £20m
No.of Employees: 21 - 50 **Product Groups:** 44

Date of Accounts	Dec 11	Dec 10	Jun 09
Sales Turnover	14m	18m	13m
Pre Tax Profit/Loss	2m	2m	1m
Working Capital	4m	4m	3m
Fixed Assets	2m	2m	2m
Current Assets	6m	6m	5m
Current Liabilities	1m	2m	1m

Motive Components Ltd
12-13 James Way Bletchley, Milton Keynes, MK1 1SU
Tel: 01908-368995 **Fax:** 01908-373722
E-mail: info@motivecomponents.co.uk
Website: http://www.motivecomponents.co.uk
Managers: T. Hartley (Sales Prom Mgr)
Immediate Holding Company: MOTIVE COMPONENTS LIMITED
Registration no: 01722280 **Date established:** 1983 **Turnover:** £2m - £5m
No.of Employees: 11 - 20 **Product Groups:** 68

Date of Accounts	Jan 12	Jan 11	Jan 10
Sales Turnover	N/A	N/A	3m
Pre Tax Profit/Loss	N/A	N/A	717
Working Capital	2m	2m	2m
Fixed Assets	115	90	88
Current Assets	3m	2m	2m
Current Liabilities	N/A	N/A	231

Multi-Contact UK Ltd
3 Presley Way Crownhill, Milton Keynes, MK8 0ES
Tel: 01908-265544 **Fax:** 01908-262080
E-mail: uk@multi-contact.com
Website: http://www.multi-contact.com
Bank(s): National Westminster Bank Plc
Directors: K. Mott (Fin), S. Horns (MD)
Managers: S. Maynard (Admin Off)
Ultimate Holding Company: STAUBLI HOLDING AG (SWITZERLAND)
Immediate Holding Company: MULTI-CONTACT (UK) LIMITED
Registration no: 00810388 **VAT No.:** GB 468 3286 13
Date established: 1964 **Turnover:** £2m - £5m **No.of Employees:** 11 - 20
Product Groups: 35, 37

Date of Accounts	Dec 11	Dec 10	Dec 09
Working Capital	2m	867	581
Fixed Assets	45	18	26
Current Assets	3m	2m	1m

Myonic Ltd
10 Warren Yard Wolverton Mill, Milton Keynes, MK12 5NW
Tel: 01908-227123 **Fax:** 01908-310427
E-mail: info.uk@myonic.com
Website: http://www.myonic.com
Managers: L. Pegg (Mgr)
Immediate Holding Company: MYONIC LIMITED
Registration no: 03497135 **Date established:** 1998 **Turnover:** £1m - £2m
No.of Employees: 1 - 10 **Product Groups:** 35, 45

Date of Accounts	Dec 08	Mar 12	Mar 11
Sales Turnover	2m	N/A	N/A
Pre Tax Profit/Loss	645	N/A	N/A
Working Capital	612	462	596
Fixed Assets	1	N/A	N/A
Current Assets	938	595	859
Current Liabilities	193	N/A	N/A

N K C Conveyors UK Ltd
30 Linford Forum Rockingham Drive, Linford Wood, Milton Keynes, MK14 6LY
Tel: 01908-695611 **Fax:** 01908-694632
E-mail: karen.dean@btconnect.com
Managers: D. Courtney (Chief Mgr)
Ultimate Holding Company: NAKANISHI METAL WORKS CO LTD (JAPAN)
Immediate Holding Company: NKC CONVEYORS (UK) LIMITED
Registration no: 02133499 **Date established:** 1987 **Turnover:** £2m - £5m
No.of Employees: 1 - 10 **Product Groups:** 35, 39, 45

Date of Accounts	Dec 11	Dec 10	Dec 09
Sales Turnover	2m	2m	5m
Pre Tax Profit/Loss	-281	-482	52
Working Capital	2m	3m	3m
Fixed Assets	17	25	37
Current Assets	3m	3m	4m
Current Liabilities	234	296	146

Nationwide Access Ltd
1 Peverel Drive Bletchley, Milton Keynes, MK1 1NL
Tel: 0845-7450000 **Fax:** 0161-790 7499
E-mail: manchester@nationwideplatforms.co.uk
Website: http://www.nationwideplatforms.co.uk
Bank(s): Lavendon Group PLC
Directors: P. Whittle (MD)
Managers: D. Roberts (District Mgr), H. Stevenson (I.T. Exec)
Registration no: 02268921 **Turnover:** £20m - £50m
No.of Employees: 21 - 50 **Product Groups:** 45, 83

Nefab Packaging UK Ltd
Technology House 151 Silbury Boulevard, Milton Keynes, MK9 1LH
Tel: 01908-424300 **Fax:** 024-7671 4828
E-mail: info@nefab.co.uk
Website: http://www.nefab.co.uk
Managers: C. Fuchs (Chief Mgr)
Immediate Holding Company: NEFAB PACKAGING UK LIMITED
Registration no: 04335687 **VAT No.:** GB 301 5469 87
Date established: 2001 **Turnover:** £1m - £2m **No.of Employees:** 1 - 10
Product Groups: 25, 27, 30, 45

Date of Accounts	Dec 11	Dec 10	Dec 09
Sales Turnover	3m	2m	1m
Pre Tax Profit/Loss	111	39	15
Working Capital	-266	-372	-411
Fixed Assets	6	1	1
Current Assets	1m	532	473
Current Liabilities	N/A	904	N/A

New City Heating Co. Ltd
4 Simpson Road Bletchley, Milton Keynes, MK2 2DD
Tel: 01908-371084 **Fax:** 01908-371084
Website: http://www.newcityheating.co.uk
Bank(s): National Westminster Bank Plc
Directors: C. Fortescue (MD)
Immediate Holding Company: NEW CITY HEATING COMPANY LIMITED
Registration no: 01163410 **VAT No.:** GB 198 4480 15
Date established: 1974 **Turnover:** £2m - £5m **No.of Employees:** 21 - 50
Product Groups: 29, 66

Date of Accounts	Apr 11	Apr 10	Apr 09
Working Capital	2m	2m	3m
Fixed Assets	1m	2m	1m
Current Assets	3m	3m	4m

Niftylift Ltd
Unit 1 Fingle Drive, Stonebridge, Milton Keynes, MK13 0ER
Tel: 01908-223456 **Fax:** 01908-312733
E-mail: info@niftylift.com
Website: http://www.niftylift.com
Directors: S. Beadle (Fin), J. Keely (MD)
Managers: S. Maher (Mktg Serv Mgr), A. Hurley (Tech Serv Mgr), J. Sizer (Purch Mgr)
Immediate Holding Company: NIFTYLIFT LIMITED
Registration no: 01264184 **Date established:** 1976
Turnover: £20m - £50m **No.of Employees:** 101 - 250
Product Groups: 35, 45

Date of Accounts	Dec 11	Dec 10	Dec 09
Sales Turnover	41m	25m	19m
Pre Tax Profit/Loss	3m	876	-1m
Working Capital	13m	11m	11m
Fixed Assets	3m	3m	3m
Current Assets	23m	20m	18m
Current Liabilities	2m	1m	2m

Omron Electronics
Opal Drive Fox Milne, Milton Keynes, MK15 0DG
Tel: 01908-258258 **Fax:** 01908-258158
E-mail: marketing@eu.omron.com
Website: http://www.eu.omron.com
Directors: D. Sanders (Fin), R. Maietti (Dir)
Ultimate Holding Company: OMRON CORP (JAPAN)
Immediate Holding Company: OMRON ELECTRONICS LIMITED
Registration no: 02602783 **Date established:** 1991
Turnover: £20m - £50m **No.of Employees:** 21 - 50 **Product Groups:** 28, 37, 38, 40, 44, 45, 52, 67, 84, 85

Date of Accounts	Mar 11	Mar 10	Mar 09
Sales Turnover	28m	23m	23m
Pre Tax Profit/Loss	544	611	-868
Working Capital	6m	6m	5m
Fixed Assets	219	258	342
Current Assets	13m	12m	10m
Current Liabilities	3m	3m	2m

Open University Worldwide
The Michael Young Building Walton Hall, Milton Keynes, MK7 6AA
Tel: 01908-858785 **Fax:** 01908-858787
E-mail: t.strudwick@open.ac.uk
Website: http://www.ouw.co.uk
Directors: A. Gribbon (MD)
Managers: M. Hedges, N. Holt, D. Andrew (Mktg Serv Mgr), D. Matthewman
Immediate Holding Company: OPEN UNIVERSITY WORLDWIDE LIMITED
Registration no: 01260275 **VAT No.:** GB 650 7489 18
Date established: 1976 **Turnover:** £5m - £10m **No.of Employees:** 21 - 50
Product Groups: 86

Date of Accounts	Jul 11	Jul 10	Jul 09
Sales Turnover	10m	10m	10m
Pre Tax Profit/Loss	2m	953	2m
Working Capital	3m	3m	3m
Current Assets	9m	8m	8m
Current Liabilities	1m	967	1m

Orien Cards LLP
37 LUNDHOLME HEELANDS, Milton Keynes, MK13 7QJ
Tel: 0845-351 9934 **Fax:** 0845-351 9941
E-mail: cards@oriengroup.co.uk
Website: http://www.oriengroup.co.uk
Directors: C. Bose (Dir)
Immediate Holding Company: BABSIBRAHEEM ENTERPRISES LIMITED
Date established: 2011 **Turnover:** Up to £250,000
No.of Employees: 1 - 10 **Product Groups:** 81

Osai UK Ltd
Mount House Bond Avenue, Bletchley, Milton Keynes, MK1 1SF
Tel: 01908-642687 **Fax:** 01908-642688
E-mail: d.hudson@osai.co.uk
Website: http://www.osai.co.uk
Directors: D. Hudson (MD)
Ultimate Holding Company: PRIMA INDUSTRIE SPA (ITALY)
Immediate Holding Company: OSAI-UK LTD
Registration no: 03323855 **VAT No.:** 690 2230 56 **Date established:** 1997
Turnover: £500,000 - £1m **No.of Employees:** 1 - 10 **Product Groups:** 37, 38, 45, 46, 48

Date of Accounts	Dec 11	Dec 10	Dec 09
Sales Turnover	927	943	872
Pre Tax Profit/Loss	37	10	-3
Working Capital	1m	1m	1m
Fixed Assets	8	22	40
Current Assets	1m	1m	1m
Current Liabilities	109	97	84

Oscar Press Ltd
Potters Lane Kiln Farm, Milton Keynes, MK11 3HQ
Tel: 01908-260333 **Fax:** 01908-560223
E-mail: sales@oscar.uk.com
Website: http://www.oscar.uk.com
Directors: M. Nash (Fin), P. Nash (MD)
Immediate Holding Company: OSCAR GROUP LIMITED
Registration no: 04395930 **Date established:** 1986
No.of Employees: 11 - 20 **Product Groups:** 28, 44, 49, 67, 79, 81, 84

Date of Accounts	Feb 12	Feb 11	Feb 10
Working Capital	3	-9	9
Fixed Assets	18	29	38
Current Assets	68	85	102

P D J Vibro Ltd
46 Barton Road Bletchley, Milton Keynes, MK2 3BB
Tel: 01908-648757 **Fax:** 01908-648766
E-mail: info@vibratoryfinishing.co.uk
Website: http://www.vibratoryfinishing.co.uk
Directors: J. Hurley (Fin)
Immediate Holding Company: PDJ VIBRO LIMITED
Registration no: 03747200 **Date established:** 1999
No.of Employees: 11 - 20 **Product Groups:** 23, 32, 33, 36, 37, 42, 44, 45, 46, 47, 48, 67, 86

Date of Accounts	Apr 11	Apr 10	Apr 09
Working Capital	198	100	96
Fixed Assets	161	169	181
Current Assets	437	256	216

P T S
Marshall Court 1-4 James Way, Bletchley, Milton Keynes, MK1 1SU
Tel: 01908-335150 **Fax:** 01908-640919
Website: http://www.ptsplumbing.co.uk
Managers: S. Wadsworth (District Mgr)
Ultimate Holding Company: TRAVIS PERKINS PLC
Immediate Holding Company: P.T.S. PLUMBING TRADE SUPPLIES LIMITED
Registration no: 01851210 **Date established:** 1984
No.of Employees: 21 - 50 **Product Groups:** 52

Date of Accounts	Dec 10	Mar 10	Mar 09
Working Capital	1m	1m	1m
Current Assets	1m	1m	1m

Panasonic Electric Works
Sunrise Parkway Linford Wood, Milton Keynes, MK14 6LF
Tel: 01908-231555 **Fax:** 01908-231599
E-mail: r.thornton@eu.pewg.panasonic.com
Website: http://www.panasonic-electric-works.co.uk

see next page

***Panasonic Electric Works** - Cont'd*
Directors: R. Thornton (MD)
Managers: G. Bandy (Personnel), H. Tooley (Fin Mgr)
Ultimate Holding Company: MATSUSHITA ELECTRIC WORKS, LTD. (JAPAN)
Immediate Holding Company: PANASONIC ELECTRIC WORKS UK LIMITED
Registration no: 01591381 **Date established:** 1981 **Turnover:** £2m - £5m **No.of Employees:** 11 - 20 **Product Groups:** 37, 38, 39, 44, 45, 49

Date of Accounts	Mar 12	Mar 11	Mar 10
Sales Turnover	1m	4m	4m
Pre Tax Profit/Loss	-219	191	70
Working Capital	411	3m	2m
Fixed Assets	774	1m	1m
Current Assets	527	3m	3m
Current Liabilities	97	331	204

Parker K V Division
Presley Way Crownhill, Milton Keynes, MK8 0HB
Tel: 01908-561515 **Fax:** 01908-561227
E-mail: info@parker.com
Website: http://www.parker.com/kvde
Registration no: 04806503 **No.of Employees:** 51 - 100
Product Groups: 36

Per Sempre Amore
PO Box 5586, Milton Keynes, MK4 1ZG
Tel: 08700-923392 **Fax:** 0870-092 3393
E-mail: michelle@persempreamore.co.uk
Website: http://www.persempreamore.co.uk
Directors: M. Caravello (Prop)
Turnover: Up to £250,000 **No.of Employees:** 1 - 10 **Product Groups:** 24, 81, 89

Pinks Syrups
86 Alston Drive Bradwell Abbey, Milton Keynes, MK13 9HF
Tel: 01908-321516 **Fax:** 01327-856766
E-mail: info@pinkssyrups.com
Website: http://www.pinkssyrups.com
Directors: F. Harcombe (Dir)
Immediate Holding Company: PINKS SYRUPS LIMITED
Registration no: 05793091 **Date established:** 2006
Turnover: Up to £250,000 **No.of Employees:** 1 - 10 **Product Groups:** 62

Date of Accounts	Oct 11	Oct 10	Oct 09
Working Capital	-9	-5	N/A
Current Assets	68	56	24

Plantation Coffee Ltd
xchange House 494 Mid Summer Boulevard, Milton Keynes, MK9 2EA
Tel: 01908-306008 **Fax:** 01908-255700
E-mail: jw@plantationcoffee.co.uk
Website: http://www.plantationcoffee.co.uk
Ultimate Holding Company: S W Holdings Ltd
Registration no: 03138975 **No.of Employees:** 1 - 10 **Product Groups:** 62

Date of Accounts	Jun 08	Jun 07	Jun 06
Working Capital	-113	-141	29
Fixed Assets	4	7	1
Current Assets	127	68	202
Current Liabilities	240	209	173

Plastics Fabrication & Printing Ltd
9 Peverel Drive Bletchley, Milton Keynes, MK1 1NL
Tel: 01908-270474 **Fax:** 01908-375628
E-mail: michael@plastics-fabrication.co.uk
Website: http://www.plasticsfabrication.co.uk
Bank(s): Barclays, Ashton House
Directors: M. Leask (MD)
Immediate Holding Company: PLASTICS FABRICATION & PRINTING LIMITED
Registration no: 00518906 **VAT No.:** GB 229 5962 27
Date established: 1953 **Turnover:** £1m - £2m **No.of Employees:** 11 - 20
Product Groups: 22, 23, 24, 28, 30, 31, 36, 48, 49, 63, 66

Date of Accounts	Mar 12	Mar 11	Mar 10
Working Capital	12	-10	12
Fixed Assets	5	7	10
Current Assets	89	76	107

The Polestar Company
Alan James Goodwin 3 Marlborough Court, Linford Wood, Milton Keynes, MK14 6DY
Tel: 01908-206800 **Fax:** 01908-206801
E-mail: alan.goodwin@polestar-group.com
Website: http://www.polestar-group.com
Directors: A. Goodwin (Co Sec)
Ultimate Holding Company: INK ACQUISITIONS LTD (CAYMAN IS)
Immediate Holding Company: TERMINUS 1 LIMITED
Registration no: FC027302 **Date established:** 2007
Turnover: £250m - £500m **No.of Employees:** 1501 & over
Product Groups: 27, 28, 30, 81

Date of Accounts	Sep 09	Sep 08	Sep 07
Sales Turnover	310m	347m	278m
Pre Tax Profit/Loss	-54m	-180m	-38m
Working Capital	-48m	-62m	-26m
Fixed Assets	231m	284m	413m
Current Assets	61m	68m	69m
Current Liabilities	42m	55m	30m

Precisa Ltd
13 Vermont Place Tongwell, Milton Keynes, MK15 8JA
Tel: 01908-211900 **Fax:** 01908-211909
E-mail: info@precisa.co.uk
Website: http://www.precisa.co.uk
Directors: A. O'mahony (Dir), C. Murphy (Co Sec), D. Buckley (MD)
Managers: D. Waller (Sales Admin)
Immediate Holding Company: Precisa Ltd
Registration no: 05997164 **VAT No.:** GB 365 9836 00
Date established: 2006 **Turnover:** £500,000 - £1m
No.of Employees: 1 - 10 **Product Groups:** 38

Date of Accounts	Dec 09	Dec 08	Dec 07
Sales Turnover	508	557	593
Pre Tax Profit/Loss	43	-71	-56
Working Capital	-163	-184	-121
Fixed Assets	86	101	106
Current Assets	189	189	183
Current Liabilities	16	24	47

Prestige Refinishing Service
65 Kirtlington Downhead Park, Milton Keynes, MK15 9AZ
Tel: 01908-665914 **Fax:** 01908-665914
E-mail: prestige@refin.freeserve.co.uk
Directors: C. Graham (Prop)
Date established: 1992 **No.of Employees:** 1 - 10 **Product Groups:** 48

Pyrotek Engineering Materials Ltd
Garamonde Drive Wymbush, Milton Keynes, MK8 8LN
Tel: 01908-561155 **Fax:** 01908-560473
E-mail: allan.roy@pyrotekeurope.com
Website: http://www.pyrotek.info
Bank(s): Barclays, Park Royal, London NW10
Directors: A. Hollis (Co Sec)
Managers: G. Smith (Tech Serv Mgr), M. Loose
Ultimate Holding Company: PYROTEK INC(USA)
Immediate Holding Company: PYROTEK ENGINEERING MATERIALS LIMITED
Registration no: 00269400 **Date established:** 1932
Turnover: £10m - £20m **No.of Employees:** 21 - 50 **Product Groups:** 27, 29, 30, 32, 33, 37, 40, 42, 46, 66

Date of Accounts	Jun 11	Jun 10	Jun 09
Sales Turnover	16m	13m	13m
Pre Tax Profit/Loss	998	46	299
Working Capital	3m	2m	2m
Fixed Assets	2m	2m	2m
Current Assets	6m	5m	4m
Current Liabilities	789	371	559

Quantitech Ltd
Unit 3 Old Wolverton Road, Old Wolverton, Milton Keynes, MK12 5NP
Tel: 01908-227722 **Fax:** 01908-227733
E-mail: info@quantitech.co.uk
Website: http://www.quantitech.co.uk
Directors: D. Duggan (Sales), J. Monaghan (Co Sec)
Immediate Holding Company: QUANTITECH LIMITED
Registration no: 02301809 **VAT No.:** GB 382 1961 41
Date established: 1988 **Turnover:** £1m - £2m **No.of Employees:** 1 - 10
Product Groups: 38, 40, 42, 84

Date of Accounts	Mar 12	Mar 11	Mar 10
Working Capital	285	218	318
Fixed Assets	181	169	171
Current Assets	954	1m	964

R A D Fabricating Co.
33 Alston Drive Bradwell Abbey, Milton Keynes, MK13 9HA
Tel: 01908-322478 **Fax:** 01908-320239
E-mail: phil@radfabricating.co.uk
Website: http://www.radfabricating.co.uk
Directors: P. Nolan (Prop)
Registration no: 01206667 **VAT No.:** GB 283 7031 58
Turnover: £500,000 - £1m **No.of Employees:** 1 - 10 **Product Groups:** 48

R & K Stockcraft
19 Vicarage Road Stony Stratford, Milton Keynes, MK11 1BN
Tel: 01908-568493 **Fax:** 01908-262472
Website: http://www.rkstockcraft.co.uk
Directors: M. King (Prop)
Date established: 1989 **No.of Employees:** 1 - 10 **Product Groups:** 36, 39, 40

R S Coatings
3 Stevens Yard Simpson Road, Bletchley, Milton Keynes, MK1 1BA
Tel: 01908-366985 **Fax:** 01908-271226
E-mail: rscoatings@aol.com
Directors: W. Hawkins (Ptnr)
Date established: 1992 **No.of Employees:** 1 - 10 **Product Groups:** 46, 48

Rack A Tier Shelving Company Ltd
39 Barton Road Water Eaton Ind Est, Milton Keynes, MK2 3HW
Tel: 01908-282842 **Fax:** 01908-282832
E-mail: sales@rackatier.co.uk
Website: http://www.rackatier.co.uk
Directors: L. Jones (Fin)
Immediate Holding Company: Rack-A-Tier Shelving Company Ltd
Registration no: 03165112 **No.of Employees:** 1 - 10 **Product Groups:** 26, 35

Date of Accounts	Mar 08	Mar 07	Mar 06
Working Capital	49	44	41
Fixed Assets	1	1	2
Current Assets	89	88	97
Current Liabilities	40	44	56

Radir Ltd
Douglas House Simpson Road, Bletchley, Milton Keynes, MK1 1BA
Tel: 01908-370000 **Fax:** 01908-370055
E-mail: ianh@radir.com
Website: http://www.radir.com
Product Groups: 37, 38, 39, 40, 41, 42, 43, 44, 45, 46, 48, 67, 83, 85, 86

Date of Accounts	Dec 11	Dec 10	Dec 09
Working Capital	54	30	31
Fixed Assets	4	8	4
Current Assets	230	262	140

Rascal Solutions Ltd
Sigma House Northfield Drive, Northfield, Milton Keynes, MK15 0DQ
Tel: 01908-695795 **Fax:** 01908-674621
E-mail: mail@escafoodsolutions.co.uk
Website: http://www.rascal-solutions.com
Directors: P. Marsden (MD)
Immediate Holding Company: RASCAL SOLUTIONS LIMITED
Registration no: 05191277 **Date established:** 2004
Turnover: £50m - £75m **No.of Employees:** 11 - 20 **Product Groups:** 20

Date of Accounts	Aug 11	Aug 10	Aug 09
Working Capital	834	927	578
Fixed Assets	1m	740	601
Current Assets	2m	2m	1m

Reed Accountancy Personnel Ltd
456 Midsummer Boulevard, Milton Keynes, MK9 2EA
Tel: 01908-660061 **Fax:** 01908-690357
E-mail: rap.miltonkeynes@reed.co.uk
Website: http://www.reed.co.uk
Managers: D. Daly (Mgr)
Immediate Holding Company: BAKER SMALL LEGAL SERVICES LTD
Registration no: 00973629 **Date established:** 2010
Turnover: £125m - £250m **No.of Employees:** 1 - 10 **Product Groups:** 80

Date of Accounts	Feb 11
Sales Turnover	82
Pre Tax Profit/Loss	-14
Working Capital	-20
Fixed Assets	6
Current Assets	16
Current Liabilities	30

Reed Finance
Exchange House Midsummer Boulevard, Milton Keynes, MK9 2EA
Tel: 01908-860606 **Fax:** 01908-690357
E-mail: d.daly@reed.co.uk
Website: http://www.reedfinance.co.uk
Managers: A. Tate (District Mgr)
Ultimate Holding Company: REED GLOBAL LTD (MALTA)
Immediate Holding Company: REED EMPLOYMENT LIMITED
Registration no: 00669854 **Date established:** 1960
Turnover: £75m - £125m **No.of Employees:** 1 - 10 **Product Groups:** 80

Date of Accounts	Jun 11	Jun 10	Dec 07
Sales Turnover	618	450	287m
Pre Tax Profit/Loss	-2m	310	8m
Working Capital	23m	28m	28m
Fixed Assets	31	36	5m
Current Assets	28m	30m	74m
Current Liabilities	37	29	21m

Reedbut Ltd
Bond Avenue Bletchley, Milton Keynes, MK1 1JJ
Tel: 01908-630200 **Fax:** 01908-630210
E-mail: sales@reedbut.com
Website: http://www.reedbut.com
Bank(s): National Westminster
Directors: M. Clarke (Fin), T. Green (MD)
Ultimate Holding Company: BOND ESTATES HOLDINGS LIMITED
Immediate Holding Company: REEDBUT LIMITED
Registration no: 04250474 **Date established:** 2001
Turnover: £10m - £20m **No.of Employees:** 21 - 50 **Product Groups:** 27

Date of Accounts	Jun 11	Jun 10	Jun 09
Working Capital	605	518	461
Fixed Assets	576	586	452
Current Assets	3m	3m	2m

Rentright Ltd
11 Warren Yard, Milton Keynes, MK12 5NW
Tel: 0870-7669056
E-mail: info@rentright.co.uk
Website: http://www.rentright.co.uk
Directors: A. Crow (Grp Chief Exec), C. Courtis (Comm)
Registration no: 05245205 **Date established:** 2004
Turnover: Up to £250,000 **No.of Employees:** 1 - 10 **Product Groups:** 80

Rig Energy Recruit
Exchange House Midsummer Boulevard, Milton Keynes, MK9 2EA
Tel: 01908-255966 **Fax:** 01908-255573
E-mail: info@rigenergy.co.uk
Website: http://www.rigenergy.co.uk
Directors: A. Langley (MD)
Immediate Holding Company: BAKER SMALL LEGAL SERVICES LTD
Registration no: 05261430 **Date established:** 2010
Turnover: £500,000 - £1m **No.of Employees:** 11 - 20 **Product Groups:** 80

Date of Accounts	Feb 11
Sales Turnover	82
Pre Tax Profit/Loss	-14
Working Capital	-20
Fixed Assets	6
Current Assets	16
Current Liabilities	30

Riskex Ltd
Sheep Lane, Milton Keynes, MK17 9HD
Tel: 0845-8800970
E-mail: sales@riskex.co.uk
Website: http://www.riskex.co.uk
Managers: J. Sharp (Develop Mgr), M. Fensham (Nat Sales Mgr), T. Phelps (Admin Off)
Registration no: 05174302 **Date established:** 1993
No.of Employees: 21 - 50 **Product Groups:** 44

Date of Accounts	Mar 08	Mar 07	Mar 06
Working Capital	24	21	12
Fixed Assets	3	1	1
Current Assets	66	40	12
Current Liabilities	41	19	N/A
Total Share Capital	2	2	2

Rockwell Automation Ltd (a division of Rockwell International Company)
Pitfield Kiln Farm, Milton Keynes, MK11 3DR
Tel: 01908-838800 **Fax:** 01908-261917
E-mail: dmolloy@ra.rockwell.com
Website: http://www.ra.rockwell.com
Bank(s): Barclays
Directors: D. Molloy (Sales)
Managers: B. Watson (Fin Mgr), T. Doyle (Personnel), C. Grasso (Purch Mgr)
Ultimate Holding Company: ROCKWELL AUTOMATION INC (USA)
Immediate Holding Company: FT TECHNOLOGY LIMITED
Registration no: 00947912 **VAT No.:** GB 111 5095 63
Date established: 1969 **Turnover:** £20m - £50m
No.of Employees: 101 - 250 **Product Groups:** 37, 38

Date of Accounts	Sep 11	Sep 10	Sep 09
Sales Turnover	77m	44m	17m
Pre Tax Profit/Loss	8m	6m	5m
Working Capital	9m	25m	19m
Fixed Assets	54m	966	1m
Current Assets	52m	35m	41m
Current Liabilities	8m	5m	7m

Rockwood Lithium (UK) Ltd
Denbigh Road Bletchley, Milton Keynes, MK1 1PB
Tel: 01908-649333 **Fax:** 01908-373939
E-mail: ukinfo@chemetall.com
Website: http://www.chemetall.com
Bank(s): Barclays
Directors: R. Rydings (Fin)
Managers: J. Schoelzel-blake (Personnel), C. Zabinski (Mktg Serv Mgr), G. Higgins (Tech Serv Mgr), S. Stanley (Purch Mgr)
Ultimate Holding Company: ROCKWOOD HOLDINGS INC (USA)
Immediate Holding Company: CHEMETALL SPECIALITY CHEMICALS LIMITED
Registration no: 01851869 **VAT No.:** GB 321 4482 86
Date established: 1984 **Turnover:** Up to £250,000
No.of Employees: 21 - 50 **Product Groups:** 17, 27, 31, 32, 34, 38, 39, 42, 48, 66

Date of Accounts	Dec 11	Dec 10	Dec 09
Sales Turnover	240	240	240
Pre Tax Profit/Loss	27	30	28
Working Capital	1m	1m	1m
Current Assets	2m	1m	1m
Current Liabilities	7	8	8

Rohan Designs Ltd
30 Maryland Road Tongwell, Milton Keynes, MK15 8HN
Tel: 01908-517900 **Fax:** 01908-211209
E-mail: post@rohan.co.uk
Website: http://www.rohan.co.uk
Bank(s): Bank of Scotland
Directors: C. Fisher (Ch), I. Palmer (Pers), M. Willison (Tech Serv), P. Parkinson (Fin)
Managers: P. Rothwell (Mktg Serv Mgr), G. Donaldson
Ultimate Holding Company: ROHAN GROUP LIMITED
Immediate Holding Company: ROHAN DESIGNS LIMITED
Registration no: 01567549 **VAT No.:** GB 679 0643 01
Date established: 1981 **Turnover:** £10m - £20m
No.of Employees: 51 - 100 **Product Groups:** 22, 24

Date of Accounts	Jan 11	Jun 10	Jun 09
Sales Turnover	14m	18m	16m
Pre Tax Profit/Loss	374	368	4m
Working Capital	791	1m	1m
Fixed Assets	2m	1m	1m
Current Assets	6m	5m	4m
Current Liabilities	4m	2m	1m

Russetts Developments Ltd
27 Burners Lane Kiln Farm, Milton Keynes, MK11 3HA
Tel: 08707-702800 **Fax:** 08707-702801
E-mail: info@russetts.co.uk
Website: http://www.russetts.co.uk
Bank(s): Lloyds TSB Bank plc
Directors: M. Leask (Fin)
Managers: D. Leask (Sales Prom Mgr)
Immediate Holding Company: RUSSETTS DEVELOPMENTS LIMITED
Registration no: 01659159 **VAT No.:** GB 382 1164 67
Date established: 1982 **Turnover:** £2m - £5m **No.of Employees:** 11 - 20
Product Groups: 23, 29, 30, 31, 35, 66

Date of Accounts	Sep 11	Sep 10	Sep 09
Working Capital	596	576	591
Fixed Assets	32	44	64
Current Assets	886	861	816

G Ryder & Co. Ltd
Denbigh Road Bletchley, Milton Keynes, MK1 1DG
Tel: 01908-375524 **Fax:** 01908-373658
E-mail: sales@ryderbox.co.uk
Website: http://www.ryderbox.co.uk
Bank(s): HSBC
Directors: C. Gear (Co Sec), D. Silverton (Fin), J. Discombe (MD)
Managers: A. Ingram (Sales & Mktg Mg)
Ultimate Holding Company: FEVORE LIMITED
Immediate Holding Company: G RYDER & CO.,LIMITED
Registration no: 00294244 **VAT No.:** GB 119 5792 41
Date established: 1934 **Turnover:** £1m - £2m **No.of Employees:** 21 - 50
Product Groups: 26, 27, 28, 49

Date of Accounts	Feb 12	Feb 11	Feb 10
Sales Turnover	1m	1m	1m
Pre Tax Profit/Loss	19	-138	29
Working Capital	376	427	457
Fixed Assets	7	11	15
Current Assets	542	583	661
Current Liabilities	64	42	89

Ryeland Tool Makers
18 Barton Road Bletchley, Milton Keynes, MK2 3JJ
Tel: 01908-647746 **Fax:** 01908-270236
E-mail: info@ryelandtoolmakers.co.uk
Website: http://www.mkp.co.uk
Bank(s): HSBC
Managers: R. Cannon (Mgr)
Immediate Holding Company: MILTON KEYNES PRESSINGS LTD
VAT No.: GB 198 5231 17 **Turnover:** £250,000 - £500,000
No.of Employees: 11 - 20 **Product Groups:** 46, 47

S S White Technologies UK Ltd
19 Heathfield Stacey Bushes, Milton Keynes, MK12 6HP
Tel: 01908-525120 **Fax:** 01908-319967
E-mail: insales@sswhite.co.uk
Website: http://www.sswhite.co.uk
Bank(s): Lloyds TSB Bank plc
Managers: S. Grimes (Chief Mgr)
Immediate Holding Company: S.S. WHITE TECHNOLOGIES UK LIMITED
Registration no: 06811482 **VAT No.:** GB 946 2689 79
Date established: 2009 **Turnover:** £1m - £2m **No.of Employees:** 11 - 20
Product Groups: 35, 45

Date of Accounts	Jul 11	Jul 10
Working Capital	244	159
Fixed Assets	43	50
Current Assets	573	449

Sansetsu UK Ltd
Bradbourne Drive Tilbrook, Milton Keynes, MK7 8AT
Tel: 01908-644660 **Fax:** 01908-367313
E-mail: info@sansetsu.co.uk
Website: http://www.sansetsu.co.uk
Bank(s): Natwest
Directors: T. Ota (Dir), I. McIlwee (Sales)
Managers: L. Williams (Personnel), S. Parmanand (Purch Mgr), D. Newlove
Immediate Holding Company: SANSETSU (U.K.) LIMITED
Registration no: 01400365 **VAT No.:** GB 322 4319 91
Date established: 1978 **Turnover:** £10m - £20m
No.of Employees: 101 - 250 **Product Groups:** 30

Date of Accounts	Dec 11	Dec 10	Dec 09
Sales Turnover	20m	23m	30m
Pre Tax Profit/Loss	-570	-2m	580
Working Capital	-2m	-2m	-2m
Fixed Assets	5m	5m	7m
Current Assets	4m	8m	8m
Current Liabilities	3m	4m	4m

Scania (Great Britain) Ltd
Delaware Drive Tongwell, Milton Keynes, MK15 8HB
Tel: 01908-210210 **Fax:** 01908-215040
E-mail: steve.wager@scania.com
Website: http://www.scania.co.uk
Bank(s): Barclays
Directors: W. Campbell (Fin), U. Perkins (Non Exec), L. Ohlsson-Leijon (Non Exec), S. Wager (Fin), P. Hirons (Supp), G. Lofgren (Ch), F. Andrew (Non Exec), D. Hoij (MD), J. Phillips (Pers)
Managers: C. Love (Mktg Serv Mgr), D. Brooks (I.T. Exec)
Ultimate Holding Company: SCANIA AB (SWEDEN)
Immediate Holding Company: SCANIA (GREAT BRITAIN) LIMITED
Registration no: 00831017 **Date established:** 1964
Turnover: £250m - £500m **No.of Employees:** 1501 & over
Product Groups: 39, 40, 68

Date of Accounts	Dec 10	Dec 09	Dec 08
Sales Turnover	472m	462m	684m
Pre Tax Profit/Loss	27m	21m	46m
Working Capital	31m	18m	40m
Fixed Assets	71m	67m	82m
Current Assets	110m	110m	136m
Current Liabilities	50m	62m	61m

Scrivens Ltd
172 Midsummer Arcade Secklow Gate East, Milton Keynes, MK9 3BA
Tel: 01908-606520
E-mail: info@scrivens.co.uk
Website: http://www.scrivens.co.uk
Ultimate Holding Company: SEAMAP LIMITED
Immediate Holding Company: SCRIVENS LIMITED
Registration no: 00377588 **Date established:** 1942
No.of Employees: 1 - 10 **Product Groups:** 37, 38, 65

Date of Accounts	Oct 10	Oct 11	Oct 08
Sales Turnover	25m	24m	33m
Pre Tax Profit/Loss	2m	2m	2m
Working Capital	-9m	-7m	-9m
Fixed Assets	11m	11m	11m
Current Assets	2m	3m	2m
Current Liabilities	2m	1m	2m

Search Optimize
161 Redbridge Stantonbury, Milton Keynes, MK14 6DL
Tel: 01908-311619 **Fax:** 01908-483939
E-mail: siteoptimise@gmail.com
Website: http://www.searchoptimize.co.uk
Managers: M. Ncube (Mgr)
Immediate Holding Company: ACAMO ACCESSORIES LIMITED
Registration no: 06360349 **Date established:** 2012
Turnover: Up to £250,000 **No.of Employees:** 1 - 10 **Product Groups:** 44

Seat UK
Delaware Drive Yeomans Drive, Blakelands, Milton Keynes, MK14 5AN
Tel: 01908-548444 **Fax:** 01908-548040
E-mail: sales@seat.co.uk
Website: http://www.seat.co.uk
Directors: P. Wyhinny (MD)
Managers: K. Cooper, M. Heath
Registration no: 00659059 **Date established:** 1988
No.of Employees: 501 - 1000 **Product Groups:** 68

Sekisui Jushi Strapping BV
N Y K Building Bradbourne Drive, Tilbrook, Milton Keynes, MK7 8BN
Tel: 01908-274464 **Fax:** 01908-274465
E-mail: sales@sekisui-jushi.co.uk
Website: http://www.sjc-strapping.com
Managers: T. Clift (Sales Prom Mgr)
Immediate Holding Company: SEKISUI JUSHI B.V.
Registration no: FC015518 **Date established:** 1990
Turnover: £10m - £20m **No.of Employees:** 1 - 10 **Product Groups:** 38, 42

Shanks
Dunedin House Auckland Park, Mount Farm, Milton Keynes, MK1 1BU
Tel: 01908-650 650 **Fax:** 01604-705554
E-mail: info@shanks.co.uk
Website: http://www.shanks.co.uk
Managers: G. Isaac (Mgr)
Immediate Holding Company: Shanks Ltd
Registration no: 02393309 **No.of Employees:** 1 - 10 **Product Groups:** 54

Shepherd Interiors
Unit 4 10 First Avenue, Bletchley, Milton Keynes, MK1 1DN
Tel: 01908-644688 **Fax:** 01908-646606
E-mail: info@rgnsltd.co.uk
Website: http://www.shepherdinteriors.co.uk
Directors: P. Shepherd (Sales), R. Shepherd (Dir), L. Castelli (Co Sec)
Immediate Holding Company: SHEPHERD INTERIORS LTD
Registration no: 05852381 **Date established:** 2006
Turnover: £500,000 - £1m **No.of Employees:** 1 - 10 **Product Groups:** 24, 25, 26, 29, 33, 35, 52, 84

Date of Accounts	Jun 08
Working Capital	39
Fixed Assets	18
Current Assets	478
Current Liabilities	439

Signs Express Milton Keynes
95 Alston Drive Bradwell Abbey, Milton Keynes, MK13 9HF
Tel: 01908-221330 **Fax:** 01908-221227
E-mail: miltonkeynes@signsexpress.co.uk
Website: http://www.signsexpress.co.uk
Managers: S. Harrison (Mgr)
Immediate Holding Company: SIGNS EXPRESS LTD
Registration no: 02375913 **No.of Employees:** 1 - 10 **Product Groups:** 30, 39, 40, 80, 81, 84

Simply Radiators
Centurion Court Brick Close, Kiln Farm, Milton Keynes, MK11 3JB
Tel: 01908-566906 **Fax:** 01908-562967
E-mail: sales@simplyradiators.co.uk
Website: http://www.simplyradiators.co.uk
Managers: T. Trott (Sales Prom Mgr)
Immediate Holding Company: SIMPLY RADIATORS LIMITED
Registration no: 05415085 **Date established:** 2005
Turnover: £250,000 - £500,000 **No.of Employees:** 1 - 10
Product Groups: 40, 66

Date of Accounts	Apr 11	Apr 10	Apr 09
Sales Turnover	361	336	267
Pre Tax Profit/Loss	-0	19	-17
Working Capital	-21	-18	-21
Fixed Assets	3	4	5
Current Assets	130	132	125
Current Liabilities	30	17	30

S J D Associates Ltd
Unit 6 Mount Avenue Mount Farm, Bletchley, Milton Keynes, MK1 1LS
Tel: 01908-632488 **Fax:** 01908-643244
E-mail: enquiries@sjd-electrical.co.uk
Website: http://www.sjd-electrical.co.uk
Directors: R. Devine (Dir)
Immediate Holding Company: S.J.D. ASSOCIATES LIMITED
Registration no: 03237560 **Date established:** 1996
Turnover: £250,000 - £500,000 **No.of Employees:** 11 - 20
Product Groups: 37, 40, 48, 52, 67, 84

Date of Accounts	Dec 11	Dec 11	Sep 11
Working Capital	73	73	73
Fixed Assets	13	13	13
Current Assets	234	234	234
Current Liabilities	133	133	133

S M C Pneumatics
Vincent Avenue Crownhill, Milton Keynes, MK8 0AN
Tel: 01908-563888 **Fax:** 01908-561185
E-mail: sales@smcpneumatics.co.uk
Website: http://www.smcpneumatics.co.uk
Directors: Y. Takada (Pres), P. Holland (Fin)
Managers: P. Humpheys, H. Walker (Personnel), P. Noble
Ultimate Holding Company: S M C Corporation (Japan)
Immediate Holding Company: SMC PNEUMATICS (U.K.) LIMITED
Registration no: 01352967 **Date established:** 1978
Turnover: £20m - £50m **No.of Employees:** 251 - 500 **Product Groups:** 38

Date of Accounts	Mar 11	Mar 10	Mar 09
Sales Turnover	42m	29m	29m
Pre Tax Profit/Loss	7m	1m	165
Working Capital	32m	26m	25m
Fixed Assets	12m	12m	13m
Current Assets	45m	35m	31m
Current Liabilities	5m	2m	2m

Sonatest Ltd
Head Office Dickens Road, Old Wolverton, Milton Keynes, MK12 5QQ
Tel: 01908-316345 **Fax:** 01908-321323
E-mail: sales@sonatest.com
Website: http://www.sonatest.com
Bank(s): National Westminster Bank Plc
Directors: W. Woodhead (MD)
Ultimate Holding Company: SONATEST NDE LIMITED
Immediate Holding Company: SONATEST NDE LIMITED
Registration no: 01961000 **Date established:** 1985
Turnover: £10m - £20m **No.of Employees:** 21 - 50 **Product Groups:** 37, 38, 39, 42, 45, 85

Date of Accounts	Dec 11	Dec 10	Dec 09
Sales Turnover	10m	16m	13m
Pre Tax Profit/Loss	3m	2m	-112
Working Capital	6m	3m	2m
Fixed Assets	896	1m	1m
Current Assets	7m	7m	7m
Current Liabilities	802	2m	2m

Stodec Products Ltd
8 James Way Bletchley, Milton Keynes, MK1 1SU
Tel: 01908-270011 **Fax:** 01908-270022
E-mail: mike@stodec.co.uk
Website: http://www.stodec.com
Directors: M. Daldry (Dir)
Immediate Holding Company: STODEC PRODUCTS LIMITED
Registration no: 02067943 **VAT No.:** GB 403 9901 61
Date established: 1986 **Turnover:** £10m - £20m **No.of Employees:** 1 - 10
Product Groups: 26, 35, 36, 45

Date of Accounts	May 11	May 10	May 09
Working Capital	307	307	382
Fixed Assets	232	241	232
Current Assets	608	658	903

Storage Direct
Garamonde Drive Wymbush, Milton Keynes, MK8 8ND
Tel: 0800-592963 **Fax:** 01908-263526
Website: http://www.storagedirect.co.uk
Managers: S. Perry (Mktg Serv Mgr), S. Perry (Mktg Serv Mgr)
Ultimate Holding Company: CHAMONIX II LP (UNITED KINGDOM)
Immediate Holding Company: APEX SPACE SOLUTIONS LIMITED
Date established: 2010 **No.of Employees:** 101 - 250 **Product Groups:** 07, 22, 23, 24, 25, 26, 27, 29, 30, 32, 33, 35, 36, 38, 39, 40, 41, 42, 44, 45, 48, 49, 63, 64, 66, 67, 68, 72, 77, 80, 84

Date of Accounts	Dec 11
Sales Turnover	18m
Pre Tax Profit/Loss	-1m
Working Capital	-44
Fixed Assets	6m
Current Assets	6m
Current Liabilities	3m

Sudpack UK Ltd
40 High Park Drive Wolverton Mill, Milton Keynes, MK12 5TT
Tel: 01908-525720 **Fax:** 01908-525721
E-mail: uk@suedpack.com
Website: http://www.suedpack.com
Directors: S. Biddiscombe (Sales)
Ultimate Holding Company: SUDPACK EUROPE (SWITZERLAND)
Immediate Holding Company: SUDPACK UK LIMITED
Registration no: 00910628 **VAT No.:** GB 302 3109 29
Date established: 1967 **Turnover:** £10m - £20m **No.of Employees:** 1 - 10
Product Groups: 30

Date of Accounts	Dec 11	Dec 10	Dec 09
Sales Turnover	13m	12m	10m
Pre Tax Profit/Loss	475	650	329
Working Capital	2m	2m	1m
Fixed Assets	88	101	104
Current Assets	4m	4m	3m
Current Liabilities	792	1m	780

Sulzer Pumps
Challenge House Sherwood Drive, Bletchley, Milton Keynes, MK3 6DP
Tel: 01908-632775 **Fax:** 01908-274957
E-mail: tim.francis@sulzer.com
Website: http://www.sulzerpumps.com
Managers: T. Francis (Sales Prom Mgr)
Date established: 2004 **No.of Employees:** 1 - 10 **Product Groups:** 40

T H K UK
1 Harrison Close Knowlhill, Milton Keynes, MK5 8PA
Tel: 01908-303050 **Fax:** 01908-303070
E-mail: sales.uk@thk.com
Website: http://www.thk.com
Managers: D. Gregory (Mktg Serv Mgr), A. Sim (District Mgr)
Ultimate Holding Company: THK , Ltd
Immediate Holding Company: THK GmbH
Registration no: FC015610 **Date established:** 1990
Turnover: £10m - £20m **No.of Employees:** 11 - 20 **Product Groups:** 35, 38, 46

Technical Software Consultants Ltd
6 Mill Square Wolverton Mill, Milton Keynes, MK12 5RB
Tel: 01908-317444 **Fax:** 01908-220959
E-mail: info@tscinspectionsystems.com
Website: http://www.tscinspectionsystems.com
Directors: D. Topp (MD)
Immediate Holding Company: TECHNICAL SOFTWARE CONSULTANTS LIMITED
Registration no: 01787682 **VAT No.:** GB 417 8475 26
Date established: 1984 **Turnover:** £2m - £5m **No.of Employees:** 11 - 20
Product Groups: 38, 85

Date of Accounts	Dec 11	Dec 10	Dec 09
Working Capital	3m	2m	1m
Fixed Assets	39	61	44
Current Assets	4m	3m	2m

Terrapin Ltd
Bond Avenue Bletchley, Milton Keynes, MK1 1JJ
Tel: 0115-907 2700 **Fax:** 0115-972 2203
E-mail: a.day@terrapin-ltd.co.uk
Website: http://www.terrapin-ltd.co.uk
Bank(s): Lloyds TSB Bank plc
Directors: N. Whitehouse (Ch), P. Howlett-White (Dir), G. Orr (Ch & MD), R. Russo (Fab), A. Day (MD), A. Allen (Fin), M. Holiday (Co Sec)
Managers: V. Cressey, R. Dunn (Purch Mgr), D. McColgan (Sales Prom Mgr)
Ultimate Holding Company: BOND ESTATES HOLDINGS LIMITED
Immediate Holding Company: TERRAPIN LIMITED
Registration no: 00687831 **Date established:** 1961 **Turnover:** £5m - £10m
No.of Employees: 21 - 50 **Product Groups:** 25, 35, 51, 52, 84

Date of Accounts	Sep 07	Sep 08	Sep 09
Sales Turnover	27m	17m	12m
Pre Tax Profit/Loss	908	-746	-2m
Working Capital	7m	961	223
Fixed Assets	2m	3m	2m
Current Assets	13m	5m	4m
Current Liabilities	4m	2m	2m

Thyssenkrupp Aerospace Ltd
Aviation House Garamonde Drive, Wymbush, Milton Keynes, MK8 8DF
Tel: 01908-556550
E-mail: sales@thyssenkrupp.com
Website: http://www.thyssenkrupp.com
Directors: J. Ferguson (Dir)
No.of Employees: 101 - 250 **Product Groups:** 34, 36

TopDrill Ltd
14 Darin Court Crownhill, Milton Keynes, MK8 0AD
Tel: 01908-666606 **Fax:** 01908-672042
E-mail: info@topdrill.co.uk
Website: http://www.topdrill.co.uk
Directors: C. Webb (MD)
Immediate Holding Company: TOPDRILL LTD
Registration no: 05930622 **Date established:** 2006
No.of Employees: 1 - 10 **Product Groups:** 45, 51, 85

Date of Accounts	Sep 11	Sep 10	Sep 09
Working Capital	188	-2	20
Fixed Assets	154	78	47
Current Assets	514	104	106

T-Systems
Futura House Bradbourne Drive, Tilbrook, Milton Keynes, MK7 8AZ
Tel: 0800-036 4656 **Fax:** 0870-121 2751
E-mail: info@t-systems.com
Website: http://www.t-systems.co.uk
Directors: R. Tracey (MD)
Ultimate Holding Company: DEUTSCHE TELEKOM AKTIENGESELLSCHAFT (GERMANY)
Immediate Holding Company: T-SYSTEMS TMT LIMITED
Registration no: 01371338 **Date established:** 1978
Turnover: £20m - £50m **No.of Employees:** 1 - 10 **Product Groups:** 44

Date of Accounts	Dec 10	Dec 09	Dec 08
Sales Turnover	369m	331m	276m
Pre Tax Profit/Loss	-10m	-23m	-50m
Working Capital	28m	8m	-2m
Fixed Assets	96m	99m	115m
Current Assets	196m	111m	95m
Current Liabilities	102m	54m	36m

U T C Fire & Security
8 Newmarket Court Kingston, Milton Keynes, MK10 0AQ
Tel: 01908-281981 **Fax:** 01908-282554
Website: http://www.ziton.com
Bank(s): Bank of Scotland
Managers: L. Dorrian (Sales Admin)
Ultimate Holding Company: GENERAL ELECTRIC COMPANY (USA)
Immediate Holding Company: UTC FIRE & SECURITY (LEGACY 2011) LIMITED
Registration no: 01386946 **VAT No.:** GB 209 8014 73
Date established: 1978 **Turnover:** £2m - £5m **No.of Employees:** 21 - 50
Product Groups: 38, 40

Date of Accounts	Dec 10	Dec 09	Dec 08
Sales Turnover	7m	7	9m
Pre Tax Profit/Loss	1m	1	4m
Working Capital	4m	2	4m
Fixed Assets	3m	3	7m
Current Assets	5m	7	14m
Current Liabilities	473	1	2m

Unifine Food & Bake Ingredients
4-5 Centurion Court Brick Close, Kiln Farm, Milton Keynes, MK11 3JB
Tel: 01908-260610 **Fax:** 01908-263213
E-mail: sales@unifine.uk.com
Website: http://www.unifine-fbi.co.uk
Managers: P. Foster (Mgr), P. Stanley (Mgr)
Immediate Holding Company: DUTCH
Registration no: 00110556 **Date established:** 2006
Turnover: £10m - £20m **No.of Employees:** 11 - 20 **Product Groups:** 20, 62

V S M Abrasives Ltd
20-21 Heathfield Stacey Bushes, Milton Keynes, MK12 6HP
Tel: 01908-310207 **Fax:** 01908-310208
E-mail: sales@vsm.co.uk
Website: http://www.vsm.co.uk
Bank(s): National Westminster Bank Plc
Directors: A. Lithgoe (MD)
Managers: I. Cooke, S. Mahoney (Fin Mgr)
Ultimate Holding Company: VEREINIGTE SCHMIRGEL & MASCHINEN - FABRI
Immediate Holding Company: VSM ABRASIVES LIMITED
Registration no: 00558460 **Date established:** 1955 **Turnover:** £2m - £5m
No.of Employees: 21 - 50 **Product Groups:** 33

Date of Accounts	Dec 11	Dec 10	Dec 09
Working Capital	2m	1m	1m
Fixed Assets	123	82	111
Current Assets	3m	2m	2m

Vass Textile Group
23 Carters Lane Kiln Farm, Milton Keynes, MK11 3HL
Tel: 01908-563804 **Fax:** 01908-563805
E-mail: mail@vass-uk.com
Website: http://www.vass-uk.com
Directors: C. Hvass (MD), M. Hvass (Fin)
Immediate Holding Company: OCEAN RAINWEAR LIMITED
Registration no: 04011112 **Date established:** 2000
No.of Employees: 1 - 10 **Product Groups:** 24, 40, 63

Date of Accounts	May 11	May 10	May 09
Working Capital	133	120	164
Fixed Assets	39	55	47
Current Assets	258	291	306

Walkergreenbank plc
Bradbourne Drive Tilbrook, Milton Keynes, MK7 8BE
Tel: 01908-658000 **Fax:** 0870-830 0364
E-mail: john_sach@walkergreenbank.com
Website: http://www.walkergreenbank.com
Bank(s): Barclays
Directors: J. Sach (Grp Chief Exec), A. Dix (Fin)
Managers: J. Smith (Tech Serv Mgr), L. Scott (Personnel)
Immediate Holding Company: WALKER GREENBANK PLC.
Registration no: 00061880 **VAT No.:** GB 419 0876 36
Date established: 1999 **Turnover:** £50m - £75m
No.of Employees: 51 - 100 **Product Groups:** 23, 25, 27, 30, 52, 63

Date of Accounts	Jan 12	Jan 11	Jan 10
Sales Turnover	74m	69m	60m
Pre Tax Profit/Loss	5m	4m	2m
Working Capital	14m	13m	10m
Fixed Assets	18m	19m	20m
Current Assets	32m	32m	26m
Current Liabilities	7m	8m	8m

Web Labs Ltd
24 Wandsworth Place, Milton Keynes, MK13 8BT
Tel: 01525-374859
E-mail: info@web-labs.co.uk
Website: http://www.web-labs.co.uk
Registration no: 4290334 **Date established:** 2001
Turnover: £500,000 - £1m **No.of Employees:** 11 - 20 **Product Groups:** 44

Date of Accounts	Sep 08	Sep 07	Sep 06
Working Capital	244	271	277
Fixed Assets	9	11	6
Current Assets	399	624	461
Current Liabilities	155	353	183

Weights
Unit A5 Greenway Business Park Winslow Road, Great Horwood, Milton Keynes, MK17 0NP
Tel: 01296-712171 **Fax:** 01296-712122
E-mail: sales@weights.uk.com
Website: http://www.weights.uk.com
Directors: J. Fenton (Prop)
No.of Employees: 1 - 10 **Product Groups:** 35, 38, 67, 85

John Weiss & Son Ltd
89 Alston Drive Bradwell Abbey, Milton Keynes, MK13 9HF
Tel: 01908-318017 **Fax:** 01908-318708
E-mail: sales@johnweiss.com
Website: http://www.johnweiss.com
Directors: S. Jacobs (Co Sec), W. Inabnit (MD)
Ultimate Holding Company: HAAG-STREIT HOLDING AG (SWITZERLAND)
Immediate Holding Company: JOHN WEISS & SON,LIMITED
Registration no: 00062893 **VAT No.:** GB 232 9448 56
Date established: 1999 **Turnover:** £2m - £5m **No.of Employees:** 11 - 20
Product Groups: 30, 38

Date of Accounts	Dec 11	Dec 10	Dec 09
Sales Turnover	2m	2m	2m
Pre Tax Profit/Loss	51	-86	100
Working Capital	771	716	793
Fixed Assets	19	25	35
Current Assets	1m	1m	1m
Current Liabilities	58	58	64

The Welders Warehouse Ltd
17 London Road, Milton Keynes, MK5 8AB
Tel: 0845-8994400 **Fax:** 0870-7518096
E-mail: help@thewelderswarehouse.com
Website: http://www.thewelderswarehouse.com
Directors: G. Rhoades (Dir)
Registration no: 4614966 **Date established:** 1993
Turnover: £250,000 - £500,000 **No.of Employees:** 1 - 10
Product Groups: 46, 67

Welwin Engineering Ltd
Church Green Road Bletchley, Milton Keynes, MK3 6BY
Tel: 01908-649700 **Fax:** 01908-649710
E-mail: swinch@welwin.freeserve.co.uk
Website: http://www.welwin.freeserve.co.uk
Directors: S. Winch (Dir)
VAT No.: GB 600 7844 59 **Date established:** 1969
Turnover: Up to £250,000 **No.of Employees:** 1 - 10 **Product Groups:** 46, 47

Gea Westfalia Seperator UK Ltd
Old Wolverton Road Old Wolverton, Milton Keynes, MK12 5PY
Tel: 01908-576500 **Fax:** 08708-305515
E-mail: barry.dumble@gea-group.com
Website: http://www.wsgb.co.uk
Bank(s): Barclays, Milton Keynes
Directors: S. Rehnert (Ch), V. Spitaleri (MD), N. Preston (Co Sec), N. Preston (Dir), B. Dumble (MD)
Ultimate Holding Company: GEA GROUP AG (GERMANY)
Immediate Holding Company: GEA MECHANICAL EQUIPMENT UK LIMITED
Registration no: 00611624 **VAT No.:** GB 119 1291 83
Date established: 1958 **Turnover:** £5m - £10m **No.of Employees:** 21 - 50
Product Groups: 36, 40, 41

Date of Accounts	Dec 10	Dec 09	Dec 08
Sales Turnover	9m	11m	10m
Pre Tax Profit/Loss	656	655	408
Working Capital	1m	5m	3m
Fixed Assets	4m	265	2m
Current Assets	5m	10m	8m
Current Liabilities	1m	1m	2m

White Clarke Group
White Clarke House Woodlands Business Park 4 Breckland, Linford Wood, Milton Keynes, MK14 6FG
Tel: 01908-576699 **Fax:** 01582-863660
E-mail: info@whiteclarkegroup.com
Website: http://www.whiteclarkegroup.com
Directors: P. Scanlon (Fin), P. Halliday (Sales), T. Puddicombe (Co Sec)
Managers: K. Day (Personnel), P. Arban (Tech Serv Mgr), A. Lepp (Mktg Serv Mgr)
Ultimate Holding Company: WHITE CLARKE TECHNOLOGIES LIMITED
Immediate Holding Company: NETWORK MANAGEMENT SERVICES UK LIMITED
Registration no: 02048558 **Date established:** 1986
No.of Employees: 101 - 250 **Product Groups:** 44

Willards Ltd
47 Newport Road New Bradwell, Milton Keynes, MK13 0AQ
Tel: 01908-225353 **Fax:** 01908-225354
E-mail: info@willards.co.uk
Website: http://www.willards.co.uk
Directors: L. Willard (Fin), T. Ray (MD)
Immediate Holding Company: WILLARDS LIMITED
Registration no: 04276075 **Date established:** 2001
No.of Employees: 1 - 10 **Product Groups:** 36, 39, 40

Date of Accounts	Mar 12	Mar 11	Mar 09
Working Capital	-5	-7	10
Fixed Assets	9	12	21
Current Assets	18	10	28

Yamaha Music Europe Ltd
Sherbourne Drive Tilbrook, Milton Keynes, MK7 8BL
Tel: 01908-366700 **Fax:** 01908-368872
E-mail: info@yamaha-music.co.uk
Website: http://www.yamaha-music.co.uk
Managers: E. McAllister
Ultimate Holding Company: YAMAHA CORPORATION (JAPAN)
Immediate Holding Company: YAMAHA MUSIC UK LIMITED
Registration no: 00911811 **Date established:** 1967
Turnover: £50m - £75m **No.of Employees:** 51 - 100 **Product Groups:** 65

Date of Accounts	Mar 09	Mar 08	Mar 07
Sales Turnover	65m	62m	62m
Pre Tax Profit/Loss	2m	4m	3m
Working Capital	17m	18m	18m
Fixed Assets	6m	6m	6m
Current Assets	22m	25m	24m
Current Liabilities	2m	3m	3m

Yaskawa Europe
Unit 3 Centurion Court Brick Close, Kiln Farm, Milton Keynes, MK11 3JB
Tel: 01908-565874 **Fax:** 01908-565938
E-mail: paul.unger@yaskawa.eu.com
Website: http://www.yaskawa.eu.com
Managers: P. Unger (Serv Mgr)
No.of Employees: 1 - 10 **Product Groups:** 37, 45

Z Design UK Ltd
33 White Alder Stacey Bushes, Milton Keynes, MK12 6HE
Tel: 01908-314914
E-mail: a.zarur@zdesignuk.com
Website: http://www.zdesign.com
Directors: A. Zarur (MD)
Immediate Holding Company: Z DESIGN UK LIMITED
Registration no: 05325116 **Date established:** 2005
Turnover: Up to £250,000 **No.of Employees:** 1 - 10 **Product Groups:** 81

Date of Accounts	Jan 11	Jan 10	Jan 09
Sales Turnover	14	8	6
Pre Tax Profit/Loss	-1	1	-1
Working Capital	-0	-0	N/A
Fixed Assets	N/A	1	1

Newport Pagnell

Access Security
9 Auden Close, Newport Pagnell, MK16 8TA
Tel: 01908-613326
E-mail: accesssecure@btinternet.com
Website: http://www.accesssecuritymk.co.uk/
Directors: R. Self (Prop)
No.of Employees: 1 - 10 **Product Groups:** 37, 38, 40, 52, 67, 81

Date of Accounts	Dec 08	Dec 07	Mar 11
Sales Turnover	19m	21m	10m
Pre Tax Profit/Loss	698	515	-210
Working Capital	1m	451	-281
Fixed Assets	194	570	78
Current Assets	4m	3m	3m
Current Liabilities	2m	2m	3m

Aston Martin Works
Tickford Street, Newport Pagnell, MK16 9AN
Tel: 01908-619264 **Fax:** 01908-216439
E-mail: ubez@astonmartin.com
Website: http://www.astonmartin.com
Bank(s): HSBC Bank plc

Directors: M. Marecki (Co Sec)
Managers: G. Darby (Chief Mgr), M. Walsh (Comptroller)
Ultimate Holding Company: ASTON MARTIN HOLDINGS (UK) LIMITED
Immediate Holding Company: ASTON MARTIN LAGONDA LIMITED
Registration no: 01199255 **VAT No.:** GB 246 4257 57
Date established: 1975 **Turnover:** £250m - £500m
No.of Employees: 51 - 100 **Product Groups:** 39

Date of Accounts	Dec 11	Dec 10	Dec 09
Sales Turnover	495m	467m	328m
Pre Tax Profit/Loss	-4m	32m	-2m
Working Capital	36m	38m	41m
Fixed Assets	184m	190m	159m
Current Assets	160m	237m	211m
Current Liabilities	106m	46m	110m

BI Worldwide

1 Vantage Court Tickford Street, Newport Pagnell, MK16 9EZ
Tel: 01908-214700 **Fax:** 01908-214777
E-mail: enquiries@eu.biworldwide.com
Website: http://www.biworldwide.com/en-uk
Bank(s): Lloyds TSB Bank Plc
Directors: R. Gibbs (Sales & Mktg), M. Truby (Fin), M. Davies (MD)
Managers: N. Burton Clausen, A. Rush, K. Minto (Personnel)
Ultimate Holding Company: SCHOENECKERS INC (USA)
Immediate Holding Company: BI WORLDWIDE LIMITED
Registration no: 01445905 **Date established:** 1979
Turnover: £10m - £20m **No.of Employees:** 101 - 250
Product Groups: 80, 81

Date of Accounts	Jun 11	Jun 10	Jun 09
Sales Turnover	19m	16m	22m
Pre Tax Profit/Loss	519	-738	-2m
Working Capital	587	-497	287
Fixed Assets	3m	3m	5m
Current Assets	6m	6m	9m
Current Liabilities	4m	4m	5m

Bridge Fuel Injection

1-3 Broad Street, Newport Pagnell, MK16 0AN
Tel: 01908-618815 **Fax:** 01908-216483
Website: http://www.bridgefuelinjection.com
Directors: I. Ledgard (Prop), I. Ledguard (Dir)
Immediate Holding Company: NEWPORT PAGNELL TESTING STATION LIMITED
Registration no: 04620422 **Date established:** 2002
Turnover: Up to £250,000 **No.of Employees:** 1 - 10 **Product Groups:** 40

Date of Accounts	Dec 10	Dec 09	Dec 08
Sales Turnover	N/A	177	155
Pre Tax Profit/Loss	N/A	11	-2
Working Capital	11	-8	-0
Fixed Assets	8	10	11
Current Assets	43	17	13

C L M Fleet Management plc

Corporate House Jenna Way, Interchange Park, Newport Pagnell, MK16 9QB
Tel: 01908-210100 **Fax:** 01908-210102
E-mail: anthony@c-l-m.co.uk
Website: http://www.clm.co.uk
Bank(s): Bank of Scotland
Directors: J. Knight (Fin), A. Hulatt (Dir)
Managers: J. Pett (Sales Prom Mgr), A. Sheppard (Personnel), R. Wentworth-james (Mktg Serv Mgr), C. Miller (Tech Serv Mgr)
Ultimate Holding Company: CLM FLEET MANAGEMENT PLC
Immediate Holding Company: CORPORATE FLEET MANAGEMENT PLC
Registration no: 01431649 **VAT No.:** GB 365 9616 14
Date established: 1979 **Turnover:** £2m - £5m **No.of Employees:** 51 - 100
Product Groups: 82

Date of Accounts	Dec 11	Dec 10	Dec 09
Sales Turnover	5m	28m	27m
Pre Tax Profit/Loss	1	232	210
Working Capital	164	3m	4m
Fixed Assets	N/A	2m	2m
Current Assets	164	7m	7m
Current Liabilities	N/A	1m	622

Castech UK Ltd

Unit 10 Manor Farm Main Road, Astwood, Newport Pagnell, MK16 9JS
Tel: 01234-391973 **Fax:** 01234-391185
E-mail: info@castech.co.uk
Website: http://www.castech.co.uk
Managers: R. Thornton (Sales Prom Mgr)
Immediate Holding Company: CASTECH (U.K.) LIMITED
Registration no: 03171292 **VAT No.:** GB 382 2541 58
Date established: 1996 **No.of Employees:** 1 - 10 **Product Groups:** 30, 34

Date of Accounts	Mar 12	Mar 11	Mar 10
Working Capital	88	75	99
Fixed Assets	6	4	2
Current Assets	206	192	162

Evatron Plastic Enclosures Ltd

Unit 24 Broughton Grounds Broughton, Newport Pagnell, MK16 0HZ
Tel: 01908-675121 **Fax:** 01908-200148
E-mail: info@evatron.com
Website: http://www.evatron.com
Directors: A. Breach (Tech Sales)
Immediate Holding Company: EVATRON LIMITED
Registration no: 05406267 **Date established:** 2005
No.of Employees: 1 - 10 **Product Groups:** 22, 26, 29, 30, 32, 35, 36, 37, 38, 39, 40, 44, 45, 46, 47, 48, 67, 84, 85

Excalibur Furniture Ltd

The Winnowing Barn High Street, Sherington, Newport Pagnell, MK16 9QP
Tel: 01908-327100 **Fax:** 01908-327101
E-mail: sales@excalibur-furniture.com
Website: http://www.excalibur-furniture.com
Directors: M. Keech (Prop)
Immediate Holding Company: EXCALIBUR FURNITURE LTD
Registration no: 03532212 **VAT No.:** 540 2505 86 **Date established:** 1998
Turnover: £2m - £5m **No.of Employees:** 1 - 10 **Product Groups:** 26, 48

Date of Accounts	Mar 11	Mar 10	Mar 09
Working Capital	30	37	19
Fixed Assets	1	N/A	1
Current Assets	150	112	50

Fenco-Aldridge Barton Ltd

Willen Works Willen Road, Newport Pagnell, MK16 0DG
Tel: 01908-614646 **Fax:** 01908-210482
E-mail: shinson@fenco.co.uk
Website: http://www.fenco.co.uk
Directors: S. Hinson (MD)
Immediate Holding Company: FENCO-ALDRIDGE (BARTON) LIMITED
Registration no: 00929023 **Date established:** 1968
Turnover: £500,000 - £1m **No.of Employees:** 1 - 10 **Product Groups:** 31, 36

Date of Accounts	Mar 12	Mar 11	Mar 10
Working Capital	198	197	143
Fixed Assets	175	174	178
Current Assets	420	514	339

H S L Engineering Co.

The Knoll Sherington, Newport Pagnell, MK16 9NZ
Tel: 01908-611869 **Fax:** 01908-211091
Directors: T. Lusted (Ptnr)
Immediate Holding Company: C.J. HAYNES & SON LIMITED
Registration no: 01851918 **Date established:** 1984
No.of Employees: 1 - 10 **Product Groups:** 35

Date of Accounts	Oct 11	Oct 10	Oct 09
Working Capital	-6	-1	-10
Fixed Assets	86	110	144
Current Assets	69	65	47

M K Trophies

21 Scott Drive, Newport Pagnell, MK16 8PW
Tel: 01908-615326 **Fax:** 01908-615326
Directors: M. Howard (Ptnr)
Turnover: Up to £250,000 **No.of Employees:** 1 - 10 **Product Groups:** 23, 33, 49, 65

M P I Ltd

109 High Street, Newport Pagnell, MK16 8EN
Tel: 01908-617222 **Fax:** 01908-617177
E-mail: info@mpi.ltd.uk
Website: http://www.mpi.ltd.uk
Managers: C. Baker (Mgr)
Ultimate Holding Company: M.P.I. (HERTS) LIMITED
Immediate Holding Company: M.P.I. LIMITED
Registration no: 02746209 **Date established:** 1992
Turnover: £500,000 - £1m **No.of Employees:** 1 - 10 **Product Groups:** 80

Date of Accounts	Sep 11	Sep 10	Sep 09
Sales Turnover	21m	19m	21m
Pre Tax Profit/Loss	313	402	1m
Working Capital	2m	2m	1m
Fixed Assets	759	827	902
Current Assets	6m	5m	5m
Current Liabilities	889	603	1m

Nampak Plastics Europe Ltd

Jenna Way Interchange Park, Newport Pagnell, MK16 9QJ
Tel: 01908-611554 **Fax:** 01908-611519
E-mail: eric.collins@eu.nampak.com
Website: http://www.eu.nampak.com
Bank(s): HSBC Bank plc
Directors: E. Collins (MD), A. Terhoven (Fin), J. Tinsley (Sales)
Managers: J. Brown, M. Wilson (Personnel), D. Conn (Tech Serv Mgr), G. Ward
Ultimate Holding Company: NAMPAK LTD (SOUTH AFRICA)
Immediate Holding Company: NAMPAK PLASTICS EUROPE LIMITED
Registration no: 00400002 **VAT No.:** GB 120 0823 31
Date established: 1945 **Turnover:** £125m - £250m
No.of Employees: 101 - 250 **Product Groups:** 30, 66

Date of Accounts	Sep 11	Sep 10	Sep 09
Sales Turnover	127m	109m	107m
Pre Tax Profit/Loss	10m	9m	5m
Working Capital	60m	58m	54m
Fixed Assets	22m	23m	24m
Current Assets	81m	73m	72m
Current Liabilities	8m	8m	8m

Schunk Intec Ltd

Unit 10 Cromwell Business Centre Howard Way, Interchange Park, Newport Pagnell, MK16 9QS
Tel: 01908-611127 **Fax:** 01908-615525
E-mail: info@gb.schunk.com
Website: http://www.gb.schunk.com
Directors: M. Kent (MD)
Immediate Holding Company: SCHUNK INTEC LTD.
Registration no: 03488643 **VAT No.:** GB 715 9191 23
Date established: 1998 **Turnover:** £1m - £2m **No.of Employees:** 1 - 10
Product Groups: 35, 36, 40, 45, 46

Date of Accounts	Dec 11	Dec 10	Dec 09
Sales Turnover	N/A	N/A	1m
Pre Tax Profit/Loss	N/A	N/A	-66
Working Capital	326	234	127
Fixed Assets	83	52	28
Current Assets	784	486	386
Current Liabilities	N/A	N/A	74

Tube Engineering

Hurst End Farm Hurst End, North Crawley, Newport Pagnell, MK16 9HS
Tel: 01234-391991 **Fax:** 01234-391991
Directors: G. Harley (Prop), G. Harvey (Prop)
Immediate Holding Company: BEDS & BUCKS PROPERTIES LIMITED
Date established: 1996 **No.of Employees:** 1 - 10 **Product Groups:** 30, 40, 46

Wholesale First Aid Supplies

24 Thomas Drive, Newport Pagnell, MK16 8TH
Tel: 01908-610093 **Fax:** 01908-610590
E-mail: sales@wholesalefirstaidsupplies.co.uk
Website: http://www.wholesalefirstaidsupplies.co.uk
Directors: D. Arnold (Dir)
Registration no: 06330958 **Date established:** 2007
Turnover: £250,000 - £500,000 **No.of Employees:** 1 - 10
Product Groups: 38

Zumbach Electronics

Unit 22 Cromwell Business Centre Howard Way, Interchange Park, Newport Pagnell, MK16 9QS
Tel: 08707-743301 **Fax:** 08707-743302
E-mail: info@zumbach.com
Website: http://www.zumbach.com
Directors: G. Canales (Co Sec)
Managers: P. Lloyd (Sales Admin)
Ultimate Holding Company: ZUMBACH ELECTRONIC AG (SWITZERLAND)
Immediate Holding Company: ZUMBACH ELECTRONICS LIMITED
Registration no: 01233358 **VAT No.:** GB 228 3185 63
Date established: 1975 **Turnover:** £250,000 - £500,000
No.of Employees: 1 - 10 **Product Groups:** 38, 85

Date of Accounts	Dec 10	Dec 09	Dec 08
Sales Turnover	343	225	372
Pre Tax Profit/Loss	-1	-8	N/A
Working Capital	-0	-1	7
Fixed Assets	2	2	2
Current Assets	191	200	206
Current Liabilities	11	19	11

Olney

Bonart Ltd

19 Stilebrook Road, Olney, MK46 5EG
Tel: 01234-711171 **Fax:** 01234-711979
E-mail: hq@bonart.co.uk
Website: http://www.bonart.co.uk
Directors: M. Maisey (MD)
Ultimate Holding Company: SWEET,HILL & GRAY LIMITED
Immediate Holding Company: BONART LIMITED
Registration no: 00696113 **VAT No.:** GB 335 2764 55
Date established: 1961 **No.of Employees:** 1 - 10 **Product Groups:** 24

Date of Accounts	Dec 11	Dec 10	Dec 09
Working Capital	771	806	829
Fixed Assets	5	9	10
Current Assets	802	894	864

H G Clarke & Son

2 High Street Weston Underwood, Olney, MK46 5JS
Tel: 01234-712047 **Fax:** 01234-712047
E-mail: info@clunch.co.uk
Website: http://www.clunch.co.uk
Directors: A. Clarke (Ptnr)
Date established: 1920 **Turnover:** Up to £250,000
No.of Employees: 1 - 10 **Product Groups:** 14, 33, 61

G & M Powder Coatings Ltd

3a Stilebrook Road, Olney, MK46 5EA
Tel: 01234-711605 **Fax:** 01234-713959
Website: http://www.ampiltd.co.uk
Directors: M. Crompton (MD), M. Holland (Fin)
Immediate Holding Company: G & M POWDER COATINGS LTD
Registration no: 07396156 **Date established:** 2010
No.of Employees: 1 - 10 **Product Groups:** 46, 48

Date of Accounts	Oct 11
Working Capital	-42
Fixed Assets	40
Current Assets	18

Jasp Design Solutions Ltd

The Old Forge Common Street, Ravenstone, Olney, MK46 5AR
Tel: 01908-551100 **Fax:** 08700-522892
E-mail: info@jaspdesign.co.uk
Website: http://www.jaspdesign.co.uk
Directors: A. Jackman (Dir), P. Smith (Fin)
Immediate Holding Company: JASP DESIGN SOLUTIONS LIMITED
Registration no: 05652280 **Date established:** 2005
Turnover: Up to £250,000 **No.of Employees:** 1 - 10 **Product Groups:** 44, 46

Date of Accounts	Dec 11	Dec 10	Dec 09
Working Capital	18	18	12
Fixed Assets	1	1	1
Current Assets	39	31	23

Logistics Education Centre Ltd

31 Carey Way, Olney, MK46 4DR
Tel: 01234-712618 **Fax:** 01234-241431
E-mail: roger@logcen.com
Website: http://www.logisticscentre.co.uk
Directors: R. Gutteridge (MD)
Immediate Holding Company: LOGISTICS EDUCATION CENTRE LIMITED
Registration no: 04073088 **Date established:** 2000
Turnover: Up to £250,000 **No.of Employees:** 1 - 10 **Product Groups:** 35, 37, 38, 44, 45, 48, 52, 54, 61, 67, 68, 77, 80, 84, 85, 86, 87

Date of Accounts	Dec 07	Dec 06	Dec 05
Sales Turnover	85	111	90
Pre Tax Profit/Loss	-3	3	10
Working Capital	8	11	6
Fixed Assets	N/A	N/A	1
Current Assets	27	40	33
Current Liabilities	19	29	27
ROCE% (Return on Capital Employed)	-29.8	25.0	138.2
ROT% (Return on Turnover)	-2.9	2.5	10.7

Olney Furniture & Collectables

5 The Galleries, Olney, MK46 4DX
Tel: 01234-713338 **Fax:** 01234-713376
E-mail: enquiries@olneyfurniture.com
Website: http://www.olneyfurniture.com
Directors: R. Wingrat (Dir), M. Kutas (Fin)
Immediate Holding Company: OLNEY FURNITURE & COLLECTABLES LLP
Registration no: OC317625 **Date established:** 2006
Turnover: Up to £250,000 **No.of Employees:** 1 - 10 **Product Groups:** 26

Scomar Ltd

Stilebrook Road, Olney, MK46 5EA
Tel: 01234-711166 **Fax:** 01234-240962
E-mail: neil.w@scorpionmouldings.co.uk
Website: http://www.scorpionmouldings.co.uk
Directors: N. Whitham (Dir), S. Whitham (Fin)
Immediate Holding Company: SCOMAR LIMITED
Registration no: 01476814 **Date established:** 1980
No.of Employees: 1 - 10 **Product Groups:** 30, 31, 48

Date of Accounts	Jul 09
Working Capital	-288
Current Assets	228

Scorpion Mouldings Ltd

Stilebrook Road, Olney, MK46 5EA
Tel: 01234-711166 **Fax:** 01234-240962
E-mail: info@scorpionmouldings.co.uk
Website: http://www.scorpionmouldings.co.uk
Bank(s): Barclays, Milton Keynes

see next page

***Scorpion Mouldings Ltd** - Cont'd*
Directors: N. Whitham (Dir)
Managers: H. Licchelli (Comptroller)
Immediate Holding Company: SCORPION ENTERPRISES LIMITED
Registration no: 01019344 **VAT No.:** GB 455 9902 12
Date established: 1971 **Turnover:** £1m - £2m **No.of Employees:** 21 - 50
Product Groups: 30, 42

Date of Accounts	Jul 11	Jul 10	Jul 09
Sales Turnover	N/A	2m	1m
Pre Tax Profit/Loss	N/A	67	-185
Working Capital	302	103	53
Fixed Assets	797	779	873
Current Assets	624	352	391
Current Liabilities	N/A	68	74

Templecoombe Ltd
The Old Maltings 102a High Street, Olney, MK46 4BE
Tel: 01234-712121 **Fax:** 01234-241888
E-mail: sales@templecoombe.co.uk
Website: http://www.templecoombe.co.uk
Directors: C. Thomsen (Sales)
Immediate Holding Company: TEMPLECOOMBE LIMITED
Registration no: 02025546 **Date established:** 1986
No.of Employees: 1 - 10 **Product Groups:** 24, 27

Date of Accounts	Jun 12	Jun 11	Jun 10
Working Capital	220	192	172
Fixed Assets	4	4	5
Current Assets	625	518	549

Princes Risborough

B E C Distribution Ltd
20 Park Street, Princes Risborough, HP27 9AH
Tel: 08454-900405 **Fax:** 0845-4900 406
E-mail: sales@bec.co.uk
Website: http://www.bec.co.uk
Bank(s): National Westminster Bank Plc
Directors: J. Dodds (MD)
Immediate Holding Company: BEC DISTRIBUTION LTD
Registration no: 06922643 **VAT No.:** GB 731 6941 31
Date established: 2009 **Turnover:** £1m - £2m **No.of Employees:** 11 - 20
Product Groups: 37

Date of Accounts	Dec 11	Dec 10	Dec 09
Working Capital	33	44	23
Fixed Assets	9	2	N/A
Current Assets	272	121	75
Current Liabilities	N/A	N/A	8

B M S Bath Renovations
Holmwood New Road, Princes Risborough, HP27 0LA
Tel: 01844-343300 **Fax:** 01844-274456
E-mail: richardhartuk@aol.com
Directors: R. Hart (Prop)
Date established: 1986 **No.of Employees:** 1 - 10 **Product Groups:** 46, 48

Birkett Electric Ltd
Bridge House Longwick Road, Princes Risborough, HP27 9RS
Tel: 01844-274480 **Fax:** 01844-274470
E-mail: info@birkett-electric.com
Website: http://www.birkett-electric.com
Directors: B. Birkett (MD), N. Birkett (Sales), C. Birkett (Co Sec)
Immediate Holding Company: BIRKETT ELECTRIC LIMITED
Registration no: 01372053 **VAT No.:** GB 302 2427 15
Date established: 1978 **Turnover:** £2m - £5m **No.of Employees:** 21 - 50
Product Groups: 37

Date of Accounts	May 12	May 11	May 10
Working Capital	349	332	327
Fixed Assets	843	869	899
Current Assets	511	503	498

Clinical Systems Ltd
63 High Street, Princes Risborough, HP27 0AE
Tel: 01844-342490 **Fax:** 01844-342940
E-mail: support@clinical-systems.co.uk
Website: http://www.clinical-systems.co.uk
Directors: A. James (Fin), G. Wilson (MD)
Immediate Holding Company: CLINICAL SYSTEMS LIMITED
Registration no: 02248783 **Date established:** 1988
Turnover: £250,000 - £500,000 **No.of Employees:** 1 - 10
Product Groups: 44

Date of Accounts	Sep 11	Sep 10	Sep 09
Working Capital	135	111	101
Fixed Assets	7	11	16
Current Assets	253	224	237

Durashine Auto Body Restoration Ltd
Unit 1 Crownfield Works Wycombe Road, Saunderton, Princes Risborough, HP27 9NR
Tel: 01844-345100 **Fax:** 01844-345101
E-mail: dab@dabrestor.co.uk
Website: http://www.dabrestor.co.uk
Directors: J. Patten (MD)
Immediate Holding Company: DURASHINE AUTO BODY RESTORATION LTD
Registration no: 05852457 **Date established:** 2006
Turnover: £250,000 - £500,000 **No.of Employees:** 1 - 10
Product Groups: 80, 81, 84

Date of Accounts	Dec 11	Dec 10	Dec 09
Working Capital	110	92	147
Fixed Assets	16	10	17
Current Assets	162	105	164

Ercol Furniture Ltd
Summerleys Road, Princes Risborough, HP27 9PX
Tel: 01844-271800 **Fax:** 01844-271888
E-mail: sales@ercol.com
Website: http://www.ercol.com
Bank(s): Lloyds TSB Bank plc
Directors: E. Tadros (Ch)
Managers: A. Sluzas (Buyer), M. Mesmain (Tech Serv Mgr), M. Lawrence, S. Martin (Cust Serv Mgr), S. Demeller (Mktg Serv Mgr)
Ultimate Holding Company: ERCOL (HOLDINGS) LIMITED
Immediate Holding Company: ERCOL FURNITURE LIMITED
Registration no: 00163292 **VAT No.:** GB 208 0138 04
Date established: 2020 **Turnover:** £10m - £20m
No.of Employees: 101 - 250 **Product Groups:** 26

Date of Accounts	Dec 11	Dec 10	Dec 09
Sales Turnover	12m	11m	10m
Pre Tax Profit/Loss	-193	9	-26
Working Capital	-1	-139	-431
Fixed Assets	4m	4m	5m
Current Assets	4m	4m	3m
Current Liabilities	721	725	560

Gommes Forge Ltd
Foundry Lane Loosley Row, Princes Risborough, HP27 0NY
Tel: 01844-345546 **Fax:** 01844-274906
Website: http://www.gommesforge.co.uk
Directors: G. Baker (Co Sec), J. Baker (MD)
Immediate Holding Company: GOMMES FORGE LIMITED
Registration no: 01191457 **Date established:** 1974
No.of Employees: 1 - 10 **Product Groups:** 26, 35

Date of Accounts	Dec 11	Dec 10	Dec 09
Working Capital	-15	-13	-13
Fixed Assets	1	1	1
Current Assets	27	28	28

Hypnos Ltd
Longwick Road, Princes Risborough, HP27 9RS
Tel: 01844-348200 **Fax:** 01844-275012
E-mail: info@hypnosbeds.com
Website: http://www.hypnosbeds.com
Bank(s): RBS
Directors: P. Keen (Ch), J. Keen (Sales), C. Ward (Mkt Research), T. Barber (Sales & Mktg), B. Eastoe (Fin)
Managers: S. Bailey, C. Quigley (Purch Mgr)
Ultimate Holding Company: KEEN & TOMS HOLDINGS LIMITED
Immediate Holding Company: HYPNOS LIMITED
Registration no: 00213405 **VAT No.:** GB 448 6014 45
Date established: 2026 **Turnover:** £20m - £50m
No.of Employees: 101 - 250 **Product Groups:** 26

Date of Accounts	Jun 09	Jun 08	Jul 10
Sales Turnover	34m	27m	22m
Pre Tax Profit/Loss	-2m	-545	148
Working Capital	-3m	-702	-3m
Fixed Assets	223	272	391
Current Assets	5m	9m	5m
Current Liabilities	2m	1m	1m

Ironcraft
Thame Road Longwick, Princes Risborough, HP27 9QU
Tel: 01844-347711 **Fax:** 01844-347711
Directors: M. Tilbury (Prop)
Date established: 1990 **No.of Employees:** 1 - 10 **Product Groups:** 26, 35

Leo Pharma
Longwick Road, Princes Risborough, HP27 9RR
Tel: 01844-347333 **Fax:** 01844-342278
E-mail: enquiries@leo-pharma.com
Website: http://www.leopharma.co.uk
Bank(s): Barclays, Whitehall, London SW1
Directors: S. Black (Dir)
Immediate Holding Company: LEO LABORATORIES LIMITED
Registration no: 00662129 **VAT No.:** GB 222 4708 88
Date established: 1960 **Turnover:** £75m - £125m
No.of Employees: 51 - 100 **Product Groups:** 31, 63

Date of Accounts	Dec 11	Dec 10	Dec 09
Sales Turnover	100m	89m	79m
Pre Tax Profit/Loss	5m	3m	3m
Working Capital	37m	36m	34m
Fixed Assets	7m	7m	7m
Current Assets	72m	78m	69m
Current Liabilities	5m	5m	3m

Risborough Agricultural Services Ltd
Woodway, Princes Risborough, HP27 0NN
Tel: 01844-275275 **Fax:** 01844-274264
E-mail: james@risag.com
Website: http://www.risag.com
Directors: J. Dance (MD), S. Dance (Fin)
Immediate Holding Company: RISBOROUGH AGRICULTURAL SERVICES LIMITED
Registration no: 01886019 **Date established:** 1985 **Turnover:** £2m - £5m
No.of Employees: 1 - 10 **Product Groups:** 41

Date of Accounts	Mar 12	Mar 11	Mar 10
Working Capital	125	-12	-66
Fixed Assets	39	42	53
Current Assets	1m	683	305

Soft Water Shop
75 Station Road, Princes Risborough, HP27 9DN
Tel: 01844-346566 **Fax:** 01844-343916
E-mail: sales@softwatershop.co.uk
Website: http://www.softwatershop.co.uk
Directors: R. Stones (Prop)
Date established: 1981 **No.of Employees:** 1 - 10 **Product Groups:** 38, 42

Solo Supplies
4 Wellington House Lower Icknield Way, Longwick, Princes Risborough, HP27 9RZ
Tel: 01844-354949 **Fax:** 01844-354022
Website: http://www.solosupplies.co.uk
Managers: T. Braginton (Mgr)
Immediate Holding Company: SOLO SUPPLIES LIMITED
Registration no: 06551862 **Date established:** 2008
No.of Employees: 1 - 10 **Product Groups:** 38, 42

Sumitomo Electric Hardmetal Ltd
50 Summerleys Road, Princes Risborough, HP27 9PW
Tel: 01844-342081 **Fax:** 01844-342415
E-mail: sue-pierce@gr.sei.co.jp
Website: http://www.sumitomo-hardmetal.co.uk
Bank(s): Barclays
Managers: T. Tolley (Chief Mgr)
Ultimate Holding Company: SUMITOMO ELECTRIC INDUSTRIES LTD (JAPAN)
Immediate Holding Company: SUMITOMO ELECTRIC HARDMETAL LIMITED
Registration no: 01307059 **VAT No.:** GB 196 1174 49
Date established: 1977 **Turnover:** £2m - £5m **No.of Employees:** 11 - 20
Product Groups: 36, 45, 46

Date of Accounts	Dec 09	Dec 08	Mar 12
Sales Turnover	3m	4m	5m
Pre Tax Profit/Loss	-40	116	296
Working Capital	1m	1m	2m
Fixed Assets	344	365	287
Current Assets	2m	2m	3m
Current Liabilities	113	186	322

CAMBRIDGESHIRE

Cambridge

Ablestik Adhesives & Sealants
Station Road Linton, Cambridge, CB21 4NW
Tel: 01223-893771 **Fax:** 01223-893546
E-mail: sales@ablestik.com
Website: http://www.henkel.com
Directors: G. Jones (Grp Chief Exec)
Managers: G. Jones (Chief Mgr), A. Winster (Tech Serv Mgr), M. Matthews (Serv Mgr)
Ultimate Holding Company: I.C.I.
Immediate Holding Company: National Starch & Chemicals Ltd
Registration no: 00226707 **Turnover:** £500,000 - £1m
No.of Employees: 11 - 20 **Product Groups:** 32, 44

Access To Export Ltd
22 Lonsdale Linton, Cambridge, CB21 4LT
Tel: 01223-890767 **Fax:** 01223-654413
E-mail: info@accesstoexport.com
Website: http://www.accesstoexport.com
Directors: C. Willers (MD)
Immediate Holding Company: ACCESS TO EXPORT LIMITED
Registration no: 05754201 **VAT No.:** GB 728 5848 88
Date established: 2006 **Turnover:** Up to £250,000
No.of Employees: 1 - 10 **Product Groups:** 61, 80, 81

Date of Accounts	Mar 11	Mar 10	Mar 09
Sales Turnover	N/A	N/A	92
Pre Tax Profit/Loss	N/A	N/A	38
Working Capital	45	43	33
Fixed Assets	N/A	2	5
Current Assets	82	50	52
Current Liabilities	N/A	N/A	18

Alfa Tail Lifts Ltd
Unit 25 South Cambridge Business Park Babraham Road, Sawston, Cambridge, CB22 3JH
Tel: 08442-098320
E-mail: cambridge@alfatailifts.co.uk
Website: http://www.alfatailifts.co.uk
Directors: P. Gibbs (MD)
Managers: P. Sapsford (Serv Mgr), P. Gibbs (Admin Off)
Immediate Holding Company: ALFA TAIL LIFTS LIMITED
Registration no: 04268864 **Date established:** 2001
No.of Employees: 11 - 20 **Product Groups:** 45, 48, 67

Date of Accounts	Oct 10	Oct 09	Oct 08
Working Capital	144	81	408
Fixed Assets	664	653	681
Current Assets	1m	1m	924

Allcontrols Ltd
William James House Cowley Road, Cambridge, CB4 0WX
Tel: 01223-223900 **Fax:** 0870-4580314
E-mail: info@allcontrols.co.uk
Website: http://www.allcontrols.co.uk
Directors: P. Mutsaerts (MD)
Registration no: 04952424 **Date established:** 2003
No.of Employees: 1 - 10 **Product Groups:** 38

Date of Accounts	Apr 10	Apr 09	Apr 08
Working Capital	111	97	86
Fixed Assets	12	15	19
Current Assets	266	187	218

AMET (Europe) Ltd
5 Cambridge Westpoint Stirling Way, Papworth Everard, Cambridge, CB23 3GY
Tel: 01480-831222 **Fax:** 08708-362 118
E-mail: info@ameteurope.co.uk
Website: http://www.ameteurope.com
Directors: D. Coaster (MD)
Registration no: 05514053 **Date established:** 2005
No.of Employees: 1 - 10 **Product Groups:** 46, 67

Date of Accounts	Jan 09	Jul 07	Jul 06
Sales Turnover	676	N/A	N/A
Pre Tax Profit/Loss	N/A	N/A	-11
Working Capital	28	-50	-11
Fixed Assets	21	31	N/A
Current Assets	418	134	60
Current Liabilities	390	184	71
Total Share Capital	25	25	N/A
ROCE% (Return on Capital Employed)			100.0

Amethyst Designs Ltd
9 Trafalgar Way Bar Hill, Cambridge, CB23 8SQ
Tel: 01954-789696 **Fax:** 01954-789662
E-mail: paul.wealleans@amethyst-designs.co.uk
Website: http://www.amethyst-designs.co.uk
Directors: P. Wealleans (MD), P. Wealleans (Chief Op Offcr)
Managers: A. Greavett (Prod Mgr)
Ultimate Holding Company: CYBERGENIC SYSTEMS LIMITED
Immediate Holding Company: AMETHYST DESIGNS LIMITED
Registration no: 01602689 **VAT No.:** GB 358 3765 16
Date established: 1981 **Turnover:** £500,000 - £1m
No.of Employees: 21 - 50 **Product Groups:** 37

Date of Accounts	Jun 11	Jun 10	Jun 09
Working Capital	290	275	295
Fixed Assets	48	59	39
Current Assets	1m	962	752

Analysis Mason Ltd
St Giles Court 24 Castle Street, Cambridge, CB3 0AJ
Tel: 08456-005244 **Fax:** 01223-460866
E-mail: enquiries@analysismason.com
Website: http://www.analysismason.com
Directors: S. Morris (Co Sec), J. Montanana (Dir)
Ultimate Holding Company: DATATEC LTD (BRITISH VIRGIN ISLANDS)
Immediate Holding Company: ANALYSYS LIMITED
Registration no: 01819989 **Date established:** 1984 **Turnover:** £1m - £2m
No.of Employees: 21 - 50 **Product Groups:** 80

Date of Accounts	Feb 12	Feb 11	Feb 10
Sales Turnover	2m	2m	2m
Pre Tax Profit/Loss	327	-406	-162
Working Capital	1m	987	1m
Current Assets	2m	2m	2m
Current Liabilities	523	1m	557

Ari Business Consultancy
5 Jordans Yard Bridge Street, Cambridge, CB2 1UG
Tel: 07977-613207
E-mail: michaeljgfjennings@yahoo.de
Directors: M. Jennings (Prop)
Turnover: Up to £250,000 **No.of Employees:** 1 - 10 **Product Groups:** 27, 40, 80

Arkex Ltd
Newnham House Cambridge Business Park, Cambridge, CB4 0WZ
Tel: 01223-427400 **Fax:** 01223-425050
E-mail: enquiries@arkex.com
Website: http://www.arkex.com
Bank(s): Barcleys
Directors: S. Gibson (Fin)
Managers: J. Siegfriad
Immediate Holding Company: ARKEX LIMITED
Registration no: 04255000 **Date established:** 2001
Turnover: £10m - £20m **No.of Employees:** 51 - 100 **Product Groups:** 34, 37

Date of Accounts	Dec 11	Dec 10	Dec 09
Sales Turnover	16m	12m	9m
Pre Tax Profit/Loss	-3m	-9m	-7m
Working Capital	-432	3m	3m
Fixed Assets	6m	7m	10m
Current Assets	7m	7m	8m
Current Liabilities	5m	3m	4m

Armtrac Ltd
70 Reach Road Burwell, Cambridge, CB25 0AH
Tel: 01638-743979 **Fax:** 01638-742578
E-mail: steve@armtrac.net
Website: http://www.armtrac.net
Directors: S. Brown (MD)
Immediate Holding Company: ARMTRAC LIMITED
Registration no: 03915015 **Date established:** 2000
No.of Employees: 1 - 10 **Product Groups:** 41

Date of Accounts	Nov 11	Nov 10	Nov 09
Working Capital	269	270	400
Fixed Assets	62	67	65
Current Assets	572	633	820
Current Liabilities	N/A	9	N/A

Art VPS Ltd
St Johns Innovation Park Cowley Road, Cambridge, CB4 0WS
Tel: 01223-424466 **Fax:** 01223-424467
E-mail: grahamw@artvps.com
Website: http://www.artvps.com
Directors: G. Wylie (Dir), D. Rossiter (Tech Serv)
Managers: B. Tyler (Sales Prom Mgr)
Immediate Holding Company: ART VPS LIMITED
Registration no: 04461295 **Date established:** 2002
Turnover: Up to £250,000 **No.of Employees:** 11 - 20 **Product Groups:** 61

Date of Accounts	Jun 11	Jun 10	Jun 09
Sales Turnover	N/A	N/A	53
Pre Tax Profit/Loss	N/A	-1	-1m
Working Capital	-6m	-5	-4m
Fixed Assets	15	N/A	10
Current Assets	75	N/A	54
Current Liabilities	N/A	N/A	4m

ATS Euromaster Ltd
143 Histon Road, Cambridge, CB4 3HZ
Tel: 01223-454631 **Fax:** 01223-454654
E-mail: ats@euromaster.com
Website: http://www.atseuromaster.co.uk
Managers: S. Billiers (Mgr)
Ultimate Holding Company: COMPAGNIE GENERALE DES ETABLISSEMENTS MICHELIN (FRANCE)
Immediate Holding Company: ATS EUROMASTER LIMITED
Registration no: 04303731 **Date established:** 2001
Turnover: £20m - £50m **No.of Employees:** 1 - 10 **Product Groups:** 29

Date of Accounts	Dec 11	Dec 10	Dec 09
Sales Turnover	295m	285m	291m
Pre Tax Profit/Loss	-3m	-5m	-29m
Working Capital	3m	11m	2m
Fixed Assets	76m	72m	71m
Current Assets	63m	60m	64m
Current Liabilities	15m	12m	13m

Aveva Solutions Ltd
High Cross Madingley Road, Cambridge, CB3 0HB
Tel: 01223-556655 **Fax:** 01223-556666
E-mail: info@aveva.com
Website: http://www.aveva.com
Bank(s): Barclays
Directors: P. Taylor (Fin)
Managers: T. Lee (I.T. Exec), H. Wright (Personnel)
Ultimate Holding Company: AVEVA GROUP PLC
Immediate Holding Company: AVEVA SOLUTIONS LIMITED
Registration no: 00803680 **VAT No.:** GB 385 9985 66
Date established: 1964 **Turnover:** £75m - £125m
No.of Employees: 101 - 250 **Product Groups:** 44

Date of Accounts	Mar 11	Mar 10	Mar 09
Sales Turnover	108m	93m	108m
Pre Tax Profit/Loss	41m	56m	64m
Working Capital	31m	53m	38m
Fixed Assets	52m	32m	30m
Current Assets	166m	155m	125m
Current Liabilities	19m	13m	19m

David Ball Group plc
Huntingdon Road Bar Hill, Cambridge, CB23 8HN
Tel: 01954-780687 **Fax:** 01954-782912
E-mail: sales@pudlo.com
Website: http://www.pudlo.com
Bank(s): National Westminster Bank Plc
Directors: D. Ball (Ch), O. Minett (Fab), J. Ball (Co Sec)
Managers: G. Wells (Sales Admin), D. McNeill (Mktg Serv Mgr)
Immediate Holding Company: DAVID BALL GROUP PUBLIC LIMITED COMPANY
Registration no: 01890135 **VAT No.:** GB 676 5207 14
Date established: 1985 **Turnover:** £2m - £5m **No.of Employees:** 11 - 20
Product Groups: 14, 31, 32, 33

Date of Accounts	Dec 11	Dec 10	Dec 09
Sales Turnover	3m	2m	2m
Pre Tax Profit/Loss	272	-103	162
Working Capital	70	233	278
Fixed Assets	2m	330	313
Current Assets	1m	560	800
Current Liabilities	252	186	121

Balsham Buildings Ltd
7 High Street Balsham, Cambridge, CB21 4DJ
Tel: 01223-894404 **Fax:** 01223-892818
Website: http://www.balsham.uk.com
Directors: M. Harris (Dir)
Ultimate Holding Company: BALSHAM HOLDINGS LIMITED
Immediate Holding Company: BALSHAM (BUILDINGS) LIMITED
Registration no: 01469747 **Date established:** 1979 **Turnover:** £5m - £10m
No.of Employees: 21 - 50 **Product Groups:** 35

Date of Accounts	Dec 11	Dec 10	Dec 09
Sales Turnover	6m	6m	8m
Pre Tax Profit/Loss	19	-476	61
Working Capital	475	358	551
Fixed Assets	53	206	269
Current Assets	2m	1m	1m
Current Liabilities	668	154	327

Baron Design Ltd
Brunswick House 61-69 Newmarket Road, Cambridge, CB5 8EG
Tel: 01223-844288 **Fax:** 01223-846787
E-mail: mail@barondesign.co.uk
Website: http://www.barondesign.co.uk
Directors: G. Baron (Dir)
Immediate Holding Company: Baron Design Holdings Ltd
Registration no: 03119127 **Date established:** 1995 **Turnover:** £2m - £5m
No.of Employees: 11 - 20 **Product Groups:** 84

Date of Accounts	Oct 08	Oct 07	Oct 06
Sales Turnover	N/A	3m	4m
Pre Tax Profit/Loss	N/A	167	150
Working Capital	640	527	391
Fixed Assets	18	24	31
Current Assets	2m	1m	1m
Current Liabilities	946	556	795
Total Share Capital	1	1	1

Barton Willmore Planning Partnership
Elizabeth House 1 High Street, Chesterton, Cambridge, CB4 1WB
Tel: 01223-345555 **Fax:** 01223-345550
E-mail: info@bartonwillmore.co.uk
Website: http://www.bartonwillmore.co.uk
Directors: A. James (Ptnr)
Registration no: 02131349 **VAT No.:** GB 537 5009 48
No.of Employees: 11 - 20 **Product Groups:** 84

Bayer Crop Science
230 Camebridge Science Park Milton Road, Cambridge, CB4 0WB
Tel: 01223-226500 **Fax:** 01223-426240
E-mail: w.welter@bayercropscience.com
Website: http://www.bayercropscience.co.uk
Directors: M. Wilkinson (Co Sec), W. Welter (Dir)
Ultimate Holding Company: BAYER AG (GERMANY)
Immediate Holding Company: BAYER CROPSCIENCE LIMITED
Registration no: 00218826 **Date established:** 2027
Turnover: £250m - £500m **No.of Employees:** 101 - 250
Product Groups: 32

Date of Accounts	Dec 11	Dec 10	Dec 09
Sales Turnover	278m	256m	261m
Pre Tax Profit/Loss	-4m	19m	9m
Working Capital	110m	32m	58m
Fixed Assets	9m	73m	71m
Current Assets	161m	132m	134m
Current Liabilities	16m	14m	16m

Beautiful Cards
Unicorn Cottage Old School Lane, Whittlesford, Cambridge, CB2 4YS
Tel: 01223-839933 **Fax:** 0870-0941215
E-mail: jo@beautifulcards.co.uk
Website: http://www.beautifulcards.co.uk
Directors: J. Dawson (MD)
Turnover: Up to £250,000 **No.of Employees:** 1 - 10 **Product Groups:** 64

Bee Mobile
8 Seymour Street, Cambridge, CB1 3DQ
Tel: 01223-246425 **Fax:** 01223-246425
Website: http://www.beemobile.co.uk
Directors: G. Wallis (Prop)
No.of Employees: 1 - 10 **Product Groups:** 38, 67

Belair Research Ltd
Broadway Bourn, Cambridge, CB23 2TA
Tel: 01954-718366 **Fax:** 01954-718355
E-mail: brl@acoustical.co.uk
Website: http://www.acoustical.co.uk
Directors: R. Collman (MD)
Immediate Holding Company: BELAIR (RESEARCH) LIMITED
Registration no: 01602951 **VAT No.:** GB 366 0045 70
Date established: 1981 **Turnover:** £250,000 - £500,000
No.of Employees: 1 - 10 **Product Groups:** 52

Date of Accounts	May 11	May 09	May 08
Working Capital	70	149	95
Fixed Assets	33	40	10
Current Assets	98	219	224

Bell International
Red Cross Lane, Cambridge, CB2 0QU
Tel: 01223-278800 **Fax:** 01223-412410
E-mail: info@bell-worldwide.com
Website: http://www.bell-worldwide.com
Directors: Y. Smith (Pers), M. Foster (Comm), L. Connon (Fin)
Managers: B. Hart (Chief Mgr), I. Danbury (Tech Serv Mgr)
Immediate Holding Company: BELL EDUCATIONAL TRUST LIMITED (THE)
Registration no: 01048465 **Date established:** 1972
Turnover: £20m - £50m **No.of Employees:** 51 - 100 **Product Groups:** 86

Bensasson & Chalmers Ltd
St Johns Innovation Centre Cowley Road, Cambridge, CB4 0WS
Tel: 01223-420048 **Fax:** 01223-420418
E-mail: sales@benc.co.uk
Website: http://www.benc.co.uk
Directors: C. Brown (Dir)
Ultimate Holding Company: MINDWORKS MANAGEMENT SYSTEMS LIMITED
Immediate Holding Company: BENSASSON & CHALMERS LIMITED
Registration no: 03188792 **Date established:** 1996
Turnover: Up to £250,000 **No.of Employees:** 1 - 10 **Product Groups:** 44

Date of Accounts	Dec 08	Dec 07	Mar 11
Sales Turnover	107	147	N/A
Pre Tax Profit/Loss	-5	14	N/A
Working Capital	-154	-147	199
Current Assets	N/A	14	311
Current Liabilities	96	86	N/A

Biochrom Ltd
22 Science Park Milton Road, Cambridge, CB4 0FJ
Tel: 01223-423723 **Fax:** 01223-420164
E-mail: sales@biochrom.co.uk
Website: http://www.biochrom.co.uk
Bank(s): Barclays
Directors: S. Luke (MD), R. Snelling (Tech Serv)
Managers: A. Moss (Personnel), N. Carter (Purch Mgr), R. Bishop (Fin Mgr)
Ultimate Holding Company: HARVARD BIOSCIENCE INC (USA)
Immediate Holding Company: SCIE-PLAS LIMITED
Registration no: 02245830 **VAT No.:** GB 731 8306 47
Date established: 1988 **Turnover:** £1m - £2m **No.of Employees:** 51 - 100
Product Groups: 38, 42

Date of Accounts	Dec 11	Dec 10	Dec 09
Sales Turnover	N/A	1m	1m
Pre Tax Profit/Loss	N/A	691	-222
Working Capital	1m	N/A	401
Fixed Assets	N/A	1m	1
Current Assets	1m	N/A	685
Current Liabilities	N/A	N/A	86

Bodycote Heat Treatments plc
2 Pembroke Avenue Denny Industrial Estate Waterbeach, Cambridge, CB25 9QR
Tel: 01223-860741 **Fax:** 01223-863498
E-mail: sales@bodycote.co.uk
Website: http://www.bodycote.com
Bank(s): HSBC, Manchester
Managers: M. Cool (Mgr)
Ultimate Holding Company: ARCAM LIMITED
Immediate Holding Company: A&R CAMBRIDGE LIMITED
Registration no: 01025652 **Date established:** 1993
Turnover: £10m - £20m **No.of Employees:** 21 - 50 **Product Groups:** 48

Date of Accounts	May 11	May 10	May 09
Sales Turnover	9m	8m	8m
Pre Tax Profit/Loss	50	75	-2m
Working Capital	840	292	187
Fixed Assets	931	953	1m
Current Assets	3m	3m	2m
Current Liabilities	1m	567	2m

Boult Wade Tennant
C P C 4 Capital Park, Fulbourn, Cambridge, CB21 5XE
Tel: 01223-883000 **Fax:** 01223-883001
E-mail: balexander@boult.com
Website: http://www.boult.com
Directors: N. Tucker (Ptnr), F. Hide (Ptnr), M. Spencer (Ptnr)
Managers: A. Frost (Mgr), B. Alexander (Mgr)
Immediate Holding Company: AUTOTECHNIQUE LIMITED
Registration no: 03536080 **Date established:** 2005
No.of Employees: 11 - 20 **Product Groups:** 44, 80, 87

Brahler I C S UK Ltd
Unit 2 The Business Centre Church End, Cambridge, CB1 3LB
Tel: 01223-411601 **Fax:** 01223-411602
E-mail: smsainsbury@brahler-ics.co.uk
Website: http://www.brahler.co.uk
Directors: S. Sainsbury (Dir)
Immediate Holding Company: BRAHLER ICS UK LIMITED
Registration no: 02220482 **VAT No.:** GB 493 0831 38
Date established: 1988 **Turnover:** £1m - £2m **No.of Employees:** 1 - 10
Product Groups: 37, 80, 81

Date of Accounts	Dec 11	Dec 10	Dec 09
Working Capital	197	164	111
Fixed Assets	254	194	214
Current Assets	787	416	287

The Burlington Press Ltd
1 Station Road Foxton, Cambridge, CB22 6SA
Tel: 01223-870266 **Fax:** 01223-872113
E-mail: info@burlingtonpress.co.uk
Website: http://www.burlingtonpress.co.uk
Bank(s): HSBC Bank plc
Directors: A. Tooke (Grp Chief Exec), J. Lindop (Sales)
Managers: G. Beattie (Sales & Mktg Mg), A. Tooke (Ops Mgr), D. Anderson (I.T. Exec)
Immediate Holding Company: BURLINGTON FINE PRINT LTD
Registration no: 06316293 **VAT No.:** GB 213 3012 34
Date established: 2007 **Turnover:** £5m - £10m **No.of Employees:** 21 - 50
Product Groups: 28

Date of Accounts	Jun 11	Jun 10	Jun 09
Working Capital	195	179	-276
Fixed Assets	729	667	2m
Current Assets	1m	797	1m

C 4 Carbides Ltd
9 Nuffield Road, Cambridge, CB4 1TF
Tel: 01223-225400 **Fax:** 01223-225405
E-mail: andrew@c4carbides.com
Website: http://www.c4carbides.com
Bank(s): Barclays
Managers: A. Grieve, A. Beynon (Eng Serv Mgr), S. Martin (Sales Prom Mgr)
Immediate Holding Company: C4 CARBIDES LIMITED
Registration no: 01902912 **VAT No.:** GB 361 4605 68
Date established: 1985 **Turnover:** £2m - £5m **No.of Employees:** 21 - 50
Product Groups: 33, 36

Date of Accounts	Dec 11	Dec 10	Dec 09
Working Capital	1m	1m	750
Fixed Assets	886	834	844
Current Assets	2m	2m	2m

C E D Group (t/a C E D)
1-2 Norman Way Industrial Estate Norman Way, Over, Cambridge, CB24 5QE
Tel: 01954-231957 **Fax:** 01954-230041
E-mail: sales@ced-packaging.co.uk
Website: http://www.ced-packaging.co.uk
Directors: J. Reader (MD), J. Reader (Fin)
Immediate Holding Company: CAMBRIDGE EXPORT DOCUMENTS LIMITED
Registration no: 01424596 **Date established:** 1979
No.of Employees: 1 - 10 **Product Groups:** 07, 20, 22, 25, 27, 29, 30, 31, 33, 34, 35, 36, 38, 42, 45, 48, 49, 61, 66, 67, 72, 74, 75, 76, 80, 84, 85

Date of Accounts	May 11	May 10	May 09
Working Capital	-69	71	42
Fixed Assets	504	471	458
Current Assets	205	229	152

C S A Cleaning Equipment
Broad Lane Cottenham, Cambridge, CB24 8SW
Tel: 01954-251573 **Fax:** 01954-206506
E-mail: sales@csacleaningstore.co.uk
Website: http://www.csacleaningstore.co.uk
Bank(s): Barclays
Directors: T. Russell (Prop)
Immediate Holding Company: EQUIPMENT SUPPORT COMPANY LIMITED
Registration no: 02572480 **VAT No.:** GB 215 4443 87
Date established: 1991 **Turnover:** £500,000 - £1m
No.of Employees: 11 - 20 **Product Groups:** 14, 33, 39, 46

Date of Accounts	Apr 12	Apr 11	Apr 10
Working Capital	209	200	198
Fixed Assets	99	74	95
Current Assets	606	450	433

Cab Glazing Services
Button End Harston, Cambridge, CB22 7GX
Tel: 01223-872400 **Fax:** 01223-872866
E-mail: sales@cabglazing.co.uk
Website: http://www.cabglazing.co.uk
Directors: J. Kivlin (Prop)
Managers: J. Welch (Chief Mgr)
Registration no: 02392041 **Turnover:** £500,000 - £1m
No.of Employees: 1 - 10 **Product Groups:** 33

Cam Com Radio (t/a) Cambridge Mobile Communications Ltd
Gusto Mills Huntingdon Road, Cambridge, CB3 0DL
Tel: 01223-277274 **Fax:** 01223-277207
E-mail: camcom@metronet.co.uk
Website: http://www.camcomradio.co.uk
Directors: K. Jones (Dir)
No.of Employees: 1 - 10 **Product Groups:** 37, 67

Cam Metric Holdings
The Pingle 85 Histon Road, Cottenham, Cambridge, CB24 8UQ
Tel: 01954-250880 **Fax:** 01954-250853
E-mail: sales@cammetric.co.uk
Website: http://www.cammetric.co.uk
Directors: P. Sexton (Prop)
VAT No.: GB 599 4165 82 **Turnover:** £250,000 - £500,000
No.of Employees: 1 - 10 **Product Groups:** 37, 38, 67

Cambio Ltd
The Irwin Centre Scotland Road, Dry Drayton, Cambridge, CB23 8AR
Tel: 01954-210200 **Fax:** 01954-210300
E-mail: support@cambio.co.uk
Website: http://www.cambio.co.uk
Directors: I. Rushton (Fin)
Immediate Holding Company: CAMBIO LIMITED
Registration no: 01964088 **Date established:** 1985
Turnover: £500,000 - £1m **No.of Employees:** 1 - 10 **Product Groups:** 84

Date of Accounts	Mar 11	Mar 10	Mar 09
Sales Turnover	855	951	840
Pre Tax Profit/Loss	-64	81	19
Working Capital	238	287	218
Fixed Assets	7	9	10
Current Assets	293	370	270
Current Liabilities	12	53	22

Cambridge Asphalt Co. Ltd
Ely Road Waterbeach, Cambridge, CB25 9PG
Tel: 01223-863000 **Fax:** 01223-440006
E-mail: info@cambridgeasphalte.co.uk
Website: http://www.cambridgeasphalte.co.uk
Bank(s): Barclays
Directors: R. Preston (MD)
Ultimate Holding Company: 03427682
Immediate Holding Company: CAMBRIDGE ASPHALTE COMPANY LIMITED
Registration no: 00461683 **VAT No.:** GB 637 1155 49
Date established: 1948 **Turnover:** £2m - £5m **No.of Employees:** 21 - 50
Product Groups: 31, 52

Cambridge Consultants
Science Park Milton Road, Cambridge, CB4 0DW
Tel: 01223-420024 **Fax:** 01223-423373
E-mail: info@cambridgeconsultants.co.uk
Website: http://www.cambridgeconsultants.co.uk
Bank(s): Barclays, Benet Street
Directors: B. Moon (Grp Chief Exec), X. Dupeyron (Grp Chief Exec), A. Richardson (Tech Serv), A. Murphy (Mkt Research)
Managers: M. Eapen, P. Donovan (Develop Mgr), P. Pordage (Mktg Serv Mgr), F. Pullen (Purch Mgr)
Ultimate Holding Company: ALTRAN TECHNOLOGIES SA (FRANCE)
Immediate Holding Company: CAMBRIDGE CONSULTANTS LIMITED
Registration no: 01036298 **Date established:** 1971
Turnover: £20m - £50m **No.of Employees:** 251 - 500
Product Groups: 38, 80, 84

Date of Accounts	Dec 11	Dec 10	Dec 09
Sales Turnover	37m	34m	32m
Pre Tax Profit/Loss	3m	6m	4m
Working Capital	21m	21m	19m
Fixed Assets	9m	9m	9m
Current Assets	28m	27m	26m
Current Liabilities	6m	5m	5m

Cambridge Education Group Ltd
Kett House Station Road, Cambridge, CB1 2JH
Tel: 01223-346180 **Fax:** 01223-346181
E-mail: cgoodwin@ceg-uk.com
Website: http://www.ceg-uk.com
Directors: R. Ball (Fin), M. Stanton (Co Sec)
Managers: B. Lee, C. Goodwin (Sales Admin), P. Boates
Ultimate Holding Company: CAMBRIDGE EDUCATION GROUP LIMITED
Immediate Holding Company: CEG PROPERTIES LIMITED
Registration no: 02354796 **Date established:** 1989 **Turnover:** £1m - £2m
No.of Employees: 21 - 50 **Product Groups:** 86

Date of Accounts	Aug 11	Aug 10	Aug 09
Pre Tax Profit/Loss	-436	471	34
Working Capital	-7m	-4m	-3m
Fixed Assets	13m	12m	11m
Current Assets	518	501	563
Current Liabilities	391	233	58

Cambridge Electro Plating Ltd
21-25 Union Lane, Cambridge, CB4 1PR
Tel: 01223-352464 **Fax:** 01223-361085
E-mail: cep@btinternet.com
Website: http://www.btinternet.com
Directors: A. Jones (Fin), M. Jones (MD)
Immediate Holding Company: CAMBRIDGE ELECTRO PLATING LIMITED
Registration no: 00491110 **VAT No.:** GB 213 2825 95
Date established: 1951 **Turnover:** £250,000 - £500,000
No.of Employees: 1 - 10 **Product Groups:** 48

Date of Accounts	Jul 11	Jul 10	Jul 09
Sales Turnover	458	370	345
Pre Tax Profit/Loss	31	-23	-53
Working Capital	-197	-231	-217
Fixed Assets	767	774	783
Current Assets	130	115	99
Current Liabilities	310	332	298

Cambridge Electronic Design
Science Park Milton Road, Cambridge, CB4 0FE
Tel: 01223-420186 **Fax:** 01223-420488
E-mail: info@ced.co.uk
Website: http://www.ced.co.uk
Bank(s): Lloyds TSB
Directors: M. Albutt (MD), P. Rice (Dir)
Immediate Holding Company: CAMBRIDGE ELECTRONIC DESIGN LIMITED
Registration no: 00972132 **VAT No.:** GB 214 2617 96
Date established: 1970 **Turnover:** £1m - £2m **No.of Employees:** 11 - 20
Product Groups: 44

Date of Accounts	Jan 11	Jan 10	Jan 09
Sales Turnover	2m	N/A	N/A
Pre Tax Profit/Loss	347	N/A	N/A
Working Capital	3m	3m	3m
Fixed Assets	8	17	27
Current Assets	4m	3m	3m
Current Liabilities	127	N/A	N/A

Cambridge Electronic Industries Ltd
Pembroke Avenue Waterbeach, Cambridge, CB25 9QR
Tel: 01223-860041 **Fax:** 01223-863625
E-mail: sales@cambridgeconnectors.com
Website: http://www.cambridgeconnectors.com
Bank(s): Barclays
Directors: A. Wilson (Co Sec), S. Smith (MD)
Ultimate Holding Company: WILSON-MOTTAZ LIMITED
Immediate Holding Company: CAMBRIDGE ELECTRONIC INDUSTRIES LIMITED
Registration no: 02106752 **VAT No.:** GB 385 9852 85
Date established: 1987 **Turnover:** £1m - £2m **No.of Employees:** 21 - 50
Product Groups: 37

Date of Accounts	May 11	May 10	May 09
Working Capital	654	510	418
Fixed Assets	30	41	41
Current Assets	1m	742	595

Cambridge Glass Blowing
Brookfield Business Centre Twentypence Road, Cottenham, Cambridge, CB24 8PS
Tel: 01954-251771 **Fax:** 01954-252028
E-mail: info@camglassblowing.co.uk
Website: http://www.prduk.com
Directors: A. Pledger (Dir)
Immediate Holding Company: CAMBRIDGE GLASSBLOWING LIMITED
Registration no: 02652662 **Date established:** 1991
Turnover: £500,000 - £1m **No.of Employees:** 1 - 10 **Product Groups:** 33, 42, 45, 63, 66

Date of Accounts	Jun 12	Jun 11	Jun 10
Working Capital	98	92	87
Fixed Assets	341	375	406
Current Assets	217	231	197

Cambridge Market Research Ltd
Unit H South Cambridge Business Park, Sawston, Cambridge, CB22 3JH
Tel: 01223-492050 **Fax:** 01223-492079
E-mail: accounts@cambridgemr.com
Website: http://www.cambridgemr.com
Bank(s): National Westminster Bank Plc
Directors: P. Beresford (MD)
Immediate Holding Company: CAMBRIDGE MARKET RESEARCH LIMITED
Registration no: 04191473 **VAT No.:** GB 561 4415 12
Date established: 2001 **Turnover:** £500,000 - £1m
No.of Employees: 11 - 20 **Product Groups:** 80, 81

Date of Accounts	Sep 11	Sep 10	Sep 09
Working Capital	971	845	504
Fixed Assets	265	323	386
Current Assets	1m	2m	863

Cambridge Marketing Communications Ltd
No 8 Randswood Industrial Units The Common, West Wratting, Cambridge, CB21 5LR
Tel: 01223-291333 **Fax:** 029-2091334
E-mail: enquiries@cmcexhibitions.co.uk
Website: http://www.cmcexhibitions.co.uk
Directors: D. Brooker (MD)
Immediate Holding Company: CAMBRIDGE MARKETING COMMUNICATIONS LIMITED
Registration no: 03835619 **Date established:** 1999
No.of Employees: 1 - 10 **Product Groups:** 26, 27, 30, 35, 49, 52, 81, 83, 84

Date of Accounts	Sep 11	Sep 10	Sep 09
Working Capital	-50	-37	-21
Fixed Assets	9	12	16
Current Assets	29	48	98

Cambridge Mobility
Unit 11 South Cambridge Business Park Babraham Road, Sawston, Cambridge, CB22 3JH
Tel: 07850-409554 **Fax:** 01223-830097
E-mail: cammobility@btconnect.com
Website: http://www.cambridgemobility.co.uk
Directors: C. Pettitt (Prop)
No.of Employees: 1 - 10 **Product Groups:** 36, 39, 45, 48, 67

Cambridge Newspapers Ltd
Winship Road Milton, Cambridge, CB24 6PP
Tel: 01223-434434 **Fax:** 01223-434222
E-mail: newsdesk@cambridge-news.co.uk
Website: http://www.cambridge-news.co.uk
Bank(s): Lloyds, Chesterton Road
Directors: G. Ayres (MD)
Managers: D. Fordham
Ultimate Holding Company: YATTENDON GROUP PLC
Immediate Holding Company: CAMBRIDGE NEWSPAPERS LIMITED
Registration no: 00240968 **VAT No.:** GB 112 4477 96
Date established: 2029 **Turnover:** £20m - £50m
No.of Employees: 251 - 500 **Product Groups:** 28

Date of Accounts	Dec 11	Dec 08	Dec 09
Sales Turnover	20m	23m	20m
Pre Tax Profit/Loss	552	-917	416
Working Capital	-1m	-233	-130
Fixed Assets	32m	38m	36m
Current Assets	3m	3m	3m
Current Liabilities	3m	3m	2m

Cambridge Online Systems Ltd
163 Cambridge Science Park Milton Road, Cambridge, CB4 0GP
Tel: 01223-422600 **Fax:** 01223-422601
E-mail: enquiries@cosl.co.uk
Website: http://www.cambridgeonline.net
Bank(s): HSBC
Directors: D. Crabb (MD)
Managers: M. Thompson, M. Queen (Ops Mgr), J. Arthur (Fin Mgr), D. Brown (Tech Serv Mgr)
Immediate Holding Company: CAMBRIDGE ONLINE SYSTEMS LIMITED
Registration no: 01381717 **VAT No.:** GB 215 3376 81
Date established: 1978 **Turnover:** £2m - £5m **No.of Employees:** 51 - 100
Product Groups: 44

Date of Accounts	Jul 11	Jul 10	Jul 09
Sales Turnover	4m	7m	10m
Pre Tax Profit/Loss	-591	-122	191
Working Capital	470	1m	1m
Fixed Assets	198	229	272
Current Assets	2m	2m	3m
Current Liabilities	903	874	797

Cambridge Power Tools
Cromwell Road, Cambridge, CB1 3YB
Tel: 01223-466154 **Fax:** 01223-466159
E-mail: cambridgepi@ridgeons.net
Website: http://www.ridgeons.net
Managers: I. Waine (Mgr)
Date established: 1991 **No.of Employees:** 1 - 10 **Product Groups:** 37

Cambridge Solar Ltd
152 NUNS WAY, Cambridge, CB4 2NS
Tel: 01223-361112
E-mail: o.morgan@cambridge-solar.co.uk
Website: http://www.cambridge-solar.co.uk
Directors: F. Eve (Dir), O. Morgan (Ptnr)
Immediate Holding Company: CAMBRIDGE SOLAR LTD
Registration no: 07013587 **Date established:** 2009
Turnover: Up to £250,000 **No.of Employees:** 1 - 10 **Product Groups:** 37

Cambridge Systems Design
1 Andersons Court Newnham Road, Cambridge, CB3 9EZ
Tel: 01223-518815
E-mail: info@cds.co.uk
Website: http://www.csd.co.uk
Directors: C. Partington (Ptnr)
No.of Employees: 1 - 10 **Product Groups:** 84

Cambridge Traditional Products
Unit 1 The Maltings Millfield, Cottenham, Cambridge, CB24 8RE
Tel: 01954-251380 **Fax:** 01954-251387
E-mail: info@bees-wax.co.uk
Website: http://www.bees-wax.co.uk
Directors: S. Whatling (MD)
Immediate Holding Company: CAMBRIDGE TRADITIONAL PRODUCTS LIMITED
Registration no: 04745586 **VAT No.:** GB 384 0944 69
Date established: 2003 **Turnover:** Up to £250,000
No.of Employees: 1 - 10 **Product Groups:** 32, 63

Date of Accounts	Dec 10	Dec 09	Dec 07
Working Capital	10	20	29
Fixed Assets	6	8	5
Current Assets	27	36	42

Cambridge University Press Holdings Ltd (Publishing Division)
The Edinburgh Building Shaftesbury Road, Cambridge, CB2 8RU
Tel: 01223-312393 **Fax:** 01223-315052
E-mail: info@cambridge.org
Website: http://www.cambridge.org/uk
Bank(s): Barclays
Directors: S. Bourne (Grp Chief Exec)
Ultimate Holding Company: UNIVERSITY OF CAMBRIDGE
Immediate Holding Company: CAMBRIDGE UNIVERSITY PRESS (HOLDINGS) LIMITED
Registration no: 04606950 **VAT No.:** GB 214 1416 14
Date established: 2002 **Turnover:** £50m - £75m
No.of Employees: 501 - 1000 **Product Groups:** 28, 64, 80

Date of Accounts	Apr 11	Apr 10	Apr 09
Sales Turnover	68m	53m	58m
Pre Tax Profit/Loss	4m	3m	-639
Working Capital	21m	18m	-251
Fixed Assets	6m	8m	8m
Current Assets	39m	44m	46m
Current Liabilities	5m	20m	6m

Cambridge Vacuum Engineering
43 Pembroke Avenue Denny Industrial Estate, Waterbeach, Cambridge, CB25 9QX
Tel: 01223-863481 **Fax:** 01223-862812
E-mail: reception@camvaceng.com
Website: http://www.camvaceng.com
Bank(s): Barclays, Churchill Place, London.
Directors: D. Maclennan (Fin)
Managers: A. Buller (Purch Mgr), C. Masters (Tech Serv Mgr)
Ultimate Holding Company: 04241498
Immediate Holding Company: AQUASIUM TECHNOLOGY LIMITED
Registration no: 04241498 **VAT No.:** GB 308 9905 31
Date established: 2001 **Turnover:** £10m - £20m
No.of Employees: 51 - 100 **Product Groups:** 38, 40, 42, 45, 46, 84

Date of Accounts	Dec 11	Dec 10	Dec 09
Sales Turnover	15m	13m	13m
Pre Tax Profit/Loss	632	-163	-137
Working Capital	4m	3m	3m
Fixed Assets	6m	6m	6m
Current Assets	8m	7m	6m
Current Liabilities	2m	2m	2m

Cambridge Vending
Unit 4-6 Crane Industrial Estate Cambridge Road Industrial Estate, Milton, Cambridge, CB24 6AZ
Tel: 01223-425522 **Fax:** 01223-425515
E-mail: info@cambridgevending.co.uk
Website: http://www.cambridgevending.co.uk
Directors: J. Handley (Fin), P. Wilson (MD)
Managers: B. Kennard
Immediate Holding Company: CAMBRIDGE VENDING LIMITED
Registration no: 04198837 **Date established:** 2001
Turnover: Up to £250,000 **No.of Employees:** 11 - 20 **Product Groups:** 40, 49, 69

Date of Accounts	Apr 12	Apr 11	Apr 10
Working Capital	344	204	80
Fixed Assets	134	142	133
Current Assets	628	481	354

Cambridge Water plc
90 Fulbourn Road, Cambridge, CB1 9JN
Tel: 01223-706050 **Fax:** 01223-214052
E-mail: info@cambridge-water.co.uk
Website: http://www.cambridge-water.co.uk
Bank(s): Barclays
Directors: S. Kay (MD)
Managers: N. Siddall, S. Dean (Personnel), F. Sandwell (Tech Serv Mgr), T. Orange (Comptroller)
Ultimate Holding Company: HUTCHISON WHAMPOA LIMITED (HONG KONG)
Immediate Holding Company: CAMBRIDGE WATER PLC
Registration no: 03175861 **VAT No.:** GB 213 2007 32
Date established: 1996 **Turnover:** £20m - £50m
No.of Employees: 51 - 100 **Product Groups:** 18

Date of Accounts	Dec 10	Dec 09	Dec 08
Sales Turnover	20m	22m	20m
Pre Tax Profit/Loss	7m	5m	3m
Working Capital	2m	-29m	-2m
Fixed Assets	50m	52m	53m
Current Assets	11m	7m	7m
Current Liabilities	7m	5m	7m

Cambs Injector Service
1-3 Green End Comberton, Cambridge, CB23 7DY
Tel: 01223-262306 **Fax:** 01223-263497
Directors: S. Davis (Prop)
Date established: 1956 **No.of Employees:** 1 - 10 **Product Groups:** 35, 36, 39

Camdata Ltd
23 Royston Road Harston, Cambridge, CB22 7NH
Tel: 0845-064 5555
E-mail: sales@camdata.co.uk
Website: http://www.camdata.co.uk
Directors: A. Lloyd (Fin), P. Cowley (MD)
Immediate Holding Company: CAMDATA LIMITED
Registration no: 03757122 **VAT No.:** GB 576 4532 16
Date established: 1999 **No.of Employees:** 1 - 10 **Product Groups:** 44

Date of Accounts	Apr 11	Apr 10	Apr 09
Working Capital	-9	N/A	7
Current Assets	52	55	43
Current Liabilities	N/A	1	1

Camlab Ltd
Unit 24 Norman Way Industrial Estate Norman Way, Over, Cambridge, CB24 5WE
Tel: 01954-233100 **Fax:** 01954-233101
E-mail: mailbox@camlab.co.uk
Website: http://www.camlab.co.uk
Bank(s): Barclays
Directors: G. Williams (MD), B. Sunderland (Grp Chief Exec), G. Minto (Ch), M. Bentata (Dir), P. Gordon (Dir)
Managers: V. Duffield (Purch Mgr), B. Carse, C. Day (Sales Prom Mgr)
Registration no: 04655447 **Date established:** 2003 **Turnover:** £5m - £10m
No.of Employees: 21 - 50 **Product Groups:** 30, 32, 38, 42, 67

Camweavers Ltd
84 Duxford Road Whittlesford, Cambridge, CB22 4NH
Tel: 01223-833338 **Fax:** 01223-833644
E-mail: enquiries@camweavers.co.uk
Website: http://www.camweavers.co.uk
Bank(s): Lloyds TSB Bank plc
Managers: M. Pauley (Chief Mgr)
Immediate Holding Company: CAMWEAVERS LIMITED
Registration no: 00556167 **VAT No.:** GB 213 3310 26
Date established: 1955 **Turnover:** £500,000 - £1m
No.of Employees: 11 - 20 **Product Groups:** 26

Date of Accounts	Apr 11	Apr 09	Apr 08
Working Capital	250	216	211
Fixed Assets	82	82	82
Current Assets	544	649	688
Current Liabilities	168	N/A	N/A

Careers In Recruitment
Sheraton House Castle Park, Cambridge, CB3 0AX
Tel: 01223-370021 **Fax:** 01223-370002
E-mail: sales@careersinrecruitment.com
Website: http://www.crac.org.uk
Directors: R. Mellors-Borne (Sales & Mktg), G. Wilson (Grp Chief Exec)
Managers: M. Elliot (Sales Admin)
Immediate Holding Company: CAREERS RESEARCH AND ADVISORY CENTRE (CRAC) LIMITED(THE)
Registration no: 00825036 **Date established:** 1964 **Turnover:** £5m - £10m
No.of Employees: 21 - 50 **Product Groups:** 80

Date of Accounts	Mar 11	Mar 10	Mar 09
Sales Turnover	4m	4m	6m
Pre Tax Profit/Loss	354	-809	481
Working Capital	703	559	931
Fixed Assets	632	586	435
Current Assets	2m	1m	2m
Current Liabilities	912	656	811

Cecil Instruments Ltd
Milton Technical Centre Cambridge Road Industrial Estate, Milton, Cambridge, CB24 6AZ
Tel: 01223-420821 **Fax:** 01223-420875
E-mail: ceciltarbet@cecilinstruments.com
Website: http://www.cecilinstruments.com
Bank(s): Lloyds TSB Bank plc
Directors: G. Chamberlain (Fin)
Managers: D. Atkinson (Buyer), A. Kujore (Sales & Mktg Mg)
Immediate Holding Company: CECIL INSTRUMENTS LIMITED
Registration no: 00909536 **VAT No.:** GB 213 2683 89
Date established: 1967 **Turnover:** £5m - £10m **No.of Employees:** 21 - 50
Product Groups: 38

Date of Accounts	May 11	May 10	May 09
Working Capital	1m	979	886
Fixed Assets	308	328	356
Current Assets	2m	2m	2m

Chemex Environmental International Ltd
Unit J Broad Lane Cottenham, Cambridge, CB24 8SW
Tel: 01954-252519 **Fax:** 01954-251764
E-mail: nread@chemex.co.uk
Website: http://www.chemex.co.uk
Directors: N. Read (MD)
Immediate Holding Company: CHEMEX ENVIRONMENTAL INTERNATIONAL LIMITED
Registration no: 04226642 **Date established:** 2001 **Turnover:** £2m - £5m
No.of Employees: 21 - 50 **Product Groups:** 84, 85

Date of Accounts	Sep 11	Sep 10	Sep 09
Working Capital	24	33	-81
Fixed Assets	143	148	191
Current Assets	439	412	327

Chubb Group Security Ltd
The Maltings Station Road, Great Shelford, Cambridge, CB22 5LR
Tel: 0870-2418536 **Fax:** 0870-2418537
E-mail: cambridge.security@chubb.co.uk
Website: http://www.chubb.co.uk
Directors: M. Lathan (Reg)
Managers: S. Cox (District Mgr)
Registration no: 00524469 **Turnover:** £10m - £20m
No.of Employees: 21 - 50 **Product Groups:** 36, 40

Citibase P LC
Sheraton House Castle Park, Cambridge, CB3 0AX
Tel: 01223-370000 **Fax:** 01223-370040
E-mail: annkessell@citibase.co.uk
Website: http://freedomatwork.com
Managers: A. Kessell (Sales Admin)
Ultimate Holding Company: WORLDMEDIACOM LIMITED
Immediate Holding Company: CITIBASE PUBLIC LIMITED COMPANY
Registration no: 02767719 **Date established:** 1992
No.of Employees: 1 - 10 **Product Groups:** 80

Date of Accounts	Feb 12	Feb 11	Feb 10
Sales Turnover	10m	10m	9m
Pre Tax Profit/Loss	15	24	24
Working Capital	-786	-877	-807
Fixed Assets	2m	2m	2m
Current Assets	4m	4m	4m
Current Liabilities	4m	3m	3m

Cleanaway Ltd
Cowley Road, Cambridge, CB4 0DN
Tel: 0845-6060460 **Fax:** 01223-566418
E-mail: information@cleanaway.com
Website: http://www.cleanaway.com
Managers: I. McLees, C. Rillstone (Mgr)
Immediate Holding Company: CLEANAWAY LIMITED
Registration no: NF002533 **VAT No.:** GB 352 1129 90
Date established: 1981 **No.of Employees:** 21 - 50 **Product Groups:** 42, 45, 54

Comar Instruments
70 Hartington Grove, Cambridge, CB1 7UH
Tel: 01223-866120 **Fax:** 01223-410033
E-mail: mail@comaroptics.com
Website: http://www.comaroptics.com
Bank(s): Abbey National plc
Directors: P. Marsh (Ptnr)
VAT No.: GB 215 0594 86 **Date established:** 1976
No.of Employees: 11 - 20 **Product Groups:** 23, 24, 27, 28, 32, 33, 37, 38, 48

Conway Pine Ltd
Unit 6b Beehive Centre Coldhams Lane, Cambridge, CB1 3ET
Tel: 01223-460664 **Fax:** 01223-329343
Website: http://www.conway-furniture.com
Managers: R. Lawrence (Mgr)
Ultimate Holding Company: CONWAY PINE HOLDINGS LIMITED
Immediate Holding Company: CONWAY PINE LIMITED
Registration no: 02286703 **Date established:** 1988 **Turnover:** £5m - £10m
No.of Employees: 1 - 10 **Product Groups:** 26, 37

Date of Accounts	Mar 11	Mar 10	Mar 09
Sales Turnover	N/A	N/A	6m
Pre Tax Profit/Loss	N/A	N/A	-320
Working Capital	-60	346	969
Fixed Assets	118	129	159
Current Assets	799	1m	1m
Current Liabilities	N/A	N/A	275

Cortex Controllers Ltd
Unit 2 The Mount Station Road, Longstanton, Cambridge, CB24 3DS
Tel: 01954-261435 **Fax:** 01223-462800
E-mail: sales@cortexcontrollers.com
Website: http://www.cortexcontrollers.com
Directors: M. Hart (Fin), N. Toop (MD), N. Toop (MD)
Immediate Holding Company: CORTEX CONTROLLERS LIMITED
Registration no: 03071960 **VAT No.:** GB 632 5658 33
Date established: 1995 **Turnover:** £250,000 - £500,000
No.of Employees: 1 - 10 **Product Groups:** 37, 38, 45, 67

Date of Accounts	Jun 12	Jun 11	Jun 10
Working Capital	129	119	-22
Fixed Assets	5	2	2
Current Assets	262	315	140

Crofton Engineering Ltd
Cambridge Road Linton, Cambridge, CB21 4NN
Tel: 01223-892138 **Fax:** 01223-893547
E-mail: info@crofton-eng.co.uk
Website: http://www.crofton-eng.co.uk
Directors: G. Godfrey (Dir), M. Mannassi (MD)
Immediate Holding Company: CROFTON ENGINEERING LIMITED
Registration no: 00521342 **VAT No.:** GB 213 3009 23
Date established: 1953 **Turnover:** £1m - £2m **No.of Employees:** 21 - 50
Product Groups: 35, 48

Date of Accounts	Sep 11	Sep 10	Sep 09
Working Capital	771	735	477
Fixed Assets	277	293	312
Current Assets	2m	1m	857

Cryosonic UK Ltd
11 Boundary Court Rathmore Road, Cambridge, CB1 7BB
Tel: 01223-720695 **Fax:** 0870-131 4500
E-mail: sales@cryosonic.co.uk
Website: http://www.cryosonic.co.uk
Directors: M. Brussee (MD), M. Brussee (Fin)
Registration no: 05267681 **Date established:** 2004
No.of Employees: 1 - 10 **Product Groups:** 47

Date of Accounts	Mar 07	Mar 06
Working Capital	-7	-3
Current Assets	3	8
Current Liabilities	10	11

Crystal Structures Ltd
Crystal Park 50 Tunbridge Lane, Bottisham, Cambridge, CB25 9EA
Tel: 01223-811451 **Fax:** 01223-11451
E-mail: info@crystalstructures.com
Website: http://www.crystalstructures.com
Directors: G. Wooster (MD)
Immediate Holding Company: CRYSTAL STRUCTURES LIMITED
Registration no: 00433246 **VAT No.:** GB 102 0138 48
Date established: 1947 **Turnover:** Up to £250,000
No.of Employees: 1 - 10 **Product Groups:** 37, 38, 42, 44, 46, 48

Date of Accounts	Dec 11	Dec 10	Dec 09
Sales Turnover	N/A	21	7
Pre Tax Profit/Loss	N/A	-2	-10
Working Capital	-177	-168	-157
Fixed Assets	320	322	317
Current Assets	23	20	34
Current Liabilities	N/A	83	187

The Cup Company Franchise Ltd
10e The Grip Linton, Cambridge, CB21 4XN
Tel: 01223-894370 **Fax:** 01223-894123
E-mail: sales@cupcompany.com
Website: http://www.cupcompany.com
Directors: S. Watson (MD)
Immediate Holding Company: THE CUP COMPANY FRANCHISE LIMITED
Registration no: 06549144 **Date established:** 2008 **Turnover:** £1m - £2m
No.of Employees: 1 - 10 **Product Groups:** 30, 49, 67

Cytocell Ltd
Unit 3-4 Cambridge Technopark Newmarket Road, Cambridge, CB5 8PB
Tel: 01223-294048 **Fax:** 01223-294986
E-mail: m.lawrie@cytocell.com
Website: http://www.cytocell.com
Directors: M. Lawrie (MD), S. Kennedy (Sales & Mktg)
Managers: T. Reeve (Sales Admin)
Immediate Holding Company: CYTOCELL LIMITED
Registration no: 04231155 **Date established:** 2001
No.of Employees: 21 - 50 **Product Groups:** 38, 67, 85

Date of Accounts	Sep 11	Sep 10	Sep 09
Working Capital	1m	722	355
Fixed Assets	173	135	156
Current Assets	2m	1m	640

D S Smith Packaging
Factory Road Burwell, Cambridge, CB25 0BN
Tel: 01638-744600 **Fax:** 01638-744613
E-mail: maggie.harris@dssp.com
Website: http://www.dssmith-packaging.com
Managers: M. Harris
Date established: 1989 **No.of Employees:** 21 - 50 **Product Groups:** 38, 42

Dalehead Foods Ltd
Cambridge Road Linton, Cambridge, CB21 4JD
Tel: 01223-891000 **Fax:** 01223-891117
E-mail: john.hughes@dalehead.co.uk
Website: http://www.flagshipfoods.co.uk
Directors: J. Hughes (MD)
Managers: W. Fairhurst (Tech Serv Mgr), R. Hawkins (Comptroller), C. Marchant (Mktg Serv Mgr), K. Collins (Sales Prom Mgr), J. Collins (Personnel), K. Cresswell
Ultimate Holding Company: DANISH CROWN AMBA (DENMARK)
Immediate Holding Company: DALEHEAD FOODS LIMITED
Registration no: 01078266 **VAT No.:** GB 424 8737 29
Date established: 1972 **Turnover:** £20m - £50m
No.of Employees: 101 - 250 **Product Groups:** 20

Date of Accounts	Oct 09	Oct 08	Oct 10
Working Capital	-460	20m	-460
Fixed Assets	460	460	460
Current Assets	N/A	20m	N/A

Datapaq Ltd
Deanland House 160 Cowley Road, Cambridge, CB4 0GU
Tel: 01223-423141 **Fax:** 01223-423306
E-mail: sales@datapaq.com
Website: http://www.datapaq.com
Directors: D. Tunley (Co Sec)
Managers: S. Powell (Mktg Serv Mgr)
Ultimate Holding Company: DANAHER CORPORATION (DELAWARE U.S.A)
Immediate Holding Company: DATAPAQ LIMITED
Registration no: 01777666 **Date established:** 1983 **Turnover:** £5m - £10m
No.of Employees: 11 - 20 **Product Groups:** 37, 38, 44, 67, 85

Date of Accounts	Dec 11	Dec 10	Dec 09
Sales Turnover	9m	8m	6m
Pre Tax Profit/Loss	3m	3m	773
Working Capital	2m	3m	3m
Fixed Assets	N/A	6	24
Current Assets	3m	5m	4m
Current Liabilities	463	592	447

De Sangosse Ltd
Hillside Mill Swaffham Bulbeck, Cambridge, CB25 0LU
Tel: 01223-811215 **Fax:** 01223-810020
E-mail: info@desangosse.co.uk
Website: http://www.desangosse.co.uk
Directors: D. Cameron (MD), C. Maquin (Mkt Research), H. Turner (Co Sec)
Ultimate Holding Company: DE SANGOSSE PARTICIPATIONS (FRANCE)
Immediate Holding Company: DE SANGOSSE LTD.
Registration no: 02871017 **Date established:** 1993 **Turnover:** £5m - £10m
No.of Employees: 1 - 10 **Product Groups:** 07, 32, 66

Date of Accounts	Aug 11	Aug 10	Aug 09
Sales Turnover	9m	8m	12m
Pre Tax Profit/Loss	2m	2m	2m
Working Capital	4m	3m	3m
Fixed Assets	60	77	43
Current Assets	8m	8m	8m
Current Liabilities	1m	870	952

De Vere University Arms Hotel
Regent Street, Cambridge, CB2 1AD
Tel: 01223-351241 **Fax:** 01223-315256
E-mail: dua.sales@devere-hotels.com
Website: http://www.devere-hotels.com
Bank(s): National Westminster, Warrington
Managers: W. Johnson (Ops Mgr), P. Wilks (Mgr), R. Lane (Maint), T. Sloan (Fin Mgr)
Ultimate Holding Company: GREENALLS
Immediate Holding Company: DEVERE HOTELS LTD
Registration no: 00418878 **Date established:** 1834 **Turnover:** £2m - £5m
No.of Employees: 51 - 100 **Product Groups:** 69

Decopierre UK Ltd
68 lyles road Cottenham, cambridge, CB24 8QR
Tel: 020-8133 8990
E-mail: info@decopierre.co.uk
Website: http://www.decopierre.co.uk
Registration no: 05844795 **Date established:** 2006
Turnover: Up to £250,000 **No.of Employees:** 1 - 10 **Product Groups:** 33

Delta T Devices
130 Low Road Burwell, Cambridge, CB25 0EJ
Tel: 01638-742922 **Fax:** 01638-743155
E-mail: lea.dodds@delta-t.co.uk
Website: http://www.delta-t.co.uk
Managers: S. Nobbs (Tech Serv Mgr), D. Harley, D. Lucas (Fin Mgr), L. Dodds (Sales & Mktg Mg), M. Soames (Personnel)
Registration no: IP22804R **VAT No.:** GB 368 3613 32
Turnover: £1m - £2m **No.of Employees:** 21 - 50 **Product Groups:** 38, 42

Dip International Ltd
Compass House Chivers Way, Histon, Cambridge, CB24 9AD
Tel: 01223-257608 **Fax:** 01223-257797
E-mail: david@dipinternational.co.uk
Website: http://www.dipinternational.co.uk
Directors: D. Greenfield (MD)
Immediate Holding Company: DIP INTERNATIONAL LIMITED
Registration no: 02982233 **Date established:** 1994
No.of Employees: 11 - 20 **Product Groups:** 37, 44, 67

Date of Accounts	Dec 11	Dec 10	Dec 09
Working Capital	2m	2m	2m
Fixed Assets	38	49	72
Current Assets	2m	2m	2m

Diverse Technologies & Systems Ltd
Zeromag House 46 Whittlesford Road, Little Shelford, Cambridge, CB22 5EW
Tel: 01223-844444
E-mail: sales@diverse-technologies.net
Website: http://www.diverse-technologies.net
Managers: S. Folds (Product)
Immediate Holding Company: DIVERSE TECHNOLOGIES AND SYSTEMS LIMITED
Registration no: 01790939 **Date established:** 1984
No.of Employees: 1 - 10 **Product Groups:** 84

Date of Accounts	Mar 12	Mar 11	Mar 10
Working Capital	225	73	21
Fixed Assets	13	12	11
Current Assets	492	171	127

Domino UK Ltd
Trafalgar Way Bar Hill, Cambridge, CB23 8TU
Tel: 01954-782551 **Fax:** 01954-782874
E-mail: sales@domino-uk.com
Website: http://www.domino-printing.com
Directors: A. Herbert (Fin), N. Bond (MD)
Immediate Holding Company: DOMINO PRINTING SCIENCES PUBLIC LIMITED COMPANY
Registration no: 01363137 **VAT No.:** GB 388 7030 22
Date established: 1978 **Turnover:** £250m - £500m
No.of Employees: 501 - 1000 **Product Groups:** 28, 32, 37, 42, 43, 44, 45, 46

Date of Accounts	Oct 11	Oct 10	Oct 09
Sales Turnover	314m	300m	256m
Pre Tax Profit/Loss	57m	52m	28m
Working Capital	60m	68m	47m
Fixed Assets	148m	116m	118m
Current Assets	133m	145m	115m
Current Liabilities	49m	56m	44m

E F S Manufacturing
1 Newmarket Road Stow-Cum-Quy, Cambridge, CB25 9AQ
Tel: 01223-813848 **Fax:** 01223-813848
E-mail: efsman@supanet.com
Managers: R. Fordham (Mgr)
Immediate Holding Company: EFS MANUFACTURING LIMITED
Registration no: 05802410 **Date established:** 2006
Turnover: £250,000 - £500,000 **No.of Employees:** 1 - 10
Product Groups: 37, 84

Date of Accounts	May 11	May 10	May 09
Working Capital	-47	-61	-45
Fixed Assets	61	86	110
Current Assets	88	82	94

E Johnson & Son
Unit 5 The Grip Linton, Cambridge, CB21 4XN
Tel: 01223-891149 **Fax:** 01223-893667
E-mail: ejohnsonandsons@hotmail.com
Directors: S. Johnson (Prop)
VAT No.: GB 214 3382 92 **Turnover:** £500,000 - £1m
No.of Employees: 1 - 10 **Product Groups:** 48

Echochoice Ltd
Cambridge Business Park Cowley Road, Cambridge, CB4 0WZ
Tel: 08456-381340 **Fax:** 0845-642 1340
E-mail: info@ecochoice.co.uk
Website: http://www.echochoice.co.uk
Managers: J. Middleton
Immediate Holding Company: ECOCHOICE LIMITED
Registration no: 05659260 **Date established:** 2005 **Turnover:** £5m - £10m
No.of Employees: 1 - 10 **Product Groups:** 25

Date of Accounts	Mar 09	Mar 08	Apr 11
Working Capital	92	49	153
Fixed Assets	N/A	N/A	1
Current Assets	220	100	305

Edale Instruments Cambridge Ltd
Gresley House Station Road Longstanton, Cambridge, CB24 3DS
Tel: 01954-260853 **Fax:** 01954-260894
Website: http://www.edale-instruments.co.uk
Directors: A. Hodgson (Prop)
Immediate Holding Company: EDALE INSTRUMENTS (CAMBRIDGE) LIMITED

Registration no: 01089550 **VAT No.:** GB 214 0545 08
Date established: 1973 **Turnover:** Up to £250,000
No.of Employees: 1 - 10 **Product Groups:** 38

Date of Accounts	May 12	May 11	May 10
Working Capital	30	35	18
Fixed Assets	212	218	139
Current Assets	31	38	19

Electrical Supplies Wholesalers
Unit A1 Atria Court Stirling Way, Papworth Everard, Cambridge, CB23 3GY
Tel: 08712-261972 **Fax:** 0871-226 1971
E-mail: sales@huntselectrical.com
Website: http://www.huintselectricalsupplies.com
Managers: H. Lean (District Mgr)
Immediate Holding Company: HUNTS ELECTRICAL SUPPLIES LIMITED
Registration no: 04359144 **Date established:** 2002
No.of Employees: 1 - 10 **Product Groups:** 37, 38, 67, 85

Date of Accounts	Jan 12	Jan 11	Jan 10
Working Capital	-117	-129	-91
Fixed Assets	287	278	296
Current Assets	171	138	156

Emre Import & Export Ltd
128 Malvern Road, Cambridge, CB1 9LH
Tel: 01223-245028 **Fax:** 01223-414862
E-mail: info@castorstockist.com
Website: http://www.castorstockist.com
Directors: A. Tiryakioglu (Ptnr)
Registration no: 03502029 **Product Groups:** 35, 39, 66, 67

Engineering & Design Plastics Ltd
84 High Street Cherry Hinton, Cambridge, CB1 9HZ
Tel: 01223-249431 **Fax:** 01223-411803
E-mail: sales@edplastics.co.uk
Website: http://www.edplastics.co.uk
Directors: C. Mason (Fin)
Managers: M. Bendall (Mgr), S. Heywood (Works Gen Mgr)
Immediate Holding Company: ENGINEERING AND DESIGN PLASTICS LTD
Registration no: 04375213 **VAT No.:** GB 215 6755 58
Date established: 2002 **Turnover:** £1m - £2m **No.of Employees:** 11 - 20
Product Groups: 48, 66

Date of Accounts	Sep 11	Sep 10	Sep 02
Current Assets	N/A	N/A	21

Eurotech International Group Ltd
The Old Coach House 56 High Street Harston, Cambridge, CB22 7PZ
Tel: 01223-875100 **Fax:** 01223-875150
E-mail: custserve@eurotech.org
Website: http://www.eurotech.org
Bank(s): Barclays Bank P.L.C., Huntingdon Business Centre
Directors: M. Hellowell (MD)
Immediate Holding Company: EUROTECH INTERNATIONAL GROUP LTD
Registration no: 04138341 **Date established:** 2001 **Turnover:** £2m - £5m
No.of Employees: 11 - 20 **Product Groups:** 84, 86

Date of Accounts	Mar 12	Mar 11	Mar 10
Working Capital	-61	-16	-6
Current Assets	1	62	63

Eurotronic Associates
46 Edinburgh Avenue Sawston, Cambridge, CB22 3DP
Tel: 01223-830620
E-mail: david.pirie@ntlworld.com
Directors: P. Pirie (Ptnr)
VAT No.: GB 599 4673 63 **Date established:** 2000
Turnover: Up to £250,000 **No.of Employees:** 1 - 10 **Product Groups:** 37

Eversheds
Kett House 1 Station Road, Cambridge, CB1 2JY
Tel: 01223-443666 **Fax:** 01223-443777
E-mail: ianmather@eversheds.com
Website: http://www.eversheds.com
Managers: I. Mather (Mgr)
Immediate Holding Company: THE RUSSELL GROUP OF UNIVERSITIES
Registration no: OC304065 **Date established:** 2007
Turnover: £250,000 - £500,000 **No.of Employees:** 51 - 100
Product Groups: 80

Date of Accounts	Dec 08	Jul 11	Jul 10
Working Capital	20	-38	N/A
Fixed Assets	7	N/A	N/A
Current Assets	23	1	N/A

F L T Training
2 Edinburgh Avenue Sawston, Cambridge, CB22 3DP
Tel: 01223-571312
E-mail: chris.sales1@ntlworld.com
Website: http://www.flttraining.co.uk
Directors: C. Sales (Prop)
Immediate Holding Company: CHRIS SALES FORK LIFT TRUCK TRAINING LIMITED
Date established: 2006 **No.of Employees:** 1 - 10 **Product Groups:** 35, 39, 45

Date of Accounts	Sep 11	Sep 10	Sep 09
Working Capital	-2	-1	-7
Fixed Assets	6	8	7
Current Assets	24	21	22

Feilden & Mawson LLP
Musgrave Farm Horningsea Road, Fen Ditton, Cambridge, CB5 8SZ
Tel: 01223-294017 **Fax:** 01223-293458
E-mail: paulrynsard@feildenandmawson.com
Website: http://www.feildenandmawson.com
Directors: P. Rynsard (Snr Part)
Immediate Holding Company: FEILDEN + MAWSON LLP
Registration no: OC300486 **Date established:** 2001
No.of Employees: 1 - 10 **Product Groups:** 84

Date of Accounts	Mar 12	Mar 11	Mar 10
Working Capital	1m	1m	1m
Fixed Assets	290	282	298
Current Assets	2m	2m	1m

First Edition Translations Ltd
6 Wellington Court Wellington Street, Cambridge, CB1 1HZ
Tel: 01223-356733 **Fax:** 01223-316232
E-mail: info@firstedit.co.uk
Website: http://www.firstedit.co.uk
Directors: J. Waller (Co Sec)
Immediate Holding Company: FIRST EDITION TRANSLATIONS LIMITED
Registration no: 02520431 **VAT No.:** GB 336 5860 38
Date established: 1990 **Turnover:** £500,000 - £1m
No.of Employees: 1 - 10 **Product Groups:** 80

Date of Accounts	Sep 11	Sep 10	Sep 09
Working Capital	153	152	112
Fixed Assets	5	4	15
Current Assets	331	286	267

Frimstone Ltd
Ely Road Waterbeach, Cambridge, CB25 9PG
Tel: 01223-860000 **Fax:** 01223-440378
E-mail: reception@frimstone.co.uk
Website: http://www.frimstone.co.uk
Bank(s): Lloyds
Directors: M. Swan (Comm), C. Faiers (Fin), G. Bell (MD)
Managers: G. Morris (Personnel)
Ultimate Holding Company: ALBORO HOLDINGS LIMITED
Immediate Holding Company: FRIMSTONE LIMITED
Registration no: 01232146 **VAT No.:** 213 5682 76 **Date established:** 1975
Turnover: £5m - £10m **No.of Employees:** 11 - 20 **Product Groups:** 14, 33, 83

Date of Accounts	Mar 12	Mar 11	Mar 10
Sales Turnover	15m	9m	6m
Pre Tax Profit/Loss	-620	252	-98
Working Capital	-531	506	1m
Fixed Assets	9m	8m	7m
Current Assets	7m	6m	4m
Current Liabilities	1m	1m	404

Fugro Aperio Ltd
Focal Point Newmarket Road, Bottisham, Cambridge, CB25 9BD
Tel: 01223-813800 **Fax:** 0870-600 8040
E-mail: info@fugro-aperio.com
Website: http://www.fugro-aperio.com
Directors: S. Dods (Dir)
Ultimate Holding Company: FUGRO NV (NETHERLANDS)
Immediate Holding Company: FUGRO APERIO LIMITED
Registration no: 03235409 **Date established:** 1996
No.of Employees: 21 - 50 **Product Groups:** 37, 38, 51, 52, 84, 85

Date of Accounts	Dec 10	Dec 09	Dec 08
Sales Turnover	3m	2m	2m
Pre Tax Profit/Loss	212	236	-13
Working Capital	463	465	276
Fixed Assets	350	203	222
Current Assets	1m	1m	902
Current Liabilities	275	180	130

G E Smallworld plc
Elizabeth House 1 High Street, Chesterton, Cambridge, CB4 1WR
Tel: 01223-301144 **Fax:** 01223-311145
E-mail: sales@gesmallworld.com
Website: http://www.gepower.com
Bank(s): Barclays
Directors: K. Simms (Fin), P. Gearing (Mkt Research)
Managers: P. McCusker (Tech Serv Mgr), D. Stonebridge (Personnel)
Immediate Holding Company: SMALLWORLDWIDE P.L.C.
Registration no: 02292791 **VAT No.:** GB 665 8845 77
Date established: 1988 **Turnover:** £20m - £50m
No.of Employees: 101 - 250 **Product Groups:** 44, 84

Givemegraphics.Net
93 Burnside, Cambridge, CB1 3PA
Tel: 01223-410818
E-mail: info@givemegraphics.net
Website: http://www.givemegraphics.net
Directors: R. Sheppard (MD), R. Sheppard (Prop)
Date established: 2001 **Turnover:** Up to £250,000
No.of Employees: 1 - 10 **Product Groups:** 64, 81

Global Graphics Software Ltd
Building 2030 Cambourne Business Park, Cambridge, CB23 6DW
Tel: 01954-283100 **Fax:** 01954-283101
Website: http://www.globalgraphics.com
Managers: V. Bibby
Ultimate Holding Company: Harlequin Group Ltd
Immediate Holding Company: Harlequin Group P.L.C.
Registration no: 02049413 **Turnover:** £10m - £20m
No.of Employees: 51 - 100 **Product Groups:** 44

Date of Accounts	Dec 09	Dec 08	Dec 07
Sales Turnover	7m	7m	9m
Pre Tax Profit/Loss	-4m	5m	1m
Working Capital	12m	16m	11m
Fixed Assets	13m	13m	13m
Current Assets	26m	29m	24m
Current Liabilities	1m	1m	765

Graphic Art Cambridge Ltd
Trinity Hall Farm Industrial Estate Nuffield Road, Cambridge, CB4 1TG
Tel: 01223-424421 **Fax:** 01223-426040
E-mail: info@graphic-art.co.uk
Website: http://www.graphic-art.co.uk
Bank(s): Lloyds TSB Bank plc
Directors: K. Jones (MD), G. Russell (Fin)
Ultimate Holding Company: MARK ONE INVESTMENTS LIMITED
Immediate Holding Company: GRAPHIC ART (CAMBRIDGE) LIMITED
Registration no: 00909006 **VAT No.:** GB 213 2837 88
Date established: 1967 **Turnover:** £2m - £5m **No.of Employees:** 21 - 50
Product Groups: 28, 30, 32, 44, 67

Date of Accounts	Aug 11	Aug 10	Aug 09
Sales Turnover	3m	3m	2m
Pre Tax Profit/Loss	-199	-283	-575
Working Capital	782	916	1m
Fixed Assets	91	159	245
Current Assets	1m	2m	2m
Current Liabilities	43	40	27

Hanworth Laboratories Ltd
Unit 2 The Grip, Linton, Cambridge, CB21 4XN
Tel: 01223-892217 **Fax:** 01223-893592
Website: http://www.HanworthLab.co.uk
Bank(s): Barclays, Saffron Walden
Directors: J. Shannon (Dir), R. Allagan (Dir), C. Taverner (Co Sec)
Managers: C. Taverner (Sales Admin)
Immediate Holding Company: HANWORTH LABORATORIES LIMITED
Registration no: 00610097 **VAT No.:** GB 283 6469 22
Date established: 1958 **Turnover:** £1m - £2m **No.of Employees:** 51 - 100
Product Groups: 31, 32, 49

Date of Accounts	Feb 09	Dec 07	Dec 06
Working Capital	86	196	239
Fixed Assets	222	300	343
Current Assets	890	1m	1m

M P Harvey
119-123 Middle Watch Swavesey, Cambridge, CB24 4RP
Tel: 01954-206113 **Fax:** 01954-206113
Directors: M. Harvey (Prop)
Date established: 1997 **No.of Employees:** 1 - 10 **Product Groups:** 37

Heffers Sound (Blackwells Retail UK)
19 Trinity Street, Cambridge, CB2 1TY
Tel: 01223-568562 **Fax:** 01223-568591
E-mail: heffers@heffers.co.uk
Website: http://www.blackwells.co.uk
Directors: B. Robinson (MD)
Managers: D. Robinson (Chief Mgr), D. Robinson (Mgr), T. McGeorge (Mgr)
Turnover: £250,000 - £500,000 **No.of Employees:** 1 - 10
Product Groups: 64

Heraeus Noble Light Analytic Ltd
3-4 Nuffield Close, Cambridge, CB4 1SS
Tel: 01223-424100 **Fax:** 01223-426338
E-mail: darren.golding@heraeus.com
Website: http://www.heraeus.com
Bank(s): National Westminster Bank Plc
Managers: D. Golding (Ops Mgr)
Ultimate Holding Company: HERAEUS HOLDING GMBH (GERMANY)
Immediate Holding Company: HERAEUS NOBLELIGHT ANALYTICS LIMITED
Registration no: 00298211 **VAT No.:** GB 599 4058 83
Date established: 1935 **Turnover:** £2m - £5m **No.of Employees:** 11 - 20
Product Groups: 37

Date of Accounts	Dec 11	Dec 10	Dec 09
Sales Turnover	3m	3m	3m
Pre Tax Profit/Loss	488	338	217
Working Capital	1m	1m	946
Fixed Assets	59	103	143
Current Assets	2m	1m	1m
Current Liabilities	196	177	149

Hewitsons
Shakespeare House 42 Newmarket Road, Cambridge, CB5 8EP
Tel: 01223-461155 **Fax:** 01223-316511
E-mail: mail@hewitsons.com
Website: http://www.hewitsons.com
Directors: S. Weaving (Mkt Research), J. Dix (Snr Part), K. Brett (Snr Part)
Managers: M. Thomas (Comptroller), A. Griffiths, J. Wilcox (Sec), C. Jones (I.T. Exec)
Immediate Holding Company: HEWITSONS LLP
Registration no: OC334689 **Date established:** 2008
Turnover: £10m - £20m **No.of Employees:** 101 - 250 **Product Groups:** 80

Date of Accounts	Apr 11	Apr 10	Apr 09
Sales Turnover	13m	13m	N/A
Pre Tax Profit/Loss	3m	3m	3m
Working Capital	3m	4m	4m
Fixed Assets	3m	375	601
Current Assets	5m	6m	6m
Current Liabilities	855	1m	1m

The Howard Group (Head Office)
93 Regent Street, Cambridge, CB2 1AW
Tel: 01223-312910 **Fax:** 01233-312911
E-mail: admin@howard-ventures.com
Website: http://www.howard-ventures.com
Directors: N. Bewes (MD)
Ultimate Holding Company: HOWARD INVESTMENT COMPANY LIMITED
Immediate Holding Company: HOWARD VENTURES LIMITED
Registration no: 05895937 **Date established:** 2006 **Turnover:** £1m - £2m
No.of Employees: 1 - 10 **Product Groups:** 80

Date of Accounts	Sep 11	Sep 10	Sep 09
Sales Turnover	1m	15m	1m
Pre Tax Profit/Loss	-786	-2m	319
Working Capital	9m	3m	9m
Fixed Assets	4m	13m	4m
Current Assets	10m	18m	9m
Current Liabilities	576	5m	517

Human Computer Interface Ltd
17 Signet Court Swann Road, Cambridge, CB5 8LA
Tel: 01223-314934 **Fax:** 01223-462562
E-mail: info@interface.co.uk
Website: http://www.interface.co.uk
Directors: D. Johnson-Davies (Dir)
Immediate Holding Company: HUMAN-COMPUTER INTERFACE LIMITED
Registration no: 02002436 **Date established:** 1986
No.of Employees: 1 - 10 **Product Groups:** 81

Date of Accounts	Jun 11	Jun 10	Jun 07
Working Capital	70	112	63
Fixed Assets	4	5	6
Current Assets	94	117	112

Hutchings & Harding Ltd
163 High Street Sawston, Cambridge, CB22 3HN
Tel: 01223-832281 **Fax:** 01223-836401
E-mail: john@chamois.com
Website: http://www.chamois.com
Directors: M. Fagan (MD)
Ultimate Holding Company: HUTCHINGS & HARDING GROUP LIMITED
Immediate Holding Company: HUTCHINGS & HARDING LIMITED
Registration no: 00185217 **Date established:** 2022
Turnover: Up to £250,000 **No.of Employees:** 21 - 50 **Product Groups:** 22

Date of Accounts	Jun 12	Jun 11	Jun 10
Working Capital	1m	1m	1m
Fixed Assets	118	159	160
Current Assets	3m	3m	2m

Hypro Eu Ltd
Station Road Longstanton, Cambridge, CB24 3DS
Tel: 01954-260097 **Fax:** 01954-260245
E-mail: info@hypro-eu.com
Website: http://hypro-eu.com
Bank(s): Bank of Scotland, Norwich

see next page

***Hypro Eu Ltd** - Cont'd*

Directors: M. Campbell (MD)
Ultimate Holding Company: PENTAIR INC (USA)
Immediate Holding Company: HYPRO EU LIMITED
Registration no: 02571559 **VAT No.:** GB 741 0617 63
Date established: 1991 **Turnover:** £2m - £5m **No.of Employees:** 21 - 50
Product Groups: 24, 30, 36, 38, 39, 40, 41, 42, 43, 45, 46

Date of Accounts	Dec 11	Dec 10	Dec 09
Sales Turnover	7m	5m	4m
Pre Tax Profit/Loss	2m	566	250
Working Capital	3m	1m	936
Fixed Assets	1m	1m	2m
Current Assets	4m	2m	2m
Current Liabilities	253	260	218

Imtech Control Services Ltd

Aqua House Rose & Crown Road, Swavesey, Cambridge, CB24 4RB
Tel: 01954-234600 **Fax:** 01954-230593
E-mail: john.wardley@imtechaqua.co.uk
Website: http://www.imtechaqua.co.uk
Directors: J. Hughes (Dir), J. Wardley (MD)
Ultimate Holding Company: IMTECH NV (NETHERLANDS)
Immediate Holding Company: IMTECH AQUA CONTROLS LTD
Registration no: 01484440 **Date established:** 1980 **Turnover:** £2m - £5m
No.of Employees: 1 - 10 **Product Groups:** 37

Date of Accounts	Dec 11	Dec 10	Dec 09
Sales Turnover	43m	32m	48m
Pre Tax Profit/Loss	1m	1m	2m
Working Capital	5m	5m	4m
Fixed Assets	2m	2m	3m
Current Assets	17m	15m	16m
Current Liabilities	3m	3m	5m

Independent Optics Ltd

20 Norman Way Industrial Estate Norman Way, Over, Cambridge, CB24 5QE
Tel: 01954-231545 **Fax:** 01954-231340
Directors: M. Kelly (Fin), P. Kelly (Dir), P. Kelly (Fin)
Immediate Holding Company: INDEPENDENT OPTICS LIMITED
Registration no: 02116735 **Date established:** 1987
No.of Employees: 1 - 10 **Product Groups:** 37, 38, 65

Date of Accounts	Jun 11	Jun 10	Jun 09
Working Capital	46	58	94
Fixed Assets	8	10	12
Current Assets	69	92	134

Industrial & Scientific Supplies

The Grip Linton, Cambridge, CB21 4XN
Tel: 01223-891953 **Fax:** 01223-894223
E-mail: sales@industrialscientific.co.uk
Website: http://www.industrialscientific.co.uk
Directors: E. Dwier (MD)
Registration no: 04484861 **Turnover:** £500,000 - £1m
No.of Employees: 1 - 10 **Product Groups:** 24, 29, 30, 37, 40

Infield Safety UK Ltd

Vanilla House Cambridge Road, Babraham, Cambridge, CB22 3GN
Tel: 01223-836222 **Fax:** 01440-705557
E-mail: info@infield-safety.co.uk
Website: http://www.infield-safety.co.uk
Directors: S. Spurdens (Dir)
Managers: A. Rodden (Mgr)
Immediate Holding Company: INFIELD SAFETY UK LIMITED
Registration no: 05607420 **Date established:** 2005
Turnover: £250,000 - £500,000 **No.of Employees:** 1 - 10
Product Groups: 40

Date of Accounts	Jul 09	Jul 08	Jul 07
Working Capital	-431	-144	65
Fixed Assets	176	186	21
Current Assets	105	215	244

Information Transfer LLP

Burleigh House 15 Newmarket Road, Cambridge, CB5 8EG
Tel: 01223-312227 **Fax:** 01223-310200
E-mail: info@intran.co.uk
Website: http://www.informationtransfer.com
Directors: N. Clayton (Co Sec), D. Ganz (Ptnr)
Immediate Holding Company: THE ACTEON CONSULTANCY LLP
Registration no: OC301093 **Date established:** 2001
Turnover: Up to £250,000 **No.of Employees:** 11 - 20 **Product Groups:** 80, 81, 82, 86

Date of Accounts	Dec 11	Dec 10	Dec 09
Working Capital	416	342	285
Fixed Assets	55	46	52
Current Assets	1m	906	641

Intumescent Seals (a division of Dixon International Group Ltd)

Brewery Road Pampisford, Cambridge, CB22 3HG
Tel: 01223-832758 **Fax:** 01223-837215
E-mail: sales@intumescentseals.co.uk
Website: http://www.intumescentseals.co.uk
Directors: E. Southern (MD), C. Malcolm-brown (Sales & Mktg)
Managers: R. Townsend (Sales Admin), D. Allen, D. Curlsey (Personnel), R. Denston (Tech Serv Mgr)
Ultimate Holding Company: DIXON INTERNATIONAL GROUP LIMITED
Immediate Holding Company: INTUMESCENT SEALS LIMITED
Registration no: 01493132 **Date established:** 1980 **Turnover:** £1m - £2m
No.of Employees: 21 - 50 **Product Groups:** 32

J S Wilson & Son Bookbinders Ltd

Unit 17 Ronald Rolph Court Wadloes Road, Cambridge, CB5 8PX
Tel: 01223-212420 **Fax:** 01223-212420
E-mail: enquiries@jswandson.co.uk
Website: http://www.cambridgebookbinding.co.uk
Directors: E. Brigham (MD)
Immediate Holding Company: JS WILSON & SON (BOOKBINDERS) LIMITED
Registration no: 06255659 **Date established:** 2007
No.of Employees: 1 - 10 **Product Groups:** 67

Date of Accounts	Jun 11	Jun 10	Jun 09
Working Capital	-27	-42	-70
Fixed Assets	125	136	149
Current Assets	19	21	21

Jewson Ltd

Mercers Row, Cambridge, CB5 8HY
Tel: 01223-356904 **Fax:** 01223-467435
E-mail: mark.hinchley@jewson.co.uk
Website: http://www.jewson.co.uk
Managers: M. Hinchley (Mgr)
Ultimate Holding Company: COMPAGNIE DE SAINT GOBAIN (FRANCE)
Immediate Holding Company: JEWSON LIMITED
Registration no: 00348407 **VAT No.:** GB 497 7184 33
Date established: 1939 **Turnover:** £2m - £5m **No.of Employees:** 1 - 10
Product Groups: 66

Date of Accounts	Dec 11	Dec 10	Dec 09
Sales Turnover	1606m	1547m	1485m
Pre Tax Profit/Loss	18m	100m	45m
Working Capital	-345m	-250m	-349m
Fixed Assets	496m	387m	481m
Current Assets	657m	1005m	1320m
Current Liabilities	66m	120m	64m

K E Developments Ltd

The Mount High Street Toft, Cambridge, CB23 2RL
Tel: 01223-263532 **Fax:** 01223-263948
E-mail: gwardall@kedev.com
Website: http://www.kedev.co.uk
Directors: G. Wardall (MD)
Ultimate Holding Company: MICRO ANALYSIS TECHNOLOGY LTD
Immediate Holding Company: K.E. DEVELOPMENTS LIMITED
Registration no: 01311528 **Date established:** 1977 **Turnover:** £1m - £2m
No.of Employees: 1 - 10 **Product Groups:** 37, 38

Date of Accounts	Jun 08	Jun 07	Jun 06
Working Capital	1790	1662	1742
Fixed Assets	155	163	169
Current Assets	2047	1981	1999
Current Liabilities	257	319	257
Total Share Capital	1	1	1

Kershaw Mechanical Services Ltd

Unit E Beadle Trading Estate Ditton Walk, Cambridge, CB5 8PD
Tel: 01223-715800 **Fax:** 01223-411061
E-mail: enquiries@kershaw-grp.co.uk
Website: http://www.kershaw-grp.co.uk
Directors: I. Greenstock (Sales), M. Finlay (MD), K. Smith (Co Sec)
Managers: I. Allan (Tech Serv Mgr), C. Blundell (Chief Buyer)
Ultimate Holding Company: KERSHAW GROUP LIMITED
Immediate Holding Company: KERSHAW MECHANICAL SERVICES LIMITED
Registration no: 00540706 **Date established:** 1954
Turnover: £10m - £20m **No.of Employees:** 51 - 100 **Product Groups:** 30

Date of Accounts	Dec 11	Dec 10	Dec 09
Sales Turnover	19m	19m	21m
Pre Tax Profit/Loss	630	1m	1m
Working Capital	534	496	545
Fixed Assets	114	149	144
Current Assets	5m	4m	5m
Current Liabilities	410	641	645

John Lawton Electronics

61 Maids Causeway, Cambridge, CB5 8DE
Tel: 01223-520604 **Fax:** 01223-566493
E-mail: design@jle.co.uk
Website: http://www.jle.co.uk
Directors: E. Hunter (Fin)
Registration no: 04712824 **Turnover:** Up to £250,000
No.of Employees: 1 - 10 **Product Groups:** 37, 38, 48, 67, 84

Date of Accounts	Apr 06
Working Capital	1
Current Assets	6
Current Liabilities	5

Leica Microsystems Cambridge Ltd

Lothbury House Newmarket Road, Cambridge, CB5 8PB
Tel: 01223-411411 **Fax:** 01223-210692
E-mail: ia-support@lis.leica.co.uk
Website: http://www.leica-microsystems.com
Bank(s): HSBC, London EC2P 2BX
Directors: C. Davis (Dir), D. Edwards (Co Sec)
Ultimate Holding Company: DANAHER CORPORATION (DELAWARE U.S.A)
Immediate Holding Company: LEICA MICROSYSTEMS CAMBRIDGE LIMITED
Registration no: 02690018 **VAT No.:** GB 290 7562 38
Date established: 1992 **Turnover:** £5m - £10m
No.of Employees: 51 - 100 **Product Groups:** 37, 44

Date of Accounts	Dec 11	Dec 10	Dec 09
Sales Turnover	9m	8m	8m
Pre Tax Profit/Loss	6m	5m	40m
Working Capital	52m	54m	49m
Fixed Assets	9m	1m	684
Current Assets	54m	56m	51m
Current Liabilities	974	1m	839

Mackay Storage Systems

85 East Road, Cambridge, CB1 1BY
Tel: 01223-517000 **Fax:** 01223- 716000
E-mail: sales@mackay.co.uk
Website: http://www.mackay.co.uk/mss
Directors: N. Mackay (Dir)
Managers: C. Twin (Tech Serv Mgr), R. Chelkowski (Buyer), S. Clemments
Immediate Holding Company: MACKAYS OF CAMBRIDGE HOLDINGS LIMITED
Registration no: 07061532 **Date established:** 2009
No.of Employees: 1 - 10 **Product Groups:** 35, 36, 37

Date of Accounts	Mar 11
Working Capital	-3m
Fixed Assets	4m
Current Assets	4

Magma Safety Products Ltd

Unit 1 Sawston Park London Road, Pampisford, Cambridge, CB22 3EE
Tel: 01223-836643 **Fax:** 01223-834648
E-mail: info@magmasafety.co.uk
Website: http://www.magmasafety.co.uk
Directors: A. Moss (MD)
Immediate Holding Company: MAGMA SAFETY PRODUCTS LIMITED
Registration no: 02711157 **Date established:** 1992
Turnover: £250,000 - £500,000 **No.of Employees:** 1 - 10
Product Groups: 29, 35, 40

Date of Accounts	May 12	May 11	May 10
Working Capital	134	116	115
Fixed Assets	42	56	35
Current Assets	220	180	203

Maplin Electronics Ltd

Ground Floor Janus House 46-48 St Andrews Street, Cambridge, CB2 3AH
Tel: 08432-277335
E-mail: customercare@maplin.co.uk
Website: http://www.maplin.co.uk
Managers: E. Hoppett
Ultimate Holding Company: MONTAGU PRIVATE EQUITY LLP
Immediate Holding Company: MAPLIN ELECTRONICS LIMITED
Registration no: 01264385 **Date established:** 1976
Turnover: £125m - £250m **No.of Employees:** 21 - 50
Product Groups: 37, 61

Date of Accounts	Dec 11	Dec 08	Dec 09
Sales Turnover	205m	204m	204m
Pre Tax Profit/Loss	25m	32m	35m
Working Capital	118m	49m	75m
Fixed Assets	27m	28m	28m
Current Assets	207m	108m	142m
Current Liabilities	78m	51m	59m

Maplin Electronics Ltd

The Beehive Centre Coldhams Lane, Cambridge, CB1 3ET
Tel: 08432-277370 **Fax:** 01223-362395
E-mail: customercare@maplin.co.uk
Website: http://www.maplin.co.uk
Managers: M. Stevens (Mgr)
Ultimate Holding Company: MONTAGU PRIVATE EQUITY LLP
Immediate Holding Company: MAPLIN ELECTRONICS LIMITED
Registration no: 01264385 **Date established:** 1976
Turnover: £125m - £250m **No.of Employees:** 1 - 10 **Product Groups:** 37, 61

Date of Accounts	Dec 11	Dec 08	Dec 09
Sales Turnover	205m	204m	204m
Pre Tax Profit/Loss	25m	32m	35m
Working Capital	118m	49m	75m
Fixed Assets	27m	28m	28m
Current Assets	207m	108m	142m
Current Liabilities	78m	51m	59m

Marshall Aerospace Cambridge Ltd

The Airport Newmarket Road, Cambridge, CB5 8RX
Tel: 01223-373737 **Fax:** 01223-321032
E-mail: info@marshallsv.com
Website: http://www.cambridgecityairport.com
Bank(s): Barclays
Directors: A. Paul (Tech Serv), R. Marshall (Prop), K. Hussey (Pers), G. Clark (Fin)
Managers: J. McKeown
Ultimate Holding Company: MARSHALL OF CAMBRIDGE (HOLDINGS) LIMITED
Immediate Holding Company: MARSHALL OF CAMBRIDGE AEROSPACE LIMITED
Registration no: 00245740 **VAT No.:** GB 432 2139 88
Date established: 1930 **Turnover:** £125m - £250m
No.of Employees: 1001 - 1500 **Product Groups:** 39, 71, 84

Date of Accounts	Dec 11	Dec 10	Dec 09
Sales Turnover	211m	197m	220m
Pre Tax Profit/Loss	4m	-8m	8m
Working Capital	22m	19m	28m
Fixed Assets	17m	19m	19m
Current Assets	83m	93m	87m
Current Liabilities	37m	48m	51m

Martek Power Ltd

Glebe Farm Campus Knapwell, Cambridge, CB23 4GG
Tel: 01954-267726 **Fax:** 01954-267626
E-mail: sales@martekpower.co.uk
Website: http://www.martekpower.co.uk
Managers: K. Ward
Ultimate Holding Company: MARTEK POWER SA (FRANCE)
Immediate Holding Company: MARTEK POWER LIMITED
Registration no: 04588863 **Date established:** 2002
Turnover: £20m - £50m **No.of Employees:** 21 - 50 **Product Groups:** 37

Date of Accounts	Dec 11	Dec 10	Dec 09
Working Capital	608	560	403
Fixed Assets	118	120	110
Current Assets	898	952	867

Micro Robotics Ltd

135 Ditton Walk, Cambridge, CB5 8QB
Tel: 01223-523100 **Fax:** 01223-524242
E-mail: sales@microrobotics.co.uk
Website: http://www.microrobotics.co.uk
Directors: E. Coyle (Co Sec), C. Keeler (Sales), K. Lam (I.T. Dir)
Immediate Holding Company: MICRO-ROBOTICS LIMITED
Registration no: 03983610 **VAT No.:** GB 393 2883 17
Date established: 2000 **Turnover:** £1m - £2m **No.of Employees:** 1 - 10
Product Groups: 37, 38, 39, 44, 45, 67, 84, 85

Date of Accounts	Mar 11	Mar 10	Mar 09
Working Capital	357	321	284
Fixed Assets	3	1	1
Current Assets	437	379	349

Microvideo Ltd

The Carthouse 1 Copley Hill Buisness Park Cambridge Road, Babraham, Cambridge, CB22 3GN
Tel: 01223-834119 **Fax:** 01223-834471
E-mail: sales@microvideo.co.uk
Website: http://www.microvideo.co.uk
Managers: I. Hudson
Ultimate Holding Company: I4B LIMITED
Immediate Holding Company: MICROVIDEO LIMITED
Registration no: 02215776 **Date established:** 1988
No.of Employees: 1 - 10 **Product Groups:** 37, 44

Date of Accounts	Apr 11	Apr 10	Apr 09
Working Capital	1	-47	-14
Fixed Assets	8	10	14
Current Assets	157	143	134

Millers Music Centre Ltd

12 Sussex Street, Cambridge, CB1 1PW
Tel: 01223-354452 **Fax:** 01223-362480
E-mail: info@millersmusic.co.uk
Website: http://www.millersmusic.co.uk
Bank(s): Barclays
Directors: B. Robinson (MD), R. Drew (Fin)
Immediate Holding Company: MILLERS MUSIC LIMITED
Registration no: 01513150 **VAT No.:** GB 213 3419 04
Date established: 1980 **No.of Employees:** 21 - 50 **Product Groups:** 49, 65

Date of Accounts	Mar 10	Mar 09	Mar 08
Working Capital	1	1	1
Current Assets	1	1	1

Mills & Reeve LLP

Francis House 112 Hills Road, Cambridge, CB2 1PH
Tel: 01223-364422 **Fax:** 01223-355848
E-mail: guy.hinchley@mills-reeve.com
Website: http://www.mills-reeve.com
Directors: G. Hinchley (MD), S. Boyle (Pers), J. Mortimer (Mkt Research)
Managers: G. Low, K. Harper (Fin Mgr)
Ultimate Holding Company: MILEX LIMITED
Immediate Holding Company: MILLS & REEVE LLP
Registration no: OC326165 **Date established:** 2007
Turnover: £250,000 - £500,000 **No.of Employees:** 101 - 250
Product Groups: 80

Date of Accounts	May 12	May 11	May 10
Sales Turnover	69m	67m	67m
Pre Tax Profit/Loss	26m	24m	24m
Working Capital	18m	19m	18m
Fixed Assets	4m	4m	4m
Current Assets	27m	28m	27m
Current Liabilities	6m	5m	N/A

Mitchams Agricultural Machinery

Berkeley House Burwell, Cambridge, CB25 0DY
Tel: 01638-741226 **Fax:** 01638-743151
E-mail: sales@mitchams.com
Website: http://www.mitchams.com
Directors: M. Mitcham (Prop)
Immediate Holding Company: MITCHAMS AGRICULTURAL MACHINERY LIMITED
Registration no: 00839325 **VAT No.:** GB 102 398 883
Date established: 1965 **Turnover:** £10m - £20m
No.of Employees: 11 - 20 **Product Groups:** 67

Date of Accounts	May 11	May 10	May 09
Sales Turnover	11m	10m	10m
Pre Tax Profit/Loss	558	75	239
Working Capital	3m	2m	2m
Fixed Assets	838	1m	959
Current Assets	16m	10m	6m
Current Liabilities	10m	5m	2m

Napp Pharmaceutical Group Ltd

Science Park Milton Road, Cambridge, CB4 0GW
Tel: 01223-424444 **Fax:** 01223-424441
E-mail: vacancies@napp.co.uk
Website: http://www.napp.co.uk
Bank(s): National Westminster Bank Plc
Directors: K. Sackler (Dir), D. Leitner (MD)
Ultimate Holding Company: NAPP PHARMACEUTICAL HOLDINGS LIMITED
Immediate Holding Company: NAPP PHARMACEUTICAL GROUP LIMITED
Registration no: 00884285 **Date established:** 1966
Turnover: £50m - £75m **No.of Employees:** 501 - 1000
Product Groups: 31, 63, 85

Date of Accounts	Dec 11	Dec 10	Dec 09
Sales Turnover	67m	70m	65m
Pre Tax Profit/Loss	34m	13m	8m
Working Capital	33m	39m	28m
Fixed Assets	5m	5m	6m
Current Assets	38m	43m	30m
Current Liabilities	5m	4m	2m

National Extension College

The Michael Young Centre Purbeck Road, Cambridge, CB2 8HN
Tel: 01223-400200 **Fax:** 01223-400399
E-mail: gavin.teasdale@nec.ac.uk
Website: http://www.nec.ac.uk
Directors: West (MD), G. Teasdale (Grp Chief Exec), A. West (Dir)
Managers: Hern (I.T. Exec), Hopwood (Sales Prom), T. Hopwood (Sales Prom)
Immediate Holding Company: NATIONAL EXTENSION COLLEGE TRUST LIMITED
Registration no: 00292829 **VAT No.:** GB 215 7137 79
Date established: 1934 **Turnover:** £2m - £5m **No.of Employees:** 21 - 50
Product Groups: 86

Date of Accounts	Jun 09	Jun 08	Jun 07
Sales Turnover	2m	3m	3m
Pre Tax Profit/Loss	-180	79	-127
Working Capital	-1m	-488	-435
Fixed Assets	7m	6m	6m
Current Assets	376	368	401
Current Liabilities	302	325	200

Noahs Ark Chemicals Ltd

39 Bosworth Road, Cambridge, CB1 8RG
Tel: 01223-471215 **Fax:** 01223-690808
E-mail: info@noahsark.eu.com
Website: http://www.noahsark.eu.com
Directors: K. Bhardwaj (Dir)
Managers: B. Bhardwaj
Immediate Holding Company: NOAHS ARK CHEMICALS LIMITED
Registration no: 04237054 **VAT No.:** GB 782 2550 25
Date established: 2001 **Turnover:** £1m - £2m **No.of Employees:** 1 - 10
Product Groups: 31, 38

Date of Accounts	Jun 11	Jun 10	Jun 09
Sales Turnover	N/A	2m	4m
Pre Tax Profit/Loss	N/A	59	90
Working Capital	382	447	428
Fixed Assets	89	66	61
Current Assets	739	850	2m
Current Liabilities	N/A	406	1m

Norwich & Peterborough Isurance Brokers

45-53 Mill Road, Cambridge, CB1 2AP
Tel: 01223-273100 **Fax:** 01223-350655
E-mail: info@npib.co.uk
Website: http://www.npib.co.uk
Bank(s): Barclays
Directors: J. Thomas (Fin), S. Kendall (Pers)
Ultimate Holding Company: YORKSHIRE BUILDING SOCIETY
Immediate Holding Company: NORWICH AND PETERBOROUGH INSURANCE BROKERS LIMITED
Registration no: 00699978 **Date established:** 1961 **Turnover:** £2m - £5m
No.of Employees: 21 - 50 **Product Groups:** 82

Date of Accounts	Dec 11	Dec 10	Dec 09
Sales Turnover	5m	5m	4m
Pre Tax Profit/Loss	2m	2m	1m
Working Capital	7m	5m	5m
Fixed Assets	978	1m	569
Current Assets	10m	9m	7m
Current Liabilities	423	787	223

Obducat Camscan Ltd

Camscan House Pembroke Avenue, Waterbeach, Cambridge, CB25 9PY
Tel: 01223-861066 **Fax:** 01223-861077
E-mail: info@camscan.com
Website: http://www.camscan.com
Bank(s): Natwest Fitzroy Street Cambridge
Directors: I. Holton (Dir)
Managers: W. Key (Sales & Mktg Mg), R. Paden (), D. Bateman (Purch Mgr)
Ultimate Holding Company: OBDUCAT AB GROUP (SWEDEN)
Immediate Holding Company: OBDUCAT CAMSCAN LIMITED
Registration no: 03589614 **VAT No.:** GB 631 8770 30
Date established: 1998 **Turnover:** £1m - £2m **No.of Employees:** 11 - 20
Product Groups: 38

Date of Accounts	Dec 09	Dec 08	Dec 07
Sales Turnover	2m	2m	1m
Pre Tax Profit/Loss	-977	-643	-546
Working Capital	852	829	771
Fixed Assets	1m	1m	1m
Current Assets	1m	1m	2m
Current Liabilities	207	279	434

1 Spatial Group Ltd

Cambridge Business Park Cowley Road, Cambridge, CB4 0WZ
Tel: 01223-420414 **Fax:** 01223-420044
E-mail: info@1spatial.com
Website: http://www.1spatial.com
Bank(s): Barclays
Directors: N. Snape (MD), C. Milverton (Fin), D. Guthrie (Sales)
Managers: R. Webb (Tech Serv Mgr), M. Couzens (Personnel), E. Gittof (Mktg Serv Mgr)
Ultimate Holding Company: 1SPATIAL HOLDINGS LIMITED
Immediate Holding Company: 1SPATIAL GROUP LIMITED
Registration no: 04785688 **Date established:** 2003 **Turnover:** £5m - £10m
No.of Employees: 51 - 100 **Product Groups:** 44

Date of Accounts	Jun 11	Jun 10	Jun 09
Sales Turnover	6m	8m	10m
Pre Tax Profit/Loss	-2m	73	539
Working Capital	627	2m	788
Fixed Assets	1m	3m	3m
Current Assets	3m	4m	3m
Current Liabilities	2m	2m	2m

Op Care Ltd

Hills Road, Cambridge, CB2 0DA
Tel: 01223-243391 **Fax:** 01223-416564
Website: http://www.opcare.co.uk
Managers: D. Peebles
Ultimate Holding Company: ABILITY TECHNOLOGY GROUP LIMITED
Immediate Holding Company: OPCARE LIMITED
Registration no: 02905086 **Date established:** 1994
No.of Employees: 1 - 10 **Product Groups:** 38, 67

Date of Accounts	Oct 11	Oct 10	Oct 09
Sales Turnover	18m	16m	17m
Pre Tax Profit/Loss	443	474	612
Working Capital	2m	2m	3m
Fixed Assets	781	468	386
Current Assets	6m	4m	5m
Current Liabilities	850	816	812

Orca Promotional Packaging

38 Histon Road, Cambridge, CB4 3LE
Tel: 01223-316603 **Fax:** 01223-305041
E-mail: sales@orcabags.co.uk
Website: http://www.orcabags.co.uk
Directors: S. Cooper (Prop)
No.of Employees: 1 - 10 **Product Groups:** 24, 27, 30, 66

Out Board

Unit 4a Church Meadows Haslingfield Road, Barrington, Cambridge, CB22 7RG
Tel: 01223-871015 **Fax:** 01223-208190
E-mail: info@outboard.co.uk
Website: http://www.outboard.co.uk
Directors: R. Whitaker (Dir)
Immediate Holding Company: GRACIE PARTNERSHIP LLP
Registration no: 04317138 **Date established:** 2012
Turnover: Up to £250,000 **No.of Employees:** 1 - 10 **Product Groups:** 67

Date of Accounts	Mar 11	Mar 10	Mar 09
Working Capital	8	15	11
Fixed Assets	356	488	503
Current Assets	8	15	11

PANalytical Ltd

7310 Iq Waterbeach, Cambridge, CB25 9AY
Tel: 01223-203480 **Fax:** 01223-203490
E-mail: info@panalytical.com
Website: http://www.panalytical.com
Directors: R. Nicholls (Dir)
Ultimate Holding Company: SPECTRIS PLC
Immediate Holding Company: PANALYTICAL LIMITED
Registration no: 01005071 **VAT No.:** GB 407 8500 60
Date established: 1971 **Turnover:** £5m - £10m **No.of Employees:** 1 - 10
Product Groups: 37

Date of Accounts	Dec 11	Dec 10	Dec 09
Sales Turnover	7m	5m	5m
Pre Tax Profit/Loss	697	568	-30
Working Capital	731	98	-493
Fixed Assets	1m	1m	2m
Current Assets	2m	4m	2m
Current Liabilities	1m	3m	1m

Papworth Furniture Ltd (Laboratory Furniture & Engineering Division)

Unit 4 Stirling Way Papworth Everard, Cambridge, CB23 3GX
Tel: 08451-308300 **Fax:** 01480-830516
E-mail: kevinsinclair@papworth-furniture.co.uk
Website: http://www.papworth-furniture.co.uk
Directors: P. Dix (MD)
Immediate Holding Company: PAPWORTH FURNITURE LIMITED
Registration no: 03145742 **Date established:** 1996 **Turnover:** £2m - £5m
No.of Employees: 11 - 20 **Product Groups:** 26, 67

Date of Accounts	Jan 12	Jan 11	Jan 10
Working Capital	376	510	361
Fixed Assets	46	60	59
Current Assets	675	1m	600

Partnertech Ltd

Unit 6-7-8 College Park Coldhams Lane, Cambridge, CB1 3HD
Tel: 01223-278850 **Fax:** 01223-244177
E-mail: angela.wootton@partnertech.co.uk
Website: http://www.partnertech.co.uk
Bank(s): Lloyds TSB Bank plc
Directors: A. Wootton (MD)
Managers: D. Majda (Personnel)
Ultimate Holding Company: PARTNERTECH AB (SWEDEN)
Immediate Holding Company: PARTNERTECH LIMITED
Registration no: 01041448 **VAT No.:** GB 105 5650 92
Date established: 1972 **Turnover:** £5m - £10m
No.of Employees: 51 - 100 **Product Groups:** 37, 47, 48, 84

Date of Accounts	Dec 11	Dec 10	Dec 09
Sales Turnover	10m	10m	10m
Pre Tax Profit/Loss	-2m	-2m	-2m
Working Capital	-2m	-1m	1m
Fixed Assets	1m	1m	1m
Current Assets	3m	4m	4m
Current Liabilities	765	691	633

Pelinda Surveillance Solutionions Ltd

Compass House Vision Park Station Road, Histon, Cambridge, CB24 9ZR
Tel: 01223-509300 **Fax:** 01223-509310
E-mail: info@telindus.com
Website: http://www.cellstack.com
Directors: W. Robinson (Sales & Mktg)
Managers: B. Mallett (Prod Mgr), J. Wille (I.T. Exec), R. Fleming (Fin Mgr), R. Coronas (Personnel)
Immediate Holding Company: SITESPHERE LIMITED
Registration no: 03093105 **VAT No.:** GB 370 3274 69
Date established: 1995 **Turnover:** £10m - £20m
No.of Employees: 21 - 50 **Product Groups:** 37, 40, 44

Pixel Power Ltd

Unit 5 College Park Coldhams Lane, Cambridge, CB1 3HD
Tel: 01223-721000 **Fax:** 01223-721111
E-mail: info@pixelpower.com
Website: http://www.pixelpower.com
Bank(s): Lloyds TSB Bank plc
Directors: J. Gilbert (MD)
Managers: E. Bertram (Mktg Serv Mgr), J. Bolbrook (Purch Mgr)
Immediate Holding Company: PIXEL POWER LIMITED
Registration no: 02154212 **VAT No.:** GB 478 7052 11
Date established: 1987 **Turnover:** £5m - £10m **No.of Employees:** 21 - 50
Product Groups: 67, 84

Date of Accounts	Jul 11	Jul 10	Jul 09
Sales Turnover	5m	5m	7m
Pre Tax Profit/Loss	-403	-318	328
Working Capital	2m	2m	3m
Fixed Assets	203	241	207
Current Assets	3m	3m	4m
Current Liabilities	386	170	664

Polar Bearings Ltd

Unit 26 Dry Drayton Industries Scotland Road, Dry Drayton, Cambridge, CB23 8AT
Tel: 01954-211643 **Fax:** 01954-210352
E-mail: cambridge@polarbearings.co.uk
Website: http://www.polarbearings.co.uk
Directors: C. Ellis (Fin), J. Constable (Sales)
Immediate Holding Company: ABREY LIMITED
Registration no: 01944599 **Date established:** 1985
No.of Employees: 1 - 10 **Product Groups:** 29, 30, 33, 34, 35, 36, 37, 38, 39, 40, 43, 45, 49, 66

Date of Accounts	May 05	May 04	May 03
Sales Turnover	N/A	N/A	645
Pre Tax Profit/Loss	N/A	N/A	6
Working Capital	1	1	68
Fixed Assets	N/A	N/A	13
Current Assets	1	1	191
Current Liabilities	N/A	N/A	18

Powertron Converters Ltd

Glebe Farm Technical Campus Knapwell, Cambridge, CB23 4GG
Tel: 01954-267726 **Fax:** 01954-267626
E-mail: sales@powertron.co.uk
Website: http://www.powertron.co.uk
Directors: T. Manquin (Fin), M. Katz (Dir)
Ultimate Holding Company: MARTEK POWER SA (FRANCE)
Immediate Holding Company: MARTEK POWER LIMITED
Registration no: 04588863 **VAT No.:** GB 215 7894 39
Date established: 2002 **Turnover:** Up to £250,000
No.of Employees: 1 - 10 **Product Groups:** 37, 44

Date of Accounts	Dec 11	Dec 10	Dec 09
Working Capital	608	560	403
Fixed Assets	118	120	110
Current Assets	898	952	867

Precision Devices Ltd

Station Road Whittlesford, Cambridge, CB22 4NL
Tel: 01223-834444 **Fax:** 01223-834589
E-mail: pmorrison@pdixtal.co.uk
Website: http://www.pdixtal.co.uk
Bank(s): HSBC
Managers: P. Morrison (Chief Mgr), S. Simper (Chief Acct)
Ultimate Holding Company: PRECISION DEVICES INC (USA)
Immediate Holding Company: PRECISION DEVICES UK LIMITED
Registration no: 01305304 **VAT No.:** GB 215 2194 92
Date established: 1977 **Turnover:** £2m - £5m **No.of Employees:** 21 - 50
Product Groups: 37

Date of Accounts	Dec 11	Dec 10	Jun 10
Sales Turnover	N/A	N/A	3m
Pre Tax Profit/Loss	N/A	N/A	263
Working Capital	547	493	997
Fixed Assets	340	291	309
Current Assets	1m	1m	2m
Current Liabilities	140	N/A	272

Prelude Ventures Ltd

Sycamore Studios New Road, Over, Cambridge, CB24 5PJ
Tel: 01954-288090 **Fax:** 01954-288099
E-mail: prelude@prelude-ventures.com
Website: http://www.prelude-ventures.co.uk
Bank(s): Barclays

see next page

Prelude Ventures Ltd - Cont'd
Directors: R. Hook (MD), R. Huck (MD), E. Reggiani (Fin)
Managers: A. Duncan (Mktg Serv Mgr), R. Haggar (I.T. Exec)
Immediate Holding Company: Prelude Technology Investment Holdings Ltd
Registration no: 01869933 **VAT No.:** GB 432 2427 83
Date established: 1986 **Turnover:** Up to £250,000
No.of Employees: 11 - 20 **Product Groups:** 82

Prior Scientific Instruments Ltd
Unit 3-4 Fielding Industrial Estate Wilbraham Road, Fulbourn, Cambridge, CB21 5ET
Tel: 01223-881711 **Fax:** 01223-881710
E-mail: stephenling@prior.com
Website: http://www.prior.com
Bank(s): HSBC Bank plc
Directors: P. Booth (Dir), S. Ling (Dir)
Managers: M. Walmsley (Mats Contrlr), P. Copeland-watts, S. Smith (Comptroller)
Immediate Holding Company: PRIOR SCIENTIFIC INSTRUMENTS LIMITED
Registration no: 00404087 **VAT No.:** GB 215 8964 39
Date established: 1946 **Turnover:** £10m - £20m
No.of Employees: 51 - 100 **Product Groups:** 37, 38, 65

Date of Accounts	Mar 11	Mar 10	Mar 09
Sales Turnover	12m	12m	12m
Pre Tax Profit/Loss	1m	2m	399
Working Capital	4m	4m	3m
Fixed Assets	2m	2m	2m
Current Assets	6m	6m	5m
Current Liabilities	813	790	633

Pulsar Light Of Cambridge Ltd
Unit 3 Coldhams Business Park Norman Way, Cambridge, CB1 3LH
Tel: 01223-403500 **Fax:** 01223-403501
E-mail: sales@pulsarlight.com
Website: http://www.pulsarlight.com
Bank(s): National Westminster
Directors: B. Daeton Brockwell (Fin), P. Mardon (MD)
Managers: J. Smith (Buyer), M. Whitley (Tech Serv Mgr)
Immediate Holding Company: PULSAR LIGHT OF CAMBRIDGE LIMITED
Registration no: 01300636 **Date established:** 1977 **Turnover:** £2m - £5m
No.of Employees: 51 - 100 **Product Groups:** 37

Date of Accounts	Dec 11	Dec 10	Dec 09
Working Capital	1m	1m	2m
Fixed Assets	359	416	477
Current Assets	2m	2m	2m

Qualitair Engineering Services
Francis Court High Ditch Road, Fen Ditton, Cambridge, CB5 8TE
Tel: 01223-295111 **Fax:** 01223-295112
E-mail: fc@qualitair.co.uk
Website: http://www.qualitair.com
Bank(s): Barclays
Managers: F. Currie
Immediate Holding Company: QUALITAIR AVIATION SERVICES LIMITED
Registration no: 02115309 **VAT No.:** GB 538 2719 26
Date established: 1987 **No.of Employees:** 11 - 20 **Product Groups:** 80

Date of Accounts	Dec 06	Dec 05
Sales Turnover	7950	4220
Pre Tax Profit/Loss	300	130
Working Capital	540	290
Fixed Assets	3440	3640
Current Assets	1700	830
Current Liabilities	1160	540
Total Share Capital	120	120
ROCE% (Return on Capital Employed)	7.5	3.3
ROT% (Return on Turnover)	3.8	3.1

Quartix Ltd
Wellington House East Road, Cambridge, CB1 1BH
Tel: 08700-136663 **Fax:** 01686-628774
E-mail: enquiries@quartix.net
Website: http://www.quartix.net
Directors: A. Kirk (MD)
Ultimate Holding Company: QUARTIX HOLDINGS LIMITED
Immediate Holding Company: QUARTIX LIMITED
Registration no: 04159907 **Date established:** 2001
Turnover: £500,000 - £1m **No.of Employees:** 1 - 10 **Product Groups:** 38, 39

Date of Accounts	Dec 11	Dec 10	Dec 09
Working Capital	3m	2m	983
Fixed Assets	51	71	101
Current Assets	5m	3m	2m

Rank Brothers Ltd (Dept K)
56 High Street Bottisham, Cambridge, CB25 9DA
Tel: 01223-811369 **Fax:** 01223-811441
E-mail: info@rankbrothers.co.uk
Website: http://www.rankbrothers.co.uk
Directors: P. Rank (MD)
Immediate Holding Company: RANK BROTHERS LIMITED
Registration no: 01838330 **VAT No.:** GB 299 9096 74
Date established: 1984 **Turnover:** £250,000 - £500,000
No.of Employees: 1 - 10 **Product Groups:** 33, 37, 38, 42, 48, 67, 85

Date of Accounts	Sep 11	Sep 10	Sep 09
Working Capital	121	119	114
Fixed Assets	71	72	87
Current Assets	179	171	173

Recover Ltd
Wellington House East Road, Cambridge, CB1 1BH
Tel: 01223-451023
E-mail: info@recoverltd.com
Website: http://www.recoverltd.com
Directors: A. Sloman (Dir), R. Webber (Dir)
Registration no: 05726475 **Date established:** 2006
Turnover: £250,000 - £500,000 **No.of Employees:** 1 - 10
Product Groups: 54

Date of Accounts	Aug 08
Working Capital	-27
Fixed Assets	1
Current Liabilities	27

Reed Accountancy Personnel Ltd
65 Regent Street, Cambridge, CB2 1AB
Tel: 01223-462857 **Fax:** 01223-329903
Website: http://www.reed.co.uk
Managers: S. Sandham (Mgr)
Immediate Holding Company: REED PERSONNEL SERVICES LTD
Registration no: 00973629 **Date established:** 1995
Turnover: £75m - £125m **No.of Employees:** 1 - 10 **Product Groups:** 80

Reed Employment Ltd
65 Regent Street, Cambridge, CB2 1AB
Tel: 01223-462872 **Fax:** 01223-462859
E-mail: cambridge@reed.co.uk
Website: http://www.reed.co.uk
Managers: M. Wilkinson (Mgr)
Ultimate Holding Company: REED GLOBAL LTD (MALTA)
Immediate Holding Company: REED EMPLOYMENT LIMITED
Registration no: 00669854 **Date established:** 1960
Turnover: £75m - £125m **No.of Employees:** 1 - 10 **Product Groups:** 80

Date of Accounts	Jun 11	Jun 10	Dec 07
Sales Turnover	618	450	287m
Pre Tax Profit/Loss	-2m	310	8m
Working Capital	23m	28m	28m
Fixed Assets	31	36	5m
Current Assets	28m	30m	74m
Current Liabilities	37	29	21m

Refrigerated Transport Information Society
140 Newmarket Road, Cambridge, CB5 8HE
Tel: 01223-461352 **Fax:** 01223-461522
E-mail: rlawton@crtech.co.uk
Website: http://www.crtech.co.uk
Directors: R. Lawton (Dir), T. Money (Fin)
Immediate Holding Company: BEADFALL LTD.
Registration no: 06082871 **Date established:** 2007
Turnover: £500,000 - £1m **No.of Employees:** 1 - 10 **Product Groups:** 38, 72, 80, 84, 86

Date of Accounts	Dec 10	Dec 09
Working Capital	-23	-22
Fixed Assets	441	463
Current Assets	50	25

Ridgeons Ltd
Trinity Hall Industrial Estate Nuffield Road, Cambridge, CB4 1TS
Tel: 01223-466000 **Fax:** 01223-466079
E-mail: angela.rushforth@ridgeons.co.uk
Website: http://www.ridgeons.net
Bank(s): HSBC, City Office, Cambridge
Directors: G. Rogers (Dir), T. Parker (MD), A. Rushforth (MD), S. Sutton (Grp Mktg), M. Ridgeon (Dir)
Managers: G. Rodgers (Mktg Serv Mgr), R. Day (Grp Sales Mgr)
Ultimate Holding Company: RIDGEON GROUP LIMITED
Immediate Holding Company: RIDGEONS LIMITED
Registration no: 02416904 **VAT No.:** GB 599 6045 82
Date established: 1989 **Turnover:** £75m - £125m
No.of Employees: 501 - 1000 **Product Groups:** 66

Date of Accounts	Dec 10	Dec 09	Dec 08
Sales Turnover	99m	99m	117m
Pre Tax Profit/Loss	-2m	-3m	-3m
Working Capital	13m	15m	14m
Fixed Assets	12m	12m	14m
Current Assets	37m	31m	29m
Current Liabilities	4m	3m	4m

Royal Society Of Chemistry
Thomas Graham House 290 Science Park Milton Road, Cambridge, CB4 0WF
Tel: 01223-420066 **Fax:** 01223-423623
E-mail: sales@rsc.org
Website: http://www.rsc.org
Directors: S. Hawthorne (Sales)
Managers: R. Parker, D. James, N. Hills
Registration no: FP051709 **VAT No.:** GB 342 1764 71
Turnover: £20m - £50m **No.of Employees:** 251 - 500
Product Groups: 28, 64

Date of Accounts	Dec 96
Sales Turnover	9843
Pre Tax Profit/Loss	2194
Working Capital	4186
Fixed Assets	34594
Current Assets	21219
Current Liabilities	17033
ROCE% (Return on Capital Employed)	5.7

S T Robotics
Orwell House Cowley Road, Cambridge, CB4 0PP
Tel: 01223-420288
E-mail: ukoffice@strobotics.com
Website: http://strobotics.com
Directors: D. Sands (MD)
Immediate Holding Company: IMAGECROFT LIMITED
Registration no: 02040832 **VAT No.:** GB 599 6952 49
Date established: 1986 **Turnover:** £250,000 - £500,000
No.of Employees: 1 - 10 **Product Groups:** 45

Date of Accounts	Mar 12	Mar 11	Mar 10
Working Capital	281	236	56
Fixed Assets	4	3	7
Current Assets	725	689	587

Sagentia
Harston Mill Royston Road, Harston, Cambridge, CB22 7GG
Tel: 01223-875200 **Fax:** 01223-875201
E-mail: info@sagentia.com
Website: http://www.sagentia.com
Directors: G. McCarthy (Co Sec)
Managers: B. Hudson
Ultimate Holding Company: SAGENTIA GROUP PUBLIC LIMITED COMPANY
Immediate Holding Company: SAGENTIA HOLDINGS LIMITED
Registration no: 02015785 **Date established:** 1986
Turnover: £20m - £50m **No.of Employees:** 101 - 250 **Product Groups:** 80

Date of Accounts	Dec 11	Dec 10	Dec 09
Pre Tax Profit/Loss	38	-444	-441
Working Capital	-8m	-9m	5m
Fixed Assets	N/A	901	8m
Current Assets	4	4	10m
Current Liabilities	4	13	10

Saica Packaging UK Ltd (Factory) UK Central Office
Villa Road Histon, Cambridge, CB24 9PA
Tel: 01223-232492 **Fax:** 01223-234526
E-mail: frayne.perkins@saica.com
Website: http://www.sca.com
Directors: F. Perkins (Fin), F. Perkins (Dir)
Managers: A. Connolly (Ops Mgr)
Immediate Holding Company: SCA PACKAGING LIMITED
Registration no: 00053913 **Date established:** 1997
No.of Employees: 51 - 100 **Product Groups:** 27

Sands Technology
Orwell House Cowley Road, Cambridge, CB4 0PP
Tel: 01223-420288 **Fax:** 01223-423291
E-mail: david@strobotics.com
Website: http://www.strobotics.com
Directors: D. Sands (MD), C. George (Fin)
Immediate Holding Company: MUSIC INFORMATION TECHNOLOGY LIMITED
Registration no: 01781726 **Date established:** 1988
No.of Employees: 1 - 10 **Product Groups:** 35, 39, 45

The Screen Company
182 High Street Cottenham, Cambridge, CB24 8RX
Tel: 01954-250139 **Fax:** 01954-252005
E-mail: thescreencompany@onetel.com
Website: http://www.thescreencompany.co.uk
Directors: P. Turner (Ptnr)
Registration no: 00253175 **Date established:** 1989
Turnover: £250,000 - £500,000 **No.of Employees:** 1 - 10
Product Groups: 38

Secure Holidays
5 Signet Court Swann Road, Cambridge, CB5 8LA
Tel: 020-3370 3810 **Fax:** 0845-290 3381
E-mail: bookings@secureholidays.co.uk
Website: http://www.secureholidays.co.uk
Managers: H. Syed (Mgr)
Immediate Holding Company: CONNECTFILMS MEDIA LIMITED
Registration no: 03809539 **Date established:** 2006
No.of Employees: 1 - 10 **Product Groups:** 26, 33, 35, 36, 41, 48, 66, 67, 81

Date of Accounts	Sep 11	Sep 10	Sep 09
Sales Turnover	58	N/A	N/A
Pre Tax Profit/Loss	-11	N/A	N/A
Working Capital	-104	-90	-100
Fixed Assets	6	3	3
Current Assets	N/A	14	2
Current Liabilities	4	N/A	N/A

Senova Ltd
49 North Road Great Abington, Abington, Cambridge, CB21 6AS
Tel: 01223-890777 **Fax:** 01223-890666
E-mail: info@senova.uk.com
Website: http://www.senova.com
Directors: C. Green (Dir)
Ultimate Holding Company: ALEXANDER HARLEY SEEDS LIMITED
Immediate Holding Company: SENOVA LIMITED
Registration no: 01584796 **Date established:** 1981
No.of Employees: 1 - 10 **Product Groups:** 02

Date of Accounts	May 11	May 10	May 09
Working Capital	3m	2m	1m
Fixed Assets	417	408	421
Current Assets	4m	4m	2m
Current Liabilities	22	N/A	N/A

Serco Consulting
Compass House 80 Newmarket Road, Cambridge, CB5 8DZ
Tel: 01223-315944 **Fax:** 01223-322565
E-mail: ann.gammie@erconsultants.co.uk
Website: http://www.erconsultants.co.uk
Bank(s): HSBC Bank plc
Directors: A. Gammie (Dir), J. Goodridge (Grp Chief Exec), D. Beresford (Dir), I. Ackroyd (Co Sec)
Managers: L. Folbrigg (Admin Off), P. Lawson (Develop Mgr)
Ultimate Holding Company: SERCO GROUP PLC
Immediate Holding Company: ER CONSULTANTS LTD.
Registration no: 02420282 **VAT No.:** GB 599 3588 59
Date established: 1989 **Turnover:** £2m - £5m **No.of Employees:** 11 - 20
Product Groups: 80, 81, 86

Date of Accounts	Dec 10	Dec 09	Dec 08
Sales Turnover	2m	2m	3m
Pre Tax Profit/Loss	-203	128	293
Working Capital	1m	2m	1m
Fixed Assets	13	28	50
Current Assets	2m	2m	2m
Current Liabilities	199	383	393

S J H Sparkes & Sons Ltd
20 Devonshire Road, Cambridge, CB1 2BH
Tel: 01223-356172 **Fax:** 01223-356172
Directors: C. Sparkes (Co Sec), C. Sparkes (Fin), K. Sparkes (MD)
Immediate Holding Company: S.J.H. SPARKES & SONS LIMITED
Registration no: 00502006 **Date established:** 1951
Turnover: Up to £250,000 **No.of Employees:** 1 - 10 **Product Groups:** 52

Date of Accounts	Dec 06	Dec 05
Working Capital	-1	3
Fixed Assets	2	2
Current Assets	17	25
Current Liabilities	18	21
Total Share Capital	2	2

Spectra Displays Ltd
194 Station Road Willingham, Cambridge, CB24 5HQ
Tel: 01954-261402 **Fax:** 01954-261403
E-mail: sales@spectra-displays.co.uk
Website: http://www.spectra-displays.co.uk
Directors: M. Boxall (MD)
Immediate Holding Company: SPECTRA DISPLAYS LIMITED
Registration no: 02428206 **VAT No.:** GB 538 2709 11
Date established: 1989 **Turnover:** £250,000 - £500,000
No.of Employees: 1 - 10 **Product Groups:** 37, 40

Date of Accounts	Oct 11	Oct 10	Oct 08
Working Capital	210	194	191
Fixed Assets	79	55	32
Current Assets	310	246	261

Speedy Asset Services Ltd
57 Cowley Road, Cambridge, CB4 0DN
Tel: 01223-423952 **Fax:** 01223-423099
Website: http://www.speedyhire.co.uk
Managers: G. Gray (Mgr)
Ultimate Holding Company: SPEEDY HIRE PLC
Immediate Holding Company: SPEEDY ASSET SERVICES LIMITED
Registration no: 06847930 **Date established:** 2009
No.of Employees: 1 - 10 **Product Groups:** 35, 39, 45

Date of Accounts	Mar 12	Mar 11	Mar 10
Sales Turnover	312m	336m	187m
Pre Tax Profit/Loss	24m	-5m	-430
Working Capital	-172m	-194m	-252m
Fixed Assets	210m	198m	268m
Current Assets	101m	144m	120m
Current Liabilities	31m	41m	33m

Summit Oxygen International Limited
Cpc1, Capital Park Fulbourn, Cambridge, CB21 5XE
Tel: 07884-006610 **Fax:** 01903-741002
E-mail: enquiries@summitoxygen.com
Website: http://www.summitoxygen.com
Directors: G. Rees (Fin), N. Greenwood (Dir)
Managers: D. Price (Sales Prom Mgr), J. Donnelly (Workshop)
Registration no: 05610446 **Date established:** 2002
Turnover: Up to £250,000 **No.of Employees:** 1 - 10 **Product Groups:** 38

Synoptics Ltd
Beacon House Nuffield Road, Cambridge, CB4 1TF
Tel: 01223-727100 **Fax:** 01223-727101
E-mail: sales@synoptics.co.uk
Website: http://www.synoptics.co.uk
Directors: P. Ellwood (MD), C. Hough (Co Sec)
Ultimate Holding Company: SCIENTIFIC DIGITAL IMAGING PLC
Immediate Holding Company: SYNOPTICS LIMITED
Registration no: 01874861 **Date established:** 1984 **Turnover:** £5m - £10m
No.of Employees: 21 - 50 **Product Groups:** 38, 44

Date of Accounts	Apr 11	Apr 10	Apr 09
Sales Turnover	5m	5m	5m
Pre Tax Profit/Loss	143	297	261
Working Capital	913	989	1m
Fixed Assets	1m	1m	1m
Current Assets	2m	2m	2m
Current Liabilities	448	580	483

System Connections Cambridge Ltd Cambridge Electronic Industries Ltd
Cambridge Connectors Pembroke Avenue, Waterbeach, Cambridge, CB25 9QR
Tel: 01223-863377 **Fax:** 01223-863625
E-mail: sales@systemconnections.co.uk
Website: http://www.cambridgeconnectors.com
Bank(s): Barclays, Bank of Scotland
Managers: S. Pepper (Chief Mgr)
Ultimate Holding Company: WILSON-MOTTAZ LIMITED
Immediate Holding Company: SYSTEM CONNECTIONS (CAMBRIDGE) LIMITED
Registration no: 02236353 **VAT No.:** GB 493 1069 40
Date established: 1988 **Turnover:** £5m - £10m **No.of Employees:** 21 - 50
Product Groups: 35, 37

T A D Precision Sheet Metal Engineers Ltd
The Mount High Street, Toft, Cambridge, CB23 2RL
Tel: 01223-263421 **Fax:** 01223-264135
E-mail: terry@tad-engineering.co.uk
Directors: T. Easey (MD)
Immediate Holding Company: TAD PRECISION SHEET METAL ENGINEERS LIMITED
Registration no: 01859284 **VAT No.:** GB 393 1495 31
Date established: 1984 **Turnover:** £250,000 - £500,000
No.of Employees: 1 - 10 **Product Groups:** 48

Date of Accounts	Dec 11	Dec 10	Dec 09
Working Capital	95	119	109
Fixed Assets	10	13	27
Current Assets	171	205	196

T W I
Granta Park Great Abington, Cambridge, CB21 6AL
Tel: 01223-891162 **Fax:** 01223-892588
E-mail: christine.wylde@twi.co.uk
Website: http://www.twi.co.uk
Directors: G. Leech (Fin), C. Weisner (Research), R. Dawkins (Fin), C. Wiesner (Grp Chief Exec)
Managers: R. John, C. Wylde, M. Lanprecht (Mktg Serv Mgr), F. Delaney (Export Sales Mg)
Ultimate Holding Company: WELDING INSTITUTE(THE)
Immediate Holding Company: WELDING INSTITUTE(THE)
Registration no: 00405555 **VAT No.:** GB 700 1708 89
Date established: 1946 **Turnover:** £50m - £75m
No.of Employees: 501 - 1000 **Product Groups:** 37, 51, 54, 80, 84, 85, 86

Date of Accounts	Dec 10	Dec 09	Dec 08
Sales Turnover	52m	48m	43m
Pre Tax Profit/Loss	14m	3m	161
Working Capital	9m	9m	7m
Fixed Assets	47m	32m	30m
Current Assets	36m	34m	32m
Current Liabilities	15m	13m	10m

Tecvac Ltd (A Wallwork Company)
Buckingway Business Park Rowles Way, Swavesey, Cambridge, CB24 4UG
Tel: 01954-233700 **Fax:** 01954-233733
E-mail: reception@tecvac.com
Website: http://www.tecvac.com
Bank(s): National Westminster Bank Plc
Directors: R. Burslem (Dir)
Managers: B. Harradence (Buyer), I. Haggan (Sales & Mktg Mg), M. Glaze (Personnel)
Immediate Holding Company: TECVAC LIMITED
Registration no: 01476898 **VAT No.:** GB 493 0461 45
Date established: 1980 **Turnover:** £2m - £5m **No.of Employees:** 51 - 100
Product Groups: 40, 42, 46, 47, 48, 84

Date of Accounts	Mar 11	Mar 10	Mar 09
Sales Turnover	4m	3m	4m
Pre Tax Profit/Loss	-312	-342	-459
Working Capital	181	2m	2m
Fixed Assets	860	726	667
Current Assets	852	3m	3m
Current Liabilities	237	435	168

Teversham Motors
5 Church Road Teversham, Cambridge, CB1 9AZ
Tel: 01223-293041
E-mail: info@tevershammotors.co.uk
Website: http://www.tevershammotors.co.uk
Managers: S. Martin (Mgr)
Date established: 1965 **Turnover:** £500,000 - £1m
No.of Employees: 1 - 10 **Product Groups:** 39

The Payroll Service Company Ltd
5 Cambridge Technopark Newmarket Road, Cambridge, CB5 8PB
Tel: 01223-506366 **Fax:** 01223-506367
E-mail: enquiries@pscpayroll.com
Website: http://www.pscpayroll.com
Bank(s): Barclays
Directors: G. Leadbeater (Dir), S. Woolston (Dir)
Managers: K. Logan
Immediate Holding Company: THE PAYROLL SERVICE COMPANY LIMITED
Registration no: 01785949 **VAT No.:** GB 214 4691 74
Date established: 1984 **Turnover:** £1m - £2m **No.of Employees:** 11 - 20
Product Groups: 44, 80

Date of Accounts	Mar 12	Mar 11	Mar 10
Working Capital	45	63	53
Fixed Assets	329	336	339
Current Assets	371	454	447

Todd Research Ltd
Unit 1 Stirling Way, Papworth Everard, Cambridge, CB23 3WA
Tel: 01480-832202 **Fax:** 01245-269409
E-mail: richard.sheil@toddresearch.co.uk
Website: http://www.toddresearch.co.uk
Directors: D. Gotts (MD), R. Sheil (Sales)
Immediate Holding Company: TODD RESEARCH LIMITED
Registration no: 00477701 **VAT No.:** GB 103 5628 00
Date established: 1950 **Turnover:** £1m - £2m **No.of Employees:** 1 - 10
Product Groups: 37

Date of Accounts	Mar 11	Mar 10	Mar 09
Sales Turnover	1m	2m	N/A
Pre Tax Profit/Loss	264	298	N/A
Working Capital	-78	1m	1m
Fixed Assets	N/A	71	108
Current Assets	8	2m	2m
Current Liabilities	86	472	493

Tomlinson Steel Fabrications
Unit 32 Industrial Estate London Road, Pampisford, Cambridge, CB22 3FX
Tel: 01223-836753 **Fax:** 01223-836753
Directors: K. Tomlinson (Prop)
Date established: 1989 **No.of Employees:** 1 - 10 **Product Groups:** 35

Torch Computers Ltd
50 South Street Comberton, Cambridge, CB23 7DZ
Tel: 01223-263818 **Fax:** 01223-264118
E-mail: sales@torchcomputers.co.uk
Website: http://www.torchcomputers.co.uk
Directors: J. Dane (MD)
Immediate Holding Company: TORCH COMPUTERS LIMITED
Registration no: 02547840 **VAT No.:** GB 589 6189 65
Date established: 1990 **Turnover:** £1m - £2m **No.of Employees:** 1 - 10
Product Groups: 44

Date of Accounts	Jul 11	Jul 10	Jul 09
Working Capital	333	337	308
Fixed Assets	3	4	5
Current Assets	381	433	349

Transcendata Europe Ltd
4 Carisbrooke Court Buckingway Business Park, Swavesey, Cambridge, CB24 4UQ
Tel: 01954-234300 **Fax:** 01954-234349
E-mail: eusales@transcendata.com
Website: http://www.transcendata.com
Bank(s): Barclays
Directors: G. Butlin (Grp Chief Exec)
Ultimate Holding Company: INTERNATIONAL TECHNEGROUP INC (USA)
Immediate Holding Company: TRANSCENDATA EUROPE LIMITED
Registration no: 01364362 **VAT No.:** GB 313 1765 84
Date established: 1978 **Turnover:** £1m - £2m **No.of Employees:** 11 - 20
Product Groups: 44

Date of Accounts	Jun 11	Jun 10	Jun 09
Sales Turnover	2m	2m	1m
Pre Tax Profit/Loss	401	265	158
Working Capital	916	631	370
Fixed Assets	24	18	21
Current Assets	2m	1m	844
Current Liabilities	683	672	343

Transico Ltd
Unit 5 Hazlewell Court Bar Road, Lolworth, Cambridge, CB23 8DS
Tel: 01954-781818 **Fax:** 01954-789305
E-mail: sales@ecoswitch.co.uk
Website: http://www.ecoswitch.co.uk
Directors: A. Pole (Fin)
Managers: C. Wright (Mgr)
Immediate Holding Company: TRANSICO LIMITED
Registration no: 03994157 **Date established:** 2000
Turnover: £500,000 - £1m **No.of Employees:** 1 - 10 **Product Groups:** 29, 37, 40, 44, 48

Date of Accounts	Dec 11	Dec 10	Dec 09
Working Capital	423	170	271
Fixed Assets	197	202	206
Current Assets	571	446	336

Tribal Education
The Paddocks 347 Cherry Hinton Road, Cambridge, CB1 8DH
Tel: 01223-470480 **Fax:** 01223-470481
E-mail: info@tribalgroup.com
Website: http://www.tribalgroup.com
Bank(s): Barclays
Managers: M. Parkin (Sales Admin)
Immediate Holding Company: BARRY'S SERVICE CENTRE LIMITED
Registration no: 01551849 **VAT No.:** GB 370 4779 34
Date established: 2003 **Turnover:** £500,000 - £1m
No.of Employees: 51 - 100 **Product Groups:** 28, 86, 89

Date of Accounts	Jul 11	Jul 10	Jul 09
Working Capital	15	21	1
Fixed Assets	73	52	54
Current Assets	62	71	67

U Q G Ltd
99-101 Cambridge Road Milton, Cambridge, CB24 6AT
Tel: 01223-420329 **Fax:** 01223-420506
E-mail: info@uqgoptics.com
Website: http://www.uqgoptics.com
Bank(s): Barclays
Directors: K. Biggs (Sales)
Immediate Holding Company: U.Q.G. LIMITED
Registration no: 01151762 **VAT No.:** GB 214 5696 59
Date established: 1973 **Turnover:** £500,000 - £1m
No.of Employees: 11 - 20 **Product Groups:** 17, 32, 33, 38, 48, 65, 85

Date of Accounts	Mar 12	Mar 11	Mar 10
Working Capital	174	129	76
Fixed Assets	680	720	673
Current Assets	576	517	395

Ultra Electronics Ltd
Vitrum Building St Johns Innovation Park Cowley Road, Cambridge, CB4 0WS
Tel: 01223-429601 **Fax:** 01223-426696
E-mail: information@ultra-electronics.com
Website: http://www.ultraquiet.com
Bank(s): Royal Bank of Scotland
Directors: K. Thomson (MD)
Ultimate Holding Company: ULTRA ELECTRONICS HOLDINGS PLC
Immediate Holding Company: ULTRA ELECTRONICS LIMITED
Registration no: 02830644 **Date established:** 1993 **Turnover:** £5m - £10m
No.of Employees: 51 - 100 **Product Groups:** 38

Date of Accounts	Dec 11	Dec 10	Dec 09
Sales Turnover	379m	313m	286m
Pre Tax Profit/Loss	59m	19m	24m
Working Capital	37m	-27m	15m
Fixed Assets	70m	76m	73m
Current Assets	208m	135m	160m
Current Liabilities	79m	68m	58m

Ultra-Violet Products Ltd
Unit 1 Trinity Hall Farm Estate Nuffield Road, Cambridge, CB4 1TG
Tel: 01223-420022 **Fax:** 01223-420561
E-mail: uvp@uvp.co.uk
Website: http://www.uvp.com
Bank(s): Barclays, Chesterton Road,
Managers: B. Sundberg (Chief Mgr), D. Wilderspin (Eng), J. Hann (Sales Prom Mgr)
Immediate Holding Company: UVP Inc (U.S.A.)
Registration no: 01182291 **Turnover:** £2m - £5m
No.of Employees: 11 - 20 **Product Groups:** 37, 38, 44, 85

Date of Accounts	Dec 11	Dec 10	Dec 09
Sales Turnover	N/A	N/A	2m
Working Capital	576	495	476
Fixed Assets	8	11	11
Current Assets	741	837	747

Valeader Pneumatics Ltd
37 Clifton Road, Cambridge, CB1 7ED
Tel: 01223-248911 **Fax:** 01223-248922
E-mail: info@valeader.co.uk
Website: http://www.valeader.co.uk
Directors: D. Newick (Dir)
Registration no: 01400273 **Turnover:** £1m - £2m
No.of Employees: 1 - 10 **Product Groups:** 30, 36, 37, 38, 40, 84

Vitral UK
17 High Street Whittlesford, Cambridge, CB22 4LT
Tel: 01223-499000 **Fax:** 01223-499001
E-mail: vitral-uk@vitral.co.uk
Website: http://www.vitral.com
Managers: V. Simpson (Chief Acct)
Ultimate Holding Company: VITRAL A/S (DENMARK)
Immediate Holding Company: VITRAL UK LIMITED
Registration no: 02047092 **Date established:** 1986 **Turnover:** £5m - £10m
No.of Employees: 1 - 10 **Product Groups:** 33, 35, 52, 66

Date of Accounts	Dec 11	Dec 10	Dec 09
Working Capital	178	160	136
Current Assets	240	276	224

Volvo Construction Equipment Ltd
Moorfield Road Duxford, Cambridge, CB22 4QX
Tel: 01223-836636 **Fax:** 01223-832357
E-mail: nick.allen@volvo.com
Website: http://www.construction.volvo.co.uk
Managers: N. Allen (Fin Mgr)
Ultimate Holding Company: AB VOLVO (SWEDEN)
Immediate Holding Company: VOLVO CONSTRUCTION EQUIPMENT LIMITED
Registration no: 01673954 **VAT No.:** GB 599 3041 08
Date established: 1982 **Turnover:** £50m - £75m
No.of Employees: 101 - 250 **Product Groups:** 41, 42, 45, 48, 67

Date of Accounts	Dec 10	Dec 09	Dec 08
Sales Turnover	N/A	70m	192m
Pre Tax Profit/Loss	N/A	2m	8m
Working Capital	26m	26m	7m
Fixed Assets	N/A	N/A	76m
Current Assets	26m	26m	57m
Current Liabilities	N/A	N/A	32m

Ware Anthony Rust Ltd
Newnham Mill Newnham Road, Cambridge, CB3 9EY
Tel: 01223-566212 **Fax:** 01223-566685
E-mail: alison.meadows@war.uk.com
Website: http://www.war.uk.com
Bank(s): H.S.B.C.
Directors: J. Keeling (Fab), A. Meadows (MD), A. Marchini (Fin), R. Bland (Dir), R. Ware (Ch)
Ultimate Holding Company: WAR HOLDINGS LIMITED
Immediate Holding Company: WARE ANTHONY RUST LIMITED
Registration no: 01890656 **VAT No.:** GB 393 2270 50
Date established: 1985 **Turnover:** £2m - £5m **No.of Employees:** 51 - 100
Product Groups: 81

Date of Accounts	Apr 11	Apr 10	Apr 09
Sales Turnover	2m	2m	3m
Pre Tax Profit/Loss	-1	-4	111
Working Capital	570	484	498
Fixed Assets	53	83	128
Current Assets	1m	1m	2m
Current Liabilities	197	258	365

Webtechy Ltd
15 Gladeside Bar Hill, Cambridge, CB23 8DY
Tel: 01954-201312 **Fax:** 0870-131 5220
E-mail: enquiries@webtechy.co.uk
Website: http://www.webtechy.co.uk
Directors: B. Weeks (MD), H. Iona (Co Sec)
Immediate Holding Company: WEBTECHY LIMITED
Registration no: 04563622 **Date established:** 2002
No.of Employees: 1 - 10 **Product Groups:** 44, 79, 80, 81

see next page

Webtechy Ltd - Cont'd

Date of Accounts	Mar 11	Mar 10	Mar 09
Working Capital	-5	-4	-7
Fixed Assets	7	4	7
Current Assets	18	20	26

L W Wedd & Son Ltd

Granta Terrace Stapleford, Cambridge, CB22 5FJ
Tel: 01223-841266 **Fax:** 01223-841013
E-mail: info@weddjoinery.co.uk
Website: http://www.lwwedd.co.uk
Bank(s): Lloyds
Directors: P. Wedd (MD), M. Wedd (Dir)
Managers: K. Royals (Sales Admin)
Immediate Holding Company: L.W. Wedd & Son Ltd
Registration no: 01336997 **VAT No.:** GB 215 3188 82
Date established: 1977 **Turnover:** £2m - £5m **No.of Employees:** 21 - 50
Product Groups: 30, 52

Date of Accounts	Dec 07	Dec 06	Dec 05
Sales Turnover	N/A	1464	1816
Pre Tax Profit/Loss	N/A	54	182
Working Capital	411	393	367
Fixed Assets	223	34	31
Current Assets	764	526	771
Current Liabilities	353	132	404
Total Share Capital	1	1	1
ROCE% (Return on Capital Employed)		12.7	45.7
ROT% (Return on Turnover)		3.7	10.0

G K Wood & Sons Ltd (t/a Fulbourn Medical)

5 Station Yard Wilbraham Road, Fulbourn, Cambridge, CB21 5ET
Tel: 01223-880909 **Fax:** 01223-880078
E-mail: info@fulbournmedical.com
Website: http://www.fulbournmedical.com
Directors: K. Wood (Dir), N. Wood (MD)
Immediate Holding Company: G.K. WOOD & SON LIMITED
Registration no: 02764966 **Date established:** 1992
Turnover: £500,000 - £1m **No.of Employees:** 11 - 20 **Product Groups:** 67

Date of Accounts	Apr 11	Apr 10	Apr 09
Working Capital	276	268	261
Fixed Assets	37	40	32
Current Assets	459	490	466

Zettlex UK Ltd

Newton Court Town Street, Newton, Cambridge, CB22 7PE
Tel: 01223-874444 **Fax:** 01223-874111
E-mail: info@zettlex.com
Website: http://www.zettlex.com
Managers: M. Howard (Chief Mgr)
Immediate Holding Company: ZETTLEX (UK) LIMITED
Registration no: 06822548 **Date established:** 2009 **Turnover:** £2m - £5m
No.of Employees: 1 - 10 **Product Groups:** 38

Date of Accounts	Feb 11	Feb 10
Working Capital	116	-52
Current Assets	205	90

Chatteris

A4 Plus Drawing Services Ltd

L25 South Fens Business Centre Fenton Way, Chatteris, PE16 6TT
Tel: 01354-691820 **Fax:** 01354-691821
E-mail: enquiries@a4plus.co.uk
Website: http://www.a4plus.co.uk
Directors: T. Wild (Fin), S. Wild (MD)
Immediate Holding Company: A4 PLUS DRAWING SERVICES LIMITED
Registration no: 03986994 **VAT No.:** GB 745 5912 12
Date established: 2000 **No.of Employees:** 1 - 10 **Product Groups:** 43, 44, 47, 48, 80, 81, 84, 85, 86

Date of Accounts	Sep 08	Sep 09	Sep 10
Working Capital	114	113	116
Fixed Assets	9	8	7
Current Assets	204	182	153

CCTV System Specialists Ltd

2 Quayside, Chatteris, PE16 6QX
Tel: 01354-691691 **Fax:** 0871-522 7876
E-mail: p.ford@cctv-systemspecialist.co.uk
Website: http://www.cctv-systemspecialist.co.uk
Directors: P. Ford (MD)
Immediate Holding Company: CCTV SYSTEM SPECIALISTS LIMITED
Registration no: 04759961 **Date established:** 2003
No.of Employees: 1 - 10 **Product Groups:** 37

Date of Accounts	Aug 11	Aug 10	Aug 08
Working Capital	-3	1	1
Fixed Assets	1	N/A	1
Current Assets	8	8	18

Connett Cable

Unit 4 South Fens Business Park Fenton Way, Chatteris, PE16 6WA
Tel: 01354-695558 **Fax:** 01354-694918
Website: http://www.jvluk.com
Directors: L. Connett (Dir)
Immediate Holding Company: JVL UK LIMITED
Registration no: 05014868 **Date established:** 2004
Turnover: £250,000 - £500,000 **No.of Employees:** 1 - 10
Product Groups: 37

Date of Accounts	Dec 11	Dec 10	Dec 09
Working Capital	-129	-267	-415
Current Assets	57	97	30

Creative Models

6-10 Industrial Estate Honeysome Road, Chatteris, PE16 6TG
Tel: 01354-760022 **Fax:** 01354-760037
E-mail: info@creativemodels.co.uk
Website: http://www.creativemodels.co.uk
Directors: S. White (Prop)
Immediate Holding Company: CREATIVE MODELS LTD
Registration no: 04671499 **Date established:** 2003 **Turnover:** £1m - £2m
No.of Employees: 1 - 10 **Product Groups:** 30, 49

Date of Accounts	Mar 11	Mar 10	Mar 09
Working Capital	693	516	413
Fixed Assets	31	35	34
Current Assets	884	617	562

Forbo Adhesives UK Ltd (a Reichhold Co.)

Bridge Street, Chatteris, PE16 6RD
Tel: 01354-692345 **Fax:** 01354-696661
Website: http://www.forbo.com
Bank(s): National Westminster
Managers: E. Norman (Chief Mgr)
Ultimate Holding Company: FORBO HOLDING AG/SA (SWITZERLAND)
Immediate Holding Company: H.B. FULLER ADHESIVES UK LTD
Registration no: 01683839 **VAT No.:** GB 226 3116 94
Date established: 1982 **Turnover:** £10m - £20m
No.of Employees: 21 - 50 **Product Groups:** 32

Date of Accounts	Dec 11	Dec 10	Dec 09
Sales Turnover	20m	14m	14m
Pre Tax Profit/Loss	881	108	638
Working Capital	2m	3m	3m
Fixed Assets	2m	2m	2m
Current Assets	8m	6m	5m
Current Liabilities	1m	842	440

Force One Ltd

L22 South Fens Business Centre Fenton Way, Chatteris, PE16 6TT
Tel: 01354-695544 **Fax:** 01354-695018
E-mail: enquiries@forceoneltd.co.uk
Website: http://www.forceoneltd.co.uk
Directors: P. Burke (Dir), M. Burke (Co Sec)
Managers: D. Perkins (Comm)
Immediate Holding Company: FORCE ONE LIMITED
Registration no: 05293964 **Date established:** 2004 **Turnover:** £5m - £10m
No.of Employees: 1 - 10 **Product Groups:** 45, 51

Date of Accounts	Nov 11	Nov 10	Nov 09
Working Capital	382	125	285
Fixed Assets	568	537	673
Current Assets	1m	850	902

Renoak Ltd

Unit 9 Honeysome Industrial Estate, Chatteris, PE16 6TG
Tel: 01354-692261 **Fax:** 01354-693462
E-mail: enquiries@renoak.co.uk
Website: http://www.renoak.co.uk
Bank(s): Midland
Directors: D. Green (MD)
Managers: D. Freeman (I.T. Exec), J. Moore (Sales Admin)
Registration no: 01355477 **Date established:** 1978
Turnover: £500,000 - £1m **No.of Employees:** 21 - 50 **Product Groups:** 48

Date of Accounts	Mar 10	Mar 09	Mar 08
Sales Turnover	752	774	755
Pre Tax Profit/Loss	-24	40	45
Working Capital	186	221	205
Fixed Assets	37	44	53
Current Assets	294	275	283
Current Liabilities	24	27	34

Stainless Metalcraft Ltd

Chatteris Engineering Works Honeysome Road, Chatteris, PE16 6SA
Tel: 01354-692391 **Fax:** 01354-695281
E-mail: p.kenny@metalcraft.co.uk
Website: http://www.metalcraft.co.uk
Bank(s): Lloyds TSB
Directors: M. James (Fin), P. Kenny (MD)
Managers: S. Gawron, D. Lenton (Tech Serv Mgr), M. Johnson (Personnel), M. Lawrence
Ultimate Holding Company: AVINGTRANS PLC
Immediate Holding Company: STAINLESS METALCRAFT (CHATTERIS) LIMITED
Registration no: 02506189 **Date established:** 1990
Turnover: £10m - £20m **No.of Employees:** 101 - 250
Product Groups: 35, 48

Date of Accounts	May 11	May 10	May 09
Sales Turnover	12m	10m	17m
Pre Tax Profit/Loss	604	-469	2m
Working Capital	2m	1m	2m
Fixed Assets	4m	4m	4m
Current Assets	7m	5m	7m
Current Liabilities	858	491	1m

Suttons Performance Packaging

16 Albert Way, Chatteris, PE16 6US
Tel: 01354-693171 **Fax:** 01354-695430
E-mail: info@suttonspp.co.uk
Website: http://www.suttonspp.co.uk
Bank(s): National Westminster Bank Plc
Directors: S. Sutton (MD), J. Little (Chief Op Offcr)
Immediate Holding Company: SUTTONS PERFORMANCE PACKAGING LIMITED
Registration no: 01887751 **VAT No.:** GB 213 5695 67
Date established: 1985 **Turnover:** £2m - £5m **No.of Employees:** 51 - 100
Product Groups: 27, 30

Ely

Anson Packaging Ltd

62 Station Road Haddenham, Ely, CB6 3XD
Tel: 01353-740990 **Fax:** 01353-741365
E-mail: sales@ansonpackaging.com
Website: http://www.ansonpackaging.com
Bank(s): Barclays
Directors: M. Tollman (Sales & Mktg), A. Osborne Smith (MD), J. Newbold (Co Sec)
Managers: C. Lupton (Personnel), P. Noyes (Tech Serv Mgr), M. Caldecoat (Fin Mgr)
Ultimate Holding Company: AVRO HOLDINGS LIMITED
Immediate Holding Company: ANSON PACKAGING LIMITED
Registration no: 01014780 **VAT No.:** GB 213 4738 80
Date established: 1971 **Turnover:** £20m - £50m
No.of Employees: 251 - 500 **Product Groups:** 30, 31, 66

Date of Accounts	Mar 09	Mar 10	Apr 11
Sales Turnover	37m	38m	35m
Pre Tax Profit/Loss	11m	341	-550
Working Capital	7m	6m	8m
Fixed Assets	10m	11m	9m
Current Assets	14m	14m	16m
Current Liabilities	3m	3m	2m

B & W Mechanical Handling

Gemini House 1 Bartholemews Walk, Ely, CB7 4EA
Tel: 01353-665001 **Fax:** 01353-666734
E-mail: blythe@bwmech.co.uk
Website: http://www.bwmech.co.uk
Bank(s): National Westminster Bank Plc
Directors: A. Blythe (MD)
Managers: M. Jones (Export Sales Mg), C. Chapman (I.T. Exec), A. Mitchell (Mgr)
Ultimate Holding Company: AUMUND HOLDING BV (NETHERLANDS)
Immediate Holding Company: B. & W. MECHANICAL HANDLING LIMITED
Registration no: 01206240 **VAT No.:** GB 215 0420 22
Date established: 1975 **Turnover:** £5m - £10m **No.of Employees:** 21 - 50
Product Groups: 39, 45, 84

Date of Accounts	Dec 10	Dec 09	Dec 08
Sales Turnover	8m	12m	11m
Pre Tax Profit/Loss	1m	2m	4m
Working Capital	3m	4m	5m
Fixed Assets	72	72	115
Current Assets	5m	7m	12m
Current Liabilities	2m	2m	4m

British Society Of Plant Breeders Ltd

Woolpack Chambers 16 Market Street, Ely, CB7 4ND
Tel: 01353-653200 **Fax:** 01353-661156
E-mail: info@bstb.co.uk
Website: http://www.bspb.co.uk
Bank(s): HSBC Bank plc
Directors: R. Summers (Dir), P. Maplestone (Co Sec)
Immediate Holding Company: BRITISH SOCIETY OF PLANT BREEDERS LIMITED(THE)
Registration no: 00876811 **Date established:** 1966
No.of Employees: 11 - 20 **Product Groups:** 07

Date of Accounts	Oct 10	Oct 09	Oct 11
Working Capital	-5	-20	111
Fixed Assets	25	33	18
Current Assets	2m	2m	3m

C C H Hose & Rubber

24 The Shade Soham, Ely, CB7 5DE
Tel: 01353-722366 **Fax:** 01353-723464
E-mail: cchhose@sales24.fsnet.co.uk
Website: http://www.cchhose.co.uk
Directors: D. Fretwell (MD)
VAT No.: GB 215 8843 51 **Date established:** 1980 **Turnover:** £2m - £5m
No.of Employees: 1 - 10 **Product Groups:** 29, 30, 36, 46

Calico Cottage

2 Haddenham Business Park Sutton Road, Haddenham, Ely, CB6 3PS
Tel: 01353-741661 **Fax:** 01353-741713
E-mail: info@calicocottage.co.uk
Website: http://www.calicocottage.co.uk
Directors: N. Baker (MD)
Date established: 1992 **No.of Employees:** 1 - 10 **Product Groups:** 20, 40, 41

Cambridge Commodities Ltd

Unit 78 Lancaster Way Business Park, Ely, CB6 3NW
Tel: 01353-667258 **Fax:** 01353-667289
E-mail: info@c-c-l.com
Website: http://www.c-c-l.com
Bank(s): Lloyds TSB Bank Plc
Directors: L. Stevens (Fin)
Immediate Holding Company: CAMBRIDGE COMMODITIES LIMITED
Registration no: 03590758 **Date established:** 1998
Turnover: £10m - £20m **No.of Employees:** 11 - 20 **Product Groups:** 01, 02, 14, 20, 31, 32, 34, 41, 61, 62

Date of Accounts	Aug 09	Aug 08	Nov 11
Sales Turnover	8m	N/A	11m
Pre Tax Profit/Loss	975	1m	-503
Working Capital	2m	2m	3m
Fixed Assets	1m	2m	868
Current Assets	4m	3m	8m
Current Liabilities	599	581	552

Cambridge Door Services Ltd

Unit A 127 Mereside Soham, Ely, CB7 5EG
Tel: 01353-725000 **Fax:** 01353-725001
E-mail: info@cambridgedoorservices.com
Website: http://www.cambridgedoorservices.com
Managers: A. Young (Mgr)
Immediate Holding Company: CAMBRIDGE DOOR SERVICES LIMITED
Registration no: 04081493 **Date established:** 2000
No.of Employees: 1 - 10 **Product Groups:** 35, 36, 48, 66

Date of Accounts	Sep 11	Sep 10	Sep 09
Working Capital	20	2	16
Fixed Assets	20	18	21
Current Assets	67	45	59

Cambridgeshire Hydraulics Ltd

97 Mereside Soham, Ely, CB7 5EE
Tel: 01353-721704 **Fax:** 01353-720653
E-mail: sales@cambshydraulics.com
Website: http://www.cambshydraulics.com
Directors: M. Neville (MD)
Ultimate Holding Company: P & N HOLDINGS LIMITED
Immediate Holding Company: CAMBRIDGESHIRE HYDRAULICS AND PNEUMATICS LIMITED
Registration no: 01833870 **Date established:** 1984
No.of Employees: 1 - 10 **Product Groups:** 29, 34, 35, 37, 38, 40, 42, 67, 85

Date of Accounts	Mar 12	Mar 11	Mar 10
Working Capital	370	328	331
Fixed Assets	341	326	333
Current Assets	621	655	581

Carmen Plumbing & Heating

20 The Borough Aldreth, Ely, CB6 3PJ
Tel: 01223-655367 **Fax:** 01223-280298
E-mail: carmenltd@msn.com
Website: http://www.carmenltd.co.uk
Directors: R. Fryer (Dir)
Immediate Holding Company: CARMEN ENTERPRISES UK LIMITED
Registration no: 03618830 **Date established:** 1998
No.of Employees: 1 - 10 **Product Groups:** 37, 40, 48, 52

Date of Accounts	Mar 11	Mar 10	Mar 09
Working Capital	-8	9	1
Fixed Assets	10	17	21
Current Assets	31	71	63

Clark & Butcher
42 High Street Soham, Ely, CB7 5HE
Tel: 01353-720237 **Fax:** 01353-720237
Directors: P. Clark (Co Sec)
Immediate Holding Company: CLARK & BUTCHER LIMITED
Registration no: 00067791 **VAT No.:** GB 215 7225 82
Date established: 2000 **Turnover:** Up to £250,000
No.of Employees: 1 - 10 **Product Groups:** 80

Date of Accounts	Jun 11	Jun 10	Jun 09
Sales Turnover	64	48	53
Pre Tax Profit/Loss	-73	-103	-119
Working Capital	1m	1m	1m
Fixed Assets	4m	4m	4m
Current Assets	1m	1m	2m
Current Liabilities	21	120	138

Clean Machine UK Ltd
The Works Barway, Ely, CB7 5UB
Tel: 01353-624888 **Fax:** 01353-624201
E-mail: sales@cleanmachine.co.uk
Website: http://www.cleanmachine.co.uk
Managers: K. Taylor (Chief Mgr)
Immediate Holding Company: CLEAN MACHINE (U.K) LIMITED
Registration no: 02017706 **Date established:** 1986
No.of Employees: 11 - 20 **Product Groups:** 40, 48, 69

Date of Accounts	Mar 11	Mar 10	Mar 09
Working Capital	186	232	226
Fixed Assets	201	151	177
Current Assets	478	632	561

David S Smith PLC
55 Ely Road Queen Adelaide, Ely, CB7 4TZ
Tel: 01353-660000 **Fax:** 01353-660011
E-mail: enquiries@dssmg.com
Website: http://www.dssmith-multigraphics.com
Bank(s): National Westminster Bank Plc
Managers: B. Pearson (Site Co-ord)
Ultimate Holding Company: DAVID S. SMITH (HOLDINGS) P.L.C.
Immediate Holding Company: DAVID S. SMITH PACKAGING LTD
Registration no: 00501594 **VAT No.:** GB 599 3782 63
Date established: 2003 **Turnover:** £5m - £10m
No.of Employees: 51 - 100 **Product Groups:** 27

Dietary Food Ltd
Cumberland House Brook Street, Soham, Ely, CB7 5BA
Tel: 01353-720791 **Fax:** 01353-721705
E-mail: graham@dietaryfoods.co.uk
Website: http://www.dietaryfoods.co.uk
Directors: R. Bright (Tech Serv), G. Bright (MD)
Managers: T. Graves, C. Grimes
Immediate Holding Company: DIETARY FOODS LIMITED
Registration no: 00807107 **Date established:** 1964 **Turnover:** £2m - £5m
No.of Employees: 21 - 50 **Product Groups:** 20, 40, 62

Date of Accounts	Sep 11	Sep 10	Sep 09
Sales Turnover	3m	N/A	N/A
Pre Tax Profit/Loss	-44	N/A	N/A
Working Capital	469	469	447
Fixed Assets	983	776	864
Current Assets	963	883	935
Current Liabilities	80	N/A	N/A

Ely Boat Chandlers
21 Waterside, Ely, CB7 4AU
Tel: 01353-663095 **Fax:** 01353-664514
E-mail: sales@elyboatchandlers.com
Website: http://www.elyboatchandlers.com
Directors: R. Alderton (Dir)
Date established: 1980 **Turnover:** Up to £250,000
No.of Employees: 1 - 10 **Product Groups:** 32, 61, 68

Ely Telecom Ltd
Unit 2 Greenham Park Common Road, Witchford, Ely, CB6 2HF
Tel: 01353-654007 **Fax:** 01353-699874
E-mail: sales@elytelecom.co.uk
Website: http://www.elytelecom.co.uk
Directors: M. Grainger (Prop)
Immediate Holding Company: ELY TELECOM LIMITED
Registration no: 05382186 **Date established:** 2005
No.of Employees: 1 - 10 **Product Groups:** 37, 44, 52

Date of Accounts	Mar 11	Mar 10	Mar 09
Working Capital	190	215	179
Fixed Assets	22	37	37
Current Assets	273	329	271

GB Innomech Ltd
The Innovation Centre Common Road, Witchford, Ely, CB6 2HZ
Tel: 01353-667394 **Fax:** 01353-663472
E-mail: sales@innomech.co.uk
Website: http://www.gbinnomech.co.uk
Directors: T. Mead (Dir)
Immediate Holding Company: GB INNOMECH SUPPORT LIMITED
Registration no: 08103112 **Date established:** 2012 **Turnover:** £2m - £5m
No.of Employees: 11 - 20 **Product Groups:** 37, 38, 40, 41, 42, 44, 45, 46, 48, 52, 54, 67, 84, 85

Date of Accounts	Jan 10	Jan 09	Jan 08
Working Capital	696	566	539
Fixed Assets	12	15	19
Current Assets	841	958	807

Glowbug Ltd (a division of Capricorn Chemicals)
Faraday Road Business Park, Littleport, Ely, CB6 1PE
Tel: 01353-863686 **Fax:** 01353-863990
E-mail: sales@capricorn.co.uk
Website: http://www.capricorn.co.uk
Directors: D. Priestley (MD)
Managers: A. Smith (Tech Serv Mgr), S. Covell (Sales Prom Mgr)
Immediate Holding Company: Dane & Co.
Registration no: 02296240 **Date established:** 1988
Turnover: £250,000 - £500,000 **No.of Employees:** 1 - 10
Product Groups: 32

G Harrison
Old Farm Westmoor Drove, Littleport, Ely, CB6 1RW
Tel: 01353-862528 **Fax:** 01353-862528
Directors: G. Harrison (Prop)
Date established: 1988 **No.of Employees:** 1 - 10 **Product Groups:** 41

Hybrid Laser Tech Ltd
Cambridgeshire Business Park Angel Drove, Ely, CB7 4EX
Tel: 01353-650835 **Fax:** 01353-650803
E-mail: info@hlt.co.uk
Website: http://www.hlt.co.uk
Directors: G. Smith (Dir), K. Gouldthorp (Dir)
Managers: K. Thompson (Sales Prom Mgr), K. Thomson (Prod Mgr), E. Spray (Quality Control)
Ultimate Holding Company: Shearline Precision Engineering Ltd
Registration no: 02176508 **VAT No.:** GB 479 8873 57
Date established: 1987 **Turnover:** £500,000 - £1m
No.of Employees: 21 - 50 **Product Groups:** 14, 31, 33, 37, 38, 40, 48

Date of Accounts	Mar 10	Mar 09	Mar 08
Working Capital	593	370	353
Fixed Assets	169	197	127
Current Assets	760	444	437

J R D Rubber Mouldings Ltd
26 Regal Drive Industrial Estate Soham, Ely, CB7 5BE
Tel: 01353-720480 **Fax:** 01353-624304
E-mail: sales@jrd-mouldings.com
Website: http://www.jrd-mouldings.com
Bank(s): Barclays Bank PLC
Directors: M. Cox (MD), T. Hooker (Dir), T. Hooker (MD)
Immediate Holding Company: JRD RUBBER MOULDINGS LIMITED
Registration no: 01309092 **VAT No.:** GB 215 1426 05
Date established: 1977 **Turnover:** £2m - £5m **No.of Employees:** 21 - 50
Product Groups: 29, 30, 36, 48, 63

Date of Accounts	Dec 11	Dec 10	Dec 09
Working Capital	483	308	437
Fixed Assets	587	670	583
Current Assets	989	937	771

Jardin Corrugated Cases Ltd
Elean Business Park Sutton, Ely, CB6 2QE
Tel: 01353-778522 **Fax:** 01353-777708
E-mail: kevin.hennessy@jccltd.com
Website: http://www.jccltd.com
Bank(s): Barclays
Directors: P. Thompson (Co Sec), R. Cameron (Sales), K. Hennessy (MD)
Managers: S. Richardson (Tech Serv Mgr)
Ultimate Holding Company: CORROPACK LIMITED (ISLE OF MAN)
Immediate Holding Company: JARDIN CORRUGATED CASES LIMITED
Registration no: 01332869 **VAT No.:** GB 344 3661 59
Date established: 1977 **Turnover:** £5m - £10m
No.of Employees: 51 - 100 **Product Groups:** 26, 27, 28

Date of Accounts	Mar 08	Apr 09	Apr 10
Sales Turnover	9m	8m	16m
Pre Tax Profit/Loss	-80	-8	-256
Working Capital	240	1m	-1m
Fixed Assets	2m	2m	2m
Current Assets	3m	4m	5m
Current Liabilities	1m	1m	3m

Michell Instruments Ltd
48 Lancaster Way Business Park, Ely, CB6 3NW
Tel: 01353-658000 **Fax:** 01353-658199
E-mail: info@michell.com
Website: http://www.michell.com
Bank(s): Lloyds TSB Bank plc
Directors: D. Leonard (Fin)
Managers: S. Lawrence (Mktg Serv Mgr), D. Mawby (Tech Serv Mgr), P. Kubietz (Mktg Serv Mgr), J. Page (Personnel), L. Stevenson (Purch Mgr)
Ultimate Holding Company: PARAMETRIC INVESTMENTS LIMITED
Immediate Holding Company: MICHELL INSTRUMENTS LIMITED
Registration no: 01183847 **VAT No.:** GB 214 7575 61
Date established: 1974 **Turnover:** £10m - £20m
No.of Employees: 51 - 100 **Product Groups:** 38, 41, 85

Date of Accounts	Dec 11	Dec 10	Jun 09
Sales Turnover	13m	16m	10m
Pre Tax Profit/Loss	1m	1m	99
Working Capital	2m	2m	542
Fixed Assets	2m	812	988
Current Assets	6m	4m	4m
Current Liabilities	468	586	315

Mini Specialists Ltd
Glebe House Wisbech Road, Littleport, Ely, CB6 1RG
Tel: 01353-861195 **Fax:** 01353-862306
E-mail: margaret.austin@minispecialists.co.uk
Website: http://www.minispecialists.co.uk
Directors: G. Kemp (MD), P. Kemp (Admin), M. Austin (Fab), M. Austin (MD)
Immediate Holding Company: MINI SPECIALISTS LIMITED
Registration no: 01564823 **VAT No.:** GB 215 5806 72
Date established: 1981 **Turnover:** Up to £250,000
No.of Employees: 1 - 10 **Product Groups:** 37, 38, 40, 49, 67

Date of Accounts	Dec 09	Dec 08	Dec 07
Sales Turnover	82	103	198
Pre Tax Profit/Loss	9	N/A	28
Working Capital	-13	-19	-18
Fixed Assets	17	17	18
Current Assets	44	44	55
Current Liabilities	4	4	9

Paragon Precision Engineering Ltd
Unit 8 Lancaster Way Business Park, Ely, CB6 3NW
Tel: 01353-662244 **Fax:** 01353-666868
E-mail: sales@paragonengineering.co.uk
Website: http://www.paragonengineering.co.uk
Directors: J. Kent (MD)
Immediate Holding Company: PARAGON PRECISION ENGINEERING LIMITED
Registration no: 03030465 **Date established:** 1995
No.of Employees: 21 - 50 **Product Groups:** 25, 26, 28, 30, 33, 34, 35, 37, 40, 45, 46, 48, 67, 84, 85

Date of Accounts	Apr 12	Apr 11	Apr 10
Working Capital	-26	-21	-65
Fixed Assets	213	243	333
Current Assets	837	765	705

Performance Packaging UK Ltd
94c Hillrow Haddenham, Ely, CB6 3TJ
Tel: 01353-741990 **Fax:** 01353-741552
E-mail: nick.robinson@ppack.co.uk
Website: http://www.ppack.co.uk
Directors: N. Robinson (MD)
Immediate Holding Company: PERFORMANCE PACKAGING (UK) LIMITED
Registration no: 03434198 **Date established:** 1997
No.of Employees: 1 - 10 **Product Groups:** 38, 42

Date of Accounts	Sep 11	Sep 10	Sep 09
Working Capital	339	276	363
Fixed Assets	48	59	62
Current Assets	578	470	601
Current Liabilities	N/A	N/A	18

Potter Group Logistics
Queen Adelaide Way Queen Adelaide, Ely, CB7 4UB
Tel: 01353-662345 **Fax:** 01353-662764
E-mail: ely@pottergroup.co.uk
Website: http://www.pottergroup.co.uk
Managers: M. Crockall (Personnel), M. Crockall (Personnel), C. Heatwole (Chief Mgr), D. Tofts (Chief Mgr), M. Griggs, E. Clark (Sales & Mktg Mg)
Ultimate Holding Company: THE POTTER GROUP (HOLDINGS) PLC
Immediate Holding Company: THE POTTER GROUP LIMITED
Registration no: 01392251 **VAT No.:** GB 557 2193 30
Date established: 1978 **Turnover:** £10m - £20m
No.of Employees: 21 - 50 **Product Groups:** 45, 72, 76, 77, 84

Date of Accounts	Apr 11	Apr 10	Apr 09
Sales Turnover	15m	15m	16m
Pre Tax Profit/Loss	447	355	28
Working Capital	7m	7m	6m
Fixed Assets	4m	3m	4m
Current Assets	11m	10m	11m
Current Liabilities	2m	1m	3m

Precision Associates Ltd
Hythe Farm The Hythe, Little Downham, Ely, CB6 2DT
Tel: 01353-699100
Website: http://www.precisionassociates.co.uk
Directors: S. Golds-Wallace (MD)
Immediate Holding Company: PRECISION ASSOCIATES LIMITED
Registration no: 03255424 **Date established:** 1996
No.of Employees: 1 - 10 **Product Groups:** 26, 35

Date of Accounts	Sep 11	Sep 10	Sep 09
Working Capital	-6	-14	-14
Fixed Assets	13	15	15
Current Assets	71	41	34

Prelude Fabrications Ltd
129 Mereside Soham, Ely, CB7 5EG
Tel: 01353-722402 **Fax:** 01353-624608
E-mail: rob.white@unicombox.com
Website: http://www.preludefabrications.com
Directors: R. White (Dir)
Immediate Holding Company: PRELUDE FABRICATIONS LIMITED
Registration no: 02533420 **VAT No.:** GB 538 5625 20
Date established: 1990 **Turnover:** £500,000 - £1m
No.of Employees: 1 - 10 **Product Groups:** 48

Date of Accounts	Aug 11	Aug 10	Aug 09
Working Capital	29	38	45
Fixed Assets	6	6	9
Current Assets	67	57	78

Prescient Engineering Ltd
25 Mereside Soham, Ely, CB7 5EE
Tel: 01353-720787 **Fax:** 01353-723356
E-mail: contact@prescientengineeringltd.co.uk
Directors: G. Bowman (Co Sec), R. Bowman (Dir)
Immediate Holding Company: PRESCIENT ENGINEERING LIMITED
Registration no: 01366595 **Date established:** 1978
Turnover: £500,000 - £1m **No.of Employees:** 1 - 10 **Product Groups:** 34, 48

Date of Accounts	Jun 11	Jun 10	Jun 09
Working Capital	470	539	545
Fixed Assets	75	80	89
Current Assets	493	564	602

Shearline Precision Engineering Ltd
Cambridgeshire Business Park Angel Drove, Ely, CB7 4EX
Tel: 01353-668668 **Fax:** 01353-668203
E-mail: sales@shearline.co.uk
Website: http://www.shearline.co.uk
Bank(s): Barclays
Directors: C. Killingworth (Fin), D. Littlechild (Ch), K. Gouldthorp (Fin)
Managers: M. Kilby (Tech Serv Mgr), H. Bacon (Personnel), L. Hughes (Buyer)
Ultimate Holding Company: SHEARLINE HOLDINGS LIMITED
Immediate Holding Company: SHEARLINE PRECISION ENGINEERING LIMITED
Registration no: 00976052 **VAT No.:** GB 214 1945 84
Date established: 1970 **Turnover:** £5m - £10m
No.of Employees: 101 - 250 **Product Groups:** 28, 48

Date of Accounts	Mar 10	Mar 09	Apr 11
Sales Turnover	5m	6m	5m
Pre Tax Profit/Loss	-728	-748	-511
Working Capital	464	430	357
Fixed Assets	2m	2m	3m
Current Assets	3m	3m	3m
Current Liabilities	2m	1m	2m

Soham Security Products Ltd
22 Regal Drive Soham, Ely, CB7 5BE
Tel: 01353-722930 **Fax:** 01353-624429
E-mail: sales@sohamsecurity.co.uk
Website: http://www.sohamsecurity.co.uk
Directors: D. Murton (Fin), S. Cooper (Sales)
Immediate Holding Company: SOHAM SECURITY PRODUCTS LIMITED
Registration no: 01964017 **Date established:** 1985
No.of Employees: 11 - 20 **Product Groups:** 26, 35

Date of Accounts	Mar 11	Mar 10	Mar 09
Working Capital	751	694	623
Fixed Assets	82	95	93
Current Assets	1m	915	863

Standen Engineering Ltd
Hereward Works 47-49 Station Road, Ely, CB7 4BP
Tel: 01353-661111 **Fax:** 01353-662370
E-mail: info@standen.co.uk
Website: http://www.standen.co.uk
Bank(s): Royal Bank of Scotland
Directors: A. Mathias (Mkt Research), A. Reedman (Sales), D. Wilson (Sales)
Managers: O. Blake, D. Rickwood (Chief Acct), E. Rickwood (Supp Mgr)
Immediate Holding Company: STANDEN ENGINEERING LIMITED
Registration no: 04315838 **Date established:** 2001
Turnover: £10m - £20m **No.of Employees:** 51 - 100 **Product Groups:** 41

Date of Accounts	Nov 11	Nov 10	Nov 09
Sales Turnover	12m	11m	10m
Pre Tax Profit/Loss	515	206	339

see next page

Standen Engineering Ltd - Cont'd

Working Capital	3m	2m	2m
Fixed Assets	274	451	200
Current Assets	5m	5m	4m
Current Liabilities	991	1m	586

Team Sprayers Ltd

Unit 3 Lancaster Way Business Park, Ely, CB6 3NW
Tel: 01353-661211 **Fax:** 01353-666642
E-mail: buyer@team-sprayers.com
Website: http://www.team-sprayers.com
Directors: D. Hubbard (MD)
Immediate Holding Company: TEAM SPRAYERS LIMITED
Registration no: 01539127 **Date established:** 1981
Turnover: £500,000 - £1m **No.of Employees:** 1 - 10 **Product Groups:** 07, 40, 41, 43, 45, 46, 48, 49, 51, 52

Date of Accounts	Nov 11	Nov 10	Nov 09
Working Capital	231	224	148
Fixed Assets	107	102	77
Current Assets	419	395	305

Techneat Engineering Ltd

2a Henry Crabb Road Littleport, Ely, CB6 1SE
Tel: 01353-862044 **Fax:** 01353-862644
E-mail: info@techneat.co.uk
Website: http://www.techneat.co.uk
Directors: O. Collins Neat (Fin), T. Neat (Dir)
Immediate Holding Company: TECHNEAT ENGINEERING LIMITED
Registration no: 01826948 **Date established:** 1984
Turnover: Up to £250,000 **No.of Employees:** 11 - 20 **Product Groups:** 41

Date of Accounts	Nov 11	Nov 10	Nov 09
Working Capital	463	353	155
Fixed Assets	330	246	238
Current Assets	788	778	487

Timbergarden

Unit 31 Lancaster Way Business Park, Ely, CB6 3NW
Tel: 01353-668333 **Fax:** 01353-668440
Website: http://www.timbergarden.co.uk
Directors: H. Fordham (Dir)
No.of Employees: 21 - 50 **Product Groups:** 08, 25, 35

Trojan Commercial Cleaning

40 High Street Aldreth, Ely, CB6 3PG
Tel: 01353-740022 **Fax:** 01353-740022
E-mail: trojan.david@virgin.net
Website: http://www.trojan-services.co.uk
Directors: D. Mills (Prop)
Immediate Holding Company: TROJAN COMMERCIAL CLEANING CONTRACTS LTD
Registration no: 06723999 **Date established:** 2008
No.of Employees: 21 - 50 **Product Groups:** 23, 24, 44, 52

Date of Accounts	Oct 10	Oct 09
Working Capital	24	-0
Current Assets	78	40

Wesley Coe Cambridge Ltd

Gas Lane, Ely, CB7 4GH
Tel: 01353-667914 **Fax:** 01223-356693
E-mail: info@wesleycoe.com
Website: http://www.wesleycoe.com
Bank(s): Barclays, Chesterton Road
Directors: A. Coe (Dir)
Managers: C. Jones (Comm)
Ultimate Holding Company: WESLEY COE (HOLDINGS) LIMITED
Immediate Holding Company: WESLEY COE (CAMBRIDGE) LIMITED
Registration no: 00502988 **VAT No.:** GB 213 5040 19
Date established: 1952 **Turnover:** £2m - £5m **No.of Employees:** 21 - 50
Product Groups: 33, 48

Date of Accounts	Mar 11	Mar 10	Mar 09
Sales Turnover	4m	4m	4m
Pre Tax Profit/Loss	92	102	139
Working Capital	2m	2m	1m
Fixed Assets	1m	2m	2m
Current Assets	2m	2m	2m
Current Liabilities	219	357	723

Whiting & Partners

George Court 6 Bartholemews Walk, Ely, CB7 4JW
Tel: 01353-662595 **Fax:** 01353-666119
E-mail: ely@whitingandpartners.co.uk
Website: http://www.whitingandpartners.co.uk
Directors: I. Piper (Snr Part)
Immediate Holding Company: HAVEN HEALTHCARE (UK) LIMITED
Registration no: OC358853 **Date established:** 2003
No.of Employees: 21 - 50 **Product Groups:** 80

Huntingdon

A T Sack Fillers

PO Box 434, Huntingdon, PE26 2RB
Tel: 01487-814002 **Fax:** 01487-814002
E-mail: sales@simplafillsystems.co.uk
Website: http://www.simplafillsystems.co.uk
Directors: B. McNish (Prop), B. McNish (MD)
Immediate Holding Company: LTE COMMUNICATIONS LIMITED
Registration no: 06688228 **Date established:** 2008
Turnover: £500,000 - £1m **No.of Employees:** 1 - 10 **Product Groups:** 42

Awg plc

Anglian House Ambury Road, Huntingdon, PE29 3NZ
Tel: 01480-323000 **Fax:** 01480-323115
Website: http://www.anglianwater.co.uk
Directors: J. Cox (Grp Chief Exec), C. Firth (Co Sec), P. Hixon (Ch), S. Longhurst (Fin)
Managers: D. Gregory (Mktg Serv Mgr)
Immediate Holding Company: AWG PLC
Registration no: 03936645 **Date established:** 2000 **Turnover:** £5m - £10m
No.of Employees: 1501 & over **Product Groups:** 18, 42

Anglia Stairlift Ltd

Unit 3 Roman Way Small Business Park London Road, Godmanchester, Huntingdon, PE29 2LN
Tel: 0845-2470907 **Fax:** 01480-810997
E-mail: enquiries@anglia-stairlifts.co.uk
Website: http://www.anglia-stairlift.co.uk
Directors: C. Jackson (Prop)
Immediate Holding Company: Anglia Stairlifts Ltd
Registration no: 05994116 **Date established:** 2006
No.of Employees: 1 - 10 **Product Groups:** 35, 39, 45

Anglian Water International Holdings Ltd (a division of Anglian Water P.L.C.)

Anlgian House Ambury Road, Huntingdon, PE29 3NZ
Tel: 01480-323000 **Fax:** 01480-326981
E-mail: admin@anglianwater.co.uk
Website: http://www.anglianwater.co.uk
Directors: G. Shepheard (Co Sec), J. Forster (Dir)
Ultimate Holding Company: ANGLIAN WATER GROUP LIMITED (JERSEY)
Immediate Holding Company: ANGLIAN WATER INTERNATIONAL HOLDINGS LIMITED
Registration no: 02024769 **Date established:** 1986
Turnover: Over £1,000m **No.of Employees:** 1 - 10 **Product Groups:** 51, 84

Date of Accounts	Mar 11	Mar 10	Mar 09
Pre Tax Profit/Loss	9	-23	10
Working Capital	-152	-152	-90
Fixed Assets	4m	4m	4m
Current Assets	226	226	255

Arch Motor Manufacturing Company Ltd

Redwongs Way, Huntingdon, PE29 7HD
Tel: 01480-459661 **Fax:** 01480-450923
E-mail: bruce@archmotor.co.uk
Website: http://www.archmotor.co.uk
Bank(s): Barclays
Directors: B. Robinson (MD)
Immediate Holding Company: ARCH MANUFACTURING COMPANY LIMITED
Registration no: 01554429 **VAT No.:** GB 119 7755 37
Date established: 1981 **No.of Employees:** 21 - 50 **Product Groups:** 48

Barrell Bearing Co Ltd

Unit G Sawtry Business Park Sawtry, Huntingdon, PE28 5GQ
Tel: 01487-834053 **Fax:** 01487-832887
Directors: H. Barrell (MD)
Registration no: 01792319 **Date established:** 1993
Turnover: Up to £250,000 **No.of Employees:** 1 - 10 **Product Groups:** 22, 23, 32, 34, 35

Black Carbon Limited

Rectory Barn Huntingdon Road, Wyton, Huntingdon, PE28 2AD
Tel: 01480-464914
E-mail: nic@blackcarbon.co.uk
Website: http://www.blackcarbon.co.uk
Directors: N. Mounteney (Prop)
Registration no: 04346653 **Date established:** 2001
Turnover: Up to £250,000 **No.of Employees:** 1 - 10 **Product Groups:** 85

Date of Accounts	Mar 09	Mar 08	Mar 07
Working Capital	-2	N/A	4
Fixed Assets	4	5	3
Current Assets	1	4	12

Bright Instrument Co. Ltd

St Margarets Way Stukeley Meadows Industrial Estate, Huntingdon, PE29 6EU
Tel: 01480-451980 **Fax:** 01480-456031
E-mail: sales@brightinstruments.com
Website: http://www.brightinstruments.com
Bank(s): Lloyds TSB
Directors: A. Bright (MD)
Immediate Holding Company: BRIGHT INSTRUMENT CO. LIMITED
Registration no: 00326019 **VAT No.:** GB 638 5106 36
Date established: 1937 **Turnover:** £1m - £2m **No.of Employees:** 21 - 50
Product Groups: 38

Date of Accounts	Mar 12	Mar 11	Mar 10
Working Capital	420	519	645
Fixed Assets	115	122	167
Current Assets	581	669	839

C Britton

The Butts Station Road, Kimbolton, Huntingdon, PE28 0HS
Tel: 01480-860943 **Fax:** 01480-860943
Website: http://www.chemsoc.org/networks/dcp
Directors: C. Britton (Prop)
Date established: 1996 **No.of Employees:** 1 - 10 **Product Groups:** 46, 48

C G C Agricultural & Motor Engineers

Five Down Puddock Road, Warboys, Huntingdon, PE28 2UB
Tel: 01487-823248 **Fax:** 01487-823248
E-mail: sales@cgcagricultural.co.uk
Website: http://www.cgcagricultural.co.uk
Directors: C. Chapfield (Prop)
Date established: 1987 **Turnover:** Up to £250,000
No.of Employees: 1 - 10 **Product Groups:** 07, 29, 48, 54, 67

C L F Packaging Ltd

Orchard House Heath Road Warboys, Huntingdon, PE28 2UW
Tel: 01487-823222 **Fax:** 01487-824011
E-mail: customercare@clfpack.co.uk
Website: http://www.clfpackaging.co.uk
Bank(s): Trustee Savings Bank
Directors: D. Lightning (MD)
Ultimate Holding Company: CLF LIMITED
Immediate Holding Company: CLF PACKAGING LIMITED
Registration no: 01192635 **VAT No.:** GB 359 9071 13
Date established: 1974 **Turnover:** £5m - £10m **No.of Employees:** 11 - 20
Product Groups: 27, 30

Date of Accounts	Apr 12	Apr 11	Apr 10
Working Capital	84	77	118
Fixed Assets	891	873	866
Current Assets	2m	2m	2m

Cambridge Transformers Ltd

Quiet Waters High Street, Earith, Huntingdon, PE28 3PN
Tel: 01487-842154 **Fax:** 01487-843445
E-mail: sales@transformers.demon.co.uk
Website: http://www.cambridgetransformers.co.uk
Directors: S. Taylor (MD), P. Norrington (MD)
Immediate Holding Company: CAMBRIDGE TRANSFORMERS LIMITED
Registration no: 06335216 **Date established:** 2007
No.of Employees: 1 - 10 **Product Groups:** 37

Date of Accounts	Oct 07	Oct 06	Oct 05
Working Capital	283	131	140
Fixed Assets	N/A	36	43
Current Assets	345	158	178
Current Liabilities	61	27	38
Total Share Capital	3	3	3

Charpack Ltd

30 St Peters Road, Huntingdon, PE29 7DG
Tel: 01480-434434 **Fax:** 01480-434545
E-mail: sales@charpak.co.uk
Website: http://www.charpak.co.uk
Bank(s): Barclays, St. Neots
Directors: P. Smith (MD), M. Smith (Co Sec)
Managers: T. Evans (Tech Serv Mgr), B. Kirk (Fin Mgr)
Registration no: 01588917 **VAT No.:** GB 455 9489 91
Turnover: £2m - £5m **No.of Employees:** 51 - 100 **Product Groups:** 30, 31, 42, 48, 49, 76

Date of Accounts	Dec 08	Dec 07	Dec 06
Working Capital	-4	2	15
Fixed Assets	2m	2m	2m
Current Assets	832	1m	892
Current Liabilities	836	1m	876

Chefaro UK Ltd (Subsidiary Of Akzo Nobel)

Unit 1 Tower Close, Huntingdon, PE29 6SZ
Tel: 01480-421800 **Fax:** 01480-434861
Website: http://www.omega-pharma.be
Bank(s): Barclays, 54 Lombard Street, EC3P 3AN
Directors: D. Gale (Fin), A. Scheepens (Dir)
Managers: B. Clements (Nat Sales Mgr)
Ultimate Holding Company: Akzo Nobel NV (Metherlands)
Immediate Holding Company: Akzo Nobel N.V.
Registration no: 00922235 **VAT No.:** GB 370 4780 49
Turnover: £20m - £50m **No.of Employees:** 21 - 50 **Product Groups:** 31, 32

Date of Accounts	Dec 09	Dec 08	Dec 07
Sales Turnover	19m	20m	24m
Pre Tax Profit/Loss	-1m	-6m	-2m
Working Capital	5m	-3m	2m
Fixed Assets	310	308	341
Current Assets	13m	14m	13m
Current Liabilities	2m	1m	3m

Components Bureau

1 Osprey Court Kingfisher Way, Hinchingbrooke Business Park, Huntingdon, PE29 6FN
Tel: 01480-412233 **Fax:** 01480-412266
E-mail: sales@componentsbureau.com
Website: http://www.componentsbureau.com
Managers: C. Wilson (Sales Off Mgr)
Immediate Holding Company: COMPONENTS BUREAU LIMITED
Registration no: 01849437 **VAT No.:** GB 393 1445 46
Date established: 1984 **Turnover:** £1m - £2m **No.of Employees:** 1 - 10
Product Groups: 67

Date of Accounts	Dec 11	Dec 10	Dec 09
Working Capital	221	155	74
Fixed Assets	85	85	89
Current Assets	850	751	456

Comtec Cables Accessories

Unit 3 Cardinal Way Godmanchester, Huntingdon, PE29 2XN
Tel: 01480-415415 **Fax:** 01480-454724
E-mail: sales@comtec-comms.com
Website: http://www.comtec-comms.com
Bank(s): Lloyds TSB Bank plc
Directors: B. Smith (Fin), D. Conway (Sales), J. Buck (MD)
Managers: M. Edwards (Tech Serv Mgr)
Ultimate Holding Company: TAYVIN 40 LIMITED
Immediate Holding Company: COMTEC CABLE ACCESSORIES LIMITED
Registration no: 01349036 **Date established:** 1978
Turnover: £10m - £20m **No.of Employees:** 21 - 50 **Product Groups:** 30, 33, 35, 36, 37, 38, 44, 45, 46

Date of Accounts	Dec 11	Dec 10	Dec 09
Sales Turnover	19m	16m	18m
Pre Tax Profit/Loss	87	6	2
Working Capital	315	330	521
Fixed Assets	884	1m	1m
Current Assets	6m	5m	5m
Current Liabilities	3m	2m	2m

Dda Shop Ltd

First Floor Office 7e High Street Fenstanton, Huntingdon, PE28 9LQ
Tel: 01480-467632
E-mail: info@ddashop.com
Website: http://www.ddashop.com
Directors: L. Morris (Prop)
Immediate Holding Company: DDA SHOP LIMITED
Registration no: 05337373 **Date established:** 2005
No.of Employees: 1 - 10 **Product Groups:** 25, 29, 35

Date of Accounts	Mar 11	Mar 10	Mar 09
Working Capital	39	31	31
Fixed Assets	4	1	1
Current Assets	79	60	60

Delta Fabrications

15 Brook Road Kimbolton, Huntingdon, PE28 0LR
Tel: 01480-861154 **Fax:** 01480-861134
E-mail: info@deltafabrications.com
Website: http://www.deltafabrications.com
Directors: R. Grice (Prop)
Turnover: £2m - £5m **No.of Employees:** 11 - 20 **Product Groups:** 35

Digital Direct Security

Unit 7 Osprey Court Kingfisher Way, Hinchingbrooke Business Park, Huntingdon, PE29 6FN
Tel: 01480-459809 **Fax:** 01480-437172
E-mail: info@digitaldirectsecurity.co.uk
Website: http://www.digitaldirectsecurity.co.uk
Directors: H. Afzal (Prop)
Registration no: 06621725 **Date established:** 2008
No.of Employees: 1 - 10 **Product Groups:** 37, 38, 40, 52, 67

Display Solutions Ltd
Osprey House 1 Osway Court Hinchingbrooke Business Park, Huntingdon, PE29 6FN
Tel: 01480-411600 **Fax:** 01480-412266
E-mail: sales@displaysolutions.co.uk
Website: http://www.displaysolutions.co.uk
Managers: M. Whitehead (Mgr)
Immediate Holding Company: DISPLAY SOLUTIONS LIMITED
Registration no: 03183367 **Date established:** 1996 **Turnover:** £2m - £5m
No.of Employees: 11 - 20 **Product Groups:** 37, 38, 44

Date of Accounts	Dec 11	Dec 10	Sep 09
Working Capital	-47	-44	-15
Fixed Assets	31	35	47
Current Assets	399	539	643

Escol Products Ltd
Windover Road, Huntingdon, PE29 7EB
Tel: 01480-454631 **Fax:** 01480-411626
E-mail: info@escolproducts.co.uk
Website: http://www.escolproducts.co.uk
Directors: R. Wates (Dir)
Ultimate Holding Company: EGE HOLDING AS (TURKEY)
Immediate Holding Company: ESCOL PRODUCTS LIMITED
Registration no: 00540240 **Date established:** 1954 **Turnover:** £5m - £10m
No.of Employees: 1 - 10 **Product Groups:** 32

Date of Accounts	Dec 11	Dec 10	Dec 09
Working Capital	-600	-565	-168
Fixed Assets	38	49	71
Current Assets	440	423	2m
Current Liabilities	N/A	N/A	228

Et 2000
Brookside Industrial Estate Sawtry, Huntingdon, PE28 5SB
Tel: 01487-830222 **Fax:** 01487-832252
Website: http://www.et2000.co.uk
Directors: S. Grice (MD)
Immediate Holding Company: P&M PUMPS LTD
Registration no: 01541080 **Date established:** 2009
No.of Employees: 21 - 50 **Product Groups:** 38, 42

Date of Accounts	Aug 11	Aug 10
Working Capital	-102	-181
Fixed Assets	244	274
Current Assets	1m	730

Express Cartons
Manchett Store Heath Road, Warboys, Huntingdon, PE28 2UW
Tel: 01487-823575 **Fax:** 01487-823923
E-mail: info@expresscartons.co.uk
Website: http://www.expresscartons.co.uk
Directors: N. Willmer (Prop)
Immediate Holding Company: BEA BUILDING PRODUCTS LIMITED
Date established: 2002 **Turnover:** £250,000 - £500,000
No.of Employees: 1 - 10 **Product Groups:** 27, 66

Fenland Rural Sports Supplies
Greenacres Farm Puddock Road, Warboys, Huntingdon, PE28 2UB
Tel: 01487-824821 **Fax:** 01487-823274
E-mail: bill@beateye.com
Website: http://www.fenlandruralsports.com
Directors: W. Hodge (Ptnr)
Registration no: 01629353 **Date established:** 1982 **Turnover:** £1m - £2m
No.of Employees: 1 - 10 **Product Groups:** 36, 40, 67

Fentex Ltd
3 Brook Farm Thrapston Road, Ellington, Huntingdon, PE28 0AE
Tel: 01480-890104 **Fax:** 01480-890105
E-mail: sales@fentex.co.uk
Website: http://www.btinternet.com
Bank(s): HSBC
Directors: D. Blanchard (MD)
Immediate Holding Company: FENTEX LIMITED
Registration no: 03665035 **VAT No.:** GB 728 5667 92
Date established: 1998 **No.of Employees:** 21 - 50 **Product Groups:** 24, 29, 30, 32, 35, 37, 38, 39, 40, 45, 54, 74

Date of Accounts	Apr 11	Apr 10	Apr 09
Working Capital	144	225	287
Fixed Assets	39	21	29
Current Assets	1m	1m	788

The First Mailing Co. Ltd
11a Glebe Road, Huntingdon, PE29 7HH
Tel: 08456-349522 **Fax:** 0845-634 9533
E-mail: leanne@firstmailing.co.uk
Website: http://www.firstmailing.co.uk
Managers: L. Carmedy (Chief Mgr)
Registration no: 03618405 **Turnover:** £500,000 - £1m
No.of Employees: 11 - 20 **Product Groups:** 27, 28, 30, 80, 81

Date of Accounts	Mar 08	Mar 07	Mar 06
Working Capital	99	152	216
Fixed Assets	117	111	103
Current Assets	246	367	417
Current Liabilities	147	215	201

Gambro Lundia A B
1-2 Ermine Centre Hurricane Close, Ermine Business Park, Huntingdon, PE29 6XX
Tel: 01480-444000 **Fax:** 01480-434084
E-mail: gordon.sutherland@gambro.co.uk
Website: http://www.gambro.com
Directors: D. Poorey (Dir)
Ultimate Holding Company: INCENTIVE AB (SWEDEN)
Immediate Holding Company: GAMBRO LUNDIA AB
Registration no: FC027429 **VAT No.:** GB 206 0009 27
Date established: 2007 **Turnover:** £10m - £20m
No.of Employees: 21 - 50 **Product Groups:** 38

Date of Accounts	Dec 10	Dec 09	Dec 08
Pre Tax Profit/Loss	N/A	N/A	1m
Working Capital	301	357	212
Fixed Assets	150	150	150
Current Assets	522	633	1m
Current Liabilities	N/A	277	821

Gema Supplies & Services
7 Deer Park Road Sawtry, Huntingdon, PE28 5TT
Tel: 01487-832321 **Fax:** 01487-832321
E-mail: gema@gemasupplies.co.uk
Website: http://www.gemasupplies.co.uk
Directors: G. Simlo (Prop)
Date established: 2005 **No.of Employees:** 1 - 10 **Product Groups:** 33, 37

Genesis Forklift Trucks Ltd
15 Warboys Airfield Industrial Estate Warboys, Huntingdon, PE28 2SH
Tel: 01487-823300 **Fax:** 01487-825214
E-mail: sales@genesisforklifts.com
Website: http://www.genesisforklifts.co.uk
Directors: G. Faulkner (MD)
Immediate Holding Company: GENESIS FORKLIFT TRUCKS LIMITED
Registration no: 04236697 **Date established:** 2001
No.of Employees: 11 - 20 **Product Groups:** 35, 39, 45

Date of Accounts	Aug 10	Aug 09	Aug 08
Working Capital	-225	-174	-228
Fixed Assets	489	524	592
Current Assets	389	314	435

Glynwed Pipe Systems Ltd (An Aliaxis Co.)
St Peter's Road, Huntingdon, PE29 7DA
Tel: 01480-52121 **Fax:** 01480-458829
E-mail: enquiries@gpsuk.com
Website: http://www.gpsuk.com
Directors: A. Catanzano (Dir), A. Wilson (Dir), M. Gisbourne (MD), R. Grately (Mkt Research), R. Smith (Dir), S. Dix (Fin)
Immediate Holding Company: GLYNWED PIPE SYSTEMS LIMITED
Registration no: 01698059 **Date established:** 1983
Turnover: £250m - £500m **No.of Employees:** 51 - 100
Product Groups: 30, 36, 45, 48

Date of Accounts	Dec 07
Sales Turnover	100000
Pre Tax Profit/Loss	12000
Working Capital	11000
Fixed Assets	29000
Current Assets	33000
Current Liabilities	22000
Total Share Capital	11000
ROCE% (Return on Capital Employed)	30.0

Goodfellow Cambridge Ltd
Units C1-C2 Ermine Business Park Spitfire Close, Ermine Business Park, Huntingdon, PE29 6WR
Tel: 01480-424800 **Fax:** 01440-730661
E-mail: info@goodfellow.com
Website: http://www.goodfellow.com
Directors: I. Doggett (Prop), I. Shirley (Fin), S. Aldersley (MD)
Managers: S. Barker (Tech Serv Mgr)
Ultimate Holding Company: GOODFELLOW HOLDINGS LIMITED
Immediate Holding Company: TECHNICAL GLASS CAMBRIDGE LIMITED
Registration no: 03947687 **VAT No.:** GB 212 8527 79
Date established: 2000 **Turnover:** £1m - £2m **No.of Employees:** 21 - 50
Product Groups: 23, 30, 31, 34, 35, 36, 37, 48, 66, 77

Date of Accounts	Mar 08	Jun 11	Jun 10
Sales Turnover	N/A	2m	1m
Pre Tax Profit/Loss	N/A	371	368
Working Capital	622	1m	1m
Fixed Assets	9	1	3
Current Assets	788	2m	1m
Current Liabilities	N/A	310	186

Greenery UK Ltd
Unit 2a Vantage Park Washingley Road, Huntingdon, PE29 6SR
Tel: 01480-422000 **Fax:** 01480-417149
E-mail: info@greeneryuk.com
Website: http://www.thegreenery.com
Bank(s): Barclays
Directors: D. Tarry (Co Sec)
Managers: A. Smith, L. Evans (Tech Serv Mgr), R. Marsh (Purch Mgr), D. Tarry (Comptroller)
Ultimate Holding Company: GREENERY BV (NETHERLANDS)
Immediate Holding Company: GREENERY UK LIMITED
Registration no: 00945702 **VAT No.:** GB 486 2975 90
Date established: 1969 **Turnover:** £75m - £125m
No.of Employees: 11 - 20 **Product Groups:** 62

Date of Accounts	Dec 08	Dec 09	Jan 11
Sales Turnover	85m	91m	107m
Pre Tax Profit/Loss	1m	525	864
Working Capital	4m	4m	4m
Fixed Assets	409	405	8m
Current Assets	11m	10m	13m
Current Liabilities	540	348	330

Hawkeye Security & Surveillance Systems Ltd
9 Blackstone Road Stukeley Meadows Industrial Estate, Huntingdon, PE29 6EF
Tel: 01480-811276 **Fax:** 01480-811256
E-mail: info@hawkeyesystems.com
Website: http://www.hawkeyesystems.com
Directors: A. King (Fin)
Immediate Holding Company: HAWKEYE SECURITY & SURVEILLANCE SYSTEMS LTD.
Registration no: 04854574 **Date established:** 2003
No.of Employees: 11 - 20 **Product Groups:** 22, 35, 36, 37, 38, 39, 40, 44, 46, 49, 52, 67, 83

Date of Accounts	Aug 11	Aug 10	Aug 09
Working Capital	15	12	8
Fixed Assets	15	8	10
Current Assets	71	41	49

House Of Flags
River Road Bicton Industrial Park, Kimbolton, Huntingdon, PE28 0LQ
Tel: 01480-861678 **Fax:** 01480-861618
E-mail: solutions@flags.co.uk
Website: http://www.flags.co.uk
Bank(s): Barclays
Directors: D. Geranio (MD)
Ultimate Holding Company: KORAMIC INDUSTRIES SA (BELGIUM)
Immediate Holding Company: HOUSE OF FLAGS LIMITED
Registration no: 02213723 **VAT No.:** GB 491 0233 70
Date established: 1988 **Turnover:** £2m - £5m **No.of Employees:** 21 - 50
Product Groups: 35, 49

Date of Accounts	Mar 12	Mar 11	Mar 10
Sales Turnover	4m	3m	N/A
Pre Tax Profit/Loss	330	214	N/A
Working Capital	1m	973	779
Fixed Assets	79	70	99
Current Assets	2m	1m	1m
Current Liabilities	689	219	N/A

Huntingdon Life Sciences
Woolley Road Alconbury, Huntingdon, PE28 4HS
Tel: 01480-892000 **Fax:** 01379-651165
E-mail: sales@ukorg.huntingdon.com
Website: http://www.huntingdon.com
Directors: A. Baker (Ch), A. Gay (Mkt Research), B. Cass (MD)
Ultimate Holding Company: LION HOLDINGS INC (USA)
Immediate Holding Company: HUNTINGDON LIFE SCIENCES LIMITED
Registration no: 01815730 **Date established:** 1984
Turnover: £75m - £125m **No.of Employees:** 501 - 1000
Product Groups: 54, 84, 85

Date of Accounts	Dec 11	Dec 10	Dec 09
Sales Turnover	82m	82m	86m
Pre Tax Profit/Loss	11m	2m	3m
Working Capital	1m	31m	34m
Fixed Assets	28m	27m	26m
Current Assets	78m	70m	74m
Current Liabilities	27m	27m	28m

Impressions
93 High Street Somersham, Huntingdon, PE28 3EE
Tel: 01487-843311 **Fax:** 01487-841133
E-mail: info@printandlabel.com
Website: http://www.printandlabel.com
Directors: R. Porter (Prop)
Date established: 1998 **Turnover:** £250,000 - £500,000
No.of Employees: 1 - 10 **Product Groups:** 27

Index Instruments Ltd
Bury Road Industrial Estate Ramsey, Huntingdon, PE26 1NF
Tel: 01487-814313 **Fax:** 01487-812789
E-mail: sales@indexinstruments.co.uk
Website: http://www.indexinstruments.com
Bank(s): Barclays Bank PLC
Directors: J. Horn (MD), D. Symonds (Fin)
Immediate Holding Company: INDEX INSTRUMENTS LIMITED
Registration no: 01514787 **VAT No.:** GB 344 3724 61
Date established: 1980 **No.of Employees:** 21 - 50 **Product Groups:** 38

Date of Accounts	Mar 12	Mar 11	Mar 10
Working Capital	639	579	555
Fixed Assets	303	287	290
Current Assets	707	629	621

Ingenion Design Ltd
Kym Road Bicton Industrial Park, Kimbolton, Huntingdon, PE28 0LW
Tel: 01480-860606 **Fax:** 01480-861122
E-mail: enquiries@ingenion.co.uk
Website: http://www.ingenion.co.uk
Directors: P. Dyke (MD), A. Wieczorek (Fin)
Immediate Holding Company: INGENION DESIGN LIMITED
Registration no: 01838951 **VAT No.:** GB 396 0193 34
Date established: 1984 **Turnover:** £500,000 - £1m
No.of Employees: 1 - 10 **Product Groups:** 84, 85

Date of Accounts	Jan 12	Jan 11	Jan 10
Working Capital	328	267	153
Fixed Assets	35	46	54
Current Assets	430	354	197

International Displays
Lancaster House Airfield Industrial Estate Warboys, Huntingdon, PE28 2SH
Tel: 01487-825050 **Fax:** 01480-414205
E-mail: sales@internationaldisplays.co.uk
Website: http://www.internationaldisplays.co.uk
Directors: C. Jenkin (Dir)
Ultimate Holding Company: H.A.G.DEVELOPMENTS LIMITED
Immediate Holding Company: KLEMETRIC DISPLAYS LIMITED
Registration no: 01012843 **Date established:** 1971 **Turnover:** £1m - £2m
No.of Employees: 11 - 20 **Product Groups:** 37

Date of Accounts	Oct 11	Oct 10	Oct 09
Working Capital	17	13	11
Fixed Assets	3	5	7
Current Assets	23	26	16

Isofast
32 Earith Business Park Meadow Drove, Earith, Huntingdon, PE28 3QF
Tel: 01487-841444 **Fax:** 01487-841440
E-mail: sales@isofast.co.uk
Website: http://www.isofast.co.uk
Directors: P. Hurst (Prop)
Immediate Holding Company: ISOFAST LIMITED
Registration no: 06257673 **Date established:** 2007
No.of Employees: 1 - 10 **Product Groups:** 22, 24, 25, 27, 29, 30, 31, 32, 33, 34, 35, 36, 37, 39, 40, 42, 43, 45, 46, 47, 49, 63, 66, 67, 83

Date of Accounts	May 11	May 09	May 08
Working Capital	-15	N/A	N/A
Fixed Assets	10	N/A	N/A
Current Assets	105	N/A	N/A

J A M Y Ltd
Unit 33 Roman Way Small Business Park London Road, Godmanchester, Huntingdon, PE29 2LN
Tel: 01480-456391 **Fax:** 01480-414959
E-mail: peter@jamy.co.uk
Website: http://www.jamy.co.uk
Directors: N. Burt (Fin), P. Burt (MD)
Immediate Holding Company: JAMY LIMITED
Registration no: 01677089 **Date established:** 1982
Turnover: £250,000 - £500,000 **No.of Employees:** 1 - 10
Product Groups: 23, 24, 25, 28, 30, 33, 35, 40, 46, 49, 65, 77, 81

Date of Accounts	Jun 11	Jun 10	Jun 09
Sales Turnover	488	424	465
Pre Tax Profit/Loss	112	50	36
Working Capital	-49	-73	-71
Fixed Assets	87	93	104
Current Assets	120	112	83
Current Liabilities	52	53	26

John Adams Leisure Ltd
Marketing House Unit 7 Blackstone Road, Stukeley Meadows Industrial Estate, Huntingdon, PE29 6EF
Tel: 01480-414361 **Fax:** 01480-414761
E-mail: sales@johnadams.co.uk
Website: http://www.johnadams.co.uk
Bank(s): HSBC, Maidenhead

see next page

John Adams Leisure Ltd - Cont'd

Directors: A. Shepherd (Co Sec), S. Pilkington (MD)
Ultimate Holding Company: TOY BROKERS HOLDINGS LIMITED
Immediate Holding Company: JOHN ADAMS LEISURE LIMITED
Registration no: 01761275 **VAT No.:** GB 199 0113 56
Date established: 1983 **Turnover:** £10m - £20m
No.of Employees: 11 - 20 **Product Groups:** 27, 49, 65

Date of Accounts	Dec 11	Dec 10	Dec 09
Sales Turnover	14m	11m	7m
Pre Tax Profit/Loss	2m	291	527
Working Capital	5m	4m	4m
Fixed Assets	200	265	198
Current Assets	13m	9m	7m
Current Liabilities	2m	2m	822

Just Digital

College Farm Thrapston Road, Ellington, Huntingdon, PE28 0AE
Tel: 01480-890056 **Fax:** 01480-896739
E-mail: adam.hill@justdigitalprint.co.uk
Website: http://www.justdigitaluk.com
Directors: A. Hill (MD)
Immediate Holding Company: JUST DIGITAL LIMITED
Registration no: 04954829 **Date established:** 2003 **Turnover:** £1m - £2m
No.of Employees: 11 - 20 **Product Groups:** 23, 26, 27, 28, 44, 49, 52, 81, 83, 84

Date of Accounts	Dec 11	Dec 10	Dec 09
Sales Turnover	2m	2m	2m
Pre Tax Profit/Loss	236	149	134
Working Capital	280	166	151
Fixed Assets	544	648	468
Current Assets	753	654	510
Current Liabilities	202	204	54

Kerry Services Ltd

6 The Walks East, Huntingdon, PE29 3AP
Tel: 01480-391504 **Fax:** 01480-386467
E-mail: info@kerrytrans.com
Website: http://www.kerrytrenf.com
Directors: P. Downhill (Dir)
Immediate Holding Company: KERRY SERVICES LTD
Registration no: 04797692 **Date established:** 2003
No.of Employees: 1 - 10 **Product Groups:** 80

Date of Accounts	Nov 11	Nov 10	Nov 09
Working Capital	239	266	210
Fixed Assets	63	5	6
Current Assets	299	333	244

Kitchen Range Foods Ltd

Hinchingbrooke Business Park Kingfisher Way Hinchingbrooke Business Park, Huntingdon, PE29 6FJ
Tel: 01480-445900 **Fax:** 01480-434555
E-mail: krf@kitchenrangefoods.co.uk
Website: http://www.kitchenrangefoods.com
Bank(s): Lloyds TSB Bank plc
Managers: P. Mccaul (Mgr)
Ultimate Holding Company: MARFRIG ALIMENTOS SA (BRAZIL)
Immediate Holding Company: KITCHEN RANGE FOODS LIMITED
Registration no: 01004539 **VAT No.:** GB 239 3617 47
Date established: 1971 **Turnover:** £20m - £50m
No.of Employees: 51 - 100 **Product Groups:** 20

Date of Accounts	Dec 11	Dec 10	Dec 09
Sales Turnover	34m	30m	32m
Pre Tax Profit/Loss	200	2m	1m
Working Capital	8m	8m	6m
Fixed Assets	4m	4m	3m
Current Assets	13m	13m	11m
Current Liabilities	1m	1m	1m

Lola Cars Ltd

12 Glebe Road St Peters Hill, Huntingdon, PE29 7DY
Tel: 01480-456722 **Fax:** 01480-482970
E-mail: lola@lolacars.com
Website: http://www.lolacars.com
Directors: M. Birrane (MD)
Ultimate Holding Company: PORTIA INVESTMENTS LTD (JERSEY)
Immediate Holding Company: LOLA CARS LIMITED
Registration no: 03500243 **VAT No.:** GB 694 7729 69
Date established: 1998 **Turnover:** £10m - £20m **No.of Employees:** 1 - 10
Product Groups: 39

Micron Workholding Ltd

Unit 5 Nene Road Kimbolton, Huntingdon, PE28 0LF
Tel: 01480-861321 **Fax:** 01480-861515
E-mail: sales@microloc.com
Website: http://www.microloc.com
Directors: M. Jenness (Dir)
Immediate Holding Company: MICRON WORKHOLDING LIMITED
Registration no: 02897976 **Date established:** 1994
No.of Employees: 1 - 10 **Product Groups:** 46

Date of Accounts	Feb 08	Feb 11	Feb 10
Working Capital	28	28	5
Fixed Assets	263	324	282
Current Assets	132	180	104
Current Liabilities	N/A	20	N/A

Munters Ltd

Blackstone Road Stukeley Meadows Industrial Estate, Huntingdon, PE29 6EE
Tel: 01480-432243 **Fax:** 01480-458333
E-mail: alistair.phillips@munters.co.uk
Website: http://www.munters.co.uk
Bank(s): Barclays
Directors: A. Ericson (Fin), A. Phillip (Div), A. Phillips (MD), L. Suffolk (Div), R. Hughes (Fin)
Managers: T. Moore (Purch Mgr), Z. Iqbal (I.T. Exec), C. Bedford (Sales Admin), C. Bye (Personnel), C. Modla (Sales Prom Mgr)
Ultimate Holding Company: MUNTERS AB (SWEDEN)
Immediate Holding Company: MUNTERS LIMITED
Registration no: 07270788 **Date established:** 2010
Turnover: £20m - £50m **No.of Employees:** 21 - 50 **Product Groups:** 42

Date of Accounts	Dec 09	Dec 08	Dec 07
Sales Turnover	26m	32m	35m
Pre Tax Profit/Loss	515	1m	3m
Working Capital	756	-329	403
Fixed Assets	2m	3m	3m
Current Assets	7m	8m	11m
Current Liabilities	2m	3m	5m

Newcom Precision Engineering Ltd

1 Earith Business Park Meadow Drove, Earith, Huntingdon, PE28 3QF
Tel: 01487-840870 **Fax:** 01487-740046
E-mail: enquiries@newcom-engineering.co.uk
Website: http://www.newcom-engineering.co.uk
Bank(s): Barclays
Directors: A. Brown (Dir)
Managers: H. Brown, M. Stokes (Purch Mgr)
Immediate Holding Company: NEWCOM PRECISION ENGINEERS LIMITED
Registration no: 05271198 **VAT No.:** GB 513 9702 52
Date established: 2004 **Turnover:** £2m - £5m **No.of Employees:** 21 - 50
Product Groups: 48

Date of Accounts	Mar 12	Mar 11	Mar 10
Working Capital	404	411	290
Fixed Assets	1m	1m	1m
Current Assets	1m	1m	1m
Current Liabilities	N/A	144	144

Nokia UK Ltd

Headland House Chord Business Park London Road, Godmanchester, Huntingdon, PE29 2NX
Tel: 01480-434343 **Fax:** 01480-445222
Website: http://www.nokia.com
Bank(s): National Westminster Bank Plc
Directors: P. Brown (MD)
Ultimate Holding Company: NOKIA CORPORATION (FINLAND)
Immediate Holding Company: NOKIA UK LIMITED
Registration no: 02212202 **Date established:** 1988
Turnover: £75m - £125m **No.of Employees:** 21 - 50 **Product Groups:** 37

Date of Accounts	Dec 11	Dec 10	Dec 09
Sales Turnover	731m	1197m	1718m
Pre Tax Profit/Loss	-12m	37m	50m
Working Capital	154m	138m	125m
Fixed Assets	62m	132m	120m
Current Assets	383m	416m	397m
Current Liabilities	105m	160m	138m

Onesat Telecommunications Equipment

34 Meadow Lane Earith, Huntingdon, PE28 3QE
Tel: 01487-741133 **Fax:** 01487-843785
E-mail: sales@one-sat.com
Website: http://www.one.co.uk
Managers: J. Stewart (Mgr)
Date established: 2001 **No.of Employees:** 1 - 10 **Product Groups:** 37, 52

Orion Automation

1 High Street Alconbury Weston, Huntingdon, PE28 4JP
Tel: 01480-891801 **Fax:** 0871-714 2130
E-mail: danmaynard@orionautomation.co.uk
Website: http://www.orionautomation.co.uk
Directors: R. Maynard (Fin), D. Maynard (Dir)
Immediate Holding Company: ORION AUTOMATION LTD
Registration no: 06159245 **Date established:** 2007
Turnover: Up to £250,000 **No.of Employees:** 1 - 10 **Product Groups:** 38

Date of Accounts	Mar 12	Mar 11	Mar 10
Working Capital	47	37	N/A
Fixed Assets	4	4	5
Current Assets	104	85	45

P I Tape Ltd

Dean Court Upper Dean, Huntingdon, PE28 0NL
Tel: 01234-708882 **Fax:** 01234-708677
E-mail: sales@pitape.co.uk
Website: http://www.pitape.co.uk
Directors: P. Cook (MD)
Immediate Holding Company: PI TAPE LIMITED
Registration no: 02545466 **Date established:** 1990
Turnover: Up to £250,000 **No.of Employees:** 1 - 10 **Product Groups:** 38

Date of Accounts	Mar 11	Mar 10	Mar 09
Sales Turnover	168	159	155
Pre Tax Profit/Loss	58	45	45
Working Capital	18	27	42
Current Assets	103	123	135
Current Liabilities	73	66	52

P & M Pumps

Unit 1 Sawtry Court Brookside Industrial Estate, Sawtry, Huntingdon, PE28 5SB
Tel: 01487-830123 **Fax:** 01487-832888
E-mail: sales@thesolidsolution.co.uk
Website: http://www.pandmpumps.co.uk
Directors: M. Harvey (Ptnr)
Immediate Holding Company: P&M PUMPS LTD
Registration no: 06996030 **Date established:** 2009 **Turnover:** £1m - £2m
No.of Employees: 1 - 10 **Product Groups:** 32, 40, 42, 45

Date of Accounts	Aug 11	Aug 10
Working Capital	-102	-181
Fixed Assets	244	274
Current Assets	1m	730

Plugtest Ltd

Red House Farm Woodwalton, Huntingdon, PE28 5YL
Tel: 01487-773777 **Fax:** 0870-063 0201
E-mail: sales@plugtest.co.uk
Website: http://www.plugtest.co.uk
Directors: P. Ippolito (Dir)
Immediate Holding Company: PLUGTEST LIMITED
Registration no: 04595515 **Date established:** 2002
No.of Employees: 11 - 20 **Product Groups:** 85

Date of Accounts	Feb 08	Feb 11	Feb 10
Working Capital	73	196	159
Fixed Assets	20	19	21
Current Assets	111	255	218

Power Gates

Walnut Tree Cottage Chapel Lane, Easton, Huntingdon, PE28 0TX
Tel: 01480-896500 **Fax:** 01480-891989
E-mail: geoff@powergates.co.uk
Website: http://www.powergates.co.uk
Directors: G. Messanger (Prop)
Date established: 1999 **No.of Employees:** 1 - 10 **Product Groups:** 26, 35

Quad Electroacoustics Ltd

I A G House Sovereign Court, Ermine Business Park, Huntingdon, PE29 6XU
Tel: 08454-580011 **Fax:** 01480-431767
E-mail: anne@quad-hifi.co.uk
Website: http://www.quad-hifi.co.uk
Bank(s): HSBC Bank plc
Directors: A. Oliver (Dir), A. Oliver (MD), T. Harris (Fin), T. Harris (MD)
Managers: R. Flane (Serv Mgr), D. Butler (I.T. Exec), D. Patching (Mktg Serv Mgr), C. O'Grady (Chief Acct), S. Macintyre (Sales Prom Mgr)
Ultimate Holding Company: IAG LIMITED (HONG KONG)
Immediate Holding Company: QUAD ELECTROACOUSTICS LIMITED
Registration no: 01388827 **VAT No.:** GB 694 8952 61
Date established: 1978 **Turnover:** £1m - £2m **No.of Employees:** 11 - 20
Product Groups: 37

Date of Accounts	Dec 10	Dec 09	Dec 08
Sales Turnover	965	1m	1m
Pre Tax Profit/Loss	-4	230	-26
Working Capital	-3m	-3m	-3m
Fixed Assets	26	39	56
Current Assets	730	581	809
Current Liabilities	46	27	220

R G E Engineering

The Avenue Godmanchester, Huntingdon, PE29 2AF
Tel: 01480-450771 **Fax:** 01480-411359
E-mail: info@rgegroup.com
Website: http://www.rgegroup.com
Directors: G. Leach (MD)
Managers: K. Reed (Purch Mgr), D. Buddle (I.T. Exec)
VAT No.: GB 486 2930 15 **Turnover:** £10m - £20m
No.of Employees: 1 - 10 **Product Groups:** 30, 46

R G S Ltd

7-8 Roman Way Small Business Park London Road, Godmanchester, Huntingdon, PE29 2LN
Tel: 01480-456556 **Fax:** 01480-456578
E-mail: sales@rgslabels.co.uk
Website: http://www.rgslabels.co.uk
Directors: P. Gudgeon (Dir)
Immediate Holding Company: RGS LIMITED
Registration no: 02947594 **Date established:** 1994
Turnover: £250,000 - £500,000 **No.of Employees:** 1 - 10
Product Groups: 22, 23, 27, 28, 29, 30, 33, 35, 36, 37, 48, 49, 76, 84

Date of Accounts	Jul 11	Jul 10	Jul 09
Working Capital	2	2	3
Current Assets	4	4	5

Riello Ltd

Ermine Centre Hurricane Close, Ermine Business Park, Huntingdon, PE29 6WX
Tel: 01480-432144 **Fax:** 01480-432191
E-mail: info@rielloburners.co.uk
Website: http://www.rielloburners.co.uk
Directors: J. Newman (Co Sec)
Managers: B. Dawson (Mktg Serv Mgr), P. Sharp (Nat Sales Mgr)
Ultimate Holding Company: RIELLO GROUP SPA (ITALY)
Immediate Holding Company: RIELLO LIMITED
Registration no: 01260734 **VAT No.:** GB 300 1191 35
Date established: 1976 **Turnover:** £20m - £50m
No.of Employees: 21 - 50 **Product Groups:** 40

Date of Accounts	Dec 11	Dec 10	Dec 09
Sales Turnover	22m	20m	18m
Pre Tax Profit/Loss	3m	2m	1m
Working Capital	5m	3m	2m
Fixed Assets	20	11	15
Current Assets	6m	6m	8m
Current Liabilities	1m	1m	723

Roder UK Ltd

Unit 16 Earith Business Park Meadow Drove, Earith, Huntingdon, PE28 3QF
Tel: 01487-840840 **Fax:** 01487-840843
E-mail: sales@roderuk.com
Website: http://www.roderuk.com
Directors: N. Lavy (Fin)
Ultimate Holding Company: RODER ZS AG (GERMANY)
Immediate Holding Company: RODER UK LTD.
Registration no: 02087541 **VAT No.:** GB 638 3590 15
Date established: 1987 **Turnover:** £1m - £2m **No.of Employees:** 1 - 10
Product Groups: 24, 35, 81

Date of Accounts	Dec 11	Dec 10	Dec 09
Working Capital	2m	2m	2m
Fixed Assets	150	137	144
Current Assets	2m	2m	2m

Romaco Holdings UK Ltd

Lake View Court Ermine Business Park, Huntingdon, PE29 6WD
Tel: 01480-435050 **Fax:** 01478-041 4220
E-mail: thomas.luken@romaco.com
Website: http://www.romaco.com
Bank(s): National Westminster
Directors: I. Ottiwell (Co Sec), T. Luken (Dir), C. Tasom (Fin), B. Moore (MD)
Managers: G. Shackels (Sales Off Mgr)
Ultimate Holding Company: ROBBINS AND MYERS INC. (USA)
Immediate Holding Company: ROBBINS & MYERS HOLDINGS UK LIMITED
Registration no: 02757423 **VAT No.:** GB 538 3113 57
Date established: 1992 **Turnover:** £75m - £125m
No.of Employees: 21 - 50 **Product Groups:** 32, 84

Date of Accounts	Aug 10	Aug 09	Aug 08
Pre Tax Profit/Loss	-37	11m	315
Working Capital	-4m	-4m	15m
Fixed Assets	15m	15m	7m
Current Assets	N/A	6	16m
Current Liabilities	80	101	39

Ruston's Engineering Co. Ltd

Brampton Road, Huntingdon, PE29 3BS
Tel: 01480-455151 **Fax:** 01480-52116
E-mail: info@reco.co.uk
Website: http://www.reco.co.uk
Bank(s): Lloyds TSB, St.Ives, Hunts
Directors: A. Ruston (MD), J. Sadler (Dir), M. Seymour (Co Sec)
Ultimate Holding Company: RECO TRADING LIMITED
Immediate Holding Company: RUSTON'S ENGINEERING COMPANY LIMITED
Registration no: 00554402 **Date established:** 1955
Turnover: £10m - £20m **No.of Employees:** 51 - 100 **Product Groups:** 41

Date of Accounts	Oct 11	Oct 10	Oct 09
Sales Turnover	12m	10m	10m
Pre Tax Profit/Loss	2m	-61	4m
Working Capital	7m	7m	7m
Fixed Assets	2m	2m	2m
Current Assets	11m	10m	10m
Current Liabilities	1m	3m	3m

Safety Works & Solutions Ltd
Unit 6 Earith Business Park Meadow Drove, Earith, Huntingdon, PE28 3QF
Tel: 01487-841400 **Fax:** 01487-841100
E-mail: info@safetyworksandsolutions.co.uk
Website: http://www.safetyworksandsolutions.co.uk
Directors: M. Norman (MD)
Managers: J. Merry
Immediate Holding Company: SAFETYWORKS & SOLUTIONS LIMITED
Registration no: 04193823 **Date established:** 2001 **Turnover:** £2m - £5m
No.of Employees: 11 - 20 **Product Groups:** 35, 40, 48, 67, 84

Date of Accounts	Sep 11	Sep 10	Sep 09
Working Capital	219	350	474
Fixed Assets	202	47	43
Current Assets	520	605	677

Savage & Hoy
78 Ramsey Road Warboys, Huntingdon, PE28 2RW
Tel: 07877-639555 **Fax:** 01487-822313
E-mail: grahamspencer@savageandhoy.co.uk
Website: http://www.savageandhoy.co.uk
Directors: G. Spencer (Prop)
VAT No.: GB 716 7239 25 **No.of Employees:** 1 - 10 **Product Groups:** 25, 49

Shelley Thermoformers International Ltd
Unit 32 Roman Way Small Business Park London Road, Godmanchester, Huntingdon, PE29 2LN
Tel: 01480-453651 **Fax:** 01480-52113
E-mail: pclarke@cannon-shelley.co.uk
Website: http://www.shelley.biz
Directors: G. Williams (Fin)
Managers: P. Clarke (Ops Mgr)
Ultimate Holding Company: CANNON SPA (ITALY)
Immediate Holding Company: SHELLEY THERMOFORMERS INTERNATIONAL LIMITED
Registration no: 00570586 **VAT No.:** GB 445 6613 41
Date established: 1956 **Turnover:** £2m - £5m **No.of Employees:** 1 - 10
Product Groups: 30, 42, 48, 67

Date of Accounts	Dec 11	Dec 10	Dec 09
Working Capital	115	79	-10
Fixed Assets	4	7	10
Current Assets	259	330	210

Smartdrive Ltd
8 Colne Road Earith, Huntingdon, PE28 3PX
Tel: 01487-843663 **Fax:** 01487-843661
E-mail: info@smartdrive.co.uk
Website: http://www.smartdrive.co.uk
Directors: D. Murphy (MD)
Immediate Holding Company: SMARTDRIVE LIMITED
Registration no: 01928089 **Date established:** 1985
No.of Employees: 1 - 10 **Product Groups:** 35, 45

Date of Accounts	Mar 11	Mar 10	Mar 09
Working Capital	541	523	506
Fixed Assets	2	3	5
Current Assets	541	688	572

Spirotech-Srd Group Ltd
Brookside Industrial Estate Sawtry, Huntingdon, PE28 5SB
Tel: 01487-833200 **Fax:** 01487-832252
E-mail: stuart@kemtech.com
Website: http://www.spirotech.co.uk
Directors: S. Darlow (MD)
Ultimate Holding Company: SRD HOLDINGS LIMITED
Immediate Holding Company: SPIROTECH SRD GROUP LIMITED
Registration no: 05021065 **Date established:** 2004
No.of Employees: 21 - 50 **Product Groups:** 35, 39, 45

Date of Accounts	Jun 12	Jun 11	Jun 10
Sales Turnover	4m	N/A	2m
Pre Tax Profit/Loss	206	N/A	72
Working Capital	-639	-696	-714
Fixed Assets	2m	1m	1m
Current Assets	912	1m	978
Current Liabilities	111	N/A	862

Staples Uk Ltd
Windover Road, Huntingdon, PE29 7EF
Tel: 01480-442222 **Fax:** 01480-442266
E-mail: sales@staplesbeds.co.uk
Website: http://www.staplesbeds.co.uk
Bank(s): National Westminster
Directors: G. Mitchell (MD)
Managers: K. Czura (Mktg Serv Mgr), S. Lever (Personnel)
Ultimate Holding Company: HORATIO MYER AND COMPANY,LIMITED
Immediate Holding Company: STAPLES & CO.LIMITED
Registration no: 00157552 **VAT No.:** GB 226 5269 59
Date established: 2019 **Turnover:** £2m - £5m
No.of Employees: 251 - 500 **Product Groups:** 26

Strata Panels UK
Lancaster House Airfield Industrial Estate, Warboys, Huntingdon, PE28 2SH
Tel: 01487-825040 **Fax:** 01487-823746
E-mail: sales@stratapanels.co.uk
Website: http://www.stratapanels.co.uk
Bank(s): Barclays
Directors: C. Jenkin (Prop), M. Garrood (Sales)
Managers: D. Spellane (Tech Serv Mgr), T. Hale
Immediate Holding Company: STRATA PANELS LIMITED
Registration no: 01334868 **VAT No.:** GB 313 0929 85
Date established: 1977 **Turnover:** £1m - £2m **No.of Employees:** 21 - 50
Product Groups: 25, 26, 27, 30, 33, 35, 42, 47, 48, 49, 52, 66, 67, 81

Date of Accounts	Oct 07	Oct 06	Oct 05
Working Capital	-152	-174	-77
Fixed Assets	94	125	142
Current Assets	137	165	170
Current Liabilities	N/A	N/A	61

T T Plastics
16 St Margarets Way Stukeley Meadows Industrial Estate, Huntingdon, PE29 6EB
Tel: 01480-434253 **Fax:** 01480-412533
E-mail: admin@ttap.com
Website: http://www.ttapgroup.com
Bank(s): Lloyds TSB
Directors: D. Leach (MD), D. Munn (Fin)
Managers: M. Tyson (Sales & Mktg Mg), S. Cox (Buyer)
Immediate Holding Company: T.T. PLASTICS (UK) LIMITED
Registration no: 03524239 **VAT No.:** GB 706 2196 49
Date established: 1998 **Turnover:** £5m - £10m **No.of Employees:** 21 - 50
Product Groups: 30, 42

Date of Accounts	Apr 11	Apr 10	Apr 09
Working Capital	-790	-751	-1m
Fixed Assets	338	443	851
Current Assets	2m	2m	946

Technical Glass Company
C1-C2 Spitfire Close, Ermine Business Park, Huntingdon, PE29 6WR
Tel: 01480-424888 **Fax:** 01440-730661
E-mail: info@goodfellow.com
Website: http://www.technicalglass.co.uk
Bank(s): RBS
Directors: S. Aldersley (MD)
Managers: I. Doggett (Sales Prom Mgr)
Immediate Holding Company: TECHNICAL GLASS CAMBRIDGE LIMITED
Registration no: 03947687 **Date established:** 2000 **Turnover:** £1m - £2m
No.of Employees: 21 - 50 **Product Groups:** 14, 17, 23, 31, 33, 35, 37, 38, 40, 48, 66, 85

Date of Accounts	Mar 08	Jun 11	Jun 10
Sales Turnover	N/A	2m	1m
Pre Tax Profit/Loss	N/A	371	368
Working Capital	622	1m	1m
Fixed Assets	9	1	3
Current Assets	788	2m	1m
Current Liabilities	N/A	310	186

Technical Resin Bonders Ltd
12 Clifton Road, Huntingdon, PE29 7EN
Tel: 01480-52381 **Fax:** 01480- 414992
E-mail: sales@trbls.co.uk
Website: http://www.trbonders.co.uk
Bank(s): HSBC
Directors: R. Hodgson (Sales), P. Martin (Fin)
Managers: J. Quirke (Mgr), L. Churchill (Purch Mgr), D. Pedley
Ultimate Holding Company: AMBER VALLEY HOLDING COMPANY LIMITED
Immediate Holding Company: TRB LIGHTWEIGHT STRUCTURES LIMITED
Registration no: 02350654 **VAT No.:** GB 507 9229 35
Date established: 1989 **Turnover:** £5m - £10m
No.of Employees: 51 - 100 **Product Groups:** 33, 39

Date of Accounts	Dec 11	Dec 10	Dec 09
Sales Turnover	7m	N/A	N/A
Pre Tax Profit/Loss	665	N/A	N/A
Working Capital	2m	1m	1m
Fixed Assets	593	267	103
Current Assets	3m	3m	2m
Current Liabilities	791	N/A	N/A

Thames Laboratories Ltd
Hollow Farm Hilton Road Fenstanton, Huntingdon, PE28 9LJ
Tel: 01480-891800 **Fax:** 01480-890008
E-mail: info@thameslabs.co.uk
Website: http://www.thameslabs.co.uk
Directors: J. Richards (MD)
Immediate Holding Company: THAMES LABORATORIES LIMITED
Registration no: 06068954 **Date established:** 2007
No.of Employees: 21 - 50 **Product Groups:** 27, 33, 40, 54, 85

Date of Accounts	Jan 09
Working Capital	1
Current Assets	1

Topper Cases Ltd
16-17 Windover Court Windover Road, Huntingdon, PE29 7EA
Tel: 01480-457251 **Fax:** 01480-452107
E-mail: sales@toppercases.co.uk
Website: http://www.toppercases.co.uk
Directors: R. Hucklesby (Sales)
Immediate Holding Company: TOPPER CASES LIMITED
Registration no: 00480775 **VAT No.:** GB 289 7271 02
Date established: 1950 **Turnover:** £1m - £2m **No.of Employees:** 11 - 20
Product Groups: 22, 24, 30, 49

Date of Accounts	May 11	May 10	May 09
Working Capital	63	44	39
Fixed Assets	43	34	37
Current Assets	253	210	170

UK Classic Parts Ltd
Low Harthay Thrapston Road, Brampton, Huntingdon, PE28 4NJ
Tel: 01480-812318
E-mail: sales@ukclassicparts.com
Website: http://www.ukclassicparts.com
Directors: M. Lenton (Dir), M. Lenton (MD)
Immediate Holding Company: UK CLASSIC PARTS LIMITED
Registration no: 04595211 **Date established:** 2002
No.of Employees: 1 - 10 **Product Groups:** 39

V I P-polymers
15 Windover Road, Huntingdon, PE29 7EB
Tel: 01480-411333 **Fax:** 01480-450430
E-mail: kim.turner@vip-polymers.com
Website: http://www.vip-polymers.com
Bank(s): Barclays
Directors: G. McCullum (Fin)
Managers: K. Turner, J. Shaw (Sales & Mktg Mg), M. Martin (Purch Mgr)
Immediate Holding Company: PART OF GLYNWED PIPE SYSTEMS LTD
Registration no: 04256307 **Turnover:** £250,000 - £500,000
No.of Employees: 101 - 250 **Product Groups:** 25, 29, 30, 31, 66, 68

Date of Accounts	Mar 08	Mar 07
Sales Turnover	13288	12678
Pre Tax Profit/Loss	922	403
Working Capital	410	-50
Fixed Assets	1293	833
Current Assets	4719	3614
Current Liabilities	4309	3663
Total Share Capital	100	100
ROCE% (Return on Capital Employed)	54.1	51.5
ROT% (Return on Turnover)	6.9	3.2

Valvetech Ltd
Unit 9 Brookside Industrial Estate Sawtry, Huntingdon, PE28 5SB
Tel: 01487-833080 **Fax:** 01487-833081
E-mail: martin@valvetech.co.uk
Website: http://www.valvetech.co.uk
Directors: M. Payne (MD)
Immediate Holding Company: VALVETECH LIMITED
Registration no: 03472366 **VAT No.:** GB 711 2492 68
Date established: 1997 **Turnover:** £500,000 - £1m
No.of Employees: 1 - 10 **Product Groups:** 30, 36, 38, 40, 67

Date of Accounts	Dec 11	Dec 10	Dec 09
Working Capital	-74	-69	-85
Fixed Assets	106	107	109
Current Assets	93	103	106

Weldlogic Europe Ltd (Diamond Ground Products Ltd)
Blackstone Road Stukeley Meadows Industrial Estate, Huntingdon, PE29 6EF
Tel: 01480-437478 **Fax:** 01480-437479
E-mail: kevin@weldlogic.co.uk
Website: http://www.weldlogic.co.uk
Bank(s): Lloyds TSB Bank plc
Directors: K. Hart (MD)
Immediate Holding Company: WELDLOGIC EUROPE LIMITED
Registration no: 03263625 **VAT No.:** GB 690 1097 37
Date established: 1996 **Turnover:** £2m - £5m **No.of Employees:** 11 - 20
Product Groups: 35, 36, 37, 42, 45, 46, 48, 67, 83, 84, 85, 86

Date of Accounts	Dec 11	Dec 10	Dec 09
Working Capital	136	123	119
Fixed Assets	135	143	125
Current Assets	347	337	280

Wharfedale International Ltd
I A G House Ermine Business Park, Huntingdon, PE29 6XU
Tel: 01480-431737 **Fax:** 01480-431767
E-mail: tim@wharfedale.co.uk
Website: http://www.columbia-tech.com
Directors: T. Harris (Prop)
Ultimate Holding Company: IAG LIMITED (HONG KONG)
Immediate Holding Company: WHARFEDALE INTERNATIONAL LIMITED
Registration no: 01648897 **VAT No.:** GB 694 8952 61
Date established: 1982 **Turnover:** £2m - £5m **No.of Employees:** 1 - 10
Product Groups: 37

Date of Accounts	Dec 10	Dec 09	Dec 08
Sales Turnover	3m	3m	3m
Pre Tax Profit/Loss	172	341	686
Working Capital	-769	-970	-1m
Fixed Assets	9	36	40
Current Assets	5m	5m	5m
Current Liabilities	195	193	164

Winter & Co UK Ltd
Stonehill Stukeley Meadows Industrial Estate, Huntingdon, PE29 6ED
Tel: 01480-377177 **Fax:** 01480-377166
E-mail: sales@winter-company.com
Website: http://www.winteruk.com
Bank(s): National Westminster Bank Plc
Directors: S. Burdett (MD), T. Edwards (Fin)
Managers: J. Landemoo (Tech Serv Mgr)
Ultimate Holding Company: WINTER HOLDING AG (SWITZERLAND)
Immediate Holding Company: WINTER & CO. UK LIMITED
Registration no: 00998715 **Date established:** 1971
Turnover: £10m - £20m **No.of Employees:** 21 - 50 **Product Groups:** 22, 23, 27, 67

Date of Accounts	Dec 11	Dec 10	Dec 09
Sales Turnover	12m	11m	10m
Pre Tax Profit/Loss	778	425	422
Working Capital	4m	4m	3m
Fixed Assets	2m	2m	2m
Current Assets	6m	5m	4m
Current Liabilities	450	355	305

Woodfield
Station Yard Station Road, Bluntisham, Huntingdon, PE28 3PA
Tel: 01487-843031 **Fax:** 01487-843342
Directors: H. Woodfield (Prop)
Date established: 1973 **No.of Employees:** 1 - 10 **Product Groups:** 41

March

A C Cartons Print Finishing
Hill View Industrial Estate Eastwood End, Wimblington, March, PE15 0PU
Tel: 01354-741884 **Fax:** 01354-741884
E-mail: alancragg@tiscali.co.uk
Website: http://www.accartons.co.uk
Directors: A. Cragg (Prop)
Date established: 2001 **No.of Employees:** 1 - 10 **Product Groups:** 23, 27, 48

Beam Structural Services Ltd
Unit 2 Foundry Way, March, PE15 0WR
Tel: 01354-660895 **Fax:** 01354-661361
E-mail: sales@bssmarchltd.co.uk
Website: http://www.bssmarchltd.co.uk
Bank(s): National Westminster Bank PLC
Directors: I. Waters (Dir), P. Melton (MD), R. Melton (Co Sec), R. Melton (Dir), K. Melton (Dir)
Immediate Holding Company: BEAM STRUCTURAL SERVICES LIMITED
Registration no: 02610752 **Date established:** 1991 **Turnover:** £5m - £10m
No.of Employees: 21 - 50 **Product Groups:** 30, 33, 34, 35, 36, 48, 49, 51, 52, 66, 80, 84

Date of Accounts	May 10	May 09	May 08
Working Capital	126	90	374
Fixed Assets	646	455	246
Current Assets	1m	877	2m

D & L Promotions Ltd
Old Bank Chambers 5-8 Dartford Road, March, PE15 8AQ
Tel: 01354-656300 **Fax:** 01354-650651
E-mail: dlpromo@btconnect.com
Website: http://www.dlpromotions.co.uk
Directors: S. Woollard (Fin), L. Fulcher (MD)
Immediate Holding Company: D & L PROMOTIONS LTD
Registration no: 03811261 **Date established:** 1999
No.of Employees: 1 - 10 **Product Groups:** 22, 23, 24, 25, 27, 28, 30, 33, 36, 37, 38, 39, 44, 49, 63, 64, 65, 66, 67

Date of Accounts	Jul 11	Jul 10	Jul 09
Working Capital	-7	-8	12
Fixed Assets	1	1	2
Current Assets	50	44	68

B Elmore
3 High Street Doddington, March, PE15 0TF
Tel: 01354-740062
E-mail: elmcottage@btinternet.com
Directors: B. Elmore (Prop)
Date established: 1978 **No.of Employees:** 1 - 10 **Product Groups:** 41

C P L Felthams
Estover Road, March, PE15 8SF
Tel: 01354-652545 **Fax:** 01354-650476
E-mail: sales@cplfelthams.co.uk
Website: http://www.cplfelthams.co.uk
Bank(s): National Westminster
Managers: C. Oswald (Chief Mgr)
Immediate Holding Company: C P L INDUSTRIES LTD
Registration no: 00375348 **Turnover:** £1m - £2m
No.of Employees: 21 - 50 **Product Groups:** 02, 22, 23, 24, 25, 27, 30, 49, 63

Fenmarc
Wisbech Road, March, PE15 0BA
Tel: 01354-662400 **Fax:** 01354-662430
E-mail: richard.anderson@fenmarc.co.uk
Website: http://www.fenmarc.co.uk
Bank(s): Lloyds TSB Bank plc
Directors: R. Anderson (Co Sec)
Managers: B. Cameron (Personnel), L. Allen (Mktg Serv Mgr), P. Bower (Tech Serv Mgr)
Ultimate Holding Company: LIFECROWN INVESTMENTS LIMITED
Immediate Holding Company: FENMARC PRODUCE LIMITED
Registration no: 02508638 **VAT No.:** GB 394 4575 12
Date established: 1990 **Turnover:** £75m - £125m
No.of Employees: 251 - 500 **Product Groups:** 20

Date of Accounts	Jun 09	Jun 08	Jun 10
Sales Turnover	83m	82m	77m
Pre Tax Profit/Loss	3m	2m	3m
Working Capital	-723	1m	2m
Fixed Assets	6m	8m	5m
Current Assets	15m	16m	17m
Current Liabilities	6m	8m	6m

Greenvale A P Ltd
Floods Ferry Road Doddington, March, PE15 0UW
Tel: 01354-672000 **Fax:** 01354-677561
E-mail: trevor.dear@greenvale.co.uk
Website: http://www.greenvale.co.uk
Bank(s): Lloyds TSB Bank plc
Directors: T. Dear (Chief Op Offcr), S. Foster (Fin)
Managers: K. Stevens, D. Huxtable, A. Broadhurst (Fin Mgr)
Ultimate Holding Company: PRODUCE INVESTMENTS PLC
Immediate Holding Company: GREENVALE HOLDINGS LIMITED
Registration no: 04412326 **VAT No.:** GB 676 5487 79
Date established: 2002 **Turnover:** £125m - £250m
No.of Employees: 251 - 500 **Product Groups:** 02

Date of Accounts	Jun 08	Jun 09	Jun 10
Working Capital	-4m	1m	1m
Fixed Assets	6m	14	14
Current Assets	3m	3m	3m

Tom Hyde & Son
30 Station Road, March, PE15 8LE
Tel: 01354-653027 **Fax:** 01354-653076
Directors: J. Hyde (Ptnr)
Date established: 1958 **No.of Employees:** 1 - 10 **Product Groups:** 38, 42

Knowles Transport Ltd
New Road Wimblington, March, PE15 0RG
Tel: 01354-740233 **Fax:** 01354-741333
E-mail: traffic@knowles-transport.co.uk
Website: http://www.knowles-transport.co.uk
Bank(s): Lloyds TSB Bank plc
Directors: A. Knowles (MD), M. Allebone (Fin)
Immediate Holding Company: KNOWLES (TRANSPORT) LIMITED
Registration no: 00446417 **VAT No.:** GB 104 6593 79
Date established: 1947 **Turnover:** £20m - £50m
No.of Employees: 101 - 250 **Product Groups:** 72, 77

Date of Accounts	Dec 11	Dec 10	Dec 09
Sales Turnover	33m	31m	30m
Pre Tax Profit/Loss	4m	4m	3m
Working Capital	6m	2m	1m
Fixed Assets	21m	22m	21m
Current Assets	12m	9m	8m
Current Liabilities	2m	1m	2m

Mondi Packaging UK Ltd
Hostmoor Avenue, March, PE15 0YZ
Tel: 01354-658626 **Fax:** 01354-652372
E-mail: sales@mondipackaging.com
Website: http://www.mondigroup.com
Directors: D. Folds (Sales), G. Fenwick (Co Sec), J. Schoonbrood (Dir), K. Leggett (Dir), M. Lapping (MD), M. Ramsey (MD)
Managers: D. Brownlow (Sales Admin)
Ultimate Holding Company: Mondi plc
Immediate Holding Company: SMURFIT KAPPA CORRUGATED LIMITED
Registration no: 03051244 **Date established:** 1995
Turnover: Up to £250,000 **No.of Employees:** 251 - 500
Product Groups: 27, 66

Plasgran Ltd
Manea Road Wimblington, March, PE15 0PE
Tel: 01354-740005 **Fax:** 01354-740933
E-mail: enquiries@plasgranltd.co.uk
Website: http://www.plasgranltd.co.uk
Directors: K. Waters (MD)
Immediate Holding Company: PLASGRAN LIMITED
Registration no: 03848053 **Date established:** 1999 **Turnover:** £2m - £5m
No.of Employees: 11 - 20 **Product Groups:** 30, 42, 66

Date of Accounts	Sep 11	Sep 10	Sep 09
Working Capital	319	118	61
Fixed Assets	1m	781	664
Current Assets	1m	849	656

Power Porter
Hill View Industrial Estate Eastwood End, Wimblington, March, PE15 0PU
Tel: 01354-741133 **Fax:** 01354-741833
E-mail: sales@easybarrow.co.uk
Website: http://www.easybarrow.co.uk
Directors: M. Evans (Prop)
Date established: 1997 **Turnover:** Up to £250,000
No.of Employees: 1 - 10 **Product Groups:** 40, 41, 45, 46

Primus Inter Pares ltd
62 Wisbech Road, March, PE15 8EB
Tel: 0845-2245782 **Fax:** 0871-9004979
E-mail: enquiries@primusinterpares.ltd.uk
Website: http://www.primusinterpares.ltd.uk
Directors: C. St John (Dir)
Registration no: 06525850 **Date established:** 2008
No.of Employees: 1 - 10 **Product Groups:** 44

Qualitetch
Century Way, March, PE15 8QW
Tel: 01354-658787 **Fax:** 01354-650385
E-mail: sales@qualitetch.co.uk
Website: http://www.qualitetch.co.uk
Directors: A. Drew (Comm), C. Garner (Fin)
Immediate Holding Company: QUALITETCH COMPONENTS LIMITED
Registration no: 02465687 **Date established:** 1990 **Turnover:** £2m - £5m
No.of Employees: 21 - 50 **Product Groups:** 32, 46, 48

Date of Accounts	Feb 11	Feb 10	Feb 09
Sales Turnover	N/A	2m	2m
Pre Tax Profit/Loss	N/A	77	37
Working Capital	359	270	261
Fixed Assets	303	344	440
Current Assets	1m	1m	981
Current Liabilities	373	224	103

Wannabox
121 Maple Grove, March, PE15 8JP
Tel: 0845-1949230
E-mail: sales@wannabox.co.uk
Website: http://www.wannabox.co.uk
Product Groups: 26, 27, 30, 66

Peterborough

A A L G Ltd
Unit 4 Chater Court Halifax Drive, Market Deeping, Peterborough, PE6 8AH
Tel: 01778-349000
E-mail: ray.crane@peli.com
Website: http://www.peli.com
Managers: R. Crane (Mgr)
Ultimate Holding Company: PELICAN PRODUCTS INC (USA)
Immediate Holding Company: AALG LIMITED
Registration no: 05463657 **Date established:** 2005 **Turnover:** £5m - £10m
No.of Employees: 11 - 20 **Product Groups:** 36, 37, 67

Date of Accounts	Dec 11	Dec 10	Dec 09
Sales Turnover	8m	8m	6m
Pre Tax Profit/Loss	1m	1m	977
Working Capital	3m	2m	791
Fixed Assets	55	46	31
Current Assets	6m	4m	2m
Current Liabilities	200	187	327

A B C Tube Systems
Empson Road, Peterborough, PE1 5UP
Tel: 01733-896341 **Fax:** 01733-315273
E-mail: alan.bostock@abcstainless.co.uk
Website: http://www.stainlesssteel-uk.com
Directors: A. Bostock (MD)
Immediate Holding Company: A.B.C. (STAINLESS) LIMITED
Registration no: 01483638 **Date established:** 1980
No.of Employees: 21 - 50 **Product Groups:** 26, 35

Date of Accounts	Sep 11	Sep 10	Sep 09
Working Capital	1m	1m	1m
Fixed Assets	28	36	46
Current Assets	2m	2m	2m

AALabels
Unit 3 Fengate Trade Park Fengate, Peterborough, PE1 5XA
Tel: 01733-348348 **Fax:** 01733-552122
E-mail: sohail@gtrecycling.com
Website: http://www.aalabels.com
Directors: A. Gilani (Mkt Research), S. Sethi (MD)
Date established: 2006 **Turnover:** Up to £250,000
No.of Employees: 1 - 10 **Product Groups:** 27

Ability International Ltd (Tower & Access Equipment)
Warmington, Peterborough, PE8 6TZ
Tel: 01832-226445 **Fax:** 01832-226398
E-mail: sales@abilityint.com
Website: http://www.abilityint.com
Bank(s): HSBC
Directors: C. Donovan (MD), B. Holborn (Co Sec)
Immediate Holding Company: ABILITY INTERNATIONAL LIMITED
Registration no: 02043599 **VAT No.:** GB 445 6618 31
Date established: 1986 **Turnover:** £500,000 - £1m
No.of Employees: 11 - 20 **Product Groups:** 24, 30, 35, 52, 66, 86

Date of Accounts	Mar 12	Mar 11	Nov 09
Working Capital	144	146	69
Fixed Assets	139	110	100
Current Assets	261	356	244

ABS Technical Services UK Ltd
7 Cardyke Drive Baston, Peterborough, PE6 9PJ
Tel: 07810-808086 **Fax:** 01778-561428
E-mail: a.coulson2@tiscali.co.uk
Website: http://www.abstechnicaluk.co.uk
Directors: S. Coulson (Co Sec)
Immediate Holding Company: ABS TECHNICAL UK LIMITED
Registration no: 05657034 **Date established:** 2005
No.of Employees: 1 - 10 **Product Groups:** 44, 48, 67

Date of Accounts	Dec 09	Dec 08	Dec 07
Working Capital	8	6	8
Current Assets	48	39	37

Acco UK Ltd
Bretton Way Bretton, Peterborough, PE3 8YE
Tel: 01733-264711 **Fax:** 01733-269910
Website: http://www.acco.co.uk
Directors: R. Valks (Fin), S. Wiliams (MD), S. Willams (MD)
Managers: R. Bull (Chief Acct)
Immediate Holding Company: Acco-Rexel Group Services Ltd
Registration no: 00197754 **Turnover:** Up to £250,000
No.of Employees: 101 - 250 **Product Groups:** 44, 64

Agricultural Industries Confederation
East of England Showground Oundle Road, Alwalton, Peterborough, PE2 6XE
Tel: 01733-385230 **Fax:** 01733-385270
E-mail: enquiries@agindustries.org.uk
Website: http://www.agindustries.org.uk
Directors: D. Caffall (Grp Chief Exec)
Ultimate Holding Company: AGRICULTURAL INDUSTRIES CONFEDERATION LIMITED
Immediate Holding Company: AGRICULTURAL INDUSTRIES CONFEDERATION SERVICES LIMITED
Registration no: 04925061 **Date established:** 2003
Turnover: £500,000 - £1m **No.of Employees:** 11 - 20 **Product Groups:** 80

Date of Accounts	Jan 12	Jan 11	Jan 10
Sales Turnover	556	566	563
Pre Tax Profit/Loss	44	42	66
Working Capital	204	168	134
Current Assets	453	407	418
Current Liabilities	227	225	233

Airblast Ltd
Unit 26 King Street Industrial Estate King Street, Langtoft, Peterborough, PE6 9QX
Tel: 01778-560650 **Fax:** 01778-560724
E-mail: sales@airblast.co.uk
Website: http://www.airblast.co.uk
Managers: R. Cox (Mgr)
Immediate Holding Company: AIRBLAST LIMITED
Registration no: 01975297 **Date established:** 1986
Turnover: £250,000 - £500,000 **No.of Employees:** 1 - 10
Product Groups: 40, 42, 45, 46

Date of Accounts	Mar 11	Mar 10	Mar 09
Working Capital	351	295	424
Fixed Assets	59	56	75
Current Assets	2m	1m	1m

Alrose Products British Gas Springs Ltd (British Gas Springs)
4 King St Industrial Estate Langtoft, Peterborough, PE6 9NF
Tel: 01778-561422 **Fax:** 01778-560400
E-mail: sales@gas-springs.com
Website: http://www.gas-springs.com
Directors: A. Rose (MD), B. Siddall (Co Sec)
Managers: J. Sharman, J. Bird (Tech Sales Mgr)
Registration no: 01924699 **VAT No.:** GB 576 4640 13
Date established: 2003 **Turnover:** £500,000 - £1m
No.of Employees: 1 - 10 **Product Groups:** 35, 39, 40

Aluminium & Glass Facades Ltd
Unit 30-31 Maxwell Road, Peterborough, PE2 7JN
Tel: 01733-230211 **Fax:** 01733-230311
Website: http://www.agf.com
Directors: M. Scotney (Fin)
Immediate Holding Company: ALUMINIUM AND GLASS FACADES LIMITED
Registration no: 02728819 **Date established:** 1992
No.of Employees: 21 - 50 **Product Groups:** 26, 35

Date of Accounts	Dec 11	Dec 10	Dec 09
Working Capital	82	14	67
Fixed Assets	213	97	95
Current Assets	853	539	405

Anglia Bearing Co. Ltd
1 & 8 Wulfric Square Bretton, Peterborough, PE3 8RF
Tel: 01733-268180 **Fax:** 01733-268156
E-mail: enquiries@angliabearings.co.uk
Website: http://www.angliabearings.co.uk
Directors: M. Thoday (MD)
Registration no: 01817624 **Turnover:** £500,000 - £1m
No.of Employees: 1 - 10 **Product Groups:** 66

Date of Accounts	Mar 08	Mar 07	Mar 06
Working Capital	160	116	86
Fixed Assets	56	19	35
Current Assets	242	214	201
Current Liabilities	82	98	115
Total Share Capital	2	2	2

Anglian Compressors & Equipment Ltd
Storeys Bar Road, Peterborough, PE1 5YS
Tel: 01733-349993 **Fax:** 01733-564983
E-mail: business@angliancomp.co.uk
Website: http://www.anglianCompressors.com
Bank(s): Lloyds TSB Bank plc
Directors: P. Skerritt (MD)
Ultimate Holding Company: M.E.P. INSTALLATIONS LIMITED
Immediate Holding Company: ANGLIAN COMPRESSORS & EQUIPMENT LIMITED
Registration no: 02544285 **VAT No.:** GB 289 7314 10
Date established: 1990 **Turnover:** £1m - £2m **No.of Employees:** 11 - 20
Product Groups: 31, 40

Date of Accounts	Aug 11	Aug 10	Aug 09
Working Capital	366	532	472
Fixed Assets	12	9	9
Current Assets	972	786	782

Anglian & Midland Sports Surfaces
Nene Valley Business Park Oundle, Peterborough, PE8 4HN
Tel: 01832-272449 **Fax:** 01832-272993
E-mail: info@amss.co.uk
Website: http://www.amss.co.uk
Directors: R. Shepherd (MD)
Managers: N. Shepherd (Sales Admin), M. Crook (Sales Prom Mgr)
Immediate Holding Company: ANGLIA & MIDLAND SPORTS LTD
Registration no: 02909126 **VAT No.:** GB 330 2845 85
Date established: 1994 **Turnover:** £1m - £2m **No.of Employees:** 1 - 10
Product Groups: 30, 52

Anglo Materials Handling
Orchardside Frognall, Deeping St James, Peterborough, PE6 8RP
Tel: 01778-342601 **Fax:** 01778-348147
Directors: P. Joyce (Ptnr)
Immediate Holding Company: KYOTO FUTONS LIMITED
Registration no: 03007974 **Date established:** 1995
No.of Employees: 1 - 10 **Product Groups:** 35, 39, 45

Date of Accounts	Mar 11	Mar 10	Jan 09
Working Capital	523	502	475
Fixed Assets	424	470	501
Current Assets	1m	1m	1m

Applied Energy Products Ltd
Morley Way, Peterborough, PE2 9JJ
Tel: 01733-456789 **Fax:** 01733-310606
E-mail: john.lee@applied-energy.com
Website: http://www.applied-energy.com
Directors: G. Collier (Fin), J. Lee (MD), N. Tunstall (Mkt Research), M. Jones (Comm), K. Stenning (Co Sec)
Managers: A. Boyden (Eng Serv Mgr), J. Hill
Immediate Holding Company: APPLIED ENERGY PRODUCTS LIMITED
Registration no: 00306008 **Date established:** 1935
Turnover: £20m - £50m **No.of Employees:** 101 - 250
Product Groups: 36, 40

Date of Accounts	Mar 10	Mar 09	Mar 08
Sales Turnover	38m	49m	48m
Pre Tax Profit/Loss	1m	2m	431
Working Capital	14m	13m	11m
Fixed Assets	1m	1m	919
Current Assets	24m	25m	23m
Current Liabilities	4m	5m	5m

Arhiann Direct
22 Saville Road Industrial Estate, Peterborough, PE3 7PR
Tel: 01733-261444
E-mail: rob@arhiann.com
Website: http://www.arhiann.com
Directors: R. Wilkinson (Prop)
Registration no: 05650058 **Date established:** 2005
Turnover: £500,000 - £1m **No.of Employees:** 1 - 10 **Product Groups:** 81

Date of Accounts	Nov 10	Nov 09	Nov 08
Sales Turnover	N/A	7m	8m
Pre Tax Profit/Loss	N/A	157	195
Working Capital	144	185	88
Fixed Assets	303	171	190
Current Assets	690	718	3m
Current Liabilities	N/A	480	2m

Arhiann Direct
29 Vere Road, Peterborough, PE1 3DZ
Tel: 01733-346739
E-mail: rob@arhiann.com
Website: http://www.arhiann.com
Directors: R. Wilkinson (Prop)
Immediate Holding Company: Arhiann Ltd
Registration no: 05774323 **Date established:** 2006
No.of Employees: 1 - 10 **Product Groups:** 28, 80, 81

Ark Communications Ltd
Hay Barn Rectory Farm Warmington, Peterborough, PE8 6UT
Tel: 01832-281003 **Fax:** 01832-281005
E-mail: info@ark-creativedesign.co.uk
Website: http://www.ark-creativedesign.co.uk
Directors: S. Mcleod (MD)
Immediate Holding Company: ARK COMMUNICATIONS LIMITED
Registration no: 02206324 **Date established:** 1987
Turnover: £500,000 - £1m **No.of Employees:** 1 - 10 **Product Groups:** 81

Date of Accounts	Apr 11	Apr 10	Apr 09
Working Capital	36	46	16
Fixed Assets	7	8	6
Current Assets	208	182	178
Current Liabilities	4	4	N/A

Array Inks Europe Ltd
Unit 6 Saracen Business Park, Newark Road, Peterborough, PE1 5WS
Tel: 01733-892691 **Fax:** 01733-892691
E-mail: sales@arrayink.com
Website: http://www.arrayinks.com
Directors: N. Stokes (Dir)
Managers: N. Weemes (Admin Off)
Registration no: 4784894 **Date established:** 2003
Turnover: Up to £250,000 **No.of Employees:** 1 - 10 **Product Groups:** 28

Date of Accounts	Nov 08	Nov 07	Nov 06
Working Capital	23	47	27
Fixed Assets	1	2	1
Current Assets	83	141	67
Current Liabilities	60	95	40

Automated Wire Bending Ltd
Padholme Road East, Peterborough, PE1 5XL
Tel: 01733-555646 **Fax:** 01733-555887
E-mail: silvio@awbl.co.uk
Website: http://www.awbl.co.uk
Directors: S. Perna (Dir)
Ultimate Holding Company: ROSE PLANT HIRE (WHITTLESEY) HOLDINGS LIMITED
Immediate Holding Company: AUTOMATED WIRE BENDING LIMITED
Registration no: 02696617 **Date established:** 1992 **Turnover:** £1m - £2m
No.of Employees: 11 - 20 **Product Groups:** 26, 35, 48, 49, 66

Date of Accounts	Jun 12	Jun 11	Jun 10
Working Capital	216	462	393
Fixed Assets	141	85	105
Current Assets	373	629	562

Aztech Engineering Ltd
Unit 37 Mere View Industrial Estate Yaxley, Peterborough, PE7 3HS
Tel: 01733-243846 **Fax:** 01733-243954
E-mail: elding.aztech@talktalkbusiness.net
Website: http://www.aztechengineeringltd.co.uk
Directors: P. Elding (MD), A. Elding (Fin)
Immediate Holding Company: AZTECH ENGINEERING LIMITED
Registration no: 03399332 **VAT No.:** GB 706 2438 51
Date established: 1997 **Turnover:** £250,000 - £500,000
No.of Employees: 1 - 10 **Product Groups:** 26

Date of Accounts	Jul 11	Jul 10	Jul 09
Sales Turnover	264	356	266
Pre Tax Profit/Loss	-8	-2	1
Working Capital	-63	-46	-31
Fixed Assets	108	124	126
Current Assets	21	51	29
Current Liabilities	36	24	11

B O C Gasses Ltd
Vicarage Farm Road, Peterborough, PE1 5TP
Tel: 01733-344422 **Fax:** 01733-568034
Website: http://www.boc.com
Managers: L. Darcy
Immediate Holding Company: INTACEPT MANAGEMENT LIMITED
Registration no: 00337663 **Date established:** 1993
No.of Employees: 1 - 10 **Product Groups:** 46

Baker Perkins Ltd
Manor Drive Paston Parkway, Peterborough, PE4 7AP
Tel: 01733-283000 **Fax:** 01733-283004
E-mail: bpltd@bakerperkinsgroup.com
Website: http://www.bakerperkinsgroup.com
Ultimate Holding Company: Invensys
Immediate Holding Company: APV Baker
Registration no: 05708493 **No.of Employees:** 251 - 500
Product Groups: 41, 42, 67

Date of Accounts	Mar 11	Mar 10	Mar 09
Sales Turnover	49m	41m	40m
Pre Tax Profit/Loss	6m	5m	2m
Working Capital	13m	11m	8m
Fixed Assets	777	N/A	N/A
Current Assets	29m	25m	24m
Current Liabilities	10m	9m	12m

J W E Banks Ltd
St Guthlacs Lodge Crowland, Peterborough, PE6 0JP
Tel: 01733-210123 **Fax:** 01733-210920
Directors: C. Banks (MD)
Immediate Holding Company: J.W.E.BANKS,LIMITED
Registration no: 00495822 **VAT No.:** GB 119 1258 81
Date established: 1951 **Turnover:** Up to £250,000
No.of Employees: 1 - 10 **Product Groups:** 84

Date of Accounts	Nov 11	Nov 10	Nov 09
Working Capital	931	663	419
Fixed Assets	3m	2m	2m
Current Assets	2m	1m	1m

Barclay & Mathieson Ltd
Oxney Road, Peterborough, PE1 5YW
Tel: 01733-312921 **Fax:** 01733-343386
E-mail: peterborough@bmsteel.co.uk
Website: http://www.bmsteel.co.uk
Managers: M. Bow (Mgr)
Ultimate Holding Company: STEMCOR HOLDINGS LIMITED
Immediate Holding Company: BARCLAY & MATHIESON LIMITED
Registration no: SC030987 **VAT No.:** GB 259 6926 05
Date established: 1955 **Turnover:** £10m - £20m **No.of Employees:** 1 - 10
Product Groups: 66

Date of Accounts	Dec 11	Dec 10	Dec 09
Sales Turnover	55m	48m	35m
Pre Tax Profit/Loss	2m	2m	-865
Working Capital	11m	13m	13m
Fixed Assets	19m	16m	18m
Current Assets	24m	25m	20m
Current Liabilities	4m	5m	713

Batt Cables plc
7 Flag Business Exchange Vicarage Farm Road, Peterborough, PE1 5TX
Tel: 01733-558485 **Fax:** 01733-562015
E-mail: paul.cocking@batt.co.uk
Website: http://www.batt.co.uk
Managers: P. Cocking (Reg Mgr)
Immediate Holding Company: BATT CABLES PLC
Registration no: 01353688 **Date established:** 1978
No.of Employees: 1 - 10 **Product Groups:** 30, 35, 36, 37, 38, 44, 66, 67

Date of Accounts	Mar 12	Mar 11	Mar 10
Sales Turnover	106m	98m	84m
Pre Tax Profit/Loss	8m	9m	5m
Working Capital	41m	36m	31m
Fixed Assets	8m	9m	8m
Current Assets	69m	60m	54m
Current Liabilities	3m	3m	2m

Baxter Avey & Co. Ltd
The Hill House Castor, Peterborough, PE5 7BS
Tel: 01733-380597 **Fax:** 01733-380365
E-mail: william.baxter@virgin.net
Directors: W. Baxter (MD)
Immediate Holding Company: BAXTER, AVEY & COMPANY LIMITED
Registration no: 02114693 **Date established:** 1987
No.of Employees: 1 - 10 **Product Groups:** 32

Date of Accounts	Jun 12	Jun 11	Jun 10
Working Capital	51	58	27
Fixed Assets	1	1	1
Current Assets	91	87	92

Beam Baking Systems Ltd
Unit 4 Barnack Business Park Sabre Way, Peterborough, PE1 5EJ
Tel: 01733-553320 **Fax:** 01733-896209
E-mail: les@beambaking.co.uk
Website: http://www.beambaking.co.uk
Directors: A. Nightingale (Sales), L. Nightingale (MD)
Immediate Holding Company: BEAM BAKING SYSTEMS LIMITED
Registration no: 02821343 **Date established:** 1993
Turnover: Up to £250,000 **No.of Employees:** 1 - 10 **Product Groups:** 67

Date of Accounts	Jul 11	Jul 10	Jul 09
Working Capital	360	299	364
Fixed Assets	55	36	56
Current Assets	565	466	613

Biffa Waste Services Ltd
Fenland District Industrial Estate Station Road, Whittlesey, Peterborough, PE7 2EY
Tel: 01733-205555 **Fax:** 01733-204555
E-mail: lee.guy@biffa.co.uk
Website: http://www.biffa.co.uk
Managers: L. Guy (Mgr)
Immediate Holding Company: BIFFA WASTE SERVICES LIMITED
Registration no: 00946107 **Date established:** 1969
No.of Employees: 1 - 10 **Product Groups:** 54, 72, 83

Date of Accounts	Mar 08	Mar 09	Apr 10
Sales Turnover	555m	574m	492m
Pre Tax Profit/Loss	23m	50m	30m
Working Capital	229m	271m	293m
Fixed Assets	371m	360m	378m
Current Assets	409m	534m	609m
Current Liabilities	50m	100m	115m

Boyriven
23 Wainman Road, Peterborough, PE2 7BU
Tel: 01733-361377 **Fax:** 01733-361334
E-mail: sales@boyriven-uk.com
Website: http://www.boyriven.com
Directors: R. Jones (MD)
Managers: C. Tipping, R. Everist (Chief Mgr), K. Brudenell-Maylin (I.T. Exec)
Ultimate Holding Company: FP052934
Immediate Holding Company: BOYRIVEN (COMMERCIAL VEHICLE COMPONENTS) LIMITED
Registration no: 00936102 **VAT No.:** GB 764 1634 26
Date established: 1968 **Turnover:** £250,000 - £500,000
No.of Employees: 1 - 10 **Product Groups:** 35, 39

Breckenridge Conservatories Ltd
78 Papyrus Road, Peterborough, PE4 5BH
Tel: 01733-575750 **Fax:** 01733-890222
E-mail: sales@breckenridgeconservatories.co.uk
Website: http://www.breckenridgeconservatories.co.uk
Directors: L. Vaughan (MD)
Immediate Holding Company: BRECKENRIDGE CONSERVATORIES (UK) LIMITED
Registration no: 06417946 **Date established:** 2007
No.of Employees: 11 - 20 **Product Groups:** 08, 25, 35

Brosch Direct Ltd
Unit E Harrier Park Southgate Way, Orton Southgate, Peterborough, PE2 6YQ
Tel: 01733-230230
E-mail: sales@broschdirect.com
Website: http://www.broschdirect.com
Directors: R. Cardell (MD)
Managers: B. Harlcok (Mktg Serv Mgr), J. Gibbons (Fin Mgr), J. Jones (Purch Mgr)
Ultimate Holding Company: BROSCH DIRECT HOLDINGS LIMITED
Immediate Holding Company: BROSCH DIRECT LIMITED
Registration no: 02382916 **Date established:** 1989
No.of Employees: 21 - 50 **Product Groups:** 24, 29, 30, 38, 67

Date of Accounts	Dec 11	Dec 10	Dec 09
Sales Turnover	7m	26m	39m
Pre Tax Profit/Loss	278	307	649
Working Capital	613	426	847
Fixed Assets	110	149	598
Current Assets	3m	2m	8m
Current Liabilities	428	375	504

Buck & Hickman
Unit 2a Welbeck Way, Peterborough, PE2 7WH
Tel: 01733-371737 **Fax:** 01733-232245
E-mail: peterborough@buckandhickman.com
Website: http://www.buckandhickman.com
Managers: J. Higgins (District Mgr)
Ultimate Holding Company: TRAVIS PERKINS PLC
Immediate Holding Company: BOSTON (2011) LIMITED
Registration no: 06028304 **Date established:** 2006
No.of Employees: 1 - 10 **Product Groups:** 24, 29, 30

Burghley Home Brew
Calamity Gulch Bridge Hill Road, Newborough, Peterborough, PE6 7SA
Tel: 01733-810259
E-mail: burghleyhomebrew@unicombox.com
Website: http://www.burghley-homebrew.com
Directors: L. Rands (Prop)
Date established: 2000 **No.of Employees:** 1 - 10 **Product Groups:** 20, 40, 41

C K Direct Peterborough Ltd
Botolph Bridge Industrial Estate Oundle Road, Peterborough, PE2 9QP
Tel: 01733-569444 **Fax:** 01733-569433
E-mail: info@ckdirect.co.uk
Website: http://www.ckdirect.co.uk
Immediate Holding Company: CK DIRECT PETERBOROUGH LTD
Registration no: 07398562 **Date established:** 2010
No.of Employees: 1 - 10 **Product Groups:** 26, 30, 33, 35, 36, 40, 52, 54, 67, 84

Date of Accounts	Mar 12
Working Capital	-50
Fixed Assets	79
Current Assets	458

City Furniture Clearance Ltd
Unit 3A 35 Benwick Road, Whittlesey, Peterborough, PE7 2HD
Tel: 01733-208111 **Fax:** 01733-205784
E-mail: sales@cityfurnitureclearance.co.uk
Website: http://www.cityfurnitureclearance.co.uk
Directors: P. Puk (MD)
Immediate Holding Company: CITY FURNITURE (CLEARANCE) LIMITED
Registration no: 05960047 **Date established:** 2006
No.of Employees: 1 - 10 **Product Groups:** 26, 67

Date of Accounts	Sep 11	Sep 10	Sep 09
Working Capital	-10	31	-52
Fixed Assets	25	33	15
Current Assets	60	104	43

Clark Drain Ltd
Station Works Broadway, Yaxley, Peterborough, PE7 3EQ
Tel: 01733-765361 **Fax:** 01733-246927
E-mail: ronald.clark@clarksteel.com
Website: http://www.clark-drain.com
Bank(s): Bank of Scotland
Directors: R. Clark (Grp Chief Exec)
Managers: D. Johnson, M. Reith (Tech Serv Mgr), S. Hughes (Sales Prom Mgr)
Ultimate Holding Company: CLARKSTEEL HOLDINGS LIMITED
Immediate Holding Company: CLARKSTEEL GALVANISING LIMITED
Registration no: 02295049 **VAT No.:** GB 478 1823 16
Date established: 1988 **Turnover:** £10m - £20m
No.of Employees: 101 - 250 **Product Groups:** 30, 33, 34, 35, 54

C M L Decorators Southern Ltd
Unit 3 The Stirling Centre Stirleing Way, Market Deeping, Peterborough, PE6 8EQ
Tel: 01778-345699 **Fax:** 01778-345687
E-mail: kevin@cmldecorators.co.uk
Website: http://www.cmldecorators.co.uk
Directors: K. Laughton (Dir), K. Laughton (Fin)
Immediate Holding Company: CML DECORATORS (SOUTHERN) LIMITED
Registration no: 04401746 **Date established:** 2002
No.of Employees: 21 - 50 **Product Groups:** 52

Date of Accounts	Mar 08	Mar 07	Mar 06
Working Capital	-24	-36	-63
Fixed Assets	1	2	4
Current Assets	298	252	371

Coloplast Ltd

Peterborough Business Park Lynch Wood, Peterborough, PE2 6FX
Tel: 01733-392000 **Fax:** 01733-233348
E-mail: skernahan@coloplast.co.uk
Website: http://www.coloplast.co.uk
Directors: A. Kjer (Fin), M. Edwards (Sales), S. Langan (Sales & Mktg), S. Sedwill (Pers)
Managers: S. Kernahan (Grp Mgr), D. Field (Purch Mgr)
Immediate Holding Company: COLOPLAST LIMITED
Registration no: 01094405 **Date established:** 1973
Turnover: £125m - £250m **No.of Employees:** 101 - 250
Product Groups: 24, 30

Date of Accounts	Sep 11	Sep 10	Sep 09
Sales Turnover	178m	165m	154m
Pre Tax Profit/Loss	7m	9m	6m
Working Capital	-8m	-11m	-18m
Fixed Assets	19m	21m	24m
Current Assets	37m	45m	37m
Current Liabilities	14m	11m	47m

Concrete Renovations

152 Park Road, Peterborough, PE1 2UB
Tel: 01733-560362
E-mail: sales@concreterenovations.co.uk
Website: http://www.concreterenovations.co.uk
Managers: G. Worraker (Mgr)
Date established: 1984 **Turnover:** Up to £250,000
No.of Employees: 1 - 10 **Product Groups:** 52

Control Design & Development

Fenlake Business Centre Fengate, Peterborough, PE1 5BQ
Tel: 01733-311566 **Fax:** 01733-312566
E-mail: enquiries@cddp.co.uk
Website: http://www.cddp.co.uk
Bank(s): Fortis Bank, 13-14 Appold Street, London, EC2A 2DP
Directors: R. Strotz (MD), I. Scott (Fin), D. Shayler (Sales & Mktg)
Managers: H. Taha, H. Williams
Ultimate Holding Company: BUHLER INTERNATIONAL (SWITZERLAND)
Immediate Holding Company: CONTROL DESIGN AND DEVELOPMENT LIMITED
Registration no: 01579088 **VAT No.:** GB 359 8876 73
Date established: 1981 **Turnover:** £5m - £10m **No.of Employees:** 21 - 50
Product Groups: 37, 38

Date of Accounts	Dec 11	Dec 10	Dec 09
Sales Turnover	7m	6m	7m
Pre Tax Profit/Loss	882	827	1m
Working Capital	1000	1m	1m
Fixed Assets	179	181	208
Current Assets	5m	5m	5m
Current Liabilities	3m	3m	3m

Conway Pine Ltd

Brotherhood Retail Park Lincoln Road, Peterborough, PE4 6LU
Tel: 01733-577910 **Fax:** 01733- 577954
Website: http://www.conway-furniture.com
Managers: A. Kendall (Mgr)
Ultimate Holding Company: CONWAY PINE HOLDINGS LIMITED
Immediate Holding Company: CONWAY PINE LIMITED
Registration no: 02286703 **Date established:** 1988 **Turnover:** £5m - £10m
No.of Employees: 1 - 10 **Product Groups:** 26, 37

Date of Accounts	Mar 11	Mar 10	Mar 09
Sales Turnover	N/A	N/A	6m
Pre Tax Profit/Loss	N/A	N/A	-320
Working Capital	-60	346	969
Fixed Assets	118	129	159
Current Assets	799	1m	1m
Current Liabilities	N/A	N/A	275

Thomas Cook Ltd

Unit 15 Coningsby Road, Peterborough, PE3 8AB
Tel: 08443-357564
E-mail: enquiries@thomascook.com
Website: http://www.thomascook.com
Directors: P. Norman (I.T. Dir), S. Robertson (Sales), M. Fontenla-Novoa (Grp Chief Exec), S. Carter (Mkt Research)
Managers: T. Hughes (District Mgr), W. Lloyd (Mktg Serv Mgr)
Ultimate Holding Company: THOMAS COOK GROUP PLC
Immediate Holding Company: THOMAS COOK LIMITED
Registration no: 03155236 **Date established:** 1996
Turnover: £75m - £125m **No.of Employees:** 1 - 10 **Product Groups:** 69

Date of Accounts	Sep 11	Sep 10	Sep 09
Working Capital	-1m	-1m	-1m
Current Liabilities	142	142	142

Crightons' Of Peterborough Ltd

Dukesmead Industrial Estate Werrington, Peterborough, PE4 6ZN
Tel: 01733-571836 **Fax:** 01733-572680
E-mail: i.crighton@crightons.co.uk
Website: http://www.crightons.co.uk
Directors: T. Crighton (Fin), I. Crighton (MD)
Immediate Holding Company: CRIGHTONS OF PETERBOROUGH LIMITED
Registration no: 00763843 **VAT No.:** GB 120 3717 15
Date established: 1963 **Turnover:** £250,000 - £500,000
No.of Employees: 11 - 20 **Product Groups:** 68

Date of Accounts	Dec 11	Dec 10	Dec 09
Working Capital	73	146	53
Fixed Assets	41	53	70
Current Assets	216	237	228

Crown Catering Equipment Ltd

41 Manasty Road Orton Southgate, Peterborough, PE2 6UP
Tel: 01733-231666 **Fax:** 01733-231636
E-mail: sales@crowncateringequipment.co.uk
Website: http://www.crowncateringequipment.co.uk
Directors: A. Chappell (Dir)
Immediate Holding Company: CROWN CATERING EQUIPMENT LIMITED
Registration no: 01977584 **Date established:** 1986
No.of Employees: 1 - 10 **Product Groups:** 02, 20, 22, 24, 27, 30, 32, 33, 35, 36, 37, 38, 40, 41, 42, 44, 45, 48, 49, 61, 62, 63, 64, 66, 67, 69

Curtis & Co Oundle Ltd

22 West Street Oundle, Peterborough, PE8 4EG
Tel: 01832-273515 **Fax:** 01832-275490
E-mail: martinleecurtis@btopenworld.com
Directors: M. Lee (MD)
Immediate Holding Company: CURTIS & CO. (OUDLE) LIMITED
Registration no: 00494352 **Date established:** 1951
No.of Employees: 1 - 10 **Product Groups:** 20

Date of Accounts	Sep 11	Sep 10	Sep 08
Working Capital	54	60	52
Fixed Assets	2	1	1
Current Assets	79	75	67

Customers Matter Ltd

3 Bridge Street Kings Cliffe, Peterborough, PE8 6XH
Tel: 01780-470003 **Fax:** 01780-470003
E-mail: info@customersmatter.co.uk
Website: http://www.customersmatter.co.uk
Directors: R. Evans (Fin), D. Pollock (MD)
Immediate Holding Company: CUSTOMERS MATTER LTD
Registration no: 04609172 **Date established:** 2002
Turnover: £250,000 - £500,000 **No.of Employees:** 1 - 10
Product Groups: 81

Date of Accounts	Dec 11	Dec 10	Dec 08
Working Capital	20	13	15
Fixed Assets	2	3	3
Current Assets	34	23	36

D L S Medical

Premier House Southgate Way, Orton Southgate, Peterborough, PE2 6YG
Tel: 01733-230700 **Fax:** 01733-230900
Website: http://www.dlsmedical.co.uk
Bank(s): HSBC Bank plc
Directors: G. Brewis (Grp), I. Partridge (Dir)
Managers: G. McAndrew
Immediate Holding Company: DANEBURY HOLDINGS LTD
Registration no: 01444401 **Turnover:** £2m - £5m
No.of Employees: 21 - 50 **Product Groups:** 24, 27, 30, 36, 38

D P H Electrical

77 Birchtree Avenue, Peterborough, PE1 4HP
Tel: 01733-701254
E-mail: dave1.hicks@ntlworld.com
Directors: D. Hicks (Prop)
No.of Employees: 1 - 10 **Product Groups:** 38, 44, 83

Lawrence David Ltd

Maxwell Road, Peterborough, PE2 7JR
Tel: 01733-397600 **Fax:** 01733-397601
E-mail: info@lawrencedavid.co.uk
Website: http://www.lawrencedavid.co.uk
Bank(s): HSBC Bank plc
Directors: L. Marshall (MD), A. Jeffs (Fin), L. Marshall (Dir)
Managers: C. Martin (Purch Mgr), S. Cashman (Tech Serv Mgr)
Immediate Holding Company: LAWRENCE DAVID LIMITED
Registration no: 01110305 **VAT No.:** GB 121 4954 87
Date established: 1973 **Turnover:** £20m - £50m
No.of Employees: 101 - 250 **Product Groups:** 39

Date of Accounts	May 11	May 10	May 09
Sales Turnover	38m	30m	35m
Pre Tax Profit/Loss	957	82	-361
Working Capital	162	311	886
Fixed Assets	7m	6m	6m
Current Assets	11m	10m	7m
Current Liabilities	2m	2m	1m

Delta Flags Ltd

Unit 7 Squirrels Lodge Deeping St James, Peterborough, PE6 8RL
Tel: 01778-349282 **Fax:** 01908-582552
E-mail: info@deltaflags.co.uk
Website: http://www.deltaflags.co.uk
Directors: R. Lavender (MD), K. Day (Fin)
Registration no: 02219212 **Date established:** 1988
No.of Employees: 11 - 20 **Product Groups:** 25, 49

Date of Accounts	Dec 08	Dec 07	Dec 06
Working Capital	-16	-10	-6
Fixed Assets	3	4	N/A
Current Assets	17	49	34
Current Liabilities	33	58	40

Document Control Services Ltd

10 Stapledon Road Orton Southgate, Peterborough, PE2 6TB
Tel: 01733-366800 **Fax:** 01733-366801
E-mail: enquiries@documentcontrolservices.co.uk
Website: http://www.documentcontrolservices.co.uk
Bank(s): National Westminster Bank Plc
Directors: E. Marshall (MD), L. Ford (Co Sec)
Ultimate Holding Company: GERALDTON SERVICES INC (USA)
Immediate Holding Company: DOCUMENT CONTROL SERVICES LIMITED
Registration no: 03386132 **VAT No.:** GB 695 0898 75
Date established: 1997 **Turnover:** £1m - £2m **No.of Employees:** 21 - 50
Product Groups: 44

Date of Accounts	Dec 11	Dec 10	Dec 09
Sales Turnover	2m	2m	3m
Pre Tax Profit/Loss	-297	-206	105
Working Capital	1m	2m	2m
Fixed Assets	55	67	104
Current Assets	2m	2m	2m
Current Liabilities	195	198	220

Elliott Group Ltd

Manor Drive, Peterborough, PE4 7AP
Tel: 01733-298700 **Fax:** 01427-718921
E-mail: hirediv@elliott-group.co.uk
Website: http://www.elliott.co.uk
Directors: M. Eburn (MD)
Ultimate Holding Company: TDR CAPITAL LLP
Immediate Holding Company: ELLIOTT GROUP HOLDINGS (UK) LIMITED
Registration no: 06344129 **VAT No.:** GB 638 6861 92
Date established: 2007 **Turnover:** £125m - £250m
No.of Employees: 51 - 100 **Product Groups:** 25, 83

Date of Accounts	Dec 10	Dec 09	Dec 08
Pre Tax Profit/Loss	-26m	-30m	-228m
Working Capital	-1m	-56m	-6m
Fixed Assets	403m	456m	456m
Current Assets	6m	6m	4m
Current Liabilities	5m	846	2m

Eltek Systems Ltd

Eltek House 38 Nene Valley Business Park, Oundle, Peterborough, PE8 4HN
Tel: 01832-277590 **Fax:** 01832-273941
E-mail: info@eltek-systems.com
Website: http://www.eltek-systems.com
Bank(s): National Westminster Bank Plc
Directors: D. Smith (Co Sec), J. Smith (MD)
Managers: M. Smith (Tech Serv Mgr)
Immediate Holding Company: ELTEK SYSTEMS LIMITED
Registration no: 01691497 **VAT No.:** GB 395 7042 26
Date established: 1983 **Turnover:** £1m - £2m **No.of Employees:** 21 - 50
Product Groups: 37

Date of Accounts	Apr 11	Apr 10	Apr 09
Working Capital	2m	2m	1m
Fixed Assets	191	143	141
Current Assets	2m	2m	2m

Empress Promotions Ltd

6 Holkham Road Orton Southgate, Peterborough, PE2 6TE
Tel: 01733-391133 **Fax:** 01733-370738
E-mail: pauline@empresspromo.com
Website: http://www.empresspromo.com
Directors: M. Smith (MD), P. Smith (Fin)
Immediate Holding Company: EMPRESS PROMOTIONS LIMITED
Registration no: 04266202 **Date established:** 2001
Turnover: £500,000 - £1m **No.of Employees:** 21 - 50
Product Groups: 48, 76

Date of Accounts	Jul 08	Jul 07	Jul 06
Working Capital	-28	-32	-32
Fixed Assets	32	37	35
Current Assets	380	328	308
Current Liabilities	408	361	340

The Enigma Encoding Company Ltd

The Laurels Southwick Road, Glapthorn, Peterborough, PE8 5BD
Tel: 01832-274963 **Fax:** 01832-274946
E-mail: admin@enigmasecurity.co.uk
Website: http://www.enigmasecurity.co.uk
Directors: J. Knowles (Dir)
Immediate Holding Company: THE ENIGMA ENCODING COMPANY LIMITED
Registration no: 02920414 **Date established:** 1994
Turnover: Up to £250,000 **No.of Employees:** 1 - 10 **Product Groups:** 37, 40, 54

Date of Accounts	Apr 11	Apr 10	Apr 09
Sales Turnover	195	291	282
Pre Tax Profit/Loss	18	41	44
Working Capital	7	2	N/A
Fixed Assets	1	1	N/A
Current Assets	35	50	41
Current Liabilities	29	48	41

Eriks UK (Peterborough Service Centre)

6 The Metro Centre, Peterborough, PE2 7UH
Tel: 01733-371616 **Fax:** 01733-371127
E-mail: peterborough@eriks.co.uk
Website: http://www.eriks.co.uk
Managers: S. Hayden (Mgr)
Turnover: £250m - £500m **No.of Employees:** 1 - 10 **Product Groups:** 66

Esscano Power Services Ltd

24 King Street Industrial Estate Langtoft, Peterborough, PE6 9NF
Tel: 01778-560562 **Fax:** 01778-561599
E-mail: service@esscano.co.uk
Website: http://www.esscano.com
Directors: D. Tilley (MD)
Immediate Holding Company: ESSCANO POWER SERVICES LIMITED
Registration no: 03850977 **Date established:** 1999
No.of Employees: 11 - 20 **Product Groups:** 29, 37, 38, 39, 40, 48, 68

Date of Accounts	Jun 11	Jun 10	Jun 09
Working Capital	101	89	104
Fixed Assets	24	38	42
Current Assets	489	171	206

Exportential

13 Beccelm Drive Crowland, Peterborough, PE6 0AG
Tel: 01733-211873
E-mail: info@exportential.co.uk
Website: http://www.exportential.co.uk
Directors: D. Stokes (Fin)
Immediate Holding Company: EXPORTENTIAL LIMITED
Registration no: 04955652 **Date established:** 2003
Turnover: Up to £250,000 **No.of Employees:** 1 - 10 **Product Groups:** 80

Date of Accounts	Mar 12	Mar 11	Mar 10
Pre Tax Profit/Loss	N/A	N/A	-2
Working Capital	-5	-3	-3
Current Assets	N/A	1	1

Fairline Boats Ltd

Nene Valley Business Park Oundle, Peterborough, PE8 4HN
Tel: 01832-273661 **Fax:** 01832-273432
E-mail: alan.bowers@fairline.com
Website: http://www.fairline.com
Bank(s): National Westminster Bank Plc
Directors: A. Bowers (Fin), A. Greenwood (Tech Serv), A. Sime (Fin)
Managers: O. Winbolt, J. Powell, I. Walters (Purch Mgr), A. Gardiner (Personnel)
Ultimate Holding Company: 62812 LIMITED
Immediate Holding Company: FAIRLINE BOATS LIMITED
Registration no: 00939223 **VAT No.:** GB 119 4135 82
Date established: 1968 **Turnover:** £75m - £125m
No.of Employees: 501 - 1000 **Product Groups:** 39

Date of Accounts	Dec 11	Dec 10	Dec 09
Sales Turnover	79m	82m	113m
Pre Tax Profit/Loss	-12m	-11m	-688
Working Capital	-37m	-30m	-20m
Fixed Assets	17m	18m	24m
Current Assets	28m	27m	34m
Current Liabilities	21m	26m	27m

Ferrus Power Ltd

6-7 Papyrus Road, Peterborough, PE4 5BH
Tel: 01733-322534 **Fax:** 01733-322535
E-mail: m.farrer@ferrus-power.co.uk
Website: http://www.ferrus-power.co.uk
Directors: C. Wilson (Co Sec), M. Farrer (Dir), A. Parkinson (MD)
Managers: G. Townsend (Transport)
Immediate Holding Company: FERRUS POWER LIMITED
Registration no: 02601096 **Date established:** 1991 **Turnover:** £1m - £2m
No.of Employees: 21 - 50 **Product Groups:** 37, 38, 40, 44, 52, 85

Date of Accounts	Oct 07	Oct 06	Oct 05
Sales Turnover	1154	N/A	N/A
Pre Tax Profit/Loss	115	N/A	N/A

Working Capital	524	433	359
Fixed Assets	172	216	240
Current Assets	528	639	520
Current Liabilities	4	206	161
Total Share Capital	100	100	100
ROCE% (Return on Capital Employed)	16.5		
ROT% (Return on Turnover)	10.0		

Fire Safety Express
Unit 43 Culley Court, Orton Southgate, Peterborough, PE2 6XD
Tel: 01733-234504 **Fax:** 08450-179624
E-mail: info@firesafetyexpress.co.uk
Website: http://www.firesafetyexpress.co.uk
Directors: P. Fredericks (MD)
Immediate Holding Company: FSE CONSULT LTD
Date established: 2007 **Turnover:** Up to £250,000
No.of Employees: 1 - 10 **Product Groups:** 40, 49, 67, 84, 86

Joseph Flach & Sons Ltd
8 Maxwell Road, Peterborough, PE2 7HU
Tel: 01733-371221 **Fax:** 01733-361323
E-mail: contact@josephflach.co.uk
Website: http://www.josephflach.co.uk
Directors: S. Flach (MD)
Immediate Holding Company: JOSEPH FLACH & SONS LIMITED
Registration no: 00218842 **VAT No.:** GB 229 3872 38
Date established: 2027 **Turnover:** Up to £250,000
No.of Employees: 1 - 10 **Product Groups:** 02, 20, 31, 32, 66

Date of Accounts	Dec 11	Dec 10	Dec 09
Working Capital	291	288	286
Fixed Assets	70	72	75
Current Assets	508	461	593

Flo Mech Ltd
Flo-Mech House Paxton Road, Orton Goldhay, Peterborough, PE2 5YA
Tel: 01733-233166 **Fax:** 01733-235200
E-mail: enquiries@flo-mech.com
Website: http://www.flo-mech.com
Directors: C. Hill (Fin), S. Elderkin (MD)
Immediate Holding Company: FLO-MECH. LIMITED
Registration no: 01190214 **Date established:** 1974
Turnover: £10m - £20m **No.of Employees:** 21 - 50 **Product Groups:** 37

Date of Accounts	Oct 11	Oct 10	Oct 09
Sales Turnover	16m	11m	10m
Pre Tax Profit/Loss	983	529	371
Working Capital	2m	716	1m
Fixed Assets	248	227	199
Current Assets	8m	5m	5m
Current Liabilities	3m	2m	2m

Ford & Slater
Newark Road, Peterborough, PE1 5YD
Tel: 01733-295000 **Fax:** 01733-295010
E-mail: enquiries@fordandslater.co.uk
Website: http://www.fordandslater.com
Bank(s): Barclays
Managers: B. Prosser (Depot Mgr)
Immediate Holding Company: CARLTON DISTRIBUTION (UK) LIMITED
Registration no: 02495131 **VAT No.:** GB 670 3219 53
Date established: 1994 **Turnover:** £500,000 - £1m
No.of Employees: 21 - 50 **Product Groups:** 39

Date of Accounts	Oct 11	Oct 10	Oct 09
Sales Turnover	1m	843	650
Pre Tax Profit/Loss	149	111	45
Working Capital	-185	-153	-112
Fixed Assets	1m	910	538
Current Assets	414	337	268
Current Liabilities	76	70	101

Fresh Produce Consortium
Minerva House Minerva Business Park, Lynch Wood, Peterborough, PE2 6FT
Tel: 01733-237117 **Fax:** 01733-237118
E-mail: infor@freshproduce.org.uk
Website: http://www.freshproduce.org.uk
Directors: N. Jenney (Grp Chief Exec)
Immediate Holding Company: THE FRESH PRODUCE CONSORTIUM (U.K.)
Registration no: 02721319 **VAT No.:** GB 628 1048 66
Date established: 1992 **No.of Employees:** 1 - 10 **Product Groups:** 62, 87

Date of Accounts	Dec 11	Dec 10	Dec 09
Working Capital	157	427	427
Fixed Assets	279	7	10
Current Assets	266	497	525

G F C UK Ltd
48 Ivatt Way, Peterborough, PE3 7PN
Tel: 01733-330000 **Fax:** 01733-330001
Website: http://www.gfc-ltd.com
Directors: G. Ahmed (Fin), T. Mahmood (MD)
Immediate Holding Company: GFC (UK) LTD
Registration no: 07292371 **Date established:** 2010
No.of Employees: 1 - 10 **Product Groups:** 35, 42, 45

Date of Accounts	Jun 12	Jun 11
Working Capital	-58	-2
Fixed Assets	214	209
Current Assets	241	310

G H Display
70 Papyrus Road, Peterborough, PE4 5BH
Tel: 01733-570222 **Fax:** 01733-320665
E-mail: mail@ghdisplay.co.uk
Website: http://www.ghdisplay.co.uk
Managers: G. Hodson (Mgr)
Turnover: £250,000 - £500,000 **No.of Employees:** 1 - 10
Product Groups: 81

G L Events Snowdens
Second Drove Industrial Estate, Peterborough, PE1 5XA
Tel: 01733-344110 **Fax:** 01733-314985
E-mail: info@snowdens.co.uk
Website: http://www.snowdens.co.uk
Bank(s): National Westminster
Directors: B. Alldread (Co Sec)
Managers: C. Coppe (Tech Serv Mgr), K. Bishop (Chief Mgr)
Immediate Holding Company: OWEN BROWN LTD
Registration no: 00505493 **Turnover:** £1m - £2m
No.of Employees: 21 - 50 **Product Groups:** 24, 83

Gilchrist & Soames
Unit 1 John Wesley Road, Werrington, Peterborough, PE4 6ZL
Tel: 01733-384100 **Fax:** 01733-384101
E-mail: sales@gilchristsoames.com
Website: http://www.gilchristsoames.com
Directors: G. Shaw (MD)
Immediate Holding Company: GILCHRIST & SOAMES UK LIMITED
Registration no: 06368196 **Date established:** 2007
Turnover: Up to £250,000 **No.of Employees:** 11 - 20 **Product Groups:** 31, 32

Date of Accounts	Dec 11	Dec 10	Dec 09
Working Capital	2m	2m	2m
Fixed Assets	410	763	1m
Current Assets	2m	3m	3m

go-displays.co.uk
Welbeck Way, Peterborough, PE2 7WH
Tel: 01733-232000 **Fax:** 01733-391825
E-mail: enquiries@go-displays.co.uk
Website: http://www.go-displays.co.uk
Directors: R. Payne (MD)
Managers: J. Payne (Sales & Mktg Mg)
Turnover: £2m - £5m **No.of Employees:** 21 - 50 **Product Groups:** 49

Graphics UK
45 Axis Park Manasty Road Orton Southgate, Peterborough, PE2 6UP
Tel: 01733-234118 **Fax:** 01733-370720
E-mail: sales@graphicsuk.com
Website: http://www.graphicsuk.com
Directors: D. Pepper (Sales)
Managers: C. Eborall (Designer)
Immediate Holding Company: GRAPHICS UK DIGITAL AND SCREEN LIMITED
Registration no: 06824892 **Date established:** 2009
No.of Employees: 1 - 10 **Product Groups:** 23, 27, 28, 29, 30, 35

Date of Accounts	Feb 10
Working Capital	-74
Fixed Assets	64
Current Assets	109

Grontmij Ltd
Winchester Place 80 Thorpe Road, Peterborough, PE3 6AP
Tel: 01733-340939 **Fax:** 01733-201970
E-mail: enquiries@grontmij.co.uk
Website: http://www.grontmij.co.uk
Directors: D. Sadler (Co Sec), J. Chubb (MD)
Ultimate Holding Company: GRONTMIJ NV (NETHERLANDS)
Immediate Holding Company: GRONTMIJ LIMITED
Registration no: 02888385 **VAT No.:** GB 418 0640 71
Date established: 1994 **Turnover:** £10m - £20m **No.of Employees:** 1 - 10
Product Groups: 80, 81, 84

Date of Accounts	Dec 10	Dec 09	Dec 08
Sales Turnover	41m	49m	62m
Pre Tax Profit/Loss	-2m	730	2m
Working Capital	1m	3m	2m
Fixed Assets	2m	2m	2m
Current Assets	13m	10m	13m
Current Liabilities	3m	4m	4m

Groupco Ltd
Unit 130 Culley Court, Orton Southgate, Peterborough, PE2 6WA
Tel: 01733-393330 **Fax:** 01733-235246
E-mail: sales@groupcoltd.co.uk
Website: http://www.groupcoltd.co.uk
Directors: J. Crittenden (MD), R. Bailey (Fin), R. Duncan (MD), D. May (Dir)
Immediate Holding Company: GROUPCO LIMITED
Registration no: 07643642 **Date established:** 2011
No.of Employees: 21 - 50 **Product Groups:** 25, 36

H M F UK Ltd
Empson Road, Peterborough, PE1 5UP
Tel: 01733-558145 **Fax:** 01733-565869
E-mail: kevin.b@hmfcranes.co.uk
Website: http://www.hmf.dk
Managers: K. Brudenell-Maylin (Comptroller)
Ultimate Holding Company: HMF HOLDING A/S (DENMARK)
Immediate Holding Company: H M F (UK) LIMITED
Registration no: 02138574 **Date established:** 1987 **Turnover:** £2m - £5m
No.of Employees: 11 - 20 **Product Groups:** 39, 41, 45, 52, 67, 72, 83

Date of Accounts	Dec 11	Dec 10	Dec 09
Sales Turnover	6m	4m	2m
Pre Tax Profit/Loss	-123	-251	-179
Working Capital	355	476	719
Fixed Assets	61	64	72
Current Assets	3m	3m	2m
Current Liabilities	302	189	102

Handling Design Ltd
12 Leofric Square, Peterborough, PE1 5TU
Tel: 01733-349062 **Fax:** 01733-568947
E-mail: handlingdes@aol.com
Website: http://www.palletconveyors.co.uk
Directors: D. Underhill (MD), V. Orme (Fin)
Immediate Holding Company: HANDLING DESIGN LTD
Registration no: 03756127 **VAT No.:** GB 728 2464 24
Date established: 1999 **Turnover:** Up to £250,000
No.of Employees: 1 - 10 **Product Groups:** 35, 41, 45

Date of Accounts	Mar 11	Mar 10	Mar 09
Working Capital	-1	-2	-3
Fixed Assets	N/A	1	1
Current Assets	7	8	3

Hereward Roofing Services
Unit 4 Benwick Road, Whittlesey, Peterborough, PE7 2HD
Tel: 01733-345679 **Fax:** 01733-345119
E-mail: info@herewardroofing.co.uk
Website: http://www.herewardroofing.co.uk
Directors: B. Rogers (Dir)
Registration no: 05126608 **Date established:** 2004 **Turnover:** £1m - £2m
No.of Employees: 11 - 20 **Product Groups:** 52

Howsafe Ltd
18-20 Challenger Way, Peterborough, PE1 5EX
Tel: 01733-560669 **Fax:** 01733-348115
E-mail: sales@howsafe.co.uk
Website: http://www.howsafe.co.uk
Bank(s): Barclays
Directors: C. Howe (MD)
Immediate Holding Company: HOWSAFE LIMITED
Registration no: 01345099 **Date established:** 1977 **Turnover:** £1m - £2m
No.of Employees: 21 - 50 **Product Groups:** 22, 24, 29, 63, 67

Date of Accounts	Apr 12	Apr 11	Apr 10
Working Capital	597	539	479
Fixed Assets	363	393	417
Current Assets	763	736	658

Hydromarque Ltd
20-21 Stapledon Road Orton Southgate, Peterborough, PE2 6TD
Tel: 01733-370545 **Fax:** 01733-361249
E-mail: mail@hydromarque.com
Website: http://www.hydromarque.com
Bank(s): Barclays
Directors: J. Mclean (MD)
Immediate Holding Company: HYDROMARQUE LIMITED
Registration no: 02127692 **Date established:** 1987 **Turnover:** £1m - £2m
No.of Employees: 11 - 20 **Product Groups:** 39, 40, 42, 43

Date of Accounts	Jun 12	Jun 11	Jun 10
Working Capital	338	310	330
Fixed Assets	67	65	37
Current Assets	934	773	729
Current Liabilities	596	N/A	N/A

Hytner Exhibitions Ltd
Bullock Road Washingley, Peterborough, PE7 3SJ
Tel: 01733-246950 **Fax:** 01733-246951
E-mail: gary@hytner.co.uk
Website: http://www.hytner.co.uk
Directors: G. Hytner (MD)
Immediate Holding Company: HYTNER EXHIBITIONS LIMITED
Registration no: 02880842 **VAT No.:** GB 638 2974 02
Date established: 1993 **Turnover:** £250,000 - £500,000
No.of Employees: 1 - 10 **Product Groups:** 81

Date of Accounts	Dec 11	Dec 10	Dec 09
Working Capital	167	190	239
Fixed Assets	242	273	337
Current Assets	239	237	297

I T W Mima Service
1 Belgic Square, Peterborough, PE1 5XF
Tel: 01733-314829 **Fax:** 01733-313140
E-mail: graham.mattacks@mimaitw.com
Website: http://www.itwmima.eu
Managers: G. Mattacks (Mgr)
Date established: 1999 **No.of Employees:** 51 - 100 **Product Groups:** 38, 42

In the Hot Seat
36 Heath Road Helpston, Peterborough, PE6 7EG
Tel: 01733-252642
E-mail: sue@inthehotseat.co.uk
Website: http://www.inthehotseat.co.uk
Directors: S. Clarke (Prop)
Date established: 2005 **Turnover:** Up to £250,000
No.of Employees: 1 - 10 **Product Groups:** 80

Indesit Company UK Ltd
Morley Way, Peterborough, PE2 9JB
Tel: 08452-235858 **Fax:** 01733-341783
E-mail: sales@gda.uk.com
Website: http://www.indesit.uk
Directors: A. Woolf (Mkt Research), S. Coochey (Pers), A. Webb (Fin), S. Jackson (Tech Serv), J. Goldsmith (Sales), I. Abernethy (Dir), A. Giubboni (Fin)
Managers: D. Ancil, D. Truss (Mgr)
Ultimate Holding Company: INDESIT COMPANY SPA (ITALY)
Immediate Holding Company: INDESIT COMPANY UK HOLDINGS LIMITED
Registration no: 04372979 **Date established:** 2002
Turnover: £500m - £1,000m **No.of Employees:** 1 - 10
Product Groups: 36

Date of Accounts	Dec 10	Dec 09	Dec 08
Sales Turnover	676m	664m	676m
Pre Tax Profit/Loss	69m	52m	2m
Working Capital	139m	121m	104m
Fixed Assets	108m	117m	106m
Current Assets	364m	343m	340m
Current Liabilities	101m	83m	44m

Inline Offline Graphics Ltd
Unit 6 Saracen Business Park, Newark Road, Peterborough, PE1 5WS
Tel: 01733-341902 **Fax:** 01733-892691
E-mail: nstokes@iographics.co.uk
Website: http://www.iographics.co.uk
Directors: N. Stokes (Dir)
Registration no: 06173907 **Date established:** 2007
No.of Employees: 1 - 10 **Product Groups:** 28, 32, 40, 44

Institute Of Export Ltd
Export House Minerva Business Park, Lynch Wood, Peterborough, PE2 6FT
Tel: 01733-404400 **Fax:** 01733-404444
E-mail: enquiries@export.org.uk
Website: http://www.export.org.uk
Directors: D. Fermie (Co Sec)
Managers: L. Batchelor
Immediate Holding Company: INSTITUTE OF EXPORT(THE)
Registration no: 00307186 **VAT No.:** GB 524 8665 24
Date established: 1935 **Turnover:** £500,000 - £1m
No.of Employees: 1 - 10 **Product Groups:** 87

Date of Accounts	Dec 11	Dec 10	Dec 09
Sales Turnover	468	562	431
Pre Tax Profit/Loss	5	65	-22
Working Capital	-138	-139	-196
Fixed Assets	325	324	318
Current Assets	72	62	63
Current Liabilities	124	96	67

Jewsons Builders Merchants
1180 Lincoln Road, Peterborough, PE4 6LA
Tel: 01733-579270 **Fax:** 01733-323092
E-mail: alan.skinner@jewson.co.uk
Website: http://www.jewson.co.uk
Directors: P. Hindle (MD)
Managers: A. Skinner (Mgr)
Immediate Holding Company: Saint Gobain
Registration no: 00348407 **VAT No.:** GB 394 1212 63
Turnover: £2m - £5m **No.of Employees:** 11 - 20 **Product Groups:** 66

John Bradshaw's Gunshop
Perio Mill Fotheringhay, Peterborough, PE8 5HU
Tel: 01832-226376 **Fax:** 01832-226272
E-mail: james@systemsaccountants.com
Website: http://www.johnbradshawguns.co.uk
Directors: M. Simpson (Ptnr)
Immediate Holding Company: JAMES BRADSHAW ASSOCIATES LIMITED
Registration no: 04238848 **Date established:** 2001
No.of Employees: 1 - 10 **Product Groups:** 36, 39, 40

Date of Accounts	Jun 11	Jun 10	Jun 09
Working Capital	-0	-0	-0

Julabo UK Ltd
34 Thorpe Wood Thorpe Wood Business Park, Peterborough, PE3 6SR
Tel: 01733-265892 **Fax:** 01733-264111
E-mail: info@julabo.co.uk
Website: http://www.julabo.co.uk
Directors: M. Juchheim (Dir), R. Juchheim (Dir)
Managers: A. Munro (Chief Mgr)
Registration no: 03876210 **VAT No.:** GB 727 9421 06
Date established: 1999 **Turnover:** £500,000 - £1m
No.of Employees: 1 - 10 **Product Groups:** 38, 40, 42, 67, 84

Date of Accounts	Dec 09	Dec 08	Dec 07
Working Capital	128	97	124
Fixed Assets	31	40	33
Current Assets	237	187	270

Keelgrove Injection Moulders Ltd
6 Stapledon Road Orton Southgate, Peterborough, PE2 6TB
Tel: 01733-235857 **Fax:** 01733-370535
E-mail: sales@keelgrove.co.uk
Website: http://www.injectionmouldings.co.uk
Bank(s): Yorkshire Bank PLC
Directors: T. Stilgrove (Dir)
Immediate Holding Company: KEELGROVE INJECTION MOULDERS LIMITED
Registration no: 01680676 **VAT No.:** GB 360 1197 78
Date established: 1982 **Turnover:** £500,000 - £1m
No.of Employees: 11 - 20 **Product Groups:** 30, 42, 48

Date of Accounts	Apr 12	Apr 11	Apr 10
Working Capital	21	38	35
Fixed Assets	181	193	206
Current Assets	77	92	88

Kin-Nex Steelwork Ltd
8 Meadow Close Stilton Stilton, Peterborough, PE7 3FG
Tel: 01733-242195 **Fax:** 01733-242195
E-mail: kinnexenquiries@aol.com
Directors: D. Cooper (Fin), S. Burton (MD)
Registration no: 04875394 **Date established:** 2003
No.of Employees: 1 - 10 **Product Groups:** 35, 51, 66

Kittiwake Procal Ltd
5 Maxwell Road, Peterborough, PE2 7HU
Tel: 01733-232495 **Fax:** 01733-235255
E-mail: post@procal.com
Website: http://www.procal.com
Bank(s): Bank of Scotland
Managers: C. Saunders (Chief Mgr), K. Canham (Sales Prom)
Ultimate Holding Company: KITTIWAKE DEVELOPMENTS LIMITED
Immediate Holding Company: KITTIWAKE PROCAL LIMITED
Registration no: 06793085 **VAT No.:** GB 678 9767 41
Date established: 2009 **Turnover:** £2m - £5m **No.of Employees:** 21 - 50
Product Groups: 38

Date of Accounts	Sep 11	Sep 10	Sep 09
Working Capital	-249	-90	N/A
Fixed Assets	177	90	N/A
Current Assets	806	243	N/A

Landis & Gyr
1 Lysander Drive Market Deeping, Peterborough, PE6 8FB
Tel: 01778-343560 **Fax:** 01778-344807
E-mail: sales.uk@landisgyr.com
Website: http://www.landisgyr.com
Managers: J. Elmer
Ultimate Holding Company: LANDIS & GYR HOLDINGS AG (SWITZERLAND)
Immediate Holding Company: LANDIS + GYR LIMITED
Registration no: 01202284 **Date established:** 1975
Turnover: £20m - £50m **No.of Employees:** 251 - 500
Product Groups: 38, 48

Date of Accounts	Dec 10	Dec 09	Dec 08
Sales Turnover	111m	43m	47m
Pre Tax Profit/Loss	3m	-2m	2m
Working Capital	-20m	-17m	7m
Fixed Assets	45m	41m	8m
Current Assets	73m	56m	18m
Current Liabilities	10m	9m	3m

Lazer Printing
65 Coniston Road, Peterborough, PE4 7UL
Tel: 01733-324404 **Fax:** 01733-324404
Directors: C. Mehdi (Dir)
Turnover: Up to £250,000 **No.of Employees:** 1 - 10 **Product Groups:** 28

Lincolnshire Fire & Safety Advisory Service
Carlton House 18 Willow Road, Yaxley, Peterborough, PE7 3HT
Tel: 01205-367465 **Fax:** 01733-248110
E-mail: info@newflame.co.uk
Website: http://www.newflame.co.uk
Directors: P. Lattimore (Sales), S. Best (MD)
Immediate Holding Company: NEWFLAME FIRE EQUIPMENT CO. LIMITED
Registration no: 05564060 **Date established:** 1981
No.of Employees: 11 - 20 **Product Groups:** 38, 42

Date of Accounts	Dec 11	Dec 10	Dec 09
Working Capital	33	33	36
Fixed Assets	187	140	165
Current Assets	226	215	234

Linden Homes
Ashurst Southgate Park Bakewell Road, Orton Southgate, Peterborough, PE2 6YS
Tel: 01733-396600 **Fax:** 01733-396669
E-mail: info@stamford-homes.co.uk
Website: http://www.lindenhomes.co.uk
Bank(s): Barclays, Birmingham
Directors: B. Maynard (I.T. Dir), F. Hopes (Fin)
Managers: A. Fysh (Purch Mgr)
Ultimate Holding Company: GALLIFORD TRY PLC
Immediate Holding Company: LINDEN MIDLANDS LIMITED
Registration no: 00409955 **VAT No.:** GB 119 7644 46
Date established: 1946 **Turnover:** £20m - £50m
No.of Employees: 21 - 50 **Product Groups:** 80

Date of Accounts	Jun 11	Jun 10	Jun 09
Sales Turnover	33m	27m	30m
Pre Tax Profit/Loss	-3m	336	3m
Working Capital	-64m	-63m	-57m
Fixed Assets	67m	65m	65m
Current Assets	75m	76m	53m
Current Liabilities	14m	16m	303

M & M Architectural Ltd
19 Leofric Square, Peterborough, PE1 5TU
Tel: 01733-339100
Website: http://www.mandmarchitectural.com
Directors: M. Galietti (Dir)
Immediate Holding Company: M&m Architectural Ltd
Registration no: 05935116 **Date established:** 2006
No.of Employees: 1 - 10 **Product Groups:** 35, 48

M & M Precision Engineering
24-25 Saville Road Industrial Estate Saville Road, Peterborough, PE3 7PR
Tel: 01733-332117 **Fax:** 01733-264424
E-mail: sales@mmpe.co.uk
Website: http://www.mmpe.co.uk
Directors: M. Szebeko (Ptnr)
VAT No.: GB 486 2909 06 **Date established:** 1987
Turnover: £250,000 - £500,000 **No.of Employees:** 1 - 10
Product Groups: 30, 48

Machine Mart Ltd
Lincoln Road, Peterborough, PE1 2PE
Tel: 01733-311770 **Fax:** 01733-893521
Website: http://www.machinemart.co.uk
Managers: M. Pryer (Mgr)
Immediate Holding Company: MACHINE MART LIMITED
Registration no: 01555925 **Date established:** 1981
Turnover: £50m - £75m **No.of Employees:** 1 - 10 **Product Groups:** 40

Date of Accounts	May 11	May 10	May 09
Sales Turnover	67m	64m	56m
Pre Tax Profit/Loss	11m	11m	9m
Working Capital	61m	53m	27m
Fixed Assets	4m	5m	5m
Current Assets	68m	59m	51m
Current Liabilities	3m	3m	21m

Manor Packaging Ltd
200 Station Road Whittlesey, Peterborough, PE7 2HA
Tel: 01733-233884 **Fax:** 01733-233885
E-mail: sale@manorpackaging.co.uk
Website: http://fencorpackaging.co.uk
Directors: T. Clifton (Dir)
Ultimate Holding Company: FENCOR PACKAGING GROUP LIMITED
Immediate Holding Company: MANOR PACKAGING LIMITED
Registration no: 02192064 **Date established:** 1987 **Turnover:** £2m - £5m
No.of Employees: 21 - 50 **Product Groups:** 38, 42

Date of Accounts	Mar 11	Mar 10	Mar 09
Sales Turnover	N/A	4m	N/A
Pre Tax Profit/Loss	N/A	56	N/A
Working Capital	503	1m	957
Fixed Assets	1m	2m	1m
Current Assets	3m	3m	2m
Current Liabilities	N/A	385	N/A

Max Wright Ltd
19 Willow Road Yaxley, Peterborough, PE7 3HT
Tel: 01733-241586 **Fax:** 01733-244519
E-mail: info@maxwright.co.uk
Website: http://www.maxwright.co.uk
Managers: D. Wright (Chief Acct), S. Cromack (Mgr)
Immediate Holding Company: MAX WRIGHT LIMITED
Registration no: 00915896 **Date established:** 1967
Turnover: £250,000 - £500,000 **No.of Employees:** 1 - 10
Product Groups: 37, 67

Date of Accounts	Sep 11	Sep 10	Sep 09
Working Capital	3m	3m	1m
Fixed Assets	2m	2m	4m
Current Assets	3m	4m	2m

Mcintyre Electrical Ltd
6 Phorpres Close Cygnet Park, Hampton, Peterborough, PE7 8FZ
Tel: 01733-898151 **Fax:** 01733-296756
E-mail: enquiries@mcintyre-electrical.co.uk
Website: http://www.mcintyre-electrical.co.uk
Directors: J. Mcintrye (Prop), J. Mcintyre (MD)
Managers: C. Salmon (Tech Serv Mgr), S. Salmon (Personnel)
Immediate Holding Company: MCINTYRE ELECTRICAL LIMITED
Registration no: 05879674 **Date established:** 2006 **Turnover:** £1m - £2m
No.of Employees: 11 - 20 **Product Groups:** 37, 52, 84

Date of Accounts	Mar 12	Mar 11	Mar 10
Working Capital	336	175	301
Fixed Assets	348	391	450
Current Assets	683	540	905

Mr Tyre Ltd
Burton Street, Peterborough, PE1 5HD
Tel: 01733-560484 **Fax:** 01733-342613
E-mail: peterborough@mrtyre.com
Website: http://www.mrtyre.com
Managers: P. Snart (Mgr)
Ultimate Holding Company: M.T. DEVELOPMENTS LIMITED
Immediate Holding Company: MR. TYRE LIMITED
Registration no: 02602575 **Date established:** 1991
Turnover: £250,000 - £500,000 **No.of Employees:** 1 - 10
Product Groups: 29, 68

Date of Accounts	Dec 11	Dec 10	Dec 09
Sales Turnover	42m	40m	41m
Pre Tax Profit/Loss	437	598	409
Working Capital	2m	2m	2m
Fixed Assets	2m	2m	2m
Current Assets	16m	15m	13m
Current Liabilities	3m	2m	2m

Nene Rubber & Plastics Ltd
43 North Street Stanground, Peterborough, PE2 8HR
Tel: 01733-894949 **Fax:** 01733-894950
E-mail: sales@nene-rubber.co.uk
Website: http://www.nene-rubber.co.uk
Directors: B. Jacobs (MD)
Immediate Holding Company: NENE RUBBER & PLASTICS LIMITED
Registration no: 01539730 **VAT No.:** GB 344 3856 44
Date established: 1981 **Turnover:** £250,000 - £500,000
No.of Employees: 1 - 10 **Product Groups:** 29

Date of Accounts	Dec 11	Dec 10	Dec 09
Working Capital	88	75	36
Fixed Assets	56	57	68
Current Assets	157	123	95

Newall UK Ltd
354 Padholme Road East, Peterborough, PE1 5XL
Tel: 01733-265566 **Fax:** 01733-843819
E-mail: sales@newall.com
Website: http://www.newall-uk.com
Directors: M. Hunt (Co Sec), C. Baxter (Sales), H. Chana (MD)
Ultimate Holding Company: DANOBAT S COOP (SPAIN)
Immediate Holding Company: NEWALL UK LIMITED
Registration no: 04714464 **Date established:** 2003 **Turnover:** £2m - £5m
No.of Employees: 21 - 50 **Product Groups:** 46

Date of Accounts	Dec 11	Dec 10	Dec 09
Working Capital	417	431	374
Fixed Assets	91	84	82
Current Assets	1m	2m	1m

Northgate H R Ltd
Thorpe Park, Peterborough, PE3 6JY
Tel: 01733-555777 **Fax:** 01733-312347
E-mail: enquiries@northgatehr.com
Website: http://www.northgatearinso.com
Bank(s): Barclays
Directors: G. Denley (Dir)
Immediate Holding Company: REBUSHR GROUP LTD
Registration no: 01587537 **Turnover:** £50m - £75m
No.of Employees: 251 - 500 **Product Groups:** 44, 80

P G Packaging Ltd
Kingsland Farm 231 March Road, Whittlesey, Peterborough, PE7 2DE
Tel: 01733-840357 **Fax:** 01733-841919
E-mail: jane.grice@pgpackagingltd.com
Website: http://www.agr-automation.com
Directors: P. Grice (Dir)
Immediate Holding Company: P. G. PACKAGING LIMITED
Registration no: 04182598 **Date established:** 2001 **Turnover:** £5m - £10m
No.of Employees: 11 - 20 **Product Groups:** 38, 42

Date of Accounts	Mar 09	Mar 08	Mar 07
Sales Turnover	8m	N/A	N/A
Pre Tax Profit/Loss	-494	499	613
Working Capital	-2m	-1m	-1m
Fixed Assets	4m	4m	3m
Current Assets	4m	3m	3m
Current Liabilities	341	426	1m

Park Air Systems Ltd
Northfields Industrial Estate Market Deeping, Peterborough, PE6 8UE
Tel: 01778-345434 **Fax:** 01778-342877
E-mail: sales@uk.parkairsystems.com
Website: http://www.parkairsystems.com
Bank(s): Barclays
Directors: S. Pilvousk (Fin), C. Houseago (MD), R. Allis (I.T. Dir)
Managers: E. Barnard, J. Draves (Personnel), F. Thompson (Tech Serv Mgr)
Ultimate Holding Company: NORTHROP GRUMMAN CORPORATION (USA)
Immediate Holding Company: PARK AIR SYSTEMS LIMITED
Registration no: 01951792 **VAT No.:** GB 551 0867 49
Date established: 1985 **Turnover:** £20m - £50m
No.of Employees: 101 - 250 **Product Groups:** 36, 37, 39

Date of Accounts	Dec 11	Dec 10	Dec 09
Sales Turnover	33m	35m	30m
Pre Tax Profit/Loss	3m	5m	4m
Working Capital	20m	18m	15m
Fixed Assets	682	460	389
Current Assets	29m	24m	23m
Current Liabilities	8m	6m	7m

Pearl Assurance plc
The Pearl Centre Peterborough Business Park, Lynch Wood, Peterborough, PE2 6FY
Tel: 08458-828121 **Fax:** 01733-475141
E-mail: enquiries@pearl.co.uk
Website: http://www.pearl.co.uk
Managers: A. Rush, D. Wright (Tech Serv Mgr), P. Benters
Immediate Holding Company: PEARL ASSURANCE (UNITFUNDS) LIMITED
Registration no: NF001913 **Date established:** 1972
Turnover: Over £1,000m **No.of Employees:** 1 - 10 **Product Groups:** 82

Date of Accounts	Dec 09	Dec 08	Dec 07
Pre Tax Profit/Loss	198m	-199m	69m
Fixed Assets	13805m	15639m	14164m
Current Assets	911m	734m	438m
Current Liabilities	67m	78m	952m

Perkins Engines Group Ltd
Eastfield, Peterborough, PE1 5NA
Tel: 01733-583000 **Fax:** 01733-582240
E-mail: purdy_claire@perkins.com
Website: http://www.perkins.com
Bank(s): The Royal Bank of Scotland
Directors: G. Henricks (Pres)
Managers: C. Mills (Personnel), D. Critchley (Mgr)
Ultimate Holding Company: CATERPILLAR INC (USA)
Immediate Holding Company: PERKINS GROUP LIMITED
Registration no: 02388892 **Date established:** 1989
Turnover: £500m - £1,000m **No.of Employees:** 1501 & over
Product Groups: 40

Date of Accounts	Dec 11	Dec 10	Dec 09
Pre Tax Profit/Loss	1m	-150	96
Working Capital	10m	5m	3m
Fixed Assets	108m	111m	111m
Current Assets	11m	7m	5m
Current Liabilities	25	88	112

Peterborough Evening Telepgraph
57 Priestgate, Peterborough, PE1 1JW
Tel: 01733-555111 **Fax:** 01733-555188
E-mail: mark.edwards@peterboroughtoday.co.uk
Website: http://www.peterboroughtoday.co.uk
Bank(s): Barclays
Directors: G. Cooper (Fin)
Managers: M. Edwards
Ultimate Holding Company: JOHNSTON PRESS PLC
Immediate Holding Company: EAST MIDLANDS NEWSPAPERS LIMITED
Registration no: 02015543 **Date established:** 1981 **Turnover:** £5m - £10m
No.of Employees: 21 - 50 **Product Groups:** 28

Date of Accounts	Dec 11	Dec 08	Jan 10
Sales Turnover	5m	7m	5m
Working Capital	N/A	100	N/A
Current Assets	N/A	100	N/A

Peterborough Tool Hire
20 Crown Street, Peterborough, PE1 3HY
Tel: 01733-890600 **Fax:** 01733-896111
E-mail: pth@nene-valley.com
Website: http://www.peterboroughtoolhire.com
Directors: K. Pateman (Dir)
No.of Employees: 1 - 10 **Product Groups:** 72, 76, 83

Portakabin Ltd
Papyrus Road, Peterborough, PE4 5ET
Tel: 01733-327444 **Fax:** 01733-327527
E-mail: peterborough.hire@portakabin.com
Website: http://www.portakabin.com
Managers: L. Valentine (Admin Off)
Immediate Holding Company: PORTAKABIN LIMITED
Registration no: 00685303 **Date established:** 1961
No.of Employees: 11 - 20 **Product Groups:** 83

Date of Accounts	Jun 11	Jun 10	Jun 09
Sales Turnover	171m	174m	202m
Pre Tax Profit/Loss	27m	26m	30m
Working Capital	35m	25m	8m
Fixed Assets	104m	103m	113m
Current Assets	79m	76m	67m
Current Liabilities	27m	35m	29m

POS Display Shop
6A Challenger Way Edgerley Drain Road, Peterborough, PE1 5EX
Tel: 01733-892815 **Fax:** 01733-558232
E-mail: info@posdisplayshop.co.uk
Website: http://www.posdisplayshop.co.uk
Product Groups: 49, 67

Potter & Moore Ltd
Lincoln Road, Peterborough, PE4 6ND
Tel: 01733-281000 **Fax:** 01733-281028
E-mail: sales@potterandmoore.com
Website: http://www.potterandmoore.co.uk
Bank(s): Barclays, Worthing
Directors: P. Forster (Fin), T. Clark (Sales & Mktg), B. Glancross (MD), A. Milne (Tech Serv), P. Foster (Fin)
Managers: C. Scott (Buyer), P. Clark, J. Babb (I.T. Exec), C. Scase
Ultimate Holding Company: CREIGHTONS PLC
Immediate Holding Company: POTTER & MOORE INNOVATIONS LIMITED
Registration no: 04645119 **VAT No.:** GB 711 7102 82
Date established: 2003 **Turnover:** £10m - £20m
No.of Employees: 101 - 250 **Product Groups:** 61

Date of Accounts	Mar 11	Mar 10	Mar 09
Sales Turnover	14m	13m	15m
Pre Tax Profit/Loss	210	375	423
Working Capital	1m	1m	768
Fixed Assets	484	531	593
Current Assets	6m	5m	4m
Current Liabilities	425	685	520

Precision Valve UK
Precision House Bakewell Road, Orton Southgate, Peterborough, PE2 6XU
Tel: 01733-238181 **Fax:** 01733-238553
E-mail: jane.butterfield@pvceu.com
Website: http://www.pvceu.com
Directors: R. Kindell (MD)
Managers: P. Helsall (Purch Mgr), J. Butterfield (Accounts), J. Butterfield
Immediate Holding Company: UK ASSOCIATION FOR ACCESSIBLE FORMATS
Registration no: 06748900 **VAT No.:** GB 395 7627 95
Date established: 2008 **Turnover:** £20m - £50m **No.of Employees:** 1 - 10
Product Groups: 30, 35

Date of Accounts	Jun 07	Jun 06
Sales Turnover	23691	22615
Pre Tax Profit/Loss	-108	-538
Working Capital	-825	1556
Fixed Assets	10903	10533
Current Assets	7829	7720
Current Liabilities	8654	6164
Total Share Capital	5220	5220
ROCE% (Return on Capital Employed)	-1.1	-4.5
ROT% (Return on Turnover)	-0.5	-2.4

Promac Precision Engineering Ltd
49 Ivatt Way, Peterborough, PE3 7PN
Tel: 01733-333000 **Fax:** 01733-333001
E-mail: management@promac.fsnet.co.uk
Website: http://www.promac.fsnet.co.uk
Directors: D. Clark (Fin), S. Lambert (MD)
Immediate Holding Company: PROMAC PRECISION ENGINEERING LIMITED
Registration no: 03719369 **VAT No.:** GB 727 7747 90
Date established: 1999 **Turnover:** £250,000 - £500,000
No.of Employees: 1 - 10 **Product Groups:** 48

Date of Accounts	Mar 12	Mar 11	Mar 10
Working Capital	154	165	157
Fixed Assets	13	11	13
Current Assets	212	236	212
Current Liabilities	49	52	43

Reed Recruitment
6a Cathedral Square, Peterborough, PE1 1XH
Tel: 01733-295880 **Fax:** 01733-564219
E-mail: peterborough@reed.co.uk
Website: http://www.reed.co.uk
Managers: S. Franklyn (Mgr)
Ultimate Holding Company: REED PERSONNEL SERVICES P.L.C.
Immediate Holding Company: REED EMPLOYMENT LIMITED
Registration no: 00669854 **Date established:** 1960
Turnover: £75m - £125m **No.of Employees:** 1 - 10 **Product Groups:** 80

Howard Richard Sales Ltd
10 Holkham Road Orton Southgate, Peterborough, PE2 6TE
Tel: 01733-237779 **Fax:** 01733-230027
E-mail: howard.jones@hrsales.co.uk
Website: http://hrsales.co.uk
Directors: D. Jones (MD), H. Jones (MD)
Managers: J. Steere (Mgr)
Immediate Holding Company: HOWARD RICHARD SALES LIMITED
Registration no: 05280722 **VAT No.:** GB 396 3981 91
Date established: 2004 **Turnover:** £1m - £2m **No.of Employees:** 1 - 10
Product Groups: 30, 35

Date of Accounts	Dec 10	Dec 09	Dec 08
Working Capital	133	173	-27
Fixed Assets	34	38	83
Current Assets	450	512	719

Rivercircle Ltd
316 Padholme Road East, Peterborough, PE1 5XL
Tel: 01733-315101 **Fax:** 01733-311595
E-mail: info@rivercircle.co.uk
Website: http://www.rivercircle.co.uk
Bank(s): National Westminster Bank Plc
Directors: J. Theobalds (MD)
Immediate Holding Company: RIVERCIRCLE LIMITED
Registration no: 01751194 **VAT No.:** GB 395 7820 04
Date established: 1983 **Turnover:** £2m - £5m **No.of Employees:** 21 - 50
Product Groups: 29, 38, 46, 48, 67

Date of Accounts	Mar 11	Mar 10	Mar 09
Working Capital	142	-2	5
Fixed Assets	266	321	395
Current Assets	1m	910	806

R A Roan & Son
22-23 Tresham Road Orton Southgate, Peterborough, PE2 6SG
Tel: 01733-238582 **Fax:** 01733-391722
E-mail: ra.roan@tiscali.co.uk
Website: http://www.roanfabricators.co.uk
Directors: R. Roan (Ptnr)
VAT No.: GB 121 2581 13 **Date established:** 1957
No.of Employees: 1 - 10 **Product Groups:** 35, 36, 48

Roe Bros & Co. Ltd
1 Fenlake Business Centre Fengate, Peterborough, PE1 5BQ
Tel: 01733-358821 **Fax:** 01733-555260
E-mail: roegroup@btconnect.com
Website: http://www.theroegroup.com
Bank(s): National Westminster
Directors: H. Whitham (MD)
Managers: C. Moorley (Sales Prom Mgr), T. Herbert (Tech Serv Mgr)
Immediate Holding Company: ROE BROS & CO (HOLDINGS) LIMITED
Registration no: 05160933 **Date established:** 2004
Turnover: £20m - £50m **No.of Employees:** 11 - 20 **Product Groups:** 34

Russell Fire Ltd
25-26 Second Drove Industrial Estate, Peterborough, PE1 5XA
Tel: 01733-310469 **Fax:** 01733-897510
E-mail: sales@russellfire.co.uk
Website: http://www.russellfire.co.uk
Directors: P. Topley (Dir)
Immediate Holding Company: CHURCHES FIRE SECURITY LTD
Registration no: 01815919 **Date established:** 1981 **Turnover:** £1m - £2m
No.of Employees: 1 - 10 **Product Groups:** 32, 33, 38, 39, 40, 52, 67, 68, 84

Date of Accounts	Jun 08	Jun 07	Jun 06
Working Capital	83	48	56
Fixed Assets	38	42	54
Current Assets	216	207	211
Current Liabilities	133	159	155
Total Share Capital	1	1	1

S J S Plastering & Partitioning Ltd
22 Second Drove, Peterborough, PE1 5XA
Tel: 01733-313588 **Fax:** 01733-313475
E-mail: steve.siggee@sjsplastering.co.uk
Website: http://www.sjsplastering.co.uk
Directors: S. Siggee (MD), S. Siggee (Grp Chief Exec)
Immediate Holding Company: S.J.S. PLASTERING AND PARTITIONING LIMITED
Registration no: 03720067 **VAT No.:** 551 0749 55 **Date established:** 1999
No.of Employees: 1 - 10 **Product Groups:** 52

Date of Accounts	Sep 08	Mar 07	Mar 06
Working Capital	610	724	348
Fixed Assets	54	132	175
Current Assets	887	984	580
Current Liabilities	277	259	232

S M W Autoblok
8 The Metro Centre, Peterborough, PE2 7UH
Tel: 01733-394394 **Fax:** 01733-394395
E-mail: sales@smwautoblok.co.uk
Website: http://www.smwautoblok.co.uk
Managers: O. Demsey (Mgr)
Immediate Holding Company: SMW-AUTOBLOK WORKHOLDING LIMITED
Registration no: 02477956 **Date established:** 1990
Turnover: £500,000 - £1m **No.of Employees:** 1 - 10 **Product Groups:** 46

Date of Accounts	Dec 11	Dec 10	Dec 09
Working Capital	567	525	515
Fixed Assets	64	70	76
Current Assets	884	762	634

S R Electromatics
511 Fulbridge Road, Peterborough, PE4 6SB
Tel: 01733-571958 **Fax:** 01733-330422
Directors: R. Lucas (Ptnr)
Date established: 1975 **Turnover:** £250,000 - £500,000
No.of Employees: 1 - 10 **Product Groups:** 48, 67

Samuk Lift Trucks
Vicarage Farm Road, Peterborough, PE1 5TP
Tel: 01733-567000 **Fax:** 01733- 310880
E-mail: enquiries@samuktrucks.co.uk
Website: http://www.samuktrucks.co.uk
Directors: N. Martin (MD)
Managers: S. Castle (Comptroller), C. Garth (Mgr)
Immediate Holding Company: SAMUK LIFT TRUCKS LIMITED
Registration no: 03042793 **Date established:** 1995
No.of Employees: 11 - 20 **Product Groups:** 35, 39, 45

Date of Accounts	Jun 11	Jun 10	Apr 09
Working Capital	-293	201	656
Fixed Assets	634	674	708
Current Assets	2m	3m	3m

Sav Fasulo Services Ltd
C3 Roundhouse Close Fengate, Peterborough, PE1 5TA
Tel: 01733-313132 **Fax:** 01733-553380
Directors: A. Fasulo (Fin), S. Fasulo (MD)
Immediate Holding Company: SAV FASULO SERVICES LIMITED
Registration no: 04051525 **Date established:** 2000
No.of Employees: 1 - 10 **Product Groups:** 35, 39, 45

Date of Accounts	Mar 11	Mar 10	Mar 09
Working Capital	127	186	262
Fixed Assets	309	230	77
Current Assets	170	252	322

Sceptre Promotions Ltd
97 Elton Road Stibbington, Peterborough, PE8 6JX
Tel: 01780-782093 **Fax:** 01780-783159
E-mail: grant@sceptre-promotions.freeserve.co.uk
Website: http://www.keyboard-cavalcade.co.uk
Directors: G. Neil (Dir)
Immediate Holding Company: SCEPTRE PROMOTIONS LIMITED
Registration no: 07033841 **Date established:** 2009
Turnover: £500,000 - £1m **No.of Employees:** 1 - 10 **Product Groups:** 28

Date of Accounts	Oct 11	Oct 10
Working Capital	31	-85
Fixed Assets	241	272
Current Assets	448	343

A B Schmidt UK Ltd
Southgate Way Orton Southgate, Peterborough, PE2 6GP
Tel: 01733-363300 **Fax:** 01733-363333
E-mail: henk.landeweerd@aebi-schmidt.co.uk
Website: http://www.schmidt.co.uk
Directors: H. Landeweerd (MD), P. Squires (Fin), H. Landeweerd (MD)
Ultimate Holding Company: AEBI SCHMIDT HOLDING AG (SWITZERLAND)
Immediate Holding Company: AEBI SCHMIDT UK LIMITED
Registration no: 00557725 **Date established:** 1955
Turnover: £20m - £50m **No.of Employees:** 51 - 100 **Product Groups:** 39, 45

Date of Accounts	Dec 11	Dec 10	Dec 09
Sales Turnover	29m	23m	31m
Pre Tax Profit/Loss	2m	-1m	744
Working Capital	3m	1m	3m
Fixed Assets	235	765	37
Current Assets	8m	8m	7m
Current Liabilities	2m	2m	2m

Sewaco Ltd
87 Eastgate Deeping St James, Peterborough, PE6 8HH
Tel: 01778-342202 **Fax:** 01778-346633
E-mail: admin@sewaco.co.uk
Website: http://www.sewaco.co.uk
Directors: J. Cox (MD)
Immediate Holding Company: SEWACO LIMITED
Registration no: 01140008 **VAT No.:** GB 330 2968 69
Date established: 1973 **Turnover:** £1m - £2m **No.of Employees:** 1 - 10
Product Groups: 42, 54

Date of Accounts	Jul 12	Jul 11	Jul 10
Working Capital	370	581	608
Fixed Assets	176	166	128
Current Assets	464	672	694

Shades Of Light
16 Broad Street Whittlesey, Peterborough, PE7 1HA
Tel: 01733-208466
Directors: J. Metcalfe (Prop)
No.of Employees: 1 - 10 **Product Groups:** 37, 67

Shanks Waste Management Ltd
Welland Road Dogsthorpe, Peterborough, PE1 3TD
Tel: 01733-310925 **Fax:** 01733-898061
Managers: I. Yorke (Mgr)
Ultimate Holding Company: SHANKS GROUP PLC
Immediate Holding Company: SHANKS WASTE MANAGEMENT LIMITED
Registration no: 02393309 **Date established:** 1989
No.of Employees: 11 - 20 **Product Groups:** 45, 54

Date of Accounts	Mar 11	Mar 10	Mar 09
Sales Turnover	153m	136m	136m
Pre Tax Profit/Loss	-18m	-954	-4m
Working Capital	-16m	16m	-1m
Fixed Assets	59m	61m	64m
Current Assets	67m	75m	48m
Current Liabilities	23m	21m	11m

Smith Brothers Stores Ltd
Empson Road, Peterborough, PE1 5UP
Tel: 01733-311711 **Fax:** 01733-345293
E-mail: david@airplants.co.uk
Website: http://www.sbs-1897.co.uk
Managers: B. Rumbelow (Mgr)
Ultimate Holding Company: SMITH BROTHERS (LEICESTER) LIMITED
Immediate Holding Company: APEX TUBE & VALVES LIMITED.
Registration no: 01915255 **Date established:** 1985 **Turnover:** £1m - £2m
No.of Employees: 1 - 10 **Product Groups:** 30, 66

Date of Accounts	Sep 11	Sep 10	Sep 09
Working Capital	1	1	1
Current Assets	1	1	1

Frederick F Smith Builders Ltd
7 The Stirling Centre Stirling Way Northfields Industrial Estate, Market Deeping, Peterborough, PE6 8EQ
Tel: 01778-342728 **Fax:** 01778-342720
E-mail: info@fredericksmithbuilders.co.uk
Website: http://www.fredericksmithbuilders.co.uk
Directors: I. Smith (Co Sec)
Immediate Holding Company: FREDERICK F.SMITH(BUILDERS)LIMITED
Registration no: 01066614 **Date established:** 1972
Turnover: £500,000 - £1m **No.of Employees:** 1 - 10 **Product Groups:** 52

see next page

Frederick F Smith Builders Ltd - *Cont'd*

Date of Accounts	Jul 11	Jul 10	Jul 09
Working Capital	256	211	191
Fixed Assets	418	420	425
Current Assets	792	652	612

Smiths Gore

Stuart House City Road, Peterborough, PE1 1QF
Tel: 01733-567231 **Fax:** 01733-568527
E-mail: shelley.cash@smithsgore.co.uk
Website: http://www.smithsgore.co.uk
Directors: K. Strong (Fin)
Managers: T. Deo (Personnel), S. Cash, A. Good, M. Markham-gebbie (Sales Admin)
Immediate Holding Company: SMITHS GORE LIMITED
Registration no: 02231331 **Date established:** 1988
Turnover: £500,000 - £1m **No.of Employees:** 51 - 100
Product Groups: 80

Solaglas Ltd

183 Fengate, Peterborough, PE1 5BZ
Tel: 01733-297800
E-mail: wayne.arthur@saint-gobain.com
Website: http://www.saint-gobain.com
Managers: D. Clarke, W. Arthur (Mgr)
Ultimate Holding Company: COMPAGNIE DE SAINT GOBAIN (FRANCE)
Immediate Holding Company: GLASSOLUTIONS SAINT-GOBAIN LIMITED
Registration no: 02442570 **Date established:** 1989
Turnover: £125m - £250m **No.of Employees:** 51 - 100
Product Groups: 17, 36, 66

Date of Accounts	Dec 11	Dec 10	Dec 09
Sales Turnover	116m	93m	97m
Pre Tax Profit/Loss	6m	-10m	-16m
Working Capital	-36m	-28m	-18m
Fixed Assets	23m	21m	15m
Current Assets	34m	33m	25m
Current Liabilities	64m	52m	15m

Spyder Cars Ltd

Fenland District Industrial Estate Station Road, Whittlesey, Peterborough, PE7 2EY
Tel: 01733-203986 **Fax:** 01733-350662
E-mail: sales@spydercars.co.uk
Website: http://www.spydercars.co.uk
Directors: S. Reeve (MD), C. Price (Fin)
Immediate Holding Company: SPECIALIST CARS ENGINEERING LIMITED
Registration no: 01296354 **VAT No.:** GB 293 9978 76
Date established: 1977 **Turnover:** Up to £250,000
No.of Employees: 1 - 10 **Product Groups:** 84

Date of Accounts	Jan 10	Jan 09	Jan 08
Working Capital	-345	-276	-206
Fixed Assets	298	303	307
Current Assets	33	106	130

Steinel UK Ltd

25 Manasty Road Orton Southgate, Peterborough, PE2 6UP
Tel: 01733-366700 **Fax:** 01733-366701
E-mail: steinel@steinel.co.uk
Website: http://www.steinel.de/en
Bank(s): HSBC
Directors: P. Lawrence (MD)
Ultimate Holding Company: STEINEL VERTRIEB GmbH & CO KG
Immediate Holding Company: STEINEL U.K. LIMITED
Registration no: 01643417 **VAT No.:** GB 514 0039 96
Date established: 1982 **Turnover:** £1m - £2m **No.of Employees:** 11 - 20
Product Groups: 37

Date of Accounts	Jun 12	Jun 11	Jun 10
Working Capital	453	455	254
Fixed Assets	211	194	164
Current Assets	1m	1m	876

Sterling Bolt & Nut Co. Ltd

25 Royce Road, Peterborough, PE1 5YB
Tel: 01733-563022 **Fax:** 01733-552115
E-mail: sales@sterlingbolt.co.uk
Website: http://www.sterlingbolt.co.uk
Directors: D. Samuel (MD)
Managers: R. Triggol
Immediate Holding Company: STERLING, BOLT AND NUT COMPANY LIMITED
Registration no: 02481273 **VAT No.:** GB 550 8286 35
Date established: 1990 **Turnover:** £500,000 - £1m
No.of Employees: 1 - 10 **Product Groups:** 22, 35, 66

Date of Accounts	Jul 11	Jul 10	Jul 09
Working Capital	168	213	216
Fixed Assets	33	18	24
Current Assets	333	254	284

Sunline Blinds

1200 Lincoln Road, Peterborough, PE4 6LA
Tel: 01733-320822 **Fax:** 01733-578732
E-mail: sales@sunlineblinds.co.uk
Website: http://www.sunlineblinds.co.uk
Directors: T. Mescall (MD), S. Mescall (Fin)
Immediate Holding Company: SUNLINE BLINDS LIMITED
Registration no: 03917930 **Date established:** 2000
Turnover: £250,000 - £500,000 **No.of Employees:** 1 - 10
Product Groups: 24, 27

T2 Studios Ltd

New Media House 79a Broadway, Peterborough, PE1 4DA
Tel: 01733-313166 **Fax:** 01733-310007
E-mail: mail@t2studios.net
Website: http://www.t2studios.net
Directors: J. Hill (Tech Serv)
Immediate Holding Company: T2 STUDIOS LIMITED
Registration no: 03546793 **Date established:** 1998
No.of Employees: 1 - 10 **Product Groups:** 28

Date of Accounts	Nov 11	Nov 10	Nov 09
Working Capital	163	87	64
Fixed Assets	1	1	7
Current Assets	350	204	180

Techno-trim (a division of Green-Tech International Ltd)

Unit 3 Fengate Trade Park Fengate, Peterborough, PE1 5XA
Tel: 01733-588 388 **Fax:** 01733-588 388
E-mail: info@technotrim.com
Website: http://www.technotrim.com
Turnover: £1m - £2m **No.of Employees:** 21 - 50 **Product Groups:** 30, 32, 44

The New Covent Garden Soup Co.

New Covent Gardens Westwood, Peterborough, PE3 9UP
Tel: 01733-843400 **Fax:** 01733-843400
E-mail: info@newcoventgardenfood.com
Website: http://www.newcoventgardenfood.com
Managers: S. Farrow
Immediate Holding Company: DANIELS P.L.C.
Registration no: 01950388 **Date established:** 1988
Turnover: £50m - £75m **No.of Employees:** 101 - 250 **Product Groups:** 20

Tom Barron Isa Ltd

Green Road Eye, Peterborough, PE6 7YP
Tel: 01733-222262 **Fax:** 01733-223345
E-mail: josie.arman@isapoultry.com
Directors: M. Delaney (Co Sec), N. Leeming (MD)
Ultimate Holding Company: TOM BARRON LIMITED
Immediate Holding Company: TOM BARRON INDEPENDENT HATCHERIES LIMITED
Registration no: 05108995 **Date established:** 2004 **Turnover:** £5m - £10m
No.of Employees: 1 - 10 **Product Groups:** 01

Date of Accounts	Jun 11	Jun 10	Jun 09
Working Capital	229	159	25
Fixed Assets	348	417	389
Current Assets	2m	2m	2m
Current Liabilities	400	150	167

Top Deal Spares

12 Peterborough Road Castor, Peterborough, PE5 7AX
Tel: 01733-380288 **Fax:** 01733-380164
E-mail: enquiries@topdealspares.co.uk
Website: http://www.topdealspares.co.uk
Directors: G. Meadows (Prop)
Turnover: Up to £250,000 **No.of Employees:** 1 - 10 **Product Groups:** 48

UK Refrigeration & Air Conditioning Ltd

32 Mere View Industrial Estate Yaxley, Peterborough, PE7 3HS
Tel: 01733-240369
E-mail: sales@uk-refrigeration.com
Website: http://www.uk-refrigeration.com
Directors: A. Steadman (Dir)
Immediate Holding Company: UK REFRIGERATION & AIR CONDITIONING LTD.
Registration no: 04188583 **Date established:** 2001
No.of Employees: 1 - 10 **Product Groups:** 40, 66

Date of Accounts	Mar 12	Mar 11	Mar 10
Working Capital	160	164	145
Fixed Assets	14	17	20
Current Assets	210	238	195

United Welding Supplies Ltd

45 Ivatt Way, Peterborough, PE3 7PN
Tel: 01733-261361 **Fax:** 01733-261300
E-mail: sales@unitedwelding.co.uk
Website: http://www.unitedwelding.co.uk
Directors: C. Allen (MD)
Immediate Holding Company: UNITED WELDING SUPPLIES LIMITED
Registration no: 02390879 **Date established:** 1989
Turnover: £500,000 - £1m **No.of Employees:** 1 - 10 **Product Groups:** 36, 38, 40

Date of Accounts	Mar 12	Mar 11	Mar 10
Working Capital	427	438	444
Fixed Assets	188	170	190
Current Assets	2m	1m	1m

Van Der Graaf UK Ltd

23 The Metro Centre, Peterborough, PE2 7UH
Tel: 01733-391777 **Fax:** 01733-391044
E-mail: sales@vandergraaf.co.uk
Website: http://www.drummotor.com
Directors: P. Bentley (MD), K. Bentley (Fin)
Immediate Holding Company: VAN DER GRAAF (U.K.) LIMITED
Registration no: 01376126 **Date established:** 1978
Turnover: £250,000 - £500,000 **No.of Employees:** 1 - 10
Product Groups: 37, 45, 48, 66, 67

Date of Accounts	Dec 11	Dec 10	Dec 09
Working Capital	-339	-303	-301
Fixed Assets	146	142	156
Current Assets	251	293	151

Westlake Tractors

West Lake Lodge Thorney Road, Peakirk, Peterborough, PE6 7NT
Tel: 01733-252185 **Fax:** 01733-252185
Directors: M. Weston (Prop)
Date established: 1971 **No.of Employees:** 1 - 10 **Product Groups:** 41

Wilcox Commercial Vehicles Ltd

Blenheim Way Market Deeping, Peterborough, PE6 8LD
Tel: 01778-345151 **Fax:** 01778-347269
E-mail: cbartlett@tippers.co.uk
Website: http://www.wilcox.uk.com
Bank(s): Barclays, Bradford
Directors: C. Bartlett (Dir), V. Ronzano (MD)
Managers: A. Welbourn
Immediate Holding Company: WILCOX COMMERCIAL VEHICLES LIMITED
Registration no: 04106720 **Date established:** 2000
Turnover: £10m - £20m **No.of Employees:** 51 - 100 **Product Groups:** 39

Date of Accounts	Nov 11	Nov 10	Nov 09
Sales Turnover	11m	10m	7m
Pre Tax Profit/Loss	242	46	-74
Working Capital	761	762	846
Fixed Assets	1m	1m	1m
Current Assets	3m	2m	2m
Current Liabilities	469	361	272

Williams Distributors

108-110 Burghley Road, Peterborough, PE1 2QE
Tel: 01733-564252 **Fax:** 01733-555275
Managers: J. Pallet (Mgr)
Date established: 1993 **No.of Employees:** 1 - 10 **Product Groups:** 37

Windsor Engineering Ltd

16 Holkham Road Orton Southgate, Peterborough, PE2 6TE
Tel: 01733-239292 **Fax:** 01733-239233
E-mail: info@windsorkomatsu.co.uk
Website: http://www.windsormaterialshandling.co.uk
Managers: M. Collin (Serv Mgr)
Immediate Holding Company: WINDSOR ENGINEERING (HULL) LIMITED
Registration no: 02371193 **Date established:** 1989
Turnover: £10m - £20m **No.of Employees:** 1 - 10 **Product Groups:** 35, 39, 45

Date of Accounts	Jul 11	Jul 10	Jul 09
Sales Turnover	10m	9m	9m
Pre Tax Profit/Loss	-44	388	420
Working Capital	-2m	-1m	-2m
Fixed Assets	7m	7m	8m
Current Assets	3m	2m	3m
Current Liabilities	366	506	361

St Ives

Acushnet Europe Ltd (Titleist & Foot-Joy Worldwide)

Caxton Road, St Ives, PE27 3LU
Tel: 01480-301114 **Fax:** 01480-492108
E-mail: ukoffice@acushnetgolf.com
Website: http://www.titleist.co.uk
Bank(s): Barclays
Directors: R. Newbery (Fin), K. Graham (Sales), H. Burling (Pers)
Managers: R. Laws (Mktg Serv Mgr), C. Collinson (Tech Serv Mgr), S. Bailey (Purch Mgr), J. Tomlinson
Ultimate Holding Company: FORTUNE BRANDS INC (USA)
Immediate Holding Company: ACUSHNET EUROPE LTD
Registration no: 01198336 **VAT No.:** GB 214 8123 91
Date established: 1975 **Turnover:** £75m - £125m
No.of Employees: 251 - 500 **Product Groups:** 22, 24, 29, 49

Date of Accounts	Dec 11	Dec 10	Dec 09
Sales Turnover	127m	85m	90m
Pre Tax Profit/Loss	12m	9m	23m
Working Capital	36m	38m	31m
Fixed Assets	8m	20m	19m
Current Assets	53m	47m	39m
Current Liabilities	6m	3m	3m

Akzo Nobel Woodcare Ltd

Meadow Lane, St Ives, PE27 4UY
Tel: 01480-496868 **Fax:** 01480-496801
E-mail: woodcare@sis.akzonobel.com
Website: http://www.akzonobel.co.uk
Bank(s): Barclays, London
Directors: A. Tarry (MD)
Managers: L. Thackray (Mktg Serv Mgr)
Ultimate Holding Company: Akzo Nobel N.V.
Immediate Holding Company: WEST ANGLIA CROSSROADS CARING FOR CARERS
Registration no: 00834700 **VAT No.:** GB 213 8725 69
Date established: 2002 **Turnover:** £10m - £20m
No.of Employees: 21 - 50 **Product Groups:** 32

Anglia C N C Engineering Ltd

Unit 4 Anglia Works Burrel Road, St Ives, PE27 3LB
Tel: 01480-464624 **Fax:** 01480-494041
E-mail: sales@ace-eng.co.uk
Website: http://www.ace-eng.co.uk
Bank(s): HSBC
Directors: A. Shaw (Fin)
Ultimate Holding Company: FENNSHAW ENGINEERING LIMITED
Immediate Holding Company: ANGLIA CNC ENGINEERING LTD
Registration no: 01124430 **VAT No.:** GB 486 2118 37
Date established: 1973 **Turnover:** £2m - £5m **No.of Employees:** 21 - 50
Product Groups: 37

Date of Accounts	Dec 11	Dec 10	Dec 09
Working Capital	2m	2m	2m
Fixed Assets	362	434	406
Current Assets	3m	2m	3m

B T M UK Automation Products

Unit 6 Stephenson Road, St Ives, PE27 3WJ
Tel: 01480-497498 **Fax:** 01480-497479
E-mail: btmautomation@btconnect.com
Website: http://www.btmcorp.com
Directors: J. Robinson (MD), M. Fermin (MD)
Managers: M. Firmin (Sales Prom Mgr)
Immediate Holding Company: BTM (UK) AUTOMATION PRODUCTS LIMITED
Registration no: 03640790 **Date established:** 1998
Turnover: £250,000 - £500,000 **No.of Employees:** 1 - 10
Product Groups: 36, 40, 45, 46, 48, 84

Date of Accounts	Oct 07
Sales Turnover	335
Pre Tax Profit/Loss	22
Working Capital	4
Fixed Assets	10
Current Assets	196
Current Liabilities	192
Total Share Capital	20
ROCE% (Return on Capital Employed)	159.3

Beamglow Ltd

Somersham Road, St Ives, PE27 3LP
Tel: 01480-465012 **Fax:** 01480-494826
E-mail: moirag@beamglow.co.uk
Website: http://www.beamglow.co.uk
Bank(s): HSBC
Directors: H. Roberts (Sales), W. Bellchamber (I.T. Dir), A. Brown (Fin), M. Griffin (MD)
Managers: C. Barnet (Personnel)
Immediate Holding Company: BEAMGLOW LIMITED
Registration no: 00889202 **VAT No.:** GB 755 4103 43
Date established: 1966 **Turnover:** £10m - £20m
No.of Employees: 101 - 250 **Product Groups:** 27

Date of Accounts	Apr 11	Apr 10	Apr 09
Sales Turnover	16m	14m	11m
Pre Tax Profit/Loss	202	242	206

Working Capital	2m	2m	2m
Fixed Assets	5m	3m	3m
Current Assets	6m	6m	5m
Current Liabilities	1m	2m	2m

Boxes & Packaging Ltd

Edison Road, St Ives, PE27 3LF
Tel: 01480-467633 **Fax:** 01480-309100
E-mail: cambridge@boxesandpackaging.co.uk
Website: http://www.boxesandpackaging.co.uk
Bank(s): Barclays
Directors: G. Troup (MD), M. Stephenson (Fin)
Managers: S. Gale (Tech Serv Mgr), S. King (Sales Off Mgr)
Ultimate Holding Company: BOXES AND PACKAGING (UK) LIMITED
Immediate Holding Company: BOXES AND PACKAGING LIMITED
Registration no: 05291434 **VAT No.:** GB 765 4155 24
Date established: 2004 **No.of Employees:** 21 - 50 **Product Groups:** 27

Cambridge Numerical Control

8-9 Royce Court Burrel Road, St Ives, PE27 3NE
Tel: 01480-468639 **Fax:** 01480-301577
E-mail: sales@cnc.uk.com
Website: http://www.cnc.uk.com
Directors: T. Collett (Ptnr)
Date established: 1981 **Turnover:** £250,000 - £500,000
No.of Employees: 1 - 10 **Product Groups:** 44

Carnhill Transformers Ltd

4 Edison Road, St Ives, PE27 3LT
Tel: 01480-462978 **Fax:** 01480-496196
E-mail: sales@carnhill.co.uk
Website: http://www.carnhill.co.uk
Bank(s): National Westminster, Cheapside, London EC4
Managers: M. Hall
Immediate Holding Company: CARNHILL TRANSFORMERS LIMITED
Registration no: 01881904 **VAT No.:** GB 410 8312 96
Date established: 1985 **Turnover:** £2m - £5m **No.of Employees:** 21 - 50
Product Groups: 37

Date of Accounts	Dec 11	Dec 10	Dec 09
Working Capital	1m	962	797
Fixed Assets	263	286	258
Current Assets	2m	1m	1m

Cle Print Ltd

Burrel Road, St Ives, PE27 3LA
Tel: 01480-465233 **Fax:** 01480-466053
E-mail: jwardley@cle.co.uk
Website: http://www.cle.co.uk
Directors: J. Souter (MD), M. Leach (Fin), D. Campion (Fab), C. Naughten (Jt MD), J. Wardley (Jt MD), J. Wardley (MD), A. Wardley (Co Sec), J. Kirk (Sales)
Managers: R. White (I.T. Exec)
Immediate Holding Company: MIMEO LIMITED
Registration no: 04122898 **Date established:** 2000 **Turnover:** £5m - £10m
No.of Employees: 51 - 100 **Product Groups:** 28, 44, 81

Date of Accounts	Dec 07	Dec 06	Dec 05
Working Capital	-50	20	-2
Fixed Assets	665	464	425
Current Assets	646	533	466
Current Liabilities	696	513	468
Total Share Capital	2	1	1

Dansac Ltd

James Hall St Ives Business Park, St Ives, PE27 4AA
Tel: 0800-581117 **Fax:** 01480-484340
E-mail: dansac.ltd@dansac.com
Website: http://www.dansac.co.uk
Bank(s): National Westminster Bank Plc
Managers: P. Newman (Mgr)
Ultimate Holding Company: JOHN DICKINSON SCHNEIDER INC (USA)
Immediate Holding Company: DANSAC LIMITED
Registration no: 01323831 **Date established:** 1977
Turnover: £20m - £50m **No.of Employees:** 11 - 20 **Product Groups:** 30

Date of Accounts	Dec 11	Dec 10	Dec 09
Sales Turnover	33m	31m	29m
Pre Tax Profit/Loss	1m	706	629
Working Capital	4m	3m	4m
Fixed Assets	130	210	246
Current Assets	8m	8m	7m
Current Liabilities	2m	2m	2m

David Smith St Ives Ltd (Gan-Nail Systems Ltd)

Marley Road, St Ives, PE27 3EX
Tel: 01480-309900 **Fax:** 01480-494832
E-mail: info@davidsmith.co.uk
Website: http://www.davidsmith.co.uk
Bank(s): HSBC Bank plc
Directors: M. Smith (MD)
Ultimate Holding Company: FLOCKLYNN LIMITED
Immediate Holding Company: DAVID SMITH,ST.IVES,LIMITED
Registration no: 00914878 **VAT No.:** GB 213 9254 77
Date established: 1967 **Turnover:** £10m - £20m
No.of Employees: 101 - 250 **Product Groups:** 25, 33

Date of Accounts	Dec 11	Dec 10	Dec 09
Sales Turnover	10m	9m	9m
Pre Tax Profit/Loss	124	-388	155
Working Capital	2m	2m	2m
Fixed Assets	871	944	1m
Current Assets	3m	3m	3m
Current Liabilities	469	354	450

Direct Communications Ltd

50-52 Edison Road, St Ives, PE27 3LH
Tel: 01480-466300 **Fax:** 01480-461044
E-mail: sales@directcoms.co.uk
Website: http://www.directcoms.co.uk
Bank(s): Barclays
Directors: P. Bailey (MD), S. Luscombe (Sales)
Immediate Holding Company: DIRECT COMMUNICATIONS RADIO SERVICES LIMITED
Registration no: 02102081 **VAT No.:** GB 213 6515 90
Date established: 1987 **Turnover:** £2m - £5m **No.of Employees:** 51 - 100
Product Groups: 37, 40, 67

Date of Accounts	Jul 11	Jul 10	Jul 09
Working Capital	486	420	267
Fixed Assets	314	371	439
Current Assets	1m	1m	945

Duckworth & Kent Precison Ltd

10 Edison Road, St Ives, PE27 3LF
Tel: 01480-467468 **Fax:** 01480-467357
E-mail: enquiries@dkpc.co.uk
Website: http://www.dkpc.co.uk
Managers: J. Bottazzi (Mgr)
Immediate Holding Company: DUCKWORTH AND KENT (PRECISION COMPONENTS) LIMITED
Registration no: 01209194 **Date established:** 1975
No.of Employees: 1 - 10 **Product Groups:** 35, 46, 47, 48, 67, 68, 85

Date of Accounts	Jan 11	Jan 10	Jan 09
Working Capital	193	245	287
Fixed Assets	149	169	205
Current Assets	248	317	401

Gray PCB Designs

62 Warren Road, St Ives, PE27 5NW
Tel: 01480-496235 **Fax:** 01480-496235
E-mail: graham@gray-pcb-designs.demon.co.uk
Website: http://www.graypcb.co.uk
Directors: G. Hudson (MD), G. Hudson (Prop)
Turnover: Up to £250,000 **No.of Employees:** 1 - 10 **Product Groups:** 37, 38, 44, 84

L H Jones & Son Ltd

Low Road, St Ives, PE27 5ET
Tel: 01480-494040 **Fax:** 01480-495280
E-mail: info@jonesboatyard.co.uk
Website: http://www.jonesboatyard.co.uk
Directors: S. Jones (Co Sec), M. Jones (MD)
Immediate Holding Company: L.H.JONES & SON (BOATBUILDERS) LIMITED
Registration no: 00996198 **VAT No.:** GB 213 4432 07
Date established: 1970 **Turnover:** £500,000 - £1m
No.of Employees: 1 - 10 **Product Groups:** 39, 74, 80

Date of Accounts	Dec 11	Dec 10	Dec 09
Working Capital	61	21	76
Fixed Assets	64	58	54
Current Assets	215	170	287

Knurr UK Ltd

Burrel Road, St Ives, PE27 3LE
Tel: 01480-496125 **Fax:** 01480-496373
E-mail: david.mcgee@knuerr.com
Website: http://www.knurr.com
Bank(s): Lloyds TSB Bank plc
Directors: D. Mcgee (MD), D. McGee (Dir), N. Heron (Fin), N. Herron (Co Sec)
Managers: A. Mills, A. Mills (), P. Anderson (Buyer), N. Ramsbottom ()
Ultimate Holding Company: EMERSON ELECTRIC CO INC (USA)
Immediate Holding Company: KNURR LTD.
Registration no: 02078922 **VAT No.:** GB 576 5070 23
Date established: 1986 **Turnover:** £5m - £10m
No.of Employees: 51 - 100 **Product Groups:** 22, 26, 30, 35, 36

Date of Accounts	Sep 11	Sep 10	Sep 09
Sales Turnover	6m	8m	7m
Pre Tax Profit/Loss	677	1m	491
Working Capital	4m	3m	2m
Fixed Assets	165	192	223
Current Assets	5m	5m	3m
Current Liabilities	334	512	346

Laser S O S Ltd

3 Burrel Road, St Ives, PE27 3LE
Tel: 01480-460990 **Fax:** 01480-469978
E-mail: toni@lasersos.com
Website: http://www.lasersos.com
Directors: A. Koszykowski (Sales)
Immediate Holding Company: LASER S.O.S. LIMITED
Registration no: 01849306 **VAT No.:** GB 395 9615 92
Date established: 1984 **Turnover:** £2m - £5m **No.of Employees:** 1 - 10
Product Groups: 28, 37, 38, 44, 46, 48, 83, 84

Date of Accounts	Oct 11	Oct 10	Oct 09
Working Capital	1m	1m	1m
Fixed Assets	382	384	430
Current Assets	2m	2m	2m

Linx Printing Technologies plc

Burrel Road, St Ives, PE27 3LA
Tel: 01480-302100 **Fax:** 01480-302116
E-mail: sales@linx.co.uk
Website: http://www.linx.co.uk
Bank(s): HSBC
Directors: T. Stafford (Fin), N. Bennett (Eng Serv), M. Verheyden (MD), C. Davis (Dir), B. Cattmull (Fab), M. Moore (Ch)
Managers: R. Wood
Ultimate Holding Company: DANAHER CORPORATION (DELAWARE U.S.A)
Immediate Holding Company: LINX PRINTING TECHNOLOGIES LIMITED
Registration no: 02066629 **Date established:** 1986
Turnover: £50m - £75m **No.of Employees:** 251 - 500
Product Groups: 37, 42, 44, 46

Date of Accounts	Dec 10	Dec 09	Dec 08
Sales Turnover	59m	51m	53m
Pre Tax Profit/Loss	17m	15m	27m
Working Capital	19m	23m	81m
Fixed Assets	4m	2m	4m
Current Assets	29m	31m	88m
Current Liabilities	2m	2m	1m

Pcme

Clearview Building Edison Road, St Ives, PE27 3GH
Tel: 01480-468200 **Fax:** 01480-463400
E-mail: sales@pcme.com
Website: http://www.pcme.co.uk
Bank(s): Lloyds
Directors: W. Averdieck (MD)
Immediate Holding Company: PCME LIMITED
Registration no: 02514486 **Date established:** 1990
No.of Employees: 21 - 50 **Product Groups:** 38, 40, 52

Date of Accounts	Mar 12	Mar 11	Mar 10
Working Capital	2m	2m	1m
Fixed Assets	208	162	67
Current Assets	3m	3m	2m

Prism Electronics Ltd

Burrel Road, St Ives, PE27 3NF
Tel: 01480-462225 **Fax:** 01480-494047
E-mail: info@prism-electronics.com
Website: http://www.prism-electronics.com
Bank(s): Barclays
Directors: D. Aspinall (MD), R. Walton (Dir)
Managers: D. Dickin (Develop Mgr), R. Vyse (Chief Acct), C. George (Personnel)
Immediate Holding Company: PRISM ELECTRONICS LIMITED
Registration no: 02562215 **VAT No.:** GB 551 0301 02
Date established: 1990 **Turnover:** £2m - £5m **No.of Employees:** 21 - 50
Product Groups: 37, 38, 48, 85

Date of Accounts	Sep 11	Sep 10	Sep 09
Working Capital	932	889	817
Fixed Assets	172	144	162
Current Assets	1m	1m	1m

Slepe Hall Hotel

Ramsey Road, St Ives, PE27 5RB
Tel: 01480-463122 **Fax:** 01480-300706
E-mail: reception@slepehallhotel.co.uk
Website: http://www.slepehall.co.uk
Bank(s): Barclays
Directors: E. Tulley (Prop)
Managers: J. Law (Mgr)
Immediate Holding Company: SLEPE SERVICES LIMITED
Registration no: 06300849 **VAT No.:** GB 445 5537 36
Date established: 2007 **Turnover:** £500,000 - £1m
No.of Employees: 11 - 20 **Product Groups:** 69, 81

Date of Accounts	Jul 09	Jul 08
Current Assets	50	25

Technical Sales Ltd

3 Harding Way, St Ives, PE27 3WR
Tel: 01480-494747 **Fax:** 020-7924 1755
E-mail: geoffrey.redhead@technicsales.co.uk
Directors: A. Rockall (Dir)
Immediate Holding Company: CAMEO PHOTOGRAPHY LIMITED
Registration no: 00777217 **Date established:** 2006
No.of Employees: 21 - 50 **Product Groups:** 32, 35, 36, 49

Date of Accounts	Dec 11	Dec 10	Dec 09
Sales Turnover	N/A	N/A	3m
Pre Tax Profit/Loss	N/A	N/A	37
Working Capital	672	690	663
Fixed Assets	184	214	246
Current Assets	2m	2m	2m
Current Liabilities	N/A	N/A	279

Tecstar Electronics Ltd

Unit 8 Bramley Road, St Ives, PE27 3WS
Tel: 01480-399499 **Fax:** 01480-399503
E-mail: sales@tecstar.co.uk
Website: http://www.starcom1.com
Directors: A. Starling (Fin), D. Kale (Dir)
Immediate Holding Company: TECSTAR ELECTRONICS LIMITED
Registration no: 03927453 **VAT No.:** GB 750 7615 31
Date established: 2000 **Turnover:** Up to £250,000
No.of Employees: 1 - 10 **Product Groups:** 37, 38, 44, 67

Date of Accounts	Mar 11	Mar 10	Mar 09
Working Capital	185	89	25
Fixed Assets	21	40	16
Current Assets	357	314	143

Teloman Products Ltd (Menu International Ltd)

3 Harding Way, St Ives, PE27 3WR
Tel: 01480-494747 **Fax:** 01480-496114
E-mail: john@teloman.com
Website: http://www.teloman.com
Bank(s): Lloyds
Directors: T. Woodroff (Co Sec), A. Rockall (Sales & Mktg), J. Dalton (Dir)
Immediate Holding Company: TELOMAN PRODUCTS LIMITED
Registration no: 01423549 **VAT No.:** GB 580 3113 70
Date established: 1979 **Turnover:** £250,000 - £500,000
No.of Employees: 21 - 50 **Product Groups:** 22

Date of Accounts	Sep 11	Sep 10	Sep 09
Working Capital	172	181	171
Fixed Assets	3	4	12
Current Assets	631	477	427

Transart Ltd

Clare Hall St Ives Business Park Parsons Green, St Ives, PE27 4WY
Tel: 01480-499200 **Fax:** 01480-499201
E-mail: sarah.dawson@transart.co.uk
Website: http://www.transart.co.uk
Bank(s): National Westminster Bank Plc
Directors: J. Price (MD), M. Dean (Dir), R. Evans (Fin), E. Price (MD), R. McConkey (Ch), S. Dawson (Dir), S. Dawson (MD), A. Woodhead (Dir)
Immediate Holding Company: TRANSART EDUCATIONAL MARKETING SYSTEMS LTD.
Registration no: 02747015 **VAT No.:** GB 638 3894 92
Date established: 1992 **Turnover:** £2m - £5m **No.of Employees:** 11 - 20
Product Groups: 86

Date of Accounts	Dec 06	Dec 05	Dec 04
Sales Turnover	N/A	1697	1383
Pre Tax Profit/Loss	N/A	31	262
Working Capital	N/A	398	2534
Fixed Assets	71	71	153
Current Assets	136	533	3162
Current Liabilities	136	136	628
Total Share Capital	34	34	34
ROCE% (Return on Capital Employed)		6.7	9.8
ROT% (Return on Turnover)		1.8	18.9

U V O 3 Ltd

Unit 25 Stephenson Road, St Ives, PE27 3WJ
Tel: 01480-355446 **Fax:** 01480-353487
E-mail: sales@uvo3.co.uk
Website: http://www.uvo3.co.uk
Directors: P. Wadsworth (MD)
Immediate Holding Company: UVO3 LTD
Registration no: 04688614 **Date established:** 2003
No.of Employees: 1 - 10 **Product Groups:** 30, 37, 38, 41, 42

Date of Accounts	Mar 12	Mar 11	Mar 10
Working Capital	330	225	133
Fixed Assets	25	30	27
Current Assets	440	307	216

Ultrapure Water Softeners

26 Stephenson Road, St Ives, PE27 3WJ
Tel: 01480-464824 **Fax:** 01480-464872
E-mail: info@ultrapure-h20.co.uk
Website: http://www.ultrapure-h20.co.uk

see next page

***Ultrapure Water Softeners** - Cont'd*

Directors: C. Boswell (Prop), P. Boswell (Fin)
Immediate Holding Company: ULTRAPURE LIMITED
Registration no: 02925972 **Date established:** 1994
No.of Employees: 1 - 10 **Product Groups:** 38, 42

Webtec Products

Nuffield Road, St Ives, PE27 3LZ
Tel: 01480-397400 **Fax:** 01480-466555
E-mail: information@webtec.co.uk
Website: http://www.webtec.co.uk
Bank(s): Barclays, St. Ives
Directors: D. Wassell (Fin), M. Cuthbert (MD)
Managers: P. Lavender, S. Cuffbert, P. Howe (Personnel), A. Cooper (Sales Prom Mgr)
Immediate Holding Company: WEBTEC PRODUCTS LIMITED
Registration no: 00832125 **VAT No.:** GB 213 8144 89
Date established: 1964 **Turnover:** £2m - £5m **No.of Employees:** 21 - 50
Product Groups: 38, 40, 46, 67

Date of Accounts	Oct 11	Oct 10	Oct 09
Working Capital	2m	1m	874
Fixed Assets	1m	2m	2m
Current Assets	3m	3m	2m

St Neots

Bailey Morris Ltd

Little End Road Eaton Socon, St Neots, PE19 8GE
Tel: 01480-216250 **Fax:** 01480-403045
E-mail: sales@baileymorris.co.uk
Website: http://www.baileymorris.co.uk
Bank(s): Barclays Bank PLC
Directors: C. Cocks (Dir)
Immediate Holding Company: BAILEY MORRIS LIMITED
Registration no: 01345726 **Date established:** 1977 **Turnover:** £2m - £5m
No.of Employees: 21 - 50 **Product Groups:** 29, 35, 36, 38, 39, 61, 67, 68

Date of Accounts	Dec 11	Dec 10	Dec 09
Working Capital	2m	2m	1m
Fixed Assets	255	226	166
Current Assets	3m	2m	2m

Bardon Contracting

18 Little End Road Eaton Socon, St Neots, PE19 8JH
Tel: 01480-213513 **Fax:** 01480- 405994
E-mail: bardon.contracting@aggregate.com
Website: http://www.aggregate.com
Directors: K. Barker (Co Sec), N. Steel (Ch), J. Taylor (Co Sec)
Managers: R. Scott (Chief Mgr)
Immediate Holding Company: AGGREGATE INDUSTRIES UK LTD
Registration no: 00870867 **Turnover:** £2m - £5m
No.of Employees: 21 - 50 **Product Groups:** 17, 51, 84

Black Teknigas & Electro Controls Ltd

Orion Court Ambuscado Road Eaton Socon, St Neots, PE19 8YX
Tel: 01480-407074 **Fax:** 01480-407076
E-mail: sales@blackteknigas.co.uk
Website: http://www.blackteknigas.com
Bank(s): National Westminster Bank Plc
Directors: P. McEntee (Sales & Mktg), S. Adams (MD)
Managers: V. Harvey (Fin Mgr), T. Foster
Ultimate Holding Company: WATTS WATER TECHNOLOGIES INC (USA)
Immediate Holding Company: ELECTRO CONTROLS LIMITED
Registration no: 01516780 **VAT No.:** GB 563 4397 21
Date established: 1980 **Turnover:** £5m - £10m
No.of Employees: 51 - 100 **Product Groups:** 36, 37, 38, 40

Date of Accounts	Dec 10	Dec 09	Dec 08
Sales Turnover	N/A	N/A	3m
Pre Tax Profit/Loss	N/A	-1	659
Working Capital	9	16	2m
Current Assets	16	16	2m
Current Liabilities	7	N/A	213

Bosch Rexroth

Cromwell Road, St Neots, PE19 2EY
Tel: 01480-223200 **Fax:** 01480-219052
E-mail: info@boschrexroth.co.uk
Website: http://www.boschrexroth.co.uk
Bank(s): Barclays Bank plc
Directors: A. Johnstone (MD), G. Rowell (Fin)
Managers: B. Best (Tech Serv Mgr), K. Nelmes (Purch Mgr), R. Benton (Mktg Serv Mgr), L. Hutchinson (Personnel)
Ultimate Holding Company: ROBERT BOSCH GMBH (GERMANY)
Immediate Holding Company: BOSCH REXROTH LIMITED
Registration no: 00768471 **VAT No.:** GB 491 2899 06
Date established: 1963 **Turnover:** £125m - £250m
No.of Employees: 101 - 250 **Product Groups:** 28, 30, 35, 36, 37, 38, 39, 40, 41, 45, 46, 48, 67, 84, 85, 86

Date of Accounts	Dec 11	Dec 10	Dec 09
Sales Turnover	168m	117m	77m
Pre Tax Profit/Loss	13m	4m	-6m
Working Capital	21m	17m	13m
Fixed Assets	15m	13m	14m
Current Assets	53m	40m	28m
Current Liabilities	7m	6m	3m

Cambridge Street Dental Practice

28 Cambridge Street, St Neots, PE19 1JL
Tel: 01480-475438
Website: http://www.cambridgestreetdentalpractice.co.uk
Managers: A. Pardesi
Immediate Holding Company: THE CAMBRIDGE STREET PRACTICE LTD
Registration no: 06855948 **Date established:** 2009
Turnover: £250,000 - £500,000 **No.of Employees:** 1 - 10
Product Groups: 31, 38, 40

Concord Lifting

10 Foundry Way Eaton Socon, St Neots, PE19 8TR
Tel: 01480-217605 **Fax:** 01480-407108
E-mail: liftingequipment@btconnect.com
Website: http://www.concordlifting.com
Directors: B. Kerrison (Ch)
Ultimate Holding Company: KFC HOLDINGS LIMITED
Immediate Holding Company: LIFTING EQUIPMENT AND SERVICES LIMITED
Registration no: 01825077 **VAT No.:** GB 395 9222 14
Date established: 1984 **Turnover:** £250,000 - £500,000
No.of Employees: 1 - 10 **Product Groups:** 39, 45

Date of Accounts	Mar 11	Mar 10	Mar 09
Working Capital	27	30	25
Fixed Assets	14	N/A	N/A
Current Assets	180	184	150

Door-Wise Ltd

3 Enterprise Court Ambuscade Road, Eaton Socon, St Neots, PE19 8YU
Tel: 01480-407645 **Fax:** 01480-407646
E-mail: doorwise@door-wise.co.uk
Website: http://www.door-wise.co.uk
Directors: E. Parker (Dir)
Immediate Holding Company: DOORWISE LIMITED
Registration no: 02295628 **Date established:** 1988
No.of Employees: 1 - 10 **Product Groups:** 26, 35

Date of Accounts	Dec 11	Dec 10	Dec 09
Working Capital	-19	17	3
Fixed Assets	18	19	21
Current Assets	81	166	115

Dorcas Engineering Ltd

17 Howard Road Eaton Socon, St Neots, PE19 8ET
Tel: 01480-213316 **Fax:** 01480-216319
E-mail: dorcaseng@tesco.net
Directors: A. Lane (MD), E. Lane (Fin)
Immediate Holding Company: DORCAS ENGINEERING LIMITED
Registration no: 01001598 **VAT No.:** GB 196 6588 94
Date established: 1971 **Turnover:** Up to £250,000
No.of Employees: 1 - 10 **Product Groups:** 35, 36, 46, 49

Date of Accounts	Apr 12	Apr 11	Apr 10
Working Capital	-1	-14	-71
Fixed Assets	42	38	39
Current Assets	41	19	12

Driftgate 2000 Ltd

Little End Road Eaton Socon, St Neots, PE19 8JH
Tel: 01480-470400 **Fax:** 01480-470401
E-mail: a.lowe@dg2k.co.uk
Website: http://www.dg2k.co.uk
Directors: A. Lowe (MD), B. Lowe (Co Sec)
Immediate Holding Company: DRIFTGATE 2000 LIMITED
Registration no: 02640452 **VAT No.:** GB 563 7831 16
Date established: 1991 **Turnover:** Up to £250,000
No.of Employees: 1 - 10 **Product Groups:** 37

Date of Accounts	Mar 11	Mar 10	Sep 08
Working Capital	47	56	68
Fixed Assets	8	9	12
Current Assets	58	70	93

Dufaylite Developments Ltd

6 Cromwell Road, St Neots, PE19 1QW
Tel: 01480-215000 **Fax:** 01480-405526
E-mail: enquiries@dufaylite.com
Website: http://www.dufaylite.com
Bank(s): Barclays, 54 Lombard Street, London, EC3P 3AH
Directors: A. Moscrop (Grp Chief Exec), M. Burnell (MD)
Managers: P. York (Prod Mgr), S. Ellis (Personnel), A. Brownhill (Mktg Serv Mgr), A. Moscrop (Sales Prom)
Ultimate Holding Company: DUFAYLITE GROUP LIMITED
Immediate Holding Company: DUFAYLITE DEVELOPMENTS LIMITED
Registration no: 00556002 **VAT No.:** GB 213 5411 10
Date established: 1955 **Turnover:** £2m - £5m **No.of Employees:** 21 - 50
Product Groups: 25, 26, 27, 30, 40, 45, 49

Date of Accounts	Sep 11	Sep 10	Sep 09
Sales Turnover	N/A	N/A	4m
Pre Tax Profit/Loss	N/A	N/A	80
Working Capital	3m	3m	3m
Fixed Assets	2m	2m	2m
Current Assets	5m	5m	5m
Current Liabilities	N/A	N/A	311

Eaton Tractors Ltd

Pitt Farm Little Paxton, St Neots, PE19 6HD
Tel: 01480-473121 **Fax:** 01480-404585
Directors: R. Saywell (MD)
Immediate Holding Company: EATON TRACTORS LIMITED
Registration no: 01256284 **VAT No.:** GB 215 3212 14
Date established: 1976 **Turnover:** £250,000 - £500,000
No.of Employees: 1 - 10 **Product Groups:** 41, 67

Date of Accounts	Mar 11	Mar 10	Mar 09
Working Capital	725	722	725
Fixed Assets	240	238	251
Current Assets	750	741	754

Finishing Aids & Tools Ltd

Little End Road Eaton Socon, St Neots, PE19 8GF
Tel: 01480-216060 **Fax:** 01480-405989
E-mail: sales@finaids.com
Website: http://www.finaids.com
Bank(s): HSBC Bank plc
Directors: R. Binham (Dir)
Immediate Holding Company: FINISHING AIDS AND TOOLS LIMITED
Registration no: 00660087 **VAT No.:** GB 216 1047 07
Date established: 1960 **Turnover:** £2m - £5m **No.of Employees:** 11 - 20
Product Groups: 33

Date of Accounts	Dec 11	Dec 10	Dec 09
Working Capital	73	100	121
Fixed Assets	347	412	377
Current Assets	862	719	594

Gates Hydraulics Ltd

Alpha Drive Eaton Socon, St Neots, PE19 8JJ
Tel: 01480-4023 00 **Fax:** 01480-402350
Website: http://www.gates.com
Directors: L. Metcalfe (Fin), V. Hainsby (Tech Serv)
Managers: R. Jones (Comptroller), S. Young (Workshop)
Ultimate Holding Company: Tomkins PLC.
Immediate Holding Company: Gates (U.K.) Ltd
Registration no: 00731970 **Date established:** 1962 **Turnover:** £2m - £5m
No.of Employees: 1 - 10 **Product Groups:** 29, 30, 36, 40

Date of Accounts	Dec 07
Working Capital	5120
Current Assets	5120
Total Share Capital	400

Glomac Engineering Ltd

Steel Close Eaton Socon, St Neots, PE19 8TT
Tel: 01480-215533 **Fax:** 01480-405952
E-mail: sales@glomac.co.uk
Website: http://www.glomac.co.uk
Directors: S. Wicks (MD)
Immediate Holding Company: GLOMAC ENGINEERING LIMITED
Registration no: 01856010 **VAT No.:** GB 393 1712 49
Date established: 1984 **Turnover:** £1m - £2m **No.of Employees:** 11 - 20
Product Groups: 35, 39, 40, 42, 45, 48, 84

Date of Accounts	Mar 12	Mar 11	Mar 10
Working Capital	49	71	63
Fixed Assets	70	40	49
Current Assets	124	126	114

Grove Electronics Ltd

26 Grove Court Rampley Lane, Little Paxton, St Neots, PE19 6PQ
Tel: 01480-382909 **Fax:** 01480-382909
E-mail: info@groveelectronics.co.uk
Website: http://www.groveelectronics.co.uk
Directors: A. Bennett (Dir)
Immediate Holding Company: GROVE ELECTRONICS LTD
Registration no: 05551615 **Date established:** 2005
Turnover: Up to £250,000 **No.of Employees:** 1 - 10 **Product Groups:** 84

Date of Accounts	Sep 11	Sep 10	Sep 09
Working Capital	199	148	164
Fixed Assets	4	5	4
Current Assets	240	166	194

Hesing Technology

41 Bushmead Road Eaton Socon, St Neots, PE19 8GN
Tel: 01480-386156 **Fax:** 01480- 386157
E-mail: hestech@dircon.co.uk
Directors: D. Hines (Ptnr)
Date established: 1994 **No.of Employees:** 1 - 10 **Product Groups:** 48, 84

Arthur Ibbett Ltd

River Lane Great Paxton, St Neots, PE19 6RD
Tel: 01480-473452 **Fax:** 01480-405026
E-mail: timibbett@ibbetts.co.uk
Website: http://www.ibbetts.co.uk
Bank(s): HSBC Bank plc
Directors: T. Ibbett (MD)
Immediate Holding Company: ARTHUR IBBETT LIMITED
Registration no: 01233660 **VAT No.:** GB 214 8975 40
Date established: 1975 **Turnover:** £1m - £2m **No.of Employees:** 11 - 20
Product Groups: 07

Date of Accounts	Dec 11	Dec 10	Dec 09
Working Capital	688	704	701
Fixed Assets	62	45	34
Current Assets	1m	1m	1m

Ibex Camping

The Lifestyle Village Great North Road, Little Paxton, St Neots, PE19 6EN
Tel: 01480-404030
E-mail: sales@ibexcamping.co.uk
Website: http://www.ibexcamping.co.uk
Directors: I. Peacock (Prop)
Immediate Holding Company: FRONTLINE ELECTRICAL SERVICES LIMITED
Registration no: 03921381 **Date established:** 2007
No.of Employees: 1 - 10 **Product Groups:** 23, 24, 49, 65

Date of Accounts	Nov 11	Nov 10	Nov 09
Sales Turnover	N/A	9	16
Pre Tax Profit/Loss	N/A	1	5
Working Capital	21	33	33
Current Assets	21	33	33

Landsmans Ltd

Brampton Road, St Neots, PE19 5UJ
Tel: 01480-810972 **Fax:** 01480-810287
E-mail: landsmans-ltd@btconnect.com
Website: http://www.landsmansloos.co.uk
Directors: G. Gilby (Fin)
Immediate Holding Company: LANDSMANS LIMITED
Registration no: 06775200 **Date established:** 2008
Turnover: £250,000 - £500,000 **No.of Employees:** 1 - 10
Product Groups: 36

Date of Accounts	Mar 11	Mar 10
Working Capital	44	-12
Fixed Assets	465	487
Current Assets	101	98

Lely UK Ltd

1-3 Station Road, St Neots, PE19 1QH
Tel: 01480-226800 **Fax:** 01480-226801
E-mail: info@lely.com
Website: http://www.lely.com
Bank(s): HSBC Bank plc
Directors: G. Dale (MD), P. Horlock (Fin)
Managers: J. Van Sehijndel (Purch Mgr), H. Jones (Mktg Serv Mgr), S. Saunders (Personnel), S. Donaldson (Tech Serv Mgr), P. Mansfield (Chief Mgr)
Ultimate Holding Company: LELY HOLDINGS SARL (LUXEMBOURG)
Immediate Holding Company: LELY (U.K.) LIMITED
Registration no: 00937578 **VAT No.:** GB 213 8916 62
Date established: 1968 **Turnover:** £20m - £50m
No.of Employees: 101 - 250 **Product Groups:** 41, 67

Date of Accounts	Dec 10	Dec 09	Dec 08
Sales Turnover	40m	36m	43m
Pre Tax Profit/Loss	-319	441	2m
Working Capital	8m	8m	8m
Fixed Assets	4m	4m	5m
Current Assets	19m	12m	17m
Current Liabilities	5m	805	992

Light Fantastic

12 Cambridge Street, St Neots, PE19 1JL
Tel: 01480-407872 **Fax:** 01480-219343
E-mail: sales@lightfan.co.uk
Website: http://www.lightfan.co.uk
Managers: S. Higgins (Sales Prom Mgr)
VAT No.: GB 440 7091 70 **Turnover:** £250,000 - £500,000
No.of Employees: 1 - 10 **Product Groups:** 22, 24, 25, 27, 29, 30, 31, 33, 35, 37, 38, 39, 40, 41, 44, 49, 67, 84

March May Ltd
Howard Road Eaton Socon, St Neots, PE19 8NZ
Tel: 01480-214444 **Fax:** 01480-405336
E-mail: sales@marchmay.co.uk
Website: http://www.marchmay.co.uk
Bank(s): Barclays
Directors: P. Boddy (Dir)
Immediate Holding Company: MARCH MAY LIMITED
Registration no: 01017563 **VAT No.:** GB 440 8993 25
Date established: 1971 **Turnover:** £2m - £5m **No.of Employees:** 11 - 20
Product Groups: 40

Date of Accounts	Aug 11	Aug 10	Aug 09
Working Capital	2m	1m	1m
Fixed Assets	366	340	357
Current Assets	2m	2m	2m

Marren
Unit 3a Oak Park Alington Road, Little Barford, St Neots, PE19 6WL
Tel: 01480-214565 **Fax:** 01480-218741
Directors: R. Loveday (MD)
Registration no: 01930017 **VAT No.:** GB 608 3500 63
Date established: 1991 **Turnover:** £1m - £2m **No.of Employees:** 1 - 10
Product Groups: 52

Mass Consultants Ltd
Enterprise House Great North Road, St Neots, PE19 6BN
Tel: 01480-222600 **Fax:** 01480-407366
E-mail: alane@mass.co.uk
Website: http://www.mass.co.uk
Directors: M. Lowes (Develop), A. Lane (MD), S. Walther (Fin)
Managers: K. Howell (Personnel), J. Water (Purch Mgr), P. Crowe (Tech Serv Mgr), A. Harris
Ultimate Holding Company: COHORT PLC
Immediate Holding Company: MASS CONSULTANTS LIMITED
Registration no: 01705804 **Date established:** 1983
Turnover: £20m - £50m **No.of Employees:** 51 - 100 **Product Groups:** 37, 38, 40, 44, 52, 67, 68, 84, 85

Date of Accounts	Apr 12	Apr 11	Apr 10
Sales Turnover	26m	24m	21m
Pre Tax Profit/Loss	4m	3m	3m
Working Capital	8m	6m	5m
Fixed Assets	5m	5m	3m
Current Assets	13m	12m	9m
Current Liabilities	4m	4m	3m

Micropump
Unit 3 Dairy Court, 97 Huntingdon Street, St Neots, PE19 1DU
Tel: 01480-356600 **Fax:** 01480-356300
E-mail: mplsales.micropump@idexcorp.com
Website: http://www.micropump.com
Bank(s): National Westminster Bank Plc
Directors: R. Epli (Fin), T. Altham (Sales)
Managers: K. Wardle (I.T. Exec)
Ultimate Holding Company: Micropump Corporation (U.S.A.)
Registration no: 03036074 **Date established:** 1995
Turnover: £500m - £1,000m **No.of Employees:** 11 - 20
Product Groups: 40, 42

Date of Accounts	Dec 07	Dec 06	Dec 05
Sales Turnover	5679	6373	5394
Pre Tax Profit/Loss	285	197	29
Working Capital	1300	1105	949
Fixed Assets	50	48	69
Current Assets	1640	1676	3756
Current Liabilities	339	572	2807
ROCE% (Return on Capital Employed)	21.1	17.1	2.8
ROT% (Return on Turnover)	5.0	3.1	0.5

L J A Miers & Co. Ltd
Hawkesden Road, St Neots, PE19 1QS
Tel: 01480-211177 **Fax:** 01480-211190
E-mail: sales@ljamiers.co.uk
Website: http://www.ljamiers.co.uk
Bank(s): Barclays, Biggleswade
Directors: A. Miers (MD), P. Curl (Co Sec)
Managers: W. Miers (Purch Mgr), M. Court
Immediate Holding Company: L.J.A.MIERS & COMPANY LIMITED
Registration no: 00538182 **VAT No.:** GB 247 7711 40
Date established: 1954 **Turnover:** £2m - £5m **No.of Employees:** 21 - 50
Product Groups: 29, 30

Date of Accounts	Sep 11	Sep 10	Sep 09
Working Capital	766	644	435
Fixed Assets	201	134	208
Current Assets	2m	1m	1m

Mindsmeet Electro Optics Ltd
12 Castle Hill Close Eaton Socon, St Neots, PE19 8HW
Tel: 01480-217083 **Fax:** 01480-217083
E-mail: prh@mindsmeet.co.uk
Website: http://www.mindsmeet.co.uk
Directors: P. Hall (Eng Serv)
Immediate Holding Company: MINDSMEET ELECTRO-OPTICS LIMITED
Registration no: 03649128 **Date established:** 1998
No.of Employees: 1 - 10 **Product Groups:** 38, 67, 84, 85

Date of Accounts	Oct 11	Oct 09	Oct 08
Working Capital	9	1	N/A
Current Assets	17	9	6

On Site Communication Ltd
179 Great North Road Eaton Socon, St Neots, PE19 8EG
Tel: 01480-405540 **Fax:** 01480-406667
E-mail: info@radio-links.co.uk
Website: http://www.radio-links.co.uk
Directors: P. Litchfield (Fin), C. Litcfiled (Dir)
Immediate Holding Company: ONSITE COMMUNICATIONS LIMITED
Registration no: 01982770 **Date established:** 1986
No.of Employees: 21 - 50 **Product Groups:** 37

Date of Accounts	Oct 11	Oct 10	Oct 06
Working Capital	N/A	N/A	219
Current Assets	N/A	N/A	219

Phoenix Optics UK Ltd
8-10 Chester Road Enterprise Court, Eaton Socon, St Neots, PE19 8YT
Tel: 01480-406024 **Fax:** 01480-470553
E-mail: steve@phoenixoptics.com
Website: http://www.phoenixoptics.com
Directors: S. Worthington (MD)
Immediate Holding Company: PHOENIX OPTICS (UK) LIMITED
Registration no: 04662845 **Date established:** 2003 **Turnover:** £2m - £5m
No.of Employees: 11 - 20 **Product Groups:** 37, 52

Date of Accounts	Sep 11	Sep 10	Sep 09
Working Capital	472	343	240
Fixed Assets	144	96	99
Current Assets	894	765	622

Photofabrication Services Ltd
14 Cromwell Road St Neots, St Neots, PE19 2HP
Tel: 01480-475831 **Fax:** 01480-475801
E-mail: sales@photofab.co.uk
Website: http://www.photofabrication.co.uk
Bank(s): T.S.B., Long Eaton
Directors: N. Shorten (Co Sec), S. Lane (MD)
Managers: K. Gray, M. Pineo (Prod Mgr), L. Allen (Buyer)
Immediate Holding Company: PHOTOFABRICATION LTD
Registration no: 01001985 **VAT No.:** GB 218 1330 00
Date established: 1971 **Turnover:** £2m - £5m **No.of Employees:** 21 - 50
Product Groups: 28, 35

Date of Accounts	Mar 11	Mar 10	Mar 09
Working Capital	386	248	372
Fixed Assets	147	129	172
Current Assets	1m	811	952

Pico Technology Ltd
James House Marlborough Road, Eaton Socon, St Neots, PE19 8YP
Tel: 01480-396395 **Fax:** 01480-396296
E-mail: post@picotech.com
Website: http://www.picotech.com
Managers: J. Percy (Sales Admin)
Ultimate Holding Company: PICO TECHNOLOGY (HOLDINGS) LIMITED
Immediate Holding Company: PICO TECHNOLOGY LIMITED
Registration no: 02626181 **Date established:** 1991
Turnover: £500,000 - £1m **No.of Employees:** 21 - 50
Product Groups: 37, 38, 39, 40, 44, 67

Date of Accounts	Jun 11	Jun 10	Jun 09
Working Capital	2m	1m	1000
Fixed Assets	2m	2m	2m
Current Assets	4m	2m	2m

Pipe Line Seal & Insulator Company Ltd
3-5 Chester Road Colmworth Business Park, Eaton Socon, St Neots, PE19 8YT
Tel: 01480-404661 **Fax:** 01480-404662
E-mail: sales@pipelineseal.co.uk
Website: http://www.pipelineseal.co.uk
Directors: A. Stevens (MD)
Ultimate Holding Company: ENPRO INDUSTRIES INC (USA)
Immediate Holding Company: PIPELINE SEAL & INSULATOR CO.LIMITED
Registration no: 00867192 **VAT No.:** GB 411 0642 12
Date established: 1965 **Turnover:** £2m - £5m **No.of Employees:** 11 - 20
Product Groups: 30

Date of Accounts	Dec 11	Dec 10	Dec 09
Sales Turnover	3m	2m	2m
Pre Tax Profit/Loss	498	303	-29
Working Capital	1m	837	509
Fixed Assets	184	181	206
Current Assets	2m	1m	860
Current Liabilities	202	118	214

Pulse Electronics
Brigade House 5a Alington Road, Little Barford, St Neots, PE19 6WG
Tel: 01480-216516 **Fax:** 01480-472428
E-mail: sales@pulse-electronics.co.uk
Website: http://www.pulse-electronics.co.uk
Managers: C. Austin (Chief Mgr), G. Pryar (Purch Mgr), C. Morgan (Sales Admin)
Immediate Holding Company: IPECO HOLDINGS LIMITED
Registration no: 00672443 **VAT No.:** GB 250 3726 82
Turnover: £2m - £5m **No.of Employees:** 21 - 50 **Product Groups:** 37

R N H Automation Ltd
Eltisley Business Park Potton Road, Abbotsley, St Neots, PE19 6TX
Tel: 01767-679114 **Fax:** 01480-880276
E-mail: sales@rnh-automation.com
Website: http://www.rnh-automation.com
Directors: R. Haynes (MD), T. Haynes (Fin)
Immediate Holding Company: RNH AUTOMATION LIMITED
Registration no: 04568350 **Date established:** 2002
No.of Employees: 1 - 10 **Product Groups:** 37, 45, 80

Date of Accounts	Dec 11	Dec 10	Dec 09
Working Capital	-4	2	-1
Fixed Assets	9	13	18
Current Assets	44	46	37

Radio Links Communications Ltd
Eaton House Great North Road, Eaton Socon, St Neots, PE19 8EG
Tel: 01480-217220 **Fax:** 01480-406667
E-mail: info@radio-links.co.uk
Website: http://www.radio-links.co.uk
Bank(s): Barclays
Directors: B. Litchfield (MD)
Immediate Holding Company: RADIO LINKS COMMUNICATIONS LIMITED
Registration no: 01184769 **Date established:** 1974 **Turnover:** £1m - £2m
No.of Employees: 21 - 50 **Product Groups:** 37, 40

Date of Accounts	Oct 11	Oct 10	Oct 09
Working Capital	393	407	478
Fixed Assets	656	644	861
Current Assets	749	851	823

St Neots Packaging Holdings Ltd
7 Howard Road Eaton Socon, St Neots, PE19 8ET
Tel: 01480-476161 **Fax:** 01480-471989
E-mail: sales@stneotspack.co.uk
Website: http://www.fastfoodpackaging.com
Directors: R. Collis (Sales), A. Ducker (Ch), A. Pealling (Fin)
Managers: S. Jacobs (Personnel), A. Lay
Ultimate Holding Company: ST NEOTS HOLDINGS LIMITED
Immediate Holding Company: ST. NEOTS PACKAGING HOLDINGS LIMITED
Registration no: 03523757 **Date established:** 1998
Turnover: £10m - £20m **No.of Employees:** 101 - 250
Product Groups: 27, 85

Date of Accounts	Jun 12	Jun 11	Jun 10
Fixed Assets	306	306	306

Salesmark Ltd
Howard Road Eaton Socon, St Neots, PE19 8ET
Tel: 01480-212888 **Fax:** 01480-218585
E-mail: sales@salesmark.co.uk
Website: http://www.salesmark.co.uk
Directors: J. Knight (Dir)
Immediate Holding Company: SALESMARK LIMITED
Registration no: 02584506 **Date established:** 1991 **Turnover:** £1m - £2m
No.of Employees: 11 - 20 **Product Groups:** 35, 36

Date of Accounts	Jun 11	Jun 10	Jun 09
Working Capital	639	589	567
Fixed Assets	935	1m	1m
Current Assets	1m	1m	1m

Simply Herbs
The Herbary 11 Town Orchard, Southoe, St Neots, PE19 5YJ
Tel: 01480-472301
E-mail: handmade@simplyherbs.co.uk
Website: http://www.simplyherbs.co.uk
Directors: M. Farmery (Prop)
Date established: 2000 **Turnover:** Up to £250,000
No.of Employees: 1 - 10 **Product Groups:** 31, 32

Tillomed Laboratories Ltd
3 Howard Road Industrial Estate Eaton Socon, St Neots, PE19 8ET
Tel: 01480-402400 **Fax:** 01480-402402
E-mail: info@tillomed.co.uk
Website: http://www.tillomed.co.uk
Directors: A. Robinson (Sales & Mktg), M. Ginai (MD)
Managers: L. Prothero (Develop Mgr), I. Walter, M. Khokhar, J. Colpin
Ultimate Holding Company: MANEESH PHARMACEUTICALS LTD (INDIA)
Immediate Holding Company: TILLOMED LABORATORIES LIMITED
Registration no: 02544103 **Date established:** 1990
Turnover: £10m - £20m **No.of Employees:** 51 - 100 **Product Groups:** 31, 63

Date of Accounts	Mar 12	Mar 11	Mar 10
Sales Turnover	13m	14m	15m
Pre Tax Profit/Loss	392	522	969
Working Capital	4m	4m	3m
Fixed Assets	4m	4m	4m
Current Assets	7m	8m	9m
Current Liabilities	1m	2m	2m

Trenton Box Co. Ltd
Marston Road, St Neots, PE19 2HF
Tel: 01480-473693 **Fax:** 01480-406225
E-mail: sales@trentonbox.co.uk
Website: http://www.trentonbox.co.uk
Bank(s): Barclays
Directors: E. Douglas (Prop), S. Douglas (Fin), Y. Woods (Fin)
Managers: A. King, K. Sherman (Maint), N. Smith (Tech Serv Mgr)
Ultimate Holding Company: TRENTON BOX COMPANY LIMITED
Immediate Holding Company: TRENTON (MILLWAY) HOLDINGS LIMITED
Registration no: 00492458 **VAT No.:** 360 1936 66 **Date established:** 1951
No.of Employees: 51 - 100 **Product Groups:** 27

Date of Accounts	Feb 10	Feb 09
Working Capital	9	9
Fixed Assets	100	100
Current Assets	9	9

Wisbech

Abtec Industries Ltd
Unit 4 Venture Court 82 Boleness Road, Wisbech, PE13 2XQ
Tel: 0800-027 1928 **Fax:** 01945-585052
E-mail: sales@abtecindustries.com
Website: http://www.abtec4abrasives.com
Directors: M. Ring (Dir)
Immediate Holding Company: ABTEC INDUSTRIES LIMITED
Registration no: 04373909 **Date established:** 2002
Turnover: £500,000 - £1m **No.of Employees:** 1 - 10 **Product Groups:** 33

Date of Accounts	Feb 08	Feb 11	Feb 10
Working Capital	-2	3	-11
Fixed Assets	7	1	2
Current Assets	87	83	91

Anglia
Sandall Road, Wisbech, PE13 2PS
Tel: 01945-474747 **Fax:** 01945-474849
E-mail: info@anglia.com
Website: http://www.anglia.com
Bank(s): The Royal Bank of Scotland
Directors: J. Bowie (Chief Op Offcr)
Managers: D. Marriott (Purch Mgr), K. Hover (Fin Mgr), S. Rawlins, J. Budnik (Tech Serv Mgr), M. Hircock (Commun Mgr)
Ultimate Holding Company: ANGLIA CORPORATION HOLDINGS LIMITED
Immediate Holding Company: ANGLIA CORPORATION HOLDINGS LIMITED
Registration no: 01188489 **VAT No.:** GB 282 0548 62
Date established: 1974 **Turnover:** Up to £250,000
No.of Employees: 101 - 250 **Product Groups:** 37, 44

Date of Accounts	Mar 11	Mar 10	Mar 09
Sales Turnover	N/A	153	32m
Pre Tax Profit/Loss	N/A	-38	1m
Working Capital	26	30	11m
Fixed Assets	N/A	N/A	2m
Current Assets	32	66	16m
Current Liabilities	7	36	1m

B R T Bearings Ltd
21-24 Regal Road, Wisbech, PE13 2RQ
Tel: 01945-461168 **Fax:** 01945-464523
E-mail: wisbech@brt-bearings.com
Website: http://www.brt-bearings.com
Directors: P. Clarke (MD)
Ultimate Holding Company: BRT (WISBECH) LIMITED
Immediate Holding Company: B.R.T. BEARINGS (ANGLIA) LIMITED
Registration no: 01260395 **Date established:** 1976
No.of Employees: 21 - 50 **Product Groups:** 35, 66

Date of Accounts	Aug 11	Aug 10	Aug 09
Working Capital	44	44	44
Current Assets	44	44	44

Barleytwist Furniture
But An Ben High Road, Wisbech St Mary, Wisbech, PE13 4RA
Tel: 01945-410557
E-mail: nicolanc23@aol.com
Website: http://www.barleytwist.coms.ph
Directors: N. Nicola (Prop)
No.of Employees: 1 - 10 **Product Groups:** 26

P A Brenchley & Sons

Clergy Farm Sutton Road Four Gotes, Tydd, Wisbech, PE13 5PH
Tel: 01945-420738 **Fax:** 01945-420788
Directors: S. Brenchley (Ptnr)
Date established: 1987 **No.of Employees:** 1 - 10 **Product Groups:** 41

C Dade

King John Bank Walpole St Andrew, Wisbech, PE14 7JT
Tel: 01945-780984 **Fax:** 01945-780006
Directors: C. Dade (Prop)
Date established: 1989 **No.of Employees:** 1 - 10 **Product Groups:** 41

Dagless Ltd

Brigstock Road, Wisbech, PE13 3JL
Tel: 01945-583826 **Fax:** 01945-582673
E-mail: info@shiregb.co.uk
Website: http://www.shiregb.co.uk
Bank(s): HSBC Bank plc
Directors: S. Sneeth (MD)
Ultimate Holding Company: DAGLESS HOLDINGS LIMITED
Immediate Holding Company: DAGLESS LIMITED
Registration no: 00399324 **Date established:** 1945 **Turnover:** £5m - £10m
No.of Employees: 51 - 100 **Product Groups:** 25

Date of Accounts	Dec 11	Dec 10	Dec 09
Sales Turnover	12m	10m	9m
Pre Tax Profit/Loss	256	251	215
Working Capital	758	649	349
Fixed Assets	5m	5m	5m
Current Assets	5m	4m	4m
Current Liabilities	406	410	518

Dawbarn & Sons Ltd

Dawbarns Harecroft Road, Wisbech, PE13 1RL
Tel: 01945-461741 **Fax:** 01945-585501
E-mail: victoria.timms@dawbarn-evertaut.co.uk
Website: http://www.dawbarn-evertaut.co.uk
Bank(s): Lloyds TSB Bank plc
Directors: S. Timms (Fin), V. Timms (Co Sec), B. Harrington (MD)
Immediate Holding Company: DAWBARN & SONS LIMITED
Registration no: 01102027 **Date established:** 1973 **Turnover:** £2m - £5m
No.of Employees: 21 - 50 **Product Groups:** 24

Date of Accounts	Mar 12	Mar 11	Mar 10
Working Capital	981	992	962
Fixed Assets	160	119	126
Current Assets	2m	2m	1m

S C Driver Opticians Ltd

4 High Street, Wisbech, PE13 1DB
Tel: 01945-582006 **Fax:** 01945-461645
E-mail: scdriveropticians@btopenworld.com
Website: http://www.driver-opticians.co.uk
Directors: R. Driver (MD), S. Driver (Fin)
Immediate Holding Company: S.C.DRIVER(OPTICIANS)LIMITED
Registration no: 00471531 **Date established:** 1949
Turnover: Up to £250,000 **No.of Employees:** 1 - 10 **Product Groups:** 65

5 Star Cases Ltd

Broadend Road, Wisbech, PE14 7BQ
Tel: 01945-427000 **Fax:** 01945-427015
E-mail: info@5star-cases.com
Website: http://www.5star-cases.com
Directors: I. Bouwhuis (Co Sec), K. Sykes (MD)
Managers: R. Jackson (Purch Mgr), J. Locks (Chief Mgr)
Ultimate Holding Company: 5 STAR GROUP HOLDINGS LIMITED
Immediate Holding Company: 5 STAR CASES LIMITED
Registration no: 02757991 **Date established:** 1992 **Turnover:** £2m - £5m
No.of Employees: 21 - 50 **Product Groups:** 22, 25, 26, 27, 49

Date of Accounts	Apr 12	Apr 11	Apr 10
Sales Turnover	3m	N/A	N/A
Pre Tax Profit/Loss	167	N/A	N/A
Working Capital	132	115	102
Fixed Assets	110	87	94
Current Assets	920	968	918
Current Liabilities	402	365	273

Grounds & Co

11 Bridge Street, Wisbech, PE13 1AE
Tel: 01945-585041 **Fax:** 01945- 474255
E-mail: enquires@grounds.co.uk
Website: http://www.grounds.co.uk
Directors: G. Brinton (Ptnr)
Managers: E. Howe (Mgr), J. Betts (Mgr)
No.of Employees: 1 - 10 **Product Groups:** 80

Fred Hartley Estates Ltd

The Offices 110 Town Street, Upwell, Wisbech, PE14 9DQ
Tel: 01945-773789 **Fax:** 01945-772928
E-mail: office@fhestates.co.uk
Website: http://www.fhestates.com
Directors: F. Hartley (Fin)
Immediate Holding Company: FRED HARTLEY (ESTATES) LIMITED
Registration no: 00438926 **Date established:** 1947
No.of Employees: 1 - 10 **Product Groups:** 62

Date of Accounts	Jan 11	Jan 10	Jan 09
Working Capital	708	641	1m
Fixed Assets	4m	4m	4m
Current Assets	2m	2m	2m

R J Herbert Engineering Ltd

Bank House Middle Drove, Marshland St James, Wisbech, PE14 8JT
Tel: 01945-430666 **Fax:** 01945-430487
E-mail: sales@rjherbert.co.uk
Website: http://www.rjherbert.co.uk
Directors: R. Herbert (MD), R. Hurbert (MD)
Immediate Holding Company: R.J. HERBERT ENGINEERING LIMITED
Registration no: 01793875 **Date established:** 1984
Turnover: £10m - £20m **No.of Employees:** 101 - 250 **Product Groups:** 41

Date of Accounts	Dec 10	Dec 09	Dec 08
Sales Turnover	12m	13m	14m
Pre Tax Profit/Loss	149	-246	309
Working Capital	-73	-116	314
Fixed Assets	1m	1m	1m
Current Assets	4m	5m	5m
Current Liabilities	1m	1m	1m

John Watts Sales & Service

Isle Road Outwell, Wisbech, PE14 8TD
Tel: 01945-773553
E-mail: jwattssales@aol.com
Directors: J. Watts (Prop)
Immediate Holding Company: M. & B. DISTRIBUTORS(CAMBS)LIMITED
Registration no: 00901240 **Date established:** 1967
Turnover: Up to £250,000 **No.of Employees:** 1 - 10 **Product Groups:** 07

Date of Accounts	May 12	May 11	May 10
Working Capital	-30	11	-9
Fixed Assets	109	16	15
Current Assets	73	65	45

John Wilson & Sons Industrial Engineer Blacksmith

High Road Wisbech St Mary, Wisbech, PE13 4RA
Tel: 01945-410238 **Fax:** 01945-410238
Directors: P. Wilson (Ptnr)
Turnover: Up to £250,000 **No.of Employees:** 1 - 10 **Product Groups:** 34, 35, 42, 48

Kier Construction Eastern

53 South Brink, Wisbech, PE14 0RQ
Tel: 01945-582121 **Fax:** 01945-588157
E-mail: martin.rayner@kier.co.uk
Website: http://www.kier.co.uk
Managers: M. Rayner (Develop Mgr)
Ultimate Holding Company: KIER GROUP PLC
Immediate Holding Company: KIER REGIONAL LTD
Registration no: 01611139 **No.of Employees:** 101 - 250
Product Groups: 51, 84

Mec A Tec Services Ltd

Boleness Road, Wisbech, PE13 2RB
Tel: 01945-474685 **Fax:** 01945-474687
E-mail: paul.framingham@mecatec.co.uk
Website: http://www.mecatec.co.uk
Directors: P. Framingham (Dir)
Managers: K. Moore (Chief Acct)
Immediate Holding Company: MEC - A - TEC SERVICES LIMITED
Registration no: 02327612 **Date established:** 1988 **Turnover:** £1m - £2m
No.of Employees: 11 - 20 **Product Groups:** 84

Date of Accounts	Dec 11	Dec 10	Dec 09
Working Capital	772	694	404
Fixed Assets	153	161	183
Current Assets	2m	3m	898

Merchant House Financial Services

Alexander House Alexandra Road, Wisbech, PE13 1HQ
Tel: 01945-585721 **Fax:** 01945-464712
E-mail: wisbech@theclarksonhillgroup.com
Website: http://www.theclarksonhillgroup.com
Directors: K. Pritchard (Dir), R. Pritchard (Grp Chief Exec), G. Withey (Fin), Pritchard (Grp Chief Exec)
Immediate Holding Company: THE CLARKSON HILL GROUP PLC
Registration no: 04310108 **Date established:** 2001
Turnover: £10m - £20m **No.of Employees:** 11 - 20 **Product Groups:** 80

Date of Accounts	Dec 09	Dec 08	Jul 07
Sales Turnover	18m	29m	18m
Pre Tax Profit/Loss	-637	-669	25
Working Capital	-143	319	661
Fixed Assets	697	785	677
Current Assets	4m	4m	4m
Current Liabilities	82	192	763

Oil-Dri UK Ltd

Bannisters Row, Wisbech, PE13 3HZ
Tel: 01945-581244 **Fax:** 01945-581250
E-mail: sales@oil-dri.co.uk
Website: http://www.oil-dri.co.uk
Bank(s): First Canadian Bank of Montreal
Managers: T. Rudge (Chief Mgr)
Ultimate Holding Company: OIL-DRI CORPORATION (USA)
Immediate Holding Company: OIL - DRI (U.K.) LIMITED
Registration no: 01224736 **Date established:** 1975 **Turnover:** £1m - £2m
No.of Employees: 11 - 20 **Product Groups:** 32

Date of Accounts	Jul 11	Jul 10	Jul 09
Sales Turnover	1m	2m	2m
Pre Tax Profit/Loss	430	-329	-377
Working Capital	-174	-609	-507
Fixed Assets	13	19	246
Current Assets	733	711	806
Current Liabilities	45	49	46

Optimum Packaging Ltd

Boleness Road, Wisbech, PE13 2RE
Tel: 01945-466060 **Fax:** 01945-580345
E-mail: sales@optimumpackaging.co.uk
Website: http://www.optimumpackaging.co.uk
Directors: P. Wilson (MD)
Immediate Holding Company: OPTIMUM PACKAGING LIMITED
Registration no: 03565381 **Date established:** 1998
Turnover: Up to £250,000 **No.of Employees:** 1 - 10 **Product Groups:** 30, 32

Date of Accounts	Mar 11	Mar 10	Mar 09
Working Capital	117	19	364
Fixed Assets	521	543	549
Current Assets	473	461	595

Peritys Greenhouses

Bona Lane Leverington, Wisbech, PE13 5JQ
Tel: 01945-410471 **Fax:** 01945-410471
E-mail: perity@peritys.co.uk
Website: http://www.peritys.co.uk
Directors: T. Perity (Ptnr)
Date established: 1987 **Turnover:** £250,000 - £500,000
No.of Employees: 1 - 10 **Product Groups:** 25

Premierchoice Ltd

3 Algores Way, Wisbech, PE13 2TQ
Tel: 01945-589558 **Fax:** 01945-587937
E-mail: info@premierchoice.co.uk
Website: http://www.premierchoice.co.uk
Directors: S. Davis (Fin), T. Pegg-paterson (MD)
Immediate Holding Company: PREMIERCHOICE LIMITED
Registration no: 05250342 **Date established:** 2004 **Turnover:** £1m - £2m
No.of Employees: 101 - 250 **Product Groups:** 63

Date of Accounts	Dec 11	Dec 10	Dec 09
Working Capital	581	601	445
Fixed Assets	2m	2m	2m
Current Assets	1m	1m	987

Priden Engineering Ltd

Algores Way, Wisbech, PE13 2TQ
Tel: 01945-588476 **Fax:** 01945-585635
E-mail: enquiries@priden.co.uk
Website: http://www.priden.co.uk
Directors: C. Prior (Prop), S. Warren (Fin)
Immediate Holding Company: PRIDEN ENGINEERING LIMITED
Registration no: 04315304 **Date established:** 2001
Turnover: £10m - £20m **No.of Employees:** 51 - 100 **Product Groups:** 30, 35

Date of Accounts	Mar 11	Mar 10	Mar 09
Sales Turnover	11m	8m	N/A
Pre Tax Profit/Loss	308	297	182
Working Capital	328	528	307
Fixed Assets	702	658	545
Current Assets	3m	2m	2m
Current Liabilities	992	502	791

Stackwell Forge

The Bank Parson Drove, Wisbech, PE13 4JD
Tel: 01945-700666 **Fax:** 01945-701242
E-mail: info@stackwellforge.com
Website: http://www.stackwellforge.com
Directors: P. Bodger (MD)
Immediate Holding Company: TAN ROSE & SONS LIMITED
Date established: 1961 **No.of Employees:** 21 - 50 **Product Groups:** 26, 35

Date of Accounts	Mar 12	Mar 11	Mar 10
Working Capital	284	282	269
Fixed Assets	27	29	24
Current Assets	303	302	295

Tanglewood Wrought Iron

36 School Road West Walton, Wisbech, PE14 7ES
Tel: 01945-466132 **Fax:** 01945-466132
E-mail: thehornets@btinternet.com
Website: http://www.tanglewoodwroughtiron.co.uk
Directors: R. Bishop (Prop)
Date established: 1998 **No.of Employees:** 1 - 10 **Product Groups:** 26, 35

TPR Resistors

Europa Way, Wisbech, PE13 2TZ
Tel: 0116-273 3633 **Fax:** 01945-464627
Website: http://www.tpr.co.uk
Directors: P. Duncan (MD)
No.of Employees: 11 - 20 **Product Groups:** 34, 37, 67

Wisbech Payroll Services

107 Norwich Road, Wisbech, PE13 2BB
Tel: 01945-464679 **Fax:** 01945-464680
E-mail: sales@wispaypayrollbureau.co.uk
Website: http://www.wispaypayrollbureau.co.uk
Directors: I. Knight (Dir)
Immediate Holding Company: WISBECH COMPUTER SERVICES LIMITED
Registration no: 01302547 **VAT No.:** GB 304 7083 81
Date established: 1977 **Turnover:** £250,000 - £500,000
No.of Employees: 1 - 10 **Product Groups:** 44, 80

Date of Accounts	Dec 09	Dec 08	Dec 07
Working Capital	-15	42	22
Fixed Assets	15	16	17
Current Assets	56	118	114

Yearsley Group

Weasenham Lane, Wisbech, PE13 2RN
Tel: 01945-474651 **Fax:** 01945-473891
E-mail: martin.talbot@yearsley.co.uk
Website: http://www.yearsley.co.uk
Bank(s): HSBC Bank plc & SG Hambros Bank and Trust Ltd
Managers: M. Talbot (Ops Mgr), R. Venemore (Chief Mgr)
Ultimate Holding Company: HUTCHINSON GROUP LIMITED
Immediate Holding Company: NORFOLK AGROCHEMICALS LIMITED
Registration no: 01616234 **Date established:** 1972
Turnover: £20m - £50m **No.of Employees:** 21 - 50 **Product Groups:** 72

Date of Accounts	Dec 03	Dec 02
Working Capital	10	10
Current Assets	10	10

CHESHIRE

Alderley Edge

Avocet Steel Strip Ltd
1 Knutsford Road, Alderley Edge, SK9 7SD
Tel: 01625-590745 **Fax:** 01625-590772
E-mail: graham@avocetsteel.co.uk
Website: http://www.avocetsteel.co.uk
Directors: G. Hall (MD), H. Hall (Fin)
Immediate Holding Company: AVOCET STEEL STRIP LIMITED
Registration no: 03255066 **Date established:** 1996
Turnover: Up to £250,000 **No.of Employees:** 1 - 10 **Product Groups:** 34, 35, 36

Date of Accounts	Sep 11	Sep 10	Sep 09
Working Capital	33	31	8
Fixed Assets	28	16	17
Current Assets	197	139	100

Emerson Management Services Ltd
Emerson House Heyes Lane, Alderley Edge, SK9 7LF
Tel: 01625-588230 **Fax:** 01625-585791
E-mail: anne.weatherby@emerson.co.uk
Website: http://www.emerson.co.uk
Bank(s): National Westminster Bank Plc & The Royal Bank of Scotland plc
Directors: A. Weatherby (Fin), P. Jones (Ch), J. Newman (Co Sec), H. Richards (Non Exec), A. Weatherby (Co Sec), T. Weatherby (Non Exec), A. White (Dir), T. Jones (MD), A. White (MD), M. Schuler (Fin)
Managers: H. Meltcalf (Mktg Serv Mgr)
Ultimate Holding Company: 01170304
Immediate Holding Company: EMERSON MANAGEMENT SERVICES LIMITED
Registration no: 01020128 **Date established:** 1971 **Turnover:** £2m - £5m
No.of Employees: 101 - 250 **Product Groups:** 80

Orbit Developments
Emerson House Heyes Lane, Alderley Edge, SK9 7LF
Tel: 01625-588400 **Fax:** 01625-585791
E-mail: info@emeson.co.uk
Website: http://www.orbit-developments.co.uk
Directors: T. Jones (Prop), P. Jones (Dir), P. Baren (Fin)
Managers: S. Wilson (Mgr)
Immediate Holding Company: ORBIT DEVELOPMENTS LIMITED
Registration no: 01186982 **Date established:** 1974 **Turnover:** £5m - £10m
No.of Employees: 101 - 250 **Product Groups:** 80

Malcolm Ross & Sons Ltd
PO Box 4, Alderley Edge, SK9 7PR
Tel: 01625-583853 **Fax:** 01625-586340
E-mail: sales@malcolmross.co.uk
Website: http://www.malcolmross.co.uk
Directors: J. Palmes (MD)
Immediate Holding Company: CROMFORD COURT PROPERTIES LIMITED
Registration no: 00299088 **VAT No.:** GB 157 9265 28
Date established: 1935 **Turnover:** £1m - £2m **No.of Employees:** 1 - 10
Product Groups: 23, 24, 27, 30, 61, 63

Date of Accounts	Mar 12	Mar 11	Mar 10
Working Capital	204	221	240
Fixed Assets	591	592	593
Current Assets	254	279	266

Altrincham

A V R Group Ltd (t/a National Monitoring)
16-24 Attenburys Park Estate Attenburys Lane, Timperley, Altrincham, WA14 5QE
Tel: 0161-905 9998 **Fax:** 0161-905 9988
E-mail: info@sonicalarm.com
Website: http://www.sonicalarm.com
Directors: V. Miller (Fin), P. Miller (MD)
Ultimate Holding Company: MONITORING LIMITED
Immediate Holding Company: A.V.R. GROUP LIMITED
Registration no: 01251842 **Date established:** 1976 **Turnover:** £2m - £5m
No.of Employees: 51 - 100 **Product Groups:** 40

Date of Accounts	Mar 11	Mar 10	Mar 09
Sales Turnover	4m	4m	N/A
Pre Tax Profit/Loss	516	-161	718
Working Capital	-553	-993	-936
Fixed Assets	3m	3m	4m
Current Assets	676	745	682
Current Liabilities	759	1m	1m

Allcode UK Ltd
Kamino House Stuart Road, Broadheath, Altrincham, WA14 5GJ
Tel: 0161-929 8158 **Fax:** 0161-929 4539
E-mail: info@allcode.co.uk
Website: http://www.allcode.co.uk
Directors: P. Holcroft (MD)
Immediate Holding Company: ALLCODE (UK) LIMITED
Registration no: 04699163 **Date established:** 2003
No.of Employees: 1 - 10 **Product Groups:** 27, 28, 30, 38, 42, 43, 44, 67, 87

Date of Accounts	Mar 11	Mar 10	Mar 09
Sales Turnover	N/A	N/A	430
Pre Tax Profit/Loss	N/A	N/A	-10
Working Capital	-4	-9	-14
Fixed Assets	6	6	6
Current Assets	91	149	124
Current Liabilities	N/A	N/A	21

Atlantic Rubber Company Ltd
Castleton Works Atlantic Street, Broadheath, Altrincham, WA14 5BX
Tel: 0161-928 3727 **Fax:** 0161-926 9755
E-mail: info@atlanticgb.co.uk
Website: http://www.atlanticrubber.co.uk
Directors: J. Anderson (MD)
Immediate Holding Company: ATLANTIC RUBBER LIMITED
Registration no: 00189846 **Date established:** 2023
Turnover: £250,000 - £500,000 **No.of Employees:** 1 - 10
Product Groups: 35, 45

Date of Accounts	Dec 11	Dec 10	Dec 09
Working Capital	47	13	13
Fixed Assets	4	5	5
Current Assets	88	72	67

Avalon and Lynwood
P.O. Box 608, Altrincham, WA15 7ZP
Tel: 0161-904 8642
E-mail: sales@avalonandlynwood.com
Website: http://www.avalonandlynwood.com
No.of Employees: 1 - 10 **Product Groups:** 22, 23, 24, 40, 42, 63

B & M Scientific
13 Goodwood Cresent Timperley, Altrincham, WA15 7BD
Tel: 0161-904 9149 **Fax:** 0161-904 9149
E-mail: info@b-mscientific.co.uk
Website: http://www.b-mscientific.co.uk
Directors: C. Walters (Prop)
Date established: 1992 **No.of Employees:** 1 - 10 **Product Groups:** 38, 67

B T T G Fire Technology Services
Unit 4b Stag Industrial Estate Atlantic Street, Broadheath, Altrincham, WA14 5DW
Tel: 0161-929 8056 **Fax:** 0161-929 8070
E-mail: paul@bttg.co.uk
Website: http://www.bttg.co.uk
Managers: P. Eaton (Mgr)
Immediate Holding Company: KEYTEQ PRESENTATION SERVICES LIMITED
Registration no: 04054830 **VAT No.:** GB 145 9206 63
Date established: 2000 **Turnover:** £5m - £10m **No.of Employees:** 1 - 10
Product Groups: 85, 86

Date of Accounts	Dec 11	Dec 10	Dec 09
Working Capital	34	55	32
Fixed Assets	24	2	N/A
Current Assets	92	72	37

C J Engineering Services
3 Mottram Drive Timperley, Altrincham, WA15 7SQ
Tel: 0161-904 8511 **Fax:** 0161-904 7620
E-mail: c.j.engineering@btconnect.com
Website: http://www.cjengineering-services.co.uk
Directors: C. Jones (Ptnr)
Date established: 1995 **No.of Employees:** 1 - 10 **Product Groups:** 35, 39, 45

C S E Ltd
Stag Industrial Estate Atlantic Street, Broadheath, Altrincham, WA14 5DW
Tel: 0161-929 8585 **Fax:** 0161-941 6182
E-mail: garry@cselimited.co.uk
Website: http://www.cseltd.co.uk
Directors: G. Lavis (MD)
Ultimate Holding Company: CSE INTERNATIONAL (HOLDINGS) LIMITED
Immediate Holding Company: CSE LTD
Registration no: 04316596 **Date established:** 2001 **Turnover:** £1m - £2m
No.of Employees: 11 - 20 **Product Groups:** 44, 79

Carbon Technology Ltd
Woodfield House Woodfield Road, Broadheath, Altrincham, WA14 4ED
Tel: 0161-941 7173 **Fax:** 0161-941 7156
E-mail: david@carbon-technology.com
Website: http://www.carbon-technology.com
Directors: D. Whitney (MD), H. Whitney (Fin)
Immediate Holding Company: CARBON TECHNOLOGY LIMITED
Registration no: 03416831 **Date established:** 1997
No.of Employees: 1 - 10 **Product Groups:** 26, 30, 33, 37, 39, 44, 46, 48

Date of Accounts	Aug 08	Aug 07	Aug 06
Working Capital	89	98	66
Fixed Assets	24	14	19
Current Assets	133	182	118
Current Liabilities	44	84	52

Cheshire Specialist Engineering Ltd
L & M Business Park Norman Road, Altrincham, WA14 4ES
Tel: 0161-928 6138 **Fax:** 0161-928 6139
E-mail: sales@cseng.co.uk
Website: http://www.cseng.co.uk
Directors: S. Evans (MD)
Immediate Holding Company: CHESHIRE SPECIALIST ENGINEERING LIMITED
Registration no: 06896108 **Date established:** 2009 **Turnover:** £1m - £2m
No.of Employees: 11 - 20 **Product Groups:** 48

Date of Accounts	Dec 11	Dec 10	May 10
Working Capital	97	N/A	N/A
Fixed Assets	26	N/A	N/A
Current Assets	253	N/A	N/A

Cheshire Tool Co. Ltd
5 Peerglow Industrial Estate Park Road, Timperley, Altrincham, WA14 5QH
Tel: 0161-969 3717 **Fax:** 0161-969 6264
E-mail: darren.leverett@ctcpressings.com
Website: http://www.ctcpressings.com
Directors: D. Leverett (Dir), P. Carr (Fin)
Ultimate Holding Company: CHESHIRE TOOL AND PRESSING COMPANY LIMITED
Immediate Holding Company: CHESHIRE TOOL COMPANY LIMITED
Registration no: 01015904 **VAT No.:** GB 144 9243 63
Date established: 1971 **Turnover:** £1m - £2m **No.of Employees:** 1 - 10
Product Groups: 30, 33, 34, 36, 37, 39, 46, 67

Date of Accounts	Dec 11	Jun 10	Jun 09
Working Capital	284	168	112
Fixed Assets	89	142	179
Current Assets	915	604	476

Concept Systems Design Ltd
1 Pacific Court Pacific Road Atlantic Street, Broadheath, Altrincham, WA14 5BJ
Tel: 0161-929 7434 **Fax:** 0161-929 0904
E-mail: sales@csd-epi.com
Website: http://www.csd-ltd.co.uk
Directors: A. Goode (MD), J. Goode (Fin)
Turnover: Up to £250,000 **No.of Employees:** 1 - 10 **Product Groups:** 37, 47, 80

Countrywide Fire Services
Gladstone House Gladstone Road, Altrincham, WA14 1NS
Tel: 0161-928 4756
Website: http://www.countrywidefireservices.co.uk
Directors: T. Smith (Prop)
Immediate Holding Company: COUNTRYWIDE VEHICLE DELIVERIES LTD
Registration no: 03487498 **Date established:** 1995
No.of Employees: 1 - 10 **Product Groups:** 38, 42

Cresta Holidays Ltd
Suite 2c Tabley Court Victoria Street, Altrincham, WA14 1EZ
Tel: 08448-007019 **Fax:** 0870-1690797
Website: http://www.crestaholidays.co.uk
Directors: E. Ferrin (MD), R. Locke (Dir), S. Kimber (MD), P. Tanner (Fin)
Managers: K. Byrne (Nat Sales Mgr), J. Willings (Mktg Serv Mgr), P. Edwards (Sec)
Ultimate Holding Company: Thomas Cook Group plc
Immediate Holding Company: CRESTA HOLIDAYS LIMITED
Registration no: 02676147 **VAT No.:** GB 437 6228 39
Date established: 1992 **Turnover:** £75m - £125m
No.of Employees: 251 - 500 **Product Groups:** 69

Datacolor International Ltd

6 St Georges Court Dairyhouse Lane, Broadheath, Altrincham, WA14 5UA
Tel: 0161-929 9441 **Fax:** 0161-929 9059
E-mail: info@datacolor.com
Website: http://www.datacolor.com
Directors: S. Dobler (Dir)
Ultimate Holding Company: EICHHOF HOLDING AG (SWITZERLAND)
Immediate Holding Company: DATACOLOR INTERNATIONAL LTD
Registration no: 00964744 **VAT No.:** GB 561 2933 45
Date established: 1969 **Turnover:** £2m - £5m **No.of Employees:** 1 - 10
Product Groups: 38

Date of Accounts	Sep 11	Sep 10	Sep 09
Sales Turnover	2m	2m	2m
Pre Tax Profit/Loss	405	135	164
Working Capital	3m	2m	2m
Fixed Assets	53	11	9
Current Assets	4m	3m	3m
Current Liabilities	682	675	526

Downs Court Business Centre

Downs Court 31 The Downs, Altrincham, WA14 2QD
Tel: 0161-941 2868 **Fax:** 0161-941 6124
E-mail: info@downscourt.co.uk
Website: http://www.downscourt.co.uk
Directors: L. Atkinson (Dir)
Immediate Holding Company: DOWNS COURT PROPERTIES LIMITED
Registration no: 01558662 **VAT No.:** GB 628 9836 83
Date established: 1981 **Turnover:** £500,000 - £1m
No.of Employees: 1 - 10 **Product Groups:** 80

Date of Accounts	Dec 05	Dec 04	Dec 03
Working Capital	-61	-209	-219
Fixed Assets	1m	333	332
Current Assets	91	53	31
Current Liabilities	23	N/A	N/A

Dulux Ltd

Aspect House Manchester Road, West Timperley, Altrincham, WA14 5PG
Tel: 0161-973 6206 **Fax:** 0161-962 9539
Website: http://www.dulux.co.uk
Directors: D. Loose (Dir), P. Kearney (Dir)
Managers: J. Hyde (Mgr), P. Brigham
Ultimate Holding Company: AKZO NOBEL NV (NETHERLANDS)
Immediate Holding Company: DULUX LIMITED
Registration no: 00967742 **VAT No.:** GB 145 0706 88
Date established: 1969 **Turnover:** £75m - £125m
No.of Employees: 1 - 10 **Product Groups:** 66

DXL Parcels

Unit 5 Oakfield Trading Estate, Altrincham, WA15 8EJ
Tel: 0161-291 9808 **Fax:** 0161-941 7383
E-mail: operations@dxlparcels.co.uk
Website: http://www.dxlparcels.co.uk
Directors: C. Churchward (MD)
Managers: M. Gallagher (Ops Mgr)
Registration no: 02908840 **Turnover:** £250,000 - £500,000
No.of Employees: 1 - 10 **Product Groups:** 79

E A B Associates (t/a E A B Associates Ltd)

3 Craven Court Craven Road, Broadheath, Altrincham, WA14 5DY
Tel: 0161-926 9077 **Fax:** 0161-927 7718
E-mail: eaball@eabassoc.co.uk
Website: http://www.eabassoc.co.uk
Directors: J. Basiurski (Dir)
Immediate Holding Company: CUMULUS SLEEPING BAGS LIMITED
Registration no: 05082800 **Date established:** 2004
No.of Employees: 1 - 10 **Product Groups:** 30, 31, 32, 33, 45, 66

Date of Accounts	Dec 11	Dec 10	Dec 09
Working Capital	9	8	7
Fixed Assets	9	12	14
Current Assets	77	75	73

Farrat Isolevel

Balmoral Road, Altrincham, WA15 8HJ
Tel: 0161-928 3654 **Fax:** 08700-111809
E-mail: rjf@farrat.com
Website: http://www.farrat.com
Bank(s): Lloyds TSB Bank plc
Directors: A. Farrell (Dir)
Immediate Holding Company: FARRAT ISOLEVEL LIMITED
Registration no: 00635283 **VAT No.:** GB 145 9515 50
Date established: 1959 **Turnover:** £500,000 - £1m
No.of Employees: 11 - 20 **Product Groups:** 29, 30, 35, 38, 39, 46

Date of Accounts	Dec 11	Dec 10	Dec 09
Working Capital	1m	2m	2m
Fixed Assets	864	213	187
Current Assets	2m	2m	2m

Gunn J C B

Atlantic Street Broadheath, Altrincham, WA14 5DN
Tel: 0161-941 2631 **Fax:** 0161-942 3399
E-mail: gordon.smith@gunn-jcb.co.uk
Website: http://www.gunn-jcb.co.uk
Bank(s): Barclays P.L.C., Altrincham
Managers: S. Nixton
Ultimate Holding Company: GUNN JCB (HOLDINGS) LIMITED
Immediate Holding Company: GUNN JCB COMPACT EQUIPMENT LIMITED
Registration no: 00200773 **VAT No.:** GB 150 9025 90
Date established: 2024 **Turnover:** £50m - £75m
No.of Employees: 101 - 250 **Product Groups:** 45, 48, 67

Date of Accounts	Dec 11	Dec 10	Dec 09
Working Capital	4	4	4
Current Assets	4	4	4

Hale Instruments Ltd

18 Atlantic Business Centre Atlantic Street, Broadheath, Altrincham, WA14 5NQ
Tel: 0161-941 4540 **Fax:** 0161-926 8597
E-mail: sales@haleinst.com
Website: http://www.haleinst.com
Directors: J. Woolley (MD)
Managers: A. French (Intern Sales En), J. Woolley (Intern Sales En)
Immediate Holding Company: HALE INSTRUMENTS LIMITED
Registration no: 01518582 **VAT No.:** GB 306 3710 88
Date established: 1980 **Turnover:** £2m - £5m **No.of Employees:** 1 - 10
Product Groups: 33, 37, 38, 39, 44, 46, 67, 84

Date of Accounts	Oct 11	Oct 10	Oct 09
Working Capital	261	273	225
Fixed Assets	17	26	26
Current Assets	427	617	370

Haven Independent Financial Advisors Ltd

2a Old Market Place, Altrincham, WA14 4NP
Tel: 0161-928 9961 **Fax:** 0161-928 9971
E-mail: sales@havenifa.co.uk
Website: http://www.havenifa.co.uk
Directors: V. Tarry (Co Sec)
Immediate Holding Company: DRIFT MEDIA LTD
Registration no: 02873345 **Date established:** 2007
No.of Employees: 1 - 10 **Product Groups:** 80

Date of Accounts	Apr 09	Apr 08
Working Capital	-4	-4
Current Assets	N/A	1

J M Heaford Ltd

9 Century Park Pacific Road Broadheath, Altrincham, WA14 5BJ
Tel: 0161-928 5679 **Fax:** 0161-927 7517
E-mail: sales@jmheaford.co.uk
Website: http://www.jmheaford.co.uk
Bank(s): National Westminster
Directors: S. Heaford (Dir), N. Heaford (Sales)
Managers: L. Taberner
Ultimate Holding Company: SEODIN LIMITED
Immediate Holding Company: J M HEAFORD LIMITED
Registration no: 01654202 **VAT No.:** GB 383 1203 77
Date established: 1982 **Turnover:** £5m - £10m **No.of Employees:** 21 - 50
Product Groups: 44

Date of Accounts	Mar 11	Mar 10	Mar 09
Working Capital	1m	1m	1m
Fixed Assets	55	39	79
Current Assets	4m	3m	3m

Heywood Ltd

2 Victoria Street, Altrincham, WA14 1ET
Tel: 0161-613 4200 **Fax:** 0161-927 7132
E-mail: enquiries@heywood.co.uk
Website: http://www.heywood.co.uk
Directors: R. Sumner (Pers), A. Trotter (Co Sec), A. Tegg (I.T. Dir)
Immediate Holding Company: HEYWOOD TRUSTEES LIMITED
Registration no: 02603663 **Date established:** 1991 **Turnover:** £2m - £5m
No.of Employees: 101 - 250 **Product Groups:** 44

Hydratron Ltd

Unit A1 Stuart Road, Broadheath, Altrincham, WA14 5GJ
Tel: 0161-928 6221 **Fax:** 0161-927 7085
E-mail: info@hydratron.co.uk
Website: http://www.hydratron.co.uk
Bank(s): Barclays
Directors: P. Sanders (MD), F. Beveridge (MD)
Managers: J. Miller (Prod Mgr), P. Watts (Sales Prom Mgr), J. Melia, C. Thorpe (Purch Mgr)
Ultimate Holding Company: PRESSURE TECHNOLOGIES PLC
Immediate Holding Company: HYDRATRON LIMITED
Registration no: 01548328 **Date established:** 1981 **Turnover:** £5m - £10m
No.of Employees: 51 - 100 **Product Groups:** 36, 38, 39, 40, 67, 85

Date of Accounts	Apr 10	Apr 09	Apr 08
Working Capital	1m	915	700
Fixed Assets	563	620	666
Current Assets	2m	2m	2m

Kennedy Street Enterprises Ltd

Kennedy House 31 Stamford Street, Altrincham, WA14 1ES
Tel: 0161-941 5151 **Fax:** 0161-928 9491
E-mail: kse@kennedystreet.com
Website: http://www.kennedystreet.com
Directors: T. Betesh (MD), D. Betesh (Fin)
Ultimate Holding Company: KENNEDY STREET HOLDINGS LIMITED
Immediate Holding Company: KENNEDY STREET ENTERPRISES LIMITED
Registration no: 00650265 **Date established:** 1960
Turnover: £10m - £20m **No.of Employees:** 1 - 10 **Product Groups:** 89

Date of Accounts	Dec 11	Dec 10	Dec 09
Sales Turnover	13m	12m	13m
Pre Tax Profit/Loss	69	-508	1m
Working Capital	3m	3m	3m
Fixed Assets	57	538	785
Current Assets	4m	4m	4m
Current Liabilities	505	971	1m

Kurt Salmon

Bruce Court 25a Hale Road, Altrincham, WA14 2EY
Tel: 020-7710 9500 **Fax:** 0161-927 7135
E-mail: manchester@kurtsalmon.com
Website: http://www.kurtsalmon.com
Directors: A. Smyth (Dir), C. Ansley (Co Sec), H. Mountney (Dep Pres)
Managers: J. Ripley (Admin Off), H. Mountliy (Mgr)
Immediate Holding Company: KURT SALMON ASSOCIATES LIMITED
Registration no: 00641077 **Date established:** 1959 **Turnover:** £2m - £5m
No.of Employees: 11 - 20 **Product Groups:** 80

Date of Accounts	Dec 10	Dec 09	Dec 08
Sales Turnover	4m	3m	3m
Pre Tax Profit/Loss	745	877	-1m
Working Capital	-6m	-6m	-7m
Fixed Assets	12	14	26
Current Assets	3m	2m	7m
Current Liabilities	861	457	793

L & M Ltd

L & M Business Park Norman Road, Altrincham, WA14 4ES
Tel: 0161-928 6131 **Fax:** 0161-927 7277
E-mail: info@landmproducts.co.uk
Bank(s): National Westminster Bank Plc
Directors: F. Bryant (Dir), J. Rattray (Dir)
Ultimate Holding Company: TIMEWILD LIMITED
Immediate Holding Company: L & M LIMITED
Registration no: 01486512 **Date established:** 1980 **Turnover:** £2m - £5m
No.of Employees: 21 - 50 **Product Groups:** 44, 48

Date of Accounts	Dec 11	Dec 10	Dec 09
Working Capital	191	185	144
Fixed Assets	7m	2m	2m
Current Assets	301	416	323

Legal & Technical Translations Ltd

16 Old Market Place, Altrincham, WA14 4DF
Tel: 0161-941 2024 **Fax:** 0161-927 7024
E-mail: joaquin.sallares@itsgroup.co.uk
Website: http://www.itsgroup.co.uk
Directors: J. Sallares (MD), G. Sallares (Ptnr), J. Sallares (Ptnr), J. Sallares (Prop)
Immediate Holding Company: LEGAL AND TECHNICAL TRANSLATIONS LTD
Registration no: 04964462 **VAT No.:** GB 359 2501 49
Date established: 2003 **Turnover:** Up to £250,000
No.of Employees: 1 - 10 **Product Groups:** 80

Date of Accounts	Dec 10	Dec 09	Dec 08
Working Capital	48	39	37
Fixed Assets	56	60	64
Current Assets	122	101	101

Lovell Partnerships Ltd

Nelson House Park Road, Timperley, Altrincham, WA14 5DL
Tel: 0161-905 1727 **Fax:** 0161-905 1645
E-mail: nigel.yates@lovell.co.uk
Website: http://www.lovell.co.uk
Directors: N. Yates (Dir)
Managers: F. Langan (Buyer), A. Cibbald (Personnel), B. Phythian (Chief Acct), J. Lowe, D. Powell (Personnel)
Ultimate Holding Company: MORGAN SINDALL GROUP PLC
Immediate Holding Company: LOVELL PARTNERSHIPS LIMITED
Registration no: 02387333 **VAT No.:** GB 208 0334 04
Date established: 1989 **Turnover:** £5m - £10m
No.of Employees: 101 - 250 **Product Groups:** 80

Date of Accounts	Dec 11	Dec 10	Dec 09
Sales Turnover	458m	382m	372m
Pre Tax Profit/Loss	13m	11m	14m
Working Capital	70m	58m	49m
Fixed Assets	37m	38m	7m
Current Assets	241m	234m	186m
Current Liabilities	107m	130m	101m

Maxa Technologies Ltd

Atlantic Street Broadheath, Altrincham, WA14 5QJ
Tel: 0161-942 7850 **Fax:** 0161-927 7664
E-mail: steve.berry@maxatec-europe.com
Website: http://www.maxatec-europe.com
Bank(s): Lloyds TSB Bank plc
Directors: S. Berry (Dir), A. Percival (MD)
Ultimate Holding Company: MAXA HOLDINGS LIMITED
Immediate Holding Company: MAXA TECHNOLOGIES LIMITED
Registration no: 01023783 **VAT No.:** GB 146 8586 26
Date established: 1971 **Turnover:** £5m - £10m **No.of Employees:** 11 - 20
Product Groups: 27, 36, 42, 43, 44, 67, 87

Date of Accounts	Aug 12	Aug 11	Aug 10
Working Capital	1m	1m	1m
Current Assets	2m	2m	2m
Current Liabilities	371	N/A	N/A

Medem UK Ltd

Unit 9 L & M Business Park Norman Road, Altrincham, WA14 4ES
Tel: 0161-233 0600 **Fax:** 0161-233 0601
E-mail: info@medem.co.uk
Website: http://www.medem.co.uk
Directors: C. Blackday (Tech Serv), C. Dearden (Tech Serv)
Immediate Holding Company: MEDEM (U.K.) LIMITED
Registration no: 01792194 **Date established:** 1984 **Turnover:** £1m - £2m
No.of Employees: 1 - 10 **Product Groups:** 37, 38, 40

Date of Accounts	Mar 12	Mar 11	Mar 10
Working Capital	495	471	460
Fixed Assets	87	98	18
Current Assets	615	620	574

Mondi Packaging Ltd

Crown House, Crown Industrial Park Canal Road, Timperley, Altrincham, WA14 1TD
Tel: 0161-976 3000 **Fax:** 0161-975 3727
E-mail: ce@mondipackaging.com
Website: http://www.mondigroup.com
Directors: A. Stewart (MD)
Managers: C. Berisford (Sales Prom Mgr)
Ultimate Holding Company: Danisco Pack AS
Immediate Holding Company: Danisco Pack Ltd
Registration no: 01846191 **Turnover:** £2m - £5m
No.of Employees: 11 - 20 **Product Groups:** 27, 28, 49, 85

Mott Macdonald

Spring Bank House 33 Stamford Street, Altrincham, WA14 1ES
Tel: 0161-926 4000 **Fax:** 01204-600661
E-mail: mail@teamwork-ms.co.uk
Website: http://www.teamwork-ms.co.uk
Directors: K. Howells (Dir), M. Lynn (Co Sec)
Ultimate Holding Company: MOTT MACDONALD GROUP LIMITED
Immediate Holding Company: TEAMWORK MANAGEMENT SERVICES LIMITED
Registration no: 02474427 **Date established:** 1990 **Turnover:** £2m - £5m
No.of Employees: 11 - 20 **Product Groups:** 84

Date of Accounts	Dec 11	Dec 10	Dec 09
Sales Turnover	N/A	N/A	2m
Pre Tax Profit/Loss	N/A	N/A	378
Working Capital	785	785	751
Fixed Assets	N/A	N/A	37
Current Assets	785	785	935
Current Liabilities	N/A	N/A	169

National Industrial Fuel Efficiency Consulting Group

Nifes House Sinderland Road, Broadheath, Altrincham, WA14 5HQ
Tel: 0161-928 5791 **Fax:** 0161-926 8718
E-mail: andy.hannah@nifes.co.uk
Website: http://www.nifes.co.uk
Bank(s): Barclays
Directors: A. Hannah (Comm), C. Sharples (Fin), L. Johnstone (Co Sec), M. Morton (Sales & Mktg)
Ultimate Holding Company: CILANTRO MIDCO LIMITED
Immediate Holding Company: NATIONAL INDUSTRIAL FUEL EFFICIENCY SERVICE LIMITED
Registration no: 01031298 **VAT No.:** GB 437 8684 03
Date established: 1971 **Turnover:** £5m - £10m
No.of Employees: 101 - 250 **Product Groups:** 54

Date of Accounts	Oct 08	Oct 07	Apr 11
Sales Turnover	9m	7m	9m
Pre Tax Profit/Loss	374	198	74
Working Capital	2m	672	2m
Fixed Assets	247	1m	N/A
Current Assets	3m	3m	2m
Current Liabilities	2m	1m	N/A

Nova Group Ltd
Norman Road, Altrincham, WA14 4EN
Tel: 0161-613 9600 **Fax:** 0161-926 8405
E-mail: it@novagroup.co.uk
Website: http://www.novagroup.co.uk
Directors: S. Felstein (MD), P. Corrie (Mkt Research)
Managers: D. East, K. Jones, I. Wootton (Tech Serv Mgr)
Ultimate Holding Company: NOVA DOUBLE GLAZING SYSTEMS LIMITED
Immediate Holding Company: NOVA GROUP LIMITED
Registration no: 01505265 **Date established:** 1980 **Turnover:** £5m - £10m
No.of Employees: 101 - 250 **Product Groups:** 36

Date of Accounts	Dec 11	Dec 10	Dec 09
Sales Turnover	8m	9m	9m
Pre Tax Profit/Loss	178	242	250
Working Capital	2m	2m	2m
Fixed Assets	3m	3m	3m
Current Assets	4m	4m	3m
Current Liabilities	856	1m	779

P I Castings Ltd
Davenport Lane Broadheath, Altrincham, WA14 5DS
Tel: 0161-928 5811 **Fax:** 0161-927 7023
E-mail: admin@pi-castings.co.uk
Website: http://www.pi-castings.co.uk
Bank(s): National Westminster Bank Plc
Directors: D. Farncombe (Sales), I. Taylor (MD), M. Robertson (Fin)
Managers: J. Bullock (Personnel), A. Darby (Mats Contrlr)
Ultimate Holding Company: TEKMET LTD.
Immediate Holding Company: P. I. CASTINGS LIMITED
Registration no: 00478116 **VAT No.:** GB 146 0704 86
Date established: 1950 **Turnover:** £5m - £10m
No.of Employees: 101 - 250 **Product Groups:** 34

Date of Accounts	Apr 12	May 09	May 10
Sales Turnover	N/A	5m	N/A
Pre Tax Profit/Loss	N/A	-103	N/A
Working Capital	204	181	-398
Fixed Assets	309	380	344
Current Assets	3m	2m	2m
Current Liabilities	N/A	211	N/A

Principal Image
Cherry Tree Lane Rostherne, Altrincham, WA14 3RZ
Tel: 01565-830213 **Fax:** 01565-830214
E-mail: info@principalimage.com
Website: http://www.principleimage.com
Directors: M. Berrisford (Prop)
Ultimate Holding Company: PRINCIPAL IMAGE UK LIMITED
Immediate Holding Company: PRINCIPAL IMAGE LIMITED
Registration no: 02462784 **VAT No.:** GB 603 3036 92
Date established: 1990 **Turnover:** £500,000 - £1m
No.of Employees: 1 - 10 **Product Groups:** 28, 44, 81, 84

Date of Accounts	Feb 12	Feb 11	Feb 10
Working Capital	101	109	93
Fixed Assets	13	4	11
Current Assets	160	177	166

Quelfire Ltd
PO Box 35, Altrincham, WA14 5QA
Tel: 0161-928 7308 **Fax:** 0161-924 1340
E-mail: stephendunbar@quelfire.co.uk
Website: http://www.quelfire.co.uk
Directors: S. Dunbar (Dir), A. Dunbar (Co Sec)
Immediate Holding Company: QUELFIRE LIMITED
Registration no: 02172353 **VAT No.:** GB 150 6701 91
Date established: 1987 **Turnover:** £1m - £2m **No.of Employees:** 1 - 10
Product Groups: 40

Sabre Instrument Valves Ltd
Golf Road Hale, Altrincham, WA15 8AH
Tel: 0161-925 4000 **Fax:** 0161-925 4021
E-mail: sales@sabreuk.com
Website: http://www.sabreuk.com
Bank(s): National Westminster Bank Plc
Directors: P. Veitch (Fin)
Ultimate Holding Company: SABRE HOLDINGS (UK) LIMITED
Immediate Holding Company: DUBLOK (UK) LIMITED
Registration no: 00880859 **VAT No.:** GB 519 7067 26
Date established: 1966 **Turnover:** £1m - £2m **No.of Employees:** 21 - 50
Product Groups: 36, 39, 40, 42

Date of Accounts	Dec 11	Dec 10	Dec 09
Working Capital	50	50	50
Current Assets	50	50	50

Sigma Engineering M C Ltd
26 Church Street, Altrincham, WA14 4DW
Tel: 0161-928 9988 **Fax:** 0161-926 8726
E-mail: office@sigmaengineering.co.uk
Website: http://www.sigmaengineering.co.uk
Directors: V. Guillemain (Dir)
Immediate Holding Company: SIGMA ENGINEERING(M/C)LIMITED
Registration no: 00924664 **Date established:** 1967
Turnover: £500,000 - £1m **No.of Employees:** 1 - 10 **Product Groups:** 39, 40

Date of Accounts	Dec 11	Dec 10	Dec 09
Working Capital	15	-38	-44
Fixed Assets	23	25	27
Current Assets	452	708	669

Silhouette Beauty Equipment
122-124 Grove Lane Timperley, Altrincham, WA15 6PL
Tel: 0161-980 1080 **Fax:** 0161-980 5040
E-mail: support@silhouetteinternational.co.uk
Website: http://www.silhouettebeauty.com
Directors: G. Birtwistle (Dir)
Registration no: 01936731 **Date established:** 1985 **Turnover:** £1m - £2m
No.of Employees: 11 - 20 **Product Groups:** 26, 28, 32, 37, 61, 63, 67, 83

Spencer Control Systems
Caidan House Canal Road, Timperley, Altrincham, WA14 1TD
Tel: 0161-975 4934
E-mail: ps@spencer-control-systems.co.uk
Website: http://www.spencer-control-systems.co.uk
Directors: P. Spencer (Prop)
Immediate Holding Company: HARROWLANE BUILDERS LIMITED
Date established: 1988 **No.of Employees:** 1 - 10 **Product Groups:** 37, 40, 45

Steelform Ltd
6b Lyon Road Atlantic Street, Broadheath, Altrincham, WA14 5EF
Tel: 0161-929 1198 **Fax:** 0161-929 1209
E-mail: cad@steelform.ltd.uk
Website: http://www.steelform.ltd.uk
Directors: G. Pulley (MD)
Immediate Holding Company: STEELFORM LIMITED
Registration no: 01212029 **Date established:** 1975
Turnover: £500,000 - £1m **No.of Employees:** 1 - 10 **Product Groups:** 26, 35

Date of Accounts	May 11	May 10	May 09
Sales Turnover	590	793	1m
Pre Tax Profit/Loss	-45	-16	11
Working Capital	69	108	105
Fixed Assets	22	29	45
Current Assets	159	186	204
Current Liabilities	34	18	32

Sterling Fluid Systems UK Ltd
Atlantic Street Broadheath, Altrincham, WA14 5DH
Tel: 0161-928 6371 **Fax:** 0161-925 2129
E-mail: uksales@sterlingfluid.com
Website: http://www.sterlingsihi.com
Directors: P. Bull (Fin), S. Hampson (Sales)
Managers: E. Mohdieck, S. Shames (Mktg Serv Mgr)
Ultimate Holding Company: TBG HOLDINGS NV (NETHERLANDS ANTILLES)
Immediate Holding Company: STERLING FLUID SYSTEMS (UK) LIMITED
Registration no: 00340267 **Date established:** 1938 **Turnover:** £5m - £10m
No.of Employees: 21 - 50 **Product Groups:** 40

Date of Accounts	Nov 11	Nov 10	Nov 09
Sales Turnover	6m	6m	6m
Pre Tax Profit/Loss	725	330	64
Working Capital	2m	2m	1m
Fixed Assets	31	34	49
Current Assets	3m	3m	2m
Current Liabilities	535	457	234

Storage Design & Services
6 Craven Court Craven Road, Broadheath, Altrincham, WA14 5DY
Tel: 0161-928 8558 **Fax:** 0161-928 2998
E-mail: andywatson2@btinternet.com
Directors: A. Watson (Prop)
Immediate Holding Company: OAKLEIGH CABINETS LTD
Registration no: 05685523 **Date established:** 2006
Turnover: £250,000 - £500,000 **No.of Employees:** 1 - 10
Product Groups: 26, 30, 35, 36, 67, 84

Sulzer Dowding & Mills
Atlantic Street Broadheath, Altrincham, WA14 5DJ
Tel: 0161-928 6444 **Fax:** 0161-926 9685
E-mail: engineering.manchester@dowdingandmills.com
Website: http://www.sulzer.com
Managers: L. Hudson (District Mgr)
Ultimate Holding Company: CASTLE SUPPORT SERVICES PLC
Immediate Holding Company: DOWDING & MILLS PLC
Registration no: SC028056 **Turnover:** £75m - £125m
No.of Employees: 21 - 50 **Product Groups:** 35, 48

Technical Silicones Ltd
6 Ambassador Place Stockport Road, Altrincham, WA15 8DB
Tel: 0161-941 5766 **Fax:** 0161-926 8722
E-mail: dkftechsil@btconnect.com
Website: http://www.technical-silicones.co.uk
Registration no: 01287849 **Turnover:** £2m - £5m
No.of Employees: 1 - 10 **Product Groups:** 31, 37, 48, 84

Date of Accounts	Oct 09	Oct 08	Oct 07
Working Capital	75	113	141
Fixed Assets	3	4	5
Current Assets	450	623	650

Themis
39 Hale Road, Altrincham, WA14 2EY
Tel: 0161-928 3500 **Fax:** 0161-929 0372
E-mail: sales@themissupport.com
Website: http://www.themissupport.com
Managers: J. Allman (Mgr)
Immediate Holding Company: THEMIS SUPPORT SERVICES LIMITED
Registration no: 05115698 **Date established:** 2004
No.of Employees: 1 - 10 **Product Groups:** 54, 61, 84, 86

Thermo Fisher Scientific
1 St Georges Court Hanover Business Park, Broadheath, Altrincham, WA14 5TP
Tel: 0161-942 3000 **Fax:** 0161-942 3001
E-mail: sales@thermolabsystems.com
Website: http://www.thermofisher.com
Managers: K. Smith (Mgr), G. Mitchell (Fin Mgr)
Ultimate Holding Company: THERMO ELECTRON CORPORATION CO.
Immediate Holding Company: THERMO INSTRUMENT SYSTEMS INC
Registration no: 03153083 **Turnover:** £20m - £50m
No.of Employees: 51 - 100 **Product Groups:** 44, 85

Turbotech Precison Products Ltd
1c Stag Industrial Estate Atlantic Street, Broadheath, Altrincham, WA14 5DW
Tel: 0161-927 7873 **Fax:** 0161-927 7023
E-mail: admin@turbotech.co.uk
Website: http://www.turbotech.co.uk
Managers: M. Sobkowiak (Workshop)
Ultimate Holding Company: TPP COMPRESSORS LIMITED
Immediate Holding Company: TURBOTECH PRECISION PRODUCTS LIMITED
Registration no: 02094056 **Date established:** 1987
No.of Employees: 1 - 10 **Product Groups:** 34

Date of Accounts	Apr 12	May 09	May 10
Working Capital	374	689	602
Fixed Assets	432	166	144
Current Assets	809	790	799

U K S Mobility (www.uksbreastscreening.com)
328 Manchester Road West Timperley, Altrincham, WA14 5NH
Tel: 0161-973 8168 **Fax:** 0161-969 4011
E-mail: uksmobility00@hotmail.com
Website: http://www.uksmobility.co.uk
Directors: G. Simister (Prop)
Registration no: 04913718 **No.of Employees:** 1 - 10 **Product Groups:** 54, 81, 82, 84, 87, 88

U P M Kymmene Ltd
2 Victoria Street, Altrincham, WA14 1ET
Tel: 0870-6000876 **Fax:** 0870-6060876
Website: http://www.upm-kymmene.com
Bank(s): Hambros
Directors: K. Lyden (MD)
Managers: K. Hodges (Chief Mgr)
Immediate Holding Company: UPM Kymmene Corporation Helsinki
Registration no: 00874773 **Turnover:** £500m - £1,000m
No.of Employees: 51 - 100 **Product Groups:** 32

U S F Blastrac
PO Box 60, Altrincham, WA14 5EP
Tel: 0161-928 6388 **Fax:** 0161-929 0381
E-mail: uk-info@wheelabrator.co.uk
Website: http://www.wheelabrator.com
Bank(s): HSBC Bank plc
Directors: V. Comer (Dir), A. Carmicheal (MD), N. Moseley (Fin)
Managers: T. Jordan (Sales Eng), C. Ward (Mktg Serv Mgr), P. Hawthorne (I.T. Exec)
Ultimate Holding Company: Vivendi SA
Immediate Holding Company: US Filter
Registration no: 00033672 **VAT No.:** GB 561 0079 67
Turnover: £10m - £20m **No.of Employees:** 51 - 100 **Product Groups:** 40, 46, 48

H Varley Ltd
Unit 5 Century Park Pacific Road Atlantic Street, Broadheath, Altrincham, WA14 5BJ
Tel: 0161-928 9817 **Fax:** 01923-245513
E-mail: sales@varley.co.uk
Website: http://www.varley.co.uk
Directors: T. Batton (MD)
Immediate Holding Company: H.VARLEY LIMITED
Registration no: 00344712 **Date established:** 1938
No.of Employees: 1 - 10 **Product Groups:** 29, 39

Date of Accounts	Dec 11	Dec 10	Dec 09
Working Capital	327	180	178
Fixed Assets	719	869	903
Current Assets	1m	973	955

Vegetarian Society UK Ltd
Parkdale Dunham Road, Altrincham, WA14 4QG
Tel: 0161-925 2000 **Fax:** 0161-926 9182
E-mail: jon@vegsoc.org
Website: http://www.vegsoc.org
Directors: A. Byatt (Co Sec), G. Thomson (Dir), J. Green (Grp Chief Exec), A. Walker (Dir), G. Fox (Grp Chief Exec), A. Pinner (Co Sec)
Managers: L. Oneill (Mktg Serv Mgr)
Immediate Holding Company: VEGETARIAN SOCIETY OF THE UNITED KINGDOM LIMITED (THE)
Registration no: 00959115 **Date established:** 1969 **Turnover:** £1m - £2m
No.of Employees: 21 - 50 **Product Groups:** 80

S Whitehead Ironfounders Ltd
Atlantic Street Broadheath, Altrincham, WA14 5DH
Tel: 0161-928 4631 **Fax:** 0161-928 4631
Directors: P. Whitehead (Dir)
Immediate Holding Company: S.WHITEHEAD(IRONFOUNDERS)LIMITED
Registration no: 00483004 **Date established:** 1950
Turnover: Up to £250,000 **No.of Employees:** 1 - 10 **Product Groups:** 34

Date of Accounts	Jan 12	Jan 11	Jan 10
Working Capital	132	107	114
Fixed Assets	6	8	10
Current Assets	147	117	129

Xpertise Group PLC
Pacific Road Atlantic Office Park, Broadheath, Altrincham, WA14 5BJ
Tel: 0161-929 2230 **Fax:** 0161-929 2250
E-mail: enquiries@xpertise.co.uk
Website: http://www.xpertise.co.uk
Directors: I. Johnson (Co Sec), W. Walker (Dir)
Ultimate Holding Company: QA-IQ HOLDINGS LIMITED
Immediate Holding Company: XPERTISE GROUP LIMITED
Registration no: 00675312 **Date established:** 1960
Turnover: £10m - £20m **No.of Employees:** 101 - 250 **Product Groups:** 86

Date of Accounts	May 09	May 10	May 12
Pre Tax Profit/Loss	-6m	N/A	N/A
Working Capital	1m	1m	1m
Current Assets	3m	3m	3m

Cheadle

Agilent Technologies Ltd
5500 Lakeside, Cheadle, SK8 3GR
Tel: 08457-125292 **Fax:** 0161-492 7013
Website: http://www.agilent.com
Directors: P. Cousins (Dir)
Managers: J. Halloran (Personnel), R. Burdsall, H. Fields (Comptroller)
Immediate Holding Company: VIRTENSYS EBT LIMITED
Registration no: 05640059 **Date established:** 2010
Turnover: Up to £250,000 **No.of Employees:** 101 - 250
Product Groups: 38, 67

Date of Accounts	Dec 07
Sales Turnover	9
Pre Tax Profit/Loss	-4m
Working Capital	2m
Fixed Assets	129
Current Assets	3m
Current Liabilities	525

Balluff Ltd
4 Oakwater Avenue Cheadle Royal Business Park, Cheadle, SK8 3SR
Tel: 0161-282 4740 **Fax:** 0161-436 5951
E-mail: sales@balluff.co.uk
Website: http://www.balluff.co.uk
Directors: J. Radford (MD), V. Geissel (Dir), J. Radford (Jt MD), C. Pavelin (Dir), G. Spearing (Co Sec)
Managers: J. Hawksworth (Mktg Serv Mgr)
Ultimate Holding Company: BALLUFF BETEILIGUNGS-GMBH AND CO (GERMANY)
Immediate Holding Company: BALLUFF LTD
Registration no: 01349404 **Date established:** 1978 **Turnover:** £5m - £10m
No.of Employees: 11 - 20 **Product Groups:** 37, 38, 39, 40, 45, 46, 49

see next page

Balluff Ltd - *Cont'd*

Date of Accounts	Dec 11	Dec 10	Dec 09
Working Capital	1m	845	361
Fixed Assets	2m	2m	2m
Current Assets	3m	2m	1m
Current Liabilities	N/A	440	N/A

Bespoke Textile Computer Systems

Sovereign House Stockport Road, Cheadle, SK8 2EA
Tel: 0161-491 8600 **Fax:** 0161-428 4495
E-mail: info@bespoke-computers.com
Website: http://www.bespoke-computers.com
Directors: P. Garner (MD), A. Rosser (Co Sec)
Ultimate Holding Company: GLOBAL BRAND INVESTMENTS LIMITED
Immediate Holding Company: BESPOKE TEXTILE COMPUTER SYSTEMS LIMITED
Registration no: 04109784 **Date established:** 2000
Turnover: £250,000 - £500,000 **No.of Employees:** 1 - 10
Product Groups: 44, 80

Date of Accounts	Dec 11	Dec 10	Dec 09
Sales Turnover	N/A	N/A	301
Working Capital	125	128	119
Fixed Assets	15	15	15
Current Assets	135	135	139

A Branthwaite

6 Ravenoak Road Cheadle Hulme, Cheadle, SK8 7DL
Tel: 0161-485 1199 **Fax:** 0161-485 1199
E-mail: abranthwaite1@aol.com
Website: http://www.abgunsmiths.co.uk
Directors: A. Branthwaite (Prop)
Date established: 1968 **No.of Employees:** 1 - 10 **Product Groups:** 36, 39, 40

Cheshire Metalcraft

Unit 25 Demmings Road, Demmings Industrial Estate, Cheadle, SK8 2PP
Tel: 0161-428 4848
E-mail: nick@cheshiremetalcraft.co.uk
Website: http://www.cheshiremetalcraft.co.uk
Directors: N. Hickman (Dir)
Immediate Holding Company: CHESHIRE METALCRAFT LIMITED
Registration no: 04883221 **Date established:** 2003
No.of Employees: 1 - 10 **Product Groups:** 26, 35

Date of Accounts	Sep 11	Sep 10	Sep 09
Working Capital	-57	-53	-60
Fixed Assets	77	78	75
Current Assets	66	34	23

Consolidated Spinners & Manufacturers Ltd

177 Stanley Road Cheadle Hulme, Cheadle, SK8 6RF
Tel: 0161-437 3295 **Fax:** 0161-436 4855
E-mail: william@hallyarns.fsnet.co.uk
Directors: F. Hall (MD), W. Hall (MD), M. Hall (Fin)
Managers: F. Hall (Sales Prom Mgr)
Immediate Holding Company: CONSOLIDATED SPINNERS AND MANUFACTURERS LIMITED
Registration no: 00416317 **Date established:** 1946
Turnover: Up to £250,000 **No.of Employees:** 1 - 10 **Product Groups:** 23

Date of Accounts	Dec 10	Dec 08	Dec 07
Working Capital	30	22	24
Fixed Assets	1	1	1
Current Assets	75	76	62

Geoffrey Culwick Wrought Iron Work

Unit 12a Brookfield Industrial Estate Brookfield Road, Cheadle, SK8 2PN
Tel: 0161-491 4237 **Fax:** 0161-491 6366
E-mail: enquiries@geoffreyculwick.co.uk
Directors: G. Culwick (Prop)
Immediate Holding Company: GEOFFREY CULWICK LIMITED
Registration no: 04433738 **Date established:** 2002
No.of Employees: 1 - 10 **Product Groups:** 26, 35

Date of Accounts	Apr 11	Apr 10	Apr 09
Sales Turnover	N/A	206	N/A
Pre Tax Profit/Loss	N/A	4	N/A
Working Capital	24	25	31
Fixed Assets	4	5	7
Current Assets	47	40	54
Current Liabilities	N/A	12	N/A

Ecolab

Duke Avenue Stanley Green Trading Estate, Cheadle, SK8 6RB
Tel: 0161-485 6166 **Fax:** 0161-488 4127
E-mail: inge.van.der.linden@ecolab.com
Website: http://www.ecolab.com
Managers: P. Brougham (Mktg Serv Mgr), R. Stone (Plant), C. Loughney, D. Walker (Sales Prom Mgr)
Registration no: 02469440 **Turnover:** £20m - £50m
No.of Employees: 51 - 100 **Product Groups:** 31, 32, 39, 48, 51, 69

James Galt & Co. Ltd

Sovereign House Stockport Road, Cheadle, SK8 2EA
Tel: 0161-428 9111 **Fax:** 0161-428 6597
E-mail: j.bolton@jamesgalt.com
Website: http://www.galttoys.com
Bank(s): The Royal Bank of Scotland
Directors: J. Mcdonnell (MD), J. Bolton (Fin)
Managers: N. Lupton (Purch Mgr), J. McNeill, M. Taylor (Tech Serv Mgr)
Ultimate Holding Company: GLOBAL BRAND INVESTMENTS LIMITED
Immediate Holding Company: JAMES GALT & CO. LIMITED
Registration no: 00135476 **VAT No.:** GB 125 6886 44
Date established: 2014 **Turnover:** £5m - £10m **No.of Employees:** 21 - 50
Product Groups: 49, 65

Date of Accounts	Dec 11	Dec 10	Dec 09
Sales Turnover	9m	10m	9m
Pre Tax Profit/Loss	499	464	979
Working Capital	2m	5m	5m
Fixed Assets	249	306	172
Current Assets	7m	7m	6m
Current Liabilities	588	618	737

HardwarePT A division of SolutionsPT

Unit 1 Oakfield Road Cheadle Royal Business Park, Cheadle, SK8 3GX
Tel: 0161-4954696 **Fax:** 0161-4954690
E-mail: hardwarept@solutionspt.com
Website: http://www.hardwarept.co.uk
Turnover: £1m - £2m **No.of Employees:** 51 - 100 **Product Groups:** 44, 67, 84

Honeywell

Countess Avenue Cheadle Hulme, Cheadle, SK8 6QS
Tel: 0161-486 3000 **Fax:** 0161-486 1267
Website: http://www.honeywell.com
Managers: P. Hill (Mgr)
Registration no: 00301598 **Date established:** 1935
No.of Employees: 101 - 250 **Product Groups:** 40

Ipt Group Ltd

The CR, Cheadle, SK8 1PS
Tel: 0161-491 4233 **Fax:** 0161- 4915864
Directors: J. Harrison (Grp Chief Exec), A. Shore (Fin)
Immediate Holding Company: IPT GROUP LIMITED
Registration no: 02991826 **Date established:** 1994
Turnover: £20m - £50m **No.of Employees:** 101 - 250 **Product Groups:** 63

Date of Accounts	Dec 11	Dec 10	Dec 09
Sales Turnover	37m	36m	30m
Pre Tax Profit/Loss	-1m	628	-1m
Working Capital	6m	7m	10m
Fixed Assets	11m	12m	10m
Current Assets	10m	12m	14m
Current Liabilities	1m	2m	2m

Jewson Ltd

Adswood Road Cheadle Hulme, Cheadle, SK8 5QY
Tel: 0161-486 9117 **Fax:** 0161-486 9946
Website: http://www.jewson.co.uk
Managers: P. Maddocks (Mgr)
Ultimate Holding Company: COMPAGNIE DE SAINT GOBAIN (FRANCE)
Immediate Holding Company: JEWSON LIMITED
Registration no: 00348407 **Date established:** 1939
Turnover: £500m - £1,000m **No.of Employees:** 1 - 10
Product Groups: 66

Date of Accounts	Dec 11	Dec 10	Dec 09
Sales Turnover	1606m	1547m	1485m
Pre Tax Profit/Loss	18m	100m	45m
Working Capital	-345m	-250m	-349m
Fixed Assets	496m	387m	461m
Current Assets	657m	1005m	1320m
Current Liabilities	66m	120m	64m

Johnson Associates

76 Elmsleigh Road Heald Green, Cheadle, SK8 3UE
Tel: 0161-498 8072 **Fax:** 0161-498 8073
Directors: D. Johnson (Prop)
Date established: 1993 **No.of Employees:** 1 - 10 **Product Groups:** 35

Multicoat Ltd

21 Turnfield Road, Cheadle, SK8 1JQ
Tel: 0161-428 7440 **Fax:** 0161-428 7440
E-mail: bruce.ikin@btconnect.com
Directors: B. Ikin (Fin), J. Bruce Ikin (Prop)
Immediate Holding Company: MULTICOAT LIMITED
Registration no: 03887014 **Date established:** 1999
No.of Employees: 1 - 10 **Product Groups:** 46, 48

Date of Accounts	Dec 11	Dec 10	Dec 09
Working Capital	17	16	24
Current Assets	19	18	27

Photo Flashback

3 Rushton Road Cheadle Hulme, Cheadle, SK8 6NS
Tel: 0161-355 3052
E-mail: glycar@aol.com
Website: http://www.retailfranchise.co.uk/flashback
Managers: G. Davies (Mgr), J. Chambers (Nat Sales Mgr)
Turnover: Up to £250,000 **No.of Employees:** 1 - 10 **Product Groups:** 81

Prior Analytics Ltd

246 Finney Lane Heald Green, Cheadle, SK8 3QD
Tel: 0845-6588121 **Fax:** 0845-6588 122
E-mail: enquiries@prior-analytics.com
Website: http://www.prior-analytics.com
Managers: R. Young (Mgr)
Registration no: 03641722 **Date established:** 2000
No.of Employees: 11 - 20 **Product Groups:** 44

Quest International UK Ltd

Unit 2 Demmings Road Industrial Road Estate, Cheadle, SK8 2PP
Tel: 0161-491 0339 **Fax:** 01233-644146
E-mail: linda.harman@givaudan.com
Website: http://www.airmanager.com
Bank(s): Barclays
Directors: D. Roseeveare (Sales), D. Roseveare (Sales), I. Parize (Grp Chief Exec), S. Senior (Dir)
Managers: R. Denham (Mgr), T. Van Der Weerdt (Research & Deve), L. Harman (Mgr)
Immediate Holding Company: Givaudan Holdings UK Ltd
Registration no: 02583389 **Turnover:** £250m - £500m
No.of Employees: 501 - 1000 **Product Groups:** 20, 32, 41

Date of Accounts	Feb 08	Feb 07	Feb 06
Working Capital	138	45	-16
Fixed Assets	63	14	1
Current Assets	298	185	67
Current Liabilities	160	140	83
Total Share Capital	171	171	171

Royal Greenland Ltd

Station Road Cheadle Hulme, Cheadle, SK8 5AF
Tel: 0161-485 8385 **Fax:** 0161-486 9106
E-mail: info@royalgreenland.com
Website: http://www.royalgreenland.com
Directors: R. Pickering (Co Sec), T. Wheatley (MD), A. Wheatley (MD)
Ultimate Holding Company: ROYAL GREENLAND A/S (GREENLAND)
Immediate Holding Company: ROYAL GREENLAND LIMITED
Registration no: 02068099 **VAT No.:** GB 787 4190 86
Date established: 1986 **Turnover:** £20m - £50m
No.of Employees: 11 - 20 **Product Groups:** 20

Date of Accounts	Sep 11	Sep 10	Sep 09
Sales Turnover	32m	38m	52m
Pre Tax Profit/Loss	-266	13	463
Working Capital	3m	3m	3m
Fixed Assets	75	54	67
Current Assets	4m	5m	6m
Current Liabilities	288	277	710

Rubert & Co. Ltd

Acru Works Demmings Road, Cheadle, SK8 2PG
Tel: 0161-428 6058 **Fax:** 0161-428 1146
E-mail: info@rubert.co.uk
Website: http://www.rubert.co.uk
Directors: P. Henshaw (Fin)
Immediate Holding Company: RUBERT & CO. LIMITED
Registration no: 00371475 **VAT No.:** GB 157 5187 42
Date established: 1941 **Turnover:** Up to £250,000
No.of Employees: 1 - 10 **Product Groups:** 38

Date of Accounts	Dec 11	Dec 10	Dec 09
Working Capital	184	181	141
Fixed Assets	475	492	514
Current Assets	301	338	262

Simon Carves Ltd

Sim Chem House Warren Road, Cheadle Hulme, Cheadle, SK8 5BR
Tel: 0161-486 4000 **Fax:** 0161-486 1302
E-mail: kiriti.bhattacharya@simoncarves.com
Website: http://www.simoncarves.com
Bank(s): Lloyds TSB Bank plc
Directors: A. Bowden (MD), D. Johnston (Chief Op Offcr), K. Bhattacharya (Grp Chief Exec), L. Chhabra (Dir), B. Waltmaier (Sales & Mktg)
Managers: R. Bowers (Chief Buyer), L. Aderson (I.T. Exec), W. Morris (Publicity)
Ultimate Holding Company: FP050409
Immediate Holding Company: SIMON CARVES LIMITED
Registration no: 04169897 **Date established:** 2001
Turnover: £20m - £50m **No.of Employees:** 101 - 250
Product Groups: 35, 38, 42, 84

Date of Accounts	Mar 10	Mar 09	Mar 08
Sales Turnover	46m	169m	177m
Pre Tax Profit/Loss	-97m	-111m	-906
Working Capital	-208m	-107m	2m
Fixed Assets	5m	14m	3m
Current Assets	64m	58m	93m
Current Liabilities	13m	40m	25m

Simply Safe Consultancy

62 Willow Avenue Cheadle Hulme, Cheadle, SK8 6AX
Tel: 0161-610 6660 **Fax:** 0161-485 8102
E-mail: simply.safe@ntlworld.com
Website: http://www.simply-safe-consultancy.co.uk
Directors: M. Nixon (Prop)
Date established: 2003 **Turnover:** Up to £250,000
No.of Employees: 1 - 10 **Product Groups:** 84, 86

Sphere Group Ltd

Brooklyn Chambers 1 Brooklyn Road, Cheadle, SK8 1BS
Tel: 0161-495 2000 **Fax:** 0161-495 2001
E-mail: info@spheregroup.com
Website: http://www.spheregroup.com
Directors: M. Douglas (Fin), G. Blackwell Frier (MD)
Immediate Holding Company: SPHERE GROUP RECRUITMENT LIMITED
Registration no: 03957572 **Date established:** 2000
No.of Employees: 11 - 20 **Product Groups:** 80

Tatham Steels Ltd

Duke Avenue Stamley Green Industrial Estate, Cheadle Hulme, Cheadle, SK8 6QZ
Tel: 0161-485 8535 **Fax:** 0161-485 7804
E-mail: cheadle@bmsteel.co.uk
Website: http://www.bmsteel.co.uk
Bank(s): Royal Bank of Scotland
Directors: R. Kyle (Sales)
Managers: D. Whitney (Depot Mgr)
Ultimate Holding Company: BARCLAY & MATHIESON LIMITED
Immediate Holding Company: TATHAM STEELS LIMITED
Registration no: 00641459 **VAT No.:** GB 723 9322 39
Date established: 1959 **Turnover:** £2m - £5m **No.of Employees:** 21 - 50
Product Groups: 34

Date of Accounts	Dec 09
Working Capital	210
Current Assets	210

Richard Thacker & Co. Ltd

Hexagon House 21-23 Gatley Road, Cheadle, SK8 1NZ
Tel: 0161-428 5232 **Fax:** 0161-491 3954
E-mail: enquiries@richardthacker.co.uk
Website: http://www.richardthacker.co.uk
Directors: H. Mayhew (MD), P. Gemmell (Co Sec)
Ultimate Holding Company: INDEMNITY INVESTMENTS LIMITED
Immediate Holding Company: RICHARD THACKER (HOLDINGS) LIMITED
Registration no: 01148242 **Date established:** 1973
No.of Employees: 11 - 20 **Product Groups:** 82

Date of Accounts	Oct 11	Oct 10	Oct 09
Fixed Assets	61	61	61

Topskips.Com

Metropolitan House Station Road, Cheadle Hulme, Cheadle, SK8 7AZ
Tel: 0800-082 1082 **Fax:** 0161-274 4113
E-mail: louise.malpas@toptriangle.com
Website: http://www.toptriangle.com
Directors: K. Attwood (MD)
Managers: L. Malpas, L. Malpass, J. Little
Immediate Holding Company: RETIREMENT SOLUTIONS (UK) LIMITED
Registration no: 01235938 **Date established:** 2007
Turnover: £10m - £20m **No.of Employees:** 21 - 50 **Product Groups:** 39, 42, 45

Date of Accounts	Mar 11	Mar 10	Mar 09
Working Capital	158	40	13
Fixed Assets	10	7	8
Current Assets	326	122	95

Umbro International Ltd

Umbro House 5400 Lakeside, Cheadle, SK8 3GQ
Tel: 0161-492 2000 **Fax:** 0161-492 2001
E-mail: david_hare@umbro.co.uk
Website: http://www.umbro.com
Bank(s): HSBC Bank plc
Directors: D. Hare (Dir)
Managers: M. Weeks (Personnel), G. Brown (Comptroller), G. Fisher
Ultimate Holding Company: NIKE INC (USA)
Immediate Holding Company: UMBRO INTERNATIONAL LIMITED
Registration no: 00198168 **VAT No.:** GB 468 1891 06
Date established: 2024 **Turnover:** £125m - £250m
No.of Employees: 101 - 250 **Product Groups:** 24

Date of Accounts	Dec 07	May 11	May 10
Sales Turnover	92m	143m	131m
Pre Tax Profit/Loss	-19m	-37m	-41m

Working Capital	-29m	-87m	-46m
Fixed Assets	98m	106m	99m
Current Assets	107m	148m	173m
Current Liabilities	19m	35m	49m

Welser Sections (UK) Ltd
Sovereign House Stockport Road, Cheadle, SK8 2EA
Tel: 0161-4915210 **Fax:** 0161-4910008
E-mail: cz@welser.com
Website: http://www.welser.com
Ultimate Holding Company: Welser Profile AG, AA-3341 Ybbsitz
Registration no: 02860346 **VAT No.:** GB 038 2891 06
Date established: 1993 **Product Groups:** 34, 36

Date of Accounts	Dec 11	Dec 10	Dec 09
Working Capital	374	318	271
Fixed Assets	7	9	18
Current Assets	446	340	284

Wienerberger Ltd
Wienerberger House Brooks Drive, Cheadle, SK8 3SA
Tel: 0161-491 8200 **Fax:** 01902-880432
E-mail: office@wienerberger.co.uk
Website: http://www.wienerberger.co.uk
Bank(s): National Westminster Bank Plc
Directors: C. Goodwin (Pers), H. Schwarzmayr (MD)
Managers: A. Forster (Mktg Serv Mgr), K. Few (Comptroller), S. Pearson, N. Hill, K. Cheatham (Grp Purch Mgr)
Ultimate Holding Company: WIENERBERGER AG (AUSTRIA)
Immediate Holding Company: BAGGERIDGE BRICK LIMITED
Registration no: 00386775 **Date established:** 1944
Turnover: £50m - £75m **No.of Employees:** 51 - 100 **Product Groups:** 33

Date of Accounts	Dec 11	Dec 10	Dec 09
Pre Tax Profit/Loss	332	287	394
Working Capital	12m	11m	11m
Current Assets	12m	11m	11m

Chester

A E Harris & Co.
Hartford Way Sealand Industrial Estate, Chester, CH1 4NT
Tel: 01244-375818 **Fax:** 01244-374596
E-mail: simon@aeharris.com
Website: http://www.aeharris.com
Directors: S. Harris (Prop)
No.of Employees: 1 - 10 **Product Groups:** 27, 32

Aaron & Partners LLP
5-7 Grosvenor Court Foregate Street, Chester, CH1 1HG
Tel: 01244-405555 **Fax:** 01244-405566
E-mail: enquiries@aaronandpartners.com
Website: http://www.aaronandpartners.com
Bank(s): The Royal Bank of Scotland
Directors: S. Edwards (Snr Part), D. Gerrard (Fin)
Managers: S. Hadden (Sales & Mktg Mg), S. Garman (Tech Serv Mgr), S. Mackie (Personnel)
Immediate Holding Company: AARON & PARTNERS LLP
Registration no: OC307122 **VAT No.:** GB 294 7924 06
Date established: 2004 **Turnover:** £2m - £5m
No.of Employees: 101 - 250 **Product Groups:** 80

Date of Accounts	Apr 11	Apr 10	Apr 09
Working Capital	2m	2m	2m
Fixed Assets	233	242	270
Current Assets	3m	3m	3m

Actioncad Ltd
Redhill House Hope Street, Chester, CH4 8BU
Tel: 01244-674977
E-mail: r.kehoe@actioncad.co.uk
Website: http://www.actioncad.co.uk
Directors: R. Kehoe (Prop)
Immediate Holding Company: ACTIONCAD LIMITED
Registration no: 05948344 **Date established:** 2006
Turnover: Up to £250,000 **No.of Employees:** 1 - 10 **Product Groups:** 86

Date of Accounts	Sep 08	Sep 07
Sales Turnover	103	83
Pre Tax Profit/Loss	39	24
Working Capital	6	5
Fixed Assets	3	3
Current Assets	28	15
Current Liabilities	22	10

Advanstar Communications
Poplar House Park West Sealand Road, Chester, CH1 4RN
Tel: 01244-378888 **Fax:** 01244-370011
E-mail: mroberts@advanstar.com
Website: http://www.advanstar.com
Directors: H. Gardener (Grp Chief Exec)
Managers: C. Connelly (Sec), N. Froster (Mgr), M. Roberts (Sales Admin), S. James (Sales Prom Mgr)
Immediate Holding Company: ADVANSTAR COMMUNICATIONS (U.K.) LIMITED
Registration no: 03287275 **Date established:** 1996 **Turnover:** £5m - £10m
No.of Employees: 21 - 50 **Product Groups:** 28

Date of Accounts	Dec 09	Dec 08	Dec 07
Sales Turnover	5m	5m	6m
Pre Tax Profit/Loss	-20	-181	-19
Working Capital	380	791	729
Fixed Assets	3m	3m	3m
Current Assets	1m	2m	2m
Current Liabilities	637	754	845

Advantage Engineering Technology Ltd
Unit 9 Capenhurst Technology Park Capenhurst, Chester, CH1 6EH
Tel: 0151-339 3830 **Fax:** 0151-339 3840
E-mail: philperry@advantage-engineering.co.uk
Website: http://www.advantage-engineering.co.uk
Directors: P. Perry (MD)
Ultimate Holding Company: INFOGAUGE LIMITED
Immediate Holding Company: ADVANTAGE ENGINEERING TECHNOLOGY LIMITED
Registration no: 03512711 **Date established:** 1998
No.of Employees: 1 - 10 **Product Groups:** 45

Date of Accounts	Apr 11	Apr 10	Apr 09
Working Capital	-0	-45	-16
Fixed Assets	22	28	36
Current Assets	123	116	63

Airbus Broughton 1898
Chester Road Broughton, Chester, CH4 0DR
Tel: 01244-524025 **Fax:** 01244-523000
Website: http://www.airbus.com
Directors: K. Davies (Co Sec), M. Stewart (Dir), C. Sparkes (Fin), B. Fleet (Vice Ch)
Managers: S. Robert (Mgr), P. Adams (Purch Mgr)
Ultimate Holding Company: BAE SYSTEMS PLC
Immediate Holding Company: AIRBUS FILTON LIMITED
Registration no: 02606556 **VAT No.:** GB 641 4071 69
Date established: 1991 **Turnover:** £250m - £500m
No.of Employees: 501 - 1000 **Product Groups:** 39

Aldford Aluminium Products Ltd
Glebe Buildings Chester Road, Aldford, Chester, CH3 6HJ
Tel: 01244-620327 **Fax:** 01244-620327
Website: http://www.aldfordaluminiumproducts-chester.co.uk
Directors: K. Pollard (Prop)
Immediate Holding Company: ALDFORD ALUMINIUM PRODUCTS LIMITED
Registration no: 08034839 **Date established:** 2012
No.of Employees: 1 - 10 **Product Groups:** 26, 35

Alembic Foods Ltd
River Lane Saltney, Chester, CH4 8RQ
Tel: 01244-680147 **Fax:** 01244-680155
E-mail: sales@alembicproducts.co.uk
Website: http://www.alembicproducts.co.uk
Directors: A. Brown (MD)
Managers: I. Wilkinson (I.T. Exec), K. Duncan (Mgr), A. Robinson (Sales Prom)
Registration no: 05240255 **Date established:** 1992 **Turnover:** £5m - £10m
No.of Employees: 1 - 10 **Product Groups:** 20, 31, 38, 66

Date of Accounts	Mar 07	Mar 06
Fixed Assets	5000	5000
Total Share Capital	1250	1250

Apple Dynamics Ltd
6 Well House Barns Chester Road, Bretton, Chester, CH4 0DH
Tel: 08707-415347 **Fax:** 01352-751565
E-mail: info@applesound.com
Website: http://www.appledynamics.com
Directors: T. Brown (MD), P. Darlington (Dir)
Immediate Holding Company: APPLE ACOUSTICS LIMITED
Registration no: 03866004 **Date established:** 2006
No.of Employees: 1 - 10 **Product Groups:** 25, 30, 31, 33, 37, 38, 39, 40, 44, 47, 48, 52, 61, 67, 80, 81, 83, 84

Date of Accounts	Nov 11	Nov 10	Nov 09
Working Capital	2m	1m	1m
Fixed Assets	17	20	19
Current Assets	3m	2m	2m

Apple Sound Ltd Apple Sound Ltd
6 Well House Barns Chester Road, Bretton, Chester, CH4 0DH
Tel: 08455-576555 **Fax:** 0870-741 0124
E-mail: info@applesound.co.uk
Website: http://www.applesound.co.uk
Directors: P. Brown (Dir), T. Brown (Dir)
Immediate Holding Company: APPLE SOUND LTD
Registration no: 03131505 **Date established:** 1995
Turnover: £500,000 - £1m **No.of Employees:** 1 - 10 **Product Groups:** 37

Date of Accounts	Dec 07	Apr 11	Apr 10
Sales Turnover	N/A	N/A	593
Pre Tax Profit/Loss	N/A	N/A	118
Working Capital	-49	-8	-38
Fixed Assets	60	47	45
Current Assets	110	40	137
Current Liabilities	N/A	N/A	41

Autolamps Online
PO Box 3154, Chester, CH1 6ZD
Tel: 01244-881961 **Fax:** 0870-133 2087
E-mail: sales@autolamps-online.com
Website: http://www.autolamps-online.com
Directors: J. Bevan (Sales)
No.of Employees: 1 - 10 **Product Groups:** 37, 39

Aviagen Turkeys
Chowley Five Chowley Oak Lane, Tattenhall, Chester, CH3 9GA
Tel: 01829-772020 **Fax:** 01829-772059
E-mail: jschlaman@aviagen.com
Website: http://www.aviagenturkeys.com
Bank(s): HSBC, 92 Kensington High St, Kensington, London W8 4SH
Directors: R. Hutchison (Sales & Mktg), J. Schlaman (Fin)
Immediate Holding Company: AVIAGEN TURKEYS LIMITED
Registration no: 00723798 **VAT No.:** GB 159 1747 38
Date established: 1962 **Turnover:** £10m - £20m
No.of Employees: 101 - 250 **Product Groups:** 01

Date of Accounts	Jun 11	Jun 10	Jun 09
Sales Turnover	19m	16m	14m
Pre Tax Profit/Loss	-1m	-1m	-1m
Working Capital	-3m	-2m	-445
Fixed Assets	214m	11m	11m
Current Assets	9m	9m	6m
Current Liabilities	3m	1m	608

Ball Packaging
Lakeside Chester Business Park, Chester, CH4 9QT
Tel: 01244-681155 **Fax:** 01244-680320
E-mail: william.robinson@ball-europe.com
Website: http://www.ball-europe.com
Bank(s): Barclays, Wrexham
Directors: W. Robinson (Pers), S. Widmann (Co Sec)
Managers: G. Courtney (Sales Prom Mgr), I. Roberts (Purch Mgr), N. Coulter (Comptroller)
Ultimate Holding Company: BALL CORPORATION (USA)
Immediate Holding Company: BALL PACKAGING EUROPE UK LTD.
Registration no: 02459095 **Date established:** 1990
Turnover: £250m - £500m **No.of Employees:** 21 - 50 **Product Groups:** 35

Date of Accounts	Dec 11	Dec 10	Dec 09
Sales Turnover	301m	303m	290m
Pre Tax Profit/Loss	32m	38m	34m
Working Capital	77m	62m	46m
Fixed Assets	51m	49m	43m
Current Assets	144m	137m	105m
Current Liabilities	29m	34m	23m

Blue Chip Technology Ltd
Chowley Oak Chowley Oak Lane, Tattenhall, Chester, CH3 9EX
Tel: 01829-772000 **Fax:** 01829-772001
E-mail: it@bluechiptechnology.co.uk
Website: http://www.bluechiptechnology.co.uk
Directors: T. Haley (Dir)
Immediate Holding Company: BLUE CHIP TECHNOLOGY LIMITED
Registration no: 03110403 **Date established:** 1995 **Turnover:** £5m - £10m
No.of Employees: 21 - 50 **Product Groups:** 44

Date of Accounts	Nov 11	Nov 10	Nov 09
Working Capital	1m	1m	1m
Fixed Assets	95	44	52
Current Assets	2m	2m	2m

Border Business Systems Ltd
Border House High Street, Farndon, Chester, CH3 6PT
Tel: 01829-270714 **Fax:** 01829-271063
E-mail: info@bbsltd.co.uk
Website: http://www.bbsltd.co.uk
Directors: C. Morgan (Sales), R. Carter (Tech Serv), S. Carter (MD)
Immediate Holding Company: BORDER BUSINESS SYSTEMS LIMITED
Registration no: 01515822 **Date established:** 1980
Turnover: £250,000 - £500,000 **No.of Employees:** 11 - 20
Product Groups: 37

Date of Accounts	Aug 11	Aug 10	Aug 09
Working Capital	156	182	184
Fixed Assets	87	60	61
Current Assets	650	635	544

Brabin & Fitz
2 Corbridge house Seller Street, Chester, CH1 3AN
Tel: 01244-314838 **Fax:** 01244-351380
E-mail: sales@brabinandfitz.co.uk
Website: http://www.brabinandfitz.co.uk
Directors: D. Mcparland (Dir)
No.of Employees: 1 - 10 **Product Groups:** 37, 67

The Business Connection
White Friars, Chester, CH1 1NZ
Tel: 0141-248 2825 **Fax:** 01244-313004
E-mail: kirsty_craig@tbc-recruit.com
Website: http://www.tbc-recruit.com
Managers: S. Horton
Immediate Holding Company: BADLEY GREEN FARM LIMITED
Registration no: 04666852 **Date established:** 1963 **Turnover:** £2m - £5m
No.of Employees: 1 - 10 **Product Groups:** 80

Date of Accounts	Mar 11	Mar 10	Mar 09
Working Capital	216	2m	2m
Fixed Assets	3m	1m	1m
Current Assets	596	3m	3m

C E S UK Ltd
Knutsford Way Sealand Industrial Estate, Chester, CH1 4NS
Tel: 01244-379279 **Fax:** 01244-371248
E-mail: melaniebray@cesuk.com
Website: http://www.cesuk.com
Bank(s): Barclays
Directors: C. Carlton (Jt MD), H. Warren (Dir), M. Warburton (Mkt Research)
Managers: J. Warren (Personnel), L. Duffy (Personnel), C. Boland, M. Harrison (Fin Mgr), M. Clements (Tech Serv Mgr), M. Harrison (Fin Mgr)
Immediate Holding Company: CES (UK) LIMITED
Registration no: 01779084 **VAT No.:** GB 406 1323 00
Date established: 1983 **Turnover:** £20m - £50m
No.of Employees: 101 - 250 **Product Groups:** 25, 39, 40, 68

Date of Accounts	Apr 11	Apr 10	Apr 09
Sales Turnover	48m	43m	37m
Pre Tax Profit/Loss	3m	3m	1m
Working Capital	4m	2m	4m
Fixed Assets	4m	4m	4m
Current Assets	17m	15m	13m
Current Liabilities	2m	4m	2m

C L S Europe
Heritage House 11 Heritage Court, Chester, CH1 1RD
Tel: 01244-313022 **Fax:** 01244-318455
E-mail: sales@clseurope.com
Website: http://www.clseurope.com
Directors: D. Young (Fin), D. Wall (Grp Chief Exec), D. Youngs (Dir)
Managers: R. Brown (Mktg Serv Mgr), J. Main (Purch Mgr)
Immediate Holding Company: CODECON LTD
Registration no: 01092333 **Turnover:** £500,000 - £1m
No.of Employees: 1 - 10 **Product Groups:** 80

Calder Industrial Materials Ltd
Jupiter Drive Chester West Employment Park, Chester, CH1 4EX
Tel: 01244-390093 **Fax:** 01244-389191
E-mail: info@caldergroup.co.uk
Website: http://www.caldergroup.co.uk
Bank(s): The Royal Bank of Scotland
Directors: A. Donald (Fin), P. Walters (Sales), B. Travers (MD), M. Bailey (Chief Op Offcr)
Managers: S. Morant (Sales Off Mgr), .. hrubiak
Ultimate Holding Company: CALDERGROUP SWISS AG (SWITZERLAND)
Immediate Holding Company: CALDER INDUSTRIAL MATERIALS LIMITED
Registration no: 00028073 **VAT No.:** GB 624 4326 58
Date established: 1989 **Turnover:** £20m - £50m
No.of Employees: 101 - 250 **Product Groups:** 25, 33, 34, 35, 37, 39, 42

Date of Accounts	May 11	May 10	May 09
Sales Turnover	36m	33m	29m
Pre Tax Profit/Loss	2m	2m	2m
Working Capital	10m	10m	8m
Fixed Assets	4m	4m	4m
Current Assets	18m	17m	21m
Current Liabilities	2m	2m	2m

Capital World Travel
Ic-Id Northgate The Pavilions, Chester Business Park, Chester, CH4 9QJ
Tel: 01244-625300 **Fax:** 01244-682197
E-mail: sales@capitalworldtravel.co.uk
Website: http://www.capitalworldtravel.co.uk
Bank(s): Bank of Scotland
Directors: P. Langlois (Dir), D. Rees (Mkt Research), G. Povey (MD)
Managers: L. O'Conner (I.T. Exec)
Ultimate Holding Company: FP002904
Immediate Holding Company: EDENRED (TRAVEL) LIMITED
Registration no: 04079050 **Date established:** 2000
Turnover: Up to £250,000 **No.of Employees:** 11 - 20 **Product Groups:** 69, 80, 81, 89

Cars For Stars Thursley Wood Limited
Suite 56 Gateway House 78 Northgate Street, Chester, CH1 2HR
Tel: 0845-226 4201 **Fax:** 01244-343522
E-mail: sales@carsforstars-chester.co.uk
Website: http://www.carsforstars-chester.co.uk
Directors: M. Woodrow (Dir), M. Woodrow (Prop)
Immediate Holding Company: ACROSEC UK LIMITED
Registration no: 06511843 **Date established:** 2008
No.of Employees: 1 - 10 **Product Groups:** 72

Central Hygiene Ltd
Red Hill House 41 Hope Street, Chester, CH4 8BU
Tel: 01244-675066 **Fax:** 01244-680129
E-mail: info@central-hygiene.co.uk
Website: http://www.central-hygiene.co.uk
Directors: M. Limited (Fin), J. Leach (Dir)
Immediate Holding Company: CENTRAL HYGIENE LIMITED
Registration no: 02050579 **VAT No.:** GB 625 4929 22
Date established: 1986 **Turnover:** £500,000 - £1m
No.of Employees: 1 - 10 **Product Groups:** 40, 84

Date of Accounts	Sep 11	Sep 10	Sep 09
Working Capital	85	73	72
Fixed Assets	25	23	24
Current Assets	108	102	97

Cheshire Agricultural Engineering Services
6 Victoria Pathway, Chester, CH4 7AG
Tel: 01244-680242
Directors: R. Gregory (Prop)
Date established: 1980 **No.of Employees:** 1 - 10 **Product Groups:** 41

Chester Chain Co. Ltd
Broughton Mills Road Bretton, Chester, CH4 0BY
Tel: 01244-663580 **Fax:** 01244-663587
E-mail: sales@chesterchain.co.uk
Website: http://www.chesterchain.co.uk
Bank(s): Barclays
Directors: B. Chambers (MD), L. Johnson (Fin)
Ultimate Holding Company: WAKEFIELD PROPERTIES LIMITED
Immediate Holding Company: CHESTER CHAIN COMPANY LIMITED
Registration no: 00798496 **VAT No.:** GB 159 1009 74
Date established: 1964 **Turnover:** £1m - £2m **No.of Employees:** 21 - 50
Product Groups: 48, 83

Date of Accounts	Mar 12	Mar 11	Mar 10
Working Capital	426	397	361
Fixed Assets	404	400	423
Current Assets	748	716	688

Chester Zoo
Cedar House Zoological Gardens Caughall Road, Upton, Chester, CH2 1LH
Tel: 01244-380280 **Fax:** 01244-371273
E-mail: guest.services@chesterzoo.org
Website: http://www.chesterzoo.org
Bank(s): Barclays, St. Werburgh St, Che
Directors: G. Reid (MD)
Managers: J. Parker (Public Relation)
Ultimate Holding Company: NORTH OF ENGLAND ZOOLOGICAL SOCIETY (THE)
Immediate Holding Company: NORTH OF ENGLAND ZOOLOGICAL SOCIETY (THE)
Registration no: 00287902 **VAT No.:** GB 595 7286 79
Date established: 1934 **Turnover:** £20m - £50m
No.of Employees: 251 - 500 **Product Groups:** 69

Date of Accounts	Dec 11	Dec 10	Dec 09
Sales Turnover	26m	24m	24m
Pre Tax Profit/Loss	-1m	493	5m
Working Capital	14m	14m	11m
Fixed Assets	14m	15m	18m
Current Assets	17m	16m	13m
Current Liabilities	2m	1m	1m

Classique Ltd
6c Chesterbank Business Park River Lane, Saltney, Chester, CH4 8SL
Tel: 01244-661113 **Fax:** 01244-345255
E-mail: info@classique.co.uk
Website: http://www.classique.co.uk
Directors: G. Butler (Dir)
Immediate Holding Company: CLASSIQUE CONSERVATORIES LIMITED
Registration no: 03578750 **Date established:** 1998
Turnover: £250,000 - £500,000 **No.of Employees:** 1 - 10
Product Groups: 08, 25, 35

Date of Accounts	Jun 11	Jun 10	Jun 09
Working Capital	-29	-34	-43
Fixed Assets	5	3	4
Current Assets	13	3	25

Climatised Coatings Ltd
105 Weston Grove Upton, Chester, CH2 1QP
Tel: 01244-378488 **Fax:** 01244-378388
E-mail: info@climatisedcoatingsuk.co.uk
Website: http://www.climatisedcoatingsuk.co.uk
Directors: V. Barlow (Contracts)
Immediate Holding Company: CLIMATISED COATINGS (U.K.) LIMITED
Registration no: 02907686 **Date established:** 1994
Turnover: Up to £250,000 **No.of Employees:** 1 - 10 **Product Groups:** 46, 48

Date of Accounts	Mar 11	Mar 10	Mar 09
Sales Turnover	N/A	208	260
Pre Tax Profit/Loss	N/A	-9	39
Working Capital	-48	-20	-11
Fixed Assets	13	13	17
Current Assets	7	6	9
Current Liabilities	N/A	7	8

Close Asset Finance Ltd
Unit D Dunkirk Trading Estate Chester Gates, Dunkirk, Chester, CH1 6LT
Tel: 01244-853430 **Fax:** 08704-437952
E-mail: sgee@closeassetfinanceltd.co.uk
Website: http://www.closeassetfinanceltd.co.uk
Directors: S. Gee (Dir)
Ultimate Holding Company: CLOSE BROTHERS GROUP PLC
Immediate Holding Company: CLOSE ASSET FINANCE LIMITED
Registration no: 02053453 **Date established:** 1986
No.of Employees: 11 - 20 **Product Groups:** 80

Date of Accounts	Jul 11	Jul 10	Jul 09
Sales Turnover	129m	103m	86m
Pre Tax Profit/Loss	31m	33m	13m
Working Capital	-10m	-22m	41m
Fixed Assets	22m	26m	28m
Current Assets	973m	789m	622m
Current Liabilities	19m	20m	11m

Colin Spofforth Studio
Stamford Mill Farm Cotton Lane, Cotton Edmunds, Chester, CH3 7QA
Tel: 01829-740890
E-mail: studio@colinspofforth.com
Website: http://www.colinspofforth.com
Product Groups: 25, 33, 35, 64, 66

Connell Consulting Engineers
Chester Road Bridge Trafford, Chester, CH2 4JR
Tel: 01244-300222
E-mail: sales@connellconsulting.co.uk
Website: http://www.connellconsulting.co.uk
Directors: P. Connell (Prop)
Immediate Holding Company: CONNELL CONSULTING ENGINEERS LIMITED
Registration no: 07583256 **Date established:** 2011
No.of Employees: 1 - 10 **Product Groups:** 35

Corks Out
21 Watergate Street, Chester, CH1 2LB
Tel: 01244-310455 **Fax:** 01244-350226
E-mail: chester@corksout.com
Website: http://www.corksout.com
Managers: J. Cowan (Mgr)
Immediate Holding Company: EX CELLAR INVESTMENTS LTD
Registration no: 00999288 **Turnover:** £500,000 - £1m
No.of Employees: 1 - 10 **Product Groups:** 62

Corporate Speak Ltd
6 St Johns Court Vicars Lane, Chester, CH1 1QE
Tel: 01244-340047 **Fax:** 01244-340048
E-mail: info@corporatespeak.co.uk
Website: http://www.corporatespeak.co.uk
Directors: D. Bradshaw (Fin), D. Bradshaw (MD)
Immediate Holding Company: CORPORATE SPEAK LIMITED
Registration no: 04443343 **Date established:** 2002
Turnover: Up to £250,000 **No.of Employees:** 1 - 10 **Product Groups:** 81

Date of Accounts	May 11	May 10	May 09
Working Capital	1	18	-3
Fixed Assets	42	46	52
Current Assets	96	94	78

Croston Engineering Ltd
Tarvin Mill Barrow Lane Tarvin Sands, Tarvin, Chester, CH3 8JF
Tel: 01829-741119 **Fax:** 01829-741169
E-mail: admin@croston-engineering.co.uk
Website: http://www.croston-engineering.co.uk
Directors: A. Croston (MD)
Immediate Holding Company: CROSTON ENGINEERING LIMITED
Registration no: 01263413 **VAT No.:** GB 163 2711 83
Date established: 1976 **Turnover:** £2m - £5m **No.of Employees:** 1 - 10
Product Groups: 45, 67

Date of Accounts	Jun 12	Jun 11	Jun 10
Working Capital	932	885	866
Fixed Assets	165	172	162
Current Assets	1m	2m	1m

Cutlass Technologies Ltd
Higher Burwardsley Burwardsley, Chester, CH3 9PG
Tel: 01829-770051
E-mail: ericjenston@aol.com
Website: http://www.cutlasstechnologies.co.uk
Directors: E. Enston (MD), J. Higton (Fin)
Immediate Holding Company: CUTLASS TECHNOLOGIES LIMITED
Registration no: 03932690 **Date established:** 2000
No.of Employees: 1 - 10 **Product Groups:** 36, 37, 38

Date of Accounts	Jun 11	Jun 09	Jun 08
Working Capital	-26	-20	3
Fixed Assets	69	29	27
Current Assets	53	58	55

Datascope
Access House Saltney Ferry, Chester, CH4 0GZ
Tel: 08454-507387 **Fax:** 0845-450 1901
E-mail: info@datascopeplc.com
Website: http://www.datascopesystems.com
Directors: J. Woodger (MD)
Immediate Holding Company: DATASCOPE LIMITED
Registration no: 04058188 **Date established:** 2000 **Turnover:** £1m - £2m
No.of Employees: 11 - 20 **Product Groups:** 44

Date of Accounts	Jun 10	Jun 09	Jun 08
Sales Turnover	1m	N/A	986
Pre Tax Profit/Loss	N/A	N/A	112
Working Capital	-202	-265	144
Fixed Assets	667	632	240
Current Assets	360	385	544
Current Liabilities	N/A	N/A	104

Dee Communications
Dutton Green Stanney Mill, Little Stanney, Chester, CH2 4SA
Tel: 0151-356 5955 **Fax:** 0121-778 3633
E-mail: arthur.ryan@deecommunications.co.uk
Website: http://www.deecommunications.co.uk
Directors: A. Ryan (MD)
Managers: P. Grant (Sales Prom Mgr)
Ultimate Holding Company: DEE RYAN LTD
Immediate Holding Company: DEE COMMUNICATIONS LIMITED
Registration no: 01366415 **VAT No.:** GB 310 1769 94
Date established: 1978 **Turnover:** £1m - £2m **No.of Employees:** 1 - 10
Product Groups: 37

Date of Accounts	Oct 10	Oct 09	Oct 08
Working Capital	477	523	468
Fixed Assets	714	726	747
Current Assets	630	665	606

Dee Fabrications
5 Silverdale Park Station Lane, Mickle Trafford, Chester, CH2 4TA
Tel: 01244-300312 **Fax:** 01244-300326
Directors: R. Willoughby (Prop)
Date established: 2003 **No.of Employees:** 1 - 10 **Product Groups:** 26, 35

Deeside Metal Company Ltd
Dragon Works Saltney, Chester, CH4 8RW
Tel: 01244-674888 **Fax:** 01244-680491
E-mail: sales@chesterskiphire.co.uk
Website: http://www.chesterskiphire.co.uk
Directors: A. Graham (MD)
Immediate Holding Company: DEESIDE METAL COMPANY LIMITED
Registration no: 02031519 **VAT No.:** GB 159 1851 43
Date established: 1986 **Turnover:** Up to £250,000
No.of Employees: 1 - 10 **Product Groups:** 66, 83

Date of Accounts	Sep 11	Sep 10	Sep 09
Working Capital	-63	-44	-94
Fixed Assets	158	185	214
Current Assets	178	116	63

Denton Clark Rentals
4 Vicars Lane, Chester, CH1 1QU
Tel: 01244-624027 **Fax:** 01244-315954
E-mail: info@dentonclarkrentals.co.uk
Website: http://www.dentonclarkrentals.co.uk
Directors: J. Dewhurst (MD)
Turnover: Up to £250,000 **No.of Employees:** 1 - 10 **Product Groups:** 80

Devaco International Ltd
Riverside House Brymau Three Trading Estate River Lane, Saltney, Chester, CH4 8RQ
Tel: 01244-671700 **Fax:** 01244-680655
E-mail: devaco@mcmail.com
Website: http://www.devaco.co.uk
Directors: J. Peacock (MD)
Managers: J. De Vera Davey (Sales Prom Mgr), A. Grimshaw (Sales Prom Mgr)
Immediate Holding Company: DEVACO INTERNATIONAL LIMITED
Registration no: 01320901 **Date established:** 1977
No.of Employees: 11 - 20 **Product Groups:** 26, 35, 36, 39, 49, 66, 67

Date of Accounts	Dec 10	Dec 09	Dec 08
Working Capital	268	260	257
Fixed Assets	344	375	353
Current Assets	348	342	424

Direct Diesel Fuel Injection Services Ltd
Broughton Mills Road Bretton, Chester, CH4 0BY
Tel: 01244-660787 **Fax:** 01244-661297
E-mail: direct.diesel@btinternet.com
Directors: T. Crofts (Fin)
Immediate Holding Company: DIRECT DIESEL INJECTION SERVICES LIMITED
Registration no: 02782747 **Date established:** 1993
No.of Employees: 1 - 10 **Product Groups:** 40

Date of Accounts	Feb 12	Feb 11	Feb 10
Working Capital	68	77	51
Fixed Assets	81	62	76
Current Assets	125	134	103

Door To Door - Garage Doors
Mannings Lane South, Chester, CH2 3RX
Tel: 01244-303119
E-mail: info@garagedoorschester.com
Website: http://www.garagedoorschester.com
Directors: Shyman (Prop)
No.of Employees: 1 - 10 **Product Groups:** 25, 30, 35

E A Technology Ltd
Capenhurst Lane Capenhurst, Chester, CH1 6ES
Tel: 0151-339 4181 **Fax:** 0151-347 2404
E-mail: sales@eatechnology.com
Website: http://www.eatechnology.com
Bank(s): National Westminster Bank Plc
Directors: C. Parry (Co Sec)
Managers: N. Harris, R. Davis, S. Parry (Tech Serv Mgr), A. Clancey (Sales & Mktg Mg)
Immediate Holding Company: EA TECHNOLOGY LIMITED
Registration no: 02566313 **VAT No.:** GB 595 5927 77
Date established: 1990 **Turnover:** £10m - £20m
No.of Employees: 101 - 250 **Product Groups:** 38, 44, 48, 80, 81, 82, 84, 85, 86

Date of Accounts	Mar 11	Mar 10	Mar 09
Sales Turnover	17m	14m	11m
Pre Tax Profit/Loss	1m	30	26
Working Capital	3m	3m	3m
Fixed Assets	2m	888	716
Current Assets	9m	8m	7m
Current Liabilities	4m	3m	4m

K Farebrother
Rowton Bridge Road Christleton, Chester, CH3 7BD
Tel: 01244-332633 **Fax:** 01244-332633
E-mail: farebrot@tiscali.co.uk
Directors: K. Farebrother (Prop)
Date established: 1983 **No.of Employees:** 1 - 10 **Product Groups:** 35, 36, 39

Edwin C Farrall Transport Ltd
Ashton Lane Ashton, Chester, CH3 8AA
Tel: 01829-751558 **Fax:** 01829-753108
E-mail: traffic@farralls.co.uk
Website: http://www.farralls.co.uk
Directors: M. Farrall (MD)
Immediate Holding Company: EDWIN C. FARRALL (TRANSPORT) LIMITED
Registration no: 01050645 **Date established:** 1972 **Turnover:** £5m - £10m
No.of Employees: 51 - 100 **Product Groups:** 77

Date of Accounts	Dec 11	Dec 10	Dec 09
Sales Turnover	7m	N/A	N/A
Pre Tax Profit/Loss	435	N/A	N/A
Working Capital	-297	-271	-242
Fixed Assets	2m	2m	2m
Current Assets	1m	1m	884
Current Liabilities	286	N/A	N/A

Flintshire Chronicle Newspapers
Chronicle House Commonhall Street, Chester, CH1 2AA
Tel: 01244-821911 **Fax:** 01244-349975
E-mail: carl.wood@cheshirenews.co.uk
Website: http://www.flintshirechronicle.co.uk

Managers: M. Green
Immediate Holding Company: MILES OF SMILES (CHESTER) LIMITED
Registration no: 03097720 **VAT No.:** GB 443 3567 67
Date established: 1995 **Turnover:** Up to £250,000
No.of Employees: 1 - 10 **Product Groups:** 28

Haltec Chester

Mollington Grange Parkgate Road, Mollington, Chester, CH1 6NP
Tel: 01244-853883 **Fax:** 01244-853892
E-mail: john.halliwell@haltec-chester.co.uk
Website: http://www.haltec-chester.co.uk
Directors: J. Halliwell (Prop)
Immediate Holding Company: W H P PROPERTIES LIMITED
Registration no: 03618133 **Date established:** 1998
No.of Employees: 1 - 10 **Product Groups:** 35

Date of Accounts	Aug 11	Aug 10	Aug 09
Working Capital	97	71	53
Fixed Assets	678	679	681
Current Assets	119	97	91

Holmes

15 Ffordd Derwyn Penyffordd, Chester, CH4 0JT
Tel: 01244-545532 **Fax:** 01244-545532
E-mail: nigel.holmes1@virgin.net
Directors: N. Holmes (Prop)
VAT No.: GB 539 4352 28 **Turnover:** Up to £250,000
No.of Employees: 1 - 10 **Product Groups:** 46

Host Von Schrader Ltd

Unit 6b Capenhurst Technology Park, Capenhurst, Chester, CH1 6EH
Tel: 0151-347 1900 **Fax:** 0151-347 1901
E-mail: mikee@hostvs.co.uk
Website: http://www.hostvonschrader.co.uk
Directors: M. Egerton (MD)
Immediate Holding Company: ALCHEMA LIMITED
Registration no: 03520126 **VAT No.:** GB 320 3678 86
Date established: 1998 **Turnover:** £250,000 - £500,000
No.of Employees: 1 - 10 **Product Groups:** 40

Ics Industrial Services Ltd

23 Brooke Avenue, Chester, CH2 1HQ
Tel: 01244-371167 **Fax:** 01244-381978
E-mail: sales@icsindustrialservices.co.uk
Website: http://www.icsindustrialservices.co.uk
Directors: S. Thomson (Fin), P. Thomson (MD)
Immediate Holding Company: ICS (INDUSTRIAL SERVICES) LIMITED
Registration no: 05177970 **Date established:** 2004
Turnover: Up to £250,000 **No.of Employees:** 1 - 10 **Product Groups:** 30, 40

Date of Accounts	Jul 11	Jul 10	Jul 09
Working Capital	-2	-4	-0
Fixed Assets	2	N/A	N/A
Current Assets	86	37	21

I R D UK Ltd

International House Aviation Park Flint Road, Saltney Ferry, Chester, CH4 0GZ
Tel: 01244-538170 **Fax:** 01244-528900
E-mail: salesuk@irdbalancing.com
Website: http://www.irdbalancing.com
Managers: P. Young (Ops Mgr)
Immediate Holding Company: IRD UK LIMITED
Registration no: 04744915 **Date established:** 2003
No.of Employees: 1 - 10 **Product Groups:** 38, 46

Date of Accounts	Sep 11	Sep 10	Sep 09
Working Capital	-426	-334	-269
Fixed Assets	4	8	14
Current Assets	365	294	344

Jewson Ltd

142 Christleton Road, Chester, CH3 5TD
Tel: 01244-342171 **Fax:** 01244-323467
Website: http://www.jewson.co.uk
Managers: H. Thomas (Mgr)
Ultimate Holding Company: COMPAGNIE DE SAINT GOBAIN (FRANCE)
Immediate Holding Company: JEWSON LIMITED
Registration no: 00348407 **VAT No.:** GB 497 7184 83
Date established: 1939 **Turnover:** £2m - £5m **No.of Employees:** 1 - 10
Product Groups: 66

Date of Accounts	Dec 11	Dec 10	Dec 09
Sales Turnover	1606m	1547m	1485m
Pre Tax Profit/Loss	18m	100m	45m
Working Capital	-345m	-250m	-349m
Fixed Assets	496m	387m	461m
Current Assets	657m	1005m	1320m
Current Liabilities	66m	120m	64m

Charles F Jones & Son

16 Grosvenor Court Foregate Street, Chester, CH1 1HN
Tel: 01244-328141 **Fax:** 01244-343232
E-mail: info@cfj.co.uk
Website: http://www.cfj.co.uk
Bank(s): Barclays, Royal Bank of Scotland
Directors: D. Gale-Hasleham (Prop)
Immediate Holding Company: CHARLES F JONES & SON LLP
Registration no: OC300815 **VAT No.:** GB 159 6586 11
Date established: 2001 **No.of Employees:** 11 - 20 **Product Groups:** 80

Date of Accounts	Sep 11	Sep 10	Sep 09
Working Capital	79	91	69
Fixed Assets	262	265	222
Current Assets	266	283	269

Kollmorgen Lift Controls Ltd

Unit 2 Office Village Sandpaper Way, Chester Business Park, Chester, CH4 9QP
Tel: 01244-678549 **Fax:** 01634-280346
E-mail: info@kollmorgen.co.uk
Website: http://www.kollmorgen.co.uk
Directors: N. Hanika (Chief Op Offcr)
Immediate Holding Company: KOLLMORGEN (UK) LIMITED
Registration no: 04088199 **Date established:** 2000
No.of Employees: 1 - 10 **Product Groups:** 35, 39, 45

Date of Accounts	Dec 11	Dec 10	Dec 09
Working Capital	10	109	260
Fixed Assets	3	1	2
Current Assets	1m	1m	1m

C J Littler

Oakbank Poplar Hall Lane, Chorlton-By-Backford, Chester, CH2 4DD
Tel: 01244-851336 **Fax:** 01244-851339
Website: http://www.cjloaded.demon.co.uk
Directors: C. Littler (Prop)
Date established: 1985 **No.of Employees:** 1 - 10 **Product Groups:** 41

Maplin Electronics Ltd

Unit 1a Boughton, Chester, CH3 5AF
Tel: 01244-315484 **Fax:** 01244-315468
Website: http://www.maplin.co.uk
Ultimate Holding Company: Maplin Electronics Group (Holdings) Ltd
Immediate Holding Company: MAPLIN ELECTRONICS LIMITED
Registration no: 01264385 **Date established:** 1976
Turnover: £125m - £250m **No.of Employees:** 1 - 10 **Product Groups:** 37, 61

Maxsound Car Security

5 Hallfield Drive Elton, Chester, CH2 4PD
Tel: 01928-726479
E-mail: laurenceharvey2@hotmail.com
Website: http://www.max-sound.co.uk
Directors: L. Harvey (Prop)
No.of Employees: 1 - 10 **Product Groups:** 40, 66, 67

Metal Improvement Co. (Subsidiary for Curtiss-Wright Corporation)

Chester Road Broughton, Chester, CH4 0BZ
Tel: 01244-534999 **Fax:** 01244-521500
E-mail: ray.lopuc@cwst.com
Website: http://www.cwst.co.uk
Bank(s): National Westminster Bank Plc
Managers: A. Bryan (Chief Acct), R. Lopuc
Ultimate Holding Company: CURTISS-WRIGHT CORPORATION USA
Registration no: FC006968 **VAT No.:** GB 126 7764 41
No.of Employees: 101 - 250 **Product Groups:** 48

Vernon Morris Utility Solutions Ltd

Chester Road Bretton, Chester, CH4 0DH
Tel: 01244-660794 **Fax:** 01244-661291
E-mail: sales@vernonmorris.co.uk
Website: http://www.vernonmorris.co.uk
Managers: W. Jones (Mgr)
Ultimate Holding Company: COMMERCIAL & INDUSTRIAL GAUGES LIMITED
Immediate Holding Company: VERNON MORRIS UTILITY SOLUTIONS LIMITED
Registration no: 06979294 **VAT No.:** GB 159 2842 39
Date established: 2009 **Turnover:** £500,000 - £1m
No.of Employees: 1 - 10 **Product Groups:** 38

Date of Accounts	Dec 11	Dec 10	Dec 09
Working Capital	116	13	-34
Fixed Assets	18	20	23
Current Assets	333	232	129

Msi Marketing Research

Viscount House River Lane, Saltney, Chester, CH4 8RH
Tel: 0800-1956756 **Fax:** 0800-1956757
E-mail: tracy@msi-marketingresearch.co.uk
Website: http://www.msi-marketingresearch.co.uk
Bank(s): Lloyds TSB
Directors: T. Gallagher-Keenan (Dir), T. Gallagher (Dir), A. Walker (Ch)
Managers: C. Owen (Sales Admin), K. Owen (Sales Admin)
Immediate Holding Company: Marketing Answers Ltd
Registration no: 03163818 **VAT No.:** GB 344 7342 55
Date established: 1980 **Turnover:** £500,000 - £1m
No.of Employees: 21 - 50 **Product Groups:** 44, 61, 80, 81, 86

Pangborn Ltd

Riverside House Brymau Three Trading Estate River Lane, Saltney, Chester, CH4 8RQ
Tel: 01244-659852 **Fax:** 01244-659853
E-mail: sales@pangborn.co.uk
Website: http://www.pangborn.com
Directors: S. Cooper (Dir), S. Cross (Co Sec)
Ultimate Holding Company: CAPITAL EQUIPMENT RESOURCES LLC (USA)
Immediate Holding Company: PANGBORN (UK) LIMITED
Registration no: 02596935 **Date established:** 1991
No.of Employees: 1 - 10 **Product Groups:** 33, 46, 48

Date of Accounts	Dec 11	Dec 10	Dec 09
Working Capital	64	65	65
Current Assets	64	65	66

Parry Crulow Ltd

35 Common Hall Street, Chester, CH1 2BJ
Tel: 01244-313151
Directors: I. Crulow (MD)
No.of Employees: 11 - 20 **Product Groups:** 38, 67

Pro Cubed UK Ltd

10 Hunters Walk Canal Street, Chester, CH1 4EB
Tel: 01244-355295 **Fax:** 01244-341488
E-mail: sales@pro-cubed.co.uk
Website: http://www.pro-cubed.co.uk
Directors: J. Hood (Fin)
Immediate Holding Company: HADGATE CLAIMS LTD
Registration no: 03243555 **Date established:** 2011
Turnover: Up to £250,000 **No.of Employees:** 1 - 10 **Product Groups:** 44

Date of Accounts	Mar 07	Mar 06
Working Capital	-22	1
Fixed Assets	23	3
Current Assets	65	28
Current Liabilities	87	26

Quality Hydraulic Power Ltd

Taylor House Minerva Avenue, Chester West Employment Park, Chester, CH1 4QL
Tel: 01244-393500
E-mail: info@qhp.co.uk
Website: http://www.qhp.co.uk
Directors: K. Brownlee (MD)
Managers: H. Frost (Fin Mgr), R. Done (Personnel)
Ultimate Holding Company: A & E HOLDINGS LIMITED
Immediate Holding Company: QUALITY HYDRAULIC POWER LIMITED
Registration no: 02131010 **VAT No.:** GB 454 0580 59
Date established: 1987 **No.of Employees:** 21 - 50 **Product Groups:** 30, 35, 38, 40, 48, 67

Date of Accounts	Dec 11	Dec 10	Dec 09
Sales Turnover	12m	7m	8m
Pre Tax Profit/Loss	937	320	455
Working Capital	2m	1m	1m
Fixed Assets	689	644	579
Current Assets	5m	3m	3m
Current Liabilities	1m	1m	1m

Rapid Newscommunications Group

Unit 2 Chowley Business Centre Chowley Oak Lane Tattenhall, Chester, CH3 9GA
Tel: 01829-770037 **Fax:** 01829-770047
E-mail: info@rapidnews.com
Website: http://www.rapidnews.com
Bank(s): Barclays
Directors: M. Blezard (MD), N. Burney (Dir), D. Wood (Dir)
Immediate Holding Company: RAPID NEWS PUBLICATIONS LIMITED
Registration no: 02721194 **VAT No.:** GB 595 8832 73
Date established: 1992 **Turnover:** £500,000 - £1m
No.of Employees: 21 - 50 **Product Groups:** 28

Date of Accounts	Dec 11	Dec 10	Dec 09
Sales Turnover	N/A	N/A	834
Pre Tax Profit/Loss	N/A	N/A	9
Working Capital	187	184	179
Fixed Assets	N/A	1	9
Current Assets	726	1m	1m
Current Liabilities	N/A	N/A	790

Rapport Creative

1 King's Buildings King Street, Chester, CH1 2AJ
Tel: 01244-328111 **Fax:** 01244-329111
E-mail: a.porter@rapport-tv.com
Website: http://www.rapportcreative.co.uk
Directors: A. Porter (Dir)
Turnover: £250,000 - £500,000 **No.of Employees:** 11 - 20
Product Groups: 81, 89

Regal Rentals

Kingfisher Court Parkgate Road Saughall, Chester, CH1 6RR
Tel: 01244-852000 **Fax:** 01244-851551
E-mail: reservations@regalrentals.com
Website: http://www.regalrentals.com
Directors: B. Hastings (Dir)
Immediate Holding Company: REGAL VEHICLE RENTALS LIMITED
Registration no: 03465480 **Date established:** 1997
No.of Employees: 1 - 10 **Product Groups:** 72

Date of Accounts	Mar 12	Mar 11	Mar 10
Sales Turnover	5m	5m	5m
Pre Tax Profit/Loss	179	194	170
Working Capital	-2m	-3m	-469
Fixed Assets	5m	6m	5m
Current Assets	1m	1m	1m
Current Liabilities	312	488	521

Safety Kleen UK

2 Broughton Industrial Estate Broughton Mills Road, Bretton, Chester, CH4 0BY
Tel: 01244-660184 **Fax:** 01244-661338
E-mail: gslater@sk-europe.com
Website: http://www.sk-europe.com
Managers: G. Slater (District Mgr)
Immediate Holding Company: SAFETY-KLEEN U.K. LIMITED
Registration no: 01190039 **Date established:** 1974
No.of Employees: 21 - 50 **Product Groups:** 38, 42

R P Shaw Fabrications

Rendova Farm Powey Lane, Mollington, Chester, CH1 6LH
Tel: 01244-881043 **Fax:** 01244-881023
E-mail: shawfabs@msn.com
Website: http://www.shawfab.co.uk
Directors: R. Shaw (Prop)
Date established: 1987 **No.of Employees:** 1 - 10 **Product Groups:** 26, 35

Sira Test & Certification Ltd

Rake Lane Eccleston, Chester, CH4 9JN
Tel: 01244-670900 **Fax:** 01244-681330
E-mail: info@siraservices.com
Website: http://www.siraservices.com
Directors: M. Shearman (MD)
Managers: J. Stobbs (Tech Serv Mgr)
Ultimate Holding Company: CANADIAN STANDARDS ASSOCIATION (CANADA)
Immediate Holding Company: SIRA TEST AND CERTIFICATION LIMITED
Registration no: 05569145 **Date established:** 2005 **Turnover:** £5m - £10m
No.of Employees: 21 - 50 **Product Groups:** 37, 38, 39, 44, 52, 65, 67, 84, 85

Date of Accounts	Dec 10	Dec 09	Dec 08
Sales Turnover	5m	4m	3m
Pre Tax Profit/Loss	885	511	30
Working Capital	762	-263	-758
Fixed Assets	159	361	608
Current Assets	4m	2m	1m
Current Liabilities	3m	2m	2m

Somac Threads Ltd

Unit 2-3 Brymau Four Trading Estate River Lane, Saltney, Chester, CH4 8RF
Tel: 01244-680506 **Fax:** 01244-680202
E-mail: info@somac.co.uk
Website: http://www.somac.co.uk
Directors: J. Webb (Dir)
Immediate Holding Company: SOMAC THREAD MANUFACTURING LIMITED
Registration no: 02061293 **Date established:** 1986
No.of Employees: 21 - 50 **Product Groups:** 23, 35

Date of Accounts	Sep 11	Sep 10	Sep 09
Working Capital	581	524	485
Fixed Assets	N/A	3	8
Current Assets	761	710	702

Stamford Agricultural Serivce

Canal Side Tattenhall Road, Tattenhall, Chester, CH3 9BD
Tel: 01829-771509 **Fax:** 01829-772509
E-mail: stamfordag@btconnect.com
Website: http://www.stamfordagricultural.co.uk
Directors: D. Whittaker (Dir), G. Foster (Fin)
Immediate Holding Company: STAMFORD AGRICULTURAL SERVICES LTD
Registration no: 04810893 **Date established:** 2003
No.of Employees: 11 - 20 **Product Groups:** 41

see next page

***Stamford Agricultural Serivce** - Cont'd*

Date of Accounts	Jun 11	Jun 10	Jun 09
Working Capital	96	48	57
Fixed Assets	9	15	17
Current Assets	1m	884	732

Strix UK Ltd
Pulford House, Bell Meadow Business Park Park Lane, Pulford, Chester, CH4 9EP
Tel: 01244-572372 **Fax:** 01244-571327
E-mail: uksales@strix.com
Website: http://www.strix.com
Bank(s): Barclays
Directors: B. Amey (Dir), E. Davies (Ch), M. Bartlett (Sales), P. Snowden (Dir)
Managers: J. Brodie (Develop Mgr), A. Holmes (Sec)
Immediate Holding Company: Strix Ltd
Registration no: 02570237 **VAT No.:** 000 0073 70 **Date established:** 2005
Turnover: £500,000 - £1m **No.of Employees:** 101 - 250
Product Groups: 38

Date of Accounts	Dec 07	Dec 06	Dec 05
Working Capital	-1351	-1468	-1388
Fixed Assets	2	12	21
Current Assets	208	88	269
Current Liabilities	1559	1555	1657
Total Share Capital	1000	1000	1000

Tecra Ltd
14 Bumpers Lane Sealand Indl-Est, Chester, CH1 4LT
Tel: 01244-377539 **Fax:** 01244-378644
E-mail: sales@tecraltd.co.uk
Website: http://www.tecra.ltd.uk
Directors: N. Walker (MD), S. Mortima (Sales & Mktg), J. O'Carroll Bailey (Dir)
Managers: K. Sherratt (Mgr)
Ultimate Holding Company: GRAFTON GROUP PUBLIC LIMITED COMPANY
Immediate Holding Company: TECRA LIMITED
Registration no: 01358241 **Date established:** 1978 **Turnover:** £2m - £5m
No.of Employees: 1 - 10 **Product Groups:** 30, 36, 40

Date of Accounts	Dec 11	Dec 10	Dec 09
Sales Turnover	N/A	3m	4m
Pre Tax Profit/Loss	N/A	91	253
Working Capital	1m	1m	744
Fixed Assets	N/A	N/A	569
Current Assets	1m	1m	2m
Current Liabilities	N/A	N/A	45

Timberwise UK plc
Suite 24v 7 Hunter Street, Chester, CH1 2HR
Tel: 01244-321366 **Fax:** 01565-621000
E-mail: chester@timberwise.co.uk
Website: http://www.timberwise.co.uk
Directors: M. Edwards (MD)
Immediate Holding Company: TIMBERWISE HOLDINGS LIMITED
Registration no: 05101213 **Date established:** 2004
No.of Employees: 1 - 10 **Product Groups:** 07, 32, 52

Date of Accounts	May 11	May 10	May 09
Working Capital	-81	-49	-3
Fixed Assets	2	3	3
Current Assets	10	6	14

Town & County Electrical Contractors Ltd
Brymau House River Lane, Saltney, Chester, CH4 8RH
Tel: 01244-675588 **Fax:** 01244-671176
E-mail: sales@town-county-electrical.co.uk
Website: http://www.town-county-electrical.co.uk
Bank(s): National Westminister
Directors: S. Crone (MD)
Immediate Holding Company: TOWN AND COUNTY ELECTRICAL CONTRACTORS LIMITED
Registration no: 00964313 **VAT No.:** 159 2137 60 **Date established:** 1969
Turnover: £1m - £2m **No.of Employees:** 21 - 50 **Product Groups:** 52

Date of Accounts	Mar 11	Mar 10	Mar 09
Working Capital	226	206	343
Fixed Assets	229	236	263
Current Assets	927	841	1m

Ungerer Ltd
Sealand Road, Chester, CH1 4LP
Tel: 01244-371711 **Fax:** 01244-380185
E-mail: kvoorhees@ungerer.co.uk
Website: http://www.ungererandcompany.com
Bank(s): Barclays, Chester
Directors: J. Percy (MD), K. Voorhees (MD)
Managers: J. Hughes (Mktg Serv Mgr), A. Southwick (Purch Mgr), G. Spencer (Sales Prom Mgr), R. Mason (Tech Serv Mgr)
Ultimate Holding Company: UNGERER INDUSTRIES INC (USA)
Immediate Holding Company: UNGERER LIMITED
Registration no: 00629190 **VAT No.:** GB 421 9909 43
Date established: 1959 **Turnover:** £20m - £50m
No.of Employees: 51 - 100 **Product Groups:** 20, 30, 31, 32, 38, 42, 63, 66

Date of Accounts	Oct 11	Oct 10	Oct 09
Sales Turnover	26m	23m	18m
Pre Tax Profit/Loss	1m	1m	889
Working Capital	4m	3m	2m
Fixed Assets	1m	1m	1m
Current Assets	12m	9m	7m
Current Liabilities	529	1m	533

University Of Chester
Parkgate Road, Chester, CH1 4BJ
Tel: 01244-511000 **Fax:** 01244-398470
E-mail: enquiries@chester.ac.uk
Website: http://www.chester.ac.uk
Directors: R. Waddington (Fin), J. Dagnall (Pers), L. Bailey (Mkt Research)
Managers: S. Vure, T. Wheeler
Immediate Holding Company: UNIVERSITY OF CHESTER TRUST
Registration no: 07828011 **Date established:** 2011
Turnover: £50m - £75m **No.of Employees:** 1501 & over
Product Groups: 86

Date of Accounts	Aug 10
Sales Turnover	11m
Pre Tax Profit/Loss	814
Working Capital	348
Fixed Assets	662
Current Assets	2m
Current Liabilities	2m

West Cheshire College
Eaton Road, Chester, CH4 7ER
Tel: 01244-656100 **Fax:** 01244-670676
E-mail: info@west-cheshire.ac.uk
Website: http://www.west-cheshire.ac.uk
Managers: N. Southern (Asst Gen Mgr)
No.of Employees: 251 - 500 **Product Groups:** 86

Wilbury Metals Ltd
Borders 2 Industrial Estate Off River Lane Saltney, Chester, CH4 8RQ
Tel: 01244-681415 **Fax:** 01244-683011
E-mail: john@wilburymetals.co.uk
Website: http://www.wilburymetals.co.uk
Directors: J. Sharples (MD)
Immediate Holding Company: WILBURY METALS LIMITED
Registration no: 02422289 **Date established:** 1989
No.of Employees: 1 - 10 **Product Groups:** 12, 31, 34, 35, 36, 66

Date of Accounts	Jan 12	Jan 11	Jan 10
Working Capital	2m	2m	1m
Fixed Assets	14	18	24
Current Assets	3m	3m	2m

Congleton

Astbury Garden Buildings Ltd
Newcastle Road Astbury, Congleton, CW12 4RL
Tel: 01260-299524 **Fax:** 01260-299119
E-mail: sales@astburygardenbuildings.co.uk
Website: http://www.comptonbuildings.co.uk
Directors: C. Milner (Dir)
Immediate Holding Company: ASTBURY GARDEN BUILDINGS LIMITED
Registration no: 05074964 **Date established:** 2004
No.of Employees: 1 - 10 **Product Groups:** 25, 33, 35, 66

Date of Accounts	Mar 11	Mar 09	Mar 08
Working Capital	-55	-67	6
Fixed Assets	12	15	16
Current Assets	83	91	105

Boalloy Industries Ltd
Radnor Park Trading Estate West Heath, Radnor Park Industrial Estate, Congleton, CW12 4QA
Tel: 01260-275151 **Fax:** 01260-279696
E-mail: sales@boalloyindustries.co.uk
Website: http://www.boalloyindustries.co.uk
Bank(s): HSBC Bank plc
Directors: C. Pickering (MD)
Ultimate Holding Company: J.M.F. LTD.
Immediate Holding Company: BOALLOY INDUSTRIES LIMITED
Registration no: 05886571 **VAT No.:** GB 611 4273 78
Date established: 2006 **Turnover:** £20m - £50m
No.of Employees: 11 - 20 **Product Groups:** 39

Date of Accounts	Dec 11	Dec 10
Working Capital	24	13
Fixed Assets	31	17
Current Assets	181	56

Clarke Cable Ltd
Varey Road Easton Bank Trading Estate, Eaton Bank Trading Estate, Congleton, CW12 1PJ
Tel: 01260-272132 **Fax:** 01260-278041
E-mail: julianb@clarkecable.co.uk
Website: http://www.clarkecable.co.uk
Directors: T. Hopper (Fin), J. Baseley (MD)
Managers: M. Beech (Buyer), D. Broadhurst (Sales Prom Mgr)
Ultimate Holding Company: EARLEX LIMITED
Immediate Holding Company: CLARKE CABLE LIMITED
Registration no: 01046138 **VAT No.:** 157 2002 95 **Date established:** 1972
Turnover: £2m - £5m **No.of Employees:** 21 - 50 **Product Groups:** 23, 37

Date of Accounts	Jul 11	Jul 09	Jul 08
Working Capital	180	180	180
Current Assets	180	180	180

Cobra Braiding Machinery
Riverdane Road Eaton Bank Trading Estate, Congleton, CW12 1PL
Tel: 01260-279326 **Fax:** 01260-299017
E-mail: office@cobrabraids.co.uk
Website: http://www.cobrabraids.co.uk
Directors: N. Hyde (Dir)
Registration no: 04267198 **Date established:** 1973
Turnover: £250,000 - £500,000 **No.of Employees:** 1 - 10
Product Groups: 29, 35, 37, 43, 45, 46

Commercial Label Products Ltd
Greenfield Industrial Estate Back Lane, Congleton, CW12 4TR
Tel: 01260-298320 **Fax:** 01260-298303
E-mail: sales@labels-uk.com
Website: http://www.labels-uk.com
Directors: S. Painton (Fin), N. Painton (MD)
Immediate Holding Company: COMMERCIAL LABEL PRODUCTS LIMITED
Registration no: 01896978 **Date established:** 1985 **Turnover:** £1m - £2m
No.of Employees: 11 - 20 **Product Groups:** 27, 28, 30, 42

Date of Accounts	May 11	May 10	May 09
Working Capital	353	388	313
Fixed Assets	795	539	587
Current Assets	625	676	546

Compact Control Design Ltd
77 Woolston Avenue, Congleton, CW12 3ED
Tel: 01260-281694 **Fax:** 01260-501196
E-mail: design@compactcontrol.co.uk
Website: http://www.compactcontrol.co.uk
Directors: A. Watts (Dir)
Immediate Holding Company: COMPACT CONTROL DESIGN LIMITED
Registration no: 05528711 **VAT No.:** GB 868 3698 55
Date established: 2005 **Turnover:** Up to £250,000
No.of Employees: 1 - 10 **Product Groups:** 37, 38, 84

Date of Accounts	Aug 11	Aug 10	Aug 09
Working Capital	9	4	-9
Fixed Assets	1	2	3
Current Assets	16	13	8

Congleton Engineering Developments Ltd
Unit 12 Daneside Business Park Riverdane Road, Congleton, CW12 1UN
Tel: 01260-278167 **Fax:** 01260-280579
Website: http://www.congleton-engineering.co.uk
Managers: A. Lathan (Mgr)
Immediate Holding Company: CONGLETON ENGINEERING DEVELOPMENTS LIMITED
Registration no: 01299199 **Date established:** 1977
No.of Employees: 11 - 20 **Product Groups:** 39, 45, 48, 49

Date of Accounts	Mar 11	Mar 10	Mar 09
Working Capital	169	93	245
Fixed Assets	298	319	363
Current Assets	1m	1m	1m

Desch Plantpak
Eaton Bank Trading Estate Varey Road, Congleton, CW12 1HD
Tel: 01260-279432 **Fax:** 01260-280856
E-mail: j.phillips@desch-plantpak.co.uk
Website: http://www.desch-plantpak.co.uk
Managers: J. Phillips (Chief Mgr)
Immediate Holding Company: SYNBRA
Registration no: 00794214 **Turnover:** £5m - £10m
No.of Employees: 21 - 50 **Product Groups:** 30, 35, 37, 40, 41, 42

Electrial Installation Supplies
Dane Mill Broadhurst Lane, Congleton, CW12 1LA
Tel: 01260-281447 **Fax:** 01260-281446
E-mail: eis@talktalkbusiness.net
Directors: A. Williams (Prop)
Immediate Holding Company: ELECTRICAL INSTALLATION SUPPLIES LIMITED
Registration no: 06520365 **Date established:** 2008
No.of Employees: 1 - 10 **Product Groups:** 36, 40

Date of Accounts	Mar 12	Mar 11	Mar 10
Working Capital	8	-18	-31
Fixed Assets	29	33	38
Current Assets	86	96	76

Findamachine Ltd (Macrotec Machine Tools Ltd)
Giantswood House Hulme Walfield, Congleton, CW12 2JJ
Tel: 01260-272172 **Fax:** 01260-298644
E-mail: richardmoss@findamachine.com
Website: http://www.findamachine.com
Directors: R. Moss (Dir)
Immediate Holding Company: FINDAMACHINE LTD
Registration no: 07258214 **Date established:** 2010
Turnover: £500,000 - £1m **No.of Employees:** 1 - 10 **Product Groups:** 40, 44, 46, 67

Date of Accounts	May 11
Working Capital	-8
Fixed Assets	9
Current Assets	2

Forkwise Training
32 Pirie Road, Congleton, CW12 2EF
Tel: 01260-280961 **Fax:** 01260-280961
Directors: G. Holmes (Prop)
Date established: 1998 **No.of Employees:** 1 - 10 **Product Groups:** 35, 39, 45

H M K Ltd
Kappa House Hatter Street, Congleton, CW12 1QJ
Tel: 01260-279411 **Fax:** 01260-281022
E-mail: sales@hmkdirect.com
Website: http://www.hmkdirect.com
Bank(s): Barclays
Directors: J. Krajewski (Fin)
Managers: A. Stafford (Comptroller)
Immediate Holding Company: HMK LIMITED
Registration no: 02778786 **VAT No.:** GB 332 1888 60
Date established: 1993 **Turnover:** £250,000 - £500,000
No.of Employees: 21 - 50 **Product Groups:** 37, 45

Date of Accounts	Jan 12	Jan 11	Jan 10
Working Capital	279	218	194
Fixed Assets	57	65	39
Current Assets	466	392	341

Hans Lingl UK Ltd
Radnor Park Industrial Estate, Congleton, CW12 4UW
Tel: 01260-277711 **Fax:** 01260-270926
E-mail: postmaster@lingl.co.uk
Website: http://www.lingl.co.uk
Directors: A. Meacham (MD), P. Moore (Co Sec)
Managers: M. Lowndes (Purch Mgr), M. Acton (Tech Serv Mgr), P. Redfern
Ultimate Holding Company: HANS LINGL ANLAGENBAU UND VERFAHRENSTECH GMBH (GERMANY)
Immediate Holding Company: HANS LINGL (U.K.) LIMITED
Registration no: 00824378 **Date established:** 1964 **Turnover:** £2m - £5m
No.of Employees: 21 - 50 **Product Groups:** 45

Date of Accounts	Dec 11	Dec 10	Dec 09
Sales Turnover	N/A	N/A	5m
Pre Tax Profit/Loss	N/A	N/A	-987
Working Capital	1m	1m	1m
Fixed Assets	965	1m	1m
Current Assets	2m	2m	3m
Current Liabilities	N/A	N/A	114

Induchem
Unit 1 Greenfield Farm Indl-Est, Congleton, CW12 4TR
Tel: 01260-277234 **Fax:** 01260-277649
E-mail: sales@induchem.biz
Website: http://www.induchem.ie
Bank(s): National Westminster Bank Plc
Directors: C. O'Mahoney (Fin), D. Carroll (Dir)
Managers: J. Brown (Chief Mgr), T. Hendzel (Mgr), A. White (Ops Mgr)
Immediate Holding Company: INDUCHEM BIO LIMITED
Registration no: 07411276 **Date established:** 2010 **Turnover:** £2m - £5m
No.of Employees: 11 - 20 **Product Groups:** 30, 36, 38, 39, 40

Investment Castings Congleton Ltd
Greenfield Farm Industrial Estate, Congleton, CW12 4TR
Tel: 01260-280181 **Fax:** 01260-298208
E-mail: dave@investment-castings.co.uk
Website: http://www.investment-castings.co.uk
Bank(s): Natwest
Directors: D. Clarkson (MD)
Immediate Holding Company: INVESTMENT CASTINGS (CONGLETON) LIMITED
Registration no: 02247501 **VAT No.:** GB 593 5919 88
Date established: 1988 **Turnover:** £250,000 - £500,000
No.of Employees: 11 - 20 **Product Groups:** 34

Date of Accounts	Apr 12	Apr 11	Apr 10
Working Capital	109	289	209
Fixed Assets	602	361	375
Current Assets	225	419	312

Macrotec Machine Tool Ltd

Giantswood House Hulme Walfield, Congleton, CW12 2JJ
Tel: 01260-272172 **Fax:** 01260-298644
E-mail: sales@macrotec.co.uk
Website: http://www.findamachine.com
Directors: S. Moss (MD)
Immediate Holding Company: Macrotec Machine Tools Ltd
Registration no: 07258214 **Date established:** 1995
Turnover: £250,000 - £500,000 **No.of Employees:** 1 - 10
Product Groups: 46

Mechandling Ltd

11b Greenfield Farm Industrial Estate, Congleton, CW12 4TR
Tel: 01260-299411 **Fax:** 01260-299032
E-mail: sales@mechandling.co.uk
Website: http://www.mechandling.co.uk
Directors: S. Young (MD)
Immediate Holding Company: MECHANDLING LIMITED
Registration no: 03591701 **Date established:** 1998
No.of Employees: 1 - 10 **Product Groups:** 35, 39, 45

Date of Accounts	Jul 11	Jul 10	Jul 09
Working Capital	72	65	82
Fixed Assets	33	48	31
Current Assets	120	127	124

John Morley Importers

Morley Drive, Congleton, CW12 3LF
Tel: 01260-299911 **Fax:** 01260-270105
E-mail: proberts@johnmorley.co.uk
Website: http://www.JOHNMORLEY.CO.UK
Bank(s): National Westminster Bank Plc
Directors: I. Hodgen (Co Sec), I. Hodgen (Fin), P. Roberts (MD)
Managers: G. Rigby (Purch Mgr)
Immediate Holding Company: JOHN MORLEY (TRADING) LIMITED
Registration no: 03927781 **VAT No.:** GB 157 7240 54
Date established: 2000 **Turnover:** £5m - £10m
No.of Employees: 101 - 250 **Product Groups:** 20

Date of Accounts	Jun 08	Jun 07	Jun 06
Sales Turnover	19119	10820	11717
Pre Tax Profit/Loss	406	116	298
Working Capital	3877	3659	3560
Fixed Assets	512	444	458
Current Assets	9403	5392	5034
Current Liabilities	5526	1733	1474
Total Share Capital	85	85	85
ROCE% (Return on Capital Employed)	9.2	2.8	7.4
ROT% (Return on Turnover)	2.1	1.1	2.5

Prism

North Rode, Congleton, CW12 2NY
Tel: 01260-223575 **Fax:** 01260-223229
E-mail: julie@prismadvertising.co.uk
Website: http://www.prismadvertising.co.uk
Directors: J. Price (Prop)
Immediate Holding Company: PRISM ADVERTISING LIMITED
Registration no: 04280574 **Date established:** 2001
No.of Employees: 1 - 10 **Product Groups:** 42, 45

Rapier Star Ltd

Bridge Row Buglawton, Congleton, CW12 2AB
Tel: 01260-285868 **Fax:** 01260-285869
E-mail: sih@rapierstar.com
Website: http://www.rapierstar.com
Directors: D. Furness (Prop)
Ultimate Holding Company: RAPIER STAR HOLDINGS LIMITED
Immediate Holding Company: RAPIER STAR LIMITED
Registration no: 02692152 **Date established:** 1992 **Turnover:** £1m - £2m
No.of Employees: 11 - 20 **Product Groups:** 35, 36, 66

Date of Accounts	Dec 10	Dec 09	Dec 08
Working Capital	2m	2m	1m
Fixed Assets	N/A	125	98
Current Assets	2m	3m	3m

Rooftherm

Dane Mill Business Centre Broadhurst Lane, Congleton, CW12 1LA
Tel: 0800-084 2887 **Fax:** 01260-295426
E-mail: info@rooftherm.co.uk
Website: http://www.rooftherm.co.uk
Managers: A. Mullings (Mgr)
Immediate Holding Company: ROMAN LODGE HOLDINGS LIMITED
Registration no: 02206515 **Date established:** 1978 **Turnover:** £2m - £5m
No.of Employees: 11 - 20 **Product Groups:** 52

Sage Zander Ltd

Triad House Mountbatten Court Worrall Street, Congleton, CW12 1DT
Tel: 01260-295264 **Fax:** 01260-295349
E-mail: sales@sagezander.com
Website: http://www.sagezander.com
Directors: P. Cockitt (Dir)
Ultimate Holding Company: THE DANE HOUSING GROUP LTD
Immediate Holding Company: SAGEZANDER LTD
Registration no: 05987698 **Date established:** 2006
Turnover: Up to £250,000 **No.of Employees:** 1 - 10 **Product Groups:** 23, 33

Date of Accounts	Nov 11	Nov 10	Nov 09
Working Capital	126	65	14
Fixed Assets	45	2	N/A
Current Assets	322	376	243

Senior Aerospace Bird Bellows

Radnor Park Industrial Estate, Congleton, CW12 4UQ
Tel: 01260-271411 **Fax:** 01260-270910
E-mail: apbird@bird-bellows.co.uk
Website: http://www.sabird-bellows.co.uk
Directors: A. Bird (MD), D. Kirkham (Fin)
Managers: C. Pate, D. Lacey (Tech Serv Mgr), G. Bevan (Personnel), R. Ratcliffe (Buyer)
Immediate Holding Company: SENIOR P.L.C.
Registration no: 01221634 **VAT No.:** GB 158 8352 32
Turnover: £5m - £10m **No.of Employees:** 101 - 250 **Product Groups:** 36

Storm Cutting Formes

Unit 2 Roe Street, Congleton, CW12 1PS
Tel: 01260-291793 **Fax:** 01260-291794
E-mail: stormcf@aol.com
Website: http://www.stormcuttingformes.co.uk
Directors: K. Mcclusky (Prop)
Date established: 2001 **Turnover:** £250,000 - £500,000
No.of Employees: 1 - 10 **Product Groups:** 27, 30, 35, 66

Surfcontrol plc

Riverside Mountbatten Way, Congleton, CW12 1DY
Tel: 01260-296200 **Fax:** 01260-296201
E-mail: sales@surfcontrol.com
Website: http://www.surfcontrol.com
Bank(s): National Westminster
Directors: M. Newman (Co Sec), P. Sueltz (Grp Chief Exec), M. Bouchard (Dir), H. Patel (Sales), D. Mendenhall (Dir), A. Martin (Mkt Research)
Managers: K. Preston (Personnel), J. Llewellwyn (Chief Mgr), A. Walker (Comptroller), A. Boardman (Purch Mgr)
Ultimate Holding Company: WEBSENSE INC (USA)
Immediate Holding Company: SURFCONTROL LIMITED
Registration no: 01566321 **Date established:** 1981 **Turnover:** £1m - £2m
No.of Employees: 101 - 250 **Product Groups:** 44

Date of Accounts	Dec 07	Jun 06	Jun 05
Sales Turnover	83m	102m	98m
Pre Tax Profit/Loss	-36m	750	8m
Working Capital	-40m	-14m	47m
Fixed Assets	219m	24m	14m
Current Assets	33m	102m	122m
Current Liabilities	73m	116m	75m
Total Share Capital	143m	5m	5m

Timcal Graphite & Carbon

PO Box 269, Congleton, CW12 3WP
Tel: 01260-276009 **Fax:** 01260-289057
E-mail: info@uk.timcal.com
Website: http://www.timcal.com
Directors: G. Nizzola (MD)
Managers: M. Minni (Purch Mgr), S. Dunn (Sales Prom Mgr)
Turnover: £20m - £50m **No.of Employees:** 1 - 10 **Product Groups:** 17, 31, 33

Vanton Pumps Europe Ltd

Unit 4 Royle Park, Congleton, CW12 1JJ
Tel: 01260-277040 **Fax:** 01260-280605
E-mail: mail@vantonpump.com
Website: http://www.vantonpump.com
Directors: A. Bould (MD), G. Lewis (MD), C. Hubert (Fin)
Immediate Holding Company: VANTON PUMPS (EUROPE) LIMITED
Registration no: 05808822 **Date established:** 2006 **Turnover:** £1m - £2m
No.of Employees: 1 - 10 **Product Groups:** 40, 43, 48

Date of Accounts	Mar 12	Mar 11	Mar 10
Working Capital	63	77	19
Fixed Assets	4	4	2
Current Assets	150	157	112

Weiale Trading Ltd

PO Box 260, Congleton, CW12 4WP
Tel: 07979-280021 **Fax:** 01260-298723
E-mail: info@weialetrading.co.uk
Website: http://www.weialetrading.co.uk
Directors: A. Rowley (Fin), W. Rowley (MD)
Immediate Holding Company: WEIALE TRADING LIMITED
Registration no: 05305077 **Date established:** 2004
No.of Employees: 1 - 10 **Product Groups:** 61

Date of Accounts	Dec 11	Dec 10	Dec 09
Working Capital	-6	1	1
Current Assets	14	14	2

Crewe

20 20 Mobile Group Ltd

Weston Road, Crewe, CW1 6BU
Tel: 01270-412020 **Fax:** 01270-412099
E-mail: support@prepaywizard.co.uk
Website: http://www.2020mobile.com
Managers: K. Sherlock (Mktg Serv Mgr)
Ultimate Holding Company: CHICAGO HOLDINGS LTD (ISLE OF MAN)
Immediate Holding Company: 20:20 MOBILE GROUP LIMITED
Registration no: 02679207 **VAT No.:** GB 319 1358 61
Date established: 1992 **Turnover:** £250m - £500m
No.of Employees: 101 - 250 **Product Groups:** 48

Date of Accounts	Dec 09	Dec 08	Dec 07
Sales Turnover	N/A	N/A	2m
Pre Tax Profit/Loss	-199m	63m	-167m
Working Capital	20m	232m	175m
Fixed Assets	34m	33m	33m
Current Assets	65m	284m	237m
Current Liabilities	3m	8m	10m

Air Products PLC (Head Office)

2 Millennium Gate Westmere Drive, Crewe, CW1 6AP
Tel: 0800-389 0202 **Fax:** 0161-223 4753
E-mail: kuhnm@airproducts.com
Website: http://www.airproducts.com
Bank(s): Barclays, 54 Lombard St, London
Managers: P. Tramver (Mktg Serv Mgr)
Ultimate Holding Company: AIR PRODUCTS & CHEMICALS INC (USA)
Immediate Holding Company: AIR PRODUCTS PUBLIC LIMITED COMPANY
Registration no: 00103881 **VAT No.:** GB 14J 3456 70
Date established: 2009 **No.of Employees:** 251 - 500 **Product Groups:** 18, 31, 34, 37, 38, 40, 41, 42, 45, 46, 47, 54, 66, 74, 75, 77, 84

Date of Accounts	Sep 11	Sep 10	Sep 09
Sales Turnover	369m	360m	422m
Pre Tax Profit/Loss	74m	56m	-5m
Working Capital	190m	122m	151m
Fixed Assets	230m	274m	248m
Current Assets	273m	254m	312m
Current Liabilities	43m	49m	56m

Burgess Food Equipment Ltd

Netherset Lane Madeley, Crewe, CW3 9PF
Tel: 01782-750471 **Fax:** 01782-750632
Website: http://www.burgessfoodequipment.co.uk
Directors: P. O'Brien (Dir), E. O'brien (Fin)
Immediate Holding Company: BURGESS FOOD EQUIPMENT LIMITED
Registration no: 04803064 **Date established:** 2003
No.of Employees: 1 - 10 **Product Groups:** 20, 40, 41

C D M Steels Ltd

Poplar Grove, Crewe, CW1 4AZ
Tel: 01270-255669 **Fax:** 01270-252670
E-mail: info@hippowash.com
Website: http://www.hippowash.com
Directors: D. Mccumesky (Co Sec)
Immediate Holding Company: HIPPOWASH LTD
Registration no: 02913494 **Date established:** 1994
No.of Employees: 21 - 50 **Product Groups:** 38, 42

Date of Accounts	Jun 11	Jun 10	Jun 09
Working Capital	173	71	72
Fixed Assets	78	64	83
Current Assets	440	233	357
Current Liabilities	N/A	11	N/A

Carillion Rail Projects

Gresty Road, Crewe, CW2 6HS
Tel: 01270-612900 **Fax:** 01270-612901
Website: http://www.carillion.com
Managers: G. Dainty (Mgr)
No.of Employees: 101 - 250 **Product Groups:** 38, 52, 81

Chamberlain Transport Ltd

Duchy Road, Crewe, CW1 6NB
Tel: 01270-502800 **Fax:** 01270-502809
E-mail: traffic@chamberlain-transport.co.uk
Website: http://www.chamberlain-transport.co.uk
Directors: S. Chamberlain (Dir)
Immediate Holding Company: CHAMBERLAIN TRANSPORT (HOLDINGS) LIMITED
Registration no: 01355738 **Date established:** 1978 **Turnover:** £2m - £5m
No.of Employees: 21 - 50 **Product Groups:** 77

Date of Accounts	Mar 11	Mar 10	Mar 09
Sales Turnover	4m	4m	4m
Pre Tax Profit/Loss	146	179	247
Working Capital	912	719	571
Fixed Assets	2m	2m	2m
Current Assets	1m	1m	1m
Current Liabilities	157	156	209

Crewe Chronicle

32-34 Victoria Street, Crewe, CW1 2JE
Tel: 01270-502400 **Fax:** 01270-502419
E-mail: newsroom@cheshirenews.co.uk
Website: http://www.iccheshire.co.uk
Managers: B. Ellans
Immediate Holding Company: TRINITY HOLDINGS
VAT No.: GB 233 3986 52 **Date established:** 2004
No.of Employees: 11 - 20 **Product Groups:** 28

Crewe Cold Food Store

Gresty Lane Shavington, Crewe, CW2 5DD
Tel: 01270-211919 **Fax:** 01270-216961
E-mail: info@crewecoldstore.co.uk
Website: http://www.gordonplantservices.co.uk
Directors: D. Plant (MD)
Immediate Holding Company: J.R. TONKS LIMITED
Registration no: 01099486 **Date established:** 1973
No.of Employees: 1 - 10 **Product Groups:** 77

Date of Accounts	Mar 12	Mar 11	Mar 10
Working Capital	535	490	495
Fixed Assets	187	199	213
Current Assets	656	597	602

Sam Dale & Son Ltd

The Forge 10 Macclesfield Road, Holmes Chapel, Crewe, CW4 7NG
Tel: 01477-532258 **Fax:** 01477-532258
Directors: E. Dale (Fin)
Immediate Holding Company: SAM DALE AND SON LIMITED
Registration no: 00555334 **Date established:** 1955
No.of Employees: 1 - 10 **Product Groups:** 41

Date of Accounts	Sep 11	Sep 10	Sep 09
Working Capital	27	35	18
Fixed Assets	4	5	5
Current Assets	76	85	72

Rodney Densem Wines Ltd

Regent House Lancaster Fields, Crewe, CW1 6FF
Tel: 01270-212200 **Fax:** 01270-212300
E-mail: sales@rdwines.com
Website: http://www.rodneydensemwines.com
Directors: N. Goodwin (Fin), S. Leonard (MD)
Managers: M. Latham (Sales Prom Mgr)
Immediate Holding Company: RODNEY DENSEM WINES LIMITED
Registration no: 03639455 **Date established:** 1998 **Turnover:** £1m - £2m
No.of Employees: 11 - 20 **Product Groups:** 21, 62

Date of Accounts	Apr 12	Apr 11	Apr 10
Working Capital	304	288	319
Fixed Assets	225	230	261
Current Assets	1m	1m	1m

Dunelm Supplies Ltd

Netherset Lane Madeley, Crewe, CW3 9PF
Tel: 01782-750884 **Fax:** 01782-751305
E-mail: sales@dunelmsupplies.co.uk
Website: http://www.dunelmsupplies.co.uk
Directors: P. Henson (Fin)
Immediate Holding Company: DUNELM SUPPLIES LIMITED
Registration no: 02345273 **VAT No.:** GB 482 5388 17
Date established: 1989 **Turnover:** £500,000 - £1m
No.of Employees: 1 - 10 **Product Groups:** 35, 41, 48

Date of Accounts	Mar 11	Mar 10	Mar 09
Working Capital	11	6	12
Fixed Assets	33	39	49
Current Assets	127	160	197

Dynamic Ceramic Ltd

Unit 10 Crewe Hall Enterprise Park Weston Road, Crewe, CW1 6UA
Tel: 01270-501000 **Fax:** 01270-501423
E-mail: sales@dynacer.com
Website: http://www.dynacer.com

see next page

Dynamic Ceramic Ltd - Cont'd

Directors: D. Smith (Fin), H. Hodgson (MD), B. Irvine (Fin)
Ultimate Holding Company: DYNAMIC-MATERIALS GROUP LIMITED
Immediate Holding Company: DYNAMIC-CERAMIC LIMITED
Registration no: 02769778 **Date established:** 1992 **Turnover:** £5m - £10m
No.of Employees: 21 - 50 **Product Groups:** 14, 23, 31, 32, 33, 34, 35, 36, 37, 40, 42, 44, 45, 46, 48, 84

Date of Accounts	Dec 11	Dec 10	Dec 09
Sales Turnover	6m	4m	4m
Pre Tax Profit/Loss	2m	953	749
Working Capital	3m	1m	588
Fixed Assets	891	696	688
Current Assets	4m	2m	1m
Current Liabilities	751	321	353

Electrical Testing & Inspection FWT Ltd

4 The Dairy Crewe Hall Farm Old Park Road, Crewe, CW1 5UE
Tel: 01270-211587 **Fax:** 01270-214467
E-mail: david@joycemontague.co.uk
Website: http://www.joycemontague.co.uk
Directors: D. Aghilli Myer (Dir)
Managers: d. aghilli-myer (Sales Admin)
Immediate Holding Company: ELECTRICAL TESTING AND INSPECTION (FWT) LTD
Registration no: 07268924 **Date established:** 2010 **Turnover:**
No.of Employees: 1 - 10 **Product Groups:** 37, 51, 52, 54, 84, 85

Fads Trading Ltd

Victoria Mill Macclesfield Road Holmes Chapel, Crewe, CW4 7PA
Tel: 01477-544544 **Fax:** 01477-535076
E-mail: info@fads.co.uk
Website: http://www.fads.co.uk
Directors: D. Mond (Fin), H. Robertson (Dir)
Managers: K. Hatton (), R. Mottershead (Personnel)
Immediate Holding Company: Strategic Retail plc
Registration no: 04233157 **Date established:** 2000
Turnover: £10m - £20m **No.of Employees:** 21 - 50 **Product Groups:** 25, 61

Date of Accounts	Feb 07	Feb 06
Sales Turnover	11198	12969
Pre Tax Profit/Loss	-422	256
Working Capital	1368	1589
Fixed Assets	407	608
Current Assets	4965	4891
Current Liabilities	3597	3302
ROCE% (Return on Capital Employed)	-23.8	11.7
ROT% (Return on Turnover)	-3.8	2.0

Fayrefield Foods Ltd

Englesea House Barthomley Road, Crewe, CW1 5UF
Tel: 01270-589311 **Fax:** 01270-582269
E-mail: info@fayrefield.com
Website: http://www.fayrefield.com
Bank(s): National Westminster Bank Plc
Directors: S. Beech (Fin)
Managers: D. Harper, M. Smith (Tech Serv Mgr), M. Reed (Comm)
Ultimate Holding Company: THE FAYREFIELD GROUP LIMITED
Immediate Holding Company: FAYREFIELD FOODS LIMITED
Registration no: 01639747 **VAT No.:** GB 338 7111 57
Date established: 1982 **Turnover:** £125m - £250m
No.of Employees: 51 - 100 **Product Groups:** 62

Date of Accounts	Dec 11	Dec 10	Dec 09
Sales Turnover	161m	154m	138m
Pre Tax Profit/Loss	2m	915	3m
Working Capital	11m	9m	8m
Fixed Assets	3m	3m	3m
Current Assets	36m	28m	31m
Current Liabilities	3m	3m	3m

Flintab Ltd

Electra House Electra Way, Crewe, CW1 6GL
Tel: 01270-251176 **Fax:** 01270-251178
Directors: P. Widgren (Co Sec)
Immediate Holding Company: FLINTAB LIMITED
Registration no: 03459873 **Date established:** 1997
No.of Employees: 1 - 10 **Product Groups:** 38, 42

Date of Accounts	Dec 11	Dec 10	Dec 09
Working Capital	N/A	-1	-2
Fixed Assets	N/A	4	9
Current Assets	64	30	42

Focus DIY Ltd

Gawsworth House Westmere Drive, Crewe, CW1 6XB
Tel: 01270-501555 **Fax:** 01270-250501
E-mail: firstname.secondname@focusdiy.co.uk
Website: http://www.focusdiy.co.uk
Directors: B. Archer (Ch), B. Grimsey (MD), S. Johnson (Grp Chief Exec), W. Grimsey (Dir), D. Wilkinson (Co Sec)
Managers: S. Thomas (Personnel), I. Roberts (Sales Prom Mgr), P. Willis (Mktg Serv Mgr), S. Cofgrove (I.T. Exec)
Ultimate Holding Company: Flp2 Ltd
Immediate Holding Company: FOCUS (DIY) LIMITED
Registration no: 01779190 **Date established:** 1983
Turnover: £75m - £125m **No.of Employees:** 251 - 500
Product Groups: 61

Date of Accounts	Feb 10	Feb 09	Feb 08
Sales Turnover	365m	371m	374m
Pre Tax Profit/Loss	-12m	-14m	-21m
Working Capital	52m	53m	61m
Fixed Assets	86m	101m	116m
Current Assets	497m	504m	526m
Current Liabilities	25m	28m	44m

G L-Tech Ltd

10 Blunstone Close, Crewe, CW2 8LS
Tel: 01270-652348 **Fax:** 01270-652348
E-mail: glafferty@gltech.co.uk
Website: http://www.gltech.co.uk
Directors: G. Lafferty (Dir)
Immediate Holding Company: GL-TECH LIMITED
Registration no: SC189992 **Date established:** 1998
Turnover: Up to £250,000 **No.of Employees:** 1 - 10 **Product Groups:** 37, 44, 79

Date of Accounts	Sep 07	Sep 06
Working Capital	6	5
Current Assets	15	9
Current Liabilities	9	4

Houston & Sons Ltd

Victoria Avenue, Crewe, CW2 7SR
Tel: 01270-500312 **Fax:** 01270-587428
E-mail: neil@houston-and-sons.co.uk
Website: http://www.houston-and-sons.co.uk
Directors: N. Tilley (MD)
Immediate Holding Company: HOUSTON AND SONS LIMITED
Registration no: 00584765 **VAT No.:** GB 278 3598 03
Date established: 1957 **Turnover:** £1m - £2m **No.of Employees:** 1 - 10
Product Groups: 42, 66

Date of Accounts	Mar 12	Mar 11	Mar 10
Working Capital	804	826	989
Fixed Assets	965	892	648
Current Assets	1m	1m	1m

Hydramatics Ltd

Unit 2b The Quantum Marshfield Bank, Crewe, CW2 8UY
Tel: 01270-500027 **Fax:** 01270-584348
E-mail: sales@hydramaticsltd.co.uk
Website: http://www.hydramaticsltd.co.uk
Directors: H. Moult (Dir)
Immediate Holding Company: HYDRAMATICS LIMITED
Registration no: 03027876 **Date established:** 1995
No.of Employees: 1 - 10 **Product Groups:** 36, 48, 84

Date of Accounts	Mar 12	Mar 11	Mar 10
Working Capital	185	187	91
Fixed Assets	70	66	54
Current Assets	298	303	186

Jewson Ltd

Victoria Avenue, Crewe, CW2 7SS
Tel: 01270-257297 **Fax:** 01270-583248
E-mail: garth.bradley@jewson.co.uk
Website: http://www.jewson.co.uk
Managers: J. Bradley (Mgr)
Ultimate Holding Company: COMPAGNIE DE SAINT GOBAIN (FRANCE)
Immediate Holding Company: JEWSON LIMITED
Registration no: 00348407 **VAT No.:** GB 394 1212 63
Date established: 1939 **Turnover:** £2m - £5m **No.of Employees:** 1 - 10
Product Groups: 66

Date of Accounts	Dec 11	Dec 10	Dec 09
Sales Turnover	1606m	1547m	1485m
Pre Tax Profit/Loss	18m	100m	45m
Working Capital	-345m	-250m	-349m
Fixed Assets	496m	387m	461m
Current Assets	657m	1005m	1320m
Current Liabilities	66m	120m	64m

Kadian Refrigeration

The Old School Wistaston Road, Crewe, CW2 7RL
Tel: 0783-670 5168 **Fax:** 01270-255500
E-mail: coldelite@hotmail.com
Website: http://www.icecreammachines.co.uk
Directors: D. O'neill (Prop)
Immediate Holding Company: KLEENACAR (CREWE) LIMITED
Registration no: 01335443 **Date established:** 1987
No.of Employees: 1 - 10 **Product Groups:** 20, 40, 41

Date of Accounts	Aug 11	Aug 10	Aug 09
Working Capital	-5	-7	-4
Fixed Assets	5	6	7
Current Assets	8	18	21

Krogab

Unit 2 Station Road Goostrey, Crewe, CW4 8PJ
Tel: 01477-544144 **Fax:** 01477-544456
E-mail: info@krogab.co.uk
Website: http://www.krogab.co.uk
Directors: S. Edwards (MD)
Immediate Holding Company: KROGAB UK LIMITED
Registration no: 02291364 **Date established:** 1988
No.of Employees: 11 - 20 **Product Groups:** 40, 49, 62

Date of Accounts	Dec 10	Dec 09	Dec 08
Working Capital	168	32	690
Fixed Assets	372	492	452
Current Assets	2m	1m	1m

Lafert Electric Motors

Electra House Electra Way, Crewe, CW1 6GL
Tel: 01270-270022 **Fax:** 01270-270023
E-mail: lafertuk@lafert.com
Website: http://www.lafert.com
Directors: N. Evenett (MD)
Immediate Holding Company: LAFERT ELECTRIC MOTORS LIMITED
Registration no: 04218919 **VAT No.:** GB 771 7215 27
Date established: 2001 **No.of Employees:** 1 - 10 **Product Groups:** 40, 67

Date of Accounts	Dec 11	Dec 10	Dec 09
Working Capital	1m	1m	1m
Fixed Assets	15	13	10
Current Assets	1m	1m	1m

Lanyards Etc

2 Duchy Road, Crewe, CW1 6ND
Tel: 01270-216369
E-mail: info@lanyardsetc.com
Website: http://www.lanyardsetc.com
Managers: J. Norman (Mgr)
Registration no: 05568378 **No.of Employees:** 21 - 50 **Product Groups:** 61

Date of Accounts	Mar 10	Mar 09	Mar 08
Sales Turnover	N/A	67	N/A
Pre Tax Profit/Loss	N/A	11	N/A
Working Capital	61	32	25
Fixed Assets	2	N/A	N/A
Current Assets	73	54	51
Current Liabilities	N/A	6	N/A

Miller Bros (Electrical) Ltd

10 Grand Junction Way, Crewe, CW1 2RP
Tel: 0870-4211097
Website: http://www.millerbros.co.uk
Managers: D. Heath (Mgr)
Immediate Holding Company: Miller Bros Electrical Ltd
Registration no: 06286179 **No.of Employees:** 1 - 10 **Product Groups:** 36, 40

Morning Foods Ltd

North Western Mills Gresty Road, Crewe, CW2 6HP
Tel: 01270-213261 **Fax:** 01270-500291
E-mail: info@morningfoods.com
Website: http://www.mornflake.com
Bank(s): Barclays, Crewe
Directors: J. Lea (MD), A. Cullom (Sales), D. Warr (Co Sec)
Ultimate Holding Company: MORNING FOODS,LIMITED
Immediate Holding Company: MORNFLAKE OATS LIMITED
Registration no: 00893231 **Date established:** 1966
Turnover: £75m - £125m **No.of Employees:** 101 - 250
Product Groups: 20, 32

Date of Accounts	Jul 11	Jul 10	Jul 09
Sales Turnover	110m	89m	90m
Pre Tax Profit/Loss	5m	4m	4m
Working Capital	13m	12m	11m
Fixed Assets	19m	17m	12m
Current Assets	29m	25m	22m
Current Liabilities	4m	4m	4m

Nantwich Chronicle

32-34 Victoria Street, Crewe, CW1 2JE
Tel: 01270-502431 **Fax:** 01270-610382
E-mail: alan.jervis@cheshirenews.co.uk
Website: http://www.crewechronicle.co.uk
Managers: A. Bowen
Ultimate Holding Company: TRINITY INTERNATIONAL HOLDINGS
Immediate Holding Company: CHESTER CHRONICAL
VAT No.: GB 655 8527 01 **Date established:** 1992
No.of Employees: 11 - 20 **Product Groups:** 28

N C C Supplies Ltd

Rose Bank Twemlow Lane, Cranage, Crewe, CW4 8EX
Tel: 01477-549484 **Fax:** 01477-533964
E-mail: sales@nccsupplies.com
Website: http://www.nccsupplies.com
Directors: R. Ling (MD)
Immediate Holding Company: NCC SUPPLIES LIMITED
Registration no: 01681368 **VAT No.:** GB 431 6034 88
Date established: 1982 **Turnover:** Up to £250,000
No.of Employees: 1 - 10 **Product Groups:** 23, 30, 36, 40, 41, 42, 46, 66, 67

Date of Accounts	Mar 12	Mar 11	Mar 10
Working Capital	-224	-219	-197
Fixed Assets	8	6	6
Current Assets	99	97	95

P R G Trailers Ltd

The Old Wood Yard Lightwood Green Avenue, Audlem, Crewe, CW3 0EN
Tel: 01270-812402 **Fax:** 01270-811293
E-mail: info@prgtrailers.co.uk
Website: http://www.prgtrailers.co.uk
Bank(s): Royal Bank Of Scotalnd
Directors: P. Grange (MD)
Immediate Holding Company: PRG TRAILERS LIMITED
Registration no: 04884868 **VAT No.:** GB 595 6163 03
Date established: 2003 **Turnover:** £500,000 - £1m
No.of Employees: 11 - 20 **Product Groups:** 68

Date of Accounts	Dec 11	Dec 10	Dec 09
Working Capital	374	332	256
Fixed Assets	194	204	217
Current Assets	495	459	549

Plasto-Sac

Goosetry Lane Cranage, Crewe, CW4 8HD
Tel: 01477-549660
Directors: J. Whitehead (MD)
No.of Employees: 1 - 10 **Product Groups:** 30, 62

Procyon Fire & Security Ltd

Electra House Electra Way, Crewe, CW1 6GL
Tel: 08700-566846 **Fax:** 01270-620350
E-mail: sales@procyonfire.com
Website: http://www.procyonfire.com
Directors: R. Cooke (Co Sec)
Immediate Holding Company: PROCYON FIRE AND SECURITY LIMITED
Registration no: 03730926 **Date established:** 1999
No.of Employees: 11 - 20 **Product Groups:** 37, 40, 67

Date of Accounts	Mar 11	Mar 10	Mar 09
Working Capital	229	165	162
Fixed Assets	4	5	6
Current Assets	650	391	343

J & H Rosenheim & Co. Ltd

Lancaster Fields, Crewe, CW1 6FF
Tel: 01270-585959 **Fax:** 01270-586611
E-mail: enquiries@rosenheim.co.uk
Website: http://www.rosenheim.co.uk
Directors: R. Pickup (MD), D. Shearsmith (Fin)
Managers: C. Wardle (Sales Prom Mgr)
Immediate Holding Company: J & H ROSENHEIM LIMITED
Registration no: 04130438 **VAT No.:** GB 771 0250 60
Date established: 2000 **Turnover:** £1m - £2m **No.of Employees:** 1 - 10
Product Groups: 35, 42, 49

Date of Accounts	May 08	May 07	May 06
Total Share Capital	1	1	1

S G World Ltd

Duchy Road, Crewe, CW1 6ND
Tel: 01270-500921 **Fax:** 01270-500220
E-mail: arnoldhaase@sgworld.com
Website: http://www.sgworld.com
Directors: A. Haase (MD), T. Mulvaney (Fin), S. Floodgate (Sales)
Managers: A. Talor (Personnel), J. Basford (Buyer), A. Coppack (Tech Serv Mgr)
Immediate Holding Company: SG WORLD LIMITED
Registration no: 03451910 **VAT No.:** GB 482 5531 38
Date established: 1997 **Turnover:** £5m - £10m
No.of Employees: 101 - 250 **Product Groups:** 28

Date of Accounts	Mar 12	Mar 11	Mar 10
Sales Turnover	9m	9m	8m
Pre Tax Profit/Loss	284	637	524
Working Capital	254	399	477
Fixed Assets	5m	1m	942
Current Assets	3m	3m	2m
Current Liabilities	525	1m	1m

Salon Beauty Supplies Ltd

Unit 2 Underwood Industrial Estate Underwood Lane, Crewe, CW1 3TJ
Tel: 01270-848535 **Fax:** 01270-848613
E-mail: suzanne@salonbeautysupplies.co.uk
Website: http://www.salonbeautysupplies.co.uk
Directors: M. Haworth (Ptnr)
Immediate Holding Company: SALON BEAUTY SUPPLIES LIMITED
Registration no: 05130316 **Date established:** 2004
Turnover: £500,000 - £1m **No.of Employees:** 1 - 10 **Product Groups:** 30, 36, 40

Date of Accounts	Jul 11	Jul 10	Jul 09
Working Capital	-10	-3	-17
Fixed Assets	20	26	32
Current Assets	50	45	65

Site Design Online
16 Drayton Crescent, Crewe, CW1 5YH
Tel: 01270-258203
E-mail: info@sitedesignonline.co.uk
Website: http://www.siteonline.co.uk
Directors: P. Bowie (Ptnr)
Date established: 1990 **Turnover:** Up to £250,000
No.of Employees: 1 - 10 **Product Groups:** 44

South Cheshire Chamber Of Commerce
Enterprise House Wistaston Road Business Centre Wistaston Ro, Crewe, CW2 7RP
Tel: 01270-504713 **Fax:** 01270-504701
E-mail: sales@southcheshirechamber.co.uk
Website: http://www.southcheshirechamber.co.uk
Directors: C. Colman (Co Sec), D. Erskine (Dir), J. Dunning (Grp Chief Exec), K. Cutler (Dir), S. Williams (Dir)
Managers: P. Coleman (Mgr), P. Colman (Mgr), M. Abbey (Sales & Mktg Mg)
Immediate Holding Company: SOUTH CHESHIRE CHAMBER OF COMMERCE AND INDUSTRY LIMITED
Registration no: 02853340 **Date established:** 1993
Turnover: £250,000 - £500,000 **No.of Employees:** 1 - 10
Product Groups: 80, 81

Wheel Wash Ltd
Pyms Lane, Crewe, CW1 3PJ
Tel: 01606-592044 **Fax:** 01606-592045
E-mail: sales@wheelwash.com
Website: http://www.wheelwash.com
Managers: I. Jolly (Chief Mgr)
Immediate Holding Company: WHEELWASH LIMITED
Registration no: 02667013 **Date established:** 1991
No.of Employees: 11 - 20 **Product Groups:** 39, 68

Date of Accounts	Sep 11	Sep 10	Sep 09
Working Capital	-200	-258	-349
Fixed Assets	770	751	1m
Current Assets	464	463	464

Dukinfield

Alpha Tube Company
Tameside Works Park Road, Dukinfield, SK16 5PT
Tel: 0161-339 8901 **Fax:** 0161-343 1750
E-mail: alpha@alphatube.freeserve.co.uk
Managers: C. Blackshaw (Mgr)
Immediate Holding Company: PIPMOOR LTD
Registration no: 01582694 **VAT No.:** GB 306 8329 58
Turnover: £500,000 - £1m **No.of Employees:** 1 - 10 **Product Groups:** 30, 46

Amiga Switchgear
5a Charles Street, Dukinfield, SK16 4SG
Tel: 0161-330 7877 **Fax:** 0161-344 1134
Website: http://www.iss-services.co.uk
No.of Employees: 1 - 10 **Product Groups:** 37, 48, 84

Cabot Plastics Ltd
Gate Street, Dukinfield, SK16 4RU
Tel: 0161-934 4500 **Fax:** 0161-934 4502
E-mail: webmaster@cabot-corp.com
Website: http://www.cabot-corp.com
Bank(s): National Westminster
Directors: M. Flegg (MD), M. Hall (Fin)
Ultimate Holding Company: CABOT CORPORATION (USA)
Immediate Holding Company: CABOT PLASTICS LIMITED
Registration no: 01329233 **VAT No.:** GB 305 0570 02
Date established: 1977 **Turnover:** £20m - £50m
No.of Employees: 51 - 100 **Product Groups:** 32

Date of Accounts	Sep 11	Sep 10	Sep 09
Sales Turnover	21m	19m	27m
Pre Tax Profit/Loss	224	486	-7m
Working Capital	-6m	-6m	-8m
Fixed Assets	N/A	16	1m
Current Assets	5m	12m	10m
Current Liabilities	327	225	353

Direct Filter Supply
1 Corn Mill Ravensfield Industrial Estate Charles Street, Dukinfield, SK16 4SD
Tel: 0161-330 5538 **Fax:** 0161-343 4826
Directors: R. Good (Prop)
Date established: 1981 **No.of Employees:** 1 - 10 **Product Groups:** 38, 42

Forbo Siegling
Unit 4 Fifth Avenue, Dukinfield, SK16 4PP
Tel: 0161-330 6521 **Fax:** 0161-308 4385
E-mail: siegling.uk@forbo.com
Website: http://www.forbo-siegling.co.uk
Bank(s): Barclays, Ashton
Directors: T. Schneider (Grp Chief Exec)
Managers: K. Walker (Fin Mgr), V. Heatley (Personnel), Y. Lawrence (Mktg Serv Mgr)
Ultimate Holding Company: FORBO HOLDING AG/SA (SWITZERLAND)
Immediate Holding Company: FORBO SIEGLING (UK) LTD.
Registration no: 00956335 **Date established:** 1969 **Turnover:** £5m - £10m
No.of Employees: 51 - 100 **Product Groups:** 22, 23, 30, 35, 43, 45, 48

Date of Accounts	Dec 11	Dec 10	Dec 09
Sales Turnover	7m	7m	6m
Pre Tax Profit/Loss	54	-227	-673
Working Capital	2m	2m	1m
Fixed Assets	23	26	59
Current Assets	3m	3m	3m
Current Liabilities	492	492	426

H B Fuller
Outram Road, Dukinfield, SK16 4XE
Tel: 0161-666 0666 **Fax:** 0161-666 0667
Website: http://www.hbfuller.com
Managers: D. Rivers (Mgr)
Ultimate Holding Company: HB FULLER INC (USA)
Immediate Holding Company: H.B.F. LIMITED
Registration no: 02849200 **Date established:** 1993 **Turnover:** £2m - £5m
No.of Employees: 1 - 10 **Product Groups:** 29, 32

Date of Accounts	Nov 08	Nov 09	Nov 10
Pre Tax Profit/Loss	-107	-33	-23
Working Capital	18m	18m	18m
Current Assets	20m	20m	20m

J W Services
3 Chapel Hill, Dukinfield, SK16 4BT
Tel: 0161-339 6664
E-mail: jwservices@ymail.com
Website: http://www.jw-services.co.uk
Directors: P. Watkins (Ptnr)
No.of Employees: 1 - 10 **Product Groups:** 40, 48, 66, 67

Microflow Europe T/A Total Celler Systems
Globe Square, Dukinfield, SK16 4RF
Tel: 0161-343 1557 **Fax:** 0161-343 3762
E-mail: william.johnston@microfloweurope.com
Website: http://www.totalcellers.com
Bank(s): National Westminster
Directors: J. Johnston (Dir), N. Walton (Sales), R. Bardsley (Ch), W. Johnson (MD), W. Johnston (MD)
Managers: C. Nicholson (I.T. Exec), D. Clarke (Buyer), K. Harrison
Immediate Holding Company: MICROFLOW EUROPE LIMITED
Registration no: 03107128 **VAT No.:** GB 589 0209 18
Date established: 1995 **Turnover:** £1m - £2m **No.of Employees:** 21 - 50
Product Groups: 36, 40

Date of Accounts	Dec 09	Dec 08	Dec 07
Working Capital	77	77	73
Fixed Assets	N/A	N/A	4
Current Assets	77	77	851

N C Engineering Services
Railway View Works Wood Street, Dukinfield, SK16 4UT
Tel: 0161-330 0855 **Fax:** 0161-343 2084
E-mail: chris.fish@btconnect.com
Website: http://www.ncengineeringservices.co.uk
Directors: C. Fish (Prop)
VAT No.: GB 306 1777 66 **Date established:** 1979
Turnover: £250,000 - £500,000 **No.of Employees:** 1 - 10
Product Groups: 48

Northpoint Ltd
Globe Lane, Dukinfield, SK16 4UY
Tel: 0161-330 4551 **Fax:** 0161-339 7169
E-mail: simon@northpoint.ltd.uk
Website: http://www.northpoint.ltd.uk
Bank(s): Barclays, Manchester
Directors: S. Quiligotti (Fin), P. Dawson (Tech Serv), H. Tomes (Sales & Mktg)
Ultimate Holding Company: NORTHPOINT GROUP LTD.
Immediate Holding Company: NORTHPOINT LIMITED
Registration no: 04707053 **VAT No.:** GB 560 8450 41
Date established: 2003 **Turnover:** £5m - £10m
No.of Employees: 51 - 100 **Product Groups:** 48

Date of Accounts	Feb 12	Feb 11	Feb 10
Sales Turnover	7m	6m	6m
Pre Tax Profit/Loss	362	195	275
Working Capital	2m	1m	1m
Fixed Assets	1m	1m	1m
Current Assets	4m	3m	3m
Current Liabilities	1m	1m	870

Parker International Ltd
Globe Works Globe Lane, Dukinfield, SK16 4RE
Tel: 0161-330 7421 **Fax:** 0161-339 2653
E-mail: info@parkerinternational.co.uk
Website: http://www.parkerinternational.co.uk
Bank(s): National Westminster Bank Plc
Directors: D. Brennand (MD)
Managers: T. Dobbins (Chief Mgr), C. Clayton
Immediate Holding Company: PARKER INTERNATIONAL LIMITED
Registration no: 05102542 **Date established:** 2004 **Turnover:** £5m - £10m
No.of Employees: 21 - 50 **Product Groups:** 77, 84

Date of Accounts	Apr 11	Apr 10	Apr 09
Working Capital	-9	89	149
Fixed Assets	233	194	178
Current Assets	638	736	812

E Preston Electrical Ltd
Unit 28 Broadway Globe Lane, Dukinfield, SK16 4UU
Tel: 0161-339 5177 **Fax:** 0161-343 1935
E-mail: sales@epreston.co.uk
Website: http://www.epreston.co.uk
Bank(s): Royal Bank of Scotland
Directors: M. Henderson (Dir)
Managers: A. North
Immediate Holding Company: E. PRESTON (ELECTRICAL) LIMITED
Registration no: 01469296 **VAT No.:** GB 306 0057 08
Date established: 1979 **Turnover:** £2m - £5m **No.of Employees:** 21 - 50
Product Groups: 33, 34, 37, 38, 39, 42, 44, 67, 68

Date of Accounts	Dec 11	Dec 10	Dec 09
Working Capital	700	466	543
Fixed Assets	749	783	706
Current Assets	2m	1m	1m

Special Piping Materials Ltd
Unit 38 Globe Lane Industrial Estate Broadway, Dukinfield, SK16 4UU
Tel: 0161-343 7005 **Fax:** 0161-343 7011
E-mail: mary@spm.co.uk
Website: http://www.spm.co.uk
Bank(s): Barclays
Managers: B. Richmond (Personnel), D. Shepherd (Sales Admin), D. Sheppard (Sales Admin), H. Muir
Immediate Holding Company: SPECIAL PIPING MATERIALS LIMITED
Registration no: 02307592 **VAT No.:** GB 508 2914 49
Date established: 1988 **Turnover:** £10m - £20m
No.of Employees: 11 - 20 **Product Groups:** 36, 52

Date of Accounts	Dec 11	Dec 10	Dec 09
Sales Turnover	30m	15m	14m
Pre Tax Profit/Loss	3m	700	782
Working Capital	11m	9m	9m
Fixed Assets	2m	2m	547
Current Assets	18m	13m	13m
Current Liabilities	1m	288	542

Surface Engineers Manchester Ltd
Unit 17 Globe Industrial Estate Off Astley Street, Dukinfield, SK16 4QZ
Tel: 0161-330 9224 **Fax:** 0161-343 2650
E-mail: gary@surface-engineers.com
Directors: L. McKeown (Fin), G. Mckeown (MD)
Immediate Holding Company: SURFACE ENGINEERS (MANCHESTER) LIMITED
Registration no: 05199615 **VAT No.:** GB 146 7060 80
Date established: 2004 **Turnover:** £1m - £2m **No.of Employees:** 21 - 50
Product Groups: 32, 48

Date of Accounts	Oct 11	Oct 10	Oct 09
Working Capital	228	225	204
Fixed Assets	50	70	77
Current Assets	469	596	558

Thermoplastic Engineering Ltd
Victoria Works Barton Road, Dukinfield, SK16 4US
Tel: 0161-339 8505 **Fax:** 0161-343 2328
E-mail: sales@thermoplasticengineering.co.uk
Website: http://www.thermoplasticengineering.co.uk
Directors: M. Townsend (MD)
Immediate Holding Company: THERMOPLASTIC ENGINEERING LIMITED
Registration no: 01478669 **Date established:** 1980
Turnover: Up to £250,000 **No.of Employees:** 1 - 10 **Product Groups:** 30, 31, 42, 46, 47, 48, 49

Date of Accounts	May 10	May 09	May 08
Working Capital	-5	-12	-14
Fixed Assets	32	20	22
Current Assets	98	58	63

Tibard Ltd
Tibard House Broadway, Dukinfield, SK16 4UU
Tel: 0161-342 1000 **Fax:** 0161-343 2016
E-mail: sales@tibard.co.uk
Website: http://www.tibard.co.uk
Directors: J. Shonfeld (Ch)
Ultimate Holding Company: TIBARD HOLDINGS LIMITED
Immediate Holding Company: TIBARD LIMITED
Registration no: 01434368 **VAT No.:** GB 331 0603 16
Date established: 1979 **Turnover:** £5m - £10m
No.of Employees: 51 - 100 **Product Groups:** 22, 23, 24, 36, 40, 41, 63, 83

Date of Accounts	Aug 11	Aug 10	Aug 09
Sales Turnover	8m	7m	7m
Pre Tax Profit/Loss	378	245	532
Working Capital	191	216	507
Fixed Assets	1m	1m	993
Current Assets	4m	3m	3m
Current Liabilities	2m	1m	1m

Tulip Ltd
Bow Street, Dukinfield, SK16 4HY
Tel: 0161-339 6000 **Fax:** 0161-214 8554
E-mail: contact@tulipltd.co.uk
Website: http://www.tulipltd.co.uk
Directors: P. Major (Site)
Managers: D. Nicholas (Site Co-ord)
Ultimate Holding Company: DANISH CROWN AMBA (DENMARK)
Immediate Holding Company: TULIP LIMITED
Registration no: 00608077 **VAT No.:** GB 44 8739 29
Date established: 1958 **Turnover:** £20m - £50m
No.of Employees: 501 - 1000 **Product Groups:** 20

Date of Accounts	Sep 08	Oct 09	Oct 10
Sales Turnover	954m	1139m	1118m
Pre Tax Profit/Loss	21m	84m	37m
Working Capital	125m	138m	200m
Fixed Assets	439m	361m	379m
Current Assets	273m	324m	304m
Current Liabilities	57m	70m	55m

Wellman Hunt Graham Ltd
Astley Street, Dukinfield, SK16 4QT
Tel: 0161-331 4400 **Fax:** 0161-330 9417
E-mail: info@wellman-thermal.com
Website: http://www.wellmanhuntgraham.com
Bank(s): The Royal Bank of Scotland
Directors: J. Edmondson (MD)
Ultimate Holding Company: INMED VENTURES LIMITED (GIBRALTAR)
Immediate Holding Company: WELLMAN HUNT GRAHAM LTD.
Registration no: 00564720 **Date established:** 1956 **Turnover:** £5m - £10m
No.of Employees: 51 - 100 **Product Groups:** 40

William Kenyon & Sons Ropes & Narrow Fabrics Ltd
Chapel Field Works Railway Street, Dukinfield, SK16 4PT
Tel: 0161-308 6000 **Fax:** 0161-308 6046
E-mail: info@williamkenyon.co.uk
Website: http://www.williamkenyon.co.uk
Bank(s): National Westminster
Managers: J. Lever, A. Barnes, J. Charlottes
Immediate Holding Company: WILLIAM KENYON & SONS LIMITED
Registration no: 00094366 **Date established:** 2007
No.of Employees: 21 - 50 **Product Groups:** 23

Frodsham

Amtec Consultants Ltd
Fraser House Bridge Lane, Frodsham, WA6 7HD
Tel: 01928-734996 **Fax:** 01928-734998
E-mail: enquiries@amteccorrosion.co.uk
Website: http://www.amteccorrosion.co.uk
Directors: L. Callow (MD), J. Lomas (Fin)
Immediate Holding Company: AMTEC ELECTROCHEM LIMITED
Registration no: 02012627 **Date established:** 1986
No.of Employees: 1 - 10 **Product Groups:** 52, 84

Date of Accounts	Mar 11	Mar 10	Mar 06
Working Capital	24	15	14
Fixed Assets	N/A	1	1
Current Assets	27	17	17

Frodsham Computers
66 Main Street, Frodsham, WA6 7AU
Tel: 01928-731692 **Fax:** 01928-731997
E-mail: sales@frodsham-computers.co.uk
Website: http://www.frodsham-computers.co.uk

see next page

Frodsham Computers - Cont'd
Directors: D. Rodgers (Ptnr)
No.of Employees: 1 - 10 **Product Groups:** 37, 40, 67

Gordon Products Ltd
100 Main Street, Frodsham, WA6 7AR
Tel: 01928-732158 **Fax:** 01928-739710
E-mail: info@gordonproducts.co.uk
Website: http://www.gordonproducts.co.uk
Directors: J. Dison (Dir)
Managers: M. Armes (Comptroller)
Ultimate Holding Company: H. GORDON & CO. LIMITED
Immediate Holding Company: GORDON PRODUCTS LIMITED
Registration no: 02401214 **VAT No.:** GB 534 6598 16
Date established: 1989 **Turnover:** £500,000 - £1m
No.of Employees: 21 - 50 **Product Groups:** 35, 46, 48, 67

Date of Accounts	Mar 12	Mar 11	Mar 10
Working Capital	766	978	838
Current Assets	1m	2m	1m

J Mallalue Consultancy
30 Foxhill Grove Helsby, Frodsham, WA6 9LQ
Tel: 01928-723599 **Fax:** 01928-724047
E-mail: jm@johnmallalueconsultancy.co.uk
Website: http://www.johnmallalueconsultancy.co.uk
Directors: J. Mallalue (Prop)
Date established: 1991 **No.of Employees:** 1 - 10 **Product Groups:** 35

C P Nield
Nields Yard Meeting House Lane, Frodsham, WA6 6TP
Tel: 01928-787868
E-mail: colin.nield@zen.co.uk
Directors: C. Nield (Prop)
Date established: 2002 **No.of Employees:** 1 - 10 **Product Groups:** 41

Pennaire Filtration Ltd
Meres Edge Chester Road, Helsby, Frodsham, WA6 0DJ
Tel: 01928-724139 **Fax:** 01928-727877
E-mail: info@pennairefiltration.com
Website: http://www.pennairefiltration.com
Directors: M. Andrews (Eng Serv)
Immediate Holding Company: PENNAIRE FILTRATION LIMITED
Registration no: 04504174 **Date established:** 2002
No.of Employees: 1 - 10 **Product Groups:** 38, 42

Date of Accounts	Dec 10	Dec 09	Dec 08
Working Capital	103	65	58
Current Assets	541	438	435

SW Distribution UK Limited
80 Church Street, Frodsham, WA6 6QU
Tel: 01928-734224 **Fax:** 01928-735410
E-mail: sales@swdistribution.co.uk
Website: http://www.swdistribution.co.uk
Directors: S. Webb (MD)
Registration no: 06245936 **No.of Employees:** 1 - 10 **Product Groups:** 37, 49, 65

Hyde

A P Patterns Ltd
Unit 7-8 Clarendon Industrial Estate, Hyde, SK14 2EW
Tel: 0161-368 6389 **Fax:** 0161-367 9669
E-mail: appatterns@btconnect.com
Website: http://www.appatterns.com
Directors: A. Mottram (Fin), P. Standen (MD), P. Standen (Dir)
Immediate Holding Company: A. P. PATTERNS LIMITED
Registration no: 03552731 **VAT No.:** GB 562 3778 20
Date established: 1998 **Turnover:** £250,000 - £500,000
No.of Employees: 21 - 50 **Product Groups:** 48

Date of Accounts	Aug 10	Aug 09	Aug 08
Working Capital	181	333	318
Fixed Assets	328	371	139
Current Assets	499	626	613

Abacus Career Wear Ltd
Unit D 6, Hyde, SK14 4EH
Tel: 0161-351 1211 **Fax:** 0161-367 8819
E-mail: abacusblf@aol.cm
Website: http://www.abacus-careerwear.co.uk
Bank(s): Yorkshire Bank PLC
Directors: A. Dingle (MD), S. Dingle (Fin)
Immediate Holding Company: ABACUS CAREERWEAR LIMITED
Registration no: 01816563 **Date established:** 1984
Turnover: £500,000 - £1m **No.of Employees:** 11 - 20 **Product Groups:** 24

Date of Accounts	Jun 11	Jun 10	Jun 09
Working Capital	277	236	247
Fixed Assets	21	27	32
Current Assets	479	517	441

Abbey Precision Polymers
4 Hattersley Industrial Estate Stockport Road, Hyde, SK14 3QT
Tel: 0161-368 9755 **Fax:** 0161-368 9767
Directors: L. Elliott (MD)
Date established: 1997 **Turnover:** £250m - £500m
No.of Employees: 11 - 20 **Product Groups:** 29

J H Ashworth & Son Ltd
Kingston Mill Manchester Road, Hyde, SK14 2BZ
Tel: 0161-368 2048 **Fax:** 0161-367 8193
E-mail: yarn@ashworth.co.uk
Website: http://www.ashworth.co.uk
Bank(s): National Westminster Bank Plc
Directors: I. Karodia (MD), L. Ashworth (Co Sec)
Immediate Holding Company: J.H.ASHWORTH & SON LIMITED
Registration no: 00416786 **VAT No.:** GB 606 5241 63
Date established: 1946 **Turnover:** £5m - £10m **No.of Employees:** 11 - 20
Product Groups: 23

Date of Accounts	Dec 11	Dec 10	Dec 09
Working Capital	948	1m	1m
Fixed Assets	32	56	71
Current Assets	1m	2m	1m

Bridge Cylinder Heads
61a Talbot Road, Hyde, SK14 4EU
Tel: 0161-368 6060 **Fax:** 0161-351 3800
E-mail: nick@cylinderheads.co.uk
Website: http://www.cylinderheads.co.uk
Directors: N. Gilfillan (Prop)
Immediate Holding Company: BRIDGE CAR COMPANY LIMITED
Registration no: 02626813 **Date established:** 1991
No.of Employees: 1 - 10 **Product Groups:** 39, 40, 68

Date of Accounts	Nov 11	Nov 10	Nov 09
Working Capital	260	233	225
Fixed Assets	79	91	100
Current Assets	360	312	309

Cheshire Ribbon Manufacturing
Kingston Mills Manchester Road, Hyde, SK14 2BZ
Tel: 0161-367 1370 **Fax:** 0161-367 1371
E-mail: sales@cheshireribbon.co.uk
Website: http://www.cheshireribbon.co.uk
Bank(s): National Westminster Bank Plc
Directors: I. Karodia (MD)
Managers: D. Pimblott (Comm), E. Ashworth (Sales Prom Mgr)
Immediate Holding Company: J.H. Ashworth & Son Ltd
Registration no: 00416786 **Turnover:** £250,000 - £500,000
No.of Employees: 11 - 20 **Product Groups:** 23, 30, 33, 67

Cosmopolitan Textile Company Ltd
Commercial Street, Hyde, SK14 2HP
Tel: 0161-367 1122 **Fax:** 0161-367 1198
E-mail: info@abcwax.co.uk
Website: http://www.cosmopolitan-textiles.co.uk
Bank(s): The Royal Bank of Scotland
Managers: W. Hill (Mgr)
Ultimate Holding Company: Cha Technologies Group plc
Immediate Holding Company: Cha Textiles Ltd
Registration no: 02727518 **VAT No.:** GB 396 7997 50
Date established: 1992 **Turnover:** £20m - £50m
No.of Employees: 101 - 250 **Product Groups:** 61

Elg Haniel Metals Ltd (North West)
Raglan Street, Hyde, SK14 2DX
Tel: 0161-368 0738 **Fax:** 0161-367 8259
E-mail: cwright@elg.co.uk
Website: http://www.elg.co.uk
Managers: C. Wright (Mgr)
Ultimate Holding Company: FRANZ HANIEL & CIE GMBH (GERMANY)
Immediate Holding Company: E.L.G. HANIEL METALS LIMITED
Registration no: 01517971 **Date established:** 1980
No.of Employees: 1 - 10 **Product Groups:** 54, 66

Date of Accounts	Dec 11	Dec 10	Dec 09
Sales Turnover	333m	309m	182m
Pre Tax Profit/Loss	8m	10m	9m
Working Capital	-7m	-4m	268
Fixed Assets	28m	26m	26m
Current Assets	63m	92m	58m
Current Liabilities	3m	3m	2m

Harviglass-Fibre Ltd
Alexandra Street, Hyde, SK14 1DX
Tel: 0161-368 2398 **Fax:** 0161-368 1508
E-mail: info@harviglass.com
Website: http://www.harviglass.com
Bank(s): National Westminster Bank Plc
Directors: J. Armstrong (Fin)
Managers: C. Hargreaves (Chief Mgr), W. Austen (Sales Eng)
Immediate Holding Company: HARVIGLASS GRP LIMITED
Registration no: 03137627 **VAT No.:** GB 589 0750 01
Date established: 1995 **Turnover:** £2m - £5m **No.of Employees:** 21 - 50
Product Groups: 26, 30, 33, 37, 38, 39, 40, 42, 48, 49, 61, 66

Date of Accounts	Dec 07	Dec 06	Dec 05
Working Capital	46	-6	28
Fixed Assets	196	196	138
Current Assets	409	333	194
Current Liabilities	362	338	166
Total Share Capital	35	35	35

Hawks Chemical Co. Ltd
2 Tower Street, Hyde, SK14 1JW
Tel: 0161-367 9441 **Fax:** 0161-367 9443
E-mail: sales@hawks-chem.com
Website: http://www.hawks-chem.com
Directors: R. Warren (MD)
Immediate Holding Company: HAWKS CHEMICAL COMPANY LIMITED
Registration no: 02253887 **Date established:** 1988 **Turnover:** £1m - £2m
No.of Employees: 1 - 10 **Product Groups:** 31

Date of Accounts	Mar 12	Mar 11	Mar 10
Working Capital	884	789	737
Fixed Assets	27	36	39
Current Assets	1m	1m	1m

Indico Rubber Co. Ltd
Unit 11-12 Meadow Street Redfern Industrial Estate, Hyde, SK14 1RE
Tel: 0161-351 9696 **Fax:** 0161-368 6363
E-mail: a.beaumont@indicorubber.co.uk
Website: http://www.indicorubber.co.uk
Bank(s): HSBC Bank plc
Managers: A. Beaumont (Sales Admin)
Immediate Holding Company: INDICO RUBBER CO. LIMITED
Registration no: 01180130 **VAT No.:** GB 158 5947 16
Date established: 1974 **Turnover:** £1m - £2m **No.of Employees:** 11 - 20
Product Groups: 29

Date of Accounts	Aug 11	Aug 10	Aug 09
Working Capital	429	336	324
Fixed Assets	44	54	65
Current Assets	575	457	417

Industrial Bulk Containers Ltd
Newton Business Park Talbot Road, Hyde, SK14 4UQ
Tel: 0161-367 8695 **Fax:** 0161-367 8685
E-mail: kevinprice@btconnect.com
Website: http://www.industrialbulkcontainers.co.uk
Directors: K. Price (MD), A. Price (Fin)
Managers: J. Kelly (Mgr)
Immediate Holding Company: INDUSTRIAL BULK CONTAINERS LIMITED
Registration no: 02588877 **Date established:** 1991
No.of Employees: 21 - 50 **Product Groups:** 30

Date of Accounts	Mar 11	Mar 10	Mar 09
Working Capital	29	9	-7
Fixed Assets	35	37	20
Current Assets	546	506	404

Involvement Packaging Ltd
Hyde Point Dunkirk Lane, Hyde, SK14 4PL
Tel: 0870-6064686 **Fax:** 0161-366 4466
E-mail: sales@invopak.co.uk
Website: http://www.involvementpkg.co.uk
Bank(s): HSBC P.L.C., Banbury, Oxon
Directors: S. Butcher (Sales), A. Cooper (MD), P. Littlehales (Mkt Research)
Managers: J. Meredith (Sales Admin), A. Windram (Chief Acct), A. Speechley (I.T. Exec)
Registration no: 01605376 **VAT No.:** GB 307 6141 80
Turnover: £5m - £10m **No.of Employees:** 21 - 50 **Product Groups:** 30, 35

Kaman Fabricated Products
Frederick House Dukinfield Road, Hyde, SK14 4QD
Tel: 0161-351 3500 **Fax:** 0161-351 3502
E-mail: paul.atherton@brookhouse.net
Website: http://www.kaman.com
Bank(s): Barclays
Directors: P. Atherton (MD)
Managers: J. Armitage (Buyer), D. Panting (Comm)
Registration no: 00163409 **No.of Employees:** 51 - 100
Product Groups: 68

Date of Accounts	Sep 07	Sep 06	Sep 05
Sales Turnover	6551	4411	3896
Pre Tax Profit/Loss	562	60	645
Working Capital	1022	710	745
Fixed Assets	357	322	242
Current Assets	2322	1878	1581
Current Liabilities	1300	1168	836
ROCE% (Return on Capital Employed)	40.8	5.8	65.3
ROT% (Return on Turnover)	8.6	1.4	16.6

William Kenyon & Sons Ropes & Narrow Fabrics Ltd
PO Box 33, Hyde, SK14 4RP
Tel: 0161-308 6030 **Fax:** 0161-308 6046
E-mail: info@williamkenyon.co.uk
Website: http://www.williamkenyon.co.uk
Bank(s): National Westminster
Directors: P. Kenyon (MD), R. Mellor (Co Sec)
Managers: A. Barnes, J. Lever (Fin Mgr)
Ultimate Holding Company: WILLIAM KENYON & SONS LIMITED
Immediate Holding Company: WILLIAM KENYON & SONS(ROPES & NARROW FABRICS)LIMITED
Registration no: 00600891 **VAT No.:** 146 3522 77 **Date established:** 1958
Turnover: £10m - £20m **No.of Employees:** 21 - 50 **Product Groups:** 23

Date of Accounts	Mar 12	Mar 11	Mar 10
Working Capital	794	2m	2m
Fixed Assets	970	145	103
Current Assets	2m	2m	2m

Kerry Foods Ltd (Golden Vale)
Godley Hill Road, Hyde, SK14 3BR
Tel: 0161-368 4080 **Fax:** 0161-351 1070
E-mail: aylesbury.sales@kerry-foodservice.co.uk
Website: http://www.kerrygroup.com
Directors: S. Wilson (Dir)
Ultimate Holding Company: KERRY GROUP PUBLIC LIMITED COMPANY
Immediate Holding Company: KERRY FOODS LIMITED
Registration no: 02604258 **Date established:** 1991
No.of Employees: 1 - 10 **Product Groups:** 62

Date of Accounts	Dec 11	Dec 10	Dec 09
Sales Turnover	679m	568m	525m
Pre Tax Profit/Loss	7m	25m	14m
Working Capital	-15m	36m	29m
Fixed Assets	121m	89m	90m
Current Assets	246m	240m	204m
Current Liabilities	6m	8m	1m

Kromachem Colours Ltd
Simpson Street, Hyde, SK14 1BJ
Tel: 0161-366 7589 **Fax:** 0161-366 8611
E-mail: stevek@kromachem.com
Website: http://www.kromachem.com
Directors: S. Kensbock (Dir)
Managers: S. Carvill, P. Constantinou
No.of Employees: 11 - 20 **Product Groups:** 29, 32, 66

Louver-Lite
Ashton Road, Hyde, SK14 4BG
Tel: 0161-882 5000 **Fax:** 0161-882 5009
E-mail: sales@louvolite.com
Website: http://www.louvolite.com
Bank(s): The Royal Bank of Scotland Plc
Directors: C. Doyle (Co Sec), R. Allsop (Ch)
Managers: S. Monk, J. Marsden (Mktg Serv Mgr), I. Cassidy (Tech Serv Mgr)
Immediate Holding Company: LOUVER-LITE LIMITED
Registration no: 01011431 **Date established:** 1971
Turnover: £20m - £50m **No.of Employees:** 251 - 500
Product Groups: 24, 25, 30, 35, 36, 46

Date of Accounts	May 12	May 11	May 10
Sales Turnover	35m	35m	35m
Pre Tax Profit/Loss	3m	3m	5m
Working Capital	25m	24m	27m
Fixed Assets	13m	13m	8m
Current Assets	28m	27m	30m
Current Liabilities	2m	1m	1m

Meredith & Eyre Ltd
Broadway, Hyde, SK14 4QF
Tel: 0161-368 6414 **Fax:** 0161-367 8702
E-mail: lesmeredith@meredithandeyre.co.uk
Website: http://www.meredithandeyre.co.uk
Directors: L. Meredith (MD), D. Meredith (Dir)
Managers: M. Carsons (Sales Prom Mgr)
Immediate Holding Company: MEREDITH AND EYRE LIMITED
Registration no: 00575149 **VAT No.:** GB 158 0900 67
Date established: 1956 **Turnover:** £5m - £10m **No.of Employees:** 11 - 20
Product Groups: 39

Date of Accounts	May 12	May 11	May 10
Working Capital	595	548	555
Fixed Assets	349	359	351
Current Assets	960	940	756

Meschia Frozen Foods
Unit 2 Hattersley Industrial Estate Stockport Road, Hyde, SK14 3QT
Tel: 0161-367 8815 **Fax:** 0161-367 8815

Directors: G. Parker (Dir), L. Meschia (Dir)
Date established: 1984 **No.of Employees:** 1 - 10 **Product Groups:** 20, 40, 41

Naylors Abrasives

Unit G7 Newton Business Park Talbot Road, Hyde, SK14 4UQ
Tel: 0161-367 1000 **Fax:** 0161-367 1012
E-mail: info@naylors-abrasives.co.uk
Website: http://www.naylors-abrasives.co.uk
Directors: G. Roberts (MD)
Registration no: 00199666 **VAT No.:** GB 157 1153 79
Turnover: £2m - £5m **No.of Employees:** 1 - 10 **Product Groups:** 33

Newland Engineering Co. Ltd

Captain Clarke Road, Hyde, SK14 4RF
Tel: 0161-368 0326 **Fax:** 0161-367 8004
E-mail: info@newland-conveyors.com
Website: http://www.newland-conveyors.com
Bank(s): Barclays
Directors: M. Holland (Fin), L. Kerfoot (Dir)
Managers: M. Kyrycz (Export Sales Mg), A. Horton
Immediate Holding Company: NEWLAND ENGINEERING COMPANY LIMITED
Registration no: 00717462 **VAT No.:** GB 142 6292 53
Date established: 1962 **Turnover:** £2m - £5m **No.of Employees:** 21 - 50
Product Groups: 38, 39, 43, 45, 83

Date of Accounts	Apr 11	Apr 10	Apr 09
Working Capital	389	364	379
Fixed Assets	63	70	87
Current Assets	817	760	687

Nordsea Ltd

Captain Clarke Road, Hyde, SK14 4QG
Tel: 0161-366 3010 **Fax:** 0161-344 1144
E-mail: nordsea@compuserve.com
Website: http://www.nordsea.ltd.uk
Directors: S. Heald (MD), P. Heald (Sales)
Managers: R. Yates (Chief Mgr)
Ultimate Holding Company: R B AIR HOLDINGS LIMITED
Immediate Holding Company: NORDSEA LIMITED
Registration no: 01780294 **VAT No.:** GB 562 6114 55
Date established: 1983 **Turnover:** £500,000 - £1m
No.of Employees: 1 - 10 **Product Groups:** 40

Date of Accounts	Oct 11	Oct 10	Oct 09
Working Capital	49	27	26
Fixed Assets	1	3	3
Current Assets	106	79	47
Current Liabilities	27	N/A	N/A

North Western Lead Company

Mill Street Newton Moor Industrial Estate, Hyde, SK14 4LJ
Tel: 0161-368 4491 **Fax:** 0161-366 5103
E-mail: sales@decraled.co.uk
Website: http://www.decraled.co.uk
Bank(s): Barclays
Directors: S. Hart (MD), S. Porter (Dir)
Immediate Holding Company: NORTH WESTERN LEAD COMPANY (HYDE) LIMITED
Registration no: 01108808 **VAT No.:** GB 298 9657 66
Date established: 1973 **Turnover:** £2m - £5m **No.of Employees:** 11 - 20
Product Groups: 30

Date of Accounts	Dec 11	Dec 10	Dec 09
Working Capital	459	128	-17
Fixed Assets	257	151	177
Current Assets	878	1m	835

Roller Shutters & Shopfronts From Mane

2 Cotton Tree Court, Hyde, SK14 1LU
Tel: 0161-320 9322
E-mail: maneshopfronts@live.co.uk
Website: http://maneshopfronts.synthasite.com
Directors: N. Wharley (Prop)
Date established: 2007 **Turnover:** Up to £250,000
No.of Employees: 1 - 10 **Product Groups:** 25, 30, 35

Ronhill Sports

Unit 4 Dawson Street Redfern Industrial Estate, Hyde, SK14 1RD
Tel: 0161-366 5020 **Fax:** 0161-366 9732
E-mail: info@ronhill.com
Website: http://www.ronhill.com
Bank(s): The Royal Bank of Scotland
Directors: M. Deegan (Grp Chief Exec)
Ultimate Holding Company: OCS LTD
Immediate Holding Company: OSC (HOLDING) LTD
Registration no: 00988970 **VAT No.:** GB 562 7262 35
Turnover: £1m - £2m **No.of Employees:** 21 - 50 **Product Groups:** 24, 63

Date of Accounts	Jun 08	Jun 07	Apr 06
Sales Turnover	9905	9684	8400
Pre Tax Profit/Loss	-23	134	-208
Working Capital	138	252	228
Fixed Assets	528	399	347
Current Assets	4747	5304	3965
Current Liabilities	4609	5052	3736
Total Share Capital	1400	1400	1400
ROCE% (Return on Capital Employed)	-3.5	20.5	-36.1
ROT% (Return on Turnover)	-0.2	1.4	-2.5

S G & P Payne Ltd

Percy House Brook Street, Hyde, SK14 2NS
Tel: 0161-367 8561 **Fax:** 0161-367 8995
E-mail: sales@sgppayne.co.uk
Website: http://www.sgppayne.co.uk
Directors: S. Payne (MD)
Immediate Holding Company: S.G. & P. PAYNE LIMITED
Registration no: 05337691 **VAT No.:** GB 298 9409 85
Date established: 2005 **Turnover:** Up to £250,000
No.of Employees: 1 - 10 **Product Groups:** 24, 30

Date of Accounts	Mar 12	Mar 11	Mar 10
Working Capital	-5	-43	-84
Fixed Assets	115	121	128
Current Assets	78	62	105

Shirley Dyeing & Finishing

Unit B6 Newton Business Park Talbot Road, Hyde, SK14 4UQ
Tel: 0161-367 9030 **Fax:** 0161-367 8845
E-mail: david.chambers@sdfonline.com
Website: http://www.sdfonline.com
Bank(s): Bank of Scotland
Managers: D. Chambers (Sales Admin)
Ultimate Holding Company: BRITISH TEXTILE TECHNOLOGY GROUP
Immediate Holding Company: SHIRLEY DYEING AND FINISHING LIMITED
Registration no: 02337403 **Date established:** 1989
Turnover: £500,000 - £1m **No.of Employees:** 11 - 20 **Product Groups:** 85

Date of Accounts	Nov 10	Sep 11	Sep 09
Sales Turnover	N/A	N/A	823
Pre Tax Profit/Loss	N/A	N/A	-113
Working Capital	93	149	43
Fixed Assets	19	11	48
Current Assets	226	291	260
Current Liabilities	N/A	N/A	65

Superior Food Machinery Ltd

Wych Fold, Hyde, SK14 5ED
Tel: 0161-366 1777 **Fax:** 0161-366 1555
E-mail: info@superiorfoodmachinery.com
Website: http://www.superiorfoodmachinery.com
Directors: P. Garner (Dir)
Managers: B. Holwil
Immediate Holding Company: SUPERIOR FOOD MACHINERY LIMITED
Registration no: 04413525 **Date established:** 2002
No.of Employees: 11 - 20 **Product Groups:** 20, 40, 41

Sweatshop

148-150 Market Street, Hyde, SK14 1EX
Tel: 0161-366 9191
E-mail: hyde@sweatshop.co.uk
Website: http://www.sweatshop.co.uk
Managers: J. Chapman
Registration no: 02741243 **VAT No.:** GB 606 4641 52
Date established: 1992 **No.of Employees:** 1 - 10 **Product Groups:** 24

3d Labelling Systems Ltd

11 Railway Street, Hyde, SK14 1DF
Tel: 0161-366 5869 **Fax:** 0161-351 1433
E-mail: info@label-systems.co.uk
Website: http://www.label-systems.co.uk
Directors: E. Donaldson (Fin)
Immediate Holding Company: 3D LABELLING SYSTEMS LIMITED
Registration no: 04392790 **VAT No.:** GB 359 3795 01
Date established: 2002 **Turnover:** Up to £250,000
No.of Employees: 1 - 10 **Product Groups:** 27, 30, 42, 43, 44, 49

Date of Accounts	May 11	May 10	May 09
Working Capital	13	13	22
Fixed Assets	3	2	2
Current Assets	64	54	42

Tiviot Prints Ltd

Lymefield Mill Broadbottom, Hyde, SK14 6AG
Tel: 01457-763297 **Fax:** 01457-765499
E-mail: info@tiviotprints.co.uk
Website: http://www.tiviotprints.co.uk
Bank(s): National Westminster
Directors: R. Taylor (Dir), S. Taylor (Co Sec)
Immediate Holding Company: TIVIOT PRINTS LIMITED
Registration no: 00685517 **VAT No.:** GB 157 7664 24
Date established: 1961 **Turnover:** £1m - £2m **No.of Employees:** 11 - 20
Product Groups: 23

Date of Accounts	Mar 12	Mar 11	Mar 10
Working Capital	579	669	718
Fixed Assets	207	208	209
Current Assets	788	897	900

Total Refrigeration Ltd

Unit 2a East Tame Business Park Rexcine Way, Hyde, SK14 4GX
Tel: 08451-272527 **Fax:** 0161-366 7374
E-mail: sales@totalrefrigeration.co.uk
Website: http://www.totalrefrigeration.co.uk
Bank(s): National Westminster Bank Plc
Directors: D. Parks (Dir), M. Lomax (Fin)
Managers: S. Grimshaw (Mktg Serv Mgr), M. Daniel (Personnel), G. Young (Buyer)
Ultimate Holding Company: UNILEVER PLC
Immediate Holding Company: TOTAL REFRIGERATION LIMITED
Registration no: 00562262 **Date established:** 1956 **Turnover:** £5m - £10m
No.of Employees: 21 - 50 **Product Groups:** 39, 40, 52, 63, 66

Date of Accounts	Dec 11	Dec 10	Dec 09
Sales Turnover	10m	9m	8m
Pre Tax Profit/Loss	471	622	205
Working Capital	635	207	-402
Fixed Assets	14	9	29
Current Assets	8m	7m	2m
Current Liabilities	741	703	628

Video Science

Unit 10 Mount Street, Hyde, SK14 1NS
Tel: 0161-351 9700 **Fax:** 0161-351 9701
Website: http://www.videoscience.co.uk
Directors: M. Harris (Dir)
No.of Employees: 1 - 10 **Product Groups:** 38, 39, 86

Welspun T/A Christy (t/a Christy)

PO Box 19, Hyde, SK14 4NR
Tel: 0161-368 1961 **Fax:** 0161-368 5148
E-mail: info@christy-towels.com
Website: http://www.christy-towels.com
Directors: K. Richardson (Co Sec), R. Walker (MD)
Ultimate Holding Company: WELSPUN INDIA LTD (INDIA)
Immediate Holding Company: CHRISTY 2004 LIMITED
Registration no: 05254268 **Date established:** 2004
Turnover: £20m - £50m **No.of Employees:** 51 - 100 **Product Groups:** 23, 24

Date of Accounts	Mar 11	Mar 10	Mar 09
Pre Tax Profit/Loss	-514	N/A	396
Working Capital	9m	12m	12m
Current Assets	13m	13m	13m

Wrapping & Converting Systems Ltd

Unit F9 Newton Business Park Talbot Road, Hyde, SK14 4UQ
Tel: 0161-366 5552 **Fax:** 0161-366 5554
E-mail: sales@shrinkwrapping.co.uk
Website: http://www.shrinkwrapping.co.uk
Directors: C. Porter (Fin), L. Wright (Dir)
Immediate Holding Company: WRAPPING & CONVERTING SYSTEMS LIMITED
Registration no: 02973501 **Date established:** 1994
Turnover: Up to £250,000 **No.of Employees:** 11 - 20 **Product Groups:** 38, 42

Date of Accounts	Oct 11	Oct 10	Oct 09
Sales Turnover	N/A	145	119
Working Capital	56	32	32
Fixed Assets	6	32	8
Current Assets	147	78	81

Knutsford

A & M Marquees Ltd

13 Thorneyholme Drive, Knutsford, WA16 8BT
Tel: 01565-633977 **Fax:** 01565-633977
E-mail: info@ammarquees.com
Website: http://www.ammarquees.com
Directors: M. Bolland (Dir)
Immediate Holding Company: A & M MARQUEES/EVENTS LTD
Registration no: 04256745 **Date established:** 2001
Turnover: Up to £250,000 **No.of Employees:** 1 - 10 **Product Groups:** 25, 30, 83

Date of Accounts	Feb 08	Feb 11	Feb 10
Working Capital	-52	-49	-38
Fixed Assets	60	28	31
Current Assets	2	3	2

Abbey England Ltd

Haig Road Parkgate Industrial Estate, Knutsford, WA16 8DX
Tel: 01565-650343 **Fax:** 01565-633825
E-mail: gb@abbeysaddlery.co.uk
Website: http://www.abbeysaddlery.co.uk
Directors: M. Phillips (Co Sec), G. Brown (MD), E. Pickering (Mkt Research)
Immediate Holding Company: ABBEY ENGLAND LIMITED
Registration no: 01638775 **Date established:** 1982
No.of Employees: 11 - 20 **Product Groups:** 22, 23, 26, 29, 35, 36, 67

Date of Accounts	Dec 11	Dec 10	Dec 09
Working Capital	1m	1m	1m
Fixed Assets	642	620	675
Current Assets	2m	2m	2m

Albis UK Ltd

2-3 Montgomery Close Parkgate Industrial Estate, Knutsford, WA16 8XW
Tel: 01565-755777 **Fax:** 01565-755196
E-mail: ian.mills@albis.com
Website: http://www.albis.com
Bank(s): Barclays, Manchester
Directors: T. Taylor (Fin), I. Mills (MD)
Managers: P. Branigan (Personnel), M. Jones (Purch Mgr), R. Fairbanks, L. Rice
Ultimate Holding Company: OTTO KRAHN GmbH & COMPANY (GERMANY)
Immediate Holding Company: ALBIS (U.K.) LIMITED
Registration no: 00886913 **VAT No.:** GB 226 8071 65
Date established: 1966 **Turnover:** £50m - £75m
No.of Employees: 101 - 250 **Product Groups:** 30

Date of Accounts	Dec 11	Dec 10	Dec 09
Sales Turnover	57m	47m	33m
Pre Tax Profit/Loss	3m	2m	951
Working Capital	9m	8m	6m
Fixed Assets	5m	5m	5m
Current Assets	18m	16m	12m
Current Liabilities	2m	1m	962

Amec Ltd

Amec Building 02 Booths Park, Knutsford, WA16 8QZ
Tel: 01565-652100 **Fax:** 01565-683200
E-mail: marketing@nnc.co.uk
Website: http://www.amec.co.uk
Bank(s): Bank of Scotland
Directors: M. Saunders (Pres), N. Watson (Pers), S. Brikho (Grp Chief Exec)
Managers: S. Timmins, I. McHoul (Comptroller)
Ultimate Holding Company: AMEC P L C
Immediate Holding Company: AMEC P L C
Registration no: 01675285 **Date established:** 1982
Turnover: Over £1,000m **No.of Employees:** 251 - 500
Product Groups: 18, 37, 38, 40, 42, 44, 45, 48, 52, 54, 80, 82, 84, 85, 86, 87

Date of Accounts	Dec 11	Dec 10	Dec 09
Sales Turnover	3261m	2951m	2539m
Pre Tax Profit/Loss	259m	258m	204m
Working Capital	576m	697m	620m
Fixed Assets	1051m	820m	656m
Current Assets	1404m	1443m	1279m
Current Liabilities	412m	343m	266m

Barrington Sports

3 Wolfe Close Parkgate Industrial Estate, Knutsford, WA16 8XJ
Tel: 01565-650269 **Fax:** 01565-634104
E-mail: customerservices@barringtonsports.com
Website: http://www.barringtonsports.com
Managers: N. Brown
No.of Employees: 11 - 20 **Product Groups:** 24, 29, 49

Businesslegal Ltd

9 Holgrave Close High Legh, Knutsford, WA16 6TX
Tel: 01925-757887 **Fax:** 01925-758611
E-mail: mike@businesslegal.ltd.uk
Website: http://www.businesslegal.ltd.uk
Directors: M. Farrell (MD)
Immediate Holding Company: BUSINESSLEGAL LTD
Registration no: 02970617 **Date established:** 1994
No.of Employees: 1 - 10 **Product Groups:** 87

Date of Accounts	Sep 11	Sep 10	Sep 09
Working Capital	6	-1	-11
Fixed Assets	2	2	1
Current Assets	26	12	13

Buzzwords Ltd

11 Rockford Lodge, Knutsford, WA16 8AH
Tel: 01565-654023
E-mail: open@buzzwords.ltd.uk
Website: http://www.buzzwords.ltd.uk
Directors: M. Beeson (Dir)
Registration no: 3501384 **Date established:** 1981
Turnover: Up to £250,000 **No.of Employees:** 1 - 10 **Product Groups:** 81

Date of Accounts	Jan 08	Jan 07	Jan 06
Working Capital	-0	-1	-0
Fixed Assets	1	N/A	N/A
Current Assets	5	3	3

C R J Services

London Road Allostock, Knutsford, WA16 9LU
Tel: 01565-723886 **Fax:** 01565-723819
E-mail: lee.taylor@crjservices.co.uk
Website: http://www.backtotheland.co.uk
Directors: L. Carter (Dir)
Immediate Holding Company: CRJ SERVICES LIMITED
Registration no: 03872602 **Date established:** 1999
No.of Employees: 11 - 20 **Product Groups:** 41, 42

Date of Accounts	Mar 11	Mar 10	Mar 09
Working Capital	87	-4	-87
Fixed Assets	3m	2m	2m
Current Assets	2m	780	700

Caspian Semiconductors

Knicker Brook Old Hall Lane, Over Tabley, Knutsford, WA16 0HT
Tel: 01565-634000 **Fax:** 01565-634051
E-mail: sales@caspiansemiconductors.com
Website: http://www.caspiansemiconductors.com
Directors: N. Gilani (Prop)
Date established: 1986 **No.of Employees:** 1 - 10 **Product Groups:** 33, 35, 37, 38, 39, 40, 42, 47, 48, 67, 84

Date of Accounts	Dec 07	Dec 06	Dec 05
Working Capital	-2	-2	-7
Fixed Assets	3	3	4
Current Assets	7	16	8
Current Liabilities	9	17	15

Edmundson Electrical Ltd

Edmonson House Tatton Street, Knutsford, WA16 6AY
Tel: 01565-700100 **Fax:** 01565-652649
E-mail: gordon.love@eel.co.uk
Website: http://www.edmundson-electrical.co.uk
Bank(s): National Westminster Bank Plc
Directors: G. Love (MD)
Ultimate Holding Company: BLACKFRIARS CORP (USA)
Immediate Holding Company: EDMUNDSON ELECTRICAL LIMITED
Registration no: 02667012 **Date established:** 1991
Turnover: £500m - £1,000m **No.of Employees:** 51 - 100
Product Groups: 67

Date of Accounts	Dec 11	Dec 10	Dec 09
Sales Turnover	1023m	852m	788m
Pre Tax Profit/Loss	57m	53m	45m
Working Capital	256m	225m	184m
Fixed Assets	17m	3m	4m
Current Assets	439m	358m	298m
Current Liabilities	59m	38m	37m

Harman Technology Ltd

Ilford Way Mobberley, Knutsford, WA16 7JL
Tel: 01565-650000 **Fax:** 01565-872734
E-mail: sales@ilfordphoto.com
Website: http://www.ilfordphoto.com
Bank(s): National Westminster Bank Plc
Directors: P. Elton (MD)
Immediate Holding Company: HARMAN TECHNOLOGY LIMITED
Registration no: 05227615 **VAT No.:** GB 511 6765 55
Date established: 2004 **Turnover:** £20m - £50m
No.of Employees: 101 - 250 **Product Groups:** 27, 32, 38

Date of Accounts	Dec 11	Dec 10	Dec 09
Sales Turnover	24m	23m	24m
Pre Tax Profit/Loss	674	2m	-1m
Working Capital	5m	5m	4m
Fixed Assets	2m	2m	2m
Current Assets	11m	9m	9m
Current Liabilities	5m	3m	4m

Heebee Designs

95 Town Lane Mobberley, Knutsford, WA16 7HH
Tel: 01565-872214 **Fax:** 01565-872239
E-mail: sales@heebeedesigns.co.uk
Website: http://www.heebeedesigns.co.uk
Directors: M. Berkin (Prop)
Turnover: £250,000 - £500,000 **No.of Employees:** 1 - 10
Product Groups: 23, 35, 63

Iron By Design

Toft Smithy Toft Road, Toft, Knutsford, WA16 9PA
Tel: 01565-634357 **Fax:** 01565-634357
E-mail: sales@iron-by-design.co.uk
Website: http://www.iron-by-design.co.uk
Directors: T. Norbury (Prop)
Date established: 1991 **No.of Employees:** 1 - 10 **Product Groups:** 26, 35

Johnson Aldridge Ltd (Chuan Soon Huat Industrial Group Singapore)

Longridge Trading Estate, Knutsford, WA16 8PR
Tel: 01565-755100 **Fax:** 01565- 755142
E-mail: sales@johnsonaldridge.co.uk
Website: http://www.johnsonaldridge.co.uk
Bank(s): HSBC Bank plc
Directors: M. Preston (Dir)
Managers: M. Preston (Ops Mgr), R. Scott (Accounts), T. Lee ()
Ultimate Holding Company: CHAUN SOON HUAT INDUSTRIAL GROUP LTD (SINGAPORE)
Immediate Holding Company: JOHNSON ALDRIDGE LIMITED
Registration no: 00463134 **VAT No.:** GB 145 5349 65
Date established: 1949 **Turnover:** £2m - £5m **No.of Employees:** 21 - 50
Product Groups: 25

Date of Accounts	Dec 08	Dec 07	Dec 06
Sales Turnover	3m	4m	4m
Pre Tax Profit/Loss	-301	141	68
Working Capital	1m	1m	-81
Fixed Assets	849	860	937
Current Assets	2m	2m	2m
Current Liabilities	64	180	116

NU Drives

Dairy House Farm Chester Road Over Tabley, Knutsford, WA16 0PN
Tel: 01565-633600 **Fax:** 01565-654101
E-mail: nudrives@aol.com
Website: http://www.nudrives.co.uk
Managers: S. Kemp (Mgr)
Immediate Holding Company: BAILEY'S TURKEYS LIMITED
Date established: 2011 **No.of Employees:** 1 - 10 **Product Groups:** 29, 30, 33, 35, 36

P E R Design UK Ltd

Booths Hall Booths Park Chelford Road, Knutsford, WA16 8GS
Tel: 01565-757810 **Fax:** 01565-650755
E-mail: info@perdesignuk.com
Website: http://www.perdesignuk.com
Directors: M. Link (MD)
Managers: M. Link (Sales Admin)
Immediate Holding Company: PER DESIGN (UK) LIMITED
Registration no: 05295846 **Date established:** 2004
No.of Employees: 1 - 10 **Product Groups:** 84

Packaging Automation Ltd

1 Montgomery Close Parkgate Industrial Estate, Knutsford, WA16 8XW
Tel: 01565-755000 **Fax:** 01565-751015
E-mail: info@pal.co.uk
Website: http://www.pal.co.uk
Directors: S. Ashton (Comm), C. Royle (MD)
Managers: A. Barlow (Tech Serv Mgr), A. Nellis, D. Wainscott (Personnel), C. Powell
Immediate Holding Company: PACKAGING AUTOMATION LIMITED
Registration no: 00761199 **VAT No.:** GB 157 5800 52
Date established: 1963 **Turnover:** £5m - £10m
No.of Employees: 51 - 100 **Product Groups:** 42, 84

Date of Accounts	Sep 11	Sep 10	Sep 09
Sales Turnover	7m	6m	5m
Pre Tax Profit/Loss	208	285	627
Working Capital	1m	1m	931
Fixed Assets	2m	2m	2m
Current Assets	3m	3m	2m
Current Liabilities	549	833	436

Stirling Lloyd Polychem Ltd

Union Bank King Street, Knutsford, WA16 6EF
Tel: 01565-633111 **Fax:** 01565-633555
E-mail: info@stirlinglloyd.com
Website: http://www.stirlinglloyd.com
Bank(s): The Royal Bank of Scotland
Directors: C. Baxter (Fin), H. Lloyd (Ch)
Managers: A. Sweetman (Tech Serv Mgr), D. Mulligan (Mktg Serv Mgr), D. Mulligan (Mktg Serv Mgr), S. Ignotus (I.T. Exec), S. Clarke (Buyer), A. Sweetman (Personnel), S. Clarke (Purch Mgr)
Ultimate Holding Company: STIRLING LLOYD PLC
Immediate Holding Company: STIRLING LLOYD POLYCHEM LIMITED
Registration no: 02401575 **Date established:** 1989
Turnover: £10m - £20m **No.of Employees:** 21 - 50 **Product Groups:** 66

Date of Accounts	Mar 12	Mar 11	Mar 10
Sales Turnover	20m	17m	13m
Pre Tax Profit/Loss	2m	914	698
Working Capital	3m	1m	1m
Fixed Assets	4m	3m	205
Current Assets	8m	8m	8m
Current Liabilities	1m	1m	3m

Terry Lifts Ltd

Longridge Trading Estate, Knutsford, WA16 8PR
Tel: 08453-655366 **Fax:** 01565-755062
E-mail: customerservices@terrylifts.net
Website: http://www.terrylifts.co.uk
Bank(s): Barclays
Directors: S. Maddox (Fin), J. McSweeny (Sales & Mktg), P. Morrey (MD)
Managers: A. Turnbull (Personnel), A. Adams (Purch Mgr), P. Dickinson (Tech Serv Mgr)
Immediate Holding Company: TERRY LIFTS LIMITED
Registration no: 04949483 **VAT No.:** GB 370 5510 73
Date established: 2003 **Turnover:** £5m - £10m
No.of Employees: 51 - 100 **Product Groups:** 26, 36, 39, 45

Voice Concepts

10 Church View, Knutsford, WA16 6DQ
Tel: 08702-460350 **Fax:** 0870-246 7712
E-mail: support@voiceconcepts.com
Website: http://www.voiceconcepts.com
Managers: S. Carter (Mgr), R. Leary (Chief Acct)
Date established: 2005 **Turnover:** £1m - £2m **No.of Employees:** 11 - 20
Product Groups: 52

Date of Accounts	Apr 08	Apr 07	Apr 06
Working Capital	-2	1	16
Fixed Assets	2	8	12
Current Assets	225	156	299
Current Liabilities	227	156	283

Lymm

Atex Explosion Hazards Ltd

Gate 2 Lymm Marina Warrington Lane, Lymm, WA13 0SW
Tel: 01925-755153 **Fax:** 01925-755892
E-mail: declan@explosionhazards.com
Website: http://www.explosionhazards.com
Directors: D. Barry (MD)
Immediate Holding Company: ATEX EXPLOSION HAZARDS LIMITED
Registration no: 01102876 **Date established:** 1973
No.of Employees: 1 - 10 **Product Groups:** 36, 40

Date of Accounts	Dec 11	Dec 10	Dec 09
Working Capital	60	65	-13
Fixed Assets	34	37	49
Current Assets	310	643	355

Elastomer Engineering Ltd

Rushgreen Works Carlton Road, Lymm, WA13 9RF
Tel: 01925-753456 **Fax:** 01925-755416
E-mail: sales@elastomer.co.uk
Website: http://www.elastomer.co.uk
Bank(s): HSBC Bank plc
Directors: P. Gardner (MD)
Managers: K. Cartwright (Sales Prom Mgr), J. Gittings (Sales Admin)
Ultimate Holding Company: Elastomer Engineering Ltd
Immediate Holding Company: ELASTOMER ENGINEERING LIMITED
Registration no: 00880807 **VAT No.:** GB 146 2707 70
Date established: 1966 **Turnover:** £1m - £2m **No.of Employees:** 21 - 50
Product Groups: 29, 31, 63

Date of Accounts	Jun 11	Jun 10	Jun 09
Working Capital	-114	-166	-212
Fixed Assets	265	289	331
Current Assets	403	343	279

Inglecliff Ltd

Unit 1 Barsbank Lane, Lymm, WA13 0ER
Tel: 01925-752471 **Fax:** 01925-755784
E-mail: admin@inglecliff.co.uk
Website: http://www.inglecliff.co.uk
Directors: J. Mandell (Fin)
Managers: R. Jones (Works Gen Mgr)
Ultimate Holding Company: MANTEK MANUFACTURING LIMITED
Immediate Holding Company: INGLECLIFF LIMITED
Registration no: 03767062 **VAT No.:** GB 738 4987 72
Date established: 1999 **Turnover:** Up to £250,000
No.of Employees: 1 - 10 **Product Groups:** 29, 63

Date of Accounts	Mar 12	Mar 11	Mar 10
Working Capital	39	21	16
Fixed Assets	53	54	56
Current Assets	85	67	58

Liber8 Ltd

The Rosebank Centre Pepper Street, Lymm, WA13 0JG
Tel: 01925-758283 **Fax:** 01925-758470
E-mail: info@liber8.co.uk
Website: http://www.liber8.co.uk
Directors: M. King (Fin), R. King (MD)
Immediate Holding Company: LIBER8 LIMITED
Registration no: 03756007 **Date established:** 1999
Turnover: £500,000 - £1m **No.of Employees:** 1 - 10 **Product Groups:** 44, 80

Date of Accounts	Mar 11	Mar 10	Mar 09
Working Capital	-27	-29	-62
Fixed Assets	14	15	15
Current Assets	31	28	45

Mobility Engineering Cheshire Ltd

Warrington Lane, Lymm, WA13 0SW
Tel: 01925-755923 **Fax:** 01925-757721
E-mail: sales@mobilityengineering.co.uk
Website: http://www.mobilityengineering.co.uk
Directors: R. Minjoot (Dir), D. Minjoot (Dir)
Immediate Holding Company: MOBILITY ENGINEERING (CHESHIRE) LIMITED
Registration no: 01180513 **Date established:** 1974 **Turnover:** £1m - £2m
No.of Employees: 11 - 20 **Product Groups:** 38, 39, 40, 43, 45, 49, 67, 84

Date of Accounts	Aug 11	Aug 10	Aug 09
Working Capital	333	120	139
Fixed Assets	286	318	350
Current Assets	814	426	243

P D A Ltd

Alder House Booths Lane, Lymm, WA13 0GH
Tel: 01925-759380 **Fax:** 01925-759320
E-mail: philipdunbavin@pdaltd.com
Website: http://www.pdaltd.com
Bank(s): HSBC, Warrington
Directors: P. Dunbavin (Prop)
Immediate Holding Company: P D A LIMITED
Registration no: 02942302 **VAT No.:** GB 483 5985 90
Date established: 1994 **Turnover:** £500,000 - £1m
No.of Employees: 11 - 20 **Product Groups:** 38, 54

Date of Accounts	Jul 11	Jul 10	Jul 09
Sales Turnover	62	77	60
Pre Tax Profit/Loss	3	6	1
Working Capital	-197	-196	-186
Fixed Assets	193	195	193
Current Assets	122	100	58
Current Liabilities	7	8	12

Quest Industrial Services Ltd

Unit 2 Barsbank Lane, Lymm, WA13 0ER
Tel: 01925-750860 **Fax:** 01925-756902
E-mail: sales@questltd.co.uk
Website: http://www.questltd.co.uk
Directors: P. Hughes (Sales), M. Jones (MD)
Immediate Holding Company: QUEST INDUSTRIAL SERVICES LTD.
Registration no: 03977511 **Date established:** 2000
No.of Employees: 21 - 50 **Product Groups:** 33, 52

Date of Accounts	May 11	May 10	May 09
Working Capital	123	108	-10
Fixed Assets	135	178	176
Current Assets	485	421	394

The Spa Group Events & Marketing Company Ltd

2 Bridgewater Court Barsbank Lane, Lymm, WA13 0ER
Tel: 01925-755590 **Fax:** 01925-757088
E-mail: hazel@communicadocreative.com
Website: http://www.spa-group.co.uk
Directors: S. Plumb (MD)
Immediate Holding Company: ANDERSON BAILLIE GROUP HOLDINGS LTD
Registration no: 02430567 **No.of Employees:** 1 - 10 **Product Groups:** 81

Sports Equipment Ltd

Poplar Park Cliff Lane, Lymm, WA13 0TD
Tel: 01925-758666 **Fax:** 01925-758577
E-mail: enquiries@sports-e-quipment.co.uk
Website: http://www.sports-e-quipment.co.uk
Directors: G. Worrall (Prop)
Immediate Holding Company: ALPHA LAND AND PROPERTY LTD
Registration no: 01134671 **Date established:** 2003
No.of Employees: 1 - 10 **Product Groups:** 49, 65

Date of Accounts	Dec 11	Dec 10	Dec 09
Working Capital	-486	-505	-460
Fixed Assets	506	527	510
Current Assets	19	35	32

Wright's Of Lymm Ltd

Wright House Crouchley Lane, Lymm, WA13 0AS
Tel: 01925-752226 **Fax:** 01925-757569
E-mail: info@wrightsoflymm.co.uk
Website: http://www.wrightsoflymm.co.uk
Directors: C. Stonehouse (Dir)
Immediate Holding Company: WRIGHT'S OF LYMM LIMITED
Registration no: 02845236 **Date established:** 1993 **Turnover:** £1m - £2m
No.of Employees: 1 - 10 **Product Groups:** 34, 49, 52, 80

Date of Accounts	Aug 12	Aug 11	Aug 10
Working Capital	929	723	701
Fixed Assets	2	2	2
Current Assets	1m	889	952

Macclesfield

Alma Sheet Metal Ltd
4 Mottram Way Hurdsfield Industrial Estate, Macclesfield, SK10 2DH
Tel: 01625-427159 **Fax:** 01625-669166
E-mail: sales@almasheetmetal.co.uk
Website: http://www.almasheetmetal.co.uk
Directors: N. Boyle (Fin)
Managers: D. Scragg (Mgr)
Ultimate Holding Company: JAMPOT HOLDINGS LIMITED
Immediate Holding Company: ALMA SHEET METAL LTD
Registration no: 01904799 **Date established:** 1985
Turnover: £500,000 - £1m **No.of Employees:** 11 - 20
Product Groups: 30, 35, 42, 45, 46, 48, 84

Date of Accounts	Apr 12	Apr 11	Apr 10
Working Capital	88	112	169
Fixed Assets	276	60	53
Current Assets	313	206	308

Architectural Design
The Courtyard 28a Great King Street, Macclesfield, SK11 6PL
Tel: 01625-615954 **Fax:** 01625-511042
E-mail: post@archdes.co.uk
Website: http://www.archdes.co.uk
Directors: C. Bailey (Prop)
Registration no: 06081436 **Date established:** 2007 **Turnover:** £2m - £5m
No.of Employees: 1 - 10 **Product Groups:** 84

Astrazeneca
Alderley Park, Macclesfield, SK10 4TF
Tel: 01625-582828 **Fax:** 01625-585022
E-mail: david.brennan@astrazeneca.co.uk
Website: http://www.astrazeneca.co.uk
Managers: D. Brennan
Immediate Holding Company: ASTRA ZENECA GROUP P.L.C.
Registration no: 03674842 **Turnover:** Over £1,000m
No.of Employees: 1 - 10 **Product Groups:** 31, 32, 81, 85

Autac Products Ltd
Bollin Cable Works London Road, Macclesfield, SK11 7RN
Tel: 01625-619277 **Fax:** 01625-619366
E-mail: info@autac.co.uk
Website: http://www.autac.co.uk
Directors: S. Phillips (Fin), S. Pearce (MD), S. Phillips (Fin)
Managers: D. Oyebande (Tech Serv Mgr)
Immediate Holding Company: AUTAC PRODUCTS LIMITED
Registration no: 00830676 **VAT No.:** GB 157 2274 62
Date established: 1964 **Turnover:** £2m - £5m **No.of Employees:** 21 - 50
Product Groups: 37

Date of Accounts	Dec 11	Dec 10	Dec 09
Working Capital	708	679	647
Fixed Assets	268	287	312
Current Assets	935	921	770

B C Transport Bollington 1991 Ltd
Cooper House Clough Bank, Bollington, Macclesfield, SK10 5NZ
Tel: 01625-572820 **Fax:** 01625-575761
E-mail: enquiries@bctransport.co.uk
Website: http://www.bctransport.co.uk
Directors: C. Goodwin (MD), C. Goodwins (MD)
Managers: A. Lowe
Immediate Holding Company: B C TRANSPORT (BOLLINGTON) 1991 LIMITED
Registration no: 02615618 **Date established:** 1991
No.of Employees: 21 - 50 **Product Groups:** 77

Date of Accounts	Sep 11	Sep 10	Sep 09
Working Capital	568	397	194
Fixed Assets	1m	967	1m
Current Assets	1m	1m	753

BASF Performance Products plc
Charter Way, Macclesfield, SK10 2NXA
Tel: 01625-665000 **Fax:** 01625-619637
E-mail: info@basf.com
Website: http://www.basf.co.uk
Directors: R. Wilkinson (Co Sec)
Managers: A. Dimery (Mgr)
Ultimate Holding Company: Ciba Specialty Chemicals Holding Inc.
Immediate Holding Company: CHEMIQUIP LIMITED
Registration no: 03249009 **VAT No.:** GB 677 3667 81
Date established: 1998 **Turnover:** £250m - £500m
No.of Employees: 1 - 10 **Product Groups:** 32

Date of Accounts	Dec 07
Sales Turnover	403940
Pre Tax Profit/Loss	21430
Working Capital	372710
Fixed Assets	170140
Current Assets	596460
Current Liabilities	223750
Total Share Capital	49990
ROCE% (Return on Capital Employed)	3.9

Bien Venue Ltd
Association House South Park Road, Macclesfield, SK11 6SH
Tel: 01625-267885 **Fax:** 01625-430500
E-mail: sam@bvevents.co.uk
Website: http://www.bvevents.co.uk
Directors: S. Elliott (Develop), S. Elliot (MD)
Managers: V. Roberts (Accounts)
Immediate Holding Company: BIEN VENUE LIMITED
Registration no: 06510519 **Date established:** 2008 **Turnover:** £1m - £2m
No.of Employees: 11 - 20 **Product Groups:** 69

Date of Accounts	Mar 11	Mar 10	Mar 09
Working Capital	-8	18	36
Fixed Assets	10	14	20
Current Assets	225	335	430

Billbo UK Ltd
Saville Street, Macclesfield, SK11 7LQ
Tel: 01625-427010 **Fax:** 01625-511481
E-mail: sales@billbo.co.uk
Website: http://www.billbo.co.uk
Bank(s): Lloyds TSB Bank plc
Directors: P. Lenton (Sales)
Immediate Holding Company: BILLBO (UK) LIMITED
Registration no: 02786207 **VAT No.:** GB 611 7245 68
Date established: 1993 **Turnover:** £500,000 - £1m
No.of Employees: 11 - 20 **Product Groups:** 49

Date of Accounts	Jun 11	Jun 10	Jun 09
Working Capital	152	210	222
Fixed Assets	56	44	55
Current Assets	233	315	351

Bodycote Macclesfield
Springwood Court Springwood Close, Tytherington Business Park, Macclesfield, SK10 2XF
Tel: 01625-505300 **Fax:** 01625-505313
E-mail: info@bodycote.com
Website: http://www.bodycote.com
Managers: G. Joiner (Tech Serv Mgr), L. Walsh (Sales & Mktg Mg), C. Davies (Personnel), S. Harris, D. Landless, P. Lee (Buyer)
Ultimate Holding Company: BODYCOTE PLC
Immediate Holding Company: BODYCOTE PLC
Registration no: 00519057 **VAT No.:** GB 553 5266 38
Date established: 1953 **Turnover:** £500m - £1,000m
No.of Employees: 21 - 50 **Product Groups:** 39, 51, 54, 84, 85

Date of Accounts	Dec 11	Dec 10	Dec 09
Sales Turnover	571m	500m	435m
Pre Tax Profit/Loss	56m	45m	-55m
Working Capital	-12m	-10m	-13m
Fixed Assets	610m	628m	642m
Current Assets	148m	144m	130m
Current Liabilities	111m	109m	108m

Broadstock Office Furniture
Brunel Road, Macclesfield, SK11 0TA
Tel: 01625-431979 **Fax:** 01625-511136
E-mail: mark@broadstock.co.uk
Website: http://www.broadstock.co.uk
Bank(s): Barclays Bank Plc
Directors: A. Meakin (Fin), A. Meakin (Co Sec), D. McGagh (Sales & Mktg)
Managers: A. Gill (Personnel), M. Meakin (Tech Serv Mgr)
Immediate Holding Company: BROADSTOCK OFFICE FURNITURE LIMITED
Registration no: 02752681 **Date established:** 1992
Turnover: £10m - £20m **No.of Employees:** 51 - 100 **Product Groups:** 26, 37, 44, 49, 52, 67, 84

Date of Accounts	Dec 11	Dec 10	Dec 09
Sales Turnover	14m	11m	12m
Pre Tax Profit/Loss	1m	1m	1m
Working Capital	686	404	168
Fixed Assets	2m	2m	3m
Current Assets	3m	2m	2m
Current Liabilities	861	827	816

Chemvac Pumps Ltd
Unit Redwood Court Tytherington Business Park, Macclesfield, SK10 2XH
Tel: 01625-443170 **Fax:** 01625-443179
E-mail: chemvacpumpsltd@btconnect.com
Website: http://www.chemvacpumps.com
Directors: G. Ikin (Dir), M. Ikin (Fin)
Immediate Holding Company: CHEMVAC PUMPS LIMITED
Registration no: 01863518 **VAT No.:** GB 670 2177 48
Date established: 1984 **No.of Employees:** 1 - 10 **Product Groups:** 39, 40, 46

Date of Accounts	Mar 12	Mar 11	Mar 10
Working Capital	8	3	45
Fixed Assets	3	5	7
Current Assets	105	155	136

Cheshire Lock & Safe Co. Ltd
Unit 3 Fence Avenue Industrial Estate, Macclesfield, SK10 1LT
Tel: 01625-614178 **Fax:** 01625-617898
E-mail: sales@cheshirelock.co.uk
Website: http://www.cheshirelock.co.uk
Directors: A. Clayton (Dir)
Immediate Holding Company: CHESHIRE LOCK & SAFE COMPANY LTD
Registration no: 06322919 **VAT No.:** GB 373 4350 56
Date established: 2007 **Turnover:** £250,000 - £500,000
No.of Employees: 1 - 10 **Product Groups:** 52

Date of Accounts	Mar 11	Mar 10	Mar 09
Working Capital	60	34	6
Fixed Assets	44	32	39
Current Assets	119	151	125

Cheshire Wrought Iron
Unit 19 Adlington Industrial Estate Adlington, Macclesfield, SK10 4NL
Tel: 01625-878866 **Fax:** 01625-878866
E-mail: cwi@hotmail.co.uk
Website: http://www.cwi.uk.com
Directors: R. Cartledge (Prop)
Date established: 2004 **No.of Employees:** 1 - 10 **Product Groups:** 26, 35

County Labels
Units 1 & 2 Ground Floor, Bollington, Macclesfield, SK10 5JB
Tel: 01625-574422 **Fax:** 01625-574425
E-mail: sales@countylabels.com
Website: http://www.countylabels.com
Bank(s): Barclays
Directors: N. Richardson (MD), P. Cash (Fin)
Immediate Holding Company: COUNTY LABELS LIMITED
Registration no: 02130404 **Date established:** 1987 **Turnover:** £1m - £2m
No.of Employees: 21 - 50 **Product Groups:** 27, 30

Date of Accounts	Mar 11	Mar 10	Mar 09
Working Capital	38	-64	-136
Fixed Assets	278	292	326
Current Assets	910	988	941

The Cubic Group
Beechfield House Winterton Way, Lyme Green Business Park, Macclesfield, SK11 0LP
Tel: 0845-463 2431 **Fax:** 01625-509121
E-mail: info@thecubicgroup.com
Website: http://www.thecubicgroup.com
Product Groups: 54, 80, 82, 84

Direct Food Ingredients
70 Waters Green, Macclesfield, SK11 6JZ
Tel: 01625-618617 **Fax:** 01625-616432
E-mail: sales@directfood.net
Website: http://www.directfood.net
Directors: S. Loake (Prop), M. Collins (Fin)
Immediate Holding Company: DIRECT FOOD INGREDIENTS LIMITED
Registration no: 03005254 **Date established:** 1994
No.of Employees: 11 - 20 **Product Groups:** 01, 09, 12, 17, 20, 21, 23, 31, 32, 34, 41, 62, 63

Date of Accounts	Dec 11	Dec 10	Dec 09
Working Capital	564	460	326
Fixed Assets	11	27	44
Current Assets	3m	2m	1m

Electroserv T C & S Ltd
PO Box 163, Macclesfield, SK11 8GA
Tel: 01260-253777 **Fax:** 01625-500746
E-mail: dh@electroserv.co.uk
Website: http://www.electroserv.co.uk
Managers: J. Ward (Admin Off)
Registration no: 03370578 **VAT No.:** GB 611 5235 81
Turnover: £500,000 - £1m **No.of Employees:** 1 - 10 **Product Groups:** 38, 49

Extruded Plastics
Hawkshead Quarry Leek Old Road, Sutton, Macclesfield, SK11 0JB
Tel: 01260-253777 **Fax:** 01260-253888
E-mail: mh@extrudedplasticsltd.com
Website: http://www.extrudedplasticsltd.com
Managers: M. Howard (Chief Mgr)
Immediate Holding Company: EXTRUDED PLASTICS LIMITED
Registration no: 02066129 **Date established:** 1986
Turnover: £250,000 - £500,000 **No.of Employees:** 1 - 10
Product Groups: 30, 66

Date of Accounts	Dec 11	Dec 10	Dec 09
Working Capital	122	110	69
Fixed Assets	63	60	70
Current Assets	233	240	161

Fabrics & Yarns Maccesfield Ltd
Charter Way, Macclesfield, SK10 2NG
Tel: 01625-427311 **Fax:** 01625-424769
E-mail: davidcrowther@fabricsandyarns.co.uk
Website: http://www.fabricsandyarns.co.uk
Directors: K. Nashar (MD)
Managers: M. Comer (Chief Acct), P. Crowther (Admin Off), D. Crowther
Immediate Holding Company: FABRICS & YARNS (MACCLESFIELD) LTD
Registration no: 02185012 **Date established:** 1987
Turnover: £10m - £20m **No.of Employees:** 11 - 20 **Product Groups:** 61

Date of Accounts	Dec 11	Dec 10	Dec 09
Sales Turnover	10m	10m	8m
Pre Tax Profit/Loss	747	656	439
Working Capital	3m	3m	4m
Fixed Assets	2m	2m	2m
Current Assets	6m	7m	6m
Current Liabilities	3m	3m	864

Fallows Associates Ltd
34 Penningtons Lane Gawsworth, Macclesfield, SK11 7US
Tel: 01625-613305 **Fax:** 0161-601 3517
E-mail: admin@fallowsassociates.co.uk
Website: http://www.fallowsassociates.co.uk
Directors: S. Fallows (Dir)
Immediate Holding Company: FALLOWS ASSOCIATES LIMITED
Registration no: 04434680 **Date established:** 2002
Turnover: Up to £250,000 **No.of Employees:** 1 - 10 **Product Groups:** 84

Date of Accounts	May 11	May 10	May 09
Working Capital	1	1	3
Current Assets	22	3	5

G Tek Systems Ltd
Adelphi Mill Grimshaw Lane, Bollington, Macclesfield, SK10 5JB
Tel: 01625-575551 **Fax:** 01625-575567
E-mail: info@g-tek.co.uk
Website: http://www.g-tek.co.uk
Directors: G. Dawson (Dir), G. Docherty (Dir), J. Grimes (MD)
Registration no: 02828452 **Date established:** 1993 **Turnover:** £1m - £2m
No.of Employees: 1 - 10 **Product Groups:** 44

Date of Accounts	Sep 09	Sep 08	Sep 07
Working Capital	-1	-1	-2
Fixed Assets	3	2	2
Current Assets	49	69	79

General Monitors UK Ltd
1 Heather Close Lyme Green Business Park, Macclesfield, SK11 0LR
Tel: 01625-619583 **Fax:** 01625-619098
E-mail: info@generalmonitors.com
Website: http://www.generalmonitors.com
Managers: B. Hill (Admin Off)
Immediate Holding Company: GENERAL MONITORS IRELAND LIMITED
Registration no: FC012599 **Date established:** 1973
No.of Employees: 1 - 10 **Product Groups:** 38, 40, 84

Gradus Accessories Ltd
Chapel Mill Park Green Park Green, Macclesfield, SK11 7LZ
Tel: 01625-428922 **Fax:** 01625-433949
E-mail: sales@gradusworld.com
Website: http://www.gradusworld.com
Bank(s): National Westminster Bank Plc
Directors: S. Watts (MD), S. Watt (MD), C. Rice (Fin), D. Tierney (Sales & Mktg)
Managers: J. Butcher, L. Thompson (Personnel), A. Lees (Chief Acct)
Registration no: 02152465 **Turnover:** £20m - £50m
No.of Employees: 21 - 50 **Product Groups:** 23, 30, 35, 36, 37, 63

A J Heapy Engineering
Unit 10 Sutton Mill Gunco Lane, Macclesfield, SK11 7JL
Tel: 01625-619639 **Fax:** 01625-425553
E-mail: andrew.heapy@btinternet.com
Directors: A. Heapy (Prop)
Immediate Holding Company: STANLEY PRESS EQUIPMENT LIMITED
Registration no: 02121318 **Date established:** 2004
No.of Employees: 1 - 10 **Product Groups:** 26, 35

Date of Accounts	Apr 12	Apr 11	Apr 10
Working Capital	174	157	94
Fixed Assets	22	36	9
Current Assets	514	470	545

Hearing Health Care
Waters Green House Waters Green, Macclesfield, SK11 6LF
Tel: 01625-614882 **Fax:** 01625-502323
E-mail: hearinghc@aol.com
Website: http://www.audiometry.co.uk

see next page

Hearing Health Care - Cont'd

Directors: R. Ten-Wolde (MD), H. Tenwelde (Prop)
Immediate Holding Company: T AND A TYRES LIMITED
Registration no: 02478549 **Date established:** 2011
Turnover: £500,000 - £1m **No.of Employees:** 1 - 10 **Product Groups:** 88

Date of Accounts	Oct 04	Oct 03
Working Capital	-19	-19
Current Liabilities	19	19
Total Share Capital	1	1

I A S Smarts Ltd

Clarence Mill Clarence Road, Bollington, Macclesfield, SK10 5JZ
Tel: 01625-578578 **Fax:** 01625-578579
E-mail: info@iasb2b.com
Website: http://www.iasb2b.com
Bank(s): National Westminster Bank Plc
Directors: A. Brandwood (Fin), R. Morrice (MD)
Managers: A. Garner (Tech Serv Mgr), C. Jackson (Personnel)
Ultimate Holding Company: MEDIA SQUARE PLC
Immediate Holding Company: IAS SMARTS LIMITED
Registration no: 01422673 **Date established:** 1979 **Turnover:** £2m - £5m
No.of Employees: 21 - 50 **Product Groups:** 28, 80, 81

Date of Accounts	Feb 08	Feb 11	Feb 10
Sales Turnover	13m	6m	5m
Pre Tax Profit/Loss	3m	364	124
Working Capital	2m	2m	3m
Fixed Assets	3m	100	112
Current Assets	6m	3m	4m
Current Liabilities	3m	876	980

Lead Precision Machine Tools Ltd

Calamine House Calamine Street, Macclesfield, SK11 7HU
Tel: 01625-434990 **Fax:** 01625-434996
E-mail: fiona@leadmachinetools.co.uk
Website: http://www.leadmachinetools.co.uk
Bank(s): Lloyds TSB
Directors: M. Heapy (MD)
Immediate Holding Company: LEAD PRECISION MACHINE TOOLS LIMITED
Registration no: 04545932 **VAT No.:** GB 593 6087 05
Date established: 2002 **Turnover:** £2m - £5m **No.of Employees:** 11 - 20
Product Groups: 46

Date of Accounts	Jun 12	Jun 11	Jun 10
Working Capital	27	-3	-1
Fixed Assets	4	6	9
Current Assets	531	676	453

R Lunn Engineering

2 Vincent Mill Vincent Street, Macclesfield, SK11 6UJ
Tel: 01625-611682 **Fax:** 01625-611682
E-mail: del@rlunnengineering.co.uk
Website: http://www.rlunnengineering.co.uk
Directors: D. Lunn (Prop)
Registration no: 01359246 **Date established:** 1978
No.of Employees: 1 - 10 **Product Groups:** 36

M S Storage Equipment Ltd

Unit 9 Normans Hall Farm Shrigley Road, Pott Shrigley, Macclesfield, SK10 5SE
Tel: 08453-888791 **Fax:** 0845-388 8792
E-mail: sales@msstorage.co.uk
Website: http://www.msstorage.co.uk
Directors: H. Simpkin (MD)
Immediate Holding Company: M.S. STORAGE EQUIPMENT LIMITED
Registration no: 01368061 **Date established:** 1978 **Turnover:** £2m - £5m
No.of Employees: 11 - 20 **Product Groups:** 26, 36

Date of Accounts	Mar 12	Mar 11	Mar 10
Working Capital	327	247	227
Fixed Assets	38	50	66
Current Assets	1m	775	1m

Mccann Manchester

Bonis Hall Bonis Hall Lane, Macclesfield, SK10 4EF
Tel: 0161-822200 **Fax:** 01625-829567
E-mail: manme.reception@europe.mccann.com
Website: http://www.mccannmanchester.com
Bank(s): Royal Bank of Scotland
Directors: M. Jackson (Fin)
Managers: J. Rothnie (Mktg Serv Mgr), P. Turnock (Tech Serv Mgr), S. Little, T. Harman
Ultimate Holding Company: INTERPUBLIC GROUP OF COMPANIES INC (USA)
Immediate Holding Company: MCCANN MANCHESTER LIMITED
Registration no: 01993425 **VAT No.:** 466 2488 18 **Date established:** 1986
Turnover: £75m - £125m **No.of Employees:** 251 - 500
Product Groups: 28, 80, 81, 87

Date of Accounts	Dec 11	Dec 10	Dec 09
Sales Turnover	80m	77m	77m
Pre Tax Profit/Loss	-2m	2m	3m
Working Capital	30m	27m	24m
Fixed Assets	8m	8m	9m
Current Assets	50m	43m	44m
Current Liabilities	8m	5m	8m

Macclesfield Chamber Of Commerce

Churchill Chambers Churchill Way, Macclesfield, SK11 6AS
Tel: 01625-665940 **Fax:** 01625-665941
E-mail: info@macclesfieldchamber.co.uk
Website: http://www.macclesfieldchamber.co.uk
Directors: J. Lamond (Grp Chief Exec)
Immediate Holding Company: MACCLESFIELD CHAMBER OF COMMERCE AND ENTERPRISE LIMITED
Registration no: 02855788 **VAT No.:** GB 611 7796 31
Date established: 1993 **Turnover:** £250,000 - £500,000
No.of Employees: 1 - 10 **Product Groups:** 80, 81

Date of Accounts	Mar 11	Mar 10	Mar 09
Working Capital	7	25	49
Fixed Assets	89	112	98
Current Assets	49	88	134

Macclesfield Stone Quarries Ltd

Bridge Quarry Windmill Lane, Kerridge, Macclesfield, SK10 5AZ
Tel: 01625-573208 **Fax:** 01625-573208
E-mail: datooth@tiscali.co.uk
Directors: D. Tooth (Dir)
Date established: 1978 **Turnover:** Up to £250,000
No.of Employees: 1 - 10 **Product Groups:** 14

Date of Accounts	Mar 08	Mar 07	Mar 06
Working Capital	-15	-18	-18
Fixed Assets	181	186	186
Current Assets	4	1	1
Current Liabilities	18	18	18

Mark Simpkin Ltd (Simply Group)

Unit F1 Adelphi Mill Grimshaw Lane, Bollington, Macclesfield, SK10 5JB
Tel: 01625-576527 **Fax:** 01625-576545
E-mail: info@simplygroupuk.co.uk
Website: http://www.simplygroupuk.co.uk
Managers: W. Knight (Chief Mgr)
Registration no: 04209008 **Date established:** 2001 **Turnover:** £2m - £5m
No.of Employees: 11 - 20 **Product Groups:** 26, 67

Date of Accounts	Aug 09	Aug 08	Aug 07
Working Capital	213	153	120
Fixed Assets	20	33	44
Current Assets	738	556	448

Mark1 Quality Assurance

53 Cedarway Bollington, Macclesfield, SK10 5NR
Tel: 0800-458 9630
E-mail: mark@mark1qa.co.uk
Website: http://www.mark1qa.co.uk
Directors: M. Nolan (Prop)
Registration no: 06311121 **No.of Employees:** 1 - 10 **Product Groups:** 38, 44, 67

Millward & Keeling

Unit 2 Bollington Lane Nether Alderley, Macclesfield, SK10 4TB
Tel: 01625-861749 **Fax:** 01625-890030
Managers: I. Bonner (Mgr)
Immediate Holding Company: MILLWARD & KEELING LIMITED
Registration no: 07737727 **Date established:** 2011
No.of Employees: 1 - 10 **Product Groups:** 41

Munsch & Co Ltd

Units Ag2/3 Clarence Mill Clarence Road, Bollington, Macclesfield, SK10 5JZ
Tel: 01625-573971 **Fax:** 01625-573250
E-mail: enquiries@wcmunsch.co.uk
Website: http://www.wcmunsch.co.uk
Directors: S. Carless (MD), K. Boycott (Fin)
VAT No.: GB 421 9017 80 **Turnover:** £250,000 - £500,000
No.of Employees: 1 - 10 **Product Groups:** 29

H Oldfield & Son Ltd

13 Mill Lane, Macclesfield, SK11 7NN
Tel: 01625-422807 **Fax:** 01625-615212
E-mail: oldfieldprinters@aol.com
Directors: I. Brooke (MD), I. Brown (Fin)
Immediate Holding Company: H.OLDFIELD & SON LIMITED
Registration no: 00732538 **Date established:** 1962
No.of Employees: 1 - 10 **Product Groups:** 28

Date of Accounts	Sep 11	Sep 10	Sep 09
Working Capital	51	43	48
Fixed Assets	26	28	30
Current Assets	89	81	70

Peak Electromagnetics Ltd

139 Bank Street, Macclesfield, SK11 7AY
Tel: 01625-269808
E-mail: sales@peak-em.co.uk
Website: http://www.peak-em.co.uk
Directors: I. Pocock (MD), A. Pocock (Co Sec)
Immediate Holding Company: PEAK ELECTROMAGNETICS LIMITED
Registration no: 05254570 **Date established:** 2004
Turnover: Up to £250,000 **No.of Employees:** 1 - 10 **Product Groups:** 37, 84

Date of Accounts	Oct 11	Oct 10	Oct 09
Working Capital	N/A	1	3
Fixed Assets	N/A	N/A	1
Current Assets	11	14	11

Polytech International

Long Lane Pott Shrigley, Macclesfield, SK10 5SD
Tel: 01625-575737 **Fax:** 01625-575720
E-mail: sales@mri-polytech.com
Website: http://www.mri-polytech.com
Directors: M. Dunkinson (MD)
Managers: K. Law (Sales Prom)
Immediate Holding Company: STONE PRODUCTS LIMITED
Registration no: 03164515 **Date established:** 1997 **Turnover:** £5m - £10m
No.of Employees: 11 - 20 **Product Groups:** 29

Date of Accounts	Mar 08	Mar 07	Mar 06
Sales Turnover	N/A	N/A	9395
Pre Tax Profit/Loss	231	N/A	95
Working Capital	1244	1059	979
Fixed Assets	1713	1734	1741
Current Assets	3684	5006	3685
Current Liabilities	2440	3946	2706
Total Share Capital	1650	1650	1650
ROCE% (Return on Capital Employed)	7.8		3.5
ROT% (Return on Turnover)			1.0

Poynton Valves Ltd

Unit 6 Snape Road, Macclesfield, SK10 2NZ
Tel: 01625-871014 **Fax:** 01625-879814
E-mail: sales@poyntonvalves.com
Website: http://www.poyntonvalves.com
Directors: D. McConnell (Fin), A. Mcconnell (MD)
Immediate Holding Company: POYNTON VALVES LIMITED
Registration no: 01509114 **VAT No.:** GB 343 7464 47
Date established: 1980 **Turnover:** £1m - £2m **No.of Employees:** 1 - 10
Product Groups: 36, 38

Date of Accounts	Mar 12	Mar 11	Mar 10
Working Capital	76	120	112
Fixed Assets	5	8	14
Current Assets	608	462	321

Prestige Systems

8 Watermill Drive, Macclesfield, SK11 7WB
Tel: 0800-5053744
E-mail: prestige_systems@btinternet.com
Directors: S. Lock (Prop)
Registration no: 06032895 **Date established:** 2006
No.of Employees: 1 - 10 **Product Groups:** 37, 40, 67

Slater Harrison & Co. Ltd

Lowerhouse Mill Bollington, Macclesfield, SK10 5HW
Tel: 01625-578900 **Fax:** 01625-578972
E-mail: c.smallwood@slater-harrison.co.uk
Website: http://www.slater-harrison.co.uk
Bank(s): National Westminster Bank Plc
Directors: B. Bogie (Sales), C. Smallwood (MD), T. Hughes (Fin)
Managers: M. Perry (Purch Mgr), P. Bowden (Mktg Serv Mgr)
Ultimate Holding Company: L.S.DIXON GROUP LIMITED
Immediate Holding Company: SLATER HARRISON & CO.LIMITED
Registration no: 00374230 **VAT No.:** GB 298 8926 70
Date established: 1942 **Turnover:** £5m - £10m
No.of Employees: 51 - 100 **Product Groups:** 27, 28, 30, 66

Date of Accounts	Dec 11	Dec 10	Dec 09
Sales Turnover	9m	9m	9m
Pre Tax Profit/Loss	38	408	353
Working Capital	3m	3m	3m
Fixed Assets	917	1m	1m
Current Assets	5m	5m	5m
Current Liabilities	478	530	617

Spectus Windows Systems

Snape Road, Macclesfield, SK10 2NZ
Tel: 01625-420400 **Fax:** 01625-501418
Website: http://www.spectussystems.com
Directors: A. Ahchinkow (MD), P. McLoughlin (Fin)
Managers: C. Powell, J. Plane (Mktg Serv Mgr), J. Webster, L. Cox
Ultimate Holding Company: BUILDING PLASTICS HOLDINGS LIMITED
Immediate Holding Company: NUS SERVICES LIMITED
Registration no: 05599269 **Date established:** 1982
Turnover: £20m - £50m **No.of Employees:** 101 - 250 **Product Groups:** 30

Date of Accounts	Jun 11	Apr 10	Apr 09
Sales Turnover	6m	4m	4m
Pre Tax Profit/Loss	834	146	2
Working Capital	1m	713	455
Fixed Assets	270	201	337
Current Assets	6m	5m	4m
Current Liabilities	3m	2m	2m

Statiflo International Ltd

Wood Street, Macclesfield, SK11 6JQ
Tel: 01625-433100 **Fax:** 01625-511376
E-mail: sales@statiflo.co.uk
Website: http://www.statiflo.net
Bank(s): National
Directors: J. Baron (Dir)
Immediate Holding Company: STATIFLO INTERNATIONAL LIMITED
Registration no: 02780638 **VAT No.:** GB 388 1205 43
Date established: 1993 **Turnover:** £1m - £2m **No.of Employees:** 11 - 20
Product Groups: 32

Date of Accounts	May 11	May 10	May 09
Working Capital	48	188	381
Fixed Assets	128	141	129
Current Assets	652	1m	1m

T S Designs Ltd

PO Box 102, Macclesfield, SK11 9EP
Tel: 01477-571357 **Fax:** 01477-571881
Website: http://www.ts-designs.com
Directors: B. Mabon (Dir)
Immediate Holding Company: TS DESIGNS LIMITED
Registration no: 03008195 **Date established:** 1995
No.of Employees: 1 - 10 **Product Groups:** 26, 35

Date of Accounts	Sep 11	Sep 10	Sep 09
Working Capital	94	37	110
Fixed Assets	4	4	3
Current Assets	219	101	186

Tablets 4 Less

Signature House Gunco Lane, Macclesfield, SK11 7JL
Tel: 01625-612170 **Fax:** 01625-508604
E-mail: sales@tablets4less.com
Website: http://www.tablets4less.com
Product Groups: 31

Technical Materials Converters

Alder Court Springwood way, Tytherington business park, Macclesfield, SK10 2XG
Tel: 01625-610441 **Fax:** 01625-613199
E-mail: sales@tmcwaterjet.co.uk
Website: http://www.tmcwaterjet.co.uk
Directors: N. Stretton (Dir)
Date established: 1990 **No.of Employees:** 1 - 10 **Product Groups:** 46, 48

Through Creative Ltd

Suite 7 Charter House Charter Way, Macclesfield, SK10 2NG
Tel: 01625-500939
E-mail: info@throughcreative.com
Website: http://www.throughcreative.com
Directors: E. Beattie (Dir)
Immediate Holding Company: THROUGH CREATIVE LIMITED
Registration no: 06389743 **Date established:** 2007
Turnover: £250,000 - £500,000 **No.of Employees:** 1 - 10
Product Groups: 44, 49, 65, 81, 89

Date of Accounts	Oct 11	Oct 10	Oct 09
Working Capital	7	4	2
Fixed Assets	4	6	7
Current Assets	66	44	34

Tullis Russell Coaters Ltd

Church Street Bollington, Macclesfield, SK10 5QF
Tel: 01625-573051 **Fax:** 01625-575525
E-mail: enquiries@trcoaters.co.uk
Website: http://www.trcoaters.co.uk
Directors: G. Miller (Co Sec), J. Smith (MD), S. McCandless (Fin)
Managers: B. Mothershaw, B. Preece, D. Hignett (Sales & Mktg Mg), H. Brady (Personnel), P. Brown (Purch Mgr), F. Davidson (Tech Serv Mgr), H. Brady (Personnel)
Ultimate Holding Company: TULLIS RUSSELL GROUP LIMITED
Immediate Holding Company: TULLIS RUSSELL COATERS LIMITED
Registration no: 01427074 **Date established:** 1979
Turnover: £20m - £50m **No.of Employees:** 101 - 250
Product Groups: 27, 30

Date of Accounts	Mar 11	Mar 10	Mar 09
Sales Turnover	27m	25m	25m
Pre Tax Profit/Loss	2m	2m	2m
Working Capital	8m	8m	8m
Fixed Assets	3m	3m	4m
Current Assets	18m	16m	15m
Current Liabilities	2m	2m	2m

UK Disability Bureau Uk-Db Ltd (UK-DB)

23 Stapleton Road, Macclesfield, SK10 3NP
Tel: 01625-432515 **Fax:** 01625-432515
E-mail: principalconsultant@uk-db.co.uk
Website: http://www.uk-db.co.uk

Managers: J. Stubbs, M. Savage, D. Townley
Registration no: 05173481 **Date established:** 2004
No.of Employees: 1 - 10 **Product Groups:** 86

W C Munsch & Co. Ltd

Clarence Mill Clarence Road, Bollington, Macclesfield, SK10 5JZ
Tel: 01625-573971 **Fax:** 01625-573250
E-mail: sales@epdm.co.uk
Website: http://www.epdm.co.uk
Directors: S. Carless (MD)
Ultimate Holding Company: MAC PANEL COMPANY (USA)
Immediate Holding Company: W.C.MUNSCH & CO. LIMITED
Registration no: 01042346 **VAT No.:** GB 157 6718 32
Date established: 1972 **Turnover:** £500,000 - £1m
No.of Employees: 11 - 20 **Product Groups:** 29

Date of Accounts	Nov 11	Nov 10	Nov 09
Working Capital	74	34	45
Fixed Assets	40	44	46
Current Assets	312	206	190

William Kenyon Macclesfield Ltd

73 Great King Street, Macclesfield, SK11 6PN
Tel: 01625-422074 **Fax:** 01625-617712
Directors: B. Kenyon (MD), B. Kenyon (Jt MD), B. Kenyon (Dir), E. Kenyon (Jt MD)
Immediate Holding Company: WILLIAM KENYON (MACCLESFIELD) LIMITED
Registration no: 00370560 **VAT No.:** GB 157 6526 41
Date established: 1941 **Turnover:** £1m - £2m **No.of Employees:** 1 - 10
Product Groups: 35, 66

Date of Accounts	Sep 09	Sep 08	Sep 07
Working Capital	12	25	33
Fixed Assets	58	60	63
Current Assets	172	237	232

Wizzoo

8 Princess Street Bollington, Macclesfield, SK10 5HZ
Tel: 0844-5048400
E-mail: info@wizzoo.com
Website: http://www.wizzoo.com
Directors: A. Watkins (MD), J. Watkins (Fin)
Immediate Holding Company: WIZZOO LIMITED
Registration no: 06386593 **Date established:** 2007
Turnover: Up to £250,000 **No.of Employees:** 1 - 10 **Product Groups:** 44

Www.Safetysignsonline.Co.Uk

5 Chelford Road, Macclesfield, SK10 3LG
Tel: 0800-288 9874 **Fax:** 01625-508261
E-mail: info@safetysignsonline.co.uk
Website: http://www.safetysignsonline.co.uk
Directors: M. Le Moignan (Prop)
Immediate Holding Company: BROKEN CROSS PAINT & WALLPAPER SUPPLIES LIMITED
Date established: 1998 **No.of Employees:** 1 - 10 **Product Groups:** 27, 30, 32, 36, 37, 39, 40, 49, 52, 66, 84

Date of Accounts	Mar 12	Mar 11	Mar 10
Working Capital	-18	-15	-34
Fixed Assets	12	16	21
Current Assets	137	134	105

Wymbs Engineering Ltd

Clarence Road Bollington, Macclesfield, SK10 5JZ
Tel: 01625-575154 **Fax:** 01625-574109
E-mail: info@wymbsengineering.com
Website: http://www.wymbsengineering.com
Directors: A. Wymbs (Fin), B. Sharples (Comm), B. Wymbs (MD)
Managers: P. Hopkins
Immediate Holding Company: WYMBS ENGINEERING LIMITED
Registration no: 01568182 **Date established:** 1981
No.of Employees: 11 - 20 **Product Groups:** 20, 40, 41

Date of Accounts	Dec 11	Dec 10	Dec 09
Working Capital	168	182	104
Fixed Assets	121	95	214
Current Assets	381	394	322

Malpas

Ace Exhibitions Displays & Installation

Church House Wrexham Road, Bulkeley, Malpas, SY14 8BW
Tel: 07767-258958
E-mail: aceexhibit@aol.com
Website: http://www.britishamericandisplays.com
Directors: P. Smith (Prop)
Date established: 1993 **Turnover:** £250,000 - £500,000
No.of Employees: 1 - 10 **Product Groups:** 26

Miles Macadam Ltd

Malpas Station Hampton Heath Industrial Estate, Hampton, Malpas, SY14 8LU
Tel: 01948-820489 **Fax:** 01948-820267
E-mail: crac@milesmacadam.co.uk
Website: http://www.milesmacadam.co.uk
Bank(s): National Westminster
Directors: C. Clarke (Dir), P. Sutton (Fin)
Immediate Holding Company: MILES MACADAM LIMITED
Registration no: 03031039 **VAT No.:** GB 482 5240 49
Date established: 1995 **Turnover:** £1m - £2m **No.of Employees:** 11 - 20
Product Groups: 51

Date of Accounts	Dec 11	Dec 10	Dec 09
Working Capital	79	92	204
Fixed Assets	175	156	61
Current Assets	2m	1m	883

Middlewich

Able Packaging Group Ltd

Unit 11b Middlewich Road, Byley, Middlewich, CW10 9NX
Tel: 01606-836161 **Fax:** 01606-836970
E-mail: info@ablepackaging.co.uk
Website: http://www.ablepackaging.co.uk
Directors: R. Pell (Dir)
Ultimate Holding Company: ABLE PACKAGING GROUP LIMITED
Immediate Holding Company: ABLE PACKAGING GROUP LIMITED
Registration no: 01223225 **Date established:** 1975 **Turnover:** £2m - £5m
No.of Employees: 1 - 10 **Product Groups:** 27, 30, 31, 42, 45, 66

Date of Accounts	Sep 11	Sep 10	Sep 09
Working Capital	125	178	170
Fixed Assets	16	23	38
Current Assets	344	436	397

Automac UK Ltd

Unit 6-7 Prosperity Court Prosperity Way, Middlewich, CW10 0GD
Tel: 01606-831113 **Fax:** 01606-831114
E-mail: sales@gruppofabbri.com
Website: http://www.gruppofabbri.com
Directors: M. Becucci (Fin), M. Govoni (MD)
Ultimate Holding Company: GRUPPO FABBRI INTERNATIONAL SA (LUXEMBOURG)
Immediate Holding Company: AUTOMAC (UK) LIMITED
Registration no: 03200331 **Date established:** 1996
No.of Employees: 1 - 10 **Product Groups:** 38, 42

Date of Accounts	Dec 11	Dec 10	Dec 09
Working Capital	398	256	278
Fixed Assets	88	94	67
Current Assets	1m	737	619

B L Farrier Supplies

Unit 1 Brooks Lane, Middlewich, CW10 0JH
Tel: 01606-837594 **Fax:** 01606-837594
Directors: R. Lee (Prop)
Immediate Holding Company: BIP ENVIRONMENTAL LTD
Date established: 2012 **No.of Employees:** 1 - 10 **Product Groups:** 36

Date of Accounts	Apr 11	Apr 10	Apr 07
Working Capital	-10	-10	-4
Fixed Assets	9	11	7
Current Assets	12	19	30

British Salt Ltd

Cledford Lane, Middlewich, CW10 0JP
Tel: 01606-832881 **Fax:** 01606-835999
E-mail: sales@british-salt.co.uk
Website: http://www.british-salt.co.uk
Bank(s): Royal Bank of Scotland, Sandbach
Directors: M. Vaughan (Fin), T. Brown (Sales)
Managers: I. Warren (Personnel), M. Vaughan (Comptroller), R. Dodd (Tech Serv Mgr)
Ultimate Holding Company: ELECTRICITE DE FRANCE SA (FRANCE)
Immediate Holding Company: CHESHIRE CAVITY STORAGE GROUP LIMITED
Registration no: 03875121 **Date established:** 1999
Turnover: £20m - £50m **No.of Employees:** 101 - 250
Product Groups: 17, 31

Date of Accounts	Dec 11	Dec 10	Dec 09
Pre Tax Profit/Loss	N/A	N/A	-20
Working Capital	-10	3	-3
Current Assets	N/A	13	7

Centec Ltd

Brooks Lane, Middlewich, CW10 0JG
Tel: 01606-737720 **Fax:** 01606-737511
E-mail: enquiry@centec.uk.com
Website: http://www.centec.uk.com
Directors: J. Blundell (MD)
Immediate Holding Company: CENTEC LIMITED
Registration no: 07104241 **Date established:** 2009
No.of Employees: 1 - 10 **Product Groups:** 32

Compuspar UK Ltd

Unit 1- Dalton Way Midpoint 18, Middlewich, CW10 0HU
Tel: 01606-738897 **Fax:** 01606-738898
E-mail: clewis@compuspar.co.uk
Website: http://www.compuspar.co.uk
Managers: D. Lewis
Registration no: 02626049 **No.of Employees:** 21 - 50 **Product Groups:** 48

Date of Accounts	Dec 07	Dec 06	Dec 05
Working Capital	-6	69	139
Fixed Assets	25	29	22
Current Assets	212	302	287

Creative Art Products Ltd (t/a Scolaquip)

10 Dalton Way, Middlewich, CW10 0HU
Tel: 01606-836076 **Fax:** 01606-841727
E-mail: orders@scolaquip.co.uk
Website: http://www.scolaquip.co.uk
Bank(s): Barclays
Directors: J. Reynard (Sales)
Immediate Holding Company: CREATIVE ART PRODUCTS LIMITED
Registration no: 02573654 **VAT No.:** GB 593 6255 10
Date established: 1991 **No.of Employees:** 11 - 20 **Product Groups:** 49

Date of Accounts	Dec 11	Dec 10	Dec 09
Working Capital	144	106	274
Fixed Assets	587	634	479
Current Assets	1m	1m	2m

E R F Ltd

E R F Way, Middlewich, CW10 0TN
Tel: 01606-843000 **Fax:** 01606-843005
E-mail: tgrove@erf.com
Website: http://www.erf.com
Bank(s): HSBC Bank plc
Directors: M. Raab (Co Sec)
Managers: M. Taylor (Buyer), D. Smith, M. Reab (Comptroller), M. Rowley, M. Walczak, C. Carr
Ultimate Holding Company: M.A.N.
Registration no: 00278235 **VAT No.:** GB 539 5309 24
Turnover: £125m - £250m **No.of Employees:** 501 - 1000
Product Groups: 39, 45, 68, 72, 87

Extronics Ltd

Unit 1 Dalton Way, Middlewich, CW10 0HU
Tel: 01260-297274 **Fax:** 01260-297280
E-mail: john@extronics.com
Website: http://www.extronics.com
Directors: P. Lazor (Sales), H. Hartley (Dir), J. Hartley (MD)
Managers: N. Saunders (Tech Serv Mgr)
Immediate Holding Company: EXTRONICS LIMITED
Registration no: 03076287 **VAT No.:** GB 611 5009 90
Date established: 1995 **Turnover:** £2m - £5m **No.of Employees:** 21 - 50
Product Groups: 36, 37, 38, 40

Date of Accounts	Oct 10	Oct 09	Oct 08
Sales Turnover	3m	N/A	N/A
Working Capital	178	124	158
Fixed Assets	252	289	51
Current Assets	1m	725	871

Hydraulic Pneumatic Services

Unit 17 King Street Trading Estate, Middlewich, CW10 9LF
Tel: 01606-835725 **Fax:** 01606-737358
E-mail: capper59@btconnect.com
Website: http://www.pressure-pumps.co.uk
Directors: D. Capper (Fin), J. Capper (MD)
Immediate Holding Company: HYDRAULIC PNEUMATIC SERVICES LTD.
Registration no: 04756248 **Date established:** 2003
Turnover: £250,000 - £500,000 **No.of Employees:** 1 - 10
Product Groups: 38, 40, 85

Date of Accounts	Apr 11	Apr 10	Apr 09
Working Capital	105	84	98
Fixed Assets	1	1	1
Current Assets	185	133	141

Manga Fu Ltd

Unit 18-19 King Street Industrial Estate, Middlewich, CW10 9LF
Tel: 0800-197 4823
E-mail: garyc@manga-fu.com
Website: http://www.manga-fu.com
Directors: G. Cronnolley (Dir)
Managers: M. LTD (I.T. Exec)
Ultimate Holding Company: VALSAVE LIMITED
Immediate Holding Company: MANGA FU LIMITED
Registration no: 05119179 **Date established:** 2004
Turnover: Up to £250,000 **No.of Employees:** 1 - 10 **Product Groups:** 34, 42, 54, 84

Date of Accounts	May 11	May 10	May 09
Working Capital	-72	-23	-15
Fixed Assets	14	17	15
Current Assets	178	349	232

P A Moston

1 Holly House Estate Middlewich Road, Cranage, Middlewich, CW10 9LT
Tel: 01606-737464 **Fax:** 01606-738300
Directors: P. Moston (Prop)
Immediate Holding Company: SMITHY GREEN APPAREL LIMITED
Date established: 1998 **No.of Employees:** 1 - 10 **Product Groups:** 41

Date of Accounts	Jun 11	Jun 10	Jun 09
Working Capital	589	595	555
Fixed Assets	25	31	25
Current Assets	2m	2m	1m

Moving Methods Ltd

Brooks Lane, Middlewich, CW10 0JH
Tel: 01606-833262 **Fax:** 01606-832304
E-mail: info@moving-methods.co.uk
Website: http://www.moving-methods.co.uk
Directors: S. Bedford (MD)
Immediate Holding Company: MOVING METHODS LIMITED
Registration no: 01017044 **Date established:** 1971
No.of Employees: 1 - 10 **Product Groups:** 35, 39, 45

Date of Accounts	Sep 11	Sep 10	Sep 09
Working Capital	86	106	125
Fixed Assets	41	42	44
Current Assets	98	131	138

M-Tech Printers

7 Maidenhills, Middlewich, CW10 9PJ
Tel: 01606-837550 **Fax:** 08721-116386
E-mail: sales@mtechprinters.co.uk
Website: http://www.mtechprinters.co.uk
Directors: G. Millman (Prop)
Date established: 2008 **Turnover:** Up to £250,000
No.of Employees: 1 - 10 **Product Groups:** 44

Northern Corrugated Cases Ltd

Unit 16 Middlewich Road Byley, Middlewich, CW10 9NX
Tel: 01606-836811 **Fax:** 01606-836088
E-mail: sales@northerncorrugatedcases.co.uk
Directors: H. Emery (MD)
Immediate Holding Company: NORTHERN CORRUGATED CASES LIMITED
Registration no: 02157272 **Date established:** 1987 **Turnover:** £2m - £5m
No.of Employees: 51 - 100 **Product Groups:** 27

Date of Accounts	Mar 12	Mar 11	Mar 10
Working Capital	464	448	375
Fixed Assets	2m	2m	2m
Current Assets	1m	1m	1m

Pochin Construction Ltd

Brooks Lane, Middlewich, CW10 0JQ
Tel: 01606-833333 **Fax:** 01606-833331
E-mail: enquiries@pochins.plc.uk
Website: http://www.pochins.plc.uk
Bank(s): National Westminster, Manchester
Directors: J. Moss (Fin), J. Pochin (MD)
Ultimate Holding Company: POCHIN'S PLC
Immediate Holding Company: POCHIN DEVELOPMENTS LIMITED
Registration no: 00740515 **VAT No.:** GB 279 4342 27
Date established: 1962 **Turnover:** £2m - £5m **No.of Employees:** 51 - 100
Product Groups: 51, 52, 84, 85

Date of Accounts	May 11	May 10	May 09
Sales Turnover	2m	1m	7m
Pre Tax Profit/Loss	-34	-390	4m
Working Capital	16m	8m	24m
Fixed Assets	N/A	8m	5m
Current Assets	25m	17m	25m
Current Liabilities	166	264	2m

Resmar Ltd
Unit 27 King Street Trading Estate, Middlewich, CW10 9LF
Tel: 08458-033399 **Fax:** 01606-841954
E-mail: sales@resmar.co.uk
Website: http://www.resmar.co.uk
Directors: R. Marco (MD), R. Barcoe (Grp Chief Exec), B. Barcoe (MD)
Managers: T. Barcoe (Purch Mgr), P. Slid (Personnel)
Immediate Holding Company: RESMAR LIMITED
Registration no: 03742894 **Date established:** 1999 **Turnover:** £2m - £5m
No.of Employees: 1 - 10 **Product Groups:** 40

Date of Accounts	Jun 11	Jun 10	Jun 09
Sales Turnover	N/A	N/A	3m
Pre Tax Profit/Loss	N/A	N/A	103
Working Capital	-386	-398	-98
Fixed Assets	123	122	146
Current Assets	678	799	793
Current Liabilities	229	340	N/A

Spanset Ltd
Telford Way, Middlewich, CW10 0HX
Tel: 01606-737494 **Fax:** 01606-737502
E-mail: customerservices@spanset.co.uk
Website: http://www.spanset.co.uk
Bank(s): National Westminster
Directors: J. Freeley (Fin)
Managers: J. Powell (Personnel), E. Williams (Mktg Serv Mgr), G. Williams (Buyer)
Ultimate Holding Company: SPANSET INTER AG (SWITZERLAND)
Immediate Holding Company: SPANSET LIMITED
Registration no: 00960688 **VAT No.:** GB 160 8518 65
Date established: 1969 **Turnover:** £2m - £5m **No.of Employees:** 51 - 100
Product Groups: 23, 30, 40

Date of Accounts	Dec 11	Dec 10	Dec 09
Sales Turnover	7m	7m	7m
Pre Tax Profit/Loss	137	262	391
Working Capital	1m	1m	1m
Fixed Assets	2m	2m	2m
Current Assets	3m	2m	2m
Current Liabilities	355	360	537

Nantwich

3I Infotech (Western Europe) Ltd
Stapeley Technology Park London Road, Nantwich, CW5 7JW
Tel: 0121-260 3300 **Fax:** 01270-625948
E-mail: marketing.we@3i-infotech.com
Website: http://www.3i-infotech.com
Directors: C. Potts (Ch)
Managers: I. Scull (Mgr), N. Ridgway (Product)
Immediate Holding Company: Misys Group
Registration no: 02760212 **VAT No.:** GB 661 5429 33
Turnover: £75m - £125m **No.of Employees:** 11 - 20 **Product Groups:** 80

Abacus Accountancy
Charles House Beam Heath Way, Nantwich, CW5 6PQ
Tel: 01270-620791 **Fax:** 0207-197 8171
E-mail: enquiries@abacusaccountants.com
Website: http://www.cheshireaccountants.com
Directors: A. Spanton (Dir)
Immediate Holding Company: ABACUS CORPORATE SERVICES LTD
Registration no: 07973265 **Date established:** 2012
No.of Employees: 1 - 10 **Product Groups:** 40

Ableworld
39 Beam Street, Nantwich, CW5 5NF
Tel: 01270-626971 **Fax:** 01270-626971
E-mail: mike@ableworld.co.uk
Website: http://www.ableworld.co.uk
Managers: B. Parker (District Mgr)
Immediate Holding Company: ABLE WORLD UK LTD
Registration no: 04048285 **Date established:** 2000
No.of Employees: 1 - 10 **Product Groups:** 20

Big Dot Media Ltd
Lindum House 44 Wellington Road, Nantwich, CW5 7BX
Tel: 01270-613310
E-mail: steve@bigdotmedia.co.uk
Website: http://www.bigdotmedia.co.uk
Directors: S. Mcgrath (Dir)
Immediate Holding Company: BIG DOT MEDIA LIMITED
Registration no: 06737238 **Date established:** 2008
Turnover: Up to £250,000 **No.of Employees:** 1 - 10 **Product Groups:** 44

Date of Accounts	Dec 11	Dec 10	Dec 09
Working Capital	N/A	-8	3
Fixed Assets	10	8	3
Current Assets	71	37	11

Bridgemere Nursery & Garden World
Bridgemere, Nantwich, CW5 7QB
Tel: 01270-521100 **Fax:** 01270-520215
E-mail: info@bridgemere.co.uk
Website: http://www.bridgemere.co.uk
Directors: A. Jenkinson (Dir)
Ultimate Holding Company: THE GARDEN CENTRE GROUP LIMITED
Immediate Holding Company: BRIDGEMERE NURSERIES TRADING LIMITED
Registration no: 03282244 **Date established:** 1996 **Turnover:** £5m - £10m
No.of Employees: 101 - 250 **Product Groups:** 28, 62, 63, 65

Date of Accounts	Dec 08	Dec 09
Sales Turnover	8m	7m
Pre Tax Profit/Loss	-206	676
Working Capital	-2m	N/A
Fixed Assets	2m	N/A
Current Assets	4m	N/A
Current Liabilities	475	N/A

Label Planet Ltd
Unit 2
Alvaston Business Park
Middlewich Road, Nantwich, CW5 6PF
Tel: 01270-668076 **Fax:** 01270-666233
E-mail: info@labelplanet.co.uk
Website: http://www.labelplanet.co.uk
Directors: D. Worgan (MD), L. Worgan (Fin)
Immediate Holding Company: LABEL PLANET LIMITED
Registration no: 04937718 **Date established:** 2003
No.of Employees: 1 - 10 **Product Groups:** 23, 27, 30, 64

Date of Accounts	Oct 11	Oct 10	Oct 09
Working Capital	80	-2	-10
Fixed Assets	13	14	12
Current Assets	207	81	58

Meadowbank Associates Ltd
42 Welsh Row, Nantwich, CW5 5EJ
Tel: 01270-629090 **Fax:** 01270-624541
E-mail: reception@meadowbankassociates.co.uk
Website: http://www.meadowbankassociates.co.uk
Managers: K. Dennis (District Mgr)
Immediate Holding Company: MEADOWBANK ASSOCIATES LIMITED
Registration no: 07868914 **VAT No.:** GB 406 2005 09
Date established: 2011 **Turnover:** £1m - £2m **No.of Employees:** 1 - 10
Product Groups: 80

Multisol Ltd
Welsh House 83 Welsh Row, Nantwich, CW5 5ET
Tel: 01270-610444 **Fax:** 01270-610555
E-mail: sales@multisolgroup.com
Website: http://www.multisolgroup.com
Bank(s): National Westminster, Liverpool
Directors: M. Rushton (Mkt Research), A. Wilkins (MD), A. Steel (Fin)
Managers: L. Hanson (Personnel), P. Kullak (Tech Serv Mgr)
Ultimate Holding Company: BRENNTAG AG (GERMANY)
Immediate Holding Company: MULTISOL LIMITED
Registration no: 00931537 **VAT No.:** GB 164 0864 62
Date established: 1968 **Turnover:** £50m - £75m
No.of Employees: 11 - 20 **Product Groups:** 31, 66

Date of Accounts	Dec 11	Mar 11	Mar 10
Sales Turnover	56m	68m	51m
Pre Tax Profit/Loss	2m	6m	3m
Working Capital	17m	17m	12m
Fixed Assets	3m	3m	3m
Current Assets	48m	41m	36m
Current Liabilities	929	3m	3m

N W F Group plc
Wardle, Nantwich, CW5 6BP
Tel: 01829-260014 **Fax:** 01829-261042
E-mail: info@nwf.co.uk
Website: http://www.nwf.co.uk
Bank(s): National Westminster Bank Plc
Directors: G. Scott (Grp Chief Exec)
Managers: P. Grundy (Sales Prom Mgr), D. Warrington (Admin Off)
Immediate Holding Company: NWF GROUP PLC
Registration no: 02264971 **VAT No.:** GB 278 8387 88
Date established: 1988 **Turnover:** £250m - £500m
No.of Employees: 1001 - 1500 **Product Groups:** 20, 62

Date of Accounts	May 12	May 11	May 10
Sales Turnover	540m	464m	380m
Pre Tax Profit/Loss	5m	8m	7m
Working Capital	8m	7m	-2m
Fixed Assets	55m	50m	46m
Current Assets	61m	61m	49m
Current Liabilities	6m	10m	17m

Noratel
Unit 7 George House, Nantwich, CW5 6GD
Tel: 01270-611368 **Fax:** 01270-611369
E-mail: info@noratel.co.uk
Website: http://www.noratel.co.uk
Directors: A. Jayasinghe (Co Sec), G. Lynock (MD)
Immediate Holding Company: NORATEL UK LTD
Registration no: 04136659 **VAT No.:** GB 595 9245 83
Date established: 2001 **Turnover:** £1m - £2m **No.of Employees:** 1 - 10
Product Groups: 37

Date of Accounts	Dec 11	Dec 10	Dec 09
Working Capital	1m	1m	733
Fixed Assets	2	13	22
Current Assets	2m	3m	2m
Current Liabilities	N/A	1m	748

Page Training Ltd
Charles House Princes Court Beam Heath Way, Nantwich, CW5 6PQ
Tel: 01270-611123
E-mail: info@pagetraining.com
Website: http://www.pagetraining.com
Directors: P. Edge (MD)
Immediate Holding Company: PAGE TRAINING LIMITED
Registration no: 03042164 **VAT No.:** GB 636 5443 30
Date established: 1995 **No.of Employees:** 1 - 10 **Product Groups:** 86

Date of Accounts	Mar 11	Mar 10	Mar 09
Working Capital	-15	-9	-21
Fixed Assets	5	13	17
Current Assets	15	26	29

Rowlinson Packaging Ltd
Unit 1 Green Lane Wardle, Nantwich, CW5 6BN
Tel: 01829-260571 **Fax:** 01829-260718
E-mail: packaging@rowlinson.co.uk
Website: http://www.rowlinsonpackaging.co.uk
Bank(s): Royal Bank of Scotland
Directors: J. Carter (Chief Op Offcr), J. Williams (MD), R. Bundock (Sales), W. Kiernan (Co Sec)
Ultimate Holding Company: ROWLINSON GROUP HOLDINGS LIMITED
Immediate Holding Company: ROWLINSON PACKAGING LIMITED
Registration no: 01176301 **Date established:** 1974
Turnover: £10m - £20m **No.of Employees:** 101 - 250
Product Groups: 22, 25, 35, 45

Date of Accounts	Apr 11	Apr 10	Apr 09
Sales Turnover	10m	8m	9m
Pre Tax Profit/Loss	323	221	466
Working Capital	8m	8m	8m
Fixed Assets	2m	2m	2m
Current Assets	11m	11m	10m
Current Liabilities	1m	1m	1m

B Shirley Fabrications
Unit 6b Cockshades Farm Stock Lane, Wybunbury, Nantwich, CW5 7HA
Tel: 01270-842023 **Fax:** 01270-842023
Directors: N. Shirley (Ptnr)
Date established: 1981 **No.of Employees:** 1 - 10 **Product Groups:** 26, 35

Stapeley Water Gardens Ltd
92 London Road Stapeley, Nantwich, CW5 7LH
Tel: 01270-611500 **Fax:** 01270-610616
E-mail: info@stapeleywg.com
Website: http://www.stapeleywg.com
Bank(s): H S B C
Directors: J. Lowe (Co Sec), K. Stretch (Fin)
Immediate Holding Company: STAPELEY WATER GARDENS LIMITED
Registration no: 01158800 **Date established:** 1974 **Turnover:** £2m - £5m
No.of Employees: 101 - 250 **Product Groups:** 02, 09, 24, 25, 26, 27, 32, 42, 62, 63

Date of Accounts	Dec 08	Dec 09	Jan 11
Pre Tax Profit/Loss	375	N/A	N/A
Working Capital	1m	1m	907
Fixed Assets	1m	1m	1m
Current Assets	2m	2m	2m
Current Liabilities	189	N/A	N/A

Bill Steele Workshop Supplies
Swanley Lane Burland, Nantwich, CW5 8QB
Tel: 01270-524278 **Fax:** 01270-524278
E-mail: ben@ben104.wanadoo.co.uk
Directors: J. Latham (Ptnr)
Date established: 1982 **No.of Employees:** 1 - 10 **Product Groups:** 35

Northwich

A & D Supplies
96 West Avenue Rudheath, Northwich, CW9 7ET
Tel: 01606-41752
Directors: J. Moores (Prop)
Date established: 1988 **No.of Employees:** 1 - 10 **Product Groups:** 36, 39, 40

A T C Semitec Ltd
Unit 14 Cosgrove Business Park Daisy Bank Lane, Anderton, Northwich, CW9 6FY
Tel: 01606-871680 **Fax:** 08709-010888
E-mail: sales@atcsemitec.co.uk
Website: http://www.atcsemitec.co.uk
Directors: M. Suzuki (Sales)
Immediate Holding Company: A.T.C. SEMITEC LIMITED
Registration no: 03369982 **Date established:** 1997
Turnover: £500,000 - £1m **No.of Employees:** 1 - 10 **Product Groups:** 37, 38

Date of Accounts	May 11	May 10	May 09
Working Capital	128	81	61
Fixed Assets	208	216	206
Current Assets	474	442	225

Artistic Fabrications
8 Frida Crescent, Northwich, CW8 1DJ
Tel: 01606-74988
Directors: A. Williamson (Prop)
No.of Employees: 1 - 10 **Product Groups:** 26, 35

Bartington Forge Ltd
Warrington Road Bartington, Northwich, CW8 4QU
Tel; 01606-851553 **Fax:** 01606-851553
E-mail: peter.bartington-forge@virgin.net
Website: http://www.bartingtonforgeblacksmith.co.uk
Directors: P. Wilson (Dir)
Immediate Holding Company: BARTINGTON FORGE LIMITED
Registration no: 04567797 **Date established:** 2002
Turnover: Up to £250,000 **No.of Employees:** 1 - 10 **Product Groups:** 26, 35

Date of Accounts	Dec 11	Dec 09	Dec 08
Sales Turnover	33	38	46
Pre Tax Profit/Loss	N/A	2	5
Working Capital	-6	-16	-17
Fixed Assets	6	13	13
Current Assets	3	2	5
Current Liabilities	N/A	1	2

Careervision Ltd
Unit 3-4 Brickfield Business Centre 60 Manchester Road, Northwich, CW9 7LS
Tel: 01606-812800 **Fax:** 01606-836977
E-mail: sales@careervision.co.uk
Website: http://www.careervision.co.uk
Bank(s): Lloyds TSB Bank plc
Directors: J. Stevens (MD), R. Norrish (Dir)
Managers: C. Fox (Develop Mgr), A. Murphy (Fin Mgr), T. Kerr (Admin Off)
Ultimate Holding Company: CAREERVISION HOLDINGS LIMITED
Immediate Holding Company: CAREERVISION LIMITED
Registration no: 01152473 **VAT No.:** GB 173 6279 42
Date established: 1973 **Turnover:** £500,000 - £1m
No.of Employees: 21 - 50 **Product Groups:** 44, 79

Date of Accounts	Mar 12	Mar 11	Mar 10
Working Capital	235	175	123
Fixed Assets	167	204	176
Current Assets	1m	657	728

Delamere Blinds & Curtains
13 Chapel Lane Acton Bridge, Northwich, CW8 3QS
Tel: 01606-854061 **Fax:** 01606-854054
E-mail: info@delamereblindsandcurtains.co.uk
Website: http://www.delamereblindsandcurtains.co.uk
Directors: K. Hand (Prop)
No.of Employees: 1 - 10 **Product Groups:** 23, 24, 63, 66

Forelink Limited
PO Box 484, Northwich, CW9 7XN
Tel: 01606-44863
E-mail: david@forelink.co.uk
Website: http://www.forelink.co.uk
Directors: D. Latter (MD)
Registration no: 3506916 **Date established:** 1998 **Turnover:**
No.of Employees: 1 - 10 **Product Groups:** 46, 86

Greensplash Ltd
308 Chester Road Hartford, Northwich, CW8 2AB
Tel: 01606-884123 **Fax:** 01606-884212
E-mail: support@greensplash.com
Website: http://www.greensplash.com
Directors: K. Spruce (Fin), A. Dunn (MD)
Immediate Holding Company: GREENSPLASH LIMITED
Registration no: 04169857 **Date established:** 2001
Turnover: £250,000 - £500,000 **No.of Employees:** 1 - 10
Product Groups: 44, 81

Date of Accounts	Mar 11	Mar 10	Mar 09
Working Capital	410	362	277
Fixed Assets	44	45	53
Current Assets	903	731	401

H & M Disinfection Systems
18 Dalby Court Gadbrook Business Centre, Rudheath, Northwich, CW9 7TN
Tel: 01606-49845 **Fax:** 01606- 330231
E-mail: sales@hm-dis.com
Website: http://www.hm-dis.com
Directors: A. Hall (Co Sec)
Immediate Holding Company: H & M DISINFECTION SYSTEMS LIMITED
Registration no: 02479852 **Date established:** 1990
No.of Employees: 1 - 10 **Product Groups:** 20, 40, 41

Date of Accounts	Mar 12	Mar 11	Mar 10
Working Capital	-55	-26	10
Fixed Assets	113	102	36
Current Assets	114	129	95

HartfordPharma
4 Kingsley Close Hartford, Northwich, CW8 1SD
Tel: 01606-79230 **Fax:** 07092- 150518
E-mail: admin@hartfordpharma.com
Website: http://www.hartfordpharma.com
Directors: T. Breeze (Prop)
No.of Employees: 1 - 10 **Product Groups:** 40, 64, 84, 86

Holidaybreak plc
Hartford Manor Greenbank Lane, Northwich, CW8 1HW
Tel: 01606-787000 **Fax:** 01606-787001
E-mail: group@holidaybreak.co.uk
Website: http://www.holidaybreak.co.uk
Directors: C. Michel (Grp Chief Exec), R. Baddeley (Fin), S. Whitfield (MD), A. Williamson (Co Sec), R. Start (Sales)
Managers: S. Howell (I.T. Exec), N. Hilton (Mktg Serv Mgr)
Immediate Holding Company: HOLIDAYBREAK PLC.
Registration no: 02305562 **Date established:** 1988
Turnover: £250m - £500m **No.of Employees:** 251 - 500
Product Groups: 69

Date of Accounts	Sep 08	Sep 07	Sep 06
Sales Turnover	455100	357900	304500
Pre Tax Profit/Loss	23400	37500	32100
Working Capital	-57400	-222000	-55000
Fixed Assets	351200	343500	126400
Current Assets	85000	97300	78100
Current Liabilities	142400	319300	133100
Total Share Capital	2400	2400	2400
ROCE% (Return on Capital Employed)	8.0	30.9	45.0
ROT% (Return on Turnover)	5.1	10.5	10.5

Incamesh Filtration Ltd
Moss Farm Occupation Lane, Antrobus, Northwich, CW9 6JS
Tel: 01565-777681 **Fax:** 01565-777 682
E-mail: sales@incamesh.co.uk
Website: http://www.incamesh.co.uk
Directors: J. Livings (MD)
Immediate Holding Company: INCAMESH FILTRATION LIMITED
Registration no: 01353975 **Date established:** 1978
Turnover: £250,000 - £500,000 **No.of Employees:** 1 - 10
Product Groups: 35, 42, 45

Date of Accounts	Apr 12	Apr 11	Apr 10
Working Capital	21	17	9
Fixed Assets	48	56	25
Current Assets	155	148	128

J E B Precision Ltd
Works Lane Lostock Gralam, Northwich, CW9 7NW
Tel: 01606-354354 **Fax:** 01606-354355
E-mail: sales@jebprecision.co.uk
Website: http://www.jebprecision.co.uk
Bank(s): Lloyds TSB Bank plc
Directors: J. Bebbington (MD), J. Bebbington (Fin)
Managers: M. Bebbington (Ops Mgr), S. Bebbington (Eng Serv Mgr)
Immediate Holding Company: J.E.B. PRECISION LIMITED
Registration no: 01142601 **VAT No.:** GB 162 5171 80
Date established: 1973 **Turnover:** £1m - £2m **No.of Employees:** 21 - 50
Product Groups: 35, 36, 40, 48, 67, 85

Date of Accounts	Dec 10	Dec 09	Dec 08
Working Capital	76	-132	-95
Fixed Assets	932	810	801
Current Assets	420	249	315

K B C Process Technology Ltd
Unit 4 Cheshire Avenue Lostock Gralam, Northwich, CW9 7UA
Tel: 01606-815100 **Fax:** 01606-815151
E-mail: info@linnhoffmarch.com
Website: http://www.kbcat.com
Directors: A. Rudman (Dir), J. Ireland (Co Sec)
Ultimate Holding Company: KBC ADVANCED TECHNOLOGIES PLC
Immediate Holding Company: KBC PROCESS TECHNOLOGY LIMITED
Registration no: 01807381 **VAT No.:** GB 403 3188 85
Date established: 1984 **Turnover:** £2m - £5m **No.of Employees:** 11 - 20
Product Groups: 44, 84

Date of Accounts	Dec 11	Dec 10	Dec 09
Sales Turnover	26m	21m	25m
Pre Tax Profit/Loss	363	-2m	-17
Working Capital	6m	8m	9m
Fixed Assets	4m	4m	4m
Current Assets	15m	16m	16m
Current Liabilities	3m	2m	3m

David Lever Ltd
9 The Coppice Cuddington, Northwich, CW8 2XF
Tel: 01606-882620
E-mail: info@david-lever.co.uk
Website: http://www.david-lever.co.uk
Directors: D. Lever (Dir), J. Lever (Co Sec)
Immediate Holding Company: DAVID LEVER LIMITED
Registration no: 04419638 **Date established:** 2002
Turnover: Up to £250,000 **No.of Employees:** 1 - 10 **Product Groups:** 80

Date of Accounts	Apr 08	Apr 07	Apr 06
Working Capital	33	55	38
Current Assets	34	61	39
Current Liabilities	1	5	N/A
Total Share Capital	1	1	1

Marvel Signs
Unit 1B Desley Heath Farm Cogshall Lane, Northwich, Northwich, CW9 6BN
Tel: 01606-891096 **Fax:** 01606-597174
E-mail: sales@marvelsigns.co.uk
Website: http://www.marvelsigns.co.uk
No.of Employees: 1 - 10 **Product Groups:** 28, 37, 49, 81

North Western Materials Handling Ltd
Chapel Street Wincham, Northwich, CW9 6DA
Tel: 01606-42999 **Fax:** 01606-43322
E-mail: rob@theforkliftpeople.co.uk
Website: http://www.theforkliftpeople.co.uk
Directors: R. Kennerley (Sales)
Immediate Holding Company: NORTH WESTERN MATERIALS HANDLING LIMITED
Registration no: 04539666 **Date established:** 2002
No.of Employees: 11 - 20 **Product Groups:** 35, 39, 45

Date of Accounts	Sep 11	Sep 10	Sep 09
Working Capital	-68	-54	-71
Fixed Assets	117	112	77
Current Assets	111	127	143

Norton Bowers Ltd
Challener House 19 Mere Bank, Davenham, Northwich, CW9 8NB
Tel: 01606-352747 **Fax:** 01605-351050
E-mail: enquiries@nortonbowers.com
Website: http://www.nortonbowers.co.uk
Directors: J. Norton (MD)
Turnover: Up to £250,000 **No.of Employees:** 1 - 10 **Product Groups:** 80

Planned Packaging Films Ltd
School Lane Sandiway, Northwich, CW8 2NH
Tel: 01606-782960 **Fax:** 01606-888223
E-mail: sales@pp-films.com
Website: http://www.pp-films.com
Directors: M. Cooper (Dir)
Immediate Holding Company: PLANNED PACKAGING FILMS LIMITED
Registration no: 05206848 **Date established:** 2004
No.of Employees: 1 - 10 **Product Groups:** 38, 42

Date of Accounts	Dec 11	Dec 10	Dec 09
Working Capital	161	114	87
Fixed Assets	10	8	5
Current Assets	373	306	284

Ratter Agricultural
Hulse House Farm Hulse Lane, Lach Dennis, Northwich, CW9 7TF
Tel: 01565-722806
E-mail: enquiries@horseboxhospital.co.uk
Website: http://www.horseboxhospital.co.uk
Directors: C. Ratter (Prop)
No.of Employees: 1 - 10 **Product Groups:** 41

Sud-Chemie UK Ltd
Drake Mews 3 Gadbrook Park Rudheath, Northwich, CW9 7XF
Tel: 01606-813060 **Fax:** 01606-813061
E-mail: info.uk@sud-chemie.com
Website: http://www.sud-chemie.com
Directors: M. Born (MD)
Ultimate Holding Company: SUD CHEMIE AG (GERMANY)
Immediate Holding Company: SUD-CHEMIE (UK) LIMITED
Registration no: 00841902 **VAT No.:** GB 146 5760 51
Date established: 1965 **Turnover:** £2m - £5m **No.of Employees:** 1 - 10
Product Groups: 66

Date of Accounts	Dec 11	Dec 10	Dec 09
Sales Turnover	4m	8m	7m
Pre Tax Profit/Loss	209	246	270
Working Capital	1m	986	816
Fixed Assets	6	12	4
Current Assets	1m	2m	2m
Current Liabilities	135	185	199

Texkimp Ltd
Swan House New Cheshire Business Park Wincham Lane, Wincham, Northwich, CW9 6GG
Tel: 01606-338748 **Fax:** 01606-40366
E-mail: info@texkimp.co.uk
Website: http://www.texkimp.co.uk
Bank(s): Royal Bank of Scotland, Wilmslow
Directors: M. Kimpton Smith (MD), P. Banham (Sales)
Managers: C. Cliffe (Tech Serv Mgr)
Ultimate Holding Company: CYGNET GROUP LIMITED
Immediate Holding Company: TEXKIMP LIMITED
Registration no: 04115619 **VAT No.:** GB 162 7081 71
Date established: 2000 **Turnover:** £10m - £20m
No.of Employees: 21 - 50 **Product Groups:** 38, 43

Date of Accounts	Nov 11	Nov 10	Nov 09
Sales Turnover	11m	6m	7m
Pre Tax Profit/Loss	1m	915	-786
Working Capital	527	-79	85
Fixed Assets	112	114	175
Current Assets	6m	3m	5m
Current Liabilities	2m	2m	3m

UK Container Maintenance Ltd
Unit 6 Avenue Engineering Park Winnington Avenue, Northwich, CW8 4FT
Tel: 01606-723020 **Fax:** 01606-872478
E-mail: refurbs@ukcm-ltd.co.uk
Website: http://www.ukcontainers.co.uk
Directors: G. Morrison (Chief Op Offcr), J. Elston (MD), e. Elston (MD), L. Wolstenholme (Fin)
Immediate Holding Company: UK CONTAINER MAINTENANCE LIMITED
Registration no: 03617405 **Date established:** 1998
No.of Employees: 51 - 100 **Product Groups:** 39, 42, 45, 48, 54, 66, 67

Date of Accounts	Aug 11	Aug 10	Aug 09
Working Capital	259	156	63
Fixed Assets	417	334	270
Current Assets	3m	2m	2m
Current Liabilities	N/A	N/A	703

Weir Engineering Services
Winnington Avenue, Northwich, CW8 4FT
Tel: 01606-782255 **Fax:** 01606- 871631
E-mail: sales@upl.weir.co.uk
Website: http://www.weir.co.uk
Managers: A. Meiklejohn (Mgr), M. Rose (), M. Rose
Ultimate Holding Company: CLYDE BLOWERS CAPITAL FUND II LP (SCOTLAND)
Immediate Holding Company: CLYDE UNION LIMITED
Registration no: SC317760 **Date established:** 2007
No.of Employees: 21 - 50 **Product Groups:** 40

Date of Accounts	Dec 10	Dec 09	Dec 08
Sales Turnover	123m	107m	84m
Pre Tax Profit/Loss	8m	3m	-9m
Working Capital	18m	3m	-463
Fixed Assets	49m	41m	39m
Current Assets	97m	54m	40m
Current Liabilities	31m	31m	29m

Runcorn

A A K Ltd
Davy Road Astmoor Industrial Estate, Runcorn, WA7 1PZ
Tel: 01928-565221 **Fax:** 01928-561172
E-mail: jon.devine@aak.com
Website: http://www.aak.com
Bank(s): National Westminster Bank Plc
Managers: J. Devine (Ops Mgr)
Ultimate Holding Company: CHINNEY HOLDINGS LTD (HONG KONG)
Immediate Holding Company: AAK LIMITED
Registration no: 02588842 **VAT No.:** GB 294 8982 84
Date established: 1991 **Turnover:** £1m - £2m
No.of Employees: 101 - 250 **Product Groups:** 20

Date of Accounts	Jun 11	Jun 10	Jun 09
Sales Turnover	8m	N/A	N/A
Pre Tax Profit/Loss	467	N/A	N/A
Working Capital	576	410	216
Fixed Assets	2m	2m	1m
Current Assets	2m	2m	2m
Current Liabilities	267	N/A	N/A

AD Aerospace Ltd (Flight Vu)
Unit 5 Monks Way, Preston Brook, Runcorn, WA7 3GH
Tel: 08704-424520 **Fax:** 0870-442 4524
E-mail: rdavies@ad-aero.com
Website: http://www.ad-aero.com
Managers: R. Davies (Mktg Serv Mgr)
Ultimate Holding Company: ANGLO DESIGN HOLDINGS PLC
Immediate Holding Company: AD AEROSPACE LIMITED
Registration no: 03034197 **Date established:** 1995
No.of Employees: 11 - 20 **Product Groups:** 37, 38, 39, 40, 67, 68

Date of Accounts	Jun 11	Jun 10	Jun 09
Sales Turnover	4m	2m	1m
Pre Tax Profit/Loss	561	143	-309
Working Capital	-4m	-5m	-5m
Fixed Assets	23	24	25
Current Assets	1m	1m	1m
Current Liabilities	89	49	59

AEL Heating Solutions Ltd
4 Berkely Court Manor Park, Runcorn, WA7 1TQ
Tel: 01928-579068 **Fax:** 01928-579523
E-mail: healey@aelheating.com
Website: http://www.aelheating.com
Registration no: 01371188 **Product Groups:** 36, 40, 66

Alias Ltd
1 Stuart Road Manor Park, Runcorn, WA7 1TS
Tel: 01928-579311 **Fax:** 01928-579389
E-mail: info@alias.ltd.uk
Website: http://www.alias.ltd.uk
Directors: D. Lott (Fin)
Managers: K. Hey (Sales Admin)
Ultimate Holding Company: HEXAGON AB (SWEDEN)
Immediate Holding Company: ALIAS LIMITED
Registration no: 02569236 **Date established:** 1990 **Turnover:** £2m - £5m
No.of Employees: 11 - 20 **Product Groups:** 44, 84

Date of Accounts	Dec 11	Dec 10	Dec 09
Sales Turnover	4m	5m	N/A
Pre Tax Profit/Loss	3m	4m	N/A
Working Capital	8m	7m	4m
Fixed Assets	690	702	720
Current Assets	9m	7m	5m
Current Liabilities	535	610	N/A

Alma Products Ltd
Unit 2 Lancer Court Astmoor Industrial Estate, Runcorn, WA7 1PN
Tel: 01928-580595 **Fax:** 01928-581022
E-mail: sales@almaproducts.co.uk
Website: http://www.almaproducts.co.uk
Bank(s): Royal Bank of Scotland
Directors: S. Dick (MD), S. Dick (MD), D. Blundell (Fin)
Managers: O. Blang (Admin Off), N. Bennett
Ultimate Holding Company: PLASTICOS HOLDINGS AG (SWITZERLAND)
Immediate Holding Company: ALMA PRODUCTS LIMITED
Registration no: 01665868 **VAT No.:** GB 372 1059 71
Date established: 1982 **Turnover:** £10m - £20m
No.of Employees: 51 - 100 **Product Groups:** 30

Date of Accounts	Dec 11	Dec 10	Dec 09
Sales Turnover	19m	15m	13m
Pre Tax Profit/Loss	-3m	-89	591
Working Capital	-1m	2m	2m
Fixed Assets	3m	4m	4m
Current Assets	4m	6m	6m
Current Liabilities	274	772	471

Arven Industrial Chemicals Ltd
12 Goddard Road Astmoor Industrial Estate, Runcorn, WA7 1QF
Tel: 01928-576262 **Fax:** 01928-575383
E-mail: info@arven.co.uk
Website: http://www.arven.co.uk
Directors: B. Jones (Co Sec), D. Naylor (MD)
Immediate Holding Company: ARVEN INDUSTRIAL CHEMICALS LIMITED
Registration no: 01606370 **Date established:** 1982
No.of Employees: 1 - 10 **Product Groups:** 32

Date of Accounts	Mar 11	Mar 10	Mar 09
Working Capital	-28	-35	-35
Fixed Assets	156	164	172
Current Assets	208	231	221

AutoCoding Systems Ltd
Cedar House Sutton Quays Business Park Clifton Road Sutton Weaver, Runcorn, WA7 3EH
Tel: 01928-790444
E-mail: janetharrison@autocodingsystems.com
Website: http://www.autocodingsystems.com
Ultimate Holding Company: BELROUTE CVA (BELGIUM)
Immediate Holding Company: AUTOCODING SYSTEMS LIMITED
Registration no: 05543560 **Date established:** 2005
No.of Employees: 11 - 20 **Product Groups:** 37

see next page

AutoCoding Systems Ltd - Cont'd

Date of Accounts	Dec 11	Dec 10	Dec 09
Working Capital	340	67	88
Fixed Assets	38	28	38
Current Assets	773	443	349

Axle Weight Technology Ltd

Picow Farm Road, Runcorn, WA7 4UN
Tel: 01928-581575 **Fax:** 01928-581574
E-mail: salesadmin@axtec.co.uk
Website: http://www.axtec.co.uk
Bank(s): National Westminster Bank Plc
Directors: K. Gresham (MD), P. Lash (Dir)
Managers: D. Hack (Mktg Serv Mgr)
Immediate Holding Company: AXLE WEIGHT TECHNOLOGY LIMITED
Registration no: 02571168 **Date established:** 1991 **Turnover:** £1m - £2m
No.of Employees: 21 - 50 **Product Groups:** 38

Date of Accounts	Dec 11	Dec 10	Dec 09
Working Capital	202	207	180
Fixed Assets	465	477	528
Current Assets	787	611	656

B I S Industrial Services Ltd

Axis House Tudor Road Manor Park, Manor Park, Runcorn, WA7 1BD
Tel: 01928-530000 **Fax:** 01928-571800
E-mail: enquiries@bis-is.co.uk
Website: http://www.bis-is.co.uk
Bank(s): Midland
Directors: P. Ashcroft (Fin), D. Hall (MD)
Managers: D. Redmond (Personnel), T. Purcell (Tech Serv Mgr), J. Price (Purch Mgr), D. Wilson (Mktg Serv Mgr)
Ultimate Holding Company: BILFINGER BERGER AG (GERMANY)
Immediate Holding Company: BIS INDUSTRIAL SERVICES LIMITED
Registration no: 05384376 **Date established:** 2005
Turnover: £75m - £125m **No.of Employees:** 51 - 100 **Product Groups:** 84

Date of Accounts	Dec 11	Dec 10	Dec 09
Sales Turnover	122m	103m	37m
Pre Tax Profit/Loss	6m	5m	2m
Working Capital	10m	6m	4m
Fixed Assets	7m	7m	2m
Current Assets	31m	31m	12m
Current Liabilities	9m	10m	3m

Banner Chemicals Ltd

Hampton Court Manor Park, Runcorn, WA7 1TU
Tel: 01928-597000 **Fax:** 01928-597001
E-mail: reception@bannerchemicals.com
Website: http://www.bannerchemicals.com
Bank(s): The Royal Bank of Scotland
Directors: C. Boyle (Fin), C. Hall (Sales)
Managers: J. Cason (Tech Serv Mgr), M. Johnson
Ultimate Holding Company: 2M GROUP LIMITED
Immediate Holding Company: BANNER CHEMICALS LIMITED
Registration no: 00072727 **VAT No.:** GB 387 2243 36
Date established: 2002 **Turnover:** £1m - £2m **No.of Employees:** 21 - 50
Product Groups: 31, 32, 48, 66, 76

Date of Accounts	Apr 12	Apr 11	Apr 10
Sales Turnover	944	1m	807
Pre Tax Profit/Loss	45	49	38
Working Capital	-8m	-8m	-8m
Fixed Assets	18m	18m	18m
Current Assets	3m	3m	3m
Current Liabilities	209	321	223

Betabite Hydraulics Ltd

Stuart Road Manor Park, Runcorn, WA7 1TS
Tel: 01928-594500 **Fax:** 01928-579818
E-mail: sales@betabite.co.uk
Website: http://www.betabite.co.uk
Bank(s): National Westminster Bank Plc
Directors: E. Drury (Fin), M. Dobson (Dir)
Immediate Holding Company: BETABITE HYDRAULICS LIMITED
Registration no: 02877457 **VAT No.:** GB 625 2266 54
Date established: 1993 **Turnover:** £1m - £2m **No.of Employees:** 21 - 50
Product Groups: 35, 36, 39, 40, 48

Date of Accounts	Apr 11	Apr 10	Apr 09
Sales Turnover	1m	1m	2m
Pre Tax Profit/Loss	25	6	21
Working Capital	362	328	294
Fixed Assets	147	159	193
Current Assets	678	667	611
Current Liabilities	84	63	48

Brooks Composites Ltd

Percival Lane, Runcorn, WA7 4DS
Tel: 01928-574776 **Fax:** 01928-577067
E-mail: sales@brooks-composites.co.uk
Website: http://www.brooks-composites.co.uk
Directors: D. Brooks (MD)
Managers: A. Parker (Sales Admin)
Immediate Holding Company: BROOKS COMPOSITES LIMITED
Registration no: 02340875 **VAT No.:** GB 534 7905 28
Date established: 1989 **Turnover:** £500,000 - £1m
No.of Employees: 11 - 20 **Product Groups:** 30, 35, 39, 40, 41, 42, 44, 46, 48, 52, 85

Date of Accounts	Mar 12	Mar 11	Mar 10
Working Capital	200	134	197
Fixed Assets	37	20	13
Current Assets	365	242	322

buytshirtsonline Ltd

1 Berkeley Court Manor Park, Runcorn, WA7 1TQ
Tel: 01928-579951
E-mail: sales@buytshirtsonline.co.uk
Website: http://www.buytshirtsonline.co.uk
Directors: G. Firth (MD)
Immediate Holding Company: BUYTSHIRTSONLINE LTD
Registration no: 06796044 **Date established:** 2009
Turnover: Up to £250,000 **No.of Employees:** 1 - 10 **Product Groups:** 24, 63, 65

Date of Accounts	Mar 11	Mar 10
Working Capital	4	-7
Fixed Assets	13	9
Current Assets	99	48

Cablofil

Unit 9 Ashville Way Sutton Weaver, Runcorn, WA7 3EZ
Tel: 01928-754380 **Fax:** 08451-304629
E-mail: salesuk@cablofil.com
Website: http://www.cablofil.co.uk
Directors: P. Courson (MD), M. Williams (Comm)
Managers: D. Eden (Buyer), G. Wilkinson (Comptroller)
Ultimate Holding Company: LEGRAND SA (FRANCE)
Immediate Holding Company: CABLOFIL UK LIMITED
Registration no: 04233437 **Date established:** 2001 **Turnover:** £5m - £10m
No.of Employees: 21 - 50 **Product Groups:** 34, 35, 36, 37, 39, 45, 51, 66

Date of Accounts	Dec 10	Dec 09	Dec 08
Sales Turnover	7m	8m	10m
Pre Tax Profit/Loss	557	50	599
Working Capital	949	549	510
Fixed Assets	5	12	22
Current Assets	3m	3m	3m
Current Liabilities	609	444	747

Capital Safety Group Ltd

7 Christleton Court Manor Park, Runcorn, WA7 1ST
Tel: 01928-571324 **Fax:** 01928-571325
E-mail: csgne@csgne.co.uk
Website: http://www.capitalsafety.com
Directors: P. Trinder (MD), M. Ali (Fin), G. Jones (Dir), D. Eaton (Dir)
Managers: M. Baldwin (Sales Prom Mgr), M. Baldwin (Mgr), Warmen (Chief Mgr), D. Biddelph (I.T. Exec)
Ultimate Holding Company: REDWING HOLDINGS SA (LUXEMBOURG)
Immediate Holding Company: CAPITAL SAFETY GROUP (NORTHERN EUROPE) LIMITED
Registration no: 01918922 **Date established:** 1985 **Turnover:** £5m - £10m
No.of Employees: 21 - 50 **Product Groups:** 40

Date of Accounts	Mar 08
Pre Tax Profit/Loss	28590
Working Capital	-10790
Fixed Assets	82200
Current Liabilities	10790
Total Share Capital	1000
ROCE% (Return on Capital Employed)	40.0

Chance & Hunt Ltd

Alexander House Crown Gate, Runcorn, WA7 2UP
Tel: 01928-793000 **Fax:** 01928-714351
E-mail: dave@chance-hunt.com
Website: http://www.chance-hunt.com
Bank(s): Bank of Scotland
Directors: D. Mccabe (Co Sec), J. Traynor (Dir), P. Fields (Grp Chief Exec)
Managers: M. Przeworski (Develop Mgr)
Immediate Holding Company: AZELIS UK LIMITED
Registration no: 03585216 **Date established:** 1998
Turnover: £50m - £75m **No.of Employees:** 51 - 100 **Product Groups:** 17, 31

Cheshire Wipes

65 Percival Lane, Runcorn, WA7 4UY
Tel: 01928-577140 **Fax:** 01928-770285
E-mail: ukman12@hotmail.com
Directors: R. Roscoe (Prop)
Turnover: Up to £250,000 **No.of Employees:** 1 - 10 **Product Groups:** 23

Clayton Thermal Products Ltd (a division of Clayton Industries)

5 Boleyn Court Manor Park, Runcorn, WA7 1SR
Tel: 01928-579009 **Fax:** 01928-571155
E-mail: gerry.rooney@claytonindustries.co.uk
Website: http://www.claytonindustries.co.uk
Managers: G. Rooney (Mgr)
Ultimate Holding Company: CLAYTON INDUSTRIES INC (USA)
Immediate Holding Company: CLAYTON THERMAL PRODUCTS LIMITED
Registration no: 01379916 **VAT No.:** GB 294 9514 **Date established:** 1978
Turnover: £1m - £2m **No.of Employees:** 1 - 10 **Product Groups:** 38, 39, 40, 66, 67, 83

Date of Accounts	Sep 11	Sep 10	Sep 09
Sales Turnover	1m	N/A	N/A
Pre Tax Profit/Loss	45	N/A	N/A
Working Capital	366	330	372
Fixed Assets	12	13	16
Current Assets	850	1m	780
Current Liabilities	164	N/A	N/A

Duni Ltd

Chester Road Preston Brook, Runcorn, WA7 3FR
Tel: 01928-712377 **Fax:** 01928-754580
E-mail: info@duni.com
Website: http://www.duni.com
Bank(s): Barclays
Directors: P. Fabian (MD), J. Beardmore (Fin)
Managers: D. Kennells (Personnel)
Ultimate Holding Company: DUNI AB (SWEDEN)
Immediate Holding Company: DUNI LIMITED
Registration no: 00897172 **VAT No.:** GB 157 1432 75
Date established: 1967 **Turnover:** £20m - £50m
No.of Employees: 11 - 20 **Product Groups:** 27, 30

Date of Accounts	Dec 11	Dec 10	Dec 09
Sales Turnover	27m	24m	19m
Pre Tax Profit/Loss	1m	859	424
Working Capital	3m	3m	2m
Fixed Assets	105	125	150
Current Assets	9m	8m	7m
Current Liabilities	3m	3m	2m

eantics Ltd

8 Lockwood View Preston Brook, Runcorn, WA7 3NB
Tel: 0845-226 2687 **Fax:** 0845-280 5440
E-mail: info@eantics.co.uk
Website: http://www.eantics.co.uk
Directors: M. Phillips (MD)
Immediate Holding Company: EANTICS LTD
Registration no: 04408161 **Date established:** 2002
Turnover: Up to £250,000 **No.of Employees:** 1 - 10 **Product Groups:** 44

Date of Accounts	Mar 11	Mar 09	Mar 08
Working Capital	14	7	-2
Fixed Assets	3	4	4
Current Assets	30	13	16

Elephante Service & Maintenance Ltd

2 Goddard Road Astmoor Industrial Estate, Runcorn, WA7 1QF
Tel: 01928-500005 **Fax:** 01928-500006
E-mail: sales@elephante-lifts.com
Website: http://www.elephante-lifts.com
Bank(s): HSBC, Prescot Merseyside
Directors: S. Bate (Sales)
Managers: D. Bate (Buyer), N. Williamson (Chief Acct)
Immediate Holding Company: ELEPHANTE SERVICE & MAINTENANCE LTD
Registration no: 05422916 **VAT No.:** GB 595 7722 85
Date established: 2005 **Turnover:** £1m - £2m **No.of Employees:** 11 - 20
Product Groups: 39, 45

Date of Accounts	Aug 11	Aug 10	Aug 09
Sales Turnover	N/A	2m	2m
Pre Tax Profit/Loss	N/A	69	107
Working Capital	-195	42	-41
Fixed Assets	3	95	95
Current Assets	312	402	319
Current Liabilities	N/A	360	233

Ellis Williams Architects Ltd

Wellfield Chester Road, Preston Brook, Runcorn, WA7 3BA
Tel: 01928-752200 **Fax:** 01928-795953
E-mail: mailbox@ewa.co.uk
Website: http://www.ewa.co.uk
Bank(s): National Westminster Bank Plc
Directors: J. Buxton (MD), A. Cain (Fin)
Managers: S. Hind, L. Sheridan
Immediate Holding Company: ELLIS WILLIAMS ARCHITECTS LIMITED
Registration no: 03818904 **VAT No.:** GB 151 7850 63
Date established: 1999 **Turnover:** £5m - £10m **No.of Employees:** 21 - 50
Product Groups: 84

Date of Accounts	Jul 11	Jul 10	Jul 09
Sales Turnover	N/A	7m	8m
Pre Tax Profit/Loss	N/A	327	310
Working Capital	1m	2m	2m
Fixed Assets	946	931	986
Current Assets	2m	3m	3m
Current Liabilities	N/A	889	946

Essential Deliveries Ltd

12 Seymour Court, Runcorn, WA7 1SY
Tel: 08452-267675 **Fax:** 0871-221 5400
E-mail: info@essentialdeliveries.co.uk
Website: http://www.essentialdeliveries.co.uk
Directors: P. Blakeley (MD), J. Blakeley (Co Sec)
Immediate Holding Company: ESSENTIAL DELIVERIES LIMITED
Registration no: 05615132 **Date established:** 2005
Turnover: Up to £250,000 **No.of Employees:** 1 - 10 **Product Groups:** 79

Date of Accounts	Nov 11	Nov 10	Nov 09
Working Capital	-12	-6	-13
Fixed Assets	12	6	16
Current Assets	111	98	82

Exel Composites

Fair Oak Lane Whitehouse Industrial Estate, Runcorn, WA7 3DU
Tel: 01928-701515 **Fax:** 01928-713572
E-mail: office.runcorn@exelcomposites.com
Website: http://www.exelcomposites.com
Bank(s): Lloyds TSB Bank plc
Directors: I. Silvanto (Fin)
Managers: J. Hartley (I.T. Exec), R. Thomas (Chief Mgr), C. Matthias (Personnel), S. Wiltson (Buyer), A. Blair (Tech Serv Mgr)
Ultimate Holding Company: LEMARNE CORPORATION LTD (AUSTRALIA)
Immediate Holding Company: FIBREFORCE COMPOSITES LIMITED
Registration no: 00240080 **VAT No.:** GB 381 3747 39
Date established: 2029 **Turnover:** £2m - £5m **No.of Employees:** 21 - 50
Product Groups: 30, 33, 66

Date of Accounts	Dec 10	Dec 09	Dec 08
Sales Turnover	5m	7m	7m
Pre Tax Profit/Loss	-75	138	173
Working Capital	2m	2m	4m
Fixed Assets	1m	1m	1m
Current Assets	5m	5m	5m
Current Liabilities	153	215	330

Express Transformers & Controls Ltd

Picow Farm Road, Runcorn, WA7 4UJ
Tel: 01928-574491 **Fax:** 01928-580693
E-mail: sales@express-transformers.co.uk
Website: http://www.express-transformers.co.uk
Bank(s): National Westminster Bank Plc
Directors: P. Hebden (MD)
Ultimate Holding Company: SOURCELONE LIMITED
Immediate Holding Company: EXPRESS TRANSFORMERS & CONTROLS LIMITED
Registration no: 00602158 **VAT No.:** GB 218 4229 71
Date established: 1958 **No.of Employees:** 21 - 50 **Product Groups:** 37

Date of Accounts	Mar 11	Mar 10	Mar 09
Working Capital	535	301	426
Fixed Assets	65	56	64
Current Assets	1m	620	635

Fibre & Furnaces Ltd

Unit 1a Ashville Way, Sutton Weaver, Runcorn, WA7 3EZ
Tel: 01928-710434 **Fax:** 01928-713432
E-mail: info@fibreandfurnaces.co.uk
Website: http://www.fibreandfurnaces.co.uk
Directors: S. Allen (Dir)
Immediate Holding Company: FIBRE & FURNACES LIMITED
Registration no: 01438050 **Date established:** 1979
No.of Employees: 1 - 10 **Product Groups:** 40, 42, 46

Date of Accounts	Aug 11	Aug 10	Aug 09
Working Capital	210	54	128
Fixed Assets	60	34	41
Current Assets	876	432	383

Global Industries North West Ltd

36 Arkwright Road Astmoor Industrial Estate, Runcorn, WA7 1NU
Tel: 01928-577846 **Fax:** 01928-560480
E-mail: info@globalindustries.co.uk
Website: http://www.globalindustries.co.uk
Directors: M. Fox (MD)
Managers: S. Goghegan (Mgr)
Immediate Holding Company: GLOBAL INDUSTRIES (NORTH WEST) LIMITED
Registration no: 01588043 **VAT No.:** GB 344 1408 81
Date established: 1981 **No.of Employees:** 1 - 10 **Product Groups:** 40, 48

Date of Accounts	Dec 11	Dec 10	Dec 09
Working Capital	46	39	28
Fixed Assets	253	203	216
Current Assets	733	570	479

Halton Fabrications Ltd

Picow Farm Road, Runcorn, WA7 4JB
Tel: 01928-572691 **Fax:** 01928-569732
E-mail: info@haltonfabrications.co.uk
Website: http://www.haltonfabrications.co.uk

Directors: C. Ditchfield (Chief Op Offcr)
Immediate Holding Company: HALTON FABRICATIONS LIMITED
Registration no: 01119506 **Date established:** 1973
No.of Employees: 11 - 20 **Product Groups:** 30, 35, 36, 37, 38, 40, 42, 48, 51, 52, 54, 80, 84

Date of Accounts	Mar 11	Mar 10	Mar 09
Working Capital	320	309	252
Fixed Assets	914	894	899
Current Assets	2m	709	676

Helsby & Longden Ltd

Unit 5 Ashville Way Sutton Weaver, Runcorn, WA7 3EZ
Tel: 01928-701555 **Fax:** 01928-718864
E-mail: info@helsby-longden.co.uk
Website: http://www.helsby-longden.co.uk
Directors: N. Jardine (MD), J. Jardine (Fin)
Immediate Holding Company: HELSBY AND LONGDEN LIMITED
Registration no: 00369221 **Date established:** 1941
No.of Employees: 51 - 100 **Product Groups:** 67, 76

Date of Accounts	Mar 11	Mar 10	Mar 09
Sales Turnover	5m	4m	N/A
Pre Tax Profit/Loss	55	-60	-128
Working Capital	337	460	571
Fixed Assets	4m	3m	3m
Current Assets	1m	1m	1m
Current Liabilities	161	117	135

Honeywell Security

Unit 8 Aston Fields Road Whitehouse Industrial Estate, Runcorn, WA7 3DL
Tel: 01928-754028 **Fax:** 01928-754050
E-mail: andrew.bull@honeywell.com
Website: http://www.honeywell.com
Directors: A. Bull (Sales)
Managers: J. Meecham, A. Cooper (Tech Serv Mgr)
Ultimate Holding Company: HONEYWELL INTERNATIONAL INC (USA)
Immediate Holding Company: HONEYWELL VIDEO SYSTEMS UK LIMITED
Registration no: 01501883 **Date established:** 1980
Turnover: £20m - £50m **No.of Employees:** 21 - 50 **Product Groups:** 36, 40

Date of Accounts	Dec 08
Working Capital	2m
Current Assets	2m

Hosokawa Micron Ltd

Rivington Road Whitehouse Industrial Estate, Whitehouse, Runcorn, WA7 3DS
Tel: 01928-755100 **Fax:** 01928-714325
E-mail: info@hmluk.hosokawa.com
Website: http://www.hosokawa.co.uk
Bank(s): National Westminster, Runcorn
Directors: I. Crosley (MD)
Managers: J. Buck (Tech Sales Eng), S. Bryan (Mktg Serv Mgr)
Ultimate Holding Company: Hosokawa Micron Corporation
Registration no: 00823762 **Date established:** 1983
Turnover: £10m - £20m **No.of Employees:** 51 - 100 **Product Groups:** 30, 35, 38, 40, 41, 42, 43, 44, 45, 54, 61, 84, 85

Date of Accounts	Sep 11	Sep 10	Sep 09
Sales Turnover	9m	8m	8m
Pre Tax Profit/Loss	511	208	289
Working Capital	438	-248	-501
Fixed Assets	1m	1m	1m
Current Assets	5m	4m	3m
Current Liabilities	2m	2m	840

Husco International Ltd

6 Rivington Road Whitehouse Industrial Estate, Runcorn, WA7 3DT
Tel: 01928-701888 **Fax:** 01928-710813
E-mail: uksales@huscointl.com
Website: http://www.huscointl.com
Bank(s): The Royal Bank of Scotland
Directors: R. Ramirez (Dir)
Ultimate Holding Company: HUSCO INTERNATIONAL INC (USA)
Immediate Holding Company: HUSCO INTERNATIONAL LIMITED
Registration no: 01924631 **Date established:** 1985
Turnover: £20m - £50m **No.of Employees:** 101 - 250
Product Groups: 38, 40, 84

Date of Accounts	Dec 11	Dec 10	Dec 09
Sales Turnover	34m	24m	16m
Pre Tax Profit/Loss	1m	454	-2m
Working Capital	2m	2m	1m
Fixed Assets	5m	5m	5m
Current Assets	12m	10m	9m
Current Liabilities	2m	2m	971

Hyloc Ltd

Unit 12 Jensen Court Astmoor Industrial Estate, Runcorn, WA7 1SQ
Tel: 01928-593100 **Fax:** 01928-590905
E-mail: sales@hyloc.com
Website: http://www.hyloc.com
Directors: A. Morley (Dir)
Immediate Holding Company: HYLOC LIMITED
Registration no: 03447848 **Date established:** 1997 **Turnover:** £2m - £5m
No.of Employees: 1 - 10 **Product Groups:** 31, 32

Date of Accounts	Dec 11	Dec 10	Dec 09
Working Capital	-1m	362	836
Fixed Assets	99	202	235
Current Assets	897	747	1m
Current Liabilities	N/A	162	N/A

I P P Mardale

Unit 5b Christleton Court Manor Park, Runcorn, WA7 1ST
Tel: 01928-580555 **Fax:** 01283-722010
E-mail: sales@ippgrp.com
Website: http://www.ippgrp.com
Bank(s): National Westminster
Directors: C. Daly (MD)
Ultimate Holding Company: SITINDUSTRIE (ITALY)
Immediate Holding Company: SITINDUSTIE S.P.A.
Registration no: 06641785 **VAT No.:** GB 145 9237 52
Date established: 1966 **Turnover:** £10m - £20m
No.of Employees: 21 - 50 **Product Groups:** 36

Ineos Compounds UK Ltd

Runcorn Site HQ South Parade PO Box 9, Runcorn, WA7 4JE
Tel: 01928-563702 **Fax:** 01928-515253
E-mail: ashley.reed@ineoschlor.com
Website: http://www.ineos.com
Directors: A. Reed (Comm), P. Nichols (Co Sec), T. Crotty (Dir)
Managers: C. Welsh (Commun Mgr)
Ultimate Holding Company: INEOS AG (SWITZERLAND)
Immediate Holding Company: INEOS COMPOUNDS UK LTD
Registration no: 02514084 **VAT No.:** GB 238 4582 41
Date established: 1990 **Turnover:** £500,000 - £1m
No.of Employees: 51 - 100 **Product Groups:** 32

Date of Accounts	Dec 11	Dec 10	Dec 09
Sales Turnover	600	600	7m
Pre Tax Profit/Loss	N/A	400	-4m
Working Capital	11m	11m	9m
Fixed Assets	500	1m	2m
Current Assets	13m	12m	13m
Current Liabilities	900	1m	2m

INEOS Enterprises Ltd

Salt Business Mersey View Road, Weston Point, Runcorn, WA7 4HB
Tel: 01928-514640 **Fax:** 01928-572261
E-mail: salt-enquiries@ineosenterprises.com
Website: http://www.INEOS.co.uk
Directors: P. Johnson (Fin), D. Goadby (MD), H. Deans (Grp Chief Exec)
Ultimate Holding Company: INEOS AG (SWITZERLAND)
Immediate Holding Company: INEOS ENTERPRISES LIMITED
Registration no: 04651437 **VAT No.:** GB 595 8036 00
Date established: 2003 **Turnover:** £125m - £250m
No.of Employees: 1 - 10 **Product Groups:** 17, 31, 32

Date of Accounts	Dec 11	Dec 10	Dec 09
Sales Turnover	217m	199m	209m
Pre Tax Profit/Loss	22m	22m	11m
Working Capital	21m	15m	21m
Fixed Assets	95m	94m	86m
Current Assets	62m	50m	49m
Current Liabilities	30m	24m	17m

Ionotec Ltd

14 Berkeley Court Manor Park, Runcorn, WA7 1TQ
Tel: 01928-579668 **Fax:** 01928-579627
E-mail: enquiries@ionotec.com
Website: http://www.ionotec.com
Directors: J. Blackburn (MD)
Immediate Holding Company: IONOTEC LTD
Registration no: 03141009 **VAT No.:** GB 678 3896 60
Date established: 1995 **Turnover:** £250,000 - £500,000
No.of Employees: 1 - 10 **Product Groups:** 33, 34, 35, 37, 42, 45, 48, 85

Date of Accounts	Mar 12	Mar 11	Mar 10
Working Capital	317	107	71
Fixed Assets	157	44	48
Current Assets	418	166	121

James Troop & Co. Ltd

4 Davy Road Astmoor Industrial Estate, Runcorn, WA7 1PZ
Tel: 01928-566170 **Fax:** 01928-577314
E-mail: sales@jamestroop.co.uk
Website: http://www.jamestroop.co.uk
Bank(s): National Westminster Bank Plc
Directors: B. Troop (MD), R. Pollock (Chief Op Offcr)
Managers: R. Troop
Immediate Holding Company: JAMES TROOP & COMPANY LIMITED
Registration no: 00149916 **VAT No.:** GB 163 7672 42
Date established: 2018 **Turnover:** Over £1,000m
No.of Employees: 21 - 50 **Product Groups:** 37, 39, 40

Date of Accounts	Aug 11	Aug 10	Aug 09
Working Capital	594	563	462
Fixed Assets	144	144	124
Current Assets	1m	2m	1m

JLT Mobile Computers Ltd

The Heath, Runcorn, WA7 4QX
Tel: 01928-515241 **Fax:** 0870-7623701
E-mail: info@cmc.org.uk
Website: http://www.jltmobile.co.uk
Managers: M. Muslek (Sales Off Mgr)
Registration no: 05094647 **No.of Employees:** 1 - 10 **Product Groups:** 44

Date of Accounts	Dec 09	Dec 08	Jun 07
Working Capital	-590	-528	-254
Fixed Assets	14	15	2
Current Assets	256	178	105

Johnson Services Group

Unit 9 Monks Way, Preston Brook, Runcorn, WA7 3GH
Tel: 01928-704600 **Fax:** 01928-704620
E-mail: enquiries@jsg.com
Website: http://www.johnsonplc.com
Directors: Y. Monaghan (Fin)
Ultimate Holding Company: Johnson Service Group plc
Immediate Holding Company: JOHNSON SERVICE GROUP PLC
Registration no: 00523335 **Date established:** 1953
Turnover: £50m - £75m **No.of Employees:** 1 - 10 **Product Groups:** 22, 23, 24, 30, 36, 40, 49, 61, 63, 66, 83

Date of Accounts	Dec 11	Dec 10	Dec 09
Sales Turnover	242m	235m	236m
Pre Tax Profit/Loss	14m	4m	21m
Working Capital	-11m	-15m	-9m
Fixed Assets	169m	169m	169m
Current Assets	49m	41m	42m
Current Liabilities	44m	39m	32m

Kawneer UK Ltd

Astmoor Road Astmoor Industrial Estate, Runcorn, WA7 1QQ
Tel: 01928-502500 **Fax:** 01928-502501
E-mail: phil.randles@alcoa.com
Website: http://www.kawneer.co.uk
Directors: P. Randles (MD)
Managers: C. Blundell (Comptroller), L. Parsons (Personnel), L. Rowlands (Purch Mgr)
Ultimate Holding Company: ALCOA INC (USA)
Immediate Holding Company: KAWNEER U.K. LIMITED
Registration no: 02917765 **Date established:** 1994
Turnover: £20m - £50m **No.of Employees:** 101 - 250
Product Groups: 34, 35

Date of Accounts	Dec 11	Dec 10	Dec 09
Sales Turnover	27m	23m	29m
Pre Tax Profit/Loss	3m	1m	2m
Working Capital	10m	10m	10m
Fixed Assets	2m	2m	2m
Current Assets	18m	18m	16m
Current Liabilities	2m	2m	2m

Klinger Ltd

21 Dewar Court Astmoor Industrial Estate, Runcorn, WA7 1PT
Tel: 01928-577030 **Fax:** 01928-575223
E-mail: enquiries@klingeruk.co.uk
Website: http://www.klingeruk.co.uk
Managers: S. Bradley (Mgr)
Ultimate Holding Company: BETAL NETHERLAND HOLDING BV (NETHERLANDS)
Immediate Holding Company: KLINGER LIMITED
Registration no: 01021936 **Date established:** 1971
No.of Employees: 1 - 10 **Product Groups:** 38, 42

Date of Accounts	Dec 11	Dec 10	Dec 09
Sales Turnover	27m	23m	24m
Pre Tax Profit/Loss	5m	4m	3m
Working Capital	8m	8m	9m
Fixed Assets	2m	1m	2m
Current Assets	11m	11m	12m
Current Liabilities	1m	1m	844

L C A Controls Ltd

1 Boleyn Court Manor Park, Runcorn, WA7 1SR
Tel: 01928-579677 **Fax:** 01928-579086
E-mail: lcacontrols@btinternet.com
Website: http://www.lcacontrols.co.uk
Directors: C. O'Brien (Dir), C. O'brien (Chief Op Offcr), L. Trotter (Fin)
Managers: V. Richards, J. Warburton (Sales Admin)
Immediate Holding Company: L C A CONTROLS LIMITED
Registration no: 02588033 **Date established:** 1991
No.of Employees: 21 - 50 **Product Groups:** 37

Date of Accounts	Apr 11	Apr 10	Apr 09
Working Capital	116	26	298
Fixed Assets	212	241	266
Current Assets	843	966	828

Metrohm UK Ltd

Evenwood Close, Runcorn, WA7 1LZ
Tel: 01928-579600 **Fax:** 01280-824800
E-mail: jkinross@metrohm.co.uk
Website: http://www.metrohm.co.uk
Directors: J. Kinross (Fin)
Managers: J. West (Sales Prom Mgr)
Ultimate Holding Company: METROHM AG (SWITZERLAND)
Immediate Holding Company: METROHM UK LIMITED
Registration no: 02949769 **Date established:** 1994 **Turnover:** £2m - £5m
No.of Employees: 21 - 50 **Product Groups:** 33, 38

Date of Accounts	Dec 11	Dec 10	Dec 09
Sales Turnover	N/A	5m	4m
Pre Tax Profit/Loss	N/A	386	-4
Working Capital	2m	2m	3m
Fixed Assets	1m	2m	434
Current Assets	4m	3m	4m
Current Liabilities	N/A	767	461

Mexichem

Accounts Payable Rocksavage Works PB 105, Runcorn, WA7 4LX
Tel: 01928-515525 **Fax:** 01928-511418
E-mail: info@mexichem.com
Website: http://www.mexichem.com
Directors: P. Breden (Co Sec)
Managers: S. Hughes, A. Ost (Comptroller), G. Lewis (Tech Serv Mgr), B. Connelly (Personnel), R. Faragher, D. McGreal (Purch Mgr)
Ultimate Holding Company: INEOS AG (SWITZERLAND)
Immediate Holding Company: INEOS FLUOR LIMITED
Registration no: 04041123 **Date established:** 2000
Turnover: £10m - £20m **No.of Employees:** 101 - 250
Product Groups: 31, 32

Date of Accounts	Dec 11	Dec 10	Dec 09
Sales Turnover	17m	26m	111m
Pre Tax Profit/Loss	9m	74m	-3m
Working Capital	135m	125m	113m
Fixed Assets	16m	25m	14m
Current Assets	241m	228m	169m
Current Liabilities	149	172	4m

Onyx Security Hardware

19 Beeston Court Stuart Road Manor Park, Runcorn, WA7 1SS
Tel: 01928-579999 **Fax:** 01928-579595
E-mail: sales@delta-hardware.co.uk
Directors: R. Bromley (Prop)
Immediate Holding Company: APPLETON HARDWARE LIMITED
Date established: 2011 **No.of Employees:** 1 - 10 **Product Groups:** 30, 36

Partner Tech UK Corp Ltd

Unit 11 Berkeley Court, Manor Park, Runcorn, WA7 1TQ
Tel: 01928-579707 **Fax:** 01928-571308
E-mail: sales@partnertech-uk.com
Website: http://www.partnertech-uk.com
Directors: C. Smith (MD)
Immediate Holding Company: PARTNER TECH UK CORP LIMITED
Registration no: 06645117 **Date established:** 2008
Turnover: £500,000 - £1m **No.of Employees:** 1 - 10 **Product Groups:** 37, 44

Date of Accounts	Dec 11	Dec 10	Jul 09
Working Capital	-24	96	117
Fixed Assets	26	22	10
Current Assets	873	1m	1m

Phoenix Medical Supplies Ltd

Rivington Road Whitehouse Industrial Estate, Runcorn, WA7 3DJ
Tel: 01928-750500 **Fax:** 01928-750750
E-mail: enquiries@phoenixmedical.co.uk
Website: http://www.myp-i-n.co.uk
Directors: K. Hudson (Fin), P. Smith (MD)
Ultimate Holding Company: PHOENIX PHARMAHANDEL AG & CO (GERMANY)
Immediate Holding Company: PHOENIX MEDICAL SUPPLIES LIMITED
Registration no: 03603234 **Date established:** 1998
Turnover: £500m - £1,000m **No.of Employees:** 251 - 500
Product Groups: 63

Date of Accounts	Jan 12	Jan 11	Jan 10
Pre Tax Profit/Loss	32m	12m	7m
Working Capital	202m	320m	269m
Fixed Assets	156m	156m	157m
Current Assets	339m	430m	427m
Current Liabilities	4m	4m	5m

Projen plc

1 Wellfield Preston Brook, Runcorn, WA7 3AZ
Tel: 01928-752500 **Fax:** 01928-752555
E-mail: enquiry@projen.co.uk
Website: http://www.projen.co.uk
Bank(s): Nat West
Directors: J. Taylor (Ch), M. Royle (Fin)
Managers: J. Bryan (Mktg Serv Mgr), I. McKay, M. Warrington, D. Elliott
Ultimate Holding Company: PROJEN HOLDINGS LIMITED
Immediate Holding Company: PROJEN PUBLIC LIMITED COMPANY
Registration no: 03085241 **Date established:** 1995
Turnover: £10m - £20m **No.of Employees:** 51 - 100 **Product Groups:** 80, 84

Date of Accounts	Apr 12	Apr 11	Apr 10
Sales Turnover	13m	11m	25m
Pre Tax Profit/Loss	604	473	697
Working Capital	1m	710	235
Fixed Assets	270	289	348
Current Assets	7m	3m	7m
Current Liabilities	1m	788	2m

Reagent Chemical Services Ltd

18 Astonfields Road Whitehouse Industrial Estate, Runcorn, WA7 3DL
Tel: 01928-716903 **Fax:** 01928-716425
E-mail: info@reagent.co.uk
Website: http://www.reagent.co.uk
Directors: R. Hudson (MD)
Managers: J. Simpson (Chief Acct)
Ultimate Holding Company: REAGENT PROPERTIES LIMITED
Immediate Holding Company: REAGENT CHEMICAL SERVICES LIMITED
Registration no: 01318854 **VAT No.:** GB 295 0375 42
Date established: 1977 **No.of Employees:** 11 - 20 **Product Groups:** 31, 66

Date of Accounts	Mar 12	Mar 11	Mar 10
Working Capital	60	80	173
Fixed Assets	192	197	131
Current Assets	431	431	478

Rinnai UK Ltd

9 Christleton Court Manor Park, Runcorn, WA7 1ST
Tel: 01928-531870 **Fax:** 01928-531880
E-mail: tonygittings@rinnaiuk.com
Website: http://www.rinnaiuk.co.uk
Directors: T. Gittings (MD)
Ultimate Holding Company: RINNAI CORPORATION (JAPAN)
Immediate Holding Company: RINNAI UK LIMITED
Registration no: 01247352 **Date established:** 1976 **Turnover:** £2m - £5m
No.of Employees: 11 - 20 **Product Groups:** 40, 63, 66

Date of Accounts	Dec 11	Dec 10	Dec 09
Working Capital	269	268	2m
Fixed Assets	11	7	8
Current Assets	2m	3m	3m

Rowland's Pharmacy

Whitehouse Industrial Estate Rivington Road, Runcorn, WA7 3DJ
Tel: 01928-750668 **Fax:** 01928-755027
E-mail: jpenn@rowlandspharmacy.co.uk
Website: http://www.rowlandspharmacy.co.uk
Bank(s): Barclays Corporate Bank
Directors: N. Topping (Sales & Mktg), J. Penn (Fin)
Managers: K. Hudson
Ultimate Holding Company: PHOENIX PHARMAHANDEL AG & CO (GERMANY)
Immediate Holding Company: L.ROWLAND & COMPANY (RETAIL) LIMITED
Registration no: 02288928 **VAT No.:** GB 741 7064 43
Date established: 1988 **Turnover:** £500m - £1,000m
No.of Employees: 1501 & over **Product Groups:** 31, 61, 62, 63, 88

Date of Accounts	Jan 12	Jan 11	Jan 10
Sales Turnover	514m	524m	527m
Pre Tax Profit/Loss	775	15m	11m
Working Capital	-303m	-314m	-333m
Fixed Assets	402m	415m	424m
Current Assets	99m	115m	110m
Current Liabilities	12m	12m	14m

Servisair UK Ltd

Servisair House Hampton Court Tudor Road, Manor Park, Runcorn, WA7 1TT
Tel: 01928-570120 **Fax:** 01928-570220
E-mail: ann.hatton@servisair.com
Website: http://www.servisair.com
Directors: A. Lelaoufir (Grp Chief Exec), J. Willis (Ch), R. Jarvis (Dir)
Managers: S. Samson (Mktg Serv Mgr), A. Hatton
Ultimate Holding Company: DERICHEBOURG SA (FRANCE)
Immediate Holding Company: SERVISAIR GROUP LIMITED
Registration no: 00924991 **Date established:** 1967 **Turnover:** £2m - £5m
No.of Employees: 51 - 100 **Product Groups:** 76

Date of Accounts	Sep 11	Sep 10	Sep 09
Pre Tax Profit/Loss	351	829	594
Working Capital	-1m	-2m	-3m
Fixed Assets	4m	4m	5m
Current Assets	292	244	101
Current Liabilities	429	242	475

Syntor Fine Chemicals Ltd

11 Boleyn Court Manor Park, Runcorn, WA7 1SR
Tel: 01928-579865
E-mail: sales@syntor.co.uk
Website: http://www.syntor.co.uk
Directors: S. Knowle (MD)
Immediate Holding Company: SYNTOR FINE CHEMICALS LIMITED
Registration no: 05177187 **Date established:** 2004
No.of Employees: 11 - 20 **Product Groups:** 31

Date of Accounts	Mar 11	Mar 10	Mar 09
Working Capital	1m	1m	1m
Fixed Assets	156	189	169
Current Assets	2m	3m	3m

System Devices UK Ltd

1 Beeston Court Stuart Road, Manor Park, Runcorn, WA7 1SS
Tel: 01928-571977 **Fax:** 01928-571988
E-mail: info@systemdevices.co.uk
Website: http://www.systemdevices.co.uk
Managers: D. Park
Immediate Holding Company: SYSTEM DEVICES UK LIMITED
Registration no: 05474715 **VAT No.:** GB 382 2768 30
Date established: 2005 **Turnover:** £1m - £2m **No.of Employees:** 1 - 10
Product Groups: 37, 45

Date of Accounts	Jan 12	Jan 11	Jan 10
Working Capital	140	96	28
Fixed Assets	348	334	337
Current Assets	362	463	250

T Q M I Ltd

The Heath Business & Technical Park, Runcorn, WA7 4QX
Tel: 01928-513171 **Fax:** 01928-513 174
E-mail: info@tqmi.co.uk
Website: http://www.tqmi.co.uk
Directors: J. Carson (Ch), G. Barnsley (Dir), J. Carson (MD)
Ultimate Holding Company: TOTAL QUALITY MANAGEMENT INTERNATIONAL LIMITED
Immediate Holding Company: TQMI LIMITED
Registration no: 03118353 **Date established:** 1995
Turnover: £500,000 - £1m **No.of Employees:** 1 - 10 **Product Groups:** 86

Thermo Fisher Scientific Scientific Instruments

112 Chadwick Road Astmoor Industrial Estate, Runcorn, WA7 1PW
Tel: 01928-581000 **Fax:** 01928-581078
E-mail: alan.wilshire@thermofisher.com
Website: http://www.thermofisher.com
Bank(s): National Westminster Bank Plc
Managers: A. Wilshire, A. Wiltshire (Quality Control), A. Wilshire (Quality Control), H. Ritchie, D. Hickey (Fin Mgr), B. Monaghan, P. Ross
Immediate Holding Company: Thermo Electron Inc (U.S.A.)
Registration no: 03466934 **Date established:** 1978
No.of Employees: 51 - 100 **Product Groups:** 31, 38, 42

Thompson & Capper Ltd

9-11 Hardwick Road Astmoor Industrial Estate, Runcorn, WA7 1PH
Tel: 01928-573734 **Fax:** 01928-580694
E-mail: enquiries@tablets2buy.com
Website: http://www.tablets2buy.com
Bank(s): National Westminster
Directors: S. O'connor (MD)
Ultimate Holding Company: DCC PUBLIC LIMITED COMPANY
Immediate Holding Company: PRIMACY HEALTHCARE LIMITED
Registration no: 00741413 **VAT No.:** GB 708 4301 50
Date established: 1962 **Turnover:** £10m - £20m
No.of Employees: 101 - 250 **Product Groups:** 20, 31, 32

Date of Accounts	Mar 11	Mar 10	Mar 09
Pre Tax Profit/Loss	-1	210	6
Working Capital	3m	3m	4m
Current Assets	4m	4m	4m
Current Liabilities	10	206	84

Ventcroft Ltd

Faraday Road Astmoor Industrial Estate, Runcorn, WA7 1PE
Tel: 01928-581098 **Fax:** 01928-581099
E-mail: sales@ventcroft.co.uk
Website: http://www.ventcroft.co.uk
Directors: A. Groves (Sales), F. Rotheram (MD), I. Rotheram (Tech Serv), L. Rotheram (Co Sec)
Managers: K. Jones (Chief Acct), H. Gabryszews (Purch Mgr)
Immediate Holding Company: VENTCROFT LIMITED
Registration no: 02600835 **Date established:** 1991
Turnover: £10m - £20m **No.of Employees:** 21 - 50 **Product Groups:** 37, 40, 66, 67

Date of Accounts	Dec 11	Sep 10	Sep 09
Sales Turnover	15m	13m	12m
Pre Tax Profit/Loss	3m	127	197
Working Capital	-521	179	-649
Fixed Assets	16m	9m	5m
Current Assets	4m	5m	5m
Current Liabilities	516	363	2m

Vibro Technical Services Ltd

23-24 Arkwright Road Astmoor Industrial Estate, Runcorn, WA7 1NU
Tel: 01928-569251 **Fax:** 01928-569252
E-mail: neilvibro@aol.com
Website: http://www.regalvibro.co.uk
Directors: N. Austin (Dir)
Immediate Holding Company: VIBRO TECHNICAL SERVICES LTD
Registration no: 07324159 **Date established:** 2010
No.of Employees: 11 - 20 **Product Groups:** 38, 42

Date of Accounts	Jul 11
Working Capital	-93
Fixed Assets	57
Current Assets	217

Whitford Ltd

10 Christleton Court Manor Park, Runcorn, WA7 1ST
Tel: 01928-571000 **Fax:** 01928-571010
E-mail: salesuk@whitfordww.co.uk
Website: http://www.whitfordww.co.uk
Bank(s): Lloyds TSB Bank plc
Directors: M. Garnett (MD), D. Johnson (Fin), D. Sydes (MD), D. Johnson (Co Sec)
Managers: M. Downing (Prod Mgr), K. Williams (Accounts), H. Dale (Cust Serv Mgr), A. Willis, T. Anderson (Purch Mgr), R. Howarth (Mktg Serv Mgr), M. Coates, M. Goddard (Fin Mgr), M. Knowles (Sales & Mktg Mg)
Ultimate Holding Company: WHITFORD WORLDWIDE CO (USA)
Immediate Holding Company: WHITFORD LIMITED
Registration no: 00959015 **VAT No.:** GB 152 2025 16
Date established: 1969 **Turnover:** £10m - £20m
No.of Employees: 51 - 100 **Product Groups:** 23, 30, 31, 32, 36, 48

Date of Accounts	Dec 10	Dec 09	Dec 08
Sales Turnover	13m	11m	10m
Pre Tax Profit/Loss	704	347	950
Working Capital	4m	2m	2m
Fixed Assets	511	594	691
Current Assets	6m	5m	3m
Current Liabilities	897	662	551

Sale

A M P M Ltd

2 Glebelands Road, Sale, M33 6LB
Tel: 0161-969 3911 **Fax:** 0161-905 2741
E-mail: enquiries@ampmsolutions.co.uk
Website: http://www.ampmsolutions.co.uk
Directors: A. Mulligan (MD), B. Dickson (Sales), G. Brockis (Dir), M. Halfpenny (Fin)
Managers: D. Mason (Mktg Serv Mgr), S. White (Factory Mgr)
Immediate Holding Company: Ampm Ltd
Registration no: 04367706 **Date established:** 2000
No.of Employees: 1 - 10 **Product Groups:** 37

Date of Accounts	Mar 08	Mar 07	Mar 06
Working Capital	73	22	-12
Fixed Assets	25	29	28
Current Assets	180	103	69
Current Liabilities	106	81	81

Advantage Technical Resorcing (Regional Office)

Stamford House Northenden Road, Sale, M33 2DH
Tel: 0161-282 1770 **Fax:** 0161-962 0316
E-mail: amanda.bevan@atlanrecruitment.com
Website: http://www.higherthinking.com
Managers: M. Summerfield (District Mgr)
Ultimate Holding Company: KRUMLIN HALL LIMITED
Immediate Holding Company: THE JOHN REYNOLDS GROUP LIMITED
Registration no: 01928564 **Date established:** 1988
Turnover: £20m - £50m **No.of Employees:** 11 - 20 **Product Groups:** 80, 81, 84, 86

Date of Accounts	Mar 09	Mar 08
Working Capital	10	10
Current Assets	10	10

Bollin Valley

2 Hampson Street, Sale, M33 3HJ
Tel: 0800-028 2557 **Fax:** 0161-962 9813
Directors: C. Brennand (Prop)
No.of Employees: 1 - 10 **Product Groups:** 40, 66

M. Buttkereit Ltd

Unit 2 Britannia Road Industrial Estate, Sale, M33 2AA
Tel: 0161-969 5418 **Fax:** 0161-969 5419
E-mail: martin@buttkereit.co.uk
Website: http://www.buttkereit.co.uk
Directors: M. Buttkereit (Dir), J. Green (Sales)
Registration no: 01875814 **Date established:** 1985
Turnover: £500,000 - £1m **No.of Employees:** 1 - 10 **Product Groups:** 29, 30, 35, 37, 39, 42, 45, 46, 47, 48, 67

Date of Accounts	Dec 11	Dec 10	Dec 09
Working Capital	390	322	171
Fixed Assets	98	102	104
Current Assets	671	566	431

Cap Gemini

Cap Gemini House 77-79 Cross Street, Sale, M33 7HG
Tel: 0161-969 3611 **Fax:** 0161-973 9016
Website: http://www.uk.capgemini.com
Directors: P. Spence (Grp Chief Exec)
Immediate Holding Company: CGS HOLDINGS LTD
Registration no: 00943935 **Turnover:** Over £1,000m
No.of Employees: 1 - 10 **Product Groups:** 44, 84, 86

Computer Box Ltd

Eaton Place Business Centre 114 Washway Road, Sale, M33 7RF
Tel: 0161-374 0770 **Fax:** 0161-374 0769
E-mail: sales@computerbox.com
Website: http://www.computerbox.com
Directors: P. Barnfield (MD), S. Barnfield (Fin)
Immediate Holding Company: COMPUTER BOX LIMITED
Registration no: 03440042 **VAT No.:** GB 694 8572 71
Date established: 1997 **Turnover:** £250,000 - £500,000
No.of Employees: 1 - 10 **Product Groups:** 44, 67

Date of Accounts	Sep 11	Sep 10	Sep 09
Sales Turnover	268	N/A	N/A
Pre Tax Profit/Loss	16	N/A	N/A
Working Capital	-45	-47	-46
Fixed Assets	176	176	176
Current Assets	45	44	86
Current Liabilities	77	N/A	N/A

Glidevale Ltd

2 Brooklands Road, Sale, M33 3SS
Tel: 0161-905 5700 **Fax:** 0161-905 2085
E-mail: info@glidevale.com
Website: http://www.glidevale.com
Directors: D. Willan (MD), M. Jackson (Sales & Mktg)
Managers: H. McMurray (I.T. Exec), R. Southern (), R. Southern
Ultimate Holding Company: BPD Holdings Ltd
Immediate Holding Company: GLIDEVALE LIMITED
Registration no: 01982225 **Date established:** 1986 **Turnover:** £2m - £5m
No.of Employees: 1 - 10 **Product Groups:** 30, 66

Going Places

22 Town Square, Sale, M33 7SN
Tel: 08443-357618 **Fax:** 0161-976 4930
Website: http://www.goingplaces.co.uk
Managers: J. Bridge (Mgr), L. Seatoney (Mgr), L. Seatonby (District Mgr)
Ultimate Holding Company: MYTRAVEL GROUP PLC
Immediate Holding Company: GOING PLACES LIMITED
Registration no: 00825955 **Date established:** 1964
No.of Employees: 1 - 10 **Product Groups:** 69

Date of Accounts	Oct 05	Oct 04	Sep 03
Working Capital	29	29	29
Current Assets	29	29	29

Ian Clarke Funeral Services

151 Northenden Road, Sale, M33 2HS
Tel: 0161-962 4141
E-mail: ianclarkefunerals@yahoo.co.uk
Website: http://www.ianclarkefunerals.co.uk
Directors: I. Clarke (Prop)
Immediate Holding Company: IAN CLARKE FUNERAL SERVICE LIMITED
Registration no: 05002263 **Date established:** 2003
No.of Employees: 1 - 10 **Product Groups:** 88

Date of Accounts	Mar 12	Mar 11	Mar 10
Working Capital	181	409	309
Fixed Assets	415	34	26
Current Assets	222	440	343

Charles Lightfoot Ltd

Orchard House Heywood Road, Brooklands, Sale, M33 3WB
Tel: 0161-973 6565 **Fax:** 0161-962 5335
E-mail: info@charleslightfoot.co.uk
Website: http://www.charleslightfoot.co.uk
Bank(s): Barclays
Directors: G. Thornton (MD)
Managers: E. Howarth (Admin Off)
Registration no: 04676049 **VAT No.:** GB 145 5774 46
Date established: 2003 **Turnover:** £250,000 - £500,000
No.of Employees: 11 - 20 **Product Groups:** 33

Date of Accounts	Mar 03	Mar 02
Sales Turnover	N/A	281
Pre Tax Profit/Loss	N/A	-30
Working Capital	-112	-51
Fixed Assets	156	171
Current Assets	24	75
Current Liabilities	136	126
Total Share Capital	9	9
ROCE% (Return on Capital Employed)		-24.7
ROT% (Return on Turnover)		-10.5

One Stop Resource Centre

Dane Road Industrial Estate, Sale, M33 7BH
Tel: 0161-283 4626 **Fax:** 0161-283 4630
E-mail: liza.alexandra@trafford.nhs.uk
Website: http://www.traffordpct.nhs.uk
Managers: L. Alexandra
Ultimate Holding Company: BETRONICS LIMITED
Immediate Holding Company: PROTECTIVE PACKAGING LIMITED
Registration no: 02312465 **Date established:** 1988
No.of Employees: 21 - 50 **Product Groups:** 38, 67

Date of Accounts	Dec 11	Dec 10	Dec 09
Sales Turnover	11m	10m	8m
Pre Tax Profit/Loss	3m	3m	2m
Working Capital	2m	2m	2m
Fixed Assets	139	139	143
Current Assets	4m	4m	4m
Current Liabilities	838	765	592

P C H Supplies

47 Washway Road, Sale, M33 7AB
Tel: 0161-976 4136 **Fax:** 0161-439 9435
E-mail: colin@pchsupplies.fsnet.co.uk
Website: http://www.pchsupplies.fsnet.co.uk
Directors: C. Hulme (Prop)
Immediate Holding Company: PCH SUPPLIES LIMITED
Registration no: 05549641 **Date established:** 2005
No.of Employees: 1 - 10 **Product Groups:** 20, 40, 41

Palletower GB Ltd

Dane Road Industrial Estate, Sale, M33 7BH
Tel: 0161-905 2233 **Fax:** 0161-972 0922
E-mail: info@palletower.com
Website: http://www.palletower.co.uk
Bank(s): Midland, Bank Sq, Wilmslow, Cheshire
Directors: P. Hutchins (MD), P. Sheldon (Fin)
Managers: I. Tate (Purch Mgr), P. Chubb (Sales Admin)
Ultimate Holding Company: PALLETOWER GROUP HOLDINGS LIMITED
Immediate Holding Company: PALLETOWER (G.B.) LIMITED
Registration no: 00908180 **VAT No.:** GB 611 7297 49
Date established: 1967 **Turnover:** £10m - £20m
No.of Employees: 21 - 50 **Product Groups:** 26, 45

Date of Accounts	Dec 11	Dec 10	Dec 09
Sales Turnover	16m	13m	10m
Pre Tax Profit/Loss	1m	1m	1m
Working Capital	4m	3m	4m
Fixed Assets	153	163	202
Current Assets	6m	5m	5m
Current Liabilities	863	N/A	692

Protective Packaging Ltd

Dane Road Industrial Estate, Sale, M33 7BH
Tel: 0161-976 2006 **Fax:** 0161-976 3330
E-mail: info@protpack.com
Website: http://www.protpack.com
Directors: S. Jolly (Sales)
Managers: T. Hawkin (Purch Mgr), C. Jones (Fin Mgr), P. Robinson (Mktg Serv Mgr), J. Budden, A. Thompson (Tech Serv Mgr)
Ultimate Holding Company: BETRONICS LIMITED
Immediate Holding Company: PROTECTIVE PACKAGING LIMITED
Registration no: 02312465 **Date established:** 1988 **Turnover:** £5m - £10m
No.of Employees: 51 - 100 **Product Groups:** 30, 34, 36

Date of Accounts	Dec 11	Dec 10	Dec 09
Sales Turnover	11m	10m	8m
Pre Tax Profit/Loss	3m	3m	2m
Working Capital	2m	2m	2m
Fixed Assets	139	139	143
Current Assets	4m	4m	4m
Current Liabilities	838	765	592

Relax Online Travel

5 Thresher Close, Sale, M33 2NQ
Tel: 0845-094 3687 **Fax:** 0161-374 0894
E-mail: enquiries@relaxonlinetravel.com
Website: http://www.relaxonlinetravel.com
Directors: V. Nicolaou (Fin)
Registration no: 06125136 **Date established:** 2006
Turnover: Up to £250,000 **No.of Employees:** 1 - 10 **Product Groups:** 69

John Reynolds Group Ltd

Stamford House Northenden Road, Sale, M33 2DH
Tel: 0161-905 5500 **Fax:** 0161-905 5510
E-mail: info@reynoldsinsure.com
Website: http://www.reynoldsinsure.com
Bank(s): HSBC Bank plc
Directors: P. Martin (MD)
Ultimate Holding Company: KRUMLIN HALL LIMITED
Immediate Holding Company: THE JOHN REYNOLDS GROUP LIMITED
Registration no: 02215326 **Date established:** 1988
No.of Employees: 11 - 20 **Product Groups:** 82

Date of Accounts	Mar 12	Mar 11	Mar 10
Working Capital	3m	2m	2m
Fixed Assets	90	101	97
Current Assets	5m	4m	3m

Stockport Shelving Equipment Ltd

5 Rivershill, Sale, M33 6JS
Tel: 0161-286 1045 **Fax:** 0161-286 1045
E-mail: sales@stockshelf.co.uk
Website: http://www.stockshelf.co.uk
Directors: D. Rowbotham (Dir), D. Rowbowtham (Dir)
Immediate Holding Company: STOCKPORT SHELVING EQUIPMENT LIMITED
Registration no: 04648168 **Date established:** 2003
Turnover: £250,000 - £500,000 **No.of Employees:** 1 - 10
Product Groups: 26

Date of Accounts	Mar 10	Mar 09	Mar 08
Working Capital	-12	-3	6
Fixed Assets	4	5	6
Current Assets	2	6	22

Survair South Manchester Ltd

17 Hawthorn Lane Ashton-On-Mersey, Sale, M33 5WW
Tel: 0161-286 9629
E-mail: brian.kiely@survair.co.uk
Website: http://www.survair.co.uk
Directors: V. Kiely (MD)
Registration no: 05221053 **Date established:** 2004
Turnover: Up to £250,000 **No.of Employees:** 1 - 10 **Product Groups:** 32, 33, 52, 66

Timberwise UK plc

Bank House 4 Wharf Road, Sale, M33 2AF
Tel: 0161-969 1526 **Fax:** 0161-972 0077
E-mail: sale@timberwise.co.uk
Website: http://www.timberwise.co.uk
Managers: J. Holt (Mgr)
Immediate Holding Company: TIMBERWISE (UK) LIMITED
Registration no: 03230356 **Date established:** 1996
No.of Employees: 1 - 10 **Product Groups:** 07, 32, 52

Willan

2 Brooklands Road, Sale, M33 3SS
Tel: 0161-973 6262 **Fax:** 0161-905 2085
E-mail: peterw@willan.co.uk
Website: http://www.willan.co.uk
Bank(s): Natwest
Directors: P. Willan (MD)
Immediate Holding Company: WILLAN GROUP LIMITED
Registration no: 03961301 **Date established:** 2000 **Turnover:** £2m - £5m
No.of Employees: 11 - 20 **Product Groups:** 25, 52

Date of Accounts	Mar 12	Apr 09	Apr 10
Sales Turnover	2m	3m	2m
Pre Tax Profit/Loss	647	50	709
Working Capital	-2m	-5m	-2m
Fixed Assets	25m	26m	27m
Current Assets	905	1m	813
Current Liabilities	2m	1m	2m

Sandbach

Armstrong Bradley Ltd

35a Middlewich Road, Sandbach, CW11 1DH
Tel: 01270-758960 **Fax:** 08459-002806
E-mail: sales@armstrongbradley.com
Website: http://www.armstrongbradley.com
Directors: J. Walker (Dir)
Immediate Holding Company: ARMSTRONG BRADLEY LIMITED
Registration no: 01490050 **VAT No.:** GB 219 3445 64
Date established: 1980 **Turnover:** £5m - £10m **No.of Employees:** 1 - 10
Product Groups: 30

Date of Accounts	Dec 11	Dec 10	Dec 09
Working Capital	4	37	32
Fixed Assets	1	1	1
Current Assets	274	199	151

Austin Broady Air Conditioning & Ventilation Ltd

58 The Hill, Sandbach, CW11 1HT
Tel: 01270-761433 **Fax:** 01270-753463
E-mail: sales@austinbroady.co.uk
Website: http://www.austinbroady.co.uk
Directors: M. Broady (Dir), K. Broady (Fin)
Immediate Holding Company: AUSTIN BROADY AIR CONDITIONING & VENTILATION LIMITED
Registration no: 03685678 **Date established:** 1998
No.of Employees: 1 - 10 **Product Groups:** 40, 52, 66, 84

Date of Accounts	Dec 10	Dec 09	Dec 08
Working Capital	20	4	1
Fixed Assets	8	10	11
Current Assets	349	198	205

Diamond Electronics Ltd

Fourways Technology Park London Road, Smallwood, Sandbach, CW11 2US
Tel: 01477-500450 **Fax:** 01477-500656
E-mail: accounts@diamondelec.co.uk
Website: http://www.diamondelec.co.uk
Bank(s): National Westminster Bank Plc
Directors: D. Hesketh (Fin), D. Hesketh (Dir), D. Spencer (Tech Serv), P. Hall (Sales & Mktg)
Immediate Holding Company: DIAMOND ELECTRONICS LIMITED
Registration no: 01374438 **Date established:** 1978 **Turnover:** £5m - £10m
No.of Employees: 21 - 50 **Product Groups:** 29, 30, 35, 37, 38, 39, 40, 44, 67, 68

Date of Accounts	Dec 11	Dec 10	Dec 09
Working Capital	641	644	522
Fixed Assets	151	171	181
Current Assets	3m	3m	2m

Ekman Cleave Films Ltd

35a Middlewich Road, Sandbach, CW11 1DH
Tel: 01270-759757 **Fax:** 01270-764797
E-mail: sales@ekmancleave.com
Website: http://www.armstrongbradley.com
Directors: J. Walker (Dir)
Immediate Holding Company: EKMAN CLEAVE FILMS LIMITED
Registration no: 04822773 **Date established:** 2003
No.of Employees: 1 - 10 **Product Groups:** 30, 31, 37

Date of Accounts	Dec 11	Dec 10	Dec 09
Working Capital	542	409	367
Fixed Assets	39	39	38
Current Assets	597	458	415

E-Signs Cheshire Ltd

Moss Lane Business Centre Moss Lane, Sandbach, CW11 3YX
Tel: 01270-759171
E-mail: sales@e-signscheshire.co.uk
Website: http://www.inspiredbysigns.co.uk
Directors: S. Miah (Dir)
Immediate Holding Company: E-SIGNS (CHESHIRE) LIMITED
Registration no: 06530521 **Date established:** 2008
Turnover: Up to £250,000 **No.of Employees:** 1 - 10 **Product Groups:** 30

Date of Accounts	Mar 11	Mar 10	Mar 09
Working Capital	-8	-4	-7
Fixed Assets	19	12	14
Current Assets	31	24	6

Flowcrete UK

Stud Green Industrial Park Booth Lane, Moston, Sandbach, CW11 3QF
Tel: 01270-753000 **Fax:** 01270-753333
E-mail: mark@flowcrete.com
Website: http://www.flowcrete.com
Directors: K. Potter (Chief Op Offcr), M. Greaves (Dir), D. Gibbins (Ch)
Managers: D. Bedwick (Purch Mgr)
Immediate Holding Company: FLOWCRETE GROUP LIMITED
Registration no: 03241647 **VAT No.:** GB 691 8998 55
Date established: 1996 **Turnover:** £10m - £20m
No.of Employees: 51 - 100 **Product Groups:** 29, 30, 32, 33, 40, 52

Date of Accounts	Dec 07
Sales Turnover	44229
Pre Tax Profit/Loss	2966
Working Capital	4967
Fixed Assets	2724
Current Assets	16027
Current Liabilities	11060
Total Share Capital	57
ROCE% (Return on Capital Employed)	38.6

Guardian Controls International Ltd

56 Crewe Road, Sandbach, CW11 4NN
Tel: 01270-760599 **Fax:** 01270-766804
E-mail: sales@guardian-controls.com
Website: http://www.guardian-controls.com
Directors: M. Murphy (MD)
Immediate Holding Company: GUARDIAN CONTROLS INTERNATIONAL LIMITED
Registration no: 04161748 **VAT No.:** 771 5030 31 **Date established:** 2001
Turnover: £1m - £2m **No.of Employees:** 1 - 10 **Product Groups:** 38

Date of Accounts	Mar 11	Mar 10	Mar 09
Working Capital	-56	-71	-79
Fixed Assets	87	87	88
Current Assets	210	247	225

Holmes Hose Ltd

Moston Road, Sandbach, CW11 3HL
Tel: 01270-753331 **Fax:** 01270-753332
E-mail: info@holmeshose.co.uk
Website: http://www.holmeshose.co.uk
Directors: R. Greenhill (MD)
Immediate Holding Company: HOLMES HOSE LIMITED
Registration no: 01474187 **VAT No.:** GB 338 2086 55
Date established: 1980 **Turnover:** £1m - £2m **No.of Employees:** 1 - 10
Product Groups: 23, 29, 30

Date of Accounts	Dec 11	Dec 10	Dec 09
Working Capital	176	162	118
Fixed Assets	56	62	69
Current Assets	344	324	236

H G Hopkins & Sons Ltd

53-55 High Street, Sandbach, CW11 1AL
Tel: 01270-762404 **Fax:** 01270-760171
Directors: J. Hopkins (MD), P. Hopkins (Fin)
Immediate Holding Company: H G HOPKINS & SONS LIMITED
Registration no: 04661036 **Date established:** 2003
No.of Employees: 1 - 10 **Product Groups:** 36, 39, 40

Date of Accounts	Feb 11	Feb 10	Feb 09
Working Capital	-18	-18	-16
Fixed Assets	41	44	47
Current Assets	33	35	30
Current Liabilities	14	20	N/A

Iauctionshop Ltd

1 The Coachouse Zan Drive Wheelock, Sandbach, CW11 4QQ
Tel: 01270-767158
E-mail: enquiry@iauctionshop.co.uk
Website: http://www.iauctionshop.co.uk
Directors: S. Russell (Fin), R. Russell (MD)
Immediate Holding Company: IAUCTIONSHOP LIMITED
Registration no: 05323126 **Date established:** 2005
Turnover: Up to £250,000 **No.of Employees:** 1 - 10 **Product Groups:** 65

Date of Accounts	Mar 11	Mar 10	Mar 09
Sales Turnover	N/A	N/A	165
Working Capital	20	2	6
Fixed Assets	15	14	2
Current Assets	30	12	6

K R Analytical

77 Forge Fields, Sandbach, CW11 3RN
Tel: 01270-763471
E-mail: info@kranalytical.co.uk
Website: http://www.kranalytical.co.uk
Directors: P. Ryan (Dir)
No.of Employees: 1 - 10 **Product Groups:** 38, 42, 67

Lawton Tools Ltd

72 The Hill, Sandbach, CW11 1LT
Tel: 01270-753636 **Fax:** 01270-753737
E-mail: accounts@lawtontools.co.uk
Website: http://www.lawtontools.co.uk
Directors: E. Horsley (MD), P. Grindley (Sales)
Immediate Holding Company: LAWTON TOOLS LIMITED
Registration no: 00958642 **VAT No.:** GB 319 1126 82
Date established: 1969 **No.of Employees:** 11 - 20 **Product Groups:** 30, 33, 35, 36, 37, 40, 45, 46, 47, 66, 67

Date of Accounts	Oct 11	Oct 10	Oct 09
Working Capital	278	287	278
Fixed Assets	61	37	45
Current Assets	506	481	383

Magus Electronics

462 Crewe Road Wheelock, Sandbach, CW11 4QD
Tel: 01270-761120 **Fax:** 01270-766626
E-mail: sales@maguselectronics.co.uk
Website: http://www.maguselectronics.co.uk
Bank(s): The Royal Bank of Scotland, Nantwich
Directors: P. Shaw (Fin)
Immediate Holding Company: MAGUS ELECTRONICS LIMITED
Registration no: 05249906 **VAT No.:** GB 439 7904 08
Date established: 2004 **No.of Employees:** 11 - 20 **Product Groups:** 37, 38, 47

Odyn Systems Ltd
111 Congleton Road, Sandbach, CW11 1DW
Tel: 01270-753562 **Fax:** 01270-753563
E-mail: sales.c@odyn.co.uk
Website: http://www.odyn.co.uk
Directors: C. Darby (Fin), S. Hewett (MD)
Immediate Holding Company: ODYN SYSTEMS LIMITED
Registration no: 03388385 **Date established:** 1997
Turnover: Up to £250,000 **No.of Employees:** 1 - 10 **Product Groups:** 44

Date of Accounts	Nov 11	Nov 10	Nov 09
Working Capital	175	174	170
Fixed Assets	2	2	3
Current Assets	237	212	206

Punch Press Services Ltd
St Georges House Dragons Wharf Dragons Lane, Moston, Sandbach, CW11 3PA
Tel: 01270-750323 **Fax:** 01270-757911
E-mail: len@punchpressuk.com
Website: http://www.punchpressuk.com
Directors: L. Holowko (Prop)
Immediate Holding Company: PUNCH PRESS SERVICES LIMITED
Registration no: 03475461 **Date established:** 1997
No.of Employees: 1 - 10 **Product Groups:** 46

Date of Accounts	Mar 11	Mar 10	Mar 09
Working Capital	-173	-171	-201
Fixed Assets	264	283	297
Current Assets	437	298	275

Sonic Drilling Supplies Ltd
Yew Tree Farm Newcastle Road, Betchton, Sandbach, CW11 4TD
Tel: 01477-500177 **Fax:** 01477-500121
E-mail: info@sonicdrill.co.uk
Website: http://www.sonicdrill.co.uk
Directors: A. Hornsby (Dir)
Immediate Holding Company: SONIC DRILLING SUPPLIES LIMITED
Registration no: 05521228 **Date established:** 2005
No.of Employees: 1 - 10 **Product Groups:** 45

Date of Accounts	Jul 11	Jul 10	Jul 09
Working Capital	-77	-114	49
Fixed Assets	332	446	493
Current Assets	451	397	471

Speck Pumpen A B C Ltd (A B C Power Tools Services Ltd)
AreenA House Moston Road, Sandbach, CW11 3HL
Tel: 08447-640632 **Fax:** 01270-580822
E-mail: admin@speck-abc.com
Website: http://www.speck-abc.com
Directors: H. Ghelani (MD)
Immediate Holding Company: SPECK PUMPEN ABC LTD
Registration no: 03208595 **Date established:** 1996
No.of Employees: 11 - 20 **Product Groups:** 40, 67

Date of Accounts	Jul 11	Jul 10	Jul 09
Working Capital	53	49	79
Fixed Assets	62	50	40
Current Assets	608	484	432

United Phosphorus Ltd
Hall Lane Rookery Bridge, Elton, Sandbach, CW11 3QQ
Tel: 01270-766666 **Fax:** 01925-766788
E-mail: info@uniphos.com
Website: http://www.uniphos.com
Bank(s): Royal Bank of Scotland, John Dalton Street, Manchester
Directors: J. Daprewalla (Fin)
Managers: M. Bell, L. Cook (Personnel)
Ultimate Holding Company: UNITED PHOSPHORUS LTD (INDIA)
Immediate Holding Company: UNITED PHOSPHORUS LIMITED
Registration no: 02844616 **Date established:** 1993
Turnover: £20m - £50m **No.of Employees:** 21 - 50 **Product Groups:** 32

Date of Accounts	Mar 12	Mar 11	Mar 10
Sales Turnover	77m	72m	70m
Pre Tax Profit/Loss	1m	8m	1m
Working Capital	28m	42m	21m
Fixed Assets	20m	20m	45m
Current Assets	104m	117m	121m
Current Liabilities	3m	5m	6m

Vacuum Pump Repair Ltd
5 Moss Lane Business Centre Moss Lane, Sandbach, CW11 3YX
Tel: 01270-753322 **Fax:** 01270-753399
E-mail: info@vacuumservices.com
Website: http://www.vacuumservices.com
Directors: M. Beale (Prop), A. Beale (Fin)
Immediate Holding Company: VACUUM PUMP REPAIR LIMITED
Registration no: 04496626 **Date established:** 2002
Turnover: Up to £250,000 **No.of Employees:** 1 - 10 **Product Groups:** 40, 42, 48, 67

Date of Accounts	Sep 11	Sep 10	Sep 09
Working Capital	-27	17	-17
Fixed Assets	7	8	8
Current Assets	15	17	15

Stalybridge

Atlas Rubber Mouldings Ltd
Grove Road Millbrook, Stalybridge, SK15 3HT
Tel: 0161-338 3598 **Fax:** 0161-303 8998
E-mail: sales@atlasrubber.com
Website: http://www.atlasrubber.com
Directors: B. Robins (MD), J. Robins (MD), M. Robins (Co Sec)
Managers: J. Hilton (Chief Mgr)
Registration no: 01141733 **Turnover:** £250,000 - £500,000
No.of Employees: 1 - 10 **Product Groups:** 29, 63

Atosina UK Ltd
Globe House Bayley Street, Stalybridge, SK15 1PY
Tel: 0161-338 4411 **Fax:** 0161-303 1908
Website: http://www.petrochemicals.atofina.com
Bank(s): Barclays
Directors: C. Dailly (Dep Pres)
Ultimate Holding Company: TOTAL SA (FRANCE)
Immediate Holding Company: TOTAL HOLDINGS UK LIMITED
Registration no: 01946658 **VAT No.:** GB 232 6481 73
Date established: 1991 **Turnover:** £75m - £125m
No.of Employees: 101 - 250 **Product Groups:** 14, 30, 31, 32, 33, 66

Bay Freight Ltd
Premier Mill Tame Street, Stalybridge, SK15 1ST
Tel: 0161-338 8700 **Fax:** 0161-338 8234
E-mail: ernest.bailey@bayfreight.co.uk
Website: http://www.bayfreight.co.uk
Directors: E. Bailey (Dir), D. Bailey (MD)
Immediate Holding Company: BAY FREIGHT LIMITED
Registration no: 01506710 **Date established:** 1980
No.of Employees: 21 - 50 **Product Groups:** 72, 84

Date of Accounts	Dec 11	Dec 10	Dec 09
Working Capital	1m	1m	960
Fixed Assets	918	3m	3m
Current Assets	3m	2m	1m

Charlestown Auto Repair Services Ltd
Bayley Street, Stalybridge, SK15 1PZ
Tel: 0161-338 6635 **Fax:** 0161-338 4884
E-mail: sales@charlestownautos.co.uk
Website: http://www.charlestownautos.co.uk
Managers: P. Nolan (Mgr)
Immediate Holding Company: CHARLESTOWN AUTO REPAIR SERVICES LTD
Registration no: 06126435 **Date established:** 2007 **Turnover:** £1m - £2m
No.of Employees: 1 - 10 **Product Groups:** 36, 48

Date of Accounts	Feb 08	Feb 11	Feb 10
Working Capital	N/A	5	7
Fixed Assets	N/A	31	30
Current Assets	N/A	29	24

Cosmo Bingo Club
62 Market Street, Stalybridge, SK15 2AB
Tel: 0161-338 5277 **Fax:** 0161-303 9163
Directors: K. Lee (Dir)
Managers: K. Lee (Chief Mgr), J. Mercer
Immediate Holding Company: SLOT WORLD LIMITED
Registration no: 01562791 **Date established:** 1981
No.of Employees: 51 - 100 **Product Groups:** 89

Date of Accounts	Mar 11	Mar 10	Mar 09
Working Capital	-42	-30	-19
Fixed Assets	28	32	47
Current Assets	22	61	63

C S F Welding Services Ltd
Unit 11 Clarence Street, Stalybridge, SK15 1QL
Tel: 0161-308 2222 **Fax:** 01457-879830
E-mail: craig@csfweldingservicesltd.co.uk
Website: http://www.csfweldingservicesltd.co.uk
Directors: C. Fitch (Prop)
Immediate Holding Company: CSF WELDING SERVICES LTD
Registration no: 06082137 **Date established:** 2007
Turnover: Up to £250,000 **No.of Employees:** 1 - 10 **Product Groups:** 39

Date of Accounts	Jan 12	Jan 11	Jan 10
Working Capital	-159	-116	-87
Fixed Assets	58	74	85
Current Assets	34	35	11

Dane Colour UK
7 Stanley Street, Stalybridge, SK15 1SS
Tel: 0161-304 4000 **Fax:** 0161-338 2611
E-mail: sharon.mcdernot@danegroup.co.uk
Website: http://www.danecolouR.co.uk
Directors: F. Mcgrath (Grp Chief Exec)
Managers: D. Stevenson (Personnel), J. Dagley (Tech Serv Mgr), S. McDermott, A. Coleman (Mktg Serv Mgr), F. Johnson (Fin Mgr)
Ultimate Holding Company: RPM INTERNATIONAL INC (USA)
Immediate Holding Company: DANE COLOR UK LIMITED
Registration no: 05974964 **VAT No.:** GB 610 1294 91
Date established: 2006 **Turnover:** £10m - £20m
No.of Employees: 21 - 50 **Product Groups:** 32

Date of Accounts	May 12	May 11	May 10
Sales Turnover	12m	12m	9m
Pre Tax Profit/Loss	4m	3m	3m
Working Capital	4m	3m	3m
Fixed Assets	6m	7m	7m
Current Assets	6m	5m	5m
Current Liabilities	1m	1m	1m

Green Engineering
Cheethams Mill Park Street, Stalybridge, SK15 2BT
Tel: 0161-303 7129 **Fax:** 0161-303 7129
Directors: A. Green (Prop)
Registration no: 05007231 **VAT No.:** GB 388 3722 13
Date established: 2004 **Turnover:** Up to £250,000
No.of Employees: 1 - 10 **Product Groups:** 48

Grip Steel Reinforcements
Atlas Works Robinson Street, Stalybridge, SK15 1TH
Tel: 0161-338 2607 **Fax:** 0161-303 0871
E-mail: gripsteel@boltblue.com
Website: http://www.gripsteel.co.uk
Directors: D. Burke (Dir)
Immediate Holding Company: GRIP STEEL (REINFORCEMENTS) LIMITED
Registration no: 01787465 **VAT No.:** GB 425 8594 23
Date established: 1984 **Turnover:** £1m - £2m **No.of Employees:** 1 - 10
Product Groups: 34, 35

Date of Accounts	Dec 11	Dec 10	Dec 09
Working Capital	184	169	158
Fixed Assets	47	48	50
Current Assets	338	256	234

Hartle I G E Ltd
Demesne Drive St Pauls Trading Estate, Stalybridge, SK15 2QF
Tel: 0161-303 7394 **Fax:** 0161-303 1110
E-mail: info@hartleige.com
Website: http://www.hartleige.com
Bank(s): National Westminster Bank Plc
Directors: K. Truter (Fin)
Managers: J. Denton
Ultimate Holding Company: CHOICESTEADY LIMITED
Immediate Holding Company: HARTLE INTERNATIONAL LIMITED
Registration no: 01128935 **VAT No.:** GB 144 9675 34
Date established: 1973 **No.of Employees:** 11 - 20 **Product Groups:** 35, 36, 40, 46

Date of Accounts	Dec 11	Dec 10	Dec 09
Working Capital	-283	-283	-283
Fixed Assets	365	365	365
Current Assets	26	22	4

Lloyd Stott
Park View Works Park Street, Stalybridge, SK15 2BT
Tel: 0161-304 8043
Directors: T. Stott (Ptnr)
Registration no: 05007231 **Date established:** 2004
Turnover: Up to £250,000 **No.of Employees:** 1 - 10 **Product Groups:** 35, 36

Mailbox Stamford Products Ltd
Bayley Street, Stalybridge, SK15 1QQ
Tel: 0161-330 5577 **Fax:** 0161-330 5576
E-mail: contacts@swift-shop.com
Website: http://www.mailboxmouldings.co.uk
Bank(s): Royal Bank of Scotland, Ashton under Lyne
Directors: J. Nugent (Ch), W. Brown (Mkt Research), S. McKenna (Sales), S. Dubyl (Comm)
Managers: V. Smith (Chief Buyer), D. Ramsdale (Mktg Serv Mgr)
Ultimate Holding Company: The Stamford Group Ltd
Registration no: 06800625 **Date established:** 1982
Turnover: £10m - £20m **No.of Employees:** 251 - 500
Product Groups: 30, 45

Micropol Ltd
Bayley Street, Stalybridge, SK15 1QQ
Tel: 0161-330 5570 **Fax:** 0161-330 5576
E-mail: j.hardacre@micropol.co.uk
Website: http://www.micropol.co.uk
Bank(s): Royal Bank of Scotland, Ashton-under-Lyne
Managers: J. Hardacre (Comm)
Ultimate Holding Company: STAMFORD GROUP LIMITED(THE)
Immediate Holding Company: MICROPOL LIMITED
Registration no: 02660478 **VAT No.:** GB 380 4811 57
Date established: 1991 **Turnover:** £2m - £5m **No.of Employees:** 21 - 50
Product Groups: 30, 31, 32, 48

Date of Accounts	Sep 11	Sep 09	Sep 08
Sales Turnover	N/A	2m	3m
Pre Tax Profit/Loss	N/A	-353	-447
Working Capital	55	55	-330
Fixed Assets	N/A	N/A	388
Current Assets	55	55	962
Current Liabilities	N/A	N/A	2

Mirfin Industrial Cleaning Services Ltd
2 Waterloo Court Waterloo Road, Stalybridge, SK15 2AU
Tel: 0161-303 2579 **Fax:** 0161-304 7713
E-mail: mirfinltd@aol.com
Directors: E. Mirfin (MD)
Ultimate Holding Company: MIRFIN HOLDINGS LIMITED
Immediate Holding Company: MIRFIN INDUSTRIAL CLEANING SERVICES LIMITED
Registration no: 02547361 **Date established:** 1990
No.of Employees: 1 - 10 **Product Groups:** 32, 33, 66

Date of Accounts	Oct 11	Oct 10	Oct 09
Working Capital	-20	-39	-37
Fixed Assets	55	71	72
Current Assets	122	104	119

MTS Occasions by Design
Inglenook House 125 Mottram Old Road, Stalybridge, SK15 2SZ
Tel: 01457-766088
E-mail: enquiries@mts-occasionsbydesign.co.uk
Website: http://www.mts-occasionsbydesign.co.uk
Product Groups: 27, 38, 49, 65

Northern Insulation Contractors
Caroline House High Street, Stalybridge, SK15 1SE
Tel: 0161-303 1899 **Fax:** 0161-303 7845
E-mail: info@northerninsulation.com
Website: http://www.northerninsulation.com
Directors: J. Castella (Prop)
Managers: P. Walsh
Immediate Holding Company: NORTHERN INSULATION CONTRACTORS LLP
Registration no: OC326083 **Date established:** 2007 **Turnover:** £2m - £5m
No.of Employees: 21 - 50 **Product Groups:** 26, 30, 33, 35, 40, 52, 54, 66, 80, 85

Date of Accounts	Mar 11	Mar 10	Feb 08
Working Capital	-122	-153	-272
Fixed Assets	298	284	637
Current Assets	801	655	832

Opto International Ltd
Stamford Mill Bayley Street, Stalybridge, SK15 1QQ
Tel: 0161-330 5577 **Fax:** 0161-343 7332
E-mail: p.moulder@optoint.co.uk
Website: http://www.stamford-products.co.uk
Bank(s): Royal Bank of Scotland, Ashton-under-Lyne
Directors: P. Moulder (Dir)
Ultimate Holding Company: STAMFORD GROUP LIMITED(THE)
Immediate Holding Company: STAMFORD DISPLAY LIMITED
Registration no: 01652684 **Date established:** 1982 **Turnover:** £1m - £2m
No.of Employees: 101 - 250 **Product Groups:** 26, 49, 52

Date of Accounts	Sep 11	Sep 09	Sep 08
Sales Turnover	N/A	1m	1m
Pre Tax Profit/Loss	N/A	-163	-260
Working Capital	53	53	-22
Fixed Assets	N/A	N/A	38
Current Assets	53	53	368
Current Liabilities	N/A	N/A	8

Stepan UK Ltd
Bridge House Bridge Street, Stalybridge, SK15 1PH
Tel: 0161-338 5511 **Fax:** 0161-303 2991
E-mail: customer.service@stepaneurope.com
Website: http://www.stepan.com
Bank(s): National Westminster
Directors: D. Mulliner (Fin), I. Davies (Fin)
Managers: P. Rigby, C. Jones (Personnel), D. Wilde (Tech Serv Mgr), G. Howgill (Plant)
Ultimate Holding Company: STEPAN INC (USA)
Immediate Holding Company: STEPAN UK LIMITED
Registration no: 03264997 **Date established:** 1996
Turnover: £50m - £75m **No.of Employees:** 101 - 250
Product Groups: 31, 66

Date of Accounts	Dec 11	Dec 10	Dec 09
Sales Turnover	81m	68m	61m
Pre Tax Profit/Loss	2m	3m	4m
Working Capital	9m	8m	6m
Fixed Assets	12m	12m	12m
Current Assets	22m	21m	15m
Current Liabilities	3m	3m	2m

The Tameside Reporter & Glossop Chronicle Ltd

Park House 5 Acres Lane, Stalybridge, SK15 2JR
Tel: 0161-304 7691 **Fax:** 0161-303 1922
E-mail: cwright@reporterandchronicle.co.uk
Website: http://www.tamesidereporter.com
Directors: C. Wright (MD), C. Wright (MD)
Immediate Holding Company: REPORTER AND CHRONICLE NEWSPAPERS LIMITED
Registration no: 03377581 **Date established:** 1997
No.of Employees: 21 - 50 **Product Groups:** 28

Date of Accounts	Dec 11	Dec 10	Dec 09
Working Capital	569	585	591
Fixed Assets	937	937	967
Current Assets	569	585	591

Stockport

A G Parfetts

Didsbury Road, Stockport, SK4 2JP
Tel: 0161-429 0429 **Fax:** 0161-480 1720
E-mail: peter.mullan@parfetts.co.uk
Website: http://www.parfetts.co.uk
Managers: P. Mullan (Chief Mgr)
Immediate Holding Company: A.G. PARFETT & SONS LIMITED
Registration no: 01472970 **Date established:** 1980
Turnover: £250m - £500m **No.of Employees:** 101 - 250
Product Groups: 61

Date of Accounts	Jun 11	Jun 10	Jun 09
Sales Turnover	301m	289m	277m
Pre Tax Profit/Loss	3m	3m	2m
Working Capital	10m	9m	7m
Fixed Assets	30m	30m	31m
Current Assets	54m	54m	44m
Current Liabilities	3m	3m	2m

Abceta Playthings Ltd (Denton Agencies-Sven Carlson Ltd)

19 Torkington Road Hazel Grove, Stockport, SK7 4RG
Tel: 0161-483 4500 **Fax:** 0161-456 6896
E-mail: sir.terry.john.denton@dicksystem.com
Website: http://www.dicksystem.com
Bank(s): National Westminster
Directors: T. Denton (Ch)
Immediate Holding Company: ABCETA PLAYTHINGS LIMITED
Registration no: 00982372 **VAT No.:** GB 157 1109 82
Date established: 1970 **Turnover:** £2m - £5m **No.of Employees:** 21 - 50
Product Groups: 28, 65

Date of Accounts	Jan 12	Jan 11	Jan 10
Working Capital	32	51	38
Fixed Assets	78	61	60
Current Assets	32	63	45

Acoustic Control Systems

64 Cromley Road High Lane, Stockport, SK6 8BU
Tel: 01663-764409 **Fax:** 01663-764409
E-mail: sales@acousticcontrol.co.uk
Website: http://www.acousticcontrol.co.uk
Directors: D. Stewart (Ptnr)
Turnover: £500,000 - £1m **No.of Employees:** 1 - 10 **Product Groups:** 54

Advanced Ripening Technologies Limited

Unit 3 Whitehill Industrial Estate, Reddish, Stockport, SK4 1NU
Tel: 0161-480 0611 **Fax:** 020-7681 1741
E-mail: info@advancedripening.co.uk
Website: http://www.advancedripening.com
Directors: D. Rodden (Dir)
Registration no: 04600499 **Date established:** 2006
Turnover: £500,000 - £1m **No.of Employees:** 1 - 10 **Product Groups:** 02

Date of Accounts	Nov 07
Working Capital	4
Fixed Assets	9
Current Assets	21
Current Liabilities	17

A.J Holmes Pump Co. Ltd

Goyt Mill Upper Hibbert Lane, Marple, Stockport, SK6 7HX
Tel: 0161-427 3888 **Fax:** 0161-427 0090
E-mail: sales@ajholmes.co.uk
Website: http://www.ajhpumps.com
Registration no: 06342795 **Date established:** 2007
No.of Employees: 1 - 10 **Product Groups:** 39

Alexandra Garage Doors

56 Kenilworth Road Cheadle Heath, Stockport, SK3 0QN
Tel: 0161-428 6992
E-mail: info@alexandragaragedoors.co.uk
Website: http://www.alexandragaragedoors.co.uk
Directors: J. Collier (MD), J. Collyer (Prop), J. Collier (Prop)
Date established: 2006 **No.of Employees:** 1 - 10 **Product Groups:** 25, 30, 35, 36

All Door Engineering

Unit 26 Chadkirk Industrial Estate Vale Road, Romiley, Stockport, SK6 3LE
Tel: 0161-427 8997 **Fax:** 0161-427 8998
E-mail: alldooreng@aol.com
Website: http://www.alldoorengineering.com
Managers: J. Stamper (Mgr)
Immediate Holding Company: ALL DOOR ENGINEERING LTD
Registration no: 05006321 **Date established:** 2004
No.of Employees: 1 - 10 **Product Groups:** 26, 35

Date of Accounts	Jul 11	Jul 10	Jul 09
Working Capital	1	-2	-40
Fixed Assets	5	7	15
Current Assets	38	27	18

Alpha Business Computers Ltd

Bentley House Newby Road Industrial Estate Newby Road, Hazel Grove, Stockport, SK7 5DA
Tel: 0161-483 5650 **Fax:** 0161-483 5576
E-mail: info@alphacom.co.uk
Website: http://www.alphacom.co.uk
Bank(s): Royal Bank of Scotland, Stockport
Directors: D. Mair (MD), H. Johnson (I.T. Dir), F. Mair (Co Sec)
Managers: J. Malabon (Sales & Mktg Mg)
Immediate Holding Company: ALPHA BUSINESS COMPUTERS LIMITED
Registration no: 01517816 **VAT No.:** GB 593 7234 13
Date established: 1980 **Turnover:** £5m - £10m **No.of Employees:** 21 - 50
Product Groups: 44

Date of Accounts	Dec 09	Dec 08	Dec 07
Working Capital	221	529	469
Fixed Assets	656	676	720
Current Assets	2m	2m	2m

API Group plc

Second Avenue Poynton, Stockport, SK12 1ND
Tel: 01625-858700 **Fax:** 01625-858701
E-mail: enquiries@apigroup.com
Website: http://www.apigroup.com
Directors: C. Smith (Fin), R. Wright (Dir)
Immediate Holding Company: API GROUP PLC
Registration no: 00169249 **VAT No.:** GB 243 2900 86
Date established: 2020 **Turnover:** £75m - £125m
No.of Employees: 1 - 10 **Product Groups:** 27

Date of Accounts	Mar 12	Mar 11	Mar 10
Sales Turnover	114m	100m	85m
Pre Tax Profit/Loss	5m	3m	-8m
Working Capital	11m	8m	7m
Fixed Assets	28m	28m	42m
Current Assets	38m	33m	31m
Current Liabilities	6m	6m	7m

Audio Design Services Ltd

St Davids House Adcroft Street, Stockport, SK1 3HW
Tel: 0161-666 6363 **Fax:** 0161-666 6366
E-mail: info@ads-worldwide.net
Website: http://www.ads-worldwide.net
Directors: D. Telford (Dir)
Immediate Holding Company: AUDIO DESIGN SERVICES LIMITED
Registration no: 02469617 **Date established:** 1990 **Turnover:** £1m - £2m
No.of Employees: 1 - 10 **Product Groups:** 26, 35, 37, 40, 67, 84

Date of Accounts	May 11	May 10	May 09
Working Capital	97	58	70
Fixed Assets	15	18	24
Current Assets	328	290	268

B 2 B International Ltd

14 Ack Lane East Bramhall, Stockport, SK7 2BY
Tel: 0161-440 6000 **Fax:** 0161-440 6006
E-mail: info@b2binternational.com
Website: http://www.b2binternational.com
Directors: P. Hague (MD), C. Morgan (Pers)
Managers: M. Harrison, C. Harrison (Mktg Serv Mgr)
Immediate Holding Company: B2B INTERNATIONAL LTD
Registration no: 03232238 **VAT No.:** GB 685 9372 75
Date established: 1996 **Turnover:** £2m - £5m **No.of Employees:** 21 - 50
Product Groups: 80, 81, 86

Date of Accounts	Dec 11	Dec 10	Dec 09
Working Capital	2m	1m	1m
Fixed Assets	326	275	223
Current Assets	2m	2m	1m

B R G International Ltd

Carrington Field Street, Stockport, SK1 3JN
Tel: 0161-429 8787 **Fax:** 0161-480 3573
E-mail: info@brginternational.co.uk
Website: http://www.brginternational.co.uk
Managers: A. Patterson (Fin Mgr)
Ultimate Holding Company: SPORTFIELD DEUTSCHLAND HOLDING GMBH (GERMANY)
Immediate Holding Company: INHOCO 564 LIMITED
Registration no: 04921903 **Date established:** 1996
No.of Employees: 21 - 50 **Product Groups:** 29, 42, 49

Date of Accounts	Dec 11	Dec 10	Dec 09
Sales Turnover	7m	7m	7m
Pre Tax Profit/Loss	293	782	293
Working Capital	9m	9m	8m
Fixed Assets	1m	1m	2m
Current Assets	9m	9m	9m
Current Liabilities	163	331	321

B S H Transit Cases

Unit 3 Brighton Road Industrial Estate, Stockport, SK4 2BE
Tel: 0161-273 2323 **Fax:** 0161-273 3531
E-mail: sales@bshtransitcases.co.uk
Website: http://www.bshtransitcases.co.uk
Directors: M. Powell (MD)
Immediate Holding Company: FISH-RA! LIMITED
Date established: 2000 **No.of Employees:** 1 - 10 **Product Groups:** 22, 25, 35, 49, 66, 67

Banner Ltd

Banner House Greg Street, Stockport, SK5 7BT
Tel: 0161-474 8000 **Fax:** 0161-474 7655
E-mail: nigel.plenderleith@bannergroup.co.uk
Website: http://www.bannergroup.co.uk
Directors: I. Parrot (MD), I. Powell (Co Sec), G. Hocking (Dir), N. Plenderleith (MD)
Managers: A. Davies (Chief Acct)
Ultimate Holding Company: 06478309
Immediate Holding Company: BANNER LIMITED
Registration no: 03386793 **Date established:** 1997
Turnover: £10m - £20m **No.of Employees:** 51 - 100 **Product Groups:** 23, 24

Date of Accounts	Nov 09	Nov 08	Oct 07
Sales Turnover	14m	17m	18m
Pre Tax Profit/Loss	-235	-2m	-409
Working Capital	8m	8m	-1m
Fixed Assets	955	1m	1m
Current Assets	10m	10m	9m
Current Liabilities	703	498	345

Bateson Trailers Ltd

Doodfield Works Windlehurst Road, Marple, Stockport, SK6 7EN
Tel: 0161-426 0500 **Fax:** 0161-426 0245
E-mail: brian@bateson-trailers.co.uk
Website: http://www.batesontrailers.com
Bank(s): National Westminster Bank Plc
Directors: D. Bateson (Fin), B. Bateson (MD)
Managers: G. Smith (Chief Mgr)
Immediate Holding Company: BATESON TRAILERS LIMITED
Registration no: 01081973 **Date established:** 1972 **Turnover:** £2m - £5m
No.of Employees: 21 - 50 **Product Groups:** 39, 41, 45

Date of Accounts	Dec 11	Dec 10	Dec 09
Working Capital	932	909	879
Fixed Assets	634	635	628
Current Assets	1m	1m	1m

Bennett Verby

7 St Petersgate, Stockport, SK1 1EB
Tel: 0161-476 9000 **Fax:** 0161-476 9001
E-mail: enquiries@bvllp.com
Website: http://www.bennettverby.co.uk
Directors: B. Verby (MD)
Immediate Holding Company: BV ACCOUNTANTS LLP
Registration no: OC304295 **Date established:** 2003 **Turnover:** £2m - £5m
No.of Employees: 51 - 100 **Product Groups:** 80

Date of Accounts	Dec 11	Mar 11	Mar 10
Working Capital	-574	-577	-505
Fixed Assets	3m	3m	3m
Current Assets	310	224	239

Beta 3 Solutions Ltd

B3S P O Box 3, Stockport, SK6 7WG
Tel: 0161-221 3331
E-mail: boyd.black@beta3solutions.com
Website: http://www.beta3solutions.com
Date established: 2002 **Turnover:** Up to £250,000
No.of Employees: 1 - 10 **Product Groups:** 40, 44, 81, 82, 83

Date of Accounts	Jan 08	Jan 07	Jan 06
Working Capital	-7	-10	11
Fixed Assets	14	14	15
Current Assets	19	6	35
Current Liabilities	26	16	24
Total Share Capital	1	1	1

George Bethell Ltd

Unit 9 Rugby Park Bletchley Road, Heaton Mersey, Stockport, SK4 3EJ
Tel: 0161-442 8805 **Fax:** 0161-442 8818
E-mail: sales@bethell.com
Website: http://www.bethell.com
Directors: G. Bethell (MD), M. Dean (Fab)
Immediate Holding Company: GEORGE BETHELL LIMITED
Registration no: 00498224 **Date established:** 1951
Turnover: £250,000 - £500,000 **No.of Employees:** 1 - 10
Product Groups: 30, 34

Date of Accounts	Sep 07	Sep 06	Sep 05
Working Capital	123	133	137
Fixed Assets	122	146	91
Current Assets	199	255	275
Current Liabilities	76	122	138
Total Share Capital	3	3	3

Bonut Engineering Ltd

Unit 12 Latham Close Bredbury, Stockport, SK6 2SD
Tel: 0161-430 4000 **Fax:** 0161-480 6173
E-mail: info@bonutengineering.co.uk
Website: http://www.bonutengineering.co.uk
Directors: B. Travis (Fin)
Ultimate Holding Company: ARBOUR HOLDINGS LIMITED
Immediate Holding Company: BONUT ENGINEERING LIMITED
Registration no: 00883368 **VAT No.:** GB 158 8671 16
Date established: 1966 **Turnover:** £250,000 - £500,000
No.of Employees: 1 - 10 **Product Groups:** 67

Date of Accounts	Mar 11	Mar 10	Mar 09
Working Capital	21	28	36
Fixed Assets	144	65	30
Current Assets	242	223	168

Boole's Tools & Pipe Fitting Ltd

Haigh Avenue, Stockport, SK4 1NU
Tel: 0161-480 7900 **Fax:** 0161-474 7142
E-mail: enquiries@booles.co.uk
Website: http://www.booles.co.uk
Bank(s): Barclays
Directors: N. Walker (MD)
Immediate Holding Company: DIAMOND SHOPFITTING LIMITED
Registration no: 00683745 **VAT No.:** GB 726 9744 92
Date established: 1994 **Turnover:** £10m - £20m
No.of Employees: 51 - 100 **Product Groups:** 30, 36, 66

Date of Accounts	Sep 11	Sep 10	Sep 09
Working Capital	87	107	47
Fixed Assets	2	3	4
Current Assets	180	189	129

Boxer Design & Manufacturing Ltd

Unit 2 Boundary Court Heaton Chapel, Stockport, SK4 5GA
Tel: 0161-975 1830 **Fax:** 0161-431 3364
E-mail: sales@boxer-design.co.uk
Website: http://www.boxer-design.co.uk
Directors: D. Horridge (MD)
Immediate Holding Company: BOXER DESIGN AND MANUFACTURING LIMITED
Registration no: 02095428 **Date established:** 1987
No.of Employees: 11 - 20 **Product Groups:** 46

Date of Accounts	Mar 11	Mar 10	Mar 09
Working Capital	502	611	591
Fixed Assets	35	32	39
Current Assets	863	914	859

Boxes & Packaging Ltd

Unit 10 Southside Bredbury Park Industrial Estate, Bredbury, Stockport, SK6 2SP
Tel: 0161-406 4200 **Fax:** 0161-406 7217
E-mail: manchester@boxesandpackaging.co.uk
Website: http://www.boxesandpackaging.co.uk
Directors: G. Hargreaves (MD)
Managers: B. Moore (Fin Mgr)
Ultimate Holding Company: BOXES AND PACKAGING (UK) LIMITED
Immediate Holding Company: BOXES AND PACKAGING LIMITED
Registration no: 05291434 **Date established:** 2004
No.of Employees: 21 - 50 **Product Groups:** 27, 28, 49

Boyco Manufacturing Company
Europa Way, Stockport, SK3 0XE
Tel: 0161-428 7077
Website: http://www.boycouk.com
Directors: D. Boyt (Ptnr)
Managers: M. Shaw (Purch Mgr)
Immediate Holding Company: BOYCO LIMITED
Registration no: 05218042 **Date established:** 2004
No.of Employees: 21 - 50 **Product Groups:** 38, 67

Date of Accounts	Aug 10	Aug 09	Aug 08
Working Capital	1	N/A	N/A
Current Assets	3	2	2

T W Bracher & Co. Ltd
Royal George Street, Stockport, SK3 8AS
Tel: 0161-480 2005 **Fax:** 0161-477 1673
E-mail: sales@tw-bracher.co.uk
Website: http://www.tw-bracher.co.uk
Directors: I. Hosfield (MD)
Immediate Holding Company: T.W.BRACHER AND COMPANY LIMITED
Registration no: 00059246 **VAT No.:** GB 157 1053 83
Date established: 1998 **Turnover:** £250,000 - £500,000
No.of Employees: 1 - 10 **Product Groups:** 22, 23

Date of Accounts	Mar 11	Mar 10	Mar 09
Working Capital	98	72	197
Fixed Assets	77	74	67
Current Assets	202	151	291

Bright Sparks
37 Carleton Road Poynton, Stockport, SK12 1TL
Tel: 01625-876716 **Fax:** 01625-630287
E-mail: installations@brightsparks-electrical.co.uk
Website: http://www.brightsparks-electrical.co.uk
Directors: R. Kay (Prop)
Date established: 1997 **No.of Employees:** 1 - 10 **Product Groups:** 07, 37, 39, 51, 52, 84

Brinksway Electro Plating Ltd
Unit 17 Latham Close Bredbury Park Industrial Estate, Bredbury, Stockport, SK6 2SD
Tel: 0161-494 6161 **Fax:** 0161-406 6447
Directors: J. Byrne (MD)
Immediate Holding Company: BRINKSWAY ELECTRO PLATING LIMITED
Registration no: 00795656 **VAT No.:** GB 157 1803 66
Date established: 1964 **Turnover:** £250,000 - £500,000
No.of Employees: 1 - 10 **Product Groups:** 48

Date of Accounts	Mar 11	Mar 10	Mar 09
Working Capital	-12	-13	-16
Fixed Assets	66	78	80
Current Assets	126	120	109

Broadstone Mill Shopping Outlet
Broadstone House Broadstone Road, Stockport, SK5 7DL
Tel: 0161-953 4470 **Fax:** 0161-953 4456
E-mail: sarah@broadstone.co.uk
Website: http://www.broadstone-shopping.co.uk
Managers: S. Moores (Mgr)
Immediate Holding Company: BROADSTONE MILL LTD
Registration no: 03386969 **VAT No.:** GB 693 6629 84
Date established: 1997 **Turnover:** £1m - £2m **No.of Employees:** 11 - 20
Product Groups: 23

Date of Accounts	Dec 11	Dec 10	Dec 09
Working Capital	-2m	-2m	-600
Fixed Assets	6m	6m	2m
Current Assets	558	891	3m
Current Liabilities	N/A	157	N/A

Cartridge Works
37 Great Portwood Street, Stockport, SK1 2DW
Tel: 0161-477 9888 **Fax:** 0161-477 9988
E-mail: sales@cartridgeworks.co.uk
Website: http://www.cartridgeworks.co.uk
Directors: A. Richings (Dir)
Immediate Holding Company: CARTRIDGE WORLD LTD
Registration no: 04124067 **Date established:** 2000 **Turnover:** £5m - £10m
No.of Employees: 1 - 10 **Product Groups:** 30, 42, 44

Centrifugal Pump Services Ltd
Pump House Bird Hall Lane, Stockport, SK3 0XX
Tel: 0161-428 0133 **Fax:** 0161-428 0188
E-mail: sales@centrifugalpumps.co.uk
Website: http://www.centrifugalpumps.co.uk
Directors: J. Shepley (Fin), G. Shepley (MD)
Immediate Holding Company: CENTRIFUGAL PUMP SERVICES LIMITED
Registration no: 03406402 **Date established:** 1997
No.of Employees: 1 - 10 **Product Groups:** 37, 39, 40

Date of Accounts	Dec 11	Dec 10	Dec 09
Working Capital	N/A	-9	11
Fixed Assets	275	244	251
Current Assets	384	117	123

Chemix Ltd
Vauxhall Industrial Estate Greg Street, Stockport, SK5 7BR
Tel: 0161-480 3487 **Fax:** 0161-480 2394
Website: http://www.chemix.com
Bank(s): TSB, Stockport
Directors: A. Tate (Develop), D. Holt (MD), M. Dolan (Sales & Tech), P. Holt (Fab)
Managers: D. Thompson (Buyer), M. Mycock (Personnel)
Registration no: 01498727 **Turnover:** £20m - £50m
No.of Employees: 101 - 250 **Product Groups:** 30

Date of Accounts	Jun 07
Pre Tax Profit/Loss	105
Working Capital	250
Fixed Assets	888
Current Assets	3948
Current Liabilities	3698
Total Share Capital	50
ROCE% (Return on Capital Employed)	9.2

Arthur W Clowes Ltd
Unit 2 Bramhall Moor Industrial Estate Pepper Road, Hazel Grove, Stockport, SK7 5BW
Tel: 0161-482 7100 **Fax:** 0161-483 1827
E-mail: sales@clowesprinters.co.uk
Website: http://www.clowesprinters.co.uk
Directors: R. Clowes (Co Sec), T. Bann (Fab), B. Sutton (Sales)
Managers: I. Allenson (Prod Mgr), S. Hearle (Accounts)
Immediate Holding Company: ARTHUR W. CLOWES LIMITED
Registration no: 00692036 **Date established:** 1961
No.of Employees: 1 - 10 **Product Groups:** 27, 28, 30, 48, 85

Date of Accounts	Mar 07	Mar 06	Mar 05
Working Capital	-223	-205	-228
Fixed Assets	560	760	928
Current Assets	1m	1m	1m

Compufit
14 Foliage Crescent, Stockport, SK5 8AP
Tel: 0161-408 4019 **Fax:** 0161-612 2363
E-mail: info@compufit.co.uk
Website: http://www.compufit.co.uk
Directors: D. Pohle (Prop)
Date established: 2008 **No.of Employees:** 1 - 10 **Product Groups:** 44, 48

Computerised Cutting Technology Services Ltd
32 Birch Tree Avenue Hazel Grove, Stockport, SK7 6AP
Tel: 0161-456 1394 **Fax:** 0161-487 3169
E-mail: james@profilerservices.co.uk
Website: http://www.profilerservices.co.uk
Directors: J. Bell (Fin), J. Bell (MD)
Immediate Holding Company: COMPUTERISED CUTTING TECHNOLOGY SERVICES LIMITED
Registration no: 03839861 **Date established:** 1999
Turnover: £500,000 - £1m **No.of Employees:** 1 - 10 **Product Groups:** 46

Date of Accounts	Sep 11	Sep 10	Sep 09
Working Capital	43	51	70
Fixed Assets	7	8	9
Current Assets	102	92	105

Connell Consulting Engineers
Baxall Business Centre Adswood Industrial Estate Adswood Road, Stockport, SK3 8LF
Tel: 0161-477 4100
E-mail: info@connellconsulting.co.uk
Website: http://www.connellconsulting.co.uk
Directors: P. Connell (Prop)
Immediate Holding Company: CONNELL CONSULTING ENGINEERS LIMITED
Registration no: 07583256 **Date established:** 2011
No.of Employees: 1 - 10 **Product Groups:** 35

Cooper Beal & Ross
33 Shaw Road, Stockport, SK4 4AG
Tel: 0161-442 9770 **Fax:** 0161-442 9775
E-mail: cooperbealross@aol.com
Directors: A. Ross (Prop)
VAT No.: GB 144 9592 38 **Turnover:** £250,000 - £500,000
No.of Employees: 1 - 10 **Product Groups:** 84

Coperion Ltd
Victoria House 19-21 Ack Lane East, Bramhall, Stockport, SK7 2BE
Tel: 0161-925 6910 **Fax:** 0161-925 6911
E-mail: info@coperion.com
Website: http://www.coperion.com
Managers: C. Sturmey
Ultimate Holding Company: COPERION GROUP GMBH (GERMANY)
Immediate Holding Company: COPERION LIMITED
Registration no: 01185424 **VAT No.:** GB 228 0260 90
Date established: 1974 **Turnover:** £250,000 - £500,000
No.of Employees: 1 - 10 **Product Groups:** 20, 41, 42, 45, 67

Date of Accounts	Dec 11	Dec 10	Dec 09
Sales Turnover	441	356	209
Pre Tax Profit/Loss	50	-21	-133
Working Capital	-271	-299	-300
Fixed Assets	22	N/A	22
Current Assets	235	173	142
Current Liabilities	36	35	81

County Gates
Unit 28 Chadkirk Cottages Vale Road, Romiley, Stockport, SK6 3LE
Tel: 0161-449 7607 **Fax:** 0161-449 7607
E-mail: sales@countygates.net
Website: http://www.countygates.net
Directors: L. Brinsley (Prop)
Date established: 1981 **No.of Employees:** 1 - 10 **Product Groups:** 26, 35

Create Solutions Ltd
Houldsworth Mill Houldsworth Street, Stockport, SK5 6DA
Tel: 0161-975 6175 **Fax:** 0161-975 6001
E-mail: info@totalinsite.co.uk
Website: http://www.createsolutions.co.uk
Directors: M. Cranny (MD), K. Cartridge (Fin)
Ultimate Holding Company: CAKE HOLDINGS LIMITED
Immediate Holding Company: CREATE SOLUTIONS LTD
Registration no: 04446616 **Date established:** 2002
No.of Employees: 1 - 10 **Product Groups:** 49

Date of Accounts	May 11	May 09	May 08
Working Capital	-3	-5	-5
Fixed Assets	4	5	6
Current Assets	33	25	24

Creighton Developments Ltd
Unit 15 Enterprise Centre Two Chester Street, Stockport, SK3 0BR
Tel: 0161-480 0668 **Fax:** 0161-480 0668
Directors: G. Robinson (Fin), N. Robinson (MD)
Immediate Holding Company: CREIGHTON DEVELOPMENTS LIMITED
Registration no: 01821667 **VAT No.:** GB 405 8241 70
Date established: 1984 **Turnover:** Up to £250,000
No.of Employees: 1 - 10 **Product Groups:** 84

Date of Accounts	Jun 12	Jun 11	Jun 10
Working Capital	66	77	69
Fixed Assets	14	15	16
Current Assets	76	100	87

Cruger Tissue Group UK Ltd
Waterside Disley, Stockport, SK12 2HW
Tel: 01663-762701 **Fax:** 01663-762421
E-mail: sales@cruger.com
Website: http://www.cruger.com
Directors: J. Krueger (Dir), R. Jones (Co Sec)
Registration no: 02925647 **VAT No.:** GB 616 2188 49
Turnover: £50m - £75m **No.of Employees:** 11 - 20 **Product Groups:** 27, 66

Davron
21 Beechfield Road, Stockport, SK3 8SF
Tel: 0161-483 5678 **Fax:** 0161-483 5678
E-mail: sales@davron.co.uk
Website: http://www.davron.co.uk
Directors: B. Goose (Prop)
Immediate Holding Company: THE ORGANISATION FOR PROFESSIONALS IN REGULATORY AFFAIRS LIMITED
Date established: 1978 **Turnover:** £250,000 - £500,000
No.of Employees: 1 - 10 **Product Groups:** 37, 39, 63, 67, 68

Ian Dayes Associates
24 Fernhill Mellor, Stockport, SK6 5AN
Tel: 0161-427 9321
E-mail: ian.dayes@id-associates.com
Website: http://www.id-associates.com
Directors: I. Dayes (Prop), J. Dayes (Dir)
No.of Employees: 1 - 10 **Product Groups:** 80

Deanprint Ltd
Cheadle Heath Works Stockport Road, Stockport, SK3 0PR
Tel: 0161-428 2236 **Fax:** 0161-428 0817
E-mail: sales@deanprint.co.uk
Website: http://www.deanprint.co.uk
Bank(s): Barclays
Directors: D. Thurrold (MD)
Managers: J. Sherlock (Sales Prom Mgr)
Ultimate Holding Company: DJK (HOLDINGS) LIMITED
Immediate Holding Company: DEAN HOLDINGS LIMITED
Registration no: 01816542 **Date established:** 1984 **Turnover:** £2m - £5m
No.of Employees: 21 - 50 **Product Groups:** 27, 28

Date of Accounts	Apr 12	Apr 11	Apr 10
Working Capital	801	357	409
Fixed Assets	531	531	531
Current Assets	842	357	425

Delta Neu Ltd
Newby Road Industrial Estate Newby Road Hazel Grove, Stockport, SK7 5DR
Tel: 0161-456 5511 **Fax:** 0161-456 2460
E-mail: mail@delta-neu.co.uk
Website: http://www.delta-neu.com
Directors: P. Dowell (Dir), M. Duffy (Co Sec)
Ultimate Holding Company: SFPI (FRANCE)
Immediate Holding Company: DELTA NEU LIMITED
Registration no: 03989637 **VAT No.:** GB 742 5101 67
Date established: 2000 **Turnover:** £2m - £5m **No.of Employees:** 1 - 10
Product Groups: 40, 42

Date of Accounts	Dec 11	Dec 10	Dec 09
Sales Turnover	3m	2m	2m
Pre Tax Profit/Loss	133	65	10
Working Capital	345	233	192
Fixed Assets	26	24	11
Current Assets	1m	993	845
Current Liabilities	280	365	212

Design Plus
Unit 15 Christie Street Industrial Estate Christie Street, Stockport, SK1 4LR
Tel: 0161-477 4414 **Fax:** 0161-477 4412
E-mail: info@designplus.co.uk
Website: http://www.designplus.co.uk
Directors: D. Barlow (Prop)
No.of Employees: 11 - 20 **Product Groups:** 23, 24, 63, 81

Direct Packaging Solutions Ltd
Grove Works Battersea Road, Stockport, SK4 3EA
Tel: 0161-975 5360 **Fax:** 0161-975 5361
E-mail: sales@dpack.co.uk
Website: http://www.dpack.co.uk
Directors: D. Leach (MD)
Immediate Holding Company: DIRECT PACKAGING SOLUTIONS LTD
Registration no: 04419905 **Date established:** 2002 **Turnover:** £2m - £5m
No.of Employees: 11 - 20 **Product Groups:** 27

Date of Accounts	May 11	May 10	May 09
Working Capital	184	118	97
Fixed Assets	816	791	798
Current Assets	901	623	550

Doorserve Ltd T/A Carrington Doors (t/a Carrington Doors)
Horton Street Higher Hillgate, Stockport, SK1 3LR
Tel: 0161-477 3391 **Fax:** 0161-477 3392
E-mail: sales@carringtondoors.co.uk
Website: http://www.carringtondoors.co.uk
Directors: S. Fielding (Dir)
Registration no: 03590801 **Date established:** 2003
Turnover: Up to £250,000 **No.of Employees:** 11 - 20 **Product Groups:** 25, 30, 35

Duscovent Engineering Ltd
86 Wellington Road North, Stockport, SK4 1HT
Tel: 0161-480 4811 **Fax:** 0161-480 6503
E-mail: sales@duscovent.co.uk
Website: http://www.duscovent.co.uk
Directors: C. Sedgeley (MD), C. Sedgley (Co Sec)
Immediate Holding Company: DUSCOVENT ENGINEERING LIMITED
Registration no: 01959966 **VAT No.:** GB 431 6206 85
Date established: 1985 **Turnover:** £1m - £2m **No.of Employees:** 1 - 10
Product Groups: 33, 40, 42

Date of Accounts	Jul 11	Jul 10	Jul 09
Working Capital	101	59	49
Fixed Assets	2	1	2
Current Assets	324	256	192

Dyer Environmental Controls Ltd
Unit 10 Lawnhurst Trading Estate Ashurst Drive, Stockport, SK3 0SD
Tel: 0161-491 4840 **Fax:** 0161-491 4841
E-mail: enquiry@dyerenvironmental.co.uk
Website: http://www.dyerenvironmental.co.uk
Directors: J. Crossley (MD), S. Richards (Co Sec)
Immediate Holding Company: DYER ENVIRONMENTAL CONTROLS LIMITED
Registration no: 02670985 **Date established:** 1991
No.of Employees: 11 - 20 **Product Groups:** 40, 66

Date of Accounts	Dec 11	Dec 10	Mar 10
Working Capital	431	426	580
Fixed Assets	6	9	8
Current Assets	853	949	1m

E & E Workwear
Church Lane Marple, Stockport, SK6 7AR
Tel: 0161-427 6522 **Fax:** 0161-426 0906
E-mail: sales@eandeworkwear.co.uk
Website: http://www.eandeworkwear.co.uk
Bank(s): Barclays
Directors: A. Ashton (Snr Part)
Turnover: £1m - £2m **No.of Employees:** 11 - 20 **Product Groups:** 24, 63

E H L Ltd
7 & 8 Broadstone Industrial Estate Gregson Road, Stockport, SK5 7SS
Tel: 0161-480 7902 **Fax:** 0161-273 8668
E-mail: nas@ehl-ingredients.co.uk
Website: http://www.ehl-ingredients.co.uk
Directors: N. Haq (Dir)
Managers: T. Backhouse
Immediate Holding Company: E.H.L. LTD.
Registration no: 03022540 **Date established:** 1995
No.of Employees: 11 - 20 **Product Groups:** 20

Date of Accounts	Jul 11	Jul 10	Jul 09
Working Capital	354	282	280
Fixed Assets	41	52	10
Current Assets	1m	819	712

Ecolab Pest Control Ltd
Falcon House Lawnhurst Industrial Estate, Stockport, SK3 0XT
Tel: 0161-491 3855 **Fax:** 0161-491 6088
Website: http://www.ecolab.com
Directors: J. Brooks (Dir)
No.of Employees: 21 - 50 **Product Groups:** 07, 32, 52, 66

Egan Reid Stationery Co. Ltd
Horsfield Way Bredbury Park Industrial Estate, Bredbury, Stockport, SK6 2SU
Tel: 0161-406 6000 **Fax:** 0161-406 6591
E-mail: sales@eganreid.co.uk
Website: http://www.eganreid.co.uk
Bank(s): Barclays P.L.C., Stockport
Directors: A. Reid (MD), B. Derbyshire (Fin)
Managers: M. Lord, P. Connor (Sales Prom Mgr), F. Trak (Mktg Serv Mgr)
Immediate Holding Company: EGAN,REID STATIONERY CO.LIMITED
Registration no: 00593651 **VAT No.:** GB 145 6026 80
Date established: 1957 **Turnover:** £5m - £10m
No.of Employees: 51 - 100 **Product Groups:** 26, 64

Date of Accounts	Mar 11	Mar 10	Mar 09
Sales Turnover	9m	9m	N/A
Pre Tax Profit/Loss	22	315	120
Working Capital	409	511	557
Fixed Assets	157	185	178
Current Assets	3m	3m	2m
Current Liabilities	419	410	332

Elastomerics
Summit House 48a Bramhall Lane South, Bramhall, Stockport, SK7 1AH
Tel: 0161-439 9116 **Fax:** 0161-440 8035
E-mail: enquiries@elastomerics.com
Website: http://www.elastomerics.com
Directors: J. Price (Fin), G. Cook (MD)
Immediate Holding Company: ELASTOMERICS LIMITED
Registration no: 01595889 **VAT No.:** 306 9525 53 **Date established:** 1981
Turnover: £20m - £50m **No.of Employees:** 1 - 10 **Product Groups:** 66, 68

Date of Accounts	Dec 11	Dec 10	Dec 09
Sales Turnover	30m	20m	15m
Pre Tax Profit/Loss	2m	1m	953
Working Capital	4m	3m	2m
Fixed Assets	70	75	68
Current Assets	7m	7m	5m
Current Liabilities	1m	723	565

Emerson Process Management Limited
Horsfield Way Bredbury, Stockport, SK6 2SU
Tel: 0870-240 1978 **Fax:** 0870-240 4389
E-mail: uksales@emersonprocess.com
Website: http://www.emersonprocess.com
Directors: J. Willson (MD)
Managers: R. Perks (Sales Prom Mgr)
Ultimate Holding Company: Roxboro
Immediate Holding Company: Solartron Mobrey
Registration no: 00671801 **VAT No.:** GB 285 1163 59
Turnover: £50m - £75m **No.of Employees:** 1 - 10 **Product Groups:** 38, 48, 52

Euromixers
PO Box 94, Stockport, SK6 6HP
Tel: 0161-449 8559 **Fax:** 0161-426 0456
E-mail: sales@euromixers.co.uk
Website: http://www.euromixers.co.uk
Directors: S. Stafford (Co Sec)
Immediate Holding Company: EURO MIXERS LIMITED
Registration no: 04002267 **Date established:** 2000
No.of Employees: 1 - 10 **Product Groups:** 27, 41, 42

Date of Accounts	May 11	May 10	May 09
Working Capital	107	88	77
Fixed Assets	6	3	2
Current Assets	232	190	184

Ferndean Fabrications
Unit 6 Chadkirk Industrial Estate Vale Road, Romiley, Stockport, SK6 3NE
Tel: 0161-426 0057 **Fax:** 0161-426 0366
E-mail: ferndeanfabs@yahoo.com
Website: http://www.ferndeanfabs.co.uk
Directors: S. Fern (Ptnr), B. Russell (Prop)
Managers: P. Butterworth (Mgr)
Date established: 1985 **No.of Employees:** 1 - 10 **Product Groups:** 38, 42

Fibrestar Drums Ltd
Redhouse Lane Disley, Stockport, SK12 2NW
Tel: 01663-764141 **Fax:** 01633-762967
E-mail: antoni.starsiak@fibrestar.co.uk
Website: http://www.fibrestar.co.uk
Directors: A. Starsiak (Ptnr), S. Hornby (Fin)
Managers: M. Holmes (Prod Mgr)
Ultimate Holding Company: BPG HOLDINGS LIMITED
Immediate Holding Company: FIBRESTAR DRUMS LIMITED
Registration no: 03928251 **Date established:** 2000 **Turnover:** £5m - £10m
No.of Employees: 51 - 100 **Product Groups:** 30, 41

Date of Accounts	Dec 07	Jun 11	Jun 10
Sales Turnover	N/A	6m	6m
Pre Tax Profit/Loss	365	130	164
Working Capital	3m	998	997
Fixed Assets	1m	706	736
Current Assets	6m	2m	3m
Current Liabilities	1m	447	464

Fichtner Consulting Engineers Ltd
Kingsgate 3rd Floor Wellington Road North, Stockport, SK4 1LW
Tel: 0161-476 0032 **Fax:** 0161-474 0618
E-mail: sales@fichtner.co.uk
Website: http://www.fichtner.co.uk
Bank(s): National Westminster Bank Plc
Directors: D. Abernethy (Develop), J. Wetherby (MD)
Managers: M. Wall (Tech Serv Mgr), L. Edgeley (Chief Acct), C. Hjoerringgaard
Immediate Holding Company: FICHTNER CONSULTING ENGINEERS LIMITED
Registration no: 02605319 **VAT No.:** GB 527 5645 27
Date established: 1991 **Turnover:** £1m - £2m **No.of Employees:** 51 - 100
Product Groups: 80, 81, 84, 85

Date of Accounts	Dec 11	Dec 10	Dec 09
Sales Turnover	8m	N/A	N/A
Pre Tax Profit/Loss	2m	N/A	N/A
Working Capital	3m	2m	2m
Fixed Assets	316	346	366
Current Assets	5m	5m	4m
Current Liabilities	2m	N/A	N/A

Firex Protection Ltd
17a Coniston Road High Lane, Stockport, SK6 8AW
Tel: 01663-763264 **Fax:** 01663-763264
E-mail: chris@firexprotection.com
Website: http://www.firexprotection.com
Directors: S. Shiels (Fin), C. Shiels (MD)
Immediate Holding Company: FIREX PROTECTION LIMITED
Registration no: 04398153 **Date established:** 2002
No.of Employees: 1 - 10 **Product Groups:** 39, 40, 52, 67, 68, 84, 86, 87

Date of Accounts	Jul 11	Jul 10	Jul 07
Working Capital	-0	-7	-24
Fixed Assets	1	1	3
Current Assets	5	6	5

Flueclean Installations Services Ltd
Lytham Street Works Lytham Street, Stockport, SK3 8JB
Tel: 0161-480 8551 **Fax:** 0161-477 7769
E-mail: enquiries@flueclean.co.uk
Website: http://www.flueclean.co.uk
Directors: D. Buller (Co Sec), A. Wallwork (MD)
Immediate Holding Company: FLUECLEAN INSTALLATIONS SERVICES LIMITED
Registration no: 01997575 **Date established:** 1986
Turnover: £500,000 - £1m **No.of Employees:** 11 - 20 **Product Groups:** 48

Date of Accounts	Sep 11	Sep 10	Sep 09
Working Capital	86	89	50
Fixed Assets	95	82	143
Current Assets	268	197	165

Forest City Export Services Ltd
Bowden Hall Bowden Lane, Marple, Stockport, SK6 6NE
Tel: 0161-449 0660 **Fax:** 0161-449 0880
E-mail: forestcity@compuserve.com
Website: http://www.forestcitygenerators.com
Directors: A. Lamb (MD)
Immediate Holding Company: FOREST CITY EXPORT SERVICES LIMITED
Registration no: 02792115 **Date established:** 1993
No.of Employees: 1 - 10 **Product Groups:** 37

Date of Accounts	Dec 11	Dec 10	Dec 09
Working Capital	256	206	136
Fixed Assets	N/A	1	1
Current Assets	716	649	523

Freestyle Hair Co. Ltd
Unit 22 Haigh Park, Stockport, SK4 1QR
Tel: 0161-476 1115 **Fax:** 0161-429 0730
E-mail: info@freestylehair.co.uk
Website: http://www.freestylehair.co.uk
Directors: A. Thompson (Fin)
Managers: L. Podmore (Sales Admin)
Immediate Holding Company: FREESTYLE HAIR COMPANY LTD.
Registration no: 02678011 **VAT No.:** GB 611 3818 67
Date established: 1992 **Turnover:** £250,000 - £500,000
No.of Employees: 1 - 10 **Product Groups:** 26, 30, 32, 33, 36, 40, 49, 61, 66, 67

Date of Accounts	Mar 11	Mar 10	Mar 09
Working Capital	-29	-2	-156
Fixed Assets	447	445	439
Current Assets	245	223	174

G S M Secure
8 Marina Road Bredbury, Stockport, SK6 2PS
Tel: 0161-660 7090 **Fax:** 0870-235 1366
E-mail: sales@gsm-secure.co.uk
Website: http://www.gsm-secure.co.uk
Directors: L. Taylor (MD)
Immediate Holding Company: GSM SECURE DISTRIBUTION LTD
Registration no: 06358080 **Date established:** 2007
No.of Employees: 1 - 10 **Product Groups:** 37, 40, 81

Garvagh Lighting
Meadow Mill Water Street, Stockport, SK1 2BY
Tel: 0161-429 8429 **Fax:** 0161-429 9547
E-mail: info@garvagh-lighting.com
Website: http://www.garvagh-lighting.com
Directors: E. Hiddleston (Fin), I. Hiddleston (MD)
Immediate Holding Company: GARVAGH LIGHTING LTD
Registration no: 04725961 **Date established:** 2003
No.of Employees: 1 - 10 **Product Groups:** 37, 84

Date of Accounts	Apr 11	Apr 10	Apr 09
Working Capital	14	6	2
Fixed Assets	9	17	25
Current Assets	100	80	65

Genesis V Systems Ltd
14 Hawthorne Grove Poynton, Stockport, SK12 1TR
Tel: 01625-879938
E-mail: sm@genesisv.com
Website: http://www.genesisv.com
Directors: S. Miall (MD)
Immediate Holding Company: GENESIS V SYSTEMS LIMITED
Registration no: 03189695 **Date established:** 1996
Turnover: Up to £250,000 **No.of Employees:** 1 - 10 **Product Groups:** 44

Date of Accounts	Jun 11	Jun 09	Jun 08
Sales Turnover	N/A	36	45
Pre Tax Profit/Loss	N/A	-3	-1
Working Capital	-3	-5	-2
Current Assets	3	8	9
Current Liabilities	N/A	13	12

Eric Gill & Co. Ltd
22 Clapgate Bradbury Green, Romiley, Stockport, SK6 3DG
Tel: 0161-430 4850 **Fax:** 0161-430 4850
E-mail: eric.gill@ntlworld.com
Directors: M. Gill (Fin), E. Gill (MD)
Immediate Holding Company: ERIC GILL & CO LIMITED
Registration no: 04567747 **Date established:** 2002
No.of Employees: 1 - 10 **Product Groups:** 61

Date of Accounts	Mar 11	Mar 10	Mar 08
Working Capital	11	19	13
Fixed Assets	1	1	1
Current Assets	13	28	17

Gradwood Ltd
Lansdown House 85 Buxton Road, Stockport, SK2 6LR
Tel: 0161-480 9629 **Fax:** 0161-474 7433
E-mail: sales@gradwood.co.uk
Website: http://www.gradwood.co.uk
Directors: N. Clark (MD), S. Foulds (Fin)
Immediate Holding Company: GRADWOOD LIMITED
Registration no: 03487628 **VAT No.:** GB 163 6897 23
Date established: 1997 **No.of Employees:** 1 - 10 **Product Groups:** 40, 52

Date of Accounts	Mar 12	Mar 11	Mar 10
Working Capital	723	672	692
Fixed Assets	114	130	147
Current Assets	2m	1m	2m

H B Ford & Co.
71-73 Wellington Road South, Stockport, SK1 3RZ
Tel: 0161-480 0177
E-mail: hbford@tiscali.co.uk
Website: http://www.h.b.ford.tripod.com
Directors: H. Jones (Prop)
Immediate Holding Company: H.B. FORD ASBESTOS SURVEYS LTD
Registration no: 05140250 **Date established:** 2004
No.of Employees: 1 - 10 **Product Groups:** 80

H B L Associates
33b Shaw Road, Stockport, SK4 4AG
Tel: 0161-432 9977 **Fax:** 0161-432 7979
Website: http://www.hblassoc.demon.co.uk
Directors: H. Long (Prop)
Date established: 1998 **No.of Employees:** 1 - 10 **Product Groups:** 35

H G Stephenson Ltd
161 Buxton Road, Stockport, SK2 6EQ
Tel: 0161-483 6256 **Fax:** 0161-483 2385
E-mail: robert@hgs.co.uk
Website: http://www.stephensons.com
Directors: R. Stephenson (Ch & MD), R. Stephenson (Ch), M. Stephenson (MD), H. Stevenson (Mkt Research), J. Lewis-Booth (Mkt Research)
Managers: J. Bennyon (I.T. Exec), S. Lyndsey (Purch Mgr)
Immediate Holding Company: H.G. STEPHENSON LIMITED
Registration no: 00065741 **Date established:** 2000 **Turnover:** £2m - £5m
No.of Employees: 21 - 50 **Product Groups:** 33, 63

Date of Accounts	Jan 12	Jan 11	Jan 10
Working Capital	66	44	171
Fixed Assets	1m	1m	1m
Current Assets	1m	1m	1m

Hall & Pickles Ltd
Second Avenue Poynton Industrial Estate, Poynton, Stockport, SK12 1NB
Tel: 01625-878787 **Fax:** 01625-855573
E-mail: sales@hallandpickles.co.uk
Website: http://www.hallandpickles.co.uk
Directors: M. Hall (MD), J. Dalton (Comm)
Managers: P. Ibberson (Comptroller), R. Woodward (Purch Mgr), T. Greaves (Personnel)
Immediate Holding Company: HALL & PICKLES 1812 LIMITED
Registration no: 03162309 **VAT No.:** GB 405 7471 58
Date established: 1996 **Turnover:** £75m - £125m
No.of Employees: 51 - 100 **Product Groups:** 34

Date of Accounts	May 11	May 10	May 09
Sales Turnover	82m	68m	94m
Pre Tax Profit/Loss	3m	2m	2m
Working Capital	9m	9m	8m
Fixed Assets	14m	14m	15m
Current Assets	33m	29m	23m
Current Liabilities	4m	3m	4m

Harriman Green & Associates
PO Box 15, Stockport, SK12 1UH
Tel: 01625-871631 **Fax:** 01625-871631
E-mail: mark@harriman-green.co.uk
Website: http://www.harriman-green.co.uk
Directors: M. Crook (Ptnr)
Turnover: Up to £250,000 **No.of Employees:** 1 - 10 **Product Groups:** 80

Harris Interactive Ltd
International House Pepper Road, Hazel Grove, Stockport, SK7 5BW
Tel: 0161-615 2300 **Fax:** 01663-762362
Website: http://www.harrisinteractive.co.uk
Bank(s): The Royal Bank of Scotland
Directors: G. Terhanian (Pres), J. White (Co Sec), R. Salvoni (MD), S. Hampson (Dir)
Managers: G. Jones (I.T. Exec)
Turnover: £2m - £5m **No.of Employees:** 101 - 250 **Product Groups:** 81

Hilti GT Britain Ltd
Bredbury Park Way Bredbury, Stockport, SK6 2SX
Tel: 0800-886100 **Fax:** 0800-886200
Website: http://www.hilti.co.uk
Ultimate Holding Company: HILTI AG (LIECHTENSTEIN)
Immediate Holding Company: HILTI (GT.BRITAIN) LIMITED
Registration no: 00479786 **Date established:** 1950
Turnover: £75m - £125m **No.of Employees:** 21 - 50 **Product Groups:** 35, 37, 48

Date of Accounts	Dec 11	Dec 10	Dec 09
Sales Turnover	87m	65m	66m
Pre Tax Profit/Loss	838	766	-379

see next page

Hilti GT Britain Ltd - *Cont'd*

Working Capital	12m	12m	15m
Fixed Assets	6m	5m	5m
Current Assets	45m	33m	25m
Current Liabilities	10m	6m	4m

Hima Sella Ltd

Carrington Field Street, Stockport, SK1 3JN
Tel: 0161-429 4500 **Fax:** 0161-476 3095
E-mail: reception@hima-sella.co.uk
Website: http://www.hima-sella.co.uk
Bank(s): Co-Operative, Manchester
Directors: E. Turnock (Sales & Mktg), J. Blackwell (Fin)
Managers: A. Marsden (Mats Contrlr), D. Brogan (Personnel), M. Chunara (Tech Serv Mgr)
Ultimate Holding Company: SELLA LIMITED
Immediate Holding Company: HIMA-SELLA LIMITED
Registration no: 02937377 **VAT No.:** GB 158 5687 16
Date established: 1994 **Turnover:** £10m - £20m
No.of Employees: 51 - 100 **Product Groups:** 35, 37, 38, 39, 40, 44, 46, 84

Date of Accounts	Mar 12	Mar 11	Mar 10
Sales Turnover	11m	11m	11m
Pre Tax Profit/Loss	1m	2m	2m
Working Capital	3m	3m	5m
Fixed Assets	443	483	456
Current Assets	5m	6m	8m
Current Liabilities	1m	2m	2m

Hi-Power Hydraulics

Unit E Bankside Business Park Coronation Street, Stockport, SK5 7PG
Tel: 0161-480 6715 **Fax:** 0161-480 4511
E-mail: hipower.hydraulics@gmail.com
Website: http://www.roquet.co.uk
Managers: S. Brown
Ultimate Holding Company: HI-POWER LTD, CORK
Immediate Holding Company: HI-POWER, CORK
Registration no: 03773128 **Date established:** 1999
Turnover: £500,000 - £1m **No.of Employees:** 1 - 10 **Product Groups:** 36, 40

E Hobby

Unit 13 Christie Street Industrial Estate Christie Street, Stockport, SK1 4LR
Tel: 0161-480 0359 **Fax:** 0161-480 0359
Directors: E. Hobby (Prop)
Date established: 1994 **No.of Employees:** 1 - 10 **Product Groups:** 46, 48

Home Security TV

2-4 Bank Road Bredbury, Stockport, SK6 1DR
Tel: 0161-430 5052
E-mail: christatham@btinternet.com
Website: http://www.pastandpresentduo.co.uk/cctvindex.html
Directors: C. Statham (Prop)
Turnover: Up to £250,000 **No.of Employees:** 1 - 10 **Product Groups:** 36, 40

Hughes Safety Showers Ltd

Whitefield Road Bredbury, Stockport, SK6 2SS
Tel: 0161-430 6618 **Fax:** 0161-430 7928
E-mail: info@hughes-safety-showers.co.uk
Website: http://www.hughes-safety-showers.co.uk
Bank(s): National Westminster Bank Plc
Directors: S. Dootson (Fin), A. Hughes (MD)
Managers: J. Mulholland (I.T. Exec), G. Powell (Mktg Serv Mgr), S. Ingham (Sales Prom Mgr), D. Grill (Sec), P. Darlington (Export Sales Mg)
Ultimate Holding Company: J.D. HUGHES GROUP PLC
Immediate Holding Company: HUGHES SAFETY SHOWERS LIMITED
Registration no: 03105656 **Date established:** 1995 **Turnover:** £5m - £10m
No.of Employees: 51 - 100 **Product Groups:** 36, 37, 39, 40, 52, 54

Date of Accounts	Dec 11	Dec 10	Dec 09
Sales Turnover	10m	9m	7m
Pre Tax Profit/Loss	625	656	510
Working Capital	1m	692	750
Fixed Assets	721	664	562
Current Assets	5m	4m	4m
Current Liabilities	1m	2m	1m

Intelligent Comfort Group Ltd

Camco House 40 Stockport Road, Stockport, SK3 0HZ
Tel: 0161-429 4800
Website: http://www.icglimited.co.uk
Directors: M. Spence (MD)
Immediate Holding Company: INTELLIGENT COMFORT GROUP LIMITED
Registration no: 05297087 **Date established:** 2004 **Turnover:** £5m - £10m
No.of Employees: 1 - 10 **Product Groups:** 40, 66

Date of Accounts	Mar 11	Mar 10	Mar 09
Working Capital	596	633	498
Fixed Assets	20	19	18
Current Assets	2m	2m	3m

Ironsides Lubricants Ltd

Shield Street, Stockport, SK3 0DS
Tel: 0161-477 5858 **Fax:** 0161-480 6203
E-mail: enquiries@ironsideslubricants.co.uk
Website: http://www.ironsideslubricants.co.uk
Bank(s): Barclays
Directors: M. Barker (Dir), D. Bell (Ch), M. Barker (MD)
Managers: K. Brocklehurst (Sales Admin), J. Mainwaring (Tech Serv Mgr), R. Haw (Sales Prom Mgr)
Ultimate Holding Company: IRONSIDES LUBRICANTS LIMITED(THE)
Immediate Holding Company: J.S.OIL COMPANY LIMITED
Registration no: 00553896 **VAT No.:** GB 157 3641 56
Date established: 1955 **Turnover:** £5m - £10m **No.of Employees:** 21 - 50
Product Groups: 31, 32, 66, 68

J T Sawyer & Co. Ltd

18 Mottram Street, Stockport, SK1 3PA
Tel: 0161-480 3366 **Fax:** 0161-480 9201
E-mail: boxes@sawyers.boxes.co.uk
Website: http://www.sawyerboxes.co.uk
Directors: M. Lee (Dir)
Managers: J. Gordon (Accounts)
Immediate Holding Company: J.T. SAWYER & COMPANY LIMITED
Registration no: 00133046 **VAT No.:** GB 157 1777 41
Date established: 2013 **Turnover:** £250,000 - £500,000
No.of Employees: 1 - 10 **Product Groups:** 27

Date of Accounts	Feb 12	Feb 11	Feb 10
Working Capital	9	12	-4
Fixed Assets	173	179	180
Current Assets	124	120	123

James Walker Townson Ltd

Unit 1B Castlehill
Hersfield Way
Bredbury Park Industrial Estate
Bredbury, Stockport, SK6 2SU
Tel: 0161-406 3350 **Fax:** 0161-430 7615
E-mail: sales.townson.uk@jameswalker.biz
Website: http://www.jameswalker.biz/townson
Directors: H. Parry (MD), C. Green (Fin), P. Wilkinson (Sales)
Immediate Holding Company: JAMES WALKER Group LTD
Registration no: 02395892 **Date established:** 1989
No.of Employees: 21 - 50 **Product Groups:** 29, 30, 35, 36, 40

Date of Accounts	Mar 08	Mar 07	Mar 06
Working Capital	-274	-396	-225
Fixed Assets	94	91	141
Current Assets	1401	1277	885
Current Liabilities	1675	1673	1110
Total Share Capital	65	65	65

Jedtec Finishing Equipment

Ann Street, Stockport, SK5 7PP
Tel: 0161-480 8087 **Fax:** 0161-429 9322
E-mail: sales@abraclean.co.uk
Website: http://www.sfeg.co.uk
Directors: I. Francis (MD)
Managers: S. Hitchin (Mktg Serv Mgr)
Registration no: 01404968 **VAT No.:** GB 322 9101 93
Date established: 1978 **Turnover:** £2m - £5m **No.of Employees:** 11 - 20
Product Groups: 33, 37, 40, 42, 45, 46, 52, 67, 83

Jedtec Finishing Equipment

4 Avondale Industrial Estate Avondale Road, Stockport, SK3 0UD
Tel: 0161-477 7052 **Fax:** 0161-429 9322
E-mail: sales@jedtec.org
Website: http://www.jedtec.org
Directors: J. Edwards (Prop)
Date established: 1993 **No.of Employees:** 1 - 10 **Product Groups:** 38, 42

Jetmarine Ltd

1 National Trading Estate Bramhall Moor Lane, Hazel Grove, Stockport, SK7 5AA
Tel: 0161-487 1648 **Fax:** 0161-483 7820
E-mail: sales@jetmarine.co.uk
Website: http://www.jetmarine.co.uk
Bank(s): The Royal Bank of Scotland
Directors: M. Thomson (Dir), P. Thomson (Dir)
Immediate Holding Company: JETMARINE LIMITED
Registration no: 02184931 **VAT No.:** GB 332 1701 05
Date established: 1987 **Turnover:** £250,000 - £500,000
No.of Employees: 21 - 50 **Product Groups:** 33, 39

Date of Accounts	Nov 11	Nov 10	Nov 09
Working Capital	-140	-122	-119
Fixed Assets	230	239	251
Current Assets	546	803	402

Jewson Ltd

Greg Street, Stockport, SK5 7NW
Tel: 0161-480 2434 **Fax:** 0161-366 6601
E-mail: g@hirepoint.co.uk
Website: http://www.jewson.co.uk
Managers: D. Conlon (Mgr)
Ultimate Holding Company: COMPAGNIE DE SAINT GOBAIN (FRANCE)
Immediate Holding Company: JEWSON LIMITED
Registration no: 00348407 **Date established:** 1939
Turnover: £500m - £1,000m **No.of Employees:** 11 - 20
Product Groups: 66

Date of Accounts	Dec 11	Dec 10	Dec 09
Sales Turnover	1606m	1547m	1485m
Pre Tax Profit/Loss	18m	100m	45m
Working Capital	-345m	-250m	-349m
Fixed Assets	496m	387m	461m
Current Assets	657m	1005m	1320m
Current Liabilities	66m	120m	64m

Krann Ltd

202 Chester Road Poynton, Stockport, SK12 1HP
Tel: 01625-850186
E-mail: info@krann.co.uk
Website: http://www.krann.co.uk
Directors: J. Shiel (MD)
Immediate Holding Company: KRANN LIMITED
Registration no: 05120573 **Date established:** 2004
No.of Employees: 1 - 10 **Product Groups:** 44

Date of Accounts	May 11	May 10	May 09
Working Capital	3	8	5
Fixed Assets	N/A	1	1
Current Assets	11	15	7

K-Tron Great Britain Ltd

4 Acorn Business Centre Acorn Business Park Heaton Lane, Stockport, SK4 1AS
Tel: 0161-209 4810 **Fax:** 0161-474 0292
E-mail: mplant@ktron.com
Website: http://www.ktron.com
Bank(s): Deutsche Bank
Managers: M. Plant (Chief Mgr)
Ultimate Holding Company: K-TRON INTERNATIONAL INC (USA)
Immediate Holding Company: K-TRON GREAT BRITAIN LIMITED
Registration no: 02139446 **Date established:** 1987
Turnover: £500,000 - £1m **No.of Employees:** 11 - 20
Product Groups: 38, 41, 45

Date of Accounts	Dec 09	Dec 08	Sep 11
Sales Turnover	1m	N/A	N/A
Pre Tax Profit/Loss	-95	N/A	N/A
Working Capital	-211	-116	-459
Current Assets	620	631	621
Current Liabilities	124	N/A	N/A

Law Print & Packaging Management Ltd

19-21 Ack Lane East Bramhall, Stockport, SK7 2BE
Tel: 0161-440 7320 **Fax:** 0161-440 7304
E-mail: carole@lawprintpack.co.uk
Website: http://www.lawprintpack.co.uk
Directors: T. Law (Dir), T. Low (Dir)
Managers: C. Gourhand (Sales Prom Mgr)
Immediate Holding Company: LAW PRINT & PACKAGING MANAGEMENT LTD
Registration no: 05016682 **Date established:** 2004 **Turnover:** £2m - £5m
No.of Employees: 1 - 10 **Product Groups:** 20, 27, 30

Date of Accounts	Dec 07	Dec 06	Dec 05
Working Capital	43	57	4
Fixed Assets	32	9	1
Current Assets	147	155	109
Current Liabilities	105	99	106

Leco Instruments UK Ltd

Newby Road Industrial Estate Hazel Grove, Stockport, SK7 5DA
Tel: 0161-487 5900 **Fax:** 0161-456 0969
E-mail: general@lecouk.com
Website: http://www.lecouk.com
Managers: K. Sever (Tech Serv Mgr), T. Hadley (Chief Mgr), B. Lee
Immediate Holding Company: LECO INSTRUMENTS (U.K.) LIMITED
Registration no: 01125402 **VAT No.:** GB 173 5832 49
Date established: 1973 **Turnover:** £2m - £5m **No.of Employees:** 21 - 50
Product Groups: 38, 46, 67

Date of Accounts	Dec 11	Dec 10	Dec 09
Working Capital	896	722	609
Fixed Assets	197	215	230
Current Assets	2m	2m	1m

Lees Walker Ltd

3 Charlesworth Street, Stockport, SK1 3UE
Tel: 0161-477 9993 **Fax:** 0161-477 9936
E-mail: leeswalkerltd@aol.com
Website: http://www.leeswalker.com
Directors: T. Walker (MD)
Immediate Holding Company: LEES WALKER PRECISION CUTTERS LIMITED
Registration no: 03543417 **Date established:** 1998
No.of Employees: 1 - 10 **Product Groups:** 46

Date of Accounts	Oct 11	Oct 10	Oct 09
Working Capital	55	-19	-80
Fixed Assets	147	151	151
Current Assets	328	212	166

Lewis's Medical Supplies

Bankside Business Park Coronation Street, Stockport, SK5 7PG
Tel: 0161-480 6797 **Fax:** 0161-480 4787
E-mail: sales@lewis-plast.co.uk
Website: http://www.lewis-plast.co.uk
Bank(s): Barclays
Directors: P. Sharp (Dir)
Immediate Holding Company: F.T. FINLEY & COMPANY LIMITED
Registration no: 01274097 **Date established:** 1976
No.of Employees: 11 - 20 **Product Groups:** 24, 31, 38

Date of Accounts	May 11	May 10	May 09
Working Capital	733	450	378
Fixed Assets	149	165	188
Current Assets	2m	1m	1m

Lighting 4 UK

37 Carleton Road Poynton, Stockport, SK12 1TL
Tel: 01625-876716 **Fax:** 01625-630287
E-mail: sales@lighting4uk.co.uk
Website: http://www.lighting4uk.co.uk
Directors: K. Kay (Dir)
Managers: R. Kay (Sales Prom Mgr)
No.of Employees: 1 - 10 **Product Groups:** 37

Loxton Foods

Rowan House, Stockport, SK5 7LW
Tel: 0161-474 1444 **Fax:** 0161-474 1222
E-mail: info@loxtonfoodco.com
Website: http://www.loxtonfoodco.com
Directors: B. Mitchell (MD), R. Rowland (Fin), D. Walker (MD)
Managers: N. Dodd (Personnel), L. Crank (Purch Mgr)
Ultimate Holding Company: LOXTON FROZEN FOODS LIMITED
Immediate Holding Company: LOXTON FOODS LIMITED
Registration no: 01905169 **Date established:** 1985
Turnover: £20m - £50m **No.of Employees:** 51 - 100 **Product Groups:** 20

Date of Accounts	Oct 11	Oct 10	Apr 09
Sales Turnover	33m	36m	9m
Pre Tax Profit/Loss	-5m	-5m	-302
Working Capital	-7m	-7m	-478
Fixed Assets	6m	6m	2m
Current Assets	8m	5m	4m
Current Liabilities	785	2m	2m

Luxaflex

Mersey Industrial Estate Battersea Road, Stockport, SK4 3EQ
Tel: 0161-432 5303 **Fax:** 0161-431 5087
E-mail: info.retail@luxaflex-sunway.co.uk
Website: http://www.luxaflex.co.uk
Bank(s): HSBC Bank plc
Directors: R. Malley (MD), C. Lapthorne (Sales & Mktg), T. Mayell (Fin)
Managers: D. Baxter (Tech Serv Mgr), S. Gloyne (Purch Mgr), J. Brace (Personnel)
Ultimate Holding Company: HUNTER DOUGLAS NV (NETHERLANDS ANTILLES)
Immediate Holding Company: HUNTER DOUGLAS LIMITED
Registration no: 02040222 **Date established:** 1986
Turnover: £20m - £50m **No.of Employees:** 51 - 100 **Product Groups:** 46, 66

Lyson Ltd

Barton Road Heaton Mersey Ind. Est., Stockport, SK4 3EG
Tel: 0161-442 2111 **Fax:** 0161-442 2001
E-mail: ukphoto@nazdar.com
Website: http://www.lyson.com
Directors: G. Ball (MD)
Managers: J. Macdonald (Sales Prom Mgr), J. Moore (Sales Prom Mgr)
Registration no: 05643509 **VAT No.:** GB 511 6671 64
Date established: 1988 **No.of Employees:** 51 - 100 **Product Groups:** 32

M & I Fabrications & Sheet Metal Works Ltd

Unit G14 Meadow Mill Water Street, Stockport, SK1 2BU
Tel: 0161-480 3217 **Fax:** 0161-480 3275
E-mail: mifabrications@btconnect.com
Directors: S. Marsh (MD)
Registration no: 02792072 **Date established:** 1993
Turnover: Up to £250,000 **No.of Employees:** 1 - 10 **Product Groups:** 26, 35

Bernard Mccartney Ltd
Unit 2 National Trading Estate Bramhall Moor Lane, Hazel Grove, Stockport, SK7 5AA
Tel: 0161-456 0102 **Fax:** 0161-483 5399
E-mail: neil@macpactor.co.uk
Website: http://www.macpactor.co.uk
Directors: N. Mccartney (Dir), H. Henigan (Co Sec)
Immediate Holding Company: BERNARD MCCARTNEY LIMITED
Registration no: 01515756 **Date established:** 1980
Turnover: £500,000 - £1m **No.of Employees:** 1 - 10 **Product Groups:** 42, 48

Date of Accounts	Sep 11	Sep 10	Sep 09
Working Capital	28	37	-136
Fixed Assets	54	57	86
Current Assets	157	217	192

Macpac Ltd
5 Barton Road, Stockport, SK4 3EG
Tel: 0161-442 1642 **Fax:** 0161-442 1643
E-mail: info@macpac.co.uk
Website: http://www.macpac.co.uk
Bank(s): Royal Bank of Scotland
Directors: G. Kershaw (MD), S. Kershaw (Co Sec), J. Kershaw (Co Sec)
Immediate Holding Company: MACPAC LIMITED
Registration no: 01107529 **Date established:** 1973 **Turnover:** £1m - £2m
No.of Employees: 21 - 50 **Product Groups:** 30, 42

Date of Accounts	Mar 11	Mar 10	Mar 09
Working Capital	324	494	320
Fixed Assets	761	656	604
Current Assets	1m	1m	1m

Man Diesel Ltd
Bramhall Moor Lane Hazel Grove, Stockport, SK7 5AQ
Tel: 0161-483 1000 **Fax:** 0161-487 1465
E-mail: adurose@mandiesel.eu
Website: http://www.manbwltd.com
Directors: A. Durose (Fin)
Managers: H. Boateng, M. Kay (Personnel), S. Whittaker (Comptroller)
Ultimate Holding Company: MAN SE (GERMANY)
Immediate Holding Company: MAN DIESEL & TURBO UK LTD
Registration no: 00759517 **Date established:** 1963
Turnover: £50m - £75m **No.of Employees:** 101 - 250
Product Groups: 35, 36, 39

Date of Accounts	Dec 11	Dec 10	Dec 09
Sales Turnover	70m	70m	72m
Pre Tax Profit/Loss	18m	21m	23m
Working Capital	47m	41m	24m
Fixed Assets	15m	15m	15m
Current Assets	58m	55m	44m
Current Liabilities	5m	7m	12m

Maple Fleet Services
Maple House Crown Royal Industrial Park Shawcross Street, Stockport, SK1 3EY
Tel: 0161-477 3476 **Fax:** 0161-477 6377
E-mail: info@maplegroup.co.uk
Website: http://www.maplegroup.co.uk
Directors: T. Orton (MD)
Immediate Holding Company: MAPLE FLEET SERVICES LIMITED
Registration no: 03335374 **Date established:** 1997 **Turnover:** £1m - £2m
No.of Employees: 21 - 50 **Product Groups:** 36, 39

Date of Accounts	Apr 11	Apr 10	Apr 09
Working Capital	440	516	533
Fixed Assets	153	213	274
Current Assets	1m	924	1m

Metalweb Ltd
Unit 20 Newby Road Industrial Estate Newby Road, Hazel Grove, Stockport, SK7 5DA
Tel: 0161-483 9662 **Fax:** 0161-483 9668
E-mail: info@metalweb.co.uk
Website: http://www.metalweb.co.uk
Directors: S. Williams (Fin), M. Benfield (Sales)
Managers: P. Darbyshire (District Mgr), A. Smith (Sales Prom Mgr)
Ultimate Holding Company: RELIANCE STEEL & ALUMINUM CO (USA)
Immediate Holding Company: METALWEB LIMITED
Registration no: 04130945 **Date established:** 2000
Turnover: £20m - £50m **No.of Employees:** 11 - 20 **Product Groups:** 34, 36, 48, 66

Date of Accounts	Dec 11	Dec 10	Dec 09
Sales Turnover	27m	23m	20m
Pre Tax Profit/Loss	740	182	413
Working Capital	5m	4m	3m
Fixed Assets	2m	3m	3m
Current Assets	13m	11m	8m
Current Liabilities	2m	2m	1m

Hans H Meyer Ltd
Unit 15 Haigh Park Haigh Avenue, Stockport, SK4 1QR
Tel: 0161-480 6464 **Fax:** 0161-480 4082
E-mail: sales@meyer-uk.com
Website: http://www.meyer-sz.de
Bank(s): HSBC Bank plc
Directors: P. Bradbury (Fin), T. Auringer (MD)
Immediate Holding Company: Hans H. Meyer Ltd
Registration no: 01903410 **VAT No.:** GB 420 7112 05
Date established: 1985 **Turnover:** £2m - £5m **No.of Employees:** 11 - 20
Product Groups: 45

Date of Accounts	Dec 08	Dec 07	Dec 06
Working Capital	-118	-205	-272
Fixed Assets	133	146	173
Current Assets	725	399	510
Current Liabilities	842	604	782
Total Share Capital	125	125	125

Mini Gears Stockport Ltd
Top Gear House Bletchley Road, Stockport, SK4 3ED
Tel: 0161-432 0222 **Fax:** 0161-432 0444
E-mail: peter@minigears.co.uk
Website: http://www.minigears.co.uk
Bank(s): National Westminster, Underbank Hall
Directors: P. Darwent (MD), P. Durkin (Dir)
Managers: H. Lewthwaite (Sales & Mktg Mg), N. Fogg (Tech Serv Mgr), C. Russell (Purch Mgr)
Immediate Holding Company: MINI-GEARS(STOCKPORT)LIMITED
Registration no: 00877735 **VAT No.:** GB 157 5974 19
Date established: 1966 **Turnover:** £5m - £10m
No.of Employees: 51 - 100 **Product Groups:** 34, 35, 40, 48, 66, 84

Date of Accounts	Apr 11	Apr 10	Apr 09
Sales Turnover	8m	8m	N/A
Pre Tax Profit/Loss	288	485	211
Working Capital	446	900	938
Fixed Assets	2m	1m	2m
Current Assets	3m	3m	3m
Current Liabilities	624	452	308

Moellers UK Ltd
Maxron House Green Lane Romiley, Romiley, Stockport, SK6 3JQ
Tel: 0161-406 9824 **Fax:** 0161-494 5982
E-mail: info@moellers.co.uk
Website: http://www.moellers.co.uk
Managers: P. Shaw (Sales Prom Mgr)
Immediate Holding Company: MOELLERS (U.K.) LIMITED
Registration no: 01409947 **Date established:** 1979 **Turnover:** £2m - £5m
No.of Employees: 1 - 10 **Product Groups:** 42, 45, 84

Date of Accounts	Dec 10	Dec 09	Dec 08
Working Capital	-445	-362	-328
Fixed Assets	4	5	7
Current Assets	67	65	100

Motor Technology Ltd
Unit 1 Motec House Chadkirk Business Centre Vale Road, Romiley, Stockport, SK6 3NE
Tel: 0161-217 7100 **Fax:** 0161-427 1306
E-mail: sales@motec.co.uk
Website: http://www.controlinmotion.com
Directors: A. Fallows (MD)
Immediate Holding Company: MOTOR TECHNOLOGY LTD.
Registration no: 01895277 **VAT No.:** GB 431 5084 78
Date established: 1985 **Turnover:** £500,000 - £1m
No.of Employees: 1 - 10 **Product Groups:** 35, 37, 38, 45, 46, 47, 84

Date of Accounts	Mar 11	Mar 10	Mar 09
Working Capital	30	26	25
Fixed Assets	2	3	5
Current Assets	164	115	151

N B Decorative Glass
209 Chestergate, Stockport, SK3 0AN
Tel: 0161-429 0779
Directors: N. Blinston (Prop)
No.of Employees: 1 - 10 **Product Groups:** 33, 35

National Tyre Service Ltd
Regent House Heaton Lane, Stockport, SK4 1BS
Tel: 0161-429 1200 **Fax:** 0161-475 3540
E-mail: customerservices@national-tyres.co.uk
Website: http://www.national.co.uk
Managers: M. Bourne (Mktg Serv Mgr), T. Neill, P. Ollerenshaw (Personnel)
Ultimate Holding Company: AXLE GROUP HOLDINGS LIMITED
Immediate Holding Company: NATIONAL TYRE SERVICE LIMITED
Registration no: 00986754 **Date established:** 1970
Turnover: £75m - £125m **No.of Employees:** 251 - 500
Product Groups: 68

Date of Accounts	Dec 11	Dec 10	Dec 09
Sales Turnover	123m	119m	114m
Pre Tax Profit/Loss	10m	11m	10m
Working Capital	94m	87m	76m
Fixed Assets	8m	6m	6m
Current Assets	111m	103m	92m
Current Liabilities	7m	6m	6m

William Nelstrop & Co. Ltd
Albion Mills Manchester Road, Stockport, SK4 1TZ
Tel: 0161-480 3071 **Fax:** 0161-480 0325
Website: http://www.nelstrop.co.uk
Bank(s): National Westminster, Barclays
Directors: A. Nelstrop (Sales & Mktg), M. Ainley (Co Sec), S. Elwood (Fin)
Managers: D. Escott (Comm)
Immediate Holding Company: WM. NELSTROP & CO. LTD
Registration no: 00260082 **VAT No.:** GB 157 6178 38
Date established: 1931 **Turnover:** £20m - £50m
No.of Employees: 51 - 100 **Product Groups:** 20, 32

Neomet Ltd
92 Cross Lane Marple, Stockport, SK6 7PZ
Tel: 0161-427 7741 **Fax:** 0161-449 0080
E-mail: richard.hammersley@sulzer.com
Website: http://www.sulzermetco.com
Bank(s): HSBC Bank plc
Directors: G. Bradwell (Fin), R. Hammersley (MD)
Ultimate Holding Company: SULZER AG (SWITZERLAND)
Immediate Holding Company: NEOMET LIMITED
Registration no: 01911415 **VAT No.:** GB 419 6997 91
Date established: 1985 **Turnover:** £2m - £5m **No.of Employees:** 21 - 50
Product Groups: 34, 35, 36, 39

Date of Accounts	Dec 11	Dec 10	Dec 09
Sales Turnover	4m	3m	3m
Pre Tax Profit/Loss	606	539	367
Working Capital	2m	2m	2m
Fixed Assets	248	189	173
Current Assets	2m	2m	2m
Current Liabilities	150	144	120

Network Print & Packaging Ltd
Unit 3 Europa Way, Stockport, SK3 0XE
Tel: 0161-476 6565 **Fax:** 0161-476 6555
E-mail: steve@networkprints.net
Directors: S. Fraser (Dir), S. Fraser (Prop)
Immediate Holding Company: NETWORK PRINT & PACKAGING LIMITED
Registration no: 04214196 **Date established:** 2001
No.of Employees: 1 - 10 **Product Groups:** 38, 42

Date of Accounts	Mar 11	Mar 10	Mar 09
Working Capital	119	134	201
Fixed Assets	23	26	361
Current Assets	211	234	420

Niplast Tanks (Offices & Factory)
187 Higher Hillgate, Stockport, SK1 3JG
Tel: 0161-477 6777 **Fax:** 0161-429 8413
E-mail: info@niplast.com
Website: http://www.niplast.com
Bank(s): National Westminster Bank Plc
Directors: A. Greenwood (Dir)
Immediate Holding Company: CMC LEASE & CONTRACTS LIMITED
Registration no: 02562309 **VAT No.:** GB 473 4371 40
Date established: 1990 **Turnover:** £1m - £2m **No.of Employees:** 11 - 20
Product Groups: 30, 35, 36, 40, 42, 45

Nnr Global Logistics UK Limited
Unit A6 Yew Street, Stockport Trading Estate, Stockport, SK4 2JW
Tel: 0161-477 4108 **Fax:** 0161-477 0780
E-mail: darren.cobb@nnruk.com
Website: http://www.nnruk.com
Managers: D. Cobb (District Mgr), L. Griffiths (Sales Prom Mgr)
Ultimate Holding Company: Nishitetsu Group
Registration no: 02661240 **Turnover:** £2m - £5m
No.of Employees: 11 - 20 **Product Groups:** 75

Nordair Niche (Northern Office)
6-14 Bean Leach Road Hazel Grove, Stockport, SK7 4LD
Tel: 0161-482 7900 **Fax:** 0161-482 7901
E-mail: sales@nordair.co.uk
Website: http://www.nordairniche.co.uk
Managers: P. Fox (Sales Prom Mgr)
Ultimate Holding Company: Ambi-Rad Ltd
Registration no: 01390934 **Turnover:** £2m - £5m
No.of Employees: 1 - 10 **Product Groups:** 38, 40, 42

Nordson UK Ltd
Ashurst Drive, Stockport, SK3 0RY
Tel: 0161-495 4200 **Fax:** 0161-428 6716
Website: http://www.nordson.com
Managers: A. Morton (Chief Mgr), D. Cundill (Mktg Serv Mgr), P. McMahon (Mgr)
Immediate Holding Company: NORDSON (U.K.) LIMITED
Registration no: 01056577 **Date established:** 1972 **Turnover:** £2m - £5m
No.of Employees: 1 - 10 **Product Groups:** 37, 42, 46

O M S UK Ltd
Omnitech House 2 Bamford Business Park, Whitehill Industrial Estate, Stockport, SK4 1PL
Tel: 0161-480 8100 **Fax:** 0161-480 0080
E-mail: anthony.southworth@omsgroup.co.uk
Website: http://www.omsgroup.co.uk
Directors: A. Southworth (MD), P. Hindson (Sales)
Immediate Holding Company: OMS (UK) LIMITED
Registration no: 02131306 **VAT No.:** GB 439 2675 22
Date established: 1987 **Turnover:** £2m - £5m **No.of Employees:** 1 - 10
Product Groups: 42, 45, 46, 48

Date of Accounts	Dec 09	Dec 08	Dec 07
Working Capital	27	47	47
Fixed Assets	23	29	36
Current Assets	412	695	594

Oliver I G D
Unit 4a Bramhall Technology Park Pepper Road, Hazel Grove, Stockport, SK7 5BW
Tel: 0161-483 1415 **Fax:** 0161-484 2345
E-mail: sales@oliver-igd.co.uk
Website: http://www.oliver-igd.co.uk
Directors: C. Peake (Co Sec), R. Oliver (Dir), A. Collier (MD)
Managers: C. Peake (Sales Prom Mgr)
Immediate Holding Company: OLIVER IGD LIMITED
Registration no: 01044944 **VAT No.:** GB 158 1027 78
Date established: 1972 **Turnover:** £1m - £2m **No.of Employees:** 11 - 20
Product Groups: 38, 84

Date of Accounts	Jan 11	Jan 10	Jan 09
Working Capital	169	178	122
Fixed Assets	120	170	213
Current Assets	457	487	669

Omniflex Ltd
67 Europa Business Park Bird Hall Lane, Stockport, SK3 0XA
Tel: 0161-491 4144 **Fax:** 0161-491 4188
E-mail: david.celine@omniflex.com
Website: http://www.omniflex.com
Directors: G. Bradshaw (Dir)
Immediate Holding Company: OMNIFLEX (UK) LIMITED
Registration no: 04238032 **Date established:** 2001
No.of Employees: 1 - 10 **Product Groups:** 37

Date of Accounts	Jun 11	Jun 10	Jun 09
Working Capital	24	9	42
Fixed Assets	N/A	1	1
Current Assets	240	335	352
Current Liabilities	2	N/A	31

P T M Wrexham Ltd
Haigh Avenue Whitehill Industrial Estate, Stockport, SK4 1NZ
Tel: 0161-477 6486 **Fax:** 0161-480 4624
E-mail: gerrym@ptmuk.co.uk
Website: http://www.ptmuk.co.uk
Directors: G. Moore (Co Sec)
Ultimate Holding Company: GOOP LIMITED
Immediate Holding Company: PTM (UK) LIMITED
Registration no: 03056448 **VAT No.:** GB 677 6262 92
Date established: 1995 **Turnover:** £5m - £10m **No.of Employees:** 1 - 10
Product Groups: 25, 27, 29, 30, 33, 36, 40, 66

Date of Accounts	Jan 11	Jan 10	Jan 08
Working Capital	2m	3m	1m
Fixed Assets	N/A	N/A	354
Current Assets	2m	3m	3m

P Z Cussons International Ltd
Cussons House Bird Hall Lane, Stockport, SK3 0XN
Tel: 0161-491 8000 **Fax:** 0161-491 8191
E-mail: anthony.green@pzcussons.com
Website: http://www.CUSSONS.COM
Bank(s): Royal Bank of Scotland
Directors: A. Green (Dir), A. Steele (Purch), D. Box (Mkt Research), K. Callan (MD), M. Campbell (Co Sec), M. Edwards (Fin), N. Craigie (Sales)
Immediate Holding Company: PZ CUSSONS (FINANCE) LIMITED
Registration no: 00954969 **Date established:** 1969
Turnover: Up to £250,000 **No.of Employees:** 251 - 500
Product Groups: 31, 32

Date of Accounts	May 08	May 07	May 06
Sales Turnover	180800	162400	147200
Pre Tax Profit/Loss	13700	3900	15800
Working Capital	115300	107600	102100
Fixed Assets	11000	33700	17500
Current Assets	180100	141100	131600
Current Liabilities	64800	33500	29500
Total Share Capital	42300	42300	42300
ROCE% (Return on Capital Employed)	10.8	2.8	11.0
ROT% (Return on Turnover)	7.6	2.4	9.0

Pac International
Bredbury Park Way Bredbury, Stockport, SK6 2SZ
Tel: 0161-406 3400 **Fax:** 0161-406 6794
E-mail: sliddy@stanleyworks.com
Website: http://www.stanleysecuritysolutions.co.uk
Bank(s): Barclays
Managers: S. Lidder (Mgr)
Immediate Holding Company: BLICK P.L.C.
Registration no: 01363776 **Date established:** 1978
Turnover: £10m - £20m **No.of Employees:** 51 - 100 **Product Groups:** 40

Date of Accounts	Dec 06	Dec 05
Sales Turnover	2601	11652
Pre Tax Profit/Loss	2508	4041
Working Capital	11325	7992
Fixed Assets	N/A	1264
Current Assets	11325	9485
Current Liabilities	N/A	1493
Total Share Capital	10	10
ROCE% (Return on Capital Employed)		43.7
ROT% (Return on Turnover)	96.4	34.7

Pama & Co. Ltd
Pama House Stockport Road East, Bredbury, Stockport, SK6 2AA
Tel: 0161-494 4245 **Fax:** 0161-494 4231
E-mail: i.farshi@pama.co.uk
Website: http://www.pama.com
Directors: I. Farshi (Dir)
Managers: M. Smithen (Tech Serv Mgr), G. Barber (Purch Mgr), L. Fowler (Mktg Serv Mgr)
Immediate Holding Company: PAMA & CO. LIMITED
Registration no: 03441841 **Date established:** 1997
Turnover: £10m - £20m **No.of Employees:** 51 - 100 **Product Groups:** 37, 67

Date of Accounts	Apr 11	Apr 10	Apr 09
Sales Turnover	15m	12m	14m
Pre Tax Profit/Loss	191	273	116
Working Capital	2m	2m	1m
Fixed Assets	326	409	511
Current Assets	5m	6m	6m
Current Liabilities	852	949	626

Parkway Plant Sales Ltd
Bredbury Park Way Bredbury, Stockport, SK6 2SN
Tel: 01942-684804 **Fax:** 0161-494 6333
E-mail: ian.wood@parkway-plant.co.uk
Website: http://www.parkwayplantsales.com
Directors: I. Wood (Dir)
Ultimate Holding Company: WESTGATE HOLDINGS LIMITED
Immediate Holding Company: PARKWAY PLANT SALES LIMITED
Registration no: 03796716 **Date established:** 1999
No.of Employees: 1 - 10 **Product Groups:** 36, 38, 39, 42, 45, 46, 48, 64, 66, 67

Date of Accounts	Dec 11	Dec 10	Dec 09
Working Capital	-50	-47	-32
Fixed Assets	19	24	33
Current Assets	442	247	250

Pennine Optical Group Ltd
Pennine House Manchester Road, Stockport, SK4 1TX
Tel: 0161-480 6468 **Fax:** 0161-477 6949
E-mail: pennine@pog.co.uk
Website: http://www.pennineoptical.co.uk
Bank(s): Barclays
Directors: A. Hornby (Fin), P. Cowan (Ch)
Immediate Holding Company: PENNINE OPTICAL GROUP LIMITED
Registration no: 01961218 **VAT No.:** GB 570 6617 34
Date established: 1985 **Turnover:** £2m - £5m **No.of Employees:** 11 - 20
Product Groups: 65

Date of Accounts	Oct 09	Oct 08	Mar 12
Sales Turnover	4m	5m	N/A
Pre Tax Profit/Loss	112	203	N/A
Working Capital	324	368	618
Fixed Assets	1m	1m	365
Current Assets	1m	1m	857
Current Liabilities	239	225	N/A

Phoenix Pipeline Products Ltd
8 Mackenzie Industrial Estate Bird Hall Lane, Stockport, SK3 0SB
Tel: 0161-428 7200 **Fax:** 0161-428 7010
E-mail: info@p3-phoenix.com
Website: http://www.p3-phoenix.com
Managers: D. Woolley (Mgr)
Immediate Holding Company: PHOENIX PIPELINE PRODUCTS LIMITED
Registration no: 03831682 **Date established:** 1999
No.of Employees: 11 - 20 **Product Groups:** 36, 66

Date of Accounts	Nov 11	Nov 10	Nov 09
Working Capital	108	70	128
Fixed Assets	20	24	8
Current Assets	317	232	439

Piggott & Whitfield Ltd
Niagara Street, Stockport, SK2 6HH
Tel: 0161-483 9438 **Fax:** 0161-487 1460
E-mail: info@piggottandwhitfield.co.uk
Website: http://www.piggottandwhitfield.co.uk
Directors: R. Speakman (MD), R. Speakman (MD), P. Williams (Fin)
Managers: V. Gee (Comptroller), R. Simons (Tech Serv Mgr), S. Bowcock
Immediate Holding Company: PIGGOTT AND WHITFIELD LIMITED
Registration no: 00438134 **VAT No.:** GB 431 5071 87
Date established: 1947 **Turnover:** £20m - £50m
No.of Employees: 21 - 50 **Product Groups:** 52

Date of Accounts	Mar 12	Mar 11	Mar 10
Sales Turnover	27m	25m	29m
Pre Tax Profit/Loss	105	203	202
Working Capital	175	64	-148
Fixed Assets	586	617	697
Current Assets	8m	9m	10m
Current Liabilities	4m	4m	5m

Polemarch Industrial Ltd
Seaton House 61 Wellington Street, Stockport, SK1 3AD
Tel: 0161-429 9217 **Fax:** 0161-480 7955
E-mail: info@polemarch.co.uk
Website: http://www.polemarch.co.uk
Directors: S. Walker (MD)
Managers: S. Walker (Fin Mgr)
Immediate Holding Company: POLEMARCH INDUSTRIAL LIMITED
Registration no: 02350537 **Date established:** 1989
No.of Employees: 1 - 10 **Product Groups:** 80

Date of Accounts	Jun 11	Jun 10	Jun 09
Working Capital	-82	-156	-492
Fixed Assets	5m	5m	6m
Current Assets	1m	917	425

Poli Chrome Engineers Moulds Ltd
Unit 10 Adswood Industrial Estate Adswood Road, Stockport, SK3 8LF
Tel: 0161-477 7370 **Fax:** 0161-477 1020
E-mail: admin@poli-chrome.co.uk
Website: http://www.poli-chrome.co.uk
Directors: I. Lusby (MD)
Immediate Holding Company: POLI-CHROME ENGINEERS (MOULDS) LIMITED
Registration no: 01235938 **VAT No.:** GB 158 8923 15
Date established: 1975 **Turnover:** £250,000 - £500,000
No.of Employees: 1 - 10 **Product Groups:** 48

Date of Accounts	Nov 11	Nov 10	Nov 09
Working Capital	106	104	101
Fixed Assets	54	56	58
Current Assets	121	123	125

Precision Controls Ltd
20 Broadhurst Street, Stockport, SK3 8JH
Tel: 0161-476 4606 **Fax:** 0161-476 5639
E-mail: sales@precisioncontrols.co.uk
Website: http://www.precisioncontrols.co.uk
Directors: J. Mckenzie (MD)
Immediate Holding Company: PRECISION CONTROLS LIMITED
Registration no: 02601605 **Date established:** 1991
No.of Employees: 1 - 10 **Product Groups:** 37, 39, 84

Date of Accounts	Mar 11	Mar 10	Mar 09
Working Capital	310	254	323
Fixed Assets	8	7	11
Current Assets	476	397	488

Premier Sacks & Packaging Ltd
Dean Farm King St Woodford, Woodford, Stockport, SK7 1RL
Tel: 01625-521971 **Fax:** 01625-521972
E-mail: info@premiersacks.co.uk
Website: http://www.premiersacks.co.uk
Directors: M. Saunders (MD)
Immediate Holding Company: PREMIER SACKS & PACKAGING LIMITED
Registration no: 02666553 **VAT No.:** GB 595 7559 70
Date established: 1991 **Turnover:** Up to £250,000
No.of Employees: 1 - 10 **Product Groups:** 27, 48

Date of Accounts	Dec 11	Dec 10	Dec 09
Working Capital	592	23	15
Fixed Assets	127	148	168
Current Assets	1m	662	621

Premier Textiles Ltd
Green Lane Industrial Estate Green Lane, Stockport, SK4 2JR
Tel: 0161-429 5770 **Fax:** 0161-429 5777
E-mail: sales@premier-textiles.com
Website: http://www.premier-textiles.com
Bank(s): Lloyds TSB Bank plc
Directors: N. Smith (Comm)
Immediate Holding Company: PREMIER TEXTILES LIMITED
Registration no: 01603882 **VAT No.:** GB 616 1515 65
Date established: 1981 **Turnover:** £10m - £20m
No.of Employees: 11 - 20 **Product Groups:** 23, 63

Date of Accounts	Jun 11	Jun 10	Jun 09
Sales Turnover	14m	11m	1m
Pre Tax Profit/Loss	818	896	-35
Working Capital	8m	7m	7m
Fixed Assets	2m	2m	2m
Current Assets	11m	9m	8m
Current Liabilities	2m	2m	678

G Priestnall & Sons Ltd
329 London Road Hazel Grove, Stockport, SK7 4PS
Tel: 0161-456 8187 **Fax:** 0161-483 9478
E-mail: stuart@g-priestnall.com
Website: http://www.g-priestnall.com
Bank(s): National Westminster Bank Plc
Directors: S. Priestnall (Dir)
Immediate Holding Company: G. PRIESTNALL & SONS LIMITED
Registration no: 03678698 **VAT No.:** GB 286 0848 26
Date established: 1998 **Turnover:** £500,000 - £1m
No.of Employees: 21 - 50 **Product Groups:** 52

Date of Accounts	Dec 11	Dec 10	Dec 09
Working Capital	114	131	30
Fixed Assets	4	1	2
Current Assets	358	420	279

Prima Doors Ltd
Unit 8a Newby Road Industrial Estate Newby Road, Hazel Grove, Stockport, SK7 5DA
Tel: 0161-487 3286
E-mail: info@primadoors.co.uk
Website: http://www.primadoors.co.uk
Directors: T. Bruce (Sales)
Managers: G. Dowell (Fin Mgr), L. Davies (Buyer)
Immediate Holding Company: PRIMA DOORS PROPERTY LTD.
Registration no: 04956916 **Date established:** 2003
No.of Employees: 21 - 50 **Product Groups:** 26, 35

Printaims Printers
Unit 24 Haigh Park Haigh Avenue, Stockport, SK4 1QR
Tel: 0161-429 9552 **Fax:** 0161-429 7662
E-mail: info@printaims.co.uk
Website: http://www.printaims.co.uk
Directors: A. Dodson (Dir), S. Bradbury (Co Sec)
No.of Employees: 1 - 10 **Product Groups:** 27, 28

Pulsation Dampers At Pulseguard Ltd
Unit 1 Greg Street Industrial Centre, Greg Street, Reddish, Stockport, SK5 7BS
Tel: 0161-480 9625 **Fax:** 0161-480 9627
E-mail: sales@pulsationdampers.co.uk
Website: http://www.pulseguard.co.uk
Registration no: 03665881 **Date established:** 1998
Turnover: £500,000 - £1m **No.of Employees:** 1 - 10 **Product Groups:** 35, 38, 39, 40

Date of Accounts	Oct 08	Oct 07	Oct 06
Working Capital	56	47	45
Current Assets	114	78	54
Current Liabilities	58	31	9

Purpoleweb Media
29 Buxton Road, Stockport, SK2 6LS
Tel: 0161-968 1830 **Fax:** 0161-968 1829
E-mail: tony@purplewebmedia.com
Website: http://www.purplewebmedia.com
Directors: A. Millward (Fab)
Managers: T. Millward (Mgr)
Immediate Holding Company: JOHN MACNAB LIMITED
Registration no: 06559803 **Date established:** 2008
No.of Employees: 1 - 10 **Product Groups:** 44

Pyramid Valley Computers
2c Heapriding Business Park Ford Street, Stockport, SK3 0BT
Tel: 0161-477 3880 **Fax:** 0161-480 8741
E-mail: andrew.mills@pyramidvalley.co.uk
Website: http://www.pyramidvalley.co.uk
Directors: T. Atkins (MD), A. Mills (Dir)
Registration no: 02710936 **VAT No.:** GB 611 5303 90
Turnover: £1m - £2m **No.of Employees:** 1 - 10 **Product Groups:** 44

Pyrometer Systems Ltd
20 Broadhurst Street, Stockport, SK3 8JH
Tel: 0161-476 4994 **Fax:** 0161-476 2656
E-mail: sales@pyrometer.co.uk
Website: http://www.pyrometer.co.uk
Directors: M. Cassidy (Fin), M. Cassidy (Co Sec), M. Slater (Sales & Mktg), J. Cassidy (MD)
Immediate Holding Company: PYROMETER SYSTEMS LIMITED
Registration no: 02610121 **VAT No.:** GB 593 6094 08
Date established: 1991 **Turnover:** £500,000 - £1m
No.of Employees: 1 - 10 **Product Groups:** 37, 38

Date of Accounts	Apr 10	Apr 09	Apr 08
Working Capital	76	70	75
Fixed Assets	1	13	16
Current Assets	142	159	172

Quirepale Ltd
Cheadle Heath Works Stockport Road, Stockport, SK3 0PR
Tel: 0161-428 3516 **Fax:** 0161-428 0817
E-mail: sales@deanprint.co.uk
Managers: J. Sherlock (Mgr)
Immediate Holding Company: DJK (HOLDINGS) LIMITED
Registration no: 01582471 **Date established:** 2011
No.of Employees: 1 - 10 **Product Groups:** 64

Date of Accounts	Mar 11	Mar 10	Mar 09
Working Capital	-15	-12	-9
Fixed Assets	10	10	10
Current Assets	59	59	18

Radar Detector Shop
437 Buxton Road Great Moor, Stockport, SK2 7HE
Tel: 0161-355 1275 **Fax:** 0161-355 5134
E-mail: info@k300.com
Website: http://www.radar-detector-shop.co.uk
Directors: S. Cookson (MD)
Managers: V. Cookson (Chief Mgr)
Registration no: 04564649 **No.of Employees:** 1 - 10 **Product Groups:** 37, 38, 39, 44, 84

F J Ratchford Ltd
Kennedy Way Green Lane, Stockport, SK4 2JX
Tel: 0161-480 8484 **Fax:** 0161-480 3679
E-mail: info@fjratchford.co.uk
Website: http://www.fjratchford.co.uk
Directors: J. Ratchford (Dir)
Immediate Holding Company: F.J.RATCHFORD LIMITED
Registration no: 00613099 **Date established:** 1958 **Turnover:** £1m - £2m
No.of Employees: 1 - 10 **Product Groups:** 28, 67

Date of Accounts	Oct 11	Oct 10	Oct 09
Working Capital	776	741	697
Fixed Assets	292	273	285
Current Assets	1m	1m	1m

Reddish Joinery Ltd
Lambeth Road, Stockport, SK5 6TW
Tel: 0161-432 7682 **Fax:** 0161-431 0183
E-mail: reddish.joinery@btconnect.com
Website: http://www.reddishjoinery.co.uk
Directors: L. Parrott (Dir), J. Parrott (Fin)
Immediate Holding Company: REDDISH JOINERY LIMITED
Registration no: 01082621 **VAT No.:** GB 157 3189 48
Date established: 1972 **Turnover:** £500,000 - £1m
No.of Employees: 21 - 50 **Product Groups:** 33

Date of Accounts	Mar 11	Mar 10	Mar 09
Working Capital	-153	-210	-202
Fixed Assets	496	569	589
Current Assets	136	147	153

Reed Employment Ltd
8th Floor Beckwith House 1 Wellington Road North, Stockport, SK4 1AF
Tel: 0161-480 0115 **Fax:** 0161-480 5733
E-mail: sue.livesey@reed.co.uk
Website: http://www.reed.co.uk
Managers: M. Roberts (Mgr)
Ultimate Holding Company: REED GLOBAL LTD (MALTA)
Immediate Holding Company: REED EMPLOYMENT LIMITED
Registration no: 00669854 **Date established:** 1960
Turnover: £75m - £125m **No.of Employees:** 1 - 10 **Product Groups:** 80

Date of Accounts	Jun 11	Jun 10	Dec 07
Sales Turnover	618	450	287m
Pre Tax Profit/Loss	-2m	310	8m
Working Capital	23m	28m	28m
Fixed Assets	31	36	5m
Current Assets	28m	30m	74m
Current Liabilities	37	29	21m

Refresh Media Design
67 Europa Business Park Bird Hall Lane, Stockport, SK3 0XA
Tel: 0161-428 2221
E-mail: nigel@refreshltd.co.uk
Website: http://www.refreshltd.co.uk
Directors: N. Walker (Fin)
Immediate Holding Company: REFRESH MEDIA DESIGN LTD
Registration no: 05805469 **Date established:** 2006
Turnover: Up to £250,000 **No.of Employees:** 1 - 10 **Product Groups:** 44, 81

Date of Accounts	May 11	May 10	May 08
Working Capital	27	29	20
Fixed Assets	5	1	4

Current Assets	57	53	32

Reisser Ltd
Pepper Road Hazel Grove, Stockport, SK7 5BW
Tel: 0161-483 5557 **Fax:** 0161-483 4631
E-mail: info@reisser.co.uk
Website: http://www.reisser.co.uk
Directors: C. Ledigo (Dir), J. O'Neill (Fin)
Managers: N. Barrat (Tech Serv Mgr)
Immediate Holding Company: REISSER LIMITED
Registration no: 01596414 **VAT No.:** GB 306 7017 82
Date established: 1981 **Turnover:** £2m - £5m **No.of Employees:** 21 - 50
Product Groups: 66

Date of Accounts	Sep 11	Sep 10	Sep 09
Working Capital	818	743	411
Fixed Assets	191	153	125
Current Assets	6m	4m	3m

Ringflex Drive Systems Ltd
4 Bankside Business Park Coronation Street, Stockport, SK5 7PG
Tel: 0161-474 0464 **Fax:** 0161-429 0272
E-mail: info@ringflex.co.uk
Website: http://www.ringflex.co.uk
Directors: P. Mcdonagh (Fin)
Immediate Holding Company: RINGFLEX DRIVE SYSTEMS LIMITED
Registration no: 02967111 **Date established:** 1994 **Turnover:** £1m - £2m
No.of Employees: 1 - 10 **Product Groups:** 29, 35, 36, 39, 40, 43, 45, 46, 66, 84

Date of Accounts	Oct 11	Oct 10	Oct 09
Working Capital	632	595	592
Fixed Assets	12	22	38
Current Assets	1m	1m	917

Robant Services Ltd
Unit 24 Mersey Street, Stockport, SK1 2HX
Tel: 0161-429 8728 **Fax:** 0161-474 7630
E-mail: sales@robant.co.uk
Website: http://www.robant.co.uk
Directors: P. Humphries (MD), J. Maddison (Co Sec), H. Humphries (Fin)
Managers: B. Newton (Sales Prom Mgr)
Immediate Holding Company: ROBANT SERVICES LIMITED
Registration no: 01684593 **VAT No.:** GB 388 1325 33
Date established: 1982 **Turnover:** £500,000 - £1m
No.of Employees: 11 - 20 **Product Groups:** 29, 44

Date of Accounts	Mar 10	Mar 09	Mar 08
Working Capital	-6	41	28
Fixed Assets	597	596	607
Current Assets	183	198	252

Robinson & Gronnow Ltd
3 Mackenzie Industrial Estate Bird Hall Lane, Stockport, SK3 0SB
Tel: 0161-428 1199 **Fax:** 0161- 4280635
E-mail: tkeane@robinson-gronnow.co.uk
Website: http://www.robinson-gronnow.co.uk
Directors: A. Keane (Fin), J. Keane (Fin), T. Keane (MD)
Immediate Holding Company: ROBINSON AND GRONNOW LIMITED
Registration no: 04334682 **VAT No.:** GB 157 8653 24
Date established: 2001 **Turnover:** £1m - £2m **No.of Employees:** 11 - 20
Product Groups: 26

Date of Accounts	Nov 09	Nov 08	Nov 07
Working Capital	37	22	23
Fixed Assets	24	29	35
Current Assets	326	260	213

Robinson Motor Rewinds
4th Floor Meadow Mill Water Street, Stockport, SK1 2BU
Tel: 0161-476 2707 **Fax:** 0161-476 2707
Directors: G. Robinson (Prop)
Immediate Holding Company: ROBINSON REWINDS LTD
Registration no: 04709418 **Date established:** 2003
No.of Employees: 1 - 10 **Product Groups:** 37, 48, 66

Date of Accounts	Mar 11	Mar 10	Mar 09
Working Capital	3	2	3
Fixed Assets	1	1	2
Current Assets	9	9	7

Rowlinson Knitwear Ltd
Woodbank Mills Turncroft Lane, Stockport, SK1 4AR
Tel: 0161-477 7791 **Fax:** 0161-480 2083
E-mail: info@rowlinson-knitwear.com
Website: http://www.rowlinson-knitwear.com
Bank(s): National Westminster Bank Plc
Directors: D. Moore (MD), C. Rowlinson (Co Sec), A. McConnell (Sales)
Managers: K. Wood (Fin Mgr), C. Brookes (Tech Serv Mgr), N. Ryan (Personnel)
Immediate Holding Company: ROWLINSON KNITWEAR LIMITED
Registration no: 01072854 **Date established:** 1972
Turnover: £10m - £20m **No.of Employees:** 51 - 100 **Product Groups:** 24

Date of Accounts	Oct 09	Oct 08	Sep 11
Sales Turnover	10m	N/A	10m
Pre Tax Profit/Loss	453	744	229
Working Capital	3m	2m	3m
Fixed Assets	2m	2m	1m
Current Assets	5m	4m	5m
Current Liabilities	398	978	255

I C Rushton central heating & plumbing Specalist
16 Rostherne Avenue High Lane, Stockport, SK6 8AR
Tel: 01663-762540
E-mail: iancrushton@aol.com
Directors: I. Rushton (Prop)
Date established: 2001 **No.of Employees:** 1 - 10 **Product Groups:** 40, 52

Rust Proofing Company Manchester Ltd
Unit 1 Vauxhall Industrial Estate Greg Street, Stockport, SK5 7BR
Tel: 0161-480 8341 **Fax:** 0161-480 8820
E-mail: hughesd4@sky.com
Directors: S. Hughes (MD)
Immediate Holding Company: RUST PROOFING COMPANY (MANCHESTER) LIMITED
Registration no: 00502375 **Date established:** 1951
Turnover: Up to £250,000 **No.of Employees:** 1 - 10 **Product Groups:** 46, 48

Date of Accounts	Dec 11	Dec 10	Dec 09
Working Capital	-17	-35	-35
Fixed Assets	9	9	22
Current Assets	37	38	30

Ryder Towing Equipment
Alvanley House Alvanley Industrial Estate Stockport Road, Bredbury, Stockport, SK6 2DJ
Tel: 0161-430 1120 **Fax:** 0161-430 8140
E-mail: d.ryder@rydertowing.co.uk
Website: http://www.rydertowing.co.uk
Directors: D. Ryder (MD)
Immediate Holding Company: KELLY CONTRACTING LIMITED
Registration no: 02222509 **VAT No.:** GB 510 1356 06
Date established: 1999 **No.of Employees:** 1 - 10 **Product Groups:** 39

Date of Accounts	Jun 11	Jun 10	Jun 09
Working Capital	-61	-61	-83
Fixed Assets	265	265	333
Current Assets	-61	126	94

S D L Atlas
PO Box 162, Stockport, SK1 3JW
Tel: 0161-480 8485 **Fax:** 0161-480 8580
E-mail: test@sdlatlas.com
Website: http://www.sdlatlas.com
Managers: G. Barker (Comptroller), W. Zielenkiewicz (Mgr)
Immediate Holding Company: SDL ATLAS LIMITED
Registration no: 02591517 **VAT No.:** GB 593 6576 87
Date established: 1991 **Turnover:** £2m - £5m **No.of Employees:** 1 - 10
Product Groups: 38, 42, 43, 85

Date of Accounts	Dec 11	Dec 10	Dec 09
Sales Turnover	N/A	N/A	5m
Pre Tax Profit/Loss	N/A	N/A	429
Working Capital	-0	974	1m
Fixed Assets	N/A	41	70
Current Assets	472	2m	2m
Current Liabilities	N/A	N/A	184

S J M Eurostat UK Ltd
Unit 4b Bramhall Moor Industrial Park, Hazel Grove, Stockport, SK7 5BW
Tel: 0161-456 6088 **Fax:** 0161-456 6089
E-mail: info.uk@eurostatgroup.com
Website: http://www.eurostatgroup.com
Managers: I. Fox (Ops Mgr)
Ultimate Holding Company: DOU YEE INTERNATIONAL PTE LTD (SINGAPORE)
Immediate Holding Company: S.J.M. EUROSTAT (U.K.) LIMITED
Registration no: 03003971 **VAT No.:** GB 616 2686 33
Date established: 1994 **Turnover:** £1m - £2m **No.of Employees:** 1 - 10
Product Groups: 32, 38

Date of Accounts	Sep 11	Sep 10	Sep 09
Working Capital	12	201	29
Fixed Assets	37	43	55
Current Assets	156	321	185

S P P Pumps Ltd
Greg Street, Stockport, SK5 7BU
Tel: 0161-480 4955 **Fax:** 0161-476 2193
E-mail: solutions@spppumps.com
Website: http://www.spppumps.com
Bank(s): National Westminster Bank Plc
Managers: T. Winstanley (Mgr), M. Copson (Mgr)
Ultimate Holding Company: KIRLOSKAR BROTHERS LIMITED (INDIA)
Immediate Holding Company: SPP PUMPS LIMITED
Registration no: 04839607 **VAT No.:** GB 243 1882 67
Date established: 2003 **Turnover:** £20m - £50m
No.of Employees: 11 - 20 **Product Groups:** 40, 48

Date of Accounts	Dec 11	Dec 10	Dec 09
Sales Turnover	69m	55m	59m
Pre Tax Profit/Loss	5m	4m	3m
Working Capital	9m	7m	6m
Fixed Assets	5m	4m	4m
Current Assets	33m	27m	27m
Current Liabilities	10m	10m	10m

Safety Glaze Ltd
Unit 10 Marsland Street Hazel Grove, Stockport, SK7 4ER
Tel: 0800-169 4083
E-mail: nick@safety-glaze.co.uk
Website: http://www.safety-glaze.co.uk
Directors: N. Moore (Dir)
Immediate Holding Company: SAFETY GLAZE LIMITED
Registration no: 05939932 **Date established:** 2006
No.of Employees: 1 - 10 **Product Groups:** 30, 35, 66

Date of Accounts	Sep 11	Sep 10	Sep 09
Sales Turnover	463	316	364
Pre Tax Profit/Loss	20	11	22
Working Capital	33	-4	N/A
Fixed Assets	24	27	36
Current Assets	84	55	54
Current Liabilities	16	16	27

Salford Translations Ltd
66 Lower Hillgate, Stockport, SK1 3AL
Tel: 0161-968 7100 **Fax:** 0161-968 7109
E-mail: info@salftrans.co.uk
Website: http://www.salftrans.co.uk
Directors: N. Rosenthal (Dir)
Immediate Holding Company: SALFORD TRANSLATIONS LIMITED
Registration no: 02268133 **VAT No.:** GB 451 4405 75
Date established: 1988 **Turnover:** £250,000 - £500,000
No.of Employees: 1 - 10 **Product Groups:** 80

Date of Accounts	Jun 12	Jun 11	Jun 10
Working Capital	18	13	10
Fixed Assets	11	14	17
Current Assets	33	30	25

Satake Europe Ltd
Horsfield Way Bredbury, Stockport, SK6 2SU
Tel: 0161-406 3800 **Fax:** 0161-406 3801
E-mail: sales@satake-europe.com
Website: http://www.satake-europe.com
Bank(s): Barclays
Managers: M. Kennedy, P. Marriott (Sales & Mktg Mg), P. Walthell (Fin Mgr), C. Dale
Ultimate Holding Company: SATAKE CORPORATION
Immediate Holding Company: SATAKE EUROPE LIMITED
Registration no: 01797595 **Date established:** 1984
No.of Employees: 21 - 50 **Product Groups:** 41

Date of Accounts	Dec 11	Dec 10	Dec 09
Sales Turnover	8m	2m	5m
Pre Tax Profit/Loss	385	-395	309

Working Capital	2m	2m	2m
Fixed Assets	381	19	18
Current Assets	9m	2m	3m
Current Liabilities	2m	120	493

L & S Schofield Ltd
Unit 11-13 Haigh Avenue, Stockport, SK4 1NU
Tel: 0161-480 3570 **Fax:** 0161-480 0836
E-mail: steve@dowelpins.fsnet.co.uk
Website: http://www.sftaylor.com
Directors: J. Schofield (Fin), P. Vokes (Sales), S. Schofield (MD)
Immediate Holding Company: L. & S. SCHOFIELD LIMITED
Registration no: 00566686 **Date established:** 1956
Turnover: £500,000 - £1m **No.of Employees:** 1 - 10 **Product Groups:** 25

Date of Accounts	Apr 11	Apr 10	Apr 09
Working Capital	4	-21	-39
Fixed Assets	25	30	35
Current Assets	159	191	132

Shackell Edwards & Co
Corrie Way Bredbury Park Industrial Estate, Bredbury, Stockport, SK6 2ST
Tel: 0161-406 7984 **Fax:** 0161-406 6233
Website: http://www.shackelledwards.com
Directors: A. Kay (Grp Chief Exec), B. Spooner (Ch), M. Cheyne (MD)
Managers: S. Findley (Mktg Serv Mgr), S. Keen
Registration no: 02861506 **Date established:** 2004 **Turnover:** £5m - £10m
No.of Employees: 21 - 50 **Product Groups:** 32

Date of Accounts	Mar 07	Mar 06
Pre Tax Profit/Loss	N/A	135
Working Capital	1320	-279
Fixed Assets	545	1754
Current Assets	3657	2516
Current Liabilities	2337	2794
Total Share Capital	1000	1000
ROCE% (Return on Capital Employed)		9.2

Shades Graphics Ltd
Stur Mill Broadstone Hall Road, Stockport, SK5 7BY
Tel: 0161-477 4688 **Fax:** 0161-474 7629
E-mail: sales@shadesgraphics.co.uk
Website: http://www.shadesgraphics.co.uk
Directors: B. Coleman (Fin), S. Dawson (MD)
Managers: I. Robertson (Buyer), M. Charlesworth (Mktg Serv Mgr)
Immediate Holding Company: SHADES (SCREEN PRINT) LIMITED
Registration no: 05156247 **VAT No.:** GB 286 0923 38
Date established: 2004 **Turnover:** £5m - £10m **No.of Employees:** 21 - 50
Product Groups: 28, 48

Date of Accounts	Dec 08	Dec 07	Sep 10
Pre Tax Profit/Loss	N/A	73	N/A
Working Capital	-119	245	-228
Fixed Assets	549	783	334
Current Assets	713	1m	609
Current Liabilities	282	292	301

Anne Shaw Consultants Ltd
26 Carrwood Road Bramhall, Stockport, SK7 3EL
Tel: 01625-576225 **Fax:** 01625-576262
E-mail: consult@anneshaw.com
Website: http://www.anneshaw.com
Directors: A. Cornforth (Co Sec), D. Regester (MD)
Immediate Holding Company: TJMN INVESTMENTS LIMITED
Registration no: 02402140 **VAT No.:** GB 548 3578 06
Date established: 1989 **Turnover:** £250,000 - £500,000
No.of Employees: 1 - 10 **Product Groups:** 80

Date of Accounts	Jan 12	Jan 11	Jan 10
Working Capital	231	231	230
Current Assets	232	231	239

Sign A Rama Ltd (Manchester)
128 London Road Hazel Grove, Stockport, SK7 4DJ
Tel: 0161-456 2003 **Fax:** 0161-456 2005
E-mail: info@signarama.uk.com
Website: http://www.signarama.com
Directors: M. Denton (Dir)
Immediate Holding Company: SIGNARAMA (BIRMINGHAM WEST) LTD
Registration no: 07106075 **Date established:** 2009
Turnover: £250,000 - £500,000 **No.of Employees:** 1 - 10
Product Groups: 30, 37

Signs & Labels
Douglas Bruce House Corrie Way, Bredbury, Stockport, SK6 2RR
Tel: 0161-494 6125 **Fax:** 0161-406 5525
E-mail: jonw@signsandlabels.co.uk
Website: http://www.signsandlabels.co.uk
Bank(s): Royal Bank of Scotland, Stockport
Managers: P. Ingleby (Chief Mgr)
Ultimate Holding Company: BRADY CORP (USA)
Registration no: 03318384 **VAT No.:** GB 148 4683 36
Date established: 1997 **Turnover:** £10m - £20m
No.of Employees: 101 - 250 **Product Groups:** 23, 27, 28, 35, 36, 37, 40, 48, 49

Simmtronic
Unit A3 Lingard Business Centre Lingard Lane, Bredbury, Stockport, SK6 2QU
Tel: 08445-617489 **Fax:** 0161-236 9313
E-mail: dave.little@simmtronic.com
Website: http://www.simmtronic.com
Managers: D. Little (Ops Mgr), D. Gillingham (Sales Prom Mgr)
No.of Employees: 1 - 10 **Product Groups:** 37, 67

Simpson Thomson Filtration
Virginia Mills 187 Higher Hillgate, Stockport, SK1 3JG
Tel: 0161-480 8991 **Fax:** 0161-429 8413
E-mail: adrian.vtc@virgin.net
Directors: A. Greenwood (Dir), A. Greenwood (Ch & MD)
Managers: J. Simmons (Chief Mgr)
Immediate Holding Company: SIMPSON THOMSON FILTRATION LIMITED
Registration no: 06749392 **Date established:** 2008
Turnover: £250,000 - £500,000 **No.of Employees:** 1 - 10
Product Groups: 23, 24, 40, 41, 42, 63

Date of Accounts	Nov 10	Nov 09
Working Capital	3	-0
Current Assets	28	24

Simulation Solutions

Unit 10 Rugby Park Bletchley Road, Stockport, SK4 3EJ
Tel: 0161-947 9113 **Fax:** 0161-947 9099
E-mail: robbie@simsol.co.uk
Website: http://www.simsol.co.uk
Directors: R. Birrell (MD)
Immediate Holding Company: BROADSTONE MILL LTD
Registration no: 01519240 **Date established:** 1997
Turnover: Up to £250,000 **No.of Employees:** 11 - 20 **Product Groups:** 72

Soul Nutrition Katie Sheen FdSc DiplON mBANT NTC registered Nutritional Therapist

19 Bramhall Lane South Bramhall, Stockport, SK7 1AL
Tel: 0161-439 9856 **Fax:** 0161-439 9856
E-mail: katiesheen@soulnutrition.co.uk
Website: http://www.soulnutrition.co.uk
Directors: K. Sheen (Prop)
No.of Employees: 1 - 10 **Product Groups:** 31, 69, 88

Sovereign Rubber Ltd

Hillgate Industrial Estate Carrington Field Street, Stockport, SK1 3JN
Tel: 0161-429 8787 **Fax:** 0161-480 3573
E-mail: salessov@sovereign-rubber.co.uk
Website: http://www.sovereign-rubber.co.uk
Managers: A. Patterson (Comptroller)
Ultimate Holding Company: SPORTFIELD DEUTSCHLAND HOLDING GMBH (GERMANY)
Immediate Holding Company: SOVEREIGN RUBBER LIMITED
Registration no: 00554644 **Date established:** 1955 **Turnover:** £5m - £10m
No.of Employees: 21 - 50 **Product Groups:** 25, 29, 30, 39, 41, 42, 49, 61, 65

Date of Accounts	Dec 11	Dec 10	Dec 09
Sales Turnover	7m	7m	7m
Pre Tax Profit/Loss	293	782	293
Working Capital	9m	9m	8m
Fixed Assets	1m	1m	2m
Current Assets	9m	9m	9m
Current Liabilities	163	331	321

Stainfab Sheet Metal Ltd

Unit 50 Offerton Industrial Estate Hempshaw Lane, Stockport, SK2 5TJ
Tel: 0161-480 5009 **Fax:** 0161-480 5509
E-mail: stainfab@hotmail.co.uk
Directors: P. White (MD)
Immediate Holding Company: STAINFAB SHEET METAL LIMITED
Registration no: 03665572 **VAT No.:** GB 616 2842 45
Date established: 1998 **Turnover:** £250,000 - £500,000
No.of Employees: 1 - 10 **Product Groups:** 26, 35, 36, 48, 67

Date of Accounts	Dec 11	Dec 10	Dec 09
Working Capital	-5	-4	-6
Fixed Assets	7	8	9
Current Assets	101	101	112

Standex International Ltd

6 Cromwell Road Bredbury, Stockport, SK6 2RF
Tel: 0161-406 4300 **Fax:** 0161-406 4301
E-mail: jim@standexuk.co.uk
Website: http://www.standex.com
Bank(s): Lloyds, London
Managers: J. Fletcher (Chief Mgr)
Ultimate Holding Company: STANDEX INTERNATIONAL CORPORATION (USA)
Immediate Holding Company: STANDEX INTERNATIONAL LIMITED
Registration no: 00094496 **VAT No.:** 157 3981 32 **Date established:** 2007
Turnover: £10m - £20m **No.of Employees:** 21 - 50 **Product Groups:** 28

Date of Accounts	Jun 11	Jun 10	Jun 09
Sales Turnover	10m	9m	8m
Pre Tax Profit/Loss	595	-356	299
Working Capital	386	-178	2m
Fixed Assets	194	227	247
Current Assets	5m	4m	4m
Current Liabilities	904	1m	674

Stannah Lift Services Ltd

Unit 12 Bamford Business Park Whitehill Industrial Estate, Stockport, SK4 1PL
Tel: 0161-477 3344 **Fax:** 0161-477 3377
E-mail: ian_ash@stannah.co.uk
Website: http://www.stannah.com
Managers: C. Bramhall (District Mgr)
Ultimate Holding Company: STANNAH LIFTS HOLDINGS LIMITED
Immediate Holding Company: STANNAH LIFT SERVICES LIMITED
Registration no: 01189799 **Date established:** 1974
No.of Employees: 21 - 50 **Product Groups:** 35, 39, 45

Date of Accounts	Dec 11	Dec 10	Dec 09
Sales Turnover	84m	82m	87m
Pre Tax Profit/Loss	191	2m	2m
Working Capital	12m	14m	15m
Fixed Assets	4m	4m	3m
Current Assets	21m	24m	24m
Current Liabilities	6m	6m	7m

Stockport Fire Extinguishers

Unit 14 Haigh Park Haigh Avenue, Stockport, SK4 1QR
Tel: 0161-476 2004 **Fax:** 0161-429 7239
E-mail: giles@stockportfire.co.uk
Directors: G. Payne (Ptnr)
Ultimate Holding Company: GOOP LIMITED
Immediate Holding Company: DIAMOND SHOPFITTING LIMITED
Registration no: 02531653 **Date established:** 1994
No.of Employees: 1 - 10 **Product Groups:** 38, 42

Date of Accounts	Sep 11	Sep 10	Sep 09
Working Capital	87	107	47
Fixed Assets	2	3	4
Current Assets	180	189	129

Stockport Metropolitan Borough Council

Town Hall, Stockport, SK1 3XE
Tel: 0161-474 3969 **Fax:** 0161-217 6032
E-mail: deryn.willock@stockport.gov.uk
Website: http://www.stockport.gov.uk
Managers: D. Willock (Sales Admin)
Turnover: Over £1,000m **No.of Employees:** 21 - 50 **Product Groups:** 87

Stockport Sheet Metal Ltd

Manor Works Coronation Street, Stockport, SK5 7PH
Tel: 0161-477 2693 **Fax:** 0161-477 0771
E-mail: derek@stockportsheetmetal.co.uk
Website: http://www.stockportsheetmetal.co.uk
Directors: D. Cox (Prop)
Immediate Holding Company: PODMORE PROPERTY LTD
Registration no: 02105101 **Date established:** 1987
Turnover: £250,000 - £500,000 **No.of Employees:** 11 - 20
Product Groups: 48

Date of Accounts	Aug 11	Aug 10	Aug 09
Working Capital	63	48	45
Fixed Assets	390	390	390
Current Assets	70	54	52

Stockport Truck Centre Ltd

Old Moor Road Bredbury, Stockport, SK6 2QE
Tel: 0161-494 9200 **Fax:** 0161-494 9433
E-mail: info@stc-uk.com
Website: http://www.stockporttrucks.co.uk
Directors: D. Hardy (Fin), G. Hardy (MD)
Ultimate Holding Company: STC HOLDINGS LIMITED
Immediate Holding Company: STOCKPORT TRUCK CENTRE LIMITED
Registration no: 03967781 **Date established:** 2000
No.of Employees: 1 - 10 **Product Groups:** 37, 39, 67

Date of Accounts	Apr 11	Apr 10	Apr 09
Working Capital	353	248	260
Fixed Assets	242	304	272
Current Assets	2m	1m	1m

T E L Engineering Ltd

Newby Road Hazel Grove, Stockport, SK7 5DA
Tel: 0161-456 6545 **Fax:** 0161-456 3810
E-mail: mail@trolexengineering.co.uk
Website: http://www.trolexengineering.co.uk
Directors: J. Pierce Jones (Dir)
Immediate Holding Company: T.E.L. ENGINEERING LIMITED
Registration no: 01341280 **Date established:** 1977
Turnover: £500,000 - £1m **No.of Employees:** 11 - 20 **Product Groups:** 37

Date of Accounts	Nov 11	Nov 10	Nov 09
Working Capital	830	713	668
Fixed Assets	134	127	149
Current Assets	1m	962	1m

Taskwear Clothing

Albert School Church Lane, Marple, Stockport, SK6 7AR
Tel: 0161-449 9449 **Fax:** 0161-426 0906
E-mail: sales@eandeworkwear.co.uk
Website: http://www.eandeworkwear.co.uk
Directors: A. Ashton (Ptnr)
Immediate Holding Company: TASKWEAR(CLOTHING)LIMITED
Registration no: 01295882 **Date established:** 1977
Turnover: Up to £250,000 **No.of Employees:** 11 - 20 **Product Groups:** 24, 63

Date of Accounts	Sep 11	Sep 10	Sep 09
Sales Turnover	N/A	N/A	96
Working Capital	1	-3	15
Fixed Assets	65	67	69
Current Assets	40	35	50
Current Liabilities	N/A	N/A	7

Tech Cell Ltd

9 Cromwell Road Bredbury, Stockport, SK6 2RF
Tel: 0161-430 2233 **Fax:** 0161-430 2626
E-mail: admin@techcell.co.uk
Website: http://www.techcell.co.uk
Directors: D. Goodwin (MD)
Immediate Holding Company: TECH-CELL LIMITED
Registration no: 03659709 **Date established:** 1998
No.of Employees: 1 - 10 **Product Groups:** 28

Date of Accounts	Oct 10	Oct 09	Oct 08
Working Capital	-201	-80	-48
Fixed Assets	599	370	411
Current Assets	220	192	239

Technical Models Ltd

Unit 10 Crosland Industrial Estate Stockport Road West, Bredbury, Stockport, SK6 2BR
Tel: 0161-494 9022 **Fax:** 0161-430 8406
E-mail: peter@technical-models.co.uk
Website: http://www.technical-models.co.uk
Directors: P. Lawson (MD), S. Lawson (Fin)
Immediate Holding Company: TECHNICAL MODELS LIMITED
Registration no: 01580805 **VAT No.:** GB 373 3232 67
Date established: 1981 **Turnover:** £250,000 - £500,000
No.of Employees: 1 - 10 **Product Groups:** 38, 49

Date of Accounts	Sep 11	Sep 10	Sep 09
Working Capital	8	16	15
Fixed Assets	12	8	10
Current Assets	171	216	182
Current Liabilities	56	66	51

Techtrol Incinerator Ltd

Gregson Road, Stockport, SK5 7SS
Tel: 0161-476 6955 **Fax:** 0161-476 2674
E-mail: mailbox@techtrol.co.uk
Website: http://www.techtrol.co.uk
Directors: J. Wharmby (Co Sec), M. Wharmby (MD)
Immediate Holding Company: TECHTROL LIMITED
Registration no: 01950671 **VAT No.:** GB 439 7902 12
Date established: 1985 **Turnover:** £2m - £5m **No.of Employees:** 1 - 10
Product Groups: 40, 42, 48, 66, 84

Date of Accounts	Mar 08	Mar 07	Mar 06
Working Capital	-18	-50	-78
Fixed Assets	52	64	71
Current Assets	1m	909	879

Timbermat Ltd

Vauxhall Industrial Estate Greg Street, Reddish, Stockport, SK5 7BR
Tel: 0844-800 9560 **Fax:** 0161-476 6253
E-mail: sales@timbermat.co.uk
Website: http://www.timbermat.co.uk
Product Groups: 35, 83

Time Controls Ltd

Unit 24 Chadkirk Industrial Estate Vale Road, Romiley, Stockport, SK6 3NE
Tel: 0161-427 4580 **Fax:** 0161-427 8730
E-mail: info@timecontrolsltd.co.uk
Website: http://www.timecontrolsltd.co.uk
Directors: A. Smith (Co Sec), M. Smith (Dir)
Immediate Holding Company: TIME CONTROLS LIMITED
Registration no: 00922481 **VAT No.:** GB 158 4018 64
Date established: 1967 **Turnover:** £250,000 - £500,000
No.of Employees: 1 - 10 **Product Groups:** 37

Date of Accounts	Mar 11	Mar 10	Mar 09
Working Capital	-27	-33	-13
Fixed Assets	5	1	1
Current Assets	69	66	56

Tool & Fastener Solutions Ltd (T/A TF Solutions Ltd)

Unit 8 Spectrum Way Cheadle Heath, Stockport, SK3 0SA
Tel: 0161-429 5917 **Fax:** 0161-429 5918
E-mail: sales@tfsolutions.co.uk
Website: http://www.tfsolutions.co.uk
Directors: P. Lynott (Dir)
Immediate Holding Company: TOOL & FASTENER SOLUTIONS LIMITED
Registration no: 04088325 **Date established:** 2000 **Turnover:** £5m - £10m
No.of Employees: 11 - 20 **Product Groups:** 40, 66

Date of Accounts	Dec 11	Dec 10	Dec 09
Sales Turnover	9m	8m	5m
Pre Tax Profit/Loss	497	211	18
Working Capital	102	-5	93
Fixed Assets	947	905	925
Current Assets	3m	2m	2m
Current Liabilities	463	418	189

Travis Perkins plc

Marcliffe Industrial Estate Macclesfield Road, Hazel Grove, Stockport, SK7 5EG
Tel: 0161-456 1616 **Fax:** 0161-487 3760
Website: http://www.travisperkins.co.uk
Directors: A. Egerton (Fin), N. Bode (Sales)
Managers: M. Rossendale (District Mgr), P. Whittaker (Sales Prom Mgr)
Immediate Holding Company: TRAVIS PERKINS PLC
Registration no: 00824821 **VAT No.:** GB 408 5567 37
Date established: 1964 **No.of Employees:** 1 - 10 **Product Groups:** 66

Date of Accounts	Dec 11	Dec 10	Dec 09
Sales Turnover	4779m	3153m	2931m
Pre Tax Profit/Loss	270m	197m	213m
Working Capital	133m	159m	248m
Fixed Assets	2771m	2749m	2108m
Current Assets	1421m	1329m	1035m
Current Liabilities	473m	412m	109m

Travis Perkins plc

Whitehill Street Whitehall Industrial Estate, Stockport, SK4 1NY
Tel: 0161-480 0881 **Fax:** 0161-477 3658
E-mail: matthew.dolan@travisperkins.co.uk
Website: http://www.travisperkins.co.uk
Managers: M. Dolan (District Mgr)
Immediate Holding Company: TRAVIS PERKINS PLC
Registration no: 00824821 **Date established:** 1964 **Turnover:** £2m - £5m
No.of Employees: 11 - 20 **Product Groups:** 66

Date of Accounts	Dec 11	Dec 10	Dec 09
Sales Turnover	4779m	3153m	2931m
Pre Tax Profit/Loss	270m	197m	213m
Working Capital	133m	159m	248m
Fixed Assets	2771m	2749m	2108m
Current Assets	1421m	1329m	1035m
Current Liabilities	473m	412m	109m

Trescal Ltd

Unit 3 Bredbury Park Way Bredbury, Stockport, SK6 2SL
Tel: 0161-406 7878 **Fax:** 0161-406 7979
E-mail: calibration.manchester@dowdingandmills.com
Website: http://www.dowdingandmills.com
Bank(s): HSBC Bank plc
Managers: K. Hancox (Mgr)
Ultimate Holding Company: FINANCIERE SERINGA III (FRANCE)
Immediate Holding Company: TRESCAL LIMITED
Registration no: 06614164 **VAT No.:** GB 109 5683 53
Date established: 2008 **No.of Employees:** 21 - 50 **Product Groups:** 37, 38, 44, 45, 48, 66, 67, 68, 84, 85

Date of Accounts	Dec 10	Dec 09	Dec 08
Sales Turnover	8m	2m	738
Pre Tax Profit/Loss	-394	-3	-512
Working Capital	703	-3m	-2m
Fixed Assets	7m	2m	1m
Current Assets	4m	901	728
Current Liabilities	1m	232	173

Trinity Computer Services Ltd

Unit 6-10 Bredbury Park Way Bredbury Park Industrial Estat, Bredbury, Stockport, SK6 2SN
Tel: 0161-406 2300 **Fax:** 0161-406 2301
E-mail: info@trinitycomputers.co.uk
Website: http://www.trinitycomputers.co.uk
Bank(s): Natwest
Directors: C. Bolus (Sales), J. Wood (Dir), L. Williams (MD), P. Heeley (I.T. Dir), P. Healy (Tech Serv)
Ultimate Holding Company: TRINITY COMPUTER HOLDINGS LIMITED
Immediate Holding Company: M-HANCE LIMITED
Registration no: 01369937 **VAT No.:** GB 545 3414 36
Date established: 1978 **Turnover:** £2m - £5m **No.of Employees:** 21 - 50
Product Groups: 44

Date of Accounts	Sep 10	Sep 09	Sep 08
Working Capital	-459	-181	-390
Fixed Assets	2m	2m	2m
Current Assets	1m	1m	1m

Trojan Engineering & Fabrication

Portwood Works Mersey Street, Stockport, SK1 2HX
Tel: 0161-480 5288 **Fax:** 0161-480 5277
Directors: P. Mcandrew (Dir)
Immediate Holding Company: TROJAN ENGINEERING (STOCKPORT) LIMITED
Registration no: 04648164 **Date established:** 2003
No.of Employees: 1 - 10 **Product Groups:** 33, 35, 48, 84

Date of Accounts	Mar 12	Mar 11	Mar 10
Working Capital	-70	-85	-95
Fixed Assets	103	119	129
Current Assets	58	62	69

Trolex Ltd

Newby Road Hazel Grove, Stockport, SK7 5DY
Tel: 0161-483 1435 **Fax:** 0161-483 5556
E-mail: sales@trolex.com
Website: http://www.trolex.com

Bank(s): National Westminster Bank Plc
Directors: D. Green (Fin), G. Christopher (Fin)
Managers: L. Murphy (Personnel), M. Dawson (Buyer), P. Brian, S. Gayle (Tech Serv Mgr), D. Barr (Mktg Serv Mgr)
Immediate Holding Company: TROLEX LIMITED
Registration no: 00644260 **Date established:** 1959 **Turnover:** £5m - £10m
No.of Employees: 51 - 100 **Product Groups:** 37, 38

Date of Accounts	Dec 11	Dec 10	Dec 09
Sales Turnover	9m	7m	7m
Pre Tax Profit/Loss	630	383	583
Working Capital	2m	1m	1m
Fixed Assets	2m	2m	2m
Current Assets	4m	3m	3m
Current Liabilities	1m	323	353

Turbo Vacuumentation Ltd

Unit 4m Pepper Road, Hazel Grove, Stockport, SK7 5BW
Tel: 0161-482 4004 **Fax:** 0161-482 4005
E-mail: info@turbo-vac.co.uk
Website: http://www.turbo-vac.co.uk
Directors: A. Downes (MD)
Immediate Holding Company: TURBO VACUUMENTATION LIMITED
Registration no: 03169336 **VAT No.:** GB 674 5809 95
Date established: 1996 **Turnover:** £1m - £2m **No.of Employees:** 1 - 10
Product Groups: 29, 37, 38, 40, 41, 42, 43, 44, 45, 47, 48, 67, 84, 86

Date of Accounts	Mar 11	Mar 10	Mar 09
Working Capital	80	64	80
Fixed Assets	27	33	47
Current Assets	493	407	399

Tyco Fire Products Manufacturing

Stockport Trading Estate Yew Street, Stockport, SK4 2JW
Tel: 0161-429 3400 **Fax:** 0161-477 6729
Website: http://www.tycofireproducts.co.uk
Directors: D. Morris (Chief Op Offcr), D. Morris (Chief Op Offcr), M. Macmichael (Fin)
Managers: L. Rose (Personnel), R. Treasure (Purch Mgr)
Immediate Holding Company: TYCO EUROPEAN METAL FRAMING LTD
Registration no: 01841522 **Date established:** 1984
Turnover: £20m - £50m **No.of Employees:** 101 - 250
Product Groups: 38, 42

Date of Accounts	Sep 07	Sep 06	Sep 05
Sales Turnover	38223	33271	30069
Pre Tax Profit/Loss	8123	6557	4677
Working Capital	36881	31750	23302
Fixed Assets	3488	2769	2624
Current Assets	41579	37364	29357
Current Liabilities	4698	5614	6055
ROCE% (Return on Capital Employed)	20.1	19.0	18.0
ROT% (Return on Turnover)	21.3	19.7	15.6

Tyre Mountain

Unit 1 New Zealand Road, Stockport, SK1 4AG
Tel: 0161-480 9991 **Fax:** 0161-480 8347
E-mail: info@tyremountain.co.uk
Website: http://www.leighautos.co.uk
Managers: D. Parkinson (Admin Off)
No.of Employees: 11 - 20 **Product Groups:** 29, 68

Verdigris

Offerton Industrial Estate Hempshaw Lane, Stockport, SK2 5TJ
Tel: 0161-429 0007
E-mail: s.hyde@verdigrismetals.co.uk
Website: http://www.verdigrismetals.co.uk
Directors: D. Hyde (Prop)
No.of Employees: 1 - 10 **Product Groups:** 26, 35

Vibrair Solids Handling

Virginia Mills 187 Higher Hillgate, Stockport, SK1 3JG
Tel: 0161-480 8991 **Fax:** 0161-474 7737
E-mail: adrian.vtc@virgin.net
Website: http://www.vibrair.com
Directors: A. Greenwood (Dir)
Immediate Holding Company: JACK GREENWOOD COMMERCIALS LIMITED
Registration no: 06452682 **Date established:** 2011
No.of Employees: 1 - 10 **Product Groups:** 35, 39, 45

Victoria Colour

Lingard Lane Bredbury, Stockport, SK6 2QT
Tel: 0161-406 6474 **Fax:** 0161-406 6550
Website: http://www.eastwicklodge.co.uk
Directors: M. Moffatt (Dir)
Immediate Holding Company: GADGETBID LIMITED
Registration no: 02271926 **Date established:** 2011
No.of Employees: 1 - 10 **Product Groups:** 32, 66

Vista Labels Ltd

349 Hempshaw Lane, Stockport, SK1 4NB
Tel: 0161-477 5151 **Fax:** 0161-477 9203
E-mail: sales@vistalabels.com
Website: http://www.vistalabels.com
Directors: R. Clarke (Co Sec), T. Grice (MD)
Immediate Holding Company: VISTA LABELS LIMITED
Registration no: 01169170 **VAT No.:** GB 158 6341 47
Date established: 1974 **Turnover:** £2m - £5m **No.of Employees:** 21 - 50
Product Groups: 27, 28, 30, 44

Date of Accounts	Mar 12	Mar 11	Mar 10
Sales Turnover	N/A	N/A	4m
Pre Tax Profit/Loss	N/A	N/A	91
Working Capital	910	698	719
Fixed Assets	837	937	1m
Current Assets	2m	2m	2m
Current Liabilities	N/A	N/A	305

F Walther Electrics Ltd

Cromwell Road Bredbury, Stockport, SK6 2RF
Tel: 0161-494 1233 **Fax:** 0161-494 5055
E-mail: mail@walther.demon.co.uk
Directors: M. Hawley (Fin)
Ultimate Holding Company: WALTHER WERKE FERDINAND WALTHER GMBH (GERMANY)
Immediate Holding Company: F. WALTHER ELECTRICS LIMITED
Registration no: 01656014 **Date established:** 1982
Turnover: £250,000 - £500,000 **No.of Employees:** 1 - 10
Product Groups: 37

Date of Accounts	Dec 11	Dec 10	Dec 09
Working Capital	1m	1m	1m
Fixed Assets	63	80	53
Current Assets	2m	1m	2m

Warehouse Handling Solutions Ltd

Unit 9 Brighton Road, Stockport, SK4 2BE
Tel: 0161-431 5010 **Fax:** 0161-431 5020
E-mail: sales@reco-group.com
Website: http://www.recohandling.com
Directors: J. Faulkner (MD)
Immediate Holding Company: RECO HANDLING LIMITED
Registration no: 03853244 **Date established:** 1999
No.of Employees: 1 - 10 **Product Groups:** 35, 39, 45

Date of Accounts	Oct 07	Oct 06	Oct 05
Working Capital	242	244	228
Fixed Assets	20	24	31
Current Assets	639	563	509

Wheatley Plastics Ltd

Reynolds Mill Newbridge Lane, Stockport, SK1 2NR
Tel: 0161-477 2800 **Fax:** 0161-480 6611
E-mail: info@wheatleyplastics.co.uk
Website: http://www.wheatleyplastics.co.uk
Bank(s): The Royal Bank of Scotland
Directors: G. Knight (MD), R. Harper (Fin)
Immediate Holding Company: WHEATLEY PLASTICS LIMITED
Registration no: 02479501 **VAT No.:** GB 570 6212 60
Date established: 1990 **Turnover:** £500,000 - £1m
No.of Employees: 11 - 20 **Product Groups:** 30

Date of Accounts	May 12	May 11	May 10
Working Capital	182	184	182
Fixed Assets	45	29	34
Current Assets	311	281	290

Woodley Engineering Stockport Ltd

Whitefield Road Bredbury, Stockport, SK6 2QR
Tel: 0161-430 7488 **Fax:** 0161-406 6061
E-mail: sales@woodley-punches.com
Website: http://www.woodley-punches.com
Directors: D. Cumings (Fin), D. Cummings (Fin)
Immediate Holding Company: WOODLEY ENGINEERING (STOCKPORT) LIMITED
Registration no: 01330011 **Date established:** 1977
No.of Employees: 21 - 50 **Product Groups:** 46

Date of Accounts	Dec 11	Dec 10	Dec 09
Working Capital	173	186	155
Fixed Assets	478	430	461
Current Assets	227	227	193

Woodstock Leabank Ltd

Corrie Way Bredbury, Stockport, SK6 2ST
Tel: 0161-494 5868 **Fax:** 0161-494 4409
E-mail: j.omalley@woodstockleabank.co.uk
Website: http://www.woodstockleabank.co.uk
Directors: L. Ryalls (Fin), T. Ingham (Sales), J. O'malley (MD)
Managers: A. Bentley (Tech Serv Mgr), T. Thomas (Mktg Serv Mgr), M. O'Malley (Purch Mgr), S. Porter
Ultimate Holding Company: MARPLACE (NUMBER 633) LIMITED
Immediate Holding Company: WOODSTOCK LEABANK OFFICE FURNITURE LIMITED
Registration no: 02861506 **VAT No.:** GB 616 4021 75
Date established: 1993 **Turnover:** £5m - £10m
No.of Employees: 51 - 100 **Product Groups:** 67

Date of Accounts	Jun 11	Jun 10	Jun 09
Sales Turnover	6m	6m	6m
Pre Tax Profit/Loss	125	213	30
Working Capital	-44	42	12
Fixed Assets	2m	2m	3m
Current Assets	2m	2m	2m
Current Liabilities	714	908	612

Zantec Hallmark Ltd

144 Dialstone Lane, Stockport, SK2 6AP
Tel: 0161-483 2359 **Fax:** 0161-483 2310
E-mail: sales@zantech.co.uk
Website: http://www.zantec.co.uk
Directors: G. Whittle (MD), J. Whittle (Fin)
Immediate Holding Company: ZANTEC CATERING & REFRIGERATION SERVICES LIMITED
Registration no: 02533485 **Date established:** 1990
No.of Employees: 1 - 10 **Product Groups:** 20, 40, 41

Date of Accounts	Aug 05	Jan 09	Jan 08
Working Capital	-62	-49	24
Fixed Assets	44	30	36
Current Assets	352	200	306

Tarporley

Collingwood Search & Selection Ltd

8 Portal Business Park Eaton Lane, Tarporley, CW6 9DL
Tel: 01829-732374
E-mail: doug.mackay@collingwoodsearch.co.uk
Website: http://www.collingwoodsearch.co.uk
Directors: D. Mackay (MD)
Immediate Holding Company: COLLINGWOOD SEARCH AND SELECTION LIMITED
Registration no: 05445136 **Date established:** 2005
No.of Employees: 1 - 10 **Product Groups:** 80

Date of Accounts	Mar 11	Mar 10	Mar 09
Working Capital	106	110	86
Fixed Assets	282	284	288
Current Assets	180	161	123

D R & M R Hallett

The Smithy Spurstow, Tarporley, CW6 9RF
Tel: 01948-830277
E-mail: linda.hallett1@btopenworld.co.uk
Directors: M. Hallett (Prop)
Immediate Holding Company: SPURSTOW LIMITED
Registration no: 05207669 **Date established:** 2004
Turnover: Up to £250,000 **No.of Employees:** 1 - 10 **Product Groups:** 26, 35

D W B Engineering

Shays Lane Little Budworth, Tarporley, CW6 9EU
Tel: 01829-760416 **Fax:** 01829-760416
Directors: D. Bloor (Prop)
Date established: 1998 **No.of Employees:** 1 - 10 **Product Groups:** 41

Morris Corfield

Bellard Court Duddon Heath, Duddon, Tarporley, CW6 0EU
Tel: 01829-749391 **Fax:** 01829-741690
E-mail: d.duppa@morriscorfield.co.uk
Managers: D. Duppa (Mgr)
Immediate Holding Company: BELLARD ELECTRONICS LIMITED
Registration no: 01309785 **Date established:** 1977
No.of Employees: 1 - 10 **Product Groups:** 41

Date of Accounts	May 11	May 10	May 09
Working Capital	97	90	57
Fixed Assets	14	7	6
Current Assets	160	186	123

Oak Exports Ltd

Unit 4 Tarporley Business Centre Nantwich Road, Tarporley, CW6 9UY
Tel: 01829-733671 **Fax:** 01829-732080
E-mail: sales@oakexports.co.uk
Website: http://www.oakexports.co.uk
Directors: R. Harvey (MD)
Immediate Holding Company: OAK EXPORTS LIMITED
Registration no: 02138599 **Date established:** 1987 **Turnover:** £5m - £10m
No.of Employees: 1 - 10 **Product Groups:** 20, 61, 62, 84

Date of Accounts	Dec 11	Dec 10	Dec 09
Working Capital	177	128	76
Fixed Assets	4	3	4
Current Assets	2m	2m	2m

R C Welding

Oaktree House Shop Lane, Little Budworth, Tarporley, CW6 9HA
Tel: 01829-760180
Directors: R. Craven (Prop)
Date established: 1998 **No.of Employees:** 1 - 10 **Product Groups:** 26, 35

Tarporley Tractors

Rode Street, Tarporley, CW6 0EF
Tel: 01829-733487 **Fax:** 01829-733606
Directors: G. Badrock (Prop)
Registration no: 03207683 **Date established:** 1996
No.of Employees: 1 - 10 **Product Groups:** 41

Warrington

A B B Ltd

Daresbury Park Daresbury, Warrington, WA4 4BT
Tel: 01925-741111 **Fax:** 01925-741212
E-mail: info@gb.abb.com
Website: http://www.abb.co.uk
Directors: B. McLaughlin (Fin), T. Gregory (MD), G. Lewis (Pers)
Ultimate Holding Company: ABB LTD (SWITZERLAND)
Immediate Holding Company: ABB LIMITED
Registration no: 03780764 **VAT No.:** GB 668 1364 13
Date established: 1999 **Turnover:** £500m - £1,000m
No.of Employees: 251 - 500 **Product Groups:** 30, 33, 37, 38, 42, 44, 45, 46, 48, 54, 66, 67, 80, 82, 84, 86

Date of Accounts	Dec 11	Dec 10	Dec 09
Sales Turnover	540m	499m	476m
Pre Tax Profit/Loss	39m	16m	13m
Working Capital	78m	139m	104m
Fixed Assets	76m	63m	62m
Current Assets	286m	342m	276m
Current Liabilities	151m	148m	122m

A B C Asbestos Ltd

Unit D Kirkstead Way Golborne, Warrington, WA3 3PY
Tel: 08444-142121 **Fax:** 01942-829805
E-mail: admin@abc-asbestos.com
Website: http://www.abc-asbestos.com
Directors: A. Davies (Dir)
Managers: L. Hesketh (Admin Off)
Immediate Holding Company: ASBESTOS BUSINESS CONTRACTORS LTD
Registration no: 05180172 **Date established:** 2004
No.of Employees: 21 - 50 **Product Groups:** 54

Date of Accounts	Jul 08	Jul 07	Jul 06
Working Capital	164	117	36
Fixed Assets	52	48	27
Current Assets	343	326	205
Current Liabilities	179	210	168

A D Y

Antrim Road, Warrington, WA2 8JT
Tel: 01925-419933 **Fax:** 01925-419944
E-mail: sales@bulkbags.co.uk
Website: http://www.bulkbags.co.uk
Directors: N. Wong (Prop)
Immediate Holding Company: A D Y PALLETS & BAGS LIMITED
Registration no: 02782160 **Date established:** 1993
Turnover: £250,000 - £500,000 **No.of Employees:** 1 - 10
Product Groups: 23, 24, 27, 30, 35, 45

Date of Accounts	Jul 11	Jul 10	Jul 08
Working Capital	28	18	84
Fixed Assets	27	29	48
Current Assets	48	50	148

A J Boxes

Woodacre Farm 78 Warrington Statham Cheshire Wa13 9bt 9 Wessex Close Woolston Warrington Cheshire Wa14dd, Woolston, Warrington, WA1 4DD
Tel: 01925-483212 **Fax:** 01925-483212
E-mail: sales@ajboxes.com
Website: http://www.ajboxes.com
Directors: A. Potter (Ptnr)
No.of Employees: 1 - 10 **Product Groups:** 25, 27, 28, 35, 44, 49, 66

Adapt Formwork Ltd

Forward Works Bridge Lane, Woolston, Warrington, WA1 4BA
Tel: 0151-345 0297
E-mail: info@adaptformwork.com
Website: http://www.adaptformwork.com
Directors: A. Gradwell (Dir)
Immediate Holding Company: ADAPT FORMWORK LIMITED
Registration no: 06899440 **Date established:** 2009
No.of Employees: 1 - 10 **Product Groups:** 25, 30

Date of Accounts	Jul 11	Jul 10
Working Capital	-2	-41
Fixed Assets	305	255

see next page

***Adapt Formwork Ltd** - Cont'd*

Current Assets	101	55

Advanced Water Technologies

Unit 39 Burtonwood Industrial Estate Phipps Lane, Burtonwood, Warrington, WA5 4HX
Tel: 01925-226411 **Fax:** 01925-220411
E-mail: info@advanced-water.co.uk
Website: http://www.advanced-water.co.uk
Managers: M. Moss (Sales Admin)
Immediate Holding Company: ADVANCED WATER TECHNOLOGIES LIMITED
Registration no: 04344970 **Date established:** 2001
No.of Employees: 11 - 20 **Product Groups:** 32, 54, 66, 67

Date of Accounts	Dec 11	Dec 10	Dec 09
Working Capital	68	36	19
Fixed Assets	44	41	22
Current Assets	378	258	240

Alexander Binzel UK Ltd

Mill Lane Winwick, Warrington, WA2 8UA
Tel: 01925-653944 **Fax:** 01925-654861
E-mail: andrew.hallows@binzel-abicor.com
Website: http://www.binzel-abicor.com
Directors: A. Hallows (Fin), S. Hallows (Dir)
Managers: K. Chudley (Tech Serv Mgr)
Immediate Holding Company: ALEXANDER BINZEL (U.K.) LIMITED
Registration no: 01618280 **Date established:** 1982 **Turnover:** £2m - £5m
No.of Employees: 21 - 50 **Product Groups:** 40, 45, 46

Date of Accounts	Dec 11	Dec 10	Dec 09
Working Capital	2m	2m	2m
Fixed Assets	583	602	614
Current Assets	3m	3m	2m

Allhire Co. Ltd

Unit 5 Kidglove Road Golborne Enterprise Park, Golborne, Warrington, WA3 3GR
Tel: 01942-715326 **Fax:** 01942-715326
Directors: P. Lamb (Dir)
Immediate Holding Company: ALLHIRE COMPANY LIMITED
Registration no: 01653541 **Date established:** 1982
No.of Employees: 1 - 10 **Product Groups:** 37

Date of Accounts	Aug 11	Aug 10	Aug 09
Working Capital	-90	-63	-33
Fixed Assets	45	45	45
Current Assets	12	15	18

Alpla UK

Yew Tree Way Golborne, Warrington, WA3 3JD
Tel: 01942-407400 **Fax:** 01942-407431
E-mail: sales@alpla.com
Website: http://www.ALPLA.COM
Ultimate Holding Company: ALPLA HOLDINGS GMBH (AUSTRIA)
Immediate Holding Company: ALPLA UK LIMITED
Registration no: 02482190 **Date established:** 1990
Turnover: £75m - £125m **No.of Employees:** 101 - 250
Product Groups: 28, 30, 66

Date of Accounts	Dec 11	Dec 10	Dec 09
Sales Turnover	143m	125m	104m
Pre Tax Profit/Loss	15m	16m	10m
Working Capital	18m	28m	17m
Fixed Assets	41m	40m	41m
Current Assets	55m	44m	35m
Current Liabilities	27m	7m	5m

American Golf

1030 Europa Boulevard Westbrook, Warrington, WA5 7YW
Tel: 01925-488400 **Fax:** 01925-488411
E-mail: ged.gould@americangolf.co.uk
Website: http://www.americangolf.co.uk
Directors: G. Gould (Fin)
Ultimate Holding Company: SUN CAPITAL PARTNERS V LP (CAYMAN ISLANDS)
Immediate Holding Company: AMERICAN GOLF DISCOUNT CENTRE LIMITED
Registration no: 01720832 **Date established:** 1983
Turnover: £50m - £75m **No.of Employees:** 1 - 10 **Product Groups:** 49, 65

Date of Accounts	Jan 10	Jan 11	Jan 12
Sales Turnover	72m	76m	94m
Pre Tax Profit/Loss	696	2m	6m
Working Capital	6m	4m	7m
Fixed Assets	5m	10m	12m
Current Assets	18m	23m	27m
Current Liabilities	2m	2m	5m

Anchor Pumps Co. Ltd

Unit C2 Taylor Business Park Risley, Warrington, WA3 6BL
Tel: 01925-761120 **Fax:** 08707-779845
E-mail: sales@anchorpumps.com
Website: http://www.anchorpumps.com
Directors: W. Holmes (MD)
Managers: G. Gardner (Sales Prom Mgr)
Immediate Holding Company: ANCHOR PUMPS COMPANY LIMITED
Registration no: 02113726 **Date established:** 1987
No.of Employees: 11 - 20 **Product Groups:** 40, 41, 42, 43, 45, 46, 48, 49, 67, 68, 83

Date of Accounts	Apr 12	Apr 11	Apr 10
Working Capital	382	330	306
Fixed Assets	58	82	99
Current Assets	1m	1m	1m

Ansell Electrical Products Ltd

Units 2 & 3 Chetham Court, Winwick Quay, Warrington, WA2 8RF
Tel: 01925-652266
Directors: M. Prince (Dir)
Registration no: 04134581 **Date established:** 2001
Turnover: £10m - £20m **No.of Employees:** 21 - 50 **Product Groups:** 37, 67

Antenna Services

74 Worsley Road Walton, Warrington, WA4 6EH
Tel: 01925-604908 **Fax:** 01925-604908
E-mail: enquiries@antennaservices.com
Website: http://www.antennaservices.com
Directors: K. Maloney (Ptnr)
Registration no: 05090463 **Date established:** 2004
No.of Employees: 1 - 10 **Product Groups:** 37

Arrow Flexible Packaging Ltd

Clarence Street Golborne, Warrington, WA3 3RR
Tel: 01942-722383 **Fax:** 01942-716502
E-mail: info@polythene.co.uk
Website: http://www.polythene.co.uk
Bank(s): National Westminster, Wigan
Directors: P. Bramich (Sales), O. Whitehead (Co Sec)
Immediate Holding Company: ARROW FLEXIBLE PACKAGING LIMITED
Registration no: 02248966 **VAT No.:** GB 437 6693 12
Date established: 1988 **Turnover:** £1m - £2m **No.of Employees:** 11 - 20
Product Groups: 30

Date of Accounts	Jul 11	Jul 10	Jul 09
Working Capital	126	143	153
Fixed Assets	343	369	388
Current Assets	305	340	318

Ashtead Plant Hire Co. Ltd

102 Dalton Avenue Birchwood, Warrington, WA3 6YE
Tel: 01925-281000 **Fax:** 01925-281001
E-mail: helpdesk@aplant.com
Website: http://www.aplant.com
Bank(s): Lloyds TSB Bank plc
Managers: P. Longmire (Mktg Serv Mgr)
Immediate Holding Company: ASHTEAD GROUP P.L.C.
Registration no: 00444569 **VAT No.:** GB 210 5687 37
No.of Employees: 51 - 100 **Product Groups:** 72, 74, 83

Atkins

Chadwick House Birchwood, Warrington, WA3 6AE
Tel: 01925-238000 **Fax:** 01925-238500
E-mail: john.mercer@atkinsglobal.com
Website: http://www.atkinsglobal.com
Directors: J. Mercer (Dir)
Immediate Holding Company: FIRST TECHNICAL RECRUITMENT LIMITED
Registration no: 00688424 **Date established:** 1997
Turnover: £500m - £1,000m **No.of Employees:** 251 - 500
Product Groups: 84

Date of Accounts	Mar 11	Mar 10	Mar 09
Working Capital	-3	16	34
Fixed Assets	14	19	19
Current Assets	72	108	148

Autoelectronix.Co.Uk

Unit 3e Parkdale Industrial Estate Wharf Street, Warrington, WA1 2HT
Tel: 01925-637330
E-mail: enquiries@autoelectronix.co.uk
Website: http://www.autoelectronix.co.uk
Directors: S. Hankinson (Dir)
Registration no: 04033454 **No.of Employees:** 1 - 10 **Product Groups:** 37, 39, 67

Avdel Metal Finishing (AMF)

43 Hardwick Grange Woolston, Warrington, WA1 4RF
Tel: 01925-856494 **Fax:** 01925-856 421
E-mail: avdelmetalfinishing@acument.com
Website: http://www.avdel-global.com
Managers: A. Mcleoud (Plant)
Date established: 2002 **No.of Employees:** 21 - 50 **Product Groups:** 46, 48, 84

Bauer Inner City Ltd

Tannery Court Tanners Lane, Warrington, WA2 7NA
Tel: 01925-428940 **Fax:** 01925-244133
E-mail: sales@bauerinnercity.co.uk
Website: http://www.bauerinnercity.co.uk
Directors: G. Lauchan (MD), H. Crouch (MD)
Ultimate Holding Company: BAUER AG (GERMANY)
Immediate Holding Company: BAUER TECHNOLOGIES LIMITED
Registration no: 02198380 **Date established:** 2009
Turnover: £250,000 - £500,000 **No.of Employees:** 1 - 10
Product Groups: 35, 48, 54, 61

Bedford Packaging

41 Burtonwood Industrial Centre Phipps Lane, Burtonwood, Warrington, WA5 4HX
Tel: 01925-291007 **Fax:** 01925-291117
E-mail: enquiries@bedfordpackaging.com
Managers: J. Dicks (Mgr)
Date established: 2004 **No.of Employees:** 1 - 10 **Product Groups:** 38, 42

Beers Timber & Building Supplies Ltd

Thelwall Lane, Warrington, WA4 1NN
Tel: 01925-634283 **Fax:** 01925-638844
E-mail: info@beersltd.co.uk
Website: http://www.beersltd.co.uk
Directors: M. Beer (MD)
Immediate Holding Company: BEERS TIMBER & BUILDING SUPPLIES LIMITED
Registration no: 04324716 **Date established:** 2001
Turnover: £10m - £20m **No.of Employees:** 51 - 100 **Product Groups:** 25, 52, 66

Date of Accounts	Dec 11	Dec 10	Dec 09
Sales Turnover	12m	11m	9m
Pre Tax Profit/Loss	58	331	315
Working Capital	2m	-2m	2m
Fixed Assets	2m	4m	4m
Current Assets	5m	3m	3m
Current Liabilities	1m	3m	314

Benbar Ltd

415 Manchester Road Paddington, Warrington, WA1 3LR
Tel: 01925-823677 **Fax:** 01925- 817718
Website: http://www.benbar.co.uk
Directors: C. Baldwin (Sales), S. Hazlehurst (Co Sec)
Immediate Holding Company: BENTLEYS MOTOR GROUP LTD
Registration no: 04833198 **Date established:** 2003
Turnover: £20m - £50m **No.of Employees:** 51 - 100 **Product Groups:** 68

Date of Accounts	Dec 11	Dec 10	Dec 09
Sales Turnover	29m	32m	31m
Pre Tax Profit/Loss	68	368	356
Working Capital	-367	126	302
Fixed Assets	2m	2m	2m
Current Assets	4m	4m	4m
Current Liabilities	3m	3m	3m

Biffa Waste Services Ltd

Rixton Old Hall Manchester Road, Rixton, Warrington, WA3 6EW
Tel: 0161-775 1011 **Fax:** 0161-775 7291
Website: http://www.biffa.co.uk
Bank(s): National Westminster Bank Plc
Directors: W. Clark (Co Sec)
Managers: J. Divine
Immediate Holding Company: BIFFA WASTE SERVICES LIMITED
Registration no: 00946107 **Date established:** 1969
Turnover: £75m - £125m **No.of Employees:** 21 - 50 **Product Groups:** 27, 54, 84

Date of Accounts	Mar 08	Mar 09	Apr 10
Sales Turnover	555m	574m	492m
Pre Tax Profit/Loss	23m	50m	30m
Working Capital	229m	271m	293m
Fixed Assets	371m	360m	378m
Current Assets	409m	534m	609m
Current Liabilities	50m	100m	115m

Bollard Tech

126 Helmsley Close Bewsey, Warrington, WA5 0GB
Tel: 01925-234363 **Fax:** 01925-234373
E-mail: kenneth.edwards@bollardtech.com
Website: http://www.bollardtech.com
Directors: K. Edwards (MD), N. Routledge (Sales)
Immediate Holding Company: BOLLARD TECH LIMITED
Registration no: 04622339 **Date established:** 2002
Turnover: £250,000 - £500,000 **No.of Employees:** 1 - 10
Product Groups: 35, 39

Date of Accounts	Dec 07	Dec 06	Dec 05
Sales Turnover	412	318	308
Pre Tax Profit/Loss	53	29	23
Working Capital	-25	46	32
Fixed Assets	438	18	15
Current Assets	192	124	81
Current Liabilities	91	34	32

Bolton Gate Services

15 Trinity Court Birchwood, Warrington, WA3 6QT
Tel: 01925-819458 **Fax:** 01925-851982
E-mail: services@boltongate.co.uk
Website: http://www.boltongateservices.co.uk
Managers: A. Hughes (Mgr)
Immediate Holding Company: PACTLIGHT LIMITED
Registration no: 02245413 **Date established:** 1988
No.of Employees: 11 - 20 **Product Groups:** 26, 35

Bonfiglioli UK Ltd

3-7 Grosvenor Grange Woolston, Warrington, WA1 4SF
Tel: 01925-852667 **Fax:** 01925-852668
E-mail: sales@bonfiglioli.com
Website: http://www.bonfiglioli.com
Directors: J. Adair (MD)
Ultimate Holding Company: BONFIGLIOLI RIDUTTORI SpA (ITALY)
Immediate Holding Company: BONFIGLIOLI U.K. LIMITED
Registration no: 01582759 **VAT No.:** GB 346 3498 32
Date established: 1981 **Turnover:** £20m - £50m **No.of Employees:** 1 - 10
Product Groups: 35, 37, 39

Date of Accounts	Dec 11	Dec 10	Dec 09
Sales Turnover	26m	24m	11m
Pre Tax Profit/Loss	217	316	276
Working Capital	2m	2m	2m
Fixed Assets	456	106	115
Current Assets	10m	11m	11m
Current Liabilities	1m	1m	419

Borregaard UK

Clayton Road Birchwood, Warrington, WA3 6QQ
Tel: 01925-285400 **Fax:** 01925-285434
E-mail: marketing_europe@borregaard.com
Website: http://www.borregaard.com
Bank(s): Citibank International plc
Directors: M. O Shea (Co Sec), M. Harlem (Dir), P. Nygren (MD)
Ultimate Holding Company: ORKLA ASA (NORWAY)
Immediate Holding Company: BORREGAARD UK LTD
Registration no: 01141222 **Date established:** 1973 **Turnover:** £5m - £10m
No.of Employees: 11 - 20 **Product Groups:** 31, 32, 62

Date of Accounts	Dec 11	Dec 10	Dec 09
Sales Turnover	8m	7m	6m
Pre Tax Profit/Loss	482	373	187
Working Capital	1m	1m	2m
Fixed Assets	536	540	566
Current Assets	2m	2m	3m
Current Liabilities	121	114	88

Brevini Power Transmissions

Planet House Centre Park, Warrington, WA1 1QX
Tel: 01925-636682 **Fax:** 01925-636682
E-mail: sales@brevini.co.uk
Website: http://www.brevini.co.uk
Bank(s): National Westminster Bank Plc
Directors: R. Brevini (Ch)
Managers: J. Norton (Eng Serv Mgr), N. Paroli, R. Marsh, D. Brown (Nat Sales Mgr)
Ultimate Holding Company: Brevini S.p.A (Italy)
Registration no: 02069720 **Turnover:** £2m - £5m
No.of Employees: 21 - 50 **Product Groups:** 35, 39, 40, 41, 42, 43, 45, 46, 48, 67

Date of Accounts	Dec 11	Dec 10	Dec 09
Sales Turnover	10m	7m	7m
Pre Tax Profit/Loss	713	599	594
Working Capital	2m	2m	2m
Fixed Assets	624	613	645
Current Assets	6m	4m	4m
Current Liabilities	2m	708	843

Britplas

18 Kingsland Grange Woolston, Warrington, WA1 4RW
Tel: 01925-577801
E-mail: office@britplas.com
Website: http://www.britplas.com
Directors: G. Hughes (Fin)
Managers: J. Blackwell (Buyer), N. Guest (Mktg Serv Mgr)
Immediate Holding Company: BRITPLAS LIMITED
Registration no: 05294170 **Date established:** 2004
No.of Employees: 21 - 50 **Product Groups:** 30, 35

Date of Accounts	Dec 11	Dec 10	Dec 09
Working Capital	230	201	123
Fixed Assets	2	5	11
Current Assets	253	306	355

Bureau Veritas
31 Kingsland Grange Woolston, Warrington, WA1 4RW
Tel: 01925-854360 **Fax:** 0161-927 7359
E-mail: jeff.percival@uk.bureauveritas.com
Website: http://www.bureauveritas.co.uk/cps
Bank(s): National Westminster Bank Plc
Managers: J. Percival (Mgr)
Ultimate Holding Company: WENDEL INVESTISSEMENT SA (FRANCE)
Immediate Holding Company: BUREAU VERITAS CONSUMER PRODUCTS SERVICES HOLDINGS UK LIMITED
Registration no: 04927383 **Date established:** 2003 **Turnover:** £2m - £5m
No.of Employees: 51 - 100 **Product Groups:** 80, 84, 85

Date of Accounts	Dec 11	Dec 10	Dec 09
Pre Tax Profit/Loss	-2m	-3m	N/A
Working Capital	-5m	-5m	N/A
Fixed Assets	3m	5m	4m

C M S Fork Trucks Ltd
Holmsfield Road Howley, Warrington, WA1 2DS
Tel: 01925-651745 **Fax:** 01925-651765
E-mail: cmsforktrucks@btconnect.com
Website: http://www.cmsfork-trucks.co.uk
Directors: N. Whiteley (Ptnr)
Immediate Holding Company: CMS FORK TRUCKS LTD
Registration no: 07713728 **Date established:** 2011
No.of Employees: 1 - 10 **Product Groups:** 35, 39, 45

C N Systems UK Ltd
Unit 1 Wellington St Workshops Wellington Street, Warrington, WA1 2DB
Tel: 01925-445190 **Fax:** 01925-445190
E-mail: info@c-nsystems.com
Website: http://www.c-nsystems.com
Directors: A. Coleman (Dir)
Immediate Holding Company: C-N SYSTEMS (U.K) LTD
Registration no: 02062531 **Date established:** 1986
Turnover: Up to £250,000 **No.of Employees:** 1 - 10 **Product Groups:** 38

Date of Accounts	Nov 11	Nov 10	Nov 09
Working Capital	19	28	45
Fixed Assets	2	2	2
Current Assets	120	138	202

C T E Supplies Ltd
697 Knutsford Road, Warrington, WA4 1JY
Tel: 01925-653132 **Fax:** 01925-658511
E-mail: sales@ctesupplies.co.uk
Website: http://www.ctesupplies.com
Directors: A. Standring (MD)
Immediate Holding Company: CTE SUPPLIES LIMITED
Registration no: 04744154 **Date established:** 2003
No.of Employees: 1 - 10 **Product Groups:** 25, 26, 30, 33, 35, 36, 37, 38, 39, 40, 45

Date of Accounts	Jun 11	Jun 10	Jun 09
Working Capital	42	-5	-17
Fixed Assets	123	140	161
Current Assets	290	271	243

Cable Systems Ltd
2-6 Gawsworth Court Risley Road, Birchwood, Warrington, WA3 6NJ
Tel: 01925-852745 **Fax:** 01925-820803
E-mail: sales@cablesystems.co.uk
Website: http://www.cablesystems.co.uk
Bank(s): HSBC Bank plc
Directors: H. Rigby (Dir), L. Bradley (Sales)
Immediate Holding Company: CABLE SYSTEMS LIMITED
Registration no: 01650681 **VAT No.:** GB 374 0134 76
Date established: 1982 **Turnover:** £2m - £5m **No.of Employees:** 11 - 20
Product Groups: 30, 37, 40

Date of Accounts	Dec 11	Dec 10	Dec 09
Working Capital	958	957	906
Fixed Assets	109	98	132
Current Assets	2m	2m	2m

Cablejog Ltd (Cable Testers)
18 Browmere Drive Croft, Warrington, WA3 7HT
Tel: 01925-764471 **Fax:** 01925-764903
E-mail: sales@cablejog.co.uk
Website: http://www.cablejog.co.uk
Directors: C. Zych (Fin), E. Zych (MD)
Immediate Holding Company: CABLEJOG LIMITED
Registration no: 04695640 **VAT No.:** GB 468 0289 22
Date established: 2003 **Turnover:** Up to £250,000
No.of Employees: 1 - 10 **Product Groups:** 38

Date of Accounts	Mar 11	Mar 10	Mar 09
Sales Turnover	N/A	31	N/A
Working Capital	46	35	34
Fixed Assets	1	1	2
Current Assets	58	40	42

Caldwell Filtration Ltd
3d Lyncastle Way Barleycastle Lane, Appleton, Warrington, WA4 4ST
Tel: 01925-267111 **Fax:** 01925-267744
E-mail: info@caldwellfiltration.co.uk
Website: http://www.caldwellfiltration.co.uk
Managers: S. Faloona (Chief Mgr)
Immediate Holding Company: CALDWELL FILTRATION LIMITED
Registration no: 01201716 **VAT No.:** GB 153 2953 66
Date established: 1975 **Turnover:** £250,000 - £500,000
No.of Employees: 1 - 10 **Product Groups:** 30, 33, 35, 37, 42, 45, 46

Date of Accounts	Aug 11	Aug 10	Aug 09
Working Capital	153	99	82
Fixed Assets	238	233	245
Current Assets	278	197	160

Camcoat Performance Coatings
129 Hoyle Street, Warrington, WA5 0LP
Tel: 01925-445003 **Fax:** 01925-444988
E-mail: info@camcoat.com
Website: http://www.camcoat.com
Managers: P. Carter (Chief Mgr)
Date established: 1988 **No.of Employees:** 1 - 10 **Product Groups:** 46, 48

Carlsberg UK
Stonecross Depot Yew Tree Way, Golborne, Warrington, WA3 3JE
Tel: 01942-408200 **Fax:** 01942-408206
E-mail: suzanne.smith@carlsberg.co.uk
Website: http://www.carlsberg.co.uk
Directors: J. Wade (Sales & Mktg), D. Grahame (Dir)
Managers: M. Cattell, L. Heeson (Sales Admin), M. Cotterel (Mgr), S. Lucus (District Mgr)
Ultimate Holding Company: CARLSBERG AS (DENMARK)
Immediate Holding Company: CARLSBERG UK LIMITED
Registration no: 00078439 **Date established:** 2003
No.of Employees: 101 - 250 **Product Groups:** 21

Carry Lift Materials Handling
Unit 113 Palatine Industrial Estate Causeway Avenue, Warrington, WA4 6QQ
Tel: 01925-411126 **Fax:** 01925-413903
E-mail: ggreen@carryliftgroup.com
Website: http://www.carryliftgroup.com
Managers: G. Green (Mgr)
Date established: 1988 **No.of Employees:** 1 - 10 **Product Groups:** 35, 39, 45

Chesire Dispersion
24 Willow Court West Quay Road, Winwick, Warrington, WA2 8UF
Tel: 01925-575678 **Fax:** 01925-575728
Website: http://www.beadmills.co.uk
Directors: J. Allen (Dir)
Registration no: 05800430 **Date established:** 2006
No.of Employees: 1 - 10 **Product Groups:** 46

Chester Chain Co. Ltd
19 Greys Court Kingsland Grange, Woolston, Warrington, WA1 4SH
Tel: 01925-838899 **Fax:** 01925-811416
E-mail: warrington@chesterchain.co.uk
Website: http://www.chesterchain.co.uk
Managers: P. Mahon (Mgr)
Ultimate Holding Company: WAKEFIELD PROPERTIES LIMITED
Immediate Holding Company: CHESTER CHAIN COMPANY LIMITED
Registration no: 00798486 **VAT No.:** GB 159 1009 74
Date established: 1964 **Turnover:** £500,000 - £1m
No.of Employees: 1 - 10 **Product Groups:** 48, 83

Date of Accounts	Mar 12	Mar 11	Mar 10
Working Capital	426	397	361
Fixed Assets	404	400	423
Current Assets	748	716	688

John Chorley & Co. Ltd
Dallam Lane, Warrington, WA2 7PZ
Tel: 01925-636552 **Fax:** 01925-415812
E-mail: sales@johnchorley.co.uk
Website: http://www.johnchorley.co.uk
Directors: T. Shanahan (Dir)
Ultimate Holding Company: CALDWELLS LIMITED
Immediate Holding Company: JOHN CHORLEY & COMPANY,LIMITED
Registration no: 00197534 **VAT No.:** GB 151 6664 65
Date established: 2024 **Turnover:** £10m - £20m
No.of Employees: 21 - 50 **Product Groups:** 48

Date of Accounts	Mar 11	Mar 10	Mar 09
Sales Turnover	12m	9m	16m
Pre Tax Profit/Loss	387	-373	444
Working Capital	1m	1m	2m
Fixed Assets	779	418	367
Current Assets	5m	4m	4m
Current Liabilities	133	150	185

Clarcor UK Ltd (UAS-Baldwin-Lockertex)
PO Box 17, Warrington, WA5 0NP
Tel: 01925-654321 **Fax:** 01925-414588
E-mail: post@clarcoruk.com
Website: http://www.clarcor.com
Directors: B. Kennedy (Co Sec), G. Shand (MD)
Managers: I. Macdonald, S. Richards (Purch Mgr)
Ultimate Holding Company: CLARCOR INC (USA)
Immediate Holding Company: CLARCOR UK LIMITED
Registration no: 00472388 **Date established:** 1949 **Turnover:** £5m - £10m
No.of Employees: 101 - 250 **Product Groups:** 40, 42, 54

Date of Accounts	Nov 11	Nov 10	Nov 09
Sales Turnover	8m	8m	6m
Pre Tax Profit/Loss	-281	-1m	-1m
Working Capital	3m	3m	3m
Fixed Assets	577	550	671
Current Assets	5m	4m	4m
Current Liabilities	355	341	282

Clear Living Ltd
Unit 3g A Lyncastle Way Barleycastle Lane, Appleton, Warrington, WA4 4ST
Tel: 01925-211430
E-mail: info@clear-living.co.uk
Website: http://www.clear-living.co.uk
Directors: K. Hansen Kolby (MD)
Immediate Holding Company: CLEAR LIVING LTD
Registration no: 06252501 **Date established:** 2007
Turnover: £250,000 - £500,000 **No.of Employees:** 1 - 10
Product Groups: 52

Date of Accounts	May 11	May 10	May 09
Working Capital	156	174	43
Fixed Assets	22	22	10
Current Assets	258	262	194

Clover Leaf Media
The White House Greenalls Avenue, Warrington, WA4 6HL
Tel: 01925-438060 **Fax:** 0161-953 4041
E-mail: enquires@cloverleafmedia.com
Website: http://www.cloverleafmedia.com
Directors: D. Addison (Dir)
Immediate Holding Company: CLOVERLEAF MEDIA LIMITED
Registration no: 04652632 **Date established:** 2003
Turnover: £500,000 - £1m **No.of Employees:** 1 - 10 **Product Groups:** 44, 81

Date of Accounts	Jan 12	Jan 11	Jan 10
Working Capital	60	55	57
Fixed Assets	2	2	1
Current Assets	102	82	86

Combined Chemical Services UK Ltd
28 Derby Road Stockton Heath, Warrington, WA4 6JR
Tel: 01925-468398 **Fax:** 01925-211436
E-mail: sales@combinedchemicalservices.co.uk
Website: http://www.combinedchemicalservices.com
Directors: A. Marshall (Fin)
Immediate Holding Company: COMBINED CHEMICAL SERVICES (UK) LTD
Registration no: 06635164 **Date established:** 2008
No.of Employees: 1 - 10 **Product Groups:** 31, 32, 66

Date of Accounts	Jul 11	Jul 10	Jul 09
Working Capital	38	20	4
Fixed Assets	1	1	1
Current Assets	77	46	20

Combined Gas Systems Ltd
13 Brookfield Road Culcheth, Warrington, WA3 4PB
Tel: 01925-767217 **Fax:** 01925-762670
E-mail: enquiries@combinedgas.com
Website: http://www.combinedgas.com
Bank(s): HSBC
Directors: P. Jackson (MD), W. Jackson (Fin)
Managers: I. Roberts (Quality Control), T. Davis (Chief Mgr)
Immediate Holding Company: COMBINED GAS SYSTEMS LIMITED
Registration no: 03327911 **VAT No.:** GB 603 4719 59
Date established: 1997 **Turnover:** £1m - £2m **No.of Employees:** 21 - 50
Product Groups: 36, 40

Date of Accounts	Jul 11	Jul 10	Jul 09
Working Capital	-20	17	N/A
Fixed Assets	865	951	N/A
Current Assets	619	479	N/A

Crest Medical
Unit 17 Chesford Grange Woolston, Warrington, WA1 4RQ
Tel: 08452-302092 **Fax:** 0845-230 2091
E-mail: sales@crestmedical.co.uk
Website: http://www.crestmedical.co.uk
Bank(s): National Westminster Bank Plc
Directors: A. Maxwell (MD)
Ultimate Holding Company: FIRST AID HOLDINGS LIMITED
Immediate Holding Company: CREST MEDICAL LIMITED
Registration no: 03876927 **VAT No.:** GB 433 6427 57
Date established: 1999 **Turnover:** £5m - £10m **No.of Employees:** 21 - 50
Product Groups: 24, 38, 63

Date of Accounts	Mar 12	Mar 11	Mar 10
Working Capital	183	399	368
Fixed Assets	155	146	176
Current Assets	2m	3m	2m

Croft Engineering Services
Unit 2 Beech Court Taylor Business Pk, Risley, Warrington, WA3 6BL
Tel: 01925-766265 **Fax:** 01925-765029
E-mail: sales@filters.co.uk
Website: http://www.filters.co.uk
Bank(s): National Westminster Bank Plc
Directors: R. Burns (Ptnr), A. Burns (Ptnr), D. Travis (Ptnr)
VAT No.: GB 437 6984 01 **Turnover:** £1m - £2m **No.of Employees:** 21 - 50
Product Groups: 23, 30, 34, 35, 36, 40, 41, 42, 44, 45, 48, 67

Dats (Holdings) Ltd
1 Springfield Street Palmyra Square, Warrington, WA1 1BB
Tel: 01925-428559 **Fax:** 01925-403801
E-mail: dats@dats.co.uk
Website: http://www.dats.co.uk
Directors: S. Nickson (MD), T. Nickson (Ch)
Immediate Holding Company: D.A.T.S. (HOLDINGS) LIMITED
Registration no: 01076937 **Date established:** 1972 **Turnover:** £5m - £10m
No.of Employees: 1 - 10 **Product Groups:** 42, 54, 80, 82, 84, 86

Date of Accounts	Mar 11	Mar 10	Mar 09
Sales Turnover	6m	6m	8m
Pre Tax Profit/Loss	-184	-351	-135
Working Capital	1m	2m	3m
Fixed Assets	3m	3m	2m
Current Assets	2m	2m	4m
Current Liabilities	284	214	258

Dedicated Micros Ltd
Unit 1200 Daresbury Park, Daresbury, Warrington, WA4 4HS
Tel: 01928-706400 **Fax:** 01928-706350
E-mail: customerservices@dmicros.com
Website: http://www.dedicatedmicros.com
Bank(s): The Royal Bank of Scotland
Managers: M. Newton
Ultimate Holding Company: ANGLO DESIGN HOLDINGS PLC
Immediate Holding Company: DEDICATED MICROS LIMITED
Registration no: 02760037 **VAT No.:** GB 659 6988 48
Date established: 1992 **Turnover:** £20m - £50m
No.of Employees: 21 - 50 **Product Groups:** 40

Date of Accounts	Jun 12	Jun 11	Jun 10
Working Capital	-3m	-3m	-3m

E C Y Holdings Ltd
Barley Castle Lane Appleton, Warrington, WA4 4RB
Tel: 01925-860000 **Fax:** 01925-861111
E-mail: sales@ecyltd.co.uk
Website: http://www.ecyltd.co.uk
Directors: R. Yarwood (MD), P. Yarwood (Fin)
Immediate Holding Company: E.C.Y. (HOLDINGS) LIMITED
Registration no: 01344471 **Date established:** 1977
No.of Employees: 21 - 50 **Product Groups:** 25, 33, 35

Date of Accounts	Dec 11	Dec 10	Dec 09
Working Capital	-73	7	-40
Fixed Assets	773	648	689
Current Assets	1m	1m	1m

E F G Office Furniture Ltd
Building 3 Clearwater Lingley Green Avenue Lingley Mere Business Park, Great Sankey, Warrington, WA5 3UZ
Tel: 08450-727600 **Fax:** 0845-604 1924
E-mail: sales@efgoffice.co.uk
Website: http://www.efgoffice.co.uk
Bank(s): HSBC
Directors: C. Howarth (MD), D. Keys (Mkt Research)
Managers: N. Williams (Sales Prom Mgr), L. Sefton (Comptroller), A. Edgeson (Purch Mgr)
Ultimate Holding Company: EFG HOLDING AB (SWEDEN)
Immediate Holding Company: EFG OFFICE FURNITURE LIMITED
Registration no: 00257489 **VAT No.:** GB 151 6840 71
Date established: 1931 **Turnover:** £5m - £10m **No.of Employees:** 21 - 50
Product Groups: 26, 38, 49

Date of Accounts	Dec 11	Dec 10	Dec 09
Sales Turnover	9m	8m	9m
Pre Tax Profit/Loss	-469	-280	-1m
Working Capital	2m	2m	3m
Fixed Assets	210	279	364
Current Assets	3m	4m	4m
Current Liabilities	324	381	333

E & I Hire Ltd
Newspaper House Tannery Lane, Penketh, Warrington, WA5 2UD
Tel: 01925-726677 **Fax:** 01925-725544
E-mail: sales@eihire.co.uk
Website: http://www.eihire.co.uk

see next page

E & I Hire Ltd - Cont'd

Directors: M. Collinson (Dir)
Immediate Holding Company: E & I HIRE LIMITED
Registration no: 02770815 **Date established:** 1992
No.of Employees: 1 - 10 **Product Groups:** 37, 38, 48, 67, 83, 85

Date of Accounts	Mar 12	Mar 11	Mar 10
Working Capital	108	106	60
Fixed Assets	54	35	38
Current Assets	186	201	143

Eagle Ottawa UK Ltd

Thelwall Lane Latchford, Warrington, WA4 1NQ
Tel: 01925-650251 **Fax:** 01925-655547
E-mail: contact@eagleottawa.com
Website: http://www.eagleottawa.com
Bank(s): National Westminster Bank Plc
Directors: C. Dunn (Dir)
Managers: D. Dixon (Purch Mgr), G. Welsh (Chief Mgr), M. Cochrane (Public Relation), M. Hughes (Comptroller), P. Schultheiss (Personnel), R. Cockane (I.T. Exec), T. Ward (I.T. Exec)
Ultimate Holding Company: ALBERT TROSTEL & SONS CO (USA)
Immediate Holding Company: Eagle Ottawa UK Ltd
Registration no: 02645641 **VAT No.:** GB 677 3561 00
Date established: 1991 **Turnover:** £20m - £50m
No.of Employees: 101 - 250 **Product Groups:** 22

Date of Accounts	Nov 03
Working Capital	5238
Current Assets	5238
Total Share Capital	2

Eiger Torrance Ltd

253 Europa Boulevard Westbrook, Warrington, WA5 7TN
Tel: 01925-232455 **Fax:** 01925-237767
E-mail: sales@eiger-torrance.com
Website: http://www.eigertorrance.com
Directors: D. Dixon (MD)
Ultimate Holding Company: CUMBERLAND GROUP HOLDINGS LIMITED
Immediate Holding Company: EIGER TORRANCE LIMITED
Registration no: 01300289 **VAT No.:** GB 231 6346 85
Date established: 1977 **Turnover:** £500,000 - £1m
No.of Employees: 1 - 10 **Product Groups:** 32, 33, 42, 48

Date of Accounts	Sep 11	Sep 10	Sep 09
Working Capital	232	233	257
Fixed Assets	8	14	24
Current Assets	528	424	427

Exova Warrington Fire

Holmesfield Road, Warrington, WA1 2DS
Tel: 01925-655116 **Fax:** 01925-655419
E-mail: john.willox@exova.com
Website: http://www.exova.com
Bank(s): National Westminster Bank Plc
Directors: J. Willox (Dir)
Managers: M. Bratt, E. Smith
Immediate Holding Company: JOHN STUART MOTOR COMPANY LIMITED
Registration no: 06088773 **Date established:** 2007 **Turnover:** £5m - £10m
No.of Employees: 51 - 100 **Product Groups:** 38, 54, 80, 84, 85

Faucets Northern

11 Cameron Court Winwick Quay, Warrington, WA2 8RE
Tel: 01925-573000 **Fax:** 01925-573001
Directors: A. Shaw (Dir)
No.of Employees: 1 - 10 **Product Groups:** 36, 49

Fenchurch Environmental Group Ltd

Dennow Farm Firs Lane, Appleton, Warrington, WA4 5LF
Tel: 01925-269111 **Fax:** 01925-269444
E-mail: general@fengroup.com
Website: http://www.fengroup.com
Directors: D. Townsend (Co Sec), F. Wood (Dir)
Managers: J. Turner (Purch Mgr), M. Rawlings (Tech Serv Mgr), M. Nicholson (Mktg Serv Mgr)
Immediate Holding Company: FENCHURCH ENVIRONMENTAL GROUP LTD
Registration no: 02645554 **Date established:** 1991
Turnover: £20m - £50m **No.of Employees:** 1 - 10 **Product Groups:** 33, 35, 42, 83

Date of Accounts	Mar 11	Mar 10	Mar 09
Sales Turnover	26m	22m	1m
Pre Tax Profit/Loss	2m	1m	662
Working Capital	1m	930	1m
Fixed Assets	4m	4m	1m
Current Assets	11m	9m	3m
Current Liabilities	3m	3m	952

Filtration Medic Ltd

Unit 4 Wellington Street Workshops Wellington Street, Warrington, WA1 2DB
Tel: 01925-453228 **Fax:** 01925-453228
E-mail: filtrationmedic@btconnect.com
Website: http://www.filtrationmedic.co.uk
Directors: R. Main (MD)
Managers: S. Conner (Sales Prom Mgr), T. Wood (Chief Acct)
Immediate Holding Company: FILTRATION MEDIC LTD
Registration no: 06375490 **Date established:** 2007
No.of Employees: 21 - 50 **Product Groups:** 34, 40, 41, 42, 48

Date of Accounts	Sep 11	Sep 10	Sep 09
Working Capital	61	48	17
Fixed Assets	28	27	21
Current Assets	98	91	71

Flangefitt Stainless Ltd

Piping House Hawleys Lane, Warrington, WA2 8JP
Tel: 01925-444807 **Fax:** 01925-445454
E-mail: sales@flangefitt.co.uk
Website: http://www.flangefitt.co.uk
Directors: J. Nulty (MD), P. Oakes (Sales)
Managers: M. Johnson (Quality Control)
Immediate Holding Company: FLANGEFITT STAINLESS LIMITED
Registration no: 01922173 **Date established:** 1985
Turnover: £10m - £20m **No.of Employees:** 21 - 50 **Product Groups:** 36

Date of Accounts	Sep 11	Sep 10	Sep 09
Sales Turnover	12m	9m	12m
Pre Tax Profit/Loss	687	358	941
Working Capital	1m	1m	1m
Fixed Assets	956	977	1m
Current Assets	5m	4m	4m
Current Liabilities	713	477	844

Foilco Ltd

Enterprise Way Lowton, Warrington, WA3 2BP
Tel: 01942-262622 **Fax:** 01942-267200
E-mail: sales@foilco.co.uk
Website: http://www.foilco.co.uk
Bank(s): The Royal Bank of Scotland
Directors: D. Hornby (Ch), P. Hornby (MD)
Ultimate Holding Company: ACCOLADE GROUP HOLDINGS LIMITED
Immediate Holding Company: FOILCO LIMITED
Registration no: 02140459 **VAT No.:** GB 468 1170 42
Date established: 1987 **Turnover:** £2m - £5m **No.of Employees:** 21 - 50
Product Groups: 27, 30, 34, 66

Date of Accounts	Jul 12	Jul 11	Jul 10
Working Capital	639	544	517
Fixed Assets	88	102	71
Current Assets	2m	2m	1m
Current Liabilities	409	451	286

Fontaine International Europe Ltd

Enterprise Way Newton Road, Lowton, Warrington, WA3 2AG
Tel: 01942-686000 **Fax:** 01942-686006
E-mail: sales@fifthwheeleurope.com
Website: http://www.fifthwheeleurope.com
Bank(s): Natwest
Managers: A. Haughton (Sales Admin), M. Swanick (Sec)
Ultimate Holding Company: BERKSHIRE HATHAWAY INC (USA)
Immediate Holding Company: Marmon Group Limited(The)
Registration no: 01062353 **Date established:** 1972 **Turnover:** £5m - £10m
No.of Employees: 21 - 50 **Product Groups:** 39

Fork Truck Wholesale & Hire

Riverside Trading Estate Cuerdley, Warrington, WA5 2UL
Tel: 01925-721366 **Fax:** 01925-721366
E-mail: forkwholesale@hotmail.com
Website: http://www.forktruckwholesale.com
Directors: I. Wilson (Prop)
No.of Employees: 11 - 20 **Product Groups:** 45, 48, 67

R E Forster Ltd

Grey Street, Warrington, WA1 2PH
Tel: 01925-634334 **Fax:** 01925-235082
Directors: C. Forster (MD)
Immediate Holding Company: R. E. FORSTER (FURNITURE) LTD
Registration no: 01278670 **Date established:** 1976
Turnover: £250,000 - £500,000 **No.of Employees:** 1 - 10
Product Groups: 34

Foss UK Ltd

730 Birchwood Boulevard Birchwood, Warrington, WA3 7QY
Tel: 01925-287700 **Fax:** 01925-287777
E-mail: info@foss.co.uk
Website: http://www.foss.co.uk
Bank(s): National Westminster Bank Plc
Directors: D. Jones (Co Sec)
Managers: C. Dale (Tech Serv Mgr), M. Wong
Ultimate Holding Company: FOSS A/S (DENMARK)
Immediate Holding Company: FOSS U.K. LIMITED
Registration no: 00694750 **VAT No.:** GB 169 2505 50
Date established: 1961 **Turnover:** £5m - £10m **No.of Employees:** 21 - 50
Product Groups: 38

Date of Accounts	Dec 11	Dec 10	Dec 09
Sales Turnover	5m	6m	5m
Pre Tax Profit/Loss	-28	-207	-160
Working Capital	2m	2m	2m
Fixed Assets	140	128	151
Current Assets	3m	3m	3m
Current Liabilities	882	897	699

Fujitsu Services Ltd

Trafalgar House Temple Court Daten Avenue, Risley, Warrington, WA3 6GD
Tel: 01925-432410 **Fax:** 01925-432233
E-mail: stuart.broadbelt@uk.fujitsu.com
Website: http://www.services.fujitsu.com
Bank(s): The Royal Bank of Scotland
Directors: S. Broadbelt (MD), R. Moseley (Co Sec)
Managers: J. Mcknight (Mktg Serv Mgr), B. Shaw (Fin Mgr), D. Clarke (Sales Prom Mgr)
Ultimate Holding Company: FUJITSU LIMITED (JAPAN)
Immediate Holding Company: FUJITSU SERVICES LIMITED
Registration no: NF000668 **Date established:** 1949
Turnover: £250m - £500m **No.of Employees:** 251 - 500
Product Groups: 67

Date of Accounts	Mar 11	Mar 10	Mar 09
Sales Turnover	1630m	1802m	1639m
Pre Tax Profit/Loss	-36m	2m	151m
Working Capital	-416m	-310m	-4m
Fixed Assets	716m	760m	919m
Current Assets	828m	869m	978m
Current Liabilities	443m	368m	302m

Fulzer Drives & Controls

14-15 Rivington Court Hardwick Grange, Woolston, Warrington, WA1 4RT
Tel: 01925-831318 **Fax:** 01925- 831317
E-mail: lee.hudson@dowdingandmills.com
Website: http://www.dowdingandmills.com
Managers: D. Clarke (District Mgr), L. Hudson (District Mgr), W. Ince (Sales Prom Mgr)
Ultimate Holding Company: CASTLE SUPPORT SERVICES PLC
Immediate Holding Company: DOWDING & MILLS PLC
Registration no: SC028056 **No.of Employees:** 11 - 20
Product Groups: 37, 39

Furmanite International Ltd

7 Colville Court Winwick Quay, Warrington, WA2 8QT
Tel: 01925-418858 **Fax:** 01925-418863
E-mail: info@furmanite.com
Website: http://www.furmanite.com
Directors: B. Van Eupen (Fin)
Managers: P. Oflanagan
Ultimate Holding Company: FURMANITE CORPORATION (USA)
Immediate Holding Company: FURMANITE INTERNATIONAL LIMITED
Registration no: 00238721 **Date established:** 2029
Turnover: Up to £250,000 **No.of Employees:** 11 - 20 **Product Groups:** 48

Date of Accounts	Dec 11	Dec 10	Dec 09
Sales Turnover	39m	34m	35m
Pre Tax Profit/Loss	5m	3m	2m
Working Capital	24m	24m	23m
Fixed Assets	3m	3m	4m
Current Assets	35m	34m	32m
Current Liabilities	2m	3m	2m

G E A Process Engineering Ltd

Leacroft House Leacroft Road, Birchwood, Warrington, WA3 6JF
Tel: 01925-812650 **Fax:** 01235-554140
E-mail: david.dubbin@niro.co.uk
Website: http://www.geaprocess.co.uk
Bank(s): Den Danske Bank
Directors: D. Dubbin (Sales)
Managers: P. Pmackie (Tech Serv Mgr), L. Billany, L. Taylor (Personnel), P. Allen
Ultimate Holding Company: GEA GROUP AG (GERMANY)
Immediate Holding Company: GEA PROCESS ENGINEERING LIMITED
Registration no: 01275022 **VAT No.:** GB 298 7688 65
Date established: 1976 **Turnover:** £10m - £20m
No.of Employees: 51 - 100 **Product Groups:** 20, 32, 37, 40, 41, 42, 67

Date of Accounts	Dec 11	Dec 10	Dec 09
Sales Turnover	27m	20m	23m
Pre Tax Profit/Loss	3m	144	-740
Working Capital	4m	2m	2m
Fixed Assets	10m	2m	2m
Current Assets	11m	11m	11m
Current Liabilities	4m	5m	3m

G & J Greenall

Distribution Point, Melbury Park Clayton Road, Birchwood, Warrington, WA3 6PH
Tel: 01925-286400 **Fax:** 01925-286485
E-mail: internet@gjgreenall.com
Website: http://www.gjgreenall.com
Bank(s): National Westminster Bank Plc
Managers: A. Robinson (Mktg Serv Mgr), D. Wardell (Purch Mgr), P. Revell (I.T. Exec), T. Sharpe (Mgr)
Ultimate Holding Company: Ahg Venice Finance No. 3 Ltd
Immediate Holding Company: De Vere Group Ltd
Registration no: 07604282 **Turnover:** £20m - £50m
No.of Employees: 51 - 100 **Product Groups:** 21

Galliford Try

Crab Lane Fearnhead, Warrington, WA2 0XR
Tel: 01925-822821 **Fax:** 01925-827924
E-mail: info@gallifordtry.co.uk
Website: http://www.gallifordtry.co.uk
Bank(s): Barclays
Managers: P. Cook (Develop Mgr), S. McCluskey (Purch Mgr), S. Walsh (Mgr)
Immediate Holding Company: GALLIMOR MEDICAL LIMITED
Registration no: 03970278 **Date established:** 2000
Turnover: £125m - £250m **No.of Employees:** 51 - 100
Product Groups: 51, 52

gatestyles

unit 44 bank quay trading estate slutchers lane, Warrington, WA1 1PG
Tel: 01925-451854
E-mail: stuartbrereton@gatestyles.co.uk
Website: http://www.gatestyles.co.uk
Directors: S. brereton (Prop)
Date established: 1994 **No.of Employees:** 1 - 10 **Product Groups:** 25, 35

GB Oils Ltd

302 Bridgewater Place Birchwood Park Birchwood, Warrington, WA3 6XG
Tel: 01925-858500 **Fax:** 0845-300 5511
E-mail: sales@cplpetroleum.co.uk
Website: http://www.cplpetroleum.co.uk
Directors: P. Vine (Dir)
Managers: G. Williams (Mktg Serv Mgr), G. Byers (Sales Prom Mgr), J. Tinon (Personnel), D. Ainsworth (Tech Serv Mgr)
Ultimate Holding Company: DCC PUBLIC LIMITED COMPANY
Immediate Holding Company: GB OILS LIMITED
Registration no: 04168225 **Date established:** 2001
Turnover: Over £1,000m **No.of Employees:** 101 - 250
Product Groups: 66

Date of Accounts	Mar 11	Mar 10	Mar 09
Sales Turnover	3027m	1993m	1928m
Pre Tax Profit/Loss	41m	20m	28m
Working Capital	-240m	-204m	-120m
Fixed Assets	1064m	233m	144m
Current Assets	371m	313m	232m
Current Liabilities	23m	23m	28m

Gefco UK Ltd

Unit 12 Yew Tree Way, Golborne, Warrington, WA3 3GY
Tel: 01942-402800 **Fax:** 01942-402826
E-mail: mervyn.hollis@gefco.net
Website: http://www.gefco.co.uk
Managers: M. Hollis (Mgr)
Ultimate Holding Company: PEUGEOT SA (FRANCE)
Immediate Holding Company: GEFCO U.K. LIMITED
Registration no: 01544410 **Date established:** 1981
No.of Employees: 11 - 20 **Product Groups:** 72, 76

Date of Accounts	Dec 10	Dec 09	Dec 08
Sales Turnover	115m	106m	138m
Pre Tax Profit/Loss	-3m	-11m	3m
Working Capital	5m	6m	13m
Fixed Assets	7m	7m	9m
Current Assets	32m	40m	35m
Current Liabilities	2m	6m	1m

G4S Security Services UK Ltd

Unit 4 Ibis Court, Centre Park, Warrington, WA1 1RL
Tel: 01925-406200 **Fax:** 01925-245320
Website: http://www.group4.co.uk
Managers: V. Bradbury (Ops Mgr), L. Ruddick (), A. Sigsworth (Comm)
Registration no: 02380900 **No.of Employees:** 11 - 20 **Product Groups:** 81

Globe Engineering Ltd

Jennetts Farm Jennetts Lane, Glazebury, Warrington, WA3 5QB
Tel: 0151-495 3759 **Fax:** 01942-608701
Directors: E. Chapman (MD)
Immediate Holding Company: GLOBE ENGINEERING LIMITED
Registration no: 06510963 **Date established:** 2008
No.of Employees: 1 - 10 **Product Groups:** 35

Date of Accounts	Aug 08	Sep 11	Sep 10
Working Capital	N/A	479	206
Fixed Assets	N/A	159	187
Current Assets	N/A	974	855

Grace Construction Products Ltd

Unit 830 Birchwood Boulevard, Birchwood, Warrington, WA3 7QZ
Tel: 01925-855330 **Fax:** 01925-824033
E-mail: andrew.meakin@grace.com
Website: http://www.grace.com

Managers: A. Meakin (Mgr)
Ultimate Holding Company: W R GRACE & COMPANY (USA)
Immediate Holding Company: GRACE CONSTRUCTION PRODUCTS LIMITED
Registration no: 00614807 **VAT No.:** GB 705 7454 02
Date established: 1958 **Turnover:** £50m - £75m **No.of Employees:** 1 - 10
Product Groups: 32, 33, 66

Date of Accounts	Dec 10	Dec 09	Dec 08
Sales Turnover	30m	40m	52m
Pre Tax Profit/Loss	-3m	-3m	2m
Working Capital	11m	14m	13m
Fixed Assets	1m	1m	5m
Current Assets	21m	30m	25m
Current Liabilities	5m	6m	2m

Graepel Perferators Ltd

5 Burtonwood Industrial Centre Phipps Lane, Burtonwood, Warrington, WA5 4HX
Tel: 01925-229795 **Fax:** 01925-228069
E-mail: sales@graepel.co.uk
Website: http://www.graepel.co.uk
Managers: A. Ledgerwood (Chief Mgr)
Immediate Holding Company: GRAEPEL PERFORATORS LIMITED
Registration no: 01074386 **Date established:** 1972
No.of Employees: 11 - 20 **Product Groups:** 33, 34, 35, 43, 45, 46

Date of Accounts	Dec 11	Dec 10	Dec 09
Working Capital	214	293	369
Fixed Assets	273	270	181
Current Assets	923	822	783

H & B Wire Fabrications Ltd

30-31 Tatton Court Kingsland Grange, Woolston, Warrington, WA1 4RR
Tel: 01925-819515 **Fax:** 01925-831773
E-mail: sales@hbwf.co.uk
Website: http://www.hbwf.co.uk
Directors: A. Ivill (Fin), R. Ivill (MD)
Immediate Holding Company: H & B. WIRE FABRICATIONS LIMITED
Registration no: 01310005 **Date established:** 1977 **Turnover:** £2m - £5m
No.of Employees: 21 - 50 **Product Groups:** 33, 35, 45, 46

Date of Accounts	Dec 11	Dec 10	Dec 09
Working Capital	2m	2m	1m
Fixed Assets	485	502	524
Current Assets	2m	2m	2m

Hamer Stevenson Ltd

1 Gateworth Industrial Estate Forrest Way, Warrington, WA5 1DF
Tel: 0161-633 6424 **Fax:** 0161-627 4797
E-mail: sales@hamer-stevenson.co.uk
Website: http://www.hamer-stevenson.co.uk
Directors: N. Dutton (Dir)
Ultimate Holding Company: MAN-FLEX LIMITED
Immediate Holding Company: HAMER STEVENSON LIMITED
Registration no: 01549546 **VAT No.:** GB 359 2714 32
Date established: 1981 **Turnover:** £500,000 - £1m
No.of Employees: 1 - 10 **Product Groups:** 23, 29, 30, 35, 36, 39, 40

Date of Accounts	Mar 11	Mar 10	Mar 09
Working Capital	141	186	246
Fixed Assets	4	15	25
Current Assets	275	343	395

Hands Industries Ltd

111 Kimberley Street, Warrington, WA5 1PA
Tel: 0870-991 7182 **Fax:** 0870-128 1665
E-mail: yvonne@hands-soap.com
Website: http://www.hands-soap.com
Directors: Y. Hands (Dir)
Registration no: 05837867 **Date established:** 2006
Turnover: Up to £250,000 **No.of Employees:** 1 - 10 **Product Groups:** 31, 32, 42, 63, 66

Henniker Scientific Ltd

Cavendish House Birchwood Park, Birchwood, Warrington, WA3 6BU
Tel: 01925-811254 **Fax:** 01925-800035
E-mail: info@henniker-scientific.com
Website: http://www.henniker-scientific.com
Directors: T. Whitmore (MD)
Immediate Holding Company: HENNIKER SCIENTIFIC LIMITED
Registration no: 06703135 **Date established:** 2008
Turnover: £250,000 - £500,000 **No.of Employees:** 1 - 10
Product Groups: 32, 38

Date of Accounts	Mar 12	Mar 11	Sep 09
Working Capital	17	1	-4
Fixed Assets	16	2	N/A
Current Assets	127	223	4

Hiden Analytical Ltd

420 Europa Boulevard Westbrook, Warrington, WA5 7UN
Tel: 01925-445225 **Fax:** 01925-416518
E-mail: info@hiden.co.uk
Website: http://www.hidenanalytical.com
Directors: R. Blacas (Fin), P. Hatton (Sales), I. Neale (Ch)
Immediate Holding Company: HIDEN ANALYTICAL LIMITED
Registration no: 01596907 **Date established:** 1981
Turnover: £10m - £20m **No.of Employees:** 51 - 100 **Product Groups:** 37, 38, 40, 45, 84, 85

Date of Accounts	Dec 11	Dec 10	Dec 09
Sales Turnover	9m	11m	9m
Pre Tax Profit/Loss	1m	2m	691
Working Capital	8m	7m	5m
Fixed Assets	794	883	887
Current Assets	11m	9m	8m
Current Liabilities	2m	2m	2m

Hilltop Products

Kirkstead Way Golborne, Warrington, WA3 3PJ
Tel: 01942-723101 **Fax:** 01942-273817
E-mail: sales@hilltop-products.co.uk
Website: http://www.hilltop-products.co.uk
Directors: S. Hill (MD)
Managers: J. Duffy, J. Walsh (Mktg Serv Mgr)
Immediate Holding Company: HILLTOP PRODUCTS (INSULATION SLEEVINGS) LIMITED
Registration no: 04464567 **Date established:** 2002 **Turnover:** £2m - £5m
No.of Employees: 21 - 50 **Product Groups:** 23, 29, 30, 42, 66

Date of Accounts	Jun 12	Jun 11	Jun 10
Working Capital	546	521	405
Fixed Assets	221	254	274
Current Assets	848	771	634

Howard George Ltd

94 Folly Lane, Warrington, WA5 0NG
Tel: 01925-444455 **Fax:** 01925-444466
E-mail: aldo.samuels@ghoward.co.uk
Directors: C. Howard (MD), C. Howard (Dir)
Managers: D. Williams (Chief Mgr), A. Pennington (I.T. Exec)
Immediate Holding Company: GEORGE HOWARD LTD
Registration no: 06686998 **VAT No.:** GB 151 8205 87
Date established: 2008 **Turnover:** £1m - £2m **No.of Employees:** 1 - 10
Product Groups: 54, 66

Date of Accounts	Apr 08	Apr 07	Apr 06
Working Capital	336	205	324
Fixed Assets	417	419	187
Current Assets	774	721	849
Current Liabilities	438	515	525
Total Share Capital	13	13	13

I E S A

Dallam Lane, Warrington, WA2 7PZ
Tel: 01925-454400 **Fax:** 0191-460 3700
E-mail: info@iesa.co.uk
Website: http://www.iesa.co.uk
Bank(s): National Westminster Bank Plc
Directors: C. Bithell (Fin)
Managers: S. Hilton (Sales Prom Mgr), M. Kitchen (Purch Mgr), L. Gregg (Tech Serv Mgr)
Ultimate Holding Company: INTEGRATED ENGINEERING STORES ASSOCIATES LIMITED
Immediate Holding Company: IESA LIMITED
Registration no: 04188491 **VAT No.:** GB 727 0084 50
Date established: 2001 **Turnover:** £20m - £50m
No.of Employees: 101 - 250 **Product Groups:** 66

Date of Accounts	Mar 12	Mar 11	Mar 10
Sales Turnover	83m	46m	39m
Pre Tax Profit/Loss	2m	559	516
Working Capital	5m	4m	3m
Fixed Assets	217	284	726
Current Assets	34m	19m	14m
Current Liabilities	9m	3m	2m

Idxtras Lanyards North West

Milner Street, Warrington, WA4 2GR
Tel: 01925-489985 **Fax:** 01925-489008
E-mail: sales@idxtras.co.uk
Website: http://www.idxtras.co.uk
Directors: C. Nightingale (Prop)
Immediate Holding Company: LANYARDS UK LTD
Registration no: 04103478 **Date established:** 2000
Turnover: £250,000 - £500,000 **No.of Employees:** 1 - 10
Product Groups: 23, 30

Imscan Systems Ltd

Imscan House Yew Tree Court Warrington Road, Risley, Warrington, WA3 6WP
Tel: 01925-761000 **Fax:** 01925-766334
E-mail: sales@imscan.co.uk
Website: http://www.imscan.co.uk
Directors: R. Cavanagh (MD)
Immediate Holding Company: IMSCAN SYSTEMS LIMITED
Registration no: 02781508 **Date established:** 1993 **Turnover:** £1m - £2m
No.of Employees: 11 - 20 **Product Groups:** 44, 80

Date of Accounts	Mar 12	Mar 11	Mar 10
Working Capital	65	133	156
Fixed Assets	157	112	121
Current Assets	237	295	479

Instrumentation Laboratory UK Ltd

Kelvin Close Birchwood, Warrington, WA3 7PB
Tel: 01925-810141 **Fax:** 01925-826708
E-mail: reception@il-uk.com
Website: http://www.il-uk.com
Bank(s): Barclays
Directors: A. Grant (Dir), S. Calderbank (Co Sec)
Ultimate Holding Company: GRUPO CH WERFEN SA (SPAIN)
Immediate Holding Company: INSTRUMENTATION LABORATORY (U K) LIMITED
Registration no: 01040034 **VAT No.:** GB 147 4470 59
Date established: 1972 **Turnover:** £20m - £50m
No.of Employees: 21 - 50 **Product Groups:** 38, 44

Date of Accounts	Dec 11	Dec 10	Dec 09
Sales Turnover	25m	27m	24m
Pre Tax Profit/Loss	-3m	-29m	3m
Working Capital	19m	12m	11m
Fixed Assets	35m	47m	78m
Current Assets	26m	19m	18m
Current Liabilities	3m	4m	3m

Isaac Ltd

2 Forrest Way Gatewarth Industrial Estate, Warrington, WA5 1DF
Tel: 01925-231899 **Fax:** 01925-655077
E-mail: stanscott.isaacltd@btinternet.com
Website: http://www.isaacltd.co.uk
Directors: S. Scott (MD)
Immediate Holding Company: ISAAC LIMITED
Registration no: 02401864 **Date established:** 1989
No.of Employees: 1 - 10 **Product Groups:** 23, 29, 30, 34, 35, 36, 37, 38, 39, 40, 41, 42, 45, 48, 49, 51, 52, 54, 66, 67

Date of Accounts	Jul 11	Jul 10	Jul 09
Working Capital	39	36	34
Fixed Assets	25	28	34
Current Assets	94	91	83

Isograph Ltd

The Malt Building Greenalls Avenue, Warrington, WA4 6HL
Tel: 01925-437000 **Fax:** 01925-437010
E-mail: sales@isograph-software.com
Website: http://www.isograph-software.com
Directors: S. Flanagan (Fin)
Immediate Holding Company: ISOGRAPH LIMITED
Registration no: 02062360 **VAT No.:** GB 444 8773 15
Date established: 1986 **Turnover:** £500,000 - £1m
No.of Employees: 1 - 10 **Product Groups:** 44

Date of Accounts	Mar 11	Mar 10	Mar 09
Working Capital	981	869	911
Fixed Assets	12	13	18
Current Assets	3m	2m	2m

J & A Plant Ltd

Nook Lane Golborne, Warrington, WA3 3NE
Tel: 01942-713511 **Fax:** 01942-713396
E-mail: j-aplantservices@structural-engineers.fsnet.co.uk
Directors: S. Knowles (Dir)
Immediate Holding Company: J & A PLANT LIMITED
Registration no: 04546686 **Date established:** 2002
No.of Employees: 1 - 10 **Product Groups:** 35

Date of Accounts	Jul 11	Jul 10	Jul 09
Working Capital	36	-55	-5
Fixed Assets	183	174	179
Current Assets	232	227	271

J S Perforated Metals Ltd

Unit 63 Burtonwood Industrial Centre Phipps Lane, Burtonwood, Warrington, WA5 4HX
Tel: 01925-292224 **Fax:** 01925-292226
E-mail: info@jsperf.co.uk
Website: http://www.jsperf.co.uk
Directors: J. Jordan (Fin), P. Jordan (MD)
Immediate Holding Company: J S PERFORATED METALS LIMITED
Registration no: 03032220 **Date established:** 1995
Turnover: £250,000 - £500,000 **No.of Employees:** 1 - 10
Product Groups: 34, 35

Date of Accounts	Mar 11	Mar 10	Mar 09
Working Capital	29	29	27
Current Assets	48	70	63

Jewson Ltd

Hood Lane Great Sankey, Warrington, WA5 1EH
Tel: 01925-650511 **Fax:** 01925-650227
E-mail: steve.daniels@jewson.co.uk
Website: http://www.jewson.co.uk
Managers: S. Daniels (District Mgr)
Ultimate Holding Company: COMPAGNIE DE SAINT GOBAIN (FRANCE)
Immediate Holding Company: JEWSON LIMITED
Registration no: 00348407 **VAT No.:** GB 394 1212 63
Date established: 1939 **Turnover:** Up to £250,000
No.of Employees: 1 - 10 **Product Groups:** 66

Date of Accounts	Dec 11	Dec 10	Dec 09
Sales Turnover	1606m	1547m	1485m
Pre Tax Profit/Loss	18m	100m	45m
Working Capital	-345m	-250m	-349m
Fixed Assets	496m	387m	461m
Current Assets	657m	1005m	1320m
Current Liabilities	66m	120m	64m

Kaba Garog

10 Eagle Park Drive, Warrington, WA2 8JA
Tel: 01925-401555 **Fax:** 01925-401551
E-mail: jobrian@kgw.kaba.com
Website: http://www.kaba-garog.co.uk
Bank(s): National Westminster Bank Plc
Directors: J. O"brian (MD)
Registration no: 00162427 **VAT No.:** GB 732 3420 68
Date established: 1990 **Turnover:** £1m - £2m **No.of Employees:** 11 - 20
Product Groups: 35, 37, 67

Karramandi

111 Kimberley Street, Warrington, WA5 1PA
Tel: 07807-083502
E-mail: yvonne@karramandi.com
Website: http://www.karramandi.com
Managers: Y. Hands (Chief Acct)
Date established: 2007 **Turnover:** Up to £250,000
No.of Employees: 1 - 10 **Product Groups:** 32

Kawasaki Robotics

Unit 4 Easter Court Europa Boulevard, Westbrook, Warrington, WA5 7ZB
Tel: 01925-713000 **Fax:** 01925-713001
E-mail: sales@kawasakirobotuk.com
Website: http://www.kawasakirobotics.co.uk
Managers: S. Pearson
Ultimate Holding Company: KAWASAKI HEAVY INDUSTRIES LTD (JAPAN)
Immediate Holding Company: KAWASAKI ROBOTICS (UK) LIMITED
Registration no: 03250611 **Date established:** 1996 **Turnover:** £1m - £2m
No.of Employees: 21 - 50 **Product Groups:** 28, 44, 45, 46, 48, 84, 86

Date of Accounts	Dec 11	Dec 10	Dec 09
Sales Turnover	2m	2m	2m
Pre Tax Profit/Loss	36	29	-62
Working Capital	2m	2m	2m
Fixed Assets	N/A	N/A	2
Current Assets	2m	2m	2m
Current Liabilities	167	138	185

Krauss Maffei UK Ltd

410 Europa Boulevard Westbrook, Warrington, WA5 7TR
Tel: 01925-644100 **Fax:** 01925-234284
E-mail: info@kraussmaffei.co.uk
Website: http://www.kraussmaffei.co.uk
Bank(s): Commerzbank, London
Directors: A. Meehan (Fin), M. Bate (MD)
Ultimate Holding Company: KRAUSS MAFFEI AG (GERMANY)
Immediate Holding Company: KRAUSS-MAFFEI (U.K.) LIMITED
Registration no: 00992565 **VAT No.:** GB 437 5214 55
Date established: 1970 **Turnover:** £2m - £5m **No.of Employees:** 21 - 50
Product Groups: 30, 42

Date of Accounts	Sep 11	Sep 10	Sep 09
Sales Turnover	5m	5m	7m
Pre Tax Profit/Loss	184	11	-1m
Working Capital	-1m	-2m	-2m
Fixed Assets	833	846	856
Current Assets	1m	1m	2m
Current Liabilities	813	775	638

Lasertech UK Ltd

Unit 5 Easter Court Europa Boulevard, Westbrook, Warrington, WA5 7ZB
Tel: 08707-872323 **Fax:** 0870-787 0708
E-mail: sales@lasertechgroup.com
Website: http://www.lasertechgroup.com
Directors: J. Williams (MD), D. Kent (Fin)
Managers: A. Wilson (Personnel), A. Lovell (Buyer)
Immediate Holding Company: LASERTECH FRANCHISING (2008) LIMITED
Registration no: 06768590 **Date established:** 2008 **Turnover:** £5m - £10m
No.of Employees: 21 - 50 **Product Groups:** 32

M B M

Unit 7 Gibson Square Talbot Street, Golborne, Warrington, WA3 3NN
Tel: 01942-721126 **Fax:** 01942- 276410
Directors: W. Knowles (Ptnr)
Date established: 1996 **No.of Employees:** 1 - 10 **Product Groups:** 35, 39, 45

Manflex Ltd
Unit 1 Gateworth Industrial Estate Forrest Way, Warrington, WA5 1DF
Tel: 01925-653215 **Fax:** 01925-416793
E-mail: sales@manflex.co.uk
Website: http://www.manflex.co.uk
Directors: A. Moody (Dir)
Immediate Holding Company: MAN-FLEX LIMITED
Registration no: 01178444 **VAT No.:** GB 153 3293 77
Date established: 1974 **Turnover:** £500,000 - £1m
No.of Employees: 1 - 10 **Product Groups:** 29, 30, 31, 32, 33, 34, 35, 36, 37, 38, 39, 40, 41, 43, 45, 46, 48, 49, 66, 67, 68

Date of Accounts	Mar 11	Mar 10	Mar 09
Working Capital	-72	-38	32
Fixed Assets	143	143	142
Current Assets	359	335	321
Current Liabilities	119	N/A	N/A

Maplin Electronics Ltd
Unit H3 Cockhedge Centre, Warrington, WA1 2QQ
Tel: 08432-277360 **Fax:** 01925-657274
E-mail: customercare@maplin.co.uk
Website: http://www.maplin.co.uk
Managers: J. England (District Mgr)
Ultimate Holding Company: MONTAGU PRIVATE EQUITY LLP
Immediate Holding Company: MAPLIN ELECTRONICS LIMITED
Registration no: 01264385 **Date established:** 1976
Turnover: £125m - £250m **No.of Employees:** 1 - 10 **Product Groups:** 37, 61

Date of Accounts	Dec 11	Dec 08	Dec 09
Sales Turnover	205m	204m	204m
Pre Tax Profit/Loss	25m	32m	35m
Working Capital	118m	49m	75m
Fixed Assets	27m	28m	28m
Current Assets	207m	108m	142m
Current Liabilities	78m	51m	59m

Mark Of Millennium Ltd
9 Saffron Close Lowton, Warrington, WA3 2GW
Tel: 01942-728000 **Fax:** 01942-728000
E-mail: info@mm-masonic.co.uk
Website: http://www.mm-masonic-regalia.co.uk
Directors: A. Huskie (Dir)
Immediate Holding Company: MARK OF MILLENNIUM LTD.
Registration no: SC192404 **Date established:** 1999
No.of Employees: 1 - 10 **Product Groups:** 22, 49

Date of Accounts	Jan 11	Jan 10	Jan 08
Working Capital	37	32	32
Fixed Assets	36	37	29
Current Assets	44	39	40

Matchless Ltd
Gilbert Wakefield Lodge 65 Bewsey Street, Warrington, WA2 7JQ
Tel: 01925-231900 **Fax:** 01925-415423
Website: http://www.unipump.co.uk
Directors: R. Entwistle (Fin)
Immediate Holding Company: MATCHLESS LIMITED
Registration no: 02673593 **Date established:** 1991
No.of Employees: 11 - 20 **Product Groups:** 40

Date of Accounts	Sep 11	Sep 10	Sep 09
Working Capital	-60	-56	-55
Fixed Assets	11	13	15
Current Assets	18	45	12

Mccarthy Recruitment Ltd
Unit 12a Olympic Way Birchwood, Warrington, WA2 0YL
Tel: 0161-828 8726 **Fax:** 0161-834 5304
E-mail: kate@mccarthyrecruitment.com
Website: http://www.mccarthyrecruitment.com
Directors: K. Mccarthy (MD)
Immediate Holding Company: MCCARTHY RECRUITMENT LIMITED
Registration no: 05235393 **Date established:** 2004
Turnover: £20m - £50m **No.of Employees:** 11 - 20 **Product Groups:** 80

Date of Accounts	Mar 12	Mar 11	Mar 10
Working Capital	313	276	209
Fixed Assets	142	115	35
Current Assets	469	596	587

Metal Doctor
Unit K2 Taylor Business Park Risley, Warrington, WA3 6BL
Tel: 01925-764579
E-mail: dave.crippin@metaldoctor.co.uk
Website: http://www.metaldoctor.co.uk
Directors: D. Crippin (Prop)
No.of Employees: 1 - 10 **Product Groups:** 26, 35

Metal Working Lubricants Ltd
Braemar House 274 Manchester Road, Woolston, Warrington, WA1 4PS
Tel: 01925-816666 **Fax:** 01925-816666
E-mail: info@mwl-uk.com
Website: http://www.mwl-uk.com
Directors: K. Freeman (MD)
Immediate Holding Company: METAL WORKING LUBRICANTS LIMITED
Registration no: 00564835 **VAT No.:** GB 160 0196 04
Date established: 1956 **Turnover:** Up to £250,000
No.of Employees: 1 - 10 **Product Groups:** 31

Date of Accounts	Jun 11	Jun 10	Jun 09
Working Capital	5	-1	-8
Fixed Assets	9	9	10
Current Assets	10	8	7

Metalflex Industrial Supplies Ltd
9 Adlington Court Birchwood, Warrington, WA3 6PL
Tel: 01925-814999 **Fax:** 01925-838999
E-mail: john.milsom@metalflex.co.uk
Website: http://www.metalflex.co.uk
Directors: E. Lawton (Co Sec), J. Milsom (Dir)
Immediate Holding Company: METALFLEX INDUSTRIAL SUPPLIES LIMITED
Registration no: 03850682 **Date established:** 1999
No.of Employees: 1 - 10 **Product Groups:** 29, 36, 38, 40

Date of Accounts	Sep 11	Sep 10	Sep 09
Working Capital	159	102	80
Fixed Assets	15	17	21
Current Assets	431	310	253

Metosa
6 Peveril Close Appleton, Warrington, WA4 5BU
Tel: 01925-211007 **Fax:** 01925-211006
E-mail: rogerwhelan@talk21.com
Website: http://www.metosa-pinacho.com
Directors: R. Whelan (Prop)
Date established: 2000 **No.of Employees:** 1 - 10 **Product Groups:** 46

Middleby UK Ltd
4 Cranford Court Hardwick Grange Woolston, Woolston, Warrington, WA1 4RX
Tel: 01925-821280 **Fax:** 01925-815653
E-mail: sales@middlebyuk.co.uk
Website: http://www.middlebyuk.co.uk
Directors: N. Maalous (MD)
Ultimate Holding Company: MIDDLEBY CORPORATION (THE) (USA)
Immediate Holding Company: MIDDLEBY UK LTD
Registration no: 02915063 **Date established:** 1994 **Turnover:** £5m - £10m
No.of Employees: 11 - 20 **Product Groups:** 40, 48, 67

Date of Accounts	Dec 11	Dec 10	Dec 09
Sales Turnover	8m	8m	6m
Pre Tax Profit/Loss	317	229	-504
Working Capital	2m	2m	2m
Fixed Assets	6	8	13
Current Assets	4m	4m	3m
Current Liabilities	637	381	252

Middleton's Spraying
7 Morley Road, Warrington, WA4 6EU
Tel: 07798-903670
E-mail: wilsonmiddleton@aol.com
Website: http://www.spraypaintingmobile.co.uk
Directors: I. Wilson (Prop)
Date established: 1988 **No.of Employees:** 1 - 10 **Product Groups:** 46, 48

Millennium Sun & Beauty Studio
4 Bruche Heath Gardens Padgate, Warrington, WA1 3TP
Tel: 01925-826935 **Fax:** 01925-828563
Directors: R. Chadwick (Prop)
Immediate Holding Company: MILLENNIUM SUPPLIES LTD
Registration no: 04618433 **Date established:** 2002
No.of Employees: 1 - 10 **Product Groups:** 46

Date of Accounts	Mar 08	Mar 07	Mar 06
Working Capital	-1	4	-1
Fixed Assets	1	1	7
Current Assets	23	32	36
Current Liabilities	23	28	37

Moorgate Ltd
2 Cedar Court Taylor Business Park, Risley, Warrington, WA3 6BT
Tel: 01925-765432 **Fax:** 01925-765422
E-mail: sales@moorgate.co.uk
Website: http://www.moorgate.co.uk
Bank(s): Royal Bank of Scotland
Directors: J. Hennessy (Dir)
Immediate Holding Company: MOORGATE LIMITED
Registration no: 02526321 **VAT No.:** GB 534 9073 37
Date established: 1990 **Turnover:** £2m - £5m **No.of Employees:** 11 - 20
Product Groups: 67

Date of Accounts	Oct 11	Oct 10	Oct 09
Working Capital	-1	72	90
Fixed Assets	28	37	38
Current Assets	414	492	452

J Murphy & Sons Ltd
Wigan Road Golborne, Warrington, WA3 3UB
Tel: 01942-725326 **Fax:** 01942-721530
Website: http://www.murphygroup.co.uk
Managers: L. Smith (Purch Mgr), G. Carney (Sales Admin), A. Lawrence (Personnel), C. Thacker (Tech Serv Mgr)
Ultimate Holding Company: MARYLAND LIMITED (ISLE OF MAN)
Immediate Holding Company: J. MURPHY & SONS LIMITED
Registration no: 00492042 **Date established:** 1951
Turnover: £125m - £250m **No.of Employees:** 101 - 250
Product Groups: 51

Date of Accounts	Dec 11	Dec 10	Dec 09
Sales Turnover	485m	401m	408m
Pre Tax Profit/Loss	26m	23m	25m
Working Capital	94m	142m	125m
Fixed Assets	94m	36m	37m
Current Assets	205m	210m	192m
Current Liabilities	65m	31m	30m

Nationwide Diesel
9 Bewsey Business Centre Bewsey Road, Warrington, WA5 0JU
Tel: 01925-418857 **Fax:** 01925-230743
E-mail: sales@nationwidediesel.co.uk
Website: http://www.nationwidediesel.co.uk
Directors: S. Mcniven (MD)
Date established: 2005 **No.of Employees:** 1 - 10 **Product Groups:** 40

Newsquest
The Academy 138 Bridge Street, Warrington, WA1 2RU
Tel: 01925-426848 **Fax:** 01925-434224
E-mail: catherine.lawler@northwest.newsquest.co.uk
Website: http://www.warringtonguardian.co.uk
Directors: C. Hughes (Reg MD)
Managers: A. Houghton (Sales Prom Mgr)
Ultimate Holding Company: Newsquest Ltd
Registration no: 03103884 **No.of Employees:** 51 - 100
Product Groups: 28

Date of Accounts	Dec 07	Dec 06
Sales Turnover	N/A	28757
Pre Tax Profit/Loss	N/A	-5157
Working Capital	9000	9000
Current Assets	9000	9000
ROT% (Return on Turnover)		-17.9

North Cheshire Windows
Unit 3a Trident Industrial Estate Warrington Road, Risley, Warrington, WA3 6AX
Tel: 01925-850022 **Fax:** 01925-850044
E-mail: sales@northcheshirewindows.com
Website: http://www.northcheshirewindows.com
Bank(s): Natwest
Directors: P. Hayes (Dir)
Immediate Holding Company: NORTH CHESHIRE HOLDINGS LIMITED
Registration no: 02828265 **VAT No.:** GB 611 6989 25
Date established: 1993 **Turnover:** £5m - £10m **No.of Employees:** 21 - 50
Product Groups: 30

Date of Accounts	Sep 11	Sep 10	Sep 09
Sales Turnover	5m	N/A	N/A
Pre Tax Profit/Loss	517	N/A	N/A
Working Capital	-35	-36	343
Fixed Assets	715	539	101
Current Assets	1m	848	977
Current Liabilities	189	N/A	N/A

North West Decoiling Trading Ltd
3 Palatine Works Causeway Avenue, Warrington, WA4 6QQ
Tel: 01925-415111 **Fax:** 01925-445134
E-mail: sales@northwestdecoiling.co.uk
Website: http://www.northwestdecoiling.co.uk
Bank(s): Co-operative Bank
Directors: R. Hassall (Dir), A. Waterfield (Fin)
Managers: N. Hudson (Sales Eng), J. Waterfield (Sales Prom Mgr)
Immediate Holding Company: North West Decoiling (Trading) Ltd
Registration no: 02628239 **VAT No.:** GB 582 0649 32
Date established: 1991 **Turnover:** £2m - £5m **No.of Employees:** 11 - 20
Product Groups: 66

Date of Accounts	Nov 07	Nov 06	Nov 05
Working Capital	-411	-273	-239
Fixed Assets	484	405	419
Current Assets	2m	2m	2m

North West Development Agency
Centre Park Warrington, Warrington, WA1 1QN
Tel: 01925-400100 **Fax:** 01925-400400
E-mail: nigel.dove@nwda.co.uk
Website: http://www.nwda.co.uk
Managers: N. Dove (Mktg Serv Mgr), N. Dove, M. Edwards (Sales & Mktg Mg), M. Hughes (Sales & Mktg Mg)
Registration no: 01910458 **Date established:** 2006 **Turnover:** £1m - £2m
No.of Employees: 251 - 500 **Product Groups:** 87

North West Steel Ltd
Mill Lane Winwick, Warrington, WA2 8QW
Tel: 01925-572201 **Fax:** 01925-413875
E-mail: sec@freeola.net
Bank(s): Natwest, Warrington
Managers: C. Taylor (District Mgr)
Immediate Holding Company: NORTH WEST STEEL LIMITED
Registration no: 02270027 **VAT No.:** GB 294 8961 92
Date established: 1988 **Turnover:** £10m - £20m
No.of Employees: 21 - 50 **Product Groups:** 30, 32, 34, 35, 45

Date of Accounts	Dec 11	Dec 10	Dec 09
Sales Turnover	11m	10m	9m
Pre Tax Profit/Loss	157	108	105
Working Capital	2m	2m	2m
Fixed Assets	766	431	486
Current Assets	5m	4m	5m
Current Liabilities	978	1m	999

Optibelt UK Ltd
5 Bishops Court Winwick Quay, Warrington, WA2 8QY
Tel: 01925-415777 **Fax:** 01925-573751
E-mail: info@optibelt.com
Website: http://www.optibelt.com
Bank(s): National Westminster Bank Plc
Directors: C. Rice (MD)
Ultimate Holding Company: ARNTZ BETEILLGUNGS GMBH & CO KG (GERMANY)
Immediate Holding Company: OPTIBELT (UK) LIMITED
Registration no: 00936602 **VAT No.:** GB 250 5103 11
Date established: 1968 **Turnover:** £2m - £5m **No.of Employees:** 11 - 20
Product Groups: 22, 23, 29, 30, 35, 38, 39, 40, 45, 66, 84

Date of Accounts	Dec 11	Dec 10	Dec 09
Sales Turnover	3m	3m	2m
Pre Tax Profit/Loss	234	139	2
Working Capital	829	593	466
Fixed Assets	27	24	27
Current Assets	1m	878	733
Current Liabilities	205	138	57

P & S Couriers Ltd
14 Thompson Avenue Culcheth, Warrington, WA3 4EB
Tel: 0773-4548560 **Fax:** 01925-767099
E-mail: uk98@btopenworld.com
Website: http://www.couriers.eng.st
Directors: P. Middleton (Dir), S. Cairns (Dir)
Registration no: 05167027 **Date established:** 2004
No.of Employees: 1 - 10 **Product Groups:** 79

Date of Accounts	Jun 07	Jun 06
Working Capital	1	1
Current Assets	4	4
Current Liabilities	3	3

Package Boiler Services Ltd
Back Forshaw Street, Warrington, WA2 7HH
Tel: 01925-411937 **Fax:** 01925-418268
E-mail: boden.j@sky.com
Directors: J. Boden (MD)
Immediate Holding Company: PACKAGE BOILER SERVICES LIMITED
Registration no: 02069306 **VAT No.:** GB 428 8834 11
Date established: 1986 **No.of Employees:** 1 - 10 **Product Groups:** 40

Date of Accounts	Dec 11	Dec 10	Dec 09
Working Capital	-12	-13	-6
Fixed Assets	14	14	15
Current Assets	19	14	23

Padgate Appliance
6-8 Marsh House Lane, Warrington, WA1 3QY
Tel: 01925-636015 **Fax:** 01925-810702
Managers: M. Zacharaasz (Mgr)
Registration no: 05870889 **No.of Employees:** 1 - 10 **Product Groups:** 36, 40

Perrite (a division of Vita Thermoplastic Compounds Ltd)
1 Kingsland Grange Woolston, Warrington, WA1 4RA
Tel: 01925-810608 **Fax:** 01925-840001
E-mail: sales@perrite.com
Website: http://www.perrite.com
Bank(s): Barclays
Managers: K. Kane (Comptroller), D. Bishop, D. Hall (Sales & Mktg Mg), D. Johnson (Comm), I. Bragg (Comptroller), J. Rochford (Sales Prom Mgr), S. Moran (Purch Mgr)
Immediate Holding Company: DOEFLEX INDUSTRIES LTD
Registration no: 01018237 **VAT No.:** GB 652 5680 26
No.of Employees: 51 - 100 **Product Groups:** 30, 31

Plastic Closures Ltd

Unit 5a New Cut Lane, Woolston, Warrington, WA1 4AG
Tel: 01925-837470 **Fax:** 01925-837460
E-mail: sales@plasticclosuresltd.com
Website: http://www.plasticclosuresltd.com
Bank(s): Clydesdale
Directors: M. Smith (Dir), J. Hargreaves (MD), A. Carrick (Dir), W. Carrick (Dir)
Managers: F. Miller (Prod Mgr), D. Merrill (Sales Admin)
Ultimate Holding Company: CARRICK HOLDINGS LIMITED
Immediate Holding Company: PLASTIC CLOSURES LIMITED
Registration no: 01941001 **VAT No.:** GB 428 8271 29
Date established: 1985 **Turnover:** £1m - £2m **No.of Employees:** 21 - 50
Product Groups: 30

Date of Accounts	Dec 11	Dec 10	Dec 09
Working Capital	895	807	790
Fixed Assets	451	438	365
Current Assets	1m	2m	2m

Poppers Senco UK Ltd

630 Europa Boul Westbrook, Warrington, WA5 7YH
Tel: 01925-445566 **Fax:** 01925-418873
E-mail: sales@poppers-senco.co.uk
Website: http://www.poppers-senco.co.uk
Bank(s): Bank of Scotland
Directors: J. Fleming (MD)
Ultimate Holding Company: C J M STRUIJK BEHEER BV (NETHERLANDS)
Immediate Holding Company: POPPERS SENCO UK LIMITED
Registration no: SC049132 **VAT No.:** GB 261 0506 01
Date established: 1971 **Turnover:** £5m - £10m **No.of Employees:** 11 - 20
Product Groups: 35, 37, 40, 42, 47

Date of Accounts	Dec 11	Dec 10	Dec 09
Sales Turnover	7m	7m	6m
Pre Tax Profit/Loss	51	-95	-1m
Working Capital	1m	1m	1m
Fixed Assets	149	130	180
Current Assets	3m	3m	4m
Current Liabilities	305	355	214

R A B Metalwork

61 Eastford Road, Warrington, WA4 6EY
Tel: 01925-650096 **Fax:** 01925-650096
Directors: R. Barker (Prop)
No.of Employees: 1 - 10 **Product Groups:** 26, 35

R P S Group Risk Management

Dalton House 105 Dalton Avenue, Birchwood, Warrington, WA3 6YF
Tel: 01925-831000 **Fax:** 01925-831231
E-mail: binnsr@rpsgroup.com
Website: http://www.rpsgroup.com
Bank(s): The Royal Bank of Scotland
Directors: A. Rigby (Co Sec)
Managers: N. Taylor (Mgr)
Ultimate Holding Company: R P S GROUP PLC
Immediate Holding Company: THE ENVIRONMENTAL CONSULTANCY LTD
Registration no: 02182945 **Date established:** 1976
Turnover: £20m - £50m **No.of Employees:** 51 - 100 **Product Groups:** 44, 54, 80, 84, 85, 86

R S J Fabrications

Unit 10c Bank Quay Trading Estate Slutchers Lane, Warrington, WA1 1PJ
Tel: 01925-575444 **Fax:** 01925-575444
Directors: A. Curran (Ptnr)
Date established: 1994 **No.of Employees:** 1 - 10 **Product Groups:** 26, 35

Renovation Seating Service

96 Stone Cross Lane North Lowton, Warrington, WA3 2SG
Tel: 07766-727811 **Fax:** 01942-723033
E-mail: renovation.seating@fsmail.net
Website: http://www.renovationseating.co.uk
Directors: G. Wilde (Ptnr), G. Wild (Ptnr)
No.of Employees: 1 - 10 **Product Groups:** 24, 26, 62

Rock Chemicals Ltd (t/a Rock Oil)

90 Priestley Street, Warrington, WA5 1ST
Tel: 01925-636191 **Fax:** 01925-632499
E-mail: sales@rockoil.co.uk
Website: http://www.rockoil.co.uk
Bank(s): National Westminster Bank Plc
Directors: C. McDonna (Pers), C. Hewitt (MD)
Managers: J. Peters (Chief Acct), R. Bower (Mktg Serv Mgr), A. Gibbs (Sales Prom Mgr), G. Tickle (Purch Mgr), G. Hewitt (Purch Mgr)
Immediate Holding Company: Rock Oil Ltd
Registration no: 00835494 **VAT No.:** GB 152 2498 70
No.of Employees: 51 - 100 **Product Groups:** 31, 32, 66

Date of Accounts	Mar 10	Mar 09	Mar 08
Sales Turnover	13m	N/A	N/A
Pre Tax Profit/Loss	257	67	106
Working Capital	1m	1m	1m
Fixed Assets	1m	1m	1m
Current Assets	4m	3m	4m
Current Liabilities	389	380	341

Rock Oil Co. Ltd

90 Priestley Street, Warrington, WA5 1ST
Tel: 01925-636191 **Fax:** 01925-632499
E-mail: sales@rockoil.co.uk
Website: http://www.rockoil.co.uk
Bank(s): National Westminster Bank Plc
Directors: C. Hewett (Dir), C. Hewitt (MD)
Immediate Holding Company: CLASSIC ROCK OIL COMPANY LIMITED
Registration no: 06988694 **VAT No.:** GB 152 2498 70
Date established: 2009 **Turnover:** £5m - £10m
No.of Employees: 51 - 100 **Product Groups:** 31, 32, 66, 68

Date of Accounts	Aug 11
Working Capital	-3
Fixed Assets	1

Rotating Maintenance Services Ltd

Forward Works Woolston, Warrington, WA1 4BA
Tel: 01925-825330 **Fax:** 01925-837303
E-mail: sales@rotatingmaintenance.com
Website: http://www.rotatingmaintenance.com
Directors: A. Dobson (MD)
Immediate Holding Company: ROTATING MAINTENANCE SERVICES LTD

Registration no: 02241384 **VAT No.:** GB 374 2140 71
Date established: 1988 **Turnover:** £250,000 - £500,000
No.of Employees: 1 - 10 **Product Groups:** 48

Date of Accounts	Mar 12	Mar 11	Mar 10
Working Capital	85	99	164
Fixed Assets	51	57	39
Current Assets	149	151	213

Rubax Lifts Ltd

Wilson House Cinnamon Park Crab Lane, Fearnhead, Warrington, WA2 0XP
Tel: 01925-849200 **Fax:** 020-8302 6644
E-mail: info@rubax.co.uk
Website: http://www.rubax.co.uk
Directors: P. Verey (MD)
Ultimate Holding Company: FROSTALL LIMITED
Immediate Holding Company: RUBAX LIFTS LIMITED
Registration no: 01509899 **Date established:** 1980 **Turnover:** £5m - £10m
No.of Employees: 1 - 10 **Product Groups:** 35, 39, 45

Date of Accounts	Dec 10	Dec 09	Dec 08
Sales Turnover	9m	8m	N/A
Pre Tax Profit/Loss	1m	1m	718
Working Capital	723	635	640
Fixed Assets	608	714	670
Current Assets	4m	3m	3m
Current Liabilities	1m	1m	1m

A & E Russell Ltd

7-9 Chetham Court Winwick Quay, Warrington, WA2 8RF
Tel: 01925-643700 **Fax:** 01925-643707
E-mail: warrington@aerussell.co.uk
Website: http://www.aerussell.co.uk
Directors: A. Russell (MD), S. Baillie (Sales), G. Black (Fin)
Managers: A. Stocker (Mgr)
Ultimate Holding Company: Bunzl plc
Immediate Holding Company: A. & E. RUSSELL LIMITED
Registration no: SC025735 **Date established:** 1947
Turnover: Up to £250,000 **No.of Employees:** 11 - 20 **Product Groups:** 23, 24, 40, 63, 67

S C C

Applied House Birchwood Boulevard, Birchwood, Warrington, WA3 7PS
Tel: 01925-819939 **Fax:** 01925-853602
E-mail: i.smith@scc.com
Website: http://www.scc.com
Bank(s): HSBC Bank plc
Managers: I. Smith (District Mgr)
Immediate Holding Company: SPECIALIST COMPUTER HOLDINGS LTD
Registration no: 01428210 **Turnover:** £250,000 - £500,000
No.of Employees: 21 - 50 **Product Groups:** 26, 44, 67, 81

Safic Alcan UK Ltd

812 Birchwood Boulevard Birchwood, Warrington, WA3 7QZ
Tel: 01925-838880 **Fax:** 01925-838883
E-mail: info@safic-alcan.co.uk
Website: http://www.safic-alcan.co.uk
Directors: P. Veal (Sales), D. Davies (Co Sec)
Ultimate Holding Company: ALCANA SAS (FRANCE)
Immediate Holding Company: SAFIC-ALCAN UK LIMITED
Registration no: 00580109 **Date established:** 1957
Turnover: £20m - £50m **No.of Employees:** 21 - 50 **Product Groups:** 32, 66

Date of Accounts	Dec 11	Dec 10	Dec 09
Sales Turnover	32m	27m	21m
Pre Tax Profit/Loss	3m	2m	982
Working Capital	4m	3m	2m
Fixed Assets	2m	2m	3m
Current Assets	10m	9m	8m
Current Liabilities	2m	1m	1m

Sky Lighting

D 20 Gough Avenue, Warrington, WA2 9QP
Tel: 01925-414411 **Fax:** 01925-414411
E-mail: enquiries@sky-lighting.co.uk
Website: http://www.sky-lighting.co.uk
Directors: I. Hamid (Prop)
No.of Employees: 1 - 10 **Product Groups:** 37, 67

Specialised Designs Ltd

Unit 2, Beech Court Taylor Business Park, Risley, Warrington, WA3 6BL
Tel: 01925-766265 **Fax:** 01925-765029
E-mail: sales@syphon-sound.co.uk
Website: http://www.syphon-sound.co.uk
Product Groups: 30, 36, 39

Spectrum Welding & Engineering

7 Tanning Court, Warrington, WA1 2HF
Tel: 01925-656546 **Fax:** 01925-656547
E-mail: spectrumwelding@btconnect.com
Directors: S. Walsh (Prop)
Immediate Holding Company: SPECTRUM WELDING AND ENGINEERING SUPPLIES LIMITED
Registration no: 04433747 **Date established:** 2002
No.of Employees: 1 - 10 **Product Groups:** 46

Date of Accounts	Mar 11	Mar 10	Mar 09
Working Capital	-90	-90	-99
Fixed Assets	27	11	13
Current Assets	198	163	96

Sterling Packaging Ltd

Unit 3-4 Catherine Street, Warrington, WA5 0LH
Tel: 01925-575520 **Fax:** 01925-575521
E-mail: sales@sterlingpackaging.co.uk
Website: http://www.sterlingpackaging.co.uk
Directors: L. Jepson (Co Sec), G. Jepson (Sales)
Immediate Holding Company: STERLING PACKAGING LIMITED
Registration no: 03333196 **Date established:** 1997
No.of Employees: 1 - 10 **Product Groups:** 38, 42

Date of Accounts	Jul 12	Jul 11	Jul 10
Working Capital	35	17	27
Fixed Assets	3	4	3
Current Assets	114	114	175

Peter Stubs Ltd

Causeway Avenue, Warrington, WA4 6QB
Tel: 01925-653939 **Fax:** 01925-413870
E-mail: sales@peterstubs.com
Website: http://www.peterstubs.com
Bank(s): Barclays
Directors: A. Baker (Co Sec), A. Shaw (Co Sec), D. Irvine (Dir), E. Bolam (Grp Chief Exec), M. Geer (MD)
Managers: A. Bentley (Fin Mgr), G. Seaman (Sales Prom Mgr)
Immediate Holding Company: ERASTEEL STUBS LIMITED
Registration no: 03966107 **VAT No.:** GB 643 6446 30
Date established: 2000 **Turnover:** £5m - £10m
No.of Employees: 51 - 100 **Product Groups:** 34

Date of Accounts	Dec 07	Dec 06	Dec 05
Sales Turnover	10617	11963	11925
Pre Tax Profit/Loss	-935	-826	-643
Working Capital	1604	2208	2029
Fixed Assets	3739	4292	5331
Current Assets	4712	5240	5129
Current Liabilities	3108	3032	3100
Total Share Capital	58	58	11808
ROCE% (Return on Capital Employed)	-17.5	-12.7	-8.7
ROT% (Return on Turnover)	-8.8	-6.9	-5.4

Taylor Wimpey Northwest Ltd

The Beacons Warrington Road, Risley, Warrington, WA3 6XU
Tel: 01925-849500 **Fax:** 01925-849501
E-mail: mark.mainwaring@taylorwimpey.com
Website: http://www.taylorwimpey.com
Directors: K. Atterbury (Co Sec), T. Mellor (Comm), G. Roberts (Fin), I. Smith (MD)
Managers: C. Fildes (Mktg Serv Mgr)
Ultimate Holding Company: TAYLOR WIMPEY PLC
Immediate Holding Company: TAYLOR WIMPEY DEVELOPMENTS LIMITED
Registration no: 00643420 **Date established:** 1959
Turnover: £50m - £75m **No.of Employees:** 21 - 50 **Product Groups:** 52, 80

Date of Accounts	Dec 11	Dec 10	Dec 09
Pre Tax Profit/Loss	2m	403m	8m
Working Capital	154m	188m	238m
Fixed Assets	1136m	1136m	586m
Current Assets	1193m	1142m	1110m
Current Liabilities	3m	200	200

Tempa Pano UK Ltd

Unit 5, Centre 21 Industrial Estate
Bridge Lane
Woolston, Warrington, WA1 4AW
Tel: 01925-811290 **Fax:** 01925-810386
E-mail: info@tempapano.co.uk
Website: http://www.tempapano.co.uk
Managers: T. Clancy (Mgr), M. Blore (Export Sales Mg)
Immediate Holding Company: TEMPA PANO UK LIMITED
Registration no: 04404553 **Date established:** 2000
No.of Employees: 1 - 10 **Product Groups:** 30, 33, 35, 36, 37, 38, 40, 44, 45, 46, 66

Date of Accounts	Dec 11	Dec 10	Dec 09
Working Capital	28	-69	-89
Fixed Assets	293	293	298
Current Assets	551	403	334

Testconsult Ltd

Ruby House 40a Hardwick Grange, Woolston, Warrington, WA1 4RF
Tel: 01925-286880 **Fax:** 01925-286881
E-mail: jo@testconsult.co.uk
Website: http://www.testconsult.co.uk
Directors: R. Stain (Fin)
Immediate Holding Company: TESTCONSULT LIMITED
Registration no: 01182561 **Date established:** 1974 **Turnover:** £2m - £5m
No.of Employees: 21 - 50 **Product Groups:** 38, 67, 85

Date of Accounts	Dec 11	Dec 10	Dec 09
Working Capital	1m	691	366
Fixed Assets	489	407	344
Current Assets	2m	1m	758

Timber Gate Manufacturers

40 Charlton Street, Warrington, WA4 1LX
Tel: 01925-652227
Directors: S. Breton (Prop)
Date established: 1999 **No.of Employees:** 1 - 10 **Product Groups:** 26, 35

Today Team

Lovell House The Quadrant, Birchwood, Warrington, WA3 6FW
Tel: 01925-202101
E-mail: info@todayteam.co.uk
Website: http://www.todayteam.com
Directors: J. Boyd (MD)
Immediate Holding Company: TODAY TEAM LIMITED
Registration no: 05329884 **Date established:** 2005
Turnover: £500,000 - £1m **No.of Employees:** 1 - 10 **Product Groups:** 79

Date of Accounts	Mar 12	Mar 11	Mar 10
Working Capital	6	-0	-7
Fixed Assets	4	7	10
Current Assets	93	42	31

Unit Pallets Ltd

Bank Street Golborne, Warrington, WA3 3RN
Tel: 01942-713501 **Fax:** 01942-722756
E-mail: sales@unit-pallets.co.uk
Website: http://www.unit-pallets.co.uk
Directors: R. Stevenson (Fin), M. March (Fin), G. Covey (MD)
Managers: M. Collopy (Sales & Mktg Mg), S. Wyatt (Purch Mgr), A. Lowe-jones (Tech Serv Mgr), J. Cawley
Ultimate Holding Company: JAMES JONES & SONS LIMITED
Immediate Holding Company: UNIT PALLETS LIMITED
Registration no: 01725860 **VAT No.:** GB 639 0889 94
Date established: 1983 **Turnover:** £10m - £20m
No.of Employees: 101 - 250 **Product Groups:** 45, 48, 76

Date of Accounts	Dec 11	Dec 10	Dec 09
Sales Turnover	16m	17m	14m
Pre Tax Profit/Loss	66	396	164
Working Capital	4m	3m	3m
Fixed Assets	978	1m	1m
Current Assets	8m	9m	8m
Current Liabilities	967	1m	931

United Utilities Water plc

Lingley Green Avenue Great Sankey, Warrington, WA5 3LP
Tel: 01925-237000 **Fax:** 01925-233360
Website: http://www.unitedutilities.co.uk
Bank(s): National Westminster
Directors: D. Morton (Dir)
Ultimate Holding Company: UNITED UTILITIES GROUP PLC
Immediate Holding Company: UNITED UTILITIES WATER PLC
Registration no: 02366678 **VAT No.:** GB 483 7973 87
Date established: 1989 **Turnover:** Over £1,000m
No.of Employees: 1501 & over **Product Groups:** 18

see next page

***United Utilities Water plc** - Cont'd*

Date of Accounts	Mar 12	Mar 11	Mar 10
Sales Turnover	1535m	1486m	1549m
Pre Tax Profit/Loss	244m	334m	439m
Working Capital	170m	-9m	-111m
Fixed Assets	8324m	8052m	7855m
Current Assets	819m	595m	592m
Current Liabilities	533m	332m	533m

Vectra Group Ltd
Europa House 310 Europa Boulevard, Westbrook, Warrington, WA5 7YQ
Tel: 01925-444648 **Fax:** 01925-444701
E-mail: info@vectragroup.co.uk
Website: http://www.vectragroup.co.uk
Bank(s): National Westminster Bank Plc
Directors: J. Morgan (Chief Op Offcr), M. Maratos (Admin), H. Brown (Co Sec), P. Flinn (MD), N. James (MD)
Managers: S. Medonos, J. Fields (Develop Mgr), J. Morgan (Develop Mgr), D. Jones (Personnel)
Ultimate Holding Company: ARCADIS NV (NETHERLANDS)
Immediate Holding Company: VECTRA GROUP LIMITED
Registration no: 01803667 **Date established:** 1984
Turnover: £10m - £20m **No.of Employees:** 51 - 100 **Product Groups:** 54, 80, 81, 84, 86

Date of Accounts	Dec 08	Dec 07	Dec 06
Sales Turnover	11m	10m	10m
Pre Tax Profit/Loss	459	440	-595
Working Capital	1m	985	592
Fixed Assets	194	189	142
Current Assets	3m	3m	3m
Current Liabilities	708	975	1m

Village Gates Ltd
10 Charnock Road Culcheth, Warrington, WA3 5SH
Tel: 01925-766629
Website: http://www.villagegates.co.uk
Directors: P. Mainwaring (MD)
Immediate Holding Company: VILLAGE GATES LIMITED
Registration no: 07205090 **Date established:** 2010
No.of Employees: 1 - 10 **Product Groups:** 26, 35

Date of Accounts	Mar 11
Working Capital	-7
Fixed Assets	7
Current Assets	3

Volvo Construction Equipment Ltd
Clayton Road Birchwood, Warrington, WA3 6PH
Tel: 01925-817330 **Fax:** 01925-838126
E-mail: william.ww.watson@volvo.com
Website: http://www.construction.volvo.co.uk
Managers: W. Watson (Mgr)
Ultimate Holding Company: AB VOLVO (SWEDEN)
Immediate Holding Company: VOLVO CONSTRUCTION EQUIPMENT LIMITED
Registration no: 01673954 **Date established:** 1982
No.of Employees: 1 - 10 **Product Groups:** 42, 45

Date of Accounts	Dec 10	Dec 09	Dec 08
Sales Turnover	N/A	70m	192m
Pre Tax Profit/Loss	N/A	2m	8m
Working Capital	26m	26m	7m
Fixed Assets	N/A	N/A	76m
Current Assets	26m	26m	57m
Current Liabilities	N/A	N/A	32m

Warrington Chamber Of Commerce
International Business Centre Delta Crescent, Westbrook, Warrington, WA5 7WQ
Tel: 01925-715150 **Fax:** 01925-715159
E-mail: info@warrington-chamber.co.uk
Website: http://www.warrington-chamber.co.uk
Directors: C. Daniels (Grp Chief Exec)
Immediate Holding Company: WARRINGTON CHAMBER OF COMMERCE & INDUSTRY
Registration no: 02964309 **VAT No.:** GB 152 4210 11
Date established: 1994 **Turnover:** Up to £250,000
No.of Employees: 1 - 10 **Product Groups:** 87

Date of Accounts	Dec 11	Dec 10	Dec 09
Working Capital	206	195	190
Fixed Assets	N/A	1	2
Current Assets	240	228	224

Welding Plant & Machinery
36 Byrom Lane Lowton, Warrington, WA3 1BL
Tel: 01942-604682 **Fax:** 01942-604682
Directors: P. Griffiths (Prop)
Date established: 1990 **No.of Employees:** 1 - 10 **Product Groups:** 46

Weldspares Ltd
50 Melford Court Hardwick Grange, Woolston, Warrington, WA1 4RZ
Tel: 01925-813288 **Fax:** 01925-817223
E-mail: sales@weldspares.co.uk
Website: http://www.weldspares-oki.com
Bank(s): The Royal Bank of Scotland
Directors: A. Underwood (Mkt Research), J. Duggan (Co Sec)
Ultimate Holding Company: FUTURIS GROUP LIMITED
Immediate Holding Company: WELDSPARES-OKI LIMITED
Registration no: 02561091 **VAT No.:** GB 696 4644 80
Date established: 1990 **Turnover:** £2m - £5m **No.of Employees:** 21 - 50
Product Groups: 24, 30, 32, 33, 34, 35, 36, 37, 38, 40, 42, 46, 67

Date of Accounts	Dec 11	Dec 10	Dec 09
Working Capital	N/A	-2m	N/A

Wetherby Building Systems
1 Kid Glove Road Golborne, Warrington, WA3 3GS
Tel: 01942-717100 **Fax:** 01299-251003
E-mail: info@wbs-ltd.co.uk
Website: http://www.wbs-ltd.co.uk
Directors: R. Dean (MD)
Immediate Holding Company: WETHERBY BUILDING SYSTEMS LIMITED
Registration no: 03621726 **Date established:** 1998
No.of Employees: 21 - 50 **Product Groups:** 30, 33, 35, 45, 52, 66, 84, 85

Date of Accounts	Oct 10	Oct 09	Oct 08
Sales Turnover	13m	9m	N/A
Pre Tax Profit/Loss	1m	395	475
Working Capital	583	381	353
Fixed Assets	1m	1m	1m
Current Assets	4m	3m	3m
Current Liabilities	967	569	589

Williams Garage Services
691-693 Warrington Road Risley, Warrington, WA3 6AY
Tel: 01925-816700 **Fax:** 01925-852961
E-mail: srwgarage@csemail.co.uk
Website: http://www.williamsgarage.co.uk
Directors: R. Nolan (Prop), G. Nolan (Dir)
Immediate Holding Company: WILLIAMS GARAGE SERVICES LTD
Registration no: 05444280 **Date established:** 2005
Turnover: Up to £250,000 **No.of Employees:** 1 - 10 **Product Groups:** 29, 37, 39

Date of Accounts	Mar 12	Mar 11	Mar 10
Working Capital	-33	-28	-30
Fixed Assets	43	31	31
Current Assets	25	22	12
Current Liabilities	N/A	41	N/A

Williams Tarr Construction Ltd
23 Bridge Road Woolston, Warrington, WA1 4AU
Tel: 01925-828877 **Fax:** 01925-817988
E-mail: info@williams-tarr.com
Website: http://www.williams-tarr.com
Directors: T. Hughes (Contracts), C. Carter (Fin), E. Wilkinson (Dir), J. Hughes (Dir)
Managers: N. Bennett (Buyer)
Ultimate Holding Company: WILLIAMS TARR HOLDINGS LTD
Immediate Holding Company: WILLIAMS TARR CONSTRUCTION LIMITED
Registration no: 00149461 **Date established:** 2018 **Turnover:** £5m - £10m
No.of Employees: 11 - 20 **Product Groups:** 51, 52, 80, 84

Date of Accounts	Dec 11	Dec 10	Dec 09
Sales Turnover	8m	8m	18m
Pre Tax Profit/Loss	-769	20	1m
Working Capital	3m	4m	4m
Fixed Assets	64	68	109
Current Assets	11m	12m	14m
Current Liabilities	594	540	980

Willow Catering Services Ltd
21 Willow Court West Quay Road, Winwick, Warrington, WA2 8UF
Tel: 01925-417594 **Fax:** 01925-418748
E-mail: service@willowcateringservices.co.uk
Website: http://www.rationalovenservice.co.uk
Directors: C. Cullen (Fin), S. Corcoran (MD)
Immediate Holding Company: WILLOW CATERING SERVICES LIMITED
Registration no: 04697554 **Date established:** 2003
No.of Employees: 1 - 10 **Product Groups:** 20, 40, 41

Date of Accounts	Mar 11	Mar 10	Mar 09
Working Capital	350	300	222
Fixed Assets	14	21	36
Current Assets	510	465	416

Wirecloth Sales & Development
11a East View Grappenhall, Warrington, WA4 2QH
Tel: 01925-268417 **Fax:** 01925-604861
E-mail: steven-hughes@wireclothsales.co.uk
Website: http://www.wireclothsales.co.uk
Directors: S. Hughes (MD)
Immediate Holding Company: WIRE CLOTH SALES & DEVELOPMENT LIMITED
Registration no: 01562420 **VAT No.:** GB 344 0419 81
Date established: 1981 **Turnover:** £500,000 - £1m
No.of Employees: 1 - 10 **Product Groups:** 35, 42, 45, 66

Date of Accounts	Jun 12	Jun 11	Jun 10
Working Capital	-4	2	3
Fixed Assets	15	16	20
Current Assets	142	90	108

Witt Gas Techniques Ltd
212 Europa Boulevard Westbrook, Warrington, WA5 7TN
Tel: 01925-234466 **Fax:** 01925-230055
E-mail: benning@wittgas.com
Website: http://www.wittgas.com
Directors: D. Benning (Fin), R. Benning (MD)
Ultimate Holding Company: WITT GMBH & CO HOLDING UND HANDELS KG (GERMANY)
Immediate Holding Company: WITT GAS TECHNIQUES LIMITED
Registration no: 01497766 **Date established:** 1980 **Turnover:** £1m - £2m
No.of Employees: 1 - 10 **Product Groups:** 30, 36, 37, 38, 39, 40, 42, 46

Date of Accounts	Mar 12	Mar 11	Mar 10
Working Capital	832	595	497
Fixed Assets	10	8	9
Current Assets	1m	816	845

Widnes

3 B Controls Ltd (Low Pressure Relief Valve Manufacturer)
Unit 4 Heron Business Park Tan House Lane, Widnes, WA8 0SW
Tel: 01928-567069 **Fax:** 01928-573069
E-mail: sales@3bcontrols.com
Website: http://www.3bcontrols.com
Directors: P. Horne (Dir)
Immediate Holding Company: 3B CONTROLS LTD
Registration no: 04653528 **Date established:** 2003
No.of Employees: 1 - 10 **Product Groups:** 36

Date of Accounts	Jun 10	Jun 09	Jun 08
Working Capital	25	36	26
Fixed Assets	30	19	15
Current Assets	265	190	188

A B M Ltd
Pitt Street, Widnes, WA8 0TG
Tel: 0151-420 2829 **Fax:** 0151-495 1689
E-mail: andrew_r@abm.ltd.uk
Website: http://www.abm.ltd.uk
Bank(s): National Westminster
Directors: A. Rogerson (Co Sec)
Managers: P. Ellens (Mgr)
Immediate Holding Company: A.B.M. LIMITED
Registration no: 01975736 **Date established:** 1986 **Turnover:** £1m - £2m
No.of Employees: 11 - 20 **Product Groups:** 37, 38, 44

Date of Accounts	Sep 11	Sep 10	Sep 09
Working Capital	152	109	129
Fixed Assets	3	6	9
Current Assets	446	324	272

Alchem Widnes Ltd
Unit 1 Shell Green Bennetts Lane, Widnes, WA8 0GW
Tel: 0151-420 3319 **Fax:** 0151-495 1688
E-mail: enquiries@alchemwidnes.com
Website: http://www.alchemwidnes.com
Bank(s): National Westminster Bank Plc
Directors: D. Parkins (Dir), L. Smedley (Fin)
Managers: R. Tunstall (Tech Serv Mgr)
Immediate Holding Company: ALCHEM WIDNES LIMITED
Registration no: 01266537 **Date established:** 1976
Turnover: £500,000 - £1m **No.of Employees:** 21 - 50
Product Groups: 52, 84

Date of Accounts	Sep 10	Sep 09	Sep 08
Sales Turnover	702	N/A	N/A
Pre Tax Profit/Loss	-247	N/A	N/A
Working Capital	-357	-120	-680
Fixed Assets	58	69	78
Current Assets	129	270	393
Current Liabilities	341	N/A	N/A

Atlantic Forklifts Ltd
Unit 2 Marshgate, Widnes, WA8 8UA
Tel: 0151-422 9192 **Fax:** 0151-257 7085
E-mail: info@atlanticforklifts.co.uk
Website: http://www.atlanticforklifts.co.uk
Directors: J. Gill (Sales), L. Whent (Co Sec)
Ultimate Holding Company: SERVACE LIMITED
Immediate Holding Company: ATLANTIC FORK LIFTS LIMITED
Registration no: 03594501 **Date established:** 1998
No.of Employees: 11 - 20 **Product Groups:** 35, 39, 45

Date of Accounts	Apr 11	Apr 10	Apr 09
Working Capital	427	383	414
Fixed Assets	403	382	435
Current Assets	1m	876	977

Bell Sons & Co. Ltd
Cheshire House Gorsey Lane, Widnes, WA8 0RP
Tel: 0151-422 1200 **Fax:** 0151-422 1211
E-mail: sales@bells-healthcare.com
Website: http://www.bells-healthcare.com
Bank(s): Barclays
Managers: D. Barlow (Comptroller)
Ultimate Holding Company: MARKSANS PHARMA LTD (INDIA)
Immediate Holding Company: BELL,SONS & CO.(DRUGGISTS)LIMITED
Registration no: 00351951 **Date established:** 1939
Turnover: £10m - £20m **No.of Employees:** 11 - 20 **Product Groups:** 31

Date of Accounts	Mar 12	Mar 11	Mar 10
Sales Turnover	14m	11m	11m
Pre Tax Profit/Loss	612	227	405
Working Capital	5m	4m	4m
Fixed Assets	3m	3m	3m
Current Assets	11m	9m	8m
Current Liabilities	685	492	451

Cellular Systems Ltd
Unit 1 Shell Green, Widnes, WA8 0GW
Tel: 0151-422 6464 **Fax:** 0151-495 1688
E-mail: enquiries@cellular-systems.co.uk
Website: http://www.cellular-systems.co.uk
Directors: J. Drinkwater (MD)
Managers: R. Kershaw (Personnel), L. Smedley (Fin Mgr), R. Tunstall (Tech Serv Mgr)
Immediate Holding Company: CELLULAR SYSTEMS LIMITED
Registration no: 03601537 **VAT No.:** GB 758 2166 11
Date established: 1998 **Turnover:** £10m - £20m
No.of Employees: 51 - 100 **Product Groups:** 37, 52, 80, 84, 85

Date of Accounts	Sep 10	Sep 09	Sep 08
Sales Turnover	13m	8m	N/A
Pre Tax Profit/Loss	1m	775	317
Working Capital	343	-368	185
Fixed Assets	3m	3m	412
Current Assets	5m	2m	2m
Current Liabilities	1m	1m	1m

Central Tool Hire
Unit 4 Alexandra Industrial Estate Moor Lane, Widnes, WA8 7AE
Tel: 0151-495 2364 **Fax:** 0151-422 0482
E-mail: sales@centraltoolhire.co.uk
Website: http://www.centraltoolhire.co.uk
Directors: K. Newport (MD)
Date established: 1995 **No.of Employees:** 1 - 10 **Product Groups:** 46

Cheshire Roof Trusses Ltd
Ditton Road, Widnes, WA8 0PA
Tel: 0151-495 2161 **Fax:** 0151-495 2163
E-mail: john@roof-trusses.co.uk
Website: http://www.roof-trusses.co.uk
Directors: I. Lewis (Dir), J. Lewis (Prop), J. Lewis (Dir)
Immediate Holding Company: CHESHIRE ROOF TRUSSES LIMITED
Registration no: 02351886 **Date established:** 1989
No.of Employees: 11 - 20 **Product Groups:** 25

Computer Junk Shop
10 Waterloo Road, Widnes, WA8 0PY
Tel: 0151-420 6671 **Fax:** 0151-420 6671
E-mail: info@computer-junkshop.co.uk
Website: http://www.computer-junkshop.co.uk
Directors: A. Couzens (Prop)
Turnover: Up to £250,000 **No.of Employees:** 1 - 10 **Product Groups:** 66

Computerised Engraving
10 Waterloo Road, Widnes, WA8 0PY
Tel: 0151-420 4590 **Fax:** 0151-495 1132
E-mail: info@computerisedengraving.com
Website: http://www.computerisedengraving.com
Directors: P. Houghton (Ptnr), K. Houghton (Ptnr), K. Hawton (Ptnr)
Managers: K. Hawton (Mgr)
VAT No.: GB 775 2360 19 **Turnover:** Up to £250,000
No.of Employees: 1 - 10 **Product Groups:** 25, 27, 28, 30, 35, 37, 39, 40, 48, 49, 65, 67, 68, 84

Conren Ltd
Ditton Road, Widnes, WA8 0PG
Tel: 0151-422 3999 **Fax:** 01246-856348
E-mail: info@conren.com
Website: http://www.conren.com
Bank(s): National Westminster Bank Plc

Directors: A. Collins (MD)
Ultimate Holding Company: VINCI SA (FRANCE)
Immediate Holding Company: CONREN LIMITED
Registration no: 01022699 **VAT No.:** GB 165 1030 03
Date established: 1971 **Turnover:** £250m - £500m
No.of Employees: 21 - 50 **Product Groups:** 29, 30, 31, 32, 33, 39, 52, 66, 85

Date of Accounts	Dec 11	Dec 10	Dec 09
Sales Turnover	5m	5m	4m
Pre Tax Profit/Loss	12	9	-260
Working Capital	-46	-108	-137
Fixed Assets	99	139	165
Current Assets	1m	1m	1m
Current Liabilities	485	410	303

Croda Europe Ltd
Foundry Lane, Widnes, WA8 8UB
Tel: 0151-423 3441 **Fax:** 0151-423 3441
E-mail: patrick.quinn@croda.com
Website: http://www.croda.com
Directors: P. Quinn (Fab)
Managers: D. Gratwick, H. Hine
Ultimate Holding Company: CRODA INTERNATIONAL PUBLIC LIMITED COMPANY
Immediate Holding Company: CRODA EUROPE LIMITED
Registration no: 00167236 **Date established:** 2020
No.of Employees: 51 - 100 **Product Groups:** 17, 20, 31, 32

Date of Accounts	Dec 11	Dec 10	Dec 09
Sales Turnover	585m	597m	566m
Pre Tax Profit/Loss	128m	22m	-37m
Working Capital	92m	118m	102m
Fixed Assets	141m	137m	99m
Current Assets	178m	217m	178m
Current Liabilities	40m	48m	41m

Delavan Ltd
Gorsey Lane, Widnes, WA8 0RJ
Tel: 0151-424 6821 **Fax:** 0151-495 1043
E-mail: dave.percival@goodrich.com
Website: http://www.delavan.co.uk
Bank(s): Barclays
Directors: D. Percival (MD), S. Geib (Fin)
Ultimate Holding Company: GOODRICH CORP (USA)
Immediate Holding Company: DELAVAN LIMITED
Registration no: 00745611 **VAT No.:** GB 294 8726 05
Date established: 1963 **Turnover:** £5m - £10m
No.of Employees: 51 - 100 **Product Groups:** 30, 36, 38, 40, 41

Date of Accounts	Dec 11	Dec 10	Dec 09
Sales Turnover	8m	7m	6m
Pre Tax Profit/Loss	2m	2m	793
Working Capital	16m	14m	12m
Fixed Assets	567	666	813
Current Assets	23m	20m	17m
Current Liabilities	814	635	360

Denca Controls Ltd
Waterloo Road, Widnes, WA8 0QR
Tel: 0151-257 9010 **Fax:** 0151-257 9020
E-mail: sales@denca.com
Website: http://www.denca.com
Directors: A. Brennan (Dir)
Managers: J. Bates (Buyer)
Immediate Holding Company: DENCA CONTROLS LIMITED
Registration no: 03078940 **Date established:** 1995 **Turnover:** £1m - £2m
No.of Employees: 21 - 50 **Product Groups:** 37, 38, 44, 85

Date of Accounts	Jul 11	Jul 10	Jul 09
Working Capital	795	736	682
Fixed Assets	3	5	10
Current Assets	1m	1m	949

Dieselprods Ltd
Finlan Road, Widnes, WA8 7RZ
Tel: 0151-495 1945 **Fax:** 0151-495 1908
E-mail: sales@dieselprods.ltd.uk
Website: http://www.dieselprods.ltd.uk
Directors: J. Meredith (Co Sec), T. Meredith (MD)
Immediate Holding Company: DIESELPRODS LIMITED
Registration no: 02295879 **VAT No.:** GB 483 6330 37
Date established: 1988 **Turnover:** £2m - £5m **No.of Employees:** 1 - 10
Product Groups: 34, 40, 68

Date of Accounts	Dec 11	Dec 10	Dec 09
Working Capital	73	70	68
Fixed Assets	30	15	7
Current Assets	832	950	721

Drivemebaby Ltd
16 Ash Priors, Widnes, WA8 4NH
Tel: 0151-420 0776 **Fax:** 0151-420 0776
E-mail: drivemebaby@hotmail.co.uk
Website: http://www.drivemebaby.com
Directors: L. Paulson (Dir)
Immediate Holding Company: DRIVEMEBABY LTD
Registration no: 06258692 **Date established:** 2007
Turnover: £250,000 - £500,000 **No.of Employees:** 1 - 10
Product Groups: 72

Date of Accounts	Nov 11	Nov 10	Nov 08
Working Capital	-69	-65	-32
Fixed Assets	54	70	51
Current Assets	24	31	18

Elg Haniel Metals Ltd (North West)
Ditton Road, Widnes, WA8 0PP
Tel: 0151-257 9203 **Fax:** 0151-257 9204
E-mail: info@elgwidnes.co.uk
Website: http://www.elghaniel.co.uk
Managers: P. Taylor (Mgr)
Ultimate Holding Company: FRANZ HANIEL & CIE GMBH (GERMANY)
Immediate Holding Company: E.L.G. HANIEL METALS LIMITED
Registration no: 01517971 **Date established:** 1980
No.of Employees: 1 - 10 **Product Groups:** 54, 66

Date of Accounts	Dec 11	Dec 10	Dec 09
Sales Turnover	333m	309m	182m
Pre Tax Profit/Loss	8m	10m	9m
Working Capital	-7m	-4m	268
Fixed Assets	28m	26m	26m
Current Assets	63m	92m	58m
Current Liabilities	3m	3m	2m

Feralco UK Ltd
Ditton Road, Widnes, WA8 0PH
Tel: 0151-802 2930 **Fax:** 0151-802 2999
E-mail: info.uk@feralco.com
Website: http://www.feralco.com
Bank(s): Barclays
Directors: S. Childs (MD)
Managers: S. Offlands (Fin Mgr), B. Lilley (Comm)
Ultimate Holding Company: FERALCO AB (SWEDEN)
Immediate Holding Company: FERALCO (UK) LIMITED
Registration no: 04052278 **VAT No.:** GB 768 0194 090 04
Date established: 2000 **Turnover:** £10m - £20m
No.of Employees: 11 - 20 **Product Groups:** 31, 32, 51, 81

Date of Accounts	Jun 12	Jun 11	Jun 10
Sales Turnover	18m	17m	17m
Pre Tax Profit/Loss	4m	5m	4m
Working Capital	554	183	-366
Fixed Assets	2m	2m	3m
Current Assets	7m	6m	5m
Current Liabilities	2m	1m	1m

Finecard International Ltd (t/a Ninja Corporation)
Topaz House Oldgate St Michaels Industrial Estate, Widnes, WA8 8TL
Tel: 0151-495 1677 **Fax:** 0151-495 1675
E-mail: admin@thepopupco.com
Website: http://www.theninjacorporation.co.uk
Directors: A. Brereton (Sales & Mktg), D. Baxter (MD)
Managers: A. Sillitoe (Ops Mgr), M. Thomson (Mktg Serv Mgr), N. Webster (), N. Webster
Ultimate Holding Company: Finecard International Ltd
Immediate Holding Company: FINECARD INTERNATIONAL LIMITED
Registration no: 01153857 **VAT No.:** GB 439 1845 28
Date established: 1973 **Turnover:** £5m - £10m **No.of Employees:** 1 - 10
Product Groups: 65

Date of Accounts	Mar 08	Mar 07	Mar 06
Working Capital	-192	-228	-68
Fixed Assets	465	472	479
Current Assets	1225	972	1351
Current Liabilities	1417	1200	1419
Total Share Capital	30	30	30

Finn Forest Ltd
Ditton Road, Widnes, WA8 0PG
Tel: 0151-552 8700 **Fax:** 0151-422 5201
E-mail: sales@finnforest.co.uk
Website: http://www.finnforest.co.uk
Directors: B. Crawley (Prop)
Managers: M. Lomas (Ops Mgr), M. Gerard (Ops Mgr), R. Kay (Sales Prom Mgr), B. Crawley (Mgr)
Immediate Holding Company: VINCI NHS PENSIONS LIMITED
Registration no: 01720295 **Date established:** 2002
No.of Employees: 101 - 250 **Product Groups:** 08, 25

Forward Chemicals Ltd
PO Box 12, Widnes, WA8 0RD
Tel: 0151-422 1000 **Fax:** 0151-422 1011
E-mail: salesandservice@forwardchem.com
Website: http://www.forwardchem.com
Bank(s): Barclays
Directors: J. Mosley (Fin), M. Doran (Sales), J. Moseley (Fin)
Managers: K. Dooley (Tech Serv Mgr), S. Jones (Purch Mgr), S. Garvie (Personnel)
Ultimate Holding Company: HALE GROUP LIMITED
Immediate Holding Company: FORWARD CHEMICALS LIMITED
Registration no: 01428569 **VAT No.:** GB 344 0633 79
Date established: 1979 **Turnover:** £2m - £5m **No.of Employees:** 51 - 100
Product Groups: 66

Date of Accounts	Dec 11	Dec 10	Dec 09
Sales Turnover	5m	5m	6m
Pre Tax Profit/Loss	244	416	236
Working Capital	2m	1m	1m
Fixed Assets	3m	2m	3m
Current Assets	3m	3m	3m
Current Liabilities	361	385	563

General Welding Supplies Ltd
GWS House 318 Hale Road, Widnes, WA8 8PX
Tel: 0151-420 6900 **Fax:** 0151-424 6728
E-mail: enquiries@generalwelding.co.uk
Website: http://www.generalwelding.co.uk
Directors: R. Twist (MD), S. Allen (MD)
Managers: M. Ward (Mktg Serv Mgr), V. Allen (Buyer)
Immediate Holding Company: GENERAL WELDING SUPPLIES (NORTH WEST) LIMITED
Registration no: 01630651 **VAT No.:** GB 373 9012 51
Date established: 1982 **Turnover:** £2m - £5m **No.of Employees:** 21 - 50
Product Groups: 24, 32, 34, 35, 37, 40

Date of Accounts	Jun 11	Jun 10	Jun 09
Working Capital	-382	-386	-402
Fixed Assets	709	664	722
Current Assets	1m	1m	863

Genlab Ltd
Tanhouse Lane, Widnes, WA8 0SR
Tel: 0151-424 5001 **Fax:** 0151-495 2197
E-mail: enquiries@genlab.co.uk
Website: http://www.genlab.co.uk
Directors: D. Crompton (Fin), B. Clarke (Tech Serv)
Managers: J. Campbell (Sales & Mktg Mg), L. Mullen (Purch Mgr)
Ultimate Holding Company: Bluetax Ltd
Registration no: 00763725 **VAT No.:** GB 151 7314 87
Date established: 1963 **Turnover:** £2m - £5m **No.of Employees:** 0
Product Groups: 26, 40, 42, 45, 48

Date of Accounts	Nov 09	Nov 08	Nov 07
Working Capital	563	510	512
Fixed Assets	69	80	77
Current Assets	867	988	950

A & A Glover Engineering Ltd
Moor Lane, Widnes, WA8 7AL
Tel: 0151-424 4015 **Fax:** 0151- 4952169
Directors: T. Conley (MD)
Immediate Holding Company: A & A GLOVER ENGINEERING LIMITED
Registration no: 01887417 **Date established:** 1985
Turnover: £20m - £50m **No.of Employees:** 1 - 10 **Product Groups:** 48

Date of Accounts	Mar 11	Mar 10	Mar 09
Working Capital	59	52	179
Fixed Assets	11	13	17
Current Assets	123	88	224

Hallmark Security
H B House Ditton Road, Widnes, WA8 0WS
Tel: 0151-257 9995 **Fax:** 0151-257 9996
E-mail: hallmarkengineer@aol.com
Website: http://www.hallmark-security.com
Directors: V. Lyon Bowes (Fin)
Immediate Holding Company: HALTON CONSTRUCTION & SURVEYING SERVICES LTD
Registration no: 04741004 **Date established:** 2003
No.of Employees: 1 - 10 **Product Groups:** 25, 26, 29, 30, 34, 35, 36, 37, 39, 45, 48, 49, 66, 67, 68, 74, 84

Date of Accounts	Mar 11	Mar 10	Mar 08
Current Assets	6	5	5

Highland Engineering Services Ltd
6 Humber Close, Widnes, WA8 3YY
Tel: 0151-420 1370 **Fax:** 0151-420 1370
E-mail: daveross50@aol.com
Directors: D. Ross (Dir), I. Ross (Dir)
Immediate Holding Company: HIGHLAND ENGINEERING SERVICES (UK) LIMITED
Registration no: 01738716 **Date established:** 1983
No.of Employees: 1 - 10 **Product Groups:** 20, 40, 41

Date of Accounts	Dec 09	Dec 08	Dec 07
Working Capital	-8	-4	-4
Fixed Assets	1	1	1
Current Assets	1	3	13

Initial Packaging Solutions Ltd
Unit 16 Off Everite Road Westgate, Widnes, WA8 8RA
Tel: 0151-420 4333 **Fax:** 0151-420 6066
E-mail: sales@initialpackaging.co.uk
Website: http://www.initialpackaging.co.uk
Bank(s): Yorkshire Bank PLC
Directors: K. Moulton (Dir), R. Croft (Sales)
Managers: K. Murphy (Prod Mgr), L. Childs, G. Croft (Purch Mgr)
Immediate Holding Company: INITIAL PACKAGING SOLUTIONS LIMITED
Registration no: 02133782 **Date established:** 1987
No.of Employees: 11 - 20 **Product Groups:** 24, 27, 30

Date of Accounts	Oct 11	Oct 10	Oct 09
Sales Turnover	10m	N/A	N/A
Pre Tax Profit/Loss	546	N/A	N/A
Working Capital	702	572	442
Fixed Assets	335	319	316
Current Assets	4m	3m	2m
Current Liabilities	2m	27	11

Keytrak Lock & Safe Company
Unit 1 Heron Business Park Tanhouse Lane, Widnes, WA8 0SW
Tel: 0151-495 5740 **Fax:** 0844-669 1293
E-mail: sales@keytrak.co.uk
Website: http://www.keytrak4security.co.uk
Directors: C. Davies (Ptnr)
Registration no: 07530640 **Turnover:** £1m - £2m
No.of Employees: 1 - 10 **Product Groups:** 22, 23, 24, 25, 26, 27, 30, 33, 35, 36, 37, 38, 39, 40, 41, 42, 44, 48, 49, 52, 63, 65, 66, 67, 68, 81, 83

Klaruw R M S Ltd
PO Box 41, Widnes, WA8 0PF
Tel: 0151-420 7377 **Fax:** 0151-495 2295
E-mail: pb-mason@klaruw.co.uk
Website: http://www.klaruw.co.uk
Managers: G. Mcghee (Contracts Mgr)
Ultimate Holding Company: BELROUTE CVA (BELGIUM)
Immediate Holding Company: KLARUW R.M.S. LIMITED
Registration no: 01975818 **VAT No.:** GB 428 8563 16
Date established: 1986 **Turnover:** £1m - £2m **No.of Employees:** 1 - 10
Product Groups: 38

Date of Accounts	Dec 11	Dec 10	Dec 09
Working Capital	-334	-233	-109
Fixed Assets	75	68	84
Current Assets	249	102	90
Current Liabilities	N/A	173	N/A

Locpac Ltd
Unit 24 Heron Business Park Tan House Lane, Widnes, WA8 0SW
Tel: 0151-423 2828 **Fax:** 0151-495 2630
E-mail: enquiries@locpac.co.uk
Website: http://www.locpac.co.uk
Directors: B. Loughnane (Dir)
Immediate Holding Company: LOCPAC LIMITED
Registration no: 07241914 **VAT No.:** GB 439 1472 41
Date established: 2010 **Turnover:** £500,000 - £1m
No.of Employees: 1 - 10 **Product Groups:** 27, 30, 42

Date of Accounts	Jun 12	Jun 11	Jun 10
Working Capital	3	1	N/A
Fixed Assets	24	25	N/A
Current Assets	94	98	N/A

Merseyside Coatings Ltd
Pickerings Road Halebank, Widnes, WA8 8XW
Tel: 0151-423 6166 **Fax:** 0151-495 1437
E-mail: info@mcl.eu.com
Website: http://www.mcl.eu.com
Bank(s): Barclays
Directors: C. Young (Co Sec), M. Young (MD)
Managers: P. Travis (Sales Admin)
Ultimate Holding Company: MERSEYSIDE COATINGS (HOLDINGS) LIMITED
Immediate Holding Company: MERSEYSIDE COATINGS LIMITED
Registration no: 03829797 **VAT No.:** GB 166 2535 59
Date established: 1999 **Turnover:** £5m - £10m
No.of Employees: 51 - 100 **Product Groups:** 48

Date of Accounts	May 10	May 09	May 08
Sales Turnover	6m	7m	6m
Pre Tax Profit/Loss	-177	358	251
Working Capital	-700	1m	1m
Fixed Assets	2m	3m	3m
Current Assets	3m	3m	3m
Current Liabilities	3m	918	1m

Nanson Brothers Plastering Contractors Ltd
259 Lunts Heath Road, Widnes, WA8 5BB
Tel: 0151-420 1567 **Fax:** 0151-420 5092
E-mail: baznanson@aol.com
Website: http://www.nansonbrothers.co.uk

see next page

Nanson Brothers Plastering Contractors Ltd - *Cont'd*

Directors: B. Nanson (Prop), T. Nanson (Dir)
Immediate Holding Company: WIDNES CORNERHOUSE LIMITED
Registration no: 04645469 **Date established:** 2003
No.of Employees: 21 - 50 **Product Groups:** 30, 45, 52, 80, 87

Date of Accounts	Mar 11	Mar 10	Mar 09
Working Capital	-220	-347	612
Fixed Assets	2m	2m	72
Current Assets	112	89	1m

Ninja Corporation Ltd

Topaz House St Michaels Industrial Estate, Widnes, WA8 8TL
Tel: 0151-495 1677 **Fax:** 0151-495 1675
E-mail: admin@thepopupco.com
Website: http://www.theninjacorporation.co.uk
Managers: M. Thompson
No.of Employees: 1 - 10 **Product Groups:** 65

P D M Group Ltd

Desoto Road Mersey Multimodal Gateway 3mg, Widnes, WA8 0PB
Tel: 0151-424 6731 **Fax:** 0151-495 1895
E-mail: aburdock@pdm-group.co.uk
Website: http://www.pdm-group.co.uk
Bank(s): Barclays
Directors: P. De Mulder (Dir), A. Birdock (Prop)
Managers: A. Burdock (Site Co-ord), A. Birdock (Ops Mgr), A. Burdock (Ops Mgr)
Immediate Holding Company: PDM GROUP LIMITED
Registration no: 04869050 **Date established:** 2003
No.of Employees: 51 - 100 **Product Groups:** 31

Pentagon Fine Chemicals Ltd

Lower Road Halebank, Widnes, WA8 8NS
Tel: 0151-424 3671 **Fax:** 0151-420 1301
E-mail: enquiries@pentagonchemicals.co.uk
Website: http://www.pentagonchemicals.co.uk
Bank(s): Barclays
Directors: A. Fullerton (Co Sec)
Managers: A. Laing
Ultimate Holding Company: CHEMTURA CORP (USA)
Immediate Holding Company: CHEMTURA UK LIMITED
Registration no: 02739552 **Date established:** 1992
Turnover: £20m - £50m **No.of Employees:** 51 - 100 **Product Groups:** 31

Date of Accounts	Dec 10	Dec 09	Dec 08
Sales Turnover	21m	14m	15m
Pre Tax Profit/Loss	8m	3m	4m
Working Capital	-12m	-17m	-20m
Current Assets	10m	11m	11m
Current Liabilities	2m	916	1m

Premier Tanker Services

2 Ditton Road, Widnes, WA8 0NE
Tel: 0151-495 9055 **Fax:** 0151-495 9066
E-mail: premiertanker@aol.com
Website: http://www.premiertankerservices.com
Directors: A. Cunliffe (Fin)
Ultimate Holding Company: GUSSION TRANSPORT LIMITED
Immediate Holding Company: PREMIER TANKER SERVICES LTD
Registration no: 04741004 **Date established:** 2003
Turnover: £250,000 - £500,000 **No.of Employees:** 1 - 10
Product Groups: 25, 29, 30, 34, 35, 36, 37, 38, 39, 40, 41, 42, 45, 48, 49, 52, 66, 67, 68, 84

Date of Accounts	Apr 08
Sales Turnover	283
Pre Tax Profit/Loss	86
Working Capital	-4
Fixed Assets	19
Current Assets	73
Current Liabilities	77
ROCE% (Return on Capital Employed)	574.0

J Preston & Son

Pitt Street, Widnes, WA8 0TG
Tel: 0151-424 3718 **Fax:** 0151-495 2360
E-mail: sales@prestonsofwidnes.co.uk
Website: http://www.prestonsofwidnes.co.uk
Bank(s): Yorkshire Bank PLC
Directors: N. Preston (Snr Part)
VAT No.: GB 152 6270 80 **Turnover:** £500,000 - £1m
No.of Employees: 11 - 20 **Product Groups:** 36, 48

Qualitank Services Ltd

Harrison Street, Widnes, WA8 8TN
Tel: 0151-495 1116 **Fax:** 0151-424 6842
E-mail: info@qualitank.co.uk
Website: http://qualitank.co.uk
Directors: S. Darnell (MD)
Immediate Holding Company: QUALITANK SERVICES LIMITED
Registration no: 02472321 **Date established:** 1990
No.of Employees: 1 - 10 **Product Groups:** 29, 30, 35, 39, 42, 45, 48, 66, 72, 76

Date of Accounts	Mar 12	Mar 11	Mar 10
Working Capital	244	216	207
Fixed Assets	1m	1m	1m
Current Assets	360	367	383

Quikshift Racing

Unit 10 Bold Industrial Estate Lunts Heath Road, Widnes, WA8 5RZ
Tel: 0151-420 3636
E-mail: enquiries@quikshiftracing.co.uk
Website: http://www.quikshiftracing.co.uk
Directors: R. Moss (Prop)
No.of Employees: 1 - 10 **Product Groups:** 38, 42

S I P Building Systems Ltd

Unit 2 Express Industrial Estate Turnall Road, Widnes, WA8 8RB
Tel: 0151-420 1404 **Fax:** 08702-248041
E-mail: sales@sipbuildingsystems.co.uk
Website: http://www.sipbuildingsystems.co.uk
Directors: L. Nixon (MD), P. Hannah (Co Sec)
Immediate Holding Company: SIP BUILDING SYSTEMS LIMITED
Registration no: 05308155 **Date established:** 2004
No.of Employees: 11 - 20 **Product Groups:** 25, 52, 66, 84

Date of Accounts	Mar 11	Mar 10	Mar 09
Working Capital	592	639	21
Fixed Assets	261	310	371
Current Assets	1m	1m	704

Scaffolding-Direct (MegaTrade Store)

Delta House, Shellgreen Estate Gorsey Lane, Widnes, WA8 0YZ
Tel: 0151-420 8208 **Fax:** 0151-420 6206
E-mail: info@scaffolding-direct.co.uk
Website: http://www.scaffolding-direct.co.uk
Registration no: 04194462 **Turnover:** £2m - £5m
No.of Employees: 1 - 10 **Product Groups:** 25, 35, 36, 39, 40, 45, 48, 52, 66, 83, 86

Severn Unival Ltd

Unit 2 Catalyst Industrial Estate Waterloo Road, Widnes, WA8 0WG
Tel: 0151-257 7227 **Fax:** 0151-257 7223
E-mail: sales@severnunival.com
Website: http://www.severnunival.com
Managers: K. Mayers (Sales Admin)
Ultimate Holding Company: SEVERN GLOCON GROUP PLC
Immediate Holding Company: SEVERN UNIVAL LIMITED
Registration no: 01564220 **Date established:** 1981
No.of Employees: 11 - 20 **Product Groups:** 36, 37, 38

Date of Accounts	Dec 11	Dec 10	Dec 09
Sales Turnover	18m	16m	18m
Pre Tax Profit/Loss	2m	2m	2m
Working Capital	4m	2m	3m
Fixed Assets	428	446	421
Current Assets	8m	5m	6m
Current Liabilities	2m	849	1m

Shepherd Widnes Ltd

Moss Bank Road, Widnes, WA8 0RU
Tel: 0151-424 9156 **Fax:** 0151-424 3539
E-mail: sales@shepwidnes.co.uk
Website: http://www.shepherdwidnes.com
Directors: J. Shepherd (MD)
Managers: G. Jones (Comptroller)
Ultimate Holding Company: THE SHEPHARD CHEMICAL COMPANY (USA)
Immediate Holding Company: SHEPHERD WIDNES LTD
Registration no: FC018633 **Date established:** 1995
Turnover: £20m - £50m **No.of Employees:** 21 - 50 **Product Groups:** 31, 32, 34, 66

Date of Accounts	Dec 11	Dec 10	Dec 09
Sales Turnover	25m	33m	22m
Pre Tax Profit/Loss	-2m	-598	-1m
Working Capital	5m	4m	3m
Fixed Assets	5m	4m	4m
Current Assets	9m	10m	8m
Current Liabilities	220	1m	820

Sorex Ltd

Oldgate, Widnes, WA8 8TJ
Tel: 0151-424 4328 **Fax:** 0151-495 1163
E-mail: info@sorexinternational.com
Website: http://www.sorex.com
Directors: R. Johnson (MD), S. Price (Dir), R. Hunt (Fin), N. May (Ch)
Managers: T. Loftrs (I.T. Exec), S. Wilson (Comm), M. Flynn (Product), R. Smith, K. Roughley (Sales Admin)
Ultimate Holding Company: FP051950
Immediate Holding Company: SOREX LIMITED
Registration no: 00469788 **VAT No.:** GB 673 4949 90
Date established: 1949 **Turnover:** £10m - £20m
No.of Employees: 51 - 100 **Product Groups:** 31, 32, 41

Date of Accounts	Dec 09	Dec 08	Dec 07
Sales Turnover	12m	18m	16m
Pre Tax Profit/Loss	-2m	869	1m
Working Capital	5m	3m	2m
Fixed Assets	6	3m	4m
Current Assets	5m	6m	7m
Current Liabilities	202	2m	1m

Sorsky Ltd

Yeoward House Dennis Road, Tanhouse Estate, Widnes, WA8 0SF
Tel: 0151-257 2222 **Fax:** 0151-257 2233
E-mail: jonathan.holt@sorsky.com
Website: http://www.sorsky.com
Directors: J. Holt (Dir), T. Heaton (MD)
Managers: K. Hogg (Sales Prom Mgr)
Ultimate Holding Company: 00631023
Immediate Holding Company: SORSKY LIMITED
Registration no: 00545534 **VAT No.:** GB 166 8470 31
Date established: 1955 **Turnover:** £5m - £10m **No.of Employees:** 21 - 50
Product Groups: 40, 63

Date of Accounts	Sep 09	Sep 08	Sep 07
Sales Turnover	9m	N/A	9m
Pre Tax Profit/Loss	69	10	20
Working Capital	274	180	142
Fixed Assets	399	461	507
Current Assets	4m	4m	4m
Current Liabilities	916	2m	571

Sovereign Cleaning & Hygiene Ltd

Brendon House Victoria Square, Widnes, WA8 6AD
Tel: 0151-257 2703 **Fax:** 0151-257 2710
E-mail: enquiries@sovereigncleaning.co.uk
Website: http://www.sovereigncleaning.co.uk
Registration no: 05549493 **Product Groups:** 52

Date of Accounts	Aug 07	Aug 06
Working Capital	12	7
Fixed Assets	9	2
Current Assets	38	21
Current Liabilities	25	14

Travis Perkins plc

Pickerings Road Halebank, Widnes, WA8 8XE
Tel: 0151-424 1444 **Fax:** 0151-424 7770
E-mail: martin.maxfield@travisperkins.co.uk
Website: http://www.travisperkins.co.uk
Managers: M. Maxfield (Mgr)
Immediate Holding Company: TRAVIS PERKINS PLC
Registration no: 00824821 **Date established:** 1964
No.of Employees: 1 - 10 **Product Groups:** 66

Date of Accounts	Dec 11	Dec 10	Dec 09
Sales Turnover	4779m	3153m	2931m
Pre Tax Profit/Loss	270m	197m	213m
Working Capital	133m	159m	248m
Fixed Assets	2771m	2749m	2108m
Current Assets	1421m	1329m	1035m
Current Liabilities	473m	412m	109m

Tudor Wrought Iron

Unit 25 St Michaels Industrial Estate, Widnes, WA8 8TL
Tel: 0151-420 3488
E-mail: steve@tudorwroughtiron.com
Website: http://www.tudorwroughtiron.com
Directors: L. Baines (Fin), S. Baines (MD)
Immediate Holding Company: TUDOR WROUGHT IRON LIMITED
Registration no: 04692336 **Date established:** 2003
No.of Employees: 1 - 10 **Product Groups:** 26, 35

Date of Accounts	Mar 07	Mar 06	Mar 05
Working Capital	-2	-4	-1
Fixed Assets	6	9	3
Current Assets	8	8	8
Current Liabilities	10	12	9

Veolia Ltd

Ditton Road, Widnes, WA8 0TH
Tel: 0151-424 5613 **Fax:** 0151-420 4504
E-mail: info@veolia.co.uk
Website: http://www.veolia.co.uk
Managers: R. Marsden (Mgr)
Immediate Holding Company: G.K.L. MANLEC LIMITED
Registration no: 01893151 **VAT No.:** GB 352 1129 90
Date established: 1978 **Turnover:** Up to £250,000
No.of Employees: 21 - 50 **Product Groups:** 54

Date of Accounts	Mar 94	Mar 93	Mar 92
Sales Turnover	126	163	153
Pre Tax Profit/Loss	-8	-41	7
Working Capital	-47	-42	N/A
Fixed Assets	15	20	13
Current Assets	36	57	57

Vivelle (U.K.) Ltd

Victoria House Croft Street, Widnes, WA8 0NQ
Tel: 0151-423 6273 **Fax:** 0151-495 1438
E-mail: vivelle@globalnet.co.uk
Website: http://www.vivelle.co.uk
Directors: C. Knight (MD)
Ultimate Holding Company: VIVELLE GMBH (GERMANY)
Immediate Holding Company: Vivelle GmbH (Germany)
Registration no: 01848761 **Date established:** 1984
Turnover: £500,000 - £1m **No.of Employees:** 1 - 10 **Product Groups:** 23, 27, 30, 49

Date of Accounts	Mar 06
Working Capital	25
Fixed Assets	23
Current Assets	156
Current Liabilities	130
Total Share Capital	1

Widnes Galvanising Ltd

Unit 2-3 Fairway Trading Park Ditton Road, Widnes, WA8 0NZ
Tel: 0151-495 1939 **Fax:** 0151-495 1956
Directors: N. Garratt (Fin)
Immediate Holding Company: WIDNES GALVANISING LIMITED
Registration no: 02206443 **Date established:** 1987
No.of Employees: 21 - 50 **Product Groups:** 46, 48

Date of Accounts	Jun 11	Jun 10	Jun 09
Working Capital	689	559	498
Fixed Assets	745	788	754
Current Assets	2m	1m	1m
Current Liabilities	N/A	6	N/A

Windes Car Centre

Moor Lane, Widnes, WA8 7AL
Tel: 0151-420 2000 **Fax:** 0151-495 1382
E-mail: gould@widnesnissan.com
Website: http://www.windesnissan.com
Directors: P. Griffies (Co Sec), J. Leach (Dir), P. Leach (Dir), C. Gould (Dir), J. Leech (MD)
Managers: K. Bramwell (I.T. Exec), D. Carr (Mktg Serv Mgr), C. Jones (Sales Prom Mgr), C. Gould (Mgr)
Immediate Holding Company: WIDNES CAR CENTRE LIMITED
Registration no: 02077711 **Date established:** 1986
Turnover: £20m - £50m **No.of Employees:** 51 - 100 **Product Groups:** 39

Date of Accounts	Dec 09	Dec 08	Dec 07
Sales Turnover	30m	31m	32m
Pre Tax Profit/Loss	-17	-80	94
Working Capital	1m	2m	1m
Fixed Assets	118	123	145
Current Assets	4m	5m	4m
Current Liabilities	480	528	614

Wilmslow

A B Supplies Ltd

130 Wilmslow Road Handforth, Wilmslow, SK9 3LQ
Tel: 01625-540023 **Fax:** 01625-526074
Website: http://www.ab-supplies.com
Directors: A. Topping (MD)
Immediate Holding Company: A B SUPPLIES LIMITED
Registration no: 03086866 **Date established:** 1995
No.of Employees: 11 - 20 **Product Groups:** 38, 42

Date of Accounts	Aug 09	Aug 08	Aug 07
Working Capital	176	136	110
Fixed Assets	51	52	68
Current Assets	393	557	466

A V Technology Ltd

Avtec House Stanley Green Trading Estate Arkle Avenue, Handforth, Wilmslow, SK9 3RW
Tel: 0161-486 3737 **Fax:** 0161-486 3747
E-mail: stevemottershead@avtechnology.co.uk
Website: http://www.avtechnology.co.uk
Directors: J. Chappell (Dir), S. Mottershead (MD)
Managers: J. Kewley
Immediate Holding Company: A V TECHNOLOGY LIMITED
Registration no: 01829338 **Date established:** 1984 **Turnover:** £2m - £5m
No.of Employees: 51 - 100 **Product Groups:** 84

Date of Accounts	Dec 11	Dec 10	Dec 09
Working Capital	546	361	533
Fixed Assets	383	354	130
Current Assets	1m	1m	1m
Current Liabilities	N/A	25	N/A

C I Research
Alderley House Alderley Road, Wilmslow, SK9 1AT
Tel: 01625-628000 **Fax:** 01625-628001
E-mail: theteam@ci-research.com
Website: http://www.ci-research.com
Bank(s): National Westminster Bank Plc
Directors: C. Auton (MD), I. Font (Fin)
Managers: G. Hodgson, R. Walker
Ultimate Holding Company: CIRL HOLDINGS LIMITED
Immediate Holding Company: CUSTOMER INSIGHT LIMITED
Registration no: 04290656 **VAT No.:** GB 638 9291 92
Date established: 2001 **Turnover:** £500,000 - £1m
No.of Employees: 21 - 50 **Product Groups:** 81

Chemquest
Summerfield Village Centre Dean Row Road, Wilmslow, SK9 2TA
Tel: 01625-528808 **Fax:** 01625-527557
E-mail: enquiries@chemquest.co.uk
Website: http://www.chemquest.co.uk
Directors: G. Hayes (Fin), Y. Hayes (MD)
Ultimate Holding Company: DEAN PROPERTY GROUP LIMITED
Immediate Holding Company: CHEMQUEST LIMITED
Registration no: 03096893 **Date established:** 1995 **Turnover:** £2m - £5m
No.of Employees: 1 - 10 **Product Groups:** 61

Date of Accounts	Sep 11	Sep 10	Sep 09
Working Capital	64	46	63
Fixed Assets	2	2	2
Current Assets	407	396	300

Corcoran Chemicals Ltd
Oak House Oak Close, Wilmslow, SK9 6DF
Tel: 01625-532731 **Fax:** 01625-539096
E-mail: john@corcoranchemicals.com
Website: http://www.corcoranchemicals.com
Directors: J. Reade (Fin)
Immediate Holding Company: CORCORAN CHEMICALS LIMITED
Registration no: 01246418 **Date established:** 1976
No.of Employees: 1 - 10 **Product Groups:** 31

Date of Accounts	Dec 11	Dec 10	Dec 09
Working Capital	454	445	471
Fixed Assets	37	28	30
Current Assets	2m	1m	1m
Current Liabilities	N/A	N/A	30

Davies Industrial Doors Ltd
32 Bramley Close, Wilmslow, SK9 6EP
Tel: 01625-529819 **Fax:** 01625-522588
E-mail: bendavis777@btinternet.com
Directors: S. Davies (Fin), B. Davies (MD)
Immediate Holding Company: DAVIES INDUSTRIAL DOORS LIMITED
Registration no: 04745352 **Date established:** 2003
Turnover: Up to £250,000 **No.of Employees:** 1 - 10 **Product Groups:** 26, 35

Date of Accounts	Jun 11	Jun 10	Jun 09
Sales Turnover	N/A	64	N/A
Working Capital	8	14	17
Fixed Assets	5	5	7
Current Assets	18	30	29

Didsbury Engineering Ltd
Unit 1b Lower Meadow Road Brooke Park, Handforth, Wilmslow, SK9 3LP
Tel: 0161-486 2200 **Fax:** 0161-486 2211
E-mail: sales@didsbury.com
Website: http://www.didsbury.com
Bank(s): Royal Bank of Scotland, Nottingham
Directors: M. Bailey (MD)
Managers: G. Kurshaw (Tech Serv Mgr), J. Cannings (Comptroller), P. Reeve (Buyer)
Ultimate Holding Company: DIDSBURY VENTURES LIMITED
Immediate Holding Company: DIDSBURY ENGINEERING CO.LIMITED
Registration no: 00371191 **Date established:** 1941 **Turnover:** £5m - £10m
No.of Employees: 21 - 50 **Product Groups:** 45, 48

Date of Accounts	Jan 12	Jan 11	Jan 10
Sales Turnover	5m	4m	4m
Pre Tax Profit/Loss	1m	602	641
Working Capital	2m	2m	2m
Fixed Assets	76	43	67
Current Assets	3m	3m	3m
Current Liabilities	588	414	415

E C F Group
Sandfield House Water Lane, Wilmslow, SK9 5AR
Tel: 01625-549652 **Fax:** 01625-549518
E-mail: lbaker@ecfplc.com
Website: http://www.ecfgroup.co.uk
Directors: B. Cartwright (Sales)
Ultimate Holding Company: MANX FINANCIAL GROUP PLC (ISLE OF MAN)
Immediate Holding Company: ECF ASSET FINANCE PLC
Registration no: 02615535 **Date established:** 1991
Turnover: £500,000 - £1m **No.of Employees:** 11 - 20 **Product Groups:** 82

Date of Accounts	Dec 10	Dec 09	Dec 08
Sales Turnover	2m	3m	3m
Pre Tax Profit/Loss	2m	-4m	265
Working Capital	-175	16m	18m
Fixed Assets	64	129	463
Current Assets	69	18m	20m
Current Liabilities	214	582	406

Four Seasons Healthcare plc
Emerson Court Alderley Road, Wilmslow, SK9 1NX
Tel: 01625-417800 **Fax:** 01625-417827
E-mail: info@fshc.co.uk
Website: http://www.fshc.co.uk
Directors: B. Taberner (Fin), P. Buckle (Pers)
Managers: P. Boden (Sales Admin), L. Summers, S. Roberts, A. Hamilton (Tech Serv Mgr)
Ultimate Holding Company: FSHC (GUERNSEY) HOLDINGS LTD
Immediate Holding Company: FOUR SEASONS HEALTH CARE LIMITED
Registration no: 05165301 **Date established:** 2004
Turnover: £250m - £500m **No.of Employees:** 11 - 20 **Product Groups:** 88

Date of Accounts	Dec 11	Dec 10	Dec 09
Sales Turnover	N/A	479m	461m
Pre Tax Profit/Loss	8m	-9m	928
Working Capital	-179m	89m	79m
Fixed Assets	367m	239m	248m
Current Assets	226m	139m	177m
Current Liabilities	111m	37m	60m

Hawthorn Group
Courthill House 60 Water Lane, Wilmslow, SK9 5AJ
Tel: 01625-419532
E-mail: power@hawthorn-group.co.uk
Website: http://www.hawthorn-group.co.uk
Directors: P. Wrigley (Prop)
Immediate Holding Company: CHEAPER CURRENCIES.COM LIMITED
Date established: 2003 **Turnover:** Up to £250,000
No.of Employees: 1 - 10 **Product Groups:** 80

Date of Accounts	Jun 11	Jun 10	Jun 09
Working Capital	-158	878	838
Fixed Assets	1m	N/A	9
Current Assets	14	1m	1m

Idox
Alderley House Alderley Road, Wilmslow, SK9 1AT
Tel: 01625-628007 **Fax:** 01625-628001
E-mail: info@idoxgroup.com
Website: http://www.idox.com
Bank(s): Natwest
Directors: J. Phillips (MD)
Ultimate Holding Company: MXDATA HOLDINGS LIMITED
Immediate Holding Company: MXDATA - TECHNOLOGIES LIMITED
Registration no: 03966740 **VAT No.:** GB 638 9291 92
Date established: 2000 **Turnover:** £2m - £5m **No.of Employees:** 21 - 50
Product Groups: 44

Date of Accounts	May 11	May 10	May 09
Working Capital	876	177	-61
Fixed Assets	1	N/A	N/A
Current Assets	1m	513	129

Kids Unlimited (t/a Kids Unlimited)
1 Summerfield Village Centre Dean Row Road, Wilmslow, SK9 2TA
Tel: 01625-540883 **Fax:** 0845-365 2196
E-mail: summerfield.manager@kidsunlimited.co.uk
Website: http://www.kidsunlimited.co.uk
Bank(s): Lloyds TSB Bank plc
Managers: U. Krystek-Walton (Mgr), A. Brandwood-Green
Ultimate Holding Company: KIDSUNLIMITED GROUP LIMITED
Immediate Holding Company: KIDS OF WILMSLOW LIMITED
Registration no: 04210086 **Date established:** 2001
Turnover: £20m - £50m **No.of Employees:** 21 - 50 **Product Groups:** 86

Date of Accounts	Apr 11	Apr 10	Apr 09
Sales Turnover	N/A	35m	33m
Pre Tax Profit/Loss	N/A	2m	3m
Working Capital	-728	1m	-2m
Fixed Assets	31m	9m	8m
Current Assets	677	10m	7m
Current Liabilities	N/A	8m	7m

Konrad Chemicals
Manchester Road, Wilmslow, SK9 2JW
Tel: 01625-531581 **Fax:** 01625-529906
E-mail: konradchemicals@ntlworld.com
Directors: S. Wilson (Dir)
Turnover: £1m - £2m **No.of Employees:** 1 - 10 **Product Groups:** 32, 54, 66

Kronos Ltd
Barons Court Manchester Road, Wilmslow, SK9 1BQ
Tel: 01625-547200 **Fax:** 01625-533123
E-mail: kronos.sales.uk@nli-usa.com
Website: http://www.kronosww.com
Directors: G. Swalwell (Dir)
Managers: J. Kelly (Chief Mgr), J. Lees (Chief Acct)
Ultimate Holding Company: VALHI INC
Immediate Holding Company: KRONOS LIMITED
Registration no: 02442679 **Date established:** 1989
Turnover: £20m - £50m **No.of Employees:** 1 - 10 **Product Groups:** 31, 32

Date of Accounts	Dec 11	Dec 10	Dec 09
Sales Turnover	34m	28m	24m
Pre Tax Profit/Loss	4m	3m	939
Working Capital	15m	12m	10m
Fixed Assets	21	34	46
Current Assets	16m	13m	11m
Current Liabilities	2m	1m	860

Mcarthur Electrical
93 Hawthorn Street, Wilmslow, SK9 5EJ
Tel: 07765-048210 **Fax:** 01625-521429
E-mail: andy@mcarthurelectrical.com
Website: http://www.mcarthurelectrical.co.uk
Directors: A. Mcarthur (Prop)
Immediate Holding Company: MCARTHUR ELECTRICAL & DATA LIMITED
Registration no: 05436328 **Date established:** 2005
Turnover: Up to £250,000 **No.of Employees:** 1 - 10 **Product Groups:** 37, 52, 84

Robert S Maynard Ltd
PO Box 8, Wilmslow, SK9 5ES
Tel: 01625-524055 **Fax:** 01625-524584
E-mail: robert.s.maynard.ltd@dial.pipex.com
Website: http://www.robertsmaynard.com
Directors: S. Maynard (MD)
Immediate Holding Company: ROBERT S.MAYNARD LIMITED
Registration no: 00693046 **VAT No.:** GB 157 5490 41
Date established: 1961 **Turnover:** £1m - £2m **No.of Employees:** 1 - 10
Product Groups: 23, 40, 43, 66, 67

Date of Accounts	May 11	May 10	May 09
Working Capital	48	44	109
Fixed Assets	245	271	280
Current Assets	236	122	191

Momentum Activating Demand Ltd Momentum Worldwide
Stanley Court Stanley Green Business Park, Handforth, Wilmslow, SK9 3RL
Tel: 0161-486 7878 **Fax:** 0161-486 7999
E-mail: rob.gleave@momentum-uk.com
Website: http://www.ndi-momentum.com
Directors: R. Gleave (MD)
Ultimate Holding Company: INTERPUBLIC GROUP OF COMPANIES INC (USA)
Immediate Holding Company: MOMENTUM ACTIVATING DEMAND LIMITED
Registration no: 07949786 **Date established:** 2012
No.of Employees: 21 - 50 **Product Groups:** 30, 80, 81

Date of Accounts	Dec 11	Dec 10	Dec 09
Sales Turnover	28m	29m	23m
Pre Tax Profit/Loss	-5m	887	-837
Working Capital	6m	6m	4m
Fixed Assets	3m	11m	12m
Current Assets	18m	15m	11m
Current Liabilities	9m	7m	6m

Norcros Plc
Ladyfield House Station Road, Wilmslow, SK9 1BU
Tel: 01625-549010 **Fax:** 01625-549011
E-mail: info@norcros.com
Website: http://www.norcros.com
Directors: D. Hamilton (Dir), N. Kelsall (Fin)
Ultimate Holding Company: NORCROS PLC
Immediate Holding Company: NORCROS GROUP (HOLDINGS) LIMITED
Registration no: 00566694 **Date established:** 1956
Turnover: £75m - £125m **No.of Employees:** 1 - 10 **Product Groups:** 80

Date of Accounts	Mar 11	Mar 10	Mar 09
Sales Turnover	115m	103m	94m
Pre Tax Profit/Loss	11m	5m	18m
Working Capital	19m	7m	13m
Fixed Assets	174m	176m	182m
Current Assets	134m	112m	114m
Current Liabilities	17m	13m	11m

Royal London Mutual Insurance Society Ltd
Royal London House Alderley Road, Wilmslow, SK9 1PF
Tel: 08708-506070 **Fax:** 01625-605406
E-mail: admin@royal-london.co.uk
Website: http://www.royal-london.co.uk
Managers: M. Ghaznavi (Personnel), B. Oxford, S. Shone, B. Young
Immediate Holding Company: ROYAL LONDON MUTUAL INSURANCE SOCIETY,LIMITED(THE)
Registration no: 00099064 **Date established:** 2008
No.of Employees: 1501 & over **Product Groups:** 80

Date of Accounts	Dec 11	Dec 10	Dec 09
Pre Tax Profit/Loss	64m	232m	461m
Fixed Assets	34594m	30719m	27922m
Current Assets	3121m	2717m	3455m
Current Liabilities	5428m	2252m	30897m

Sales Point
75 Wilmslow Road Handforth, Wilmslow, SK9 3EN
Tel: 01625-525226 **Fax:** 01625-533307
E-mail: info@salespoint.co.uk
Website: http://www.salespoint.co.uk
Directors: A. Ward (Ptnr)
Date established: 2005 **Turnover:** Up to £250,000
No.of Employees: 1 - 10 **Product Groups:** 81

Therma Float Ltd
Beech Lane House Beech Lane, Wilmslow, SK9 5ER
Tel: 01625-251000 **Fax:** 01625-524584
E-mail: sales@robertsmaynard.com
Website: http://www.therma-foil.co.uk
Directors: M. Howard (Sales), S. Maynard (MD)
Registration no: 03476144 **VAT No.:** GB 707 7822 19
Date established: 1997 **No.of Employees:** 1 - 10 **Product Groups:** 30

Date of Accounts	Dec 03	Dec 02
Working Capital	7	1
Fixed Assets	1	N/A
Current Assets	8	15
Current Liabilities	1	14

Version One Ltd
Pentland House Village Way, Wilmslow, SK9 2GH
Tel: 01625-856500 **Fax:** 01625-856501
E-mail: info@versionone.co.uk
Website: http://www.versionone.co.uk
Directors: J. Buck (Dir), P. Gibson (Co Sec)
Ultimate Holding Company: REDAC HOLDINGS LTD (GUERNSEY)
Immediate Holding Company: VERSION ONE LIMITED
Registration no: 02443078 **Date established:** 1989 **Turnover:** £5m - £10m
No.of Employees: 21 - 50 **Product Groups:** 44

Date of Accounts	Mar 09	Feb 12	Feb 11
Sales Turnover	5m	5m	5m
Pre Tax Profit/Loss	1m	2m	2m
Working Capital	2m	6m	4m
Fixed Assets	97	79	91
Current Assets	4m	9m	7m
Current Liabilities	2m	3m	3m

Winsford

Advanced Medical Solutions Group plc
Premiere Park 33 Road One Winsford Industrial Estate, Winsford, CW7 3RT
Tel: 01606-863500 **Fax:** 01606-863600
E-mail: info@admedsol.com
Website: http://www.admedsol.com
Directors: M. Tavener (Fin)
Managers: K. Ellison (Purch Mgr), S. Coates (Tech Serv Mgr), R. Walton
Ultimate Holding Company: ADVANCED MEDICAL SOLUTIONS GROUP PLC
Immediate Holding Company: ADVANCED MEDICAL SOLUTIONS LIMITED
Registration no: 02666957 **VAT No.:** GB 636 555 12
Date established: 1991 **Turnover:** £20m - £50m
No.of Employees: 101 - 250 **Product Groups:** 85

Date of Accounts	Dec 11	Dec 10	Dec 09
Sales Turnover	22m	21m	19m
Pre Tax Profit/Loss	5m	3m	3m
Working Capital	12m	9m	8m
Fixed Assets	11m	10m	8m
Current Assets	16m	12m	12m
Current Liabilities	966	2m	2m

Ambassador Packaging Ltd
Road One Winsford Industrial Estate, Winsford, CW7 3QB
Tel: 01606-567000 **Fax:** 01606-567001
E-mail: ambassador@ambassador-antalis.co.uk
Website: http://www.ambassador-antalis.co.uk
Bank(s): HSBC, Poultry and Princes St, London EC2 2BX
Directors: F. Motamed (Tech Serv), G. Ladley (MD)
Managers: C. Stamper (Buyer), B. Rolfe (Personnel), S. McCue, K. Ladley (Mktg Serv Mgr)

see next page

Ambassador Packaging Ltd - *Cont'd*
Ultimate Holding Company: AEA INVESTORS LP (USA)
Immediate Holding Company: PREGIS PROTECTIVE PACKAGING LTD.
Registration no: 00104001 **Date established:** 2009
Turnover: £20m - £50m **No.of Employees:** 51 - 100 **Product Groups:** 25, 27, 30

Date of Accounts	Dec 10	Dec 09	Dec 08
Sales Turnover	26m	22m	24m
Pre Tax Profit/Loss	486	468	986
Working Capital	6m	5m	4m
Fixed Assets	3m	3m	3m
Current Assets	12m	10m	9m
Current Liabilities	1m	1m	1m

Britton Taco Ltd
20 Road One Winsford Industrial Estate, Winsford, CW7 3RD
Tel: 01606-593434 **Fax:** 01606-866436
E-mail: stephen.goodman@britton-group.com
Website: http://www.brittontaco.com
Bank(s): National Westminster Bank Plc
Directors: D. Dean (MD), P. Toby (Gen Sec), S. Goodman (Fin)
Managers: G. Stanley, P. Thompson (Tech Serv Mgr), L. Urwin (Personnel)
Ultimate Holding Company: BRAVO BIDCO LIMITED
Immediate Holding Company: BRITTON TACO LIMITED
Registration no: 02233869 **VAT No.:** GB 682 6224 26
Date established: 1988 **Turnover:** £75m - £125m
No.of Employees: 101 - 250 **Product Groups:** 30

Date of Accounts	Apr 11	Apr 10	Apr 09
Sales Turnover	85m	68m	65m
Pre Tax Profit/Loss	5m	2m	2m
Working Capital	3m	-52	-1m
Fixed Assets	14m	13m	14m
Current Assets	27m	21m	17m
Current Liabilities	8m	5m	7m

Cleaning Supplies 2 U (Ki Chem UK Ltd)
3 Wallace Court Road Three, Winsford Industrial Estate, Winsford, CW7 3PD
Tel: 0800-652 3118 **Fax:** 01606-552288
E-mail: info@cleaningsupplies2u.co.uk
Website: http://www.cleaningsupplies2u.co.uk
Directors: J. Hargreaves (Fin), J. Hargreaves (MD)
Immediate Holding Company: KI-CHEM UK LIMITED
Registration no: 03133147 **Date established:** 1995
Turnover: £500,000 - £1m **No.of Employees:** 1 - 10 **Product Groups:** 32, 52, 63, 64, 66

Date of Accounts	Nov 11	Nov 10	Nov 09
Working Capital	-138	-118	-95
Fixed Assets	10	11	16
Current Assets	27	27	29

Contour Showers Ltd
Siddorn Street, Winsford, CW7 2BA
Tel: 01606-592586 **Fax:** 01606-861260
E-mail: tim.robinson@contour-showers.co.uk
Website: http://www.contour-showers.co.uk
Directors: D. Whitehead (Dir)
Managers: M. Smith (Mktg Serv Mgr)
Ultimate Holding Company: ELFREED LTD
Immediate Holding Company: CONTOUR SHOWERS LIMITED
Registration no: 01347879 **Date established:** 1978 **Turnover:** £5m - £10m
No.of Employees: 51 - 100 **Product Groups:** 26, 30, 35, 36, 86

Date of Accounts	Jan 12	Jan 11	Jan 10
Sales Turnover	6m	5m	N/A
Pre Tax Profit/Loss	446	360	528
Working Capital	4m	3m	3m
Fixed Assets	1m	958	1m
Current Assets	5m	4m	4m
Current Liabilities	459	406	510

D S Services
10 Buckingham Drive, Winsford, CW7 1FA
Tel: 01606-551594 **Fax:** 01606-590860
E-mail: info@thirstbustersofwantage.co.uk
Website: http://www.thirstbustersofwantage.co.uk
Directors: K. Burns (Ptnr)
No.of Employees: 1 - 10 **Product Groups:** 35, 39, 45

Essential Cuisine Ltd
Browning Way Woodford Park Industrial Estate, Winsford, CW7 2RH
Tel: 01606-541490 **Fax:** 0870-050 1143
E-mail: alan@essentialcuisine.com
Website: http://www.essentialcuisine.com
Directors: A. Metcalf (Dir)
Immediate Holding Company: ESSENTIAL CUISINE LIMITED
Registration no: 03169326 **Date established:** 1996
No.of Employees: 21 - 50 **Product Groups:** 20

Date of Accounts	Jun 12	Jun 11	Jun 10
Working Capital	589	500	423
Fixed Assets	266	180	119
Current Assets	1m	1m	842

Flexfilm Ltd
Road One Winsford Industrial Estate, Winsford, CW7 3QE
Tel: 01606-550100 **Fax:** 01606-551111
E-mail: enquiries@flexfilm.co.uk
Website: http://www.flexfilm.co.uk
Directors: J. Hughes (Co Sec), J. Stanley (Dir)
Immediate Holding Company: FLEXFILM LIMITED
Registration no: 03379307 **Date established:** 1997
Turnover: £10m - £20m **No.of Employees:** 21 - 50 **Product Groups:** 30

Date of Accounts	Dec 11	Dec 10	Dec 09
Sales Turnover	14m	12m	10m
Pre Tax Profit/Loss	708	416	234
Working Capital	3m	2m	2m
Fixed Assets	1m	2m	2m
Current Assets	5m	5m	3m
Current Liabilities	587	341	199

Gardner Denver Nash UK
Road One Winsford Industrial Estate, Winsford, CW7 3PL
Tel: 01606-542400 **Fax:** 01606-542434
E-mail: sales@nashpumps.co.uk
Website: http://www.gdnash.com
Bank(s): HSBC, Manchester
Directors: M. Roughsedge (Dir)
Ultimate Holding Company: GD FIRST UK LTD
Immediate Holding Company: POWERED ACCESS PLATFORMS LTD
Registration no: 00256827 **VAT No.:** GB 159 6764 13
Turnover: £5m - £10m **No.of Employees:** 21 - 50 **Product Groups:** 40

Date of Accounts	Dec 07
Sales Turnover	960
Pre Tax Profit/Loss	150
Total Share Capital	150

Isys International
Meridian House Road One, Winsford Industrial Estate, Winsford, CW7 3QG
Tel: 08707-771130 **Fax:** 08707-061731
E-mail: jbetts@isys-int.com
Website: http://www.isys-int.com
Managers: G. Holland (Gen Contact), J. Betts, G. Holland (Mgr)
Immediate Holding Company: HOWARTH COMMUNICATIONS LIMITED
Registration no: 03036004 **Date established:** 1995 **Turnover:** £1m - £2m
No.of Employees: 1 - 10 **Product Groups:** 80

Date of Accounts	Jun 11	Jun 10	Jun 09
Working Capital	76	78	79
Fixed Assets	30	34	40
Current Assets	128	151	224

Iveco UK Ltd
Road One Winsford Industrial Estate, Winsford, CW7 3QP
Tel: 01606-541000 **Fax:** 01606-541126
E-mail: alan.coppin@iveco.com
Website: http://www.iveco.com
Bank(s): National Westminster Bank Plc
Directors: A. Coppin (MD)
Managers: D. Power (Mktg Serv Mgr), J. Clark (Fin Mgr)
Ultimate Holding Company: FORD
Registration no: 01975271 **Turnover:** £1m - £2m
No.of Employees: 101 - 250 **Product Groups:** 39, 40, 68

J D Doors
Nat Lane, Winsford, CW7 3BS
Tel: 01606-550529 **Fax:** 01606-552326
E-mail: richard@jddoors.co.uk
Directors: R. Gilbert (MD)
Immediate Holding Company: J. D. DOORS LIMITED
Registration no: 04554730 **Date established:** 2002
No.of Employees: 1 - 10 **Product Groups:** 26, 35

Date of Accounts	Dec 11	Dec 10	Dec 09
Working Capital	279	309	280
Fixed Assets	25	25	81
Current Assets	793	795	317

Jiffy Packaging Company Ltd
9 Road Four Winsford Industrial Estate, Winsford, CW7 3QR
Tel: 01606-867200 **Fax:** 01606-592634
E-mail: sales@jiffy.co.uk
Website: http://www.jiffy.co.uk
Bank(s): HSBC Bank plc
Directors: M. Weller (MD)
Ultimate Holding Company: AEA INVESTORS LP (USA)
Immediate Holding Company: JIFFY PACKAGING COMPANY LIMITED
Registration no: 00796167 **VAT No.:** GB 150 5834 77
Date established: 1964 **Turnover:** £10m - £20m
No.of Employees: 101 - 250 **Product Groups:** 27, 30

Date of Accounts	Dec 10	Dec 09	Dec 08
Sales Turnover	17m	15m	19m
Pre Tax Profit/Loss	-1m	-2m	-436
Working Capital	9m	10m	6m
Fixed Assets	9m	8m	8m
Current Assets	12m	14m	9m
Current Liabilities	1m	2m	2m

Milestone Services
8 Turnberry Close, Winsford, CW7 2SW
Tel: 01606-553519
E-mail: ian_milestone@hotmail.com
Directors: I. Milestone (Prop)
No.of Employees: 1 - 10 **Product Groups:** 38, 42

Collins Stewart & Minchem Ltd (a division of Amcol International Inc)
Weaver Valley Road, Winsford, CW7 3BU
Tel: 01606-868200 **Fax:** 01606-868268
E-mail: csm@csminchem.co.uk
Website: http://www.csminchem.co.uk
Directors: A. Newbold (Mkt Research), J. Waddicer (MD)
Ultimate Holding Company: AMCOL INTERNATIONAL CORP (USA)
Immediate Holding Company: AMCOL EUROPE LIMITED
Registration no: 02347184 **Date established:** 1989
Turnover: £20m - £50m **No.of Employees:** 51 - 100 **Product Groups:** 14, 17, 31, 32, 33, 48, 61, 66, 76, 77

Date of Accounts	Dec 07	Dec 06	Dec 05
Sales Turnover	23345	24548	23380
Pre Tax Profit/Loss	218	1352	2251
Working Capital	5232	8856	9515
Fixed Assets	12992	3195	3718
Current Assets	14057	12901	13634
Current Liabilities	8825	4045	4119
Total Share Capital	49	49	49
ROCE% (Return on Capital Employed)	1.2	11.2	17.0
ROT% (Return on Turnover)	0.9	5.5	9.6

Prismatape UK
Road One Winsford Industrial Estate, Winsford, CW7 3RW
Tel: 01606-596600 **Fax:** 01606-596611
E-mail: prismatape.uk@btconnect.com
Website: http://www.prismatape.com
Directors: T. Mangano (MD)
Immediate Holding Company: PRISMATAPE U.K. LIMITED
Registration no: 02647508 **Date established:** 1991
No.of Employees: 1 - 10 **Product Groups:** 38, 42

Date of Accounts	Feb 12	Feb 11	Feb 10
Working Capital	7	15	13
Fixed Assets	45	57	50
Current Assets	1m	971	888
Current Liabilities	N/A	N/A	357

S M S Mevac UK Ltd
Road Four Winsford Industrial Estate, Winsford, CW7 3RS
Tel: 01606-551421 **Fax:** 01606-553078
E-mail: mail@sms-mevac.co.uk
Website: http://www.sms-mevac.co.uk
Bank(s): National Westminster
Directors: C. Priday (MD)
Ultimate Holding Company: SMS DEMAG AG (GERMANY)
Immediate Holding Company: SMS MEVAC UK LIMITED
Registration no: 00542562 **VAT No.:** GB 000 5425 26
Date established: 1954 **Turnover:** £5m - £10m **No.of Employees:** 21 - 50
Product Groups: 84

Date of Accounts	Dec 11	Dec 10	Dec 09
Sales Turnover	7m	7m	10m
Pre Tax Profit/Loss	355	137	966
Working Capital	277	1m	1m
Fixed Assets	429	534	499
Current Assets	6m	7m	7m
Current Liabilities	5m	5m	6m

Sandersons T C M
Unit 4-5 Wallace Court Road Three, Winsford Industrial Estate, Winsford, CW7 3PD
Tel: 01606-550668
E-mail: paul.sandersonstcm@yahoo.co.uk
Website: http://www.sandersons-tcm.co.uk
Directors: P. Peacock (Ptnr)
No.of Employees: 1 - 10 **Product Groups:** 26, 35

Thermo Electrical
Ion Path Road Three, Winsford, CW7 3BX
Tel: 01606-548100 **Fax:** 01606-552588
Website: http://www.thermo.com
Directors: P. Sigsworth (Mkt Research)
Managers: A. Cliffe (Buyer)
Ultimate Holding Company: THERMO ELECTRON GROUP
Registration no: 02085582 **Date established:** 1984
Turnover: £20m - £50m **No.of Employees:** 51 - 100 **Product Groups:** 38, 47

Thermo Onix Ltd
Factory One Ion Path Road Three, Winsford Industrial Estate, Winsford, CW7 3GA
Tel: 01606-548700 **Fax:** 01606-548711
E-mail: eurosales@thermofisher.com
Website: http://www.thermo.com
Bank(s): Barclays, Crawley
Directors: A. Crawford (MD), P. Warburton (Mkt Research), N. Ward (Co Sec)
Immediate Holding Company: Onix Holdings Ltd
Registration no: 03284171 **Date established:** 1974
Turnover: £10m - £20m **No.of Employees:** 51 - 100 **Product Groups:** 38

Wachs UK
Units 4 & 5 Navigation Park, Road One, Winsford Industrial Estate, Winsford, CW7 3RL
Tel: 01606-861423 **Fax:** 01606-556364
E-mail: dravenscroft@ehwachs.com
Website: http://www.ehwachs.com
Ultimate Holding Company: E.H. Wachs Co. (USA)
Immediate Holding Company: E.H. Wachs
Registration no: 02728094 **Product Groups:** 38, 45, 46, 48, 54

Date of Accounts	Dec 07
Working Capital	617
Fixed Assets	48
Current Assets	709
Current Liabilities	92
Total Share Capital	1

Winsford Sawmills Ltd
Smoke Hall Lane Industrial Estate Smoke Hall Lane, Winsford, CW7 3BE
Tel: 01606-555500 **Fax:** 01606-555511
E-mail: mail@winsfordsawmills.co.uk
Website: http://www.winsfordsawmills.co.uk
Bank(s): Bank of Scotland
Directors: A. Massey (Sales), M. Smee (Prop), S. Williams (Fin)
Managers: I. Mcfarlane (Sales Admin), J. Dilger (I.T. Exec), R. Weighill (Mktg Serv Mgr)
Immediate Holding Company: Smee Holdings Ltd
Registration no: 02733662 **Date established:** 1992
Turnover: £10m - £20m **No.of Employees:** 21 - 50 **Product Groups:** 25, 39, 48, 66

CLEVELAND

Billingham

B & S Rentals Ltd
Unit 9b Royce Avenue, Billingham, TS23 4BX
Tel: 01642-371025 **Fax:** 01642-563821
Website: http://www.bs-forklifts.co.uk
Directors: J. Gaynor (Co Sec)
Managers: S. Young (Chief Mgr), A. Robinson (Sales Prom Mgr), S. Robinson, K. Williams (Sales Prom Mgr)
Immediate Holding Company: B & S (RENTALS) LIMITED
Registration no: 02688951 **Date established:** 1992
No.of Employees: 21 - 50 **Product Groups:** 35, 39, 45

Date of Accounts	Sep 11	Sep 10	Sep 09
Working Capital	-111	-160	-189
Fixed Assets	287	345	349
Current Assets	287	141	184

Billingham Press Ltd
155 Central Avenue, Billingham, TS23 1LF
Tel: 01642-550067 **Fax:** 01642-550957
E-mail: info@billinghampress.co.uk
Website: http://www.billinghampress.co.uk
Bank(s): Barclays
Directors: I. Dodds (MD)
Immediate Holding Company: BILLINGHAM PRESS,LIMITED
Registration no: 00375599 **Date established:** 1942 **Turnover:** £1m - £2m
No.of Employees: 11 - 20 **Product Groups:** 28, 80

Date of Accounts	Dec 11	Dec 10	Dec 09
Working Capital	101	143	168
Fixed Assets	666	784	901
Current Assets	396	332	379

Doncasters Paralloy Ltd
Paralloy House Nuffield Road, Cowpen Lane Industrial Estate, Billingham, TS23 4DA
Tel: 01642-370686 **Fax:** 01642-564811
E-mail: paralloysales@doncasters.com
Website: http://www.doncasters.com
Bank(s): National Westminster, Birmingham City Office
Directors: R. Farnworth (Fin), H. Jackson (Co Sec)
Managers: D. Vaughan (Tech Serv Mgr), R. Sykes (Purch Mgr), N. Halliday (Personnel)
Immediate Holding Company: DONCASTERS LTD
Registration no: 00260752 **VAT No.:** GB 389 1553 14
Date established: 1954 **Turnover:** £20m - £50m
No.of Employees: 101 - 250 **Product Groups:** 34, 40

Elland Steel
Building A The Grange Business Centre Belasis Avenue, Billingham, TS23 1LG
Tel: 01642-361256 **Fax:** 01642-555916
E-mail: northeast@ellandsteel.com
Website: http://www.ellandsteel.com
Managers: B. Paulett (Mgr)
Immediate Holding Company: JAYVEE BUILDING SERVICES LIMITED
Registration no: OC339997 **Date established:** 2009
No.of Employees: 1 - 10 **Product Groups:** 35

Date of Accounts	Jul 11	Jul 10
Working Capital	-0	N/A
Current Assets	2	3

Frutarom (UK) Ltd formerly H.E. Daniel Ltd
Belasis Ave, Billingham, TS23 1LQ
Tel: 01642-379900 **Fax:** 01642-379901
E-mail: fandf@uk.frutarom.com
Website: http://www.frutarom.com
Bank(s): Barclays
Directors: M. Gujral (MD)
Managers: N. Blanchard (Accounts), M. Copley (Comm), S. Ayles (Sales Prom Mgr), E. Reeves (Purch Mgr)
Ultimate Holding Company: ICC Industries Inc.
Immediate Holding Company: Frutarom Ltd
Registration no: 02628890 **VAT No.:** GB 596 2112 34
Turnover: £10m - £20m **No.of Employees:** 51 - 100 **Product Groups:** 20, 31, 32, 62, 66

Date of Accounts	Dec 09	Dec 08	Dec 07
Sales Turnover	36m	30m	24m
Pre Tax Profit/Loss	4m	3m	-473
Working Capital	5m	8m	-3m
Fixed Assets	30m	26m	27m
Current Assets	18m	16m	12m
Current Liabilities	4m	3m	2m

Glamal Engineering Ltd
Pegasus House Wynyard Avenue, Wynyard, Billingham, TS22 5TB
Tel: 01740-645040 **Fax:** 01642-565831
E-mail: sales@glamal.co.uk
Website: http://www.glamal.co.uk
Directors: N. Pentland (MD), A. Thompson (Sales), T. Thompson (Sales), P. Veitch (MD)
Managers: S. Hopes (Sales Prom Mgr), I. Giddings (Buyer), C. Mitchell (Sales Admin)
Ultimate Holding Company: LFF HOLDINGS LIMITED
Immediate Holding Company: GLAMAL ENGINEERING LIMITED
Registration no: 02166918 **VAT No.:** GB 257 5075 45
Date established: 1987 **Turnover:** £5m - £10m **No.of Employees:** 1 - 10
Product Groups: 36

Date of Accounts	Dec 11	Dec 10	Dec 09
Sales Turnover	33m	34m	30m
Pre Tax Profit/Loss	186	178	633
Working Capital	1m	1m	1m
Current Assets	10m	13m	5m
Current Liabilities	1m	448	1m

Hautin Tarpaulins Ltd
8b Royce Avenue, Billingham, TS23 4BX
Tel: 01642-370094 **Fax:** 01642-563813
E-mail: info@hautintarpaulins.com
Website: http://www.hautintarpaulins.com
Directors: B. Whitfield (Dir)
Immediate Holding Company: HAUTIN TARPAULINS LIMITED
Registration no: 05613799 **Date established:** 2005
No.of Employees: 1 - 10 **Product Groups:** 23, 24, 29, 30

Date of Accounts	Oct 11	Oct 10	Oct 09
Working Capital	-3	-13	10
Fixed Assets	29	20	24
Current Assets	57	57	113

Magnum Packaging
Haverton Hill Industrial Estate Haverton Hill, Billingham, TS23 1PZ
Tel: 01642-370044 **Fax:** 01642-373429
E-mail: info@magnumpackaging.co.uk
Website: http://www.magnumpackaging.co.uk
Directors: S. Younis (Fin), M. Younis (MD)
Immediate Holding Company: MAGNUM PACKAGING (N.E.) LIMITED
Registration no: 01764041 **Date established:** 1983 **Turnover:** £5m - £10m
No.of Employees: 21 - 50 **Product Groups:** 27, 30, 66

Date of Accounts	Mar 12	Mar 10	Mar 09
Sales Turnover	7m	10m	N/A
Pre Tax Profit/Loss	446	331	647
Working Capital	3m	1m	535
Fixed Assets	186	981	2m
Current Assets	4m	2m	2m
Current Liabilities	236	246	346

Mesh Supplies & Fabrications
Unit B2 Bentley Avenue Cowpen Lane Industrial Estate, Billingham, TS23 4BU
Tel: 01642-370777 **Fax:** 01642-371088
E-mail: info@meshsupplies.co.uk
Website: http://www.meshsupplies.co.uk
Directors: M. Stansfield (Prop)
Date established: 1991 **No.of Employees:** 1 - 10 **Product Groups:** 35

North East Truck & Van
Cowpen Bewley Road, Billingham, TS23 4EX
Tel: 01642-370555 **Fax:** 01642-370021
E-mail: a.mcdonald@netvltd.co.uk
Website: http://www.northeasttruckandvan.com
Directors: A. McDonald (MD), A. Nicholson (Fin), B. Beadnel (Ch)
Managers: A. Kidd (Sales Prom Mgr), A. Peat (I.T. Exec), M. Leahy (Mktg Serv Mgr)
Ultimate Holding Company: NORTH EAST TRUCK & VAN LIMITED
Immediate Holding Company: NORTH EAST TRUCK & VAN (IMMINGHAM) LIMITED
Registration no: 03201319 **VAT No.:** GB 602 2480 84
Date established: 1996 **No.of Employees:** 101 - 250 **Product Groups:** 68

P D Logistics
Cowpen Lane, Billingham, TS23 4DB
Tel: 01642-560456 **Fax:** 01642-564061
E-mail: frank.antropik@pdports.co.uk
Website: http://www.pdports.co.uk
Directors: F. Antropik (Prop)
Ultimate Holding Company: BROOKFIELD PORTS UK LTD
Immediate Holding Company: PD PORTCO LTD
Registration no: 01422772 **VAT No.:** GB 601 8534 63
No.of Employees: 1 - 10 **Product Groups:** 72, 76, 77

Date of Accounts	Jun 08	Jun 07	Jun 06
Working Capital	48144	43955	41486
Current Assets	55581	51019	47056
Current Liabilities	7437	7064	5570
Total Share Capital	4000	4000	4000

Geoffrey Robinson Ltd
Macklin Avenue Cowpen Lane Industrial Estate, Billingham, TS23 4ET
Tel: 01642-370500 **Fax:** 01642-370600
E-mail: enquiry@geoffreyrobinson.co.uk
Website: http://www.geoffreyrobinson.co.uk
Bank(s): Co-Operative Bank, Middlesborough
Directors: F. Sweeney (Fin), G. Robinson (MD), F. Sweeney (Fin)
Managers: A. Collinson (Sales Prom Mgr)
Immediate Holding Company: GEOFFREY ROBINSON LIMITED
Registration no: 01042638 **VAT No.:** GB 257 8930 16
Date established: 1972 **Turnover:** £10m - £20m
No.of Employees: 51 - 100 **Product Groups:** 52

Date of Accounts	Dec 11	Dec 10	Dec 09
Sales Turnover	10m	12m	16m
Pre Tax Profit/Loss	299	153	319
Working Capital	2m	2m	2m
Fixed Assets	2m	2m	2m
Current Assets	4m	4m	4m
Current Liabilities	1m	1m	1m

Speedy Asset Services
Unit A2 Bentley Avenue Cowpen Lane Industrial Estate, Billingham, TS23 4BU
Tel: 01642-457357 **Fax:** 01642-566032
E-mail: teeside@lgh.co.uk
Website: http://www.lgh.co.uk
Managers: G. Foster (District Mgr), G. Foster (Mgr)
Ultimate Holding Company: L.G.H. Group Ltd
Immediate Holding Company: LIFTING GEAR HIRE LIMITED
Registration no: 05566506 **Date established:** 2005
No.of Employees: 1 - 10 **Product Groups:** 35, 37, 38, 39, 45, 48, 83

Tomlinson Hall & Company Ltd (Factory)
Lagonda Road Cowpen Lane Industrial Estate, Billingham, TS23 4JA
Tel: 01642-379500 **Fax:** 01642-379502
E-mail: enquiries@tomlinson-hall.co.uk
Website: http://www.tomlinson-hall.co.uk
Bank(s): Barclays
Directors: T. Keville (MD), P. Dixon (Fin)
Immediate Holding Company: TOMLINSON,HALL & COMPANY LIMITED
Registration no: 00531097 **VAT No.:** GB 257 7679 03
Date established: 1954 **Turnover:** £2m - £5m **No.of Employees:** 21 - 50
Product Groups: 39, 40, 67

Date of Accounts	Mar 11	Mar 10	Mar 09
Working Capital	657	568	672
Fixed Assets	1m	1m	1m
Current Assets	1m	1m	1m

World Of Wrought Iron
1 Langton Avenue, Billingham, TS22 5DS
Tel: 01642-896013
E-mail: brian@worldofwroughtiron.com
Website: http://www.worldofwroughtiron.com
Directors: B. Fagan (Prop)
Date established: 1969 **No.of Employees:** 1 - 10 **Product Groups:** 26, 35

Guisborough

Euremica Ltd
Instrument House Morgan Drive, Guisborough, TS14 7DG
Tel: 01287-204020 **Fax:** 01287-204021
E-mail: sales@euremica.com
Website: http://www.euremica.com
Bank(s): Barclays, Guisborough
Directors: M. Baty (Ch), N. Linford (Fin)
Managers: J. Allen (Sales Prom Mgr)
Immediate Holding Company: EUREMICA LIMITED
Registration no: 00907523 **VAT No.:** GB 368 2052 51
Date established: 1967 **Turnover:** £1m - £2m **No.of Employees:** 21 - 50
Product Groups: 38

Date of Accounts	May 12	May 11	May 10
Working Capital	321	291	98
Fixed Assets	584	595	597
Current Assets	516	536	500

Guisborough Dental Laboratory
4 Redcar Road, Guisborough, TS14 6DB
Tel: 01287-635555 **Fax:** 01287-634902
Directors: D. Lambert (Prop)
Date established: 1978 **No.of Employees:** 11 - 20 **Product Groups:** 38, 67, 88

Hartlepool

A M I Exchangers Ltd Of Diesel Marine International
Apex Workshops Graythorp Industrial Estate, Hartlepool, TS25 2DF
Tel: 01429-860187 **Fax:** 01429-860673
E-mail: sales@ami-exchangers.co.uk
Website: http://www.ami-exchangers.co.uk
Bank(s): Barclays Bank Plc
Directors: J. Wiffen (MD), N. Welford (Sales), N. Welford (Sales)
Ultimate Holding Company: DIESEL MARINE INTERNATIONAL LIMITED
Immediate Holding Company: A M I EXCHANGERS LIMITED
Registration no: 02329014 **VAT No.:** GB 499 4067 90
Date established: 1988 **Turnover:** £2m - £5m **No.of Employees:** 21 - 50
Product Groups: 36, 40, 48

Date of Accounts	Dec 11	Dec 10	Dec 09
Sales Turnover	4m	4m	4m
Pre Tax Profit/Loss	697	756	695
Working Capital	769	390	609
Fixed Assets	802	845	903
Current Assets	1m	1m	1m
Current Liabilities	163	419	194

Advanced Techniks Ltd
28 Relton Way, Hartlepool, TS26 0BB
Tel: 01429-231839 **Fax:** 01429-231839
E-mail: kenkirbyatl@yahoo.co.uk
Website: http://www.advancedtechniks.co.uk
Directors: C. Kirby (Fin), K. Kirby (MD)
Immediate Holding Company: ADVANCED TECHNIKS LIMITED
Registration no: 03253709 **Date established:** 1996
No.of Employees: 1 - 10 **Product Groups:** 46

Date of Accounts	Dec 11	Dec 10	Dec 09
Working Capital	14	6	11
Fixed Assets	4	6	8
Current Assets	31	23	29

Atlas Industrial Services Ltd
Tofts Farm Industrial Estate East Brenda Road, Hartlepool, TS25 2BS
Tel: 01429-233018 **Fax:** 01429-863316
E-mail: m.gcoop@tiscali.co.uk
Website: http://www.atlasclensol.co.uk
Bank(s): HSBC
Directors: M. Coop (Dir), P. Kaye (Co Sec)
Immediate Holding Company: ATLAS INDUSTRIAL SERVICES LIMITED
Registration no: 04577167 **VAT No.:** 802 8819 25 **Date established:** 2002
Turnover: £1m - £2m **No.of Employees:** 21 - 50 **Product Groups:** 52, 66

Date of Accounts	Nov 11	Nov 10	Nov 09
Working Capital	60	-4	-7
Fixed Assets	135	138	145
Current Assets	367	286	334

Bearing Traders Ltd
1e Longhill Industrial Estate Ullswater Road, Hartlepool, TS25 1UE
Tel: 01429-862555 **Fax:** 01429-862533
E-mail: hpsales@bearingtraders.com
Website: http://www.bearingtraders.com
Managers: R. Kirton (District Mgr)
Immediate Holding Company: BEARING TRADERS LIMITED
Registration no: 01994643 **Date established:** 1986
No.of Employees: 1 - 10 **Product Groups:** 35, 36

Britton Decoflex
Skerne Road, Hartlepool, TS24 0RH
Tel: 01429-272102 **Fax:** 01429-860388
E-mail: simon.rowe@britton-group.com
Website: http://www.decoflex-flexibles.co.uk
Bank(s): National Westminster Bank Plc
Directors: M. Duff (Fin)
Managers: A. Heaton (Personnel), S. Rowe (Mgr), J. Rikkerink (Tech Serv Mgr)
Ultimate Holding Company: BRITTON FLEXIBLES LTD
Immediate Holding Company: BRITTON GROUP LIMITED
Registration no: 03541144 **VAT No.:** GB 226 5685 45
Date established: 1998 **Turnover:** £10m - £20m
No.of Employees: 51 - 100 **Product Groups:** 27, 30

Date of Accounts	Apr 08	Apr 07	Apr 06
Sales Turnover	18542	12809	12472
Pre Tax Profit/Loss	371	-143	1073
Working Capital	944	1466	2232
Fixed Assets	2826	2898	1586
Current Assets	11568	9240	6092
Current Liabilities	10624	7774	3860
Total Share Capital	60	60	60
ROCE% (Return on Capital Employed)	9.8	-3.3	28.1
ROT% (Return on Turnover)	2.0	-1.1	8.6

Cecil M Yuill Ltd
Cecil House Loyalty Road, Hartlepool, TS25 5BD
Tel: 01429-266620 **Fax:** 01429-231359
E-mail: david.mullins@yuill.co.uk
Website: http://www.yuillhomes.co.uk
Directors: S. Latimer (Sales & Mktg), D. McNaught (Grp Chief Exec), D. Mullins (MD)
Managers: N. Bell, L. Kenny (I.T. Exec)
Ultimate Holding Company: NEWBRIDGE ENTERPRISES LIMITED
Immediate Holding Company: CECIL M. YUILL LIMITED
Registration no: 01765648 **VAT No.:** GB 602 1631 94
Date established: 1983 **Turnover:** £20m - £50m
No.of Employees: 21 - 50 **Product Groups:** 52

Date of Accounts	Dec 09	Dec 08	Dec 07
Sales Turnover	26m	28m	61m
Pre Tax Profit/Loss	2m	-378	9m
Working Capital	39m	38m	38m
Fixed Assets	473	1m	954
Current Assets	47m	53m	64m
Current Liabilities	569	1m	3m

Enetgate
3 Moffat Road, Hartlepool, TS25 3QN
Tel: 01429-286182
E-mail: design@enetgate.com
Website: http://www.enetgate.co.uk
Managers: R. Carevic (Consultant), R. Carevic (Mgr)
Date established: 2006 **No.of Employees:** 1 - 10 **Product Groups:** 44

Expamet Building Products Ltd
Longhill Industrial Estate North Greatham Street, Hartlepool, TS25 1PU
Tel: 01429-866688 **Fax:** 01429-866633
E-mail: sales@expamet.net
Website: http://www.expamet.co.uk
Directors: J. Knowles (MD)
Ultimate Holding Company: HILL & SMITH HOLDINGS PLC
Immediate Holding Company: EXPAMET BUILDING PRODUCTS LIMITED
Registration no: 01836369 **VAT No.:** GB 472 0768 39
Date established: 1984 **Turnover:** £20m - £50m
No.of Employees: 101 - 250 **Product Groups:** 33, 34, 35

Date of Accounts	Dec 11	Dec 10	Dec 09
Working Capital	-324	-324	-324
Current Assets	33	33	33
Current Liabilities	7	7	7

The Expanded Metal Company
Stranton Works Longhill Industrial Estate, Hartlepool, TS25 1PR
Tel: 01429-867366 **Fax:** 01429-867355
E-mail: fencing@exmesh.co.uk
Website: http://www.expandedmetalcompany.co.uk
Directors: C. Bates (MD)
Managers: C. Bates (Sales Prom Mgr), I. Hutchinson (Sales Prom Mgr)
Immediate Holding Company: EXPAMET FENCING LIMITED
Registration no: 04549115 **Date established:** 2002
No.of Employees: 101 - 250 **Product Groups:** 34, 35, 36, 37, 41, 49, 66

Date of Accounts	Dec 10	Dec 09	Dec 08
Sales Turnover	19m	19m	23m
Pre Tax Profit/Loss	-716	282	2m
Working Capital	6m	6m	5m
Fixed Assets	8m	9m	10m
Current Assets	10m	9m	9m
Current Liabilities	525	532	567

Exwold Technology
Brenda Road, Hartlepool, TS25 2BW
Tel: 01429-230340 **Fax:** 01429-232996
E-mail: kevin@exwold.com
Website: http://www.exwold.com
Bank(s): National Westminster Bank Plc
Directors: A. Coyne (Co Sec), J. Robson (Fin), K. Martin (MD), S. Price (Comm)
Managers: M. Druce (Purch Mgr)
Ultimate Holding Company: HARTLEPOOL INVESTMENTS LIMITED
Immediate Holding Company: EXWOLD TECHNOLOGY LIMITED
Registration no: 02735432 **Date established:** 1992 **Turnover:** £1m - £2m
No.of Employees: 51 - 100 **Product Groups:** 32, 33

Date of Accounts	Sep 11	Sep 10	Sep 09
Working Capital	136	39	23
Fixed Assets	1m	1m	959
Current Assets	2m	1m	2m

Factorycover
Eamont Park Toft Farm West Indl-Est, Hartlepool, TS25 2BQ
Tel: 01429-863366 **Fax:** 01429-263188
Directors: J. Elders (Ch), J. Elders (MD)
Ultimate Holding Company: F.C. INVESTMENTS LTD
Immediate Holding Company: F.C. INVESTMENTS LTD
Registration no: 02467819 **VAT No.:** GB 409 1295 58
Turnover: Up to £250,000 **No.of Employees:** 1 - 10 **Product Groups:** 52

Flex Ability Ltd
Prospect Way Park View West Industrial Estate, Park View Industrial Estate, Hartlepool, TS25 1UD
Tel: 01429-860233 **Fax:** 01429-869696
E-mail: dmills@flex-ability.co.uk
Website: http://www.flex-ability.co.uk
Bank(s): Barclays
Directors: D. Mills (MD), N. Wass (Tech Serv)
Managers: A. McCloskey, C. Wall (Sales Prom Mgr)
Immediate Holding Company: FLEX-ABILITY LIMITED
Registration no: 02122310 **Date established:** 1987 **Turnover:** £2m - £5m
No.of Employees: 21 - 50 **Product Groups:** 37, 44, 84

Date of Accounts	Mar 08	Mar 07	Sep 05
Working Capital	-235	-206	38
Fixed Assets	681	748	593
Current Assets	938	895	1287
Current Liabilities	1172	1101	1249
Total Share Capital	20	20	26

Frutarom UK Ltd
Zinc Works Road Seaton Carew, Hartlepool, TS25 2DT
Tel: 01429-863222 **Fax:** 01429-867567
E-mail: sales@uk.frutarom.com
Website: http://www.frutarom.com
Bank(s): Midland
Managers: L. Catchpole (Purch Mgr), A. Weston (Chief Mgr), K. Hanson (Tech Serv Mgr), A. Burnhope (Personnel)
Ultimate Holding Company: YULE CATTO & CO PUBLIC LIMITED COMPANY
Immediate Holding Company: TEMPLE FIELDS 534 LIMITED
Registration no: 02201740 **Date established:** 1987 **Turnover:** £5m - £10m
No.of Employees: 51 - 100 **Product Groups:** 32

Date of Accounts	Dec 11	Dec 10	Dec 09
Sales Turnover	N/A	N/A	772
Pre Tax Profit/Loss	N/A	-10	4m
Working Capital	8m	8m	8m
Current Assets	8m	8m	8m

J J Hardy & Sons Ltd
Brenda Road, Hartlepool, TS25 2BL
Tel: 01429-279837 **Fax:** 01429-860182
E-mail: sales@jjhardy.co.uk
Website: http://www.jjhardy.co.uk
Bank(s): Barclays
Directors: A. Pailor (MD), E. Pailor (Fin)
Immediate Holding Company: J.J.HARDY & SONS LIMITED
Registration no: 00182491 **VAT No.:** GB 257 9492 09
Date established: 2022 **Turnover:** £1m - £2m **No.of Employees:** 11 - 20
Product Groups: 39, 48

Date of Accounts	May 11	May 10	May 09
Working Capital	136	202	2m
Fixed Assets	405	245	264
Current Assets	517	498	358

Heerema Hartlepool Ltd
Greenland Road, Hartlepool, TS24 0RQ
Tel: 01642-340200 **Fax:** 01642-340208
E-mail: info@heerema.com
Website: http://www.heerema.com
Bank(s): Barclays
Directors: D. Neil (Fin)
Managers: P. Self (Sales & Mktg Mg), T. Stewart (Tech Serv Mgr), S. Groom (Personnel), A. Lloyd, D. Grant (Purch Mgr)
Ultimate Holding Company: HEEREMA FABRICATION GROUP BV (NETHERLAND
Immediate Holding Company: HEEREMA HARTLEPOOL LIMITED
Registration no: 01287666 **Date established:** 1976
Turnover: £50m - £75m **No.of Employees:** 101 - 250 **Product Groups:** 51

Date of Accounts	Dec 11	Dec 10	Dec 09
Sales Turnover	63m	26m	61m
Pre Tax Profit/Loss	6m	-18m	-816
Working Capital	-11m	-16m	1m
Fixed Assets	7m	9m	4m
Current Assets	25m	8m	15m
Current Liabilities	30m	22m	6m

Hydrochem UK Ltd
1 Graythorp Industrial Estate Tees Road, Hartlepool, TS25 2DF
Tel: 01429-860836 **Fax:** 01429-868832
E-mail: info@hydrochemgroup.co.uk
Website: http://www.hydrochemgroup.co.uk
Bank(s): National Westminster Bank Plc
Directors: W. Abbott (Dir)
Immediate Holding Company: HYDROCHEM (U.K.) LIMITED
Registration no: 02562697 **Date established:** 1990
No.of Employees: 11 - 20 **Product Groups:** 32, 39, 41, 42, 52, 54, 66, 67

Date of Accounts	Dec 11	Dec 10	Dec 09
Working Capital	91	12	-50
Fixed Assets	50	48	49
Current Assets	261	265	243

Infotech 24 7 Ltd
Hartlepool Innovation Centre Venture Court, Queens Meadow Business Park, Hartlepool, TS25 5TG
Tel: 03337-000247 **Fax:** 08700-111558
E-mail: sales@infotech247.com
Website: http://www.infotech247.com
Directors: M. Siddle (Dir)
Immediate Holding Company: INFOTECH 24 7 LIMITED
Registration no: 04366886 **Date established:** 2002
Turnover: £250,000 - £500,000 **No.of Employees:** 1 - 10
Product Groups: 44

Date of Accounts	Feb 08	Feb 11	Feb 10
Working Capital	16	72	53
Fixed Assets	20	28	24
Current Assets	63	132	112

Northdale Rotary Engineering Ltd
Tofts Farm Industrial Estate West Brenda Road, Hartlepool, TS25 2BQ
Tel: 01429-276891 **Fax:** 01429-864421
E-mail: northdalecent@btconnect.com
Website: http://www.northdaleeng.co.uk
Directors: H. Cassidy (Fin)
Managers: A. Nixon (Mgr)
Immediate Holding Company: NORTHDALE ROTARY ENGINEERING LIMITED
Registration no: 01550158 **VAT No.:** GB 360 4996 33
Date established: 1981 **No.of Employees:** 11 - 20 **Product Groups:** 41, 42

Date of Accounts	Nov 11	Nov 10	Nov 09
Working Capital	510	630	758
Fixed Assets	142	137	143
Current Assets	842	937	1m

Palmer UK Ltd
Tofts Farm Industrial Estate West Brenda Road, Hartlepool, TS25 2BQ
Tel: 01429-268076 **Fax:** 01429-223726
E-mail: info@palmerint.com
Website: http://www.palmerint.com
Directors: D. Brown (MD), D. Crowe (MD)
Managers: D. Craw (Ops Mgr), M. Hall (Sales Admin), S. Logan (Sales Admin)
Ultimate Holding Company: PALMER INTERNATIONAL INC (USA)
Immediate Holding Company: PALMER (U.K.) LIMITED
Registration no: 01565731 **VAT No.:** GB 360 5930 58
Date established: 1981 **No.of Employees:** 1 - 10 **Product Groups:** 33, 40

Date of Accounts	Dec 11	Dec 10	Dec 09
Working Capital	608	516	754
Fixed Assets	298	311	300
Current Assets	1m	1m	1m
Current Liabilities	N/A	228	169

R J B Coatings
Tofts Farm Industrial Estate East Brenda Road, Hartlepool, TS25 2BS
Tel: 01429-222270
E-mail: info@rjbcoatings.co.uk
Website: http://www.rjbcoatings.co.uk
Directors: R. Brackscone (Prop)
Immediate Holding Company: RJB COATINGS LTD
Registration no: 06560662 **Date established:** 2008
No.of Employees: 1 - 10 **Product Groups:** 46, 48

Date of Accounts	Feb 12	Feb 11	Feb 09
Working Capital	-64	-17	15
Fixed Assets	138	76	49
Current Assets	30	35	56

R Lambert
Dental Surgery 4 Grange Road, Hartlepool, TS26 8JA
Tel: 01429-864555 **Fax:** 01429-860159
E-mail: lambert@speedinternet.co.uk
Managers: M. Lambert
No.of Employees: 11 - 20 **Product Groups:** 38, 67

S C A Packaging Ltd (Factory) UK Central Office
Oakesway, Hartlepool, TS24 0RB
Tel: 01429-272192 **Fax:** 01429-223720
E-mail: sales@scapackaging.com
Website: http://www.scapackaging.co.uk
Directors: D. Wilbraham (Sales), J. Beadle (MD)
Managers: S. Moore (I.T. Exec), T. Griffiths (Comptroller), J. Jackson (Ops Mgr)

Immediate Holding Company: SCA PACKAGING LIMITED
Registration no: 00053913 **Date established:** 1997
No.of Employees: 101 - 250 **Product Groups:** 27, 28, 30, 49

Seaton Blinds

Unit 10 Hartlepool Enterprise Centre Brougham Terrace, Hartlepool, TS24 8EY
Tel: 01429-262565 **Fax:** 01429-264304
E-mail: info@seatonblinds.co.uk
Website: http://www.seatonblinds.co.uk
Managers: D. King (Chief Mgr)
Date established: 2004 **Turnover:** Up to £250,000
No.of Employees: 1 - 10 **Product Groups:** 23, 24, 25, 30, 35, 63

Stadium Consumer Products

Stadium North Tofts Farm Industrial Estate East, Hartlepool, TS25 2DH
Tel: 01429-862616 **Fax:** 01429-272126
E-mail: julie.morrisey@stadiumcp.co.uk
Website: http://www.stadiumcp.co.uk
Bank(s): National Westminister
Directors: S. Morrisey (MD)
Managers: A. Kelsey (Sales Admin), S. Douglas
Immediate Holding Company: STADIUM CONSUMER PRODUCTS LIMITED
Registration no: 04315373 **VAT No.:** GB 220 4153 22
Date established: 2001 **Turnover:** £1m - £2m **No.of Employees:** 51 - 100
Product Groups: 37, 38, 40, 46, 47

Date of Accounts	Dec 11	Dec 10	Dec 09
Working Capital	489	446	439
Fixed Assets	21	36	24
Current Assets	894	1m	1m

Ta T/A Steel UK Ltd

42 Inch Mill Tube Works, Hartlepool, TS25 2EF
Tel: 01429-266611 **Fax:** 01429-527283
Website: http://www.tatasteel.com
Managers: M. Coull (Tech Serv Mgr), N. Scott (Mgr), N. Ashton (Personnel), S. Mason (Chief Acct), A. Knox, N. Duffey (Personnel)
Ultimate Holding Company: TATA STEEL LIMITED (INDIA)
Immediate Holding Company: TATA STEEL UK LIMITED
Registration no: 02280000 **VAT No.:** GB 238 7122 60
Date established: 1988 **No.of Employees:** 101 - 250 **Product Groups:** 36

Date of Accounts	Mar 12	Mar 11	Mar 10
Sales Turnover	5206m	4907m	4175m
Pre Tax Profit/Loss	-429m	-140m	-567m
Working Capital	29m	917m	973m
Fixed Assets	2746m	2684m	2435m
Current Assets	2004m	3101m	2509m
Current Liabilities	291m	336m	382m

Traditional Steel

Lower Oxford Street, Hartlepool, TS25 1PT
Tel: 01429-291600 **Fax:** 01429-291600
Directors: G. Filby (Prop)
Date established: 1998 **No.of Employees:** 1 - 10 **Product Groups:** 26, 35

Travis Perkins plc

Belle Vue Way, Hartlepool, TS25 1JZ
Tel: 01429-221133 **Fax:** 01429-863357
E-mail: hartlepool@travisperkins.co.uk
Website: http://www.travisperkins.co.uk
Bank(s): National Westminster
Managers: P. Johnstone (Mgr)
Immediate Holding Company: TRAVIS PERKINS PLC
Registration no: 00824821 **VAT No.:** GB 456 5069 30
Date established: 1964 **Turnover:** £1m - £2m **No.of Employees:** 11 - 20
Product Groups: 08, 25, 66

Date of Accounts	Dec 11	Dec 10	Dec 09
Sales Turnover	4779m	3153m	2931m
Pre Tax Profit/Loss	270m	197m	213m
Working Capital	133m	159m	248m
Fixed Assets	2771m	2749m	2108m
Current Assets	1421m	1329m	1035m
Current Liabilities	473m	412m	109m

Middlesbrough

Aveco Teesside Ltd

The Slipways Dockside Road, Middlesbrough, TS3 8AT
Tel: 01642-224994 **Fax:** 01642-248138
E-mail: aveco.teesside@ntl.com
Website: http://www.aveco.co.uk
Bank(s): HSBC Bank plc
Directors: D. Aveling (MD), J. Rutherford (Fin)
Managers: P. Conwell (Mgr)
Ultimate Holding Company: M.J. SCAIFE LIMITED
Immediate Holding Company: AVECO (TEESSIDE) LIMITED
Registration no: 01299573 **VAT No.:** GB 360 4371 73
Date established: 1977 **Turnover:** £500,000 - £1m
No.of Employees: 11 - 20 **Product Groups:** 48

Date of Accounts	Apr 11	Apr 10	Apr 09
Working Capital	-113	-52	-54
Fixed Assets	324	330	338
Current Assets	16	99	96

Ayton Fire Protection

2 Moorland View Dikes Lane, Great Ayton, Middlesbrough, TS9 6HG
Tel: 01642-722520 **Fax:** 01642-722520
Directors: I. Brown (Prop)
Date established: 1984 **No.of Employees:** 1 - 10 **Product Groups:** 38, 42

Balfour Beatty Utility Solutions

Sotherby Road South Bank, Middlesbrough, TS6 6LP
Tel: 01642-468431 **Fax:** 01642-440628
Website: http://www.bbusl.com
Bank(s): National Westminster Bank Plc
Managers: A. Smith
Ultimate Holding Company: BALFOUR BEATTY PLC
Immediate Holding Company: BALFOUR BEATTY GROUP LTD
Registration no: 02067112 **Date established:** 2001
No.of Employees: 101 - 250 **Product Groups:** 37, 43

F J Booth & Partners Ltd

Dockside Road, Middlesbrough, TS3 8AT
Tel: 01642-241581 **Fax:** 01642-223398
E-mail: christon@boothandpartners.co.uk
Website: http://www.boothandpartners.co.uk
Bank(s): National Westminster Bank Plc
Directors: H. Hare (MD), S. Muir (MD), S. Muir (Dir)
Managers: L. Robson (Admin Off)
Ultimate Holding Company: M.J. SCAIFE LIMITED
Immediate Holding Company: F.J. BOOTH & PARTNERS LIMITED
Registration no: 01188419 **VAT No.:** GB 654 2308 49
Date established: 1974 **Turnover:** £10m - £20m
No.of Employees: 51 - 100 **Product Groups:** 35, 51

Date of Accounts	Dec 09	Dec 08	Dec 07
Sales Turnover	19m	N/A	N/A
Pre Tax Profit/Loss	649	826	1m
Working Capital	-210	385	581
Fixed Assets	2m	2m	676
Current Assets	3m	7m	4m
Current Liabilities	1m	2m	1m

Steve Brettle Fabrications

5a Bowes Road, Middlesbrough, TS2 1LU
Tel: 01642-219998 **Fax:** 01642-249213
E-mail: steve@brettlefabs.co.uk
Website: http://www.brettlefabs.co.uk
Directors: S. Brettle (Prop)
Immediate Holding Company: STEVE BRETTLE FABRICATIONS LTD.
Registration no: 03751161 **Date established:** 1999
No.of Employees: 11 - 20 **Product Groups:** 35

Date of Accounts	Mar 12	Mar 11	Mar 10
Working Capital	119	87	53
Fixed Assets	63	76	71
Current Assets	353	274	591

James Brown & Sons Ltd

92 The Grove Marton-in-Cleveland, Middlesbrough, TS7 8AP
Tel: 01642-318370 **Fax:** 01642-318370
Directors: C. Widmer (MD), A. Widmer (Fin)
Immediate Holding Company: JAMES BROWN & SONS LIMITED
Registration no: 01371135 **VAT No.:** GB 317 5371 61
Date established: 1978 **Turnover:** Up to £250,000
No.of Employees: 1 - 10 **Product Groups:** 30, 36

Date of Accounts	Apr 11	Apr 10	Apr 09
Working Capital	42	32	38
Current Assets	44	36	41

Buck & Hickman Ltd

7 Cannon Park Way Cannon Park Industrial Estate, Middlesbrough, TS1 5JU
Tel: 01642-240116 **Fax:** 01642-245299
E-mail: middlesbrough@buckhickmaninone.com
Website: http://www.buckhickman.co.uk
Managers: A. Mcgee
Ultimate Holding Company: TRAVIS PERKINS PLC
Immediate Holding Company: BOSTON (2011) LIMITED
Registration no: 06028304 **Date established:** 2006
No.of Employees: 1 - 10 **Product Groups:** 24, 29, 30, 33, 36, 37, 41, 46

Date of Accounts	Dec 10	Mar 10	Mar 09
Working Capital	6m	6m	6m
Current Assets	27m	27m	27m

Bureau Of Analysed Samples Ltd

Newham Hall Stokesley Road, Newby, Middlesbrough, TS8 9EA
Tel: 01642-300500 **Fax:** 01642-315209
E-mail: rpmeeres@basrid.co.uk
Website: http://www.basrid.co.uk
Bank(s): Barclays
Directors: G. Flintoft (Dir), R. Meeres (MD)
Immediate Holding Company: BUREAU OF ANALYSED SAMPLES LIMITED
Registration no: 00307549 **VAT No.:** GB 258 0944 39
Date established: 1935 **Turnover:** £1m - £2m **No.of Employees:** 21 - 50
Product Groups: 31, 38

Date of Accounts	Nov 11	Nov 10	Nov 09
Working Capital	4m	4m	3m
Fixed Assets	103	90	88
Current Assets	4m	4m	4m

C & M Electrical Contracts & Maintenance Ltd

2f Vaughan Court Stapylton Street, Middlesbrough, TS6 7BJ
Tel: 01642-440640 **Fax:** 01642-460595
E-mail: jd@cmelec.co.uk
Website: http://www.cmelec.co.uk
Managers: B. Campbell (Sales Admin), J. Davies (Mgr)
Immediate Holding Company: C & M ELECTRICAL CONTRACTORS & MAINTENANCE LIMITED
Registration no: 02946297 **VAT No.:** GB 633 3779 25
Date established: 1994 **Turnover:** £250,000 - £500,000
No.of Employees: 1 - 10 **Product Groups:** 52

Carillion

Webb Road Skippers Lane Industrial Estate, Middlesbrough, TS6 6HD
Tel: 01642-459000 **Fax:** 01642- 454111
Website: http://www.carillionplc.com
Directors: S. Law (Dir)
Ultimate Holding Company: CARILLION PLC
Immediate Holding Company: CARILLION HOLDINGS LIMITED
Registration no: 03783019 **VAT No.:** GB 222 8311 95
Date established: 1999 **No.of Employees:** 251 - 500 **Product Groups:** 48, 52

Cartridge World Ltd

40 Borough Road, Middlesbrough, TS1 5DW
Tel: 01642-230025 **Fax:** 01642-656000
Website: http://www.cartridgeworld.co.uk
Managers: C. Gould (Mgr)
Immediate Holding Company: CARTRIDGE WORLD LIMITED
Registration no: 04124067 **Date established:** 2000 **Turnover:** £5m - £10m
No.of Employees: 1 - 10 **Product Groups:** 28, 30, 44

Date of Accounts	Dec 11	Dec 10	Dec 09
Sales Turnover	6m	7m	8m
Pre Tax Profit/Loss	373	164	210
Working Capital	1m	967	878
Fixed Assets	403	455	524
Current Assets	7m	7m	6m
Current Liabilities	4m	1m	2m

Cleveland Cable Co. Ltd

Riverside Park Road, Middlesbrough, TS2 1QW
Tel: 01642-254234 **Fax:** 01642-226171
E-mail: a-powell@clevelandcable.com
Website: http://www.clevelandcable.com
Bank(s): Midland
Directors: A. Powell (MD)
Immediate Holding Company: CLEVELAND CABLE COMPANY LIMITED
Registration no: 05538824 **VAT No.:** 317 4462 63 **Date established:** 2005
Turnover: £125m - £250m **No.of Employees:** 251 - 500
Product Groups: 37

Date of Accounts	Apr 11	Apr 10	Apr 09
Sales Turnover	213m	166m	191m
Pre Tax Profit/Loss	23m	26m	6m
Working Capital	142m	125m	105m
Fixed Assets	16m	16m	17m
Current Assets	162m	140m	120m
Current Liabilities	7m	6m	4m

Cleveland Croming Co.

Snowdon Road, Middlesbrough, TS2 1DY
Tel: 01642-244911 **Fax:** 01642-251975
Website: http://www.clevelandchroming.co.uk
Directors: A. Turner (MD)
Immediate Holding Company: LADRIM LIMITED
Registration no: 02111410 **Date established:** 1987
No.of Employees: 1 - 10 **Product Groups:** 46, 48

Date of Accounts	Sep 11	Sep 10	Sep 09
Working Capital	-18	-26	-30
Fixed Assets	66	70	74
Current Assets	88	83	91

Cleveland Sitesafe

Riverside Works Dockside Road, Middlesbrough, TS3 8AT
Tel: 01642-244663 **Fax:** 01642-244664
E-mail: sales@cleveland-sitesafe.ltd.uk
Website: http://www.cleveland-sitesafe.ltd.uk
Directors: M. Scaife (MD)
Ultimate Holding Company: M.J. SCAIFE LIMITED
Immediate Holding Company: CLEVELAND SITESAFE LIMITED
Registration no: 02189415 **Date established:** 1987 **Turnover:** £1m - £2m
No.of Employees: 1 - 10 **Product Groups:** 26, 35, 36, 67

Date of Accounts	Sep 11	Sep 10	Sep 09
Working Capital	777	819	744
Fixed Assets	51	340	354
Current Assets	958	1m	1m

Cleveland Up & Over Door Company Ltd

7 Metcalfe Road Skippers Lane Industrial Estate, Middlesbrough, TS6 6PT
Tel: 01642-440920 **Fax:** 01642-456106
E-mail: osssystems@hotmail.co.uk
Website: http://www.clevelandupover.co.uk
Directors: A. Knight (Co Sec), P. Knight (MD)
Immediate Holding Company: CLEVELAND UP & OVER DOORS LIMITED
Registration no: 04727994 **Date established:** 2003
No.of Employees: 1 - 10 **Product Groups:** 25, 30, 35, 36

Date of Accounts	Mar 11	Mar 10	Mar 09
Working Capital	-25	-23	-26
Fixed Assets	30	26	32
Current Assets	72	62	59

Cockfield Knight & Co. Ltd

Dinsdale House Riverside Park Road, Middlesbrough, TS2 1UT
Tel: 01642-230111 **Fax:** 01642-231651
E-mail: agency@cockfieldknight.com
Website: http://www.cockfieldknight.com
Managers: R. Booth (Mgr)
Immediate Holding Company: COCKFIELD, KNIGHT & COMPANY LIMITED
Registration no: 07204485 **Date established:** 2010
Turnover: £250,000 - £500,000 **No.of Employees:** 1 - 10
Product Groups: 74, 76, 82, 84

Coldtec Refrigeration

11 Lawson Way, Middlesbrough, TS3 6LN
Tel: 01642-270111 **Fax:** 01642-270011
E-mail: coldtech@onyxnet.co.uk
Website: http://www.onyxnet.co.uk
Directors: G. Marron (Ptnr)
Date established: 1984 **Turnover:** Up to £250,000
No.of Employees: 1 - 10 **Product Groups:** 40, 41, 66, 67

Corus Metal Shops

1 Startforth Road Riverside Park Industrial Estate, Middlesbrough, TS2 1PT
Tel: 01642-243777 **Fax:** 01642-243888
E-mail: peter.mcphillips@corusgroup.com
Website: http://www.corusgroup.com
Managers: P. McPhillips (Comm), P. McPhillips (Mgr)
Registration no: SC029016 **Turnover:** Over £1,000m
No.of Employees: 1 - 10 **Product Groups:** 34, 66

Cowie Technology Group Ltd

Ridgeway Coulby Newham, Middlesbrough, TS8 0TQ
Tel: 01642-599190 **Fax:** 01642-596810
E-mail: enquiries@cowie-tech.com
Website: http://www.cowie-tech.com
Directors: J. Cowie (MD), S. Price (Co Sec)
Managers: J. Morgan
Immediate Holding Company: COWIE TECHNOLOGY GROUP LIMITED
Registration no: 00850954 **VAT No.:** GB 275 6043 53
Date established: 1965 **Turnover:** £2m - £5m **No.of Employees:** 51 - 100
Product Groups: 30

Date of Accounts	Jun 11	Jun 10	Jun 09
Sales Turnover	4m	4m	3m
Pre Tax Profit/Loss	957	529	532
Working Capital	4m	3m	3m
Fixed Assets	1m	1m	1m
Current Assets	5m	4m	4m
Current Liabilities	431	242	204

D B Grinding

Station Road Stokesley, Middlesbrough, TS9 7AB
Tel: 01642-711695
Directors: D. Bearshaw (Prop)
Date established: 1984 **No.of Employees:** 1 - 10 **Product Groups:** 36

Direct Business Supplies
Unit 7 Terry Dicken Industrial Estate Stokesley, Middlesbrough, TS9 7AE
Tel: 01642-714715 **Fax:** 01642-713291
E-mail: sales@directinabox.co.uk
Website: http://www.directinabox.co.uk
Directors: J. Barber (MD)
Immediate Holding Company: TERRY DICKEN LIMITED
Date established: 2003 **No.of Employees:** 1 - 10 **Product Groups:** 27, 28, 44

N Duckworth
Unit 24 Bessemer Court Bolckow Industrial Estate, Middlesbrough, TS6 7EB
Tel: 01642-461027
Directors: N. Duckworth (Prop)
Date established: 1989 **No.of Employees:** 1 - 10 **Product Groups:** 35

Ecco Finishing Supplies
Unit 5-9 Letitia Industrial Estate, Middlesbrough, TS5 4BE
Tel: 01642-219760 **Fax:** 01642-248379
E-mail: sales@eccofinishingsupplies.com
Website: http://www.eccofinishingsupplies.co.uk
Directors: C. Miller (Fin), K. Miller (MD)
Immediate Holding Company: ECCO FINISHING SUPPLIES LIMITED
Registration no: 03112795 **Date established:** 1995
No.of Employees: 11 - 20 **Product Groups:** 38, 42

Date of Accounts	Nov 11	Nov 10	Nov 09
Working Capital	365	191	40
Fixed Assets	153	110	99
Current Assets	2m	990	1m

Engineering Installation Teesside Ltd
Owens Road, Middlesbrough, TS6 6HX
Tel: 01642-452471 **Fax:** 01642-462005
E-mail: les@enginst.co.uk
Website: http://www.enginst.co.uk
Directors: L. Dickons (MD), N. Foster (Fin)
Immediate Holding Company: ENGINEERING INSTALLATIONS (TEESSIDE) LIMITED
Registration no: 00929483 **VAT No.:** GB 547 1310 64
Date established: 1968 **Turnover:** £1m - £2m **No.of Employees:** 1 - 10
Product Groups: 52

Date of Accounts	Mar 12	Mar 11	Mar 10
Working Capital	307	299	256
Fixed Assets	38	36	19
Current Assets	688	726	700

Eriks UK (Middlesbrough Service Centre)
5 Newport Way, Middlesbrough, TS1 5JW
Tel: 01642-240056 **Fax:** 01642-224358
E-mail: middlesbrough@eriks.co.uk
Website: http://www.eriks.co.uk
Managers: A. Gurski (Mgr)
Turnover: £250m - £500m **No.of Employees:** 1 - 10 **Product Groups:** 66

Fairless Engineering
Webb Road Skippers Lane Industrial Estate, Middlesbrough, TS6 6HD
Tel: 01642-676070 **Fax:** 01642-606401
E-mail: enquiries@fairless.co.uk
Website: http://www.fairless.co.uk
Bank(s): Lloyds TSB Bank plc
Directors: V. Scott (Fin), M. Howe (Dir)
Immediate Holding Company: FAIRLESS ENGINEERING LIMITED
Registration no: 06776092 **VAT No.:** GB 329 3483 41
Date established: 2008 **Turnover:** £500,000 - £1m
No.of Employees: 11 - 20 **Product Groups:** 37

Date of Accounts	Feb 12	Feb 11	Feb 10
Working Capital	-5	4	-1
Fixed Assets	39	30	39
Current Assets	241	272	96

Fast Graphics & Signs
11 Brass Castle Lane Marton-In-Cleveland, Middlesbrough, TS8 9EF
Tel: 01642-440884
Directors: C. Horner (Prop)
No.of Employees: 1 - 10 **Product Groups:** 30, 81, 84

Fleet Factors Ltd
Unit 3 Wallis Road, Skippers Lane Industrial Estate, Middlesbrough, TS6 6JB
Tel: 01642-770664 **Fax:** 01642-455900
E-mail: middlesbrough@fleetfactors.co.uk
Website: http://www.fleetfactors.co.uk
Bank(s): Barclays
Directors: G. Norris (MD), B. Hunter (Fin)
Managers: M. Gordon (Depot Mgr), C. McManus
Immediate Holding Company: FLEET FACTORS LIMITED
Registration no: 01231325 **VAT No.:** GB 441 4825 60
Date established: 1975 **Turnover:** £20m - £50m
No.of Employees: 21 - 50 **Product Groups:** 39

Date of Accounts	Oct 11	Oct 10	Oct 09
Sales Turnover	34m	31m	28m
Pre Tax Profit/Loss	975	2m	403
Working Capital	5m	5m	4m
Fixed Assets	1m	1m	791
Current Assets	13m	12m	10m
Current Liabilities	1m	1m	761

Gaffney Industrial & Supplies Ltd
Brewsdale Road, Middlesbrough, TS3 6LJ
Tel: 01642-223466 **Fax:** 01642-230224
Bank(s): National Westminster Bank Plc
Directors: P. Chapman (Dir), R. Walker (Tech Serv)
Managers: C. Richardson (Sales Prom Mgr), S. Myers (Sales Admin)
Ultimate Holding Company: LINDE AG (GERMANY)
Immediate Holding Company: GAFFNEY INDUSTRIAL & WELDING SUPPLIES LTD
Registration no: 03474867 **VAT No.:** GB 708 0919 33
Date established: 1997 **Turnover:** £2m - £5m **No.of Employees:** 21 - 50
Product Groups: 33, 35, 67

Date of Accounts	Dec 11	Dec 10	Dec 09
Sales Turnover	7m	5m	4m
Pre Tax Profit/Loss	290	91	40
Working Capital	687	528	499
Fixed Assets	423	357	345
Current Assets	2m	2m	1m
Current Liabilities	210	143	61

Gazette Media Company
Borough Road, Middlesbrough, TS1 3AZ
Tel: 01642-245401 **Fax:** 01642-254915
E-mail: news@gazettemedia.co.uk
Website: http://www.gazettelive.co.uk
Bank(s): Barclays
Directors: B. Green (Fin), S. Edgley (MD), P. Quinn (Tech Serv)
Managers: J. Purvis (Personnel), C. Moore
Ultimate Holding Company: TRINITY MIRROR PLC
Immediate Holding Company: DAILY POST OVERSEAS LTD
Registration no: 03441979 **VAT No.:** GB 654 2978 04
Turnover: £20m - £50m **No.of Employees:** 101 - 250 **Product Groups:** 28

Date of Accounts	Dec 07	Dec 06
Sales Turnover	23400	23850
Pre Tax Profit/Loss	8370	7810
Working Capital	20	-4870
Fixed Assets	32150	31250
Current Assets	52220	44730
Current Liabilities	52200	49600
Total Share Capital	22050	22050
ROCE% (Return on Capital Employed)	26.0	29.6
ROT% (Return on Turnover)	35.8	32.7

Greenbank Compactors LLP
Ginnington House Sotherby Road, Middlesbrough, TS3 8BT
Tel: 01642-249924 **Fax:** 01642-249926
E-mail: sales@compactorsuk.co.uk
Website: http://www.greenbankgroup.net
Bank(s): National Westminster Bank Plc
Directors: R. Evershed (Ptnr), S. Evershed (Ptnr)
Immediate Holding Company: GREENBANK COMPACTORS LLP
Registration no: OC374593 **VAT No.:** GB 327 9100 65
Date established: 2012 **Turnover:** £500,000 - £1m
No.of Employees: 21 - 50 **Product Groups:** 41, 42, 43, 44

Hawk Fasteners Ltd
Brunel Road Skippers Lane Industrial Estate, Middlesbrough, TS6 6JA
Tel: 01642-468581 **Fax:** 01642-440880
E-mail: sales@hawkfast.com
Website: http://www.hawkfast.com
Bank(s): Barclays
Directors: J. Dodds (MD)
Immediate Holding Company: HAWK FASTENERS LIMITED
Registration no: 01597125 **Date established:** 1981
Turnover: £500,000 - £1m **No.of Employees:** 11 - 20 **Product Groups:** 35

Date of Accounts	Sep 11	Sep 10	Sep 09
Working Capital	797	748	719
Fixed Assets	69	76	82
Current Assets	893	838	783

Industrial & Marine Hydraulics Ltd
2 Snowdon Road, Middlesbrough, TS2 1LP
Tel: 01642-802700 **Fax:** 01642-802701
E-mail: info@imh-uk.com
Website: http://www.imh-uk.com
Bank(s): National Westminster Bank Plc
Directors: P. Griffiths (MD)
Immediate Holding Company: INDUSTRIAL AND MARINE HYDRAULICS LIMITED
Registration no: 01731698 **VAT No.:** GB 391 8306 37
Date established: 1983 **Turnover:** £2m - £5m **No.of Employees:** 21 - 50
Product Groups: 18, 35, 36, 38, 39, 40, 42, 45, 48, 67, 84

Date of Accounts	Jun 11	Jun 10	Jun 09
Working Capital	607	545	601
Fixed Assets	292	305	299
Current Assets	854	973	723

Javac UK Ltd
6 Drake Court, Middlesbrough, TS2 1RS
Tel: 01642-232880 **Fax:** 01642-232870
E-mail: sales@javac.co.uk
Website: http://www.javac.co.uk
Directors: K. Davies (Fin)
Immediate Holding Company: JAVAC (UK) LIMITED
Registration no: 01129173 **VAT No.:** GB 189 4749 95
Date established: 1973 **Turnover:** £1m - £2m **No.of Employees:** 1 - 10
Product Groups: 40

Date of Accounts	Jun 12	Jun 11	Jun 10
Working Capital	525	403	401
Fixed Assets	55	57	59
Current Assets	869	743	863

Jewson Ltd
Station Road Stokesley, Middlesbrough, TS9 7AB
Tel: 01642-711730 **Fax:** 01642-712686
E-mail: david.ball@jewson.co.uk
Website: http://www.jewson.co.uk
Managers: D. Ball (Mgr)
Ultimate Holding Company: COMPAGNIE DE SAINT GOBAIN (FRANCE)
Immediate Holding Company: JEWSON LIMITED
Registration no: 00348407 **VAT No.:** GB 394 1212 63
Date established: 1939 **Turnover:** £5m - £10m **No.of Employees:** 1 - 10
Product Groups: 66

Date of Accounts	Dec 11	Dec 10	Dec 09
Sales Turnover	1606m	1547m	1485m
Pre Tax Profit/Loss	18m	100m	45m
Working Capital	-345m	-250m	-349m
Fixed Assets	496m	387m	461m
Current Assets	657m	1005m	1320m
Current Liabilities	66m	120m	64m

Klinger Ltd
2 Drake Court, Middlesbrough, TS2 1RS
Tel: 01642-220289 **Fax:** 01642-220290
Website: http://www.klingeruk.co.uk
Managers: K. Housam
Ultimate Holding Company: BETAL NETHERLAND HOLDING BV (NETHERLANDS)
Immediate Holding Company: KLINGER LIMITED
Registration no: 01021936 **Date established:** 1971
No.of Employees: 1 - 10 **Product Groups:** 38, 42

Date of Accounts	Dec 11	Dec 10	Dec 09
Sales Turnover	27m	23m	24m
Pre Tax Profit/Loss	5m	4m	3m
Working Capital	8m	8m	9m
Fixed Assets	2m	1m	2m
Current Assets	11m	11m	12m
Current Liabilities	1m	1m	844

Labman Automation Ltd
Seamer Hill Seamer, Middlesbrough, TS9 5NQ
Tel: 01642-710580 **Fax:** 01642-710667
E-mail: mailroom@labman.co.uk
Website: http://www.labman.co.uk
Directors: C. Smith (Fin)
Immediate Holding Company: LABMAN AUTOMATION LIMITED
Registration no: 02765790 **Date established:** 1992
Turnover: £500,000 - £1m **No.of Employees:** 21 - 50
Product Groups: 28, 37, 40, 44, 45, 67, 84, 85

Date of Accounts	Oct 11	Oct 10	Oct 09
Working Capital	-160	-65	4
Fixed Assets	1m	1m	882
Current Assets	1m	1m	2m

Lotus Electrical & Mechanical Ltd
36b High Street Stokesley, Middlesbrough, TS9 5DQ
Tel: 01642-713366 **Fax:** 01642-713365
Directors: M. Hartley (Dir), J. Hartley (Fin)
Immediate Holding Company: LOTUS ELECTRICAL & MECHANICAL LIMITED
Registration no: 05109836 **Date established:** 2004
Turnover: £500,000 - £1m **No.of Employees:** 1 - 10 **Product Groups:** 37, 51, 84

Date of Accounts	Mar 11	Mar 10	Mar 09
Sales Turnover	713	722	2m
Pre Tax Profit/Loss	133	15	305
Working Capital	168	127	187
Fixed Assets	22	25	26
Current Assets	215	178	289
Current Liabilities	29	36	98

Maplin Electronics Ltd
Unit 1 The Forbes Building 309-321 Linthorpe Road, Middlesbrough, TS1 4AW
Tel: 08432-277314 **Fax:** 01642-242909
E-mail: customercare@maplin.co.uk
Website: http://www.maplin.co.uk
Managers: D. Cathey (Mgr)
Ultimate Holding Company: MONTAGU PRIVATE EQUITY LLP
Immediate Holding Company: MAPLIN ELECTRONICS LIMITED
Registration no: 01264385 **Date established:** 1976
Turnover: £125m - £250m **No.of Employees:** 1 - 10 **Product Groups:** 37, 61

Date of Accounts	Dec 11	Dec 08	Dec 09
Sales Turnover	205m	204m	204m
Pre Tax Profit/Loss	25m	32m	35m
Working Capital	118m	49m	75m
Fixed Assets	27m	28m	28m
Current Assets	207m	108m	142m
Current Liabilities	78m	51m	59m

B Marshall Engineering Ltd
Dockside Road, Middlesbrough, TS3 8AT
Tel: 01642-211234 **Fax:** 01642-213050
E-mail: info@marshallengineering.co.uk
Website: http://www.marshallengineering.co.uk
Directors: J. Marshall (Fin), B. Marshall (MD)
Immediate Holding Company: B MARSHALL ENGINEERING LIMITED
Registration no: 06126993 **Date established:** 2007
No.of Employees: 1 - 10 **Product Groups:** 35

Date of Accounts	Feb 12	Feb 11	Feb 10
Working Capital	-234	-235	-271
Fixed Assets	316	332	350
Current Assets	155	156	219

Middlesborough Football Club
Riverside Stadium Middlehaven Way, Middlesbrough, TS3 6RS
Tel: 08444-996789 **Fax:** 01642-877840
E-mail: enquiries@mfc.co.uk
Website: http://www.mfc.co.uk
Managers: M. Smith, Y. Ferguson (Personnel), B. Brown (Tech Serv Mgr), A. Beige (Comptroller)
Immediate Holding Company: MFC.CO.UK LIMITED
Registration no: 03904202 **Date established:** 2000
Turnover: £50m - £75m **No.of Employees:** 101 - 250 **Product Groups:** 87

Date of Accounts	Dec 09	Dec 08	Dec 07
Sales Turnover	120	122	170
Pre Tax Profit/Loss	-105	-78	-50
Working Capital	-287	-180	-104
Fixed Assets	1	N/A	2
Current Assets	100	90	49
Current Liabilities	386	266	153

Mitie Property Services UK Ltd
3 Redesdale Court, Middlesbrough, TS2 1RL
Tel: 01642-247956 **Fax:** 01642-223378
E-mail: prop@mitie.co.uk
Website: http://www.mitie.com
Directors: W. Robson (Dir)
Ultimate Holding Company: MITIE GROUP PLC
Immediate Holding Company: MITIE PROPERTY SERVICES (UK) LIMITED
Registration no: 02935593 **VAT No.:** GB 633 4665 35
Date established: 1994 **Turnover:** £125m - £250m
No.of Employees: 1 - 10 **Product Groups:** 52

Date of Accounts	Mar 12	Mar 11	Mar 10
Sales Turnover	228m	148m	150m
Pre Tax Profit/Loss	8m	11m	12m
Working Capital	12m	19m	17m
Fixed Assets	7m	496	733
Current Assets	93m	72m	56m
Current Liabilities	9m	9m	10m

M P Storage & Banner Chemicals
Deepwater Wharf Dockside Road, Middlesbrough, TS3 8AS
Tel: 01642-244125 **Fax:** 01642-231780
E-mail: sales@mpstorage.com
Website: http://www.mpstorage.co.uk
Directors: H. Appleton (Co Sec)
Managers: M. Goodwin (Mgr)
Ultimate Holding Company: 2M HOLDINGS LTD
Immediate Holding Company: BANNER CHEMICALS LTD
Registration no: 02237196 **Turnover:** Up to £250,000
No.of Employees: 21 - 50 **Product Groups:** 32

Date of Accounts	Apr 08	Dec 06	Apr 06
Sales Turnover	2053	1039	N/A
Pre Tax Profit/Loss	56	212	N/A

Working Capital	687	578	385
Fixed Assets	878	931	968
Current Assets	870	834	568
Current Liabilities	183	256	183
Total Share Capital	2	2	2
ROCE% (Return on Capital Employed)	3.6	14.1	
ROT% (Return on Turnover)	2.7	20.4	

North East Countries Fire Protection Ltd

Yard Premises West Lane, Grangetown, Middlesbrough, TS6 7AA
Tel: 01642-466190 **Fax:** 01642-463882
E-mail: dconnor355@hotmail.co.uk
Directors: D. Connor (Fin)
Immediate Holding Company: NORTH EAST COUNTIES FIRE PROTECTION ENGINEERS LIMITED
Registration no: 04766597 **Date established:** 2003
No.of Employees: 1 - 10 **Product Groups:** 38, 42

Date of Accounts	May 11	May 10	May 09
Working Capital	15	27	42
Fixed Assets	21	30	38
Current Assets	35	50	70

Office Options

Sotherby Road, Middlesbrough, TS3 8BS
Tel: 01642-211100 **Fax:** 01642-227878
E-mail: sales@officeoptionsuk.com
Website: http://www.officeoptionsuk.com
Directors: A. Owen (Ptnr)
Date established: 2002 **No.of Employees:** 1 - 10 **Product Groups:** 52

Parson & Crosland Ltd

PO Box 10, Middlesbrough, TS2 1HG
Tel: 01642-244161 **Fax:** 01642-230487
E-mail: sales@parsonandcrosland.com
Website: http://www.parsonandcrosland.com
Bank(s): Barclays, Lea Valley, Hertford
Directors: A. Smith (Dir)
Managers: P. Bird (Sales Prom Mgr)
Ultimate Holding Company: MURRAY INTERNATIONAL HOLDINGS LIMITED
Immediate Holding Company: PARSON & CROSLAND LIMITED
Registration no: 08049085 **VAT No.:** GB 234 5397 55
Date established: 2012 **Turnover:** £5m - £10m **No.of Employees:** 21 - 50
Product Groups: 66

Date of Accounts	Jan 08	Jun 11	Jun 10
Sales Turnover	N/A	17m	13m
Pre Tax Profit/Loss	40	-809	-522
Working Capital	-118	3m	4m
Fixed Assets	2m	2m	2m
Current Assets	5	8m	7m
Current Liabilities	N/A	310	402

Paul J Watson Solicitors

The Vanguard Suite Broadcasting House, Middlesbrough, TS1 5JA
Tel: 01642-293427 **Fax:** 01642-293429
E-mail: jongouder@hotmail.com
Website: http://www.pauljwatson.com
Managers: G. Gouder (Sales Admin)
Immediate Holding Company: AZTEC TELECOM LTD
Registration no: 06523852 **Date established:** 2002
No.of Employees: 1 - 10 **Product Groups:** 80

Date of Accounts	Jun 07	Jun 06	Jun 04
Working Capital	13	5	-1
Current Assets	23	13	3

Profile Analysis Ltd (t/a Rocket Science)

3 Startforth Road Riverside Park Industrial Estate, Middlesbrough, TS2 1PJ
Tel: 01642-808888 **Fax:** 01642-249049
E-mail: alan.timothy@profile-analysis.com
Website: http://www.rocketscience.uk.com
Bank(s): National Westminster Bank Plc
Directors: A. Timothy (MD), J. Adams (Co Sec)
Immediate Holding Company: PROFILE ANALYSIS LIMITED
Registration no: 02579269 **Date established:** 1991 **Turnover:** £1m - £2m
No.of Employees: 21 - 50 **Product Groups:** 81

Date of Accounts	Oct 11	Oct 10	Oct 09
Working Capital	526	485	777
Fixed Assets	2	1	39
Current Assets	640	623	897

Q A Weldtech Ltd

Bowes Road, Middlesbrough, TS2 1LU
Tel: 01642-222831 **Fax:** 01642-242003
E-mail: quality@qaweldtech.co.uk
Website: http://www.qaweldtech.co.uk
Directors: C. Tighe (MD)
Managers: A. Dean, T. Elston (Purch Mgr), C. Roberts (Sales Admin), M. Brazier
Immediate Holding Company: Q.A. (WELD TECH) LIMITED
Registration no: 01479089 **Date established:** 1980 **Turnover:** £5m - £10m
No.of Employees: 51 - 100 **Product Groups:** 48

Date of Accounts	Feb 12	Feb 11	Feb 10
Sales Turnover	6m	7m	N/A
Pre Tax Profit/Loss	-186	342	N/A
Working Capital	1m	1m	1m
Fixed Assets	802	797	636
Current Assets	3m	3m	3m
Current Liabilities	687	517	N/A

R J Development & Regeneration Consultants Ltd

Springboard Business Centre Ellerbeck Way, Stokesley, Middlesbrough, TS9 5JZ
Tel: 01642-715345 **Fax:** 01642-715344
E-mail: office@audio-experts.co.uk
Website: http://www.audio-experts.co.uk
Directors: S. Brennan (Dir), T. Goldspink (Ptnr), R. Johnson (MD)
Immediate Holding Company: R J DEVELOPMENT & REGENERATION CONSULTANTS LIMITED
Registration no: 07055249 **Date established:** 2009
Turnover: Up to £250,000 **No.of Employees:** 1 - 10 **Product Groups:** 80

Richardson

Courville House 1 Ellerbeck Court, Stokesley, Middlesbrough, TS9 5PT
Tel: 01642-714791 **Fax:** 01642-714387
E-mail: enquiries@pcrichardson.co.uk
Website: http://www.pcrichardson.co.uk
Directors: J. Richardson (Ch), P. Richardson (MD), B. Jackson (Dir & Co Sec)
Managers: D. Richardson (Mktg Serv Mgr)
Ultimate Holding Company: PCR HOLDINGS LIMITED
Immediate Holding Company: RICHARDSON BROTHERS LIMITED
Registration no: 00247767 **VAT No.:** GB 258 5157 37
Date established: 1930 **Turnover:** £5m - £10m **No.of Employees:** 1 - 10
Product Groups: 35, 51, 52

Date of Accounts	Dec 10	Oct 09	Oct 08
Working Capital	1m	1m	1m
Current Assets	1m	1m	1m

Richardson's Shelving

Unit 6 Collingwood Court Riverside Park Industrial Estate, Middlesbrough, TS2 1RP
Tel: 01642-242228 **Fax:** 01642-242259
E-mail: sales@richardsonsuk.co.uk
Website: http://www.richardsonsuk.co.uk
Directors: L. Richardson (Ptnr)
VAT No.: GB 441 3169 73 **Date established:** 1986 **Turnover:** £1m - £2m
No.of Employees: 1 - 10 **Product Groups:** 26, 67

S B V Fabrication & Site Services Ltd

Dormor Way South Bank, Middlesbrough, TS6 6XH
Tel: 01642-253366 **Fax:** 01642-254466
E-mail: info@sbvfabrications.co.uk
Website: http://www.sbvfabrications.co.uk
Bank(s): Barclays
Directors: D. Geary (MD), S. Condren (Fin)
Managers: A. Bridgewater (Sales Prom Mgr), J. Betts (Projects), P. Craig (Personnel)
Ultimate Holding Company: ZENITH HOLDINGS LIMITED
Immediate Holding Company: SBV FABRICATION AND SITE SERVICES LIMITED
Registration no: 02532371 **VAT No.:** GB 499 2428 94
Date established: 1990 **Turnover:** £5m - £10m
No.of Employees: 51 - 100 **Product Groups:** 48

Date of Accounts	Dec 10	Dec 09	Dec 08
Sales Turnover	4m	4m	N/A
Pre Tax Profit/Loss	-250	93	N/A
Working Capital	2m	2m	2m
Fixed Assets	1m	1m	981
Current Assets	3m	3m	3m
Current Liabilities	927	602	N/A

S T D Engineering Services Ltd

104 High Street Eston, Middlesbrough, TS6 9EJ
Tel: 01642-454973
E-mail: office@std_eng.co.uk
Website: http://www.std-eng.co.uk
Directors: S. Dauncey (MD), M. Dauncey (Co Sec)
Immediate Holding Company: STD ENGINEERING SERVICES LIMITED
Registration no: 04466143 **Date established:** 2002
No.of Employees: 1 - 10 **Product Groups:** 46

Date of Accounts	Jun 11	Jun 10	Jun 09
Working Capital	29	28	49
Fixed Assets	N/A	N/A	6
Current Assets	42	38	66

Walter Smith Joinery Ltd

Westerby Road East Middlesbrough Industrial Estate, Middlesbrough, TS3 8BQ
Tel: 01642-221171 **Fax:** 01642-231342
Website: http://www.waltersmithjoineryltd.co.uk
Bank(s): HSBC
Directors: D. Gould (Dir), R. Jones (Dir), A. Hancocks (MD)
Managers: K. Readman (Sales Admin), P. Cheason (Sales Prom Mgr)
Ultimate Holding Company: B.I.E. HOLDINGS LIMITED
Immediate Holding Company: WALTER SMITH (JOINERY) LIMITED
Registration no: 00766163 **VAT No.:** GB 258 0706 55
Date established: 1963 **Turnover:** £500,000 - £1m
No.of Employees: 21 - 50 **Product Groups:** 08, 48, 52

Date of Accounts	Dec 10	Dec 09	Dec 08
Working Capital	75	84	251
Fixed Assets	38	34	44
Current Assets	159	163	336

Steel Benders

Dockside Road Industrial Estate Cochranes Wharf, Middlesbrough, TS3 6AU
Tel: 01642-244428 **Fax:** 01642-244429
E-mail: m.cooper@steelbenders.co.uk
Website: http://www.steelbenders.co.uk
Directors: M. Cooper (MD)
Immediate Holding Company: STEEL BENDERS (UK) LIMITED
Registration no: 04400578 **Date established:** 2002
No.of Employees: 11 - 20 **Product Groups:** 34, 66

Date of Accounts	Mar 12	Mar 11	Mar 10
Working Capital	182	89	34
Fixed Assets	203	193	223
Current Assets	467	364	201

Sulzer Dowding & Mills

Vulcan Works Lower East Street, Middlesbrough, TS2 1QQ
Tel: 01642-248451 **Fax:** 01642-232577
E-mail: carl.mudd@dowdingandmills.com
Website: http://www.sulzer.com
Managers: C. Mudd (District Mgr), T. Kay (Buyer)
Ultimate Holding Company: CASTLE SUPPORT SERVICES PLC
Immediate Holding Company: DOWDING & MILLS PLC
Registration no: SC028056 **Turnover:** £125m - £250m
No.of Employees: 21 - 50 **Product Groups:** 37, 44, 45, 48, 84, 85

T & D Alstom Ltd

4a Brighouse Business Village Brighouse Road, Middlesbrough, TS2 1RT
Tel: 01642-254280 **Fax:** 01642-254287
Website: http://www.areva-td.com
Managers: A. Green (Mgr)
No.of Employees: 1 - 10 **Product Groups:** 34, 37, 52, 84

Teesside Precision Engineering Ltd

Skippers Lane Industrial Estate Skippers Lane, Middlesbrough, TS6 6HA
Tel: 01642-455295 **Fax:** 01642-440465
E-mail: enquiry@tpe-ltd.com
Website: http://www.tpe-ltd.com
Managers: S. Dean (Sales Admin)
Registration no: 07113748 **Date established:** 2010 **Turnover:**
No.of Employees: 11 - 20 **Product Groups:** 46, 48, 67, 81

Teesside Technology Solutions Ltd

Suite 29 Enterprise Court Puddlers Court, Middlesbrough, TS6 6TL
Tel: 01642-438401 **Fax:** 0870-766 8570
E-mail: sales@applaud.uk.com
Website: http://www.applaud.uk.com
Directors: P. Hassock (Co Sec)
Immediate Holding Company: TEESSIDE TECHNOLOGY SOLUTIONS LIMITED
Registration no: 05398627 **Date established:** 2005
Turnover: £500,000 - £1m **No.of Employees:** 1 - 10 **Product Groups:** 44

Date of Accounts	Mar 11	Mar 10	Mar 09
Working Capital	25	38	36
Fixed Assets	37	6	1
Current Assets	84	84	74

Teesside Trailer Hire

Unit B Skippers Lane Industrial Estate, Middlesbrough, TS6 6JB
Tel: 01642-206558 **Fax:** 01642-460873
E-mail: corner625@yahoo.co.uk
Website: http://www.teesidetrailorhire.co.uk
Directors: S. Grant (Fin), K. Hunter (MD), R. Corner (Prop)
Managers: P. Blewitt (Grp Mgr), P. Jackson (Comm)
Immediate Holding Company: FARRELL FABRICATIONS LIMITED
Registration no: 04205548 **Date established:** 1996 **Turnover:** £2m - £5m
No.of Employees: 1 - 10 **Product Groups:** 86

Date of Accounts	Mar 11	Mar 10	Mar 09
Working Capital	103	117	118
Fixed Assets	69	68	76
Current Assets	302	265	350

Timber Packing Cases

Barnes & Woodhouseferndale One Commercial St, Middlesbrough, TS2 1JT
Tel: 01642-224092 **Fax:** 01642-251272
E-mail: enquiries@timberpackingcases.com
Website: http://www.timberpackingcases.com
Managers: C. Woodhouse (Sales Prom Mgr)
Date established: 1955 **Turnover:** £500,000 - £1m
No.of Employees: 1 - 10 **Product Groups:** 25, 66

Weschenfelder

North Road, Middlesbrough, TS2 1DD
Tel: 01642-247524 **Fax:** 01642-249336
E-mail: tim.wesch@weschenfelder.co.uk
Website: http://www.weschenfelder.co.uk
Directors: T. Weschenfelder (MD), T. Weschenfelder (Dir), J. Weschenfelder (Dir)
Ultimate Holding Company: WESCHENFELDER (SALES) LIMITED
Immediate Holding Company: DIXONS OF DARLINGTON LIMITED
Registration no: 00878173 **Date established:** 1966
Turnover: £500,000 - £1m **No.of Employees:** 1 - 10 **Product Groups:** 30, 33, 40, 67

Zemira Designs

26 Fairwood Park Marton-in-Cleveland, Middlesbrough, TS8 9XP
Tel: 01642-271440
E-mail: zemiradesigns@hotmail.com
Directors: J. Harrison (Prop)
Immediate Holding Company: DB10 ENGINEERING LIMITED
Date established: 2010 **No.of Employees:** 1 - 10 **Product Groups:** 52

Date of Accounts	Dec 11
Working Capital	23
Fixed Assets	1
Current Assets	45

Redcar

Allendale Components Ltd

28 Allendale Tee New Marske, Redcar, TS11 8HN
Tel: 01642-478738 **Fax:** 01642-272683
E-mail: t.wall@ntlworld.com
Directors: P. Wall (Fin), A. Wall (MD)
Immediate Holding Company: ALLENDALE COMPONENTS LIMITED
Registration no: 04810638 **VAT No.:** GB 499 3315 05
Date established: 2003 **Turnover:** Up to £250,000
No.of Employees: 1 - 10 **Product Groups:** 48

Date of Accounts	Apr 12	Apr 11	Apr 10
Working Capital	-75	-80	-46
Fixed Assets	314	261	289
Current Assets	43	15	42

Connect 2 Technology Ltd

Longbeck Road Marske-by-the-sea, Redcar, TS11 6HQ
Tel: 01642-492220 **Fax:** 01642-492223
E-mail: enquiries@connect2t.co.uk
Website: http://www.connect2t.co.uk
Directors: A. Gleghorn (MD), K. Harding (Chief Op Offcr), G. Cook (Fin), G. Nossiter (Sales)
Managers: J. Walker (Tech Serv Mgr), A. Rock (Personnel)
Ultimate Holding Company: CLEVELAND CIRCUITS LIMITED
Immediate Holding Company: CONNECT-2 TECHNOLOGY LIMITED
Registration no: 03028919 **VAT No.:** GB 602 2019 06
Date established: 1995 **Turnover:** £2m - £5m **No.of Employees:** 51 - 100
Product Groups: 37, 48, 67

Containerships UK Ltd

The Wilton Centre Wilton, Redcar, TS10 4RF
Tel: 01642-468592 **Fax:** 01642-770737
E-mail: sales@containerships.co.uk
Website: http://www.containerships.co.uk
Directors: C. Patton (MD)
Managers: M. Colledge (Comptroller), W. Hall (Personnel), L. Warren (Sales Prom Mgr)
Ultimate Holding Company: CONTAINER FINANCE LTD OY (FINLAND)
Immediate Holding Company: CONTAINERSHIPS (UK) LTD
Registration no: 02237324 **Date established:** 1988
Turnover: £20m - £50m **No.of Employees:** 101 - 250 **Product Groups:** 76

Date of Accounts	Dec 11	Dec 10	Dec 09
Sales Turnover	37m	36m	34m
Pre Tax Profit/Loss	34	17	9
Working Capital	1m	1m	1m
Fixed Assets	251	274	270
Current Assets	3m	4m	3m
Current Liabilities	205	319	218

D J Tucker Ltd
Longbeck Trading Estate Marske-By-The-Sea, Redcar, TS11 6HS
Tel: 01642-471361 **Fax:** 01642-471369
Directors: D. Tucker (MD)
Immediate Holding Company: D.J. TUCKER LIMITED
Registration no: 01496967 **Date established:** 1980
Turnover: £250,000 - £500,000 **No.of Employees:** 1 - 10
Product Groups: 52

Date of Accounts	Aug 11	Aug 10	Aug 09
Working Capital	116	372	369
Fixed Assets	412	272	300
Current Assets	233	581	594

H Jarvis Ltd
Longbeck Estate Marske-By-The-Sea, Redcar, TS11 6HH
Tel: 01642-482366 **Fax:** 01642-484015
E-mail: c.jarvis@hjarvisandson.co.uk
Website: http://www.hjarvis.co.uk
Bank(s): Barclays
Directors: C. Jarvis (Prop), D. Glendinning (MD)
Immediate Holding Company: H. JARVIS LTD
Registration no: 00419975 **VAT No.:** GB 257 7299 13
Date established: 1946 **Turnover:** £2m - £5m **No.of Employees:** 21 - 50
Product Groups: 30

Date of Accounts	Dec 11	Dec 10	Dec 09
Working Capital	2m	2m	2m
Fixed Assets	1m	2m	925
Current Assets	2m	2m	2m

Inshore Fisheries Ltd
Inshore Fisheries House Tod Point Road, Redcar, TS10 5AU
Tel: 01642-484125 **Fax:** 01642-486749
E-mail: sales@inshore.co.uk
Website: http://www.inshore.co.uk
Directors: M. Rogerson (Dir), P. Lowery (Dir), H. Cook (Dir)
Immediate Holding Company: INSHORE FISHERIES LIMITED
Registration no: 05296983 **Date established:** 2004
Turnover: £10m - £20m **No.of Employees:** 11 - 20 **Product Groups:** 62

Date of Accounts	Dec 09	Dec 08	Mar 11
Working Capital	116	360	152
Fixed Assets	16	21	18
Current Assets	1m	1m	967

R J Fabrications
Unit 5 Garbutt Business Park Longbeck Estate, Marske-By-The-Sea, Redcar, TS11 6HB
Tel: 01642-484422
Directors: R. Ross (Prop)
Immediate Holding Company: PIPELINE PROFILE COMPANY LIMITED
Date established: 2005 **No.of Employees:** 1 - 10 **Product Groups:** 35

Date of Accounts	Oct 11	Oct 10	Oct 09
Working Capital	131	112	69
Fixed Assets	33	42	42
Current Assets	375	259	198

Redcar & Cleveland Youth Inclusion Project
Redcar Station Business Centre Station Road, Redcar, TS10 1RD
Tel: 01642-495735 **Fax:** 01642-495735
Website: http://www.cleveland.ac.uk
Managers: T. Basche (Mgr)
Immediate Holding Company: REDCAR AND CLEVELAND MIND
Registration no: 07626797 **Date established:** 2011
Turnover: £250,000 - £500,000 **No.of Employees:** 1 - 10
Product Groups: 86

Stellar Consultancy (UK) Limited
64 Newmarket Road, Redcar, TS10 2JA
Tel: 01642-285655 **Fax:** 0871-9004967
E-mail: steve.jones@stellarconsultancy.com
Website: http://www.stellarconsultancy.com
Directors: S. Jones (MD)
Registration no: 06683430 **Date established:** 2008
Turnover: Up to £250,000 **No.of Employees:** 1 - 10 **Product Groups:** 80

Typhoon International Ltd
Limerick Road, Redcar, TS10 5JU
Tel: 01642-486104 **Fax:** 01642-487204
E-mail: sales@typhoon-int.co.uk
Website: http://www.typhoon-int.co.uk
Bank(s): HSBC Bank plc
Directors: S. Ward (MD)
Managers: H. Coupe (Mktg Serv Mgr), H. Scanlon (Fin Mgr)
Ultimate Holding Company: TYPHOON HOLDINGS LIMITED
Immediate Holding Company: TYPHOON INTERNATIONAL LIMITED
Registration no: 00462364 **VAT No.:** GB 438 7530 29
Date established: 1948 **Turnover:** £5m - £10m
No.of Employees: 51 - 100 **Product Groups:** 24, 40

Date of Accounts	Oct 11	Oct 10	Oct 09
Sales Turnover	7m	7m	8m
Pre Tax Profit/Loss	106	150	144
Working Capital	2m	2m	2m
Fixed Assets	554	452	442
Current Assets	4m	4m	4m
Current Liabilities	227	243	216

Weyfringe Labelling Systems
Longbeck Road Marske-by-the-Sea, Redcar, TS11 6HQ
Tel: 01642-490121 **Fax:** 01642-490385
E-mail: sales@weyfringe.co.uk
Website: http://www.weyfringe.co.uk
Bank(s): Barclays Bank
Directors: A. Gleghorn (Fin), G. Nossiter (Fin)
Ultimate Holding Company: CLEVELAND CIRCUITS LIMITED
Immediate Holding Company: WEYFRINGE LIMITED
Registration no: 00825319 **Date established:** 1964 **Turnover:** £2m - £5m
No.of Employees: 11 - 20 **Product Groups:** 27, 28, 42, 43, 44

Saltburn By The Sea

Cleveland Circuits Ltd
Skelton Industrial Estate Skelton-In-Cleveland, Saltburn By The Sea, TS12 2LQ
Tel: 01287-651991 **Fax:** 01287-652898
E-mail: sales@pcb.co.uk
Website: http://www.pcb.co.uk
Bank(s): Barclays
Directors: A. Chiles (Dir), A. Gleghorn (Dir)
Ultimate Holding Company: CLEVELAND CIRCUITS LIMITED
Immediate Holding Company: CLEVELAND CIRCUITS (SKELTON) LIMITED
Registration no: 02775373 **Date established:** 1993 **Turnover:** £1m - £2m
No.of Employees: 51 - 100 **Product Groups:** 37, 44, 84

Consteel Technical Services Ltd
Clarens House Milton Street, Saltburn By The Sea, TS12 1EW
Tel: 01287-623378 **Fax:** 01287-624779
E-mail: ken.clewes@consteel.co.uk
Website: http://www.consteel.co.uk
Directors: D. Hirshfeld (Fin), J. Hall (Co Sec), C. Joy (Dir)
Ultimate Holding Company: HIRSCHFELD INC (USA)
Immediate Holding Company: CONSTEEL TECHNICAL SERVICES LIMITED
Registration no: 01266415 **Date established:** 1976
No.of Employees: 21 - 50 **Product Groups:** 07, 35, 42, 44, 48, 51, 52, 54, 80, 84, 85

Date of Accounts	Dec 11	Dec 10	Dec 09
Working Capital	-47	285	494
Fixed Assets	14	30	69
Current Assets	310	495	554

Marske Machine Co
Flat 1 The Zetland Marine Parade, Saltburn By The Sea, TS12 1BU
Tel: 01642-713388 **Fax:** 01642-718 929
E-mail: enquiries@marske.com
Website: http://www.marske.com
Directors: T. McCullagh (Ptnr), T. McCullogh (MD)
Managers: A. Burton (Admin Off), R. Fox
Immediate Holding Company: MARSKE SITE SERVICES UK LIMITED
Registration no: 01831529 **VAT No.:** GB 546 8202 38
Date established: 2005 **Turnover:** £2m - £5m **No.of Employees:** 1 - 10
Product Groups: 48, 80

Mold In Graphic Systems
Skelton Industrial Estate Skelton-In-Cleveland, Saltburn By The Sea, TS12 2NW
Tel: 01287-623332 **Fax:** 01287-625664
E-mail: info@moldinggraphics.com
Website: http://www.moldinggraphics.com
Directors: N. Moldan (Sales), P. Clark (MD), D. Horsall (Dir)
Turnover: £2m - £5m **No.of Employees:** 1 - 10 **Product Groups:** 30, 42, 66, 67

Morr Laminat
Exeter Street, Saltburn By The Sea, TS12 1BN
Tel: 01287-624954 **Fax:** 01287-205931
E-mail: phildove@f2s.com
Website: http://www.morr-laminat.co.uk
Directors: P. Dove (Prop)
Date established: 2004 **Turnover:** Up to £250,000
No.of Employees: 1 - 10 **Product Groups:** 30, 52, 66

Peel Jones Copper Products Ltd
Maynard Foundry Kilton Lane, Carlin How, Saltburn By The Sea, TS13 4EY
Tel: 01287-640658 **Fax:** 01287-642906
E-mail: ian@peeljonescopper.com
Website: http://www.peeljones.sageweb.co.uk
Bank(s): Barclays
Directors: A. Young (Tech Serv), I. Young (Ch), P. Garner (MD)
Managers: A. Sibills (Purch Mgr), A. Whittaker (Fin Mgr), B. Dowey (Sales Prom Mgr)
Immediate Holding Company: PEEL JONES COPPER PRODUCTS LIMITED
Registration no: 00929198 **VAT No.:** GB 258 0938 34
Date established: 1968 **Turnover:** £2m - £5m **No.of Employees:** 51 - 100
Product Groups: 34, 46

Date of Accounts	Oct 11	Oct 10	Oct 09
Working Capital	1m	1m	1m
Fixed Assets	389	427	467
Current Assets	2m	2m	1m

Stockton On Tees

A B Fabrications Ltd
Unit 2 Carrol Street, Stockton On Tees, TS18 2SE
Tel: 01642-608822 **Fax:** 01642-608822
Directors: D. Umplby (Dir)
Immediate Holding Company: AB FABRICATIONS LIMITED
Registration no: 05460772 **Date established:** 2005
No.of Employees: 1 - 10 **Product Groups:** 35

Date of Accounts	Mar 11	Mar 10	Mar 09
Working Capital	15	4	19
Fixed Assets	15	18	22
Current Assets	71	37	57

Access Ladders
208 Durham Road, Stockton On Tees, TS19 0PT
Tel: 01642-355308 **Fax:** 01642-675240
E-mail: sales@accessladdersuk.com
Website: http://www.accessladdersuk.com
Directors: J. Dobbing (Dir)
Immediate Holding Company: ACCESS LADDERS (UK) LIMITED
Registration no: 02983939 **Date established:** 1994
No.of Employees: 1 - 10 **Product Groups:** 35

Date of Accounts	May 11	May 10	May 09
Working Capital	12	14	10
Fixed Assets	9	13	19
Current Assets	44	50	70

Acquistions International
Redheugh House Thornaby Place, Thornaby, Stockton On Tees, TS17 6SG
Tel: 01642-607204 **Fax:** 01642-671749
E-mail: phil@acquisitionsinternational.com
Website: http://www.acquisitionsinternational.com
Directors: P. Monaghan (Dir)
Turnover: £1m - £2m **No.of Employees:** 11 - 20 **Product Groups:** 80

Aker Kvaerner Engineering Services Ltd
Phoenix House 3 Surtees Way, Surtees Business Park, Stockton On Tees, TS18 3HR
Tel: 01642-334000 **Fax:** 01642-334001
E-mail: bus.dev@akersolutions.com
Website: http://www.akersolutions.com
Managers: C. Milewood (I.T. Exec), J. Turner (Personnel), N. Routledge (Sales Prom Mgr)
Ultimate Holding Company: Kvaernar Enc
Immediate Holding Company: Kvaernar P.L.C.
Registration no: 04967961 **VAT No.:** GB 441 4341 82
Turnover: £125m - £250m **No.of Employees:** 1001 - 1500
Product Groups: 42, 45, 54

Date of Accounts	Dec 08
Sales Turnover	101380
Pre Tax Profit/Loss	8960
Working Capital	19380
Current Assets	46630
Current Liabilities	27250
Total Share Capital	51000
ROCE% (Return on Capital Employed)	46.2

Amos Swift Co. Ltd
Boathouse Lane, Stockton On Tees, TS18 3AW
Tel: 01642-675241 **Fax:** 01642-675241
E-mail: john.hingley@ntlworld.com
Directors: J. Hingley (MD)
Immediate Holding Company: AMOS SWIFT & COMPANY,LIMITED
Registration no: 00217084 **VAT No.:** GB 257 5332 57
Date established: 2026 **Turnover:** Up to £250,000
No.of Employees: 1 - 10 **Product Groups:** 63

Date of Accounts	Jun 11	Jun 10	Jun 09
Working Capital	34	39	38
Fixed Assets	6	6	7
Current Assets	79	61	58

Andrews Sykes Hire Ltd
Salters Lane Sedgefield, Stockton On Tees, TS21 3EE
Tel: 01740-620141 **Fax:** 01740-622753
E-mail: sedgefield@andrews-sykes.com
Website: http://www.andrews-sykes.com
Managers: J. Christian (Mgr)
Immediate Holding Company: ANDREWS SYKES HIRE LIMITED
Registration no: 02985657 **VAT No.:** GB 100 4295 24
Date established: 1994 **Turnover:** £5m - £10m **No.of Employees:** 11 - 20
Product Groups: 40

Date of Accounts	Dec 11	Dec 10	Dec 09
Sales Turnover	35m	36m	34m
Pre Tax Profit/Loss	10m	10m	8m
Working Capital	8m	6m	2m
Fixed Assets	7m	7m	9m
Current Assets	33m	35m	35m
Current Liabilities	7m	7m	5m

Appleyard Locksmith
24 Norton Road, Stockton On Tees, TS18 2BS
Tel: 01642-880777 **Fax:** 01642-670298
E-mail: info@lockout-tagout.co.uk
Website: http://www.lockout-tagout.co.uk
Directors: P. Appleyard (Prop)
Immediate Holding Company: LOCKOUT TAGOUT SAFETY LIMITED
Registration no: 06863995 **Date established:** 2009
Turnover: £500,000 - £1m **No.of Employees:** 1 - 10 **Product Groups:** 40

Arco Stockton Ltd
Malleable Way, Stockton On Tees, TS18 2QX
Tel: 01642-617441 **Fax:** 01642-617025
E-mail: arco.teesside@arco.co.uk
Website: http://www.arco.co.uk
Managers: N. Marshall
Ultimate Holding Company: AGILE GROUP LIMITED
Immediate Holding Company: AGILE COMMUNICATIONS LIMITED
Registration no: 00820957 **Date established:** 2006
Turnover: £125m - £250m **No.of Employees:** 21 - 50
Product Groups: 24, 29, 30, 40

Date of Accounts	Dec 11	Dec 10	Dec 09
Working Capital	-41	-31	-11
Current Assets	3	13	22

Atkins Consultants Ltd
Dunedin House Riverside Columbia Drive, Thornaby, Stockton On Tees, TS17 6BJ
Tel: 01642-525200 **Fax:** 01642-525201
E-mail: paul.hinley@atkinsglobal.com
Website: http://www.atkinsglobal.com
Managers: P. Hinley
Ultimate Holding Company: WS ATKINS PLC
Immediate Holding Company: ATKINS CONSULTANTS LIMITED
Registration no: 00755613 **VAT No.:** GB 209 8612 53
Date established: 1963 **Turnover:** Up to £250,000
No.of Employees: 51 - 100 **Product Groups:** 84

Date of Accounts	Mar 12	Mar 11	Mar 10
Sales Turnover	N/A	N/A	73
Pre Tax Profit/Loss	N/A	-1	-1
Working Capital	248	248	247
Current Assets	285	285	286

Barwick Dental Services
6 Myton Road Ingleby Barwick, Stockton On Tees, TS17 0WA
Tel: 01642-751887 **Fax:** 01642-751887
Directors: A. Robinson (Fin), C. Robinson (MD)
Immediate Holding Company: BARWICK DENTAL LABORATORY SERVICES LIMITED
Registration no: 04512337 **Date established:** 2002
Turnover: £500,000 - £1m **No.of Employees:** 11 - 20
Product Groups: 38, 67

Date of Accounts	Aug 11	Aug 10	Aug 09
Working Capital	314	283	250
Fixed Assets	55	52	42
Current Assets	427	399	348

Batt Cables plc
Wellington House Falcon Court, Preston Farm Industrial Estate, Stockton On Tees, TS18 3TS
Tel: 01642-678633 **Fax:** 01642-674487
E-mail: kate.williams@batt.co.uk
Website: http://www.batt.co.uk
Managers: K. Williams (Mgr)
Immediate Holding Company: BATT CABLES PLC
Registration no: 01353688 **Date established:** 1978
No.of Employees: 1 - 10 **Product Groups:** 30, 35, 36, 37, 38, 44, 66, 67

Date of Accounts	Mar 12	Mar 11	Mar 10
Sales Turnover	106m	98m	84m
Pre Tax Profit/Loss	8m	9m	5m
Working Capital	41m	36m	31m
Fixed Assets	8m	9m	8m
Current Assets	69m	60m	54m
Current Liabilities	3m	3m	2m

Beta Electronics
Dukesway Teesside Industrial Estate, Stockton On Tees, TS17 9LT
Tel: 01642-765321 **Fax:** 01642-760155
E-mail: steve@betaelectronics.co.uk
Website: http://www.betaelectronics.co.uk
Bank(s): National Westminster Bank Plc
Directors: S. Kclincke (Prop), S. Klincke (Prop)
VAT No.: GB 441 3409 79 **Turnover:** £5m - £10m
No.of Employees: 11 - 20 **Product Groups:** 45, 67

Bodycote Heat Treatment
Stillington, Stockton On Tees, TS21 1LD
Tel: 01740-630353 **Fax:** 01740-630075
E-mail: barry.maven@bodycoteheat.com
Website: http://www.bodycoteheat.com
Bank(s): National Westminster
Managers: B. Maven (Mgr)
Ultimate Holding Company: WEIR GROUP P.L.C.
Immediate Holding Company: DARCHEM ENG LTD
Registration no: 00146396 **VAT No.:** GB 602 2424 94
Date established: 1968 **Turnover:** £1m - £2m **No.of Employees:** 11 - 20
Product Groups: 48, 85

Carroll & Meynell Transformers Ltd
5 Guisley Way Durham Lane Industrial Park, Eaglescliffe, Stockton On Tees, TS16 0RF
Tel: 01642-617406 **Fax:** 01642-614178
E-mail: enquiries@carroll-meynell.com
Website: http://www.carroll-meynell.com
Bank(s): National Westminster
Directors: M. Meynell (MD)
Managers: P. McGurr (Comm), D. Simpson (Personnel), J. Shippey
Immediate Holding Company: CARROLL & MEYNELL TRANSFORMERS LIMITED
Registration no: 05533078 **VAT No.:** GB 259 3615 37
Date established: 2005 **No.of Employees:** 21 - 50 **Product Groups:** 37

Date of Accounts	Sep 11	Sep 10	Sep 09
Working Capital	-76	-235	-290
Fixed Assets	565	584	622
Current Assets	3m	2m	2m

Carter Steel Ltd
Yarm Road, Stockton On Tees, TS18 3SA
Tel: 01642-679831 **Fax:** 01642-670346
E-mail: david.carter@cartersteel.co.uk
Website: http://www.cartersteelltd.co.uk
Bank(s): Barclays
Directors: D. Carter (MD), J. Carter (Sales)
Immediate Holding Company: CARTER STEEL LIMITED
Registration no: 00982504 **VAT No.:** GB 247 5453 39
Date established: 1970 **Turnover:** £1m - £2m **No.of Employees:** 11 - 20
Product Groups: 66

Date of Accounts	May 12	May 11	May 10
Working Capital	1m	1m	1m
Fixed Assets	119	145	257
Current Assets	1m	1m	1m

Caterpillar Stockton Ltd
2 Handley Close Preston Farm Industrial Estate, Stockton On Tees, TS18 3SD
Tel: 01642-625500 **Fax:** 01642-612445
E-mail: info@worthygroup.co.uk
Website: http://www.caterpilliar.com
Directors: A. Johnston (Fin), N. Burroughs (Dir)
Managers: A. McKay (Fin Mgr)
Ultimate Holding Company: CATERPILLAR UK GROUP LTD
Immediate Holding Company: EASTFIELD NO 24 LIMITED
Registration no: 02153095 **VAT No.:** GB 661 5461 37
Date established: 1987 **No.of Employees:** 51 - 100 **Product Groups:** 45

Chubb Fire & Security Limited
Concorde House Concorde Way, Preston Farm Business Park, Stockton On Tees, TS18 3RB
Tel: 0844-8791820 **Fax:** 01642-602023
E-mail: info@chubb.co.uk
Website: http://www.chubb.co.uk
Managers: M. Rodger (District Mgr), M. Rodgers (District Mgr), C. Harrington (District Mgr)
Immediate Holding Company: Chubb Group Security Ltd
Registration no: 00524469 **Date established:** 1969
Turnover: £50m - £75m **No.of Employees:** 101 - 250 **Product Groups:** 81

Ray Clark
3 St Marys Gate Business Park Station Street, Stockton On Tees, TS20 2AB
Tel: 01642-614446 **Fax:** 01642-604333
E-mail: ray@catering87.freeserve.co.uk
Website: http://www.rayclark.co.uk
Directors: R. Clark (Ptnr)
No.of Employees: 1 - 10 **Product Groups:** 20, 40, 41

Cleveland Biotech
3 Vanguard Court Preston Farm Business Park, Preston Farm Industrial Estate, Stockton On Tees, TS18 3TR
Tel: 01642-647267 **Fax:** 01642-606040
E-mail: bugs@clevebio.com
Website: http://www.clevebio.com
Directors: B. Hoskins (MD), C. Maclean (Dir), E. Winfield (Co Sec), K. Hazley (Sales)
Immediate Holding Company: CLEVELAND BIOTECH LIMITED
Registration no: 02775682 **VAT No.:** GB 602 1892 66
Date established: 1992 **No.of Employees:** 1 - 10 **Product Groups:** 31, 32, 54

Date of Accounts	Mar 11	Mar 10	Mar 09
Working Capital	961	739	676
Fixed Assets	54	62	84
Current Assets	1m	884	855

Conveyors Direct Online Ltd
Unit 6 Fishburn Industrial Estate Fishburn, Stockton On Tees, TS21 4AJ
Tel: 01740-623338 **Fax:** 01740-622504
E-mail: sales@conveyorsdirect.co.uk
Website: http://www.conveyorsdirect.co.uk
Directors: S. Spoors (MD), A. Worrall (Fin)
Immediate Holding Company: AUTOVEYTION (UK) LTD
Registration no: 04332638 **Date established:** 2001
Turnover: £250,000 - £500,000 **No.of Employees:** 1 - 10
Product Groups: 35, 39, 45

Date of Accounts	Dec 09	Dec 08	Dec 07
Sales Turnover	466	579	629
Pre Tax Profit/Loss	3	-215	292
Working Capital	-118	-104	168
Fixed Assets	7	10	13
Current Assets	182	238	429
Current Liabilities	233	281	190

Crossling
Portrack Grange Road, Stockton On Tees, TS18 2PF
Tel: 01642-616996 **Fax:** 01642-616231
E-mail: stockton@crossling.co.uk
Website: http://www.crossling.co.uk
Bank(s): Lloyds
Managers: G. Turner (District Mgr)
Immediate Holding Company: T. CROSSLING & CO. LTD
Registration no: 02749235 **VAT No.:** GB 176 0964 39
Date established: 1885 **Turnover:** £20m - £50m
No.of Employees: 21 - 50 **Product Groups:** 30, 36

D M V UK
PO Box 876, Stockton On Tees, TS19 1HU
Tel: 01642-646687 **Fax:** 01642-646687
E-mail: sales@dmv-uk.com
Website: http://www.dmv-uk.com
Directors: M. Cottle (Prop)
No.of Employees: 1 - 10 **Product Groups:** 67, 85

Dacrylate Paints Ltd
44 Norton Road, Stockton On Tees, TS18 2BS
Tel: 01642-616429
Website: http://www.dacrylate.co.uk
Managers: G. Dalby (Mgr)
Ultimate Holding Company: DACRYLATE LIMITED
Immediate Holding Company: DACRYLATE PAINTS LIMITED
Registration no: 01744820 **Date established:** 1983
No.of Employees: 1 - 10 **Product Groups:** 46, 48

Date of Accounts	Aug 11	Aug 10	Aug 09
Working Capital	2m	2m	1m
Fixed Assets	92	50	64
Current Assets	2m	2m	2m

Dplan Ltd
Freeman House Thornaby Road, Thornaby, Stockton On Tees, TS17 8AA
Tel: 01642-803454 **Fax:** 01642-803454
E-mail: orders@dplan.co.uk
Website: http://www.dplan.co.uk
Directors: L. Blackburn (MD)
Registration no: 04681992 **Turnover:** Up to £250,000
No.of Employees: 1 - 10 **Product Groups:** 62

Dual Brown & Sons Ltd
Ross Road, Stockton On Tees, TS18 2NH
Tel: 01642-602226 **Fax:** 01642-602227
Directors: J. Allen (Dir)
Immediate Holding Company: DUAL BROWN & SONS LIMITED
Registration no: 02432035 **VAT No.:** GB 547 0734 39
Date established: 1989 **Turnover:** Up to £250,000
No.of Employees: 1 - 10 **Product Groups:** 48

Date of Accounts	Apr 11	Apr 10	Apr 09
Working Capital	227	211	179
Fixed Assets	463	400	419
Current Assets	312	279	226

Esab Group UK Ltd
Logistics Centre Durham Lane, Eaglescliffe, Stockton On Tees, TS16 0RW
Tel: 01642-785374 **Fax:** 01642-785371
Website: http://www.esab.co.uk
Directors: B. Wise (Sales)
Ultimate Holding Company: CHARTER INTERNATIONAL PLC (JERSEY)
Immediate Holding Company: ESAB GROUP (UK) LTD
Registration no: 00275947 **Date established:** 1933
No.of Employees: 1 - 10 **Product Groups:** 46

Date of Accounts	Dec 10	Dec 09	Dec 08
Sales Turnover	33m	31m	35m
Pre Tax Profit/Loss	2m	-920	4m
Working Capital	72m	40m	43m
Fixed Assets	169	226	330
Current Assets	88m	56m	58m
Current Liabilities	3m	4m	3m

Fibox Ltd
Suite 25 Durham Tees Valley Business Centre Orde Wingate Way, Stockton On Tees, TS19 0GD
Tel: 01642-604400 **Fax:** 01642-604600
E-mail: sales@fibox.co.uk
Website: http://www.fibox.com
Directors: S. Gallon (MD)
Ultimate Holding Company: FIBOX OY AB (FINLAND)
Immediate Holding Company: FIBOX LIMITED
Registration no: 03218542 **Date established:** 1996
No.of Employees: 11 - 20 **Product Groups:** 30, 35, 37

Date of Accounts	Dec 11	Dec 10	Dec 09
Working Capital	312	347	340
Fixed Assets	4	7	8
Current Assets	692	709	648

Filter Services Ltd
Unit 8 Orde Wingate Way, Stockton On Tees, TS19 0GA
Tel: 01642-604752 **Fax:** 01642-618740
E-mail: sales@filterservices.co.uk
Website: http://www.filterservices.co.uk
Directors: J. Yeouart (MD)
Ultimate Holding Company: D R M LIMITED
Immediate Holding Company: FILTER SERVICES LIMITED
Registration no: 01611206 **Date established:** 1982
No.of Employees: 1 - 10 **Product Groups:** 38, 42

Date of Accounts	Dec 11	Dec 10	Dec 09
Working Capital	174	154	138
Fixed Assets	27	23	13
Current Assets	227	203	207

Flanges Ltd
PO Box 1, Stockton On Tees, TS18 2PL
Tel: 01642-672626 **Fax:** 01642-617574
E-mail: sales@flanges-ltd.co.uk
Website: http://www.flanges-ltd.co.uk
Bank(s): HSBC Bank plc
Directors: A. Thompson (Sales), J. Inch (Dir)
Managers: P. Parker (Admin Off)
Immediate Holding Company: FLANGES LIMITED
Registration no: 00735863 **VAT No.:** GB 257 5813 35
Date established: 1962 **Turnover:** £1m - £2m **No.of Employees:** 21 - 50
Product Groups: 34, 36, 48

Date of Accounts	Sep 11	Sep 10	Sep 09
Working Capital	673	668	785
Fixed Assets	464	437	311
Current Assets	1m	1m	1m

H P F Energy Services
99 Sadler Forster Way Teesside Industrial Estate, Stockton On Tees, TS17 9JY
Tel: 01642-750009 **Fax:** 01642-750044
E-mail: thornaby@hpf-energy.com
Website: http://www.hpf-energy.com
Directors: L. Hopper (Prop)
Immediate Holding Company: MARLA TUBE FITTINGS LTD
Registration no: 00709160 **Turnover:** £20m - £50m
No.of Employees: 1 - 10 **Product Groups:** 36

Harrison Packaging
Easter Park Teesside Industrial Estate, Stockton On Tees, TS17 9NT
Tel: 01642-754600 **Fax:** 01642-769900
E-mail: sales@harrisonpack.com
Website: http://www.harrisonpack.com
Bank(s): Barclays
Directors: M. Caffry (Fin), H. Whitehead (MD)
Managers: R. Mawson (Tech Serv Mgr), R. French (Purch Mgr), M. Baum
Registration no: 00108064 **VAT No.:** GB 317 5644 52
Turnover: £2m - £5m **No.of Employees:** 101 - 250 **Product Groups:** 27

Date of Accounts	Jan 08	Jan 07	Jan 06
Sales Turnover	12137	11040	8514
Pre Tax Profit/Loss	1190	1144	593
Working Capital	1133	1009	861
Fixed Assets	2466	2690	2742
Current Assets	4961	4230	3526
Current Liabilities	3827	3221	2665
Total Share Capital	37	37	37
ROCE% (Return on Capital Employed)	33.1	30.9	16.5
ROT% (Return on Turnover)	9.8	10.4	7.0

C A Hields Engineers Ltd
9 Wass Way Eaglescliffe, Stockton On Tees, TS16 0RG
Tel: 01642-782407 **Fax:** 01642-785502
E-mail: hieldseng@aol.com
Directors: C. Hields (Dir)
Immediate Holding Company: C.A.HIELDS(ENGINEERS)LIMITED
Registration no: 00962074 **Date established:** 1969
Turnover: Up to £250,000 **No.of Employees:** 1 - 10 **Product Groups:** 48

Date of Accounts	Sep 11	Sep 10	Sep 09
Working Capital	378	420	457
Fixed Assets	265	223	228
Current Assets	526	592	499

Hosch GB Ltd
97 Sadler Forster Way Teesside Industrial Estate, Stockton On Tees, TS17 9JY
Tel: 01642-751100 **Fax:** 01642-751448
E-mail: mail@hosch.co.uk
Website: http://www.hosch.co.uk
Managers: D. Patterson (Chief Mgr)
Ultimate Holding Company: HOSCH COMPANY (USA)
Immediate Holding Company: HOSCH (G.B.) LIMITED
Registration no: 01753435 **VAT No.:** GB 499 1452 05
Date established: 1983 **Turnover:** £1m - £2m **No.of Employees:** 1 - 10
Product Groups: 45

Date of Accounts	Dec 11	Dec 10	Dec 09
Working Capital	416	608	591
Fixed Assets	34	36	35
Current Assets	924	896	741

Implants International Simco 708 Ltd
71 Jay Avenue Teesside Industrial Estate, Stockton On Tees, TS17 9LZ
Tel: 01642-769080 **Fax:** 01642-765848
E-mail: enquiries@implantsinternational.com
Website: http://www.implantsinternational.com
Directors: N. Emmanuel (Fin)
Immediate Holding Company: IMPLANTS INTERNATIONAL LIMITED
Registration no: 05467946 **Date established:** 2005
No.of Employees: 11 - 20 **Product Groups:** 38, 67

Date of Accounts	Jun 11	Jun 10	Jun 09
Working Capital	375	260	561
Fixed Assets	337	376	168
Current Assets	2m	2m	1m
Current Liabilities	N/A	60	257

Interserve Construction Ltd
Ross Road, Stockton On Tees, TS18 2NN
Tel: 01642-675125 **Fax:** 01642-601970
E-mail: stockton.office@interserve.com
Website: http://www.interserve.com
Bank(s): HSBC Bank plc
Directors: D. Flewker (MD)
Ultimate Holding Company: INTERSERVE PLC
Immediate Holding Company: INTERSERVE CONSTRUCTION LIMITED
Registration no: 00303359 **Date established:** 1935
Turnover: £500m - £1,000m **No.of Employees:** 21 - 50
Product Groups: 51, 52

Date of Accounts	Dec 11	Dec 10	Dec 09
Sales Turnover	734m	740m	825m
Pre Tax Profit/Loss	16m	23m	14m

see next page

Interserve Construction Ltd - Cont'd

Working Capital	80m	71m	66m
Fixed Assets	9m	8m	10m
Current Assets	331m	331m	339m
Current Liabilities	53m	59m	72m

John Clark Valves

Portrack Grange Road, Stockton On Tees, TS18 2PH
Tel: 01642-602288 **Fax:** 01642-603388
E-mail: sales@jcvltd.com
Website: http://www.jcvltd.com
Directors: T. Roberts (Dir), J. Roberts (Fin)
Immediate Holding Company: JOHN CLARK VALVES LIMITED
Registration no: 01901208 **VAT No.:** GB 422 5492 64
Date established: 1985 **Turnover:** £500,000 - £1m
No.of Employees: 1 - 10 **Product Groups:** 36, 38

Date of Accounts	Mar 11	Mar 10	Mar 09
Working Capital	523	408	304
Fixed Assets	150	153	167
Current Assets	1m	913	1m

K D Flavell & Sons Welding Specialists Co. Ltd

Robert Street Thornaby, Stockton On Tees, TS17 6AN
Tel: 01642-678808 **Fax:** 01642-618375
E-mail: sales@flavellwelding.co.uk
Website: http://www.flavellwelding.co.uk
Bank(s): National Westminster Bank Plc
Directors: M. Flavell (Dir)
Immediate Holding Company: K.D. FLAVELL & SONS WELDING SPECIALISTS COMPANY LIMITED
Registration no: 01339713 **VAT No.:** GB 258 4824 29
Date established: 1977 **Turnover:** £1m - £2m **No.of Employees:** 21 - 50
Product Groups: 48

Date of Accounts	Dec 11	Dec 10	Dec 09
Working Capital	261	232	252
Fixed Assets	159	157	170
Current Assets	351	294	311

K R G Industries Ltd

Church Road, Stockton On Tees, TS18 2HN
Tel: 01642-675001 **Fax:** 01642-672164
Website: http://www.krgindustries.com
Bank(s): National Westminster Bank Plc
Directors: K. Hughes (MD), P. Cowe (Fin)
Immediate Holding Company: KRG INDUSTRIES LIMITED
Registration no: SC083045 **Date established:** 1983
Turnover: £5m - £10m **No.of Employees:** 21 - 50 **Product Groups:** 48

Date of Accounts	May 09	Mar 12	Nov 10
Sales Turnover	19m	20m	11m
Pre Tax Profit/Loss	374	2m	-141
Working Capital	-161	-145	-949
Fixed Assets	4m	4m	4m
Current Assets	5m	5m	4m
Current Liabilities	2m	2m	2m

L H Quarry Plant Ltd (Incorporating H R Marsden Ltd)

Earlsway Teesside Industrial Estate, Thornaby, Stockton On Tees, TS17 9JU
Tel: 01642-769735 **Fax:** 01642-760293
E-mail: pc@lhgroup.co.uk
Website: http://www.lhgroup.co.uk
Bank(s): Barclays
Directors: J. Caswell (Jt MD), L. Caswell (Ch), N. Caswell (I.T. Dir)
Managers: L. Shepherd (Accounts)
Immediate Holding Company: L.H. (Quarry Plant) Ltd
Registration no: 01515326 **VAT No.:** GB 360 6887 28
Date established: 1980 **No.of Employees:** 21 - 50 **Product Groups:** 45

Date of Accounts	Mar 10	Mar 09	Mar 08
Working Capital	189	202	148
Fixed Assets	143	125	152
Current Assets	1m	1m	1m

LD Pipework Services Ltd

1 Regency Park Ingleby Barwick, Stockton On Tees, TS17 0QR
Tel: 01642-769998 **Fax:** 01642-769998
E-mail: ldpipework@btinternet.com
Product Groups: 20, 25, 27, 29, 30, 31, 33, 34, 35, 36, 37, 38, 39, 40, 41, 42, 45, 46, 48, 51, 52, 54, 80, 84

Date of Accounts	Oct 07	Oct 06	Oct 05
Working Capital	104	72	26
Fixed Assets	28	17	17
Current Assets	126	96	58
Current Liabilities	22	24	33

Lindy Electronics Ltd

Sadler Forster Way Teesside Industrial Estate, Stockton On Tees, TS17 9JY
Tel: 01642-754000 **Fax:** 01642-754027
E-mail: info@lindy.co.uk
Website: http://www.lindy.co.uk
Directors: D. Casey (MD), G. Casey (Co Sec)
Managers: A. Lane (Tech Serv Mgr), S. Griffths (Fin Mgr), M. Baker (Sales Prom Mgr), M. O'Connor (Mktg Serv Mgr), N. Franklin (Purch Mgr)
Ultimate Holding Company: LINDY ELECTRONICS LIMITED
Registration no: 02132710 **Date established:** 1987 **Turnover:** £2m - £5m
No.of Employees: 21 - 50 **Product Groups:** 35, 37, 44

Date of Accounts	Mar 12	Mar 11	Mar 10
Working Capital	2m	2m	2m
Fixed Assets	1m	1m	1m
Current Assets	3m	3m	2m

M B Tech Fabrications Ltd

Unit 2 Boathouse Lane, Stockton On Tees, TS18 3AW
Tel: 01642-633355 **Fax:** 01642-633358
E-mail: s.mcdonald@mb-tech.co.uk
Website: http://www.mb-tech.co.uk
Directors: S. McDonald (MD)
Immediate Holding Company: MB TECH FABRICATIONS LIMITED
Registration no: 06450695 **Date established:** 2007
No.of Employees: 11 - 20 **Product Groups:** 34, 35, 36, 46, 48

Date of Accounts	Apr 10	Apr 09	Apr 08
Working Capital	-5	-3	-5
Fixed Assets	12	14	7
Current Assets	2	176	58

M C E Group plc

Pennine House Hurricane Court, Preston Farm Industrial Estate, Stockton On Tees, TS18 3TL
Tel: 01642-882211 **Fax:** 01642-882233
E-mail: reception@mceplc.com
Website: http://www.mceplc.com
Managers: G. Brooks (Sales Prom Mgr), J. Reilly, M. Putson (Tech Serv Mgr), P. Fernie (Mktg Serv Mgr), L. Dunstan (Comptroller)
Ultimate Holding Company: VALVTECHNOLOGIES INC (USA)
Immediate Holding Company: MCE GROUP PLC
Registration no: 02477325 **Date established:** 1990 **Turnover:** £2m - £5m
No.of Employees: 21 - 50 **Product Groups:** 36, 37, 38

Date of Accounts	Jul 11	Jul 10	Jul 09
Sales Turnover	5m	4m	6m
Pre Tax Profit/Loss	152	-402	276
Working Capital	813	522	1m
Fixed Assets	45	74	74
Current Assets	2m	1m	2m
Current Liabilities	330	145	559

M C S Computers Ltd (Hewcrest Ltd)

Martinet Road Thornaby, Stockton On Tees, TS17 0AS
Tel: 01642-765757 **Fax:** 01642-750850
E-mail: enquiries@mcs-computers.co.uk
Website: http://www.mcs-computers.co.uk
Directors: S. Byrne (MD)
Immediate Holding Company: MCS COMPUTERS LIMITED
Registration no: 05269663 **Date established:** 2004
Turnover: £500,000 - £1m **No.of Employees:** 1 - 10 **Product Groups:** 84

Malton Gates

10 Mary Street, Stockton On Tees, TS18 4AN
Tel: 01642-673884
E-mail: les.stockton@malton-gates.co.uk
Website: http://www.malton-gates.co.uk
Directors: L. Stockton (Prop)
Turnover: Up to £250,000 **No.of Employees:** 1 - 10 **Product Groups:** 35, 49

Meditek Ltd

Unit 1-4 Fishburn Industrial Estate Fishburn, Stockton On Tees, TS21 4AJ
Tel: 01740-623823 **Fax:** 01740-623923
E-mail: info@meditek.net
Website: http://www.meditek.net
Directors: P. Rice (Dir), R. Kirk (Co Sec)
Immediate Holding Company: MEDITEK LIMITED
Registration no: 03039760 **Date established:** 1995
No.of Employees: 21 - 50 **Product Groups:** 35, 39, 45

Date of Accounts	Apr 11	Apr 10	Apr 09
Working Capital	1m	920	837
Fixed Assets	56	12	6
Current Assets	2m	2m	1m

Mercia Lifting Gear Ltd

44a Dukesway Teesside Industrial Estate, Stockton On Tees, TS17 9LT
Tel: 01642-760990 **Fax:** 01642-761200
E-mail: enquiries@mercialiftinggear.com
Website: http://www.mercialiftinggear.com
Managers: A. Blacklock (District Mgr)
Immediate Holding Company: MERCIA LIFTING GEAR LIMITED
Registration no: 01611229 **Date established:** 1982
No.of Employees: 1 - 10 **Product Groups:** 35, 39, 45

Date of Accounts	Feb 08	Feb 11	Feb 10
Working Capital	17	71	61
Fixed Assets	55	38	56
Current Assets	1m	854	628
Current Liabilities	151	303	226

Metabrasive Ltd

Ironmasters Way Stillington, Stockton On Tees, TS21 1LE
Tel: 01740-630212 **Fax:** 01740-630555
E-mail: claire-louise.foster@metabrasive.com
Website: http://www.metabrasive.com
Bank(s): Barclays
Managers: C. Foster
Ultimate Holding Company: WHEELABRATOR ALLEVARD
Immediate Holding Company: METABRASIVE LIMITED
Registration no: 01477523 **VAT No.:** GB 559 7454 88
Date established: 1980 **Turnover:** £2m - £5m **No.of Employees:** 21 - 50
Product Groups: 34

Date of Accounts	Dec 11	Dec 10	Dec 09
Sales Turnover	17m	16m	15m
Pre Tax Profit/Loss	2m	1m	2m
Working Capital	10m	8m	7m
Fixed Assets	573	595	631
Current Assets	12m	11m	10m
Current Liabilities	870	976	836

Mitre Plastics

Moss Way Preston Farm Industrial Estate, Stockton On Tees, TS18 3TF
Tel: 01642-633366 **Fax:** 01642-633377
E-mail: sylvia.breckon@mitreplastics.co.uk
Website: http://www.mitreplastics.co.uk
Directors: S. Breckon (MD)
Immediate Holding Company: MITRE PLASTICS
Registration no: 01114860 **Date established:** 1973
No.of Employees: 51 - 100 **Product Groups:** 30

Date of Accounts	Mar 95	Mar 94	Mar 93
Working Capital	-323	-167	N/A
Fixed Assets	1m	612	548
Current Assets	1m	676	478

John Morfield Ltd

Unit 98 Sadler Forster Way Teesside Industrial Estate, Stockton On Tees, TS17 9JY
Tel: 01642-760555 **Fax:** 01642-750391
E-mail: enquiries@johnmorfield.co.uk
Website: http://www.johnmorfield.co.uk
Bank(s): Barclays, Albert Rd, Middlesbrough
Directors: S. Johnston (MD)
Immediate Holding Company: JOHN MORFIELD LIMITED
Registration no: 00742887 **Date established:** 1962 **Turnover:** £2m - £5m
No.of Employees: 21 - 50 **Product Groups:** 36, 38, 40

Date of Accounts	Mar 11	Mar 10	Mar 09
Working Capital	617	685	613
Fixed Assets	356	206	304
Current Assets	3m	3m	2m

Nifco UK Ltd

Yarm Road, Stockton On Tees, TS18 3RX
Tel: 01642-672299 **Fax:** 01642-611004
E-mail: matthewsm@nifcoeu.com
Website: http://www.nifcoeu.com
Bank(s): Barclays
Directors: M. Matthews (MD)
Managers: A. McDowall (Sales & Mktg Mg), F. Hoy (Personnel), D. Binks, J. Tinkler (Tech Serv Mgr)
Ultimate Holding Company: NIFCO INC (JAPAN)
Immediate Holding Company: NIFCO UK LIMITED
Registration no: 01392769 **Date established:** 1978
Turnover: £20m - £50m **No.of Employees:** 101 - 250
Product Groups: 30, 39

Date of Accounts	Dec 11	Dec 10	Dec 09
Sales Turnover	32m	28m	22m
Pre Tax Profit/Loss	4m	5m	4m
Working Capital	6m	11m	6m
Fixed Assets	14m	4m	4m
Current Assets	15m	18m	12m
Current Liabilities	1m	2m	2m

Oceaneering Asset Integrity

109 Bowesfield Lane, Stockton On Tees, TS18 3HF
Tel: 01642-604661 **Fax:** 01642-670300
E-mail: jwatkinson@oceaneering.com
Website: http://www.oceaneering.com
Directors: J. Watkinson (Grp Chief Exec)
Managers: C. Bradford, M. Carlin (Tech Serv Mgr), A. Husband (Personnel)
Ultimate Holding Company: OCEANEERING INTERNATIONAL INC (USA)
Immediate Holding Company: OIS PLC
Registration no: 01676689 **VAT No.:** GB 377 0558 28
Date established: 1982 **Turnover:** £250,000 - £500,000
No.of Employees: 51 - 100 **Product Groups:** 37, 38, 44, 48, 51, 54, 85

Onyx Group

9 Cheltenham Road Portrack Interchange Business Park, Stockton On Tees, TS18 2AD
Tel: 01642-216200 **Fax:** 01642-216201
E-mail: sales@onyx.net
Website: http://www.onyx.net
Directors: T. Clark (Fin), S. Clark (Co Sec), H. Gillen (Sales & Mktg)
Managers: N. Stephenson, Z. Bewick (Personnel), G. Bowe (Buyer), S. Woodward
Ultimate Holding Company: ONYX INFORMATION TECHNOLOGY HOLDINGS LIMITED
Immediate Holding Company: ONYX INTERNET LIMITED
Registration no: 04061967 **Date established:** 2000 **Turnover:** £2m - £5m
No.of Employees: 51 - 100 **Product Groups:** 79

Date of Accounts	Dec 11	Dec 10	Dec 09
Sales Turnover	4m	4m	4m
Pre Tax Profit/Loss	438	166	150
Working Capital	42	-419	-554
Fixed Assets	4m	3m	3m
Current Assets	5m	4m	3m
Current Liabilities	2m	2m	2m

Pickerings Lifts Ltd

PO Box 19, Stockton On Tees, TS20 2AD
Tel: 01642-607161 **Fax:** 01642-677638
E-mail: info@pickeringslifts.co.uk
Website: http://www.pickerings.co.uk
Directors: R. Middleton (Fin), K. Armstrong (Comm)
Managers: K. Workman (Mktg Serv Mgr), N. Reiley (Personnel)
Ultimate Holding Company: KIPLUN LIMITED
Immediate Holding Company: PICKERINGS EUROPE LIMITED
Registration no: 03217853 **Date established:** 1996
Turnover: £20m - £50m **No.of Employees:** 251 - 500
Product Groups: 35, 39, 45

Date of Accounts	Dec 11	Dec 10	Dec 09
Sales Turnover	22m	20m	23m
Pre Tax Profit/Loss	3m	35m	5m
Working Capital	25m	25m	19m
Fixed Assets	11m	9m	9m
Current Assets	31m	30m	24m
Current Liabilities	4m	4m	3m

Plant & Consumables Services Ltd

2 Reed Street Thornaby, Stockton On Tees, TS17 7AF
Tel: 01642-605555 **Fax:** 01642-671814
E-mail: sales@pacs.uk.com
Website: http://www.pacs.uk.com
Directors: A. Shaw (MD), M. Evans (Fin)
Ultimate Holding Company: P & I DESIGN LIMITED
Immediate Holding Company: P & I DESIGN LIMITED
Registration no: 01596778 **Date established:** 1978
No.of Employees: 11 - 20 **Product Groups:** 46

Date of Accounts	Jul 11	Jul 10	Jul 09
Working Capital	1	1	1
Current Assets	1	1	1

Process Control Equipment

45 Dukesway Teesside Industrial Estate, Stockton On Tees, TS17 9LT
Tel: 01642-768250
E-mail: enquiries@processcontrolequipment.co.uk
Website: http://www.processcontrolequipment.co.uk
Directors: B. Jackson (MD)
Immediate Holding Company: PROCESS CONTROL EQUIPMENT LIMITED
Registration no: 01490723 **Date established:** 1980
No.of Employees: 21 - 50 **Product Groups:** 36, 37, 38

Date of Accounts	Jun 11	Jun 10	Jun 09
Working Capital	2m	1m	1m
Fixed Assets	74	103	162
Current Assets	4m	4m	4m

Radiographic Accessories Ltd

Guisley Way Durham Lane Industrial Park, Eaglescliffe, Stockton On Tees, TS16 0RF
Tel: 01642-790580 **Fax:** 01642-790420
E-mail: jack@radac.demon.co.uk
Website: http://www.radac.demon.co.uk
Bank(s): Lloyds
Directors: J. Hadwin (Dir)
Immediate Holding Company: RADIOGRAPHIC ACCESSORIES LIMITED
Registration no: 02904032 **VAT No.:** GB 633 2768 35
Date established: 1994 **Turnover:** £500,000 - £1m
No.of Employees: 11 - 20 **Product Groups:** 37

Date of Accounts	Apr 12	Apr 11	Apr 10
Working Capital	537	549	469
Fixed Assets	41	3	5

Current Assets	826	745	749

R B G

35f Dukesway Teesside Industrial Estate, Stockton On Tees, TS17 9LT
Tel: 01642-769906 **Fax:** 01642-760059
E-mail: jasonpavitt@rbgltd.com
Website: http://www.rbgltd.com
Bank(s): Lloyds TSB Bank plc
Directors: B. Chisholm (Dir), J. Ray (Dir), P. Prior (MD)
Managers: D. Dakers (Mgr), K. Collitor (Mgr)
Ultimate Holding Company: VALMONT INDUSTRIES INC (USA)
Immediate Holding Company: STAINTON METAL COMPANY LIMITED
Registration no: 04264876 **VAT No.:** GB 384 6027 40
Date established: 2001 **Turnover:** £2m - £5m **No.of Employees:** 51 - 100
Product Groups: 38, 48, 85

Date of Accounts	Oct 10	Oct 09	May 08
Working Capital	-269	-252	-195
Fixed Assets	265	185	462
Current Assets	133	81	262

Serco UK Europe

Cavendish House Princes Wharf Thornaby, Stockton On Tees, TS17 6QY
Tel: 01642-636700 **Fax:** 01642-636701
Website: http://www.serco.com
Bank(s): National Westminster
Directors: C. Bax (MD)
Immediate Holding Company: TEES VALLEY REGENERATION LIMITED
Registration no: 00242246 **VAT No.:** GB 207 5233 88
Date established: 2002 **Turnover:** £20m - £50m
No.of Employees: 101 - 250 **Product Groups:** 44

Shopmobility

3-5 Bridge Road, Stockton On Tees, TS18 1BH
Tel: 01642-861211 **Fax:** 01642-615436
Website: http://www.stocktonshopmobility.co.uk
Directors: R. Campbell (Grp Chief Exec), T. Scott (Co Sec)
Immediate Holding Company: STOCKTON SHOPMOBILITY LIMITED
Registration no: 03061335 **Date established:** 1995
Turnover: Up to £250,000 **No.of Employees:** 1 - 10 **Product Groups:** 26, 39, 45

Date of Accounts	Mar 11	Mar 10	Mar 09
Sales Turnover	109	87	75
Pre Tax Profit/Loss	8	2	4
Working Capital	23	14	11
Fixed Assets	5	6	7
Current Assets	39	30	27
Current Liabilities	15	15	15

Spie WHS Ltd

21 Allensway Thornaby, Stockton On Tees, TS17 9HA
Tel: 01642-769085 **Fax:** 01642-761137
E-mail: gwilliams@eiwhs.co.uk
Website: http://www.spiewhs.com
Bank(s): Royal Bank of Scotland, Croydon
Managers: D. Gunn (Purch Mgr), M. Walden (Chief Mgr)
Ultimate Holding Company: FINANCIERE SPIE (FRANCE)
Immediate Holding Company: SPIE WHS LIMITED
Registration no: 05211611 **VAT No.:** GB 239 3550 53
Date established: 2004 **Turnover:** £10m - £20m
No.of Employees: 21 - 50 **Product Groups:** 52

Date of Accounts	Dec 11	Dec 10	Dec 09
Sales Turnover	48m	56m	21m
Pre Tax Profit/Loss	3m	4m	832
Working Capital	8m	6m	2m
Fixed Assets	1m	1m	1m
Current Assets	24m	19m	23m
Current Liabilities	6m	6m	3m

Stockton Casting Co.

Ross Road, Stockton On Tees, TS18 2NP
Tel: 01642-607486 **Fax:** 01642-611484
E-mail: info@stockton-castings.co.uk
Website: http://www.stockton-castings.co.uk
Bank(s): HSBC
Directors: S. Keelan (Dir), R. York (Dir), C. Laverick (Fin), A. Ramsay (Tech Serv)
Ultimate Holding Company: TEESCRAFT ENGINEERING LIMITED
Immediate Holding Company: STOCKTON CASTING COMPANY LIMITED(THE)
Registration no: 00443377 **VAT No.:** GB 258 0954 36
Date established: 1947 **Turnover:** £2m - £5m **No.of Employees:** 21 - 50
Product Groups: 34, 42, 48

Date of Accounts	Dec 11	Mar 11	Mar 10
Working Capital	675	580	498
Fixed Assets	460	471	450
Current Assets	1m	917	786

Stream

39 Front Street Fishburn, Stockton On Tees, TS21 4AA
Tel: 01740-623311 **Fax:** 01740-623311
E-mail: enquiries@streamsupplies.f2s.com
Website: http://www.streamsupplies.co.uk
Directors: D. Gatiss (Prop), S. St Juste (Ptnr)
No.of Employees: 1 - 10 **Product Groups:** 25, 30, 52, 63, 64

T J Thomson & Son Ltd

Millfield Works Grangefield Road, Stockton On Tees, TS18 4AE
Tel: 01642-672551 **Fax:** 01642-672556
E-mail: postbox@tjthomson.co.uk
Website: http://www.tjthomson.co.uk
Bank(s): National Westminster Bank Plc
Directors: R. Turner (Dir)
Managers: D. Turner, R. Winterschladen
Immediate Holding Company: T.J.THOMSON & SON LIMITED
Registration no: 00638347 **VAT No.:** GB 258 2369 37
Date established: 1959 **Turnover:** £20m - £50m
No.of Employees: 51 - 100 **Product Groups:** 42, 66

Date of Accounts	Mar 12	Mar 11	Mar 10
Sales Turnover	31m	25m	19m
Pre Tax Profit/Loss	837	2m	474
Working Capital	7m	7m	6m
Fixed Assets	1m	874	499
Current Assets	16m	12m	11m
Current Liabilities	704	2m	1m

J G Tinkler Ltd

Bowesfield Lane, Stockton On Tees, TS18 3HJ
Tel: 01642-675797 **Fax:** 01642-673193
E-mail: jgtinklerltd@aol.com
Directors: S. Hamilton (Fin), R. Thomas (MD), S. Thomas (Contracts)
Ultimate Holding Company: 02396673
Immediate Holding Company: J.G. TINKLER LIMITED
Registration no: 00482990 **VAT No.:** GB 329 2014 81
Date established: 1950 **Turnover:** £1m - £2m **No.of Employees:** 1 - 10
Product Groups: 35, 36, 39, 45, 48

Date of Accounts	Dec 08	Dec 07	Dec 06
Working Capital	413	481	501
Fixed Assets	246	279	262
Current Assets	611	600	653

Towne Lifting & Testing

Pennine Avenue North Tees Industrial Estate, Stockton On Tees, TS18 2RJ
Tel: 01642-611035 **Fax:** 01642-611036
E-mail: stockton@towne.co.uk
Website: http://www.towne.co.uk
Managers: S. Strike (Works Gen Mgr)
Ultimate Holding Company: NETA TRAINING TRUST
Immediate Holding Company: NETA TRAINING CONSULTANCY LIMITED
Registration no: 02700788 **Date established:** 1990
No.of Employees: 1 - 10 **Product Groups:** 35, 39, 45

UK Web.Solutions Direct Ltd

Lakeside House Kingfisher Way, Stockton On Tees, TS18 3NB
Tel: 0845-862 0300 **Fax:** 0845-862 0275
E-mail: sales@ukwsd.com
Website: http://ukwebsolutionsdirect.co.uk
Bank(s): Lloyds TSB
Directors: M. Perry (MD), A. Roberts (Chief Op Offcr), N. Fairhead (Sales & Mktg), N. Mincher (Dir)
Managers: S. Fish (Purch Mgr)
Immediate Holding Company: Asteelflash (Bedford) Ltd
Registration no: 05667819 **Date established:** 1987
Turnover: £10m - £20m **No.of Employees:** 21 - 50 **Product Groups:** 37

Date of Accounts	Sep 07	Sep 06	Sep 05
Sales Turnover	11364	9363	8458
Pre Tax Profit/Loss	231	242	253
Working Capital	823	559	339
Fixed Assets	1372	1685	1379
Current Assets	3514	4219	2612
Current Liabilities	2690	3661	2274
Total Share Capital	50	50	50
ROCE% (Return on Capital Employed)	10.5	10.8	14.7
ROT% (Return on Turnover)	2.0	2.6	3.0

Valco Self Adhesive

6-7 Navigator Court Preston Farm Industrial Estate, Stockton On Tees, TS18 3TQ
Tel: 01642-617536 **Fax:** 01642-617541
E-mail: sales@self-adhesive.co.uk
Website: http://www.self-adhesive.co.uk
Directors: R. Sutton (Dir)
Immediate Holding Company: VALCO SELF ADHESIVE LIMITED
Registration no: 01389018 **Date established:** 1978
Turnover: £250,000 - £500,000 **No.of Employees:** 1 - 10
Product Groups: 27

Date of Accounts	Mar 11	Mar 10	Mar 09
Working Capital	33	61	85
Fixed Assets	69	81	94
Current Assets	129	144	162

Vixen Surface Treatments Ltd

73 Jay Avenue Teesside Industrial Estate, Stockton On Tees, TS17 9LZ
Tel: 01642-769333 **Fax:** 01642-769441
E-mail: a.mallon@vixen.co.uk
Website: http://www.vixen.co.uk
Directors: A. Mallon (MD)
Managers: D. Smith, D. Relph (Buyer)
Immediate Holding Company: LAKESIDE HOUSE (NO 26) LIMITED
Registration no: 02488790 **Date established:** 1990 **Turnover:** £2m - £5m
No.of Employees: 51 - 100 **Product Groups:** 38, 42

Date of Accounts	Apr 10	Apr 09	Apr 08
Sales Turnover	3m	3m	3m
Pre Tax Profit/Loss	235	187	201
Working Capital	-162	-60	-265
Fixed Assets	2m	1m	1m
Current Assets	1m	1m	953
Current Liabilities	534	437	408

CORNWALL

Bodmin

Bardon Concrete Ltd
2 Lucknow Road, Bodmin, PL31 1DR
Tel: 01208-74321 **Fax:** 01208-74327
Website: http://www.aggregateindustries.com
Bank(s): National Westminster, London
Managers: S. Curley (Chief Mgr)
Ultimate Holding Company: AGGREGATE INDUSTRIES HOLDINGS LIMITED
Immediate Holding Company: BARDON CONCRETE LIMITED
Registration no: 04553003 **VAT No.:** GB 222 8284 72
Date established: 2002 **No.of Employees:** 11 - 20 **Product Groups:** 52

Blue Fish
Coldrennick Farm Offices Helland, Bodmin, PL30 4QE
Tel: 08456-440725 **Fax:** 0845-644 0726
E-mail: sales@bluefishpromo.com
Website: http://www.bluefishpromo.com
Directors: M. Penn (Prop), M. Penn (Mkt Research)
Immediate Holding Company: CASTLEMAN (UK) LTD
Registration no: 04613646 **Date established:** 2008
No.of Employees: 1 - 10 **Product Groups:** 65

Date of Accounts	Feb 08	Feb 07	Feb 06
Working Capital	-130	-188	-118
Fixed Assets	19	25	38
Current Assets	112	77	107
Current Liabilities	242	264	225

Cornish Lime Company Ltd
Brims Park Old Callywith Road, Bodmin, PL31 2DZ
Tel: 01208-79779 **Fax:** 01208-73744
E-mail: sales@cornishlime.co.uk
Website: http://www.cornishlime.co.uk
Directors: K. Brown (Fin), P. Brown (MD)
Immediate Holding Company: CORNISH LIME COMPANY LIMITED
Registration no: 04391187 **Date established:** 2002 **Turnover:** £1m - £2m
No.of Employees: 1 - 10 **Product Groups:** 25, 33, 35, 52, 66

Date of Accounts	Mar 11	Mar 10	Mar 09
Working Capital	195	74	92
Fixed Assets	299	314	290
Current Assets	550	384	379

Electro-Diesel Rcjltd
Unit 4b Cooksland Industrial Estate, Bodmin, PL31 2QB
Tel: 01208-77511 **Fax:** 01208-78885
E-mail: bodmin@electro-diesel.co.uk
Website: http://www.electro-diesel.co.uk
Directors: R. Mather (MD)
Immediate Holding Company: ELECTRO-DIESEL (RCJ) LTD.
Registration no: 03052097 **Date established:** 1995
No.of Employees: 1 - 10 **Product Groups:** 40

Date of Accounts	Apr 11	Apr 10	Apr 09
Working Capital	387	325	365
Fixed Assets	508	528	212
Current Assets	626	558	535

The General Packaging Company Ltd
Unit 3 Cooksland Indl-Est, Bodmin, PL31 2QB
Tel: 01208-265870 **Fax:** 01208-72457
E-mail: enquiries@generalpackaging.co.uk
Website: http://www.generalpackaging.co.uk
Directors: C. Crocker (MD)
Managers: C. Harding (Mgr), S. Dean (Sales Prom Mgr), D. Marshall (Develop Mgr)
Immediate Holding Company: THE GENERAL PACKAGING COMPANY LIMITED
Registration no: 01683918 **Date established:** 1982
No.of Employees: 1 - 10 **Product Groups:** 23, 24, 27, 28, 30, 45, 66

Date of Accounts	Dec 07	Dec 06	Dec 05
Sales Turnover	N/A	N/A	1884
Pre Tax Profit/Loss	N/A	N/A	-22
Working Capital	30	46	91
Fixed Assets	172	138	89
Current Assets	672	628	599
Current Liabilities	642	582	508
Total Share Capital	10	10	10
ROCE% (Return on Capital Employed)			-12.3
ROT% (Return on Turnover)			-1.2

Gul Watersports Ltd
Callywith Gate Industrial Estate Launceston Road, Bodmin, PL31 2RQ
Tel: 01208-262400 **Fax:** 01208-262474
E-mail: gul@gul.com
Website: http://www.gul.com
Bank(s): National Westminster Bank Plc
Directors: M. Flavelle (MD), M. Flavelle (MD)
Managers: M. Pickering (Nat Sales Mgr)
Immediate Holding Company: GUL INTERNATIONAL LIMITED
Registration no: 04706430 **VAT No.:** GB 326 6931 43
Date established: 2003 **Turnover:** £5m - £10m **No.of Employees:** 11 - 20
Product Groups: 24

Date of Accounts	Dec 07	Dec 06	Jan 10
Sales Turnover	7m	6m	6m
Pre Tax Profit/Loss	-164	-56	1m
Working Capital	356	692	677
Fixed Assets	759	498	847
Current Assets	3m	2m	2m
Current Liabilities	954	953	664

Interior Iron
Unit 4 10 Normandy Way, Bodmin, PL31 1EX
Tel: 01208-72244 **Fax:** 01208-79192
Website: http://www.interioriron.towp.com
Directors: M. Chalk (Prop)
Date established: 1999 **No.of Employees:** 1 - 10 **Product Groups:** 26, 35

J & N Engineering Services
Unit 9a Callywith Gate Industrial Estate Launceston Road, Bodmin, PL31 2RQ
Tel: 01208-77886 **Fax:** 01208-77116
E-mail: jon@jn-engineering.co.uk
Website: http://www.jn-engineering.co.uk
Directors: J. Rawson (Prop)
Immediate Holding Company: YOUR POWER NO 24 LIMITED
Date established: 2011 **No.of Employees:** 1 - 10 **Product Groups:** 37, 46

P J Cleaning
Unit 3 St Kew Highway, Bodmin, PL30 3ED
Tel: 01208-841166
E-mail: paul@pjcleaning.biz
Website: http://www.pjcleaning.biz
Directors: P. Heath (Prop)
No.of Employees: 11 - 20 **Product Groups:** 23, 40, 52, 63

P P T Services
Unit 1 19 Paardeberg Road, Bodmin, PL31 1EY
Tel: 01208-78677 **Fax:** 01208-73450
E-mail: ppt.services@btconnect.com
Website: http://www.pptservices.org.uk
Managers: P. Sullivan (Mgr)
Date established: 1990 **No.of Employees:** 1 - 10 **Product Groups:** 38, 42

Phil Tucker
Treliver Farm St Wenn, Bodmin, PL30 5PQ
Tel: 01726-890286 **Fax:** 01726-890286
Directors: P. Tucker (Prop)
No.of Employees: 1 - 10 **Product Groups:** 35

Tulip Ltd
Newtons Margate Industrial Estate, Bodmin, PL31 1HF
Tel: 01208-262626 **Fax:** 01208-262662
E-mail: admin@tulipltd.co.uk
Website: http://www.tulipltd.co.uk
Directors: H. Gensen (Fin), P. Judge (MD), T. Brown (Tech Serv), K. Wilkins (Pers)
Ultimate Holding Company: DANISH CROWN AMBA (DENMARK)
Immediate Holding Company: TULIP LIMITED
Registration no: 00608077 **Date established:** 1958
Turnover: £125m - £250m **No.of Employees:** 1501 & over
Product Groups: 20

Date of Accounts	Sep 08	Oct 09	Oct 10
Sales Turnover	954m	1139m	1118m
Pre Tax Profit/Loss	21m	84m	37m
Working Capital	125m	138m	200m
Fixed Assets	439m	361m	379m
Current Assets	273m	324m	304m
Current Liabilities	57m	70m	55m

Walker Lines Motor Sport
10 Normandy Way Walker Lines Ind. Est., Bodmin, PL31 1EX
Tel: 07971-593994
E-mail: mike@walkerlinesmotorsport.co.uk
Website: http://www.walkerlinesmotorsport.co.uk
Product Groups: 35, 39, 68

West Pharmaceutical Services
Unit 15 Cooksland Business Park, Bodmin, PL31 2QB
Tel: 01208-73122 **Fax:** 01208-77792
Website: http://www.westpharma.com
Bank(s): National Westminster Bank Plc
Managers: P. Dunn (District Mgr)
Ultimate Holding Company: WEST PHARMACEUTICAL SERVICES INC
Registration no: 00930319 **VAT No.:** GB 132 3077 06
No.of Employees: 21 - 50 **Product Groups:** 42, 48

The Wool Company
Higher Hill Farm Cardinham, Bodmin, PL30 4EG
Tel: 01208-821113 **Fax:** 0845-686 8015
E-mail: help@thewoolcompany.co.uk
Website: http://www.thewoolcompany.co.uk
Directors: H. Mayman (Prop)
Immediate Holding Company: THE WOOL COMPANY LIMITED
Registration no: 07393778 **Date established:** 2010
No.of Employees: 1 - 10 **Product Groups:** 22, 24, 26, 63

Wovina Woven Labels
1-3 Omaha Road, Bodmin, PL31 1ER
Tel: 01208-73484 **Fax:** 01208-78158
E-mail: m.flowerdew@wovina.com
Website: http://www.wovina.com
Directors: M. Flowerdew (Ptnr)
Date established: 1971 **Turnover:** £500,000 - £1m
No.of Employees: 11 - 20 **Product Groups:** 23

Bude

Bott Ltd
Unit 8 Bude-Stratton Business Park, Bude, EX23 8LY
Tel: 01288-357788 **Fax:** 01288-352692
E-mail: clivew@bottltd.co.uk
Website: http://www.bottltd.co.uk
Bank(s): Barclays
Directors: S. Fry (Fin), C. Woodwood (MD)
Managers: M. Loudwill (Tech Serv Mgr), A. Crossley (Personnel), A. Vines (Sales Prom Mgr), G. Wright, B. Rotheray (Mktg Serv Mgr)
Ultimate Holding Company: WILHELM BOTT, GMBH & CO KG (GERMANY)
Immediate Holding Company: BOTT LIMITED
Registration no: 01325869 **VAT No.:** GB 313 2034 21
Date established: 1977 **Turnover:** £20m - £50m
No.of Employees: 101 - 250 **Product Groups:** 26, 30, 35, 36, 45, 46, 66

Date of Accounts	Dec 11	Dec 10	Dec 09
Sales Turnover	30m	22m	18m
Pre Tax Profit/Loss	2m	1m	627
Working Capital	4m	3m	3m
Fixed Assets	9m	9m	8m
Current Assets	11m	9m	8m
Current Liabilities	2m	2m	2m

Mobbs Electrical Contractors Ltd
59 Victoria Road, Bude, EX23 8RH
Tel: 01288-359823 **Fax:** 01288-359824
E-mail: info@bude-electrician.co.uk
Website: http://www.bude-electrician.co.uk
Directors: D. Mobbs (Dir)
Immediate Holding Company: MOBBS ELECTRONIC REPAIRS LIMITED
Registration no: 04186421 **Date established:** 2001
No.of Employees: 1 - 10 **Product Groups:** 36, 40

Date of Accounts	Jun 11	Jun 10	Jun 09
Working Capital	-79	-77	-78
Fixed Assets	17	20	23
Current Assets	23	13	19

Pritchard Plastics Ltd
Kings Hill Industrial Estate, Bude, EX23 8QN
Tel: 01288-353211 **Fax:** 01288-355686
E-mail: admin@pritchard-plastics.co.uk
Website: http://www.pritchard-plastics.co.uk
Bank(s): National Westminster
Directors: I. Stallard (Dir)
Immediate Holding Company: PRITCHARD (PLASTICS) LIMITED
Registration no: 00967567 **VAT No.:** GB 143 4281 86
Date established: 1969 **Turnover:** £1m - £2m **No.of Employees:** 21 - 50
Product Groups: 30, 66

Date of Accounts	Mar 11	Mar 10	Mar 09
Working Capital	135	116	175
Fixed Assets	157	160	224

Current Assets	200	214	283

Sara's

5 Belle Vue Lane, Bude, EX23 8BR
Tel: 01288-352610 **Fax:** 01288-352610
Directors: B. Grand (Dir)
Date established: 1994 **No.of Employees:** 1 - 10 **Product Groups:** 36, 39, 40

Stairlifts South West

Budds Cottage Titson, Marhamchurch, Bude, EX23 0HQ
Tel: 01288-361113 **Fax:** 01288-361113
Website: http://www.stairliftssouthwest.co.uk
Directors: J. Hackwell (Dir), S. Crowther (Fin), I. Hackwell (Prop)
Immediate Holding Company: STAIRLIFTS SOUTH WEST LTD
Registration no: 06090651 **Date established:** 2007
Turnover: Up to £250,000 **No.of Employees:** 1 - 10 **Product Groups:** 35, 39, 45

Date of Accounts	Mar 11	Mar 10	Mar 09
Sales Turnover	N/A	103	129
Pre Tax Profit/Loss	N/A	-2	-8
Working Capital	-35	-35	-32
Fixed Assets	24	24	24
Current Assets	15	23	39
Current Liabilities	N/A	1	7

Technical Instrument Casting Co.

Kings Hill Industrial Estate, Bude, EX23 8QN
Tel: 01288-353150 **Fax:** 01288-353783
E-mail: office@tic-castings.co.uk
Website: http://www.btinternet.com
Bank(s): Lloyds TSB Bank plc
Managers: K. Starr (Works Gen Mgr)
Immediate Holding Company: TECHNICAL AND INSTRUMENT CASTING CO LIMITED
Registration no: 00975673 **Date established:** 1970
No.of Employees: 11 - 20 **Product Groups:** 34, 48

Date of Accounts	Aug 11	Aug 10	Aug 09
Working Capital	-28	-78	-84
Fixed Assets	9	9	10
Current Assets	538	461	440

Callington

Bibby Engineers Ltd

Granite Way Moss Side Industrial Estate, Callington, PL17 7EB
Tel: 01579-382277 **Fax:** 01579-383977
E-mail: enquiries@bibbyengineers.com
Website: http://www.bibbyengineers.com
Bank(s): Barclays
Directors: G. Crowle (MD)
Immediate Holding Company: BIBBY ENGINEERS LIMITED
Registration no: 00463661 **VAT No.:** GB 143 0520 17
Date established: 1949 **Turnover:** £250,000 - £500,000
No.of Employees: 11 - 20 **Product Groups:** 30, 66

Date of Accounts	Apr 12	Apr 11	Apr 10
Working Capital	89	67	77
Fixed Assets	260	214	231
Current Assets	227	218	187

Camborne

Advanced Recycling Solutions Ltd

The Factory Boswithian Road Tolvaddon, Camborne, TR14 0EJ
Tel: 01209-611898 **Fax:** 01209-712888
E-mail: sales@ars-chs.co.uk
Website: http://www.ars-chs.co.uk
Directors: E. Hattam (Fin), B. Hattam (MD)
Immediate Holding Company: ADVANCED RECYCLING SYSTEMS LIMITED
Registration no: 04741596 **Date established:** 2003 **Turnover:** £1m - £2m
No.of Employees: 1 - 10 **Product Groups:** 48, 67

C & R Plastics Ltd

Unit E9 Formal Industrial Estate Treswithian, Camborne, TR14 0PY
Tel: 01209-613992 **Fax:** 01209-711895
E-mail: crplastics2000@yahoo.co.uk
Website: http://www.candrplasticsltd.co.uk
Directors: M. Roberts (MD)
Immediate Holding Company: C & R PLASTICS LIMITED
Registration no: 04805425 **Date established:** 2003
Turnover: £250,000 - £500,000 **No.of Employees:** 1 - 10
Product Groups: 30

Date of Accounts	Jun 12	Jun 11	Jun 10
Working Capital	-65	-70	-74
Fixed Assets	73	79	85
Current Assets	27	41	72

Grosvenor Pumps Ltd

Trevoole Praze, Camborne, TR14 0PJ
Tel: 01209-831500 **Fax:** 01209-831939
E-mail: sales@grosvenorpumps.com
Website: http://www.grosvenorpumps.com
Bank(s): Barclays
Directors: D. Handley (MD)
Immediate Holding Company: GROSVENOR PUMPS LIMITED
Registration no: 02345508 **VAT No.:** GB 531 5217 62
Date established: 1989 **Turnover:** £500,000 - £1m
No.of Employees: 11 - 20 **Product Groups:** 22, 29, 30, 31, 33, 34, 35, 36, 37, 38, 39, 40, 41, 42, 43, 45, 46, 48, 49, 67, 68, 83

Date of Accounts	May 11	May 10	May 09
Working Capital	22	-1	-1
Fixed Assets	40	40	40
Current Assets	100	99	84

Martin Andrew Kearney

Fairview Croft-Mitchell, Troon, Camborne, TR14 9JH
Tel: 01209-831662 **Fax:** 01209-831662
Directors: M. Kearney (Prop)
Registration no: 01325242 **Turnover:** £500,000 - £1m
No.of Employees: 11 - 20 **Product Groups:** 39, 65

Pump International Ltd (Head Office)

Trevool Praze, Camborne, TR14 0PJ
Tel: 01209-831937 **Fax:** 01209-831939
E-mail: admin@pumpinternational.com
Website: http://www.pumpinternational.com
Directors: D. Handley (MD), M. Blair (Sales)
Immediate Holding Company: PUMP INTERNATIONAL LIMITED
Registration no: 00581799 **VAT No.:** GB 385 6080 30
Date established: 1957 **Turnover:** £500,000 - £1m
No.of Employees: 1 - 10 **Product Groups:** 39, 40

Date of Accounts	Jul 11	Jul 10	Jul 09
Working Capital	90	15	-144
Fixed Assets	178	187	378
Current Assets	167	147	134

Vi2dus Limited

Race Court Treswithian, Camborne, TR14 0PU
Tel: 0844-8002722 **Fax:** 01209-719561
E-mail: info@vi2dus.co.uk
Website: http://www.sneddonmanagement.co.uk
Directors: T. Sneddon (Prop)
Registration no: 06072703 **No.of Employees:** 1 - 10 **Product Groups:** 80

W & S Measuring Systems Ltd

Race Court Treswithian Downs, Camborne, TR14 0PU
Tel: 01209-712135 **Fax:** 01490-413014
E-mail: info.uk@globalencoder.com
Website: http://www.globalencoder.com
Directors: K. Hinzwaber (MD)
Immediate Holding Company: W + S MEASURING SYSTEMS LIMITED
Registration no: 03419454 **VAT No.:** GB 691 7491 94
Date established: 1997 **Turnover:** £1m - £2m **No.of Employees:** 1 - 10
Product Groups: 38

Date of Accounts	Dec 11	Dec 10	Dec 09
Working Capital	58	37	60
Fixed Assets	2	1	N/A
Current Assets	102	100	79
Current Liabilities	N/A	60	7

Camelford

Nelson Stokes Ltd

Highfield Road, Camelford, PL32 9RA
Tel: 01840-213711 **Fax:** 01840-213338
E-mail: enquiries@nelsonstokes.com
Website: http://www.nelsonstokes.com
Bank(s): Lloyds TSB Bank plc
Directors: H. Stokes (MD), M. Stokes (Fin)
Managers: M. Bullen, P. Martin
Immediate Holding Company: NELSON STOKES LIMITED
Registration no: 01250857 **VAT No.:** GB 464 8321 36
Date established: 1976 **Turnover:** £2m - £5m **No.of Employees:** 21 - 50
Product Groups: 39

Date of Accounts	Dec 11	Dec 10	Dec 09
Working Capital	217	86	-469
Fixed Assets	377	444	441
Current Assets	570	578	501

Trewhella Bros

The Mead Tremail, Camelford, PL32 9YQ
Tel: 01840-261179 **Fax:** 01840-261187
Managers: P. Saywell (Mgr)
Date established: 2000 **No.of Employees:** 1 - 10 **Product Groups:** 35, 39, 45

Falmouth

Better Balance Coaching

Orchard Cottages Flushing, Falmouth, TR11 5TR
Tel: 01326-374114
E-mail: info@betterbalance.co.uk
Website: http://www.betterbalance.co.uk
Directors: J. Gill (Dir)
Date established: 1996 **No.of Employees:** 1 - 10 **Product Groups:** 80

Coastal Diesel & Transmission

The Docks, Falmouth, TR11 4NR
Tel: 01326-313332 **Fax:** 01326-313334
Directors: R. Warren (Ptnr)
Immediate Holding Company: PENDENNIS SHIPYARD (HOLDINGS) LIMITED
Registration no: 06838243 **Date established:** 1988
Turnover: £10m - £20m **No.of Employees:** 1 - 10 **Product Groups:** 35, 36, 39

Date of Accounts	Dec 11	Dec 10	Dec 09
Sales Turnover	31m	26m	25m
Pre Tax Profit/Loss	2m	1m	722
Working Capital	-1m	-3m	-3m
Fixed Assets	7m	8m	8m
Current Assets	6m	4m	4m
Current Liabilities	5m	5m	6m

L P Dawe

Meneer House 22 Berkeley Vale, Falmouth, TR11 3PA
Tel: 01326-316233
E-mail: lpdawe@btconnect.com
Website: http://www.lpdawe.co.uk
Directors: T. Meneer (Snr Part)
Registration no: 00029485 **Date established:** 1963
No.of Employees: 1 - 10 **Product Groups:** 80, 82, 87

Earth Energy

Falmouth Business Park Bickland Water Road, Falmouth, TR11 4SZ
Tel: 01326-310650 **Fax:** 01326-211071
E-mail: enquiries@earthenergy.co.uk
Website: http://www.earthenergy.co.uk
Directors: B. Carnelly (MD), R. Curtis (Tech Serv)
Managers: D. Johnson (Sales Prom Mgr), P. Ledingham (I.T. Exec)
Immediate Holding Company: EARTHENERGY LIMITED
Registration no: 03163262 **Date established:** 1996
Turnover: £500,000 - £1m **No.of Employees:** 1 - 10 **Product Groups:** 66, 84

Date of Accounts	Dec 09	Dec 08	Dec 07
Working Capital	2	450	162
Fixed Assets	2m	2m	1m
Current Assets	2m	2m	1m
Current Liabilities	444	N/A	N/A

Falmouth Boat Construction Ltd

Little Falmouth Flushing, Falmouth, TR11 5TJ
Tel: 01326-374309 **Fax:** 01326-377689
E-mail: bernie@fal-boat.demon.co.uk
Website: http://www.falmouthboatconstruction.com
Bank(s): Lloyds TSB Birmingham
Directors: B. Bagley (MD)
Ultimate Holding Company: BAGLEY MARINE LIMITED
Immediate Holding Company: FALMOUTH BOAT CONSTRUCTION LIMITED
Registration no: 00985592 **VAT No.:** GB 131 9991 49
Date established: 1970 **No.of Employees:** 11 - 20 **Product Groups:** 39

Date of Accounts	May 11	May 10	May 09
Working Capital	201	202	304
Fixed Assets	180	202	195
Current Assets	297	249	400

Fibrefusion Ltd

Unit 9e Spencer Carter Works Tregoniggie Industrial Estate, Falmouth, TR11 4SN
Tel: 01326-378787 **Fax:** 01326-377065
E-mail: info@fibrefusion.com
Website: http://www.fibrefusion.com
Directors: S. Neal (MD)
Immediate Holding Company: FIBREFUSION LIMITED
Registration no: 04353452 **Date established:** 2002
Turnover: Up to £250,000 **No.of Employees:** 1 - 10 **Product Groups:** 48

Date of Accounts	Mar 12	Mar 11	Mar 10
Working Capital	90	55	50
Fixed Assets	33	40	44
Current Assets	150	120	88

Geoscience Ltd

Unit 2 Falmouth Business Park Bickland Water Road, Falmouth, TR11 4SZ
Tel: 01326-211070 **Fax:** 01326-212754
E-mail: batchelor@geoscience.co.uk
Website: http://www.geoscience.co.uk
Bank(s): Bank of Scotland
Directors: A. Batchelor (Dir), P. Ledingham (Dir)
Managers: M. Mervill, R. Pearson (Mktg Serv Mgr)
Immediate Holding Company: GEOSCIENCE LIMITED
Registration no: 01930745 **Date established:** 1985 **Turnover:** £5m - £10m
No.of Employees: 21 - 50 **Product Groups:** 51, 52, 54, 84, 85

Date of Accounts	Dec 11	Dec 10	Dec 09
Sales Turnover	N/A	6m	7m
Pre Tax Profit/Loss	N/A	-499	-1m
Working Capital	2m	2m	3m
Fixed Assets	510	3m	3m
Current Assets	2m	3m	4m
Current Liabilities	N/A	635	671

Hirst Magnetic Instruments Ltd

Pesla House Tregoniggie Industrial Estate, Falmouth, TR11 4SN
Tel: 01326-372734 **Fax:** 01326-378069
E-mail: sales@hirst-magnetics.com
Website: http://www.hirst-magnetics.com
Directors: J. Dudding (MD)
Immediate Holding Company: HIRST MAGNETIC INSTRUMENTS LIMITED
Registration no: 01564814 **Date established:** 1981
Turnover: £500,000 - £1m **No.of Employees:** 11 - 20
Product Groups: 37, 38, 48, 67, 85

Date of Accounts	Jun 11	Jun 10	Jun 09
Working Capital	-3	-55	-98
Fixed Assets	861	864	829
Current Assets	401	410	366
Current Liabilities	N/A	44	33

International Paints

Building 450 5 The Docks, Falmouth, TR11 4NJ
Tel: 01326-212974 **Fax:** 01326- 212974
Managers: M. Young (Mgr)
Ultimate Holding Company: VENEZOLANOS HOLDINGS SA (BAHAMAS)
Immediate Holding Company: RIGHTHALT LIMITED
Registration no: 02025285 **Date established:** 1986
Turnover: £500,000 - £1m **No.of Employees:** 1 - 10 **Product Groups:** 46, 48

Marine Trak Engineering

Mylor Yacht Harbour Mylor Churchtown, Falmouth, TR11 5UF
Tel: 01326-376588 **Fax:** 01326-378258
E-mail: nathan.percival@mylor.com
Website: http://www.mylor.com
Managers: N. Percival (Mgr)
Date established: 1973 **No.of Employees:** 1 - 10 **Product Groups:** 35, 36, 39

P T Marine & General Fabrications Ltd

21 North Parade, Falmouth, TR11 2TD
Tel: 01326-311004 **Fax:** 01326-311004
Directors: P. Tonkin (Prop)
Immediate Holding Company: CHACE KENDRICK LTD
Registration no: 04544429 **Date established:** 2007
No.of Employees: 1 - 10 **Product Groups:** 35

Research Instruments Ltd

Bickland Industrial Park, Falmouth, TR11 4TA
Tel: 01326-372753 **Fax:** 01326-378783
E-mail: sales@research-instruments.com
Website: http://www.research-instruments.com
Bank(s): Barclays
Directors: D. Lansdowne (Fin), W. Brown (MD)
Immediate Holding Company: RESEARCH INSTRUMENTS LIMITED
Registration no: 03419143 **VAT No.:** 750 4247 49 **Date established:** 1997
Turnover: £500,000 - £1m **No.of Employees:** 51 - 100
Product Groups: 37

Date of Accounts	Mar 11	Mar 10	Mar 09
Working Capital	2m	2m	2m
Fixed Assets	1m	1m	1m
Current Assets	4m	3m	2m

Keith Rolleston Associates
38b High Street, Falmouth, TR11 2AF
Tel: 01326-210490 **Fax:** 01326-210976
E-mail: kr@krastructures.co.uk
Directors: K. Rolleston (Prop)
Date established: 1998 **No.of Employees:** 1 - 10 **Product Groups:** 35

South West Ict
6 Florence Place, Falmouth, TR11 3NJ
Tel: 01326-317797 **Fax:** 01326-318810
E-mail: helpdesk@southwestict.com
Website: http://www.southwestict.com
Directors: S. Leek (Dir), J. Hudson (Fin)
Immediate Holding Company: SOUTH WEST ICT LIMITED
Registration no: 06059445 **Date established:** 2007
No.of Employees: 1 - 10 **Product Groups:** 44, 80, 86

Date of Accounts	Dec 11	Dec 10	Dec 09
Working Capital	-24	-1	9
Fixed Assets	36	9	2
Current Assets	58	12	24

Spencer Carter Ltd
Tregoniggie Industrial Estate, Falmouth, TR11 4SN
Tel: 01326-373423 **Fax:** 01326-373571
E-mail: reception@spencercarter.com
Website: http://www.spencercarter.com
Directors: R. Carter (Fin)
Ultimate Holding Company: SPENCER-CARTER HOLDINGS LIMITED
Immediate Holding Company: SPENCER-CARTER LIMITED
Registration no: 03433308 **Date established:** 1997
No.of Employees: 11 - 20 **Product Groups:** 35, 39, 45

Date of Accounts	Mar 12	Mar 11	Mar 10
Working Capital	304	301	293
Fixed Assets	97	74	68
Current Assets	490	412	427

Splash-Tec
2 Empire Way Tregoniggie Industrial Estate, Falmouth, TR11 4RX
Tel: 01326-375610 **Fax:** 01326-375610
E-mail: info@splash-tec.co.uk
Website: http://www.splash-tec.co.uk
Directors: J. Ellis (Dir)
No.of Employees: 1 - 10 **Product Groups:** 30, 32, 36, 37, 38, 49

Sub Marine Services Ltd
Falmouth Docks, Falmouth, TR11 4NR
Tel: 01326-211517 **Fax:** 01326-212757
E-mail: morwenna@submarineservices.com
Website: http://www.submarineservices.com
Directors: A. Richards (MD)
Immediate Holding Company: SUB MARINE SERVICES LIMITED
Registration no: 02128038 **Date established:** 1987
Turnover: £10m - £20m **No.of Employees:** 1 - 10 **Product Groups:** 39

Date of Accounts	Mar 12	Mar 11	Mar 10
Working Capital	29	-132	-151
Fixed Assets	717	755	806
Current Assets	366	178	206

T R G Marine Engineers
Unit 3 Chough Close Tregoniggie Industrial Estate, Falmouth, TR11 4SN
Tel: 01326-313777 **Fax:** 01326-313777
Directors: M. Taylor (Prop)
Immediate Holding Company: WILSHAW DENTAL LABORATORY LTD
Date established: 2006 **No.of Employees:** 1 - 10 **Product Groups:** 35, 36, 39

Watson Marlow Pumps Ltd
Bickland Water Road, Falmouth, TR11 4RU
Tel: 01326-370370 **Fax:** 01326-376009
E-mail: info@watson-marlow.co.uk
Website: http://www.wmpg.co.uk
Bank(s): Barclays
Directors: J. Whalen (Dir), S. Godzicz (Ch)
Managers: J. Harvey (Buyer), M. Sullivan (Grp Mktg Mgr), W. Hamilton (Tech Serv Mgr), F. Pasco (Sales Prom Mgr)
Ultimate Holding Company: SPIRAX-SARCO ENGINEERING PLC
Immediate Holding Company: WATSON-MARLOW LIMITED
Registration no: 02481019 **VAT No.:** GB 527 0966 32
Date established: 1990 **Turnover:** £20m - £50m
No.of Employees: 101 - 250 **Product Groups:** 29, 40

Date of Accounts	Dec 11	Dec 10	Dec 09
Sales Turnover	33m	30m	25m
Pre Tax Profit/Loss	8m	6m	5m
Working Capital	4m	4m	3m
Fixed Assets	12m	12m	13m
Current Assets	10m	8m	7m
Current Liabilities	2m	2m	2m

Fowey

Fowey Harbour Marine Engineers
The Workshop Passage Lane, Fowey, PL23 1JS
Tel: 01726-832806 **Fax:** 01726-832806
E-mail: info@fhme.co.uk
Website: http://www.fhme.co.uk
Directors: N. Beard (Ptnr)
Date established: 1997 **No.of Employees:** 1 - 10 **Product Groups:** 35, 36, 39

Marine Electronics Of Fowey
23-25 Station Road, Fowey, PL23 1DF
Tel: 01726-833101 **Fax:** 01726-833101
E-mail: sales@marineelectronicsuk.com
Website: http://www.marineelectronicsuk.com
Directors: M. Millar (Ptnr)
No.of Employees: 1 - 10 **Product Groups:** 35, 36, 39

South Coast UK
The Docks, Fowey, PL23 1AL
Tel: 01726-833161 **Fax:** 01726-833474
E-mail: ben.jones@denholm-barwil.com
Website: http://www.imerys.com
Managers: B. Jones (Chief Mgr)
Ultimate Holding Company: IMERYS MINERALS LTD
Registration no: 00344734 **Turnover:** £1m - £2m
No.of Employees: 1 - 10 **Product Groups:** 61, 76

Gunnislake

Magnum Venus Plastech Ltd
Chilsworthy Beam, Gunnislake, PL18 9AT
Tel: 01822-832621 **Fax:** 01822-833999
E-mail: rtm@plastech.co.uk
Website: http://www.plastech.co.uk
Bank(s): Royal Bank of Scotland
Directors: A. Harper (MD)
Immediate Holding Company: MAGNUM VENUS PLASTECH LIMITED
Registration no: 03978164 **VAT No.:** GB 760 5292 32
Date established: 2000 **Turnover:** £1m - £2m **No.of Employees:** 11 - 20
Product Groups: 42, 48

Date of Accounts	Dec 11	Dec 10	Dec 09
Sales Turnover	1m	N/A	1m
Pre Tax Profit/Loss	-146	N/A	8
Working Capital	612	-55	-72
Fixed Assets	41	43	141
Current Assets	750	685	610
Current Liabilities	30	N/A	137

Hayle

Prosharp Sharpening Service
29 Prospect Place, Hayle, TR27 4LU
Tel: 01736-756162
E-mail: sales@prosharp.co.uk
Website: http://www.prosharp.co.uk
Directors: T. Arnull (Prop)
Date established: 1997 **No.of Employees:** 1 - 10 **Product Groups:** 36

Rigibore Ltd
Guildford Road Industrial Estate, Hayle, TR27 4BA
Tel: 01736-755355 **Fax:** 01736-756100
E-mail: info@rigibore.com
Website: http://www.rigibore.com
Directors: R. Bassett (Dir), S. Bennet (Co Sec)
Managers: T. Negus (Chief Mgr)
Immediate Holding Company: Bassett Group Ltd
Registration no: 01465509 **Date established:** 1979
No.of Employees: 21 - 50 **Product Groups:** 46

Date of Accounts	Jun 08	Jun 07	Jun 06
Sales Turnover	N/A	N/A	1190
Pre Tax Profit/Loss	N/A	N/A	-6
Working Capital	-6	247	199
Fixed Assets	1552	1056	1210
Current Assets	1484	1553	1273
Current Liabilities	1490	1306	1074
Total Share Capital	450	450	450
ROCE% (Return on Capital Employed)			-0.4
ROT% (Return on Turnover)			-0.5

Symons Agricultural Services Ltd
3a Guildford Road Industrial Estate Guildford Road, Hayle, TR27 4QZ
Tel: 01736-755010 **Fax:** 01736-756044
Directors: L. Symons (Co Sec), P. Symons (MD)
Immediate Holding Company: SYMONS AGRICULTURAL SERVICES LIMITED
Registration no: 01660817 **Date established:** 1982
No.of Employees: 1 - 10 **Product Groups:** 41

Date of Accounts	Nov 11	Nov 10	Nov 08
Working Capital	43	44	48
Fixed Assets	14	18	30
Current Assets	96	106	241

Helston

A P Valves (t/a A P Valves)
Water-Ma-Trout, Helston, TR13 0LW
Tel: 01326-561040 **Fax:** 01326-573605
E-mail: sales@apvalves.com
Website: http://www.apvalvesdirect.com
Directors: M. Parker (MD)
Managers: A. Wall (Tech Serv Mgr), D. Jackson (Personnel), J. Parker, S. Coobe, A. Clarke (Sales Prom Mgr), A. Clarke (Sales Prom Mgr)
Ultimate Holding Company: CLIPPER DATA LIMITED
Immediate Holding Company: PARKER DIVING LIMITED
Registration no: 02785572 **VAT No.:** GB 591 3535 31
Date established: 1993 **Turnover:** £250,000 - £500,000
No.of Employees: 51 - 100 **Product Groups:** 35, 36, 40, 84

Date of Accounts	Jan 12	Jan 11	Jan 10
Working Capital	607	539	-236
Fixed Assets	207	258	307
Current Assets	1m	956	731

Abstract Arcs
Unit 3 Trannack Mill Industrial Estate Coverack Bridges, Helston, TR13 0SW
Tel: 01326-564455
E-mail: paul@abstractarcs.com
Website: http://www.abstractarcs.com
Directors: P. Hoskin (Prop)
Date established: 2000 **No.of Employees:** 1 - 10 **Product Groups:** 26, 35

The Big Beautiful Bunting Co.
Trembraze Farmhouse St.Keverne, Helston, TR12 6PG
Tel: 01326-281513
E-mail: info@bigbeautifulbunting.co.uk
Website: http://www.bigbeautifulbunting.co.uk
Managers: G. Kirby (Mgr)
Date established: 2007 **No.of Employees:** 1 - 10 **Product Groups:** 83

Cellar Marine Ltd
Porthallow St Keverne, Helston, TR12 6PP
Tel: 01326-280214 **Fax:** 01326-280334
Directors: J. Skewes (Dir)
Immediate Holding Company: CELLAR MARINE LIMITED
Registration no: 05129893 **Date established:** 2004
No.of Employees: 1 - 10 **Product Groups:** 35, 36, 39

Date of Accounts	May 11	May 10	May 08
Working Capital	217	202	127
Fixed Assets	49	55	66
Current Assets	302	293	245

Celtic Engineering Helston Ltd
Water-Ma-Trout, Helston, TR13 0LW
Tel: 01326-561857 **Fax:** 01326-565007
E-mail: celticeng@btconnect.com
Website: http://www.celticengineering.co.uk
Directors: A. Trewhella (MD)
Immediate Holding Company: CELTIC ENGINEERING (HELSTON) LTD
Registration no: 04430920 **Date established:** 2002
No.of Employees: 1 - 10 **Product Groups:** 46, 48

Date of Accounts	Jun 12	Jun 11	Jun 10
Working Capital	17	-9	-40
Fixed Assets	26	36	46
Current Assets	85	76	74

Helston Diesel
St Johns Business Park Penzance Road, Helston, TR13 8HN
Tel: 01326-561977 **Fax:** 01326-565146
E-mail: enquiries@helstondiesel.co.uk
Directors: R. Atkinson (Prop)
Date established: 1998 **No.of Employees:** 1 - 10 **Product Groups:** 40

R Kueck
Trenoweth Farm St Keverne, Helston, TR12 6QQ
Tel: 01326-280230 **Fax:** 01326-280230
E-mail: rogerkueck@btconnect.com
Directors: R. Kueck (Prop)
Date established: 1972 **No.of Employees:** 1 - 10 **Product Groups:** 41

Kuggar Stoves
Unit 5 St Johns Business Park Penzance Road, Helston, TR13 8HN
Tel: 01326-573643 **Fax:** 01326-573653
Website: http://www.kuggar-stoves.co.uk
Directors: R. Priest (Ptnr)
Date established: 1983 **No.of Employees:** 1 - 10 **Product Groups:** 40

Prestige Firearms
Glendevon Trenear, Helston, TR13 0HA
Tel: 01326-572130 **Fax:** 01326-572130
Directors: J. Williams (Prop)
Immediate Holding Company: PENGERSICK HISTORIC & EDUCATION TRUST
Date established: 2011 **No.of Employees:** 1 - 10 **Product Groups:** 36, 39, 40

Launceston

Armada Tube
Tube & Service Centre Lowley Road, Pennygillam Industrial Estate, Launceston, PL15 7PY
Tel: 01566-776699 **Fax:** 01566-776500
E-mail: sales@armadatube.co.uk
Website: http://www.armadatube.co.uk
Directors: D. Whitehouse (Fin)
Ultimate Holding Company: ARMADA INDUSTRIAL LIMITED
Immediate Holding Company: ARMADA TUBE LIMITED
Registration no: 02657922 **VAT No.:** GB 557 7325 14
Date established: 1991 **Turnover:** £5m - £10m **No.of Employees:** 11 - 20
Product Groups: 36, 66

Date of Accounts	Sep 10	Sep 09	Sep 08
Sales Turnover	6m	N/A	6m
Pre Tax Profit/Loss	80	N/A	302
Working Capital	-266	-251	-32
Fixed Assets	1m	2m	2m
Current Assets	4m	2m	4m
Current Liabilities	2m	775	1m

Celtic Solar Ltd
The Shipon Egloskerry, Launceston, PL15 8RZ
Tel: 01566-781509 **Fax:** 01566-781509
E-mail: info@celticsolar.co.uk
Website: http://www.celticsolar.co.uk
Directors: J. Turner (MD)
Immediate Holding Company: CELTIC RENEWABLE ENERGY LIMITED
Registration no: 04772098 **Date established:** 2003
No.of Employees: 1 - 10 **Product Groups:** 37, 40

Date of Accounts	Apr 12	Apr 11	Apr 10
Working Capital	162	68	6
Fixed Assets	30	19	14
Current Assets	257	198	121

D S Smith Packaging Ltd
Hurdon Road, Launceston, PL15 9HN
Tel: 01566-772303 **Fax:** 01566-774489
Website: http://www.dssmith-packaging.com
Bank(s): National Westminster Bank Plc
Directors: S. Owens (Dir)
Managers: S. Martyn (Comptroller), C. Hume (Personnel), S. Hampshire (Tech Serv Mgr), P. Ingerson, R. Carle (Sales Prom Mgr)
Ultimate Holding Company: DS SMITH PLC
Immediate Holding Company: DS SMITH PACKAGING LIMITED
Registration no: 00630681 **VAT No.:** GB 557 6159 10
Date established: 1959 **Turnover:** £10m - £20m
No.of Employees: 101 - 250 **Product Groups:** 27, 28

Date of Accounts	Apr 11	Apr 10	Apr 09
Sales Turnover	513m	427m	434m
Pre Tax Profit/Loss	17m	29m	18m
Working Capital	22m	24m	30m
Fixed Assets	125m	127m	137m
Current Assets	123m	116m	104m
Current Liabilities	15m	21m	19m

Harrison Fork Trucks Launceston
Quarry Cresent Pennygillam Industrial Estate, Launceston, PL15 7PF
Tel: 01566-777707 **Fax:** 01566-772541
E-mail: sales@harrisonforktrucks.co.uk
Website: http://www.harrisonforktrucks.co.uk
Directors: D. Harrison (Prop)
Immediate Holding Company: HARRISON FORK TRUCKS LIMITED
Registration no: 06638128 **Date established:** 2008
No.of Employees: 1 - 10 **Product Groups:** 35, 39, 45

Launceston Stoves
5 Newport Square, Launceston, PL15 8EN
Tel: 01566-773046 **Fax:** 01566-773046
Directors: D. Hawkins (Prop)
Date established: 1996 **No.of Employees:** 1 - 10 **Product Groups:** 40

Markrite Ltd
Compass Business Park Pipers Close, Pennygillam Industrial Estate, Launceston, PL15 7EB
Tel: 01566-774268 **Fax:** 01566-774268
E-mail: bill.hodgetts@btconnect.com
Directors: W. Hodgetts (Prop)
Immediate Holding Company: MARKRITE LIMITED
Registration no: 05549000 **Date established:** 2005
No.of Employees: 1 - 10 **Product Groups:** 37

Date of Accounts	Sep 11	Sep 10	Sep 09
Working Capital	-54	-61	-69
Fixed Assets	118	138	166
Current Assets	95	67	51

Safari Tech Services Ltd
Unit 27f Pennygillam Way, Pennygillam Industrial Estate, Launceston, PL15 7ED
Tel: 01566-779774 **Fax:** 01566-779773
E-mail: office@cpnitro.com
Website: http://www.safaribars.co.uk
Directors: M. Barnes (MD)
Immediate Holding Company: SAFARI TECH SERVICES LTD
Registration no: 04460805 **Date established:** 2002
No.of Employees: 1 - 10 **Product Groups:** 20, 40, 41

Date of Accounts	Jan 12	Jan 11	Jan 10
Working Capital	-17	-64	-147
Fixed Assets	1	69	173
Current Assets	31	65	30

Tarps UK
9 Fair Field Park Five Lanes, Launceston, PL15 7RQ
Tel: 01566-880116 **Fax:** 01566-880116
E-mail: john@tarps.co.uk
Website: http://www.canvas-tarps.co.uk
Directors: J. Hurkett (Prop)
No.of Employees: 21 - 50 **Product Groups:** 23, 24, 63

Liskeard

Audio Medical Services Ltd
Trevecca Industrial Park Culverland Road, Trevecca, Liskeard, PL14 6RE
Tel: 01579-348435 **Fax:** 01579-346960
E-mail: info@audiomedical.uk.com
Website: http://www.audiomedical.uk.com
Directors: E. Nickson (MD)
Immediate Holding Company: AUDIO MEDICAL SERVICES LIMITED
Registration no: 02776030 **Date established:** 1992
Turnover: £500,000 - £1m **No.of Employees:** 1 - 10 **Product Groups:** 84

Date of Accounts	Mar 11	Mar 10	Mar 09
Working Capital	-142	-87	-54
Fixed Assets	12	15	18
Current Assets	30	28	36

Barxtras
5 Addington South, Liskeard, PL14 3EQ
Tel: 01579-348834 **Fax:** 01579-342661
Directors: A. Lightfoot (Prop)
Date established: 1998 **No.of Employees:** 1 - 10 **Product Groups:** 20, 40, 41

Drinkmaster Ltd
Plymouth Road, Liskeard, PL14 3PG
Tel: 01579-342082 **Fax:** 01579-342591
E-mail: sales@drinkmaster.co.uk
Website: http://www.drinkmaster.co.uk
Bank(s): Bank of Scotland
Directors: P. Vickers (MD)
Ultimate Holding Company: SNACKTIME PLC
Immediate Holding Company: DRINKMASTER HOLDINGS LIMITED
Registration no: 02663746 **VAT No.:** GB 591 1282 44
Date established: 1991 **Turnover:** £5m - £10m
No.of Employees: 101 - 250 **Product Groups:** 49

Date of Accounts	Dec 09	Dec 08	Dec 07
Pre Tax Profit/Loss	250	N/A	N/A
Working Capital	-5m	-5m	-5m
Fixed Assets	6m	6m	6m
Current Assets	318	318	318

Hotline Chimneys Ltd
Moorswater Industrial Estate Moorswater, Liskeard, PL14 4LG
Tel: 01579-324232 **Fax:** 01579-324741
E-mail: sales@hotline-chimneys.co.uk
Website: http://www.hotline-chimneys.co.uk
Registration no: 07147247 **Product Groups:** 25, 33, 35, 66

Jewson Ltd
Moorswater Industrial Estate Moorswater, Liskeard, PL14 4LN
Tel: 01579-342021 **Fax:** 01579-347149
Website: http://www.jewson.co.uk
Managers: P. Williams (Mgr)
Ultimate Holding Company: COMPAGNIE DE SAINT GOBAIN (FRANCE)
Immediate Holding Company: JEWSON LIMITED
Registration no: 00348407 **VAT No.:** GB 394 1216 30
Date established: 1939 **Turnover:** £500m - £1,000m
No.of Employees: 1 - 10 **Product Groups:** 66

Date of Accounts	Dec 11	Dec 10	Dec 09
Sales Turnover	1606m	1547m	1485m
Pre Tax Profit/Loss	18m	100m	45m
Working Capital	-345m	-250m	-349m
Fixed Assets	496m	387m	461m
Current Assets	657m	1005m	1320m
Current Liabilities	66m	120m	64m

Kee Engineering
Unit 14a Miller Business Park Station Road, Liskeard, PL14 4DA
Tel: 01579-344285 **Fax:** 01579-348635
E-mail: chris@kee.co.uk
Website: http://www.kee.co.uk
Directors: C. Edwards (Prop)
Turnover: £250,000 - £500,000 **No.of Employees:** 1 - 10
Product Groups: 46, 48

Pearce's
The Show Site Dobwalls, Liskeard, PL14 6JN
Tel: 01579-350111 **Fax:** 01579- 320898
E-mail: sales@compton-buildings.co.uk
Website: http://www.comptonbuildings.co.uk
Directors: J. Pearce (Prop)
Date established: 1973 **No.of Employees:** 1 - 10 **Product Groups:** 25, 33, 35, 66

Puckator Ltd
Lowman Works East Tap House, East Taphouse, Liskeard, PL14 4NQ
Tel: 01579-321550 **Fax:** 01579-321520
E-mail: customerservices@puckator.co.uk
Website: http://www.puckator.co.uk
Directors: C. Howard (Fin), M. Howard (Fin), M. Shaw (Dir)
Managers: S. Thomas (Sales Admin), E. Pellia
Ultimate Holding Company: PUCKATOR HOLDINGS LIMITED
Immediate Holding Company: PUCKATOR LIMITED
Registration no: 03413131 **Date established:** 1997
No.of Employees: 21 - 50 **Product Groups:** 49

Date of Accounts	Dec 11	Dec 10	Dec 09
Working Capital	482	286	162
Fixed Assets	792	796	801
Current Assets	1m	980	819

Red Snapper Design
Chapel Row Tremar Coombe, Liskeard, PL14 5EY
Tel: 01579-348540
E-mail: enquiries@redsnapperdesign.co.uk
Website: http://www.redsnapperdesign.co.uk
Managers: R. Morton
No.of Employees: 1 - 10 **Product Groups:** 44, 81

South West One Ltd
Foxhill Herodsfoot, Liskeard, PL14 4QX
Tel: 01579-321300 **Fax:** 01579-320586
E-mail: swonewebsiteenquiries@tauntondeane.gov.uk
Website: http://www.southwestone.co.uk
Directors: D. Porter (Ch), J. Porter (Dir)
Ultimate Holding Company: South West One Ltd
Immediate Holding Company: South West One Ltd
Registration no: 06373780 **VAT No.:** GB 462 8366 26
Date established: 1987 **Turnover:** Up to £250,000
No.of Employees: 1 - 10 **Product Groups:** 81

T M A Engineering
Unit 14 Miller Business Park Station Road, Liskeard, PL14 4DA
Tel: 01579-343883 **Fax:** 01579-343884
E-mail: tmaengineering@btopenworld.com
Website: http://www.outdoorfeatures.co.uk
Directors: A. Smith (Prop)
Date established: 1991 **No.of Employees:** 1 - 10 **Product Groups:** 26, 35

Thrussell & Thrussell
Colquite Farm St Neot, Liskeard, PL14 6PZ
Tel: 01208-821692
E-mail: info@thrussellandthrussell.com
Website: http://www.thrussellandthrussell.com
Directors: G. Thrussell (Prop)
No.of Employees: 1 - 10 **Product Groups:** 26, 35, 66

Tiflex Ltd (James Walker Group)
Tiflex House Treburgie Water, Liskeard, PL14 4NB
Tel: 01579-320808 **Fax:** 01579-320802
E-mail: sales@tiflex.co.uk
Website: http://www.tiflex.co.uk
Bank(s): HSBC Bank plc
Directors: R. Spearman (MD), P. Caulfield (Fin), N. Spearman (MD), P. Collins (Co Sec)
Managers: M. Hargraves (Comm), A. Diamond (Personnel), N. Yew (Tech Serv Mgr)
Ultimate Holding Company: JAMES WALKER GROUP LIMITED
Immediate Holding Company: TIFLEX LIMITED
Registration no: 00394614 **VAT No.:** GB 211 6452 03
Date established: 1945 **Turnover:** £10m - £20m
No.of Employees: 101 - 250 **Product Groups:** 25, 27, 29, 30, 32, 35, 39, 49

Date of Accounts	Mar 12	Mar 11	Mar 10
Sales Turnover	12m	14m	10m
Pre Tax Profit/Loss	676	2m	979
Working Capital	5m	5m	3m
Fixed Assets	928	848	906
Current Assets	6m	7m	4m
Current Liabilities	402	684	555

Looe

Jewson Ltd
Polean Trading Estate, Looe, PL13 2HR
Tel: 01503-262141 **Fax:** 01503-265015
Website: http://www.jewson.co.uk
Managers: P. Richardson (Mgr)
Ultimate Holding Company: COMPAGNIE DE SAINT GOBAIN (FRANCE)
Immediate Holding Company: JEWSON LIMITED
Registration no: 00348407 **Date established:** 1939 **Turnover:** £2m - £5m
No.of Employees: 1 - 10 **Product Groups:** 66

Date of Accounts	Dec 11	Dec 10	Dec 09
Sales Turnover	1606m	1547m	1485m
Pre Tax Profit/Loss	18m	100m	45m
Working Capital	-345m	-250m	-349m
Fixed Assets	496m	387m	461m
Current Assets	657m	1005m	1320m
Current Liabilities	66m	120m	64m

Weightcheck
Pickney House Killigarth, Looe, PL13 2JQ
Tel: 01503-272636 **Fax:** 01503-272636
E-mail: enquiries@weightcheck.co.uk
Website: http://www.weightcheck.co.uk
Directors: K. Davies (MD)
Turnover: £500,000 - £1m **No.of Employees:** 11 - 20
Product Groups: 38, 67

Lostwithiel

Cornwall Furniture Restoration
Unit 9a 4 Restormel Industrial Estate, Lostwithiel, PL22 0HG
Tel: 01208-871444
E-mail: iantiques@btinternet.com
Website: http://www.cornwallfurniturerestoration.co.uk
Directors: I. Marshall (Prop)
Immediate Holding Company: RESTORMEL ESTATES LIMITED
Registration no: 06675868 **Date established:** 1992
Turnover: Up to £250,000 **No.of Employees:** 1 - 10 **Product Groups:** 26

Date of Accounts	Jun 11	Jun 10	Jun 09
Sales Turnover	N/A	N/A	304
Working Capital	-74	-57	-46
Fixed Assets	102	135	169
Current Assets	184	138	212

Newquay

Celtic Sheepskin Company Ltd
Unit B Treloggan Industrial Estate, Newquay, TR7 2SX
Tel: 01637-871605 **Fax:** 01637-851989
E-mail: support@celtic-sheepskin.co.uk
Website: http://www.celtic-sheepskin.co.uk
Bank(s): HSBC Bank plc
Directors: N. Whitworth (MD), K. Whitworth (Dir)
Managers: C. Cole (Sec)
Ultimate Holding Company: THE CELTIC SHEEPSKIN CO (HOLDINGS) LIMITED
Immediate Holding Company: THE CELTIC SHEEPSKIN CO LTD
Registration no: 03265058 **VAT No.:** GB 557 6498 85
Date established: 1996 **Turnover:** £250,000 - £500,000
No.of Employees: 21 - 50 **Product Groups:** 22

Date of Accounts	Jan 11	Jan 10	Jan 09
Working Capital	2m	2m	936
Fixed Assets	279	158	179
Current Assets	3m	3m	2m

Clinton Ironworks
14 Trevemper Road, Newquay, TR7 2HR
Tel: 01637-871760 **Fax:** 01637-871760
Directors: J. Clinton (Ptnr)
Date established: 1994 **No.of Employees:** 1 - 10 **Product Groups:** 26, 35

Dimensions Electrical
3 St Georges Road, Newquay, TR7 1RE
Tel: 01637-874343 **Fax:** 01637-871417
Website: http://www.cornwallappliances.co.uk
Directors: B. Coombes (Ptnr)
Date established: 1968 **No.of Employees:** 1 - 10 **Product Groups:** 43

Forged Originals
Sunny Cottage Mount Joy, Newquay, TR8 4LN
Tel: 01726-860119
Directors: D. Studden (Prop)
No.of Employees: 1 - 10 **Product Groups:** 26, 35

Higman Windows
Westways Lane, Newquay, TR8 4QB
Tel: 01637-879343 **Fax:** 01637-879342
E-mail: clive.higmanwindows@tiscali.co.uk
Website: http://www.higman-windows.co.uk
Directors: C. Bicknell (Prop)
Immediate Holding Company: HIGMAN WINDOWS LIMITED
Registration no: 05316012 **Date established:** 2004
No.of Employees: 1 - 10 **Product Groups:** 33, 35, 40, 52

Date of Accounts	Dec 11	Dec 10	Dec 09
Working Capital	107	143	140
Fixed Assets	57	63	57
Current Assets	156	218	207

Jewson Ltd
Pargolla Road, Newquay, TR7 1RP
Tel: 01637-871234 **Fax:** 01637-850883
E-mail: gordoncree@graham-group.co.uk
Website: http://www.jewson.co.uk
Managers: C. Matthais (District Mgr)
Ultimate Holding Company: COMPAGNIE DE SAINT GOBAIN (FRANCE)
Immediate Holding Company: JEWSON LIMITED
Registration no: 00348407 **VAT No.:** GB 394 1212 63
Date established: 1939 **Turnover:** £20m - £50m **No.of Employees:** 1 - 10
Product Groups: 66

Date of Accounts	Dec 11	Dec 10	Dec 09
Sales Turnover	1606m	1547m	1485m
Pre Tax Profit/Loss	18m	100m	45m
Working Capital	-345m	-250m	-349m
Fixed Assets	496m	387m	461m
Current Assets	657m	1005m	1320m
Current Liabilities	66m	120m	64m

M J D Accountancy Services
31 St Annes Road, Newquay, TR7 2SA
Tel: 01637-851949 **Fax:** 01637-851949
E-mail: mjd@mjdservices.co.uk
Website: http://www.mjdservices.co.uk

see next page

***M J D Accountancy Services** - Cont'd*
Directors: M. Derbyshire (Prop)
Turnover: Up to £250,000 **No.of Employees:** 1 - 10 **Product Groups:** 44, 80

Mid Cornwall Metal Fabrications
Treloggan Industrial Estate, Newquay, TR7 2SX
Tel: 01637-879474 **Fax:** 01637-877278
E-mail: mike@mcmf.co.uk
Website: http://www.mcmf.co.uk
Directors: M. Wilton (Prop)
Ultimate Holding Company: R T JULIAN & SON (HOLDINGS) LIMITED
Immediate Holding Company: R T JULIAN & SON (HOLDINGS) LIMITED
Registration no: 04216674 **Date established:** 2001
No.of Employees: 21 - 50 **Product Groups:** 26, 35

Date of Accounts	Apr 11	Apr 10	Apr 09
Working Capital	74	263	366
Fixed Assets	181	60	69
Current Assets	86	321	574

Optical Works Ltd
Ealing Science Centre Treloggan Lane, Newquay, TR7 1HX
Tel: 01637-870100 **Fax:** 01637-877211
E-mail: sales@opticalworks.co.uk
Website: http://www.opticalworks.co.uk
Directors: E. Frisk (MD), P. Frisk (MD)
Managers: I. Johnson (I.T. Exec)
Immediate Holding Company: Optical Works,Limited
Registration no: 00363402 **VAT No.:** GB 226 7076 60
Date established: 1940 **Turnover:** £250,000 - £500,000
No.of Employees: 1 - 10 **Product Groups:** 38, 65

Date of Accounts	Sep 08	Sep 07	Sep 06
Working Capital	-92	-92	-78
Fixed Assets	218	221	223
Current Assets	54	58	68
Current Liabilities	147	150	146
Total Share Capital	50	50	50

Par

Fowey Pilots
Par Harbour 2 Harbour Road, Par, PL24 2BD
Tel: 01726-815777
Website: http://www.foweypilots.com
Directors: C. Woods (Dir)
No.of Employees: 11 - 20 **Product Groups:** 35, 36, 39

Penryn

Allen & Heath Ltd
Kernick Industrial Estate, Penryn, TR10 9LU
Tel: 01326-372070 **Fax:** 01326-377097
E-mail: glenn.rogers@dmh-global.com
Website: http://www.allen-heath.com
Bank(s): HSBC Bank plc
Directors: G. Rogers (MD), D. Jones (Fin)
Managers: M. Clarke (Purch Mgr), N. Dickey (Personnel), M. Hitchman, D. Kirk (Mktg Serv Mgr), D. Maxted (Sales Prom Mgr)
Ultimate Holding Company: D&M HOLDINGS INC (JAPAN)
Immediate Holding Company: ALLEN & HEATH LIMITED
Registration no: 04163451 **VAT No.:** GB 491 9810 13
Date established: 2001 **Turnover:** £20m - £50m
No.of Employees: 101 - 250 **Product Groups:** 37

Date of Accounts	Mar 11	Mar 10	Mar 09
Sales Turnover	30m	23m	19m
Pre Tax Profit/Loss	6m	5m	2m
Working Capital	8m	6m	4m
Fixed Assets	4m	4m	5m
Current Assets	13m	8m	7m
Current Liabilities	2m	2m	1m

Discount Appliances
46 Kernick Road, Penryn, TR10 9DQ
Tel: 01326-373122
Directors: R. Hathaway (Prop)
No.of Employees: 1 - 10 **Product Groups:** 36, 40

Ecostat Direct
19 Lanoweth, Penryn, TR10 8RP
Tel: 01326-378654 **Fax:** 01326-378539
E-mail: audreychallingsworth@fsmail.net
Website: http://www.ecostat-direct.co.uk
Directors: A. Challingsworth (Prop)
Registration no: 03664639 **Turnover:** Up to £250,000
No.of Employees: 1 - 10 **Product Groups:** 41

Elegant Homes Ltd (t/a kilian craft)
The Praze, Penryn, TR10 8AA
Tel: 01326-377113 **Fax:** 01326-378691
E-mail: kilian.craft@lineone.net
Website: http://www.eleganthomescornwall.co.uk
Directors: M. Fenton (Dir)
Immediate Holding Company: TASTE KITCHEN STUDIO LIMITED
Registration no: 03874129 **VAT No.:** GB 717 6105 45
Date established: 1999 **Turnover:** £250,000 - £500,000
No.of Employees: 1 - 10 **Product Groups:** 26, 63

Date of Accounts	Jun 11	Jun 10	Jun 09
Sales Turnover	562	580	620
Pre Tax Profit/Loss	6	20	-34
Working Capital	-160	88	120
Fixed Assets	61	72	90
Current Assets	133	142	211
Current Liabilities	238	14	39

Keefe Engineering
Islington Wharf, Penryn, TR10 8AT
Tel: 01326-374869
Directors: R. Keefe (Prop)
Date established: 1978 **No.of Employees:** 1 - 10 **Product Groups:** 35, 36, 39

Kernow Coatings Ltd
Kernick Road, Penryn, TR10 9DQ
Tel: 01326-373147 **Fax:** 01326-376614
E-mail: pnewell@kernowcoatings.com
Website: http://www.sensitisers.com
Bank(s): National Westminster Bank Plc
Directors: P. Knewell (Fin), P. Newell (Dir)
Managers: S. Chaple (Mgr)
Ultimate Holding Company: SENSITISERS GROUP LTD.
Immediate Holding Company: KERNOW COATINGS LIMITED
Registration no: 01092182 **VAT No.:** GB 337 0321 87
Date established: 1973 **Turnover:** £10m - £20m
No.of Employees: 51 - 100 **Product Groups:** 27, 30, 66

Date of Accounts	Mar 11	Mar 10	Mar 09
Sales Turnover	13m	11m	N/A
Pre Tax Profit/Loss	1m	226	411
Working Capital	4m	4m	3m
Fixed Assets	2m	2m	2m
Current Assets	7m	6m	5m
Current Liabilities	827	550	462

Powerfal Ltd
Unit 9 Kernick Industrial Estate Kernick, Penryn, TR10 9EP
Tel: 01326-377160 **Fax:** 01326-377161
E-mail: service@powerfal.co.uk
Website: http://www.powerfal.co.uk
Directors: C. Hough (MD)
Immediate Holding Company: POWERFAL LIMITED
Registration no: 03005316 **Date established:** 1995
No.of Employees: 11 - 20 **Product Groups:** 35, 36, 39

Date of Accounts	Mar 12	Mar 11	Jan 10
Working Capital	51	23	36
Fixed Assets	341	334	270
Current Assets	294	237	239

Simon Caddy Marine Engineers
31 Bronescombe Close, Penryn, TR10 8LE
Tel: 01326-372682 **Fax:** 01326-372682
E-mail: caddymarine@tiscali.co.uk
Website: http://www.simoncaddy-marineengineers.co.uk
Directors: S. Caddy (Prop)
Date established: 1978 **No.of Employees:** 1 - 10 **Product Groups:** 35, 36, 39

Wills Ridley Ltd
Unit 1 Kernick Business Park, Penryn, TR10 9EW
Tel: 01326-376015 **Fax:** 01326-376212
E-mail: info@wills-ridley.com
Website: http://www.wills-ridley.com
Directors: P. Kitchener (MD)
Immediate Holding Company: WILLS RIDLEY LIMITED
Registration no: 02729805 **VAT No.:** GB 591 1779 13
Date established: 1992 **Turnover:** £250,000 - £500,000
No.of Employees: 1 - 10 **Product Groups:** 39, 84

Date of Accounts	Oct 11	Oct 10	Oct 09
Working Capital	135	129	132
Fixed Assets	50	62	71
Current Assets	211	225	199

Penzance

Biffa Waste Services Ltd
Long Rock Industrial Estate Long Rock, Penzance, TR20 8HX
Tel: 01736-360737 **Fax:** 01736-351661
E-mail: marketing@biffa.co.uk
Website: http://www.biffa.co.uk
Managers: D. Tilby (Mgr), P. Richards (Chief Mgr), A. Sugg (Mgr)
Immediate Holding Company: BIFFA WASTE SERVICES LIMITED
Registration no: 00946107 **Date established:** 1969
No.of Employees: 21 - 50 **Product Groups:** 54

Date of Accounts	Mar 08	Mar 09	Apr 10
Sales Turnover	555m	574m	492m
Pre Tax Profit/Loss	23m	50m	30m
Working Capital	229m	271m	293m
Fixed Assets	371m	360m	378m
Current Assets	409m	534m	609m
Current Liabilities	50m	100m	115m

Castle Gates
Borea Farm Borea, Nancledra, Penzance, TR20 8AZ
Tel: 01736-363605
Directors: S. Carter (Prop)
Date established: 1992 **No.of Employees:** 1 - 10 **Product Groups:** 26, 35

Cottage Thimbles
Unit 8a The Old Dairy Sancreed, Penzance, TR20 8QP
Tel: 01736-332342 **Fax:** 01736-351272
E-mail: cottage@thimbles.co.uk
Website: http://www.thimbles.com
Directors: C. Church (Ptnr)
Immediate Holding Company: THE GREEN BEAN COFFEE COMPANY LIMITED
Registration no: 06271542 **Date established:** 2007
Turnover: £500,000 - £1m **No.of Employees:** 1 - 10 **Product Groups:** 30, 33, 35, 40, 49

Dolphin Stairlifts Ltd
Lamorna House Trewelloe Road, Praa Sands, Penzance, TR20 9SU
Tel: 01736-763580
E-mail: info@dolphinstairlifts.co.uk
Website: http://www.dolphinstairlifts.co.uk
Directors: S. Harper (Ptnr)
Immediate Holding Company: DOLPHIN STAIRLIFTS CORNWALL LIMITED
Registration no: 04143693 **Date established:** 2001
No.of Employees: 1 - 10 **Product Groups:** 35, 39, 45

Date of Accounts	Jan 12	Jan 11	Jan 10
Working Capital	49	78	122
Fixed Assets	8	26	26
Current Assets	141	174	176

E S Hocking
Truthwall Crowlas, Penzance, TR20 9BW
Tel: 01736-740579 **Fax:** 01736-740579
Directors: E. Hocking (Prop)
Date established: 1987 **No.of Employees:** 1 - 10 **Product Groups:** 41

Mounts Bay Engineering Co.
North Pier Newlyn, Penzance, TR18 5JB
Tel: 01736-363095 **Fax:** 01736-332010
Managers: D. Ryeland (Chief Mgr)
Registration no: 01593185 **No.of Employees:** 1 - 10 **Product Groups:** 35, 36, 39

Netpack Mail Order Shopping
Long Rock, Penzance, TR93 0XX
Tel: 01736-360036 **Fax:** 01736-364636
E-mail: tim@netpack.co.uk
Website: http://www.netpack.co.uk
Directors: F. Evans (Fin), C. Evans (Dir), T. Drawn (MD)
Managers: A. Richards (Cust Serv Mgr)
Date established: 1998 **No.of Employees:** 21 - 50 **Product Groups:** 77

R Johns Fabrications
2 Strand Stores Harbour Road, Newlyn, Penzance, TR18 5HA
Tel: 01736-333412
E-mail: info@macace.net
Website: http://www.macace.net
Directors: R. Johns (Prop)
Date established: 1991 **No.of Employees:** 1 - 10 **Product Groups:** 35

Seagems Ltd
Long Rock Industrial Estate Long Rock, Penzance, TR20 8HX
Tel: 01736-335840 **Fax:** 01736-332033
E-mail: marcusprice@seagems.co.uk
Website: http://www.seagems.co.uk
Directors: T. Price (Dir)
Ultimate Holding Company: BMT NV (BELGIUM)
Immediate Holding Company: SEA GEMS LIMITED
Registration no: 00744915 **VAT No.:** GB 131 6286 85
Date established: 1962 **Turnover:** £2m - £5m **No.of Employees:** 11 - 20
Product Groups: 49

Date of Accounts	Dec 11	Dec 10	Dec 09
Working Capital	965	1m	1m
Fixed Assets	657	671	675
Current Assets	2m	2m	2m

Simpsons
Queens Buildings 4 Promenade, Penzance, TR18 4HH
Tel: 01736-361110 **Fax:** 01736-361876
E-mail: alan@simpsonsmultimedia.co.uk
Website: http://www.simpsonsmultimedia.co.uk
Directors: A. Simpson (Prop)
No.of Employees: 1 - 10 **Product Groups:** 37

Taylor Foodservice Facilities
Truthwall Mill Crowlas, Penzance, TR20 9BL
Tel: 01736-711310 **Fax:** 01736-711317
E-mail: tffc_ian_taylor@compuserve.com
Website: http://www.taylorfoodservice.com
Directors: I. Taylor (Prop), I. Taylor (Ptnr), H. Taylor (Dir), S. Taylor (Dir)
Date established: 1984 **Turnover:** £500,000 - £1m
No.of Employees: 1 - 10 **Product Groups:** 40, 49

Perranporth

Kernowcraft Rocks & Gems Ltd
Penwartha Road Bolingey, Perranporth, TR6 0DH
Tel: 01872-573888 **Fax:** 01872-573704
E-mail: info@kernowcraft.com
Website: http://www.kernowcraft.com
Directors: H. Hodge (MD)
Immediate Holding Company: KERNOWCRAFT ROCKS AND GEMS LIMITED
Registration no: 00984779 **Date established:** 1970
Turnover: £250,000 - £500,000 **No.of Employees:** 1 - 10
Product Groups: 47, 49

Date of Accounts	Mar 11	Mar 10	Mar 09
Working Capital	213	179	147
Fixed Assets	57	62	77
Current Assets	249	227	182

Port Isaac

I V O C M S
9 Trewetha Lane, Port Isaac, PL29 3RN
Tel: 01208-881056 **Fax:** 01208-881055
E-mail: ivocms@aol.com
Website: http://www.ivocms.co.uk
Directors: C. Raynor (Fin), D. Raynor (MD)
Immediate Holding Company: IVO CMS CONTROLS LIMITED
Registration no: 02985591 **Date established:** 1994
Turnover: Up to £250,000 **No.of Employees:** 1 - 10 **Product Groups:** 38, 44

Date of Accounts	Dec 11	Dec 10	Dec 09
Sales Turnover	22	24	27
Pre Tax Profit/Loss	-0	1	-2
Working Capital	20	20	19
Fixed Assets	N/A	N/A	1
Current Assets	55	57	62
Current Liabilities	1	N/A	1

Redruth

Alarm & Lock Doc
13 Roskrow Close Four Lanes, Redruth, TR16 6NG
Tel: 01209-314960 **Fax:** 01209-314960
E-mail: sales@alarmandlocdoc.fsnet.co.uk
Website: http://www.alarmandlocdoc.fsnet.co.uk
Directors: D. Strickland (Prop)
Date established: 2001 **No.of Employees:** 1 - 10 **Product Groups:** 37, 40, 67

Alternature
The Old Grammar School West Park, Redruth, TR15 3AJ
Tel: 0781-080 7859
E-mail: alternature@hotmail.com
Website: http://www.alternature.biz
Directors: T. Harris (Prop)
Immediate Holding Company: CORNISH MEDIA INDUSTRIES LIMITED
Date established: 2009 **No.of Employees:** 1 - 10 **Product Groups:** 26

Date of Accounts	Dec 11	Dec 10	Dec 09
Sales Turnover	52	62	64
Pre Tax Profit/Loss	1	-15	13
Working Capital	13	13	28
Current Assets	15	22	40
Current Liabilities	1	6	8

S J Andrew & Sons
South Turnpike, Redruth, TR15 2LZ
Tel: 01209-213171 **Fax:** 01209-219459
E-mail: accounts@sjandrew.com
Website: http://www.sjandrew.com
Bank(s): Barclays
Managers: N. Andrew (Mgr)
Ultimate Holding Company: SJ ANDREW HOLDINGS LIMITED
Immediate Holding Company: SJ ANDREW HOLDINGS LIMITED
Registration no: 07201902 **VAT No.:** GB 131 6069 93
Date established: 2010 **Turnover:** £2m - £5m **No.of Employees:** 21 - 50
Product Groups: 34, 35, 36, 66

Date of Accounts	Mar 12	Mar 11
Working Capital	384	454
Fixed Assets	1m	1m
Current Assets	608	691

Aquamacs
Moorgrove Tolgullow, St Day, Redruth, TR16 5PD
Tel: 03003-651250 **Fax:** 01209-821796
E-mail: info@aquamacs.co.uk
Website: http://www.aquamacs.co.uk
Directors: S. Mackenzie (Prop)
Immediate Holding Company: AQUAMACS (UK) LTD
Registration no: 07757600 **Date established:** 2011
Turnover: Up to £250,000 **No.of Employees:** 1 - 10 **Product Groups:** 62

R S Berry
1 Coach Lane, Redruth, TR15 2TP
Tel: 01209-313261 **Fax:** 01209-313261
Directors: R. Berry (Prop)
Date established: 2000 **No.of Employees:** 1 - 10 **Product Groups:** 46, 48

Brewer & Bunney
Unit 9 Barncoose Industrial Estate, Redruth, TR15 3XX
Tel: 01752-266444 **Fax:** 01209-313057
E-mail: enquiries@brewerandbunney.co.uk
Website: http://www.brewerandbunney.co.uk
Directors: C. Trustcott (Fin), D. Hayes (MD)
Managers: L. Harris (Comptroller)
Immediate Holding Company: BREWER & BUNNEY LIMITED
Registration no: 03636372 **Date established:** 1998
Turnover: £500,000 - £1m **No.of Employees:** 11 - 20
Product Groups: 40, 63

Date of Accounts	Nov 11	Nov 10	Nov 09
Working Capital	273	340	253
Fixed Assets	518	405	440
Current Assets	734	878	787

Broad Agri
Unit 5 United Downs Industrial Park St Day, Redruth, TR16 5HY
Tel: 01209-821841 **Fax:** 01209-820019
E-mail: sales@broad-agri.co.uk
Website: http://www.broad-agri.co.uk
Directors: R. Broadbank (Ptnr)
Date established: 1996 **No.of Employees:** 1 - 10 **Product Groups:** 41

CFS Fibreglass Supplies
United Downs Industrial Park, Redruth, TR16 5HY
Tel: 01209-821028 **Fax:** 01209-822192
E-mail: sales@cfsnet.co.uk
Website: http://www.cfsnet.co.uk
Directors: A. McGovan (Ptnr)
Date established: 1974 **No.of Employees:** 11 - 20 **Product Groups:** 30, 66

Cornish Welding Supplies
United Downs Industrial Park St Day, Redruth, TR16 5HY
Tel: 01209-822588 **Fax:** 01209-822112
Directors: D. Roberts (Prop)
Date established: 2004 **No.of Employees:** 1 - 10 **Product Groups:** 46

Eriks UK (Redruth Service Centre)
Unit 16c Pool Industrial Estate, Pool, Redruth, TR15 3RH
Tel: 01209-216839 **Fax:** 01209-219793
E-mail: redruth@eriks.co.uk
Website: http://www.eriks.co.uk
Managers: R. Martin (District Mgr)
Immediate Holding Company: WYKO HOLDINGS LTD
Registration no: 00917112 **No.of Employees:** 1 - 10 **Product Groups:** 66

Fellside Plastics Ltd
Wilson Way Pool, Redruth, TR15 3RX
Tel: 01209-212917 **Fax:** 01209-212919
E-mail: fellside@blowit.fsbusiness.co.uk
Directors: D. Beharall (MD)
Immediate Holding Company: FELLSIDE (PLASTICS) LIMITED
Registration no: 02984901 **Date established:** 1994
Turnover: Up to £250,000 **No.of Employees:** 11 - 20 **Product Groups:** 30, 42, 66

Date of Accounts	Nov 09	Nov 08	Nov 07
Working Capital	118	125	94
Fixed Assets	69	76	76
Current Assets	262	395	296

Frame Homes South West
Jenson House Cardrew Industrial Estate, Redruth, TR15 1SS
Tel: 01209-310560 **Fax:** 01209-310561
E-mail: info@frameuk.com
Website: http://www.frameuk.com
Bank(s): Lloyds TSB Bank plc
Directors: R. Pepper (Prop), R. Smith (MD)
Managers: M. Pepper (Personnel), N. Stevens (Sales Prom Mgr), A. Welsh (Tech Serv Mgr), A. Walsall, R. Chapman (Mktg Serv Mgr)
Immediate Holding Company: FRAME HOMES LIMITED
Registration no: 03405502 **VAT No.:** GB 132 7414 91
Date established: 1997 **Turnover:** £10m - £20m
No.of Employees: 51 - 100 **Product Groups:** 25

Gloveman Supplies Ltd
Vision House, Redruth, TR16 4AX
Tel: 01209-314759
E-mail: david@gloveman.co.uk
Website: http://www.gloveman.co.uk
Managers: D. Dinneen (Mgr)
Immediate Holding Company: GLOVEMAN SUPPLIES LIMITED
Registration no: 04862122 **Date established:** 2003
No.of Employees: 11 - 20 **Product Groups:** 27, 29, 38

Date of Accounts	Mar 12	Mar 11	Mar 10
Working Capital	494	317	-56
Fixed Assets	39	46	36
Current Assets	2m	1m	1m

Hardmetal Engineering Cornwall Ltd
Treleigh Industrial Estate Jon Davey Drive, Redruth, TR16 4AX
Tel: 01209-202800 **Fax:** 01209-202819
E-mail: sales@tungsten-carbide.com
Website: http://www.tungsten-carbide.com
Bank(s): The Royal Bank of Scotland
Directors: A. Hosking (MD), S. Hosking (Fin)
Ultimate Holding Company: WELDING ELECTRODE STORE LIMITED
Immediate Holding Company: HARDMETAL ENGINEERING (CORNWALL) LIMITED
Registration no: 04902425 **VAT No.:** 337 2525 61 **Date established:** 2003
Turnover: £250,000 - £500,000 **No.of Employees:** 11 - 20
Product Groups: 34, 35, 36, 48

Date of Accounts	Mar 11	Mar 10	Mar 09
Sales Turnover	405	N/A	N/A
Pre Tax Profit/Loss	27	N/A	N/A
Working Capital	61	37	74
Fixed Assets	67	75	79
Current Assets	194	161	217
Current Liabilities	97	N/A	78

Jewson Ltd
Agar Road Illogan Highway, Redruth, TR15 3ED
Tel: 01209-213030 **Fax:** 01209-216288
Website: http://www.jewson.co.uk
Managers: J. Westley (Mgr)
Ultimate Holding Company: COMPAGNIE DE SAINT GOBAIN (FRANCE)
Immediate Holding Company: JEWSON LIMITED
Registration no: 00348407 **Date established:** 1939
No.of Employees: 21 - 50 **Product Groups:** 66

Date of Accounts	Dec 11	Dec 10	Dec 09
Sales Turnover	1606m	1547m	1485m
Pre Tax Profit/Loss	18m	100m	45m
Working Capital	-345m	-250m	-349m
Fixed Assets	496m	387m	461m
Current Assets	657m	1005m	1320m
Current Liabilities	66m	120m	64m

Jolly's L W C
Wilson Way Pool, Redruth, TR15 3JD
Tel: 01209-213504 **Fax:** 01209-210342
E-mail: robin.gray@lwc-drinks.co.uk
Website: http://www.lwc-drinks.co.uk
Directors: R. Gray (Prop)
Managers: D. Jolly (Mgr)
Registration no: 01351047 **VAT No.:** GB 133 2270 11
Date established: 1979 **Turnover:** £5m - £10m **No.of Employees:** 21 - 50
Product Groups: 21, 62

Kemp Engineering & Surveying Ltd
8 Barncoose Industrial Estate Barncoose, Redruth, TR15 3RQ
Tel: 01209-214687 **Fax:** 01209-215189
E-mail: office@kempengineering.co.uk
Website: http://www.kempengineeringsurvey.co.uk
Directors: S. Kemp (MD)
Managers: L. Jones
Ultimate Holding Company: UKRD GROUP LIMITED
Immediate Holding Company: KEMP ENGINEERING AND SURVEYING LTD.
Registration no: 03275853 **Date established:** 1996
Turnover: £500,000 - £1m **No.of Employees:** 11 - 20 **Product Groups:** 84

Date of Accounts	Feb 12	Feb 11	Feb 10
Working Capital	7	-67	-79
Fixed Assets	58	92	124
Current Assets	198	198	222

Laird King Ltd
Roseland Lanner Moor, Redruth, TR16 6JA
Tel: 01209-216912 **Fax:** 01209-216913
E-mail: info@lairdking.co.uk
Website: http://www.lairdking.co.uk
Directors: C. Stewart (Fin), C. King (MD)
Immediate Holding Company: DAVID KING TECHNOLOGIES LIMITED
Registration no: 03450991 **Date established:** 1997
No.of Employees: 1 - 10 **Product Groups:** 25, 35, 45

Mitchell & Webber Ltd
The Fuel Depot Scorrier, Redruth, TR16 5UT
Tel: 01209-821881 **Fax:** 01209-820750
E-mail: robert.weedon@mitweb.co.uk
Website: http://www.mitweb.co.uk
Directors: R. Weedon (Dir)
Immediate Holding Company: MITCHELL & WEBBER LIMITED
Registration no: 00892461 **Date established:** 1966
Turnover: £20m - £50m **No.of Employees:** 21 - 50 **Product Groups:** 31, 39, 40, 42, 52, 66

Date of Accounts	Nov 11	Nov 10	Nov 09
Sales Turnover	38m	25m	19m
Pre Tax Profit/Loss	133	296	342
Working Capital	789	1m	778
Fixed Assets	3m	3m	3m
Current Assets	6m	5m	3m
Current Liabilities	440	223	187

Movevirgo Ltd
New Portreath Road, Redruth, TR16 4QL
Tel: 01209-843484 **Fax:** 01209-843488
E-mail: stephen@movevirgo.co.uk
Website: http://www.movevirgo.co.uk
Directors: P. Williams (Fin), S. Wilkinson (MD)
Ultimate Holding Company: SWELL SURF PRODUCTS LIMITED
Immediate Holding Company: MOVEVIRGO LIMITED
Registration no: 01619880 **Date established:** 1982
No.of Employees: 1 - 10 **Product Groups:** 30, 31, 45, 48, 49

Date of Accounts	Mar 11	Mar 10	Mar 09
Working Capital	-50	-61	-18
Fixed Assets	33	43	44
Current Assets	205	312	207

New Life Health
Rose Cottage Ting Tang, Carharrack, Redruth, TR16 5SF
Tel: 01209-822207 **Fax:** 01209-822207
E-mail: info@newlifehealth.co.uk
Website: http://www.newlifehealth.co.uk
Directors: M. Sallis (Prop)
No.of Employees: 1 - 10 **Product Groups:** 31, 32

Opto Electronic Manufacturing Corporation Ltd (t/a OMC UK Ltd)
Candela House Cardrew Industrial Estate, Redruth, TR15 1SS
Tel: 01209-215424 **Fax:** 01209-215197
E-mail: heaths@omc-uk.com
Website: http://www.omc-uk.com
Bank(s): Barclays
Directors: W. Heath (Dir)
Managers: C. Rowland (Chief Acct), P. Ault
Immediate Holding Company: BOB PEPPER HOLDINGS LIMITED
Registration no: 03405502 **Date established:** 2012 **Turnover:** £2m - £5m
No.of Employees: 21 - 50 **Product Groups:** 37, 38, 45

Date of Accounts	Mar 08	Mar 07	Mar 06
Working Capital	1149	1005	1131
Fixed Assets	122	143	147
Current Assets	1416	1190	1427
Current Liabilities	267	185	295
Total Share Capital	2	2	2

P W F Fhe Forklift Doctor
The Old Corporation Yard Dudnance Lane Pool, Redruth, TR15 3QY
Tel: 01209-711166 **Fax:** 01209-711166
E-mail: p.weight@theforkliftdoctor.co.uk
Website: http://www.theforkliftdoctor.co.uk
Directors: P. Waite (Prop)
Immediate Holding Company: HEARTLANDS TRUST
Registration no: 06706027 **Date established:** 2010
No.of Employees: 1 - 10 **Product Groups:** 35, 39, 45

Parker Hannifin Ltd
1 Treleigh Industrial Estate Jon Davey Drive, Redruth, TR16 4AX
Tel: 01209-712712 **Fax:** 01209-713579
E-mail: parkerpneumatic@parker.com
Website: http://www.parker.com
Bank(s): Lloyds, Camborne
Directors: M. Vadgama (Co Sec), R. Arthur (Dir)
Managers: D. Tripconey (Prod Mgr), S. Webber (Plant), J. Griffith (Plant)
Immediate Holding Company: PARKER HANNIFIN LIMITED
Registration no: 07595632 **VAT No.:** GB 131 6348 89
Date established: 2011 **Turnover:** Up to £250,000
No.of Employees: 101 - 250 **Product Groups:** 33, 38, 40, 84

Date of Accounts	Jun 07	Jun 06
Working Capital	1940	1940
Current Assets	1940	1940
Total Share Capital	5990	5990

Premier Signs
Unit 9a Barncoose Industrial Estate, Barncoose, Redruth, TR15 3RQ
Tel: 01209-213695 **Fax:** 01209-219113
E-mail: cliffshaw50@aol.com
Website: http://www.premiersignssw.com
Directors: C. Shaw (Prop)
Registration no: 04692771 **Date established:** 2003
Turnover: Up to £250,000 **No.of Employees:** 1 - 10 **Product Groups:** 30, 39, 40

Nigel Rafferty
12 Trevelthan Road, Redruth, TR16 4DX
Tel: 01209-215829 **Fax:** 01209-215829
Directors: N. Rafferty (Prop)
Date established: 2000 **No.of Employees:** 1 - 10 **Product Groups:** 41

Rosewithian Catering & Gas Engineers
Unit 2 Wilson Way, Pool, Redruth, TR15 3RX
Tel: 01209-210677 **Fax:** 01209-210585
E-mail: rosewithian2@tiscali.co.uk
Website: http://www.rosewithiancatering.co.uk
Directors: T. Prisk (Ptnr)
Date established: 1998 **No.of Employees:** 1 - 10 **Product Groups:** 20, 40, 41

Sanders Pepper Smith Ltd
Unit 14 Cardrew Industrial Estate, Redruth, TR15 1SS
Tel: 01209-202170 **Fax:** 01209-310561
E-mail: enquiries@sanderspeppersmith.com
Website: http://www.sanderspeppersmith.com
Directors: A. Sanders (Dir)
Immediate Holding Company: FRAME HOMES LIMITED
Registration no: 6919938 **Date established:** 1997 **Turnover:**
No.of Employees: 1 - 10 **Product Groups:** 81, 84

Spraychem Ltd
Cardrew Industrial Estate, Redruth, TR15 1ST
Tel: 01209-312123 **Fax:** 01209-314333
E-mail: vernon.holmes@contico.co.uk
Website: http://www.spraychem.co.uk

see next page

Spraychem Ltd - *Cont'd*
Directors: S. Wiseman (Sales), V. Holmes (MD)
Managers: N. Davies (Mktg Serv Mgr), P. Haggerty (Purch Mgr)
Immediate Holding Company: SPRAYCHEM LIMITED
Registration no: 01670517 **VAT No.:** GB 438 4462 35
Date established: 1982 **Turnover:** £5m - £10m **No.of Employees:** 1 - 10
Product Groups: 30, 36, 40, 45, 63

G T Stone & Son
Dudnance Lane Pool, Redruth, TR15 3QZ
Tel: 01209-713862 **Fax:** 01209-710285
Directors: L. Stone (Co Sec), G. Stone (MD)
VAT No.: GB 131 9764 60 **Turnover:** £250,000 - £500,000
No.of Employees: 1 - 10 **Product Groups:** 72

Stralfors plc
Unit 1 Cardre Industrial Estcardre Way, Redruth, TR15 1SH
Tel: 01209-312800 **Fax:** 01209-312900
E-mail: tony.plummer@stralfors.com
Website: http://www.stralfors.com
Bank(s): Barclays
Directors: R. Olver (Fin), T. Plummer (MD)
Managers: S. Thompson (Sales & Mktg Mg), D. Glogley (Personnel), E. Swindale (Tech Serv Mgr)
Ultimate Holding Company: POSTNORD AB (SWEDEN)
Immediate Holding Company: STRALFORS PLC
Registration no: 01626027 **VAT No.:** GB 136 6001 30
Date established: 1982 **Turnover:** £10m - £20m
No.of Employees: 51 - 100 **Product Groups:** 27, 44, 79

Date of Accounts	Dec 11	Dec 10	Dec 09
Sales Turnover	19m	20m	31m
Pre Tax Profit/Loss	-3m	-525	-2m
Working Capital	-3m	-1m	27
Fixed Assets	6m	7m	6m
Current Assets	3m	3m	5m
Current Liabilities	2m	2m	3m

Wellington Welding Supplies Ltd
Unit 7c Pool Industrial Estate Pool, Redruth, TR15 3RH
Tel: 01209-213544 **Fax:** 01209-213556
E-mail: redruth@wellyweld.co.uk
Website: http://www.wellyweld.co.uk
Managers: P. Spargo (District Mgr)
Immediate Holding Company: WELLINGTON WELDING SUPPLIES LIMITED
Registration no: 00821066 **Date established:** 1964
No.of Employees: 1 - 10 **Product Groups:** 46

Date of Accounts	Dec 11	Dec 10	Dec 09
Working Capital	231	252	355
Fixed Assets	587	587	522
Current Assets	1m	1m	1m

West Cornwall Hose & Hydraulics
15a Treleigh Industrial Estate Jon Davey Drive, Redruth, TR16 4AX
Tel: 01209-313594 **Fax:** 01209-313595
Website: http://www.hoseandhydraulicsgroup.co.uk
Managers: C. George (Mgr)
Immediate Holding Company: EURO TOOL HIRE AND SALES (SOUTH WEST) LIMITED
Date established: 2006 **No.of Employees:** 1 - 10 **Product Groups:** 30, 36

Yates Structural Design
Studio 9 & 10 Bosleake Row Shops Bosleake, Redruth, TR15 3YG
Tel: 01209-610826 **Fax:** 01209-610826
Directors: B. Yates (Ptnr)
Date established: 2000 **No.of Employees:** 1 - 10 **Product Groups:** 35

Saltash

Access Engineering
Unit 9 Sellick Industrial Units Gilston Road, Saltash, PL12 6TW
Tel: 01752-841327
Directors: S. Johnson (Prop)
No.of Employees: 1 - 10 **Product Groups:** 45, 48, 83

Appleby Westward Group Ltd
PO Box 3, Saltash, PL12 6LX
Tel: 01752-854000 **Fax:** 01752-854067
Website: http://www.swspar.com
Directors: J. Findlay (Pers), T. Gummow (Fin), M. McCammond (MD)
Managers: N. Vivian
Ultimate Holding Company: BWG GROUP
Immediate Holding Company: APPLEBY WESTWARD GROUP LIMITED
Registration no: 01791158 **VAT No.:** GB 700 6444 72
Date established: 1984 **Turnover:** £125m - £250m
No.of Employees: 101 - 250 **Product Groups:** 49, 77

Date of Accounts	Dec 11	Dec 10	Dec 09
Sales Turnover	135m	136m	136m
Pre Tax Profit/Loss	2m	2m	3m
Working Capital	10m	10m	8m
Fixed Assets	6m	7m	8m
Current Assets	25m	27m	26m
Current Liabilities	2m	1m	2m

Spinnaker International Ltd
Spinnaker House Saltash Parkway, Saltash, PL12 6LF
Tel: 01752-850300 **Fax:** 01752-850301
E-mail: info@spinnaker.co.uk
Website: http://www.spinnakerinternational.com
Directors: J. Yandel (MD), J. Yandell (Ch), M. Pascoe (Co Sec)
Managers: D. Milner (Mktg Serv Mgr), T. Gullis (Purch Mgr)
Ultimate Holding Company: Spinnaker International Ltd
Immediate Holding Company: Spinnaker Group Ltd
Registration no: 02516654 **Date established:** 1990 **Turnover:** £5m - £10m
No.of Employees: 51 - 100 **Product Groups:** 22, 36

Date of Accounts	Apr 08
Pre Tax Profit/Loss	2050
Working Capital	1659
Fixed Assets	554
Current Assets	5190
Current Liabilities	3531
ROCE% (Return on Capital Employed)	92.6

St Agnes

Finisterre UK Ltd
Wheal Kitty Studios, St Agnes, TR5 0RD
Tel: 01872-554481 **Fax:** 01872-554482
E-mail: sarah@finisterreuk.com
Website: http://www.finisterreuk.com
Managers: S. Milligan
Immediate Holding Company: FINISTERRE UK LIMITED
Registration no: 04444480 **Date established:** 2002
No.of Employees: 1 - 10 **Product Groups:** 24

Date of Accounts	Apr 11	Apr 10	Apr 09
Working Capital	93	132	45
Fixed Assets	22	22	7
Current Assets	218	307	65

St Austell

Cuddra Aquatics
Holmebush Road, St Austell, PL25 3RQ
Tel: 01726-76686 **Fax:** 01726-76602
E-mail: robsharman@hotmail.co.uk
Website: http://www.cuddraaquatics.co.uk
Directors: R. Charman (Prop)
Turnover: £250,000 - £500,000 **No.of Employees:** 1 - 10
Product Groups: 09, 30, 40, 42, 45, 52, 62

Edmundson Electrical Ltd
Unit 3, St Austell, PL25 3RF
Tel: 01726-812211 **Fax:** 01726-816614
Website: http://www.edmundson-electrical.co.uk/
Managers: C. Jones (District Mgr)
Ultimate Holding Company: BLACKFRIARS CORP (USA)
Immediate Holding Company: EDMUNDSON ELECTRICAL LIMITED
Registration no: 02667012 **Date established:** 1991
No.of Employees: 1 - 10 **Product Groups:** 36, 40

Date of Accounts	Dec 11	Dec 10	Dec 09
Sales Turnover	1023m	852m	788m
Pre Tax Profit/Loss	57m	53m	45m
Working Capital	256m	225m	184m
Fixed Assets	17m	3m	4m
Current Assets	439m	358m	298m
Current Liabilities	59m	38m	37m

B Gardiner
Lower Bodella Trerice, St Dennis, St Austell, PL26 8EG
Tel: 01726-860743 **Fax:** 01726-860743
Directors: B. Gardiner (Prop)
Date established: 1980 **No.of Employees:** 1 - 10 **Product Groups:** 26, 35

Hentland
3 Bojea Indl-Est Trethowel, St Austell, PL25 5RJ
Tel: 01726-627070 **Fax:** 08707-772923
Website: http://www.hentland.com
Managers: C. Bidmead (Contracts Mgr)
Immediate Holding Company: COASTAL SPECIALIST IRONMONGERY
Date established: 2008 **No.of Employees:** 11 - 20 **Product Groups:** 38, 42

Date of Accounts	Dec 11	Dec 10	Dec 09
Sales Turnover	N/A	2m	1m
Pre Tax Profit/Loss	N/A	395	301
Working Capital	106	246	90
Fixed Assets	643	56	29
Current Assets	735	823	586
Current Liabilities	N/A	143	102

Hewaswater Engineering Ltd
Hewas Water, St Austell, PL26 7JF
Tel: 01726-885200 **Fax:** 01726-885212
E-mail: info@hewaswater.co.uk
Website: http://www.hewaswater.co.uk
Bank(s): National Westminster Bank Plc
Directors: R. James (MD)
Managers: S. Prout (Tech Serv Mgr)
Ultimate Holding Company: HEWASWATER HOLDINGS LIMITED
Immediate Holding Company: HEWASWATER ENGINEERING LTD
Registration no: 01957026 **VAT No.:** GB 447 3864 19
Date established: 1985 **Turnover:** £2m - £5m **No.of Employees:** 51 - 100
Product Groups: 25, 35

Date of Accounts	Mar 12	Mar 11	Mar 10
Working Capital	1m	1m	527
Fixed Assets	183	211	741
Current Assets	2m	2m	674

Knight Security
11b Victoria Road, St Austell, PL25 4QF
Tel: 01726-71386
E-mail: jkc@knight-security.co.uk
Website: http://www.knight-security.co.uk
Directors: J. Clemes (Prop)
No.of Employees: 1 - 10 **Product Groups:** 40, 52, 67

Lavrean Projects
Unit N2 West Haul Park Par Moor Road, St Austell, PL25 3RF
Tel: 01726-816564 **Fax:** 01726-815387
Directors: C. Commons (Prop)
Immediate Holding Company: MID CORNWALL ENTERPRISE TRUST LIMITED
Registration no: 01576151 **Date established:** 2007
No.of Employees: 1 - 10 **Product Groups:** 35

Liftman
Pengarth Foxhole Lane, Gorran Haven, St Austell, PL26 6JP
Tel: 01726-844994 **Fax:** 01726-844011
E-mail: info@liftman.co.uk
Website: http://www.liftman.co.uk
Directors: J. Stokes (Prop)
Date established: 1998 **No.of Employees:** 1 - 10 **Product Groups:** 35, 39, 45

MentOrg Ltd ETC (SW) Limited
Cornwall Enterprise Centre St. Austell Bay Business Park, Par Moor Road, St Austell, PL25 3RF
Tel: 07761-425635
E-mail: contact@mentorg.co.uk
Website: http://www.mentorg.co.uk
Directors: M. Baker (Co Sec), D. Baker (MD)
Registration no: 07233768 **Date established:** 2006
No.of Employees: 1 - 10 **Product Groups:** 86

Ocean Sports
17 West End Pentewan, St Austell, PL26 6BX
Tel: 01726-842817
E-mail: sales@ocean-sports.co.uk
Website: http://www.ocean-sports.co.uk
Directors: M. Avery (Prop)
Date established: 1988 **No.of Employees:** 1 - 10 **Product Groups:** 24, 40, 49, 74

D C Ould
Mount Pleasant Roche, St Austell, PL26 8LH
Tel: 01726-890349 **Fax:** 01726-890910
Directors: D. Ould (Prop)
No.of Employees: 1 - 10 **Product Groups:** 66

Partech Electronics Ltd
Charlestown Road, St Austell, PL25 3NN
Tel: 01726-879800 **Fax:** 01726-879801
E-mail: info@partech.co.uk
Website: http://www.partech.co.uk
Bank(s): HSBC
Directors: R. Henderson (Tech Serv), A. Fosten (Sales & Mktg)
Managers: R. Brinckley (Comptroller)
Immediate Holding Company: PARTECH (ELECTRONICS) LIMITED
Registration no: 00804340 **VAT No.:** GB 131 7966 58
Date established: 1964 **Turnover:** £500,000 - £1m
No.of Employees: 11 - 20 **Product Groups:** 67

Date of Accounts	Dec 11	Dec 10	Dec 09
Working Capital	347	424	595
Fixed Assets	112	96	94
Current Assets	641	664	804

Plastestrip Profiles Ltd
Unit 1-4 St Austell Enterprise Park Treverbyn Road, Carclaze, St Austell, PL25 4EJ
Tel: 01726-74771 **Fax:** 01726-69238
E-mail: sales@plastestrip.com
Website: http://www.plastestrip.com
Bank(s): National Westminster Bank Plc
Managers: P. Hennelly (Mgr)
Ultimate Holding Company: BLACKFRIARS CORP (USA)
Immediate Holding Company: PLASTESTRIP (PROFILES) LIMITED
Registration no: 01347169 **VAT No.:** GB 337 0378 58
Date established: 1978 **Turnover:** Up to £250,000
No.of Employees: 11 - 20 **Product Groups:** 23, 30

Date of Accounts	Dec 10	Dec 09	Dec 08
Working Capital	1	621	621
Current Assets	1	621	621

Rubber Flooring Online
Unit 6 St. Austell Bay Business Park Par Moor Road, St Austell, PL25 3RF
Tel: 01726-817563 **Fax:** 01726-817563
E-mail: administrator@rubberflooringonline.co.uk
Website: http://www.rubberflooringonline.co.uk
Directors: E. Whetter (Dir)
Registration no: 01576151 **Date established:** 2003
No.of Employees: 1 - 10 **Product Groups:** 29

St Austell Brewery Co. Ltd
63 Trevarthian Road, St Austell, PL25 4BY
Tel: 01726-74444 **Fax:** 01726- 627209
E-mail: info@staustellbrewery.co.uk
Website: http://www.staustellbrewery.co.uk
Bank(s): Barclays
Directors: J. Staughton (MD)
Immediate Holding Company: ST.AUSTELL BREWERY COMPANY LIMITED
Registration no: 00107021 **VAT No.:** GB 131 6038 07
Date established: 2010 **Turnover:** £75m - £125m
No.of Employees: 101 - 250 **Product Groups:** 20, 21

Date of Accounts	Dec 11	Dec 08	Jan 10
Sales Turnover	99m	87m	93m
Pre Tax Profit/Loss	10m	7m	8m
Working Capital	2m	1m	3m
Fixed Assets	92m	71m	74m
Current Assets	17m	18m	16m
Current Liabilities	6m	4m	5m

St Merryn Food
Talgarrek House Victoria Industrial Estate, Roche, St Austell, PL26 8LX
Tel: 01726-891000 **Fax:** 01726-891213
E-mail: enquiries@stmerryn.co.uk
Directors: J. Allan (Pers)
Managers: S. Buckingham (Fin Mgr), L. Cooper (Purch Mgr), I. Woods
Immediate Holding Company: VION FOOD WALES & WEST ENGLAND LIMITED
Registration no: 02169077 **Date established:** 1987
Turnover: £250m - £500m **No.of Employees:** 21 - 50 **Product Groups:** 62

Date of Accounts	May 07	May 06
Sales Turnover	342920	345510
Pre Tax Profit/Loss	4600	10660
Working Capital	3230	2140
Fixed Assets	45610	56630
Current Assets	40680	36700
Current Liabilities	37450	34560
Total Share Capital	1360	1360
ROCE% (Return on Capital Employed)	9.4	18.1
ROT% (Return on Turnover)	1.3	3.1

Teddington Appliance Controls Ltd
Daniels Lane, St Austell, PL25 3HG
Tel: 01726-74400 **Fax:** 01726-67953
E-mail: info@tedcon.com
Website: http://www.tedcon.com
Bank(s): HSBC Bank plc
Directors: P. Henderson (Ch), T. Wyatt (MD), G. Mitchell (Fin)
Managers: J. Burbank (Sales & Mktg Mg), L. Wyatt (Purch Mgr), P. Dean (Tech Serv Mgr)

Ultimate Holding Company: HENDERSON INDUSTRIES LIMITED
Immediate Holding Company: TEDDINGTON CONTROLS LIMITED
Registration no: 00533304 **VAT No.:** GB 383 8763 04
Date established: 1954 **Turnover:** £5m - £10m **No.of Employees:** 21 - 50
Product Groups: 36, 37, 38, 39, 40, 42, 43, 44, 48, 49, 63, 67, 72

Date of Accounts	Sep 10	Sep 09	Sep 08
Working Capital	-11	-11	-11
Current Assets	25	25	14
Current Liabilities	N/A	36	N/A

White River Outdoor

Kingswood London Apprentice, St Austell, PL26 7AR
Tel: 01726-874100 **Fax:** 01726-67448
E-mail: sales@mountcaravans.co.uk
Website: http://www.mountcaravans.co.uk
Directors: W. Hoddinott (Prop)
Immediate Holding Company: MOUNT CARAVANS LIMITED
Registration no: 00907449 **VAT No.:** GB 133 1594 87
Date established: 1967 **Turnover:** £500,000 - £1m
No.of Employees: 1 - 10 **Product Groups:** 24, 31, 39, 49, 63, 65, 74

Date of Accounts	Oct 11	Oct 10	Oct 09
Working Capital	188	248	120
Fixed Assets	N/A	N/A	188
Current Assets	201	296	262

St Columb

European Springs Ltd

1 Indian Queens Industrial Estate Lodge Way, Indian Queens, St Columb, TR9 6TF
Tel: 01726-861444 **Fax:** 01726-861555
E-mail: cornwallsales@europeansprings.com
Website: http://www.europeansprings.com
Directors: M. Gibbs (MD)
Immediate Holding Company: EUROPEAN SPRINGS LTD
Registration no: 00548932 **Date established:** 1948 **Turnover:** £5m - £10m
No.of Employees: 21 - 50 **Product Groups:** 35, 38, 66

Golant Fire & Security

8 Moorland Road Moorland Industrial Park, Indian Queens, St Columb, TR9 6HJ
Tel: 01726-861116 **Fax:** 01637-852153
E-mail: info@gfsfire.co.uk
Website: http://www.gfsfire.co.uk
Directors: M. Berresford (Ptnr)
Ultimate Holding Company: WESTLANDS HOLDINGS LIMITED
Immediate Holding Company: WESSEX SLATE AND TILE ROOFING SERVICES LTD
Date established: 1988 **No.of Employees:** 1 - 10 **Product Groups:** 38, 42

Date of Accounts	Mar 11	Mar 10	Mar 09
Working Capital	155	142	171
Fixed Assets	41	42	49
Current Assets	446	353	302

Ocean Magic Surf Boards

Unit 6c St Columb Industrial Estate, St Columb, TR9 6SF
Tel: 01637-880421 **Fax:** 01637-852042
E-mail: info@nsboards.co.uk
Website: http://www.nsboards.co.uk
Directors: N. Semmens (Prop)
Immediate Holding Company: OCEAN MAGIC LIMITED
Registration no: 04664716 **VAT No.:** 526 9713 22 **Date established:** 2003
Turnover: Up to £250,000 **No.of Employees:** 1 - 10 **Product Groups:** 49

Date of Accounts	Mar 11	Mar 10	Mar 09
Sales Turnover	N/A	211	153
Pre Tax Profit/Loss	N/A	11	-26
Working Capital	-97	-139	-154
Fixed Assets	24	29	34
Current Assets	81	75	73
Current Liabilities	N/A	198	220

Trevithick Supplies

1d Newquay Road St Columb Road, St Columb, TR9 6PZ
Tel: 01726-862800 **Fax:** 01726- 861392
E-mail: info@trevithicksupplies.co.uk
Website: http://www.trevithicksupplies.co.uk
Directors: P. Lawther (Prop)
Date established: 2001 **No.of Employees:** 1 - 10 **Product Groups:** 35

St Ives

Bioproducts Technology Consultant

'Poldhune' Parc Owles Carbis Bay, St Ives, TR26 2RE
Tel: 01736-796847 **Fax:** 01736-798209
E-mail: sbrewer@bptc.co.uk
Website: http://www.bptc.co.uk
Directors: S. Brewer (Dir)
Date established: 1996 **No.of Employees:** 1 - 10 **Product Groups:** 84

Torpoint

A M S Fabrications Ltd

Unit 3a Trevol Business Park, Torpoint, PL11 2TB
Tel: 01752-814488 **Fax:** 01752-814488
Directors: J. Shattock (Fin), A. Shattock (MD)
Immediate Holding Company: AMS FABRICATIONS LTD
Registration no: 04897819 **Date established:** 2003
No.of Employees: 1 - 10 **Product Groups:** 26, 35

Date of Accounts	Sep 11	Sep 10	Sep 09
Working Capital	-0	41	19
Fixed Assets	2	2	N/A
Current Assets	56	41	58
Current Liabilities	18	N/A	N/A

Mashfords

Shipbuilding Yard Cremyll, Torpoint, PL10 1HY
Tel: 01752-822232 **Fax:** 01752-823059
E-mail: mashfords@btconnect.com
Website: http://www.mashfordsofcremyll.co.uk
Bank(s): National Westminster
Managers: R. Porter (Chief Mgr)
Immediate Holding Company: APPLEDORE SHIP BUILDERS
Registration no: 05236018 **Date established:** 1999 **Turnover:** £1m - £2m
No.of Employees: 21 - 50 **Product Groups:** 30, 39

S C A Packaging

near Millbrook, Torpoint, PL11 3AX
Tel: 01752-822551 **Fax:** 01752-823551
E-mail: julia.nodder@sca.com
Website: http://www.sca.com
Bank(s): National Westminster
Managers: J. Clarkson, J. Nodder (Plant)
Immediate Holding Company: OMNIPACK LTD
Registration no: 00548992 **Date established:** 1958
No.of Employees: 21 - 50 **Product Groups:** 30, 31

Truro

Arcol UK Ltd

Threemilestone Industrial Estate Threemilestone, Truro, TR4 9LG
Tel: 01872-277431 **Fax:** 01872-222002
E-mail: mpritchard@arcolresistors.com
Website: http://www.arcol.com
Bank(s): Bank of Scotland
Directors: M. Pritchard (MD), A. Morgan (Dir)
Managers: A. Bone, T. Daly (Sales Prom Mgr), J. Adams (Purch Mgr), A. King (Personnel)
Ultimate Holding Company: ARCOL (HOLDINGS) LIMITED
Immediate Holding Company: ARCOL U.K. LIMITED
Registration no: 00503996 **VAT No.:** GB 229 1852 54
Date established: 1952 **Turnover:** £1m - £2m **No.of Employees:** 21 - 50
Product Groups: 37

Date of Accounts	Jan 12	Jan 11	Jan 10
Working Capital	1m	1m	532
Fixed Assets	275	258	850
Current Assets	2m	2m	772

P S Bray

Nancorras St Mawes, Truro, TR2 5AD
Tel: 01326-270011 **Fax:** 01326-270024
E-mail: psbray@aol.com
Directors: P. Bray (Prop)
Immediate Holding Company: PURITI LIMITED
Registration no: 03956339 **Date established:** 2000
No.of Employees: 1 - 10 **Product Groups:** 38, 42

C A W Cornwall Ltd

Threemilestone Industrial Estate Threemilestone, Truro, TR4 9LD
Tel: 01872-271491 **Fax:** 01872-222310
E-mail: cawcornwall@line1.net
Website: http://www.cawcornwall.com
Directors: C. Pascoe (Dir)
Ultimate Holding Company: CORNWALL ALUMINIUM WINDOW CO. LIMITED
Immediate Holding Company: C.A.W. (CORNWALL) LIMITED
Registration no: 02177346 **VAT No.:** GB 679 5934 62
Date established: 1987 **Turnover:** £2m - £5m **No.of Employees:** 21 - 50
Product Groups: 30, 35

Date of Accounts	Sep 11	Sep 10	Sep 09
Sales Turnover	3m	3m	3m
Pre Tax Profit/Loss	101	72	170
Working Capital	133	166	160
Fixed Assets	88	51	66
Current Assets	731	731	818
Current Liabilities	139	195	241

C R D Records Ltd

Trelissa Farmhouse Philleigh Truro Cornwall Philleigh, Truro, TR2 5NE
Tel: 01872-580000 **Fax:** 01872-580002
E-mail: info@crdrecords.com
Website: http://www.crdrecords.com
Directors: G. Pauncefort (MD), S. Collings (Fin)
Immediate Holding Company: CRD RECORDS LIMITED
Registration no: 01172240 **VAT No.:** GB 228 5227 63
Date established: 1974 **Turnover:** £250,000 - £500,000
No.of Employees: 1 - 10 **Product Groups:** 65

Date of Accounts	Jul 11	Jul 10	Jul 09
Working Capital	48	47	54
Fixed Assets	1	1	2
Current Assets	122	127	126

Cornwall Batteries Ltd

Unit 34 Threemilestone Industrial Estate Threemilestone, Truro, TR4 9LD
Tel: 01872-270011 **Fax:** 01872-264250
E-mail: truro@bristolbatteries.com
Website: http://www.bristolbatteries.com
Managers: M. James (Mgr)
Immediate Holding Company: BRISTOL BATTERIES LTD
VAT No.: GB 138 6316 60 **Date established:** 1972
No.of Employees: 1 - 10 **Product Groups:** 37, 39, 67, 68

Date of Accounts	Sep 11	Sep 10	Sep 09
Working Capital	1	1	1
Current Assets	1	1	1

Domestic Parts & Services

Pannier Market Lemon Quay, Truro, TR1 2LW
Tel: 01872-222615 **Fax:** 01872-222615
Website: http://www.dps.freeola.com
Directors: M. Dockree (Ptnr)
Immediate Holding Company: MDRB INKS LIMITED
Date established: 2009 **No.of Employees:** 1 - 10 **Product Groups:** 43

Date of Accounts	May 12	Sep 11	Sep 10
Working Capital	-16	-15	-14
Fixed Assets	4	5	6

Current Assets	8	11	9

E P Mitchell

Greenbottom House Greenbottom, Chacewater, Truro, TR4 8QL
Tel: 07850-153860 **Fax:** 01872-560353
Directors: E. Mitchell (Prop)
Date established: 1944 **No.of Employees:** 1 - 10 **Product Groups:** 38, 42

Exhibitions South West Ltd

Glenthorne House Truro Business Park, Threemilestone, Truro, TR3 6BW
Tel: 01872-245220 **Fax:** 01872-572551
E-mail: peter.sugden@expowestexhibitions.com
Website: http://www.expowestexhibition.com
Directors: P. Sugden (MD)
Immediate Holding Company: EXHIBITIONS SOUTH WEST LIMITED
Registration no: 01734940 **VAT No.:** GB 337 3578 84
Date established: 1983 **Turnover:** £250,000 - £500,000
No.of Employees: 1 - 10 **Product Groups:** 81

Date of Accounts	Jun 11	Jun 10	Jun 09
Sales Turnover	418	444	431
Pre Tax Profit/Loss	22	69	58
Working Capital	339	339	287
Fixed Assets	642	649	671
Current Assets	359	396	379
Current Liabilities	8	26	24

Holman Wilfley Ltd

Wheal Jane Baldhu, Truro, TR3 6EE
Tel: 01872-561163 **Fax:** 01872-561162
E-mail: chris.bailey@holmanwilfley.co.uk
Website: http://www.holmanwilfley.co.uk
Directors: C. Bailey (MD), C. Aldag (Co Sec)
Immediate Holding Company: SGS MINERALS SERVICES UK LTD
Registration no: 04356791 **Date established:** 2002
Turnover: £500,000 - £1m **No.of Employees:** 1 - 10 **Product Groups:** 36, 37, 42

Date of Accounts	Aug 08	Aug 07	Aug 06
Working Capital	535	586	439
Fixed Assets	85	52	48
Current Assets	844	695	669
Current Liabilities	309	109	230
Total Share Capital	517	517	517

Key Wear

9 Frances Street, Truro, TR1 3DN
Tel: 01872-242233 **Fax:** 01872-262390
E-mail: keywearuniforms@btconnect.com
Website: http://www.keywear.co.uk
Directors: A. Montgomery (Prop)
No.of Employees: 1 - 10 **Product Groups:** 24, 63

Kier Western

1 Victoria Wharf Malpas Road, Truro, TR1 1QH
Tel: 01872-274373 **Fax:** 01872- 223900
E-mail: enquiries@kier.co.uk
Website: http://www.kier.co.uk
Directors: P. Young (MD)
Managers: J. Fox (Mgr), M. Williams (Sales Admin)
Registration no: 00000397 **Turnover:** £5m - £10m
No.of Employees: 11 - 20 **Product Groups:** 07, 52

J Lee

Newham Road Newham, Truro, TR1 2SU
Tel: 01872-260932
Directors: J. Lee (Prop)
Date established: 1992 **No.of Employees:** 1 - 10 **Product Groups:** 35, 36, 39

Malcomp

North Downs Bodrean, Truro, TR4 9AF
Tel: 07971-901783 **Fax:** 01872-272394
E-mail: sales@malcomp.com
Website: http://www.malcomp.com
Directors: I. Mallison (Prop)
Immediate Holding Company: SOUTH TO SOUTH UK LIMITED
Registration no: 05723329 **Date established:** 2006
Turnover: Up to £250,000 **No.of Employees:** 1 - 10 **Product Groups:** 44, 48, 84

Stephen Richards

Chy Vista St Clement, Truro, TR1 1TD
Tel: 01872-270592
Directors: S. Richards (Ptnr)
Date established: 1975 **No.of Employees:** 1 - 10 **Product Groups:** 41

Spiritus Consulting

PO Box 23, Truro, TR1 2ZT
Tel: 08708-507169 **Fax:** 01872-225053
E-mail: info@spiritusgroup.com
Website: http://www.spiritusgroup.com
Directors: J. Raquet (MD)
Managers: M. Jakt (), M. Jakt
No.of Employees: 1 - 10 **Product Groups:** 84

Staeng Ltd

Unit 1a Goonhavern Industrial Estate, Goonhavern, Truro, TR4 9QL
Tel: 01872-572071 **Fax:** 01872-571335
E-mail: sales@staeng.co.uk
Website: http://www.staeng.co.uk
Bank(s): HSBC
Directors: T. Jones (Fin)
Managers: S. Mcdonald (Chief Mgr)
Ultimate Holding Company: HELLERMANN TYTON SARL (LUXEMBOURG)
Immediate Holding Company: STAENG LIMITED
Registration no: 01182252 **VAT No.:** GB 276 3607 40
Date established: 1974 **Turnover:** £500,000 - £1m
No.of Employees: 11 - 20 **Product Groups:** 35, 37

Date of Accounts	Dec 09	Dec 08
Working Capital	9	9
Current Assets	9	9

Wadebridge

Camel Refridgeration

13 Cleaveland, Wadebridge, PL27 7PT
Tel: 01208-816878 **Fax:** 01208-816878
Directors: G. Hoare (Prop), G. Hawke (Prop)
Date established: 2003 **No.of Employees:** 1 - 10 **Product Groups:** 36, 40

Cornish Crabbers LLP

Pityme St Minver, Wadebridge, PL27 6NT
Tel: 01208-862666 **Fax:** 01208-862375
E-mail: info@cornishcrabbers.co.uk
Website: http://www.cornishcrabbers.co.uk
Bank(s): National Westminster Bank Plc
Directors: C. Colam (Fin), P. Thomas (MD)
Immediate Holding Company: CORNISH CRABBERS ROCK LIMITED
Registration no: 07283787 **VAT No.:** GB 143 2052 14
Date established: 2010 **Turnover:** £5m - £10m **No.of Employees:** 21 - 50
Product Groups: 39

Date of Accounts	Dec 11	Dec 10
Working Capital	-95	-163
Fixed Assets	180	180
Current Assets	160	34

Daften Diecasting Ltd

Trevilling Quay, Wadebridge, PL27 6EB
Tel: 01208-812148 **Fax:** 01208-814092
E-mail: guy@daften.co.uk
Website: http://www.daften.co.uk
Bank(s): HSBC Bank plc
Directors: M. Weedon (Dir), G. Weedon (Dir)
Managers: A. Parsons, E. Bennett (Fin Mgr)
Immediate Holding Company: DAFTEN DIE-CASTING LIMITED
Registration no: 00679033 **VAT No.:** GB 131 6926 75
Date established: 1960 **Turnover:** £1m - £2m **No.of Employees:** 21 - 50
Product Groups: 34, 48

Date of Accounts	Jun 11	Jun 10	Jun 09
Working Capital	191	190	-320
Fixed Assets	1m	1m	1m
Current Assets	845	695	593

Irons Bros Ltd

The Foundry St Breock, Wadebridge, PL27 7JP
Tel: 01208-812635 **Fax:** 01208-814884
E-mail: sales@ironsbrothers.com
Website: http://www.ironsbrothers.com
Bank(s): Barclays
Directors: J. Sutton (MD), M. Robinson (Ch), N. Burt (Dir), R. Eason (Dir)
Immediate Holding Company: IRONS BROTHERS,LIMITED
Registration no: 00248168 **VAT No.:** GB 131 7151 06
Date established: 1930 **Turnover:** £1m - £2m **No.of Employees:** 21 - 50
Product Groups: 34, 39, 48

Date of Accounts	Dec 11	Dec 10	Dec 09
Working Capital	1m	1m	1m
Fixed Assets	436	454	469
Current Assets	1m	1m	1m

Jewson Ltd

Bodieve Business Park Gonvena Hill, Wadebridge, PL27 6BN
Tel: 01208-812451 **Fax:** 01208-815272
E-mail: jeff.varcoe@jewson.co.uk
Website: http://www.jewson.co.uk
Bank(s): Barclays
Managers: J. Varcoe (Mgr)
Ultimate Holding Company: COMPAGNIE DE SAINT GOBAIN (FRANCE)
Immediate Holding Company: JEWSON LIMITED
Registration no: 00348407 **Date established:** 1939
No.of Employees: 11 - 20 **Product Groups:** 66

Date of Accounts	Dec 11	Dec 10	Dec 09
Sales Turnover	1606m	1547m	1485m
Pre Tax Profit/Loss	18m	100m	45m
Working Capital	-345m	-250m	-349m
Fixed Assets	496m	387m	461m
Current Assets	657m	1005m	1320m
Current Liabilities	66m	120m	64m

M G C Engineering Ltd

Bradfords Quay, Wadebridge, PL27 6DB
Tel: 01208-812585 **Fax:** 01208-814066
E-mail: mgceng@tiscali.co.uk
Website: http://www.mgcengineering.co.uk
Bank(s): Lloyds TSB Bank plc
Directors: G. Bragg (Fin), T. Irons (Dir)
Immediate Holding Company: M. G. C. ENGINEERING LIMITED
Registration no: 01158108 **VAT No.:** GB 132 7350 96
Date established: 1974 **Turnover:** £500,000 - £1m
No.of Employees: 11 - 20 **Product Groups:** 07, 51

Date of Accounts	Apr 12	Apr 11	Apr 10
Working Capital	318	382	413
Fixed Assets	41	45	46
Current Assets	428	454	492

CUMBRIA

Alston

Bonds Precision Casting Ltd
Clitheroe Works Potters Loaning, Alston, CA9 3TP
Tel: 01434-381228 **Fax:** 01434-381038
E-mail: andrew.dodd@bondsprecisioncastings.com
Website: http://www.bondsprecisioncastings.com
Bank(s): Barclays Bank P.L.C.
Managers: A. Dodd (Site Co-ord), D. Keillor (Personnel), V. Keillor (Fin Mgr)
Ultimate Holding Company: BONDSHOLD LIMITED
Immediate Holding Company: BONDS PRECISION CASTINGS LIMITED
Registration no: 06663688 **VAT No.:** GB 374 9409 18
Date established: 2008 **Turnover:** £2m - £5m **No.of Employees:** 51 - 100
Product Groups: 34, 40, 48

Date of Accounts	Sep 11	Sep 10	Sep 09
Working Capital	795	379	162
Fixed Assets	669	628	238
Current Assets	2m	2m	1m
Current Liabilities	694	534	378

Robert Gascoyne Consulting Ltd
Holmsfoot House Nenthead Nenthead, Alston, CA9 3LR
Tel: 07841-341757
Website: http://www.robertgascoyne.com
Directors: R. Gascoyne (Fin), R. Gascoyne (MD)
Immediate Holding Company: ROBERT GASCOYNE CONSULTING LTD
Registration no: 05277526 **Date established:** 2004
Turnover: Up to £250,000 **No.of Employees:** 1 - 10 **Product Groups:** 80, 84, 85, 86

Date of Accounts	Nov 11	Nov 10	Nov 09
Sales Turnover	N/A	N/A	57
Pre Tax Profit/Loss	N/A	N/A	9
Working Capital	8	24	10
Fixed Assets	13	2	1
Current Assets	39	54	37
Current Liabilities	N/A	N/A	21

Total Post Services plc
1 Skelgillside, Alston, CA9 3TR
Tel: 08454-900360 **Fax:** 01434-382035
E-mail: sales@totalpost.com
Website: http://www.totalpost.com
Directors: D. Hymers (MD)
Immediate Holding Company: TOTALPOST SERVICES PLC
Registration no: 04532416 **VAT No.:** GB 437 5239 39
Date established: 2002 **Turnover:** £2m - £5m **No.of Employees:** 1 - 10
Product Groups: 38, 44

Date of Accounts	Dec 11	Dec 10	Dec 09
Sales Turnover	2m	2m	2m
Pre Tax Profit/Loss	137	66	107
Working Capital	394	112	55
Fixed Assets	356	383	390
Current Assets	881	989	818
Current Liabilities	114	566	N/A

Appleby In Westmorland

The Feel Good Factory
3-5 Boroughgate, Appleby In Westmorland, CA16 6XF
Tel: 01768-354129 **Fax:** 01768-354129
Directors: L. Petty (Prop)
No.of Employees: 1 - 10 **Product Groups:** 31, 32

Highblade Cables
Shire Hall The Sands, Appleby In Westmorland, CA16 6XN
Tel: 01768-352560 **Fax:** 01768-352960
E-mail: info@highblade-cables.co.uk
Website: http://www.highblade.com
Directors: N. Dowden (Fin), S. Marsh (MD)
Immediate Holding Company: HIGHBLADE LIMITED
Registration no: 01967338 **VAT No.:** GB 410 4723 95
Date established: 1985 **Turnover:** £250,000 - £500,000
No.of Employees: 1 - 10 **Product Groups:** 33, 35, 37, 38, 44, 48, 52, 67

Date of Accounts	Mar 12	Mar 11	Mar 10
Working Capital	223	164	173
Fixed Assets	27	30	33
Current Assets	323	219	196

A E & F A Longstaff
Ascot House Murton, Appleby In Westmorland, CA16 6ND
Tel: 01768-351273 **Fax:** 01768-351273
E-mail: brian.longstaff@btconnect.com
Directors: B. Longstaff (Ptnr)
Date established: 1958 **No.of Employees:** 1 - 10 **Product Groups:** 41

Penrith Survival Equipment
Sandale Coupland Beck, Appleby In Westmorland, CA16 6LN
Tel: 01768-351666 **Fax:** 01768-353666
E-mail: colin.westgarth@penrithsurvival.co.uk
Website: http://www.penrithsurvival.co.uk
Directors: C. Westgarth (MD)
Immediate Holding Company: PENRITH SURVIVAL EQUIPMENT LIMITED
Registration no: 04701063 **VAT No.:** GB 621 1613 88
Date established: 2003 **Turnover:** £500,000 - £1m
No.of Employees: 1 - 10 **Product Groups:** 22, 24, 40

Date of Accounts	Mar 12	Mar 11	Mar 10
Working Capital	122	136	123
Fixed Assets	5	6	7
Current Assets	206	223	220

Pigney H Son Agricultural Engineers
Chapel Street, Appleby In Westmorland, CA16 6QR
Tel: 01768-351240 **Fax:** 01768-353033
E-mail: pigney@pigney.co.uk
Directors: D. Pigney (Prop)
Immediate Holding Company: H PIGNEY & SON LIMITED
Registration no: 04428587 **Date established:** 2002
Turnover: Up to £250,000 **No.of Employees:** 11 - 20 **Product Groups:** 39

Date of Accounts	Dec 11	Dec 10	Dec 09
Working Capital	494	472	438
Fixed Assets	192	195	205
Current Assets	723	666	607

Taylor & Braithwaite Ltd
Dyke Nook Sandford, Appleby In Westmorland, CA16 6NS
Tel: 01768-341400 **Fax:** 01768-341488
E-mail: sales@notjusttractors.co.uk
Website: http://www.notjusttractors.co.uk
Managers: P. Taylor
Immediate Holding Company: TAYLOR & BRAITHWAITE LIMITED
Registration no: 04510044 **Date established:** 2002
No.of Employees: 21 - 50 **Product Groups:** 41

Date of Accounts	Oct 11	Oct 10	Oct 09
Working Capital	158	52	21
Fixed Assets	755	761	737
Current Assets	2m	2m	1m

Town Head Farm Cottages
Town Head Farm Great Asby, Appleby In Westmorland, CA16 6EX
Tel: 01768-351499 **Fax:** 01768-353771
E-mail: sales@westmorlandfurniture.co.uk
Website: http://www.westmorlandfurniture.co.uk
Directors: S. Lucas (Prop)
Date established: 1982 **No.of Employees:** 1 - 10 **Product Groups:** 26

Barrow In Furness

Bostik Sovereign Chemicals
Park Road Industrial Estate Park Road, Barrow In Furness, LA14 4EQ
Tel: 01229-870800 **Fax:** 01229-870500
E-mail: henry@sovchem.co.uk
Website: http://www.sovchem.co.uk
Managers: D. Wright (Ops Mgr)
Ultimate Holding Company: TOTAL SAFETY INC (USA)
Immediate Holding Company: SOVEREIGN CHEMICALS LIMITED
Registration no: 03281228 **Date established:** 1996 **Turnover:** £5m - £10m
No.of Employees: 1 - 10 **Product Groups:** 31, 32

Date of Accounts	Dec 11	Dec 10	Dec 09
Sales Turnover	10m	10m	10m
Pre Tax Profit/Loss	226	602	287
Working Capital	13m	14m	18m
Fixed Assets	3m	3m	3m
Current Assets	15m	15m	20m
Current Liabilities	373	415	425

Centrica R P S Ltd
Rooscote Power Station Roose, Barrow In Furness, LA13 0PQ
Tel: 01229-845600 **Fax:** 01229-813808
E-mail: anne-marie.burrell@centrica.co.uk
Website: http://www.centrica.com
Bank(s): HSBC Bank plc
Directors: J. Watts (Dir)
Managers: D. Knight, A. Paxton, D. Higginson
Ultimate Holding Company: CENTRICA PLC
Immediate Holding Company: CENTRICA RPS LIMITED
Registration no: 04713745 **VAT No.:** GB 621 1593 68
Date established: 2003 **Turnover:** £10m - £20m
No.of Employees: 21 - 50 **Product Groups:** 18

Date of Accounts	Dec 11	Dec 10	Dec 09
Sales Turnover	17m	19m	23m
Pre Tax Profit/Loss	7m	-18m	8m
Working Capital	35m	30m	20m
Fixed Assets	3m	867	27m
Current Assets	37m	31m	23m
Current Liabilities	1m	613	3m

Classic Drinks Ltd
Unit 5a Peter Green Way Furness Business Park, Barrow In Furness, LA14 2PE
Tel: 01229-870100 **Fax:** 01229-813922
Managers: P. Low (Mgr)
Ultimate Holding Company: BOOKER GROUP PLC
Immediate Holding Company: CLASSIC DRINKS LIMITED
Registration no: 07462412 **VAT No.:** GB 154 6109 75
Date established: 2010 **No.of Employees:** 1 - 10 **Product Groups:** 21

Deltawaite Ltd
Old Dairy Roose Road, Barrow In Furness, LA13 0EP
Tel: 01229-821959 **Fax:** 01229-820377
E-mail: info@safetydirect.co.uk
Website: http://www.safetydirect.co.uk
Bank(s): National Westminster Bank Plc
Directors: G. Brocklebank (Fin), K. Brocklebank (Dir)
Immediate Holding Company: DELTAWAITE LIMITED
Registration no: 03352573 **VAT No.:** GB 153 6121 91
Date established: 1997 **Turnover:** £2m - £5m **No.of Employees:** 11 - 20
Product Groups: 24, 33, 34, 35, 36, 38, 40, 46

Date of Accounts	Dec 11	Dec 10	Dec 09
Working Capital	2m	2m	2m
Fixed Assets	413	397	521
Current Assets	3m	3m	2m

Etyres
Settle Street, Barrow In Furness, LA14 5HR
Tel: 01229-550050
E-mail: cumbria1@etyres.co.uk
Website: http://www.etyres.co.uk
Managers: C. Cullingford (Mgr)
Immediate Holding Company: ETYRES LIMITED
Registration no: 03445634 **Date established:** 1997
No.of Employees: 1 - 10 **Product Groups:** 29, 35, 68

Date of Accounts	Dec 11	Dec 10	Dec 09
Working Capital	1m	1m	848
Fixed Assets	7	57	37
Current Assets	2m	3m	2m

Furness Building Society
51-55 Duke Street, Barrow In Furness, LA14 1RT
Tel: 01229-824560 **Fax:** 01229-837043
E-mail: avril.willis@furness-bs.co.uk
Website: http://www.furnessbs.co.uk
Directors: A. Willis (Dir), B. Ryninks (Fin), P. Lake (Co Sec)
Managers: M. Carlisle (Personnel), A. Smith (Tech Serv Mgr), M. Cutbill (Sales & Mktg Mg)
Immediate Holding Company: FURNESS MORTGAGE SERVICES LIMITED
Registration no: 02948076 **Date established:** 1994
Turnover: Up to £250,000 **No.of Employees:** 101 - 250
Product Groups: 82

Date of Accounts	Dec 11	Dec 10	Dec 09
Sales Turnover	N/A	N/A	158
Pre Tax Profit/Loss	287	385	196
Working Capital	-121	-84	-60
Fixed Assets	8m	9m	10m
Current Assets	30	12	26
Current Liabilities	151	96	85

Furness Heat Treatment
Unit 47 Salthouse Mills Industrial Estate Salthouse Road, Barrow In Furness, LA13 0DH
Tel: 01229-831881 **Fax:** 01229-831881

see next page

Furness Heat Treatment - *Cont'd*

Directors: S. Ainsworth (Prop)
Date established: 1994 **No.of Employees:** 1 - 10 **Product Groups:** 46, 48

Furness Newspapers (North West Evening Mail)

Newspaper House Abbey Road, Barrow In Furness, LA14 5QS
Tel: 01229-821835 **Fax:** 01229-832141
E-mail: news@nwemail.co.uk
Website: http://www.nwemail.co.uk
Bank(s): HSBC Bank plc
Directors: J. Lee (Publishing)
Managers: A. Holmes (Sales Prom Mgr), C. Harker, K. Whittle (Personnel)
Ultimate Holding Company: CN GROUP LIMITED
Immediate Holding Company: FURNESS NEWSPAPERS LIMITED
Registration no: 01155841 **Date established:** 1974 **Turnover:** £5m - £10m
No.of Employees: 51 - 100 **Product Groups:** 28

Date of Accounts	Dec 11	Dec 10	Dec 09
Sales Turnover	N/A	N/A	6m
Pre Tax Profit/Loss	N/A	N/A	-5m
Working Capital	-2m	-2m	-2m
Fixed Assets	134	196	269
Current Assets	1m	1m	1m
Current Liabilities	N/A	N/A	188

Furness Property Letting & Management Ltd

76 Duke Street, Barrow In Furness, LA14 1RX
Tel: 01229-870022 **Fax:** 01229-870022
E-mail: enquiries@fplm.co.uk
Website: http://www.furnesspropertyletting.co.uk
Directors: C. Metcalfe (Fin)
Immediate Holding Company: FURNESS PROPERTY LETTING AND MANAGEMENT LIMITED
Registration no: 04511657 **Date established:** 2002
No.of Employees: 1 - 10 **Product Groups:** 80

Date of Accounts	Mar 11	Mar 10	Mar 09
Working Capital	-1	-2	8
Fixed Assets	71	78	84
Current Assets	20	26	44

B L Gilbert Barrow Ltd

St Andrews Street, Barrow In Furness, LA14 2SU
Tel: 01229-823456 **Fax:** 01229-826976
E-mail: sales@gilbar.co.uk
Website: http://www.gilbert-tools.co.uk
Directors: V. Gilbert (MD)
Immediate Holding Company: B.L.GILBERT(BARROW)LIMITED
Registration no: 00827152 **VAT No.:** GB 153 9050 73
Date established: 1964 **Turnover:** £1m - £2m **No.of Employees:** 1 - 10
Product Groups: 67

Date of Accounts	Dec 11	Dec 10	Dec 09
Working Capital	223	222	224
Fixed Assets	54	54	31
Current Assets	377	418	471

Handmark Engineering Co. Ltd

Unit 4 Park Road Industrial Estate Park Road, Barrow In Furness, LA14 4EQ
Tel: 01229-835922 **Fax:** 01229-870074
E-mail: tony@handmarkengineering.co.uk
Website: http://www.handmarkengineering.co.uk
Bank(s): Barclays Bank PLC
Directors: T. Marklew (MD), S. Powell (Fin), A. Marklew (MD), J. Bell (Dir)
Immediate Holding Company: HANDMARK ENGINEERING COMPANY LIMITED
Registration no: 01680897 **VAT No.:** GB 364 0743 58
Date established: 1982 **Turnover:** £1m - £2m **No.of Employees:** 51 - 100
Product Groups: 35, 48

Date of Accounts	Jan 12	Jan 11	Jan 10
Working Capital	598	746	630
Fixed Assets	1m	636	684
Current Assets	2m	2m	1m

Handmark Engineering Co. Ltd

Cavendish Dock Road, Barrow In Furness, LA14 2LA
Tel: 01229-829616 **Fax:** 01229-870074
E-mail: tony@handmarkengineering.co.uk
Website: http://www.handmarkengineering.co.uk
Directors: T. Marklew (Dir), M. Marklew (Co Sec)
Immediate Holding Company: HANDMARK ENGINEERING COMPANY LIMITED
Registration no: 01680897 **Date established:** 1982
No.of Employees: 21 - 50 **Product Groups:** 35, 42, 45

Date of Accounts	Jan 11	Jan 10	Jan 09
Working Capital	746	630	859
Fixed Assets	636	684	636
Current Assets	2m	1m	2m

J H P Training

College House Howard Street, Barrow In Furness, LA14 1NB
Tel: 01229-813202 **Fax:** 01229-430818
E-mail: joe.reynolds@jhptraining.com
Website: http://www.jhptraining.com
Managers: J. Reynolds (Mgr)
Immediate Holding Company: JHP TRAINING LIMITED
Registration no: 03247918 **Date established:** 1996
No.of Employees: 11 - 20 **Product Groups:** 86

James Fisher plc

Fisher House Michaelson Road, Barrow In Furness, LA14 1HR
Tel: 01229-615400 **Fax:** 01229-836761
E-mail: michael.shields@james-fisher.co.uk
Website: http://www.james-fisher.co.uk
Directors: S. Kilpatick (MD), S. Kilpatrick (Fin)
Managers: H. Savage (Tech Serv Mgr), P. Hogan, J. Dufour (Purch Mgr), R. Harvey
Ultimate Holding Company: JAMES FISHER AND SONS PUBLIC LIMITED COMPANY
Immediate Holding Company: JAMES FISHER (GIBRALTAR) LIMITED
Registration no: FC017850 **Date established:** 1994 **Turnover:** £2m - £5m
No.of Employees: 51 - 100 **Product Groups:** 74

Date of Accounts	Dec 99	Dec 98	Dec 01
Sales Turnover	5m	7m	2m
Pre Tax Profit/Loss	-800	130	-530
Working Capital	5m	-3m	7m
Fixed Assets	10m	19m	8m
Current Assets	6m	675	7m
Current Liabilities	907	522	56

Jewson Ltd

Central Sawmill Hibbert Road, Barrow In Furness, LA14 5AF
Tel: 01229-820108 **Fax:** 01229-870438
Website: http://www.jewson.co.uk
Managers: T. Errington (District Mgr)
Ultimate Holding Company: COMPAGNIE DE SAINT GOBAIN (FRANCE)
Immediate Holding Company: JEWSON LIMITED
Registration no: 00348407 **VAT No.:** GB 497 7184 33
Date established: 1939 **Turnover:** £50m - £75m **No.of Employees:** 1 - 10
Product Groups: 66

Date of Accounts	Dec 11	Dec 10	Dec 09
Sales Turnover	1606m	1547m	1485m
Pre Tax Profit/Loss	18m	100m	45m
Working Capital	-345m	-250m	-349m
Fixed Assets	496m	387m	461m
Current Assets	657m	1005m	1320m
Current Liabilities	66m	120m	64m

Nimbus Industrial Sewing Services

67 Greengate Street, Barrow In Furness, LA14 1EZ
Tel: 01229-829615 **Fax:** 01229-826797
E-mail: info@nimbusindustrialsewing.co.uk
Website: http://www.nimbusindustrialsewing.co.uk
Directors: P. Thomas (Prop)
Date established: 2000 **No.of Employees:** 1 - 10 **Product Groups:** 43

Optech Fibres Ltd (North West)

Andrews Way, Barrow In Furness, LA14 2UD
Tel: 01229-825018 **Fax:** 01229-814640
E-mail: jamie.frankland@optechfibres.co.uk
Website: http://www.optechfibres.co.uk
Directors: J. Frankland (Dir)
Managers: R. Horrocks (Develop Mgr)
Immediate Holding Company: OPTECH FIBRES LIMITED
Registration no: 05442069 **Date established:** 2005 **Turnover:** £1m - £2m
No.of Employees: 21 - 50 **Product Groups:** 37

Date of Accounts	Mar 11	Mar 10	Mar 09
Working Capital	311	213	348
Fixed Assets	53	64	50
Current Assets	691	496	673

Ottley

45 Andreas Avenue Walney, Barrow In Furness, LA14 3JN
Tel: 01229-470700 **Fax:** 01229- 475029
Directors: C. Ottley (Prop)
Immediate Holding Company: OTTLEY ELECTRICAL WALNEY LIMITED
Registration no: 07329925 **Date established:** 2010
No.of Employees: 1 - 10 **Product Groups:** 46

Date of Accounts	Sep 11
Working Capital	1
Current Assets	9

St Andrews Engineering Barrow-In-Furness Ltd

St Andrews Crossing, Barrow In Furness, LA14 2SS
Tel: 01229-826029 **Fax:** 01229-870069
E-mail: enquiries@standrewsengineering.co.uk
Website: http://www.standrewsengineering.co.uk
Directors: A. Keen (MD)
Immediate Holding Company: ST. ANDREWS ENGINEERING (BARROW-IN-FURNESS) LIMITED
Registration no: 01188270 **VAT No.:** 156 0757 58 **Date established:** 1974
Turnover: £500,000 - £1m **No.of Employees:** 1 - 10 **Product Groups:** 46

Date of Accounts	Dec 11	Dec 10	Dec 09
Working Capital	158	215	232
Fixed Assets	71	37	51
Current Assets	251	263	312

Structured Software Systems Ltd 3sl

Suite 2 22a Duke Street, Barrow In Furness, LA14 1HH
Tel: 01229-838867 **Fax:** 01229-870096
E-mail: mark.walker@threesl.com
Website: http://www.threefl.com
Bank(s): Lloyds
Directors: M. Walker (Dir)
Immediate Holding Company: STRUCTURED SOFTWARE SYSTEMS LIMITED
Registration no: 02153654 **VAT No.:** GB 473 2757 28
Date established: 1987 **Turnover:** £1m - £2m **No.of Employees:** 21 - 50
Product Groups: 44

Date of Accounts	Sep 11	Sep 10	Sep 09
Working Capital	1m	1m	1m
Fixed Assets	30	40	52
Current Assets	1m	1m	1m

Brampton

Clive Walton Engineering Ltd

Rivendell Cumrew, Heads Nook, Brampton, CA8 9DD
Tel: 01768-896232 **Fax:** 01768-896451
E-mail: sales@clivewaltonengineering.com
Website: http://www.clivewaltonengineering.com
Directors: C. Walton (MD)
Immediate Holding Company: CLIVE WALTON ENGINEERING LIMITED
Registration no: 04799460 **VAT No.:** GB 288 1441 39
Date established: 2003 **Turnover:** £250,000 - £500,000
No.of Employees: 1 - 10 **Product Groups:** 48

Date of Accounts	Aug 11	Aug 10	Aug 09
Working Capital	139	71	39
Fixed Assets	135	139	187
Current Assets	311	250	162

Dawkins

Romanway Gilsland, Brampton, CA8 7AA
Tel: 01697-747252 **Fax:** 01697-747252
Directors: T. Dawkins (Prop)
Date established: 1997 **No.of Employees:** 1 - 10 **Product Groups:** 20, 40, 41

Horn UK Ltd

Townfoot Industrial Estate, Brampton, CA8 1SW
Tel: 01697-741080 **Fax:** 01697-741022
E-mail: enq@cumbrian.co.uk
Website: http://www.cumbrian.co.uk
Directors: D. Smales (MD)
Managers: D. Graham-battersby (Comm)
Ultimate Holding Company: STALKERS TRANSPORT SERVICES LTD
Immediate Holding Company: PALL-EX (NORTHERN) LIMITED
Registration no: 02886999 **VAT No.:** GB 598 2628 84
Date established: 1996 **No.of Employees:** 11 - 20 **Product Groups:** 27, 30

Priory Products

Townfoot Industrial Estate, Brampton, CA8 1TB
Tel: 01697-72944 **Fax:** 01697- 741017
E-mail: priory.products@btconnect.com
Managers: S. Long (Sales Prom Mgr)
Ultimate Holding Company: RICAL GROUP
VAT No.: GB 110 2038 47 **Turnover:** Up to £250,000
No.of Employees: 1 - 10 **Product Groups:** 65

W C F Ltd

Craw Hall, Brampton, CA8 1TN
Tel: 01697-745050 **Fax:** 01697-745090
E-mail: lanark@wcfcountrycentres.co.uk
Website: http://www.wcf.co.uk
Managers: M. Parker, T. Cannon (Mktg Serv Mgr), D. Brimicombe, D. Thompson (Tech Serv Mgr), J. Ritzema (Comptroller)
Immediate Holding Company: WCF LTD.
Registration no: 02263148 **Date established:** 1988
Turnover: £75m - £125m **No.of Employees:** 51 - 100
Product Groups: 31, 61, 66

Date of Accounts	May 09	May 10	May 11
Sales Turnover	124m	131m	123m
Pre Tax Profit/Loss	4m	4m	4m
Working Capital	22m	24m	26m
Fixed Assets	8m	6m	7m
Current Assets	35m	37m	38m
Current Liabilities	2m	3m	3m

Carlisle

A S D Metal Services

Unit C Kingmoor Park, Carlisle, CA6 4RP
Tel: 01228-674766 **Fax:** 01228-674197
E-mail: carlisle@asdmetalservices.co.uk
Website: http://www.asdmetalservices.co.uk
Bank(s): Barclays
Managers: S. Tyrer (Chief Mgr)
Immediate Holding Company: A.S.D P.L.C.
Registration no: 01117743 **VAT No.:** GB 412 1831 95
Turnover: £500,000 - £1m **No.of Employees:** 11 - 20 **Product Groups:** 34

A Steadman & Son Ltd (t/a Steadmans)

Warnell Welton, Carlisle, CA5 7HH
Tel: 01697-478277 **Fax:** 01697-478530
E-mail: info@steadmans.co.uk
Website: http://www.steadmans.co.uk
Directors: A. Wilson (Fin), R. Monro (Co Sec), C. Williams (Dir)
Managers: I. Hogdson (Sales & Mktg Mg), S. McLnally, C. Steadman (Personnel), S. Iverson (Tech Serv Mgr)
Ultimate Holding Company: SIG PLC
Immediate Holding Company: A. STEADMAN & SON LIMITED
Registration no: 02161849 **Date established:** 1987 **Turnover:** £5m - £10m
No.of Employees: 101 - 250 **Product Groups:** 30, 35, 49

Date of Accounts	Dec 10	Dec 09	Dec 08
Sales Turnover	N/A	N/A	29m
Pre Tax Profit/Loss	N/A	29m	4m
Working Capital	75	75	-4m
Fixed Assets	N/A	N/A	6m
Current Assets	75	75	18m
Current Liabilities	N/A	N/A	1m

A W Communication Systems Ltd

Crook Barn The Crook Rowelton, Roweltown, Carlisle, CA6 6LH
Tel: 01697-748777
E-mail: adrian@awcsl.com
Website: http://www.awcsl.com
Directors: A. Charlton (MD)
Immediate Holding Company: A.W. COMMUNICATION SYSTEMS LIMITED
Registration no: 04891652 **Date established:** 2003
No.of Employees: 1 - 10 **Product Groups:** 37, 67

Date of Accounts	Sep 11	Sep 10	Sep 09
Working Capital	353	238	39
Fixed Assets	333	319	259
Current Assets	431	325	549

Abacus

243 Green Lane Belle Vue, Carlisle, CA2 7RB
Tel: 01228-530967 **Fax:** 01228-530967
E-mail: abacusbuildings@tiscali.co.uk
Website: http://www.discountsectionalgarages.com
Directors: G. Dixon (Prop)
Date established: 1984 **No.of Employees:** 1 - 10 **Product Groups:** 25, 33, 35, 66

Arco Ltd

Kingstown Broadway Kingstown Industrial Estate, Carlisle, CA3 0HA
Tel: 01228-591100 **Fax:** 01228-404200
E-mail: sean.churchill@arco.co.uk
Website: http://www.arco.co.uk
Managers: S. Churchill (Reg Mgr)
Immediate Holding Company: ARCO LIMITED
Registration no: 00133804 **Date established:** 2014
Turnover: Up to £250,000 **No.of Employees:** 1 - 10 **Product Groups:** 24, 63

Date of Accounts	Jun 11	Jun 10	Jun 09
Sales Turnover	229m	216m	214m
Pre Tax Profit/Loss	8m	6m	260
Working Capital	32m	27m	29m
Fixed Assets	19m	21m	23m
Current Assets	82m	67m	62m
Current Liabilities	12m	13m	8m

Benfield Motor Group

Auchinlek Drive Rosehill Industrial Estate, Carlisle, CA1 2UR
Tel: 01228-525555 **Fax:** 01228-554554
E-mail: vw.morpeth@benfield-motors.co.uk
Website: http://www.benfield-motors.co.uk

Managers: D. Robinson, S. Trickett (Sales Prom Mgr), D. Bagley
Ultimate Holding Company: ADDISON MOTORS LIMITED
Immediate Holding Company: BENFIELD MOTOR GROUP LIMITED
Registration no: 06844413 **Date established:** 2009
No.of Employees: 51 - 100 **Product Groups:** 68

Biffa Waste Services Ltd
St Ninians Road, Carlisle, CA2 4LR
Tel: 01228-532244 **Fax:** 01228-514200
E-mail: marketing@biffa.co.uk
Website: http://www.biffa.co.uk
Managers: J. Walmsley (Mgr)
Immediate Holding Company: BIFFA WASTE SERVICES LIMITED
Registration no: 00946107 **Date established:** 1969
No.of Employees: 21 - 50 **Product Groups:** 32, 54

Date of Accounts	Mar 08	Mar 09	Apr 10
Sales Turnover	555m	574m	492m
Pre Tax Profit/Loss	23m	50m	30m
Working Capital	229m	271m	293m
Fixed Assets	371m	360m	378m
Current Assets	409m	534m	609m
Current Liabilities	50m	100m	115m

Border Steelwork Structures Ltd
58 Warwick Road, Carlisle, CA1 1DR
Tel: 01228-548744 **Fax:** 01228-511073
E-mail: admin@bordersteelwork.co.uk
Website: http://www.bordersteelwork.co.uk
Bank(s): HSBC Bank plc
Directors: D. Downie (MD), D. Milne (Dir)
Managers: I. Reeves (Sales Admin), M. Downie (Buyer)
Immediate Holding Company: BORDER STEELWORK STRUCTURES LIMITED
Registration no: SC066172 **VAT No.:** GB 293 2876 22
Date established: 1978 **Turnover:** £5m - £10m **No.of Employees:** 21 - 50
Product Groups: 30, 35, 48, 52

Date of Accounts	Oct 11	Oct 10	Oct 09
Sales Turnover	6m	9m	5m
Pre Tax Profit/Loss	109	312	-58
Working Capital	2m	2m	643
Fixed Assets	887	878	1m
Current Assets	3m	4m	3m
Current Liabilities	828	802	852

A Brown Sporting Guns
254 Kingstown Road, Carlisle, CA3 0BW
Tel: 01228-541205 **Fax:** 01228-541205
E-mail: adrian@absportingguns.co.uk
Website: http://www.absportingguns.co.uk
Directors: A. Brown (Prop)
Date established: 1985 **No.of Employees:** 1 - 10 **Product Groups:** 36, 39, 40

Byers Brothers Ltd
Rigg Street, Carlisle, CA2 5TN
Tel: 01228-523304 **Fax:** 01228-810198
Website: http://www.byersbros.co.uk
Bank(s): Barclays
Directors: R. Byers (MD)
Immediate Holding Company: BYERS BROTHERS LIMITED
Registration no: 01511435 **VAT No.:** GB 330 5455 83
Date established: 1980 **Turnover:** £500,000 - £1m
No.of Employees: 11 - 20 **Product Groups:** 48

Date of Accounts	Mar 12	Mar 11	Mar 10
Working Capital	37	17	35
Fixed Assets	15	19	24
Current Assets	191	137	175

C N Group Ltd
Newspaper House Dalston Road, Carlisle, CA2 5UA
Tel: 01228-612600 **Fax:** 01228-600601
Website: http://www.cngroup.co.uk
Bank(s): HSBC Bank plc
Directors: T. Hall (Mkt Research), C. Bisco (MD), R. Burgess (Grp Chief Exec)
Managers: W. Allardes (Personnel), B. Pennington (I.T. Exec)
Registration no: 01931452 **Turnover:** £10m - £20m
No.of Employees: 251 - 500 **Product Groups:** 28

Date of Accounts	Dec 09	Dec 08	Dec 07
Sales Turnover	29m	35m	38m
Pre Tax Profit/Loss	-7m	-6m	4m
Working Capital	4m	3m	5m
Fixed Assets	14m	22m	27m
Current Assets	6m	7m	9m
Current Liabilities	1m	2m	2m

Carlisle Refrigeration
Brunthill Road Kingstown Industrial Estate, Carlisle, CA3 0EH
Tel: 01228-531449 **Fax:** 01228-511514
E-mail: david.thompson@carlislerefrigeration.co.uk
Website: http://www.carlislerefrigeration.co.uk
Bank(s): The Royal Bank of Scotland
Directors: D. Thompson (Fin), D. Lowe (Sales)
Ultimate Holding Company: CARLISLE REFRIGERATION (HOLDINGS) LIMITED
Immediate Holding Company: CARLISLE REFRIGERATION LIMITED
Registration no: 01844394 **VAT No.:** GB 257 3344 54
Date established: 1984 **Turnover:** £10m - £20m
No.of Employees: 51 - 100 **Product Groups:** 39, 40, 72

Date of Accounts	Mar 11	Mar 10	Mar 09
Sales Turnover	13m	10m	11m
Pre Tax Profit/Loss	612	390	301
Working Capital	2m	1m	1m
Fixed Assets	2m	2m	2m
Current Assets	4m	3m	3m
Current Liabilities	976	982	699

Carrs Billington Agriculture Sales Ltd
Montgomery Way Rosehill Industrial Estate, Carlisle, CA1 2UY
Tel: 01228-520212 **Fax:** 01228-512572
E-mail: rae.tomlinson@carrs-billington.com
Website: http://www.carrs-billington.com
Bank(s): The Royal Bank of Scotland
Directors: R. Tomlinson (Fin), K. Dixon (Fin)
Managers: B. Bell (District Mgr), G. Alison, I. Oliver (Sales & Mktg Mg)
Ultimate Holding Company: CARR'S MILLING INDUSTRIES PUBLIC LIMITED COMPANY
Immediate Holding Company: CARRS AGRICULTURE LIMITED
Registration no: 00480342 **VAT No.:** GB 269 0523 50
Date established: 1950 **Turnover:** £10m - £20m
No.of Employees: 51 - 100 **Product Groups:** 32, 41

Date of Accounts	Aug 08	Aug 09	Aug 10
Sales Turnover	89m	69m	73m
Pre Tax Profit/Loss	8m	990	4m
Working Capital	2m	-2m	-6m
Fixed Assets	4m	4m	9m
Current Assets	31m	13m	17m
Current Liabilities	5m	1m	3m

Carrs Milling Industries plc
Old Croft Stanwix, Carlisle, CA3 9BA
Tel: 01228-554600 **Fax:** 01228-554602
E-mail: reception@cmiplc.co.uk
Website: http://www.carrs-milling.com
Bank(s): Clydesdale Bank PLC
Directors: R. Wood (Fin)
Managers: N. Macguiness (Tech Serv Mgr)
Ultimate Holding Company: CARR'S MILLING INDUSTRIES PUBLIC LIMITED COMPANY
Immediate Holding Company: CARRS MILLING LIMITED
Registration no: 02475619 **Date established:** 1990
Turnover: £10m - £20m **No.of Employees:** 21 - 50 **Product Groups:** 20, 32

Cavaghan & Gray Group (Northern Foods)
Brunel House Brunel Way, Durranhill Industrial Estate, Carlisle, CA1 3NQ
Tel: 01228-518200 **Fax:** 01228-518215
E-mail: mark.murray@cavaghan-and-gray.co.uk
Website: http://www.northernfoods.com
Directors: S. Henderson (Fin), W. Duncanson (MD)
Managers: M. Murray, L. Cooke (Personnel), E. Routledge (Fin Mgr)
Ultimate Holding Company: NORTHERN FOODS LIMITED
Immediate Holding Company: CAVAGHAN & GRAY GROUP LIMITED
Registration no: 01357837 **Date established:** 1978 **Turnover:** £5m - £10m
No.of Employees: 501 - 1000 **Product Groups:** 20

Date of Accounts	Mar 08	Mar 09	Apr 10
Sales Turnover	22m	23m	23m
Pre Tax Profit/Loss	-3m	-229	-2m
Working Capital	13m	14m	14m
Fixed Assets	8m	7m	5m
Current Assets	19m	18m	17m
Current Liabilities	1m	795	641

Chip-It
Unit 28 Chapel Place Dentonholme Trading Estate, Carlisle, CA2 5DF
Tel: 01228-590033 **Fax:** 01228-590033
E-mail: info@chip-it.org.uk
Website: http://www.chip-it.org.uk
Directors: D. Seabrook (Ptnr)
Immediate Holding Company: SOAKS LIMITED
Registration no: 05014986 **Date established:** 2004
Turnover: Up to £250,000 **No.of Employees:** 1 - 10 **Product Groups:** 39

Clark Door Limited
Unit F Central Kingmoor Park, Carlisle, CA6 4SJ
Tel: 01228-522321 **Fax:** 01228-401854
E-mail: mail@clarkdoor.com
Website: http://www.clarkdoor.com
Bank(s): Barclays Bank
Directors: P. Ashley (MD)
Managers: B. Payne (Sales Prom Mgr), C. Johnstone (Tech Serv Mgr), B. Paine (Mktg Serv Mgr), M. College (Buyer), M. Collidge (Buyer), W. Jonhson (Mktg Serv Mgr)
Immediate Holding Company: Amountindex Ltd
Registration no: SC046648 **Date established:** 2005
Turnover: £250,000 - £500,000 **No.of Employees:** 51 - 100
Product Groups: 35, 40

Date of Accounts	Mar 08
Working Capital	20
Fixed Assets	688
Current Assets	1089
Current Liabilities	1069
Total Share Capital	10

Cowens Ltd
Ellers Mill Dalston, Carlisle, CA5 7QJ
Tel: 01228-710205 **Fax:** 01228-710331
E-mail: info@cowens.co.uk
Website: http://www.cowens.co.uk
Bank(s): HSBC Bank plc
Directors: J. Coulthard (Prop)
Immediate Holding Company: COWENS LIMITED
Registration no: 03790634 **VAT No.:** GB 257 4463 41
Date established: 1999 **Turnover:** £1m - £2m **No.of Employees:** 11 - 20
Product Groups: 23, 24, 26, 38, 42, 63

Date of Accounts	Dec 11	Dec 10	Dec 09
Working Capital	1m	782	472
Fixed Assets	140	162	139
Current Assets	1m	1m	926

Crossling Plumbers' Merchants
Kingstown Broadway Kingstown Industrial Estate, Carlisle, CA3 0HA
Tel: 01228-541101 **Fax:** 01228-539288
E-mail: carlisle@crossling.co.uk
Website: http://www.crossling.co.uk
Bank(s): Lloyds TSB Bank plc
Managers: S. Goad (Mgr)
Immediate Holding Company: PENFOLD BOOK & BIBLE HOUSE LIMITED
Registration no: 01071230 **Date established:** 1998
Turnover: £20m - £50m **No.of Employees:** 11 - 20 **Product Groups:** 30, 35, 36

Date of Accounts	Nov 08	Nov 07	Nov 06
Working Capital	102	79	89
Fixed Assets	3	4	3
Current Assets	245	226	246

Crown Packaging UK plc
PO Box 28, Carlisle, CA1 2TL
Tel: 01228-811200 **Fax:** 01228-811290
E-mail: david.watling@eur.crowncork.com
Website: http://www.crowncork.com
Managers: P. Brear, M. Constable (Sales & Mktg Mg), D. Watling (I.T. Exec), L. Campbell (Personnel), K. Simons (Purch Mgr)
Ultimate Holding Company: CROWN HOLDINGS INC (USA)
Immediate Holding Company: CROWN PACKAGING UK PLC
Registration no: 00178090 **VAT No.:** GB 274 7764 16
Date established: 2021 **Turnover:** £500m - £1,000m
No.of Employees: 251 - 500 **Product Groups:** 35

Date of Accounts	Dec 11	Dec 10	Dec 09
Sales Turnover	502m	510m	493m
Pre Tax Profit/Loss	-27m	11m	11m
Working Capital	128m	123m	109m
Fixed Assets	122m	152m	158m
Current Assets	348m	384m	356m
Current Liabilities	20m	67m	76m

Cumberland Building Society
67a English Street, Carlisle, CA3 8JZ
Tel: 01228-515175 **Fax:** 01228-596694
E-mail: executives@cumberland.co.uk
Website: http://www.cumberland.co.uk
Managers: C. Graham (Mgr)
Ultimate Holding Company: CUMBERLAND BUILDING SOCIETY
Immediate Holding Company: CUMBERLAND BUILDING SOCIETY CHARITABLE FOUNDATION
Registration no: FP021297 **VAT No.:** GB 708 1214 66
Date established: 1998 **Turnover:** Up to £250,000
No.of Employees: 11 - 20 **Product Groups:** 82

Date of Accounts	Mar 12	Mar 11	Mar 10
Sales Turnover	28	25	31
Pre Tax Profit/Loss	-8	-7	-5
Working Capital	4	12	19
Current Assets	4	12	19

Cumbria Limoscene
17 Punton Road, Carlisle, CA3 9BB
Tel: 01228-537058
E-mail: enquiries@cumbrialimoscene.co.uk
Website: http://www.cumbrialimoscene.co.uk
Managers: S. Lee (Chief Mgr)
Date established: 2006 **Turnover:** Up to £250,000
No.of Employees: 1 - 10 **Product Groups:** 72

Cumbria Newspapers
Newspaper House Dalston Road, Carlisle, CA2 5UA
Tel: 01228-612600 **Fax:** 01228-612601
E-mail: robinburgess@cngroup.co.uk
Website: http://www.newsandstar.co.uk
Directors: T. Hall (MD)
Ultimate Holding Company: CN GROUP LIMITED
Immediate Holding Company: WEST CUMBERLAND ADVERTISER LIMITED
Registration no: 01679975 **Date established:** 1982
Turnover: £10m - £20m **No.of Employees:** 251 - 500 **Product Groups:** 28

Cumbria Plating Services Ltd
Unit 5 Currock Road Trade Centre Currock Road, Carlisle, CA2 5AD
Tel: 01228-819324 **Fax:** 01228-819324
Website: http://www.cumbriaplatingservices.co.uk
Directors: B. Morris (MD)
Immediate Holding Company: CUMBRIA PLATING SERVICES CARLISLE LIMITED
Registration no: 07100784 **Date established:** 2009
No.of Employees: 1 - 10 **Product Groups:** 46, 48

Date of Accounts	Dec 11	Dec 10
Working Capital	2	8
Fixed Assets	52	45
Current Assets	21	24

D D Fabrications Ltd
Blackdyke Road Kingstown Industrial Estate, Carlisle, CA3 0PJ
Tel: 01228-536595 **Fax:** 01228-536595
E-mail: enquiries@ddfabrications.co.uk
Website: http://www.ddfabrications.co.uk
Directors: M. Blaylock (MD)
Immediate Holding Company: D. D. FABRICATIONS LIMITED
Registration no: 05776681 **VAT No.:** GB 257 4936 24
Date established: 2006 **Turnover:** £250,000 - £500,000
No.of Employees: 1 - 10 **Product Groups:** 39

Date of Accounts	Dec 11	Dec 10	Dec 09
Working Capital	-244	-258	-273
Fixed Assets	258	285	310
Current Assets	100	120	106

John Davidson Pipes Ltd
Townfoot Longtown, Carlisle, CA6 5LY
Tel: 01228-791503 **Fax:** 01228-791682
E-mail: iain.mcguiness@jdpipes.co.uk
Website: http://www.jdpipes.co.uk
Bank(s): Lloyds TSB Bank plc
Directors: S. Mclellan (MD)
Managers: L. Bell (Personnel), I. McGuiness (Fin Mgr)
Ultimate Holding Company: TESSENDERLO CHEMIE NV (BELGIUM)
Immediate Holding Company: JOHN DAVIDSON (PIPES) LIMITED
Registration no: SC050397 **Date established:** 1972
Turnover: £20m - £50m **No.of Employees:** 21 - 50 **Product Groups:** 30

Date of Accounts	Dec 11	Dec 10	Dec 09
Sales Turnover	41m	37m	37m
Pre Tax Profit/Loss	759	586	454
Working Capital	3m	4m	3m
Fixed Assets	2m	2m	3m
Current Assets	12m	10m	9m
Current Liabilities	1m	2m	2m

Delta Refrigeration & Air Conditioning Delta Refrigeration
Kingstown Road, Carlisle, CA3 0AX
Tel: 01228-830020
E-mail: sales@deltarefrigeration.co.uk
Website: http://www.deltarefrigeration.co.uk
Directors: M. Cosham (Dir)
No.of Employees: 1 - 10 **Product Groups:** 37, 48, 67, 83

Electro Mechanical Engineering Services Ltd
12 Allenbrook Road Rosehill Industrial Estate, Carlisle, CA1 2UT
Tel: 01228-518100 **Fax:** 01228-597989
E-mail: sales@emeservices.co.uk
Website: http://www.eme-group.co.uk
Directors: G. Mooney (Fin)
Immediate Holding Company: ELECTRO-MECHANICAL ENGINEERING SERVICES LIMITED
Registration no: 03522702 **Date established:** 1998
No.of Employees: 1 - 10 **Product Groups:** 35, 39, 45

Date of Accounts	Mar 12	Mar 11	Mar 10
Working Capital	2m	1m	1m
Fixed Assets	191	213	230
Current Assets	2m	2m	2m
Current Liabilities	N/A	275	N/A

EnviroMech Design Ltd
Viloet House Cumrew, Carlisle, CA8 9DD
Tel: 01768-896800 **Fax:** 01228-830100
E-mail: info@envirornechdesign.com
Website: http://www.envirornechdesign.com
Date established: 1997 **Turnover:** £500,000 - £1m
No.of Employees: 1 - 10 **Product Groups:** 40

Date of Accounts	Sep 07	Sep 06	Sep 05
Working Capital	39	31	22
Fixed Assets	5	5	3
Current Assets	76	67	43
Current Liabilities	37	37	22

Furmanite International Ltd
Parkhill Road Kingstown Industrial Estate, Carlisle, CA3 0EX
Tel: 01228-536396 **Fax:** 01228-515374
Website: http://www.furmanite.co.uk
Managers: B. Irving, G. Jenkinson (Tech Supp Eng)
Ultimate Holding Company: FURMANITE CORPORATION (USA)
Immediate Holding Company: FURMANITE INTERNATIONAL LIMITED
Registration no: 00238721 **Date established:** 2029 **Turnover:** £1m - £2m
No.of Employees: 21 - 50 **Product Groups:** 48

Date of Accounts	Dec 11	Dec 10	Dec 09
Sales Turnover	39m	34m	35m
Pre Tax Profit/Loss	5m	3m	2m
Working Capital	24m	24m	23m
Fixed Assets	3m	3m	4m
Current Assets	35m	34m	32m
Current Liabilities	2m	3m	2m

Graham
Lancaster Street, Carlisle, CA1 1TG
Tel: 01228-525426 **Fax:** 01228-515632
E-mail: keithrobinson@graham-group.co.uk
Website: http://www.graham-group.co.uk
Managers: K. Robinson (Mgr)
Immediate Holding Company: JEWSONS
Registration no: 00066738 **Turnover:** Over £1,000m
No.of Employees: 1 - 10 **Product Groups:** 66

J H P Training Ltd
Broadacre House 16-20 Lowther Street, Carlisle, CA3 8DA
Tel: 01228-536373 **Fax:** 01228-591236
E-mail: carlisle.business.centre@jhp-group.com
Website: http://www.jhptraining.com
Managers: R. Smith (Mgr)
Immediate Holding Company: JHP TRAINING LIMITED
Registration no: 03247918 **Date established:** 1996
Turnover: £10m - £20m **No.of Employees:** 1 - 10 **Product Groups:** 86

Jewson Ltd
Stephenson Road Durranhill Industrial Estate, Carlisle, CA1 3NU
Tel: 01228-536401 **Fax:** 01228-515401
Website: http://www.jewson.co.uk
Managers: I. Coupland (District Mgr)
Ultimate Holding Company: COMPAGNIE DE SAINT GOBAIN (FRANCE)
Immediate Holding Company: JEWSON LIMITED
Registration no: 00348407 **Date established:** 1939
Turnover: £500m - £1,000m **No.of Employees:** 1 - 10
Product Groups: 66

Date of Accounts	Dec 11	Dec 10	Dec 09
Sales Turnover	1606m	1547m	1485m
Pre Tax Profit/Loss	18m	100m	45m
Working Capital	-345m	-250m	-349m
Fixed Assets	496m	387m	461m
Current Assets	657m	1005m	1320m
Current Liabilities	66m	120m	64m

K H S
Telford Road Durranhill Industrial Estate, Carlisle, CA1 3NW
Tel: 07767-464203 **Fax:** 01228-596700
E-mail: sales@karaokehire.biz
Website: http://www.karaokehire.biz
Directors: D. Klein (Prop)
Immediate Holding Company: KLEIN HANDLING SYSTEMS LIMITED
Registration no: 05797789 **Date established:** 2006
No.of Employees: 1 - 10 **Product Groups:** 35, 39, 45

Date of Accounts	Apr 11	Apr 10	Apr 09
Working Capital	-36	-95	-123
Fixed Assets	108	135	219
Current Assets	138	48	84

W A Kennedy & Son
Low Hesket, Carlisle, CA4 0ET
Tel: 01697-473307
Directors: M. Kennedy (Prop)
Date established: 1977 **No.of Employees:** 1 - 10 **Product Groups:** 41

Lawson Engineers Ltd
Barras Lane Dalston, Carlisle, CA5 7ND
Tel: 01228-711470 **Fax:** 01228-711255
E-mail: anne.duckworth@lawson-engineers.com
Website: http://www.lawson-engineers.com
Directors: A. Duckworth (Fin)
Managers: N. Summers (Mktg Serv Mgr), D. Wood (Tech Serv Mgr)
Immediate Holding Company: LAWSON ENGINEERS LIMITED
Registration no: 01797799 **Date established:** 1984 **Turnover:** £1m - £2m
No.of Employees: 11 - 20 **Product Groups:** 45, 84

Date of Accounts	Jul 11	Jul 10	Jul 09
Working Capital	318	191	441
Fixed Assets	131	145	159
Current Assets	2m	1m	2m

Linton Tweeds Ltd
Shaddon Mills Shaddongate, Carlisle, CA2 5TZ
Tel: 01228-527569 **Fax:** 01228-512062
E-mail: info@lintondirect.com
Website: http://www.lintondirect.com
Bank(s): HSBC
Directors: K. Walker (MD), K. Carruthers (Fin), R. Irvine (Sales)
Immediate Holding Company: LINTON TWEEDS LIMITED
Registration no: 00125406 **VAT No.:** GB 256 6552 38
Date established: 2012 **Turnover:** £2m - £5m **No.of Employees:** 51 - 100
Product Groups: 23

Date of Accounts	Feb 12	Feb 11	Feb 10
Working Capital	1m	1m	924
Fixed Assets	1m	1m	1m
Current Assets	2m	1m	1m

Lloyd Ltd (Head Office)
Kingstown Broadway Kingstown Industrial Estate, Carlisle, CA3 0EF
Tel: 01228-517100 **Fax:** 01228-531212
E-mail: derek.marlborough@lloyd.co.uk
Website: http://www.lloyd.ltd.uk
Bank(s): HSBC Bank plc
Managers: S. Miller
Immediate Holding Company: LLOYD LIMITED
Registration no: 00786404 **VAT No.:** GB 256 3281 58
Date established: 1964 **Turnover:** £50m - £75m
No.of Employees: 21 - 50 **Product Groups:** 39, 41, 45, 67, 83

Date of Accounts	Dec 11	Dec 10	Dec 09
Sales Turnover	67m	56m	61m
Pre Tax Profit/Loss	2m	962	576
Working Capital	7m	6m	7m
Fixed Assets	6m	6m	6m
Current Assets	23m	20m	21m
Current Liabilities	3m	2m	4m

Keith Mason Agricultural Engineers
Broadacres Chapel Hill Road, Wreay, Carlisle, CA4 0RP
Tel: 01697-473886 **Fax:** 01697-473886
Directors: K. Mason (Prop)
Immediate Holding Company: KEITH MASON AGRICULTURAL ENGINEER LIMITED
Registration no: 04553491 **Date established:** 2002
No.of Employees: 1 - 10 **Product Groups:** 41

Date of Accounts	Feb 11	Feb 10	Feb 09
Working Capital	-41	-40	-38
Fixed Assets	48	49	47
Current Assets	37	58	55

W Moses
43a Milbrook Road Kingstown Industrial Estate, Carlisle, CA3 0EU
Tel: 01228-401374 **Fax:** 01228-510427
Directors: W. Moses (Prop)
Date established: 1991 **No.of Employees:** 1 - 10 **Product Groups:** 40

Mountelm Ltd
8 Junction Street, Carlisle, CA2 5XH
Tel: 01228-523136 **Fax:** 01228-530550
E-mail: m.liddle@btconnect.com
Directors: M. Hepworth (Dir)
Ultimate Holding Company: CHESTNUT GROUP LIMITED
Immediate Holding Company: MOUNTELM LIMITED
Registration no: 01195569 **VAT No.:** 391 0180 73 **Date established:** 1975
No.of Employees: 11 - 20 **Product Groups:** 51, 66

Date of Accounts	Jul 11	Jul 10	Jul 09
Working Capital	159	100	39
Current Assets	773	506	276

J Nicholson & Sons
The Forge Kirkandrews-on-Eden, Carlisle, CA5 6DJ
Tel: 01228-576245 **Fax:** 01228-576016
E-mail: info@edenforge.co.uk
Website: http://www.edenforge.co.uk
Directors: R. Nicholson (Prop)
Immediate Holding Company: NIGEL SPRINGER LIMITED
Date established: 2010 **No.of Employees:** 1 - 10 **Product Groups:** 41

Date of Accounts	Dec 11
Working Capital	-7
Fixed Assets	1

Nixon Engineering Ltd
7 Peterfield Road Kingstown Industrial Estate, Carlisle, CA3 0EY
Tel: 01228-523956 **Fax:** 01228-401919
E-mail: sales@nixonengltd.freeserve.co.uk
Website: http://www.nixonengineering.com
Directors: E. Nixon (MD), D. Cockett (Fin)
Immediate Holding Company: NIXON ENGINEERING LIMITED
Registration no: 00695038 **VAT No.:** GB 256 6062 55
Date established: 1961 **Turnover:** £250,000 - £500,000
No.of Employees: 1 - 10 **Product Groups:** 48

Date of Accounts	Aug 11	Aug 10	Aug 09
Working Capital	-40	-22	-25
Fixed Assets	263	275	291
Current Assets	77	93	76

M J Park
Ross Villa Westlinton, Carlisle, CA6 6AW
Tel: 01228-674550 **Fax:** 01228-674550
Directors: M. Park (Prop)
Date established: 2002 **No.of Employees:** 1 - 10 **Product Groups:** 41

Penney Packaging Ltd
The Old Chapel Warwick-On-Eden, Carlisle, CA4 8PG
Tel: 01228-561704 **Fax:** 01228-561646
E-mail: ian.penney@btconnect.com
Directors: I. Penney (MD)
Date established: 1981 **No.of Employees:** 1 - 10 **Product Groups:** 38, 42

Garry Phillips Agricultural Engineers
Roughsyke Roadhead, Carlisle, CA6 6NL
Tel: 01697-748227 **Fax:** 01697-748227
E-mail: garry.phillips1@btopenworld.com
Website: http://www.quadbikescumbria.co.uk
Directors: G. Phillips (Prop)
Date established: 1986 **No.of Employees:** 1 - 10 **Product Groups:** 41

Pioneer Food Services Ltd
Pioneer House Montgomery Way Rosehill Estate, Carlisle, CA1 2RR
Tel: 01228-523474 **Fax:** 01228-512906
E-mail: g.jenkins@pioneerfoods.co.uk
Website: http://www.pioneerfoods.co.uk
Bank(s): National Westminster
Directors: K. Abbott (Co Sec)
Managers: G. Jenkins (Mgr), M. Elliott (Tech Serv Mgr), S. Dhesi (Personnel)
Immediate Holding Company: P.F.D.(CARLISLE)LIMITED
Registration no: 00557210 **VAT No.:** GB 533 4457 50
Date established: 1955 **Turnover:** £20m - £50m
No.of Employees: 101 - 250 **Product Groups:** 20, 62

Date of Accounts	Apr 11	Apr 10	Apr 09
Sales Turnover	30m	30m	29m
Pre Tax Profit/Loss	743	1m	1m

Working Capital	5m	5m	4m
Fixed Assets	5m	5m	5m
Current Assets	9m	8m	8m
Current Liabilities	1m	1m	1m

Precise Solutions
Cote House Wetheral, Carlisle, CA4 8HZ
Tel: 01228-562234 **Fax:** 01228-501912
E-mail: derekjohnston@precise-solutions.co.uk
Website: http://www.precise-solutions.co.uk
Immediate Holding Company: PRECISE SOLUTIONS GPS LIMITED
Registration no: 06246353 **Date established:** 2007
No.of Employees: 1 - 10 **Product Groups:** 37, 38, 39, 67

Date of Accounts	Mar 11	Mar 10	Mar 09
Working Capital	202	245	217
Fixed Assets	58	35	36
Current Assets	667	812	669
Current Liabilities	9	8	N/A

Rickerby Ltd
Currock Road, Carlisle, CA2 4AU
Tel: 01228-527521 **Fax:** 01228-533008
E-mail: info@rickerby.net
Website: http://www.rickerby.net
Directors: N. Platton (Fin)
Managers: M. Henderson (Sales Prom Mgr), J. Humphries
Ultimate Holding Company: RICKERBY HOLDINGS LIMITED
Immediate Holding Company: RICKERBY HOLDINGS LIMITED
Registration no: 00149685 **Date established:** 2018
Turnover: £20m - £50m **No.of Employees:** 101 - 250 **Product Groups:** 41

Date of Accounts	Sep 11	Sep 10	Sep 09
Sales Turnover	44m	42m	39m
Pre Tax Profit/Loss	1m	1m	1m
Working Capital	6m	5m	5m
Fixed Assets	4m	3m	3m
Current Assets	15m	13m	13m
Current Liabilities	2m	1m	5m

Robson Medical & Mobility
4 Brunswick Street, Carlisle, CA1 1PP
Tel: 01228-510044 **Fax:** 01228-510055
Directors: A. Robson (Ptnr)
Immediate Holding Company: ROBSON MEDICAL AND MOBILITY LIMITED
Registration no: 08148508 **Date established:** 2012
No.of Employees: 1 - 10 **Product Groups:** 38, 39, 83

Scot J C B Ltd
Millbrook Road Kingstown Industrial Estate, Carlisle, CA3 0EU
Tel: 01228-536331 **Fax:** 01228-514698
E-mail: enquiries@scot-jcb.co.uk
Website: http://www.scot-jcb.co.uk
Directors: D. Donoghue (MD)
Ultimate Holding Company: SCOT JCB (HOLDINGS) LIMITED
Immediate Holding Company: SCOT J C B LIMITED
Registration no: SC051692 **Date established:** 1972
No.of Employees: 11 - 20 **Product Groups:** 48

Date of Accounts	Dec 11	Dec 10	Dec 09
Sales Turnover	78m	60m	52m
Pre Tax Profit/Loss	3m	2m	2m
Working Capital	9m	8m	6m
Fixed Assets	2m	2m	2m
Current Assets	22m	15m	13m
Current Liabilities	1m	1m	4m

Smith & Co Carlisle Ltd
Junction Street, Carlisle, CA2 5UQ
Tel: 01228-522213 **Fax:** 01228-515388
E-mail: sales@smithandcompany.co.uk
Directors: M. Smith (Jt MD), N. Smith (Jt MD), I. Carruthers (Co Sec)
Immediate Holding Company: SMITH & CO. (CARLISLE) LTD
Registration no: 02322727 **VAT No.:** GB 698 2588 62
Date established: 1988 **No.of Employees:** 21 - 50 **Product Groups:** 48, 52

Date of Accounts	Mar 07	Mar 06
Working Capital	250	228
Fixed Assets	73	66
Current Assets	620	601
Current Liabilities	370	373
Total Share Capital	15	15

Speedy Asset Services
Unit 9 Long Island Park, Carlisle, CA2 5AS
Tel: 01228-599766 **Fax:** 01228-599788
Website: http://www.speedyhire.co.uk
Managers: N. Sparks (Mgr)
Ultimate Holding Company: SPEEDY HIRE PLC
Immediate Holding Company: SPEEDY LIFTING LIMITED
Registration no: 04529136 **Date established:** 2002
Turnover: £20m - £50m **No.of Employees:** 1 - 10 **Product Groups:** 35, 37, 38, 39, 45, 48, 83

Date of Accounts	Mar 11	Mar 10	Mar 09
Sales Turnover	N/A	21m	62m
Pre Tax Profit/Loss	N/A	4m	11m
Working Capital	20m	20m	-3m
Fixed Assets	N/A	N/A	22m
Current Assets	20m	21m	17m
Current Liabilities	N/A	N/A	11m

Stagecoach Ltd
Broadacre House 16-20 Lowther Street, Carlisle, CA3 8DA
Tel: 01228-597222 **Fax:** 01228-597888
E-mail: christopher.bowles@stagecoachbus.com
Website: http://www.stagecoachbus.com
Directors: C. Bowles (MD)
Ultimate Holding Company: STAGECOACH GROUP PLC
Immediate Holding Company: STAGECOACH LIMITED
Registration no: 03092390 **Date established:** 1995
Turnover: £10m - £20m **No.of Employees:** 1 - 10 **Product Groups:** 72

Date of Accounts	Apr 11	Apr 10	Apr 09
Pre Tax Profit/Loss	-251	-240	-531
Working Capital	-13	203	412
Current Assets	2m	2m	2m

Stead Mcalpin & Co. Ltd
Cummersdale Print Works Cummersdale, Carlisle, CA2 6BT
Tel: 01228-525224 **Fax:** 01228-512070
E-mail: enquiries@steadmcalpin.co.uk
Website: http://www.steadmcalpin.co.uk
Bank(s): National Westminster, Cavendish Square, London W.1.

Directors: A. Queen (Fin), J. Kidd (Dir)
Managers: P. Whitaker (Tech Serv Mgr), L. Spence (Sales Prom Mgr)
Ultimate Holding Company: APEX TEXTILES LTD.
Immediate Holding Company: LUPFAWSMA LIMITED
Registration no: 00198535 **Date established:** 2024 **Turnover:** £5m - £10m
No.of Employees: 101 - 250 **Product Groups:** 23, 63

Date of Accounts	Sep 07	Jan 05	Jan 06
Sales Turnover	7m	14m	12m
Pre Tax Profit/Loss	296	-11m	-6m
Working Capital	4m	-26m	-31m
Fixed Assets	930	1m	2m
Current Assets	5m	9m	5m
Current Liabilities	135	1m	2m

Steele Fabrications
Unit J Kingmoor Park Heathlands Estate, Carlisle, CA6 4RE
Tel: 01228-672212 **Fax:** 01228-672212
Website: http://www.steelfabrications.co.uk
Directors: T. Steele (Prop)
Date established: 2001 **No.of Employees:** 1 - 10 **Product Groups:** 35

Terris Electrical Co. Ltd
Unit 6 Long Island Park, Carlisle, CA2 5AS
Tel: 01228-539555 **Fax:** 01228-514707
E-mail: admin@terris-electrical.co.uk
Website: http://www.terris-electrical.co.uk
Bank(s): Barclays
Directors: J. Pattinson (Co Sec)
Immediate Holding Company: TERRIS ELECTRICAL & CO. LIMITED
Registration no: 02676309 **VAT No.:** GB 288 2197 19
Date established: 1992 **Turnover:** £500,000 - £1m
No.of Employees: 11 - 20 **Product Groups:** 52

Date of Accounts	Sep 11	Sep 10	Sep 09
Sales Turnover	561	661	644
Pre Tax Profit/Loss	70	116	97
Working Capital	115	136	336
Fixed Assets	10	14	125
Current Assets	219	271	452
Current Liabilities	42	48	39

Thomas Graham & Sons
The Maltings Shaddongate, Carlisle, CA2 5UT
Tel: 01228-525364 **Fax:** 01524-841076
E-mail: roger@thomas-graham.co.uk
Website: http://www.thomas-graham.co.uk
Bank(s): HSBC
Managers: M. Singleton (Mgr)
Immediate Holding Company: THOMAS GRAHAM & SONS (IRON & STEEL) LIMITED
Registration no: 00656879 **VAT No.:** GB 288 2379 13
Date established: 1960 **Turnover:** £20m - £50m
No.of Employees: 11 - 20 **Product Groups:** 66

Date of Accounts	May 11	May 10	May 09
Sales Turnover	21m	18m	18m
Pre Tax Profit/Loss	2m	1m	891
Working Capital	8m	7m	7m
Fixed Assets	3m	3m	3m
Current Assets	12m	11m	8m
Current Liabilities	1m	950	645

Tudor Metalcraft
Scaleby Hill, Carlisle, CA6 4LY
Tel: 01228-675117 **Fax:** 01228-675117
Directors: M. Barry (Prop)
Immediate Holding Company: GRAHAM STEEL ERECTORS LIMITED
Registration no: 04268160 **Date established:** 2001
No.of Employees: 1 - 10 **Product Groups:** 26, 35

Date of Accounts	Aug 11	Aug 10	Aug 09
Working Capital	107	115	125
Fixed Assets	45	50	48
Current Assets	137	142	142

Vortex Hydra UK Ltd
Kingmoor Industrial Estate Kingmoor Road, Carlisle, CA3 9QJ
Tel: 01228-510800 **Fax:** 01228-510808
E-mail: matt_mccaffrey@vortexhydra.com
Website: http://www.vortexhydra.com
Managers: M. Mccaffrey (Ops Mgr)
Immediate Holding Company: VORTEX HYDRA (UK) LIMITED
Registration no: 04009093 **Date established:** 2000
Turnover: £20m - £50m **No.of Employees:** 1 - 10 **Product Groups:** 33, 45

Date of Accounts	Dec 11	Dec 10	Dec 09
Working Capital	263	246	283
Fixed Assets	36	41	28
Current Assets	590	539	592

Geoff Wilson Practical Gunsmith
36 Portland Place, Carlisle, CA1 1RL
Tel: 01228-531542 **Fax:** 01228-531542
E-mail: ppwilson2@aol.com
Website: http://www.geoffwilsons.co.uk
Directors: P. Wilson (Prop)
Date established: 1982 **No.of Employees:** 1 - 10 **Product Groups:** 36, 39, 40

Cleator

Bollman Headwear Europe Ltd
Cleator Mills, Cleator, CA23 3DJ
Tel: 01946-810312 **Fax:** 01946-811087
E-mail: enquiries@kangolheadwareeurope.com
Website: http://www.bollmanhats.com
Directors: C. Corlett (Fin), C. Fitterling (Fin), R. Tanti (MD)
Managers: D. Lewis-Dalby (Mktg Serv Mgr)
Ultimate Holding Company: BOLLMAN HAT COMPANY (USA)
Registration no: 04315464 **VAT No.:** GB 256 5240 62
Date established: 2001 **Turnover:** £2m - £5m **No.of Employees:** 51 - 100
Product Groups: 23, 24

Date of Accounts	Dec 07	Dec 06	Dec 05
Sales Turnover	4234	4856	6052
Pre Tax Profit/Loss	-319	115	-608
Working Capital	492	789	757
Fixed Assets	384	415	497
Current Assets	1879	1957	1977
Current Liabilities	1387	1168	1220
ROCE% (Return on Capital Employed)	-36.4	9.6	-48.5
ROT% (Return on Turnover)	-7.5	2.4	-10.0

Miami Lights
The Forge, Cleator, CA23 3AD
Tel: 01946-817700 **Fax:** 01946-599266
E-mail: info@miamilights.co.uk
Directors: I. Statter (Prop)
Date established: 2003 **No.of Employees:** 1 - 10 **Product Groups:** 26, 35

Cleator Moor

Capalex
, Cleator Moor, CA25 5QB
Tel: 01946-811771 **Fax:** 01946-813681
E-mail: enquiries@capalex.com
Website: http://www.capalex.co.uk
Bank(s): Bank of Scotland, Kilmarnock
Directors: P. Beasley (MD)
Managers: G. Foster (Sales Prom Mgr)
Registration no: 03218112 **Date established:** 1979 **Turnover:** £5m - £10m
No.of Employees: 51 - 100 **Product Groups:** 14, 32, 34, 35, 36, 40, 46, 48, 49, 66

Cockermouth

P Chuter Ltd
High Gate Bewaldeth, Cockermouth, CA13 9SU
Tel: 01768-776137 **Fax:** 01768-776137
Website: http://www.paulchuter.co.uk
Directors: P. Chuter (Prop), D. Chuter (Prop)
Immediate Holding Company: PAUL CHUTER AGRICULTURAL SERVICES LIMITED
Registration no: 04745334 **Date established:** 2003
No.of Employees: 1 - 10 **Product Groups:** 41

Date of Accounts	Apr 11	Apr 10	Apr 09
Working Capital	17	25	38
Fixed Assets	63	76	80
Current Assets	149	161	127

Cumbria Saw Service Ltd
Low Road Brigham, Cockermouth, CA13 0XH
Tel: 01900-827720 **Fax:** 01900-827720
Directors: S. Marsh (Fin), S. Marsh (MD)
Immediate Holding Company: CUMBRIA SAW SERVICE LIMITED
Registration no: 04852624 **Date established:** 2003
No.of Employees: 1 - 10 **Product Groups:** 46, 48

Date of Accounts	Jul 11	Jul 10	Jul 09
Working Capital	-51	-42	-10
Fixed Assets	192	175	195
Current Assets	33	19	73

Herbs & Helpers
6 Butts Fold, Cockermouth, CA13 9HY
Tel: 01900-826392 **Fax:** 01900-826392
E-mail: info@herbalmedicineuk.com
Website: http://www.herbalmedicineuk.com
Directors: L. Hodgkinson (Prop)
Date established: 1993 **No.of Employees:** 1 - 10 **Product Groups:** 31

Thermoforce Ltd
Wakefield Road, Cockermouth, CA13 0HS
Tel: 01900-823231 **Fax:** 01900-825965
E-mail: sales@thermoforce.co.uk
Website: http://www.thermoforce.co.uk
Bank(s): National Westminster
Directors: A. Cole (MD)
Immediate Holding Company: THERMOFORCE LIMITED
Registration no: 00397449 **VAT No.:** GB 675 2331 34
Date established: 1945 **Turnover:** £250,000 - £500,000
No.of Employees: 11 - 20 **Product Groups:** 67

Date of Accounts	Jun 11	Jun 10	Jun 09
Sales Turnover	N/A	N/A	323
Pre Tax Profit/Loss	N/A	N/A	-60
Working Capital	33	69	55
Fixed Assets	2m	2m	1m
Current Assets	192	316	165
Current Liabilities	N/A	N/A	26

James Walker & Co. Ltd
Gote Brow, Cockermouth, CA13 0NH
Tel: 01900-823555 **Fax:** 01900-898354
E-mail: cockermouth@jameswalker.biz
Website: http://www.jameswalker.biz
Directors: P. Hall (MD)
Managers: L. Washington (Sales Admin)
Registration no: 02432592 **Date established:** 1882
No.of Employees: 251 - 500 **Product Groups:** 23, 25, 27, 29, 30, 32, 33, 36, 38, 40

Coniston

Duddon Electronics Ltd
Hazel Hall Torver, Coniston, LA21 8BU
Tel: 01539-441437
E-mail: enquiries@duddon-electronics.co.uk
Website: http://www.duddon-electronics.co.uk
Directors: J. Clunan (MD)
Immediate Holding Company: DUDDON ELECTRONICS LIMITED
Registration no: 01404736 **Date established:** 1978
Turnover: £500,000 - £1m **No.of Employees:** 1 - 10 **Product Groups:** 38

Date of Accounts	Mar 12	Mar 11	Mar 10
Working Capital	-0	-1	-1
Fixed Assets	1	1	1
Current Assets	40	21	17

Dalton In Furness

Baskets & Bows Fingers & Toes
22 Queen Street, Dalton In Furness, LA15 8EG
Tel: 01229-467868 **Fax:** 01229-467868
E-mail: susanburns@tiscali.co.uk
Website: http://www.basketsandbows-fingersandtoes.co.uk
Directors: S. Burns (Prop)
Registration no: 05070616 **Date established:** 2004
Turnover: Up to £250,000 **No.of Employees:** 1 - 10 **Product Groups:** 30, 61, 63

Egremont

A-Plant Ltd
Unit 8 Bridge End, Egremont, CA22 2RE
Tel: 01946-823073 **Fax:** 01946-821792
E-mail: egremont@aplant.com
Website: http://www.aplant.com
Directors: J. Cotton (MD)
Managers: C. Mann ()
Immediate Holding Company: A.PLANT LIMITED
Registration no: 05407712 **VAT No.:** GB 209 5687 37
Date established: 2005 **Turnover:** Up to £250,000
No.of Employees: 1 - 10 **Product Groups:** 83

Kendal

Axetec Guitar Pickups & Parts
Heath Close, Kendal, LA9 5BW
Tel: 01539-755015
E-mail: info@axetec.co.uk
Website: http://www.axetec.co.uk
Directors: K. Jolley (Dir)
Immediate Holding Company: AXETEC LIMITED
Registration no: 07156827 **Date established:** 2010
No.of Employees: 1 - 10 **Product Groups:** 49

Date of Accounts	Feb 12	Feb 11
Working Capital	32	25
Fixed Assets	4	1
Current Assets	92	94
Current Liabilities	57	66

G C Bell
12-16 Ann Street, Kendal, LA9 6AA
Tel: 01539-741080
Directors: G. Bell (Prop)
Date established: 1976 **No.of Employees:** 1 - 10 **Product Groups:** 40

C E M Catering Equipment
Unit 3b Boundary Bank Underbarrow Road, Kendal, LA9 5RR
Tel: 01539-445939 **Fax:** 01539-733243
E-mail: info@cemcateringequipment.co.uk
Website: http://www.cemcateringequipment.co.uk
Directors: A. Attrill (Fin), R. Attrill (Dir)
Immediate Holding Company: C E M CATERING EQUIPMENT LIMITED
Registration no: 04615536 **Date established:** 2002
No.of Employees: 1 - 10 **Product Groups:** 20, 40, 41

Date of Accounts	Jan 11	Jan 10	Jan 09
Working Capital	-26	11	26
Fixed Assets	256	273	278
Current Assets	127	196	167
Current Liabilities	39	42	38

Charter House Windows
Unit 9 Gatebeck Farm Gatebeck, Kendal, LA8 0HW
Tel: 01539-567979
E-mail: info@charterhousewindows.co.uk
Website: http://www.charterhousewindows.co.uk
Directors: R. Barrett (Prop)
Immediate Holding Company: THE WESTMORLAND COUNTY AGRICULTURAL SOCIETY LTD
Registration no: 03146325 **Date established:** 1996
Turnover: £500,000 - £1m **No.of Employees:** 1 - 10 **Product Groups:** 25, 35

Cooper Engraving
Unit 12-13 Staveley Mill Yard Back Lane, Staveley, Kendal, LA8 9LR
Tel: 01539-822220 **Fax:** 01539-822221
E-mail: cooper.engraving@ic24.net
Website: http://https://picasaweb.google.com/108687054354567654863/engravedwork
Directors: A. Marsh (Prop)
Turnover: Up to £250,000 **No.of Employees:** 1 - 10 **Product Groups:** 32, 48, 49

James Cropper plc
Burneside Mills Burneside, Kendal, LA9 6PZ
Tel: 01539-722002 **Fax:** 01539-818239
E-mail: info@cropper.com
Website: http://www.cropper.com
Bank(s): Barclays
Directors: N. Read (Sales & Mktg), J. Denman (Fin), I. Kindness (Sales)
Managers: A. Ripley (Buyer), C. Newton, D. Nicholson (Personnel)
Ultimate Holding Company: JAMES CROPPER PUBLIC LIMITED COMPANY
Immediate Holding Company: JAMES CROPPER PUBLIC LIMITED COMPANY
Registration no: 00030226 **Date established:** 1989
Turnover: £75m - £125m **No.of Employees:** 251 - 500
Product Groups: 27

Date of Accounts	Mar 12	Mar 09	Mar 10
Sales Turnover	78m	75m	76m
Pre Tax Profit/Loss	971	858	2m

see next page

James Cropper plc - Cont'd

Working Capital	20m	15m	15m
Fixed Assets	21m	23m	19m
Current Assets	31m	26m	30m
Current Liabilities	7m	7m	9m

1st Frame Cumbria Ltd
Old Parkers Building Stockbeck, Kendal, LA9 6HP
Tel: 01539-739486 **Fax:** 01539-739487
E-mail: office@1stframe.co.uk
Website: http://www.1stframe.co.uk
Directors: I. Meadowcroft (MD), C. James (Fin)
Immediate Holding Company: 1ST FRAME (CUMBRIA) LIMITED
Registration no: 04164993 **Date established:** 2001
No.of Employees: 11 - 20 **Product Groups:** 30

Date of Accounts	Apr 11	Apr 10	Apr 09
Working Capital	100	122	90
Fixed Assets	37	65	86
Current Assets	272	327	331

Furmanite International Ltd
Furman House Shap Road, Kendal, LA9 6RU
Tel: 01539-729009 **Fax:** 01642-465692
E-mail: infouk@furmanite.co.uk
Website: http://www.furmanite.co.uk
Bank(s): National Westminster Bank Plc
Directors: S. Berriman (Pers)
Managers: J. Jarvis
Ultimate Holding Company: FURMANITE CORPORATION (USA)
Immediate Holding Company: FURMANITE INTERNATIONAL LIMITED
Registration no: 00238721 **VAT No.:** GB 378 5218 21
Date established: 2029 **Turnover:** £20m - £50m
No.of Employees: 21 - 50 **Product Groups:** 48, 54

Date of Accounts	Dec 11	Dec 10	Dec 09
Sales Turnover	39m	34m	35m
Pre Tax Profit/Loss	5m	3m	2m
Working Capital	24m	24m	23m
Fixed Assets	3m	3m	4m
Current Assets	35m	34m	32m
Current Liabilities	2m	3m	2m

Gilbert Gilkes & Gordon Ltd
Canal Iron Works, Kendal, LA9 7BZ
Tel: 01539-720028 **Fax:** 01539-732110
E-mail: enquiries@gilkes.com
Website: http://www.gilkes.com
Bank(s): Barclays, 9 Highgate, Kendal
Directors: K. Rowland (Fin), A. Poole (Dir)
Managers: S. Cartmell (Purch Mgr), S. James (Sales Prom), R. Nixon (Tech Serv Mgr), S. Jones (Personnel)
Immediate Holding Company: GILBERT GILKES & GORDON LIMITED
Registration no: 00173768 **Date established:** 2021
Turnover: £20m - £50m **No.of Employees:** 101 - 250
Product Groups: 18, 37, 39, 40, 41, 45, 48, 67

Date of Accounts	Sep 11	Sep 10	Sep 09
Sales Turnover	26m	23m	22m
Pre Tax Profit/Loss	800	1m	1m
Working Capital	1m	2m	1m
Fixed Assets	4m	3m	3m
Current Assets	13m	10m	5m
Current Liabilities	9m	6m	4m

Heinz (Farley Health Products)
Mint Bridge Road, Kendal, LA9 6NL
Tel: 01539-723815 **Fax:** 01539-733324
E-mail: damian.cullen@heinz.co.uk
Website: http://www.heinz.com
Directors: G. Price (Fin)
Managers: P. Nelms (Mktg Serv Mgr), T. Lawrence (Purch Mgr), R. Chinoy (Personnel), D. Cullen (Mgr), L. Barbosa (Tech Serv Mgr)
Ultimate Holding Company: H.J. HEINZ
Registration no: 00147624 **Turnover:** £75m - £125m
No.of Employees: 101 - 250 **Product Groups:** 20

Kentmere Ltd
Kentmere Mills Staveley, Kendal, LA8 9PB
Tel: 01539-821365 **Fax:** 01539-821399
E-mail: sales@kentmere.sale.co.uk
Website: http://www.kentmere.co.uk
Bank(s): National Westminster Bank Plc
Directors: C. Chambers (Ch), G. Hume (Sales & Mktg), S. Mulvaney (MD)
Managers: S. Jones (Mgr), H. Hughes (Accounts)
Ultimate Holding Company: Kentmere Ltd
Registration no: 00087803 **VAT No.:** GB 153 9192 53
Date established: 2006 **Turnover:** £5m - £10m **No.of Employees:** 21 - 50
Product Groups: 27

Date of Accounts	Dec 09	Dec 08	Dec 07
Pre Tax Profit/Loss	N/A	N/A	554
Working Capital	2m	2m	1m
Fixed Assets	911	916	944
Current Assets	2m	2m	3m
Current Liabilities	N/A	N/A	1m

The Key Network
Low House Barn Old Hutton, Kendal, LA8 0NH
Tel: 01539-730890
E-mail: sales@thekeynetwork.co.uk
Website: http://www.thekeynetwork.co.uk
Directors: S. Mcelroy (Prop)
Date established: 1998 **No.of Employees:** 1 - 10 **Product Groups:** 80, 86

Millenium Polymeric Systems
Unit 28 Lake District Business Park Mint Bridge Road, Kendal, LA9 6NH
Tel: 01539-733701 **Fax:** 01539-733701
E-mail: mscott.mpsltd@virgin.net
Managers: M. Scott (Mgr)
Immediate Holding Company: MILLENNIUM POLYMERIC SYSTEMS LIMITED
Registration no: 03332059 **Date established:** 1997
No.of Employees: 1 - 10 **Product Groups:** 46, 48

Date of Accounts	Mar 11	Mar 10	Mar 09
Working Capital	-37	-41	-28
Fixed Assets	12	12	22
Current Assets	43	58	44

Northern Power Tools & Accessories Ltd
Unit 6 Shap Road Industrial Estate, Kendal, LA9 6NZ
Tel: 01539-735687 **Fax:** 01539-735687
E-mail: info@northern-powertools.co.uk
Website: http://www.northern-powertools.co.uk
Directors: M. Bewsher (MD), J. Warriner (Fin)
Immediate Holding Company: NORTHERN POWER TOOLS & ACCESSORIES LIMITED
Registration no: 04158037 **Date established:** 2001
No.of Employees: 1 - 10 **Product Groups:** 37

Date of Accounts	Feb 08	Feb 11	Feb 10
Working Capital	74	40	40
Fixed Assets	3	11	13
Current Assets	210	231	231

E H Penny
Fowl Ing Works Fowl Ing Lane, Kendal, LA9 6PH
Tel: 01539-721605 **Fax:** 01539-721605
Directors: C. Penny (Ptnr)
Turnover: Up to £250,000 **No.of Employees:** 1 - 10 **Product Groups:** 30, 35, 37, 40, 41, 42

Slewtic Ltd
6 Shap Road Industrial Estate, Kendal, LA9 6NZ
Tel: 01539-733114 **Fax:** 01539-733247
E-mail: sales@slewtic.co.uk
Website: http://www.slewtic.co.uk
Directors: J. Hadwin (Fin), S. Dodgson (MD)
Immediate Holding Company: SLEWTIC LIMITED
Registration no: 04253779 **Date established:** 2001
No.of Employees: 11 - 20 **Product Groups:** 41

Date of Accounts	Apr 12	Apr 11	Apr 09
Working Capital	147	118	-152
Fixed Assets	601	608	544
Current Assets	593	525	348

The Sunlight Service Group Ltd
Shap Road, Kendal, LA9 6DQ
Tel: 01539-723378 **Fax:** 01539-740921
E-mail: kendal@sunlight.co.uk
Website: http://www.sunlight.co.uk
Bank(s): HSBC Bank plc
Managers: K. Bakhat (Mgr)
Ultimate Holding Company: BERENDSEN PLC
Immediate Holding Company: THE SUNLIGHT SERVICE GROUP LIMITED
Registration no: 00228604 **Date established:** 2028 **Turnover:** £2m - £5m
No.of Employees: 101 - 250 **Product Groups:** 83

Date of Accounts	Dec 10	Dec 09	Dec 08
Sales Turnover	352m	351m	359m
Pre Tax Profit/Loss	14m	24m	17m
Working Capital	30m	18m	-2m
Fixed Assets	452m	481m	504m
Current Assets	118m	106m	91m
Current Liabilities	52m	47m	48m

T F M Engineering
1 Ghyll Mill Beehive Lane, New Hutton, Kendal, LA8 0AJ
Tel: 01539-733881 **Fax:** 01539-721616
E-mail: sales@tfmengineering.co.uk
Website: http://www.tfmengineering.co.uk
Directors: T. Mcfarlane (MD), R. McFarlen (Ptnr)
Immediate Holding Company: TFM ENGINEERING LIMITED
Registration no: 05426710 **Date established:** 2005
No.of Employees: 1 - 10 **Product Groups:** 41

Date of Accounts	May 11	May 10	May 09
Working Capital	63	57	45
Fixed Assets	49	54	63
Current Assets	126	131	127

Transtec Equipment Ltd
High Yews Crosthwaite, Kendal, LA8 8JB
Tel: 01539-568789 **Fax:** 01539-568678
E-mail: mail@transtecequipment.com
Website: http://www.transtecequipment.com
Directors: K. Jones (MD)
Immediate Holding Company: WEST HIGHLAND LEISURE LTD
Registration no: 03720984 **Date established:** 1999
No.of Employees: 1 - 10 **Product Groups:** 35, 39, 45

Date of Accounts	Mar 11	Mar 10	Mar 09
Working Capital	135	159	174
Fixed Assets	365	472	457
Current Assets	327	348	749

Travis Perkins plc
Mintsfeet Trading Estate, Kendal, LA9 6RX
Tel: 01539-731166 **Fax:** 01539-723338
E-mail: tony.fiddler@travisperkins.co.uk
Website: http://www.travisperkins.co.uk
Managers: T. Fiddler (Mgr)
Immediate Holding Company: TRAVIS PERKINS PLC
Registration no: 00824821 **Date established:** 1964
No.of Employees: 21 - 50 **Product Groups:** 33, 39

Date of Accounts	Dec 11	Dec 10	Dec 09
Sales Turnover	4779m	3153m	2931m
Pre Tax Profit/Loss	270m	197m	213m
Working Capital	133m	159m	248m
Fixed Assets	2771m	2749m	2108m
Current Assets	1421m	1329m	1035m
Current Liabilities	473m	412m	109m

Neil Webster & Co. Ltd
14 Finkle Street, Kendal, LA9 4AB
Tel: 01539-731518 **Fax:** 01539-725602
E-mail: neil@websterco.freeserve.co.uk
Website: http://www.websterco.freeserve.co.uk
Directors: N. Webster (MD)
Immediate Holding Company: NEIL WEBSTER & CO LTD
Registration no: 04394229 **Date established:** 2002
No.of Employees: 1 - 10 **Product Groups:** 80

Date of Accounts	Apr 08	Apr 07	Apr 06
Working Capital	-14	-6	-96
Fixed Assets	137	143	132
Current Assets	26	32	33
Current Liabilities	40	39	129

The Westmorland Gazette Newspaper
1 Wainwright Yard, Kendal, LA9 4DP
Tel: 01539-720555 **Fax:** 01539-723618
E-mail: andrew.thomas@kendal.newsquest.co.uk
Website: http://www.thisisthelakedistrict.co.uk
Bank(s): Lloyds TSB
Managers: A. Thomas
Immediate Holding Company: NEWSQUEST MEDIA GROUP
VAT No.: GB 667 8301 08 **Date established:** 1813 **Turnover:** £2m - £5m
No.of Employees: 21 - 50 **Product Groups:** 28

Westmorland Glass Kendal Ltd
Shap Road, Kendal, LA9 6LX
Tel: 01539-730000 **Fax:** 01539-740076
Directors: R. Farrar (Fin)
Ultimate Holding Company: PR BOOKS LIMITED
Immediate Holding Company: WESTMORLAND GLASS (KENDAL) LIMITED
Registration no: 01028553 **VAT No.:** GB 155 1492 69
Date established: 1971 **Turnover:** Up to £250,000
No.of Employees: 1 - 10 **Product Groups:** 30, 52, 66

Date of Accounts	Oct 07	Jan 11	Jan 10
Working Capital	194	147	62
Fixed Assets	171	1m	1m
Current Assets	317	233	132

Westmorland Packaging Ltd
Mintsfeet Road Estate Mintsfeet Road, Kendal, LA9 6LU
Tel: 01539-727300 **Fax:** 01539-731150
E-mail: sales@westpac.uk.com
Website: http://www.wespacpackaging.co.uk
Directors: S. Carter (Dir)
Immediate Holding Company: WESTMORLAND PACKAGING LIMITED
Registration no: 03643537 **Date established:** 1998
No.of Employees: 1 - 10 **Product Groups:** 27, 30, 67

Date of Accounts	Jul 11	Jul 10	Jul 09
Working Capital	-49	-56	-59
Fixed Assets	60	71	77
Current Assets	282	312	256
Current Liabilities	46	52	63

Keswick

Armathwaite Hall Hotel
Bassenthwaite, Keswick, CA12 4RE
Tel: 01768-776551 **Fax:** 01768-776220
E-mail: reservations@armathwaite-hall.com
Website: http://www.armathwaite-hall.com
Directors: C. Graves (Dir)
Managers: L. Lennox (Mktg Serv Mgr), S. Steele (Chief Mgr)
Immediate Holding Company: ARMATHWAITE HALL HOTEL LIMITED
Registration no: 01279666 **Date established:** 1976 **Turnover:** £2m - £5m
No.of Employees: 51 - 100 **Product Groups:** 69, 84, 89

Date of Accounts	Mar 11	Mar 10	Mar 09
Sales Turnover	4m	4m	N/A
Pre Tax Profit/Loss	397	436	-149
Working Capital	-2m	-4m	-8m
Fixed Assets	17m	17m	16m
Current Assets	264	287	344
Current Liabilities	916	2m	2m

Castlerigg Engineering Co. Ltd
Browfoot Works Penrith Road, Keswick, CA12 4LH
Tel: 01768-772876 **Fax:** 01768-772885
E-mail: tony@castlerigg-eng.co.uk
Directors: A. Stephenson (MD), S. Stephenson (Co Sec)
Immediate Holding Company: CASTLERIGG ENGINEERING COMPANY LIMITED
Registration no: 04564720 **VAT No.:** GB 442 7481 45
Date established: 2002 **Turnover:** Up to £250,000
No.of Employees: 1 - 10 **Product Groups:** 48

Date of Accounts	Dec 11	Dec 10	Dec 09
Working Capital	57	98	184
Fixed Assets	22	33	45
Current Assets	166	160	286

Crosthwaite Garage
Crosthwaite Road, Keswick, CA12 5PR
Tel: 01768-772606 **Fax:** 01768-772606
E-mail: zen58411@zen.co.uk
Website: http://www.crosthwaitegarage.co.uk
Directors: K. Taylor (Prop)
Immediate Holding Company: LAKELAND GUILD (HOLDINGS) COMPANY LIMITED
Date established: 2005 **Turnover:** Up to £250,000
No.of Employees: 1 - 10 **Product Groups:** 39

Date of Accounts	Sep 11	Sep 10	Sep 08
Working Capital	-14	-14	-14
Current Liabilities	14	14	N/A

Cumberland Pencil Museum
Southey Works Main Street, Keswick, CA12 5NG
Tel: 01768-773626 **Fax:** 01768-774679
E-mail: museum@acco-uk.co.uk
Website: http://www.pencils.co.uk
Managers: A. Farthing (Mgr)
Ultimate Holding Company: Fortune Brands Inc. (U.S.A.)
Immediate Holding Company: ACCO UK Ltd
VAT No.: GB 232 4189 79 **No.of Employees:** 11 - 20 **Product Groups:** 49, 64

Pitlochry In Lakeland
63-71 Main Street, Keswick, CA12 5DZ
Tel: 01768-772642 **Fax:** 01768-772642
Website: http://www.ewm.co.uk
Managers: S. Langcake
No.of Employees: 1 - 10 **Product Groups:** 23, 24

Kirkby In Furness

Burlington Slate Ltd (Head Office)
Cavendish House, Kirkby In Furness, LA17 7UN
Tel: 01229-889661 **Fax:** 01229-889466
E-mail: sales@burlingtonstone.co.uk
Website: http://www.burlingtonstone.co.uk
Bank(s): Barclays Bank PLC, London

Directors: N. Williams (Sales & Mktg), R. Irwin (MD)
Ultimate Holding Company: BURLINGTON SLATE LIMITED
Immediate Holding Company: BURLINGTON SLATE LIMITED
Registration no: 01781765 **VAT No.:** GB 312 2159 07
Date established: 1984 **Turnover:** £5m - £10m
No.of Employees: 101 - 250 **Product Groups:** 14, 26, 33

Date of Accounts	Dec 10	Dec 09	Dec 08
Sales Turnover	9m	7m	N/A
Pre Tax Profit/Loss	300	-7	132
Working Capital	3m	3m	879
Fixed Assets	2m	2m	992
Current Assets	4m	4m	2m
Current Liabilities	702	796	660

Kirkby Stephen

Brockhill Enterprises Ltd

Hobsons Lane, Kirkby Stephen, CA17 4RN
Tel: 01768-372027 **Fax:** 01768-372049
E-mail: sales@brockcom.co.uk
Website: http://www.brockcom.co.uk
Directors: A. Purnell (MD)
Immediate Holding Company: BROCKHILL ENTERPRISES LIMITED
Registration no: 02080001 **Date established:** 1986
Turnover: £500,000 - £1m **No.of Employees:** 11 - 20 **Product Groups:** 37

Date of Accounts	Mar 11	Mar 10	Mar 09
Working Capital	27	-46	-18
Fixed Assets	307	312	322
Current Assets	166	130	125

Ian Carrick

Unit 1 Hartley Fold Hartley, Kirkby Stephen, CA17 4JH
Tel: 01768-372600 **Fax:** 01768-372600
Directors: I. Carrick (Prop)
Registration no: 04440338 **Date established:** 2002
No.of Employees: 1 - 10 **Product Groups:** 40

Lakeland Laser Ltd

Crossfield Mill Hobson Lane Hobson Lane, Kirkby Stephen, CA17 4RN
Tel: 01768-372200 **Fax:** 01768-374030
E-mail: stephenreay@lakelandlaser.co.uk
Website: http://www.lakelandlaser.co.uk
Directors: J. Reay (Fin), S. Reay (MD)
Immediate Holding Company: LAKELAND LASER LIMITED
Registration no: 03405513 **Date established:** 1997
Turnover: £10m - £20m **No.of Employees:** 1 - 10 **Product Groups:** 24, 28, 34, 43, 45, 46, 47, 48, 84, 85, 89

Date of Accounts	Apr 11	Apr 10	Apr 09
Working Capital	402	339	376
Fixed Assets	25	20	24
Current Assets	656	580	566

Maryport

Elite Supplies

25c Solway Trading Estate, Maryport, CA15 8NF
Tel: 01900-810111 **Fax:** 01900-810222
E-mail: sales@elite-supplies.co.uk
Website: http://www.elite-supplies.co.uk
Managers: P. Evans (Mgr)
No.of Employees: 1 - 10 **Product Groups:** 24, 63

Grants Smoke House Ltd

Unit 14 Solway Trading Estate, Maryport, CA15 8NF
Tel: 01900-818585 **Fax:** 01900-819717
E-mail: sales@grantssmokehouse.com
Website: http://www.grantssmokehouse.com
Directors: A. Mcmorran (MD), A. Murphy (Fin), J. Wood (Fin), N. Hill (Sales)
Managers: T. Hamer (Purch Mgr), J. White (Sales Prom Mgr)
Ultimate Holding Company: CUMBRIAN HOLDINGS LIMITED
Immediate Holding Company: CSL REALISATIONS 2011 LIMITED
Registration no: 04104794 **Date established:** 2000
Turnover: £125m - £250m **No.of Employees:** 51 - 100
Product Groups: 20

Date of Accounts	Mar 08	Mar 09	Mar 10
Sales Turnover	128m	146m	155m
Pre Tax Profit/Loss	-2m	-7m	3m
Working Capital	-1m	-11m	-8m
Fixed Assets	16m	17m	15m
Current Assets	22m	24m	21m
Current Liabilities	5m	13m	12m

Support In Sport Ltd

Glasson Industrial Estate, Maryport, CA15 8NT
Tel: 01900-812796 **Fax:** 01900-815509
E-mail: sales@supportinsport.com
Website: http://www.supportinsport.com
Bank(s): Bank of Scotland
Managers: P. Nichols (Mgr)
Ultimate Holding Company: SUPPORT IN SPORT GROUP LIMITED
Immediate Holding Company: SUPPORT IN SPORT (UK) LIMITED
Registration no: 04174873 **Date established:** 2001 **Turnover:** £2m - £5m
No.of Employees: 21 - 50 **Product Groups:** 26, 30, 49, 66

Date of Accounts	Dec 11	Dec 10	Dec 09
Sales Turnover	N/A	3m	4m
Working Capital	225	226	258
Fixed Assets	120	81	26
Current Assets	2m	1m	999

Thomas Armstrong Aggregates Ltd

Workington Road Flimby, Maryport, CA15 8RY
Tel: 01900-68114 **Fax:** 01900-66136
E-mail: aggregates@thomasarmstrong.co.uk
Website: http://www.thomasarmstrong.co.uk
Directors: F. Harkness (Dir), J. Denham (MD), P. Armstrong (Fin)
Managers: T. Bennett (Tech Serv Mgr), J. Baliff (Personnel)
Ultimate Holding Company: THOMAS ARMSTRONG (HOLDINGS) LIMITED
Immediate Holding Company: THOMAS ARMSTRONG (AGGREGATES) LIMITED
Registration no: 01278704 **Date established:** 1976
Turnover: £10m - £20m **No.of Employees:** 101 - 250
Product Groups: 14, 45, 66

Date of Accounts	Sep 08	Sep 09	Oct 10
Sales Turnover	21m	17m	17m
Pre Tax Profit/Loss	2m	2m	1m
Working Capital	3m	5m	3m
Fixed Assets	6m	5m	5m
Current Assets	8m	8m	7m
Current Liabilities	2m	2m	2m

Thomas Armstrong Holdings Ltd

Workington Road Flimby, Maryport, CA15 8RY
Tel: 01900-68211 **Fax:** 01900- 602672
E-mail: david.atkinson@thomasarmstrong.co.uk
Website: http://www.thomasarmstrong.co.uk
Directors: P. Armstrong (Fin)
Managers: D. Atkinson, J. Bailiff (Personnel), S. Jay (Tech Serv Mgr), J. Wilson (Chief Buyer)
Immediate Holding Company: THOMAS ARMSTRONG (HOLDINGS) LIMITED
Registration no: 00244751 **VAT No.:** GB 533 7245 50
Date established: 1930 **Turnover:** £75m - £125m
No.of Employees: 101 - 250 **Product Groups:** 51, 52

Date of Accounts	Sep 08	Sep 09	Oct 10
Sales Turnover	144m	107m	110m
Pre Tax Profit/Loss	6m	6m	8m
Working Capital	32m	38m	44m
Fixed Assets	51m	47m	45m
Current Assets	55m	58m	67m
Current Liabilities	13m	12m	13m

Millom

Drum Closures Ltd

Borwick Rails, Millom, LA18 4JT
Tel: 01229-772101 **Fax:** 01229-774972
E-mail: timc@drum-closures.co.uk
Website: http://www.drum-closures.co.uk
Bank(s): Barclays Bank PLC, Pall Mall
Directors: T. Clark (Tech Serv), T. Clark (Tech Serv), S. Lupton (Fin)
Ultimate Holding Company: METAL RINGS CO LIMITED
Immediate Holding Company: DRUM CLOSURES LIMITED
Registration no: 00500963 **Date established:** 1951 **Turnover:** £2m - £5m
No.of Employees: 11 - 20 **Product Groups:** 35

Date of Accounts	Aug 11	Aug 10	Aug 09
Working Capital	408	397	384
Fixed Assets	134	357	371
Current Assets	792	714	634

P J Woodhouse & Co.

Bootle Station, Millom, LA19 5XB
Tel: 01229-718359 **Fax:** 01229-718358
E-mail: pwoodhouse1@btconnect.com
Directors: P. Woodhouse (Prop)
Date established: 1993 **No.of Employees:** 1 - 10 **Product Groups:** 41

Milnthorpe

C M Signs

Leighton Beck Road Hazelwood, Slack Head, Milnthorpe, LA7 7AX
Tel: 01539-563000
Directors: C. Merckel (Prop)
No.of Employees: 1 - 10 **Product Groups:** 30, 49, 52

John Dobson Milnthorpe Ltd

Bela Mill, Milnthorpe, LA7 7QP
Tel: 01539-563528 **Fax:** 01539-562481
E-mail: sbrown@combs.co.uk
Website: http://www.combs.co.uk
Bank(s): Barclays, Kendal
Directors: S. Brown (Dir)
Immediate Holding Company: JOHN DOBSON (MILNTHORPE) LIMITED
Registration no: 00205983 **VAT No.:** GB 153 6767 43
Date established: 2025 **Turnover:** £1m - £2m **No.of Employees:** 11 - 20
Product Groups: 22, 24, 29, 30, 33, 35, 36, 49

Date of Accounts	Dec 11	Dec 10	Dec 09
Working Capital	151	173	202
Fixed Assets	41	50	59
Current Assets	327	348	456

Moor Row

Atkins Ltd

Wastwater Pavilion Ingwell Drive, Westlakes Science & Technology Park, Moor Row, CA24 3JZ
Tel: 01946-692345 **Fax:** 01946-692139
E-mail: michael.robertson@atkinsglobal.com
Website: http://www.atkinsglobal.com
Managers: M. Robertson (Mgr)
Ultimate Holding Company: WS ATKINS PLC
Immediate Holding Company: ATKINS LIMITED
Registration no: 00688424 **VAT No.:** GB 209 8612 53
Date established: 1961 **Turnover:** £75m - £125m
No.of Employees: 51 - 100 **Product Groups:** 51, 84

Date of Accounts	Mar 12	Mar 11	Mar 10
Sales Turnover	791m	844m	872m
Pre Tax Profit/Loss	46m	25m	55m
Working Capital	265m	266m	251m
Fixed Assets	166m	191m	234m
Current Assets	652m	654m	612m
Current Liabilities	214m	231m	243m

Penrith

Age UK Carlisle & Eden

Sandgate, Penrith, CA11 7TP
Tel: 01768-863618 **Fax:** 01768-863792
E-mail: office@ageukcarlisleandeden.org.uk
Website: http://www.ageuk.org.uk
Managers: A. Murray
Immediate Holding Company: AGE UK CARLISLE AND EDEN
Registration no: 06785041 **Date established:** 2009
No.of Employees: 11 - 20 **Product Groups:** 38, 67

Date of Accounts	Mar 11	Mar 10
Sales Turnover	1m	1m
Pre Tax Profit/Loss	25	139
Working Capital	781	717
Fixed Assets	924	954
Current Assets	847	775
Current Liabilities	52	48

A K Bell

Dunroamin Cross Dormont, Howtown, Penrith, CA10 2NA
Tel: 01768-486537 **Fax:** 01768-486537
E-mail: library@pkc.gov.uk
Website: http://www.pkc.gov.uk
Directors: A. Bell (Prop)
Date established: 1969 **No.of Employees:** 1 - 10 **Product Groups:** 41

Beqacon Edge Specialised Nursing Home

Beacon Edge Home, Penrith, CA11 8BN
Tel: 01768-866885 **Fax:** 01768-210758
E-mail: admin@beaconinterim.co.uk
Website: http://www.beaconinterin.co.uk/
Managers: D. Byrne (Mgr)
Date established: 2005 **Turnover:** £250,000 - £500,000
No.of Employees: 21 - 50 **Product Groups:** 80, 87

Frank Bird Poultry Ltd

Underlyne Langwathby, Penrith, CA10 1NB
Tel: 01768-881555 **Fax:** 01768-881868
E-mail: frankbird@frankbirdpoultry.co.uk
Website: http://www.frankbirdpoultry.co.uk
Directors: F. Bird (Prop)
Ultimate Holding Company: F AND N ONE LIMITED
Immediate Holding Company: BALINGOUR LIMITED
Registration no: 01264817 **Date established:** 1976
Turnover: £10m - £20m **No.of Employees:** 101 - 250
Product Groups: 20, 62

Date of Accounts	Jan 10	Jan 09	Jan 11
Sales Turnover	10m	9m	11m
Pre Tax Profit/Loss	336	364	200
Working Capital	706	346	955
Fixed Assets	1m	1m	979
Current Assets	2m	1m	2m
Current Liabilities	120	120	28

Colin Dawson Ltd

High Mill Langwathby, Penrith, CA10 1NB
Tel: 01768-889084 **Fax:** 01768-889083
E-mail: dawson@xlninternet.co.uk
Directors: C. Dawson (MD)
Immediate Holding Company: COLIN DAWSON LIMITED
Registration no: 04220175 **Date established:** 2001
No.of Employees: 1 - 10 **Product Groups:** 41

Date of Accounts	Oct 11	Oct 10	Oct 09
Working Capital	61	46	11
Fixed Assets	22	21	28
Current Assets	230	311	190

Emersons Commercial Services Ltd

Unit 39 Stalker Road, Gilwilly Industrial Estate, Penrith, CA11 9BG
Tel: 01768-864531 **Fax:** 01768-899367
Directors: A. Emerson (MD)
Immediate Holding Company: EMERSON'S COMMERCIAL SERVICES LIMITED
Registration no: 03565458 **Date established:** 1998
No.of Employees: 1 - 10 **Product Groups:** 38, 42

Date of Accounts	Sep 11	Sep 10	Sep 09
Working Capital	294	302	266
Fixed Assets	41	46	55
Current Assets	361	407	367

Four Square PR

Lowther Estate Office Lowther, Penrith, CA10 2HG
Tel: 01931-712999 **Fax:** 01768-864151
E-mail: tony@4-sq.com
Website: http://www.4-sq.com
Directors: K. Morton (Fin), S. Wilson (Chief Op Offcr), C. Higgins (Fin), R. Brunskill (MD), T. Brunskill (MD)
Immediate Holding Company: Four Square PR Ltd
Registration no: 04004458 **Date established:** 2000
No.of Employees: 1 - 10 **Product Groups:** 81

Date of Accounts	Oct 08	Oct 07	Oct 06
Working Capital	45	36	24
Fixed Assets	1	1	4
Current Assets	74	57	53
Current Liabilities	29	21	29

Primasonics International Ltd

North Lakes Business Park Flusco, Penrith, CA11 0JG
Tel: 01768-480372 **Fax:** 01768-480374
E-mail: sound@primasonics.com
Website: http://www.primasonics.com
Managers: K. Fox (Fin Mgr)
Immediate Holding Company: PRIMASONICS INTERNATIONAL LIMITED
Registration no: 03557946 **Date established:** 1998
No.of Employees: 1 - 10 **Product Groups:** 40, 67

Date of Accounts	Oct 11	Oct 10	Oct 09
Working Capital	87	49	77
Fixed Assets	20	19	21
Current Assets	152	124	142

D E & J E Raine

4 Hopper Hill Crosby Ravensworth, Penrith, CA10 3JN
Tel: 01931-715223 **Fax:** 01931-715099

see next page

D E & J E Raine - Cont'd
Directors: D. Raine (Ptnr)
Date established: 1982 **No.of Employees:** 1 - 10 **Product Groups:** 35

Replenergy Limited
7 Brookside Tirril, Penrith, CA10 2JG
Tel: 01768-892027 **Fax:** 01768-892027
E-mail: info@replenergy.co.uk
Website: http://replenergy.co.uk
Directors: I. Cleasby (Dir)
Registration no: 5911290 **Date established:** 2006
Turnover: Up to £250,000 **No.of Employees:** 1 - 10 **Product Groups:** 37

Date of Accounts	Aug 09	Aug 08	Aug 07
Working Capital	-27	-16	-7
Fixed Assets	7	5	N/A
Current Assets	19	29	17

Rickerby Ltd
Harvester House Greenbank Road, Gilwilly Industrial Estate, Penrith, CA11 9FB
Tel: 01768-863718 **Fax:** 01768-899117
E-mail: sales@rickerby.net
Website: http://www.rickerby.net
Managers: K. Connoly (Mgr)
Ultimate Holding Company: RICKERBY HOLDINGS LIMITED
Immediate Holding Company: RICKERBY LIMITED
Registration no: 04985069 **Date established:** 2003
No.of Employees: 11 - 20 **Product Groups:** 41

Date of Accounts	Sep 11	Sep 10	Sep 09
Sales Turnover	44m	42m	39m
Pre Tax Profit/Loss	949	755	1m
Working Capital	4m	3m	3m
Fixed Assets	936	693	688
Current Assets	14m	12m	13m
Current Liabilities	2m	1m	4m

Soft- Apeth Ltd
7 Brookside Tirril, Penrith, CA10 2JG
Tel: 01768-892027 **Fax:** 01768-892027
E-mail: enquiries@soft-apeth.co.uk
Website: http://www.soft-apeth.co.uk
Directors: E. Cleasby (Dir), E. Cleasby (Fin), I. Cleasby (Dir), I. Cleasby (MD)
Managers: J. Jackson (Sales Prom Mgr)
Immediate Holding Company: SOFT- APETH LIMITED
Registration no: 05006212 **Date established:** 2004
No.of Employees: 1 - 10 **Product Groups:** 61

Date of Accounts	Jan 08	Jan 07	Jan 06
Working Capital	19	25	23
Fixed Assets	1	2	1
Current Assets	22	41	38
Current Liabilities	3	16	15

Charles R Sykes
4 Great Dockray, Penrith, CA11 7BL
Tel: 01768-862418 **Fax:** 01768-862418
E-mail: info@charlesrsykes.co.uk
Website: http://www.charlesrsykes.co.uk
Directors: T. Rosling (Prop)
Date established: 1946 **No.of Employees:** 1 - 10 **Product Groups:** 36, 39, 40

The Wood Workshop
Units 7-8 Redhills Business Park Redhills Lane, Redhills, Penrith, CA11 0DT
Tel: 01768-899895 **Fax:** 01768-899895
E-mail: enquiries@woodworkshop.co.uk
Website: http://www.woodworkshop.co.uk
Directors: R. Harrison (Prop)
No.of Employees: 1 - 10 **Product Groups:** 25

Seascale

Cumbrian Goat Experience
Woodhow Farm Wasdale, Seascale, CA20 1ET
Tel: 01946-726246
E-mail: info@cumbrian-goat-experience.co.uk
Website: http://www.cumbrian-goat-experience.co.uk
Directors: R. Scrivener (Ptnr)
Date established: 2007 **No.of Employees:** 1 - 10 **Product Groups:** 01

Sedbergh

J J Martin Commercial Catering
Norcroft House Joss Lane, Sedbergh, LA10 5AS
Tel: 01539-620400 **Fax:** 01539-621271
E-mail: angela@jj-martin.co.uk
Website: http://www.catering-appliance.com
Directors: A. Wearmouth (Prop)
No.of Employees: 1 - 10 **Product Groups:** 36, 40

Mudd Farm Equipment
Park View Marthwaite, Sedbergh, LA10 5HS
Tel: 01539-620704 **Fax:** 01539-621573
Directors: M. Mudd (Prop)
Immediate Holding Company: MICHAEL MUDD LIMITED
Registration no: 04634044 **Date established:** 2003
No.of Employees: 1 - 10 **Product Groups:** 41

Date of Accounts	Mar 12	Mar 11	Mar 10
Working Capital	225	189	172
Fixed Assets	74	84	80
Current Assets	296	267	293

Henry Shine UK Holdings Ltd
Kings Yard Main Street, Sedbergh, LA10 5BJ
Tel: 01539-620778
Managers: P. Clough (Mgr)
No.of Employees: 11 - 20 **Product Groups:** 38, 67

Ulverston

Acrastyle Ltd
North Lonsdale Road, Ulverston, LA12 9EB
Tel: 01229-583232 **Fax:** 01229-582586
E-mail: sales@acrastyle.co.uk
Website: http://www.acrastyle.co.uk
Managers: K. Fenwick (Personnel), W. Wilson (Comptroller), J. Brown (Comm), S. Baldwin
Ultimate Holding Company: S & S POWER SWITCHGEAR (INDIA)
Immediate Holding Company: ACRASTYLE LIMITED
Registration no: 00728049 **Date established:** 1962 **Turnover:** £5m - £10m
No.of Employees: 51 - 100 **Product Groups:** 35, 37, 38, 39, 40

Date of Accounts	Mar 12	Mar 11	Sep 09
Sales Turnover	5m	9m	8m
Pre Tax Profit/Loss	22	-801	-160
Working Capital	-519	-511	432
Fixed Assets	846	878	1m
Current Assets	2m	2m	3m
Current Liabilities	704	2m	2m

Chromtechmic Ltd
Unit 6 Low Mill Business Park, Ulverston, LA12 9EE
Tel: 01229-581551
E-mail: edavidson@chromatechnic.com
Website: http://www.chromatechnic.com
Managers: E. Davison (Mgr)
Immediate Holding Company: I.T. SHAW LIMITED
Registration no: 05529261 **VAT No.:** GB 149 2793 33
Date established: 1994 **Turnover:** £500,000 - £1m
No.of Employees: 1 - 10 **Product Groups:** 37, 38

Date of Accounts	Sep 11	Sep 10	Sep 09
Working Capital	338	213	133
Fixed Assets	453	458	376
Current Assets	628	449	260
Current Liabilities	48	43	N/A

Cross Services Engineering Ltd
North Lonsdale Road, Ulverston, LA12 9DR
Tel: 01229-588600 **Fax:** 01229-588600
Website: http://www.crossgroup.co.uk
Managers: T. Jones (Mgr)
Ultimate Holding Company: Cross Group Ltd
Immediate Holding Company: Profit Bank Ltd
Registration no: 05624965 **Date established:** 2005
No.of Employees: 11 - 20 **Product Groups:** 37, 52, 84

Dry Ice Solution
The Rusland Pool Hotel Haverthwaite, Ulverston, LA12 8AA
Tel: 07710-939010 **Fax:** 01229-861425
E-mail: sales@dryicesolutions.co.uk
Website: http://www.dryicesolutions.co.uk
Directors: B. Pound (Prop)
Date established: 2008 **Turnover:** Up to £250,000
No.of Employees: 11 - 20 **Product Groups:** 20, 21, 46

Forge Europa Ltd
35 Princes Street, Ulverston, LA12 7NQ
Tel: 01229-580000 **Fax:** 01229-586890
E-mail: info@forge-europa.co.uk
Website: http://www.forge-europa.co.uk
Directors: R. Barton (MD)
Managers: I. Dixon (Sales Prom Mgr)
Immediate Holding Company: FORGE EUROPA LTD
Registration no: 02902591 **Date established:** 1994
No.of Employees: 21 - 50 **Product Groups:** 27, 37, 48

Date of Accounts	Nov 11	Nov 10	Nov 09
Working Capital	2m	2m	2m
Fixed Assets	775	643	167
Current Assets	2m	2m	2m

Furness Winding Co. Ltd
Kings Works Kings Road, Ulverston, LA12 0BT
Tel: 01229-586041 **Fax:** 01229-586391
E-mail: sales@furnesswinding.co.uk
Directors: D. Smith (MD)
Immediate Holding Company: FURNESS WINDING COMPANY LTD
Registration no: 01464925 **Date established:** 1979
Turnover: Up to £250,000 **No.of Employees:** 1 - 10 **Product Groups:** 48

Hill Foot Garden Centre
County Road, Ulverston, LA12 7SE
Tel: 01229-587282 **Fax:** 01229-586633
E-mail: sales@hillfootgc.co.uk
Website: http://www.hillfoot-gardencentre.co.uk
Directors: J. Dodd (Prop)
No.of Employees: 1 - 10 **Product Groups:** 25, 33, 35, 66

J G Black Polymers Ltd
Unit 2 Cross Lane Court Cross Lane, Ulverston, LA12 9DQ
Tel: 01229-580512 **Fax:** 01229-580515
E-mail: john@jgblackpolymers.co.uk
Website: http://www.jgblackpolymers.co.uk
Directors: J. Black (Dir), R. Black (Co Sec)
Immediate Holding Company: J.G. BLACK POLYMERS LIMITED
Registration no: 02753600 **VAT No.:** GB 442 8880 26
Date established: 1992 **Turnover:** £250,000 - £500,000
No.of Employees: 1 - 10 **Product Groups:** 30

Date of Accounts	Dec 11	Dec 10	Dec 09
Working Capital	277	9	535
Fixed Assets	463	805	439
Current Assets	327	316	736

Marl International Ltd
Morecambe Road, Ulverston, LA12 9BN
Tel: 01229-582430 **Fax:** 01229-585155
E-mail: sales@marl.co.uk
Website: http://www.leds.co.uk
Bank(s): HSBC Bank plc
Directors: D. Ford (Comm), A. Rawlinson (MD)
Managers: G. Round (Nat Sales Mgr), H. Thurgood (Tech Serv Mgr), A. Rawlinson, K. Procter
Ultimate Holding Company: MARL INTERNATIONAL HOLDINGS LIMITED
Immediate Holding Company: MARL INTERNATIONAL LIMITED
Registration no: 01109955 **VAT No.:** GB 155 7230 69
Date established: 1973 **Turnover:** £5m - £10m
No.of Employees: 51 - 100 **Product Groups:** 30, 37, 38, 39, 40, 45, 51, 52, 54

Date of Accounts	May 11	May 10	May 09
Sales Turnover	8m	4m	5m
Pre Tax Profit/Loss	958	180	370
Working Capital	926	126	186
Fixed Assets	426	2m	2m
Current Assets	3m	2m	1m
Current Liabilities	1m	494	598

Oxley Developments Company Ltd
Priory Park, Ulverston, LA12 9QG
Tel: 01229-582621 **Fax:** 01229-585090
E-mail: sales@oxleygroup.com
Website: http://www.oxleygroup.com
Bank(s): HSBC Bank plc
Directors: A. Bednarek (Sales & Mktg), M. Pritchard (Co Sec), P. Cotterill (MD), J. Waddington (Fin)
Ultimate Holding Company: OXLEY INTERNATIONAL INC (PANAMA)
Immediate Holding Company: OXLEY GROUP LIMITED
Registration no: 00964834 **VAT No.:** GB 154 4140 91
Date established: 1969 **Turnover:** £10m - £20m
No.of Employees: 101 - 250 **Product Groups:** 33, 37, 38

Date of Accounts	Sep 11	Sep 10	Sep 09
Sales Turnover	14m	17m	16m
Pre Tax Profit/Loss	-1m	312	-202
Working Capital	3m	3m	3m
Fixed Assets	1m	1m	1m
Current Assets	6m	7m	6m
Current Liabilities	428	658	717

Playdale Playgrounds Ltd
Haverthwaite, Ulverston, LA12 8AE
Tel: 01539-531561 **Fax:** 01539-531539
E-mail: enquiries@playdale.co.uk
Website: http://www.playdale.co.uk
Bank(s): Barclays
Directors: G. Croasdale (Fin), B. Leahey (Sales & Mktg)
Managers: J. Nicholson (Personnel), R. Beach, J. Caldwell (Purch Mgr), B. Rooney (Tech Serv Mgr)
Immediate Holding Company: PLAYDALE PLAYGROUNDS LIMITED
Registration no: 00525615 **VAT No.:** GB 155 6253 62
Date established: 1953 **Turnover:** £10m - £20m
No.of Employees: 101 - 250 **Product Groups:** 49

Date of Accounts	Dec 11	Dec 10	Dec 09
Sales Turnover	13m	15m	12m
Pre Tax Profit/Loss	508	477	283
Working Capital	1m	696	347
Fixed Assets	434	493	471
Current Assets	3m	3m	4m
Current Liabilities	1m	1m	1m

Tronic Ltd
Low Mill Business Park, Ulverston, LA12 9EE
Tel: 01229-580500 **Fax:** 01229-586604
E-mail: sales@tronic.co.uk
Website: http://www.tronicweb.com
Directors: L. Mcalister (Co Sec), L. McAlister (Fin), M. Jones (MD)
Managers: W. Jackson (Develop Mgr), C. McKenzie (Sales Prom Mgr), M. Bell (I.T. Exec)
Ultimate Holding Company: EXPRO INTERNATIONAL GROUP LIMITED
Immediate Holding Company: TRONIC LIMITED
Registration no: 01415875 **VAT No.:** GB 698 6018 83
Date established: 1979 **Turnover:** £50m - £75m **No.of Employees:** 1 - 10
Product Groups: 37

Whitehaven

Ashtead Plant Hire Ltd
Red Lonning Industrial Estate, Whitehaven, CA28 6SJ
Tel: 01946-64613 **Fax:** 01946- 691267
E-mail: whitehaven@aplant.com
Website: http://www.aplant.com
Bank(s): Lloyds TSB Bank plc
Managers: S. Carruthers (Mgr)
Immediate Holding Company: ASHTEAD PLANT HIRE
Registration no: 00000444 **Turnover:** £10m - £20m
No.of Employees: 11 - 20 **Product Groups:** 83

J Dixon & Son Ltd
10 Lowther Street, Whitehaven, CA28 7AL
Tel: 01946-692351 **Fax:** 01946-66657
E-mail: wrcs_dixon@hotmail.com
Website: http://www.sjdixon.co.uk
Directors: D. Dixon (MD)
Immediate Holding Company: J.DIXON & SON,LIMITED
Registration no: 00584915 **Date established:** 1957 **Turnover:** £2m - £5m
No.of Employees: 21 - 50 **Product Groups:** 24

Date of Accounts	Jan 09	Jan 10	Jan 11
Sales Turnover	8m	6m	4m
Pre Tax Profit/Loss	-12	-944	-249
Working Capital	-270	-321	2m
Fixed Assets	9m	8m	8m
Current Assets	1m	1m	3m
Current Liabilities	258	191	212

Jewson Ltd
Timber Yard Coach Road, Whitehaven, CA28 7TB
Tel: 01946-692257 **Fax:** 01946-691449
E-mail: briancoulthard@jewsons.co.uk
Website: http://www.jewson.co.uk
Managers: B. Coulthard (District Mgr)
Ultimate Holding Company: COMPAGNIE DE SAINT GOBAIN (FRANCE)
Immediate Holding Company: JEWSON LIMITED
Registration no: 00348407 **VAT No.:** GB 497 7184 83
Date established: 1939 **No.of Employees:** 1 - 10 **Product Groups:** 66

Date of Accounts	Dec 11	Dec 10	Dec 09
Sales Turnover	1606m	1547m	1485m
Pre Tax Profit/Loss	18m	100m	45m
Working Capital	-345m	-250m	-349m
Fixed Assets	496m	387m	461m
Current Assets	657m	1005m	1320m
Current Liabilities	66m	120m	64m

Konecranes
Unit A24 Haig Enterprise Park, Whitehaven, CA28 9AN
Tel: 01946-61667 **Fax:** 01946- 693219
E-mail: paul.sellers@konecranes.com
Website: http://www.konecranes.com
Managers: M. Mcgarry (Reg Mgr), P. Sellars (Reg Mgr)
Registration no: 00969869 **No.of Employees:** 1 - 10 **Product Groups:** 38, 39, 84

Smurfit Kappa Composites
Richmond Works Moresby Road, Hensingham, Whitehaven, CA28 8TS
Tel: 01946-61671 **Fax:** 01946- 592281
E-mail: marketing@smurfitkappa.co.uk
Website: http://www.smurfitkappa.co.uk
Bank(s): SEB
Managers: G. Frazer (Purch Mgr), K. Nichol (Mgr), N. Bridge (Sales Prom Mgr), T. Scott (Tech Serv Mgr), T. McCooey (Comptroller), C. Monkhouse (Personnel)
Ultimate Holding Company: ASSIDOMAN (SWEDEN)
Immediate Holding Company: ASSIDOMAN PACKAGING UK LTD
Registration no: 03566845 **Turnover:** £20m - £50m
No.of Employees: 51 - 100 **Product Groups:** 27, 45, 84

Wigton

Contract Fencing
Unit 16 Station Yard Station Road, Wigton, CA7 9BA
Tel: 01697-344405 **Fax:** 01697-344259
E-mail: info@contractfencing.ltd.uk
Website: http://www.contractfencing.ltd.uk
Directors: T. Davison (MD)
No.of Employees: 1 - 10 **Product Groups:** 35, 48, 52

Innovia Films Ltd
Station Road, Wigton, CA7 9BG
Tel: 01697-342281 **Fax:** 01697-341417
E-mail: filmsinfo@innoviafilms.com
Website: http://www.innoviafilms.com
Bank(s): Barclays Bank PLC
Directors: D. Horton (Fin)
Ultimate Holding Company: INNOVIA FILMS (HOLDING 1) LIMITED
Immediate Holding Company: INNOVIA FILMS LIMITED
Registration no: 00271998 **VAT No.:** GB 845 4559 96
Date established: 1933 **Turnover:** £125m - £250m
No.of Employees: 501 - 1000 **Product Groups:** 30

Date of Accounts	Dec 11	Dec 10	Dec 09
Sales Turnover	230m	225m	204m
Pre Tax Profit/Loss	10m	26m	21m
Working Capital	82m	84m	61m
Fixed Assets	135m	138m	139m
Current Assets	136m	135m	108m
Current Liabilities	7m	9m	8m

J K M Services
19 Kirkbride Airfield Kirkbride, Wigton, CA7 5HP
Tel: 01697-352017 **Fax:** 01697-352177
Directors: K. Matterson (Prop)
Date established: 1998 **No.of Employees:** 1 - 10 **Product Groups:** 41

Robinson Fork Trucks
Brookside, Wigton, CA7 9AW
Tel: 01697-342328 **Fax:** 01697-345055
E-mail: info@robinsonforktrucks.co.uk
Website: http://www.robinsonforktrucks.co.uk
Managers: M. Robinson (Mgr)
Immediate Holding Company: ROBINSON FORK TRUCKS LIMITED
Registration no: 04900215 **Date established:** 2003
No.of Employees: 1 - 10 **Product Groups:** 35, 39, 45

Date of Accounts	Sep 11	Sep 10	Sep 09
Working Capital	-17	-19	-27
Fixed Assets	65	59	63
Current Assets	66	90	49

Ian Steel
Gate House Bothel, Wigton, CA7 2JA
Tel: 01697-320616
Directors: I. Steel (Prop)
Date established: 1976 **No.of Employees:** 1 - 10 **Product Groups:** 41

Travis Perkins plc
Bog Farm Off Station Road, Wigton, CA7 9AX
Tel: 01697-342286 **Fax:** 01697-344712
E-mail: chris.foster@travisperkins.co.uk
Website: http://www.travisperkins.co.uk
Managers: C. Foster (Mgr)
Immediate Holding Company: TRAVIS PERKINS PLC
Registration no: 00824821 **VAT No.:** GB 456 5069 30
Date established: 1964 **Turnover:** £1m - £2m **No.of Employees:** 11 - 20
Product Groups: 08, 25, 66

Date of Accounts	Dec 11	Dec 10	Dec 09
Sales Turnover	4779m	3153m	2931m
Pre Tax Profit/Loss	270m	197m	213m
Working Capital	133m	159m	248m
Fixed Assets	2771m	2749m	2108m
Current Assets	1421m	1329m	1035m
Current Liabilities	473m	412m	109m

Woodrow Services
Woodrow Hall Woodrow, Wigton, CA7 0AT
Tel: 01697-344905
E-mail: hazel@woodrowservices.co.uk
Website: http://www.woodrowservices.co.uk
Directors: H. Duhy (Prop)
No.of Employees: 1 - 10 **Product Groups:** 28, 44, 79, 81

T Wilson & Sons
The Barracks Abbeytown, Wigton, CA7 4SY
Tel: 01697-361628 **Fax:** 01697-361622
E-mail: darren@twilsonandsons.biz
Website: http://www.twilsonandsons.biz
Directors: D. Graham (Ptnr)
Immediate Holding Company: TRAVELOLOGY COMPANY LIMITED
Registration no: 05644751 **Date established:** 2005
No.of Employees: 1 - 10 **Product Groups:** 41

Windermere

Lakeland
Alexandra Buildings, Windermere, LA23 1BQ
Tel: 01539-488200 **Fax:** 01224-620961
E-mail: sam.rayner@lakeland.co.uk
Website: http://www.lakeland.co.uk
Bank(s): Barclays
Directors: S. Rayner (MD)
Immediate Holding Company: LAKELAND LIMITED
Registration no: 00809688 **Date established:** 1964
Turnover: £125m - £250m **No.of Employees:** 101 - 250
Product Groups: 61, 63

Date of Accounts	Dec 11	Dec 10	Dec 09
Sales Turnover	151m	148m	142m
Pre Tax Profit/Loss	7m	11m	10m
Working Capital	7m	4m	3m
Fixed Assets	50m	50m	48m
Current Assets	32m	28m	23m
Current Liabilities	16m	16m	14m

Windemere Auto Centre
3 Victoria Forge Victoria Street, Windermere, LA23 1AD
Tel: 01539-488955 **Fax:** 01539-488864
E-mail: nick@kankku.co.uk
Website: http://www.windermereautocentre.co.uk
Directors: N. Fieldhouse (Prop)
Managers: K. Fieldhouse (Sec)
Immediate Holding Company: ELLERAY BANK (WINDERMERE) FLAT MANAGEMENT CO LIMITED
Date established: 1982 **No.of Employees:** 1 - 10 **Product Groups:** 39

Workington

C P L Petroleum
Terminal 2 Prince of Wales Dock, Northside, Workington, CA14 1BN
Tel: 01900-61292 **Fax:** 01900-68862
E-mail: workington@cplpetroleum.co.uk
Website: http://www.cplpetroleum.co.uk
Managers: D. Mossom (Mgr)
Ultimate Holding Company: CPL INDUSTRIES HOLDINGS LIMITED
Immediate Holding Company: CPL PETROLEUM LIMITED
Registration no: 03003860 **VAT No.:** GB 721 5764 39
Date established: 1994 **No.of Employees:** 1 - 10 **Product Groups:** 66

Date of Accounts	Mar 12	Mar 11	Mar 10
Pre Tax Profit/Loss	N/A	878	904
Working Capital	31	30m	30m
Fixed Assets	26	26m	26m
Current Assets	57	56m	56m
Current Liabilities	26	246	253

Cumbria Fabrications
Main Street Distington, Workington, CA14 5XJ
Tel: 01946-833331 **Fax:** 01946-824831
Directors: D. Rushton (Ptnr)
Date established: 1979 **No.of Employees:** 1 - 10 **Product Groups:** 35

Dowson Blades Ltd
6 West Cumbria Business Park Dewent Howe, Derwent Howe Industrial Estate, Workington, CA14 3YW
Tel: 01900-64516 **Fax:** 01900-64187
E-mail: dowsonblades@talk21.com
Website: http://www.dowsonblades.co.uk
Bank(s): Cleysdale
Directors: R. Duckitt (MD)
Immediate Holding Company: DOWSON BLADES LIMITED
Registration no: 01994721 **VAT No.:** GB 447 5999 83
Date established: 1986 **Turnover:** £1m - £2m **No.of Employees:** 21 - 50
Product Groups: 36, 40, 41

Date of Accounts	Mar 12	Mar 11	Mar 10
Working Capital	375	127	104
Fixed Assets	677	446	486
Current Assets	813	732	656

Fellside Recordings Ltd
PO Box 40, Workington, CA14 3GJ
Tel: 01900-61556 **Fax:** 01900-61585
E-mail: info@fellside.com
Website: http://www.fellside.com
Directors: L. Adams (Fin), P. Adams (MD)
Immediate Holding Company: FELLSIDE RECORDINGS LIMITED
Registration no: 03958499 **VAT No.:** GB 257 4623 45
Date established: 2000 **Turnover:** £2m - £5m **No.of Employees:** 1 - 10
Product Groups: 61, 79, 89

Date of Accounts	Apr 12	Apr 11	Apr 10
Working Capital	266	255	256
Fixed Assets	27	30	35
Current Assets	319	283	276

Graham
Enterprise Court Lakes Road, Derwent Howe Industrial Estate, Workington, CA14 3YP
Tel: 01900-605599 **Fax:** 01900-871566
E-mail: nick.hensby@graham-group.co.uk
Website: http://www.jewson.co.uk
Managers: N. Hensby (Mgr)
Ultimate Holding Company: SAINT-GOBAIN PLC
Immediate Holding Company: GRAHAM GROUP LTD
Registration no: 00066738 **Turnover:** £20m - £50m
No.of Employees: 1 - 10 **Product Groups:** 66

Hydro Ellay Enfield Ltd
Lillyhall Industrial Estate Joseph Noble Road, Lillyhall, Workington, CA14 4JX
Tel: 01900-601166 **Fax:** 01900-601110
E-mail: fiona.mcdonald@hydro.com
Website: http://www.hydro.com
Bank(s): Barclays, Ipswich
Directors: F. Mcdonald (MD)
Managers: M. Tarrant-rhodes (Fin Mgr), A. Wightman (Purch Mgr)
Ultimate Holding Company: NORSK HYDRO ASA (NORWAY)
Immediate Holding Company: HYDRO ELLAY ENFIELD LIMITED
Registration no: 00371989 **VAT No.:** GB 302 1119 31
Date established: 1942 **Turnover:** £10m - £20m
No.of Employees: 21 - 50 **Product Groups:** 36, 39, 40

Date of Accounts	Dec 11	Dec 10	Dec 09
Sales Turnover	15m	15m	10m
Pre Tax Profit/Loss	106	120	-79
Working Capital	967	861	678
Fixed Assets	1m	1m	1m
Current Assets	4m	5m	4m
Current Liabilities	508	1m	563

Iggesund Paperboard Ltd (division of The Holmen Group)
Siddick, Workington, CA14 1JX
Tel: 01900-601000 **Fax:** 01900-605000
E-mail: info.as@iggesundpaperboard.com
Website: http://www.iggesund.com
Bank(s): HSBC
Directors: R. Giezen (Fin), O. Aksnes (Sales), O. Schultz-Eklund (MD)
Managers: S. Sharpe (Transport)
Ultimate Holding Company: HOLMEN AB (SWEDEN)
Immediate Holding Company: IGGESUND PAPERBOARD EUROPE LIMITED
Registration no: 00959670 **VAT No.:** GB 473 3424 50
Date established: 1969 **Turnover:** £1m - £2m
No.of Employees: 251 - 500 **Product Groups:** 27

Date of Accounts	Dec 11	Dec 10	Dec 09
Sales Turnover	N/A	973	1m
Pre Tax Profit/Loss	N/A	51	47
Working Capital	55	55	9
Current Assets	55	387	405
Current Liabilities	N/A	136	211

A J Johnson Ltd
Units 9-10 Peart Road, Derwent Howe Industrial Estate, Workington, CA14 3YT
Tel: 01900-67065 **Fax:** 01900-67133
E-mail: ajjohnson@aol.com
Website: http://www.ajjohnsonwelding.co.uk
Directors: A. Johnson (MD), C. Johnson (I.T. Dir)
Immediate Holding Company: A.J. JOHNSON LIMITED
Registration no: 04693127 **Date established:** 2003
No.of Employees: 1 - 10 **Product Groups:** 42, 45

Date of Accounts	Mar 12	Mar 11	Mar 10
Working Capital	30	-5	3
Fixed Assets	29	23	11
Current Assets	113	70	109

Lakeland Guns
50 Finkle Street, Workington, CA14 2AZ
Tel: 01900-872005 **Fax:** 01900-872005
Website: http://www.blakelandguns.co.uk
Directors: I. Bell (Prop)
Date established: 1999 **No.of Employees:** 1 - 10 **Product Groups:** 36, 39, 40

K Mossop
2 Sunnyside Seaton, Workington, CA14 1LQ
Tel: 01900-604955 **Fax:** 01900-604955
Directors: K. Mossop (Prop)
Date established: 1990 **No.of Employees:** 1 - 10 **Product Groups:** 40

Port Of Workington
Prince of Wales Dock, Workington, CA14 2JH
Tel: 01900-602301 **Fax:** 01900-604696
E-mail: jlihou@portofworkington.co.uk
Website: http://www.portofworkington.co.uk
Bank(s): National Westminster
Managers: J. Lihou (Chief Mgr)
Immediate Holding Company: CUMBRIA COUNTY COUNCIL
VAT No.: GB 257 1771 45 **No.of Employees:** 11 - 20 **Product Groups:** 71

Waste Recycling Group Ltd
Joseph Noble Road Lillyhall Indl-Est, Lillyhall, Workington, CA14 4JH
Tel: 01900-602205 **Fax:** 01900-601886
Website: http://www.wrj.co.uk
Bank(s): HSBC Bank plc
Directors: H. Walker (Ch), T. Sharpe (MD)
Managers: P. Weatherell (Site Co-ord), J. Shaw (Chief Mgr), J. Foley (Sales & Mktg Mg), I. Griffiths (District Mgr), J. Fawley (Sales & Mktg Mg)
Ultimate Holding Company: FOMENTO DE CONSTRUCCIONES Y CONTRATAS SA (SPAIN)
Immediate Holding Company: FCC ENVIRONMENT (UK) LIMITED
Registration no: 02902416 **Date established:** 1994 **Turnover:** £2m - £5m
No.of Employees: 21 - 50 **Product Groups:** 54

Date of Accounts	Dec 10	Dec 09	Dec 08
Sales Turnover	497m	553m	524m
Pre Tax Profit/Loss	12m	-16m	-19m
Working Capital	-117m	-227m	-217m
Fixed Assets	800m	826m	836m
Current Assets	85m	112m	115m
Current Liabilities	168m	188m	142m

Wulfsport
Joseph Noble Road Lillyhall, Workington, CA14 4JX
Tel: 01900-873456 **Fax:** 01900-870663
E-mail: wulfstores2@yahoo.co.uk
Website: http://www.wulfsport.com
Managers: L. Tubman (Admin Off)
Immediate Holding Company: S B ENGINEERING LIMITED
Registration no: 06281583 **VAT No.:** GB 686 3608 96
Date established: 2001 **No.of Employees:** 1 - 10 **Product Groups:** 24, 40

Date of Accounts	Feb 08	Feb 11	Feb 10
Working Capital	-21	-14	-17
Fixed Assets	23	17	18
Current Assets	106	83	153

DERBYSHIRE

Alfreton

2 K Polymer Systems Ltd
Venture Crescent Nixs Hill Indl-Est, Alfreton, DE55 7RA
Tel: 01773-540440 **Fax:** 01773-607638
E-mail: info@2kps.net
Website: http://www.2kps.net
Bank(s): HSBC
Directors: P. Devonport (Sales), L. Macnamara (MD), M. Ball (Grp Chief Exec)
Managers: A. Wright (I.T. Exec), L. MacKnamara (Mktg Serv Mgr), P. Fearnley (Sales Off Mgr)
Ultimate Holding Company: SEALWOOD GROUP LIMITED
Immediate Holding Company: 2K POLYMER SYSTEMS LIMITED
Registration no: 06085634 **VAT No.:** GB 243 7851 48
Date established: 2007 **Turnover:** £10m - £20m
No.of Employees: 21 - 50 **Product Groups:** 32, 35

Date of Accounts	Dec 10	Dec 09	Dec 08
Sales Turnover	11m	12m	N/A
Pre Tax Profit/Loss	617	870	N/A
Working Capital	1m	774	-271
Fixed Assets	2m	2m	2m
Current Assets	5m	5m	4m
Current Liabilities	3m	2m	N/A

A C Engineering Services Ltd
1 Quarry Road Somercotes, Alfreton, DE55 4HY
Tel: 01773-603516 **Fax:** 01773-528135
E-mail: sales@acengineeringservicesltd.co.uk
Website: http://www.acengineeringservicesltd.co.uk
Directors: D. Coxhead (Dir)
Immediate Holding Company: AC ENGINEERING SERVICES LIMITED
Registration no: 04231514 **Date established:** 2001
Turnover: £250,000 - £500,000 **No.of Employees:** 1 - 10
Product Groups: 39, 45, 48, 68, 83

Date of Accounts	Jun 11	Jun 10	Jun 09
Working Capital	314	305	311
Fixed Assets	230	245	256
Current Assets	365	343	335

Alfreton Fabrications Ltd
Unit 5b Wimsey Way Somercotes, Alfreton, DE55 4LS
Tel: 01773-608163 **Fax:** 01773-300471
E-mail: admin@alfretonfabs.co.uk
Website: http://www.alfretonfabs.co.uk
Directors: S. Rainford (MD)
Immediate Holding Company: ALFRETON FABRICATIONS LIMITED
Registration no: 05379647 **Date established:** 2005
Turnover: Up to £250,000 **No.of Employees:** 1 - 10 **Product Groups:** 48

Date of Accounts	Aug 11	Aug 10	Aug 09
Working Capital	50	35	5
Fixed Assets	65	95	151
Current Assets	155	150	124

Amberol Ltd
The Plantation King Street, Alfreton, DE55 7TT
Tel: 01773-830930 **Fax:** 01773-834191
E-mail: sales@amberol.co.uk
Website: http://www.selfwateringplanters.co.uk
Bank(s): National Westminster
Directors: P. Atkinson-Gregory (MD)
Managers: J. Williamson (Mktg Serv Mgr)
Immediate Holding Company: AMBEROL LIMITED
Registration no: 00950595 **VAT No.:** 126 6416 75 **Date established:** 1969
Turnover: £500,000 - £1m **No.of Employees:** 11 - 20
Product Groups: 26, 30, 45

Date of Accounts	Dec 11	Dec 10	Dec 09
Working Capital	1m	1m	1m
Fixed Assets	827	873	704
Current Assets	1m	1m	1m

Ashland UK
Wimsey Way Somercotes, Alfreton, DE55 4LR
Tel: 01773-604321 **Fax:** 01773-606901
Website: http://www.ashland.com
Bank(s): National Westminster Bank Plc
Directors: C. Harding (MD), A. Coe (Fin)
Managers: L. Marples (Chief Mgr), M. Turvey (Mktg Serv Mgr), K. Young (Prod Mgr)
Ultimate Holding Company: ASHLAND INC (USA)
Immediate Holding Company: ASHLAND INDUSTRIES UK LIMITED
Registration no: 07050037 **Date established:** 2009
Turnover: £50m - £75m **No.of Employees:** 21 - 50 **Product Groups:** 32, 38, 42

Date of Accounts	Sep 11	Sep 10
Sales Turnover	53m	24m
Pre Tax Profit/Loss	1m	862
Working Capital	127	5m
Fixed Assets	12m	5m
Current Assets	16m	14m
Current Liabilities	1m	2m

Autochair
Wood Street North, Alfreton, DE55 7JR
Tel: 01773-830222 **Fax:** 01773-830444
E-mail: info@autochair.co.uk
Website: http://www.autochair.co.uk
Directors: M. Walker (MD)
Managers: A. Clewlow (Ops Mgr), F. Atkin (Mktg Serv Mgr), A. Hall (Chief Acct)
Immediate Holding Company: AUTOCHAIR LIMITED
Registration no: 02533881 **Date established:** 1990 **Turnover:** £1m - £2m
No.of Employees: 21 - 50 **Product Groups:** 26

Date of Accounts	Dec 11	Dec 10	Dec 09
Working Capital	153	154	163
Fixed Assets	308	279	180
Current Assets	986	639	472
Current Liabilities	28	N/A	N/A

G Bopp & Co. Ltd (Registered Office)
Grange Close Clover Nook Industrial Park, Somercotes, Alfreton, DE55 4QT
Tel: 01773-521266 **Fax:** 01773-521163
E-mail: info@gbopp.com
Website: http://www.boppmesh.co.uk
Bank(s): National Westminster Bank Plc
Managers: A. Moss (Chief Mgr), P. Moss (Tech Serv Mgr), C. Machen
Ultimate Holding Company: G BOPP & CO AG (SWITZERLAND)
Immediate Holding Company: G.BOPP & CO.LIMITED
Registration no: 00762927 **Date established:** 1963 **Turnover:** £2m - £5m
No.of Employees: 21 - 50 **Product Groups:** 23, 34, 35, 42

Date of Accounts	Dec 11	Dec 10	Dec 09
Working Capital	2m	1m	1m
Fixed Assets	153	175	170
Current Assets	3m	3m	3m

Border Office Equipment
Unit 4 Block 14 Amber Business Centre Greenhill Lane, Riddings, Alfreton, DE55 4BR
Tel: 01773-608039 **Fax:** 01773-609145
E-mail: borderofficeriddings@btinternet.com
Directors: D. Cooper (Ptnr)
Turnover: Up to £250,000 **No.of Employees:** 1 - 10 **Product Groups:** 49, 64

Bridge Thermo Plastics Ltd
1 Old Colliery Yard Main Road, Morton, Alfreton, DE55 6HL
Tel: 01773-590022 **Fax:** 01773-590033
E-mail: sales@bridgeplastics.co.uk
Website: http://www.bridgeplastics.co.uk
Directors: M. Spray (MD)
Immediate Holding Company: BRIDGE THERMOPLASTICS LIMITED
Registration no: 02086404 **VAT No.:** GB 457 3593 17
Date established: 1986 **Turnover:** £500,000 - £1m
No.of Employees: 11 - 20 **Product Groups:** 30

Date of Accounts	Jun 11	Jun 10	Jun 09
Working Capital	314	255	294
Fixed Assets	168	189	212
Current Assets	492	418	425

Bridgeshire Packaging Ltd
1 Wimsey Way Alfreton Trading Estate, Somercotes, Alfreton, DE55 4LS
Tel: 01773-601000 **Fax:** 01773-606075
E-mail: michelle.turnbull@bridgeshire.co.uk
Website: http://www.bridgeshire.co.uk
Directors: M. Turnbull (Fin), B. Trigg (Dir)
Managers: M. Bridgers (Sales Prom Mgr)
Immediate Holding Company: BRIDGESHIRE PACKAGING LIMITED
Registration no: 02780044 **Date established:** 1993 **Turnover:** £2m - £5m
No.of Employees: 21 - 50 **Product Groups:** 27

Date of Accounts	Nov 11	Nov 10	Nov 09
Working Capital	-72	-171	-236
Fixed Assets	2m	2m	2m
Current Assets	1m	1m	901

Celebrity Motion Furniture Ltd
Unit 1 Wimsey Way Somercotes, Alfreton, DE55 4LS
Tel: 01773-604607 **Fax:** 01773-541408
E-mail: info@celebrity-furniture.co.uk
Website: http://www.celebrity-furniture.co.uk
Bank(s): National Westminster Bank Plc
Directors: W. Hollis (Fab), R. Nicolson (MD), R. Nicolson (MD)
Managers: J. Dyer (Chief Acct), M. Steel (Buyer)
Ultimate Holding Company: JDP FURNITURE GROUP LIMITED
Immediate Holding Company: CELEBRITY MOTION FURNITURE LIMITED
Registration no: 04012089 **VAT No.:** GB 572 3239 43
Date established: 2000 **Turnover:** £10m - £20m
No.of Employees: 101 - 250 **Product Groups:** 26

Date of Accounts	Sep 08	Sep 09	Oct 10
Sales Turnover	N/A	15m	16m
Pre Tax Profit/Loss	2m	2m	2m
Working Capital	8m	9m	11m
Fixed Assets	142	127	134
Current Assets	10m	11m	13m
Current Liabilities	648	781	1m

Cherry Blossom Ltd
Grange Close Clover Nook Industrial Park, Alfreton, DE55 4QT
Tel: 01773-521521 **Fax:** 01773-521262
E-mail: davew@grangers.co.uk
Website: http://www.cherryblossom.co.nz
Directors: C. Jones (MD)
Managers: J. Bissell (Sales Off Mgr)
Registration no: 02838546 **VAT No.:** GB 354 0171 84
Turnover: £250,000 - £500,000 **No.of Employees:** 21 - 50
Product Groups: 32

City Electrical Factors Ltd
Unit 4c Monk Road Industrial Estate Nottingham Road, Alfreton, DE55 7RL
Tel: 01773-831698 **Fax:** 01773-520848
E-mail: neil.bettle@cef.co.uk
Website: http://www.cef.co.uk
Managers: N. Bettle (District Mgr)
Ultimate Holding Company: CEF HOLDINGS LIMITED
Immediate Holding Company: CITY ELECTRICAL FACTORS LIMITED
Registration no: 00336408 **Date established:** 1938
No.of Employees: 1 - 10 **Product Groups:** 37, 67

Date of Accounts	Apr 11	Apr 10	Apr 09
Sales Turnover	439m	406m	444m
Pre Tax Profit/Loss	22m	26m	34m
Working Capital	53m	172m	164m
Fixed Assets	13m	17m	18m
Current Assets	179m	250m	227m
Current Liabilities	53m	23m	20m

Coal Merchants Federation
7 Swanwick Court, Alfreton, DE55 7AS
Tel: 01773-835400 **Fax:** 01773-834351
E-mail: wilma@solidfuel.co.uk
Website: http://www.coalmerchants.co.uk
Directors: W. Brooks (Co Sec)
Immediate Holding Company: COAL MERCHANTS FEDERATION (GREAT BRITAIN) LIMITED
Registration no: 02076497 **VAT No.:** GB 233 8946 39
Date established: 1986 **Turnover:** £500,000 - £1m
No.of Employees: 1 - 10 **Product Groups:** 87

Date of Accounts	Dec 11	Dec 10	Dec 09
Working Capital	649	698	698
Fixed Assets	1	1	N/A
Current Assets	733	802	782

D C Engineering
Lydford Road Meadow Lane Industrial Estate, Alfreton, DE55 7RQ
Tel: 01773-520108
Directors: Castledine (Prop)
Ultimate Holding Company: RT HOLDINGS GMBH (GERMANY)
Immediate Holding Company: J & H RENTALS LIMITED
Registration no: 04525775 **Date established:** 2000 **Turnover:** £5m - £10m
No.of Employees: 1 - 10 **Product Groups:** 35

Date of Accounts	Feb 08	Feb 11	Feb 10
Working Capital	859	893	769
Fixed Assets	35	31	165
Current Assets	889	1m	806

Derwent Upholstery Ltd
Amber Business Centre Greenhill Lane, Riddings, Alfreton, DE55 4BR
Tel: 01773-604121 **Fax:** 01773-540813
E-mail: richard.sowter@derwentupholstery.com
Website: http://www.derwentupholstery.com
Bank(s): Barclays, Cardiff

Directors: J. Wakeman (MD), A. Miles (Works), A. Kennaugh (Sales), M. Steventon (Fin), R. Sowter (Fin), A. Walker (Sales), B. Stitfall (Fin), R. Sowter (MD), K. Stevenson (Works)
Immediate Holding Company: DERWENT UPHOLSTERY LIMITED
Registration no: 01121102 **VAT No.:** GB 133 4836 74
Date established: 1973 **Turnover:** £10m - £20m
No.of Employees: 101 - 250 **Product Groups:** 26

Dicom Ltd (Waste Compaction & Baling Systems)

Lydford Road Meadow Lane Industrial Estate, Alfreton, DE55 7RQ
Tel: 01773-520565 **Fax:** 01773-520881
E-mail: sales@dicom.ltd.uk
Website: http://www.dicom.ltd.uk
Bank(s): Barclays
Directors: J. Greatorex (Sales), S. Lenton (Fin), C. Heley (MD)
Ultimate Holding Company: RT HOLDINGS GMBH (GERMANY)
Immediate Holding Company: DICOM LIMITED
Registration no: 03937313 **VAT No.:** GB 342 9851 36
Date established: 2000 **Turnover:** £5m - £10m **No.of Employees:** 21 - 50
Product Groups: 42, 44

Date of Accounts	Dec 11	Dec 10	Dec 09
Sales Turnover	8m	5m	5m
Pre Tax Profit/Loss	253	123	-139
Working Capital	-220	-275	-1m
Fixed Assets	1m	2m	2m
Current Assets	1m	1m	747
Current Liabilities	947	960	1m

E P C UK

Rough Close Works Carnfield Hill, South Normanton, Alfreton, DE55 2BE
Tel: 01773-832253 **Fax:** 01726-828826
Website: http://www.exchem-explosives.co.uk
Managers: D. Bridge (Mgr)
Immediate Holding Company: EXOR EXPLOSIVES LIMITED
Registration no: 00084170 **Date established:** 2002
Turnover: £10m - £20m **No.of Employees:** 1 - 10 **Product Groups:** 32

Date of Accounts	Dec 11	Dec 10	Dec 09
Sales Turnover	1m	996	1m
Pre Tax Profit/Loss	10	-129	-142
Working Capital	789	683	747
Fixed Assets	119	218	312
Current Assets	942	887	998
Current Liabilities	151	188	190

Elastogran UK Ltd

Wimsey Way Somercotes, Alfreton, DE55 4NL
Tel: 01773-607161 **Fax:** 01773-602089
E-mail: elastogran-uk@elastogran.co.uk
Website: http://www.elastogran.co.uk
Bank(s): HSBC Bank plc
Directors: C. Dunn (Dir), S. Hatton (Fin)
Ultimate Holding Company: BASF SOCIETAS EUROPAEA (GERMANY)
Immediate Holding Company: BASF POLYURETHANES U.K. LIMITED
Registration no: 00702844 **VAT No.:** GB 696 4771 73
Date established: 1961 **Turnover:** £20m - £50m
No.of Employees: 51 - 100 **Product Groups:** 26, 30, 31, 32, 39, 40, 48

Date of Accounts	Dec 11	Dec 10	Dec 09
Sales Turnover	55	45m	35m
Pre Tax Profit/Loss	3	4m	2m
Working Capital	3	4m	3m
Fixed Assets	2	2m	3m
Current Assets	11	11m	9m
Current Liabilities	1	2m	1m

Eurocell Building Plastics Ltd

Cheeseboroughclover Nook Road Cotes Park Industrial Estate, Somercotes, Alfreton, DE55 4RF
Tel: 01773-842300 **Fax:** 01773-842399
E-mail: marketing@eurocell.co.uk
Website: http://www.eurocell.co.uk
Managers: D. Salt (Sales & Mktg Mg), J. Gran (Buyer), S. Heathcote (Transport)
Ultimate Holding Company: TESSENDERLO CHEMIE SA (BELGIUM)
Immediate Holding Company: EUROCELL BUILDING PLASTICS LIMITED
Registration no: 03071407 **Date established:** 1995
Turnover: £50m - £75m **No.of Employees:** 251 - 500
Product Groups: 25, 29, 30, 32, 33, 34, 35, 36, 38, 40, 41, 66, 67

Date of Accounts	Dec 09	Dec 08	Dec 07
Sales Turnover	68m	59m	55m
Pre Tax Profit/Loss	4m	5m	3m
Working Capital	7m	5m	5m
Fixed Assets	5m	3m	2m
Current Assets	20m	19m	13m
Current Liabilities	3m	1m	3m

Eurocell Profiles Ltd

Fairbrook House Clover Nook Road Somercotes, Alfreton, DE55 4RF
Tel: 01773-842100 **Fax:** 01773-842109
E-mail: info@eurocell.co.uk
Website: http://www.eurocell.co.uk
Bank(s): National Westminster Bank Plc
Directors: D. Lang (MD)
Immediate Holding Company: EUROCELL PROFILES LIMITED
Registration no: 02649790 **VAT No.:** GB 616 7517 31
Date established: 1991 **Turnover:** £75m - £125m
No.of Employees: 501 - 1000 **Product Groups:** 30, 35, 36, 52

Date of Accounts	Dec 09	Dec 08	Dec 07
Sales Turnover	80m	69m	75m
Pre Tax Profit/Loss	-574	-3m	3m
Working Capital	12m	8m	6m
Fixed Assets	20m	19m	18m
Current Assets	25m	25m	19m
Current Liabilities	829	1m	1m

Filigree Ltd

South Normanton, Alfreton, DE55 2EG
Tel: 01773-811630 **Fax:** 01773-862777
E-mail: tmulligan@filigree.org
Website: http://www.filigreeholdings.co.uk
Bank(s): Barclays, Leicester
Directors: M. Willey (MD), P. Richards (Sales), P. Richardson (Sales), S. Walkley (Mkt Research), T. Mulligan (Dir), T. Mulligan (MD)
Immediate Holding Company: FILIGREE LIMITED
Registration no: 02523169 **VAT No.:** GB 570 8813 24
Date established: 1990 **Turnover:** £5m - £10m **No.of Employees:** 21 - 50
Product Groups: 23, 24

Date of Accounts	Dec 08	Dec 07	Dec 06
Working Capital	-14	-29	-207
Fixed Assets	N/A	167	175
Current Assets	N/A	1570	1418
Current Liabilities	14	1599	1625
Total Share Capital	745	745	745

Geaco Automotive

Pye Bridge Industrial Estate Pye Bridge, Alfreton, DE55 4NX
Tel: 01773-541707 **Fax:** 01905-381050
E-mail: info@geaco.freeserve.co.uk
Managers: G. Ace (Mgr)
No.of Employees: 1 - 10 **Product Groups:** 30, 42, 48

Grangers International Ltd

Grange Close Clover Nook Industrial Park, Somercotes, Alfreton, DE55 4QT
Tel: 01773-521521 **Fax:** 01773-521262
E-mail: neil@grangers.co.uk
Website: http://www.grangers.co.uk
Bank(s): National Westminster Bank Plc
Directors: N. George (Co Sec), D. Watkins (Sales), K. Jones (I.T. Dir)
Managers: N. Holloway, R. Randall, H. Ogilvie
Ultimate Holding Company: MARTYN ROSE LIMITED
Immediate Holding Company: GRANGERS INTERNATIONAL LIMITED
Registration no: 00327936 **Date established:** 1937 **Turnover:** £5m - £10m
No.of Employees: 21 - 50 **Product Groups:** 32

Date of Accounts	Sep 11	Sep 10	Sep 09
Sales Turnover	8m	6m	5m
Pre Tax Profit/Loss	834	479	79
Working Capital	1m	744	564
Fixed Assets	955	854	653
Current Assets	3m	2m	2m
Current Liabilities	798	591	636

Granwood Flooring Ltd

Greenhill Lane Riddings, Alfreton, DE55 4AT
Tel: 01773-602341 **Fax:** 01773-540043
E-mail: sales@granwood.co.uk
Website: http://www.granwood.co.uk
Directors: C. Blythe (Fin)
Managers: S. Vickers
Ultimate Holding Company: GRANWOOD HOLDINGS LIMITED
Immediate Holding Company: GRANWOOD FLOORING LIMITED
Registration no: 00566174 **VAT No.:** GB 125 5228 87
Date established: 1956 **Turnover:** £2m - £5m **No.of Employees:** 1 - 10
Product Groups: 25

Date of Accounts	Dec 11	Dec 10	Dec 09
Sales Turnover	2m	4m	3m
Pre Tax Profit/Loss	104	406	667
Working Capital	3m	3m	3m
Fixed Assets	2m	2m	2m
Current Assets	5m	5m	4m
Current Liabilities	915	1m	974

Griffith Laboratories Ltd

Cotes Park Estate Somercotes, Alfreton, DE55 4NN
Tel: 01773-837000 **Fax:** 01773-837001
E-mail: info@griffithlaboratories.com
Website: http://www.griffithlaboratories.com
Bank(s): Barclays
Directors: S. Paschalidis (Co Sec), D. Richmond (Purch)
Managers: I. Smith (Site Co-ord), J. Smith (Personnel), H. Smith (Sales Prom Mgr), J. Ward (Tech Serv Mgr)
Ultimate Holding Company: GRIFFITH LABORATORIES INC (USA)
Immediate Holding Company: GRIFFITH LABORATORIES LIMITED
Registration no: 00954742 **Date established:** 1969
Turnover: £20m - £50m **No.of Employees:** 101 - 250
Product Groups: 20, 32

Date of Accounts	Sep 11	Sep 10	Sep 09
Sales Turnover	33m	30m	29m
Pre Tax Profit/Loss	-302	1m	402
Working Capital	4m	4m	3m
Fixed Assets	5m	5m	5m
Current Assets	12m	11m	11m
Current Liabilities	549	836	847

Guilford Europe Ltd

Cotes Park Lane Somercotes, Alfreton, DE55 4NJ
Tel: 01773-547200 **Fax:** 01773-547315
E-mail: dturner@eu.gfd.com
Website: http://www.guilfordproducts.com
Directors: D. Turner (MD), O. Suarez (Fin)
Ultimate Holding Company: GMI HOLDING CORP (USA)
Immediate Holding Company: GUILFORD EUROPE LIMITED
Registration no: 00385595 **VAT No.:** GB 118 3438 75
Date established: 1944 **Turnover:** £75m - £125m
No.of Employees: 251 - 500 **Product Groups:** 36, 43

Date of Accounts	Sep 08	Sep 09	Oct 10
Sales Turnover	87m	77m	97m
Pre Tax Profit/Loss	5m	-5m	-795
Working Capital	3m	7m	2m
Fixed Assets	6m	6m	8m
Current Assets	36m	26m	23m
Current Liabilities	861	818	2m

Havelock Europa

3 Swanwick Court, Alfreton, DE55 7AS
Tel: 01773-543300 **Fax:** 01773-543301
E-mail: andrew.mcmenzie@havelockeuropa.com
Website: http://www.havelockeuropa.com
Directors: G. Carruthers (Tech Serv), R. McDonald (Sales)
Managers: L. Wallace (Purch Mgr), G. Harkes (Personnel), A. Mcmenzie, G. Findlay
Immediate Holding Company: HAVELOCK EUROPA PLC
Registration no: 00782546 **Date established:** 1963
Turnover: £75m - £125m **No.of Employees:** 501 - 1000
Product Groups: 52

Date of Accounts	Dec 11	Dec 10	Dec 09
Sales Turnover	99m	99m	108m
Pre Tax Profit/Loss	-5m	-5m	-6m
Working Capital	4m	17m	15m
Fixed Assets	17m	25m	28m
Current Assets	41m	42m	41m
Current Liabilities	9m	8m	8m

Izax offshore

2 Littlemoor Lane Newton, Alfreton, DE55 5TY
Tel: 01773-875986 **Fax:** 01773-875986
E-mail: matt_izax@hotmail.com
Website: http://www.izax-offshore.co.uk
Directors: M. Ward (Co Sec)
Registration no: 06925629 **No.of Employees:** 1 - 10 **Product Groups:** 37, 39, 68, 74

J K S Boyles Ltd

Unit 9 Salcombe Road, Alfreton, DE55 7RG
Tel: 01773-835323 **Fax:** 01773-521377
E-mail: sales@jks-boyles-ltd.co.uk
Website: http://www.jksboyles.co.uk
Bank(s): Barclays
Directors: S. Jones (Dir)
Ultimate Holding Company: ROCBORE INTERNATIONAL LIMITED
Immediate Holding Company: ROCBORE LIMITED
Registration no: 02484790 **VAT No.:** GB 385 8147 14
Date established: 1990 **Turnover:** £1m - £2m **No.of Employees:** 11 - 20
Product Groups: 45

Date of Accounts	Jul 11	Jul 10	Jul 09
Sales Turnover	N/A	N/A	1m
Pre Tax Profit/Loss	N/A	N/A	-4
Working Capital	76	76	71
Current Assets	104	135	266
Current Liabilities	28	N/A	41

Gavin Kenning Engineering

Whites Close, Alfreton, DE55 7RB
Tel: 01773-607505 **Fax:** 01773-540505
E-mail: sales@tradersupplies.co.uk
Website: http://www.tradersupplies.co.uk
Directors: G. Kenning (Prop)
Immediate Holding Company: GAVIN KENNING ENGINEERING LTD
Registration no: 07728778 **Date established:** 2011 **Turnover:** £2m - £5m
No.of Employees: 1 - 10 **Product Groups:** 34

Leengate Valves

Unit2 Grange Close Somercotes, Alfreton, DE55 4QT
Tel: 01773-521555 **Fax:** 01773-521591
E-mail: info@leengatevalves.co.uk
Website: http://www.leengatevalves.co.uk
Bank(s): National Westminster Bank Plc
Directors: S. Pickering (MD)
Ultimate Holding Company: LEENGATE WELDING GROUP LTD
Immediate Holding Company: GAS INSTRUMENT SERVICES LD
Registration no: 01880211 **VAT No.:** GB 419 7551 29
Date established: 1985 **Turnover:** £2m - £5m **No.of Employees:** 11 - 20
Product Groups: 30, 36, 38, 39, 40, 42

Link-A-Bord Ltd

Colliery Industrial Estate Main Road, Morton, Alfreton, DE55 6HL
Tel: 01773-590566 **Fax:** 01773-590681
E-mail: sales@link-a-bord.co.uk
Website: http://www.armillatox.co.uk
Directors: P. Godfrey (MD)
Immediate Holding Company: LINK-A-BORD LIMITED
Registration no: 03905570 **VAT No.:** GB 127 2161 96
Date established: 2000 **Turnover:** £500,000 - £1m
No.of Employees: 1 - 10 **Product Groups:** 30, 32

M M D Mining Machinery Developments

Cotes Park Lane Cotes Park Industrial Estate, Somercotes, Alfreton, DE55 4NJ
Tel: 01773-835533 **Fax:** 01773-835593
E-mail: reception@mmdsizers.com
Website: http://www.mmdsizers.com
Bank(s): HSBC Bank plc
Directors: A. Potts (Ch)
Immediate Holding Company: MMD MINERAL SIZING (EUROPE) LIMITED
Registration no: 01447376 **VAT No.:** GB 345 8387 22
Date established: 1979 **Turnover:** £20m - £50m
No.of Employees: 251 - 500 **Product Groups:** 45, 48

Date of Accounts	Feb 08	Feb 11	Feb 10
Working Capital	323	657	605
Fixed Assets	94	128	126
Current Assets	3m	5m	3m

Maun Motors

Berristow Lane South Normanton, Alfreton, DE55 2FH
Tel: 01773-810007 **Fax:** 01773-511599
E-mail: andrew@maunmotors.co.uk
Website: http://www.maunmotors.co.uk
Directors: A. Kennedy (Prop)
Immediate Holding Company: UDG (NO.2) LIMITED
Registration no: 02018805 **Date established:** 1996
Turnover: £20m - £50m **No.of Employees:** 11 - 20 **Product Groups:** 72

Metmachex Engineering Ltd

Unit 9 Monk Road, Alfreton, DE55 7RL
Tel: 01773-836241 **Fax:** 01773-520109
E-mail: info@metmachex.net
Website: http://www.metmachex.net
Bank(s): Yorkshire
Directors: H. Ryde (Fin), W. Ryde (MD)
Immediate Holding Company: METMACHEX ENGINEERING LIMITED
Registration no: 04399565 **VAT No.:** GB 309 6061 66
Date established: 2002 **Turnover:** £250,000 - £500,000
No.of Employees: 11 - 20 **Product Groups:** 68

Date of Accounts	Apr 11	Apr 10	Apr 09
Working Capital	178	238	115
Fixed Assets	124	103	128
Current Assets	231	343	229

Morrison McConnell Ltd (t/a British Van Heusen Co. Ltd)

Keys Road, Alfreton, DE55 7SQ
Tel: 01773-727500 **Fax:** 01773-727501
Website: http://www.m2c2.co.uk
Directors: G. Towne (MD)
Immediate Holding Company: Coates Viyella P.L.C.
No.of Employees: 101 - 250 **Product Groups:** 24

N F T Distribution Operation Ltd

Unit 1 Azalea Close Somercotes, Alfreton, DE55 4QX
Tel: 01773-523523 **Fax:** 01773-831740
E-mail: david.frankish@nft.co.uk
Website: http://www.nft.co.uk
Directors: S. Dennison (Fin), M. Ferguson (Pers), D. Fiddy (Sales & Mktg)
Managers: S. Szikora (Tech Serv Mgr), A. Knyhynckyj (Purch Mgr), D. Frankish

see next page

N F T Distribution Operation Ltd - Cont'd

Ultimate Holding Company: NFT DISTRIBUTION HOLDINGS LIMITED
Immediate Holding Company: NFT DISTRIBUTION HOLDINGS LIMITED
Registration no: 05844617 **Date established:** 2006
Turnover: £125m - £250m **No.of Employees:** 101 - 250
Product Groups: 72

Date of Accounts	Mar 12	Mar 11	Mar 10
Sales Turnover	152m	141m	128m
Pre Tax Profit/Loss	3m	2m	-2m
Working Capital	-35m	-9m	-9m
Fixed Assets	63m	61m	61m
Current Assets	21m	19m	23m
Current Liabilities	19m	19m	24m

David Nieper

Nottingham Road, Alfreton, DE55 7LE
Tel: 01773-833335 **Fax:** 01773-520246
E-mail: angela.durose@davidnieper.co.uk
Website: http://www.davidnieper.co.uk
Managers: A. Durose
Immediate Holding Company: DAVID NIEPER LTD
Registration no: 00687485 **Turnover:** £2m - £5m
No.of Employees: 101 - 250 **Product Groups:** 24, 61, 63

Date of Accounts	Mar 08	Mar 07	Mar 06
Pre Tax Profit/Loss	1558	907	981
Working Capital	4403	3710	3502
Fixed Assets	841	849	875
Current Assets	6305	5129	5187
Current Liabilities	1902	1419	1685
Total Share Capital	1	1	1
ROCE% (Return on Capital Employed)	29.7	19.9	22.4

Pilkington Plyglass Ltd

Cotes Park Somercotes, Pye Bridge, Alfreton, DE55 4PX
Tel: 01773-520000 **Fax:** 01773-520052
E-mail: derren.gittins@pilkington.com
Website: http://www.pilkington.com
Managers: M. Metcalfe (Sales Prom Mgr), A. Swain (Fin Mgr), A. Swain (Fin Mgr), D. Gittins (Mgr), I. Godber (Mats Contrlr), M. Metcalfe (Sales Prom Mgr)
Ultimate Holding Company: PILKINGTON P.L.C.
Immediate Holding Company: PILKINGTON UK LTD
Registration no: 01417048 **Turnover:** £10m - £20m
No.of Employees: 101 - 250 **Product Groups:** 33

R P T Engineering Ltd

Wimsey Way Somercotes, Alfreton, DE55 4LS
Tel: 01773-609982 **Fax:** 01773-609435
E-mail: rptengineeringltd@tiscali.co.uk
Directors: L. May (Fin)
Immediate Holding Company: R.P.T. ENGINEERING LIMITED
Registration no: 02960535 **Date established:** 1994
Turnover: £250,000 - £500,000 **No.of Employees:** 1 - 10
Product Groups: 29

Date of Accounts	Jun 11	Jun 10	Jun 09
Sales Turnover	N/A	N/A	297
Pre Tax Profit/Loss	N/A	N/A	21
Working Capital	143	141	102
Fixed Assets	35	26	30
Current Assets	211	197	142
Current Liabilities	N/A	N/A	21

Regal Paints Ltd

Dunsford Road Meadow Lane Industrial Estate, Alfreton, DE55 7RH
Tel: 01773-830700 **Fax:** 01773-832652
E-mail: regalpaintslimited@tiscali.co.uk
Website: http://www.regalpaintslimited.co.uk
Directors: A. Adkins (MD)
Immediate Holding Company: REGAL PAINTS LIMITED
Registration no: 02833626 **VAT No.:** GB 598 3570 84
Date established: 1993 **Turnover:** £250,000 - £500,000
No.of Employees: 1 - 10 **Product Groups:** 32

Date of Accounts	Aug 11	Aug 10	Aug 09
Working Capital	15	9	12
Fixed Assets	5	5	7
Current Assets	66	80	87

Rock Fall UK Ltd

Major House Wimsey Way Alfreton Trading Estate, Somercotes, Alfreton, DE55 4LS
Tel: 01773-608616 **Fax:** 01773-608614
E-mail: stephen@rockfall.co.uk
Website: http://www.rockfall.co.uk
Directors: S. Noon (MD)
Immediate Holding Company: ROCKFALL UK LIMITED
Registration no: 03436704 **Date established:** 1997
No.of Employees: 1 - 10 **Product Groups:** 63

Date of Accounts	Sep 11	Sep 10	Sep 09
Working Capital	601	581	572
Fixed Assets	48	55	42
Current Assets	1m	1m	885

Rotrex Winches

Griffon Works Wimsey Way, Somercotes, Alfreton, DE55 4LS
Tel: 01773-603997 **Fax:** 01773-540566
E-mail: sales@rotrexwinches.co.uk
Website: http://www.rotrexwinches.co.uk
Bank(s): HSBC Bank plc
Managers: A. Coxon, I. Bunting (Comm), M. Maher (Sales Prom Mgr), P. Eley (Buyer)
Ultimate Holding Company: HB FULLER INC (USA)
Immediate Holding Company: H.B. FULLER U.K. LIMITED
Registration no: 03468967 **Date established:** 1997 **Turnover:** £2m - £5m
No.of Employees: 21 - 50 **Product Groups:** 35, 37, 38, 39, 45, 48, 83

S T M Healthcare

Azalea Close Clover Nook Industrial Park, Somercotes, Alfreton, DE55 4QX
Tel: 01773-830426 **Fax:** 01773-830427
E-mail: p@recticel.co.uk
Website: http://www.stm-healthcare.co.uk
Managers: P. Howes (Nat Sales Mgr), P. Howse (Nat Sales Mgr)
Ultimate Holding Company: NFT DISTRIBUTION HOLDINGS LIMITED
Immediate Holding Company: NFT DISTRIBUTION OPERATIONS LIMITED
Registration no: 05813752 **Date established:** 2006
Turnover: Up to £250,000 **No.of Employees:** 21 - 50 **Product Groups:** 38, 67

Date of Accounts	Mar 12	Mar 11	Mar 10
Pre Tax Profit/Loss	-1	-2	-2
Working Capital	19m	19m	18m
Fixed Assets	5m	5m	5m
Current Assets	19m	19m	18m

Sapa Profiles Ltd

Unit 1-4 Tibshelf Business Park Sawpit Lane, Tibshelf, Alfreton, DE55 5NH
Tel: 01773-872761 **Fax:** 01773-874389
E-mail: info@sapagroup.com
Website: http://www.sapagroup.com
Bank(s): Barclays
Directors: A. Couturier (MD)
Ultimate Holding Company: ORKLA ASA (NORWAY)
Immediate Holding Company: SAPA PROFILES LIMITED
Registration no: 02448020 **Date established:** 1989
Turnover: £50m - £75m **No.of Employees:** 101 - 250
Product Groups: 32, 34, 36

Date of Accounts	Dec 11	Dec 10	Dec 09
Sales Turnover	99m	85m	70m
Pre Tax Profit/Loss	3m	2m	-58
Working Capital	17m	14m	13m
Fixed Assets	28m	25m	26m
Current Assets	38m	31m	25m
Current Liabilities	4m	2m	2m

Severnside Recycling

Pye Bridge Industrial Estate Pye Bridge, Alfreton, DE55 4NX
Tel: 01773-607381 **Fax:** 01773-607704
E-mail: mark.jones@severnside.com
Website: http://www.severnside.com
Bank(s): National Westminster
Directors: J. Malone (Sales), P. McGuinness (MD), F. Patel (Pers), D. Malone (Sales)
Managers: D. Stewart (Mgr), M. Jones (Mgr), A. Briggs (Ops Mgr)
Immediate Holding Company: RAINBRIDGE TIMBER 2001 LIMITED
Registration no: 00489560 **VAT No.:** 479 5202 22 **Date established:** 1983
Turnover: £5m - £10m **No.of Employees:** 21 - 50 **Product Groups:** 66

Sherwood Truck & Van Ltd

Berristow Lane South Normanton, Alfreton, DE55 2FH
Tel: 01773-863311 **Fax:** 01773-580271
E-mail: enquiries@sherwoodtruckandvan.com
Website: http://www.sherwoodtruckandvan.com
Bank(s): HSBC
Directors: R. Spittle (MD), M. Lancaster (Sales), D. Smith (Co Sec)
Managers: M. Rourke
Ultimate Holding Company: IAN GUEST HOLDINGS LIMITED
Immediate Holding Company: SHERWOOD TRUCK AND VAN LTD
Registration no: 01866003 **VAT No.:** GB 116 2918 78
Date established: 1984 **Turnover:** £20m - £50m
No.of Employees: 101 - 250 **Product Groups:** 39, 68, 72, 82

Date of Accounts	Dec 11	Apr 10	Apr 09
Sales Turnover	22m	24m	35m
Pre Tax Profit/Loss	119	34	-232
Working Capital	981	1m	1m
Fixed Assets	245	224	279
Current Assets	10m	8m	14m
Current Liabilities	1m	5m	8m

Sia Abrafoam Ltd

Keys Road Nixs Hill Industrial Estate, Alfreton, DE55 7FQ
Tel: 01773-832524 **Fax:** 01773-520776
E-mail: info@sia-abrafoam.co.uk
Website: http://www.sia-abrafoam.co.uk
Directors: R. Eberle (Dir), R. Motteram (Co Sec)
Ultimate Holding Company: ROBERT BOSCH GMBH (GERMANY)
Immediate Holding Company: SIA ABRAFOAM LIMITED
Registration no: 02954615 **Date established:** 1994 **Turnover:** £5m - £10m
No.of Employees: 101 - 250 **Product Groups:** 33

Date of Accounts	Dec 10	Dec 09	Dec 08
Sales Turnover	7m	6m	7m
Pre Tax Profit/Loss	-192	-405	62
Working Capital	1m	1m	2m
Fixed Assets	530	571	515
Current Assets	3m	2m	3m
Current Liabilities	399	245	259

Siliconepak Ltd

Birchwood Way Somercotes, Alfreton, DE55 4QQ
Tel: 01773-607967 **Fax:** 01773-540283
E-mail: richard.smith@siliconpak.co.uk
Website: http://www.siliconpak.co.uk
Directors: R. Smith (MD)
Ultimate Holding Company: CHARAPAK SPECIALITY PACKAGING LIMITED
Immediate Holding Company: SILICONPAK LIMITED
Registration no: 01729156 **Date established:** 1983 **Turnover:** £2m - £5m
No.of Employees: 11 - 20 **Product Groups:** 27

Date of Accounts	Dec 11	Dec 10	Dec 09
Sales Turnover	2m	3m	2m
Pre Tax Profit/Loss	64	209	-83
Working Capital	140	385	222
Fixed Assets	79	10	12
Current Assets	751	923	581
Current Liabilities	89	135	48

Solid Fuel Association

7 Swanwick Court, Alfreton, DE55 7AS
Tel: 08456-014406 **Fax:** 01773-834351
E-mail: martyn@solidfuel.co.uk
Website: http://www.solidfuel.co.uk
Managers: M. Buckley (Chief Mgr)
Immediate Holding Company: SOLID FUEL ASSOCIATION
Registration no: 02895640 **Date established:** 1994
Turnover: £250,000 - £500,000 **No.of Employees:** 1 - 10
Product Groups: 84

Date of Accounts	Dec 11	Dec 10	Dec 09
Working Capital	57	48	47
Fixed Assets	2	3	4
Current Assets	90	90	80

Specialist Refractory Services Ltd

Amber Business Centre Riddings, Alfreton, DE55 4BR
Tel: 01773-608969 **Fax:** 01773-540105
E-mail: sales@srs-ltd.co.uk
Website: http://www.srs-ltd.co.uk
Directors: G. Davis (Dir), H. Davis (Dir), P. Ashley (Co Sec), P. Ashley (Fin)
Ultimate Holding Company: Goodwin plc
Immediate Holding Company: GOODWIN REFRACTORY SERVICES LIMITED
Registration no: 06404024 **VAT No.:** GB 401 6501 07
Date established: 1984 **Turnover:** £5m - £10m **No.of Employees:** 21 - 50
Product Groups: 34, 47

Speeds Ltd

Hallfield Farm Hallfieldgate Lane, Shirland, Alfreton, DE55 6AA
Tel: 01773-520820 **Fax:** 01773-520643
Website: http://www.speeds.co.uk
Directors: G. Fayward (Fin), M. Speed (MD)
Managers: S. Parkin
Ultimate Holding Company: SPEEDS LIMITED
Immediate Holding Company: SPEEDS MOTOR GROUP LIMITED
Registration no: 00609024 **VAT No.:** GB 295 2723 35
Date established: 1958 **Turnover:** £1m - £2m **No.of Employees:** 1 - 10
Product Groups: 68

Date of Accounts	Dec 10	Dec 09	Dec 08
Working Capital	178	178	178
Current Assets	178	178	178

Storm

Nixs Hill Nixs Hill Industrial Estate, Alfreton, DE55 7GN
Tel: 01773-521309 **Fax:** 01773-521430
E-mail: sales@stormwaterproofing.com
Website: http://www.stormwaterproofing.com
Managers: F. Horne (Sales Admin)
Ultimate Holding Company: STORMDFX LIMITED
Immediate Holding Company: STORM SOLUTION LIMITED
Registration no: 05917165 **Date established:** 2006
No.of Employees: 1 - 10 **Product Groups:** 32

Date of Accounts	Dec 11	Dec 10	Dec 09
Working Capital	-34	7	-59
Fixed Assets	N/A	N/A	108
Current Assets	4	178	237

Thorntons plc Head Office

Thornton Park Somercotes, Alfreton, DE55 4XJ
Tel: 0845-0757565 **Fax:** 01773-540757
E-mail: michael.holton@thorntons.co.uk
Website: http://www.thorntons.co.uk
Directors: C. Brown (Pers), M. Henson (Dir), M. Davies (Grp Chief Exec), J. Von Spreckleson (Ch), D. Prendergast (Sales)
Managers: T. Baines (I.T. Exec), T. Mansfield (Purch Mgr), J. Wall (Fin Mgr), J. Mercer (Mktg Serv Mgr), B. Blumer (Ops Mgr)
Immediate Holding Company: THORNTONS PLC
Registration no: 00174706 **VAT No.:** GB 172 8413 60
Date established: 1921 **Turnover:** £125m - £250m
No.of Employees: 1501 & over **Product Groups:** 62

Transvac Systems

Monsal House 1 Bramble Way, Somercotes, Alfreton, DE55 4RH
Tel: 01773-831100 **Fax:** 01773-831123
E-mail: sales@transvac.co.uk
Website: http://www.transvac.co.uk
Bank(s): National Westminster
Directors: D. Ainge (Dir), D. Redgate (Dir)
Managers: P. Ainge (Tech Serv Mgr), K. Cornwell (Purch Mgr)
Immediate Holding Company: TRANSVAC SYSTEMS LIMITED
Registration no: 01526398 **VAT No.:** GB 353 4344 65
Date established: 1980 **Turnover:** £1m - £2m **No.of Employees:** 21 - 50
Product Groups: 84

Date of Accounts	Dec 11	Dec 10	Dec 09
Working Capital	498	290	277
Fixed Assets	610	574	311
Current Assets	2m	2m	1m

Ashbourne

Aggregate Industries Ltd

Smithhall Lane Hulland Ward, Ashbourne, DE6 3ET
Tel: 01335-372222 **Fax:** 01909-568780
E-mail: alan.smith@aggregate.com
Website: http://www.brookeconcrete.co.uk
Directors: G. Bolsover (Dir), M. Ford (Co Sec)
Ultimate Holding Company: HOLCIM LTD (SWITZERLAND)
Immediate Holding Company: AGGREGATE INDUSTRIES LIMITED
Registration no: 05655952 **VAT No.:** GB 533 2605 71
Date established: 2005 **Turnover:** £1m - £2m **No.of Employees:** 21 - 50
Product Groups: 14, 17, 31, 33

Date of Accounts	Dec 11	Dec 10	Dec 09
Pre Tax Profit/Loss	3m	49m	251m
Working Capital	N/A	2m	2m
Fixed Assets	421m	421m	351m
Current Assets	N/A	2m	2m

Ashbourne Agricultural Engineers

Honeysuckle Cottage Sandybrook, Ashbourne, DE6 2AQ
Tel: 01335-344076 **Fax:** 01335-344076
Directors: R. Wright (Prop)
Date established: 1981 **No.of Employees:** 1 - 10 **Product Groups:** 41

CIS Street Furniture

Albany Court Blenhiem Road, Airfield Industrial Estate, Ashbourne, DE6 1HA
Tel: 01335-300234 **Fax:** 01335-300353
Website: http://www.cis-streetfurniture.co.uk
Managers: P. Dury (Mgr)
Ultimate Holding Company: 03121036
Immediate Holding Company: CIS STREET FURNITURE LIMITED
Registration no: 03120963 **Date established:** 1995
No.of Employees: 11 - 20 **Product Groups:** 26, 35

D A Pak Ltd

Brittania House Blenheim Road, Airfield Industrial Estate, Ashbourne, DE6 1HA
Tel: 01335-344215 **Fax:** 01335-346834
E-mail: sales@dapak.co.uk
Website: http://www.dapak.co.uk
Managers: K. Middleton (Comptroller)
Immediate Holding Company: D.A. PAK LIMITED
Registration no: 03546924 **Date established:** 1998
No.of Employees: 1 - 10 **Product Groups:** 38, 42

Date of Accounts	Mar 12	Mar 11	Mar 10
Working Capital	179	259	224
Fixed Assets	556	572	587
Current Assets	1m	1m	1m

G K General Engineering Ltd

Blenheim Road Airfield Industrial Estate, Ashbourne, DE6 1HA
Tel: 01335-346272 **Fax:** 01335-300361
E-mail: ray@gk-general-eng.co.uk
Website: http://www.gk-general-eng.co.uk
Directors: J. Clowes (Fin), K. Renshaw (MD)
Immediate Holding Company: G.K. GENERAL ENGINEERING LIMITED
Registration no: 01697708 **Date established:** 1983
No.of Employees: 1 - 10 **Product Groups:** 35, 42, 45

Date of Accounts	Feb 12	Feb 11	Feb 10
Working Capital	20	-3	-60
Fixed Assets	177	178	175
Current Assets	327	320	157

H G V Direct

Moor Farm Road Airfield Industrial Estate, Ashbourne, DE6 1HD
Tel: 01335-346236 **Fax:** 01335-346056
E-mail: sales@hgvdirect.co.uk
Website: http://www.hgvdirect.co.uk
Managers: D. Moxon (Mgr)
Immediate Holding Company: HGV DIRECT LIMITED
Registration no: 01857034 **Date established:** 1984 **Turnover:** £5m - £10m
No.of Employees: 1 - 10 **Product Groups:**

Date of Accounts	Dec 11	Dec 10	Dec 09
Sales Turnover	7m	N/A	6m
Pre Tax Profit/Loss	81	N/A	-18
Working Capital	-143	10	-45
Fixed Assets	430	326	347
Current Assets	2m	2m	2m
Current Liabilities	1000	N/A	823

H & H Industrial Fasteners Midlands Ltd

The Paddocks Somersal Herbert, Ashbourne, DE6 5PD
Tel: 01283-585473 **Fax:** 01283-585625
E-mail: kathleen@h-hfasteners.com
Website: http://www.h-hfasteners.com
Directors: J. Harris (MD)
Immediate Holding Company: H & H INDUSTRIAL FASTENERS (MIDLANDS) LIMITED
Registration no: 02407573 **Date established:** 1989
Turnover: £500,000 - £1m **No.of Employees:** 1 - 10 **Product Groups:** 35, 66

Date of Accounts	Oct 11	Oct 10	Oct 09
Working Capital	127	170	187
Fixed Assets	10	13	8
Current Assets	186	230	229

Homelux Nenplas

Blenheim Road Airfield Industrial Estate, Ashbourne, DE6 1HA
Tel: 01335-347300 **Fax:** 01335-340271
E-mail: enquiries@homeluxnenplas.co.uk
Website: http://www.homelux.co.uk
Bank(s): Lloyds TSB Bank plc
Directors: R. Lumb (Fin)
Managers: J. Hillyer (Tech Serv Mgr), M. Gyles (Personnel), B. Firth (Mktg Serv Mgr)
Immediate Holding Company: HOMELUX NENPLAS LIMITED
Registration no: 05743422 **VAT No.:** GB 738 0874 08
Date established: 2006 **Turnover:** £10m - £20m
No.of Employees: 101 - 250 **Product Groups:** 25, 26, 30, 33, 35, 36

Date of Accounts	May 11	May 10	May 09
Sales Turnover	16m	13m	N/A
Pre Tax Profit/Loss	2m	1m	624
Working Capital	3m	2m	1m
Fixed Assets	6m	4m	4m
Current Assets	7m	6m	5m
Current Liabilities	2m	2m	2m

Howardson Ltd

Howardson Works Ashbourne Road, Kirk Langley, Ashbourne, DE6 4NJ
Tel: 01332-824777 **Fax:** 01332-824525
E-mail: ian@dennisuk.com
Website: http://www.dennisuk.com
Managers: I. Howard (Mgr)
Immediate Holding Company: HOWARDSON LIMITED
Registration no: 00641526 **VAT No.:** GB 345 9918 12
Date established: 1959 **Turnover:** £500,000 - £1m
No.of Employees: 11 - 20 **Product Groups:** 40, 41, 48

Date of Accounts	Dec 11	Dec 10	Dec 09
Working Capital	611	895	807
Fixed Assets	823	480	373
Current Assets	2m	1m	925

Mastermover International Ltd

The Limes Moor Farm Road Airfield Industrial Estate, Ashbourne, DE6 1HD
Tel: 01335-348797 **Fax:** 01335-347711
E-mail: info@mastermover.com
Website: http://www.mastermover.com
Directors: A. Owen (Dir)
Ultimate Holding Company: M-MOVER HOLDINGS LIMITED
Immediate Holding Company: MASTERMOVER INTERNATIONAL LIMITED
Registration no: 02981115 **Date established:** 1994
No.of Employees: 11 - 20 **Product Groups:** 35, 39, 45

Date of Accounts	Dec 11	Dec 10	Dec 09
Working Capital	104	104	546
Fixed Assets	N/A	N/A	181
Current Assets	107	107	1m

Nu Star Material Handling Ltd

Hollington Lane Ednaston, Ashbourne, DE6 3AE
Tel: 08704-435646 **Fax:** 08704-435647
E-mail: steve@nu-starmhl.com
Website: http://www.nu-starmhl.com
Directors: S. Mather (Dir)
Immediate Holding Company: NU-STAR MATERIAL HANDLING LIMITED
Registration no: 04233846 **Date established:** 2001
No.of Employees: 1 - 10 **Product Groups:** 39, 45, 67

Date of Accounts	Nov 11	Nov 10	Nov 09
Working Capital	319	357	271
Fixed Assets	19	17	19
Current Assets	380	460	353

Red Crow Events Management

Hackwood Farm Radbourne, Ashbourne, DE6 4LZ
Tel: 07707-552931
E-mail: ally@redcrow.info
Website: http://www.redcrow.info
Managers: A. McClelland (Mgr)
Date established: 1993 **No.of Employees:** 1 - 10 **Product Groups:** 89

Roston Castings Ltd

Mill Lane Ellastone, Ashbourne, DE6 2HF
Tel: 01335-324368 **Fax:** 01335-324544
E-mail: info@rostoncastings.co.uk
Website: http://www.rostoncastings.co.uk
Directors: P. Woolley (Co Sec), M. Hooley (MD)
Immediate Holding Company: ROSTON CASTINGS LIMITED
Registration no: 01063617 **VAT No.:** GB 126 1810 96
Date established: 1972 **Turnover:** £1m - £2m **No.of Employees:** 21 - 50
Product Groups: 34, 35

Date of Accounts	Jul 11	Jul 10	Jul 09
Working Capital	292	337	498
Fixed Assets	87	91	99
Current Assets	755	615	691

P Spencer

Tudor House Farm Church Lane, Kirk Langley, Ashbourne, DE6 4NG
Tel: 01332-824216 **Fax:** 01332-824216
Directors: P. Spencer (Prop)
Immediate Holding Company: FAIRMONT AUTOS LIMITED
Registration no: 01199065 **Date established:** 1975
No.of Employees: 1 - 10 **Product Groups:** 26, 35

Tarmac Topfloor Ltd

Weston Underwood, Ashbourne, DE6 4PH
Tel: 01335-360601 **Fax:** 01332-868401
E-mail: will.spur@tarmac.co.uk
Website: http://www.tarmac.co.uk
Directors: W. Spurr (MD)
Ultimate Holding Company: ANGLO AMERICAN PLC
Immediate Holding Company: TARMAC TOPFLOOR LIMITED
Registration no: 03231391 **VAT No.:** GB 532 3679 43
Date established: 1996 **Turnover:** £20m - £50m
No.of Employees: 101 - 250 **Product Groups:** 33

Termodeck

Weston Underwood, Ashbourne, DE6 4PH
Tel: 01332-868510 **Fax:** 01332-868511
E-mail: termodeck@tarmac.co.uk
Website: http://www.termodeck.co.uk
Managers: G. Russell-smith (Chief Mgr), G. Russell Smith (Chief Mgr)
Immediate Holding Company: TARMAC GROUP P.L.C.
Registration no: 02840754 **Date established:** 1998
No.of Employees: 1 - 10 **Product Groups:** 52

Bakewell

Brocklehurst Bakewell

Beeches Matlock Street, Bakewell, DE45 1EE
Tel: 01629-812089 **Fax:** 01629-814777
E-mail: sales@brocklehursts.com
Website: http://www.brocklehursts.com
Directors: M. Brocklehurst (MD)
Immediate Holding Company: INTERIOR DECORATIONS OF BROOMHILL LIMITED
Registration no: 04264264 **Date established:** 1959
Turnover: £500,000 - £1m **No.of Employees:** 11 - 20 **Product Groups:** 61

Date of Accounts	Dec 11	Dec 10	Dec 09
Sales Turnover	2m	2m	2m
Pre Tax Profit/Loss	60	19	32
Working Capital	523	483	462
Fixed Assets	287	276	283
Current Assets	647	639	592
Current Liabilities	116	132	102

Codel International Ltd

Station Building Station Road, Bakewell, DE45 1GE
Tel: 01629-814351 **Fax:** 0870-056 6307
E-mail: david.coe@codel.co.uk
Website: http://www.codel.co.uk
Bank(s): National Westminster Bank Plc
Directors: D. Coe (MD), D. Fairbrother (Dir), P. Coe (Co Sec)
Managers: D. Wilmot (Purch Mgr), N. Plum (Sales Prom Mgr)
Immediate Holding Company: CODEL INTERNATIONAL LIMITED
Registration no: 01606652 **VAT No.:** GB 379 1096 23
Date established: 1982 **Turnover:** £2m - £5m **No.of Employees:** 21 - 50
Product Groups: 38, 40, 54

Date of Accounts	Mar 11	Mar 10	Mar 09
Working Capital	1m	1m	933
Fixed Assets	784	774	770
Current Assets	3m	3m	2m

E F C O Steel Shutters UK

Ashford Road Deepdale Business Park, Bakewell, DE45 1GT
Tel: 01629-815232 **Fax:** 01629-815241
E-mail: info@efcoforms.com
Website: http://www.efcoforms.com
Managers: G. Brown (Mgr)
Immediate Holding Company: PEAK ASSOCIATES LIMITED
Date established: 2005 **No.of Employees:** 1 - 10 **Product Groups:** 35, 52, 66

Date of Accounts	Jan 11	Jan 09	Jan 08
Pre Tax Profit/Loss	N/A	N/A	-9
Working Capital	-1	-1	-0
Fixed Assets	231	225	213
Current Assets	N/A	N/A	1
Current Liabilities	N/A	1	1

Holdsworth Chocolate Ltd

Unit 2a-2b Station Yard Station Road, Bakewell, DE45 1GE
Tel: 01629-813573 **Fax:** 01629-813850
E-mail: catherine@holdsworthchocolates.co.uk
Website: http://www.holdsworthchocolates.co.uk
Bank(s): The Royal Bank of Scotland
Directors: D. Sharple (MD)
Immediate Holding Company: HOLDSWORTH CHOCOLATE LIMITED
Registration no: 03984917 **VAT No.:** GB 509 1033 80
Date established: 2000 **Turnover:** £250,000 - £500,000
No.of Employees: 11 - 20 **Product Groups:** 20

Date of Accounts	May 11	May 10	May 09
Sales Turnover	N/A	N/A	295
Pre Tax Profit/Loss	N/A	N/A	-49
Working Capital	-58	-64	-73
Fixed Assets	2	2	2
Current Assets	92	90	100
Current Liabilities	N/A	N/A	68

Pinelog Ltd

Riverside Business Park Buxton Road, Bakewell, DE45 1GS
Tel: 01629-814481 **Fax:** 01629-814634
E-mail: admin@pinelog.co.uk
Website: http://www.pinelog.co.uk
Bank(s): Lloyds TSB
Directors: N. Grayson (MD), P. Daly (Fin), K. Cooper (Purch), I. Grant (Sales & Mktg)
Ultimate Holding Company: PINELOG GROUP LIMITED
Immediate Holding Company: PINELOG LIMITED
Registration no: 02587185 **VAT No.:** GB 593 4498 91
Date established: 1991 **Turnover:** £5m - £10m
No.of Employees: 51 - 100 **Product Groups:** 25

Date of Accounts	Oct 10	Oct 11	Nov 08
Sales Turnover	7m	6m	12m
Pre Tax Profit/Loss	-87	-318	755
Working Capital	874	436	1m
Fixed Assets	318	488	459
Current Assets	2m	2m	4m
Current Liabilities	454	361	1m

Roche Violins

Main Street Youlgrave, Bakewell, DE45 1UW
Tel: 01629-630099 **Fax:** 01629-630099
E-mail: brian@rocheviolins.com
Website: http://www.rocheviolins.com
Directors: B. Roche (Prop)
Date established: 2005 **Turnover:** Up to £250,000
No.of Employees: 1 - 10 **Product Groups:** 49

Super-Tec Machine Tools Ltd

Cross Lane Monyash, Bakewell, DE45 1JN
Tel: 01629-810108 **Fax:** 0162-981 4333
E-mail: mileshutchinson@btconnect.com
Website: http://www.supertecmachinetools.com
Directors: M. Hutchinson (MD), M. Hutchison (Dir), D. Hutchinson (Co Sec)
Managers: B. McEnery (Works Eng)
Immediate Holding Company: ORT (Thread Rolling) Ltd
Registration no: 06859135 **VAT No.:** GB 116 9899 21
Date established: 1997 **Turnover:** £500,000 - £1m
No.of Employees: 1 - 10 **Product Groups:** 46

Suresafe Electrical Services

7 Pinfold View, Bakewell, DE45 1GR
Tel: 01629-810241
E-mail: lee@suresafe.org.uk
Website: http://www.suresafe.org.uk
Directors: L. Hodgkinson (Prop)
Date established: 2007 **Turnover:** Up to £250,000
No.of Employees: 1 - 10 **Product Groups:** 85

Tony Team

Unit 6 Station Yard Station Road, Bakewell, DE45 1GE
Tel: 01629-813859 **Fax:** 01629-814334
E-mail: sales@tonyteam.co.uk
Website: http://www.tonyteam.co.uk
Directors: V. Head (MD)
Immediate Holding Company: TONY TEAM LIMITED
Registration no: 05759343 **Date established:** 2006 **Turnover:** £2m - £5m
No.of Employees: 11 - 20 **Product Groups:** 38, 42

Date of Accounts	Apr 12	Apr 11	Apr 10
Working Capital	131	123	139
Fixed Assets	140	106	48
Current Assets	549	555	562

Trelleborg Forsheda Pipe Seals

Vantage House Station Road, Bakewell, DE45 1GE
Tel: 01629-813835 **Fax:** 01629-814658
E-mail: mike.chambers@trelleborg.com
Website: http://www.trelleborg.com/pipeseals
Managers: M. Chambers (Mgr)
Ultimate Holding Company: SMITHS GROUP PLC
Immediate Holding Company: TISPP LTD
Registration no: 00446036 **Date established:** 1985 **Turnover:** £2m - £5m
No.of Employees: 1 - 10 **Product Groups:** 29, 30

Zanogen UK Ltd

Unit 12 Riverside Business Park Buxton Road, Bakewell, DE45 1GS
Tel: 01629-812582 **Fax:** 01629-814494
E-mail: zanogen@yahoo.co.uk
Website: http://www.zanogenuk.com
Directors: A. Morgan (MD)
Immediate Holding Company: ZANOGEN (UK) LIMITED
Registration no: 04132875 **Date established:** 2000
No.of Employees: 11 - 20 **Product Groups:** 46

Date of Accounts	Mar 12	Mar 11	Mar 10
Working Capital	147	161	83
Fixed Assets	9	3	5
Current Assets	310	413	320

Belper

Abru Ltd

Derwentside Industrial Park Derby Road, Belper, DE56 1WE
Tel: 01773-525730 **Fax:** 01773-828059
E-mail: sales@abru.co.uk
Website: http://www.abruladders.co.uk
Bank(s): National Westminster Bank Plc
Directors: S. Brown (Fin), C. Ball (MD), M. Law (Sales), P. Bruton (Mkt Research)
Managers: H. Basi (Tech Serv Mgr), C. Taylor (Personnel), C. Weedon
Ultimate Holding Company: NEW WERNER HOLDING CO INC (UNITED STATES OF AMERICA)
Immediate Holding Company: ABRU LIMITED
Registration no: 00939028 **VAT No.:** GB 501 3617 92
Date established: 1968 **Turnover:** £20m - £50m
No.of Employees: 101 - 250 **Product Groups:** 35, 36

Date of Accounts	Dec 11	Dec 10	Dec 09
Sales Turnover	20m	21m	21m
Pre Tax Profit/Loss	34	204	750

see next page

Abru Ltd - Cont'd

Working Capital	3m	3m	4m
Fixed Assets	1m	1m	2m
Current Assets	7m	8m	8m
Current Liabilities	1m	1m	1m

Adshead Ratcliffe & Co. Ltd

Derby Road, Belper, DE56 1WJ
Tel: 01773-826661 **Fax:** 01773-821215
E-mail: julian.miller@arbo.co.uk
Website: http://www.arbo.co.uk
Bank(s): Barclays Bank Plc
Directors: L. Bailey (MD), R. Sheehan (Chief Op Offcr), M. Blunden (Tech Sales), B. Ratcliffe (Ch), A. Newton (Sales), M. Bullen (Tech Sales)
Managers: S. Brown, J. Miller (Comptroller), C. Sheehan (Prod Mgr)
Ultimate Holding Company: ARBO (HOLDINGS) LIMITED
Immediate Holding Company: ADSHEAD RATCLIFFE & COMPANY,LIMITED
Registration no: 00388288 **VAT No.:** GB 295 2020 69
Date established: 1944 **Turnover:** £5m - £10m
No.of Employees: 51 - 100 **Product Groups:** 27, 30, 31, 32, 35, 37, 42, 66

Date of Accounts	Jan 11	Jan 10	Jan 09
Sales Turnover	8m	8m	N/A
Pre Tax Profit/Loss	306	165	59
Working Capital	1m	1m	1m
Fixed Assets	61	72	130
Current Assets	4m	4m	4m
Current Liabilities	475	390	575

B B Beresford

Goods Road, Belper, DE56 1UU
Tel: 01773-825959 **Fax:** 01773-821213
E-mail: beresford@btconnect.com
Website: http://www.beresford.uk.com
Directors: B. Beresford (MD)
Immediate Holding Company: NELSON DISTRIBUTION LTD
Registration no: 05879632 **VAT No.:** GB 401 5834 82
Date established: 1986 **Turnover:** £1m - £2m **No.of Employees:** 11 - 20
Product Groups: 30, 33

Bowmer & Kirkland Ltd

High Edge Court Church Street, Heage, Belper, DE56 2BW
Tel: 01773-853131 **Fax:** 01773-856710
E-mail: john.kirkland@bandk.co.uk
Website: http://www.bandk.co.uk
Bank(s): Lloyds TSB Bank plc
Directors: C. Stirland (Tech Serv), J. Kirkland (MD), M. Sheldon (Fin), R. Jones (Sales & Mktg)
Managers: M. Robinson (Buyer), E. Lord (Personnel)
Ultimate Holding Company: BOWMER AND KIRKLAND LIMITED
Immediate Holding Company: BOWMER AND KIRKLAND LIMITED
Registration no: 00701982 **VAT No.:** GB 125 7674 54
Date established: 1961 **Turnover:** £500m - £1,000m
No.of Employees: 251 - 500 **Product Groups:** 87

Date of Accounts	Aug 11	Aug 10	Aug 09
Sales Turnover	708m	667m	870m
Pre Tax Profit/Loss	45m	33m	29m
Working Capital	104m	96m	78m
Fixed Assets	182m	149m	143m
Current Assets	448m	440m	435m
Current Liabilities	175m	199m	181m

Brick & Stone Cosmetics Western Ltd

56 Pinewood Road, Belper, DE56 2TS
Tel: 01773-826160
Directors: S. Oldknown (MD)
Registration no: 05213032 **Date established:** 2004
No.of Employees: 1 - 10 **Product Groups:** 31, 32, 48, 66

D S Smith Speciality Packaging Ltd

Derby Road, Belper, DE56 1WL
Tel: 01773-822811 **Fax:** 01773-820633
E-mail: sales.support@dssp.com
Website: http://www.dssmith-packaging.com
Bank(s): National Westminster Bank Plc
Directors: T. Nelson (I.T. Dir), G. Tattam (MD)
Managers: D. Greaves (Tech Serv Mgr), C. Munro, C. Monroe, J. Sloan (Comptroller), C. Norton (Sales Prom Mgr), A. Platts (Sales Prom Mgr), J. Hitchcock (Comptroller)
Immediate Holding Company: DAVID S. SMITH GROUP
Registration no: 00001437 **VAT No.:** GB 570 9211 47
Turnover: Over £1,000m **No.of Employees:** 101 - 250
Product Groups: 27

Derbyshire Building Society

Duffield Hall St Ronans Avenue, Duffield, Belper, DE56 4HG
Tel: 08456-004005 **Fax:** 01332-840350
E-mail: customerservices@thederbyshire.co.uk
Website: http://www.thederbyshire.co.uk
Directors: J. Paul (Co Sec), A. Thorpe (Sales), S. Breakspear (Dir)
Managers: P. Richardson
Immediate Holding Company: DERBYSHIRE IFS LTD
Registration no: 02170056 **Date established:** 1987 **Turnover:** £2m - £5m
No.of Employees: 1 - 10 **Product Groups:** 82

Date of Accounts	Dec 07	Dec 06	Dec 05
Sales Turnover	3520	1682	1319
Pre Tax Profit/Loss	924	234	104
Working Capital	766	103	-155
Fixed Assets	87	107	195
Current Assets	1516	430	337
Current Liabilities	750	327	492
Total Share Capital	10	10	10
ROCE% (Return on Capital Employed)	108.3	111.4	256.8
ROT% (Return on Turnover)	26.3	13.9	7.9

Fisher Consultants Derbyshire Ltd

8 Parkside, Belper, DE56 1HY
Tel: 08453-707760
Website: http://www.fisherconsultants.co.uk
Directors: S. Fisher (Fin), D. Fisher (Dir), D. Fisher (Prop), D. Fisher (MD)
Immediate Holding Company: FISHER CONSULTANTS (DERBYSHIRE) LIMITED
Registration no: 05859767 **VAT No.:** GB 395 6666 90
Date established: 2006 **Turnover:** Up to £250,000
No.of Employees: 1 - 10 **Product Groups:** 85

Date of Accounts	May 11	May 10	May 09
Working Capital	12	15	16
Fixed Assets	N/A	N/A	1
Current Assets	12	15	16

Grant M S M Ltd

Goods Road, Belper, DE56 1UU
Tel: 01773-827268 **Fax:** 01773-880884
E-mail: sales@grantmsm.co.uk
Website: http://www.grantmsm.co.uk
Bank(s): Lloyds TSB Bank plc
Directors: K. Hallsworth (Sales), N. Hunt (Fin), B. Barge (Co Sec)
Ultimate Holding Company: NIC GROUP LIMITED
Immediate Holding Company: GRANT M.S.M. LIMITED
Registration no: 06353779 **VAT No.:** GB 706 0820 64
Date established: 2007 **Turnover:** £1m - £2m **No.of Employees:** 21 - 50
Product Groups: 22, 24, 40

Heatcall Group Services

Nottingham Road, Belper, DE56 1JT
Tel: 01773-828100 **Fax:** 01773-828123
Website: http://www.vaillant.co.uk
Managers: K. Mathers (Mgr)
Ultimate Holding Company: VAILLANT GMBH (GERMANY)
Immediate Holding Company: VAILLANT INDUSTRIAL UK LIMITED
Registration no: 01064184 **Date established:** 1972
Turnover: £125m - £250m **No.of Employees:** 501 - 1000
Product Groups: 40

Date of Accounts	Dec 11	Dec 10	Dec 09
Sales Turnover	102m	119m	115m
Pre Tax Profit/Loss	5m	6m	5m
Working Capital	40m	42m	38m
Fixed Assets	6m	4m	4m
Current Assets	77m	81m	79m
Current Liabilities	20m	28m	25m

L B Plastics Ltd

Firs Works Heage Firs, Nether Heage, Belper, DE56 2JJ
Tel: 01773-852311 **Fax:** 01773-857080
E-mail: info@lbplastics.co.uk
Website: http://www.litchfield-group.co.uk
Bank(s): Barclays, Nottingham
Directors: D. Strang (Mkt Research), L. Litchfield (Ch), M. Llewellyn (Fin)
Managers: N. Bird (Personnel), S. Woodward (Tech Serv Mgr), R. Erridge (Purch Mgr)
Immediate Holding Company: L. B. PLASTICS LIMITED
Registration no: 00559700 **Date established:** 1956
Turnover: £50m - £75m **No.of Employees:** 501 - 1000
Product Groups: 26, 30, 39, 66

Date of Accounts	Dec 11	Dec 10	Dec 09
Sales Turnover	50m	51m	55m
Pre Tax Profit/Loss	-4m	-5m	-4m
Working Capital	13m	16m	21m
Fixed Assets	20m	21m	22m
Current Assets	22m	26m	26m
Current Liabilities	1m	954	2m

Litchfield Bros Ltd

Ripley Road Ambergate, Belper, DE56 2EP
Tel: 01773-852435 **Fax:** 01773-852661
E-mail: info@lbplastics.co.uk
Website: http://www.litchfield-group.co.uk
Bank(s): Barclays, Nottingham
Managers: A. Simmonds (Mgr)
Ultimate Holding Company: L. B. PLASTICS LIMITED
Immediate Holding Company: LITCHFIELD BROS. LIMITED
Registration no: 00495416 **Date established:** 1951
Turnover: £250,000 - £500,000 **No.of Employees:** 11 - 20
Product Groups: 35, 36

Date of Accounts	Dec 11	Dec 10	Dec 09
Sales Turnover	N/A	438	514
Pre Tax Profit/Loss	N/A	-71	-87
Working Capital	3m	3m	3m
Fixed Assets	17	6	5
Current Assets	3m	3m	3m
Current Liabilities	N/A	22	17

Snake Lane Design Ltd

2 Snake Lane Duffield, Belper, DE56 4FF
Tel: 01332-840889 **Fax:** 08717-333764
E-mail: ian.slater@snakelane.co.uk
Website: http://www.snakelane.co.uk
Directors: F. Ford (Fin), I. Slater (MD)
Immediate Holding Company: SNAKE LANE DESIGN LIMITED
Registration no: 04855818 **Date established:** 2003
Turnover: Up to £250,000 **No.of Employees:** 1 - 10 **Product Groups:** 44, 81, 84

Date of Accounts	Aug 11	Aug 10	Aug 09
Working Capital	-42	-61	-38
Fixed Assets	6	7	7
Current Assets	11	12	7

Sound Dynamics Ltd

Avenue House Sunny Bank Gardens, Belper, DE56 1WD
Tel: 01773-828486 **Fax:** 01773-828475
E-mail: stuartw@sound-dynamics.co.uk
Website: http://www.sound-dynamics.co.uk
Directors: S. Wilkinson (Dir)
Immediate Holding Company: SOUND DYNAMICS LIMITED
Registration no: 02288871 **Date established:** 1988
Turnover: £500,000 - £1m **No.of Employees:** 1 - 10 **Product Groups:** 26, 37, 44, 49, 65, 67

Date of Accounts	Aug 11	Aug 10	Aug 09
Working Capital	88	84	39
Fixed Assets	1	2	2
Current Assets	183	184	122

T W Titterton

Field View 181 Ashbourne Road, Turnditch, Belper, DE56 2LH
Tel: 01773-550401
Directors: T. Titterton (Prop)
Date established: 1966 **No.of Employees:** 1 - 10 **Product Groups:** 41

Buxton

A B & Sons Ltd

15a Batham Gate Road Peak Dale, Buxton, SK17 8AH
Tel: 01298-23607 **Fax:** 01298-72087
Directors: D. Birch (Dir)
Immediate Holding Company: A B & SONS LIMITED
Registration no: 04293408 **Date established:** 2001
No.of Employees: 1 - 10 **Product Groups:** 38, 42

Date of Accounts	Sep 11	Sep 10	Sep 09
Working Capital	29	36	19
Fixed Assets	44	39	39
Current Assets	132	136	105

Belle Engineering Sheen Ltd

Sheen, Buxton, SK17 0EU
Tel: 01298-84606 **Fax:** 01298-84722
E-mail: sales@belle-group.co.uk
Website: http://www.belle-group.co.uk
Bank(s): The Royal Bank of Scotland
Directors: R. Neilson (Dir)
Managers: B. Gill (Tech Serv Mgr), I. Smith (Comptroller)
Ultimate Holding Company: ALTRAD INVESTMENT AUTHORITY (FRANCE)
Immediate Holding Company: BELLE ENGINEERING (SHEEN) LIMITED
Registration no: 00682892 **VAT No.:** GB 278 7948 79
Date established: 1961 **Turnover:** £20m - £50m
No.of Employees: 101 - 250 **Product Groups:** 45

Date of Accounts	Dec 08	Aug 11	Aug 10
Sales Turnover	42m	27m	25m
Pre Tax Profit/Loss	-8m	2m	547
Working Capital	994	6m	5m
Fixed Assets	2m	2m	2m
Current Assets	15m	15m	13m
Current Liabilities	2m	1m	657

Bradbury & Son Buxton Ltd

Staden Business Park Staden Lane, Buxton, SK17 9SZ
Tel: 01298-23180 **Fax:** 01298-27302
E-mail: richard.paul@bradburyscheese.co.uk
Website: http://www.bradburyandson.co.uk
Directors: G. Paul (Fin)
Managers: R. Paul
Immediate Holding Company: BRADBURY & SON (BUXTON) LIMITED
Registration no: 00363223 **Date established:** 1940
Turnover: £50m - £75m **No.of Employees:** 51 - 100 **Product Groups:** 20, 62

Date of Accounts	Apr 08	Apr 07	Apr 06
Sales Turnover	50478	N/A	N/A
Pre Tax Profit/Loss	457	-186	527
Working Capital	1083	956	1360
Fixed Assets	4315	4188	3038
Current Assets	9837	8168	8196
Current Liabilities	8753	7212	6836
Total Share Capital	3	3	3
ROCE% (Return on Capital Employed)	8.5	-3.6	12.0
ROT% (Return on Turnover)	0.9		

Buxton Press Ltd

Palace Road, Buxton, SK17 6AE
Tel: 01298-212000 **Fax:** 01298-212001
E-mail: kirkgalloway@buxpress.co.uk
Website: http://www.buxtonpress.co.uk
Bank(s): The Royal Bank of Scotland
Directors: M. Williams (I.T. Dir), K. Galloway (MD), B. Galloway (Ch), B. Galloway (MD), G. Briddon (MD), K. Gallaway (Works)
Ultimate Holding Company: 05494895
Immediate Holding Company: BUXTON PRESS LIMITED
Registration no: 00662586 **VAT No.:** GB 157 2459 50
Date established: 1960 **Turnover:** £10m - £20m
No.of Employees: 101 - 250 **Product Groups:** 28

Date of Accounts	Sep 09	Sep 08	Sep 07
Pre Tax Profit/Loss	859	1m	1m
Working Capital	1m	763	347
Fixed Assets	3m	4m	5m
Current Assets	4m	4m	3m
Current Liabilities	405	691	581

D S F Refractories & Minerals Ltd

Friden Newhaven, Buxton, SK17 0DX
Tel: 01629-636271 **Fax:** 01629-636892
E-mail: info@dsf.co.uk
Website: http://www.dsf.co.uk
Bank(s): Bank of Scotland, Edinburgh
Directors: N. Parkin (MD), P. Hutchinson (Sales & Mktg)
Managers: P. Bearn (Comptroller), P. Bearn (Comptroller), P. Llanwarne (Purch Mgr), J. Flower (Personnel), J. Flower (Personnel), I. Gould (Tech Serv Mgr)
Ultimate Holding Company: DSF HOLDINGS LIMITED
Immediate Holding Company: DSF REFRACTORIES & MINERALS LIMITED
Registration no: SC144005 **VAT No.:** GB 611 6814 60
Date established: 1993 **Turnover:** £5m - £10m
No.of Employees: 101 - 250 **Product Groups:** 33

Date of Accounts	May 11	May 10	May 09
Sales Turnover	20m	17m	20m
Pre Tax Profit/Loss	904	1m	2m
Working Capital	4m	4m	3m
Fixed Assets	5m	4m	4m
Current Assets	11m	8m	10m
Current Liabilities	768	1m	2m

Elliott & Wragg Ltd

Elliott & Wragg Buxton Road, Tideswell, Buxton, SK17 8PQ
Tel: 01298-871582 **Fax:** 01298-871785
Directors: C. Wragg (Dir)
Immediate Holding Company: ELLIOTT AND WRAGG LTD
Registration no: 06408331 **Date established:** 2007
No.of Employees: 1 - 10 **Product Groups:** 35, 51

Date of Accounts	Mar 11	Mar 10	Mar 09
Working Capital	-132	-131	-90
Fixed Assets	156	135	95
Current Assets	344	255	171
Current Liabilities	N/A	161	130

Flowflex Components Ltd
Samuel Blaser Works Tongue Lane Industrial Estate, Buxton, SK17 7LR
Tel: 01298-77211 **Fax:** 01298-72362
E-mail: sales@flowflex.com
Website: http://www.flowflex.com
Bank(s): Barclays
Directors: P. Cull (Fin), G. Croll (I.T. Dir)
Ultimate Holding Company: FLOWFLEX HOLDINGS LIMITED
Immediate Holding Company: FLOWFLEX COMPONENTS LIMITED
Registration no: 00530070 **VAT No.:** GB 511 5793 55
Date established: 1954 **Turnover:** £10m - £20m
No.of Employees: 51 - 100 **Product Groups:** 36, 37

Date of Accounts	Mar 11	Mar 10	Mar 09
Sales Turnover	16m	14m	N/A
Pre Tax Profit/Loss	-132	359	21
Working Capital	1m	1m	2m
Fixed Assets	1	3	5
Current Assets	9m	8m	7m
Current Liabilities	1m	2m	230

Greengages Limited
105 Fairfield Road, Buxton, SK17 7EZ
Tel: 0845-6588984
E-mail: info@greengages.com
Website: http://www.gogreengages.com
Directors: M. Timms (Dir)
Registration no: 06469195 **Date established:** 2008
Turnover: Up to £250,000 **No.of Employees:** 1 - 10 **Product Groups:** 69

Heathylee House Farm
Hollinsclough, Buxton, SK17 0RD
Tel: 01298-83659
E-mail: karen@heathylee.co.uk
Website: http://www.heathylee.co.uk
Managers: K. Ballington (Mgr)
Date established: 2003 **Turnover:** Up to £250,000
No.of Employees: 1 - 10 **Product Groups:** 66

Jayplas Extrusions Ltd
Unit 4 Whitecross Road Tideswell, Buxton, SK17 8NY
Tel: 01298-872161 **Fax:** 01298-872429
E-mail: enquiries@jayplas-extrusions.co.uk
Website: http://www.jayplas-extrusions.co.uk
Directors: J. Hallows (MD), A. Gregory (Fin)
Managers: A. Gregory (Sales Prom Mgr)
Immediate Holding Company: JAYPLAS EXTRUSIONS LIMITED
Registration no: 03724529 **VAT No.:** GB 438 9036 27
Date established: 1999 **Turnover:** £250,000 - £500,000
No.of Employees: 1 - 10 **Product Groups:** 30, 31, 42, 48, 66

Date of Accounts	Mar 11	Mar 10	Mar 09
Working Capital	-51	-50	-35
Fixed Assets	41	36	47
Current Assets	181	188	134

Lea Manufacturing Co.
Tongue Lane, Buxton, SK17 7LN
Tel: 01298-25335 **Fax:** 01298-79945
E-mail: info@lea.co.uk
Website: http://www.lea.co.uk
Bank(s): Royal Bank of Scotland, 1 Cavendish Circus, Buxton
Directors: R. Kennington (Fin), K. Thurlow (MD)
Ultimate Holding Company: PROFESSIONAL FINISHING LIMITED
Immediate Holding Company: GRESKETH LIMITED
Registration no: 00572541 **VAT No.:** GB 764 6576 86
Date established: 2003 **Turnover:** £2m - £5m **No.of Employees:** 11 - 20
Product Groups: 23, 25, 32, 33, 42, 45, 46

Lhoist UK
Hindlow, Buxton, SK17 0EL
Tel: 01298-768666 **Fax:** 01298-768667
E-mail: sales@lhoist.co.uk
Website: http://www.lhoist.co.uk
Managers: S. Baker (Purch Mgr), G. Watkins (Sales Prom Mgr), D. Patigny (Chief Mgr)
Ultimate Holding Company: Lhoist Group
Registration no: 04056154 **Turnover:** Over £1,000m
No.of Employees: 51 - 100 **Product Groups:** 14, 31, 32, 33, 66

Date of Accounts	Dec 11	Dec 10	Dec 09
Sales Turnover	26m	22m	19m
Pre Tax Profit/Loss	3m	945	-444
Working Capital	1m	3m	-15m
Fixed Assets	25m	27m	28m
Current Assets	7m	8m	7m
Current Liabilities	4m	4m	20m

Litton Logs
Dale House Farm Litton Dale, Litton, Buxton, SK17 8QL
Tel: 01298-872806
E-mail: markotter@btinternet.com
Website: http://www.littonlogs.co.uk
Directors: R. Otter (Prop)
Immediate Holding Company: LITTON LOGS LIMITED
Registration no: 07383106 **Date established:** 2010
No.of Employees: 11 - 20 **Product Groups:** 40

Otter Controls Ltd
Hardwick Square South, Buxton, SK17 6LA
Tel: 01298-762300 **Fax:** 01298-72664
E-mail: sales@ottercontrols.com
Website: http://www.ottercontrols.com
Bank(s): National Westminster Bank Plc
Directors: D. Smith (Dir), J. Preece (Grp Chief Exec), N. Salt (Dir), R. Hough (Co Sec)
Managers: K. Bradd (Purch Mgr), M. Gostick (I.T. Exec), R. Palmer (Sales & Mktg Mg)
Registration no: 00406954 **VAT No.:** GB 157 5881 26
Date established: 1946 **Turnover:** £20m - £50m
No.of Employees: 501 - 1000 **Product Groups:** 37, 38, 40

Date of Accounts	Dec 07
Sales Turnover	37510
Pre Tax Profit/Loss	2150
Working Capital	3750
Fixed Assets	13840
Current Assets	11440
Current Liabilities	7690
Total Share Capital	410
ROCE% (Return on Capital Employed)	12.2

Peak Traditional Ironwork
7b Meverill Road Tideswell, Buxton, SK17 8PY
Tel: 01298-872353 **Fax:** 01298-872353
E-mail: info@peakironwork.co.uk
Website: http://www.peakironwork.co.uk
Directors: J. Cartilage (Prop)
Date established: 1990 **No.of Employees:** 1 - 10 **Product Groups:** 26, 35

Plasma Biotal Ltd
Unit 3 Meverill Road, Tideswell, Buxton, SK17 8PY
Tel: 01298-872348 **Fax:** 01299-873708
E-mail: info@plasma-group.co.uk
Website: http://www.plasma-group.co.uk
Bank(s): Barclays
Directors: P. Stephenson (MD), P. Steverson (Fin), D. Anderson (MD)
Immediate Holding Company: PLASMA BIOTAL LIMITED
Registration no: 02490949 **VAT No.:** GB 593 6035 24
Date established: 1990 **Turnover:** £1m - £2m **No.of Employees:** 11 - 20
Product Groups: 38, 48

Date of Accounts	Mar 12	Mar 11	Mar 10
Working Capital	657	672	549
Fixed Assets	10	49	86
Current Assets	742	799	651

Rainer Schneider & Ayres
3 Hereford Close, Buxton, SK17 9PH
Tel: 01298-79903 **Fax:** 01298-72124
E-mail: rsa_bxt@btconnect.com
Website: http://www.rainer-schneider-ayres.co.uk
Directors: R. Ayres (Prop)
VAT No.: GB 350 5256 75 **Turnover:** £500,000 - £1m
No.of Employees: 1 - 10 **Product Groups:** 37, 38

Selden Research Ltd
Bradshaws Yard Staden Lane, Buxton, SK17 9RZ
Tel: 01298-26226 **Fax:** 01298-26540
E-mail: sales@selden.co.uk
Website: http://www.selden.co.uk
Bank(s): The Royal Bank of Scotland
Directors: M. Woodhead (MD), E. Woodhead (MD)
Managers: G. Overton (Tech Serv Mgr), Y. Watson (Personnel), G. Overton (I.T. Exec)
Immediate Holding Company: SELDEN RESEARCH LIMITED
Registration no: 00984285 **VAT No.:** GB 157 5116 65
Date established: 1970 **Turnover:** £10m - £20m
No.of Employees: 101 - 250 **Product Groups:** 31, 32, 66

Date of Accounts	Mar 12	Mar 11	Mar 10
Sales Turnover	17m	19m	19m
Pre Tax Profit/Loss	331	1m	705
Working Capital	2m	2m	2m
Fixed Assets	9m	9m	8m
Current Assets	6m	6m	6m
Current Liabilities	904	944	1m

Swift Catering Equipment
Unit 30 Harpur Hill Business Park, Buxton, SK17 9JL
Tel: 01298-79381 **Fax:** 01298-72212
Directors: G. Kitchen (Ptnr)
No.of Employees: 1 - 10 **Product Groups:** 20, 40, 41

Tarmac
Tunstead Quarry Tunstead, Buxton, SK17 8TG
Tel: 01298-768555 **Fax:** 01298-72195
E-mail: info@tarmac.co.uk
Website: http://www.tarmac.co.uk
Bank(s): Barclays
Managers: T. Last
Ultimate Holding Company: ANGLO AMERICAN PLC
Immediate Holding Company: TARMAC LTD
Registration no: 02649831 **Turnover:** £50m - £75m
No.of Employees: 101 - 250 **Product Groups:** 14, 33

Date of Accounts	Dec 10	Dec 09	Dec 08
Sales Turnover	1069m	1247m	1566m
Pre Tax Profit/Loss	75m	-47m	-29m
Working Capital	-24m	25m	2m
Fixed Assets	1244m	1391m	1434m
Current Assets	321m	431m	447m
Current Liabilities	93m	168m	213m

William Moss & Sons Stockport Ltd
Unit 15 Harpur Hill Business Park, Buxton, SK17 9JL
Tel: 01298-74988 **Fax:** 01298-74989
E-mail: alastairnmoss@msn.com
Website: http://www.williammoss.co.uk
Directors: A. Moss (MD)
Immediate Holding Company: WILLIAM MOSS & SONS (STOCKPORT) LIMITED
Registration no: 00207730 **Date established:** 2025
Turnover: £250,000 - £500,000 **No.of Employees:** 1 - 10
Product Groups: 34, 46, 48, 84

Date of Accounts	Sep 11	Sep 10	Sep 09
Working Capital	24	144	117
Fixed Assets	11	13	15
Current Assets	93	196	180

Chesterfield

A G W Electronics Ltd
Adelphi Way
Ireland Industrial Estate
Staveley, Chesterfield, S43 3LS
Tel: 01246-473086 **Fax:** 01246-280082
E-mail: kompass@agw.co.uk
Website: http://www.agw.co.uk
Bank(s): National Westminster Bank Plc
Directors: N. Godwin (MD), T. Godwin (Prop)
Managers: K. Vadhia (Sales Prom Mgr), K. Vadhia (Mgr), J. Taylor (Fin Mgr), K. Vadhia (Mktg Serv Mgr), P. Gillott (Prod Mgr), S. Orton (Purch Mgr), M. Mooney (Research & Deve), J. Walters (Tech Serv Mgr)
Ultimate Holding Company: AGW HOLDINGS LIMITED
Immediate Holding Company: A.G.W. ELECTRONICS LIMITED
Registration no: 01194670 **VAT No.:** GB 127 5652 62
Date established: 1974 **Turnover:** £2m - £5m **No.of Employees:** 51 - 100
Product Groups: 37, 48

Date of Accounts	Dec 11	Dec 10	Dec 09
Working Capital	1m	1m	1m
Fixed Assets	159	177	192
Current Assets	2m	2m	1m

Abel Demountable Systems Ltd
Station Road Old Tupton, Chesterfield, S42 6DA
Tel: 01246-851175 **Fax:** 01246-855506
E-mail: sales@abelsystems.co.uk
Website: http://www.abelsystems.co.uk
Bank(s): HSBC Bank plc
Directors: M. Brown (MD), S. Pickles (MD)
Managers: A. Farley (Purch Mgr), G. Taylor (Chief Acct)
Ultimate Holding Company: WHEELBASE HOLDINGS LIMITED
Immediate Holding Company: ABEL SYSTEMS LIMITED
Registration no: 01912556 **VAT No.:** GB 580 9592 02
Date established: 1985 **Turnover:** £2m - £5m **No.of Employees:** 21 - 50
Product Groups: 39

Date of Accounts	Aug 10	Aug 09	Aug 08
Working Capital	739	940	1m
Fixed Assets	153	163	144
Current Assets	1m	2m	2m

Alton Fork Truck Services
Pottery Lane East, Chesterfield, S41 9BH
Tel: 01246-455015 **Fax:** 01246-452020
E-mail: altonforks@aol.com
Directors: A. Oliver (MD), J. Oliver (Fin)
Immediate Holding Company: ALTON FORK TRUCK SERVICES LIMITED
Registration no: 04711997 **Date established:** 2003
No.of Employees: 1 - 10 **Product Groups:** 35, 39, 45

Date of Accounts	Sep 11	Sep 10	Sep 09
Working Capital	3	-4	-30
Fixed Assets	101	88	107
Current Assets	201	163	138

Amber Instruments Ltd
Dunston House Sheepbridge Works Dunston Road, Chesterfield, S41 9QD
Tel: 01246-260250 **Fax:** 01246-260955
E-mail: sales@amberinstruments.com
Website: http://amberinstruments.com
Directors: P. Armstrong (Dir)
Immediate Holding Company: AMBER INSTRUMENTS LIMITED
Registration no: 02184659 **VAT No.:** GB 593 3297 09
Date established: 1987 **Turnover:** £250,000 - £500,000
No.of Employees: 1 - 10 **Product Groups:** 35, 37, 38, 44

Date of Accounts	Mar 11	Mar 10	Mar 09
Working Capital	5	6	-6
Fixed Assets	3	3	4
Current Assets	77	61	52

Amber Plastics Ltd
Broombank Road, Chesterfield, S41 9QJ
Tel: 01246-453544 **Fax:** 01246-450339
E-mail: reception@amberplastics.co.uk
Website: http://www.amberplastics.co.uk
Bank(s): Yorkshire Bank PLC
Directors: D. Round (MD), R. Greenwood (Fin)
Managers: J. Siddell (Purch Mgr)
Immediate Holding Company: AMBER PLASTICS LIMITED
Registration no: 01553309 **VAT No.:** GB 295 5787 91
Date established: 1981 **Turnover:** £1m - £2m **No.of Employees:** 21 - 50
Product Groups: 26, 30, 39, 45, 66

Date of Accounts	Apr 11	Apr 10	Apr 09
Working Capital	32	-5	-70
Fixed Assets	283	249	288
Current Assets	635	573	506

Amies W E & Co. Ltd
Quarry Lane, Chesterfield, S40 3AT
Tel: 01246-568046 **Fax:** 01246-569811
E-mail: sales@amiesplastics.co.uk
Website: http://www.amiesplastics.co.uk
Bank(s): National Westminster Bank Plc
Directors: R. Ball (MD)
Managers: D. Shepley (Prod Mgr)
Immediate Holding Company: W E AMIES HOLDINGS LIMITED
Registration no: 07276098 **VAT No.:** GB 706 5346 41
Date established: 2010 **Turnover:** £500,000 - £1m
No.of Employees: 21 - 50 **Product Groups:** 30, 66

Date of Accounts	Dec 11	Dec 10
Working Capital	21	N/A
Fixed Assets	50	N/A
Current Assets	48	N/A

Andrew Engineering Ltd
1a Foxwood Way, Chesterfield, S41 9RA
Tel: 01246-261422 **Fax:** 08451-267874
E-mail: sales@andrew-eng.co.uk
Website: http://www.andrew-eng.co.uk
Managers: S. Skinner (Chief Acct)
Immediate Holding Company: ANDREW ENGINEERING LIMITED
Registration no: 01598495 **Date established:** 1981 **Turnover:** £1m - £2m
No.of Employees: 1 - 10 **Product Groups:** 40, 52, 84

Date of Accounts	Mar 12	Mar 11	Mar 10
Working Capital	116	230	269
Fixed Assets	60	25	22
Current Assets	216	362	369

Anixter Ltd
Brimington Road North, Chesterfield, S41 9BE
Tel: 01246-459300 **Fax:** 01246-455778
E-mail: chris.tyrrell@anixter.com
Website: http://www.anixter.com
Directors: C. Tyrrell (MD)
Ultimate Holding Company: ANIXTER INTERNATIONAL INC (USA)
Immediate Holding Company: ANIXTER LIMITED
Registration no: 00248952 **Date established:** 1930
No.of Employees: 51 - 100 **Product Groups:** 30, 32, 35

Date of Accounts	Jun 11	Jun 10	Jun 09
Working Capital	330	148	133
Fixed Assets	28	37	50
Current Assets	1m	1m	1m

Applied Laser Solutions Ltd
Unit 4 Broombank Park, Chesterfield, S41 9RT
Tel: 01246-268662 **Fax:** 01246-268657
E-mail: sales@appliedlaser.fsnet.co.uk
Website: http://www.appliedlasersolutions.co.uk

see next page

***Applied Laser Solutions Ltd** - Cont'd*

Directors: S. Roe (MD)
Immediate Holding Company: APPLIED LASER SOLUTIONS LIMITED
Registration no: 04016448 **Date established:** 2000
No.of Employees: 1 - 10 **Product Groups:** 38, 42, 46

Date of Accounts	Aug 11	Aug 10	Aug 09
Working Capital	3	5	-7
Fixed Assets	5	6	8
Current Assets	36	44	48

Ariel Plastics Ltd

Speedwell Industrial Estate Staveley, Chesterfield, S43 3JP
Tel: 01246-281111 **Fax:** 01246-561115
E-mail: pat.williams@brettmartin.com
Website: http://www.arielplastics.com
Bank(s): Barclays
Directors: J. Taylor (Fin), M. Porter (MD)
Managers: P. Bingham (Buyer), D. Walker
Ultimate Holding Company: BRETT MARTIN HOLDINGS LTD
Immediate Holding Company: ARIEL PLASTICS LIMITED
Registration no: 02257976 **Date established:** 1988
Turnover: £10m - £20m **No.of Employees:** 51 - 100 **Product Groups:** 30, 52

Date of Accounts	Dec 11	Dec 10	Dec 09
Sales Turnover	13m	12m	12m
Pre Tax Profit/Loss	-854	-471	-426
Working Capital	-7m	-6m	-6m
Fixed Assets	718	966	617
Current Assets	7m	7m	6m
Current Liabilities	3m	1m	918

Arrow Butler Castings

Station Road Whittington Moor, Chesterfield, S41 9ES
Tel: 01246-450027 **Fax:** 01246-261913
E-mail: sales@arrowbutlercastings.co.uk
Website: http://www.arrowbutlercastings.co.uk
Bank(s): National Westminster
Directors: G. Robertshaw (Dir), V. Robertshaw (Co Sec)
Managers: P. Roberts
Immediate Holding Company: ARROW BUTLER CASTINGS LIMITED
Registration no: 02377673 **Date established:** 1989 **Turnover:** £1m - £2m
No.of Employees: 21 - 50 **Product Groups:** 34

Date of Accounts	Mar 12	Mar 11	Mar 10
Working Capital	78	63	94
Fixed Assets	49	61	74
Current Assets	566	585	432

Arrowhead Rockdrill Co. Ltd

Hema Works Station Lane, Old Whittington, Chesterfield, S41 9QX
Tel: 01246-260012 **Fax:** 01246-260013
E-mail: info@arrowheadrockdrill.com
Website: http://www.arrowheadrockdrill.co.uk
Directors: B. Johnson (Sales)
Ultimate Holding Company: HYDRODYNE SYSTEMS LIMITED
Immediate Holding Company: ARROWHEAD ROCKDRILL COMPANY LIMITED
Registration no: 03246725 **Date established:** 1996
No.of Employees: 21 - 50 **Product Groups:** 45, 46, 48, 83, 84

Date of Accounts	Apr 11	Apr 10	Apr 09
Working Capital	1m	2m	2m
Current Assets	3m	3m	3m

Arthritis Research UK

Copeman House St Marys Court St Marys Gate, Chesterfield, S41 7TD
Tel: 01246-558033 **Fax:** 01246-558007
E-mail: enquiries@arthritisresearchuk.org
Website: http://www.arthritisresearchuk.org
Directors: L. O'toole (Dir)
Immediate Holding Company: ARTHRITIS RESEARCH UK
Registration no: 00490500 **Date established:** 1951
Turnover: £20m - £50m **No.of Employees:** 51 - 100 **Product Groups:** 81, 85

Date of Accounts	Jul 11	Jul 10	Jul 09
Sales Turnover	36m	39m	38m
Pre Tax Profit/Loss	11m	15m	-3m
Working Capital	5m	6m	13m
Fixed Assets	106m	94m	72m
Current Assets	18m	20m	22m
Current Liabilities	13m	14m	10m

Arthur Cottam & Co.

Carnwood Road, Chesterfield, S41 9QB
Tel: 01246-453672 **Fax:** 01246-260274
E-mail: info@cottamhorseshoes.com
Website: http://www.cottamhorseshoes.com
Directors: P. Cottam (MD)
Managers: G. Wilson (Fin Mgr), K. Gill (Sales Prom Mgr)
Immediate Holding Company: ARTHUR COTTAM & CO.(HORSE SHOES)LIMITED
Registration no: 00753241 **Date established:** 1963
Turnover: £250,000 - £500,000 **No.of Employees:** 11 - 20
Product Groups: 29, 30, 35, 36

Date of Accounts	Apr 12	Apr 11	Apr 10
Working Capital	244	338	292
Fixed Assets	968	1m	1m
Current Assets	996	999	1m

Aspire Gates

Unit 2 Broombank Park, Chesterfield, S41 9RT
Tel: 01246-454505
E-mail: richbrear@hotmail.co.uk
Website: http://www.aspiregates.co.uk
Directors: R. Brear (MD)
Immediate Holding Company: ASPIRE GATES LIMITED
Registration no: 04805598 **Date established:** 2003
No.of Employees: 1 - 10 **Product Groups:** 26, 35

Date of Accounts	Jul 11	Jul 10	Jul 09
Working Capital	-7	-8	-6
Fixed Assets	9	9	10
Current Assets	11	12	17

AvantiGas

P.O. Box 1100, Chesterfield, S44 5YQ
Tel: 0808-208 0000 **Fax:** 0870-830 1101
E-mail: enquiries@avantigas.com
Website: http://www.avantigas.com
Managers: A. Mann (Mktg Serv Mgr)
Registration no: 481121 **Date established:** 1962
No.of Employees: 1501 & over **Product Groups:** 18, 31, 35, 39, 40, 42, 52, 63, 68, 77

Band-It Co. Ltd

Telford Crescent Speedwell Industrial Estate, Staveley, Chesterfield, S43 3PF
Tel: 01246-477333 **Fax:** 01246-476324
E-mail: jbowmer@idexcorp.com
Website: http://www.band-it-idex.eu
Directors: J. Bowmer (Sales & Mktg)
Managers: K. Allsopp (Fin Mgr), S. Furness (Buyer), T. Parker (Tech Serv Mgr)
Ultimate Holding Company: IDEX CORPORATION (USA)
Immediate Holding Company: BAND-IT COMPANY LIMITED
Registration no: 00763442 **Date established:** 1963
Turnover: £10m - £20m **No.of Employees:** 51 - 100 **Product Groups:** 35, 36, 37, 39

Date of Accounts	Dec 11	Dec 10	Dec 09
Sales Turnover	13m	12m	11m
Pre Tax Profit/Loss	3m	3m	4m
Working Capital	20m	17m	15m
Fixed Assets	852	1m	1m
Current Assets	21m	19m	16m
Current Liabilities	493	373	590

Peter J Bates

105 Whitecotes Lane, Chesterfield, S40 3HJ
Tel: 01246-279538 **Fax:** 01246-279539
E-mail: peter.bates@ratiolink.org
Website: http://www.ratiolink.org
Directors: P. Bates (Prop)
No.of Employees: 1 - 10 **Product Groups:** 35

BeaconMedaes

Telford Crescent Staveley, Chesterfield, S43 3PE
Tel: 01246-474242 **Fax:** 01246-472982
E-mail: gbn.info@beaconmedaes.com
Website: http://www.beaconmedaes.com
Directors: J. Tapkas (Pres), S. Parkinson (MD)
Registration no: 59861259 **Date established:** 1994
Turnover: £10m - £20m **No.of Employees:** 21 - 50 **Product Groups:** 26, 31, 37, 38, 40, 42, 48, 67, 84, 85

Bembridges Portable Buildings

53 Lordsmill Street, Chesterfield, S41 7RS
Tel: 01246-273969 **Fax:** 01246-273969
Directors: T. Bembridge (Ptnr)
Date established: 1937 **No.of Employees:** 1 - 10 **Product Groups:** 35

Biffa Waste Services Ltd

20 Station Road Clowne, Chesterfield, S43 4PE
Tel: 0800-307307 **Fax:** 01235- 521842
E-mail: info@biffa.co.uk
Website: http://www.biffa.co.uk
Managers: D. Mann
Immediate Holding Company: BIFFA WASTE SERVICES LIMITED
Registration no: 00946107 **Date established:** 1969
No.of Employees: 51 - 100 **Product Groups:** 32, 54

Date of Accounts	Mar 08	Mar 09	Apr 10
Sales Turnover	555m	574m	492m
Pre Tax Profit/Loss	23m	50m	30m
Working Capital	229m	271m	293m
Fixed Assets	371m	360m	378m
Current Assets	409m	534m	609m
Current Liabilities	50m	100m	115m

Bodycote H I P Ltd

Carlisle Close Sheffield Road, Chesterfield, S41 9ED
Tel: 01246-260888 **Fax:** 01246-260889
E-mail: lance.tidbury@bodycote.com
Website: http://www.bodycote.com
Bank(s): HSBC
Managers: L. Tidbury
Ultimate Holding Company: BODYCOTE PLC
Immediate Holding Company: BODYCOTE H.I.P. LIMITED
Registration no: 01276450 **VAT No.:** GB 593 6330 22
Date established: 1976 **Turnover:** £10m - £20m
No.of Employees: 21 - 50 **Product Groups:** 46

Date of Accounts	Dec 11	Dec 10	Dec 09
Sales Turnover	5m	5m	7m
Pre Tax Profit/Loss	1m	417	1m
Working Capital	2m	3m	242
Fixed Assets	9m	10m	11m
Current Assets	4m	4m	3m
Current Liabilities	1m	1m	2m

British Rema Manufacturing Co. Ltd

The Image Works Foxwood Industrial Park, Chesterfield, S41 9RN
Tel: 01246-269955 **Fax:** 01246-269944
E-mail: sales@britishrema.co.uk
Website: http://www.britishrema.com
Directors: W. Mcbride (Fin), S. Cuthbert (MD)
Managers: A. Hooley (Purch Mgr), M. Cunningham (Sales Prom Mgr), J. Kemp (Tech Sales Mgr), B. Tomlinson, A. Belega (Mktg Serv Mgr)
Immediate Holding Company: DASU LIMITED
Registration no: 01491606 **VAT No.:** GB 172 3758 51
Date established: 2011 **Turnover:** £1m - £2m **No.of Employees:** 1 - 10
Product Groups: 32, 33, 41, 42, 84

Date of Accounts	Mar 12	Mar 11	Mar 10
Working Capital	905	1m	739
Fixed Assets	2m	2m	2m
Current Assets	2m	2m	1m

Bryan Donkin R M G Gas Controls Ltd

Enterprise Drive Holmewood, Chesterfield, S42 5UZ
Tel: 01246-501501 **Fax:** 01246-501500
E-mail: sales@bdrmg.co.uk
Website: http://www.bdrmg.co.uk
Bank(s): HSBC
Directors: G. Lloyd (Co Sec), A. Clark (MD)
Ultimate Holding Company: HONEYWELL INTERNATIONAL INC (USA)
Immediate Holding Company: BRYAN DONKIN RMG GAS CONTROLS LIMITED
Registration no: 03123056 **VAT No.:** 657 8647 76 **Date established:** 1995
Turnover: £10m - £20m **No.of Employees:** 51 - 100 **Product Groups:** 38

Date of Accounts	Dec 11	Dec 10	Dec 09
Sales Turnover	12m	10m	11m
Pre Tax Profit/Loss	50	882	1m
Working Capital	4m	4m	3m
Fixed Assets	247	246	259
Current Assets	7m	6m	5m
Current Liabilities	1m	372	741

Bulroc Ltd

Station Lane Old Whittington, Chesterfield, S41 9QX
Tel: 01246-450608 **Fax:** 01246-454621
E-mail: info@bulroc.com
Website: http://www.bulroc.com
Bank(s): HSBC Bank plc
Directors: J. Hurt (MD), J. Hurt (Ch)
Managers: S. Wagstaff (Purch Mgr), D. Pieris
Immediate Holding Company: BULROC (UK) LIMITED
Registration no: 01139416 **VAT No.:** GB 127 3317 86
Date established: 1973 **Turnover:** £5m - £10m **No.of Employees:** 21 - 50
Product Groups: 45

Date of Accounts	Mar 11	Mar 10	Mar 09
Working Capital	2m	2m	1m
Fixed Assets	2m	1m	1m
Current Assets	4m	3m	3m

C C S Media Ltd

Old Birdholme House Derby Road, Chesterfield, S40 2EX
Tel: 01246-200200 **Fax:** 01246-207048
E-mail: terry.betts@ccsmedia.com
Website: http://www.ccsmedia.com
Directors: R. Omar (Sales)
Ultimate Holding Company: CCS MEDIA HOLDINGS LIMITED
Immediate Holding Company: CCS MEDIA LIMITED
Registration no: 01693516 **Date established:** 1983
Turnover: £50m - £75m **No.of Employees:** 51 - 100 **Product Groups:** 26, 37, 38, 44

Date of Accounts	Dec 11	Dec 10	Dec 09
Sales Turnover	68m	60m	53m
Pre Tax Profit/Loss	677	665	126
Working Capital	1m	838	912
Fixed Assets	1m	1m	1m
Current Assets	16m	14m	12m
Current Liabilities	3m	3m	1m

C & J Supplies

First Stage House Brimington Road North, Chesterfield, S41 9BE
Tel: 01246-205271 **Fax:** 01246-206045
Directors: J. Sanderson (MD)
Immediate Holding Company: R HICKS (HOLDINGS) LIMITED
Registration no: 04071332 **Date established:** 1990
No.of Employees: 1 - 10 **Product Groups:** 36, 40

C P L Distribution

Mill Lane Wingerworth, Chesterfield, S42 6NG
Tel: 01246-277001 **Fax:** 01246-212212
E-mail: info@cpldistribution.co.uk
Website: http://www.coals2u.co.uk
Bank(s): National Westminster
Managers: J. Carter (Mktg Serv Mgr)
Ultimate Holding Company: CPL INDUSTRIES HOLDINGS LIMITED
Immediate Holding Company: CPL DISTRIBUTION LIMITED
Registration no: 00544782 **Date established:** 1955
Turnover: £50m - £75m **No.of Employees:** 51 - 100 **Product Groups:** 11, 25, 31, 45

Date of Accounts	Mar 12	Mar 11	Mar 10
Sales Turnover	63m	72m	72m
Pre Tax Profit/Loss	997	2m	2m
Working Capital	27m	28m	27m
Fixed Assets	16m	16m	16m
Current Assets	45m	37m	35m
Current Liabilities	2m	2m	2m

C Y L Liners Ltd

Whitting Valley Road Old Whittington, Chesterfield, S41 9EY
Tel: 01246-456133 **Fax:** 01246-456134
E-mail: cyl-liners@btconnect.com
Website: http://www.cyl-liners.co.uk
Directors: N. Ingman (MD), T. Ingman (Fin)
Immediate Holding Company: CYL-LINERS LIMITED
Registration no: 01213275 **Date established:** 1975
No.of Employees: 1 - 10 **Product Groups:** 35, 36, 39

Date of Accounts	Jun 11	Jun 10	Jun 09
Working Capital	103	95	92
Fixed Assets	1	1	3
Current Assets	159	152	166

Caldic UK Ltd

Stainsby Close Holmewood Industrial Estate, Holmewood, Chesterfield, S42 5UG
Tel: 01246-854111 **Fax:** 01246-856222
E-mail: j.mitchell@caldic.com
Website: http://www.caldic.com
Bank(s): Lloyds TSB Bank plc
Directors: J. Mitchell (Co Sec)
Ultimate Holding Company: CALDIC BV (NETHERLANDS)
Immediate Holding Company: CALDIC (UK) LTD
Registration no: 02084881 **VAT No.:** GB 603 6935 43
Date established: 1986 **Turnover:** £20m - £50m
No.of Employees: 21 - 50 **Product Groups:** 31, 87

Date of Accounts	Dec 11	Dec 10	Dec 09
Sales Turnover	33m	22m	18m
Pre Tax Profit/Loss	3m	1m	806
Working Capital	3m	573	778
Fixed Assets	2m	1m	922
Current Assets	8m	6m	4m
Current Liabilities	1m	834	680

Capital Refractories Ltd

2 Station Road Clowne, Chesterfield, S43 4AB
Tel: 01246-811163 **Fax:** 01246-819573
E-mail: info@capital-refractories.com
Website: http://www.capital-refractories.com
Bank(s): Lloyds TSB Bank plc
Directors: J. Newsome (MD), N. Robson (Sales), D. Newsome (Co Sec)
Managers: C. Wragg (Mgr), L. Denman (Tech Serv Mgr)
Immediate Holding Company: CAPITAL REFRACTORIES LIMITED
Registration no: 01101489 **VAT No.:** GB 354 4598 28
Date established: 1973 **Turnover:** £20m - £50m
No.of Employees: 21 - 50 **Product Groups:** 66

Date of Accounts	Nov 11	Nov 10	Nov 09
Sales Turnover	22m	18m	15m
Pre Tax Profit/Loss	2m	863	412

Working Capital	3m	2m	2m
Fixed Assets	3m	3m	3m
Current Assets	9m	7m	6m
Current Liabilities	820	924	977

Castle Container Services
3 Sheepbridge Centre Sheepbridge Lane, Chesterfield, S41 9RX
Tel: 01246-456522 **Fax:** 01246-456523
E-mail: kbe@castleskips.co.uk
Website: http://www.skipunits.co.uk
Bank(s): The Royal Bank of Scotland
Directors: M. Hampson (Sales), R. Wake (Fin), A. Muirhead (MD)
Ultimate Holding Company: RAMSHORN LIMITED
Immediate Holding Company: CASTLE CONTAINER SERVICES LIMITED
Registration no: 03084743 **VAT No.:** GB 646 6161 28
Date established: 1995 **No.of Employees:** 21 - 50 **Product Groups:** 42, 45, 54

Date of Accounts	May 11	May 10	May 09
Working Capital	228	924	959
Fixed Assets	43	71	99
Current Assets	1m	4m	4m

Cathelco Ltd
18 Hipper Street South, Chesterfield, S40 1SS
Tel: 01246-277656 **Fax:** 01246-206519
E-mail: sales@cathelco.co.uk
Website: http://www.cathelco.co.uk
Directors: P. Smith (Dir), J. Salisbury (Dir), J. Hollis (Fin)
Immediate Holding Company: CATHELCO LIMITED
Registration no: 00562740 **VAT No.:** GB 125 2759 71
Date established: 1956 **Turnover:** £10m - £20m
No.of Employees: 51 - 100 **Product Groups:** 37, 52

Date of Accounts	Mar 11	Mar 10	Mar 09
Sales Turnover	15m	14m	N/A
Pre Tax Profit/Loss	2m	1m	2m
Working Capital	7m	7m	7m
Fixed Assets	5m	5m	3m
Current Assets	13m	13m	12m
Current Liabilities	3m	3m	3m

CB's Aerials
Glendale Heath Road, Holmewood, Chesterfield, S42 5RB
Tel: 01246-852667
E-mail: carlboulter@aol.com
Directors: C. Boulter (Prop)
Date established: 1992 **No.of Employees:** 1 - 10 **Product Groups:** 26, 37, 39, 67

CE+T UK Ltd
151 Nethermoor Road New Tupton, Chesterfield, S42 6LF
Tel: 01246-251111 **Fax:** 01246-251133
E-mail: info@cetuk.co.uk
Website: http://www.cet.be
Directors: O. Bomboir (Sales), L. Willis (Dir), K. Willis (Fin)
Managers: K. Willis (Sec), A. Pirotte (Purch Mgr)
Immediate Holding Company: CE+T UK LIMITED
Registration no: 03435185 **Date established:** 1997 **Turnover:** £2m - £5m
No.of Employees: 1 - 10 **Product Groups:** 37

Date of Accounts	Dec 07	Dec 06	Dec 05
Working Capital	8	-0	-5
Current Assets	35	53	82

Chesterfield P C Support
9 Rufford Close, Chesterfield, S40 2PB
Tel: 0800-955 6968
E-mail: info@chesterfieldpcsupport.com
Website: http://www.chesterfieldcomputers.com
Managers: B. Bas (Mgr)
Date established: 2002 **Turnover:** Up to £250,000
No.of Employees: 1 - 10 **Product Groups:** 44, 48

Clear Plastic Supplies
Sydney Street, Chesterfield, S40 1DA
Tel: 01246-270992 **Fax:** 01246-270992
E-mail: sales@clearplasticsupplies.co.uk
Website: http://www.clearplasticsupplies.co.uk
Directors: P. Ostler (Ptnr)
No.of Employees: 1 - 10 **Product Groups:** 30, 66, 67

Convertex Ltd
Unit G Coney Green Networkcentre Wingfield View, Clay Cross, Chesterfield, S45 9HX
Tel: 08712-000205 **Fax:** 0871-200 0206
E-mail: sales@convertex.co.uk
Website: http://www.convertex.co.uk
Directors: C. Moss (MD)
Immediate Holding Company: CONVERTEX LIMITED
Registration no: 03711350 **VAT No.:** GB 727 9399 77
Date established: 1999 **No.of Employees:** 1 - 10 **Product Groups:** 23, 27, 29, 30, 31, 33, 37, 49, 66, 68

Date of Accounts	Dec 11	Dec 10	Dec 09
Working Capital	44	44	43
Fixed Assets	60	70	76
Current Assets	163	160	179

Croftsure Engineering
Troughbrook Road Hollingwood, Chesterfield, S43 2JP
Tel: 01246-472156 **Fax:** 01246-472176
E-mail: chris.thorneycroft@croftsure.co.uk
Directors: C. Thorneycroft (Prop)
No.of Employees: 1 - 10 **Product Groups:** 30, 34, 35

Cup Alloys Ltd
15 Sandstone Avenue Walton, Chesterfield, S42 7NS
Tel: 01909-547248 **Fax:** 01246-567288
Website: http://www.cupalloys.com
Directors: J. Buchan (Fin), K. Hale (MD)
Immediate Holding Company: CUP ALLOYS LIMITED
Registration no: 04462063 **Date established:** 2002
No.of Employees: 1 - 10 **Product Groups:** 46

Date of Accounts	Jul 12	Jul 11	Jul 10
Working Capital	66	61	33
Current Assets	101	134	103
Current Liabilities	28	52	N/A

D O R Electrical Rewinds & Installations
Carrwood Road Chesterfield Trading Estate, Chesterfield, S41 9QB
Tel: 01246-260055 **Fax:** 01246-456104
Website: http://www.dorelectrical.co.uk
Bank(s): Yorkshire Bank PLC
Managers: R. Dart (Contracts Mgr)
Immediate Holding Company: D.O.R. ELECTRICAL LIMITED
Registration no: 07509539 **Date established:** 2011
No.of Employees: 21 - 50 **Product Groups:** 48

Derbyshire Times
37 Station Road, Chesterfield, S41 7XD
Tel: 01246-504500 **Fax:** 01246-504580
E-mail: mark.ashton@derbyshiretimes.co.uk
Website: http://www.derbyshiretimes.co.uk
Bank(s): The Royal Bank of Scotland
Directors: M. Ashton (Co Sec)
Managers: E. Wilde, S. Jarvis (Tech Serv Mgr)
Ultimate Holding Company: JOHNSTON PRESS PLC
Immediate Holding Company: WILFRED EDMUNDS,LIMITED
Registration no: 00061775 **VAT No.:** GB 125 6897 39
Date established: 1999 **Turnover:** £2m - £5m
No.of Employees: 101 - 250 **Product Groups:** 28

Date of Accounts	Dec 11	Dec 08	Jan 10
Sales Turnover	3m	4m	4m
Pre Tax Profit/Loss	-10	-8	-6
Working Capital	4m	4m	4m
Fixed Assets	48	69	63
Current Assets	4m	4m	4m

Derim Steels Ltd
Station Road Industrial Estate Clowne, Chesterfield, S43 4AB
Tel: 01246-811456 **Fax:** 01246-810107
E-mail: sales@derimsteels.co.uk
Website: http://www.derimsteels.co.uk
Directors: C. Mottram (MD), J. Mottram (Fin)
Immediate Holding Company: DERIM STEELS LIMITED
Registration no: 01365140 **VAT No.:** GB 295 5309 30
Date established: 1978 **Turnover:** £2m - £5m **No.of Employees:** 1 - 10
Product Groups: 34

Date of Accounts	Mar 12	Mar 11	Mar 10
Working Capital	294	226	134
Fixed Assets	15	24	33
Current Assets	1m	847	722

Direct Engineering & Site Services Ltd
Unit 1-3 Foxwood Industrial Park, Chesterfield, S41 9RN
Tel: 01246-260058
E-mail: info@directeng.co.uk
Website: http://www.directeng.co.uk
Directors: R. Woolley (MD), L. Woolley (Co Sec)
Immediate Holding Company: DIRECT ENGINEERING & SITE SERVICES LTD
Registration no: 04983141 **Date established:** 2003
No.of Employees: 11 - 20 **Product Groups:** 35, 36

Date of Accounts	Jan 12	Jan 11	Jan 10
Working Capital	81	72	51
Fixed Assets	167	147	124
Current Assets	375	268	134

Eco Technology Ltd
East Field Astwith, Pilsley, Chesterfield, S45 8AN
Tel: 01246-857076 **Fax:** 01246-857349
E-mail: kgoodchap@ecotechnology.ltd.uk
Website: http://www.ecotechnology.ltd.uk
Directors: K. Goodchap (Fin)
Immediate Holding Company: ECO TECHNOLOGY LTD.
Registration no: 02832828 **Date established:** 1993
Turnover: £250,000 - £500,000 **No.of Employees:** 21 - 50
Product Groups: 54

Date of Accounts	Jul 11	Jul 10	Jul 09
Working Capital	-227	218	205
Fixed Assets	948	468	242
Current Assets	1m	930	697

Electraplas Ltd
Unit 8 Devonshire Industrial Hemlet Station Road Brimington, Chesterfield, S43 1JU
Tel: 01246-550305 **Fax:** 01246-550236
E-mail: info@huddlestone.co.uk
Website: http://www.huddlestone.co.uk
Directors: C. Toyne (Fin), C. Toyne (MD)
Immediate Holding Company: ELECTRAPLAS LIMITED
Registration no: 01788827 **Date established:** 1984
Turnover: £500,000 - £1m **No.of Employees:** 11 - 20 **Product Groups:** 46

Date of Accounts	Mar 12	Mar 11	Mar 10
Working Capital	137	80	48
Fixed Assets	206	221	238
Current Assets	245	212	169

Elliott Aerial Systems
167 Chesterfield Road Holmewood, Chesterfield, S42 5TD
Tel: 01246-850854 **Fax:** 01246-850456
E-mail: elliott.aerials@btinternet.com
Website: http://www.elliottaerials.co.uk
Directors: P. Elliott (Ptnr)
Turnover: Up to £250,000 **No.of Employees:** 1 - 10 **Product Groups:** 37

Eve Trakway Ltd
Bramley Vale, Chesterfield, S44 5GA
Tel: 01246-858600 **Fax:** 08700-737373
E-mail: mail@evetrakway.co.uk
Website: http://www.evetrakway.co.uk
Directors: C. Lowton (Fin), R. Barnett (MD)
Managers: D. Mosley (Tech Serv Mgr)
Ultimate Holding Company: ACCESSION GROUP LIMITED
Immediate Holding Company: EVE TRAKWAY LIMITED
Registration no: 02207643 **Date established:** 1987
Turnover: £10m - £20m **No.of Employees:** 101 - 250
Product Groups: 35, 45, 83

Date of Accounts	Mar 11	Mar 10	Mar 09
Sales Turnover	19m	17m	17m
Pre Tax Profit/Loss	3m	3m	4m
Working Capital	11m	8m	5m
Fixed Assets	8m	8m	9m
Current Assets	14m	11m	8m
Current Liabilities	2m	2m	2m

Everbright Stainless
Brimington Road North, Chesterfield, S41 9BE
Tel: 01246-451600 **Fax:** 01246-451611
E-mail: chris.tyrrell@anixter.com
Website: http://www.anixter.com
Directors: C. Tyrrell (Prop)
Ultimate Holding Company: F.S.M. HOLDINGS LIMITED
Immediate Holding Company: FIRST STAGE MACHINING CO LTD
Registration no: 04071332 **VAT No.:** GB 222 5219 01
Date established: 2000 **No.of Employees:** 21 - 50 **Product Groups:** 35, 36, 37

Date of Accounts	Jun 11	Jun 10	Jun 09
Working Capital	330	148	133
Fixed Assets	28	37	50
Current Assets	1m	1m	1m

F A W Electronics Ltd
Stand Park Sheffield Road, Chesterfield, S41 8JT
Tel: 01246-233632 **Fax:** 01246-201193
E-mail: irene@fawelectronics.co.uk
Website: http://www.fawelectronics.co.uk
Bank(s): National Westminster Bank Plc
Directors: I. Wilkinson (MD)
Immediate Holding Company: F A W ELECTRONICS LIMITED
Registration no: 04524627 **VAT No.:** GB 295 6334 26
Date established: 2002 **Turnover:** £250,000 - £500,000
No.of Employees: 21 - 50 **Product Groups:** 37, 38

Date of Accounts	Sep 07	Sep 06	Sep 05
Working Capital	-64	11	-53
Fixed Assets	174	111	89
Current Assets	673	385	418
Current Liabilities	738	373	471

Fa-St Filtration Analysis Services Technology Ltd
41 Heaton Street, Chesterfield, S40 3AQ
Tel: 01246-268900 **Fax:** 01246-200679
E-mail: info@fa-st.co.uk
Website: http://www.oilfiltration.co.uk
Directors: A. Fraser (MD)
Immediate Holding Company: FA-ST FILTRATION ANALYSIS SERVICES TECHNOLOGY LTD
Registration no: 05525184 **Date established:** 2005
No.of Employees: 1 - 10 **Product Groups:** 36

Date of Accounts	Jul 12	Jul 11	Jul 10
Working Capital	61	N/A	14
Fixed Assets	19	24	19
Current Assets	101	N/A	51

Far East Europe
Coney Green Farm Market Street, Clay Cross, Chesterfield, S45 9NE
Tel: 01246-251177 **Fax:** 01246-251199
E-mail: sales@fareasteurope.com
Website: http://www.fareasteurope.com
Directors: B. Liu (MD), F. Liu (MD)
Immediate Holding Company: FAR EAST EUROPE LIMITED
Registration no: 04513486 **Date established:** 2002
No.of Employees: 11 - 20 **Product Groups:** 20, 40, 41

Date of Accounts	Jul 11	Jul 10	Jul 09
Working Capital	181	140	144
Fixed Assets	13	23	21
Current Assets	628	625	629

Fast Track Recruitment Ltd
Coney Green Business Centre Wingfield View, Clay Cross, Chesterfield, S45 9JW
Tel: 08448-002851 **Fax:** 01246-252351
E-mail: info@fasttrack-recruitment.co.uk
Website: http://www.fasttrack-recruitment.co.uk
Directors: P. Diver (MD)
Immediate Holding Company: FAST TRACK RECRUITMENT LIMITED
Registration no: 05959006 **Date established:** 2006 **Turnover:** £1m - £2m
No.of Employees: 1 - 10 **Product Groups:** 80

Date of Accounts	Nov 10	Nov 09	Nov 08
Working Capital	89	37	36
Fixed Assets	19	13	18
Current Assets	431	96	113

Fire Trade Supplies
90 Newbridge Lane Old Whittington, Chesterfield, S41 9JF
Tel: 01246-268949
Website: http://www.firetradesupplies.co.uk
Directors: R. Baker (Prop)
Date established: 1998 **No.of Employees:** 1 - 10 **Product Groups:** 38, 42

Flaretec Alloys & Equipment Ltd
Hardwick View Road Holmewood, Chesterfield, S42 5SA
Tel: 01246-853522 **Fax:** 01246-852415
E-mail: office@flaretec.com
Website: http://www.flaretec.com
Bank(s): Yorkshire Bank PLC
Directors: I. Manuel (MD)
Immediate Holding Company: FLARETEC ALLOYS & EQUIPMENT LIMITED
Registration no: 01557884 **Date established:** 1981 **Turnover:** £1m - £2m
No.of Employees: 21 - 50 **Product Groups:** 35, 37, 38, 41, 42

Date of Accounts	Apr 11	Apr 10	Apr 09
Working Capital	134	82	55
Fixed Assets	171	168	184
Current Assets	391	373	976

Frank Guy
Bidston House Astwith Close, Holmewood, Chesterfield, S42 5UR
Tel: 01246-851222 **Fax:** 01246-851225
E-mail: sales@frank-guy.co.uk
Website: http://www.frank-guy.co.uk
Bank(s): National Westminster Bank Plc
Managers: P. Revell (Buyer), P. Trennan (Comm), L. Mills (Mgr)
Registration no: 01258632 **VAT No.:** GB 289 2175 23
Turnover: £1m - £2m **No.of Employees:** 21 - 50 **Product Groups:** 22, 23, 26, 32, 39

Date of Accounts	Dec 06	Dec 05
Working Capital	-488	-94
Fixed Assets	257	210
Current Assets	259	252
Current Liabilities	746	347
Total Share Capital	100	100

Fred Armstrong Glass Ltd
49 Brimington Road North, Chesterfield, S41 9BE
Tel: 01246-450827

see next page

Fred Armstrong Glass Ltd - Cont'd

Directors: R. Gadd (MD)
Immediate Holding Company: FRED ARMSTRONG (GLASS) LIMITED
Registration no: 00525273 **Date established:** 1953
No.of Employees: 1 - 10 **Product Groups:** 33, 35, 52

Date of Accounts	Dec 11	Dec 10	Dec 09
Working Capital	22	13	10
Fixed Assets	18	18	18
Current Assets	35	28	22

Furnival Steel Co. Ltd
7 Hardwick Court Hardwick View Road Holmewood, Chesterfield, S42 5SA
Tel: 01246-855589 **Fax:** 01246-855572
E-mail: info@furnivalsteel.co.uk
Website: http://www.furnivalsteel.co.uk
Directors: A. Ottewell (MD)
Immediate Holding Company: FURNIVAL STEEL COMPANY LIMITED
Registration no: 06654785 **Date established:** 2008
Turnover: £250,000 - £500,000 **No.of Employees:** 1 - 10
Product Groups: 34

Date of Accounts	Mar 11	Mar 10	Mar 09
Working Capital	4	20	-54
Fixed Assets	61	61	66
Current Assets	126	72	60

G K Group
Chatsworth Road, Chesterfield, S40 2BJ
Tel: 01246-209999 **Fax:** 01246-220711
E-mail: info@gmarshall.co.uk
Website: http://www.gk-group.co.uk
Directors: M. Hamer (MD)
Managers: G. Baxter (Personnel), P. Murdoch (Mktg Serv Mgr), S. Hawkings (Tech Serv Mgr), D. Kenning
Immediate Holding Company: G K GROUP LIMITED
Registration no: 02086705 **Date established:** 1987
Turnover: £125m - £250m **No.of Employees:** 101 - 250
Product Groups: 68

Date of Accounts	Dec 11	Dec 10	Dec 09
Sales Turnover	146m	156m	205m
Pre Tax Profit/Loss	121	36	65
Working Capital	-2m	-1m	-910
Fixed Assets	12m	13m	13m
Current Assets	41m	49m	56m
Current Liabilities	807	3m	1m

The Garden Buildings Centre
Sheffield Road, Chesterfield, S41 7LX
Tel: 01246-220301 **Fax:** 08707-460204
E-mail: nicp@thediyconservatorycentre.co.uk
Website: http://www.greenhousesupply.co.uk
Directors: N. Paice (MD)
Immediate Holding Company: GARDEN BUILDINGS CENTRE (CHESTERFIELD) LIMITED
Registration no: 06235570 **Date established:** 2007 **Turnover:** £1m - £2m
No.of Employees: 1 - 10 **Product Groups:** 33

Date of Accounts	May 11	May 10	May 08
Working Capital	-3	-3	N/A
Fixed Assets	N/A	5	N/A
Current Assets	6	38	N/A

Glapwell Contracting Services Ltd
Newbridge Works Whitting Valley Road, Old Whittington, Chesterfield, S41 9EY
Tel: 01246-454444 **Fax:** 01246-260384
E-mail: admin@glapwell.co.uk
Website: http://www.glapwell.co.uk
Bank(s): Yorkshire Bank PLC
Directors: J. Harrison (MD)
Ultimate Holding Company: GLAPWELL LIMITED
Immediate Holding Company: GLAPWELL CONTRACTING SERVICES LIMITED
Registration no: 01620686 **VAT No.:** GB 598 5194 76
Date established: 1982 **Turnover:** £2m - £5m **No.of Employees:** 21 - 50
Product Groups: 30, 32, 35, 36, 37, 38, 40, 42, 52, 71

Date of Accounts	Jul 11	Jul 10	Jul 09
Sales Turnover	4m	5m	5m
Pre Tax Profit/Loss	134	401	181
Working Capital	766	665	633
Fixed Assets	135	94	120
Current Assets	2m	2m	2m
Current Liabilities	106	295	494

Gould Alloys Ltd
Carrwood Industrial Park Carrwood Road, Chesterfield, S41 9QB
Tel: 01246-263300 **Fax:** 01246-260999
E-mail: sales@gouldalloys.co.uk
Website: http://www.gouldalloys.co.uk
Bank(s): Barclays
Directors: C. Fairman (Fin), J. Bradshaw (MD)
Managers: M. North (Personnel), J. Wereteinikow (Tech Serv Mgr), P. Chruscinski
Ultimate Holding Company: HENLEY MANAGEMENT COMPANY (USA)
Immediate Holding Company: GOULD ALLOYS LTD
Registration no: 01854699 **VAT No.:** GB 419 7239 31
Date established: 1984 **Turnover:** £10m - £20m
No.of Employees: 51 - 100 **Product Groups:** 34

Date of Accounts	Dec 11	Dec 10	Dec 09
Sales Turnover	18m	18m	22m
Pre Tax Profit/Loss	804	1m	2m
Working Capital	5m	5m	8m
Fixed Assets	92	67	89
Current Assets	10m	10m	12m
Current Liabilities	823	1m	995

Granwood Holdings Ltd
Stubben Edge Hall Ashover, Chesterfield, S45 0EU
Tel: 01246-590543 **Fax:** 01246-590449
Directors: M. Pass (Ch)
Ultimate Holding Company: GRANWOOD HOLDINGS LIMITED
Immediate Holding Company: GRANWOOD FLOORING GROUP LIMITED
Registration no: 03573722 **VAT No.:** GB 125 5228 87
Date established: 1998 **No.of Employees:** 1 - 10 **Product Groups:** 80

Date of Accounts	Dec 11	Dec 10	Dec 09
Working Capital	-2m	-2m	-1m
Fixed Assets	4m	4m	4m
Current Assets	1m	1m	2m

Graphoidal Developments
Broombank Road, Chesterfield, S41 9QJ
Tel: 01246-266000 **Fax:** 01246-269269
E-mail: sales@graphoidal.com
Website: http://www.graphoidal.com
Bank(s): Yorkshire Bank PLC
Directors: M. Johnston (MD), C. Crewes (Co Sec)
Immediate Holding Company: GRAPHOIDAL DEVELOPMENTS LIMITED
Registration no: 00604606 **VAT No.:** GB 126 8782 40
Date established: 1958 **Turnover:** £2m - £5m **No.of Employees:** 21 - 50
Product Groups: 32, 36, 40, 45, 46, 67

Date of Accounts	Dec 11	Dec 10	Dec 09
Working Capital	1m	891	822
Fixed Assets	36	82	88
Current Assets	2m	1m	1m
Current Liabilities	3	3	3

Greenhouse Supply Ltd
The Garden Buildings Centre Sheffield Road, Chesterfield, S41 7LX
Tel: 01246-220301 **Fax:** 01246-271110
E-mail: nicp@conservatorycentre.co.uk
Website: http://www.greenhousesupply.co.uk
Directors: N. Paice (MD)
Managers: N. Paice (Chief Mgr)
Date established: 1999 **Turnover:** £1m - £2m **No.of Employees:** 1 - 10
Product Groups: 25, 30, 33, 35

H G Systems Ltd
Dunston House Sheepbridge Works Dunston Road, Chesterfield, S41 9QD
Tel: 01246-263700 **Fax:** 01246-450323
E-mail: sales@hgsystems.co.uk
Website: http://www.hgsystems.co.uk
Bank(s): Lloyds TSB
Directors: A. Rahman (Sales), G. Stevens (MD), K. Thompson (Fin)
Managers: M. Edwards, S. Swirles (Sales & Mktg Mg), N. Dudley (Sales Prom Mgr)
Ultimate Holding Company: H G HOLDINGS LIMITED
Immediate Holding Company: HG SYSTEMS LIMITED
Registration no: 03902739 **VAT No.:** 745 4766 02 **Date established:** 2000
No.of Employees: 51 - 100 **Product Groups:** 38, 44, 52, 84

Date of Accounts	Dec 11	Dec 10	Dec 09
Working Capital	355	131	374
Fixed Assets	581	489	279
Current Assets	3m	3m	2m

H P C Gears Ltd
Unit 14 Foxwood Industrial Park, Chesterfield, S41 9RN
Tel: 01246-268080 **Fax:** 01246-260003
E-mail: sales@hpcgears.com
Website: http://www.hpcgears.com
Bank(s): National Westminster Bank Plc
Directors: P. Hinchliffe (Co Sec), T. Hinchliffe (MD)
Ultimate Holding Company: HPC CORPORATION LIMITED
Immediate Holding Company: HPC GEARS LIMITED
Registration no: 03262229 **VAT No.:** GB 684 1312 42
Date established: 1996 **Turnover:** £2m - £5m **No.of Employees:** 21 - 50
Product Groups: 25, 29, 30, 31, 33, 34, 35, 36, 37, 38, 39, 40, 43, 45, 46, 48, 49, 66, 68

Date of Accounts	Mar 12	Mar 11	Mar 10
Working Capital	351	479	274
Fixed Assets	1m	537	467
Current Assets	2m	2m	2m

Hi-Fli Banners & Flags Ltd
Adelphi Way Ireland Industrial Estate, Staveley, Chesterfield, S43 3LS
Tel: 01246-472 949 **Fax:** 01246-280 476
E-mail: sales@hi-fli.com
Website: http://www.hi-fli.com
Directors: B. Low (MD)
Managers: B. Haldane (Sales Prom Mgr), R. Haldean (Mgr)
Registration no: SC048739 **No.of Employees:** 1 - 10 **Product Groups:** 25, 33, 35, 49

Impac Infrared Ltd
Thompson House Thompson Close, Chesterfield, S41 9AZ
Tel: 01246-269066 **Fax:** 01246-269564
E-mail: info@impac-infrared.com
Website: http://www.impac-infrared.com
Directors: M. Bell (Co Sec), M. Welling (MD)
Ultimate Holding Company: MIKRON Infrared Inc. Oakland USA
Immediate Holding Company: IMPAC Infrared GmbH. Frankfurt Germany
Registration no: 03624461 **VAT No.:** GB 732 4376 40
Date established: 1998 **Turnover:** £500,000 - £1m
No.of Employees: 1 - 10 **Product Groups:** 38

Date of Accounts	Dec 08	Dec 07	Oct 06
Sales Turnover	770	478	94
Pre Tax Profit/Loss	-110	-45	-16
Working Capital	-171	-61	-16
Fixed Assets	2	2	2
Current Assets	200	243	21
Current Liabilities	371	305	38
Total Share Capital	20	20	20
ROCE% (Return on Capital Employed)	65.2	76.5	116.1
ROT% (Return on Turnover)	-14.3	-9.4	-17.1

Inspirepac
Carrwood Road, Chesterfield, S41 9QB
Tel: 01246-572000 **Fax:** 01246-454769
Website: http://www.inspirepac.com
Directors: C. Munroe (Fin), M. Hawkins (MD)
Managers: D. Aris (Personnel), E. Beer (Mktg Serv Mgr)
Ultimate Holding Company: LOGSON LIMITED
Immediate Holding Company: INSPIREPAC LIMITED
Registration no: 06028714 **Date established:** 2006
Turnover: £20m - £50m **No.of Employees:** 51 - 100 **Product Groups:** 27, 28, 49, 85

Date of Accounts	Dec 11	Dec 10	Dec 09
Sales Turnover	36m	32m	28m
Pre Tax Profit/Loss	2m	1m	1m
Working Capital	-4m	-2m	-3m
Fixed Assets	7m	6m	7m
Current Assets	10m	9m	9m
Current Liabilities	2m	2m	1m

Internet Consultancy & Management Ltd
12 Sycamore Avenue Glapwell, Chesterfield, S44 5LH
Tel: 0800-043 1057 **Fax:** 0870-127 0965
E-mail: support@icamltd.co.uk
Website: http://www.icamltd.co.uk
Directors: A. Russell (MD)
Immediate Holding Company: INTERNET CONSULTANCY AND MANAGEMENT LIMITED
Registration no: 04914139 **Date established:** 2003
Turnover: Up to £250,000 **No.of Employees:** 1 - 10 **Product Groups:** 44

Date of Accounts	Sep 11	Sep 10	Sep 09
Working Capital	17	23	16
Current Assets	38	23	22

Jacksons Building Centres
Newbold Road, Chesterfield, S41 7PB
Tel: 01246-203201 **Fax:** 01246-208985
E-mail: paulsharman@jacksonbc.co.uk
Website: http://www.jacksonbc.co.uk
Bank(s): Lloyds TSB Bank plc
Managers: P. Sharman (Mgr), S. Marriot (Sales & Mktg Mg)
Immediate Holding Company: JUNCTION ARTS LIMITED
Registration no: 00413760 **VAT No.:** GB 128 2526 76
Date established: 1984 **No.of Employees:** 21 - 50 **Product Groups:** 66, 67

Date of Accounts	Mar 11	Mar 10	Mar 09
Sales Turnover	178	187	187
Pre Tax Profit/Loss	-35	-41	-33
Working Capital	117	71	73
Fixed Assets	5	86	125
Current Assets	143	89	84
Current Liabilities	27	18	11

Jemelec
39-41 High Street Clay Cross, Chesterfield, S45 9DX
Tel: 08707-871769 **Fax:** 0844-873 1830
E-mail: sales@jemelec.com
Website: http://www.jemelec.com
Directors: M. Daniels (Prop)
Immediate Holding Company: JEMELEC LIMITED
Registration no: 06190798 **Date established:** 2007
No.of Employees: 1 - 10 **Product Groups:** 37

Date of Accounts	Mar 11	Mar 09	Mar 08
Working Capital	-6	-8	13
Fixed Assets	6	8	2
Current Assets	27	20	13

Johnson Field Sports
Unit 5 Ireland Close Staveley, Chesterfield, S43 3PE
Tel: 01246-477666 **Fax:** 01246-475566
E-mail: sales@field-sports.co.uk
Website: http://www.field-sports.co.uk
Directors: N. Ward (Prop)
Date established: 1993 **No.of Employees:** 1 - 10 **Product Groups:** 36, 39, 40

Joseph Clayton & Sons Ltd
Clayton Street, Chesterfield, S41 0DU
Tel: 01246-232863 **Fax:** 01246-207807
E-mail: sales@claytonleather.com
Website: http://www.claytonleather.com
Bank(s): National Westminster Bank Plc
Directors: C. Douglas (Co Sec)
Managers: M. Abbott (Sales Prom Mgr), P. Stevens (Chief Mgr), C. Silcock (Mktg Serv Mgr)
Ultimate Holding Company: CLAYTON OF CHESTERFIELD LIMITED
Immediate Holding Company: CLAYTON OF CHESTERFIELD LIMITED
Registration no: 02912896 **VAT No.:** GB 125 4359 77
Date established: 1994 **Turnover:** £1m - £2m **No.of Employees:** 21 - 50
Product Groups: 22, 66

Date of Accounts	Dec 11	Dec 10	Dec 09
Working Capital	287	335	352
Fixed Assets	904	845	867
Current Assets	420	366	383

George Jowitt & Sons Ltd
Bridgeway Broombank Road, Chesterfield, S41 9QJ
Tel: 01246-572230 **Fax:** 01246-572249
E-mail: sales@jowitt.com
Website: http://www.jowitt.com
Bank(s): Yorkshire Bank PLC
Directors: A. Henderson (Sales), R. Orme (MD)
Managers: T. Gee (Tech Serv Mgr), V. Dent
Immediate Holding Company: GEORGE JOWITT & SONS,LIMITED
Registration no: 00169714 **Date established:** 2020
No.of Employees: 21 - 50 **Product Groups:** 33

Date of Accounts	Mar 11	Mar 10	Mar 09
Working Capital	749	525	688
Fixed Assets	393	438	403
Current Assets	1m	1m	1m

John Jowitt
105 Slayley View Road Barlborough, Chesterfield, S43 4UQ
Tel: 01246-811118 **Fax:** 01246-811118
E-mail: john.jowitt@virgin.net
Directors: J. Jowitt (Prop)
Date established: 2001 **No.of Employees:** 1 - 10 **Product Groups:** 37, 67

The Jump Shop Ltd
225 Old Hall Road, Chesterfield, S40 1HQ
Tel: 07939-030339 **Fax:** 01246-203487
E-mail: sales@thejumpshop.co.uk
Website: http://www.thejumpshop.co.uk
Directors: S. Hewitt (Dir), N. Halls (Fin)
Immediate Holding Company: THE JUMP SHOP LTD
Registration no: 06625880 **Date established:** 2008
No.of Employees: 1 - 10 **Product Groups:** 24, 40, 63

Date of Accounts	Mar 12	Mar 11	Mar 10
Working Capital	-2	1	-2
Fixed Assets	3	5	5
Current Assets	32	39	24

K T Machining
3 Clayton Street, Chesterfield, S41 0DW
Tel: 01246-208098 **Fax:** 01246-208098
Directors: C. Smith (Prop)
Date established: 1987 **No.of Employees:** 1 - 10 **Product Groups:** 35

L J Specialities Ltd
Holmewood Industrial Park Holmewood, Chesterfield, S42 5UW
Tel: 01246-593000 **Fax:** 01246-857810
E-mail: info@lj-specialities.co.uk
Website: http://www.lj-specialities.co.uk

Directors: A. Lee (MD), M. Drabble (Fin), S. Oldham (Sales)
Managers: C. Briscoe (Personnel), G. Smedley (Tech Serv Mgr)
Ultimate Holding Company: ITOCHU CORPORATION (JAPAN)
Immediate Holding Company: L. J. SPECIALITIES LIMITED
Registration no: 01498517 **Date established:** 1980
Turnover: £10m - £20m **No.of Employees:** 11 - 20 **Product Groups:** 32, 43

Date of Accounts	Dec 10	Dec 09	Dec 08
Sales Turnover	11m	6m	8m
Pre Tax Profit/Loss	325	-189	78
Working Capital	1m	1m	2m
Fixed Assets	773	772	724
Current Assets	5m	4m	5m
Current Liabilities	433	374	349

Laser Trader Ltd

Hillhouse Court New Road, Wingerworth, Chesterfield, S42 6TD
Tel: 01246-238670 **Fax:** 01246-269381
E-mail: sales@lasertrader.co.uk
Website: http://www.lasertrader.co.uk
Directors: J. Cocker (MD), J. Firminger (Fin)
Immediate Holding Company: LASER TRADER LIMITED
Registration no: 04112559 **Date established:** 2000
No.of Employees: 1 - 10 **Product Groups:** 37, 38, 42, 43, 46, 47, 48

Date of Accounts	Mar 12	Mar 11	Mar 10
Working Capital	53	29	29
Fixed Assets	34	3	4
Current Assets	195	149	161

Lloyd Loom Ltd

Foxwood Industrial Park Foxwood Road, Chesterfield, S41 9RN
Tel: 01246-264600 **Fax:** 01246-264609
E-mail: lloyd.loom.nova@dsl.pipex.com
Bank(s): National Westminster
Directors: S. Buchanan (MD)
Managers: J. Buchanan (), J. Buchanan, L. Willis (Sales Admin)
Immediate Holding Company: LLOYD LOOM LIMITED
Registration no: 02074593 **VAT No.:** GB 533 9283 32
Date established: 1986 **No.of Employees:** 11 - 20 **Product Groups:** 26

Date of Accounts	Mar 07	Mar 06	Mar 05
Working Capital	N/A	1	1
Current Assets	N/A	12	9

Mallatite Ltd

Hardwick View Road Holmewood, Chesterfield, S42 5SA
Tel: 01246-593280 **Fax:** 01246-593281
E-mail: sales@mallatite.co.uk
Website: http://www.mallatite.co.uk
Bank(s): Co-operative
Directors: A. Paterson (MD), N. Clark (Fin), N. Clarke (Fin)
Managers: D. Beckett (Tech Serv Mgr), M. Allcroft (Personnel), J. Nettle (Sales Prom Mgr)
Ultimate Holding Company: HILL & SMITH HOLDINGS PLC
Immediate Holding Company: MALLATITE LIMITED
Registration no: 02621328 **Date established:** 1991 **Turnover:** £2m - £5m
No.of Employees: 51 - 100 **Product Groups:** 30, 39, 45, 48

Date of Accounts	Dec 11	Dec 10	Dec 09
Sales Turnover	11m	10m	9m
Pre Tax Profit/Loss	1m	810	901
Working Capital	5m	4m	3m
Fixed Assets	1m	1m	1m
Current Assets	7m	7m	6m
Current Liabilities	772	669	2m

Martec Of Whitwell Ltd

Unit 12 Midway Business Centre Bridge St Industria Bridge Street, Clay Cross, Chesterfield, S45 9NU
Tel: 01246-860855 **Fax:** 01246-860877
E-mail: sales@martec-conservation.com
Website: http://www.martec-conservation.com
Directors: J. Harper (MD)
Immediate Holding Company: MARTEC OF WHITWELL LIMITED
Registration no: 03366643 **Date established:** 1997
No.of Employees: 1 - 10 **Product Groups:** 37, 38, 42, 45, 51, 54, 85

Date of Accounts	Apr 11	Apr 10	Apr 09
Working Capital	1	-130	-125
Fixed Assets	33	40	43
Current Assets	196	64	27

Mastercut Cutting Systems Ltd

Unit 9 Upper Mantle Close Bridge Street Industrial Estate, Clay Cross, Chesterfield, S45 9NU
Tel: 01246-860811 **Fax:** 01246-866928
E-mail: info@mastercut.co.uk
Website: http://www.mastercut.co.uk
Bank(s): Lloyds TSB
Directors: S. Fern (Fin), M. Fern (MD)
Immediate Holding Company: MASTERCUT CUTTING SYSTEMS LIMITED
Registration no: 04420747 **Date established:** 2002
Turnover: £500,000 - £1m **No.of Employees:** 11 - 20
Product Groups: 23, 36, 42, 43, 44, 46, 47, 48, 67

Date of Accounts	Sep 11	Sep 10	Sep 09
Working Capital	133	75	84
Fixed Assets	174	186	213
Current Assets	308	253	238

Geoff Matthews Engineers

Unit 17, Pavillion Workshops Park Road, Holmewood Industrial Park, Chesterfield, S42 5UY
Tel: 01246-851118 **Fax:** 01246-855502
E-mail: enquiries@gmengineers.co.uk
Website: http://www.gmengineers.co.uk
Managers: J. Matthews (Mgr)
No.of Employees: 1 - 10 **Product Groups:** 40, 41, 67

Mayfly Containers Ltd

Bridge Street Industrial Estate Bridge Street, Clay Cross, Chesterfield, S45 9NU
Tel: 01246-862456 **Fax:** 01246-862711
E-mail: contact@mayfly.co.uk
Website: http://www.mayfly.co.uk
Directors: C. Hall (Sales), D. Hall (MD)
Ultimate Holding Company: MAYFLY WASTE ENGINEERING LIMITED
Immediate Holding Company: MAYFLY CONTAINERS LIMITED
Registration no: 01722388 **Date established:** 1983
Turnover: £10m - £20m **No.of Employees:** 51 - 100 **Product Groups:** 35, 36, 45

Date of Accounts	Mar 11	Mar 10	Mar 09
Sales Turnover	15m	11m	N/A
Pre Tax Profit/Loss	306	288	191
Working Capital	-74	-135	157
Fixed Assets	2m	2m	2m
Current Assets	5m	4m	3m
Current Liabilities	1m	2m	966

Mentor F L T Training Ltd

Mentor House Burley Close, Chesterfield, S40 2UB
Tel: 01246-555222 **Fax:** 01246-234184
E-mail: info@mentortraining.co.uk
Website: http://www.mentortraining.co.uk
Directors: R. Shore (MD)
Immediate Holding Company: MENTOR F.L.T. TRAINING LIMITED
Registration no: 04341326 **Date established:** 2001
No.of Employees: 11 - 20 **Product Groups:** 86

Date of Accounts	Mar 12	Mar 11	Mar 10
Working Capital	127	-413	-396
Fixed Assets	1m	1m	1m
Current Assets	2m	1m	1m

Metapic Ltd

Brimington Road North, Chesterfield, S41 9BG
Tel: 01246-451710 **Fax:** 01246-455999
E-mail: sales@metapic.co.uk
Website: http://www.metapic.co.uk
Directors: D. Stevenson (MD)
Ultimate Holding Company: ASCENTRA LIMITED
Immediate Holding Company: METAPIC LIMITED
Registration no: 00677296 **Date established:** 1960
No.of Employees: 11 - 20 **Product Groups:** 46, 48

Date of Accounts	Oct 11	Oct 10	Oct 09
Working Capital	84	116	119
Fixed Assets	14	18	22
Current Assets	281	186	198

Mitchell & Proctor

Sunnybank 12 Albion Road, Chesterfield, S40 1LJ
Tel: 01246-275107 **Fax:** 01246-279252
E-mail: tim@mitchellproctor.co.uk
Website: http://www.mitchellproctor.fsnet.co.uk
Directors: S. Haslam (Ptnr)
Immediate Holding Company: INSPIRE PERMANENT RESOURCING LIMITED
Date established: 2012 **No.of Employees:** 1 - 10 **Product Groups:** 84

Mollart-Cox Engineering Limited

Unit 1 Broombank Road, Chesterfield, S41 9QJ
Tel: 01246-458090 **Fax:** 01246-458091
E-mail: christophercox@mollartcox.co.uk
Website: http://www.mollartcox.co.uk
Directors: C. Cox (MD)
Date established: 1995 **Turnover:** £2m - £5m **No.of Employees:** 21 - 50
Product Groups: 46, 48, 84

Motan Colortronic Ltd

Matilda House Carrwood Road, Chesterfield, S41 9QB
Tel: 01246-260222 **Fax:** 01246-455420
E-mail: sales@motan-colortronic.co.uk
Website: http://www.motan-colortronic.co.uk
Bank(s): National Westminster Bank Plc
Directors: K. Miller (MD)
Immediate Holding Company: COLORTRONIC (U.K.) LIMITED
Registration no: 01160948 **Date established:** 1974 **Turnover:** £5m - £10m
No.of Employees: 21 - 50 **Product Groups:** 38, 42, 84

Date of Accounts	Dec 11	Dec 10	Sep 09
Working Capital	4m	4m	3m
Fixed Assets	76	76	87
Current Assets	4m	5m	4m

Nhbb Europe

Tapton Park Innovation Centre Brimington Road, Tapton, Chesterfield, S41 0TZ
Tel: 01246-541907 **Fax:** 01246-541942
E-mail: info@nhbb.com
Website: http://www.nhbb.com
Managers: D. Clark (Mgr)
Ultimate Holding Company: TECHNOGYM GROUP SPA (ITALY)
Registration no: 02782468 **Date established:** 1993
Turnover: £20m - £50m **No.of Employees:** 1 - 10 **Product Groups:** 35, 45

Nitec UK Ltd

Hardwick View Road Holmewood, Chesterfield, S42 5SA
Tel: 01246-859200 **Fax:** 01246-859300
E-mail: info@nitec-enp.co.uk
Website: http://www.nitec-enp.co.uk
Directors: D. Brown (MD)
Ultimate Holding Company: WILLIAM BELFIT LIMITED
Immediate Holding Company: NITEC (UK) LIMITED
Registration no: 02036655 **Date established:** 1986 **Turnover:** £2m - £5m
No.of Employees: 21 - 50 **Product Groups:** 28, 29, 32, 34, 35, 36, 40, 46, 48, 84

Date of Accounts	Aug 11	Aug 10	Aug 09
Working Capital	111	11	-55
Fixed Assets	756	724	719
Current Assets	879	1m	884

Palamatic Ltd

Unit 8 Cobnar Wood Close, Chesterfield, S41 9RQ
Tel: 01246-452054 **Fax:** 01246-451379
E-mail: stewart.bennison@palamatic.com
Website: http://www.palamatic.com
Bank(s): National Westminster Bank Plc
Directors: S. Bennison (Dir)
Managers: R. Fincham, A. Fincham (Personnel), K. Webster, M. Partridge (Tech Serv Mgr)
Immediate Holding Company: PHS REALISATIONS LIMITED
Registration no: 01900578 **Date established:** 1985 **Turnover:** £2m - £5m
No.of Employees: 51 - 100 **Product Groups:** 44, 45, 46, 47, 61, 67, 84

Date of Accounts	Jun 08	Jun 07	Jun 06
Working Capital	-218	-86	-92
Fixed Assets	969	942	951
Current Assets	2m	2m	2m

Parsons Contracting Ltd

36 Brimington Road, Chesterfield, S41 7UL
Tel: 01246-276536 **Fax:** 01246-203315
E-mail: info@parsonscontracting.co.uk
Website: http://www.parsonscontracting.co.uk
Directors: R. Parsons (MD)
Immediate Holding Company: PARSONS CONTRACTING (CHESTERFIELD) LIMITED
Registration no: 01306377 **Date established:** 1977
No.of Employees: 21 - 50 **Product Groups:** 52

Date of Accounts	Mar 11	Mar 10	Mar 09
Working Capital	2m	2m	2m
Fixed Assets	82	102	105
Current Assets	3m	3m	2m

Peak Sensors Ltd

Unit 25-27 Beresford Way, Chesterfield, S41 9FG
Tel: 01246-261999 **Fax:** 01246-261888
E-mail: p.smith@peaksensors.co.uk
Website: http://www.peaksensors.com
Directors: P. Smith (MD)
Immediate Holding Company: PEAK SENSORS LIMITED
Registration no: 03386191 **VAT No.:** GB 695 0256 18
Date established: 1997 **Turnover:** £1m - £2m **No.of Employees:** 1 - 10
Product Groups: 38

Date of Accounts	Mar 12	Mar 11	Mar 10
Sales Turnover	1m	N/A	N/A
Pre Tax Profit/Loss	233	N/A	N/A
Working Capital	571	544	451
Fixed Assets	578	581	589
Current Assets	774	793	596
Current Liabilities	98	N/A	N/A

Penny Hydraulics Ltd

Station Road Industrial Estate Station Road, Clowne, Chesterfield, S43 4AB
Tel: 01246-811475 **Fax:** 01246-810403
E-mail: sales@pennyhydraulics.com
Website: http://www.pennyhydraulics.com
Bank(s): Barclays
Directors: D. Battrum (Fin), R. Short (Sales), R. Penny (Fab)
Managers: K. Wootton (Develop Mgr), L. White
Immediate Holding Company: PENNY HYDRAULICS LIMITED
Registration no: 01380206 **VAT No.:** GB 295 5936 03
Date established: 1978 **Turnover:** £1m - £2m **No.of Employees:** 51 - 100
Product Groups: 45

Date of Accounts	Jun 12	Jun 11	Jun 10
Sales Turnover	5m	5m	N/A
Pre Tax Profit/Loss	266	294	N/A
Working Capital	2m	2m	2m
Fixed Assets	773	660	680
Current Assets	3m	3m	3m
Current Liabilities	633	587	N/A

Permafast Ltd

Derby Road Clay Cross, Chesterfield, S45 9AG
Tel: 01246-250150 **Fax:** 01246-250085
E-mail: info@permafast.co.uk
Website: http://www.permafast.co.uk
Bank(s): Barclays
Directors: P. Beardsley (Ch)
Immediate Holding Company: PERMAFAST LIMITED
Registration no: 02105973 **VAT No.:** GB 457 3984 02
Date established: 1987 **Turnover:** £1m - £2m **No.of Employees:** 11 - 20
Product Groups: 35, 66

Date of Accounts	Mar 12	Mar 11	Mar 10
Working Capital	130	132	147
Fixed Assets	29	39	41
Current Assets	446	413	328

Power System Services Ltd

Carrwood Road, Chesterfield, S41 9QB
Tel: 01246-268800 **Fax:** 01246-268811
E-mail: info@powersystemservices.co.uk
Website: http://www.pss-uk.com
Bank(s): Barclays, Birmingham
Directors: P. Beauchamp (Dir)
Managers: D. Howie (Sales Prom Mgr), P. Edwards (Factory Mgr), D. Lock
Immediate Holding Company: POWER SYSTEM SERVICES LIMITED
Registration no: 02962766 **VAT No.:** GB 471 3458 45
Date established: 1994 **Turnover:** £2m - £5m **No.of Employees:** 21 - 50
Product Groups: 40

Date of Accounts	Mar 12	Mar 11	Mar 10
Working Capital	158	69	422
Fixed Assets	2m	2m	2m
Current Assets	1m	1m	913

Precision Products Ltd

Unit 1 Cobnar Wood Close, Chesterfield, S41 9RQ
Tel: 01246-261621 **Fax:** 01246-261622
E-mail: sales@ringleader.net
Website: http://www.precisionproductsuk.com
Directors: G. Simonds (Fin), G. Whiting (Sales), P. Rowlands (MD)
Immediate Holding Company: PRECISION PRODUCTS LIMITED
Registration no: 02928395 **Date established:** 1994 **Turnover:** £5m - £10m
No.of Employees: 51 - 100 **Product Groups:** 33, 40, 52

Date of Accounts	Dec 11	Dec 10	Dec 09
Sales Turnover	6m	5m	5m
Pre Tax Profit/Loss	701	435	193
Working Capital	1m	1m	1m
Fixed Assets	3m	3m	3m
Current Assets	3m	2m	2m
Current Liabilities	390	243	213

Pronto Industrial Paints Ltd

Stainsby Close Holmewood, Chesterfield, S42 5UG
Tel: 01246-857777 **Fax:** 01246-857978
Website: http://www.prontopaints.co.uk
Directors: D. Beckford (Dir), L. Harris (Dir)
Immediate Holding Company: PRONTO INDUSTRIAL PAINTS LIMITED
Registration no: 02978626 **Date established:** 1994
No.of Employees: 21 - 50 **Product Groups:** 32, 35, 48

Date of Accounts	Mar 11	Mar 10	Mar 09
Working Capital	196	243	277
Fixed Assets	1m	2m	1m
Current Assets	1m	1m	880

Propex Concrete Systems Ltd Synthetic Industries Europe Limited

Propex House 9 Royal Court Basil Close, Chesterfield, S41 7SL
Tel: 01246-564200 **Fax:** 01246-564201
E-mail: enquiries@propexinc.co.uk
Website: http://www.fibermesh.com

see next page

***Propex Concrete Systems Ltd Synthetic Industries Europe Limited** - Cont'd*

Directors: P. Combier (MD)
Managers: A. Lind
Ultimate Holding Company: THE STERLING GROUP LP (USA)
Immediate Holding Company: PROPEX CONCRETE SYSTEMS LIMITED
Registration no: 02772124 **Date established:** 1992
Turnover: £10m - £20m **No.of Employees:** 21 - 50 **Product Groups:** 23, 29, 30, 32, 33, 34, 35, 51, 63, 66

Date of Accounts	Dec 11	Dec 10	Dec 09
Sales Turnover	10m	13m	10m
Pre Tax Profit/Loss	-186	171	336
Working Capital	5m	5m	5m
Fixed Assets	44	60	90
Current Assets	6m	6m	6m
Current Liabilities	554	450	595

Proteus Fittings Ltd

Unit 6 Stonegravels Lane, Chesterfield, S41 7LF
Tel: 01246-211303 **Fax:** 01246-209700
E-mail: info@proteusfittings.co.uk
Website: http://www.proteusfittings.co.uk
Directors: P. Oxspring (Fin)
Immediate Holding Company: PROTEUS FITTINGS LIMITED
Registration no: 02897455 **VAT No.:** GB 598 4683 66
Date established: 1994 **Turnover:** Up to £250,000
No.of Employees: 1 - 10 **Product Groups:** 30, 36, 37

Date of Accounts	Feb 12	Feb 11	Feb 10
Working Capital	-3	22	31
Fixed Assets	26	16	7
Current Assets	229	222	195

Protex

22 The Green Hasland, Chesterfield, S41 0LJ
Tel: 01246-556806 **Fax:** 01246-556806
E-mail: toldboy@aol.co.uk
Website: http://www.protex.gbr.com
Directors: L. Silkstone (Prop)
Date established: 2000 **Turnover:** Up to £250,000
No.of Employees: 1 - 10 **Product Groups:** 26, 35

J Pugh Lewis Ltd

The Old Saw Mills Morton Road, Pilsley, Chesterfield, S45 8EE
Tel: 01773-872362 **Fax:** 01773-874763
E-mail: info@pugh-lewis.co.uk
Website: http://www.pugh-lewis.co.uk
Directors: R. Pugh Lewis (Dir), J. Pugh Lewis (MD)
Immediate Holding Company: J.PUGH-LEWIS LIMITED
Registration no: 00881861 **Date established:** 1966 **Turnover:** £2m - £5m
No.of Employees: 21 - 50 **Product Groups:** 35, 52, 66

Date of Accounts	Mar 11	Mar 10	Mar 09
Sales Turnover	3m	3m	3m
Pre Tax Profit/Loss	166	56	29
Working Capital	-122	-237	-176
Fixed Assets	512	581	609
Current Assets	613	378	646
Current Liabilities	86	72	83

Quartex Components Ltd

2c Carrwood Road Chesterfield Trading Estate, Chesterfield, S41 9QB
Tel: 01246-450273 **Fax:** 01246-450321
E-mail: keith.gill@greatbritain.co.uk
Website: http://www.quartexcomponents.co.uk
Bank(s): Yorkshire
Directors: K. Gill (MD)
Immediate Holding Company: QUARTEX COMPONENTS LIMITED
Registration no: 01910675 **VAT No.:** GB 419 8406 33
Date established: 1985 **Turnover:** £500,000 - £1m
No.of Employees: 11 - 20 **Product Groups:** 30

Date of Accounts	Dec 11	Dec 10	Dec 09
Working Capital	142	109	87
Fixed Assets	65	75	78
Current Assets	290	283	232

R Wilson & Co. Ltd Zachrome Works

Zachrome Works Sheffield Road, Chesterfield, S41 8NH
Tel: 01246-450387 **Fax:** 01246-455875
E-mail: office@zachrome.com
Website: http://www.zachrome.com
Directors: J. Colton (MD)
Ultimate Holding Company: EARLYSTATE LIMITED
Immediate Holding Company: R.WILSON & CO.(PLATERS)LIMITED
Registration no: 00449802 **Date established:** 1948
No.of Employees: 21 - 50 **Product Groups:** 48

Date of Accounts	Dec 11	Dec 10	Oct 09
Working Capital	635	440	1m
Fixed Assets	1m	1m	849
Current Assets	1m	950	2m

Realstone Ltd

Bolehill Quarry Bolehill, Wingerworth, Chesterfield, S42 6RG
Tel: 01246-270244 **Fax:** 01246-220095
E-mail: info@realstone.co.uk
Website: http://www.realstone.co.uk
Bank(s): Barclays
Directors: S. Wright (Co Sec), J. Gregory (MD), I. Kennedy (MD)
Managers: J. Busby (Tech Serv Mgr)
Immediate Holding Company: REALSTONE LIMITED
Registration no: 00557167 **VAT No.:** GB 125 3441 00
Date established: 1955 **Turnover:** £2m - £5m **No.of Employees:** 51 - 100
Product Groups: 14

Date of Accounts	Dec 11	Dec 10	Dec 09
Sales Turnover	5m	4m	5m
Pre Tax Profit/Loss	-112	-181	-440
Working Capital	1m	271	1m
Fixed Assets	1m	1m	1m
Current Assets	3m	2m	3m
Current Liabilities	957	698	1m

Remploy Health Care

Remploy House Sheffield Road, Chesterfield, S41 8NJ
Tel: 08451-460600 **Fax:** 01685-881755
E-mail: sales@remployhealthcare.com
Website: http://www.remployhealthcare.com
Managers: S. Jones (Chief Mgr)
Immediate Holding Company: REMPLOY,LIMITED
Registration no: 00394532 **No.of Employees:** 51 - 100
Product Groups: 38, 67

Renforce Reinforcements Ltd

Staveley Lane Staveley, Chesterfield, S43 3YQ
Tel: 01246-432597 **Fax:** 01246-431563
E-mail: sales@renforce.co.uk
Website: http://www.renforce.co.uk
Managers: D. Rotherham (Mgr)
Immediate Holding Company: RENFORCE REINFORCEMENTS LIMITED
Registration no: 06734499 **Date established:** 2008
No.of Employees: 11 - 20 **Product Groups:** 35

Date of Accounts	Feb 11	Feb 10
Working Capital	80	11
Fixed Assets	35	23
Current Assets	1m	298

Rent A Ramp Ltd

Unit 37 Station Lane Indl-Est Station Lane, Old Whittington, Chesterfield, S41 9QX
Tel: 01246-260602 **Fax:** 01246-260493
E-mail: johnm@thorworld.co.uk
Website: http://www.rentaramp.com
Directors: J. Meale (MD)
Immediate Holding Company: RENT-A-RAMP LIMITED
Registration no: 02066488 **Date established:** 1986
No.of Employees: 11 - 20 **Product Groups:** 35, 39, 45

Right For Staff

Draefern House Dunston Court, Dunston Road, Chesterfield, S41 8NL
Tel: 01246-267021 **Fax:** 01246-267001
E-mail: info@right4staff.com
Website: http://www.right4staff.com
Bank(s): Barclays
Directors: J. Hardy (Fin), J. Watts (Ch), P. Smith (MD), M. Carflake (MD)
Managers: D. Knight (I.T. Exec), I. Thornley (Comm)
Ultimate Holding Company: RIGHT4STAFF HOLDINGS LIMITED
Immediate Holding Company: EPOCH 2 LIMITED
Registration no: 01949160 **Date established:** 1985
Turnover: £75m - £125m **No.of Employees:** 21 - 50 **Product Groups:** 80

Rock & Mine Engineering Ltd

High Street Clay Cross, Chesterfield, S45 9PF
Tel: 01246-252000 **Fax:** 01246-865077
E-mail: hausherr@btconnect.com
Website: http://www.hausherr.co.uk
Directors: K. Fiander (MD), M. Blunden (Co Sec)
Immediate Holding Company: ROCK AND MINE ENGINEERING LIMITED
Registration no: 07629530 **Date established:** 2011 **Turnover:** £1m - £2m
No.of Employees: 1 - 10 **Product Groups:** 40, 45

Date of Accounts	Dec 94	Dec 93	Dec 92
Working Capital	39	296	N/A
Fixed Assets	N/A	322	313
Current Assets	39	818	1m
Current Liabilities	N/A	522	957
Total Share Capital	100	100	N/A

Rompa International

Goyt Side Road, Chesterfield, S40 2PH
Tel: 01246-211777 **Fax:** 01246-221802
E-mail: reception@rompa.com
Website: http://www.rompa.com
Directors: S. Cooke (MD)
Ultimate Holding Company: FLAGHOUSE INC (USA)
Immediate Holding Company: ROMPA LIMITED
Registration no: 04011415 **Date established:** 2000
Turnover: £20m - £50m **No.of Employees:** 21 - 50 **Product Groups:** 40, 49, 65, 86

Date of Accounts	Dec 11	Dec 10	Dec 09
Sales Turnover	7m	7m	7m
Pre Tax Profit/Loss	277	-47	466
Working Capital	973	1m	859
Fixed Assets	507	559	595
Current Assets	2m	2m	2m
Current Liabilities	597	404	523

Sarclad Ltd

Broombank Park, Chesterfield, S41 9RT
Tel: 01246-457000 **Fax:** 01246-457010
E-mail: sarclad@sarclad.com
Website: http://www.sarclad.com
Directors: K. Shillam (MD), M. Sorby (MD), S. Meadows (Co Sec)
Managers: J. Morris (Sales Prom Mgr), M. Crinks (Purch Mgr)
Immediate Holding Company: SARCLAD LIMITED
Registration no: 03913109 **Date established:** 2000
Turnover: £10m - £20m **No.of Employees:** 21 - 50 **Product Groups:** 39, 46

Date of Accounts	Dec 11	Dec 10	Dec 09
Sales Turnover	10m	8m	15m
Pre Tax Profit/Loss	714	814	4m
Working Capital	4m	4m	6m
Fixed Assets	11	N/A	N/A
Current Assets	9m	9m	12m
Current Liabilities	1m	3m	3m

Scaglia Indeva Ltd

Unit 37 Coney Green Business Centre Clay Cross, Chesterfield, S45 9JW
Tel: 01246-252333 **Fax:** 01246-252334
E-mail: info@uk.indevagroup.com
Website: http://www.indevagroup.com
Registration no: 04122641 **Date established:** 1838 **Turnover:** £5m - £10m
No.of Employees: 1 - 10 **Product Groups:** 40, 41, 43, 44, 45, 46, 48, 67, 84

Date of Accounts	Dec 09	Dec 08	Dec 07
Working Capital	-162	-44	20
Fixed Assets	102	108	81
Current Assets	1m	1m	590

Schmolz & Bick En Bach

Stephenson Road Staveley, Chesterfield, S43 3JW
Tel: 01246-280280 **Fax:** 01246- 280445
E-mail: paul.roberts@schmolz-bickenbach.co.uk
Website: http://www.tkspecialsteels.co.uk
Directors: C. Staffell (MD), E. Kirk (MD)
Managers: G. Hide (Sales Prom Mgr), P. Roberts (Chief Acct)
Ultimate Holding Company: SCHMOLZ & BICKENBACH DISTRIBUTIONS (GERMANY)
Immediate Holding Company: SCHMOLZ+BICKENBACH (UK) LIMITED
Registration no: 00616108 **Date established:** 1958
Turnover: £20m - £50m **No.of Employees:** 21 - 50 **Product Groups:** 34

Date of Accounts	Dec 10	Dec 09	Dec 08
Sales Turnover	48m	40m	49m
Pre Tax Profit/Loss	735	-929	261
Working Capital	1m	283	1m
Fixed Assets	6m	6m	6m
Current Assets	26m	19m	29m
Current Liabilities	2m	1m	5m

Sealtight Gaskets Ltd

Unit 15 Calow Brook Drive Hasland, Chesterfield, S41 0DR
Tel: 01246-222400 **Fax:** 01246-222401
E-mail: harveyrslack@btconnect.com
Website: http://www.sealtightgaskets.co.uk
Directors: H. Slack (MD), R. Slack (Co Sec)
Immediate Holding Company: SEALTIGHT GASKETS LIMITED
Registration no: 02802400 **VAT No.:** GB 598 3257 88
Date established: 1993 **Turnover:** Up to £250,000
No.of Employees: 1 - 10 **Product Groups:** 27, 29, 30, 33, 36, 37

Date of Accounts	May 11	May 10	May 09
Working Capital	9	1	2
Fixed Assets	34	17	20
Current Assets	49	33	33

Serrations Ltd

Unit 5 Cobnar Wood Close, Chesterfield, S41 9RQ
Tel: 01246-456595 **Fax:** 01246-453377
E-mail: james@serrations.com
Website: http://www.serrations.com
Directors: J. Hartley (Dir), M. Hartley (Co Sec)
Immediate Holding Company: SERRATIONS LIMITED
Registration no: 03953139 **VAT No.:** GB 600 1740 00
Date established: 2000 **No.of Employees:** 1 - 10 **Product Groups:** 38

Date of Accounts	Apr 12	Apr 11	Apr 10
Working Capital	449	384	355
Fixed Assets	141	155	163
Current Assets	543	433	414

Sidetracker Engineering Ltd

Station Road Industrial Estate Station Road, Clowne, Chesterfield, S43 4AB
Tel: 01246-810655 **Fax:** 01246-812015
E-mail: info@sidetracker.co.uk
Website: http://www.sidetracker.co.uk
Bank(s): Lloyds TSB Bank plc
Directors: D. Dobson (MD)
Managers: B. Eastman (Sales Prom Mgr)
Immediate Holding Company: SIDETRACKER ENGINEERING LIMITED
Registration no: 00758051 **VAT No.:** GB 126 6498 47
Date established: 1963 **Turnover:** £1m - £2m **No.of Employees:** 11 - 20
Product Groups: 45, 67, 83

Date of Accounts	Apr 11	Apr 10	Apr 09
Working Capital	390	314	551
Fixed Assets	590	592	594
Current Assets	788	607	817

Franke Sissons Ltd

Carrwood Road, Chesterfield, S41 9QB
Tel: 01246-450255 **Fax:** 01246-451276
E-mail: ian.king@sissons.co.uk
Website: http://www.franke-sissons.co.uk
Bank(s): HSBC, Sheffield
Directors: J. Padfield (Fin)
Managers: K. Pugh (Buyer), L. Hartshorn (Personnel), V. Himsworth (Mktg Serv Mgr), P. Urszovics (Tech Serv Mgr), R. Stewart
Ultimate Holding Company: FRANKE HOLDING AG (SWITZERLAND)
Immediate Holding Company: FRANKE SISSONS LIMITED
Registration no: 02078694 **VAT No.:** GB 126 2517 89
Date established: 1986 **Turnover:** £5m - £10m
No.of Employees: 101 - 250 **Product Groups:** 26, 30, 35, 36, 40, 41, 45, 48, 66, 67

Date of Accounts	Dec 11	Dec 10	Dec 09
Sales Turnover	9m	10m	10m
Pre Tax Profit/Loss	-583	-425	-1m
Working Capital	957	1m	1m
Fixed Assets	5m	5m	6m
Current Assets	3m	3m	3m
Current Liabilities	381	442	545

Sixt Rent A Car

Durant House Holywell Street, Chesterfield, S41 7SH
Tel: 01246-220111 **Fax:** 0116-285 4546
E-mail: admin@e-sixt.co.uk
Website: http://www.sixt.co.uk
Bank(s): Barclays, Colemore Row, Birmingham
Managers: C. Hope
Ultimate Holding Company: SIXT AG (GERMANY)
Immediate Holding Company: SIXT PLC
Registration no: 03401066 **VAT No.:** GB 646 9183 03
Date established: 1997 **Turnover:** £20m - £50m
No.of Employees: 21 - 50 **Product Groups:** 72, 82

Date of Accounts	Dec 11	Dec 10	Dec 09
Sales Turnover	33m	27m	27m
Pre Tax Profit/Loss	3m	3m	1m
Working Capital	-27m	-23m	-25m
Fixed Assets	38m	31m	29m
Current Assets	12m	14m	9m
Current Liabilities	4m	3m	3m

Speed Plastics Ltd

Wheatbridge Road, Chesterfield, S40 2AB
Tel: 01246-276510 **Fax:** 01246-245400
E-mail: mikeh@speedplastics.co.uk
Website: http://www.speedplastics.co.uk
Bank(s): Bank of Scotland
Directors: A. Lauder (Dir), M. Hutson (MD)
Immediate Holding Company: SPEED PLASTICS LIMITED
Registration no: 02335046 **Date established:** 1989 **Turnover:** £2m - £5m
No.of Employees: 21 - 50 **Product Groups:** 26, 29, 30, 37, 38, 39, 40, 48, 49, 66, 67

Date of Accounts	Sep 08	Dec 07	Dec 06
Working Capital	1435	1217	890
Fixed Assets	380	384	485
Current Assets	1998	1893	1805
Current Liabilities	563	676	915
Total Share Capital	3	3	3

Stafford Catering Equipment

63 Clay Lane Clay Cross, Chesterfield, S45 9EW
Tel: 01246-251065 **Fax:** 01246-251065
E-mail: staffordcatering@talktalk.net
Directors: M. Stafford (Prop)
Date established: 2001 **No.of Employees:** 1 - 10 **Product Groups:** 20, 40, 41

Stainless Steel Fasteners Ltd

Broombank Road, Chesterfield, S41 9QJ
Tel: 01246-451818 **Fax:** 01246-455268
E-mail: sales@ssf.co.uk
Website: http://www.ssfast.co.uk
Bank(s): Barclays, Lombard St, London
Directors: S. Wilkinson (MD), D. Barber (Sales), K. Ridgeway (Fin)
Managers: J. McDonald (Chief Buyer), M. Tongue (Tech Serv Mgr)
Ultimate Holding Company: IMI PLC
Immediate Holding Company: STAINLESS STEEL FASTENERS LIMITED
Registration no: 00996214 **VAT No.:** GB 509 2782 34
Date established: 1970 **Turnover:** £5m - £10m
No.of Employees: 51 - 100 **Product Groups:** 35, 66

Date of Accounts	Dec 11	Dec 10	Dec 09
Sales Turnover	8m	7m	7m
Pre Tax Profit/Loss	1m	1m	1m
Working Capital	1m	5m	4m
Fixed Assets	348	180	217
Current Assets	3m	7m	6m
Current Liabilities	501	515	449

Stemcor Special Steels

Pottery Lane, Chesterfield, S41 9BH
Tel: 01246-451666 **Fax:** 01246-260092
E-mail: adrian@chesterfieldsteels.co.uk
Website: http://www.stemcorspecialsteels.com
Bank(s): Nat West
Managers: A. Cole
Immediate Holding Company: SIDDALL'S PROPERTY LTD
Registration no: 04559783 **VAT No.:** GB 125 7954 48
Date established: 2012 **Turnover:** £5m - £10m **No.of Employees:** 21 - 50
Product Groups: 34, 46

Date of Accounts	Aug 07	Aug 06
Sales Turnover	12453	12140
Pre Tax Profit/Loss	252	537
Working Capital	2779	2503
Fixed Assets	1470	1288
Current Assets	10039	9712
Current Liabilities	7260	7209
Total Share Capital	2	2
ROCE% (Return on Capital Employed)	5.9	14.2
ROT% (Return on Turnover)	2.0	4.4

Sterling Hydrotech Ltd

Freshwaters Park Road, Holmewood, Chesterfield, S42 5UY
Tel: 01246-857000 **Fax:** 01246-852200
E-mail: enquiries@sterling-hydrotech.co.uk
Website: http://www.sterling-hydrotech.co.uk
Bank(s): National Westminster Bank Plc
Directors: D. Gleeson (Sales), S. Thompson (Dir)
Immediate Holding Company: STERLING HYDROTECH LIMITED
Registration no: 02275897 **VAT No.:** GB 487 5244 11
Date established: 1988 **Turnover:** £2m - £5m **No.of Employees:** 11 - 20
Product Groups: 32, 38, 40, 41, 42, 48, 52, 54

Date of Accounts	Mar 12	Mar 11	Mar 10
Working Capital	232	118	66
Fixed Assets	3	7	18
Current Assets	715	529	415

Storm Studios

Unit 3 Old Brick Works Lane, Chesterfield, S41 7JD
Tel: 01246-293012 **Fax:** 01246-293019
E-mail: info@stormstudios.co.uk
Website: http://www.stormstudios.co.uk
Directors: S. France (Dir)
Immediate Holding Company: STORM STUDIOS MARKETING LIMITED
Registration no: 07070959 **Date established:** 2009
No.of Employees: 1 - 10 **Product Groups:** 44, 81

T C Richards & Sons

Calow Green Calow, Chesterfield, S44 5XQ
Tel: 01246-275612 **Fax:** 01246-237202
Directors: C. Richards (Ptnr)
Immediate Holding Company: CALOW GREEN FARMS LTD
No.of Employees: 1 - 10 **Product Groups:** 07

Tchibo Coffee International Ltd

1 Foxwood Road Dunston Trading Estate, Chesterfield, S41 9RF
Tel: 01246-455503 **Fax:** 01246-260506
E-mail: sales@tchibocoffee.co.uk
Website: http://www.tchibocoffee.co.uk
Managers: D. Garner (Mgr)
Ultimate Holding Company: MAXINGVEST AG (GERMANY)
Immediate Holding Company: TCHIBO COFFEE INTERNATIONAL LIMITED
Registration no: 00761849 **VAT No.:** GB 564 2125 58
Date established: 1963 **No.of Employees:** 21 - 50 **Product Groups:** 20

Date of Accounts	Dec 11	Dec 10	Dec 09
Sales Turnover	22m	20m	20m
Pre Tax Profit/Loss	1m	997	2m
Working Capital	12m	12m	12m
Fixed Assets	6m	5m	4m
Current Assets	14m	15m	15m
Current Liabilities	1m	1m	2m

Tennant Metallurgical Group Ltd

Suite 4 Venture House Venture Way Dunston Technology Park, Chesterfield, S41 8NR
Tel: 01246-263000 **Fax:** 01246-263001
E-mail: ross.convery@tenmet.co.uk
Website: http://www.tenmet.co.uk
Bank(s): Midland, Courtwood House, Sheffield
Directors: I. Cunningham (Mkt Research), J. Cunningham (Ch), I. Cunningham (MD), M. Lee (Dir), M. Midgley (Dir), R. Rastrick (Co Sec), I. Howe (Sales)
Managers: R. Convery (Mgr), R. Convery (I.T. Exec)
Immediate Holding Company: TENNANT METALLURGICAL GROUP LIMITED
Registration no: 00646646 **Date established:** 1960
Turnover: £20m - £50m **No.of Employees:** 11 - 20 **Product Groups:** 33, 34

Trans Tronic

Whitting Valley Road Old Whittington, Chesterfield, S41 9EY
Tel: 01246-264260 **Fax:** 01246-455281
E-mail: enquiries@trans-tronic.co.uk
Website: http://www.trans-tronic.co.uk
Bank(s): Barclays
Directors: D. Goater (MD)
Immediate Holding Company: GLAPWELL CONTRACTING SERVICES HOLDINGS LIMITED
Registration no: 02616086 **VAT No.:** GB 295 6479 00
Date established: 2012 **Turnover:** £2m - £5m **No.of Employees:** 21 - 50
Product Groups: 37

Truckmixer UK Ltd

Stainsby Close Holmewood, Chesterfield, S42 5UG
Tel: 01246-854339 **Fax:** 01246-854339
Directors: G. Tagg (Dir)
Immediate Holding Company: GTKV ENGINEERING LIMITED
Registration no: 02519293 **Date established:** 1990
Turnover: Up to £250,000 **No.of Employees:** 1 - 10 **Product Groups:** 42, 45

Date of Accounts	Jul 09	Jul 08	Jul 07
Working Capital	-28	-14	26
Fixed Assets	40	47	14
Current Assets	94	161	237

UK Industrial Knife Ltd

P.O. Box 597, Chesterfield, S40 9EG
Tel: 0870-712 0663 **Fax:** 0870-135 5343
E-mail: sales@industrialknife.co.uk
Website: http://www.industrialknife.co.uk
Product Groups: 36, 37, 40, 41, 42, 43, 44, 46, 47, 49, 66

Date of Accounts	Jun 07
Working Capital	23
Current Assets	62
Current Liabilities	38

Universal Hydraulics Ltd

Carrwood Road, Chesterfield, S41 9QB
Tel: 01246-451711 **Fax:** 01246-450399
E-mail: sales@universalhydraulics.co.uk
Website: http://www.universalhydraulics.co.uk
Directors: V. Mee (Fin), C. Cantral (MD)
Managers: Y. Montague (Sales Admin), V. Mee (Sales Admin)
Immediate Holding Company: UNIVERSAL HYDRAULICS LIMITED
Registration no: 01183511 **VAT No.:** GB 173 8838 22
Date established: 1974 **Turnover:** £500,000 - £1m
No.of Employees: 1 - 10 **Product Groups:** 35, 36, 40, 46

Date of Accounts	Dec 11	Dec 10	Dec 09
Working Capital	163	150	86
Fixed Assets	115	119	127
Current Assets	418	338	210

Universal Weighing Services

5 Winders Corner Barlborough, Chesterfield, S43 4WH
Tel: 01246-813333
E-mail: universalweigh@btconnect.com
Managers: J. Bushell (Mgr)
No.of Employees: 1 - 10 **Product Groups:** 38, 42

Valley Spring Co. Ltd

Pottery Lane East, Chesterfield, S41 9BH
Tel: 01246-451981 **Fax:** 01246-454327
E-mail: sales@valleyspring.com
Website: http://www.valleyspring.com
Bank(s): HSBC, Redditch
Directors: C. Roberts (Co Sec), J. Hewitt (Dir)
Ultimate Holding Company: SPRINGMASTERS LIMITED
Immediate Holding Company: VALLEY SPRING COMPANY LIMITED(THE)
Registration no: 00595524 **VAT No.:** GB 126 4991 51
Date established: 1957 **Turnover:** £500,000 - £1m
No.of Employees: 21 - 50 **Product Groups:** 35, 36, 39, 66

Date of Accounts	May 11	May 10	May 09
Working Capital	-86	16	43
Fixed Assets	412	392	442
Current Assets	585	548	493

Vecstar Ltd

Unit 11-12 Dunston Trading Estate Foxwood Road, Chesterfield, S41 9RF
Tel: 01246-260094 **Fax:** 01246-450213
E-mail: sales@vecstar.com
Website: http://www.vecstar.com
Directors: A. Duggan (Sales), C. Cadywould (Co Sec)
Immediate Holding Company: VECSTAR LIMITED
Registration no: 05016570 **Date established:** 2004
No.of Employees: 1 - 10 **Product Groups:** 35, 40, 42, 46

Date of Accounts	Jan 12	Jan 11	Jan 10
Working Capital	295	270	220
Fixed Assets	32	42	43
Current Assets	395	385	328

Walker & Partners Ltd

Inkersall Road Industrial Estate Speedwell Industrial Estate, Staveley, Chesterfield, S43 3JN
Tel: 01246-472147 **Fax:** 01246-473913
E-mail: sales@walkerandpartners.co.uk
Website: http://www.walkerandpartners.co.uk
Directors: J. Walker (MD)
Immediate Holding Company: WALKER & PARTNERS LIMITED
Registration no: 00657165 **Date established:** 1960 **Turnover:** £2m - £5m
No.of Employees: 1 - 10 **Product Groups:** 22, 25, 30, 33, 34, 35, 36, 37, 39, 40, 41, 42, 45, 46, 47, 48, 67, 84

Date of Accounts	Mar 12	Mar 11	Mar 10
Working Capital	220	182	166
Fixed Assets	1m	1m	1m
Current Assets	288	224	213

Weightron UK Ltd

Broombank Road, Chesterfield, S41 9QJ
Tel: 01246-260062 **Fax:** 01246-260844
E-mail: reception@weightroncb.co.uk
Website: http://www.weightron.com
Bank(s): National Westminster
Directors: N. Catt (MD)
Managers: E. Roberts (Tech Serv Mgr), S. Ducker (Chief Mgr)
Ultimate Holding Company: SOCIETA COOPERATIVA BILANCIAI CAMPOGALLIANO ARL (ITALY)
Immediate Holding Company: WEIGHTRON BILANCIAI LIMITED
Registration no: 02154099 **VAT No.:** GB 458 2230 52
Date established: 1987 **Turnover:** £5m - £10m **No.of Employees:** 11 - 20
Product Groups: 38, 48

Date of Accounts	Dec 11	Dec 10	Dec 09
Sales Turnover	7m	N/A	N/A
Pre Tax Profit/Loss	341	N/A	N/A
Working Capital	474	351	335
Fixed Assets	2m	2m	1m
Current Assets	2m	2m	1m
Current Liabilities	667	N/A	N/A

Willett Bros Chesterfield Ltd

King Street North, Chesterfield, S41 9BA
Tel: 01246-455101 **Fax:** 01246-454568
E-mail: sales@willettssweet.co.uk
Website: http://www.willetts-sweets.com
Bank(s): National Westminster Bank Plc
Directors: R. Willett (MD)
Immediate Holding Company: WILLETT BROTHERS (CHESTERFIELD) LIMITED
Registration no: 00694592 **Date established:** 1961 **Turnover:** £2m - £5m
No.of Employees: 21 - 50 **Product Groups:** 20

Date of Accounts	Dec 11	Dec 10	Dec 09
Working Capital	-275	-177	-84
Fixed Assets	536	545	555
Current Assets	554	603	742

Wooden Products Ltd

Unit 18 Whitting Valley Road, Old Whittington, Chesterfield, S41 9EY
Tel: 01246-453577 **Fax:** 01246-454954
E-mail: admin@wooden-boxes.co.uk
Website: http://www.wooden-boxes.co.uk
Directors: J. Woolhouse (Dir)
Immediate Holding Company: WOODEN PRODUCTS LIMITED
Registration no: 06920092 **Date established:** 2009
Turnover: £250,000 - £500,000 **No.of Employees:** 1 - 10
Product Groups: 25, 45, 46, 66

Date of Accounts	May 11	May 10
Working Capital	-10	-7
Fixed Assets	11	2
Current Assets	42	30

Xtratherm

Park Road Holmewood Industrial Park, Holmewood, Chesterfield, S42 5UY
Tel: 01246-858100 **Fax:** 01246-857447
E-mail: info@xtratherm.com
Website: http://www.xtratherm.com
Directors: B. Ratterty (Fab)
Managers: K. Westlake (Sales & Mktg Mg), N. Lomas (Personnel)
Ultimate Holding Company: LEANORT LIMITED
Immediate Holding Company: XTRATHERM UK LIMITED
Registration no: 04404208 **Date established:** 2002
Turnover: £20m - £50m **No.of Employees:** 51 - 100 **Product Groups:** 30, 33, 66

Date of Accounts	Dec 11	Dec 10	Dec 09
Sales Turnover	56m	36m	29m
Pre Tax Profit/Loss	2m	1m	387
Working Capital	262	-2m	-118
Fixed Assets	16m	17m	7m
Current Assets	14m	11m	6m
Current Liabilities	2m	2m	1m

W Yeomans Ltd

11 Midland Way Barlborough, Chesterfield, S43 4XA
Tel: 01246-571270 **Fax:** 01246-571271
E-mail: customerservices@wyeomans.com
Website: http://www.yeomansoutdoors.co.uk
Bank(s): National Westminster Bank Plc
Directors: R. Milner (Chief Op Offcr)
Managers: K. Orwin, C. Boardman (Buyer), T. Pickering (Personnel)
Ultimate Holding Company: YEOMANS INVESTMENTS LIMITED
Immediate Holding Company: W.YEOMANS (CHESTERFIELD) LIMITED
Registration no: 00357326 **VAT No.:** GB 125 9600 73
Date established: 1939 **Turnover:** £20m - £50m
No.of Employees: 21 - 50 **Product Groups:** 24, 49, 65

Date of Accounts	Jan 10	Jan 09	Jan 08
Sales Turnover	19m	15m	N/A
Pre Tax Profit/Loss	304	2m	730
Working Capital	4m	5m	2m
Fixed Assets	1m	659	2m
Current Assets	7m	7m	3m
Current Liabilities	1m	825	834

Derby

A S G Group Ltd

997 London Road Alvaston, Derby, DE24 8PX
Tel: 01332-753333 **Fax:** 01332-756333
E-mail: info@asg-group.co.uk
Website: http://www.asg-group.co.uk
Directors: V. Allman (Fin), A. Toothill (Fin), J. Allman (MD)
Managers: P. Rowden (Sales & Mktg Mg), S. Eccarius
Ultimate Holding Company: ASG GROUP ASSOCIATES LIMITED
Immediate Holding Company: ASG GROUP LIMITED
Registration no: 00957576 **Date established:** 1969
Turnover: £10m - £20m **No.of Employees:** 21 - 50 **Product Groups:** 22, 24, 26, 29, 30, 35, 36, 39, 45, 54, 61, 68

Date of Accounts	Feb 08	Feb 11	Feb 10
Sales Turnover	N/A	12m	5m
Pre Tax Profit/Loss	987	878	83
Working Capital	2m	3m	2m
Fixed Assets	3m	1m	1m
Current Assets	4m	5m	3m
Current Liabilities	646	687	294

Aburnet Ltd

Walter Street Draycott, Derby, DE72 3NU
Tel: 01332-874797 **Fax:** 01332-875284
E-mail: info@aburnet.co.uk
Website: http://www.aburnet.co.uk
Bank(s): National Westminster Bank Plc
Directors: R. Burnet (MD)
Immediate Holding Company: ABURNET LIMITED
Registration no: 00202702 **VAT No.:** GB 116 2716 90
Date established: 2024 **Turnover:** £1m - £2m **No.of Employees:** 21 - 50
Product Groups: 23, 24

Date of Accounts	Dec 11	Dec 10	Dec 09
Working Capital	1m	1m	894
Fixed Assets	219	164	169
Current Assets	2m	2m	1m

Advanced Vending Services Ltd
7 Fosbrook Drive Castle Donington, Derby, DE74 2UW
Tel: 08454-307123
E-mail: info@advancedvending.co.uk
Website: http://www.advancedvending.co.uk
Directors: G. Davidson (Dir)
Immediate Holding Company: ADVANCED VENDING SERVICES LIMITED
Registration no: 04846914 **Date established:** 2003 **Turnover:** £1m - £2m
No.of Employees: 51 - 100 **Product Groups:** 20, 48

Date of Accounts	Mar 11	Mar 10	Mar 09
Sales Turnover	200	N/A	N/A
Pre Tax Profit/Loss	21	N/A	N/A
Working Capital	-7	-20	-25
Fixed Assets	24	21	26
Current Assets	15	15	19
Current Liabilities	5	N/A	N/A

Aida S R L (UK Branch)
City Road, Derby, DE1 3RP
Tel: 01332-648200 **Fax:** 01332-648223
E-mail: info@aida-uk.com
Website: http://www.aida-europe.com
Managers: S. Farrell, F. Brown (Fin Mgr), L. Mount (Chief Mgr)
Immediate Holding Company: AIDA SAS
Registration no: FC024799 **VAT No.:** GB 824 5513 20
Date established: 2003 **Turnover:** £10m - £20m **No.of Employees:** 1 - 10
Product Groups: 37, 38, 45, 46, 48, 67

Allenbuild Ltd
Stoney Gate Road Spondon, Derby, DE21 7RY
Tel: 01332-680400 **Fax:** 01332-680444
E-mail: east.midland@allenbuild.co.uk
Website: http://www.allenbuild.co.uk
Directors: E. Carlisle (Fin)
Managers: M. Gallagher (Reg Mgr)
Immediate Holding Company: ALLENBUILD LIMITED
Registration no: 01248351 **VAT No.:** GB 151 6295 70
Date established: 1976 **Turnover:** £75m - £125m
No.of Employees: 251 - 500 **Product Groups:** 52

Allways Fork Trucks Services Ltd
Wincanton Close, Derby, DE24 8NB
Tel: 01332-755442 **Fax:** 01332-755442
E-mail: info@allways-forktrucks.co.uk
Website: http://www.allways-forktrucks.co.uk
Directors: L. Pilkington (Fin), A. Pilkington (MD)
Immediate Holding Company: ALLWAYS MANUFACTURING LIMITED
Registration no: 03310391 **Date established:** 1997
No.of Employees: 11 - 20 **Product Groups:** 35, 39, 45

Date of Accounts	Feb 12	Feb 11	Feb 10
Working Capital	27	27	27
Current Assets	27	27	27

Alpha Construction Ltd
Alpha House Hilton, Derby, DE65 5GE
Tel: 01283-733688 **Fax:** 01283-734546
E-mail: rob.smith@alphaconstruction.co.uk
Website: http://www.alphaconstruction.co.uk
Bank(s): National Westminster Bank Plc
Directors: R. Smith (MD)
Managers: G. Knight (Sales Admin), S. McLeod (Purch Mgr)
Ultimate Holding Company: ALPHA CONSTRUCTION (GROUP) LIMITED
Immediate Holding Company: ALPHA CONSTRUCTION (HOLDINGS) LIMITED
Registration no: 03052910 **VAT No.:** GB 380 1144 85
Date established: 1995 **Turnover:** £5m - £10m
No.of Employees: 51 - 100 **Product Groups:** 33, 42, 51, 52, 84

Date of Accounts	Dec 11	Dec 10	Dec 09
Pre Tax Profit/Loss	300	100	N/A
Working Capital	-157	-157	-157
Fixed Assets	347	347	347
Current Assets	210	10	10

Anixter Industrial - Derby
Fastener House Canal Street, Derby, DE1 2RJ
Tel: 08456-001430 **Fax:** 01332-297348
Website: http://www.anixter.com
Managers: R. Thurtell
Turnover: Up to £250,000 **No.of Employees:** 11 - 20 **Product Groups:** 30

Appor Ltd
Duffield Road Industrial Estate Little Eaton, Derby, DE21 5EG
Tel: 01332-832455 **Fax:** 01332-834427
E-mail: info@appor.com
Website: http://www.appor.com
Bank(s): Bank of Scotland, Birmingham
Directors: P. Bott (MD)
Managers: M. Lander (Sales Prom Mgr), J. Doughty (Purch Mgr), K. Atkinson
Immediate Holding Company: DEB Group Ltd
Registration no: 00853355 **VAT No.:** GB 570 9365 20
Date established: 1965 **Turnover:** £2m - £5m **No.of Employees:** 21 - 50
Product Groups: 30, 40, 42

Ascott Weighing Services Ltd
81 Collingham Gardens, Derby, DE22 4FQ
Tel: 01332-364597 **Fax:** 01332-364597
E-mail: sales@ascottweighing.co.uk
Website: http://www.ascottweighing.co.uk
Directors: A. Lawton (Fin), S. Roberts (MD)
Immediate Holding Company: ASCOTT WEIGHING SERVICES LTD
Registration no: 04978706 **Date established:** 2003
No.of Employees: 1 - 10 **Product Groups:** 38, 42

Date of Accounts	Sep 11	Sep 10	Sep 07
Working Capital	8	7	7
Fixed Assets	3	3	3
Current Assets	18	20	13

Ashfield Screen Printing Ltd (Head Office)
Unit 10b Stoney Cross Industrial Estate Station Road, Spondon, Derby, DE21 7RX
Tel: 01332-662026 **Fax:** 01332-668620
E-mail: sales@ashfieldsp.co.uk
Website: http://www.ashfieldsp.com
Bank(s): National Westminster Bank Plc
Directors: C. Henry (MD), S. Henry (Fin)
Immediate Holding Company: ASHFIELD SCREEN PRINTING LIMITED
Registration no: 00559110 **VAT No.:** GB 126 1415 05
Date established: 1955 **Turnover:** £500,000 - £1m
No.of Employees: 11 - 20 **Product Groups:** 27, 28, 30, 35, 44, 49, 81

Date of Accounts	Mar 11	Mar 10	Mar 09
Working Capital	-126	-67	7
Fixed Assets	381	405	256
Current Assets	275	230	208

Ashton & Morris Engineering
6 Reginald Road South Chaddesden, Derby, DE21 6ND
Tel: 01332-670779 **Fax:** 01332-664332
E-mail: eddiemorris51199@aol.com
Directors: E. Morris (Prop), A. Tierney (Fin)
Immediate Holding Company: ASHTON & MORRIS (STRUCTURAL ENGINEERS) LIMITED
Registration no: 01745783 **Date established:** 1983
No.of Employees: 1 - 10 **Product Groups:** 40

Date of Accounts	Jan 10	Jan 09	Jan 08
Working Capital	1	-1	-8
Fixed Assets	9	11	13
Current Assets	105	100	79

B O B Stevenson Ltd
5 Coleman Street, Derby, DE24 8NL
Tel: 01332-574112 **Fax:** 01332-757286
E-mail: l.perrott@bobstevenson.co.uk
Website: http://www.bobstevenson.co.uk
Directors: L. Perrott (MD)
Immediate Holding Company: B.O.B. STEVENSON LIMITED
Registration no: 01881804 **Date established:** 1985
No.of Employees: 11 - 20 **Product Groups:** 40, 43, 48

Date of Accounts	Oct 11	Oct 10	Oct 09
Working Capital	95	104	148
Fixed Assets	8	16	29
Current Assets	146	204	246

B S S Group Ltd
Riverside Road Pride Park, Derby, DE24 8HH
Tel: 01332-685600 **Fax:** 01332-685601
E-mail: 1450.mgr@bssgroup.com
Website: http://www.bssgroup.com
Managers: A. Lawrence (District Mgr)
Immediate Holding Company: BUSINESS SUPPORT SERVICES UK LTD
Registration no: 03106393 **No.of Employees:** 11 - 20 **Product Groups:** 40

Balfour Beatty Plant & Fleet Services
Main Office, Derby, DE21 7BG
Tel: 01332-661491 **Fax:** 01332-288590
Website: http://www.bbpnl.com
Managers: L. Shacklock
Ultimate Holding Company: BALFOUR BEATTY PLC
Immediate Holding Company: BALFOUR BEATTY GROUP LTD
Registration no: 02067112 **Date established:** 1979
No.of Employees: 251 - 500 **Product Groups:** 67, 76, 84

Balfour Beatty Rail Projects Ltd
Midland House 1 Nelson Street, Derby, DE1 2SA
Tel: 01332-262666 **Fax:** 01332-262295
E-mail: peter.anderson@bbrail.com
Website: http://www.bbrail.com
Directors: A. Mccarthy-Wyper (Dir), S. Edgington (Tech Serv), T. Fossey (Fin), J. Webb (Pers)
Immediate Holding Company: BALFOUR BEATTY PLC
Registration no: 00395826 **Date established:** 1945
Turnover: Over £1,000m **No.of Employees:** 51 - 100 **Product Groups:** 37, 39, 51, 71

Date of Accounts	Dec 11	Dec 10	Dec 09
Sales Turnover	9494m	9236m	8954m
Pre Tax Profit/Loss	246m	187m	267m
Working Capital	-646m	-490m	-468m
Fixed Assets	3817m	2910m	2818m
Current Assets	2755m	2469m	2576m
Current Liabilities	2218m	1930m	1894m

Baxi Group
16 Stanier Way Wyvern Business Park, Chaddesden, Derby, DE21 6BF
Tel: 01332-545400 **Fax:** 01332-545410
E-mail: info@baxipotterton.co.uk
Website: http://www.baxigroup.com
Bank(s): The Royal Bank of Scotland
Directors: A. Darling (Fin), A. Newington (Non Exec), F. Loredan (Non Exec), H. Mumford (Non Exec), J. Burgess (Ch), M. Croffey (Grp Chief Exec), M. Davies (Non Exec), M. Edwards (Grp Chief Exec)
Managers: A. Hannah, D. Basile, R. Nash, L. Barratt
Ultimate Holding Company: Baxi Holdings Ltd
Immediate Holding Company: Heating Finance plc
Registration no: 04061959 **VAT No.:** GB 604 6658 37
Date established: 2000 **Turnover:** £500m - £1,000m
No.of Employees: 21 - 50 **Product Groups:** 36, 37, 40, 48

Date of Accounts	Dec 09	Dec 08	Dec 07
Pre Tax Profit/Loss	49m	21m	22m
Working Capital	-74m	-79m	-84m
Fixed Assets	160m	160m	160m
Current Assets	888m	768m	658m
Current Liabilities	5m	6m	5m

Bemrose Booth
PO Box 18, Derby, DE21 6XG
Tel: 01332-294242 **Fax:** 01332-290366
E-mail: enquiries@bemrose.co.uk
Website: http://www.bemrosebooth.com
Bank(s): Barclays
Directors: L. Levie (Fin), M. Richards (Grp Chief Exec)
Managers: A. Rigg (Buyer)
Ultimate Holding Company: 06661704
Immediate Holding Company: BEMROSE GROUP LIMITED
Registration no: 03978230 **VAT No.:** GB 745 7849 80
Date established: 2000 **Turnover:** £50m - £75m
No.of Employees: 501 - 1000 **Product Groups:** 28, 81

Binder Creations Ltd
Unit 22 Shaftesbury Street South, Derby, DE23 8YH
Tel: 01332-297575 **Fax:** 01332-384625
E-mail: karen.smith@bindercreations.co.uk
Website: http://www.bindercreations.co.uk
Directors: K. Smith (Dir), G. Freestone (Fin)
Immediate Holding Company: BINDER CREATIONS LIMITED
Registration no: 06275704 **Date established:** 2007
No.of Employees: 1 - 10 **Product Groups:** 27, 28, 30, 80

Date of Accounts	Jul 12	Jul 11	Jul 10
Working Capital	9	18	27
Fixed Assets	5	8	11
Current Assets	60	98	118

Blatchs T V & Electrical
6 Market Place Melbourne, Derby, DE73 8DS
Tel: 01332-862607 **Fax:** 01332-862607
E-mail: tb@blatchs.co.uk
Website: http://www.blatchs.co.uk
Directors: T. Blatch (Prop)
Date established: 1991 **No.of Employees:** 1 - 10 **Product Groups:** 40, 41, 67

Bodycote Heat Treatment Ltd
Wilmore Road, Derby, DE24 9HZ
Tel: 01332-275800 **Fax:** 01332-767785
E-mail: philip.lee@bodycote.com
Website: http://www.bodycote.com
Directors: P. Lee (Dir)
Immediate Holding Company: BODYCOTE PLC
Registration no: 00519057 **Date established:** 1953
No.of Employees: 11 - 20 **Product Groups:** 46, 48

Date of Accounts	Dec 11	Dec 10	Dec 09
Sales Turnover	571m	500m	435m
Pre Tax Profit/Loss	56m	45m	-55m
Working Capital	-12m	-10m	-13m
Fixed Assets	610m	628m	642m
Current Assets	148m	144m	130m
Current Liabilities	111m	109m	108m

Bombardier Transportation Rolling Stock UK Ltd
Derby Carriage Works Litchurch Lane, Derby, DE24 8AD
Tel: 01332-257500 **Fax:** 01332-266271
E-mail: heidi.lee@uk.transport.bombardier.com
Website: http://www.bombardier.com
Managers: D. Moss (Chief Mgr)
Ultimate Holding Company: BOMBARDIER INC (CANADA)
Immediate Holding Company: BOMBARDIER TRANSPORTATION (ROLLING STOCK) UK LTD
Registration no: 02988520 **Date established:** 1994
Turnover: £20m - £50m **No.of Employees:** 51 - 100 **Product Groups:** 84

Date of Accounts	Dec 11	Dec 10	Dec 09
Sales Turnover	34m	18m	N/A
Pre Tax Profit/Loss	-475	-6m	N/A
Working Capital	16m	16m	496
Fixed Assets	532	1m	13m
Current Assets	21m	25m	7m
Current Liabilities	3m	2m	N/A

British Wood Preserving & Damp Proofing Association
1 Gleneagles House Vernon Gate, Derby, DE1 1UP
Tel: 01332-225100 **Fax:** 01332-225101
E-mail: enquiry@bpca.org.uk
Website: http://www.bwpda.co.uk
Directors: K. Higgins (Dir), Y. Chopin (Fin), L. Meikle (MD), D. Lovell (Sales), O. Madge (Co Sec)
Managers: L. Norton (Sales Admin), A. Howitt (Sales Admin)
Immediate Holding Company: THE BRITISH WOOD PRESERVING AND DAMP-PROOFING ASSOCIATION
Registration no: 03280875 **Date established:** 1996
Turnover: £500,000 - £1m **No.of Employees:** 1 - 10 **Product Groups:** 41, 52

Date of Accounts	Dec 08	Dec 07	Dec 06
Sales Turnover	N/A	N/A	413
Pre Tax Profit/Loss	N/A	18	58
Working Capital	106	110	94
Fixed Assets	N/A	N/A	10
Current Assets	115	119	142
Current Liabilities	N/A	9	36

Brookes Machine Tools Ltd
Derby Road Kegworth, Derby, DE74 2EN
Tel: 01509-672256 **Fax:** 01509-674502
E-mail: bmtlimited@aol.com
Directors: P. Brookes (Dir)
Immediate Holding Company: BROOKES MACHINE TOOLS LIMITED
Registration no: 04596677 **Date established:** 2002 **Turnover:** £1m - £2m
No.of Employees: 1 - 10 **Product Groups:** 67

Date of Accounts	Dec 11	Dec 10	Dec 09
Working Capital	-3	8	-5
Fixed Assets	3	3	3
Current Assets	61	72	66
Current Liabilities	57	N/A	N/A

Owen Brown
Station Road Castle Donington, Derby, DE74 2NL
Tel: 01332-850000 **Fax:** 01332-850005
E-mail: info@owen-brown.co.uk
Website: http://www.owen-brown.co.uk
Bank(s): National Westminster Bank Plc
Directors: A. Robertson (MD), M. Chapman (Fin)
Managers: K. Soutar (Mktg Serv Mgr), C. Coppe (Tech Serv Mgr), H. Newton
Ultimate Holding Company: POLYGONE SA (FRANCE)
Immediate Holding Company: OWEN BROWN LIMITED
Registration no: 00392279 **Date established:** 1945
Turnover: £20m - £50m **No.of Employees:** 51 - 100 **Product Groups:** 24, 83

Date of Accounts	Dec 11	Dec 10	Dec 09
Sales Turnover	20m	16m	13m
Pre Tax Profit/Loss	1m	508	648
Working Capital	2m	1m	2m
Fixed Assets	9m	9m	9m
Current Assets	16m	5m	4m
Current Liabilities	11m	1m	1m

Business Link East Midlands
Innovation House Riverside Park Raynesway Spondon, Derby, DE21 7BF
Tel: 08450-586644 **Fax:** 01332-280792
E-mail: info@businesslinkem.co.uk
Website: http://www.businesslink.gov.uk/EastMidlands
Directors: T. McEwen (Grp Chief Exec)
Managers: J. Kersey (Mktg Serv Mgr)
Ultimate Holding Company: APICA LIMITED
Immediate Holding Company: NORTHWEST BUSINESS LINK
Registration no: 06060925 **Date established:** 2007
Turnover: £500,000 - £1m **No.of Employees:** 1 - 10 **Product Groups:** 80, 81

Date of Accounts	Mar 11	Mar 10	Mar 09
Sales Turnover	24m	30m	27m
Pre Tax Profit/Loss	-588	174	-209

Working Capital	4m	3m	4m
Fixed Assets	N/A	931	1m
Current Assets	5m	4m	5m
Current Liabilities	1m	690	2m

C S S Asbestos Surveys

Suite 3 Keynes House Chester Park Alfreton Road, Derby, DE21 4AS
Tel: 01332-204074 **Fax:** 01332-207915
E-mail: enquiries@css-surveys.com
Website: http://www.css-surveys.com
Directors: B. Halloran (Prop)
Immediate Holding Company: A.R.C. TRAINING CONSULTANCY LTD
Registration no: 06413261 **Date established:** 2007
No.of Employees: 11 - 20 **Product Groups:** 85

Celanece Acetate Ltd

PO Box 5, Derby, DE21 7BP
Tel: 01332-661422 **Fax:** 01332-681786
Website: http://www.celanece.com
Bank(s): Barclays Bank PLC
Directors: A. Poulsom (Dir)
Managers: P. Newing (Personnel)
Ultimate Holding Company: ACORDIS BV (NETHERLANDS)
Immediate Holding Company: ACETATE PRODUCTS LIMITED
Registration no: 00217201 **VAT No.:** GB 817 3666 12
Date established: 2026 **Turnover:** Up to £250,000
No.of Employees: 51 - 100 **Product Groups:** 23, 31, 49, 66

Date of Accounts	Dec 11	Dec 10	Dec 09
Sales Turnover	28	1m	2m
Pre Tax Profit/Loss	-726	-678	-855
Working Capital	3m	4m	5m
Current Assets	3m	4m	7m
Current Liabilities	332	415	1m

Central Training

Unit 14 Robinsons Industrial Estate Shaftesbury Street, Derby, DE23 8NL
Tel: 01332-369933 **Fax:** 01332-833998
E-mail: enquiries@central-training.com
Website: http://www.central-training.com
Directors: R. Eyden (Prop)
Date established: 1989 **No.of Employees:** 1 - 10 **Product Groups:** 35, 39, 45

Charles Blyth & Company Ltd

Carnival Way Castle Donington, Derby, DE74 2NJ
Tel: 01332-810283 **Fax:** 01332-855810
E-mail: nab@charlesblyth-co.co.uk
Website: http://www.charlesblyth-co.co.uk
Bank(s): Midland Bank
Directors: C. Blyth (MD), N. Blyth (Dir)
Ultimate Holding Company: CHARLES BLYTH (HOLDINGS) LIMITED
Immediate Holding Company: CHARLES BLYTH & CO LIMITED
Registration no: 00348644 **VAT No.:** GB 125 5413 92
Date established: 1939 **No.of Employees:** 11 - 20 **Product Groups:** 26, 35

Date of Accounts	Jun 11	Jun 10	Jun 09
Working Capital	196	239	105
Fixed Assets	1m	1m	1m
Current Assets	814	1m	985

Charterhouse Holdings plc

Trent Lane Castle Donington, Derby, DE74 2PY
Tel: 01332-855050 **Fax:** 01332-858383
E-mail: head.office@charterhouse-holdings.co.uk
Website: http://www.charterhouse-holdings.co.uk
Directors: M. Clayton (Ch), R. Horbuckle (Mkt Research), S. Ellis (Fin)
Managers: M. Williams (Buyer), A. Mears (Tech Serv Mgr), D. Clayton, K. Tomlinson (Personnel)
Immediate Holding Company: CHARTERHOUSE HOLDINGS PUBLIC LIMITED COMPANY
Registration no: 00981987 **VAT No.:** GB 114 4123 22
Date established: 1970 **Turnover:** £20m - £50m
No.of Employees: 51 - 100 **Product Groups:** 67, 87

Date of Accounts	Dec 11	Dec 10	Dec 09
Sales Turnover	22m	22m	19m
Pre Tax Profit/Loss	4m	3m	3m
Working Capital	14m	12m	11m
Fixed Assets	4m	4m	4m
Current Assets	18m	15m	14m
Current Liabilities	3m	3m	3m

Choc-A-Block Drainage Services

120a Western Road Mickleover, Derby, DE3 9GR
Tel: 0800-019 9512 **Fax:** 01332-510144
E-mail: pennyandlance@fsmail.net
Managers: P. Russell (Sec)
Registration no: 06873520 **Date established:** 2009
No.of Employees: 1 - 10 **Product Groups:** 54

Date of Accounts	May 07	May 06
Sales Turnover	163	88
Pre Tax Profit/Loss	6	12
Working Capital	8	6
Fixed Assets	11	10
Current Assets	15	9
Current Liabilities	8	4
ROCE% (Return on Capital Employed)	31.2	77.6
ROT% (Return on Turnover)	3.6	13.8

Coe's Derby Ltd Engineers in GRP

Thirsk Place, Derby, DE24 8JL
Tel: 01332-299412 **Fax:** 01332-340774
E-mail: info@coesofderby.co.uk
Website: http://www.coesofderby.co.uk
Directors: P. Harrison (Fin), R. Harrison (MD)
Immediate Holding Company: COE S(DERBY)LIMITED
Registration no: 00496838 **VAT No.:** GB 125 4068 88
Date established: 1951 **Turnover:** £250,000 - £500,000
No.of Employees: 1 - 10 **Product Groups:** 30, 33, 35, 39, 40, 48, 52, 66

Date of Accounts	May 11	May 10	May 09
Sales Turnover	496	359	N/A
Pre Tax Profit/Loss	49	-85	N/A
Working Capital	54	7	73
Fixed Assets	10	12	46
Current Assets	127	136	139
Current Liabilities	42	74	N/A

Thomas Coleman Engineering Ltd

Alfreton Road, Derby, DE21 4AL
Tel: 01332-345519 **Fax:** 01332-343436
E-mail: sales@colemaneng.co.uk
Website: http://www.colemaneng.co.uk
Directors: C. Rushbrook (Fin)
Immediate Holding Company: THOMAS COLEMAN ENGINEERING LTD
Registration no: 02287955 **VAT No.:** GB 125 2376 87
Date established: 1988 **Turnover:** £250,000 - £500,000
No.of Employees: 1 - 10 **Product Groups:** 40, 45, 48

Date of Accounts	Dec 10	Dec 09	Dec 08
Working Capital	-384	-341	-311
Fixed Assets	2	2	3
Current Assets	28	25	49

Competition Logistics Ltd

Unit 1 Castle Lane Industrial Estate Castle Lane Melbourne, Derby, DE73 8JB
Tel: 01332-695258 **Fax:** 01332-695259
E-mail: sarah@complog.co.uk
Website: http://www.complog.co.uk
Directors: S. Roberts (Fin)
Immediate Holding Company: COMPETITION LOGISTICS LIMITED
Registration no: SC256012 **Date established:** 2003
No.of Employees: 1 - 10 **Product Groups:** 29, 39

Date of Accounts	Jan 12	Jan 11	Jan 10
Working Capital	178	221	178
Fixed Assets	185	202	201
Current Assets	515	405	379

Cooper Parry

3 Centro Place Pride Park, Derby, DE24 8RF
Tel: 01332-295544 **Fax:** 01332-295600
E-mail: advice@cooperparry.com
Website: http://www.cooperparry.com
Directors: O. Parrish (Pers), A. Geer (Ptnr), C. Nurden (Fin), J. Bowler (Grp Chief Exec)
Managers: D. Wilson, M. Campbell (Mktg Serv Mgr)
Ultimate Holding Company: COOPER PARRY LLP
Immediate Holding Company: COOPER PARRY LLP
Registration no: OC301728 **Date established:** 2002
Turnover: £10m - £20m **No.of Employees:** 251 - 500 **Product Groups:** 80

Date of Accounts	Apr 12	Apr 11	Apr 10
Sales Turnover	16m	14m	15m
Pre Tax Profit/Loss	5m	4m	5m
Working Capital	2m	2m	3m
Fixed Assets	394	368	454
Current Assets	6m	5m	6m
Current Liabilities	2m	2m	2m

Cott Beverages Ltd

Citrus Grove Sideley, Kegworth, Derby, DE74 2FJ
Tel: 01509-674915 **Fax:** 01977-791735
E-mail: reception@cott.co.uk
Website: http://www.cott.com
Bank(s): Lloyds TSB Bank plc
Directors: M. Turner (Tech Serv)
Managers: K. Mills
Ultimate Holding Company: COTT CORPORATION INC (CANADA)
Immediate Holding Company: COTT LIMITED
Registration no: 02186825 **VAT No.:** GB 629 7872 83
Date established: 1987 **Turnover:** £125m - £250m
No.of Employees: 251 - 500 **Product Groups:** 21

Date of Accounts	Dec 07	Dec 08	Jan 10
Working Capital	1	N/A	N/A
Current Assets	1	N/A	N/A

The Countryman Of Derby

Unit 15 Prime Enterprise Park Prime Park Way, Derby, DE1 3QB
Tel: 01332-360357 **Fax:** 01332-720959
E-mail: martyn@the-countryman.com
Website: http://www.countrymanofderby.co.uk
Directors: C. Bray (Fin), M. Bray (MD)
Immediate Holding Company: COUNTRYMAN OF DERBY LIMITED
Registration no: 04753842 **Date established:** 2003
No.of Employees: 1 - 10 **Product Groups:** 36, 39, 40

Date of Accounts	Jun 11	Jun 10	Jun 09
Working Capital	155	119	118
Fixed Assets	263	38	47
Current Assets	240	170	182

Peter Cox Ltd

Chester Park Alfreton Road, Derby, DE21 4AS
Tel: 01332-299222 **Fax:** 01332-200066
Website: http://www.petercox.com
Directors: K. Mesterton (MD)
Managers: G. Bartram (Mgr)
Ultimate Holding Company: FP051617
Immediate Holding Company: PETER COX LIMITED
Registration no: 02438126 **Date established:** 1989
No.of Employees: 11 - 20 **Product Groups:** 07, 32, 52, 66

Creative Steel

6 Prime Industrial Estate Shaftesbury Street South, Derby, DE23 8YH
Tel: 07958-699315 **Fax:** 01332-772714
E-mail: steve@creativesteel.co.uk
Website: http://www.creativesteel.co.uk
Directors: S. Aukett (Prop)
Immediate Holding Company: CREATIVE STEEL LTD
Registration no: 06060246 **Date established:** 1996
No.of Employees: 1 - 10 **Product Groups:** 49

D S Fabrications

5 Briar Lea Close Sinfin, Derby, DE24 9PB
Tel: 01332-721414 **Fax:** 01332-721414
Directors: D. Faund (Prop)
Date established: 1995 **No.of Employees:** 1 - 10 **Product Groups:** 26, 35

Datapath Ltd

Alfreton Road, Derby, DE21 4AD
Tel: 01332-294441 **Fax:** 01332-290667
E-mail: sales@datapath.co.uk
Website: http://www.datapath.co.uk
Bank(s): National Westminster Bank Plc
Directors: C. Anderson (Mkt Research), N. Fasey (Fin), S. De'ath (Co Sec), S. Mikos (Sales), T. Jones (Chief Op Offcr)
Ultimate Holding Company: DATAPATH GROUP LIMITED
Immediate Holding Company: DATAPATH LIMITED
Registration no: 01609392 **VAT No.:** GB 354 4986 19
Date established: 1982 **Turnover:** £10m - £20m
No.of Employees: 21 - 50 **Product Groups:** 44

Date of Accounts	Mar 12	Mar 11	Mar 10
Sales Turnover	13m	10m	8m
Pre Tax Profit/Loss	4m	4m	2m
Working Capital	15m	12m	9m
Fixed Assets	70	51	48
Current Assets	16m	13m	10m
Current Liabilities	897	735	326

Davis Derby Ltd

Chequers Lane, Derby, DE21 6AW
Tel: 01332-341671 **Fax:** 01332-372190
E-mail: enquiries@davisderby.com
Website: http://www.davisderby.com
Bank(s): Lloyds TSB
Directors: G. Beetles (MD), A. Cooper (Fin)
Managers: G. Ball (Personnel), L. Owen, D. Randle, A. Stevenson, J. Kennedy
Ultimate Holding Company: DAVIS DERBY HOLDINGS LIMITED
Immediate Holding Company: DAVIS DERBY LIMITED
Registration no: 02701771 **VAT No.:** GB 610 3579 65
Date established: 1992 **Turnover:** £5m - £10m
No.of Employees: 51 - 100 **Product Groups:** 36, 37, 38

Date of Accounts	Dec 11	Dec 10	Dec 09
Sales Turnover	7m	6m	9m
Pre Tax Profit/Loss	6	23	1m
Working Capital	2m	2m	2m
Fixed Assets	124	158	119
Current Assets	3m	3m	4m
Current Liabilities	439	420	1m

Davpack

Charlton House Riverside Park, Spondon, Derby, DE21 7BF
Tel: 01332-821200 **Fax:** 01332-821209
E-mail: sales@davpack.co.uk
Website: http://www.davpack.co.uk
Directors: C. Davenport (Fin)
Immediate Holding Company: DAVENPORT PAPER CO LIMITED
Registration no: 02012280 **Date established:** 1986
No.of Employees: 11 - 20 **Product Groups:** 24, 25, 26, 27, 29, 30, 34, 35, 38, 40, 42, 44, 45, 49, 63, 66, 67

Date of Accounts	Apr 11	Apr 10	Apr 09
Working Capital	946	688	683
Fixed Assets	285	133	136
Current Assets	2m	2m	1m

Deaf Alerter plc

Enfield House 303 Burton Road, Derby, DE23 6AG
Tel: 01332-363981 **Fax:** 01332-293267
E-mail: steveh@deaf-alerter.com
Website: http://www.deaf-alerter.co.uk
Bank(s): Barclays, Derby
Directors: C. Presland (Dir), C. Haseldine (Sales), S. Haseldine (MD), K. Haseldine (Fin)
Managers: J. Wallace (Tech Serv Mgr), M. Nicholson (Sales Admin)
Immediate Holding Company: DEAF ALERTER PLC
Registration no: 04078512 **Date established:** 2000 **Turnover:** £1m - £2m
No.of Employees: 21 - 50 **Product Groups:** 44, 49, 84

Date of Accounts	Dec 11	Dec 10	Dec 09
Sales Turnover	2m	2m	2m
Pre Tax Profit/Loss	4	41	38
Working Capital	-37	-98	58
Fixed Assets	846	922	717
Current Assets	732	745	668
Current Liabilities	274	310	196

Deltarail Group Ltd

Hudson House 2 Hudson Way Pride Park, Derby, DE24 8HS
Tel: 01332-221000 **Fax:** 0870-1901008
E-mail: lawrence.roberts@deltarail.com
Website: http://www.deltarail.com
Managers: L. Roberts ()
Date established: 2006 **Turnover:** £50m - £75m **Product Groups:** 39, 44, 52, 68

Date of Accounts	Sep 11	Sep 10	Sep 09
Sales Turnover	29m	34m	40m
Pre Tax Profit/Loss	2m	-4m	2m
Working Capital	-124	-1m	3m
Fixed Assets	14m	15m	15m
Current Assets	9m	11m	15m
Current Liabilities	9m	11m	7m

Derby Box Co. Ltd

Unit 2 Endland Industrial Estate Parcel Terrace, Derby, DE1 1LY
Tel: 01332-372191 **Fax:** 01332-372191
E-mail: derbyboxco@aol.com
Website: http://www.derbyboxcompany.co.uk
Directors: S. Roome (Co Sec)
Immediate Holding Company: DERBY BOX COMPANY LIMITED
Registration no: 04419356 **VAT No.:** GB 745 5990 89
Date established: 2002 **No.of Employees:** 1 - 10 **Product Groups:** 25, 30, 45, 66, 76

Date of Accounts	Apr 12	Apr 11	Apr 10
Working Capital	-4	-11	-25
Fixed Assets	41	52	60
Current Assets	54	40	36

Derby Telegraph Media Group

Northcliffe House Meadow Road, Derby, DE1 2BH
Tel: 01332-291111 **Fax:** 01332-253011
E-mail: newsdesk@derbytelegraph.co.uk
Website: http://www.thisisderbyshire.co.uk
Bank(s): National Westminster Bank Plc
Managers: C. Smith (Fin Mgr), E. Hillyer
Ultimate Holding Company: ROTHERMERE CONTINUATION LTD (BERMUDA)
Immediate Holding Company: NORTHCLIFFE NEWSPAPERS GROUP LTD
Registration no: 00218661 **Turnover:** £20m - £50m
No.of Employees: 101 - 250 **Product Groups:** 28

Derbyshire Forklifts

Bakeacre Lane Findern, Derby, DE65 6BH
Tel: 01332-510670 **Fax:** 01332-510136
E-mail: info@derbyshireforklifts.co.uk
Website: http://www.derbyshireforklifts.co.uk
Directors: A. Penny (Prop)
Date established: 1972 **No.of Employees:** 1 - 10 **Product Groups:** 35, 39, 45

Derwent Enamellers Derby Ltd
Kingsway Industrial Park Kingsway Park Close, Derby, DE22 3FP
Tel: 01332-340971 **Fax:** 01332-292179
E-mail: wayne@derwentenamellers.co.uk
Website: http://www.derwentenamellers.co.uk
Directors: D. Castledine (Co Sec)
Immediate Holding Company: DERWENT ENAMELLERS (DERBY) LIMITED
Registration no: 01526589 **Date established:** 1980
No.of Employees: 1 - 10 **Product Groups:** 46, 48

Date of Accounts	Mar 12	Mar 11	Mar 10
Working Capital	-1	-5	13
Fixed Assets	345	346	351
Current Assets	107	84	103

Diamond Compresser Services
23 Mayfield Road Chaddesden, Derby, DE21 6FX
Tel: 01332-677835 **Fax:** 01332-677835
E-mail: ap@diamondcompressor.fsnet.co.uk
Website: http://www.diamondcompressor.fsnet.co.uk
Directors: A. Pritchard (Dir), D. Wallace (MD)
Turnover: £500,000 - £1m **No.of Employees:** 1 - 10 **Product Groups:** 39, 40

Drug-Aware Ltd
20 Tuxford Close Oakwood, Derby, DE21 2HH
Tel: 01332-232820 **Fax:** 01332-738414
E-mail: info@drug-aware.com
Website: http://www.drug-aware.com
Directors: C. Evans (Dir)
Immediate Holding Company: DRUG-AWARE LTD
Registration no: 04160376 **Date established:** 2001
No.of Employees: 1 - 10 **Product Groups:** 31

Date of Accounts	Feb 12	Feb 11	Feb 10
Working Capital	-1	92	50
Fixed Assets	4	4	3
Current Assets	113	192	111

E G G
Riverside Road Pride Park, Derby, DE99 3GG
Tel: 01332-335127
Website: http://www.egg.com
Managers: A. Deller (Sales Prom Mgr), M. Nancarrow, P. Gratton
Turnover: £2m - £5m **No.of Employees:** 1 - 10 **Product Groups:** 82

East Midland Computers Ltd
Downing Road West Meadows Industrial Estate, Derby, DE21 6HA
Tel: 01332-362481 **Fax:** 01332-291272
E-mail: info@emc.cc
Website: http://www.emc.cc
Directors: S. Abbey (MD)
Immediate Holding Company: XUPER LIMITED
Registration no: 01722490 **Date established:** 1983 **Turnover:** £1m - £2m
No.of Employees: 11 - 20 **Product Groups:** 44

Date of Accounts	Jul 11	Jul 10	Jul 09
Working Capital	476	204	299
Fixed Assets	430	466	435
Current Assets	1m	1m	1m

Edge Tools & Equipment Ltd
Victoria Way Pride Park, Derby, DE24 8AN
Tel: 01332-210212 **Fax:** 01332-210211
E-mail: sales@edge.com
Website: http://www.edgediamond.com
Directors: I. Clarke (Grp Chief Exec)
Immediate Holding Company: EDGE TOOLS & EQUIPMENT LIMITED
Registration no: 03899210 **Date established:** 1999
Turnover: Up to £250,000 **No.of Employees:** 1 - 10 **Product Groups:** 49

Date of Accounts	May 08	Sep 11	Sep 10
Working Capital	295	251	317
Fixed Assets	1m	829	834
Current Assets	818	783	915

Eggleston Steel Ltd
Centurion Way Business Park Alfreton Road, Derby, DE21 4AY
Tel: 01332-341536 **Fax:** 01332-295715
E-mail: info@egglestonsteel.co.uk
Website: http://www.egglestonsteel.co.uk
Bank(s): National Westminster Bank Plc
Directors: R. Hewitt (MD)
Immediate Holding Company: EGGLESTON STEEL LIMITED
Registration no: 00797154 **VAT No.:** GB 125 4285 80
Date established: 1964 **Turnover:** £2m - £5m **No.of Employees:** 21 - 50
Product Groups: 66

Date of Accounts	Apr 12	Apr 11	Apr 10
Sales Turnover	2m	N/A	N/A
Pre Tax Profit/Loss	140	N/A	N/A
Working Capital	538	589	471
Fixed Assets	2m	2m	2m
Current Assets	3m	3m	2m
Current Liabilities	59	N/A	N/A

Eley Metrology Ltd (Incorporating Crown Windley)
Beaufort House Mansfield Road, Derby, DE21 4FS
Tel: 01332-367475 **Fax:** 01332-371435
E-mail: sales@eleymet.com
Website: http://www.eleymet.com
Bank(s): HSBC, Malmesbury
Directors: J. Eley (Ch)
Immediate Holding Company: ELEY METROLOGY LIMITED
Registration no: 01285862 **VAT No.:** GB 179 7332 23
Date established: 1976 **Turnover:** £500,000 - £1m
No.of Employees: 11 - 20 **Product Groups:** 38, 46, 48, 85

Date of Accounts	Mar 11	Mar 10	Mar 09
Working Capital	540	467	405
Fixed Assets	760	872	801
Current Assets	817	716	623

Ellison Industrial Products Ltd
Unit 3 & 4 Bemrose Park Wayzgoose Drive, Derby, DE21 6XQ
Tel: 01332-340002 **Fax:** 01332-383128
E-mail: mcargill@ellisonip.co.uk
Website: http://www.ellisonip.co.uk
Bank(s): National Westminster Bank plc
Directors: J. Heathcote (Co Sec)
Managers: M. Cargill (Sales Admin)
Immediate Holding Company: ELLISON METAL PRODUCTS LIMITED
Registration no: 00595152 **VAT No.:** GB 125 2175 00
Date established: 1957 **Turnover:** £5m - £10m **No.of Employees:** 21 - 50
Product Groups: 35, 36, 49

Date of Accounts	Mar 08	Mar 07	Mar 06
Pre Tax Profit/Loss	-915	197	170
Working Capital	453	588	882
Fixed Assets	2m	2m	2m
Current Assets	3m	3m	4m
Current Liabilities	134	458	280

Energas Ltd
Haslams Lane, Derby, DE22 1EB
Tel: 01332-364121 **Fax:** 01332-291590
E-mail: derby@engworld.co.uk
Website: http://www.energas.co.uk
Directors: T. Howitt (Snr Part), G. Beech (Sales)
Ultimate Holding Company: ENERGAS HOLDINGS LIMITED
Immediate Holding Company: ENERGAS LIMITED
Registration no: 01603643 **Date established:** 1981 **Turnover:** £2m - £5m
No.of Employees: 21 - 50 **Product Groups:** 31

Date of Accounts	Sep 11	Sep 10	Sep 09
Sales Turnover	22m	18m	18m
Pre Tax Profit/Loss	5m	3m	5m
Working Capital	5m	10m	10m
Fixed Assets	9m	9m	10m
Current Assets	7m	12m	13m
Current Liabilities	1m	638	2m

Engineering Welding Supplies Ltd
Haslams Lane, Derby, DE22 1EB
Tel: 01332-363251 **Fax:** 01332-291590
E-mail: derby@engweld.co.uk
Website: http://www.engweld.co.uk
Bank(s): Lloyds TSB Bank plc
Directors: C. Moore (Pers), M. Wright (I.T. Dir)
Managers: T. Howitt
Immediate Holding Company: ENGINEERING AND WELDING SUPPLIES LIMITED
Registration no: 00815796 **Date established:** 1964 **Turnover:** £5m - £10m
No.of Employees: 11 - 20 **Product Groups:** 46, 47, 67, 83

Date of Accounts	Sep 11	Sep 10	Sep 09
Sales Turnover	18m	15m	14m
Pre Tax Profit/Loss	2m	1m	1m
Working Capital	8m	7m	6m
Fixed Assets	3m	3m	3m
Current Assets	10m	9m	8m
Current Liabilities	627	423	470

Eriks Industrial Distribution (Derby Service Centre)
Unit 4 Shaftesbury Street South, Derby, DE23 8YH
Tel: 01332-364453 **Fax:** 01332-291330
E-mail: wid.derby@wyko.co.uk
Website: http://www.eriks.co.uk
Managers: P. Baker
Immediate Holding Company: WYKO HOLDINGS LTD
Registration no: 03142338 **Turnover:** £250m - £500m
No.of Employees: 1 - 10 **Product Groups:** 66

Ewart Chain Ltd
Colombo Street, Derby, DE23 8LX
Tel: 01332-345451 **Fax:** 01332-371753
E-mail: sales@ewartchain.co.uk
Website: http://www.ewartchain.co.uk
Bank(s): Bank of Scotland
Directors: M. Horton (Ch), W. Harrison (Fin)
Managers: J. Heath (Chief Buyer), C. Sweeney (Sales Prom Mgr)
Ultimate Holding Company: EWART INTERNATIONAL HOLDINGS LIMITED
Immediate Holding Company: EWART CHAIN LTD.
Registration no: 00152385 **VAT No.:** GB 125 7121 95
Date established: 2018 **Turnover:** £2m - £5m **No.of Employees:** 51 - 100
Product Groups: 30, 35, 41, 42, 45

Date of Accounts	Jun 11	Jun 10	Jun 09
Sales Turnover	N/A	5m	6m
Pre Tax Profit/Loss	N/A	188	-146
Working Capital	2m	2m	2m
Fixed Assets	40	79	103
Current Assets	4m	4m	4m
Current Liabilities	N/A	814	935

Fairfax Meadow Ltd
6 Newmarket Drive, Derby, DE24 8SW
Tel: 01332-861200 **Fax:** 01332-861290
E-mail: enquiries@fairfaxmeadow.co.uk
Website: http://www.fairfaxmeadow.co.uk
Bank(s): The Royal Bank of Scotland
Directors: A. Barnes (Fin), G. Wensley (Dir)
Ultimate Holding Company: FLETCHER BAY GROUP LIMITED
Immediate Holding Company: ARGENT MEAT TRADERS LIMITED
Registration no: 00368420 **VAT No.:** GB 694 8896 45
Date established: 1941 **Turnover:** Up to £250,000
No.of Employees: 251 - 500 **Product Groups:** 62

Date of Accounts	Dec 11	Dec 10	Dec 09
Sales Turnover	178	N/A	N/A
Pre Tax Profit/Loss	231	91	241
Working Capital	4m	2m	3m
Fixed Assets	2m	1m	500
Current Assets	4m	4m	3m
Current Liabilities	N/A	2m	257

Fast React Systems Ltd
Evolution House Wyvern Business Park, Chaddesden, Derby, DE21 6LY
Tel: 01332-668942 **Fax:** 0115-914 9873
E-mail: sales@fastreact.com
Website: http://www.fastreact.com
Directors: A. Hinton (Sales), P. Jennings (Fin), A. Brown (MD), P. Rudd (Comm)
Immediate Holding Company: FAST REACT SYSTEMS LIMITED
Registration no: 03698622 **Date established:** 1999
No.of Employees: 21 - 50 **Product Groups:** 44

Date of Accounts	Mar 11	Mar 10	Mar 09
Working Capital	310	440	408
Fixed Assets	76	81	103
Current Assets	2m	2m	2m

Feel For Hair Ltd
PO Box 184, Derby, DE65 5BU
Tel: 01283-585656 **Fax:** 01283-585866
E-mail: sales@feelforhair.co.uk
Website: http://www.feelforhair.co.uk
Directors: N. Scillabeer (MD)
Immediate Holding Company: FEEL FOR HAIR LIMITED
Registration no: 04588059 **Date established:** 2002
No.of Employees: 1 - 10 **Product Groups:** 30, 36

Date of Accounts	Mar 11	Mar 10	Mar 09
Working Capital	394	225	158
Fixed Assets	47	62	79
Current Assets	756	358	275

Fives Fletcher Ltd
Brunel Parkway Pride Park, Derby, DE24 8HR
Tel: 01332-636000 **Fax:** 01332-636020
E-mail: alan.mclean@fivesgroup.com
Website: http://www.fivesgroup.com
Bank(s): National Westminster, Derby
Directors: D. Hamilton (Sales), A. McLean (Comm)
Ultimate Holding Company: FL INVESTCO (FRANCE)
Immediate Holding Company: FIVES FLETCHER LIMITED
Registration no: 01639932 **VAT No.:** GB 380 1052 90
Date established: 1982 **Turnover:** £5m - £10m **No.of Employees:** 11 - 20
Product Groups: 41

Date of Accounts	Dec 11	Dec 10	Dec 09
Sales Turnover	8m	10m	11m
Pre Tax Profit/Loss	671	926	1m
Working Capital	512	1m	1m
Fixed Assets	19	25	29
Current Assets	4m	6m	6m
Current Liabilities	3m	4m	3m

Flamepro UK Ltd
32 Longbridge Lane Ascot Business Park, Derby, DE24 8UJ
Tel: 01332-758510 **Fax:** 01332-757938
E-mail: philip@flame-pro.co.uk
Website: http://www.flame-pro.com
Directors: P. Johnson (MD)
Immediate Holding Company: FLAMEPRO (UK) LTD
Registration no: 05737793 **VAT No.:** GB 695 1130 35
Date established: 2006 **Turnover:** Up to £250,000
No.of Employees: 1 - 10 **Product Groups:** 24

Date of Accounts	Aug 11	Aug 10	Aug 09
Working Capital	8	-42	-53
Fixed Assets	4	9	11
Current Assets	213	121	222

Flint Bishop Solicitors
St Michaels Court St Michaels Lane, Derby, DE1 3HQ
Tel: 01332-340211 **Fax:** 01332-347107
E-mail: marketing@flintbishop.co.uk
Website: http://www.flintbishop.com
Directors: C. Weston (Mkt Research), K. Dixon (MD)
Immediate Holding Company: FLINT BISHOP LLP
Registration no: OC317931 **VAT No.:** GB 125 4538 77
Date established: 2006 **Turnover:** £5m - £10m
No.of Employees: 101 - 250 **Product Groups:** 80

Date of Accounts	Apr 11	Apr 10	Feb 09
Sales Turnover	9m	8m	N/A
Pre Tax Profit/Loss	1m	1m	N/A
Working Capital	2m	2m	N/A
Fixed Assets	535	203	N/A
Current Assets	5m	4m	N/A
Current Liabilities	794	752	N/A

Freshfood Systems Ltd
Units 26 & 27 Willow Road Trent Lane Industrial Estate Castle Donington, Derby, DE74 2NP
Tel: 01332-850468 **Fax:** 01332-850749
E-mail: uk@easiyo.com
Website: http://www.easiyo.com
Bank(s): HSBC
Managers: R. Scott (Sales Admin)
Ultimate Holding Company: EASIYO PRODUCTS LTD (NEW ZEALAND)
Immediate Holding Company: FRESHFOOD SYSTEMS LIMITED
Registration no: 03590257 **VAT No.:** GB 331 527 75
Date established: 1998 **Turnover:** £250,000 - £500,000
No.of Employees: 11 - 20 **Product Groups:** 30, 39

Date of Accounts	Jan 08	Jan 07	Jan 06
Working Capital	2	5	2
Fixed Assets	6	5	5
Current Assets	499	412	276
Current Liabilities	497	408	274
Total Share Capital	3	3	3

G & T Electrical Services
46 Bren Way Hilton, Derby, DE65 5HP
Tel: 01283-730832
E-mail: ian@gntelectrical.co.uk
Website: http://www.gntelectrical.co.uk
Directors: I. Godlington (Prop)
Date established: 2001 **No.of Employees:** 1 - 10 **Product Groups:** 38, 85

Genic Ltd
113 Duffield Road, Derby, DE22 1AE
Tel: 01332-342514 **Fax:** 01332-342514
E-mail: breadcrumbs@btconnect.com
Directors: J. Nicholson (Fin), W. Nicholson (MD)
Immediate Holding Company: GENIC LIMITED
Registration no: 00359465 **Date established:** 1940
No.of Employees: 1 - 10 **Product Groups:** 20

Date of Accounts	Dec 11	Dec 10	Dec 09
Working Capital	33	37	49
Current Assets	50	66	80

Geoquip Ltd
Little Eaton, Derby, DE21 5DR
Tel: 01629-824891 **Fax:** 01629-824896
E-mail: info@geoquip.com
Website: http://www.geoquip.com
Bank(s): The Royal Bank of Scotland
Directors: S. Midani (MD)
Managers: L. Gerrard (Sales Admin), P. Cork (Tech Serv Mgr), B. Alphonso (Sales Prom Mgr), M. Donoher (Buyer)
Ultimate Holding Company: CRH PUBLIC LIMITED COMPANY
Immediate Holding Company: GEOQUIP LIMITED
Registration no: 01526375 **VAT No.:** GB 706 4475 35
Date established: 1980 **Turnover:** £5m - £10m **No.of Employees:** 21 - 50
Product Groups: 40

Date of Accounts	Dec 11	Dec 10	Dec 09
Sales Turnover	7m	6m	6m
Pre Tax Profit/Loss	1m	497	474
Working Capital	7m	7m	6m
Fixed Assets	123	78	186
Current Assets	10m	8m	7m
Current Liabilities	585	1m	301

Gordon Ellis & Co

Trent Lane Castle Donington, Derby, DE74 2PY
Tel: 01332-810504 **Fax:** 01332-850830
E-mail: enquiries@gordonellis.co.uk
Website: http://www.gordonellis.com
Bank(s): HSBC. Castle Donington
Directors: S. Evanson (Mkt Research), S. King (Co Sec), W. Ellis (Ch), F. Ellis-Winkfield (Dir)
Managers: A. Walters (Purch Mgr)
Immediate Holding Company: GORDON ELLIS & CO.
Registration no: 00231734 **VAT No.:** GB 428 4666 26
Date established: 1893 **Turnover:** £5m - £10m
No.of Employees: 101 - 250 **Product Groups:** 25, 26, 28, 29, 30, 33, 34, 35, 36, 38, 42, 45, 47, 48, 49, 67

Green Tube

St. Katherine's House St. Mary's Wharf, Derby, DE1 3TQ
Tel: 01332-294350
Website: http://www.relux.co.uk
Directors: D. Powell (Dir)
Registration no: 04927216 **No.of Employees:** 1 - 10 **Product Groups:** 37, 67

J & E Hall Ltd

Hansard Gate West Meadows Industrial Estate, Derby, DE21 6JN
Tel: 01332-253400 **Fax:** 01332-371061
E-mail: graham.chamberlain@jehall.co.uk
Website: http://www.jehall.co.uk
Directors: G. Chamberlain (Dir), I. Creasey (Co Sec)
Managers: H. Jerram (Mktg Serv Mgr), J. Archer (Purch Mgr)
Ultimate Holding Company: DAIKIN INDUSTRIES LTD (JAPAN)
Immediate Holding Company: J & E HALL LIMITED
Registration no: 03120673 **VAT No.:** GB 663 3447 296
Date established: 1995 **Turnover:** £20m - £50m
No.of Employees: 101 - 250 **Product Groups:** 52

Date of Accounts	Dec 11	Dec 10	Dec 09
Sales Turnover	40m	36m	34m
Pre Tax Profit/Loss	672	-159	-251
Working Capital	4m	2m	2m
Fixed Assets	4m	4m	4m
Current Assets	17m	14m	13m
Current Liabilities	7m	6m	6m

Hammerhead Wrought Ironwork

B Markeaton Craft Village Markeaton Park, Derby, DE22 3BG
Tel: 01332-207259
E-mail: andrew@mccallum1632.fsworld.com
Website: http://www.mccallum1632.fsworld.com
Directors: A. McCallum (Prop)
Date established: 1997 **No.of Employees:** 1 - 10 **Product Groups:** 26, 35

Howarth Timber & Building Supplies Ltd

12 Old Nottingham Road, Derby, DE1 3QT
Tel: 01332-360233 **Fax:** 01332-291874
E-mail: sales.derby@howarth-timber.co.uk
Website: http://www.howarth-timber.co.uk
Managers: P. Nuttall (Chief Mgr)
Ultimate Holding Company: HOWARTH TIMBER GROUP LIMITED
Immediate Holding Company: HOWARTH TIMBER & BUILDING SUPPLIES LIMITED
Registration no: 00201929 **Date established:** 2024
No.of Employees: 11 - 20 **Product Groups:** 08, 25

Date of Accounts	Mar 12	Mar 11	Mar 10
Sales Turnover	55m	55m	52m
Pre Tax Profit/Loss	2m	611	47
Working Capital	12m	11m	10m
Fixed Assets	2m	2m	2m
Current Assets	22m	21m	19m
Current Liabilities	4m	4m	3m

Indespension Ltd

Ascot Drive, Derby, DE24 8ST
Tel: 01332-348555 **Fax:** 01332-294614
E-mail: sales@indespension.co.uk
Website: http://www.indespension.co.uk
Managers: D. Ransome (Mgr)
Ultimate Holding Company: D.R.A. LTD
Immediate Holding Company: INDESPENSION LTD
Registration no: 02125263 **Date established:** 1987 **Turnover:** £2m - £5m
No.of Employees: 1 - 10 **Product Groups:** 39

Date of Accounts	Jun 11	Jun 10	Jun 09
Sales Turnover	17m	15m	19m
Pre Tax Profit/Loss	550	192	137
Working Capital	2m	1m	2m
Fixed Assets	4m	5m	6m
Current Assets	8m	8m	8m
Current Liabilities	3m	527	783

Industrial Measurements Ltd

Unit 6 Willow Road Castle Donington, Derby, DE74 2NP
Tel: 01332-810240 **Fax:** 01332-812440
E-mail: mail@indmeas.co.uk
Website: http://www.indmeas.co.uk
Directors: D. Corby (Co Sec), P. Everitt (MD)
Ultimate Holding Company: COBCO 812 LIMITED
Immediate Holding Company: INDUSTRIAL MEASUREMENTS LIMITED
Registration no: 01579603 **Date established:** 1981
Turnover: £500,000 - £1m **No.of Employees:** 1 - 10 **Product Groups:** 37, 38

Date of Accounts	Nov 11	Nov 10	Sep 09
Sales Turnover	628	618	N/A
Pre Tax Profit/Loss	71	73	N/A
Working Capital	343	294	236
Fixed Assets	12	4	6
Current Assets	410	359	314
Current Liabilities	26	27	N/A

Infomill Ltd

Pentagon House Sir Frank Whittle Road, Derby, DE21 4XA
Tel: 01332-253170 **Fax:** 01332-295360
E-mail: info@infomill.com
Website: http://www.infomill.com
Directors: J. Ralphs (Grp Chief Exec)
Immediate Holding Company: INFOMILL LIMITED
Registration no: 03203522 **Date established:** 1996
Turnover: Up to £250,000 **No.of Employees:** 21 - 50 **Product Groups:** 44

Date of Accounts	Jun 12	Jun 11	Jun 10
Working Capital	1m	840	402
Fixed Assets	110	137	171
Current Assets	1m	1m	564

Interlevin Refrigeration Ltd

Unit 6a West Meadow Rise, Castle Donington, Derby, DE74 2HL
Tel: 01332-850090 **Fax:** 01332-810685
E-mail: trade.sales@interlevin.co.uk
Website: http://www.interlevin.co.uk
Directors: C. Barwick (Fin), P. Mcewan (Purch)
Managers: J. Allfree (Sales & Mktg Mg)
Ultimate Holding Company: INTERLEVIN HOLDINGS LIMITED
Immediate Holding Company: INTERLEVIN REFRIGERATION LIMITED
Registration no: 00908993 **VAT No.:** GB 468 3062 35
Date established: 1967 **Turnover:** £10m - £20m
No.of Employees: 21 - 50 **Product Groups:** 36, 38, 40, 41, 42, 48, 52, 63, 66

Date of Accounts	Dec 11	Dec 10	Dec 09
Sales Turnover	17m	19m	21m
Pre Tax Profit/Loss	577	1m	1m
Working Capital	3m	3m	3m
Fixed Assets	162	186	138
Current Assets	6m	6m	7m
Current Liabilities	1m	1m	1m

Isys Interactive Systems Ltd

45 Brunel Parkway Pride Park, Derby, DE24 8HR
Tel: 01332-380311 **Fax:** 01332-342975
E-mail: richard.bowers@isys-waste.com
Website: http://www.isys-waste.com
Bank(s): Barclays, Derby
Directors: R. Bowers (Fin)
Immediate Holding Company: ISYS INTERACTIVE SYSTEMS LTD
Registration no: 03451721 **Date established:** 1997 **Turnover:** £1m - £2m
No.of Employees: 11 - 20 **Product Groups:** 44

Date of Accounts	Mar 12	Mar 11	Mar 10
Working Capital	779	518	652
Fixed Assets	69	94	117
Current Assets	2m	1m	2m

Jubilee Machine Tools Ltd

Unit 4 Centurion Way Business Park Alfreton Road, Derby, DE21 4AY
Tel: 01332-348749 **Fax:** 01332-342416
E-mail: pope@jubileemactools.com
Website: http://www.jubileemactools.com
Directors: A. Pope (MD)
Immediate Holding Company: POPE MACHINERY LIMITED
Registration no: 01763317 **VAT No.:** GB 395 5380 16
Date established: 1983 **Turnover:** £250,000 - £500,000
No.of Employees: 1 - 10 **Product Groups:** 46

Date of Accounts	Dec 11	Dec 10	Dec 09
Working Capital	88	94	119
Fixed Assets	25	21	27
Current Assets	215	203	174

K Line Logistics UK Ltd

Building 100 East Midlands Airport, Castle Donington, Derby, DE74 2SA
Tel: 01332-850888 **Fax:** 01332-812185
E-mail: ema@uk.klinelogistics.com
Managers: D. Kendrick (Mgr)
Ultimate Holding Company: KAWASAKI KISEN KAISHA LTD (JAPAN)
Immediate Holding Company: K LINE LOGISTICS (UK) LIMITED
Registration no: 02318517 **VAT No.:** GB 417 1539 61
Date established: 1988 **Turnover:** £1m - £2m **No.of Employees:** 1 - 10
Product Groups: 39, 75, 76

Date of Accounts	Dec 11	Dec 10	Dec 09
Working Capital	459	553	439
Fixed Assets	92	88	100
Current Assets	1m	1m	911

Key Personnel Ltd

10 Old Blacksmiths Yard Sadler Gate, Derby, DE1 3PD
Tel: 01332-296256 **Fax:** 01332-341124
E-mail: derby@key-personnel.co.uk
Website: http://www.key-personnel.co.uk
Managers: J. Keighron (District Mgr)
Immediate Holding Company: BARMINE LTD
Registration no: 06318947 **Date established:** 2007
No.of Employees: 1 - 10 **Product Groups:** 80, 86

Kuehne Nagel Drinks Logistics

2300 Park Avenue Dove Valley Park, Foston, Derby, DE65 5BY
Tel: 01283-586200 **Fax:** 01283-586419
Website: http://www.kuehne-nagel.com
Managers: J. Moscrop (Chief Mgr)
Ultimate Holding Company: HAYS P.L.C.
Registration no: 00172216 **Turnover:** £10m - £20m
No.of Employees: 51 - 100 **Product Groups:** 26, 52, 77

La Systems Ltd

Old Hall Mill Business Park Alfreton Road, Little Eaton, Derby, DE21 5EJ
Tel: 01332-830005 **Fax:** 01332-833225
E-mail: info@la-systems.co.uk
Website: http://www.la-systems.co.uk
Managers: S. Duffield (Comptroller)
Ultimate Holding Company: Q HOLDINGS LIMITED
Immediate Holding Company: L.A.SYSTEMS LIMITED
Registration no: 04239576 **Date established:** 2001 **Turnover:** £1m - £2m
No.of Employees: 11 - 20 **Product Groups:** 20, 67

Date of Accounts	Dec 10	Dec 09	Dec 08
Sales Turnover	2m	1m	641
Pre Tax Profit/Loss	19	374	89
Working Capital	240	214	-159
Fixed Assets	118	125	105
Current Assets	576	443	438
Current Liabilities	74	71	405

Litho Supplies (Midlands Region)

D R G Building Longmoor Lane, Breaston, Derby, DE72 3BQ
Tel: 01332-873921 **Fax:** 020-8575 6252
E-mail: eddie.williams@litho.co.uk
Website: http://www.litho.co.uk
Bank(s): Bank of Scotland
Directors: M. Hammond (Dir), E. Williams (MD), E. Williams (Reg), E. Willams (Reg)
Managers: K. Galer (Mgr), C. Hughes (Ops Mgr)
Ultimate Holding Company: HILCO TRADING LLC (UNITED STATES OF AMERICA)
Immediate Holding Company: LITHO SUPPLIES (UK) LIMITED
Registration no: 07088832 **VAT No.:** GB 567 5624 07
Date established: 2009 **Turnover:** £75m - £125m
No.of Employees: 21 - 50 **Product Groups:** 28, 38, 44

Date of Accounts	Dec 10
Sales Turnover	14m
Pre Tax Profit/Loss	-408
Working Capital	-491
Fixed Assets	83
Current Assets	4m
Current Liabilities	3m

M & D Engineering

Heath Top Farm Business Park Church Broughton, Derby, DE65 5AY
Tel: 01283-584866 **Fax:** 01335-330055
Website: http://www.manddengineering.co.uk
Directors: M. Malia (Dir)
No.of Employees: 1 - 10 **Product Groups:** 34, 40, 48, 84

M W Polymer Products Ltd

The Sidings Duffield Road Industrial Estate, Little Eaton, Derby, DE21 5EG
Tel: 01332-835001 **Fax:** 01332-835051
E-mail: admin@mwpolymers.co.uk
Website: http://www.mwpolymers.co.uk
Bank(s): National Westminster Bank Plc
Directors: M. Wild (Dir)
Immediate Holding Company: M.W. (POLYMER PRODUCTS) LIMITED
Registration no: 02772147 **Date established:** 1992
Turnover: £500,000 - £1m **No.of Employees:** 11 - 20 **Product Groups:** 32

Date of Accounts	Aug 11	Aug 10	Aug 09
Working Capital	-285	-233	-247
Fixed Assets	888	891	893
Current Assets	127	151	145

Mcconnells Midlands Ltd

49 Uttoxeter New Road, Derby, DE22 3NL
Tel: 01332-222900 **Fax:** 01332-222901
E-mail: info@mccgp.co.uk
Website: http://www.mccgp.co.uk
Bank(s): National Westminster
Directors: E. Cheeseman (Fin)
Immediate Holding Company: MCCONNELL'S (MIDLANDS) LIMITED
Registration no: 00596621 **Date established:** 1958 **Turnover:** £2m - £5m
No.of Employees: 21 - 50 **Product Groups:** 81

Date of Accounts	Dec 11	Dec 10	Dec 09
Working Capital	671	611	586
Fixed Assets	170	197	198
Current Assets	1m	1m	1m

Mccroft Lighting

2 Pontefract Street, Derby, DE24 8JD
Tel: 01332-299100 **Fax:** 01332-200365
E-mail: keith@mccroftlighting.co.uk
Directors: K. Mccroft (Prop)
Ultimate Holding Company: HELIOS INVESTMENT COMPANY LIMITED(THE)
Immediate Holding Company: ATLAS ENGINEERING LIMITED
VAT No.: GB 284 1824 47 **Date established:** 1972
Turnover: Up to £250,000 **No.of Employees:** 1 - 10 **Product Groups:** 37, 67

Date of Accounts	Mar 11	Mar 10	Mar 09
Working Capital	88	94	53
Fixed Assets	53	77	37
Current Assets	140	152	101

Marshall Sewing Machines

7 Wellesley Avenue Sunnyhill, Derby, DE23 1GQ
Tel: 01332-771716 **Fax:** 01332-771716
E-mail: sales@marshalltextiles.co.uk
Website: http://www.marshalltextiles.co.uk
Directors: S. Marshall (Prop)
Immediate Holding Company: MARSHALL TEXTILES LIMITED
Registration no: 05724517 **Date established:** 2006
No.of Employees: 1 - 10 **Product Groups:** 43

Mclean & Associates Consulting Engineers

Unit 27 Perkins Way Mansfield Road, Derby, DE21 4AW
Tel: 01332-363339 **Fax:** 01332-363339
E-mail: mcl_assoc@internetpost.co.uk
Directors: J. McClean (Prop), J. Mcleans (Prop), J. McLean (Head)
Date established: 1978 **No.of Employees:** 1 - 10 **Product Groups:** 35

Meakin & Son Derby Ltd

270 Abbey Street, Derby, DE22 3SX
Tel: 01332-344144 **Fax:** 01332-292420
E-mail: metalwork@dial.pipex.com
Directors: A. Ellis (MD), K. Ellis (Fin)
Immediate Holding Company: MEAKIN AND SON (DERBY) LIMITED
Registration no: 01159774 **VAT No.:** GB 127 5494 54
Date established: 1974 **No.of Employees:** 1 - 10 **Product Groups:** 48

Date of Accounts	Mar 11	Mar 10	Mar 09
Working Capital	137	111	138
Fixed Assets	58	54	59
Current Assets	233	185	203

Med-Lab International Ltd

Copeland Street, Derby, DE1 2PU
Tel: 01332-349094 **Fax:** 01332-371237
E-mail: sales@med-lab.co.uk
Website: http://www.med-lab.co.uk
Bank(s): Lloyds TSB
Directors: M. Knight (MD), S. Bowers (Co Sec)
Ultimate Holding Company: UMECO LIMITED
Immediate Holding Company: MED-LAB INTERNATIONAL LIMITED
Registration no: 01554340 **VAT No.:** GB 125 7931 60
Date established: 1981 **Turnover:** £250,000 - £500,000
No.of Employees: 11 - 20 **Product Groups:** 39

Date of Accounts	Mar 12	Mar 11	Mar 10
Sales Turnover	N/A	N/A	325
Pre Tax Profit/Loss	425	336	325
Working Capital	-51	-51	-51
Fixed Assets	52	52	52
Current Assets	11	11	11

Melbourne Tackle & Gun
64 Church Street Melbourne, Derby, DE73 8EJ
Tel: 01332-862091 **Fax:** 01332-863090
Website: http://www.melbournegun.com
Directors: A. Williams (Prop)
Date established: 1988 **No.of Employees:** 1 - 10 **Product Groups:** 36, 39, 40

Metal Improvement Co. (Derby Division) (Subsidiary of Curtiss-Wright Corporation)
Ascot Drive, Derby, DE24 8ST
Tel: 01332-756076 **Fax:** 01332-754392
E-mail: steve_panther@metalimprovemtn.com
Website: http://www.metalimprovement.co.uk
Bank(s): HSBC Bank plc
Managers: N. Sheward, S. Panther (Div Mgr), R. Walker (Personnel)
Immediate Holding Company: METAL IMPROVEMENT COMPANY LLC
Registration no: FC006968 **VAT No.:** GB 126 7764 41
Date established: 1971 **Turnover:** £125m - £250m
No.of Employees: 51 - 100 **Product Groups:** 30, 31, 48

Midland Marine UK Ltd
Park Lane Castle Donington, Derby, DE74 2RS
Tel: 01332-850088 **Fax:** 01332-814780
E-mail: info@midland-marine-uk.com
Website: http://www.midland-marine-uk.com
Directors: J. McCafferty (Fin), M. McCafferty (Mkt Research)
Immediate Holding Company: MIDLAND MARINE UK LIMITED
Registration no: 04115908 **Date established:** 2000
No.of Employees: 1 - 10 **Product Groups:** 35, 36, 39

Date of Accounts	Nov 11	Nov 10	Nov 09
Working Capital	-45	-17	-5
Fixed Assets	2	1	2
Current Assets	53	95	130

Minelco Ltd
Mica Works Raynesway, Derby, DE21 7BE
Tel: 01332-673131 **Fax:** 01332-677590
E-mail: jane.potts@minelco.com
Website: http://www.minelco.com
Directors: R. Day (Sales), J. Potts (Fin)
Managers: S. Banaham, A. Meakin (Personnel), S. Creedon (Mktg Serv Mgr)
Ultimate Holding Company: LKAB (SWEDEN)
Immediate Holding Company: MINELCO SPECIALITIES LTD
Registration no: 01151578 **Date established:** 1973
Turnover: £20m - £50m **No.of Employees:** 21 - 50 **Product Groups:** 12, 14, 17, 31, 32, 33, 66

Date of Accounts	Dec 11	Dec 10	Dec 09
Pre Tax Profit/Loss	122	N/A	-100
Working Capital	471	147	142
Fixed Assets	N/A	223	228
Current Assets	471	147	142

Mirage Machines
10 Enterprise Way Jubilee Business Park, Derby, DE21 4BB
Tel: 01332-291767 **Fax:** 01332-370356
E-mail: sales@miragemachines.com
Website: http://www.miragemachines.com
Bank(s): Barclays
Directors: R. Silk (MD)
Managers: E. Monck, S. Tilsley (Purch Mgr), S. Gormley (Sales Prom Mgr)
Ultimate Holding Company: FR X OFFSHORE GP LIMITED (CAYMAN ISLANDS)
Immediate Holding Company: MIRAGE MACHINES LIMITED
Registration no: 02788205 **VAT No.:** GB 616 6140 57
Date established: 1993 **Turnover:** £500,000 - £1m
No.of Employees: 21 - 50 **Product Groups:** 46, 67

Date of Accounts	Dec 10	Dec 09	Dec 08
Working Capital	80	-316	-521
Fixed Assets	471	565	706
Current Assets	996	926	880

Mitec Cad Ltd
2nd Floor Kings Chambers 1 Cathedral Road, Derby, DE1 3PA
Tel: 01332-298282 **Fax:** 01332-298282
E-mail: mt@miteccad.com
Website: http://www.miteccad.com
Directors: M. Tory (MD)
Immediate Holding Company: MITEC CAD LIMITED
Registration no: 07751928 **Date established:** 2011
No.of Employees: 1 - 10 **Product Groups:** 35

Moore Large & Co. Ltd
Grampian Buildings Sinfin Lane, Derby, DE24 9GL
Tel: 01332-274200 **Fax:** 01332-270635
E-mail: sales@moorelarge.co.uk
Website: http://www.moorelarge.co.uk
Bank(s): HSBC
Directors: N. Moore (MD), S. Caunt (Fin)
Managers: D. Smith, D. Jack (Purch Mgr), M. Peberdy (Tech Serv Mgr), L. Vanderplank (Mktg Serv Mgr)
Ultimate Holding Company: J.H. MOORE & SON (RICKMANSWORTH) LIMITED
Immediate Holding Company: MOORE LARGE & CO. LIMITED
Registration no: 01163012 **VAT No.:** GB 746 2925 12
Date established: 1974 **Turnover:** £20m - £50m
No.of Employees: 51 - 100 **Product Groups:** 68

Date of Accounts	Jan 11	Jan 10	Jan 09
Sales Turnover	23m	24m	20m
Pre Tax Profit/Loss	2m	1m	2m
Working Capital	10m	9m	8m
Fixed Assets	4m	4m	4m
Current Assets	14m	13m	11m
Current Liabilities	3m	3m	3m

Newlook Ceilings Ltd
57 Uttoxeter Road Mickleover, Derby, DE3 9GF
Tel: 01332-523718
Directors: R. O'Shea (Dir)
Immediate Holding Company: NEWLOOK CEILINGS LIMITED
Registration no: 04928751 **Date established:** 2003
No.of Employees: 1 - 10 **Product Groups:** 37, 67

Date of Accounts	Mar 11	Mar 09	Mar 08
Working Capital	N/A	20	10
Fixed Assets	1	11	9
Current Assets	82	76	36

O G P UK Ltd
Faraday House Woodyard Lane, Foston, Derby, DE65 5DJ
Tel: 01283-585933 **Fax:** 01283-585181
E-mail: sales@ogpuk.com
Website: http://www.ogpuk.com
Directors: A. Fulton (MD)
Immediate Holding Company: OGP UK LIMITED
Registration no: 02596148 **Date established:** 1991
Turnover: Over £1,000m **No.of Employees:** 11 - 20 **Product Groups:** 38

Date of Accounts	Sep 11	Sep 10	Sep 09
Working Capital	83	100	106
Fixed Assets	44	44	43
Current Assets	1m	1m	813

Obara UK
1 Tomlinson Industrial Estate Alfreton Road, Derby, DE21 4ED
Tel: 01332-297868
E-mail: sales@obara.co.uk
Website: http://www.obara.co.uk
Managers: S. Flowers (Buyer), D. Hatfield (Sales Prom Mgr)
Immediate Holding Company: OBARA CORPORATION OF JAPAN
Registration no: 00025749 **VAT No.:** GB 614 9162 44
Date established: 2005 **No.of Employees:** 1 - 10 **Product Groups:** 35, 46

Omya UK Ltd
Stephensons Way Wyvern Business Park, Chaddesden, Derby, DE21 6LY
Tel: 01332-674000 **Fax:** 01332-544700
E-mail: suzanne.bunting@omya.com
Website: http://www.omya.co.uk
Bank(s): National Westminster Bank Plc
Directors: G. Dixon (Fin), B. Cardew (Sales)
Managers: S. Bunting, H. Shepherd (Personnel)
Ultimate Holding Company: OMYA AG (SWITZERLAND)
Immediate Holding Company: OMYA LIMITED
Registration no: 01602362 **VAT No.:** GB 356 7319 31
Date established: 1981 **Turnover:** £75m - £125m
No.of Employees: 51 - 100 **Product Groups:** 14, 17, 20, 31, 32, 33

Maurice Parker Ltd
Alfred House Alfreton Road, Derby, DE21 4AF
Tel: 01332-363422 **Fax:** 01332-293455
E-mail: sales@mauriceparker.co.uk
Website: http://www.squaredeal.co.uk
Directors: D. Parker (MD)
Immediate Holding Company: MAURICE PARKER LIMITED
Registration no: 01137507 **Date established:** 1973
No.of Employees: 1 - 10 **Product Groups:** 33

Date of Accounts	Apr 11	Apr 10	Apr 09
Working Capital	-23	-355	-284
Fixed Assets	522	686	696
Current Assets	271	209	250

Parkes & Son Ltd
234 Kedleston Old Road, Derby, DE22 1GA
Tel: 07762-943483
E-mail: info@parkesandson.co.uk
Website: http://www.parkesandson.co.uk
Directors: M. Parkes (Grp Chief Exec)
Immediate Holding Company: PARKES & SON LIMITED
Registration no: 03471465 **Date established:** 1997
No.of Employees: 1 - 10 **Product Groups:** 80

Date of Accounts	Nov 11	Nov 10	Nov 07
Working Capital	-6	-9	-6
Fixed Assets	1	1	1
Current Assets	9	5	9

Pektron
Alfreton Road, Derby, DE21 4AP
Tel: 01332-832424 **Fax:** 01332-833270
E-mail: info@pektron.co.uk
Website: http://www.pektron.co.uk
Bank(s): Barclays
Directors: B. Morgan (Fin), J. Potts (Sales), N. Morgan (MD), P. Morgan (Fin)
Managers: R. Smith (Tech Serv Mgr), J. Hatton (Purch Mgr)
Immediate Holding Company: PEKTRON GROUP LIMITED
Registration no: 00823259 **VAT No.:** GB 354 5187 44
Date established: 1964 **Turnover:** £20m - £50m
No.of Employees: 101 - 250 **Product Groups:** 37

Date of Accounts	Dec 11	Dec 10	Dec 09
Sales Turnover	27m	23m	20m
Pre Tax Profit/Loss	5m	3m	2m
Working Capital	17m	18m	15m
Fixed Assets	7m	5m	5m
Current Assets	22m	21m	18m
Current Liabilities	4m	2m	1m

Pendragon Contracts Ltd
Sir Frank Whittle Road, Derby, DE21 4AZ
Tel: 01332-292777 **Fax:** 01332-364270
E-mail: neal.francis@pendragon.uk.com
Website: http://www.pendragon-contracts.uk.com
Bank(s): Lloyds TSB
Directors: A. Hillier (Mkt Research), J. Given (Sales), N. Francis (MD), S. Daldorph (Fin)
Ultimate Holding Company: PENDRAGON PLC
Immediate Holding Company: PENDRAGON CONTRACTS LIMITED
Registration no: 00141388 **Date established:** 2015
Turnover: £10m - £20m **No.of Employees:** 51 - 100 **Product Groups:** 72, 82

Date of Accounts	Dec 11	Dec 10	Dec 09
Sales Turnover	16m	14m	19
Pre Tax Profit/Loss	3m	964	2
Working Capital	25m	13m	12
Fixed Assets	4m	4m	7
Current Assets	41m	31m	31
Current Liabilities	13m	14m	10

Pentagon Vauxhall
Pentagon Island Nottingham Road, Derby, DE21 6HB
Tel: 01332-362661 **Fax:** 01332-292736
E-mail: dave.white@pentagon-group.co.uk
Website: http://www.pentagon-chevrolet.co.uk
Bank(s): Royal Bank of Scotland
Directors: T. Reeve (MD)
Managers: D. White (Chief Mgr)
Immediate Holding Company: PENTAGON DEVELOPMENT SERVICES LIMITED
Registration no: 03380944 **VAT No.:** GB 558 5544 06
Date established: 1997 **Turnover:** Up to £250,000
No.of Employees: 251 - 500 **Product Groups:** 68

Date of Accounts	Mar 11	Mar 10	Mar 09
Sales Turnover	114	133	129
Pre Tax Profit/Loss	26	5	4
Working Capital	-165	-203	-151
Fixed Assets	386	399	384
Current Assets	400	78	166
Current Liabilities	105	248	294

Personalized 4 U
1 Oxford Street Off London Road,, Derby, DE1 2TE
Tel: 01332-204030 **Fax:** 01332-204030
E-mail: info@personalized4u.co.uk
Website: http://www.personalized4u.webs.com
Directors: L. Sanders (Prop)
Registration no: 06650326 **Date established:** 2008
Turnover: Up to £250,000 **No.of Employees:** 1 - 10 **Product Groups:** 23, 24, 63

Plant & Consumable Services Ltd
9b Pond End Castle Donington, Derby, DE74 2UB
Tel: 01332-813300 **Fax:** 01332-813301
E-mail: tr@pacs.uk.com
Website: http://www.pax.uk.com
Managers: D. Bramhill (Mgr)
Ultimate Holding Company: SCAP HOLDINGS LIMITED
Immediate Holding Company: PLANT AND CONSUMABLE SERVICES LIMITED
Registration no: 04132575 **Date established:** 2000
Turnover: £10m - £20m **No.of Employees:** 51 - 100 **Product Groups:** 33, 37

Date of Accounts	Mar 11	Mar 10	Mar 09
Sales Turnover	18m	15m	N/A
Pre Tax Profit/Loss	1m	1m	1m
Working Capital	770	624	296
Fixed Assets	7m	7m	6m
Current Assets	12m	11m	7m
Current Liabilities	6m	6m	3m

Porterbrook Leasing Co Mebo Ltd
Burdett House Becket Street, Derby, DE1 1JP
Tel: 01332-262405 **Fax:** 01332-262451
E-mail: paul.francis@porterbrook.co.uk
Website: http://www.porterbrook.co.uk
Bank(s): Lloyds, 43 Irongate, Derby
Directors: W. Day (Fin), P. Francis (MD)
Managers: S. Tonks (Tech Serv Mgr), K. Jackson (Mktg Serv Mgr), K. North (Personnel)
Ultimate Holding Company: BANCO SANTANDER SA (SPAIN)
Immediate Holding Company: SANTANDER SECRETARIAT SERVICES LIMITED
Registration no: 03072288 **VAT No.:** GB 648 2729 08
Date established: 1995 **Turnover:** £250,000 - £500,000
No.of Employees: 51 - 100 **Product Groups:** 72, 84

Date of Accounts	Dec 09	Dec 08
Sales Turnover	393	N/A
Pre Tax Profit/Loss	393	438m
Working Capital	N/A	76m
Current Assets	N/A	76m

Positive Id Labelling
Castle Lane Melbourne, Derby, DE73 8JB
Tel: 01332-864895 **Fax:** 01332-864315
E-mail: sales@pid-labelling.co.uk
Website: http://www.pid-labelling.co.uk
Directors: J. Mayers (MD)
Immediate Holding Company: CHAUFFEURLINE CONNECTIONS LIMITED
Registration no: 03431590 **Date established:** 2011
No.of Employees: 1 - 10 **Product Groups:** 38, 42

Poxon Engineering Ltd
Egginton, Derby, DE65 6GU
Tel: 01283-730111 **Fax:** 01283-730222
Website: http://www.poxonengineeringltd.co.uk
Directors: T. Poxon (MD)
No.of Employees: 1 - 10 **Product Groups:** 35

Pro Live Audio
19 Blakelow Drive Etwall, Derby, DE65 6NN
Tel: 01283-730925
E-mail: hire@proliveaudio.co.uk
Website: http://www.proliveaudio.co.uk
Directors: D. Chapman (Dir), J. Knapp (Dir)
Immediate Holding Company: PRO LIVE AUDIO LIMITED
Registration no: 06009970 **Date established:** 2006
No.of Employees: 1 - 10 **Product Groups:** 83

Date of Accounts	Dec 10	Dec 09	Dec 08
Working Capital	-50	-53	-88
Fixed Assets	70	75	94
Current Assets	N/A	1	1

Protrade
Unit 2 Riverside Road Pride Park, Derby, DE24 8HY
Tel: 01332-680120 **Fax:** 08452-306071
E-mail: burton@protrade.co.uk
Website: http://www.protrade.co.uk
Directors: S. Rooney (Fin), S. Lovatt (Fin)
Managers: O. Flint (Tech Serv Mgr), T. Lambert (Buyer), D. Kerry
Immediate Holding Company: PROTRADE LTD
Registration no: 05408392 **Date established:** 2005
No.of Employees: 21 - 50 **Product Groups:** 37

Date of Accounts	Dec 11	Dec 10	Dec 09
Working Capital	-100	-98	-119
Fixed Assets	72	72	66
Current Assets	570	452	530

Quadralene Ltd
Bateman Street, Derby, DE23 8JL
Tel: 01332-292500 **Fax:** 01332-295941
E-mail: info@quadralene.co.uk
Website: http://www.quadralene.co.uk
Bank(s): HSBC
Directors: H. Wigglesworth (Dir), R. Newsome (Sales)
Managers: I. McDonald (Tech Serv Mgr)
Immediate Holding Company: QUADRALENE LIMITED
Registration no: 00246955 **VAT No.:** GB 125 3366 85
Date established: 1930 **Turnover:** £2m - £5m **No.of Employees:** 21 - 50
Product Groups: 32, 68

Date of Accounts	Dec 11	Dec 10	Dec 09
Working Capital	2m	2m	2m
Fixed Assets	169	151	116

Current Assets	2m	2m	2m

Quinton Crane Electronics Ltd

Carnival Way Castle Donington, Derby, DE74 2HP
Tel: 01332-810955 **Fax:** 01332-810475
E-mail: caroline.richards@systekcontrols.com
Website: http://www.systekcontrols.com
Bank(s): Lloyds TSB
Directors: C. Thompson (Purch), J. Thompson (Dir), C. Richards (Fin)
Ultimate Holding Company: ELDERAY LIMITED
Immediate Holding Company: QUINTON CRANE ELECTRONICS LIMITED
Registration no: 04053843 **VAT No.:** GB 746 2511 39
Date established: 2000 **No.of Employees:** 21 - 50 **Product Groups:** 37, 38

Date of Accounts	Sep 11	Sep 10	Sep 09
Working Capital	557	572	423
Fixed Assets	28	11	19
Current Assets	2m	999	815

R G C Support Services Ltd

Parker Centre Parker Industrial Estate Mansfield Road, Derby, DE21 4SZ
Tel: 08453-700742 **Fax:** 0845-370 1742
E-mail: rob.lewis@tidyco.co.uk
Website: http://www.rgcsupportservices.co.uk
Directors: R. Lewis (MD)
Immediate Holding Company: R.G.C. SUPPORT SERVICES LIMITED
Registration no: 04185931 **Date established:** 2001
Turnover: £500,000 - £1m **No.of Employees:** 1 - 10 **Product Groups:** 66

Date of Accounts	Jul 11	Jul 10	Jul 09
Working Capital	55	25	13
Fixed Assets	N/A	3	4
Current Assets	217	167	166

R L M International Ltd

Unit 1 Cargo Terminal 4, Beverley Road East Midlands Airport, Castle Donington, Derby, DE74 2SA
Tel: 01332-853040 **Fax:** 01332-850404
E-mail: d.orme@mies.co.uk
Website: http://www.rlm-ema.co.uk
Directors: R. Mould (MD)
Managers: L. Henderson (District Mgr), K. Hill (Sales Prom Mgr), C. Thompson (Chief Mgr)
Ultimate Holding Company: Rennies Freight Services Ltd
Immediate Holding Company: R.L.M. International Ltd
Registration no: 04193459 **VAT No.:** 455 7740 22 **Date established:** 1986
Turnover: £1m - £2m **No.of Employees:** 1 - 10 **Product Groups:** 76

Date of Accounts	Dec 07	Dec 06	Dec 05
Working Capital	-20	-28	-36
Fixed Assets	34	44	51
Current Assets	177	180	184
Current Liabilities	196	208	220
Total Share Capital	10	10	10

Reeve (Derby) Ltd

Pentagon Island Nottingham Road, Derby, DE21 6HB
Tel: 01332-362661 **Fax:** 01332-292736
E-mail: info@pentagon-group.co.uk
Website: http://www.pentagon-group.co.uk
Directors: T. Reeve (Dir), S. Reeve (Dir)
Managers: R. Sissons (Sales Prom Mgr)
Registration no: 04120259 **Turnover:** £50m - £75m
No.of Employees: 101 - 250 **Product Groups:** 68

Riley Automation Ltd

Foresters Business Park Sinfin Lane, Derby, DE23 8AG
Tel: 01332-275850 **Fax:** 01332-275855
E-mail: sales@rileyautomation.com
Website: http://www.rileyautomation.com
Directors: A. Clarke (Eng Serv), D. Collinge (Comm)
Immediate Holding Company: RILEY AUTOMATION LIMITED
Registration no: 03955728 **Date established:** 2000
No.of Employees: 11 - 20 **Product Groups:** 35, 39, 45

Date of Accounts	Jun 11	Jun 10	Jun 09
Working Capital	558	512	488
Fixed Assets	21	12	22
Current Assets	985	1000	797

Robbins & Myers UK Ltd

7 Cranmer Road West Meadows Industrial Estate, Derby, DE21 6XT
Tel: 01332-363175 **Fax:** 01332-290323
E-mail: ian.ottiwell@robn.com
Website: http://www.chemineer.com
Bank(s): The Royal Bank of Scotland
Directors: I. Ottiwell (Fin), N. Cathie (MD)
Managers: I. Fisher (Buyer), N. Davies (Chief Mgr)
Ultimate Holding Company: ROBBINS AND MYERS INC. (USA)
Immediate Holding Company: CHEMINEER, LIMITED
Registration no: 01073590 **Date established:** 1972 **Turnover:** £2m - £5m
No.of Employees: 21 - 50 **Product Groups:** 40, 41, 42, 43, 44, 45

Robinsons

20 Parker House Mansfield Road, Derby, DE21 4SZ
Tel: 01332-679898 **Fax:** 01332-671717
E-mail: tony@wsrobinson.com
Website: http://www.biscuitmachines.co.uk
Directors: T. Robinson (MD)
Immediate Holding Company: ROBINSONS OF DERBY LIMITED
Registration no: 07641591 **VAT No.:** GB 728 3576 08
Date established: 2011 **Turnover:** £1m - £2m **No.of Employees:** 1 - 10
Product Groups: 67

Rolls Royce plc

Moore Lane, Derby, DE24 8BJ
Tel: 01332-242424 **Fax:** 01332-249936
Website: http://www.rolls-royce.com
Directors: M. King (Pres)
Managers: P. Ottewell (Comm)
Ultimate Holding Company: ROLLS-ROYCE GROUP PLC
Immediate Holding Company: ROLLS-ROYCE (FRANCE) LIMITED
Registration no: 00353321 **Date established:** 1939
No.of Employees: 21 - 50 **Product Groups:** 39

Date of Accounts	Dec 10	Dec 09	Dec 08
Sales Turnover	N/A	N/A	140
Pre Tax Profit/Loss	N/A	-46	222
Working Capital	106	106	2m
Current Assets	106	106	2m
Current Liabilities	N/A	N/A	55

Rotadata Ltd

Bateman Street, Derby, DE23 8JQ
Tel: 01332-348008 **Fax:** 01332-331023
E-mail: simon.taylor@roscom.com
Website: http://www.rotadata.com
Bank(s): Barclays
Directors: S. Taylor (MD)
Immediate Holding Company: ROTADATA LIMITED
Registration no: 01347216 **VAT No.:** GB 295 4818 14
Date established: 1978 **Turnover:** £2m - £5m **No.of Employees:** 21 - 50
Product Groups: 37, 80

Date of Accounts	Apr 11	Apr 10	Apr 09
Working Capital	1m	1m	1m
Fixed Assets	628	646	670
Current Assets	2m	2m	2m

The Royal Crown Derby Porcelain Company Ltd

194 Osmaston Road, Derby, DE23 8JZ
Tel: 01332-712800 **Fax:** 01332-712863
E-mail: stuart.hughes@royal-crown-derby.co.uk
Website: http://www.royal-crown-derby.co.uk
Directors: S. Willis (Sales & Mktg), S. Hughes (Co Sec)
Managers: D. Lightfoot (Tech Serv Mgr), K. Howell (Purch Mgr), P. Ridguard (Personnel)
Immediate Holding Company: THE ROYAL CROWN DERBY PORCELAIN COMPANY LIMITED
Registration no: 03981291 **Date established:** 2000 **Turnover:** £5m - £10m
No.of Employees: 251 - 500 **Product Groups:** 33

Date of Accounts	Jun 07	Jun 08	Dec 09
Sales Turnover	9m	8m	10m
Pre Tax Profit/Loss	-296	-1m	-3m
Working Capital	1m	758	124
Fixed Assets	9m	8m	6m
Current Assets	4m	4m	3m
Current Liabilities	899	969	547

Rykneld Tean Ltd

Hansard Gate West Meadows Industrial Estate, Derby, DE21 6RR
Tel: 01332-542700 **Fax:** 01332-542710
E-mail: sales@rykneldtean.co.uk
Website: http://www.rykneldtean.co.uk
Directors: T. Wilkinson (MD), C. Jones (Fin)
Ultimate Holding Company: RYKNELD TEAN (HOLDINGS) LIMITED
Immediate Holding Company: RYKNELD TEAN LIMITED
Registration no: 00366190 **VAT No.:** GB 274 1764 46
Date established: 1941 **Turnover:** £5m - £10m **No.of Employees:** 1 - 10
Product Groups: 23, 63, 66

Date of Accounts	Mar 11	Mar 10	Mar 09
Pre Tax Profit/Loss	N/A	N/A	126
Working Capital	2m	2m	2m
Fixed Assets	324	333	396
Current Assets	3m	2m	3m
Current Liabilities	N/A	N/A	632

Scientifics Ltd

500 London Rd, Derby, DE24 8BQ
Tel: 01332-268440 **Fax:** 01332-268495
E-mail: sales@scientifics.com
Website: http://www.scientifics.com
Bank(s): Royal Bank of Scotland
Directors: A. Gibson (MD), M. Jones (Fin), D. Watson (Div)
Managers: D. Brayshaw (Mktg Serv Mgr), M. Barke (Purch Mgr)
Immediate Holding Company: Inspicio PLC
Registration no: 03204613 **VAT No.:** GB 684 1685 03
Turnover: £10m - £20m **No.of Employees:** 251 - 500
Product Groups: 38, 48, 54, 81, 83, 84, 85, 86, 87

Date of Accounts	Dec 09	Dec 08	Dec 07
Sales Turnover	20m	22m	22m
Pre Tax Profit/Loss	-452	3m	1m
Working Capital	4m	-2m	-2m
Fixed Assets	5m	6m	4m
Current Assets	9m	8m	5m
Current Liabilities	3m	2m	1m

Secure Alarm Co.

Lincoln House Malcolm Street, Derby, DE23 8LT
Tel: 08446-331999 **Fax:** 08700-420099
E-mail: info@securealarm.co.uk
Website: http://www.securealarm.co.uk
Immediate Holding Company: SECURE ALARM COMPANY LIMITED
Registration no: 03815151 **Date established:** 1999
No.of Employees: 11 - 20 **Product Groups:** 37, 40, 81

Date of Accounts	Jan 11	Jan 10	Jan 09
Working Capital	-122	-92	-50
Fixed Assets	314	326	346
Current Assets	51	148	196

Seddon Design Ltd

Gelscoe Farm Diseworth, Derby, DE74 2QQ
Tel: 01530-223777 **Fax:** 01530-223666
E-mail: mike@seddon-design.co.uk
Website: http://www.seddon-design.co.uk
Directors: M. Seddon (MD)
Immediate Holding Company: SEDDON DESIGN LIMITED
Registration no: 02897475 **Date established:** 1994
Turnover: £250,000 - £500,000 **No.of Employees:** 1 - 10
Product Groups: 49

Date of Accounts	Mar 12	Mar 11	Mar 09
Working Capital	1	1	-18
Fixed Assets	1	1	N/A
Current Assets	41	16	8

Shaws Metals Ltd

Hartland Works Haydock Park Road, Derby, DE24 8HW
Tel: 01332-362836 **Fax:** 01332-294085
E-mail: sales@shawsmetals.co.uk
Website: http://www.shawsmetals.co.uk
Directors: J. Shaw (Fin)
Immediate Holding Company: SHAWS METALS LIMITED
Registration no: 00638175 **VAT No.:** GB 125 3609 85
Date established: 1959 **Turnover:** £1m - £2m **No.of Employees:** 11 - 20
Product Groups: 23, 34, 35, 36, 40, 45, 48, 66, 72

Date of Accounts	Sep 11	Sep 10	Sep 09
Working Capital	260	139	116
Fixed Assets	5	8	18
Current Assets	503	504	494

Skip Units Ltd

Block D Industrial Estate Sinfin Lane, Derby, DE24 9GL
Tel: 01332-761361 **Fax:** 01332-270013
E-mail: enquiries@skipunits.co.uk
Website: http://www.skipunits.co.uk
Bank(s): The Royal Bank of Scotland
Directors: A. Muirhead (MD), M. Hampson (Sales), R. Wake (Co Sec)
Managers: H. Neilson
Ultimate Holding Company: RAMSHORN LIMITED
Immediate Holding Company: SKIP UNITS LIMITED
Registration no: 03068281 **VAT No.:** GB 289 8230 11
Date established: 1995 **Turnover:** £2m - £5m **No.of Employees:** 51 - 100
Product Groups: 42, 45, 54

Date of Accounts	May 12	May 11	May 10
Sales Turnover	N/A	N/A	3m
Pre Tax Profit/Loss	N/A	N/A	-4
Working Capital	2m	2m	2m
Fixed Assets	802	786	809
Current Assets	13m	8m	7m
Current Liabilities	N/A	N/A	155

Smith Of Derby Ltd

112 Alfreton Road, Derby, DE21 4AU
Tel: 01332-345569 **Fax:** 01332-290642
E-mail: enquiries@smithofderby.com
Website: http://www.smithofderby.com
Bank(s): HSBC Bank plc
Directors: J. Foster (Sales), N. Smith (Fin)
Managers: N. Weir, P. Barry (Fin Mgr)
Immediate Holding Company: SMITH OF DERBY LIMITED
Registration no: 01395408 **VAT No.:** GB 125 6772 59
Date established: 1978 **Turnover:** £2m - £5m **No.of Employees:** 51 - 100
Product Groups: 30, 34, 35, 38, 48, 49, 66, 81

Date of Accounts	Dec 10	Dec 09	Dec 08
Sales Turnover	4m	N/A	N/A
Pre Tax Profit/Loss	-166	N/A	N/A
Working Capital	977	101	669
Fixed Assets	151	1	93
Current Assets	2m	237	2m
Current Liabilities	535	N/A	N/A

John Smith & Sons

112 Alfreton Road, Derby, DE21 4AU
Tel: 01332-345569 **Fax:** 01332-290642
E-mail: val.soar@smithofderby.com
Website: http://www.smithofderby.com
Bank(s): HSBC Plc
Directors: N. Smith (Fin), J. Smith (Ch), J. Foster (Sales), B. Betts (MD), S. Williams (Fin)
Ultimate Holding Company: SMITH OF DERBY GROUP LIMITED
Immediate Holding Company: SMITH OF DERBY (SCANDINAVIA) LIMITED
Registration no: 00252492 **VAT No.:** GB 125 6772 59
Date established: 2003 **Turnover:** £2m - £5m **No.of Employees:** 51 - 100
Product Groups: 30, 40, 49

Speedy Assets Services

Unit 2 Pentagon Island Nottingham Road, Derby, DE21 6BW
Tel: 01332-200330 **Fax:** 01332-202464
E-mail: craig.knowles@speedyservices.com
Website: http://www.speedyservices.com
Directors: B. Leaver (Dir)
Managers: C. Knowles (Site Co-ord)
Ultimate Holding Company: ULC CO.
Immediate Holding Company: HEWDEN STUART LTD
Registration no: SC046005 **No.of Employees:** 1 - 10 **Product Groups:** 35, 39, 45

Star Micronics GB Ltd

Chapel Street Melbourne, Derby, DE73 8JF
Tel: 01332-864455 **Fax:** 01332-864005
E-mail: sales@stargb.com
Website: http://www.stargb.com
Directors: R. Hunt (MD)
Ultimate Holding Company: STAR MICRONICS CO LTD (JAPAN)
Immediate Holding Company: STAR MICRONICS GB LIMITED
Registration no: 02671978 **Date established:** 1991 **Turnover:** £5m - £10m
No.of Employees: 11 - 20 **Product Groups:** 46, 47

Date of Accounts	Dec 09	Dec 08	Dec 07
Sales Turnover	5m	8m	9m
Pre Tax Profit/Loss	55	-167	888
Working Capital	3m	3m	3m
Fixed Assets	36	63	98
Current Assets	4m	4m	5m
Current Liabilities	287	230	478

Swindell & Pearson Ltd

48 Friar Gate, Derby, DE1 1GY
Tel: 01332-367051 **Fax:** 0800-977 8701
E-mail: info@patents.co.uk
Website: http://www.patents.co.uk
Bank(s): HSBC
Managers: P. Mulchinock
Immediate Holding Company: SWINDELL & PEARSON LIMITED
Registration no: 01616604 **Date established:** 1982 **Turnover:** £1m - £2m
No.of Employees: 21 - 50 **Product Groups:** 80

Date of Accounts	Dec 11	Dec 10	Dec 09
Sales Turnover	N/A	N/A	1m
Pre Tax Profit/Loss	N/A	N/A	10
Working Capital	160	426	232
Fixed Assets	3m	3m	47
Current Assets	2m	1m	318
Current Liabilities	N/A	N/A	28

T Clarke Midlands Ltd

Ascot Drive, Derby, DE24 8GZ
Tel: 01332-332177 **Fax:** 01332-374769
E-mail: david.peck@tclarke.co.uk
Website: http://www.tclarke.co.uk
Directors: D. Peck (Dir), K. Bones (MD)
Ultimate Holding Company: T CLARKE PUBLIC LIMITED COMPANY
Immediate Holding Company: MITCHELL AND HEWITT LIMITED
Registration no: 01455864 **Date established:** 1979
Turnover: £10m - £20m **No.of Employees:** 101 - 250
Product Groups: 35, 37, 40

Date of Accounts	Dec 11	Dec 10	Dec 09
Sales Turnover	10m	12m	13m
Pre Tax Profit/Loss	-401	-289	56

see next page

T Clarke Midlands Ltd - Cont'd

Working Capital	551	585	714
Fixed Assets	N/A	261	397
Current Assets	3m	3m	4m
Current Liabilities	228	523	561

T Q Education & Training Ltd
Garden Court Lockington HallMain Street, Lockington, Derby, DE74 2SJ
Tel: 01509-678 400 **Fax:** 01509-678 401
E-mail: enquiries@tq.com
Website: http://www.tq.com
Bank(s): Barclays, Alfreton Road
Directors: J. Murray (Fin), R. Davies (Grp Chief Exec), R. Edwards (Grp MD), H. Milsom (Dir)
Managers: S. Lamley (Export Sales Mg)
Ultimate Holding Company: TQ Holdings Ltd
Immediate Holding Company: TQ Group Ltd
Registration no: 00604934 **Date established:** 1958
Turnover: £20m - £50m **No.of Employees:** 101 - 250 **Product Groups:** 28

Date of Accounts	Sep 08	Sep 07	Sep 06
Sales Turnover	18361	21147	18360
Pre Tax Profit/Loss	2763	7268	4711
Working Capital	4411	3021	5165
Fixed Assets	804	1703	2239
Current Assets	11139	10710	13747
Current Liabilities	6728	7689	8582
Total Share Capital	594	594	594
ROCE% (Return on Capital Employed)	53.0	153.9	63.6
ROT% (Return on Turnover)	15.0	34.4	25.7

T R S Boiler Makers
Greenacres Station Road, Melbourne, Derby, DE73 8BQ
Tel: 01332-865616
E-mail: info@trs-welding.co.uk
Website: http://www.trs-welding.co.uk
Directors: T. Statham (Prop)
Date established: 1993 **No.of Employees:** 1 - 10 **Product Groups:** 37, 40, 48

Tatem Industrial Automation Ltd
Unit 4a Derby Small Business Centre Canal Street, Derby, DE1 2RJ
Tel: 01332-204850 **Fax:** 01332-204851
E-mail: info@tatem.co.uk
Website: http://www.tatem.co.uk
Directors: J. Tatem (Fin), S. Tatem (MD)
Immediate Holding Company: TATEM INDUSTRIAL AUTOMATION LIMITED
Registration no: 03446828 **VAT No.:** GB 705 7408 41
Date established: 1997 **Turnover:** £500,000 - £1m
No.of Employees: 1 - 10 **Product Groups:** 37, 38, 45, 46, 48, 84, 86

Date of Accounts	Mar 12	Mar 11	Mar 10
Working Capital	-29	-57	-67
Fixed Assets	6	2	4
Current Assets	108	123	67

Teamlink Sports Tours
Victoria Buildings 138-152 Uttoxeter New Road, Derby, DE22 3WZ
Tel: 0808-149 3787 **Fax:** 01332-384222
E-mail: info@teamlink.co.uk
Website: http://www.teamlink.co.uk
Directors: M. Gardner (Dir), J. Walter (Co Sec), H. Cooper (Co Sec)
Immediate Holding Company: Tui Travel plc
Registration no: 02493474 **Date established:** 2008 **Turnover:** £2m - £5m
No.of Employees: 1 - 10 **Product Groups:** 69

Date of Accounts	Mar 08	Dec 06	Dec 05
Working Capital	353	365	145
Fixed Assets	17	21	24
Current Assets	1478	798	652
Current Liabilities	1125	433	507
Total Share Capital	100	100	100

Tecnograv Ltd
Nottingham Road Spondon, Derby, DE21 7GX
Tel: 01332-662416 **Fax:** 01332-660135
Bank(s): National Westminster
Directors: Hartley (Fin), T. Wrigley (MD)
Ultimate Holding Company: TRESSANDA LIMITED
Immediate Holding Company: TECNOGRAV LIMITED
Registration no: 01102828 **VAT No.:** 694 7399 64 **Date established:** 1973
Turnover: £5m - £10m **No.of Employees:** 21 - 50 **Product Groups:** 28, 30, 44

Date of Accounts	Apr 11	Apr 10	Apr 09
Working Capital	-171	-106	-385
Fixed Assets	13	18	46
Current Assets	687	659	544

Tekmat Ltd
Ryan House Trent Lane, Castle Donington, Derby, DE74 2PY
Tel: 01332-853443 **Fax:** 01332-853424
E-mail: sales@tekmat.co.uk
Website: http://www.tekmat.co.uk
Directors: A. Barnes (MD)
Immediate Holding Company: TEKMAT LIMITED
Registration no: 02447920 **VAT No.:** GB 439 4179 24
Date established: 1989 **Turnover:** £10m - £20m **No.of Employees:** 1 - 10
Product Groups: 36, 46

Date of Accounts	Sep 11	Sep 10	Sep 09
Working Capital	236	274	269
Fixed Assets	1	1	1
Current Assets	295	333	304

Tex Industrial Plastics Ltd
Wetherby Road, Derby, DE24 8HL
Tel: 01332-363249 **Fax:** 01332-292186
E-mail: info@texip.co.uk
Website: http://www.tex-plastics.co.uk
Bank(s): National Westminster Bank Plc
Directors: C. Varley (MD), M. Mansell (Fin)
Ultimate Holding Company: TEX HOLDINGS PLC
Immediate Holding Company: TEX PLASTICS (DERBY) LIMITED
Registration no: 01286373 **Date established:** 1976
Turnover: £10m - £20m **No.of Employees:** 101 - 250
Product Groups: 30, 66

Date of Accounts	Dec 11	Dec 10	Dec 09
Sales Turnover	12m	10m	9m
Pre Tax Profit/Loss	237	34	-234
Working Capital	2m	2m	2m
Fixed Assets	3m	2m	3m
Current Assets	4m	4m	4m
Current Liabilities	340	510	413

Thorpe's George Pollard
45 The Green Castle Donington, Derby, DE74 2JX
Tel: 01332-810038 **Fax:** 01332-810038
Directors: G. Pollard (Prop), G. Pollard (Head)
Date established: 1994 **Turnover:** Up to £250,000
No.of Employees: 1 - 10 **Product Groups:** 84

Trimlace Ltd
Unit D4 Bridge Field Breaston, Derby, DE72 3DS
Tel: 01332-874848 **Fax:** 01332-875102
E-mail: sales@trimlace.co.uk
Website: http://www.trimlace.co.uk
Bank(s): The Royal Bank of Scotland
Directors: S. Wright (MD)
Immediate Holding Company: TRIMLACE LIMITED
Registration no: 01751856 **VAT No.:** GB 395 5556 05
Date established: 1983 **No.of Employees:** 11 - 20 **Product Groups:** 23

Date of Accounts	Dec 11	Dec 10	Dec 09
Working Capital	-13	-2	103
Fixed Assets	47	115	107
Current Assets	157	203	305

Trueweld Ltd Derby
Alfreton Road, Derby, DE21 4AP
Tel: 01332-365130 **Fax:** 01332-296302
E-mail: malcolm.prentice@garrandale.co.uk
Website: http://www.trueweld.co.uk
Directors: A. Millington (Fin), S. Rowley (Sales)
Managers: M. Prentice
Ultimate Holding Company: GARRANDALE GROUP LIMITED
Immediate Holding Company: TRUE WELD (DERBY) LIMITED
Registration no: 01345820 **Date established:** 1977
No.of Employees: 51 - 100 **Product Groups:** 24, 32, 33, 34, 35, 45, 46, 67, 83

Date of Accounts	Oct 11	Oct 10	Oct 09
Working Capital	69	70	59
Fixed Assets	14	17	27
Current Assets	164	165	193

Veolia Environmental Services Ltd
971a London Road Alvaston, Derby, DE24 8PX
Tel: 01332-861900 **Fax:** 01332-861911
Website: http://www.onyxgroup.co.uk
Managers: A. Howe
Immediate Holding Company: VEOLIA ES HOLDINGS UK PLC
Registration no: 02215767 **VAT No.:** GB 530 0088 93
Turnover: £75m - £125m **No.of Employees:** 21 - 50 **Product Groups:** 39, 42, 54

Watermark Systems UK Ltd
18 Cotton Brook Road, Derby, DE23 8YJ
Tel: 01332-366000 **Fax:** 01332-372006
E-mail: sales@watermark-uk.com
Website: http://www.watermark-uk.com
Bank(s): National Westminster
Directors: M. Roberts (Fin)
Immediate Holding Company: WATERMARK SYSTEMS UK LIMITED
Registration no: 03004901 **VAT No.:** GB 598 6766 52
Date established: 1994 **Turnover:** £1m - £2m **No.of Employees:** 21 - 50
Product Groups: 48

Date of Accounts	Apr 11	Apr 10	Apr 09
Working Capital	287	276	361
Fixed Assets	93	79	99
Current Assets	624	500	564

Woodgrow Horticulture
Burton Road Findern, Derby, DE65 6BE
Tel: 01332-517600 **Fax:** 01332-511481
E-mail: sales@woodgrow.com
Website: http://www.woodgrow.com
Directors: M. Woodhouse (Dir), S. Meecham (Fin)
Immediate Holding Company: WOODGROW HORTICULTURE LIMITED
Registration no: 01152068 **VAT No.:** GB 127 3917 62
Date established: 1973 **Turnover:** £250,000 - £500,000
No.of Employees: 1 - 10 **Product Groups:** 25

Date of Accounts	Sep 11	Sep 10	Sep 09
Working Capital	-53	-72	-5
Fixed Assets	65	74	84
Current Assets	107	69	78

Wordcraft International Ltd
Park Hill Hilton Road, Egginton, Derby, DE65 6GU
Tel: 01283-731400 **Fax:** 01283-731401
E-mail: sales@wordcraft.com
Website: http://www.wordcraft.com
Directors: A. Roach (MD)
Immediate Holding Company: WORDCRAFT INTERNATIONAL LIMITED
Registration no: 02043431 **Date established:** 1986 **Turnover:** £2m - £5m
No.of Employees: 1 - 10 **Product Groups:** 35, 37, 38, 39, 44, 45, 46, 48, 49, 67, 71, 83

Date of Accounts	Dec 11	Dec 10	Dec 09
Working Capital	278	306	314
Fixed Assets	4	4	7
Current Assets	350	359	369

Workplatform Ltd
The Old Vicarage Market Street, Castle Donington, Derby, DE74 2JB
Tel: 01332-856359 **Fax:** 01332-810769
E-mail: info@workplatformltd.co.uk
Website: http://www.workplatformltd.co.uk
Directors: J. Hull (Dir)
Immediate Holding Company: WORKPLATFORM LIMITED
Registration no: 06598369 **Date established:** 2008
Turnover: £500,000 - £1m **No.of Employees:** 1 - 10 **Product Groups:** 35, 36, 40, 45

Date of Accounts	Jun 12	Jun 11	Jun 10
Working Capital	449	254	161
Fixed Assets	101	87	66
Current Assets	2m	1m	613

F E Worthington
5 Beaufort Court, Derby, DE21 4FA
Tel: 01332-364809 **Fax:** 01332-364809
Directors: F. Worthington (Prop)
Date established: 1989 **No.of Employees:** 1 - 10 **Product Groups:** 35

XN Hotel Systems Ltd
The Old Vicarage Market Street, Castle Donington, Derby, DE74 2JB
Tel: 0845-0942220 **Fax:** 0845-0942221
E-mail: sales@xnhotels.com
Website: http://www.xnhotels.com
Managers: P. Willmott, M. Davey (I.T. Exec)
Ultimate Holding Company: Checkout Holdings Ltd
Immediate Holding Company: Checkout Computer Systems Ltd
Registration no: 05961437 **No.of Employees:** 101 - 250
Product Groups: 44

Date of Accounts	Dec 09	Dec 08	Dec 07
Sales Turnover	2m	2m	2m
Pre Tax Profit/Loss	274	203	638
Working Capital	-197	-525	-502
Fixed Assets	1m	1m	1m
Current Assets	546	927	1m
Current Liabilities	415	398	360

Dronfield

A & H Lift Services Ltd
15 Cruck Close Dronfield Woodhouse, Dronfield, S18 8QX
Tel: 01246-419708 **Fax:** 01246-291900
E-mail: info@ahlifts.co.uk
Website: http://www.ahlifts.co.uk
Directors: A. Wilson (Dir)
Immediate Holding Company: A. & H. LIFT SERVICES LTD.
Registration no: 02204658 **Date established:** 1987
No.of Employees: 1 - 10 **Product Groups:** 35, 39, 45

Date of Accounts	May 12	May 11	May 10
Working Capital	19	20	32
Fixed Assets	29	22	14
Current Assets	114	98	125

Admiral
39 Chesterfield Road, Dronfield, S18 2XG
Tel: 01246-411764 **Fax:** 01246-290294
E-mail: admin@admiralconstruction.co.uk
Website: http://www.admiralconstruction.co.uk
Bank(s): Lloyds TSB Bank plc
Directors: K. Roebuck (Fin), S. Savage (MD)
Ultimate Holding Company: AC HOLDINGS LIMITED
Immediate Holding Company: ADMIRAL CONSTRUCTION LIMITED
Registration no: 01642646 **Date established:** 1982
No.of Employees: 21 - 50 **Product Groups:** 51

Date of Accounts	Jun 11	Jun 10	Jun 09
Pre Tax Profit/Loss	63	90	466
Working Capital	879	810	1m
Fixed Assets	64	84	112
Current Assets	3m	2m	3m
Current Liabilities	514	260	605

Armeg Ltd
Callywhite Lane, Dronfield, S18 2XJ
Tel: 01246-411081 **Fax:** 01246-411882
E-mail: sales@armeg.co.uk
Website: http://www.armeg.co.uk
Bank(s): Midland bank
Directors: C. Pugh (Fin), M. Goodison (MD)
Managers: G. Wall (Sales & Mktg Mg), A. Slater Senior (Prod Mgr)
Immediate Holding Company: ARMEG LIMITED
Registration no: 03827176 **VAT No.:** GB 173 3399 47
Date established: 1999 **Turnover:** £2m - £5m **No.of Employees:** 51 - 100
Product Groups: 46

Date of Accounts	Dec 11	Dec 10	Dec 09
Working Capital	472	381	325
Fixed Assets	154	200	306
Current Assets	1m	1m	983
Current Liabilities	295	295	295

Banner Plant Ltd
Callywhite Lane, Dronfield, S18 2XS
Tel: 01246-299400 **Fax:** 01246-290253
E-mail: dronfield@bannerplant.co.uk
Website: http://www.bannerplant.co.uk
Bank(s): Barclays
Directors: G. Boot (MD)
Ultimate Holding Company: HENRY BOOT PLC
Immediate Holding Company: BANNER PLANT LIMITED
Registration no: 00607575 **VAT No.:** GB 125 3854 72
Date established: 1958 **Turnover:** £2m - £5m **No.of Employees:** 11 - 20
Product Groups: 83

Date of Accounts	Dec 11	Dec 10	Dec 09
Sales Turnover	10m	9m	9m
Pre Tax Profit/Loss	190	212	-105
Working Capital	-2m	-2m	-3m
Fixed Assets	7m	7m	8m
Current Assets	2m	2m	2m
Current Liabilities	4	8	N/A

British Rema Process Equipment Ltd
Unit 4, Traso Business Park Cally Lane, Dronfield, S18 2XR
Tel: 01246-269955 **Fax:** 01246-269944
E-mail: sales@britishrema.com
Website: http://www.britishrema.co.uk
Bank(s): Barclays Plc
Directors: S. McBride (MD), D. Bugler (Sales)
Managers: S. Abbott (Prod Mgr)
Registration no: 05556424 **VAT No.:** GB 872 0080 45
Date established: 1980 **Turnover:** £2m - £5m **No.of Employees:** 21 - 50
Product Groups: 12, 14, 17, 30, 32, 33, 34, 40, 41, 42, 45, 47, 67, 85

Chans Cooker Ltd
Unit 4 Bridge Works Mill Lane, Dronfield, S18 2XL
Tel: 01246-292527 **Fax:** 01246-292521
Website: http://www.chanscookers.com
Directors: B. Chan (MD)
Immediate Holding Company: CHAN'S COOKER LTD
Registration no: 05180782 **Date established:** 2004
No.of Employees: 1 - 10 **Product Groups:** 20, 40, 41

Date of Accounts	Apr 11	Apr 10	Apr 09
Working Capital	51	57	18
Fixed Assets	1	2	1
Current Assets	236	153	124

Cobal Cranes Ltd
Callywhite Lane, Dronfield, S18 2XR
Tel: 01246-292984 **Fax:** 0114-261 9003
E-mail: sam@cobalcranes.com
Website: http://www.cobalcranes.com
Bank(s): National Westminster Bank Plc
Directors: S. Sowerby (Dir), J. Hides (Fin)
Ultimate Holding Company: COBAL CRANES (UK) LIMITED
Immediate Holding Company: COBAL (CRANES) LTD.
Registration no: 01261011 **VAT No.:** GB 308 4054 79
Date established: 1976 **Turnover:** £1m - £2m **No.of Employees:** 11 - 20
Product Groups: 45, 48

Date of Accounts	Mar 11	Mar 10	Mar 09
Working Capital	394	437	564
Fixed Assets	41	47	61
Current Assets	529	547	760

Custom Candles Ltd
14 Cross Lane Coal Aston, Dronfield, S18 3AL
Tel: 01246-414740 **Fax:** 01246-290012
E-mail: sales@customcandles.co.uk
Website: http://www.customcandles.co.uk
Directors: T. Hudson (MD), D. Hudson (Fin)
Immediate Holding Company: CUSTOM CANDLES LIMITED
Registration no: 01214805 **Date established:** 1975
Turnover: Up to £250,000 **No.of Employees:** 1 - 10 **Product Groups:** 32

Date of Accounts	Aug 11	Aug 10	Aug 08
Working Capital	169	165	179
Fixed Assets	271	277	278
Current Assets	185	181	189

Hallam Polymer Engineering Ltd
Traso House Callywhite Lane, Dronfield, S18 2XR
Tel: 01246-415511 **Fax:** 01246-414818
E-mail: martin@hallampolymer.com
Website: http://www.hallampolymer.com
Bank(s): HSBC, Church St
Directors: S. Cooper (Co Sec), M. Cooper (MD)
Immediate Holding Company: HALLAM POLYMER ENGINEERING LIMITED
Registration no: 01928595 **VAT No.:** GB 125 5224 95
Date established: 1985 **Turnover:** £1m - £2m **No.of Employees:** 21 - 50
Product Groups: 29, 30, 31, 39, 48

Date of Accounts	Mar 11	Mar 10	Mar 09
Working Capital	1m	1m	960
Fixed Assets	161	161	89
Current Assets	1m	1m	1m

Hamilton Acorn Ltd
2c Callywhite Lane, Dronfield, S18 2XP
Tel: 01246-418306 **Fax:** 01246-410334
E-mail: keith@hamilton-acorn.co.uk
Website: http://www.hamilton-acorn.co.uk
Managers: K. Davies (Mgr)
Registration no: 03149785 **VAT No.:** GB 558 4073 24
Turnover: £2m - £5m **No.of Employees:** 1 - 10 **Product Groups:** 35, 36, 49

Harrison Silverdale Ltd
Unit 1 Traso Business Park Callywhite Lane, Dronfield, S18 2XR
Tel: 01246-296930 **Fax:** 01246-296940
E-mail: fasteners@harrisonsilverdale.co.uk
Website: http://www.harrisonsilverdale.co.uk
Directors: M. Harrison (Sales)
Immediate Holding Company: HARRISON - SILVERDALE LIMITED
Registration no: 01686821 **Date established:** 1982
No.of Employees: 11 - 20 **Product Groups:** 25, 30, 34, 35, 36, 38, 39, 42, 44, 46, 48, 66

Date of Accounts	Dec 11	Dec 10	Dec 09
Working Capital	365	261	210
Fixed Assets	68	39	23
Current Assets	892	788	594

Idea Showcases Ltd
32 Hallowes Lane, Dronfield, S18 1SS
Tel: 01246-415535 **Fax:** 01246-415535
E-mail: mail@ideashowcases.co.uk
Website: http://www.ideashowcases.co.uk
Directors: L. Grayson (MD)
Immediate Holding Company: IDEA SHOWCASES LIMITED
Registration no: 05028338 **Date established:** 2004
No.of Employees: 11 - 20 **Product Groups:** 52, 67

Date of Accounts	Dec 10	Dec 09	Dec 08
Working Capital	34	31	13
Fixed Assets	2	2	1
Current Assets	76	76	27

Jays Refractory Specialists Ltd
Callywhite Lane, Dronfield, S18 2XR
Tel: 01246-410241 **Fax:** 01246-290221
E-mail: info@jrsuk.com
Website: http://www.jrsuk.com
Bank(s): National Westminster Bank Plc
Directors: M. Turner (MD)
Immediate Holding Company: JAY'S REFRACTORY SPECIALISTS LIMITED
Registration no: 01853599 **VAT No.:** GB 391 1683 42
Date established: 1984 **No.of Employees:** 11 - 20 **Product Groups:** 14, 17, 27, 33, 66

Date of Accounts	Dec 11	Dec 10	Dec 09
Working Capital	968	948	789
Fixed Assets	426	414	435
Current Assets	2m	2m	1m

Kilner Vacuumation Co. Ltd
Callywhite Lane, Dronfield, S18 2XR
Tel: 01246-416441 **Fax:** 01246-290573
E-mail: sales@kilner-vacuum-lifting.com
Website: http://www.kilner-vacuum-lifting.com
Bank(s): National Westminster Bank Plc
Directors: A. Kilner (MD)
Immediate Holding Company: KILNER VACUUMATION COMPANY LIMITED
Registration no: 00829473 **VAT No.:** GB 126 0570 95
Date established: 1964 **Turnover:** £500,000 - £1m
No.of Employees: 11 - 20 **Product Groups:** 38, 40, 42, 43, 45, 46, 48, 84

Date of Accounts	Mar 12	Mar 11	Mar 10
Working Capital	267	205	228
Fixed Assets	169	164	170
Current Assets	330	281	269

Land-Surv eGeomatics Limited
Mill Lane, Dronfield, S18 2XL
Tel: 08456-432832 **Fax:** 08456-432842
E-mail: enquiries@land-surv.co.uk
Website: http://www.land-surv.co.uk
Registration no: 07536262 **Turnover:** £250,000 - £500,000
No.of Employees: 1 - 10 **Product Groups:** 38, 80, 85

William Lee Ltd (a subsidiary of Castings P.L.C.)
Callywhite Lane, Dronfield, S18 2XU
Tel: 01246-416155 **Fax:** 01246-292194
E-mail: sales@wmlee.co.uk
Website: http://www.wmlee.co.uk
Bank(s): HSBC Bank plc
Directors: M. Whelpton (Foundry), G. Cooper (MD), A. Roddis (Sales), T. Carannante (Eng Serv)
Managers: S. Smith (Sales Prom), C. Hodson (Sales Prom Mgr)
Ultimate Holding Company: Castings P.L.C.
Registration no: 02575974 **Date established:** 1901
Turnover: £20m - £50m **No.of Employees:** 251 - 500
Product Groups: 34, 48, 66

Date of Accounts	Mar 11	Mar 10	Mar 09
Sales Turnover	45m	27m	35m
Pre Tax Profit/Loss	5m	3m	1m
Working Capital	5m	2m	-2m
Fixed Assets	27m	26m	27m
Current Assets	16m	11m	9m
Current Liabilities	3m	2m	2m

Lubeline Lubricating Equipment
4 Collins Yard Mill Lane, Dronfield, S18 2XL
Tel: 01246-292333 **Fax:** 01246-292444
E-mail: sales@lubeline.co.uk
Website: http://www.lubeline.co.uk
Directors: D. Shepherd (Prop), N. Orford (Fin)
Immediate Holding Company: LUBELINE LIMITED
Registration no: 04257869 **Date established:** 2001
No.of Employees: 1 - 10 **Product Groups:** 31, 32, 36, 39, 40, 45, 48, 66, 67

Neville Instruments
14 Garth Way, Dronfield, S18 1RL
Tel: 01246-414551 **Fax:** 01246-414551
E-mail: neville_dental@msn.com
Website: http://www.nevilleforceps.co.uk
Directors: F. Lee (Snr Part)
VAT No.: GB 125 8898 27 **Date established:** 1959
Turnover: Up to £250,000 **No.of Employees:** 1 - 10 **Product Groups:** 38, 67

Noble Abrasives Ltd
12 Carr Lane Dronfield Woodhouse, Dronfield, S18 8XG
Tel: 01246-291953 **Fax:** 01246-298109
E-mail: peter@noble-abrasives.co.uk
Website: http://www.noble-abrasives.com
Directors: P. Noble (Prop)
Immediate Holding Company: NOBLE ABRASIVES LIMITED
Registration no: 05419144 **Date established:** 2005
No.of Employees: 1 - 10 **Product Groups:** 27, 32, 33, 45

Date of Accounts	Mar 11	Mar 10	Mar 09
Working Capital	1	1	8
Fixed Assets	6	8	1
Current Assets	49	39	36

Padley & Venables Ltd
Callywhite Lane, Dronfield, S18 2XT
Tel: 01246-299100 **Fax:** 01246-290354
E-mail: darren.bradwell@padley-venables.com
Website: http://www.padley-venables.com
Bank(s): National Westminster Bank Plc
Directors: D. Bradwell (Fin)
Managers: J. Perrite (Personnel), Y. Salat (Sales Admin), L. Barnsley (Purch Mgr), B. Roddie (Tech Serv Mgr), J. Whitehouse
Ultimate Holding Company: BRUNNER & LAY INTERNATIONAL LTD (CAYMAN ISLANDS)
Immediate Holding Company: PADLEY & VENABLES LIMITED
Registration no: 02778086 **Date established:** 1993
Turnover: £10m - £20m **No.of Employees:** 101 - 250
Product Groups: 34, 36, 37, 40, 45, 46, 51

Date of Accounts	Dec 11	Dec 10	Dec 09
Sales Turnover	19m	19m	13m
Pre Tax Profit/Loss	3m	4m	663
Working Capital	15m	13m	10m
Fixed Assets	9m	7m	7m
Current Assets	17m	16m	12m
Current Liabilities	1m	2m	596

Phillips Kiln Services Europe Ltd
Unit 4 Traso Business Park Callywhite Lane, Dronfield, S18 2XR
Tel: 01246-292700 **Fax:** 01246-292400
E-mail: sales@phillipsrema.co.uk
Website: http://www.phillipsrema.co.uk
Directors: J. Cameron (Dir), A. Hunter (Co Sec)
Immediate Holding Company: PHILLIPS KILN SERVICES (EUROPE) LTD
Registration no: 02750412 **Date established:** 1992
Turnover: £500,000 - £1m **No.of Employees:** 11 - 20 **Product Groups:** 84

Date of Accounts	Jun 12	Jun 11	Jun 10
Working Capital	371	9	-58
Fixed Assets	87	101	119
Current Assets	1m	740	631

Phoenix Machinery Ltd
Riverside Studios Mill Lane, Dronfield, S18 2XL
Tel: 01246-290027 **Fax:** 01246-290093
Directors: D. Brierley (MD)
Immediate Holding Company: PHOENIX MACHINERY LIMITED
Registration no: 01723531 **Date established:** 1983
Turnover: £250,000 - £500,000 **No.of Employees:** 1 - 10
Product Groups: 46

Date of Accounts	Jun 11	Jun 09	Jun 08
Working Capital	108	107	106
Fixed Assets	21	8	15
Current Assets	199	162	177

Radius Solutions Ltd
Manor House High Street, Dronfield, S18 1PY
Tel: 01246-290331 **Fax:** 01246-412401
E-mail: david.taylor@radiussolutions.com
Website: http://www.radiussolutions.com
Bank(s): HSBC
Directors: D. Taylor (Dir), L. Bland (Fin), R. Wyllie (MD)
Managers: D. Moore (I.T. Exec), R. Upton (Sales Prom Mgr)
Immediate Holding Company: RADIUS SOLUTIONS LIMITED
Registration no: 05076818 **VAT No.:** GB 347 8084 28
Date established: 2004 **Turnover:** £2m - £5m **No.of Employees:** 51 - 100
Product Groups: 44

Date of Accounts	Dec 09	Dec 08	Dec 07
Pre Tax Profit/Loss	N/A	N/A	-4
Working Capital	46	46	46
Fixed Assets	4m	4m	4m
Current Assets	46	46	56

Rillatech Ltd
16 Callywhite Lane, Dronfield, S18 2XP
Tel: 01246-291488 **Fax:** 01246-291227
E-mail: enquiries@rillatech.co.uk
Website: http://www.rillatech.co.uk
Directors: T. Pickford (MD)
Immediate Holding Company: RILLATECH LIMITED
Registration no: 01674358 **Date established:** 1982 **Turnover:** £5m - £10m
No.of Employees: 21 - 50 **Product Groups:** 38, 42

Date of Accounts	Jan 11	Jan 10	Jan 09
Sales Turnover	7m	7m	N/A
Working Capital	843	836	816
Fixed Assets	198	191	210
Current Assets	2m	2m	2m

Saxon Steels Ltd
Callywhite Lane, Dronfield, S18 2XR
Tel: 01246-418363 **Fax:** 01246-290309
E-mail: enquiries@saxonsteels.com
Website: http://www.saxonsteels.com
Bank(s): The Royal Bank of Scotland
Directors: D. Kitchin (MD)
Immediate Holding Company: SAXON STEELS LIMITED
Registration no: 01084027 **Date established:** 1972
No.of Employees: 11 - 20 **Product Groups:** 34

Date of Accounts	Jun 11	Jun 10	Jun 09
Working Capital	3m	855	809
Fixed Assets	278	292	327
Current Assets	3m	2m	2m

Standall Tools Ltd
Mickley Lane Dronfield Woodhouse, Dronfield, S18 8XB
Tel: 0114-262 0626 **Fax:** 0114-262 0520
E-mail: jse@standall.com
Website: http://www.standall.com
Bank(s): National Westminster Bank Plc
Directors: G. Atkinson (Ch), J. Ellison (Fin), R. Bremner (Sales)
Managers: A. Duke, D. Pope (Export Sales Mg), D. Taylor (Mgr)
Ultimate Holding Company: Dengel & Barker Ltd
Immediate Holding Company: STANDALL TOOLS LIMITED
Registration no: 03925163 **VAT No.:** GB 438 9255 15
Date established: 2000 **Turnover:** £5m - £10m **No.of Employees:** 21 - 50
Product Groups: 36, 37, 46, 47

Date of Accounts	Mar 10	Mar 09	Mar 08
Working Capital	500	643	687
Fixed Assets	816	796	824
Current Assets	1m	2m	2m

Thomas Turton Ltd
Callywhite Lane, Dronfield, S18 2XT
Tel: 01246-290000 **Fax:** 01246-291144
E-mail: bradwell@padley-venables.com
Website: http://www.thomas-turton.co.uk
Bank(s): National Westminster Bank Plc
Directors: D. Bradwell (Co Sec)
Managers: J. Parret (Personnel), J. Whitehouse
Immediate Holding Company: THOMAS TURTON LIMITED
Registration no: 03860515 **Date established:** 1999
No.of Employees: 101 - 250 **Product Groups:** 36, 37, 40, 45

West Brook Resources Ltd
West Brook House Wreakes Lane, Dronfield, S18 1LY
Tel: 01246-292292 **Fax:** 01246-292293
Website: http://www.wbrl.co.uk
Bank(s): HSBC
Directors: S. Walton (MD)
Ultimate Holding Company: WESTBROOK HOLDINGS LIMITED
Immediate Holding Company: WESTBROOK RESOURCES LIMITED
Registration no: 04057615 **VAT No.:** GB 598 3245 95
Date established: 2000 **Turnover:** £20m - £50m
No.of Employees: 21 - 50 **Product Groups:** 34

Date of Accounts	Dec 08	Dec 07	Dec 06
Sales Turnover	112m	106m	113m
Pre Tax Profit/Loss	8m	2m	2m
Working Capital	8m	8m	10m
Fixed Assets	2m	2m	260
Current Assets	28m	36m	36m
Current Liabilities	21m	28m	27m
Total Share Capital	200	200	200

Glossop

A O M L Packaging Ltd
Unit A Brookfield Industrial Estate Peakdale Road, Glossop, SK13 6LQ
Tel: 01457-862800
E-mail: m.white@aomlpackaging.co.uk
Website: http://www.aomlpackaging.co.uk
Directors: M. White (Prop)
Immediate Holding Company: A O M L PACKAGING LIMITED
Registration no: 05393472 **Date established:** 2005
No.of Employees: 1 - 10 **Product Groups:** 27, 30, 48

Date of Accounts	Mar 11	Mar 10	Mar 09
Working Capital	87	79	12
Fixed Assets	183	59	60
Current Assets	411	350	166

Accutest A Division Of Trimble

Wren Nest Road, Glossop, SK13 8HB
Tel: 01457-866613 **Fax:** 01457-856789
E-mail: david.sudworth@accutest.co.uk
Website: http://www.accutest.co.uk
Directors: D. Sudworth (Co Sec)
Immediate Holding Company: NICASH LTD
Registration no: 02958713 **Date established:** 2003
No.of Employees: 21 - 50 **Product Groups:** 44, 80

Date of Accounts	Mar 08	Aug 07	Aug 06
Working Capital	208	-93	-89
Fixed Assets	43	145	142
Current Assets	1024	461	461
Current Liabilities	816	554	550

Ashton Steel Stockholders Ltd

Station Yard Station Road, Hadfield, Glossop, SK13 1AA
Tel: 01457-862438 **Fax:** 01457-861325
Bank(s): Barclays, 190 Stamford St, Ashton Under Lyme, OL6 7NZ
Directors: A. Dest (Prop)
Ultimate Holding Company: ASHTON STEEL HOLDINGS LIMITED
Immediate Holding Company: ASHTON STEEL STOCKHOLDERS LIMITED
Registration no: 00970970 **VAT No.:** GB 145 1574 74
Date established: 1970 **Turnover:** £2m - £5m **No.of Employees:** 11 - 20
Product Groups: 66

Date of Accounts	Dec 11	Dec 10	Dec 09
Working Capital	397	462	405
Fixed Assets	242	246	251
Current Assets	2m	1m	1m

Birchfield Sheet Metal

15 Hadfield Industrial Estate Waterside, Hadfield, Glossop, SK13 1BS
Tel: 01457-865536 **Fax:** 01457-865536
E-mail: birchfieldsheetmetal@hotmail.co.uk
Website: http://www.birchfieldsheetmetal.co.uk
Directors: G. Castree (MD)
Immediate Holding Company: BIRCHFIELD SHEET METAL ENGINEERING COMPANY LIMITED
Registration no: 06476591 **VAT No.:** GB 298 9514 88
Date established: 2008 **Turnover:** Up to £250,000
No.of Employees: 1 - 10 **Product Groups:** 48

Date of Accounts	Mar 12	Mar 11	Mar 10
Working Capital	69	42	14
Fixed Assets	15	16	9
Current Assets	136	102	57

Brass Fittings & Supplies Ltd

Hawkshead Hope Street, Glossop, SK13 7SS
Tel: 01457-854415 **Fax:** 01457-855403
E-mail: philbfs@btinternet.com
Bank(s): Barclays
Directors: P. Brookes (MD)
Immediate Holding Company: BRASS FITTINGS AND SUPPLIES LIMITED
Registration no: 00971875 **VAT No.:** GB 157 3605 60
Date established: 1970 **Turnover:** £2m - £5m **No.of Employees:** 11 - 20
Product Groups: 35, 36, 38, 40

Date of Accounts	Mar 12	Mar 11	Mar 10
Working Capital	67	95	-1
Fixed Assets	27	34	85
Current Assets	344	360	339

British Rigid Urethane Foam Manufacturers Association Limited

12a High Street East, Glossop, SK13 8DA
Tel: 01457-855 884 **Fax:** 0161-236 9292
E-mail: brufma@brufma.co.uk
Website: http://www.brufma.co.uk
Directors: G. Ball (Gen Sec), H. Roberts (Co Sec), J. Roberts (Co Sec)
Managers: M. Price (Personnel)
Immediate Holding Company: British Rigid Urethane Foam Manufacturers Association Ltd
Registration no: 01369401 **VAT No.:** GB 305 7710 74
Date established: 2001 **Turnover:** Up to £250,000
No.of Employees: 1 - 10 **Product Groups:** 87

Date of Accounts	Dec 08	Dec 07	Dec 06
Sales Turnover	121	109	124
Pre Tax Profit/Loss	N/A	-2	-2
Working Capital	46	47	48
Fixed Assets	1	1	1
Current Assets	153	170	178
Current Liabilities	107	123	130
ROCE% (Return on Capital Employed)		-4.3	-3.8
ROT% (Return on Turnover)		-1.9	-1.5

Cell Ltd

Unit 9 Graphite Way Rossington Park Industrial Estate Hadfield, Glossop, SK13 1QH
Tel: 01457-865444 **Fax:** 01457-861162
E-mail: enquire@cell-limited.co.uk
Website: http://www.cell-limited.co.uk
Directors: C. Townsend (MD)
Managers: M. Johnson (Sales Prom Mgr), D. Golden (Sales Prom), S. Milner (Sales Prom Mgr)
Immediate Holding Company: CELL LIMITED
Registration no: 01676049 **Date established:** 1982 **Turnover:** £5m - £10m
No.of Employees: 1 - 10 **Product Groups:** 27

Date of Accounts	Dec 11	Dec 10	Dec 09
Sales Turnover	9m	N/A	N/A
Pre Tax Profit/Loss	164	N/A	N/A
Working Capital	271	190	-77
Fixed Assets	180	106	116
Current Assets	3m	4m	2m
Current Liabilities	2m	N/A	N/A

John R Crossland Construction Ltd

18-20 New Road Tintwistle, Glossop, SK13 1JN
Tel: 01457-868642 **Fax:** 01457-862161
E-mail: enquiries@crossties.co.uk
Website: http://www.connectfree.co.uk
Directors: J. Crossland (MD)
Immediate Holding Company: JOHN R. CROSSLAND CONSTRUCTION LIMITED
Registration no: 01807722 **Date established:** 1984
Turnover: Up to £250,000 **No.of Employees:** 11 - 20 **Product Groups:** 52

Date of Accounts	Apr 12	Apr 11	Apr 10
Sales Turnover	N/A	175	147
Pre Tax Profit/Loss	N/A	6	-13
Working Capital	-76	-85	-89
Fixed Assets	153	158	163
Current Assets	7	11	5
Current Liabilities	27	23	21

Design House North West Ltd

110 Padfield Main Road Padfield, Glossop, SK13 1ET
Tel: 01457-868380 **Fax:** 01457-868809
E-mail: info@designhousenw.co.uk
Website: http://www.designhousenw.co.uk
Directors: E. Reeve (MD), M. Hather (Fin), L. Hather (Comm)
Immediate Holding Company: DESIGN HOUSE NORTHWEST LTD
Registration no: 04403733 **Date established:** 2002
No.of Employees: 1 - 10 **Product Groups:** 28, 81

Date of Accounts	Mar 12	Mar 11	Mar 10
Working Capital	-14	-9	-7
Fixed Assets	N/A	N/A	1
Current Assets	9	15	21
Current Liabilities	N/A	20	22

Esu Ltd

E S U Ltd Peakdale Road, Glossop, SK13 6XE
Tel: 01457-863511 **Fax:** 01457-867820
E-mail: enquiries@esucannon.co.uk
Website: http://www.esucannon.co.uk
Directors: P. O'Mara (Dir), P. Sleigh (Co Sec), S. Ashton (Dir), S. Martin (Dir), I. Froehlich (Dir), P. Martin (Ch), J. Bevan (Dir)
Managers: B. Cheyne (Mktg Serv Mgr), P. Harris (Purch Mgr)
Immediate Holding Company: DELPRO LIMITED
Registration no: 01215595 **VAT No.:** GB 606 6110 73
Date established: 1975 **Turnover:** £2m - £5m **No.of Employees:** 1 - 10
Product Groups: 30, 42, 46, 48, 66, 67, 68

Date of Accounts	Mar 11	Mar 10	Mar 09
Working Capital	508	418	488
Fixed Assets	341	359	361
Current Assets	666	864	555

Firth Rixson Metals Ltd

Meadow Mills Shepley Street, Glossop, SK13 9SA
Tel: 0114-219 3006 **Fax:** 01457-855529
E-mail: lbrierley@firthrixson.com
Website: http://www.firthrixson.com
Directors: J. Hart (Fin), P. Kirkham (MD), P. Bland (Fin), J. Bergin (Dir), J. Males (Sales), J. Hart (Co Sec)
Managers: M. Toole, N. Harris (Purch Mgr), K. Barton (Nat Sales Mgr)
Ultimate Holding Company: FIRTH RIXSON (CYPRUS) LIMITED (CYPRUS).
Immediate Holding Company: FIRTH RIXSON METALS LIMITED
Registration no: 00138691 **VAT No.:** GB 173 7004 76
Date established: 2014 **Turnover:** £5m - £10m **No.of Employees:** 1 - 10
Product Groups: 34, 85

Date of Accounts	Sep 11	Sep 10	Sep 09
Sales Turnover	90m	70m	72m
Pre Tax Profit/Loss	10m	4m	8m
Working Capital	31m	21m	22m
Fixed Assets	32m	32m	32m
Current Assets	76m	59m	51m
Current Liabilities	2m	876	217

Fluorochem Ltd

Wesley Street, Glossop, SK13 7RY
Tel: 01457-865698 **Fax:** 01457-869360
E-mail: martinw@fluorochem.co.uk
Website: http://www.oceanchemicals.co.uk
Bank(s): HSBC Bank plc
Directors: D. Birch (Co Sec), D. Birch (Fin), M. Woolley (Dir), M. Woolley (MD)
Managers: M. Wooley (Sales Prom Mgr)
Ultimate Holding Company: SYNTHETIC TECHNOLOGIES LTD
Immediate Holding Company: FLUOROCHEM LIMITED
Registration no: 02049362 **VAT No.:** GB 693 4408 13
Date established: 1986 **Turnover:** £5m - £10m **No.of Employees:** 21 - 50
Product Groups: 31, 32

Date of Accounts	Mar 08	Mar 07	Mar 06
Pre Tax Profit/Loss	748	N/A	N/A
Working Capital	2930	3275	2929
Fixed Assets	159	188	183
Current Assets	4632	5108	4384
Current Liabilities	1701	1834	1455
ROCE% (Return on Capital Employed)	24.2		

G D L Air Systems Ltd

Air Diffusion Works Woolley Bridge Road, Hadfield, Glossop, SK13 1AB
Tel: 01457-861538 **Fax:** 01457-866010
E-mail: sales@grille.co.uk
Website: http://www.grille.co.uk
Bank(s): Barclays, Altrincham
Directors: P. Callaghan (Dir), L. Callaghan (Mkt Research)
Managers: S. Jackson (Chief Acct), S. Wilson (Tech Serv Mgr)
Immediate Holding Company: GDL AIR SYSTEMS LIMITED
Registration no: 05075986 **Date established:** 2004 **Turnover:** £2m - £5m
No.of Employees: 21 - 50 **Product Groups:** 35, 40

Date of Accounts	Jun 11	Jun 10	Jun 09
Working Capital	459	483	424
Fixed Assets	245	233	271
Current Assets	2m	1m	1m
Current Liabilities	548	104	N/A

Garie Bevan Coatings

Chunal Works Charlestown, Glossop, SK13 8LF
Tel: 01457-865676 **Fax:** 01457-862323
E-mail: enquiries@gariebevancoatings.co.uk
Website: http://www.gariebevancoatings.co.uk
Directors: G. Bevan (Prop)
Registration no: 03131557 **Date established:** 1995
No.of Employees: 1 - 10 **Product Groups:** 46, 48

High Peak Steels Ltd

Thornfield House Brookfield Industrial Estate Peakdale Road, Glossop, SK13 6LQ
Tel: 01457-866911 **Fax:** 01457-869178
E-mail: sales@highpeaksteels.com
Website: http://www.highpeaksteels.com
Directors: M. Thornley (MD)
Immediate Holding Company: HIGH PEAK STEELS LIMITED
Registration no: 01878509 **VAT No.:** GB 419 5872 19
Date established: 1985 **Turnover:** £2m - £5m **No.of Employees:** 21 - 50
Product Groups: 34, 66

Date of Accounts	Feb 12	Feb 11	Feb 10
Working Capital	552	425	336
Fixed Assets	256	259	287
Current Assets	2m	2m	1m

Kingpak Plastic Sheeting Supplies

Unit 11-12 Waterside Business Park, Hadfield, Glossop, SK13 1BE
Tel: 01457-862521 **Fax:** 01457-862138
E-mail: enquiries@kingpak.co.uk
Website: http://www.kingpak.co.uk
Managers: P. King (Mgr)
Turnover: £1m - £2m **No.of Employees:** 1 - 10 **Product Groups:** 30

Lynton Trailers UK Ltd

Unit 16 Graphite Way Hadfield, Glossop, SK13 1QH
Tel: 0161-223 8211 **Fax:** 0161-223 0933
E-mail: darran.reynolds@lyntontrailers.co.uk
Website: http://www.lyntontrailers.co.uk
Bank(s): National Westminster
Directors: D. Reynolds (MD)
Managers: N. McKay (Buyer), T. Morgan (Sales & Mktg Mg), J. Burney
Ultimate Holding Company: LYNTON SHOWPOINT (UK) LIMITED
Immediate Holding Company: LYNTON TRAILERS (UK) LIMITED
Registration no: 03789362 **VAT No.:** GB 732 7509 32
Date established: 1999 **Turnover:** £5m - £10m **No.of Employees:** 21 - 50
Product Groups: 39, 45

Date of Accounts	Nov 08	Nov 09	Nov 10
Working Capital	-105	-140	-160
Fixed Assets	2m	2m	2m
Current Assets	608	358	464

Metal Fabrication

Unit 13 Waterside Business Park Waterside, Hadfield, Glossop, SK13 1BE
Tel: 01457-862043 **Fax:** 01457-868961
Website: http://www.metalfabs.com
Directors: R. Grahamslaw (Prop)
Immediate Holding Company: METAL FABRICATION (GLOSSOP) LTD
Registration no: 07291627 **Date established:** 2010
No.of Employees: 1 - 10 **Product Groups:** 26, 35

Date of Accounts	Jun 11
Working Capital	3
Fixed Assets	63
Current Assets	107

Pressure Tech Ltd

Unit 24 Graphite Way, Hadfield, Glossop, SK13 1QH
Tel: 01457-899307 **Fax:** 01457-899308
E-mail: info@pressure-tech.com
Website: http://www.pressure-tech.com
Bank(s): Barclays Bank
Directors: S. York-Robinson (MD)
Immediate Holding Company: PRESSURE TECH LIMITED
Registration no: 04088229 **VAT No.:** GB 776 7408 83
Date established: 2000 **Turnover:** Up to £250,000
No.of Employees: 11 - 20 **Product Groups:** 38, 42

Date of Accounts	Oct 11	Oct 10	Oct 09
Working Capital	13	-13	23
Fixed Assets	322	196	187
Current Assets	416	253	222

Prisma Colour Ltd

Hole House Mill Marple Road, Chisworth, Glossop, SK13 5DH
Tel: 01457-856505 **Fax:** 01457-856505
E-mail: sales@prismacolour.com
Website: http://www.prismacolour.com
Directors: M. Wood (Sales)
Managers: S. Furlong (Chief Acct), R. Heap (Purch Mgr)
Immediate Holding Company: PRISMA COLOUR LIMITED
Registration no: 02658661 **VAT No.:** GB 551 0301 02
Date established: 1991 **No.of Employees:** 21 - 50 **Product Groups:** 32, 48

Date of Accounts	Nov 11	Nov 10	Nov 09
Working Capital	763	644	462
Fixed Assets	437	453	426
Current Assets	2m	2m	1m

Springvale E P S Ltd

Dinting Vale Works Dinting Vale Industrial Estate, Glossop, SK13 6LG
Tel: 01457-863211 **Fax:** 01457-869269
E-mail: sales@springvale.com
Website: http://www.springvale.com
Directors: T. France (MD), A. France (MD), S. McGreevy (Fin)
Managers: N. Tebbett
Ultimate Holding Company: CRH PUBLIC LIMITED COMPANY
Immediate Holding Company: SPRINGVALE EPS LIMITED
Registration no: NI001043 **VAT No.:** GB 562 7540 33
Date established: 1936 **No.of Employees:** 21 - 50 **Product Groups:** 30

Date of Accounts	Dec 10	Dec 09	Dec 08
Sales Turnover	17m	14m	16m
Pre Tax Profit/Loss	-1m	289	906
Working Capital	102	8m	7m
Fixed Assets	2m	2m	2m
Current Assets	8m	22m	21m
Current Liabilities	2m	2m	2m

Trace Basement Systems

Unit 7 Graphite Way, Hadfield, Glossop, SK13 1QH
Tel: 01457-865165 **Fax:** 01457-866253
E-mail: enquiries@traceremedial.co.uk
Website: http://www.TRACEBASEMENTSYSTEMS.CO.UK
Directors: G. Hockey (Dir), J. Hockey (Dir), G. Hockey (Prop)
Ultimate Holding Company: LYNTON SHOWPOINT (UK) LIMITED
Immediate Holding Company: LYNTON TRAILERS (UK) LIMITED
Date established: 1999 **No.of Employees:** 1 - 10 **Product Groups:** 40, 52, 66, 67

Date of Accounts	Nov 08	Nov 09	Nov 10
Working Capital	-105	-140	-160
Fixed Assets	2m	2m	2m
Current Assets	608	358	464

Unitrak Powderflight Ltd

Unit 20 Dinting Lane Industrial Estate, Glossop, SK13 7NU
Tel: 01457-865038 **Fax:** 01457-869776
E-mail: info@unitrak.co.uk
Website: http://www.unitrak.co.uk
Directors: D. Snoddon (Fin)
Ultimate Holding Company: UNITRAK CORP LIMITED (USA)
Immediate Holding Company: UNITRAK POWDERFLIGHT LIMITED
Registration no: 01612523 **Date established:** 1982
Turnover: £500,000 - £1m **No.of Employees:** 1 - 10 **Product Groups:** 67

Date of Accounts	Mar 12	Mar 11	Mar 10
Working Capital	198	180	195
Fixed Assets	17	25	36

Current Assets	332	399	280

E G L Vaughan Ltd
Brook Street, Glossop, SK13 8BG
Tel: 01457-866614 **Fax:** 01457-869364
E-mail: admin@eglvaughan.co.uk
Website: http://www.eglvaughan.co.uk
Directors: D. Robertson (MD), C. Robertson (Fin)
Immediate Holding Company: EGL VAUGHAN LIMITED
Registration no: 05352296 **VAT No.:** GB 606 5895 16
Date established: 2005 **Turnover:** £250,000 - £500,000
No.of Employees: 1 - 10 **Product Groups:** 48

Date of Accounts	Feb 12	Feb 11	Feb 10
Working Capital	-10	-0	-1
Fixed Assets	94	84	71
Current Assets	186	224	148

Visilume Ltd
High Street West, Glossop, SK13 8ER
Tel: 01457-865700 **Fax:** 01923-211432
E-mail: sales@visilume.com
Website: http://www.visilume.com
Directors: A. Green (MD), V. Green (Fin)
Immediate Holding Company: VISILUME LIMITED
Registration no: 01607816 **VAT No.:** GB 410 8719 66
Date established: 1982 **Turnover:** £500,000 - £1m
No.of Employees: 1 - 10 **Product Groups:** 33, 37, 38

Date of Accounts	Dec 11	Dec 10	Dec 09
Working Capital	360	179	77
Fixed Assets	6	8	12
Current Assets	502	383	287

Wise Owl Business Solutions Ltd
PO Box 57, Glossop, SK13 7GA
Tel: 01457-858877 **Fax:** 01457-869957
E-mail: sales@wiseowl.co.uk
Website: http://www.wiseowl.co.uk
Directors: A. Brown (Dir)
Immediate Holding Company: WISE OWL BUSINESS SOLUTIONS LIMITED
Registration no: 05110386 **Date established:** 2004
Turnover: Up to £250,000 **No.of Employees:** 1 - 10 **Product Groups:** 44

Date of Accounts	Apr 12	Apr 11	Apr 10
Working Capital	2	1	11
Fixed Assets	64	73	85
Current Assets	116	103	130

Wray Mechanical & Acoustics Ltd
Unit 11 Etherow Industrial Estate Woolley Bridge Road, Hadfield, Glossop, SK13 2NS
Tel: 01457-852540 **Fax:** 01457-860598
E-mail: wray@wraymechanical.com
Directors: J. Wray (Ptnr)
Immediate Holding Company: WRAY MECHANICAL AND ACOUSTICS LIMITED
Registration no: 01666139 **VAT No.:** GB 373 4564 37
Date established: 1982 **Turnover:** £1m - £2m **No.of Employees:** 11 - 20
Product Groups: 37

Date of Accounts	Aug 11	Aug 10	Aug 09
Working Capital	287	227	202
Fixed Assets	137	146	147
Current Assets	802	615	417

Heanor

Bowers Electricals Ltd
Slack Lane, Heanor, DE75 7GX
Tel: 01773-531531 **Fax:** 01773-716171
E-mail: enquiries@bowerselec.co.uk
Website: http://www.bowerselec.co.uk
Bank(s): Royal Bank of Scotland
Directors: M. Bowers (MD)
Managers: R. Radford (Tech Serv Mgr), A. Barnett (Chief Acct)
Immediate Holding Company: BOWERS ELECTRICALS LIMITED
Registration no: 01955004 **VAT No.:** GB 416 3613 71
Date established: 1985 **Turnover:** £5m - £10m
No.of Employees: 51 - 100 **Product Groups:** 37, 48

Date of Accounts	Mar 11	Sep 09	Sep 08
Sales Turnover	9m	8m	N/A
Pre Tax Profit/Loss	-4	154	214
Working Capital	913	1m	1m
Fixed Assets	1m	1m	1m
Current Assets	3m	3m	3m
Current Liabilities	167	664	653

Concept Plastic Packaging
40 Adams Close Heanor Gate Industrial Estate, Heanor, DE75 7SW
Tel: 01773-763321 **Fax:** 01773-763646
E-mail: sales@conceptpp.co.uk
Website: http://www.conceptpp.co.uk
Directors: I. Marlow (MD)
Managers: A. Thomas (Sales Prom Mgr)
Immediate Holding Company: CONCEPT PLASTIC PACKAGING LTD
Registration no: 03491928 **VAT No.:** GB 125 8912 59
Date established: 1998 **Turnover:** £5m - £10m **No.of Employees:** 1 - 10
Product Groups: 39, 46, 48, 84

Date of Accounts	Dec 11	Dec 10	Dec 09
Sales Turnover	9m	7m	N/A
Pre Tax Profit/Loss	156	10	N/A
Working Capital	-2m	-1m	-764
Fixed Assets	3m	2m	1m
Current Assets	2m	2m	1m
Current Liabilities	782	2m	N/A

Eastwood Lighting
Unit 1 Taylor Lane Indl-Est, Loscoe, Heanor, DE75 7TA
Tel: 01773-712978 **Fax:** 01773-713438
Managers: G. Simpson (Mgr)
Immediate Holding Company: WITTO FREIGHT & LOGISTICS LTD
Date established: 2011 **No.of Employees:** 1 - 10 **Product Groups:** 37, 67

Four D Rubber Co. Ltd
Delves Rd Heanor Gate Industrial Estate, Heanor, DE75 7SJ
Tel: 01773-763134 **Fax:** 01773-763136
E-mail: sales@fourdrubber.com
Website: http://www.fourdrubber.com
Bank(s): Co-Op Bank, Birmingham
Directors: B. Ralley (Ch), P. Tonks (MD)
Managers: S. Slinn (Sales Off Mgr), S. Longdon (Prod Mgr)
Registration no: 04197962 **VAT No.:** GB 772 1239 37
Date established: 1965 **Turnover:** £2m - £5m **No.of Employees:** 21 - 50
Product Groups: 24, 29, 38, 49, 66

Date of Accounts	Dec 11	Dec 10	Dec 09
Sales Turnover	4m	N/A	N/A
Pre Tax Profit/Loss	262	N/A	N/A
Working Capital	16	226	154
Fixed Assets	2m	2m	3m
Current Assets	1m	928	949
Current Liabilities	425	N/A	N/A

Harlite Installations Ltd
Midesco House Burns Street, Heanor, DE75 7FY
Tel: 01773-712321 **Fax:** 01773-530513
E-mail: harlite@btconnect.com
Directors: R. Aplin (MD)
Ultimate Holding Company: SYMANHIRE (EAST MIDLANDS) LIMITED
Immediate Holding Company: HARLITE INSTALLATIONS LIMITED
Registration no: 01142326 **VAT No.:** GB 118 4396 60
Date established: 1973 **Turnover:** £1m - £2m **No.of Employees:** 21 - 50
Product Groups: 37

Date of Accounts	Dec 11	Dec 10	Dec 09
Working Capital	121	-379	5m
Fixed Assets	74	767	852
Current Assets	431	1m	5m

M R N Fabrications
Unit 2 Adams Close Heanor Gate Industrial Estate, Heanor, DE75 7SW
Tel: 01773-710411 **Fax:** 01773-710411
Directors: M. Neail (Ptnr)
Date established: 1995 **No.of Employees:** 1 - 10 **Product Groups:** 35

R & F D Castings
Taylor Lane Loscoe, Heanor, DE75 7TA
Tel: 01773-760432 **Fax:** 01773-760432
E-mail: lee.delrosso@btconnect.com
Directors: L. Delrosso (Ptnr)
Immediate Holding Company: R & F D CASTINGS LIMITED
Registration no: 04661862 **Date established:** 2003
No.of Employees: 1 - 10 **Product Groups:** 46

Umeco
Sinclair Close, Heanor, DE75 7SP
Tel: 01773-766200 **Fax:** 01773-530245
E-mail: structural@umeco.com
Website: http://www.advanced-composites.co.uk
Bank(s): Lloyds TSB
Directors: M. Malitskie (Fin), J. Stowell (Mkt Research), J. Mabbitt (MD)
Managers: M. Murney (Tech Serv Mgr), A. Bird (Personnel), D. Smith
Immediate Holding Company: D. B. BROOKS LIMITED
Registration no: 02264869 **VAT No.:** GB 411 1698 77
Date established: 1974 **Turnover:** £20m - £50m
No.of Employees: 101 - 250 **Product Groups:** 30, 31, 32, 33, 42, 48

Date of Accounts	May 11	May 10	May 09
Working Capital	1m	1m	1m
Fixed Assets	133	125	131
Current Assets	3m	3m	3m

High Peak

Arden Control Systems Ltd
Unit 3 Swindells Yard Arden Street, New Mills, High Peak, SK22 4NS
Tel: 01663-746060 **Fax:** 01663-746189
E-mail: ibrown@ardencontrolsystems.co.uk
Website: http://www.ardencontrols.co.uk
Directors: I. Brown (Dir)
Immediate Holding Company: ARDEN CONTROLS & ELECTRICAL LIMITED
Registration no: 01507421 **Date established:** 1980 **Turnover:** £1m - £2m
No.of Employees: 1 - 10 **Product Groups:** 37

Date of Accounts	Sep 11	Sep 10	Sep 09
Working Capital	157	158	99
Fixed Assets	4	6	7
Current Assets	293	323	139

Ascott Clark
42 Western Lane Buxworth, High Peak, SK23 7NS
Tel: 01663-734221 **Fax:** 01663-734318
E-mail: c.clark@ascottclark.com
Website: http://www.ascottclark.com
Directors: C. Clark (MD)
Date established: 1990 **Turnover:** £2m - £5m **No.of Employees:** 21 - 50
Product Groups: 33, 54, 61, 80, 84

C J K Packaging Ltd
Bridgeholme Industrial Estate Bridgeholme, Chinley, High Peak, SK23 6DU
Tel: 01663-750222 **Fax:** 01663-750333
E-mail: sales@cjk.co.uk
Website: http://www.cjk.co.uk
Directors: C. Sizeland (MD)
Immediate Holding Company: CJK PACKAGING LIMITED
Registration no: 04721061 **Date established:** 2003
Turnover: Up to £250,000 **No.of Employees:** 1 - 10 **Product Groups:** 07, 30, 35, 36, 42, 66

Date of Accounts	Apr 11	Apr 10	Apr 09
Working Capital	335	267	249
Fixed Assets	38	50	61
Current Assets	604	639	485

Chronicle Accountants Ltd
1 Market Street Whaley Bridge, High Peak, SK23 7AA
Tel: 01663-734736 **Fax:** 01663-734736
E-mail: enquiries@chronicleaccountants.co.uk
Website: http://www.chronicleaccountants.co.uk
Directors: G. Leathley (MD), C. Leathley (Co Sec)
Immediate Holding Company: CHRONICLE ACCOUNTANTS LTD
Registration no: 04346639 **Date established:** 2002
No.of Employees: 1 - 10 **Product Groups:** 80

Date of Accounts	Dec 11	Dec 09	Dec 08
Working Capital	-6	-0	-1
Fixed Assets	7	1	2
Current Assets	17	17	9

Dilworth & Morris Engineering Ltd
Hyde Bank Road New Mills, High Peak, SK22 4BP
Tel: 01663-746383 **Fax:** 01663-744230
E-mail: dillworth.morris@btconnect.com
Directors: S. Jebb (MD)
Immediate Holding Company: DILWORTH & MORRIS ENGINEERING LIMITED
Registration no: 04261464 **Date established:** 2001
No.of Employees: 1 - 10 **Product Groups:** 46

Date of Accounts	Nov 10	Nov 09	Nov 08
Working Capital	-28	-4	33
Fixed Assets	14	26	38
Current Assets	81	108	171

Dow Hyperlast
Station Road Birch Vale, High Peak, SK22 1BR
Tel: 01663-746518 **Fax:** 01663-746605
E-mail: info@dow.com
Website: http://www.dow.com
Directors: G. Mueller (Tech Serv)
Managers: G. Alderley
Ultimate Holding Company: The Dow Chemical Company
Registration no: 02947247 **VAT No.:** GB 616 3267 48
Turnover: £20m - £50m **No.of Employees:** 1 - 10 **Product Groups:** 30, 31, 32, 37, 39, 85

Dugdill Fabrications
Unit 14 Bingswood Trading Estate, Whaley Bridge, High Peak, SK23 7LY
Tel: 01663-719519 **Fax:** 0871-256 3258
E-mail: john.dugdill@vacflo.com
Website: http://www.vacflo.com
Directors: J. Dugdill (Prop)
Immediate Holding Company: NDB (UK) LIMITED
VAT No.: GB 388 1440 33 **Date established:** 2007
Turnover: Up to £250,000 **No.of Employees:** 1 - 10 **Product Groups:** 46

Federal Mogul Friction Products
Hayfield Road Chapel-E N-Le-Frith, Chapel-En-Le-Frith, High Peak, SK23 0JP
Tel: 01298-811200 **Fax:** 01298-811319
E-mail: santino.lammond@federalmogul.com
Website: http://www.federalmogul.com
Bank(s): National Westminster Bank Plc
Directors: S. Lammond (Dir)
Managers: D. Evans (Sales Prom Mgr), W. Brown, H. Moon (Tech Serv Mgr), S. Lomas (Fin Mgr), S. Milner (Fin Mgr)
Immediate Holding Company: FEDERAL-MOGUL FRICTION PRODUCTS LTD
Registration no: 00851194 **VAT No.:** GB 145 2609 76
Date established: 1897 **Turnover:** £75m - £125m
No.of Employees: 251 - 500 **Product Groups:** 33, 35, 39

Flowguard
Watford Bridge Road New Mills, High Peak, SK22 4HJ
Tel: 01663-745976 **Fax:** 01663-742788
E-mail: swheatley@coorstek.com
Website: http://www.flowguard.com
Bank(s): National Westminster Bank Plc
Directors: J. Cole (Fin)
Managers: A. Hay (Mgr), L. Hill (Buyer)
Ultimate Holding Company: GENERAL ELECTRIC COMPANY (USA)
Immediate Holding Company: HYDRIL PCB LIMITED
Registration no: 01418491 **Date established:** 1979
Turnover: £10m - £20m **No.of Employees:** 21 - 50 **Product Groups:** 36, 40, 84

Date of Accounts	Dec 11	Dec 10	Dec 09
Sales Turnover	18m	15m	22m
Pre Tax Profit/Loss	2m	6m	5m
Working Capital	17m	14m	8m
Fixed Assets	N/A	N/A	260
Current Assets	30m	19m	14m
Current Liabilities	1m	2m	2m

H D Sharman Ltd
High Peak Works Chapel-en-le-Frith, High Peak, SK23 0HW
Tel: 01298-812371 **Fax:** 01298-812237
E-mail: info@hdsharman.co.uk
Website: http://www.hdsharman.co.uk
Directors: L. Hartley (Ptnr), M. Bullen (Sales)
Immediate Holding Company: H.D.SHARMAN LIMITED
Registration no: 00945570 **Date established:** 1969
Turnover: £500,000 - £1m **No.of Employees:** 11 - 20 **Product Groups:** 29

Date of Accounts	Dec 11	Dec 10	Dec 09
Working Capital	2m	2m	1m
Fixed Assets	156	163	171
Current Assets	3m	2m	2m

Induction Heat Treatment Ltd
Station Works Station Road, New Mills, High Peak, SK22 3JB
Tel: 01663-742483 **Fax:** 01663-746223
E-mail: info@inductionheat.co.uk
Website: http://www.inductionheat.co.uk
Directors: A. Barker (MD)
Immediate Holding Company: INDUCTION HEAT TREATMENTS (MANCHESTER) LIMITED
Registration no: 00981276 **VAT No.:** GB 157 1097 63
Date established: 1970 **Turnover:** £500,000 - £1m
No.of Employees: 1 - 10 **Product Groups:** 48

Date of Accounts	Jun 11	Jun 10	Jun 09
Working Capital	-14	-59	10
Fixed Assets	168	175	182
Current Assets	122	99	161

Industrial Clutch Parts Ltd
Unit 11 Bingswood Trading Estate Whaley Bridge, High Peak, SK23 7LY
Tel: 01663-734627 **Fax:** 01663-733023
E-mail: sales@icpltd.co.uk
Website: http://www.icpltd.co.uk
Directors: C. Holmes (MD)
Immediate Holding Company: INDUSTRIAL CLUTCH PARTS LIMITED
Registration no: 02763370 **Date established:** 1992
No.of Employees: 1 - 10 **Product Groups:** 33, 35, 36

Date of Accounts	Dec 11	Dec 10	Dec 09
Working Capital	440	446	329
Fixed Assets	62	90	67
Current Assets	1m	1m	936
Current Liabilities	N/A	15	N/A

R E Knowles Ltd
Buxton Road Furness Vale, High Peak, SK23 7PJ
Tel: 01663-744127 **Fax:** 01663-741562
E-mail: fred@hesmith.co.uk
Directors: F. Smith (Dir)
Immediate Holding Company: R.E. KNOWLES LIMITED
Registration no: 00386921 **VAT No.:** GB 157 1842 56
Date established: 1944 **Turnover:** £250,000 - £500,000
No.of Employees: 1 - 10 **Product Groups:** 14, 17, 33

Date of Accounts	Feb 08	Feb 11	Feb 10
Working Capital	1m	2m	2m
Fixed Assets	501	646	453
Current Assets	2m	2m	2m

Leo Engineering Ltd
Bingswood Industrial Estate Whaley Bridge, High Peak, SK23 7LY
Tel: 01663-735344 **Fax:** 01663-735352
E-mail: info@minibusoptions.co.uk
Website: http://www.minibusoptions.co.uk
Bank(s): National Westminster Bank Plc
Directors: S. Moore (MD)
Managers: D. Moore (Tech Serv Mgr), R. Davis (Chief Acct), F. James (Sales Prom Mgr)
Ultimate Holding Company: MINIBUS OPTIONS LIMITED
Immediate Holding Company: LEO ENGINEERING LIMITED
Registration no: 02454151 **Date established:** 1989 **Turnover:** £1m - £2m
No.of Employees: 21 - 50 **Product Groups:** 39

Date of Accounts	Mar 11	Mar 10	Mar 09
Working Capital	210	196	199
Fixed Assets	214	225	238
Current Assets	655	622	657

Minibus Options Ltd
Unit 1 Bingswood Trading Estate Whaley Bridge, High Peak, SK23 7LY
Tel: 01663-735355 **Fax:** 01663-735352
E-mail: info@minibusoptions.co.uk
Website: http://www.minibusoptions.co.uk
Directors: S. Moore (Dir)
Immediate Holding Company: MINIBUS OPTIONS LIMITED
Registration no: 02080895 **Date established:** 1986 **Turnover:** £1m - £2m
No.of Employees: 11 - 20 **Product Groups:** 39

Date of Accounts	Mar 11	Mar 10	Mar 09
Working Capital	208	97	-8
Fixed Assets	2m	2m	2m
Current Assets	2m	1m	2m

Morgan Ward NDT Ltd
Dale Road New Mills, High Peak, SK22 4NW
Tel: 01663-747061 **Fax:** 01663-746837
E-mail: admin@morganward.co.uk
Website: http://www.morganward.co.uk
Directors: S. Wright (MD)
Managers: B. Wright (Sales & Mktg Mg), K. Buckley (Chief Acct)
Immediate Holding Company: MORGAN-WARD (NON-DESTRUCTIVE TESTING) LIMITED
Registration no: 01127975 **VAT No.:** 158 5369 30 **Date established:** 1973
Turnover: £500,000 - £1m **No.of Employees:** 21 - 50
Product Groups: 34, 38, 54, 85, 86

Date of Accounts	Oct 11	Oct 10	Oct 09
Working Capital	68	59	42
Fixed Assets	341	607	624
Current Assets	442	518	402

Neiman Packaging Ltd
Brunswick Works Albion Road, New Mills, High Peak, SK22 3HB
Tel: 01663-743924 **Fax:** 01663-741078
E-mail: enquiries@neimanpackaging.com
Website: http://www.neimanpackaging.com
Bank(s): Barclays
Directors: I. Walker (Fin), M. Franklin (Fin)
Managers: A. Unsworth (Tech Serv Mgr), P. Steel (Chief Mgr)
Ultimate Holding Company: SWIZZELS MATLOW LIMITED
Immediate Holding Company: NEIMAN PACKAGING LIMITED
Registration no: 01573614 **Date established:** 1981 **Turnover:** £2m - £5m
No.of Employees: 51 - 100 **Product Groups:** 30, 48

Date of Accounts	Dec 11	Dec 10	Dec 09
Sales Turnover	4m	4m	5m
Pre Tax Profit/Loss	27	-108	303
Working Capital	1m	1m	1m
Fixed Assets	522	584	587
Current Assets	2m	2m	2m
Current Liabilities	130	212	197

Peak Translations Ltd
Shepherds Bank Macclesfield Road, Kettleshulme, High Peak, SK23 7QU
Tel: 01663-732074 **Fax:** 01663-735499
E-mail: enquiries@peak-translations.co.uk
Website: http://www.peak-translations.co.uk
Directors: D. Gordon (Fin)
Registration no: 02906009 **VAT No.:** GB 527 5261 45
Date established: 1978 **No.of Employees:** 1 - 10 **Product Groups:** 28, 44, 80

Date of Accounts	Dec 09	Dec 08	Dec 07
Working Capital	131	108	48
Fixed Assets	9	12	14
Current Assets	159	130	82

Rotaflow F V Ltd
Rotec House Bingswood Trading Estate, Whaley Bridge, High Peak, SK23 7LY
Tel: 01663-735003 **Fax:** 01663-735006
E-mail: sales@rotaflow.com
Website: http://www.rotaflow.com
Directors: I. Watt (MD), V. Watt (Fin)
Immediate Holding Company: ROTAFLOW FV LIMITED
Registration no: 01851533 **VAT No.:** GB 373 4375 40
Date established: 1984 **Turnover:** £250,000 - £500,000
No.of Employees: 11 - 20 **Product Groups:** 36, 40, 42

Date of Accounts	Oct 11	Oct 10	Oct 09
Working Capital	992	846	436
Fixed Assets	93	58	46
Current Assets	1m	1m	618

Rotational Mouldings Ltd
Knowles Industrial Estate Furness Vale, High Peak, SK23 7PH
Tel: 01663-742897 **Fax:** 01663-747584
E-mail: sales@rotationalmouldings.co.uk
Website: http://www.rotationalmouldings.co.uk
Bank(s): Barclays, Buxton
Directors: J. Rowbotham (MD)
Immediate Holding Company: ROTATIONAL MOULDINGS LIMITED
Registration no: 01147334 **Date established:** 1973 **Turnover:** £2m - £5m
No.of Employees: 21 - 50 **Product Groups:** 30, 39, 40, 41, 45, 48, 66

Date of Accounts	Nov 10	Nov 09	Nov 08
Working Capital	2m	2m	1m
Fixed Assets	117	195	334
Current Assets	3m	3m	2m

Shannon R. & D. Ltd
Shannon House, Botany Business Park Macclesfield Road, Whaley Bridge, High Peak, SK23 7DQ
Tel: 01663-736260 **Fax:** 01633-719933
E-mail: sales@shannon.co.uk
Website: http://www.shannon.co.uk
Registration no: 00774324 **Turnover:** £2m - £5m
No.of Employees: 1 - 10 **Product Groups:** 23, 30, 35, 36, 39, 40, 45, 66, 68, 85

Date of Accounts	Dec 08	Dec 07	Dec 06
Working Capital	347	281	243
Fixed Assets	68	75	70
Current Assets	566	649	693
Current Liabilities	219	368	450
Total Share Capital	10	10	10

Street Crane Ltd
Townend Works Chapel-En-Le-Frith, High Peak, SK23 0PH
Tel: 01298-812456 **Fax:** 01298-814945
E-mail: admin@streetcrane.co.uk
Website: http://www.streetcrane.co.uk
Bank(s): Royal Bank of Scotland, Bakewell
Directors: C. Lindley-smith (Sales), G. Zona (Sales), I. Jackson (Fin)
Managers: K. Stainer, S. Hale (Personnel), T. Partridge (Tech Serv Mgr)
Ultimate Holding Company: STREASON LIMITED
Immediate Holding Company: STREASON LIMITED
Registration no: 00733435 **Date established:** 1962
Turnover: £20m - £50m **No.of Employees:** 101 - 250
Product Groups: 35, 39, 41, 45, 52, 67

Date of Accounts	Mar 11	Mar 10	Mar 09
Sales Turnover	21m	15m	N/A
Pre Tax Profit/Loss	666	659	N/A
Working Capital	4m	3m	600
Fixed Assets	2m	2m	270
Current Assets	10m	7m	603
Current Liabilities	2m	2m	1

Swizzels Matlow Ltd
Carlton House Albion Road, New Mills, High Peak, SK22 3HA
Tel: 01663-744144 **Fax:** 01663-742800
E-mail: info@swizzels-matlow.com
Website: http://www.swizzels-matlow.com
Bank(s): Barclays
Directors: B. Dee (Purch), I. Walker (Co Sec), M. Walker (Sales), N. Matlow (Pers)
Managers: A. Unsworth, S. Heslop (Mktg Serv Mgr)
Immediate Holding Company: SWIZZELS MATLOW LIMITED
Registration no: 00562269 **VAT No.:** GB 158 0100 02
Date established: 1956 **Turnover:** £20m - £50m
No.of Employees: 501 - 1000 **Product Groups:** 20

Date of Accounts	Dec 11	Dec 10	Dec 09
Sales Turnover	50m	48m	47m
Pre Tax Profit/Loss	5m	3m	2m
Working Capital	17m	16m	13m
Fixed Assets	13m	13m	14m
Current Assets	26m	24m	20m
Current Liabilities	5m	5m	4m

T W Marine Ltd
The Marina Station Road, Furness Vale, High Peak, SK23 7QA
Tel: 01663-745757 **Fax:** 01663-741891
E-mail: info@twmarine.co.uk
Website: http://www.twmarine.co.uk
Directors: P. Webb (Fin), S. Webb (MD)
Immediate Holding Company: T. W. MARINE LIMITED
Registration no: 01600970 **Date established:** 1981
No.of Employees: 1 - 10 **Product Groups:** 35, 36, 39

Date of Accounts	Nov 10	Nov 09	Nov 08
Working Capital	80	79	72
Fixed Assets	2	2	2
Current Assets	134	133	125

Hope Valley

Ballington Brothers Ltd
Glenmoor Maynard Road, Grindleford, Hope Valley, S32 2JD
Tel: 01433-630581 **Fax:** 01433-630581
Directors: M. Ballington (MD)
Immediate Holding Company: BALLINGTON BROTHERS LIMITED
Registration no: 01412036 **Date established:** 1979
No.of Employees: 1 - 10 **Product Groups:** 33, 34, 36, 49, 61, 65, 66

Date of Accounts	Mar 11	Mar 10	Mar 07
Working Capital	N/A	N/A	1
Current Assets	3	3	4

Buxo Plas
Quarters Farm Hazle Badge, Bradwell, Hope Valley, S33 9HX
Tel: 01433-620175 **Fax:** 01433-620047
E-mail: sales@buxoplas.co.uk
Website: http://www.buxoplas.co.uk
Directors: J. Mycock (Ptnr)
VAT No.: GB 286 0670 41 **Turnover:** £250,000 - £500,000
No.of Employees: 21 - 50 **Product Groups:** 30

Corbolite Ltd
Parsons Lane Hope, Hope Valley, S33 6RB
Tel: 01433-620011 **Fax:** 01433-621193
E-mail: info@carbolite.com
Website: http://www.carbolite.com
Directors: J. Bailey (MD)
Managers: W. Hope (Purch Mgr), S. Chapman (Mktg Serv Mgr), A. Bear (Fin Mgr), A. Ramsdale (Personnel), A. Ramsdale (Personnel), P. Haigh (I.T. Exec), M. Baggaley (Tech Serv Mgr), D. Turner (Sales Prom Mgr), A. Beare (Fin Mgr), A. Street (Mktg Serv Mgr), B. Thompson (Chief Mgr)
Ultimate Holding Company: NOVA BOXER LP (GUERNSEY)
Immediate Holding Company: CARBOLITE LIMITED
Registration no: 01371507 **Date established:** 1978
No.of Employees: 101 - 250 **Product Groups:** 38, 40, 42, 44, 45, 46, 47, 48

Date of Accounts	Sep 11	Sep 10	Sep 09
Sales Turnover	13m	11m	11m
Pre Tax Profit/Loss	2m	2m	2m
Working Capital	3m	2m	541
Fixed Assets	4m	4m	4m
Current Assets	9m	7m	5m
Current Liabilities	3m	2m	2m

Craft Supplies Ltd
Newburgh Works Netherside, Bradwell, Hope Valley, S33 9JL
Tel: 01433-622550 **Fax:** 01433-622552
E-mail: sales@craft-supplies.co.uk
Website: http://www.craft-supplies.co.uk
Bank(s): National Westminster
Directors: N. Davison (MD)
Immediate Holding Company: CRAFT SUPPLIES LIMITED
Registration no: 01582293 **VAT No.:** GB 373 3388 36
Date established: 1981 **No.of Employees:** 11 - 20 **Product Groups:** 36, 66

Date of Accounts	Apr 11	Apr 10	Apr 09
Working Capital	44	73	-947
Fixed Assets	36	45	49
Current Assets	306	365	362

Derbyshire Dales Engineering
Cavendish Mill Farnsley Lane, Stoney Middleton, Hope Valley, S32 4TH
Tel: 01433-639374
E-mail: email@cavendishengineering.com
Website: http://www.derbyshiredalesengineering.co.uk
Directors: B. Wright (Fin)
Immediate Holding Company: DERBYSHIRE DALES ENGINEERING LIMITED
Registration no: 05609079 **Date established:** 2005
No.of Employees: 1 - 10 **Product Groups:** 35, 52

Date of Accounts	Jan 11	Jan 09	Jan 08
Working Capital	7	7	7
Current Assets	7	7	11

Lenton Thermal Designs Ltd
PO Box 2031, Hope Valley, S33 6BW
Tel: 01433-621515 **Fax:** 01433-623600
E-mail: sales@lentonfurnaces.com
Website: http://www.lentonfurnaces.com
Bank(s): HSBC Bank plc
Directors: M. Leadbetter (MD)
Managers: A. Beare (Accounts), B. Baxter (Comptroller), B. Thomson (Chief Mgr), D. Evans (Comm), P. Birbhmore (Sales Prom Mgr), P. Birchmore (Sales Prom Mgr), R. Turner (Admin Off), W. Hope (Buyer)
Immediate Holding Company: LENTON THERMAL DESIGNS LIMITED
Registration no: 01263305 **Date established:** 1976 **Turnover:** £1m - £2m
No.of Employees: 101 - 250 **Product Groups:** 40, 42, 46

Date of Accounts	Sep 05	Sep 04	Sep 03
Working Capital	93	93	93
Current Assets	93	93	93

Lindley Educational Trust
Hollowford Centre Castleton, Hope Valley, S33 8WB
Tel: 01433-620377 **Fax:** 01433-621717
E-mail: enquiries@hollowford.org
Website: http://www.lindleyeducationaltrust.org
Bank(s): Barclays
Managers: V. Card (Fin Mgr), M. Williams
Immediate Holding Company: LINDLEY EDUCATIONAL TRUST LIMITED
Registration no: 00867065 **VAT No.:** GB 114 6086 89
Date established: 1965 **Turnover:** £1m - £2m **No.of Employees:** 11 - 20
Product Groups: 87, 89

Date of Accounts	Mar 12	Mar 11	Mar 10
Sales Turnover	1m	1m	1m
Pre Tax Profit/Loss	55	28	18
Working Capital	416	333	298
Fixed Assets	801	828	885
Current Assets	712	600	608
Current Liabilities	271	242	283

Nashmead Structural Engineers Ltd
The Old Manse Back Lane, Hathersage, Hope Valley, S32 1AR
Tel: 01433-650979 **Fax:** 01433-651820
E-mail: keith@nashmead.co.uk
Website: http://www.nashmead.co.uk
Directors: K. Groom (MD)
Immediate Holding Company: NASHMEAD LIMITED
Registration no: 06791117 **Date established:** 2009
No.of Employees: 1 - 10 **Product Groups:** 35

Date of Accounts	Mar 11	Mar 10
Working Capital	60	26
Fixed Assets	18	24
Current Assets	113	65

Newburgh Engineering Co. Ltd
Newburgh Works Bradwell, Hope Valley, S33 9NT
Tel: 01709-724260 **Fax:** 01433-620771
E-mail: sales@newburgh.co.uk
Website: http://www.newburgh.co.uk
Bank(s): National Westminster Bank Plc
Directors: A. Cutts (Co Sec), D. Greenan (Chief Op Offcr), P. Middleton (Pres)
Managers: M. Jewitt (Sales & Mktg Mg)
Immediate Holding Company: Newburgh Holdings Ltd
Registration no: 00371040 **Date established:** 1938
Turnover: £10m - £20m **No.of Employees:** 21 - 50 **Product Groups:** 34, 35, 36, 37, 39, 40, 41, 42, 45, 46, 48

The Needham Group (Inkjet Division)
Unit 11 Brough Busines Park Brough, Bradwell, Hope Valley, S33 9HG
Tel: 01433-621361 **Fax:** 01433-623354
E-mail: info@needham-group.com
Website: http://www.rnsl.co.uk
Managers: P. Buckley (Tech Sales Mgr)
Ultimate Holding Company: CHARTAN HOLDINGS LIMITED
Immediate Holding Company: CHARTAN PRODUCTS LIMITED
Date established: 1981 **No.of Employees:** 1 - 10 **Product Groups:** 28, 32, 44, 46, 80

Date of Accounts	Sep 11	Sep 10	Sep 09
Working Capital	608	522	535
Fixed Assets	20	29	40
Current Assets	843	756	706

Wearnes Cambion Ltd
Mill Bridge Castleton, Hope Valley, S33 8WR
Tel: 01433-621555 **Fax:** 01433-621290
E-mail: sales@cambion.com
Website: http://www.cambion.com
Bank(s): National Westminster Bank Plc
Directors: W. Rowland (Fin), M. Stoneman (MD)
Managers: J. Bowers (Personnel)
Ultimate Holding Company: WBL CORPORATION LIMITED (SINGAPORE)
Immediate Holding Company: WEARNES CAMBION LIMITED
Registration no: 00703283 **VAT No.:** GB 157 2418 64
Date established: 1961 **Turnover:** £2m - £5m **No.of Employees:** 51 - 100
Product Groups: 35, 37

Date of Accounts	Sep 11	Sep 10	Sep 09
Sales Turnover	4m	4m	4m
Pre Tax Profit/Loss	242	383	776
Working Capital	2m	2m	2m
Fixed Assets	716	725	714
Current Assets	3m	3m	3m
Current Liabilities	250	314	319

Ilkeston

Amcor Flexibles UK Ltd
Digby Street, Ilkeston, DE7 5TS
Tel: 0115-932 4391 **Fax:** 0115-932 7506
E-mail: paul.rodger@amcor.com
Website: http://www.amcor.com
Bank(s): Clydesdale
Directors: D. Seel (Sales & Mktg)
Managers: M. Lee, D. Newman (Fin Mgr), P. Rodger (Chief Mgr), C. Ackernley (Purch Mgr), A. Gwilliam (Personnel)
Ultimate Holding Company: AMCOR LTD (AUSTRALIA)
Immediate Holding Company: AMCOR FLEXIBLES UK LIMITED
Registration no: 02808801 **VAT No.:** 268 6302 42 **Date established:** 1993
No.of Employees: 101 - 250 **Product Groups:** 25, 27, 30

Date of Accounts	Jun 11	Jun 10	Jun 09
Sales Turnover	119m	124m	138m
Pre Tax Profit/Loss	16m	2m	285
Working Capital	16m	6m	10m
Fixed Assets	52m	60m	58m
Current Assets	102m	82m	86m
Current Liabilities	7m	8m	8m

J B Armstrong & Co. Ltd
Middleton Street, Ilkeston, DE7 5TT
Tel: 0115-932 4913 **Fax:** 0115-930 0083
E-mail: jacqueline@armstrongsmill.co.uk
Directors: J. Dodsley (Co Sec), K. Armstrong (MD), O. Armstrong (Dir)
Immediate Holding Company: J.B. ARMSTRONG & CO. LIMITED
Registration no: 00657414 **Date established:** 1960 **Turnover:** £2m - £5m
No.of Employees: 1 - 10 **Product Groups:** 24

Date of Accounts	Jan 08
Sales Turnover	6823
Pre Tax Profit/Loss	117
Working Capital	600
Fixed Assets	1519
Current Assets	3137
Current Liabilities	2537
Total Share Capital	3
ROCE% (Return on Capital Employed)	5.5

B J Supplies Ltd
10 Merlin Way Quarry Hill Industrial Estate, Ilkeston, DE7 4RA
Tel: 0115-932 9902 **Fax:** 0115-944 1945
E-mail: enquiries@bjsupplies.co.uk
Website: http://www.bjsupplies.co.uk
Directors: B. Smith (MD)
Immediate Holding Company: W.R.EVANS(CHEMIST)LIMITED
Registration no: 05593221 **VAT No.:** GB 706 3263 55
Date established: 1960 **Turnover:** £50m - £75m **No.of Employees:** 1 - 10
Product Groups: 61

Date of Accounts	Jul 11	Jul 10	Jul 09
Sales Turnover	76m	76m	74m
Pre Tax Profit/Loss	3m	3m	4m
Working Capital	1m	1m	726
Fixed Assets	58m	58m	57m
Current Assets	19m	15m	15m
Current Liabilities	648	1m	1m

Bardini Plastics
Unit 4 Ellesmere Manners Industrial Estate, Ilkeston, DE7 8EF
Tel: 0115-944 2733 **Fax:** 0115-944 2723
E-mail: t-hubbard@bardini.freeuk.com
Website: http://www.bardini.freeuk.com
Directors: J. Hubbard (Ptnr), T. Hubbard (Ptnr)
Registration no: 03064075 **VAT No.:** GB 580 8381 20
Date established: 1995 **No.of Employees:** 1 - 10 **Product Groups:** 30

Bath Flair
31 Wood Lane Horsley Woodhouse, Ilkeston, DE7 6BN
Tel: 01332-882017
E-mail: bathflair@msn.com
Website: http://www.bathflair.com
Directors: G. Glover (Prop)
Date established: 2005 **No.of Employees:** 1 - 10 **Product Groups:** 46, 48

Brundlefly Spraying
Buxton Court Manners Avenue, Manners Industrial Estate, Ilkeston, DE7 8EF
Tel: 0115-930 9328 **Fax:** 0115-930 9328
Directors: J. Gregory (Prop)
Ultimate Holding Company: SKYMARK PACKAGING INTERNATIONAL LIMITED
Immediate Holding Company: SKYMARK PERFORMANCE FILMS LIMITED
Registration no: 01450486 **Date established:** 1993
No.of Employees: 1 - 10 **Product Groups:** 46, 48

Date of Accounts	Dec 11	Dec 10	Dec 09
Sales Turnover	34m	34m	25m
Pre Tax Profit/Loss	841	3m	6m
Working Capital	7m	7m	9m
Fixed Assets	16m	17m	14m
Current Assets	12m	14m	18m
Current Liabilities	1m	976	2m

Cluny Lace Company Ltd
Belper Street Works, Ilkeston, DE7 5FJ
Tel: 0115-932 5031 **Fax:** 0115-944 0590
E-mail: sales@clunylace.co.uk
Website: http://www.clunylace.co.uk
Directors: C. Mason (Dir)
Managers: K. Knight (Sales Prom Mgr), K. Hendrix (Fin Mgr)
Immediate Holding Company: CLUNY LACE COMPANY LIMITED
Registration no: 01235472 **Date established:** 1975
Turnover: £500,000 - £1m **No.of Employees:** 21 - 50 **Product Groups:** 23

Date of Accounts	Mar 12	Mar 11	Mar 10
Working Capital	339	335	274
Fixed Assets	269	276	302
Current Assets	452	459	450

County Lifts
Merlin Way Quarry Hill Industrial Estate, Ilkeston, DE7 4RA
Tel: 0115-944 5095 **Fax:** 0115-944 1674
Directors: C. Taylor (Fin), K. Taylor (MD)
Immediate Holding Company: COUNTY LIFTS LIMITED
Registration no: 04514126 **Date established:** 2002
Turnover: £50m - £75m **No.of Employees:** 1 - 10 **Product Groups:** 35, 39, 45

Date of Accounts	Aug 11	Aug 10	Aug 09
Working Capital	3	7	6
Fixed Assets	19	15	17
Current Assets	19	25	39
Current Liabilities	N/A	N/A	31

Custompak Ltd
Denmark House Furnace Road, Ilkeston, DE7 5EP
Tel: 0115-930 1578 **Fax:** 0115-930 9659
E-mail: sales@custompak.co.uk
Website: http://www.custompak.co.uk
Directors: J. Baldwin (MD)
Immediate Holding Company: CUSTOMPAK LTD
Registration no: 04658357 **Date established:** 2003
No.of Employees: 11 - 20 **Product Groups:** 27, 30, 44

Date of Accounts	Mar 11	Mar 10	Mar 09
Working Capital	-63	-16	-72
Fixed Assets	252	170	157
Current Assets	606	551	585

Dewbar Fabrications
4 Eagle Road Quarry Hill Industrial Estate, Ilkeston, DE7 4RB
Tel: 0115-944 4275 **Fax:** 0115-944 4297
E-mail: psp.fabrications@virgin.net
Directors: P. Barber (Dir)
Date established: 1994 **No.of Employees:** 1 - 10 **Product Groups:** 26, 35

James Dring Power Plant Ltd
8 Eagle Road Quarry Hill Industrial Estate, Ilkeston, DE7 4RB
Tel: 0115-944 0072 **Fax:** 0115-944 0235
E-mail: enquiries@jamesdring.co.uk
Website: http://www.jamesdring.co.uk
Directors: J. Martindale (Fin), S. Martindale (MD)
Immediate Holding Company: JAMES DRING POWER PLANT LIMITED
Registration no: 01157422 **Date established:** 1974 **Turnover:** £2m - £5m
No.of Employees: 11 - 20 **Product Groups:** 35, 37

Date of Accounts	Feb 11	Feb 10	Feb 09
Working Capital	22	-35	-56
Fixed Assets	112	114	120
Current Assets	2m	481	859

F H Brundle
Condor Road Quarry Hill Industrial Estate, Ilkeston, DE7 4RE
Tel: 0115-930 2070 **Fax:** 0115-951 2455
E-mail: sales@brundle.com
Website: http://www.fhbrundle.co.uk
Managers: C. Taylor (Transport)
Ultimate Holding Company: F.H. Brundle (London)
Immediate Holding Company: F H BRUNDLE
Registration no: 07168270 **Date established:** 2010 **Turnover:** £5m - £10m
No.of Employees: 21 - 50 **Product Groups:** 30, 32, 34, 35, 36, 39, 46, 49, 66, 67

Flagpole Express
Unit 1 Heron Court Merlin Way, Quarry Hill Industrial Estate, Ilkeston, DE7 4RA
Tel: 0115-944 2255 **Fax:** 0115-944 2255
E-mail: sales@flagpoleexpress.co.uk
Website: http://www.flagpoleexpress.co.uk
Managers: S. Bou (Mgr)
Immediate Holding Company: FLAGPOLE EXPRESS LIMITED
Registration no: 06006635 **Date established:** 2006
No.of Employees: 1 - 10 **Product Groups:** 23, 24, 28, 49

Date of Accounts	Dec 11	Dec 10	Dec 09
Working Capital	74	33	30
Fixed Assets	70	66	77
Current Assets	203	102	80

Gardner Group
Cotmanhay Road, Ilkeston, DE7 8LL
Tel: 0115-944 5913 **Fax:** 0115-989 8801
E-mail: ilkeston@gardner-aerospace.com
Website: http://www.gardner-aerospace.com
Bank(s): The Royal Bank of Scotland
Directors: C. Morris (Dir)
Ultimate Holding Company: BECAP VIVAT LIMITED
Immediate Holding Company: GARDNER GROUP LIMITED
Registration no: 04672639 **Date established:** 2003
Turnover: £50m - £75m **No.of Employees:** 101 - 250
Product Groups: 33, 34, 36, 39

Date of Accounts	Aug 11	Aug 10	Aug 09
Sales Turnover	55m	53m	60m
Pre Tax Profit/Loss	-9m	-4m	-2m
Working Capital	11m	10m	8m
Fixed Assets	21m	13m	12m
Current Assets	26m	21m	18m
Current Liabilities	5m	5m	3m

Gladex Ltd
Unit 2 Elizabeth Court Manners Avenue, Manners Industrial Estate, Ilkeston, DE7 8EF
Tel: 0115-944 5511 **Fax:** 0115-944 5050
E-mail: colin.lamb@gladex.co.uk
Website: http://www.gladex.co.uk
Managers: C. Lamb (Mgr)
Immediate Holding Company: GLADEX LIMITED
Registration no: 01787426 **Date established:** 1984
Turnover: £250,000 - £500,000 **No.of Employees:** 1 - 10
Product Groups: 26, 30, 40, 45

Date of Accounts	May 11	May 10	May 09
Working Capital	-2	-1	52
Fixed Assets	51	64	65
Current Assets	22	38	101

Intern Transport Systems UK Ltd
421 Nottingham Road, Ilkeston, DE7 5BP
Tel: 0115-930 7724 **Fax:** 0115-930 1742
E-mail: gjones@itsuk.org.uk
Website: http://www.itsuk.org.uk
Directors: G. Jones (Dir), J. Jones (Fin)
Managers: J. Peel (I.T. Exec), R. Jones (Chief Mgr)
Immediate Holding Company: ITS-INTERN TRANSPORT SYSTEM (U.K.) LTD
Registration no: 01657415 **Date established:** 1982 **Turnover:** £2m - £5m
No.of Employees: 1 - 10 **Product Groups:** 45

International Spray Jets Ltd
Furnace Road, Ilkeston, DE7 5EP
Tel: 0115-944 4069
Website: http://www.internationalspray-jets.com
Managers: J. Houghton (Comm)
Immediate Holding Company: International Spray-Jets Ltd
Registration no: 05818182 **Date established:** 2006
No.of Employees: 1 - 10 **Product Groups:** 30, 33, 45

J Reeves Industrial Sewing Ltd
Unit G Soloman Road, Cossall Industrial Estate, Ilkeston, DE7 5UA
Tel: 0115-944 3232 **Fax:** 0115-944 3234
E-mail: martin@jreevessewing.fsnet.co.uk
Directors: J. Reeves (Prop)
Immediate Holding Company: J. REEVES SEWING LIMITED
Registration no: 01998390 **Date established:** 1986
No.of Employees: 1 - 10 **Product Groups:** 43

Date of Accounts	Sep 11	Sep 10	Sep 09
Sales Turnover	N/A	N/A	161
Pre Tax Profit/Loss	N/A	N/A	117
Working Capital	2m	2m	2m
Fixed Assets	960	968	897
Current Assets	2m	2m	2m
Current Liabilities	N/A	N/A	32

J W Engineering Ltd
Barker Gate, Ilkeston, DE7 8DS
Tel: 0115-877 0444 **Fax:** 0115-877 0791
E-mail: jrankers@declegg.co.uk
Website: http://www.espgroup.co.uk
Bank(s): Barclays
Directors: A. Grant (Comm), J. Ankers (Co Sec)
Managers: A. Filipowicz (Prod Mgr)
Ultimate Holding Company: CLEGG HOLDINGS LIMITED
Immediate Holding Company: J.W.ENGINEERING LIMITED
Registration no: 00978885 **VAT No.:** GB 116 6535 74
Date established: 1970 **Turnover:** £2m - £5m **No.of Employees:** 11 - 20
Product Groups: 34, 35

Date of Accounts	Dec 11	Dec 10	Dec 09
Sales Turnover	2m	2m	5m
Pre Tax Profit/Loss	-370	-409	-47
Working Capital	25	292	576
Fixed Assets	127	150	177
Current Assets	823	1m	2m
Current Liabilities	58	823	122

Jpen John Patrick Engineering Ltd
Merlin Way Quarry Hill Industrial Park, Quarry Hill Industrial Estate, Ilkeston, DE7 4RA
Tel: 0115-944 0360 **Fax:** 0115-944 0373
E-mail: info@jpen.co.uk
Website: http://www.jpen.co.uk
Bank(s): National Westminster Bank Plc
Directors: J. Patrick (MD)
Managers: A. Fox (Comm), G. Webber (Contracts Mgr)
Immediate Holding Company: JOHN PATRICK ENGINEERING LIMITED
Registration no: 01629576 **VAT No.:** GB 385 2021 66
Date established: 1982 **Turnover:** £1m - £2m **No.of Employees:** 11 - 20
Product Groups: 35, 36

Date of Accounts	Dec 10	Dec 09	Dec 08
Working Capital	-3	178	-23
Fixed Assets	42	52	48
Current Assets	536	655	637

K P P Converters Ltd
Units 1-4 Manners Industrial Estate Manners Industrial Estate, Ilkeston, DE7 8EF
Tel: 0115-930 5777 **Fax:** 0115-932 9184
E-mail: enquiries@kpptissue.co.uk
Website: http://www.kpptissue.co.uk
Bank(s): National Westminster Bank Plc
Directors: D. Vaughan (Dir), C. Arnold (MD)
Ultimate Holding Company: INTERTRADE CORPORATE SERVICES LIMITED
Immediate Holding Company: K.P.P. CONVERTERS LIMITED
Registration no: 02978262 **VAT No.:** GB 648 6745 87
Date established: 1994 **Turnover:** £2m - £5m **No.of Employees:** 11 - 20
Product Groups: 27

Date of Accounts	Dec 11	Dec 10	Dec 09
Working Capital	717	670	649
Fixed Assets	211	300	354
Current Assets	1m	1m	1m

M B Welding
Unit7-8 Enterprise Court Manners Avenue, Manners Industrial Estate, Ilkeston, DE7 8EF
Tel: 0115-944 4575 **Fax:** 0115-944 4673
E-mail: john.wilkinson@uktool.co.uk
Website: http://www.uktool.co.uk
Directors: J. Wilkinson (MD)
Ultimate Holding Company: SKYMARK PACKAGING INTERNATIONAL LIMITED
Immediate Holding Company: IBC LINERS LIMITED
Registration no: 02120023 **Date established:** 1992 **Turnover:** £1m - £2m
No.of Employees: 1 - 10 **Product Groups:** 46

Date of Accounts	Dec 11	Dec 10	Dec 09
Sales Turnover	34m	34m	25m
Pre Tax Profit/Loss	841	3m	6m

see next page

M B Welding - Cont'd

Working Capital	7m	7m	9m
Fixed Assets	16m	17m	14m
Current Assets	12m	14m	18m
Current Liabilities	1m	976	2m

M L Automotive Ltd

Merlin Way Quarry Hill Industrial Estate, Ilkeston, DE7 4RA
Tel: 0115-944 2009 **Fax:** 0115-944 1910
E-mail: sales@mlafilters.co.uk
Website: http://www.mlautomotive.co.uk
Directors: M. Mitchell (MD)
Immediate Holding Company: M.L. AUTOMOTIVE LIMITED
Registration no: 05333155 **Date established:** 2005
Turnover: £500,000 - £1m **No.of Employees:** 1 - 10 **Product Groups:** 38, 42

Date of Accounts	Jan 12	Jan 11	Jan 10
Working Capital	155	148	148
Fixed Assets	42	57	52
Current Assets	249	212	196

Marriott Breadsall Priory Hotel & Golf & Country Club

Moor Road Morley, Ilkeston, DE7 6DL
Tel: 01332-832235 **Fax:** 01332-833509
E-mail: nick.dumbell@marriotthotel.com
Website: http://www.marriott.co.uk
Managers: B. Sales (Tech Serv Mgr), L. Williams (Personnel), N. Dumbell (Chief Mgr), G. Jones (Fin Mgr), K. Lee (Buyer), N. Lathwell (Sales & Mktg Mg), L. Whitaker
Immediate Holding Company: WHITBREAD HOTEL CO.
Registration no: 00029423 **VAT No.:** GB 243 2928 64
Turnover: £5m - £10m **No.of Employees:** 101 - 250 **Product Groups:** 69

Metool Products Ltd

Mercian Close, Ilkeston, DE7 8HG
Tel: 0115-922 5931 **Fax:** 0115-922 4578
E-mail: postmaster@metool.com
Website: http://www.kabelschlepp.co.uk
Bank(s): Barclays
Directors: M. Blunden (Co Sec), O. Huebner (Dir)
Ultimate Holding Company: TSUBAKIMOTO CHAIN CO. (JAPAN)
Immediate Holding Company: METOOL PRODUCTS LIMITED
Registration no: 00368091 **VAT No.:** GB 116 6915 64
Date established: 1941 **Turnover:** £5m - £10m **No.of Employees:** 11 - 20
Product Groups: 30, 35, 36, 37, 40, 45, 46

Date of Accounts	Dec 11	Dec 10	Dec 09
Working Capital	104	196	258
Fixed Assets	39	40	63
Current Assets	1m	1m	2m

Metreel Ltd

Cossall Industrial Estate, Ilkeston, DE7 5UA
Tel: 0115-932 7010 **Fax:** 0115-930 6263
E-mail: admin@metreel.co.uk
Website: http://www.metreel.co.uk
Bank(s): Lloyds TSB Bank plc
Directors: D. Tacey (Fin), S. Cullingworth (MD)
Managers: D. Leverton (Purch Mgr)
Ultimate Holding Company: CARIOCA ASSETS LIMITED
Immediate Holding Company: METREEL LIMITED
Registration no: 00949482 **VAT No.:** GB 116 9685 40
Date established: 1969 **Turnover:** £2m - £5m **No.of Employees:** 21 - 50
Product Groups: 35, 36, 45, 67

Date of Accounts	Mar 12	Mar 11	Mar 10
Sales Turnover	6m	N/A	N/A
Pre Tax Profit/Loss	776	N/A	N/A
Working Capital	1m	752	842
Fixed Assets	1m	907	1m
Current Assets	3m	3m	3m
Current Liabilities	666	N/A	N/A

Norton Plastics

The Old Gasworks Belfield Street, Ilkeston, DE7 8DU
Tel: 0115-944 1245 **Fax:** 0115-932 8975
E-mail: norton.plastics@vigin.net
Bank(s): Midland
Directors: R. Squires (MD), A. Robinson (Dir)
Managers: G. McIntyre (Works Gen Mgr), S. Moore (Chief Mgr)
Immediate Holding Company: SAFE ACCESS SCAFFOLDING (MIDLANDS) LIMITED
Registration no: 01328175 **VAT No.:** 116 9208 74 **Date established:** 2000
Turnover: £1m - £2m **No.of Employees:** 11 - 20 **Product Groups:** 30

Date of Accounts	Oct 11	Oct 10	Oct 09
Working Capital	114	78	33
Fixed Assets	61	58	67
Current Assets	199	201	98

Peveril Machinery Supply Co.

Merlin Way Quarry Hill Industrial Estate, Ilkeston, DE7 4RA
Tel: 0115-930 9068 **Fax:** 0115-932 7460
Directors: P. Sawell (Ptnr), T. Bradford (Prop)
Immediate Holding Company: INTERGRAND UK LIMITED
Registration no: 04119805 **Date established:** 2008
No.of Employees: 1 - 10 **Product Groups:** 35, 42, 45

Premier Ribbon Ltd

Manners Avenue Manners Industrial Estate, Ilkeston, DE7 8EF
Tel: 0115-930 8699 **Fax:** 0115-930 4555
E-mail: chris@fashionribbon.co.uk
Website: http://www.fashionribbonww.co.uk
Directors: C. Rosenzweig (Dir), P. Butler (Co Sec)
Immediate Holding Company: FASHION RIBBON LIMITED
Registration no: 00943118 **Date established:** 1968 **Turnover:** £2m - £5m
No.of Employees: 1 - 10 **Product Groups:** 23

Date of Accounts	Dec 11	Dec 10	Dec 09
Working Capital	-40	-50	-44
Fixed Assets	121	125	129
Current Assets	14	6	213

Safety Signs & Notices

Unit C & D Digby Street, Ilkeston, DE7 5TG
Tel: 0115-727 0172 **Fax:** 0115-727 0173
E-mail: info@safetysignsandnotices.co.uk
Website: http://www.safetysignsandnotices.co.uk
Directors: S. Froggatt (Snr Part)
Immediate Holding Company: A & D PLASTICS RECYCLING LIMITED
VAT No.: GB 945 1205 41 **Date established:** 2000
No.of Employees: 1 - 10 **Product Groups:** 30, 37, 39, 40, 45, 49, 68, 84

Date of Accounts	May 11	May 10	May 09
Working Capital	156	193	169
Fixed Assets	83	69	84
Current Assets	259	281	301

Saint Gobain P A M UK

PO Box 9, Ilkeston, DE7 4QU
Tel: 0115-930 5000 **Fax:** 0115-932 9513
E-mail: paul.minchin@saint-gobain-pam.co.uk
Website: http://www.saint-gobain-pam.co.uk
Bank(s): HSBC, Darlaston
Directors: R. Wall (Fin), P. Minchin (MD), S. Wallbanks (Pers)
Managers: V. Meldrom
Ultimate Holding Company: COMPAGNIE DE SAINT GOBAIN (FRANCE)
Immediate Holding Company: SAINT-GOBAIN PAM UK LIMITED
Registration no: 00056433 **VAT No.:** GB 416 3969 32
Date established: 1998 **Turnover:** £50m - £75m
No.of Employees: 51 - 100 **Product Groups:** 34, 35

Date of Accounts	Dec 11	Dec 10	Dec 09
Sales Turnover	76m	70m	88m
Pre Tax Profit/Loss	20m	-83	5m
Working Capital	-21m	-21m	-9m
Fixed Assets	71m	70m	63m
Current Assets	26m	27m	38m
Current Liabilities	8m	10m	12m

Shed Express

Roberts Yard Off Crompton Road, Ilkeston, DE7 4BG
Tel: 0115-877 6696 **Fax:** 0115-930 8500
E-mail: terry@shedexpress.com
Website: http://www.shedexpress.com
Directors: T. Mellard (MD), T. Mellard (Prop)
Ultimate Holding Company: HILLBRIDGE INVESTMENTS LIMITED
Immediate Holding Company: M PLUS RECYCLING LIMITED
Registration no: 03764114 **Date established:** 2000
No.of Employees: 1 - 10 **Product Groups:** 25, 35, 41

Date of Accounts	Sep 11	Sep 10	Sep 09
Sales Turnover	2m	2m	2m
Pre Tax Profit/Loss	73	67	71
Working Capital	583	472	432
Fixed Assets	522	587	574
Current Assets	949	897	631
Current Liabilities	149	80	33

Shipley Blinds

20-22 Lower Stanton Road, Ilkeston, DE7 4LN
Tel: 0115-930 8488 **Fax:** 0115-930 8488
Website: http://www.shipleyblinds.com
Managers: C. Scottney (Mgr)
Immediate Holding Company: SHIPLEY BLINDS LIMITED
Registration no: 04900789 **Date established:** 2003
No.of Employees: 1 - 10 **Product Groups:** 24, 30, 35

Date of Accounts	Sep 11	Sep 10	Sep 09
Working Capital	33	27	24
Fixed Assets	N/A	N/A	1
Current Assets	80	61	50

Signs Direct Ltd

Unit 13 Soloman Road, Cossall Industrial Estate, Ilkeston, DE7 5UA
Tel: 0115-944 2065
E-mail: sales@signsdirect-uk.com
Website: http://www.signsdirect-uk.com
Directors: I. Wright (Dir)
Immediate Holding Company: SIGNS DIRECT LTD
Registration no: 04600303 **Date established:** 2002
Turnover: Up to £250,000 **No.of Employees:** 1 - 10 **Product Groups:** 30, 40, 44, 49

Date of Accounts	Feb 12	Feb 11	Feb 10
Working Capital	-17	-8	-12
Fixed Assets	47	34	21
Current Assets	59	35	30

Skymark Packaging Solutions Ltd

Manners Avenue Manners Industrial Estate, Ilkeston, DE7 8EF
Tel: 0115-930 2020 **Fax:** 0115-907 1525
E-mail: admin@skymark.co.uk
Website: http://www.skymark.co.uk
Bank(s): Royal Bank of Scotland
Directors: P. Styles (Sales), J. Lambert (Fin), J. Turner (MD)
Managers: O. Summers, P. Holder (Personnel)
Ultimate Holding Company: SKYMARK PACKAGING INTERNATIONAL LIMITED
Immediate Holding Company: SKYMARK PACKAGING SOLUTIONS LIMITED
Registration no: 01450486 **VAT No.:** GB 762 7632 12
Date established: 1979 **Turnover:** £10m - £20m
No.of Employees: 51 - 100 **Product Groups:** 30, 31

Date of Accounts	Dec 11	Dec 10	Dec 09
Sales Turnover	N/A	N/A	14m
Pre Tax Profit/Loss	N/A	N/A	832
Working Capital	2m	2m	2m
Current Assets	2m	2m	2m

Stanton Bonna Concrete Ltd

Littlewell Lane Stanton-by-dale, Ilkeston, DE7 4QW
Tel: 0115-944 1448 **Fax:** 0115-944 1466
E-mail: b.wilson@stanton-bonna.co.uk
Website: http://www.stanton-bonna.co.uk
Bank(s): HSBC Bank plc
Directors: B. Cooper (Grp Chief Exec), B. Wilson (Fin)
Managers: S. Hopewell, M. Howitt (Mktg Serv Mgr)
Ultimate Holding Company: CONSOLIS SAS (FRANCE)
Immediate Holding Company: STANTON BONNA CONCRETE LIMITED
Registration no: 02263795 **VAT No.:** GB 520 5843 65
Date established: 1988 **Turnover:** £10m - £20m
No.of Employees: 101 - 250 **Product Groups:** 33, 66

Date of Accounts	Dec 11	Dec 10	Dec 09
Sales Turnover	18m	17m	21m
Pre Tax Profit/Loss	494	331	1m
Working Capital	3m	2m	2m
Fixed Assets	5m	5m	5m
Current Assets	8m	8m	8m
Current Liabilities	3m	4m	5m

Technifab Engineering

Unit 3-4 Kingfisher Court Kestrel Close, Quarry Hill Industrial Estate, Ilkeston, DE7 4RD
Tel: 0115-944 2227 **Fax:** 0115-944 5222
E-mail: sales@technifab.co.uk
Directors: N. Phillips (Ptnr)
Immediate Holding Company: TECHNIFAB ENGINEERING (MIDLANDS) LTD
Registration no: 07572058 **Date established:** 2011
No.of Employees: 1 - 10 **Product Groups:** 26, 35

Travis Perkins plc

Thurman Street, Ilkeston, DE7 4BY
Tel: 0115-932 4278 **Fax:** 0115-944 1338
E-mail: david.brock@travisperkins.co.uk
Website: http://www.travisperkins.co.uk
Managers: D. Brock (District Mgr)
Immediate Holding Company: TRAVIS PERKINS PLC
Registration no: 00824821 **Date established:** 1964 **Turnover:** £1m - £2m
No.of Employees: 1 - 10 **Product Groups:** 66

Date of Accounts	Dec 11	Dec 10	Dec 09
Sales Turnover	4779m	3153m	2931m
Pre Tax Profit/Loss	270m	197m	213m
Working Capital	133m	159m	248m
Fixed Assets	2771m	2749m	2108m
Current Assets	1421m	1329m	1035m
Current Liabilities	473m	412m	109m

Tuthill UK

Birkdale Close Manners Industrial Estate, Ilkeston, DE7 8YA
Tel: 0115-932 5226 **Fax:** 0115-932 4816
E-mail: tuthilluk@tuthill.com
Website: http://www.tuthill.com
Bank(s): Barclays
Directors: M. Todd (MD), M. Binch (Sales)
Managers: M. Crinks (Comptroller)
Ultimate Holding Company: TUTHILL CORPORATION (USA)
Immediate Holding Company: TUTHILL U.K. LIMITED
Registration no: 00912417 **VAT No.:** GB 190 9375 83
Date established: 1967 **Turnover:** £5m - £10m **No.of Employees:** 21 - 50
Product Groups: 38, 39, 40

Date of Accounts	Dec 11	Dec 10	Dec 09
Sales Turnover	7m	10m	9m
Pre Tax Profit/Loss	940	1m	-884
Working Capital	5m	8m	5m
Fixed Assets	1m	1m	3m
Current Assets	6m	9m	7m
Current Liabilities	855	560	402

Weleda UK Ltd

Heanor Road, Ilkeston, DE7 8DR
Tel: 0115-944 8200 **Fax:** 0115-944 8210
E-mail: robert.ballard@weleda.co.uk
Website: http://www.weleda.co.uk
Bank(s): HSBC Bank plc
Directors: R. Ballard (MD), S. Spibey (Fin)
Managers: I. Bent (Personnel), J. Stirland (Sales & Mktg Mg), C. Roland, J. Pheasant (Tech Serv Mgr)
Ultimate Holding Company: WELEDA AG (SWITZERLAND)
Immediate Holding Company: WELEDA (U.K.) LIMITED
Registration no: 00203230 **Date established:** 2025 **Turnover:** £5m - £10m
No.of Employees: 51 - 100 **Product Groups:** 31, 32

Date of Accounts	Dec 11	Dec 10	Dec 09
Sales Turnover	6m	6m	6m
Pre Tax Profit/Loss	-212	2	98
Working Capital	1m	756	955
Fixed Assets	2m	3m	3m
Current Assets	3m	2m	3m
Current Liabilities	400	420	369

Matlock

Autochair Ltd

Unit 143 Brookfield Industrial Estate Tansley, Matlock, DE4 5ND
Tel: 01629-581122 **Fax:** 01629-581123
Website: http://www.autochair.co.uk
Registration no: 02533881 **Date established:** 1990
No.of Employees: 21 - 50 **Product Groups:** 39, 45, 67

Brownwood Engineering Fabrication Ltd

Tansley Wood Mills Lower Lumsdale, Matlock, DE4 5EX
Tel: 01629-55850 **Fax:** 01629- 580470
Directors: S. Myers (Fin), G. Myers (MD)
Immediate Holding Company: BROWNWOOD ENGINEERING & FABRICATION CO. LTD
Registration no: 04432330 **Date established:** 2002
No.of Employees: 1 - 10 **Product Groups:** 41

Date of Accounts	Jul 11	Jul 10	Jul 09
Working Capital	149	134	129
Fixed Assets	3	4	6
Current Assets	170	185	158
Current Liabilities	N/A	11	6

Derwent Castings Ltd

Derwent Foundry Derby Road, Whatstandwell, Matlock, DE4 5HG
Tel: 01773-852173 **Fax:** 01773-856632
E-mail: info@derwent-foundry.co.uk
Website: http://www.derwent-foundry.co.uk
Bank(s): Royal Bank of Scotland, King St, Belper, Derbyshir
Directors: M. Mackrell (MD), P. Donnelly (Dir)
Immediate Holding Company: DERWENT CASTINGS LIMITED
Registration no: 04507267 **Date established:** 2002
Turnover: £500,000 - £1m **No.of Employees:** 11 - 20 **Product Groups:** 34

Date of Accounts	Aug 11	Aug 10	Aug 09
Working Capital	285	263	276
Fixed Assets	11	15	20
Current Assets	433	383	416

H J Enthoven & Sons Ltd

Darley Dale Smelter South Darley, Matlock, DE4 2LP
Tel: 01629-733291 **Fax:** 01629-733092
E-mail: info@hjenthoven.co.uk
Website: http://www.hjenthoven.co.uk
Bank(s): Lloyds TSB Bank plc
Directors: G. Cummins (Fin)
Managers: A. Dalton (Personnel), J. Coulombeau (Purch Mgr), R. Fisher (Tech Serv Mgr), C. Myers (Fin Mgr), L. Mellor (Sales & Mktg Mg)
Ultimate Holding Company: EB HOLDINGS II INC (NEVADA)
Immediate Holding Company: H.J. ENTHOVEN & SONS LIMITED
Registration no: 02903069 **Date established:** 1994
Turnover: £20m - £50m **No.of Employees:** 101 - 250 **Product Groups:** 34

Date of Accounts	Dec 11	Dec 10	Dec 09
Pre Tax Profit/Loss	-30	3m	2m
Working Capital	-1m	-1m	-1m
Fixed Assets	1m	1m	1m

Expertise Ltd
25 Warmbrook Wirksworth, Matlock, DE4 4EA
Tel: 01629-826482
E-mail: enquiries@expertise-limited.co.uk
Website: http://www.expertise-limited.co.uk
Directors: S. Moran (MD)
Registration no: 03819104 **Date established:** 1999
No.of Employees: 1 - 10 **Product Groups:** 84

Date of Accounts	Mar 10	Mar 09	Mar 08
Working Capital	-3	3	24
Fixed Assets	1	1	1
Current Assets	9	16	45

Greenhill Joinery
Unit 6 Via Gellia Mill Via Gellia Road, Bonsall, Matlock, DE4 2AJ
Tel: 01629-822392 **Fax:** 01629-825424
E-mail: info@greenhilljoinery.com
Website: http://www.greenhillcountrycoops.co.uk
Directors: C. Ellis (Prop)
Date established: 1990 **No.of Employees:** 1 - 10 **Product Groups:** 49

Harrington Generators International Ltd
Ravenstor Road Wirksworth, Matlock, DE4 4FY
Tel: 01629-824284 **Fax:** 01629-824613
E-mail: enquiries@hgigenerators.com
Website: http://www.hgigenerators.com
Bank(s): The Royal Bank of Scotland
Directors: G. Barnes (Co Sec)
Managers: M. Smith, R. Young (Fin Mgr), C. Coulton (Tech Serv Mgr), D. Clay (Mktg Serv Mgr), B. Kimber (Sales Prom Mgr), R. Moor (Personnel)
Ultimate Holding Company: MELROSE PLC
Immediate Holding Company: HARRINGTON GENERATORS INTERNATIONAL LIMITED
Registration no: 02184794 **VAT No.:** GB 295 5866 95
Date established: 1987 **Turnover:** £5m - £10m
No.of Employees: 51 - 100 **Product Groups:** 37, 46

Date of Accounts	Dec 11	Dec 10	Dec 09
Sales Turnover	9m	7m	7m
Pre Tax Profit/Loss	607	173	477
Working Capital	3m	2m	2m
Fixed Assets	154	101	127
Current Assets	5m	4m	3m
Current Liabilities	956	447	486

Ideagen Software Ltd
Lime Tree Business Park Lime Tree Road, Matlock, DE4 3EJ
Tel: 01629-761590 **Fax:** 01629-56060
E-mail: sales@ideagenplc.com
Website: http://www.ideagen.co.uk
Bank(s): National Westminster Bank Plc
Managers: J. Ogden (Sales Admin)
Ultimate Holding Company: IDEAGEN PLC
Immediate Holding Company: IDEAGEN SOFTWARE LIMITED
Registration no: 03505254 **VAT No.:** GB 598 3699 56
Date established: 1998 **Turnover:** £500,000 - £1m
No.of Employees: 11 - 20 **Product Groups:** 44

Date of Accounts	Jul 10	Jul 09	Jul 08
Working Capital	468	503	413
Fixed Assets	31	33	36
Current Assets	1m	1m	1m

Lifetile Traditional Ltd
Unit 11 Molyneux Business Park Whitworth Road, Darley Dale, Matlock, DE4 2HJ
Tel: 08452-004959 **Fax:** 0845-200 4969
E-mail: sales@lifetile.co.uk
Website: http://www.lifetile.co.uk
Directors: G. Edwards (MD)
Immediate Holding Company: LIFETILE LIMITED
Registration no: 04008140 **Date established:** 2000
No.of Employees: 1 - 10 **Product Groups:** 33

Date of Accounts	Jun 11	Jun 10	Jun 03
Working Capital	6	6	-0
Current Assets	6	6	N/A

Longcliffe Quarries Ltd
Longcliffe Brassington, Matlock, DE4 4BZ
Tel: 01629-540284 **Fax:** 01629-540569
E-mail: sales@longcliffe.co.uk
Website: http://www.longcliffe.co.uk
Bank(s): HSBC Bank plc
Directors: I. Gorbould (Fin)
Ultimate Holding Company: LONGCLIFFE GROUP LIMITED
Immediate Holding Company: LONGCLIFFE QUARRIES LIMITED
Registration no: 00273400 **Date established:** 1933
Turnover: £20m - £50m **No.of Employees:** 101 - 250
Product Groups: 14, 20, 31, 32, 33

Date of Accounts	Mar 12	Mar 11	Mar 10
Sales Turnover	21m	20m	18m
Pre Tax Profit/Loss	N/A	1m	453
Working Capital	2m	2m	1m
Fixed Assets	14m	15m	14m
Current Assets	8m	7m	6m
Current Liabilities	2m	2m	2m

Moto-Racing
11 Pinewood Road, Matlock, DE4 3HN
Tel: 01629-581552 **Fax:** 01629-584394
E-mail: info@moto-racing.co.uk
Website: http://www.moto-racing.co.uk
Directors: M. Riley (Prop)
Turnover: Up to £250,000 **No.of Employees:** 1 - 10 **Product Groups:** 30, 39, 68

Platts Harris Ltd
Dale Road North Darley Dale, Matlock, DE4 2HX
Tel: 01629-734807 **Fax:** 01629-733884
E-mail: johnmarsden@plattsharris.co.uk
Website: http://www.plattsharris.co.uk
Managers: J. Marsden (District Mgr)
Ultimate Holding Company: LOOKERS PUBLIC LIMITED COMPANY
Immediate Holding Company: PLATTS HARRIS LIMITED
Registration no: 01726323 **Date established:** 1983
Turnover: Up to £250,000 **No.of Employees:** 1 - 10 **Product Groups:** 41

Date of Accounts	Dec 11	Dec 10	Dec 09
Sales Turnover	18m	15m	15m
Pre Tax Profit/Loss	160	181	231
Working Capital	355	449	240
Fixed Assets	492	277	359
Current Assets	6m	4m	5m
Current Liabilities	313	227	345

S J Tech Stephen James Technologies Ltd
Ground Floor Bentley Bridge House Upper Lumsdale, Matlock, DE4 5LB
Tel: 01629-581899 **Fax:** 01629-581899
E-mail: asl@stephenjames.biz
Website: http://www.stephenjames.biz
Directors: A. Link (MD)
Immediate Holding Company: STEPHEN JAMES TECHNOLOGIES LIMITED
Registration no: 04082347 **Date established:** 2000
Turnover: Up to £250,000 **No.of Employees:** 1 - 10 **Product Groups:** 84

Date of Accounts	Oct 11	Oct 10	Oct 09
Working Capital	45	33	31
Fixed Assets	14	12	12
Current Assets	132	122	97

Salisbury & Wood Ltd
Old Coach Road Tansley, Matlock, DE4 5FY
Tel: 01629-582272 **Fax:** 01629-583989
E-mail: ken@salswood.co.uk
Website: http://www.salswood.co.uk
Bank(s): Royal Bank of Scotland
Directors: K. Bowmer (MD), E. Cooper (Co Sec)
Immediate Holding Company: SALISBURY & WOOD LIMITED
Registration no: 00223173 **Date established:** 2027 **Turnover:** £1m - £2m
No.of Employees: 11 - 20 **Product Groups:** 14, 17, 31, 33, 66

Date of Accounts	Mar 12	Mar 11	Mar 10
Working Capital	133	127	113
Fixed Assets	446	384	400
Current Assets	575	650	520

Savox Ltd
Sandy Hill Park Middleton, Matlock, DE4 4LR
Tel: 01629-820820 **Fax:** 01629-820800
E-mail: savox@savox.com
Website: http://www.savox.com
Bank(s): HSBC
Managers: A. Mclachlan (Chief Mgr)
Immediate Holding Company: SAVOX LIMITED
Registration no: 07182371 **VAT No.:** GB 295 2732 34
Date established: 2010 **Turnover:** £2m - £5m **No.of Employees:** 11 - 20
Product Groups: 37

John Smedley Ltd
Lea Mills Lea Bridge, Matlock, DE4 5AG
Tel: 01629-534571 **Fax:** 01629-534691
E-mail: enquiries@johnsmedley.com
Website: http://www.johnsmedley.com
Directors: J. Hope (Fin), J. Irving (Tech Serv)
Managers: M. Richards (Personnel)
Immediate Holding Company: JOHN SMEDLEY LIMITED
Registration no: 00040000 **Date established:** 1993
Turnover: £10m - £20m **No.of Employees:** 251 - 500 **Product Groups:** 24

Date of Accounts	Dec 10	Dec 09	Dec 08
Sales Turnover	16m	15m	15m
Pre Tax Profit/Loss	-2m	32	988
Working Capital	5m	7m	8m
Fixed Assets	2m	2m	2m
Current Assets	7m	9m	11m
Current Liabilities	2m	2m	2m

Tansley Teak
2 Holly Lane Tansley, Matlock, DE4 5FF
Tel: 01629-593893
E-mail: info@tansleyteak.co.uk
Website: http://www.tansleyteak.co.uk
Directors: S. Coxon (Prop)
Immediate Holding Company: J.W.L. 105 LIMITED
Date established: 2004 **Turnover:** Up to £250,000
No.of Employees: 1 - 10 **Product Groups:** 26

Technolog Ltd
Technolog House Ravenstor Road, Wirksworth, Matlock, DE4 4FY
Tel: 01629-823611 **Fax:** 01629-824283
E-mail: sdrury@technolog.com
Website: http://www.technolog.com
Directors: B. James (Fin), J. Bignall (Co Sec), S. Drury (Dir), S. Howard (Comm)
Managers: A. Oliver (Tech Serv Mgr), P. Madeley (Purch Mgr), J. Goodlad (Personnel)
Ultimate Holding Company: ROPER INDUSTRIES INC (USA)
Immediate Holding Company: TECHNOLOG LIMITED
Registration no: 01574170 **Date established:** 1981
Turnover: £20m - £50m **No.of Employees:** 51 - 100 **Product Groups:** 38, 44

Date of Accounts	Dec 11	Dec 10	Dec 09
Sales Turnover	29m	23m	22m
Pre Tax Profit/Loss	10m	5m	6m
Working Capital	8m	8m	6m
Fixed Assets	2m	3m	2m
Current Assets	18m	20m	13m
Current Liabilities	6m	5m	5m

Viaton Industries Ltd
Brassington, Matlock, DE4 4ES
Tel: 01629-540373 **Fax:** 01629-540289
E-mail: sales@viaton.com
Website: http://www.viaton.com
Bank(s): National Westminster Bank Plc
Directors: C. Bell (Tech Serv), J. Bestwick (Fin), J. Beswick (Fin), R. Edwards (Sales), J. Prime (Pers)
Ultimate Holding Company: ELLASTONE INVESTMENTS LIMITED
Immediate Holding Company: VIATON INDUSTRIES LIMITED
Registration no: 00213795 **Date established:** 2026 **Turnover:** £5m - £10m
No.of Employees: 21 - 50 **Product Groups:** 17, 32

Date of Accounts	Dec 11	Dec 10	Dec 09
Sales Turnover	9m	8m	7m
Pre Tax Profit/Loss	471	367	-143
Working Capital	2m	2m	2m
Fixed Assets	381	492	610
Current Assets	5m	5m	3m
Current Liabilities	549	544	190

Ripley

Howard Berkin
Victoria Road, Ripley, DE5 3FX
Tel: 01773-513800 **Fax:** 01773-513600
E-mail: howardberkin@tiscalli.co.uk
Directors: H. Berkin (Prop)
Immediate Holding Company: HOWARD BERKIN STEEL FABRICATION & WELDING LIMITED
Registration no: 04942815 **Date established:** 2003
No.of Employees: 1 - 10 **Product Groups:** 35, 48

Date of Accounts	Oct 11	Oct 10	Oct 09
Working Capital	-47	-45	-17
Fixed Assets	17	24	29
Current Assets	30	37	48

Codnor Horticultural Ltd
Cherry Tree Cottage Farm 210 Peasehill, Ripley, DE5 3JQ
Tel: 01773-742847 **Fax:** 01773-512120
E-mail: info@gro-welldirect.co.uk
Website: http://www.gro-welldirect.co.uk
Directors: A. Shaw (MD)
Immediate Holding Company: CODNOR HORTICULTURAL (WHOLESALE) SUPPLIES LIMITED
Registration no: 02704405 **VAT No.:** GB 119 0254 94
Date established: 1992 **Turnover:** £250,000 - £500,000
No.of Employees: 1 - 10 **Product Groups:** 27, 32

Date of Accounts	Apr 12	Apr 11	Apr 10
Working Capital	191	209	215
Fixed Assets	81	84	111
Current Assets	348	353	354

Crown Ceramics
8 Mill Lane Codnor, Ripley, DE5 9QF
Tel: 01773-749278 **Fax:** 01773-749278
E-mail: info@crown-ceramics.co.uk
Website: http://www.crown-ceramics.co.uk
Directors: B. Swindell (Ptnr)
Date established: 1992 **No.of Employees:** 1 - 10 **Product Groups:** 38, 67, 88

Deb R & D Ltd
Denby Hall Way Denby, Ripley, DE5 8JZ
Tel: 01773-855300 **Fax:** 01773-855107
E-mail: enquiry@debgroup.com
Website: http://www.debgroup.com
Managers: D. Limbert (Sales Admin)
Ultimate Holding Company: DEB GROUP HOLDINGS LIMITED
Immediate Holding Company: DEB HOLDINGS LIMITED
Registration no: 04113118 **Date established:** 2000
Turnover: £20m - £50m **No.of Employees:** 1 - 10 **Product Groups:** 30, 31, 32

Date of Accounts	Dec 11	Dec 10	Dec 09
Pre Tax Profit/Loss	7m	38m	-14m
Working Capital	43m	36m	2m
Fixed Assets	69m	69m	76m
Current Assets	60m	40m	3m
Current Liabilities	2m	581	76

Evans Concrete Products Ltd
Pease Hill Road, Ripley, DE5 3HZ
Tel: 01773-748026 **Fax:** 01773-570354
E-mail: evans@evansconcreteproducts.co.uk
Website: http://www.evansconcreteproducts.co.uk
Directors: G. McBride (Ch)
Managers: C. Foster (Eng Serv Mgr), B. Greenhough (Comptroller)
Immediate Holding Company: Vitram Ltd
Registration no: 02517363 **Date established:** 1990 **Turnover:** £2m - £5m
No.of Employees: 1 - 10 **Product Groups:** 33

Date of Accounts	Sep 08	Sep 07	Sep 06
Working Capital	381	115	80
Fixed Assets	151	137	85
Current Assets	1336	876	867
Current Liabilities	955	762	786

H L Plastics Ltd
Flamstead House Denby Hall Business Park, Marehay, Ripley, DE5 8JX
Tel: 01332-883800 **Fax:** 01332-830867
E-mail: sales@hlplastics.co.uk
Website: http://www.hlplastics.co.uk
Directors: M. Sims (Sales), E. Arrell (Fin), R. Cheetham (Mkt Research), D. Chambers (Tech Serv)
Managers: W. Zoladkiewicz (Purch Mgr), L. Brown (Personnel)
Ultimate Holding Company: FLAMSTEAD HOLDINGS LIMITED
Immediate Holding Company: H L PLASTICS LIMITED
Registration no: 03360857 **VAT No.:** GB 616 7517 31
Date established: 1997 **Turnover:** £20m - £50m
No.of Employees: 101 - 250 **Product Groups:** 30, 45, 48, 66

Date of Accounts	Dec 11	Dec 10	Dec 09
Sales Turnover	29m	20m	10m
Pre Tax Profit/Loss	710	51	137
Working Capital	-3m	-3m	-890
Fixed Assets	11m	11m	8m
Current Assets	8m	7m	6m
Current Liabilities	979	764	1m

Linden Signs Ltd
Linden House 73 Upper Marehay, Ripley, DE5 8JF
Tel: 01773-741500 **Fax:** 01773-741555
E-mail: info@lindensigns.org
Website: http://www.lindensigns.org
Directors: K. Bradley (MD)
Immediate Holding Company: LINDEN SIGNS LTD
Registration no: 04951321 **Date established:** 2003
No.of Employees: 1 - 10 **Product Groups:** 28, 30, 39, 40, 49, 67, 68

Date of Accounts	Nov 11	Nov 10	Nov 09
Working Capital	457	420	336
Fixed Assets	12	16	21
Current Assets	548	509	424

Machine Building Systems Ltd
Heage Road Industrial Estate, Ripley, DE5 3GH
Tel: 01773-749330 **Fax:** 01773-749560
E-mail: sales@mbsitem.co.uk
Website: http://www.mbsitem.co.uk

see next page

***Machine Building Systems Ltd** - Cont'd*
Bank(s): Barclays
Directors: S. Mitchell (MD)
Managers: H. Kearney (Sales Prom Mgr)
Immediate Holding Company: MACHINE BUILDING SYSTEMS LIMITED
Registration no: 02415581 **VAT No.:** GB 543 6524 44
Date established: 1989 **Turnover:** £1m - £2m **No.of Employees:** 11 - 20
Product Groups: 34, 45, 84

Date of Accounts	Oct 11	Oct 10	Oct 09
Working Capital	2m	2m	1m
Fixed Assets	2m	2m	2m
Current Assets	3m	3m	2m

Manthorpe Building Products
Unit 3 Forty Horse Close Brittain Drive Codnor Gate Industrial Estate, Ripley, DE5 3ND
Tel: 01773-514200 **Fax:** 01773-514261
E-mail: sales@manthorpe.co.uk
Website: http://www.manthorpe.co.uk
Bank(s): Royal Bank of Scotland, Nottingham
Directors: A. Steele (Sales & Mktg), M. Elliott (Chief Op Offcr)
Managers: M. Tivey (Buyer), L. Wylie (Personnel), A. Smith (Fin Mgr)
Ultimate Holding Company: MANTHORPE LIMITED
Immediate Holding Company: MANTHORPE ENGINEERING LIMITED
Registration no: 01810526 **Date established:** 1984
Turnover: £10m - £20m **No.of Employees:** 11 - 20 **Product Groups:** 33, 40

Date of Accounts	Apr 12	Apr 11	Apr 10
Sales Turnover	15m	13m	11m
Pre Tax Profit/Loss	116	-273	-1m
Working Capital	-272	-115	-186
Fixed Assets	5m	6m	6m
Current Assets	8m	8m	9m
Current Liabilities	1m	783	2m

Peak Plastics Ltd
Derwent Business Park Heage Road, Ripley, DE5 3GH
Tel: 01773-743152 **Fax:** 01773-513478
E-mail: enquiries@peakplastics.co.uk
Website: http://www.peakplastics.co.uk
Bank(s): Barclays
Directors: C. Lindley (Fin), D. Lindley (MD)
Immediate Holding Company: PEAK PLASTICS LIMITED
Registration no: 01002314 **Date established:** 1971
Turnover: £500,000 - £1m **No.of Employees:** 11 - 20 **Product Groups:** 30

Date of Accounts	Aug 12	Aug 11	Aug 10
Working Capital	174	184	173
Fixed Assets	228	160	124
Current Assets	281	252	229

Q C Packaging Films Ltd
Technology House Heage Road Industrial Estate, Ripley, DE5 3GH
Tel: 01773-740300 **Fax:** 01773-740301
E-mail: info@qcpackagingfilms.com
Bank(s): Yorkshire Bank, Derby
Directors: B. Singh (Dir)
Immediate Holding Company: QC PACKAGING FILMS LIMITED
Registration no: 04431892 **VAT No.:** GB 660 5034 62
Date established: 2002 **Turnover:** £1m - £2m **No.of Employees:** 11 - 20
Product Groups: 30

Date of Accounts	May 12	May 11	May 10
Working Capital	2m	2m	1m
Fixed Assets	243	265	270
Current Assets	2m	2m	2m

Ross Ceramics Ltd
Derby Road Denby, Ripley, DE5 8NX
Tel: 01773-570800 **Fax:** 01773-570152
E-mail: tcox@rossceramics.co.uk
Website: http://www.rossceramics.co.uk
Bank(s): Lloyds TSB Bank plc
Directors: P. Cooper (Fin), T. Cox (MD), K. Waldron (Co Sec)
Managers: B. Eyre (Personnel), J. Bamford (Sales & Mktg Mg), J. Stanton (Purch Mgr), P. Bain (Tech Serv Mgr)
Ultimate Holding Company: ROLLS-ROYCE HOLDINGS PLC
Immediate Holding Company: ROSS CERAMICS LIMITED
Registration no: 02220030 **VAT No.:** GB 509 1131 80
Date established: 1988 **Turnover:** £10m - £20m
No.of Employees: 101 - 250 **Product Groups:** 33, 42, 48

Date of Accounts	Dec 11	Dec 10	Dec 09
Sales Turnover	13m	12m	15m
Pre Tax Profit/Loss	471	570	539
Working Capital	3m	3m	3m
Fixed Assets	3m	3m	3m
Current Assets	5m	5m	5m
Current Liabilities	839	942	1m

S B Wrought Iron Ltd
Unit 2b Bradley Park High Holborn Road, Ripley, DE5 3NW
Tel: 01773-741416 **Fax:** 01773-741417
E-mail: steve@sbwroughtiron.orangehome.co.uk
Website: http://www.sbwroughtiron.co.uk
Directors: S. Bunting (Dir)
Immediate Holding Company: S B WROUGHT IRON LIMITED
Registration no: 04730440 **Date established:** 2003
No.of Employees: 1 - 10 **Product Groups:** 26, 35

Date of Accounts	Mar 11	Mar 10	Mar 09
Working Capital	-41	-27	-27
Fixed Assets	5	6	8
Current Assets	7	13	14

Schades Ltd
Brittain Drive Codnor Gate Industrial Estate, Ripley, DE5 3RZ
Tel: 01773-748721 **Fax:** 01773-745061
E-mail: jack@schades.co.uk
Website: http://www.schades.com
Bank(s): HSBC Bank plc
Directors: G. Butler (Sales), P. Moller (Dir)
Managers: E. Haynes (Chief Acct)
Ultimate Holding Company: SCHADES HOLDINGS A/S (DENMARK)
Immediate Holding Company: SCHADES LIMITED
Registration no: 02213725 **VAT No.:** GB 509 1061 75
Date established: 1988 **Turnover:** £20m - £50m
No.of Employees: 21 - 50 **Product Groups:** 27

Date of Accounts	Dec 11	Dec 10	Dec 09
Sales Turnover	20m	18m	17m
Pre Tax Profit/Loss	972	261	494
Working Capital	5m	4m	4m
Fixed Assets	1m	1m	2m
Current Assets	7m	7m	6m
Current Liabilities	731	600	507

E N Snape
The College Derby Road, Denby, Ripley, DE5 8NJ
Tel: 01773-748063 **Fax:** 01773-748063
E-mail: nicksnape@msn.com
Directors: E. Snape (Prop)
Immediate Holding Company: JACKSDALE & DISTRICT INSTITUTE,LIMITED
Registration no: 00134658 **Date established:** 1914
No.of Employees: 1 - 10 **Product Groups:** 46, 48

Tarpey-Harris Ltd
Flamstead House Denby Hall Business Park Hall Road, Marehay, Ripley, DE5 8JX
Tel: 01332-883950 **Fax:** 01332-883951
E-mail: stevej@tarpey-harris.co.uk
Website: http://www.tarpey-harris.co.uk
Bank(s): Natwest
Directors: S. Jones (MD), E. Arrell (Fin)
Managers: J. Haywood (Tech Serv Mgr), L. Brown (Personnel)
Ultimate Holding Company: FLAMSTEAD HOLDINGS LIMITED
Immediate Holding Company: TARPEY-HARRIS LIMITED
Registration no: 00958369 **VAT No.:** GB 616 7517 31
Date established: 1969 **Turnover:** £2m - £5m **No.of Employees:** 21 - 50
Product Groups: 42, 46, 48

Date of Accounts	Dec 11	Dec 10	Dec 09
Sales Turnover	3m	2m	N/A
Pre Tax Profit/Loss	148	-7	N/A
Working Capital	181	17	-103
Fixed Assets	763	863	1m
Current Assets	2m	823	1m
Current Liabilities	544	175	N/A

Tubesheet Ltd
High Holborn Road, Ripley, DE5 3NW
Tel: 01773-744755 **Fax:** 01773-747273
E-mail: enquiries@tubesheet.co.uk
Website: http://www.tubesheet.co.uk
Directors: A. Vaughan (MD)
Immediate Holding Company: TUBESHEET LIMITED
Registration no: 01843861 **VAT No.:** GB 389 2763 95
Date established: 1984 **Turnover:** £2m - £5m **No.of Employees:** 1 - 10
Product Groups: 34, 35, 36, 40, 48

Date of Accounts	Aug 11	Aug 10	Aug 09
Working Capital	666	2m	1m
Fixed Assets	421	552	443
Current Assets	1m	2m	2m

Turner Refrigeration
9 Devonshire Avenue, Ripley, DE5 3SS
Tel: 01773-744328 **Fax:** 01773-745067
E-mail: trna705@aol.com
Directors: J. Turner (Prop)
Immediate Holding Company: TURNER REFRIGERATION LTD
Registration no: 06401672 **Date established:** 2007
No.of Employees: 1 - 10 **Product Groups:** 36, 40

W J B Welding & Fabrication
Unit 3 Butterley Park, Ripley, DE5 3QW
Tel: 07774-601528 **Fax:** 01773-570590
E-mail: wjbwelding@aol.com
Website: http://www.wjbwelding.com
Directors: W. Bryant (Prop)
Immediate Holding Company: BLOCK PLANT LIMITED
Date established: 1999 **No.of Employees:** 1 - 10 **Product Groups:** 35

Date of Accounts	Dec 10	Dec 09	Dec 08
Working Capital	-64	-67	-63
Fixed Assets	76	78	80
Current Assets	N/A	1	1

Zycomm Electronics Ltd
51 Nottingham Road, Ripley, DE5 3AS
Tel: 01773-570123 **Fax:** 01773-570155
E-mail: sales@zycomm.co.uk
Website: http://www.zycomm.co.uk
Bank(s): National Westminster
Directors: R. Dixon (MD), C. Pass (Co Sec)
Managers: C. Price
Ultimate Holding Company: ZYCOMM HOLDINGS LIMITED
Immediate Holding Company: ZYCOMM ELECTRONICS LIMITED
Registration no: 01412033 **Date established:** 1979 **Turnover:** £2m - £5m
No.of Employees: 11 - 20 **Product Groups:** 37

Date of Accounts	Jan 11	Jan 10	Jan 09
Working Capital	160	72	101
Fixed Assets	6	19	38
Current Assets	661	844	630

Swadlincote

Airetool UK Ltd
Park House 4 Orchard Street, Newhall, Swadlincote, DE11 0JS
Tel: 01283-218885 **Fax:** 01283-215692
Directors: S. Bartlam (Fin), R. Delaney (MD)
Immediate Holding Company: AIRETOOL (UK) LIMITED
Registration no: 03154741 **Date established:** 1996
No.of Employees: 1 - 10 **Product Groups:** 37

Date of Accounts	Mar 12	Mar 11	Mar 10
Working Capital	352	309	274
Fixed Assets	17	27	27
Current Assets	400	350	323

Assured Solutions Ltd
Unit H Westminster Industrial Estate Measham, Swadlincote, DE12 7DS
Tel: 01530-272922 **Fax:** 01530-272921
E-mail: sales@assuredsolutionsltd.co.uk
Website: http://www.chemicalsuppliers.uk.com
Bank(s): National Westminster Bank Plc
Directors: P. Chamberlain (MD)
Immediate Holding Company: ASSURED SOLUTIONS LIMITED
Registration no: 02238356 **VAT No.:** GB 507 9360 37
Date established: 1988 **Turnover:** £1m - £2m **No.of Employees:** 11 - 20
Product Groups: 32

Date of Accounts	Mar 12	Mar 11	Mar 10
Working Capital	311	275	247
Fixed Assets	37	32	26
Current Assets	641	637	553

Autoclenz
Stanhope Road, Swadlincote, DE11 9BE
Tel: 01283-550033 **Fax:** 01283-550298
E-mail: customers@autoclenz.co.uk
Website: http://www.autoclenz.co.uk
Directors: T. Clingo (Fin), G. Rummery (Dir)
Managers: K. Dyche, L. Johnson (Purch Mgr), L. Thompson (Personnel)
Ultimate Holding Company: AUTOCLENZ HOLDINGS PLC
Immediate Holding Company: AUTOCLENZ LIMITED
Registration no: 00956430 **Date established:** 1969
Turnover: £20m - £50m **No.of Employees:** 21 - 50 **Product Groups:** 39

Date of Accounts	Dec 11	Dec 10	Dec 09
Sales Turnover	22m	22m	21m
Pre Tax Profit/Loss	609	1m	2m
Working Capital	5m	5m	4m
Fixed Assets	446	387	447
Current Assets	9m	8m	7m
Current Liabilities	2m	3m	2m

B B C S Ltd
Unit 9 Riverside Court Westminster Industrial Estate, Measham, Swadlincote, DE12 7DS
Tel: 01530-274933 **Fax:** 01530-515292
E-mail: john.blount@bbcs-ltd.com
Website: http://www.bbcs-ltd.com
Directors: J. Blount (Prop)
Immediate Holding Company: B.B.C.S. LIMITED
Registration no: 04994605 **Date established:** 2003
No.of Employees: 1 - 10 **Product Groups:** 48

Date of Accounts	Dec 11	Dec 10	Dec 09
Working Capital	2	-14	22
Fixed Assets	16	34	31
Current Assets	142	108	90

Baker Technilock Ltd
Unit 5c Boardman Industrial Estate Boardman Road, Swadlincote, DE11 9DL
Tel: 01283-222202 **Fax:** 01283-222203
E-mail: sales@technilock.co.uk
Website: http://www.cast-iron-repair.com
Directors: D. Baker (MD)
Immediate Holding Company: BAKER TECHNILOCK LTD
Registration no: 05585105 **Date established:** 2005
No.of Employees: 1 - 10 **Product Groups:** 34, 35, 37, 39, 40, 42, 46, 48, 66, 68, 84, 85

Date of Accounts	Mar 11	Mar 10	Mar 09
Working Capital	1	N/A	5
Fixed Assets	N/A	N/A	2
Current Assets	46	30	27

Bikers Motorcycles Ltd
Unit 11 Boardmans Road, Swadlincote, DE11 9DL
Tel: 01283-558282 **Fax:** 01283-551129
E-mail: sales@bikersjersey.com
Website: http://www.bikersmotorcycles.co.uk
Managers: I. Smith (Mgr)
Immediate Holding Company: BIKERS MOTORCYCLES LIMITED
Registration no: 04654926 **Date established:** 2003
No.of Employees: 1 - 10 **Product Groups:** 39, 40

Date of Accounts	Aug 11	Aug 10	Aug 09
Sales Turnover	N/A	577	349
Pre Tax Profit/Loss	N/A	46	5
Working Capital	46	55	42
Fixed Assets	31	32	16
Current Assets	315	256	118
Current Liabilities	N/A	20	7

Bloor Homes Ltd
Ashby Road Measham, Swadlincote, DE12 7JP
Tel: 01530-270100 **Fax:** 01530-273665
E-mail: hq@bloorhomes.com
Website: http://www.bloorhomes.com
Directors: J. Bloor (Prop)
Ultimate Holding Company: BLOOR HOLDINGS LIMITED
Immediate Holding Company: J.S.BLOOR (SWINDON) LIMITED
Registration no: 02300003 **VAT No.:** GB 125 4938 61
Date established: 1988 **Turnover:** £20m - £50m
No.of Employees: 51 - 100 **Product Groups:** 39, 52, 84

Date of Accounts	Jun 11	Jun 10	Jun 09
Sales Turnover	N/A	44m	50m
Pre Tax Profit/Loss	N/A	455	-2m
Working Capital	-3m	-646	-5m
Fixed Assets	N/A	789	822
Current Assets	44m	67m	64m
Current Liabilities	N/A	178	69

J S Bloor Measham Ltd
Ashby Road Measham, Swadlincote, DE12 7JP
Tel: 01530-270100 **Fax:** 01530-273665
E-mail: hq@bloorhomes.com
Website: http://www.bloorhomes.com
Bank(s): National Westminster Bank Plc
Directors: J. Bloor (Ch), J. Bloor (Prop), R. Dodson (MD)
Managers: D. Southall (Accounts), M. Bradley (Tech Serv Mgr)
Immediate Holding Company: J.S. BLOOR (MEASHAM) LIMITED
Registration no: 00511568 **VAT No.:** GB 125 4938 61
Date established: 1952 **Turnover:** £20m - £50m
No.of Employees: 51 - 100 **Product Groups:** 52

Date of Accounts	Jun 10	Jun 09	Jun 08
Sales Turnover	34m	31m	25m
Pre Tax Profit/Loss	1m	-8m	-8m
Working Capital	8m	8m	17m
Fixed Assets	85	103	116
Current Assets	72m	72m	79m
Current Liabilities	363	296	212

Bowfran Component Anodising
Unit 1b Boardman Industrial Estate Boardman Road, Swadlincote, DE11 9DL
Tel: 01283-215060 **Fax:** 01283-218571
E-mail: admin@bowfran.co.uk
Managers: D. Jarvis (Mgr)
Registration no: 04476588 **Turnover:** Up to £250,000
No.of Employees: 1 - 10 **Product Groups:** 48

Date of Accounts	Jul 05	Jul 04	Jul 03
Working Capital	N/A	2	-13
Fixed Assets	18	18	20

Current Assets	N/A	26	21
Current Liabilities	N/A	24	34

C M S Pozament

Swainspark Industrial Estate Overseal, Swadlincote, DE12 6JT
Tel: 01283-554800 **Fax:** 01283-552923
E-mail: cmspozament@tarmac.co.uk
Website: http://www.tarmac.co.uk/cmspozament
Managers: B. Gill (Mgr)
Ultimate Holding Company: ANGLO AMERICAN P.L.C.
Immediate Holding Company: TARMAC SOUTH LTD
Registration no: 01822564 **Turnover:** £5m - £10m
No.of Employees: 1 - 10 **Product Groups:** 33, 66

D G Controls (DeeGee)

Cadley Hill Road, Swadlincote, DE11 9TB
Tel: 01283-550850 **Fax:** 01283-550776
E-mail: mail@beaconlamps.com
Website: http://www.beaconlamps.com
Bank(s): Barclays
Directors: W. Whiten (Dir & Co Sec), W. Whiten (MD)
Managers: M. Gibson (Sales Prom Mgr)
Immediate Holding Company: SALTATION LTD
Registration no: 00911313 **VAT No.:** GB 813 0477 54
Date established: 1967 **No.of Employees:** 11 - 20 **Product Groups:** 37, 38, 39, 40

Dyson Thermal Technologies

Mount Pleasant Works Moira Road, Woodville, Swadlincote, DE11 8EZ
Tel: 01283-217081 **Fax:** 01283-550774
E-mail: enq@dysontt.com
Website: http://www.dysontt.com
Directors: B. Llewellyn (MD)
No.of Employees: 1 - 10 **Product Groups:** 33, 35

Gega Lotz Ltd

Kiln Way Woodville, Swadlincote, DE11 8EA
Tel: 01283-214281 **Fax:** 01283-222108
E-mail: reception@gega.co.uk
Website: http://www.gegalotz.co.uk
Bank(s): Lloyds TSB Bank plc
Directors: R. Manning (Co Sec), G. Manning (MD), H. Lotz (Ch)
Managers: P. Fowler (Tech Serv Mgr), P. Mottram
Immediate Holding Company: GEGA LOTZ LIMITED
Registration no: 00986924 **VAT No.:** GB 126 0343 09
Date established: 1970 **Turnover:** £50m - £75m
No.of Employees: 51 - 100 **Product Groups:** 46

Date of Accounts	Dec 11	Dec 10	Dec 09
Sales Turnover	50m	N/A	N/A
Pre Tax Profit/Loss	35	N/A	N/A
Working Capital	361	608	852
Fixed Assets	2m	2m	660
Current Assets	2m	2m	2m
Current Liabilities	186	142	72

General Trailer Engineering

Bridge Street Church Gresley, Swadlincote, DE11 8EL
Tel: 01283-210800 **Fax:** 01283-224067
E-mail: sales@generaltrailerengineering.co.uk
Website: http://www.generaltrailerengineering.co.uk
Directors: D. Allen (Prop)
Immediate Holding Company: GENERAL TRAILER ENGINEERING LIMITED
Registration no: 03739460 **Date established:** 1999
No.of Employees: 1 - 10 **Product Groups:** 45, 48, 67, 68

H R International Crushing & Screening Ltd

Huntingdon Court Huntingdon Way, Measham, Swadlincote, DE12 7NQ
Tel: 01530-272799 **Fax:** 01530-272787
E-mail: nigel@hr-int.co.uk
Website: http://www.hewittrobins.co.uk
Directors: N. Wileman (Dir)
Ultimate Holding Company: HEWITT ROBINS INTERNATIONAL HOLDINGS LIMITED
Immediate Holding Company: HEWITT ROBINS INTERNATIONAL LTD
Registration no: 01552299 **VAT No.:** GB 343 3855 52
Date established: 1981 **Turnover:** £5m - £10m **No.of Employees:** 1 - 10
Product Groups: 42, 45, 46

Date of Accounts	Mar 12	Mar 11	Mar 10
Working Capital	3m	2m	2m
Fixed Assets	67	23	227
Current Assets	4m	3m	3m

Hewitt Robins International Ltd

Huntingdon Court Huntingdon Way, Measham, Swadlincote, DE12 7NQ
Tel: 01530-272799 **Fax:** 01530-272787
E-mail: sales@hr-int.co.uk
Website: http://www.hewittrobins.co.uk
Directors: G. Pratt (Dir)
Managers: D. Stevenson (Sales Prom Mgr)
Immediate Holding Company: Hewitt Robins International Holdings Ltd
Registration no: 01552299 **Date established:** 1891
No.of Employees: 51 - 100 **Product Groups:** 14, 31, 45

Ig Ltd

Ryder Close, Swadlincote, DE11 9EU
Tel: 01633-486486 **Fax:** 01633-486492
E-mail: info@igltd.co.uk
Website: http://www.igltd.co.uk
Bank(s): Barclays
Directors: D. McFarlan (MD), D. Mcfarlind (MD), J. Cole (Mkt Research)
Managers: M. Thomas (Systems Mgr), L. Cann (Personnel)
Immediate Holding Company: IG LIMITED
Registration no: 05881523 **VAT No.:** GB 543 0449 62
Date established: 2006 **Turnover:** £5m - £10m **No.of Employees:** 21 - 50
Product Groups: 30, 35

Date of Accounts	Mar 08	Mar 07
Pre Tax Profit/Loss	-756	-414
Working Capital	483	1001

Fixed Assets	681	1956
Current Assets	5285	6447
Current Liabilities	4803	5446
ROCE% (Return on Capital Employed)	-65.0	-14.0

Intec Foams

7 Fenton Avenue Blackfordby, Swadlincote, DE11 8AR
Tel: 01283-225796 **Fax:** 08714-719827
E-mail: info@intecfoams.co.uk
Website: http://www.intecfoams.co.uk
Directors: S. Challoner (Prop)
Immediate Holding Company: INTEC FOAMS LIMITED
Registration no: 06583479 **Date established:** 2008
No.of Employees: 1 - 10 **Product Groups:** 27, 29, 30

Integrex

Portwood Industrial Estate Church Gresley, Swadlincote, DE11 9PT
Tel: 01283-550880 **Fax:** 01283-552028
E-mail: sales@integrex.co.uk
Website: http://www.integrex.co.uk
Directors: A. Kightley (MD), A. Haywood (Dir), J. Portus (Co Sec)
Managers: A. Langley (Tech Serv Mgr), G. Simons (Sales Prom)
Immediate Holding Company: INTEGREX LIMITED
Registration no: 00968810 **Date established:** 1969 **Turnover:** £2m - £5m
No.of Employees: 11 - 20 **Product Groups:** 44

Date of Accounts	Jun 11	Jun 10	Jun 09
Working Capital	605	509	511
Fixed Assets	172	189	199
Current Assets	1m	948	918

Lecky Metal Ornaments

Unit 1 Tetron Point William Nadin Way, Swadlincote, DE11 0BB
Tel: 01283-552950 **Fax:** 01283-220241
E-mail: sales@lecky.co.uk
Website: http://www.lecky.co.uk
Managers: G. Lyne (Chief Mgr), J. Gregory (Develop Mgr)
Immediate Holding Company: LECKY METAL ORNAMENTS LIMITED
Registration no: 04314427 **Date established:** 2001
No.of Employees: 1 - 10 **Product Groups:** 26, 35

Date of Accounts	Dec 11	Dec 10	Dec 09
Working Capital	649	884	663
Fixed Assets	71	122	162
Current Assets	905	1m	1m

Mavitta Division Morson Projects Mavitta Division

Unit 8 Furnace Lane Moira, Swadlincote, DE12 6AT
Tel: 01283-211711 **Fax:** 01283-226868
E-mail: info@mavitta.com
Website: http://www.mavitta.com
Directors: T. Kent Chapman (Co Sec)
Managers: P. Meakin (Mgr)
Immediate Holding Company: THE MOIRA FURNACE MUSEUM TRUST LIMITED
Registration no: 02860200 **VAT No.:** GB 643 0267 60
Date established: 1989 **No.of Employees:** 1 - 10 **Product Groups:** 44, 81, 84

Date of Accounts	Mar 11	Mar 10	Mar 09
Sales Turnover	75	70	76
Pre Tax Profit/Loss	9	1	-11
Working Capital	17	8	6
Fixed Assets	1	2	3
Current Assets	25	14	12
Current Liabilities	6	6	5

Micron Stainless Steel Hygienics

Unit 5n Boardman Industrial Estate Boardman Road, Swadlincote, DE11 9DL
Tel: 01283-552191 **Fax:** 01283-229129
Directors: M. Nemec (Prop)
Date established: 1991 **No.of Employees:** 1 - 10 **Product Groups:** 35

Microsystems Technology

12 Paradise Close Moira, Swadlincote, DE12 6EE
Tel: 01283-225890
E-mail: pete.shaw@microtechsoftware.com
Website: http://www.microtechsoftware.co.uk
Directors: P. Shaw (MD), P. Shaw (Prop)
Immediate Holding Company: MICROSYSTEMS TECHNOLOGY (MICROTECH) LIMITED
Registration no: 01446703 **VAT No.:** GB 678 3902 91
Date established: 1979 **Turnover:** £250,000 - £500,000
No.of Employees: 1 - 10 **Product Groups:** 44

P H Flexible Packaging Ltd

Boardman Industrial Estate Boardman Road, Swadlincote, DE11 9DL
Tel: 01283-551050 **Fax:** 01283-551647
E-mail: paul.horobin@phflexible.co.uk
Website: http://www.packaginggb.co.uk
Directors: P. Horobin (Fin)
Immediate Holding Company: P H FLEXIBLE PACKAGING LIMITED
Registration no: 03088908 **Date established:** 1995
Turnover: £500,000 - £1m **No.of Employees:** 11 - 20
Product Groups: 38, 42

Date of Accounts	Sep 11	Sep 10	Sep 09
Working Capital	170	108	109
Fixed Assets	262	304	343
Current Assets	443	425	399

Phoenix Weighing Services Ltd

Unit 9 Lower Rectory Farm
Snarestone Road
Appleby Magna, Swadlincote, DE12 7AJ
Tel: 07866-772394
E-mail: info@phoenixweigh.com
Website: http://www.phoenixweigh.com
Registration no: 05307592 **Product Groups:** 33, 37, 38, 40, 45, 85

Date of Accounts	Mar 10	Mar 09	Mar 08
Working Capital	51	61	74
Fixed Assets	22	28	21
Current Assets	87	96	126

David Redpath

Catton Hall Catton Park, Catton, Swadlincote, DE12 8LN
Tel: 01283-713430
Directors: D. Redpath (Prop)
Date established: 1992 **No.of Employees:** 1 - 10 **Product Groups:** 41

Rose House Funeral Supplies Ltd

Unit 1a Boardman Industrial Estate, Swadlincote, DE11 9DL
Tel: 01283-819922 **Fax:** 01283-819947
E-mail: sales@rosehousegroup.co.uk
Website: http://www.funeral-supplies.co.uk
Directors: M. Wilson (Dir)
Immediate Holding Company: ROSE HOUSE FUNERAL SUPPLIES LTD
Registration no: 06257759 **Date established:** 2007
No.of Employees: 11 - 20 **Product Groups:** 26, 30, 36, 40, 49, 66, 67

Date of Accounts	Apr 12	Apr 11	Apr 10
Working Capital	-25	-38	-30
Fixed Assets	7	11	13
Current Assets	63	88	63

Secura Labels Ltd

Unit L2 Westminster Industrial Estate Measham, Swadlincote, DE12 7DS
Tel: 01530-515170 **Fax:** 01530-515171
E-mail: sales@securalabels.co.uk
Website: http://www.securalabels.co.uk
Bank(s): Fortis
Directors: M. Budz (MD)
Ultimate Holding Company: PEMBERSTONE VENTURES LIMITED
Immediate Holding Company: SECURA LABELS LIMITED
Registration no: 06648431 **VAT No.:** GB 371 7589 18
Date established: 2008 **Turnover:** £5m - £10m **No.of Employees:** 11 - 20
Product Groups: 23, 27, 28, 30, 32, 35, 66

Date of Accounts	Dec 11	Dec 10	Mar 10
Sales Turnover	N/A	1m	N/A
Pre Tax Profit/Loss	N/A	108	N/A
Working Capital	-6	-23	N/A
Fixed Assets	905	851	N/A
Current Assets	584	626	N/A
Current Liabilities	58	412	N/A

Surfair

Unit 5 Mount Pleasant Works Occupation Lane, Woodville, Swadlincote, DE11 8EX
Tel: 01283-228528 **Fax:** 01283-214381
E-mail: transport@oneworldlogistics.co.uk
Website: http://www.surfair.co.uk
Managers: P. Cannon (Sales Prom Mgr)
Immediate Holding Company: United Global Logistics Ltd
Registration no: 07537120 **VAT No.:** GB 485 5299 95
Date established: 2008 **Turnover:** £2m - £5m **No.of Employees:** 1 - 10
Product Groups: 76

Date of Accounts	May 08	May 07
Working Capital	185	162
Fixed Assets	37	59
Current Assets	765	714
Current Liabilities	581	552
Total Share Capital	1	1

Swadlincote Diesel Fuel Injection Services Co. Ltd

Unit 1 Ryder Close, Swadlincote, DE11 9EU
Tel: 01283-217951 **Fax:** 01283-551198
E-mail: shane.swad@btconnect.com
Website: http://www.swadlincotediesel.co.uk
Bank(s): Bank of Scotland
Directors: S. Richins (MD), M. Watson (Fin), M. Richins (Co Sec)
Immediate Holding Company: SWADLINCOTE DIESEL FUEL INJECTION SERVICES LIMITED
Registration no: 01107591 **VAT No.:** GB 127 1989 47
Date established: 1973 **Turnover:** Up to £250,000
No.of Employees: 21 - 50 **Product Groups:** 40

Date of Accounts	May 11	May 10	May 09
Working Capital	65	65	64
Fixed Assets	118	85	105
Current Assets	192	189	173

R Swain & Sons

Ocupation Lane Woodville, Swadlincote, DE11 8EU
Tel: 01283-217051 **Fax:** 01283-551334
E-mail: shaunbaker@rswaingroup.com
Website: http://www.rswain.com
Bank(s): HSBC Bank plc
Managers: S. Baker
Ultimate Holding Company: ENSOR HOLDINGS P.L.C.
Registration no: 00666100 **Date established:** 2000 **Turnover:** £2m - £5m
No.of Employees: 21 - 50 **Product Groups:** 72

T Musk Engineering Ltd

Unit 3 Astron Business Park Hearthcote Road, Swadlincote, DE11 9DW
Tel: 01283-200400 **Fax:** 01283-200444
E-mail: k.booth@musk-eng.co.uk
Website: http://www.musk-eng.co.uk
Bank(s): Barclays
Directors: K. Booth (MD)
Ultimate Holding Company: W.T. PARKER GROUP LTD.
Immediate Holding Company: T. MUSK ENGINEERING LIMITED
Registration no: 02183496 **VAT No.:** GB 289 1784 03
Date established: 1987 **Turnover:** £10m - £20m
No.of Employees: 51 - 100 **Product Groups:** 34, 36

Date of Accounts	Feb 12	Feb 11	Feb 10
Sales Turnover	15m	11m	9m
Pre Tax Profit/Loss	649	453	219
Working Capital	1m	784	934
Fixed Assets	515	434	101
Current Assets	5m	4m	2m
Current Liabilities	2m	2m	796

Trelleborg Sealing Solutions

Cadley Hill Industrial Estate, Swadlincote, DE11 9EU
Tel: 01283-222145 **Fax:** 01283-222911
E-mail: james.douglas@trelleborg.com
Website: http://www.trelleborg.com
Bank(s): HSBC, Cheltenham
Managers: C. Charteris (Personnel), K. Jones (Buyer), A. Buck (Fin Mgr), J. Douglas (Chief Mgr)
Immediate Holding Company: EMPIRE ACCOUNTANCY SERVICES LIMITED
Registration no: 05434133 **Date established:** 2007
Turnover: £20m - £50m **No.of Employees:** 101 - 250 **Product Groups:** 29

Date of Accounts	Mar 11	Mar 10	Mar 09
Working Capital	35	25	4
Fixed Assets	10	5	5
Current Assets	65	55	29

W T I Fasteners

Unit 7 Marquis Court Marquis Drive, Moira, Swadlincote, DE12 6EJ
Tel: 01283-215588 **Fax:** 01283-212020
E-mail: sales@wti-fasteners.co.uk
Website: http://www.wireinserts.com
Directors: J. Mason (MD)
Immediate Holding Company: W.T.I. FASTENERS LTD
Registration no: 02417598 **Date established:** 1989
Turnover: £500,000 - £1m **No.of Employees:** 1 - 10 **Product Groups:** 35

Date of Accounts	Oct 11	Oct 10	Oct 09
Working Capital	847	742	514
Fixed Assets	182	120	106
Current Assets	1m	976	645

DEVON

Axminster

Air Control Industries Ltd
Weycroft Avenue, Axminster, EX13 5HU
Tel: 08455-000501 **Fax:** 0845-500 0502
E-mail: sales@aircontrolindustries.com
Website: http://www.aircontrolindustries.com
Directors: M. Forknall (Mkt Research), S. Gale (Fin)
Managers: N. Wilson (Purch Mgr)
Immediate Holding Company: AIR CONTROL INDUSTRIES LIMITED
Registration no: 00959711 **VAT No.:** GB 185 3096 46
Date established: 1969 **Turnover:** £5m - £10m **No.of Employees:** 21 - 50
Product Groups: 40, 41, 42, 43, 66, 84

Date of Accounts	Mar 12	Mar 09	Apr 11
Sales Turnover	N/A	7m	N/A
Pre Tax Profit/Loss	N/A	469	N/A
Working Capital	1m	2m	2m
Fixed Assets	337	41	78
Current Assets	3m	3m	3m
Current Liabilities	N/A	432	N/A

Axminster Carpets Ltd
Woodmead Road, Axminster, EX13 5PQ
Tel: 01297-32244 **Fax:** 01297-35241
E-mail: sales@axminster-carpets.co.uk
Website: http://www.axminster-carpets.co.uk
Bank(s): HSBC
Directors: A. Biggs (Fin), D. McKelvey (Fin), G. Humphries (Sales), J. Dutfield (MD)
Managers: A. Pinn (Purch Mgr), D. Jeffries (Personnel), G. Larcombe (Tech Serv Mgr), S. Upton
Ultimate Holding Company: AXMINSTER CARPETS HOLDINGS LIMITED
Immediate Holding Company: AXMINSTER CARPETS,LIMITED
Registration no: 00324654 **VAT No.:** GB 185 3543 47
Date established: 1937 **Turnover:** £20m - £50m
No.of Employees: 251 - 500 **Product Groups:** 23

Date of Accounts	Dec 10	Dec 09	Dec 08
Sales Turnover	33m	32m	32m
Pre Tax Profit/Loss	415	206	1m
Working Capital	6m	9m	9m
Fixed Assets	13m	11m	11m
Current Assets	19m	16m	17m
Current Liabilities	2m	2m	2m

Axminster Tool Centre
Unit 10 Weycroft Avenue Millwey Rise Industrial Estate, Axminster, EX13 5PH
Tel: 0800-371822 **Fax:** 01297-35254
E-mail: email@axminster.co.uk
Website: http://www.axminster.co.uk
Directors: A. Parkhouse (Mkt Research), A. Thomas (Fin)
Managers: K. Styles (Personnel), D. Norcombe (Tech Serv Mgr), I. Styles, L. Forino (Sales Prom Mgr), A. Styles
Ultimate Holding Company: STYLES & BROWN LTD
Immediate Holding Company: AXMINSTER TOOL CENTRE LTD
Registration no: 03326979 **Date established:** 1997
Turnover: £20m - £50m **No.of Employees:** 101 - 250 **Product Groups:** 37

Date of Accounts	Apr 12	Apr 11	Apr 10
Sales Turnover	31m	29m	27m
Pre Tax Profit/Loss	419	890	1m
Working Capital	1m	1m	1m
Fixed Assets	3m	3m	2m
Current Assets	10m	12m	10m
Current Liabilities	2m	2m	1m

BriMarc Tools & Machinery
Unit 10 Weycroft Avenue, Axminster, EX13 5PH
Tel: 0300-100 1008 **Fax:** 0300-100 1009
E-mail: email@brimarc.com
Website: http://www.brimarc.com
Product Groups: 36, 40, 46, 47

M D Broom
4 Chestnut View Membury, Axminster, EX13 7AD
Tel: 01404-881784 **Fax:** 01404-881349
Directors: D. Broom (Prop), M. Broom (Prop)
Date established: 1991 **No.of Employees:** 1 - 10 **Product Groups:** 41

Doncasters Amtech (Part of Doncasters Ltd)
Weycroft Avenue, Axminster, EX13 5HU
Tel: 01297-34567 **Fax:** 01297-631110
E-mail: d.gage@doncasters.com
Website: http://www.doncasters.com
Managers: D. Gage (Mgr)
Immediate Holding Company: AXMINSTER ELECTRONICS LIMITED
Registration no: 01908981 **VAT No.:** GB 389 1553 14
Date established: 1985 **Turnover:** £500,000 - £1m
No.of Employees: 1 - 10 **Product Groups:** 40, 48

Date of Accounts	Mar 11	Mar 10	Mar 08
Working Capital	23	11	-15
Fixed Assets	1	1	1
Current Assets	47	55	18

GB Windpumps Ltd
Willowbrook Kilmington, Axminster, EX13 7SH
Tel: 01297-631672 **Fax:** 01297-631672
E-mail: sales@windpumps.co.uk
Website: http://www.windpumps.co.uk
Directors: C. Thorne (MD)
Immediate Holding Company: GB WINDPUMPS LIMITED
Registration no: 03680437 **Date established:** 1998
No.of Employees: 1 - 10 **Product Groups:** 40

Date of Accounts	Dec 11	Dec 10	Dec 09
Working Capital	93	86	68
Fixed Assets	12	15	16
Current Assets	106	121	77

Goulds Pumps a Division of ITT Industries Ltd
Millwey Rise Industrial Estate, Axminster, EX13 5HU
Tel: 01297-639100 **Fax:** 01297-630476
E-mail: axminster.sales@itt.com
Website: http://www.gouldspumps.com
Directors: T. Allsopp (MD)
Immediate Holding Company: AXMINSTER ELECTRONICS LIMITED
Registration no: 01908981 **Date established:** 1985 **No.of Employees:** 22
Product Groups: 40

Date of Accounts	Mar 11	Mar 10
Working Capital	29	7
Fixed Assets	1m	1m
Current Assets	61	157

Logical Energy Ltd
Ondine Horslears, Axminster, EX13 5JX
Tel: 0800-458 4148 **Fax:** 01297-631227
E-mail: julian@logicalenergy.co.uk
Website: http://www.logicalenergy.co.uk
Directors: J. Lack (Fin)
Immediate Holding Company: LOGICAL ENERGY LTD
Registration no: 05981073 **Date established:** 2006
No.of Employees: 1 - 10 **Product Groups:** 37

Date of Accounts	Dec 11	Dec 10	Dec 09
Working Capital	-27	-63	-42
Fixed Assets	7	10	3
Current Assets	154	51	35

Nu-Type Ltd
Millwey Rise Industrial Estate, Axminster, EX13 5HU
Tel: 01297-33114 **Fax:** 01297-34935
E-mail: nu-type@telinco.co.uk
Website: http://www.nu-type.co.uk
Bank(s): National Westminster
Managers: P. Deen (Tech), A. Hellier
Ultimate Holding Company: DATACARD CORPORATION (USA)
Immediate Holding Company: NU-TYPE LIMITED
Registration no: 02165728 **Date established:** 1987
Turnover: £500,000 - £1m **No.of Employees:** 21 - 50
Product Groups: 44, 48

Date of Accounts	Dec 08	Dec 07	Mar 11
Sales Turnover	N/A	N/A	919
Pre Tax Profit/Loss	N/A	N/A	102
Working Capital	144	148	166
Fixed Assets	7	2	6
Current Assets	216	217	272
Current Liabilities	N/A	N/A	102

P E M S Butler Ltd
The Red House, Axminster, EX13 5SE
Tel: 01297-631435 **Fax:** 01297-631437
E-mail: pems.butler@btopenworld.com
Website: http://www.superquick.co.uk
Directors: R. Butler (MD)
Immediate Holding Company: PEMS BUTLER LIMITED
Registration no: 00808618 **VAT No.:** 685 7295 77 **Date established:** 1964
Turnover: £250,000 - £500,000 **No.of Employees:** 1 - 10
Product Groups: 28, 49

Date of Accounts	Apr 11	Apr 10	Apr 09
Working Capital	163	155	169
Fixed Assets	522	535	545
Current Assets	178	158	173

Rob Perry Marine
The Boating Centre Charmouth Road, Axminster, EX13 5ST
Tel: 01297-631314 **Fax:** 01297-631409
E-mail: robert@robperrymarine.co.uk
Website: http://www.robperrymarine.co.uk
Directors: R. Perry (Prop)
Date established: 2001 **No.of Employees:** 1 - 10 **Product Groups:** 35, 36, 39

Barnstaple

4mation Educational Software Ltd
PO Box 282, Barnstaple, EX31 1HG
Tel: 01271-325353 **Fax:** 01271-322974
E-mail: rob@4mation.co.uk
Website: http://www.4mation.co.uk
Directors: R. McKay (MD)
VAT No.: GB 385 0699 15 **Turnover:** Up to £250,000
No.of Employees: 1 - 10 **Product Groups:** 44

Date of Accounts	Oct 05
Pre Tax Profit/Loss	-4
Working Capital	51
Current Assets	51
Total Share Capital	150

Aero Stanrew Ltd
Gratton Way Roundswell Business Park, Barnstaple, EX31 3AR
Tel: 01271-341300 **Fax:** 01271-341301
E-mail: sales@aerostanrew.co.uk
Website: http://www.aerostanrew.co.uk
Directors: C. Evans (Dir)
Ultimate Holding Company: ARLE COURT INDUSTRIES LIMITED
Immediate Holding Company: AERO STANREW LIMITED
Registration no: 00464848 **VAT No.:** GB 229 2280 68
Date established: 1949 **Turnover:** £5m - £10m
No.of Employees: 101 - 250 **Product Groups:** 37

Date of Accounts	Feb 12	Feb 11	Feb 10
Sales Turnover	11m	10m	8m
Pre Tax Profit/Loss	2m	1m	1m
Working Capital	7m	6m	5m
Fixed Assets	475	431	441
Current Assets	11m	10m	8m
Current Liabilities	2m	533	2m

Arma Products Building Materials
10 Riverside Units Riverside Road, Pottington Business Park, Barnstaple, EX31 1QN
Tel: 01271-373322 **Fax:** 01271-891139
E-mail: arthur@armaproducts.co.uk
Website: http://www.armaproducts.co.uk
Directors: A. Goozee (Prop)
Date established: 1989 **No.of Employees:** 1 - 10 **Product Groups:** 35

R J Dallyn
South Hill West Buckland, Barnstaple, EX32 0SE
Tel: 01598-760503 **Fax:** 01598-760654
E-mail: info@robertdallyn.co.uk
Directors: R. Dallyn (Prop)
Turnover: £250,000 - £500,000 **No.of Employees:** 1 - 10
Product Groups: 41

Danaher Motion UK Company
Fishleigh Road Roundswell Business Park, Barnstaple, EX31 3UD
Tel: 01271-334500 **Fax:** 01271-334502
E-mail: information@tiblmail.com
Website: http://www.danahermotion.com

see next page

Danaher Motion UK Company - Cont'd

Directors: K. Wallis (Co Sec)
Managers: R. Caddick, R. Davis (Transport)
Ultimate Holding Company: THOMSON INDUSTRIES INC (USA)
Immediate Holding Company: Launchchange Instrumentation Ltd
Registration no: 02071151 **Date established:** 1945
Turnover: £10m - £20m **No.of Employees:** 11 - 20 **Product Groups:** 30, 35, 37, 38, 45, 46

Date of Accounts	Dec 09	Dec 08	Dec 01
Sales Turnover	4m	6m	12m
Pre Tax Profit/Loss	577	-80	-290
Working Capital	-5m	-4m	1m
Fixed Assets	3m	5m	2m
Current Assets	1m	2m	10m
Current Liabilities	213	309	477

Devon Building Services Ltd

Unit 4a Upcott Avenue, Pottington Business Park, Barnstaple, EX31 1HN
Tel: 01271-374019 **Fax:** 01271-375977
E-mail: sales@dbsltd.eclipse.co.uk
Website: http://www.devonbuildingservices.co.uk
Managers: R. Mills (Sales Admin)
Immediate Holding Company: DEVON BUILDING SERVICES LTD
Registration no: 06643314 **Date established:** 2008 **Turnover:** £2m - £5m
No.of Employees: 21 - 50 **Product Groups:** 48

Date of Accounts	Jul 11	Jul 10	Jul 09
Working Capital	-155	-95	-54
Fixed Assets	153	148	171
Current Assets	518	557	312

Dolphin Tool Supplies

27 Bear Street, Barnstaple, EX32 7BX
Tel: 01271-325205 **Fax:** 07092-172204
E-mail: sales@dolphintools.biz
Website: http://www.dolphintools.biz
Directors: S. Macey (Prop)
Date established: 1996 **No.of Employees:** 1 - 10 **Product Groups:** 35, 36, 37, 41

Eriks UK (Leeds Service Centre)

Unit 10 Gratton Court, Roundswell Business Park, Barnstaple, EX31 3NL
Tel: 01271-371929 **Fax:** 01271-323915
E-mail: stuart.clement@eriks.co.uk
Website: http://www.eriks.co.uk
Managers: S. Clement
No.of Employees: 1 - 10 **Product Groups:** 29, 30, 35, 36

Forks2u

Pottington Business Park, Barnstaple, EX31 1QN
Tel: 01271-349898 **Fax:** 01271-349898
E-mail: forks2u@ukf.net
Directors: D. Phillips (MD)
Immediate Holding Company: FORKS 2 U LIMITED
Registration no: 07086668 **Date established:** 2009
No.of Employees: 1 - 10 **Product Groups:** 35, 39, 45

Date of Accounts	Nov 10
Fixed Assets	1

Terence Richard Hamley

Sunnydean Middle Marwood, Barnstaple, EX31 4EG
Tel: 01271-850468 **Fax:** 01271-850468
Directors: M. Hamley (Ptnr)
Date established: 1970 **No.of Employees:** 1 - 10 **Product Groups:** 41

Havana Coffee Co.

Barbican Close, Barnstaple, EX32 9HE
Tel: 01271-374376 **Fax:** 01271-374376
E-mail: info@havanacoffeeco.com
Website: http://www.havanacoffeeco.com
Managers: N. Shapland (Sales Prom Mgr)
Turnover: Up to £250,000 **No.of Employees:** 21 - 50 **Product Groups:** 40, 67

Ideal Power Ltd

14 Larks Way Tree Beech Rural Enterprise Park Gunn, Goodleigh, Barnstaple, EX32 7NZ
Tel: 01271-831299 **Fax:** 01271-831522
E-mail: info@idealpower.co.uk
Website: http://www.idealpower.co.uk
Directors: B. Gouldbourne (MD)
Immediate Holding Company: IDEAL POWER LIMITED
Registration no: 04063412 **Date established:** 2000
Turnover: £250,000 - £500,000 **No.of Employees:** 1 - 10
Product Groups: 37, 39, 67

Date of Accounts	Sep 11	Sep 10	Sep 09
Working Capital	274	110	148
Fixed Assets	7	6	5
Current Assets	791	694	596

J & S Ltd

Riverside Road Pottington Business Park, Barnstaple, EX31 1LY
Tel: 01271-337500 **Fax:** 01271-337501
E-mail: headoffice@jands.co.uk
Website: http://www.jands.co.uk
Bank(s): National Westminster
Directors: D. Jeffries (MD)
Immediate Holding Company: J+S LIMITED
Registration no: 03753462 **Date established:** 1999
Turnover: £10m - £20m **No.of Employees:** 101 - 250
Product Groups: 37, 84

Date of Accounts	Sep 11	Sep 10	Sep 09
Sales Turnover	13m	10m	11m
Pre Tax Profit/Loss	1m	964	721
Working Capital	1m	1m	809
Fixed Assets	1m	1m	954
Current Assets	4m	4m	4m
Current Liabilities	1m	1m	1m

Jewson Ltd

Upcott Avenue Pottington Business Park, Barnstaple, EX31 1HN
Tel: 01271-345891 **Fax:** 01271-378917
E-mail: kevin.betts@jewson.co.uk
Website: http://www.jewson.co.uk
Managers: K. Betts (Mgr)
Ultimate Holding Company: COMPAGNIE DE SAINT GOBAIN (FRANCE)
Immediate Holding Company: JEWSON LIMITED
Registration no: 00348407 **Date established:** 1939
No.of Employees: 1 - 10 **Product Groups:** 66

Date of Accounts	Dec 11	Dec 10	Dec 09
Sales Turnover	1606m	1547m	1485m
Pre Tax Profit/Loss	18m	100m	45m
Working Capital	-345m	-250m	-349m
Fixed Assets	496m	387m	461m
Current Assets	657m	1005m	1320m
Current Liabilities	66m	120m	64m

Labeline

The Old Aerodrome Chivenor, Barnstaple, EX31 4AY
Tel: 01271-817677 **Fax:** 0870-240 8072
E-mail: sales@labeline.com
Website: http://www.labeline.com
Managers: M. Brice (Sales Prom Mgr)
No.of Employees: 1 - 10 **Product Groups:** 27

N D Precision Products

Braunton Road, Barnstaple, EX31 1GE
Tel: 01271-345496 **Fax:** 01271-344188
E-mail: sales@ndprecisionproducts.co.uk
Website: http://www.ndprecisionproducts.co.uk
Directors: D. Squire (Fin)
Immediate Holding Company: ELECTRICZONE LIMITED
Registration no: 05231991 **Date established:** 2004
No.of Employees: 11 - 20 **Product Groups:** 36

North Devon Journal

96 High Street, Barnstaple, EX31 1HT
Tel: 01271-343064 **Fax:** 01271-323165
E-mail: advertising@northdevon.journal.co.uk
Website: http://www.thisisnorthdevon.co.uk
Bank(s): National Westminster
Managers: A. Cooper (Mgr), D. Sawyer, H. Saunders (Bldg Mgr)
Ultimate Holding Company: DAILY MAIL & GENERAL TRUST
Immediate Holding Company: NORTHCLIFFE NEWSPAPERS GROUP LTD
Registration no: 00392494 **VAT No.:** GB 143 1354 03
Date established: 1952 **Turnover:** £1m - £2m **No.of Employees:** 51 - 100
Product Groups: 28

North Devon Steel Services

5 Riverside Units Riverside Road Pottington Industrial Estate, Pottington Business Park, Barnstaple, EX31 1QN
Tel: 01271-323001 **Fax:** 01271-323001
Website: http://www.northdevonsteelservices.co.uk
Directors: D. Gordon (Ptnr)
Date established: 1988 **No.of Employees:** 1 - 10 **Product Groups:** 35

Parker Hannifin plc (Instrumentation Products Division)

Riverside Road Pottington Business Park, Barnstaple, EX31 1NP
Tel: 01271-313131 **Fax:** 01271-373636
E-mail: ipd@parker.com
Website: http://www.parker.com
Bank(s): Lloyds TSB Bank plc
Directors: A. Sibbald (Tech Serv), D. Tozer (Pers), S. Garratt (Fin)
Managers: D. Bailey (Chief Mgr), P. Ager (I.T. Exec), R. Roebuck (Personnel), N. Jakes (Fin Mgr)
Immediate Holding Company: PARKER HANNIFIN (HOLDINGS) LIMITED
Registration no: 03922924 **Date established:** 2000
No.of Employees: 251 - 500 **Product Groups:** 36, 40

Date of Accounts	Jun 11	Jun 10	Jun 09
Pre Tax Profit/Loss	-123	-3m	-2
Working Capital	-3m	-3m	195
Fixed Assets	200m	200m	200m
Current Assets	459	196	195

Pearce Construction Barnstaple Ltd

Brannam Crescent Roundswell Industrial Estate Roundswell Business Park, Barnstaple, EX31 3TD
Tel: 01271-345261 **Fax:** 01271-322164
E-mail: coleys@pearcebarnstaple.co.uk
Website: http://www.pearcebarnstaple.co.uk
Bank(s): Lloyds, Cross St, Barnstaple
Managers: S. Coley (Personnel)
Ultimate Holding Company: PCBL LIMITED
Immediate Holding Company: PEARCE CONSTRUCTION (BARNSTAPLE) LIMITED
Registration no: 00408163 **Date established:** 1946
Turnover: £10m - £20m **No.of Employees:** 21 - 50 **Product Groups:** 51, 52, 84

Date of Accounts	Apr 12	Apr 11	Apr 10
Sales Turnover	13m	14m	13m
Pre Tax Profit/Loss	5	2	-143
Working Capital	3m	2m	2m
Fixed Assets	2m	2m	2m
Current Assets	5m	5m	4m
Current Liabilities	1m	1m	1m

Phillip Merrell Agency

51 Cleave Road Sticklepath, Barnstaple, EX31 2DU
Tel: 01271-322175 **Fax:** 01271-325414
E-mail: pma@p-m-a.freeserve.co.uk
Website: http://www.p-m-a.freeserve.co.uk
Directors: P. Merrell (Prop)
Immediate Holding Company: PHILLIP MERRELL AGENCY LIMITED
Registration no: 04462833 **Date established:** 2002
No.of Employees: 1 - 10 **Product Groups:** 20, 40, 41

Date of Accounts	Jun 11	Jun 10	Jun 09
Working Capital	N/A	8	8
Current Assets	N/A	9	10
Current Liabilities	N/A	1	N/A

Sandpark Service Station

Kentisbury, Barnstaple, EX31 4NF
Tel: 01271-883320 **Fax:** 01271-883320
Directors: W. Camp (Prop)
No.of Employees: 1 - 10 **Product Groups:** 41

Smallridge Bros

East Collabear Tawstock, Barnstaple, EX31 3JZ
Tel: 01271-858426 **Fax:** 01271-858615
E-mail: sales@smallridgebros.co.uk
Website: http://www.smallridgebros.co.uk
Directors: D. Smallridge (Ptnr)
Immediate Holding Company: SMALLRIDGE BROS LIMITED
Registration no: 06509382 **Date established:** 2008 **Turnover:** £5m - £10m
No.of Employees: 21 - 50 **Product Groups:** 41

Date of Accounts	Mar 11	Mar 10	Mar 09
Sales Turnover	9m	9m	N/A
Pre Tax Profit/Loss	612	735	590
Working Capital	2m	2m	1m
Fixed Assets	577	533	572
Current Assets	8m	5m	5m
Current Liabilities	1m	450	629

Smurfit Kappa

Pottington Industrial Estate Pottington Business Park, Barnstaple, EX31 1LX
Tel: 01271-345011 **Fax:** 01271-346665
E-mail: mike.reed@smurfitkappa.co.uk
Website: http://www.smurfitkappa.co.uk
Managers: G. Mason (Plant)
Ultimate Holding Company: SMURFIT GROUP UK
Registration no: 01017013 **No.of Employees:** 21 - 50 **Product Groups:** 27

M Stone

2 Higher Elmwood Roundswell, Barnstaple, EX31 3SG
Tel: 01271-329243
Directors: M. Stone (Prop)
Date established: 1998 **No.of Employees:** 1 - 10 **Product Groups:** 20, 40, 41

Tex Plastics Barnstaple Ltd

Unit 1 Aviemore Industrial Estate Sticklepath, Barnstaple, EX31 2EU
Tel: 01271-378528 **Fax:** 01271-379230
E-mail: info@tex.co.uk
Website: http://www.tex-holdings.co.uk
Bank(s): National Westminster Bank Plc
Directors: A. Clarke (Tech Serv), C. Varley (MD), J. Davies (Sales), C. Wilcox (Fin)
Managers: K. Payne (Purch Mgr)
Ultimate Holding Company: TEX HOLDINGS PLC
Immediate Holding Company: TEX PLASTICS (BARNSTAPLE) LIMITED
Registration no: 00309549 **VAT No.:** GB 510 5070 04
Date established: 1936 **Turnover:** £5m - £10m
No.of Employees: 51 - 100 **Product Groups:** 30, 39, 48

Date of Accounts	Dec 11	Dec 10	Dec 09
Sales Turnover	8m	9m	7m
Pre Tax Profit/Loss	361	353	250
Working Capital	1m	1m	906
Fixed Assets	615	776	874
Current Assets	3m	3m	2m
Current Liabilities	662	907	456

Tilt Master

Mill Road, Barnstaple, EX31 1JQ
Tel: 01271-321232 **Fax:** 01271-344355
E-mail: info@tiltmaster.co.uk
Website: http://www.tiltmaster.co.uk
Directors: C. Lidstone (Prop)
Immediate Holding Company: BARNSTAPLE FC SOCIAL CLUB LIMITED
Registration no: 07150089 **Date established:** 2012
No.of Employees: 1 - 10 **Product Groups:** 20, 40, 41

Date of Accounts	May 11
Working Capital	-13
Current Assets	3

Tinting Express Ltd

New Estate House Old School Lane, Fremington, Barnstaple, EX31 3AZ
Tel: 01271-322857 **Fax:** 01271-326346
E-mail: mail@tintingexpress.co.uk
Website: http://www.tintingexpress.co.uk
Directors: B. Cornish (MD)
Immediate Holding Company: WINDSCREEN & TINTING EXPRESS LTD
Registration no: 05510048 **Date established:** 2005
No.of Employees: 1 - 10 **Product Groups:** 30, 52, 63, 66

Date of Accounts	Nov 11	Nov 10	Nov 09
Working Capital	-3	-0	-4
Fixed Assets	4	5	7
Current Assets	18	19	13

W Y K O Industrial Distribution Ltd Barnstaple Service Centre

Unit 10 Gratton Court Gratton Way Roundswell Industrial Estate, Roundswell Business Park, Barnstaple, EX31 3NL
Tel: 01271-371929 **Fax:** 01271-323915
E-mail: wid.barnstaple@wyko.co.uk
Website: http://www.wyko.co.uk
Managers: J. Clements (Mgr)
Immediate Holding Company: BRIAN HOCKIN ACCOUNTANTS LIMITED
Registration no: 00917112 **Date established:** 2009
Turnover: £250m - £500m **No.of Employees:** 1 - 10 **Product Groups:** 83

Date of Accounts	Dec 11	Dec 10
Working Capital	-48	-52
Fixed Assets	60	63
Current Assets	37	49

Wellington Welding Supplies Ltd

Unit 21 Oakwood Close Brannam Business Park, Roundswell Business Park, Barnstaple, EX31 3NJ
Tel: 01271-325333 **Fax:** 01271-325334
Website: http://www.wellingtonweldingsupplies.co.uk
Managers: M. Hayward (District Mgr)
Immediate Holding Company: WELLINGTON WELDING SUPPLIES LIMITED
Registration no: 00821066 **Date established:** 1964
No.of Employees: 1 - 10 **Product Groups:** 46

Date of Accounts	Dec 11	Dec 10	Dec 09
Working Capital	231	252	355
Fixed Assets	587	587	522
Current Assets	1m	1m	1m

West Of England Fire Protection Ltd

Unit 4 Taw Trade Park Braunton Road, Barnstaple, EX31 1JZ
Tel: 01271-377394 **Fax:** 01271-321711
E-mail: info@westfire.co.uk
Website: http://www.westfire.co.uk
Directors: C. Payne (MD)
Immediate Holding Company: WEST OF ENGLAND FIRE PROTECTION LIMITED
Registration no: 03923800 **Date established:** 2000
No.of Employees: 1 - 10 **Product Groups:** 38, 42

Date of Accounts	Jul 11	Jul 10	Jul 09
Working Capital	28	19	18
Fixed Assets	36	44	34
Current Assets	105	103	101

Guy Winsor Metalcrafts
Netherby Roundswell, Barnstaple, EX31 3NS
Tel: 01271-327183 **Fax:** 01271-327183
Directors: G. Winsor (Prop)
Date established: 1981 **No.of Employees:** 1 - 10 **Product Groups:** 26, 35

Bideford

B X R Ballscrews Ltd BXR Group
Unit 5 Harton Way Industrial Park, Hartland, Bideford, EX39 6AG
Tel: 01237-479069 **Fax:** 01237-424527
E-mail: info@bxrballscrews.co.uk
Website: http://www.bxrballscrews.co.uk
Directors: K. McCormick (MD)
Managers: L. McCormick (Chief Acct), K. Mccormick (Mgr)
Immediate Holding Company: BXR BALLSCREWS LTD
Registration no: 06672294 **Date established:** 2008
Turnover: Up to £250,000 **No.of Employees:** 1 - 10 **Product Groups:** 48

Britton Valves Ltd
Kynochs Nuttaberry, Bideford, EX39 4DT
Tel: 01237-477465 **Fax:** 01237-421459
E-mail: post@britton.dowsongroup.com
Website: http://www.dowsongroup.com
Managers: J. Lewis (Chief Mgr)
Registration no: 05869826 **Date established:** 2006
No.of Employees: 1 - 10 **Product Groups:** 36, 37, 38

Greendoor Design caroline bale
16 Northdown Road, Bideford, EX39 3LP
Tel: 01237-425532 **Fax:** 01237-425532
E-mail: greendoordesign@btinternet.com
Website: http://www.greendoordesign.co.uk
Directors: B. Scoines (Dir)
No.of Employees: 1 - 10 **Product Groups:** 32, 52, 84

Joslings Lighting
Nuttaberry Hill, Bideford, EX39 4EA
Tel: 01237-475106
Website: http://www.lightingrmbideford.co.uk
Directors: S. Cook (Ptnr)
No.of Employees: 1 - 10 **Product Groups:** 37, 67

Living Space
60 Bay View Road Northam, Bideford, EX39 1BH
Tel: 01237-424424 **Fax:** 01237-424424
E-mail: sales@compton-buildings.co.uk
Website: http://www.comptonbuildings.co.uk
Directors: L. Shelley (Prop)
No.of Employees: 1 - 10 **Product Groups:** 25, 33, 35, 66

Marine Electronics
Putridge Buckland Brewer, Bideford, EX39 5LZ
Tel: 01271-860001 **Fax:** 01271-860001
Website: http://www.marineelectronicsystems.co.uk
Directors: J. Rice (Prop)
Date established: 1998 **No.of Employees:** 1 - 10 **Product Groups:** 35, 36, 39

North Devon Tooling
Haven Dean Horns Cross, Bideford, EX39 5QG
Tel: 01237-451347
Directors: D. Hicks (Ptnr), A. Hicks (Ptnr)
Date established: 1976 **No.of Employees:** 1 - 10 **Product Groups:** 36

Notts Contractors Ltd
Barton Yards Abbotsham, Bideford, EX39 5AP
Tel: 01237-421066 **Fax:** 01237-478800
Website: http://www.nottscontractorsltd.co.uk
Bank(s): Barclays
Directors: P. Jury (MD), K. Shapland (Fin), K. Davies (Dir)
Immediate Holding Company: NOTTS CONTRACTORS LIMITED
Registration no: 03106260 **VAT No.:** GB 666 3394 06
Date established: 1995 **Turnover:** £1m - £2m **No.of Employees:** 21 - 50
Product Groups: 14, 54, 67

Date of Accounts	Oct 11	Oct 10	Oct 09
Working Capital	2m	2m	2m
Fixed Assets	464	573	596
Current Assets	2m	3m	2m

Pot Black UK
Bowden Green Clovelly, Bideford, EX39 5TH
Tel: 01237-478061 **Fax:** 01237-471044
Directors: P. Vickery (MD), S. Husband (Fin)
Immediate Holding Company: TANDEM GROUP PLC
Registration no: 02096209 **Turnover:** £5m - £10m
No.of Employees: 1 - 10 **Product Groups:** 49

Safety Services Direct Ltd
Units 7-8 Danver Court Clovelly Road Industrial Estate, Bideford, EX39 3HN
Tel: 01237-477931
E-mail: info@safetyservicesdirect.com
Website: http://www.safetyservicesdirect.com
Directors: O. Whitfield (Dir)
Immediate Holding Company: SAFETY SERVICES DIRECT LIMITED
Registration no: 05216927 **Date established:** 2004
Turnover: £500,000 - £1m **No.of Employees:** 1 - 10 **Product Groups:** 84

Date of Accounts	Dec 11	Dec 10	Dec 09
Working Capital	629	417	133
Fixed Assets	204	546	589
Current Assets	636	537	250

Swallow Field plc
Alverdiscott Road, Bideford, EX39 4LQ
Tel: 01237-471771 **Fax:** 01237-477240
E-mail: ruth.clifton@swallowfield.com
Website: http://www.swallowfield.com
Bank(s): National Westminster Bank Plc
Directors: C. Hume (Co Sec)
Managers: I. Kraze (Personnel), R. Clifton (Prod Mgr), C. Denton (Mktg Serv Mgr), S. Miller (Chief Acct), R. Lewis (I.T. Exec), G. Moore, L. Davis
Immediate Holding Company: SWALLOWFIELD PLC
Registration no: 01975376 **VAT No.:** GB 429 2206 64
Date established: 1986 **Turnover:** £5m - £10m
No.of Employees: 101 - 250 **Product Groups:** 32

Date of Accounts	Jun 11	Jun 10	Jun 09
Sales Turnover	57m	52m	49m
Pre Tax Profit/Loss	1m	1m	1m
Working Capital	5m	5m	5m
Fixed Assets	12m	11m	12m
Current Assets	24m	21m	18m
Current Liabilities	6m	2m	3m

Terry Josling
Nuttaberry Hill, Bideford, EX39 4EA
Tel: 01237-475106
Directors: S. Cook (Ptnr)
Immediate Holding Company: NECULAU LOGISTICS LTD
Date established: 2010 **No.of Employees:** 1 - 10 **Product Groups:** 37, 67

Date of Accounts	Mar 11
Working Capital	2
Current Assets	2

Voicethrower Ltd
3 Springfield Terrace Northam, Bideford, EX39 1DN
Tel: 01237-425770 **Fax:** 01237-424637
E-mail: info@voicethrower.com
Website: http://www.voicethrower.com
Directors: D. Carpenter (Fin), R. Carpenter (MD)
Immediate Holding Company: VOICETHROWER LTD
Registration no: 04389042 **Date established:** 2002
No.of Employees: 1 - 10 **Product Groups:** 37

Date of Accounts	May 11	May 10	May 09
Working Capital	-120	-149	-161
Fixed Assets	61	66	72
Current Assets	1	N/A	1

Zymax Lightning & Surge Protection Devices
9 Caddsdown Industrial Park Clovelly Road, Bideford, EX39 3DX
Tel: 01237-479797 **Fax:** 01237-476600
E-mail: sales@zymax.com
Website: http://www.zymax.com
Managers: R. Elgar (Sales Prom Mgr)
Immediate Holding Company: ZYMAX INTERNATIONAL LIMITED
Registration no: 02881817 **Date established:** 1993
No.of Employees: 1 - 10 **Product Groups:** 33, 37, 38, 44, 67, 84

Date of Accounts	Dec 11	Dec 10	Dec 09
Working Capital	2	-21	-5
Fixed Assets	16	15	17
Current Assets	68	43	56

Braunton

A4 Apparel Ltd
Unit 1 Velator, Braunton, EX33 2DX
Tel: 01271-816158 **Fax:** 01905-755885
E-mail: info@a4apparel.co.uk
Website: http://www.a4apparel.co.uk
Directors: A. Lambert (MD)
Immediate Holding Company: A4 APPAREL LIMITED
Registration no: 05383501 **Date established:** 2005
Turnover: £500,000 - £1m **No.of Employees:** 1 - 10 **Product Groups:** 24, 49

Date of Accounts	Mar 11	Mar 10	Mar 09
Working Capital	32	25	19
Fixed Assets	29	26	37
Current Assets	179	130	118

Butler & Yeo
Unit 3 Knowle Trading Estate Knowle, Braunton, EX33 2NA
Tel: 01271-812941 **Fax:** 01271-812941
Directors: M. Bulled (Prop)
Date established: 1969 **No.of Employees:** 1 - 10 **Product Groups:** 35

North Devon Electronics Ltd
Velator, Braunton, EX33 2DX
Tel: 01271-813553 **Fax:** 01271-816171
E-mail: ralf@nde.co.uk
Website: http://www.nde.co.uk
Bank(s): HSBC Bank plc
Directors: R. Gordon (Dir)
Managers: T. Lockwood (Prod Mgr), F. Gordon (Sales Admin), J. Hams (Sales & Mktg Mg), B. Morgan (Mats Contrlr)
Ultimate Holding Company: N.D. THORNLEY LIMITED
Immediate Holding Company: NORTH DEVON ELECTRONICS LIMITED
Registration no: 01109299 **VAT No.:** GB 144 7824 53
Date established: 1973 **Turnover:** £2m - £5m **No.of Employees:** 51 - 100
Product Groups: 37

Date of Accounts	Mar 11	Mar 10	Mar 09
Pre Tax Profit/Loss	N/A	N/A	330
Working Capital	2m	2m	2m
Fixed Assets	260	170	210
Current Assets	4m	3m	2m
Current Liabilities	N/A	N/A	181

Perrigo UK
Staggers Lane Wrafton, Braunton, EX33 2DL
Tel: 01271-815815 **Fax:** 01283-228328
E-mail: russell.howard@perrigouk.com
Website: http://www.perrigouk.com
Bank(s): Lloyds
Directors: R. Howard (MD), K. Spurling (Pers)
Managers: M. Tucker, G. Clark, M. Rogers (Purch Mgr)
Ultimate Holding Company: PERRIGO COMPANY (USA)
Immediate Holding Company: PERRIGO UK ACQUISITION LIMITED
Registration no: 04235859 **Date established:** 2001
Turnover: £10m - £20m **No.of Employees:** 251 - 500 **Product Groups:** 31

Date of Accounts	May 09	May 08	May 10
Sales Turnover	N/A	71m	N/A
Pre Tax Profit/Loss	-1m	832	25
Working Capital	13m	-38m	13m
Fixed Assets	65m	66m	65m
Current Assets	13m	35m	14m
Current Liabilities	N/A	7m	17

Ruda Holiday Park Ltd
Croyde Bay Croyde, Braunton, EX33 1NY
Tel: 01271-890477 **Fax:** 01271-890656
E-mail: info@ruda.co.uk
Website: http://www.ruda.co.uk
Directors: S. Irvine (Dir), J. Waterworth (MD)
Managers: S. Ion (Site Co-ord), S. Irvine (District Mgr)
Ultimate Holding Company: PARKDEAN HOLIDAYS LIMITED
Immediate Holding Company: RUDA HOLIDAY PARK LIMITED
Registration no: 01347793 **Date established:** 1978
No.of Employees: 21 - 50 **Product Groups:** 69

Brixham

C F Bowles
Overgang Road, Brixham, TQ5 8AR
Tel: 01803-853670 **Fax:** 01803-855514
Directors: C. Bowles (Prop)
Immediate Holding Company: C F BOWLES MARINE ENGINEERS LTD
Registration no: 04820673 **Date established:** 2003
No.of Employees: 1 - 10 **Product Groups:** 35, 36, 39

Brixham Steel Constructional
Furze Lane Pump Street, Brixham, TQ5 8EE
Tel: 01803-852080
Directors: R. Coopman (Prop)
Date established: 1950 **No.of Employees:** 1 - 10 **Product Groups:** 35

Hubbard Engineering
Furze Lane Pump Street, Brixham, TQ5 8EE
Tel: 01803-853327 **Fax:** 01803-882734
Directors: S. Hubbard (Ptnr)
Date established: 1946 **No.of Employees:** 1 - 10 **Product Groups:** 35, 36, 39

J B Packaging
Unit 7 Northfields Industrial Estate, Brixham, TQ5 8UA
Tel: 01803-882034 **Fax:** 01803-882053
E-mail: enquiries@jbpackaging.co.uk
Website: http://www.jbpackaging.co.uk
Managers: M. Stansbie (Mgr)
Date established: 1982 **No.of Employees:** 1 - 10 **Product Groups:** 38, 42

Marine Engineering Looe
Unit 1 The Dart Building Dartside Quay, Galmpton, Brixham, TQ5 0GA
Tel: 01803-844777 **Fax:** 01803-845684
E-mail: torbay@marine-engineering-looe.co.uk
Website: http://www.marine-engineering-looe.co.uk
Managers: M. Northbrook (Ops Mgr)
Date established: 2001 **No.of Employees:** 1 - 10 **Product Groups:** 35, 36, 39

Northfield Foundry Ltd
Northfields Lane, Brixham, TQ5 8NU
Tel: 01803-853222 **Fax:** 01803-855776
E-mail: info@northfieldfoundry.co.uk
Bank(s): Alliance & Leicester
Directors: P. Spencer (MD)
Managers: M. Hughes (Sales Admin)
Ultimate Holding Company: W.G.THURSFIELD(PATTERN MAKERS)LIMITED
Immediate Holding Company: NORTHFIELD FOUNDRY LIMITED
Registration no: 00435134 **VAT No.:** 141 1036 29 **Date established:** 1947
No.of Employees: 21 - 50 **Product Groups:** 34

Date of Accounts	Jun 11	Jun 10	Jun 09
Working Capital	837	803	796
Fixed Assets	15	28	41
Current Assets	1m	937	953

Protec Fire
29 Summer Lane, Brixham, TQ5 0DL
Tel: 01803-858048 **Fax:** 01803-858048
E-mail: sales@protecfire.co.uk
Website: http://www.protecfire.co.uk
Directors: D. Passmore (Prop)
Date established: 1991 **No.of Employees:** 1 - 10 **Product Groups:** 38, 42

Ultrasonic Cleaning Services Ltd
Unit 2 Metherell Avenue Industrial Estate, Brixham, TQ5 9QL
Tel: 01803-857500 **Fax:** 08704-871755
E-mail: info@ucs-brixham.co.uk
Website: http://www.ucs-brixham.co.uk
Directors: M. Dodd (MD)
Date established: 2005 **No.of Employees:** 1 - 10 **Product Groups:** 35, 36, 39

Upton Electronics
25 Horsepool Street, Brixham, TQ5 9LF
Tel: 07855-800540
E-mail: u.e.installations@gmail.com
Website: http://www.uptonelectronics.co.uk
Managers: D. Woods (Mgr)
No.of Employees: 1 - 10 **Product Groups:** 37, 67, 83

Buckfastleigh

D C E Holne Ltd
Mardle Way Industrial Estate, Buckfastleigh, TQ11 0NS
Tel: 01364-643862 **Fax:** 01364-643025
E-mail: enquiries@dce-holne.co.uk
Website: http://www.dce-holne.co.uk
Bank(s): Lloyds TSB Bank plc
Directors: P. Chapman (MD)
Ultimate Holding Company: D.C.E. HOLDINGS LIMITED
Immediate Holding Company: D.C.E. HOLNE LIMITED
Registration no: 01449688 **VAT No.:** GB 339 6136 40
Date established: 1979 **Turnover:** £1m - £2m **No.of Employees:** 11 - 20
Product Groups: 48

Date of Accounts	Oct 11	Oct 10	Oct 09
Working Capital	160	145	285
Current Assets	447	313	434

Green Batteries
71 Barn Park, Buckfastleigh, TQ11 0AT
Tel: 0781-7975025
E-mail: battery@ukf.net
Website: http://www.battery.ukf.net
Directors: S. White (MD)
Product Groups: 37

Hoist Hire Services Ltd
Mardle Way, Buckfastleigh, TQ11 0JS
Tel: 01364-644101 **Fax:** 01364-644080
E-mail: info@hoisthire.co.uk
Website: http://www.hoisthire.co.uk
Directors: J. Douce (MD)
Ultimate Holding Company: HOIST HIRE HOLDINGS LIMITED
Immediate Holding Company: HOIST HIRE SERVICES LIMITED
Registration no: 02398442 **Date established:** 1989 **Turnover:** £1m - £2m
No.of Employees: 11 - 20 **Product Groups:** 35, 39, 45

Date of Accounts	May 11	May 10	May 09
Sales Turnover	N/A	1m	N/A
Pre Tax Profit/Loss	N/A	-41	N/A
Working Capital	-128	-90	-259
Fixed Assets	1m	1m	2m
Current Assets	431	449	401
Current Liabilities	N/A	228	N/A

Budleigh Salterton

Creative Chrome
Unit 7 South Farm Court South Farm Road, Budleigh Salterton, EX9 7AY
Tel: 01395-446009 **Fax:** 01395-446009
E-mail: enquiries@creativechrome.co.uk
Website: http://www.creativechrome.co.uk
Directors: S. King (Ptnr)
No.of Employees: 1 - 10 **Product Groups:** 31, 34, 38, 88

Chulmleigh

Malcolm Vile
Lamorna Lama Cross, Wembworthy, Chulmleigh, EX18 7SA
Tel: 01837-83681
Directors: M. Vile (Prop)
Date established: 1980 **No.of Employees:** 1 - 10 **Product Groups:** 41

Colyton

Ceramtec UK Ltd
Sidmouth Road, Colyton, EX24 6JP
Tel: 01297-552707 **Fax:** 01297-553325
E-mail: info@ceramtec.co.uk
Website: http://www.ceramtec.co.uk
Bank(s): Lloyds TSB Bank plc
Directors: J. Langer (MD), N. Bygrave (Fin)
Managers: K. Taylor
Ultimate Holding Company: ROCKWOOD HOLDINGS INC (USA)
Immediate Holding Company: CERAMTEC UK LTD
Registration no: 00851165 **VAT No.:** GB 409 0496 53
Date established: 1965 **Turnover:** £2m - £5m **No.of Employees:** 51 - 100
Product Groups: 14, 33, 37, 38

Date of Accounts	Dec 11	Dec 10	Dec 09
Sales Turnover	4m	4m	3m
Pre Tax Profit/Loss	-227	-125	-288
Working Capital	925	1m	1m
Fixed Assets	688	689	459
Current Assets	2m	2m	2m
Current Liabilities	162	224	141

Telesiseagle Ltd
Dolphin Street, Colyton, EX24 6LU
Tel: 01297-551313 **Fax:** 01297-551319
E-mail: marianne.jones@telesis.com
Website: http://www.telesiseagle.com
Directors: P. Rowlands (MD), M. Jones (Co Sec)
Immediate Holding Company: TELESISEAGLE LIMITED
Registration no: 01745452 **Date established:** 1983 **Turnover:** £2m - £5m
No.of Employees: 1 - 10 **Product Groups:** 42, 46, 47

Date of Accounts	Dec 07	Dec 06	Dec 05
Working Capital	-270	-497	80
Fixed Assets	292	306	141
Current Assets	818	733	1229
Current Liabilities	1089	1229	1148
Total Share Capital	12	12	12

Crediton

Advance Fire Technology
Tucking Mill Zeal Monachorum, Crediton, EX17 6DF
Tel: 01363-82825 **Fax:** 01363-82243
Directors: G. Hocking (Prop)
Date established: 1990 **No.of Employees:** 1 - 10 **Product Groups:** 38, 42

Crediton Sewing Machine Services
5 Golden Joy, Crediton, EX17 1EA
Tel: 01363-774852 **Fax:** 01363-774852
E-mail: info@csms.uk.net
Directors: M. Jordan (Prop)
Date established: 1987 **No.of Employees:** 1 - 10 **Product Groups:** 43

Dolphin Lifts South West
Forge House Coldridge, Crediton, EX17 6AX
Tel: 01363-83892 **Fax:** 01363-83745
Website: http://www.dolphins.co.uk
Directors: S. Carpenter (Prop)
Date established: 2001 **No.of Employees:** 1 - 10 **Product Groups:** 35, 39, 45

Farmco Agricultural Engineers
Station House Lapford, Crediton, EX17 6QU
Tel: 01363-83434 **Fax:** 01363- 884288
Directors: S. Harvey (Ptnr)
Date established: 1975 **No.of Employees:** 1 - 10 **Product Groups:** 41

Ferryman Polytunnels Ltd
Bridge Road Lapford, Crediton, EX17 6AE
Tel: 01363-83444 **Fax:** 01363-83050
E-mail: info@ferryman.uk.com
Website: http://www.ferryman-polytunnels.co.uk
Directors: G. Bruce (Dir), S. Briant Evans (Co Sec)
Immediate Holding Company: FERRYMAN POLYTUNNELS LIMITED
Registration no: 05020172 **Date established:** 2004
No.of Employees: 1 - 10 **Product Groups:** 26, 35

Date of Accounts	May 11	May 10	May 09
Working Capital	-74	-87	-204
Fixed Assets	262	317	315
Current Assets	112	90	64

Graphic plc
Down End Lords Meadow Industrial Estate, Crediton, EX17 1HN
Tel: 01363-774874 **Fax:** 01363-775753
E-mail: sales@graphic.plc.uk
Website: http://www.graphic.plc.uk
Directors: R. Rozario (Ch), T. Sanders (Sales), P. Di Giuseppe (Fin)
Managers: S. Keeping (Purch Mgr), J. Kelsey (Tech Serv Mgr), A. Good (Personnel)
Immediate Holding Company: GRAPHIC PLC
Registration no: 01036230 **Date established:** 1971
Turnover: £10m - £20m **No.of Employees:** 101 - 250 **Product Groups:** 37

Date of Accounts	Sep 11	Sep 10	Sep 09
Sales Turnover	15m	13m	12m
Pre Tax Profit/Loss	2m	2m	290
Working Capital	2m	760	498
Fixed Assets	8m	8m	7m
Current Assets	6m	5m	4m
Current Liabilities	1m	1m	905

Ernest Jackson & Co. Ltd
29 High Street, Crediton, EX17 3AP
Tel: 01363-636000 **Fax:** 01363-636063
E-mail: dave.walter@craftfoods.com
Website: http://www.ejackson.co.uk
Bank(s): Lloyds TSB
Directors: C. Evans (Pers), P. Franics (Comm), S. Hill (Fin), D. Walter (MD)
Managers: S. Camm, K. Trowbridge (Personnel), L. Hodges (Nat Sales Mgr), S. Trowbridge
Ultimate Holding Company: KRAFT FOODS INC (USA)
Immediate Holding Company: ERNEST JACKSON & CO. LIMITED
Registration no: 00144133 **Date established:** 2016
Turnover: £10m - £20m **No.of Employees:** 101 - 250
Product Groups: 20, 31

Date of Accounts	Dec 11	Dec 10	Dec 09
Sales Turnover	12m	N/A	N/A
Pre Tax Profit/Loss	1m	N/A	N/A
Working Capital	8m	1m	1m
Fixed Assets	5m	N/A	N/A
Current Assets	14m	1m	1m
Current Liabilities	3m	N/A	N/A

Kirton Kayaks Ltd
Marsh Lane Lords Meadow Industrial Estate, Crediton, EX17 1ES
Tel: 01363-773295 **Fax:** 01363-775908
E-mail: sales@kirton-kayaks.co.uk
Website: http://www.kirton-kayaks.co.uk
Directors: D. Green (Fin), P. Cockram (MD)
Immediate Holding Company: KIRTON KAYAKS LIMITED
Registration no: 01200267 **VAT No.:** GB 142 4808 78
Date established: 1975 **Turnover:** £250,000 - £500,000
No.of Employees: 1 - 10 **Product Groups:** 24, 30, 39, 49

Date of Accounts	Oct 11	Oct 10	Oct 09
Working Capital	67	33	31
Fixed Assets	8	4	4
Current Assets	151	117	90

South West Chimney Services SWCS Ltd
20 Greenaway Morchard Bishop, Crediton, EX17 6PA
Tel: 01363-877644
E-mail: mail@southwestchimneyservices.co.uk
Website: http://www.southwestchimneyservices.co.uk
Directors: A. McPherson (Fin), P. McPherson (Dir)
Immediate Holding Company: EXCELSIOR WHOLESALE LTD.
Registration no: 05754735 **Date established:** 2011
No.of Employees: 1 - 10 **Product Groups:** 36, 40, 49, 52

Sunnybank Engineering
East Begbeer Spreyton, Crediton, EX17 5AR
Tel: 01363-82545 **Fax:** 01363-82478
E-mail: sunnybankeng@yahoo.co.uk
Directors: A. Palfrey (MD)
Immediate Holding Company: SUNNYBANK ENGINEERING LIMITED
Registration no: 04507801 **Date established:** 2002
Turnover: £500,000 - £1m **No.of Employees:** 1 - 10 **Product Groups:** 41

Date of Accounts	Dec 11	Dec 09	Dec 08
Sales Turnover	N/A	N/A	648
Pre Tax Profit/Loss	N/A	N/A	108
Working Capital	61	51	30
Fixed Assets	9	13	16
Current Assets	166	164	156
Current Liabilities	N/A	N/A	23

Western Spray
2 Ash Buildings Down End, Lords Meadow Industrial Estate, Crediton, EX17 1HN
Tel: 01363-775467 **Fax:** 01363-776276
E-mail: westernspray@sosi.net
Website: http://www.westernspray.co.uk
Managers: P. Heal (Mgr)
Immediate Holding Company: GRAPHIC PLC
Registration no: 03931359 **Date established:** 2000
No.of Employees: 1 - 10 **Product Groups:** 38, 42

Cullompton

Access Electrical Services Ltd
4 Kingsmill Industrial Estate Saunders Way, Cullompton, EX15 1BS
Tel: 01884-34445 **Fax:** 01884-32194
E-mail: sales@access-electrical.co.uk
Website: http://www.access-electrical.co.uk
Managers: D. Hornsey (District Mgr)
Immediate Holding Company: ACCESS ELECTRICAL (SERVICES) LIMITED
Registration no: 01084120 **VAT No.:** GB 224 3599 60
Date established: 1972 **Turnover:** £1m - £2m **No.of Employees:** 1 - 10
Product Groups: 37

Date of Accounts	Apr 12	Apr 11	Apr 10
Working Capital	454	439	452
Fixed Assets	13	12	12
Current Assets	618	603	637

CPS - Construction Plant Services
Construction Plant Services Ltd
Unit 6 Kingsford Rural Business Park Kentisbeare, Cullompton, EX15 2AU
Tel: 08452-705630 **Fax:** 01884-266 088
E-mail: info@cpsltd.co.uk
Website: http://www.cpsltd.co.uk
Registration no: 06440669 **Product Groups:** 45, 67

Culm Valley Farm Buildings
Bridge Works Bridge Street, Uffculme, Cullompton, EX15 3AX
Tel: 01884-841557 **Fax:** 01884-841341
E-mail: hillstan@btinternet.com
Directors: S. Hill (Prop)
Immediate Holding Company: CULM VALLEY FARM & INDUSTRIAL BUILDINGS LIMITED
Registration no: 04369964 **Date established:** 2002
No.of Employees: 1 - 10 **Product Groups:** 35

Date of Accounts	Dec 11	Dec 10	Dec 09
Working Capital	15	-26	44
Fixed Assets	14	15	17
Current Assets	235	168	198

Double S Exhausts Ltd
Station House Station Road, Cullompton, EX15 1BW
Tel: 01884-33454 **Fax:** 01884-32829
E-mail: info@stainlesssteelexhausts.co.uk
Website: http://www.stainlesssteelexhausts.co.uk
Bank(s): National Westminster Bank Plc
Directors: A. Goddard (MD), C. Goddard (Fin)
Immediate Holding Company: DOUBLE S EXHAUSTS LIMITED
Registration no: 01139040 **Date established:** 1973
Turnover: £500,000 - £1m **No.of Employees:** 11 - 20
Product Groups: 39, 40

Date of Accounts	Dec 11	Dec 10	Dec 09
Working Capital	156	128	81
Fixed Assets	246	142	156
Current Assets	436	264	194

Independent Agri Parts
Rodleigh Farm Hemyock, Cullompton, EX15 3RU
Tel: 01823-681131 **Fax:** 01823-681424
E-mail: sales@independentagriparts.co.uk
Website: http://www.tractorsparesonline.co.uk
Directors: P. Clist (Prop)
Turnover: Up to £250,000 **No.of Employees:** 1 - 10 **Product Groups:** 39, 40, 48, 61, 67, 68

Industrial Coating Supplies
Unit 2 Simmons Place, Cullompton, EX15 1BH
Tel: 01884-34506 **Fax:** 01884-35878
Website: http://www.industrialcoatingsupplies.co.uk
Managers: P. Tucker (Mgr)
Date established: 1989 **No.of Employees:** 1 - 10 **Product Groups:** 46, 48

Off Zero Ltd
Unit 4-5 Farthings Lodge Plymtree, Cullompton, EX15 2JY
Tel: 01884-277394 **Fax:** 01884-277371
Website: http://www.offzero.co.uk
Directors: K. Brooks (Fin)
Immediate Holding Company: OFF ZERO LIMITED
Registration no: 02970709 **Date established:** 1994
No.of Employees: 1 - 10 **Product Groups:** 40, 41

Date of Accounts	Mar 12	Mar 11	Mar 10
Working Capital	177	182	179
Fixed Assets	9	8	9
Current Assets	298	293	312

Phoenix Cellar Services Ltd
Unit 3a Dulford Business Park Dulford, Cullompton, EX15 2DY
Tel: 01884-266818 **Fax:** 01884-266819
E-mail: info@pxcs.co.uk
Website: http://www.pxcs.co.uk
Directors: M. Scott (Dir)
Immediate Holding Company: PHOENIX CELLAR SERVICES LIMITED
Registration no: 04975182 **Date established:** 2003
No.of Employees: 11 - 20 **Product Groups:** 20, 40, 41

Date of Accounts	Nov 11	Nov 10	Nov 09
Working Capital	136	134	50
Fixed Assets	123	113	114
Current Assets	258	249	149

Pressure Washers South West
Devon Business Park Saunders Way, Cullompton, EX15 1BS
Tel: 01884-33703 **Fax:** 01884-34037
E-mail: peterbuxton@pressurewashersw.co.uk
Website: http://www.pressurewasherssw.co.uk
Directors: P. Buxton (Dir)
Ultimate Holding Company: PRESSURE WASHERS SW LIMITED
Immediate Holding Company: PRESSURE WASHERS SW LIMITED
Registration no: 01853276 **Date established:** 1984
Turnover: Up to £250,000 **No.of Employees:** 1 - 10 **Product Groups:** 39, 40, 48

Date of Accounts	Nov 11	Nov 10	Nov 09
Working Capital	616	562	511
Fixed Assets	152	149	151
Current Assets	845	790	722

Rayda Plastics Ltd
Unit 3 South View Estate Willand, Cullompton, EX15 2QW
Tel: 01884-820955 **Fax:** 01884-821544
E-mail: enquiries@rayda.co.uk
Website: http://www.rayda.co.uk
Directors: R. Vincent (MD), D. Vincent (Fin)
Immediate Holding Company: RAYDA PLASTICS LIMITED
Registration no: 01265143 **Date established:** 1976
Turnover: Up to £250,000 **No.of Employees:** 1 - 10 **Product Groups:** 30, 66

Date of Accounts	Aug 11	Aug 10	Aug 09
Working Capital	389	317	337
Fixed Assets	176	189	160
Current Assets	504	559	446

St Regis Paper Co. Ltd
Higher Kings Mill, Cullompton, EX15 1QJ
Tel: 01884-836300 **Fax:** 01884-836333
E-mail: sales@stregis.co.uk
Website: http://www.stregis.co.uk
Bank(s): National Westminster Bank Plc
Directors: A. Kennedy (MD)
Managers: F. Parsons (Personnel)
Ultimate Holding Company: DS SMITH PLC
Immediate Holding Company: HIGHER KINGS MILL LIMITED
Registration no: 00518152 **Date established:** 2011
Turnover: £10m - £20m **No.of Employees:** 101 - 250 **Product Groups:** 66

Date of Accounts	Mar 12
Sales Turnover	9m
Pre Tax Profit/Loss	920
Working Capital	5m
Fixed Assets	1m
Current Assets	10m
Current Liabilities	1m

Thermal Engineering Systems Ltd
Langlands Business Park Uffculme, Cullompton, EX15 3DA
Tel: 01884-840216 **Fax:** 01884-840197
E-mail: sales@thermal-eng.co.uk
Website: http://www.thermal-eng.co.uk
Bank(s): National Westminster Bank Plc
Directors: J. Gasan (MD), K. Keyte (Fin)
Managers: S. Jones (Sales Prom Mgr), S. Wade (Purch Mgr)
Ultimate Holding Company: J2AMP LIMITED
Immediate Holding Company: THERMAL ENGINEERING SYSTEMS LIMITED
Registration no: 01541473 **VAT No.:** GB 357 2319 50
Date established: 1981 **Turnover:** £2m - £5m **No.of Employees:** 21 - 50
Product Groups: 31, 35, 37, 38, 40, 41, 42, 43, 44, 45, 46, 48, 52, 68, 84

Date of Accounts	Dec 08	Dec 07	Mar 11
Working Capital	254	161	345
Fixed Assets	209	246	80
Current Assets	867	726	2m

2 Sisters Food Group
Lloyd Maunder Road Willand, Cullompton, EX15 2PJ
Tel: 01884-820534 **Fax:** 01884-821404
E-mail: ranjit.boparan@2sfg.com
Website: http://www.2sfg.com
Directors: V. Dicussa (Pers), J. Roberts (Fin)
Managers: G. Pugsley (Chief Mgr), R. Walker (Mktg Serv Mgr), R. Groke (Tech Serv Mgr)
Ultimate Holding Company: BOPARAN HOLDINGS LIMITED
Immediate Holding Company: LLOYD MAUNDER LIMITED
Registration no: 00234992 **VAT No.:** 129 9284 33 **Date established:** 2028
Turnover: £20m - £50m **No.of Employees:** 501 - 1000
Product Groups: 62

Date of Accounts	Jul 10	Aug 08	Aug 09
Sales Turnover	N/A	80m	26m
Pre Tax Profit/Loss	N/A	-2m	-2m
Working Capital	419	-1m	419
Fixed Assets	N/A	4m	N/A
Current Assets	419	10m	419
Current Liabilities	N/A	5m	N/A

West Country Door & Gate
11 Somerville Close Willand, Cullompton, EX15 2PN
Tel: 01884-821403 **Fax:** 01884-33335
Directors: R. Payne (Ptnr)
Immediate Holding Company: GALLOPER LIMITED
Date established: 2010 **No.of Employees:** 1 - 10 **Product Groups:** 26, 35

Dawlish

Red Rcok Electrical A division of Red Rock Utilities Ltd
12 Pinewood Close, Dawlish, EX7 0AJ
Tel: 01626-895105 **Fax:** 01626-895105
E-mail: info@redrockelectrical.co.uk
Website: http://www.redrockelectrical.co.uk
Turnover: £250,000 - £500,000 **No.of Employees:** 1 - 10
Product Groups: 37, 52, 84

Exeter

A C Mobile Services
32 Fairfield Road, Exeter, EX2 8UF
Tel: 01392-206454
Directors: A. Carpenter (Prop)
Date established: 2005 **No.of Employees:** 1 - 10 **Product Groups:** 26, 35

A G T Electrical Ltd
Francis Close, Exeter, EX4 1HD
Tel: 01392-411120 **Fax:** 01392-420088
E-mail: admin@agt.co.uk
Website: http://www.agt.co.uk
Directors: M. Ireland (Dir)
Immediate Holding Company: A.G.T. ELECTRICAL (EXETER) LIMITED
Registration no: 01176584 **VAT No.:** GB 142 4803 88
Date established: 1974 **Turnover:** £500,000 - £1m
No.of Employees: 1 - 10 **Product Groups:** 52

Date of Accounts	Dec 11	Dec 10	Dec 09
Working Capital	305	299	290
Fixed Assets	3	4	4
Current Assets	340	368	326

Allwood Buildings Ltd
Talewater Works Talaton, Exeter, EX5 2RT
Tel: 01404-850977 **Fax:** 01404-850946
E-mail: terry@allwoodtimber.co.uk
Website: http://www.allwoodtimber.co.uk
Directors: T. Kingdon (Dir), S. Kingdon (Dir)
Immediate Holding Company: ALLWOOD BUILDINGS LTD
Registration no: 02676458 **Date established:** 1992 **Turnover:** £1m - £2m
No.of Employees: 21 - 50 **Product Groups:** 35, 52

Date of Accounts	Dec 11	Dec 10	Dec 09
Working Capital	345	343	293
Fixed Assets	33	31	106
Current Assets	1m	1m	924

B Y Gone Baths
Newcourt Road Topsham, Exeter, EX3 0BT
Tel: 01392-876517
E-mail: c.fuller@bygonebaths.co.uk
Website: http://www.bygonebaths.co.uk
Directors: C. Fuller (Prop)
Date established: 2003 **No.of Employees:** 1 - 10 **Product Groups:** 46, 48

Be I.T Services Ltd
8 Taddyforde Court Mansions, Exeter, EX4 4AS
Tel: 01392-279377
E-mail: info@beitservices.com
Website: http://www.beitservices.com
Directors: T. Harding (Dir)
Immediate Holding Company: TADDYFORDE COURT MANSIONS MANAGEMENT COMPANY LIMITED
Registration no: 06603647 **Date established:** 1988
No.of Employees: 1 - 10 **Product Groups:** 44

Date of Accounts	Mar 11	Mar 10	Mar 09
Sales Turnover	7	6	6
Pre Tax Profit/Loss	2	N/A	-1
Working Capital	2	1	N/A
Fixed Assets	2	2	2
Current Assets	3	1	N/A

Beach Bros Ltd
Western Road, Exeter, EX4 1EQ
Tel: 01392-257891 **Fax:** 01392-412834
E-mail: steve@woodentops.co.uk
Website: http://www.beachbros.co.uk
Bank(s): HSBC, Lloyds TSB
Directors: S. Beach (MD), S. Kingsnorth (Dir)
Immediate Holding Company: BEACH BROS. LIMITED
Registration no: 00372166 **VAT No.:** GB 140 7091 94
Date established: 1942 **Turnover:** £5m - £10m **No.of Employees:** 21 - 50
Product Groups: 25

Date of Accounts	Mar 11	Mar 10	Mar 09
Sales Turnover	N/A	N/A	5m
Pre Tax Profit/Loss	N/A	N/A	76
Working Capital	2m	2m	2m
Fixed Assets	547	626	709
Current Assets	2m	2m	3m
Current Liabilities	N/A	N/A	146

Besley & Copp Ltd
Unit 7 Orchard Court Heron Road, Sowton Industrial Estate, Exeter, EX2 7LL
Tel: 01392-477137 **Fax:** 01392-432046
E-mail: sales@besleyandcopp.co.uk
Website: http://www.besleyandcopp.co.uk
Directors: S. Tout (Chief Op Offcr)
Immediate Holding Company: BESLEY & COPP LIMITED
Registration no: 00059148 **VAT No.:** GB 140 7156 92
Date established: 1998 **Turnover:** £2m - £5m **No.of Employees:** 1 - 10
Product Groups: 27, 28

Date of Accounts	Mar 12	Mar 11	Mar 10
Working Capital	57	53	-7
Fixed Assets	229	299	389
Current Assets	384	507	592

Bishop's Blatchpack
Kestrel Way Sowton Industrial Estate, Exeter, EX2 7PA
Tel: 01392-202040 **Fax:** 01392-201251
E-mail: blatchpack@bishops-move.co.uk
Website: http://www.bishopsmove.com
Bank(s): The Royal Bank of Scotland
Directors: K. O'sullivan (Fin)
Managers: E. Hall (Chief Mgr), P. Laverick (Shipping Mgr), H. Hughes ()
Ultimate Holding Company: Bishop & Sons Depositories Ltd
VAT No.: GB 140 8443 84 **Date established:** 1993
No.of Employees: 11 - 20 **Product Groups:** 72, 76, 77

Boc Ltd
Alphinbrook Road Marsh Barton Trading Estate, Exeter, EX2 8RG
Tel: 01392-437410 **Fax:** 01392-434257
E-mail: glyn.hopkins@boc.com
Website: http://www.bocindustrial.com
Managers: G. Hopkin (Mgr)
Ultimate Holding Company: LINDE AG (GERMANY)
Immediate Holding Company: BOC LIMITED
Registration no: 00337663 **Date established:** 1938
No.of Employees: 1 - 10 **Product Groups:** 46

Date of Accounts	Dec 11	Dec 10	Dec 08
Sales Turnover	726m	691m	721m
Pre Tax Profit/Loss	122m	125m	67m
Working Capital	409m	278m	-219m
Fixed Assets	480m	492m	538m
Current Assets	724m	578m	371m
Current Liabilities	64m	68m	73m

Bramdean School
47-51 Homefield Road, Exeter, EX1 2QR
Tel: 01392-273387 **Fax:** 01392-439330
E-mail: info@bramdeanschool.co.uk
Website: http://www.bramdeanschool.co.uk
Directors: D. Stoneman (Prop)
Managers: S. Coaker, T. Connett
Date established: 1976 **No.of Employees:** 21 - 50 **Product Groups:** 86

Bridger Marine
The Boat Shed City Industrial Estate Michael Browning Way, Exeter, EX2 8DD
Tel: 01392-250970 **Fax:** 01392-410955
E-mail: bridgermarine@btconnect.com
Website: http://www.johnbridgermarine.co.uk
Directors: P. Bridger (Prop)
Immediate Holding Company: BRIDGER MARINE LIMITED
Registration no: 06734703 **VAT No.:** GB 320 9518 72
Date established: 2008 **Turnover:** £500,000 - £1m
No.of Employees: 1 - 10 **Product Groups:** 24, 40, 74

Date of Accounts	Dec 11	Dec 10	Dec 09
Sales Turnover	630	770	N/A
Working Capital	1	-6	N/A
Fixed Assets	2	2	N/A
Current Assets	170	174	N/A
Current Liabilities	N/A	180	N/A

C C Welders
28 Raglans, Exeter, EX2 8XN
Tel: 01392-255653
E-mail: chriscoombes@hotmail.co.uk
Directors: C. Coombes (Prop)
Date established: 1977 **No.of Employees:** 1 - 10 **Product Groups:** 26, 35

C P Shipping Ltd
19 Flexi Units Budlake Road, Marsh Barton Trading Estate, Exeter, EX2 8PY
Tel: 01392-216022 **Fax:** 01392-251891
E-mail: admin@cpshipping.co.uk
Website: http://www.cpshipping.co.uk
Directors: M. Pegley (MD)
Immediate Holding Company: CP SHIPPING LIMITED
Registration no: 04882425 **VAT No.:** GB 365 8821 18
Date established: 2003 **No.of Employees:** 1 - 10 **Product Groups:** 76

Date of Accounts	Aug 11	Aug 10	Aug 09
Working Capital	64	62	60
Fixed Assets	21	33	48
Current Assets	217	239	227

Capricorn Imports Ltd
Unit 1 Greendale Business Park Woodbury Salterton, Exeter, EX5 1EW
Tel: 01395-233320 **Fax:** 01395-233554
E-mail: sales@capricornimports.co.uk
Website: http://www.capricornimports.co.uk
Directors: B. Male (MD), B. Pengelly (Fin)
Immediate Holding Company: CAPRICORN IMPORTS LIMITED
Registration no: 03409733 **Date established:** 1997 **Turnover:** £2m - £5m
No.of Employees: 11 - 20 **Product Groups:** 26

Date of Accounts	Jul 11	Jul 10	Jul 09
Working Capital	2m	2m	2m
Fixed Assets	217	249	318
Current Assets	2m	2m	2m

Certus Technology Associates Ltd
86 Longbrook Street, Exeter, EX4 6AP
Tel: 01392-270930
E-mail: mail@certus-tech.com
Website: http://www.certus-tech.com
Directors: I. Bamsey (MD), R. Pumphrey (I.T. Dir)
Immediate Holding Company: CERTUS TECHNOLOGY ASSOCIATES LIMITED
Registration no: 04109464 **VAT No.:** GB 668 4603 06
Date established: 2000 **No.of Employees:** 1 - 10 **Product Groups:** 44, 80

Date of Accounts	Nov 11	Nov 10	Nov 09
Working Capital	29	37	32
Fixed Assets	2	3	5
Current Assets	101	97	132

Classic Gates & Railings
Badgers Meadow Clapham, Exeter, EX2 9UN
Tel: 01392-832828 **Fax:** 01392-832828
Website: http://www.classicgatesandrailings.co.uk
Directors: P. Clay (Prop)
Date established: 1999 **No.of Employees:** 1 - 10 **Product Groups:** 26, 35

M J N Colston
Passmore House Grace Road Central, Marsh Barton Trading Estate, Exeter, EX2 8QA
Tel: 01392-277352 **Fax:** 01392-253150
Website: http://www.mjncolston.co.uk
Directors: S. Elford (Fin), R. Pearce (MD), P. Churchart (MD), A. Salway (Contracts)
Managers: N. Drury (Reg Mgr), M. Pickton (Mgr), B. Glastonbury, S. Mogg (Buyer)
Ultimate Holding Company: STAVELEY INDUSTRIES P.L.C.
Immediate Holding Company: FRAME WAREHOUSE UK LIMITED
Registration no: 04713645 **VAT No.:** GB 239 3550 53
Date established: 2003 **Turnover:** £125m - £250m
No.of Employees: 21 - 50 **Product Groups:** 52

Curtis Holt S W
Toolbank House Bittern Road, Sowton Indl-Est, Exeter, EX2 7LW
Tel: 08444-636080 **Fax:** 01392-412235
E-mail: pangell@toolbank.com
Website: http://www.toolbank.com
Managers: P. Angell (Mgr)
Immediate Holding Company: SHORT RUN PRESS LIMITED
Date established: 1980 **No.of Employees:** 21 - 50 **Product Groups:** 32, 35, 36, 72, 80

Date of Accounts	Apr 11	Apr 10	Apr 09
Working Capital	-277	-258	-262
Fixed Assets	290	300	266
Current Assets	549	330	318
Current Liabilities	N/A	N/A	84

Devon Contractors Ltd
Clyst Court Hill Barton Business Park, Clyst St Mary, Exeter, EX5 1SA
Tel: 01395-234280 **Fax:** 01395-234281
E-mail: pete.alderson@devoncontractors.co.uk
Website: http://www.devoncontractors.com
Bank(s): National Westminster Bank Plc
Directors: D. Hunt (Dir), P. Alderson (Dir), S. Bennington (Fin)
Managers: S. Buckland (Comm)
Ultimate Holding Company: CLYST HOLDINGS LIMITED
Immediate Holding Company: DEVON CONTRACTORS LIMITED
Registration no: 00533232 **VAT No.:** GB 141 0171 28
Date established: 1954 **Turnover:** £5m - £10m **No.of Employees:** 11 - 20
Product Groups: 51, 52

see next page

Devon Contractors Ltd - Cont'd

Date of Accounts	May 11	May 10	May 09
Sales Turnover	9m	11m	11m
Pre Tax Profit/Loss	261	384	377
Working Capital	995	858	670
Fixed Assets	71	53	63
Current Assets	3m	4m	5m
Current Liabilities	2m	752	991

Drain Centre (Plastics Branch)

Unit C1 Eagle Way, Sowton Industrial Estate, Exeter, EX2 7HY
Tel: 01392-445588 **Fax:** 01392-445599
E-mail: simon.smith@wolseley.co.uk
Website: http://www.wolseley.co.uk
Managers: S. Smith (Mgr)
Immediate Holding Company: HANDLE WITH CARE LTD
Registration no: 00424702 **Date established:** 1994
Turnover: £500,000 - £1m **No.of Employees:** 1 - 10 **Product Groups:** 30

Date of Accounts	Aug 11	Aug 10	Aug 09
Working Capital	-7	-12	46
Fixed Assets	213	246	36
Current Assets	219	226	237

Duke Manufacturing UK Ltd

Unit 10 Greendale Business Park, Woodbury Salterton, Exeter, EX5 1EW
Tel: 01395-234140 **Fax:** 01392-360236
E-mail: paul@duke-emea.com
Website: http://www.dukemfg.com
Managers: P. Stephens, J. Clapworthy (Sales Prom Mgr)
Immediate Holding Company: DUKE MANUFACTURING-UK, LTD.
Registration no: 05022558 **Date established:** 2004 **Turnover:** £2m - £5m
No.of Employees: 1 - 10 **Product Groups:** 20, 40, 41

Date of Accounts	Dec 11	Dec 10	Dec 09
Sales Turnover	1m	1m	N/A
Pre Tax Profit/Loss	73	70	N/A
Working Capital	195	147	91
Fixed Assets	32	24	31
Current Assets	233	212	149
Current Liabilities	38	65	N/A

Eriks UK (Forco Exeter)

Manaton Close Matford Business Park, Marsh Barton Trading Estate, Exeter, EX2 8PF
Tel: 01392-274935 **Fax:** 01392-210619
E-mail: exeter@eriks.co.uk
Website: http://www.wyko.co.uk
Managers: B. Miles (Mgr)
Immediate Holding Company: BESLEY & COPP LIMITED
Date established: 1998 **No.of Employees:** 1 - 10 **Product Groups:** 66

Date of Accounts	Oct 10	Oct 09	Oct 08
Working Capital	86	85	96
Fixed Assets	40	60	42
Current Assets	106	104	135

Evans Transport Ltd

Peamore Truck Centre Alphington, Exeter, EX2 9SL
Tel: 01392-833030 **Fax:** 01392-833540
E-mail: sales@palletforce.com
Website: http://www.evanstransport.co.uk
Bank(s): HSBC
Directors: N. Evans (Prop)
Ultimate Holding Company: E T HOLDINGS LIMITED
Immediate Holding Company: EVANS TRANSPORT LIMITED
Registration no: 00437864 **VAT No.:** GB 631 2633 70
Date established: 1947 **Turnover:** £20m - £50m
No.of Employees: 101 - 250 **Product Groups:** 72

Date of Accounts	Mar 11	Mar 10	Mar 09
Sales Turnover	16m	13m	13m
Pre Tax Profit/Loss	150	12	-53
Working Capital	-2m	-2m	-2m
Fixed Assets	8m	8m	7m
Current Assets	4m	4m	3m
Current Liabilities	1m	3m	360

The Exe Engineering Company Limited

60-64 Alphington Road St Thomas, Exeter, EX2 8HX
Tel: 01392-275186 **Fax:** 01392-260336
E-mail: sales@exeengineering.co.uk
Website: http://www.exeengineering.co.uk
Directors: A. Goldsworthy (Fin), N. Goldsworthy (MD)
Immediate Holding Company: EXE ENGINEERING COMPANY,LIMITED(THE)
Registration no: 00176496 **VAT No.:** GB 141 4507 01
Date established: 2021 **Turnover:** £500,000 - £1m
No.of Employees: 1 - 10 **Product Groups:** 46, 48, 84

Date of Accounts	Jun 11	Jun 10	Jun 09
Working Capital	47	56	67
Fixed Assets	48	52	54
Current Assets	143	127	135

Exeter Chamber Of Commerce

4-5 Southernhay West, Exeter, EX1 1JG
Tel: 01392-431133 **Fax:** 01392-278804
E-mail: enquiries@exeterchamber.co.uk
Website: http://www.exeterchamber.co.uk
Managers: L. Vanstone (Mgr)
Immediate Holding Company: NU SOLAR LIMITED
Registration no: 00270612 **VAT No.:** GB 585 6814 92
Date established: 2005 **Turnover:** Up to £250,000
No.of Employees: 1 - 10 **Product Groups:** 87

Date of Accounts	Jul 11	Jul 10	Jul 09
Working Capital	149	175	288
Fixed Assets	3	2	4
Current Assets	377	326	434

Exeter Stove & Chimneys (Devon)

Unit 5 Bakers Yard Alphinbrook Road, Marsh Barton Trading Estate, Exeter, EX2 8RG
Tel: 01392-410903 **Fax:** 01392-410903
E-mail: info@exeterstoves.co.uk
Website: http://www.exeterstoves.co.uk
Directors: R. Wilson (Prop)
Date established: 1996 **No.of Employees:** 1 - 10 **Product Groups:** 40

The Express & Echo

Heron Road Sowton Industrial Estate, Exeter, EX2 7NF
Tel: 01392-442211 **Fax:** 01392-442298
Website: http://www.thisisexeter.co.uk
Bank(s): National Westminster
Directors: P. Powles (Pers), S. Carpenter (I.T. Dir), A. Blair (MD), J. Perrett (Fin)
Managers: A. Phelan, J. Beesley (Fin Mgr), D. Calvert (Tech Serv Mgr)
Ultimate Holding Company: DAILY MAIL & GENERAL TRUST P.L.C.
Immediate Holding Company: SOUTH WEST MEDIA GROUP LTD
Registration no: 00070992 **Turnover:** £10m - £20m
No.of Employees: 51 - 100 **Product Groups:** 28

Fingle Farm Buildings

West Fingle Crockernwell, Exeter, EX6 6NJ
Tel: 01647-281226 **Fax:** 01647-281226
Website: http://www.finglefarmbuildings.co.uk
Directors: J. Loram (Prop)
Immediate Holding Company: FINGLE FARM BUILDINGS LTD
Registration no: 05405183 **Date established:** 2005
No.of Employees: 1 - 10 **Product Groups:** 35

Date of Accounts	Dec 11	Dec 10	Dec 09
Working Capital	150	74	97
Fixed Assets	75	95	114
Current Assets	219	161	164

First Databank Europe Ltd

Swallowtail House Grenadier Road, Exeter Business Park, Exeter, EX1 3LH
Tel: 01392-440100 **Fax:** 01392-440192
E-mail: info@fdbhealth.com
Website: http://www.fdbhealth.co.uk
Directors: R. Arnold (Fin), D. Nichols (Dir), M. Treleaven (Sales & Mktg)
Managers: C. Zumseldy (Mktg Serv Mgr), I. Jones (Tech Serv Mgr)
Ultimate Holding Company: HEARST CORPORATION (USA)
Immediate Holding Company: FIRST DATABANK EUROPE LIMITED
Registration no: 01880682 **Date established:** 1985 **Turnover:** £5m - £10m
No.of Employees: 51 - 100 **Product Groups:** 44

Date of Accounts	Dec 11	Dec 10	Dec 09
Sales Turnover	9m	10m	9m
Pre Tax Profit/Loss	3m	4m	4m
Working Capital	7m	5m	5m
Fixed Assets	349	500	516
Current Assets	10m	7m	8m
Current Liabilities	2m	2m	3m

Flybe

Jack Walker House Clyst Honiton, Exeter, EX5 2HL
Tel: 01392-366669 **Fax:** 01392-366151
E-mail: caroline.fletcher@flybe.com
Website: http://www.flybe.com
Directors: S. Lilley (Mkt Research), A. Knuckey (Fin), R. Knuckey (Co Sec), S. Charles (Pers)
Ultimate Holding Company: FLYBE GROUP PLC
Immediate Holding Company: FLYBE LIMITED
Registration no: 02769768 **Date established:** 1992
Turnover: £500,000 - £1m **No.of Employees:** 1501 & over
Product Groups: 75

Date of Accounts	Mar 12	Mar 11	Mar 10
Sales Turnover	615m	596m	571m
Pre Tax Profit/Loss	-3m	-3m	4m
Working Capital	2m	21m	-72m
Fixed Assets	135m	105m	95m
Current Assets	244m	261m	179m
Current Liabilities	129m	127m	144m

Gazco Ltd

Osprey Road Sowton Industrial Estate, Exeter, EX2 7JG
Tel: 01392-261999 **Fax:** 01392-444148
E-mail: sales@gazco.com
Website: http://www.stovax.com
Bank(s): HSBC
Directors: M. Sage (MD)
Managers: M. Brookman (Purch Mgr)
Ultimate Holding Company: STOVAX GROUP LIMITED
Immediate Holding Company: GAZCO LIMITED
Registration no: 02228426 **VAT No.:** GB 675 7628 83
Date established: 1988 **Turnover:** £10m - £20m
No.of Employees: 101 - 250 **Product Groups:** 30, 33, 35, 40

Date of Accounts	May 11	May 10	May 09
Sales Turnover	15m	14m	14m
Pre Tax Profit/Loss	2m	1m	762
Working Capital	5m	5m	5m
Fixed Assets	368	416	486
Current Assets	7m	7m	6m
Current Liabilities	965	955	516

D J Golightly

11a Wardrew Road, Exeter, EX4 1HB
Tel: 01392-411733 **Fax:** 01392-411733
Directors: D. Golightly (Prop)
Date established: 2005 **No.of Employees:** 1 - 10 **Product Groups:** 35

Good Wood Cellars

16-17 The Quay, Exeter, EX2 4AP
Tel: 01392-498030 **Fax:** 01392-202252
Website: http://www.goodwoodcellars.co.uk
Directors: R. Williams (Prop)
Date established: 1992 **Turnover:** Up to £250,000
No.of Employees: 1 - 10 **Product Groups:** 25, 26, 63

Graham

Alphin Brook Road Marsh Barton Trading Estate, Exeter, EX2 8RF
Tel: 01392-434341 **Fax:** 01392-421474
Website: http://www.graham-group.co.uk
Managers: G. Darke (District Mgr)
Immediate Holding Company: JEWSONS
Registration no: 00066738 **No.of Employees:** 1 - 10 **Product Groups:** 66

Gun & Sport Shop

76 Fore Street Heavitree, Exeter, EX1 2RR
Tel: 01392-271701 **Fax:** 01392-209013
E-mail: gunandsport@hotmail.com
Managers: N. Chard (Mgr)
Date established: 1963 **No.of Employees:** 1 - 10 **Product Groups:** 36, 39, 40

H V P Security Shutters

4 Grace Parade Grace Road West, Marsh Barton Trading Estate, Exeter, EX2 8PU
Tel: 01392-270218 **Fax:** 01392-278548
E-mail: info@hvpshutters.co.uk
Website: http://www.hvpshutters.co.uk
Directors: A. Keating (Dir)
Managers: G. Oliver (Mktg Serv Mgr)
Immediate Holding Company: H.V.P. SECURITY SHUTTERS LIMITED
Registration no: 01406952 **VAT No.:** GB 320 8417 83
Date established: 1978 **Turnover:** Up to £250,000
No.of Employees: 11 - 20 **Product Groups:** 25, 35, 36

Date of Accounts	Mar 11	Mar 10	Mar 09
Sales Turnover	N/A	1m	N/A
Pre Tax Profit/Loss	N/A	117	N/A
Working Capital	169	149	151
Fixed Assets	277	278	280
Current Assets	516	444	447
Current Liabilities	N/A	96	N/A

N C Hamlyn

Paynes Farm Broadclyst, Exeter, EX5 3BJ
Tel: 01392-466720
E-mail: nchamlyn@fsbdial.co.uk
Website: http://www.paynes-farm.co.uk
Directors: N. Hamlyn (Prop)
Date established: 1996 **No.of Employees:** 1 - 10 **Product Groups:** 41

Hanover Lifts

8 Harrier Court Exeter Airport, Clyst Honiton, Exeter, EX5 2DR
Tel: 01392-461061 **Fax:** 01392-461007
E-mail: info@hanoverlifts.co.uk
Website: http://www.hanoverlifts.co.uk
Directors: C. Martin (Ptnr)
Date established: 1993 **No.of Employees:** 1 - 10 **Product Groups:** 35, 39, 45

Heaver Brothers Ltd

Exeter Airport Industrial Estate Clyst Honiton, Exeter, EX5 2LJ
Tel: 01392-446678 **Fax:** 01392-444324
E-mail: info@heaverbros.co.uk
Website: http://www.heaverbros.co.uk
Directors: B. Heaver (Dir), M. Heaver (Dir)
Immediate Holding Company: HEAVER BROTHERS LIMITED
Registration no: 04429051 **Date established:** 2002
No.of Employees: 21 - 50 **Product Groups:** 35, 42, 45

Date of Accounts	May 11	May 10	May 09
Working Capital	177	221	166
Fixed Assets	339	284	320
Current Assets	637	608	474

Howmet Ltd

Kestrel Way Sowton Industrial Estate, Exeter, EX2 7LG
Tel: 01392-429700 **Fax:** 01392-429701
E-mail: lluis.fargasmas@howmet.com
Website: http://www.howmet.com
Bank(s): Barclays
Directors: L. Fargas Mas (Dir), J. Camino (Co Sec)
Managers: S. Woods (Comptroller), L. Ives (Personnel), K. Bond (Purch Mgr), A. Hume (Sales Prom Mgr), E. Deacon (Tech Serv Mgr)
Ultimate Holding Company: ALCOA INC (USA)
Immediate Holding Company: HOWMET LIMITED
Registration no: 02659893 **VAT No.:** GB 140 9060 95
Date established: 1991 **Turnover:** £75m - £125m
No.of Employees: 501 - 1000 **Product Groups:** 34, 39, 40, 68

Date of Accounts	Dec 11	Dec 10	Dec 09
Sales Turnover	94m	95m	123m
Pre Tax Profit/Loss	-2m	539	3m
Working Capital	13m	16m	15m
Fixed Assets	14m	14m	14m
Current Assets	32m	36m	41m
Current Liabilities	1m	7m	8m

Ian Leach Plumbing & Heating

1 Walnut Cottage Oil Mill Lane, Clyst St Mary, Exeter, EX5 1AH
Tel: 07879-066065
E-mail: ianleach.plumbing@googlemail.com
Directors: I. Leach (Prop)
Date established: 2003 **Turnover:** Up to £250,000
No.of Employees: 1 - 10 **Product Groups:** 52

Interserve Construction Ltd

Interserve House Oberon Road, Exeter Business Park, Exeter, EX1 3QD
Tel: 01392-203350 **Fax:** 01392-203347
E-mail: richard.ellis@interserve.com
Website: http://www.interserve.com
Bank(s): HSBC Bank plc
Directors: R. Ellis (Reg)
Managers: D. Ash
Ultimate Holding Company: INTERSERVE PLC
Immediate Holding Company: INTERSERVE CONSTRUCTION LIMITED
Registration no: 00303359 **Date established:** 1935
Turnover: £500m - £1,000m **No.of Employees:** 21 - 50
Product Groups: 51, 52

Date of Accounts	Dec 11	Dec 10	Dec 09
Sales Turnover	734m	740m	825m
Pre Tax Profit/Loss	16m	23m	14m
Working Capital	80m	71m	66m
Fixed Assets	9m	8m	10m
Current Assets	331m	331m	339m
Current Liabilities	53m	59m	72m

Jackaman Welding Supplies

28 Aldrin Road, Exeter, EX4 5DN
Tel: 01392-676447 **Fax:** 01392-676447
Directors: A. Jackaman (Prop)
Date established: 1979 **No.of Employees:** 1 - 10 **Product Groups:** 46

Llexeter Ltd

Units 15 - 18 Greendale Business Park Woodbury Salterton, Exeter, EX5 1EW
Tel: 0845-459 2369 **Fax:** 0845-4592374
E-mail: S.Ward@llexeter.co.uk
Website: http://www.llexeter.co.uk
Managers: P. Wakely (Sales Prom Mgr), S. Ward (Sales Prom)
Registration no: 04940600 **Date established:** 2004
Turnover: £250,000 - £500,000 **No.of Employees:** 21 - 50
Product Groups: 39

Date of Accounts	Oct 07	Oct 06	Oct 05
Working Capital	647	283	163
Fixed Assets	110	112	45
Current Assets	1708	1059	912
Current Liabilities	1061	776	749

Maker Coating Systems Ltd
5 Oak Business Units 18 Thorverton Road, Exeter, EX2 8FS
Tel: 01392-822600 **Fax:** 01392-829479
E-mail: sales@makercoating.com
Website: http://www.makercoating.com
Directors: P. Grierson (MD)
Ultimate Holding Company: P & W GRIERSON HOLDING COMPANY LTD.
Immediate Holding Company: MAKER COATING SYSTEMS LIMITED
Registration no: 01448795 **Date established:** 1979
No.of Employees: 1 - 10 **Product Groups:** 46, 48

Date of Accounts	Mar 12	Mar 11	Mar 10
Working Capital	79	55	61
Fixed Assets	171	162	128
Current Assets	380	320	294

Mantracourt Electronics Ltd
The Drive Farringdon, Exeter, EX5 2JB
Tel: 01395-232020 **Fax:** 01395-233190
E-mail: info@mantracourt.co.uk
Website: http://www.mantracourt.co.uk
Bank(s): National Westminster Bank Plc
Directors: D. Willmington (MD), C. Willmington (Fin)
Managers: A. Connelly, M. Nicholas (Tech Serv Mgr), K. Voysey (Sales & Mktg Mg)
Immediate Holding Company: MANTRACOURT ELECTRONICS LIMITED
Registration no: 01749118 **Date established:** 1983 **Turnover:** £2m - £5m
No.of Employees: 21 - 50 **Product Groups:** 37, 38, 44, 67

Date of Accounts	Dec 11	Dec 10	Dec 09
Working Capital	3m	2m	2m
Fixed Assets	213	228	288
Current Assets	4m	3m	2m

Multifoil Ltd
Alphinbrook Road Marsh Barton Trading Estate, Exeter, EX2 8RG
Tel: 01392-221255 **Fax:** 01392-420868
E-mail: info@multifoil.co.uk
Website: http://www.multifoil.co.uk
Bank(s): Bank of Scotland, Exeter
Directors: S. Willingham (Dir), J. Benn (Sales), P. Di Giuseppe (Fin)
Ultimate Holding Company: ISCA FOIL LIMITED
Immediate Holding Company: MULTIFOIL LIMITED
Registration no: 01158652 **Date established:** 1974 **Turnover:** £2m - £5m
No.of Employees: 21 - 50 **Product Groups:** 34

Date of Accounts	Jan 12	Jan 11	Jan 10
Working Capital	1m	1m	1m
Fixed Assets	751	72	87
Current Assets	2m	2m	2m

G H Newbery & Son Ltd
4 Ashton Road Marsh Barton Industrial Estate, Marsh Barton Trading Estate, Exeter, EX2 8LN
Tel: 01392-275377 **Fax:** 01392-435249
E-mail: ghnewbery@btconnect.com
Website: http://www.ghnewbery.co.uk
Directors: R. Toghill (MD)
Ultimate Holding Company: TOGS LIMITED
Immediate Holding Company: G.H. NEWBERY & SON LIMITED
Registration no: 00563681 **Date established:** 1956
Turnover: £20m - £50m **No.of Employees:** 11 - 20 **Product Groups:** 66

Date of Accounts	Dec 11	Dec 10	Dec 09
Sales Turnover	25m	22m	13m
Pre Tax Profit/Loss	1m	2m	2m
Working Capital	2m	-86	2m
Fixed Assets	916	956	495
Current Assets	7m	8m	6m
Current Liabilities	207	408	469

Newey & Eyre Ltd
Cofton Road Marsh Barton Trading Estate, Exeter, EX2 8QW
Tel: 01392-257135 **Fax:** 01392-410358
Website: http://www.neweysonline.co.uk
Managers: C. Sowden (Mgr)
Immediate Holding Company: NEWEY & EYRE LIMITED
Registration no: 00216596 **VAT No.:** GB 614 2136 80
Date established: 2026 **Turnover:** £1m - £2m **No.of Employees:** 1 - 10
Product Groups: 63, 77

Date of Accounts	Dec 11	Dec 10	Dec 09
Pre Tax Profit/Loss	N/A	N/A	387
Working Capital	15m	15m	15m
Fixed Assets	265	265	265
Current Assets	15m	15m	15m

NewZapp
7 Park Five Business Centre Harrier Way, Exeter, EX2 7HU
Tel: 0845-6125544
E-mail: sales@newzapp.co.uk
Website: http://www.newzapp.co.uk
Directors: D. Hepburn (Sales)
Date established: 1998 **No.of Employees:** 11 - 20 **Product Groups:** 44

Parker Merchanting Ltd
Cofton Road Marsh Barton Trading Estate, Exeter, EX2 8QW
Tel: 01392-288900 **Fax:** 01392-288901
E-mail: info.parker@hagemeyer.co.uk
Website: http://www.parker-direct.com
Managers: C. Spokes (Mgr)
Ultimate Holding Company: RAY INVESTMENT SARL (LUXEMBOURG)
Immediate Holding Company: PARKER MERCHANTING LIMITED
Registration no: 00224779 **VAT No.:** GB 614 2136 80
Date established: 2027 **Turnover:** £75m - £125m
No.of Employees: 21 - 50 **Product Groups:** 22, 23, 24, 29, 30, 33, 37, 39, 40, 45, 63, 66, 68

Date of Accounts	Dec 10	Dec 09	Dec 08
Working Capital	51	51	51
Current Assets	51	51	51

Pennon Group
Peninsula House Rydon Lane, Exeter, EX2 7HR
Tel: 01392-446688 **Fax:** 01392-434966
E-mail: kwoodier@pennon-group.co.uk
Website: http://www.pennon-group.co.uk
Managers: M. Billinghay (Personnel), M. Davies (Purch Mgr), K. Woodier, C. Mills, T. Hooper, K. Nankivell (Tech Serv Mgr)
Ultimate Holding Company: PENNON GROUP PLC
Immediate Holding Company: VIRIDOR WASTE 2 LIMITED
Registration no: 02298543 **Date established:** 1988
Turnover: £500m - £1,000m **No.of Employees:** 251 - 500
Product Groups: 54

Date of Accounts	Mar 11	Mar 10	Mar 09
Pre Tax Profit/Loss	N/A	N/A	1
Working Capital	278m	278m	278m
Fixed Assets	6m	6m	6m
Current Assets	278m	278m	278m

Pickfords Business Moving
11 Cofton Road Marsh Barton Trading Estate, Exeter, EX2 8QW
Tel: 08456-121008 **Fax:** 01392-425298
E-mail: enquiries6@pickfords.com
Website: http://www.pickfords.com
Managers: M. Herrington (Chief Mgr)
Ultimate Holding Company: Moving Services Group Holdings Ltd
Immediate Holding Company: PICKFORDS LIMITED
Registration no: 05025126 **Date established:** 2004
Turnover: £500,000 - £1m **No.of Employees:** 1 - 10 **Product Groups:** 36, 72, 77, 84

William Pollard & Company Ltd
Oak House Falcon Road, Sowton Industrial Estate, Exeter, EX2 7NU
Tel: 01392-445333 **Fax:** 01392-276503
E-mail: info@pollardsprint.co.uk
Website: http://www.pollardsprint.co.uk
Bank(s): Natwest
Directors: D. Mace (Fin)
Managers: M. Burnett, M. Makinen (Tech Serv Mgr)
Immediate Holding Company: WILLIAM POLLARD & COMPANY LIMITED
Registration no: 00065337 **VAT No.:** GB 141 2857 81
Date established: 2000 **Turnover:** £2m - £5m **No.of Employees:** 51 - 100
Product Groups: 27, 28, 81

Date of Accounts	Mar 12	Mar 11	Mar 10
Sales Turnover	5m	4m	4m
Pre Tax Profit/Loss	190	174	-330
Working Capital	83	20	197
Fixed Assets	6m	6m	6m
Current Assets	1m	1m	2m
Current Liabilities	421	542	347

Red Baron Couriers Ltd
2 Forrest Unit Hennock Road East, Marsh Barton Trading Estate, Exeter, EX2 8RJ
Tel: 07973-287202 **Fax:** 01392-823223
E-mail: admin@redbaroncouriers.co.uk
Directors: M. Gratland (Fin)
Immediate Holding Company: RED BARON COURIERS LIMITED
Registration no: 07454702 **Date established:** 2010
No.of Employees: 1 - 10 **Product Groups:** 72

Date of Accounts	Jul 08
Working Capital	-2
Fixed Assets	4
Current Assets	4
Current Liabilities	6

Revill Industrial Finishes Ltd
Exeter Airport Business Park Clyst Honiton, Exeter, EX5 2UL
Tel: 01392-366574 **Fax:** 01392-366318
E-mail: revills@eicgroup.co.uk
Website: http://www.eicgroup.co.uk
Directors: J. Jacobs (Dir)
Ultimate Holding Company: E.I.C. GROUP LIMITED
Immediate Holding Company: REVILL INDUSTRIAL FINISHES LIMITED
Registration no: 00855057 **VAT No.:** GB 141 7305 95
Date established: 1965 **Turnover:** £500,000 - £1m
No.of Employees: 11 - 20 **Product Groups:** 48

Date of Accounts	Mar 11	Mar 10	Mar 09
Working Capital	576	551	751
Fixed Assets	324	340	347
Current Assets	675	694	1m

Robson Liddle Ltd
Building3 Capital Court Sowton Industrial Estate, Exeter, EX2 7LW
Tel: 01392-351200 **Fax:** 01291-645894
E-mail: mail@robsonliddle.com
Website: http://www.robsonliddle.com
Bank(s): National Westminster Bank Plc
Directors: I. Robson (Dir), I. Robson (MD), M. Liddle (Dir), M. Liddle (Fin)
Managers: S. Milum (Sec)
Ultimate Holding Company: NORSE GROUP LIMITED
Immediate Holding Company: ROBSON LIDDLE LIMITED
Registration no: 03240492 **VAT No.:** GB 585 4030 39
Date established: 1996 **Turnover:** £1m - £2m **No.of Employees:** 11 - 20
Product Groups: 84

Date of Accounts	Mar 08	Jan 11	Jan 10
Sales Turnover	N/A	1m	1m
Pre Tax Profit/Loss	N/A	64	39
Working Capital	119	-13	-94
Fixed Assets	493	446	501
Current Assets	545	343	367
Current Liabilities	N/A	117	171

S A S Europe Ltd
Kingstag House Cheriton Bishop, Exeter, EX6 6JE
Tel: 01647-24620 **Fax:** 01647-24020
E-mail: sales@sas-europe.com
Website: http://www.sas-europe.com
Directors: P. Nickells (MD)
Managers: W. Nickells (Prod Mgr)
Immediate Holding Company: SAS (EUROPE) LIMITED
Registration no: 04264226 **Date established:** 2001
No.of Employees: 11 - 20 **Product Groups:** 33

Date of Accounts	Dec 11	Dec 10	Dec 09
Working Capital	317	402	375
Fixed Assets	125	107	144
Current Assets	1m	887	926

S M C Wholesale
1 Budlake Unit Budlake Road, Marsh Barton Trading Estate, Exeter, EX2 8PY
Tel: 01392-217635 **Fax:** 01392-259291
E-mail: sales@smcwholesale.co.uk
Website: http://www.smcwholesale.co.uk
Directors: F. Scriven (Dir)
No.of Employees: 1 - 10 **Product Groups:** 35, 36

Safecar Security Services Ltd
Bittern Road Sowton Industrial Estate, Exeter, EX2 7LW
Tel: 01392-257333 **Fax:** 01392-423869
E-mail: krjohns@hotmail.com
Website: http://www.securestorage.co.uk
Directors: B. Johns (Fin), K. Johns (MD)
Immediate Holding Company: SAFECAR SECURITY SERVICES LIMITED
Registration no: 01012057 **Date established:** 1971 **Turnover:** £1m - £2m
No.of Employees: 1 - 10 **Product Groups:** 72, 77, 81

Date of Accounts	Apr 12	Apr 11	Apr 10
Working Capital	1m	1m	998
Fixed Assets	1m	1m	1m
Current Assets	868	830	840

Sca Packaging Limited
Kingfisher Way Sowton Industrial Estate, Exeter, EX2 7LE
Tel: 01392-445141 **Fax:** 01392-445125
E-mail: sales@scapackaging.co.uk
Website: http://www.scapackaging.co.uk
Managers: S. Lockett (Sales Prom Mgr), J. Woolley (Plant)
Immediate Holding Company: FBA
Registration no: 00053913 **Turnover:** £2m - £5m
No.of Employees: 21 - 50 **Product Groups:** 27, 28, 30, 49

Short Run Press
25 Bittern Road Sowton Industrial Estate, Exeter, EX2 7LW
Tel: 01392-211909 **Fax:** 01392-444134
E-mail: rob@shortrunpress.co.uk
Website: http://www.shortrunpress.co.uk
Directors: M. Couch (Dir), R. Gliddon (Dir)
Immediate Holding Company: SHORT RUN PRESS LIMITED
Registration no: 01526157 **Date established:** 1980
No.of Employees: 11 - 20 **Product Groups:** 28, 67, 81

Date of Accounts	Apr 11	Apr 10	Apr 09
Working Capital	-277	-258	-262
Fixed Assets	290	300	266
Current Assets	549	330	318
Current Liabilities	N/A	N/A	84

South West Business Centre Ltd
Queensgate House 48 Queen Street, Exeter, EX4 3SR
Tel: 01392-215541 **Fax:** 01392-410436
E-mail: info@swbus.co.uk
Website: http://www.swbus.co.uk
Directors: G. Purton (Fin), M. Purton (MD)
Immediate Holding Company: THE SOUTH WEST BUSINESS CENTRE LIMITED
Registration no: 03099112 **Date established:** 1995
Turnover: £250,000 - £500,000 **No.of Employees:** 1 - 10
Product Groups: 80

Date of Accounts	Sep 11	Sep 10	Sep 09
Working Capital	N/A	N/A	27
Current Assets	34	N/A	27

South West Metal Finishing Ltd
Alphinbrook Road Marsh Barton Trading Estate, Exeter, EX2 8TJ
Tel: 01392-258234 **Fax:** 01392-421538
E-mail: paul@eicgroup.co.uk
Website: http://www.eicgroup.co.uk
Bank(s): Lloyds, Exeter
Directors: P. Jacobs (Dir), J. Jacobs (Fin)
Managers: A. Prouse
Ultimate Holding Company: E.I.C. GROUP LIMITED
Immediate Holding Company: SOUTH WEST METAL FINISHING LIMITED
Registration no: 02246273 **VAT No.:** GB 510 6265 81
Date established: 1988 **Turnover:** £2m - £5m **No.of Employees:** 51 - 100
Product Groups: 48

Date of Accounts	Mar 11	Mar 10	Mar 09
Sales Turnover	4m	4m	4m
Pre Tax Profit/Loss	208	117	217
Working Capital	1m	1m	1m
Fixed Assets	1m	1m	1m
Current Assets	3m	2m	2m
Current Liabilities	898	621	555

South West Water Ltd
Peninsula House Rydon Lane, Exeter, EX2 7HR
Tel: 0800-169 1144 **Fax:** 01392-434966
Website: http://www.southwestwater.co.uk
Bank(s): Lloyds
Directors: S. Davy (Fin)
Managers: P. Cameron
Ultimate Holding Company: PENNON GROUP PLC
Immediate Holding Company: SOUTH WEST WATER LIMITED
Registration no: 02366665 **Date established:** 1989
Turnover: £250m - £500m **No.of Employees:** 1001 - 1500
Product Groups: 18

Date of Accounts	Mar 12	Mar 11	Mar 10
Sales Turnover	475m	449m	445m
Pre Tax Profit/Loss	141m	129m	128m
Working Capital	183m	186m	53m
Fixed Assets	2546m	2472m	2430m
Current Assets	383m	395m	339m
Current Liabilities	74m	96m	94m

Sparex International Ltd
Exeter Airport Devon, Clyst Honiton, Exeter, EX5 2LJ
Tel: 01392-368892 **Fax:** 01392-369904
E-mail: theunis.stortenbeker@sparex.co.uk
Website: http://www.sparex.co.uk
Directors: T. Stortenbeker (Dir)
Ultimate Holding Company: RUBICON PARTNERS INDUSTRIES LLP
Immediate Holding Company: SPAREX INTERNATIONAL LIMITED
Registration no: 01750165 **VAT No.:** GB 754 8199 87
Date established: 1983 **Turnover:** £20m - £50m **No.of Employees:** 1 - 10
Product Groups: 41, 67

Spenco Engineering Co. Ltd
Clyst Honiton, Exeter, EX5 2DX
Tel: 01392-369795 **Fax:** 01392-364439
E-mail: post@spenco.co.uk
Website: http://www.spenco.co.uk
Bank(s): Royal Bank of Scotland Plc, London
Directors: D. Bray (MD)
Managers: A. Clarke (Buyer), I. McLelland
Ultimate Holding Company: AGCO CORP (USA)
Immediate Holding Company: SPENCO ENGINEERING CO. LIMITED
Registration no: 01242155 **Date established:** 1976 **Turnover:** £2m - £5m
No.of Employees: 21 - 50 **Product Groups:** 41, 48, 67

Date of Accounts	Dec 11	Dec 10	Dec 09
Sales Turnover	4m	3m	3m
Pre Tax Profit/Loss	278	390	202

see next page

Spenco Engineering Co. Ltd - Cont'd

Working Capital	5m	5m	4m
Fixed Assets	198	123	140
Current Assets	5m	5m	4m
Current Liabilities	192	182	204

Stovax Ltd

Falcon Road Sowton Industrial Estate, Exeter, EX2 7LF
Tel: 01392-474011 **Fax:** 01392-219932
E-mail: info@stovax.com
Website: http://www.stovax.com
Bank(s): HSBC Bank plc
Directors: A. Walker (Co Sec), R. Crabb (Dir)
Ultimate Holding Company: STOVAX GROUP LIMITED
Immediate Holding Company: STOVAX LIMITED
Registration no: 01572550 **Date established:** 1981
Turnover: £20m - £50m **No.of Employees:** 51 - 100 **Product Groups:** 33, 40

Date of Accounts	May 11	May 10	May 09
Sales Turnover	20m	17m	20m
Pre Tax Profit/Loss	5m	3m	4m
Working Capital	7m	6m	5m
Fixed Assets	276	348	216
Current Assets	9m	7m	7m
Current Liabilities	1m	1m	1m

Tag Plastic Extrusions Ltd

21 Marsh Green Road North Marsh Barton Trading Estate, Exeter, EX2 8NY
Tel: 01392-479036 **Fax:** 01392-432835
Website: http://www.tagplastics.co.uk
Directors: G. Sergides (Jt MD), M. Belcher (Jt MD), C. Sergides (MD)
Ultimate Holding Company: DRAKEMEAD LIMITED
Immediate Holding Company: TAG PLASTIC EXTRUSIONS LIMITED
Registration no: 01800102 **VAT No.:** GB 391 3715 45
Date established: 1984 **Turnover:** £500,000 - £1m
No.of Employees: 1 - 10 **Product Groups:** 29, 30

Date of Accounts	Mar 12	Mar 11	Mar 10
Working Capital	117	114	104
Fixed Assets	101	90	103
Current Assets	303	250	241

Tamar Specialist Brushes Ltd

PO Box 286, Exeter, EX2 8WW
Tel: 01392-491818 **Fax:** 01392-491818
E-mail: enquiries@tamarbrushes.co.uk
Website: http://www.tamarbrushes.co.uk
Directors: C. Best (MD)
Immediate Holding Company: TAMAR SPECIALIST BRUSHES LIMITED
Registration no: 07830765 **Date established:** 2011
Turnover: Up to £250,000 **No.of Employees:** 1 - 10 **Product Groups:** 24, 30, 36, 40

James Townsend & Sons Ltd

PO Box 12, Exeter, EX1 2AB
Tel: 01392-849000 **Fax:** 01392-849001
E-mail: thomas.gregory@james-townsend.co.uk
Website: http://www.james-townsend.co.uk
Bank(s): National Westminster Bank Plc
Directors: N. Goodall (Sales & Mktg), T. Gregory (Fin), A. Coles (Ch & MD), C. Jone (Sales & Mktg), C. Jones (Sales)
Managers: G. Coles (I.T. Exec), L. Coles (Admin Off)
Ultimate Holding Company: 04331809
Immediate Holding Company: JAMES TOWNSEND & SONS LIMITED
Registration no: 00367549 **VAT No.:** GB 140 7458 76
Date established: 1941 **Turnover:** £5m - £10m
No.of Employees: 51 - 100 **Product Groups:** 28

Date of Accounts	Mar 08	Mar 07	Mar 06
Pre Tax Profit/Loss	279	-381	-690
Working Capital	1009	1789	1740
Fixed Assets	5461	5831	5623
Current Assets	5981	6154	6249
Current Liabilities	4972	4365	4508
Total Share Capital	192	192	192
ROCE% (Return on Capital Employed)	4.3	-5.0	-9.4

Tremlett Ski Craft Ltd

Odhams Wharf Ebford, Exeter, EX3 0PD
Tel: 01392-873680 **Fax:** 01392-876277
Directors: M. Tremlett (MD)
Immediate Holding Company: TREMLETTS (SKICRAFT) LIMITED
Registration no: 00675169 **VAT No.:** GB 142 9439 58
Date established: 1960 **Turnover:** £500,000 - £1m
No.of Employees: 1 - 10 **Product Groups:** 39

Date of Accounts	Nov 11	Nov 10	Nov 09
Working Capital	-13	-25	-9
Fixed Assets	470	471	468
Current Assets	123	125	157

Trump Engineering

23 Charwell Meadow Bradninch, Exeter, EX5 4QQ
Tel: 01392-881402 **Fax:** 01392-881402
Directors: S. Trump (Prop)
Date established: 1994 **No.of Employees:** 1 - 10 **Product Groups:** 41

UK Vehicle Contracts

Unit 9 Sandpiper Court Harrington Lane, Exeter, EX4 8NS
Tel: 01392-331200 **Fax:** 01392-331201
E-mail: andywoodward@ukvehiclecontracts.com
Website: http://www.ukcommercialvehicles.com
Managers: A. Woodward (Mgr)
Immediate Holding Company: CPM (EXETER) LIMITED
Registration no: 04297315 **Date established:** 2012
No.of Employees: 11 - 20 **Product Groups:** 81

Date of Accounts	Mar 09	Mar 08	Mar 07
Working Capital	-101	9	-30
Fixed Assets	292	292	336
Current Assets	426	997	1m

The Vapormatic Co. Ltd

PO Box 58, Exeter, EX2 7NB
Tel: 01392-435461 **Fax:** 01392-438445
E-mail: peter.brennan@vapormatic.com
Website: http://www.vapormatic.co.uk
Bank(s): Lloyds TSB Bank plc
Directors: P. Brennan (MD)
Ultimate Holding Company: DEERE & COMPANY (USA)
Immediate Holding Company: VAPORMATIC COMPANY LIMITED(THE)
Registration no: 00538655 **VAT No.:** GB 362 0233 93
Date established: 1954 **Turnover:** £20m - £50m
No.of Employees: 51 - 100 **Product Groups:** 41, 45

Date of Accounts	Oct 11	Oct 10	Oct 09
Sales Turnover	23m	21m	20m
Pre Tax Profit/Loss	2m	239	112
Working Capital	9m	7m	4m
Fixed Assets	4m	4m	4m
Current Assets	12m	10m	10m
Current Liabilities	1m	932	806

W G Grace & Son Ltd

Unit 8 Gidleys Meadow Christow, Exeter, EX6 7QB
Tel: 01647-252995 **Fax:** 01647-252995
E-mail: grace.greenhouses@virgin.net
Directors: W. Grace (Dir)
Immediate Holding Company: W G GRACE & SON LIMITED
Registration no: 04747979 **Date established:** 2003
No.of Employees: 1 - 10 **Product Groups:** 26, 35

Date of Accounts	Mar 12	Mar 11	Mar 10
Working Capital	-67	-67	-66
Fixed Assets	72	71	73
Current Assets	12	11	14

J Wippell & Co. Ltd

PO Box 1, Exeter, EX4 1DQ
Tel: 01392-254234 **Fax:** 01392-250868
E-mail: richardson@jwippell.co.uk
Website: http://www.wippell.co.uk
Bank(s): National Westminster
Directors: C. Morrish (Dir), R. Richardson (Ch)
Immediate Holding Company: J. WIPPELL & COMPANY LIMITED
Registration no: 00074973 **VAT No.:** 141 1210 39 **Date established:** 2002
Turnover: £2m - £5m **No.of Employees:** 51 - 100 **Product Groups:** 24, 26

Date of Accounts	Jan 12	Jan 11	Jan 10
Sales Turnover	4m	3m	3m
Pre Tax Profit/Loss	417	143	125
Working Capital	617	480	619
Fixed Assets	2m	2m	2m
Current Assets	1m	978	1m
Current Liabilities	409	356	369

Wood & Wood International Signs Ltd

Heron Road Sowton Industrial Estate, Exeter, EX2 7LX
Tel: 01392-444501 **Fax:** 01392-252358
E-mail: info@wwsigns.co.uk
Website: http://www.wwsigns.co.uk
Bank(s): National Westminster Bank Plc
Directors: N. Jeal (Dir)
Managers: M. Jephtha (Tech Serv Mgr), G. Adam (Purch Mgr)
Ultimate Holding Company: GILHOME LIMITED (BVI)
Immediate Holding Company: WOOD & WOOD INTERNATIONAL SIGNS LIMITED
Registration no: 00926425 **Date established:** 1968 **Turnover:** £2m - £5m
No.of Employees: 21 - 50 **Product Groups:** 37, 40, 49, 84

Date of Accounts	Dec 11	Dec 10	Dec 09
Sales Turnover	5m	5m	6m
Pre Tax Profit/Loss	173	-40	299
Working Capital	3m	2m	2m
Fixed Assets	87	89	120
Current Assets	4m	3m	4m
Current Liabilities	400	351	754

Z M T Services Ltd

Unit 2 Dart Business Park Clyst St George, Exeter, EX3 0QH
Tel: 01392-873788 **Fax:** 01392-873474
E-mail: kenneth.goddard@zmtservices.co.uk
Website: http://www.zmtservices.co.uk
Directors: K. Goddard (MD)
Immediate Holding Company: ZMT SERVICES LTD
Registration no: 03750113 **Date established:** 1999
Turnover: Up to £250,000 **No.of Employees:** 1 - 10 **Product Groups:** 46

Date of Accounts	Jun 07	Jun 06
Sales Turnover	150	179
Pre Tax Profit/Loss	25	31
Working Capital	24	28
Fixed Assets	1	1
Current Assets	35	43
Current Liabilities	11	15
ROCE% (Return on Capital Employed)	100.2	107.5
ROT% (Return on Turnover)	16.7	17.3

Exmouth

Devon Metalcrafts Ltd

2 Victoria Way, Exmouth, EX8 1EW
Tel: 01395-272846 **Fax:** 01395-276688
E-mail: trevor@devonmetalcrafts.co.uk
Website: http://www.devonmetalcrafts.co.uk
Directors: S. Lendon (MD), T. Ford (Fin)
Immediate Holding Company: DEVON METALCRAFTS LIMITED
Registration no: 01681207 **Date established:** 1982
Turnover: Up to £250,000 **No.of Employees:** 1 - 10 **Product Groups:** 34, 36

Date of Accounts	Mar 11	Mar 10	Mar 09
Working Capital	39	27	27
Fixed Assets	8	10	11
Current Assets	78	54	61

Exmouth Power Tools Ltd

4 Pound Lane Office Suite Pound Lane, Exmouth, EX8 4NP
Tel: 01395-269209 **Fax:** 01395-269209
E-mail: gary@exmouthpowertools.com
Website: http://www.exmouthpowertools.com
Directors: G. Wright (Prop)
Immediate Holding Company: EXMOUTH POWER TOOLS LIMITED
Registration no: 04860600 **Date established:** 2003
No.of Employees: 1 - 10 **Product Groups:** 37

Date of Accounts	Aug 11	Aug 10	Aug 09
Working Capital	-16	-10	-23
Fixed Assets	26	39	49
Current Assets	136	146	141

Jewson Ltd

Fore Street, Exmouth, EX8 1HX
Tel: 01395-264373 **Fax:** 01395-222420
E-mail: tim.evans@jewson.co.uk
Website: http://www.jewson.co.uk
Directors: S. Long (Prop)
Ultimate Holding Company: COMPAGNIE DE SAINT GOBAIN (FRANCE)
Immediate Holding Company: JEWSON LIMITED
Registration no: 00348407 **Date established:** 1939
No.of Employees: 1 - 10 **Product Groups:** 66

Date of Accounts	Dec 11	Dec 10	Dec 09
Sales Turnover	1606m	1547m	1485m
Pre Tax Profit/Loss	18m	100m	45m
Working Capital	-345m	-250m	-349m
Fixed Assets	496m	387m	461m
Current Assets	657m	1005m	1320m
Current Liabilities	66m	120m	64m

Vetaphone

2b Cranford Avenue, Exmouth, EX8 2HT
Tel: 01395-264144 **Fax:** 01395-227335
E-mail: ashcroft@vetaphone.com
Website: http://www.vetaphone.com
Managers: S. Ashcroft (Mgr)
No.of Employees: 1 - 10 **Product Groups:** 42, 49

Holsworthy

B S Y Group

Oakwood Dunsland Cross, Brandis Corner, Holsworthy, EX22 7YT
Tel: 01409-220400 **Fax:** 01409-220401
E-mail: info@bsygroup.co.uk
Website: http://www.bsygroup.co.uk
Directors: A. Williams (Head)
No.of Employees: 21 - 50 **Product Groups:** 86

Date of Accounts	Dec 10	Dec 09	Dec 08
Working Capital	69	-18	119
Fixed Assets	25	49	112
Current Assets	264	200	317

D & M Tractors

Week Close Burnhards House Bude Road, Pancrasweek, Holsworthy, EX22 7JB
Tel: 01409-254306
Directors: D. Jones (Ptnr)
Date established: 1996 **No.of Employees:** 1 - 10 **Product Groups:** 41

Tom Hannaford

Moorview Whitstone, Holsworthy, EX22 6LB
Tel: 01288-341526 **Fax:** 01288-341526
Directors: S. Hannaford (Ptnr)
Immediate Holding Company: TOM HANNAFORD BUILDINGS LTD
Registration no: 06846570 **Date established:** 2009
No.of Employees: 1 - 10 **Product Groups:** 35

Date of Accounts	Mar 11	Mar 10
Working Capital	-11	-124
Fixed Assets	247	225
Current Assets	143	129

Jco Goods

5 Fore Street, Holsworthy, EX22 6EB
Tel: 01409-254455 **Fax:** 01409-254469
E-mail: petersmith666@yahoo.co.uk
Directors: P. Smith (Prop)
Date established: 1997 **No.of Employees:** 1 - 10 **Product Groups:** 36, 40

Passive Components Ltd

1 The Cottages Chilsworthy, Holsworthy, EX22 7BQ
Tel: 01409-254728 **Fax:** 01409-254728
E-mail: sales@pascomp.com
Website: http://www.pascomp.com
Directors: J. Borsay (MD)
Immediate Holding Company: PASSIVE COMPONENTS LTD
Registration no: 05145002 **Date established:** 2004
No.of Employees: 1 - 10 **Product Groups:** 33, 37

Date of Accounts	Jun 11	Jun 10	Jun 09
Sales Turnover	19	20	19
Pre Tax Profit/Loss	1	-0	N/A
Working Capital	-11	-12	-12
Fixed Assets	1	1	1
Current Assets	6	5	9
Current Liabilities	16	13	17

Robert Cole Agricultural Engineers Ltd

Unit 4b Neet Way, Holsworthy Industrial Estate, Holsworthy, EX22 6ES
Tel: 01409-253629 **Fax:** 01409-254544
E-mail: sales@robertcole.co.uk
Website: http://www.robertcole.co.uk
Directors: R. Cole (MD)
Immediate Holding Company: ROBERT COLE AGRICULTURAL ENGINEERS LIMITED
Registration no: 04736404 **Date established:** 2003
No.of Employees: 21 - 50 **Product Groups:** 41

Date of Accounts	Oct 10	Oct 09	Oct 08
Working Capital	432	330	238
Fixed Assets	103	128	97
Current Assets	2m	2m	1m

Short & Abbott Ltd

Agricultural Workshop Bridge Mill, Bridgerule, Holsworthy, EX22 7EL
Tel: 01288-381485 **Fax:** 01288-381486
E-mail: gary@shortandabbott.fsnet.co.uk
Website: http://www.shortandabbott.co.uk
Directors: C. Short (MD), G. Abbott (Fin)
Immediate Holding Company: SHORT & ABBOTT LIMITED
Registration no: 04188097 **Date established:** 2001
Turnover: £500,000 - £1m **No.of Employees:** 1 - 10 **Product Groups:** 41

Date of Accounts	Mar 12	Mar 11	Mar 10
Working Capital	135	106	129
Fixed Assets	35	32	33
Current Assets	278	195	263

J Weston & Partners Ltd

East Putford, Holsworthy, EX22 7XR
Tel: 01237-451838 **Fax:** 01237-451553
E-mail: n.j.moulder@btconnect.com
Directors: N. Moulder (MD)
Immediate Holding Company: J.WESTON & PARTNERS LIMITED
Registration no: 00794134 **VAT No.:** GB 205 8458 61
Date established: 1964 **Turnover:** Up to £250,000
No.of Employees: 1 - 10 **Product Groups:** 36, 46

Date of Accounts	Feb 08	Feb 11	Feb 10
Working Capital	20	21	-3
Fixed Assets	62	60	61
Current Assets	67	74	61

Honiton

Aylward Engineering & Pneumatics Ltd
Devonshire Road Heathpark Industrial Estate, Honiton, EX14 1SG
Tel: 01404-548000 **Fax:** 01404-548005
E-mail: info@aep-ltd.co.uk
Website: http://www.aep-ltd.co.uk
Bank(s): Barclays
Directors: D. Harris (MD)
Ultimate Holding Company: THE WEST GROUP (FLUID POWER) LIMITED
Immediate Holding Company: AYLWARD ENGINEERING AND PNEUMATICS LIMITED
Registration no: 01227271 **Date established:** 1975 **Turnover:** £1m - £2m
No.of Employees: 11 - 20 **Product Groups:** 30, 34, 36, 39, 40

Date of Accounts	Aug 11	Aug 10	Aug 09
Working Capital	320	200	154
Fixed Assets	465	478	492
Current Assets	2m	1m	638

T Broom
10 Mount Pleasant Workshops Offwell, Honiton, EX14 9RP
Tel: 01404-44521
Directors: T. Broom (Prop), T. Broome (Prop)
Date established: 1998 **No.of Employees:** 1 - 10 **Product Groups:** 35

C C L Group
18 Durham Way, Honiton, EX14 1SQ
Fax: 01404-540333
E-mail: south@computercomponents.com
Website: http://www.computercomponents.com
Product Groups: 33, 61, 67, 84

Computer Components Ltd
18 Durham Way Heathpark Industrial Estate, Honiton, EX14 1SQ
Tel: 01404-540300 **Fax:** 01404-540333
E-mail: info@computercomponents.com
Website: http://www.computercomponents.com
Directors: A. Chinery (Dir), M. Upsher (Co Sec), V. Osborn (Sales)
Immediate Holding Company: COMPUTER COMPONENTS LIMITED
Registration no: 03425090 **Date established:** 1997
No.of Employees: 11 - 20 **Product Groups:** 33, 61, 67, 84

Date of Accounts	Dec 11	Dec 10	Dec 09
Working Capital	14	41	30
Fixed Assets	76	35	44
Current Assets	420	350	310

Coziers
Flight Way Business Park Dunkeswell, Honiton, EX14 4RJ
Tel: 01404-891990 **Fax:** 01404-891990
E-mail: sales@coziers.eu.com
Website: http://www.coziers.eu.com
Directors: C. Cozier (Prop)
No.of Employees: 1 - 10 **Product Groups:** 37, 38

Goonvean Fibres Ltd
Bramble Hill Industrial Estate, Honiton, EX14 1BW
Tel: 01404-44194 **Fax:** 01404-45102
E-mail: office@goonveanfibres.co.uk
Website: http://www.goonveanfibres.com
Bank(s): Barclays
Directors: J. Opie (MD)
Managers: D. Chaplin (Fin Mgr), J. Mumgeam
Ultimate Holding Company: GOONVEAN HOLDINGS LIMITED
Immediate Holding Company: GOONVEAN FIBRES LIMITED
Registration no: 04735337 **VAT No.:** GB 130 2788 87
Date established: 2003 **Turnover:** £1m - £2m **No.of Employees:** 21 - 50
Product Groups: 20, 23, 30, 32

Date of Accounts	Sep 11	Sep 10	Sep 09
Working Capital	2m	2m	2m
Fixed Assets	749	789	490
Current Assets	3m	3m	3m
Current Liabilities	N/A	179	137

Lynch Motor Company Ltd
Unit 8 Park Court Devonshire Road, Heathpark Indl-Est, Honiton, EX14 1SW
Tel: 01404-549940 **Fax:** 01404-549546
E-mail: sales@lmcltd.net
Website: http://www.lmcltd.net
Directors: T. Lees (MD), T. Leef (MD)
Ultimate Holding Company: MAXINI AG (SWITZERLAND)
Immediate Holding Company: LEES MOTOR COMPANY LIMITED
Registration no: 04555463 **Date established:** 2002
Turnover: £500,000 - £1m **No.of Employees:** 1 - 10 **Product Groups:** 37

Date of Accounts	Mar 11	Mar 10	Mar 09
Working Capital	-68	-43	-108
Fixed Assets	66	58	56
Current Assets	149	136	130

Playways
Maidengreen Upottery, Honiton, EX14 9QT
Tel: 01404-861379
E-mail: enquiries@playways.co.uk
Website: http://www.playways.co.uk
Directors: M. Killick (Prop)
Immediate Holding Company: DEVON PLAYWAYS LIMITED
Registration no: 05701480 **Date established:** 2006
Turnover: Up to £250,000 **No.of Employees:** 1 - 10 **Product Groups:** 49, 52

Roberts Warr Electronics Ltd
The Old Vcge Broadhembury, Honiton, EX14 3ND
Tel: 01404-841648 **Fax:** 01404-841575
E-mail: sales@robertswarr.com
Website: http://www.robertswarr.com
Directors: S. Carter (MD)
Immediate Holding Company: ROBERTS WARR ELECTRONICS LIMITED
Registration no: 01771033 **Date established:** 1983
No.of Employees: 1 - 10 **Product Groups:** 37, 39, 40, 44

Date of Accounts	Apr 11	Apr 10	Apr 09
Working Capital	-8	11	11
Fixed Assets	4	6	7
Current Assets	95	179	196

Sheerspeed Shelters Ltd
Diamond House Reme Drive Heathpark Industrial Estate, Heathpark Industrial Estate, Honiton, EX14 1SE
Tel: 01404-46006 **Fax:** 01404-45520
E-mail: sales@sheerspeed.com
Website: http://www.sheerspeed.com
Directors: A. Horobin (Fin)
Managers: P. Fernandez
Immediate Holding Company: SHEERSPEED SHELTERS LIMITED
Registration no: 03493192 **VAT No.:** 768 5442 88 **Date established:** 1998
Turnover: £500,000 - £1m **No.of Employees:** 1 - 10 **Product Groups:** 23, 24, 25, 29, 30, 46, 49, 63, 83

Date of Accounts	Dec 11	Dec 09	Dec 08
Sales Turnover	N/A	773	884
Working Capital	286	-57	329
Fixed Assets	1m	1m	1m
Current Assets	563	297	493

Supacat
The Airfield, Honiton, EX14 4LF
Tel: 01404-891777 **Fax:** 01404-891776
E-mail: generalenquiries@supacat.com
Website: http://www.supacat.com
Bank(s): National Westminster
Directors: A. Mitchell (Fin), N. Jones (MD)
Managers: C. Butler (Buyer), L. Beard-lowe (Personnel), L. Parfitt (Tech Serv Mgr), J. Clarke (Sales & Mktg Mg)
Immediate Holding Company: SUPACAT LIMITED
Registration no: 01514084 **Date established:** 1980
Turnover: £20m - £50m **No.of Employees:** 101 - 250 **Product Groups:** 67

Date of Accounts	Aug 11	Aug 10	Aug 09
Sales Turnover	22m	108m	50m
Pre Tax Profit/Loss	2m	8m	3m
Working Capital	5m	5m	3m
Fixed Assets	4m	5m	3m
Current Assets	10m	22m	39m
Current Liabilities	4m	6m	17m

T W M Technology Ltd
Heathpark Way Heathpark Industrial Estate, Honiton, EX14 1BB
Tel: 01404-46737 **Fax:** 01404-46718
E-mail: sales@twmtech.co.uk
Website: http://www.twmtech.co.uk
Directors: D. Douglas (Dir)
Ultimate Holding Company: THE EUROTECH GROUP PLC
Immediate Holding Company: TWM TECHNOLOGY LIMITED
Registration no: 02696553 **Date established:** 1992
Turnover: £500,000 - £1m **No.of Employees:** 11 - 20
Product Groups: 46, 48

Date of Accounts	Jun 11	Jun 10	Jun 09
Sales Turnover	959	633	819
Pre Tax Profit/Loss	24	-41	-30
Working Capital	507	383	453
Fixed Assets	136	163	197
Current Assets	675	484	522
Current Liabilities	5	13	6

Tracmac Ltd
Tower Cross, Honiton, EX14 9UY
Tel: 01404-46655 **Fax:** 01404-46677
E-mail: export@tracmac.co.uk
Website: http://www.tracmac.co.uk
Directors: W. Mccormick (Dir)
Immediate Holding Company: TRACMAC LIMITED
Registration no: 02897751 **Date established:** 1994
Turnover: £500,000 - £1m **No.of Employees:** 1 - 10 **Product Groups:** 29, 39, 41

Date of Accounts	Jan 11	Jan 10	Jan 09
Working Capital	6	-1	-4
Fixed Assets	1	1	1
Current Assets	29	25	13

Ilfracombe

Combe Martin Post Office
High Street Combe Martin, Ilfracombe, EX34 0EN
Tel: 01271-882266
E-mail: sales@combemartinmodels.com
Website: http://www.combemartinmodels.com
Managers: C. Lincoln
No.of Employees: 1 - 10 **Product Groups:** 40, 45

Glo-Marka
Beeches Westminster Villas, Ilfracombe, EX34 9NX
Tel: 01271-865528 **Fax:** 01271-864664
E-mail: sales@glo-marka.co.uk
Website: http://www.glo-marka.co.uk
Directors: A. Kino (Ptnr)
VAT No.: GB 384 2265 44 **Turnover:** Up to £250,000
No.of Employees: 1 - 10 **Product Groups:** 24

Investacast Ltd
Mullacott Cross Industrial Estate, Ilfracombe, EX34 8PL
Tel: 01271-866200 **Fax:** 01271-867148
E-mail: chris@investacast.com
Website: http://www.investacast.com
Bank(s): National Westminster Bank Plc
Directors: C. Thompson (Ptnr), C. Thompson (MD)
Immediate Holding Company: INVESTACAST LIMITED
Registration no: 01238636 **VAT No.:** GB 365 8652 15
Date established: 1975 **Turnover:** £2m - £5m **No.of Employees:** 51 - 100
Product Groups: 34

Date of Accounts	Sep 11	Sep 10	Sep 09
Working Capital	2m	1m	1m
Fixed Assets	539	460	477
Current Assets	4m	3m	2m

John Fowler Holidays
Marlborough Road, Ilfracombe, EX34 8PF
Tel: 01271-866766 **Fax:** 01271-866791
E-mail: admin@jfhols.co.uk
Website: http://www.johnfowlerholidays.com
Directors: J. Fowler (Grp Chief Exec)
Managers: S. Hastings
Immediate Holding Company: JOHN FOWLER HOLIDAYS LIMITED
Registration no: 00834652 **Date established:** 1965
Turnover: £20m - £50m **No.of Employees:** 51 - 100 **Product Groups:** 69, 89

Date of Accounts	Dec 11	Dec 10	Dec 09
Sales Turnover	19m	21m	21m
Pre Tax Profit/Loss	14	2m	3m
Working Capital	-1m	159	-4m
Fixed Assets	59m	59m	60m
Current Assets	3m	3m	4m
Current Liabilities	1m	2m	2m

Pall Ilfracombe
Station Road, Ilfracombe, EX34 8BH
Tel: 01271-395111 **Fax:** 01271-395208
Website: http://www.pall.com
Directors: E. Casswell (MD)
Managers: Coles (I.T. Exec)
No.of Employees: 501 - 1000 **Product Groups:** 38, 67

South West Office Supplies
Oak Cottage High Street, Combe Martin, Ilfracombe, EX34 0HS
Tel: 01271-889337 **Fax:** 01271-828193
E-mail: sales@swofficesupplies.co.uk
Website: http://www.swofficesupplies.co.uk
Directors: S. Rice (Dir)
Registration no: 07181877 **Date established:** 0002 **Turnover:**
No.of Employees: 1 - 10 **Product Groups:** 26, 27, 28, 30, 32, 38, 44, 49

T D K Lambda UK Ltd
Kingsley Avenue, Ilfracombe, EX34 8ES
Tel: 01271-856600 **Fax:** 01271-856632
E-mail: adam.rawicz@lambdaeu.com
Website: http://www.uk.tdk-lambda.com
Directors: M. Southam (Sales), W. Davies (Fin), A. Rawicz (MD)
Managers: H. Owen (Mktg Serv Mgr), D. Moss (Purch Mgr), L. Gillingham (Personnel), C. Davies (Tech Serv Mgr)
Ultimate Holding Company: TDK CORPORATION (JAPAN)
Immediate Holding Company: TDK-LAMBDA UK LIMITED
Registration no: 00634143 **Date established:** 1959
Turnover: £20m - £50m **No.of Employees:** 251 - 500
Product Groups: 38, 40, 45, 65, 67

Date of Accounts	Mar 11	Mar 10	Mar 09
Sales Turnover	39m	24m	26m
Pre Tax Profit/Loss	3m	631	-1m
Working Capital	8m	6m	5m
Fixed Assets	4m	4m	5m
Current Assets	15m	10m	8m
Current Liabilities	2m	1m	909

Tanzanite Gemstone
27 Saint Brannocks Road, Ilfracombe, EX34 8EQ
Tel: 020-8123 3785
E-mail: josh@tanzanite-gemstone.com
Website: http://www.tanzanite-gemstone.com
Directors: J. Robbins (Dir)
Date established: 1983 **Turnover:** £250,000 - £500,000
No.of Employees: 1 - 10 **Product Groups:** 65

Ivybridge

B R C
Unit C East Way, Lee Mill Industrial Estate, Ivybridge, PL21 9GE
Tel: 01752-894660 **Fax:** 01752-896761
E-mail: pat.mcculloch@brc.ltd.uk
Website: http://www.brc.ltd.uk
Managers: P. Mcculloch (Mgr)
Immediate Holding Company: BRC LIMITED
Registration no: 06662824 **Date established:** 2008
No.of Employees: 11 - 20 **Product Groups:** 25, 29, 30, 31, 32, 33, 34, 35, 36, 45, 66

Esterlam International Ltd
East Way Lee Mill Industrial Estate, Ivybridge, PL21 9GE
Tel: 01752-690691 **Fax:** 01752-690436
E-mail: info@esterlam.com
Website: http://www.esterlam.com
Directors: J. Hailey (MD)
Immediate Holding Company: ESTERLAM INTERNATIONAL LIMITED
Registration no: 01797022 **VAT No.:** GB 409 5132 66
Date established: 1984 **Turnover:** £500,000 - £1m
No.of Employees: 1 - 10 **Product Groups:** 44

Date of Accounts	Aug 11	Aug 10	Aug 09
Working Capital	260	233	197
Fixed Assets	35	40	25
Current Assets	904	1m	871

Fire Retardent Servicesinternational Passive Fire Ltd
Unit 12a Kingsley Close Lee Mill Industrial Estate, Ivybridge, PL21 9LL
Tel: 01752-690997 **Fax:** 01752-690927
E-mail: gary@fireproofpaint.co.uk
Website: http://www.fireproofpaint.co.uk
Directors: G. Bryan (Prop)
Immediate Holding Company: INTERNATIONAL PASSIVE FIRE LIMITED
Registration no: 07599268 **Date established:** 2011
No.of Employees: 1 - 10 **Product Groups:** 32, 33

Date of Accounts	May 12
Working Capital	24
Fixed Assets	28
Current Assets	137

Land Machinery Ltd
Redlake Trading Estate, Ivybridge, PL21 0EZ
Tel: 01752-891336 **Fax:** 01752-891338
E-mail: info@pottingeruk.co.uk
Website: http://www.landmecpottinger.co.uk

see next page

Land Machinery Ltd - Cont'd
Bank(s): Lloyds TSB Bank plc
Directors: D. Jones (MD), R. Phillimore (Dir), S. Metcalfe (Fin)
Managers: J. Squires (Sales & Mktg Mg), K. Butcher (Tech Serv Mgr), P. Craig (Personnel)
Immediate Holding Company: LAND MACHINERY LTD
Registration no: 00447678 **VAT No.:** GB 705 3141 75
Date established: 1948 **Turnover:** £5m - £10m **No.of Employees:** 21 - 50
Product Groups: 67

Date of Accounts	Sep 11	Sep 10	Sep 09
Sales Turnover	8m	7m	8m
Pre Tax Profit/Loss	6	106	170
Working Capital	2m	2m	2m
Fixed Assets	62	56	58
Current Assets	4m	4m	4m
Current Liabilities	1m	656	773

Lapmaster International Ltd
North Road Lee Mill Industrial Estate, Ivybridge, PL21 9EN
Tel: 01752-893191 **Fax:** 01752-896355
E-mail: sales@lapmaster.co.uk
Website: http://www.lapmaster.co.uk
Managers: M. Nicholas (I.T. Exec)
Immediate Holding Company: LAPMASTER INTERNATIONAL LIMITED
Registration no: 00537328 **VAT No.:** GB 143 4567 68
Date established: 1954 **Turnover:** £5m - £10m **No.of Employees:** 21 - 50
Product Groups: 29, 33, 38, 40, 45, 46, 47, 48, 67

Date of Accounts	Dec 11	Dec 10	Dec 09
Working Capital	821	544	471
Fixed Assets	1m	3m	3m
Current Assets	2m	1m	1m

Meddings Machine Tools
Kingsley Close Lee Mill Industrial Estate, Ivybridge, PL21 9LL
Tel: 01752-313323 **Fax:** 01752-313333
E-mail: sales@meddings.co.uk
Website: http://www.meddings.co.uk
Bank(s): T.S.B.
Directors: S. Luckman (Sales)
Managers: S. Atrill, K. Adams (Grp Sales Mgr)
Immediate Holding Company: MEDDINGS THERMALEC LIMITED
Registration no: 00950992 **VAT No.:** GB 207 8137 69
Date established: 1969 **Turnover:** £500,000 - £1m
No.of Employees: 11 - 20 **Product Groups:** 40, 46, 47

Date of Accounts	Mar 11	Mar 10	Mar 09
Working Capital	404	-13	-26
Fixed Assets	109	120	146
Current Assets	1m	948	892

Permaban Ltd
Mill Close Lee Mill Industrial Estate, Ivybridge, PL21 9GL
Tel: 01752-895288 **Fax:** 01752-690535
E-mail: info@permaban.com
Website: http://www.permaban.com
Directors: J. Tarrant (Fin)
Ultimate Holding Company: FLORCON LIMITED
Immediate Holding Company: PERMABAN LIMITED
Registration no: 02815314 **Date established:** 1993 **Turnover:** £5m - £10m
No.of Employees: 21 - 50 **Product Groups:** 29, 30, 32, 33, 35, 52

Date of Accounts	Dec 11	Oct 10	Oct 09
Sales Turnover	7m	5m	7m
Pre Tax Profit/Loss	342	-132	612
Working Capital	2m	2m	2m
Fixed Assets	717	803	890
Current Assets	3m	3m	4m
Current Liabilities	362	189	325

Peter Hill Agricultural Engineer
17 Greenfield Drive, Ivybridge, PL21 0UG
Tel: 01752-690346 **Fax:** 01752-690346
Directors: P. Hill (Prop)
Date established: 1992 **No.of Employees:** 1 - 10 **Product Groups:** 41

Schuf UK Ltd
Unit 3 East Way Lee Mill Industrial Estate, Ivybridge, PL21 9GE
Tel: 020-3355 2012 **Fax:** 020-8943 3898
E-mail: sales@schuf.co.uk
Website: http://www.schuf.co.uk
Directors: S. Ogle (MD)
Registration no: 01047274 **VAT No.:** GB 222 8784 52
Date established: 1972 **Turnover:** £500,000 - £1m
No.of Employees: 1 - 10 **Product Groups:** 36, 38

Date of Accounts	Dec 07	Dec 06	Dec 05
Working Capital	21	77	33
Fixed Assets	37	16	22
Current Assets	333	404	260
Current Liabilities	312	327	228

Steve Oborne Maintenance
3 Marshall Drive, Ivybridge, PL21 0UQ
Tel: 07789-712712
E-mail: info@steveoborne.com
Website: http://www.steveoborne.com
Directors: J. Oborne (Fin), S. Oborne (Prop)
Registration no: 03327699 **Turnover:** Up to £250,000
No.of Employees: 1 - 10 **Product Groups:** 20, 40, 41

Date of Accounts	Mar 06	Mar 05
Sales Turnover	84	136
Pre Tax Profit/Loss	-8	-9
Working Capital	-5	3
Fixed Assets	1	1
Current Assets	2	12
Current Liabilities	7	9
ROCE% (Return on Capital Employed)	207.7	-203.2
ROT% (Return on Turnover)	-9.9	-6.5

The Gun Room
4 Western Road, Ivybridge, PL21 9AN
Tel: 01752-893344 **Fax:** 01752-893344
E-mail: tony.bennett@thegunroom.co.uk
Website: http://www.thegunroom.co.uk
Directors: J. Rogers (Prop)
Date established: 1986 **No.of Employees:** 1 - 10 **Product Groups:** 36, 39, 40

Thermalec Products
Kingsley Close Lee Mill Industrial Estate, Ivybridge, PL21 9LL
Tel: 01752-313343 **Fax:** 01752-313353
E-mail: info@thermalec.co.uk
Website: http://www.thermalec.co.uk
Managers: S. Luckman (Chief Mgr)
Ultimate Holding Company: W.J. MEDDINGS (HOLDINGS) LIMITED
Immediate Holding Company: THERMALEC PRODUCTS LIMITED
Registration no: 00892338 **VAT No.:** GB 197 6295 06
Date established: 1966 **Turnover:** £250,000 - £500,000
No.of Employees: 1 - 10 **Product Groups:** 29

Westcountry Training Services
1 New Mills Industrial Estate Modbury, Ivybridge, PL21 0TP
Tel: 01752-872167 **Fax:** 01752-872999
E-mail: fjfurzeland@aol.com
Website: http://www.westcountrytrainingservices.com
Directors: F. Furzeland (Prop)
No.of Employees: 1 - 10 **Product Groups:** 35, 39, 45

Westmac Ltd
Redlake Trading Estate, Ivybridge, PL21 0EZ
Tel: 01752-891299 **Fax:** 01752-891346
E-mail: info@westmac.co.uk
Website: http://www.westmac.co.uk
Bank(s): Lloyds TSB Bank plc
Directors: D. Jones (MD), J. Squires (Sales), K. Tuck (Sales), R. Phillimore (Dir), S. Medcalfe (Fin), S. Metcalfe (Fin)
Managers: K. Butcher (I.T. Exec), M. Holden (Sales Prom Mgr), L. Jeffery (Cr Control)
Immediate Holding Company: WESTMAC LIMITED
Registration no: 01064972 **VAT No.:** GB 705 3141 75
Date established: 1972 **Turnover:** £10m - £20m
No.of Employees: 21 - 50 **Product Groups:** 41

Kingsbridge

E Dawes & Sons
Unit 4h South Hams Business Park, Churchstow, Kingsbridge, TQ7 3QH
Tel: 01548-857654
Directors: G. Luscombe (Prop)
Date established: 2001 **No.of Employees:** 1 - 10 **Product Groups:** 36

Fairford Electronics Ltd
Derby Road, Kingsbridge, TQ7 1JL
Tel: 01548-857494 **Fax:** 01548-853118
E-mail: julian.tope@fairford.co.uk
Website: http://www.fairford.co.uk
Bank(s): Lloyds TSB Bank plc
Directors: J. Tope (Dir), M. Shepherd (MD)
Managers: D. Anstey (Sales Prom Mgr), M. Thong (Purch Mgr)
Immediate Holding Company: FAIRFORD ELECTRONICS LIMITED
Registration no: 01559267 **VAT No.:** GB 367 2844 24
Date established: 1981 **Turnover:** £2m - £5m **No.of Employees:** 21 - 50
Product Groups: 37, 67

Date of Accounts	Mar 10	Mar 09	Mar 08
Sales Turnover	3m	3m	2m
Pre Tax Profit/Loss	88	734	33
Working Capital	1m	906	390
Fixed Assets	56	70	31
Current Assets	1m	2m	746
Current Liabilities	44	369	32

Jades Components Ltd
Derby Road, Kingsbridge, TQ7 1JL
Tel: 01548-853377 **Fax:** 01548-856820
E-mail: jades@jadescomponents.co.uk
Website: http://www.jadescomponents.co.uk
Bank(s): National Westminster Bank Plc
Directors: S. Edmonds (Dir)
Immediate Holding Company: JADES COMPONENTS LTD
Registration no: 01639802 **VAT No.:** GB 367 2271 45
Date established: 1982 **Turnover:** £2m - £5m **No.of Employees:** 21 - 50
Product Groups: 37

Date of Accounts	May 11	May 10	May 09
Working Capital	126	95	53
Fixed Assets	209	228	243
Current Assets	930	778	686

Jewson Ltd
New Quay Embankment Road, Kingsbridge, TQ7 1JY
Tel: 01548-857424 **Fax:** 01548-854244
E-mail: simon.neal@jewson.co.uk
Website: http://www.jewson.co.uk
Managers: J. Smith (District Mgr)
Ultimate Holding Company: COMPAGNIE DE SAINT GOBAIN (FRANCE)
Immediate Holding Company: JEWSON LIMITED
Registration no: 00348407 **VAT No.:** GB 394 1212 63
Date established: 1939 **Turnover:** £2m - £5m **No.of Employees:** 1 - 10
Product Groups: 66

Date of Accounts	Dec 11	Dec 10	Dec 09
Sales Turnover	1606m	1547m	1485m
Pre Tax Profit/Loss	18m	100m	45m
Working Capital	-345m	-250m	-349m
Fixed Assets	496m	387m	461m
Current Assets	657m	1005m	1320m
Current Liabilities	66m	120m	64m

Nick Walker Printing
The Old Workhouse Higher Union Road, Kingsbridge, TQ7 1EQ
Tel: 01548-852812 **Fax:** 01548-854320
E-mail: mail@nwprint.co.uk
Website: http://www.nwprint.co.uk
Directors: N. Walker (Prop)
No.of Employees: 1 - 10 **Product Groups:** 28, 80

R T Farm & Industrial Buildings
Avon Bridge The Workshop Aveton Gifford, Kingsbridge, TQ7 4NT
Tel: 01548-550003
Website: http://www.rtfarmbuildings.co.uk
Directors: R. Triggs (Prop)
Immediate Holding Company: WEST COUNTRY STOVES LIMITED
Date established: 2012 **No.of Employees:** 11 - 20 **Product Groups:** 35

Sound & Secure
Robins Park Loddiswell, Kingsbridge, TQ7 4RT
Tel: 07967-033718
E-mail: jason@soundandsecure.freeserve.co.uk
Website: http://www.soundandsecure.freeserve.co.uk
Directors: J. Sidebottom (Prop)
Turnover: Up to £250,000 **No.of Employees:** 1 - 10 **Product Groups:** 37, 39, 67

South Hams Electrical Supplies
Springfield Clarks Barn Road, Loddiswell, Kingsbridge, TQ7 4EL
Tel: 01548-559001 **Fax:** 01548-550093
E-mail: colinjarvis@netlineuk.net
Website: http://www.netlineuk.net
Directors: C. Jarvis (Prop)
Date established: 2003 **No.of Employees:** 1 - 10 **Product Groups:** 36, 40

Lifton

V Mounce & Sons
Colmans Farm, Lifton, PL16 0HD
Tel: 01566-784696 **Fax:** 01566-784696
E-mail: mail@vmounce.f2s.com
Directors: R. Mounce (Prop)
Date established: 1989 **No.of Employees:** 1 - 10 **Product Groups:** 41

Newton Abbot

A1 Extraction
Wentsworth Road Heathfield Industrial Estate, Liverton, Newton Abbot, TQ12 6PL
Tel: 01626-832007 **Fax:** 01626-834590
Bank(s): Lloyds TSB Bank plc
Directors: J. Coleman (MD), J. Coleman (MD)
Immediate Holding Company: A1 EXTRACTION LIMITED
Registration no: 03709842 **VAT No.:** GB 510 5599 57
Date established: 1999 **Turnover:** £500,000 - £1m
No.of Employees: 11 - 20 **Product Groups:** 40

Date of Accounts	May 11	May 10	May 09
Working Capital	111	85	112
Fixed Assets	29	35	46
Current Assets	242	245	268

Abbey Plastics Southwest Ltd
Unit 3 Forde Road, Newton Abbot, TQ12 4AD
Tel: 01626-337755
Directors: S. Khairdque (Fin), P. King (MD)
Immediate Holding Company: ABBEY PLASTICS LIMITED
Registration no: 01891825 **Date established:** 1985
No.of Employees: 1 - 10 **Product Groups:** 30, 31

Date of Accounts	Sep 08	Sep 07	Sep 06
Sales Turnover	N/A	N/A	2m
Pre Tax Profit/Loss	N/A	N/A	15
Working Capital	-228	-42	-57
Fixed Assets	135	156	167
Current Assets	371	574	550
Current Liabilities	N/A	N/A	82

Astra Building Supplies
Unit A & H Minerva Building Minerva Way, Newton Abbot, TQ12 4PJ
Tel: 01626-335072 **Fax:** 01626-335172
Website: http://www.askastra.co.uk
Directors: S. Ellis (Prop)
Immediate Holding Company: ASTRA BUILDING SUPPLIES LIMITED
Registration no: 05240401 **Date established:** 2004
No.of Employees: 1 - 10 **Product Groups:** 37

B T Marine Propellers Ltd
Swift Industrial Units Canal Road, Kingsteignton, Newton Abbot, TQ12 3RZ
Tel: 01626-368484 **Fax:** 01626-368485
E-mail: info@btmarinepropellers.co.uk
Website: http://www.btmarinepropellers.co.uk
Directors: M. Hamilton (Fin)
Immediate Holding Company: BT MARINE PROPELLERS LIMITED
Registration no: 04782255 **Date established:** 2003
No.of Employees: 1 - 10 **Product Groups:** 35, 36, 39

Date of Accounts	Dec 11	Dec 10	Jun 10
Working Capital	400	191	184
Fixed Assets	100	97	105
Current Assets	642	496	481

C & O Engineering
Unit 11 The Old Cider Works Abbotskerswell, Newton Abbot, TQ12 5NF
Tel: 01626-367782 **Fax:** 01626-334410
Managers: G. Lentern (Mgr)
Immediate Holding Company: PETER BOOTH KITCHENS LIMITED
Registration no: 07226871 **Date established:** 2002
No.of Employees: 1 - 10 **Product Groups:** 35, 36, 39

C2 Composites Ltd
Nam House Bradley Lane, Newton Abbot, TQ12 1JP
Tel: 01626-356611 **Fax:** 01626-356659
E-mail: info@c2-composites.com
Website: http://www.c2-composites.com
Directors: J. Crouchen (Dir), M. Crouchen (MD)
Managers: S. Roberts (Sales Prom Mgr)
Immediate Holding Company: B/E AEROSPACE COMPOSITES LIMITED
Registration no: 02229527 **Date established:** 1988 **Turnover:** £2m - £5m
No.of Employees: 51 - 100 **Product Groups:** 23, 30, 33, 43, 44

Centristic Ltd
Cavalier Road Heathfield Industrial Estate, Newton Abbot, TQ12 6TQ
Tel: 01626-834310 **Fax:** 01626-834681
E-mail: info@centristic.co.uk
Website: http://www.centristic.co.uk
Bank(s): Barclays, Brixham
Directors: A. Grant (MD)
Ultimate Holding Company: WALDEGRAVE (RG) LIMITED
Immediate Holding Company: CENTRISTIC LIMITED
Registration no: 01549267 **VAT No.:** GB 354 9790 11
Date established: 1981 **Turnover:** £1m - £2m **No.of Employees:** 21 - 50
Product Groups: 35, 45, 67

Date of Accounts	Mar 12	Mar 11	Mar 10
Working Capital	1m	933	930
Fixed Assets	574	566	554
Current Assets	2m	2m	2m

Corroless Southern Ltd
Jetty Marsh Road, Newton Abbot, TQ12 2SL
Tel: 01626-331000 **Fax:** 01626-356582
E-mail: sales@makercoating.com
Website: http://www.makercoating.com
Directors: C. Bower (MD)
Ultimate Holding Company: Lemon Tree Garden Designs Ltd
Immediate Holding Company: CORROLESS SOUTHERN LIMITED
Registration no: 02383884 **Date established:** 1989
No.of Employees: 1 - 10 **Product Groups:** 46, 48

D Sign's
Pottery Road Bovey Tracey, Newton Abbot, TQ13 9DS
Tel: 01626-835000
E-mail: sales@dsigns.me.uk
Website: http://www.dsigns.me.uk
Directors: R. Such (Prop)
Ultimate Holding Company: THE PLASTIC SURGEON HOLDINGS LIMITED
Immediate Holding Company: THE PLASTIC SURGEON LIMITED
Date established: 1999 **No.of Employees:** 1 - 10 **Product Groups:** 37, 40, 81

Date of Accounts	Mar 11	Mar 10	Mar 09
Working Capital	23	-12	-32
Fixed Assets	8	12	20
Current Assets	135	83	99

Devlex Newton Abbot Ltd
Silverhills Road Decoy Industrial Estate, Newton Abbot, TQ12 5ND
Tel: 01626-362255 **Fax:** 01626-331108
E-mail: devlex@decoy.freeserve.co.uk
Directors: J. Veale (Dir)
Immediate Holding Company: DEVLEX (NEWTON ABBOT) LIMITED
Registration no: 01420430 **VAT No.:** 385 0643 42 **Date established:** 1979
Turnover: £1m - £2m **No.of Employees:** 1 - 10 **Product Groups:** 48

Date of Accounts	Jan 08	Jan 07	Jan 06
Working Capital	57	50	40
Fixed Assets	400	400	400
Current Assets	77	71	59

Devon Engineering Services Ltd
6 Silverhills Buildings Silverhills Road, Decoy Industrial Estate, Newton Abbot, TQ12 5LZ
Tel: 01626-333598 **Fax:** 01626-333598
E-mail: t.pollard@btinternet.com
Directors: T. Pollard (MD)
Immediate Holding Company: DEVON ENGINEERING SERVICES LIMITED
Registration no: 04844076 **Date established:** 2003
No.of Employees: 1 - 10 **Product Groups:** 20, 40, 41

Date of Accounts	Jul 11	Jul 10	Jul 09
Working Capital	-11	-17	3
Fixed Assets	15	18	10
Current Assets	91	94	72

James Halldron
Wessex House Teign Road, Newton Abbot, TQ12 4AA
Tel: 01626-204842 **Fax:** 01626-204843
Directors: J. Halldron (Prop)
Immediate Holding Company: SILVERWOOD TRADING LLP
Date established: 2007 **No.of Employees:** 1 - 10 **Product Groups:** 35

Date of Accounts	Mar 11	Mar 10	Mar 09
Working Capital	138	138	113
Fixed Assets	59	67	86
Current Assets	150	150	150

Hallons
Riverside Works Forde Road, Newton Abbot, TQ12 4AD
Tel: 01626-358700 **Fax:** 01626-358701
E-mail: sales@hallons.co.uk
Website: http://www.hallons.co.uk
Managers: C. Lee (Sales Admin)
Ultimate Holding Company: T.S.P. (SERVICES) LIMITED
Immediate Holding Company: HALLONS LTD.
Registration no: 02279652 **VAT No.:** GB 525 0070 89
Date established: 1988 **Turnover:** £1m - £2m **No.of Employees:** 1 - 10
Product Groups: 49

Date of Accounts	Mar 11	Mar 09	Mar 08
Working Capital	1	1	1
Current Assets	1	1	1

Hammer & Tongs
Unit 14 Milber Trading Estate, Newton Abbot, TQ12 4SG
Tel: 01626-367556
Directors: D. Cockran (Prop)
Date established: 1970 **No.of Employees:** 1 - 10 **Product Groups:** 26, 35

Hanbury Autogil
Bradley Lane, Newton Abbot, TQ12 1LZ
Tel: 01626-333366 **Fax:** 01626-333388
E-mail: sales@hanbury-autogil.co.uk
Website: http://www.hanbury-autogil.co.uk
Bank(s): Lloyds TSB Bank plc
Directors: R. Hanbury (MD)
Immediate Holding Company: HANBURY-AUTOGIL LIMITED
Registration no: 05267374 **Date established:** 2004 **Turnover:** £1m - £2m
No.of Employees: 11 - 20 **Product Groups:** 42, 43, 46, 47, 48, 66

Date of Accounts	Feb 12	Feb 11	Feb 10
Working Capital	93	74	28
Fixed Assets	85	35	50
Current Assets	425	265	216

House Of Marbles
The Old Pottery Pottery Street, Bovey Tracey, Newton Abbot, TQ13 9DS
Tel: 01626-835358 **Fax:** 01626-835315
E-mail: uk@houseofmarbles.com
Website: http://www.houseofmarbles.com
Bank(s): HSBC Bank plc
Directors: S. Campbell (Sales)
Managers: J. Taylor (Personnel), A. Harkin (Mktg Serv Mgr), W. McCollun (Fin Mgr), W. Mccollum (Fin Mgr)
Immediate Holding Company: HOUSE OF MARBLES LIMITED
Registration no: 01994465 **VAT No.:** GB 320 7485 71
Date established: 1986 **No.of Employees:** 51 - 100 **Product Groups:** 33

Date of Accounts	Nov 08
Working Capital	-4
Current Liabilities	4

Jewson Ltd
Forde Road, Newton Abbot, TQ12 4AD
Tel: 01626-331333 **Fax:** 01626-331024
E-mail: colin.poulter@jewson.co.uk
Website: http://www.jewson.co.uk
Bank(s): HSBC Bank plc
Managers: C. Poulter (District Mgr)
Ultimate Holding Company: COMPAGNIE DE SAINT GOBAIN (FRANCE)
Immediate Holding Company: JEWSON LIMITED
Registration no: 00348407 **Date established:** 1939
Turnover: £500m - £1,000m **No.of Employees:** 21 - 50
Product Groups: 66

Date of Accounts	Dec 11	Dec 10	Dec 09
Sales Turnover	1606m	1547m	1485m
Pre Tax Profit/Loss	18m	100m	45m
Working Capital	-345m	-250m	-349m
Fixed Assets	496m	387m	461m
Current Assets	657m	1005m	1320m
Current Liabilities	66m	120m	64m

K B Reinforcements Western Ltd
Unit 4 Roundhead Road, Heathfield Industrial Estate, Newton Abbot, TQ12 6GY
Tel: 01626-833861 **Fax:** 01626-832825
E-mail: sales@kbreinforcements.co.uk
Website: http://www.kbreinforcements.co.uk
Bank(s): Lloyds TSB
Directors: S. Lewis (MD)
Ultimate Holding Company: BOWMER AND KIRKLAND LIMITED
Immediate Holding Company: K.B. REINFORCEMENTS (WESTERN) LIMITED
Registration no: 01188903 **VAT No.:** GB 305 2764 76
Date established: 1974 **No.of Employees:** 11 - 20 **Product Groups:** 34, 35

Date of Accounts	Aug 11	Aug 10	Aug 09
Working Capital	1m	1m	1m
Fixed Assets	430	454	509
Current Assets	2m	2m	2m

Keith Darch Wrought Iron
7 Oakland Road, Newton Abbot, TQ12 4EA
Tel: 01626-361040
Directors: S. Darch (Ptnr)
Registration no: 06651422 **Date established:** 2008
Turnover: Up to £250,000 **No.of Employees:** 1 - 10 **Product Groups:** 26, 35

Kwik-Fit GB Ltd
The Avenue, Newton Abbot, TQ12 2BY
Tel: 01626-333212
Website: http://www.kwik-fit.com
Managers: S. Packham (Mgr)
Ultimate Holding Company: FINANCIERE DAUNOU 2 SA (LUXEMBOURG)
Immediate Holding Company: KWIK-FIT (GB) LIMITED
Registration no: 01009184 **Date established:** 1971
No.of Employees: 1 - 10 **Product Groups:** 29, 39, 85

Date of Accounts	Dec 10	Dec 09	Dec 08
Sales Turnover	527m	495m	449m
Pre Tax Profit/Loss	269m	56m	97m
Working Capital	197m	201m	154m
Fixed Assets	106m	115m	110m
Current Assets	375m	368m	329m
Current Liabilities	36m	36m	38m

Launa Windows
Bradley Mill Bradley Lane, Newton Abbot, TQ12 1LZ
Tel: 01626-367666 **Fax:** 01626-367668
E-mail: info@launa.co.uk
Website: http://www.launa.co.uk
Directors: H. Rushton (Prop), P. Green (Sales), A. Mahon (Mkt Research), T. Freeman (Fin), H. Rushden (MD)
Immediate Holding Company: FRUGAL GENERATION LIMITED
Registration no: 02716674 **Date established:** 1992
Turnover: £250,000 - £500,000 **No.of Employees:** 1 - 10
Product Groups: 25, 30

Lorient Polyproducts Ltd
Endeavour House Fairfax Road, Heathfield Industrial Estate, Newton Abbot, TQ12 6UD
Tel: 01626-834252 **Fax:** 01626-833166
E-mail: jwilliams@lorientuk.com
Website: http://www.lorientuk.com
Bank(s): Midland
Directors: J. Williams (Dir)
Managers: K. Hicks (Nat Sales Mgr), M. Pickford (Tech Serv Mgr), T. Kingdon, A. Binmore (Mktg Serv Mgr), K. Kyte (Personnel), R. McCormack (Purch Mgr)
Ultimate Holding Company: MJT LENTUS LIMITED
Immediate Holding Company: LORIENT HOLDINGS LIMITED
Registration no: 02993498 **VAT No.:** GB 335 4867 35
Date established: 1994 **Turnover:** £500,000 - £1m
No.of Employees: 51 - 100 **Product Groups:** 30, 33, 40

Date of Accounts	Dec 11	Dec 10	Dec 09
Sales Turnover	911	898	812
Pre Tax Profit/Loss	486	795	802
Working Capital	829	937	696
Fixed Assets	3m	3m	3m
Current Assets	1m	2m	1m
Current Liabilities	152	166	94

Metals South West Ltd
Unit 6b International House Battle Road, Heathfield Industrial Estate, Newton Abbot, TQ12 6RY
Tel: 01626-362026 **Fax:** 01626-332220
E-mail: info@metalsw.co.uk
Website: http://www.metalsW.CO.UK
Directors: P. Rowse (Dir)
Immediate Holding Company: METALS SOUTH WEST LTD
Registration no: 07745560 **Date established:** 2011
Turnover: £250,000 - £500,000 **No.of Employees:** 1 - 10
Product Groups: 66

Mill Horticultural Decco Ltd
Old Newton Road Heathfield, Newton Abbot, TQ12 6GN
Tel: 01626-832010 **Fax:** 01626-837716
E-mail: newtonabbot.051@decco.co.uk
Website: http://www.decco.co.uk
Managers: K. Willey (Mgr)
No.of Employees: 21 - 50 **Product Groups:** 36

Moreton Forge
The Forge 27 Cross Street, Moretonhampstead, Newton Abbot, TQ13 8NL
Tel: 01647-440331
E-mail: gregabel@moretonforge.co.uk
Website: http://www.moretonforge.co.uk
Directors: G. Abel (Prop)
No.of Employees: 1 - 10 **Product Groups:** 26, 35

Ornamental Metalcraft
1 Ropewalk East Street, Newton Abbot, TQ12 2LE
Tel: 01626-362928
Directors: G. Brown (Prop)
Date established: 1999 **No.of Employees:** 1 - 10 **Product Groups:** 26, 35

Pirongs Ltd
Silverhills Road Decoy Industrial Estate, Newton Abbot, TQ12 5NA
Tel: 01626-352655 **Fax:** 01626-336574
E-mail: mail@pirongs.co.uk
Website: http://www.pirongs.co.uk
Directors: R. Pirongs (Dir)
Immediate Holding Company: PIRONGS LIMITED
Registration no: 00656792 **VAT No.:** GB 141 3197 92
Date established: 1960 **Turnover:** £500,000 - £1m
No.of Employees: 1 - 10 **Product Groups:** 28

Date of Accounts	Aug 11	Aug 10	Aug 09
Working Capital	286	343	353
Fixed Assets	14	16	18
Current Assets	428	505	508

Pow Processes Of Water Ltd
Conitor House Denbury Road, Newton Abbot, TQ12 6AD
Tel: 01626-361490 **Fax:** 01626-333359
E-mail: sales@powplastics.co.uk
Website: http://www.powplastics.co.uk
Directors: D. Crossman (MD), R. Crossman (Fin)
Immediate Holding Company: POW PROCESSES OF WATER LIMITED
Registration no: 06950480 **VAT No.:** GB 321 0226 27
Date established: 2009 **Turnover:** £1m - £2m **No.of Employees:** 1 - 10
Product Groups: 30, 54

Quality Marking Services Ltd
6 Cannon Road Heathfield Industrial Estate, Newton Abbot, TQ12 6SG
Tel: 01626-836777 **Fax:** 01626-836774
E-mail: info@qmarkings.co.uk
Website: http://www.qmarkings.co.uk
Managers: M. Llewellyn, P. Lequeux (Fin Mgr)
Immediate Holding Company: QUALITY MARKING SERVICES LIMITED
Registration no: 04238367 **Date established:** 2001
No.of Employees: 11 - 20 **Product Groups:** 51

Date of Accounts	Dec 11	Dec 10	Dec 09
Working Capital	123	67	136
Fixed Assets	217	215	215
Current Assets	699	436	395

H Rorke
Teign Crest Mount Pleasant Road, Newton Abbot, TQ12 1AS
Tel: 01626-202981
Directors: H. Rorke (Prop)
No.of Employees: 1 - 10 **Product Groups:** 43

Sapphire Windows
Bradley House Two Mile Oak, Newton Abbot, TQ12 6DF
Tel: 01803-814299
E-mail: info@sapphirewindows.fsnet.co.uk
Website: http://www.sapphirewindowsystems.com
Directors: A. Barnes (Dir)
Registration no: 03861002 **Date established:** 1999
No.of Employees: 1 - 10 **Product Groups:** 46

Skaigh Engineering Company Ltd
Old Gas Works Oldway, Chudleigh, Newton Abbot, TQ13 0JA
Tel: 01626-852159 **Fax:** 01626-853495
E-mail: sales@skaigh.co.uk
Website: http://www.skaigh.co.uk
Bank(s): Lloyds
Directors: S. Ripley (Dir)
Immediate Holding Company: SKAIGH ENGINEERING CO.LIMITED
Registration no: 00869410 **VAT No.:** GB 141 5707 85
Date established: 1966 **Turnover:** £2m - £5m **No.of Employees:** 21 - 50
Product Groups: 34

Date of Accounts	Apr 12	Apr 11	Apr 10
Working Capital	611	557	463
Fixed Assets	626	583	630
Current Assets	826	841	628

Tata Steel Metal Centre
Fairfax Road Heathfield Industrial Estate, Newton Abbot, TQ12 6UD
Tel: 01626-835008 **Fax:** 01626-835009
E-mail: shaun.harraway@corusgroup.com
Website: http://www.tatasteelautomotive.com/en/
Managers: S. Harraway (Comm)
Immediate Holding Company: CANNON COMMERCIALS LIMITED
Registration no: 04808608 **Date established:** 2003
No.of Employees: 1 - 10 **Product Groups:** 66

Date of Accounts	Feb 12	Feb 11	Feb 10
Working Capital	135	242	198
Fixed Assets	640	528	581
Current Assets	447	427	372

Teignbridge Propellers International
Great Western Way Forde Road, Newton Abbot, TQ12 4AW
Tel: 01626-333377 **Fax:** 01626-360783
E-mail: sales@teignbridge.co.uk
Website: http://www.teignbridge.co.uk
Bank(s): Bank of Scotland
Directors: D. Duncan (MD)
Managers: C. Hutton
Ultimate Holding Company: DUNCAN PROPELLERS HOLDINGS LIMITED
Immediate Holding Company: DUNCAN PROPELLERS LIMITED
Registration no: 05284615 **VAT No.:** GB 699 0815 81
Date established: 2004 **Turnover:** £2m - £5m **No.of Employees:** 51 - 100
Product Groups: 39

Date of Accounts	Dec 11	Dec 10	Dec 09
Sales Turnover	N/A	N/A	3m
Pre Tax Profit/Loss	N/A	N/A	455

see next page

Teignbridge Propellers International - Cont'd

Working Capital	828	596	-1m
Fixed Assets	1m	1m	1m
Current Assets	1m	901	836
Current Liabilities	N/A	N/A	908

The Educational Warehouse

66 Queen Street, Newton Abbot, TQ12 2ER
Tel: 01626-331166 **Fax:** 08451-700333
E-mail: info@furniturewise.net
Website: http://www.furniturewise.net
Managers: J. Malton (Mgr)
Immediate Holding Company: SRP MEDIA LIMITED
Date established: 2010 **No.of Employees:** 1 - 10 **Product Groups:** 26, 28, 30, 52, 67

Date of Accounts	Jan 08	Feb 07
Working Capital	-14	-22
Current Assets	53	69
Current Liabilities	66	91

Toolfix Ltd

Unit 8 Riverside 2 Quay Road, Newton Abbot, TQ12 4DZ
Tel: 01626-362129 **Fax:** 01626-333744
Managers: S. Crook (Mgr)
Immediate Holding Company: TOOLFIX LIMITED
Registration no: 03896962 **Date established:** 1999
No.of Employees: 1 - 10 **Product Groups:** 37

Date of Accounts	Dec 11	Dec 10	Dec 09
Working Capital	32	54	38
Fixed Assets	4	7	10
Current Assets	59	78	54

W R Refrigeration Ltd

5 Zealley Estate Greenhill Way, Kingsteignton, Newton Abbot, TQ12 3TD
Tel: 01626-336565 **Fax:** 01626-336868
E-mail: torbaybranch@wrref.com
Website: http://www.wrref.com
Managers: M. Peck (District Mgr)
Ultimate Holding Company: HUURRE GROUP OY (FINLAND)
Immediate Holding Company: WR REFRIGERATION LIMITED
Registration no: 00594746 **VAT No.:** GB 485 4284 16
Date established: 1957 **No.of Employees:** 1 - 10 **Product Groups:** 52

Date of Accounts	Dec 11	Dec 10	Dec 09
Sales Turnover	45m	44m	57m
Pre Tax Profit/Loss	412	-2m	1m
Working Capital	29m	21m	23m
Fixed Assets	3m	4m	3m
Current Assets	52m	45m	36m
Current Liabilities	4m	2m	2m

Watermota Ltd

Cavalier Road Heathfield Industrial Estate, Newton Abbot, TQ12 6TQ
Tel: 01626-830910 **Fax:** 01626-830911
E-mail: info@watermota.co.uk
Website: http://www.watermota.co.uk
Bank(s): Barclays
Directors: M. Beacham (MD)
Immediate Holding Company: WATERMOTA LIMITED
Registration no: 00627154 **VAT No.:** GB 384 9747 88
Date established: 1959 **Turnover:** £1m - £2m **No.of Employees:** 11 - 20
Product Groups: 37, 84

Date of Accounts	Dec 11	Jul 10	Jul 09
Working Capital	276	189	148
Fixed Assets	113	86	85
Current Assets	2m	910	911

Wessex Products

Wessex House Teign Road, Newton Abbot, TQ12 4AA
Tel: 01626-204800 **Fax:** 01626-204801
E-mail: sales@wessexproducts.co.uk
Website: http://www.wessexproducts.co.uk
Directors: M. Hentsehel (Dir)
Immediate Holding Company: SILVERWOOD TRADING LLP
Registration no: 03230409 **Date established:** 2007
No.of Employees: 11 - 20 **Product Groups:** 20, 40, 41

Date of Accounts	Mar 11	Mar 10	Mar 09
Working Capital	138	138	113
Fixed Assets	59	67	86
Current Assets	150	150	150

West Country Cases

7 Cavalier Road Heathfield Industrial Estate, Newton Abbot, TQ12 6TQ
Tel: 01626-201068 **Fax:** 01626-201069
E-mail: sales@westcountrycases.co.uk
Website: http://www.westcountrycases.co.uk
Directors: A. Heckford (MD)
Ultimate Holding Company: WALDEGRAVE (RG) LIMITED
Immediate Holding Company: WESTCOUNTRY CASES LTD
Registration no: 04663056 **Date established:** 2003
Turnover: £500,000 - £1m **No.of Employees:** 11 - 20
Product Groups: 25, 76

Date of Accounts	Sep 11	Sep 10	Sep 09
Working Capital	-23	24	73
Fixed Assets	110	97	110
Current Assets	155	117	187

Westomatic Vending Services Ltd

Units 7-8 Forde Court Forde Road, Newton Abbot, TQ12 4BT
Tel: 01626-323100 **Fax:** 01626-332828
E-mail: sales@westomatic.com
Website: http://www.westomatic.com
Directors: A. Brinsley (Fin), R. Brinsley (MD)
Managers: B. Craig, B. Bonehill (Comptroller)
Ultimate Holding Company: BRINTOR GROUP LIMITED
Immediate Holding Company: WESTOMATIC VENDING SERVICES LIMITED
Registration no: 00873813 **Date established:** 1966 **Turnover:** £2m - £5m
No.of Employees: 21 - 50 **Product Groups:** 49

Date of Accounts	Sep 11	Oct 08	Oct 09
Sales Turnover	N/A	6m	4m
Pre Tax Profit/Loss	N/A	-882	-937
Working Capital	558	927	664
Fixed Assets	3m	4m	3m
Current Assets	1m	3m	2m
Current Liabilities	N/A	613	735

Williams & Triggs

The Avenue Stone Works The Avenue, Newton Abbot, TQ12 2DD
Tel: 01626-201157 **Fax:** 01626-201156
E-mail: enquiries@williamsandtriggs.co.uk
Website: http://www.williamsandtriggs.co.uk
Directors: R. Williams (Snr Part)
Date established: 1850 **Turnover:** £250,000 - £500,000
No.of Employees: 1 - 10 **Product Groups:** 33

North Tawton

Agrispares Devon

Unit 10 & 10a Moorview Industrial Estate, North Tawton, EX20 2HW
Tel: 01837-810230 **Fax:** 01837-810242
E-mail: tcook@agrispares.eclipse.co.uk
Directors: T. Cook (Prop)
Registration no: 03784999 **Turnover:** £1m - £2m
No.of Employees: 1 - 10 **Product Groups:** 30, 35, 37, 40, 41, 42

C H Jones & Son

1 The Square, North Tawton, EX20 2EW
Tel: 01837-82237 **Fax:** 01837-82526
E-mail: admin@chjonesandson.co.uk
Website: http://www.chjonesandson.co.uk
Directors: T. Bramston (Ptnr)
VAT No.: GB 140 9248 77 **Date established:** 1920
Turnover: Up to £250,000 **No.of Employees:** 1 - 10 **Product Groups:** 07

Okehampton

Ashridge Engineering Ltd

Unit 1a 58 North Road Industrial Estate, Okehampton, EX20 1BQ
Tel: 01837-53381 **Fax:** 01837-55022
E-mail: sales@ash-eng.co.uk
Website: http://www.ash-eng.co.uk
Directors: A. Orchard (Dir)
Immediate Holding Company: ASHRIDGE ENGINEERING LIMITED
Registration no: 01468514 **Date established:** 1979
Turnover: £500,000 - £1m **No.of Employees:** 1 - 10 **Product Groups:** 38, 67

Date of Accounts	Dec 11	Dec 10	Dec 09
Working Capital	337	194	220
Fixed Assets	161	134	160
Current Assets	449	365	354

Brookite Ltd

Brightley Mill, Okehampton, EX20 1RR
Tel: 01837-53315 **Fax:** 01837-53223
E-mail: amanda.harrison@brookite.com
Website: http://www.brookite.com
Directors: A. Harrison (MD)
Immediate Holding Company: BROOKITE LIMITED
Registration no: 00395108 **VAT No.:** GB 229 1076 72
Date established: 1945 **Turnover:** £500,000 - £1m
No.of Employees: 1 - 10 **Product Groups:** 49

Date of Accounts	Sep 11	Sep 10	Sep 09
Working Capital	384	356	365
Fixed Assets	119	122	118
Current Assets	634	439	436

M Crocker

Coryton, Okehampton, EX20 4PQ
Tel: 01822-820588 **Fax:** 01822-820588
Directors: M. Crocker (Prop)
Date established: 1996 **No.of Employees:** 1 - 10 **Product Groups:** 35

Elemental Microanalysis Ltd

Hameldown Road Exeter Road Industrial Estate, Okehampton, EX20 1UB
Tel: 01837-54446 **Fax:** 01837-54454
E-mail: info@microanalysis.co.uk
Website: http://www.microanalysis.co.uk
Bank(s): National Westminster
Directors: G. Wardall (Sales & Mktg), I. Smith (MD)
Ultimate Holding Company: MICRO ANALYSIS TECHNOLOGY LTD
Immediate Holding Company: ELEMENTAL MICRO-ANALYSIS LIMITED
Registration no: 01281028 **VAT No.:** GB 217 5194 65
Date established: 1976 **Turnover:** £1m - £2m **No.of Employees:** 21 - 50
Product Groups: 31, 84

Date of Accounts	Jun 11	Jun 10	Jun 09
Working Capital	763	684	511
Fixed Assets	177	143	117
Current Assets	1m	941	681

Jewson Ltd

Unit 22 North Road Industrial Estate, Okehampton, EX20 1BQ
Tel: 01837-52356 **Fax:** 01837-54038
E-mail: george.jays@graham.co.uk
Website: http://www.jewson.co.uk
Managers: G. Friend, G. Jays (District Mgr), M. Waldridge (Sales Prom Mgr)
Ultimate Holding Company: COMPAGNIE DE SAINT GOBAIN (FRANCE)
Immediate Holding Company: JEWSON LIMITED
Registration no: 00348407 **VAT No.:** GB 394 1212 63
Date established: 1939 **No.of Employees:** 1 - 10 **Product Groups:** 66

Date of Accounts	Dec 11	Dec 10	Dec 09
Sales Turnover	1606m	1547m	1485m
Pre Tax Profit/Loss	18m	100m	45m
Working Capital	-345m	-250m	-349m
Fixed Assets	496m	387m	461m
Current Assets	657m	1005m	1320m
Current Liabilities	66m	120m	64m

Lighting Infocus

The Old Rectory Jacobstowe, Okehampton, EX20 3RQ
Tel: 01837-851436
E-mail: info@lighting-infocus.co.uk
Website: http://www.lighting-infocus.co.uk
Product Groups: 37, 67

Quantum Production

Units 1-3 Hatherleigh Industrial Estate Hatherleigh, Okehampton, EX20 3LP
Tel: 01844-339993 **Fax:** 01844-339996
E-mail: info@quantumproduction.co.uk
Website: http://www.quantumproduction.co.uk
Directors: D. Thorntonwood (Dir)
Registration no: 01538194 **VAT No.:** GB 348 4028 52
No.of Employees: 11 - 20 **Product Groups:** 38, 39

Date of Accounts	Mar 08	Mar 07	Mar 06
Working Capital	238	175	101
Fixed Assets	47	31	32
Current Assets	364	394	338
Current Liabilities	126	219	237

Ottery St Mary

E M & F Group Ltd

3 Cornhill, Ottery St Mary, EX11 1DW
Tel: 01404-813762 **Fax:** 01404-815236
E-mail: devdor@emfgroup.com
Website: http://www.emfgroup.com
Directors: K. Carr (Dir)
Immediate Holding Company: EM & F GROUP LIMITED
Registration no: 03035561 **Date established:** 1995
No.of Employees: 1 - 10 **Product Groups:** 80

Date of Accounts	Mar 11	Mar 10	Mar 09
Working Capital	226	214	189
Fixed Assets	6	8	10
Current Assets	251	237	214

Western Saw & Tool Service

Knightstone House Knightstone, Ottery St Mary, EX11 1PP
Tel: 01404-814414
Directors: S. Tallack (Prop)
Registration no: 04960553 **Date established:** 2003
No.of Employees: 1 - 10 **Product Groups:** 36

Paignton

Claron Plastics Ltd

Alders Way Yalberton Industrial Estate, Paignton, TQ4 7QL
Tel: 01803-528677 **Fax:** 01803-525134
E-mail: sales@claron.co.uk
Website: http://www.claron.co.uk
Directors: D. Stanley (Fin)
Immediate Holding Company: CLARON (PLASTICS) LIMITED
Registration no: 01792799 **Date established:** 1984 **Turnover:** £1m - £2m
No.of Employees: 1 - 10 **Product Groups:** 30, 31, 66

Date of Accounts	Mar 11	Mar 10	Mar 09
Working Capital	851	812	824
Fixed Assets	11	13	16
Current Assets	1m	992	1m

Crown Sports Lockers UK Ltd

Units 2 & 3 Torbay Business Park Woodview Road, Paignton, TQ4 7HP
Tel: 01803-555885 **Fax:** 01803-556767
E-mail: mailbox@crownlockers.co.uk
Website: http://www.crownlockers.co.uk
Managers: S. Parmer (Mgr)
Immediate Holding Company: CROWN SPORTS LOCKERS (UK) LIMITED
Registration no: 02521770 **Date established:** 1990
No.of Employees: 11 - 20 **Product Groups:** 26, 49, 66

Date of Accounts	Mar 12	Mar 11	Mar 10
Working Capital	-168	-110	-213
Fixed Assets	207	179	217
Current Assets	267	460	196

Devon Microwave Specialists

The Vault 353 Torquay Road, Paignton, TQ3 2BT
Tel: 01803-551363 **Fax:** 01803-520349
E-mail: sales@microwaveshop.co.uk
Website: http://www.microwaveshop.co.uk
Directors: N. Crowe (Prop)
Date established: 1976 **No.of Employees:** 1 - 10 **Product Groups:** 36, 40

Doran Packaging Co.

Unit 2 Moorview Industrial Park Kemmings Close, Paignton, TQ4 7TW
Tel: 01803-522513 **Fax:** 01803-521616
E-mail: sales@packagingplus.co.uk
Website: http://www.doranpackaging.co.uk
Directors: M. Smith (MD)
Immediate Holding Company: FOUR CROSS GARAGE LIMITED
Registration no: 03865008 **Date established:** 2010
No.of Employees: 1 - 10 **Product Groups:** 38, 42

Date of Accounts	Mar 11
Sales Turnover	319
Pre Tax Profit/Loss	138
Working Capital	148
Fixed Assets	464
Current Assets	148

E Shop Supplies Ltd

222 Torquay Road, Paignton, TQ3 2HN
Tel: 01803-520088 **Fax:** 01803-520088
E-mail: sales@eshopsupplies.co.uk
Website: http://www.eshopsupplies.co.uk
Directors: B. Amer (MD)
No.of Employees: 1 - 10 **Product Groups:** 30, 64, 66

G S Catering

Aspen Way, Paignton, TQ4 7QR
Tel: 01803-528586 **Fax:** 01803-554338
E-mail: gmassey@gsgroup.co.uk
Website: http://www.gsgroup.co.uk
Directors: G. Massey (Co Sec)
Immediate Holding Company: G.S. CATERING EQUIPMENT LIMITED
Registration no: 01702374 **Date established:** 1983
No.of Employees: 11 - 20 **Product Groups:** 20, 40, 41

Date of Accounts	Mar 11	Mar 10	Mar 09
Working Capital	402	389	352
Fixed Assets	32	42	69

Current Assets	1m	1m	2m

Horsehage Manufacturers Mark Westaway & Son

Love Lane Farm Marldon, Paignton, TQ3 1SP
Tel: 01803-527257 **Fax:** 01803-528010
E-mail: sales@horsehage.co.uk
Website: http://www.horsehage.co.uk
Directors: M. Westaway (Prop)
Immediate Holding Company: HORSEHAGE LIMITED
Registration no: 02666259 **VAT No.:** 354 8667 15 **Date established:** 1991
Turnover: Up to £250,000 **No.of Employees:** 1 - 10 **Product Groups:** 14, 20

Jewson Ltd

Aspen Way, Paignton, TQ4 7QU
Tel: 01803-559293 **Fax:** 01803-555044
Website: http://www.jewson.co.uk
Managers: N. Massey (District Mgr)
Ultimate Holding Company: Saint-Gobain Ltd
Immediate Holding Company: JEWSON LIMITED
Registration no: 00348407 **Date established:** 1939
Turnover: £500m - £1,000m **No.of Employees:** 1 - 10
Product Groups: 66

Julie's Payroll Service

5 Gibson Road, Paignton, TQ4 7AG
Tel: 01803-844860 **Fax:** 01803-844860
E-mail: juliespayrollservices@yahoo.co.uk
Website: http://www.juliespayrollservices.co.uk
Directors: J. Tancock (Prop)
Turnover: Up to £250,000 **No.of Employees:** 1 - 10 **Product Groups:** 80

Mexboro Concrete Ltd

Yalberton Tor Industrial Estate Alders Way, Paignton, TQ4 7QQ
Tel: 01803-558025 **Fax:** 01803-524717
E-mail: sales@mexboroconcrete.com
Website: http://www.mexboroconcrete.co.uk
Bank(s): Barclays
Directors: M. Vallance (MD)
Ultimate Holding Company: W.L.VALLANCE (HOLDINGS) LIMITED
Immediate Holding Company: MEXBORO CONCRETE LIMITED
Registration no: 00652279 **VAT No.:** GB 441 2759 57
Date established: 1960 **No.of Employees:** 21 - 50 **Product Groups:** 33

Date of Accounts	Sep 11	Sep 10	Sep 09
Working Capital	252	234	247
Fixed Assets	110	121	167
Current Assets	677	663	564

New & Used Catering Equipment

28a The Mews Elmbank Road, Paignton, TQ4 5NG
Tel: 01803-525389 **Fax:** 01803- 525389
Directors: J. Thompson (Dir)
Date established: 1996 **No.of Employees:** 1 - 10 **Product Groups:** 20, 40, 41

Oak Tree Forge

Oak Tree Yard Upper Manor Road, Paignton, TQ3 2TP
Tel: 01803-550436 **Fax:** 01803-529277
Directors: C. Tilbrook (Prop), K. Hadfield (Prop)
Date established: 1977 **No.of Employees:** 1 - 10 **Product Groups:** 26, 35

Robinson Arc Rescue Services

Landfall Brixham Road, Paignton, TQ4 7BQ
Tel: 01803-843512
Directors: P. Robinson (Prop)
Date established: 1971 **No.of Employees:** 1 - 10 **Product Groups:** 35

Torbay Steel Fabrications

Unit 2b Miglo Industrial Estate Yalberton Road, Paignton, TQ4 7QW
Tel: 01803-555355 **Fax:** 01803-555455
E-mail: torsteel@blueyonder.co.uk
Website: http://www.torbaysteelfabrications.co.uk
Directors: D. Langler (Prop)
Date established: 2002 **No.of Employees:** 1 - 10 **Product Groups:** 35

Weldquip Welding Equipment

8 Battersway Road, Paignton, TQ4 7EX
Tel: 01803-553738 **Fax:** 01803-553738
E-mail: david.adcock3@btinternet.com
Website: http://www.weldquip.co.uk
Directors: D. Adcock (Ptnr)
Date established: 1996 **No.of Employees:** 1 - 10 **Product Groups:** 46

Plymouth

ADT Fire & Security plc

Security House Estover Industrial Estate Estover Close, Plymouth, PL6 7PL
Tel: 0800-542 3108 **Fax:** 01752-738985
E-mail: mharvey@adt.co.uk
Website: http://www.adt.co.uk
Directors: A. McNutt (MD), A. Alphonsus (Co Sec)
Ultimate Holding Company: TYCO INTERNATIONAL LIMITED (SWITZERLAND)
Immediate Holding Company: ADT FIRE AND SECURITY PLC
Registration no: 01161045 **Date established:** 1974
No.of Employees: 1501 & over **Product Groups:** 37, 38, 39, 40, 47, 52, 81

Date of Accounts	Sep 11	Sep 08	Sep 09
Sales Turnover	363m	414m	384m
Pre Tax Profit/Loss	18m	4m	10m
Working Capital	450m	618m	561m
Fixed Assets	120m	193m	171m
Current Assets	710m	765m	722m
Current Liabilities	81m	57m	42m

A G S Electronics

16 May Terrace, Plymouth, PL4 8PP
Tel: 01752-224947 **Fax:** 01752- 254447
E-mail: sales@agselectronics.fsnet.co.uk
Website: http://www.ags-electronics.fsnet.co.uk
Directors: A. Spry (Prop)
Date established: 1979 **No.of Employees:** 1 - 10 **Product Groups:** 67

Aalco

Unit B Armada Point Estover Road, Plymouth, PL6 7PY
Tel: 01752-770877 **Fax:** 01752-770844
E-mail: plymouth@aalco.co.uk
Website: http://www.aalco.co.uk
Managers: W. Kelly
Registration no: 02794687 **Turnover:** £1m - £2m
No.of Employees: 11 - 20 **Product Groups:** 34, 35, 36, 66

Abbey Lifts Ltd

194 Saltash Road Keyham, Plymouth, PL2 2BD
Tel: 01752-559855 **Fax:** 01752-559850
E-mail: admin@abbeylifts.co.uk
Website: http://www.abbeylifts.co.uk
Directors: C. Morgan (MD)
Immediate Holding Company: ABBEY LIFTS LIMITED
Registration no: 01667840 **Date established:** 1982
No.of Employees: 11 - 20 **Product Groups:** 35, 39, 45

Date of Accounts	Feb 12	Feb 11	Feb 10
Working Capital	-4	-6	136
Fixed Assets	16	14	20
Current Assets	112	117	253

Algram Groups

Eastern Wood Road Langage Business Park, Plympton, Plymouth, PL7 5ET
Tel: 01752-342388 **Fax:** 01752-342482
E-mail: stephen.brown@algram.com
Website: http://www.algram.com
Bank(s): Barclays
Directors: S. Brown (MD), S. Emson (Sales), C. Harris (Chief Op Offcr), J. Rowe (Co Sec)
Managers: M. Hallwell (Tech Serv Mgr), R. Bishop (Purch Mgr), G. Mayhew (Sales Prom Mgr)
Ultimate Holding Company: OLYMPUS CORPORATION (JAPAN)
Immediate Holding Company: ALGRAM GROUP LIMITED
Registration no: 02189247 **Date established:** 1987 **Turnover:** £5m - £10m
No.of Employees: 101 - 250 **Product Groups:** 30, 48, 66

Date of Accounts	Mar 11	Mar 10	Mar 09
Sales Turnover	7m	7m	7m
Pre Tax Profit/Loss	-58	10	104
Working Capital	1m	1m	1m
Fixed Assets	2m	2m	2m
Current Assets	2m	2m	2m
Current Liabilities	385	465	409

Autotech Robotics Ltd

20 Darklake View Estover, Plymouth, PL6 7TL
Tel: 01752-202600 **Fax:** 01752-202601
E-mail: sales@autotech-robotics.com
Website: http://www.autotech-robotics.com
Directors: K. Gilbert (Co Sec), G. Gilbert (MD)
Ultimate Holding Company: GILL & GILBERT LIMITED
Immediate Holding Company: AUTOTECH ROBOTICS LIMITED
Registration no: 02387261 **Date established:** 1989
No.of Employees: 11 - 20 **Product Groups:** 45, 48, 84

Date of Accounts	Oct 11	Oct 10	Oct 09
Working Capital	-60	-65	23
Fixed Assets	246	227	233
Current Assets	178	87	144

Bakare Beds Ltd

Unit 1a Engineering Resource Centre Bell Close Plympton, Plymouth, PL7 4JH
Tel: 01752-512222 **Fax:** 01752-511117
E-mail: dgibbons@bakare.co.uk
Website: http://www.bakare.co.uk
Directors: D. Gibbons (MD)
Immediate Holding Company: BAKARE BEDS LIMITED
Registration no: 02813000 **Date established:** 1993
No.of Employees: 21 - 50 **Product Groups:** 26

Date of Accounts	Mar 11	Mar 10	Mar 09
Working Capital	280	237	209
Fixed Assets	14	11	26
Current Assets	818	696	701

Barden Corporation (UK) Limited

Plymbridge Rd Estover, Plymouth, PL6 7LH
Tel: 01752-735555 **Fax:** 01752-733481
E-mail: bardenbearings@schaeffler.com
Website: http://www.bardenbearings.co.uk
Bank(s): National Westminster Bank Plc
Directors: I. Burnage (MD), R. Globe (Sales & Mktg)
Managers: D. Woodward (Buyer), C. Evans (Mktg Serv Mgr)
Immediate Holding Company: Schaeffler AG
Registration no: 00450577 **Date established:** 1948
Turnover: £20m - £50m **No.of Employees:** 251 - 500
Product Groups: 33, 34, 35, 39, 48

Date of Accounts	Dec 11	Dec 10	Dec 09
Sales Turnover	47m	35m	26m
Pre Tax Profit/Loss	12m	6m	2m
Working Capital	18m	9m	5m
Fixed Assets	11m	11m	12m
Current Assets	24m	15m	11m
Current Liabilities	6m	4m	273

Bathroom Lifestyle

16 Spinnaker Quay, Plymouth, PL9 9SA
Tel: 08450-745778 **Fax:** 0870-758 5877
E-mail: sales@bathroomlifestyle.com
Website: http://www.bathroomlifestyle.com
Directors: K. Heppell (MD)
Registration no: 05514838 **Date established:** 2005
Turnover: £250,000 - £500,000 **No.of Employees:** 1 - 10
Product Groups: 26, 30, 63, 66

Date of Accounts	Sep 07	Sep 06
Working Capital	-16	-3
Fixed Assets	15	4
Current Assets	83	38
Current Liabilities	99	41

Bel Cher Mobile Locksmiths & Safe Engineers Bel-Cher Locksmiths & Safe Engineers

26 Valletort Road Stoke Damerel, Plymouth, PL1 5PH
Tel: 01752-567222 **Fax:** 01752-550888
E-mail: c-belcher@btconnect.com
Website: http://www.chrisbelcher.com
Directors: C. Bel Cher (Ptnr)
No.of Employees: 1 - 10 **Product Groups:** 36, 38, 52

Birch Valley Plastics Ltd

Darklake View Estover, Plymouth, PL6 7TL
Tel: 01752-696515 **Fax:** 01752-696724
E-mail: info@birchvalley.co.uk
Website: http://www.birchvalley.co.uk
Bank(s): HSBC
Directors: R. Jennings (Dir)
Immediate Holding Company: BIRCH VALLEY PLASTICS LIMITED
Registration no: 02316354 **VAT No.:** GB 557 7944 98
Date established: 1988 **Turnover:** £1m - £2m **No.of Employees:** 21 - 50
Product Groups: 30

Date of Accounts	Jun 11	Jun 10	Jun 09
Working Capital	389	341	324
Fixed Assets	512	527	559
Current Assets	575	499	461

Boatcoat

Unit 3 Garden Close Langage Business Park, Plympton, Plymouth, PL7 5EU
Tel: 01752-227333 **Fax:** 01752-227333
E-mail: sales@boatcoat.co.uk
Website: http://www.boatcoat.com
Directors: E. Lake (Fin), A. Kingsbury (Dir), E. Lake (Dir)
Managers: B. Kirkham, B. Kirkham (Mgr)
Immediate Holding Company: BOATCOAT LIMITED
Registration no: 05710534 **Date established:** 2006 **Turnover:** £1m - £2m
No.of Employees: 1 - 10 **Product Groups:** 48

Brandon Loadtite

Sutton Road, Plymouth, PL4 0HN
Tel: 01752-665335 **Fax:** 01752-254726
Website: http://www.brandonhire.co.uk
Managers: M. Holland (Mgr)
Date established: 2002 **No.of Employees:** 1 - 10 **Product Groups:** 35, 39, 45

British Filters Ltd

11-12 Porsham Close Roborough, Plymouth, PL6 7DB
Tel: 01752-703900 **Fax:** 01752-703901
E-mail: sales@britishfilters.co.uk
Website: http://www.britishfilters.co.uk
Bank(s): National Westminster Bank Plc
Directors: P. Denyer (MD)
Immediate Holding Company: BRITISH FILTERS LIMITED
Registration no: 03839960 **VAT No.:** GB 272 8016 62
Date established: 1999 **Turnover:** £500,000 - £1m
No.of Employees: 11 - 20 **Product Groups:** 42

Date of Accounts	Feb 12	Feb 11	Feb 10
Working Capital	450	366	328
Fixed Assets	78	73	75
Current Assets	542	441	366

Brittany Ferries

Millbay Docks, Plymouth, PL1 3EW
Tel: 08712-441400 **Fax:** 0870-902 0300
E-mail: enquiries@brittanyferries.com
Website: http://www.brittanyferries.com
Bank(s): National Westminster Bank Plc
Directors: D. Longdon (Mkt Research), J. Mapton (Fin)
Managers: M. Hammett (Chief Mgr), R. Price (Sales Prom Mgr), M. Bevens
Ultimate Holding Company: BAI SA
Immediate Holding Company: BAI SA FRANCE
Registration no: 01080495 **VAT No.:** GB 143 6026 92
Turnover: £10m - £20m **No.of Employees:** 51 - 100 **Product Groups:** 74

Business Link For Devon Cornwall & Somerset

5 Research Way, Plymouth, PL6 8BT
Tel: 08456-009966 **Fax:** 01752-770925
Website: http://www.bldc.co.uk
Managers: A. Chambers
Immediate Holding Company: COAST BUSINESS SOLUTIONS LTD
Registration no: 06860980 **Date established:** 2003 **Turnover:** £5m - £10m
No.of Employees: 51 - 100 **Product Groups:** 80, 81

Carval Computing Ltd

Innovation & Technology Transfer Centre Tamar Science Park, Plymouth, PL6 8BX
Tel: 01752-764290 **Fax:** 01752-764291
E-mail: c.sweby@carval.co.uk
Website: http://www.carval.co.uk
Directors: C. Sweby (Dir)
Immediate Holding Company: CARVAL COMPUTING LIMITED
Registration no: 02038457 **VAT No.:** GB 447 4298 21
Date established: 1986 **Turnover:** £500,000 - £1m
No.of Employees: 11 - 20 **Product Groups:** 44

Date of Accounts	Sep 11	Sep 10	Sep 09
Working Capital	224	108	81
Fixed Assets	22	8	8
Current Assets	486	378	200

Coinage Limited

91 Mayflower Street, Plymouth, PL1 1SB
Tel: 0870-1600992 **Fax:** 0845-0532884
E-mail: sales@coinage.co.uk
Website: http://www.coinage.co.uk
Bank(s): National Westminster Bank Plc
Directors: C. Hailes (MD)
Registration no: 00757004 **VAT No.:** GB 130 0072 43
Turnover: £500,000 - £1m **No.of Employees:** 11 - 20 **Product Groups:** 49

Continental Engravers Precision Ltd

Unit 3 Huxley Close Plympton, Plymouth, PL7 4JN
Tel: 01752-344474 **Fax:** 01752-342938
E-mail: cepsigns@btopenworld.com
Website: http://www.continentalengravers.co.uk
Directors: R. Thomson (MD)
Ultimate Holding Company: THOMSON INDEPENDENT TRADERS LIMITED
Immediate Holding Company: CONTINENTAL ENGRAVERS (PRECISION) LIMITED
Registration no: 00819854 **VAT No.:** GB 143 7780 53
Date established: 1964 **Turnover:** £500,000 - £1m
No.of Employees: 1 - 10 **Product Groups:** 28

see next page

***Continental Engravers Precision Ltd** - Cont'd*

Date of Accounts	Aug 11	Aug 10	Aug 09
Working Capital	-1	157	205
Fixed Assets	14	25	36
Current Assets	119	255	270

D S G Canusa GmbH & Co.

Sales Bergstrand House Parkwood Close, Plymouth, PL6 7SG
Tel: 01752-209880 **Fax:** 01752-209850
E-mail: info-uk@dsgcanusa.com
Website: http://www.dsgcanusa.shawcor.com
Bank(s): HSBC Bank plc
Directors: H. McColl (Co Sec)
Managers: T. Schminke (Mgr), C. Willgress (Site Co-ord)
Ultimate Holding Company: SHAWCOR LTD (CANADA)
Immediate Holding Company: DSG-CANUSA UK LIMITED
Registration no: 02282421 **VAT No.:** GB 209 6401 61
Date established: 1988 **Turnover:** £1m - £2m **No.of Employees:** 11 - 20
Product Groups: 30, 31, 35, 37, 38, 66

Date of Accounts	Dec 10	Dec 09	Dec 08
Sales Turnover	1m	1m	1m
Pre Tax Profit/Loss	102	111	109
Working Capital	-545	-643	-744
Fixed Assets	290	322	354
Current Assets	289	336	1m
Current Liabilities	90	40	134

D S Smith Recycling PLC

Wallsend Industrial Estate Cattedown Road, Plymouth, PL4 0RW
Tel: 01752-261312 **Fax:** 01752-226062
E-mail: athonykingman@severnside.com
Website: http://www.dssmithrecycling.com
Bank(s): National Westminster Bank Plc
Managers: J. Warner (Depot Mgr)
Immediate Holding Company: INTERFISH PRODUCER ORGANISATION LIMITED
Registration no: 00489560 **VAT No.:** GB 479 5202 22
Date established: 2008 **No.of Employees:** 21 - 50 **Product Groups:** 66

Date of Accounts	Jan 11	Jan 10
Working Capital	48	N/A
Current Assets	49	1

Dac Handling Solutions

Unit 9a Bell Close Plympton, Plymouth, PL7 4JH
Tel: 08456-013529 **Fax:** 08701-662904
Website: http://www.dac-handling.co.uk
Managers: P. White (Mgr)
No.of Employees: 11 - 20 **Product Groups:** 45, 48, 67, 83, 86

Davies Turner & Co. Ltd

Langage Park Office Campus Ashleigh Way, Plympton, Plymouth, PL7 5JX
Tel: 01752-348822 **Fax:** 01752-348833
E-mail: alancorson@daviesturner.co.uk
Website: http://www.daviesturneraircargo.com
Managers: A. Corson (Mgr)
Ultimate Holding Company: DAVIES TURNER HOLDINGS PLC
Immediate Holding Company: DAVIES TURNER & CO. LIMITED
Registration no: 04345197 **VAT No.:** GB 235 6746 45
Date established: 2001 **Turnover:** £500,000 - £1m
No.of Employees: 1 - 10 **Product Groups:** 76

Date of Accounts	Mar 12	Mar 11	Mar 10
Sales Turnover	50m	48m	41m
Pre Tax Profit/Loss	2m	1m	952
Working Capital	6m	5m	5m
Fixed Assets	365	433	436
Current Assets	16m	15m	13m
Current Liabilities	4m	4m	3m

Deep Blue Sound Ltd

6 Elizabeth Court Higher Lane, Plymouth, PL1 2AN
Tel: 01752-601462 **Fax:** 01752-453901
E-mail: sales@deepbluesound.co.uk
Website: http://www.deepbluesound.co.uk
Directors: N. Burt (Dir)
Managers: A. Steer (Tech Serv Mgr)
Immediate Holding Company: DEEP BLUE SOUND LIMITED
Registration no: 03593215 **Date established:** 1998
Turnover: £500,000 - £1m **No.of Employees:** 21 - 50
Product Groups: 37, 89

Date of Accounts	Jul 11	Jul 10	Jul 09
Working Capital	110	91	54
Fixed Assets	352	369	402
Current Assets	251	213	207

Eagle Signs Ltd

Unit 12 Barn Close Langage Business Park, Plympton, Plymouth, PL7 5HQ
Tel: 01752-345400
E-mail: mark.carter@eaglesigns.co.uk
Website: http://www.eaglesigns.co.uk
Directors: J. Carter (Dir), R. Carter (Co Sec)
Immediate Holding Company: EAGLE SIGNS LIMITED
Registration no: 00760468 **Date established:** 1963
No.of Employees: 21 - 50 **Product Groups:** 37, 84

Date of Accounts	May 11	May 10	May 09
Working Capital	13	-25	45
Fixed Assets	805	845	872
Current Assets	988	909	990

Eriks Industrial Distribution Ltd (Plymouth Service Centre)

Cattewater Road, Plymouth, PL4 0SP
Tel: 01752-255077 **Fax:** 01752-250523
E-mail: wayne.luke@wyko.co.uk
Website: http://www.wyko.co.uk
Managers: W. Luke (Mgr)
Immediate Holding Company: HJ MOTORS PLYMOUTH LTD
Date established: 2011 **Turnover:** £250m - £500m
No.of Employees: 1 - 10 **Product Groups:** 66

Fire Co

The Barn Great Woodford Drive, Plympton, Plymouth, PL7 4RP
Tel: 01752-512777 **Fax:** 01752-512777
Managers: A. Freeman (Eng Serv Mgr), R. Thornton (Mgr)
Date established: 2001 **No.of Employees:** 1 - 10 **Product Groups:** 38, 42

Fringes

Strode Road Newnham Industrial Estate, Plympton, Plymouth, PL7 4AY
Tel: 01752-345464 **Fax:** 01752-345464
E-mail: info@fringesrugs.co.uk
Website: http://www.fringesrugs.co.uk
Directors: T. Stevens (Prop)
Immediate Holding Company: FRINGES RUGS LTD
Registration no: 05846166 **Date established:** 2006
No.of Employees: 1 - 10 **Product Groups:** 23, 24, 39

Geocel Ltd

Western Wood Way Langage Business Park, Plympton, Plymouth, PL7 5BG
Tel: 01752-202060 **Fax:** 01752-202065
E-mail: sales@geocel.co.uk
Website: http://www.geocel.co.uk
Directors: W. Barclay (MD), G. Thomas (Sales), G. Wilkins (Co Sec)
Managers: R. Von Oven (Tech Serv Mgr), L. Drummond (Personnel), L. John (Fin Mgr)
Ultimate Holding Company: GEOCEL CORP (USA)
Immediate Holding Company: GEOCEL LIMITED
Registration no: 02539551 **VAT No.:** GB 492 8921 03
Date established: 1990 **Turnover:** £20m - £50m
No.of Employees: 51 - 100 **Product Groups:** 32

Date of Accounts	Dec 11	Dec 10	Dec 09
Sales Turnover	22m	21m	19m
Pre Tax Profit/Loss	1m	839	719
Working Capital	4m	4m	3m
Fixed Assets	2m	1m	1m
Current Assets	8m	8m	6m
Current Liabilities	1m	1m	1m

Graphicomm Digital Ltd

17 Willow Court St Modwen Road, Plymouth, PL6 8LQ
Tel: 01752-670099 **Fax:** 01752-265700
E-mail: sales@graphicomm.co.uk
Website: http://www.graphicomm.co.uk
Directors: J. Hardaker (MD)
Immediate Holding Company: GRAPHICOMM DIGITAL LIMITED
Registration no: 06385500 **VAT No.:** GB 750 2383 51
Date established: 2007 **Turnover:** £250,000 - £500,000
No.of Employees: 1 - 10 **Product Groups:** 28

Date of Accounts	Apr 11	Apr 10	Apr 09
Working Capital	-6	-13	-7
Fixed Assets	25	26	28
Current Assets	31	20	30

Handy Plastics

Unit 3 The Rope Walk Beech Avenue, Plymouth, PL4 0QQ
Tel: 01752-205295 **Fax:** 01752-205295
E-mail: handyplastic@aol.com
Directors: A. Patterson (Prop)
No.of Employees: 1 - 10 **Product Groups:** 30

Harris Cox Woodcraft Ltd

Belliver Way Roborough, Plymouth, PL6 7BP
Tel: 01752-788333 **Fax:** 01752-788337
E-mail: services@harriscox.co.uk
Website: http://www.harriscox.co.uk
Directors: P. Higgins (Comm), D. Moore (Fin)
Managers: S. Arries (Tech Serv Mgr), S. Peters
Immediate Holding Company: HARRIS COX WOODCRAFT LIMITED
Registration no: 02401751 **Date established:** 1989
No.of Employees: 51 - 100 **Product Groups:** 26, 49, 67

Date of Accounts	Nov 11	Nov 10	Nov 09
Pre Tax Profit/Loss	-840	321	236
Working Capital	540	1m	1m
Fixed Assets	330	455	285
Current Assets	2m	4m	3m
Current Liabilities	819	2m	828

F E Harris Ltd

Barn Close Langage Business Park, Plympton, Plymouth, PL7 5HQ
Tel: 01752-338311 **Fax:** 01752-340748
E-mail: feharris@btconnect.com
Bank(s): Lloyds TSB Bank plc
Directors: S. Jukes (Prop)
Ultimate Holding Company: JUKES HOLDINGS LIMITED
Immediate Holding Company: F.E. HARRIS LIMITED
Registration no: 02386239 **VAT No.:** GB 527 0838 41
Date established: 1989 **Turnover:** £1m - £2m **No.of Employees:** 11 - 20
Product Groups: 49

Date of Accounts	Dec 11	Dec 10	Dec 09
Working Capital	274	237	192
Fixed Assets	48	59	59
Current Assets	684	623	483

Hex Holdings Ltd

3 Bell Park Bell Close, Plympton, Plymouth, PL7 4TA
Tel: 01752-347600 **Fax:** 01752-347790
Website: http://www.hex.co.uk
Managers: R. Wharton (Mgr)
Immediate Holding Company: HEX HOLDINGS LIMITED
Registration no: 01285161 **VAT No.:** GB 507 7607 39
Date established: 1976 **Turnover:** £250,000 - £500,000
No.of Employees: 1 - 10 **Product Groups:** 32, 34

Date of Accounts	Apr 10	Apr 09	Apr 08
Sales Turnover	20m	21m	N/A
Pre Tax Profit/Loss	32	105	23
Working Capital	1m	767	771
Fixed Assets	3m	3m	3m
Current Assets	11m	11m	9m
Current Liabilities	3m	3m	4m

Hyder Consulting UK Ltd

680 Budshead Road, Plymouth, PL6 5XR
Tel: 01752-769675 **Fax:** 01752-769677
Website: http://www.hyderconsulting.com
Managers: J. Baron (Sales Admin)
Ultimate Holding Company: HYDER CONSULTING PLC
Immediate Holding Company: HYDER CONSULTING (UK) LIMITED
Registration no: 02212959 **Date established:** 1988
No.of Employees: 51 - 100 **Product Groups:** 84

Date of Accounts	Mar 12	Mar 11	Mar 10
Sales Turnover	70m	88m	96m
Pre Tax Profit/Loss	2m	5m	2m
Working Capital	24m	25m	23m
Fixed Assets	7m	8m	10m
Current Assets	41m	49m	45m
Current Liabilities	9m	11m	13m

Icology Research Solutions

25a Alexandra Road Ford, Plymouth, PL2 1JX
Tel: 07866-052021
E-mail: mail@icology.co.uk
Website: http://www.icology.co.uk
Directors: R. Burton (Prop)
Date established: 2006 **No.of Employees:** 1 - 10 **Product Groups:** 81, 86

Impact Industrial Support Services

Devonport Dockyard, Plymouth, PL2 2BG
Tel: 01752-552515 **Fax:** 01752-554607
Website: http://www.fendercare.com
Directors: D. Storey (MD)
Date established: 2000 **No.of Employees:** 21 - 50 **Product Groups:** 35, 36, 39

Date of Accounts	Jul 08	Jul 07	Jul 06
Working Capital	177	189	173
Fixed Assets	79	102	114
Current Assets	300	276	245
Current Liabilities	123	87	73

Interdive Services Ltd

Unit 3 Stoke Damerel Business Centre 5 Church Street, Plymouth, PL3 4DT
Tel: 01752-558080 **Fax:** 01752-569090
E-mail: admin@interdive.co.uk
Website: http://www.interdive.co.uk
Directors: J. Rabone (MD)
Immediate Holding Company: INTERDIVE SERVICES LIMITED
Registration no: 04449522 **VAT No.:** GB 643 4682 28
Date established: 2002 **Turnover:** Up to £250,000
No.of Employees: 1 - 10 **Product Groups:** 39, 51, 86

Date of Accounts	May 11	May 10	May 09
Working Capital	548	447	403
Fixed Assets	15	18	23
Current Assets	632	513	554

Interlube Systems Ltd

85 St Modwen Road, Plymouth, PL6 8LH
Tel: 01752-676000 **Fax:** 01752-676001
E-mail: info@interlubesystems.co.uk
Website: http://www.interlubesystems.com
Bank(s): Bank of Scotland
Directors: K. Horner (Dir), M. Boyd (Fin), M. Cusack (MD)
Managers: G. Perring (Mats Contrlr), K. Pring (Tech Serv Mgr)
Immediate Holding Company: INTERLUBE SYSTEMS LIMITED
Registration no: 03999847 **Date established:** 2000 **Turnover:** £5m - £10m
No.of Employees: 51 - 100 **Product Groups:** 29, 30, 36, 39, 40, 48, 84

Date of Accounts	Mar 11	Mar 10	Mar 09
Sales Turnover	8m	7m	8m
Pre Tax Profit/Loss	951	398	17
Working Capital	1m	706	-513
Fixed Assets	955	1m	1m
Current Assets	3m	3m	2m
Current Liabilities	796	820	2m

Invensys Controls UK Ltd

Southway Drive, Plymouth, PL6 6QT
Tel: 01752-737166 **Fax:** 01752-739246
E-mail: pavel.dolezel@invensyscontrols.com
Website: http://www.invensys.com
Directors: G. Haywood (I.T. Dir), D. McFadyen (Sales)
Managers: J. Hawkin (Fin Mgr), F. Riggall (Personnel), D. Walker (Purch Mgr), N. Parsons (Personnel), T. Bray (Tech Serv Mgr), M. Barratt, R. Pena (Plant)
Ultimate Holding Company: INVENSYS PLC
Immediate Holding Company: INVENSYS CONTROLS UK LTD
Registration no: 00739180 **Date established:** 1962
Turnover: £125m - £250m **No.of Employees:** 251 - 500
Product Groups: 38

Date of Accounts	Mar 12	Mar 11	Mar 10
Sales Turnover	41m	47m	45m
Pre Tax Profit/Loss	1m	2m	960
Working Capital	43m	41m	39m
Fixed Assets	5m	5m	5m
Current Assets	52m	51m	48m
Current Liabilities	5m	4m	4m

Joce Electrical Electric Contractor

Regent Street, Plymouth, PL4 8BG
Tel: 01752-668381 **Fax:** 01752-227146
Directors: B. Joce (MD)
Ultimate Holding Company: W.H. JOCE & SONS (HOLDINGS) LIMITED
Immediate Holding Company: W.H.JOCE & SONS,LIMITED
Registration no: 00372430 **VAT No.:** GB 144 8997 17
Date established: 1951 **Turnover:** £500,000 - £1m
No.of Employees: 1 - 10 **Product Groups:** 52

Date of Accounts	Mar 11	Mar 10	Mar 09
Working Capital	61	47	-239
Fixed Assets	22	15	20
Current Assets	117	107	139
Current Liabilities	N/A	N/A	37

K 2 Medical Systems Ltd

7 Research Way, Plymouth, PL6 8BT
Tel: 01752-764800 **Fax:** 01752-674899
E-mail: enquiries@k2ms.com
Website: http://www.k2ms.com
Directors: G. Weeks (Co Sec), R. Keith (MD), I. Crozier (Dir), J. Meeson (Dir)
Ultimate Holding Company: K2 MEDICAL SYSTEMS HOLDINGS LIMITED
Immediate Holding Company: K2 MEDICAL SYSTEMS LIMITED
Registration no: 03809089 **Date established:** 1999
No.of Employees: 11 - 20 **Product Groups:** 38, 81, 88

Date of Accounts	Jun 11	Jun 10	Jun 09
Working Capital	520	148	-37
Fixed Assets	2m	2m	1m
Current Assets	973	668	446

Kawasaki Precision Machinery UK Ltd

Ernesettle Lane, Plymouth, PL5 2SA
Tel: 01752-364394 **Fax:** 01752-364816
E-mail: sales@kpm-uk.co.uk
Website: http://www.kpm-eu.com
Bank(s): National Westminster Bank Plc
Directors: K. Hida (Dir)
Managers: R. Morton (Comptroller), S. Bendall (Purch Mgr), N. Crawford (Tech Serv Mgr), J. Whetter, R. Davies (Personnel)
Ultimate Holding Company: KAWASAKI HEAVY INDUSTRIES LTD (JAPAN)
Immediate Holding Company: KAWASAKI PRECISION MACHINERY (UK) LIMITED

Registration no: 02833215 **VAT No.:** GB 591 4961 09
Date established: 1993 **Turnover:** £75m - £125m
No.of Employees: 251 - 500 **Product Groups:** 40

Date of Accounts	Dec 11	Dec 10	Dec 09
Sales Turnover	83m	51m	36m
Pre Tax Profit/Loss	4m	4m	1m
Working Capital	3m	-2m	-8
Fixed Assets	12m	12m	11m
Current Assets	44m	33m	16m
Current Liabilities	3m	2m	2m

Keyline Builders Merchants

Lister Close Newnham Industrial Estate, Plympton, Plymouth, PL7 4BA
Tel: 01752-335956 **Fax:** 01752-342895
E-mail: ply0235@keyline.co.uk
Website: http://www.keyline.co.uk
Managers: D. Pote (Asst Gen Mgr)
Immediate Holding Company: HEAVENLY LEISURE LTD
Registration no: 02711617 **VAT No.:** GB 408 5567 37
Date established: 2007 **No.of Employees:** 1 - 10 **Product Groups:** 25, 66

Date of Accounts	Jun 11	Jun 10	Jun 09
Working Capital	-1	-4	-21
Fixed Assets	9	10	12
Current Assets	19	16	11
Current Liabilities	N/A	N/A	5

Kier Western

27-37 Martin Street, Plymouth, PL1 3NE
Tel: 01752-201123 **Fax:** 01392- 261789
E-mail: info.plymouth@kier.co.uk
Website: http://www.kier.co.uk
Bank(s): Barclays
Directors: R. Moretti (Co Sec), P. Sheffield (Dir), J. French (Ch), P. Young (MD)
Managers: K. McLoud (Mktg Serv Mgr), M. Parker (Mgr)
Ultimate Holding Company: KIER GROUP
Immediate Holding Company: KIER REGIONAL LTD
Registration no: 02099533 **Turnover:** £20m - £50m
No.of Employees: 51 - 100 **Product Groups:** 51, 52

Knight Scientific Ltd

Unit 15 Wolseley Business Park Wolseley Close, Plymouth, PL2 3BY
Tel: 01752-565676 **Fax:** 01752-561672
E-mail: info@knightscientific.com
Website: http://www.knightscientific.com
Directors: J. Knight (MD)
Immediate Holding Company: KNIGHT SCIENTIFIC LIMITED
Registration no: 02487800 **VAT No.:** GB 526 9352 28
Date established: 1990 **Turnover:** Up to £250,000
No.of Employees: 1 - 10 **Product Groups:** 31

Date of Accounts	Mar 11	Mar 10	Mar 09
Working Capital	29	46	15
Fixed Assets	78	82	72
Current Assets	51	116	65

Kwik-Fit GB Ltd

Tavistock Road, Plymouth, PL5 3DG
Tel: 01752-777704
Website: http://www.kwik-fit.com
Managers: K. Robinson (Mgr)
Ultimate Holding Company: FINANCIERE DAUNOU 2 SA (LUXEMBOURG)
Immediate Holding Company: KWIK-FIT (GB) LIMITED
Registration no: 01009184 **Date established:** 1971
No.of Employees: 1 - 10 **Product Groups:** 29, 39, 85

Date of Accounts	Dec 10	Dec 09	Dec 08
Sales Turnover	527m	495m	449m
Pre Tax Profit/Loss	269m	56m	97m
Working Capital	197m	201m	154m
Fixed Assets	106m	115m	110m
Current Assets	375m	368m	329m
Current Liabilities	36m	36m	38m

Lamerton Engineering Services

52 Clarence Place Morice Town, Plymouth, PL2 1SF
Tel: 01752-509707 **Fax:** 01752-509707
Directors: D. Lamerton (Prop)
Date established: 1978 **No.of Employees:** 1 - 10 **Product Groups:** 35, 36, 39

Lanes For Drains plc

Unit 11 Bell Park Bell Close Newnham Industrial Estate, Plympton, Plymouth, PL7 4TA
Tel: 01752-334280 **Fax:** 01752-600292
E-mail: michelle.ringland@lanesfordrains.co.uk
Website: http://www.lanesfordrains.co.uk
Managers: D. Tafner (Reg Mgr)
No.of Employees: 11 - 20 **Product Groups:** 37, 54, 84

Langdon Transport

Hursley Business Park Blackeven Road, Roborough, Plymouth, PL6 7AX
Tel: 01752-777110 **Fax:** 01752-777220
E-mail: sales@palletforce.com
Website: http://www.palletforce.com
Directors: S. Langdon (MD)
Immediate Holding Company: LANGDON TRANSPORT LIMITED
Registration no: 04661798 **Date established:** 2003
No.of Employees: 1 - 10 **Product Groups:** 77

Date of Accounts	Jul 08	Jul 07	Jul 06
Working Capital	-688	-643	-442
Fixed Assets	1216	797	693
Current Assets	990	704	564
Current Liabilities	1678	1347	1006

Martin Luck Group Ltd

Rowdown House Rowdown Close Langage Business Park, Plympton, Plymouth, PL7 5EY
Tel: 01752-336699 **Fax:** 01752-330022
E-mail: sales@martinluck.co.uk
Website: http://www.martinluck.co.uk
Directors: B. Jones (Fin)
Managers: D. Dobson (Chief Mgr), R. Lambourne (Tech Serv Mgr), C. Timmins (Sales Prom Mgr), R. Street (Purch Mgr)
Immediate Holding Company: MARTIN LUCK GROUP LIMITED
Registration no: 07032735 **Date established:** 2009
Turnover: £10m - £20m **No.of Employees:** 21 - 50 **Product Groups:** 22, 23, 26, 27, 28, 30, 81

Date of Accounts	Jun 11	Jun 10
Sales Turnover	6m	1m
Pre Tax Profit/Loss	155	304
Working Capital	-1m	-2m
Fixed Assets	2m	2m
Current Assets	2m	2m
Current Liabilities	3m	3m

M R Gas Services

6 Elm Grove Plympton, Plymouth, PL7 2BW
Tel: 01752-346482
Website: http://www.mrgasservices.co.uk
Directors: M. Rodd (Prop)
Immediate Holding Company: MR GAS SERVICES LTD
Registration no: 07346063 **Date established:** 2010
No.of Employees: 1 - 10 **Product Groups:** 40, 52, 66

Mcarthur Group Ltd

Unit D3-D4 Cot Hill Trading Estate, Plymouth, PL7 1SR
Tel: 01752-339851 **Fax:** 01752-342588
E-mail: marketing@mcarthur-group.com
Website: http://www.mcarthur-group.com
Managers: K. Rose (Chief Mgr)
Immediate Holding Company: MCARTHUR GROUP LIMITED
Registration no: 00394222 **VAT No.:** GB 138 3754 51
Date established: 1945 **Turnover:** £2m - £5m **No.of Employees:** 11 - 20
Product Groups: 66

Date of Accounts	Dec 11	Dec 10	Dec 09
Sales Turnover	82m	79m	79m
Pre Tax Profit/Loss	-1m	-529	-2m
Working Capital	-1m	144	10
Fixed Assets	13m	14m	15m
Current Assets	25m	26m	22m
Current Liabilities	1m	2m	11m

Marine Systems

9 Thornville Terrace, Plymouth, PL9 7LG
Tel: 07979-804681
E-mail: support@marinetrades.co.uk
Website: http://www.marinetrades.co.uk
Directors: P. Brian (Prop)
Registration no: 04394890 **Turnover:** Up to £250,000
No.of Employees: 1 - 10 **Product Groups:** 84

Marine Wise UK Ltd

Breakwater Road Plymstock, Plymouth, PL9 7HJ
Tel: 01752-407575 **Fax:** 01752-484374
E-mail: info@marinewise.co.uk
Website: http://www.marinewise.co.uk
Directors: S. Lethbridge (Dir)
Immediate Holding Company: MARINE WISE U.K. LIMITED
Registration no: 05371791 **Date established:** 2005
No.of Employees: 1 - 10 **Product Groups:** 35, 36, 39

Date of Accounts	Jul 11	Jul 10	Jul 09
Working Capital	-19	8	30
Fixed Assets	14	17	14
Current Assets	178	189	199

Metal Solutions South West Ltd

Darklake View Estover, Plymouth, PL6 7TL
Tel: 01752-770555 **Fax:** 01752-775444
E-mail: info@metal-solutions.co.uk
Website: http://www.metal-solutions.co.uk
Managers: W. Waterson (Admin Off)
Immediate Holding Company: J D RACING LIMITED
Registration no: 02706178 **Date established:** 2010
No.of Employees: 21 - 50 **Product Groups:** 35

Date of Accounts	Dec 10
Working Capital	-13
Fixed Assets	12
Current Assets	14

More Than Mobility

139 Cornwall Street, Plymouth, PL1 1PA
Tel: 01752-673367
E-mail: marcy@morethanmobility.com
Website: http://www.morethanmobility.com
Managers: M. Lashbrook (Mgr)
Date established: 2001 **Turnover:** £75m - £125m
No.of Employees: 1 - 10 **Product Groups:** 39

N B N International Ltd

10 Estover Road, Plymouth, PL6 7PY
Tel: 01752-202301 **Fax:** 01752-202330
E-mail: orders@nbninternational.com
Website: http://www.nbninternational.com
Bank(s): Midland
Directors: I. Myers (Dir), I. Wordsworth (Chief Op Offcr)
Managers: L. Nunn (Mktg Serv Mgr), T. Woodley (Chief Acct), J. Wildash (Personnel)
Ultimate Holding Company: RIIB LIMITED
Immediate Holding Company: HITCHINGS & MASON LIMITED
Registration no: 04957045 **VAT No.:** GB 526 9593 06
Date established: 1963 **Turnover:** £2m - £5m **No.of Employees:** 51 - 100
Product Groups: 64

Date of Accounts	Mar 11	Mar 10
Working Capital	-236	-218
Fixed Assets	272	278
Current Assets	382	396

Nicobond Plymouth

Unit C1 Cot Hill Trading Estate, Plymouth, PL7 1SR
Tel: 01752-339724 **Fax:** 01752-342746
E-mail: steve.moore@nichollsandclarke.com
Website: http://www.ncdirect.co.uk
Bank(s): National Westminster Bank Plc
Managers: S. Moore (Mgr)
Registration no: 00000140 **Turnover:** £2m - £5m
No.of Employees: 11 - 20 **Product Groups:** 30, 32, 33, 66

Olympia Foods Ltd

Unit 6 Estover Road, Plymouth, PL6 7PF
Tel: 01752-201685 **Fax:** 01752-201769
E-mail: info@olympiafoods.co.uk
Website: http://www.olympiafoods.co.uk
Directors: H. Nairne (Prop)
Immediate Holding Company: OLYMPIA FOODS (SOUTHWEST) LIMITED
Registration no: 06804381 **Date established:** 2009
Turnover: £500,000 - £1m **No.of Employees:** 11 - 20
Product Groups: 20, 40, 62

Date of Accounts	Mar 11	Mar 10
Working Capital	-236	-218
Fixed Assets	272	278
Current Assets	382	396

P H C Management Ltd

19 Mary Seacole Road, Plymouth, PL1 3JY
Tel: 01752-257678 **Fax:** 01752-666804
E-mail: info@phc-management.com
Website: http://www.phc-management.com
Directors: M. Postle-Hacon (MD)
Immediate Holding Company: PHC MANAGEMENT LIMITED
Registration no: 04601615 **Date established:** 2002
No.of Employees: 1 - 10 **Product Groups:** 80

Date of Accounts	Nov 11	Nov 10	Nov 09
Working Capital	-109	-66	-33
Fixed Assets	8	10	12
Current Assets	297	306	476

Paper Converting Machine Company Ltd

1 Bush Park, Plymouth, PL6 7RG
Tel: 01752-735881 **Fax:** 01752-733290
E-mail: markfowler@pcmc.com
Website: http://pcmc.com
Bank(s): National Westminster Bank Plc
Directors: M. Fowler (Comm)
Managers: C. Jenkin (Purch Mgr), S. Vosper
Ultimate Holding Company: BARRY WEHMILLER INC (USA)
Immediate Holding Company: PAPER CONVERTING MACHINE COMPANY LIMITED
Registration no: 00745399 **VAT No.:** GB 143 4625 80
Date established: 1962 **Turnover:** £5m - £10m **No.of Employees:** 21 - 50
Product Groups: 42, 43, 44, 45

Date of Accounts	Sep 11	Sep 10	Sep 09
Sales Turnover	6m	7m	4m
Pre Tax Profit/Loss	346	418	-193
Working Capital	11m	11m	11m
Fixed Assets	38	51	63
Current Assets	12m	14m	13m
Current Liabilities	722	713	382

Passionate For Presents

186 Tailyour Road, Plymouth, PL6 5DJ
Tel: 01752-212954
E-mail: info@passionateforpresents.co.uk
Website: http://www.passionateforpresents.co.uk
Directors: C. Rapson (Ptnr)
Date established: 2004 **No.of Employees:** 1 - 10 **Product Groups:** 49

Plus Organisation Ltd

Plymouth Industrial Services Clittaford Road, Plymouth, PL6 6DF
Tel: 01752-306630 **Fax:** 01752-696225
E-mail: plus@pluss.org.uk
Website: http://www.pluss.org.uk
Directors: M. Davies (MD)
Managers: M. Shillingford (Mktg Serv Mgr), L. Greenslade
No.of Employees: 11 - 20 **Product Groups:** 39, 45, 67, 85

Plymartech

7 Melbourne Cotts, Plymouth, PL1 5HG
Tel: 01752-222944 **Fax:** 01752-310490
Directors: J. Waters (Dir)
Date established: 2006 **No.of Employees:** 1 - 10 **Product Groups:** 35, 36, 39

Date of Accounts	Jul 07
Working Capital	-3
Fixed Assets	14
Current Assets	18
Current Liabilities	21

Plymouth Metal Polishing & Finishing

12 & 14 Haxter Close Roborough, Plymouth, PL6 7DD
Tel: 01752-517104 **Fax:** 01752-517105
E-mail: info@plymouthmetalpolishing.co.uk
Website: http://www.plymouthmetalpolishing.co.uk
Directors: S. Kelly (Prop)
Date established: 1989 **No.of Employees:** 11 - 20 **Product Groups:** 46, 48

Plymouth Packaging Services Ltd

Darklake Close Estover, Plymouth, PL6 7TJ
Tel: 01752-696330 **Fax:** 01752-695589
E-mail: lesley@plymouthpackaging.co.uk
Website: http://www.plymouthpackaging.co.uk
Directors: J. Edington (Fin), L. Foster (Dir)
Immediate Holding Company: PLYMOUTH PACKAGING SERVICES LIMITED
Registration no: 00920703 **VAT No.:** GB 143 6993 41
Date established: 1967 **Turnover:** Up to £250,000
No.of Employees: 1 - 10 **Product Groups:** 48

Date of Accounts	Dec 11	Dec 10	Dec 09
Working Capital	5	19	-5
Fixed Assets	19	22	24
Current Assets	45	57	72

Power Tool Services

9 Cathcart Avenue, Plymouth, PL4 9QF
Tel: 01752-268413 **Fax:** 01752-268413
Directors: I. Kirby (Prop)
Date established: 1999 **No.of Employees:** 1 - 10 **Product Groups:** 36, 37

Princess Yachts International plc

Newport Street, Plymouth, PL1 3QG
Tel: 01752-203888 **Fax:** 01752-203777
E-mail: info@princessyachts.com
Website: http://www.princessyachts.com
Bank(s): National Westminster
Directors: D. King (Ch), D. Pyle (Sales), I. Duffin (Fin), R. Gale (Co Sec)
Managers: S. Clare, E. Vanjaarsveldt (Personnel), G. Hooper, B. Saunders (Tech Serv Mgr)
Ultimate Holding Company: RNO GROUP SCA (LUXEMBOURG)
Immediate Holding Company: PRINCESS YACHTS INTERNATIONAL PLC
Registration no: 00856633 **VAT No.:** GB 143 4285 78
Date established: 1965 **Turnover:** £125m - £250m
No.of Employees: 1501 & over **Product Groups:** 39

Date of Accounts	Dec 11	Dec 10	Dec 09
Sales Turnover	208m	206m	214m
Pre Tax Profit/Loss	15m	21m	18m
Working Capital	61m	54m	44m
Fixed Assets	35m	34m	34m
Current Assets	169m	152m	129m
Current Liabilities	87m	77m	61m

Promarine UK Ltd
Unit 6 Tamar Building Queen Anne Battery, Plymouth, PL4 0LP
Tel: 01752-267984
E-mail: mail@promarineuk.com
Website: http://www.promarineuk.com
Directors: C. Dark (Dir)
Immediate Holding Company: PROMARINE (UK) LIMITED
Registration no: 04512732 **Date established:** 2002
No.of Employees: 1 - 10 **Product Groups:** 35, 36, 39

Date of Accounts	Aug 11	Aug 10	Aug 09
Working Capital	5	11	11
Fixed Assets	30	40	48
Current Assets	113	59	69

Proweld UK Ltd
Field House Estover, Plymouth, PL6 7TL
Tel: 01752-695522 **Fax:** 01752-695848
E-mail: sales@proweld.co.uk
Website: http://www.proweld.co.uk
Directors: P. Valente (Dir)
Immediate Holding Company: PROWELD UK LIMITED
Registration no: 02618352 **Date established:** 1991
No.of Employees: 11 - 20 **Product Groups:** 46

Date of Accounts	May 11	May 10	May 09
Working Capital	-39	-59	-21
Fixed Assets	10	18	23
Current Assets	277	326	382

Pyropress Engineering Co. Ltd
Bell Close Newnham Industrial Estate, Plympton, Plymouth, PL7 4JH
Tel: 01752-339866 **Fax:** 01752-336681
E-mail: carol@pyropress.com
Website: http://www.pyropress.com
Bank(s): National Westminster Bank Plc
Managers: C. Ruttledge (Fin Mgr)
Ultimate Holding Company: PYROBAN GROUP LIMITED
Immediate Holding Company: PYROPRESS ENGINEERING COMPANY LIMITED(THE)
Registration no: 00502781 **VAT No.:** GB 196 9196 96
Date established: 1951 **Turnover:** £1m - £2m **No.of Employees:** 21 - 50
Product Groups: 35, 36, 37, 38, 39, 40, 46, 49, 52

Date of Accounts	Dec 11	Dec 09	Jun 11
Sales Turnover	1m	N/A	N/A
Pre Tax Profit/Loss	185	N/A	N/A
Working Capital	719	720	1m
Fixed Assets	1m	926	910
Current Assets	1m	1m	1m
Current Liabilities	156	N/A	N/A

Quarterdeck Marine
10 East Street, Plymouth, PL1 3NU
Tel: 01752-224567 **Fax:** 01752-224567
Directors: M. Strutt (Prop)
Date established: 1973 **No.of Employees:** 1 - 10 **Product Groups:** 35, 36, 39

Rowse Electrical Wholsales Ltd
Unit 5 Estover Estover, Plymouth, PL6 7PS
Tel: 01752-674100 **Fax:** 01752-673990
E-mail: jrowse@rowse-electrical.co.uk
Website: http://www.rowseelectrical.co.uk
Directors: J. Rowse (Prop)
Immediate Holding Company: Rowse Electrical Wholesalers Ltd
Registration no: 05220551 **Date established:** 2004
No.of Employees: 1 - 10 **Product Groups:** 36, 40

Date of Accounts	Sep 08	Sep 07	Sep 06
Working Capital	77	21	-7
Fixed Assets	13	13	13
Current Assets	320	278	213
Current Liabilities	243	257	220

S D Plastering
50 Chudleigh Road, Plymouth, PL4 7HU
Tel: 07875-460912
E-mail: sdanplastering@yahoo.co.uk
Website: http://www.plasterersinplymouth.co.uk
Directors: S. Dan (Prop)
Date established: 2000 **Turnover:** Up to £250,000
No.of Employees: 1 - 10 **Product Groups:** 33

S L D Pumps & Power
Breakwater Road Plymstock, Plymouth, PL9 7HJ
Tel: 01752-481661 **Fax:** 01752-484122
E-mail: plymouth@sldpumpspower.co.uk
Website: http://www.sldpumpspower.co.uk
Managers: D. Matheron (Mgr)
Immediate Holding Company: SOUTHWEST RIB CENTRE LTD
Registration no: 03991063 **Date established:** 2011
No.of Employees: 1 - 10 **Product Groups:** 40

S L Powder Coatings
1 Parkwood Close Broadley Industrial Park, Plymouth, PL6 7SG
Tel: 01752-696970 **Fax:** 01752-696980
E-mail: info@slpowdercoating.co.uk
Website: http://www.slpowdercoating.co.uk
Managers: S. Leach (Mgr)
Immediate Holding Company: S L POWDER COATINGS LTD
Registration no: 05448619 **Date established:** 2005
No.of Employees: 1 - 10 **Product Groups:** 46, 48

Date of Accounts	May 11	May 09	May 08
Working Capital	189	180	113
Fixed Assets	57	67	76
Current Assets	298	293	271

S M B Plating Ltd
Emma Place Stonehouse, Plymouth, PL1 3QX
Tel: 01752-669853 **Fax:** 01752-665434
E-mail: jim.gallagher@smbplating.co.uk
Website: http://www.smbplating.co.uk
Bank(s): Lloyds TSB
Directors: J. Gallagher (MD)
Immediate Holding Company: SMB PLATING LIMITED
Registration no: 04406453 **VAT No.:** GB 143 6210 02
Date established: 2002 **No.of Employees:** 11 - 20 **Product Groups:** 48

Date of Accounts	Mar 11	Mar 10	Mar 09
Working Capital	72	10	-17
Fixed Assets	374	390	404
Current Assets	443	415	260

S M Group Europe Ltd
Mercator House 22 Brest Road, Plymouth, PL6 5XP
Tel: 01752-241000 **Fax:** 01752-241040
E-mail: sales@smgeurope.com
Website: http://www.smgeurope.com
Bank(s): National Westminster
Directors: C. Northmore (Dir), S. Stubbs (Fin)
Managers: A. Johnson (Sales Prom Mgr)
Immediate Holding Company: SM GROUP (EUROPE) LTD.
Registration no: 01306320 **VAT No.:** GB 291 4596 30
Date established: 1977 **Turnover:** £2m - £5m **No.of Employees:** 11 - 20
Product Groups: 39, 49

Date of Accounts	Oct 11	Oct 10	Oct 09
Working Capital	2m	1m	2m
Fixed Assets	350	292	200
Current Assets	3m	3m	3m

S M S Plymouth
Marine House Commercial Road, Plymouth, PL4 0LE
Tel: 01752-666333 **Fax:** 01752-666016
E-mail: parts@sm4.co.uk
Website: http://www.sm4.co.uk
Directors: J. Bowyer (MD)
Registration no: 04518397 **Date established:** 2002
No.of Employees: 1 - 10 **Product Groups:** 35, 36, 39

Sea Chest
Dolphin Building Queen Anne Battery, Plymouth, PL4 0LP
Tel: 01752-222012 **Fax:** 01752-252679
E-mail: sales@seachest.co.uk
Website: http://www.seachest.co.uk
Directors: R. Boyns (Prop)
No.of Employees: 1 - 10 **Product Groups:** 37, 38, 39, 44, 49, 67

Sea Wind
2 Ensign House Parkway Court Longbridge Road, Marsh Mills, Plymouth, PL6 8LR
Tel: 01752-268835 **Fax:** 01752- 268836
Website: http://www.seawindmarine.com
Directors: J. Adams (Prop)
Date established: 2003 **No.of Employees:** 1 - 10 **Product Groups:** 35, 36, 39

Seymour Signs
216 Mannamead Road, Plymouth, PL3 5RF
Tel: 01752-290000
E-mail: paul@seymoursigns.co.uk
Directors: P. Hands (Ptnr)
No.of Employees: 1 - 10 **Product Groups:** 30, 49, 52

Shoreheat Ltd
9 Pomphlett Farm Industrial Estate Broxton Drive, Plymouth, PL9 7BG
Tel: 01752-481122 **Fax:** 01752-484070
Website: http://www.shoreheat.co.uk
Directors: G. Holton (MD), R. Terry (Sales), A. Maxwell (Dir)
Managers: J. Cresswell (District Mgr), A. Perkins (Sales Prom Mgr), A. Fursman (Mgr), D. Clarkson (Mgr)
Immediate Holding Company: SHOREHEAT LIMITED
Registration no: 01566154 **VAT No.:** GB 484 6088 12
Date established: 1981 **Turnover:** £5m - £10m **No.of Employees:** 1 - 10
Product Groups: 36, 38, 40

Silverstall
The Armada Centre Armada Way, Plymouth, PL1 1LE
Tel: 01752-250066 **Fax:** 01752-660584
E-mail: j-hall@silverstall.com
Website: http://www.silverstall.com
Directors: J. Hall (Prop), J. Hall (Grp Chief Exec)
Date established: 1994 **No.of Employees:** 1 - 10 **Product Groups:** 65

Source
Unit13c Barn Close Plympton, Plymouth, PL7 5HQ
Tel: 01752-698698 **Fax:** 01752-698001
E-mail: info@cable-accessories.com
Website: http://www.cable-accessories.com
Directors: A. Dunkerley (Dir)
Ultimate Holding Company: MYRNA LTD
Immediate Holding Company: J.G. BUSINESS MACHINES LIMITED
Registration no: 04561647 **Date established:** 1979 **Turnover:** £1m - £2m
No.of Employees: 21 - 50 **Product Groups:** 30, 35, 37

Date of Accounts	Apr 11	Apr 10	Apr 09
Sales Turnover	N/A	8m	N/A
Pre Tax Profit/Loss	N/A	366	N/A
Working Capital	684	340	261
Fixed Assets	699	673	691
Current Assets	3m	2m	2m
Current Liabilities	N/A	1m	N/A

Stoke Potteries
30 Devonport Road, Plymouth, PL3 4DH
Tel: 01752-551425 **Fax:** 01752-551425
Directors: V. Morran (Ptnr)
Date established: 1990 **No.of Employees:** 1 - 10 **Product Groups:** 20, 40, 41

Tamerton Wrought Ironwork
23 Commercial Road, Plymouth, PL4 0LE
Tel: 01752-228163 **Fax:** 01752-256213
Website: http://www.tamertonwroughtironwork.com
Directors: P. Back (Dir), P. Back (MD), K. Back (Fin)
Immediate Holding Company: TAMERTON WROUGHT IRON WORKS LTD
Registration no: 05615291 **Date established:** 2005
No.of Employees: 1 - 10 **Product Groups:** 26, 35

Tecalemit Garage Equipment Co. Ltd
Eagle Road Plympton, Plymouth, PL7 5JY
Tel: 01752-219111 **Fax:** 01752-219128
E-mail: sales@tecalemit.co.uk
Website: http://www.tecalemit.co.uk
Bank(s): Lloyds TSB Bank plc
Directors: P. Cledwyn (Sales), J. Devonport (MD)
Managers: J. Porter (Purch Mgr), J. Brown, N. Walke (Personnel)
Ultimate Holding Company: PENTA SPA (ITALY)
Immediate Holding Company: TECALEMIT GARAGE EQUIPMENT COMPANY LIMITED
Registration no: 01099738 **Date established:** 1973
Turnover: £10m - £20m **No.of Employees:** 21 - 50 **Product Groups:** 36, 38, 39, 40, 46

Date of Accounts	Dec 11	Dec 10	Dec 09
Sales Turnover	11m	11m	10m
Pre Tax Profit/Loss	7	43	-18
Working Capital	4m	4m	4m
Fixed Assets	109	70	64
Current Assets	7m	6m	6m
Current Liabilities	2m	1m	1m

Telecom Protection Technologies Ltd
1a Garden Close Langage Business Park, Plympton, Plymouth, PL7 5EU
Tel: 01752-346096 **Fax:** 01752-338493
E-mail: sales@tpt.uk.com
Website: http://www.tpt.uk.com
Directors: J. Eaton (MD), W. Greenwood (Co Sec)
Ultimate Holding Company: GREENWOODS GROUP LIMITED
Immediate Holding Company: TELECOM PROTECTION TECHNOLOGIES LIMITED
Registration no: 02851605 **VAT No.:** GB 591 4653 20
Date established: 1993 **Turnover:** £1m - £2m **No.of Employees:** 1 - 10
Product Groups: 37

Date of Accounts	Dec 11	Dec 10	Dec 09
Sales Turnover	N/A	N/A	1m
Pre Tax Profit/Loss	N/A	N/A	-109
Working Capital	-2m	-1m	-1m
Fixed Assets	N/A	118	97
Current Assets	2	648	1m
Current Liabilities	N/A	N/A	138

Tufcoat
Unit 3 Garden Close Langage Business Park, Plympton, Plymouth, PL7 5EU
Tel: 01752-227333 **Fax:** 01752-227333
E-mail: sales@tufcoat.co.uk
Website: http://www.boatcoat.com
Directors: E. Lake (Fin)
Managers: B. Kirkham
Immediate Holding Company: BOATCOAT LIMITED
Registration no: 05710534 **Date established:** 2006
Turnover: £250,000 - £500,000 **No.of Employees:** 11 - 20
Product Groups: 30

Two Four Productions
Bush Park, Plymouth, PL6 7RG
Tel: 020-7438 1800 **Fax:** 01752-727450
E-mail: enquiries@twofour.co.uk
Website: http://www.twofour.co.uk
Bank(s): Barclays
Directors: A. Hughes (Fin), C. Mills (Mkt Research), C. Wace (MD), C. White (MD)
Managers: J. Lourie
Registration no: 02351132 **VAT No.:** GB 462 9728 13
Turnover: £5m - £10m **No.of Employees:** 101 - 250 **Product Groups:** 86, 89

Date of Accounts	Dec 07	Dec 06	Dec 05
Sales Turnover	14880	8431	8401
Pre Tax Profit/Loss	201	19	302
Working Capital	264	335	329
Fixed Assets	236	N/A	N/A
Current Assets	3031	2286	2698
Current Liabilities	2767	1951	2370
Total Share Capital	100	100	100
ROCE% (Return on Capital Employed)	40.2	5.7	91.9
ROT% (Return on Turnover)	1.4	0.2	3.6

University Of Plymouth
Drake Circus, Plymouth, PL4 8AA
Tel: 01752-600600 **Fax:** 01752-232155
Website: http://www.plymouth.ac.uk
Bank(s): HSBC
Directors: V. Matthews (Pers)
Managers: S. Jones, G. Bouch, W. Purcell, J. Chafer, J. Bushrod
Immediate Holding Company: UNIVERSITY OF PLYMOUTH ENTERPRISE LIMITED
Registration no: 03707827 **VAT No.:** GB 526 7104 57
Date established: 1999 **Turnover:** £2m - £5m
No.of Employees: 1501 & over **Product Groups:** 07, 54, 80, 81, 84

Date of Accounts	Jul 11	Jul 10	Jul 09
Sales Turnover	3m	2m	2m
Pre Tax Profit/Loss	142	173	201
Working Capital	186	122	-98
Fixed Assets	280	257	96
Current Assets	2m	1m	1m
Current Liabilities	902	792	289

Vending Matters Ltd
Lee Mill Industrial Estate Westway, Plymouth, PL9 9RL
Tel: 01752-892563 **Fax:** 01752-892581
E-mail: sales@romacoffee.co.uk
Website: http://www.kgvending.co.uk
Directors: G. Clements (Dir)
Immediate Holding Company: VENDING MATTERS LTD
Registration no: 05533376 **Date established:** 2005
No.of Employees: 1 - 10 **Product Groups:** 20, 40, 62, 67

Date of Accounts	Mar 11	Mar 10	Mar 09
Working Capital	-69	-122	-83
Fixed Assets	60	78	81
Current Assets	80	73	80

Vi Spring Ltd
Ernesettle Lane, Plymouth, PL5 2TT
Tel: 01752-366311 **Fax:** 01752-355109
E-mail: sales@vispring.co.uk
Website: http://www.vi-spring.co.uk
Bank(s): Royal Bank of Scotland
Directors: J. Johnson (Fin), F. McArthur (Mkt Research), M. Meehan (MD)
Managers: A. Soughcotp (Purch Mgr), P. Tasker (Sales & Mktg Mg), J. Gerety (Sales Prom Mgr), D. Ketley (I.T. Exec), L. Smith (Personnel), M. Tasker (Sales & Mktg Mg), D. Ketley (Tech Serv Mgr)
Ultimate Holding Company: FLEX EQUIPOS DE DESCANSO SA (SPAIN)
Immediate Holding Company: VI - SPRING LIMITED
Registration no: 00071430 **Date established:** 2001
Turnover: £20m - £50m **No.of Employees:** 101 - 250 **Product Groups:** 26

Date of Accounts	Dec 11	Dec 10	Dec 09
Sales Turnover	35m	32m	29m
Pre Tax Profit/Loss	4m	4m	3m
Working Capital	6m	5m	3m
Fixed Assets	2m	2m	2m
Current Assets	13m	12m	10m
Current Liabilities	2m	2m	3m

Voiceovers Ltd
PO Box 326, Plymouth, PL4 9YQ
Tel: 020-7099 2264 **Fax:** 01752-227141
E-mail: info@voiceovers.co.uk
Website: http://www.voiceovers.co.uk
Managers: P. Bridge
Immediate Holding Company: VOICEOVERS LIMITED
Registration no: 05460172 **Date established:** 2005
Turnover: Up to £250,000 **No.of Employees:** 1 - 10 **Product Groups:** 89

Date of Accounts	**May 11**	**May 10**	**May 09**
Working Capital	113	71	43
Fixed Assets	8	9	9
Current Assets	206	148	155

Vortok International
3 Western Wood Way Langage Science Park, Plymouth, PL7 5BG
Tel: 01752-349200 **Fax:** 01752-338855
E-mail: sales@vortok.co.uk
Website: http://www.vortok.co.uk
Directors: P. Shropshall (Dir), P. Shrubsall (MD), P. Shrubsall (Dir & Gen Mgr)
Managers: R. Goldsmith (Buyer)
Ultimate Holding Company: Pandrol International
Immediate Holding Company: Multiclip Ltd
Registration no: 01212929 **Turnover:** £1m - £2m
No.of Employees: 1 - 10 **Product Groups:** 39

W D Tamlyn & Company Ltd
Atlantic Building Queen Anne Battery, Plymouth, PL4 0LP
Tel: 01752-663444 **Fax:** 01752-221979
Website: http://www.wdtamlyn.co.uk
Managers: B. Jones (Mgr)
Immediate Holding Company: LIBERTY YACHTS LTD.
Registration no: 02907786 **VAT No.:** GB 591 5432 31
Date established: 1986 **Turnover:** £250,000 - £500,000
No.of Employees: 1 - 10 **Product Groups:** 74, 76

Date of Accounts	**Nov 11**	**Nov 10**	**Nov 09**
Working Capital	8	2	-6
Fixed Assets	1	4	7
Current Assets	96	37	39

Western Morning News Co. Ltd
17 Brest Road Derriford, Plymouth, PL6 5AA
Tel: 01752-765500 **Fax:** 01752-765515
E-mail: plymouthfrontcounter@westcountrypublications.co.uk
Website: http://www.thisisplymouth.co.uk
Bank(s): National Westminster
Directors: D. Currall (MD), P. Collins (Co Sec)
Managers: R. Woodwood (Mktg Serv Mgr), S. Carpenter (I.T. Exec)
Immediate Holding Company: WESTERN MORNING NEWS & MEDIA LIMITED
Registration no: 00194502 **Date established:** 2023
Turnover: £20m - £50m **No.of Employees:** 251 - 500 **Product Groups:** 28

Date of Accounts	**Sep 07**
Sales Turnover	34790
Pre Tax Profit/Loss	4270
Working Capital	-11070
Fixed Assets	15610
Current Assets	53400
Current Liabilities	64470
Total Share Capital	250
ROCE% (Return on Capital Employed)	94.1

Westwise Manufacturing
Hawthorn House Darklake View, Estover, Plymouth, PL6 7TL
Tel: 01752-695557 **Fax:** 01752-695558
E-mail: info@westwise.co.uk
Website: http://www.westwise.co.uk
Directors: M. Potter (Dir)
Immediate Holding Company: ASTAR FABRICATION (S.W.) LIMITED
Registration no: 06469914 **Date established:** 2008
No.of Employees: 1 - 10 **Product Groups:** 36, 40, 66

Date of Accounts	**Oct 11**	**Jun 11**	**Jun 10**
Working Capital	-12	-9	-29
Fixed Assets	12	47	57
Current Assets	34	51	31

Wilts Wholesale Electrical
513 Lifton Road, Plymouth, PL4 0NT
Tel: 01752-669788 **Fax:** 01752-601386
E-mail: plymouth@wilts.co.uk
Website: http://www.wilts.co.uk
Managers: N. Spencer (Mgr)
Immediate Holding Company: WILTS WHOLESALE ELECTRICAL COMPANY,LIMITED
Registration no: 00679117 **VAT No.:** GB 422 9006 79
Date established: 1960 **Turnover:** Up to £250,000
No.of Employees: 1 - 10 **Product Groups:** 77

Wrigley Co. Ltd
Estover, Plymouth, PL6 7PR
Tel: 01752-701107 **Fax:** 01752-778850
E-mail: ukinfo@wrigley.com
Website: http://www.wrigley.com
Bank(s): National Westminster
Directors: M. Lancaster (Fin)
Managers: G. Chubb, R. Challifour, L. Birch, H. Thomson (Chief Mgr)
Ultimate Holding Company: MARS INC (USA)
Immediate Holding Company: WRIGLEY COMPANY LIMITED(THE)
Registration no: 00210533 **Date established:** 2025
Turnover: £125m - £250m **No.of Employees:** 251 - 500
Product Groups: 20

Date of Accounts	**Dec 11**	**Dec 09**	**Dec 08**
Sales Turnover	194m	189m	199m
Pre Tax Profit/Loss	40m	31m	30m
Working Capital	33m	23m	35m
Fixed Assets	129m	36m	41m
Current Assets	83m	60m	64m
Current Liabilities	18m	12m	14m

Salcombe

S M S Salcombe Ltd
Lincombe Boatyard, Salcombe, TQ8 8NQ
Tel: 01548-843655 **Fax:** 01548-843006
E-mail: info@sm4.co.uk
Website: http://www.sm4.co.uk
Directors: J. Bower (MD), L. Dingley (Fin)
Immediate Holding Company: S.M.S. (SALCOMBE) LIMITED
Registration no: 04558962 **Date established:** 2002
Turnover: £500,000 - £1m **No.of Employees:** 1 - 10 **Product Groups:** 35, 36, 39

Date of Accounts	**Nov 11**	**Nov 10**	**Nov 09**
Sales Turnover	723	700	606
Pre Tax Profit/Loss	14	-12	-5
Working Capital	20	48	64
Fixed Assets	18	19	35
Current Assets	150	144	170
Current Liabilities	13	22	21

Sailing Marine Engineers
Island Street, Salcombe, TQ8 8DP
Tel: 01548-842094 **Fax:** 01548-842094
E-mail: sailing.salcombe@btopenworld.com
Website: http://www.sailingmarine.co.uk
Directors: B. Carter (Prop)
Immediate Holding Company: WOOLSTON MANAGEMENT LIMITED
Registration no: 04211550 **Date established:** 2010
Turnover: Up to £250,000 **No.of Employees:** 1 - 10 **Product Groups:** 35, 36, 39

Date of Accounts	**Aug 11**	**Aug 10**	**Aug 09**
Working Capital	N/A	3	2
Current Assets	N/A	4	3

Seaton

Peco Publications & Publicity Ltd
Underleys Beer, Seaton, EX12 3NA
Tel: 01297-20580 **Fax:** 01297-20229
E-mail: sales.peco@btconnect.com
Website: http://www.peco-uk.com
Directors: C. Pritchard (Ch), D. Peach (Purch)
Managers: J. King (Chief Mgr), S. Haynes (Sales & Mktg Mg)
Ultimate Holding Company: PRITCHARD PATENT PRODUCT COMPANY (2001) LIMITED
Immediate Holding Company: PECO PUBLICATIONS & PUBLICITY,LIMITED
Registration no: 00501541 **Date established:** 1951
Turnover: £250,000 - £500,000 **No.of Employees:** 1 - 10
Product Groups: 28

Date of Accounts	**Apr 11**	**Apr 10**	**Apr 09**
Working Capital	2m	2m	2m
Fixed Assets	18	10	5
Current Assets	2m	2m	2m

Pritchard Patent Product Co. Ltd
Underleys Beer, Seaton, EX12 3NA
Tel: 01297-21542 **Fax:** 01297-20229
Website: http://www.peco-uk.com
Bank(s): Lloyds, Sidmouth
Directors: P. Lawlor (MD)
Ultimate Holding Company: PRITCHARD PATENT PRODUCT COMPANY (2001) LIMITED
Immediate Holding Company: PRITCHARD PATENT PRODUCT CO. LIMITED
Registration no: 00408782 **Date established:** 1946 **Turnover:** £5m - £10m
No.of Employees: 51 - 100 **Product Groups:** 49

Date of Accounts	**Apr 11**	**Apr 10**	**Apr 09**
Sales Turnover	6m	6m	5m
Pre Tax Profit/Loss	508	586	-45
Working Capital	3m	3m	2m
Fixed Assets	2m	2m	2m
Current Assets	4m	4m	3m
Current Liabilities	270	406	200

South Brent

Devon & Cornwall Fire Protection Ltd
2 Church Street, South Brent, TQ10 9AB
Tel: 01364-728220 **Fax:** 01364-728220
E-mail: paul@dcfire.entadsl.com
Website: http://dcfire.co.uk
Directors: J. Bannister (Fin)
Immediate Holding Company: DEVON AND CORNWALL FIRE PROTECTION LTD.
Registration no: 04431013 **Date established:** 2002
Turnover: £250,000 - £500,000 **No.of Employees:** 1 - 10
Product Groups: 32, 40, 67

Date of Accounts	**May 11**	**May 10**	**May 09**
Working Capital	5	8	-2
Fixed Assets	25	14	14
Current Assets	23	27	13
Current Liabilities	N/A	N/A	2

P D Devices Ltd
Unit 1-2 Old Station Yard, South Brent, TQ10 9AL
Tel: 01364-649248 **Fax:** 01364-649250
E-mail: sales@pddevices.co.uk
Website: http://www.pddevices.co.uk
Directors: D. Flower (I.T. Dir), M. Rendell (MD), A. Rendell (Co Sec), J. Rendell (Co Sec)
Managers: T. Kuhl (Tech Serv Mgr)
Immediate Holding Company: PD DEVICES LIMITED
Registration no: 04253515 **Date established:** 2001
No.of Employees: 11 - 20 **Product Groups:** 33, 36, 37, 38, 44, 84

Date of Accounts	**Sep 11**	**Sep 10**	**Sep 09**
Working Capital	30	78	95
Fixed Assets	331	375	351

Current Assets	537	412	340

South Molton

Andrew Symons Ltd
Borners Bridge Works Borners Bridge, South Molton, EX36 3LZ
Tel: 01769-574455 **Fax:** 01769-579100
E-mail: courtney@andrewsymons.co.uk
Website: http://www.andrewsymons.co.uk
Directors: A. Symons (Prop)
Immediate Holding Company: ANDREW SYMONS LIMITED
Registration no: 06180428 **Date established:** 2007
No.of Employees: 11 - 20 **Product Groups:** 41

Date of Accounts	**Mar 11**	**Mar 10**	**Mar 09**
Sales Turnover	9m	9m	N/A
Pre Tax Profit/Loss	203	236	N/A
Working Capital	288	113	-89
Fixed Assets	306	321	384
Current Assets	3m	3m	3m
Current Liabilities	995	433	N/A

Bluemay Weston Ltd
Pathfields Business Park, South Molton, EX36 3LH
Tel: 01769-574574 **Fax:** 01769-572944
E-mail: sales@bluemayweston.co.uk
Website: http://www.bluemayweston.co.uk
Bank(s): Barclays
Managers: P. Hughes (Chief Mgr)
Immediate Holding Company: BLUEMAY WESTON LIMITED
Registration no: 03754478 **Date established:** 1999 **Turnover:** £2m - £5m
No.of Employees: 11 - 20 **Product Groups:** 29, 30

Date of Accounts	**Jun 11**	**Jun 10**	**Jun 09**
Working Capital	119	117	78
Fixed Assets	2m	2m	2m
Current Assets	305	322	265

Norbord Europe Ltd
Hill Village Nadder Lane, South Molton, EX36 4HP
Tel: 01769-572991 **Fax:** 01769-574848
E-mail: sales@norbord.com
Website: http://www.norbord.com
Bank(s): National Westminster
Directors: W. Hovord (MD), D. Wilson (Fin)
Ultimate Holding Company: BROOKFIELD ASSET MANAGEMENT INC (CANADA)
Immediate Holding Company: NORBORD LIMITED
Registration no: 00357722 **VAT No.:** GB 607 3100 85
Date established: 1939 **Turnover:** £125m - £250m
No.of Employees: 251 - 500 **Product Groups:** 25

Date of Accounts	**Dec 11**	**Dec 10**	**Dec 09**
Sales Turnover	251m	190m	180m
Pre Tax Profit/Loss	5m	3m	869
Working Capital	-8m	12m	5m
Fixed Assets	80m	71m	75m
Current Assets	47m	67m	49m
Current Liabilities	24m	27m	22m

Rubber & Plastic Profiles Co. (Bluemay Weston Limited)
High Meadow Pathfields Business Park, South Molton, EX36 3LH
Tel: 01769-574574 **Fax:** 01769-572944
E-mail: sales@bluemayweston.co.uk
Website: http://www.rubberandplasticprofiles.co.uk
Directors: A. Mogg (Grp Chief Exec)
Managers: A. Mogg (Mgr)
Immediate Holding Company: Mogal Properties Ltd
Registration no: 03754478 **Date established:** 1967
Turnover: Up to £250,000 **No.of Employees:** 1 - 10 **Product Groups:** 29, 30

Simmette Ltd
Cooks Cross Horsepond Meadow, South Molton, EX36 4EJ
Tel: 01769-572871 **Fax:** 01769-572871
Bank(s): Barclays, Bristol
Directors: A. Simmons (Fin), N. Simmons (MD)
Immediate Holding Company: SIMMETTE LIMITED
Registration no: 00381721 **VAT No.:** GB 138 2405 81
Date established: 1943 **Turnover:** £1m - £2m **No.of Employees:** 11 - 20
Product Groups: 32, 63

Date of Accounts	**Dec 11**	**Dec 10**	**Dec 09**
Working Capital	77	99	190
Fixed Assets	24	90	92
Current Assets	92	104	194

Tavistock

Antex Electronics Ltd
2 Westbridge Industrial Estate, Tavistock, PL19 8DE
Tel: 01822-613565 **Fax:** 01822-617598
E-mail: sales@antex.co.uk
Website: http://www.antex.co.uk
Bank(s): National Westminster Bank Plc
Directors: A. Owen (MD), I. Lockhart (MD)
Managers: J. Tomkies (Sales Prom Mgr), T. Chilvers (Comptroller)
Immediate Holding Company: ANTEX (ELECTRONICS) LIMITED
Registration no: 04762632 **VAT No.:** GB 339 6099 20
Date established: 2003 **Turnover:** £1m - £2m **No.of Employees:** 21 - 50
Product Groups: 27, 35, 37, 44, 46, 47, 66

Date of Accounts	**Dec 11**	**Dec 10**	**Jun 10**
Sales Turnover	2m	1m	2m
Pre Tax Profit/Loss	-503	13	-9
Working Capital	4	233	216
Fixed Assets	360	666	684
Current Assets	656	871	695
Current Liabilities	319	252	249

Biffa Waste Services Ltd
Haye Down, Tavistock, PL19 0NN
Tel: 01822-860297 **Fax:** 01822-860382
E-mail: tavistock@biffa.co.uk
Website: http://www.biffa.co.uk

see next page

***Biffa Waste Services Ltd** - Cont'd*
Managers: S. Price (Mgr)
Immediate Holding Company: BIFFA WASTE SERVICES LIMITED
Registration no: 00946107 **Date established:** 1969
No.of Employees: 1 - 10 **Product Groups:** 32, 54

Date of Accounts	Mar 08	Mar 09	Apr 10
Sales Turnover	555m	574m	492m
Pre Tax Profit/Loss	23m	50m	30m
Working Capital	229m	271m	293m
Fixed Assets	371m	360m	378m
Current Assets	409m	534m	609m
Current Liabilities	50m	100m	115m

C N C Machinery Ltd
Wilminstone Industrial Estate, Tavistock, PL19 0JP
Tel: 01822-617791 **Fax:** 01822-611137
E-mail: cncmachineryltd@btconnect.com
Website: http://www.cncmachineryltd.co.uk
Directors: D. Hoar (Dir)
Immediate Holding Company: CNC MACHINERY LIMITED
Registration no: 04274703 **Date established:** 2001
Turnover: £250,000 - £500,000 **No.of Employees:** 1 - 10
Product Groups: 20, 40, 41

Date of Accounts	Sep 11	Sep 10	Sep 09
Sales Turnover	N/A	N/A	362
Working Capital	238	238	186
Fixed Assets	25	12	15
Current Assets	358	393	263

Superwinch Ltd
Union Mine Road, Tavistock, PL19 0NS
Tel: 01822-614101 **Fax:** 01822-615204
E-mail: sales@superwinch.net
Website: http://www.superwinch.com
Bank(s): HSBC Bank plc
Directors: L. Blackmore (Dir)
Immediate Holding Company: SUPERWINCH LIMITED
Registration no: 02708737 **VAT No.:** GB 143 5169 75
Date established: 1992 **Turnover:** £5m - £10m **No.of Employees:** 21 - 50
Product Groups: 35, 39, 45

Date of Accounts	Dec 11	Dec 10	Aug 09
Working Capital	883	557	526
Fixed Assets	92	98	127
Current Assets	2m	2m	1m

Teignmouth

P & P Lifts Ltd
Kempston Mill Lane, Teignmouth, TQ14 9BB
Tel: 01626-773761 **Fax:** 01626-773761
E-mail: info@pandplifts.co.uk
Website: http://www.pandplifts.com
Directors: B. Pile (MD)
Immediate Holding Company: P & P LIFTS LIMITED
Registration no: 04446657 **Date established:** 2002
No.of Employees: 1 - 10 **Product Groups:** 35, 39, 45

Date of Accounts	Sep 11	Sep 10	Sep 09
Working Capital	68	42	34
Fixed Assets	52	44	36
Current Assets	119	78	62

Robin Catering Equipment Ltd
19 Lower Brook Street, Teignmouth, TQ14 8HR
Tel: 01626-776465 **Fax:** 01626-773500
Website: http://www.robincateringequipment.com
Directors: S. Newbury (MD)
Immediate Holding Company: ROBIN CATERING EQUIPMENT LIMITED
Registration no: 01162466 **Date established:** 1974
No.of Employees: 1 - 10 **Product Groups:** 20, 40, 41

Date of Accounts	Jul 11	Jul 10	Jul 09
Working Capital	-7	-13	-20
Fixed Assets	2	3	4
Current Assets	28	32	29

Seaworthy Marine
Riverside Bishopsteignton Road, Teignmouth, TQ14 9PH
Tel: 01626-879977 **Fax:** 01626-879977
E-mail: stuart.williams@seaworthymarine.co.uk
Website: http://www.seaworthymarine.co.uk
Directors: S. Williams (Prop)
Date established: 1999 **No.of Employees:** 1 - 10 **Product Groups:** 35, 36, 39

Timberwise UK Ltd
PO Box 65, Teignmouth, TQ14 9WR
Tel: 01626-777595 **Fax:** 01935-814436
E-mail: devon@timberwise.co.uk
Website: http://www.timberwise.co.uk
Ultimate Holding Company: TIMBERWISE HOLDINGS LIMITED
Immediate Holding Company: TIMBERWISE (UK) LIMITED
Registration no: 03230356 **Date established:** 1996
No.of Employees: 1 - 10 **Product Groups:** 07, 32, 52

Date of Accounts	Dec 11	Dec 10	Dec 09
Sales Turnover	N/A	N/A	5m
Pre Tax Profit/Loss	N/A	N/A	214
Working Capital	397	343	326
Fixed Assets	265	291	301
Current Assets	1m	1m	1m
Current Liabilities	N/A	N/A	585

Wilson Services
Unit 2 Broadmeadow Indl-Est, Teignmouth, TQ14 9AE
Tel: 01626-775794 **Fax:** 01626- 775794
Directors: G. Wilson (Prop)
Date established: 1985 **No.of Employees:** 1 - 10 **Product Groups:** 26, 35

Yacht Electrical Services
4 Higher Yannon Drive, Teignmouth, TQ14 9JQ
Tel: 01626-870167
E-mail: service@yachtelectricalservices.co.uk
Website: http://yachtelectricalservices.co.uk
No.of Employees: 1 - 10 **Product Groups:** 37, 38, 39, 67, 84

Tiverton

Bush & Wilton Ltd
Unit 1 Millennium Place, Tiverton, EX16 6SB
Tel: 01884-242233 **Fax:** 01884-252555
E-mail: sales@bushandwilton.com
Website: http://www.bushandwilton.com
Directors: S. Swales (Fin)
Ultimate Holding Company: ROTOLOK (HOLDINGS) LIMITED
Immediate Holding Company: BUSH & WILTON LIMITED
Registration no: 04142146 **Date established:** 2001 **Turnover:** £1m - £2m
No.of Employees: 1 - 10 **Product Groups:** 36

Date of Accounts	May 11	May 10	May 09
Working Capital	87	75	88
Current Assets	233	191	151

Fraser Anti Static Techniques Ltd
Scotts Business Park Woodland Close, Bampton, Tiverton, EX16 9DN
Tel: 01398-331114 **Fax:** 01398-331411
E-mail: sales@fraser-antistatic.co.uk
Website: http://www.fraser-antistatic.co.uk
Bank(s): Barclays
Directors: R. Fraser (Dir)
Managers: S. Robinson (Ops Mgr), L. Harvey
Immediate Holding Company: FRASER ANTI-STATIC TECHNIQUES LIMITED
Registration no: 02642741 **VAT No.:** GB 586 0698 92
Date established: 1991 **Turnover:** £2m - £5m **No.of Employees:** 11 - 20
Product Groups: 30

Date of Accounts	Nov 11	Nov 10	Nov 09
Working Capital	337	275	136
Fixed Assets	648	465	442
Current Assets	707	663	388

Heathcoat Fabrics Ltd
Westexe, Tiverton, EX16 5LL
Tel: 01884-254949 **Fax:** 01884-252897
E-mail: cameron@heathcoat.co.uk
Website: http://www.heathcoat.co.uk
Bank(s): National Westminster Bank Plc
Directors: S. Waddington (Fin), C. Harvie (MD), A. Cockram (MD), J. Hayman (Co Sec)
Managers: A. Govey, P. Hill, R. Frost (Buyer), A. Cockram
Immediate Holding Company: HEATHCOAT FABRICS LIMITED
Registration no: 00450787 **Date established:** 1948
Turnover: £20m - £50m **No.of Employees:** 251 - 500
Product Groups: 23, 24

Date of Accounts	May 11	May 10	May 09
Sales Turnover	46m	38m	33m
Pre Tax Profit/Loss	2m	1m	1m
Working Capital	16m	15m	15m
Fixed Assets	6m	6m	6m
Current Assets	25m	21m	19m
Current Liabilities	3m	1m	926

Hepco Motion
Lowermoor Business Park Tiverton Way, Tiverton, EX16 6TG
Tel: 01884-243400 **Fax:** 01884-243399
E-mail: enquiries@hepco.co.uk
Website: http://www.hepcomotion.com
Bank(s): Barclays
Directors: A. Gordon (Co Sec)
Managers: K. Barber (Cust Serv Mgr), S. Hudd (Purch Mgr), H. O'Leary (Tech Serv Mgr), A. Blackmore (Sales Admin)
Immediate Holding Company: HEPCO (HOLDINGS) LIMITED
Registration no: 02422332 **VAT No.:** GB 634 6073 44
Date established: 1989 **Turnover:** £20m - £50m
No.of Employees: 251 - 500 **Product Groups:** 45, 46

Date of Accounts	Dec 11	Dec 10	Dec 09
Sales Turnover	24m	20m	17m
Pre Tax Profit/Loss	3m	3m	396
Working Capital	16m	15m	13m
Fixed Assets	11m	10m	11m
Current Assets	22m	20m	17m
Current Liabilities	2m	1m	722

Kaba Ltd Head Office
Lower Moor Way Tiverton Industrial Estate, Tiverton, EX16 6SS
Tel: 08700-005625 **Fax:** 01884-234415
E-mail: info@kaba.co.uk
Website: http://www.kaba.co.uk
Bank(s): National Westminster Bank Plc
Directors: W. Gillies (Fin), H. Anoyrkatis (Fin)
Managers: N. Head (Tech Serv Mgr), P. Humphries (Purch Mgr), P. Spencer, P. Prior (Sales Off Mgr), S. Childs (Personnel)
Ultimate Holding Company: KABA HOLDING AG (SWITZERLAND)
Immediate Holding Company: KABA LIMITED
Registration no: 03792985 **Date established:** 1999
Turnover: £10m - £20m **No.of Employees:** 101 - 250
Product Groups: 34, 35, 36, 37, 39, 40, 44, 52, 66, 81, 84, 86

Date of Accounts	Jun 11	Jun 10	Jun 09
Sales Turnover	16m	14m	15m
Pre Tax Profit/Loss	371	-283	569
Working Capital	5m	4m	4m
Fixed Assets	2m	2m	2m
Current Assets	7m	6m	7m
Current Liabilities	1m	1m	990

Kap Engineering & Fabrication
4 Gooding Rise, Tiverton, EX16 5BX
Tel: 01884-259951
E-mail: info@kap-engineering.co.uk
Website: http://www.kap-engineering.co.uk
Directors: P. Smith (Prop)
Immediate Holding Company: KAP ENGINEERING & FABRICATION LIMITED
Registration no: 07315410 **Date established:** 2010
No.of Employees: 1 - 10 **Product Groups:** 35

Date of Accounts	Jul 11
Working Capital	-6
Fixed Assets	10
Current Assets	12

Norfloat International Ltd
Unit 3a Woodlands Business Park Burlescombe, Tiverton, EX16 7LL
Tel: 01823-672772 **Fax:** 01823-672773
E-mail: info@norfloat.com
Website: http://www.norfloat.com
Directors: R. Owen (Fin)
Ultimate Holding Company: INTERNATIONAL MARINE HOLDINGS LIMITED
Immediate Holding Company: NORFLOAT INTERNATIONAL LIMITED
Registration no: 04654964 **Date established:** 2003 **Turnover:** £1m - £2m
No.of Employees: 1 - 10 **Product Groups:** 25, 30, 35, 37, 39, 67

Date of Accounts	Sep 11	Sep 10	Sep 09
Working Capital	-231	-152	-105
Current Assets	128	126	106

Original Forgery Ltd
Lodfin Farm Morebath, Tiverton, EX16 9DD
Tel: 01398-331400 **Fax:** 01398-331400
E-mail: info@originalforgery.co.uk
Website: http://www.originalforgery.co.uk
Directors: E. Goodwin (Fin), J. Goodwin (MD)
Immediate Holding Company: ORIGINAL FORGERY LIMITED
Registration no: 04305653 **Date established:** 2001
Turnover: Up to £250,000 **No.of Employees:** 1 - 10 **Product Groups:** 26, 35

Date of Accounts	Dec 11	Dec 10	Dec 09
Working Capital	14	2	-3
Fixed Assets	23	31	35
Current Assets	39	28	26

Oyster Assets
Lower Bradley Withleigh, Tiverton, EX16 8LA
Tel: 01884-255150 **Fax:** 01884-255080
E-mail: brokers@oysterassets.com
Website: http://www.oysterassets.com
Directors: K. Keane (Fin)
Immediate Holding Company: KEANE OFFSHORE LIMITED
Registration no: 6122729 **Date established:** 2000
Turnover: Up to £250,000 **No.of Employees:** 1 - 10 **Product Groups:** 42, 67, 74

B G Phillips
Prospect Cottage Rackenford, Tiverton, EX16 8DS
Tel: 07710-850220 **Fax:** 01884-881512
Directors: B. Phillips (Prop)
Date established: 1990 **No.of Employees:** 1 - 10 **Product Groups:** 41

Stags
19 Bampton Street, Tiverton, EX16 6AA
Tel: 01884-256331 **Fax:** 01884-258401
E-mail: tiverton@stags.co.uk
Website: http://www.stags.co.uk
Bank(s): HSBC
Directors: J. Seaner (Snr Part)
Date established: 1899 **No.of Employees:** 21 - 50 **Product Groups:** 80

Twose of Tiverton Ltd
6 Chinon Court Lower Moor Way, Tiverton, EX16 6SS
Tel: 01884-253691 **Fax:** 01884-255189
E-mail: tcoleridge@twose.com
Website: http://www.twose.com
Managers: T. Coleridge
Ultimate Holding Company: ALAMO GROUP INC (USA)
Immediate Holding Company: TWOSE OF TIVERTON LIMITED
Registration no: 02258559 **VAT No.:** GB 133 8747 53
Date established: 1988 **Turnover:** £2m - £5m **No.of Employees:** 1 - 10
Product Groups: 41

Date of Accounts	Dec 11	Dec 10	Dec 09
Sales Turnover	5m	4m	4m
Pre Tax Profit/Loss	507	514	545
Working Capital	3m	2m	2m
Fixed Assets	118	118	119
Current Assets	3m	3m	2m
Current Liabilities	302	238	264

X Y Z Machine Tools Ltd
Woodlands Business Park Burlescombe, Tiverton, EX16 7LL
Tel: 01823-674200 **Fax:** 07000-999584
E-mail: sales@xyzmachinetools.com
Website: http://www.xyzmachinetools.com
Bank(s): Royal Bank of Scotland
Directors: N. Atherton (Dir)
Managers: G. Harris (Fin Mgr), J. Sanders (Sales & Mktg Mg)
Immediate Holding Company: XYZ MACHINE TOOLS LIMITED
Registration no: 01765883 **Date established:** 1983
Turnover: £10m - £20m **No.of Employees:** 21 - 50 **Product Groups:** 36, 47

Date of Accounts	Apr 11	Apr 10	Apr 09
Sales Turnover	16m	10m	17m
Pre Tax Profit/Loss	3m	2m	3m
Working Capital	11m	9m	9m
Fixed Assets	3m	3m	3m
Current Assets	13m	11m	10m
Current Liabilities	1m	547	755

Torquay

A & J Audio
61 Warbro Road, Torquay, TQ1 3PP
Tel: 01803-324589 **Fax:** 01803- 324589
E-mail: sales@ajaudio.co.uk
Website: http://www.ajaudio.co.uk
Directors: A. Mathew (Prop)
Turnover: Up to £250,000 **No.of Employees:** 1 - 10 **Product Groups:** 38, 81, 83

Ace Repairs
47 Teignmouth Road, Torquay, TQ1 4EG
Tel: 01803-311775 **Fax:** 01803-311775
Directors: R. Messer (Prop)
Date established: 1998 **No.of Employees:** 1 - 10 **Product Groups:** 20, 40, 41

Applestone Music & Sound Ltd
197 Union Street, Torquay, TQ1 4BY
Tel: 01803-297297 **Fax:** 01803-297297
E-mail: admin@theacademy.uk.com
Website: http://www.theacademy.uk.com
Directors: C. McGugan (MD)
Immediate Holding Company: ESCAPE ARTISTS LIMITED
Registration no: 04598685 **Date established:** 2002
Turnover: Up to £250,000 **No.of Employees:** 1 - 10 **Product Groups:** 49, 61, 89

Date of Accounts	Mar 11	Mar 10	Mar 09
Working Capital	-92	-98	-99
Fixed Assets	74	82	91
Current Assets	4	7	6

Automatic Gate Co.
Woodland Business Park Woodland Road, Torquay, TQ2 7AT
Tel: 01803-616858 **Fax:** 01803-616187
Website: http://www.hewettelectrical.co.uk
Directors: J. Hewett (Prop)
Immediate Holding Company: BCS COMPUTERS LIMITED
Registration no: 03139144 **Date established:** 1995
No.of Employees: 1 - 10 **Product Groups:** 36, 40

Date of Accounts	Apr 11	Apr 10	Apr 09
Working Capital	147	113	91
Fixed Assets	1	N/A	N/A
Current Assets	214	193	169

B N A British Nursing Association
Tor Lodge 15 Park Hill Road, Torquay, TQ1 2AL
Tel: 08718-733324 **Fax:** 01803-299161
E-mail: info@bna.co.uk
Website: http://www.bna.co.uk
Managers: J. Cousins (District Mgr)
Ultimate Holding Company: A24 GROUP LIMITED
Immediate Holding Company: THE NURSING SERVICES OF THE UK LIMITED
Registration no: 06038061 **VAT No.:** GB 235 4135 84
Date established: 2006 **Turnover:** £2m - £5m **No.of Employees:** 1 - 10
Product Groups: 80

Bay Tool & Equipment Services
121 Teignmouth Road, Torquay, TQ1 4HA
Tel: 01803-311177 **Fax:** 01803-311177
E-mail: steve@baytools.co.uk
Directors: S. Harrison (Prop)
Immediate Holding Company: REMI LIMITED
Registration no: 03073492 **Date established:** 2012
No.of Employees: 1 - 10 **Product Groups:** 37

Date of Accounts	Mar 11	Mar 10	Mar 09
Working Capital	3	3	-792
Fixed Assets	N/A	N/A	619
Current Assets	3	3	42

Blinding Ideas
Lansdowne Lane, Torquay, TQ2 5BS
Tel: 01803-299880 **Fax:** 01803-299880
E-mail: fran_kim@feaves.freeserve.co.uk
Website: http://www.blindingideas.co.uk
Directors: F. Eaves (Prop)
Immediate Holding Company: BLINDING IDEAS INTERIORS
Turnover: Up to £250,000 **No.of Employees:** 1 - 10 **Product Groups:** 23, 24, 30, 63, 66

D S Safety
123 St Marychurch Road, Torquay, TQ1 3HL
Tel: 01803-327543 **Fax:** 08450-941229
E-mail: sales@dssafety.co.uk
Website: http://www.dssafety.co.uk
Directors: P. Nixon (Dir)
Registration no: 02137733 **Date established:** 1987
No.of Employees: 1 - 10 **Product Groups:** 22

Edmundson Electrical Ltd
Unit D Broomhill Way Industrial Estate, Torquay, TQ2 7QL
Tel: 01803-616372 **Fax:** 01803-616377
E-mail: torquay.227@eel.co.uk
Website: http://www.edmundson-electrical.co.uk/
Managers: S. Lovegrove (District Mgr)
Ultimate Holding Company: BLACKFRIARS CORP (USA)
Immediate Holding Company: EDMUNDSON ELECTRICAL LIMITED
Registration no: 02667012 **VAT No.:** GB 579 9948 39
Date established: 1991 **No.of Employees:** 1 - 10 **Product Groups:** 67

Date of Accounts	Dec 11	Dec 10	Dec 09
Sales Turnover	1023m	852m	788m
Pre Tax Profit/Loss	57m	53m	45m
Working Capital	256m	225m	184m
Fixed Assets	17m	3m	4m
Current Assets	439m	358m	298m
Current Liabilities	59m	38m	37m

Emmerson Ross Recruitment
The White House Broomhill Way, Torquay, TQ2 7QL
Tel: 01803-618888 **Fax:** 01803-618889
E-mail: jobs@erjobs.co.uk
Website: http://www.erjobs.co.uk
Directors: G. Ross (Prop)
Immediate Holding Company: CHELSTON ELECTRICAL SERVICES LIMITED
Registration no: 04988528 **Date established:** 2003
Turnover: Up to £250,000 **No.of Employees:** 1 - 10 **Product Groups:** 80

Date of Accounts	Jun 11	Jun 10	Jun 09
Working Capital	99	80	56
Fixed Assets	91	97	106
Current Assets	195	162	145

Jewson Ltd
Lymington Road, Torquay, TQ1 4AS
Tel: 01803-314100 **Fax:** 01803-322472
Website: http://www.jewson.co.uk
Managers: D. Bailey (District Mgr)
Ultimate Holding Company: COMPAGNIE DE SAINT GOBAIN (FRANCE)
Immediate Holding Company: JEWSON LIMITED
Registration no: 00348407 **Date established:** 1939
Turnover: Over £1,000m **No.of Employees:** 11 - 20 **Product Groups:** 66

Date of Accounts	Dec 11	Dec 10	Dec 09
Sales Turnover	1606m	1547m	1485m
Pre Tax Profit/Loss	18m	100m	45m
Working Capital	-345m	-250m	-349m
Fixed Assets	496m	387m	461m
Current Assets	657m	1005m	1320m
Current Liabilities	66m	120m	64m

Meditech 2000 Ltd
98a Union Street, Torquay, TQ2 5PY
Tel: 01803-290566 **Fax:** 01803- 290560
Directors: S. Austin (MD)
No.of Employees: 11 - 20 **Product Groups:** 38, 42

MILK & TWO Graphic Design
15 Lower Thurlow Road, Torquay, TQ1 3EL
Tel: 01803-326648
E-mail: hello@milkand2.co.uk
Website: http://www.milkand2.co.uk
Directors: M. McCully (MD)
Date established: 2004 **Turnover:** £250,000 - £500,000
No.of Employees: 1 - 10 **Product Groups:** 81

Mill Auto Supplies
Unit 1-2-3 Minerva Court Woodland Close, Torquay, TQ2 7BD
Tel: 01803-613063 **Fax:** 01803-618119
Website: http://www.autoquipgroup.co.uk
Bank(s): National Westminster Bank Plc
Managers: D. Mcmahon (District Mgr)
Immediate Holding Company: DAVIS MANAGEMENT LIMITED
Registration no: 01866386 **VAT No.:** GB 418 1682 50
Date established: 2011 **No.of Employees:** 21 - 50 **Product Groups:** 68

The Pension Drawdown Company
Highfield Middle Warberry Road, Torquay, TQ1 1RS
Tel: 01803-211214 **Fax:** 01803-293443
E-mail: info@pension-drawdown.co.uk
Website: http://www.pension-drawdown.co.uk
Directors: J. Walker (MD)
Registration no: 04483515 **Date established:** 2002
No.of Employees: 1 - 10 **Product Groups:** 82

Powercraft Engineering
3-5 Walnut Road, Torquay, TQ2 6QG
Tel: 07780-636751 **Fax:** 01803-556930
E-mail: info@powercraftengineering.com
Website: http://www.powercraftengineering.com
Directors: A. Weller (Prop), C. Watson (Ch & MD), M. Watson (MD)
No.of Employees: 1 - 10 **Product Groups:** 34, 39, 68

Sabre Leisure
Home Orchard Brim Hill, Maidencombe, Torquay, TQ1 4TR
Tel: 01803-316655
Directors: N. Davis (Prop)
Immediate Holding Company: SABRE LEISURE LTD
Registration no: 06721362 **Turnover:** Up to £250,000
No.of Employees: 1 - 10 **Product Groups:** 30, 32, 33, 40

Stephen P Wales Ltd
The Old Brewery Works Lower Ellacombe Church Road, Torquay, TQ1 1JH
Tel: 01803-295430 **Fax:** 01803-212819
E-mail: sales@stephenpwales.co.uk
Website: http://www.stephenpwales.co.uk
Directors: S. Wales (Prop)
Immediate Holding Company: STEPHEN P. WALES LIMITED
Registration no: 05383565 **Date established:** 2005
No.of Employees: 1 - 10 **Product Groups:** 35, 36, 37, 38, 67

Date of Accounts	Mar 11	Mar 10	Mar 09
Working Capital	364	315	254
Fixed Assets	21	19	19
Current Assets	485	405	371

Taylor Made Gates
8 Coventry Farm Newton Road, Torquay, TQ2 7HX
Tel: 01803-875084
Directors: M. Lange (Prop)
Date established: 1995 **No.of Employees:** 1 - 10 **Product Groups:** 26, 35

Thaistyle Apparel Ltd
Ground Floor 23 Fleet Street, Torquay, TQ1 1DB
Tel: 01803-898333 **Fax:** 0845-226 9949
E-mail: bluesarong@gmail.com
Website: http://www.thaistyle.co.uk
Directors: A. Matthews (Ptnr)
Immediate Holding Company: THAISTYLE APPAREL LIMITED
Registration no: 06019029 **Date established:** 2006
No.of Employees: 1 - 10 **Product Groups:** 23, 24, 63

Date of Accounts	Dec 11	Dec 10	Dec 09
Working Capital	13	12	10
Fixed Assets	7	12	17
Current Assets	14	13	11

Tool & Fixing Centre
Tormohun House Barton Hill Road, Torquay, TQ2 8JJ
Tel: 01803-324095 **Fax:** 01803-324095
E-mail: sales@toolandfixingcentre.co.uk
Website: http://www.toolandfixingcentre.co.uk
Directors: C. Thompson (MD)
Date established: 1980 **No.of Employees:** 1 - 10 **Product Groups:** 37

Typing Solutions
8 Camden Road, Torquay, TQ1 1NZ
Tel: 01803-392653
E-mail: enquiries@typingsolutions.org.uk
Website: http://www.typingsolutions.org.uk
Directors: L. Sheppard (Prop)
Date established: 2006 **No.of Employees:** 1 - 10 **Product Groups:** 80

Torrington

Alco Engineering Company Sheet Metal Ltd
High Bullen, Torrington, EX38 7JA
Tel: 01805-622461 **Fax:** 01805-624011
E-mail: sales@alcoeng.co.uk
Website: http://www.alcoeng.co.uk
Directors: S. Cooke (MD)
Immediate Holding Company: ALCO ENGINEERING COMPANY (SHEET METAL) LIMITED
Registration no: 00697425 **VAT No.:** GB 144 3387 69
Date established: 1961 **Turnover:** £500,000 - £1m
No.of Employees: 1 - 10 **Product Groups:** 48

Date of Accounts	Dec 11	Dec 10	Dec 09
Working Capital	34	44	5
Fixed Assets	274	228	224
Current Assets	169	173	134

Dartington Crystal Ltd (a division of Enesco Ltd)
Linden Close, Torrington, EX38 7AN
Tel: 01805-626244 **Fax:** 01805-626263
E-mail: enquiries@dartington.co.uk
Website: http://www.dartington.co.uk
Directors: N. Hughes (MD)
Immediate Holding Company: DARTINGTON CRYSTAL LIMITED
Registration no: 07049952 **VAT No.:** GB 631 2845 55
Date established: 2009 **Turnover:** £5m - £10m **No.of Employees:** 1 - 10
Product Groups: 33

Plaster Craft Interiors
1a Hoopers Way, Torrington, EX38 7NS
Tel: 01805-623235
E-mail: mail@plastercraftinteriors.co.uk
Website: http://www.plastercraftinteriors.co.uk
Directors: D. arkell (Prop)
Date established: 1991 **Turnover:** Up to £250,000
No.of Employees: 1 - 10 **Product Groups:** 45

R W Simon Ltd
Hatchmoor Industrial Estate, Torrington, EX38 7HP
Tel: 01805-623721 **Fax:** 01805-624578
E-mail: info@rwsimon.co.uk
Website: http://www.rwsimon.co.uk
Bank(s): Lloyds TSB Bank plc
Directors: T. Hitchins (Co Sec), H. Woolley (Dir)
Immediate Holding Company: R.W.SIMON LIMITED
Registration no: 00615240 **VAT No.:** GB 231 4161 10
Date established: 1958 **Turnover:** £5m - £10m
No.of Employees: 51 - 100 **Product Groups:** 30, 40

Date of Accounts	Mar 11	Mar 10	Mar 09
Sales Turnover	6m	5m	N/A
Pre Tax Profit/Loss	156	-54	18
Working Capital	2m	2m	2m
Fixed Assets	983	968	1m
Current Assets	3m	3m	2m
Current Liabilities	364	369	340

C F Smithers
31 Fore Street Langtree, Torrington, EX38 8NG
Tel: 01805-601297 **Fax:** 01805-601297
Directors: C. Smithy (Prop)
Date established: 1983 **No.of Employees:** 1 - 10 **Product Groups:** 46

Travis Perkins plc
Stibb Cross, Torrington, EX38 8LJ
Tel: 01805-601204 **Fax:** 01805-601561
E-mail: torrington@travisperkins.co.uk
Website: http://www.travisperkins.co.uk
Managers: P. Flinn (District Mgr)
Immediate Holding Company: TRAVIS PERKINS PLC
Registration no: 00824821 **VAT No.:** 143 9200 87 **Date established:** 1964
Turnover: £2m - £5m **No.of Employees:** 1 - 10 **Product Groups:** 66

Date of Accounts	Dec 11	Dec 10	Dec 09
Sales Turnover	4779m	3153m	2931m
Pre Tax Profit/Loss	270m	197m	213m
Working Capital	133m	159m	248m
Fixed Assets	2771m	2749m	2108m
Current Assets	1421m	1329m	1035m
Current Liabilities	473m	412m	109m

Totnes

Nick Allday
Broadley Works Stoke Gabriel, Totnes, TQ9 6PU
Tel: 01803-782742 **Fax:** 01803-782742
E-mail: nick@nickallday.plus.com
Website: http://www.nickallday.plus.com
Directors: N. Allday (Prop)
Date established: 1998 **No.of Employees:** 1 - 10 **Product Groups:** 41

Andrews & Hughes
Bridge Farm Harberton, Totnes, TQ9 7PP
Tel: 01803-867105
Directors: G. Hughes (Ptnr)
Date established: 1997 **No.of Employees:** 1 - 10 **Product Groups:** 35

Association Of Professional Recording Services Ltd
PO Box 22, Totnes, TQ9 7YZ
Tel: 01803-868600 **Fax:** 01803-868444
E-mail: sales@atrs.co.uk
Website: http://www.atrs.co.uk
Directors: D. Harries (I.T. Dir)
Managers: F. Smith
Immediate Holding Company: THE ASSOCIATION OF PROFESSIONAL RECORDING SERVICES LIMITED

see next page

Association Of Professional Recording Services Ltd - Cont'd

Registration no: 00502532 **VAT No.:** GB 196 5406 34
Date established: 1951 **Turnover:** Up to £250,000
No.of Employees: 1 - 10 **Product Groups:** 37, 79, 87, 89

Date of Accounts	Dec 11	Dec 10	Dec 09
Sales Turnover	N/A	49	67
Pre Tax Profit/Loss	N/A	-3	1
Working Capital	-1	2	5
Fixed Assets	N/A	N/A	1
Current Assets	24	15	20
Current Liabilities	N/A	12	15

Baltic Wharf Boatyard Ltd

Baltic Wharf Business Centre St Peters Quay, Totnes, TQ9 5EW
Tel: 01803-867922 **Fax:** 01803-866795
E-mail: enquiries@balticwharf.co.uk
Website: http://www.balticwharf.co.uk
Bank(s): Lloyds TSB
Directors: I. Dennis (MD)
Managers: P. Simms (Comptroller), S. Wharton
Immediate Holding Company: BALTIC WHARF LIMITED
Registration no: 05887604 **VAT No.:** GB 631 2050 94
Date established: 2006 **Turnover:** Up to £250,000
No.of Employees: 11 - 20 **Product Groups:** 39, 80

Date of Accounts	Aug 11	Aug 10	Aug 09
Working Capital	-579	-628	-707
Fixed Assets	789	875	945
Current Assets	129	219	635

Clayton Munroe

2b Burke Road, Totnes, TQ9 5XL
Tel: 01803-865700 **Fax:** 01803-840720
E-mail: sales@claytonmunroe.com
Website: http://www.claytonmunroe.com
Directors: S. Hagger (Sales)
Immediate Holding Company: CLAYTON-MUNROE LIMITED
Registration no: 01814914 **Date established:** 1984
Turnover: Over £1,000m **No.of Employees:** 1 - 10 **Product Groups:** 36

Date of Accounts	Dec 11	Dec 10	Dec 09
Working Capital	184	41	32
Fixed Assets	8	10	10
Current Assets	332	345	348

Daco Engineering

5 Wills Road, Totnes, TQ9 5XN
Tel: 01803-864079 **Fax:** 01803-864919
Directors: A. Cox (Prop)
Date established: 1980 **No.of Employees:** 1 - 10 **Product Groups:** 35, 38, 42

Exact Engineering Ltd

1-4 Burke Road, Totnes, TQ9 5XL
Tel: 01803-866464 **Fax:** 01803-866385
E-mail: sales@exact-eng.co.uk
Website: http://www.exact-eng.co.uk
Bank(s): HSBC
Directors: B. Floyd (Co Sec), J. Vincent (MD)
Managers: I. Grout (Sales Prom Mgr)
Immediate Holding Company: EXACT ENGINEERING (HOSE & FITTINGS) COMPANY LIMITED
Registration no: 03068520 **Date established:** 1995
Turnover: Up to £250,000 **No.of Employees:** 21 - 50 **Product Groups:** 29, 30

Foundry Fabrications Totnes Ltd

Foundry Fabrication Totne Babbage Road, Totnes, TQ9 5JD
Tel: 01803-869400 **Fax:** 01803-869410
E-mail: darren@foundryfabrication.co.uk
Website: http://www.foundryfabrication.co.uk
Bank(s): HSBC Bank plc
Directors: M. Francis (MD), D. Francis (MD)
Managers: D. Francis, G. Sewell
Immediate Holding Company: FOUNDRY & FABRICATION (TOTNES) LIMITED
Registration no: 00736055 **Date established:** 1962 **Turnover:** £2m - £5m
No.of Employees: 51 - 100 **Product Groups:** 34, 48

Graphic Controls

St Peters Quay, Totnes, TQ9 5XH
Tel: 01803-860100 **Fax:** 01803-863838
E-mail: tslatter@graphiccontrols.com
Website: http://www.graphiccontrols.co.uk
Directors: T. Slatter (Fin)
Managers: P. Goss, M. Hunt (Buyer)
Ultimate Holding Company: GRAPHIC CONTROLS HOLDINGS INC (UNITED STATES)
Immediate Holding Company: GRAPHIC CONTROLS LTD
Registration no: 05999241 **VAT No.:** GB 141 2252 18
Date established: 2006 **Turnover:** £2m - £5m **No.of Employees:** 21 - 50
Product Groups: 27, 38, 44

Date of Accounts	Dec 11	Dec 10	Dec 09
Working Capital	-2m	494	370
Fixed Assets	3m	1m	1m
Current Assets	7m	2m	1m

Ron Greet

Bickaton Broadhempston, Totnes, TQ9 6BY
Tel: 01803-812269 **Fax:** 01803-813613
E-mail: info@rongreet.co.uk
Website: http://www.rongreet.co.uk
Directors: R. Greet (Prop)
Immediate Holding Company: CENTRAL CITY SOFTWARE LIMITED
Registration no: 04876054 **Date established:** 1996
No.of Employees: 1 - 10 **Product Groups:** 41

Date of Accounts	Sep 11	Sep 10	Sep 09
Working Capital	2	2	2
Current Assets	3	4	6

Isotemp Ltd

2b Burke Road, Totnes, TQ9 5XL
Tel: 01803-840405 **Fax:** 01803- 840407
E-mail: isotempsw@isotemp.co.uk
Website: http://www.isotemp.co.uk
Managers: J. Nixon (Mgr)
No.of Employees: 1 - 10 **Product Groups:** 35, 38, 40

Jewson Ltd

Babbage Road, Totnes, TQ9 5JA
Tel: 01803-863881 **Fax:** 01803-866426
Website: http://www.jewson.co.uk
Managers: S. McKinnell (Mgr)
Ultimate Holding Company: COMPAGNIE DE SAINT GOBAIN (FRANCE)
Immediate Holding Company: JEWSON LIMITED
Registration no: 00348407 **Date established:** 1939
No.of Employees: 11 - 20 **Product Groups:** 66

Date of Accounts	Dec 11	Dec 10	Dec 09
Sales Turnover	1606m	1547m	1485m
Pre Tax Profit/Loss	18m	100m	45m
Working Capital	-345m	-250m	-349m
Fixed Assets	496m	387m	461m
Current Assets	657m	1005m	1320m
Current Liabilities	66m	120m	64m

R Soper & Sons

Pandora Dartmouth Road, East Allington, Totnes, TQ9 7QX
Tel: 01548-521222 **Fax:** 01548-521415
E-mail: terry.soper@btconnect.com
Directors: C. Soper (Ptnr)
Date established: 1969 **No.of Employees:** 1 - 10 **Product Groups:** 41

Specialty Fasteners & Components Ltd

Seymour Wharf Steamer Quay Road, Totnes, TQ9 5AL
Tel: 01803-868677 **Fax:** 01803-868678
E-mail: sales@specialty-fasteners.co.uk
Website: http://www.specialty-fasteners.co.uk
Directors: P. Boote (MD)
Immediate Holding Company: SPECIALTY FASTENERS AND COMPONENTS LIMITED
Registration no: 02666902 **Date established:** 1991 **Turnover:** £2m - £5m
No.of Employees: 11 - 20 **Product Groups:** 29, 30, 35, 36, 39, 66

Date of Accounts	Dec 11	Dec 10	Dec 09
Working Capital	919	740	561
Fixed Assets	163	191	194
Current Assets	2m	2m	2m

Tideford Organic Foods Ltd

5 The Alpha Centre Babbage Road, Totnes, TQ9 5JA
Tel: 01803-840555 **Fax:** 01803-840551
E-mail: tideford@btconnect.com
Website: http://www.tidefordorganics.com
Directors: L. Sinclaire (MD), L. Sinclair (MD)
Managers: P. Camden-woodley
Immediate Holding Company: TIDEFORD ORGANIC FOODS LIMITED
Registration no: 03279974 **Date established:** 1996 **Turnover:** £1m - £2m
No.of Employees: 11 - 20 **Product Groups:** 62

Date of Accounts	Mar 12	Mar 11	Mar 10
Working Capital	-21	-111	-119
Fixed Assets	93	106	129
Current Assets	155	119	108

UK Sire Services Ltd

Venton Stud Dartington, Totnes, TQ9 6DP
Tel: 01803-863560 **Fax:** 01803-863560
E-mail: geoff.corke@uksireservices.com
Website: http://www.uksireservices.com
Directors: G. Corke (Fin)
Immediate Holding Company: UK SIRE SERVICES LIMITED
Registration no: 04313671 **Date established:** 2001
Turnover: £250,000 - £500,000 **No.of Employees:** 1 - 10
Product Groups: 01

Date of Accounts	Mar 12	Mar 11	Mar 10
Working Capital	-125	-148	-233
Fixed Assets	39	24	35
Current Assets	324	274	216

Valeport Ltd

St. Peters Quay, Totnes, TQ9 5EW
Tel: 01803-869292 **Fax:** 01803-869293
E-mail: sales@valeport.co.uk
Website: http://www.valeport.co.uk
Bank(s): HSBC Bank plc
Directors: M. Quartley (MD)
Managers: K. Edwards (Sales Prom Mgr), T. Cole (Purch Mgr)
Registration no: 01950444 **VAT No.:** GB 430 4453 84
Date established: 1969 **Turnover:** £2m - £5m **No.of Employees:** 21 - 50
Product Groups: 37, 38, 39, 42, 67

Date of Accounts	Nov 11	Nov 10	Nov 09
Working Capital	3m	2m	2m
Fixed Assets	1m	1m	1m
Current Assets	5m	3m	3m

W B Muddeman & Son Ltd

The Scope Complex Wills Road, Totnes, TQ9 5XN
Tel: 01803-862058 **Fax:** 01803-866273
E-mail: su4555@eclipse.co.uk
Website: http://www.muddemans.com
Directors: R. Muddeman (MD), F. Muddeman (MD)
Immediate Holding Company: W.B. Muddeman & Son Ltd
Registration no: 00443045 **VAT No.:** 141 2417 12 **Date established:** 1947
Turnover: £250,000 - £500,000 **No.of Employees:** 1 - 10
Product Groups: 65

Date of Accounts	Mar 07	Mar 06
Working Capital	206	202
Fixed Assets	9	9
Current Assets	257	249
Current Liabilities	51	47
Total Share Capital	5	5

Umberleigh

Rawle Gammon & Baker Holdings Ltd

Chapelton Sawmills Chapelton, Umberleigh, EX37 9DZ
Tel: 01769-560235 **Fax:** 01769-560074
E-mail: peter.haimes@rgbltd.co.uk
Website: http://www.rgbltd.co.uk
Bank(s): National Westminster Bank Plc
Managers: P. Haimes (Mgr)
Immediate Holding Company: RAWLE GAMMON & BAKER HOLDINGS LIMITED
Registration no: 00308273 **VAT No.:** GB 143 0119 18
Date established: 1935 **Turnover:** £10m - £20m
No.of Employees: 21 - 50 **Product Groups:** 25, 66

Date of Accounts	Mar 12	Mar 11	Mar 10
Sales Turnover	39m	39m	35m
Pre Tax Profit/Loss	2m	2m	1m
Working Capital	8m	7m	7m
Fixed Assets	12m	12m	12m
Current Assets	13m	13m	12m
Current Liabilities	1m	2m	1m

Winkleigh

Devon Cattle Breeders Society

Wisteria Cottage Iddesleigh, Winkleigh, EX19 8BG
Tel: 01837-810942 **Fax:** 01837-810942
E-mail: lane@dcbf.fsbusiness.co.uk
Website: http://www.redrubydevon.co.uk
Directors: A. Lane (Co Sec)
Immediate Holding Company: DEVON CATTLE BREEDERS SOCIETY
Registration no: 00019605 **Date established:** 1984
Turnover: Up to £250,000 **No.of Employees:** 1 - 10 **Product Groups:** 87

Date of Accounts	Dec 10	Dec 09	Dec 08
Sales Turnover	80	77	77
Pre Tax Profit/Loss	18	9	16
Working Capital	199	182	172
Fixed Assets	2	1	1
Current Assets	202	185	175

Woolacombe

Jacky Derham

Wellfield House Springfield Road, Woolacombe, EX34 7BX
Tel: 07966-313233
Website: http://www.foreverknowledge.info
Product Groups: 02, 20, 31, 63

Yelverton

Drake Lifts

Euro House Bere Ferrers, Yelverton, PL20 7JX
Tel: 01752-696054 **Fax:** 01752-696054
E-mail: info@euro-lifts.co.uk
Website: http://www.euro-lifts.co.uk
Managers: G. Harding (Mgr)
Immediate Holding Company: EURO LIFTS LIMITED
Date established: 1989 **No.of Employees:** 11 - 20 **Product Groups:** 35, 39, 45

Date of Accounts	Mar 11	Mar 10	Mar 09
Working Capital	434	337	319
Fixed Assets	43	42	56
Current Assets	597	448	562

H 4 Marine Ltd

7 Richmond Terrace Buckland Monachorum, Yelverton, PL20 7LU
Tel: 01822-852466 **Fax:** 01822-853179
E-mail: sales@h4marine.com
Website: http://www.h4marine.com
Directors: M. Ahlstrom (Fin), N. Young (MD)
Immediate Holding Company: H4 MARINE LIMITED
Registration no: 05027965 **Date established:** 2004
No.of Employees: 1 - 10 **Product Groups:** 39

Date of Accounts	Apr 12	Apr 11	Apr 10
Working Capital	26	13	5
Current Assets	39	25	19
Current Liabilities	8	7	5

PR Dogs Ltd

1 Walkham Terrace Horrabridge, Yelverton, PL20 7TR
Tel: 01822-859294 **Fax:** 01822-859295
E-mail: prdogs@prdogs.com
Website: http://www.prdogs.com
Directors: C. Taynton (Fin), J. Taynton (Dir)
Registration no: 05150635 **Date established:** 2004
No.of Employees: 1 - 10 **Product Groups:** 81

Date of Accounts	Aug 08	Aug 07	Aug 06
Working Capital	-1	-14	-14
Fixed Assets	13	10	5
Current Assets	50	17	14
Current Liabilities	52	32	27

S W L Panda Lifts Ltd

Brilanda Vineyard Beer Ferrers, Bere Ferrers, Yelverton, PL20 7JX
Tel: 01822-841178 **Fax:** 01872-225725
E-mail: info@euro-lifts.co.uk
Website: http://www.euro-lifts.co.uk
Directors: G. Harding (Dir)
Immediate Holding Company: EURO LIFTS LIMITED
Registration no: 02374225 **Date established:** 1989
No.of Employees: 11 - 20 **Product Groups:** 35, 39, 45

Date of Accounts	Mar 11	Mar 10	Mar 09
Working Capital	434	337	319
Fixed Assets	43	42	56
Current Assets	597	448	562

South West Consulting Ltd

8 Leather Tor Close, Yelverton, PL20 6EQ
Tel: 07769-912117 **Fax:** 01822-859314
E-mail: gcgoddard@southwestconsulting.co.uk
Website: http://www.southwestconsulting.co.uk
Directors: G. Goddard (Dir), J. Goddard (Fin)
Registration no: 04455784 **Date established:** 2002
Turnover: Up to £250,000 **No.of Employees:** 1 - 10 **Product Groups:** 80

Date of Accounts	Jun 10	Jun 09	Jun 08
Working Capital	-9	2	2
Fixed Assets	2	2	2
Current Assets	2	2	2
Current Liabilities	11	N/A	N/A

DORSET

Beaminster

Per Pro

Cambrian House Whitesheet Hill, Beaminster, DT8 3SF
Tel: 01308-861145 **Fax:** 0118-973 5629
E-mail: perpro@perprolimited.com
Website: http://www.perprolimited.com
Directors: D. Wootton (Dir), M. Wootton (MD)
Immediate Holding Company: Per Pro Ltd
Registration no: 02745017 **VAT No.:** GB 614 5615 53
Date established: 1974 **Turnover:** £1m - £2m **No.of Employees:** 1 - 10
Product Groups: 80

Date of Accounts	Nov 08	Nov 07	Nov 06
Working Capital	65	114	142
Fixed Assets	4	6	3
Current Assets	108	194	403
Current Liabilities	43	80	261
Total Share Capital	1	1	1

Trans European Plastics Ltd

Bakers Arms South Perrott, Beaminster, DT8 3HS
Tel: 01935-891881
Website: http://www.transeuroplastics.co.uk
Directors: J. Thackwell (MD)
Immediate Holding Company: TRANS EUROPEAN PLASTICS LIMITED
Registration no: 02255234 **Date established:** 1988
No.of Employees: 1 - 10 **Product Groups:** 30

Date of Accounts	Mar 12	Mar 11	Mar 10
Working Capital	161	142	137
Fixed Assets	17	27	37
Current Assets	417	588	510

Blandford Forum

A C Shooting School

9 Portman Road Pimperne, Blandford Forum, DT11 8UJ
Tel: 01258-459161 **Fax:** 01258-459161
E-mail: cochrane@tinyworld.co.uk
Website: http://www.acshootingschool.com
Directors: A. Cochrane (Prop)
Date established: 1987 **No.of Employees:** 1 - 10 **Product Groups:** 36, 39, 40

Blandford Engineering

Unit 7 Littletowns Estate Blandford Heights, Blandford Forum, DT11 7UR
Tel: 01258-454222 **Fax:** 01258-480433
E-mail: blandfordpumps@btinternet.com
Directors: A. Meyer (Dir)
Immediate Holding Company: BLANDFORD ENGINEERING LTD
Registration no: 05233868 **VAT No.:** GB 186 5511 44
Date established: 2004 **Turnover:** Up to £250,000
No.of Employees: 1 - 10 **Product Groups:** 39, 40

Date of Accounts	Dec 09	Dec 08	Dec 07
Sales Turnover	85	77	110
Pre Tax Profit/Loss	4	-27	-11
Working Capital	-82	-88	-67
Fixed Assets	7	9	15
Current Assets	13	3	11
Current Liabilities	68	58	47

Boost Energy Systems Limited

Unit 2, Milborne Business Centre Milborne, St. Andrew, Blandford Forum, DT11 0HZ
Tel: 01258-837 266 **Fax:** 01258-837 496
E-mail: info@boost-energy.com
Website: http://www.boost-energy.com
Directors: D. Sharman (Dir), P. Burton (Fin), M. Vangestel (Sales & Mktg)
Immediate Holding Company: Boost Energy Systems Ltd
Registration no: 04937610 **Date established:** 2003
Turnover: £500,000 - £1m **No.of Employees:** 1 - 10 **Product Groups:** 37

Date of Accounts	Dec 08	Dec 07	Dec 06
Working Capital	-184	3	33
Fixed Assets	415	348	294
Current Assets	261	334	196
Current Liabilities	33	N/A	N/A

Bristol Maid Hospital Equipment (t/a Bristol Maid)

Blandford Heights, Blandford Forum, DT11 7TG
Tel: 01258-451338 **Fax:** 01258-455056
E-mail: sales@bristolmaid.com
Website: http://www.bristolmaid.com
Bank(s): HSBC, 17 Market Place, Blandford Forum
Directors: S. Davis (MD), A. Davis (Fin)
Immediate Holding Company: BRISTOL MAID LIMITED
Registration no: 04102554 **VAT No.:** GB 137 5867 34
Date established: 2000 **Turnover:** £20m - £50m
No.of Employees: 101 - 250 **Product Groups:** 26, 36, 38

Burford Controls Ltd

Unit 18 Applins Park Farrington, Blandford Forum, DT11 8RA
Tel: 01747-811173 **Fax:** 01747-811171
E-mail: info@burfordcontrols.co.uk
Website: http://www.burfordcontrols.co.uk
Directors: S. Latham (Dir)
Immediate Holding Company: BURFORD CONTROLS LIMITED
Registration no: 02803486 **Date established:** 1993
Turnover: £250,000 - £500,000 **No.of Employees:** 1 - 10
Product Groups: 38, 40, 67

Date of Accounts	Aug 11	Aug 10	Aug 09
Working Capital	16	6	6
Fixed Assets	N/A	1	1
Current Assets	110	27	26
Current Liabilities	2	N/A	N/A

Alan Butcher Components Ltd

1 Beechwood Clump Farm Industrial Estate Tinpot Lane Shaftesbury Lane, Blandford Forum, DT11 7TD
Tel: 01258-456360 **Fax:** 01258-459194
E-mail: sales@abcomponents.co.uk
Website: http://www.abcomponents.co.uk
Directors: W. Butcher (Fin), P. Butcher (MD)
Immediate Holding Company: ALAN BUTCHER COMPONENTS LIMITED
Registration no: 03433635 **VAT No.:** GB 711 8465 41
Date established: 1997 **Turnover:** £500,000 - £1m
No.of Employees: 1 - 10 **Product Groups:** 37, 67

Date of Accounts	Apr 12	Apr 11	Apr 10
Working Capital	269	227	147
Fixed Assets	8	16	25
Current Assets	423	439	284

C L P Computer Supplies Ltd

Unit 2 Uplands Park, Blandford Forum, DT11 7UZ
Tel: 01258-459544 **Fax:** 01258-459565
E-mail: info@clp.co.uk
Website: http://www.clp.co.uk
Directors: S. Rigby (Dir)
Registration no: 02123158 **VAT No.:** GB 453 7179 31
Date established: 1987 **Turnover:** £500,000 - £1m
No.of Employees: 1 - 10 **Product Groups:** 27, 44, 61

R M Doble & Sons

Applins Farm Business Units Farrington, Blandford Forum, DT11 8RA
Tel: 01747-811510 **Fax:** 01747-811510
Directors: R. Doble (Prop)
Immediate Holding Company: R M DOBLE & SONS LIMITED
Registration no: 04683927 **Date established:** 2003
No.of Employees: 1 - 10 **Product Groups:** 35

Date of Accounts	Mar 11	Mar 10	Mar 09
Working Capital	9	1	4
Fixed Assets	3	2	3
Current Assets	16	2	8

Dometic UK Ltd

Dometic House The Brewery, Blandford Forum, DT11 9LS
Tel: 01582-494111 **Fax:** 01582-490197
E-mail: sales@dometic.co.uk
Website: http://www.dometic.co.uk
Directors: A. Sutton (Fin)
Managers: A. Diamond (Mktg Serv Mgr), M. Fry (Tech Serv Mgr), I. Clarke (Personnel), T. Bowler (Sales Prom Mgr)
Ultimate Holding Company: FINA COLD 1 SA (LUXEMBOURG)
Immediate Holding Company: DOMETIC UK LIMITED
Registration no: 04190363 **Date established:** 2001
Turnover: £10m - £20m **No.of Employees:** 21 - 50 **Product Groups:** 26, 33, 36, 41

Date of Accounts	Dec 11	Dec 10	Dec 09
Sales Turnover	21m	19m	17m
Pre Tax Profit/Loss	-377	480	-545
Working Capital	10m	9m	8m
Fixed Assets	9m	10m	12m
Current Assets	20m	19m	19m
Current Liabilities	4m	5m	4m

Iracroft Ltd

Blandford Heights, Blandford Forum, DT11 7TE
Tel: 01258-486300 **Fax:** 01258-486301
E-mail: info@iracroft.demon.co.uk
Website: http://www.iracroft.co.uk
Bank(s): Barclays, Uttoxeter
Directors: J. Harrison (MD)
Managers: P. Bray
Immediate Holding Company: IRACROFT LIMITED
Registration no: 01055419 **Date established:** 1972
Turnover: £10m - £20m **No.of Employees:** 101 - 250
Product Groups: 40, 48

Date of Accounts	Dec 11	Dec 10	Dec 09
Sales Turnover	14m	10m	6m
Pre Tax Profit/Loss	998	461	-731
Working Capital	1m	1m	531
Fixed Assets	4m	17m	4m
Current Assets	4m	3m	2m
Current Liabilities	1m	812	410

JEC Industrial Equipment Ltd

Unit 5 Vanguard Works, Blandford Forum, DT11 7TE
Tel: 01258-488398 **Fax:** 01258-488711
E-mail: sales@jecltd.com
Website: http://www.jecltd.com
Directors: P. Natolie (MD)
Immediate Holding Company: J.E.C. INDUSTRIAL EQUIPMENT LIMITED
Registration no: 03767290 **VAT No.:** GB 737 1536 29
Date established: 1999 **No.of Employees:** 1 - 10 **Product Groups:** 22, 24, 26, 29, 30, 35, 36, 39, 40, 41, 45, 49, 63, 66, 67

Date of Accounts	Apr 12	Apr 11	Apr 10
Working Capital	-23	-63	17
Fixed Assets	15	18	19
Current Assets	149	174	292
Current Liabilities	2	N/A	54

Leisure Controls International Ltd

Clump Farm Industrial Estate Higher Shaftesbury Road, Blandford Forum, DT11 7TD
Tel: 01258-489075 **Fax:** 01258-488526
E-mail: info@lcigb.com
Website: http://www.lci.gb.com
Directors: A. Cole (I.T. Dir), L. Fairhurst (Dir)
Immediate Holding Company: LEISURE CONTROLS INTERNATIONAL LIMITED
Registration no: 02527144 **VAT No.:** GB 834 8704 09
Date established: 2004 **Turnover:** £500,000 - £1m
No.of Employees: 1 - 10 **Product Groups:** 40, 49, 65

Date of Accounts	Oct 11	Oct 10	Oct 09
Sales Turnover	N/A	N/A	790
Pre Tax Profit/Loss	N/A	N/A	15
Working Capital	171	154	130
Fixed Assets	43	47	237
Current Assets	312	297	265
Current Liabilities	N/A	N/A	38

Telesoft Technologies Ltd

Observatory House Stour Park, Blandford St Mary, Blandford Forum, DT11 9LQ
Tel: 01258-480880 **Fax:** 01258-486598
E-mail: sales@telesoft-technologies.com
Website: http://www.telesoft-technologies.com
Directors: J. Gordon (Pers), A. Evripides (Sales), B. Markham (MD)
Managers: P. Lewis (Chief Acct)
Immediate Holding Company: TELESOFT TECHNOLOGIES LIMITED
Registration no: 02344740 **Date established:** 1989
Turnover: £10m - £20m **No.of Employees:** 101 - 250
Product Groups: 37, 38, 67

Date of Accounts	Sep 11	Sep 10	Sep 09
Sales Turnover	14m	14m	13m
Pre Tax Profit/Loss	2m	560	1m
Working Capital	6m	5m	6m
Fixed Assets	3m	3m	4m
Current Assets	11m	10m	10m
Current Liabilities	4m	3m	3m

M G Trevett Ltd (t/a Valley Fabrications & Winterbourne Horsebox Co.)

West Street Winterborne Stickland, Blandford Forum, DT11 0NT
Tel: 01258-880490 **Fax:** 01258-880470

see next page

***M G Trevett Ltd (t/a Valley Fabrications & Winterbourne Horsebox Co.)** - Cont'd*

Directors: G. Trevett (MD)
Immediate Holding Company: M.G. TREVETT LIMITED
Registration no: 01397439 **Date established:** 1978
Turnover: £250,000 - £500,000 **No.of Employees:** 1 - 10
Product Groups: 39

Date of Accounts	Nov 11	Nov 10	Nov 09
Working Capital	133	135	137
Fixed Assets	21	16	23
Current Assets	179	221	209

Tri Metals Ltd

Sunrise Business Park Higher Shaftesbury Road, Blandford Forum, DT11 8ST
Tel: 01258-459441 **Fax:** 01258-480408
E-mail: sales@trimetals.co.uk
Website: http://www.trimetals.co.uk
Bank(s): HSBC, Blandford
Directors: A. Smith (Mkt Research), G. Smith (Co Sec), M. Bennett (Dir)
Immediate Holding Company: TRIMETALS LIMITED
Registration no: 00897439 **VAT No.:** GB 207 9354 56
Date established: 1967 **Turnover:** £1m - £2m **No.of Employees:** 21 - 50
Product Groups: 35, 48

Date of Accounts	Jan 12	Jan 11	Jan 10
Working Capital	1m	1m	930
Fixed Assets	363	392	418
Current Assets	1m	1m	1m

Volts Auto Electrical

9 Chettle Chettle, Blandford Forum, DT11 8DB
Tel: 01258-808283
E-mail: m3wvh@hotmail.com
Website: http://www.volts.org.uk
Directors: W. Hemmings (Prop)
No.of Employees: 51 - 100 **Product Groups:** 40, 48

Woodhouse Inns

The Brewery, Blandford Forum, DT11 9LS
Tel: 01258-452141 **Fax:** 01258-452122
Website: http://www.hall-woodhouse.co.uk
Bank(s): National Westminster
Directors: A. Rockley (Prop), M. Scott (Fin)
Managers: R. Payne (Mktg Serv Mgr), S. Lacey (Tech Serv Mgr), S. Hodder (Personnel)
Ultimate Holding Company: HALL & WOODHOUSE LIMITED
Immediate Holding Company: WOODHOUSE INNS LIMITED
Registration no: 00625878 **VAT No.:** GB 185 6836 17
Date established: 1959 **Turnover:** £50m - £75m
No.of Employees: 1001 - 1500 **Product Groups:** 21

Date of Accounts	Jan 09	Jan 10	Jan 11
Sales Turnover	50m	51m	52m
Pre Tax Profit/Loss	7m	6m	7m
Working Capital	-3m	-2m	-2m
Fixed Assets	3m	2m	2m

Bournemouth

Abbey Life Assurance Co. Ltd

Abbey Life Centre PO Box 33 100 Holdenhurst Road, Bournemouth, BH8 8AL
Tel: 01202-292373 **Fax:** 01202-296158
E-mail: neil.tointon@abbeylife.co.uk
Website: http://www.abbeylife.co.uk
Directors: A. Bartlett (Co Sec), N. Tointon (Dir)
Ultimate Holding Company: DEUTSCHE BANK AG (GERMANY)
Immediate Holding Company: ABBEY LIFE ASSURANCE COMPANY LIMITED
Registration no: 00710383 **Date established:** 1961
Turnover: Over £1,000m **No.of Employees:** 21 - 50 **Product Groups:** 82

Date of Accounts	Dec 10	Dec 09	Dec 08
Pre Tax Profit/Loss	133m	177m	17m
Fixed Assets	11300m	10878m	10141m
Current Assets	290m	243m	N/A
Current Liabilities	38m	4285m	10980m

Above Board Components Ltd

3 Osmund Walk Old Sarum, Bournemouth, SP4 6NE
Tel: 01202-313665 **Fax:** 01722-325 827
E-mail: sales@aboveboardcomp.com
Website: http://www.aboveboardcomp.com
Directors: S. Marchant (MD)
Registration no: 05694221 **No.of Employees:** 21 - 50
Product Groups: 37, 38, 44, 61, 67

Date of Accounts	Feb 07
Working Capital	10
Current Assets	40
Current Liabilities	31

Aim Aviation Jecco Ltd

Jecco House Boscombe Grove Road, Bournemouth, BH1 4PD
Tel: 01202-397388 **Fax:** 01202-398706
E-mail: e-mail@aim-aviation.co.uk
Website: http://www.aim-aviation.co.uk
Bank(s): National Westminster, London
Directors: D. Ward (Fin), M. Tappenden (Dir)
Managers: N. Brown, S. Beynon (Purch Mgr)
Ultimate Holding Company: AIM AVIATION LIMITED
Immediate Holding Company: AIM AVIATION (JECCO) LIMITED
Registration no: 01004276 **VAT No.:** 185 9888 90 **Date established:** 1971
Turnover: £20m - £50m **No.of Employees:** 251 - 500
Product Groups: 24, 39

Date of Accounts	Apr 12	Apr 11	Apr 10
Sales Turnover	39m	31m	27m
Pre Tax Profit/Loss	9m	6m	5m
Working Capital	7m	7m	13m
Fixed Assets	2m	2m	2m
Current Assets	20m	14m	19m
Current Liabilities	3m	3m	2m

Air O Ducts Contracts Ltd

Unit 10 Drewitt Industrial Estate 865 Ringwood Road, Bournemouth, BH11 8LL
Tel: 01202-576511 **Fax:** 01202-570511
E-mail: admin@airoducts.co.uk
Website: http://www.airoducts.co.uk
Directors: W. Craggs (MD), P. Phipps (Fin)
Ultimate Holding Company: AIR-O-DUCTS (WESSEX) LIMITED
Immediate Holding Company: AIR-O-DUCTS (CONTRACTS) LIMITED
Registration no: 01449860 **VAT No.:** GB 423 5412 82
Date established: 1979 **Turnover:** £250,000 - £500,000
No.of Employees: 1 - 10 **Product Groups:** 52

Date of Accounts	Jun 05	Jun 04	Jun 03
Working Capital	22	61	73
Fixed Assets	3	4	3
Current Assets	49	111	170

Amtec Ltd

Throop Business Park Throop Road, Bournemouth, BH8 0DW
Tel: 01202-533557 **Fax:** 01202-533567
E-mail: liz@amtec.uk.com
Website: http://www.amtec.co.uk
Directors: T. McManus (Co Sec)
Managers: J. Watton (Sales Admin)
Immediate Holding Company: AMTEC LTD
Registration no: 03036386 **Date established:** 1995
No.of Employees: 11 - 20 **Product Groups:** 30, 52

Date of Accounts	Sep 11	Sep 10	Sep 09
Working Capital	156	107	85
Fixed Assets	113	63	82
Current Assets	525	384	469

B M S Technology Ltd

10 Sandringham Close, Bournemouth, BH9 3QP
Tel: 0701-070 0020 **Fax:** 0701-070 0021
E-mail: info@bmstech.com
Website: http://www.bmstech.com
Directors: J. Cook (Fin)
Immediate Holding Company: BMS TECHNOLOGY LIMITED
Registration no: 02710065 **VAT No.:** GB 596 2891 81
Date established: 1992 **No.of Employees:** 1 - 10 **Product Groups:** 84

Date of Accounts	May 12	May 11	May 10
Working Capital	68	62	60
Current Assets	70	64	61

Base Model

PO Box 6709, Bournemouth, BH11 0BW
Tel: 08452-255015 **Fax:** 01202-301156
E-mail: info@basemodels.co.uk
Website: http://www.basemodels.co.uk
Directors: H. Hawkins (Fin)
Registration no: 02529614 **Date established:** 1998
Turnover: Up to £250,000 **No.of Employees:** 1 - 10 **Product Groups:** 89

Bighead Bonding Fasteners Ltd

Units 15-16 Elliott Road, Bournemouth, BH11 8LZ
Tel: 01202-574601 **Fax:** 01202-578300
E-mail: info@bighead.co.uk
Website: http://www.bighead.co.uk
Bank(s): National Westminster Bank Plc
Directors: M. Cowell (Sales)
Ultimate Holding Company: BIGHEAD HOLDINGS LIMITED
Immediate Holding Company: BIGHEAD BONDING FASTENERS LIMITED
Registration no: 00722335 **Date established:** 1962
No.of Employees: 11 - 20 **Product Groups:** 35, 39

Date of Accounts	Dec 11	Dec 10	Dec 09
Working Capital	1m	928	657
Fixed Assets	236	255	323
Current Assets	2m	1m	1m

The Bizxchange

13 Lansdowne Road, Bournemouth, BH1 1RZ
Tel: 08452-607515 **Fax:** 08452-607516
E-mail: info@thebizxchange.net
Website: http://www.thebizxchange.net
Directors: G. Fitzgerald (Prop)
Managers: E. Fitzgerald (Comm)
Registration no: 06944632 **Date established:** 2009
Turnover: Up to £250,000 **No.of Employees:** 1 - 10 **Product Groups:** 80

Boscombe Beds & Suites

40 Ashley Road, Bournemouth, BH1 4LJ
Tel: 01202-300909 **Fax:** 01202-720888
E-mail: info@loungearound.co.uk
Website: http://www.boscombebeds.com
Directors: G. Stephenson (Prop)
No.of Employees: 1 - 10 **Product Groups:** 26, 48, 63

Bournemouth Stained Glass

790 Wimborne Road, Bournemouth, BH9 2DX
Tel: 01202-514734 **Fax:** 01202-250239
E-mail: shop@stainedglass.co.uk
Website: http://www.stainedglass.co.uk
Directors: E. Law (Ptnr)
Turnover: Up to £250,000 **No.of Employees:** 1 - 10 **Product Groups:** 40, 45, 46

Bournetech

3 Bower Road, Bournemouth, BH8 9HQ
Tel: 01202-729031 **Fax:** 01202-729032
Managers: R. Jones (Mgr)
Date established: 1978 **No.of Employees:** 1 - 10 **Product Groups:** 36

Burder Films

37 Braidley Road, Bournemouth, BH2 6JY
Tel: 01202-295395 **Fax:** 01202-589089
E-mail: j.burder@johnburder.co.uk
Website: http://www.johnburder.co.uk
Directors: J. Burder (Ptnr)
Date established: 1968 **Turnover:** £500,000 - £1m
No.of Employees: 1 - 10 **Product Groups:** 28, 89

C G Agencies

24 Hillcrest Road, Bournemouth, BH9 3HX
Tel: 07906-879009 **Fax:** 01202-525085
E-mail: clive.gill1@ntworld.com
Directors: C. Gill (Prop)
No.of Employees: 1 - 10 **Product Groups:** 26

Coastal Dry Wall Ltd

85 Littledown Avenue, Bournemouth, BH7 7AX
Tel: 08717-128694
E-mail: info@coastaldrywall.co.uk
Website: http://www.coastaldrywall.co.uk
Directors: M. Mccann (Dir)
Immediate Holding Company: COASTAL DRYWALL LTD
Registration no: 05985978 **Date established:** 2006
No.of Employees: 1 - 10 **Product Groups:** 52

Date of Accounts	Nov 11	Nov 10	Nov 09
Working Capital	-33	-24	-20
Fixed Assets	4	5	8
Current Assets	12	9	10
Current Liabilities	38	N/A	N/A

Connect PC Services

8 Lea Way, Bournemouth, BH11 9NF
Tel: 0781-585 6314
E-mail: info@connectpcservices.co.uk
Website: http://www.connectpcservices.co.uk
Directors: M. Davis (Dir)
Date established: 2007 **Turnover:** Up to £250,000
No.of Employees: 1 - 10 **Product Groups:** 44

Date of Accounts	May 08
Working Capital	-1
Fixed Assets	1
Current Assets	7
Current Liabilities	8

Copycare Office Equipment Ltd

9 Dorset Road, Bournemouth, BH4 9LB
Tel: 01202-761111 **Fax:** 01202-766101
E-mail: info@copycareoffice.co.uk
Website: http://www.copycareoffice.co.uk
Directors: T. Callaway (Dir), T. Callaway (MD)
Immediate Holding Company: COPYCARE OFFICE EQUIPMENT LIMITED
Registration no: 05105586 **Date established:** 2004
No.of Employees: 1 - 10 **Product Groups:** 27, 28, 32, 44, 48, 67, 80, 83

Date of Accounts	Jun 11	Jun 10	Jun 09
Working Capital	49	18	30
Fixed Assets	83	91	98
Current Assets	125	83	81

Craft Decor

19 Glenroyd Gardens, Bournemouth, BH6 3JN
Tel: 01202-434131 **Fax:** 01202-433844
E-mail: sales@craftdecor.co.uk
Website: http://www.craftdecor.co.uk
Directors: G. Underhill (Ptnr)
Date established: 1979 **No.of Employees:** 1 - 10 **Product Groups:** 25, 33, 36, 52, 84

D-Ray Marine

36 Cherford Road, Bournemouth, BH11 8SU
Tel: 07799-406669
E-mail: sales@d-raymarine.co.uk
Website: http://www.d-raymarine.co.uk
Directors: D. Ray (Prop)
Date established: 2003 **No.of Employees:** 1 - 10 **Product Groups:** 35, 36, 39

Discovery Fine Chemicals Ltd

29 Nursery Road, Bournemouth, BH9 3AT
Tel: 01202-521225 **Fax:** 0845-094 4385
E-mail: pjc@discofinechem.com
Website: http://discofinechem.com
Directors: J. Bell (Co Sec)
Immediate Holding Company: DISCOVERY FINE CHEMICALS LIMITED
Registration no: 05971945 **Date established:** 2006
Turnover: Up to £250,000 **No.of Employees:** 1 - 10 **Product Groups:** 85

Date of Accounts	Dec 11	Dec 10	Dec 09
Working Capital	394	116	63
Fixed Assets	3	2	1
Current Assets	577	309	164

Door & Gatecraft

812 Wimborne Road, Bournemouth, BH9 2DT
Tel: 01202-526361 **Fax:** 01202-519193
E-mail: sales@doorandgatecraft.co.uk
Website: http://www.doorandgatecraft.co.uk
Directors: P. Ralph (Prop)
Date established: 1990 **No.of Employees:** 1 - 10 **Product Groups:** 26, 35

Dorset Enterprises

Elliott Road West Howe, Bournemouth, BH11 8JP
Tel: 01202-577966 **Fax:** 01202-570049
E-mail: paul.white@bournemouth.gov.uk
Website: http://www.deckchairsuk.com
Bank(s): HSBC Bank plc
Managers: P. White (Factory Mgr)
Immediate Holding Company: D.W. ENTERPRISES LTD
Registration no: 06937133 **VAT No.:** GB 187 3025 57
Date established: 2009 **Turnover:** Up to £250,000
No.of Employees: 21 - 50 **Product Groups:** 26, 63

Emap Glenigan

41-47 Seabourne Road, Bournemouth, BH5 2HU
Tel: 01202-432121 **Fax:** 01202-431204
E-mail: mike.woolfrey@glenigan.emap.com
Website: http://www.glenigan.com
Directors: R. Mcinally (Sales), M. Hogg (Co Sec), P. Angell (MD), M. Woolfrey (MD), P. Brown (Dir)
Managers: M. Baker (), V. Mcewen (Personnel), V. Mcewen, A. Murray (Nat Sales Mgr), P. Angel (Mktg Serv Mgr)
Immediate Holding Company: EMAP INTERNATIONAL LTD
Registration no: 03154512 **Turnover:** £5m - £10m
No.of Employees: 51 - 100 **Product Groups:** 44, 81

Energy Advice Line Ltd

Post Office Buildings Cardigan Road, Bournemouth, BH9 1BJ
Tel: 01202-517489 **Fax:** 0845-094 2518
E-mail: jullian.morgan@energyadviceline.org.uk
Website: http://www.energyadviceline.org.uk
Directors: J. Morgan (Dir)
Immediate Holding Company: ENERGY ADVICE LINE LIMITED
Registration no: 05774275 **Date established:** 2006
No.of Employees: 1 - 10 **Product Groups:** 18

Date of Accounts	Mar 11	Mar 10	Mar 09
Working Capital	2	-3	6
Fixed Assets	3	3	5
Current Assets	49	24	34

Erro Tool Co. Ltd
70 Iddesleigh Road, Bournemouth, BH3 7NH
Tel: 01202-466447 **Fax:** 01202-466447
E-mail: sales@holtwaterloo.com
Website: http://www.holtwaterloo.com
Directors: G. Waters (Dir)
Date established: 2006 **Turnover:** **No.of Employees:** 1 - 10
Product Groups: 22, 26, 30, 39, 45

Escor Toys Limited
St Stephens Road, Bournemouth, BH2 6DY
Tel: 01202-451451 **Fax:** 01202-454690
E-mail: enquiries@bournemouth.gov.uk
Website: http://www.bournemouth.gov.uk
Bank(s): HSBC Bank plc
Directors: W. Gaskins (MD)
Managers: B. Gaskins (Mgr), S. Atkins (Sales & Mktg Mg)
Immediate Holding Company: Bournemouth Borough Council
Registration no: 00412703 **VAT No.:** GB 187 3025 57
Turnover: £250,000 - £500,000 **No.of Employees:** 21 - 50
Product Groups: 26, 65

Date of Accounts	Mar 06
Working Capital	17
Fixed Assets	190
Current Assets	26
Current Liabilities	9
Total Share Capital	11

Excelsior Tours Ltd
Central Business Park, Bournemouth, BH1 3SJ
Tel: 01202-652222 **Fax:** 01202-652223
E-mail: info@videostudio.co.uk
Website: http://www.excelsior-coaches.com
Directors: K. Tilberry (MD)
Immediate Holding Company: EXCELSIOR TRANSPORT LTD
Registration no: 04329645 **Date established:** 2001
Turnover: £500,000 - £1m **No.of Employees:** 1 - 10 **Product Groups:** 69

Date of Accounts	Dec 11	Dec 10	Nov 09
Sales Turnover	N/A	666	771
Pre Tax Profit/Loss	N/A	-91	11
Working Capital	-930	4	-38
Fixed Assets	3m	2m	159
Current Assets	85	11	98
Current Liabilities	N/A	2	123

fashy UK Ltd
192 Alma Road, Bournemouth, BH9 1AJ
Tel: 01202-515251 **Fax:** 01202-531409
E-mail: alan@fashy.co.uk
Website: http://www.fashy.com
Directors: A. Gardener (MD), A. gardner (MD)
Immediate Holding Company: FASHY UK LIMITED
Registration no: 04021967 **Date established:** 2000
Turnover: £50m - £75m **No.of Employees:** 1 - 10 **Product Groups:** 30

Date of Accounts	Dec 09	Dec 08	Dec 07
Working Capital	-7	1	6
Fixed Assets	28	33	14
Current Assets	14	20	19

Fortuna Scafolding
23 Glenville Road, Bournemouth, BH10 5DD
Tel: 01202-526758 **Fax:** 01202-518274
E-mail: enquiries@fortunascaffolding.co.uk
Website: http://www.fortunascaffolding.co.uk
Directors: L. Butt (MD), R. Butt (Fin)
Immediate Holding Company: FORTUNA SCAFFOLDING LTD
Registration no: 03644605 **Date established:** 1998
Turnover: Up to £250,000 **No.of Employees:** 1 - 10 **Product Groups:** 52

G J Services
13 Albemarle Road, Bournemouth, BH3 7LZ
Tel: 01202-529589 **Fax:** 01202-530923
E-mail: info@gjsdiamondtools.co.uk
Website: http://www.gjsdiamondtools.co.uk
Directors: G. Jones (Snr Part)
Date established: 1989 **No.of Employees:** 1 - 10 **Product Groups:** 36

Global Optics UK Ltd
30 Brockley Road, Bournemouth, BH10 6JN
Tel: 01202-530609 **Fax:** 01202-547209
E-mail: info@globalopticsuk.com
Website: http://www.globalopticsuk.com
Directors: D. Read (MD)
Immediate Holding Company: GLOBAL OPTICS (UK) LIMITED
Registration no: 03509979 **Date established:** 1998
No.of Employees: 1 - 10 **Product Groups:** 16, 17, 32, 33, 37, 38, 45, 48, 49

Date of Accounts	Feb 08	Feb 11	Feb 10
Working Capital	652	504	420
Fixed Assets	40	31	25
Current Assets	724	685	513

Gray Campling Ltd
91a Southcote Road, Bournemouth, BH1 3SN
Tel: 01202-291828 **Fax:** 01202-297304
E-mail: sales@graycampling.co.uk
Website: http://www.graycampling.co.uk
Directors: P. Blake (Sales)
Immediate Holding Company: GRAY-CAMPLING LIMITED
Registration no: 00783370 **VAT No.:** GB 185 5678 14
Date established: 1963 **Turnover:** £500,000 - £1m
No.of Employees: 1 - 10 **Product Groups:** 46

Date of Accounts	Nov 11	Nov 10	Nov 09
Working Capital	105	135	227
Fixed Assets	382	389	394
Current Assets	199	254	332

Hanson Quality Management Ltd
11 Hendford Road, Bournemouth, BH10 5AT
Tel: 01202-469251 **Fax:** 01202-469251
E-mail: sales@hqm-ltd.co.uk
Website: http://www.hqm-ltd.co.uk
Directors: L. Hanson (Fin), A. Hanson (MD)
Immediate Holding Company: HANSON QUALITY MANAGEMENT LIMITED
Registration no: 04420646 **Date established:** 2002
No.of Employees: 1 - 10 **Product Groups:** 80

Date of Accounts	Apr 11	Apr 10	Apr 09
Working Capital	1	-1	1
Fixed Assets	3	3	3
Current Assets	11	9	13

Hants & Dorset Signs
112 Kimberley Road, Bournemouth, BH6 5DA
Tel: 01202-423362 **Fax:** 01202-417131
E-mail: sales@hantsanddorsetsigns.co.uk
Website: http://www.hantsanddorsetsigns.co.uk
Directors: A. Bird (Dir)
Turnover: Up to £250,000 **No.of Employees:** 1 - 10 **Product Groups:** 37, 39

Head 2 Toe Security & Workwear
298 Charminster Road, Bournemouth, BH8 9RT
Tel: 01202-532465 **Fax:** 01202-532465
E-mail: info@head2toesecurity.co.uk
Website: http://www.head2toesecurity.co.uk
Directors: L. Stephenson (Dir)
No.of Employees: 1 - 10 **Product Groups:** 24, 63

Headboards UK
40-42 Ashley Road, Bournemouth, BH1 4LJ
Tel: 01722-744616
E-mail: sales@headboardsuk.co.uk
Website: http://www.headboardsuk.co.uk
Directors: Stephenson (Prop), M. Stephenson (Prop)
Managers: M. Stephenson (Sales Prom Mgr)
Date established: 2007 **No.of Employees:** 1 - 10 **Product Groups:** 26

Hermitage Hotel
Exeter Road, Bournemouth, BH2 5AH
Tel: 01202-557363 **Fax:** 01202-559173
E-mail: info@hermitage-hotel.co.uk
Website: http://www.hermitage-hotel.co.uk
Managers: S. Moss (Chief Mgr)
Date established: 1996 **No.of Employees:** 51 - 100 **Product Groups:** 69

Hilken Design
114 Stewart Road, Bournemouth, BH8 8NX
Tel: 07779-094330
E-mail: louise@hilkendesign.com
Website: http://www.hilkendesign.com
Directors: L. Hilken (Prop)
Turnover: Up to £250,000 **No.of Employees:** 1 - 10 **Product Groups:** 24, 63, 81

Hobs Reprographics plc
178 Old Christchurch Road, Bournemouth, BH1 1NU
Tel: 01202-553233 **Fax:** 01202-557616
E-mail: bournemouth@hobsrepro.com
Website: http://www.hobsrepro.com
Managers: M. Pragnell (Mgr)
Ultimate Holding Company: OBETT HOLDINGS LIMITED
Immediate Holding Company: HOBS REPROGRAPHICS PLC
Registration no: 00511368 **Date established:** 1952
Turnover: £75m - £125m **No.of Employees:** 1 - 10 **Product Groups:** 28, 81

Date of Accounts	Apr 12	Apr 11	Apr 10
Sales Turnover	18m	18m	18m
Pre Tax Profit/Loss	555	547	415
Working Capital	2m	2m	5m
Fixed Assets	7m	6m	4m
Current Assets	10m	10m	10m
Current Liabilities	1m	1m	1m

Honeycomb Computer Technology
31 Cranleigh Road, Bournemouth, BH6 5JT
Tel: 01202-432053
Website: http://www.worka-b.com
Directors: R. Woodward (Ptnr)
VAT No.: GB 580 2225 64 **Date established:** 1991
Turnover: Up to £250,000 **No.of Employees:** 1 - 10 **Product Groups:** 44

Igloo Ice
Kimberley Road Southbourne, Bournemouth, BH6 5EX
Tel: 01202-419690 **Fax:** 01202-419690
E-mail: sales@iglooice.co.uk
Website: http://www.iglooice.co.uk
Managers: M. Laxton (District Mgr)
Date established: 2006 **Turnover:** Up to £250,000
No.of Employees: 1 - 10 **Product Groups:** 21

Ironage Wrought Ironwork
9 Yeomans Industrial Park Yeomans Way, Bournemouth, BH8 0BJ
Tel: 01202-519729 **Fax:** 01202-519729
Directors: J. Sweetman (Prop)
Immediate Holding Company: D B ELECTRICAL WHOLESALE LTD
Date established: 1998 **No.of Employees:** 1 - 10 **Product Groups:** 26, 35

Date of Accounts	Dec 11	Dec 10	Dec 09
Working Capital	36	22	9
Fixed Assets	18	10	17
Current Assets	159	170	166

Just Diaries
17 Albemarle Road, Bournemouth, BH3 7LZ
Tel: 01202-248494
E-mail: paul@justdiaries.co.uk
Website: http://www.justdiaries.co.uk
Directors: P. Buck (Mkt Research)
Registration no: 04629645 **Date established:** 2003
Turnover: Up to £250,000 **No.of Employees:** 1 - 10 **Product Groups:** 22, 28

Date of Accounts	Apr 08	Apr 07	Apr 06
Sales Turnover	N/A	60	N/A
Pre Tax Profit/Loss	N/A	7	-1
Working Capital	6	2	N/A
Fixed Assets	3	4	1
Current Assets	13	11	N/A
Current Liabilities	7	9	N/A
Total Share Capital	1	1	N/A
ROCE% (Return on Capital Employed)		105.0	
ROT% (Return on Turnover)		10.9	

Lasermet
137 Hankinson Road, Bournemouth, BH9 1HR
Tel: 01202-770740 **Fax:** 01202-770730
E-mail: office@lasermet.com
Website: http://www.lasermet.com
Directors: P. Tozer (MD)
Immediate Holding Company: LASERMET LIMITED
Registration no: 02084778 **Date established:** 1986
Turnover: £500,000 - £1m **No.of Employees:** 21 - 50
Product Groups: 38, 40, 44, 46, 54, 84, 85

Date of Accounts	Mar 12	Mar 11	Mar 10
Working Capital	776	93	573
Fixed Assets	20	499	511
Current Assets	921	716	739

Chris Lewis
Faraday House 38 Poole Road, Bournemouth, BH4 9DW
Tel: 01202-751599 **Fax:** 01202-759500
E-mail: sales@chrislewissecurity.co.uk
Website: http://www.chrislewissecurity.co.uk
Directors: A. Lewis (Sales & Mktg), C. Lewis (MD), J. Anderson (Sales & Mktg)
Managers: G. Richards (District Mgr)
Immediate Holding Company: NOEL BROTHERS (U.K.) LIMITED
Registration no: 01327379 **VAT No.:** GB 423 7399 38
Date established: 1985 **Turnover:** £1m - £2m **No.of Employees:** 1 - 10
Product Groups: 40, 52

Date of Accounts	Sep 86
Fixed Assets	10
Current Assets	19

Lexis Information Systems Ltd
Melbury House 1-3 Oxford Road, Bournemouth, BH8 8ES
Tel: 0845-2607518
E-mail: info@lexisclick.com
Website: http://www.lexisclick.com
Directors: S. Bavister (MD)
Managers: P. Adkins (Consultant)
Registration no: 05451946 **Date established:** 2005
No.of Employees: 1 - 10 **Product Groups:** 44

Date of Accounts	May 10	May 09	May 08
Working Capital	-24	-33	-9
Fixed Assets	14	3	4
Current Assets	36	31	17

Liverpool Victoria
County Gates, Bournemouth, BH1 2NF
Tel: 01202-292333 **Fax:** 01202-292253
E-mail: sales@liverpoolvictoria.co.uk
Website: http://www.lv.com
Bank(s): Lloyds
Directors: M. Rogers (Grp Chief Exec)
Ultimate Holding Company: LIVERPOOL VICTORIA FRIENDLY SOCIETY LIMITED
Immediate Holding Company: LIVERPOOL VICTORIA ASSET MANAGEMENT LIMITED
Registration no: 03287943 **Date established:** 1996 **Turnover:** £2m - £5m
No.of Employees: 1501 & over **Product Groups:** 82

Date of Accounts	Dec 11	Dec 10	Dec 09
Pre Tax Profit/Loss	-4m	-5m	-5m
Working Capital	-206m	-203m	-200m
Fixed Assets	684m	680m	621m
Current Liabilities	183m	N/A	183m

M B S
53-59 Southcote Road, Bournemouth, BH1 3SH
Tel: 01202-589314 **Fax:** 01202-587974
Directors: S. Srajapour (Prop)
Date established: 2002 **No.of Employees:** 1 - 10 **Product Groups:** 35

Maplin Electronics Ltd
102 Commercial Road, Bournemouth, BH2 5LR
Tel: 08432-277348 **Fax:** 01202-311007
E-mail: customercare@maplin.co.uk
Website: http://www.maplin.co.uk
Managers: S. Coventry (Mgr)
Ultimate Holding Company: MONTAGU PRIVATE EQUITY LLP
Immediate Holding Company: MAPLIN ELECTRONICS LIMITED
Registration no: 01264385 **Date established:** 1976
Turnover: £125m - £250m **No.of Employees:** 21 - 50
Product Groups: 37, 61

Date of Accounts	Dec 11	Dec 08	Dec 09
Sales Turnover	205m	204m	204m
Pre Tax Profit/Loss	25m	32m	35m
Working Capital	118m	49m	75m
Fixed Assets	27m	28m	28m
Current Assets	207m	108m	142m
Current Liabilities	78m	51m	59m

Mccarthy & Stone Ltd
26-32 Oxford Road, Bournemouth, BH8 8EZ
Tel: 01202-292480 **Fax:** 01202-557261
E-mail: info@mccarthyandstone.co.uk
Website: http://www.mccarthyandstone.co.uk
Bank(s): National Westminster Bank Plc
Directors: T. Green (Co Sec)
Ultimate Holding Company: MANDARIN 1 LIMITED
Immediate Holding Company: MCCARTHY & STONE LIMITED
Registration no: 06622199 **VAT No.:** GB 370 0308 93
Date established: 2008 **Turnover:** £250m - £500m
No.of Employees: 1001 - 1500 **Product Groups:** 52

Date of Accounts	Aug 11	Aug 10	Aug 09
Sales Turnover	231m	203m	99m
Pre Tax Profit/Loss	5m	-9m	-400
Working Capital	473m	466m	483m
Fixed Assets	87m	93m	101m
Current Assets	640m	592m	529m
Current Liabilities	160m	119m	40m

Modern & Antique Firearms Ltd
147b Tuckton Road, Bournemouth, BH6 3JZ
Tel: 01202-429369 **Fax:** 01202-426926
Website: http://www.modernandantiquefirearms.co.uk
Directors: G. Howe (MD), J. Ryall (Fin)
Immediate Holding Company: MODERN & ANTIQUE FIREARMS LIMITED
Registration no: 04169494 **Date established:** 2001
No.of Employees: 1 - 10 **Product Groups:** 36, 39, 40

Date of Accounts	Dec 11	Dec 10	Dec 09
Working Capital	-15	-21	-5
Current Assets	22	25	33

Morlands
581 Charminster Road Charminster, Bournemouth, BH8 9RQ
Tel: 01202-513787 **Fax:** 01202-510500
E-mail: thepartnership@morlands.demon.co.uk
Website: http://www.emorlands.com
Directors: B. Morland (Ptnr)
Date established: 2002 **No.of Employees:** 1 - 10 **Product Groups:** 36, 37

Motion Control Products Ltd
11-15 Francis Avenue, Bournemouth, BH11 8NX
Tel: 01202-599922 **Fax:** 01202-599955
E-mail: enquiries@motioncontrolproducts.com
Website: http://www.motioncontrolproducts.com
Bank(s): National Westminster Bank Plc
Directors: S. Mckay (MD)
Managers: M. Rudkin
Immediate Holding Company: MOTION CONTROL PRODUCTS LIMITED
Registration no: 02910074 **VAT No.:** GB 651 2816 48
Date established: 1994 **Turnover:** £1m - £2m **No.of Employees:** 11 - 20
Product Groups: 35, 36, 37, 38, 39, 44, 45, 46, 47

Date of Accounts	Jul 11	Jul 10	Jul 09
Working Capital	112	127	169
Fixed Assets	92	96	65
Current Assets	569	429	417

Nova Contract Cleaners
12 Smithfield Place, Bournemouth, BH9 2QJ
Tel: 01202-536770 **Fax:** 01202-520475
E-mail: sales@nova-cleaners.co.uk
Website: http://www.nova-cleaners.co.uk
Managers: S. Ferguson (Chief Mgr)
Registration no: 1480625 **Date established:** 1968 **Turnover:** £1m - £2m
No.of Employees: 101 - 250 **Product Groups:** 52

Openings
325-327 Holdenhurst Road, Bournemouth, BH8 8BT
Tel: 01202-301267 **Fax:** 01202-727071
E-mail: sales@openings.co.uk
Website: http://www.openings.co.uk
Directors: D. Hall (Dir)
Managers: M. Tyreman (Sales Prom Mgr)
Registration no: 02236021 **Date established:** 1988 **Turnover:** £1m - £2m
No.of Employees: 1 - 10 **Product Groups:** 35, 36, 37, 45, 66

Oswald Bailey Group
72-74 Palmerston Road, Bournemouth, BH1 4JT
Tel: 01202-397273 **Fax:** 01202-397274
E-mail: sales@oswaldbailey.co.uk
Website: http://www.oswaldbailey.co.uk
Bank(s): National Westminster Bank Plc
Directors: S. Bailey (MD)
Managers: C. Bailey, R. Williams (Personnel), S. Osbourne (Buyer), S. Sinkinson (Fin Mgr)
Ultimate Holding Company: OSWALD BAILEY GROUP LIMITED
Immediate Holding Company: OSWALD BAILEY LIMITED
Registration no: 00559815 **VAT No.:** GB 392 7947 95
Date established: 1956 **Turnover:** £5m - £10m **No.of Employees:** 11 - 20
Product Groups: 22, 24, 63, 65

Date of Accounts	Jan 12	Jan 11	Jan 10
Sales Turnover	5m	7m	7m
Pre Tax Profit/Loss	-810	-162	-24
Working Capital	-722	-68	33
Fixed Assets	104	138	177
Current Assets	440	3m	2m
Current Liabilities	290	308	303

Parvalux Electric Motors Ltd
490-492 Wallisdown Road, Bournemouth, BH11 8PU
Tel: 01202-512575 **Fax:** 01202-530885
E-mail: sales@parvalux.co.uk
Website: http://www.parvalux.co.uk
Bank(s): National Westminster
Directors: N. Spech (Comm)
Managers: A. Hunt (Purch Mgr), C. Reynolds (I.T. Exec)
Ultimate Holding Company: PARVALUX LIMITED
Immediate Holding Company: EMD DRIVE SYSTEMS LIMITED
Registration no: 07308170 **VAT No.:** GB 185 9522 25
Date established: 2010 **Turnover:** £5m - £10m
No.of Employees: 101 - 250 **Product Groups:** 37, 40

Portman Building Society
Richmond Hill, Bournemouth, BH2 6EP
Tel: 08456-090600 **Fax:** 01202-563800
Website: http://www.portman.co.uk
Managers: J. Gully
Immediate Holding Company: BLS BUILDING SPECIALISTS LTD
Registration no: 09000125 **Date established:** 1846
No.of Employees: 1 - 10 **Product Groups:** 82

Qualitech Filters
5 Abbott Close, Bournemouth, BH9 1EX
Tel: 01202-249642
Directors: A. Hawkes (Prop)
Registration no: 03955093 **Date established:** 2000
No.of Employees: 1 - 10 **Product Groups:** 38, 42

Quiller Holdings Ltd
2 Pailsey Road, Bournemouth, BH6 5EU
Tel: 01202-436777 **Fax:** 01202-421255
E-mail: sales@quiller.co.uk
Website: http://www.quiller.co.uk
Directors: J. Clarke (Dir), P. Allen (Dir), R. Sadowski (Dir), T. Barker (MD)
Managers: J. Cox (Sec)
Ultimate Holding Company: Abacus Group Ltd
Immediate Holding Company: Deltron Electronics Ltd
Registration no: 03611347 **VAT No.:** GB 568 4011 39
Date established: 1998 **Turnover:** £5m - £10m **No.of Employees:** 1 - 10
Product Groups: 37, 38, 39, 40, 44

Date of Accounts	Dec 05
Fixed Assets	596
Current Assets	614
Current Liabilities	614
Total Share Capital	69

Ranger Fixings Ltd
8 Central Business Park Southcote Road, Bournemouth, BH1 3SJ
Tel: 01202-297125 **Fax:** 01202-294087
E-mail: ranger.fixings@tiscali.co.uk
Directors: J. Maddox (Fin), M. Lock (MD)
Immediate Holding Company: RANGER FIXINGS LIMITED
Registration no: 02593329 **VAT No.:** GB 579 9564 57
Date established: 1991 **Turnover:** Up to £250,000
No.of Employees: 1 - 10 **Product Groups:** 66

Date of Accounts	Dec 11	Dec 10	Dec 09
Working Capital	234	237	273
Fixed Assets	44	64	42
Current Assets	406	398	380

Read Fabrications Ltd
Rear of 51 Columbia Road, Bournemouth, BH10 4EA
Tel: 01202-517920 **Fax:** 01202-517920
E-mail: info@readfabrications.co.uk
Website: http://www.readfabrications.co.uk
Directors: S. Read (MD)
Immediate Holding Company: READ FABRICATIONS LIMITED
Registration no: 04575800 **Date established:** 2002
No.of Employees: 1 - 10 **Product Groups:** 26, 35

Date of Accounts	Nov 11	Nov 10	Nov 09
Working Capital	47	40	28
Fixed Assets	75	79	88
Current Assets	92	94	101

Safatech Ltd
6 Ferris Place, Bournemouth, BH8 0AU
Tel: 01202-392772 **Fax:** 01202-392760
E-mail: office@safatech.co.uk
Website: http://www.safatech.co.uk
Managers: E. Sanger (Ops Mgr)
Immediate Holding Company: SAFATECH LIMITED
Registration no: 04014418 **Date established:** 2000
Turnover: Up to £250,000 **No.of Employees:** 1 - 10 **Product Groups:** 80, 81, 85

Date of Accounts	Mar 12	Mar 11	Mar 10
Sales Turnover	82	68	59
Pre Tax Profit/Loss	24	21	10
Working Capital	25	8	-9
Fixed Assets	7	4	5
Current Assets	40	31	20
Current Liabilities	13	13	10

Sembcorp Bournemouth Water Ltd
George Jessell House Francis Avenue, Bournemouth, BH11 8NX
Tel: 01202-591111 **Fax:** 01202-597022
E-mail: itmanager@bwhwater.co.uk
Website: http://www.bwhwater.co.uk
Bank(s): Lloyds TSB Bank plc
Managers: T. Macey (Mgr)
Ultimate Holding Company: SEMBCORP INDUSTRIES LTD (SINGAPORE)
Immediate Holding Company: WEST HAMPSHIRE WATER LIMITED
Registration no: 05598453 **VAT No.:** GB 619 7841 04
Date established: 2005 **Turnover:** £20m - £50m
No.of Employees: 101 - 250 **Product Groups:** 18, 52, 54, 84

Signage Store
362 Charminster Road, Bournemouth, BH8 9RX
Tel: 01202-528588 **Fax:** 01202-528583
E-mail: enquiries@thesignagestore.co.uk
Website: http://www.thesignagestore.co.uk
Directors: L. Warrington (Prop)
No.of Employees: 1 - 10 **Product Groups:** 28, 30, 49, 52, 67

Signex UK Ltd
21a Hankinson Road, Bournemouth, BH9 1HJ
Tel: 01202-247000 **Fax:** 01202-247001
E-mail: jon@signex.com
Website: http://www.signex.com
Directors: K. Finney (Fin), J. Finney (MD)
Immediate Holding Company: SIGNEX UK LIMITED
Registration no: 04730470 **Date established:** 2003
Turnover: Up to £250,000 **No.of Employees:** 1 - 10 **Product Groups:** 37

Date of Accounts	Dec 11	Dec 10	Dec 09
Working Capital	28	32	39
Fixed Assets	24	23	23
Current Assets	48	45	67

Solid Contracts Ltd
Bristol & West House Post Office Road, Bournemouth, BH1 1BL
Tel: 01202-314444
E-mail: asorrell@solidcontracts.co.uk
Website: http://www.solidcontracts.co.uk
Managers: A. Sorrell (Mgr)
Immediate Holding Company: SOLID CONTRACTS LTD
Registration no: 06601172 **Date established:** 2008
No.of Employees: 1 - 10 **Product Groups:** 44

Date of Accounts	Jul 10	Jul 09	Mar 11
Working Capital	16	5	14
Fixed Assets	1	N/A	1
Current Assets	57	43	87

The Suncliff
29 East Overcliff Drive, Bournemouth, BH1 3AG
Tel: 01202-291711 **Fax:** 01202-293788
E-mail: reception@suncliffbournemouth.co.uk
Website: http://www.suncliffbournemouth.co.uk
Managers: R. Carley (Chief Mgr), P. Winskill
Immediate Holding Company: CALOTELS GROUP
Turnover: £2m - £5m **No.of Employees:** 51 - 100 **Product Groups:** 69

Technical Paint Services Ltd
The Paint Centre 27 Southcote Road, Bournemouth, BH1 3SH
Tel: 01202-295570 **Fax:** 08452-301255
E-mail: info@technicalpaintservices.com
Website: http://www.technicalpaintservices.com
Directors: R. Peacop (Dir)
Immediate Holding Company: NEATCROSS LIMITED
Registration no: 01570359 **Date established:** 1981
Turnover: Up to £250,000 **No.of Employees:** 1 - 10 **Product Groups:** 32

Date of Accounts	Jun 11	Jun 10	Jun 09
Sales Turnover	206	189	149
Pre Tax Profit/Loss	-12	-44	-16
Working Capital	-24	-116	-73
Fixed Assets	3	4	5
Current Assets	47	42	69
Current Liabilities	N/A	157	N/A

The Bournemouth Daily Echo (Newscom & Media P.L.C.)
Richmond Hill, Bournemouth, BH2 6HH
Tel: 01202-411411 **Fax:** 01202-292115
E-mail: advertising@bournemouthecho.co.uk
Website: http://www.advertiseseries.co.uk
Bank(s): Lloyds TSB Bank plc
Directors: V. Boni (MD), A. Sullivan (Fin)
Managers: P. Davidson (Mgr)
Immediate Holding Company: POETS (10) LLP
Registration no: 05834822 **VAT No.:** GB 188 4831 19
Date established: 2009 **Turnover:** £2m - £5m
No.of Employees: 101 - 250 **Product Groups:** 28

Date of Accounts	Mar 11	Mar 10
Working Capital	60	-2m
Fixed Assets	3m	2m
Current Assets	122	1

Thinking Juice Advertising Ltd
Burlington House Burlington Arcade, Bournemouth, BH1 2HZ
Tel: 01202-294114 **Fax:** 01202-201145
E-mail: ideas@thinkingjuice.co.uk
Website: http://www.thinkingjuice.co.uk
Directors: G. Watt (MD)
Immediate Holding Company: THINKING JUICE LIMITED
Registration no: 05419447 **Date established:** 2005 **Turnover:** £1m - £2m
No.of Employees: 11 - 20 **Product Groups:** 28, 44, 81, 87

Date of Accounts	May 11	Nov 10	Nov 09
Working Capital	-80	-4	-57
Fixed Assets	11	12	10
Current Assets	48	54	-57
Current Liabilities	40	N/A	N/A

UK Fire & Security Services Ltd
55 Monks Way, Bournemouth, BH11 9TP
Tel: 08716-629966 **Fax:** 07053-611338
E-mail: sales@ukfireandsecurityservicesltd.co.uk
Website: http://www.ukfireandsecurityservicesltd.co.uk
Directors: I. Jones (MD)
Immediate Holding Company: UK FIRE & SECURITY SERVICES LTD
Registration no: 06015449 **Date established:** 2006
No.of Employees: 1 - 10 **Product Groups:** 38, 42

Date of Accounts	Nov 11	Nov 10	Nov 09
Working Capital	-10	-2	N/A
Fixed Assets	1	2	2
Current Assets	1	4	12

Vitcom Engineering Ltd
26 East Avenue, Bournemouth, BH3 7BZ
Tel: 01202-589190
E-mail: antonas@vitcom.com
Website: http://vitcom.com
Directors: I. Antonas (Fin)
Immediate Holding Company: VITCOM GLOBAL SOLUTIONS LTD
Registration no: 03684093 **Date established:** 1998
No.of Employees: 1 - 10 **Product Groups:** 32, 37, 38, 40, 42, 44, 46, 48, 52, 66, 67, 80, 84, 85, 86

Date of Accounts	Dec 09	Dec 08	Dec 07
Working Capital	-9	-16	28
Fixed Assets	3	2	2
Current Assets	12	9	72

Xpress Blinds Ltd
37 Cedar Manor 19-21 Poole Road, Bournemouth, BH4 9DE
Tel: 0800-5200967
E-mail: support@xpressblinds.net
Website: http://www.xpressblinds.net
Directors: P. Cornelius (MD)
Registration no: 05149047 **Date established:** 2004
Turnover: Up to £250,000 **No.of Employees:** 1 - 10 **Product Groups:** 25, 30

Date of Accounts	Jun 08	Jun 07	Jun 06
Working Capital	-6	5	-4
Fixed Assets	12	4	2
Current Assets	8	39	5
Current Liabilities	14	34	8

Zintech Ltd
Gild House 70 Norwich Avenue West, Bournemouth, BH2 6AW
Tel: 01202-755733
E-mail: andy@zintech.co.uk
Website: http://www.zintech.co.uk
Directors: A. Anderson (Dir)
Immediate Holding Company: ZINTECH LIMITED
Registration no: 05598587 **Date established:** 2005
Turnover: Up to £250,000 **No.of Employees:** 1 - 10 **Product Groups:** 37

Date of Accounts	Mar 11	Mar 10	Mar 09
Working Capital	-21	-10	-10
Fixed Assets	31	17	18
Current Assets	3	4	3

Bridport

Amsafe Bridport
The Court West Street, Bridport, DT6 3QU
Tel: 01308-456666 **Fax:** 01308-456605
E-mail: reception@amsafe.com
Website: http://www.amsafe.com
Directors: L. White (Fin), M. Brooks (Fin)
Managers: M. Homewood (Personnel), T. Athulathmudali (Tech Serv Mgr), F. Duce (Purch Mgr), H. Smith
Ultimate Holding Company: AMSAFE GLOBAL HOLDINGS INC (USA)
Immediate Holding Company: AMSAFE BRIDPORT LIMITED
Registration no: 00140449 **VAT No.:** GB 291 9330 43
Date established: 2015 **Turnover:** £20m - £50m
No.of Employees: 101 - 250 **Product Groups:** 23

Date of Accounts	Dec 11	Dec 10	Dec 09
Sales Turnover	41m	39m	37m
Pre Tax Profit/Loss	1m	3m	2m
Working Capital	31m	31m	29m
Fixed Assets	6m	8m	6m
Current Assets	37m	38m	40m
Current Liabilities	2m	2m	2m

Bridec
West Bay Road, Bridport, DT6 4EH
Tel: 01308-456684 **Fax:** 01308-424255
E-mail: general@bridec.co.uk
Website: http://www.bridec.co.uk
Bank(s): Lloyds TSB Bank plc
Directors: A. Pollard (Dir), A. Fowkes (MD)
Managers: J. Mackay (Buyer)
Immediate Holding Company: BRIDEC LIMITED
Registration no: 03460212 **Date established:** 1997
Turnover: Up to £250,000 **No.of Employees:** 21 - 50 **Product Groups:** 30

Date of Accounts	Mar 11	Mar 09	Mar 08
Working Capital	-58	-64	-48
Fixed Assets	N/A	1	1
Current Assets	1	N/A	N/A

Curtis Wright
Napoleon House Gore Cross Business Park Corbin Way, Bradpole, Bridport, DT6 3UX
Tel: 01308-422256 **Fax:** 01308-427760
E-mail: dtucker@curtisswright.com
Website: http://www.cwfc.com
Directors: S. Bowler (Tech Serv), M. Breese (Sales & Mktg), D. Tucker (MD)
Managers: M. Donnan (Comptroller), C. Thurston (Mats Contrlr)
Ultimate Holding Company: CURTISS WRIGHT CORPORATION (U.S.A)
Immediate Holding Company: CURTISS-WRIGHT FLOW CONTROL (UK) LIMITED
Date established: 2001 **No.of Employees:** 51 - 100 **Product Groups:** 36, 37, 38

Date of Accounts	Dec 11	Dec 10	Dec 09
Sales Turnover	30m	11m	17m
Pre Tax Profit/Loss	10	-493	2m
Working Capital	11m	5m	5m
Fixed Assets	12m	6m	6m
Current Assets	21m	7m	8m
Current Liabilities	3m	400	1m

Deben Group Industries Ltd
Gore Cross Business Park Corbin Way, Bradpole, Bridport, DT6 3UX
Tel: 01308-423576 **Fax:** 01308-425912
E-mail: johnp@deben.com
Website: http://www.deben.com
Directors: P. Walker (MD), J. Pask (Dir)
Managers: J. Pask (Mgr)
Immediate Holding Company: DEBEN GROUP INDUSTRIES LIMITED
Registration no: 02813799 **VAT No.:** GB 637 7376 03
Date established: 1993 **Turnover:** £2m - £5m **No.of Employees:** 1 - 10
Product Groups: 23

Date of Accounts	May 08	May 07	May 06
Working Capital	1912	1869	1414
Fixed Assets	2800	2535	1410
Current Assets	3018	2778	2190
Current Liabilities	1106	909	775

M C Harvey
4 Crepe Farm Business Park Symondsbury, Bridport, DT6 6EX
Tel: 07977-141196
E-mail: mc66h@hotmail.com
Directors: M. Harvey (Prop)
Date established: 1997 **No.of Employees:** 1 - 10 **Product Groups:** 35

Huck Nets UK Ltd
Gore Cross Business Park Corbin Way, Bradpole, Bridport, DT6 3UX
Tel: 01308-425100 **Fax:** 01308-458109
E-mail: sales@hucknetting.co.uk
Website: http://www.hucknetting.co.uk
Bank(s): Barclays Bank Plc
Directors: S. Davis (Co Sec), J. Legg-bagg (Sales)
Managers: R. Raybould (Factory Mgr)
Immediate Holding Company: HUCK NETS (U.K.) LIMITED
Registration no: 03276081 **VAT No.:** GB 684 4852 92
Date established: 1996 **Turnover:** £5m - £10m **No.of Employees:** 21 - 50
Product Groups: 22, 23, 26, 29, 30, 35, 39, 41, 49, 52, 63, 65

Date of Accounts	Dec 11	Dec 10	Dec 09
Sales Turnover	N/A	6m	6m
Pre Tax Profit/Loss	N/A	123	82
Working Capital	1m	1m	1m
Fixed Assets	1m	1m	1m
Current Assets	3m	3m	3m
Current Liabilities	N/A	394	440

Lay Gard Ltd
West Road, Bridport, DT6 5JT
Tel: 01308-456232 **Fax:** 01308-458101
E-mail: sales@seawinch.co.uk
Website: http://www.seawinch.co.uk
Directors: S. Lambert (Fin), W. Bowell (MD), G. Lambert (MD)
Registration no: 01451928 **Date established:** 1979
Turnover: Up to £250,000 **No.of Employees:** 1 - 10 **Product Groups:** 35, 36, 39

Par Louvre Systems
St Andrews House St Andrews Trading Estate, Bridport, DT6 3EX
Tel: 01308-455920 **Fax:** 01308-425958
E-mail: tony.colborne@parlouvre.com
Website: http://www.parlouvre.com
Directors: T. Colborne (Dir)
Immediate Holding Company: PAR LOUVRE SYSTEMS LIMITED
Registration no: 04112478 **Date established:** 2000
No.of Employees: 11 - 20 **Product Groups:** 35, 37, 40

Date of Accounts	Nov 07	Nov 06	Nov 05
Working Capital	23	-43	-100
Fixed Assets	17	13	28
Current Assets	800	562	483
Current Liabilities	777	605	583

Preset Calibration Services Ltd
94A East Street, Bridport, DT6 3LL
Tel: 01308-456539 **Fax:** 01308-421676
E-mail: info@preset.com
Website: http://www.preset.com
Directors: S. Kick (MD)
Immediate Holding Company: PRESET CALIBRATION SERVICES LIMITED
Registration no: 02077066 **VAT No.:** 378 8491 85 **Date established:** 1986
Turnover: £500,000 - £1m **No.of Employees:** 1 - 10 **Product Groups:** 37, 38, 44, 85

Date of Accounts	Dec 11	Dec 10	Dec 09
Working Capital	-25	-15	-12
Fixed Assets	91	89	86
Current Assets	154	236	174

Retail Display Solutions
St Andrew House St Andrews Trading Estate, Bridport, DT6 3EX
Tel: 01308-459950 **Fax:** 01308-424410
E-mail: info@retaildisplaysolutions.co.uk
Website: http://www.retaildisplaysolutions.co.uk
Directors: T. Clark (Dir)
No.of Employees: 21 - 50 **Product Groups:** 40, 48, 49

Rotorflush Filters Ltd
Langmoor Manor Charmouth, Bridport, DT6 6BU
Tel: 01297-560229 **Fax:** 01297-560110
E-mail: sales@rotorflush.com
Website: http://www.rotorflush.com
Directors: J. Hosford (MD)
Immediate Holding Company: ROTORFLUSH FILTERS LIMITED
Registration no: 07472511 **Date established:** 2010
No.of Employees: 1 - 10 **Product Groups:** 14, 41, 42

Date of Accounts	Mar 12
Working Capital	-8
Fixed Assets	60
Current Assets	36

Broadstone

Dorset Lifts Ltd
3 Arrowsmith Court Station Approach, Broadstone, BH18 8AX
Tel: 01202-650361 **Fax:** 01202-658647
E-mail: sales@dorsetlifts.com
Website: http://www.dorsetlifts.com
Directors: C. Wing (Dir)
Immediate Holding Company: DORSET LIFTS LIMITED
Registration no: 03699485 **Date established:** 1999
No.of Employees: 11 - 20 **Product Groups:** 35, 39, 45

Date of Accounts	Jan 11	Jan 10	Jan 09
Working Capital	14	-0	-35
Fixed Assets	N/A	1	1
Current Assets	269	183	215

I S T Ltd
11 Moor Road, Broadstone, BH18 8AZ
Tel: 01202-692775 **Fax:** 01202-605588
E-mail: sales@ist-limited.com
Website: http://www.ist.gb.net
Directors: A. Shepherd (Sales)
Immediate Holding Company: NEW DRIVER SCHOOLS OF MOTORING (REGISTRY AND ADMINISTRATION) LIMITED
Registration no: 02219906 **Date established:** 1988
No.of Employees: 1 - 10 **Product Groups:** 38, 42

Date of Accounts	Mar 12	Mar 11	Mar 10
Working Capital	78	133	179
Fixed Assets	14	17	19
Current Assets	113	159	241

Christchurch

A D Labels
14 Turnberry Close, Christchurch, BH23 1LQ
Tel: 01202-482434
E-mail: graham@ad-labels.co.uk
Website: http://www.ad-labels.co.uk
Directors: G. Kerwood (Prop)
Turnover: Up to £250,000 **No.of Employees:** 1 - 10 **Product Groups:** 27, 28, 30, 32, 42, 49

Absolute Corporate Events
7b Somerford Road, Christchurch, BH23 3PH
Tel: 01202-485500 **Fax:** 01202-487200
E-mail: paul@acevenues.com
Website: http://www.absolutecoporateevents.com
Directors: A. Mason (MD)
Turnover: £2m - £5m **No.of Employees:** 1 - 10 **Product Groups:** 37, 67, 69, 89

Adept Safety
14 Holme Road Highcliffe, Christchurch, BH23 5LJ
Tel: 01425-276719
E-mail: adeptsafety@yahoo.com
Website: http://www.adeptsafety.com
Directors: J. Carpenter (Dir)
No.of Employees: 1 - 10 **Product Groups:** 80, 84

Aeroflex Hose & Engineering Ltd
11a Aviation Park West Bournemouth International Airport, Hurn, Christchurch, BH23 6EW
Tel: 01202-895660 **Fax:** 01202-891177
E-mail: sales@aeroflex.co.uk
Website: http://www.aeroflex.co.uk
Directors: D. Murphy (MD), M. Murphy (Fin)
Immediate Holding Company: AEROFLEX HOSE AND ENGINEERING LIMITED
Registration no: 01506555 **Date established:** 1980
Turnover: Up to £250,000 **No.of Employees:** 21 - 50 **Product Groups:** 29, 30, 36

Date of Accounts	Dec 11	Dec 10	Dec 09
Working Capital	590	527	447
Fixed Assets	125	101	86
Current Assets	1m	1m	946

Aim Aviation Ltd
Building 138 Bournemouth International, Hurn, Christchurch, BH23 6NW
Tel: 01202-599666 **Fax:** 01202-599677
E-mail: email@aim-aviation.co.uk
Website: http://www.aim-aviation.co.uk
Directors: J. Thorpe (MD)
Immediate Holding Company: AIM AVIATION LIMITED
Registration no: 07275471 **VAT No.:** GB 185 9883 90
Date established: 2010 **No.of Employees:** 101 - 250 **Product Groups:** 39

Date of Accounts	Apr 12	Apr 11
Sales Turnover	86m	64m
Pre Tax Profit/Loss	7m	3m
Working Capital	22m	24m
Fixed Assets	43m	45m
Current Assets	45m	41m
Current Liabilities	11m	8m

Atkinson Bailey Ceramics Ltd
3a Groveley Road, Christchurch, BH23 3HB
Tel: 01202-473330 **Fax:** 01202-480686
Website: http://www.abceramics.co.uk
Directors: A. Bailey (Dir)
Date established: 1984 **No.of Employees:** 1 - 10 **Product Groups:** 38, 67

Aviation Rentals Ltd
North East Sector Bournemouth International Airport, Hurn, Christchurch, BH23 6NE
Tel: 01202-573331 **Fax:** 01202-576709
E-mail: mail@av-rentals.co.uk
Website: http://www.av-rentals.co.uk
Directors: S. Stilton (MD)
Immediate Holding Company: AVIATION RENTALS LIMITED
Registration no: 03437513 **Date established:** 1997
Turnover: £75m - £125m **No.of Employees:** 11 - 20 **Product Groups:** 39

Date of Accounts	Mar 11	Mar 10	Mar 09
Working Capital	59	90	84
Fixed Assets	33	N/A	N/A
Current Assets	182	215	191

Avon Plastics Ltd
Unit 15 Silver Business Park Airfield Way, Christchurch, BH23 3TA
Tel: 01202-470888
E-mail: sales@avonplastics.co.uk
Website: http://www.avonplastics.co.uk
Directors: M. Parkes (Fin)
Immediate Holding Company: AVON PLASTICS LIMITED
Registration no: 04361452 **Date established:** 2002
No.of Employees: 1 - 10 **Product Groups:** 30, 32

Date of Accounts	Mar 11	Mar 10	Mar 09
Working Capital	20	48	39
Fixed Assets	6	7	9
Current Assets	179	170	129

B F Component Solutions Ltd
4a Wilverley Road, Christchurch, BH23 3RU
Tel: 01202-488202 **Fax:** 01202-474442
E-mail: sales@bfcgroupltd.com
Website: http://www.bfcgroupltd.com
Bank(s): National Westminster Bank Plc
Directors: K. Pond (MD)
Immediate Holding Company: THE SLIMMING COACH LIMITED
Registration no: 06312514 **VAT No.:** GB 285 1261 59
Date established: 2004 **No.of Employees:** 11 - 20 **Product Groups:** 30, 35, 66

Date of Accounts	Dec 11	Dec 10	Dec 09
Working Capital	-31	-25	-16
Fixed Assets	17	21	25
Current Assets	3	5	4
Current Liabilities	20	N/A	N/A

Bath Travel
4 High Street, Christchurch, BH23 1AY
Tel: 01202-484247 **Fax:** 01202-487144
Website: http://www.bathtravel.com
Managers: K. Wearn (Mgr)
Ultimate Holding Company: R.E. BATH TRAVEL SERVICE LIMITED(THE)
Immediate Holding Company: TAPPERS TRAVEL SERVICE LIMITED
Registration no: 00785141 **Date established:** 1963 **Turnover:** £1m - £2m
No.of Employees: 1 - 10 **Product Groups:** 69

Date of Accounts	Oct 10	Oct 09	Oct 07
Sales Turnover	N/A	N/A	1m
Pre Tax Profit/Loss	N/A	N/A	227
Working Capital	50	50	50
Current Assets	50	50	50

Boyland Joinery Ltd
Stony Lane, Christchurch, BH23 1EZ
Tel: 01202-499499 **Fax:** 01202-499037
E-mail: enquiries@boylandjoinery.co.uk
Website: http://www.boylandjoinery.co.uk
Bank(s): National Westminster Bank Plc
Directors: C. Thrumble (MD), C. Thrumble (MD)
Managers: J. Hammond (Sales & Mktg Mg)
Immediate Holding Company: BOYLAND JOINERY LIMITED
Registration no: 00698872 **Date established:** 1961 **Turnover:** £2m - £5m
No.of Employees: 21 - 50 **Product Groups:** 25, 33

Date of Accounts	Jan 12	Jan 11	Jan 10
Working Capital	-84	-97	-142
Fixed Assets	310	256	203
Current Assets	591	504	475

Bridgeworks Ltd
135 Summerford Road, Christchurch, BH23 3PY
Tel: 01425-478811 **Fax:** 0870-121 0709
E-mail: sales@4bridgeworks.com
Website: http://www.4bridgeworks.com
Directors: W. Eykyn (Co Sec)
Immediate Holding Company: BRIDGEWORKS LTD.
Registration no: 02155954 **VAT No.:** GB 355 9489 02
Date established: 1987 **Turnover:** £1m - £2m **No.of Employees:** 1 - 10
Product Groups: 44

Date of Accounts	Dec 11	Dec 10	Dec 09
Working Capital	-36	-247	-2m
Fixed Assets	48	46	37
Current Assets	271	197	126

Burning Media
Yonder House Derritt Lane, Bransgore, Christchurch, BH23 8AR
Tel: 01425-674937 **Fax:** 01425-674938
E-mail: info@burningmedia.com
Website: http://www.burningmedia.com
Directors: F. Preece (MD)
Immediate Holding Company: BURNING MEDIA LIMITED
Registration no: 04661432 **Date established:** 2003
No.of Employees: 1 - 10 **Product Groups:** 44, 89

Date of Accounts	Feb 08	Feb 11	Feb 10
Working Capital	N/A	1	2
Fixed Assets	8	4	5
Current Assets	4	5	4

C S E Citation Centre
Hanger 100 North West Sector Bournemouth International Airport, Hurn, Christchurch, BH23 6NW
Tel: 01202-573243 **Fax:** 01202-581579
E-mail: info@csecitationcentre.com
Website: http://www.csecitationcentre.co.uk
Directors: M. Gooding (Co Sec), P. Lammiman (MD), S. Adams (Pers), A. Wilson (I.T. Dir)
Ultimate Holding Company: BBA AVIATION
Immediate Holding Company: OXFORD AVIATION
Registration no: 01474814 **VAT No.:** GB 342 6517 63
Turnover: £2m - £5m **No.of Employees:** 21 - 50 **Product Groups:** 39

Roy Cobb
Merlie Cottage Croft Road, Neacroft, Christchurch, BH23 8JS
Tel: 01425-673252 **Fax:** 01425-673252
E-mail: roy.cobb@btconnect.com
Directors: R. Cobb (Prop)
Date established: 1979 **No.of Employees:** 1 - 10 **Product Groups:** 41

Coulton Instrumentation Ltd
Unit 17 Somerford Business Park Wilverley Road, Christchurch, BH23 3RU
Tel: 01202-480303 **Fax:** 01202-480808
E-mail: admin@coulton.com
Website: http://www.coulton.com
Directors: M. Jones (Mkt Research)
Ultimate Holding Company: RYE PALA (UK) LTD
Immediate Holding Company: COULTON INSTRUMENTATION LIMITED
Registration no: 04179308 **Date established:** 2001 **Turnover:** £1m - £2m
No.of Employees: 1 - 10 **Product Groups:** 37, 45

Date of Accounts	Apr 11	Apr 10	Apr 09
Working Capital	75	59	28
Fixed Assets	3	1	4
Current Assets	455	414	288

Data Track Technology plc
153 Somerford Road, Christchurch, BH23 3TY
Tel: 01425-270333 **Fax:** 01425-270433
E-mail: sales@dtrack.com
Website: http://www.datatrackpi.com
Bank(s): Lloyds TSB Bank plc
Directors: P. Staddon (Dir)
Immediate Holding Company: DATA TRACK TECHNOLOGY PLC
Registration no: 01414963 **Date established:** 1979 **Turnover:** £2m - £5m
No.of Employees: 51 - 100 **Product Groups:** 37, 38, 80

Date of Accounts	May 11	May 10	May 09
Sales Turnover	4m	4m	4m
Pre Tax Profit/Loss	-237	-281	114
Working Capital	539	678	956
Fixed Assets	223	291	357
Current Assets	1m	1m	2m
Current Liabilities	613	435	516

Distec Display Technology Ltd
1 Sea Vixen Industrial Estate Wilverley Road, Christchurch, BH23 3RU
Tel: 01202-470196 **Fax:** 01202-471446
E-mail: v_sutherland@btconnect.com
Website: http://www.distecdisplay.co.uk
Directors: C. Sutherland (Fin), V. Sutherland (MD)
Immediate Holding Company: DISTEC DISPLAY TECHNOLOGY LIMITED
Registration no: 03972061 **Date established:** 2000
Turnover: Up to £250,000 **No.of Employees:** 1 - 10 **Product Groups:** 23, 24, 26, 27, 28, 29, 30, 32, 35, 37, 38, 39, 40, 43, 44, 45, 49, 52, 63, 66, 67, 68, 80, 81

Date of Accounts	May 11	May 10	May 09
Working Capital	-0	3	-11
Fixed Assets	4	3	3
Current Assets	19	40	25

Dorset Metal Spinning Services
Building 107 Aviation Business Park Hurn, Christchurch, BH23 6NW
Tel: 01202-593670 **Fax:** 01202-593670
Directors: A. Dunesby (Prop)
VAT No.: GB 504 5133 86 **Date established:** 1988
Turnover: Up to £250,000 **No.of Employees:** 1 - 10 **Product Groups:** 48

Ellesco Ltd
6 Airfield Road, Christchurch, BH23 3TG
Tel: 01202-499400 **Fax:** 01202-484202
E-mail: general@ellesco.co.uk
Website: http://www.ellesco.co.uk
Directors: V. Simonis (Dir)
Immediate Holding Company: ELLESCO LIMITED
Registration no: 02895297 **Date established:** 1994 **Turnover:** £1m - £2m
No.of Employees: 11 - 20 **Product Groups:** 33, 42, 46, 49

Date of Accounts	Jun 12	Jun 11	Jun 10
Working Capital	350	426	364
Fixed Assets	44	38	56
Current Assets	915	763	1m

Exitflex UK Ltd
5 Airfield Road, Christchurch, BH23 3TG
Tel: 01202-478334 **Fax:** 01202-488110
E-mail: sales@exitflex.co.uk
Website: http://www.exitflex.co.uk
Directors: M. Whibley (MD)
Immediate Holding Company: EXITFLEX (UK) LIMITED
Registration no: 01972709 **VAT No.:** GB 423 4617 69
Date established: 1985 **Turnover:** £500,000 - £1m
No.of Employees: 1 - 10 **Product Groups:** 30

Date of Accounts	Dec 11	Dec 10	Dec 09
Working Capital	567	488	444
Fixed Assets	146	143	143
Current Assets	929	744	552

Fastener Network Holdings Ltd
5 Ambassador Industrial Estate 9 Airfield Road, Christchurch, BH23 3TG
Tel: 01202-479621 **Fax:** 01202-477222
E-mail: sales@fastenernetwork.co.uk
Website: http://www.fastenernetwork.co.uk
Directors: L. Lammas (Co Sec)
Managers: J. Ellis (Chief Mgr)
Immediate Holding Company: FASTENER NETWORK HOLDINGS LIMITED
Registration no: 06688655 **VAT No.:** GB 504 5364 67
Date established: 2008 **Turnover:** £2m - £5m **No.of Employees:** 11 - 20
Product Groups: 35, 66

Date of Accounts	Dec 11	Dec 10	Dec 09
Working Capital	459	434	38
Fixed Assets	54	70	86
Current Assets	2m	18m	2m

Hda Associates Ltd (Head Office)
Avon Wharf 23 Bridge Street, Christchurch, BH23 1DY
Tel: 01202-481811 **Fax:** 01202-499654
E-mail: llb@hda.co.uk
Website: http://www.hda.co.uk
Bank(s): Lloyds TSB Bank plc
Directors: P. Dicks (Ch), P. Dicks (Dir), L. Battson (Fin), P. Hilborn (MD), C. Glen (Grp Chief Exec), C. Glen (Chief Op Offcr)
Immediate Holding Company: HDA (UK) LTD.
Registration no: 04204238 **Date established:** 2001 **Turnover:** £1m - £2m
No.of Employees: 11 - 20 **Product Groups:** 80, 86

Honeywell Aerospace Bournemouth
Enterprise Way Aviation Park, Hurn, Christchurch, BH23 6EW
Tel: 01202-581818 **Fax:** 01202-581919
E-mail: webmaster.ssec@honeywell.com
Website: http://www.honeywell.com
Bank(s): Barclays
Managers: T. Erb (Mgr)
Immediate Holding Company: ALLIED SIGNAL AEROSPACE
VAT No.: GB 100 3286 30 **No.of Employees:** 101 - 250
Product Groups: 39

Insight Marketing Servivces Ltd
10 Valiant Way, Christchurch, BH23 4TW
Tel: 01425-276303 **Fax:** 01425-276384
E-mail: sales@i-marketing.uk.com
Website: http://www.insightmarketing.com
Directors: D. Edgar (MD)
Immediate Holding Company: I - MARKETING SERVICES LIMITED
Registration no: 05254520 **Date established:** 2004
Turnover: Up to £250,000 **No.of Employees:** 1 - 10 **Product Groups:** 81

Date of Accounts	Oct 11	Oct 10	Oct 08
Working Capital	2	N/A	7
Current Assets	4	1	19

ITX Warehouse Centretek Limited
Unit 81 Basepoint Business Centre Aviation Park West, Enterprise Way, Christchurch, BH23 6NX
Tel: 0870-3500277 **Fax:** 01202-232937
E-mail: info@itx-warehouse.co.uk
Website: http://www.itx-warehouse.co.uk
Directors: A. Grimstead (Dir)
Registration no: 04901816 **Date established:** 2004
No.of Employees: 1 - 10 **Product Groups:** 44, 67

K N G Developments
Building 196 North East Sector Bournemouth International Airport, Hurn, Christchurch, BH23 6NE
Tel: 01202-581856 **Fax:** 01202-581856
E-mail: administrator@kngdevelopments.com
Website: http://www.kngdevelopments.com
Directors: K. Gilson (Prop)
No.of Employees: 1 - 10 **Product Groups:** 22, 25, 26, 30, 33, 39, 40, 48, 66, 67

Charles Kendall Freight Ltd
2 South East Sector Bournemouth Int Airport, Hurn, Christchurch, BH23 6SE
Tel: 01202-593949 **Fax:** 01202-593940
E-mail: ckfbournemouth@charleskendall.com
Website: http://www.charleskendallfreight.com
Managers: T. Messer (Mgr)
Ultimate Holding Company: CHARLES KENDALL GROUP LIMITED
Immediate Holding Company: CHARLES KENDALL FREIGHT LIMITED
Registration no: 00540121 **VAT No.:** GB 238 4062 67
Date established: 1954 **No.of Employees:** 1 - 10 **Product Groups:** 76

Date of Accounts	Dec 11	Dec 10	Dec 09
Sales Turnover	19m	21m	20m
Pre Tax Profit/Loss	445	248	107
Working Capital	3m	2m	2m
Current Assets	13m	9m	7m
Current Liabilities	167	150	95

Linpol Metal Polishing
Building 352 Aviation Park West Bournemouth International Airp, Hurn, Christchurch, BH23 6NW
Tel: 01202-582778 **Fax:** 01202-582778
Directors: C. Robinson (Prop)
Immediate Holding Company: M & P LEASING LIMITED
Registration no: 01344118 **Date established:** 2008 **Turnover:** £2m - £5m
No.of Employees: 1 - 10 **Product Groups:** 46, 48

Date of Accounts	Mar 11	Mar 10	Mar 09
Working Capital	50	69	42
Fixed Assets	67	73	53
Current Assets	172	197	178

Logo Bugs Plus Ltd
9 Airfield Way, Christchurch, BH23 3PE
Tel: 01202-588500 **Fax:** 01202-487177
E-mail: sales@logobugsplus.co.uk
Website: http://www.logobugsplus.co.uk
Directors: D. Grace (MD)
Immediate Holding Company: LOGOBUGS LIMITED
Registration no: 03222827 **Date established:** 1996 **Turnover:** £1m - £2m
No.of Employees: 11 - 20 **Product Groups:** 24, 25, 27, 28, 30, 33, 37, 38, 49, 65

M P M Mouldings Ltd
7 7 Airfield Road, Christchurch, BH23 3TQ
Tel: 01202-470405 **Fax:** 01202-470405
E-mail: sales@mpmmouldings.com
Website: http://www.mpmmouldings.com
Directors: D. Wright (MD), J. Kingsley (Prop), K. Wright (Fin)
Immediate Holding Company: MPM MOULDINGS LIMITED
Registration no: 04808931 **VAT No.:** GB 423 6397 47
Date established: 2003 **Turnover:** Up to £250,000
No.of Employees: 1 - 10 **Product Groups:** 66

Date of Accounts	Sep 08	Sep 07	Sep 06
Working Capital	13	9	12
Fixed Assets	7	14	22
Current Assets	44	58	38
Current Liabilities	32	49	26

Meggitt plc
Atlantic House Aviation Park West, Hurn, Christchurch, BH23 6EW
Tel: 01202-597597 **Fax:** 01202-597555
E-mail: executive@meggitt.com
Website: http://www.meggitt.com
Bank(s): HSBC, Bournemouth
Directors: S. Young (Fin), T. Twigger (Grp Chief Exec)
Managers: F. Greig, V. Ramsden (Personnel)
Ultimate Holding Company: MEGGITT PLC
Immediate Holding Company: MEGGITT PLC
Registration no: 00432989 **VAT No.:** GB 185 6535 31
Date established: 1947 **Turnover:** Over £1,000m
No.of Employees: 21 - 50 **Product Groups:** 34

Date of Accounts	Dec 11	Dec 10	Dec 09
Sales Turnover	1455m	1162m	1151m
Pre Tax Profit/Loss	226m	173m	181m
Working Capital	226m	168m	178m
Fixed Assets	3290m	2765m	2735m
Current Assets	696m	536m	515m
Current Liabilities	320m	271m	249m

N F F Precision Ltd
4 Enterprise Way Aviation Park West Bournemouth International Airport, Hurn, Christchurch, BH23 6EW
Tel: 01202-583000 **Fax:** 01202-583058
E-mail: sales@nff.uk.com
Website: http://www.nff.uk.com
Directors: A. Rogers (MD), B. Oldrey (Fin)
Managers: W. Keynes (Personnel)
Ultimate Holding Company: NFF HOLDINGS LIMITED
Immediate Holding Company: N.F.F. PRECISION LIMITED
Registration no: 01563804 **VAT No.:** Gb 392 7871 05
Date established: 1981 **Turnover:** £2m - £5m **No.of Employees:** 21 - 50
Product Groups: 84

Date of Accounts	Dec 11	Dec 10	Dec 09
Working Capital	201	167	193
Fixed Assets	147	71	83
Current Assets	984	950	733

Nevis Marketing Ltd
Unit 12 Priory Industrial Park Airspeed Road, Christchurch, BH23 4HD
Tel: 01425-273344 **Fax:** 01425-273311
E-mail: info@nevis.uk.com
Website: http://www.nevis.uk.com
Directors: K. Culverwell (Dir)
Registration no: 02327895 **Date established:** 1988
No.of Employees: 11 - 20 **Product Groups:** 22, 24, 39, 40

P C Fabrication
Rossiters Boat Yard Bridge Street, Christchurch, BH23 1DZ
Tel: 01202-485385 **Fax:** 01202-485385
E-mail: petecouch304@aol.com
Website: http://www.pcfabrications.org.uk
Directors: P. Couch (Prop)
Ultimate Holding Company: CHRISTCHURCH MARINE LIMITED
Immediate Holding Company: ROSSITER YACHTS LIMITED
Registration no: 02845467 **Date established:** 1947
Turnover: Up to £250,000 **No.of Employees:** 1 - 10 **Product Groups:** 35

Date of Accounts	Nov 11	Nov 10	Nov 09
Working Capital	-21	-11	-17
Current Assets	6	7	9

P G Drive Technology
1 Airspeed Road, Christchurch, BH23 4HD
Tel: 01425-271444 **Fax:** 01425-272655
E-mail: sales@pgdt.com
Website: http://www.pgdt.com
Bank(s): HSBC Bank plc
Directors: H. Chenhall (MD), L. Thomas (Fin)
Ultimate Holding Company: SPIRENT COMMUNICATIONS PLC
Immediate Holding Company: PG INTERNATIONAL LTD
Registration no: 02279804 **No.of Employees:** 101 - 250
Product Groups: 37, 38, 39

Date of Accounts	Dec 07	Dec 06	Dec 05
Working Capital	10	10	10
Current Assets	10	10	10
Total Share Capital	10	10	10

Penny & Giles Controls Ltd
15 Airfield Road, Christchurch, BH23 3TG
Tel: 01202-409409 **Fax:** 01202-409410
E-mail: sales@pennyandgiles.com
Website: http://www.pennyandgiles.com
Bank(s): HSBC Bank plc
Directors: R. Storer (Tech Serv), N. Jones (Fin), B. Smith (Pers)
Managers: S. Leaper (Sales & Mktg Mg), L. Cavaco (Admin Off), L. Stammas (Purch Mgr)
Ultimate Holding Company: CURTISS WRIGHT CORPORATION (U.S.A)
Immediate Holding Company: PENNY & GILES CONTROLS LIMITED
Registration no: 00843903 **VAT No.:** GB 682 4436 21
Date established: 1965 **Turnover:** £20m - £50m
No.of Employees: 251 - 500 **Product Groups:** 37, 38, 45

Date of Accounts	Dec 11	Dec 10	Dec 09
Sales Turnover	37m	31m	25m
Pre Tax Profit/Loss	2m	3m	2m
Working Capital	27m	26m	28m
Fixed Assets	2m	1m	1m
Current Assets	34m	31m	31m
Current Liabilities	3m	3m	2m

Precision Fabrications Ltd
Units 8-9 Sea Vixen Industrial Estate 3 Wilverley Road, Christchurch, BH23 3RU
Tel: 01202-474406 **Fax:** 01202-473821
E-mail: enquiries@precisionfabricationsltd.co.uk
Website: http://www.precisionfabricationsltd.co.uk
Directors: D. Hewitt (Fin), P. Hewitt (MD)
Immediate Holding Company: PRECISION FABRICATIONS LIMITED
Registration no: 01743572 **VAT No.:** GB 392 7475 13
Date established: 1983 **Turnover:** Up to £250,000
No.of Employees: 1 - 10 **Product Groups:** 48

Date of Accounts	Aug 11	Aug 10	Aug 09
Working Capital	3	13	29
Fixed Assets	28	36	48
Current Assets	44	51	63

Presentation Media Ltd
1 Canberra Close, Christchurch, BH23 2FD
Tel: 01202-483883 **Fax:** 01202-483884
E-mail: sales@presentationmedia.co.uk
Website: http://www.presentationmedia.co.uk

Directors: J. Mooney (MD)
Immediate Holding Company: PRESENTATION MEDIA LIMITED
Registration no: 04327737 **Date established:** 2001
Turnover: £250,000 - £500,000 **No.of Employees:** 1 - 10
Product Groups: 28, 37, 38, 44, 81, 83, 86

Date of Accounts	Dec 11	Dec 10	Dec 09
Working Capital	50	56	51
Fixed Assets	2	2	3
Current Assets	145	132	147

Pulse Computing
96 Purewell, Christchurch, BH23 1EU
Tel: 01202-476888 **Fax:** 01202-475060
E-mail: info@pulsecomputing.co.uk
Website: http://www.pulsecomputing.co.uk
Directors: G. Mooney (Dir)
Managers: D. Kemp (I.T. Exec), J. Mooney (Mktg Serv Mgr)
Date established: 1988 **Turnover:** £2m - £5m **No.of Employees:** 1 - 10
Product Groups: 86

Pure Flow Water Systems Ltd
Unit C 16 Arthur Road, Christchurch, BH23 1PU
Tel: 01202-470829 **Fax:** 01202-388900
E-mail: nigelpcook@hotmail.co.uk
Website: http://www.pureflowsofteners.co.uk
Directors: N. Cook (MD), E. Cook (Fin)
Immediate Holding Company: PUREFLOW WATER SYSTEMS LIMITED
Registration no: 04712361 **Date established:** 2003
No.of Employees: 1 - 10 **Product Groups:** 38, 42

Date of Accounts	Mar 11	Mar 10	Mar 09
Working Capital	-27	-23	-21
Fixed Assets	30	35	41
Current Assets	4	3	5

R E Atkins Precision Engineering
Rear of 59 Fairmile Road, Christchurch, BH23 2LA
Tel: 01202-478824
Directors: R. Atkins (Prop)
Date established: 1983 **No.of Employees:** 1 - 10 **Product Groups:** 36

R I B S Marine
Little Avon Marina Stony Lane South, Christchurch, BH23 1HW
Tel: 01202-477327 **Fax:** 01202-471456
E-mail: simon@ribsmarine.co.uk
Website: http://www.ribsmarine.co.uk
Directors: S. Chapman (Prop)
Date established: 1978 **No.of Employees:** 1 - 10 **Product Groups:** 35, 36, 39

S F P Services Ltd
Unit 12 Sea Vixen Industrial Estate 3 Wilverley Road, Christchurch, BH23 3RU
Tel: 01202-496313 **Fax:** 01202-496363
E-mail: info@sfpservices.com
Website: http://www.sfpservices.com
Directors: D. Fiveash (Dir)
Immediate Holding Company: SFP SERVICES LTD
Registration no: 03964563 **Date established:** 2000
No.of Employees: 1 - 10 **Product Groups:** 38, 42

Date of Accounts	Mar 12	Mar 11	Mar 10
Sales Turnover	N/A	N/A	261
Working Capital	-3	-14	-12
Fixed Assets	14	14	14
Current Assets	212	175	155

Siemens plc
Loewy House 11 Aviation Park West, Hurn, Christchurch, BH23 6EW
Tel: 01202-331000 **Fax:** 01202-581851
E-mail: sales@vai.co.at
Website: http://www.vai.co.at
Directors: R. Tazzyman (MD)
Managers: A. McDonald (Purch Mgr), D. Hill, G. Wingrove, J. Evans, M. Neville (Sales Prom Mgr)
Ultimate Holding Company: VA Tech
Immediate Holding Company: SIEMENS PUBLIC LIMITED COMPANY
Registration no: 00727817 **Date established:** 1962
Turnover: £75m - £125m **No.of Employees:** 101 - 250
Product Groups: 37, 45, 46, 48

Date of Accounts	Sep 09	Sep 08	Sep 07
Sales Turnover	251m	246m	150m
Pre Tax Profit/Loss	-5m	15m	-6m
Working Capital	13m	340	10m
Fixed Assets	38m	39m	30m
Current Assets	224m	204m	116m
Current Liabilities	179m	159m	87m

Signs Express
Unit 20 Priory Industrial Park, Christchurch, BH23 4HD
Tel: 01425-277676 **Fax:** 01425-277694
E-mail: bournemouth@signsexpress.co.uk
Website: http://www.signsexpress.co.uk
Directors: J. Sharp (MD)
Immediate Holding Company: SIGNS EXPRESS LIMITED
Registration no: 02375913 **Date established:** 1989
Turnover: Up to £250,000 **No.of Employees:** 1 - 10 **Product Groups:** 28, 30, 37, 40

Sopley Forge
Ringwood Road Sopley, Christchurch, BH23 7BE
Tel: 01425-673316
Directors: D. Pitt (Prop)
Date established: 1978 **No.of Employees:** 1 - 10 **Product Groups:** 26, 35

Stone Catering Equipment
301 Aviation Park West Bournemouth International Airport, Hurn, Christchurch, BH23 6NW
Tel: 01202-593880 **Fax:** 01202-593880
Website: http://www.stonecateringequipment.com
Directors: A. Stone (MD)
Ultimate Holding Company: STONE CATERING EQUIPMENT LIMITED
Immediate Holding Company: STONE CATERING EQUIPMENT LIMITED
Registration no: 02989794 **Date established:** 1994
No.of Employees: 1 - 10 **Product Groups:** 20, 40, 41

Date of Accounts	Dec 11	Dec 10	Dec 09
Working Capital	-1	5	13
Fixed Assets	7	8	5
Current Assets	29	26	35

T A L Shooting & Scuba Diving
8 St Catherines Parade Fairmile Road, Christchurch, BH23 2LQ
Tel: 01202-473030 **Fax:** 01202-479600
E-mail: sales@go-diving.co.uk
Website: http://www.go-diving.co.uk
Managers: K. Burnell (Mgr), K. Burnett (Mgr)
Registration no: 04692654 **Date established:** 2003
No.of Employees: 1 - 10 **Product Groups:** 36, 39, 40

Unreal Wheels
1 Preston Way, Christchurch, BH23 4QT
Tel: 07931-521001
Directors: S. Smith (Prop)
No.of Employees: 1 - 10 **Product Groups:** 29, 35, 39

Vendredi Screen Print
23 Airfield Road, Christchurch, BH23 3TG
Tel: 01202-470570 **Fax:** 01202-470570
E-mail: vendredi@btconnect.com
Directors: C. Pitt (Ptnr)
VAT No.: GB 580 2513 59 **Date established:** 1983
Turnover: Up to £250,000 **No.of Employees:** 1 - 10 **Product Groups:** 23, 28

Dorchester

Acrogen Ltd
Westfield House Puncknowle, Dorchester, DT2 9BP
Tel: 01308-897734 **Fax:** 01308-897734
E-mail: raymond.peto@acrogen.com
Website: http://www.acrogen.com
Directors: M. Peto (Fin), R. Peto (MD)
Immediate Holding Company: ACROGEN LIMITED
Registration no: 03087650 **VAT No.:** GB 663 1309 39
Date established: 1995 **Turnover:** £250,000 - £500,000
No.of Employees: 1 - 10 **Product Groups:** 37, 38, 40, 54, 67, 84, 85

Date of Accounts	Jan 11	Jan 10	Jan 09
Working Capital	3	-1	-4
Fixed Assets	N/A	N/A	5
Current Assets	74	64	37

Casterbridge Fires Ltd
15 Casterbridge Industrial Estate London Road, Dorchester, DT1 1PL
Tel: 01305-262829 **Fax:** 01305-257483
E-mail: contact@casterbridgefires.co.uk
Website: http://www.casterbridgefires.co.uk
Directors: A. Bradbeer (MD)
Immediate Holding Company: CASTERBRIDGE FIRES LIMITED
Registration no: 07091521 **Date established:** 2009
No.of Employees: 1 - 10 **Product Groups:** 40, 66

Date of Accounts	Dec 11	Dec 10
Working Capital	-28	-37
Fixed Assets	36	42
Current Assets	148	137

Michael Clapp
Stable Court Bradford Peverell, Dorchester, DT2 9SF
Tel: 01305-267267
Directors: M. Clapp (Prop)
Date established: 1995 **No.of Employees:** 1 - 10 **Product Groups:** 35, 36, 39

Combined Electrical & Engineering Services
12 Wyvern Buildings Grove Trading Estate, Dorchester, DT1 1ST
Tel: 01305-251177 **Fax:** 01243-536056
Website: http://www.ceesltd.co.uk
Directors: S. Taylor (MD)
Immediate Holding Company: COMBINED ELECTRICAL AND ENGINEERING SERVICES LIMITED
Registration no: 02515950 **Date established:** 1990
No.of Employees: 11 - 20 **Product Groups:** 37, 44, 84

Date of Accounts	Jun 11	Jun 10	Jun 09
Working Capital	436	147	161
Fixed Assets	602	554	560
Current Assets	2m	620	826

Cygnus Instruments Ltd
Cygnus House 30 Prince of Wales Road, Dorchester, DT1 1PW
Tel: 01305-265533 **Fax:** 01305-269960
E-mail: sales@cygnus-instruments.com
Website: http://www.cygnus-instruments.com
Bank(s): Lloyds TSB Bank plc
Directors: G. Haines (Dir)
Managers: C. Andrews
Immediate Holding Company: CYGNUS INSTRUMENTS LIMITED
Registration no: 01699180 **VAT No.:** GB 469 6424 06
Date established: 1983 **Turnover:** £1m - £2m **No.of Employees:** 11 - 20
Product Groups: 31, 34, 37, 38, 39, 48, 67, 68, 84, 85, 86, 87

Date of Accounts	Dec 11	Dec 10	Dec 09
Working Capital	1m	1m	909
Fixed Assets	96	91	26
Current Assets	1m	1m	1m

Dorchester Saddlery
The Granary Warmwell, Dorchester, DT2 8HQ
Tel: 01305-852270
E-mail: admin@dorchestersaddlery.co.uk
Website: http://www.equestrian-dorchester.co.uk
Directors: M. Hemingway (Prop)
No.of Employees: 1 - 10 **Product Groups:** 22, 24, 35, 41, 49, 63, 65

Dynamic Display Ltd
Unit 9a Hybris Business Park Warmwell Road, Crossways, Dorchester, DT2 8BF
Tel: 01305-854999 **Fax:** 01305-854999
E-mail: sales@dynamic-display.co.uk
Website: http://www.dynamic-display.co.uk
Directors: B. Dilevski (Fin), R. Spence (MD)
Immediate Holding Company: DYNAMIC DISPLAY LIMITED
Registration no: 03634133 **Date established:** 1998
Turnover: £500,000 - £1m **No.of Employees:** 1 - 10 **Product Groups:** 37

Date of Accounts	Sep 11	Sep 10	Sep 09
Working Capital	-52	-62	-58
Fixed Assets	138	144	151
Current Assets	48	13	7

Glasmaster Ltd
20 Enterprise Park Piddlehinton, Dorchester, DT2 7UA
Tel: 01305-848758 **Fax:** 01305-848942
E-mail: dickgain@aol.com
Website: http://www.signmasterdirect.co.uk
Bank(s): National Westminster Bank Plc
Directors: R. Gain (MD), P. Gain (Fin)
Immediate Holding Company: GLASMASTER LIMITED
Registration no: 02651203 **VAT No.:** GB 355 6733 32
Date established: 1991 **Turnover:** £500,000 - £1m
No.of Employees: 11 - 20 **Product Groups:** 30

Date of Accounts	Oct 11	Oct 10	Oct 09
Working Capital	-275	-272	-230
Fixed Assets	8	10	12
Current Assets	82	58	58
Current Liabilities	N/A	124	N/A

Highwood
Higher Woodsford, Dorchester, DT2 8BL
Tel: 01305-853900 **Fax:** 01305-852838
E-mail: nick.green@highwood-ag.co.uk
Website: http://www.highwood-ag.co.uk
Managers: N. Green (Chief Mgr)
No.of Employees: 1 - 10 **Product Groups:** 07, 41, 45

Henry Ling Ltd
23 High East Street, Dorchester, DT1 1HD
Tel: 01305-251066 **Fax:** 01305-251908
E-mail: production@henryling.co.uk
Website: http://www.henryling.co.uk
Bank(s): Lloyds TSB Bank plc
Directors: M. Kennett (Fin), H. Kennett (MD)
Ultimate Holding Company: DORSET PRESS LIMITED(THE)
Immediate Holding Company: HENRY LING LIMITED
Registration no: 00224715 **Date established:** 2027 **Turnover:** £5m - £10m
No.of Employees: 101 - 250 **Product Groups:** 27, 28, 44

Date of Accounts	Jun 11	Jun 10	Jun 09
Sales Turnover	9m	9m	9m
Pre Tax Profit/Loss	566	597	59
Working Capital	3m	3m	3m
Fixed Assets	3m	3m	3m
Current Assets	5m	5m	5m
Current Liabilities	554	486	734

M A Rainback Ltd
5 Moreton Road Owermoigne, Dorchester, DT2 8HT
Tel: 01305-853737 **Fax:** 01305-853737
E-mail: mrainback@gmail.com
Directors: M. Rainback (MD)
Immediate Holding Company: M A RAINBACK LIMITED
Registration no: 04453657 **Date established:** 2002
No.of Employees: 1 - 10 **Product Groups:** 36, 39, 40

Date of Accounts	Jul 11	Jul 10	Jul 09
Working Capital	-14	-15	-15
Fixed Assets	22	22	23
Current Assets	20	26	14

Marine Inspection Services Ltd
Unit 10, Mellstock Business Park Higher Bockhampton, Dorchester, DT2 8QJ
Tel: 01305-257438 **Fax:** 01305-259 573
E-mail: info@marinspec.com
Website: http://www.marinspec.com
Directors: S. Ruddick (Dir)
Registration no: 05697638 **Date established:** 2006
No.of Employees: 1 - 10 **Product Groups:** 74

On The Table Ltd
28 South Street, Dorchester, DT1 1BY
Tel: 01305-257258 **Fax:** 01305-257258
E-mail: shop@onthetable.co.uk
Website: http://www.onthetable.co.uk
Directors: G. Bridge (MD), V. Bridge (Fin)
Immediate Holding Company: ON THE TABLE LIMITED
Registration no: 04801160 **Date established:** 2003
Turnover: Up to £250,000 **No.of Employees:** 1 - 10 **Product Groups:** 25, 30, 33, 36, 63

Date of Accounts	Jan 12	Jan 11	Feb 07
Working Capital	19	23	-20
Fixed Assets	7	7	10
Current Assets	54	59	42

Quill Productions
Manor Farm Pulham, Dorchester, DT2 7EE
Tel: 01258-818239 **Fax:** 01258-817261
E-mail: sales@quillprod.com
Website: http://www.quillprod.com
Directors: G. Crocker (Prop)
Immediate Holding Company: CLAY BOX LIMITED
Registration no: 05697837 **Date established:** 2008
No.of Employees: 11 - 20 **Product Groups:** 32, 41

Date of Accounts	Mar 11	Mar 10	Mar 09
Working Capital	66	39	-73
Fixed Assets	77	85	101
Current Assets	258	262	208

Selections Mail Order Ltd
Southover House Tolpuddle, Dorchester, DT2 7YG
Tel: 01305-848725 **Fax:** 01305-848516
E-mail: sales@selections.com
Website: http://www.selections.com
Directors: M. Slocock (Prop)
Immediate Holding Company: SELECTIONS MAIL ORDER LIMITED
Registration no: 05072379 **Date established:** 2004
Turnover: £250m - £500m **No.of Employees:** 11 - 20
Product Groups: 02, 26, 30, 41, 45

Date of Accounts	Jun 12	Jun 11	Jun 10
Working Capital	107	80	68
Fixed Assets	82	88	92
Current Assets	473	384	872
Current Liabilities	140	120	110

Snashall Steel Fabrications
Pulham Business Park Pulham, Dorchester, DT2 7DX
Tel: 01300-345588 **Fax:** 01300-345533
E-mail: dawn@snashallsteel.co.uk
Website: http://www.snashallsteel.co.uk
Bank(s): Lloyds TSB
Directors: D. Snashall (Dir)
Managers: A. Horne
Immediate Holding Company: SNASHALL STEEL FABRICATIONS COMPANY LIMITED
Registration no: 01224537 **VAT No.:** 187 6964 93 **Date established:** 1975
Turnover: £2m - £5m **No.of Employees:** 11 - 20 **Product Groups:** 35

Date of Accounts	Sep 11	Sep 10	Sep 09
Sales Turnover	N/A	N/A	5m
Pre Tax Profit/Loss	N/A	N/A	-24
Working Capital	643	612	687
Fixed Assets	381	421	537
Current Assets	2m	2m	2m
Current Liabilities	N/A	N/A	170

Sportarm Of Dorchester
Princes Street, Dorchester, DT1 1TW
Tel: 01305-268001 **Fax:** 01305-261002
E-mail: enquiries@sportarm.com
Website: http://www.sportarm.com
Directors: K. Phillips (Dir)
Immediate Holding Company: SPORTARM LIMITED
Registration no: 04134274 **Date established:** 2000
No.of Employees: 1 - 10 **Product Groups:** 36, 39, 40

Date of Accounts	Mar 11	Mar 10	Mar 09
Working Capital	78	113	-57
Fixed Assets	66	63	69
Current Assets	762	679	918

Sportsman Gun Centre
Wardon Hill, Dorchester, DT2 9PW
Tel: 01935-83099 **Fax:** 01935-83077
Website: http://www.sportsmanguncentre.com
Managers: E. Blunden (Mgr)
No.of Employees: 1 - 10 **Product Groups:** 36, 39, 40

Spring Grove Forge Ltd
Spring Grove Forge Coombe Road, Puddletown, Dorchester, DT2 8RZ
Tel: 01305-848328 **Fax:** 01305-848328
Directors: R. Lovett (MD)
Immediate Holding Company: SPRING GROVE FORGE LIMITED(THE)
Registration no: 00482669 **Date established:** 1950
Turnover: Up to £250,000 **No.of Employees:** 1 - 10 **Product Groups:** 26, 35

Date of Accounts	May 11	May 10	May 07
Sales Turnover	N/A	N/A	144
Working Capital	40	40	38
Fixed Assets	3	3	6
Current Assets	174	174	156
Current Liabilities	N/A	N/A	51

Top Turf Supplies Ltd
2 Winton Cottages Corscombe, Dorchester, DT2 0NX
Tel: 01935-891475 **Fax:** 01935-891680
E-mail: inf@topturfsupplies.co.uk
Website: http://www.topturfsupplies.co.uk
Directors: J. Puzey (Dir)
Immediate Holding Company: TOP TURF SUPPLIES LIMITED
Registration no: 05823860 **Date established:** 2006
No.of Employees: 1 - 10 **Product Groups:** 02, 07, 32

Date of Accounts	Jul 11	Jul 10	Jul 08
Working Capital	-38	-37	-38
Fixed Assets	11	13	15
Current Assets	13	13	8

Tritex NDT Ltd
Unit 10 Mellstock Business Park Higher Bockhampton, Dorchester, DT2 8QJ
Tel: 01305-257160 **Fax:** 01305-259573
E-mail: sales@tritexndt.com
Website: http://www.tritexndt.com
Managers: J. Sharland (Sales Prom Mgr)
Immediate Holding Company: TRITEX NDT LIMITED
Registration no: 05685071 **Date established:** 2006
No.of Employees: 1 - 10 **Product Groups:** 37, 38, 85

Date of Accounts	Mar 11	Mar 10	Mar 09
Working Capital	-22	-18	-27
Fixed Assets	4	12	20
Current Assets	82	88	86

Vaughan Agri
Yellowham Wood, Dorchester, DT2 8FA
Tel: 01305-849000 **Fax:** 01305-849222
E-mail: j.hicken@westernharvesters.co.uk
Website: http://www.vaughanagri.co.uk
Managers: J. Hicken (Mgr)
Date established: 1993 **No.of Employees:** 11 - 20 **Product Groups:** 41

Window Blinds Centres Ltd (North Devon Blinds Ltd)
29a High East Street, Dorchester, DT1 1HF
Tel: 01305-261271 **Fax:** 01305-261271
E-mail: sales@northdevonblinds.co.uk
Website: http://www.northdevonblinds.co.uk
Directors: P. Denton (Prop)
Registration no: 04798812 **No.of Employees:** 1 - 10 **Product Groups:** 24, 35, 63

Wright Pugson Chain Ltd
Unit D2 Roman Hill Business Park Broadmayne, Dorchester, DT2 8LY
Tel: 01305-851514
Website: http://www.wpchain.co.uk
Directors: N. Whitaker (MD)
Registration no: 03994850 **Date established:** 2000
No.of Employees: 1 - 10 **Product Groups:** 30, 45

Ferndown

Ash Associates (TOGA Group Partnership)
PO Box 5374, Ferndown, BH22 0ZX
Tel: 08451-232701 **Fax:** 0845-123 2702
E-mail: recruit@ash-associates.com
Website: http://www.ash-associates.com
Directors: J. Hunt (Snr Part)
Date established: 2000 **Turnover:** £250,000 - £500,000
No.of Employees: 1 - 10 **Product Groups:** 80

Dixon Mechanical Services Ltd
59 Ringwood Road, Ferndown, BH22 9AA
Tel: 01202-581000 **Fax:** 01202-578899
E-mail: admin@dixonmechanical.com
Website: http://www.dixonmechanical.com
Directors: D. Dixon (Dir)
Immediate Holding Company: DIXON MECHANICAL SERVICES LIMITED
Registration no: 06459486 **VAT No.:** GB 186 5397 16
Date established: 2007 **No.of Employees:** 1 - 10 **Product Groups:** 52

Date of Accounts	Dec 11	Dec 10	Dec 09
Working Capital	92	48	-48
Fixed Assets	52	73	102
Current Assets	545	472	611

Garden Building Centre
Unit 1 Haskins Garden Centre Longham, Ferndown, BH22 9DG
Tel: 01202-577745 **Fax:** 01202-581925
E-mail: ferndown@gbcgroup.co.uk
Website: http://www.gbcgroup.co.uk
Managers: K. Garrett (Asst Gen Mgr)
Date established: 2003 **No.of Employees:** 1 - 10 **Product Groups:** 25, 33, 35, 66

Network Telex UK Ltd
Kingsland House 512 Wimborne Road East, Ferndown, BH22 9NG
Tel: 01202-877780 **Fax:** 01202-897827
E-mail: sales@telex-net.com
Website: http://www.telex-net.com
Directors: P. Clarke (MD)
Immediate Holding Company: TELEX-NET LIMITED
Registration no: 03043718 **VAT No.:** GB 580 1737 42
Date established: 1995 **Turnover:** £1m - £2m **No.of Employees:** 1 - 10
Product Groups: 37, 79

Date of Accounts	Sep 11	Sep 10	Sep 09
Working Capital	74	72	75
Fixed Assets	2	6	9
Current Assets	111	137	150

Style South
Consort House Princes Road, Ferndown, BH22 9JG
Tel: 01202-874044 **Fax:** 01202-874844
E-mail: south@style-partitions.co.uk
Website: http://www.style-partitons.co.uk
Directors: J. Sargent (Dir)
Managers: J. Mosley (Mktg Serv Mgr)
Immediate Holding Company: STYLE DOOR SYSTEMS LTD.
Registration no: 03693137 **Date established:** 1999
Turnover: £500,000 - £1m **No.of Employees:** 11 - 20
Product Groups: 24, 25, 26, 33, 35, 36, 40, 48, 52, 66, 67

Date of Accounts	Mar 12	Mar 11	Mar 10
Working Capital	424	381	229
Fixed Assets	14	18	24
Current Assets	1m	1m	2m

www.secretgarden.uk.com
85 Severn Road, Ferndown, BH22 8XB
Tel: 01202-861192
E-mail: enquiries@secretgarden.uk.com
Website: http://www.secretgarden.uk.com
Directors: V. Lapage-Norris (MD), V. Lapage Norris (MD)
No.of Employees: 1 - 10 **Product Groups:** 30, 32, 41, 66

Gillingham

Chester Jefferies Ltd
Buckingham Road, Gillingham, SP8 4QE
Tel: 01747-822629 **Fax:** 01747-824092
E-mail: enquiry@chesterjefferies.co.uk
Website: http://www.chesterjefferies.co.uk
Bank(s): National Westminster Bank Plc
Directors: P. Kelly (Fin)
Immediate Holding Company: CHESTER JEFFERIES LIMITED
Registration no: 00333841 **VAT No.:** GB 185 5708 31
Date established: 1937 **Turnover:** £500,000 - £1m
No.of Employees: 11 - 20 **Product Groups:** 24

Date of Accounts	Oct 11	Oct 10	Oct 09
Working Capital	226	227	243
Fixed Assets	26	29	33
Current Assets	429	428	452

Dextra Lighting Systems plc
Unit 17-20 Brickfields Business Park, Gillingham, SP8 4PX
Tel: 01747-858100 **Fax:** 01747-858119
E-mail: keith.brownhill@dextralighting.co.uk
Website: http://www.dextra-lighting-systems.co.uk
Directors: K. Brownhill (Fin), D. Ward (Tech Serv)
Managers: N. Ward (Mktg Serv Mgr), T. Archer (Sales Prom Mgr), K. Gill (Personnel), G. Trevitt (Purch Mgr)
Ultimate Holding Company: DEXTRA GROUP PLC
Immediate Holding Company: DEXTRA LIGHTING LIMITED
Registration no: 06460114 **VAT No.:** GB 323 2439 85
Date established: 2007 **Turnover:** £20m - £50m
No.of Employees: 251 - 500 **Product Groups:** 37

Date of Accounts	Dec 11	Dec 10	Dec 09
Sales Turnover	43m	48m	46m
Pre Tax Profit/Loss	5m	4m	3m
Working Capital	5m	6m	4m
Current Assets	11m	13m	11m
Current Liabilities	5m	6m	5m

Littlemore Scientific
Gutch Pool Farm, Gillingham, SP8 5QP
Tel: 01747-835550 **Fax:** 01747-835552
E-mail: elsec@elsec.co.uk
Website: http://www.elsec.com
Directors: W. Hall (MD)
VAT No.: GB 194 7984 93 **Date established:** 1957
Turnover: £500,000 - £1m **No.of Employees:** 1 - 10 **Product Groups:** 38

Magdalen Metalwork
14 Manor Farm Trading Estate Fifehead Magdalen, Gillingham, SP8 5RR
Tel: 01258-821118 **Fax:** 01258-821118
E-mail: enquiries@magdalenmetalwork.co.uk
Website: http://www.magdalenmetalwork.co.uk
Directors: N. Hicks (Prop)
No.of Employees: 1 - 10 **Product Groups:** 35, 46, 84

Pasta Reale Ltd
Station Road, Gillingham, SP8 4QA
Tel: 01747-826332 **Fax:** 01747-826828
E-mail: r.herbert@pastareale.com
Website: http://www.pastareale.com
Directors: R. Herbert (Dir)
Immediate Holding Company: PASTA REALE LIMITED
Registration no: 01963438 **Date established:** 1985
Turnover: £10m - £20m **No.of Employees:** 51 - 100 **Product Groups:** 20, 40, 41

Date of Accounts	Sep 11	Sep 10	Sep 09
Sales Turnover	28m	33m	35m
Pre Tax Profit/Loss	-444	-162	735
Working Capital	989	2m	2m
Fixed Assets	9m	9m	10m
Current Assets	6m	7m	9m
Current Liabilities	1m	1m	2m

Sherman Chemicals Ltd
Brickfields Business Park, Gillingham, SP8 4PX
Tel: 01747-823293 **Fax:** 01747-825383
E-mail: info@sherchem.co.uk
Website: http://www.sherchem.co.uk
Directors: J. Hurst (MD), J. Clasby (Fin)
Immediate Holding Company: SHERMAN CHEMICALS LIMITED
Registration no: 00596365 **VAT No.:** GB 456 0085 57
Date established: 1958 **Turnover:** £1m - £2m **No.of Employees:** 1 - 10
Product Groups: 31, 32, 34, 66

Date of Accounts	Dec 11	Dec 10	Dec 09
Working Capital	340	352	355
Fixed Assets	7	9	8
Current Assets	452	570	485

Lyme Regis

Eagland Machine Tools Ltd
The Studio Hill Road, Lyme Regis, DT7 3PG
Tel: 01297-446000 **Fax:** 01297-446001
E-mail: sales@eagland.co.uk
Website: http://www.eagland.co.uk
Directors: R. Eagland (MD), P. Eagland (Fin)
Immediate Holding Company: EAGLAND MACHINE TOOLS LIMITED
Registration no: 01225720 **VAT No.:** GB 189 8109 14
Date established: 1975 **Turnover:** £250,000 - £500,000
No.of Employees: 1 - 10 **Product Groups:** 48

Date of Accounts	Dec 11	Dec 10	Dec 09
Working Capital	-5	-2	1
Fixed Assets	149	153	157
Current Assets	14	22	14

Precision Waterjet Ltd
Unit 1 Uplyme Business Park Uplyme Road, Lyme Regis, DT7 3LS
Tel: 01297-444456 **Fax:** 05601-135290
E-mail: sales@precisionwaterjet.co.uk
Website: http://www.precisionwaterjet.co.uk
Directors: P. Davis (MD)
Immediate Holding Company: PRECISION WATERJET LIMITED
Registration no: 05972035 **Date established:** 2006
No.of Employees: 1 - 10 **Product Groups:** 23, 25, 27, 28, 33, 34, 35, 36, 39, 42, 44, 45, 48, 49, 51, 52, 66, 84

Date of Accounts	Mar 12	Mar 11	Mar 10
Working Capital	-4	-17	-44
Fixed Assets	131	190	153
Current Assets	209	147	77

Southern Filters Ltd
Carnbrae Woodhouse Hill, Uplyme, Lyme Regis, DT7 3SL
Tel: 01297-444558 **Fax:** 01297- 444558
Directors: A. Turner (MD)
Immediate Holding Company: SOUTHERN FILTERS LIMITED
Registration no: 04044665 **Date established:** 2000
No.of Employees: 1 - 10 **Product Groups:** 38, 42

Date of Accounts	Aug 11	Aug 10	Aug 09
Working Capital	834	796	767
Fixed Assets	241	253	280
Current Assets	980	927	921

Poole

21st Century Tints
15 Morris Road Nuffield Industrial Estate, Poole, BH17 0GG
Tel: 01202-677848 **Fax:** 01202-677848
Directors: H. Wilson (Fin)
Immediate Holding Company: 21ST CENTURY TINTS LIMITED
Registration no: 05551203 **Date established:** 2005
No.of Employees: 1 - 10 **Product Groups:** 30, 39, 80

A B Precision Poole Ltd
1 Fleets Lane, Poole, BH15 3BZ
Tel: 01202-665000 **Fax:** 01202-675965
E-mail: enquiries@abprecision.co.uk
Website: http://www.abprecision.co.uk
Bank(s): Lloyds TSB Bank plc

Directors: A. Mullins (Fin)
Managers: N. Allgood (Tech Serv Mgr), S. Maycock, K. Cross (Mgr), H. Hill (Personnel), L. Betreen (Purch Mgr)
Ultimate Holding Company: HWH INVESTMENTS LIMITED
Immediate Holding Company: A.B. PRECISION (POOLE) LIMITED
Registration no: 00889363 **VAT No.:** GB 580 0839 39
Date established: 1966 **Turnover:** £10m - £20m
No.of Employees: 51 - 100 **Product Groups:** 35, 37, 47, 48, 84

Date of Accounts	Mar 11	Mar 10	Mar 09
Sales Turnover	13m	9m	8m
Pre Tax Profit/Loss	2m	694	485
Working Capital	3m	3m	3m
Fixed Assets	144	163	187
Current Assets	5m	5m	4m
Current Liabilities	1m	1m	793

A E T Transport Services Ltd
51 Holton Road Holton Heath Trading Park, Poole, BH16 6LT
Tel: 01202-632221 **Fax:** 01202-678256
E-mail: aetrotter@aet-transport.co.uk
Website: http://www.aet-transport.co.uk
Bank(s): National Westminster Bank Plc
Directors: A. Trotter (MD)
Immediate Holding Company: A.E.T. TRANSPORT SERVICES LIMITED
Registration no: 02391217 **VAT No.:** GB 541 7012 78
Date established: 1989 **Turnover:** £1m - £2m **No.of Employees:** 21 - 50
Product Groups: 72

Date of Accounts	Aug 11	Aug 10	Aug 09
Working Capital	-578	-763	-781
Fixed Assets	5m	6m	6m
Current Assets	1m	979	507

A First Wave
5 Mayfield Avenue, Poole, BH14 9NY
Tel: 01202-747979
Directors: B. Leah (Prop)
No.of Employees: 1 - 10 **Product Groups:** 36, 40

A K Controls
Unit 17 Fleetsbridge Business Centre Upton Road, Poole, BH17 7AF
Tel: 01202-660061 **Fax:** 01202-660200
E-mail: info@akcontrols.com
Website: http://www.akcontrols.com
Directors: J. King (Fin), D. King (MD)
Immediate Holding Company: A K CONTROLS LTD
Registration no: 04635869 **Date established:** 2003 **Turnover:** £1m - £2m
No.of Employees: 11 - 20 **Product Groups:** 37

Date of Accounts	Mar 12	Mar 11	Mar 10
Working Capital	292	298	268
Fixed Assets	109	120	126
Current Assets	422	465	410

Abbey Fire Safety Ltd
42 Banbury Road Nuffield Industrial Estate, Poole, BH17 0GA
Tel: 01202-679461 **Fax:** 01202-679461
E-mail: caroline.abbeyfire@ntlworld.com
Website: http://www.abbeyfiresafety.co.uk
Directors: C. Naven-Lowey (MD)
Immediate Holding Company: ABBEY FIRE LTD.
Registration no: 04693663 **Date established:** 2003
Turnover: £500,000 - £1m **No.of Employees:** 11 - 20
Product Groups: 29, 30, 33, 35, 36, 37, 38, 39, 40, 52, 67, 68, 84, 85, 86, 87

Date of Accounts	Mar 09	Mar 08	Mar 07
Working Capital	-39	4	14
Fixed Assets	4	4	6
Current Assets	59	62	56

Accurate Controls Ltd
25 Cowley Road Nuffield Industrial Estate, Poole, BH17 0UJ
Tel: 01202-678108 **Fax:** 01202-670161
E-mail: info@accurate-controls.ltd.uk
Website: http://www.accurate-controls.ltd.uk
Bank(s): Bank of Scotland
Directors: M. Spreadbury (Dir)
Immediate Holding Company: ACCURATE CONTROLS LIMITED
Registration no: 02427774 **VAT No.:** GB 541 7860 35
Date established: 1989 **Turnover:** £1m - £2m **No.of Employees:** 11 - 20
Product Groups: 38

Date of Accounts	Oct 08	Oct 07	Mar 11
Working Capital	250	131	299
Fixed Assets	28	44	1
Current Assets	385	369	435

Aeronautical & General Instruments Ltd
Fleets Point Willis Way, Poole, BH15 3SS
Tel: 01202-685661 **Fax:** 01202-685670
E-mail: sales@agiltd.co.uk
Website: http://www.agiltd.co.uk
Bank(s): Barclays
Directors: S. Maycock (Fin), J. Harris (MD)
Managers: H. Hill (Personnel), S. Sims (Mats Contrlr), J. Sawyer (Sales & Mktg Mg), J. Howarth (Tech Serv Mgr)
Ultimate Holding Company: HWH INVESTMENTS LIMITED
Immediate Holding Company: AERONAUTICAL & GENERAL INSTRUMENTS LIMITED
Registration no: 00138853 **VAT No.:** GB 541 8181 50
Date established: 2015 **Turnover:** £20m - £50m
No.of Employees: 101 - 250 **Product Groups:** 38, 39

Date of Accounts	Mar 11	Mar 10	Mar 09
Sales Turnover	21m	21m	14m
Pre Tax Profit/Loss	5m	5m	2m
Working Capital	9m	8m	7m
Fixed Assets	476	380	343
Current Assets	14m	11m	12m
Current Liabilities	3m	3m	3m

Aish Electro-Mechanical Services
Unit 2b 8 Cowley Road, Nuffield Industrial Estate, Poole, BH17 0UJ
Tel: 01202-677100 **Fax:** 01202-677233
E-mail: service@aishpumps.co.uk
Website: http://www.aishpumps.co.uk
Directors: K. Sloyan (MD)
Immediate Holding Company: AISH ELECTRO-MECHANICAL SERVICES LTD
Registration no: 05165446 **Turnover:** Up to £250,000
No.of Employees: 1 - 10 **Product Groups:** 48, 52

Albert Waeschle
11 Balena Close, Poole, BH17 7DB
Tel: 01202-601177 **Fax:** 01202-650022
E-mail: albert@albertwaeschle.co.uk
Website: http://www.aw-online.com
Directors: A. Waeschle (Prop)
Managers: W. Little (Purch Mgr), J. Hall (Mktg Serv Mgr)
Immediate Holding Company: ALBERT WAESCHLE LIMITED
Registration no: 01675355 **Date established:** 1982
No.of Employees: 21 - 50 **Product Groups:** 37, 38

Date of Accounts	Aug 11	Aug 10	Aug 09
Working Capital	552	543	500
Fixed Assets	812	826	847
Current Assets	1m	993	1m

Alfatronix Ltd
29 Newtown Business Park Albion Close, Poole, BH12 3LL
Tel: 01202-715517 **Fax:** 01202-715122
E-mail: sales@alfatronix.co.uk
Website: http://www.alfatronix.co.uk
Bank(s): Lloyds TSB Bank plc
Directors: K. Reilly (MD)
Ultimate Holding Company: ALFATRONIX (HOLDINGS) LIMITED
Immediate Holding Company: ALFATRONIX LIMITED
Registration no: 01416679 **VAT No.:** GB 423 3612 84
Date established: 1979 **Turnover:** £1m - £2m **No.of Employees:** 21 - 50
Product Groups: 37

Date of Accounts	Nov 11	Nov 10	Nov 09
Working Capital	2m	2m	2m
Fixed Assets	114	57	80
Current Assets	3m	3m	2m

Alform Extrusions Ltd (Head Office)
Units 6 & 7 Holton Heath Trading Park, Holton Heath, Poole, BH16 6LG
Tel: 01202-624830 **Fax:** 01202-624976
E-mail: mike@alform.co.uk
Website: http://www.alform.co.uk
Bank(s): Lloyds TSB Bank plc
Directors: M. Willshire (Dir), L. Wells (Dir)
Registration no: 02580618 **VAT No.:** GB 684 7620 01
Date established: 1978 **Turnover:** £2m - £5m **No.of Employees:** 11 - 20
Product Groups: 34, 35, 36, 37

Date of Accounts	Apr 11	Apr 10	Apr 09
Working Capital	542	624	602
Fixed Assets	105	121	84
Current Assets	1m	1m	964

Allfix Distributors
2 Leyland Road, Poole, BH12 5HB
Tel: 01202-522506 **Fax:** 01202-518353
E-mail: sales@allfix.co.uk
Website: http://www.allfix.co.uk
Directors: T. Wild (Dir), M. Davis (Tech Serv), M. Wild (MD)
Managers: A. Trim (Mgr), A. Trim (Asst Gen Mgr), M. Matthews (Asst Gen Mgr), M. Russell (Sales Prom Mgr), P. Bridge (Buyer)
Immediate Holding Company: ALLFIX LIMITED
Registration no: 04487184 **Date established:** 2002
No.of Employees: 21 - 50 **Product Groups:** 30, 32, 35, 36, 37, 42, 47, 66

Date of Accounts	Aug 09	Aug 08	Aug 07
Working Capital	430	524	571
Fixed Assets	156	182	179
Current Assets	1m	2m	2m

Alpha Design & Engineering Services Ltd
1 Didcot Road Nuffield Industrial Estate, Poole, BH17 0GD
Tel: 01202-606050 **Fax:** 01202-666190
E-mail: info@alphadesign-poole.co.uk
Website: http://www.alphadesign-poole.co.uk
Directors: B. Thornley (Dir), B. Thornley (Dir)
Managers: P. Mead (Chief Mgr)
Immediate Holding Company: ALPHA DESIGN & ENGINEERING SERVICES LIMITED
Registration no: 07484515 **Date established:** 2011
Turnover: £250,000 - £500,000 **No.of Employees:** 1 - 10
Product Groups: 37

Andrew Witt Estate Agents Lettings
335 Wallisdown Road, Poole, BH12 5BU
Tel: 01202-524444 **Fax:** 01202-530222
E-mail: sales@andrewwitt.co.uk
Website: http://www.andrewwitt.co.uk
Directors: A. Witt (Dir)
Immediate Holding Company: ANDREW WITT ESTATE AGENTS LTD.
Registration no: 05899673 **Date established:** 2006
Turnover: Up to £250,000 **No.of Employees:** 1 - 10 **Product Groups:** 80

Date of Accounts	Aug 11	Aug 10	Aug 09
Working Capital	-14	-2	-22
Fixed Assets	8	10	11
Current Assets	17	26	9

Applied Truck & Trolley Ltd
32 Holton Road Holton Heath Trading Park, Poole, BH16 6LT
Tel: 01202-632210 **Fax:** 01202-632570
E-mail: steve@appliedtruck.co.uk
Website: http://www.appliedtruck.co.uk
Directors: S. Hyne (MD)
Immediate Holding Company: APPLIED TRUCK & TROLLEY LIMITED
Registration no: 01183733 **VAT No.:** GB 187 5439 20
Date established: 1974 **Turnover:** Up to £250,000
No.of Employees: 1 - 10 **Product Groups:** 35, 39, 41, 45

Date of Accounts	Mar 11	Mar 10	Mar 09
Working Capital	33	30	28
Fixed Assets	10	12	13
Current Assets	59	61	51
Current Liabilities	7	8	6

Argon Welding Services
Unit 11 Manor Park 35 Willis Way, Poole, BH15 3SZ
Tel: 01202-660665 **Fax:** 01202-649659
E-mail: argonwelding@btconnect.com
Website: http://www.argonweldingservices.co.uk
Directors: S. Pickering (Prop)
Immediate Holding Company: ARGON WELDING LTD
Registration no: 06619514 **Date established:** 2008
Turnover: Up to £250,000 **No.of Employees:** 1 - 10 **Product Groups:** 34, 35, 46, 48

Date of Accounts	Sep 11	Sep 10	Sep 09
Working Capital	-23	-31	-33
Fixed Assets	33	35	47
Current Assets	46	61	62

Ascii Software Ltd
PO BOX 4174,, Poole, BH15 4PF
Tel: 01202-258041 **Fax:** 023-9220 0833
E-mail: sales@asciisoftware.com
Website: http://www.asciisoftware.com
Directors: D. Patrick (Dir)
Immediate Holding Company: ASCII SOFTWARE LIMITED
Registration no: 03910650 **Date established:** 2000
Turnover: Up to £250,000 **No.of Employees:** 1 - 10 **Product Groups:** 44

Date of Accounts	Mar 10	Mar 09	Mar 08
Working Capital	-1	-18	-23
Current Assets	13	4	10

Ashley Power Ltd
580-586 Ashley Road, Poole, BH14 0AQ
Tel: 01202-746031 **Fax:** 01202-741108
E-mail: sales@ashleypower.co.uk
Website: http://www.ashleypower.co.uk
Directors: C. Hayward (Fin), G. Tate (MD)
Immediate Holding Company: ASHLEY POWER LIMITED
Registration no: 03642510 **Date established:** 1998
No.of Employees: 1 - 10 **Product Groups:** 22, 29, 30, 34, 35, 36, 39

Date of Accounts	Dec 11	Dec 10	Dec 09
Working Capital	85	83	74
Fixed Assets	142	159	180
Current Assets	214	223	177

B P Systems Barvick Process Systems Ltd
Dacombe Drive, Poole, BH16 5JN
Tel: 01202-256017 **Fax:** 0845-127 4303
E-mail: enq2bps@aol.com
Website: http://www.bpsystems-eu.com
Directors: J. Hodges (MD)
No.of Employees: 1 - 10 **Product Groups:** 30, 35, 36, 41, 42, 45, 63

Bakbone Software Ltd
Merck House Seldown Road, Poole, BH15 1TD
Tel: 01202-241000 **Fax:** 01202-249000
E-mail: info@bakbone.com
Website: http://www.bakbone.com
Bank(s): National Westminster
Directors: C. Barnes (Sales), C. Ross (Dir), D. Parkin (MD), F. Helliker (Dir), H. Brayne (Dir), V. Gamlin (Mkt Research)
Registration no: 03825597 **VAT No.:** 754 7029 20 **Date established:** 1995
Turnover: £5m - £10m **No.of Employees:** 51 - 100 **Product Groups:** 44

Date of Accounts	Mar 08	Mar 07	Mar 06
Sales Turnover	8442	7477	6108
Pre Tax Profit/Loss	233	83	-1163
Working Capital	-2417	-2488	-3987
Fixed Assets	503	586	756
Current Assets	5331	4540	3101
Current Liabilities	7748	7028	7089
Total Share Capital	97	97	97
ROCE% (Return on Capital Employed)	-12.2	-4.4	36.0
ROT% (Return on Turnover)	2.8	1.1	-19.0

Batchelor Electrical Ltd
Unit 15 Albany Business Park Cabot Lane, Poole, BH17 7BX
Tel: 01202-266200 **Fax:** 01202-266201
E-mail: info@batchelor-electrical.co.uk
Website: http://www.batchelor-electrical.co.uk
Directors: I. Batchelor (MD)
Immediate Holding Company: BATCHELOR ELECTRICAL LIMITED
Registration no: 02679096 **Date established:** 1992
No.of Employees: 1 - 10 **Product Groups:** 52

Date of Accounts	Jan 12	Jan 11	Jan 10
Working Capital	219	193	130
Fixed Assets	90	56	71
Current Assets	987	387	387

Beckox Plastic Fabrications Ltd
4-6 Wool Road, Poole, BH12 4NG
Tel: 01202-736725 **Fax:** 01202-738352
E-mail: reg@beckox.co.uk
Website: http://www.beckox.co.uk
Directors: R. Wilcox (MD), C. Wilcox (Fin)
Immediate Holding Company: BECKOX PLASTIC FABRICATIONS LIMITED
Registration no: 01629459 **VAT No.:** GB 355 7637 23
Date established: 1982 **No.of Employees:** 1 - 10 **Product Groups:** 30, 46

Date of Accounts	Apr 11	Apr 10	Apr 09
Working Capital	318	384	424
Fixed Assets	18	12	15
Current Assets	457	794	547

Bell Plastics Ltd
450 Blandford Road, Poole, BH16 5BN
Tel: 01202-625596 **Fax:** 01202-739285
E-mail: mail@bellplastics.co.uk
Website: http://www.bellplastics.co.uk
Bank(s): Barclays
Directors: D. Kavanagh (MD), R. Vessey (Fin)
Ultimate Holding Company: PLASTICS CAPITAL TRADING LIMITED
Immediate Holding Company: BELL PLASTICS LIMITED
Registration no: 02095777 **VAT No.:** GB 423 7723 55
Date established: 1987 **Turnover:** £2m - £5m **No.of Employees:** 11 - 20
Product Groups: 30, 31, 35, 48

Date of Accounts	Mar 11	Mar 10	Mar 09
Sales Turnover	4m	2m	2m
Pre Tax Profit/Loss	1m	274	611
Working Capital	3m	2m	2m
Fixed Assets	634	537	444
Current Assets	5m	4m	3m
Current Liabilities	786	421	370

Blakell Europlacer Ltd (Electronics Assembly Equipment & Gas Monitoring Division)
30 Factory Road, Poole, BH16 5SL
Tel: 01202-266500 **Fax:** 01202-266599
E-mail: info@europlacer.co.uk
Website: http://www.europlacer.com
Bank(s): Bank of Scotland

see next page

Blakell Europlacer Ltd (Electronics Assembly Equipment & Gas Monitoring Division) - Cont'd

Directors: J. Boardman (Fin)
Managers: C. White (Tech Serv Mgr), W. Smith, C. Steven
Ultimate Holding Company: BLAKELL EUROPLACER LIMITED
Immediate Holding Company: BLAKELL EUROPLACER LIMITED
Registration no: 00984064 **VAT No.:** GB 755 1201 58
Date established: 1970 **Turnover:** £10m - £20m
No.of Employees: 21 - 50 **Product Groups:** 30, 37, 44, 47, 48, 84

Date of Accounts	Dec 11	Dec 10	Dec 09
Sales Turnover	14m	16m	14m
Pre Tax Profit/Loss	2m	1m	-1m
Working Capital	6m	5m	4m
Fixed Assets	341	908	1m
Current Assets	9m	11m	9m
Current Liabilities	2m	4m	3m

Bourne Steel Ltd

Ferguson House 11 Church Road, Poole, BH14 8UF
Tel: 01202-710000 **Fax:** 01202-710012
Website: http://www.bournesteel.co.uk
Directors: D. Sanns (Dir)
Ultimate Holding Company: Bourne Group Holdings Ltd
Immediate Holding Company: BOURNE STEEL LTD
Registration no: 05982913 **Date established:** 2006
No.of Employees: 11 - 20 **Product Groups:** 35

Bourne Steel

St Clements House St Clements Road, Poole, BH12 4GP
Tel: 01202-746666 **Fax:** 0117-957 9933
E-mail: howard.davis@bournegroup.eu
Website: http://www.bournegroup.eu
Bank(s): Lloyds, High Street
Directors: N. Hatton (MD)
Immediate Holding Company: BOURNE STEEL LTD
Registration no: 05982913 **VAT No.:** GB 580 1240 73
Date established: 2006 **Turnover:** £20m - £50m
No.of Employees: 101 - 250 **Product Groups:** 26, 35, 48

Bournemouth University

Poole House Talbot Campus Fern Barrow, Poole, BH12 5BB
Tel: 01202-524111 **Fax:** 01202-513293
E-mail: vlewis@bournemouth.ac.uk
Website: http://www.bournemouth.ac.uk
Bank(s): Barclays
Managers: S. Clarke, V. Lewis
Immediate Holding Company: FEELPRIME LIMITED
Registration no: 00497624 **VAT No.:** GB 504 4921 66
Date established: 2000 **Turnover:** Up to £250,000
No.of Employees: 501 - 1000 **Product Groups:** 86

Date of Accounts	Jul 11	Jul 10	Jul 09
Working Capital	11	10	7
Current Assets	46	22	74

British Diamond Wire Die Co. Ltd

66 Old Wareham Road, Poole, BH12 4QS
Tel: 01202-745104 **Fax:** 01202-746125
E-mail: sales@bdwd.freeserve.co.uk
Website: http://www.balloffetdie.com
Bank(s): HSBC Bank plc
Directors: R. Jarratt (Sales), S. Romeo (MD)
Ultimate Holding Company: SOCIETE DE FILIERES BALLOFFET (FRANCE)
Immediate Holding Company: BRITISH DIAMOND WIRE DIE COMPANY LIMITED
Registration no: 00205665 **Date established:** 2025 **Turnover:** £1m - £2m
No.of Employees: 21 - 50 **Product Groups:** 46, 65

Date of Accounts	Dec 11	Dec 10	Dec 09
Working Capital	593	469	417
Fixed Assets	10	15	27
Current Assets	742	587	501

C & B Consultants Ltd

194 Stanley Green Road, Poole, BH15 3AH
Tel: 01202-673666 **Fax:** 01202-671776
E-mail: accounts@candbcomposites.com
Website: http://www.candbcomposites.com
Directors: S. Salmon (MD)
Immediate Holding Company: CB CONSULTANTS LTD
Registration no: 03186418 **No.of Employees:** 1 - 10 **Product Groups:** 38, 85

C Brewer & Sons

76-88 Old Wareham Road, Poole, BH12 4QR
Tel: 01202-741666 **Fax:** 01202-741777
Managers: A. Faulkner (Mgr)
Immediate Holding Company: C.BREWER & SONS LIMITED
Registration no: 00203852 **VAT No.:** GB 196 1565 70
Date established: 1925 **Turnover:** £500m - £1,000m
No.of Employees: 1 - 10 **Product Groups:** 27, 30, 32

C T Production Ltd

39 Harwell Road Nuffield Industrial Estate, Poole, BH17 0GE
Tel: 01202-687633 **Fax:** 01202-680788
E-mail: alan@ctproduction.co.uk
Website: http://www.ctproduction.co.uk
Directors: C. Trevarton (Fin), A. Trevarton (MD)
Managers: C. Trevarton (Mats Contrlr)
Ultimate Holding Company: SOLARSHAPE LIMITED
Immediate Holding Company: C.T. PRODUCTION LIMITED
Registration no: 01678483 **VAT No.:** GB 355 6502 51
Date established: 1982 **Turnover:** £2m - £5m **No.of Employees:** 21 - 50
Product Groups: 37

Date of Accounts	Dec 11	Dec 10	Dec 09
Working Capital	-81	-143	-131
Fixed Assets	278	353	289
Current Assets	557	589	628

Cable First Ltd

32-40 Harwell Road Nuffield Industrial Estate, Poole, BH17 0GE
Tel: 01202-687337 **Fax:** 01202-672501
E-mail: sales@cablefirst.co.uk
Website: http://www.cablefirst.co.uk
Bank(s): National Westminster Bank Plc
Directors: A. Lodge (MD), A. Lodge (MD)
Managers: D. Barlett (Purch Mgr)
Ultimate Holding Company: GEMACO HOLDINGS LIMITED
Immediate Holding Company: CABLE FIRST LIMITED
Registration no: 03254437 **VAT No.:** GB 704 5656 38
Date established: 1996 **Turnover:** £1m - £2m **No.of Employees:** 21 - 50
Product Groups: 30, 37, 66

Date of Accounts	Dec 11	Dec 10	Dec 09
Working Capital	130	123	105
Fixed Assets	300	209	174
Current Assets	1m	959	806

Callender Design

Unit 2 Birch Copse Technology Road, Poole, BH17 7FH
Tel: 01202-692007 **Fax:** 01202-603347
E-mail: info@callenderdesigns.com
Website: http://www.callenderdesigns.com
Directors: C. Callender (Prop)
Immediate Holding Company: CALLENDER DESIGNS LIMITED
Registration no: 03733026 **Date established:** 1999
No.of Employees: 1 - 10 **Product Groups:** 30, 52, 81, 84

Date of Accounts	Mar 12	Mar 11	Mar 10
Working Capital	-8	1	-9
Fixed Assets	4	7	10
Current Assets	13	23	16

Caparo Testing Technologies

Unit 18 Dawkins Road, Poole, BH15 4JY
Tel: 01202-681971 **Fax:** 01202-680845
E-mail: poole@caparotesting.com
Website: http://www.caparotesting.com
Managers: S. Richardson (Mgr)
Ultimate Holding Company: SURECHECK SOUTHERN LTD
Date established: 1981 **Turnover:** £5m - £10m **No.of Employees:** 1 - 10
Product Groups: 38, 85

Capital Hair & Beauty

Unit 1 Old Generator House Bourne Valley Road, Poole, BH12 1DZ
Tel: 01202-763442 **Fax:** 01202-762009
E-mail: bournemouth@capitalhb.co.uk
Website: http://www.capitalhairandbeauty.co.uk
Managers: S. Fowler (Mgr)
Immediate Holding Company: CAPITAL (HAIR AND BEAUTY) LIMITED
Registration no: 00530201 **Date established:** 1954
No.of Employees: 1 - 10 **Product Groups:** 32, 40, 63, 67

Date of Accounts	Dec 11	Dec 10	Dec 09
Sales Turnover	32m	28m	24m
Pre Tax Profit/Loss	4m	749	2m
Working Capital	7m	4m	3m
Fixed Assets	3m	3m	2m
Current Assets	13m	8m	7m
Current Liabilities	4m	3m	3m

Chalwyn Estates Ltd

Unit 1c Chalwyn Industrial Estate St Clements Road, Poole, BH12 4PE
Tel: 01202-744418 **Fax:** 01202-715600
E-mail: sales@chalwyn.co.uk
Website: http://www.chalwyn.co.uk
Directors: T. Long (Fin)
Immediate Holding Company: CHALWYN ESTATES LIMITED
Registration no: 05151519 **VAT No.:** GB 186 1608 49
Date established: 2004 **Turnover:** £2m - £5m **No.of Employees:** 1 - 10
Product Groups: 35, 39, 40, 45

Date of Accounts	Jun 11	Jun 10	Jun 09
Working Capital	744	364	-43
Fixed Assets	5m	5m	5m
Current Assets	1m	2m	1m

Charnwood Healthcare Ltd

Unit B7 46 Holton Heath Training Park Holton Road, Holton Heath Trading Park, Poole, BH16 6LT
Tel: 01202-620839 **Fax:** 01202-620839
E-mail: paul.mclintic@charnwoodhealthcare.com
Website: http://www.charnwoodhealthcare.co.uk
Directors: P. Mclintic (Dir), R. McLintic (Co Sec)
Immediate Holding Company: CHARNWOOD HEALTHCARE LIMITED
Registration no: 01726104 **Date established:** 1983
No.of Employees: 1 - 10 **Product Groups:** 26, 38

Date of Accounts	Dec 10	Dec 08	Dec 07
Working Capital	-57	-57	-56
Fixed Assets	60	64	58
Current Assets	35	27	29

Chilltech Refrigeration Equipment

14 Manor Park 35 Willis Way, Poole, BH15 3SZ
Tel: 01202-668844 **Fax:** 01202-661111
Website: http://www.chilltech.co.uk
Directors: A. Shea (Ptnr)
No.of Employees: 1 - 10 **Product Groups:** 38, 40, 45, 83

Coastal Aluminium

D'Oriel House Blackhill Road West, Holton Heath Trading Park, Poole, BH16 6LE
Tel: 01202-624011 **Fax:** 01202-622465
E-mail: sales@coastalwindows.co.uk
Website: http://www.coastalaluminium.co.uk
Bank(s): Lloyds TSB Bank plc
Directors: D. Locke (MD)
Ultimate Holding Company: A. & B. GLASS COMPANY LIMITED
Immediate Holding Company: COASTAL WINDOWS LIMITED
Registration no: 05034162 **VAT No.:** GB 119 7195 49
Date established: 2004 **Turnover:** £20m - £50m
No.of Employees: 21 - 50 **Product Groups:** 30, 35

Coil Winding International

PO Box 936 Alder Hills, Poole, BH12 4YD
Tel: 01202-380661 **Fax:** 01202-736018
E-mail: coilwind@bournemouth-net.co.uk
Website: http://www.bournemouth-net.co.uk
Directors: T. House (Prop), T. House (MD), J. Gale (Co Sec)
Managers: R. Gale, J. Gale (Accounts), J. Gails (Mgr)
Immediate Holding Company: COIL WINDING INTERNATIONAL LTD
Registration no: 03419433 **Date established:** 1997
Turnover: Up to £250,000 **No.of Employees:** 1 - 10 **Product Groups:** 37

Connexions 4 London

7th Floor County Gates House 300 Poole Road, Branksome, Poole, BH12 1AZ
Tel: 0800-047 0481 **Fax:** 08707-061094
E-mail: sales@c4l.co.uk
Website: http://www.c4l.co.uk
Directors: P. Hawkings (Fin), M. Hawkings (MD)
Managers: I. Miller (Sales Prom Mgr)
Immediate Holding Company: CONNEXIONS4LONDON LTD
Registration no: 05237920 **Date established:** 2004
No.of Employees: 21 - 50 **Product Groups:** 79

Date of Accounts	Oct 11	Oct 10	Oct 09
Working Capital	-368	9	-328
Fixed Assets	2m	1m	947
Current Assets	2m	2m	2m
Current Liabilities	N/A	2m	N/A

Conoflow Ltd

87-89 Sterte Avenue West, Poole, BH15 2AL
Tel: 01202-660090
E-mail: sales@conoflow.co.uk
Website: http://www.conoflow.co.uk
Directors: E. Parry (Prop)
Immediate Holding Company: CONOFLOW LIMITED
Registration no: 01528200 **Date established:** 1980
No.of Employees: 1 - 10 **Product Groups:** 36, 37, 38

Date of Accounts	Apr 11	Apr 10	Apr 09
Working Capital	-64	-69	-67
Fixed Assets	33	28	33
Current Assets	84	83	95

Corhaven Sheet Metal Fabrications Ltd

Unit 8 Alder Hills Industrial Estate 16 Alder Hills, Poole, BH12 4AR
Tel: 01202-741166 **Fax:** 01202-741166
E-mail: corhaven@tiscali.co.uk
Website: http://www.corhaven.co.uk
Directors: S. Roberts (Dir)
Immediate Holding Company: CORHAVEN SHEET METAL FABRICATIONS LIMITED
Registration no: 04634335 **Date established:** 2003
Turnover: £250,000 - £500,000 **No.of Employees:** 1 - 10
Product Groups: 35, 48, 66

Date of Accounts	Jan 11	Jan 10	Jan 09
Working Capital	94	99	102
Fixed Assets	22	23	31
Current Assets	181	158	169

Alan Courtenay Ltd

Fleetsbridge Business Centre Upton Road, Poole, BH17 7AF
Tel: 01202-666383 **Fax:** 01202-666384
E-mail: sales@alancourtenay.co.uk
Website: http://www.alancourtenay.co.uk
Bank(s): TSB, Bournemouth
Directors: A. Courtenay (MD)
Immediate Holding Company: ALAN COURTENAY LIMITED
Registration no: 01828365 **Date established:** 1984 **Turnover:** £1m - £2m
No.of Employees: 11 - 20 **Product Groups:** 26, 40

Date of Accounts	Jun 12	Jun 11	Jun 10
Working Capital	458	351	270
Fixed Assets	272	278	228
Current Assets	948	732	487

Crusherform Grinding & Engineering Ltd

30 Kennington Road Nuffield Industrial Estate, Poole, BH17 0GF
Tel: 01202-679363 **Fax:** 01202-682970
Directors: P. Blake (MD)
Immediate Holding Company: CRUSHERFORM GRINDING & ENGINEERING LTD
Registration no: 05997664 **VAT No.:** GB 185 6637 23
Date established: 2006 **Turnover:** Up to £250,000
No.of Employees: 1 - 10 **Product Groups:** 27, 29, 48

Date of Accounts	Dec 11	Dec 10	Dec 09
Working Capital	14	-1	-12
Fixed Assets	27	33	38
Current Assets	37	21	23

Custom Coatings Ltd

2 Allens Lane, Poole, BH16 5DA
Tel: 01202-632989 **Fax:** 01202-627622
E-mail: stuart@customcoatings.eu
Website: http://www.customcoatings.eu
Managers: S. Forsyth (Ops Mgr)
Ultimate Holding Company: JET INDUSTRIAL HOLDINGS LIMITED
Immediate Holding Company: CUSTOM COATINGS LIMITED
Registration no: 01993614 **Date established:** 1986
Turnover: £250,000 - £500,000 **No.of Employees:** 1 - 10
Product Groups: 46

Date of Accounts	Mar 11	Mar 10	Jan 09
Working Capital	-19	21	354
Fixed Assets	23	27	N/A
Current Assets	139	120	413

Custom Micro Products Ltd

450 Blandford Road, Poole, BH16 5BN
Tel: 01202-631733 **Fax:** 01202-632036
E-mail: sales@custom-micro.com
Website: http://www.custom-micro.com
Bank(s): HSBC
Directors: M. Rapoport (Pres)
Ultimate Holding Company: NEWMARK SECURITY PLC
Immediate Holding Company: CUSTOM MICRO PRODUCTS LIMITED
Registration no: 01015185 **VAT No.:** GB 185 6789 00
Date established: 1971 **Turnover:** £2m - £5m **No.of Employees:** 11 - 20
Product Groups: 40, 44, 49

Date of Accounts	Apr 11	Apr 10	Apr 09
Pre Tax Profit/Loss	N/A	-1	-1
Working Capital	28	28	28
Current Assets	28	28	28

Cyclone Power Ltd

48 Hatch Pond Road Nuffield Industrial Estate, Poole, BH17 0JZ
Tel: 01202-649411 **Fax:** 01202-666002
E-mail: enquiries@cyclonepowerltd.co.uk
Directors: K. Banyard (MD), C. Banyard (Fin)
Immediate Holding Company: CYCLONE POWER LIMITED
Registration no: 04631728 **Date established:** 2003
Turnover: Up to £250,000 **No.of Employees:** 1 - 10 **Product Groups:** 39, 40

Date of Accounts	Dec 10	Dec 09	Dec 07
Working Capital	6	5	219
Fixed Assets	127	143	29
Current Assets	11	8	225

D P Seals Ltd

6 Dawkins Road, Poole, BH15 4JY
Tel: 01202-674671 **Fax:** 01202-665581
E-mail: sales@dpseals.com
Website: http://www.dpseals.com
Directors: A. Piper (Tech Serv), B. Piper (Co Sec)
Immediate Holding Company: D. P. SEALS LIMITED
Registration no: 00739542 **Date established:** 1962 **Turnover:** £1m - £2m
No.of Employees: 21 - 50 **Product Groups:** 29, 35, 49, 63

Date of Accounts	Dec 11	Dec 10	Dec 09
Working Capital	158	160	217
Fixed Assets	1m	861	825
Current Assets	569	562	457

De Monchy Aromatics Ltd

Blackhill Road Holton Heath Trading Park, Poole, BH16 6LS
Tel: 01202-620888 **Fax:** 01202-620999
E-mail: sales@demonchyaromatics.com
Website: http://www.demonchyaromatics.com
Bank(s): Lloyds TSB Bank plc
Directors: M. Gill (MD), S. Gill (Fin)
Immediate Holding Company: DE MONCHY AROMATICS LIMITED
Registration no: 01615220 **VAT No.:** GB 355 7338 33
Date established: 1982 **Turnover:** £2m - £5m **No.of Employees:** 11 - 20
Product Groups: 20, 31, 66

Date of Accounts	Dec 11	Dec 08	Mar 11
Working Capital	2m	1m	2m
Fixed Assets	72	166	78
Current Assets	3m	2m	3m

Denholm Barwil Ltd

Unit N4 New Quay New Harbour Road, Poole, BH15 4BB
Tel: 01202-673831 **Fax:** 01202-666225
E-mail: denholm.poole@dial.pipex.com
Website: http://www.denholm-shipping.co.uk
Managers: A. Savory (Sales Admin)
Immediate Holding Company: DENHOLM BARWIL LIMITED
Registration no: SC032785 **Date established:** 1958
No.of Employees: 1 - 10 **Product Groups:** 72, 74

Dorset Chamber Of Commerce

Unit B Acorn Office Park Ling Road, Poole, BH12 4NZ
Tel: 01202-714800 **Fax:** 01202-747862
E-mail: peter.scott@dcci.co.uk
Website: http://www.dcci.co.uk
Directors: P. Scott (Grp Chief Exec)
Immediate Holding Company: DORSET CHAMBER OF COMMERCE AND INDUSTRY
Registration no: 00503870 **VAT No.:** GB 291 8986 94
Date established: 1952 **Turnover:** £500,000 - £1m
No.of Employees: 11 - 20 **Product Groups:** 87

Date of Accounts	Mar 11	Mar 10	Mar 09
Sales Turnover	753	822	749
Pre Tax Profit/Loss	7	23	11
Working Capital	-115	-102	-98
Fixed Assets	592	604	618
Current Assets	163	252	118
Current Liabilities	239	288	166

Dorset Lake Shipyard Ltd

Lake Drive, Poole, BH15 4DT
Tel: 01202-674532 **Fax:** 01202-677518
E-mail: office@lakeyard.com
Website: http://www.bostonwhaler.co.uk
Directors: T. Shroder (Co Sec), R. Culpan (Dir)
Ultimate Holding Company: SQUADRON MARINE LIMITED
Immediate Holding Company: DORSET LAKE SHIPYARD LIMITED
Registration no: 00324125 **VAT No.:** GB 185 5204 59
Date established: 1937 **Turnover:** Up to £250,000
No.of Employees: 1 - 10 **Product Groups:** 39

Date of Accounts	Nov 11	Nov 10	Nov 09
Working Capital	80	68	-44
Fixed Assets	881	885	901
Current Assets	280	330	176

Dorset Yacht Company Ltd

Lake Drive, Poole, BH15 4DT
Tel: 01202-674534 **Fax:** 01202-677518
E-mail: sales@lakeyard.co.uk
Website: http://www.lakeyard.co.uk
Directors: R. Culpan (MD)
Ultimate Holding Company: SQUADRON MARINE LIMITED
Immediate Holding Company: DORSET YACHT CO. LIMITED
Registration no: 00907476 **VAT No.:** GB 291 9296 17
Date established: 1967 **Turnover:** £250,000 - £500,000
No.of Employees: 1 - 10 **Product Groups:** 39, 68

Date of Accounts	Nov 11	Nov 10	Nov 09
Working Capital	-204	-210	-159
Fixed Assets	5	8	11
Current Assets	166	205	273

Dorsetware Ltd

Unit 1-2 Dawkins Road, Poole, BH15 4JP
Tel: 01202-677939 **Fax:** 01202-665537
E-mail: sales@dorsetware.com
Website: http://www.dorsetware.com
Bank(s): The Royal Bank of Scotland plc
Directors: A. Thomas (Fin), C. Long (MD)
Immediate Holding Company: DORSETWARE LIMITED
Registration no: 05427214 **VAT No.:** GB 185 7416 34
Date established: 2005 **Turnover:** £500,000 - £1m
No.of Employees: 11 - 20 **Product Groups:** 48

Date of Accounts	Mar 11	Mar 10	Mar 09
Working Capital	4	4	15
Fixed Assets	66	43	46
Current Assets	194	129	129

R Dyke Structural Services Ltd

53 Nansen Avenue, Poole, BH15 3DD
Tel: 01202-676701 **Fax:** 01202-676701
Directors: R. Dyke (MD)
Immediate Holding Company: R DYKE STRUCTURAL SERVICES LIMITED
Registration no: 04741378 **Date established:** 2003
No.of Employees: 1 - 10 **Product Groups:** 35

Date of Accounts	Mar 12	Mar 11	Mar 10
Working Capital	11	11	10
Fixed Assets	1	1	1
Current Assets	21	22	20

E S E Engineering UK Llp

14 Cowley Road Nuffield Industrial Estate, Poole, BH17 0UJ
Tel: 01202-683441 **Fax:** 01202-666408
E-mail: info@eseengineering.co.uk
Website: http://www.eseengineering.com
Directors: P. Regan (Fin), T. Saunders (Fin)
Managers: C. Justice (Chief Mgr)
Immediate Holding Company: ESE ENGINEERING LIMITED
Registration no: 03751586 **VAT No.:** GB 542 0327 82
Date established: 1999 **Turnover:** £1m - £2m **No.of Employees:** 21 - 50
Product Groups: 35, 48

Date of Accounts	Apr 11	Apr 10	Apr 09
Working Capital	-183	-183	-183
Current Assets	25	370	368
Current Liabilities	N/A	498	N/A

Edmundson Electrical Ltd

Unit 25 Wessex Trade Centre, Poole, BH12 3PF
Tel: 01202-747241 **Fax:** 01202-682785
Website: http://www.edmundson-electrical.co.uk
Managers: L. Cooper (District Mgr)
Ultimate Holding Company: BLACKFRIARS CORP (USA)
Immediate Holding Company: EDMUNDSON ELECTRICAL LIMITED
Registration no: 02667012 **VAT No.:** GB 579 9948 39
Date established: 1991 **Turnover:** £20m - £50m **No.of Employees:** 1 - 10
Product Groups: 87

Date of Accounts	Dec 11	Dec 10	Dec 09
Sales Turnover	1023m	852m	788m
Pre Tax Profit/Loss	57m	53m	45m
Working Capital	256m	225m	184m
Fixed Assets	17m	3m	4m
Current Assets	439m	358m	298m
Current Liabilities	59m	38m	37m

English Ford

1 Yarrow Road, Poole, BH12 4QA
Tel: 01202-715577 **Fax:** 01202-715973
E-mail: brettsanstleben@evanshalshaw.com
Website: http://www.ford.co.uk
Directors: P. Hopkinson (I.T. Dir), C. Yoxon (Prop), K. Davies (Sales)
Managers: C. Sansom (Nat Sales Mgr), D. Maidment (Chief Acct), J. Pearson (Sec), J. Pearson, M. Bingham (Personnel)
Immediate Holding Company: PENDRAGON MOTOR GROUP
Turnover: £20m - £50m **No.of Employees:** 51 - 100 **Product Groups:** 68

Eriks UK Ltd (Poole Service Centre)

Unit 20 Albany Park Cabot Lane, Poole, BH17 7BX
Tel: 01202-699922 **Fax:** 01202-691844
E-mail: poole@eriks.co.uk
Website: http://www.wyko.co.uk
Managers: M. Iverson (Mgr)
Immediate Holding Company: FRANK WAINWRIGHT & SON LIMITED
Date established: 1941 **Turnover:** £250m - £500m
No.of Employees: 1 - 10 **Product Groups:** 66

Eventscape Corporate Entertainment

Discovery Court Business Centre 551-553 Wallisdown Road, Poole, BH12 5AG
Tel: 01202-853202 **Fax:** 07050-654383
E-mail: enquiries@eventscape.co.uk
Website: http://www.eventscape.co.uk
Directors: L. Davis (Chief Op Offcr)
Immediate Holding Company: EVENTSCAPE LTD.
Registration no: 04228465 **Date established:** 2001
No.of Employees: 1 - 10 **Product Groups:** 29, 49, 68, 89

Date of Accounts	Nov 11	Nov 10	Nov 09
Working Capital	17	14	19
Fixed Assets	N/A	1	1
Current Assets	64	51	49

Fineline Fabrications Ltd

184-186 Stanlet Green Road, Poole, BH15 3AH
Tel: 01202-669026 **Fax:** 01202-669026
E-mail: info@finelinefabs.co.uk
Website: http://www.finelinefabs.com
Directors: A. Bailey (Fin), M. Jupe (MD)
Immediate Holding Company: FINELINE FABRICATIONS LIMITED
Registration no: 04655443 **Date established:** 2003
No.of Employees: 1 - 10 **Product Groups:** 26, 35

Date of Accounts	Mar 11	Mar 10	Mar 09
Working Capital	193	225	175
Fixed Assets	88	93	83
Current Assets	275	335	267

Form Waterjet

42 Harwell Road Nuffield Industrial Estate, Poole, BH17 0GE
Tel: 01202-660440 **Fax:** 01202-660550
E-mail: info@formwaterjet.co.uk
Website: http://www.formwaterjet.co.uk
Directors: D. Freer (Dir)
No.of Employees: 1 - 10 **Product Groups:** 41, 42, 45, 46, 47, 48

G P & J Baker Ltd (incorporating Parker Fabrics)

PO Box 30, Poole, BH17 0SW
Tel: 01202-266999 **Fax:** 01202-266701
E-mail: sales@gpjbaker.com
Website: http://www.gpjbaker.com
Bank(s): Lloyds TSB Bank plc
Directors: A. Grafton (Prop), G. Coote (Sales)
Managers: C. Partridge, S. Bigmore (Personnel), S. Jackson, D. Beard (Tech Serv Mgr), V. Manuel (Mktg Serv Mgr)
Ultimate Holding Company: KRAVET FABRICS INC (USA)
Immediate Holding Company: GP & J BAKER LIMITED
Registration no: 03761709 **Date established:** 1999
Turnover: £10m - £20m **No.of Employees:** 101 - 250 **Product Groups:** 63

Date of Accounts	Dec 11	Dec 10	Dec 09
Sales Turnover	18m	17m	15m
Pre Tax Profit/Loss	346	616	303
Working Capital	2m	2m	1m
Fixed Assets	259	153	274
Current Assets	7m	8m	7m
Current Liabilities	N/A	621	320

Griffin International Associates Ltd

15 Springfield Crescent, Poole, BH14 0LL
Tel: 01202-730535 **Fax:** 01202-730535
E-mail: ckentrichardson@tiscali.co.uk
Website: http://www.griffininternational.co.uk
Directors: C. Richardson (Prop)
Immediate Holding Company: GIA INTERNATIONAL LIMITED
Registration no: 01635565 **VAT No.:** GB 355 8886 94
Date established: 1982 **Turnover:** Up to £250,000
No.of Employees: 1 - 10 **Product Groups:** 61

Date of Accounts	Mar 11	Mar 10	Mar 09
Sales Turnover	N/A	22	59
Pre Tax Profit/Loss	N/A	-1	-1
Working Capital	6	9	11
Current Assets	6	9	12

Hamworthy Combustion Engineering Ltd

Fleets Corner, Poole, BH17 0LA
Tel: 01202-662700 **Fax:** 01202-669875
E-mail: info@hamworthy-combustion.com
Website: http://www.hamworthy-combustion.com
Bank(s): National Westminster Bank Plc
Directors: R. Lee (Fin)
Managers: G. Wright (Mgr), T. Buchanan (Personnel), D. Miller (Tech Serv Mgr), T. Saia
Ultimate Holding Company: CITIGROUP INC (USA)
Immediate Holding Company: HAMWORTHY COMBUSTION ENGINEERING LIMITED
Registration no: 00713226 **VAT No.:** GB 504 2409 86
Date established: 1962 **Turnover:** £50m - £75m
No.of Employees: 251 - 500 **Product Groups:** 39, 40, 66

Date of Accounts	Dec 11	Apr 11	Apr 10
Sales Turnover	26m	53m	50m
Pre Tax Profit/Loss	-4m	5m	3m
Working Capital	4m	6m	5m
Fixed Assets	16m	17m	17m
Current Assets	37m	36m	35m
Current Liabilities	22m	13m	6m

Hamworthy Heating Ltd

Fleets Corner, Poole, BH17 0HH
Tel: 01202-662500 **Fax:** 01202-662550
E-mail: sales@hamworthy-heating.com
Website: http://www.hamworthy-heating.com
Bank(s): National Westminster Bank Plc
Directors: A. Moore (MD)
Ultimate Holding Company: HEATING HOLDINGS LIMITED
Immediate Holding Company: HAMWORTHY HEATING LIMITED
Registration no: 02223589 **VAT No.:** GB 504 2409 86
Date established: 1988 **No.of Employees:** 51 - 100 **Product Groups:** 35, 40

Hamworthy Waste Water plc

Fleets Corner, Poole, BH17 0JT
Tel: 01202-662600 **Fax:** 01202-666363
E-mail: info@hamworthy.com
Website: http://www.hamworthy.com
Bank(s): National Westminster Bank Plc
Directors: K. Derrick (Grp Chief Exec), G. Page (Ch), P. Crompton (Fin), J. Wilding (Fin)
Managers: G. Lockyer (Mktg Serv Mgr), R. Edmondson (Personnel), N. Levkouskis (Purch Mgr), M. Turner (I.T. Exec), L. Jackson (Purch Mgr), A. White (Sales Prom Mgr), M. Maidment (Works Gen Mgr)
Ultimate Holding Company: HAMWORTHY PLC
Immediate Holding Company: WARTSILA HAMWORTHY LIMITED
Registration no: 00713225 **Date established:** 1962
Turnover: £125m - £250m **No.of Employees:** 501 - 1000
Product Groups: 36, 39, 40, 42

Date of Accounts	Mar 11	Mar 10	Mar 09
Sales Turnover	182m	214m	253m
Pre Tax Profit/Loss	14m	21m	22m
Working Capital	77m	72m	57m
Fixed Assets	45m	45m	39m
Current Assets	173m	164m	191m
Current Liabilities	81m	78m	114m

Hoare Lea Ltd

Yarmouth Road, Poole, BH12 1TP
Tel: 01202-545800 **Fax:** 01202-545801
E-mail: annestickland@hoarelea.com
Website: http://www.hoarelea.com
Managers: A. Stickland (Sales Admin)
Immediate Holding Company: HOARE LEA LIMITED
Registration no: 07088478 **Date established:** 2009
Turnover: £10m - £20m **No.of Employees:** 21 - 50 **Product Groups:** 84

Holes Bay Marine

25-28 Cobbs Quay, Poole, BH15 4EL
Tel: 01202-667202 **Fax:** 01202-667202
E-mail: richard@holesbaymarine.co.uk
Website: http://www.holesbaymarine.co.uk
Managers: R. Moore (Mgr)
Immediate Holding Company: BOATYLICIOUS MARINE LIMITED
Date established: 2011 **No.of Employees:** 1 - 10 **Product Groups:** 35, 36, 39

Date of Accounts	Jun 08	Jun 07	Jun 06
Working Capital	48	36	38
Fixed Assets	23	19	23
Current Assets	152	98	103
Current Liabilities	104	62	65

Holton Crest Ltd

10 Cowley Road Nuffield Industrial Estate, Poole, BH17 0UJ
Tel: 01202-681501 **Fax:** 01202-681502
E-mail: info@holtoncrest.com
Website: http://www.holtoncrest.com
Directors: P. Barker (Dir)
Immediate Holding Company: HOLTON CREST LIMITED
Registration no: 05777787 **Date established:** 2006
No.of Employees: 1 - 10 **Product Groups:** 34, 40, 46, 48, 67

Date of Accounts	Apr 11	Apr 10	Apr 09
Working Capital	336	222	80
Fixed Assets	15	17	15
Current Assets	648	702	1m

Honeywell Analytics Ltd
Hatch Pond House 4 Stinsford Road, Poole, BH17 0RZ
Tel: 01202-645577 **Fax:** 01202-678011
E-mail: info@zellweger-analytics.co.uk
Website: http://www.honeywellanalytics.com
Managers: T. Jack (Comm)
Ultimate Holding Company: HONEYWELL INTERNATIONAL INC (USA)
Immediate Holding Company: HONEYWELL ANALYTICS LIMITED
Registration no: 00412070 **VAT No.:** GB 392 8347 17
Date established: 1946 **Turnover:** £500m - £1,000m
No.of Employees: 101 - 250 **Product Groups:** 38, 40, 45, 84

Date of Accounts	Dec 11	Dec 10	Dec 09
Sales Turnover	18m	10m	9m
Pre Tax Profit/Loss	-2m	2m	2m
Working Capital	15m	6m	3m
Fixed Assets	1m	12m	12m
Current Assets	24m	19m	16m
Current Liabilities	1m	602	839

Hyphose Ltd
2 Witney Road Nuffield Industrial Estate, Poole, BH17 0GH
Tel: 01202-673333 **Fax:** 01202-687788
E-mail: sales@hyphose.com
Website: http://www.hyphose.com
Bank(s): HSBC Bank plc
Directors: A. Barwick (Fin), D. Johnson (Dir)
Managers: K. Pullen (District Mgr)
Immediate Holding Company: HYPHOSE LIMITED
Registration no: 01472439 **Date established:** 1980
No.of Employees: 21 - 50 **Product Groups:** 30

Date of Accounts	Mar 12	Mar 11	Mar 10
Working Capital	269	270	368
Fixed Assets	1m	948	908
Current Assets	2m	2m	2m

Ibcos Computers Ltd
Abacus House Acorn Business Park, Poole, BH12 4NZ
Tel: 01202-714200 **Fax:** 01202-733552
E-mail: info@ibcos.co.uk
Website: http://www.ibcos.co.uk
Directors: A. Scothern (Fin), J. Vulcher (Sales & Mktg)
Managers: J. Machin (Buyer)
Ultimate Holding Company: IBCOS HOLDINGS LIMITED
Immediate Holding Company: IBCOS HOLDINGS LIMITED
Registration no: 01984987 **VAT No.:** GB 634 3689 20
Date established: 1986 **Turnover:** £2m - £5m **No.of Employees:** 21 - 50
Product Groups: 44

Date of Accounts	Mar 12	Mar 11	Mar 10
Working Capital	15	15	15
Fixed Assets	5	5	5
Current Assets	15	15	15

Inrekor Ltd
Unit 1c Chalwyd Industrial Estate St Clements Road, Poole, BH12 4PE
Tel: 01202-721211
E-mail: fpr@inrekor.co.uk
Website: http://www.inrekor.com
Directors: F. Page Roberts (Sales)
Immediate Holding Company: INREKOR LIMITED
Registration no: 07212868 **Date established:** 2010
No.of Employees: 1 - 10 **Product Groups:** 25, 30, 35, 39

Date of Accounts	Dec 11	Dec 10
Working Capital	-842	-641
Fixed Assets	264	248
Current Assets	51	7

Ishida Europe Ltd
Unit 1 19 Willis Way, Poole, BH15 3SS
Tel: 01202-466300 **Fax:** 01202-466302
E-mail: info@ishidaeurope.com
Website: http://www.ishidaeurope.com
Bank(s): Barclays, Poole
Managers: C. Witheford (Mgr)
Ultimate Holding Company: ISHIDA COMPANY LTD (JAPAN)
Immediate Holding Company: ISHIDA EUROPE LTD.
Registration no: 01832141 **Date established:** 1984 **Turnover:** £5m - £10m
No.of Employees: 21 - 50 **Product Groups:** 41, 42

Date of Accounts	Mar 12	Mar 11	Mar 10
Sales Turnover	95m	78m	67m
Pre Tax Profit/Loss	6m	5m	203
Working Capital	29m	24m	20m
Fixed Assets	4m	5m	5m
Current Assets	73m	50m	44m
Current Liabilities	30m	15m	11m

J Motor Components Ltd (Head Office)
Unit K The Fulcrum Centre Vantage Way, Poole, BH12 4NU
Tel: 01202-711177 **Fax:** 01202-535777
E-mail: sales@jmotorcomponents.com
Website: http://www.jmotorcomponents.co.uk
Bank(s): Lloyds, 45 Old X Church Rd, Bournemouth
Directors: J. Hicks (Fin)
Immediate Holding Company: J MOTOR COMPONENTS LIMITED
Registration no: 05106204 **VAT No.:** GB 185 6712 35
Date established: 2004 **Turnover:** £2m - £5m **No.of Employees:** 11 - 20
Product Groups: 39

J & T Tubes Ltd
Unit 3 -6 Ventura Centre Ventura Place, Poole, BH16 5SW
Tel: 01202-625007 **Fax:** 01202-622989
E-mail: info@jandttubes.com
Website: http://www.jandttubes.com
Directors: J. Fletcher (MD)
Immediate Holding Company: J & T TUBES LIMITED
Registration no: 03874635 **VAT No.:** GB 423 8664 40
Date established: 1999 **Turnover:** £500,000 - £1m
No.of Employees: 1 - 10 **Product Groups:** 48

Date of Accounts	Apr 11	Apr 10	Apr 09
Working Capital	82	81	65
Fixed Assets	115	140	163
Current Assets	138	132	98

James Bros Hamworthy Ltd
3 Fleets Lane, Poole, BH15 3AJ
Tel: 01202-673815 **Fax:** 01202-684033
E-mail: inquiries@james-bros.co.uk
Website: http://www.james-bros.co.uk
Bank(s): Lloyds TSB Bank plc
Directors: M. Pryke (MD), J. Charles (MD), S. Dyke (MD)
Immediate Holding Company: James Bros.(Hamworthy)Limited
Registration no: 00381971 **VAT No.:** GB 185 7489 07
Date established: 1943 **No.of Employees:** 11 - 20 **Product Groups:** 26, 30, 35, 36, 48, 52, 66

JM Decorating
107, Princess Road Westbourne, Poole, BH12 1BQ
Tel: 07939-620650
E-mail: info@decoratingdorset.co.uk
Website: http://www.Jmdecorating.com
Directors: J. Martin (Dir)
Date established: 1993 **No.of Employees:** 1 - 10 **Product Groups:** 52

K E S Tools
262 Ashley Road, Poole, BH14 9BZ
Tel: 01202-742393 **Fax:** 01202-722042
Directors: K. Sibbert (Prop)
Date established: 1988 **No.of Employees:** 1 - 10 **Product Groups:** 37

K W Engineering Poole Ltd
Unit 1 Ency Park 7 Abingdon Road, Nuffield Industrial Estate, Poole, BH17 0UH
Tel: 01202-677990 **Fax:** 01202-666355
E-mail: sales@kw-eng.co.uk
Website: http://www.kw-eng.co.uk
Bank(s): Lloyds TSB Bank plc
Directors: B. McGuiness (Fin), G. Docking (Dir)
Immediate Holding Company: K.W. ENGINEERING (POOLE) LIMITED
Registration no: 01750240 **VAT No.:** GB 392 7783 02
Date established: 1983 **Turnover:** £500,000 - £1m
No.of Employees: 21 - 50 **Product Groups:** 38

Date of Accounts	Nov 11	Nov 10	Nov 09
Working Capital	-17	10	-20
Fixed Assets	557	545	696
Current Assets	800	737	515

Kerry Foods Ltd (t/a Kerry Foods - Poole)
10-20 Sterte Avenue, Poole, BH15 2AS
Tel: 01202-666000 **Fax:** 01202-666352
E-mail: peter.richards@kerryfoods.co.uk
Website: http://www.kerryfoods.co.uk
Bank(s): National Westminster Bank Plc
Managers: P. Richards (Chief Mgr), R. Eustace (Comptroller), S. Wootten (Personnel)
Ultimate Holding Company: KERRY GROUP PUBLIC LIMITED COMPANY
Immediate Holding Company: KERRY FOODS LIMITED
Registration no: 02604258 **VAT No.:** GB 635 8381 17
Date established: 1991 **No.of Employees:** 501 - 1000 **Product Groups:** 20

Date of Accounts	Dec 11	Dec 10	Dec 09
Sales Turnover	679m	568m	525m
Pre Tax Profit/Loss	7m	25m	14m
Working Capital	-15m	36m	29m
Fixed Assets	121m	89m	90m
Current Assets	246m	240m	204m
Current Liabilities	6m	8m	1m

Lilys Leds
19 Balena Close, Poole, BH17 7DU
Tel: 01202-605010 **Fax:** 01202-605010
Website: http://www.lilysleds.co.uk
Directors: R. Coulson (Ptnr)
Immediate Holding Company: LILYS LEDS LTD
Registration no: 04472111 **Date established:** 2002
No.of Employees: 1 - 10 **Product Groups:** 32, 81

M & P Electronics
54 Ringwood Road, Poole, BH14 0RN
Tel: 01202-672358 **Fax:** 01202-677271
Directors: M. Smith (Dir)
Date established: 1993 **No.of Employees:** 1 - 10 **Product Groups:** 37, 40, 67

Machine Sales & Services Ltd (Poole)
23 Cowley Road Nuffield Industrial Estate, Poole, BH17 0UJ
Tel: 01202-686238 **Fax:** 01202-686661
E-mail: adrian@msstools.com
Website: http://www.machinesalesandservices.co.uk
Directors: M. Mosley (Dir)
Immediate Holding Company: MACHINE SALES AND SERVICES (POOLE) LIMITED
Registration no: 01715998 **VAT No.:** GB 355 9965 93
Date established: 1983 **Turnover:** £500,000 - £1m
No.of Employees: 1 - 10 **Product Groups:** 37, 48, 67

Date of Accounts	Jun 11	Jun 10	Jun 09
Sales Turnover	N/A	N/A	507
Pre Tax Profit/Loss	N/A	N/A	20
Working Capital	54	29	3
Fixed Assets	10	12	16
Current Assets	253	221	198
Current Liabilities	N/A	N/A	39

Majestic Transformer Co.
245 Rossmore Road Parkstone, Poole, BH12 2HQ
Tel: 01202-734463 **Fax:** 01202-733793
E-mail: info@transformers.uk.com
Website: http://www.transformers.uk.com
Bank(s): National Westminster, Westbourne
Managers: K. Arnold (Chief Mgr), D. Cole (Sales Prom Mgr)
VAT No.: GB 423 7188 51 **Date established:** 1942
Turnover: £250,000 - £500,000 **No.of Employees:** 11 - 20
Product Groups: 37, 67

Maplin Electronics Ltd
Unit 1ba Wessexgate East Retail Park Willis Way, Poole, BH15 3TF
Tel: 08432-277389
E-mail: customercare@maplin.co.uk
Website: http://www.maplin.co.uk
Ultimate Holding Company: MONTAGU PRIVATE EQUITY LLP
Immediate Holding Company: MAPLIN ELECTRONICS LIMITED
Registration no: 01264385 **Date established:** 1976
Turnover: £125m - £250m **No.of Employees:** 1 - 10 **Product Groups:** 37, 61

Date of Accounts	Dec 11	Dec 08	Dec 09
Sales Turnover	205m	204m	204m
Pre Tax Profit/Loss	25m	32m	35m
Working Capital	118m	49m	75m
Fixed Assets	27m	28m	28m
Current Assets	207m	108m	142m
Current Liabilities	78m	51m	59m

Marinautic Marine Engineers
1b Cobbs Quay, Poole, BH15 4EL
Tel: 01202-678085 **Fax:** 01202-678085
Website: http://www.marinautic.ltd.uk
Directors: R. Edmonds (Ptnr)
Immediate Holding Company: BOATYLICIOUS MARINE LIMITED
Date established: 2011 **No.of Employees:** 1 - 10 **Product Groups:** 35, 36, 39

Mathmos Ltd
Unit 4 Holton Road Holton Heath Trading Park, Poole, BH16 6LG
Tel: 01202-620114 **Fax:** 01202-669440
E-mail: cressida@mathmos.co.uk
Website: http://www.mathmos.co.uk
Directors: C. Granger (MD)
Immediate Holding Company: MATHMOS LIMITED
Registration no: 02526274 **Date established:** 1990
No.of Employees: 1 - 10 **Product Groups:** 37, 67

Date of Accounts	Jun 11	Jun 10	Jun 09
Working Capital	153	204	294
Fixed Assets	48	67	45
Current Assets	342	503	637

Matt Black Systems
Unit D Broom Road Business Park Broom Road, Poole, BH12 4PA
Tel: 01202-307884 **Fax:** 01202-736736
E-mail: mail@mattblacksystems.com
Website: http://www.mattblacksystems.com
Managers: A. Furnell (Projects)
Immediate Holding Company: CRYSTRAN LIMITED
Registration no: 02863378 **Date established:** 1993
No.of Employees: 11 - 20 **Product Groups:** 37, 38, 44

Date of Accounts	Oct 11	Oct 10	Oct 09
Working Capital	1m	1m	1m
Fixed Assets	1m	1m	1m
Current Assets	2m	1m	1m
Current Liabilities	N/A	3	N/A

D J Mellor
3 Dawkins Business Centre Dawkins Road, Poole, BH15 4JY
Tel: 01202-668424 **Fax:** 01202-661732
E-mail: djmtoolmaking@googlemail.com
Website: http://www.toolmaking.freeserve.co.uk
Directors: D. Mellor (Prop)
Date established: 1996 **No.of Employees:** 1 - 10 **Product Groups:** 36

Mercom
5 Cowley Road Nuffield Industrial Estate, Poole, BH17 0UJ
Tel: 01202-661210 **Fax:** 01202-661216
E-mail: sales@mercom.org
Website: http://www.mercom.org
Bank(s): National Westminster Bank Plc
Directors: M. Alcock (MD)
Managers: S. Alcock (Fin Mgr), M. Stanfield (Sales Prom Mgr), D. Pye (Tech Serv Mgr), S. Walpole (Ops Mgr)
Date established: 1982 **Turnover:** £1m - £2m
No.of Employees: 101 - 250 **Product Groups:** 44

Merlin Entertainments Group Ltd
3 Market Close, Poole, BH15 1NQ
Tel: 01202-666900 **Fax:** 01202-440018
E-mail: enquiries@merlinentertainments.biz
Website: http://www.merlinentertainments.biz
Directors: S. Williamson (Mkt Research)
Managers: A. Carr (Comptroller), C. Armstrong, S. Owens (Personnel)
Ultimate Holding Company: MERLIN ENTERTAINMENTS GROUP INTERNATIONAL LIMITED
Immediate Holding Company: MERLIN ENTERTAINMENTS GROUP OPERATIONS LIMITED
Registration no: 03671093 **Date established:** 1998 **Turnover:** £2m - £5m
No.of Employees: 21 - 50 **Product Groups:** 89

Date of Accounts	Dec 11	Dec 08	Dec 09
Sales Turnover	5m	N/A	N/A
Pre Tax Profit/Loss	-1m	-2m	-2m
Working Capital	-11m	-6m	-2m
Fixed Assets	11m	9m	5m
Current Assets	5m	2m	4m
Current Liabilities	1m	323	130

Mermaid Marine
The Mews 14-17 West Quay ROAD, Poole, BH15 1JD
Tel: 01202-677776 **Fax:** 01202-677777
E-mail: engines@mermaid-marine.co.uk
Website: http://www.mermaid-marine.co.uk/contact-us
Managers: E. Nugent (District Mgr)
Ultimate Holding Company: MMH (DORSET) LTD
Immediate Holding Company: MML (DORSET) LTD
Registration no: 07195114 **VAT No.:** GB 211 7818 79
Date established: 2005 **Turnover:** £1m - £2m **No.of Employees:** 1 - 10
Product Groups: 39, 40

Date of Accounts	Oct 08	Oct 07	Oct 06
Working Capital	255	301	233
Fixed Assets	20	42	57
Current Assets	434	393	406
Current Liabilities	179	92	173

Mike Wills Marine
Cobbs Quay Ltd Cobbs Quay, Poole, BH15 4EJ
Tel: 01202-679756 **Fax:** 01202-649759
E-mail: mikewills2@aol.com
Directors: M. Wills (Prop)
Immediate Holding Company: BOATYLICIOUS MARINE LIMITED
Date established: 2011 **No.of Employees:** 1 - 10 **Product Groups:** 35, 36, 39

Moore International Ltd
Unit 9 Cortry Close, Poole, BH12 4BQ
Tel: 01202-743222 **Fax:** 01202-739955
E-mail: mark@moore-international.com
Website: http://www.mooreinternational.co.uk
Bank(s): Lloyds TSB Bank plc

Directors: B. Moore (Fin), C. Moore (Sales), M. Moore (MD)
Immediate Holding Company: MOORE INTERNATIONAL LIMITED
Registration no: 03902244 **Date established:** 2000
Turnover: £500,000 - £1m **No.of Employees:** 11 - 20
Product Groups: 25, 35, 36, 37, 39, 45, 46

Date of Accounts	Mar 12	Mar 11	Mar 10
Working Capital	195	192	123
Fixed Assets	97	9	12
Current Assets	428	332	280

Moore Speed Racing Ltd

Unit 12 Cortry Close, Poole, BH12 4BQ
Tel: 01202-746141 **Fax:** 01202-739955
E-mail: colin@moore-international.com
Website: http://www.moore-speed-racing.co.uk
Directors: C. Moore (MD), B. Moore (Co Sec)
Immediate Holding Company: MOORE SPEED RACING LIMITED
Registration no: 04806424 **Date established:** 2003
Turnover: £250,000 - £500,000 **No.of Employees:** 1 - 10
Product Groups: 29, 39, 68

Date of Accounts	Mar 11	Mar 10	Mar 09
Sales Turnover	N/A	N/A	402
Pre Tax Profit/Loss	N/A	N/A	24
Working Capital	48	45	36
Fixed Assets	8	11	13
Current Assets	137	135	113
Current Liabilities	N/A	N/A	47

Multisuite Software

1 Winchester Place North Street, Poole, BH15 1NX
Tel: 01202-678191 **Fax:** 01202-678448
E-mail: customer.services@multisuite.com
Website: http://www.multisuite.com
Directors: C. Bevan (Fin)
Managers: R. Harding (Sales Admin)
Immediate Holding Company: MULTISUITE SOFTWARE LIMITED
Registration no: 04629967 **Date established:** 2003
Turnover: £500,000 - £1m **No.of Employees:** 1 - 10 **Product Groups:** 44

Date of Accounts	Mar 11	Mar 10	Mar 08
Working Capital	6	-0	25
Fixed Assets	3	3	2
Current Assets	327	149	297

N B Spraying

15 Balena Close, Poole, BH17 7DB
Tel: 01202-600635 **Fax:** 01202-697700
E-mail: nbspraying@btconnect.com
Directors: N. Fear (MD)
Date established: 1986 **No.of Employees:** 1 - 10 **Product Groups:** 46, 48

National Oilwell Varco

Holton Road Holton Heath Trading Park, Poole, BH16 6LT
Tel: 01202-631817 **Fax:** 01202-631708
E-mail: training.uk@nov.com
Website: http://www.varco.com
Bank(s): Barclays
Managers: B. Carter (Mgr), C. Harcourt (Sales Prom Mgr), P. Vollands (Mgr), R. Norris (Gen Contact), T. Alner (I.T. Exec), M. Groombridge (Admin Off)
Immediate Holding Company: Varco Co
Registration no: 00873028 **VAT No.:** GB 582 8958 76
Date established: 1985 **Turnover:** £2m - £5m **No.of Employees:** 21 - 50
Product Groups: 45

Norco Group Ltd

Unit 33 Holton Road Holton Heath Trading Park, Poole, BH16 6LT
Tel: 01202-623934 **Fax:** 01202-621940
E-mail: m.northey@norco.co.uk
Website: http://www.norco.co.uk
Directors: M. Northey (MD)
Managers: A. Watkins (Purch Mgr), K. Northey (Personnel)
Immediate Holding Company: NORCO GROUP LIMITED
Registration no: SC235198 **Date established:** 2002 **Turnover:** £2m - £5m
No.of Employees: 51 - 100 **Product Groups:** 24, 26, 30, 33, 37, 38, 39, 48, 61, 66, 68, 81, 84, 86

Date of Accounts	Sep 09	Sep 08	Sep 11
Working Capital	-130	-347	-333
Fixed Assets	2m	2m	2m
Current Assets	1m	847	2m

NTE Vacuum Technology Ltd

190-192 Stanley Green Road, Poole, BH15 3AH
Tel: 01202-677715 **Fax:** 01202-677723
E-mail: sales@ntevacuum.co.uk
Website: http://www.ntevacuum.co.uk
Bank(s): National Westminster
Directors: A. Bailey (Dir)
Managers: T. Raik
Immediate Holding Company: NTE VACUUM TECHNOLOGY LTD
Registration no: 02699445 **VAT No.:** GB 580 1489 35
Date established: 1992 **Turnover:** £1m - £2m **No.of Employees:** 21 - 50
Product Groups: 40

Date of Accounts	Mar 11	Mar 10	Mar 09
Working Capital	237	78	-14
Fixed Assets	466	421	450
Current Assets	612	561	479

Orbis Software Ltd

3 Bourne Gate 25 Bourne Valley Road, Poole, BH12 1DY
Tel: 01202-241115 **Fax:** 01202-241116
E-mail: enquiries@orbis-software.com
Website: http://www.orbis-software.com
Directors: J. Bucknell (MD)
Managers: K. Lavender (Personnel)
Immediate Holding Company: ORBIS SOFTWARE LIMITED
Registration no: 03704171 **Date established:** 1999
No.of Employees: 51 - 100 **Product Groups:** 44

Date of Accounts	Sep 11	Sep 10	Sep 09
Working Capital	-89	-134	-155
Fixed Assets	273	201	200
Current Assets	413	302	416

Outboard Care Centre

56 Panorama Road, Poole, BH13 7RE
Tel: 01202-708971 **Fax:** 01202-708971
Directors: A. Stacey (Ptnr)
Date established: 1978 **No.of Employees:** 1 - 10 **Product Groups:** 35, 36, 39

P R F Composite Materials

3 Upton Road, Poole, BH17 7AA
Tel: 01202-680022 **Fax:** 01202-680077
E-mail: mail@prfcomposites.com
Website: http://www.prfcomposites.com
Bank(s): Lloyds TSB Bank plc
Directors: R. Burnell (MD)
Immediate Holding Company: PLASTIC REINFORCEMENT FABRICS LIMITED
Registration no: 01858229 **Date established:** 1984 **Turnover:** £1m - £2m
No.of Employees: 11 - 20 **Product Groups:** 23, 30, 31, 33, 63

Date of Accounts	Dec 11	Dec 10	Dec 09
Working Capital	966	799	1m
Fixed Assets	414	297	173
Current Assets	2m	2m	2m

Parkway Marine

202 Sandbanks Road, Poole, BH14 8HA
Tel: 01202-745568 **Fax:** 01202-742978
E-mail: sales@parkwaymarine.co.uk
Website: http://www.parkwaymarine.co.uk
Directors: R. King (Prop)
Immediate Holding Company: BLUE LAGOON BOAT YARD LIMITED
Registration no: 00793972 **Date established:** 2011
No.of Employees: 1 - 10 **Product Groups:** 74

Pelilites4less.Com

UNIT 9 HOLES BAY PARK, STERTE AVENUE WEST, Poole, BH152AA
Tel: 01202-667770 **Fax:** 01202-671047
E-mail: info@pelilites4less.co.uk
Website: http://pelilites4less.co.uk
Managers: P. Kitchen (Chief Mgr)
Turnover: Up to £250,000 **No.of Employees:** 1 - 10 **Product Groups:** 37, 44, 67

Pilkington UK Ltd

10-12 Alder Hills, Poole, BH12 4AL
Tel: 01202-742700 **Fax:** 01202-736155
Website: http://www.pilkingtons.com
Bank(s): Natwest
Managers: P. Tuck (Chief Mgr), B. Hendon (Works Gen Mgr)
Immediate Holding Company: PILKINGTON UNITED KINGDOM LIMITED
Registration no: 01417048 **Date established:** 1979 **Turnover:** £5m - £10m
No.of Employees: 51 - 100 **Product Groups:** 33, 52, 66

Poole Diesel

75d Ringwood Road, Poole, BH14 0RG
Tel: 01202-749071 **Fax:** 01202-749071
Directors: A. Tubbs (Ptnr)
Date established: 1973 **No.of Employees:** 1 - 10 **Product Groups:** 40

Poole Lighting Ltd

Cabot Lane, Poole, BH17 7BY
Tel: 01202-690945 **Fax:** 01202-600166
E-mail: trevor.hodder@poolelighting.com
Website: http://www.poolelighting.com
Bank(s): Lloyds TAB
Directors: T. Hodder (MD), J. Cooper (Fin), L. Walters (Fin)
Managers: A. Vujevic (Tech Serv Mgr), A. Shawcross (Purch Mgr), B. Marshall (I.T. Exec)
Ultimate Holding Company: THE NATIONAL LIGHTING COMPANY LIMITED
Immediate Holding Company: POOLE LIGHTING LIMITED
Registration no: 04740426 **Date established:** 2003
Turnover: £10m - £20m **No.of Employees:** 101 - 250 **Product Groups:** 37

Date of Accounts	Dec 11	Dec 10	Dec 09
Sales Turnover	21m	19m	22m
Pre Tax Profit/Loss	2m	1m	4m
Working Capital	3m	15m	12m
Fixed Assets	5m	5m	6m
Current Assets	18m	32m	23m
Current Liabilities	6m	11m	9m

Poole Technical Plating Services Ltd

Unit 32-33 Dawkins Business Centre Dawkins Road, Poole, BH15 4JY
Tel: 01202-673640 **Fax:** 01202-682414
E-mail: sales@ptpuk.com
Website: http://www.ptpuk.com
Bank(s): Lloyds TSB
Directors: M. Eaton (Fin)
Managers: C. Scott (Product)
Immediate Holding Company: POOLE TECHNICAL PLATING SERVICES LIMITED
Registration no: 01116843 **VAT No.:** 187 0503 62 **Date established:** 1973
Turnover: £2m - £5m **No.of Employees:** 21 - 50 **Product Groups:** 48

Date of Accounts	Jun 12	Jun 11	Jun 10
Sales Turnover	3m	2m	2m
Pre Tax Profit/Loss	338	352	174
Working Capital	449	499	331
Fixed Assets	625	631	608
Current Assets	831	965	836
Current Liabilities	184	192	114

PooleCool

11 Gwenlyn Road, Poole, BH16 5HA
Tel: 01202-772999
E-mail: info@poolecool.co.uk
Website: http://www.poolecool.co.uk
Directors: I. Belchanber (Prop)
No.of Employees: 1 - 10 **Product Groups:** 38, 39, 52, 66

Powder Tec

Chalwyn Industrial Estate St Clements Road, Poole, BH12 4PE
Tel: 01202-716248 **Fax:** 01202-733026
E-mail: info@vent.co.uk
Website: http://www.powdercoat-uk.com
Directors: L. Jones (MD)
No.of Employees: 1 - 10 **Product Groups:** 35, 39, 48, 67

Precision Disc Castings Ltd

16 Mannings Heath Road, Poole, BH12 4NJ
Tel: 01202-715050 **Fax:** 01202-715068
E-mail: reception@pdcastings.co.uk
Website: http://www.pdcastings.co.uk
Directors: S. Humphrey (Sales), G. Rushton (Fin)
Managers: J. Grazebrook (Chief Acct), S. Lindsfield (Purch Mgr), C. Keeps (Personnel), J. Perett (Tech Serv Mgr)
Ultimate Holding Company: EURAC HOLDINGS LIMITED
Immediate Holding Company: PRECISION DISC CASTINGS LTD
Registration no: 02687523 **VAT No.:** 580 1332 68 **Date established:** 1992
Turnover: £20m - £50m **No.of Employees:** 101 - 250 **Product Groups:** 34

Date of Accounts	Dec 11	Mar 11	Mar 10
Sales Turnover	26m	34m	29m
Pre Tax Profit/Loss	2m	3m	2m
Working Capital	8m	6m	4m
Fixed Assets	4m	4m	4m
Current Assets	14m	13m	9m
Current Liabilities	3m	3m	2m

Precision Units Dorset Ltd

2a Gloucester Road, Poole, BH12 2AP
Tel: 01202-741664 **Fax:** 01202-716473
E-mail: steve@precisionunits.co.uk
Website: http://www.precisionunits.co.uk
Bank(s): Lloyds
Directors: S. Lumber (MD), S. Lumber (MD)
Immediate Holding Company: PRECISION UNITS (DORSET) LIMITED
Registration no: 00488181 **VAT No.:** GB 185 5910 36
Date established: 1950 **Turnover:** £500,000 - £1m
No.of Employees: 11 - 20 **Product Groups:** 28

Date of Accounts	Oct 11	Oct 10	Oct 09
Working Capital	468	468	483
Fixed Assets	214	220	217
Current Assets	597	618	692
Current Liabilities	94	112	162

Quay Surface Engineering Metalblast Ltd

11 Cowley Road Nuffield Industrial Estate, Poole, BH17 0UJ
Tel: 01202-684231 **Fax:** 01202-675470
E-mail: metalblast@onetel.com
Website: http://www.quaysurface.co.uk
Directors: J. Black (Fin), S. Black (Dir), M. Trim (Fab)
Managers: F. Black (Sales Prom Mgr)
Registration no: 01575024 **Date established:** 1981
Turnover: £500,000 - £1m **No.of Employees:** 1 - 10 **Product Groups:** 30, 32, 35, 46, 48

Date of Accounts	Jun 09	Jun 08	Jun 07
Working Capital	222	136	106
Fixed Assets	102	103	76
Current Assets	433	338	289

Re-Nu Kitchens Ltd

60 Nuffield Road Nuffield Industrial Estate, Poole, BH17 0RT
Tel: 01202-687642 **Fax:** 01202-671773
E-mail: sales@re-nukitchens.co.uk
Website: http://www.re-nukitchens.co.uk
Directors: J. Elkins (MD)
Managers: J. Snowdon (Ops Mgr)
Registration no: 04561102 **Turnover:** £1m - £2m
No.of Employees: 11 - 20 **Product Groups:** 25

Robton Engineering

28 Balena Close, Poole, BH17 7EB
Tel: 01202-695480 **Fax:** 01202-658899
E-mail: solutions@robton.co.uk
Website: http://www.robton.co.uk
Bank(s): Lloyds
Directors: A. O'callaghan (Ptnr)
VAT No.: GB 187 9393 95 **Date established:** 1973
Turnover: £250,000 - £500,000 **No.of Employees:** 11 - 20
Product Groups: 27, 29, 48

Rovic Engineering

1 Allens Lane, Poole, BH16 5DA
Tel: 01202-683446 **Fax:** 01202-684824
E-mail: rovic@roviceng.co.uk
Website: http://www.roviceng.co.uk
Directors: T. Denison (Dir)
Immediate Holding Company: M B WELDING LIMITED
VAT No.: GB 187 1498 24 **Date established:** 2008
No.of Employees: 11 - 20 **Product Groups:** 67

Date of Accounts	Mar 11	Mar 10
Working Capital	38	34
Fixed Assets	13	13
Current Assets	56	60
Current Liabilities	3	4

S S Tool & Welding Supplies

41 Redwood Road, Poole, BH16 5QG
Tel: 01202-631224 **Fax:** 01202-624442
Directors: S. Battell (Prop)
Date established: 1988 **No.of Employees:** 1 - 10 **Product Groups:** 46

SAFI Ltd

35 Holton Road Holton Heath Trading Park, Poole, BH16 6LT
Tel: 01202-624618 **Fax:** 01202-632225
E-mail: sales@safi-limited.com
Website: http://www.safi-valves.com
Bank(s): Lloyds TSB
Directors: S. Moison (Dir), M. Ralph (Co Sec)
Managers: S. Cook (Chief Mgr)
Ultimate Holding Company: SOCIETE ANONYME DE FABRICATIONS INDUSTRIELLES (FRANCE)
Immediate Holding Company: S.A.F.I. LTD
Registration no: 01146568 **VAT No.:** 230 7544 82 **Date established:** 1973
Turnover: £1m - £2m **No.of Employees:** 21 - 50 **Product Groups:** 30, 36, 38, 40, 66

Date of Accounts	Dec 11	Dec 10	Dec 09
Working Capital	3m	3m	3m
Fixed Assets	727	786	877
Current Assets	3m	3m	3m

Sandbanks & Harbourside Marine Ltd

Turks Lane, Poole, BH14 8EW
Tel: 01202-746824 **Fax:** 01202-746824
Directors: P. Savage (Fin)
Immediate Holding Company: SANDBANKS AND HARBOURSIDE MARINE LTD
Registration no: 04987828 **Date established:** 2003
No.of Employees: 1 - 10 **Product Groups:** 35, 36, 39

Date of Accounts	Feb 12	Feb 11	Feb 10
Working Capital	14	18	8
Fixed Assets	4	5	1
Current Assets	19	25	17

Shrinkwrap Machinery Co. Ltd
145 Sterte Road Sterte Industrial Estate, Poole, BH15 2AF
Tel: 01202-674944 **Fax:** 01202-671891
E-mail: peter@shrinkwrap.co.uk
Website: http://www.shrinkwrap.co.uk
Directors: P. Frith (MD), D. Frith (Co Sec)
Immediate Holding Company: SHRINKWRAP MACHINERY CO.LIMITED
Registration no: 00918708 **Date established:** 1967
No.of Employees: 11 - 20 **Product Groups:** 38, 42

Date of Accounts	Dec 11	Dec 10	Dec 09
Working Capital	189	188	293
Fixed Assets	15	20	28
Current Assets	267	249	356

Shuttertechnik Roller Shutter Mnfrs
87 Lake Drive, Poole, BH15 4LR
Tel: 01202-673050
E-mail: office@shuttertechnik.demon.co.uk
Website: http://www.shuttertechnik.co.uk
Directors: K. Wadham (Prop)
Date established: 1996 **No.of Employees:** 1 - 10 **Product Groups:** 26, 35

Siemens plc
Sopers Lane, Poole, BH17 7ER
Tel: 01202-782978 **Fax:** 01202-782331
E-mail: admin@siemenstraffic.com
Website: http://www.siemens.co.uk/traffic
Directors: D. Carter (MD), D. McIntosh (Chief Op Offcr), T. Macmorran (Sales & Mktg)
Ultimate Holding Company: SIEMENS AG (GERMANY)
Immediate Holding Company: SIEMENS PUBLIC LIMITED COMPANY
Registration no: 00727817 **Date established:** 1962
Turnover: £20m - £50m **No.of Employees:** 251 - 500
Product Groups: 39, 40, 45, 49, 51

SmartGauge Electronics Power Conversion Technology
C/O Merlin Equipment Ltd Unit 3 & 4, Cabot Business Village, Holyrood Close, Cabot Lane, Poole, BH17 7BA
Tel: 01202-697979 **Fax:** 01202-691919
E-mail: david.small@merlinequipment.com
Website: http://www.smartgauge.co.uk
No.of Employees: 1 - 10 **Product Groups:** 38, 67

Standard & Pochin Ltd
Unit 7-9 Dawkins Road, Poole, BH15 4JP
Tel: 01202-677244 **Fax:** 01929-556726
E-mail: sales@mvm-uk.com
Website: http://www.mvm-uk.com
Managers: M. Andrews (Comm)
Immediate Holding Company: STANDARD AND POCHIN LIMITED
Registration no: 01514707 **Date established:** 1980
No.of Employees: 21 - 50 **Product Groups:** 35, 36, 39, 40

Date of Accounts	Dec 07	Dec 06	Dec 05
Working Capital	-136	-271	-278
Fixed Assets	571	708	848
Current Assets	1m	2m	2m

Sunseeker Poole Ltd
Sunseeker Wharf West Quay Road, Poole, BH15 1HW
Tel: 01202-666060 **Fax:** 01202-382222
E-mail: simon.gennery@sunseekerpoole.com
Website: http://www.sunseekerpoole.com
Bank(s): Lloyds
Managers: S. Gennery (Fin Mgr)
Ultimate Holding Company: SUNSEEKER INTERNATIONAL (HOLDINGS) LIMITED
Immediate Holding Company: SUNSEEKER POOLE LIMITED
Registration no: 06738406 **VAT No.:** GB 186 1308 61
Date established: 2008 **Turnover:** £250m - £500m
No.of Employees: 11 - 20 **Product Groups:** 39

Date of Accounts	Nov 11	Nov 10	Nov 09
Sales Turnover	10m	N/A	N/A
Pre Tax Profit/Loss	-61	N/A	N/A
Working Capital	-1m	-1m	882
Fixed Assets	1m	1m	2m
Current Assets	6m	9m	5m
Current Liabilities	5m	N/A	N/A

T & G Sheet Metal & Fabrication
20 Kennington Road Nuffield Industrial Estate, Poole, BH17 0GF
Tel: 01202-668084 **Fax:** 01202-668093
E-mail: garry@tandg-promech.co.uk
Website: http://www.tandg-promech.co.uk
Directors: G. Powell (Ptnr)
Date established: 1998 **No.of Employees:** 1 - 10 **Product Groups:** 35

Taymar Precision Grinding Ltd
6 Benson Road Nuffield Industrial Estate, Poole, BH17 0GB
Tel: 01202-674967 **Fax:** 01202-675167
E-mail: enquiries@taymar.co.uk
Website: http://www.taymar.co.uk
Directors: D. Belcher (MD)
Ultimate Holding Company: BOWMILL ENGINEERING LIMITED
Immediate Holding Company: TAYMAR PRECISION GRINDING LIMITED
Registration no: 03795167 **Date established:** 1999
No.of Employees: 1 - 10 **Product Groups:** 46, 48

Date of Accounts	Dec 11	Dec 10	Dec 09
Working Capital	-43	-5	-40
Fixed Assets	83	104	149
Current Assets	98	144	162

TechDraw Ltd (Design & Drafting)
Applemead New Road Lytchett Minster, Poole, BH16 6JQ
Tel: 01202-622300 **Fax:** 01202-622300
E-mail: graham.cummins@techdraw.co.uk
Directors: C. Cummins (Fin), G. Cummins (MD)
Immediate Holding Company: TECHDRAW LIMITED
Registration no: 03439835 **Date established:** 1997
Turnover: Up to £250,000 **No.of Employees:** 1 - 10 **Product Groups:** 80, 81

Date of Accounts	Mar 11	Mar 10	Mar 09
Working Capital	-0	-0	-1
Fixed Assets	9	9	10
Current Assets	4	4	5
Current Liabilities	1	1	4

Telsonic UK Ltd
Unit 14-15 Birch Copse Technology Road, Poole, BH17 7FH
Tel: 01202-697340 **Fax:** 01202-693674
E-mail: sales@telsonic.co.uk
Website: http://www.telsonic.co.uk
Directors: D. Norton (MD)
Ultimate Holding Company: VIEBE HOLDINGS AG (SWITZERLAND)
Immediate Holding Company: TELSONIC (U.K.) LIMITED
Registration no: 01405707 **Date established:** 1978
No.of Employees: 1 - 10 **Product Groups:** 46

Date of Accounts	Dec 11	Dec 10	Dec 09
Working Capital	629	657	652
Fixed Assets	108	79	65
Current Assets	2m	2m	1m

Total Product
Unit 16j Chalwyn Industrial Estate St Clements Road, Poole, BH12 4PE
Tel: 01202-722606 **Fax:** 01202-732525
E-mail: info@totalproduct.co.uk
Website: http://www.totalproduct.co.uk
Directors: R. Futcher (MD)
Immediate Holding Company: TOTAL PRODUCT SUPPLIES LIMITED
Registration no: 02864691 **Date established:** 1993
No.of Employees: 1 - 10 **Product Groups:** 46

Date of Accounts	Nov 11	Nov 10	Nov 09
Working Capital	-1	-2	-4
Fixed Assets	4	5	7
Current Assets	60	34	39

TRI Catering Equipment Ltd
C8, Hailey Centre, 46 Holton Road Holton Heath Trading Park, Poole, BH16 6LT
Tel: 01202-630123 **Fax:** 01202-630123
E-mail: info@tri-cateringequipment.com
Website: http://www.tri-cateringequipment.com
Registration no: 05946067 **No.of Employees:** 1 - 10 **Product Groups:** 20, 40, 41

Date of Accounts	Dec 07
Working Capital	-23
Fixed Assets	31
Current Assets	13
Current Liabilities	36

Trickett Marine Products
44 Old Wareham Road, Poole, BH12 4QR
Tel: 01202-748180 **Fax:** 01202-731538
E-mail: sales@trickettmarineproducts.co.uk
Website: http://www.trickettmarineproducts.co.uk
Directors: P. Trickett (MD)
Immediate Holding Company: TRICKETT MARINE PRODUCTS LTD
Registration no: 07876678 **Date established:** 2011
Turnover: Up to £250,000 **No.of Employees:** 1 - 10 **Product Groups:** 37, 40, 67

Triton Marine
Unit 1 Cobbs Quay, Poole, BH15 4EJ
Tel: 01202-667668 **Fax:** 01202-667668
Directors: S. Weeden (Prop)
Date established: 1986 **No.of Employees:** 1 - 10 **Product Groups:** 35, 36, 39

Trucut Tools
The White House 2 Broom Road, Poole, BH12 4NL
Tel: 01202-717110 **Fax:** 01202-743034
E-mail: sales@trucuttools.co.uk
Directors: J. Cooper (Prop)
Date established: 1993 **No.of Employees:** 1 - 10 **Product Groups:** 46

Twickenham Plating Group Ltd
12-13 Balena Close, Poole, BH17 7DB
Tel: 01202-692416 **Fax:** 01202-600628
E-mail: info@twickenham.co.uk
Website: http://www.twickenham.co.uk
Bank(s): HSBC Bank plc
Directors: D. Quick (Sales), D. Hill (MD), R. Dearing (Fin), J. Hill (MD)
Managers: J. Lemarinel (Purch Mgr)
Ultimate Holding Company: TWICKENHAM PLATING LIMITED
Immediate Holding Company: TWICKENHAM PLATING GROUP LIMITED
Registration no: 00436536 **Date established:** 1947 **Turnover:** £2m - £5m
No.of Employees: 51 - 100 **Product Groups:** 34, 48

Date of Accounts	Dec 11	Dec 10	Dec 09
Working Capital	1m	911	679
Fixed Assets	233	189	185
Current Assets	2m	2m	1m

Typographix
Flat 2 177 Bournemouth Road, Poole, BH14 9HT
Tel: 07904-153638
E-mail: bisibord@hotmail.com
Directors: J. Noades (Dir), J. Noades (Prop)
No.of Employees: 1 - 10 **Product Groups:** 25, 28, 49

Ultra Plastics Ltd
Unit 39 Wessex Trade Centre Ringwood Road, Poole, BH12 3PG
Tel: 01202-715557 **Fax:** 01202-745899
Directors: J. Brewster (Prop)
Immediate Holding Company: ULTRA PLASTICS LTD
Registration no: 05976392 **Date established:** 2006
No.of Employees: 1 - 10 **Product Groups:** 30, 32

Date of Accounts	Feb 12	Feb 11	Feb 10
Working Capital	-33	-41	-45
Fixed Assets	19	20	23
Current Assets	110	125	98

Upton Oil Company Ltd
Blandford Road North Upton, Poole, BH16 6AA
Tel: 01202-622257 **Fax:** 01202-632578
E-mail: sales@uptonoil.co.uk
Website: http://www.uptonoil.co.uk
Bank(s): National Westminster Bank Plc
Directors: A. Stacey (Prop)
Managers: C. Staines (Sales Prom Mgr), D. Langley (Chief Acct)
Immediate Holding Company: UPTON OIL COMPANY LIMITED
Registration no: 00374600 **VAT No.:** GB 186 0717 49
Date established: 1942 **Turnover:** £5m - £10m **No.of Employees:** 21 - 50
Product Groups: 31, 66

Date of Accounts	Mar 11	Mar 10	Mar 09
Working Capital	655	834	669
Fixed Assets	581	533	490
Current Assets	3m	3m	2m

Us 4 Slush
8-9 Morris Road Nuffield Industrial Estate, Poole, BH17 0GG
Tel: 01202-666922
E-mail: sales@us4slush.com
Website: http://www.us4slush.com/
Directors: D. Fish (Dir)
Registration no: 05153930 **Turnover:** £500,000 - £1m
No.of Employees: 1 - 10 **Product Groups:** 21

Date of Accounts	Sep 07	Sep 06	Sep 05
Working Capital	18	39	4
Fixed Assets	19	8	7
Current Assets	36	70	20
Current Liabilities	17	31	15

V R Technology
Blackhill Road West Holton Heath, Poole, BH16 6LU
Tel: 01202-624478 **Fax:** 01202-625308
Website: http://www.vr3.co.uk
Directors: K. Gurr (MD)
No.of Employees: 1 - 10 **Product Groups:** 39, 40, 44

Vent Engineering
Unit 16c Chalwyn Industrial Estate St Clements Road, Poole, BH12 4PE
Tel: 01202-744958 **Fax:** 01202-733026
E-mail: info@vent.co.uk
Website: http://www.vent.co.uk
Directors: L. Jones (MD)
Immediate Holding Company: VENT ENGINEERING LTD
Registration no: 05269735 **Date established:** 2004 **Turnover:** £1m - £2m
No.of Employees: 21 - 50 **Product Groups:** 30, 35, 37, 38, 39, 40, 48, 84

Date of Accounts	Oct 10	Oct 09	Oct 08
Working Capital	41	19	7
Fixed Assets	N/A	1	1
Current Assets	73	48	35

Vsi Automation UK
26 Holton Road Holton Heath Trading Park, Poole, BH16 6LT
Tel: 01202-624727 **Fax:** 01202-624569
E-mail: vsi.uk@virgin.net
Bank(s): Lloyds TSB
Directors: M. Taylor (MD)
Immediate Holding Company: VSI AUTOMATION (UK) LIMITED
Registration no: 03165343 **VAT No.:** GB 619 7066 20
Date established: 1996 **Turnover:** £1m - £2m **No.of Employees:** 21 - 50
Product Groups: 42, 45, 47

Date of Accounts	Jan 10	Jan 09	Jan 08
Working Capital	-123	-217	-213
Fixed Assets	1	1	1
Current Assets	119	195	195

Watkins & Watson Ltd
141 Blandford Road, Poole, BH15 4AT
Tel: 01202-679920 **Fax:** 01202-675463
E-mail: info@watkinsandwatson.co.uk
Website: http://www.watkinsandwatson.co.uk
Directors: C. Drake (MD)
Immediate Holding Company: WATKINS AND WATSON LIMITED
Registration no: 02985135 **VAT No.:** GB 619 8947 80
Date established: 1994 **Turnover:** £250,000 - £500,000
No.of Employees: 1 - 10 **Product Groups:** 40, 49

Date of Accounts	Sep 11	Sep 10	Sep 09
Working Capital	39	17	-1
Fixed Assets	13	22	33
Current Assets	137	119	124

Wessex Dental Laboratory
Unit 10 Holes Bay Park Sterte Avenue West, Poole, BH15 2AA
Tel: 01202-674486 **Fax:** 01202-674486
E-mail: wessex.dental@virgin.net
Directors: P. Law (Ptnr)
Immediate Holding Company: WESSEX DENTAL LABORATORY LIMITED
Registration no: 07695853 **Date established:** 2011
No.of Employees: 11 - 20 **Product Groups:** 38, 67

Wessex Filters
87 Warburton Road, Poole, BH17 8SD
Tel: 01202-671671 **Fax:** 01202-671671
Directors: H. Horne (Prop)
Ultimate Holding Company: LAITA SA (FRANCE)
Immediate Holding Company: EURILAIT LIMITED
Date established: 1991 **Turnover:** Up to £250,000
No.of Employees: 1 - 10 **Product Groups:** 38, 42

Wessex Rope & Packaging
6 20 Abingdon Road Nuffield Industrial Estate, Poole, BH17 0UG
Tel: 01202-661066 **Fax:** 01202-661077
E-mail: accounts@wrp-poole.co.uk
Website: http://www.wrp-poole.co.uk
Directors: M. Worley (Prop)
Immediate Holding Company: WESSEX ROPE & PACKAGING LIMITED
Registration no: 05281987 **Date established:** 2004
Turnover: £250,000 - £500,000 **No.of Employees:** 1 - 10
Product Groups: 38, 42

Date of Accounts	Dec 11	Dec 10	Dec 09
Working Capital	285	220	187
Fixed Assets	163	86	21
Current Assets	354	291	256

Williams Harris Optical Supplies
Unit 4 Stanley Green Industrial Estate Stanley Green Crescent, Poole, BH15 3TH
Tel: 01202-686622 **Fax:** 01202-674020
E-mail: williamsharris@hotmail.co.uk
Website: http://www.williamharris.co.uk
Directors: N. Harris (Ptnr)
Immediate Holding Company: WILLIAMS-HARRIS OPTICAL SUPPLIES LIMITED
Registration no: 01233084 **Date established:** 1975
Turnover: £250,000 - £500,000 **No.of Employees:** 1 - 10
Product Groups: 38

Date of Accounts	Dec 11	Dec 10	Dec 09
Working Capital	42	51	56
Fixed Assets	49	39	35
Current Assets	96	109	99

Wireless Data Services Ltd
1st Floor Forelle House Upton Road, Poole, BH17 7AG
Tel: 01202-713700 **Fax:** 01202-712025
E-mail: info@wds.co
Website: http://www.wds.co
Directors: D. Ffoukes Jones (MD)
Managers: I. Tomlinson (Tech Serv Mgr), M. Bateman (Comptroller)
Immediate Holding Company: WIRELESS DATA SERVICES LIMITED
Registration no: 01714719 **Date established:** 1983
Turnover: £50m - £75m **No.of Employees:** 251 - 500 **Product Groups:** 44

Date of Accounts	Dec 11	Dec 10	Dec 09
Sales Turnover	62m	56m	62m
Pre Tax Profit/Loss	3m	-3m	3m
Working Capital	3m	2m	4m
Fixed Assets	8m	9m	8m
Current Assets	14m	14m	14m
Current Liabilities	6m	5m	5m

Woodward H R T
Unit 6 Upton Industrial Estate Factory Road, Poole, BH16 5SL
Tel: 01202-628100 **Fax:** 01242-511398
E-mail: stephen.beresford@woodward.com
Website: http://woodwardhrt.woodward.com
Bank(s): HSBC Bank plc
Managers: S. Beresford (Chief Mgr), L. Holley (Chief Acct)
Immediate Holding Company: WOODWARD (U.K.) LIMITED
Registration no: 06829573 **VAT No.:** GB 449 4657 07
Date established: 2009 **Turnover:** £50m - £75m
No.of Employees: 21 - 50 **Product Groups:** 37, 38, 39, 40

Date of Accounts	Sep 11	Sep 10	Sep 09
Working Capital	2m	1m	1m
Fixed Assets	6m	6m	6m
Current Assets	2m	2m	2m

Wound Components
Unit 12 Stanley Green Industrial Estate Stanley Green Esc, Poole, BH15 3TH
Tel: 01202-682828 **Fax:** 01202-682828
E-mail: geoffbudden@btconnect.com
Website: http://www.woundcomponents.co.uk
Directors: G. Perks (Fin), G. Budden (MD)
Immediate Holding Company: S P WOUND COMPONENTS LTD
Registration no: 03540634 **VAT No.:** GB 580 0437 59
Date established: 1998 **Turnover:** £250,000 - £500,000
No.of Employees: 1 - 10 **Product Groups:** 37

Date of Accounts	Apr 11	Apr 10	Apr 09
Working Capital	-106	-2	-3
Fixed Assets	1	3	4
Current Assets	81	112	110

Wyvern Cargo Distribution Ltd (Southern Distribution Centre)
Broom Road, Poole, BH12 4NR
Tel: 01202-307500 **Fax:** 01202-715066
E-mail: sales@wyverncargo.com
Website: http://www.wyverncargo.com
Bank(s): Barclays
Directors: S. Bennett (Fin), E. Sparrowhawk (MD)
Managers: L. Waldie (Tech Serv Mgr), J. Madgewick
Ultimate Holding Company: WYVERN HOLDINGS LIMITED
Immediate Holding Company: WYVERN CARGO DISTRIBUTION LTD
Registration no: 03654831 **VAT No.:** GB 355 9257 23
Date established: 1998 **Turnover:** £10m - £20m
No.of Employees: 51 - 100 **Product Groups:** 76

Date of Accounts	Mar 10	Mar 09
Pre Tax Profit/Loss	N/A	-29
Working Capital	-1	-1

Yellow Penguin Y P Ltd
Parkstone Bay Marina Turks Lane, Poole, BH14 8EW
Tel: 01202-710448
E-mail: info@yellowpenguin.co.uk
Website: http://www.yellowpenguin.co.uk
Directors: N. Reed (Fin), P. Reed (Prop)
Immediate Holding Company: YELLOW PENGUIN (YP) LIMITED
Registration no: 06359539 **Date established:** 2007
No.of Employees: 1 - 10 **Product Groups:** 35, 36, 39

Date of Accounts	Oct 11	Oct 10	Oct 09
Working Capital	-12	1	25
Fixed Assets	32	23	14
Current Assets	254	353	240

Portland

Cirrus Systems Ltd
136 South Way Southwell Business Park, Portland, DT5 2NL
Tel: 01305-822659 **Fax:** 08707-064558
E-mail: sales@cirrus-systems.co.uk
Website: http://www.cirrus-systems.co.uk
Directors: M. Cribley (Prop), M. Cribley (Dir)
Immediate Holding Company: CIRRUS SYSTEMS LIMITED
Registration no: 05958999 **Date established:** 2006
No.of Employees: 1 - 10 **Product Groups:** 32, 37

Date of Accounts	Mar 08
Working Capital	6
Fixed Assets	1
Current Assets	26
Current Liabilities	21

Eurotubes UK Ltd
Park House Park Road, Portland, DT5 2AD
Tel: 01305-823932 **Fax:** 01305-861106
E-mail: sales@eurotubes.co.uk
Website: http://www.eurotubes-uk.com
Directors: S. Bedford (Fin), R. Bedford (MD)
Immediate Holding Company: EUROTUBES UK LIMITED
Registration no: 03019560 **Date established:** 1995
Turnover: £500,000 - £1m **No.of Employees:** 11 - 20
Product Groups: 40, 41, 42, 44, 46, 47, 67

Date of Accounts	Feb 12	Feb 11	Feb 10
Sales Turnover	N/A	N/A	504
Working Capital	-30	59	138
Fixed Assets	551	440	385
Current Assets	333	372	341

Perryfields Ltd
Easton Lane, Portland, DT5 1BW
Tel: 01305-820447 **Fax:** 01305-861081
E-mail: perryfieldsltd@aol.com
Website: http://www.perryfieldsltd.co.uk
Directors: J. Langrish (MD), L. Watton (Fin)
Immediate Holding Company: PERRYFIELDS LIMITED
Registration no: 04736229 **Date established:** 2003
Turnover: Up to £250,000 **No.of Employees:** 1 - 10 **Product Groups:** 46, 48

Date of Accounts	Jun 11	Jun 10	Jun 09
Working Capital	159	239	59
Fixed Assets	145	143	156
Current Assets	228	408	201

Portland Engineering Co. Ltd
Wide Street, Portland, DT5 2JP
Tel: 01305-821273 **Fax:** 01305-821499
E-mail: office@portlandengineering.com
Website: http://www.portlandengineering.com
Bank(s): HSBC
Directors: I. Strong (Fab), R. Strong (MD)
Immediate Holding Company: PORTLAND ENGINEERING COMPANY LIMITED
Registration no: 00771581 **Date established:** 1963 **Turnover:** £1m - £2m
No.of Employees: 21 - 50 **Product Groups:** 39, 48

Date of Accounts	Sep 11	Sep 10	Sep 09
Working Capital	370	374	237
Fixed Assets	951	990	1m
Current Assets	666	765	745

Shaftesbury

Johnson Baker
Longmead, Shaftesbury, SP7 8PU
Tel: 01747-853445 **Fax:** 01747-853444
E-mail: johnsonbaker@btclick.com
Bank(s): Lloyds TSB Bank plc
Managers: S. Carther (Chief Acct), R. Brickell (Mgr)
Immediate Holding Company: JOHNSON BAKER & COMPANY LTD
Registration no: 00290616 **Turnover:** £500,000 - £1m
No.of Employees: 21 - 50 **Product Groups:** 22, 25, 27, 49

Pork Farms Riverside Ltd
Longmead Indl-Est Longmead, Shaftesbury, SP7 8PL
Tel: 01749-851511 **Fax:** 01747-853401
Website: http://www.porkfarmsltd.uk.com
Bank(s): HSBC Bank plc
Directors: M. Godley (MD), J. Heydon (Dir), S. Hart (Pers)
Managers: M. Deol (Mgr), J. Haydon (Ops Mgr), J. Heydon (Site Co-ord)
Immediate Holding Company: PORK FARMS LIMITED
Registration no: 05998346 **VAT No.:** GB 168 7433 30
Date established: 2006 **No.of Employees:** 101 - 250 **Product Groups:** 20

Seaway Powell Marine Ltd
Unit 24k Wincombe Business Park, Shaftesbury, SP7 9QJ
Tel: 01747-858585 **Fax:** 01747-858305
E-mail: info@seawaypowell.com
Website: http://www.seawaypowell.com
Managers: G. Thwaites (Chief Mgr)
Immediate Holding Company: SEAWAY POWELL (IMH) LIMITED
Registration no: 05624751 **Date established:** 2005
No.of Employees: 1 - 10 **Product Groups:** 35, 36, 39

Date of Accounts	Dec 11	Dec 10	Dec 09
Working Capital	73	112	22
Fixed Assets	N/A	1	13
Current Assets	76	176	79

Shaftesbury Tractors
6 Wincombe Business Park, Shaftesbury, SP7 9QJ
Tel: 01747-850050 **Fax:** 01747-850055
E-mail: geoffsnell@shaftesburytractors.co.uk
Website: http://www.shaftesburytractors.co.uk
Managers: G. Snell (Mgr)
Ultimate Holding Company: TRAKM8 HOLDINGS PLC
Immediate Holding Company: CARELINE CC LIMITED
Registration no: 04415597 **Date established:** 2006 **Turnover:** £2m - £5m
No.of Employees: 1 - 10 **Product Groups:** 41

Date of Accounts	Mar 11	Mar 10	Mar 09
Working Capital	-35	-30	-1
Fixed Assets	78	68	72
Current Assets	90	117	98

Sonoscan Ultrasonic Equipment Mnfrs
Wincombe Business Park, Shaftesbury, SP7 9QJ
Tel: 01747-855988 **Fax:** 01747-855938
E-mail: info@sonoscan.com
Website: http://www.sonoscan.com
Directors: A. Basterfield (Prop)
Ultimate Holding Company: TRAKM8 HOLDINGS PLC
Immediate Holding Company: TRAKM8 LIMITED
Registration no: 04415597 **Date established:** 2002 **Turnover:** £2m - £5m
No.of Employees: 1 - 10 **Product Groups:** 38, 44, 85

Southern Filter Co.
Unit 22j Wincombe Business Park, Shaftesbury, SP7 9QJ
Tel: 01747-853670 **Fax:** 01747-852619
E-mail: david@southernfilters.co.uk
Website: http://www.southernfilters.co.uk
Directors: D. Sherlock (Prop)
Immediate Holding Company: TRAKM8 HOLDINGS PLC
Registration no: 04327499 **Date established:** 2001
Turnover: Up to £250,000 **No.of Employees:** 1 - 10 **Product Groups:** 40, 42, 66, 67

J Webber
Coles Lane Farm, Shaftesbury, SP7 0PY
Tel: 01747-851717 **Fax:** 01747-855635
E-mail: john@webberengineering.co.uk
Directors: J. Webber (Prop)
Date established: 1985 **No.of Employees:** 1 - 10 **Product Groups:** 41

Wessex Electricals Ltd
Wincombe Lane, Shaftesbury, SP7 8PJ
Tel: 01747-852878 **Fax:** 01747-855117
E-mail: general@wessex.org
Website: http://www.wessex.org
Bank(s): Midland, Shaftesbury
Directors: A. Brunt (MD)
Managers: R. Nikos (Mktg Serv Mgr), S. Wilkinson (Tech Serv Mgr), R. Revell (Personnel)
Ultimate Holding Company: WESSEX GROUP LIMITED
Immediate Holding Company: WESSEX GROUP LIMITED
Registration no: 02457125 **Date established:** 1990
Turnover: £20m - £50m **No.of Employees:** 251 - 500 **Product Groups:** 52

Date of Accounts	Feb 12	Feb 11	Feb 10
Sales Turnover	31m	24m	24m
Pre Tax Profit/Loss	1m	600	1m
Working Capital	3m	3m	3m
Fixed Assets	3m	3m	3m
Current Assets	13m	10m	11m
Current Liabilities	4m	3m	3m

Sherborne

Ace Fibreglass Mouldings
The Railway Shed South Western Business Park, Sherborne, DT9 3PS
Tel: 01935-816437
E-mail: ian@acegrp.fsbusiness.co.uk
Website: http://www.fibreglass.com
Directors: I. Gay (Prop)
Immediate Holding Company: R.E. PEARCE PROPERTIES LIMITED
Date established: 1984 **Turnover:** Up to £250,000
No.of Employees: 1 - 10 **Product Groups:** 30

Date of Accounts	Mar 12	Mar 11	Mar 10
Working Capital	695	332	374
Fixed Assets	447	385	387
Current Assets	1m	2m	1m

Compton Engineering
Unit 1 Old Yarn Mills Westbury, Sherborne, DT9 3RQ
Tel: 01935-389779
Website: http://www.comptonengineering.co.uk
Directors: K. Hannam (Prop)
Immediate Holding Company: COMPTON ENGINEERING SHERBORNE LIMITED
Registration no: 07621917 **Date established:** 2011
No.of Employees: 1 - 10 **Product Groups:** 35

Crocker Engineering
Folke, Sherborne, DT9 5HP
Tel: 01963-210467 **Fax:** 01963-210467
E-mail: the.crockers@virgin.net
Directors: C. Crocker (Prop)
Date established: 1978 **No.of Employees:** 1 - 10 **Product Groups:** 41

J P Fabrications Ltd
Stourton Leaze Farm Holnest, Sherborne, DT9 6HX
Tel: 01963-210800 **Fax:** 01963-210310
Directors: J. Parkinson (Prop)
Immediate Holding Company: JP FABRICATIONS LIMITED
Registration no: 06582790 **Date established:** 2008
No.of Employees: 1 - 10 **Product Groups:** 35, 84

Date of Accounts	May 11	May 10	May 09
Working Capital	-181	-195	-168
Fixed Assets	215	224	246
Current Assets	97	90	108

P D Interglas Technologies Ltd
Westbury, Sherborne, DT9 3RB
Tel: 01935-813722 **Fax:** 01935-811800
E-mail: shane.cherrington@interglas-technologies.com
Website: http://www.pd-fibreglass.com
Bank(s): Barclays; Standard Chartered
Directors: H. Urban (MD)
Managers: M. Mitchell (Personnel), S. Massey (Purch Mgr), R. Andrews (Tech Serv Mgr), K. Loader (Fin Mgr), C. Burt
Ultimate Holding Company: F-D MANAGEMENT INDUSTRIES - TECHNOLOGIES GMBH (GERMANY)
Immediate Holding Company: P-D INTERGLAS TECHNOLOGIES LIMITED
Registration no: 02189095 **VAT No.:** GB 469 7513 02
Date established: 1987 **Turnover:** £10m - £20m
No.of Employees: 101 - 250 **Product Groups:** 23, 33, 66

Date of Accounts	Dec 11	Dec 10	Dec 09
Sales Turnover	17m	16m	17m
Pre Tax Profit/Loss	3m	2m	1m
Working Capital	9m	7m	6m
Fixed Assets	4m	4m	4m
Current Assets	11m	9m	8m
Current Liabilities	903	887	547

Perennis Ltd
807 Staffords Green Corton Denham, Sherborne, DT9 4LY
Tel: 020-7482 5920 **Fax:** 020-7482 5964
E-mail: perennisltd@msn.com
Directors: M. Suckle (MD)
Immediate Holding Company: PERENNIS LIMITED
Registration no: 01491902 **Date established:** 1980
Turnover: Up to £250,000 **No.of Employees:** 1 - 10 **Product Groups:** 81

Date of Accounts	Dec 11	Dec 10	Dec 09
Working Capital	76	70	91
Fixed Assets	2	3	3
Current Assets	167	135	198

Symms Fabrications Ltd
Adber, Sherborne, DT9 4SG
Tel: 01935-851243 **Fax:** 01935-851113
E-mail: davidsymms@btconnect.com
Website: http://www.symmsfabrication.co.uk
Directors: D. Symms (Prop)
Immediate Holding Company: SYMMS FABRICATIONS LIMITED
Registration no: 05469650 **Date established:** 2005
No.of Employees: 1 - 10 **Product Groups:** 41

Date of Accounts	Jun 11	Jun 10	Jun 09
Working Capital	262	22	119
Fixed Assets	303	275	119

see next page

Symms Fabrications Ltd - Cont'd

Current Assets	417	124	226

Titan Enterprises Ltd
Unit 2 5a Coldharbour Business Park, Sherborne, DT9 4JW
Tel: 01935-812790 **Fax:** 01935-812890
E-mail: john@flowmeters.co.uk
Website: http://www.slowmeters.co.uk
Directors: J. Forster (MD)
Immediate Holding Company: TITAN ENTERPRISES LIMITED
Registration no: 01599477 **Date established:** 1981
Turnover: £500,000 - £1m **No.of Employees:** 11 - 20 **Product Groups:** 38

Date of Accounts	Mar 11	Mar 10	Mar 09
Working Capital	583	309	402
Fixed Assets	74	55	273
Current Assets	583	576	551

Y S E Ltd
Church House Abbey Close, Sherborne, DT9 3LQ
Tel: 08451-221414 **Fax:** 0845-122 1415
E-mail: sales@yseski.co.uk
Website: http://www.yseski.co.uk
Directors: F. Easdale (Prop)
Immediate Holding Company: YSE LIMITED
Registration no: 02573425 **Date established:** 1991
No.of Employees: 1 - 10 **Product Groups:** 80

Date of Accounts	May 12	May 11	May 10
Working Capital	-209	-121	-32
Fixed Assets	778	822	815
Current Assets	476	395	428

Sturminster Newton

A S D
Station Road Stalbridge, Sturminster Newton, DT10 2RW
Tel: 01963-362646 **Fax:** 01963-363260
E-mail: storage@asdmetalservices.co.uk
Website: http://www.asdmetalservices.co.uk
Bank(s): Barclays
Directors: B. Kent (Fin)
Managers: J. Wakefield (Chief Mgr)
Ultimate Holding Company: Klockner & Co.
Immediate Holding Company: A.S.D. PLC
Registration no: 01370600 **VAT No.:** GB 412 1831 95
Turnover: £500,000 - £1m **No.of Employees:** 21 - 50 **Product Groups:** 34

Adbruf Ltd
Gibbs Marsh Trading Estate Stalbridge, Sturminster Newton, DT10 2RX
Tel: 01963-362640 **Fax:** 01963-363762
E-mail: stephen@adbruf.com
Website: http://www.adbruf.com
Bank(s): Lloyds TSB Bank plc
Directors: P. Chandaman (I.T. Dir), S. Goodwin (Fin), S. McGilchrist (Sales)
Ultimate Holding Company: BRUF CONTRACT HOLDINGS LIMITED
Immediate Holding Company: ADBRUF LIMITED
Registration no: 00815828 **VAT No.:** GB 188 3317 38
Date established: 1964 **Turnover:** £1m - £2m **No.of Employees:** 21 - 50
Product Groups: 29, 30, 32

Date of Accounts	Mar 11	Mar 10	Mar 09
Working Capital	1m	1m	1m
Fixed Assets	77	88	97
Current Assets	2m	2m	2m
Current Liabilities	228	226	260

Caleva Process Solutions Ltd
Unit 4b Butts Pond Industrial Estate, Sturminster Newton, DT10 1AZ
Tel: 01258-471122 **Fax:** 01258-471133
E-mail: info@caleva.co.uk
Website: http://www.caleva.com
Directors: S. Robinson (MD)
Immediate Holding Company: CALEVA PROCESS SOLUTIONS LTD.
Registration no: 03073156 **Date established:** 1995
Turnover: £500,000 - £1m **No.of Employees:** 1 - 10 **Product Groups:** 84

Date of Accounts	Mar 11	Jun 10	Jun 09
Working Capital	447	376	441
Fixed Assets	5	6	15
Current Assets	595	428	553
Current Liabilities	88	N/A	N/A

William Hughes Ltd
Station Road Stalbridge, Sturminster Newton, DT10 2RZ
Tel: 01963-363377 **Fax:** 01963-363538
E-mail: chughes@wmhughes.co.uk
Website: http://www.wmhughes.co.uk
Bank(s): National Westminster Bank Plc
Directors: C. Hughes (Fin)
Managers: E. Burgon (Tech Serv Mgr), B. Chappel (Sales Prom Mgr), D. Tovey (Personnel)
Ultimate Holding Company: HIGH TENSION WIRES LIMITED
Immediate Holding Company: WILLIAM HUGHES LIMITED
Registration no: 00243035 **VAT No.:** GB 233 0787 73
Date established: 2029 **Turnover:** £5m - £10m
No.of Employees: 51 - 100 **Product Groups:** 35, 66

Date of Accounts	Dec 11	Dec 10	Dec 09
Sales Turnover	6m	6m	5m
Pre Tax Profit/Loss	-132	67	12
Working Capital	657	767	729
Fixed Assets	31	44	39
Current Assets	3m	3m	2m
Current Liabilities	811	486	346

L K M Direct Ltd
Unit 2 Gibbs Marsh Farm Stalbridge, Sturminster Newton, DT10 2RU
Tel: 01963-363521 **Fax:** 01963-364429
Website: http://www.quickreactionforce.co.uk
Managers: E. Dowgent (Mgr), S. Waggott (Mgr)
No.of Employees: 1 - 10 **Product Groups:** 35

M Richards
Back Lane Kingston, Sturminster Newton, DT10 2DT
Tel: 01258-817372 **Fax:** 01258-817185
E-mail: sales@tractorsuk.co.uk
Website: http://www.tractorsuk.co.uk
Directors: M. Richards (Prop)
No.of Employees: 1 - 10 **Product Groups:** 41

Yachting Instruments Ltd
Mappowder, Sturminster Newton, DT10 1EH
Tel: 01258-817662
E-mail: office@tidemaster.co.uk
Website: http://www.tidemaster.co.uk
Directors: W. Woodhouse (MD), A. Woodhouse (Co Sec)
Immediate Holding Company: YACHTING INSTRUMENTS LIMITED
Registration no: 01103322 **Date established:** 1973
Turnover: Up to £250,000 **No.of Employees:** 1 - 10 **Product Groups:** 24, 49, 74

Date of Accounts	Jun 11	Jun 10	Jun 09
Working Capital	-24	-21	-18
Fixed Assets	N/A	1	1
Current Assets	5	5	7
Current Liabilities	N/A	1	1

Swanage

English Stamp Co.
Kingston Road Worth Matravers, Swanage, BH19 3JP
Tel: 01929-439117 **Fax:** 01929-439150
E-mail: sales@englishstamp.com
Website: http://www.englishstamp.com
Directors: J. Dorey (Ptnr)
Date established: 1992 **Turnover:** £500,000 - £1m
No.of Employees: 1 - 10 **Product Groups:** 30, 49, 64

R J Simpson Ornamental Ironwork
Unit 4b Swanage Industrial Estate Off Victoria Avenue, Swanage, BH19 1AU
Tel: 01929-427672 **Fax:** 01929-427672
Directors: R. Simpson (Prop)
Date established: 1991 **No.of Employees:** 1 - 10 **Product Groups:** 26, 35

Sutronics
62 Park Road, Swanage, BH19 2AE
Tel: 01929-426400
E-mail: sales@sutronics.com
Website: http://www.sutronics.com
Directors: C. Davidson (Prop)
Immediate Holding Company: SUTRONICS LIMITED
Registration no: 04458486 **Date established:** 2002
Turnover: £250,000 - £500,000 **No.of Employees:** 1 - 10
Product Groups: 38

Verwood

Dayfold Ltd
Unit 4-6 27 Black Moor Road, Ebblake Industrial Estate, Verwood, BH31 6BE
Tel: 01202-827401 **Fax:** 01202-825841
E-mail: enquiries@dayfold.com
Website: http://www.dayfold.com
Bank(s): HSBC Bank plc
Directors: M. Shier (Comm), P. Scott Oldfield (Co Sec)
Immediate Holding Company: DAYFOLD LIMITED
Registration no: 01487784 **Date established:** 1980
No.of Employees: 21 - 50 **Product Groups:** 28

Date of Accounts	Jul 11	Jul 10	Jul 09
Working Capital	197	217	160
Fixed Assets	457	562	660
Current Assets	963	1m	1m

Flux Pumps
Unit 12 Enterprise Park Black Moor Road Ebblake Industrial Estate, Verwood, BH31 6YS
Tel: 01202-823304 **Fax:** 01202-813387
E-mail: info@flux-pumps.co.uk
Website: http://www.flux-pumps.co.uk
Managers: J. Phillips (Sales Prom Mgr)
Immediate Holding Company: FLUX PUMPS INTERNATIONAL UK LTD
Registration no: 02029429 **Turnover:** £2m - £5m
No.of Employees: 1 - 10 **Product Groups:** 38, 40

Date of Accounts	Dec 07	Dec 06	Dec 05
Working Capital	-66	-51	-25
Fixed Assets	50	15	27
Current Assets	170	92	121
Current Liabilities	236	143	146
Total Share Capital	200	200	200

Global Filters Ltd
25 Blackmoor Road Ebblake Industrial Estate, Verwood, BH31 6BE
Tel: 01202-828109 **Fax:** 01202-813400
Website: http://www.globalfilters.co.uk
Bank(s): The Royal Bank of Scotland
Directors: J. Cobby (Co Sec), R. Cobby (MD)
Managers: P. Lasky (Sales Prom Mgr)
Registration no: 03239555 **Date established:** 1988 **Turnover:** £2m - £5m
Product Groups: 23, 35, 36, 38, 39, 40, 41, 42, 47, 67, 68

Date of Accounts	Mar 11	Mar 10	Mar 09
Working Capital	353	385	233
Fixed Assets	335	299	353
Current Assets	995	691	742

Key Industrial Equipment
35 Black Moor Road Ebblake Industrial Estate, Verwood, BH31 6AT
Tel: 0800-652 6000 **Fax:** 0800-373030
E-mail: sales@key.co.uk
Website: http://www.key.co.uk
Bank(s): Lloyds TSB Bank plc & National Westminster Bank Plc
Directors: M. Luddington (MD), J. Guichard (MD)
Ultimate Holding Company: MANUTAN INTERNATIONAL SA (FRANCE)
Immediate Holding Company: KEY INDUSTRIAL EQUIPMENT LIMITED
Registration no: 01092975 **VAT No.:** GB 323 6086 72
Date established: 1973 **Turnover:** £20m - £50m
No.of Employees: 51 - 100 **Product Groups:** 07, 22, 23, 24, 26, 27, 29, 30, 32, 33, 35, 36, 37, 38, 39, 40, 41, 42, 45, 46, 49, 52, 61, 64, 66, 67, 77, 80, 83, 84, 85, 87

Date of Accounts	Sep 11	Sep 10	Sep 09
Sales Turnover	24m	23m	24m
Pre Tax Profit/Loss	265	360	-294
Working Capital	4m	4m	5m
Fixed Assets	6m	6m	7m
Current Assets	10m	10m	9m
Current Liabilities	1m	940	504

Manitou Site Lift Ltd
Black Moor Road Ebblake Industrial Estate, Verwood, BH31 6BB
Tel: 01202-825331 **Fax:** 01202-813027
E-mail: info@manitou.com
Website: http://www.manitou.com
Bank(s): Societe Generale, 60 Gracechurch St, London
Directors: P. Streatfield (Co Sec), M. Braud (Ch), J. Tapp (Sales)
Managers: P. Bidwell (Mktg Serv Mgr), J. Bowl, D. Gould (Tech Serv Mgr)
Ultimate Holding Company: MANITOU BF SA (FRANCE)
Immediate Holding Company: MANITOU UK LIMITED
Registration no: 01049338 **Date established:** 1972
Turnover: £50m - £75m **No.of Employees:** 21 - 50 **Product Groups:** 36, 45, 48, 67, 71

Date of Accounts	Dec 10	Dec 09	Dec 08
Sales Turnover	50m	51m	76m
Pre Tax Profit/Loss	1m	1m	473
Working Capital	7m	10m	12m
Fixed Assets	4m	4m	4m
Current Assets	16m	14m	24m
Current Liabilities	2m	2m	3m

Surtees Southern Ltd
63 Moorlands Road, Verwood, BH31 7PD
Tel: 01202-821485 **Fax:** 0845-652 6677
E-mail: avml@surtees.co.uk
Website: http://www.surtees.co.uk
Directors: A. Slightam (Dir)
Immediate Holding Company: SURTEES (SOUTHERN) LIMITED
Registration no: 04380541 **Date established:** 2002
Turnover: £250,000 - £500,000 **No.of Employees:** 1 - 10
Product Groups: 83

Date of Accounts	May 11	May 10	May 09
Working Capital	-42	-29	-7
Current Assets	50	30	47

Tennco Distribution Ltd
Unit A1-A2 Forelle Centre 30 Blackmoor Road, Ebblake Industrial Estate, Verwood, BH31 6BB
Tel: 01202-824433 **Fax:** 01202-814500
E-mail: matt@tennconet.com
Website: http://www.tennconet.com
Managers: M. Smith (Mgr)
Immediate Holding Company: TENNCO DISTRIBUTION LIMITED
Registration no: 03301534 **Date established:** 1997
No.of Employees: 1 - 10 **Product Groups:** 23, 25, 30, 31, 32, 33, 34, 35, 36, 37, 38, 39, 40, 41, 42, 44, 45, 46, 47, 48, 49, 63, 65, 66, 67, 68, 84

Date of Accounts	Apr 12	Apr 11	Apr 10
Sales Turnover	N/A	812	581
Pre Tax Profit/Loss	N/A	1	1
Working Capital	64	61	60
Fixed Assets	3	3	4
Current Assets	231	271	211
Current Liabilities	N/A	151	8

Weldcare Services Ltd
Unit 4-7 25 Black Moor Road, Ebblake Industrial Estate, Verwood, BH31 6BE
Tel: 01202-829390 **Fax:** 01202-828935
E-mail: john@weldcareservices.co.uk
Website: http://www.weldcareservices.co.uk
Directors: I. Orbell (Dir), J. Orbell (Prop)
Immediate Holding Company: WELDCARE SERVICES LIMITED
Registration no: 01370652 **Date established:** 1978
No.of Employees: 1 - 10 **Product Groups:** 46

Wareham

Anglo American Oil Co. Ltd
Holly Close Sandford, Wareham, BH20 7QE
Tel: 01929-551557 **Fax:** 01929-551567
E-mail: info@aaoil.co.uk
Website: http://www.aaoil.co.uk
Directors: A. Hildebrand (MD), E. Hildebrand (Fin)
Immediate Holding Company: ANGLO AMERICAN OIL COMPANY LIMITED
Registration no: 03777822 **Date established:** 1999
Turnover: £10m - £20m **No.of Employees:** 1 - 10 **Product Groups:** 31

Date of Accounts	Dec 11	Dec 10	Dec 09
Working Capital	167	249	315
Fixed Assets	124	91	107
Current Assets	483	524	534

C B I Equipment Ltd Shotblasting & Degreasing Machinery
5 Tyneham Close Sandford, Wareham, BH20 7BE
Tel: 01929-550669 **Fax:** 01929-554423
E-mail: marc@cbiequipment.co.uk
Website: http://www.cbiequipment.co.uk
Directors: M. Ross (MD)
Immediate Holding Company: CBI EQUIPMENT LTD
Registration no: 05925516 **Date established:** 2006
Turnover: £250,000 - £500,000 **No.of Employees:** 1 - 10
Product Groups: 52

Date of Accounts	Sep 11	Sep 09	Sep 08
Working Capital	44	-10	-3
Fixed Assets	1	N/A	N/A
Current Assets	44	15	19

C S M Electronics
Ryan Business Park Sandford Lane, Wareham, BH20 4DY
Tel: 01929-554099 **Fax:** 01929-554106
E-mail: sales@csmelectronics.co.uk
Website: http://www.csmelectronics.co.uk
Directors: J. Amos (Sales & Mktg), G. Davies (I.T. Dir), S. Gamage (Fin)
Managers: S. Keeley (Sales & Mktg Mg), J. Turner (Purch Mgr), D. Barton (Chief Mgr), A. Burgess (Tech Serv Mgr)
Immediate Holding Company: C.S.M. ELECTRONICS LIMITED
Registration no: 02447134 **Date established:** 1989 **Turnover:** £1m - £2m
No.of Employees: 21 - 50 **Product Groups:** 37, 48

Date of Accounts	Oct 11	Oct 10	Oct 09
Working Capital	716	1m	1m
Fixed Assets	1m	1m	1m

Current Assets	2m	3m	3m

Charter Tech Ltd

Sandford Lane, Wareham, BH20 4DY
Tel: 01929-553000 **Fax:** 01929-550022
E-mail: enquiries@charter-tech.com
Website: http://www.charter-tech.com
Directors: A. Baker (MD)
Immediate Holding Company: CHARTER TECH LIMITED
Registration no: 02491318 **VAT No.:** GB 542 0006 05
Date established: 1990 **Turnover:** £5m - £10m **No.of Employees:** 1 - 10
Product Groups: 38, 44

Date of Accounts	Jan 12	Jan 11	Jan 10
Working Capital	903	760	542
Fixed Assets	17	20	19
Current Assets	1m	959	766

Darglow Engineering Ltd

6 Justin Business Park Sandford Lane, Wareham, BH20 4DY
Tel: 01929-556512 **Fax:** 01929-551956
E-mail: mail@darglow.co.uk
Website: http://www.darglow.co.uk
Directors: C. Hares (Dir)
Immediate Holding Company: DARGLOW ENGINEERING LTD
Registration no: 02752286 **Date established:** 1992
No.of Employees: 1 - 10 **Product Groups:** 35, 36, 39

Date of Accounts	Oct 11	Oct 10	Oct 09
Working Capital	52	27	28
Fixed Assets	17	16	14
Current Assets	145	149	138

Ensign Communications Ltd

Unit 20-21 Sandford Lane Industrial Estate Sandford Lane, Wareham, BH20 4DY
Tel: 01929-556553 **Fax:** 01929-554516
E-mail: call@ensign-net.co.uk
Website: http://www.ensign-net.co.uk
Bank(s): Lloyds TSB Bank plc
Directors: P. Hookey (Sales & Mktg), W. South (Tech Serv), W. South (Tech Serv), G. Sadler (Fin)
Managers: L. Batten
Immediate Holding Company: ENSIGN COMMUNICATIONS (HOLDINGS) LIMITED
Registration no: 07354000 **VAT No.:** GB 355 8658 10
Date established: 2010 **Turnover:** £2m - £5m **No.of Employees:** 21 - 50
Product Groups: 44

Date of Accounts	Dec 11
Working Capital	-435
Fixed Assets	917

Geedev Ltd

21 Barndale Drive, Wareham, BH20 5BX
Tel: 01929-551122 **Fax:** 01929-552936
E-mail: brian.g@dial.pipex.com
Website: http://www.geedev.co.uk
Directors: B. Groome (MD)
Immediate Holding Company: GEEDEV LIMITED
Registration no: 01438466 **VAT No.:** GB 335 4858 36
Date established: 1979 **Turnover:** £250,000 - £500,000
No.of Employees: 1 - 10 **Product Groups:** 37, 44, 67

Date of Accounts	Sep 11	Sep 10	Sep 09
Working Capital	7	N/A	7
Fixed Assets	1	2	2
Current Assets	11	18	29

A E Griffin & Son

10 North Street Bere Regis, Wareham, BH20 7LA
Tel: 01929-471253 **Fax:** 01929-472208
E-mail: aegriffinandson@aol.com
Directors: R. Griffin (Ptnr)
Turnover: Up to £250,000 **No.of Employees:** 1 - 10 **Product Groups:** 52

Hood Sailmakers (Kemp Sail Ltd)

Unit 16 Sandford Lane Industrial Estate Sandford Lane, Wareham, BH20 4DY
Tel: 01929-554308 **Fax:** 01590-673797
E-mail: sales@hoodsails.com
Website: http://www.hood-sails.com
Bank(s): Bank of Ireland
Directors: J. Woodhouse Iii (Pres), M. Atkins (MD), R. Kemp (Dir)
Managers: M. Rose (Comptroller)
Immediate Holding Company: NATIONWIDE HOME INNOVATIONS LIMITED
Registration no: 00889213 **VAT No.:** GB 188 0313 61
Date established: 2008 **Turnover:** £500,000 - £1m
No.of Employees: 21 - 50 **Product Groups:** 23, 24, 35

Date of Accounts	Aug 10	Aug 09	Aug 08
Working Capital	85	95	95
Fixed Assets	34	36	40
Current Assets	247	285	233

Magnetic Fields Ltd

6 Keysworth Drive, Wareham, BH20 7BD
Tel: 01202-632886 **Fax:** 01202-632886
E-mail: dominique.williams@btinternet.com
Website: http://www.gowiththeflow.org
Directors: D. Williams (MD)
Immediate Holding Company: MAGNETIC FIELDS LIMITED
Registration no: 02661658 **VAT No.:** GB 580 0580 54
Date established: 1991 **Turnover:** Up to £250,000
No.of Employees: 1 - 10 **Product Groups:** 37

Date of Accounts	Nov 11	Nov 10	Nov 09
Working Capital	27	26	21
Fixed Assets	1	2	2
Current Assets	42	39	39

Nationwide Home Innovations Ltd

Unit 4-5 Omega Centre Sandford Lane, Wareham, BH20 4DY
Tel: 01929-554901 **Fax:** 01929-551023
E-mail: sales@nationwideltd.co.uk
Website: http://www.nationwideltd.co.uk
Directors: O. Fallon (Dir)
Immediate Holding Company: NATIONWIDE SECURITY BLINDS LIMITED
Registration no: 02171020 **Date established:** 1987
No.of Employees: 11 - 20 **Product Groups:** 26, 35

Date of Accounts	Sep 07	Sep 06	Sep 05
Working Capital	-201	-51	-19
Fixed Assets	23	30	38
Current Assets	1m	1m	1m
Current Liabilities	N/A	625	N/A

Newring Electronics Ltd

Unit 7-8 Justin Business Park Sandford Lane, Wareham, BH20 4DY
Tel: 01929-554790 **Fax:** 01929-554789
E-mail: mail@newring.co.uk
Website: http://www.newring.co.uk
Directors: A. Werring (Fin), P. Hicks (MD)
Immediate Holding Company: NEWRING ELECTRONICS LIMITED
Registration no: 03952282 **VAT No.:** GB 541 6164 60
Date established: 2000 **Turnover:** £250,000 - £500,000
No.of Employees: 1 - 10 **Product Groups:** 37

Date of Accounts	Apr 11	Apr 10	Apr 09
Working Capital	38	86	64
Fixed Assets	14	19	38
Current Assets	72	152	103

Polish Inc

4 Justin Business Park Sandford Lane, Wareham, BH20 4DY
Tel: 01929-554037 **Fax:** 01929-555262
Directors: P. Williams (Ptnr)
Date established: 1989 **No.of Employees:** 1 - 10 **Product Groups:** 46, 48

Relec Electronics Ltd

Sandford Lane, Wareham, BH20 4DY
Tel: 01929-555700 **Fax:** 01929-555701
E-mail: sales@relec.co.uk
Website: http://www.relec.co.uk
Directors: P. Lappin (Dir)
Immediate Holding Company: RELEC ELECTRONICS LIMITED
Registration no: 01389153 **VAT No.:** GB 320 5205 16
Date established: 1978 **Turnover:** £1m - £2m **No.of Employees:** 11 - 20
Product Groups: 29, 30, 37, 38, 40, 44, 85

Date of Accounts	Dec 10	Dec 09	Dec 08
Working Capital	1m	1m	1m
Fixed Assets	208	89	501
Current Assets	2m	2m	2m

Weymouth

Acrogen Ltd

14a Cambridge Road Granby Industrial Estate, Weymouth, DT4 9TJ
Tel: 01305-769754 **Fax:** 01305- 784555
E-mail: acrogen@acrogen.com
Website: http://www.acrogen.com
Directors: R. Peto (MD)
Immediate Holding Company: ACROGEN LIMITED
Registration no: 03087650 **Date established:** 1995
Turnover: £250,000 - £500,000 **No.of Employees:** 1 - 10
Product Groups: 37

Date of Accounts	Jan 11	Jan 10	Jan 09
Working Capital	3	-1	-4
Fixed Assets	N/A	N/A	5
Current Assets	74	64	37

Amerson Ltd

9 Albany Road Granby Industrial Estate, Weymouth, DT4 9TH
Tel: 01305-206101 **Fax:** 01305-206106
E-mail: amersonsales@amerson.co.uk
Website: http://www.amerson.co.uk
Bank(s): Coutts
Directors: S. Farrer (Sales), A. Smith (MD), T. Blundell (Dir)
Managers: A. Perrett (I.T. Exec), H. Stockley (Sales & Mktg Mg)
Immediate Holding Company: AMERSON LIMITED
Registration no: 00530142 **VAT No.:** GB 137 4301 89
Date established: 1954 **Turnover:** £500,000 - £1m
No.of Employees: 11 - 20 **Product Groups:** 49

Date of Accounts	Mar 10	Mar 09	Mar 08
Sales Turnover	694	856	904
Pre Tax Profit/Loss	44	30	66
Working Capital	58	40	39
Fixed Assets	1	1	1
Current Assets	164	138	186
Current Liabilities	85	16	114

Aston Mortgage Services Ltd

Aston House Verne Road, Weymouth, DT4 0RX
Tel: 01305-830300 **Fax:** 01305-830300
E-mail: contact@astonmortgages.co.uk
Website: http://www.astonmortgages.co.uk
Directors: Y. White (Fin), P. White (MD)
Immediate Holding Company: ASTON MORTGAGE SERVICES LIMITED
Registration no: 05117455 **Date established:** 2004
Turnover: Up to £250,000 **No.of Employees:** 1 - 10 **Product Groups:** 82

Date of Accounts	Mar 11	Mar 10	Mar 09
Working Capital	-5	-4	-5
Fixed Assets	2	2	2
Current Assets	N/A	2	3
Current Liabilities	N/A	6	N/A

Blue Water Horizons

Ferrymans Way, Weymouth, DT4 9YU
Tel: 01305-782080 **Fax:** 01305-786010
E-mail: admin@blue-horizons.co.uk
Website: http://www.blue-horizons.co.uk
Directors: P. Stevens (Co Sec), P. Stevens (Fin)
Managers: L. Clamp
Immediate Holding Company: BLUE WATER HORIZONS LIMITED
Registration no: 02856152 **Date established:** 1993
No.of Employees: 1 - 10 **Product Groups:** 35, 36, 39

Date of Accounts	May 08	May 07	May 06
Working Capital	330	478	133
Fixed Assets	729	744	797
Current Assets	1668	1395	1086
Current Liabilities	1338	917	953

Blundell Harling Ltd (Incorporating Magpie Furniture)

Granby Industrial Estate Albany Road, Weymouth, DT4 9TH
Tel: 01305-206000 **Fax:** 01305-760598
E-mail: sales@blundellharling.co.uk
Website: http://www.blundellharling.co.uk
Bank(s): Barclays
Directors: A. Smith (MD)
Managers: G. Scriven (Purch Mgr), S. Phillips (Personnel), J. King (Sales Prom Mgr), A. Perrett (Tech Serv Mgr)
Immediate Holding Company: BLUNDELL HARLING LIMITED
Registration no: 00449650 **VAT No.:** GB 185 3392 42
Date established: 1948 **Turnover:** £2m - £5m **No.of Employees:** 21 - 50
Product Groups: 26, 27, 38, 39, 49

Date of Accounts	Mar 11	Mar 10	Mar 09
Sales Turnover	2m	2m	3m
Pre Tax Profit/Loss	77	76	-239
Working Capital	260	274	43
Fixed Assets	2m	2m	2m
Current Assets	650	605	595
Current Liabilities	116	119	147

Coda Octopus Martech

14 Albany Road Granby Industrial Estate, Weymouth, DT4 9TH
Tel: 01305-770440 **Fax:** 01305-784555
E-mail: paul.baxter@codaoctopus.com
Website: http://www.martechsystems.co.uk
Bank(s): National Westminster, Weymouth
Directors: P. Baxter (MD)
Ultimate Holding Company: CODA OCTOPUS GROUP INC (UNITED STATES OF AMERICA)
Immediate Holding Company: CODA OCTOPUS MARTECH LIMITED
Registration no: 02300406 **VAT No.:** GB 510 8925 55
Date established: 1988 **Turnover:** £250,000 - £500,000
No.of Employees: 11 - 20 **Product Groups:** 84

Date of Accounts	Oct 11	Oct 10	Oct 09
Sales Turnover	1m	2m	2m
Pre Tax Profit/Loss	44	-327	-52
Working Capital	311	94	-40
Fixed Assets	63	84	109
Current Assets	1m	871	566
Current Liabilities	596	N/A	350

Cooknell Electronics Ltd

17 Cambridge Road Granby Industrial Estate, Weymouth, DT4 9TJ
Tel: 01305-773744 **Fax:** 01305-779527
E-mail: info@cooknell-electronics.co.uk
Website: http://www.cooknell-electronics.co.uk
Directors: F. Cooknell (MD), K. Hinde (I.T. Dir)
Immediate Holding Company: COOKNELL ELECTRONICS LIMITED
Registration no: 02377961 **VAT No.:** GB 529 7132 34
Date established: 1989 **Turnover:** £250,000 - £500,000
No.of Employees: 1 - 10 **Product Groups:** 84

Date of Accounts	Mar 11	Mar 10	Mar 09
Sales Turnover	N/A	272	441
Pre Tax Profit/Loss	N/A	3	113
Working Capital	268	433	430
Fixed Assets	155	6	7
Current Assets	292	462	491
Current Liabilities	N/A	19	47

Dek Printing Machines Ltd

11 Albany Road Granby Industrial Estate, Weymouth, DT4 9TH
Tel: 01305-760760 **Fax:** 01305-760123
E-mail: pdavey@dek.com
Website: http://www.dek.com
Bank(s): HSBC, Dorchester
Directors: J. Knowles (Dir), C. Shaw (Co Sec), R. Campion (Co Sec), J. Hartner (MD), A. Fisher (Fin), J. Knowles (Ch)
Managers: R. Burton (Sales Off Mgr), M. Danby (Mgr), J. McShane (Ops Mgr)
Ultimate Holding Company: DOVER CORPORATION (U.S.A.)
Immediate Holding Company: DEK PRINTING MACHINES LIMITED
Registration no: 00921662 **VAT No.:** GB 185 7388 13
Date established: 1967 **Turnover:** £10m - £20m
No.of Employees: 251 - 500 **Product Groups:** 28, 44

Date of Accounts	Dec 10	Dec 09	Dec 08
Sales Turnover	17m	11m	15m
Pre Tax Profit/Loss	2m	1m	1m
Working Capital	6m	5m	4m
Fixed Assets	3m	2m	2m
Current Assets	11m	6m	5m
Current Liabilities	2m	935	1m

E T R Metal Finishing Ltd

11 Cambridge Road Granby Industrial Estate, Weymouth, DT4 9TJ
Tel: 01305-789088 **Fax:** 01305-789099
E-mail: etrmetalfin@aol.com
Directors: A. Topp (MD)
Immediate Holding Company: ETR METAL FINISHING LIMITED
Registration no: 07374764 **Date established:** 2010
No.of Employees: 1 - 10 **Product Groups:** 46, 48

Date of Accounts	Sep 11
Working Capital	64
Fixed Assets	107
Current Assets	107

Edmundson B C E

Unit 1 Granby Court Granby Industrial Estate, Weymouth, DT4 9XB
Tel: 01305-780396 **Fax:** 01305-760104
Website: http://www.edmundson-electrical.co.uk/
Managers: J. Diaz (District Mgr)
Immediate Holding Company: EDMUNDSON ELECTRICAL LIMITED
Registration no: 02667012 **VAT No.:** GB 579 9948 39
Date established: 1991 **No.of Employees:** 1 - 10 **Product Groups:** 66, 67

Elcontrol Ltd

5 Regulus Works 79 Lynch Lane, Weymouth, DT4 9DW
Tel: 01305-773426 **Fax:** 01305-760539
E-mail: sales@elcontrol.co.uk
Website: http://www.elcontrol.co.uk
Directors: R. Jenkins (MD)
Immediate Holding Company: ELCONTROL LIMITED
Registration no: 01614036 **VAT No.:** GB 196 8737 93
Date established: 1982 **Turnover:** £250,000 - £500,000
No.of Employees: 1 - 10 **Product Groups:** 37, 38, 45

Date of Accounts	Mar 12	Mar 11	Mar 10
Working Capital	79	78	82
Fixed Assets	1	1	1
Current Assets	133	132	143
Current Liabilities	N/A	N/A	25

Steve Hill Associates LLP

16 Mount Pleasant Avenue North, Weymouth, DT3 5HW
Tel: 01305-773092 **Fax:** 01305-773092
E-mail: tracey@iso-9001.biz
Website: http://www.iso-9001.biz

see next page

Steve Hill Associates LLP - Cont'd

Directors: T. Hill (Dir)
Immediate Holding Company: STEVE HILL ASSOCIATES LLP
Registration no: OC301889 **Date established:** 2002
Turnover: Up to £250,000 **No.of Employees:** 1 - 10 **Product Groups:** 80, 82

Date of Accounts	Mar 11	Mar 10	Mar 09
Sales Turnover	63	N/A	N/A
Pre Tax Profit/Loss	52	N/A	N/A
Working Capital	24	34	13
Fixed Assets	3	3	4
Current Assets	28	36	14
Current Liabilities	4	N/A	N/A

innovations-tech Ltd.
28 Osprey Road, Weymouth, DT4 9BU
Tel: 020-3286 2626
E-mail: info@innovations-tech.com
Website: http://innovations-tech.com
Directors: W. Edwards (MD)
Registration no: 6728051 **Date established:** 2008
Turnover: £125m - £250m **No.of Employees:** 1 - 10 **Product Groups:** 37, 38, 44, 47, 51, 84

Kingfisher Marine
10a Custom House Quay, Weymouth, DT4 8BG
Tel: 01305-766595 **Fax:** 01305-766502
E-mail: sales@kingfishermarine.co.uk
Website: http://www.kingfishermarine.co.uk
Directors: D. Caddy (Prop)
Date established: 1989 **No.of Employees:** 1 - 10 **Product Groups:** 35, 36, 39

M W Legal Services
26 Bryn Road, Weymouth, DT4 0NP
Tel: 01305-774786
E-mail: matt@mattwalk.com
Website: http://www.mattwalk.com
Directors: M. Walkden (Prop)
Immediate Holding Company: WESTCOUNTRY ONLINE LIMITED
Registration no: 06459849 **Date established:** 2007
Turnover: Up to £250,000 **No.of Employees:** 1 - 10 **Product Groups:** 80

Date of Accounts	Mar 12	Mar 11	Mar 10
Working Capital	-3	-3	N/A
Current Assets	1	1	3

Noble Manhattan Coaching Ltd
105 The Esplanade, Weymouth, DT4 7EA
Tel: 01305-769411 **Fax:** 0870-706 4313
E-mail: info@noble-manhattan.com
Website: http://www.noble-manhattan.com
Directors: G. O'Donovan (Co Sec), G. O'donovan (MD)
Immediate Holding Company: NOBLE MANHATTAN COACHING LTD
Registration no: 04363413 **Date established:** 2002
No.of Employees: 11 - 20 **Product Groups:** 86

Date of Accounts	Dec 11	Dec 10	Dec 09
Working Capital	76	83	84
Fixed Assets	2	2	1
Current Assets	167	245	252

H W Smith & Son Contracting Ltd
24 Cambridge Rdgranby Industrial Estate Granby Industrial Estate, Weymouth, DT4 9TJ
Tel: 01305-786501 **Fax:** 01305-774959
E-mail: djs@hws24.co.uk
Website: http://www.hws24.co.uk
Directors: D. Smith (MD), H. Smith (Ch), M. Smith (Dir)
Managers: A. Birch (Accounts), R. Hill (I.T. Exec)
Immediate Holding Company: H.W. SMITH & SON (CONTRACTING) LIMITED
Registration no: 01130105 **VAT No.:** GB 187 8392 05
Date established: 1973 **Turnover:** £5m - £10m **No.of Employees:** 1 - 10
Product Groups: 37, 40, 52

Date of Accounts	Apr 10	Apr 09	Apr 08
Working Capital	368	700	693
Fixed Assets	48	44	37
Current Assets	736	1m	1m

Tecan Ltd
Tecan Way Granby Industrial Estate, Weymouth, DT4 9TU
Tel: 01305-765432 **Fax:** 01305-780194
E-mail: info@tecan.co.uk
Website: http://www.tecan.co.uk
Directors: S. Aitken (MD)
Managers: D. Worsdell (Mktg Serv Mgr), J. Edwards (Fin Mgr), P. Stalley, K. O'Leary (Personnel), S. Honeybun (Purch Mgr)
Immediate Holding Company: P L CANE INVESTMENTS LIMITED
Registration no: 00988383 **VAT No.:** GB 212 3378 95
Date established: 1970 **Turnover:** £5m - £10m
No.of Employees: 51 - 100 **Product Groups:** 48, 49

Date of Accounts	Dec 11	Dec 10	Dec 09
Working Capital	-15	-117	4m
Fixed Assets	4m	4m	N/A
Current Assets	N/A	N/A	4m

Ultimate Roofing LLP
45 Broughton Crescent, Weymouth, DT4 9AR
Tel: 07828-507956 **Fax:** 01305-785244
E-mail: info@ultimateroofingllp.co.uk
Website: http://www.ultimateroofingllp.co.uk
Directors: J. Smith (Prop)
Immediate Holding Company: ULTIMATE ROOFING LLP
Registration no: OC341962 **Date established:** 2008
No.of Employees: 1 - 10 **Product Groups:** 30, 31, 52

Date of Accounts	Mar 11	Mar 10
Working Capital	-14	-15
Fixed Assets	4	17
Current Assets	3	N/A
Current Liabilities	3	3

Weymouth Pin Manufacturing Ltd
83 Lynch Lane, Weymouth, DT4 9DN
Tel: 01305-767174 **Fax:** 01305-767074
E-mail: gerry.byze@weypin.co.uk
Website: http://www.weypin.co.uk
Directors: V. Gough (Co Sec), D. Taylor (Fin), G. Vize (Dir)
Immediate Holding Company: PANKL ENGINE SYSTEMS WEYMOUTH PIN LIMITED
Registration no: 02923248 **Date established:** 1994 **Turnover:** £1m - £2m
No.of Employees: 1 - 10 **Product Groups:** 35, 36, 39

Date of Accounts	Sep 08	Sep 07	Sep 06
Sales Turnover	2402	1926	1893
Pre Tax Profit/Loss	6	-70	240
Working Capital	340	102	141
Fixed Assets	357	259	447
Current Assets	824	557	458
Current Liabilities	484	455	316
Total Share Capital	53	53	53
ROCE% (Return on Capital Employed)	0.8	-19.3	40.8
ROT% (Return on Turnover)	0.2	-3.6	12.7

Wimborne

A C Electrical Wholesale ltd
Schlumberger Building Cobham Road, Ferndown Industrial Estate, Wimborne, BH21 7SJ
Tel: 01202-851800 **Fax:** 01202-851818
E-mail: admin@ac-electrical.co.uk
Website: http://www.ac-electrical.co.uk
Directors: D. Bell (Dir), J. Kelly (MD)
Managers: J. Head
Registration no: 01204867 **No.of Employees:** 51 - 100
Product Groups: 63

Aish Electro
22 Bailie Gate Industrial Estate Sturminster Marshall, Wimborne, BH21 4DB
Tel: 01258-858478
Website: http://www.aishem.co.uk
Managers: G. Legg (Mgr)
No.of Employees: 1 - 10 **Product Groups:** 40, 48, 84

Apt Conservatories Ltd
Bailey Gate Industrial Estate Sturminster Marshall, Wimborne, BH21 4DB
Tel: 01258-858243 **Fax:** 01258-857879
E-mail: sales@aptroofs.co.uk
Website: http://www.aptroofs.co.uk
Directors: P. Turner (Fin), A. Turner (MD), P. Turner (Prop)
Immediate Holding Company: APT CONSERVATORIES LIMITED
Registration no: 05506889 **Date established:** 2005
Turnover: £250,000 - £500,000 **No.of Employees:** 1 - 10
Product Groups: 30, 35

AR Bearings & Transmissions
Unit B14 Arena Business Centre 9 Nimrod Way East Dorset Trade Park, Wimborne, BH21 7UH
Tel: 01202-862730 **Fax:** 01202-862734
E-mail: sales@arbearings.co.uk
Website: http://www.arbearings.co.uk
Directors: R. Fry (Ptnr)
Registration no: 06302279 **Date established:** 2007
Turnover: £10m - £20m **No.of Employees:** 1 - 10 **Product Groups:** 35, 45

Automatic Windings Ltd
Unit 40 Azura Close Woolsbridge Industrial Estate Three Legged Cross, Wimborne, BH21 6SZ
Tel: 01202-814532 **Fax:** 01202-814533
E-mail: sales@automatic-windings.co.uk
Website: http://www.automatic-windings.co.uk
Directors: M. Bright (MD)
Immediate Holding Company: AUTOMATIC WINDINGS LIMITED
Registration no: 03306544 **Date established:** 1997
Turnover: £500,000 - £1m **No.of Employees:** 1 - 10 **Product Groups:** 37

Date of Accounts	Sep 11	Sep 10	Sep 09
Working Capital	130	123	113
Fixed Assets	128	129	132
Current Assets	196	148	140

B I S Valves Ltd
Unit 17-23 Kingfisher Park Collingwood Road, West Moors, Wimborne, BH21 6US
Tel: 01202-896322 **Fax:** 01202-896718
E-mail: salesadmin@bisvalves.co.uk
Website: http://www.bisvalves.co.uk
Bank(s): National Westminster Bank Plc
Directors: D. Kelly (MD), T. Thompson (Fin), J. Kelly (Sales)
Managers: S. Balson (Prod Mgr)
Immediate Holding Company: BIS VALVES LIMITED
Registration no: 00826821 **VAT No.:** GB 186 7458 12
Date established: 1964 **Turnover:** £1m - £2m **No.of Employees:** 51 - 100
Product Groups: 35, 36, 37, 38, 39, 40, 67

Date of Accounts	Dec 11	Dec 10	Dec 09
Working Capital	1m	2m	1m
Fixed Assets	725	672	573
Current Assets	2m	2m	2m

Beavin Engineering Ltd
33 Haviland Road Ferndown Industrial Estate, Wimborne, BH21 7SA
Tel: 01202-894404 **Fax:** 01202-894404
E-mail: beavineng@btconnect.com
Website: http://www.beavinengineering.co.uk
Directors: T. Brown (Dir)
Immediate Holding Company: BEAVIN ENGINEERING LIMITED
Registration no: 05216397 **Date established:** 2004
Turnover: Up to £250,000 **No.of Employees:** 1 - 10 **Product Groups:** 30, 42

Date of Accounts	Sep 11	Sep 10	Sep 09
Working Capital	47	37	-18
Fixed Assets	216	231	237
Current Assets	71	67	82

Biffa Waste Services Ltd
Arrowsmith Road, Wimborne, BH21 3BQ
Tel: 01202-841496 **Fax:** 01202-841500
E-mail: whitepit@biffa.co.uk
Website: http://www.biffa.co.uk
Managers: K. Bennett (Mgr)
Immediate Holding Company: BIFFA WASTE SERVICES LIMITED
Registration no: 00946107 **Date established:** 1969
No.of Employees: 1 - 10 **Product Groups:** 54

Date of Accounts	Mar 08	Mar 09	Apr 10
Sales Turnover	555m	574m	492m
Pre Tax Profit/Loss	23m	50m	30m
Working Capital	229m	271m	293m
Fixed Assets	371m	360m	378m
Current Assets	409m	534m	609m
Current Liabilities	50m	100m	115m

Brights Of Nettlebed Ltd
61-63 Leigh Road, Wimborne, BH21 1AE
Tel: 01202-884613 **Fax:** 01202-885679
E-mail: wimborne@brights-interiors.com
Website: http://www.brights-interiors.com
Managers: R. Fisher (Mgr)
Immediate Holding Company: ROBERT STAMP & ASSOCIATES LTD
Registration no: 01777421 **No.of Employees:** 1 - 10 **Product Groups:** 25, 26, 63

Carford Group Ltd
Units 1-4 Mitchell Road, Ferndown Industrial Estate, Wimborne, BH21 7SG
Tel: 01202-851900 **Fax:** 01202-851921
E-mail: sales@carford.co.uk
Website: http://www.carford.co.uk
Directors: N. Aubin (Fin), N. Oryino (MD), S. Carter (Co Sec)
Managers: I. Bryan (Sales Prom Mgr), J. Baulch
Ultimate Holding Company: CARFORD HOLDINGS LIMITED
Immediate Holding Company: CARFORD GROUP LIMITED
Registration no: 03006635 **VAT No.:** GB 292 0841 57
Date established: 1995 **Turnover:** £10m - £20m
No.of Employees: 101 - 250 **Product Groups:** 67

Date of Accounts	Nov 11	Nov 10	Nov 09
Sales Turnover	12m	13m	12m
Pre Tax Profit/Loss	305	510	442
Working Capital	362	343	458
Fixed Assets	993	1m	1m
Current Assets	4m	4m	4m
Current Liabilities	2m	2m	2m

Chambar Engineering Ltd
3 Telford Road Ferndown Industrial Estate, Wimborne, BH21 7QN
Tel: 01202-871143 **Fax:** 01202-897045
E-mail: info@chambar.co.uk
Website: http://www.chambar.co.uk
Directors: S. Chamberlain (MD)
Immediate Holding Company: CHAMBAR ENGINEERING LTD
Registration no: 06000550 **VAT No.:** GB 291 9153 39
Date established: 2006 **No.of Employees:** 1 - 10 **Product Groups:** 46, 48

Date of Accounts	Oct 11	Oct 10	Oct 09
Working Capital	-109	-77	-65
Fixed Assets	55	49	58
Current Assets	91	90	119

Cobham plc
Brook Road, Wimborne, BH21 2BJ
Tel: 01202-882020 **Fax:** 01202-880096
E-mail: communications@cobham.com
Website: http://www.cobham.com
Directors: D. Harrison (Fin)
Managers: A. Stevens
Ultimate Holding Company: COBHAM PLC
Immediate Holding Company: COBHAM LEASING LIMITED
Registration no: 02941915 **Date established:** 1994 **Turnover:** £5m - £10m
No.of Employees: 251 - 500 **Product Groups:** 35, 68

Date of Accounts	Dec 11	Dec 10	Dec 09
Sales Turnover	7m	6m	7m
Pre Tax Profit/Loss	1m	704	1m
Working Capital	13m	12m	12m
Fixed Assets	7m	9m	10m
Current Assets	17m	17m	15m
Current Liabilities	3m	3m	2m

Cobham Mission Equipment Ltd (F R Hitemp Division)
Brook Road, Wimborne, BH21 2BJ
Tel: 01202-882121 **Fax:** 01202-880096
E-mail: communications@cobham.com
Website: http://www.cobham.com
Bank(s): Midland Bank
Directors: M. Burke (Develop)
Immediate Holding Company: COBHAM PLC
Registration no: 00030470 **VAT No.:** GB 185 8738 07
Date established: 1989 **Turnover:** Over £1,000m
No.of Employees: 251 - 500 **Product Groups:** 48

Date of Accounts	Dec 11	Dec 10	Dec 09
Sales Turnover	1854m	1903m	1880m
Pre Tax Profit/Loss	234m	189m	245m
Working Capital	235m	295m	60m
Fixed Assets	1300m	1448m	1479m
Current Assets	984m	1123m	963m
Current Liabilities	532m	407m	405m

Copyrite Ltd
Unit 15 Riverside Park Station Road, Wimborne, BH21 1QU
Tel: 01202-848866 **Fax:** 01202-849567
E-mail: sales@copyrite.co.uk
Website: http://www.copyrite.co.uk
Directors: P. Ford (Dir), I. Stewart (Fin)
Managers: M. Burden (Tech Serv Mgr), D. Beale (Mktg Serv Mgr), J. Gregory (Fin Mgr), D. Littlecott (Mgr)
Immediate Holding Company: COPYRITE BUSINESS SOLUTIONS LIMITED
Registration no: 03255320 **Date established:** 1996
No.of Employees: 21 - 50 **Product Groups:** 44

Date of Accounts	Sep 11	Sep 10	Sep 09
Working Capital	-72	93	105
Fixed Assets	339	112	85
Current Assets	1m	765	750

Cranborne Forge
Little Haythorne Haythorne, Horton, Wimborne, BH21 7JG
Tel: 01258-841140 **Fax:** 01725-517888
E-mail: richard@cranborneforge.co.uk
Website: http://www.cranborneforge.co.uk
Directors: R. Rideout (Prop)
Date established: 1974 **No.of Employees:** 1 - 10 **Product Groups:** 26, 35

Cynergy3 Components Ltd
7 Cobham Road Ferndown Industrial Estate, Wimborne, BH21 7PE
Tel: 01202-897969 **Fax:** 01202-891918
E-mail: sales@cynergy3.com
Website: http://www.cynergy3.com
Bank(s): National Westminster Bank Plc
Directors: D. Bailey (Pers)
Ultimate Holding Company: CNGY4 INVESTMENTS LIMITED (JERSEY)
Immediate Holding Company: CYNERGY3 COMPONENTS LIMITED
Registration no: 03049081 **VAT No.:** GB 619 8026 27
Date established: 1995 **Turnover:** £2m - £5m **No.of Employees:** 51 - 100
Product Groups: 37, 38

Date of Accounts	Dec 11	Dec 10	Dec 09
Sales Turnover	6m	6m	4m
Pre Tax Profit/Loss	1m	549	-481
Working Capital	2m	3m	710
Fixed Assets	612	595	953
Current Assets	4m	4m	3m
Current Liabilities	600	515	2m

Dolphin Care Stairlifts Ltd
47 Haviland Road Ferndown Industrial Estate, Wimborne, BH21 7RY
Tel: 01202-873730 **Fax:** 01202-873730
E-mail: jaustindcs@aol.com
Directors: P. Austin (Fin), J. Austin (MD)
Immediate Holding Company: DOLPHIN CARE STAIRLIFTS LIMITED
Registration no: 04261932 **Date established:** 2001
No.of Employees: 1 - 10 **Product Groups:** 35, 39, 45

Date of Accounts	Jul 11	Jul 10	Jul 09
Working Capital	41	48	45
Fixed Assets	15	25	33
Current Assets	74	83	75

Dorset Sheet Metal Products Ltd
Unit 2a 27 Brook Road, Wimborne, BH21 2BH
Tel: 01202-841276 **Fax:** 01202-842648
E-mail: sales@dsmp.co.uk
Website: http://www.dsmp.co.uk
Directors: J. Chapman (Fin)
Immediate Holding Company: DORSET SHEET METAL PRODUCTS LIMITED
Registration no: 01857070 **VAT No.:** GB 392 9554 07
Date established: 1984 **Turnover:** £250,000 - £500,000
No.of Employees: 1 - 10 **Product Groups:** 36, 48

Date of Accounts	Sep 11	Sep 10	Sep 09
Working Capital	35	42	42
Fixed Assets	38	43	45
Current Assets	148	187	172

Dowding & Mills Engineering Services Ltd
5 Maple Business Park Cobham Road, Ferndown Industrial Estate, Wimborne, BH21 7RS
Tel: 01202-877900 **Fax:** 01202-877992
E-mail: laurie.melville@sulzer.com
Website: http://www.dowdingandmills.com
Managers: L. Melville (District Mgr)
Ultimate Holding Company: CASTLE SUPPORT SERVICES PLC
Immediate Holding Company: DOWDING & MILLS PLC
Registration no: SC028056 **No.of Employees:** 1 - 10 **Product Groups:** 37, 44, 45, 48, 84, 85

Electronic Technicians Ltd
41 Cobham Road Ferndown Industrial Estate, Wimborne, BH21 7QZ
Tel: 01202-897722 **Fax:** 01202-892922
E-mail: sales@etluk.co.uk
Website: http://www.etluk.co.uk
Bank(s): National Westminster Bank Plc
Managers: S. Crook (Fin Mgr), J. Arnold (Sales Prom Mgr)
Immediate Holding Company: ELECTRONIC TECHNICIANS LIMITED
Registration no: 01575674 **VAT No.:** GB 392 7572 15
Date established: 1981 **Turnover:** £2m - £5m **No.of Employees:** 21 - 50
Product Groups: 37, 48, 80, 85

Date of Accounts	Jun 12	Jun 11	Jun 10
Working Capital	161	247	241
Fixed Assets	456	387	368
Current Assets	926	1m	1m

Epoxy Products Ltd
7 Haviland Road Ferndown Industrial Estate, Wimborne, BH21 7RZ
Tel: 01202-891899 **Fax:** 01202-896983
E-mail: sales@epoxyproducts.co.uk
Website: http://www.epoxyproducts.co.uk
Directors: T. Langrish (MD)
Immediate Holding Company: EPOXY PRODUCTS LIMITED
Registration no: 01800264 **VAT No.:** GB 355 9334 31
Date established: 1984 **Turnover:** £500,000 - £1m
No.of Employees: 1 - 10 **Product Groups:** 30, 31, 32, 52

Date of Accounts	Mar 11	Mar 10	Mar 09
Sales Turnover	761	632	630
Pre Tax Profit/Loss	-19	26	-1
Working Capital	-32	-18	-44
Fixed Assets	9	9	17
Current Assets	133	176	96
Current Liabilities	67	70	47

Eurotecno Spray Booths
Unit A3 6 Nimrod Way East Dorset Trade Park, Wimborne, BH21 7SH
Tel: 01202-897672
E-mail: sales@eurotecno.co.uk
Website: http://www.eurotecno.co.uk
Directors: J. Compiani (Dir)
No.of Employees: 1 - 10 **Product Groups:** 26, 40, 46

Ferndown Fabrications Ltd
69 Haviland Road Ferndown Industrial Estate, Wimborne, BH21 7PY
Tel: 01202-896415 **Fax:** 01202-877290
E-mail: fernfab@hotmail.co.uk
Website: http://www.kellysearch.com/partners/ferndownfabrications.asp
Directors: L. Sims (Dir), E. Sims (Fin)
Immediate Holding Company: FERNDOWN FABRICATIONS LIMITED
Registration no: 01848053 **Date established:** 1984
No.of Employees: 1 - 10 **Product Groups:** 35, 36, 37, 40, 43, 45, 46, 47, 48, 49, 66, 67, 84

Date of Accounts	Sep 11	Sep 10	Sep 09
Working Capital	-89	-64	-47
Fixed Assets	29	35	41
Current Assets	73	67	76

Garden Retreat Ltd
14 Poole Road, Wimborne, BH21 1QG
Tel: 01202-885663 **Fax:** 01202-881933
E-mail: jim.parker@garden-retreat.co.uk
Website: http://www.garden-retreat.co.uk
Directors: J. Parker (Works), J. Parker (Dir)
Immediate Holding Company: GARDEN RETREAT LIMITED
Registration no: 06400293 **Date established:** 2007
Turnover: Up to £250,000 **No.of Employees:** 1 - 10 **Product Groups:** 25, 35, 83

Date of Accounts	Oct 10	Oct 09	Oct 08
Working Capital	-46	-54	-46
Fixed Assets	46	29	18
Current Assets	31	19	5

GB Lifts Ltd
Suite G12-14 10 Whittle Road, Ferndown Industrial Estate, Wimborne, BH21 7RL
Tel: 01202-871012 **Fax:** 01202-894345
E-mail: dorset@gblifts.co.uk
Website: http://www.gblifts.co.uk
Directors: A. Barnicoat (Ptnr)
Managers: P. Middleton (Mgr)
Immediate Holding Company: G.B. LIFTS LIMITED
Registration no: 02339916 **Date established:** 1989
No.of Employees: 1 - 10 **Product Groups:** 35, 39, 45

Date of Accounts	Mar 11	Mar 10	Mar 09
Sales Turnover	814	N/A	N/A
Pre Tax Profit/Loss	-142	N/A	N/A
Working Capital	-141	30	107
Fixed Assets	N/A	72	59
Current Assets	288	283	742
Current Liabilities	130	N/A	N/A

The Hand Made Sofa Company
Unit 4 Manor Farm Business Centre Gussage St Michael, Wimborne, BH21 5HT
Tel: 01258-841414 **Fax:** 01258-841490
E-mail: info@handmadesofacompany.co.uk
Website: http://www.handmadesofacompany.co.uk
Directors: A. Davies (Prop)
Immediate Holding Company: THE HANDMADE SOFA COMPANY LTD
Registration no: 05900991 **Date established:** 2006
Turnover: Up to £250,000 **No.of Employees:** 1 - 10 **Product Groups:** 26

Date of Accounts	Aug 11	Aug 10	Aug 08
Working Capital	14	15	12
Fixed Assets	N/A	1	1
Current Assets	68	77	66

Hi-Tec Welding & Fabrication Ltd
23 Whittle Road Ferndown Industrial Estate, Wimborne, BH21 7RP
Tel: 01202-870660 **Fax:** 01202-870662
E-mail: info@hi-tec-welding.co.uk
Website: http://www.hi-tec-welding.co.uk
Bank(s): National Westminster Bank Plc
Managers: M. Goodhand, H. Herrington
Immediate Holding Company: HI-TEC WELDING AND FABRICATION SERVICES LIMITED
Registration no: 03719580 **VAT No.:** GB 423 5001 06
Date established: 1999 **Turnover:** £2m - £5m **No.of Employees:** 11 - 20
Product Groups: 35

Date of Accounts	Jul 11	Jul 10	Jul 09
Working Capital	134	128	485
Fixed Assets	158	185	185
Current Assets	414	310	627

Ion Enterprises Ltd
Arena C15 9 Nimrod Way East Dorset Trade Park, Wimborne, BH21 7SH
Tel: 01202-862560 **Fax:** 01202-862561
E-mail: harveybuchanan@scalebuster.com
Website: http://www.scalebuster.com
Managers: H. Buchanan (Chief Mgr)
Immediate Holding Company: ION ENTERPRISES LIMITED
Registration no: 02502463 **Date established:** 1990
No.of Employees: 1 - 10 **Product Groups:** 32, 35, 36, 37, 39, 40, 42, 48, 54, 66, 67, 84, 85

Date of Accounts	Dec 11	Dec 10	Dec 09
Working Capital	323	335	243
Fixed Assets	6	4	1
Current Assets	381	406	289

Jason's Cradle
Unit 6 Ariel Park Uddens Trading Estate, Wimborne, BH21 7NL
Tel: 01202-874365 **Fax:** 01202-876296
E-mail: suematthews@jasonscradle.co.uk
Website: http://www.jasonscradle.co.uk
Directors: S. Matthews (Prop)
Registration no: 1866976 **Date established:** 1980 **Turnover:**
No.of Employees: 1 - 10 **Product Groups:** 23

Kroll
49 Azura Close Woolsbridge Industrial Estate Three Legged Cross, Wimborne, BH21 6SZ
Tel: 01202-822221 **Fax:** 01202-822222
E-mail: sales@krolluk.com
Website: http://www.krolluk.com
Managers: J. Groves (Mgr)
Ultimate Holding Company: KROLL GMBH (GERMANY)
Immediate Holding Company: KROLL (U.K.) LIMITED
Registration no: 02674620 **VAT No.:** GB 580 1256 58
Date established: 1991 **Turnover:** £250,000 - £500,000
No.of Employees: 1 - 10 **Product Groups:** 40

Date of Accounts	Mar 12	Mar 11	Mar 10
Working Capital	71	101	56
Current Assets	191	268	167

Lewis Concrete Products Ltd
Old Barn Farm Road Woolbridge Industrial Estate, Three Legged Cross, Wimborne, BH21 6SF
Tel: 01202-821895 **Fax:** 01202-820672
E-mail: info@lewisconcrete.net
Website: http://www.lewisconcrete.co.uk
Bank(s): Barclays
Directors: S. Lewis (MD), S. Lweis (MD)
Managers: B. Small (Sales Prom Mgr)
Immediate Holding Company: LEWIS CONCRETE PRODUCTS LIMITED
Registration no: 06760447 **VAT No.:** GB 186 0129 66
Date established: 2008 **Turnover:** £500,000 - £1m
No.of Employees: 11 - 20 **Product Groups:** 33, 35, 66

Little Green Nursery
117 Middlehill Road, Wimborne, BH21 2HL
Tel: 01202-884527
E-mail: info@little-green-nursery.co.uk
Website: http://www.little-green-nursery.co.uk
Directors: D. Green (Prop)
Turnover: Up to £250,000 **No.of Employees:** 1 - 10 **Product Groups:** 31, 32

Marden Edwards Ltd
2 Nimrod Way East Dorset Trade Park, Wimborne, BH21 7SH
Tel: 01202-861200 **Fax:** 01202-842632
E-mail: sales@wrapsuk.com
Website: http://www.mardenedwards.com
Bank(s): Lloyds TSB Bank Plc
Directors: J. Edwards (MD)
Managers: S. Williamson, P. Daniel (Purch Mgr), J. Phillips (Personnel), M. Gray (Sales Prom Mgr), P. Evans (Tech Serv Mgr)
Ultimate Holding Company: MARDEN EDWARDS LIMITED
Immediate Holding Company: WRAPS (UK) LIMITED
Registration no: 02541223 **VAT No.:** GB 185 3238 52
Date established: 1990 **Turnover:** £10m - £20m
No.of Employees: 101 - 250 **Product Groups:** 20, 41, 42, 45, 67

Date of Accounts	Apr 11	Apr 10	Apr 09
Working Capital	146	85	48
Fixed Assets	6	8	10
Current Assets	413	356	360

New Forest Instrument Control Ltd
84 Cobham Road Ferndown Indl-Est, Wimborne, BH21 7RW
Tel: 01202-875308 **Fax:** 01202-893462
E-mail: info@newforestinstruments.co.uk
Website: http://www.newforestinstruments.co.uk
Directors: G. Simpson (Dir), G. Sitmpson (Dir), G. Stimpson (Prop), P. Stimpson (MD)
Immediate Holding Company: NEW FOREST INSTRUMENT CONTROL LIMITED
Registration no: 01070841 **VAT No.:** GB 186 9150 30
Date established: 1972 **Turnover:** Up to £250,000
No.of Employees: 21 - 50 **Product Groups:** 48

Date of Accounts	May 11	May 10	May 09
Working Capital	26	-52	169
Fixed Assets	879	866	657
Current Assets	418	369	404

Otto Kampf
46-54 Leigh Road, Wimborne, BH21 1AQ
Tel: 01202-883136 **Fax:** 01202-880352
E-mail: ottokampf@btconnect.com
Website: http://www.ottokampf.co.uk
Directors: S. Sheppard (Dir)
Immediate Holding Company: OTTO KAMPF LIMITED
Registration no: 06211525 **Date established:** 2007
No.of Employees: 11 - 20 **Product Groups:** 46, 48

P A L Electrical Wholesale Ltd
2 Victory Close Woolsbridge Industrial Estate, Three Legged Cross, Wimborne, BH21 6SX
Tel: 01202-813783 **Fax:** 01202-813875
E-mail: palelectrical@btconnect.com
Website: http://www.palelectrical.co.uk
Directors: D. Lane (MD), P. Lane (Fin)
Immediate Holding Company: PAL ELECTRICAL WHOLESALE LIMITED
Registration no: 02426413 **VAT No.:** GB 541 9818 24
Date established: 1989 **Turnover:** £250,000 - £500,000
No.of Employees: 1 - 10 **Product Groups:** 37

Date of Accounts	Dec 07	Dec 06	Dec 05
Working Capital	115	88	111
Fixed Assets	26	20	19
Current Assets	206	183	186
Current Liabilities	91	95	75
Total Share Capital	1	1	1

P C S Cables & Connectors Ltd
14-16 Kingfisher Park Three Cross Road, West Moors, Wimborne, BH21 6US
Tel: 01202-871924 **Fax:** 01202-895661
E-mail: enquiries@pcscables.com
Website: http://www.pcscables.com
Directors: A. Bates (MD), C. Bates (Co Sec)
Immediate Holding Company: PCS CABLES & CONNECTORS LIMITED
Registration no: 02800687 **Date established:** 1993 **Turnover:** £1m - £2m
No.of Employees: 1 - 10 **Product Groups:** 37, 39, 68

Date of Accounts	Jul 11	Jul 10	Jul 09
Working Capital	-8	-43	-53
Fixed Assets	213	214	197
Current Assets	138	118	110

P D L Engineering Ltd
5 Whittle Road Ferndown Industrial Estate, Wimborne, BH21 7RJ
Tel: 01202-871188 **Fax:** 01202-892499
Directors: P. Axon (Fin)
Immediate Holding Company: P.D.L. ENGINEERING LIMITED
Registration no: 02199489 **VAT No.:** GB 186 2635 39
Date established: 1987 **Turnover:** £250,000 - £500,000
No.of Employees: 1 - 10 **Product Groups:** 48

Date of Accounts	Nov 11	Nov 10	Nov 09
Working Capital	229	225	165
Fixed Assets	110	125	116
Current Assets	285	305	210

Powertech Solar Ltd
86 Cobham Road Ferndown Industrial Estate, Wimborne, BH21 7PQ
Tel: 01202-890234
Website: http://www.solar.org.uk
Managers: J. Mortby (Sales Prom Mgr)
Registration no: 04131978 **Date established:** 2000
No.of Employees: 1 - 10 **Product Groups:** 37, 40

Purley Plastics
41 Haviland Road Ferndown Industrial Estate, Wimborne, BH21 7RY
Tel: 01202-892255 **Fax:** 01202-892255
Directors: R. Fendley (Ptnr)
VAT No.: GB 542 0179 71 **Date established:** 1990
No.of Employees: 1 - 10 **Product Groups:** 30

Quad Vision Ltd
Unit C17 Arena Business Centre 9 Nimrod Way, Wimborne, BH21 7SH
Tel: 01202-862325 **Fax:** 01202-862326
E-mail: enquiries@quadvision.co.uk
Website: http://www.quadvision.co.uk
Directors: R. Hughes (Dir)
Immediate Holding Company: QUAD VISION LIMITED
Registration no: 02970561 **VAT No.:** GB 474 4587 11
Date established: 1994 **Turnover:** £500,000 - £1m
No.of Employees: 1 - 10 **Product Groups:** 44

Date of Accounts	Jul 11	Jul 10	Jul 09
Working Capital	174	113	80
Fixed Assets	5	7	6
Current Assets	313	237	220

R J W Sheet Metal Ltd

40 Cobham Road Ferndown Industrial Estate, Wimborne, BH21 7NP
Tel: 01202-875852 **Fax:** 01202-893953
E-mail: enquiries@rjwsheetmetal.com
Website: http://www.rjwsheetmetal.com
Directors: A. Weight (Dir), C. Weight (Dir)
Immediate Holding Company: R J W SHEET METAL LIMITED
Registration no: 00868857 **VAT No.:** GB 185 8456 17
Date established: 1966 **Turnover:** £1m - £2m **No.of Employees:** 21 - 50
Product Groups: 48

Date of Accounts	Mar 11	Mar 10	Mar 09
Working Capital	409	326	323
Fixed Assets	559	607	642
Current Assets	747	667	761

R M Fabrications

Unit 1-4 Ashley Heath Industrial Estate Ringwood Road, Three Legged Cross, Wimborne, BH21 6UZ
Tel: 01202-828240 **Fax:** 01202-828250
E-mail: enquiries@rmfabrications.co.uk
Website: http://www.rmfabrications.co.uk
Directors: R. Mills (MD)
Date established: 2004 **No.of Employees:** 11 - 20 **Product Groups:** 35

R B S Electronics

55 Azura Close Three Legged Cross, Wimborne, BH21 6SZ
Tel: 01202-826262 **Fax:** 01202-826263
E-mail: sales@rbselectronics.co.uk
Website: http://www.rbselectronics.co.uk
Directors: J. Hitchens (Prop)
Turnover: £250,000 - £500,000 **No.of Employees:** 1 - 10
Product Groups: 37

Renntec

Unit 65-69 Azura Close Woolsbridge Industrial Estate, Three Legged Cross, Wimborne, BH21 6SZ
Tel: 01202-826722 **Fax:** 01202-826747
E-mail: sales@technicaltubes.com
Website: http://www.renntec.co.uk
Bank(s): Lloyds TSB Bank plc
Directors: D. Morley (MD)
Immediate Holding Company: TUBULAR MARINE PRODUCTS LTD
Registration no: 02788437 **VAT No.:** GB 355 9420 38
Turnover: £1m - £2m **No.of Employees:** 21 - 50 **Product Groups:** 22, 24, 29, 35, 68

Date of Accounts	Jan 06
Working Capital	1
Current Assets	1
Total Share Capital	1

Rollalong Ltd

309 Old Barn Farm Road Three Legged Cross, Wimborne, BH21 6SF
Tel: 01202-824541 **Fax:** 01202-826525
E-mail: enquiries@rollalong.co.uk
Website: http://www.rollalong.co.uk
Bank(s): National Westminster
Directors: A. Bale (Co Sec), M. Sayers (MD), T. Woodley (Chief Op Offcr)
Managers: J. Mills (Comptroller)
Ultimate Holding Company: ROLLALONG HOLDINGS LIMITED
Immediate Holding Company: ROLLALONG LIMITED
Registration no: 03683003 **VAT No.:** GB 730 3987 28
Date established: 1998 **Turnover:** £20m - £50m
No.of Employees: 51 - 100 **Product Groups:** 25, 35, 36, 39

Date of Accounts	Dec 11	Dec 10	Dec 09
Sales Turnover	30m	35m	23m
Pre Tax Profit/Loss	3m	2m	3m
Working Capital	6m	4m	2m
Fixed Assets	253	237	525
Current Assets	18m	15m	9m
Current Liabilities	5m	3m	2m

Rowland Sandwith Ltd

32 Canford Bottom, Wimborne, BH21 2HD
Tel: 01202-882323 **Fax:** 01202-842815
E-mail: office@rowland-sandwith.co.uk
Website: http://www.h-h-hancock.co.uk
Bank(s): HSBC, St Peters Port, Guernsey
Directors: P. Sandwith (MD)
Ultimate Holding Company: HORACE H HANCOCK LIMITED (GUERNSEY)
Immediate Holding Company: ROWLAND SANDWITH LIMITED
Registration no: 00422430 **VAT No.:** GB 186 3657 26
Date established: 1946 **No.of Employees:** 11 - 20 **Product Groups:** 49, 64

Date of Accounts	Dec 11	Dec 10	Dec 09
Working Capital	113	87	149
Fixed Assets	198	198	114
Current Assets	199	164	190

Sabre Engines Ltd

22 Cobham Road Ferndown Industrial Estate, Wimborne, BH21 7PW
Tel: 01202-893720 **Fax:** 01202-851700
E-mail: post@sabre-engines.co.uk
Website: http://www.perkins-sabre.com
Bank(s): Barclays
Directors: P. Freeman (MD), J. Nicholls (Co Sec)
Managers: A. Freeman (Mktg Serv Mgr), G. Trefman (I.T. Exec), T. Suttle (Purch Mgr), C. Creelman (Accounts)
Ultimate Holding Company: Caterpillar UK Group Ltd
Immediate Holding Company: Caterpillar UK Holdings Ltd
Registration no: 00940053 **VAT No.:** GB 186 0634 53
Date established: 1968 **Turnover:** £20m - £50m
No.of Employees: 51 - 100 **Product Groups:** 40

Date of Accounts	Dec 07	Dec 06	Dec 05
Sales Turnover	20012	16034	14903
Pre Tax Profit/Loss	1010	555	343
Working Capital	3490	2813	2499
Fixed Assets	530	482	421
Current Assets	6039	4916	4732
Current Liabilities	2549	2103	2233
Total Share Capital	1092	1092	1092
ROCE% (Return on Capital Employed)	25.1	16.8	11.7
ROT% (Return on Turnover)	5.0	3.5	2.3

Saturn Spraying Systems Ltd

Unit 3 13 Cobham Road Ferndown Industrial Estate, Wimborne, BH21 7PE
Tel: 01202-891863 **Fax:** 01202-871543
E-mail: sales@saturnspraying.com
Website: http://www.saturnspraying.com
Directors: J. Beesley (MD)
Immediate Holding Company: SATURN SPRAYING SYSTEMS LTD
Registration no: 03239668 **Date established:** 1996
Turnover: £500m - £1,000m **No.of Employees:** 1 - 10
Product Groups: 20, 41, 45, 84

Date of Accounts	Sep 11	Sep 10	Sep 09
Working Capital	-47	-53	-78
Fixed Assets	30	23	24
Current Assets	138	103	75

Saxon Forge

Silver Snaffles Verwood Road, Three Legged Cross, Wimborne, BH21 6RR
Tel: 01202-826375 **Fax:** 01202-826375
Directors: Z. Haigh (Ptnr)
Immediate Holding Company: SAXON FORGE LIMITED
Registration no: 03084307 **Date established:** 1995
No.of Employees: 1 - 10 **Product Groups:** 26, 35

Date of Accounts	Jul 11	Jul 10	Jul 09
Working Capital	-2	-3	N/A
Fixed Assets	2	3	4
Current Assets	4	3	5

Sherwood Tinning

Unit 5a Bailey Gate Industrial Estate, Sturminster Marshall, Wimborne, BH21 4DB
Tel: 01258-857703 **Fax:** 01258-858383
E-mail: sales@sherwoodtinning.co.uk
Website: http://www.sherwoodtinning.co.uk
Directors: N. Stevenson (Dir)
Immediate Holding Company: SHERWOOD TINNING LIMITED
Registration no: 04844016 **Date established:** 2003
Turnover: Up to £250,000 **No.of Employees:** 1 - 10 **Product Groups:** 46, 48

Date of Accounts	Mar 11	Mar 10	Mar 09
Sales Turnover	N/A	N/A	52
Pre Tax Profit/Loss	N/A	N/A	23
Working Capital	11	10	8
Fixed Assets	9	11	14
Current Assets	21	17	17
Current Liabilities	N/A	N/A	8

Sitest Ltd

Unit 8 Minster Park Collingwood Road, West Moors, Wimborne, BH21 6QF
Tel: 01202-861733 **Fax:** 01202-861734
E-mail: info@sitest.co.uk
Website: http://www.sitest.co.uk
Directors: A. Langridge (MD), L. Langridge (Fin)
Immediate Holding Company: SI TEST LIMITED
Registration no: 01974658 **Date established:** 1986
No.of Employees: 11 - 20 **Product Groups:** 38

Date of Accounts	Dec 11	Dec 10	Jun 09
Working Capital	26	24	8
Fixed Assets	1	2	5
Current Assets	75	236	145

David Smith Motors

21 Telford Road Ferndown Industrial Estate, Wimborne, BH21 7QS
Tel: 01202-871858 **Fax:** 01202-891329
E-mail: david@dsmuk.fsnet.co.uk
Website: http://www.davidsmithmotors.co.uk
Directors: D. Smith (Prop)
Date established: 1998 **No.of Employees:** 1 - 10 **Product Groups:** 80

Solent Products

Unit 1 Minster Park Collingwood Road, West Moors, Wimborne, BH21 6QF
Tel: 01202-855855 **Fax:** 01202-518887
E-mail: salessolent@aol.com
Website: http://www.solentproducts.co.uk
Directors: T. Deegan (Ptnr)
Date established: 1995 **No.of Employees:** 1 - 10 **Product Groups:** 35

Keith Spicer Ltd

5 Cobham Road Ferndown Industrial Estate, Wimborne, BH21 7PN
Tel: 01202-863800 **Fax:** 01202-863801
E-mail: andypepper@keith-spicer.co.uk
Website: http://www.keith-spicer.co.uk
Bank(s): National Westminster Bank Plc
Directors: S. Bryant (Fin), A. Lee (Sales & Mktg), A. Pepper (Chief Op Offcr)
Ultimate Holding Company: HARRRIS FREEMAN & CO INC (USA)
Immediate Holding Company: KEITH SPICER LIMITED
Registration no: 00348565 **VAT No.:** GB 185 6409 36
Date established: 1939 **Turnover:** £10m - £20m
No.of Employees: 101 - 250 **Product Groups:** 20, 40, 62

Date of Accounts	Dec 11	Dec 10	Dec 09
Sales Turnover	19m	19m	21m
Pre Tax Profit/Loss	-940	2m	-235
Working Capital	4m	4m	2m
Fixed Assets	1m	2m	4m
Current Assets	10m	10m	9m
Current Liabilities	297	307	577

Superior Seals Ltd

East Dorset Trade Park 7 Nimrod Way, Wimborne, BH21 7SH
Tel: 01202-891180 **Fax:** 01202-894468
E-mail: sales@superiorltd.com
Website: http://www.superiorltd.com
Directors: M. Wallis (Fin), P. Barat (Sales & Mktg), T. Brown (Dir)
Managers: H. Griffiths (Personnel), V. Northcott (Buyer)
Ultimate Holding Company: SUPERIOR GROUP LIMITED
Immediate Holding Company: SUPERIOR SPECIALS LIMITED
Registration no: 02353516 **Date established:** 1989 **Turnover:** £5m - £10m
No.of Employees: 51 - 100 **Product Groups:** 29, 63

Date of Accounts	May 11	May 10	May 09
Sales Turnover	6m	5m	4m
Pre Tax Profit/Loss	714	478	144
Working Capital	2m	2m	2m
Fixed Assets	2m	2m	2m
Current Assets	5m	4m	3m
Current Liabilities	682	448	385

Techniflow Hand Driers Ltd

Unit 6a Uddens Trading Estate Wimborne Road West, Stape Hill, Wimborne, BH21 7LQ
Tel: 01202-870770 **Fax:** 01425-470167
E-mail: techniflow@btinternet.com
Website: http://www.handdriers.co.uk
Directors: P. Barker (Fin), E. Barker (MD)
Immediate Holding Company: HAND DRIERS LIMITED
Registration no: 04873015 **Date established:** 2003
No.of Employees: 1 - 10 **Product Groups:** 26, 36, 38, 40, 41, 42, 61, 64, 66, 83

Thermo Packs

Unit 70 Condor Close, Three Legged Cross, Wimborne, BH21 6SU
Tel: 01202-828277 **Fax:** 01202-826766
E-mail: sales@thermopacks.com
Website: http://www.thermopacks.com
Managers: F. Nally (Sales Prom Mgr)
Immediate Holding Company: THERMO PACKS SOUTHERN LIMITED
Registration no: 06193727 **VAT No.:** GB 619 6392 12
Date established: 2007 **Turnover:** Up to £250,000
No.of Employees: 1 - 10 **Product Groups:** 49

Date of Accounts	Mar 11	Mar 10	Mar 09
Working Capital	17	-32	-92
Fixed Assets	N/A	80	95
Current Assets	76	89	79

Total Laminate Systems Ltd

1 Nimrod Way East Dorset Trade Park, Wimborne, BH21 7SH
Tel: 01202-868900 **Fax:** 01202-861638
E-mail: sales@total-laminate.co.uk
Website: http://www.total-laminate.co.uk
Directors: J. Andrews (MD), J. Andrews (Prop)
Managers: C. Nunn (Sales Prom)
Ultimate Holding Company: TLS GROUP HOLDINGS LIMITED
Immediate Holding Company: TOTAL LAMINATE SYSTEMS LTD
Registration no: 02793768 **Date established:** 1993
Turnover: £10m - £20m **No.of Employees:** 51 - 100 **Product Groups:** 23, 25

Date of Accounts	Mar 11	Mar 10	Mar 09
Sales Turnover	13m	11m	12m
Pre Tax Profit/Loss	498	247	637
Working Capital	1m	1m	1m
Fixed Assets	310	383	496
Current Assets	4m	4m	4m
Current Liabilities	748	456	709

Universal Pipeline Controls Ltd

3 Cobham Road Ferndown Industrial Estate, Wimborne, BH21 7PE
Tel: 01202-896001 **Fax:** 01202-861900
E-mail: martinread@upcfiltration.co.uk
Website: http://www.upcfiltration.co.uk
Directors: M. Read (MD)
Immediate Holding Company: UNIVERSAL PIPELINE CONTROLS LIMITED
Registration no: 03993356 **Date established:** 2000
No.of Employees: 1 - 10 **Product Groups:** 38, 42

Date of Accounts	Sep 11	Sep 10	Sep 09
Working Capital	-75	-55	16
Fixed Assets	4	4	4
Current Assets	113	170	202

Vital Sines Ltd

16 Cedar Drive, Wimborne, BH21 2JH
Tel: 01202-887702 **Fax:** 01202-887702
E-mail: design@vitalsines.co.uk
Website: http://www.vitalsines.co.uk
Directors: P. Ramsey (MD)
Immediate Holding Company: VITAL SINES LIMITED
Registration no: 05568322 **Date established:** 2005
No.of Employees: 1 - 10 **Product Groups:** 84

Date of Accounts	Sep 11	Sep 10	Sep 09
Working Capital	1	-4	-3
Current Assets	11	N/A	1

West Pharmaservices Ltd

Gundrymoor Trading Estate Collingwood Road, West Moors, Wimborne, BH21 6QQ
Tel: 01202-870890 **Fax:** 01202-870873
E-mail: sales@westpharmaservices.co.uk
Website: http://www.westpharmaservices.co.uk
Directors: J. Jeffery (MD), S. Jeffery (Fin)
Immediate Holding Company: WEST PHARMASERVICES LIMITED
Registration no: 04017755 **Date established:** 2000
No.of Employees: 1 - 10 **Product Groups:** 38, 42

Date of Accounts	Jun 11	Jun 10	Jun 09
Working Capital	-79	-66	-83
Fixed Assets	276	231	231
Current Assets	178	73	76

P J White

Horton Heath Horton, Wimborne, BH21 7JP
Tel: 01202-822664
Directors: P. White (Prop)
Date established: 1977 **No.of Employees:** 1 - 10 **Product Groups:** 41

Wimborne Engineering

58 Cobham Road Ferndown Industrial Estate, Wimborne, BH21 7QH
Tel: 01202-893043
E-mail: knud@moldtechnik.co.uk
Website: http://www.moldtechnik.co.uk
Directors: K. Morgan (Prop)
Registration no: 02677151 **Turnover:** Up to £250,000
No.of Employees: 1 - 10 **Product Groups:** 42, 48

Wimborne Engraving

Unit 14a Mill Lane, Wimborne, BH21 1LN
Tel: 01202-886373 **Fax:** 01202-886373
Directors: K. Short (Prop)
Date established: 1979 **No.of Employees:** 1 - 10 **Product Groups:** 46, 48

DURHAM

Barnard Castle

Fillpack Ltd
Kenya Lodge Laneside, Middleton-in-Teesdale, Barnard Castle, DL12 0RY
Tel: 01833-640820 **Fax:** 01833-640237
E-mail: info@fillpack.co.uk
Website: http://www.fillpack.co.uk
Directors: L. Robinson (Fin), K. Robinson (MD)
Immediate Holding Company: FILLPACK LIMITED
Registration no: 03352779 **Date established:** 1997
No.of Employees: 1 - 10 **Product Groups:** 38, 42

Date of Accounts	Jul 11	Jul 10	Jul 09
Working Capital	1m	1m	1m
Fixed Assets	84	58	73
Current Assets	1m	1m	1m

S & A Fabrications
Harmire Enterprise Park, Barnard Castle, DL12 8EH
Tel: 01833-690379 **Fax:** 01833-690040
E-mail: g.simpson@s-and-a.co.uk
Website: http://www.s-and-a.co.uk
Directors: G. Simpson (Ptnr)
Ultimate Holding Company: SIMPSON & ALLINSON LIMITED
Immediate Holding Company: SIMPSON & ALLINSON LIMITED
Registration no: 03506452 **VAT No.:** GB 317 4694 42
Date established: 1998 **No.of Employees:** 21 - 50 **Product Groups:** 35, 66

Date of Accounts	Apr 11	Apr 10	Apr 09
Working Capital	687	614	492
Fixed Assets	749	801	785
Current Assets	2m	2m	2m
Current Liabilities	2m	N/A	N/A

Bishop Auckland

ACE Cleaning Equipment
Armond Carr Farm Tow Law, Bishop Auckland, DL13 4HH
Tel: 01388-731854 **Fax:** 01388-731854
E-mail: jacrammond@aol.com
Website: http://www.acecleaningequipment.com
Directors: J. Crammond (Prop)
No.of Employees: 1 - 10 **Product Groups:** 32, 40, 41, 46, 48, 52

Aptec Textiles Ltd
Darlington Road West Auckland, Bishop Auckland, DL14 9PD
Tel: 01388-832321 **Fax:** 01388-832200
E-mail: enquiries@aptecproducts.co.uk
Website: http://www.aptecproducts.co.uk
Directors: M. Wilcox (Fin), T. Robthan (MD)
Managers: K. Nelson (Buyer)
Immediate Holding Company: Automotive Products Group Ltd
Registration no: 03029115 **Turnover:** £2m - £5m
No.of Employees: 21 - 50 **Product Groups:** 43, 66

Date of Accounts	Dec 03
Sales Turnover	2438
Pre Tax Profit/Loss	29
Working Capital	469
Fixed Assets	807
Current Assets	836
Current Liabilities	367
Total Share Capital	5700
ROCE% (Return on Capital Employed)	2.3

B S & P Ltd
Unit 3a Hatfield Way Southchurch Enterprise Park, South Church Enterprise Park, Bishop Auckland, DL14 6XF
Tel: 01388-776666 **Fax:** 01388-776585
E-mail: n.peters@bs-p.co.uk
Website: http://www.bs-p.co.uk
Directors: N. Peters (MD)
Immediate Holding Company: BS&P LTD
Registration no: 06945131 **VAT No.:** GB 654 1974 17
Date established: 2009 **Turnover:** £250,000 - £500,000
No.of Employees: 1 - 10 **Product Groups:** 30, 35, 36, 45, 66

Date of Accounts	Jun 11	Jun 10
Sales Turnover	N/A	405
Pre Tax Profit/Loss	N/A	-14
Working Capital	-1	-19
Fixed Assets	6	6
Current Assets	106	131
Current Liabilities	N/A	71

Barkair Ltd
Auckland House 66 Kingsway, Bishop Auckland, DL14 7JF
Tel: 01388-607874 **Fax:** 01388-603050
E-mail: paulbarker@barkair.co.uk
Website: http://www.barkair.co.uk
Directors: P. Barker (Dir), M. Wilson (Sales)
Immediate Holding Company: BARKAIR LIMITED
Registration no: 06302556 **Date established:** 2007 **Turnover:** £2m - £5m
No.of Employees: 1 - 10 **Product Groups:** 36, 38, 40, 61, 84

Date of Accounts	Jul 10	Jul 09	Jul 08
Working Capital	-10	-14	N/A
Fixed Assets	12	16	N/A
Current Assets	131	54	17

Bonds Foundry Co. Ltd
North Road Tow Law, Bishop Auckland, DL13 4JS
Tel: 01388-730328 **Fax:** 01388-731034
E-mail: mike.best@bondsfoundry.com
Website: http://www.bondsfoundry.com
Directors: M. Best (MD)
Managers: B. Tinkler (Purch Mgr), S. Hind (Sales Eng), J. Machin, J. Carr (Fin Mgr)
Ultimate Holding Company: BONDS LIMITED
Immediate Holding Company: BONDS FOUNDRY COMPANY LIMITED
Registration no: 03968831 **VAT No.:** GB 257 5895 07
Date established: 2000 **Turnover:** £5m - £10m
No.of Employees: 51 - 100 **Product Groups:** 34

Date of Accounts	Sep 11	Sep 10	Sep 09
Sales Turnover	10m	8m	7m
Pre Tax Profit/Loss	576	472	477
Working Capital	1m	638	251
Fixed Assets	518	532	600
Current Assets	5m	4m	3m
Current Liabilities	3m	2m	1m

Brandon Hire plc
St Helen Way St Helen Auckland, Bishop Auckland, DL14 9AX
Tel: 01388-663085 **Fax:** 01388-607264
Website: http://www.brandonhire.co.uk
Managers: Smith (Mgr)
Ultimate Holding Company: BRANDON HIRE GROUP HOLDINGS LIMITED
Immediate Holding Company: BRANDON HIRE LIMITED
Registration no: 01008351 **Date established:** 1971
No.of Employees: 1 - 10 **Product Groups:** 35, 39, 45

Date of Accounts	Dec 11	Dec 10	Jul 09
Sales Turnover	75m	103m	87m
Pre Tax Profit/Loss	11m	7m	-28m
Working Capital	2m	-11m	-23m
Fixed Assets	27m	29m	37m
Current Assets	22m	21m	30m
Current Liabilities	7m	8m	10m

Castle Fencing Services
Newton Cap House Toronto, Bishop Auckland, DL14 7SB
Tel: 01388-450200 **Fax:** 01388-450200
E-mail: mick@castlefencing.fsbusiness.co.uk
Website: http://www.horse-shelters.com
No.of Employees: 1 - 10 **Product Groups:** 25, 35, 41, 52

Crosby Weighing Machine Services
Unit 1a Agl Business Park Coundon Industrial Estate, Coundon, Bishop Auckland, DL14 8NR
Tel: 01388-450623 **Fax:** 01388-450755
E-mail: enquiries@crosbyweighing.co.uk
Website: http://www.crosby-weighing.co.uk
Directors: P. Crosby (MD)
Immediate Holding Company: CROSBY WEIGHING LIMITED
Registration no: 07636842 **Date established:** 2011
No.of Employees: 1 - 10 **Product Groups:** 38, 42

Ebac (Dehumidifier/Industrial Division)
St Helen Trading Estate, Bishop Auckland, DL14 9AL
Tel: 01388-605061 **Fax:** 01388-609845
E-mail: info@ebac.com
Website: http://www.ebac.co.uk
Bank(s): HSBC Bank plc
Directors: A. Hird (Co Sec)
Ultimate Holding Company: EBAC GROUP LIMITED
Immediate Holding Company: EBAC LIMITED
Registration no: 01089991 **VAT No.:** GB 258 6233 42
Date established: 1973 **Turnover:** £10m - £20m
No.of Employees: 101 - 250 **Product Groups:** 40, 42, 43, 52

Date of Accounts	Dec 11	Dec 10	Dec 09
Sales Turnover	15m	13m	13m
Pre Tax Profit/Loss	167	872	3m
Working Capital	8m	6m	8m
Fixed Assets	2m	3m	4m
Current Assets	24m	23m	24m
Current Liabilities	871	961	780

Electrix International Ltd
1a-1b Dovecot Hill South Church Enterprise Park, Bishop Auckland, DL14 6XP
Tel: 01388-774455 **Fax:** 01388-777359
E-mail: malcolm@electrix.co.uk
Website: http://www.electrix.co.uk
Directors: C. Thompson (Chief Op Offcr), M. Thompson (MD), M. Craggs (Fin), D. Thompson (Co Sec)
Managers: H. Brown (Sales Admin), S. Beer (Factory Mgr)
Immediate Holding Company: ELECTRIX INTERNATIONAL LIMITED
Registration no: 01570249 **VAT No.:** GB 353 9980 12
Date established: 1981 **Turnover:** £5m - £10m
No.of Employees: 51 - 100 **Product Groups:** 35, 36, 37

Date of Accounts	Jan 12	Jan 11	Jan 10
Sales Turnover	7m	6m	5m
Pre Tax Profit/Loss	2m	2m	1m
Working Capital	1m	1m	832
Fixed Assets	3m	2m	3m
Current Assets	3m	3m	2m
Current Liabilities	505	616	559

G N P Equipment
44 Greenfields Road, Bishop Auckland, DL14 9TQ
Tel: 01388-665317 **Fax:** 01388-665317
E-mail: info@gnpequipment.co.uk
Website: http://www.gnpequipment.co.uk
Directors: T. Mattimoe (Prop)
Date established: 2000 **No.of Employees:** 1 - 10 **Product Groups:** 38, 42

Geological Engineering Ltd
Far Cornriggs Cowshill Upper Weardale, Cowshill, Bishop Auckland, DL13 1AF
Tel: 01388-537070 **Fax:** 01388-537070
Directors: P. Yates (MD)
Immediate Holding Company: GEOLOGICAL ENGINEERING LIMITED
Registration no: 05184387 **Date established:** 2004
Turnover: Up to £250,000 **No.of Employees:** 1 - 10 **Product Groups:** 84

Date of Accounts	Aug 11	Aug 10	Aug 09
Working Capital	-2	-6	1
Fixed Assets	2	2	3
Current Assets	28	21	22
Current Liabilities	N/A	20	17

Hercules Security Fabrications Ltd
Coundon Industrial Estate Coundon, Bishop Auckland, DL14 8NR
Tel: 01388-458794 **Fax:** 01388-458806
E-mail: info@hercules-security.co.uk
Website: http://www.hercules-security.co.uk
Directors: V. Golightly (MD)
Immediate Holding Company: HERCULES SECURITY FABRICATIONS LIMITED
Registration no: 01512302 **VAT No.:** GB 322 7700 81
Date established: 1980 **Turnover:** £1m - £2m **No.of Employees:** 1 - 10
Product Groups: 35

Date of Accounts	Nov 11	Nov 10	Nov 09
Working Capital	-320	-339	-359
Fixed Assets	2	3	4
Current Assets	48	124	69

Industrial Anodising Services
Unit 12-14 Nuns Close, South Church Enterprise Park, Bishop Auckland, DL14 6XD
Tel: 01388-774528 **Fax:** 01388-773093
E-mail: sales@almitgroup.co.uk
Website: http://www.almitgroup.co.uk
Directors: S. Mitchell (Dir)
Date established: 1998 **No.of Employees:** 1 - 10 **Product Groups:** 46, 48

L P C Elements Ltd
Coundon Industrial Estate Coundon, Bishop Auckland, DL14 8NR
Tel: 01388-608270 **Fax:** 01388-450048
E-mail: enquiries@lpcholdings.co.uk
Website: http://www.lpcholdings.co.uk
Managers: S. Thompson (Chief Mgr)
Immediate Holding Company: LPC HOLDINGS LIMITED
Registration no: 00232245 **VAT No.:** GB 226 5398 48
Date established: 2028 **Turnover:** £2m - £5m **No.of Employees:** 11 - 20
Product Groups: 37

Date of Accounts	Dec 10	Dec 09	Dec 08
Working Capital	716	790	771
Fixed Assets	N/A	7	7
Current Assets	791	896	872

Mechetronics Ltd
Hatfield Way South Church Enterprise Park, Bishop Auckland, DL14 6XF
Tel: 01388-771200 **Fax:** 01388-772490
E-mail: enquiries@mechetronics.co.uk
Website: http://www.mechetronics.co.uk
Bank(s): Lloyds
Directors: M. Wolfe (Ch), D. Sharp (MD)
Managers: G. Wright (Develop Mgr)
Ultimate Holding Company: CURTISS WRIGHT CORPORATION (U.S.A)
Immediate Holding Company: Mechetronics Holdings Ltd
Registration no: 02916339 **Date established:** 1994 **Turnover:** £5m - £10m
No.of Employees: 51 - 100 **Product Groups:** 30, 36, 37, 38, 39, 40, 67

Date of Accounts	Dec 09	Dec 08	Jul 07
Sales Turnover	4m	7m	N/A
Pre Tax Profit/Loss	-977	-267	N/A
Working Capital	-2m	597	838
Fixed Assets	30	193	210
Current Assets	851	2m	2m
Current Liabilities	17	409	N/A

Orbital Maintenance Services Ltd
56 Dene Hall Drive, Bishop Auckland, DL14 6UG
Tel: 01388-664464 **Fax:** 01388-664614
E-mail: sales@orbital.org.uk
Website: http://www.orbital.org.uk
Directors: C. Pickering (Fin), G. Pickering (MD)
Registration no: 05163901 **Turnover:** £250,000 - £500,000
No.of Employees: 1 - 10 **Product Groups:** 36, 38, 40

Robert Simpson
Hartford House 48 Darlington Road, West Auckland, Bishop Auckland, DL14 9HT
Tel: 01388-832380
E-mail: robsimpsonironwork@hotmail.co.uk
Directors: R. Simpson (Prop)
Date established: 1979 **No.of Employees:** 1 - 10 **Product Groups:** 26, 35

Smurfit Kappa West Auckland
Darlington Road West Auckland, Bishop Auckland, DL14 9PE
Tel: 01388-832531 **Fax:** 01388-833766
Website: http://www.smurfitkappa.com
Directors: A. Innes (Purch), J. Moody (Fin), N. Bagshaw (Sales), A. Burrows (Reg)
Managers: W. Brumley (Tech Serv Mgr), J. McDermott (Personnel)
Ultimate Holding Company: SMURFIT KAPPA PACKAGING LIMITED
Immediate Holding Company: SMURFIT CORRUGATED LIMITED
Registration no: 00675273 **Date established:** 1960
Turnover: £50m - £75m **No.of Employees:** 101 - 250 **Product Groups:** 27

Date of Accounts	Dec 99	Dec 98	Dec 97
Working Capital	12m	12m	12m
Current Assets	12m	12m	12m

Solaglas Ltd Solaglas Ltd (part of the Saint-Gobain group)
Catkin Way Greenfields Industrial Estate, Bishop Auckland, DL14 9TF
Tel: 01388-603667 **Fax:** 01388-600594
E-mail: solaglas.gpd@saint-gobain-glass.com
Website: http://www.saint-gobain.com
Bank(s): Lloyds TSB
Directors: J. Lawrenson (MD)
Ultimate Holding Company: COMPAGNIE DE SAINT GOBAIN (FRANCE)
Immediate Holding Company: GLASSOLUTIONS SAINT-GOBAIN LIMITED
Registration no: 02442570 **VAT No.:** GB 544 9390 18
Date established: 1989 **Turnover:** £10m - £20m
No.of Employees: 101 - 250 **Product Groups:** 33

Date of Accounts	Dec 11	Dec 10	Dec 09
Sales Turnover	116m	93m	97m
Pre Tax Profit/Loss	6m	-10m	-16m
Working Capital	-36m	-28m	-18m
Fixed Assets	23m	21m	15m
Current Assets	34m	33m	25m
Current Liabilities	64m	52m	15m

South Durham Structures
South Church Enterprise Park Dovecot Hill South Church Enterprise Park, Bishop Auckland, DL14 6XR
Tel: 01388-777350 **Fax:** 01388-775225
E-mail: contact@southdurhamstructures.co.uk
Website: http://www.south-durham-structures.co.uk
Bank(s): Barclays
Managers: D. Gregory (Sales Admin)
Immediate Holding Company: SOUTH DURHAM STRUCTURES LIMITED
Registration no: 01560481 **VAT No.:** GB 360 4760 62
Date established: 1981 **Turnover:** £1m - £2m **No.of Employees:** 21 - 50
Product Groups: 35, 51

Date of Accounts	May 11	May 10	May 09
Working Capital	200	196	291
Fixed Assets	805	825	831
Current Assets	867	835	737

Steel Pro Services Ltd
Unit 8 Longfield Road, South Church Enterprise Park, Bishop Auckland, DL14 6XB
Tel: 01388-776513
E-mail: enquiries@steelproservicesltd.co.uk
Website: http://www.steelproservicesltd.co.uk
Directors: E. Bruce (Dir)
Immediate Holding Company: STEELPRO SERVICES LIMITED
Registration no: 06070056 **Date established:** 2007
Turnover: £20m - £50m **No.of Employees:** 1 - 10 **Product Groups:** 46, 48

Date of Accounts	Mar 12	Mar 11	Mar 10
Working Capital	43	33	18
Fixed Assets	15	22	27
Current Assets	99	92	75

Tomlinson Longstaff Ltd
9 Chapel Street West Auckland, Bishop Auckland, DL14 9HP
Tel: 01388-833836 **Fax:** 01388-834593
E-mail: tony@tomlinsonlongstaff.co.uk
Website: http://www.themail.co.uk
Bank(s): HSBC Bank plc
Directors: A. Kirkup (MD), J. O Hare (Fin), J. O'Hare (Fin)
Immediate Holding Company: TOMLINSON LONGSTAFF LIMITED
Registration no: 01206464 **VAT No.:** GB 259 4337 34
Date established: 1975 **Turnover:** £1m - £2m **No.of Employees:** 11 - 20
Product Groups: 52

Date of Accounts	May 11	May 10	May 09
Working Capital	133	175	190
Fixed Assets	87	124	139
Current Assets	317	466	363

Wear Valley Aerosols
Unit 7 Hatfield Way South Church Enterprise Park, Bishop Auckland, DL14 6XF
Tel: 01388-772250 **Fax:** 01388-772263
E-mail: sales@gpaerosols.co.uk
Website: http://www.stevens-sis.co.uk
Managers: A. Douglas (Mgr)
Ultimate Holding Company: ROOSTER ENTERPRISES LIMITED
Immediate Holding Company: WV ASSOCIATES LIMITED
Registration no: 01798981 **Date established:** 1984
No.of Employees: 21 - 50 **Product Groups:** 35, 45

Date of Accounts	Mar 09	Mar 08	Apr 11
Working Capital	722	759	746
Fixed Assets	77	142	324
Current Assets	2m	2m	3m

Chester le Street

A E I Cables
Durham Road Birtley, Chester le Street, DH3 2RA
Tel: 0191-410 3111 **Fax:** 0191-410 8312
E-mail: info@aeicables.co.uk
Website: http://www.aeicables.co.uk
Directors: J. Duffy (Fin), M. Guel (Fin)
Managers: P. Hemsley (Buyer), N. Wallace (Tech Serv Mgr), N. Searle (I.T. Exec), K. Scott (Personnel), C. Sharp
Ultimate Holding Company: PARAMOUNT COMMUNICATIONS LIMITED
Immediate Holding Company: AEI CABLES LIMITED
Registration no: 06196375 **Date established:** 2007
Turnover: £50m - £75m **No.of Employees:** 11 - 20 **Product Groups:** 37

Date of Accounts	Aug 09	Aug 08	Mar 11
Sales Turnover	40m	56m	55m
Pre Tax Profit/Loss	-1m	4m	-3m
Working Capital	5m	7m	2m
Fixed Assets	445	471	385
Current Assets	21m	20m	23m
Current Liabilities	3m	12m	3m

Ace Microwave Services
20 Crathie Birtley, Chester le Street, DH3 1QJ
Tel: 0191-410 3326 **Fax:** 0191-410 3326
Directors: P. Clarke (Prop)
Date established: 1994 **No.of Employees:** 1 - 10 **Product Groups:** 36, 40

B A E Land Systems
George Street Birtley, Chester le Street, DH3 1QY
Tel: 0191-410 2241
Website: http://www.baesystems.com
Managers: L. Smurthwiatte (Mgr)
No.of Employees: 1 - 10 **Product Groups:** 36, 39, 40

Bradford Stalker
Ouston Bank Farm Birtley, Chester le Street, DH2 1BB
Tel: 0191-410 0565 **Fax:** 0191-410 8888
E-mail: contact@bradfordstalker.co.uk
Website: http://www.bradfordstalker.co.uk
Directors: P. Bradford (Prop)
Immediate Holding Company: BRADFORD STALKER LTD
Registration no: 04497749 **Date established:** 2002
No.of Employees: 1 - 10 **Product Groups:** 36, 39, 40

Date of Accounts	Sep 11	Sep 10	Sep 09
Working Capital	197	138	76
Fixed Assets	142	141	151
Current Assets	368	329	213

Carpet & Tiles Unlimited
2 Penshaw Way Birtley, Chester le Street, DH3 2SA
Tel: 0191-492 1500 **Fax:** 0191-492 1501
Website: http://brightfloors.co.uk
Directors: D. Bright (Snr Part)
No.of Employees: 1 - 10 **Product Groups:** 25, 30, 33

Chester-Le-Street Community Centre (Economic Development Service)
Newcastle Road, Chester le Street, DH3 3TS
Tel: 0191-388 4752 **Fax:** 0191-389 3058
E-mail: clscentre@fsmail.net
Website: http://www.clscommcentre.com
Directors: W. Stephenson (Grp Chief Exec)
Immediate Holding Company: CHESTER-LE-STREET CRICKET CLUB LIMITED
Registration no: 04173318 **Date established:** 2006
Turnover: Up to £250,000 **No.of Employees:** 1 - 10 **Product Groups:** 87

Date of Accounts	May 08	Nov 11	Nov 10
Working Capital	28	-56	-29
Fixed Assets	169	379	370
Current Assets	61	37	70

Hoofmark UK Ltd
Suite C Rickleton 2 Lambton Park, Chester le Street, DH3 4AN
Tel: 0191-385 3238 **Fax:** 0191-584 5577
E-mail: info@hoofmark.co.uk
Website: http://www.hoofmark.co.uk
Directors: P. Sykes (Dir), R. Sykes (Dir)
Managers: B. Scott (Sales Off Mgr)
Immediate Holding Company: HOOFMARK (U.K.) LIMITED
Registration no: 02990274 **Date established:** 1994
No.of Employees: 1 - 10 **Product Groups:** 30, 35, 42, 54

Date of Accounts	Jun 11	Jun 10	Jun 09
Working Capital	41	73	48
Fixed Assets	84	78	75
Current Assets	696	722	848

Hydro Aluminium Extrusion
Durham Road Birtley, Chester le Street, DH3 2AH
Tel: 0191-301 1200 **Fax:** 0191-301 1234
E-mail: sales@hydro.com
Website: http://www.hydro.com/extrusion/uk
Directors: P. Randle (Fin), C. Vitsch (MD), N. James (Sales)
Managers: G. Dougan (Personnel), T. Gifford (Mktg Serv Mgr), J. Norman (Contracts Mgr)
Ultimate Holding Company: NORSK HYDRO ASA
Immediate Holding Company: HYDRO ALUMINIUM GROUP
Registration no: 00961843 **Turnover:** £75m - £125m
No.of Employees: 101 - 250 **Product Groups:** 34, 46, 48, 84

Ibstock Building Products Ltd
Station Lane Birtley, Chester le Street, DH2 1AW
Tel: 0191-411 3900 **Fax:** 0191-492 0601
E-mail: rjohnson@ibstockbricks.co.uk
Website: http://www.ibstock.co.uk
Bank(s): National Westminster Bank Plc
Managers: R. Johnson (Factory Mgr)
Ultimate Holding Company: CRH PUBLIC LIMITED COMPANY
Immediate Holding Company: IBSTOCK BUILDING PRODUCTS LIMITED
Registration no: 00784339 **Date established:** 1963
Turnover: £75m - £125m **No.of Employees:** 21 - 50 **Product Groups:** 33, 66

Date of Accounts	Dec 11	Dec 10	Dec 09
Sales Turnover	3m	3m	2m
Pre Tax Profit/Loss	2m	7m	2m
Working Capital	22m	20m	16m
Fixed Assets	191m	191m	192m
Current Assets	22m	20m	16m

Jewson Ltd
Durham Road Birtley, Chester le Street, DH3 2QY
Tel: 0191-410 2522 **Fax:** 0191-410 3294
Website: http://www.jewson.co.uk
Managers: K. Brown (District Mgr)
Ultimate Holding Company: COMPAGNIE DE SAINT GOBAIN (FRANCE)
Immediate Holding Company: JEWSON LIMITED
Registration no: 00348407 **Date established:** 1939
Turnover: £500m - £1,000m **No.of Employees:** 11 - 20
Product Groups: 66

Date of Accounts	Dec 11	Dec 10	Dec 09
Sales Turnover	1606m	1547m	1485m
Pre Tax Profit/Loss	18m	100m	45m
Working Capital	-345m	-250m	-349m
Fixed Assets	496m	387m	461m
Current Assets	657m	1005m	1320m
Current Liabilities	66m	120m	64m

Keyline Builders Merchants
Station Lane Birtley, Chester le Street, DH2 1AW
Tel: 0191-410 2708 **Fax:** 0191-492 2104
E-mail: george.campbell@keyline.co.uk
Website: http://www.keyline.co.uk
Managers: G. Campbell (Mgr)
Ultimate Holding Company: COUPE GROUP LIMITED
Immediate Holding Company: COUPE CONSTRUCTION LIMITED
Registration no: 02711617 **Date established:** 1984 **Turnover:** £5m - £10m
No.of Employees: 1 - 10 **Product Groups:** 66

Date of Accounts	Apr 12	Apr 11	Apr 10
Sales Turnover	N/A	5m	8m
Pre Tax Profit/Loss	N/A	29	83
Working Capital	2m	2m	947
Fixed Assets	806	841	2m
Current Assets	2m	4m	3m
Current Liabilities	N/A	655	1m

Komatsu UK Ltd
Durham Road Birtley, Chester le Street, DH3 2QX
Tel: 0191-410 3155 **Fax:** 0191-410 8156
E-mail: enquiries@komatsuuk.com
Website: http://www.komatsuuk.com
Directors: P. Howe (Dir), S. Reid (Fin)
Ultimate Holding Company: KOMATSU LTD (JAPAN)
Immediate Holding Company: KOMATSU UK LIMITED
Registration no: 01948743 **VAT No.:** GB 440 9386 41
Date established: 1985 **Turnover:** £125m - £250m
No.of Employees: 251 - 500 **Product Groups:** 67, 83, 84

Date of Accounts	Mar 12	Mar 11	Mar 10
Sales Turnover	176m	115m	71m
Pre Tax Profit/Loss	5m	8m	-839
Working Capital	51m	55m	48m
Fixed Assets	13m	11m	13m
Current Assets	97m	83m	63m
Current Liabilities	14m	12m	10m

Magden P V C UK Products Ltd
Unit 26 Third Avenue Drum Industrial Estate, Chester Le Street, DH2 1AG
Tel: 0191-492 0042 **Fax:** 0191-492 0043
Website: http://www.magdenltd.com
Directors: A. Robinson (Dir)
No.of Employees: 1 - 10 **Product Groups:** 30, 66

Date of Accounts	May 11	May 10	May 09
Sales Turnover	8m	8m	8m
Pre Tax Profit/Loss	243	-282	-286
Working Capital	783	543	813
Fixed Assets	200	211	214
Current Assets	2m	2m	2m
Current Liabilities	402	384	214

Marian Engineering Ltd
Birtley Business Centre Station Lane Imex Business Centre, Birtley, Chester Le Street, DH3 1QT
Tel: 0191-410 2200 **Fax:** 0191-491 0891
E-mail: sales@mariandoors.co.uk
Website: http://www.mariandoors.co.uk

Directors: J. Mcdonnell (MD), S. McDonnell (Fin)
Immediate Holding Company: MARIAN ENGINEERING LIMITED
Registration no: 01369278 **VAT No.:** GB 322 6785 52
Date established: 1978 **Turnover:** £250,000 - £500,000
No.of Employees: 21 - 50 **Product Groups:** 35

Date of Accounts	Mar 12	Mar 11	Mar 10
Working Capital	357	322	302
Fixed Assets	79	77	89
Current Assets	771	638	690

Midland Steel Traders Ltd

Shadon Way Birtley, Chester le Street, DH3 2SW
Tel: 0191-410 5311 **Fax:** 0191-410 0482
E-mail: rw@msttracks.com
Website: http://www.msttracks.com
Directors: L. Whitehall (Fin), R. Whitehall (Sales & Mktg)
Managers: A. Clarke (Purch Mgr), G. Hall (Comptroller), C. Lamb (Chief Mgr)
Immediate Holding Company: MIDLAND STEEL TRADERS LIMITED,
Registration no: 00768729 **Date established:** 1963
Turnover: £10m - £20m **No.of Employees:** 101 - 250
Product Groups: 29, 45, 67

Date of Accounts	Mar 12	Mar 11	Mar 10
Sales Turnover	12m	12m	11m
Pre Tax Profit/Loss	129	146	550
Working Capital	537	502	324
Fixed Assets	726	923	1m
Current Assets	6m	6m	5m
Current Liabilities	623	721	534

Parker Dominick Hunter (Process Division)

Durham Road Birtley, Chester le Street, DH3 2SF
Tel: 0191-410 5121 **Fax:** 0191-410 4497
E-mail: dhprocess@parker.com
Website: http://www.domnickhunter.com
Directors: G. Ellinor (Co Sec), I. Molyneux (Dir)
Managers: S. Masters (Tech Serv Mgr), A. Nichols (Personnel), D. Smith, C. Roast (Sales Prom Mgr), D. Ridealgh (Mktg Serv Mgr), G. Bradford (Comptroller)
Ultimate Holding Company: PARKER HANNIFIN CORP (USA)
Immediate Holding Company: DOMNICK HUNTER GROUP LIMITED
Registration no: 02422827 **Date established:** 1989
No.of Employees: 251 - 500 **Product Groups:** 33, 34, 38, 40, 41, 42

Date of Accounts	Jun 11	Jun 10	Jun 09
Pre Tax Profit/Loss	N/A	149m	-11
Working Capital	8m	23m	3m
Fixed Assets	26m	26m	41m
Current Assets	21m	29m	8m

Peak Test Services

152a Front Street, Chester le Street, DH3 3AY
Tel: 0191-387 1923 **Fax:** 0191-387 1994
E-mail: f.nuttall@thepeakgroup.com
Website: http://www.thepeakgroup.com
Directors: F. Nuttall (Co Sec)
Immediate Holding Company: PEAK TEST SERVICES LIMITED
Registration no: 02303254 **VAT No.:** 514 6627 49 **Date established:** 1988
Turnover: £2m - £5m **No.of Employees:** 1 - 10 **Product Groups:** 38, 84

Date of Accounts	Aug 11	Aug 10	Aug 09
Working Capital	110	113	105
Fixed Assets	N/A	1	1
Current Assets	550	639	544

Rockwood Pigments

Birtley, Chester Le Street, DH3 1QX
Tel: 0191-410 2361 **Fax:** 0191-410 6005
E-mail: info@elementis.com
Website: http://www.rockwoodpigments.com
Bank(s): Nat West
Directors: R. Lysons (Fab)
Managers: H. Alprovich (Personnel)
Ultimate Holding Company: ELEMENTIS UK LTD
Immediate Holding Company: ELEMENTIS PLC
Registration no: 00656457 **VAT No.:** GB 317 4846 45
Turnover: £20m - £50m **No.of Employees:** 21 - 50 **Product Groups:** 31, 32, 42, 66

Simpson Brothers Tyneside Ltd

Drum Industrial Estate, Chester Le Street, DH2 1ST
Tel: 0191-492 4343 **Fax:** 0191-492 4345
E-mail: traffic@simpson-bros.co.uk
Website: http://www.simpson-bros.co.uk
Directors: G. Simpson (MD)
Managers: J. Stafford, T. Whiteman
Immediate Holding Company: SIMPSON BROS. (TYNESIDE) LIMITED
Registration no: 01492967 **Date established:** 1980
Turnover: £10m - £20m **No.of Employees:** 101 - 250 **Product Groups:** 77

Date of Accounts	Apr 11	Apr 10	Apr 09
Sales Turnover	12m	10m	N/A
Pre Tax Profit/Loss	162	252	225
Working Capital	-542	-456	-463
Fixed Assets	3m	3m	3m
Current Assets	3m	2m	2m
Current Liabilities	2m	1m	373

Stanley Towbar Centre

2 Station Road, Chester le Street, DH3 3DY
Tel: 0191-387 1422 **Fax:** 0191-387 1422
E-mail: sales@stanleytowbars.co.uk
Website: http://www.stanleytowbars.co.uk
Directors: B. Rowlands (Prop)
Date established: 1983 **Turnover:** Up to £250,000
No.of Employees: 1 - 10 **Product Groups:** 39

Steelcraft Ltd

Unit 2-6 Drum Industrial Estate, Chester Le Street, DH2 1AG
Tel: 0191-410 9996 **Fax:** 0191-410 9228
E-mail: sales@steelcraft.ltd.uk
Website: http://www.steelcraft.ltd.uk
Bank(s): Barclays
Directors: D. Armstrong (MD), J. Armstrong (Ch), M. Rodgers (Dir)
Immediate Holding Company: STEELCRAFT LIMITED
Registration no: 02339892 **VAT No.:** GB 514 6757 36
Date established: 1989 **Turnover:** £500,000 - £1m
No.of Employees: 21 - 50 **Product Groups:** 35, 49

Date of Accounts	Feb 12	Feb 11	Feb 10
Working Capital	255	297	164
Fixed Assets	116	108	200
Current Assets	501	486	469

Straughans

Hadrian House Front Street, Chester le Street, DH3 3DB
Tel: 0191-388 3377 **Fax:** 0191-387 1745
E-mail: mtait@straughans.co.uk
Website: http://www.straughans.co.uk
Directors: M. Tate (Snr Part), M. Tait (Fin)
Managers: P. Allon
Immediate Holding Company: STRAUGHANS LIMITED
Registration no: 03574727 **Date established:** 1998
No.of Employees: 21 - 50 **Product Groups:** 80

Date of Accounts	Mar 11	Mar 10	Mar 09
Working Capital	276	222	102
Fixed Assets	885	975	1m
Current Assets	440	416	368

Thermal Energy

1 Pinetree Centre Durham Road, Birtley, Chester le Street, DH3 2TD
Tel: 0191-492 1976 **Fax:** 0191-410 0916
Managers: B. Robinson (Mgr)
No.of Employees: 1 - 10 **Product Groups:** 40, 48

Tor Coatings Ltd

Shadon Way Birtley, Chester le Street, DH3 2RE
Tel: 0191-410 6611 **Fax:** 0191-492 0125
E-mail: enquiries@tor-coatings.com
Website: http://www.tor-coatings.com
Bank(s): Lloyds
Directors: C. Carter (Dir), P. Tompkins (Co Sec), S. Robson (Fin)
Managers: D. Kennedy (Purch Mgr), P. Waller (Mktg Serv Mgr)
Ultimate Holding Company: RPM INTERNATIONAL INC (USA)
Immediate Holding Company: TOR COATINGS LIMITED
Registration no: 04503854 **VAT No.:** GB 514 6241 71
Date established: 2002 **Turnover:** £20m - £50m
No.of Employees: 101 - 250 **Product Groups:** 32

Date of Accounts	May 12	May 11	May 10
Sales Turnover	28m	25m	20m
Pre Tax Profit/Loss	4m	4m	3m
Working Capital	9m	8m	6m
Fixed Assets	20m	20m	22m
Current Assets	21m	18m	12m
Current Liabilities	2m	3m	2m

Consett

A A Flags

Unit 4b Park Road Industrial Estate, Consett, DH8 5PY
Tel: 01207-582665 **Fax:** 01207-581560
E-mail: mandy@aaflags.co.uk
Website: http://www.aaflags.co.uk
Directors: R. Armstrong (Fin), A. Scott (Prop)
Immediate Holding Company: A A FLAGS LIMITED
Registration no: 03941647 **Date established:** 2000 **Turnover:** £2m - £5m
No.of Employees: 11 - 20 **Product Groups:** 49

Date of Accounts	Apr 11	Apr 10	Apr 09
Working Capital	188	133	283
Fixed Assets	183	188	6
Current Assets	260	196	323

Bescol Ltd

Delves Lane, Consett, DH8 7ES
Tel: 01207-582555 **Fax:** 01207-583951
E-mail: name@btconnect.com
Directors: P. Chapman (Dir)
Immediate Holding Company: BESCOL LIMITED
Registration no: 01806690 **VAT No.:** GB 532 6538 46
Date established: 1984 **Turnover:** £250,000 - £500,000
No.of Employees: 1 - 10 **Product Groups:** 30, 63, 66

Date of Accounts	Dec 11	Dec 10	Dec 09
Working Capital	-247	-282	-306
Fixed Assets	472	484	508
Current Assets	284	277	263
Current Liabilities	N/A	8	N/A

Consett Steel Services Ltd

Bradley Workshops, Consett, DH8 6HG
Tel: 01207-590171 **Fax:** 01207-592086
E-mail: sales@consett-steel.co.uk
Website: http://www.consett-steel.co.uk
Bank(s): HSBC Bank plc
Directors: A. Robinson (MD)
Managers: P. Chasney
Immediate Holding Company: CONSETT STEEL SERVICES LIMITED
Registration no: 02762751 **VAT No.:** GB 633 4223 67
Date established: 1992 **Turnover:** £2m - £5m **No.of Employees:** 11 - 20
Product Groups: 66

Date of Accounts	Sep 08
Working Capital	1
Current Assets	1

E C A Lifts

Unit 44 Derwentside Business Centre Consett Business Park, Villa Real, Consett, DH8 6BP
Tel: 08456-005215 **Fax:** 01207-508717
E-mail: info@ecalifts.co.uk
Website: http://www.ecalifts.co.uk
Directors: K. Lewcock (Dir)
No.of Employees: 1 - 10 **Product Groups:** 30, 39, 45

Electrak Holdings Ltd

Number One Industrial Estate Medomsley Road, Consett, DH8 6SR
Tel: 01207-503400 **Fax:** 01207-501799
E-mail: sales@electrak.co.uk
Website: http://www.electrak.co.uk
Bank(s): National Westminster Bank Plc
Directors: A. Greig (Dir), P. Swales (Sales), P. Middlemast (Fin), G. McCann (MD), J. McCann (MD)
Managers: E. Holden
Ultimate Holding Company: LEGRAND SA (FRANCE)
Immediate Holding Company: ELECTRAK OVERSEAS LIMITED
Registration no: 01569484 **VAT No.:** GB 318 3144 76
Date established: 1981 **Turnover:** £5m - £10m
No.of Employees: 51 - 100 **Product Groups:** 37, 38

Date of Accounts	Dec 10	Dec 09	Dec 08
Sales Turnover	N/A	N/A	10m
Pre Tax Profit/Loss	N/A	N/A	1m
Working Capital	3m	3m	3m
Current Assets	3m	3m	3m

Ionbond Ltd (a Berna Group Co.)

Factory 36 Number One Industrial Estate Medomsley Road, Consett, DH8 6TS
Tel: 01207-500823 **Fax:** 01207-590254
E-mail: info@ionbond.com
Website: http://www.ionbond.com
Directors: A. Frost (Comm)
Ultimate Holding Company: INDIGO TOPCO LIMITED
Immediate Holding Company: IONBOND UK LIMITED
Registration no: 01665506 **Date established:** 1982 **Turnover:** £2m - £5m
No.of Employees: 11 - 20 **Product Groups:** 48

Date of Accounts	Dec 11	Dec 10	Dec 09
Sales Turnover	3m	2m	2m
Pre Tax Profit/Loss	22	26	153
Working Capital	420	1m	1m
Fixed Assets	2m	902	1m
Current Assets	1m	1m	2m
Current Liabilities	270	199	170

Jewson Ltd

Knitsley Lane, Consett, DH8 7NN
Tel: 01207-504581 **Fax:** 01207-581447
Website: http://www.jewsonltd.com
Managers: E. Taylor (Mgr)
Ultimate Holding Company: COMPAGNIE DE SAINT GOBAIN (FRANCE)
Immediate Holding Company: JEWSON LIMITED
Registration no: 00348407 **VAT No.:** GB 497 7184 33
Date established: 1939 **Turnover:** £2m - £5m **No.of Employees:** 1 - 10
Product Groups: 66

Date of Accounts	Dec 11	Dec 10	Dec 09
Sales Turnover	1606m	1547m	1485m
Pre Tax Profit/Loss	18m	100m	45m
Working Capital	-345m	-250m	-349m
Fixed Assets	496m	387m	461m
Current Assets	657m	1005m	1320m
Current Liabilities	66m	120m	64m

K C Engineering Ltd

Hownsgill Drive, Consett, DH8 9HU
Tel: 01207-583100 **Fax:** 01207-581900
E-mail: miranda.lee@kceng.com
Website: http://www.kceng.com
Bank(s): HSBC Bank plc
Directors: M. Chester (Dir), K. Chester (MD), P. Chester (MD), J. Carr (Works), K. Chester (Grp Chief Exec)
Managers: M. Lee (Sales Admin)
Immediate Holding Company: K.C. ENGINEERING LIMITED
Registration no: 01675949 **VAT No.:** GB 369 0988 95
Date established: 1982 **Turnover:** £1m - £2m **No.of Employees:** 21 - 50
Product Groups: 35

Date of Accounts	Dec 10	Dec 09	Apr 09
Working Capital	-283	-352	-300
Fixed Assets	775	892	962
Current Assets	700	811	841

Lam Plas Durham Ltd

Castleside Industrial Estate, Consett, DH8 8JA
Tel: 01207-502474 **Fax:** 01207-500407
E-mail: k.siddle@lamplas.co.uk
Website: http://www.lamplas.co.uk
Bank(s): Barclays
Directors: J. Hamilton (Fin), K. Siddle (Fab)
Managers: M. Coulson (Purch Mgr), M. Gallagher (Develop Mgr)
Immediate Holding Company: LAM-PLAS (DURHAM) LIMITED
Registration no: 00997279 **VAT No.:** GB 176 7040 54
Date established: 1970 **Turnover:** £2m - £5m **No.of Employees:** 21 - 50
Product Groups: 39

Date of Accounts	Sep 11	Sep 10	Sep 09
Working Capital	567	547	176
Fixed Assets	733	710	754
Current Assets	1m	1m	1m

M I S

Eden House Watling Street, Consett, DH8 6TA
Tel: 01207-500463 **Fax:** 01603-633844
E-mail: info@mis-environmental.co.uk
Website: http://www.mis-environmental.co.uk
Bank(s): Lloyds
Managers: J. Madrell, A. Nairn (Chief Mgr), B. Gilespie (Mktg Serv Mgr), G. Kirby (Tech Serv Mgr), M. Hunter (Cr Control)
Immediate Holding Company: MIS MECHANICAL LIMITED
Registration no: 06712173 **VAT No.:** 334 7800 58 **Date established:** 2008
Turnover: £1m - £2m **No.of Employees:** 21 - 50 **Product Groups:** 85

Date of Accounts	Nov 11	Nov 10	Nov 09
Working Capital	282	210	73
Fixed Assets	385	411	429
Current Assets	1m	1m	820

Merc Millipore (Bio Process Division)

Unit 31 Number One Industrial Estate, Consett, DH8 6SZ
Tel: 01207-581555 **Fax:** 01207-500944
E-mail: lesley_wallace@millipore.com
Website: http://www.millipore.com
Bank(s): HSBC
Managers: L. Wallace (Ops Mgr)
Ultimate Holding Company: BIOPROCESSING CORP LTD
Registration no: 01658867 **VAT No.:** GB 369 0619 29
Date established: 2001 **No.of Employees:** 21 - 50 **Product Groups:** 63

Metaltech Ltd

Unit 1-5 Hownsgill Drive, Consett, DH8 9HU
Tel: 01207-500937 **Fax:** 01207-580743
E-mail: rs@metaltech.co.uk
Website: http://www.metaltech.co.uk
Directors: G. Foster (MD)
Immediate Holding Company: METALTECH SERVICES LIMITED
Registration no: 01803148 **VAT No.:** GB 353 9656 21
Date established: 1984 **Turnover:** £500,000 - £1m
No.of Employees: 1 - 10 **Product Groups:** 48, 81, 84

Date of Accounts	Jun 11	Jun 10	Jun 09
Working Capital	29	31	16
Fixed Assets	25	6	3
Current Assets	46	35	16

Paul & Loughran Ltd
Unit 2 Number One Industrial Estate, Consett, DH8 6SR
Tel: 01207-507237 **Fax:** 01207-590140
E-mail: jburrell@paul-loughran.com
Website: http://www.paul-loughran.com
Directors: L. Burrell (Fin), J. Burrell (Dir)
Immediate Holding Company: PAUL AND LOUGHRAN LIMITED
Registration no: 01359089 **VAT No.:** GB 322 6024 03
Date established: 1978 **No.of Employees:** 11 - 20 **Product Groups:** 35, 40, 42, 48

Date of Accounts	Mar 12	Mar 11	Mar 10
Working Capital	1m	1m	1m
Fixed Assets	20	46	63
Current Assets	2m	2m	2m

Persuasion PR
38 Derwentside Business Centre Consett Business Park, Villa Real, Consett, DH8 6BP
Tel: 0845-0710678 **Fax:** 0191-214 0240
E-mail: paul.dobbie@persuasion-pr.com
Website: http://www.persuasion-pr.com
Directors: P. Dobbie (MD), J. Cowell (Dir)
Registration no: 04878594 **VAT No.:** GB 569 5698 63
Date established: 1994 **Turnover:** Up to £250,000
No.of Employees: 1 - 10 **Product Groups:** 81

Phileas Fogg
Unit 46 Number One Industrial Estate, Consett, DH8 6TX
Tel: 01207-580999 **Fax:** 01207-580970
Website: http://www.unitedbiscuits.com
Directors: A. Blidman (Dir)
Managers: P. Hinsley (Comptroller), P. Gland (Personnel), J. O'Leary
Immediate Holding Company: UNITED BISCUITS
No.of Employees: 101 - 250 **Product Groups:** 51, 52, 80, 84

R S Conveyors
4 G Industrial Estate Park Road North, Blackhill, Consett, DH8 5UN
Tel: 01207-591453 **Fax:** 01207-504274
E-mail: curryrsconveyors@aol.com
Website: http://www.rsconveyors.com
Directors: R. Curry (Prop)
Turnover: Up to £250,000 **No.of Employees:** 1 - 10 **Product Groups:** 35, 45, 47

Rand Rocket Ltd
Abcare House Hownsgill Industrial Park Knitsley Lane, Consett, DH8 7NU
Tel: 01207-591099 **Fax:** 01207-591098
E-mail: sales@rand-rocket.co.uk
Website: http://www.randrocket.com
Directors: D. Vickers (MD)
Immediate Holding Company: RAND ROCKET LIMITED
Registration no: 02086506 **VAT No.:** GB 335 1534 77
Date established: 1986 **Turnover:** £2m - £5m **No.of Employees:** 1 - 10
Product Groups: 31, 32, 33, 36, 38, 49

Date of Accounts	Mar 11	Mar 10	Mar 09
Working Capital	248	280	315
Fixed Assets	11	1	2
Current Assets	1m	1m	1m
Current Liabilities	N/A	N/A	287

Roberts Forge Lift Ltd
1 C Park Road Industrial Estate, Consett, DH8 5PY
Tel: 01207-590163 **Fax:** 01207-591600
E-mail: robertsdm@btconnect.com
Website: http://www.robertsforgelift.co.uk
Directors: D. Roberts (MD)
Immediate Holding Company: ROBERTS FORGE-LIFT LIMITED
Registration no: 01805283 **VAT No.:** GB 407 9524 41
Date established: 1984 **Turnover:** Up to £250,000
No.of Employees: 1 - 10 **Product Groups:** 35, 36, 45, 48

Date of Accounts	Dec 11	Dec 10	Dec 09
Sales Turnover	N/A	210	287
Pre Tax Profit/Loss	N/A	-5	16
Working Capital	23	22	51
Fixed Assets	2	3	4
Current Assets	61	57	88
Current Liabilities	N/A	11	12

Romag Ltd
Leadgate Industrial Estate, Consett, DH8 7RN
Tel: 01207-500000 **Fax:** 01207-591979
E-mail: info@romag.co.uk
Website: http://www.romag.co.uk
Bank(s): Lloyds TSB Bank plc
Directors: K. Morrison (Sales), P. Murray (MD)
Managers: F. Robson (Purch Mgr), T. Scott, J. Ross, L. Sloan (Personnel)
Ultimate Holding Company: ROMAG HOLDINGS PLC
Immediate Holding Company: ROM REALISATIONS LIMITED
Registration no: 01549869 **VAT No.:** GB 532 6128 65
Date established: 1981 **Turnover:** £10m - £20m
No.of Employees: 101 - 250 **Product Groups:** 33, 35, 37, 40, 44

Date of Accounts	Sep 09	Sep 08	Sep 07
Sales Turnover	20m	34m	17m
Pre Tax Profit/Loss	1m	4m	3m
Working Capital	7m	14m	5m
Fixed Assets	28m	26m	24m
Current Assets	24m	20m	16m
Current Liabilities	458	1m	989

Thomas Swan & Co. Ltd
Rotary Way, Consett, DH8 7ND
Tel: 01207-505131 **Fax:** 01207-590467
E-mail: sales@thomas-swan.co.uk
Website: http://www.thomas-swan.co.uk
Bank(s): Midland Bank
Directors: D. Cavet (Fin)
Managers: D. Thorpe, M. Davison (Tech Serv Mgr)
Immediate Holding Company: THOMAS SWAN & CO.LIMITED
Registration no: 00210794 **VAT No.:** GB 532 6071 68
Date established: 2025 **Turnover:** £20m - £50m
No.of Employees: 101 - 250 **Product Groups:** 31, 32

Date of Accounts	Mar 11	Mar 10	Mar 09
Sales Turnover	24m	21m	18m
Pre Tax Profit/Loss	1m	2m	-908
Working Capital	7m	6m	2m
Fixed Assets	5m	5m	7m
Current Assets	11m	10m	6m
Current Liabilities	2m	1m	2m

Winsund Intrenational Limited
Priory Farm Muggleswick, Consett, DH8 9DW
Tel: 01207-255365 **Fax:** 01207-255683
E-mail: info@winsund.com
Website: http://www.winsund.com
Directors: M. Seeley (MD), M. Seely (Dir)
Immediate Holding Company: Hugh Jennings Ltd
Registration no: 04135693 **VAT No.:** GB 425 9671 26
Date established: 2001 **Turnover:** £1m - £2m **No.of Employees:** 1 - 10
Product Groups: 37

Crook

Blue Teal Tackle & Guns
20 High Grange, Crook, DL15 8AS
Tel: 01388-766263
Directors: J. Dodd (Ptnr)
Date established: 1982 **No.of Employees:** 1 - 10 **Product Groups:** 36, 39, 40

Colourfast Decorating - French Polish
Prospect Terrace Willington, Crook, DL15 0DT
Tel: 07971-980927
E-mail: info@colourfastdecorating.co.uk
Website: http://www.colourfastdecorating.co.uk/
Managers: I. Ahmad (Mgr)
Date established: 1985 **Turnover:** Up to £250,000
No.of Employees: 11 - 20 **Product Groups:** 26

E S P Plastics Ltd
Prospect Road, Crook, DL15 8JL
Tel: 01388-765400 **Fax:** 01388-765300
E-mail: operations@esp-plastics.co.uk
Website: http://www.esp-plastics.co.uk
Directors: A. Freeman (Chief Op Offcr), T. Smith (Co Sec), P. Ritson (Dir)
Immediate Holding Company: E.S.P. PLASTICS LTD
Registration no: 01877977 **Date established:** 1985 **Turnover:** £1m - £2m
No.of Employees: 11 - 20 **Product Groups:** 24, 26, 30, 39, 40, 42, 48, 49, 66

Date of Accounts	Mar 11	Mar 10	Mar 09
Working Capital	47	-7	-30
Fixed Assets	212	237	273
Current Assets	440	357	365

Darlington

A M P Consultants
Morton House Morton Road, Darlington, DL1 4PT
Tel: 01325-481941 **Fax:** 01325-366930
E-mail: admin@ampconsultants.com
Website: http://www.ampconsultants.com
Directors: D. Hodson (Dir), M. Harding (Co Sec)
Immediate Holding Company: AMP (NORTH EAST) LIMITED
Registration no: 00705164 **Date established:** 1992
Turnover: £10m - £20m **No.of Employees:** 1 - 10 **Product Groups:** 35

Date of Accounts	Aug 11	Aug 10	Aug 09
Sales Turnover	7m	9m	11m
Pre Tax Profit/Loss	316	617	-780
Working Capital	3m	3m	2m
Fixed Assets	672	766	783
Current Assets	4m	4m	6m
Current Liabilities	660	987	3m

Amdega Ltd
Faverdale Industrial Estate, Darlington, DL3 0PW
Tel: 01325-468522 **Fax:** 01325-489209
E-mail: info@amdega.co.uk
Website: http://www.amdega.co.uk
Bank(s): Barclays, Newcastle
Directors: C. Redfern (Chief Op Offcr), C. Taylor (MD), M. Willink (Chief Op Offcr), L. Robson (Co Sec)
Managers: G. Sutton (Sales Prom Mgr), L. Skoropinski (I.T. Exec), P. Craig (Personnel), W. Wilkinson (Purch Mgr)
Immediate Holding Company: AMDEGA LIMITED
Registration no: 03367115 **Date established:** 1997
Turnover: £10m - £20m **No.of Employees:** 101 - 250
Product Groups: 25, 36

Date of Accounts	Sep 09	Dec 08	Dec 07
Sales Turnover	16m	27m	29m
Pre Tax Profit/Loss	74	-997	41
Working Capital	-4m	-4m	-3m
Fixed Assets	6m	6m	6m
Current Assets	6m	6m	7m
Current Liabilities	8m	9m	8m

Bowes & Raine
15 Edward Street Industrial Estate, Darlington, DL1 2UP
Tel: 01325-288071
Directors: L. Raine (Prop)
Date established: 1984 **No.of Employees:** 1 - 10 **Product Groups:** 41

Breedon & Gell
200 Back Haughton Road, Darlington, DL1 2PH
Tel: 01325-381088 **Fax:** 01325-381088
Website: http://www.dieseldarlington1.fsnet.co.uk
Directors: J. Gell (Ptnr)
Date established: 1976 **No.of Employees:** 1 - 10 **Product Groups:** 40

C G Fixings Ltd
Morton Park Way, Darlington, DL1 4PJ
Tel: 01325-462299 **Fax:** 01325-460949
E-mail: chris@cgfixings.co.uk
Website: http://www.cgfixings.co.uk
Directors: C. Guy (MD)
Immediate Holding Company: C.G. FIXINGS LIMITED
Registration no: 04666779 **Date established:** 2003
No.of Employees: 1 - 10 **Product Groups:** 26, 30, 32, 35, 36, 37, 41, 42, 46, 66, 67, 83

Date of Accounts	Mar 12	Mar 11	Mar 10
Working Capital	-10	-18	-38
Fixed Assets	139	135	138
Current Assets	230	231	172

Coats Ltd
Lingfield House Lingfield Point, Darlington, DL1 1YJ
Tel: 08456-030150 **Fax:** 08702-431855
E-mail: consumer.services@coats.com
Website: http://www.coats.com
Directors: D. McMillan (Chief Op Offcr)
Managers: H. Lewis (Mktg Serv Mgr), D. Shaffer (Mktg Serv Mgr)
Ultimate Holding Company: COATS VIYELLA P.L.C.
Immediate Holding Company: COATS EUROPE
Registration no: 00516691 **VAT No.:** GB 556 7662 02
Turnover: £20m - £50m **No.of Employees:** 1 - 10 **Product Groups:** 23, 80

The Coffee Machine Company
8 The Woodlands Millbank Road, Darlington, DL3 9UB
Tel: 01325-461215
E-mail: sarduno@ntlworld.com
Website: http://www.rancilio.it
Managers: A. Pala (Mgr)
No.of Employees: 1 - 10 **Product Groups:** 40, 67

The Consumer Council For Water
Northgate House St Augustines Way, Darlington, DL1 1XA
Tel: 01325-464222 **Fax:** 01325-369269
E-mail: yorkshire@ccwater.org.uk
Website: http://www.ccwater.org.uk
Managers: D. Freeman (Asst Gen Mgr), D. Beattie (Mgr), L. Walker (District Mgr)
Registration no: 04673100 **Date established:** 2002
Turnover: Up to £250,000 **No.of Employees:** 1 - 10 **Product Groups:** 84

Crete Text Systems (Lauder Paving)
Unit 1 Nestfield Industrial Estate, Darlington, DL1 2NW
Tel: 01325-360269 **Fax:** 01325-362348
E-mail: sales@ukpavingservices.co.uk
Website: http://www.cretetextsystems.co.uk
Directors: A. Lauder (Prop)
Turnover: Up to £250,000 **No.of Employees:** 1 - 10 **Product Groups:** 32, 51, 52, 83

Cummins
Yarm Road, Darlington, DL1 4PW
Tel: 01325-556000 **Fax:** 01325-359380
E-mail: mike.d.mccabe@cummins.com
Website: http://www.cummins.com
Directors: J. Herrington (Pers)
Managers: R. Osbaldestone (Purch Mgr), A. Robson (Comptroller), D. Mcmenamin (Plant), S. Clapham (Tech Serv Mgr), S. Nendick
Ultimate Holding Company: CUMMINS INC (USA)
Immediate Holding Company: CUMMINS LTD.
Registration no: 00573951 **Date established:** 1956
Turnover: Over £1,000m **No.of Employees:** 501 - 1000
Product Groups: 40

Date of Accounts	Dec 11	Dec 10	Dec 09
Sales Turnover	1886m	1374m	802m
Pre Tax Profit/Loss	377m	239m	89m
Working Capital	443m	220m	336m
Fixed Assets	250m	234m	75m
Current Assets	1104m	683m	676m
Current Liabilities	239m	67m	26m

D F L Material Handling Ltd
Unit 5-8 St Nicholas Industrial Estate, Darlington, DL1 2NL
Tel: 01325-483104 **Fax:** 01325-483104
Directors: D. Render (Dir)
Immediate Holding Company: DFL MATERIALS HANDLING LIMITED
Registration no: 02986901 **Date established:** 1994
No.of Employees: 1 - 10 **Product Groups:** 35, 39, 45

Date of Accounts	Nov 11	Nov 10	Nov 09
Working Capital	76	90	64
Fixed Assets	66	65	65
Current Assets	126	143	119

Epcot Leisure Ltd
Unit 1 Whessoe Road, Darlington, DL3 0QP
Tel: 01325-366666
E-mail: sales@epcotleisure.com
Website: http://www.epcotleisure.com
Directors: L. Curtain (MD)
Managers: J. Binks (Chief Mgr)
Ultimate Holding Company: RED DOT LEISURE LIMITED
Immediate Holding Company: EPCOT LEISURE LIMITED
Registration no: 01971564 **Date established:** 1985
No.of Employees: 1 - 10 **Product Groups:** 36, 40

Date of Accounts	Dec 11	Dec 10	Dec 09
Working Capital	45	68	106
Fixed Assets	204	195	166
Current Assets	109	118	143

Ernest Bennett & Co Darlington Ltd
Aviation Way Durham Tees Valley Airport, Darlington, DL2 1NA
Tel: 01325-332656 **Fax:** 01325-333137
E-mail: david@ernestbennett.co.uk
Website: http://www.ernestbennett.co.uk
Bank(s): HSBC Bank plc
Directors: D. Maxey (MD), S. Maxey (Fin)
Immediate Holding Company: PARAGON RAPID TECHNOLOGIES LTD
Registration no: 00822990 **VAT No.:** GB 257 6516 36
Date established: 2003 **Turnover:** £1m - £2m **No.of Employees:** 21 - 50
Product Groups: 37, 41

Date of Accounts	Jul 11	Jul 10	Jul 09
Working Capital	552	371	253
Fixed Assets	84	100	116
Current Assets	994	775	502

European Process Equipment Ltd
PO Box 336, Darlington, DL3 8WD
Tel: 01325-353539 **Fax:** 01325-460878
E-mail: sales@epe-ltd.com
Website: http://www.epe-ltd.com
Directors: M. Bruffell (MD), L. Ross Bruffell (Co Sec)
Immediate Holding Company: EUROPEAN PROCESS EQUIPMENT LIMITED
Registration no: 03099026 **Date established:** 1995
No.of Employees: 1 - 10 **Product Groups:** 38, 42

Date of Accounts	Jan 11	Jan 10	Jan 09
Working Capital	56	111	112
Fixed Assets	7	8	17

Current Assets	179	198	171

F P E Ltd (Fluid Power)

2 Kellaw Road, Darlington, DL1 4YA
Tel: 01325-282732 **Fax:** 01325-381815
E-mail: sales@fpe-ltd.co.uk
Website: http://www.fpe-ltd.co.uk
Managers: H. Kelly (Sales & Mktg Mg), C. Hickson (Buyer), S. Harrison
Ultimate Holding Company: DIPLOMA PLC
Immediate Holding Company: FPE LIMITED
Registration no: 03725829 **Date established:** 1999 **Turnover:** £5m - £10m
No.of Employees: 21 - 50 **Product Groups:** 29, 30, 33, 36, 37, 39, 40, 48

Date of Accounts	Sep 11	Sep 10	Sep 09
Sales Turnover	5m	4m	3m
Pre Tax Profit/Loss	1m	1m	826
Working Capital	2m	2m	3m
Fixed Assets	744	837	745
Current Assets	3m	3m	3m
Current Liabilities	486	371	296

Farmway Ltd

Cock Lane Piercebridge, Darlington, DL2 3TJ
Tel: 01325-504600 **Fax:** 01325-374094
E-mail: k.shaw@farmway.co.uk
Website: http://www.farmway.co.uk
Bank(s): Barclays
Managers: J. Richardson (Fin Mgr), K. Shaw (Chief Buyer), S. Champbers (Tech Serv Mgr), C. Gibson (Mktg Serv Mgr), H. Forbes (Personnel)
Immediate Holding Company: FARMWAY MACHINERY LIMITED
Registration no: 03275563 **VAT No.:** GB 258 4954 16
Date established: 1996 **No.of Employees:** 51 - 100 **Product Groups:** 84

Glen Office Supplies Ltd

Unit 3 Faverdale Industrial Estate, Darlington, DL3 0PP
Tel: 01325-382020 **Fax:** 01325-380988
E-mail: sales@glenoffice.co.uk
Website: http://www.glenofficesupplies.co.uk
Managers: M. Glen (Sales Admin)
Immediate Holding Company: GLEN OFFICE SUPPLIES LIMITED
Registration no: 05388654 **Date established:** 2005
No.of Employees: 1 - 10 **Product Groups:** 27, 44, 61

Date of Accounts	Dec 11	Dec 10	Dec 09
Working Capital	163	224	253
Fixed Assets	47	60	76
Current Assets	301	355	424

Granada Architectural Aluminium

Unit 2 Lakeland Estate Business Park Faverdale North, Darlington, DL3 0PH
Tel: 01325-355351 **Fax:** 01325-353428
E-mail: nigel.bainbridge@granada-aluminium.co.uk
Website: http://www.granada-aluminium.co.uk
Directors: N. Bainbridge (MD)
Immediate Holding Company: GRANADA ALUMINIUM (HOLDINGS) LIMITED
Registration no: 01371854 **Date established:** 1978
No.of Employees: 11 - 20 **Product Groups:** 26, 35

Date of Accounts	Sep 08	Sep 07	Sep 06
Working Capital	23	-6	-25
Fixed Assets	29	34	40
Current Assets	340	403	362

Heinzmann UK Ltd

Durham Tees Valley Airport, Darlington, DL2 1PD
Tel: 01325-332805 **Fax:** 01325-333631
E-mail: info@heinzmannuk.com
Website: http://www.heinzmann.de
Managers: C. Shore (Chief Mgr)
Ultimate Holding Company: FRITZ HEINZMANN GMBH & CO (GERMANY)
Immediate Holding Company: HEINZMANN UK LIMITED
Registration no: 01777894 **Date established:** 1983
No.of Employees: 11 - 20 **Product Groups:** 37, 38, 40

Date of Accounts	Dec 11	Dec 10	Dec 09
Working Capital	2m	2m	2m
Fixed Assets	236	244	249
Current Assets	3m	4m	3m

Ironworld

Eastmount Road, Darlington, DL1 1LE
Tel: 01325-488095 **Fax:** 01325-482224
E-mail: ironworldmandy@yahoo.co.uk
Website: http://www.ironworld.co.uk
Directors: A. Petch (Ptnr), M. Potts (Ptnr)
Registration no: 04865178 **Date established:** 2003
No.of Employees: 1 - 10 **Product Groups:** 26, 35

Jewson Ltd

Valley Street North, Darlington, DL1 1LF
Tel: 01325-356141 **Fax:** 01325-351249
E-mail: graeme.wilson@jewson.co.uk
Website: http://www.jewson.co.uk
Bank(s): Barclays
Managers: G. Wilson (District Mgr)
Ultimate Holding Company: COMPAGNIE DE SAINT GOBAIN (FRANCE)
Immediate Holding Company: JEWSON LIMITED
Registration no: 00348407 **Date established:** 1939
Turnover: £500m - £1,000m **No.of Employees:** 21 - 50
Product Groups: 66

Date of Accounts	Dec 11	Dec 10	Dec 09
Sales Turnover	1606m	1547m	1485m
Pre Tax Profit/Loss	18m	100m	45m
Working Capital	-345m	-250m	-349m
Fixed Assets	496m	387m	461m
Current Assets	657m	1005m	1320m
Current Liabilities	66m	120m	64m

M C Products Ironcraft

Home Farm Cliffe Piercebridge, Darlington, DL2 3SS
Tel: 01325-374676
E-mail: info@mcproductsironcraft.co.uk
Website: http://www.mcproductsironcraft.co.uk
Directors: D. Magill (Ptnr)
Date established: 1976 **No.of Employees:** 1 - 10 **Product Groups:** 26, 35

M Machine

Unit 6 Forge Way, Darlington, DL1 2PJ
Tel: 01325-381300 **Fax:** 01325-381300
E-mail: sales@m-machine.co.uk
Website: http://www.m-machine.co.uk
Directors: D. Myers (Prop)
No.of Employees: 1 - 10 **Product Groups:** 36, 39, 48

Mech Tool Engineering Ltd

Whessoe Road, Darlington, DL3 0QT
Tel: 01325-355141 **Fax:** 01325-487053
E-mail: mail@mechtool.co.uk
Website: http://www.mechtool.co.uk
Bank(s): National Westminster Bank Plc
Directors: K. Bell (MD), J. Swain (Fin), J. Swain (Fin)
Managers: P. Lacey (Tech Serv Mgr), J. Banham (Chief Buyer), M. Camp (Develop Mgr)
Immediate Holding Company: MECH-TOOL ENGINEERING LIMITED
Registration no: 04087377 **VAT No.:** GB 340 8052 83
Date established: 2000 **Turnover:** £10m - £20m
No.of Employees: 101 - 250 **Product Groups:** 37, 38, 40, 52, 54

Date of Accounts	Mar 12	Mar 11	Mar 10
Sales Turnover	16m	14m	16m
Pre Tax Profit/Loss	606	501	507
Working Capital	2m	828	973
Fixed Assets	1m	1m	847
Current Assets	6m	6m	5m
Current Liabilities	2m	2m	1m

N S Hygiene

Unit 21 Nestfield Industrial Estate, Darlington, DL1 2NW
Tel: 01325-364616 **Fax:** 01325-362025
E-mail: daniel.ogilvie@nshygiene.fsbusiness.co.uk
Website: http://www.nshygiene.fsbusiness.co.uk
Directors: S. Ogilvie (Fin), N. Ogilvie (MD)
Immediate Holding Company: N.S. HYGIENE LIMITED
Registration no: 04593711 **Date established:** 2002
Turnover: £250,000 - £500,000 **No.of Employees:** 1 - 10
Product Groups: 27, 30

Date of Accounts	Dec 10	Dec 09	Dec 08
Working Capital	3	-0	-2
Fixed Assets	6	9	13
Current Assets	73	74	76

Neville Pybus Associates

19 Neville Road, Darlington, DL3 8HZ
Tel: 01325-269627 **Fax:** 01325-269627
E-mail: neville-pybus@ntlworld.com
Directors: N. Pybus (Prop)
Date established: 2000 **No.of Employees:** 1 - 10 **Product Groups:** 37

News Quest Yorkshire & North Eeast Ltd

Priestgate, Darlington, DL1 1NF
Tel: 01325-381313 **Fax:** 01325-486222
E-mail: tracey.dowson@nne.co.uk
Website: http://www.nothernecho.co.uk
Bank(s): Lloyds TSB Bank plc
Directors: D. Coates (MD), D. Brown (MD), A. Brown (Fin)
Managers: D. Kelly (Mgr), D. Frankland, P. Masheder (Sales & Mktg Mg), S. Tailor (Publishing), T. Dowson
Immediate Holding Company: THE MEDIA FACTORY LIMITED
Registration no: 03000664 **VAT No.:** GB 667 8301 08
Date established: 1994 **Turnover:** £20m - £50m
No.of Employees: 101 - 250 **Product Groups:** 28

Date of Accounts	Dec 07	Dec 06	Dec 05
Sales Turnover	25087	24958	25508
Pre Tax Profit/Loss	8171	8702	9117
Working Capital	11869	12004	14504
Fixed Assets	48562	48619	48863
Current Assets	13674	16105	18503
Current Liabilities	1805	4101	3999
ROCE% (Return on Capital Employed)	13.5	14.4	14.4
ROT% (Return on Turnover)	32.6	34.9	35.7

T Norman Civil Engineering Services

Royal Oak Works Royal Oak, Heighington, Darlington, DL2 2UJ
Tel: 01388-833338
Directors: T. Norman (Prop)
Date established: 1985 **No.of Employees:** 1 - 10 **Product Groups:** 35

Northgate Vehicle Hire Ltd

Norflex House Allington Way, Darlington, DL1 4DY
Tel: 01325-467558 **Fax:** 01325-381009
E-mail: marketing@northgateplc.com
Website: http://www.northgateonline.co.uk
Bank(s): The Royal Bank of Scotland
Directors: J. Piers (Mkt Research), J. Smith (Tech Serv), M. Bertrand (Pers)
Managers: C. Gould (Mktg Serv Mgr)
Ultimate Holding Company: NORTHGATE PLC
Immediate Holding Company: NORTHGATE VEHICLE HIRE LIMITED
Registration no: 01434157 **Date established:** 1979
Turnover: £250m - £500m **No.of Employees:** 101 - 250
Product Groups: 72

Date of Accounts	Apr 11	Apr 10	Apr 09
Sales Turnover	307m	301m	411m
Pre Tax Profit/Loss	88m	56m	-60m
Working Capital	114m	78m	42m
Fixed Assets	499m	472m	462m
Current Assets	192m	152m	111m
Current Liabilities	23m	33m	25m

Robin Finnegan

27 Post House Wynd, Darlington, DL3 7LP
Tel: 01325-489820 **Fax:** 01325-357674
E-mail: diamondmerchants@btopenworld.com
Website: http://www.militarybadges.co.uk
Directors: R. Finnegan (Prop)
No.of Employees: 1 - 10 **Product Groups:** 23, 24, 49

Ruck Engineering

Kellaw Road, Darlington, DL1 4YA
Tel: 01325-286081 **Fax:** 01325-480722
E-mail: sales@ruckengineering.co.uk
Website: http://www.ruckengineering.co.uk
Directors: S. Ruck (Prop)
Immediate Holding Company: C. P. OFFSET LIMITED
Registration no: 01011151 **Date established:** 1971 **Turnover:** £1m - £2m
No.of Employees: 11 - 20 **Product Groups:** 35, 40, 46, 47, 52

Date of Accounts	Sep 07	Sep 06	Sep 05
Sales Turnover	1m	1m	1m
Pre Tax Profit/Loss	-57	-60	3
Working Capital	-10	24	114
Fixed Assets	296	338	383
Current Assets	287	270	380
Current Liabilities	84	60	85

S W Ironcraft

Unit 4 Drinkfield Business Park, Darlington, DL3 0RY
Tel: 01325-485589 **Fax:** 01325-247411
E-mail: swelshgates@aol.com
Website: http://www.swironcraft.co.uk
Directors: S. Welch (Prop), S. Welsh (Prop)
Date established: 1999 **No.of Employees:** 1 - 10 **Product Groups:** 26, 35

Sherwoods Darlington Ltd

Chesnut Street, Darlington, DL1 1RJ
Tel: 01325-466155 **Fax:** 01325-376030
E-mail: amac@sherwoods-vauxhall.co.uk
Website: http://www.sherwoodsgroup.co.uk
Bank(s): Barclays
Directors: A. Macconachie (MD)
Ultimate Holding Company: GENERAL MOTORS CORP (USA)
Immediate Holding Company: SHERWOODS (DARLINGTON) LIMITED
Registration no: 02876229 **VAT No.:** GB 633 2385 51
Date established: 1993 **Turnover:** £20m - £50m
No.of Employees: 51 - 100 **Product Groups:** 68

Date of Accounts	Dec 11	Dec 10	Dec 09
Sales Turnover	51m	50m	45m
Pre Tax Profit/Loss	205	362	377
Working Capital	408	509	679
Fixed Assets	4m	4m	4m
Current Assets	10m	9m	9m
Current Liabilities	746	1m	920

Tees Valley Fire Protection Ltd

Unit 5 Nestfield Industrial Estate, Darlington, DL1 2NW
Tel: 01325-365555 **Fax:** 01325-365555
Website: http://www.teesvalleyfire.com
Directors: M. Clegg (Dir)
Immediate Holding Company: TEES VALLEY FIRE PROTECTION LIMITED
Registration no: 03031291 **Date established:** 1995
No.of Employees: 1 - 10 **Product Groups:** 38, 42

Date of Accounts	Mar 11	Mar 10	Mar 08
Working Capital	-3	2	28
Fixed Assets	5	6	7
Current Assets	32	29	46

Whessoe Oil & Gas Ltd

Whessoe Technology Centre Morton Palms, Darlington, DL1 4WB
Tel: 01325-390000 **Fax:** 01325-390001
E-mail: wilf.mcnaughton@whessoe.co.uk
Website: http://www.whessoe.co.uk
Managers: W. Mcnaughton (Chief Mgr)
Ultimate Holding Company: AL RUSHAID INVESTMENT CO LTD (SAUDI ARABIA)
Immediate Holding Company: WHESSOE OIL & GAS LIMITED
Registration no: 05081024 **VAT No.:** GB 378 4031 42
Date established: 2004 **Turnover:** £2m - £5m **No.of Employees:** 51 - 100
Product Groups: 42, 45, 48

Date of Accounts	Dec 10	Dec 09	Dec 08
Sales Turnover	4m	11m	72m
Pre Tax Profit/Loss	11	797	4m
Working Capital	8m	8m	2m
Fixed Assets	40	69	876
Current Assets	16m	20m	21m
Current Liabilities	2m	7m	15m

Henry Williams Darlington Ltd

Dodsworth Street, Darlington, DL1 2NJ
Tel: 01325-462722 **Fax:** 01325-381744
E-mail: sales@hwilliams.co.uk
Website: http://www.hwilliams.co.uk
Bank(s): National Westminster Bank Plc
Directors: D. Neil (Fin), P. Knowles (Fin)
Managers: J. Whitney (Project Eng), W. Mallett (Personnel), S. Marriott, L. Smith (Purch Mgr), B. Blareau (Sales Prom Mgr), B. Blareau (Sales Prom Mgr)
Ultimate Holding Company: CON MECH GROUP LIMITED
Immediate Holding Company: HENRY WILLIAMS LIMITED
Registration no: 02326847 **VAT No.:** GB 499 5051 03
Date established: 1988 **Turnover:** £5m - £10m
No.of Employees: 51 - 100 **Product Groups:** 34, 35, 37, 38, 39, 48, 51, 52

Date of Accounts	Dec 11	Dec 10	Dec 09
Sales Turnover	9m	8m	7m
Pre Tax Profit/Loss	666	555	178
Working Capital	2m	1m	713
Fixed Assets	2m	2m	2m
Current Assets	4m	3m	3m
Current Liabilities	492	653	808

Yorkshire Storage Systems Ltd

Edelweiss West Lane, Dalton on Tees, Darlington, DL2 2PP
Tel: 01325-378621 **Fax:** 01325-378705
Directors: A. Wilkinson (MD), A. Wilkinson (Fin)
Immediate Holding Company: YORKSHIRE STORAGE SYSTEMS LIMITED
Registration no: 01736045 **Date established:** 1983
No.of Employees: 1 - 10 **Product Groups:** 41

Date of Accounts	Sep 11	Sep 10	Sep 09
Working Capital	126	-11	-24
Fixed Assets	55	43	44
Current Assets	769	82	83

Durham

Barbican Armoury

Brancepeth Castle Brancepeth, Durham, DH7 8DE
Tel: 0191-378 2880 **Fax:** 0191-378 2880
Directors: L. Tully (Prop)
Date established: 1985 **No.of Employees:** 1 - 10 **Product Groups:** 36, 39, 40

C D S Security Ltd

8-9 Dragonville Industrial Park Dragon Lane, Durham, DH1 2XH
Tel: 0191-384 0079 **Fax:** 0191-384 0071
Website: http://www.cdssecurity.co.uk

see next page

C D S Security Ltd - Cont'd
Directors: S. Dunn (Dir), S. Northcote (Dir), E. Dunn (Dir)
Ultimate Holding Company: CDS SECURITY & FIRE LIMITED
Immediate Holding Company: C.D.S. SECURITY LIMITED
Registration no: 02621153 **Date established:** 1991
No.of Employees: 21 - 50 **Product Groups:** 36, 37, 40, 52

Date of Accounts	Jul 11	Jul 10	Jul 09
Working Capital	68	60	65
Fixed Assets	8	8	11
Current Assets	486	500	363

Cathedral Pallet Trucks Ltd
Damson House Damson Way, Dragonville, Durham, DH1 2YN
Tel: 0191-383 0456 **Fax:** 0191-383 9736
E-mail: sales@cathedralpallettrucks.co.uk
Website: http://www.pallettrucks.tv
Directors: P. Trott (MD), S. Trott (Fin)
Immediate Holding Company: CATHEDRAL PALLET TRUCKS LIMITED
Registration no: 03190391 **Date established:** 1996
No.of Employees: 1 - 10 **Product Groups:** 35, 39, 45

Date of Accounts	Apr 11	Apr 10	Apr 09
Working Capital	206	98	173
Fixed Assets	43	51	49
Current Assets	426	344	317

Durham Flooring
45 Brackendale Road, Durham, DH1 2AB
Tel: 0191-384 7447 **Fax:** 0191-384 7447
E-mail: sam@durhamflooring.co.uk
Website: http://www.durhamflooring.co.uk
Directors: S. Watson (Ptnr)
Date established: 2002 **Turnover:** Up to £250,000
No.of Employees: 1 - 10 **Product Groups:** 23, 30, 33, 66

Durham Pumps Ltd
Unit 23a Damson Way, Dragonville, Durham, DH1 2XL
Tel: 0191-383 2472 **Fax:** 0191-383 1638
E-mail: mark-jones@durhampumps.co.uk
Website: http://www.durhampumps.co.uk
Directors: M. Jones (MD)
Immediate Holding Company: DURHAM PUMPS LIMITED
Registration no: 04263652 **Date established:** 2001
No.of Employees: 1 - 10 **Product Groups:** 39, 40, 42, 43, 45, 46, 48, 49, 54, 67, 68, 83, 84

Date of Accounts	Aug 11	Aug 10	Aug 09
Working Capital	25	17	35
Fixed Assets	11	12	5
Current Assets	192	156	158

Elliott Hire
Bowburn South Industrial Estate Bowburn, Durham, DH6 5AD
Tel: 0191-377 8788 **Fax:** 0191-377 8770
E-mail: info@elliotthire.co.uk
Website: http://www.elliotthire.co.uk
Directors: P. Blake (Dir)
Immediate Holding Company: ELLIOTT GROUP HOLDINGS (UK) LIMITED
Registration no: 06344129 **Date established:** 2007
Turnover: Up to £250,000 **No.of Employees:** 11 - 20 **Product Groups:** 35, 39

Date of Accounts	Dec 10	Dec 09	Dec 08
Pre Tax Profit/Loss	-26m	-30m	-228m
Working Capital	-1m	-56m	-6m
Fixed Assets	403m	456m	456m
Current Assets	6m	6m	4m
Current Liabilities	5m	846	2m

Food Technologists
55 Moor Crescent, Durham, DH1 1DA
Tel: 0191-386 6401
E-mail: info@food-technologists.co.uk
Website: http://www.food-technologists.co.uk
Directors: K. Driver (Prop)
Date established: 1992 **Turnover:** Up to £250,000
No.of Employees: 1 - 10 **Product Groups:** 80

Harrison & Harrison Ltd
St Johns Road Meadowfield, Durham, DH7 8YH
Tel: 0191-378 2222 **Fax:** 0191-378 3388
E-mail: h.h@btinternet.com
Website: http://www.harrisorgans.co.uk
Bank(s): National Westminster Bank Plc
Directors: C. Batchelor (MD), J. Conlon (Co Sec)
Managers: N. Radford (Admin Off)
Immediate Holding Company: HARRISON & HARRISON LIMITED
Registration no: 00351508 **VAT No.:** GB 175 9439 19
Date established: 1939 **Turnover:** £500,000 - £1m
No.of Employees: 21 - 50 **Product Groups:** 49

Date of Accounts	Dec 11	Dec 10	Dec 09
Working Capital	225	252	230
Fixed Assets	996	946	973
Current Assets	1m	1m	1m

P C Henderson Ltd
Unit 1 Durham Road, Bowburn, Durham, DH6 5NG
Tel: 0191-377 0701 **Fax:** 0191-377 1309
E-mail: sales@pchenderson.com
Website: http://www.pchenderson.com
Directors: D. Moncrieff (Dir), D. Moncreiff (MD), D. Moncreiss (MD)
Managers: A. Collins (Tech Serv Mgr), M. Lumsden (Purch Mgr), G. Smith (Mktg Serv Mgr)
Ultimate Holding Company: CARDO AB (SWEDEN)
Immediate Holding Company: P.C. HENDERSON LIMITED
Registration no: 01188468 **Date established:** 1974 **Turnover:** £5m - £10m
No.of Employees: 51 - 100 **Product Groups:** 25, 30, 35, 36, 37

Date of Accounts	Dec 11	Dec 10	Dec 09
Sales Turnover	8m	8m	7m
Pre Tax Profit/Loss	950	437	-231
Working Capital	2m	1m	847
Fixed Assets	4m	4m	4m
Current Assets	4m	5m	3m
Current Liabilities	354	3m	549

International Marine Survey
Abbey Road Business Centre Abbey Road, Durham, DH1 5JZ
Tel: 0191-645 0095
E-mail: info@internationalmarinesurvey.com
Website: http://Internationalmarinesurvey.com
Managers: K. farthing (Consultant)
Date established: 2008 **No.of Employees:** 1 - 10 **Product Groups:** 74

J H P Training Ltd (J H P Training)
4-5 North Road, Durham, DH1 4SH
Tel: 0191-383 9958 **Fax:** 0191- 3866212
Website: http://www.jhptraining.com
Directors: S. Williams (MD), W. Sheppard (Prop)
Immediate Holding Company: JHP TRAINING LIMITED
Registration no: 03247918 **Date established:** 1996
No.of Employees: 1 - 10 **Product Groups:** 86

N J C Wrought Iron
16 Springwell Avenue Langley Park, Durham, DH7 9XT
Tel: 0191-373 9714
Directors: N. Cassidy (Prop)
Date established: 2002 **No.of Employees:** 1 - 10 **Product Groups:** 26, 35

Nation Wide Platforms
Damson Way Dragonville, Durham, DH1 2YN
Tel: 0191-384 7227 **Fax:** 0191-383 9297
E-mail: durham@nationwideplatforms.co.uk
Website: http://www.nationwideplatforms.co.uk
Managers: G. Stephenson (Depot Mgr)
Immediate Holding Company: Lavendon Group P.L.C.
Registration no: 02268921 **Turnover:** £20m - £50m
No.of Employees: 11 - 20 **Product Groups:** 45, 83

Date of Accounts	Apr 11	Apr 10	Apr 09
Working Capital	206	98	173
Fixed Assets	43	51	49
Current Assets	426	344	317

Ness Furniture Ltd
Croxdale, Durham, DH6 5HT
Tel: 01388-816109 **Fax:** 01388-812416
E-mail: johnwilliams@nessfurniture.co.uk
Website: http://www.nessfurniture.co.uk
Bank(s): Barclays
Directors: J. Williams (MD), R. Sugden (Co Sec)
Ultimate Holding Company: NEW EQUIPMENT HOLDINGS LIMITED
Immediate Holding Company: NESS FURNITURE LIMITED
Registration no: 00402191 **VAT No.:** GB 408 0162 88
Date established: 1945 **Turnover:** £5m - £10m
No.of Employees: 101 - 250 **Product Groups:** 67

Date of Accounts	Dec 11	Dec 10	Dec 09
Sales Turnover	9m	11m	6m
Pre Tax Profit/Loss	20	501	68
Working Capital	4m	4m	3m
Fixed Assets	1m	1m	1m
Current Assets	8m	9m	7m
Current Liabilities	870	1m	494

North East Assemblies Ltd
The Works Station Road, Ushaw Moor, Durham, DH7 7QA
Tel: 0191-373 6000 **Fax:** 0191-373 7000
E-mail: enquiries@nea.co.uk
Website: http://www.nea.co.uk
Bank(s): Lloyds TSB Bank plc
Directors: J. Smith (MD), S. Smith (Fin)
Immediate Holding Company: NORTH EAST ASSEMBLIES LIMITED
Registration no: 03042648 **VAT No.:** GB 633 5826 32
Date established: 1995 **No.of Employees:** 11 - 20 **Product Groups:** 35, 42, 48, 66

Date of Accounts	Sep 11	Sep 10	Sep 09
Working Capital	38	8	-22
Fixed Assets	153	174	35
Current Assets	180	238	165

North East Mobility Warehouse
Unit 1-5 Front Street Industrial Estate Front Street, South Hetton, Durham, DH6 2UZ
Tel: 0191-520 8880 **Fax:** 0191-520 8814
E-mail: sales@northeastmob.com
Website: http://www.northeastmob.com
Directors: I. Morrell (MD)
Immediate Holding Company: THE NORTH EAST MOBILITY WAREHOUSE LTD
Registration no: 04933414 **Date established:** 2003
No.of Employees: 1 - 10 **Product Groups:** 26, 37, 39

Date of Accounts	Sep 11	Sep 10	Sep 09
Working Capital	-109	-116	-113
Fixed Assets	48	32	34
Current Assets	100	72	67

P H S Datashred Ltd
Rennys Lane, Durham, DH1 2RW
Tel: 0800-376 4422 **Fax:** 0191-370 9850
E-mail: info@phs.co.uk
Website: http://www.shredding.info
Managers: R. Tucker (Depot Mgr)
Registration no: 00770813 **No.of Employees:** 11 - 20 **Product Groups:** 44

P S I Global Ltd
Bowburn South Industrial Estate Bowburn, Durham, DH6 5AD
Tel: 0191-377 7000 **Fax:** 0191-377 0769
E-mail: sales@psiglobal.co.uk
Website: http://www.psiglobal.co.uk
Directors: D. Hunter (Co Sec), S. Hunter (Dir)
Managers: M. Kay (Buyer)
Immediate Holding Company: PSI GLOBAL LTD
Registration no: 01252181 **VAT No.:** GB 017 0113 70
Date established: 1976 **Turnover:** £2m - £5m **No.of Employees:** 21 - 50
Product Groups: 67

Date of Accounts	Apr 11	Apr 09	Apr 08
Working Capital	543	244	457
Fixed Assets	1m	993	922
Current Assets	2m	2m	2m

Persimmon
Charles Church House Bowburn North Industrial Estate, Bowburn, Durham, DH6 5PF
Tel: 0191-377 4000 **Fax:** 0191-377 4001
E-mail: reception.ccne@charleschurch.com
Website: http://www.persimmonhomes.com
Directors: N. Foster (MD), C. Cooper (Sales)
Managers: A. Hill (Purch Mgr), M. Tilford (Chief Acct)
Ultimate Holding Company: VESTBROWN LIMITED
Immediate Holding Company: ESH DEVELOPMENTS LIMITED
Registration no: 05022849 **Date established:** 1993
No.of Employees: 21 - 50 **Product Groups:** 52

Date of Accounts	Dec 10	Dec 09	Dec 08
Sales Turnover	23m	13m	22m
Pre Tax Profit/Loss	-4m	-6m	-12m
Working Capital	31m	-12m	-7m
Fixed Assets	141	221	462
Current Assets	34m	45m	62m
Current Liabilities	1m	1m	2m

Red Strawberry Solutions Ltd
9 Wesley Terrace Chester Le Street, Durham, DH3 3EJ
Tel: 0844-8700517 **Fax:** 0844-8700518
E-mail: sales@redstrawberry.co.uk
Website: http://www.redstrawberry.co.uk
Registration no: 07490857 **Product Groups:** 23, 35, 49

S M S Fabweld
Colliery Road Bearpark, Durham, DH7 7AU
Tel: 0191-383 9833 **Fax:** 0191-383 9833
Directors: S. Shippen (Prop)
Immediate Holding Company: ELVET SCIENTIFIC LIMITED
Registration no: 01355607 **Date established:** 1983
No.of Employees: 1 - 10 **Product Groups:** 35

Date of Accounts	Mar 11	Mar 10	Mar 08
Working Capital	10	10	27
Current Assets	16	16	49
Current Liabilities	N/A	N/A	23

Sagittarian Embroidery
27 Durham Road Sacriston, Durham, DH7 6LN
Tel: 0191-371 9371 **Fax:** 0191-371 2288
E-mail: sagittarianemb@clara.co.uk
Website: http://www.sagemb.co.uk
Directors: A. Willis (Fin), K. Willis (Dir)
Immediate Holding Company: SAGITTARIAN EMBROIDERY LIMITED
Registration no: 03565911 **VAT No.:** GB 605 6711 53
Date established: 1998 **Turnover:** Up to £250,000
No.of Employees: 1 - 10 **Product Groups:** 23

Tarmac Topblock Ltd (Eastern)
Littleburn Industrial Estate Langley Moor, Durham, DH7 8HJ
Tel: 0191-378 0406 **Fax:** 0191-378 2160
E-mail: enquiries@tarmac.co.uk
Website: http://www.topblock.co.uk
Managers: W. Hinet (I.T. Exec)
Immediate Holding Company: TARMAC TOPBLOCK LIMITED
Registration no: 03224202 **Date established:** 1996
Turnover: £20m - £50m **No.of Employees:** 11 - 20 **Product Groups:** 33

Travis Perkins plc
Dragon Lane Gilsgate Moor, Durham, DH1 2XD
Tel: 0191-386 0060 **Fax:** 0191-386 2713
Website: http://www.travisperkins.co.uk
Bank(s): HSBC
Managers: N. Lowes (District Mgr)
Immediate Holding Company: TRAVIS PERKINS PLC
Registration no: 00824821 **VAT No.:** GB 456 5069 30
Date established: 1964 **No.of Employees:** 11 - 20 **Product Groups:** 08, 25, 26, 66

Date of Accounts	Dec 11	Dec 10	Dec 09
Sales Turnover	4779m	3153m	2931m
Pre Tax Profit/Loss	270m	197m	213m
Working Capital	133m	159m	248m
Fixed Assets	2771m	2749m	2108m
Current Assets	1421m	1329m	1035m
Current Liabilities	473m	412m	109m

Ferryhill

H J Banks & Co. Ltd (The Banks Group Ltd)
Thrislington Indl-Est West Cornforth, Ferryhill, DL17 9EU
Tel: 01740-651915 **Fax:** 01740-658520
Website: http://www.hjbanks.com
Bank(s): HSBC Bank plc
Directors: D. Martin (Co Sec), J. Dickenson (Dir), J. Banks (Ch), J. Banks (Prop), H. Banks (MD)
Managers: N. Brown (Sales Prom Mgr), K. Farrow (Mktg Serv Mgr), A. Sherwen (I.T. Exec)
Immediate Holding Company: BANKS RENEWABLES (CROFT HILL WIND FARM) LIMITED
Registration no: 02903354 **VAT No.:** GB 569 3236 14
Date established: 2010 **Turnover:** £10m - £20m
No.of Employees: 101 - 250 **Product Groups:** 51, 66, 80

Cater Tech
Unit 1d Dean & Chapter Industrial Estate, Ferryhill, DL17 8LN
Tel: 01740-650777 **Fax:** 01740-650888
Website: http://www.cater-tech.co.uk
Directors: T. Dartnall (Prop)
Immediate Holding Company: CATERTECH (NORTH EAST) LIMITED
Registration no: 06486159 **Date established:** 2008
No.of Employees: 1 - 10 **Product Groups:** 20, 40, 41

Express Motor Factors
48 North Street, Ferryhill, DL17 8HX
Tel: 01740-652926 **Fax:** 01740-655113
E-mail: expressmotorfactors@fsmail.net
Managers: A. Ratcliffe (Mgr)
Immediate Holding Company: EXPRESS MOTOR FACTORS(NE) LTD
Registration no: 05197458 **VAT No.:** GB 317 4343 71
Date established: 2004 **No.of Employees:** 1 - 10 **Product Groups:** 39

Date of Accounts	Sep 10	Sep 09	Sep 08
Working Capital	-10	-6	-21
Fixed Assets	18	21	26
Current Assets	76	67	88

Metal Drum
Denebridge Chilton, Ferryhill, DL17 0NU
Tel: 01388-720391 **Fax:** 01388-721880
E-mail: sales@metal-drum.co.uk
Website: http://www.metal-drum.co.uk

Directors: J. Britton (MD)
Managers: J. Sheppard (Sales & Mktg Mg)
Ultimate Holding Company: METAL DRUM COMPANY LIMITED(THE)
Immediate Holding Company: METAL DRUM COMPANY LIMITED(THE)
Registration no: 00703681 **Date established:** 1961 **Turnover:** £5m - £10m
No.of Employees: 21 - 50 **Product Groups:** 35, 85

Date of Accounts	May 11	May 10	May 09
Pre Tax Profit/Loss	806	271	68
Working Capital	3m	2m	2m
Fixed Assets	2m	2m	2m
Current Assets	5m	4m	4m
Current Liabilities	795	579	511

Parnaby Cyclones International Ltd

Avenue One Chilton, Ferryhill, DL17 0SH
Tel: 01388-720849 **Fax:** 01388-721415
E-mail: enquiries@parnaby.co.uk
Website: http://www.parnaby.co.uk
Bank(s): Barclays
Directors: K. Parnaby (Co Sec), A. Parnaby (MD), P. Telford (Dir), P. Lerigo (Dir)
Managers: J. Walton (Purch Mgr)
Immediate Holding Company: DEREK PARNABY CYCLONES INTERNATIONAL LIMITED
Registration no: 01124062 **VAT No.:** GB 259 4281 35
Date established: 1973 **Turnover:** £5m - £10m
No.of Employees: 51 - 100 **Product Groups:** 42, 45

Date of Accounts	Sep 11	Sep 10	Sep 09
Sales Turnover	20m	9m	10m
Pre Tax Profit/Loss	7m	1m	2m
Working Capital	9m	4m	3m
Fixed Assets	1m	1m	1m
Current Assets	14m	7m	5m
Current Liabilities	3m	1m	612

Newton Aycliffe

A P O Materials Management Ltd

PO Box 11, Newton Aycliffe, DL5 6YD
Tel: 01325-301594 **Fax:** 01325-307461
E-mail: info@apomgt.co.uk
Website: http://www.apomgt.co.uk
Directors: C. Cruddace (Fin)
Immediate Holding Company: APO MATERIALS MANAGEMENT LIMITED
Registration no: 02426961 **Date established:** 1989
Turnover: Up to £250,000 **No.of Employees:** 1 - 10 **Product Groups:** 86

Date of Accounts	Apr 12	Apr 11	Apr 10
Working Capital	25	16	71
Fixed Assets	8	9	13
Current Assets	280	351	304

A S V Vehicle Systems

Calibration House Ketton Way, Aycliffe Business Park, Newton Aycliffe, DL5 6SG
Tel: 01325-319943 **Fax:** 01325-320077
E-mail: ashley.meson@vehiclesystems.org.uk
Website: http://www.vehiclesystems.org.uk
Directors: A. Meson (Prop)
Managers: A. Meson (Sales Prom Mgr)
Immediate Holding Company: VEHICLE SYSTEMS LTD
Registration no: 05623183 **Turnover:** Up to £250,000
No.of Employees: 1 - 10 **Product Groups:** 39

Aclet Electronics Ltd

Unit B2 Whinbank Park Whinbank Road, Aycliffe Business Park, Newton Aycliffe, DL5 6AY
Tel: 01325-300983 **Fax:** 01325-300983
E-mail: sales@aclet.co.uk
Website: http://www.aclet.co.uk
Bank(s): National Westminster Bank Plc
Directors: D. Taylor (Comm), D. Taylor (Purch), P. Bellis (Fab)
Managers: N. Bellis (Sales Admin)
Immediate Holding Company: ACLET ELECTRONICS LIMITED
Registration no: 03913808 **VAT No.:** GB 532 7986 14
Date established: 2000 **Turnover:** £250,000 - £500,000
No.of Employees: 21 - 50 **Product Groups:** 37

Date of Accounts	Apr 11	Apr 10	Apr 09
Working Capital	87	-121	-14
Fixed Assets	393	412	397
Current Assets	502	646	215

Almit Metal Finishing

Whinfield Drive Aycliffe Industrial Estate, Aycliffe Business Park, Newton Aycliffe, DL5 6AU
Tel: 01325-311777 **Fax:** 01325-316472
E-mail: enquiries@almitgroup.co.uk
Website: http://www.almitgroup.co.uk
Directors: S. Mitchell (Tech Serv)
Immediate Holding Company: ALMIT METAL FINISHING LTD
Registration no: 05318317 **VAT No.:** GB 360 5747 49
Date established: 2004 **Turnover:** £1m - £2m **No.of Employees:** 1 - 10
Product Groups: 48

Date of Accounts	Mar 12	Mar 11	Mar 10
Working Capital	17	-31	-35
Fixed Assets	107	69	72
Current Assets	431	377	433

Appletree Joinery Products Ltd

Howden Road Aycliffe Industrial Estate, Aycliffe Business Park, Newton Aycliffe, DL5 6EU
Tel: 01325-300445 **Fax:** 01325-311299
E-mail: shirley@appletreejoinery.co.uk
Website: http://www.appletreejoinery.co.uk
Directors: S. Pardoe (Dir), J. Pardoe (Dir)
Managers: J. Miller (Sales Admin), J. Dunn (Prod Mgr)
Immediate Holding Company: APPLETREE JOINERY PRODUCTS LIMITED
Registration no: 01931775 **Date established:** 1985
No.of Employees: 51 - 100 **Product Groups:** 23, 25, 26, 32, 35, 61, 63, 67

Date of Accounts	Apr 11	Apr 10	Apr 09
Working Capital	-216	-183	-9
Fixed Assets	1m	977	696
Current Assets	1m	893	718

Aycliffe Engineering Ltd

Beaumont Way Aycliffe Business Park, Newton Aycliffe, DL5 6SN
Tel: 01325-300223 **Fax:** 01325-300233
E-mail: kaltringham@aycliffeengineering.co.uk
Website: http://www.aycliffe-engineering.co.uk
Bank(s): Barclays
Directors: K. Altringham (MD), K. Altringham (MD)
Managers: K. Altringham
Immediate Holding Company: AYCLIFFE ENGINEERING LIMITED
Registration no: 00443976 **VAT No.:** GB 329 4379 31
Date established: 1947 **Turnover:** £2m - £5m **No.of Employees:** 21 - 50
Product Groups: 48

Date of Accounts	Sep 11	Sep 10	Sep 09
Working Capital	220	210	230
Fixed Assets	409	432	440
Current Assets	496	557	470

Aycliffe Fabrications Ltd

Unit 10-12 Leaside, Aycliffe Business Park, Newton Aycliffe, DL5 6HX
Tel: 01325-310000 **Fax:** 01325-301987
E-mail: info@aycliffefabrications.co.uk
Website: http://www.aycliffefabrications.co.uk
Directors: D. Spensley (Dir)
Immediate Holding Company: AYCLIFFE FABRICATIONS LIMITED
Registration no: 04310888 **VAT No.:** GB 329 3166 53
Date established: 2001 **Turnover:** £250,000 - £500,000
No.of Employees: 1 - 10 **Product Groups:** 48

Date of Accounts	Dec 11	Dec 10	Dec 09
Working Capital	-50	-52	-54
Fixed Assets	34	27	34
Current Assets	93	106	77

Columbus Cleaning Machines (North East) Ltd

Columbus House Unit 1 Ridgeway, Aycliffe Industrial Park, Newton Aycliffe, DL5 6SP
Tel: 01325-379000 **Fax:** 01325-327114
E-mail: tanny@columbusne.co.uk
Website: http://www.columbusne.co.uk
No.of Employees: 1 - 10 **Product Groups:** 23, 28, 40, 46

Date of Accounts	May 08	May 07
Working Capital	-53	-23
Fixed Assets	114	96
Current Assets	101	159
Current Liabilities	154	182

T W & G Corner

Rye Close Farm Ricknall Lane, Aycliffe, Newton Aycliffe, DL5 6JJ
Tel: 01325-311900 **Fax:** 01325-310559
E-mail: ryeclosefarm@sky.com
Directors: G. Corner (Ptnr)
Date established: 1975 **No.of Employees:** 1 - 10 **Product Groups:** 41

D B S

Unit 15 Ies Centre Horndale Avenue, Aycliffe Business Park, Newton Aycliffe, DL5 6DS
Tel: 01325-307230 **Fax:** 01325-307123
E-mail: enquiries@dbs-fabrication.co.uk
Website: http://www.dbs-centres.co.uk
Directors: J. Knight (Ptnr)
Date established: 1996 **No.of Employees:** 1 - 10 **Product Groups:** 35

Doriflon Ltd

Unit 5 Cumbie Way Aycliffe Business Park, Newton Aycliffe, DL5 6YA
Tel: 01325-300533 **Fax:** 01325-320231
E-mail: info@doriflon.co.uk
Website: http://www.doriflon.co.uk
Bank(s): Barclays
Directors: J. Towell (Fin), D. Towell (Dir)
Immediate Holding Company: DORIFLON LIMITED
Registration no: 01365572 **Date established:** 1978
Turnover: £500,000 - £1m **No.of Employees:** 11 - 20
Product Groups: 30, 40, 66

Date of Accounts	Dec 11	Dec 10	Dec 09
Working Capital	276	230	193
Fixed Assets	26	13	16
Current Assets	329	280	234

Endress & Hauser

Unit 30 Northfield Way Aycliffe Business Park, Newton Aycliffe, DL5 6UF
Tel: 01325-329801 **Fax:** 01325-300840
E-mail: workshop@uk.endress.com
Website: http://www.uk.endress.com
Directors: P. Endress (MD)
Ultimate Holding Company: ENDRESS + HAUSER
Immediate Holding Company: WHESSOE P.L.C.
Registration no: 03783794 **VAT No.:** GB 257 5820 38
Turnover: £10m - £20m **No.of Employees:** 1 - 10 **Product Groups:** 38, 40

Gilgen Door Systems UK Ltd

Unit 4 Woodham Road Aycliffe Business Park, Newton Aycliffe, DL5 6HT
Tel: 01325-303700 **Fax:** 01325-303701
E-mail: info@gilgendoorsystems.co.uk
Website: http://www.gilgendoorsystems.co.uk
Managers: H. Jukes-Jones (Mktg Serv Mgr)
Ultimate Holding Company: KABA HOLDING AG (SWITZERLAND)
Immediate Holding Company: GILGEN DOOR SYSTEMS UK LIMITED
Registration no: 03762371 **Date established:** 1999 **Turnover:** £2m - £5m
No.of Employees: 21 - 50 **Product Groups:** 33, 35, 40, 66, 81

Date of Accounts	Dec 11	Jun 10	Jun 09
Sales Turnover	21m	17m	21m
Pre Tax Profit/Loss	-2m	-779	-424
Working Capital	378	1m	2m
Fixed Assets	353	406	607
Current Assets	5m	5m	6m
Current Liabilities	1m	2m	2m

Haldex Ltd

Unit 1 Durham Way South, Aycliffe Business Park, Newton Aycliffe, DL5 6XN
Tel: 01325-310110 **Fax:** 01325-311834
E-mail: info.gbay@haldex.com
Website: http://www.haldex.com
Managers: L. Johansson (Comptroller), Y. Lockhart
Ultimate Holding Company: ICC INDUSTRIES INC (USA)
Immediate Holding Company: HALDEX LIMITED
Registration no: 01522328 **Date established:** 1980
Turnover: £500,000 - £1m **No.of Employees:** 1 - 10 **Product Groups:** 35, 37, 39, 40, 45

Date of Accounts	Dec 11	Dec 10	Dec 09
Sales Turnover	801	791	1m
Pre Tax Profit/Loss	-2m	-4m	-741
Working Capital	-6m	-5m	-582
Fixed Assets	3	3	4
Current Assets	2m	3m	7m
Current Liabilities	54	163	109

Hydro Polymers Ltd

Aycliffe Industrial Park, Newton Aycliffe, DL5 6EA
Tel: 01325-300555 **Fax:** 01325-300215
Website: http://www.hydro.com
Bank(s): National Westminster Bank Plc
Directors: G. Shaw (Pers), Z. Bird (Fin)
Managers: C. Welton (Publicity)
Immediate Holding Company: Norsk Hydro A.S. (Oslo)
Registration no: 01631120 **VAT No.:** GB 339 3496 25
Date established: 1950 **Turnover:** £125m - £250m
No.of Employees: 251 - 500 **Product Groups:** 31

Itec North East Ltd

The Digital Factory Durham Way South, Aycliffe Business Park, Newton Aycliffe, DL5 6XP
Tel: 01325-320052 **Fax:** 01325-317530
E-mail: info@itecne.co.uk
Website: http://www.itecne.co.uk
Managers: S. Wright
Ultimate Holding Company: ITEC NORTH EAST LIMITED
Immediate Holding Company: ITEC NORTH EAST LIMITED
Registration no: 02045777 **Date established:** 1986 **Turnover:** £1m - £2m
No.of Employees: 11 - 20 **Product Groups:** 87

Date of Accounts	Mar 12	Mar 11	Mar 10
Sales Turnover	1m	1m	1m
Pre Tax Profit/Loss	77	6	38
Working Capital	385	281	252
Fixed Assets	29	59	86
Current Assets	584	369	353
Current Liabilities	81	57	36

Lacegold Electrical & Mechanical Services

1 Aerial House School Aycliffe, Newton Aycliffe, DL5 6QF
Tel: 01325-315316 **Fax:** 01325-329940
E-mail: jupex@lacegoldems@upexgroup.co.uk
Website: http://www.upexgroup.co.uk
Bank(s): Lloyds TSB Bank plc
Directors: A. Upex (Fin), L. Upex (MD)
Immediate Holding Company: LACEGOLD ELECTRICAL AND MECHANICAL SERVICES LIMITED
Registration no: 01821581 **VAT No.:** GB 409 1982 39
Date established: 1984 **Turnover:** £1m - £2m **No.of Employees:** 21 - 50
Product Groups: 35, 37, 40

Date of Accounts	Jun 11	Jun 10	Jun 09
Working Capital	785	778	663
Fixed Assets	118	102	113
Current Assets	998	1m	973

Linden Group Ltd

1 Leaside North Aycliffe Industrial Estate, Aycliffe Business Park, Newton Aycliffe, DL5 6DU
Tel: 01325-311331 **Fax:** 01325-300128
E-mail: cb@lindengroup.co.uk
Website: http://www.lindengroup.co.uk
Directors: C. Billany (MD), E. Bradley (MD)
Immediate Holding Company: LINDEN GROUP LIMITED
Registration no: 02170634 **VAT No.:** GB 495 9368 25
Date established: 1987 **Turnover:** £500m - £1,000m
No.of Employees: 21 - 50 **Product Groups:** 29, 30, 36, 48

Date of Accounts	Dec 11	Dec 10	Dec 09
Sales Turnover	875m	743m	609m
Pre Tax Profit/Loss	82	54	84
Working Capital	371	348	333
Fixed Assets	231	187	199
Current Assets	10m	7m	6m
Current Liabilities	116	4m	4m

Lucite International Speciality Polymers & Resins Ltd

Horndale Avenue Aycliffe Industrial Estate, Aycliffe Business Park, Newton Aycliffe, DL5 6YE
Tel: 01325-300990 **Fax:** 01325-314925
E-mail: ann-marie.stannard@lucite.com
Website: http://www.luciteinternational.com/resins
Managers: M. Easton (Purch Mgr), A. Stannard (Chief Mgr)
Ultimate Holding Company: MITSUBISHI CHEMICAL HOLDINGS CORPORATION (JAPAN)
Immediate Holding Company: LUCITE INTERNATIONAL SPECIALITY POLYMERS AND RESINS LIMITED
Registration no: 00272076 **Date established:** 1933
Turnover: £10m - £20m **No.of Employees:** 51 - 100 **Product Groups:** 31

Date of Accounts	Dec 11	Dec 10	Dec 09
Sales Turnover	11m	10m	9m
Pre Tax Profit/Loss	1m	800	900
Working Capital	-300	-1m	-2m
Fixed Assets	4m	4m	4m
Current Assets	4m	3m	3m
Current Liabilities	4m	4m	4m

M F Engineering Ltd

12 Hurworth Road Aycliffe Industrial Estate, Aycliffe Business Park, Newton Aycliffe, DL5 6UD
Tel: 01325-320256 **Fax:** 01325-300323
E-mail: andrew@mfengineering.co.uk
Website: http://www.mfengineering.co.uk
Bank(s): Barclays
Directors: A. Fisher (MD), M. Fisher (Dir), A. Fisher (Grp Chief Exec)
Managers: I. Stoker (Mgr), P. Bradley (Mgr)
Immediate Holding Company: M/F ENGINEERING LIMITED
Registration no: 01700414 **VAT No.:** GB 391 7163 38
Date established: 1983 **Turnover:** £250,000 - £500,000
No.of Employees: 21 - 50 **Product Groups:** 28, 30, 35, 37, 39, 40, 44, 45, 46, 48, 49, 52, 67, 68, 80, 81, 84

Date of Accounts	Mar 09	Mar 08	Mar 07
Working Capital	-53	-59	-50
Fixed Assets	137	161	166
Current Assets	210	248	214
Current Liabilities	263	306	264

P W S Distributors
PO Box 20, Newton Aycliffe, DL5 6XJ
Tel: 01325-505555 **Fax:** 01325-505500
E-mail: mail@pws.co.uk
Website: http://www.pws.co.uk
Bank(s): Barclays.
Directors: M. Elgood (MD)
Ultimate Holding Company: DANESMOOR LIMITED
Immediate Holding Company: PWS DISTRIBUTORS LIMITED
Registration no: 02214406 **VAT No.:** GB 285 0089 50
Date established: 1988 **Turnover:** £50m - £75m
No.of Employees: 251 - 500 **Product Groups:** 36

Date of Accounts	Apr 11	Apr 10	Apr 09
Sales Turnover	53m	55m	59m
Pre Tax Profit/Loss	4m	3m	5m
Working Capital	8m	5m	12m
Fixed Assets	10m	13m	15m
Current Assets	21m	22m	25m
Current Liabilities	4m	2m	2m

Perry Process Equipment Ltd
Station Road Aycliffe Business Park, Newton Aycliffe, DL5 6EQ
Tel: 01325-315111 **Fax:** 01325-301496
E-mail: info@perryprocess.co.uk
Website: http://www.perryprocess.co.uk
Bank(s): National Westminster Bank Plc
Directors: D. Bentham (Dir)
Ultimate Holding Company: PERRY MACHINERY CORPORATION (USA)
Immediate Holding Company: PERRY PROCESS EQUIPMENT LIMITED
Registration no: 02459771 **VAT No.:** GB 566 2818 15
Date established: 1990 **Turnover:** £5m - £10m **No.of Employees:** 11 - 20
Product Groups: 35, 40, 41, 42, 44, 45, 61, 66, 67

Date of Accounts	Dec 11	Dec 10	Dec 09
Working Capital	1m	2m	2m
Fixed Assets	494	515	539
Current Assets	4m	3m	3m

Plasmor Ltd
Groat Avenue Aycliffe Industrial Estate, Aycliffe Business Park, Newton Aycliffe, DL5 6HB
Tel: 01325-312328 **Fax:** 01325-320838
E-mail: sarby@plasmor.co.uk
Website: http://www.plasmor.co.uk
Directors: K. Knaggs (Co Sec), A. Slater (MD)
Immediate Holding Company: PLASMOR LIMITED
Registration no: 00642173 **Date established:** 1959
No.of Employees: 11 - 20 **Product Groups:** 14, 33

Date of Accounts	Aug 11	Aug 10	Aug 09
Sales Turnover	49m	47m	41m
Pre Tax Profit/Loss	-795	514	-1m
Working Capital	15m	16m	14m
Fixed Assets	22m	22m	23m
Current Assets	24m	25m	21m
Current Liabilities	3m	3m	3m

Promotional Handling Logistics
Woodham Road Aycliffe Business Park, Newton Aycliffe, DL5 6HT
Tel: 01325-304052 **Fax:** 01325-304063
Managers: A. Mcdonald (Mgr)
Immediate Holding Company: PROMOTIONAL HANDLING LOGISTICS LTD
Registration no: 04446638 **Date established:** 2002
No.of Employees: 1 - 10 **Product Groups:** 35, 39, 45

Date of Accounts	May 07	May 06	May 05
Working Capital	-43	-43	-34
Fixed Assets	7	8	9
Current Assets	9	22	10

Protech Direct (Flame Exports & Imports Ltd)
Blue Bridge Centre Horndale Avenue, Aycliffe Business Park, Newton Aycliffe, DL5 6DS
Tel: 01325-310520 **Fax:** 01480-300670
E-mail: bbb@protechdirect.co.uk
Website: http://www.protechdirect.co.uk
Directors: B. Bermingham (MD), S. Bermingham (Co Sec)
Ultimate Holding Company: THE B.B. GROUP LIMITED
Immediate Holding Company: PROTECH DIRECT LIMITED
Registration no: 04876947 **VAT No.:** GB 330 2350 15
Date established: 2003 **No.of Employees:** 1 - 10 **Product Groups:** 30, 37, 40, 67

Robinson Engineering Ltd
Durham Way North Aycliffe Business Park, Newton Aycliffe, DL5 6HP
Tel: 01325-304070 **Fax:** 01325-304088
E-mail: info@robinson-engineering.com
Website: http://www.robinson-engineering.com
Directors: A. Robinson (MD)
Immediate Holding Company: ROBINSON ENGINEERING LIMITED
Registration no: 03991356 **VAT No.:** GB 440 9611 60
Date established: 2000 **No.of Employees:** 1 - 10 **Product Groups:** 48

Date of Accounts	Apr 11	Apr 10	Apr 09
Working Capital	42	17	36
Fixed Assets	117	148	166
Current Assets	146	89	107

S M K UK Ltd
Northfield Way Aycliffe Industrial Estate, Aycliffe Business Park, Newton Aycliffe, DL5 6UF
Tel: 01325-300770 **Fax:** 01325-300556
Website: http://www.smk.co.jp
Directors: T. Ishibashi (MD)
Managers: M. Thurlbeck (Purch Mgr), W. Osborne
Ultimate Holding Company: SMK CORPORATION (JAPAN)
Immediate Holding Company: SMK (U.K.) LIMITED
Registration no: 02181284 **Date established:** 1987
No.of Employees: 51 - 100 **Product Groups:** 35, 38

Date of Accounts	Mar 11	Mar 10	Mar 09
Working Capital	-14	-225	-2m
Fixed Assets	224	286	686
Current Assets	1m	1m	1m

S W D T Ltd
Durham Way South Aycliffe Business Park, Newton Aycliffe, DL5 6AT
Tel: 01325-313194 **Fax:** 01325-318249
E-mail: admin@swdt.co.uk
Website: http://www.swdt.co.uk
Bank(s): HSBC
Directors: J. Crowther (Co Sec)
Managers: A. Cant, K. Davey (Admin Off), S. Lamb
Immediate Holding Company: S.W. DURHAM TRAINING LIMITED
Registration no: 00918178 **VAT No.:** GB 258 4739 20
Date established: 1967 **Turnover:** £2m - £5m **No.of Employees:** 21 - 50
Product Groups: 86

Date of Accounts	Aug 11	Aug 10	Aug 09
Sales Turnover	5m	2m	3m
Pre Tax Profit/Loss	3m	-194	-309
Working Capital	401	382	287
Fixed Assets	6m	3m	3m
Current Assets	839	528	653
Current Liabilities	177	121	212

Siesta Blinds Ltd
1 Brighouse Courts Burtree Road, Aycliffe Business Park, Newton Aycliffe, DL5 6HZ
Tel: 08450-953411 **Fax:** 01325-318779
E-mail: sales@siestablinds.com
Website: http://www.siestablinds.com
Directors: J. Forbes (Sales), L. Robb (Co Sec), J. Forbes (Prop), L. Robb (Fin)
Managers: D. Shaw (Sales Prom Mgr), S. Forbes (Nat Sales Mgr)
Immediate Holding Company: SIESTA BLINDS LTD
Registration no: 04547233 **Date established:** 2002
Turnover: £500,000 - £1m **No.of Employees:** 11 - 20
Product Groups: 25, 30, 35

Date of Accounts	Oct 06	Oct 05
Working Capital	17	6
Fixed Assets	35	4
Current Assets	130	118
Current Liabilities	113	112

Stairlift Solutions
19 Whitworth Drive Aycliffe Business Park, Newton Aycliffe, DL5 6SZ
Tel: 01325-307473 **Fax:** 01325-307476
Website: http://www.stairliftsolution.co.uk
Managers: D. Patrick (Mgr)
Date established: 2001 **No.of Employees:** 1 - 10 **Product Groups:** 35, 39, 45

Starlight Windows Ltd
Leaside North Aycliffe Industrial Estate, Aycliffe Business Park, Newton Aycliffe, DL5 6DU
Tel: 01325-321301 **Fax:** 01325-321302
E-mail: sales@starlightwindows.co.uk
Website: http://www.starlightwindows.co.uk
Directors: J. Moodie (MD)
Immediate Holding Company: STARLIGHT WINDOWS LIMITED
Registration no: 03468757 **Date established:** 1997
No.of Employees: 1 - 10 **Product Groups:** 26, 35

Date of Accounts	Dec 11	Dec 10	Dec 09
Working Capital	31	92	99
Fixed Assets	138	134	143
Current Assets	98	195	186

Teeside Fluid System Technologies
Whinbank Road Aycliffe Business Park, Newton Aycliffe, DL5 6AY
Tel: 01325-316468 **Fax:** 01325-300559
E-mail: barry.waller@swagelokteeside.co.uk
Website: http://www.swagelok.com
Directors: B. Waller (MD)
Immediate Holding Company: S.C.H. SITE SERVICES LTD
Registration no: 06446507 **Date established:** 2005
No.of Employees: 11 - 20 **Product Groups:** 29, 30, 34, 36, 38, 40, 46, 66

Date of Accounts	Dec 11	Dec 10	Dec 09
Working Capital	1m	1m	710
Fixed Assets	690	585	593
Current Assets	2m	2m	2m

Total Partition Solutions Ltd
Ies Centre Horndale Avenue, Aycliffe Business Park, Newton Aycliffe, DL5 6DS
Tel: 01325-301333 **Fax:** 01325-301444
E-mail: sales@thrislington.co.uk
Website: http://www.thrislington.co.uk
Directors: P. Beecroft (MD)
Immediate Holding Company: TOTAL PARTITION SOLUTIONS LIMITED
Registration no: 07371583 **VAT No.:** GB 675 3721 16
Date established: 2010 **Turnover:** £5m - £10m **No.of Employees:** 1 - 10
Product Groups: 35

Date of Accounts	Jun 12	Jun 11
Working Capital	-24	-20
Fixed Assets	67	40
Current Assets	182	134

Tyne Tees Packaging
Grindon Way Heighington Lane Business Park, Newton Aycliffe, DL5 6DQ
Tel: 01325-311114 **Fax:** 01325-311301
E-mail: sales@tyneteespackaging.co.uk
Website: http://www.tyneteespackaging.co.uk
Bank(s): Midland
Directors: L. Donald (Fin), G. Wiper (MD)
Managers: E. Williams
Immediate Holding Company: TYNE TEES PACKAGING LIMITED
Registration no: 01646511 **VAT No.:** GB 360 7081 67
Date established: 1982 **Turnover:** £2m - £5m **No.of Employees:** 21 - 50
Product Groups: 27

Date of Accounts	Oct 11	Apr 11	Apr 10
Working Capital	-937	-984	-787
Fixed Assets	4m	3m	4m
Current Assets	2m	2m	2m

Upex Electrical Distributors Ltd
2 Aerial House School Aycliffe, Newton Aycliffe, DL5 6QF
Tel: 01325-315315 **Fax:** 01325-318315
E-mail: upexelectrical@upexgroup.co.uk
Website: http://www.upexelectrical.co.uk
Directors: G. Monk (MD)
Immediate Holding Company: UPEX ELECTRICAL DISTRIBUTORS LIMITED
Registration no: 02091132 **Date established:** 1987
Turnover: £250,000 - £500,000 **No.of Employees:** 1 - 10
Product Groups: 36, 37, 39, 44, 46

Date of Accounts	Dec 11	Dec 10	Dec 09
Working Capital	192	138	120
Fixed Assets	7	9	18
Current Assets	445	284	294

W Y K O Industrial Distribution Ltd (Newton Aycliffe Service Centre)
10 Gurney Way Aycliffe Industrial Estate, Aycliffe Business Park, Newton Aycliffe, DL5 6UJ
Tel: 01325-307007 **Fax:** 01325-307555
E-mail: newton-aycliffe@eriks.co.uk
Website: http://www.wyko.co.uk
Managers: B. Walker (Mgr)
Immediate Holding Company: WYKO HOLDINGS LTD
Registration no: 00917112 **Turnover:** £250m - £500m
No.of Employees: 1 - 10 **Product Groups:** 66

Peterlee

A W C Fabrications
15 Whitworth Road South West Industrial Estate, Peterlee, SR8 2LY
Tel: 0191-586 5252 **Fax:** 0191-586 5252
Directors: A. Clark (Prop)
Date established: 1995 **No.of Employees:** 1 - 10 **Product Groups:** 26, 35

Actem UK Ltd
2 Sea View Industrial Estate, Peterlee, SR8 4TQ
Tel: 0191-518 0235 **Fax:** 0191-586 1139
E-mail: kevin.harris@actem.co.uk
Website: http://www.actem.co.uk
Bank(s): Coop, Newcastle
Directors: K. Harris (Dir)
Managers: P. Watson (Sales Admin)
Immediate Holding Company: ACTEM (UK) LIMITED
Registration no: 02115283 **VAT No.:** GB 459 8741 88
Date established: 1987 **Turnover:** £1m - £2m **No.of Employees:** 51 - 100
Product Groups: 48

Date of Accounts	Dec 09	Dec 08	Oct 11
Sales Turnover	1m	N/A	N/A
Pre Tax Profit/Loss	-357	N/A	N/A
Working Capital	-46	294	-140
Fixed Assets	431	475	791
Current Assets	405	841	1m
Current Liabilities	142	166	N/A

Aldona Seals
1 Brindley Road South West Industrial Estate, Peterlee, SR8 2LT
Tel: 0191-518 1555 **Fax:** 0191-518 0555
E-mail: gtsm@gtgroup.co.uk
Website: http://www.gtsm.co.uk
Bank(s): National Westminster Bank Plc
Directors: S. Turnbull (Fin), G. Turnbull (Ch), S. Conley (Fin)
Ultimate Holding Company: G.T. GROUP LTD
Immediate Holding Company: ALDONA SEALS LTD
Registration no: 02282241 **Date established:** 1988 **Turnover:** £2m - £5m
No.of Employees: 21 - 50 **Product Groups:** 36

Date of Accounts	Oct 11	Oct 10	Oct 09
Working Capital	179	-31	-83
Fixed Assets	52	78	115
Current Assets	562	567	329

Alpha Process Controls (International) Ltd
3 Traynor Way Whitehouse Business Park, Peterlee, SR8 2RU
Tel: 0191-586 2366 **Fax:** 0191-587 2111
E-mail: alpha.sales@gtgroup.co.uk
Website: http://www.alphaprocess.co.uk
Bank(s): Barclays
Directors: G. Turnbull (Ch), J. Lamb (MD)
Managers: C. Gibson (Mktg Serv Mgr)
Immediate Holding Company: G T Group
Registration no: 01383443 **VAT No.:** GB 301 3819 96
Turnover: £1m - £2m **No.of Employees:** 11 - 20 **Product Groups:** 36, 39, 48

Date of Accounts	Oct 07	Oct 06	Oct 05
Sales Turnover	N/A	N/A	542
Pre Tax Profit/Loss	N/A	N/A	45
Working Capital	378	299	325
Fixed Assets	14	18	9
Current Assets	485	390	615
Current Liabilities	107	91	290
Total Share Capital	95	95	95
ROCE% (Return on Capital Employed)			13.5
ROT% (Return on Turnover)			8.3

B & H Exchangers Ltd
9 Sea View Indl-Est, Peterlee, SR8 4TQ
Tel: 0191-586 6964 **Fax:** 0191- 5861334
E-mail: whill@bhexchangers.com
Website: http://www.bhexchangers.com
Directors: H. Green (Co Sec), W. Hill (Dir)
Managers: B. Marshall (Fin Mgr), S. Henderson (Mgr)
Registration no: 02017049 **VAT No.:** GB 441 0436 91
Date established: 1986 **Turnover:** £1m - £2m **No.of Employees:** 1 - 10
Product Groups: 40

Carillion Energy Services
Unit 4 Traynor Way Whitehouse Business Park, Peterlee, SR8 2RT
Tel: 0191-288 9920 **Fax:** 0191-385 9288
E-mail: terri.wilson@eaga.com
Website: http://www.eaga.com
Managers: T. Wilson
Date established: 1982 **Turnover:** £20m - £50m **No.of Employees:** 1 - 10
Product Groups: 30, 33, 45, 52, 66, 84

Caterpillar Peterlee Ltd
North West Industrial Estate, Peterlee, SR8 2HX
Tel: 0191-569 2200 **Fax:** 0191-569 2298
Website: http://www.cat.com
Bank(s): TSB Lloyds, Grey Street, Manchester
Directors: R. Cooper (MD), P. Handley (MD)
Managers: S. Avis (Prod Mgr), S. Kreiger (Comm), J. Dickson (Ops Mgr), D. Powell (Mgr)
Ultimate Holding Company: CATERPILLAR INC (USA)
Immediate Holding Company: Eastfield No 23 Ltd
Registration no: 01923368 **VAT No.:** GB 661 5461 37
Date established: 1985 **Turnover:** £75m - £125m
No.of Employees: 501 - 1000 **Product Groups:** 39, 41, 45

Conder Products Ltd

2 Whitehouse Way South West Industrial Estate, Peterlee, SR8 2RA
Tel: 0191-587 8650 **Fax:** 0191-586 1274
E-mail: sales@conderproducts.co.uk
Website: http://www.conderproducts.com
Directors: A. Varney (Dir), D. Cox (Dir), A. Balmer (MD)
Managers: P. Gilan (Mktg Serv Mgr)
Immediate Holding Company: CONDER SOLUTIONS LIMITED
Registration no: 06698049 **Date established:** 2008
Turnover: £10m - £20m **No.of Employees:** 51 - 100 **Product Groups:** 30, 48

Date of Accounts	Apr 07
Sales Turnover	11790
Pre Tax Profit/Loss	-308
Working Capital	205
Fixed Assets	2419
Current Assets	3393
Current Liabilities	3188
Total Share Capital	10
ROCE% (Return on Capital Employed)	-11.7

Continental Chef Supplies Ltd

2 Swan Road South West Industrial Estate, Peterlee, SR8 2HS
Tel: 0191-518 8080 **Fax:** 08081-002777
E-mail: sales@chefs.net
Website: http://www.chefs.net
Directors: J. Hindmarsh (Fin), P. Brown (MD)
Managers: A. Ward (Mktg Serv Mgr)
Ultimate Holding Company: BUNZL PUBLIC LIMITED COMPANY
Immediate Holding Company: CONTINENTAL CHEF SUPPLIES LIMITED
Registration no: 03392672 **Date established:** 1997
No.of Employees: 21 - 50 **Product Groups:** 20, 22, 24, 27, 30, 32, 33, 35, 36, 37, 38, 40, 41, 42, 44, 45, 48, 62, 63, 64, 66, 67, 69, 83

Date of Accounts	Dec 11	Dec 10	Dec 09
Working Capital	110	110	1m
Current Assets	110	110	1m

D W Marshall

3b Gresley Road South West Industrial Estate, Peterlee, SR8 2LU
Tel: 0191-586 2693 **Fax:** 0191-518 0509
E-mail: dwm@talk21.com
Website: http://www.dwmarshall.co.uk
Directors: M. Bowler (MD), K. Wilson (MD)
Immediate Holding Company: D.W. MARSHALL AND CO. LIMITED
Registration no: 01468740 **VAT No.:** GB 334 7005 80
Date established: 1979 **Turnover:** £1m - £2m **No.of Employees:** 21 - 50
Product Groups: 66

Date of Accounts	Sep 11	Sep 10	Sep 09
Working Capital	299	353	333
Fixed Assets	521	494	519
Current Assets	1m	896	774

DevilWear Ltd

1 Cotsford Lane, Peterlee, SR8 4JJ
Tel: 0191-587 9835 **Fax:** 0191-527 9427
E-mail: sales@devilwear.co.uk
Website: http://www.devilwear.co.uk
Directors: K. Smith (MD), J. Seager (Fin)
Immediate Holding Company: DEVILWEAR LIMITED
Registration no: 05006651 **Date established:** 2004
No.of Employees: 1 - 10 **Product Groups:** 61

Date of Accounts	Jan 11	Jan 10	Jan 09
Working Capital	86	27	36
Current Assets	135	103	95

East Durham Business Service

Novus Business Centre Judson Road, North West Industrial Estate, Peterlee, SR8 2QJ
Tel: 0191-586 3366 **Fax:** 0191-518 0332
E-mail: peter.chapman@edbs.co.uk
Website: http://www.edbs.co.uk
Bank(s): HSBC Bank plc
Directors: P. Chapman (Grp Chief Exec)
Managers: D. Hart, S. Wardle, D. Fielding (Fin Mgr)
Immediate Holding Company: EAST DURHAM BUSINESS SERVICE LTD.
Registration no: 02050252 **Date established:** 1986 **Turnover:** £1m - £2m
No.of Employees: 11 - 20 **Product Groups:** 80

Date of Accounts	Mar 11	Mar 10	Mar 09
Sales Turnover	2m	2m	784
Pre Tax Profit/Loss	87	112	-9
Working Capital	465	378	266
Fixed Assets	3	3	5
Current Assets	522	517	306
Current Liabilities	56	73	32

Manual Lifting Products Ltd

PO Box 21, Peterlee, SR8 2II
Tel: 0191-586 2228 **Fax:** 0191-586 2228
Directors: D. Hart (Prop), D. Hart (Fin)
Immediate Holding Company: MANUAL LIFTING PRODUCTS LIMITED
Registration no: 02983612 **Date established:** 1994
No.of Employees: 1 - 10 **Product Groups:** 35, 39, 45

Date of Accounts	Oct 06	Oct 05
Working Capital	-2	3
Current Assets	18	19
Current Liabilities	20	16

Peterlee Glass Co. Ltd

28 Lister Road North West Industrial Estate, Peterlee, SR8 2RB
Tel: 0191-586 4626 **Fax:** 0191-518 0459
E-mail: sales@peterleeglass.com
Website: http://www.peterleeglass.com
Bank(s): Barclays
Directors: G. Hawes (MD), G. Stephenson (Dir)
Managers: S. Burlison (Sales Prom Mgr)
Immediate Holding Company: PETERLEE GLASS COMPANY LIMITED
Registration no: 01334681 **Date established:** 1977 **Turnover:** £1m - £2m
No.of Employees: 21 - 50 **Product Groups:** 33

Date of Accounts	Mar 12	Mar 11	Mar 10
Working Capital	58	79	65
Fixed Assets	880	896	984
Current Assets	445	595	430

Sotech Ltd

Unit 2 Traynor Way, Whitehouse Business Park, Peterlee, SR8 2RU
Tel: 0191-587 2287 **Fax:** 0191-518 0703
E-mail: mail@sotech-optima.co.uk
Website: http://www.sotech-optima.co.uk
Directors: J. Eggington (MD), C. Egginton (Fin)
Managers: C. McLaughlin (Mktg Serv Mgr), R. Egginton (Personnel)
Immediate Holding Company: SOTECH LIMITED
Registration no: 01651304 **Date established:** 1982 **Turnover:** £2m - £5m
No.of Employees: 21 - 50 **Product Groups:** 35

Date of Accounts	Jun 11	Jun 10	Jun 09
Working Capital	289	337	7
Fixed Assets	675	695	703
Current Assets	2m	1m	981

Sotralentz UK Ltd

5 Mill Hill North West Industrial Estate, Peterlee, SR8 2HR
Tel: 0191-586 0577 **Fax:** 0191-586 7542
E-mail: sales@sotralentz.com
Website: http://www.sotralentz.com
Directors: C. Brown (Co Sec), N. Poerschke (Grp Chief Exec), P. Lentz (Dir), S. Solyom (Fin)
Managers: H. Poerschke (Chief Mgr), J. Balmforth (Prod Mgr)
Ultimate Holding Company: Sotralentz SA
Registration no: 01943809 **VAT No.:** 440 9945 31 **Date established:** 2009
Turnover: £500,000 - £1m **No.of Employees:** 1 - 10 **Product Groups:** 30

The Seaward Group (a division of Seaward Electronic Ltd)

15-18 Bracken Hill South West Industrial Estate, Peterlee, SR8 2SW
Tel: 0191-586 3511 **Fax:** 0191-586 0227
E-mail: info@seaward.co.uk
Website: http://www.seaward.co.uk
Bank(s): Bank of Scotland
Directors: R. Taylor (MD), M. Marsh (Fin), A. Upton (Sales), I. West (Chief Op Offcr)
Managers: S. Sweeney, C. Gaffney, W. Chaplin
Ultimate Holding Company: SEAWARD HOLDING COMPANY LIMITED
Immediate Holding Company: SEAWARD ELECTRONIC LIMITED
Registration no: 01674384 **VAT No.:** GB 219 6938 26
Date established: 1982 **Turnover:** £10m - £20m
No.of Employees: 101 - 250 **Product Groups:** 38, 39, 67

Date of Accounts	Mar 12	Mar 11	Mar 10
Sales Turnover	12m	12m	1m
Pre Tax Profit/Loss	923	719	678
Working Capital	4m	3m	3m
Fixed Assets	2m	2m	1m
Current Assets	8m	7m	7m
Current Liabilities	572	773	733

U S G UK Ltd

1 Swan Road South West Industrial Estate, Peterlee, SR8 2HS
Tel: 0191-518 8600 **Fax:** 0191-586 0097
E-mail: pdauwe@usg.com
Website: http://www.usg.uk.com
Directors: C. Neil (Fin)
Managers: M. Allinson (Purch Mgr), P. Dauwe, A. Baker, D. Hoyle (Sales & Mktg Mg), A. Manser (Personnel)
Ultimate Holding Company: USG CORPORATION (U.S.A.)
Immediate Holding Company: USG (UK) LIMITED
Registration no: 01139974 **Date established:** 1973 **Turnover:** £5m - £10m
No.of Employees: 11 - 20 **Product Groups:** 30, 33, 35, 40, 52, 66

Date of Accounts	Dec 11	Dec 10	Dec 09
Sales Turnover	7m	7m	9m
Pre Tax Profit/Loss	82	-499	-2m
Working Capital	1m	456	2m
Fixed Assets	161	390	385
Current Assets	4m	3m	4m
Current Liabilities	2m	2m	2m

Seaham

3 T Ltd (Thermal Transfer Technology)

Hall Dene Way Seaham Grange Industrial Estate, Seaham, SR7 0PU
Tel: 0191-523 8002 **Fax:** 0191-523 8342
E-mail: sales@three-t.co.uk
Bank(s): Barclays
Directors: A. Thomas (MD), D. Hill (Sales), I. Pearson (Fin)
Managers: J. Greenwood (Personnel)
Immediate Holding Company: ENLUCO LIMITED
Registration no: 05150676 **Date established:** 2004
No.of Employees: 51 - 100 **Product Groups:** 36, 38, 40

A G & P

Unit 7a Cold Hesledon Industrial Estate Cold Hesledon, Seaham, SR7 8ST
Tel: 0191-513 1010 **Fax:** 0191-513 1515
E-mail: agp2print@yahoo.co.uk
Website: http://www.agandp.co.uk
Managers: L. Parker (), L. Parker
Immediate Holding Company: AG&P LIMITED
Registration no: 07106588 **Date established:** 2009 **Turnover:** £1m - £2m
No.of Employees: 1 - 10 **Product Groups:** 24, 25, 27, 28, 30, 33, 35, 37, 39, 40, 49, 51, 52, 64, 68, 80, 81, 83, 84

Amundsen & Smith

Cargodurham Distribution Centre, Seaham, SR7 7NZ
Tel: 0191-581 2315 **Fax:** 0191-581 7360
E-mail: enquiries@amundsen-smith.co.uk
Website: http://www.amundsen-smith.co.uk
Managers: N. Kelly
Immediate Holding Company: SAVICK LIMITED
Registration no: 00993225 **Date established:** 1970
Turnover: £500,000 - £1m **No.of Employees:** 1 - 10 **Product Groups:** 74, 76

Date of Accounts	Mar 08	Mar 07	Mar 06
Working Capital	34	32	16
Fixed Assets	2	3	2
Current Assets	117	77	123
Current Liabilities	84	46	107
Total Share Capital	5	5	5

John Calvert Electrical Ltd

60-62 Church Street, Seaham, SR7 7HF
Tel: 0191-581 2731 **Fax:** 0191-513 0047
E-mail: john@calvertselectrical.co.uk
Website: http://www.calverts.org.uk
Directors: J. Calvert (MD)
Immediate Holding Company: JOHN CALVERT (ELECTRICAL) LIMITED
Registration no: 00532674 **VAT No.:** GB 176 1764 42
Date established: 1954 **Turnover:** £1m - £2m **No.of Employees:** 11 - 20
Product Groups: 77

Date of Accounts	Sep 11	Sep 10	Sep 09
Working Capital	248	218	228
Fixed Assets	95	111	54
Current Assets	538	538	658

Dynamic Arc Ltd

Unit 5a Chipchase Court, Seaham Grange Industrial Estate, Seaham, SR7 0PP
Tel: 0191-521 1501
E-mail: peter@dynamicarc.co.uk
Directors: P. Greaves (MD)
Immediate Holding Company: DYNAMIC ARC LIMITED
Registration no: 03553204 **Date established:** 1998
No.of Employees: 1 - 10 **Product Groups:** 46

Date of Accounts	May 11	May 10	May 09
Working Capital	14	9	34
Fixed Assets	22	5	6
Current Assets	163	91	108

East Durham Signs

Greenhills Gray Road, Murton, Seaham, SR7 9LN
Tel: 0191-526 3333 **Fax:** 0191-526 3333
E-mail: info@eastdurham.co.uk
Website: http://www.eastdurhamsigns.co.uk
Directors: B. Singh (Prop)
No.of Employees: 1 - 10 **Product Groups:** 27, 28, 30, 37, 39, 40, 44, 45, 49, 67, 80

Date of Accounts	Jan 08	Jan 07
Working Capital	6	-4
Fixed Assets	7	9
Current Assets	22	9
Current Liabilities	15	13

Industrial Deep Cleaning Ltd

8 Adelaide Row, Seaham, SR7 7EF
Tel: 0191-513 0158 **Fax:** 0191-513 0158
E-mail: leeidc@aol.com
Website: http://www.deep-cleaning.net
Directors: L. Bryan (MD)
Immediate Holding Company: INDUSTRIAL DEEP CLEANING LIMITED
Registration no: 04991099 **Date established:** 2003
No.of Employees: 1 - 10 **Product Groups:** 40, 48, 52

Date of Accounts	Dec 11	Dec 10	Dec 09
Working Capital	36	17	29
Fixed Assets	43	29	34
Current Assets	103	85	82

M B Air Systems Ltd

Woodland House Unit 2 Hall Dene Way, Seaham Grange Industrial Estate, Seaham, SR7 0PU
Tel: 0191-521 4111 **Fax:** 0191-521 1616
E-mail: sales@mbairsystems.co.uk
Website: http://www.mbairsystems.co.uk
Bank(s): Clydesdale, London
Directors: R. Donalson (Dir)
Immediate Holding Company: MB AIR SYSTEMS LIMITED
Registration no: SC210643 **VAT No.:** GB 556 5568 04
Date established: 2000 **No.of Employees:** 11 - 20 **Product Groups:** 40, 46, 52

Date of Accounts	Dec 11	Dec 10	Dec 09
Sales Turnover	16m	14m	14m
Pre Tax Profit/Loss	604	540	530
Working Capital	965	632	390
Fixed Assets	1m	1m	1m
Current Assets	6m	4m	4m
Current Liabilities	3m	3m	2m

M & K Services Northern Ltd

George Street Industrial Estate, Seaham, SR7 7SL
Tel: 0191-581 7291
E-mail: maurice@mandk.co.uk
Website: http://www.mandkservices.com
Managers: M. Trainor (Mgr)
Immediate Holding Company: M + K SERVICES (NORTHERN) LIMITED
Registration no: 04654817 **Date established:** 2003
No.of Employees: 1 - 10 **Product Groups:** 35

Date of Accounts	Jul 11	Jul 10	Jul 09
Working Capital	319	311	301
Fixed Assets	64	44	34
Current Assets	487	416	365

Geoffrey Maskell Engineering Ltd

Londonderry Works, Seaham, SR7 7SL
Tel: 0191-581 3244 **Fax:** 0191-581 0273
E-mail: info@maskelleng.co.uk
Website: http://www.maskelleng.co.uk
Bank(s): Barclays
Directors: G. Maskell (Prop)
Managers: A. Byrom (Chief Mgr)
Ultimate Holding Company: GEOFFREY MASKELL ENGINEERING LIMITED
Immediate Holding Company: GEOFFREY MASKELL ENGINEERING LIMITED
Registration no: 00509173 **Date established:** 1978 **Turnover:** £1m - £2m
No.of Employees: 11 - 20 **Product Groups:** 32, 33, 34, 35, 36, 37, 38, 39, 40, 41, 42, 44, 45, 46, 48, 49, 52, 61, 63, 66, 67, 76

Date of Accounts	Mar 10	Mar 09	Mar 08
Working Capital	315	395	238
Fixed Assets	421	461	504
Current Assets	786	1m	1m

Northern Machine Tool Repairs

81 Weymouth Drive, Seaham, SR7 8DF
Tel: 07855-265429 **Fax:** 0191-581 6348
E-mail: joe.salts@btconnect.com
Website: http://www.nmtr.co.uk
Directors: J. Salt (Prop)
Date established: 2003 **No.of Employees:** 1 - 10 **Product Groups:** 46

Northern Remedials

61 Beadnell Drive, Seaham, SR7 7WG
Tel: 0800-148 8346 **Fax:** 0191-552 8932
E-mail: enquiries@northern-remedials.co.uk
Website: http://www.northern-remedials.co.uk
Directors: T. Donkin (Dir)
Immediate Holding Company: NORTHERN REMEDIALS LTD
Registration no: 06059813 **Date established:** 2007
Turnover: £250,000 - £500,000 **No.of Employees:** 1 - 10
Product Groups: 52

R S H
Unit 2a Chipchase Court Seaham Grange Industrial Estate, Seaham, SR7 0PP
Tel: 0191-523 8989 **Fax:** 0191-523 8890
E-mail: rshseaham@aol.com
Managers: K. Collings (District Mgr)
No.of Employees: 1 - 10 **Product Groups:** 29, 63, 66

Seaham Safety Services Ltd
Unit 12c Enterprise Court, Seaham Grange Industrial Estate, Seaham, SR7 0PS
Tel: 0191-581 8400 **Fax:** 0191-521 4793
E-mail: info@seahamsafetyservicesltd.com
Website: http://www.seahamsafetyservicesltd.com
Managers: G. Macpherson Jnr
Immediate Holding Company: SEAHAM SAFETY SERVICES LTD
Registration no: 06004656 **VAT No.:** GB 916 3825 16
Date established: 2006 **No.of Employees:** 1 - 10 **Product Groups:** 54, 80, 84, 86

Date of Accounts	Oct 11	Oct 10	Oct 09
Working Capital	2	20	77
Fixed Assets	22	24	25
Current Assets	43	76	134

Shildon

Brancepeth Engineering Ltd
Unit 14 Hackworth Industrial Park, Shildon, DL4 1HF
Tel: 01388-777134 **Fax:** 01388-776194
E-mail: mail@brancepethengineering.co.uk
Website: http://www.brancepethengineering.co.uk
Directors: C. Haggie (Fin)
Managers: L. Firbanks (Purch Mgr)
Immediate Holding Company: BRANCEPETH ENGINEERING LIMITED
Registration no: 05446726 **Date established:** 2005
No.of Employees: 21 - 50 **Product Groups:** 46

Date of Accounts	Oct 11	Oct 10	Oct 09
Working Capital	17	31	-80
Fixed Assets	153	189	214
Current Assets	251	246	159

C R D Devices Ltd
3 All Saints Industrial Estate Darlington Road, Shildon, DL4 2RD
Tel: 01388-778400 **Fax:** 01388-778800
E-mail: sales@crd-devices.co.uk
Website: http://www.crd-devices.co.uk
Directors: S. Cockrill (MD)
Immediate Holding Company: C.R.D. DEVICES LTD.
Registration no: 03110347 **Date established:** 1995 **Turnover:** £5m - £10m
No.of Employees: 1 - 10 **Product Groups:** 36, 37, 38, 40, 48, 67

Date of Accounts	Dec 08	Dec 07	Mar 11
Working Capital	58	53	224
Fixed Assets	16	11	11
Current Assets	428	381	840

D J Camp Ltd
Unit 10 Furnace Industrial Estate, Shildon, DL4 1QB
Tel: 01388-777393 **Fax:** 01388-776232
E-mail: robert@djcamp.co.uk
Website: http://www.djcamp.co.uk
Directors: R. Camp (Dir)
Immediate Holding Company: DJ CAMP LTD
Registration no: 05632718 **Date established:** 2005
No.of Employees: 1 - 10 **Product Groups:** 35

Date of Accounts	Dec 11	Dec 10	Dec 09
Working Capital	90	61	38
Fixed Assets	53	64	49
Current Assets	231	215	165

Magneco Metrel UK Ltd
Hackworth Industrial Park, Shildon, DL4 1HG
Tel: 01388-777484 **Fax:** 01388-776286
E-mail: colleen@magneco-metrel.com
Website: http://www.magnaco-metrel.com
Managers: M. Taylor, D. Parks (Tech Serv Mgr)
Ultimate Holding Company: MAGNECO METREL INC (USA)
Immediate Holding Company: MAGNECO METREL U.K. LIMITED
Registration no: 02501896 **Date established:** 1990 **Turnover:** £5m - £10m
No.of Employees: 1 - 10 **Product Groups:** 33

Date of Accounts	Dec 11	Dec 10	Dec 09
Sales Turnover	5m	6m	4m
Pre Tax Profit/Loss	336	621	-379
Working Capital	2m	2m	2m
Fixed Assets	292	325	371
Current Assets	3m	3m	3m
Current Liabilities	237	191	91

P P G Industries UK
Darlington Road, Shildon, DL4 2QP
Tel: 01388-772541 **Fax:** 01388-774373
E-mail: jallison@ppg.com
Website: http://www.ppg.com
Directors: S. Clarkson (Fin)
Managers: J. Allison (Admin Off), K. Punshon (Personnel), J. Carroll
No.of Employees: 101 - 250 **Product Groups:** 46, 48

PPG Aerospace
Darlington Road, Shildon, DL4 2QP
Tel: 01388-770222 **Fax:** 01388-770288
Website: http://www.ppg.com
Managers: K. Ramsey (Comm)
Immediate Holding Company: P.P.G.
Registration no: 02895435 **Date established:** 1928
Turnover: £20m - £50m **No.of Employees:** 1 - 10 **Product Groups:** 31, 32

Specialist Coating Ltd
All Saints Industrial Estate Darlington Road, Shildon, DL4 2RD
Tel: 01388-774034 **Fax:** 01388-777010
E-mail: admitchell@almitgroup.co.uk
Website: http://www.almitgroup.co.uk
Managers: A. Mitchell (Chief Mgr)
Immediate Holding Company: SPECIALIST COATINGS LIMITED
Registration no: 02792107 **Date established:** 1993
Turnover: £250,000 - £500,000 **No.of Employees:** 21 - 50
Product Groups: 46, 48

Date of Accounts	Mar 12	Mar 11	Mar 10
Working Capital	70	-242	-994
Fixed Assets	341	528	1m
Current Assets	2m	1m	2m

Winston Fabrications Ltd
Unit 4 Hackworth Industrial Park, Shildon, DL4 1HF
Tel: 01388-777989 **Fax:** 01388-776296
E-mail: anthony@winstonfabrications.co.uk
Directors: A. Hauxwell (MD)
Ultimate Holding Company: AKV HOLDINGS LTD
Immediate Holding Company: WINSTON FABRICATIONS LIMITED
Registration no: 06895695 **VAT No.:** GB 425 9667 17
Date established: 2009 **Turnover:** Up to £250,000
No.of Employees: 1 - 10 **Product Groups:** 35, 67

Date of Accounts	May 12	May 11	May 10
Working Capital	-9	-13	-1
Fixed Assets	1	1	N/A
Current Assets	16	39	59

Spennymoor

Advance Automated Systems Ltd
Unit 12 Enterprise City Meadowfield Avenue, Spennymoor, DL16 6JF
Tel: 01388-811122 **Fax:** 01388-811133
E-mail: sales@advanceautomation.co.uk
Website: http://www.advanceautomation.co.uk
Directors: B. Roberts (MD), I. Slack (Fin)
Managers: S. Graham (Sales & Mktg Mg)
Immediate Holding Company: ADVANCE AUTOMATED SYSTEMS LIMITED
Registration no: 04905449 **Date established:** 2003
Turnover: £500,000 - £1m **No.of Employees:** 11 - 20 **Product Groups:** 67

Date of Accounts	Sep 11	Sep 10	Sep 09
Working Capital	52	29	15
Fixed Assets	21	16	15
Current Assets	366	247	205

Alto Bollards UK Ltd
Unit 1b Tudhoe Industrial Estate, Spennymoor, DL16 6TL
Tel: 01388-810782 **Fax:** 0800-4715242
E-mail: paul@altobollards.com
Website: http://www.altobollards.com
Directors: G. Styles (Grp Chief Exec), P. Rickelton (MD), P. Rickelton (Prop)
Managers: G. King (Purch Mgr), S. Linsay (Personnel)
Immediate Holding Company: ALTO BOLLARDS LIMITED
Registration no: 04410918 **Date established:** 2002
Turnover: £500,000 - £1m **No.of Employees:** 1 - 10 **Product Groups:** 26, 33, 39, 66, 84

Date of Accounts	Mar 08	Mar 07	Mar 06
Working Capital	-15	-2	-1
Fixed Assets	8	9	11
Current Assets	151	81	80
Current Liabilities	166	83	81

Black & Decker Factory Outlet
Green Lane, Spennymoor, DL16 6JG
Tel: 08707-521270 **Fax:** 08707-521261
Website: http://www.blackanddecker.com
Directors: S. Swaddle (Dir)
Ultimate Holding Company: STANLEY BLACK & DECKER CORPORATION (USA)
Immediate Holding Company: BLACK & DECKER
Registration no: 00291547 **Date established:** 1934
No.of Employees: 1 - 10 **Product Groups:** 36, 37

Date of Accounts	Dec 10	Dec 09	Dec 08
Sales Turnover	23m	79m	100m
Pre Tax Profit/Loss	-3m	-19m	-10m
Working Capital	61m	131m	152m
Fixed Assets	296m	297m	299m
Current Assets	121m	198m	269m
Current Liabilities	2m	9m	8m

Deerness Rubber Co. Ltd
Coulson Street, Spennymoor, DL16 7RS
Tel: 01388-420301 **Fax:** 01388-420284
E-mail: sales@deerness-rubber.co.uk
Website: http://www.deerness-rubber.co.uk
Directors: P. McKenna (Sales), S. McKenna (Dir)
Immediate Holding Company: DEERNESS RUBBER COMPANY LIMITED
Registration no: 01402935 **VAT No.:** GB 322 7429 69
Date established: 1978 **Turnover:** £500,000 - £1m
No.of Employees: 21 - 50 **Product Groups:** 29, 30, 35, 49, 63

Date of Accounts	Mar 11	Mar 10	Mar 09
Working Capital	951	859	824
Fixed Assets	523	540	542
Current Assets	1m	1m	1m

Design & Security Services Ltd
Enterprise City Meadowfield Avenue, Spennymoor, DL16 6JF
Tel: 01388-811155 **Fax:** 01388-811155
E-mail: mark.kelly@dandss.co.uk
Website: http://www.designsecurity.co.uk
Directors: M. Kelly (Dir)
Immediate Holding Company: DESIGN AND SECURITY SERVICES LIMITED
Registration no: 05025344 **Date established:** 2004
No.of Employees: 1 - 10 **Product Groups:** 35

Date of Accounts	Mar 11	Mar 10	Mar 09
Working Capital	27	27	4
Fixed Assets	22	20	24
Current Assets	125	157	128

Enviromental Lighting
21 Stratton Street, Spennymoor, DL16 7TW
Tel: 01388-812181 **Fax:** 01388-812181
Directors: C. Bateman (MD)
Immediate Holding Company: CB LIGHTING DISTRIBUTORS LIMITED
Date established: 2004 **No.of Employees:** 1 - 10 **Product Groups:** 37, 67

Date of Accounts	Mar 11	Mar 10	Mar 09
Working Capital	51	25	14
Current Assets	113	84	51

Howell Cummings Catering Equipment Ltd
Unit 5 Enterprise City Green Lane Industrial Estate, Spennymoor, DL16 6JF
Tel: 01388-816555 **Fax:** 01388-816444
E-mail: sales@howellcummings.co.uk
Website: http://www.howellcummings.co.uk
Directors: P. Surtees (MD)
Immediate Holding Company: HOWELL CUMMINGS CATERING EQUIPMENT LIMITED
Registration no: 07532181 **Date established:** 2011
No.of Employees: 1 - 10 **Product Groups:** 20, 40, 41

Date of Accounts	Mar 10	Mar 09	Mar 08
Working Capital	-26	-33	-32
Fixed Assets	34	40	50
Current Assets	412	616	399

C C Jensen Ltd
Unit 26 Enterprise City Meadowfield Avenue, Spennymoor, DL16 6JF
Tel: 01388-420721 **Fax:** 01388-420718
E-mail: bl@cjcuk.co.uk
Website: http://www.cjc.dk
Managers: B. Lee (Mgr)
Ultimate Holding Company: CC JENSEN A/S (DENMARK)
Immediate Holding Company: C. C. JENSEN LIMITED
Registration no: 02504210 **Date established:** 1990 **Turnover:** £2m - £5m
No.of Employees: 1 - 10 **Product Groups:** 38, 42

Date of Accounts	Dec 11	Dec 10	Dec 09
Working Capital	181	96	139
Fixed Assets	42	46	39
Current Assets	734	1m	427

Katem Logistics Ltd
Unit 9 Merrington Lane Industrial Estate, Spennymoor, DL16 7XL
Tel: 01388-810999 **Fax:** 01388-813733
E-mail: trevor@katem.co.uk
Website: http://www.katem.co.uk
Directors: C. Wood (MD)
Ultimate Holding Company: KATEM LOGISTICS LIMITED
Immediate Holding Company: KATEM HIRE LIMITED
Registration no: 03053229 **Date established:** 1995
Turnover: £500,000 - £1m **No.of Employees:** 11 - 20 **Product Groups:** 77

Date of Accounts	May 08	Mar 11	Mar 10
Working Capital	710	1	1
Fixed Assets	434	N/A	N/A
Current Assets	2m	77	286

R Taylor & Sons Ltd
12 Cheapside, Spennymoor, DL16 6DJ
Tel: 01388-815426 **Fax:** 01388-801477
E-mail: barriebt@yahoo.co.uk
Directors: B. Taylor (MD)
Managers: B. Knox (Mgr), L. Brack (I.T. Exec)
Immediate Holding Company: R. TAYLOR & SONS LIMITED
Registration no: 00605687 **Date established:** 1958 **Turnover:** £2m - £5m
No.of Employees: 1 - 10 **Product Groups:** 61

T A Plastics Ltd
Tudhoe Industrial Estate, Spennymoor, DL16 6TL
Tel: 01388-814858 **Fax:** 01388-819534
E-mail: general@taplastics.co.uk
Website: http://www.taplastics.co.uk
Directors: J. Humphreys (MD)
Ultimate Holding Company: T.A.P. LIMITED
Immediate Holding Company: T.A. PLASTIC SUPPLIES LIMITED
Registration no: 01326610 **VAT No.:** GB 569 4681 85
Date established: 1977 **No.of Employees:** 11 - 20 **Product Groups:** 30

Date of Accounts	Dec 11	Dec 10	Dec 09
Working Capital	239	207	183
Fixed Assets	50	53	48
Current Assets	718	580	494
Current Liabilities	N/A	70	136

T P Enterprises Ltd
Meadowfield Avenue Green Lane Industrial Estate, Spennymoor, DL16 6YJ
Tel: 01388-420555 **Fax:** 01388-420777
E-mail: adam@taylor-packaging.co.uk
Directors: A. Taylor (Sales)
Immediate Holding Company: T.P. ENTERPRISES LIMITED
Registration no: 01999397 **Date established:** 1986
No.of Employees: 11 - 20 **Product Groups:** 38, 42

Date of Accounts	Mar 11	Mar 10	Mar 09
Working Capital	-204	-115	71
Fixed Assets	414	439	410
Current Assets	471	399	540
Current Liabilities	N/A	132	N/A

Thorn Lighting Ltd
House of Light Butchers Race, Spennymoor, DL16 6HL
Tel: 01388-420042 **Fax:** 01388-420156
E-mail: terry.carmichael@thornlighting.com
Website: http://www.thornlighting.co.uk
Bank(s): National Westminster
Directors: T. Carmichael (Chief Op Offcr), J. Derweduwe (Mkt Research), K. Herrick (Mkt Research), D. Johnston (Chief Op Offcr)
Managers: T. Lawson (Sales Prom Mgr), J. Goodwin (Personnel), P. Houghton (Comptroller), M. Simpson (Tech Serv Mgr), J. Goodwin (Personnel), P. Arthy
Ultimate Holding Company: ZUMTOBEL AG (AUSTRIA)
Immediate Holding Company: THORN LIGHTING LIMITED
Registration no: 00263866 **VAT No.:** GB 626 8664 06
Date established: 1932 **Turnover:** £250m - £500m
No.of Employees: 501 - 1000 **Product Groups:** 36, 37

Date of Accounts	Apr 12	Apr 11	Apr 10
Sales Turnover	112m	105m	108m
Pre Tax Profit/Loss	-8m	-13m	-11m
Working Capital	3m	-3m	-3m
Fixed Assets	51m	55m	59m
Current Assets	36m	33m	28m
Current Liabilities	11m	7m	6m

Stanley

B L S Electronics Ltd
14 Morrison Industrial Estate North, Stanley, DH9 7RU
Tel: 01207-234018 **Fax:** 01207-238201
E-mail: s.williams@btconnect.com
Website: http://www.blselectronics.co.uk
Bank(s): Lloyds TSB Bank plc
Directors: F. Williams (MD)
Immediate Holding Company: B.L.S. ELECTRONICS LIMITED
Registration no: 01090671 **VAT No.:** GB 178 1422 58
Date established: 1973 **Turnover:** £250,000 - £500,000
No.of Employees: 11 - 20 **Product Groups:** 37

Date of Accounts	May 11	May 10	May 09
Working Capital	38	46	61
Fixed Assets	88	31	33
Current Assets	184	152	149

B S & A Power Press
Unit 7-8 Tanfield Lea Industrial Estate South Tanfield Lea, Stanley, DH9 9QX
Tel: 01207-283377 **Fax:** 01207-283366
E-mail: bsassociates@aol.com
Directors: R. Fay (Dir), V. Dee (Dir), B. Smith (Co Sec), B. Smith (MD), M. Newton (Dir)
Immediate Holding Company: B.S. & A POWER PRESS LIMITED
Registration no: 03951094 **VAT No.:** GB 733 9172 25
Date established: 2000 **Turnover:** £500,000 - £1m
No.of Employees: 1 - 10 **Product Groups:** 48

Con Mech Engineers Ltd
Hare Law Industrial Estate, Stanley, DH9 8UR
Tel: 01207-230621 **Fax:** 01207-290100
E-mail: sales@conmecheng.co.uk
Website: http://www.conmecheng.co.uk
Bank(s): National Westminster Bank Plc
Directors: R. Dilley (Dir)
Ultimate Holding Company: CON MECH GROUP LIMITED
Immediate Holding Company: CON MECH ENGINEERS LIMITED
Registration no: 00677804 **Date established:** 1960
Turnover: £10m - £20m **No.of Employees:** 51 - 100 **Product Groups:** 41

Date of Accounts	Dec 11	Dec 10	Dec 09
Sales Turnover	11m	9m	8m
Pre Tax Profit/Loss	932	282	357
Working Capital	2m	2m	1m
Fixed Assets	2m	2m	2m
Current Assets	4m	5m	4m
Current Liabilities	362	238	250

Cox Agri
Unit 1 Greencroft Industrial Park Greencroft Industrial Park, Stanley, DH9 7YA
Tel: 08456-008081 **Fax:** 01207-529966
E-mail: sales@coxagri.com
Website: http://www.coxagri.com
Bank(s): National Westminster Bank Plc
Managers: S. Goodfellow (Mktg Serv Mgr), D. Thompson (Comptroller), I. Spore (Buyer), J. Leedham (Tech Serv Mgr), A. Thwaite
Ultimate Holding Company: COX AGRI LIMITED
Immediate Holding Company: ALLIGATOR SHEEP HANDLING LIMITED
Registration no: 02561875 **VAT No.:** GB 217 8268 47
Date established: 1990 **Turnover:** £2m - £5m **No.of Employees:** 21 - 50
Product Groups: 30, 32, 35, 36, 38, 41, 67

Dyer Engineering Ltd
Unit 3-5 Morrison Industrial Estate Nort, Stanley, DH9 7RU
Tel: 01207-288020 **Fax:** 01207-282834
E-mail: paul@dyer-engineering.ltd.uk
Website: http://www.dyer.co.uk
Bank(s): Lloyds TSB Bank plc
Directors: R. Bradley (Fin), P. Dyer (Ch)
Managers: M. Bick
Immediate Holding Company: DYER ENGINEERING LTD.
Registration no: 02186740 **VAT No.:** GB 495 9194 82
Date established: 1987 **Turnover:** £5m - £10m
No.of Employees: 51 - 100 **Product Groups:** 48

Date of Accounts	May 11	May 10	May 09
Sales Turnover	7m	6m	N/A
Pre Tax Profit/Loss	101	-384	504
Working Capital	856	670	1m
Fixed Assets	1m	2m	2m
Current Assets	2m	2m	3m
Current Liabilities	453	471	604

Greencroft Bottling
Greencroft Industrial Estate, Stanley, DH9 7XP
Tel: 01207-521400 **Fax:** 01207-521444
E-mail: veronica@lanchesterwines.co.uk
Website: http://www.greencroftbottling.co.uk
Directors: V. Cleary (Dir), A. Close (Fin)
Managers: R. Mitchell (Ops Mgr), A. Armstrong (Prod Mgr)
Immediate Holding Company: GREENCROFT BOTTLING COMPANY LIMITED
Registration no: 04768870 **Date established:** 2003
Turnover: £10m - £20m **No.of Employees:** 51 - 100 **Product Groups:** 38, 42

Date of Accounts	Jun 11	Jun 10	Jun 09
Sales Turnover	14m	N/A	6m
Pre Tax Profit/Loss	1m	N/A	326
Working Capital	-372	-944	-471
Fixed Assets	3m	2m	2m
Current Assets	4m	3m	3m
Current Liabilities	944	N/A	2m

Power Tools Services
The Chapel Cheviot View Front Street, Dipton, Stanley, DH9 9DQ
Tel: 01207-571500
Directors: R. Nicks (Prop)
Date established: 1995 **No.of Employees:** 1 - 10 **Product Groups:** 36

Rasmi Electronics Ltd
Morrison Road, Stanley, DH9 7RX
Tel: 01207-291300 **Fax:** 01207-291304
E-mail: accounts@rasmi.com
Website: http://www.rasmi.com
Bank(s): Barclays
Directors: A. Hampton (Dir)
Immediate Holding Company: RASMI ELECTRONICS LIMITED
Registration no: 01179123 **VAT No.:** GB 178 4527 29
Date established: 1974 **Turnover:** £10m - £20m
No.of Employees: 21 - 50 **Product Groups:** 37

Date of Accounts	Dec 11	Dec 10	Dec 09
Working Capital	-212	-329	-319
Fixed Assets	775	813	864
Current Assets	964	1m	1m
Current Liabilities	198	N/A	N/A

Schmitz Cargobull UK Ltd
North Road, Stanley, DH9 8HJ
Tel: 01207-282882 **Fax:** 01207-232479
E-mail: info@cargobull.com
Website: http://www.cargobull.com
Directors: A. Joyce (Purch), N. Summers (Sales), C. Skinner (Tech Serv)
Managers: P. Avery (Ops Mgr), A. Corr (Mktg Serv Mgr), S. Huntsman (Personnel), P. Gill (I.T. Exec), D. Sidlow (Ops Mgr), C. Gill (Sales Prom Mgr), W. Barr (Chief Acct)
Ultimate Holding Company: SCHMITZ CARGOBULL AG (GERMANY)
Immediate Holding Company: SCHMITZ CARGOBULL (U.K.) LIMITED
Registration no: 02657467 **VAT No.:** GB 569 6458 66
Date established: 1991 **Turnover:** £20m - £50m **No.of Employees:** 1 - 10
Product Groups: 39

Date of Accounts	Mar 11	Mar 10	Mar 09
Sales Turnover	48m	36m	65m
Pre Tax Profit/Loss	-1m	-9m	5m
Working Capital	-1m	-343	7m
Fixed Assets	2m	3m	7m
Current Assets	15m	9m	17m
Current Liabilities	2m	846	2m

Spectrum Lighting N E Ltd
58 Front Street, Stanley, DH9 0HU
Tel: 01207-280907
Managers: C. Lowery (Mgr)
Immediate Holding Company: SPECTRUM LIGHTING (N.E.) LIMITED
Registration no: 04036877 **Date established:** 2000
No.of Employees: 1 - 10 **Product Groups:** 37, 67

Date of Accounts	Oct 11	Oct 10	Oct 09
Working Capital	146	99	101
Fixed Assets	26	18	15
Current Assets	621	592	547

Trimdon Station

D L I Engineering Ltd
Trimdon Grange Industrial Estate Trimdon Grange, Trimdon Station, TS29 6PA
Tel: 01429-880454 **Fax:** 01429-880369
E-mail: info@dlipe.plus.com
Website: http://www.dlipe.plus.com
Directors: B. Wells (MD)
Managers: A. Sutton (Tech Serv Mgr), C. Starling (Fin Mgr), S. Quinn (Buyer)
Immediate Holding Company: DLI ENGINEERING LIMITED
Registration no: 06587952 **Date established:** 2008 **Turnover:** £1m - £2m
No.of Employees: 21 - 50 **Product Groups:** 46, 48

Date of Accounts	Apr 12	Apr 11	Apr 10
Working Capital	34	-125	-138
Fixed Assets	358	261	280
Current Assets	1m	943	555
Current Liabilities	250	294	197

D L I Seals Ltd
Trimdon Grange Industrial Estate Trimdon Grange, Trimdon Station, TS29 6EW
Tel: 01429-881660 **Fax:** 01429-882299
E-mail: malcolm.purdy@dliseals.co.uk
Website: http://www.dliseals.com
Bank(s): National Westminster Bank Plc
Directors: G. Purdy (Dir)
Managers: M. Purdy (Mgr)
Immediate Holding Company: DLI SEALS LIMITED
Registration no: 01436831 **Date established:** 1979 **Turnover:** £1m - £2m
No.of Employees: 21 - 50 **Product Groups:** 27, 29, 30, 33, 36, 40, 66

Date of Accounts	Dec 11	Dec 10	Dec 09
Working Capital	396	256	196
Fixed Assets	262	287	309
Current Assets	771	671	550

Halcyon Building Systems
Unit 2f Trimdon Grange Industrial Estate Trimdon Grange, Trimdon Station, TS29 6PA
Tel: 01429-882555 **Fax:** 01429-882666
E-mail: halcyon.bs@ntlworld.com
Website: http://www.halcyonbuildingsystems.co.uk
Directors: A. Richardson (MD)
Immediate Holding Company: HALCYON BUILDING SYSTEMS LIMITED
Registration no: 04435383 **Date established:** 2002
Turnover: £500,000 - £1m **No.of Employees:** 11 - 20
Product Groups: 24, 25, 26, 27, 30, 33, 34, 35, 39, 40, 45, 48, 52, 66

Date of Accounts	May 11	May 10	May 09
Working Capital	304	308	486
Fixed Assets	112	110	28
Current Assets	3m	1m	1m

Wingate

Fidgeon Ltd
Unit 3 Wingate Grange Industrial Estate, Wingate, TS28 5AH
Tel: 01429-836655 **Fax:** 01429-837766
E-mail: sales@fidgeon.co.uk
Website: http://www.fidgeon.com
Directors: P. Fidgeon (MD)
Immediate Holding Company: FIDGEON LIMITED
Registration no: 01224694 **VAT No.:** GB 259 4596 10
Date established: 1975 **Turnover:** £2m - £5m **No.of Employees:** 1 - 10
Product Groups: 27, 37, 38

Date of Accounts	Sep 11	Sep 10	Sep 09
Working Capital	16	701	17
Fixed Assets	144	138	145
Current Assets	660	701	652

ESSEX

Barking

A M Forktrucks Ltd
Unit 1-4 Riverside Industrial Estate Thames Road, Barking, IG11 0ND
Tel: 020-8594 5313 **Fax:** 020-8507 7776
E-mail: allan@amforktrucks.com
Website: http://www.amforktrucks.com
Directors: A. Pickton (MD)
Immediate Holding Company: A.M. FORKTRUCKS LIMITED
Registration no: 03622865 **Date established:** 1998
No.of Employees: 11 - 20 **Product Groups:** 35, 39, 45

Date of Accounts	Aug 11	Aug 10	Aug 09
Working Capital	117	104	111
Fixed Assets	266	245	264
Current Assets	336	374	466

A & M Security Co.
First Floor Pacific House Hertford Road, Barking, IG11 8BL
Tel: 020-8591 8181 **Fax:** 020-8591 8585
E-mail: info@amsecuritycompany.co.uk
Website: http://www.amsecuritycompany.co.uk
Directors: S. Hayden (MD)
Managers: J. Hayden (Personnel)
No.of Employees: 1 - 10 **Product Groups:** 44, 81

Adler & Allan Ltd
Container Base Box Lane Renwick Road, Barking, IG11 0SQ
Tel: 020-8555 7111 **Fax:** 020-8519 3090
E-mail: sales@adlerandallan.co.uk
Website: http://www.adlerandallan.co.uk
Bank(s): National Westminster, 116 Fenchurch St, EC3M 5AN
Directors: G. Gibson (Co Sec), M. Calvert (Dir)
Managers: P. Cunliffe (Personnel)
Ultimate Holding Company: ADLER & ALLAN HOLDINGS LIMITED
Immediate Holding Company: ADLER & ALLAN LIMITED
Registration no: 00318460 **VAT No.:** GB 232 2474 90
Date established: 1936 **Turnover:** £20m - £50m
No.of Employees: 101 - 250 **Product Groups:** 39, 52, 54

Date of Accounts	Sep 11	Sep 10	Sep 09
Sales Turnover	35m	28m	24m
Pre Tax Profit/Loss	3m	2m	654
Working Capital	5m	3m	189
Fixed Assets	8m	7m	10m
Current Assets	11m	6m	5m
Current Liabilities	1m	1m	2m

All Metal Products Ltd
30 Thames Road, Barking, IG11 0HZ
Tel: 020-8594 5666 **Fax:** 020-8594 3967
E-mail: clarksmetalproducts@yahoo.com
Directors: B. Offord (MD)
Immediate Holding Company: ALL METAL PRODUCTS LIMITED
Registration no: 07041171 **Date established:** 2009
No.of Employees: 1 - 10 **Product Groups:** 35

Amba Forwarding London Ltd
Unit 6 Trafalgar Business Centre River Road, Barking, IG11 0JU
Tel: 020-8591 1600 **Fax:** 020-8591 1700
E-mail: info@ambaforwarding.com
Website: http://www.ambaforwarding.com
Directors: K. Patel (Fin), K. Shah (MD)
Immediate Holding Company: AMBA FORWARDING (LONDON) LIMITED
Registration no: 01281193 **VAT No.:** GB 249 6201 56
Date established: 1976 **Turnover:** £1m - £2m **No.of Employees:** 1 - 10
Product Groups: 72, 75, 76

Date of Accounts	Dec 11	Dec 10	Dec 09
Working Capital	13	-2	-7
Fixed Assets	197	201	200
Current Assets	191	159	175

Architype Metal Work
4 Rippleside Commercial Estate Ripple Road, Barking, IG11 0RJ
Tel: 020-8517 4216 **Fax:** 020-8517 4216
Website: http://www.architypemetalwork.co.uk
Directors: N. Stapley (Ptnr)
Date established: 2003 **No.of Employees:** 1 - 10 **Product Groups:** 35

Barking & Dagenham Council Events Department
4th Floor Maritime House 1 Linton Road, Barking, IG11 8HG
Tel: 020-8227 3591 **Fax:** 020-8594 1576
E-mail: info@bdchamber.co.uk
Website: http://www.bdchamber.co.uk
Managers: J. Hunte
Immediate Holding Company: BARKING AND DAGENHAM CHAMBER OF COMMERCE LIMITED
Registration no: 03038503 **Date established:** 1995
Turnover: Up to £250,000 **No.of Employees:** 1 - 10 **Product Groups:** 87

Date of Accounts	Mar 11	Mar 10	Mar 09
Working Capital	26	19	28
Fixed Assets	104	94	86
Current Assets	54	34	47

Brighthouse Ltd
Focal House 12-18 Station Parade, Barking, IG11 8DN
Tel: 020-8594 9194 **Fax:** 020-8594 3171
Website: http://www.brighthouse.co.uk
Managers: R. Malling (Mgr)
Ultimate Holding Company: VISION CAPITAL PARTNERS VI B LP
Immediate Holding Company: BRIGHTHOUSE LIMITED
Registration no: 06073794 **Date established:** 2007
No.of Employees: 1 - 10 **Product Groups:** 36, 40

Date of Accounts	Mar 12	Mar 11	Mar 10
Sales Turnover	266m	228m	197m
Pre Tax Profit/Loss	29m	25m	20m
Working Capital	57m	49m	68m
Fixed Assets	171m	161m	123m
Current Assets	97m	87m	98m
Current Liabilities	29m	26m	22m

Brownings Electric Co. Ltd
11 Thames Road, Barking, IG11 0HG
Tel: 020-8591 3030 **Fax:** 020-8591 3030
E-mail: enquiries@browningselectric.co.uk
Website: http://www.browningselectric.co.uk
Bank(s): Barclays
Directors: J. Lake (MD)
Ultimate Holding Company: BEC (LONDON) LIMITED
Immediate Holding Company: BROWNINGS ELECTRIC COMPANY LIMITED
Registration no: 00362699 **Date established:** 1940 **Turnover:** £5m - £10m
No.of Employees: 51 - 100 **Product Groups:** 48

Date of Accounts	Dec 11	Dec 10	Dec 09
Sales Turnover	7m	7m	7m
Pre Tax Profit/Loss	868	398	586
Working Capital	2m	2m	3m
Fixed Assets	938	979	996
Current Assets	4m	3m	4m
Current Liabilities	811	846	538

Bullman Marine Supplies & Containers Ltd
84 River Road, Barking, IG11 0DS
Tel: 020-8594 6930 **Fax:** 020-8595 1837
E-mail: info@bullmans.co.uk
Website: http://www.bullmans.co.uk
Directors: S. Bullman (Dir), S. Bullman (MD)
Immediate Holding Company: BULLMAN MARINE SUPPLIES & CONTAINERS LIMITED
Registration no: 01220886 **Date established:** 1975
No.of Employees: 21 - 50 **Product Groups:** 35, 36, 40, 45, 48, 72

Date of Accounts	Jul 11	Jul 10	Jul 09
Working Capital	230	544	552
Fixed Assets	438	257	195
Current Assets	1m	1m	1m

Concorde Glass Ltd
111 River Road, Barking, IG11 0EG
Tel: 020-8507 9001 **Fax:** 020-8591 6771
E-mail: concordeglassltd@hotmail.co.uk
Website: http://www.concordeglass.co.uk
Bank(s): Lloyds TSB Bank plc
Directors: K. Walczak (MD), K. Walczak (Fin), P. Drummond (Dir)
Immediate Holding Company: CONCORDE GLASS LIMITED
Registration no: 01220255 **Date established:** 1987 **Turnover:** £5m - £10m
No.of Employees: 11 - 20 **Product Groups:** 66

Date of Accounts	Dec 10	Dec 09	Dec 08
Working Capital	1m	1m	1m
Fixed Assets	100	90	119
Current Assets	2m	2m	2m

Coral
Glebe House Vicarage Drive, Barking, IG11 7NS
Tel: 020-8591 5151 **Fax:** 020-8591 8761
Website: http://www.galacoral.co.uk
Directors: G. Hughes (Dir), J. Cronk (Dir), J. Hart (Dir), N. Gordon (Grp Chief Exec), S. Jones (Dir), W. Walsh (MD)
Ultimate Holding Company: Gala Coral Group Ltd
Immediate Holding Company: CORAL GROUP TRADING LIMITED
Registration no: 03674996 **Date established:** 1998 **Turnover:** £5m - £10m
No.of Employees: 1501 & over **Product Groups:** 89

Cosco UK Ltd
Cosco House Vicarage Drive, Barking, IG11 7NA
Tel: 020-8594 8688 **Fax:** 020-8594 7234
E-mail: reception@coscon.co.uk
Website: http://www.cosco.co.uk
Directors: M. Dong (Grp Chief Exec)
Managers: J. Lawrence (Personnel), R. Mendoza, A. Lewis (Tech Serv Mgr)
Ultimate Holding Company: CHINA OCEAN SHIPPING COMPANY (CHINA)
Immediate Holding Company: COSCO (UK) LIMITED
Registration no: 02216271 **VAT No.:** GB 494 2167 29
Date established: 1988 **Turnover:** £20m - £50m
No.of Employees: 21 - 50 **Product Groups:** 76

Date of Accounts	Dec 11	Dec 10	Dec 09
Sales Turnover	29m	35m	25m
Pre Tax Profit/Loss	1m	4m	1m
Working Capital	12m	11m	8m
Fixed Assets	5m	5m	5m
Current Assets	20m	17m	15m
Current Liabilities	7m	4m	5m

W E Deane Ltd
Mayesbrook House Lyon Business Park, Barking, IG11 0EU
Tel: 020-8532 6400 **Fax:** 020-8532 6497
E-mail: info@deanefreight.com
Website: http://www.deanefreight.com
Bank(s): Barclays
Directors: A. Doctors (Co Sec)
Immediate Holding Company: W.E. DEANE LIMITED
Registration no: 00768571 **VAT No.:** 246 3465 55 **Date established:** 1963
Turnover: £20m - £50m **No.of Employees:** 21 - 50 **Product Groups:** 72, 74, 75, 76

Date of Accounts	Jul 11	Jul 10	Jul 09
Sales Turnover	27m	20m	20m
Pre Tax Profit/Loss	415	316	68
Working Capital	2m	2m	2m
Fixed Assets	394	409	372
Current Assets	6m	5m	4m
Current Liabilities	981	405	318

Driscoll & Crowley
47a Suffolk Road, Barking, IG11 7QP
Tel: 020-7474 0777 **Fax:** 020-7473 3019
E-mail: info@driscollcrowley.co.uk
Website: http://www.driscollcrowley.co.uk
Directors: L. Austin (Dir)
Immediate Holding Company: DRISCOLL & CROWLEY LIMITED
Registration no: 07042127 **Date established:** 2009
Turnover: Up to £250,000 **No.of Employees:** 1 - 10 **Product Groups:** 52

Date of Accounts	Oct 11	Oct 10
Working Capital	-13	-11
Fixed Assets	3	4
Current Assets	N/A	1

E L G Haniel Metals Ltd (South East)
12-14 River Road, Barking, IG11 0DG
Tel: 020-8591 8444 **Fax:** 020-8594 0786
E-mail: cook@elg.co.uk
Website: http://www.elghanielmetals.co.uk
Managers: D. Cook (Mgr)
Ultimate Holding Company: FRANZ HANIEL & CIE GMBH (GERMANY)
Immediate Holding Company: E.L.G. HANIEL METALS LIMITED
Registration no: 01517971 **Date established:** 1980
No.of Employees: 1 - 10 **Product Groups:** 54, 66

Date of Accounts	Dec 11	Dec 10	Dec 09
Sales Turnover	333m	309m	182m
Pre Tax Profit/Loss	8m	10m	9m
Working Capital	-7m	-4m	268
Fixed Assets	28m	26m	26m
Current Assets	63m	92m	58m
Current Liabilities	3m	3m	2m

Electrical & Associated Services Ltd
Ashton House 1 Bankside Park Industrial Estate, Barking, IG11 0HZ
Tel: 01634-827751 **Fax:** 01634-821129
E-mail: ian.wright@eas.co.uk
Website: http://www.eas.co.uk
Directors: I. Wright (Dir & Buyer), S. Colyer (Co Sec), I. Wright (Dir), C. Stedman (MD), J. Dunham (Fin)
Immediate Holding Company: R DUNHAM UK SERVICES LIMITED
Registration no: 01230012 **Date established:** 1975
Turnover: £500,000 - £1m **No.of Employees:** 11 - 20 **Product Groups:** 52

Date of Accounts	Apr 11	Apr 10	Apr 09
Sales Turnover	392	770	1m
Pre Tax Profit/Loss	36	-79	-263
Working Capital	51	-23	3
Fixed Assets	2	36	49
Current Assets	310	271	275
Current Liabilities	24	28	22

Enterprise Liner Agencies Ltd
Unit 20 77-87 Trafalgar Business Centre River Road, Barking, IG11 0JU
Tel: 020-8591 8787 **Fax:** 020- 85911502
E-mail: malcolm@elaltd.demon.co.uk
Website: http://www.ela-uk.com
Bank(s): Lloyds TSB Bank plc
Directors: D. Roche (Dir), G. Haddow (Sales), M. Spencer (MD)
Immediate Holding Company: ENTERPRISE LINER AGENCIES LIMITED
Registration no: 01663949 **VAT No.:** GB 597 2678 75
Date established: 1982 **Turnover:** £1m - £2m **No.of Employees:** 11 - 20
Product Groups: 72, 76

Date of Accounts	Mar 08	Mar 07	Mar 06
Working Capital	383	359	340
Fixed Assets	175	203	220
Current Assets	930	913	954
Current Liabilities	547	554	614

G & G Powder Coatings Ltd
Unit 3 Rippleside Commercial Estate Ripple Road, Barking, IG11 0RJ
Tel: 020-8592 4555 **Fax:** 020-8592 4777
E-mail: info@gg-powdercoating.com
Website: http://www.gg-powdercoating.com
Bank(s): HSBC
Directors: G. Langford (MD)
Ultimate Holding Company: G & G HOLDINGS LIMITED
Immediate Holding Company: G & G POWDER COATINGS LIMITED
Registration no: 03667269 **VAT No.:** GB 454 4970 26
Date established: 1998 **Turnover:** £500,000 - £1m
No.of Employees: 11 - 20 **Product Groups:** 37, 48

Date of Accounts	Jun 12	Jun 11	Jun 10
Sales Turnover	N/A	911	892
Pre Tax Profit/Loss	N/A	2	1
Working Capital	79	78	77
Current Assets	79	407	334
Current Liabilities	N/A	20	13

Herald Plastics Ltd
Anglian Industrial Estate Atcost Road, Barking, IG11 0EQ
Tel: 020-8507 7900 **Fax:** 020-8507 2914
E-mail: sales@heraldplastics.com
Website: http://www.heraldplastics.com
Directors: R. Patel (Fin), B. Patel (MD)
Immediate Holding Company: HERALD PLASTIC LIMITED
Registration no: 03471741 **Date established:** 1997
No.of Employees: 1 - 10 **Product Groups:** 24, 25, 29, 30

Date of Accounts	Mar 12	Mar 11	Mar 10
Working Capital	283	275	314
Fixed Assets	479	494	487
Current Assets	1m	1m	1m

Jaymar Freight Ltd
Container Base Box Lane Renwick Road, Barking, IG11 0SQ
Tel: 020-8984 8030 **Fax:** 020-8984 7379
E-mail: shipping@jaymarfreight.co.uk
Website: http://www.jaymarfreight.co.uk
Directors: T. Kelly (Co Sec), D. Buffrey (Dir)
Immediate Holding Company: JAYMAR FREIGHT LIMITED
Registration no: 05184573 **VAT No.:** GB 685 3977 71
Date established: 2004 **Turnover:** Up to £250,000
No.of Employees: 1 - 10 **Product Groups:** 39

Date of Accounts	Jul 11	Jul 10	Jul 09
Working Capital	-121	-126	-84
Fixed Assets	1	2	2
Current Assets	137	155	124

Longvalley Packaging Ltd
6 Atcost Road, Barking, IG11 0EQ
Tel: 020-8591 2760 **Fax:** 020-8594 7001
E-mail: lalji@longvalley.co.uk
Website: http://www.longvalley.co.uk
Bank(s): Barclays
Directors: D. Bhudia (Dir), L. Bhudia (MD)
Managers: V. Bhudia (Sales Prom Mgr)
Immediate Holding Company: LONGVALLEY PACKAGING LIMITED
Registration no: 01401927 **VAT No.:** GB 249 9428 13
Date established: 1978 **Turnover:** £1m - £2m **No.of Employees:** 21 - 50
Product Groups: 30

Date of Accounts	Mar 11	Mar 10	Mar 09
Working Capital	132	137	97
Fixed Assets	89	87	98
Current Assets	452	391	346

Manor Croft Door Systems Ltd
Manor House 6-8 Creek Road, Barking, IG11 0TA
Tel: 020-8591 3300 **Fax:** 020-8591 3338
E-mail: enquiries@mdsdoors.co.uk
Website: http://www.mdsdoors.co.uk
Bank(s): Barclays
Directors: W. Croft (MD)
Immediate Holding Company: MANORCROFT DOOR SYSTEMS LIMITED
Registration no: 07660561 **VAT No.:** GB 597 2288 88
Date established: 2011 **Turnover:** £1m - £2m **No.of Employees:** 11 - 20
Product Groups: 25

Date of Accounts	Oct 11
Working Capital	-31
Fixed Assets	34
Current Assets	13

Mather Engineering Co. Ltd
73 River Road, Barking, IG11 0DR
Tel: 020-8594 1092 **Fax:** 020-8594 9247
E-mail: email@mather-engineering.co.uk
Bank(s): Barclays
Directors: I. Mather (Fin)
Immediate Holding Company: MATHER ENGINEERING LIMITED
Registration no: 01109209 **VAT No.:** GB 247 1727 55
Date established: 1973 **Turnover:** Up to £250,000
No.of Employees: 11 - 20 **Product Groups:** 31, 48

Date of Accounts	Oct 11	Oct 10	Oct 09
Working Capital	190	155	102
Fixed Assets	78	98	123
Current Assets	356	285	232

Online Lubricants
20 The I O Centre 59-71 River Road, Barking, IG11 0DR
Tel: 020-8507 0123 **Fax:** 020-8593 0234
E-mail: john@online-lubricants.co.uk
Website: http://www.online-lubricants.co.uk
Directors: C. Collings (Fin), J. Collings (Dir)
Immediate Holding Company: ONLINE LUBRICANTS LIMITED
Registration no: 02936230 **Date established:** 1994
Turnover: £500,000 - £1m **No.of Employees:** 11 - 20
Product Groups: 31, 32, 33, 66, 68

Date of Accounts	Jul 11	Jul 10	Jul 09
Working Capital	605	521	318
Fixed Assets	50	42	39
Current Assets	1m	1m	983

P G C S Partnership
62a River Road, Barking, IG11 0DS
Tel: 0844-9155000 **Fax:** 01277-630157
E-mail: robert@pgcspartnership.com
Website: http://www.pgcspartnership.co.uk
Directors: C. Coles (Ptnr), C. Cole (Ptnr), R. Syms (Ptnr)
Date established: 1995 **No.of Employees:** 11 - 20 **Product Groups:** 35

P & I Protection
Thames Road, Barking, IG11 0JA
Tel: 020-8594 0578 **Fax:** 020-8507 3981
Directors: M. Bass (Prop), P. Churchyard (Ptnr)
Turnover: Up to £250,000 **No.of Employees:** 1 - 10 **Product Groups:** 25, 30, 35, 36, 39, 66

Poulten & Graf Ltd
1 Alfreds Way Alfreds Way, Barking, IG11 0AS
Tel: 020-8594 4256 **Fax:** 020-8594 8419
E-mail: jason.robson@poulten-graf.com
Website: http://www.poulten-graf.com
Bank(s): Barclays
Directors: J. Robson (Fin)
Managers: L. Bedwell, L. Proudfoot
Immediate Holding Company: POULTEN & GRAF LIMITED
Registration no: 01303932 **Date established:** 1977 **Turnover:** £2m - £5m
No.of Employees: 21 - 50 **Product Groups:** 33, 42, 66

Date of Accounts	Dec 11	Dec 10	Dec 09
Working Capital	331	332	209
Fixed Assets	1m	1m	1m
Current Assets	714	803	864

R N B Industrial Door Service Ltd
6 Davenport Centre Renwick Road, Barking, IG11 0SH
Tel: 020-8595 1242 **Fax:** 020-8595 3849
Website: http://www.rnbdoors.co.uk
Directors: R. Finch (MD), H. Finch (Fin)
Immediate Holding Company: R.N.B. INDUSTRIAL DOOR SERVICES LIMITED
Registration no: 01721201 **Date established:** 1983
Turnover: £500,000 - £1m **No.of Employees:** 11 - 20
Product Groups: 26, 35

Rascal Confectionery Ltd
Samal House Loxford Road, Barking, IG11 8PU
Tel: 020-8591 7777 **Fax:** 020-8594 3645
E-mail: rascal@supanet.com
Website: http://www.rascal-chocolate.com
Bank(s): Allied Irish
Directors: A. Malyon (MD), S. Malyon-Davies (Dir), C. Malyon (Dir)
Managers: D. Cole (I.T. Exec), D. White (Purch Mgr)
Ultimate Holding Company: M D Estates Ltd
Immediate Holding Company: Bonnevale Ltd
Registration no: 00916510 **VAT No.:** GB 248 0052 83
Date established: 1967 **Turnover:** £1m - £2m **No.of Employees:** 21 - 50
Product Groups: 20

Date of Accounts	Jul 08	Jul 07	Oct 06
Working Capital	638	759	724
Fixed Assets	1154	1034	1038
Current Assets	1553	2089	2101
Current Liabilities	916	1330	1377

Saunders Displays UK Ltd
Unit 10 Buzzard Creek Industrial Estate River Road, Barking, IG11 0EL
Tel: 020-8594 7221 **Fax:** 020-8594 7216
E-mail: sales@saundersdisplays.co.uk
Website: http://www.saundersdisplays.co.uk
Directors: M. Saunders (Dir), N. Saunders (Fin)
Immediate Holding Company: SAUNDERS DISPLAYS (UK) LIMITED
Registration no: 06660903 **Date established:** 2008
No.of Employees: 1 - 10 **Product Groups:** 30, 49, 81

Date of Accounts	Jul 11	Jul 10	Jul 09
Working Capital	3	35	21
Current Assets	76	106	131

Sentinal Lifts
Trocall House Wakering Road, Barking, IG11 8PD
Tel: 020-8594 1461 **Fax:** 020-8507 1427
E-mail: info@sentinal-lifts.co.uk
Website: http://www.sentinal-lifts.co.uk
Directors: G. Redwood (MD)
Immediate Holding Company: SENTINAL LIFTS LIMITED
Registration no: 01714459 **Date established:** 1983
No.of Employees: 1 - 10 **Product Groups:** 35, 39, 45

Date of Accounts	Mar 09	Mar 08	Mar 07
Working Capital	-48	-25	2
Fixed Assets	32	43	25
Current Assets	308	199	235
Current Liabilities	3	N/A	N/A

Shipco Transport Ltd
Box Lane, Barking, IG11 0SE
Tel: 020-8984 9399 **Fax:** 020-8593 7641
E-mail: info@shipco.com
Website: http://www.shipco.com
Managers: C. Jensen (Chief Mgr), D. Pannall (Comptroller), C. Burch (Mgr)
Ultimate Holding Company: SCAN SHIPPING AS (DENMARK)
Immediate Holding Company: SHIPCO TRANSPORT LIMITED
Registration no: 02298865 **Date established:** 1988
No.of Employees: 21 - 50 **Product Groups:** 75, 76

Date of Accounts	Dec 11	Dec 10	Dec 09
Working Capital	522	579	427
Fixed Assets	19	9	30
Current Assets	2m	2m	2m

Sita Recycling Limited
72-76 River Road, Barking, IG11 0DS
Tel: 020-8594 7477 **Fax:** 020-8594 7486
Website: http://www.sita.co.uk
Bank(s): Lloyds TSB Bank plc
Directors: J. Knight (Dir)
Managers: K. Smith (Depot Mgr)
Ultimate Holding Company: A & G Ball Group
Immediate Holding Company: Sita South East Ltd
Registration no: 00517576 **Turnover:** £125m - £250m
No.of Employees: 21 - 50 **Product Groups:** 27, 42, 80

Solutions For Seating Ltd
8 Lyon Business Park River Road, Barking, IG11 0JS
Tel: 020-8594 4774 **Fax:** 020-8594 5775
Website: http://www.solutions4interiors.co.uk
Directors: I. Burns (Fin), P. Burns (MD)
Immediate Holding Company: SOLUTIONS FOR SEATING LIMITED
Registration no: 03640324 **Date established:** 1998
No.of Employees: 11 - 20 **Product Groups:** 26, 52

Date of Accounts	Sep 11	Sep 10	Sep 09
Working Capital	56	60	66
Current Assets	61	61	68
Current Liabilities	N/A	N/A	1

Squibb Grup
62 River Road, Barking, IG11 0DS
Tel: 020-8594 7143 **Fax:** 020-8594 5617
E-mail: paul@squibbgroup.co.uk
Website: http://www.squibbgroup.co.uk
Managers: K. Butcher (Comptroller), P. Blanks (Chief Mgr), E. Boileau (Mktg Serv Mgr)
Immediate Holding Company: SQUIBB DEMOLITION LIMITED
Registration no: 07368894 **Date established:** 2010
Turnover: £20m - £50m **No.of Employees:** 21 - 50 **Product Groups:** 32, 35, 36, 40, 45, 48, 51, 52, 54, 72, 83, 84, 85

United Fork Trucks 1992 Ltd
37 River Road, Barking, IG11 0DA
Tel: 020-8591 2950 **Fax:** 020-8591 2952
Website: http://www.unitedforktrucks.co.uk
Managers: B. Carrott (Mgr)
Immediate Holding Company: United Forktrucks (1992) Ltd
Registration no: 02693495 **No.of Employees:** 11 - 20
Product Groups: 35, 39, 45

Well Trade Services Ltd
Media Park 40 River Road, Barking, IG11 0DW
Tel: 020-8594 3336 **Fax:** 020-8594 3338
E-mail: sales@wtsbroadcast.com
Website: http://www.wtsbroadcast.com
Directors: S. Foot (Fin)
Managers: B. Murphy (Mktg Serv Mgr), M. Byrne (Tech Serv Mgr)
Ultimate Holding Company: WTS INTERNATIONAL HOLDINGS LIMITED (CYPRUS)
Immediate Holding Company: WELLTRADE SERVICES LIMITED
Registration no: 03133829 **Date established:** 1995
Turnover: £20m - £50m **No.of Employees:** 11 - 20 **Product Groups:** 37, 38

Date of Accounts	Dec 11	Dec 10	Dec 09
Sales Turnover	41m	26m	18m
Pre Tax Profit/Loss	3m	2m	314
Working Capital	5m	2m	2m
Fixed Assets	2m	3m	3m
Current Assets	11m	29m	16m
Current Liabilities	3m	23m	8m

L H Wigzell Ltd
96 Abbey Road, Barking, IG11 7BT
Tel: 020-8594 4314 **Fax:** 020-8507 8329
E-mail: machineryenquiries@btconnect.com
Website: http://www.liquidationmachinery.com
Directors: J. Bolton (Prop)
Immediate Holding Company: L.H.WIGZELL LIMITED
Registration no: 00972784 **Date established:** 1970
Turnover: Up to £250,000 **No.of Employees:** 1 - 10 **Product Groups:** 46

Date of Accounts	Mar 11	Mar 10	Mar 07
Sales Turnover	N/A	N/A	54
Pre Tax Profit/Loss	N/A	N/A	-47
Working Capital	-428	-164	-117
Current Assets	160	387	318
Current Liabilities	N/A	N/A	435

Basildon

4site Implementation Ltd
22 Hemmells, Basildon, SS15 6ED
Tel: 01268-540081 **Fax:** 01268-541624
E-mail: sales@4site-implementation.com
Website: http://www.4site-implementation.com
Directors: D. Reeson (Dir), S. Baker (MD)
Immediate Holding Company: 4SITE IMPLEMENTATION LIMITED
Registration no: 05794829 **Date established:** 2006
Turnover: £500,000 - £1m **No.of Employees:** 11 - 20
Product Groups: 37, 49, 52

Date of Accounts	Apr 12	Apr 11	Apr 10
Working Capital	-38	-46	-19
Fixed Assets	69	82	57
Current Assets	331	198	291

Abbott Fasteners Ltd
Unit 4B The Gloucesters Luckyn Lane, Basildon, SS14 3AX
Tel: 01268-532434 **Fax:** 01268-532435
E-mail: clive@helicoil.co.uk
Website: http://www.abbottfasteners.co.uk

see next page

***Abbott Fasteners Ltd** - Cont'd*

Bank(s): Barclays
Directors: C. Clark (MD), S. Brand (Fin)
Immediate Holding Company: ABBOTT FASTENERS LIMITED
Registration no: 01627240 **VAT No.:** 368 7385 96 **Date established:** 1982
Turnover: £1m - £2m **No.of Employees:** 11 - 20 **Product Groups:** 30, 35

Date of Accounts	May 11	May 10	May 09
Working Capital	713	614	582
Fixed Assets	9	14	16
Current Assets	1m	810	741
Current Liabilities	N/A	13	N/A

Ace Signs Group

1 Bentalls, Basildon, SS14 3BS
Tel: 01268-706800 **Fax:** 01702-294325
E-mail: enquiries@asg.co.uk
Website: http://www.acesigns.co.uk
Directors: J. Cook (MD), R. Eldridge (Fin)
Managers: A. Debnam (Prod Mgr), M. Baker (Tech Serv Mgr), N. Norey (Personnel)
Ultimate Holding Company: ASGH LIMITED
Immediate Holding Company: NOTSALLOW 280 LIMITED
Registration no: 06201392 **VAT No.:** GB 250 3314 08
Date established: 2007 **Turnover:** £5m - £10m
No.of Employees: 101 - 250 **Product Groups:** 26, 30, 37, 39, 49, 52, 81

Date of Accounts	Jun 11	Jun 10	Jun 09
Pre Tax Profit/Loss	N/A	N/A	-2m
Working Capital	N/A	N/A	-1m
Fixed Assets	N/A	N/A	2m
Current Assets	N/A	N/A	4m
Current Liabilities	N/A	N/A	2m

Action EPC Ltd

Unit 14 Adams Business Centre Cranes Farm Road, Basildon, SS14 3JF
Tel: 01268-288387 **Fax:** 01268-288956
E-mail: actionplating@fsmail.net
Website: http://www.actionplating.co.uk
Directors: M. Wisbey (MD), J. Meade (Fin)
Immediate Holding Company: ACTION EPC LIMITED
Registration no: 04590511 **Date established:** 2002
Turnover: £500,000 - £1m **No.of Employees:** 1 - 10 **Product Groups:** 48

Date of Accounts	Dec 11	Dec 10	Dec 09
Working Capital	105	99	76
Fixed Assets	33	38	37
Current Assets	261	247	217

Alexander's Machinery Ltd

6 Angel Close Vange, Basildon, SS16 4RF
Tel: 01268-557383 **Fax:** 01268-470783
E-mail: info@alexanders-machinery.co.uk
Website: http://www.alexanders-machinery.co.uk
Directors: C. Smith (Dir)
Immediate Holding Company: Alexander's Machinery Ltd
Registration no: 06176866 **Date established:** 2007
No.of Employees: 1 - 10 **Product Groups:** 38, 42

Date of Accounts	Mar 10	Mar 09	Mar 08
Working Capital	-7	-14	-16
Fixed Assets	8	9	11
Current Assets	17	21	6

Allison Engineering Ltd

2 Capricorn Centre Cranes Farm Road, Basildon, SS14 3JA
Tel: 01268-526161 **Fax:** 01268-533144
E-mail: sharwood@allison.co.uk
Website: http://www.allison.co.uk
Directors: J. Harwood (Co Sec), S. Harwood (Sales)
Immediate Holding Company: ALLISON ENGINEERING LIMITED
Registration no: 01391860 **VAT No.:** GB 328 4678 27
Date established: 1978 **Turnover:** £1m - £2m **No.of Employees:** 1 - 10
Product Groups: 38

Date of Accounts	Sep 11	Sep 10	Sep 09
Sales Turnover	N/A	N/A	2m
Pre Tax Profit/Loss	N/A	N/A	-11
Working Capital	-3	21	-67
Fixed Assets	282	217	459
Current Assets	382	295	358
Current Liabilities	39	N/A	30

Allthread Plastics Ltd

Ridley Road Burnt Mills Industrial Estate, Basildon, SS13 1EG
Tel: 01268-726559 **Fax:** 01268-725287
E-mail: sales@allthread.co.uk
Website: http://www.allthread.co.uk
Bank(s): Lloyds TSB Bank plc
Directors: J. Hampson (Dir)
Immediate Holding Company: ALLTHREAD PLASTICS LIMITED
Registration no: 01654820 **VAT No.:** GB 251 4479 62
Date established: 1982 **Turnover:** £500,000 - £1m
No.of Employees: 11 - 20 **Product Groups:** 30

Date of Accounts	Oct 11	Oct 10	Oct 09
Working Capital	199	197	149
Fixed Assets	37	27	26
Current Assets	390	306	274

Amari Plastics plc

Amari House Paycocke Road, Basildon, SS14 3NW
Tel: 01268-884444
Managers: T. Cobbett (District Mgr)
Ultimate Holding Company: BLACKFRIARS CORP (USA)
Immediate Holding Company: AMARI PLASTICS PUBLIC LIMITED COMPANY
Registration no: 01220776 **Date established:** 1975
Turnover: £75m - £125m **No.of Employees:** 21 - 50 **Product Groups:** 30, 31, 66

Date of Accounts	Dec 11	Dec 10	Dec 09
Sales Turnover	101m	93m	79m
Pre Tax Profit/Loss	7m	5m	2m
Working Capital	17m	12m	4m
Fixed Assets	3m	3m	8m
Current Assets	33m	30m	24m
Current Liabilities	5m	5m	3m

Andrews Sykes Hire Ltd

Archers Fields Burnt Mills Industrial Estate, Basildon, SS13 1DH
Tel: 01268-284440 **Fax:** 01603-766284
E-mail: basildon@andrews-sykes.com
Website: http://www.andrews-sykes.com
Managers: D. Baker (Mgr)
Immediate Holding Company: ANDREWS SYKES HIRE LIMITED
Registration no: 02985657 **VAT No.:** GB 100 4295 24
Date established: 1994 **Turnover:** £1m - £2m **No.of Employees:** 1 - 10
Product Groups: 40

Date of Accounts	Dec 11	Dec 10	Dec 09
Sales Turnover	35m	36m	34m
Pre Tax Profit/Loss	10m	10m	8m
Working Capital	8m	6m	2m
Fixed Assets	7m	7m	9m
Current Assets	33m	35m	35m
Current Liabilities	7m	7m	5m

Azbern Ltd

1 Seax Way, Basildon, SS15 6SW
Tel: 01268-494300 **Fax:** 01268-545244
Website: http://www.beerflow.co.uk
Directors: D. Watson (MD), T. Watson (Fin)
Immediate Holding Company: BEERFLOW LIMITED
Registration no: 04145003 **Date established:** 2001
No.of Employees: 21 - 50 **Product Groups:** 20, 40, 41

Date of Accounts	Mar 07	Mar 06	Mar 05
Working Capital	39	-41	-16
Fixed Assets	34	39	43
Current Assets	229	178	170
Current Liabilities	190	220	186

Bannerbridge

22-24 Hornsby Square Southfields Business Park, Basildon, SS15 6SD
Tel: 01268-419101 **Fax:** 01268-886609
E-mail: sales@bannerbridge.co.uk
Website: http://www.bannerbridge.co.uk
Directors: D. Holyfield (Dir), P. Buttress (Fin), P. Wheeler (MD)
Managers: K. Godfrey (Sales Admin), J. Foote (Tech Serv Mgr)
Immediate Holding Company: BANNERBRIDGE PLC
Registration no: 01554709 **VAT No.:** GB 345 6780 30
Date established: 1981 **Turnover:** £2m - £5m **No.of Employees:** 51 - 100
Product Groups: 44

Date of Accounts	Dec 11	Dec 10	Dec 09
Sales Turnover	4m	5m	5m
Pre Tax Profit/Loss	192	200	251
Working Capital	1m	1m	912
Fixed Assets	114	134	155
Current Assets	2m	2m	2m
Current Liabilities	117	253	237

Barford Engineering Ltd

11 Capricorn Centre Cranes Farm Road, Basildon, SS14 3JJ
Tel: 08456-442486 **Fax:** 08451-232931
E-mail: r-heatherill@xrtraining.co.uk
Website: http://www.barford-engineering.co.uk
Directors: R. Heatherill (MD)
Immediate Holding Company: BARFORD ENGINEERING (UK) LIMITED
Registration no: 04504035 **Date established:** 2002
No.of Employees: 1 - 10 **Product Groups:** 34, 44, 48

Date of Accounts	Aug 11	Aug 10	Aug 09
Working Capital	-221	-177	-155
Fixed Assets	590	413	361
Current Assets	704	543	158

Beaver 84

Ellencroft House Harvey Road, Basildon, SS13 1EP
Tel: 08704-238584 **Fax:** 01268-727184
E-mail: sales@beaver84.co.uk
Website: http://www.beaver84.co.uk
Directors: S. Tyso (MD)
Ultimate Holding Company: ALTRAD INVESTMENT AUTHORITY (FRANCE)
Immediate Holding Company: ALTRAD BEAVER 84 LIMITED
Registration no: 01808583 **Date established:** 1984
Turnover: £10m - £20m **No.of Employees:** 1 - 10 **Product Groups:** 83

Date of Accounts	Feb 12	Feb 11	Feb 10
Working Capital	145	134	121
Fixed Assets	3	4	5
Current Assets	185	174	160

Bespoke Packaging Ltd

17 Southfields Industrial Park Hornsby Square, Southfields Business Park, Basildon, SS15 6SD
Tel: 01268-412255 **Fax:** 01268-412822
E-mail: chris@bespokepack.fsnet.co.uk
Website: http://www.bespokepack.fsnet.co.uk
Directors: B. Cowell (Fin), C. Thirkell (MD)
Immediate Holding Company: BESPOKE PACKAGING LIMITED
Registration no: 04200148 **VAT No.:** GB 645 0930 43
Date established: 2001 **Turnover:** Up to £250,000
No.of Employees: 1 - 10 **Product Groups:** 27, 28, 84

Date of Accounts	Apr 09	Apr 08	Apr 07
Working Capital	103	117	39
Fixed Assets	5	7	10
Current Assets	230	225	254

C B T Packaging Ltd (a division of C B T Packaging Ltd)

Unit D2 Zenith Paycocke Road, Basildon, SS14 3DW
Tel: 01268-247380 **Fax:** 01268-271979
E-mail: sales@cbtpackaging.co.uk
Website: http://www.cbtpackaging.co.uk
Bank(s): HSBC Bank plc
Directors: C. Corrigan (MD)
Immediate Holding Company: CBT PACKAGING LIMITED
Registration no: 00891861 **Date established:** 1966
Turnover: £500,000 - £1m **No.of Employees:** 11 - 20 **Product Groups:** 27

Date of Accounts	Dec 11	Dec 10	Dec 09
Working Capital	1m	1m	1m
Fixed Assets	104	124	170
Current Assets	2m	1m	2m

C M R Controls Ltd

22 Repton Court Repton Close, Basildon, SS13 1LN
Tel: 01268-287222 **Fax:** 01268-287099
E-mail: sales@cmr.co.uk
Website: http://www.cmr.co.uk
Bank(s): National Westminster Bank Plc
Directors: C. Richter (MD), L. Richter (Fin)
Immediate Holding Company: CMR CONTROLS LIMITED
Registration no: 01372356 **VAT No.:** GB 324 6125 82
Date established: 1978 **Turnover:** £2m - £5m **No.of Employees:** 11 - 20
Product Groups: 37, 38, 40

Date of Accounts	Dec 11	Dec 10	Dec 09
Working Capital	472	578	439
Fixed Assets	449	474	429
Current Assets	701	925	978

Circuit Electronics Services

10 Paycocke Close, Basildon, SS14 3HS
Tel: 01268-273470 **Fax:** 01268-273475
E-mail: cesbas@aol.com
Website: http://www.circuit-electronics.com
Directors: L. Atkins (Fin), S. Atkins (MD)
Immediate Holding Company: CIRCUIT ELECTRONIC SERVICES LTD
Registration no: 04055898 **Date established:** 2000
No.of Employees: 1 - 10 **Product Groups:** 37, 48, 84

Date of Accounts	Oct 07	Oct 06	Oct 05
Working Capital	-5	-9	-7
Fixed Assets	9	11	12
Current Assets	46	32	41

Crowley Saws Ltd

Bentalls Pipps Hill Industrial Estate, Basildon, SS14 3BY
Tel: 01268-293605 **Fax:** 01268-285452
E-mail: enquiries@crowleysaws.com
Website: http://www.thecrowleygroup.com
Directors: R. Crowley (MD), D. Crowley (Fin)
Immediate Holding Company: E.CROWLEY AND SON LIMITED
Registration no: 00576621 **Date established:** 1957
Turnover: £500,000 - £1m **No.of Employees:** 1 - 10 **Product Groups:** 31, 34, 36

Date of Accounts	Dec 11	Dec 10	Dec 09
Working Capital	118	115	94
Fixed Assets	721	725	700
Current Assets	174	191	180

D H Industries Ltd

Sullivan House Fenton Way, Southfields Business Park, Basildon, SS15 6TD
Tel: 01268-410666 **Fax:** 01268-410777
E-mail: dh@dhi.co.uk
Website: http://www.dhi.co.uk
Bank(s): National Westminster Bank Plc
Directors: P. Sullivan (MD), A. Sheard (Fin)
Managers: B. Williams (Tech Serv Mgr), L. Consiglio (Purch Mgr)
Ultimate Holding Company: PAMASOL WILLI MAEDER AG (SWITZERLAND)
Immediate Holding Company: D.H. INDUSTRIES LIMITED
Registration no: 01485632 **VAT No.:** GB 342 2874 59
Date established: 1980 **Turnover:** £2m - £5m **No.of Employees:** 21 - 50
Product Groups: 32, 42, 84

Date of Accounts	Dec 11	Dec 10	Dec 09
Sales Turnover	9m	5m	8m
Pre Tax Profit/Loss	381	-597	413
Working Capital	4m	3m	4m
Fixed Assets	2m	2m	2m
Current Assets	7m	6m	6m
Current Liabilities	2m	2m	1m

D S Smith Recycling

Hovefields Avenue, Basildon, SS13 1EB
Tel: 01268-591300 **Fax:** 01268-591303
E-mail: paul.read@dssmithrecycling.com
Website: http://www.dssmithrecycling.com
Bank(s): The Royal Bank of Scotland
Directors: P. Reid (Fin)
Managers: P. Mcgreavy (District Mgr)
Immediate Holding Company: BPB BRITISH GYPSON
Registration no: 06313803 **Turnover:** £2m - £5m
No.of Employees: 11 - 20 **Product Groups:** 27, 42, 54, 66

Denmans Electrical Wholesalers Ltd

Unit E2 The Hemmells Laindon Trading Centre, Basildon, SS15 6ED
Tel: 01268-418181 **Fax:** 01268-541277
Website: http://www.denmans.co.uk
Managers: P. Hayward (Mgr)
Ultimate Holding Company: REXEL SA (FRANCE)
Immediate Holding Company: DENMANS ELECTRICAL WHOLESALERS LIMITED
Registration no: 00291521 **VAT No.:** GB 112 4242 26
Date established: 1934 **Turnover:** £1m - £2m **No.of Employees:** 1 - 10
Product Groups: 77

Date of Accounts	Dec 11	Dec 10	Dec 09
Sales Turnover	40m	68m	67m
Pre Tax Profit/Loss	4m	6m	5m
Working Capital	8m	22m	24m
Fixed Assets	N/A	5m	5m
Current Assets	10m	35m	37m
Current Liabilities	N/A	4m	4m

E S L Engineers

Woolaston Way Burnt Mills Industrial Estate, Basildon, SS13 1DJ
Tel: 01268-727777 **Fax:** 01268-728866
E-mail: sales@eslengineers.co.uk
Website: http://www.eslengineers.co.uk
Bank(s): Barclays
Directors: B. Townsend (MD)
Immediate Holding Company: E.S.L. (BASILDON) HOLDINGS LTD
Registration no: 00723927 **VAT No.:** GB 719 1659 15
Turnover: £2m - £5m **No.of Employees:** 21 - 50 **Product Groups:** 25, 35, 39, 48, 49

Eriks Industrial Distribution Ltd (Basildon Service Centre)

Unit 23 Bakers Court Paycocke Road, Basildon, SS14 3EH
Tel: 01268-533002 **Fax:** 01268-522891
E-mail: basildon@eriks.co.uk
Website: http://www.eriks.co.uk
Managers: R. Varnals (Chief Mgr)
Immediate Holding Company: SAFFRON PLASTICS LIMITED
Registration no: 02585270 **Date established:** 1990
Turnover: £250m - £500m **No.of Employees:** 1 - 10 **Product Groups:** 66

Date of Accounts	Apr 12	Apr 11	Apr 10
Working Capital	210	124	104
Fixed Assets	22	26	33
Current Assets	1m	1m	981

F D R Ltd

F D R House Christopher Martin Road, Basildon, SS14 9AA
Tel: 01268-296431 **Fax:** 01268-296352
Website: http://www.firstdatacorp.co.uk

Directors: E. Caddle (Fin), R. Rayman (Fin)
Managers: S. Winiberg (Personnel), H. Owen (Mktg Serv Mgr)
Ultimate Holding Company: FIRST DATA CORPORATION (USA)
Immediate Holding Company: FDR U.K. LIMITED
Registration no: 02134777 **Date established:** 1987 **Turnover:** £2m - £5m
No.of Employees: 1501 & over **Product Groups:** 82

Date of Accounts	Dec 11	Dec 10	Dec 09
Pre Tax Profit/Loss	488	608	-8m
Working Capital	6m	7m	3m
Fixed Assets	2m	2m	451
Current Assets	7m	9m	6m
Current Liabilities	414	200	749

Fast International Inc
31 Saffron Court Southfields Business Park, Basildon, SS15 6SS
Tel: 01268-544000 **Fax:** 01268-544500
E-mail: gkoether@fastinc.com
Website: http://www.fastinc.com
Directors: J. Koether (Fin), G. Koether (MD)
Immediate Holding Company: (FAST.) INTERNATIONAL INC.
Registration no: FC013920 **Date established:** 1982
Turnover: £500,000 - £1m **No.of Employees:** 1 - 10 **Product Groups:** 38, 40, 67

Date of Accounts	Dec 98	Dec 97	Dec 04
Sales Turnover	837	769	777
Pre Tax Profit/Loss	55	-17	172
Working Capital	344	285	361
Fixed Assets	48	66	28
Current Assets	619	545	589
Current Liabilities	110	120	72

Fibresports
10 Bowlers Croft, Basildon, SS14 3ED
Tel: 01268-282723 **Fax:** 01268-282273
E-mail: fibresports@aol.com
Website: http://www.fibresports.co.uk
Managers: H. Garwood (Mgr)
Turnover: £500,000 - £1m **No.of Employees:** 1 - 10 **Product Groups:** 30, 31, 33

Finnforest UK Ltd
Mayne House Juniper Park Fenton Way, Basildon, SS15 6RZ
Tel: 08456-012401 **Fax:** 01268-364617
E-mail: derek.wilkie@finnforest.com
Website: http://www.finnforest.co.uk
Directors: N. Wijesooriya (Fin), J. Tong (Sales), T. Tong (Mkt Research), W. Clason (MD)
Managers: D. Wilkie (Prod Mgr), T. Chrisostomou (I.T. Exec)
Ultimate Holding Company: METSALIITTO OSUUSKUNTA (FINLAND)
Immediate Holding Company: FINNFOREST UK LIMITED
Registration no: 03071064 **Date established:** 1995
Turnover: £125m - £250m **No.of Employees:** 51 - 100
Product Groups: 33, 39, 66

Date of Accounts	Dec 10	Dec 09	Dec 08
Sales Turnover	218m	218m	249m
Pre Tax Profit/Loss	4m	5m	3m
Working Capital	28m	40m	42m
Fixed Assets	23m	21m	23m
Current Assets	53m	63m	66m
Current Liabilities	9m	7m	12m

Fusion Four Telecoms Ltd
Unit 7 Saffron Court Southfields Business Park, Basildon, SS15 6SS
Tel: 01268-417500 **Fax:** 01268-543355
E-mail: williambutler@fusiontelecom.co.uk
Website: http://www.fusiontelecom.co.uk
Directors: W. Butler (MD)
Immediate Holding Company: FUSION FOUR TELECOMS LIMITED
Registration no: 04026523 **Date established:** 2000
No.of Employees: 1 - 10 **Product Groups:** 37, 67

Date of Accounts	Dec 11	Dec 10	Dec 09
Working Capital	-17	-20	-2
Fixed Assets	34	43	51
Current Assets	275	275	265

G E Energy Services
Basildon Service Centre Crompton Close, Basildon, SS14 3AY
Tel: 01268-287654 **Fax:** 01268-520274
E-mail: basildon.reception@ge.com
Website: http://www.ge.com
Bank(s): Barclays
Directors: L. Fenech (Fin)
Managers: S. Beeson (Buyer), S. Downey, A. Gagliardi (Tech Serv Mgr)
Ultimate Holding Company: GENERAL ELECTRIC (USA)
Immediate Holding Company: G.E. INTERNATIONAL INC
Registration no: 01182449 **Turnover:** £10m - £20m
No.of Employees: 101 - 250 **Product Groups:** 37, 48, 67

G M S Co.
35 Southfields Industrial Park Hornsby Square, Southfields Business Park, Basildon, SS15 6SD
Tel: 01268-419909 **Fax:** 01268-544346
E-mail: office@gamasco.co.uk
Website: http://www.gamasco.co.uk
Directors: T. Oliver (Prop)
Ultimate Holding Company: KERAMAB (BELGIUM)
Registration no: 04091693 **VAT No.:** GB 367 7190 20
Date established: 1982 **Turnover:** £1m - £2m **No.of Employees:** 1 - 10
Product Groups: 23, 24, 33, 37, 39, 40, 48, 52, 66, 67, 83

G S L Ltd
1 Nevendon Trading Estate Harvey Road, Basildon, SS13 1DA
Tel: 01268-590248 **Fax:** 01268-590256
E-mail: b.skinner@gslltd.co.uk
Website: http://www.gslltd.co.uk
Directors: B. Skinner (Dir)
Ultimate Holding Company: G4S 308 (UK) LIMITED
Immediate Holding Company: GSL LIMITED
Registration no: 03799262 **Date established:** 1999
No.of Employees: 1 - 10 **Product Groups:** 35, 39, 45

Galvoptics Optical Goods
Harvey Road, Basildon, SS13 1ES
Tel: 01268-728077 **Fax:** 01268-590445
E-mail: info@galvoptics.fsnet.co.uk
Website: http://www.galvoptics.fsnet.co.uk
Directors: R. Wale (MD)
Immediate Holding Company: GALVOPTICS LIMITED
Registration no: 01116562 **Date established:** 1973
No.of Employees: 1 - 10 **Product Groups:** 32, 33, 37, 38

Date of Accounts	Aug 11	Aug 10	Aug 09
Working Capital	933	727	470
Fixed Assets	194	210	223
Current Assets	2m	2m	1m

Gardner Aerospace Ltd
Wollaston House Wollaston Way, Burnt Mills Industrial Estate, Basildon, SS13 1DJ
Tel: 01268-729311 **Fax:** 01268-728951
E-mail: info@gardner-aerospace-basildon.com
Website: http://www.gardner-aerospace.com
Directors: K. Fowler (Fin), M. Pittman (MD)
Immediate Holding Company: GARDNER AEROSPACE - BASILDON LIMITED
Registration no: 03921668 **VAT No.:** GB 676 0040 49
Date established: 2000 **Turnover:** £10m - £20m
No.of Employees: 101 - 250 **Product Groups:** 39, 48

Date of Accounts	Aug 11	Aug 10	Aug 09
Sales Turnover	11m	11m	13m
Pre Tax Profit/Loss	695	2m	-9m
Working Capital	6m	6m	102
Fixed Assets	2m	2m	6m
Current Assets	9m	8m	6m
Current Liabilities	689	458	402

Gilbarco Veeder-Root
Crompton Close, Basildon, SS14 3BA
Tel: 01268-533090 **Fax:** 01268-524214
E-mail: sales@gilbarco.com
Website: http://www.gilbarco.com
Directors: J. Vincent (Pers), S. Flowerday (Fin), M. Clayton (Sales), J. Tierney (Mkt Research), D. Coombe (MD)
Managers: J. Dear (Personnel), A. Hayter (Chief Acct), L. Chapman
Ultimate Holding Company: DANAHER CORPORATION (DELAWARE U.S.A)
Immediate Holding Company: GILBARCO LIMITED
Registration no: 00253120 **Date established:** 1930
No.of Employees: 51 - 100 **Product Groups:** 11, 31, 32

Date of Accounts	Dec 10	Dec 09	Dec 08
Pre Tax Profit/Loss	481	939	3m
Working Capital	42m	41m	20m
Fixed Assets	103m	103m	18m
Current Assets	46m	45m	20m
Current Liabilities	6	3	N/A

H & B Scaffolding Ltd
Harvey Road, Basildon, SS13 1QJ
Tel: 01268-727175 **Fax:** 01268-725291
E-mail: sales@h-bscaffoldinggroupplc.co.uk
Website: http://www.h-bscaffoldingltd.co.uk
Directors: D. Blackwell (Dir), J. Cobb (Dir)
Managers: S. Harris (Sales & Mktg Mg)
Immediate Holding Company: H & B Scaffolding Group plc
Registration no: 01193356 **Date established:** 1974 **Turnover:** £5m - £10m
No.of Employees: 21 - 50 **Product Groups:** 52

H L C Engineering Ltd
4 Harvey Road Burnt Mills Industrial Estate, Basildon, SS13 1QJ
Tel: 01268-590080 **Fax:** 01268-590141
E-mail: steelwork@hlcengineering.com
Website: http://www.hlcengineering.com
Bank(s): Royal Bank of Scotland, Basildon
Directors: D. Moran (Dir), D. Moran (MD), G. Williamson (MD)
Immediate Holding Company: H.L.C. ENGINEERING LIMITED
Registration no: 01376936 **VAT No.:** GB 251 6800 75
Date established: 1978 **Turnover:** £1m - £2m **No.of Employees:** 21 - 50
Product Groups: 35, 51

Date of Accounts	Jul 09	Jul 08	Jul 07
Working Capital	16	-0	-9
Fixed Assets	111	117	141
Current Assets	288	470	430

The Ideal Group
8 Wollaston Cresent Burnt Mills, Basildon, SS13 1QD
Tel: 01268-590590 **Fax:** 01268-728203
E-mail: info@idealgroupuk.co.uk
Website: http://www.idealgroup.co.uk
Directors: M. Leckenby (MD), N. Dingley (Fin), Y. Kobayashi (Dir)
Managers: L. Davis (Sales Admin), G. Kempston (I.T. Exec), I. Smith (Mktg Serv Mgr)
Immediate Holding Company: Konica Minolta Business Solutions UK Ltd
Registration no: 05124822 **Date established:** 1980 **Turnover:** £1m - £2m
No.of Employees: 1 - 10 **Product Groups:** 44, 67

Date of Accounts	Mar 08	Apr 07
Sales Turnover	1650	1916
Pre Tax Profit/Loss	270	273
Working Capital	74	22
Fixed Assets	26	34
Current Assets	491	611
Current Liabilities	417	589
Total Share Capital	8	8
ROCE% (Return on Capital Employed)	269.9	491.6
ROT% (Return on Turnover)	16.4	14.3

Image Optics Components
Harvey Road, Basildon, SS13 1ES
Tel: 01268-728477 **Fax:** 01268-590445
E-mail: sales@image-optics.fsnet.co.uk
Website: http://www.image-optics.fsnet.co.uk
Directors: S. Wale (Co Sec)
Immediate Holding Company: IMAGE OPTICS COMPONENTS LIMITED
Registration no: 02067966 **Date established:** 1986
No.of Employees: 11 - 20 **Product Groups:** 33, 37, 38, 39, 40, 45, 48, 49

Date of Accounts	Dec 11	Dec 10	Dec 09
Working Capital	452	315	275
Fixed Assets	3	4	5
Current Assets	561	387	476

Intacab Ltd
Service House West Mayne, Basildon, SS15 6RW
Tel: 01268-545454 **Fax:** 01268-886707
E-mail: mgreenaway@toomey.uk.com
Website: http://www.intacabessex.co.uk
Directors: M. Greenaway (Dir)
Ultimate Holding Company: LAINDON HOLDINGS LIMITED
Immediate Holding Company: INTACAB LIMITED
Registration no: 01212625 **Date established:** 1975
Turnover: £500,000 - £1m **No.of Employees:** 21 - 50 **Product Groups:** 79

Date of Accounts	Dec 11	Dec 10	Dec 09
Sales Turnover	544	638	660
Pre Tax Profit/Loss	-104	-128	-118
Working Capital	5	59	144
Fixed Assets	75	149	110
Current Assets	357	389	399
Current Liabilities	23	37	18

Integrated Metal Solutions Ltd
17b Bakers Court Paycocke Road, Basildon, SS14 3EH
Tel: 01268-534133 **Fax:** 01268-534134
E-mail: info@integratedmetalsolutions.com
Website: http://www.integratedmetalsolutions.com
Directors: L. Anderson (Dir), R. Sharpless (MD)
Immediate Holding Company: INTEGRATED METAL SOLUTIONS LIMITED
Registration no: 06565309 **VAT No.:** 247 4960 34 **Date established:** 2008
Turnover: £1m - £2m **No.of Employees:** 1 - 10 **Product Groups:** 35, 40, 42, 84

Date of Accounts	Jun 11	Jun 10	Jun 09
Sales Turnover	801	N/A	N/A
Pre Tax Profit/Loss	-195	N/A	N/A
Working Capital	-28	49	93
Fixed Assets	11	129	172
Current Assets	164	317	224
Current Liabilities	104	N/A	N/A

J C Y Steel Supplies Ltd
35 Hovefield Avenue Burnt Mills Industrial Area, Basildon, SS13 1EB
Tel: 01268-729886 **Fax:** 01268-725262
E-mail: sales@jcysteel.com
Website: http://www.jcysteel.com
Directors: B. Nattey (Sales), R. England (MD)
Managers: R. Vere (I.T. Exec)
Immediate Holding Company: J.C.Y. (Steel Supplies) Ltd
Registration no: 00868330 **Turnover:** £2m - £5m
No.of Employees: 21 - 50 **Product Groups:** 23, 34

J W Froehlich UK Ltd
Sable Way Laindon, Basildon, SS15 6TU
Tel: 01268-469000 **Fax:** 01268-469001
E-mail: sales@jwf.co.uk
Website: http://www.jwf.co.uk
Directors: D. Wells (MD), G. Brinkley (Tech Serv), J. Froehlich (Ch)
Managers: M. Outhwaite (Purch Mgr), S. Bannister
Ultimate Holding Company: J W FROEHLICH MASCHINENFABRIK GMBH (GERM
Immediate Holding Company: JW FROEHLICH UK LIMITED
Registration no: 01212505 **VAT No.:** GB 251 3601 96
Date established: 1975 **Turnover:** £10m - £20m **No.of Employees:** 1 - 10
Product Groups: 38, 40, 45, 46, 47, 49, 67, 84, 85

Date of Accounts	Dec 11	Dec 10	Dec 09
Sales Turnover	9m	11m	8m
Pre Tax Profit/Loss	282	338	10
Working Capital	5m	5m	4m
Fixed Assets	1m	1m	1m
Current Assets	6m	10m	5m
Current Liabilities	N/A	181	197

Jalite plc
1 Bentalls, Basildon, SS14 3BS
Tel: 01268-242300 **Fax:** 01268-274148
E-mail: info@jalite.com
Website: http://www.jalite.com
Directors: D. Henderson (Dir)
Immediate Holding Company: JALITE PUBLIC LIMITED COMPANY
Registration no: 01756315 **VAT No.:** GB 394 9834 86
Date established: 1983 **Turnover:** £1m - £2m **No.of Employees:** 21 - 50
Product Groups: 32, 39, 40

Date of Accounts	Dec 11	Dec 10	Dec 09
Sales Turnover	2m	2m	2m
Pre Tax Profit/Loss	-51	-53	20
Working Capital	873	427	454
Fixed Assets	228	210	247
Current Assets	1m	1m	1m
Current Liabilities	132	538	405

Jonathan Lee Recruitment
3 Silvan Court Silvan Way, Laindon, Basildon, SS15 6TU
Tel: 01268-455520
E-mail: southfields@jonlee.co.uk
Website: http://www.jonlee.co.uk
Directors: M. Sanchez (Reg)
Date established: 1978 **No.of Employees:** 11 - 20 **Product Groups:** 80

Jordan Reflectors Ltd
9-10 Seax Way, Basildon, SS15 6SW
Tel: 01268-415828 **Fax:** 01268-410985
E-mail: bmartin@jordanreflectors.co.uk
Website: http://www.jordanreflectors.co.uk
Directors: B. Martin (Fin), P. Shoobridge (Sales)
Managers: S. Knight
Immediate Holding Company: JORDAN REFLECTORS LIMITED
Registration no: 02844015 **VAT No.:** GB 627 8135 27
Date established: 1993 **Turnover:** £5m - £10m **No.of Employees:** 21 - 50
Product Groups: 30, 37

Date of Accounts	Dec 11	Dec 10	Dec 09
Sales Turnover	8m	N/A	N/A
Pre Tax Profit/Loss	450	N/A	N/A
Working Capital	2m	250	72
Fixed Assets	479	863	893
Current Assets	3m	1m	720
Current Liabilities	375	275	N/A

Kearsley Precision Engineering
Unit 8 9 Herons Gate Trading Estate, Basildon, SS14 3EU
Tel: 01268-289422 **Fax:** 01268-282318
E-mail: sales@kearsleyprecision.com
Website: http://www.kearsleyprecision.com
Directors: A. Dhruva (Prop)
Immediate Holding Company: KEARSLEY PRECISION ENGINEERING CO. LIMITED
Registration no: 05361061 **Date established:** 2005
Turnover: £250,000 - £500,000 **No.of Employees:** 1 - 10
Product Groups: 35

Date of Accounts	Dec 11	Dec 10	Dec 09
Working Capital	-23	-23	235
Fixed Assets	24	6	55
Current Assets	195	111	355
Current Liabilities	N/A	24	N/A

Keycolour Ltd
10 Basildon Business Centre Bentalls, Basildon, SS14 3FT
Tel: 01268-522007 **Fax:** 01268-522007
Directors: L. Newell (MD), E. Newell (Fin)
Immediate Holding Company: KEYCOLOUR LIMITED
Registration no: 03067123 **Date established:** 1995
No.of Employees: 1 - 10 **Product Groups:** 46, 48

Date of Accounts	Jul 11	Jul 10	Jul 09
Working Capital	202	250	241
Fixed Assets	27	14	7
Current Assets	217	292	292

Lea Valley Packaging Ltd
1 Lords Way, Basildon, SS13 1TN
Tel: 01268-885858 **Fax:** 01992-626328
E-mail: sales@packer-products.co.uk
Website: http://www.leapack.com
Bank(s): Lloyds TSB Bank plc
Directors: M. Alston (Sales)
Managers: J. Sweeney (Mgr)
Immediate Holding Company: LEA VALLEY PACKAGING LIMITED
Registration no: 01600414 **VAT No.:** GB 247 0877 41
Date established: 1981 **Turnover:** £2m - £5m **No.of Employees:** 51 - 100
Product Groups: 23, 27, 30

Date of Accounts	Dec 10	Dec 09	Dec 08
Working Capital	120	82	129
Fixed Assets	3	4	5
Current Assets	235	161	216

Linear Systems & Equipment Ltd
Unit 9 Samson House Arterial Road, Laindon, Basildon, SS15 6DR
Tel: 01268-419558 **Fax:** 01268-417034
E-mail: linsys@btconnect.com
Directors: T. Hibbert (MD), K. Hibbert (Fin)
Immediate Holding Company: LINEAR SYSTEMS & EQUIPMENT LIMITED
Registration no: 01493674 **Date established:** 1980
Turnover: Up to £250,000 **No.of Employees:** 1 - 10 **Product Groups:** 35, 46, 84

Date of Accounts	Mar 11	Mar 10	Mar 09
Working Capital	-4	-5	-6
Fixed Assets	4	5	6
Current Assets	7	6	25
Current Liabilities	N/A	N/A	6

M D M Timber Ltd
6 Howard Chase Pipps Hill Industrial Estate, Basildon, SS14 3BE
Tel: 01268-530550 **Fax:** 0845-130 4696
E-mail: sales@mdmtimber.co.uk
Website: http://www.mdmtimber.co.uk
Bank(s): Barclays Bank
Directors: M. Alum (MD)
Immediate Holding Company: MDM TIMBER LIMITED
Registration no: 02348881 **VAT No.:** GB 507 5208 63
Date established: 1989 **Turnover:** £20m - £50m
No.of Employees: 11 - 20 **Product Groups:** 25, 48, 61, 66

Date of Accounts	Apr 11	Apr 10	Apr 09
Sales Turnover	41m	31m	30m
Pre Tax Profit/Loss	1m	1m	1m
Working Capital	4m	3m	3m
Fixed Assets	181	184	190
Current Assets	15m	14m	10m
Current Liabilities	5m	6m	5m

M G & A Engineering Ltd
6 Swinbourne Court Swinbourne Road, Burnt Mills Industrial Estate, Basildon, SS13 1QA
Tel: 01268-590222 **Fax:** 01268-590666
E-mail: mgaengineering@yahoo.co.uk
Website: http://www.gearmanufacture.co.uk
Directors: A. Gardner (MD)
Immediate Holding Company: M G & A ENGINEERING LIMITED
Registration no: 04995740 **Date established:** 2003
No.of Employees: 1 - 10 **Product Groups:** 35, 45

Date of Accounts	Mar 11	Mar 10	Mar 09
Working Capital	32	36	37
Fixed Assets	21	28	36
Current Assets	58	61	71

M K Electric Ltd
Paycocke Road, Basildon, SS14 3EA
Tel: 01268-563000 **Fax:** 01268-563563
E-mail: jeff.stacey@honeywell.com
Website: http://www.mkelectric.co.uk
Bank(s): National Westminster Bank Plc
Directors: C. White (Fin), T. Marston (Sales)
Managers: J. Stacey (Sales Admin), R. Ghelani (Mktg Serv Mgr), S. Mitchell (Purch Mgr), E. Jack, J. Trickett
Immediate Holding Company: M&K ELECTRIC LTD
Registration no: 08135240 **VAT No.:** GB 220 3449 06
Date established: 2012 **Turnover:** £5m - £10m
No.of Employees: 251 - 500 **Product Groups:** 30, 35, 37, 38, 39, 40, 49, 67, 68

Manor House (t/a Manor House Kitchens)
Manor House Heron Court Cranes Farm Road, Basildon, SS14 3DF
Tel: 01268-288444 **Fax:** 01268-534265
E-mail: info@manor-design.co.uk
Website: http://www.manor-design.com
Directors: C. Harvey (MD), L. Usselman (Co Sec), S. Tristran (Dir)
Immediate Holding Company: APPS MARKETING LTD
Registration no: 02545045 **VAT No.:** GB 583 1472 34
Date established: 2012 **Turnover:** £500,000 - £1m
No.of Employees: 1 - 10 **Product Groups:** 26, 61

Meadows Forklifts
Ridley Road Burnt Mills Industrial Estate, Basildon, SS13 1EG
Tel: 01268-724422 **Fax:** 01268-725282
E-mail: lee@meadowsforklifts.com
Website: http://www.meadowsforklifts.co.uk
Directors: L. Meadows (Ptnr), K. Dormer (Ptnr)
Immediate Holding Company: ALLTHREAD PLASTICS LIMITED
Registration no: 01654820 **Date established:** 1982
No.of Employees: 11 - 20 **Product Groups:** 35, 39, 45

Date of Accounts	Oct 11	Oct 10	Oct 09
Working Capital	199	197	149
Fixed Assets	37	27	26
Current Assets	390	306	274

Mountfield Services Ltd
Harvey Road, Basildon, SS13 1EP
Tel: 01268-724996 **Fax:** 01268-451887
E-mail: sales@mountfieldservices.co.uk
Website: http://www.mountfieldservices.co.uk
Directors: M. Anderson (MD), P. Chandler (Fin)
Immediate Holding Company: MOUNTFIELD SERVICES LIMITED
Registration no: 03152847 **Date established:** 1996
Turnover: £500,000 - £1m **No.of Employees:** 11 - 20
Product Groups: 35, 39, 45

Date of Accounts	Jan 11	Jan 10	Jan 09
Sales Turnover	782	1m	2m
Pre Tax Profit/Loss	1	-128	20
Working Capital	282	276	400
Fixed Assets	15	20	26
Current Assets	326	344	459
Current Liabilities	11	5	19

Mulhouse Ltd
36 Nobel Square Burnt Mills Industrial Estate, Basildon, SS13 1LT
Tel: 01268-726222 **Fax:** 01268-590424
E-mail: info@mulhouseltd.com
Website: http://www.mulhouseltd.com
Directors: G. Arnold (MD)
Immediate Holding Company: MULHOUSE LIMITED
Registration no: 01473069 **Date established:** 1980
No.of Employees: 11 - 20 **Product Groups:** 35, 39, 45

Date of Accounts	Jun 11	Jun 10	Jun 09
Working Capital	1m	912	675
Fixed Assets	58	74	98
Current Assets	1m	1m	903

Musto Ltd
Unit 4 Juniper West Fenton Way, Basildon, SS15 6SJ
Tel: 01268-491555 **Fax:** 01268-491440
E-mail: customerservices@musto.co.uk
Website: http://www.musto.co.uk
Directors: D. Cook (Fin), N. Musto (Dir)
Ultimate Holding Company: MUSTO TOPCO LIMITED
Immediate Holding Company: MUSTO LIMITED
Registration no: 01004420 **Date established:** 1971
Turnover: £20m - £50m **No.of Employees:** 51 - 100 **Product Groups:** 24

Date of Accounts	Dec 11	Dec 10	Dec 09
Sales Turnover	32m	31m	26m
Pre Tax Profit/Loss	-89	2m	-4m
Working Capital	6m	6m	5m
Fixed Assets	8m	8m	7m
Current Assets	15m	14m	13m
Current Liabilities	3m	2m	2m

Newsquest Essex Ltd (Newsquest (Essex) Ltd)
Newspaper House Chester Hall Lane, Basildon, SS14 3BL
Tel: 01268-522792 **Fax:** 01268-532060
E-mail: michael.harper@nqe.com
Website: http://www.echo-news.co.uk
Bank(s): Lloyds TSB Bank plc
Directors: M. Harper (MD), M. Good (Fin)
Managers: G. White, J. O'Rawa (Sales & Mktg Mg), S. Head-anderson
Ultimate Holding Company: GANNETT CO INC (USA)
Immediate Holding Company: NEWSQUEST (ESSEX) LIMITED
Registration no: 03102787 **VAT No.:** GB 667 8301 08
Date established: 1995 **Turnover:** £10m - £20m
No.of Employees: 101 - 250 **Product Groups:** 28

Date of Accounts	Dec 08	Dec 09	Dec 10
Sales Turnover	34m	26m	24m
Pre Tax Profit/Loss	-29m	3m	3m
Working Capital	-25m	8m	13m
Fixed Assets	44m	44m	43m
Current Assets	11m	13m	16m
Current Liabilities	3m	2m	2m

Onforme Dies Ltd
Unit 3g Nevendon Trading Estate Harvey Road, Basildon, SS13 1DA
Tel: 01268-729811 **Fax:** 01268-590017
E-mail: onform@hotmail.com
Directors: R. Pope (MD), P. Hickford (Co Sec)
Immediate Holding Company: ONFORM (DIES) LIMITED
Registration no: 01917688 **Date established:** 1985
No.of Employees: 1 - 10 **Product Groups:** 44

Date of Accounts	Aug 11	Aug 10	Aug 09
Working Capital	49	38	7
Fixed Assets	9	13	29
Current Assets	76	60	53

P M S International Group plc
International House Cricketers Way, Basildon, SS13 1ST
Tel: 01268-505050 **Fax:** 01268-505000
E-mail: info@pmsinternational.com
Website: http://www.pmsinternational.com
Directors: T. Goding (Sales), P. Beverley (MD), M. Benson (Fin)
Managers: P. Smith (Tech Serv Mgr), D. Eagling (Purch Mgr)
Ultimate Holding Company: KARUSSEL HOLDINGS LIMITED (BVI)
Immediate Holding Company: PMS INTERNATIONAL HOLDINGS PLC
Registration no: 01969212 **Date established:** 1985
Turnover: £20m - £50m **No.of Employees:** 251 - 500 **Product Groups:** 49

Date of Accounts	Nov 08	Nov 09	Nov 10
Sales Turnover	36m	46m	47m
Pre Tax Profit/Loss	-946	3m	4m
Working Capital	8m	9m	3m
Fixed Assets	15m	11m	11m
Current Assets	24m	25m	28m
Current Liabilities	1m	3m	7m

Panel Supplies
Harvey Road, Basildon, SS13 1ES
Tel: 01268-729100 **Fax:** 01268-729700
E-mail: sales@panelsupplies.co.uk
Website: http://www.panelsupplies.co.uk
Managers: L. O'brien (Chief Mgr)
Registration no: 01116562 **Date established:** 1973 **Turnover:** £1m - £2m
No.of Employees: 11 - 20 **Product Groups:** 25, 45, 52

Phillips Foils Ltd
1 Olympic Business Centre Paycocke Road, Basildon, SS14 3ET
Tel: 01268-288955 **Fax:** 01268-286080
E-mail: info@pfl.uk.com
Website: http://www.pfl.uk.com
Bank(s): Barclays
Directors: A. Man (MD), T. Wilson (Fin)
Ultimate Holding Company: PFL UK LIMITED
Immediate Holding Company: PHILLIPS FOILS LIMITED
Registration no: 02207448 **Date established:** 1987 **Turnover:** £1m - £2m
No.of Employees: 11 - 20 **Product Groups:** 34, 44, 48

Date of Accounts	Apr 11	Apr 10	Apr 09
Working Capital	289	226	186
Fixed Assets	490	499	525
Current Assets	783	702	622

Powell
Chester Hall Lane, Basildon, SS14 3DQ
Tel: 01708-448877 **Fax:** 01708-700007
E-mail: info@rodwell-powell.com
Website: http://www.rodwell-powell.com
Bank(s): Barclays
Directors: C. Washington (Fin)
Ultimate Holding Company: NORAM INTERNATIONAL INC (NEVIS)
Immediate Holding Company: RODWELL ENGINEERING GROUP LIMITED
Registration no: 00502926 **VAT No.:** GB 406 3416 80
Date established: 1951 **Turnover:** £5m - £10m
No.of Employees: 51 - 100 **Product Groups:** 30, 33, 34, 39, 46, 48, 84

Date of Accounts	Dec 11	Dec 10	Dec 09
Sales Turnover	5m	6m	5m
Pre Tax Profit/Loss	-160	-132	-428
Working Capital	-153	-759	-773
Fixed Assets	800	863	900
Current Assets	2m	2m	2m
Current Liabilities	266	248	380

Power Adhesives Ltd
1 Lords Way, Basildon, SS13 1TN
Tel: 01268-885800 **Fax:** 01268-885810
E-mail: s.sweeney@poweradhesives.com
Website: http://www.poweradhesives.com
Bank(s): Lloyds TSB, Romford
Directors: R. Colbert (Fin), S. Sweeny (Tech Serv), S. Sweeney (Tech Serv)
Managers: L. Hart (Mktg Serv Mgr), S. Edmeades (Tech Serv Mgr)
Immediate Holding Company: POWER ADHESIVES LIMITED
Registration no: 01193164 **VAT No.:** GB 228 0776 55
Date established: 1974 **Turnover:** £2m - £5m **No.of Employees:** 21 - 50
Product Groups: 32, 37

Date of Accounts	Aug 11	Aug 10	Aug 09
Working Capital	1m	1m	925
Fixed Assets	4m	4m	4m
Current Assets	3m	3m	2m

Precision Louvre Co. Ltd
Swinbourne Road Burnt Mills Industrial Estate, Basildon, SS13 1EH
Tel: 01268-729554 **Fax:** 01268-729563
E-mail: sales@precision-louvre.co.uk
Website: http://www.precision-louvre.co.uk
Directors: P. O'sullivan (Co Sec), T. Butcher (Dir)
Managers: A. Cheethim (I.T. Exec), P. Saunders (Sales Prom Mgr)
Immediate Holding Company: PRECISION LOUVRE COMPANY LIMITED
Registration no: 02827919 **Date established:** 1993
Turnover: £250,000 - £500,000 **No.of Employees:** 51 - 100
Product Groups: 37

Professional Fee Protection Ltd
Sylvan Way Southfields Business Park, Basildon, SS15 6TW
Tel: 08453-071177 **Fax:** 01277-622475
E-mail: f.pons@pfp.uk.com
Website: http://www.pfponline.com
Bank(s): Midland
Directors: F. Pons (MD)
Managers: J. Howell, J. Wynn, A. Riley (Sales Admin)
Immediate Holding Company: PROFESSIONAL FEE PROTECTION LIMITED
Registration no: 01971993 **Date established:** 1985 **Turnover:** £2m - £5m
No.of Employees: 21 - 50 **Product Groups:** 82

Date of Accounts	Apr 11	Apr 10	Apr 09
Sales Turnover	N/A	4m	3m
Pre Tax Profit/Loss	N/A	166	27
Working Capital	793	343	278
Fixed Assets	263	204	144
Current Assets	2m	1m	966
Current Liabilities	N/A	598	26

Q P P Ltd
33 Bowlers Croft, Basildon, SS14 3DZ
Tel: 01268-288192 **Fax:** 01268-293453
E-mail: qpp.ltd@gmail.com
Website: http://www.nationaltrust.org.uk
Directors: S. Smith (Fin), S. Smith (MD)
Immediate Holding Company: Q. P. P. LIMITED
Registration no: 02762394 **Date established:** 1992
No.of Employees: 1 - 10 **Product Groups:** 46, 48

Date of Accounts	Nov 11	Nov 10	Nov 09
Working Capital	-5	-1	-14
Fixed Assets	11	13	15
Current Assets	51	54	45

Rawley Event Toilets
Burnt Mills Industrial Estate Harvey Road, Basildon, SS13 1RP
Tel: 01268-722311 **Fax:** 01268-722313
E-mail: marketing@rawley.co.uk
Website: http://www.rawley.co.uk
Directors: C. Rawley (Ch)
Managers: M. Capps (Mktg Serv Mgr), T. Mitchell
Immediate Holding Company: TCC HIRE LLP
Registration no: OC344353 **Date established:** 2009
No.of Employees: 21 - 50 **Product Groups:** 30, 36, 66

Date of Accounts	Dec 11	Dec 10	Mar 10
Working Capital	68	90	81
Fixed Assets	80	19	32
Current Assets	109	153	118

Rawley Plant Ltd
Burnt Mills Industrial Estate Harvey Road, Basildon, SS13 1RP
Tel: 01268-722300 **Fax:** 01268-722313
E-mail: marketing@rawley.co.uk
Website: http://www.rawley.co.uk
Directors: C. Rawley (Ch)
Managers: M. Capps (Mktg Serv Mgr), T. Mitchell
Ultimate Holding Company: J.H. RAWLEY GROUP LIMITED
Immediate Holding Company: RAWLEY PLANT LTD.
Registration no: 00939976 **Date established:** 1968
No.of Employees: 21 - 50 **Product Groups:** 36, 66, 67, 83

Date of Accounts	Dec 11	Dec 10	Dec 09
Working Capital	-191	-322	-429
Fixed Assets	2m	2m	2m
Current Assets	490	429	360

Redhead Freight Ltd

Unit E Zenith Business Park Paycocke Road, Basildon, SS14 3DW
Tel: 01268-884488 **Fax:** 01268-884489
E-mail: ros@redhead-int.com
Website: http://www.redhead-int.com
Managers: R. Meshkova (Mgr)
Ultimate Holding Company: REDHEAD HOLDINGS LIMITED
Immediate Holding Company: REDHEAD FREIGHT LIMITED
Registration no: 01355753 **VAT No.:** GB 697 4297 69
Date established: 1978 **Turnover:** £2m - £5m **No.of Employees:** 1 - 10
Product Groups: 76

Date of Accounts	Mar 12	Mar 11	Mar 10
Sales Turnover	31m	29m	25m
Pre Tax Profit/Loss	1m	1m	1m
Working Capital	3m	2m	2m
Fixed Assets	3m	3m	2m
Current Assets	12m	11m	11m
Current Liabilities	773	1m	1m

Rhenus Logistics Ltd

Rhenus House Courtauld Road, Basildon, SS13 1RW
Tel: 01268-596620 **Fax:** 01268-592181
E-mail: martin.cleary@uk.rhenus.com
Website: http://www.rhenus.com
Directors: M. Cleary (Dir)
Ultimate Holding Company: RETHMANN AG & CO KG (GERMANY)
Immediate Holding Company: RHENUS LOGISTICS LIMITED
Registration no: 04401654 **VAT No.:** GB 146 8926 28
Date established: 2002 **Turnover:** £2m - £5m **No.of Employees:** 21 - 50
Product Groups: 76

Date of Accounts	Dec 11	Dec 10	Dec 09
Sales Turnover	52m	45m	39m
Pre Tax Profit/Loss	2m	461	1m
Working Capital	1m	2m	2m
Fixed Assets	7m	2m	2m
Current Assets	11m	11m	10m
Current Liabilities	2m	2m	1m

Rim Plastics Technology Ltd

1 Wollaston Way Burnt Mills Industrial Estate, Basildon, SS13 1DJ
Tel: 01268-729679 **Fax:** 01268-729031
E-mail: sales@rimplas.co.uk
Website: http://www.rimplas.co.uk
Bank(s): Nat West
Directors: J. Elliott (Fin), K. Whyte (MD), R. Whyte (MD)
Managers: I. Cook (Sales Prom Mgr)
Immediate Holding Company: RIM PLASTICS TECHNOLOGY LIMITED
Registration no: 02073596 **VAT No.:** GB 451 9186 36
Date established: 1986 **Turnover:** £2m - £5m **No.of Employees:** 51 - 100
Product Groups: 30

Date of Accounts	Dec 11	Dec 10	Dec 09
Working Capital	602	587	254
Fixed Assets	2m	712	772
Current Assets	2m	2m	1m

Rodwell H T B Ltd

Bentalls, Basildon, SS14 3SD
Tel: 01268-286646 **Fax:** 01268-287799
E-mail: sales@rodwell-autoclave.com
Website: http://www.rodwell-htb.com
Directors: A. Rodwell (MD)
Managers: J. Granger (Fin Mgr), J. Goodall (Sales Prom Mgr)
Ultimate Holding Company: NORAM INTERNATIONAL INC (NEVIS)
Immediate Holding Company: RODWELL - H T B LIMITED
Registration no: 01010432 **Date established:** 1971 **Turnover:** £1m - £2m
No.of Employees: 21 - 50 **Product Groups:** 40

Rodwell Powell

Chester Hall Lane, Basildon, SS14 3DQ
Tel: 01268-286641 **Fax:** 01268-286644
E-mail: steve.brough@rodwell-powell.com
Website: http://www.rodwell-powell.com
Directors: S. Brough (MD)
No.of Employees: 21 - 50 **Product Groups:** 38, 46, 85

H & L Russell

Russel House Hornsby Way, Southfields Business Park, Basildon, SS15 6TF
Tel: 01268-889000 **Fax:** 01268-889100
E-mail: pauls@russel.co.uk
Website: http://www.russell.co.uk
Bank(s): Lloyds TSB Bank plc
Managers: C. Waller (Purch Mgr), R. Warland (Sales Prom Mgr), P. Sharp (Chief Mgr), C. Hargraves
Immediate Holding Company: L C H GROUP
Registration no: 00299128 **VAT No.:** GB 350 6479 50
Turnover: £10m - £20m **No.of Employees:** 21 - 50 **Product Groups:** 61

S K Sales

Unit 31 33 Nobel Square, Burnt Mills Industrial Estate, Basildon, SS13 1LT
Tel: 01268-596760 **Fax:** 01268-590766
Website: http://www.sksales.co.uk
Managers: B. Taylor (Mgr)
No.of Employees: 1 - 10 **Product Groups:** 40, 66

Sculpture Studios

3 Hornsby Square Southfields Industrial Park, Laindon West, Basildon, SS15 6SD
Tel: 01268-418837 **Fax:** 01268-414118
E-mail: aden.hynes@virgin.net
Website: http://www.sculpturestudios.co.uk
Directors: A. Hynes (MD)
Turnover: Up to £250,000 **No.of Employees:** 1 - 10 **Product Groups:** 25, 26, 30, 33, 35, 49, 52, 86, 89

Seal UK Ltd

Unit 1 Watkins Close Burnt Mill Industrial Estate, Burnt Mills Industrial Estate, Basildon, SS13 1TL
Tel: 01268-722400 **Fax:** 01268-725864
Website: http://www.sealgraphics.com
Bank(s): National Westminster, 21 Lombard Street, London EC3

Directors: M. Triggs (MD), J. McMahon (Fin)
Ultimate Holding Company: NESCHEN AG (GERMANY)
Immediate Holding Company: NESCHEN COATING UK LTD
Registration no: 04276307 **VAT No.:** GB 583 2047 44
Date established: 2001 **Turnover:** £500,000 - £1m
No.of Employees: 21 - 50 **Product Groups:** 27, 30, 42, 48

Date of Accounts	Dec 11	Dec 10	Dec 09
Sales Turnover	969	2m	2m
Pre Tax Profit/Loss	-2m	-801	5m
Working Capital	-2m	-739	N/A
Fixed Assets	163	234	295
Current Assets	440	415	349
Current Liabilities	200	102	150

Selex Communications

Lambda House Christopher Martin Road, Basildon, SS14 3EL
Tel: 01268-823400 **Fax:** 01245-287125
E-mail: info@selex-comms.com
Website: http://www.selex-comms.com
Bank(s): National Westminster Bank Plc
Directors: A. Piolao (Fin), J. Archbold (Pers)
Managers: L. Powell (Purch Mgr), M. Watson-lee (Tech Serv Mgr), P. Robinson (Mgr)
Ultimate Holding Company: FINMECCANICA SPA (ITALY)
Immediate Holding Company: SELEX ELSAG LIMITED
Registration no: 00964533 **Date established:** 1969
Turnover: £75m - £125m **No.of Employees:** 251 - 500
Product Groups: 37

Date of Accounts	Dec 11	Dec 10	Dec 09
Sales Turnover	100m	116m	112m
Pre Tax Profit/Loss	4m	10m	14m
Working Capital	81m	77m	68m
Fixed Assets	33m	35m	36m
Current Assets	162m	162m	159m
Current Liabilities	26m	38m	35m

Shalam Containers UK Shalam Packaging International Shalam Packaging International

Plastic Container Division Honeywood Business Park, Basildon, SS14 3DS
Tel: 0870-516 8324 **Fax:** 0870-516 8325
E-mail: sales@shalam.net
Website: http://www.shalam.co.il
Registration no: 06578674 **Product Groups:** 30, 67

Skyline Elevators

Unit 2 Wrexham Road, Basildon, SS15 6PX
Tel: 01268-414295 **Fax:** 01268-545883
E-mail: m.philpin@skylineelevators.co.uk
Website: http://www.skylineelevators.co.uk
Directors: K. Ford (Prop), M. Philpin (Ptnr)
Immediate Holding Company: BUTTONHOLE LIMITED
Date established: 1982 **No.of Employees:** 1 - 10 **Product Groups:** 35, 39, 45

Date of Accounts	Jul 10	Jul 09	Jul 08
Working Capital	-100	-109	-134
Fixed Assets	113	114	116
Current Assets	40	46	30

Stanton Hope

11 Seax Court, Basildon, SS15 6LY
Tel: 01268-419141 **Fax:** 01268-545992
E-mail: sales@stantonhope.co.uk
Website: http://www.stantonhope.co.uk
Directors: A. Morris (Sales)
Immediate Holding Company: STANTON HOPE LIMITED
Registration no: 01023434 **VAT No.:** GB 250 4979 48
Date established: 1971 **Turnover:** £1m - £2m **No.of Employees:** 1 - 10
Product Groups: 24, 37, 41, 67

Date of Accounts	Dec 11	Dec 10	Dec 09
Working Capital	189	188	193
Fixed Assets	6	7	8
Current Assets	318	318	346

Sun Changing Rooms Ltd

Unit E Enterprise Centre Paycocke Road, Basildon, SS14 3DY
Tel: 01268-285343 **Fax:** 01268-281440
E-mail: s-himpfen@sunchangingrooms.co.uk
Website: http://www.sunchangingrooms.co.uk
Directors: S. Himpfen (Dir), S. Himpfen (MD)
Immediate Holding Company: SUN CHANGING ROOMS LIMITED
Registration no: 02700668 **Date established:** 1992
No.of Employees: 1 - 10 **Product Groups:** 35, 42, 45

Date of Accounts	Mar 10	Mar 09	Mar 08
Working Capital	-44	-54	-58
Fixed Assets	115	121	104
Current Assets	56	51	37

T N T Document Services

Unit 3a Festival Way Festival Leisure Park, Basildon, SS14 3WB
Tel: 01268-247800 **Fax:** 020-7250 0602
E-mail: chris.wright@tnt.co.uk
Website: http://www.tnt.co.uk
Bank(s): Barclays
Managers: C. Wright (Ops Mgr), P. Taylor (Buyer)
Ultimate Holding Company: TPG GROUP
Registration no: 00977839 **VAT No.:** GB 417 6746 31
Date established: 1970 **Turnover:** £50m - £75m
No.of Employees: 51 - 100 **Product Groups:** 28, 44, 80, 81

Timesco Of London Ltd

Unit 3 Carnival Park Carnival Close, Basildon, SS14 3WN
Tel: 01268-297700 **Fax:** 01268-297800
E-mail: info@timesco.com
Website: http://www.timesco.com
Bank(s): Midland
Directors: S. Fayyaz (MD), K. Rashaid (Fin)
Managers: A. Boylett (Chief Mgr), T. McCormick (Personnel), A. Massey (Mktg Serv Mgr), A. Lobo, R. McDowall (Tech Serv Mgr)
Immediate Holding Company: TIMESCO HEALTHCARE LIMITED
Registration no: 03346938 **VAT No.:** GB 233 1987 60
Date established: 1997 **Turnover:** £5m - £10m **No.of Employees:** 21 - 50
Product Groups: 38, 67

The Transformer & Electrical Co. (Engineering) Ltd

Honywood Road, Basildon, SS14 3DT
Tel: 01268-520491 **Fax:** 01268-530344
E-mail: carcher@teccoltd.com
Website: http://www.teccoltd.com
Bank(s): National Westminster Bank Plc
Directors: I. Rowley (Dir), J. McIlfactrick (Co Sec), J. McLifatrick (Dir & Gen Mgr), K. Spooner (MD), L. Whitehead (Dir), W. Lyons (Dir)
Managers: C. Archer (I.T. Exec), W. Cox (Sales Admin)
Immediate Holding Company: Claude Lyons Ltd
Registration no: 00365546 **Date established:** 1988 **Turnover:** £1m - £2m
No.of Employees: 21 - 50 **Product Groups:** 37

U T I Worldwide Ltd

Acorn House Great Oaks, Basildon, SS14 1LL
Tel: 01268-289501 **Fax:** 01268-530295
E-mail: bsn@go2uti.com
Website: http://www.go2uti.com
Bank(s): Barclays
Managers: R. Reedes (Mgr)
Ultimate Holding Company: UTI WORLDWIDE INC (BRITISH VIRGIN ISLANDS)
Immediate Holding Company: UTI WORLDWIDE (UK) LIMITED
Registration no: 02402322 **VAT No.:** 641 9441 37 **Date established:** 1989
Turnover: £20m - £50m **No.of Employees:** 11 - 20 **Product Groups:** 72, 74, 76, 77

Date of Accounts	Jan 12	Jan 11	Jan 10
Sales Turnover	135m	95m	75m
Pre Tax Profit/Loss	-816	-3m	-3m
Working Capital	-972	-325	-1m
Fixed Assets	878	849	2m
Current Assets	15m	20m	16m
Current Liabilities	5m	4m	3m

Universal Cycles

Unit 8a Festival Way Festival Leisure Park, Basildon, SS14 3WB
Tel: 08448-888484 **Fax:** 01268-247047
E-mail: sarah.markscheffel@universalcycles.plc.uk
Website: http://www.universalcycles.plc.uk
Bank(s): HSBC
Directors: R. Mellors (Fin)
Managers: T. Pritchard (Mgr)
Ultimate Holding Company: MASH HOLDINGS LIMITED
Immediate Holding Company: UNIVERSAL CYCLES LIMITED
Registration no: 01339667 **VAT No.:** GB 583 0217 55
Date established: 1977 **Turnover:** £10m - £20m
No.of Employees: 51 - 100 **Product Groups:** 39, 68

Date of Accounts	Apr 11	Apr 10	Apr 09
Sales Turnover	16m	18m	23m
Pre Tax Profit/Loss	-1m	-1m	-2m
Working Capital	-9m	-8m	-7m
Fixed Assets	5m	5m	5m
Current Assets	8m	8m	10m
Current Liabilities	16m	1m	7m

Vulcan Shot Blasting & Powder Coating

6 Cranes Close, Basildon, SS14 3JB
Tel: 01268-282662 **Fax:** 01268-282651
E-mail: vulcanshotblasting@mac.com
Website: http://www.vulcanshotblasting.com
Directors: S. Elman (Dir)
Registration no: 02942421 **VAT No.:** GB 646 2524 38
Date established: 1994 **Turnover:** £500,000 - £1m
No.of Employees: 1 - 10 **Product Groups:** 14, 32, 48, 52

Date of Accounts	Jun 08	Jun 07	Jun 06
Working Capital	-9	45	71
Fixed Assets	128	132	131
Current Assets	175	170	165
Current Liabilities	183	125	93

Waymade Health Care plc

Soverign House Miles Gray Road, Basildon, SS14 3FR
Tel: 01268-535200 **Fax:** 01268-535299
E-mail: reception@waymade.co.uk
Website: http://www.waymade.co.uk
Bank(s): National Westminster
Directors: B. Patel (MD), A. Beck (Fin)
Managers: D. Wilson (Personnel), S. Brown (Sales Prom Mgr), G. Lees (Purch Mgr), D. Sartain (Tech Serv Mgr), G. Hapley (Mktg Serv Mgr)
Ultimate Holding Company: VERDOT LIMITED (JERSEY)
Immediate Holding Company: WAYMADE HEALTHCARE PLC
Registration no: 01856320 **VAT No.:** GB 420 5410 07
Date established: 1984 **Turnover:** Up to £250,000
No.of Employees: 101 - 250 **Product Groups:** 63

Date of Accounts	Dec 10	Dec 09	Dec 08
Sales Turnover	127m	123m	137m
Pre Tax Profit/Loss	2m	682	4m
Working Capital	68m	71m	71m
Fixed Assets	11m	6m	5m
Current Assets	186m	153m	168m
Current Liabilities	10m	3m	4m

Welding Equipment Repair

22 Bourne Close, Basildon, SS15 6DZ
Tel: 01268-490765 **Fax:** 01268- 490765
E-mail: sales@weldingonline.co.uk
Website: http://www.weldingonline.co.uk
Directors: S. Beacham (Prop)
No.of Employees: 1 - 10 **Product Groups:** 46

Xchanging Resourcing Services

Endeavour Drive, Basildon, SS14 3WF
Tel: 01268-643868 **Fax:** 01268-643872
E-mail: info@xchanging.com
Website: http://www.rebusis.com
Managers: T. Woods Taylor (Admin Off)
Ultimate Holding Company: VSL GROUP HOLDINGS LIMITED
Immediate Holding Company: ROWAN INTERNATIONAL LIMITED
Registration no: 02477215 **VAT No.:** GB 359 9330 15
Date established: 1990 **Turnover:** £20m - £50m **No.of Employees:** 1 - 10
Product Groups: 44

Date of Accounts	Dec 11	Dec 10	Dec 09
Sales Turnover	53m	48m	47m
Pre Tax Profit/Loss	3m	2m	3m
Working Capital	2m	685	750
Fixed Assets	6m	6m	6m
Current Assets	11m	9m	8m
Current Liabilities	4m	3m	4m

Yellow Advertiser Newspaper Group Ltd
Acorn House Great Oaks, Basildon, SS14 1AH
Tel: 01268-503400 **Fax:** 01268-503404
E-mail: Basildon@YellowAd.co.uk
Website: http://www.yellowadvertiser-today.co.uk
Bank(s): National Westminster Bank Plc
Directors: S. Wood (Publishing)
Managers: J. Curtis (Tech Serv Mgr), M. Jenkinson (I.T. Exec), K. Todd
Ultimate Holding Company: TRINITY MIRROR PLC
Immediate Holding Company: TRINITY MIRROR SOUTHERN LTD
Registration no: 01167453 **VAT No.:** GB 216 2339 07
Turnover: £10m - £20m **No.of Employees:** 51 - 100 **Product Groups:** 28

Benfleet

Aero Dart Ltd
5 Brook Road, Benfleet, SS7 5JB
Tel: 01268-566111 **Fax:** 01268-565222
E-mail: direct@aerodart.ndirect.co.uk
Directors: F. Patel (Co Sec), M. Patel (Dir)
Registration no: 01295004 **Date established:** 1977
Turnover: Up to £250,000 **No.of Employees:** 1 - 10 **Product Groups:** 67

Date of Accounts	Aug 06
Sales Turnover	175
Pre Tax Profit/Loss	-4
Working Capital	4
Current Assets	13
Current Liabilities	9
Total Share Capital	3
ROCE% (Return on Capital Employed)	-89.1

Anchor Marine Plastics Ltd
231 Church Road, Benfleet, SS7 4QW
Tel: 01268-566666
E-mail: info@rwo-marine.com
Website: http://www.rwo-marine.com
Directors: S. Phillips (Sales)
Immediate Holding Company: ANCHOR MARINE PLASTICS LIMITED
Registration no: 01356272 **Date established:** 1978
No.of Employees: 11 - 20 **Product Groups:** 30, 39

Aztec Information Technology Ltd
30 Meadow Road Hadleigh, Benfleet, SS7 2DN
Tel: 01702-557998
E-mail: info@aztec-it.co.uk
Website: http://www.aztec-it.co.uk
Directors: G. Eyers (I.T. Dir)
Registration no: 05761625 **Date established:** 2006
Turnover: £250,000 - £500,000 **No.of Employees:** 1 - 10
Product Groups: 44, 67

Castle Locks
318-320 London Road, Benfleet, SS7 5XR
Tel: 01268-794848 **Fax:** 01268-794848
E-mail: castle.locks@btinternet.com
Website: http://www.castlelocks.co.uk
Directors: M. Cairns (Ptnr)
No.of Employees: 1 - 10 **Product Groups:** 36, 52

City Special Metals Ltd
122 Hart Road, Benfleet, SS7 3PS
Tel: 01268-774261 **Fax:** 0870-241 3443
E-mail: info@cityspecialmetals.co.uk
Website: http://www.cityspecialmetals.co.uk
Directors: K. Ingle (MD)
Immediate Holding Company: CITY SPECIAL METALS LTD
Registration no: 04276827 **Date established:** 2001
Turnover: £500,000 - £1m **No.of Employees:** 1 - 10 **Product Groups:** 77

Date of Accounts	Dec 11	Dec 10	Dec 09
Working Capital	743	482	315
Fixed Assets	11	9	10
Current Assets	1m	615	462

Connect Packaging
6-8 Brunel Road Manor Trading Estate, Benfleet, SS7 4PS
Tel: 01268-565656 **Fax:** 01268-565980
E-mail: info@connectpackaging.com
Website: http://www.connectpackaging.com
Bank(s): Barclays, Great Tarpots, Benfleet
Directors: J. Newton (Sales & Mktg), P. Lewis (Chief Op Offcr), R. Davidson (Dir), R. Davison (Comm), R. Essex (MD)
Ultimate Holding Company: C.A. Coutts Holdings P.L.C.
Immediate Holding Company: Writtle Holdings Ltd
Registration no: 00582559 **VAT No.:** GB 250 4157 90
Date established: 1957 **Turnover:** £5m - £10m
No.of Employees: 51 - 100 **Product Groups:** 85

Date of Accounts	Dec 09	Dec 08	Dec 07
Sales Turnover	7m	8m	9m
Pre Tax Profit/Loss	-93	-318	9
Working Capital	168	291	534
Fixed Assets	3m	3m	3m
Current Assets	2m	2m	3m
Current Liabilities	901	376	395

Elevation Lift Services Ltd
76 High Street Hadleigh, Benfleet, SS7 2PB
Tel: 01702-555916 **Fax:** 01702-553594
E-mail: rdebenham@elevationlifts.com
Website: http://www.elevationlifts.co.uk
Directors: R. Debenham (MD)
Immediate Holding Company: ELEVATION LIFT SERVICES LIMITED
Registration no: 03342834 **Date established:** 1997 **Turnover:** £1m - £2m
No.of Employees: 11 - 20 **Product Groups:** 26, 39, 45, 48, 67, 84, 85

Date of Accounts	Mar 11	Mar 10	Mar 09
Working Capital	66	87	-91
Fixed Assets	21	25	23
Current Assets	696	698	439

W Farthing & Sons Ltd
Units 2 & 4 B Block Fulton Road Manor Trading Estate, Benfleet, SS7 4PZ
Tel: 01268-794103 **Fax:** 01268-756094
E-mail: steve@wfarthingandsons.com
Website: http://www.wfarthingandsons.com
Directors: S. Hillis (Dir)
Immediate Holding Company: W FARTHING & SONS LIMITED
Registration no: 04589559 **Date established:** 2002
No.of Employees: 1 - 10 **Product Groups:** 26, 35

Date of Accounts	Dec 11	Dec 10	Dec 09
Working Capital	-4	-14	5
Fixed Assets	189	180	187
Current Assets	87	82	105

Huff 'N' Puff
34 Jotmans Lane, Benfleet, SS7 5BH
Tel: 01702-478329 **Fax:** 01702-716762
E-mail: sales@huffnpuff.co.uk
Website: http://www.huffnpuff.co.uk
Directors: K. Meager (Prop)
Turnover: £250,000 - £500,000 **No.of Employees:** 1 - 10
Product Groups: 49, 65, 75, 81

Date of Accounts	Jun 08	Jun 07	Jun 06
Sales Turnover	36	72	54
Pre Tax Profit/Loss	-7	13	-3
Working Capital	-45	-40	-49
Fixed Assets	7	10	5
Current Assets	47	53	58
Current Liabilities	92	93	107
ROCE% (Return on Capital Employed)	18.0	-43.8	6.7
ROT% (Return on Turnover)	-18.6	18.4	-5.4

Masterlite Double Glazing
296 Church Road, Benfleet, SS7 3HJ
Tel: 01268-752978 **Fax:** 01268-758600
E-mail: sales@masterlite.co.uk
Website: http://www.masterlite.co.uk
Directors: R. Sagrott (Prop)
VAT No.: GB 546 0763 38 **Date established:** 2001
Turnover: Up to £250,000 **No.of Employees:** 1 - 10 **Product Groups:** 30, 35, 52

Project Skills Solution
Lloyds House Kents Hill Road, Benfleet, SS7 5PN
Tel: 08451-307411 **Fax:** 01268-754520
E-mail: info@projss.co.uk
Website: http://www.projss.co.uk
Managers: A. Aa (Trng Mgr)
Immediate Holding Company: PROJECT SKILLS SOLUTIONS LTD
Registration no: 05262497 **Date established:** 2004 **Turnover:** £1m - £2m
No.of Employees: 11 - 20 **Product Groups:** 33, 37, 44, 45, 52, 54, 80, 84, 86

Date of Accounts	Mar 07	Mar 06
Working Capital	19	1
Fixed Assets	23	2
Current Assets	96	18
Current Liabilities	77	17

Proplate Metal Finishing Co.
17 Manor Trading Estate Armstrong Road, Benfleet, SS7 4PW
Tel: 01268-752037 **Fax:** 01268-755862
E-mail: proplate@btconnect.com
Directors: R. Lamb (Prop)
Managers: R. Pattell (Mgr)
Date established: 1996 **No.of Employees:** 1 - 10 **Product Groups:** 46, 48

R T E UK Ltd
101a Hall Farm Road, Benfleet, SS7 5JW
Tel: 01268-569393 **Fax:** 01268-751753
E-mail: rte-uk@lineone.net
Website: http://www.rte-timberengineering.co.uk
Directors: F. Mcgarry (MD), J. McGarry (Fin)
Immediate Holding Company: RTE (UK) LIMITED
Registration no: 03182025 **VAT No.:** GB 247 9487 09
Date established: 1996 **Turnover:** £500,000 - £1m
No.of Employees: 1 - 10 **Product Groups:** 25, 52

Date of Accounts	Mar 11	Mar 10	Mar 09
Working Capital	-9	-9	-1
Current Assets	4	3	7

R W O Marine Equipment Ltd
231 Church Road, Benfleet, SS7 4QW
Tel: 01268-566666 **Fax:** 01268-795118
E-mail: info@rwo-marine.com
Website: http://www.rwo-marine.com
Directors: D. Wahl (Works), M. Owen (Jt MD), R. Owen (MD), S. Phillips (Sales)
Managers: J. Wahl (I.T. Exec), L. Coulson (Purch Mgr), S. Phillips (Sales & Mktg Mg)
Ultimate Holding Company: INTERNATIONAL MARINE HOLDINGS LIMITED
Immediate Holding Company: RWO (MARINE EQUIPMENT) LIMITED
Registration no: 02057210 **VAT No.:** GB 250 3611 02
Date established: 1986 **Turnover:** £5m - £10m **No.of Employees:** 21 - 50
Product Groups: 84

Date of Accounts	Sep 11	Sep 10	Sep 09
Working Capital	14	23	14
Current Assets	570	625	626

T R Robb
316 High Road, Benfleet, SS7 5HB
Tel: 01268-752888
E-mail: terry.trobb@s9.co.uk
Website: http://www.trobb.s9.co.uk
Directors: T. Robb (Prop)
Date established: 1979 **No.of Employees:** 1 - 10 **Product Groups:** 36, 39, 40

S & J Contractors
81 Vicarage Hill, Benfleet, SS7 1PD
Tel: 01268-755761
Directors: S. McGown (Fin), J. Clarke (MD)
Immediate Holding Company: S & J CONTRACTORS LIMITED
Registration no: 03277315 **Date established:** 1996
No.of Employees: 11 - 20 **Product Groups:** 35

Date of Accounts	Mar 11	Mar 10	Mar 09
Working Capital	43	56	80
Fixed Assets	12	16	22
Current Assets	93	98	144

A J Smith & Son Benfleet Ltd
242 High Road, Benfleet, SS7 5LA
Tel: 01268-792771 **Fax:** 01268-750780
E-mail: info@ajsmith.uk.com
Website: http://www.ajsmith.uk.com
Bank(s): HSBC Bank plc
Directors: G. Smith (MD), T. Copsey (Sales)
Immediate Holding Company: A.J.SMITH AND SON(BENFLEET)LIMITED
Registration no: 00482542 **VAT No.:** GB 660 4871 29
Date established: 1950 **Turnover:** £1m - £2m **No.of Employees:** 11 - 20
Product Groups: 25, 66

Date of Accounts	Dec 11	Dec 10	Dec 09
Working Capital	243	236	221
Fixed Assets	44	51	41
Current Assets	428	410	397

Thames Loose Leaf
289 Kiln Road, Benfleet, SS7 1QS
Tel: 01268-775555 **Fax:** 01702-559068
E-mail: info@thamesgroup.co.uk
Website: http://www.thamescardtechnology.co.uk
Bank(s): Barclays
Directors: P. Underwood (MD), T. Hood (Fin)
Immediate Holding Company: THAMES LOOSE LEAF LIMITED
Registration no: 02670813 **VAT No.:** GB 583 2449 24
Date established: 1991 **Turnover:** £2m - £5m **No.of Employees:** 21 - 50
Product Groups: 28, 30, 42, 48

Date of Accounts	May 09	Nov 11	Nov 10
Sales Turnover	4m	N/A	N/A
Pre Tax Profit/Loss	106	N/A	N/A
Working Capital	37	136	138
Fixed Assets	862	727	759
Current Assets	596	1m	1m
Current Liabilities	115	N/A	N/A

Billericay

Acketts Group Ltd
Molyneux Court 4 Radford Way, Billericay, CM12 0BT
Tel: 01277-655178 **Fax:** 01277-632121
E-mail: info@ackettsgl.co.uk
Website: http://www.ackettsgl.co.uk
Directors: H. Fearn (Fin), K. Acketts (Dir)
Immediate Holding Company: ACKETTS GROUP LIMITED
Registration no: 02722832 **Date established:** 1992
No.of Employees: 1 - 10 **Product Groups:** 36, 66

Date of Accounts	Feb 11	Feb 10	Feb 09
Working Capital	293	289	400
Fixed Assets	16	17	22
Current Assets	465	438	566

Bow Shutters & Blinds
196 Stock Road, Billericay, CM12 0SH
Tel: 01277-624296
E-mail: val.ives@yahoo.co.uk
Directors: K. Ives (Prop)
No.of Employees: 1 - 10 **Product Groups:** 26, 35

Butyl Products Ltd
11 Radford Crescent, Billericay, CM12 0DW
Tel: 01277-653281 **Fax:** 01277-657921
E-mail: rodney@butylproducts.co.uk
Website: http://butylproducts.co.uk
Bank(s): Barclays
Directors: G. Mitchell (MD), R. Martin (MD)
Managers: L. Arney (Purch Mgr)
Immediate Holding Company: BUTYL PRODUCTS LIMITED
Registration no: 03141465 **VAT No.:** GB 668 3740 01
Date established: 1995 **Turnover:** £2m - £5m **No.of Employees:** 21 - 50
Product Groups: 29

Date of Accounts	Dec 11	Dec 10	Dec 09
Working Capital	2m	2m	2m
Fixed Assets	939	876	872
Current Assets	3m	3m	2m

Direct Insurance Agency Ltd
Cumberland House 129 High Street, Billericay, CM12 9AH
Tel: 01277-844360 **Fax:** 01277-844399
E-mail: info@direct-ins.co.uk
Website: http://www.direct-ins.co.uk
Directors: D. Bearman (MD)
Immediate Holding Company: DIRECT INSURANCE GROUP PLC
Registration no: 03149879 **Date established:** 1996
No.of Employees: 11 - 20 **Product Groups:** 82

Date of Accounts	Dec 11	Dec 10	Dec 09
Sales Turnover	1m	1m	1m
Pre Tax Profit/Loss	150	38	74
Working Capital	215	155	143
Fixed Assets	47	42	77
Current Assets	986	998	1m
Current Liabilities	75	63	162

Estelle Electrical Contractors Ltd
51 High Street, Billericay, CM12 9AX
Tel: 01277-651320 **Fax:** 01277-630608
Bank(s): Lloyds TSB Bank plc
Directors: R. Greaves (MD)
Immediate Holding Company: ESTELLE ELECTRICAL CONTRACTORS LTD
Registration no: 01068318 **VAT No.:** GB 250 4088 83
Date established: 1972 **Turnover:** £500,000 - £1m
No.of Employees: 11 - 20 **Product Groups:** 38, 52

First Byte Micro
5 Radford Business Centre Radford Crescent, Billericay, CM12 0DP
Tel: 01277-634200 **Fax:** 01277-631439
E-mail: sales@firstbytemicro.com
Website: http://www.firstbytemicro.com
Directors: H. Peacock (Dir)
No.of Employees: 1 - 10 **Product Groups:** 37, 67, 84

Glyn Ltd
172 Norsey Road, Billericay, CM11 1BU
Tel: 01277-634200 **Fax:** 01277-631439
E-mail: sales@glyn.com
Website: http://www.glyn.com
Directors: S. Rutter (MD)
Registration no: 02411343 **Turnover:** £5m - £10m
No.of Employees: 1 - 10 **Product Groups:** 37, 44

Date of Accounts	Dec 07	Dec 06	Dec 05
Working Capital	92	132	104
Fixed Assets	62	81	91
Current Assets	417	578	550
Current Liabilities	325	446	446
Total Share Capital	30	30	30

Ground Control Ltd

The Stables London Road, Billericay, CM12 9HS
Tel: 01277-650697 **Fax:** 01277-630746
E-mail: info@ground-control.co.uk
Website: http://www.ground-control.co.uk
Directors: J. Coote (Co Sec)
Managers: P. Trehern
Ultimate Holding Company: GROUND CONTROL HOLDINGS LIMITED
Immediate Holding Company: GROUND CONTROL LIMITED
Registration no: 01795094 **Date established:** 1984
Turnover: £20m - £50m **No.of Employees:** 21 - 50 **Product Groups:** 07, 84

Date of Accounts	Mar 11	Mar 10	Mar 09
Sales Turnover	N/A	346	620
Pre Tax Profit/Loss	N/A	-350	339
Working Capital	-1m	-1m	-1m
Fixed Assets	3m	4m	9m
Current Assets	19	21	30
Current Liabilities	N/A	473	683

Jetform Services Ltd

Heath Road Ramsden Heath, Billericay, CM11 1HU
Tel: 01268-711700 **Fax:** 01268-711600
E-mail: mail@jetformpools.co.uk
Website: http://www.jetformpools.co.uk
Bank(s): Barclays
Directors: R. Wakefield (MD), R. Thorogood (MD)
Immediate Holding Company: JETFORM SERVICES LIMITED
Registration no: 02739147 **VAT No.:** GB 583 3874 04
Date established: 1992 **Turnover:** £1m - £2m **No.of Employees:** 21 - 50
Product Groups: 52

Date of Accounts	Jan 12	Jan 11	Jan 10
Working Capital	375	289	202
Fixed Assets	82	62	27
Current Assets	586	534	476

Killby & Gayford Ltd (t/a Killby-Tann)

30 Radford Way, Billericay, CM12 0DA
Tel: 01277-655921 **Fax:** 01277-630193
Website: http://www.killbygayford.co.uk
Bank(s): Barclays; National Westminster
Directors: C. Chivers (MD), C. Chivers (Grp Chief Exec), T. Smith (Dir), G. Hamer (Co Sec)
Ultimate Holding Company: KILLBY & GAYFORD GROUP LIMITED
Immediate Holding Company: KILLBY & GAYFORD LIMITED
Registration no: 00628491 **Date established:** 1959
Turnover: £20m - £50m **No.of Employees:** 51 - 100 **Product Groups:** 66, 84

Date of Accounts	Dec 10	Dec 09	Dec 08
Sales Turnover	78m	74m	87m
Pre Tax Profit/Loss	2m	2m	4m
Working Capital	10m	9m	9m
Current Assets	47m	43m	36m
Current Liabilities	4m	3m	2m

Total Stripping

Oak Lane Crays Hill, Billericay, CM11 2YH
Tel: 0791-635 4450
E-mail: stevec563@msn.com
Website: http://www.totalstripping.co.uk
Directors: S. Christie (Prop)
Immediate Holding Company: EURO LINE STRIPING LIMITED
Date established: 2011 **No.of Employees:** 1 - 10 **Product Groups:** 32, 33, 39, 48, 51, 52, 54

Tropicool

3 Weir Cottage Hardings Elms Road, Crays Hill, Billericay, CM11 2UH
Tel: 020-8592 6123 **Fax:** 020-8592 6123
E-mail: sales@tropicool.co.uk
Website: http://www.tropicool.co.uk
Directors: A. Langley (MD), V. Abraham (Prop)
Registration no: 05475843 **Date established:** 2004
No.of Employees: 1 - 10 **Product Groups:** 40, 52, 66, 83

Unbar Rothon Ltd

2 Radford Crescent, Billericay, CM12 0DR
Tel: 01277-632211 **Fax:** 01277-630151
E-mail: prothon@unbarrothon.co.uk
Website: http://www.unbarrothon.co.uk
Bank(s): Barclays, Brentwood
Directors: P. Rothon (Purch), W. Rothon (Dir)
Managers: D. Freeman (Personnel), R. Rothon (Mgr)
Immediate Holding Company: UNBAR ROTHON LIMITED
Registration no: 00173381 **VAT No.:** GB 250 3521 03
Date established: 2021 **Turnover:** £2m - £5m **No.of Employees:** 21 - 50
Product Groups: 20, 32

Date of Accounts	Feb 12	Feb 11	Feb 10
Sales Turnover	5m	4m	4m
Pre Tax Profit/Loss	211	274	238
Working Capital	3m	3m	2m
Fixed Assets	2m	2m	2m
Current Assets	3m	3m	3m
Current Liabilities	121	151	113

Uniter Group Ltd

3 Radford Way, Billericay, CM12 0DX
Tel: 08458-112000 **Fax:** 0845-811 2001
E-mail: jo.klingen@uniter.co.uk
Website: http://www.unitergroup.co.uk
Bank(s): National Westminster
Directors: C. Jawed (MD), J. Klingen (MD)
Managers: J. Bridge
Immediate Holding Company: UNITER GROUP LTD
Registration no: 04794421 **VAT No.:** GB 632 4931 46
Date established: 2003 **Turnover:** £2m - £5m **No.of Employees:** 51 - 100
Product Groups: 79

Date of Accounts	Mar 11	Mar 10	Mar 09
Sales Turnover	5m	5m	4m
Pre Tax Profit/Loss	-547	95	-261
Working Capital	-599	-166	282
Fixed Assets	620	692	780
Current Assets	3m	4m	2m
Current Liabilities	1m	796	756

Universal Air Products Ltd

Unit 5ardley Works London Road, Billericay, CM12 9HP
Tel: 01277-634637 **Fax:** 01277-632655
E-mail: sales@universalair.net
Website: http://www.universalair.net
Directors: M. Johnson (MD), A. Norwood (Fin)
Immediate Holding Company: UNIVERSAL AIR PRODUCTS LIMITED
Registration no: 03464294 **Date established:** 1997
Turnover: £500,000 - £1m **No.of Employees:** 1 - 10 **Product Groups:** 38, 42

Date of Accounts	Mar 12	Mar 11	Mar 10
Working Capital	-2	1	-6
Fixed Assets	5	6	7
Current Assets	131	134	129

Used Fork Lifts

107 Perry Street, Billericay, CM12 0NH
Tel: 01277-624608 **Fax:** 01277- 656108
Directors: J. Salmons (Dir)
Date established: 1994 **No.of Employees:** 1 - 10 **Product Groups:** 35, 39, 45

World Of Spice Ltd

Bebington Close, Billericay, CM12 0DT
Tel: 01277-633303 **Fax:** 01277-633036
E-mail: sales@worldofspice.co.uk
Website: http://www.worldofspice.co.uk
Managers: M. Rothon (Chief Mgr), D. Painter (Comm), M. Berry (Ops Mgr)
Ultimate Holding Company: UNBAR ROTHON LIMITED
Immediate Holding Company: WORLD OF SPICE LIMITED
Registration no: 02762118 **Date established:** 1992
Turnover: £500,000 - £1m **No.of Employees:** 21 - 50 **Product Groups:** 20

Date of Accounts	Feb 12	Feb 11	Feb 10
Working Capital	648	566	350
Fixed Assets	116	121	136
Current Assets	1m	813	705

Zeelandia Ltd

Unit 4 Radford Way, Billericay, CM12 0DX
Tel: 01277-651966 **Fax:** 01277-630074
E-mail: info@zeelandia.co.uk
Website: http://www.zeelandia.co.uk
Bank(s): Lloyds TSB
Directors: R. Schrama (MD)
Ultimate Holding Company: KONINKLIJKE ZEELANDIA GROEP BV (HOLLAND)
Immediate Holding Company: ZEELANDIA HOLDINGS (UK) LIMITED
Registration no: 02451997 **VAT No.:** GB 583 2163 42
Date established: 1989 **No.of Employees:** 11 - 20 **Product Groups:** 20, 31, 32

Date of Accounts	Dec 11	Dec 08	Jan 10
Fixed Assets	100	100	100

Braintree

A A T I Ltd

11 Swinbourne Drive Springwood Industrial Estate, Braintree, CM7 2YP
Tel: 01376-346278 **Fax:** 01376-348480
E-mail: info@aati.co.uk
Website: http://www.aati.co.uk
Directors: D. Bisset (MD), G. Elshaw (Co Sec)
Ultimate Holding Company: ENFIELD HOLDINGS LIMITED
Immediate Holding Company: AATI LIMITED
Registration no: 01841189 **VAT No.:** GB 759 9188 57
Date established: 1984 **Turnover:** £500,000 - £1m
No.of Employees: 1 - 10 **Product Groups:** 29, 30, 33, 34, 35, 36, 39, 40

Date of Accounts	Mar 11	Mar 10	Mar 09
Working Capital	26	80	127
Fixed Assets	87	75	58
Current Assets	511	479	578

Alphatemp Technology Ltd

Network House 300-302 Cressing Road, Braintree, CM7 3PG
Tel: 01376-344679 **Fax:** 01376-348976
E-mail: jim@alphatemptech.co.uk
Website: http://www.alphatemptech.co.uk
Product Groups: 29, 30, 35, 38, 40, 49

Date of Accounts	Dec 09	Dec 08	Dec 07
Working Capital	1	9	16
Fixed Assets	13	17	N/A
Current Assets	44	57	59

Atlantic Microwave Ltd

40a Springwood Drive, Braintree, CM7 2YN
Tel: 01376-550220 **Fax:** 01376-552145
E-mail: sales@atlanticmicrowave.co.uk
Website: http://www.amrf.co.uk
Managers: P. Grimmett (Sales Prom Mgr)
Immediate Holding Company: ATLANTIC MICROWAVE LIMITED
Registration no: 02412885 **Date established:** 1989
Turnover: £500,000 - £1m **No.of Employees:** 1 - 10 **Product Groups:** 37, 38

Date of Accounts	Dec 11	Dec 10	Dec 09
Working Capital	642	393	335
Fixed Assets	199	177	112
Current Assets	947	628	623

Aveat Heating Ltd

Lambert House 7 Driberg Way, Braintree, CM7 1NB
Tel: 01376-325670 **Fax:** 01376-551210
E-mail: enquiries@aveat.co.uk
Website: http://www.aveat.co.uk
Directors: R. Lewis (Co Sec)
Ultimate Holding Company: AVH BUILDING SERVICES LIMITED
Immediate Holding Company: AVEAT HEATING LIMITED
Registration no: 01380758 **Date established:** 1978
No.of Employees: 11 - 20 **Product Groups:** 40, 42, 52

Date of Accounts	Jun 11	Jun 10	Jun 09
Working Capital	110	238	188
Fixed Assets	54	65	85
Current Assets	969	954	2m

B C G Creative FX

10 Bocking End, Braintree, CM7 9AA
Tel: 01376-323461
E-mail: creativefx@virgin.net
Directors: B. Godden (Prop)
Turnover: £250,000 - £500,000 **No.of Employees:** 1 - 10
Product Groups: 44

B W T Ltd

Suite 3 Unit F Warners Mill Silks Way, Braintree, CM7 3GB
Tel: 01376-334200 **Fax:** 01376-334201
E-mail: enquiries@bwt-uk.co.uk
Website: http://www.bwt-uk.co.uk
Bank(s): National Westminster Bank Plc
Managers: S. Dines (Fin Mgr)
Immediate Holding Company: STERLING WASHROOM SERVICES LIMITED
Registration no: 01386074 **VAT No.:** GB 318 4924 45
Date established: 2012 **Turnover:** £2m - £5m **No.of Employees:** 21 - 50
Product Groups: 30, 32

Barlow Tyrie Ltd

Springwood Industrial Estate, Braintree, CM7 2RN
Tel: 01376-557600 **Fax:** 01376-557610
E-mail: info@teak.com
Website: http://www.teak.com
Bank(s): HSBC Bank plc
Directors: J. Tyrie (Fin), P. Tyrie (MD)
Managers: V. Read (Sales Admin), D. Evans (Mktg Serv Mgr), R. Chinnery (Tech Serv Mgr)
Immediate Holding Company: BARLOW TYRIE LIMITED
Registration no: 00573243 **VAT No.:** GB 102 0346 41
Date established: 1956 **Turnover:** £2m - £5m **No.of Employees:** 21 - 50
Product Groups: 24, 26

Date of Accounts	Sep 11	Sep 10	Sep 09
Sales Turnover	5m	N/A	N/A
Pre Tax Profit/Loss	333	N/A	N/A
Working Capital	636	327	257
Fixed Assets	11m	11m	11m
Current Assets	3m	4m	3m
Current Liabilities	2m	626	628

Barnes Packaging Ltd

8 Broomhills Industrial Estate Rayne Road, Braintree, CM7 2RG
Tel: 01376-347838 **Fax:** 01376-329128
E-mail: sales@barnespackaging.co.uk
Website: http://www.barnespackaging.co.uk
Directors: M. Sussex (Fin)
Immediate Holding Company: BARNES PACKAGING (BRAINTREE) LTD
Registration no: 01601949 **VAT No.:** GB 368 5545 13
Date established: 1981 **Turnover:** £1m - £2m **No.of Employees:** 11 - 20
Product Groups: 27

Date of Accounts	Aug 11	Feb 11	Feb 10
Working Capital	42	31	24
Fixed Assets	28	21	24
Current Assets	267	222	191

Braintree Electro Platers Ltd

12-13 Springwood Drive, Braintree, CM7 2YN
Tel: 01376-344265 **Fax:** 01376-328927
Bank(s): Lloyds TSB Bank plc
Directors: A. Joyce (Prop), L. Joyce (Co Sec)
Ultimate Holding Company: XPECT LEISURE LIMITED
Immediate Holding Company: BRAINTREE ELECTRO PLATERS LIMITED
Registration no: 01004632 **Date established:** 1971 **Turnover:** £1m - £2m
No.of Employees: 11 - 20 **Product Groups:** 48

Date of Accounts	Oct 11	Oct 09	Oct 08
Working Capital	199	66	77
Fixed Assets	222	231	242
Current Assets	276	119	136

Buildbase Ltd

Manor Street, Braintree, CM7 3HS
Tel: 01376-322944 **Fax:** 01376-550046
E-mail: leigh.ford@buildbase.co.uk
Website: http://www.buildbase.co.uk
Bank(s): National Westminster Bank Plc
Managers: L. Ford (Mgr)
Ultimate Holding Company: GRAFTON GROUP PUBLIC LIMITED COMPANY
Immediate Holding Company: GRAFTON MERCHANTING GB LIMITED
Registration no: 04725313 **Date established:** 2003 **Turnover:** £1m - £2m
No.of Employees: 11 - 20 **Product Groups:** 25, 48, 66

Date of Accounts	Dec 11	Dec 10	Dec 09
Sales Turnover	904m	854m	538m
Pre Tax Profit/Loss	12m	14m	-6m
Working Capital	226m	185m	288m
Fixed Assets	359m	364m	348m
Current Assets	483m	456m	531m
Current Liabilities	21m	18m	16m

C M J Mould Tools Ltd

New Walthambury House Anglia Way, Braintree, CM7 3RG
Tel: 01376-347776 **Fax:** 01376-347776
E-mail: sales@cmjmouldtools.co.uk
Website: http://www.cmjmouldtools.co.uk
Directors: C. Roberts (MD)
Immediate Holding Company: C.M.J. MOULD TOOLS LIMITED
Registration no: 01857517 **Date established:** 1984
Turnover: £250,000 - £500,000 **No.of Employees:** 11 - 20
Product Groups: 48

Date of Accounts	Apr 11	Apr 10	Apr 09
Working Capital	-61	-75	-96
Fixed Assets	84	90	179
Current Assets	177	134	39

Clingbrook Ltd

Unit 10 Lakes Industrial Park Lower Chapel Hill, Braintree, CM7 3RU
Tel: 01376-327206 **Fax:** 01376-330755
E-mail: enquiries@clingbrook.com
Website: http://www.clingbrook.com
Directors: C. Joyner (Co Sec)
Immediate Holding Company: CLINGBROOK LIMITED
Registration no: 01430149 **VAT No.:** GB 341 6818 55
Date established: 1979 **Turnover:** £250,000 - £500,000
No.of Employees: 1 - 10 **Product Groups:** 29

Date of Accounts	Mar 12	Mar 11	Mar 10
Working Capital	64	44	33
Fixed Assets	100	103	83
Current Assets	182	151	127

Crest Designs

11 Bradford Street, Braintree, CM7 9AS
Tel: 01376-325430 **Fax:** 01376-343863
E-mail: crest.designs@talk21.com
Website: http://www.crestdesigns.co.uk
Directors: R. Hughes (MD)
No.of Employees: 1 - 10 **Product Groups:** 23, 49, 65

Econoprint UK Ltd

3 Cooper Drive Springwood Industrial Estate, Braintree, CM7 2RF
Tel: 01376-349955 **Fax:** 01376-346853
E-mail: sales@econoprint.co.uk
Website: http://www.econoprint.co.uk
Directors: B. Siebert (Fin), N. Siebert (Dir)
Immediate Holding Company: ECONOPRINT (U.K.) LIMITED
Registration no: 01604452 **VAT No.:** GB 367 3953 14
Date established: 1981 **Turnover:** £1m - £2m **No.of Employees:** 11 - 20
Product Groups: 27, 28, 44

Date of Accounts	Mar 12	Mar 11	Mar 10
Working Capital	272	171	162
Fixed Assets	65	51	66
Current Assets	522	382	357

Essex Pat Testing

Tabor Avenue, Braintree, CM7 2SX
Tel: 01634-305962 **Fax:** 01634-308749
E-mail: info@pat-testing-essex.com
Website: http://www.pat-testing-essex.com
Directors: P. Abbott (Dir)
Date established: 2002 **No.of Employees:** 1 - 10 **Product Groups:** 85

Flow Control Company Ltd

Cooper Drive Springwood Industrial Estate, Braintree, CM7 2RF
Tel: 01376-321211 **Fax:** 01376-321222
E-mail: sales@flowcontrol.co.uk
Website: http://www.flowcontrol.co.uk
Directors: T. Blunden (Fin)
Immediate Holding Company: FLOW CONTROL COMPANY LIMITED
Registration no: 02673885 **Date established:** 1991
No.of Employees: 1 - 10 **Product Groups:** 38, 48

Date of Accounts	Mar 11	Mar 10	Mar 09
Working Capital	1m	1m	1m
Fixed Assets	9	9	25
Current Assets	2m	2m	2m

Foremost Electronics Ltd

Bluegate Hall Braintree Road, Great Bardfield, Braintree, CM7 4PZ
Tel: 01371-811171 **Fax:** 01371-810933
E-mail: info@4most.co.uk
Website: http://www.4most.co.uk
Directors: A. Cook (Dir)
Immediate Holding Company: FOREMOST ELECTRONICS LIMITED
Registration no: 03151126 **Date established:** 1996
Turnover: £250,000 - £500,000 **No.of Employees:** 1 - 10
Product Groups: 29, 37, 38, 63, 67

Date of Accounts	Apr 11	Apr 10	Apr 09
Working Capital	55	62	73
Fixed Assets	38	42	57
Current Assets	832	651	530

Freeola

92-102 East Street, Braintree, CM7 3JW
Tel: 08712-109977 **Fax:** 0871-210 9988
E-mail: tony.donovan@freeola.co.uk
Website: http://www.freeola.com
Managers: T. Donovan (Chief Mgr)
Immediate Holding Company: FREEOLA LIMITED
Registration no: 05335999 **Date established:** 2005 **Turnover:** £1m - £2m
No.of Employees: 11 - 20 **Product Groups:** 79

Date of Accounts	May 11	May 10	May 09
Sales Turnover	2m	2m	2m
Pre Tax Profit/Loss	40	31	12
Working Capital	294	218	149
Fixed Assets	163	207	246
Current Assets	483	366	332
Current Liabilities	128	120	120

F C Frost Ltd

7 Benfield Way, Braintree, CM7 3YS
Tel: 01376-329111 **Fax:** 01376-347002
E-mail: info@fcfrost.com
Website: http://www.fcfrost.com
Bank(s): HSBC Bank plc
Directors: D. Frost (Dir)
Immediate Holding Company: F.C. FROST LIMITED
Registration no: 01024973 **VAT No.:** GB 102 5796 82
Date established: 1971 **Turnover:** £2m - £5m **No.of Employees:** 21 - 50
Product Groups: 35, 36, 66

Date of Accounts	May 11	May 10	May 09
Working Capital	52	-10	14
Fixed Assets	951	2m	2m
Current Assets	542	526	778

Futureglass

Park Drive Industrial Estate Unit 8 Park Drive, Braintree, CM7 1AW
Tel: 01376-330300 **Fax:** 01376-440414
E-mail: gareth.phillips@futureglass.co.uk
Website: http://www.futureglass.com
Directors: G. Phillips (MD)
Ultimate Holding Company: DEMOS CICLITIRA LIMITED
Immediate Holding Company: FUTUREGLASS LIMITED
Registration no: 04419899 **Date established:** 2002
Turnover: £250,000 - £500,000 **No.of Employees:** 1 - 10
Product Groups: 26, 30

Date of Accounts	Aug 11	Apr 10
Working Capital	-237	N/A
Fixed Assets	161	N/A
Current Assets	45	N/A

G&M Loft Conversions

White House Farm, Braintree, CM7 4HF
Tel: 0800-328 7216
E-mail: enqs@gmloftconversions.com
Website: http://www.gmloftconversions.com
Directors: B. Martin (MD)
Registration no: 04655164 **Date established:** 1990
No.of Employees: 11 - 20 **Product Groups:** 52

Date of Accounts	Mar 10	Mar 09	Mar 08
Working Capital	7	56	73
Fixed Assets	20	22	22
Current Assets	129	196	222

Greengate Fabrications Ltd

Unit 3 Park Drive, Braintree, CM7 1AP
Tel: 01376-346040
E-mail: info@greengatefab.co.uk
Website: http://www.greengatefab.co.uk
Directors: K. Daden (Dir)
Immediate Holding Company: GREENGATE FABRICATIONS LIMITED
Registration no: 02301416 **Date established:** 1988
No.of Employees: 11 - 20 **Product Groups:** 30, 33, 34, 35

Date of Accounts	Jul 11	Jul 10	Jul 09
Working Capital	315	385	367
Fixed Assets	481	492	508
Current Assets	546	670	623

Handleyoursecurity

470 Avenue West Great Notley, Braintree, CM77 7AA
Tel: 01376-557557 **Fax:** 01376-557550
E-mail: info@handleyoursecurity.co.uk
Website: http://www.handleyoursecurity.co.uk
No.of Employees: 1 - 10 **Product Groups:** 30, 33, 36, 66

Handmade Gates & Garage Doors

51 Blackwater Way, Braintree, CM7 9BX
Tel: 01376-347789
Directors: N. French (Prop)
Date established: 1988 **No.of Employees:** 1 - 10 **Product Groups:** 26, 35

If 6 Was 9 Design Ltd

2 Elizabeth Lockhart Way, Braintree, CM7 9RH
Tel: 01376-322357
E-mail: info@if6was9design.com
Website: http://www.if6was9design.com
Directors: C. Gillman (Dir)
Immediate Holding Company: IF6WAS9 DESIGN LIMITED
Registration no: 05177664 **Date established:** 2004
No.of Employees: 1 - 10 **Product Groups:** 44, 81

Date of Accounts	Jul 11	Jul 10	Jul 09
Sales Turnover	N/A	92	58
Pre Tax Profit/Loss	N/A	50	33
Working Capital	51	25	18
Fixed Assets	4	4	2
Current Assets	94	44	28
Current Liabilities	43	14	8

The Incentive Works Ltd

Shendeck House 13 Harold Road, Braintree, CM7 2RU
Tel: 01376-550442
E-mail: sales@theincentiveworks.co.uk
Website: http://www.theincentiveworks.co.uk
Directors: S. Fields (Dir)
Registration no: 05679582 **Date established:** 2005
No.of Employees: 1 - 10 **Product Groups:** 49

IsoCool Ltd

Urban Hive, 460 Avenue West Skyline 120, Great Notley, Braintree, CM77 7AA
Tel: 01376-928455 **Fax:** 01376-328873
E-mail: info@isocool.ltd.uk
Website: http://www.isocool.ltd.uk
Directors: N. Hallett (MD)
Registration no: 04417519 **No.of Employees:** 1 - 10 **Product Groups:** 38, 40, 42, 49, 54, 63, 66, 76, 83, 84

Date of Accounts	Mar 08	Dec 06	Dec 05
Working Capital	25	18	-12
Fixed Assets	413	406	21
Current Assets	367	696	160
Current Liabilities	342	678	173

Kalestead Ltd

Network House Cressing Road, Braintree, CM7 3PG
Tel: 01376-349036 **Fax:** 01376-348976
E-mail: terence@kalestead.co.uk
Website: http://www.kalestead.co.uk
Bank(s): National Westminster Bank Plc
Directors: T. Hewitt (MD)
Managers: C. Lowe, C. Haven (Sales Prom Mgr), R. Patterson
Ultimate Holding Company: KALESTEAD HOLDINGS LIMITED
Immediate Holding Company: KALESTEAD LIMITED
Registration no: 01498292 **VAT No.:** GB 341 7417 68
Date established: 1980 **Turnover:** £2m - £5m **No.of Employees:** 51 - 100
Product Groups: 35, 37, 44, 67

Date of Accounts	Jun 11	Jun 10	Jun 09
Working Capital	379	297	47
Fixed Assets	67	75	217
Current Assets	630	537	473

Karikool Ltd

Hedingham Road Wethersfield, Braintree, CM7 4EQ
Tel: 01371-851606 **Fax:** 01371-850404
E-mail: info@karikool.co.uk
Website: http://www.karikool.co.uk
Directors: A. Waterman (Prop)
Immediate Holding Company: KARIKOOL LIMITED
Registration no: 05443502 **Date established:** 2005
No.of Employees: 1 - 10 **Product Groups:** 36, 40

Date of Accounts	Jun 11	Jun 10	Jun 09
Working Capital	-72	-90	-107
Fixed Assets	72	90	109
Current Assets	47	64	76

Kemtron Ltd

19-21 Finch Drive, Braintree, CM7 2SF
Tel: 01376-348115 **Fax:** 01376-345885
E-mail: info@kemtron.co.uk
Website: http://www.kemtron.co.uk
Bank(s): Barclays, Southend-on-Sea
Directors: D. Wall (MD)
Immediate Holding Company: KEMTRON LIMITED
Registration no: 03548932 **VAT No.:** GB 719 9711 96
Date established: 1998 **No.of Employees:** 21 - 50 **Product Groups:** 23, 29, 30, 32, 33, 34, 37, 38, 48

Date of Accounts	Sep 11	Sep 10	Sep 09
Working Capital	879	767	653
Fixed Assets	247	179	158
Current Assets	1m	1m	955

Lactosan UK Ltd

Lacsan House 5 Swinbourne Drive, Braintree, CM7 2YP
Tel: 01376-342226 **Fax:** 01376-342132
E-mail: enquiries@lactosan.co.uk
Website: http://www.lactosan.com
Managers: C. Morfin
Ultimate Holding Company: THORNICO A/S (DENMARK)
Immediate Holding Company: LACTOSAN HOLDINGS LIMITED
Registration no: 02773030 **Date established:** 1992
Turnover: Up to £250,000 **No.of Employees:** 1 - 10 **Product Groups:** 20

Date of Accounts	Dec 11	Dec 10	Dec 09
Pre Tax Profit/Loss	-256	-256	-256
Working Capital	-2m	-2m	-1m
Fixed Assets	6m	6m	6m
Current Assets	2	2	2
Current Liabilities	3	3	3

London Pressed Hinge Co. Ltd

6 Swinborne Drive Springwood Industrial Estate, Braintree, CM7 2YG
Tel: 01376-347074 **Fax:** 01376-340347
E-mail: sales@lph-uk.co.uk
Website: http://www.lph-uk.co.uk
Directors: J. Blackaby (Co Sec)
Immediate Holding Company: LONDON PRESSED HINGE COMPANY LIMITED
Registration no: 00219276 **VAT No.:** GB 248 2218 65
Date established: 2027 **Turnover:** £500,000 - £1m
No.of Employees: 1 - 10 **Product Groups:** 35, 36

Date of Accounts	Sep 11	Sep 10	Sep 09
Working Capital	615	608	628
Fixed Assets	118	119	118
Current Assets	697	677	672

W J Morray Engineering Ltd

Anglia Way, Braintree, CM7 3RG
Tel: 01376-322722 **Fax:** 01376-323277
E-mail: kevin@morray.com
Website: http://www.moray.com
Bank(s): National Westminster Bank Plc
Directors: I. Golds (Dir), K. Jackman (MD), K. Monk (Dir), K. Monk (Sales), T. Kato (Co Sec)
Managers: R. Martin (Purch Mgr)
Ultimate Holding Company: STAHLS INC (USA)
Immediate Holding Company: W. J. MORRAY ENGINEERING LIMITED
Registration no: 00844008 **VAT No.:** GB 102 4931 10
Date established: 1965 **Turnover:** £2m - £5m **No.of Employees:** 21 - 50
Product Groups: 42

Date of Accounts	Mar 10	Mar 09	Mar 08
Sales Turnover	N/A	3m	4m
Pre Tax Profit/Loss	N/A	-131	-173
Working Capital	85	200	141
Fixed Assets	837	279	298
Current Assets	945	1m	1m
Current Liabilities	N/A	277	494

Motor Parts Direct Ltd

Cooper Drive Springwood Indl-Est, Braintree, CM7 2RF
Tel: 01376-347542 **Fax:** 01376-340646
E-mail: info@mpdonline.co.uk
Website: http://www.mpdonline.co.uk
Bank(s): National Westminster Bank Plc
Directors: M. Shah (MD), R. Abadee (Sales), D. Wykes (Asst MD), M. Shah (Prop), P. Chen (MD)
Managers: R. Moss (Product)
Immediate Holding Company: MOTOR PARTS DIRECT LIMITED
Registration no: 03604992 **Date established:** 1998
Turnover: £10m - £20m **No.of Employees:** 21 - 50 **Product Groups:** 38, 39, 68

Nordair Niche (Southern Office)

Unit 4 Chilford Court Rayne Road, Braintree, CM7 2QS
Tel: 01376-332200 **Fax:** 01376-332201
E-mail: mail@nordairniche.co.uk
Website: http://www.nordairniche.co.uk
Bank(s): Barclays Bank Plc, High Street, Worcester
Managers: A. Wilshaw (Mgr)
Registration no: 01413321 **Turnover:** £2m - £5m
No.of Employees: 11 - 20 **Product Groups:**

E J Owen Engineering

2 The Mazes East Street, Braintree, CM7 3JJ
Tel: 01376-345631 **Fax:** 01376-345631
E-mail: oweneng@hotmail.co.uk
Website: http://www.oweneng.co.uk
Directors: E. Owen (Prop)
VAT No.: GB 418 4850 40 **Turnover:** Up to £250,000
No.of Employees: 1 - 10 **Product Groups:** 48

Pacepacker Services

Unit 16 Bluegate Hall Braintree Road, Great Bardfield, Braintree, CM7 4PZ
Tel: 01371-811544 **Fax:** 01371-811621
E-mail: mail@pacepackerservices.com
Website: http://www.pacepackerservices.com
Bank(s): Lloyds TSB Bank plc
Managers: M. Hiley-Thomas (Sales Admin)
Immediate Holding Company: PACEPACKER SERVICES LIMITED
Registration no: 05141363 **VAT No.:** GB 711 5899 23
Date established: 2004 **Turnover:** £500,000 - £1m
No.of Employees: 11 - 20 **Product Groups:** 42

Date of Accounts	Jul 11	Jul 10	Jul 09
Working Capital	183	144	113
Fixed Assets	66	71	63
Current Assets	815	966	530

Peerless Europe Ltd

Cardinals Court Bradford Street, Braintree, CM7 9AT
Tel: 01376-556059 **Fax:** 01376-556059
E-mail: sales@peerlesseurope.com
Website: http://www.peerlesseurope.com
Bank(s): Lloyds
Managers: D. Barker (Sales Prom Mgr), L. Henderson (Comptroller), S. Cooley (Tech Serv Mgr), H. Barton (Personnel)
Ultimate Holding Company: PEERLESS MFG CO (USA)
Immediate Holding Company: PEERLESS EUROPE LTD.
Registration no: 02627558 **VAT No.:** GB 594 7631 94
Date established: 1991 **Turnover:** £5m - £10m **No.of Employees:** 21 - 50
Product Groups: 31, 40, 42

Date of Accounts	Jun 11	Jun 10	Jun 09
Sales Turnover	11m	8m	9m
Pre Tax Profit/Loss	831	178	992

Working Capital	3m	2m	2m
Fixed Assets	125	115	141
Current Assets	13m	10m	8m
Current Liabilities	4m	3m	2m

Permex Systems Ltd
PO Box 7747, Braintree, CM7 4WP
Tel: 08453-451603 **Fax:** 08453-451604
E-mail: enquiries@permexsystems.com
Website: http://www.permexsystems.com
Directors: A. Piper (Fin), M. Shingleton (MD)
Immediate Holding Company: PERMEX SYSTEMS LIMITED
Registration no: 04836845 **Date established:** 2003
No.of Employees: 1 - 10 **Product Groups:** 35, 36, 45

Date of Accounts	Jul 11	Jul 10	Jul 09
Working Capital	39	27	66
Fixed Assets	14	17	11
Current Assets	221	173	203

Power Lift Plant
The Garage Panfield Lane, Braintree, CM7 5RN
Tel: 01376-320245 **Fax:** 01376-341742
Website: http://www.power-lift-plant.co.uk
Directors: S. Thompson (Prop)
Date established: 1984 **No.of Employees:** 1 - 10 **Product Groups:** 35, 39, 45

R V L Fabrications
3 Albert Road, Braintree, CM7 3JQ
Tel: 01376-342988 **Fax:** 01376-342988
Directors: C. Barnard (Dir)
Date established: 1998 **No.of Employees:** 1 - 10 **Product Groups:** 37, 40, 48

Sassi Lift Systems Ltd
5 Blackwell Drive, Braintree, CM7 2QJ
Tel: 01376-550666 **Fax:** 01376-341219
E-mail: info@sls-ltd.co.uk
Website: http://www.sls-ltd.co.uk
Directors: K. Hogan (MD)
Immediate Holding Company: SASSI LIFT SYSTEMS LIMITED
Registration no: 01062171 **Date established:** 1972 **Turnover:** £2m - £5m
No.of Employees: 11 - 20 **Product Groups:** 35, 39, 45

Date of Accounts	Dec 11	Dec 10	Dec 09
Sales Turnover	4m	4m	4m
Pre Tax Profit/Loss	462	590	555
Working Capital	1m	1m	1m
Fixed Assets	12	13	16
Current Assets	2m	2m	2m
Current Liabilities	730	643	666

Shielding Solutions Ltd
Braintree Enterprise Centre Springwood Drive, Braintree, CM7 2YN
Tel: 01376-330033 **Fax:** 01376-339163
E-mail: info@shielding-solutions.com
Website: http://www.shielding-solutions.com
Directors: R. Claydon (Dir)
Immediate Holding Company: SHIELDING SOLUTIONS LIMITED
Registration no: 05418526 **VAT No.:** GB 873 7067 93
Date established: 2005 **Turnover:** £5m - £10m **No.of Employees:** 1 - 10
Product Groups: 29, 30, 32, 33, 36, 37, 39, 48

Date of Accounts	Mar 12	Mar 11	Mar 10
Working Capital	221	128	71
Fixed Assets	10	4	5
Current Assets	377	247	168

Softeners Services
Unit 3 Concord Farm School Road, Rayne, Braintree, CM77 6SP
Tel: 01376-553777 **Fax:** 01376-340004
Website: http://www.softeners-filters.co.uk
Directors: K. Goodwin (MD)
Date established: 1999 **No.of Employees:** 11 - 20 **Product Groups:** 38, 42

Swann Engineering Ltd
6 Springwood Drive, Braintree, CM7 2YN
Tel: 01376-324809 **Fax:** 01376-552296
E-mail: engineering@swanngroupltd.com
Website: http://www.swanngroupltd.com
Directors: G. Randle (Fin)
Managers: M. Parrett (Comptroller)
Ultimate Holding Company: SWANN GROUP LTD
Immediate Holding Company: SWANN ENGINEERING LIMITED
Registration no: 06521885 **VAT No.:** GB 103 2332 36
Date established: 2008 **Turnover:** £1m - £2m **No.of Employees:** 21 - 50
Product Groups: 35, 37

Date of Accounts	Mar 10	Mar 09
Working Capital	N/A	-0

Target Transfers Ltd
Anglia Way, Braintree, CM7 3RG
Tel: 01376-326351 **Fax:** 01376-345876
E-mail: info@targettransfers.com
Website: http://www.targettransfers.com
Bank(s): Barclays
Directors: R. Tubbs (Fin), R. Bull (MD)
Managers: C. Tredway (Sales Prom Mgr)
Ultimate Holding Company: STAHLS INC (USA)
Immediate Holding Company: TARGET TRANSFERS LIMITED
Registration no: 04071002 **Date established:** 2000 **Turnover:** £2m - £5m
No.of Employees: 21 - 50 **Product Groups:** 23, 24, 28, 43, 44

Date of Accounts	Jun 11	Jun 10	Jun 09
Working Capital	35	38	111
Fixed Assets	159	122	139
Current Assets	584	594	541

Telerelay Sales Ltd
Park Drive Industrial Estate, Braintree, CM7 1AW
Tel: 01376-321216 **Fax:** 01376-347910
E-mail: brucegriffin@telerelay.co.uk
Directors: B. Griffin (Ch), B. Griffin (MD), C. Griffin (Co Sec), C. Griffin (Fin)
Managers: G. Lowe (Chief Mgr)
Ultimate Holding Company: DEMOS CICLITIRA LIMITED
Immediate Holding Company: TELERELAY (SALES) LIMITED
Registration no: 00577492 **VAT No.:** GB 103 8038 06
Date established: 1957 **Turnover:** £250,000 - £500,000
No.of Employees: 1 - 10 **Product Groups:** 37

Date of Accounts	Jan 08	Jan 07	Jan 06
Working Capital	153	141	97
Fixed Assets	11	16	4

Current Assets	196	199	142
Current Liabilities	43	58	46
Total Share Capital	5	5	5

Zahra Art Foundries Ltd
9 Swinbourne Drive, Braintree, CM7 2YP
Tel: 01376-529797 **Fax:** 01376-529797
E-mail: jim@zmaf.co.uk
Website: http://www.msaf.co.uk
Directors: J. Guy (MD)
Immediate Holding Company: ZAHRA ART FOUNDRIES LIMITED
Registration no: 07271277 **VAT No.:** GB 759 9188 57
Date established: 2010 **Turnover:** £500,000 - £1m
No.of Employees: 1 - 10 **Product Groups:** 25, 34, 35, 48, 49

Date of Accounts	Jun 11
Working Capital	-280
Fixed Assets	30
Current Assets	108

Zipp Ltd
7a Cooper Drive Springwood Industrial Estate, Braintree, CM7 2RF
Tel: 01376-330833 **Fax:** 01376-343983
E-mail: sales@zippoffice.co.uk
Website: http://www.zippoffice.co.uk
Directors: S. Cochrane (Fin)
Immediate Holding Company: ZIPP LIMITED
Registration no: 03660017 **Date established:** 1998 **Turnover:** £1m - £2m
No.of Employees: 1 - 10 **Product Groups:** 27

Date of Accounts	Dec 09	Dec 08	Dec 07
Working Capital	4	-12	22
Fixed Assets	3	1	6
Current Assets	212	165	202

Brentwood

A D M Milling Ltd
Kingsgate 1 King Edward Road, Brentwood, CM14 4HG
Tel: 01277-262525 **Fax:** 0151-933 4504
Website: http://www.allied-mills.co.uk
Bank(s): HSBC Bank plc
Directors: D. McCarthy (Fin), I. Pinner (MD), J. Cottrell (Tech Serv), T. Cook (Sales)
Managers: A. Lovett (I.T. Exec), J. Hastwell (Mktg Serv Mgr), C. Gill (Personnel)
Ultimate Holding Company: ARCHER DANIELS MIDLAND COMPANY INC (USA)
Immediate Holding Company: ADM MILLING LIMITED
Registration no: 02445197 **VAT No.:** GB 508 0382 66
Date established: 1989 **Turnover:** £125m - £250m
No.of Employees: 21 - 50 **Product Groups:** 20

Date of Accounts	Dec 11	Dec 10	Dec 09
Sales Turnover	213m	174m	186m
Pre Tax Profit/Loss	-850	-930	3m
Working Capital	55m	57m	56m
Fixed Assets	25m	25m	28m
Current Assets	81m	86m	73m
Current Liabilities	3m	4m	5m

Ab Fab Catering
9 The Gardens Doddinghurst, Brentwood, CM15 0LU
Tel: 01277-822066 **Fax:** 01277-822066
E-mail: abfabcatering@live.com
Website: http://www.abfabcateringsolutions.co.uk
Directors: K. Lane (Prop)
Immediate Holding Company: AB FAB CATERING LIMITED
Registration no: 06728326 **Date established:** 2008
No.of Employees: 1 - 10 **Product Groups:** 69, 80, 89

Allister Welding Co. Ltd
30 Horndon Industrial Park West Horndon, Brentwood, CM13 3XL
Tel: 01277-812534 **Fax:** 01277-812616
E-mail: steve.moore@allister.co.uk
Website: http://www.allister.co.uk
Directors: S. Moore (Dir), P. McAllister (MD), S. Moore (MD)
Managers: J. Hawkins (Works Gen Mgr)
Immediate Holding Company: ALLISTER WELDING COMPANY LIMITED(THE)
Registration no: 00645722 **Date established:** 1959 **Turnover:** £2m - £5m
No.of Employees: 21 - 50 **Product Groups:** 48

Amstrad Ltd
130 Kings Road, Brentwood, CM14 4EQ
Tel: 01277-228888 **Fax:** 01277-211350
E-mail: info@amstrad.com
Website: http://www.amstrad.com
Bank(s): Lloyds TSB Bank plc
Directors: D. Gormley (Co Sec), S. Askey (Sales & Mktg), A. Sugar (Ch & MD)
Managers: D. Berry (I.T. Exec)
Ultimate Holding Company: British Sky Broadcasting Group plc
Immediate Holding Company: Sky Digital Supplies Ltd
Registration no: 00955321 **Turnover:** £75m - £125m
No.of Employees: 51 - 100 **Product Groups:** 37, 79, 84

Brentwood Burners & Bathrooms
3-9 Coxtie Green Road Pilgrims Hatch, Brentwood, CM14 5PN
Tel: 01277-374247 **Fax:** 01277-374949
E-mail: admin@brent-wood-burners.co.uk
Website: http://www.brent-wood-burners.co.uk
Directors: W. Mccann (MD)
Date established: 1980 **No.of Employees:** 1 - 10 **Product Groups:** 40

British Gaskets Ltd
Unit 7 Childerditch Industrial Estate Childerditch Hall Drive, Little Warley, Brentwood, CM13 3HD
Tel: 01277-815300 **Fax:** 01277-815350
E-mail: sales@british-gaskets.co.uk
Website: http://www.british-gaskets.co.uk
Bank(s): National Westminster Bank Plc
Directors: R. Jones (MD), R. Jones (Dir & Co Sec), A. Thurlbourn (MD), A. Therbourne (MD)
Managers: G. Print (Sales Admin), K. Stroud (Sales & Mktg Mg), R. Edwards (Inspect Mgr), J. Ditmore (Accounts)
Ultimate Holding Company: MASTER INDUSTRIES JERSEY LTD (JERSEY)
Immediate Holding Company: BRITISH GASKETS LIMITED
Registration no: 00431728 **VAT No.:** GB 311 7341 96
Date established: 1947 **Turnover:** £5m - £10m **No.of Employees:** 11 - 20
Product Groups: 29, 40

Date of Accounts	Nov 10	Nov 09	Nov 08
Sales Turnover	3m	2m	3m
Pre Tax Profit/Loss	29	-62	180
Working Capital	314	256	291
Fixed Assets	101	143	163
Current Assets	2m	1m	1m
Current Liabilities	967	764	717

C C S Catercare Ltd
133a Ongar Road, Brentwood, CM15 9DL
Tel: 01277-200500 **Fax:** 01277-849249
E-mail: ccscatercareltd@btconnect.com
Directors: T. Potton (MD)
Immediate Holding Company: C.C.S. (CATERCARE) LIMITED
Registration no: 03088826 **Date established:** 1995
No.of Employees: 1 - 10 **Product Groups:** 20, 40, 41

Date of Accounts	Aug 11	Aug 10	Aug 09
Working Capital	8	13	-6
Fixed Assets	55	74	98
Current Assets	133	133	103

Camlar Ltd
5 Osborne Road Pilgrims Hatch, Brentwood, CM15 9LE
Tel: 07970-238215 **Fax:** 0203-236789
E-mail: info@camlar.co.uk
Website: http://www.camlar.co.uk
Directors: S. Ball (Dir)
Immediate Holding Company: CAMLAR LIMITED
Registration no: 05667554 **Date established:** 2006
Turnover: £250,000 - £500,000 **No.of Employees:** 1 - 10
Product Groups: 52

Date of Accounts	Jan 11	Jan 10	Jan 09
Working Capital	14	18	24
Fixed Assets	4	6	2
Current Assets	49	70	70

Cleanaway Ltd
Warley Hill Business Park The Drive, Great Warley, Brentwood, CM13 3BE
Tel: 01277-262002 **Fax:** 01277-230067
E-mail: information@cleanaway.com
Website: http://www.cleanaway.com
Directors: W. Payne (I.T. Dir)
Managers: M. Tyler (Mktg Serv Mgr), P. Jackson (Sales Prom Mgr)
Immediate Holding Company: CLEANAWAY LIMITED
Registration no: NF002533 **VAT No.:** GB 352 1129 90
Date established: 1981 **Turnover:** £75m - £125m
No.of Employees: 1 - 10 **Product Groups:** 54

Date of Accounts	Dec 07	Dec 06
Sales Turnover	N/A	612220
Pre Tax Profit/Loss	N/A	7900
Working Capital	41770	50620
Fixed Assets	51210	179410
Current Assets	79400	166050
Current Liabilities	37630	115430
Total Share Capital	89530	89530
ROCE% (Return on Capital Employed)		3.4
ROT% (Return on Turnover)		1.3

D H Fork Trucks UK Ltd
Place Farm Place Farm Lane, Doddinghurst, Brentwood, CM15 0JA
Tel: 01277-372411 **Fax:** 01277-372412
E-mail: info@dhforktrucks.com
Website: http://www.forkliftwarehouse.co.uk
Directors: V. Demetriades (MD), G. Kyriacou (Fin)
Immediate Holding Company: DEMETRIADES HANDLING UK LIMITED
Registration no: 04215161 **Date established:** 2001
No.of Employees: 1 - 10 **Product Groups:** 35, 39, 45

Date of Accounts	Jun 11	Jun 10	Jun 09
Working Capital	27	37	35
Fixed Assets	7	9	12
Current Assets	223	212	232

Digital Technology International Ltd
4-6 Crescent Road Warley, Brentwood, CM14 5JR
Tel: 01277-246000 **Fax:** 01277-228767
E-mail: info@dtint.com
Website: http://www.dtint.com
Bank(s): Natwest
Directors: P. Gillogaley (Dir)
Ultimate Holding Company: DTI HOLDING COMPANY (DELAWARE)
Immediate Holding Company: DIGITAL TECHNOLOGY INTERNATIONAL LIMITED
Registration no: 01876409 **Date established:** 1985 **Turnover:** £1m - £2m
No.of Employees: 21 - 50 **Product Groups:** 28, 44

Date of Accounts	Dec 11	Dec 10	Dec 09
Sales Turnover	2m	2m	3m
Pre Tax Profit/Loss	-1m	-1m	-822
Working Capital	-3m	-2m	-638
Fixed Assets	55	78	110
Current Assets	3m	3m	3m
Current Liabilities	1m	1m	1m

Drakefield Ltd
Unit 60 West Hornden Industrial Estate, West Horndon, Brentwood, CM13 3XL
Tel: 01277-814060 **Fax:** 01277-814070
E-mail: webmaster@abstroubleshooting.com
Website: http://www.drakefield.com
Directors: A. Beckers (Dir)
Immediate Holding Company: DRAKEFIELD LIMITED
Registration no: 01555626 **Date established:** 1981 **Turnover:** £2m - £5m
No.of Employees: 1 - 10 **Product Groups:** 35, 39

Date of Accounts	May 11	May 10	May 09
Working Capital	457	535	546
Fixed Assets	69	44	38
Current Assets	1m	1m	1m

Equity Insurance
Library House New Road, Brentwood, CM14 4GD
Tel: 01277-200100 **Fax:** 01277-206283
E-mail: info@equitygroup.co.uk
Website: http://www.equitygroup.co.uk
Directors: J. Morley (Fin), N. Utley (Grp Chief Exec), N. Utley (Ch)
Managers: F. King (Personnel), G. Robertshaw (Sales & Mktg Mg), E. Forbes-Fitzsimmons (Purch Mgr), K. Gill (Sales & Mktg Mg)

see next page

Equity Insurance - Cont'd
Immediate Holding Company: EQUITY INSURANCE MANAGEMENT LIMITED
Registration no: 00170558 **Date established:** 1920
Turnover: £10m - £20m **No.of Employees:** 1 - 10 **Product Groups:** 82

Date of Accounts	Jun 09	Jun 08	Jun 07
Pre Tax Profit/Loss	-26m	-24m	37m
Working Capital	-63m	-45m	-28m
Fixed Assets	90m	91m	91m
Current Assets	190m	207m	217m
Current Liabilities	N/A	N/A	4

Essex Hinge Co. Ltd
Tallon Rd, Hutton Industrial Estate Hutton, Brentwood, CM13 1TP
Tel: 01277-211993 **Fax:** 01277-261902
E-mail: info@hinge.co.uk
Website: http://www.hinge.co.uk
Bank(s): National Westminster Bank plc
Directors: A. Moore (Co Sec), A. Reid (Dir), E. Reid (Dir)
Managers: K. Maynard (Tech Serv Mgr)
Registration no: 00312826 **VAT No.:** GB 246 0930 69
Date established: 1936 **Turnover:** £1m - £2m **No.of Employees:** 21 - 50
Product Groups: 30, 35, 36, 49

Date of Accounts	Mar 08	Mar 07	Mar 06
Working Capital	878	846	646
Fixed Assets	408	438	471
Current Assets	1083	1044	884
Current Liabilities	204	198	238
Total Share Capital	3	3	3

Firehorse Embroidery Ltd
16 Hallam Close Doddinghurst, Brentwood, CM15 0NW
Tel: 01277-822889
E-mail: sales@firehorseltd.org.uk
Website: http://www.firehorseltd.org.uk
Directors: A. Robson (Dir)
Registration no: 05418555 **Date established:** 2005
Turnover: Up to £250,000 **No.of Employees:** 1 - 10 **Product Groups:** 23, 24, 30, 44, 49, 63, 65, 81, 84

Date of Accounts	Mar 08	Mar 07
Sales Turnover	16	8
Pre Tax Profit/Loss	4	1
Working Capital	-3	2
Fixed Assets	6	7
Current Assets	N/A	4
Current Liabilities	3	2
Total Share Capital	1	1
ROCE% (Return on Capital Employed)	142.4	12.4
ROT% (Return on Turnover)	24.9	14.1

Ford Motor Company Ltd
Central Office Eagle Way, Great Warley, Brentwood, CM13 3BW
Tel: 01277-253000
Website: http://www.ford.co.uk
Directors: J. Miles (Tech Serv), M. Ovenden (MD), D. Lowe (Fin), J. Ball (Pers)
Ultimate Holding Company: FORD MOTOR COMPANY (USA)
Immediate Holding Company: FORD MOTOR COMPANY LIMITED
Registration no: 00235446 **VAT No.:** GB 246 4257 57
Date established: 2028 **Turnover:** Over £1,000m
No.of Employees: 1501 & over **Product Groups:** 39, 40

Date of Accounts	Dec 11	Dec 10	Dec 09
Sales Turnover	9084m	8378m	6980m
Pre Tax Profit/Loss	253m	306m	-27m
Working Capital	-396m	-338m	-743m
Fixed Assets	1212m	1253m	1371m
Current Assets	1727m	1863m	2025m
Current Liabilities	728m	442m	537m

Inka Presswood Pallets Ltd
1 Horndon Industrial Park Station Road, West Horndon, Brentwood, CM13 3XL
Tel: 01277-811085 **Fax:** 01277-811971
E-mail: sales@inkapallets.co.uk
Website: http://www.inkapallets.co.uk
Directors: J. Graham Campbell (Co Sec), M. Springham (MD)
Ultimate Holding Company: INKA HOLDINGS (UK) LIMITED
Immediate Holding Company: INKA PRESSWOOD PALLETS LIMITED
Registration no: 01863766 **VAT No.:** GB 815 0057 64
Date established: 1984 **Turnover:** £1m - £2m **No.of Employees:** 1 - 10
Product Groups: 25, 27, 30, 45, 66, 67, 76

Date of Accounts	Dec 11	Dec 10	Dec 09
Working Capital	242	218	177
Fixed Assets	14	2	5
Current Assets	448	417	429

Millard & Partners
Millfields Business Centre Ashwells Road, Pilgrims Hatch, Brentwood, CM15 9ST
Tel: 01277-375888 **Fax:** 01277-375889
E-mail: office@millard-partners.co.uk
Directors: F. Millard (Prop)
Ultimate Holding Company: MARTIN MCCOLL RETAIL GROUP LIMITED
Immediate Holding Company: ANTHONY JAMES D'AMATO LIMITED
Registration no: 01024564 **Date established:** 2006
No.of Employees: 1 - 10 **Product Groups:** 35

Date of Accounts	Nov 10	Nov 09	Nov 08
Working Capital	32	67	65
Fixed Assets	25	31	33
Current Assets	57	89	91

N V Tools Ltd
28 Wash Road Hutton, Brentwood, CM13 1TB
Tel: 01277-214455 **Fax:** 01277-227341
E-mail: enquiries@nvtools.co.uk
Website: http://www.nvtools.co.uk
Bank(s): Barclays
Directors: N. Sutton (Purch), N. Snape (Fin), P. Bennett (MD)
Immediate Holding Company: N.V.TOOLS LIMITED
Registration no: 00528701 **VAT No.:** GB 246 4318 63
Date established: 1954 **Turnover:** £2m - £5m **No.of Employees:** 51 - 100
Product Groups: 30, 34, 35, 36, 37, 42, 43, 44, 48

Date of Accounts	Jan 11	Jan 10	Jan 09
Sales Turnover	2m	3m	N/A
Pre Tax Profit/Loss	17	33	N/A
Working Capital	1m	1m	1m
Fixed Assets	308	313	292
Current Assets	2m	2m	2m
Current Liabilities	320	91	N/A

Navestock Metalworks
Horseman Side, Brentwood, CM14 5SU
Tel: 07753-565469 **Fax:** 01708-703505
Directors: D. Gray (Prop)
Date established: 2003 **No.of Employees:** 1 - 10 **Product Groups:** 26, 35

Onsite Specialist Spraying Ltd
Unit 44a Horndon Industrial Park, West Horndon, Brentwood, CM13 3XS
Tel: 01277-812145 **Fax:** 01277-812475
E-mail: trevor@powderpainting.com
Website: http://www.powderpainting.com
Bank(s): Barclays
Directors: T. Riley (MD)
Managers: T. Riley (Mgr)
Immediate Holding Company: ONSITE SPECIALIST SPRAYING LIMITED
Registration no: 06590568 **VAT No.:** GB 583 1171 48
Date established: 2008 **Turnover:** £250,000 - £500,000
No.of Employees: 11 - 20 **Product Groups:** 25, 32, 37, 46

Pawle & Co
3 Horndon Industrial Park West Horndon, Brentwood, CM13 3XL
Tel: 01277-811005 **Fax:** 01277-811002
Website: http://www.pawleandco.co.uk
Directors: R. Ashby (MD), G. Arnold (MD)
Immediate Holding Company: PAWLE & CO LIMITED
Registration no: 02740708 **Date established:** 1992
No.of Employees: 1 - 10 **Product Groups:** 35, 39, 45

Date of Accounts	Mar 11	Mar 10	Mar 09
Working Capital	79	49	110
Fixed Assets	25	53	74
Current Assets	191	178	237

Pensteel Ltd
Unit 1 Horndon Industrial Park West Horndon, Brentwood, CM13 3XL
Tel: 01277-810211 **Fax:** 01277-811971
E-mail: richard.edwards@pensteel.co.uk
Website: http://www.pensteel.co.uk
Directors: R. Edwards (Dir), R. Edwards (MD)
Managers: M. Pickton (Chief Mgr)
Immediate Holding Company: PENSTEEL LIMITED
Registration no: 01780172 **VAT No.:** GB 406 3441 81
Date established: 1983 **Turnover:** £2m - £5m **No.of Employees:** 1 - 10
Product Groups: 30, 35, 45, 76

Date of Accounts	Apr 10	Apr 09	Apr 08
Working Capital	395	437	447
Fixed Assets	25	20	11
Current Assets	659	642	965

Pipe Center
Childerditch Lane Little Warley, Brentwood, CM13 3ED
Tel: 020-8338 0240 **Fax:** 01277-810077
E-mail: pipe.surfs@walleys.co.uk
Website: http://www.pipecenter.co.uk
Managers: D. Woodbury (Mgr)
Registration no: 00124326 **Turnover:** Over £1,000m
No.of Employees: 51 - 100 **Product Groups:** 66

Date of Accounts	Jun 11	Jun 10	Jun 09
Sales Turnover	87m	96m	96m
Pre Tax Profit/Loss	-2m	5m	5m
Working Capital	-2m	1m	4m
Fixed Assets	36m	34m	26m
Current Assets	34m	33m	45m
Current Liabilities	9m	7m	9m

Pont Packaging UK
51 Woodway Hutton, Brentwood, CM13 2JR
Tel: 07795-978669
E-mail: b.jones@pont.nl
Website: http://www.ponteurope.com
Directors: B. Jones (Prop)
Date established: 2002 **No.of Employees:** 1 - 10 **Product Groups:** 30

Stockfit Ltd
Unit 1 Cockridden Farm Industrial Estate Brentwood Road, Herongate, Brentwood, CM13 3LH
Tel: 01277-812323 **Fax:** 01277-812333
E-mail: sales@stockfit.co.uk
Website: http://www.stockfit.co.uk
Directors: C. Leo (Dir)
Immediate Holding Company: STOCKFIT LIMITED
Registration no: 03194523 **Date established:** 1996
No.of Employees: 1 - 10 **Product Groups:** 63, 66

Turner Packaging Ltd
Unit 42 Horndon Industrial Park West Horndon, Brentwood, CM13 3HW
Tel: 01277-810846 **Fax:** 01277-810191
E-mail: service@turnerpack.co.uk
Website: http://www.turnerpack.co.uk
Bank(s): National Westminster Bank Plc
Directors: G. Carter (MD)
Immediate Holding Company: TURNER PACKAGING LIMITED
Registration no: 01224346 **Date established:** 1975 **Turnover:** £1m - £2m
No.of Employees: 21 - 50 **Product Groups:** 27, 28, 30, 84

Date of Accounts	Dec 11	Dec 10	Dec 09
Working Capital	328	308	231
Fixed Assets	392	352	339
Current Assets	1m	1m	799

Buckhurst Hill

Biddle & Mumford Gears Ltd
8-18 Kings Place, Buckhurst Hill, IG9 5EA
Tel: 020-8505 4615 **Fax:** 020-8505 3718
E-mail: mahendra@biddleandmumford.co.uk
Website: http://www.biddleandmumford.co.uk
Directors: M. Tailor (MD)
Immediate Holding Company: BIDDLE & MUMFORD GEARS LIMITED
Registration no: 02647279 **Date established:** 1991 **Turnover:** £1m - £2m
No.of Employees: 21 - 50 **Product Groups:** 35, 49, 66

Date of Accounts	Apr 12	Apr 11	Apr 10
Working Capital	171	83	67
Fixed Assets	144	161	101
Current Assets	738	539	443

London Fire Protection
37 Starling Close, Buckhurst Hill, IG9 5TN
Tel: 020-8506 2360 **Fax:** 020-8506 2360
Website: http://www.londonfire.net
Directors: V. Finney (Prop)
Date established: 2002 **No.of Employees:** 1 - 10 **Product Groups:** 38, 42

May Of London Gunmakers Ltd
21-23 Cherry Tree Rise, Buckhurst Hill, IG9 6EU
Tel: 020-8504 5946 **Fax:** 020-8505 6664
Website: http://www.mayoflondon.co.uk
Directors: C. Gamblin (MD)
Immediate Holding Company: MAY OF LONDON (GUN MAKERS) LIMITED
Registration no: 00898112 **Date established:** 1967
Turnover: £250,000 - £500,000 **No.of Employees:** 1 - 10
Product Groups: 36, 39, 40

Date of Accounts	Mar 11	Mar 10	Mar 09
Working Capital	173	171	162
Fixed Assets	21	22	23
Current Assets	192	210	249

Pira Ltd
Warwick House 116 Palmerston Road, Buckhurst Hill, IG9 5LQ
Tel: 01279-508111 **Fax:** 01279-508550
E-mail: sales@pira.info
Website: http://www.pira.info
Directors: J. Kelly (Fin), S. Platt (MD)
Immediate Holding Company: PIRA LIMITED
Registration no: 00708549 **Date established:** 1961
Turnover: Up to £250,000 **No.of Employees:** 1 - 10 **Product Groups:** 61, 63

Date of Accounts	Feb 11	Feb 10	Feb 09
Working Capital	-32	-26	-5
Fixed Assets	2	3	3
Current Assets	24	30	62

Sheen Publishing Ltd
50a Queens Road, Buckhurst Hill, IG9 5DD
Tel: 020-8504 1661 **Fax:** 020-8505 4336
E-mail: c.titmuss@sheenpublishing.co.uk
Website: http://www.sheenpublishing.co.uk
Bank(s): National Westminster Bank Plc
Directors: C. Titmuss (MD)
Immediate Holding Company: SHEEN PUBLISHING LIMITED
Registration no: 01546195 **VAT No.:** GB 354 3903 54
Date established: 1981 **Turnover:** £2m - £5m **No.of Employees:** 11 - 20
Product Groups: 28

Date of Accounts	Feb 12	Feb 11	Feb 10
Working Capital	62	65	106
Fixed Assets	9	11	13
Current Assets	112	116	149

Supadance Ltd
159 Queens Road, Buckhurst Hill, IG9 5BA
Tel: 020-8505 8888 **Fax:** 020-8504 4536
E-mail: sales@supadance.com
Website: http://www.supadance.com
Bank(s): Barclays
Directors: M. Free (Fin), M. Free (MD)
Immediate Holding Company: SUPADANCE INTERNATIONAL LIMITED
Registration no: 01379256 **VAT No.:** GB 342 2190 89
Date established: 1978 **Turnover:** £250,000 - £500,000
No.of Employees: 11 - 20 **Product Groups:** 22

Date of Accounts	Dec 11	Dec 10	Dec 09
Working Capital	-855	-325	171
Fixed Assets	2m	1m	468
Current Assets	1m	1m	1m

Burnham On Crouch

Anglia Rubber Burnham Ltd
Private Road Side of 148 Station Road, Burnham On Crouch, CM0 8HQ
Tel: 01621-783468 **Fax:** 01621-786087
E-mail: sue@angliarubber.co.uk
Directors: J. Ward (Fin), S. Hill (MD)
Immediate Holding Company: ANGLIA RUBBER (BURNHAM) LIMITED
Registration no: 01572079 **Date established:** 1981
Turnover: £500,000 - £1m **No.of Employees:** 1 - 10 **Product Groups:** 29

Date of Accounts	Nov 09	Nov 08	Nov 07
Working Capital	23	-3	6
Fixed Assets	1	1	1
Current Assets	64	44	53

Ceetex Ltd
Burnham Business Park Springfield Road, Burnham On Crouch, CM0 8TE
Tel: 01621-784684 **Fax:** 01621-784558
E-mail: info@ceetex.co.uk
Website: http://www.ceetex.co.uk
Bank(s): Midland, HSBC
Directors: A. Gray (Fin), C. Gray (MD)
Managers: D. Moule (Chief Mgr), S. Dukelow (Sales Admin)
Immediate Holding Company: CEETEX (LEISURE) LIMITED
Registration no: 01723007 **VAT No.:** GB 386 8543 00
Date established: 1983 **Turnover:** £500,000 - £1m
No.of Employees: 21 - 50 **Product Groups:** 49

Date of Accounts	Jul 11	Jul 10	May 09
Working Capital	-58	-52	-76
Fixed Assets	222	165	169
Current Assets	567	517	290

Flag Paints
Unit 8 Springfield Industrial Estate Springfield Road, Burnham On Crouch, CM0 8UA
Tel: 01621-785173 **Fax:** 01621-785393
E-mail: sales@flagfinishes.co.uk
Website: http://www.flagfinishes.co.uk
Bank(s): National Westminster Bank Plc
Directors: T. Grover (MD)
Immediate Holding Company: FLAG PAINTS LIMITED
Registration no: 00353436 **VAT No.:** GB 549 9680 76
Date established: 1939 **No.of Employees:** 11 - 20 **Product Groups:** 32

Date of Accounts	May 12	May 11	May 10
Working Capital	262	269	201
Fixed Assets	291	261	219

Current Assets	788	616	525

Hardy Engineering Ltd (Factory)

Unit D Foundry Lane, Burnham On Crouch, CM0 8SH
Tel: 01621-782726 **Fax:** 01621-785645
E-mail: email@hardyengineering.com
Website: http://www.hardyengineering.com
Directors: J. Hardy (MD)
Immediate Holding Company: HARDY ENGINEERING LIMITED
Registration no: 04033626 **Date established:** 2000
Turnover: £250,000 - £500,000 **No.of Employees:** 1 - 10
Product Groups: 39, 45

Date of Accounts	Dec 11	Dec 10	Dec 09
Working Capital	109	122	145
Fixed Assets	27	33	24
Current Assets	349	357	337

Holt Marine Limited

10 Burnham Business Park, Burnham On Crouch, CM0 8TE
Tel: 01621-787080 **Fax:** 020-8789 8365
E-mail: sales@holtallen.com
Website: http://www.holt.eu
Bank(s): National Westminster Bank Plc
Directors: B. Dunton (Sales & Mktg), C. Beecher-Moore (MD), M. Sharpe (Fin)
Managers: J. Daryanani (Mgr)
Immediate Holding Company: K L PROPERTIES (UK) LIMITED
Registration no: 07163804 **VAT No.:** GB 216 0774 78
Date established: 2003 **Turnover:** £2m - £5m **No.of Employees:** 11 - 20
Product Groups: 35, 39, 74

Petticrows Ltd

Petticrows Boat Yard The Quay, Burnham On Crouch, CM0 8AT
Tel: 01621-782115 **Fax:** 01621-785389
E-mail: tim@petticrows.com
Website: http://www.petticrows.com
Directors: S. Jensen (Co Sec), T. Tavinor (MD)
Immediate Holding Company: PETTICROWS LIMITED
Registration no: 05457569 **VAT No.:** GB 623 0474 69
Date established: 2005 **Turnover:** £1m - £2m **No.of Employees:** 1 - 10
Product Groups: 39

Date of Accounts	Jun 11	Jun 10	Jun 09
Working Capital	-103	-115	-178
Fixed Assets	228	234	250
Current Assets	415	524	377

R J Prior & Sons Burnham Ltd

The Quayside, Burnham On Crouch, CM0 8AS
Tel: 01621-782160 **Fax:** 01621-784367
E-mail: sales@priorsboatyard.com
Website: http://www.priorsboatyard.com
Directors: R. Prior (MD)
Immediate Holding Company: R.J. PRIOR & SON (BURNHAM) LIMITED
Registration no: 00393574 **Date established:** 1945
Turnover: £250,000 - £500,000 **No.of Employees:** 1 - 10
Product Groups: 51, 68, 74, 80, 84

Taker Products

Unit 12 Dammerwick Farm Marsh Road, Burnham On Crouch, CM0 8NB
Tel: 01621-783355
Directors: R. Symmonds (Prop)
No.of Employees: 1 - 10 **Product Groups:** 20, 40, 41

Teer Mouldings Ltd

8-9 Springfield Nursery Site Springfield Road, Burnham On Crouch, CM0 8TA
Tel: 01621-784280 **Fax:** 01621-784280
E-mail: trevatteer@hotmail.com
Website: http://www.teermouldings.co.uk
Directors: T. Richardson (Dir)
Immediate Holding Company: TEER MOULDINGS LIMITED
Registration no: 03191635 **VAT No.:** GB 759 8551 69
Date established: 1996 **Turnover:** Up to £250,000
No.of Employees: 1 - 10 **Product Groups:** 30

Date of Accounts	Apr 12	Apr 11	Apr 10
Working Capital	-1	-11	-9
Fixed Assets	1	1	N/A
Current Assets	21	3	3

Tri Ark Ltd

Burnham Business Park Springfield Road, Burnham On Crouch, CM0 8TE
Tel: 01621-781144 **Fax:** 01621-781155
E-mail: sales@tri-ark.com
Website: http://www.tri-ark.com
Directors: D. Rozee (MD)
Immediate Holding Company: TRI-ARK LIMITED
Registration no: 01854311 **Date established:** 1984 **Turnover:** £1m - £2m
No.of Employees: 1 - 10 **Product Groups:** 29, 49

Date of Accounts	Sep 11	Sep 10	Sep 09
Working Capital	-52	-40	-52
Fixed Assets	189	197	207
Current Assets	156	156	146

Canvey Island

Alert Alarms

16 Church Parade, Canvey Island, SS8 9RQ
Tel: 01268-696534 **Fax:** 01268-680785
E-mail: alertadmin@gmail.com
Directors: T. Kemsley (Co Sec)
Ultimate Holding Company: ALFA LAVAL AB (SWEDEN)
Immediate Holding Company: ALFA LAVAL LIMITED
Date established: 2023 **No.of Employees:** 1 - 10 **Product Groups:** 40, 52, 67

C Y B Ltd

Unit 2 Mulberry Road, Canvey Island, SS8 0PR
Tel: 01268-696094 **Fax:** 01268-684040
E-mail: support@cybglassfibre.co.uk
Website: http://www.cybglassfibre.co.uk
Directors: A. Lipscombe (Dir)
Immediate Holding Company: CYB LIMITED
Registration no: 02493304 **Date established:** 1990
No.of Employees: 1 - 10 **Product Groups:** 30, 33, 66

Date of Accounts	Apr 12	Apr 11	Apr 10
Working Capital	61	64	65
Fixed Assets	40	23	21
Current Assets	145	159	133

Cambridge Electronic Industries

1b Beatrice Avenue, Canvey Island, SS8 9DN
Tel: 01268-691351 **Fax:** 01268-691351
E-mail: grahamk@cambridgeelectronics.com
Website: http://www.cambridgeconnectors.com
Managers: G. Keith (Mgr)
No.of Employees: 1 - 10 **Product Groups:** 37, 67

Duration Windows

Unit 4-5 Charfleets Road, Canvey Island, SS8 0PQ
Tel: 01268-681612 **Fax:** 01268-510058
E-mail: sales@duration.co.uk
Website: http://www.duration.co.uk
Directors: B. Chelton (Prop), D. Mitchell (Fin)
Managers: D. Roberts (Buyer), J. Smith (Personnel), T. Cook (Tech Serv Mgr), A. Arnold (Sales Prom Mgr)
Immediate Holding Company: DURATION WINDOWS LIMITED
Registration no: 02360810 **Date established:** 1989
No.of Employees: 51 - 100 **Product Groups:** 30

Epic Marketing Services

Point Road, Canvey Island, SS8 7RT
Tel: 01268-514290 **Fax:** 01268-695891
E-mail: info@epictelemarketing.co.uk
Website: http://www.epictelemarketing.co.uk
Bank(s): National Westminster Bank Plc
Directors: J. Clark (Fin), K. Clark (MD)
Immediate Holding Company: EPIC MARKETING SERVICES LIMITED
Registration no: 04435231 **VAT No.:** GB 626 4202 64
Date established: 2002 **Turnover:** Up to £250,000
No.of Employees: 11 - 20 **Product Groups:** 81

Date of Accounts	Mar 11	Mar 10	Mar 09
Working Capital	-24	-14	-4
Fixed Assets	29	31	31
Current Assets	87	81	107

Final Finish & Polishing Ltd

8 Cambria Close, Canvey Island, SS8 0JX
Tel: 01268-692225 **Fax:** 01268-692131
Directors: D. Benson (Dir)
Immediate Holding Company: FINAL FINISH & POLISHING LTD
Registration no: 06649943 **Date established:** 2008
No.of Employees: 1 - 10 **Product Groups:** 46, 48

Grant & Livingston Ltd

Kings Road Charsleets Industrial Estate, Canvey Island, SS8 0RA
Tel: 01268-696855 **Fax:** 01268-697018
E-mail: gandl.canvey@btconnect.com
Website: http://www.grantandlivingstonltd.com
Bank(s): Barclays, Canvey Island
Directors: E. Fawkes (MD)
Immediate Holding Company: GRANT & LIVINGSTON LIMITED
Registration no: 00794410 **VAT No.:** GB 246 1571 66
Date established: 1964 **Turnover:** £2m - £5m **No.of Employees:** 51 - 100
Product Groups: 34, 35

Date of Accounts	Mar 11	Mar 10	Mar 09
Working Capital	504	599	671
Fixed Assets	651	646	663
Current Assets	1m	1m	1m

H S M Services

Site 7 Kings Road, Canvey Island, SS8 0QY
Tel: 01268-660300 **Fax:** 01268-660301
E-mail: info@hsm-services.com
Website: http://www.hsm-services.com
Bank(s): Barclays
Directors: M. Prowse (Prop)
Registration no: 03292466 **VAT No.:** GB 246 6145 58
Turnover: £250,000 - £500,000 **No.of Employees:** 11 - 20
Product Groups: 23, 26, 30, 32, 35, 37, 38, 39, 42, 43, 45, 46, 48, 67

Date of Accounts	Dec 07	Dec 06	Dec 05
Working Capital	-62	-48	-106
Fixed Assets	613	585	475
Current Assets	321	357	231
Current Liabilities	382	405	337
Total Share Capital	25	25	25

J P Polishing

Charfleet Industrial Estate Kings Close, Canvey Island, SS8 0QZ
Tel: 01268-680245 **Fax:** 01268-685706
E-mail: johnthepolish@tiscali.co.uk
Website: http://www.jppolishing.co.uk
Directors: J. Blamey (Prop)
Immediate Holding Company: SOUTH EASTERN ROAD TANKERS LIMITED
Registration no: 01634580 **Date established:** 1982
No.of Employees: 1 - 10 **Product Groups:** 46, 48

Date of Accounts	May 11	May 10	May 09
Working Capital	188	184	242
Fixed Assets	28	34	26
Current Assets	300	302	341

Neale Dataday Ltd

3 Neale Courtyard Shannon Way, Canvey Island, SS8 0PD
Tel: 01268-510123 **Fax:** 01268-510125
E-mail: stephen.treacy@ndpublishing.co.uk
Website: http://www.netcomuk.co.uk
Bank(s): HSBC, Cardiff
Directors: S. Treacy (Publishing), S. Treacy (Publishing)
Managers: M. Seagar, C. Page, H. Poulter, L. Hayter
Ultimate Holding Company: ND PUBLISHING LIMITED
Immediate Holding Company: NEALE DATADAY LIMITED
Registration no: 02063071 **VAT No.:** GB 645 2478 25
Date established: 1986 **Turnover:** £2m - £5m **No.of Employees:** 21 - 50
Product Groups: 22, 28, 49

Date of Accounts	Dec 11	Dec 10	Dec 09
Sales Turnover	N/A	N/A	3m
Pre Tax Profit/Loss	N/A	N/A	71
Working Capital	630	609	597
Fixed Assets	39	60	83
Current Assets	1m	2m	2m
Current Liabilities	N/A	N/A	600

Oikos Storage Ltd

Hull Haven Wharf Haven Road, Canvey Island, SS8 0NR
Tel: 01268-682206 **Fax:** 01268-510095
E-mail: info@oikos.co.uk
Website: http://www.oikos.co.uk
Directors: C. Horton (MD)
Ultimate Holding Company: CHALLENGER FINANCIAL SERVICES GROUP LTD (AUSTRALIA)
Immediate Holding Company: OIKOS STORAGE LIMITED
Registration no: 00315280 **Date established:** 1936 **Turnover:** £1m - £2m
No.of Employees: 11 - 20 **Product Groups:** 39, 54, 77

Date of Accounts	Jun 11	Jun 10	Jun 09
Sales Turnover	1m	4m	5m
Pre Tax Profit/Loss	-4m	-1m	6m
Working Capital	7m	8m	11m
Fixed Assets	31m	11m	3m
Current Assets	10m	12m	14m
Current Liabilities	2m	491	2m

Powell Auto & Marine

G 2 Prout Industrial Estate Point Road, Canvey Island, SS8 7TJ
Tel: 01268-515078 **Fax:** 01268-515078
Directors: E. Powell (Prop)
Date established: 1999 **No.of Employees:** 1 - 10 **Product Groups:** 35, 36, 39

Savage Gate Automation

8 Mulberry Road, Canvey Island, SS8 0PR
Tel: 01268-698182 **Fax:** 01268-511722
Directors: J. Savage (Prop)
Date established: 1995 **No.of Employees:** 1 - 10 **Product Groups:** 26, 35

Vikon Constuction Ltd

8 Runwood Road, Canvey Island, SS8 0PL
Tel: 01268-691525 **Fax:** 01268-683468
Website: http://www.vikonconstructions.co.uk
Directors: R. Fedelmesi (Dir)
No.of Employees: 1 - 10 **Product Groups:** 35

Willis Machine Tool Services

180 Thissett Road, Canvey Island, SS8 9BL
Tel: 01268-680360 **Fax:** 01268-680360
E-mail: sales@willismachinetoolservices.co.uk
Website: http://www.willismachinetoolservices.co.uk
Directors: S. Willis (Prop)
Date established: 2006 **No.of Employees:** 1 - 10 **Product Groups:** 46

Chelmsford

A T B Plastics Ltd

52 Bancrofts Road South Woodham Ferrers, Chelmsford, CM3 5UQ
Tel: 01245-328693 **Fax:** 01245-321492
E-mail: sales@atbplastics.com
Website: http://www.atbplastics.com
Directors: A. Baron (MD), T. Baron (Fin)
Immediate Holding Company: A.T.B. PLASTICS LIMITED
Registration no: 02147062 **VAT No.:** GB 463 5253 48
Date established: 1987 **Turnover:** £1m - £2m **No.of Employees:** 1 - 10
Product Groups: 30, 42

Date of Accounts	Aug 11	Aug 10	Aug 09
Working Capital	55	49	6
Fixed Assets	22	20	24
Current Assets	248	290	234

Abbotts Countrywide Lettings

17 Duke Street, Chelmsford, CM1 1HP
Tel: 01245-898693 **Fax:** 01245-358280
E-mail: julian.irby@crldirect.co.uk
Website: http://www.abbotts.co.uk
Directors: C. Hazel (Dir)
Managers: N. Miller (Mgr)
Immediate Holding Company: ABBOTTS ESTATE AGENTS LTD
Registration no: 02598868 **VAT No.:** GB 212 5511 12
Date established: 1991 **Turnover:** Up to £250,000
No.of Employees: 1 - 10 **Product Groups:** 80

Date of Accounts	Dec 11	Dec 10	Dec 09
Pre Tax Profit/Loss	11m	51m	-3m
Working Capital	-188m	-202m	-146m
Fixed Assets	443m	443m	363m
Current Assets	135m	113m	121m
Current Liabilities	14m	12m	8m

A C O Scaffolding Ltd

32 Downleaze South Woodham Ferrers, Chelmsford, CM3 5SN
Tel: 01245-322894 **Fax:** 01245-322894
E-mail: coxaco@aol.com
Directors: S. Cox (Fin)
Immediate Holding Company: ACO SCAFFOLDING LIMITED
Registration no: 03452367 **Date established:** 1997
No.of Employees: 11 - 20 **Product Groups:** 52

Date of Accounts	Oct 11	Oct 10	Oct 09
Working Capital	79	103	96
Fixed Assets	48	51	53
Current Assets	137	166	150

ACS Agricultural Supplies Ltd

Rosehill Hatchery Creephedge Lane, East Hanningfield, Chelmsford, CM3 8BP
Tel: 01245-401005 **Fax:** 01245-401006
E-mail: info@acsupplies.co.uk
Website: http://www.acsupplies.co.uk
Directors: R. Moss (Ch), K. Moss (Co Sec), K. Short (MD)
Registration no: 01522247 **Date established:** 1980
No.of Employees: 1 - 10 **Product Groups:** 25, 66

Date of Accounts	Oct 09	Oct 08	Oct 07
Working Capital	-345	-371	-375
Fixed Assets	749	783	812
Current Assets	111	91	102

Adcock Refrigeration & Air Conditioning Ltd

Unit 5 Suffolk Drive, Chelmsford, CM2 6UN
Tel: 01245-359595 **Fax:** 01245-490864
E-mail: chelmsford@adcock.co.uk
Website: http://www.adcock.co.uk
Directors: N. Claydon (Dir)
Immediate Holding Company: ADCOCK REFRIGERATION AND AIR CONDITIONING LIMITED
Registration no: 01307597 **Date established:** 1977
No.of Employees: 11 - 20 **Product Groups:** 40, 66

Date of Accounts	Jan 12	Jan 11	Jan 10
Sales Turnover	34m	29m	26m
Pre Tax Profit/Loss	2m	2m	2m
Working Capital	7m	6m	6m
Fixed Assets	5m	5m	4m
Current Assets	12m	11m	10m
Current Liabilities	2m	2m	2m

Anglia Ruskin University Chelmsford Campus

Bishop Hall Lane, Chelmsford, CM1 1SQ
Tel: 08452-713333
E-mail: answers@anglia.ac.uk
Website: http://www.anglia.ac.uk
Bank(s): Barclays
Managers: L. Collett (Admin Off)
Immediate Holding Company: ANGLIA RUSKIN DEVELOPMENT LTD
Registration no: 02740672 **Date established:** 1992 **Turnover:** £1m - £2m
No.of Employees: 501 - 1000 **Product Groups:** 86

Date of Accounts	Jul 11	Jul 10	Jul 09
Sales Turnover	1m	1m	1m
Pre Tax Profit/Loss	172	132	-177
Working Capital	956	588	185
Fixed Assets	16m	16m	17m
Current Assets	7m	6m	6m
Current Liabilities	242	223	204

Aon Ltd

County House 100 New London Road, Chelmsford, CM2 0RG
Tel: 01245-261811 **Fax:** 01245-269496
E-mail: debbie.seton@ars.aon.co.uk
Website: http://www.aon.co.uk
Bank(s): National Westminster Bank Plc
Directors: R. Broekhuizen (Div)
Ultimate Holding Company: AON CORPORATION INC (USA)
Immediate Holding Company: A1 VENTURES LIMITED
Registration no: 04578543 **VAT No.:** GB 508 9239 26
Date established: 2002 **Turnover:** £20m - £50m
No.of Employees: 11 - 20 **Product Groups:** 82

Arbor Trading Ltd

7-11 Haltwhistle Road South Woodham Ferrers, Chelmsford, CM3 5ZA
Tel: 01245-326210 **Fax:** 01245-326211
E-mail: sales@arbortrading.co.uk
Website: http://www.arbortrading.co.uk
Directors: A. Hillman (MD)
Immediate Holding Company: ARBOR TRADING LIMITED
Registration no: 02331842 **Date established:** 1988
No.of Employees: 1 - 10 **Product Groups:** 26, 36, 37, 67

Date of Accounts	Mar 11	Mar 10	Mar 09
Working Capital	2m	2m	2m
Fixed Assets	169	70	88
Current Assets	3m	2m	2m

Arc Services

45 Maldon Road Danbury, Chelmsford, CM3 4QL
Tel: 01245-226565 **Fax:** 01245-227859
Directors: R. Cunningham (Prop)
Date established: 1996 **No.of Employees:** 1 - 10 **Product Groups:** 46

Averine

7-9 Broomfield Road, Chelmsford, CM1 1SY
Tel: 01245-290205
Website: http://www.averine.co.uk
Directors: J. Holloway (MD)
No.of Employees: 1 - 10 **Product Groups:** 32, 37, 67

B A E Systems

Eastwood House Glebe Road, Chelmsford, CM1 1QW
Tel: 01245-702702 **Fax:** 01245-702700
E-mail: terry.soame@baesystems.com
Website: http://www.baesystems.com
Bank(s): National Westminster Bank Plc
Managers: T. Soame (Site Co-ord)
Ultimate Holding Company: FINMECCANICA SPA (ITALY)
Immediate Holding Company: SELEX COMMUNICATIONS HOLDINGS LIMITED
Registration no: 04365710 **VAT No.:** GB 239 1370 65
Date established: 2002 **Turnover:** £1m - £2m
No.of Employees: 251 - 500 **Product Groups:** 37, 38, 39

Beanstalk Marketing Services

Moulsham Mill Parkway, Chelmsford, CM2 7PX
Tel: 0845-4742047
E-mail: info@beanstalkmarketing.co.uk
Website: http://www.beanstalkmarketing.co.uk
Directors: G. Burt (Jt MD), P. Swanson (Jt MD)
Registration no: 06982898 **Date established:** 2009 **Turnover:**
No.of Employees: Unknown **Product Groups:** 81

Biffa Waste Services Ltd (Chelmsford Customer Centre)

Drakes Lane Boreham, Chelmsford, CM3 3BE
Tel: 01245-360088 **Fax:** 01245-362342
E-mail: info@biffawasteservices.co.uk
Website: http://www.biffa.co.uk
Managers: K. Steward (District Mgr)
Immediate Holding Company: BIFFA WASTE SERVICES LIMITED
Registration no: 00946107 **Date established:** 1969 **Turnover:** £5m - £10m
No.of Employees: 21 - 50 **Product Groups:** 54, 72

Date of Accounts	Mar 08	Mar 09	Apr 10
Sales Turnover	555m	574m	492m
Pre Tax Profit/Loss	23m	50m	30m
Working Capital	229m	271m	293m
Fixed Assets	371m	360m	378m
Current Assets	409m	534m	609m
Current Liabilities	50m	100m	115m

Bremins

66 Imperial Avenue Mayland, Chelmsford, CM3 6AH
Tel: 01621-742735 **Fax:** 08450-542541
E-mail: contact@bremins.co.uk
Website: http://www.bremins.co.uk
Directors: B. Guiliano (MD)
Immediate Holding Company: BREMINS LIMITED
Registration no: 07210119 **Date established:** 2010
No.of Employees: 1 - 10 **Product Groups:** 38, 85, 87

Britvic Soft Drinks Ltd

Britvic House Broomfield Road, Chelmsford, CM1 1TU
Tel: 01245-261871 **Fax:** 01245-267147
E-mail: john.gibney@britvic.co.uk
Website: http://www.britvic.co.uk
Bank(s): HSBC Bank plc
Directors: J. Gibney (Fin), S. Stewart (Mkt Research), D. Frost (Pers), D. Price (Co Sec), P. Moody (Sales)
Managers: M. Rose
Ultimate Holding Company: BRITVIC PLC
Immediate Holding Company: BRITANNIA SOFT DRINKS LIMITED
Registration no: 00047094 **Date established:** 1996
Turnover: £500m - £1,000m **No.of Employees:** 1501 & over
Product Groups: 21, 62

Date of Accounts	Sep 08	Sep 09	Oct 10
Pre Tax Profit/Loss	-31m	229m	-17m
Working Capital	-657m	-516m	-533m
Fixed Assets	804m	784m	784m
Current Assets	8m	9m	5m

Bullus & Co

Rumbolds House Hammonds Road, Sandon, Chelmsford, CM2 7RS
Tel: 01245-474035 **Fax:** 01245-477175
E-mail: search@bullus.co.uk
Website: http://www.bullus.co.uk
Directors: R. Bullus (Prop), R. Bullus (Grp Chief Exec), D. Rogers (Dir)
Managers: C. Byron (Consultant), C. Milton (Consultant), C. Bullus (Mktg Serv Mgr)
VAT No.: GB 406 9811 44 **Date established:** 1983
No.of Employees: 1 - 10 **Product Groups:** 80

C D C Ltd

18 Baynes Place, Chelmsford, CM1 2QX
Tel: 01245-253420 **Fax:** 01245-253421
E-mail: sales@cdcuk.com
Website: http://www.cdcuk.com
Directors: P. Curry (MD)
Immediate Holding Company: CDC LIMITED
Registration no: 03855059 **Date established:** 1999
No.of Employees: 11 - 20 **Product Groups:** 25, 27, 30, 35, 36, 46, 49

Date of Accounts	Dec 09	Dec 08
Working Capital	-0	-0
Current Assets	-0	-0

Cannon Piling

Main Road Rettendon Common, Chelmsford, CM3 8DZ
Tel: 01245-401333 **Fax:** 01245-401111
E-mail: sales@cannonpiling.com
Website: http://www.cannonpiling.com
Directors: J. Newton (MD), C. Ford (Fin)
Immediate Holding Company: CANNON PILING LIMITED
Registration no: 04412631 **Date established:** 2002 **Turnover:** £5m - £10m
No.of Employees: 21 - 50 **Product Groups:** 34, 51, 66, 67, 84

Carmo Ltd (Ultraplast)

11-19 Bancrofts Road South Woodham Ferrers, Chelmsford, CM3 5UG
Tel: 01245-322130 **Fax:** 01245-328695
E-mail: ann@carno.co.uk
Website: http://www.carmo.co.uk
Managers: A. Krelle (Mgr)
Immediate Holding Company: CARMO LIMITED
Registration no: 01165915 **VAT No.:** GB 249 2171 59
Date established: 1974 **No.of Employees:** 1 - 10 **Product Groups:** 30

Date of Accounts	Dec 11	Dec 10	Dec 09
Working Capital	195	169	173
Fixed Assets	113	115	119
Current Assets	389	204	202

Cavendish Laboratories

Bush House 294 Ongar Road, Writtle, Chelmsford, CM1 3NZ
Tel: 01245-422800 **Fax:** 01245-422501
E-mail: info@cavendishlaboratories.com
Website: http://www.cavendishlaboratories.com
Directors: P. Jarvis (Dir)
Immediate Holding Company: CAVENDISH LABORATORIES LIMITED
Registration no: 03128776 **Date established:** 1995
No.of Employees: 11 - 20 **Product Groups:** 31, 85

Date of Accounts	Nov 11	Nov 10	Nov 09
Working Capital	198	176	205
Fixed Assets	61	72	77
Current Assets	338	313	299

Cento Engineering Co. Ltd

Baddow Park West Hanningfield Road, Great Baddow, Chelmsford, CM2 7SY
Tel: 01245-477708 **Fax:** 01245-477748
E-mail: info@cento.co.uk
Website: http://www.cento.co.uk
Directors: T. Murphy (Co Sec), B. Murphy (MD)
Immediate Holding Company: CENTO ENGINEERING COMPANY LIMITED
Registration no: 03069251 **VAT No.:** 637 1698 11 **Date established:** 1995
Turnover: £1m - £2m **No.of Employees:** 1 - 10 **Product Groups:** 35, 39

Date of Accounts	Nov 11	Nov 10	Nov 09
Sales Turnover	2m	2m	3m
Pre Tax Profit/Loss	225	164	181
Working Capital	727	615	541
Fixed Assets	16	7	22
Current Assets	1m	755	1m
Current Liabilities	188	97	291

The Chocolate Truffle Company

43 Rookes Crescent, Chelmsford, CM1 3GL
Tel: 01245-257628
E-mail: christine@thechocolatetrufflecompany.co.uk
Website: http://www.thechocolatetrufflecompany.co.uk
Directors: C. Moss (Prop)
Date established: 2006 **No.of Employees:** 1 - 10 **Product Groups:** 20

Clifford Thames Group Ltd

Springfield Lyons House Springfield Lyons Approach, Springfield, Chelmsford, CM2 5TH
Tel: 01245-236600 **Fax:** 01245-236611
E-mail: sales@clifford-thames.com
Website: http://www.cliffordthames.com
Directors: R. Raffell (Co Sec), R. Raffel (Fin), R. Barber (MD)
Managers: S. Christie (I.T. Exec), P. Abrey (Personnel), B. Schneider, C. Barnett (Chief Mgr)
Immediate Holding Company: CLIFFORD THAMES GROUP LIMITED
Registration no: 06864880 **Date established:** 2009
Turnover: £20m - £50m **No.of Employees:** 101 - 250
Product Groups: 28, 44, 79, 81

Date of Accounts	Mar 11	Mar 10
Sales Turnover	34m	5m
Pre Tax Profit/Loss	2m	293
Working Capital	3m	3m
Fixed Assets	17m	16m
Current Assets	9m	10m
Current Liabilities	2m	2m

Cloakroom Solutions Ltd

Unit 9, Beehive Business Centre Beehive Lane, Chelmsford, CM2 9TE
Tel: 01245-490333 **Fax:** 01245-490111
E-mail: info@cloakroomsolutions.co.uk
Website: http://www.cloakroomsolutions.co.uk
Registration no: 03000622 **Product Groups:** 25, 26, 30, 33, 35, 36, 40, 44, 49, 52, 61, 64, 66, 67, 84

Date of Accounts	Aug 08	Aug 07	Aug 06
Working Capital	246	233	200
Fixed Assets	N/A	1	2
Current Assets	321	292	236
Current Liabilities	76	59	37

Communications Express Ltd

7 Grafton Place Dukes Park Industrial Estate, Chelmsford, CM2 6TG
Tel: 01245-459490 **Fax:** 0845-200 0257
E-mail: sales@comms-express.com
Website: http://www.comms-express.com
Managers: A. Boyce (Cust Serv Mgr)
Immediate Holding Company: COMMS EXPRESS LIMITED
Registration no: 04359914 **Date established:** 2002 **Turnover:** £5m - £10m
No.of Employees: 21 - 50 **Product Groups:** 37, 45

Date of Accounts	Dec 11	Dec 10	Dec 09
Working Capital	585	253	25
Fixed Assets	114	148	155
Current Assets	2m	1m	1m

Craintern UK Ltd

13-17 Haltwhistle Road South Woodham Ferrers, Chelmsford, CM3 5ZA
Tel: 01245-322438 **Fax:** 01245-328926
E-mail: mailbox@ctlmedical.co.uk
Website: http://www.ctlmedical.co.uk
Directors: T. Catling (MD)
Immediate Holding Company: CRAINTERN (UK) LIMITED
Registration no: 04942848 **Date established:** 2003 **Turnover:** £2m - £5m
No.of Employees: 21 - 50 **Product Groups:** 48

Date of Accounts	Mar 12	Mar 11	Mar 10
Working Capital	286	214	151
Fixed Assets	56	72	80
Current Assets	582	591	547

C V C Chelmer Valve Co. Ltd

Scatterbrook Farm Rectory Lane, Latchingdon, Chelmsford, CM3 6HB
Tel: 01621-745450 **Fax:** 01245-241309
E-mail: sales@chelmervalve.com
Website: http://www.chelmervalve.com
Managers: B. Adams (Mgr)
Immediate Holding Company: CVC CHELMER VALVE COMPANY LTD
Registration no: 04600230 **VAT No.:** GB 102 0017 60
Date established: 2002 **Turnover:** £1m - £2m **No.of Employees:** 1 - 10
Product Groups: 33, 35, 37, 38, 40, 44, 67

Date of Accounts	Mar 12	Mar 11	Mar 10
Working Capital	211	55	103
Fixed Assets	125	127	4
Current Assets	396	352	146

D L Products Ltd

13 Redhills Road South Woodham Ferrers, Chelmsford, CM3 5UL
Tel: 01245-426001 **Fax:** 01245-320040
E-mail: sales@dlproducts.co.uk
Website: http://www.auto-bar.co.uk
Directors: L. Hart (MD)
Ultimate Holding Company: CRASHTENT LIMITED
Immediate Holding Company: D L PRODUCTS LIMITED
Registration no: 01795438 **Date established:** 1984
No.of Employees: 11 - 20 **Product Groups:** 48

Date of Accounts	Apr 11	Apr 10	Apr 09
Working Capital	178	131	122
Fixed Assets	41	57	50
Current Assets	940	875	899

D W B Anglia Ltd Gang-Nail Systems Ltd

Mapledean Industrial Estate Maldon Road Maldon Road, Latchingdon, Chelmsford, CM3 6LG
Tel: 01621-744455 **Fax:** 01621-744976
E-mail: trevor.t@dwbgroup.co.uk
Website: http://www.dwbgroup.co.uk
Directors: T. Tween (MD)
Immediate Holding Company: D.W.B. (ANGLIA) LIMITED
Registration no: 03065754 **Date established:** 1995 **Turnover:** £2m - £5m
No.of Employees: 11 - 20 **Product Groups:** 30, 31, 33, 35, 66

Date of Accounts	Jan 12	Jan 11	Jan 10
Working Capital	-13	-81	-70
Fixed Assets	970	997	914
Current Assets	430	215	190

Danbury Electronics
20 Cutlers Road Saltcoats Industrial Estate, South Woodham Ferrers, Chelmsford, CM3 5XJ
Tel: 01245-328174 **Fax:** 01245-328963
E-mail: sales@danburyelectronics.co.uk
Website: http://www.danburyelectronics.co.uk
Managers: D. Brooks (Mgr)
VAT No.: GB 386 7931 93 **Date established:** 1983
Turnover: £250,000 - £500,000 **No.of Employees:** 1 - 10
Product Groups: 37

Demeter Windings
Unit 8 Beehive Business Centre Beehive Lane, Chelmsford, CM2 9TE
Tel: 01245-344544 **Fax:** 01245-265344
E-mail: demeterw@lycos.co.uk
Website: http://www.demeterwindings.com
Directors: K. Ward (Prop)
Ultimate Holding Company: DRAINAGE AND HYGIENE SERVICES LIMITED
Immediate Holding Company: CLEAN DRAIN LIMITED
Registration no: 01299030 **VAT No.:** GB 594 5524 08
Date established: 1980 **Turnover:** £250,000 - £500,000
No.of Employees: 1 - 10 **Product Groups:** 37

Denward Manufacturing
Denward House 50 Writtle Road, Chelmsford, CM1 3BU
Tel: 01245-492986 **Fax:** 01245-496939
E-mail: sales@denward.com
Website: http://www.denward.com
Directors: D. Halfhide (Fin), S. Halfhide (MD)
Immediate Holding Company: DENWARD MANUFACTURING LIMITED
Registration no: 03955314 **Date established:** 2000
No.of Employees: 1 - 10 **Product Groups:** 38, 42

Date of Accounts	Mar 11	Mar 10	Mar 09
Working Capital	261	243	174
Fixed Assets	84	85	38
Current Assets	384	323	239

Discount Leisure UK ltd
Carlton House 101 New London Road, Chelmsford, CM2 0PP
Tel: 01245-477333 **Fax:** 01245-477888
E-mail: sales@discount-leisure.com
Website: http://www.discountleisure.co.uk
Directors: C. NICHOLLS (Dir), T. BULLOCK (Sales)
Immediate Holding Company: DISCOUNT LEISURE (UK) LIMITED
Registration no: 05401694 **Date established:** 2005
Turnover: £250,000 - £500,000 **No.of Employees:** 1 - 10
Product Groups: 29, 30, 33, 35, 37, 40, 42, 52, 65

Date of Accounts	Mar 08	Mar 07	Mar 06
Working Capital	-11	-1	-1
Fixed Assets	8	2	2
Current Assets	44	26	10
Current Liabilities	56	27	11

Duplex Telecom Ltd
The Widford Hall Widford Hall Lane, Chelmsford, CM2 8TD
Tel: 08707-481408 **Fax:** 08707-481407
E-mail: sales@duplex.co.uk
Website: http://www.duplex.co.uk
Bank(s): Barclays, Chelmsford
Directors: L. Richards (Asst MD), S. Last (MD), P. McGuinness (Fin)
Managers: L. Suddards (Sales Prom Mgr)
Ultimate Holding Company: TRIO APPLIED TECHNOLOGIES LIMITED
Immediate Holding Company: DUPLEX TELECOM LIMITED
Registration no: 02141994 **VAT No.:** GB 507 1721 71
Date established: 1987 **Turnover:** £1m - £2m **No.of Employees:** 21 - 50
Product Groups: 37

Date of Accounts	Sep 10	Sep 09	Sep 08
Working Capital	-76	-44	-22
Fixed Assets	53	71	91
Current Assets	233	371	438

E 2 V Technologies Ltd
106 Waterhouse Lane, Chelmsford, CM1 2QU
Tel: 01245-493493 **Fax:** 01245-492492
E-mail: keith.attwood@e2vtechnologies.com
Website: http://www.e2v.com
Bank(s): Lloyds, Lombard St, EC3
Directors: C. Parmenter (Co Sec), K. Attwood (Grp Chief Exec)
Managers: P. Casey, R. Hindson
Ultimate Holding Company: E2V TECHNOLOGIES PLC
Immediate Holding Company: E2V TECHNOLOGIES (UK) LIMITED
Registration no: 00432014 **VAT No.:** 795 9843 47 **Date established:** 1947
Turnover: £75m - £125m **No.of Employees:** 501 - 1000
Product Groups: 37, 38

Date of Accounts	Mar 12	Mar 11	Mar 10
Sales Turnover	119m	105m	105m
Pre Tax Profit/Loss	19m	8m	19m
Working Capital	19m	17m	32m
Fixed Assets	25m	22m	22m
Current Assets	58m	57m	67m
Current Liabilities	11m	12m	11m

E D S Engineering Ltd
Rivermead North Bishop Hall Lane, Chelmsford, CM1 1PW
Tel: 01245-355351 **Fax:** 01245-358022
E-mail: info@edseng.co.uk
Website: http://www.edseng.co.uk
Bank(s): Natwest
Directors: J. Cloughton (Works), S. Clarke (MD)
Ultimate Holding Company: E D S Co. Ltd
Registration no: 02142541 **Turnover:** £2m - £5m
No.of Employees: 21 - 50 **Product Groups:** 46, 48, 84

Date of Accounts	Sep 09	Sep 08	Sep 07
Working Capital	454	722	526
Fixed Assets	829	985	689
Current Assets	2m	2m	1m

Eastern Compressors Ltd
1-9 Drapers Road South Woodham Ferrers, Chelmsford, CM3 5UH
Tel: 01245-320624 **Fax:** 01245-328700
E-mail: sales@easterncompressors.com
Website: http://www.easterncompressors.com
Bank(s): Barclays
Directors: D. Lowe (Fin)
Ultimate Holding Company: ACTIV-AIR AUTOMATION LIMITED
Immediate Holding Company: EASTERN COMPRESSORS LIMITED
Registration no: 00837369 **VAT No.:** GB 102 4860 07
Date established: 1965 **Turnover:** £1m - £2m **No.of Employees:** 11 - 20
Product Groups: 38, 40

Date of Accounts	Mar 11	Mar 10	Mar 09
Working Capital	138	126	121
Fixed Assets	74	76	75
Current Assets	457	417	434

Emerson Network Power Connectivity Solutions Ltd
7-13 Russell Way, Chelmsford, CM1 3AA
Tel: 01245-342060 **Fax:** 01245-358938
E-mail: connectivityeurope@emerson.com
Website: http://www.emersonconnectivity.co.uk
Directors: W. Malcolm (MD)
Managers: A. Malcolm, J. Malcolm
Ultimate Holding Company: EMERSON ELECTRIC CO INC (USA)
Immediate Holding Company: MIDWEST MICROWAVE LTD
Registration no: 04817100 **Date established:** 2003
No.of Employees: 51 - 100 **Product Groups:** 37

Date of Accounts	Sep 11	Sep 09	Sep 08
Working Capital	1	1	1
Current Assets	1	1	1

Endicott Interconnect UK Ltd
Unit 62 Waterhouse Business Centre 2 Cormar Way, Chelmsford, CM1 7GB
Tel: 01245-392500 **Fax:** 01245-443193
E-mail: steve.payne@eitny.com
Website: http://endicottinterconnect.com
Directors: S. Payne (Dir), T. Taro (Dir)
Date established: 2002 **No.of Employees:** 1501 & over
Product Groups: 37, 44, 47, 48, 84, 85

Essex Chronicle Media Group
Westway, Chelmsford, CM1 3BE
Tel: 01245-600700
E-mail: switchboard@essexchronicle.co.uk
Website: http://www.thisistotalessex.co.uk
Bank(s): National Westminster Bank Plc
Directors: D. Hobden (Chief Op Offcr), J. Bennett (Fin), J. Walker (MD), T. Newton (Comm)
Managers: P. Humphrey (Sales Admin), L. Patterson
Immediate Holding Company: MID ESSEX ENTERPRISE AGENCY LIMITED
Registration no: 00184465 **Date established:** 1987 **Turnover:** £5m - £10m
No.of Employees: 101 - 250 **Product Groups:** 28

Date of Accounts	Mar 11	Mar 10	Mar 09
Working Capital	41	71	100
Fixed Assets	2	3	4
Current Assets	46	80	114

Essex Scale Services
259 Springfield Road, Chelmsford, CM1 7RA
Tel: 01245-258543 **Fax:** 01245-258543
E-mail: bob.smith23855@hotmail.co.uk
Directors: R. Smith (MD)
Immediate Holding Company: ESSEX SCALE SERVICES LTD
Registration no: 04901135 **Date established:** 2003
No.of Employees: 1 - 10 **Product Groups:** 38, 42

Date of Accounts	Sep 11	Sep 10	Sep 09
Working Capital	-2	-1	-1
Fixed Assets	6	7	1
Current Assets	13	16	17

Eurolag Group Ltd
The Coach House Baddow Park West Hanningfield Road, Great Baddow, Chelmsford, CM2 7SY
Tel: 01245-478901 **Fax:** 01708-723524
E-mail: info@eurolag.com
Website: http://www.eurolag-group.co.uk
Directors: J. Sharpe (Chief Op Offcr)
Ultimate Holding Company: EUROLAG HOLDINGS LIMITED
Immediate Holding Company: EUROLAG GROUP LIMITED
Registration no: 02887941 **Date established:** 1994 **Turnover:** £2m - £5m
No.of Employees: 11 - 20 **Product Groups:** 40, 54

Date of Accounts	Aug 11	Aug 10	Aug 09
Working Capital	232	147	214
Fixed Assets	329	404	276
Current Assets	1m	1m	1m

Express Reinforcements
18 Barlows Reach, Chelmsford, CM2 6SN
Tel: 01245-460667
Directors: E. Sibey (Prop)
No.of Employees: 1 - 10 **Product Groups:** 34, 37, 44

Frost Windows
10 Skylark Walk, Chelmsford, CM2 8BB
Tel: 01245-259121 **Fax:** 01245-357680
E-mail: enquiries@frostwindows.co.uk
Website: http://www.frostwindows.co.uk
Directors: M. Frost (Prop)
No.of Employees: 1 - 10 **Product Groups:** 25, 30, 35, 66

Galliford Try Partnership Ltd
50 Rainsford Road, Chelmsford, CM1 2XB
Tel: 01245-494849 **Fax:** 01245-493494
E-mail: davinder.nandra@gallifordtry.co.uk
Website: http://www.gallifordtry.co.uk
Directors: D. Nandra (Fin)
Managers: N. Brooks (Develop Mgr), R. Bullen (Reg Sales Mgr), C. Richardson (Chief Buyer), G. Taylor (Personnel)
Ultimate Holding Company: GALLIFORD TRY PLC
Immediate Holding Company: GALLIFORD TRY PARTNERSHIPS LIMITED
Registration no: 00800384 **Date established:** 1964
Turnover: £75m - £125m **No.of Employees:** 51 - 100 **Product Groups:** 51

Date of Accounts	Jun 11	Jun 10	Jun 09
Sales Turnover	83m	61m	71m
Pre Tax Profit/Loss	3m	3m	1m
Working Capital	9m	23m	23m
Fixed Assets	2m	2m	233
Current Assets	105m	64m	56m
Current Liabilities	43m	34m	29m

Global Enterprises
The Old Stores Penny Royal Road, Danbury, Chelmsford, CM3 4ED
Tel: 01245-226004 **Fax:** 01245-225995
E-mail: stephaniehoulden@globalheatseal.com
Website: http://www.globalheatseal.com
Managers: S. Houlden (Mgr)
Immediate Holding Company: MODITA LIMITED
Registration no: 03555707 **VAT No.:** GB 720 1795 54
Date established: 1999 **Turnover:** £250,000 - £500,000
No.of Employees: 1 - 10 **Product Groups:** 30, 42, 67

Date of Accounts	Jun 11	Jun 10	Jun 07
Working Capital	1	-30	8
Fixed Assets	36	N/A	N/A
Current Assets	10	2	10

Global Marine Systems Investments Ltd
New Saxon House 1 Winsford Way Boreham Interchange, Chelmsford, CM2 5PD
Tel: 01245-702000 **Fax:** 01245-703045
E-mail: beverley.pinborough@globalmarinesystems.com
Website: http://www.globalmarinesystems.com
Directors: B. Pinborough (MD)
Ultimate Holding Company: BRIDGEHOUSE MARINE LIMITED
Immediate Holding Company: GLOBAL MARINE SYSTEMS (INVESTMENTS) LIMITED
Registration no: 03917661 **Date established:** 2000
No.of Employees: 1 - 10 **Product Groups:** 51, 74, 84

Date of Accounts	Dec 10	Dec 09	Dec 08
Working Capital	-4m	-4m	-4m

Golding Catering Equipment
47 Chignal Road, Chelmsford, CM1 2JA
Tel: 01245-252800
E-mail: sales@gcs.uk.co
Website: http://www.gcs.uk.co
Directors: M. Golding (Prop)
Date established: 1996 **No.of Employees:** 1 - 10 **Product Groups:** 20, 40, 41

Grabern Engraving ltd
Oyster Place 28 Montrose Road, Chelmsford, CM2 6TX
Tel: 01245-468223 **Fax:** 01245-469121
E-mail: info@grabernengraving.com
Website: http://www.grabernengraving.com
Directors: K. Troubridge (Sales)
Immediate Holding Company: Grabern Engraving Ltd
Registration no: 05395583 **VAT No.:** GB 312 4282 95
Date established: 2005 **Turnover:** £250,000 - £500,000
No.of Employees: 1 - 10 **Product Groups:** 27, 28, 35, 48

Date of Accounts	Apr 09	Apr 08	Apr 07
Working Capital	-4	-4	5
Fixed Assets	4	5	6
Current Assets	28	33	41
Current Liabilities	N/A	N/A	13

H S Powder Coating
Mapledean Chase Maldon Road, Latchingdon, Chelmsford, CM3 6LG
Tel: 01621-742779 **Fax:** 01621-742779
Directors: J. Hurd (Prop)
Immediate Holding Company: D.W.B. (ANGLIA) LIMITED
VAT No.: GB 623 3498 40 **Date established:** 1995
Turnover: Up to £250,000 **No.of Employees:** 1 - 10 **Product Groups:** 48

Date of Accounts	Jan 12	Jan 11	Jan 10
Working Capital	-13	-81	-70
Fixed Assets	970	997	914
Current Assets	430	215	190

Heaths Lambert Consulting
Duke Street Saxon House, Chelmsford, CM1 1HT
Tel: 01245-293300 **Fax:** 01245-490558
E-mail: rnoble@heathlambert.com
Website: http://www.heathlambert.com
Directors: R. Noble (Dir)
Managers: R. Noble (Mgr), L. Simmons (District Mgr)
Ultimate Holding Company: FLYING BRANDS LTD (JERSEY)
Immediate Holding Company: BELLBOURNE PROPERTIES LIMITED
Registration no: 02061404 **Date established:** 1986
No.of Employees: 21 - 50 **Product Groups:** 80, 82

I S & G Steel Stockholders Ltd
Temple Wood Stock Road West Hanningfield, Chelmsford, CM2 8LL
Tel: 01277-840471 **Fax:** 01277-840234
E-mail: ricky.page@isgsteel.co.uk
Website: http://www.isg-steel.co.uk
Bank(s): HSBC Bank plc
Managers: R. Paige (Warehouse Mgr)
Ultimate Holding Company: I S & G (HOLDINGS) LIMITED
Immediate Holding Company: I. S. & G. STEEL STOCKHOLDERS LIMITED
Registration no: 00251016 **VAT No.:** GB 205 6860 68
Date established: 1930 **Turnover:** £1m - £2m **No.of Employees:** 21 - 50
Product Groups: 66

Date of Accounts	Mar 11	Mar 10	Mar 09
Sales Turnover	9m	8m	12m
Pre Tax Profit/Loss	298	-236	132
Working Capital	2m	1m	1m
Fixed Assets	358	302	378
Current Assets	4m	4m	4m
Current Liabilities	462	1m	1m

IDT Laser (ID & T GmbH)
17 Galleywood Road Great Baddow Great Baddow, Chelmsford, CM2 8DH
Tel: 01245-471046 **Fax:** 01245-471046
E-mail: uk@idtlaser.com
Website: http://www.idtlaser.com
Managers: J. Walton (Mgr)
Date established: 2008 **No.of Employees:** 1 - 10 **Product Groups:** 36, 38, 45, 48

Industrial Training Services Ltd
52-54 Hullbridge Road South Woodham Ferrers, Chelmsford, CM3 5NH
Tel: 01245-321130 **Fax:** 01245-328277
E-mail: info@industrial-training-services.co.uk
Website: http://www.industrial-training-services.co.uk
Ultimate Holding Company: CAPITAL ENGINEERING GROUP HOLDINGS LTD
Immediate Holding Company: INDUSTRIAL TRAINING SERVICES LTD
Registration no: 02382479 **Date established:** 1989
Turnover: £250,000 - £500,000 **No.of Employees:** 1 - 10
Product Groups: 80, 86, 87

Date of Accounts	Mar 11	Mar 10	Mar 09
Sales Turnover	1m	2m	2m
Pre Tax Profit/Loss	364	546	608

see next page

***Industrial Training Services Ltd** - Cont'd*

Working Capital	620	544	787
Fixed Assets	90	100	105
Current Assets	724	807	1m
Current Liabilities	89	238	320

John O'Donnell Ltd

Victoria Road, Chelmsford, CM1 1NZ
Tel: 01245-256112 **Fax:** 01245-492854
E-mail: sales@johnodonnell.com
Website: http://www.johnodonnell.com
Directors: J. O'donnell (MD)
Immediate Holding Company: JOHN O DONNELL LIMITED
Registration no: 01132571 **VAT No.:** GB 104 2331 32
Date established: 1973 **Turnover:** £1m - £2m **No.of Employees:** 21 - 50
Product Groups: 63

Date of Accounts	Dec 11	Dec 10	Dec 09
Working Capital	461	454	425
Fixed Assets	5	22	38
Current Assets	669	614	579

Johnson Controls Automotive UK Ltd

Ford Buiness Union The Hampton Centre, Chelmsford, CM1 3BY
Tel: 01245-292200 **Fax:** 01245-292309
E-mail: enquiries@jca.com
Website: http://www.jca.com
Directors: J. Bell (Dir)
Ultimate Holding Company: JOHNSON CONTROLS INC (USA)
Immediate Holding Company: JOHNSON CONTROLS AUTOMOTIVE (UK) LTD.
Registration no: 00443687 **Date established:** 1947
Turnover: £250m - £500m **No.of Employees:** 1501 & over
Product Groups: 22, 39, 84

Date of Accounts	Sep 11	Sep 10	Sep 09
Sales Turnover	499m	571m	442m
Pre Tax Profit/Loss	25m	20m	-32m
Working Capital	77m	70m	52m
Fixed Assets	42m	40m	42m
Current Assets	195m	188m	195m
Current Liabilities	32m	32m	35m

K C K Engineering

Unit 2 Baddow Park West Hanningfield Road, Great Baddow, Chelmsford, CM2 7SY
Tel: 01245-478488 **Fax:** 01245-473148
E-mail: garycornwall@tiscali.co.uk
Directors: G. Cornwall (Prop)
Immediate Holding Company: COURT DEVELOPMENTS LIMITED
Registration no: 06203242 **Date established:** 2008
No.of Employees: 1 - 10 **Product Groups:** 37, 40, 48

Date of Accounts	Dec 11	Dec 10	Dec 09
Working Capital	-29	-29	-29
Fixed Assets	23	23	23
Current Assets	128	128	128
Current Liabilities	158	N/A	N/A

Kay-Metzeler Ltd (Polystyrene Division)

Brook Street, Chelmsford, CM1 1UQ
Tel: 01245-342100 **Fax:** 01245-342123
E-mail: epssales@vcfuk.com
Website: http://www.kay-metzeler.com
Bank(s): Lloyds
Directors: D. Hughes (Mkt Research), M. Sheilds (MD)
Managers: M. Shields (Comm)
Immediate Holding Company: British Vita P.L.C.
Registration no: 00621497 **VAT No.:** GB 606 3424 65
Date established: 1950 **Turnover:** £5m - £10m
No.of Employees: 51 - 100 **Product Groups:** 30, 51

Robert Keen Ltd

Unit 2 Bilton Road, Chelmsford, CM1 2UP
Tel: 01245-355541 **Fax:** 01245-492403
E-mail: sales@robert-keen.co.uk
Website: http://www.robert-keen.co.uk
Bank(s): HSBC
Directors: R. Nicks (Jt MD), R. Nicks (MD), V. Trew (Jt MD)
Immediate Holding Company: R One K Ltd
Registration no: 00475621 **VAT No.:** GB 594 7838 72
Date established: 1949 **Turnover:** £2m - £5m **No.of Employees:** 21 - 50
Product Groups: 48

Date of Accounts	Jul 07	Jul 06
Working Capital	20	326
Fixed Assets	934	961
Current Assets	761	993
Current Liabilities	741	667
Total Share Capital	4	4

L S Francis Ltd

Unit 12a Mayfair Industrial Estate Maldon Road, Latchingdon, Chelmsford, CM3 6LF
Tel: 01621-740924 **Fax:** 01621-740924
Website: http://www.lsfrancislabels.co.uk
Directors: L. Francis (Fin), L. Francis (MD)
Immediate Holding Company: L S FRANCIS LTD.
Registration no: 04717054 **Date established:** 2003
Turnover: Up to £250,000 **No.of Employees:** 1 - 10 **Product Groups:** 27

Date of Accounts	Jun 12	Jun 11	Jun 10
Working Capital	N/A	-3	-8
Fixed Assets	24	31	38
Current Assets	26	29	23

Lighting & Ceiling Louvres Ltd

7-13 Cutlers Road South Woodham Ferrers, Chelmsford, CM3 5WA
Tel: 01245-321561 **Fax:** 01245-325034
E-mail: sales@lcll.co.uk
Website: http://www.lcll.co.uk
Bank(s): TSB, City Office, London
Directors: G. Elms (Mkt Research), L. Parris (Fin), P. Deal (Purch), N. Yates (MD), U. Vester (Pers)
Immediate Holding Company: LIGHTING AND CEILING LOUVRES LIMITED
Registration no: 01416881 **VAT No.:** GB 360 2439 75
Date established: 1979 **Turnover:** £2m - £5m **No.of Employees:** 51 - 100
Product Groups: 37

Date of Accounts	Sep 11	Sep 10	Sep 09
Sales Turnover	3m	3m	3m
Pre Tax Profit/Loss	313	261	76
Working Capital	569	406	244
Fixed Assets	1m	1m	1m
Current Assets	1m	916	718
Current Liabilities	293	302	265

Lumisphere Products Ltd

14 Heralds Way South Woodham Ferrers, Chelmsford, CM3 5TQ
Tel: 01245-329999 **Fax:** 01245-322600
E-mail: sales@lumisphere.co.uk
Website: http://www.lumisphere.co.uk
Managers: K. Knight (Mgr)
Immediate Holding Company: LUMISPHERE PRODUCTS LTD.
Registration no: 02335636 **Date established:** 1989
No.of Employees: 1 - 10 **Product Groups:** 37, 67

Date of Accounts	Mar 12	Mar 11	Mar 10
Working Capital	200	187	130
Fixed Assets	37	19	24
Current Assets	287	271	202

M C M Ltd

22 Bancrofts Road South Woodham Ferrers, Chelmsford, CM3 5UQ
Tel: 01245-329818 **Fax:** 01245-329468
E-mail: mc.m@talk21.com
Website: http://www.tak21.com
Directors: M. Zarb Cousin (Dir)
Immediate Holding Company: MCM LIMITED
Registration no: 05896200 **VAT No.:** GB 594 8705 86
Date established: 2006 **Turnover:** £250,000 - £500,000
No.of Employees: 1 - 10 **Product Groups:** 30

M T T Ltd

Gazelle House Old Wickford Road, South Woodham Ferrers, Chelmsford, CM3 5QT
Tel: 01245-320782 **Fax:** 01245-324785
E-mail: stuart@molyandtantalum.com
Website: http://www.molyandtantalum.com
Directors: S. Alexander (Dir)
Managers: S. alexander (Chief Acct)
Immediate Holding Company: MTT LIMITED
Registration no: 06936844 **Date established:** 2009
No.of Employees: 1 - 10 **Product Groups:** 66

Date of Accounts	Jun 10	Jun 09
Working Capital	11	1
Fixed Assets	8	1
Current Assets	28	9

Maplin Electronics Ltd

32-42 Springfield Road The Meadows, Chelmsford, CM2 6JX
Tel: 08432-277374 **Fax:** 01245-346814
E-mail: customercare@maplin.co.uk
Website: http://www.maplin.co.uk
Ultimate Holding Company: MONTAGU PRIVATE EQUITY LLP
Immediate Holding Company: MAPLIN ELECTRONICS LIMITED
Registration no: 01264385 **Date established:** 1976
Turnover: £125m - £250m **No.of Employees:** 1 - 10 **Product Groups:** 37, 61

Date of Accounts	Dec 11	Dec 08	Dec 09
Sales Turnover	205m	204m	204m
Pre Tax Profit/Loss	25m	32m	35m
Working Capital	118m	49m	75m
Fixed Assets	27m	28m	28m
Current Assets	207m	108m	142m
Current Liabilities	78m	51m	59m

Mells Roofing Ltd

Beehive Lane Works Beehive Lane, Chelmsford, CM2 9JY
Tel: 0800-298 3251 **Fax:** 01245-260060
E-mail: info@mellsroofing.co.uk
Website: http://www.mellsroofing.co.uk
Bank(s): Bank of Scotland
Directors: P. Fitzgerald (MD)
Immediate Holding Company: MELLS ROOFING LIMITED
Registration no: 02552588 **VAT No.:** GB 583 0517 43
Date established: 1990 **Turnover:** £500,000 - £1m
No.of Employees: 11 - 20 **Product Groups:** 52

Date of Accounts	Dec 11	Dec 10	Dec 09
Working Capital	76	93	81
Fixed Assets	57	22	22
Current Assets	372	309	255

Metalas UK Ltd

White Cottages Fuller Street, Fairstead, Chelmsford, CM3 2AY
Tel: 01245-233715 **Fax:** 01245-381866
E-mail: admin@metalas.co.uk
Website: http://www.metalas.co.uk
Managers: R. Watson (Mgr)
Immediate Holding Company: METALAS (U.K.) LIMITED
Registration no: 01418747 **VAT No.:** GB 325 6946 36
Date established: 1979 **Turnover:** £1m - £2m **No.of Employees:** 1 - 10
Product Groups: 32, 37, 38, 39, 40, 41, 42, 44, 45, 46

Date of Accounts	Dec 11	Dec 10	Dec 09
Working Capital	38	42	178
Fixed Assets	41	46	25
Current Assets	57	67	226

Midwest Microwave International Ltd Emerson Network Power Connectivity Solutions

9-11 Russell Way, Chelmsford, CM1 3AA
Tel: 01245-359515 **Fax:** 01245-358938
E-mail: sales@midwest-microwave.ltd.uk
Website: http://www.emersonconnectivity.co.uk
Bank(s): The Royal Bank of Scotland
Directors: D. Hazell (MD)
Managers: J. Pennick (Quality Control), J. Moores, C. Victory, S. Hearn (Purch Mgr), S. Greenhill (Sales Prom Mgr), S. Groves
Immediate Holding Company: MIDWEST MICROWAVE LTD
Registration no: 04817100 **VAT No.:** GB 450 3498 53
Date established: 2003 **Turnover:** £2m - £5m **No.of Employees:** 21 - 50
Product Groups: 37, 38

Date of Accounts	Sep 08	Sep 07	Sep 06
Sales Turnover	4739	2332	2439
Pre Tax Profit/Loss	227	76	317
Working Capital	-421	-1041	757
Fixed Assets	2002	2035	158
Current Assets	2796	1425	1231
Current Liabilities	3217	2466	474
Total Share Capital	1	1	1
ROCE% (Return on Capital Employed)	14.4	7.6	34.6
ROT% (Return on Turnover)	4.8	3.3	13.0

Objective Computing Ltd

The Old Brewery 47 Church Street, Great Baddow, Chelmsford, CM2 7JA
Tel: 01245-330360 **Fax:** 01268-413353
E-mail: interested@objectiveit.com
Website: http://www.objectiveit.com
Directors: C. Fox (MD)
Managers: A. Clouter (Commun Mgr), K. Harding (Mktg Serv Mgr)
Immediate Holding Company: Objective Computing Ltd
Registration no: 02287416 **Date established:** 1988
No.of Employees: 21 - 50 **Product Groups:** 44

Date of Accounts	Mar 10	Mar 09	Mar 08
Working Capital	126	115	130
Fixed Assets	32	41	53
Current Assets	435	428	337

Opie's The Stove Shop

The Street Hatfield Peverel, Chelmsford, CM3 2DY
Tel: 01245-380471 **Fax:** 01245-381606
E-mail: opiesstoveshop@googlemail.com
Website: http://www.opie-woodstoves.co.uk
Directors: G. Cater (Prop)
Date established: 1984 **No.of Employees:** 1 - 10 **Product Groups:** 40

Packaging 4 Less Ltd

6 Drakes Lane Industrial Estate Drakes Lane, Boreham, Chelmsford, CM3 3BE
Tel: 01245-362363 **Fax:** 01245-362364
E-mail: sales@packaging4less.co.uk
Website: http://www.packaging4less.co.uk
Directors: E. Quick (Fin), P. Quick (MD)
Immediate Holding Company: LIME PACKAGING LIMITED
Registration no: 03119498 **Date established:** 1995
No.of Employees: 1 - 10 **Product Groups:** 38, 42

Date of Accounts	Jul 07	Jul 06	Jul 05
Working Capital	-4	-9	-9
Fixed Assets	8	12	15
Current Assets	201	194	175
Current Liabilities	N/A	31	38

R M & T M Pegram

Rose Hill Farm Creephedge Lane, East Hanningfield, Chelmsford, CM3 8BP
Tel: 01245-400363 **Fax:** 01245-400627
E-mail: robertpegram@btconnect.com
Website: http://www.secondarycrushing.co.uk
Directors: R. Pegram (Ptnr)
Turnover: £250,000 - £500,000 **No.of Employees:** 1 - 10
Product Groups: 14, 33, 42, 45, 61

Pennweld Fabrications

Oakford Farm Nounsley Road, Hatfield Peverel, Chelmsford, CM3 2NG
Tel: 01245-382505
Directors: G. Penn (Prop)
Date established: 1997 **No.of Employees:** 1 - 10 **Product Groups:** 35

Philip Grahame International Ltd

Dukes Park Industrial Estate Montrose Road, Chelmsford, CM2 6TE
Tel: 01245-451717 **Fax:** 01245-451870
E-mail: sales@pgrahame.com
Website: http://www.pgrahame.com
Bank(s): National Westminster Bank Plc
Directors: D. Harding (Fin), P. Harding (MD)
Ultimate Holding Company: AMARYLLIS GROUP HOLDINGS LTD
Immediate Holding Company: PHILIP GRAHAME INTERNATIONAL LIMITED
Registration no: 01622534 **Date established:** 1982 **Turnover:** £5m - £10m
No.of Employees: 21 - 50 **Product Groups:** 36, 37

Date of Accounts	May 11	May 10	May 09
Sales Turnover	5m	5m	5m
Pre Tax Profit/Loss	767	613	685
Working Capital	410	273	273
Fixed Assets	516	463	433
Current Assets	2m	2m	2m
Current Liabilities	953	718	839

Pillarhouse International Ltd

Rodney Way, Chelmsford, CM1 3BY
Tel: 01245-491333 **Fax:** 01245-491331
E-mail: n.monk@pillarhouse.co.uk
Website: http://www.pillarhouse.co.uk
Bank(s): National Westminster Bank Plc
Directors: D. Johnson (Sales), N. Monk (MD), J. Wray (Dir)
Managers: N. Wray (Tech Serv Mgr), P. White (Purch Mgr)
Immediate Holding Company: PILLARHOUSE INTERNATIONAL LIMITED
Registration no: 01201305 **VAT No.:** GB 448 9891 77
Date established: 1975 **Turnover:** £5m - £10m **No.of Employees:** 21 - 50
Product Groups: 46, 47, 48

Date of Accounts	Dec 11	Dec 10	Dec 09
Working Capital	2m	2m	2m
Fixed Assets	2m	2m	2m
Current Assets	4m	2m	2m

Precision Test Systems Ltd

40 Holkham Avenue South Woodham Ferrers, Chelmsford, CM3 7AU
Tel: 01245-329608
E-mail: martyn@ptsyst.com
Website: http://www.ptsyst.com
Directors: M. Smith (MD)
Immediate Holding Company: PRECISION TEST SYSTEMS LTD
Registration no: 04177141 **Date established:** 2001
Turnover: Up to £250,000 **No.of Employees:** 1 - 10 **Product Groups:** 38, 48, 85

Date of Accounts	Mar 12	Mar 11	Mar 10
Working Capital	114	111	82
Fixed Assets	3	5	6
Current Assets	143	137	113
Current Liabilities	N/A	23	19

Reed Accountancy Personnel Ltd

3 New London Road, Chelmsford, CM2 0NA
Tel: 01245-245500 **Fax:** 01245-351737
E-mail: rapchelmsford@reed.co.uk
Website: http://www.reed.co.uk

Managers: M. Browne (Mgr)
Immediate Holding Company: REED PERSONNEL SERVICES LTD
Registration no: 00973629 **Date established:** 1990
Turnover: £75m - £125m **No.of Employees:** 1 - 10 **Product Groups:** 80

Reed Employment Ltd

3 New London Road, Chelmsford, CM2 0NA
Tel: 01245-352332 **Fax:** 01245-496327
E-mail: vicki.mullin@reedglobal.com
Website: http://www.reed.co.uk
Managers: V. Mullin (Mgr)
Ultimate Holding Company: REED GLOBAL LTD (MALTA)
Immediate Holding Company: REED EMPLOYMENT LIMITED
Registration no: 00669854 **Date established:** 1960
Turnover: £75m - £125m **No.of Employees:** 1 - 10 **Product Groups:** 80

Date of Accounts	Jun 11	Jun 10	Dec 07
Sales Turnover	618	450	287m
Pre Tax Profit/Loss	-2m	310	8m
Working Capital	23m	28m	28m
Fixed Assets	31	36	5m
Current Assets	28m	30m	74m
Current Liabilities	37	29	21m

Reef Engineering

Unit 2 Mayfair Industrial Estate Maldon Road, Latchingdon, Chelmsford, CM3 6LF
Tel: 01621-744689 **Fax:** 01621-744285
E-mail: reefengineering@btconnect.com
Website: http://www.reef-engineering.com
Directors: D. Rogers (Ptnr)
Immediate Holding Company: REEF AUTOMATION LIMITED
Registration no: 02075199 **VAT No.:** GB 367 8600 22
Date established: 1986 **Turnover:** £500,000 - £1m
No.of Employees: 1 - 10 **Product Groups:** 32, 46

Reliance Security Group Limited

Unit 72, Waterhouse Business Centre No 2 Cromar Way, Chelmsford, CM1 2QE
Tel: 0870-6068999 **Fax:** 01245-392189
E-mail: info@reliancesecurity.co.uk
Website: http://www.reliancesecurity.co.uk
Bank(s): National Westminster
Directors: K. Allison (Ch), R. Ban (Fin)
Managers: C. Rugg (Chief Mgr)
Registration no: 01473721 **Turnover:** Up to £250,000
No.of Employees: 11 - 20 **Product Groups:** 81

S D Tooling UK Ltd

Manor Lodge Tabors Hill, Great Baddow, Chelmsford, CM2 7BP
Tel: 01245-471807 **Fax:** 01245-475884
E-mail: steve@sdtools.freeserve.co.uk
Website: http://www.sdtools.freeserve.co.uk
Directors: S. Dunster (Fin), S. Dunster (MD)
Immediate Holding Company: S D TOOLING (UK) LIMITED
Registration no: 03016692 **Date established:** 1995
No.of Employees: 1 - 10 **Product Groups:** 46

Date of Accounts	Oct 11	Oct 10	Oct 08
Working Capital	-4	-5	-0
Fixed Assets	10	6	4
Current Assets	145	123	93

Safety Lighting Systems

49 Cutlers Road South Woodham Ferrers, Chelmsford, CM3 5WA
Tel: 01245-325000 **Fax:** 01245- 327177
E-mail: sales@safetylighting.co.uk
Website: http://www.safetylighting.co.uk
Directors: S. Whiteley (Fin)
Immediate Holding Company: ENPHOS HOLDINGS LTD
Registration no: 04751643 **Turnover:** Up to £250,000
No.of Employees: 1 - 10 **Product Groups:** 37, 39

Date of Accounts	Apr 07	Apr 06
Working Capital	-20	5
Fixed Assets	5	1
Current Assets	112	209
Current Liabilities	132	204
Total Share Capital	1	1

Scott Wilson Ltd

Alexandra Court Church Street, Great Baddow, Chelmsford, CM2 7HY
Tel: 01245-243700 **Fax:** 020-8309 2401
E-mail: gary.freeman@scottwilson.com
Website: http://www.scottwilson.com
Directors: G. Smith (Co Sec), G. Freeman (Dir), J. Johncock (Dir), M. Grindle (Dir)
Immediate Holding Company: SCOTT WILSON LTD
Registration no: 00880328 **Date established:** 1966 **Turnover:** £2m - £5m
No.of Employees: 21 - 50 **Product Groups:** 42, 54, 84

Shelfspan Shelving Systems

The Cart Lodge Mayland Hall Farm, Mayland, Chelmsford, CM3 6EA
Tel: 08450-722385 **Fax:** 08450-722386
E-mail: info@shelfspan.co.uk
Website: http://www.shelfspan.co.uk
Directors: G. Morris (Prop)
No.of Employees: 1 - 10 **Product Groups:** 26, 40, 41, 45, 66, 67

A E Simmons Ltd

9 Bilton Road, Chelmsford, CM1 2UJ
Tel: 01245-352480 **Fax:** 01245-359733
E-mail: sales@simmonsprinters.com
Website: http://www.simmonsprinters.com
Directors: A. Ritchie (Dir)
Managers: A. Watts, N. Bullen-bell (Sales Prom Mgr), A. Goward (Personnel)
Immediate Holding Company: A.E.SIMMONS LIMITED
Registration no: 00416128 **Date established:** 1946 **Turnover:** £2m - £5m
No.of Employees: 21 - 50 **Product Groups:** 23, 28

Date of Accounts	Sep 11	Sep 10	Sep 09
Working Capital	533	499	490
Fixed Assets	431	604	789
Current Assets	1m	1m	931

Smiths Environmental Products Ltd

Unit 1-2 Blackall Industrial Estate Hamberts Road, South Woodham Ferrers, Chelmsford, CM3 5UW
Tel: 01245-324900 **Fax:** 01245-324422
E-mail: info@smiths-env.com
Website: http://www.smiths-env.com
Bank(s): Barclays, Epping
Directors: J. Bennett (Mkt Research), J. Bennett (Mkt Research), A. Goldsmith (Admin), A. Kirton (Admin)
Managers: B. Cockran (I.T. Exec), D. Rolston (Chief Acct), R. Luxton (Sales Prom Mgr), L. Townsend (Buyer)
Immediate Holding Company: SMITH'S ENVIRONMENTAL PRODUCTS LIMITED
Registration no: 02607831 **VAT No.:** GB 594 6122 23
Date established: 1991 **Turnover:** £2m - £5m **No.of Employees:** 51 - 100
Product Groups: 37, 38, 40

Date of Accounts	Dec 11	Dec 10	Dec 09
Working Capital	1m	1m	1m
Fixed Assets	438	360	313
Current Assets	2m	2m	2m

Stacarac UK Ltd

Marine House 6-8 Industrial Estate Steeple Road, Mayland, Chelmsford, CM3 6AX
Tel: 01621-741250 **Fax:** 01621-742768
E-mail: richard@stacarac.com
Website: http://www.stacarac.com
Directors: L. Kehoe (Fin), R. Kehoe (MD)
Immediate Holding Company: STACARAC (UK) LIMITED
Registration no: 01921395 **VAT No.:** GB 415 6562 53
Date established: 1985 **No.of Employees:** 1 - 10 **Product Groups:** 26, 40, 45, 67

Date of Accounts	Mar 12	Mar 11	Mar 10
Working Capital	-17	-19	-30
Fixed Assets	31	38	26
Current Assets	151	181	169

Surface Development & Engineering Ltd

Alpha Kitchener Road, North Fambridge, Chelmsford, CM3 6NJ
Tel: 01621-744900 **Fax:** 01621-744 900
E-mail: enquiries@surfdev.co.uk
Website: http://www.surfdev.co.uk
Directors: N. Williams (Dir)
Immediate Holding Company: SURFACE DEVELOPMENT & ENGINEERING LTD
Registration no: 04085142 **Date established:** 2000
No.of Employees: 1 - 10 **Product Groups:** 44

Date of Accounts	Mar 11	Mar 10	Mar 09
Working Capital	-27	-23	23
Fixed Assets	30	23	44
Current Assets	39	87	90

Sutch & Searle Shipping

Highwood Road Writtle, Chelmsford, CM1 3PT
Tel: 01245-421770 **Fax:** 01245-422734
E-mail: enquiries@sutchandsearle.com
Website: http://www.sutchandsearle.com
Bank(s): Barclays
Directors: K. Davis (Dir), D. Ryan (Fin)
Managers: D. Totty (Tech Serv Mgr), P. Eaton (Chief Mgr)
Ultimate Holding Company: RVL HOLDINGS PLC
Immediate Holding Company: SUTCH & SEARLE SHIPPING LIMITED
Registration no: 00912551 **VAT No.:** GB 243 5369 59
Date established: 1967 **Turnover:** £2m - £5m **No.of Employees:** 11 - 20
Product Groups: 72, 74, 75, 76, 77

Date of Accounts	Mar 11	Mar 10	Mar 09
Sales Turnover	4m	5m	2m
Pre Tax Profit/Loss	-719	29	329
Working Capital	-492	613	1m
Fixed Assets	228	228	241
Current Assets	388	2m	2m
Current Liabilities	33	166	168

Thyssenkrupp Elevator UK Ltd

26a High Street Great Baddow, Chelmsford, CM2 7HQ
Tel: 01245-478048 **Fax:** 01245-478063
E-mail: barry.nash@tke-uk-thyssenkrupp.com
Website: http://www.tke-uk-thyssenkrupp.com
Managers: B. Nash (Mgr)
Immediate Holding Company: THYSSENKRUPP ELEVATOR UK LIMITED
Registration no: 00688790 **Date established:** 1961
No.of Employees: 11 - 20 **Product Groups:** 35, 39, 45

Town & Country Ltd

41 Beehive Lane, Chelmsford, CM2 9TQ
Tel: 01245-295600 **Fax:** 01245-496818
Website: http://www.kwik-fit.com
Directors: S. Watson (Dir)
Registration no: 02171521 **Date established:** 1987
No.of Employees: 1 - 10 **Product Groups:** 29, 39, 68, 85

TS Control Systems

Medway Farm Southminster Road, Althorne, Chelmsford, CM3 6EN
Tel: 01621-743123 **Fax:** 01621-743126
Website: http://www.tscontrol.co.uk
Directors: D. Philip (Prop)
Registration no: 03868775 **Date established:** 1999
No.of Employees: 1 - 10 **Product Groups:** 37, 38, 84

Wenbar Plastics

Great Hayes Business Park Lower Road, Stow Maries, Chelmsford, CM3 6SQ
Tel: 01245-322444 **Fax:** 01245-322456
E-mail: wcastle@wenbarplastics.co.uk
Website: http://www.wenbarplastics.co.uk
Directors: W. Castle (Co Sec)
Immediate Holding Company: WENBAR PLASTICS LIMITED
Registration no: 06034193 **Date established:** 2006
No.of Employees: 11 - 20 **Product Groups:** 28, 30, 42, 48

Date of Accounts	Dec 11	Dec 10	Dec 09
Working Capital	21	48	-0
Fixed Assets	386	446	477
Current Assets	771	928	613

Wilson Machinery International

Maplefield Marlpits Road, Purleigh, Chelmsford, CM3 6RB
Tel: 01245-221200
E-mail: nigelwilson1@btconnect.com
Website: http://www.wilsonmachinery.co.uk
Directors: N. Wilson (MD)
Registration no: 01137989 **VAT No.:** GB 247 4529 44
Turnover: £500,000 - £1m **No.of Employees:** 1 - 10 **Product Groups:** 46

Date of Accounts	Aug 07	Aug 06	Aug 05
Working Capital	-41	-8	-19
Fixed Assets	64	19	24
Current Assets	47	101	44
Current Liabilities	88	108	63

Ziehl Abegg Ltd

Unit 1 Lonebarn Link, Chelmsford, CM2 5AR
Tel: 01245-449010 **Fax:** 01245-449011
Website: http://www.ziehl-abegg.co.uk
Directors: L. Fish (MD)
Ultimate Holding Company: ZIEHL ABEGG AG (GERMANY)
Immediate Holding Company: ZIEHL-ABEGG UK LIMITED
Registration no: 05414030 **Date established:** 2005
Turnover: £10m - £20m **No.of Employees:** 11 - 20 **Product Groups:** 40, 66

Date of Accounts	Dec 11	Dec 10	Dec 09
Sales Turnover	12m	11m	9m
Pre Tax Profit/Loss	740	453	256
Working Capital	1m	735	1m
Fixed Assets	16	27	45
Current Assets	5m	3m	3m
Current Liabilities	581	385	207

Chigwell

Catering Investments Ltd

1 Taylors Business Park Gravel Lane, Chigwell, IG7 6DQ
Tel: 020-8501 5353 **Fax:** 020-8501 5454
E-mail: davcateng@btconnect.com
Website: http://www.cateringinvestments.com
Directors: R. Mccormack (Ptnr)
Immediate Holding Company: CATERING INVESTMENTS LIMITED
Registration no: 04507454 **Date established:** 2002
Turnover: £500,000 - £1m **No.of Employees:** 1 - 10 **Product Groups:** 20, 25, 26, 30, 32, 33, 36, 37, 38, 39, 40, 41, 42, 45, 46, 48, 49, 62, 63, 66, 67, 69, 80

Date of Accounts	Dec 09	Dec 08	Dec 07
Sales Turnover	N/A	N/A	621
Pre Tax Profit/Loss	N/A	N/A	29
Working Capital	46	68	100
Fixed Assets	7	3	4
Current Assets	336	277	284
Current Liabilities	N/A	N/A	138

Jolly Learning Ltd

Tailours 59 High Road, Chigwell, IG7 6DL
Tel: 020-8501 0405 **Fax:** 020-8500 1619
E-mail: info@jollylearning.co.uk
Website: http://www.jollylearning.co.uk
Bank(s): HSBC Bank plc
Directors: C. Jolly (Dir)
Immediate Holding Company: JOLLY LEARNING LIMITED
Registration no: 02178683 **VAT No.:** GB 466 7636 04
Date established: 1987 **Turnover:** £2m - £5m **No.of Employees:** 11 - 20
Product Groups: 28

Date of Accounts	Mar 11	Mar 10	Mar 09
Sales Turnover	3m	3m	3m
Pre Tax Profit/Loss	1m	1m	2m
Working Capital	2m	714	2m
Fixed Assets	30	29	34
Current Assets	2m	1m	3m
Current Liabilities	435	393	466

London Gate Co

Lambourne Road, Chigwell, IG7 6ET
Tel: 020-8500 2001
Directors: C. Golding (Prop)
No.of Employees: 1 - 10 **Product Groups:** 40, 52

Ken Whiffin Plumbing & Heating

248 Brocket Way, Chigwell, IG7 4LT
Tel: 07971-857516 **Fax:** 0870-762 5957
E-mail: plumberken@hotmail.com
Website: http://www.kenwhiffinplumbingandheating.co.uk
Directors: K. Whiffin (Prop)
No.of Employees: 1 - 10 **Product Groups:** 52

Clacton On Sea

Ace Catering Engineers Ltd

Unit 10 Dudley Court Jessop Close, Clacton On Sea, CO15 4LY
Tel: 01255-224004 **Fax:** 01255-225514
E-mail: info@acecateringengineers.co.uk
Website: http://www.acecateringengineers.co.uk
Directors: J. Williams (MD)
Immediate Holding Company: ACE CATERING ENGINEERS LTD
Registration no: 04842114 **Date established:** 2003
No.of Employees: 1 - 10 **Product Groups:** 20, 40, 41

Date of Accounts	Mar 12	Mar 11	Mar 10
Working Capital	112	151	162
Fixed Assets	40	34	32
Current Assets	231	321	275

Advanced Medical Products Clacton Ltd

10 Brindley Road, Clacton On Sea, CO15 4XL
Tel: 01255-421634 **Fax:** 01255-432149
E-mail: advancedmed@btconnect.com
Directors: P. Garner (Fin), J. Denman (Dir), P. Garner (Co Sec)
Managers: S. Moule (Chief Mgr)
Ultimate Holding Company: BUNZL PUBLIC LIMITED COMPANY
Immediate Holding Company: ADVANCED MEDICAL PRODUCTS (CLACTON) LIMITED
Registration no: 05838394 **Date established:** 2006
No.of Employees: 11 - 20 **Product Groups:** 38, 67

Date of Accounts	Dec 10	Dec 09	Dec 08
Sales Turnover	1m	1m	1m
Pre Tax Profit/Loss	-201	-201	-36
Working Capital	-441	-299	-154
Fixed Assets	3	6	5
Current Assets	313	460	312
Current Liabilities	30	41	52

Apex Publishing Ltd
PO Box 7086, Clacton On Sea, CO15 5WN
Tel: 01255-428500 **Fax:** 0870-046 6536
E-mail: chris@apexpublishing.co.uk
Website: http://www.apexpublishing.co.uk
Directors: C. Martin (Dir)
Immediate Holding Company: APEX PUBLISHING LTD
Registration no: 04441614 **Date established:** 2002
No.of Employees: 1 - 10 **Product Groups:** 28

Date of Accounts	May 11	May 10	May 09
Working Capital	-6	-9	-18
Fixed Assets	28	31	38
Current Assets	1	1	1

Assemtech Europe Ltd
Ricebridge Industrial Estate Station Road, Thorpe-Le-Soken, Clacton On Sea, CO16 0HL
Tel: 01255-862236 **Fax:** 01255-862014
E-mail: sales@assemtech.co.uk
Website: http://www.assemtech.co.uk
Bank(s): Lloyds TSB Bank plc
Managers: A. Wood (Sales Off Mgr)
Immediate Holding Company: ASSEMTECH EUROPE LIMITED
Registration no: 02407546 **VAT No.:** GB 549 9266 86
Date established: 1989 **Turnover:** £1m - £2m **No.of Employees:** 21 - 50
Product Groups: 29, 37, 38

Date of Accounts	Jul 11	Jul 10	Jul 09
Working Capital	401	289	275
Fixed Assets	73	56	66
Current Assets	790	700	695
Current Liabilities	66	N/A	N/A

Booker Cash & Carry Ltd
Bull Hill Road, Clacton On Sea, CO15 4AU
Tel: 01255-421123 **Fax:** 01255-428711
E-mail: andrewdavies@booker.co.uk
Website: http://www.booker.co.uk
Managers: A. Davies (Mgr)
Ultimate Holding Company: BOOKER GROUP PLC
Immediate Holding Company: BOOKER CASH & CARRY LIMITED
Registration no: 05355306 **Date established:** 2005
No.of Employees: 11 - 20 **Product Groups:** 61

Bowens International Ltd
355 Old Road, Clacton On Sea, CO15 3RH
Tel: 01255-422807 **Fax:** 01255-475503
E-mail: info@bowens.co.uk
Website: http://www.bowensinternational.co.uk
Bank(s): Lloyds TSB Bank plc
Directors: L. Lankester (Fin), L. Smith (Fin)
Managers: S. Hoadley (Purch Mgr)
Ultimate Holding Company: RUBICON PARTNERS INDUSTRIES LLP
Immediate Holding Company: BOWENS INTERNATIONAL LIMITED
Registration no: 00754171 **VAT No.:** GB 362 0233 93
Date established: 1963 **Turnover:** £10m - £20m
No.of Employees: 51 - 100 **Product Groups:** 38

Date of Accounts	Dec 11	Dec 10	Dec 09
Sales Turnover	10m	11m	10m
Pre Tax Profit/Loss	830	208	606
Working Capital	10m	9m	9m
Fixed Assets	1m	949	980
Current Assets	13m	12m	11m
Current Liabilities	366	575	691

Bruntons Propellers Ltd
Oakwood Business Park Stephenson Road West, Clacton On Sea, CO15 4TL
Tel: 01255-420005 **Fax:** 01255-427775
E-mail: sales@bruntons-propellers.com
Website: http://www.bruntons-propellers.com
Directors: A. Miles (MD), W. Cowley (Co Sec)
Ultimate Holding Company: LANGHAM INDUSTRIES LIMITED
Immediate Holding Company: BRUNTON'S PROPELLERS LIMITED
Registration no: 00156484 **VAT No.:** 102 2770 18 **Date established:** 2019
Turnover: £2m - £5m **No.of Employees:** 1 - 10 **Product Groups:** 39, 48

Date of Accounts	Dec 11	Dec 10	Dec 09
Sales Turnover	1m	2m	2m
Pre Tax Profit/Loss	-3	14	55
Working Capital	128	127	136
Fixed Assets	35	34	26
Current Assets	1m	676	1m
Current Liabilities	197	255	515

Castle Services
Acorn House Alpha Road, St Osyth, Clacton On Sea, CO16 8NP
Tel: 01255-822103 **Fax:** 01255-822103
E-mail: sandra@castlesecurity.com
Website: http://www.castlesecurity.com
Directors: S. Jordan (Prop)
Date established: 1998 **No.of Employees:** 1 - 10 **Product Groups:** 26, 35

Dalau Ltd
Ford Road, Clacton On Sea, CO15 3DZ
Tel: 01255-220220 **Fax:** 01255-221122
E-mail: sales@dalau.com
Website: http://www.dalau.com
Bank(s): Barclays
Directors: D. Sage (MD), G. Jaggs (Fin)
Immediate Holding Company: DALAU LIMITED
Registration no: 00609539 **VAT No.:** GB 312 5469 74
Date established: 1958 **Turnover:** £5m - £10m
No.of Employees: 51 - 100 **Product Groups:** 23, 30, 31, 35, 48

Date of Accounts	Mar 11	Mar 10	Mar 09
Sales Turnover	8m	5m	N/A
Pre Tax Profit/Loss	728	-265	183
Working Capital	2m	1m	1m
Fixed Assets	589	658	830
Current Assets	3m	2m	3m
Current Liabilities	254	286	266

Dyvig Metalwork Design
The Forge Botany Lane, Weeley, Clacton On Sea, CO16 9EG
Tel: 01255-831199 **Fax:** 01255-831199
E-mail: shop@dyvig.co.uk
Website: http://www.dyvig.co.uk
Directors: M. Dyvig (Prop)
Date established: 1991 **No.of Employees:** 1 - 10 **Product Groups:** 26, 35

Easifix
7 Oakwood Business Park Stephenson Road West, Clacton On Sea, CO15 4TL
Tel: 08456-018291 **Fax:** 01255-436852
E-mail: info@easifix.co.uk
Website: http://www.easifix.co.uk
Directors: W. Huckle (MD)
Immediate Holding Company: PRESCRIPTION2YOU (DOVERCOURT) LIMITED
Registration no: 02248080 **VAT No.:** GB 512 3842 72
Date established: 2011 **Turnover:** Up to £250,000
No.of Employees: 1 - 10 **Product Groups:** 30, 33, 66

East Anglian Food Ingredients Ltd
Wade Road, Clacton On Sea, CO15 4LT
Tel: 01255-433124 **Fax:** 01255-220091
E-mail: steve@eafi.co.uk
Website: http://www.eafi.co.uk
Directors: V. Wallace (Fin), S. Clemenson (MD), C. Church (Sales)
Immediate Holding Company: SEBENCO LIMITED
Registration no: 01408267 **Date established:** 1979 **Turnover:** £5m - £10m
No.of Employees: 21 - 50 **Product Groups:** 02, 20, 31, 62, 66

Date of Accounts	Jan 10	Jan 09	Jan 08
Working Capital	2m	2m	2m
Fixed Assets	1m	1m	1m
Current Assets	2m	3m	2m

East Essex Toolmakers
4 Telford Road, Clacton On Sea, CO15 4LP
Tel: 01255-425555 **Fax:** 01255-475222
Directors: J. Spooner (Ptnr)
Immediate Holding Company: EAST ESSEX TOOLMAKERS LIMITED
Registration no: 07973025 **Date established:** 2012
No.of Employees: 1 - 10 **Product Groups:** 36

Holland UK Ltd
12 Conway Units Stephenson Road, Clacton On Sea, CO15 4XA
Tel: 01255-431773 **Fax:** 01255-221393
E-mail: david@hollanduk.co.uk
Website: http://www.hollanduk.co.uk
Directors: G. Nursey (MD), P. Wood (Fin)
Immediate Holding Company: HOLLAND U.K. LIMITED
Registration no: 01555905 **VAT No.:** GB 360 2668 60
Date established: 1981 **Turnover:** £500,000 - £1m
No.of Employees: 1 - 10 **Product Groups:** 20, 54, 62

Date of Accounts	Mar 12	Feb 11	Feb 10
Working Capital	34	38	46
Fixed Assets	20	19	30
Current Assets	95	76	98

International Marketing & Distrubution
11c Stephenson Road, Clacton On Sea, CO15 4XA
Tel: 01255-479864 **Fax:** 01255-474705
E-mail: markcoulter@indfulfilment.com
Website: http://www.indfulfilment.com
Managers: M. Coulter (Ops Mgr)
Registration no: 06672704 **Date established:** 2008
No.of Employees: 11 - 20 **Product Groups:** 30, 49, 61, 66, 81

Date of Accounts	Dec 07	Dec 06	Dec 05
Working Capital	-15	-20	-33
Fixed Assets	40	46	1
Current Assets	258	230	36
Current Liabilities	273	250	69

Lennox Pet Supplies
Telford Road, Clacton On Sea, CO15 4LP
Tel: 01255-429973 **Fax:** 01255-429533
E-mail: lennoxpets@aol.com
Website: http://www.lennoxrawhide.com
Managers: R. Poly (Chief Mgr)
Immediate Holding Company: CAN-CAN COVERS LTD
Date established: 2001 **No.of Employees:** 1 - 10 **Product Groups:** 20, 62

Mantair
13 Baker Close Oakwood Business Park Stephenson Road West, Clacton On Sea, CO15 4TL
Tel: 01255-476376 **Fax:** 01255-476817
E-mail: enquiries@mantair.com
Website: http://www.mantair.com
Directors: A. Skilling (MD)
Immediate Holding Company: MANTAIR LTD
Registration no: 03658897 **Date established:** 1998
No.of Employees: 1 - 10 **Product Groups:** 30, 33, 42, 51, 54

Date of Accounts	Oct 11	Oct 10	Oct 09
Working Capital	-45	-6	-6
Fixed Assets	66	69	34
Current Assets	100	95	105

Nantmor Blinds
1 Brindley Road, Clacton On Sea, CO15 4XL
Tel: 01255-475044 **Fax:** 01255-434242
E-mail: info@nantmorblinds.com
Website: http://www.nantmorblinds.com
Directors: T. Feek (Snr Part)
Managers: A. Finch (Tech Serv Mgr)
Registration no: 01827319 **Date established:** 1982
Turnover: £500,000 - £1m **No.of Employees:** 21 - 50
Product Groups: 24, 25, 30, 33, 63, 66

Nico Manufacturing Co. Ltd
109 Oxford Road, Clacton On Sea, CO15 3TJ
Tel: 01255-422333 **Fax:** 01255-432909
E-mail: sales@nico.co.uk
Website: http://www.nico.co.uk
Bank(s): RBS, Colmore Row, Birmingham
Directors: G. Hagger (Fin), G. Hagger (Fin)
Managers: T. Warren (Purch Mgr), S. Dalton (Personnel), G. Pateman (Sales Prom Mgr)
Ultimate Holding Company: JBS INDUSTRIES LIMITED
Immediate Holding Company: NICO MANUFACTURING LIMITED
Registration no: 02826971 **Date established:** 1993 **Turnover:** £5m - £10m
No.of Employees: 51 - 100 **Product Groups:** 30, 35, 36, 49

Date of Accounts	Nov 08	Nov 07	Feb 11
Sales Turnover	5m	6m	7m
Pre Tax Profit/Loss	-99	87	572
Working Capital	826	1m	926
Fixed Assets	1m	1m	1m
Current Assets	2m	2m	2m
Current Liabilities	164	379	193

Pickering Electronics Ltd
Stephenson Road, Clacton On Sea, CO15 4NL
Tel: 01255-428141 **Fax:** 01255-475058
E-mail: graham.dale@pickeringrelay.com
Website: http://www.pickeringrelay.com
Directors: G. Dale (Dir)
Managers: J. Boggas, J. Powel (Sales & Mktg Mg), J. Benson (Purch Mgr)
Immediate Holding Company: PICKERING ELECTRONICS LIMITED
Registration no: 00857509 **VAT No.:** GB 103 5366 04
Date established: 1965 **No.of Employees:** 101 - 250 **Product Groups:** 37

Date of Accounts	Jun 11	Jun 10	Jun 09
Working Capital	2m	1m	1m
Fixed Assets	363	392	407
Current Assets	3m	2m	1m

Prestige Welding & Powder Coating Ltd
3 Spring Valley Units Stephenson Road, Clacton On Sea, CO15 4XA
Tel: 01255-225273
E-mail: info@prestigeweld.co.uk
Website: http://www.prestigeweld.co.uk
Directors: K. Reid (MD)
Immediate Holding Company: PRESTIGE WELDING AND POWDER COATING LTD
Registration no: 06447533 **Date established:** 2007
No.of Employees: 1 - 10 **Product Groups:** 35, 66, 84

Date of Accounts	Nov 11	Nov 10	Nov 09
Working Capital	50	27	10
Fixed Assets	45	41	39
Current Assets	121	84	64

Protection Security Systems
5 Conway Units Stephenson Road, Clacton On Sea, CO15 4XA
Tel: 01255-221924 **Fax:** 01255-221924
E-mail: info@protectionsecuritysystems.com
Website: http://www.protectionsecuritysystems.com
Directors: J. Myers (Prop)
No.of Employees: 1 - 10 **Product Groups:** 35, 37, 40, 52, 67

Sabreglaze Window Repairs
7 Oakwood Business Park Stephenson Road West, Clacton On Sea, CO15 4TL
Tel: 01255-436852 **Fax:** 01255-436852
E-mail: w.huckle@easifix.co.uk
Website: http://www.sabresharp.co.uk
Directors: W. Huckle (Fin), R. Pearson (MD)
Immediate Holding Company: SABREGLAZE LIMITED
Registration no: 02661779 **VAT No.:** GB 594 8124 09
Date established: 1991 **Turnover:** Up to £250,000
No.of Employees: 1 - 10 **Product Groups:** 52

Date of Accounts	Apr 10	Apr 09	Apr 07
Sales Turnover	N/A	N/A	23
Pre Tax Profit/Loss	-0	-0	1
Working Capital	-1	-1	-2
Current Assets	N/A	1	10
Current Liabilities	2	2	2

Town & Country Gates
12b Ford Road, Clacton On Sea, CO15 3DS
Tel: 01255-224007
Directors: D. Merlini (Prop)
No.of Employees: 1 - 10 **Product Groups:** 26, 35

Zeus Products
Unit D1 Seaden Court, Clacton On Sea, CO15 4XN
Tel: 01255-220996 **Fax:** 01255-429991
E-mail: zeusproducts@uko2.co.uk
Directors: S. Fearis (Ptnr)
Date established: 1984 **No.of Employees:** 1 - 10 **Product Groups:** 36

Colchester

24-7 Boxes & Packaging
St Ives Road Peldon, Colchester, CO5 7QD
Tel: 01206-736187
E-mail: sales@247boxes.co.uk
Website: http://www.247boxes.co.uk
Directors: S. Jeffrey (Prop)
Registration no: 04591584 **Date established:** 2002
Turnover: £500,000 - £1m **No.of Employees:** 1 - 10 **Product Groups:** 25

Adhere Industrial Tapes Ltd
Unit 1 Whitehall Road Whitehall Industrial Estate, Colchester, CO2 8WA
Tel: 01206-871999
E-mail: sales@adhere.co.uk
Website: http://www.adhere.co.uk
Directors: A. Shepherd (Dir)
Managers: T. Woodard (Chief Acct)
Immediate Holding Company: ADHERE INDUSTRIAL TAPES LIMITED
Registration no: 04015255 **Date established:** 2000 **Turnover:** £1m - £2m
No.of Employees: 11 - 20 **Product Groups:** 27, 30

Date of Accounts	Apr 11	Apr 10	Apr 09
Working Capital	-29	430	416
Fixed Assets	596	661	707
Current Assets	1m	1m	1m

Albea UK Ltd
De Novo House Newcomen Way, Colchester, CO4 9AE
Tel: 01206-753400 **Fax:** 01206-844002
E-mail: kaye.stevens@betts-uk.com
Website: http://www.betts-group.com
Directors: A. Spears (Co Sec)
Managers: I. McDonnell (Fin Mgr), R. Mackay (Personnel)
Ultimate Holding Company: SUN CAPITAL PARTNERS V LP (CAYMAN ISLANDS)
Immediate Holding Company: ALBEA UK LIMITED
Registration no: 00061652 **Date established:** 1999
Turnover: £20m - £50m **No.of Employees:** 101 - 250 **Product Groups:** 30

Date of Accounts	Dec 11	Dec 10	Mar 10
Sales Turnover	36m	24m	35m
Pre Tax Profit/Loss	807	307	295
Working Capital	17m	19m	18m
Fixed Assets	9m	5m	6m
Current Assets	37m	37m	27m
Current Liabilities	4m	3m	2m

Alberta Springs
Unit 17 Notley Enterprise Park Raydon Road, Great Wenham, Colchester, CO7 6QD
Tel: 01473-311783
E-mail: sales@albertasprings.co.uk
Website: http://www.albertasprings.co.uk
Directors: G. Jennings (Prop)
Date established: 1996 **No.of Employees:** 1 - 10 **Product Groups:** 35

Albion Valve Company Ltd
Bouchiers Grange Warehouse Markshall Estate, Coggeshall, Colchester, CO6 1TE
Tel: 01708-523715 **Fax:** 01376-562530
Directors: B. Riordan (Dir), A. Riordan (Dir)
Immediate Holding Company: ALBION VALVE COMPANY LIMITED
Registration no: 03161020 **VAT No.:** GB 342 2927 64
Date established: 1996 **No.of Employees:** 1 - 10 **Product Groups:** 66

Date of Accounts	Mar 08	Mar 07	Mar 06
Working Capital	12	30	33
Fixed Assets	9	11	18
Current Assets	59	74	89
Current Liabilities	47	45	55

Almag Components Ltd
32 Church Street Coggeshall, Colchester, CO6 1TX
Tel: 01376-563264 **Fax:** 01376-563143
E-mail: almag@btconnect.com
Directors: R. Ryder (Fin), J. Ryder (MD)
Immediate Holding Company: ALMAG COMPONENTS LTD
Registration no: 04999567 **VAT No.:** GB 434 7375 39
Date established: 2003 **Turnover:** £250,000 - £500,000
No.of Employees: 1 - 10 **Product Groups:** 37

Date of Accounts	Dec 11	Dec 10	Dec 09
Working Capital	204	192	136
Fixed Assets	10	12	5
Current Assets	276	277	308

Alpha Finishing Supplies Ltd
Unit C4 Cowdray Centre Cowdray Avenue, Colchester, CO1 1BN
Tel: 01206-760500 **Fax:** 01206-767313
E-mail: alpha.finishing@btconnect.com
Directors: G. Eastaugh (Dir), A. Eastaugh (Fin)
Immediate Holding Company: ALPHA FINISHING SUPPLIES LIMITED
Registration no: 02723441 **Date established:** 1992
Turnover: £250,000 - £500,000 **No.of Employees:** 1 - 10
Product Groups: 33

Date of Accounts	Jul 10	Jul 09	Jul 08
Working Capital	15	24	45
Fixed Assets	4	5	7
Current Assets	99	109	118

Alpha Lift Engineering Services Ltd
Honeylands Farm Elm Lane, Marks Tey, Colchester, CO6 1HU
Tel: 01206-211160 **Fax:** 0871-714 3992
E-mail: office@alphalift.co.uk
Website: http://www.alphalift.co.uk
Managers: Y. Newton (Sales Admin)
Immediate Holding Company: ALPHA LIFT ENGINEERING SERVICES LIMITED
Registration no: 04573634 **Date established:** 2002
Turnover: £20m - £50m **No.of Employees:** 1 - 10 **Product Groups:** 35, 39, 45

Date of Accounts	Dec 11	Dec 10	Dec 09
Sales Turnover	263	223	222
Pre Tax Profit/Loss	62	90	89
Working Capital	32	34	22
Fixed Assets	9	10	13
Current Assets	73	69	57
Current Liabilities	26	32	29

Alstons Upholstery Ltd
Albro Works Gosbecks Road, Colchester, CO2 9JU
Tel: 01206-765343 **Fax:** 01206-763401
E-mail: david.alston@alstons.co.uk
Website: http://www.alstons.co.uk
Bank(s): Lloyds TSB Bank plc
Directors: D. Alston (MD), T. Cramphorn (Fin), I. Bickers (Co Sec), A. Kennaugh (Sales)
Managers: S. Johnson (Personnel), H. Alston, B. Reeve, N. Hall (Tech Serv Mgr)
Immediate Holding Company: ALSTONS (UPHOLSTERY) LIMITED
Registration no: 00491171 **Date established:** 1951
Turnover: £20m - £50m **No.of Employees:** 101 - 250 **Product Groups:** 26

Date of Accounts	Mar 11	Mar 10	Mar 09
Sales Turnover	22m	23m	N/A
Pre Tax Profit/Loss	1m	1m	255
Working Capital	5m	4m	5m
Fixed Assets	3m	4m	4m
Current Assets	9m	8m	8m
Current Liabilities	2m	2m	2m

Anglian Electrics
60-62 Barrack Street, Colchester, CO1 2LS
Tel: 01206-791894 **Fax:** 01206-794944
E-mail: sales@anglianelectrics.co.uk
Website: http://www.anglianelectrics.co.uk
Directors: T. Noy (Ptnr)
Immediate Holding Company: ANGLIAN ELECTRICS LIMITED
Registration no: 06047842 **VAT No.:** GB 341 7193 64
Date established: 2007 **Turnover:** £1m - £2m **No.of Employees:** 1 - 10
Product Groups: 52, 63

Aquatech - Pressmain Ltd
A G M House London Road, Copford, Colchester, CO6 1GT
Tel: 01206-215121
Website: http://www.aquatechpressmain.co.uk
Directors: M. Taylor (MD)
Ultimate Holding Company: AQUATRONIC GROUP MANAGEMENT PLC
Immediate Holding Company: AQUATECH PRESSMAIN LIMITED
Registration no: 01677940 **Date established:** 1982 **Turnover:** £5m - £10m
No.of Employees: 21 - 50 **Product Groups:** 35, 38

Date of Accounts	Sep 11	Sep 10	Sep 09
Sales Turnover	5m	5m	5m
Pre Tax Profit/Loss	546	450	457
Working Capital	1m	1m	877
Fixed Assets	95	75	104
Current Assets	3m	3m	2m
Current Liabilities	267	274	253

Bartech Marine Engineering
11-12 Rushmere Close West Mersea, Colchester, CO5 8QQ
Tel: 01206-384677 **Fax:** 01206-385329
E-mail: info@bartechmarine.com
Website: http://www.bartechmarine.com
Directors: G. Barnett (MD), J. Barnett (Fin)
Registration no: 02154196 **Turnover:** £500,000 - £1m
No.of Employees: 11 - 20 **Product Groups:** 37, 40, 48, 52, 68, 84

Bentley Fire Shop
Unit 4 Plough Road Centre Plough Road, Great Bentley, Colchester, CO7 8LG
Tel: 01206-251118 **Fax:** 01206-252145
E-mail: sales@bentleyfireshop.co.uk
Website: http://www.bentleyfireshop.co.uk
Directors: G. Bennett (Ptnr), S. Bennett (Ptnr)
Immediate Holding Company: BENTLEY FIRE SHOP LIMITED
Registration no: 05814293 **Date established:** 2006
No.of Employees: 11 - 20 **Product Groups:** 46, 48

Blossom & Berry
Spindrift Way Wivenhoe, Colchester, CO7 9GW
Tel: 07958-626933
E-mail: info@blossomandberry.com
Website: http://www.blossomandberry.com
Product Groups: 24, 26, 38, 61

Bowling Garrard Electrical Ltd
1a Crowhurst Road, Colchester, CO3 3JN
Tel: 01206-542285 **Fax:** 01206-578832
E-mail: sales@bowlinggarrard.co.uk
Website: http://www.bowlinggarrard.co.uk
Directors: A. Stokes (Fin), P. Stokes (MD)
Immediate Holding Company: BOWLING GARRARD ELECTRICAL LIMITED
Registration no: 01004946 **Date established:** 1971 **Turnover:** £1m - £2m
No.of Employees: 1 - 10 **Product Groups:** 52

Date of Accounts	Feb 12	Feb 11	Feb 10
Working Capital	23	134	166
Fixed Assets	76	68	91
Current Assets	440	517	499

Brantham Electronics
The Gattinetts Unit 2b Hadleigh Road, East Bergholt, Colchester, CO7 6QT
Tel: 01206-298951
E-mail: sales@branthamelectronics.co.uk
Website: http://www.branthamelectronics.co.uk
Directors: P. Oliver (Prop)
Immediate Holding Company: EAST BERGHOLT OUT OF SCHOOL CLUB
Registration no: 05824615 **VAT No.:** GB 529 4051 49
Date established: 2012 **Turnover:** Up to £250,000
No.of Employees: 1 - 10 **Product Groups:** 37, 44, 81

Brochure Holders International Ltd
Victor Unit Earls Colne Business Park, Earls Colne, Colchester, CO6 2NS
Tel: 01787-220700 **Fax:** 01787-220701
E-mail: tracy.partridge@brochureholders.co.uk
Website: http://www.brochureholders.com
Directors: T. Partridge (Dir)
Immediate Holding Company: BROCHURE HOLDERS INTERNATIONAL LIMITED
Registration no: 02225635 **VAT No.:** GB 496 6028 11
Date established: 1988 **Turnover:** £2m - £5m **No.of Employees:** 1 - 10
Product Groups: 49, 81

Date of Accounts	Dec 11	Dec 10	Dec 09
Working Capital	3m	2m	2m
Fixed Assets	112	68	95
Current Assets	4m	4m	3m

C A Blackwell Construction Ltd
Coggeshall Road Earls Colne, Colchester, CO62 2JX
Tel: 01787-223131 **Fax:** 01787-224391
E-mail: steve.clarke@cablackwell.co.uk
Website: http://www.cablackwell.co.uk
Directors: K. Gooday (Fin), S. Clarke (Dir)
Ultimate Holding Company: C.A. BLACKWELL GROUP LIMITED
Immediate Holding Company: BLACKWELL MASTERTON INTERNATIONAL LTD
Registration no: 01260837 **VAT No.:** GB 102 0443 43
Date established: 1976 **Turnover:** £50m - £75m **No.of Employees:** 1 - 10
Product Groups: 51

R J Cannon Ltd
Maldon Road Tiptree, Colchester, CO5 0PH
Tel: 01621-815396 **Fax:** 01621-817939
E-mail: info@rjcannon.co.uk
Directors: H. Cannon (Fin), R. Cannon (MD)
Immediate Holding Company: R.J. CANNON CRANE AND PLANT HIRE LIMITED
Registration no: 03978074 **Date established:** 2000
Turnover: £250,000 - £500,000 **No.of Employees:** 1 - 10
Product Groups: 41

Date of Accounts	Apr 11	Apr 10	Apr 09
Sales Turnover	N/A	305	360
Pre Tax Profit/Loss	N/A	76	110
Working Capital	568	527	666
Fixed Assets	480	488	294
Current Assets	603	571	708
Current Liabilities	N/A	39	38

Cautrac Used Construction Machinery Ltd
Domus The Causeway, Great Horkesley, Colchester, CO6 4EJ
Tel: 01206-273881 **Fax:** 01206-273120
E-mail: sales@cautrac.com
Website: http://www.cautrac.com
Directors: J. Hillman (MD)
Immediate Holding Company: TATE COMPLIANCE LIMITED
Date established: 2005 **No.of Employees:** 11 - 20 **Product Groups:** 29, 36, 40, 41, 42, 45, 48, 61, 67, 83, 84

Date of Accounts	Oct 11	Oct 10	Oct 09
Working Capital	-0	-7	-4
Fixed Assets	38	45	56
Current Assets	54	48	39

Chandos Records
Chandos House 1 Commerce Park Commerce Way, Colchester, CO2 8HX
Tel: 01206-225200 **Fax:** 01206-225201
E-mail: enquiries@chandos.net
Website: http://www.chandos.net
Directors: R. Couzens (MD)
Immediate Holding Company: CHANDOS MUSIC LIMITED
Registration no: 00860192 **Date established:** 1965
No.of Employees: 11 - 20 **Product Groups:** 61

Date of Accounts	Mar 12	Mar 11	Mar 10
Working Capital	277	295	274
Current Assets	279	337	359

Chris Loader Welding Supplies
Unit 14 Peartree Business Centre Peartree Road, Stanway, Colchester, CO3 0JN
Tel: 01206-548424 **Fax:** 01206-546141
Directors: D. Loader (Prop)
Registration no: 01615702 **Date established:** 1982
No.of Employees: 1 - 10 **Product Groups:** 46

Coastdigital
Beacon End Courtyard London Road, Stanway, Colchester, CO3 0NU
Tel: 01206-369696 **Fax:** 01206-369697
E-mail: info@coastdigital.co.uk
Website: http://www.coastdigital.co.uk
Directors: M. Frost (Fin), J. Frost (MD)
Managers: A. Jones (Mktg Serv Mgr), M. Jackson (Sales Admin)
Immediate Holding Company: COAST DIGITAL LIMITED
Registration no: 04432211 **Date established:** 2002 **Turnover:** £2m - £5m
No.of Employees: 21 - 50 **Product Groups:** 81, 84

Date of Accounts	Apr 12	Apr 11	Apr 10
Working Capital	272	361	317
Fixed Assets	22	30	29
Current Assets	584	1m	1m

Codeway Ltd
13 Telford Way Severalls Industrial Park, Colchester, CO4 9QP
Tel: 01206-751300 **Fax:** 01206-756705
E-mail: ian.russell@codeway.com
Website: http://www.codeway.com
Bank(s): National Westminster Bank Plc
Directors: J. Russell (MD), M. Russell (Fin)
Immediate Holding Company: CODEWAY LIMITED
Registration no: 01713564 **VAT No.:** GB 386 7792 81
Date established: 1983 **Turnover:** £2m - £5m **No.of Employees:** 21 - 50
Product Groups: 28, 44, 67

Date of Accounts	Apr 12	Apr 11	Apr 10
Sales Turnover	4m	3m	3m
Pre Tax Profit/Loss	97	-36	-16
Working Capital	905	910	1m
Fixed Assets	316	311	312
Current Assets	1m	1m	1m
Current Liabilities	143	116	111

Colchester Engineering Systems
Unit 5 Chancers Farm Fossetts Lane, Fordham, Colchester, CO6 3NY
Tel: 01206-240788 **Fax:** 01206-240099
E-mail: tfilby@bowcott.com
Website: http://www.colchesterengineering.com
Directors: J. Jephcott (Dir)
Immediate Holding Company: COLCHESTER ENGINEERING SYSTEMS LIMITED
Registration no: 05946869 **VAT No.:** GB 638 041254
Date established: 2006 **Turnover:** £500,000 - £1m
No.of Employees: 1 - 10 **Product Groups:** 40

Colchester English Study Centre Ltd
19 Lexden Road, Colchester, CO3 3PW
Tel: 01206-544422 **Fax:** 01206-761849
E-mail: info@cesc.co.uk
Website: http://www.cesc.co.uk
Bank(s): Coutts & Co.
Directors: S. Greatoren (Head)
Managers: J. Dunn (Personnel)
Immediate Holding Company: LEXDEN CENTRE(OXFORD)LIMITED
Registration no: 00955201 **VAT No.:** GB 102 9180 04
Date established: 1969 **Turnover:** £1m - £2m **No.of Employees:** 21 - 50
Product Groups: 86

Date of Accounts	Dec 11	Dec 10	Dec 09
Working Capital	143	237	397
Fixed Assets	873	848	832
Current Assets	686	821	1m

Colchester Fuel Injection Ltd
Haven Road, Colchester, CO2 8HT
Tel: 01206-862049 **Fax:** 01206-861771
E-mail: paul.goldsmith@colfuel.co.uk
Website: http://www.colfuel.co.uk
Bank(s): HSBC Bank plc
Managers: P. Goldsmith (Mgr)
Immediate Holding Company: COLCHESTER FUEL INJECTION LIMITED
Registration no: 01272093 **Date established:** 1976 **Turnover:** £2m - £5m
No.of Employees: 21 - 50 **Product Groups:** 48

Date of Accounts	Nov 11	Nov 10	Nov 09
Working Capital	548	579	454
Fixed Assets	279	220	310
Current Assets	1m	1m	1m

Colchester Motor Factors
3a Hawkins Road, Colchester, CO2 8JY
Tel: 01206-799503 **Fax:** 01206-790915
Managers: J. Everett (Mgr)
VAT No.: GB 386 7343 13 **Turnover:** £500,000 - £1m
No.of Employees: 1 - 10 **Product Groups:** 67

Colchester Rewind & Repairs Ltd
Moss Road Stanway, Colchester, CO3 0LE
Tel: 01206-768886 **Fax:** 01206-768915
E-mail: sales@colchesterrewinds.co.uk
Website: http://www.colchesterrewinds.co.uk
Bank(s): Barclays
Directors: D. Bond (MD)
Ultimate Holding Company: COLCHESTER REWINDS AND REPAIRS LIMITED
Immediate Holding Company: COLCHESTER REWINDS PLANT AND ENGINEERING LIMITED
Registration no: 01515748 **VAT No.:** GB 360 2131 06
Date established: 1980 **Turnover:** £250,000 - £500,000
No.of Employees: 11 - 20 **Product Groups:** 52

Date of Accounts	Mar 12	Mar 11	Mar 10
Sales Turnover	384	296	327
Pre Tax Profit/Loss	32	12	-34

see next page

Colchester Rewind & Repairs Ltd - Cont'd

Working Capital	143	118	116
Fixed Assets	55	36	22
Current Assets	245	215	204
Current Liabilities	23	15	18

W H Collier Ltd

Brick Works Church Lane, Marks Tey, Colchester, CO6 1LN
Tel: 01206-210301 **Fax:** 01206-212540
E-mail: maurice@thebrickbusiness.com
Website: http://www.whcollier.co.uk
Directors: M. Page (MD)
Immediate Holding Company: W.H.COLLIER LIMITED
Registration no: 00706704 **Date established:** 1961
Turnover: £250,000 - £500,000 **No.of Employees:** 1 - 10
Product Groups: 33, 66

Date of Accounts	Dec 11	Dec 10	Dec 09
Working Capital	158	157	162
Fixed Assets	23	28	34
Current Assets	229	208	215

Company Packaging Ltd

Unit 14 Riverside Business Park Station Road, Earls Colne, Colchester, CO6 2ER
Tel: 01787-224969 **Fax:** 01787-224273
Directors: A. Turner (Dir)
Immediate Holding Company: COMPANY PACKAGING LIMITED
Registration no: 04114028 **Date established:** 2000
No.of Employees: 1 - 10 **Product Groups:** 38, 42

Date of Accounts	Jan 11	Jan 10	Jan 09
Working Capital	-9	-7	-9
Fixed Assets	13	13	18
Current Assets	159	129	107

Concurrent Technologies plc

Gilberd Court Newcomen Way, Severalls Industrial Park, Colchester, CO4 9WN
Tel: 01206-752626 **Fax:** 01206-751116
E-mail: info@cct.co.uk
Website: http://www.cct.co.uk
Directors: G. Fawcett (MD)
Immediate Holding Company: CONCURRENT TECHNOLOGIES PLC
Registration no: 01919979 **Date established:** 1985
Turnover: £10m - £20m **No.of Employees:** 51 - 100 **Product Groups:** 44

Date of Accounts	Dec 11	Dec 10	Dec 09
Sales Turnover	14m	13m	13m
Pre Tax Profit/Loss	3m	2m	3m
Working Capital	8m	8m	8m
Fixed Assets	7m	5m	4m
Current Assets	10m	10m	10m
Current Liabilities	560	560	761

Cowells Small Machine Tools Ltd

Tendring Road Little Bentley, Colchester, CO7 8SH
Tel: 01206-251792 **Fax:** 01206-251792
E-mail: sales@cowells.com
Website: http://www.cowells.com
Directors: C. Childs (MD), M. Childs (Fin)
Immediate Holding Company: COWELLS SMALL MACHINE TOOLS LIMITED
Registration no: 03343890 **Date established:** 1997
No.of Employees: 1 - 10 **Product Groups:** 46

Date of Accounts	Mar 11	Mar 10	Mar 09
Working Capital	15	17	19
Current Assets	32	40	37

Cpa Europe

Eastbridge House East Street, Colchester, CO1 2TX
Tel: 01206-227688 **Fax:** 01206-227687
E-mail: thinking@cpaeurope.com
Website: http://www.cpaeurope.com
Directors: S. Alexander (MD)
Managers: B. Morling (Mktg Serv Mgr)
Registration no: 04375666 **Date established:** 2002
Turnover: £250,000 - £500,000 **No.of Employees:** 1 - 10
Product Groups: 61, 80, 81

Craftsman Welding Alloys

The Boat Yard Shipyard Estate, Brightlingsea, Colchester, CO7 0AR
Tel: 01206-303519 **Fax:** 01206-305439
E-mail: enquiries@morganmarine.com
Website: http://www.morganmarine.com
Directors: S. Morgan (Prop)
Ultimate Holding Company: L H MORGAN & SONS (MARINE) LIMITED
Immediate Holding Company: CRAFTSMAN WELDING ALLOYS LIMITED
Registration no: 01161360 **Date established:** 1974
No.of Employees: 11 - 20 **Product Groups:** 46

Date of Accounts	Oct 11	Oct 10	Oct 03
Working Capital	1	1	1
Current Assets	1	1	1

Curtis Machine Tools Ltd

Martells Pit Slough Lane Ardleigh, Colchester, CO7 7RU
Tel: 01206-230032 **Fax:** 01206-231426
E-mail: alan.wilkinson@douglascurtis.co.uk
Website: http://www.curtisgrinding.com
Bank(s): National Westminster Bank Plc
Directors: A. Wilkinson (MD)
Managers: M. Boley, N. Spurgeon
Ultimate Holding Company: DOUGLAS CURTIS MACHINE TOOLS (COLCHESTER) LIMITED
Immediate Holding Company: CURTIS MACHINE TOOLS LIMITED
Registration no: 03820802 **Date established:** 1999 **Turnover:** £1m - £2m
No.of Employees: 21 - 50 **Product Groups:** 46, 48, 85

Date of Accounts	Jul 11	Jul 10	Jul 09
Working Capital	-710	-966	-897
Fixed Assets	46	141	157
Current Assets	2m	2m	2m

D B Marine

Shipyard Estate Brightlingsea, Colchester, CO7 0AR
Tel: 01206-304391 **Fax:** 01206-304391
E-mail: info@dbmarine.co.uk
Website: http://www.dbmarine.co.uk
Directors: D. Beeston (Prop)
Immediate Holding Company: L H MORGAN & SONS (MARINE) LIMITED
Registration no: 01260235 **Date established:** 1976
No.of Employees: 1 - 10 **Product Groups:** 35, 36, 39

Date of Accounts	Oct 11	Oct 10	Oct 09
Working Capital	501	429	454
Fixed Assets	323	369	352
Current Assets	951	1m	957

D J Az Productions

9 Duffield Drive, Colchester, CO4 3YQ
Tel: 07990-626729
E-mail: djazproductions@toucansurf.com
Website: http://www.djazproductions.co.cc
Directors: A. Hobson (Prop)
Registration no: 4563634766 **Date established:** 2004
Turnover: Up to £250,000 **No.of Employees:** 1 - 10 **Product Groups:** 28, 49

Davey & Co London Ltd

1 Commerce Way, Colchester, CO2 8HR
Tel: 01206-500945 **Fax:** 01206-500949
E-mail: peter@davey.co.uk
Website: http://www.davey.co.uk
Directors: P. Tracey (MD)
Immediate Holding Company: DAVEY AND COMPANY LONDON LIMITED
Registration no: 00107693 **VAT No.:** GB 214 8015 67
Date established: 2010 **Turnover:** £1m - £2m **No.of Employees:** 1 - 10
Product Groups: 33, 36, 39

Date of Accounts	Dec 11	Dec 10	Dec 09
Working Capital	253	219	200
Fixed Assets	18	28	37
Current Assets	375	321	317

Day Impex Ltd

Station Road Earls Colne, Colchester, CO6 2ER
Tel: 01787-223232 **Fax:** 01787-224171
E-mail: info@day-impex.co.uk
Website: http://www.day-impex.co.uk
Bank(s): Lloyds TSB Bank plc
Directors: G. Berger (MD)
Immediate Holding Company: DAY-IMPEX LIMITED
Registration no: 00415552 **VAT No.:** GB 102 0500 57
Date established: 1946 **Turnover:** £2m - £5m **No.of Employees:** 21 - 50
Product Groups: 33, 38, 49, 66

Date of Accounts	Jul 11	Jul 10	Jul 09
Working Capital	458	468	483
Fixed Assets	926	882	824
Current Assets	583	577	639

Designed For Sound Ltd

61-67 Rectory Road Wivenhoe, Colchester, CO7 9ES
Tel: 01206-827171 **Fax:** 01206-826936
E-mail: info@d4s.co.uk
Website: http://www.d4s.co.uk
Bank(s): Barclays, 9 High Street
Directors: C. Dickinson (Co Sec)
Immediate Holding Company: DESIGNED FOR SOUND LIMITED
Registration no: 01313518 **VAT No.:** GB 299 7320 08
Date established: 1977 **Turnover:** £2m - £5m **No.of Employees:** 11 - 20
Product Groups: 29, 30, 33, 35, 37, 38, 39, 40, 42, 54, 67, 84

Date of Accounts	Dec 11	Dec 10	Dec 09
Working Capital	528	491	259
Fixed Assets	398	415	393
Current Assets	665	769	888

Direct Lift Co

16 Orchard Road Alresford, Colchester, CO7 8DX
Tel: 01206-827555 **Fax:** 01206-827335
E-mail: D.Embling@directlifts.co.uk
Website: http://www.directlifts.co.uk
Directors: D. Embling (Prop)
No.of Employees: 1 - 10 **Product Groups:** 35, 39, 45

Doe Sport Ltd

Unit 4 Threshelfords Business Park Inworth Road, Feering, Colchester, CO5 9SE
Tel: 01376-572555 **Fax:** 01376-572666
E-mail: sarah.swanick@doesport.co.uk
Website: http://www.doesport.co.uk
Directors: S. Swanick (MD)
Immediate Holding Company: DOE SPORT LIMITED
Registration no: 01869361 **VAT No.:** GB 418 3750 49
Date established: 1984 **Turnover:** £2m - £5m **No.of Employees:** 1 - 10
Product Groups: 49

Date of Accounts	Dec 11	Dec 10	Dec 09
Working Capital	35	105	149
Fixed Assets	515	478	505
Current Assets	490	824	818

Dominion I.T Solutions

4 Brunel Court Brunel Way Severalls Park, Severalls Industrial Park, Colchester, CO4 9FG
Tel: 01206-500016 **Fax:** 01206-752782
E-mail: info@dii.co.uk
Website: http://www.dii.co.uk
Directors: R. Brooks (Dir), S. Gregory (Co Sec)
Immediate Holding Company: DOMINION IT SOLUTIONS LIMITED
Registration no: 02993277 **Date established:** 1994
Turnover: Up to £250,000 **No.of Employees:** 1 - 10 **Product Groups:** 44, 79

Date of Accounts	Dec 10	Dec 09	Dec 08
Working Capital	-1	-2	-18
Current Assets	2	1	9

Double Three Motorcycles

Unit C12 Plough Road Business Centre, Great Bentley, Colchester, CO7 8LG
Tel: 01206-251066 **Fax:** 05602-056050
E-mail: bill@doublethreemotorcycles.com
Website: http://www.doublethreemotorcycles.co.uk
Directors: B. Warren (Prop)
No.of Employees: 1 - 10 **Product Groups:** 24, 39, 86

Dr C C Richardson - University Of Essex Health Centre

Wivenhoepark Wivenhoe Park, Colchester, CO4 3SQ
Tel: 01206-794484 **Fax:** 01206-873598
E-mail: info@wivenhoehousehotel.co.uk
Website: http://www.rowhedgesurgery.co.uk
Directors: R. Murphy (I.T. Dir), I. Crewe (Ch)
Managers: C. Riordan, C. Riordan, J. Pittis, M. Phillips, K. Mason (Purch Mgr), J. Grinter
Immediate Holding Company: UNIVERSITY OF ESSEX ENTERPRISES LIMITED
Registration no: 02533347 **Date established:** 1990
No.of Employees: 11 - 20 **Product Groups:** 86

Date of Accounts	Jul 11	Jul 10	Jul 09
Sales Turnover	4m	1m	2m
Pre Tax Profit/Loss	73	-333	-23
Working Capital	530	-350	-47
Fixed Assets	227	3	33
Current Assets	2m	549	143
Current Liabilities	242	16	98

The Drain Centre a division of Woseley UK Ltd

Unit A Axis One Severalls Industrial Park, Colchester, CO4 9QX
Tel: 01206-853853 **Fax:** 01206-855228
E-mail: mick.tucker@wolseley.co.uk
Website: http://www.capperplastics.com
Managers: M. Tucker (Mgr)
Turnover: Over £1,000m **No.of Employees:** 1 - 10 **Product Groups:** 30, 31, 36, 39, 40, 42, 48, 66

Eastcom Engineers Ltd

Unit 3a Haven Road, Colchester, CO2 8HT
Tel: 01206-794114 **Fax:** 01206-792749
E-mail: admin@eastcomengineering.co.uk
Directors: P. Bayley (MD)
Immediate Holding Company: EASTCOM ENGINEERS LTD
Registration no: 07101966 **VAT No.:** GB 623 1154 82
Date established: 2009 **No.of Employees:** 1 - 10 **Product Groups:** 48

Date of Accounts	Dec 10
Working Capital	17
Current Assets	24

Eastern Plastics Machinery Ltd

1 Priors Way Coggeshall, Colchester, CO6 1TW
Tel: 01376-562288 **Fax:** 01376-561385
E-mail: info@easternplastics.co.uk
Website: http://www.easternplastics.co.uk
Directors: C. Siddall (MD)
Immediate Holding Company: EASTERN PLASTICS MACHINERY LIMITED
Registration no: 01280521 **VAT No.:** GB 289 6883 73
Date established: 1976 **Turnover:** £2m - £5m **No.of Employees:** 1 - 10
Product Groups: 38, 42, 45, 46, 48, 84

Date of Accounts	Dec 11	Dec 10	Dec 09
Working Capital	-48	-63	-1
Fixed Assets	138	270	275
Current Assets	192	85	128
Current Liabilities	N/A	N/A	2

Electro Gear Ltd

14 Davey Close, Colchester, CO1 2XL
Tel: 01206-862062 **Fax:** 01206-862053
E-mail: enquiries@electrogear.co.uk
Website: http://www.electrogear.co.uk
Directors: A. Barge (Dir)
Immediate Holding Company: ELECTRO GEAR LIMITED
Registration no: 02182117 **VAT No.:** GB 466 0186 44
Date established: 1987 **Turnover:** £500,000 - £1m
No.of Employees: 1 - 10 **Product Groups:** 37, 38

Date of Accounts	Dec 11	Dec 10	Dec 09
Working Capital	73	68	61
Fixed Assets	12	14	16
Current Assets	221	251	278

Essex Chambers Of Commerce (North Essex Office)

8-9 St Peters Court Middleborough, Colchester, CO1 1WD
Tel: 01206-765277 **Fax:** 01206-578073
E-mail: info@essexchambers.co.uk
Website: http://www.essexchambers.co.uk
Directors: E. Oddie (Fin), D. Rossiter (Grp Chief Exec)
Immediate Holding Company: ESSEX CHAMBERS OF COMMERCE & INDUSTRY LIMITED
Registration no: 02981688 **Date established:** 1994
Turnover: £500,000 - £1m **No.of Employees:** 11 - 20
Product Groups: 80, 87

Date of Accounts	Dec 11	Dec 10	Dec 09
Sales Turnover	N/A	N/A	928
Pre Tax Profit/Loss	N/A	N/A	11
Working Capital	168	149	134
Fixed Assets	17	5	5
Current Assets	291	334	292
Current Liabilities	N/A	N/A	99

Essex Governor Services Ltd

Wormingford Road Fordham, Colchester, CO6 3NS
Tel: 01206-242000 **Fax:** 01206-242021
E-mail: info@egsgov.com
Website: http://www.egsgov.com
Directors: W. Ward (Fin), A. Whyte (MD)
Ultimate Holding Company: ESSEX ENGINEERING (HOLDINGS) LIMITED
Immediate Holding Company: ESSEX GOVERNOR SERVICES LIMITED
Registration no: 01876943 **Date established:** 1985 **Turnover:** £2m - £5m
No.of Employees: 21 - 50 **Product Groups:** 35, 36, 39

Date of Accounts	Jan 12	Jan 11	Jan 10
Sales Turnover	N/A	N/A	2m
Pre Tax Profit/Loss	N/A	N/A	319
Working Capital	1m	1m	1m
Fixed Assets	163	188	186
Current Assets	2m	2m	1m
Current Liabilities	N/A	N/A	184

Essex Shooting Supplies Ltd

Cantfields Farm Easthorpe, Colchester, CO5 9HH
Tel: 01206-331238 **Fax:** 01206-331238
Directors: J. Brown (Dir)
Immediate Holding Company: ESSEX SHOOTING SUPPLIES LIMITED
Registration no: 02264630 **Date established:** 1988
Turnover: £250,000 - £500,000 **No.of Employees:** 1 - 10
Product Groups: 36, 39, 40

Date of Accounts	May 12	May 11	May 10
Sales Turnover	N/A	N/A	443
Pre Tax Profit/Loss	N/A	N/A	28
Working Capital	28	44	55
Fixed Assets	7	10	15
Current Assets	217	215	229
Current Liabilities	N/A	N/A	11

Eurotex International Ltd
Unit 20 Shipyard Estate Brightlingsea, Colchester, CO7 0AR
Tel: 01206-304063 **Fax:** 01206-304026
E-mail: info@eurotex-int.com
Website: http://www.eurotex-intl.com
Directors: S. Codd (MD), S. Lamb (Dir)
Ultimate Holding Company: TEX HOLDINGS PLC
Immediate Holding Company: EUROTEX INTERNATIONAL LIMITED
Registration no: 01453734 **VAT No.:** GB 434 7275 43
Date established: 1979 **Turnover:** £2m - £5m **No.of Employees:** 21 - 50
Product Groups: 39, 40, 48, 84

Date of Accounts	Dec 11	Dec 10	Dec 09
Sales Turnover	3m	2m	3m
Pre Tax Profit/Loss	248	169	231
Working Capital	978	943	860
Fixed Assets	89	93	104
Current Assets	1m	2m	1m
Current Liabilities	208	420	257

Evergreen Office Supplies
Evergreen Turnpike Close, Ardleigh, Colchester, CO7 7QW
Tel: 01206-231111 **Fax:** 01206-231476
E-mail: sales@evergreen.co.uk
Website: http://www.evergreen.co.uk
Directors: J. Alston (MD)
Immediate Holding Company: EVERGREEN OFFICE SUPPLIES LIMITED
Registration no: 04279365 **VAT No.:** GB 448 9560 03
Date established: 2001 **Turnover:** £500,000 - £1m
No.of Employees: 1 - 10 **Product Groups:** 64

F V Conservatories & Windows
Colchester Road Elmstead Market Elmstead, Colchester, CO7 7EA
Tel: 01206-825374 **Fax:** 01206-825405
E-mail: sales@fvconservatories.co.uk
Website: http://www.fvconservatories.co.uk
Directors: R. Vaughan (Dir)
Immediate Holding Company: FV CONSERVATORIES & WINDOWS LTD
Registration no: 05895900 **Date established:** 2006 **Turnover:** £1m - £2m
No.of Employees: 1 - 10 **Product Groups:** 35, 52

Date of Accounts	Oct 11	Oct 10	Oct 09
Working Capital	-44	-49	-63
Fixed Assets	10	13	16
Current Assets	114	66	55

Fenn Wright Residential Lettings
146 High Street, Colchester, CO1 1PW
Tel: 01206-764499 **Fax:** 01206-760571
E-mail: alj@fennwright.co.uk
Website: http://www.fennwright.co.uk
Bank(s): Barclays
Directors: A. Jones (Co Sec)
Immediate Holding Company: FENN WRIGHT LIMITED
Registration no: 02427639 **VAT No.:** GB 102 4163 29
Date established: 1989 **Turnover:** £2m - £5m **No.of Employees:** 21 - 50
Product Groups: 52, 80, 82, 84

Flakt Woods Ltd
Axial Way, Colchester, CO4 5ZD
Tel: 01206-222555 **Fax:** 01206-222777
E-mail: marketing.uk@flaktwoods.com
Website: http://www.flaktwoods.com
Bank(s): HSBC - London
Directors: A. Herdle (MD), A. Hurdle (MD)
Managers: S. Lee (Comptroller), H. Gilfillan (Personnel)
Ultimate Holding Company: STROMBOLI INVESTISSEMENTS SAS (FRANCE)
Immediate Holding Company: FLAKT WOODS LIMITED
Registration no: 00233771 **VAT No.:** GB 759 9121 98
Date established: 2028 **Turnover:** £50m - £75m
No.of Employees: 251 - 500 **Product Groups:** 35, 37, 38, 39, 40, 41, 48, 49, 66, 68

Date of Accounts	Dec 11	Dec 10	Dec 09
Sales Turnover	66m	62m	63m
Pre Tax Profit/Loss	1m	4m	4m
Working Capital	8m	7m	5m
Fixed Assets	6m	7m	7m
Current Assets	37m	38m	32m
Current Liabilities	3m	3m	3m

Gamet Bearings
Hythe Station Road, Colchester, CO2 8LD
Tel: 01206-862121 **Fax:** 01206-868690
E-mail: sales@gamet-bearings.co.uk
Website: http://www.gamet-bearings.com
Bank(s): National Westminster Bank Plc
Directors: T. Tankard (Fab)
Ultimate Holding Company: 600 GROUP LTD
Immediate Holding Company: 600 UK LTD
Registration no: 00144979 **VAT No.:** GB 226 5185 65
Date established: 1954 **Turnover:** £2m - £5m **No.of Employees:** 11 - 20
Product Groups: 35, 45, 46

Geosynthetic Technology Ltd
Nags Corner Wiston Road, Nayland, Colchester, CO6 4LT
Tel: 01206-262676 **Fax:** 01206-262998
E-mail: sales@geosynthetic.co.uk
Website: http://www.geosynthetic.co.uk
Directors: D. Alexander (Dir)
Immediate Holding Company: GEOSYNTHETIC TECHNOLOGY LIMITED
Registration no: 02522950 **Date established:** 1990 **Turnover:** £1m - £2m
No.of Employees: 1 - 10 **Product Groups:** 30

Date of Accounts	Jun 12	Jun 11	Jun 10
Working Capital	273	284	233
Fixed Assets	145	173	121
Current Assets	600	657	831

Golding Audio
8 Peartree Business Centre Peartree Road, Stanway, Colchester, CO3 0JN
Tel: 01206-762462 **Fax:** 01206-762633
E-mail: info@goldingaudio.co.uk
Website: http://www.goldingaudio.co.uk
Directors: J. Patrick (MD)
Immediate Holding Company: GOLDING AUDIO LIMITED
Registration no: 00949331 **VAT No.:** 102 5645 06 **Date established:** 1969
Turnover: £500,000 - £1m **No.of Employees:** 1 - 10 **Product Groups:** 37, 61, 83

Date of Accounts	Mar 12	Mar 11	Mar 10
Working Capital	234	247	277
Fixed Assets	14	14	18
Current Assets	385	361	508

Gowen Ocean Sailmakers Ltd
130 Coast Road West Mersea, Colchester, CO5 8PG
Tel: 01206-384412 **Fax:** 01206-382834
E-mail: sales@gosails.com
Website: http://www.gosails.com
Bank(s): Barclays
Directors: F. Vincent (MD)
Immediate Holding Company: GOWEN OCEAN SAILMAKERS LIMITED
Registration no: 01929584 **VAT No.:** GB 102 3620 32
Date established: 1985 **Turnover:** Up to £250,000
No.of Employees: 11 - 20 **Product Groups:** 24

Date of Accounts	Oct 11	Oct 10	Oct 09
Working Capital	N/A	25	57
Current Assets	N/A	25	57

R Gray
Hall Barns Hall Road, West Bergholt, Colchester, CO6 3DU
Tel: 01206-243588
Directors: R. Gray (Prop)
Date established: 2001 **No.of Employees:** 1 - 10 **Product Groups:** 35

Great Tey Metalcraft Ltd
Elm Farm Elm Lane, Marks Tey, Colchester, CO6 1HU
Tel: 01206-210747 **Fax:** 01206-212155
Directors: J. Tatam (MD)
Immediate Holding Company: GREAT TEY METALCRAFT LIMITED
Registration no: 06788091 **Date established:** 2009
No.of Employees: 1 - 10 **Product Groups:** 26, 35

Date of Accounts	Jan 11	Jan 10
Working Capital	-26	-19
Fixed Assets	101	105
Current Assets	49	78

Greenmill
16 Cowdray Centre Mason Road, Colchester, CO1 1BX
Tel: 01206-541155 **Fax:** 0870-9508908
Directors: N. Millar (Ptnr), N. Millar (Prop)
Immediate Holding Company: GREENMILL SUPPLY COMPANY LIMITED
Registration no: 07205837 **Date established:** 2010
No.of Employees: 1 - 10 **Product Groups:** 40, 66

Hammerton Metal Craft
North View Cottages Coach Road, Great Horkesley, Colchester, CO6 4AT
Tel: 01206-271020
Directors: D. Hammerton (Prop)
Date established: 2001 **No.of Employees:** 1 - 10 **Product Groups:** 26, 35

Hawker Softeners Ltd
47 Station Road Tiptree, Colchester, CO5 0BL
Tel: 01621-817395
E-mail: janet.hawker@hawkersofteners.co.uk
Website: http://www.hawkersofteners.co.uk
Directors: J. Hawker (Fin), A. Hawker (MD)
Immediate Holding Company: HAWKER SOFTENERS LIMITED
Registration no: 04503280 **Date established:** 2002
No.of Employees: 1 - 10 **Product Groups:** 38, 42

Date of Accounts	Mar 11	Mar 09	Mar 08
Working Capital	2	-3	-1
Fixed Assets	11	3	4
Current Assets	29	13	25

Hermes Abrasives Ltd
Wyncolls Road Severalls Industrial Park, Colchester, CO4 9LW
Tel: 01206-754400 **Fax:** 01206-754401
E-mail: j.mcwilliams@hermes-abrasives.com
Website: http://www.hermes-abrasives.com
Bank(s): National Westminster Bank Plc
Directors: P. Matthews (Fin), J. Mcwilliams (MD)
Managers: D. Holmes, P. Seargent (Chief Acct), V. Clark, J. Macwilliams (Ops Mgr)
Ultimate Holding Company: HERMES SCHLEIFMITTEL GMBH & CO KG (GERMANY)
Immediate Holding Company: HERMES ABRASIVES LIMITED
Registration no: 01858788 **VAT No.:** GB 418 4147 57
Date established: 1984 **Turnover:** £10m - £20m
No.of Employees: 21 - 50 **Product Groups:** 33

Date of Accounts	Dec 11	Dec 10
Sales Turnover	6m	N/A
Current Assets	1m	N/A
Current Liabilities	314	N/A

Hydrocut Ltd
PO Box 2926, Colchester, CO6 2QP
Tel: 01787-222266 **Fax:** 01787-222210
E-mail: info@hydrocut.co.uk
Website: http://www.hydrocut.co.uk
Directors: J. Chamberlain (MD)
Immediate Holding Company: HYDROCUT LIMITED
Registration no: 00621641 **VAT No.:** GB 102 7233 19
Date established: 1959 **No.of Employees:** 1 - 10 **Product Groups:** 67

Date of Accounts	Oct 11	Oct 10	Oct 07
Working Capital	207	216	136
Fixed Assets	7	9	12
Current Assets	233	241	179

I S Enterprises International
Clement House Commerce Way, Colchester, CO2 8HY
Tel: 01206-798131 **Fax:** 01206-791186
E-mail: jgranger@isenterprises.co.uk
Website: http://www.isenterprisesintl.co.uk
Directors: R. Clayton (Co Sec), J. Granger (Sales)
Immediate Holding Company: IS ENTERPRISES INTERNATIONAL LIMITED
Registration no: 03549601 **VAT No.:** GB 285 3875 14
Date established: 1998 **Turnover:** £2m - £5m **No.of Employees:** 51 - 100
Product Groups: 24, 49, 81

Date of Accounts	May 11	May 10	May 09
Sales Turnover	4m	N/A	N/A
Pre Tax Profit/Loss	99	N/A	N/A
Working Capital	2m	2m	2m
Fixed Assets	43	58	86
Current Assets	3m	2m	3m
Current Liabilities	116	N/A	N/A

Identilabel Ltd
Unit 2a The Gattinetts Hadleigh Road, East Bergholt, Colchester, CO7 6QT
Tel: 01206-299777 **Fax:** 01206-299007
E-mail: sales@identilabel.co.uk
Website: http://www.identilabel.co.uk
Directors: A. Chumbley (Fin), B. Chumbley (MD), R. Chumbley (MD)
Immediate Holding Company: IDENTILABEL LIMITED
Registration no: 03846073 **VAT No.:** GB 325 7911 50
Date established: 1999 **Turnover:** Up to £250,000
No.of Employees: 1 - 10 **Product Groups:** 22, 23, 27, 28, 29, 30, 33, 35, 36, 37, 39, 40, 43, 44, 45, 49, 64, 67, 68

Date of Accounts	Jul 11	Jul 10	Jul 09
Working Capital	62	58	55
Fixed Assets	12	14	14
Current Assets	86	87	81

Imagine Transfers
Teybrook Centre Brook Road, Great Tey, Colchester, CO6 1JE
Tel: 01206-210221 **Fax:** 01206-213613
E-mail: jlmassoc@aol.com
Website: http://www.imagine-transfers.co.uk
Directors: W. Janssen (Dir)
Date established: 1993 **No.of Employees:** 1 - 10 **Product Groups:** 23

Imofa UK Ltd
New Coach House 21 Grange Way, Colchester, CO2 8HF
Tel: 01206-505909 **Fax:** 01206-794095
E-mail: sales@imofa.co.uk
Website: http://www.imofa.co.uk
Directors: G. Baldwin (Dir), A. Rushmer (Fin)
Ultimate Holding Company: BEHEER EN BELEGGINGSMAATSCHAPPIJ HONING BV (HOLLAND)
Immediate Holding Company: IMOFA (UK) LIMITED
Registration no: 02818848 **Date established:** 1993
Turnover: £500,000 - £1m **No.of Employees:** 1 - 10 **Product Groups:** 37, 66

Date of Accounts	Dec 11	Dec 10	Dec 09
Sales Turnover	1m	N/A	N/A
Pre Tax Profit/Loss	81	N/A	N/A
Working Capital	237	175	207
Fixed Assets	19	12	17
Current Assets	381	316	339
Current Liabilities	31	N/A	N/A

Inchcape East Properties Ltd
Osbourne Corner Ipswich Road, Colchester, CO4 9TF
Tel: 01206-855455 **Fax:** 01206-845868
E-mail: info.honda-colchester@ir.inchcape.co.uk
Website: http://www.inchcapecolchester.volkswagen.co.uk
Directors: M. Wheatley (Fin)
Managers: K. Walters (Chief Mgr)
Ultimate Holding Company: INCHCAPE PLC
Immediate Holding Company: INCHCAPE EAST (PROPERTIES) LIMITED
Registration no: 00921802 **VAT No.:** GB 103 2204 45
Date established: 1967 **Turnover:** £50m - £75m **No.of Employees:** 1 - 10
Product Groups: 68

Date of Accounts	Dec 10	Dec 09	Dec 08
Pre Tax Profit/Loss	N/A	N/A	12
Working Capital	7	18m	18m
Current Assets	7	18m	18m

Indasa Abrasives UK Ltd
Viking Works Greenstead Road, Colchester, CO1 2ST
Tel: 01206-870366 **Fax:** 01206-860525
E-mail: andrew@indasa.co.uk
Website: http://www.indasaabrasives.com
Bank(s): Lloyds TSB Bank plc
Directors: D. Dell (Pers), A. Tindall (MD), J. Babbs (Fin)
Managers: P. Blowers (Sales Prom Mgr), R. Evans, R. Todd
Ultimate Holding Company: INDASA - INDUSTRIA DE ABRASIVOS SA (PORTUGAL)
Immediate Holding Company: INDASA ABRASIVES (UK) LTD
Registration no: 02392535 **Date established:** 1989
No.of Employees: 21 - 50 **Product Groups:** 27, 32, 33, 45

Date of Accounts	Dec 11	Dec 10	Dec 09
Working Capital	2m	3m	2m
Fixed Assets	1m	161	124
Current Assets	3m	4m	4m

Indulgence Patisserie Ltd
20 Clough Road Severalls Industrial Park, Colchester, CO4 9QS
Tel: 01206-843397 **Fax:** 01206-842577
E-mail: angus@indulgence.co.uk
Website: http://www.indulgence.co.uk
Bank(s): National Westminster Bank Plc
Directors: S. Allan (Chief Op Offcr), A. Allan (MD)
Ultimate Holding Company: CARSTAIRS HOLDINGS LIMITED
Immediate Holding Company: INDULGENCE PATISSERIE LIMITED
Registration no: 03320474 **VAT No.:** GB 466 0551 47
Date established: 1997 **Turnover:** £2m - £5m **No.of Employees:** 21 - 50
Product Groups: 20

Date of Accounts	May 11	May 10	May 09
Working Capital	805	594	486
Fixed Assets	2m	2m	1m
Current Assets	2m	2m	983

Informa UK Ltd
Sheepen Place, Colchester, CO3 3LT
Tel: 020-7017 5000
E-mail: headoffice@informa.com
Website: http://www.informa.com
Bank(s): National Westminster
Directors: R. Richman (Tech Serv), T. Humphris (Pers), C. Chesher (Grp Sales), I. Peck (Grp Mktg)
Managers: C. Higgin (Buyer), A. Walker
Ultimate Holding Company: INFORMA PLC (JERSEY)
Immediate Holding Company: INFORMA UK LIMITED
Registration no: 01072954 **Date established:** 1972
Turnover: £20m - £50m **No.of Employees:** 251 - 500 **Product Groups:** 28

Date of Accounts	Dec 11	Dec 10	Dec 09
Sales Turnover	343m	333m	323m
Pre Tax Profit/Loss	42m	31m	9m
Working Capital	-706m	-732m	-770m
Fixed Assets	560m	567m	597m
Current Assets	132m	80m	171m
Current Liabilities	198m	178m	165m

Integer Micro Systems Ltd
Dugard House Peartree Road, Stanway, Colchester, CO3 0UL
Tel: 01206-564600 **Fax:** 01206-369620
E-mail: sales@ims-integer.com
Website: http://www.ims-integer.com
Bank(s): Barclays

see next page

Integer Micro Systems Ltd - Cont'd

Directors: M. Goodchild (Dir)
Immediate Holding Company: INTEGER MICRO SYSTEMS LIMITED
Registration no: 02453620 **Date established:** 1989 **Turnover:** £1m - £2m
No.of Employees: 11 - 20 **Product Groups:** 44

Date of Accounts	Sep 11	Sep 10	Sep 09
Working Capital	29	32	23
Fixed Assets	515	509	520
Current Assets	354	341	304

International Timber

Haven Road, Colchester, CO2 8HT
Tel: 01206-866822 **Fax:** 01206-878000
E-mail: neil.salmon@internationaltimber.com
Website: http://www.internationaltimber.co.uk
Managers: N. Salmon (Transport)
Ultimate Holding Company: METSALIITTO COOPERATIVE (FINLAND)
Immediate Holding Company: TIMBERA LIMITED
Registration no: 00441153 **VAT No.:** GB 145 8472 47
Date established: 1947 **Turnover:** Up to £250,000
No.of Employees: 1 - 10 **Product Groups:** 61

Date of Accounts	Dec 11	Dec 10	Dec 09
Working Capital	500	500	500
Current Assets	500	500	500

Iron Works Earls Colne

Unit 5 Riverside Business Park Station Road, Earls Colne, Colchester, CO6 2ER
Tel: 01787-222335
E-mail: riversideforge@hotmail.co.uk
Website: http://www.freewebs.com
Directors: S. Skeggs (Prop)
Immediate Holding Company: IRONWORKS-EARLS COLNE LIMITED
Registration no: 04674887 **Date established:** 2003
No.of Employees: 1 - 10 **Product Groups:** 26, 35

Date of Accounts	Mar 11	Mar 10	Mar 07
Working Capital	-32	-35	-29
Fixed Assets	32	35	29
Current Assets	16	2	3

Jewson Ltd

Hawkins Road, Colchester, CO2 8LH
Tel: 01206-799169 **Fax:** 01206-799844
Website: http://www.jewson.co.uk
Managers: C. Jones (District Mgr), K. Hopkins (Admin Off)
Ultimate Holding Company: COMPAGNIE DE SAINT GOBAIN (FRANCE)
Immediate Holding Company: JEWSON LIMITED
Registration no: 00348407 **Date established:** 1939
Turnover: Up to £250,000 **No.of Employees:** 11 - 20 **Product Groups:** 66

Date of Accounts	Dec 11	Dec 10	Dec 09
Sales Turnover	1606m	1547m	1485m
Pre Tax Profit/Loss	18m	100m	45m
Working Capital	-345m	-250m	-349m
Fixed Assets	496m	387m	461m
Current Assets	657m	1005m	1320m
Current Liabilities	66m	120m	64m

K G Composits & Mouldings

Unit 10a Grange Way Business Park Grange Way, Colchester, CO2 8HF
Tel: 01206-795073 **Fax:** 01206-795069
E-mail: kgcomposits@btconnect.com
Website: http://www.kgcomposits.co.uk
Directors: J. Thomson (Dir)
Immediate Holding Company: GRAHAM RICHARDSON & SON LIMITED
Registration no: 04291467 **Date established:** 2000
Turnover: Up to £250,000 **No.of Employees:** 11 - 20 **Product Groups:** 30, 48

E W King & Co. Ltd

Monks Farm Kelvedon, Colchester, CO5 9PG
Tel: 01376-570000 **Fax:** 01376-571189
E-mail: sales@kingsseeds.com
Website: http://www.kingsseeds.com
Directors: A. Ward (Sales & Mktg), L. Day (MD)
Managers: P. Miller (Purch Mgr)
Immediate Holding Company: E.W. KING & CO LIMITED
Registration no: 00162896 **VAT No.:** GB 102 7974 74
Date established: 2020 **No.of Employees:** 21 - 50 **Product Groups:** 02

Date of Accounts	Jun 11	Jun 10	Jun 09
Working Capital	1m	1m	1m
Fixed Assets	838	744	793
Current Assets	2m	2m	1m

Kirvin Tubeform

4 Surrex Farm Units Colchester Road, Coggeshall, Colchester, CO6 1RR
Tel: 01376-563784 **Fax:** 01376-564819
E-mail: clive@kirvintubeform.co.uk
Directors: C. Hilzbrich (Prop)
Date established: 1992 **No.of Employees:** 1 - 10 **Product Groups:** 35

Krantz Systems

61-67 Rectory Road Wivenhoe, Colchester, CO7 9ES
Tel: 01206-827171 **Fax:** 01206-826936
E-mail: rs@krantz.uk.com
Website: http://www.krantz.uk.com
Bank(s): Barclays
Directors: C. Dickinson (Co Sec), K. Ross (MD)
Managers: R. Scales (Sales Prom Mgr)
Registration no: 01313518 **Turnover:** £2m - £5m
No.of Employees: 11 - 20 **Product Groups:** 29, 33, 35, 37, 38, 40, 42, 67, 84

Lyteze Products Ltd

8 Colne Road Brightlingsea, Colchester, CO7 0DL
Tel: 01206-302699 **Fax:** 01206-302699
E-mail: anne@lyteze.com
Website: http://www.lyteze.com
Directors: A. Cook (MD), A. Cook (Fin)
Immediate Holding Company: LYTEZE PRODUCTS LIMITED
Registration no: 00316970 **VAT No.:** GB 386 7368 94
Date established: 1936 **Turnover:** Up to £250,000
No.of Employees: 1 - 10 **Product Groups:** 36, 37

Date of Accounts	Mar 11	Mar 10	Mar 09
Working Capital	10	12	7
Current Assets	24	26	24

M G Electric

Wyncolls Road Severalls Industrial Park, Colchester, CO4 9HX
Tel: 01206-842244 **Fax:** 01206-853889
E-mail: sales@mgelectric.co.uk
Website: http://www.mgeworldwide.com
Bank(s): The Royal Bank of Scotland
Directors: S. Martin (Tech Serv)
Managers: M. Warriner, M. Withrington, S. Edwards
Immediate Holding Company: MARTIN MANAGEMENT LTD
Registration no: 00880470 **VAT No.:** GB 368 5808 07
Date established: 1963 **Turnover:** £1m - £2m **No.of Employees:** 21 - 50
Product Groups: 40, 46

M K Design Solutions

40 Titus Way, Colchester, CO4 5GD
Tel: 01206-248612
Directors: H. Pearce (Fin), M. Pearce (Dir)
Registration no: 06345577 **No.of Employees:** 1 - 10 **Product Groups:** 38, 44, 84

Marketing Assistance Ltd

5 Inworth Grange Grange Road, Tiptree, Colchester, CO5 0QQ
Tel: 01621-818555 **Fax:** 01621-810884
E-mail: kevin@marketing-assistance.co.uk
Website: http://www.marketing-assistance.co.uk
Directors: K. Norman (Comm)
Immediate Holding Company: MARKETING ASSISTANCE LIMITED
Registration no: 02879729 **Date established:** 1993
Turnover: Up to £250,000 **No.of Employees:** 1 - 10 **Product Groups:** 80, 81

Date of Accounts	Sep 11	Sep 10	Sep 09
Sales Turnover	N/A	N/A	153
Pre Tax Profit/Loss	N/A	N/A	35
Working Capital	18	4	5
Fixed Assets	4	5	4
Current Assets	52	26	21
Current Liabilities	N/A	N/A	12

Medical Equipment Rental

24 Worthington Way, Colchester, CO3 4LA
Tel: 01206-561571 **Fax:** 01206-364974
E-mail: services@merlimited.co.uk
Website: http://www.merlimited.co.uk
Directors: K. Norman (Fin), M. Norman (MD)
Immediate Holding Company: MEDICAL EQUIPMENT RENTAL LIMITED
Registration no: 04252064 **Date established:** 2001
Turnover: Up to £250,000 **No.of Employees:** 1 - 10 **Product Groups:** 83

Date of Accounts	Jul 11	Jul 10	Jul 09
Working Capital	-31	-24	-27
Fixed Assets	46	22	7
Current Assets	1	1	N/A

Meklift Fork Trucks Ltd

Unit 11 Grange Farm Road Whitehall Industrial Estate, Colchester, CO2 8JW
Tel: 01206-795111 **Fax:** 01206-795123
E-mail: info@meklift.co.uk
Website: http://www.meklift.co.uk
Directors: R. Vost (MD)
Immediate Holding Company: MEKLIFT LTD
Registration no: 03881687 **Date established:** 1999
No.of Employees: 1 - 10 **Product Groups:** 45, 48, 67, 83

Date of Accounts	Dec 11	Dec 10	Dec 09
Working Capital	16	23	7
Fixed Assets	59	67	69
Current Assets	100	50	54

Milfab Engineering Ltd

Heckworth Close Severalls Industrial Park, Colchester, CO4 9TB
Tel: 01206-751211 **Fax:** 01206-841110
E-mail: info@milfab.co.uk
Website: http://www.milfab.co.uk
Managers: L. Lovelock (Prod Mgr)
Immediate Holding Company: MILFAB ENGINEERING LIMITED
Registration no: 02202934 **VAT No.:** GB 360 3178 72
Date established: 1987 **No.of Employees:** 11 - 20 **Product Groups:** 48

Date of Accounts	May 12	May 11	May 10
Working Capital	520	447	408
Fixed Assets	325	376	336
Current Assets	734	701	565

D K Moriarty Ltd

East Gates Industrial Park Moorside, Colchester, CO1 2TJ
Tel: 01206-867141 **Fax:** 01206-867613
E-mail: sales@dk-moriarty.ltd.uk
Website: http://www.dk-moriarty.ltd.uk
Bank(s): Lloyds TSB Bank plc
Directors: S. Moriarty (Comm), T. Moriarty (Fin)
Managers: D. Kitson (Sales Eng)
Immediate Holding Company: D.K. MORIARTY LIMITED
Registration no: 00977186 **VAT No.:** GB 102 6403 25
Date established: 1970 **Turnover:** £1m - £2m **No.of Employees:** 21 - 50
Product Groups: 37

Date of Accounts	Apr 11	Apr 10	Apr 09
Working Capital	950	817	764
Fixed Assets	453	428	450
Current Assets	1m	1m	1m

Mower & Saw Services Ltd

2 Vale View Business Units Crown Lane South, Ardleigh, Colchester, CO7 7PL
Tel: 01206-230180 **Fax:** 01206-230833
E-mail: s.hart@mowerandsaw.co.uk
Website: http://www.mowerandsaw.co.uk
Directors: S. Hart (Dir)
Immediate Holding Company: MOWER & SAW SERVICES LIMITED
Registration no: 03501436 **Date established:** 1998
No.of Employees: 1 - 10 **Product Groups:** 41

Date of Accounts	Sep 11	Sep 10	Sep 09
Working Capital	37	35	41
Fixed Assets	7	10	2
Current Assets	139	132	147

National Federation Of Fishmongers

PO Box 9639, Colchester, CO5 9WR
Tel: 01376-571391 **Fax:** 01376-571391
Directors: G. Sage (Pres), G. Hooper (Pres)
Managers: H. Leftwich (Sec)
Immediate Holding Company: ABBEYCOM LIMITED
Registration no: 03585080 **Date established:** 1998
No.of Employees: 1 - 10 **Product Groups:** 87

Date of Accounts	Sep 08	Sep 07	Sep 06
Sales Turnover	N/A	N/A	13
Pre Tax Profit/Loss	N/A	N/A	2
Working Capital	96	92	89
Fixed Assets	337	335	327
Current Assets	112	109	102
Current Liabilities	16	17	13
ROCE% (Return on Capital Employed)			0.4
ROT% (Return on Turnover)			14.1

North Essex Signs

15 Clough Road Severalls Industrial Park, Colchester, CO4 9QS
Tel: 01206-841250 **Fax:** 01206-845090
E-mail: jon@nes-solutions.co.uk
Website: http://www.nes-solutions.co.uk
Bank(s): Royal Bank of Scotland
Directors: J. Baker (Dir), J. Baker (Prop), D. Irwin (Fin), A. Irwin (MD)
Managers: B. Hiskett (Sales Prom Mgr)
Immediate Holding Company: GUILFORM LIMITED
Registration no: 02971093 **VAT No.:** GB 740 9738 12
Date established: 2001 **Turnover:** £5m - £10m **No.of Employees:** 21 - 50
Product Groups: 26, 28, 30, 35, 37, 44, 49, 84

Date of Accounts	Dec 07	Dec 06	Dec 05
Working Capital	202	502	413
Fixed Assets	489	539	433
Current Assets	1235	1133	681
Current Liabilities	1034	631	268

P M R Electrical

8 School Farm Buildings School Road Langham, Colchester, CO4 5PB
Tel: 01206-231894 **Fax:** 01206-231895
E-mail: tony@pmrelec.fsnet.co.uk
Website: http://www.pmrelectrical.co.uk
Directors: K. Mills (Prop)
Immediate Holding Company: P.M.R. (ELECTRICAL) LIMITED
Registration no: 00698009 **VAT No.:** 103 4939 85 **Date established:** 1961
Turnover: £500,000 - £1m **No.of Employees:** 1 - 10 **Product Groups:** 52

Date of Accounts	Jun 11	Jun 10	Jun 09
Working Capital	104	90	123
Fixed Assets	13	18	8
Current Assets	166	166	166

Pago Ltd

7 Crown Gate Wyncolls Road, Severalls Industrial Park, Colchester, CO4 9HZ
Tel: 01206-755206 **Fax:** 01206-755210
E-mail: sales@pago.co.uk
Website: http://www.pago.com
Directors: C. Peachy (MD)
Immediate Holding Company: PAGO LIMITED
Registration no: 02625502 **VAT No.:** GB 594 6511 12
Date established: 1991 **Turnover:** £5m - £10m **No.of Employees:** 11 - 20
Product Groups: 27, 30

Date of Accounts	Dec 11	Dec 10	Dec 09
Working Capital	-298	84	400
Fixed Assets	51	82	130
Current Assets	730	741	833

Parkinson Motorcycles Ltd

Block C5 Cowdray Centre, Colchester, CO1 1BN
Tel: 01206-368500 **Fax:** 01206-368599
E-mail: info@parkinsonmotorcycles.co.uk
Website: http://www.parkinsonmotorcycles.co.uk
Directors: N. Moore (Dir)
Immediate Holding Company: PARKINSON MOTORCYCLES LIMITED
Registration no: 05328307 **Date established:** 2005
No.of Employees: 1 - 10 **Product Groups:** 39, 40

Date of Accounts	Jan 12	Jan 11	Jan 10
Working Capital	123	153	192
Fixed Assets	4	5	8
Current Assets	401	619	804

Permatex Protective Coatings UK Ltd

The Colchester Centre Hawkins Road, Colchester, CO2 8JX
Tel: 01206-266867 **Fax:** 01708-378868
E-mail: permatexpcltd@hotmail.co.uk
Website: http://www.permatexpcukltd.co.uk
Directors: S. Holland (MD)
Immediate Holding Company: PERMATEX PROTECTIVE COATINGS (U.K.) LIMITED
Registration no: 03666917 **VAT No.:** GB 726 2377 31
Date established: 1998 **Turnover:** £50m - £75m **No.of Employees:** 1 - 10
Product Groups: 29, 30, 32, 52, 66, 85

Date of Accounts	Nov 11	Nov 10	Nov 09
Working Capital	-2	3	2
Fixed Assets	3	3	3
Current Assets	40	98	100

Pertwee Estates Ltd

Lodge Lane Langham, Colchester, CO4 5NE
Tel: 01206-231000 **Fax:** 01206-231132
E-mail: mail@pertwee.co.uk
Website: http://www.pertwee.co.uk
Directors: M. Pertwee (MD)
Immediate Holding Company: PERTWEE ESTATES LTD
Registration no: 00289726 **VAT No.:** GB 102 4519 16
Date established: 1934 **Turnover:** £500,000 - £1m
No.of Employees: 1 - 10 **Product Groups:** 80

Date of Accounts	Jan 12	Jan 11	Jan 10
Sales Turnover	551	N/A	N/A
Pre Tax Profit/Loss	38	N/A	N/A
Working Capital	921	990	977
Fixed Assets	511	414	424
Current Assets	1m	1m	1m
Current Liabilities	503	N/A	N/A

Philips Speech Processing

6 The Courtyards Wyncolls Road, Severalls Industrial Park, Colchester, CO4 9PE
Tel: 01206-755755 **Fax:** 01206-755888
E-mail: mark.burns@philips.com
Website: http://www.speech.philips.com
Directors: M. Burns (Dir)
Immediate Holding Company: PHILIPS ELECTRONIC & ASSOCIATED INDUSTRIES
Registration no: 00446897 **Turnover:** £10m - £20m
No.of Employees: 1 - 10 **Product Groups:** 37, 44

Playle Engineering Co.

Home Farm Works Birch Park, Birch, Colchester, CO2 0LS
Tel: 01206-330315 **Fax:** 01206-330138
E-mail: sales@playleengineering.com
Website: http://www.playleengineering.co.uk
Bank(s): HSBC
Directors: J. Clarke (Fin), N. Clarke (MD)
Immediate Holding Company: PLAYLE ENGINEERING COMPANY LTD
Registration no: 01478700 **VAT No.:** GB 341 7203 87
Date established: 1980 **Turnover:** £250,000 - £500,000
No.of Employees: 11 - 20 **Product Groups:** 35, 48

Date of Accounts	May 12	May 11	May 10
Working Capital	492	341	347
Fixed Assets	46	45	50
Current Assets	871	757	529

Polestar Colchester Ltd

Wyncolls Road Severalls Industrial Park, Colchester, CO4 9HU
Tel: 01206-849500 **Fax:** 01206-224629
Website: http://www.polestar-group.com
Bank(s): National Westminster
Directors: C. Bellinger (Fin), J. Algar (MD)
Managers: J. Bolton (Purch Mgr), S. Francis (Personnel), B. Hugo (Tech Serv Mgr)
Immediate Holding Company: POLESTAR COLCHESTER LIMITED
Registration no: 00478774 **VAT No.:** 637 0168 45 **Date established:** 1950
Turnover: £20m - £50m **No.of Employees:** 101 - 250
Product Groups: 28, 48

Powerfix

19 Peartree Business Centre Peartree Road, Stanway, Colchester, CO3 0JN
Tel: 01206-762882 **Fax:** 01206-571775
E-mail: steve@powerfix-colchester.co.uk
Directors: S. Brooker (Ptnr)
Date established: 1989 **No.of Employees:** 1 - 10 **Product Groups:** 37

Powerplus Engineering Ltd

School Road Langham, Colchester, CO4 5PB
Tel: 01206-271266 **Fax:** 01206-271208
E-mail: scott.comiskey@powerpluseng.co.uk
Website: http://www.powerpluseng.co.uk
Bank(s): Barclays
Directors: S. Comiskey (Dir), T. Clayfield (MD)
Ultimate Holding Company: POWERPLUS HOLDINGS LIMITED
Immediate Holding Company: POWERPLUS ENGINEERING LIMITED
Registration no: 03031875 **VAT No.:** GB 651 1612 69
Date established: 1995 **Turnover:** £1m - £2m **No.of Employees:** 21 - 50
Product Groups: 35, 37, 40, 48, 54

Date of Accounts	Apr 12	Apr 11	Apr 10
Working Capital	-37	209	151
Fixed Assets	419	443	445
Current Assets	1m	2m	2m

The Promotional Gift Superstore

Wick House 15 Abbots Road, Old Heath, Colchester, CO2 8BE
Tel: 0845-3701022 **Fax:** 0845-3701033
E-mail: sales@nostrano-uk.com
Website: http://www.promotionalgift-superstore.com
Directors: A. Stephenson (Ptnr)
Registration no: 07092889 **Date established:** 2001
No.of Employees: 1 - 10 **Product Groups:** 24, 28, 49, 81

Regulateurs Europa Ltd

Port Lane, Colchester, CO1 2NX
Tel: 01206-799556 **Fax:** 01206-792685
E-mail: sales@regulateurseuropa.com
Website: http://www.regulateurseuropa.com
Directors: M. Congdon (Dir)
Managers: C. Jeggo
Ultimate Holding Company: FRITZ HEINZMANN GMBH & CO (GERMANY)
Immediate Holding Company: REGULATEURS EUROPA LIMITED
Registration no: 05576851 **VAT No.:** GB 531 9423 54
Date established: 2005 **Turnover:** £2m - £5m **No.of Employees:** 21 - 50
Product Groups: 37, 38, 40, 44, 48, 84

Date of Accounts	Dec 11	Dec 10	Dec 09
Working Capital	2m	2m	2m
Fixed Assets	615	641	732
Current Assets	3m	3m	3m

Rose Of Colchester Ltd

Clough Road Severalls Industrial Park, Colchester, CO4 9QT
Tel: 01206-844500 **Fax:** 01206-845872
E-mail: sales@rosecalendars.co.uk
Website: http://www.rosecalendArs.co.uk
Bank(s): Lloyds, Colchester
Directors: A. Clement (Fin), A. Clement (Fin), M. Rose (MD)
Managers: G. Paige (Sales & Mktg Mg)
Immediate Holding Company: ROSE OF COLCHESTER LIMITED
Registration no: 00575231 **VAT No.:** GB 102 5842 04
Date established: 1956 **Turnover:** £5m - £10m **No.of Employees:** 21 - 50
Product Groups: 28

Date of Accounts	Sep 11	Sep 10	Sep 09
Sales Turnover	6m	5m	5m
Pre Tax Profit/Loss	448	311	290
Working Capital	3m	3m	2m
Fixed Assets	2m	2m	2m
Current Assets	4m	3m	3m
Current Liabilities	450	304	255

S E S Mechanical Services Ltd

Telford Way Severalls Industrial Park, Colchester, CO4 9QP
Tel: 01206-845333 **Fax:** 01206-844601
E-mail: accounts@sesmechanical.co.uk
Website: http://www.sesmechanical.co.uk
Bank(s): H.S.B.C.
Directors: P. Hazelton (Dir)
Immediate Holding Company: SES MECHANICAL SERVICES LIMITED
Registration no: 04002638 **VAT No.:** GB 249 9233 28
Date established: 2000 **Turnover:** £1m - £2m **No.of Employees:** 11 - 20
Product Groups: 52, 84

Date of Accounts	May 12	May 11	May 10
Working Capital	378	326	345
Fixed Assets	185	191	212
Current Assets	798	641	923

Sanab Ltd

29 Grantham Road Great Horkesley, Colchester, CO6 4TU
Tel: 01206-271810 **Fax:** 01206-273075
E-mail: gladys@sanabltd.co.uk
Website: http://www.sanabltd.co.uk
Directors: G. Smith (Dir)
Immediate Holding Company: SANAB LIMITED
Registration no: 02863358 **Date established:** 1993
No.of Employees: 1 - 10 **Product Groups:** 32, 34, 66

Date of Accounts	Apr 12	Apr 11	Apr 10
Working Capital	-25	107	64
Fixed Assets	221	2	2
Current Assets	120	267	259

Sequis Design Engineers

30 Old Ferry Road Wivenhoe, Colchester, CO7 9SW
Tel: 01206-828003
E-mail: rick@motherload.co.uk
Website: http://www.motherload.co.uk
Directors: R. Cawley (Prop)
No.of Employees: 1 - 10 **Product Groups:** 37, 67

Sirus UK

Unit 8a Lodge Lane, Langham, Colchester, CO4 5NE
Tel: 01206-231103 **Fax:** 01245-464669
E-mail: sales@hosequip.co.uk
Website: http://www.hosequip.co.uk
Directors: J. Greenwood (Prop)
Immediate Holding Company: FJM CONSULTING LIMITED
Date established: 2011 **No.of Employees:** 1 - 10 **Product Groups:** 35, 36

Date of Accounts	Dec 11	Dec 10	Dec 09
Sales Turnover	5m	15m	3m
Pre Tax Profit/Loss	2m	2m	2m
Working Capital	2m	1m	927
Fixed Assets	279	177	46
Current Assets	8m	7m	6m
Current Liabilities	947	982	1m

A Smith Great Bentley Ltd

Clacton Road Frating, Colchester, CO7 7DL
Tel: 01206-250380 **Fax:** 01206-250509
E-mail: info@asgb.co.uk
Website: http://www.asgb.co.uk
Bank(s): Barclays, Clacton-On-Sea
Directors: S. Magnin (Fin), S. Hare (Ch)
Ultimate Holding Company: BOLD LIMITED
Immediate Holding Company: A. SMITH GT. BENTLEY LIMITED
Registration no: 01112118 **VAT No.:** GB 103 3380 20
Date established: 1973 **Turnover:** £5m - £10m
No.of Employees: 101 - 250 **Product Groups:** 30, 37, 38, 39, 40, 84

Date of Accounts	Mar 12	Mar 11	Mar 10
Sales Turnover	10m	7m	10m
Pre Tax Profit/Loss	657	-592	375
Working Capital	3m	3m	3m
Fixed Assets	3m	3m	3m
Current Assets	5m	5m	5m
Current Liabilities	1m	1m	838

Sovereign Labelling Systems Ltd

28 Morses Lane Brightlingsea, Colchester, CO7 0SF
Tel: 01206-304182 **Fax:** 01206-306100
E-mail: sovereign@sovereignlabellingsystems.co.uk
Website: http://www.sovereignlabellingsystems.co.uk
Directors: K. McCarthy (Fin), K. McCarthy (MD)
Immediate Holding Company: SOVEREIGN LABELLING SYSTEMS LIMITED
Registration no: 03189707 **Date established:** 1996
No.of Employees: 11 - 20 **Product Groups:** 38, 42

Date of Accounts	Jun 11	Jun 10	Jun 09
Working Capital	377	330	382
Fixed Assets	50	52	65
Current Assets	517	539	561

J E Spalding

112 East Road West Mersea, Colchester, CO5 8SA
Tel: 01206-382477 **Fax:** 01206-382477
Directors: J. Spalding (Prop)
Date established: 1969 **No.of Employees:** 1 - 10 **Product Groups:** 36, 39, 40

Sticks & Stones

Colchester Main Road Alresford, Colchester, CO7 8DD
Tel: 01206-826835 **Fax:** 01206-827655
E-mail: info@stixandstones.co.uk
Website: http://www.stixandstones.co.uk
Directors: P. Neal (Dir), C. Neal (Fin)
No.of Employees: 1 - 10 **Product Groups:** 25, 33, 35, 41

Syntema East Ltd

Block C Commerce Way, Colchester, CO2 8HH
Tel: 01206-868400 **Fax:** 01206-868455
E-mail: sales@syntemaeast.co.uk
Website: http://www.syntema.co.uk
Directors: S. Williams (MD)
Ultimate Holding Company: EAST ANGLIAN HOLDINGS LIMITED
Immediate Holding Company: SYMPHONY COATINGS (EAST) LIMITED
Registration no: 00239886 **Date established:** 2029 **Turnover:** £1m - £2m
No.of Employees: 1 - 10 **Product Groups:** 46, 48

Date of Accounts	Dec 11	Dec 10	Dec 09
Working Capital	370	279	204
Fixed Assets	170	108	63
Current Assets	1m	941	821

Systemair G M P H (t/a Matthews & Yates)

Suite 2 Lodge Lane Langham, Colchester, CO4 5NE
Tel: 01206-543311 **Fax:** 01206-760497
E-mail: sales@matthews-yates.co.uk
Website: http://www.systemair.com
Managers: R. Sexton (Mgr)
Immediate Holding Company: FJM CONSULTING LIMITED
Date established: 2011 **Turnover:** £5m - £10m **No.of Employees:** 1 - 10
Product Groups: 40, 41

Date of Accounts	Dec 11	Dec 10	Dec 09
Sales Turnover	5m	15m	3m
Pre Tax Profit/Loss	2m	2m	2m
Working Capital	2m	1m	927
Fixed Assets	279	177	46
Current Assets	8m	7m	6m
Current Liabilities	947	982	1m

John Tatam

The Forge Colchester Road, Wakes Colne, Colchester, CO6 2BY
Tel: 01787-222356
E-mail: sales@tatam-blacksmith.co.uk
Website: http://www.tatam-blacksmith.co.uk
Directors: J. Tatam (Prop)
Date established: 1923 **No.of Employees:** 1 - 10 **Product Groups:** 26, 35

T D T Enterprises Ltd

Unit 24 Wryneck Close, Colchester, CO4 5XH
Tel: 01206-853599 **Fax:** 08715-289983
E-mail: trevor@tdtenterprises.co.uk
Website: http://www.tdtenterprises.co.uk
Directors: T. Trood (Dir)
Immediate Holding Company: TDT ENTERPRISES LIMITED
Registration no: 04536966 **Date established:** 2002
Turnover: Up to £250,000 **No.of Employees:** 1 - 10 **Product Groups:** 40, 67

Date of Accounts	Feb 12	Feb 11	Feb 10
Working Capital	-33	76	78
Fixed Assets	235	1	1
Current Assets	29	91	95

Thorogood Timber plc

Colchester Road Ardleigh, Colchester, CO7 7PQ
Tel: 01206-233100 **Fax:** 01206-233115
E-mail: sales@thorogood.co.uk
Website: http://www.thorogood.co.uk
Bank(s): HSBC Bank plc
Directors: D. Mayhew (Mkt Research), P. Thorogood (MD), R. Thorogood (Fin)
Immediate Holding Company: THOROGOOD TIMBER PLC
Registration no: 00746503 **VAT No.:** GB 102 0514 46
Date established: 1963 **Turnover:** £2m - £5m **No.of Employees:** 21 - 50
Product Groups: 08, 25, 48

Date of Accounts	Jan 12	Jan 11	Jan 10
Sales Turnover	5m	5m	4m
Pre Tax Profit/Loss	265	283	268
Working Capital	2m	2m	2m
Fixed Assets	831	753	822
Current Assets	2m	2m	2m
Current Liabilities	280	377	283

Titon Hardware Ltd (Head Office)

International House Peartree Road, Stanway, Colchester, CO3 0JL
Tel: 01206-713800 **Fax:** 01206-543126
E-mail: enquiries@titon.co.uk
Website: http://www.titon.co.uk
Directors: T. Gearey (Tech Serv), T. Anderson (Sales & Mktg), D. Ruffell (Grp Chief Exec), C. Martin (Sales)
Managers: T. Hunter (Personnel)
Ultimate Holding Company: TITON HOLDINGS PLC
Immediate Holding Company: TITON HARDWARE LIMITED
Registration no: 01071731 **VAT No.:** GB 676 6864 00
Date established: 1972 **Turnover:** £10m - £20m
No.of Employees: 21 - 50 **Product Groups:** 36

Date of Accounts	Sep 11	Sep 10	Sep 09
Sales Turnover	13m	14m	13m
Pre Tax Profit/Loss	-152	464	-169
Working Capital	369	738	210
Fixed Assets	1m	1m	1m
Current Assets	5m	5m	5m
Current Liabilities	575	625	561

Turner Process Equipment Ltd

Unit 2 Oakford Place Tog Lane, Great Horkesley, Colchester, CO6 4BX
Tel: 01206-272272 **Fax:** 01206-272998
E-mail: sales@turnerprocessequipment.co.uk
Website: http://www.turnerprocessequipment.co.uk
Directors: C. Giles (Dir)
Immediate Holding Company: TURNER PROCESS EQUIPMENT LIMITED
Registration no: 04829765 **Date established:** 2003
No.of Employees: 1 - 10 **Product Groups:** 36, 40

Date of Accounts	Jul 11	Jul 10	Jul 09
Working Capital	38	35	29
Fixed Assets	11	13	14
Current Assets	137	120	124

Vacuumatic Ltd

8 Brunel Way Severalls Industrial Park, Colchester, CO4 9QX
Tel: 01206-841100 **Fax:** 01206-841166
E-mail: sales@vacuumatic.com
Website: http://www.vacuumatic.com
Bank(s): National Westminster Bank Plc
Directors: S. Boyd (Ch), J. Lewis (Sales & Mktg), N. Millard (Fin), D. Long (Tech Serv)
Managers: C. Page (Personnel), P. Delabruyere (Chief Buyer)
Immediate Holding Company: VACUUMATIC LIMITED
Registration no: 05812970 **VAT No.:** GB 637 0368 37
Date established: 2006 **Turnover:** £5m - £10m **No.of Employees:** 21 - 50
Product Groups: 44

Date of Accounts	Sep 11	Sep 10	Sep 09
Working Capital	905	811	877
Fixed Assets	60	32	31
Current Assets	2m	2m	2m

Wallis Shipping Services Ltd

4 Brunel Way Severalls Industrial Park, Colchester, CO4 9QX
Tel: 01206-751133 **Fax:** 01788-553646
E-mail: info@wssl.co.uk
Website: http://www.wssl.co.uk
Bank(s): Barclays
Managers: K. Barton (Mgr)
Ultimate Holding Company: WSS HOLDINGS LIMITED
Immediate Holding Company: WALLIS SHIPPING SERVICES LIMITED
Registration no: 02074902 **Date established:** 1986 **Turnover:** £1m - £2m
No.of Employees: 11 - 20 **Product Groups:** 74

Date of Accounts	Dec 11	Dec 10	Dec 09
Working Capital	153	108	108
Fixed Assets	26	50	40
Current Assets	777	729	849

White Formula Ltd

14 Regent Road Brightlingsea, Colchester, CO7 0NL
Tel: 01206-302724 **Fax:** 01206-305434
E-mail: info@whiteformula.com
Website: http://www.whiteformula.com

see next page

White Formula Ltd - Cont'd

Directors: M. Fry (Dir), R. White (Fin)
Immediate Holding Company: WHITE FORMULA LIMITED
Registration no: 02994497 **Date established:** 1994
Turnover: £250,000 - £500,000 **No.of Employees:** 11 - 20
Product Groups: 29, 39

Date of Accounts	Mar 10	Mar 09	Mar 08
Working Capital	-167	-181	-111
Fixed Assets	N/A	N/A	11
Current Assets	N/A	6	120
Current Liabilities	167	N/A	N/A

Wilkin & Sons Ltd

Brook Road Tiptree, Colchester, CO5 0RF
Tel: 01621-815407 **Fax:** 01621-814555
E-mail: peter.wilkin@qad.com
Website: http://www.tiptree.com
Bank(s): Barclays, Witham
Directors: P. Wilkin (Ch), S. James (Fin)
Managers: N. Smith (Tech Serv Mgr), S. Cook (Personnel), E. Brothers (Purch Mgr), J. Watkins (Sales Prom Mgr), K. Munford (Mktg Serv Mgr)
Immediate Holding Company: WILKIN & SONS LIMITED
Registration no: 00026233 **VAT No.:** GB 102 3008 46
Date established: 1988 **Turnover:** £20m - £50m
No.of Employees: 101 - 250 **Product Groups:** 01, 20

Date of Accounts	Dec 10	Dec 09	Dec 08
Sales Turnover	28m	25m	22m
Pre Tax Profit/Loss	2m	543	1m
Working Capital	8m	6m	6m
Fixed Assets	7m	7m	5m
Current Assets	12m	9m	9m
Current Liabilities	2m	938	1m

Wood & Mott Ltd

29 Morses Lane Brightlingsea, Colchester, CO7 0SF
Tel: 01206-303929 **Fax:** 01206-304925
E-mail: info@wood-and-mott.co.uk
Website: http://www.wood-and-mott.co.uk
Bank(s): Barclays
Directors: S. Simons (MD), K. Wood (Dir)
Immediate Holding Company: WOOD & MOTT LIMITED
Registration no: 01341914 **VAT No.:** GB 312 5190 95
Date established: 1977 **Turnover:** £500,000 - £1m
No.of Employees: 11 - 20 **Product Groups:** 26

Date of Accounts	Mar 11	Mar 10	Mar 09
Working Capital	83	93	109
Fixed Assets	95	46	58
Current Assets	237	250	246

Dagenham

A W Phillips Ltd

Unit L O Y O Business Units Hindmans Way, Dagenham, RM9 6LN
Tel: 020-8517 0902 **Fax:** 020-8517 0832
E-mail: sales@awphillips.co.uk
Website: http://www.awphillips.co.uk
Directors: E. Cardy (Dir)
Immediate Holding Company: A.W. PHILLIPS LIMITED
Registration no: 04328277 **Date established:** 2001
Turnover: £500,000 - £1m **No.of Employees:** 1 - 10 **Product Groups:** 38, 40, 48, 67, 83

Date of Accounts	Apr 11	Apr 10	Apr 09
Sales Turnover	N/A	N/A	506
Pre Tax Profit/Loss	N/A	N/A	80
Working Capital	6	12	-8
Fixed Assets	241	256	263
Current Assets	127	109	143
Current Liabilities	N/A	N/A	91

Abbey Gauge Company Ltd

139 Becontree Avenue, Dagenham, RM8 2UL
Tel: 020-8590 3233 **Fax:** 020-8590 5082
E-mail: sales@abbeygauge.co.uk
Website: http://www.abbeygauge.co.uk
Directors: A. Williams (MD), J. Clarke (Fin)
Immediate Holding Company: ABBEY GAUGE COMPANY LIMITED
Registration no: 00731308 **VAT No.:** GB 246 2712 69
Date established: 1962 **Turnover:** £250,000 - £500,000
No.of Employees: 1 - 10 **Product Groups:** 36, 38

Date of Accounts	Jul 11	Jul 10	Jul 09
Working Capital	-3	-2	-3
Fixed Assets	4	3	4
Current Assets	49	43	30

Athena Training UK

Suite 3 13 Sheppey Gardens, Dagenham, RM9 4LD
Tel: 020-8596 9768 **Fax:** 020-8517 0007
E-mail: enquiries@athenatraininguk.net
Website: http://www.athenatraininguk.net
Managers: M. Wear (Mgr)
Turnover: Up to £250,000 **No.of Employees:** 11 - 20 **Product Groups:** 26, 28, 64, 86

Capital Hair & Beauty

Unit 1 Cromwell Centre Selinas Lane, Dagenham, RM8 1QH
Tel: 020-8593 1883 **Fax:** 020-8593 7462
E-mail: dagenham@capitalhairandbeauty.co.uk
Website: http://www.capitalhairandbeauty.co.uk
Directors: P. Vanfagnew (Dir)
Immediate Holding Company: CAPITAL (HAIR AND BEAUTY) LIMITED
Registration no: 00530201 **Date established:** 1954
No.of Employees: 1 - 10 **Product Groups:** 32, 40, 63, 67

Date of Accounts	Dec 11	Dec 10	Dec 09
Sales Turnover	32m	28m	24m
Pre Tax Profit/Loss	4m	749	2m
Working Capital	7m	4m	3m
Fixed Assets	3m	3m	2m
Current Assets	13m	8m	7m
Current Liabilities	4m	3m	3m

Carona Reuter

Unit 13 Coppen Road, Dagenham, RM8 1HN
Tel: 020-8592 2576 **Fax:** 020-8595 8024
E-mail: nick@carona-reuter.com
Website: http://www.carona-reuter.com
Bank(s): The Royal Bank of Scotland
Directors: N. Roberts (Dir)
Immediate Holding Company: CARONA REUTER INDUSTRIAL LIMITED
Registration no: 03044187 **VAT No.:** GB 657 1282 28
Date established: 1995 **Turnover:** £1m - £2m **No.of Employees:** 11 - 20
Product Groups: 35, 63, 66

Date of Accounts	Oct 11	Oct 10	Oct 09
Working Capital	-92	-105	-70
Fixed Assets	115	127	144
Current Assets	465	375	462

Containers4sale UK Ltd

27 Goring Road, Dagenham, RM10 8BL
Tel: 020-8517 5524
E-mail: sales@containrs4saleuk.com
Website: http://www.containers4saleuk.com
Directors: L. Smallwood (Fin)
Immediate Holding Company: CONTAINERS4SALE UK LTD
Registration no: 06499642 **Date established:** 2008
No.of Employees: 1 - 10 **Product Groups:** 25

Date of Accounts	May 11	May 10	May 09
Working Capital	-41	-23	-15
Fixed Assets	187	151	96
Current Assets	119	86	79

Continental Shutters Ltd

1 Heathway Industrial Estate Manchester Way, Dagenham, RM10 8PN
Tel: 020-8517 8877 **Fax:** 020-8593 5721
E-mail: sales@continentalshutters.com
Website: http://www.continentalshutters.com
Directors: R. Gell (Sales & Mktg), S. Davidson (Dir)
Managers: S. Jones (Sales Prom Mgr), M. Gell (Mgr), J. Mace ()
Registration no: 01056899 **No.of Employees:** 11 - 20
Product Groups: 30, 35, 36, 49

Date of Accounts	Jun 08	Jun 07	Jun 06
Working Capital	192	219	214
Fixed Assets	58	33	44
Current Assets	433	469	493
Current Liabilities	241	250	279
Total Share Capital	1	1	1

Earlswood Lift Gates & Shutters Ltd

7 Mirravale Trading Estate Selinas Lane, Dagenham, RM8 1QD
Tel: 020-8595 3060 **Fax:** 020-8596 9345
E-mail: info@earlswood.co.uk
Website: http://www.earlswood.co.uk
Directors: A. Revell (Fin)
Managers: A. Lloyd
Ultimate Holding Company: BGC HOLDINGS LIMITED
Immediate Holding Company: EARLSWOOD INDUSTRIAL SERVICES LIMITED
Registration no: 02241291 **Date established:** 1988
No.of Employees: 11 - 20 **Product Groups:** 26, 35

Date of Accounts	Dec 11	Dec 10	Dec 09
Working Capital	-222	-51	-52
Fixed Assets	504	518	537
Current Assets	380	444	521

Essex Wrought Iron Ltd

Unit 6 Midis Industrial Estate Wantz Road, Dagenham, RM10 8PS
Tel: 020-8592 9619 **Fax:** 020-8517 1085
E-mail: sales@essexwroughtiron.co.uk
Website: http://www.essexwroughtiron.co.uk
Directors: F. Marnham (MD)
Immediate Holding Company: ESSEX WROUGHT IRON LIMITED
Registration no: 02775791 **Date established:** 1992
No.of Employees: 1 - 10 **Product Groups:** 35, 36, 37, 39, 40, 45, 49, 66

Date of Accounts	Dec 11	Dec 10	Dec 09
Working Capital	-26	-46	16
Fixed Assets	74	99	36
Current Assets	167	95	85

A J S Group Services Ltd

22-42 Freshwater Road, Dagenham, RM8 1RY
Tel: 020-8597 7000 **Fax:** 020-8597 7300
E-mail: info@ajsgroupservices.com
Website: http://www.ajsgroupservices.com
Bank(s): Barclays
Directors: K. Barnard (Dir)
Immediate Holding Company: AJS GROUP SERVICES LTD
Registration no: 06299457 **VAT No.:** GB 646 1358 34
Date established: 2007 **Turnover:** £2m - £5m **No.of Employees:** 21 - 50
Product Groups: 52

F W Hipkin Ltd

Coppen Road, Dagenham, RM8 1NU
Tel: 020-8984 1000 **Fax:** 020-8984 0101
Directors: S. Hipkin (Dir)
Managers: S. Walker (Mgr)
Ultimate Holding Company: HIPKIN HOLDINGS LIMITED
Immediate Holding Company: F W HIPKIN LIMITED
Registration no: 00322577 **Date established:** 1937
Turnover: £500,000 - £1m **No.of Employees:** 21 - 50 **Product Groups:** 66

Date of Accounts	Dec 11	Dec 10	Dec 09
Working Capital	1m	1m	1m
Fixed Assets	899	673	640
Current Assets	3m	2m	2m

Hyrdrovane Air Compressor Services

Unit L O Y O Business Units Hindmans Way, Dagenham, RM9 6LN
Tel: 020-8517 0902 **Fax:** 020-7511 0194
E-mail: sales@awphillips.co.uk
Website: http://www.awphillips.co.uk
Directors: E. Cardy (Dir)
Turnover: £1m - £2m **No.of Employees:** 1 - 10 **Product Groups:** 38, 40, 48, 67, 83

J M R Section Benders Ltd

Sterling Industrial Estate Rainham Road South, Dagenham, RM10 8TX
Tel: 020-8593 7324 **Fax:** 020-8595 6139
E-mail: roger@jmrsectionbenders.co.uk
Website: http://www.jmrsectionbenders.co.uk
Bank(s): Barclays, Barking
Directors: R. Jeffreys (MD), R. Jeffries (MD)
Immediate Holding Company: JMR SECTION BENDERS LTD
Registration no: 00526837 **VAT No.:** GB 597 0002 45
Date established: 1953 **Turnover:** £500,000 - £1m
No.of Employees: 11 - 20 **Product Groups:** 34, 35, 45, 48

Date of Accounts	Apr 11	Apr 10	Apr 09
Working Capital	5	-54	13
Fixed Assets	79	75	73
Current Assets	225	169	231

L B S Group

6 Sterling Industrial Estate Rainham Road South, Dagenham, RM10 8TX
Tel: 020-8517 6655 **Fax:** 020-8984 0378
E-mail: martin.olsen@lbsgroup.co.uk
Website: http://www.lbsgroup.co.uk
Directors: M. Cordell (Fin), L. Bird (MD)
Managers: M. Olsen (Mgr)
Turnover: £1m - £2m **No.of Employees:** 51 - 100 **Product Groups:** 30, 35, 36, 48

Lockson Services Ltd

Heath Park Industrial Estate Freshwater Road, Dagenham, RM8 1RX
Tel: 020-8597 2889 **Fax:** 020-8597 5265
E-mail: enquiries@lockson.co.uk
Website: http://www.lockson.co.uk
Bank(s): National Westminster
Directors: B. King (MD)
Immediate Holding Company: LOCKSON SERVICES LIMITED
Registration no: 00391428 **VAT No.:** GB 243 6328 68
Date established: 1944 **Turnover:** £1m - £2m **No.of Employees:** 11 - 20
Product Groups: 76

Date of Accounts	Jun 11	Jun 10	Jun 09
Working Capital	120	71	141
Fixed Assets	2m	2m	2m
Current Assets	872	899	984

Nomico Electrical Co. Ltd

817 Dagenham Road, Dagenham, RM10 7UP
Tel: 020-8595 1119 **Fax:** 020-8593 7099
Website: http://www.lineone.com
Directors: J. Briggs (MD)
Immediate Holding Company: NOMICO ELECTRICAL COMPANY LIMITED
Registration no: 01114330 **VAT No.:** GB 247 4329 52
Date established: 1973 **Turnover:** £500,000 - £1m
No.of Employees: 1 - 10 **Product Groups:** 52

Date of Accounts	Jun 11	Jun 10	Jun 09
Working Capital	674	589	529
Fixed Assets	29	202	203
Current Assets	842	829	725
Current Liabilities	N/A	42	N/A

Online Technology Ltd

240 Freshwater Road, Dagenham, RM8 1RX
Tel: 020-8599 6992 **Fax:** 020-7983 8948
E-mail: sales@palletforce.com
Website: http://www.onlinetech.co.uk
Directors: G. Lane (Fin)
Immediate Holding Company: ONLINE TECHNOLOGY INTERNATIONAL LTD.
Registration no: 03391974 **Date established:** 1997
Turnover: £250,000 - £500,000 **No.of Employees:** 101 - 250
Product Groups: 77

Date of Accounts	Dec 08	Dec 07	Jan 11
Sales Turnover	292	132	N/A
Pre Tax Profit/Loss	35	1	N/A
Working Capital	-281	-318	117
Fixed Assets	N/A	1	1
Current Assets	98	32	178
Current Liabilities	322	284	N/A

Ruban d'Or

Crescent Road, Dagenham, RM10 7HR
Tel: 020-8491 9147
E-mail: info@rubandor.co.uk
Website: http://www.rubandor.co.uk
Directors: L. Gordon (Prop)
No.of Employees: 1 - 10 **Product Groups:** 36, 67, 69

Russell Shutters Ltd (Part of the LBS Group)

Unit 6 Sterling Trading Estate Rainham Road South, Dagenham, RM10 8TX
Tel: 020-8517 6655 **Fax:** 020-8984 0378
E-mail: sales@lbsgroup.co.uk
Website: http://www.lbsgroup.co.uk
Bank(s): Barclays
Directors: L. Bird (Prop)
Managers: D. Salter (Sales Prom Mgr), I. Dejoudt (Chief Mgr)
Registration no: 02724171 **VAT No.:** GB 387 8342 04
Turnover: £2m - £5m **No.of Employees:** 51 - 100 **Product Groups:** 35, 36, 49

Sanofi Aventis

Rainham Road South, Dagenham, RM10 7XS
Tel: 020-8919 3060 **Fax:** 020-8919 2140
Website: http://www.sanofi.com
Directors: D. Nicholls (Fin), D. Rees (Dir)
Immediate Holding Company: PHONE POULENC S.A.
Registration no: 01535640 **No.of Employees:** 251 - 500
Product Groups: 32

W F Electrical

301-311 Rainham Road South, Dagenham, RM10 8SX
Tel: 020-8596 7200 **Fax:** 020-8984 9400
E-mail: peter.warsap@hagemeyer.co.uk
Website: http://www.wf-online.com
Managers: J. Evetts (Mgr)
Ultimate Holding Company: RAY INVESTMENT SARL (LUXEMBOURG)
Immediate Holding Company: WF ELECTRICAL LIMITED
Registration no: 00085004 **VAT No.:** GB 466 6077 19
Date established: 2005 **Turnover:** £5m - £10m **No.of Employees:** 11 - 20
Product Groups: 37

Date of Accounts	Dec 11	Dec 10	Dec 09
Pre Tax Profit/Loss	N/A	-1	2
Working Capital	25m	25m	25m
Current Assets	38m	38m	38m

Whitaker & Sawyer Brushes Ltd

Unit 17 Midas Business Centre Wantz Road, Dagenham, RM10 8PS
Tel: 020-8593 7204 **Fax:** 020-8595 7353
E-mail: info@wsbrushes.co.uk
Website: http://www.wsbrushes.co.uk
Directors: N. Forbes (MD)
Ultimate Holding Company: BROOKLINK LIMITED
Immediate Holding Company: WHITAKER & SAWYER (BRUSHES) LIMITED

Registration no: 02472949 **VAT No.:** GB 504 2109 79
Date established: 1990 **Turnover:** £500,000 - £1m
No.of Employees: 1 - 10 **Product Groups:** 49

Date of Accounts	Dec 11	Dec 10	Dec 09
Working Capital	128	115	120
Fixed Assets	1	10	16
Current Assets	196	179	176

Dunmow

The Active Spring Company Ltd

Sibleys Green Sibleys Lane, Thaxted, Dunmow, CM6 2NU
Tel: 01371-830557 **Fax:** 01371-831151
E-mail: sales@tascuk.com
Website: http://www.tascuk.com
Directors: J. Crane (MD), A. Crane (Fin)
Managers: T. McKay (Mktg Serv Mgr)
Immediate Holding Company: THE ACTIVE SPRING COMPANY LIMITED
Registration no: 01598903 **Date established:** 1981
Turnover: £250,000 - £500,000 **No.of Employees:** 11 - 20
Product Groups: 35

Date of Accounts	Mar 11	Mar 10	Mar 09
Working Capital	-74	11	-160
Fixed Assets	893	773	894
Current Assets	779	537	453

Associated Joinery Techniques Ltd

Marks Hall Marks Hall Lane, Margaret Roding, Dunmow, CM6 1QT
Tel: 01245-231881 **Fax:** 01245-231818
E-mail: kyoung@ajtlabfurniture.com
Website: http://www.ajtlabfurniture.com
Directors: A. Polan (MD)
Immediate Holding Company: ASSOCIATED JOINERY TECHNIQUES LIMITED
Registration no: 00911907 **VAT No.:** GB 246 6364 76
Date established: 1967 **Turnover:** £1m - £2m **No.of Employees:** 1 - 10
Product Groups: 26

Date of Accounts	Sep 11	Sep 10	Sep 09
Working Capital	33	10	82
Fixed Assets	23	29	38
Current Assets	250	204	417

Atlas Winch & Hoist Services

Martels Works High Easter Road, Barnston, Dunmow, CM6 1NA
Tel: 01371-859555 **Fax:** 01371-859567
E-mail: info@winchhire.com
Website: http://www.winchhire.com
Directors: A. Lavery (Prop)
Ultimate Holding Company: WESTBURY GARDEN ROOMS LIMITED
Immediate Holding Company: HIGH PROFILE SYSTEMS LIMITED
Date established: 1985 **No.of Employees:** 1 - 10 **Product Groups:** 35, 39, 45

Date of Accounts	Mar 94	Mar 93	Mar 92
Working Capital	110	N/A	N/A
Fixed Assets	55	49	63
Current Assets	895	604	473

Base Design Ltd

Bigods Hall Bigods Lane, Dunmow, CM6 3BE
Tel: 01371-876479
E-mail: mark@base-design.co.uk
Website: http://base-design.co.uk
Managers: M. Foyle (Ops Mgr)
Immediate Holding Company: BASE DESIGN LTD
Registration no: 06401438 **Date established:** 2007
No.of Employees: 1 - 10 **Product Groups:** 38, 67

Date of Accounts	Oct 08	May 11	May 09
Working Capital	-19	-35	-17
Fixed Assets	8	11	7
Current Assets	21	37	29

C J Skilton Aquarist

Willow Thatch Stebbing Green, Gt Dunmow, Dunmow, CM6 3TE
Tel: 01371-856257 **Fax:** 01245-400585
E-mail: cjskilton@aquaskil.co.uk
Website: http://www.aquaskil.co.uk
Directors: C. Skilton (Prop), S. Skilton (MD)
Turnover: Up to £250,000 **No.of Employees:** 1 - 10 **Product Groups:** 02, 30, 38, 49, 62, 84

Colter Products Ltd

Unit 7 Zone C Chelmsford Road Industrial Estate Chelmsford Road, Dunmow, CM6 1HD
Tel: 01371-876887 **Fax:** 01371-875638
E-mail: sales@coltergroup.co.uk
Website: http://www.coltergroup.co.uk
Directors: P. Fox (MD), P. Fox (Fin)
Immediate Holding Company: COLTER PRODUCTS LIMITED
Registration no: 03112388 **VAT No.:** GB 550 0240 02
Date established: 1995 **Turnover:** £1m - £2m **No.of Employees:** 1 - 10
Product Groups: 37

Date of Accounts	Sep 11	Sep 10	Sep 09
Working Capital	130	102	142
Fixed Assets	7	8	9
Current Assets	170	152	162

Complus Teltronic Ltd

Sibleys Green Thaxted, Dunmow, CM6 2NU
Tel: 01371-830326 **Fax:** 01371-831096
E-mail: enquiries@complus.co.uk
Website: http://www.complusteltronic.co.uk
Bank(s): Lloyds TSB Bank plc
Directors: B. Richardson (Tech Serv), G. Gregoriou (Sales), J. Davies (Fin), W. Stogdon (MD)
Immediate Holding Company: Commend UK Ltd
Registration no: 06654371 **VAT No.:** GB 213 5987 54
Date established: 2008 **Turnover:** £2m - £5m **No.of Employees:** 51 - 100
Product Groups: 37, 40, 67

Essex X-Ray & Medical Equipment Ltd

Flitch Industrial Estate Chelmsford Road, Dunmow, CM6 1XJ
Tel: 01371-875661 **Fax:** 01371-875665
E-mail: peter.smith@essexxray.com
Website: http://www.essex-x-ray.com
Directors: P. Smith (Sales & Mktg)
Managers: P. Smith (Chief Mgr)
Ultimate Holding Company: HEICO ELECTRONIC TECHNOLOGIES GROUP INC (USA)
Immediate Holding Company: ESSEX X-RAY AND MEDICAL EQUIPMENT LIMITED
Registration no: 02624214 **Date established:** 1991 **Turnover:** £2m - £5m
No.of Employees: 21 - 50 **Product Groups:** 37

Date of Accounts	Oct 11	Oct 10	Oct 09
Working Capital	888	935	691
Fixed Assets	287	317	337
Current Assets	1m	2m	1m

Fleuroma Ltd

Unit 5 Flitch Industrial Estate Chelmsford Road, Dunmow, CM6 1XJ
Tel: 01371-874116 **Fax:** 01371-876975
E-mail: ted@fleuroma.demon.co.uk
Website: http://www.fleuroma.com
Directors: E. Satchell (MD)
Immediate Holding Company: FLEUROMA LIMITED
Registration no: 02880440 **Date established:** 1993
Turnover: £250,000 - £500,000 **No.of Employees:** 1 - 10
Product Groups: 31, 32, 61, 63, 66

Date of Accounts	Mar 11	Mar 10	Mar 08
Working Capital	15	16	72
Fixed Assets	2	2	4
Current Assets	72	74	141

High Voltage Technology Limited

Flitch Industrial Estate Chelmsford Road, Great Dunmow, Dunmow, CM6 1XJ
Tel: 01371-875668 **Fax:** 01371-875665
E-mail: hvt@essex-x-ray.com
Website: http://www.essex-x-ray.com
Bank(s): Natwest
Directors: J. De Fries (MD)
Managers: S. Mountain (Chief Mgr)
Immediate Holding Company: High Voltage Technology Ltd
Registration no: 02643431 **VAT No.:** GB 594 6294 91
Date established: 1991 **Turnover:** £2m - £5m **No.of Employees:** 21 - 50
Product Groups: 29, 33, 37, 38

Hospitality A V

Unit 2 Martels High Easter Road, Barnston, Dunmow, CM6 1NA
Tel: 01371-872288 **Fax:** 01371-875881
E-mail: sales@hospitalityav.com
Website: http://www.hospitalityav.com
Directors: J. Came (Prop)
Registration no: 2639963 **Turnover:** £1m - £2m **No.of Employees:** 1 - 10
Product Groups: 26, 28, 30, 36, 37, 39, 49, 64, 65, 67, 69

J W F

Hales Farm High Cross Lane, Little Canfield, Dunmow, CM6 1TQ
Tel: 01371-878383 **Fax:** 01371-878393
Directors: M. Walker (Ptnr)
Immediate Holding Company: THE ESSEX HUNT
Registration no: 04405538 **Date established:** 2004
No.of Employees: 1 - 10 **Product Groups:** 35

Date of Accounts	Apr 11	Apr 10	Apr 08
Sales Turnover	93	90	80
Pre Tax Profit/Loss	-10	-13	-13
Working Capital	-12	19	28
Fixed Assets	20	N/A	13
Current Assets	4	38	31
Current Liabilities	16	19	1

Molecular Properties Ltd

Mill End Thaxted, Dunmow, CM6 2LT
Tel: 01371-830676 **Fax:** 01371-830998
E-mail: info@molecularproducts.co.uk
Website: http://www.molecularproducts.co.uk
Bank(s): Lloyds TSB Bank plc
Directors: A. McKernan (MD), R. Ignatius (Co Sec)
Managers: E. Knight, J. Lomas (Personnel), R. Wright (Tech Serv Mgr)
Ultimate Holding Company: MOLECULAR PRODUCTS GROUP PLC
Immediate Holding Company: MOLECULAR PROPERTIES LIMITED
Registration no: 01065581 **VAT No.:** GB 249 3111 72
Date established: 1972 **Turnover:** Up to £250,000
No.of Employees: 51 - 100 **Product Groups:** 31, 32, 42, 54

Date of Accounts	Mar 12	Mar 11	Mar 10
Sales Turnover	182	182	132
Pre Tax Profit/Loss	106	110	48
Working Capital	125	161	-16
Fixed Assets	1m	1m	2m
Current Assets	398	239	69
Current Liabilities	18	23	30

Peta UK Ltd

Marks Hall Marks Hall Lane, Margaret Roding, Dunmow, CM6 1QT
Tel: 01245-231118 **Fax:** 01245-231811
E-mail: peta@peta-uk.com
Website: http://www.peta-uk.com
Directors: G. Crockett (MD)
Managers: L. Fairman (Sales Prom Mgr)
Immediate Holding Company: PETA (UK) LIMITED
Registration no: 00504011 **Date established:** 1952
Turnover: £250,000 - £500,000 **No.of Employees:** 1 - 10
Product Groups: 30, 41

Date of Accounts	Dec 09	Dec 08	Dec 07
Working Capital	213	180	171
Fixed Assets	40	44	36
Current Assets	260	219	214

Plasmold Precision

8 Oak Industrial Park Chelmsford Road, Dunmow, CM6 1XN
Tel: 01371-876445 **Fax:** 01708-732691
E-mail: lee@plasmoldplastics.co.uk
Website: http://www.plasmoldplastics.co.uk
Directors: F. Hallinan (Dir)
Immediate Holding Company: PLASMOLD PRECISION LIMITED
Registration no: 03667700 **Date established:** 1998
Turnover: £500,000 - £1m **No.of Employees:** 1 - 10 **Product Groups:** 30, 42, 48, 67, 84

Precision Moulded Products Ltd

Riclyn House Flitch Industrial Estate Chelmsford Road, Dunmow, CM6 1XJ
Tel: 01371-876681 **Fax:** 01371-874900
E-mail: simon.lane@hookergroup.co.uk
Website: http://www.pmpessex.co.uk
Bank(s): Barclays, Clacton-On-Sea
Directors: M. Pineo (Fin), S. Lane (MD)
Managers: C. Beales (Sales Admin), W. Baldwin (Chief Mgr)
Immediate Holding Company: PRECISION MOULDED PRODUCTS (ESSEX) LIMITED
Registration no: 01342732 **VAT No.:** GB 490 3748 28
Date established: 1977 **Turnover:** £1m - £2m **No.of Employees:** 11 - 20
Product Groups: 30, 84

Date of Accounts	Mar 11	Mar 10	Mar 09
Working Capital	147	247	107
Fixed Assets	117	186	298
Current Assets	585	572	690

R G H Rubber & Plastics

Acorn House 2 Oak Industrial Park Chelmsford Road, Dunmow, CM6 1XN
Tel: 01371-875941 **Fax:** 01371-873804
E-mail: sales@rghrubber.co.uk
Website: http://www.rghrubber.co.uk
Bank(s): Barclays Great Dunmow
Directors: R. Hildrow (Co Sec)
Immediate Holding Company: R G H RUBBER AND PLASTICS LIMITED
Registration no: 02501493 **Date established:** 1990
No.of Employees: 11 - 20 **Product Groups:** 27, 29, 30, 31, 49

Date of Accounts	Apr 12	Apr 11	Apr 10
Working Capital	434	385	329
Fixed Assets	281	229	139
Current Assets	966	734	598

Results Consortium Ltd

Melville House High Street, Dunmow, CM6 1AF
Tel: 01371-859344 **Fax:** 01371-878414
E-mail: paul.caffery@resultsresults.co.uk
Website: http://www.resultsresults.co.uk
Directors: P. Caffery (MD)
Immediate Holding Company: RESULTS CONSORTIUM LIMITED
Registration no: 04372425 **VAT No.:** GB 937 5671 84
Date established: 2002 **Turnover:** £250,000 - £500,000
No.of Employees: 1 - 10 **Product Groups:** 86

Date of Accounts	Mar 11	Mar 10	Mar 09
Sales Turnover	356	346	348
Pre Tax Profit/Loss	-49	-45	-40
Working Capital	-139	-91	-47
Fixed Assets	12	13	14
Current Assets	23	83	150
Current Liabilities	5	5	5

Russell Stone Fixing Ltd

Unit D Marks Hall Farm Marks Hall Lane White Roding, Dunmow, CM6 1RT
Tel: 01279-877777 **Fax:** 01279-877777
E-mail: info@russellstonefixing.com
Website: http://www.russellstonefixing.com
Directors: A. Russell (Dir)
Managers: D. Curbishley (Comm)
Immediate Holding Company: RUSSELL STONE FIXING LTD
Registration no: 05054387 **Date established:** 2004
Turnover: £125m - £250m **No.of Employees:** 1 - 10 **Product Groups:** 14, 26, 33, 49, 66

Date of Accounts	Feb 08	Feb 07	Feb 06
Working Capital	7	9	1
Fixed Assets	58	2	4
Current Assets	148	22	10
Current Liabilities	141	14	9

Paul Tuckwell Ltd

Chelmsford Road Industrial Estate Chelmsford Road, Dunmow, CM6 1HD
Tel: 01371-875751 **Fax:** 01371-874636
E-mail: dunmow@tuckwell.co.uk
Website: http://www.tuckwell.co.uk
Directors: O. Poulson (Dir)
Registration no: 00607392 **Turnover:** £10m - £20m
No.of Employees: 11 - 20 **Product Groups:** 67, 84

Date of Accounts	Nov 07	Nov 06	Nov 05
Pre Tax Profit/Loss	1191	339	379
Working Capital	1849	1111	911
Fixed Assets	957	932	961
Current Assets	8101	7102	6436
Current Liabilities	6252	5991	5524
Total Share Capital	1	1	1
ROCE% (Return on Capital Employed)	42.4	16.6	20.2

Viking Mouldings

Unit 11 Ongar Road Trading Estate Ongar Road, Dunmow, CM6 1EU
Tel: 01371-875214 **Fax:** 01371-873826
E-mail: info@vikingcruisers.com
Website: http://www.vikingcruisers.com
Bank(s): Lloyds
Directors: V. Clayden (Ptnr)
Date established: 1972 **Turnover:** £250,000 - £500,000
No.of Employees: 11 - 20 **Product Groups:** 39, 68

Washtec UK Ltd

14a Oak Industrial Park Chelmsford Road, Dunmow, CM6 1XN
Tel: 01371-878800 **Fax:** 01371-878810
E-mail: sales@washtec-uk.com
Website: http://www.washtec-uk.com
Managers: C. Sampson, D. Halls (Comptroller), K. Pratt (Buyer), D. Fraizer (Mktg Serv Mgr)
Ultimate Holding Company: WASHTEC AG (GERMANY)
Immediate Holding Company: WASHTEC (UK) LIMITED
Registration no: 02040161 **VAT No.:** GB 448 9736 89
Date established: 1986 **Turnover:** £10m - £20m
No.of Employees: 51 - 100 **Product Groups:** 39, 45

Date of Accounts	Dec 11	Dec 10	Dec 09
Sales Turnover	8m	11m	11m
Pre Tax Profit/Loss	-896	549	661
Working Capital	889	2m	2m
Fixed Assets	405	538	649
Current Assets	3m	4m	4m
Current Liabilities	1m	2m	2m

Weldair Stansted Ltd

The Rise Brick End, Broxted, Dunmow, CM6 2BJ
Tel: 01279-850076 **Fax:** 01279-850073
Directors: R. Webb (MD)
Immediate Holding Company: WELDAIR STANSTED LIMITED
Registration no: 02468463 **Date established:** 1990
No.of Employees: 1 - 10 **Product Groups:** 46

Date of Accounts	Feb 08	Feb 11	Feb 10
Working Capital	-17	23	36
Fixed Assets	47	36	45
Current Assets	95	74	97

Epping

Arthur Branwell & Co. Ltd
58-62 High Street, Epping, CM16 4AE
Tel: 01992-577333 **Fax:** 01992-561138
E-mail: colincooper@branwell.com
Website: http://www.branwell.com
Directors: B. Denyar (Dir)
Immediate Holding Company: ARTHUR BRANWELL & CO. LIMITED
Registration no: 00079908 **Date established:** 2004
Turnover: £10m - £20m **No.of Employees:** 11 - 20 **Product Groups:** 32, 33

Date of Accounts	Sep 11	Sep 10	Sep 09
Sales Turnover	12m	12m	10m
Pre Tax Profit/Loss	220	207	233
Working Capital	2m	2m	1m
Fixed Assets	3m	3m	3m
Current Assets	6m	5m	5m
Current Liabilities	208	633	531

Clarke International
Hemnall Street, Epping, CM16 4LG
Tel: 01992-565300 **Fax:** 01992-561562
E-mail: info@clarkeinternational.com
Website: http://www.clarkeinternational.com
Bank(s): National Westminster Bank Plc
Directors: J. Clarke (Dir), T. Aiken (Sales), S. Clarke (Fin)
Immediate Holding Company: CLARKE INTERNATIONAL LIMITED
Registration no: 00972660 **VAT No.:** GB 220 4213 30
Date established: 1970 **Turnover:** £20m - £50m
No.of Employees: 101 - 250 **Product Groups:** 37, 39, 40

Date of Accounts	May 11	May 10	May 09
Sales Turnover	34m	31m	28m
Pre Tax Profit/Loss	2m	847	65
Working Capital	19m	17m	16m
Fixed Assets	4m	4m	4m
Current Assets	73m	61m	54m
Current Liabilities	51m	41m	36m

CLT Innovations Ltd
Tawney Barn Yawney Common, Epping, CM16 7PX
Tel: 01992-524991
E-mail: john@gallowayfarms.org
Website: http://www.scarem.co.uk
Directors: J. Galloway (Dir)
Registration no: 06690051 **Date established:** 2001
Turnover: £250,000 - £500,000 **No.of Employees:** 1 - 10
Product Groups: 67

Eagle Automation Systems Ltd
Newhouse Farm Vicarage Lane, North Weald, Epping, CM16 6AP
Tel: 01992-524800 **Fax:** 01992-522208
E-mail: info@eagleautogate.co.uk
Website: http://www.eagleautogate.co.uk
Directors: D. Ashby (MD)
Immediate Holding Company: EAGLE AUTOMATION SYSTEMS LIMITED
Registration no: 03307848 **Date established:** 1997
Turnover: £500,000 - £1m **No.of Employees:** 11 - 20
Product Groups: 35, 36, 37, 38, 39, 40, 45, 49, 52, 66, 67, 81

Date of Accounts	Apr 11	Apr 10	Apr 09
Working Capital	606	615	446
Fixed Assets	92	98	99
Current Assets	1m	1m	938

Emwood Catering Equipment Engineers
8 Elm Gardens North Weald, Epping, CM16 6DR
Tel: 01992-524742 **Fax:** 01992-524584
E-mail: em.wood@yahoo.co.uk
Directors: M. Wood (Prop)
Registration no: 01635632 **Date established:** 1982
No.of Employees: 1 - 10 **Product Groups:** 20, 40, 41

Kardex Systems UK Ltd
Kestrel House Falconry Court Bakers Lane, Epping, CM16 5LL
Tel: 01992-566200 **Fax:** 0870-240 0420
E-mail: richard.price@kardex.co.uk
Website: http://www.kardex-remstar.co.uk
Bank(s): The Royal Bank of Scotland, London
Directors: N. Tuggey (Mkt Research), R. Price (Sales)
Managers: R. Pandya (Personnel), A. Joslin, M. Davidson, R. Short (Purch Mgr)
Ultimate Holding Company: KARDEX AG (SWITZERLAND)
Immediate Holding Company: KARDEX SYSTEMS (UK) LIMITED
Registration no: 00960163 **Date established:** 1969 **Turnover:** £5m - £10m
No.of Employees: 11 - 20 **Product Groups:** 35, 36, 37, 44, 49, 84

Date of Accounts	Dec 11	Dec 10	Dec 09
Sales Turnover	10m	10m	8m
Pre Tax Profit/Loss	-436	266	-84
Working Capital	229	717	544
Fixed Assets	54	74	34
Current Assets	4m	5m	5m
Current Liabilities	3m	3m	2m

King Carbon Ltd
Richmond Farm Parsloe Road, Epping Green, Epping, CM16 6QB
Tel: 01279-641111
E-mail: info@kingcarbon.co.uk
Website: http://www.kingcarbon.co.uk
Directors: L. Gudgeon (Dir)
Ultimate Holding Company: BAXTER INTERNATIONAL INC
Immediate Holding Company: KING CARBON LIMITED
Registration no: 06771333 **VAT No.:** GB 103 2224 39
Date established: 2008 **Turnover:** £20m - £50m **No.of Employees:** 1 - 10
Product Groups: 30, 38

Date of Accounts	Apr 11	Apr 10
Working Capital	-17	-13
Fixed Assets	21	21
Current Assets	23	26

Moores Forklifts Ltd
Unit 9 Esgors Farm High Road, Thornwood, Epping, CM16 6LY
Tel: 01992-575761 **Fax:** 020-7511 7636
E-mail: info@mooresforklifts.co.uk
Directors: H. Moore (Fin), R. Moore (MD)
Immediate Holding Company: MOORES FORKLIFTS LIMITED
Registration no: 04093399 **Date established:** 2000
Turnover: £250,000 - £500,000 **No.of Employees:** 1 - 10
Product Groups: 35, 39, 45

Date of Accounts	Sep 11	Sep 10	Sep 09
Working Capital	-1	27	16
Fixed Assets	12	10	16
Current Assets	80	83	75

Steiner Hops Ltd
319a High Street, Epping, CM16 4DA
Tel: 01992-572331 **Fax:** 01992-573780
E-mail: enquiries@hopsteiner.co.uk
Website: http://www.hopsteiner.com
Directors: T. Roberts (Fin)
Managers: L. Gimbel
Ultimate Holding Company: S S STEINER INC (USA)
Immediate Holding Company: STEINER HOPS LIMITED
Registration no: 01166845 **Date established:** 1974
No.of Employees: 1 - 10 **Product Groups:** 20, 40, 41

Date of Accounts	Dec 11	Dec 10	Dec 09
Working Capital	985	1000	968
Fixed Assets	35	42	49
Current Assets	2m	3m	2m

Frinton On Sea

Gardencast
Estate House 143 Connaught Avenue, Frinton On Sea, CO13 9AB
Tel: 01255-679600 **Fax:** 01255-679825
E-mail: enquiries@gardencast.co.uk
Website: http://www.gardencast.co.uk
Directors: R. Eason (Prop)
Immediate Holding Company: JAYGATE (CAMBRIDGE) LIMITED
Registration no: 03889887 **VAT No.:** GB 749 0394 09
Date established: 2011 **Turnover:** £2m - £5m **No.of Employees:** 1 - 10
Product Groups: 34, 61, 63, 67

Date of Accounts	Mar 12	Mar 11
Working Capital	-1m	-1m
Fixed Assets	1m	1m
Current Assets	16	34

Loxford Equipment Co. Ltd
Wood Hall Church Lane, Great Holland, Frinton On Sea, CO13 0JS
Tel: 01255-851555 **Fax:** 01255-851051
E-mail: enquiries@loxford-equipment.co.uk
Website: http://www.loxford-equipment.co.uk
Directors: M. Poulten (MD), S. Nicoll (MD)
Immediate Holding Company: Loxford Equipment Co.Limited
Registration no: 00785981 **VAT No.:** GB 597 1479 83
Turnover: Up to £250,000 **No.of Employees:** 1 - 10 **Product Groups:** 37, 84

Date of Accounts	Mar 08	Mar 07	Mar 06
Working Capital	169	160	160
Fixed Assets	3	4	4
Current Assets	208	193	193
Current Liabilities	40	33	33

Robin C Rolfe
35 Queens Road, Frinton On Sea, CO13 9BL
Tel: 01255-672564 **Fax:** 01255-672564
E-mail: robinrolfe@btconnect.com
Directors: R. Rolfe (Prop)
Date established: 1999 **No.of Employees:** 1 - 10 **Product Groups:** 35

Grays

Ashby & Croft
Yard 5 Oliver Road, Grays, RM20 3ED
Tel: 01708-869600 **Fax:** 01708-867200
E-mail: sales@ashbyandcroft.co.uk
Website: http://www.ashbyandcroft.co.uk
Directors: D. Langford (MD)
Immediate Holding Company: QUEST ENVIROMENTAL LTD
Registration no: 05820729 **Date established:** 2010
No.of Employees: 11 - 20 **Product Groups:** 25, 30, 33, 35, 66, 83, 84

Date of Accounts	Oct 11
Working Capital	-2
Fixed Assets	4
Current Assets	12
Current Liabilities	14

Atlas Diesel Services
Unit B Criton Industrial Estate Stanford Road, Orsett, Grays, RM16 3DH
Tel: 01375-891045
Directors: J. Buckhorn (Prop)
Date established: 1957 **No.of Employees:** 1 - 10 **Product Groups:** 40

Philip Beadle
56 Mayfields, Grays, RM16 2XL
Tel: 01375-386197
E-mail: philipbeadle@talktalk.net
Directors: P. Beadle (Prop)
Date established: 1993 **No.of Employees:** 1 - 10 **Product Groups:** 35

Blount Shutters Ltd
734 London Road, Grays, RM20 3NL
Tel: 01708-860000 **Fax:** 01708-861271
E-mail: sales@blountshutters.co.uk
Website: http://www.blountshutters.co.uk
Directors: P. Blount (Fin)
Managers: C. Brennan (Mktg Serv Mgr), P. Robertson (Personnel), J. Turner, B. Weston (Ops Mgr), P. White (Purch Mgr)
Immediate Holding Company: BLOUNT SHUTTERS LIMITED
Registration no: 01849492 **Date established:** 1984 **Turnover:** £1m - £2m
No.of Employees: 51 - 100 **Product Groups:** 30, 34, 35, 36, 37, 40, 48, 49, 66

Date of Accounts	Mar 11	Mar 10	Mar 09
Working Capital	803	683	545
Fixed Assets	135	195	277
Current Assets	1m	1m	1m

C E D Ltd
728 London Road, Grays, RM20 3LU
Tel: 01708-867237 **Fax:** 01708-867230
E-mail: michaelheap@ced.ltd.uk
Website: http://www.ced.ltd.uk
Directors: G. Heap (Dir), M. Heap (MD)
Managers: D. Maughn (Tech Serv Mgr)
Immediate Holding Company: CED LIMITED
Registration no: 00624843 **Date established:** 1959
Turnover: £10m - £20m **No.of Employees:** 21 - 50 **Product Groups:** 33, 66

Date of Accounts	Jun 11	Jun 10	Jun 09
Sales Turnover	12m	11m	11m
Pre Tax Profit/Loss	210	101	-348
Working Capital	183	173	158
Fixed Assets	3m	4m	4m
Current Assets	5m	4m	4m
Current Liabilities	880	344	230

Cartridge World Ltd
92 Orsett Road, Grays, RM17 5EL
Tel: 01375-377751 **Fax:** 01375-377752
Website: http://www.cartridgeworld.org
Managers: M. Drake (Mgr)
Registration no: 04124067 **Date established:** 2000 **Turnover:** £5m - £10m
No.of Employees: 1 - 10 **Product Groups:** 28, 30, 44, 64

Chemviron Carbon Ltd (Sales Office)
434 London Road, Grays, RM20 4DH
Tel: 01375-381711 **Fax:** 01375-389644
E-mail: info@calgoncarbon.com
Website: http://www.chemvironcarbon.com
Bank(s): Barclays, 9 High St, Grays
Directors: L. Ball (Fin)
Managers: M. Harrison (Mgr)
Ultimate Holding Company: CALGON CARBON CORPORATION (USA)
Immediate Holding Company: CHEMVIRON CARBON LIMITED
Registration no: 02208285 **Date established:** 1987
Turnover: £20m - £50m **No.of Employees:** 11 - 20 **Product Groups:** 31, 33, 40, 42

Date of Accounts	Dec 11	Dec 10	Dec 09
Sales Turnover	33m	28m	24m
Pre Tax Profit/Loss	4m	2m	988
Working Capital	8m	9m	7m
Fixed Assets	7m	5m	6m
Current Assets	15m	12m	10m
Current Liabilities	2m	2m	1m

E C Group Ltd
Europa Park London Road, Grays, RM20 4DN
Tel: 01375-484555 **Fax:** 01375-484556
E-mail: info@ecgroup.co.uk
Website: http://www.ecgroup.co.uk
Directors: M. Rowlands (Tech Serv), C. Long (MD), L. Bishop (Fin)
Managers: C. Tillin, S. Burch (I.T. Exec), D. Vapiwala (Personnel)
Ultimate Holding Company: E. CHRISTIAN & COMPANY (HOLDINGS) LIMITED
Immediate Holding Company: EC LOGISTICS LIMITED
Registration no: 02598770 **Date established:** 1991
Turnover: £10m - £20m **No.of Employees:** 51 - 100 **Product Groups:** 44, 61, 72, 77, 80, 81, 84

Date of Accounts	Mar 11	Mar 10	Mar 09
Working Capital	-876	-516	-395
Fixed Assets	5m	5m	5m
Current Assets	113	111	126

E T Marine & Industrial Engineering Co. Ltd
Unit 1 Manor Way Industrial Estate Curzon Drive, Grays, RM17 6BG
Tel: 01375-378282 **Fax:** 01375-385804
E-mail: ggaler@etmarine.com
Website: http://www.etmarine.com
Directors: L. Emson (Dir), G. Galer (MD), G. Galer (MD)
Ultimate Holding Company: ET MANAGEMENT LTD.
Immediate Holding Company: E.T. MARINE & INDUSTRIAL ENGINEERING COMPANY LIMITED
Registration no: 02431765 **VAT No.:** GB 542 3087 61
Date established: 1989 **No.of Employees:** 21 - 50 **Product Groups:** 84

Date of Accounts	Feb 12	Feb 11	Feb 10
Working Capital	595	610	564
Fixed Assets	151	145	138
Current Assets	845	877	917

Essex Diesel Injection Services
Unit 1-2 The Chase, Grays, RM20 4XF
Tel: 01375-390143 **Fax:** 01375-390869
E-mail: sales@essexdiesel.co.uk
Website: http://www.essexdiesel.co.uk
Directors: A. Evans (Ptnr)
Date established: 1987 **No.of Employees:** 1 - 10 **Product Groups:** 40

Essex Laser Job Shop Ltd
Unit D4 Frogmore Estate Trading Estate Motherwell Way, Grays, RM20 3XD
Tel: 01708-689658 **Fax:** 01708-865953
E-mail: sales@essexlaser.co.uk
Website: http://www.essexlaser.co.uk
Directors: S. Millar (Fin)
Managers: M. Millar (Chief Mgr)
Ultimate Holding Company: DSM GROUP LIMITED
Immediate Holding Company: ESSEX LASER JOB SHOP LIMITED
Registration no: 03675601 **Date established:** 1998
No.of Employees: 1 - 10 **Product Groups:** 24, 48

Date of Accounts	Jun 11	Jun 10	Jun 09
Working Capital	-323	-344	-349
Fixed Assets	9	6	12
Current Assets	346	307	377

Euro Engines
4 Cliffside Industrial Estate Askew Farm Lane, Grays, RM17 5XR
Tel: 01375-371188 **Fax:** 01375-377388
Directors: M. Sibley (Ptnr)
No.of Employees: 1 - 10 **Product Groups:** 40, 68

First Personnel Group plc
1 Cromwell Road, Grays, RM17 5HF
Tel: 01375-391111 **Fax:** 01375-390151
E-mail: contactus@firstpersonnel.co.uk
Website: http://www.firstpersonnel.co.uk
Managers: D. Ashworth
Immediate Holding Company: FIRST PERSONNEL LIMITED
Registration no: 02698188 **Date established:** 1989
No.of Employees: 1 - 10 **Product Groups:** 80

Grays Packaging Ltd
PO Box 237, Grays, RM17 6WL
Tel: 01375-399128
E-mail: sales@grayspackaging.co.uk
Website: http://www.grayspackaging.co.uk
Directors: N. Dobie (Dir)
Immediate Holding Company: GRAYS PACKAGING LTD.
Registration no: 01853487 **Date established:** 1984
Turnover: £250,000 - £500,000 **No.of Employees:** 1 - 10
Product Groups: 30

Date of Accounts	Mar 12	Mar 11	Mar 10
Sales Turnover	N/A	414	N/A
Working Capital	33	30	43
Fixed Assets	2	2	3
Current Assets	114	110	114

Harsco
609 London Road, Grays, RM20 3BJ
Tel: 01708-681666 **Fax:** 01708-869560
E-mail: ncolloss@harsco.com
Website: http://www.harsco.com
Managers: N. Colloss (District Mgr)
Ultimate Holding Company: BALSPEED AG (SWITZERLAND)
Immediate Holding Company: ANGLO OVERSEAS (HOLDINGS) LIMITED
Date established: 1985 **Turnover:** £2m - £5m **No.of Employees:** 51 - 100
Product Groups: 30, 35

Date of Accounts	Dec 08
Sales Turnover	20

Industrial Flow Control Ltd
Unit 1 Askews Farm Lane, Grays, RM17 5XR
Tel: 01375-387155 **Fax:** 01375-387420
E-mail: carl@inflow.co.uk
Website: http://www.inflow.co.uk
Managers: K. Shaw (Ops Mgr)
Ultimate Holding Company: FLOWMAX HOLDINGS LIMITED (BVI)
Immediate Holding Company: INDUSTRIAL FLOW CONTROL LIMITED
Registration no: 02111157 **VAT No.:** GB 452 0326 85
Date established: 1987 **Turnover:** £2m - £5m **No.of Employees:** 1 - 10
Product Groups: 38, 42

Date of Accounts	Apr 12	Apr 11	Apr 10
Working Capital	149	151	108
Fixed Assets	18	17	13
Current Assets	338	577	438
Current Liabilities	86	176	80

Lafarge Cement
Oliver Close, Grays, RM20 3EE
Tel: 01708-685300 **Fax:** 01708-685302
E-mail: john.cox@lefargecement.co.uk
Website: http://www.lafargecement.co.uk
Managers: J. Cox (Mgr)
Immediate Holding Company: M.G. COSGROVE CONSTRUCTION LIMITED
Registration no: 02182762 **Date established:** 1996
No.of Employees: 21 - 50 **Product Groups:** 33

Date of Accounts	Jul 11	Jul 10	Jul 09
Working Capital	-145	-104	-64
Fixed Assets	8	7	10
Current Assets	133	66	56

Maplins
Lakeside Retail Park, Grays, RM20 1WN
Tel: 01708-867976 **Fax:** 01708-865517
E-mail: customercare@maplins.co.uk
Website: http://www.maplins.co.uk
Managers: M. Dalgarno (Mgr)
Ultimate Holding Company: MAPLIN ELECTRONICS GROUP (HOLDINGS) LTD
Immediate Holding Company: MAPLIN ELECTRONICS (HOLDINGS) LTD
Registration no: 01264385 **Date established:** 1976
Turnover: £125m - £250m **No.of Employees:** 11 - 20
Product Groups: 37, 61

Metropolitan Weighing Machine Co. Ltd
Unit 113 Foxton Road, Grays, RM20 4XX
Tel: 01375-390140 **Fax:** 01375-390140
E-mail: nickwatts@metroweigh.co.uk
Website: http://www.metroweigh.com
Directors: N. Watts (Sales), C. Tomlin (Dir), R. Watts (MD)
Managers: N. Watts (Sales & Mktg Mg)
Immediate Holding Company: TCS CHANDLERY LIMITED
Registration no: 04577671 **VAT No.:** GB 292 3911 47
Date established: 2002 **Turnover:** £500,000 - £1m
No.of Employees: 1 - 10 **Product Groups:** 38, 48, 83

N R C Plant Ltd
Neagron House Stanford Road, Orsett, Grays, RM16 3BX
Tel: 01375-361616 **Fax:** 01375-361818
E-mail: sales@nrcplant.co.uk
Website: http://www.nrcplant.co.uk
Bank(s): hsbc
Directors: R. Abbott (Dir), W. Parker (Co Sec)
Managers: D. Wheeler (Serv Mgr), S. Marsh, S. Morum (I.T. Exec), S. Morum (Tech Serv Mgr)
Ultimate Holding Company: JOSEPH GALLAGHER GROUP LIMITED
Immediate Holding Company: N.R.C. PLANT LIMITED
Registration no: 03303686 **VAT No.:** GB 685 2876 82
Date established: 1997 **Turnover:** £2m - £5m **No.of Employees:** 21 - 50
Product Groups: 35, 45, 67

Date of Accounts	Sep 11	Sep 10	Sep 09
Sales Turnover	N/A	N/A	6m
Pre Tax Profit/Loss	N/A	N/A	697
Working Capital	711	-129	-195
Fixed Assets	6m	6m	6m
Current Assets	3m	3m	2m
Current Liabilities	N/A	N/A	767

Perrys Refridgeration
22 Hayes Close Parsonage Road, Grays, RM20 4AX
Tel: 07729-378294 **Fax:** 01375-377120
Directors: M. Perry (Prop)
Date established: 1999 **No.of Employees:** 1 - 10 **Product Groups:** 20, 40, 41

Safe Lifting Gear Ltd
Unit 10 Thurrock Enterprise Centre Maidstone Road, Grays, RM17 6NF
Tel: 01375-396059 **Fax:** 01375-396875
E-mail: safeliftinggear@btconnect.com
Website: http://www.safeliftinggear.co.uk
Directors: P. Tibble (Dir)
Immediate Holding Company: SAFE LIFTING GEAR LIMITED
Registration no: 03071478 **Date established:** 1995
No.of Employees: 1 - 10 **Product Groups:** 35, 39, 45

Date of Accounts	Jun 11	Jun 10	Jun 09
Working Capital	69	31	30
Fixed Assets	7	8	9
Current Assets	129	60	63

Saybolt UK Ltd
Unit A4 Motherwell Way, Grays, RM20 3XD
Tel: 01708-862611 **Fax:** 01708-867401
Website: http://www.corelab.com
Bank(s): National Westminster Bank Plc
Directors: D. Bleser (MD)
Ultimate Holding Company: CORE LABORATORIES NV (NETHERLANDS)
Immediate Holding Company: SAYBOLT UNITED KINGDOM LIMITED
Registration no: 00896844 **Date established:** 1967 **Turnover:** £2m - £5m
No.of Employees: 11 - 20 **Product Groups:** 51, 82, 85

Date of Accounts	Dec 11	Dec 10	Dec 09
Sales Turnover	3m	3m	3m
Pre Tax Profit/Loss	736	878	578
Working Capital	4m	3m	3m
Fixed Assets	761	743	766
Current Assets	5m	4m	3m
Current Liabilities	350	367	406

Senator Welding Engineering Supplies Ltd
Hedley Avenue, Grays, RM20 4EL
Tel: 01375-396646 **Fax:** 01375-375370
E-mail: turtlewelding@hotmail.co.uk
Directors: M. Gray (MD)
Immediate Holding Company: SENATOR WELDING & ENGINEERING SUPPLIES LIMITED
Registration no: 02737297 **Date established:** 1992
Turnover: £250,000 - £500,000 **No.of Employees:** 1 - 10
Product Groups: 46

Date of Accounts	Dec 11	Dec 10	Dec 09
Sales Turnover	327	348	272
Pre Tax Profit/Loss	27	33	34
Working Capital	53	54	55
Fixed Assets	9	11	15
Current Assets	114	109	102
Current Liabilities	12	13	13

Skyline Tower Crane Services Ltd
27a Oliver Close, Grays, RM20 3EE
Tel: 01708-860534 **Fax:** 01708-861553
E-mail: info@skylinetcs.com
Website: http://www.skylinetcs.com
Managers: P. Whitford (Mgr)
Immediate Holding Company: SKYLINE TOWER CRANE SERVICES LTD
Registration no: 05101808 **Date established:** 2004
No.of Employees: 1 - 10 **Product Groups:** 45, 48, 67, 83, 85

Date of Accounts	Mar 11	Mar 10	Mar 09
Working Capital	-162	-174	-74
Fixed Assets	632	554	646
Current Assets	345	334	462

Stamford Fabrications Ltd
Stamford House Oliver Close, Grays, RM20 3EE
Tel: 01708-861665 **Fax:** 01708-864123
E-mail: info@stamfordfabs.co.uk
Website: http://www.stamfordfabs.com
Directors: R. Bowyer (MD)
Immediate Holding Company: STAMFORD FABRICATIONS LIMITED
Registration no: 01486233 **Date established:** 1980
No.of Employees: 11 - 20 **Product Groups:** 35, 42, 45

Date of Accounts	Mar 11	Mar 10	Mar 09
Working Capital	-415	-371	-263
Fixed Assets	850	854	860
Current Assets	485	585	608

Sykes Marine Hydromaster Ltd
B6 Fleet House Trading Estate Motherwell Way, Grays, RM20 3XD
Tel: 01708-862651 **Fax:** 01708-867905
E-mail: info@sykeshydromaster.com
Website: http://www.sykeshydromaster.com
Managers: J. Packham (Fin Mgr)
Immediate Holding Company: SYKES MARINE (HYDROMASTER) LIMITED
Registration no: 02133966 **Date established:** 1987 **Turnover:** £2m - £5m
No.of Employees: 1 - 10 **Product Groups:** 39

Date of Accounts	Jun 11	Jun 10	Jun 09
Working Capital	495	428	492
Fixed Assets	83	76	15
Current Assets	728	801	904

Thameside Electrical Ltd
713 London Road, Grays, RM20 3HX
Tel: 01708-867191 **Fax:** 01708-866295
E-mail: dennis@thamesideelec.co.uk
Website: http://www.thamesideelec.co.uk
Bank(s): HSBC
Directors: D. Wakeling (MD)
Immediate Holding Company: THAMESIDE ELECTRICAL LIMITED
Registration no: 00927033 **VAT No.:** GB 246 7102 71
Date established: 1968 **Turnover:** £1m - £2m **No.of Employees:** 21 - 50
Product Groups: 52

Date of Accounts	Dec 10	Dec 09	Dec 08
Working Capital	110	149	144
Fixed Assets	5	7	9
Current Assets	373	412	444

Titan Arcticstore A/S
Europa Trading Estate London Road, Grays, RM20 4DB
Tel: 01375-396456
E-mail: INFO@ARCTICSTORE.CO.UK
Website: http://www.arcticstore.co.uk
Product Groups: 45, 48, 76, 83

Date of Accounts	Sep 10	Sep 09	Sep 08
Working Capital	-241	-184	-284
Fixed Assets	2m	2m	3m
Current Assets	468	373	268

Trelleborg Stanton Ltd
853 London Road, Grays, RM20 3NL
Tel: 01708-685685 **Fax:** 01708-685686
E-mail: sales@trelleborg.com
Website: http://www.trelleborg.com
Directors: C. Stead (Comm), F. Lacrioix (MD), F. Lacroix (MD), I. Elcock (Co Sec)
Managers: E. Howson (Sales & Tech Mg)
Immediate Holding Company: Trelleborg Holdings UK Ltd
Registration no: 01491903 **VAT No.:** GB 506 9526 35
Date established: 1990 **Turnover:** £10m - £20m
No.of Employees: 101 - 250 **Product Groups:** 38

Date of Accounts	Dec 07	Dec 06	Dec 05
Sales Turnover	19000	17560	22290
Pre Tax Profit/Loss	-10410	-4870	-2870
Working Capital	1180	720	-2630
Fixed Assets	80	720	3320
Current Assets	10750	6750	8020
Current Liabilities	9570	6030	10650
Total Share Capital	380	380	380
ROCE% (Return on Capital Employed)	-826.2	-338.2	-415.9
ROT% (Return on Turnover)	-54.8	-27.7	-12.9

Victor Marine
Cosgrove Road, Grays, RM20 3EE
Tel: 01708-899780 **Fax:** 01708-890599
E-mail: info@victormarine.com
Website: http://www.victormarine.com
Bank(s): National Westminster, Bishopsgate
Managers: K. Taylor (Ops Mgr)
Immediate Holding Company: SAMUEL HODGE HOLDINGS LTD
Registration no: 01341187 **VAT No.:** GB 246 3644 55
Turnover: £10m - £20m **No.of Employees:** 11 - 20 **Product Groups:** 39, 40, 54

Watts Industrial Tyres plc
3 Acorn Trading Centre Gumley Road, Grays, RM20 4XB
Tel: 01375-378055 **Fax:** 01375-390265
Website: http://www.wattstyreservices.co.uk
Directors: A. Gissing (MD), J. Game (Dir)
Managers: C. Elves (District Mgr)
Ultimate Holding Company: Watts Of Lydney Group Ltd
Immediate Holding Company: WATTS INDUSTRIAL TYRES LIMITED
Registration no: 01434811 **Date established:** 1979
Turnover: £10m - £20m **No.of Employees:** 1 - 10 **Product Groups:** 29, 68

Wilmurten Manufacturing
Manor Way Industrial Estate, Grays, RM17 6BJ
Tel: 01375-373984 **Fax:** 01375-391867
E-mail: wilmurten@aol.com
Website: http://www.wilmurten.co.uk
Directors: H. Bond (MD)
Immediate Holding Company: WILMURTEN MANUFACTURING COMPANY LIMITED
Registration no: 00689320 **Date established:** 1961
Turnover: Up to £250,000 **No.of Employees:** 1 - 10 **Product Groups:** 29

Date of Accounts	Sep 11	Sep 10	Sep 09
Working Capital	51	61	61
Fixed Assets	14	18	23
Current Assets	97	79	76

Halstead

Anglia Fixing Ltd
28a First Avenue, Halstead, CO9 2EX
Tel: 01787-479017
E-mail: sales@angliafixing.co.uk
Website: http://www.angliafixing.co.uk
Directors: C. Fitch (Prop)
Immediate Holding Company: ANGLIA FIXING LTD.
Registration no: 02943625 **Date established:** 1994
No.of Employees: 11 - 20 **Product Groups:** 35, 48, 52

Date of Accounts	Jun 12	Jun 11	Jun 10
Working Capital	150	164	186
Fixed Assets	76	87	77
Current Assets	571	470	561

Autron Products Ltd
17 Second Avenue, Halstead, CO9 2SU
Tel: 01787-473964 **Fax:** 01787-474061
E-mail: sales@autron.co.uk
Website: http://www.autron.co.uk
Directors: P. Keyes (MD), P. Keys (MD)
Ultimate Holding Company: AQUATRONIC GROUP MANAGEMENT PLC
Immediate Holding Company: AUTRON PRODUCTS LIMITED
Registration no: 00983440 **Date established:** 1970 **Turnover:** £1m - £2m
No.of Employees: 11 - 20 **Product Groups:** 37, 40

Date of Accounts	Sep 11	Sep 10	Sep 09
Sales Turnover	2m	2m	2m
Pre Tax Profit/Loss	218	282	320
Working Capital	1m	1m	1m
Fixed Assets	103	120	138
Current Assets	2m	2m	2m
Current Liabilities	173	141	164

Brooks Transport Services Ltd
15 Second Avenue, Halstead, CO9 2SU
Tel: 01787-476624 **Fax:** 01787-474879
E-mail: sales@brooks-transport.co.uk
Website: http://www.brooks-transport.co.uk
Directors: S. Brooks (Fin)
Ultimate Holding Company: R.G. BROOKS LIMITED
Immediate Holding Company: BROOKS TRANSPORT SERVICES LIMITED

see next page

Brooks Transport Services Ltd - *Cont'd*

Registration no: 02808253 **Date established:** 1993
No.of Employees: 21 - 50 **Product Groups:** 77, 84

Date of Accounts	Apr 11	Apr 10	Apr 09
Working Capital	516	484	430
Fixed Assets	376	364	365
Current Assets	1m	932	724

Centurion Packaging

Suite 5a Enterprise House Rippers Court, Sible Hedingham, Halstead, CO9 3PY
Tel: 01787-237535 **Fax:** 01787-238326
Website: http://www.centurionbulkbags.co.uk
Managers: D. Garnham (Mgr)
Immediate Holding Company: VIRTUALPUBS.COM LIMITED
Registration no: 04293897 **Date established:** 2000
No.of Employees: 1 - 10 **Product Groups:** 38, 42

Date of Accounts	Feb 12	Feb 11	Feb 10
Working Capital	-21	4	-1
Fixed Assets	8	7	9
Current Assets	2	8	1
Current Liabilities	1	1	N/A

Checkmate Industries Ltd

Bridge House 12 Bridge Street, Halstead, CO9 1HT
Tel: 01787-477272 **Fax:** 01787-476334
E-mail: checkmatecarpets@btconnect.com
Bank(s): Barclays
Directors: D. Whybrow (MD)
Immediate Holding Company: CHECKMATE INDUSTRIES LIMITED
Registration no: 01150695 **VAT No.:** GB 282 8480 30
Date established: 1973 **Turnover:** £2m - £5m **No.of Employees:** 11 - 20
Product Groups: 23

Date of Accounts	Mar 11	Mar 10	Mar 09
Working Capital	1m	1m	999
Fixed Assets	20	35	54
Current Assets	1m	1m	1m

Coda Systems Ltd

Oak Road Little Maplestead, Halstead, CO9 2RT
Tel: 01787-478678 **Fax:** 01376-342266
E-mail: sales@coda-systems.co.uk
Website: http://www.coda-systems.co.uk
Directors: H. Davis (MD)
Immediate Holding Company: CODA SYSTEMS LIMITED
Registration no: 01470428 **Date established:** 1980 **Turnover:** £1m - £2m
No.of Employees: 1 - 10 **Product Groups:** 37, 38

Date of Accounts	Jan 12	Jan 11	Jan 10
Working Capital	336	316	248
Fixed Assets	368	380	386
Current Assets	537	727	410

The Copy Box

37 Tilbury Road Great Yeldham, Halstead, CO9 4JG
Tel: 01787-238161
E-mail: info@thecopybox.com
Website: http://www.thecopybox.com
Managers: L. James (Mgr)
No.of Employees: 1 - 10 **Product Groups:** 81

D I S East Anglia Ltd

9 Ripper Court Sible Hedingham, Halstead, CO9 3PY
Tel: 01787-462322 **Fax:** 01787-460626
E-mail: sales@diseastanglia.com
Website: http://www.diseastanglia.com
Directors: S. Blore (Dir)
Immediate Holding Company: DIS (EAST ANGLIA) LIMITED
Registration no: 03520414 **Date established:** 1998
Turnover: £500,000 - £1m **No.of Employees:** 1 - 10 **Product Groups:** 29, 30, 31, 35, 36, 37, 40, 66

Date of Accounts	May 12	May 11	May 10
Sales Turnover	575	486	408
Working Capital	293	212	272
Fixed Assets	21	28	18
Current Assets	293	300	272

Dee Jay Services

6 New England Sible Hedingham, Halstead, CO9 3HY
Tel: 01787-461083 **Fax:** 01787-461083
Directors: D. Murray (Prop)
Date established: 2000 **No.of Employees:** 1 - 10 **Product Groups:** 46

Elmsett Engineering

Southey Green Sible Hedingham, Halstead, CO9 3RN
Tel: 01787-461806
E-mail: jaygrey@btinternet.com
Directors: G. Smith (Prop)
Date established: 1984 **No.of Employees:** 1 - 10 **Product Groups:** 41

Essex Tool Sharpening Services

21 Ridgewell Road Great Yeldham, Halstead, CO9 4RG
Tel: 01787-237905 **Fax:** 07092-110455
E-mail: peter.etss@btconnect.com
Directors: P. Bevan (Prop)
Date established: 1984 **No.of Employees:** 1 - 10 **Product Groups:** 36

Finning UK Ltd

19 Fourth Avenue Colchester Road, Halstead, CO9 2SY
Tel: 01787-272000 **Fax:** 01787-474968
E-mail: lynnreeve@finning.co.uk
Website: http://www.finning.co.uk
Directors: C. Thomas (Fin)
Managers: A. Langdale (Mgr), J. Burton (Sales Prom Mgr)
Ultimate Holding Company: FINNING INTERNATIONAL INC (CANADA)
Immediate Holding Company: FINNING (UK) LTD.
Registration no: 00367090 **VAT No.:** GB 100 5160 42
Date established: 1941 **No.of Employees:** 1 - 10 **Product Groups:** 45

Date of Accounts	Dec 11	Dec 10	Dec 09
Sales Turnover	522m	413m	334m
Pre Tax Profit/Loss	31m	10m	8m
Working Capital	98m	79m	49m
Fixed Assets	71m	81m	77m
Current Assets	236m	207m	170m
Current Liabilities	70m	38m	34m

Halstead Plating Services Ltd

48 Broton Drive, Halstead, CO9 1HB
Tel: 01787-476783 **Fax:** 01787-475861
Directors: S. Anbouche (Fin)
Immediate Holding Company: HALSTEAD PLATING SERVICES LIMITED
Registration no: 01524683 **Date established:** 1980
No.of Employees: 1 - 10 **Product Groups:** 46, 48

Date of Accounts	Apr 11	Apr 10	Apr 09
Working Capital	-23	-35	-30
Fixed Assets	148	154	159
Current Assets	42	22	23

Hunwick Engineering Ltd

Kings Road, Halstead, CO9 1HD
Tel: 01787-474547 **Fax:** 01787-475741
E-mail: sales@plc-hunwick.co.uk
Website: http://www.hunwick-engineering.co.uk
Directors: K. Ripper (MD), V. Burrell (Co Sec)
Immediate Holding Company: HUNWICK ENGINEERING LIMITED
Registration no: 04437451 **Date established:** 2002 **Turnover:** £1m - £2m
No.of Employees: 51 - 100 **Product Groups:** 34, 35, 48

Date of Accounts	Mar 11	Mar 10	Mar 09
Working Capital	2m	553	694
Fixed Assets	1m	961	1m
Current Assets	4m	896	1m

Hygiplas Containers Ltd

Unit 27 5th Avenue Bluebridge Industrial Estate, Halstead, CO9 2SZ
Tel: 01787-472308 **Fax:** 01787-474290
E-mail: sales@hygiplas.co.uk
Website: http://www.hygiplas.co.uk
Directors: M. Beill (MD), M. Beille (MD)
Managers: C. Newton (Mgr)
Immediate Holding Company: HYGIPLAS (CONTAINERS) LIMITED
Registration no: 01347004 **VAT No.:** GB 302 1494 05
Date established: 1978 **Turnover:** £500,000 - £1m
No.of Employees: 1 - 10 **Product Groups:** 30, 45

Landline Ltd

1 First Avenue, Halstead, CO9 2EX
Tel: 01787-476699 **Fax:** 01787-472507
E-mail: sales@landline.co.uk
Website: http://www.landline.co.uk
Bank(s): National Westminster Bank Plc
Directors: S. Quill (MD)
Managers: T. Willson (Fin Mgr), A. Cox (Tech Serv Mgr)
Immediate Holding Company: LANDLINE LIMITED
Registration no: 01618248 **VAT No.:** GB 368 5544 15
Date established: 1982 **No.of Employees:** 21 - 50 **Product Groups:** 30

Date of Accounts	Nov 11	Nov 10	Nov 09
Working Capital	341	262	262
Fixed Assets	496	538	574
Current Assets	949	628	709
Current Liabilities	N/A	111	N/A

Omega Laser Systems

2 Oak Road Little Maplestead, Halstead, CO9 2RT
Tel: 01787-477551 **Fax:** 01787-477510
E-mail: info@omegalaser.co.uk
Website: http://www.omegalaser.co.uk
Managers: J. Nelson (Chief Mgr)
Immediate Holding Company: OMEGA LASER SYSTEMS LIMITED
Registration no: 02644421 **VAT No.:** GB 564 4082 40
Date established: 1991 **Turnover:** £500,000 - £1m
No.of Employees: 1 - 10 **Product Groups:** 88

Date of Accounts	Mar 08	Jun 11	Jun 10
Working Capital	5	121	17
Fixed Assets	19	14	18
Current Assets	217	290	248

Premaberg Manufacturing Ltd

22-24 High Street, Halstead, CO9 2AP
Tel: 01787-475651 **Fax:** 01787-475046
E-mail: julian.durrant@premaberg.com
Website: http://www.premaberg.com
Bank(s): National Westminster Plc
Directors: G. Wadley (MD)
Managers: J. Durrant (Div Mgr)
Ultimate Holding Company: PREMABERG HOLDINGS LIMITED
Immediate Holding Company: PREMABERG LIMITED
Registration no: 01346774 **VAT No.:** GB 29 5071 55
Date established: 1978 **Turnover:** £2m - £5m **No.of Employees:** 51 - 100
Product Groups: 35, 40, 42

Date of Accounts	Dec 11	Dec 10	Dec 09
Sales Turnover	4m	3m	3m
Pre Tax Profit/Loss	334	350	75
Working Capital	2m	2m	1m
Fixed Assets	70	52	45
Current Assets	2m	2m	2m
Current Liabilities	128	77	75

R P C Containers Ltd

Fourth Avenue Colchester Road, Halstead, CO9 2SY
Tel: 01787-473224 **Fax:** 01787-474151
E-mail: sales@rpc-halstead.co.uk
Website: http://www.rpc-containers.co.uk
Managers: J. Suckling (Fin Mgr), P. Goodwin, R. Sells (Chief Mgr), R. Windsor
Ultimate Holding Company: RPC GROUP PLC
Immediate Holding Company: RPC CONTAINERS LIMITED
Registration no: 02786492 **Date established:** 1993
No.of Employees: 51 - 100 **Product Groups:** 30

Date of Accounts	Mar 11	Mar 10	Mar 09
Sales Turnover	189m	175m	183m
Pre Tax Profit/Loss	14m	15m	-1m
Working Capital	21m	17m	-37m
Fixed Assets	81m	77m	79m
Current Assets	76m	66m	68m
Current Liabilities	17m	13m	14m

Sound Security Ltd

Jasmine Cottage Drury Lane, Ridgewell, Halstead, CO9 4SL
Tel: 01440-788255 **Fax:** 01440-788014
E-mail: info@sound-security.co.uk
Website: http://www.sound-security.co.uk
Directors: N. Branston (Fin)
Managers: H. Bester (Sales Admin)
Immediate Holding Company: SOUND SECURITY LIMITED
Registration no: 06489257 **Date established:** 2008
Turnover: Up to £250,000 **No.of Employees:** 1 - 10 **Product Groups:** 81

Date of Accounts	Jan 11	Jan 10	Jan 09
Sales Turnover	N/A	N/A	4
Pre Tax Profit/Loss	N/A	N/A	-31
Working Capital	-73	-62	-50
Fixed Assets	11	15	20
Current Assets	N/A	N/A	1
Current Liabilities	N/A	N/A	44

Travis Perkins plc

11 Second Avenue Blue Bridge Industrial Estate, Halstead, CO9 2SU
Tel: 01787-477882 **Fax:** 01787-473761
E-mail: paul.ainsworth@travisperkins.co.uk
Website: http://www.travisperkins.co.uk
Managers: P. Ainsworth (Mgr)
Immediate Holding Company: TRAVIS PERKINS PLC
Registration no: 00824821 **Date established:** 1964
Turnover: Over £1,000m **No.of Employees:** 1 - 10 **Product Groups:** 66

Date of Accounts	Dec 11	Dec 10	Dec 09
Sales Turnover	4779m	3153m	2931m
Pre Tax Profit/Loss	270m	197m	213m
Working Capital	133m	159m	248m
Fixed Assets	2771m	2749m	2108m
Current Assets	1421m	1329m	1035m
Current Liabilities	473m	412m	109m

Wade International Ltd

Third Avenue, Halstead, CO9 2SX
Tel: 01787-475151 **Fax:** 01787-475579
E-mail: sales@wade.eu
Website: http://www.wade.eu
Bank(s): Barclays
Directors: R. Thomas (MD), D. Lewis (Fin)
Managers: M. Woodward (Tech Serv Mgr), M. Everitt (Prod Mgr), P. Bartlett (Buyer)
Ultimate Holding Company: WADE INTERNATIONAL LIMITED
Immediate Holding Company: WADE INTERNATIONAL LIMITED
Registration no: 04398143 **VAT No.:** GB 103 7734 88
Date established: 2002 **Turnover:** £5m - £10m
No.of Employees: 51 - 100 **Product Groups:** 35

Date of Accounts	Jun 11	Jun 10	Jun 09
Sales Turnover	6m	6m	7m
Pre Tax Profit/Loss	1m	2m	2m
Working Capital	5m	4m	3m
Fixed Assets	4m	3m	3m
Current Assets	7m	7m	6m
Current Liabilities	806	2m	3m

Harlow

A Knight Errant In Fire Protection

New Horizon Business Centre Barrows Road, Harlow, CM19 5FN
Tel: 01279-626000 **Fax:** 01279-730505
Website: http://www.sawbridgeworthdirectory.com/fse.htm
Directors: G. Peterson (Prop)
No.of Employees: 1 - 10 **Product Groups:** 38, 42

A W A Refiners Ltd

10 Mead Industrial Park Riverway, Harlow, CM20 2SE
Tel: 01279-423743 **Fax:** 01279-422243
E-mail: sales@awarefiners.com
Website: http://www.awarefiners.com
Bank(s): National Westminster Bank Plc
Directors: S. Warrin (Dir)
Immediate Holding Company: A.W.A. REFINERS LIMITED
Registration no: 02596483 **VAT No.:** GB 573 0625 47
Date established: 1991 **Turnover:** £5m - £10m **No.of Employees:** 11 - 20
Product Groups: 34, 48, 65, 66

Date of Accounts	May 11	May 10	May 09
Working Capital	789	506	467
Fixed Assets	68	41	38
Current Assets	1m	854	729

Abbey Engraving

Unit 15 New Horizon Business Centre Barrows Road, Harlow, CM19 5FN
Tel: 01279-626277 **Fax:** 01279-626277
E-mail: info@abbeyengraving.co.uk
Website: http://www.abbeyengraving.co.uk
Directors: D. Court (Prop)
Immediate Holding Company: PERCEPTION INTERNATIONAL LIMITED
VAT No.: GB 632 5118 65 **Date established:** 2003
Turnover: Up to £250,000 **No.of Employees:** 1 - 10 **Product Groups:** 28, 49, 65

Active Security Group Ltd

5-7 Horsecroft Place, Harlow, CM19 5BT
Tel: 01279-420016 **Fax:** 01279-444491
E-mail: administration@activesecuritygroup.co.uk
Website: http://www.activesecuritygroup.com
Bank(s): Royal Bank of Scotland
Directors: B. Miles (MD), R. Lemonde (MD)
Managers: P. Weirich (Sales Admin), G. Pooke (Sales & Mktg Mg)
Immediate Holding Company: ACTIVE SECURITY GROUP LIMITED
Registration no: 01218831 **VAT No.:** GB 240 2857 79
Date established: 1975 **Turnover:** £500,000 - £1m
No.of Employees: 21 - 50 **Product Groups:** 52

Date of Accounts	Jun 12	Jun 11	Jun 10
Working Capital	103	-73	-168
Fixed Assets	204	323	459
Current Assets	1m	1m	1m

Air Industrial Co. Ltd

Greenway Harlow Business Park, Harlow, CM19 5QJ
Tel: 01279-454999 **Fax:** 01279-454997
E-mail: info@airindust.com
Website: http://www.aiedirect.co.uk
Directors: R. Weaver (MD)
Registration no: 01478518 **Turnover:** £1m - £2m
No.of Employees: 1 - 10 **Product Groups:** 40, 46, 83

Akhter Computers Ltd

Akhter House Perry Road, Harlow, CM18 7PN
Tel: 01279-821200 **Fax:** 01279-821300
E-mail: sales@akhter.co.uk
Website: http://www.akhter.co.uk
Bank(s): Lloyds TSB Bank plc
Directors: J. Oakley (Sales), A. Laffoley (Tech Serv), H. Mughal (MD), D. Nuttall (Co Sec)

Managers: A. Upton, M. Edib, C. Ahmed
Ultimate Holding Company: AKHTER GROUP LIMITED
Immediate Holding Company: AKHTER COMPUTERS PUBLIC LIMITED COMPANY
Registration no: 02253061 **VAT No.:** GB 532 2629 63
Date established: 1988 **Turnover:** £10m - £20m
No.of Employees: 51 - 100 **Product Groups:** 44

Date of Accounts	Jun 11	Jun 10	Jun 09
Sales Turnover	13m	6m	7m
Pre Tax Profit/Loss	1m	209	360
Working Capital	3m	2m	1m
Fixed Assets	178	189	205
Current Assets	5m	3m	3m
Current Liabilities	1m	71	299

Albert Packing Case Co. Ltd

Unit 2 New Horizon Business Centre Barrows Road, Harlow, CM19 5FN
Tel: 01279-419012 **Fax:** 01279-419013
E-mail: enquiries@albertpackingcase.com
Website: http://www.albertpackingcase.com
Directors: K. Burnand (MD), P. Pettet (Dir), H. Burnand (MD)
Managers: J. McBeth (Factory Mgr)
Immediate Holding Company: ALBERT PACKING CASE CO. LIMITED
Registration no: 00474962 **Date established:** 1949
Turnover: £250,000 - £500,000 **No.of Employees:** 1 - 10
Product Groups: 25

Date of Accounts	Sep 10	Sep 09	Sep 08
Working Capital	15	23	37
Fixed Assets	353	356	357
Current Assets	72	65	86

Alcad

5 Astra Centre Edinburgh Way, Harlow, CM20 2BN
Tel: 01279-772555 **Fax:** 01279-420696
E-mail: carter.sarah@alcad.com
Website: http://www.alcad.com
Directors: J. Taylor (Sales)
Ultimate Holding Company: DOUGHTY HANSON
Immediate Holding Company: SAFT LTD
Registration no: 00407689 **No.of Employees:** 1 - 10 **Product Groups:** 37

Applied Scintillation Technologies

Unit 7-8 Roydenbury Industrial Estate Horsecroft Road, Harlow, CM19 5BZ
Tel: 01279-641234 **Fax:** 01279-413679
E-mail: rhawkins@appscintech.com
Website: http://www.appscintech.com
Bank(s): H S B C
Directors: R. Hawkins (Dir), S. Quinn (Co Sec)
Immediate Holding Company: APPLIED SCINTILLATION TECHNOLOGIES LIMITED
Registration no: 01773459 **VAT No.:** GB 404 4566 68
Date established: 1983 **Turnover:** £2m - £5m **No.of Employees:** 51 - 100
Product Groups: 37, 38, 80, 85

Date of Accounts	Mar 11	Mar 10	Mar 09
Sales Turnover	N/A	3m	3m
Pre Tax Profit/Loss	N/A	341	500
Working Capital	2m	2m	1m
Fixed Assets	469	364	413
Current Assets	4m	2m	2m
Current Liabilities	N/A	295	282

Avery Dennison

7 Astra Centre Edinburgh Way, Harlow, CM20 2BN
Tel: 01279-786000 **Fax:** 01279-786100
E-mail: declan.quinn@eu.avery.dennison.com
Website: http://www.monarch.averydennison.com
Bank(s): National Westminster Bank Plc
Managers: D. Quinn (Comptroller)
Ultimate Holding Company: PAXAR CORP - USA
Immediate Holding Company: PAXAR EUROPE LTD
Registration no: 02330305 **VAT No.:** GB 732 1179 57
Turnover: £20m - £50m **No.of Employees:** 51 - 100 **Product Groups:** 27, 28, 30, 42, 44

Brookfield Viscometers Ltd

Brookfield Technical Centre Stadium Way, Harlow, CM19 5GX
Tel: 01279-451774 **Fax:** 01279-451775
E-mail: sales@brookfield.co.uk
Website: http://www.brookfield.co.uk
Bank(s): Lloyds TSB Bank plc
Managers: J. Rye (Sales Prom Mgr)
Ultimate Holding Company: BROOKFIELD ENGINEERING LABORATORIES INC (USA)
Immediate Holding Company: BROOKFIELD VISCOMETERS LIMITED
Registration no: 02382054 **VAT No.:** GB 542 5834 40
Date established: 1989 **No.of Employees:** 11 - 20 **Product Groups:** 38

Date of Accounts	Dec 11	Dec 10	Dec 09
Sales Turnover	4m	N/A	N/A
Pre Tax Profit/Loss	166	N/A	N/A
Working Capital	4m	4m	4m
Fixed Assets	796	681	717
Current Assets	4m	4m	5m
Current Liabilities	437	N/A	N/A

Leonard Brooks Harlow Ltd

17 Wych Elm, Harlow, CM20 1QR
Tel: 01279-417501
E-mail: brookpaint@aol.com
Website: http://www.leonardbrooks.co.uk
Directors: R. Groves (MD)
Immediate Holding Company: LEONARD BROOKS (HARLOW) LIMITED
Registration no: 01568725 **Date established:** 1981
No.of Employees: 1 - 10 **Product Groups:** 38, 42

Date of Accounts	Sep 11	Sep 10	Sep 09
Working Capital	81	42	-12
Fixed Assets	13	9	2
Current Assets	181	115	52

Bureau Veritas

130 Sandringham Avenue Sandringham Avenue, Harlow, CM19 5QA
Tel: 01279-634000 **Fax:** 020-8335 3056
Website: http://www.bureauveritas.co.uk
Bank(s): Bank of Scotland
Managers: K. Crompton-Cook, K. Compton Cook (Sales Prom Mgr)
Immediate Holding Company: BUREAU VERITAS
Registration no: FC000718 **VAT No.:** GB 528 0765 36
Date established: 2008 **Turnover:** £2m - £5m **No.of Employees:** 21 - 50
Product Groups: 54, 84

C C Hydrosonics Ltd

Units 1-4 Italstyle Buildings Cambridge Road, Harlow, CM20 2HE
Tel: 01279-418942 **Fax:** 01279-453926
E-mail: sales@cchydrosonics.com
Website: http://www.cchydrosonics.com
Directors: D. Casey (MD), L. Casey (Fin)
Ultimate Holding Company: CREST GROUP INC (USA)
Immediate Holding Company: C. C. HYDROSONICS LIMITED
Registration no: 01108860 **Date established:** 1973 **Turnover:** £1m - £2m
No.of Employees: 21 - 50 **Product Groups:** 32, 37, 46, 48

Date of Accounts	Jun 11	Jun 10	Jun 09
Working Capital	803	871	757
Fixed Assets	60	46	57
Current Assets	2m	2m	2m

Clement Clarke International Ltd

Unit A Cartel Business Estate Edinburgh Way, Harlow, CM20 2TT
Tel: 01279-414969 **Fax:** 01279-456339
E-mail: info@c3headsets.com
Website: http://www.clementclarke.com
Bank(s): Barclays P.L.C., PO Box 12, Harlow, Essex CM20 2ED
Directors: M. Sanders (MD)
Managers: J. Hopkins (Tech Serv Mgr), M. Dutch (Purch Mgr), S. Jacobs (Fin Mgr), K. Reed (Personnel), H. Mander (Mktg Serv Mgr)
Ultimate Holding Company: HAAG-STREIT HOLDING AG (SWITZERLAND)
Immediate Holding Company: CLEMENT CLARKE INTERNATIONAL LIMITED
Registration no: 00377748 **VAT No.:** GB 213 2506 14
Date established: 1942 **Turnover:** £5m - £10m
No.of Employees: 51 - 100 **Product Groups:** 37, 38

Date of Accounts	Dec 11	Dec 10	Dec 09
Sales Turnover	7m	7m	6m
Pre Tax Profit/Loss	-547	-69	-448
Working Capital	-207	614	1m
Fixed Assets	573	323	336
Current Assets	4m	4m	4m
Current Liabilities	559	519	473

Connectors Cables Specialists Ltd

Unit 6 Stort Mill River Way, Harlow, CM20 2SN
Tel: 01279-639251 **Fax:** 01279-641118
E-mail: sales@ccsukltd.co.uk
Website: http://www.ccsukltd.co.uk
Directors: J. Elwood (Fin), P. Elwood (MD)
Ultimate Holding Company: CCS CONNECTORS LIMITED
Immediate Holding Company: CONNECTORS CABLES SPECIALISTS (CCS) LIMITED
Registration no: 01740235 **Date established:** 1983
Turnover: £500,000 - £1m **No.of Employees:** 1 - 10 **Product Groups:** 37

Date of Accounts	Aug 11	Aug 10	Aug 09
Working Capital	783	763	788
Fixed Assets	52	26	23
Current Assets	891	854	881

D J Sports Cars International Ltd

2 Edinburgh Place, Harlow, CM20 2DJ
Tel: 01279-442661 **Fax:** 01279-434956
E-mail: post@daxcars.co.uk
Website: http://www.daxcars.co.uk
Directors: S. Johns (Sales), B. Johns (MD), S. Johns (Dir)
Managers: P. Johns (Accounts)
Immediate Holding Company: D.J. SPORTSCARS INTERNATIONAL LIMITED
Registration no: 01345817 **VAT No.:** GB 215 2545 89
Date established: 1977 **Turnover:** £1m - £2m **No.of Employees:** 1 - 10
Product Groups: 39

Dalon International Ltd

12 The Spire Green Centre, Harlow, CM19 5TR
Tel: 01279-453823 **Fax:** 01279-453824
E-mail: longdalon@aol.com
Directors: L. Fox (Fin)
Immediate Holding Company: DALON INTERNATIONAL LIMITED
Registration no: 02151647 **VAT No.:** GB 506 1580 69
Date established: 1987 **Turnover:** £250,000 - £500,000
No.of Employees: 1 - 10 **Product Groups:** 33, 36

Date of Accounts	Apr 11	Apr 10	Apr 09
Sales Turnover	N/A	337	N/A
Working Capital	259	268	279
Fixed Assets	17	13	9
Current Assets	502	516	495

Dencon Accessories Ltd

Lyden House South Road, Harlow, CM20 2BS
Tel: 01279-433533 **Fax:** 01279-433633
E-mail: info@vernons.co.uk
Website: http://www.dencon.co.uk
Bank(s): HSBC
Managers: Z. Vgr (Buyer)
Immediate Holding Company: DENCON ACCESSORIES LIMITED
Registration no: 00834335 **Date established:** 1965 **Turnover:** £5m - £10m
No.of Employees: 21 - 50 **Product Groups:** 37

Date of Accounts	Jun 11	Jun 10	Jun 09
Sales Turnover	7m	7m	7m
Pre Tax Profit/Loss	99	45	182
Working Capital	890	843	860
Fixed Assets	3m	3m	3m
Current Assets	4m	3m	3m
Current Liabilities	875	235	202

Ductwork Environmental Services Ltd

Unit 10 Stort Mill River Way, Harlow, CM20 2SN
Tel: 01279-438889
Directors: M. Williams (Fin), A. Williams (MD)
Immediate Holding Company: DUCTWORK ENVIRONMENTAL SERVICES LIMITED
Registration no: 03825150 **Date established:** 1999
No.of Employees: 1 - 10 **Product Groups:** 37, 40, 48

Date of Accounts	Aug 11	Aug 10	Aug 09
Working Capital	13	7	2
Current Assets	42	37	36

European Water Care Ltd

Regal House South Road, Harlow, CM20 2BL
Tel: 01279-780250 **Fax:** 01279-780268
E-mail: info@watercare.co.uk
Website: http://www.watercare.co.uk
Managers: G. Pomfrey (Chief Mgr), M. Shields
Ultimate Holding Company: EWC GROUP LIMITED
Immediate Holding Company: EUROPEAN WATER CARE LIMITED
Registration no: 03114221 **Date established:** 1995 **Turnover:** £1m - £2m
No.of Employees: 21 - 50 **Product Groups:** 41, 42

Date of Accounts	Oct 11	Oct 10	Oct 09
Working Capital	-368	-227	-455
Fixed Assets	799	856	1m
Current Assets	3m	3m	2m

Foodmaster Group

13 Burnett Park, Harlow, CM19 4SD
Tel: 01279-419131 **Fax:** 01279-421251
E-mail: sales@refrigeration-freezers.com
Website: http://www.refrigeration-freezers.com
Directors: S. Slyth (Prop)
No.of Employees: 1 - 10 **Product Groups:** 40, 66

Fusion Automation Inc

Barrows Road, Harlow, CM19 5FD
Tel: 01279-443122 **Fax:** 01279-424057
E-mail: info@fusion-inc.com
Website: http://www.fusion-inc.com
Bank(s): Barclays
Managers: L. Schafferova (Admin Off), D. Wright (Prod Mgr), K. Poiser
Ultimate Holding Company: FUSION INC. {U.S.A}
Immediate Holding Company: FUSION AUTOMATION INC.
Registration no: FC013211 **VAT No.:** GB 424 7983 23
Date established: 1984 **Turnover:** £2m - £5m **No.of Employees:** 21 - 50
Product Groups: 32, 34, 46, 48, 66, 67

Date of Accounts	Dec 11	Dec 10	Dec 09
Sales Turnover	5m	5m	3m
Pre Tax Profit/Loss	179	135	-102
Working Capital	578	434	314
Fixed Assets	32	42	66
Current Assets	846	855	797
Current Liabilities	185	318	222

Golf Electric

Unit 10 R024 Greenway Harlow Business Park, Harlow, CM19 5QB
Tel: 01279-423977 **Fax:** 01279-439309
E-mail: stuart@golfelectrics.com
Website: http://www.golfelectrics.co.uk
Directors: S. Daniels (Prop)
Immediate Holding Company: GOLF ELECTRICS LIMITED
Registration no: 05259392 **Date established:** 2004
No.of Employees: 1 - 10 **Product Groups:** 37, 38, 44

Date of Accounts	Mar 11	Mar 10	Mar 09
Working Capital	58	51	34
Fixed Assets	4	5	26
Current Assets	99	104	74

Gratnells Ltd

8 Howard Way, Harlow, CM20 2SU
Tel: 01279-401550 **Fax:** 01279-419127
E-mail: nevilleh@gratnells.co.uk
Website: http://www.gratnells.co.uk
Bank(s): Barclays
Directors: M. Hudson (Dir), N. Hudson (MD), P. Mayo (Ch)
Immediate Holding Company: GRATNELLS LIMITED
Registration no: 00359473 **VAT No.:** 248 1485 47 **Date established:** 1940
Turnover: £5m - £10m **No.of Employees:** 21 - 50 **Product Groups:** 26, 38

Date of Accounts	Jun 11	Jun 10	Jun 09
Sales Turnover	9m	9m	9m
Pre Tax Profit/Loss	574	1m	300
Working Capital	1m	2m	1m
Fixed Assets	5m	5m	6m
Current Assets	4m	5m	5m
Current Liabilities	883	1m	2m

Green Book Electrical plc

West Road, Harlow, CM20 2BG
Tel: 01279-772772 **Fax:** 01279-635285
E-mail: meters@rdluk.com
Website: http://www.greenbrook.co.uk
Directors: S. Appleyard (MD), D. Green (Prop), R. Shaw (Grp Chief Exec)
Managers: D. Tomkins (Personnel)
Immediate Holding Company: GREENBROOK ELECTRICAL PLC
Registration no: 00512045 **Date established:** 1952 **Turnover:** £1m - £2m
No.of Employees: 51 - 100 **Product Groups:** 37, 38

Hales Freight Ltd

Horseshoe Farm London Road, Harlow, CM17 9LH
Tel: 01279-421122 **Fax:** 01279-439144
E-mail: info@halesfreight.com
Website: http://www.halesfreight.com
Managers: P. Veltom (Mgr)
Immediate Holding Company: HALES FREIGHT LIMITED
Registration no: FC010958 **VAT No.:** GB 166 3374 52
Date established: 1981 **Turnover:** £5m - £10m **No.of Employees:** 1 - 10
Product Groups: 72, 77

Harlow Spraytech

St James Centre 7 East Road, Harlow, CM20 2BJ
Tel: 01279-414665 **Fax:** 01279- 416828
Website: http://www.harlow-group.com
Bank(s): Barclays
Managers: D. Russell (Mgr)
Immediate Holding Company: HARLOW FABRICATIONS P.L.C.
Registration no: 05431685 **Date established:** 2005 **Turnover:** £5m - £10m
No.of Employees: 11 - 20 **Product Groups:** 28, 48

Harlow Springs Ltd

Housham Hall Farm Harlow Road, Matching Tye, Harlow, CM17 0PB
Tel: 01279-429004 **Fax:** 01279-635953
E-mail: sales@harlowsprings.co.uk
Website: http://www.harlowsprings.co.uk
Managers: S. Whatley (Mgr)
Ultimate Holding Company: BLUEBRIDGE HOLDINGS LIMITED
Immediate Holding Company: HARLOW SPRINGS LIMITED
Registration no: 06126014 **VAT No.:** GB 213 4812 94
Date established: 2007 **No.of Employees:** 1 - 10 **Product Groups:** 35

Date of Accounts	Mar 11	Mar 10	Mar 09
Working Capital	-101	-94	-164
Fixed Assets	71	42	53
Current Assets	200	183	139

Hire Power Contracts Ltd

Horseshoe House London Road, Harlow, CM17 9LH
Tel: 01279-428915 **Fax:** 01279-439297
E-mail: gary@hirepowerc.co.uk
Website: http://www.hirepower.co.uk
Bank(s): Barclays
Directors: G. Sando (Prop)
Immediate Holding Company: HIRE POWER CONTRACTS LIMITED
Registration no: 02222626 **VAT No.:** GB 572 9317 19
Date established: 1988 **Turnover:** £2m - £5m **No.of Employees:** 11 - 20
Product Groups: 72, 74, 76, 77

Date of Accounts	Oct 09	Oct 08	Jul 11
Working Capital	-433	-406	-184
Fixed Assets	675	892	596
Current Assets	318	443	307

International Lamps & Components

Stadium Way, Harlow, CM19 5FG
Tel: 01279-442266 **Fax:** 01279-442222
E-mail: sales@internationallamps.co.uk
Website: http://www.internationallamps.co.uk
Bank(s): Lloyds TSB Bank plc
Directors: A. Gorie (Co Sec)
Ultimate Holding Company: INTERNATIONAL LAMP GROUP
Immediate Holding Company: INTERNATIONAL LAMPS LIMITED
Registration no: 00994025 **VAT No.:** GB 213 2103 36
Date established: 1970 **Turnover:** £2m - £5m **No.of Employees:** 21 - 50
Product Groups: 36, 37, 38, 39, 44, 49, 67

Date of Accounts	Nov 11	Nov 10	Nov 09
Working Capital	2m	2m	2m
Fixed Assets	756	785	800
Current Assets	3m	3m	2m

Interstyle Group

Reeves Lane Roydon Hamlet, Roydon, Harlow, CM19 5DE
Tel: 01279-793366 **Fax:** 01279-836637
E-mail: deanfoster@interstyle.co.uk
Website: http://www.interstyle.co.uk
Directors: D. Foster (Prop)
Immediate Holding Company: INTERSTYLE GROUP LIMITED
Registration no: 04018254 **Date established:** 2000
Turnover: £250,000 - £500,000 **No.of Employees:** 1 - 10
Product Groups: 33, 35, 52, 66

Date of Accounts	Jun 11	Jun 10	Jun 09
Working Capital	-48	-39	-39
Fixed Assets	14	2	6
Current Assets	96	71	73

J M W Ltd

Warwick House Perry Road, Harlow, CM18 7NF
Tel: 01279-307100 **Fax:** 01279-307101
E-mail: sales@jmwlimited.co.uk
Website: http://www.jmwlimited.co.uk
Directors: C. Manley (MD)
Immediate Holding Company: J.M.W. LIMITED
Registration no: 02680024 **VAT No.:** GB 573 2388 25
Date established: 1992 **Turnover:** £1m - £2m **No.of Employees:** 1 - 10
Product Groups: 38, 85

Date of Accounts	Mar 11	Mar 10	Mar 09
Working Capital	60	-0	-2
Fixed Assets	1	3	3
Current Assets	384	259	192

Jumo Instrument Co. Ltd

Temple Bank River Way, Harlow, CM20 2DY
Tel: 01279-635533 **Fax:** 01279-635262
E-mail: sales@jumo.co.uk
Website: http://www.jumo.co.uk
Directors: M. Juchheim (Dir)
Managers: S. Sawkins
Ultimate Holding Company: JUMO GMBH & CO (GERMANY)
Immediate Holding Company: JUMO INSTRUMENT COMPANY LIMITED
Registration no: 01410418 **Date established:** 1979 **Turnover:** £1m - £2m
No.of Employees: 1 - 10 **Product Groups:** 37, 38

Date of Accounts	Dec 11	Dec 10	Dec 09
Working Capital	255	139	-47
Fixed Assets	691	708	709
Current Assets	492	395	349

Kenex Electro Medical Ltd

24 Burnt Mill Industrial Estate Elizabeth Way, Harlow, CM20 2HS
Tel: 01279-417241 **Fax:** 01279-443749
E-mail: ken.hunt@kenex.co.uk
Website: http://www.kenex.co.uk
Bank(s): Lloyds TSB Bank plc
Directors: K. Hunt (MD)
Immediate Holding Company: KENEX (ELECTRO-MEDICAL) LIMITED
Registration no: 00982587 **Date established:** 1970 **Turnover:** £2m - £5m
No.of Employees: 11 - 20 **Product Groups:** 24, 26, 27, 29, 30, 33, 37, 38, 40, 42, 63

Date of Accounts	Jun 11	Jun 10	Jun 09
Working Capital	1m	741	526
Fixed Assets	32	40	41
Current Assets	2m	1m	1m

Leitz Tooling UK Ltd

Flex Meadow The Pinnacles, Harlow, CM19 5TN
Tel: 01279-454530 **Fax:** 01279-454509
E-mail: salesuk@leitz.org
Website: http://www.leitz.org
Bank(s): Barclays, London
Directors: I. Milligan (Dir), R. Milligan (MD)
Managers: A. Grant (Comptroller), Grant (Comptroller), D. Statham (Works Gen Mgr), B. Maddox (Purch Mgr)
Immediate Holding Company: LEITZ TOOLING UK LIMITED
Registration no: 00093766 **VAT No.:** GB 220 3778 84
Date established: 2007 **Turnover:** £2m - £5m **No.of Employees:** 21 - 50
Product Groups: 36, 47

Date of Accounts	Dec 10	Dec 09	Dec 08
Pre Tax Profit/Loss	N/A	-9	5
Working Capital	1m	1m	1m
Fixed Assets	1m	1m	1m
Current Assets	2m	2m	2m
Current Liabilities	N/A	276	248

Lesney Industries Ltd

Norwood House Temple Bank, Harlow, CM20 2DY
Tel: 01279-260130 **Fax:** 01279-413100
E-mail: sales@lesney.co.uk
Website: http://www.lesney.co.uk
Bank(s): HSBC Bank plc
Directors: M. James (MD)
Immediate Holding Company: LESNEY INDUSTRIES LIMITED
Registration no: 01645658 **VAT No.:** GB 415 0126 06
Date established: 1982 **Turnover:** £1m - £2m **No.of Employees:** 51 - 100
Product Groups: 30, 34, 66

Date of Accounts	Jan 10	Jan 11	Jan 08
Sales Turnover	1m	2m	4m
Pre Tax Profit/Loss	-319	-160	42
Working Capital	-44	-240	247
Fixed Assets	818	842	644
Current Assets	399	515	939
Current Liabilities	257	305	472

Luminescence International Ltd

The Fairway, Harlow, CM18 6NG
Tel: 01279-453711 **Fax:** 01279-421142
E-mail: sales@luminescence.co.uk
Website: http://www.luminescence.co.uk
Bank(s): National Westminster Bank Plc
Directors: A. Cooper (Dir)
Immediate Holding Company: LUMINESCENCE INTERNATIONAL LTD
Registration no: 03735854 **VAT No.:** GB 432 2555 74
Date established: 1999 **Turnover:** £5m - £10m **No.of Employees:** 21 - 50
Product Groups: 32

Date of Accounts	May 11	May 10	May 09
Sales Turnover	8m	7m	6m
Pre Tax Profit/Loss	2m	2m	2m
Working Capital	3m	2m	360
Fixed Assets	2m	2m	3m
Current Assets	5m	5m	4m
Current Liabilities	125	410	627

Lynar Manufacturing Ltd

4 Edinburgh Place, Harlow, CM20 2DJ
Tel: 01279-418604 **Fax:** 01279-432015
E-mail: sales@lynar.co.uk
Website: http://www.lynar.co.uk
Bank(s): Barclays
Managers: S. Richens (Mgr)
Ultimate Holding Company: SPR LYNAR HOLDINGS LTD
Immediate Holding Company: LYNAR MANUFACTURING LIMITED
Registration no: 07824267 **VAT No.:** GB 213 7143 96
Date established: 2011 **Turnover:** £1m - £2m **No.of Employees:** 11 - 20
Product Groups: 46, 48

Date of Accounts	Dec 10	Dec 09	Dec 08
Working Capital	321	375	341
Fixed Assets	53	76	107
Current Assets	702	735	725

M&ES Flexilope

Campions Cottage 129 Sheering Road, Harlow, CM17 0JP
Tel: 01279-454500 **Fax:** 01279-435400
E-mail: sales@flexilope.co.uk
Website: http://www.flexilope.co.uk
No.of Employees: 1 - 10 **Product Groups:** 27, 30, 64

Majestic Shower Co

1 North Place Edinburgh Way, Harlow, CM20 2SL
Tel: 01279-443644 **Fax:** 01279-635074
E-mail: jean@majesticshowers.com
Website: http://www.majesticshowers.com
Directors: J. King (Dir), J. Fairhurst (Fin)
Immediate Holding Company: MAJESTIC SHOWER COMPANY LIMITED
Registration no: 01313470 **Date established:** 1977 **Turnover:** £1m - £2m
No.of Employees: 21 - 50 **Product Groups:** 30, 35, 36

Date of Accounts	Sep 07	Sep 06	Sep 05
Working Capital	864	489	472
Fixed Assets	565	584	163
Current Assets	1684	1188	1148
Current Liabilities	820	698	676

Manor Garage Doors

37 Canons Gate, Harlow, CM20 1QG
Tel: 01279-452628 **Fax:** 01279-320664
E-mail: info@manorgaragedoors.co.uk
Website: http://www.manorgaragedoors.co.uk
Directors: R. Scott (Prop)
Immediate Holding Company: MANOR GARAGE DOORS LTD
Registration no: 03833722 **Date established:** 1999
No.of Employees: 1 - 10 **Product Groups:** 25, 30, 35

M C S Flooring & Fabric Cleaning

39 Rundells, Harlow, CM18 7HB
Tel: 07802-448871
E-mail: info@mcs-clean.co.uk
Website: http://www.mcs-clean.co.uk
Directors: M. Lane - Matthews (Prop)
Immediate Holding Company: MCS STONECARE LIMITED
Date established: 2009 **No.of Employees:** 1 - 10 **Product Groups:** 23, 32, 52

Date of Accounts	Nov 10
Working Capital	-41
Fixed Assets	33
Current Assets	2

Merial Animal Health Ltd

PO Box 327, Harlow, CM19 5TG
Tel: 01279-775858 **Fax:** 01279-775888
Website: http://www.merial.com
Directors: H. Nalle (Co Sec)
Ultimate Holding Company: SANOFI-AVENTIS SA (FRANCE)
Immediate Holding Company: MERIAL LIMITED
Registration no: 03332751 **Date established:** 1997
Turnover: Over £1,000m **No.of Employees:** 21 - 50 **Product Groups:** 07

Date of Accounts	Dec 08	Dec 07	Dec 06
Sales Turnover	3m	2466m	2195m
Pre Tax Profit/Loss	660	653m	498m
Working Capital	680	625m	604m
Fixed Assets	1m	1263m	1167m
Current Assets	1m	1328m	1264m
Current Liabilities	580	703m	660m
Total Share Capital	590	585m	585m

Morplan

PO Box 54, Harlow, CM20 2TS
Tel: 01279-435333 **Fax:** 01279-451928
E-mail: sales@morplan.com
Website: http://www.morplan.com
Directors: W. Edwards (MD), N. Haynes (Mkt Research), K. Simmons (Fin), T. Ghandour (Fin)
Managers: V. Justice (Sales Prom Mgr), L. Thorpe (Personnel), J. Pemble (Purch Mgr), J. Pickett (Tech Serv Mgr)
Ultimate Holding Company: TERENA SPAS (FRANCE)
Immediate Holding Company: MORPLAN LIMITED
Registration no: 03801026 **Date established:** 1999
Turnover: £10m - £20m **No.of Employees:** 101 - 250
Product Groups: 22, 25, 26, 27, 30, 33, 35, 37, 40, 45, 49, 52, 66, 67

Date of Accounts	Dec 11	Dec 10	Dec 09
Sales Turnover	19m	19m	16m
Pre Tax Profit/Loss	2m	996	-339
Working Capital	4m	7m	6m
Fixed Assets	2m	3m	3m
Current Assets	7m	10m	8m
Current Liabilities	1m	1m	540

N L B Engineering

1-3 Cedar House Stonehall Business Park Downhall Road, Matching Green, Harlow, CM17 0RA
Tel: 01279-730363 **Fax:** 01279-730353
E-mail: admin@nlbengineering.co.uk
Website: http://www.nlbengineering.co.uk
Directors: J. Heffernan (Dir)
Immediate Holding Company: NLB ENGINEERING LIMITED
Registration no: 04360141 **Date established:** 2002
Turnover: Up to £250,000 **No.of Employees:** 1 - 10 **Product Groups:** 30, 36

Date of Accounts	Jan 12	Jan 11	Jan 10
Sales Turnover	N/A	N/A	95
Pre Tax Profit/Loss	N/A	N/A	-112
Working Capital	-72	2	-7
Fixed Assets	45	29	26
Current Assets	51	102	125
Current Liabilities	N/A	N/A	5

Orridge & Co. Ltd

Astra Centre Edinburgh Way, Harlow, CM20 2BN
Tel: 01279-775600 **Fax:** 01279-620806
E-mail: contact@orridge.co.uk
Website: http://www.orridge.co.uk
Directors: P. Harding (Dir)
Immediate Holding Company: ORRIDGE GROUP LTD
Registration no: 04605119 **VAT No.:** GB 238 9273 29
Turnover: £5m - £10m **No.of Employees:** 1 - 10 **Product Groups:** 80

Parsons Brinckerhoff

Crown House River Way, Harlow, CM20 2DL
Tel: 01279-450900 **Fax:** 01279-450898
E-mail: info@pbworld.com
Website: http://www.pbworld.com
Directors: R. Bird (Tech Serv), T. Mathews (MD), T. O'Neil (Ch)
Immediate Holding Company: Balfour Beatty plc
Registration no: 02554514 **Turnover:** £20m - £50m
No.of Employees: 11 - 20 **Product Groups:** 84

P D S Design Solutions Ltd

Greenway Business Centre Harlow Busines Park, Harlow, CM19 5QE
Tel: 01279-406960 **Fax:** 01279-406961
E-mail: colinw@whatpowersupply.com
Website: http://www.whatpowersupply.com
Directors: C. Watkins (Dir)
Managers: S. Billson (Nat Sales Mgr)
Immediate Holding Company: PDS DESIGN SOLUTIONS LIMITED
Registration no: 03465624 **Date established:** 1997
Turnover: £500,000 - £1m **No.of Employees:** 1 - 10 **Product Groups:** 37, 44, 67

Date of Accounts	Aug 10	Aug 09	Aug 08
Working Capital	-31	-16	-31
Fixed Assets	2	2	2
Current Assets	56	30	65

Pearson Eduction Ltd

Edinburgh Gate Edinburgh Way, Harlow, CM20 2JE
Tel: 01279-623623 **Fax:** 01279-431059
E-mail: john.fallon@pearsoned-ema.com
Website: http://www.pearsoneducation.co.uk
Directors: J. Knight (Fin)
Managers: L. Wilson (Sales Admin), J. Fallon, B. Maurer (Personnel)
Ultimate Holding Company: PEARSON PLC
Immediate Holding Company: PEARSON EDUCATION LIMITED
Registration no: 00872828 **Date established:** 1966
Turnover: £250m - £500m **No.of Employees:** 251 - 500
Product Groups: 28, 64

Date of Accounts	Dec 11	Dec 10	Dec 09
Sales Turnover	511m	258m	243m
Pre Tax Profit/Loss	70m	-9m	-18m
Working Capital	112m	-207m	-210m
Fixed Assets	175m	423m	434m
Current Assets	502m	177m	200m
Current Liabilities	185m	24m	24m

Phasa Developments

International House Horsecroft Road, Harlow, CM19 5SU
Tel: 01279-630200 **Fax:** 01279-630222
E-mail: sales@phasa.co.uk
Website: http://www.phasa.co.uk
Bank(s): Bank of Scotland, Haymarket, London
Managers: T. Woods (Chief Mgr)
Ultimate Holding Company: U I S, USA
Immediate Holding Company: FLEXIBLE LAMPS LTD
Registration no: 00195431 **Turnover:** £1m - £2m
No.of Employees: 11 - 20 **Product Groups:** 42, 46, 48, 67

Pinnacle Partitions

6 Cawley Hatch, Harlow, CM19 5AN
Tel: 01279-641317 **Fax:** 01279-641329
E-mail: sales@pinnacle-partitions.co.uk
Website: http://www.pinnacle-partitions.co.uk
Directors: J. Diffey (Fin), V. Langhelt (MD)
Immediate Holding Company: NORTH CORNWALL SERVICES LIMITED
Registration no: 03117465 **Date established:** 1995
Turnover: Up to £250,000 **No.of Employees:** 1 - 10 **Product Groups:** 33, 35, 52

Date of Accounts	Oct 07	Jun 11	Jun 09
Sales Turnover	N/A	N/A	1
Pre Tax Profit/Loss	N/A	N/A	8
Working Capital	244	150	288
Fixed Assets	156	140	146
Current Assets	322	150	290
Current Liabilities	N/A	N/A	1

Power Connections
Unit 5 Harold Close, Harlow, CM19 5TH
Tel: 01279-422022 **Fax:** 01279-626304
E-mail: info@powerconnections.co.uk
Website: http://www.powerconnections.co.uk
Directors: V. Redmond (Dir)
Date established: 1996 **No.of Employees:** 11 - 20 **Product Groups:** 36, 40

S & J Juniper & Co.
7 Potter Street, Harlow, CM17 9AD
Tel: 01279-422456 **Fax:** 01279-438095
E-mail: info@sjjuniper.com
Website: http://www.sjjuniper.com
Directors: B. Juniper (MD)
Immediate Holding Company: S.& J.JUNIPER & CO.
Registration no: 00902516 **Date established:** 1967
Turnover: £250,000 - £500,000 **No.of Employees:** 1 - 10
Product Groups: 33, 37, 38, 40, 42, 46

Date of Accounts	Mar 10	Mar 09	Mar 08
Sales Turnover	266	283	N/A
Pre Tax Profit/Loss	18	41	N/A
Working Capital	414	443	441
Fixed Assets	37	14	15
Current Assets	442	486	473
Current Liabilities	8	16	N/A

S M S Technologies Ltd
St James Centre East Road, Harlow, CM20 2SX
Tel: 01279-406000 **Fax:** 01279-406001
E-mail: admin@smstl.com
Website: http://www.smstl.com
Bank(s): Barclays
Directors: C. Sandland (Co Sec), S. Sandland (Ch)
Managers: R. Shail (Chief Acct)
Immediate Holding Company: SMS TECHNOLOGIES LIMITED
Registration no: 02159350 **VAT No.:** GB 493 2243 45
Date established: 1987 **Turnover:** £2m - £5m **No.of Employees:** 21 - 50
Product Groups: 38, 48, 67

Date of Accounts	Sep 09	Sep 08	Oct 10
Working Capital	131	24	123
Fixed Assets	265	295	281
Current Assets	456	337	452

S R S Product plc
19 Mead Industrial Park Riverway, Harlow, CM20 2SE
Tel: 01279-635500 **Fax:** 01279-635282
E-mail: sales@srs-products.co.uk
Website: http://www.srs-products.co.uk
Bank(s): National Westminster Bank Plc
Directors: B. Gunning (Tech Serv), D. Ryan (Fin), M. Deards (MD)
Managers: G. Phillips (Buyer)
Immediate Holding Company: SRS PRODUCTS PLC
Registration no: 02014206 **VAT No.:** GB 432 1007 13
Date established: 1986 **Turnover:** £1m - £2m **No.of Employees:** 21 - 50
Product Groups: 26, 30, 34, 35, 37, 38

Date of Accounts	Dec 11	Dec 10	Dec 09
Sales Turnover	1m	1m	980
Pre Tax Profit/Loss	123	173	76
Working Capital	567	534	465
Fixed Assets	42	52	59
Current Assets	711	695	565
Current Liabilities	70	99	47

Salco Group plc
Salco House 5 Central Road, Harlow, CM20 2ST
Tel: 01279-439991 **Fax:** 01279-410984
E-mail: sales@salcogroup.com
Website: http://www.salcogroup.com
Bank(s): Nat West
Directors: H. Chow (Fin)
Ultimate Holding Company: SALCO HOLDINGS LIMITED
Immediate Holding Company: SALCO GROUP LIMITED
Registration no: 00439970 **Date established:** 1947
Turnover: £10m - £20m **No.of Employees:** 51 - 100 **Product Groups:** 61

Date of Accounts	Dec 11	Dec 10	Dec 09
Sales Turnover	17m	18m	19m
Pre Tax Profit/Loss	-481	-161	63
Working Capital	3m	4m	3m
Fixed Assets	2m	2m	3m
Current Assets	6m	7m	6m
Current Liabilities	381	883	525

Scooter Stores Ltd
Unit 11 Italstyle Buildings Cambridge Road, Harlow, CM20 2HE
Tel: 01279-453565 **Fax:** 01279-454030
E-mail: albertwass@site-safe.co.uk
Website: http://www.site-safe.co.uk
Directors: A. Wass (Dir)
Immediate Holding Company: SCOOTER STORE LIMITED
Registration no: 03141502 **VAT No.:** GB 731 9986 91
Date established: 1995 **Turnover:** £500,000 - £1m
No.of Employees: 1 - 10 **Product Groups:** 36

Date of Accounts	Dec 11	Dec 10	Dec 09
Working Capital	-7	-6	-29
Fixed Assets	31	27	36
Current Assets	39	20	56

Sheardown Engineering Ltd
15 South Road, Harlow, CM20 2AP
Tel: 01279-421788 **Fax:** 01279-435642
E-mail: info@sheardown.co.uk
Website: http://www.sheardown.co.uk
Bank(s): Barclays
Directors: N. Sheardown (MD)
Immediate Holding Company: SHEARDOWN ENGINEERING LIMITED
Registration no: 01140673 **VAT No.:** GB 214 4800 95
Date established: 1973 **Turnover:** £1m - £2m **No.of Employees:** 11 - 20
Product Groups: 36

Date of Accounts	Nov 11	Nov 10	Nov 09
Working Capital	158	187	189
Fixed Assets	51	56	61
Current Assets	199	230	215

Spray Finishes Of Harlow
Unit 16 Capital Place, Harlow, CM19 5AS
Tel: 01279-454160 **Fax:** 01279-454161
E-mail: keith.kingett@spray-finishes.co.uk
Website: http://www.spray-finishes.co.uk
Directors: K. Kinggett (Prop)
Date established: 1999 **No.of Employees:** 1 - 10 **Product Groups:** 46, 48

Stansted Fluid Power Ltd
Unit 5 New Horizon Business Centre Barrows Road, Harlow, CM19 5FN
Tel: 01279-813459 **Fax:** 01279-815180
E-mail: admin@sfp.uk.com
Website: http://www.sfp.uk.com
Bank(s): Barclays, Bishop Stortford
Directors: A. Freeman (MD), M. Freeman (Sales)
Immediate Holding Company: STANSTED FLUID POWER (PRODUCTS) LIMITED
Registration no: 01172803 **Date established:** 1974
Turnover: £250,000 - £500,000 **No.of Employees:** 11 - 20
Product Groups: 32, 36, 38, 40, 41, 42, 46, 85

Date of Accounts	Dec 10	Dec 09	Dec 08
Working Capital	69	45	48
Fixed Assets	19	32	41
Current Assets	88	73	65

Robert Stuart plc
10-11 Edinburgh Way, Harlow, CM20 2DH
Tel: 01279-442931 **Fax:** 01279-626063
E-mail: enquiries@robertstuart.plc.uk
Website: http://www.robertstuart.plc.uk
Directors: J. Hammett (Co Sec)
Managers: J. Searle (Sales Prom Mgr), S. Canfield (Buyer)
Immediate Holding Company: ROBERT STUART LTD.
Registration no: 00398525 **Date established:** 1945 **Turnover:** £2m - £5m
No.of Employees: 1 - 10 **Product Groups:** 48

Date of Accounts	Jul 09	Jul 08	Nov 11
Sales Turnover	4m	5m	4m
Pre Tax Profit/Loss	327	895	33
Working Capital	1m	1m	1m
Fixed Assets	1m	1m	926
Current Assets	2m	2m	2m
Current Liabilities	403	636	255

Teknequip Ltd
Horsecroft Road, Harlow, CM19 5BP
Tel: 01279-439761 **Fax:** 01279-635456
E-mail: sales@teknequip.co.uk
Website: http://www.teknequip.co.uk
Directors: H. Kinmond (Fin)
Managers: J. Hunt (Chief Mgr)
Ultimate Holding Company: SAMUEL HODGE HOLDINGS LIMITED
Immediate Holding Company: TEKNEQUIP LIMITED
Registration no: 00709252 **Date established:** 1961 **Turnover:** £1m - £2m
No.of Employees: 21 - 50 **Product Groups:** 38, 42

Date of Accounts	Mar 12	Mar 11	Mar 10
Sales Turnover	N/A	2m	2m
Pre Tax Profit/Loss	N/A	-103	-248
Working Capital	202	549	647
Fixed Assets	487	97	74
Current Assets	1m	869	767
Current Liabilities	N/A	58	35

Top Office Equipment Ltd
14 West Place West Road, Harlow, CM20 2GY
Tel: 020-8519 3330 **Fax:** 020-8519 5142
E-mail: sales@hogplc.com
Website: http://www.topofficebrochure.co.uk
Bank(s): Barclays
Directors: K. Harris (MD)
Ultimate Holding Company: HOG PLC
Immediate Holding Company: TOP OFFICE LIMITED
Registration no: 04115575 **Date established:** 2000 **Turnover:** £2m - £5m
No.of Employees: 11 - 20 **Product Groups:** 26, 49, 67

Total Communications Training Ltd
Cawley Hatch, Harlow, CM19 5AN
Tel: 0870-760 6824 **Fax:** 01279-426625
E-mail: info@totalcommstraining.com
Website: http://www.totalcommstraining.com
Directors: C. Atkin (Dir)
Managers: D. Brown (Accounts), R. Lovegrove (Sales Admin), S. Harris (Sales Prom Mgr)
Immediate Holding Company: TOTAL COMMS TRAINING LIMITED
Registration no: 07382050 **Date established:** 2010
No.of Employees: 1 - 10 **Product Groups:** 86

Date of Accounts	Sep 11
Working Capital	20
Fixed Assets	9
Current Assets	54

W E Marson & Company Ltd
Roding House Flex Meadow, Harlow, CM19 5TJ
Tel: 01279-451288 **Fax:** 01279-451422
E-mail: sales@wemarson.co.uk
Website: http://www.wemarson.co.uk
Bank(s): HSBC Bank plc
Directors: J. Marson (MD), A. Delaney (Co Sec)
Ultimate Holding Company: MARSON HOLDINGS LIMITED
Immediate Holding Company: W.E.MARSON AND COMPANY LIMITED
Registration no: 00328990 **VAT No.:** GB 220 3303 34
Date established: 1937 **Turnover:** £1m - £2m **No.of Employees:** 11 - 20
Product Groups: 26, 42

Date of Accounts	Dec 11	Dec 10	Dec 09
Working Capital	528	547	416
Fixed Assets	124	107	118
Current Assets	943	1m	895

David Webster Ltd
Field House Station Approach, Harlow, CM20 2FB
Tel: 01279-645100 **Fax:** 01279-645101
E-mail: info@dwlimited.co.uk
Website: http://www.dwlimited.co.uk
Bank(s): National Westminster Bank Plc
Directors: D. Webster (Prop), W. Hall (Chief Op Offcr), V. Ladougne (Dir), R. Thompson (MD), M. Webster (Dir), J. Barker (Asst MD), M. Thomson (MD)
Managers: S. Robinson (Mktg Serv Mgr), R. Gilbert (Sales Prom Mgr), C. Newman (Purch Mgr)
Ultimate Holding Company: BOUYGUES S.A. (FRANCE)
Immediate Holding Company: ETDE INFRASTRUCTURE LIMITED
Registration no: 00707875 **Date established:** 1961
Turnover: £20m - £50m **No.of Employees:** 51 - 100 **Product Groups:** 52

Date of Accounts	Dec 10	Dec 09	Dec 08
Sales Turnover	44m	39m	53m
Pre Tax Profit/Loss	-1m	-3m	-3m
Working Capital	5m	-1m	5m
Fixed Assets	2m	2m	3m
Current Assets	19m	21m	25m
Current Liabilities	10m	17m	14m

Young & Woods Ltd
13 Burnt Mill Industrial Estate Elizabeth Way, Harlow, CM20 2HS
Tel: 01279-443247 **Fax:** 01279-420698
E-mail: antony@young-woods.com
Website: http://www.young-woods.com
Bank(s): Barclays
Managers: C. Kirk (Fin Mgr)
Immediate Holding Company: YOUNG & WOODS LIMITED
Registration no: 00937948 **VAT No.:** GB 213 3242 17
Date established: 1968 **Turnover:** Up to £250,000
No.of Employees: 21 - 50 **Product Groups:** 46, 48

Date of Accounts	Sep 11	Sep 10	Sep 09
Working Capital	463	443	476
Fixed Assets	297	335	363
Current Assets	701	679	643

Yule Catto & Co plc
Central Road, Harlow, CM20 2BH
Tel: 01279-442791 **Fax:** 01279-641360
E-mail: info@yulecatto.com
Website: http://www.yulecatto.com
Bank(s): Barclays, National Westminster, Morgan Grenfell
Directors: R. Atkinson (Co Sec)
Ultimate Holding Company: YULE CATTO & CO PUBLIC LIMITED COMPANY
Immediate Holding Company: YULE CATTO OVERSEAS
Registration no: 00281773 **VAT No.:** GB 213 8287 67
Date established: 1933 **Turnover:** £250m - £500m
No.of Employees: 21 - 50 **Product Groups:** 32, 33, 66

Date of Accounts	Dec 11	Dec 10	Dec 09
Pre Tax Profit/Loss	3	-3m	-6m
Working Capital	271m	271m	275m
Current Assets	271m	271m	275m

Harwich

Access All Areas
33 Hewitt Road Ramsey, Harwich, CO12 5DY
Tel: 01255-242777
E-mail: rojaxuk@aol.com
Website: http://www.access-auditing.com
Directors: R. Kettle (Dir)
No.of Employees: 1 - 10 **Product Groups:** 80

Gordon Equipments Ltd
Durite Works Valley Road, Harwich, CO12 4RX
Tel: 01255-555200 **Fax:** 01255-555222
E-mail: sales@durite.co.uk
Website: http://www.durite.co.uk
Directors: A. Leviston (Mkt Research), J. Carr (MD)
Managers: S. Cooper, S. Thurlow, M. Flatt (Works Gen Mgr), A. Currell (Tech Serv Mgr)
Ultimate Holding Company: GORDON EQUIPMENTS LIMITED
Immediate Holding Company: GORDON EQUIPMENTS LIMITED
Registration no: 00373113 **VAT No.:** GB 102 5785 87
Date established: 1942 **Turnover:** £5m - £10m
No.of Employees: 51 - 100 **Product Groups:** 39, 68

Date of Accounts	Mar 11	Mar 10	Mar 09
Sales Turnover	10m	9m	N/A
Pre Tax Profit/Loss	2m	2m	2m
Working Capital	5m	4m	5m
Fixed Assets	1m	633	2m
Current Assets	6m	5m	6m
Current Liabilities	695	578	357

M & D Drainage Ltd
Unit 2 Friths Farm Colchester Road, Stones Green, Harwich, CO12 5DF
Tel: 01255-870993 **Fax:** 01255-870393
E-mail: suzanne@mddrainage.co.uk
Website: http://www.mddrainage.co.uk
Directors: S. Roberts (Dir)
Immediate Holding Company: M & D DRAINAGE LIMITED
Registration no: 05345154 **Date established:** 2005
No.of Employees: 1 - 10 **Product Groups:** 33, 34, 35, 37, 40, 48, 51, 52, 54, 66, 84

Date of Accounts	Feb 12	Feb 11	Feb 10
Working Capital	-30	8	-9
Fixed Assets	49	63	66
Current Assets	118	154	173

Premier Labellers
Unit 2 Bathside The Old Mercedes Building, Harwich, CO12 4LT
Tel: 01255-553822 **Fax:** 01255-241638
E-mail: sales@premierlabellers.co.uk
Website: http://www.premierlabellers.co.uk
Bank(s): National Westminster Bank plc
Directors: T. White (Fin)
Immediate Holding Company: PREMIER LABELLERS LIMITED
Registration no: 04422121 **VAT No.:** GB 638 0086 41
Date established: 2002 **Turnover:** £2m - £5m **No.of Employees:** 21 - 50
Product Groups: 07, 20, 23, 27, 28, 37, 42, 43, 44, 48, 66, 67, 76, 77

Date of Accounts	Mar 11	Mar 10	Mar 09
Working Capital	2	24	39
Fixed Assets	21	23	25
Current Assets	153	72	150

Sato UK Ltd
Valley Road, Harwich, CO12 4RR
Tel: 01255-240000 **Fax:** 01255-240111
E-mail: pwilkinson@satouk.com
Website: http://www.satouk.com
Bank(s): Lloyds TSB
Directors: N. Batchelor (MD), D. Joyce (Fin)
Managers: M. Lewis (Purch Mgr), P. Wilkinson (Personnel), L. Heath (Fin Mgr), J. Pratt (Tech Serv Mgr)
Ultimate Holding Company: SATO CORPORATION (JAPAN)
Immediate Holding Company: SATO UK LIMITED
Registration no: 00604144 **VAT No.:** GB 278 4006 49
Date established: 1958 **Turnover:** £10m - £20m
No.of Employees: 101 - 250 **Product Groups:** 23, 27, 28, 37, 42, 43, 44

Date of Accounts	Mar 12	Mar 11	Mar 10
Sales Turnover	12m	13m	14m
Pre Tax Profit/Loss	-189	-165	-650

see next page

Sato UK Ltd - Cont'd

Working Capital	-818	-315	-300
Fixed Assets	588	520	715
Current Assets	4m	5m	5m
Current Liabilities	1m	1m	1m

Hockley

Auto Plas International Ltd
90 Main Road Hawkwell, Hockley, SS5 4JH
Tel: 01702-202795 **Fax:** 01702-203499
E-mail: info@auto-plas.co.uk
Website: http://www.auto-plas.co.uk
Bank(s): National Westminster Bank Plc
Directors: K. Harris (Prop)
Immediate Holding Company: AUTO-PLAS (INTERNATIONAL) LIMITED
Registration no: 00665717 **VAT No.:** GB 250 5693 61
Date established: 1960 **Turnover:** £2m - £5m **No.of Employees:** 21 - 50
Product Groups: 30, 39

Date of Accounts	Dec 11	Oct 10	Oct 09
Sales Turnover	N/A	N/A	3m
Pre Tax Profit/Loss	N/A	N/A	-43
Working Capital	1m	1m	1m
Fixed Assets	3m	2m	2m
Current Assets	1m	2m	2m
Current Liabilities	N/A	N/A	36

C P Engineering Services
Central Avenue Hullbridge, Hockley, SS5 6AU
Tel: 07712-308316 **Fax:** 01702-230446
E-mail: info@cp-engineering-services.co.uk
Website: http://www.cp-engineering-services.co.uk
Directors: C. Parasram (Prop)
Immediate Holding Company: GOODSPEED LIMITED
Registration no: 02262265 **Date established:** 2003
No.of Employees: 1 - 10 **Product Groups:** 48

Date of Accounts	Apr 12	Apr 11	Apr 10
Working Capital	28	28	28
Fixed Assets	N/A	N/A	1
Current Assets	34	36	32
Current Liabilities	6	8	4

Doge Contracting Services
Thorpe Nurseries Thorpe Road, Hockley, SS5 4JT
Tel: 01702-204953 **Fax:** 01702-204953
Directors: G. House (Prop)
No.of Employees: 1 - 10 **Product Groups:** 35

Essex Catering Services
43 Greensward Lane, Hockley, SS5 5HG
Tel: 0783-672 9752
E-mail: essexcatering@hotmail.co.uk
Managers: M. Morgan (Serv Eng)
Turnover: Up to £250,000 **No.of Employees:** 1 - 10 **Product Groups:** 20, 40, 41

Excalibur Screwbolts Ltd
Gate 3 New Hall Nursery Lower Road, Hockley, SS5 5JU
Tel: 01702-206962 **Fax:** 01702-207918
E-mail: info@screwbolt.com
Website: http://www.screwbolt.com
Directors: C. Bickford (MD), R. Bickford (Fin)
Immediate Holding Company: EXCALIBUR SCREWBOLTS LTD
Registration no: 01996840 **VAT No.:** GB 451 8492 34
Date established: 1986 **Turnover:** £500,000 - £1m
No.of Employees: 1 - 10 **Product Groups:** 35, 36, 39

Date of Accounts	Sep 11	Sep 10	Sep 09
Working Capital	586	524	457
Fixed Assets	24	27	30
Current Assets	702	679	589

Gould Upholstery
30 Eldon Way Industrial Estate Eldon Way, Hockley, SS5 4AD
Tel: 01702-200229 **Fax:** 01702-200500
E-mail: info@gouldupholstery.com
Website: http://www.gouldupholstery.com
Directors: J. Duce (Fin)
Immediate Holding Company: THE ALAN GOULD UPHOLSTERY COMPANY LIMITED
Registration no: 04447946 **Date established:** 2002
No.of Employees: 11 - 20 **Product Groups:** 22, 25, 26, 63, 67

Kolorsol
31 Eldon Way Industrial Estate Eldon Way, Hockley, SS5 4AD
Tel: 01702-200050 **Fax:** 01702-200025
E-mail: steve@kolorsol.com
Website: http://www.kolorsol.com
Managers: S. Lee (Chief Mgr)
Date established: 2003 **No.of Employees:** 1 - 10 **Product Groups:** 46, 48

Prodek Roofing
26 White Hart Lane, Hockley, SS5 4DQ
Tel: 01702-202123 **Fax:** 01702- 202932
E-mail: linbjol@aol.com
Website: http://www.prodekroofing.co.uk
Directors: L. Thompson (Prop)
Registration no: 05048515 **No.of Employees:** 11 - 20 **Product Groups:** 52

Date of Accounts	Mar 08	Mar 07	Mar 06
Working Capital	38	-1	-12
Fixed Assets	124	25	17
Current Assets	276	172	81
Current Liabilities	238	173	93

Seetec
75-77 Main Road, Hockley, SS5 4RG
Tel: 01702-201070 **Fax:** 01702-201224
E-mail: info@seetec.co.uk
Website: http://www.seetec.co.uk
Bank(s): Barclays
Directors: L. Barry (Fin), A. Bunney (Mkt Research), P. Cooper (MD), J. Baumback (Tech Serv), A. Conway (Pers)
Managers: E. Cole, M. Hall
Immediate Holding Company: SEETEC BUSINESS TECHNOLOGY CENTRE LIMITED
Registration no: 02291188 **VAT No.:** GB 546 0957 25
Date established: 1988 **Turnover:** £50m - £75m
No.of Employees: 51 - 100 **Product Groups:** 44, 80, 86

Date of Accounts	Mar 11	Mar 10	Mar 09
Sales Turnover	53m	38m	21m
Pre Tax Profit/Loss	15m	5m	2m
Working Capital	13m	4m	4m
Fixed Assets	3m	3m	2m
Current Assets	36m	20m	6m
Current Liabilities	22m	15m	2m

Swyft Plastic Moulding Ltd
22 Eldon Way, Hockley, SS5 4AD
Tel: 01702-200203 **Fax:** 01702-200204
E-mail: info@swyftplastics.co.uk
Website: http://www.swyftplastics.co.uk
Directors: M. Payne (MD)
Immediate Holding Company: SWYFT PLASTIC MOULDINGS LIMITED
Registration no: 06105284 **Date established:** 2007
Turnover: £500,000 - £1m **No.of Employees:** 1 - 10 **Product Groups:** 30, 48

Date of Accounts	Feb 08	Feb 11	Feb 10
Sales Turnover	390	N/A	N/A
Pre Tax Profit/Loss	48	N/A	N/A
Working Capital	7	-72	-58
Fixed Assets	34	31	34
Current Assets	100	112	148
Current Liabilities	51	N/A	N/A

Hornchurch

Firstford Ltd
King House Broadway Parade, Hornchurch, RM12 4RS
Tel: 01708-470351 **Fax:** 01708-477991
E-mail: sales@firstfordltd.co.uk
Website: http://www.firstfordltd.co.uk
Bank(s): Lloyds TSB Bank plc
Directors: B. Buckler (MD)
Immediate Holding Company: FIRSTFORD LIMITED
Registration no: 01828919 **Date established:** 1984 **Turnover:** £1m - £2m
No.of Employees: 21 - 50 **Product Groups:** 38, 39, 40

Date of Accounts	Jul 12	Jul 11	Jul 10
Working Capital	74	75	82
Fixed Assets	5	6	8
Current Assets	111	122	136

Pip Lift Service Ltd
Stafford Avenue, Hornchurch, RM11 2ER
Tel: 01708-460130 **Fax:** 01708-441337
E-mail: sales@pip-group.co.uk
Website: http://www.pip-group.co.uk
Directors: J. Masterson (Fin), P. Masterson (Dir), P. Masterson (MD)
Immediate Holding Company: P.I.P. LIFT SERVICE LIMITED
Registration no: 02746163 **Date established:** 1992
No.of Employees: 21 - 50 **Product Groups:** 35, 39, 45

Date of Accounts	Dec 09	Dec 08	Dec 07
Working Capital	506	421	284
Fixed Assets	80	94	88
Current Assets	1m	1m	1m

Ukap
Stirling House 21-25 Station Lane, Hornchurch, RM12 6JL
Tel: 01708-447788 **Fax:** 01708-441111
E-mail: sales@ukap.co.uk
Website: http://www.ukap.co.uk
Directors: R. Howard (Fin), L. Welsh (MD)
Managers: D. Phillips, J. Kelly (Sales Prom Mgr), I. Byatt (Comm), S. Shepherd (Quality Control)
Ultimate Holding Company: BLACKFRIARS CORP (USA)
Immediate Holding Company: UKAP LIMITED
Registration no: 01579960 **VAT No.:** GB 398 6301 15
Date established: 1981 **Turnover:** £1m - £2m **No.of Employees:** 1 - 10
Product Groups: 30

Date of Accounts	Dec 10	Dec 09	Dec 08
Working Capital	50	2m	2m
Current Assets	50	2m	2m

Ilford

A & H Commercial Printers
153 Ley Street, Ilford, IG1 4BL
Tel: 020-8478 2558 **Fax:** 020-8514 6848
E-mail: info@ahprinters.com
Website: http://www.ahprinters.com
Managers: A. Mehta (Mgr)
Immediate Holding Company: A&H PRINTERS LIMITED
Date established: 2010 **No.of Employees:** 1 - 10 **Product Groups:** 28, 44, 81

Abbey Metalworks
2 Austin House Abbey Road, Ilford, IG2 7ND
Tel: 020-8554 8917
Directors: P. Hassell (Prop)
Date established: 1996 **No.of Employees:** 1 - 10 **Product Groups:** 26, 35

Aquanile UK Ltd
62 Daffodil Gardens, Ilford, IG1 2JW
Tel: 020-8262 2429
E-mail: sales@aquanile.com
Website: http://www.aquanile.com
Directors: N. Nigam (MD)
Immediate Holding Company: AQUANILE UK LIMITED
Registration no: 04641324 **Date established:** 2003
No.of Employees: 1 - 10 **Product Groups:** 44

Date of Accounts	Jan 12	Jan 11	Jan 10
Pre Tax Profit/Loss	-0	N/A	N/A
Working Capital	N/A	-0	N/A

Archant London
Recorder House 539 High Road, Ilford, IG1 1UD
Tel: 020-8478 4444 **Fax:** 020-8478 6606
E-mail: enzo.testa@archant.co.uk
Website: http://www.london24.com
Directors: P. Watling (Fin), E. Testa (MD), P. Curran (Fin)
Managers: M. Cutler (Sales Admin), S. Fenton, T. Little, L. Head (Personnel), P. Brennan
Immediate Holding Company: ARCHANT REGIONAL LIMITED
Registration no: 00019300 **Date established:** 1984
Turnover: £10m - £20m **No.of Employees:** 101 - 250 **Product Groups:** 28

Date of Accounts	Dec 07	Dec 06	Dec 05
Sales Turnover	13488	14201	11342
Pre Tax Profit/Loss	-1177	-1002	3754
Working Capital	-1060	-312	-572
Fixed Assets	13943	15248	16861
Current Assets	2488	3134	3581
Current Liabilities	3548	3445	4153
Total Share Capital	8000	8000	8000
ROCE% (Return on Capital Employed)	-9.1	-6.7	23.0
ROT% (Return on Turnover)	-8.7	-7.1	33.1

Arkle Bros Ltd
5 Herbert Road, Ilford, IG3 8AL
Tel: 020-8590 3321 **Fax:** 020-8590 3349
E-mail: info@arklebros.co.uk
Website: http://www.arklebros.co.uk
Directors: R. Mathers (Co Sec)
No.of Employees: 1 - 10 **Product Groups:** 37, 44, 52, 85

Armourfend Ltd
Unit 1, 24/26 Fowler Road Hainault Business Park, Hainault, Ilford, IG6 3UT
Tel: 020-8501 6346 **Fax:** 020-8501 6349
Website: http://www.armourfend.co.uk
Directors: C. Scott (Dir)
Registration no: 02956335 **No.of Employees:** 1 - 10 **Product Groups:** 46, 48

Date of Accounts	May 08	May 07	May 06
Working Capital	-108	-120	-85
Fixed Assets	15	30	24
Current Assets	34	30	47
Current Liabilities	142	150	132

Bombardier Transportation UK
Ley Street, Ilford, IG1 4BP
Tel: 020-7465 9525 **Fax:** 020-7465 9536
Website: http://www.transport.bombardier.com
Managers: J. Carey (Chief Mgr)
No.of Employees: 101 - 250 **Product Groups:** 41

Burton Engineering Ltd
621 Eastern Avenue, Ilford, IG2 6PN
Tel: 020-8554 0920 **Fax:** 020-8554 4828
E-mail: sales@burtonpower.com
Website: http://www.burtonpower.com
Directors: D. Burton (Prop), G. Burton (Co Sec)
Immediate Holding Company: AVENUE CORPORATE PLANNING LTD
Registration no: 01057517 **VAT No.:** GB 506 1939 50
Date established: 1963 **Turnover:** £2m - £5m **No.of Employees:** 1 - 10
Product Groups: 35, 40, 68

Date of Accounts	Apr 11	Apr 10	Apr 09
Working Capital	710	690	604
Fixed Assets	54	60	45
Current Assets	1m	1m	1m

Doma Electrical Goods
89 Green Lane, Ilford, IG1 1XJ
Tel: 020-8514 2551 **Fax:** 020-8478 2552
Directors: G. Mcgrath (Ptnr)
Date established: 2000 **No.of Employees:** 1 - 10 **Product Groups:** 36, 40

Excel Plastering Ilford Ltd
1 Natal Road, Ilford, IG1 2HA
Tel: 020-8553 2244 **Fax:** 020-8553 4489
E-mail: info@excelplastering.com
Website: http://www.excelplastering.com
Bank(s): AIB Group
Directors: J. Brewer (MD), L. Brewer (Dir), P. Brewer (Dir)
Managers: A. Brewer (Admin Off)
Immediate Holding Company: EXCEL PLASTERING (ILFORD) LIMITED
Registration no: 02653230 **VAT No.:** GB 685 2462 2
Date established: 1991 **Turnover:** £2m - £5m **No.of Employees:** 21 - 50
Product Groups: 33, 52

Date of Accounts	Aug 11	Aug 10	Aug 09
Sales Turnover	N/A	N/A	3m
Pre Tax Profit/Loss	N/A	N/A	102
Working Capital	-22	-34	-34
Fixed Assets	34	36	42
Current Assets	555	262	301
Current Liabilities	N/A	N/A	120

friends textiles
23 Merrivale Avanue South Woodford, Ilford, IG4 5PQ
Tel: 0778-9961635
E-mail: sales@friendstextiles.com
Website: http://www.friendstextiles.com
Managers: F. syed (Mgr)
Date established: 1975 **Turnover:** Up to £250,000
No.of Employees: 1 - 10 **Product Groups:** 24

Fujichem Sonneborn Ltd
Jaxa Works 91-95 Peregrine Road, Ilford, IG6 3XH
Tel: 020-8500 0251 **Fax:** 020-8500 3696
E-mail: sales@fcsonneborn.com
Website: http://www.fcsonneborn.co.uk
Bank(s): National Westminster Bank Plc
Directors: E. Cox (Fin), R. Sheppard (Dir)
Managers: A. Flanagan (Buyer), K. Snow (Personnel)
Immediate Holding Company: FUJICHEM SONNEBORN LIMITED
Registration no: 00437672 **VAT No.:** GB 701 8761 44
Date established: 1947 **Turnover:** £20m - £50m
No.of Employees: 21 - 50 **Product Groups:** 30, 32, 34, 48, 68

Date of Accounts	Dec 11	Dec 10	Jun 10
Sales Turnover	24m	10m	20m
Pre Tax Profit/Loss	-551	-2m	-1m
Working Capital	-4m	-3m	-510
Fixed Assets	6m	5m	5m
Current Assets	8m	8m	9m
Current Liabilities	3m	4m	5m

Heventech Mechanical Service Ltd
3 Redbridge Enterprise Centre Thompson Close, Ilford, IG1 1TY
Tel: 08451-298565
E-mail: brian@heventech.co.uk
Website: http://www.heventech.co.uk
Directors: L. Ash (MD), B. Almond (Dir), B. Almond (Fin)
Managers: C. Wilkinson (Serv Mgr)
Immediate Holding Company: HEVENTECH MECHANICAL SERVICES LIMITED
Registration no: 02258560 **VAT No.:** GB 488 2879 74
Date established: 1988 **Turnover:** £1m - £2m **No.of Employees:** 1 - 10
Product Groups: 40, 52

Date of Accounts	Jun 11	Jun 10	Jun 09
Working Capital	-15	N/A	N/A
Fixed Assets	13	21	14
Current Assets	51	63	88

Kelvin Hughes Ltd (Charts & Maritime Supplies)
New North Road Hainault, Ilford, IG6 2UR
Tel: 020-8502 6887 **Fax:** 020-8559 8535
E-mail: marketing@kelvinhughes.co.uk
Website: http://www.kelvinhughes.com
Bank(s): Lloyds TSB Bank plc
Directors: C. Eastdal (Fin), R. Gould (Grp Chief Exec), S. Hughes (Sales)
Managers: D. Bowden (Tech Serv Mgr), J. Davis (Mktg Serv Mgr), M. Bundy (Personnel)
Ultimate Holding Company: ECI PARTNERS LLP
Immediate Holding Company: KELVIN HUGHES LIMITED
Registration no: 01030135 **VAT No.:** GB 226 6019 77
Date established: 1971 **Turnover:** £50m - £75m
No.of Employees: 251 - 500 **Product Groups:** 28, 37, 39, 49, 64

Date of Accounts	Jul 11	Jul 10	Jul 09
Sales Turnover	57m	54m	59m
Pre Tax Profit/Loss	6m	3m	1m
Working Capital	14m	8m	6m
Fixed Assets	11m	11m	11m
Current Assets	43m	33m	29m
Current Liabilities	1m	3m	2m

L P L Commercial Investigations
890-900 Eastern Avenue, Ilford, IG2 7HH
Tel: 020-8597 2229 **Fax:** 020-8597 1180
E-mail: info@lplgroup.com
Website: http://www.lplgroup.com
Directors: S. Lewis (Ptnr)
Immediate Holding Company: LPL COMMERCIAL SERVICES LIMITED
Registration no: 04935222 **Date established:** 2003
Turnover: £250,000 - £500,000 **No.of Employees:** 11 - 20
Product Groups: 81, 82

Date of Accounts	Nov 11	Nov 10	Nov 09
Sales Turnover	472	414	692
Pre Tax Profit/Loss	N/A	-86	16
Working Capital	-247	-282	-189
Fixed Assets	20	25	33
Current Assets	74	77	184
Current Liabilities	N/A	255	301

Lanbourne Refrigerators & Freezers
51-55 Fowler Road Hainault Business Park, Ilford, IG6 3XE
Tel: 020-8501 0500 **Fax:** 020-8501 5500
Website: http://www.lanbournerefrigeration.co.uk
Directors: P. Tipley (Ptnr)
Immediate Holding Company: BOND SECURITY SERVICES LTD
Date established: 2011 **No.of Employees:** 1 - 10 **Product Groups:** 36, 40

Date of Accounts	Dec 10	Dec 09	Dec 08
Working Capital	-303	-242	62
Fixed Assets	758	872	563
Current Assets	785	679	754

LatestSol Website Design & Development
72a Ilford Lane, Ilford, IG1 2LA
Tel: 020-8478 5532
E-mail: info@latestsol.co.uk
Website: http://www.latestsol.co.uk
Directors: A. Azam (Grp Chief Exec)
Date established: 2000 **Turnover:** Up to £250,000
No.of Employees: 21 - 50 **Product Groups:** 44

Maplin Electronics Ltd
302-304 Green Lane, Ilford, IG1 1XT
Tel: 08432-277312 **Fax:** 020-8599 5169
E-mail: customercare@maplin.co.uk
Website: http://www.maplin.co.uk
Managers: A. Ali
Ultimate Holding Company: MONTAGU PRIVATE EQUITY LLP
Immediate Holding Company: MAPLIN ELECTRONICS LIMITED
Registration no: 01264385 **Date established:** 1976
Turnover: £125m - £250m **No.of Employees:** 1 - 10 **Product Groups:** 37, 61

Date of Accounts	Dec 11	Dec 08	Dec 09
Sales Turnover	205m	204m	204m
Pre Tax Profit/Loss	25m	32m	35m
Working Capital	118m	49m	75m
Fixed Assets	27m	28m	28m
Current Assets	207m	108m	142m
Current Liabilities	78m	51m	59m

A J Middleton & Co. Ltd
45 York Road, Ilford, IG1 3AD
Tel: 020-8478 1501 **Fax:** 020-8478 1501
E-mail: geoff612phillips@googlemail.com
Directors: G. Phillips (MD)
Immediate Holding Company: A.J. MIDDLETON AND COMPANY LIMITED
Registration no: 00594813 **VAT No.:** GB 246 6733 41
Date established: 1957 **Turnover:** £250,000 - £500,000
No.of Employees: 1 - 10 **Product Groups:** 35, 36, 37, 39, 46

Date of Accounts	Dec 11	Dec 10	Dec 09
Sales Turnover	357	N/A	589
Pre Tax Profit/Loss	8	N/A	34
Working Capital	18	2	-2
Fixed Assets	32	32	32
Current Assets	231	143	157
Current Liabilities	N/A	N/A	117

Pettex Ltd
62-70 Fowler Road, Ilford, IG6 3UT
Tel: 020-8501 1033 **Fax:** 020-8501 3943
E-mail: enquiries@pettex.co.uk
Website: http://www.pettex.co.uk
Bank(s): TSB
Directors: K. Cornell (Dir), T. Fisher (Dir), S. O'Brien (MD), S. Bolton (Dir)
Immediate Holding Company: PETTEX LIMITED
Registration no: 00695155 **VAT No.:** GB 246 5311 72
Date established: 1961 **Turnover:** £2m - £5m **No.of Employees:** 21 - 50
Product Groups: 62

Date of Accounts	Jul 11	Jul 10	Jul 09
Working Capital	2m	1m	1m
Fixed Assets	1m	1m	1m
Current Assets	3m	2m	2m

Plaut International
Heron Mews House 1a Balfour Road, Ilford, IG1 4HP
Tel: 020-8553 3471 **Fax:** 020-8478 1876
E-mail: john@plautint.co.uk
Website: http://www.plautint.co.uk
Directors: I. Burbidge (Co Sec), J. Yates (MD)
Immediate Holding Company: PLAUT INTERNATIONAL LIMITED
Registration no: 02329905 **VAT No.:** GB 506 5039 66
Date established: 1988 **Turnover:** £10m - £20m
No.of Employees: 11 - 20 **Product Groups:** 25, 26

Date of Accounts	May 11	May 10	May 09
Working Capital	1m	1m	1m
Fixed Assets	268	229	213
Current Assets	7m	6m	4m

Radar Signs
12 High View Parade Woodford Avenue, Ilford, IG4 5EP
Tel: 020-8551 0216 **Fax:** 020-8551 1458
E-mail: radarsigns@btclick.com
Directors: B. Cohen (Ch & MD), B. Cohens (Ptnr)
Managers: M. Buffy (I.T. Exec)
VAT No.: GB 597 1726 95 **Turnover:** Up to £250,000
No.of Employees: 1 - 10 **Product Groups:** 30, 52

Raught Ltd
117 The Drive, Ilford, IG1 3JE
Tel: 020-8554 9921 **Fax:** 020-8554 8337
E-mail: raughtltd@aol.com
Website: http://www.raught.co.uk
Directors: J. Lessman (MD), I. Lassman (Dir), S. Lassman (Grp Chief Exec)
Managers: S. Sidom (I.T. Exec)
Immediate Holding Company: RAUGHT LIMITED
Registration no: 01125158 **VAT No.:** GB 247 4461 52
Date established: 1973 **No.of Employees:** 1 - 10 **Product Groups:** 31

Date of Accounts	Jul 11	Jul 10	Jul 09
Working Capital	5	21	19
Fixed Assets	3	3	3
Current Assets	89	114	114

Reed Employment Ltd
35 Cranbrook Road, Ilford, IG1 4PA
Tel: 020-8514 3777 **Fax:** 020-8911 0403
E-mail: ilford@reed.co.uk
Website: http://www.reed.co.uk
Managers: H. Fontaine (Mgr)
Ultimate Holding Company: REED GLOBAL LTD (MALTA)
Immediate Holding Company: REED EMPLOYMENT LIMITED
Registration no: 00669854 **Date established:** 1960
Turnover: £500m - £1,000m **No.of Employees:** 1 - 10
Product Groups: 80

Date of Accounts	Jun 11	Jun 10	Dec 07
Sales Turnover	618	450	287m
Pre Tax Profit/Loss	-2m	310	8m
Working Capital	23m	28m	28m
Fixed Assets	31	36	5m
Current Assets	28m	30m	74m
Current Liabilities	37	29	21m

Resolve HR Consultancy
603-605 CRANBROOK ROAD GANTS HILL, Ilford, IG2 6SU
Tel: 0845-8339830
E-mail: rosemary@resolveandevolve.co.uk
Website: http://www.resolvehr.co.uk
Managers: R. Martin (Consultant)
Registration no: 04119555 **Date established:** 2003
No.of Employees: 1 - 10 **Product Groups:** 80

S & S Trading Co.
2 Thornton Road, Ilford, IG1 2ER
Tel: 020-8553 2830 **Fax:** 020-8220 5584
E-mail: snstradingco786@hotmail.com
Directors: S. Shaikh (Prop)
Turnover: Up to £250,000 **No.of Employees:** 1 - 10 **Product Groups:** 61

Salon Connect
Connect House 1 Connect Lane Barkingside, Ilford, IG6 2AN
Tel: 020-8418 2490 **Fax:** 020-8551 5719
E-mail: salon@salonconnect.co.uk
Website: http://www.salonconnect.co.uk
Directors: G. Kaymakam (Snr Part)
Turnover: £250,000 - £500,000 **No.of Employees:** 1 - 10
Product Groups: 30, 36, 40

UK County Couriers Ltd
21 Malvern Drive, Ilford, IG3 9DP
Tel: 08704-460810 **Fax:** 0870-446 0740
E-mail: ukcountycouriers@btinternet.com
Website: http://www.ukcountycouriers.co.uk
Turnover: Up to £250,000 **No.of Employees:** 1 - 10 **Product Groups:** 24, 64, 71, 75, 79

Wallis Office Furniture Ltd
8-18 Fowler Road Hainault Industrial Estate, Ilford, IG6 3UT
Tel: 020-8500 9991 **Fax:** 020-8500 1949
E-mail: info@wallisoffice.com
Website: http://www.wallisoffice.com
Bank(s): Lloyds TSB Bank plc
Directors: J. Old (Co Sec), A. Old (Grp Chief Exec)
Managers: A. Old (Sales Prom Mgr), J. Low (Sales Admin)
Ultimate Holding Company: WALLIS OFFICE HOLDINGS LIMITED
Immediate Holding Company: WALLIS OFFICE FURNITURE LIMITED
Registration no: 01206974 **VAT No.:** GB 244 6959 27
Date established: 1975 **Turnover:** £5m - £10m **No.of Employees:** 21 - 50
Product Groups: 67

Date of Accounts	Mar 11	Mar 10	Mar 09
Working Capital	758	984	1m
Fixed Assets	72	93	2m
Current Assets	1m	1m	2m

Websouls Limited
94-Endsleigh Gardens, Ilford, IG1 3EG
Tel: 020-8252 2497 **Fax:** 020-8816 7871
E-mail: info@websouls.co.uk
Website: http://www.websouls.co.uk
Managers: A. Rafiq (Mktg Serv Mgr)
Registration no: 05213704 **Date established:** 2003
No.of Employees: 1 - 10 **Product Groups:** 79

Westrow Control Systems
33 Westrow Gardens, Ilford, IG3 9NF
Tel: 020-8590 2798 **Fax:** 020-8220 2442
E-mail: sales@westrowcontrolsystems.co.uk
Website: http://www.westrowcontrolsystems.co.uk
Directors: J. Newton (Prop)
Date established: 1984 **No.of Employees:** 1 - 10 **Product Groups:** 26, 35

Ingatestone

Eurostand Display Ltd
The Barn Writtle Road, Margaretting, Ingatestone, CM4 0EL
Tel: 01277-350925 **Fax:** 01277-356732
E-mail: sales@eurostanddisplay.com
Website: http://www.eurostanddisplay.com
Directors: G. Neile (Fin)
Immediate Holding Company: EUROSTAND DISPLAY LIMITED
Registration no: 04966334 **Date established:** 2003
Turnover: £250,000 - £500,000 **No.of Employees:** 1 - 10
Product Groups: 26

Date of Accounts	Apr 11	Apr 10	Apr 09
Working Capital	83	81	77
Fixed Assets	9	8	5
Current Assets	426	363	346
Current Liabilities	N/A	N/A	14

Grassform Plant Hire Ltd
Little Woodbarns Farm Green Street, Ingatestone, CM4 0NT
Tel: 01277-353686 **Fax:** 01277-355504
E-mail: sales@grassform.co.uk
Website: http://www.grassform.co.uk
Directors: M. Dunning (Prop)
Immediate Holding Company: GRASSFORM PLANT HIRE LIMITED
Registration no: 05185169 **Date established:** 2004
No.of Employees: 1 - 10 **Product Groups:** 51

Date of Accounts	Feb 11	Feb 10	Feb 09
Working Capital	-280	-257	-206
Fixed Assets	507	455	370
Current Assets	38	55	51

R H Horwitz Associates
23 High Street, Ingatestone, CM4 9DU
Tel: 01277-356311 **Fax:** 01277-356683
E-mail: richard@rhorwitz.co.uk
Website: http://www.rhorwitz.co.uk
Directors: R. Horwitz (Prop)
Registration no: 03713056 **Date established:** 1999
No.of Employees: 1 - 10 **Product Groups:** 35

Leigh On Sea

Allen Bros Ltd
724 London Road, Leigh On Sea, SS9 3NL
Tel: 01702-475255 **Fax:** 01702-470420
E-mail: allenbros@btopenworld.com
Website: http://www.lightstore.uk.com
Directors: C. Allen (MD), M. Allen (Fin)
Immediate Holding Company: ALLEN BROS. (ELECTRICAL FACTORS) LIMITED
Registration no: 01039794 **VAT No.:** GB 250 2475 86
Date established: 1972 **Turnover:** £250,000 - £500,000
No.of Employees: 1 - 10 **Product Groups:** 77

Date of Accounts	Jul 11	Jul 10	Jul 09
Working Capital	449	455	505
Fixed Assets	61	92	58
Current Assets	737	728	755

Brook Systems
9 Ellenbrook Close, Leigh On Sea, SS9 3DY
Tel: 01702-480608 **Fax:** 01702-716080
E-mail: john@brooksystems.co.uk
Website: http://www.brooksystems.co.uk
Directors: J. Healy (Ptnr)
No.of Employees: 1 - 10 **Product Groups:** 37, 48, 67, 79

1st 4 Carpet Cleaning
64 The Ryde, Leigh On Sea, SS9 4TN
Tel: 01702-473700
E-mail: doug@1st4carpetcleaning.com
Website: http://www.1st4carpetcleaning.com
Directors: D. Holloway (Prop)
No.of Employees: 1 - 10 **Product Groups:** 23, 32, 52

Guardian Industrial Doors Ltd
45 Progress Road, Leigh On Sea, SS9 5PR
Tel: 01702-512424 **Fax:** 01702-510015
E-mail: mail@guardiandoors.com
Website: http://www.guardiandoors.net
Bank(s): The Royal Bank of Scotland
Directors: E. Everitt (Fin)
Managers: R. Everitt (Mgr)
Immediate Holding Company: GUARDIAN INDUSTRIAL DOORS LIMITED
Registration no: 01447746 **VAT No.:** GB 328 5339 44
Date established: 1979 **Turnover:** £1m - £2m **No.of Employees:** 21 - 50
Product Groups: 35, 36

Date of Accounts	Mar 11	Mar 10	Mar 09
Working Capital	291	242	147
Fixed Assets	55	73	85
Current Assets	804	725	604

Hometec UK
401 Rayleigh Road, Leigh On Sea, SS9 5JG
Tel: 01702-421421 **Fax:** 01702-521521
E-mail: nigel@hometec.co.uk
Website: http://www.hometech.co.uk
Directors: N. Jackson (Dir)
Immediate Holding Company: CALMINSTER LIMITED
Registration no: 02747699 **Date established:** 1992
No.of Employees: 21 - 50 **Product Groups:** 30, 52

Date of Accounts	Dec 11	Dec 10	Dec 09
Working Capital	-8	3	2
Fixed Assets	37	43	56
Current Assets	321	389	266

Jegs Electrical Ltd
20 Progress Road, Leigh On Sea, SS9 5PR
Tel: 01702-421555 **Fax:** 01702-420363
E-mail: sales@jegs.co.uk
Website: http://www.jegs.co.uk
Directors: E. Gibbins (MD)
Immediate Holding Company: JEGS ELECTRICAL LIMITED
Registration no: 06190390 **Date established:** 2007 **Turnover:** £5m - £10m
No.of Employees: 51 - 100 **Product Groups:** 77

Date of Accounts	Jul 11	Jul 10	Jul 09
Sales Turnover	8m	8m	7m
Pre Tax Profit/Loss	634	420	213
Working Capital	2m	-177	-315
Fixed Assets	737	855	643
Current Assets	2m	2m	2m
Current Liabilities	405	2m	2m

Monometer Holdings Ltd
Monometer House Rectory Grove, Leigh On Sea, SS9 2HN
Tel: 01702-472201 **Fax:** 01702-715112
E-mail: david.hall@monometer.com
Website: http://www.monometer.co.uk
Directors: Y. Hall (MD)
Immediate Holding Company: MONOMETER HOLDINGS LIMITED
Registration no: 00251890 **Date established:** 1930
No.of Employees: 1 - 10 **Product Groups:** 40, 42, 46

Date of Accounts	Dec 11	Dec 10	Dec 09
Working Capital	99	121	122
Fixed Assets	235	210	213
Current Assets	210	216	230

1 A Plumber
Gravel Road, Leigh On Sea, SS9 5AS
Tel: 01702-523947 **Fax:** 01702-523947
E-mail: sales@1aplumber.com
Website: http://www.1aplumber.com
Directors: D. Jenkins (Prop)
No.of Employees: 1 - 10 **Product Groups:** 52

Overton Vehicles
370 Rayleigh Road, Leigh On Sea, SS9 5PT
Tel: 01702-526152 **Fax:** 01702-510489
E-mail: tedo.bentleyboys@virgin.net
Website: http://www.bentleyboys.com
Directors: T. Overton (Prop)
Registration no: 04054368 **VAT No.:** GB 250 9838 41
Turnover: £250,000 - £500,000 **No.of Employees:** 1 - 10
Product Groups: 39

Porta Tool Fixings Ltd
Units 6-8 Brunel Road, Leigh On Sea, SS9 5JL
Tel: 01702-510080 **Fax:** 01702-510030
E-mail: portatools@btconnect.com
Bank(s): TSB P.L.C., Southend On Sea
Directors: D. Little (MD)
Immediate Holding Company: PORTA TOOL FIXINGS (BASILDON) LIMITED
Registration no: 01463294 **VAT No.:** Gb 352 0421 02
Date established: 1979 **Turnover:** £500,000 - £1m
No.of Employees: 11 - 20 **Product Groups:** 24, 66

Date of Accounts	Jul 11	Jul 10	Jul 09
Working Capital	390	400	377
Fixed Assets	20	19	15
Current Assets	612	549	563

H Portsmouth & Son
1033-1043 London Road, Leigh On Sea, SS9 3JY
Tel: 01702-478255 **Fax:** 01702-473640
E-mail: print@hportsmouth.plus.com
Website: http://www.affordablecolourprint.co.uk
Directors: A. Portsmouth (Ptnr)
Turnover: £500,000 - £1m **No.of Employees:** 1 - 10 **Product Groups:** 27, 28, 49, 64, 66

Reliable Fire Protection
56 Glendale Gardens, Leigh On Sea, SS9 2AS
Tel: 01702-715226 **Fax:** 01702-475122
E-mail: info@reliablefire.co.uk
Website: http://www.reliablefire.co.uk
Directors: A. Weinling (Sales)
Date established: 1985 **No.of Employees:** 11 - 20 **Product Groups:** 38, 42

S X Environmental Supplies Ltd
Unit 4 Airborne Industrial Estate Arterial Road, Leigh On Sea, SS9 4EX
Tel: 0800-085 1451 **Fax:** 0800-085 1451
E-mail: info@pestcontrolonline.com
Website: http://www.pestcontrolonline.com
Directors: R. Bye (Fin), R. Lund (MD)
Immediate Holding Company: SX ENVIRONMENTAL SUPPLIES LTD
Registration no: 03226765 **Date established:** 1996 **Turnover:** £1m - £2m
No.of Employees: 11 - 20 **Product Groups:** 32, 37, 41, 52

Date of Accounts	Dec 11	Mar 11	Mar 10
Working Capital	632	498	527
Fixed Assets	155	211	94
Current Assets	2m	1m	1m

Safefire Protection Ltd
14 Kendal Way, Leigh On Sea, SS9 5QS
Tel: 01702-522183
E-mail: enquiries@safefireprotection.co.uk
Website: http://www.safefireprotection.co.uk
Directors: S. Lesley (Dir), P. Coltman (Fin)
Immediate Holding Company: Safe Fire Protection Ltd
Registration no: 03677493 **Date established:** 1998
No.of Employees: 1 - 10 **Product Groups:** 38, 42

Date of Accounts	Dec 06	Dec 05
Working Capital	12	12
Fixed Assets	N/A	2
Current Assets	26	33
Current Liabilities	14	21

Sign Factory
1333 London Road, Leigh On Sea, SS9 2AD
Tel: 01702-716161 **Fax:** 01702-716141
E-mail: louise@signfactory.demon.co.uk
Website: http://www.signmakersouthend.co.uk
Directors: L. Willis (Prop)
Turnover: Up to £250,000 **No.of Employees:** 1 - 10 **Product Groups:** 27, 30, 37, 40, 49, 52, 67, 81, 84

Solo Sprayers Ltd
4 Brunel Road, Leigh On Sea, SS9 5JN
Tel: 01702-525740 **Fax:** 01702-522752
E-mail: solo.sprayers@fsbdial.co.uk
Website: http://www.solosprayers.co.uk
Directors: J. Vale (Works), R. Vale (MD)
Immediate Holding Company: SOLO SPRAYERS LIMITED
Registration no: 00474992 **VAT No.:** GB 250 4309 73
Date established: 1949 **Turnover:** £250,000 - £500,000
No.of Employees: 11 - 20 **Product Groups:** 41

Date of Accounts	Mar 06	Mar 05	Mar 02
Working Capital	43	31	36
Fixed Assets	7	8	9
Current Assets	336	312	185

Loughton

Aeon Electronics Protection Systems Ltd
Unit 7 York House Langston Road, Loughton, IG10 3TQ
Tel: 020-8502 4400 **Fax:** 020-8502 3366
E-mail: info@aeonsystems.co.uk
Website: http://www.aeonsystems.co.uk
Directors: T. Wilkinson (Fin)
Immediate Holding Company: AEON ELECTRONIC PROTECTION SYSTEMS LTD
Registration no: 03793381 **Date established:** 1999
No.of Employees: 1 - 10 **Product Groups:** 36, 40, 52

Date of Accounts	Jun 11	Jun 10	Jun 09
Working Capital	652	456	716
Fixed Assets	46	46	69
Current Assets	1m	1m	1m

Aerzen Machines Ltd
Aerzen House Langston Road, Loughton, IG10 3SL
Tel: 020-8502 8100 **Fax:** 020-8502 8109
E-mail: sales@aerzen.co.uk
Website: http://www.aerzen.co.uk
Directors: M. Morey (MD), F. Dickinson (Co Sec)
Ultimate Holding Company: AERZENER MASCHINENFABRIK GMBH (GERMANY)
Immediate Holding Company: AERZEN MACHINES LIMITED
Registration no: 01134139 **VAT No.:** GB 230 6942 75
Date established: 1973 **Turnover:** £5m - £10m **No.of Employees:** 21 - 50
Product Groups: 38, 40

Date of Accounts	Dec 11	Dec 10	Dec 09
Sales Turnover	7m	6m	6m
Pre Tax Profit/Loss	139	303	343
Working Capital	858	917	836
Fixed Assets	2m	2m	2m
Current Assets	3m	3m	2m
Current Liabilities	399	454	363

Antler Office Furniture Ltd
Seedbed Centre Langston Road, Loughton, IG10 3TQ
Tel: 020-8787 7097 **Fax:** 020-8787 7066
E-mail: enquiries@antleroffice.co.uk
Website: http://www.antleroffice.co.uk
Directors: B. Swistak (Jt MD)
Managers: K. Southgate (Sec), T. Webb (Admin Off)
Immediate Holding Company: PROJECT 26 (SITE MANAGEMENT SERVICES) LIMITED
Registration no: 02154237 **Date established:** 2004
Turnover: Up to £250,000 **No.of Employees:** 1 - 10 **Product Groups:** 26, 30, 36, 49, 67, 83

M K Associates
38 Chigwell Lane, Loughton, IG10 3NY
Tel: 020-8508 4001 **Fax:** 01494-775090
E-mail: enquiries@mkcarlton.com
Website: http://www.giffardnewton.com
Bank(s): National Westminster Bank Plc
Directors: B. Virk (MD), S. Virk (MD)
Immediate Holding Company: M K ASSOCIATES LIMITED
Registration no: 02878813 **VAT No.:** GB 342 9340 61
Date established: 1993 **Turnover:** £2m - £5m **No.of Employees:** 11 - 20
Product Groups: 22

Date of Accounts	Mar 11	Mar 10	Mar 09
Sales Turnover	N/A	4m	2m
Pre Tax Profit/Loss	N/A	163	-319
Working Capital	454	30	124
Fixed Assets	2m	2m	2m
Current Assets	2m	1m	1m
Current Liabilities	N/A	721	570

Birthdays Retail Ltd
The Crystal Building Langston Road, Loughton, IG10 3TH
Tel: 020-8502 8293 **Fax:** 0161-763 7354
E-mail: reception@birthdays.co.uk
Website: http://www.birthdays.co.uk
Directors: S. Holsten (MD)
Managers: S. Williamson (Mktg Serv Mgr), J. Wright, J. Sedgwick
Registration no: 06924509 **Date established:** 1988
Turnover: £75m - £125m **No.of Employees:** 21 - 50 **Product Groups:** 27, 49

Date of Accounts	Aug 10
Sales Turnover	61m
Pre Tax Profit/Loss	6m
Working Capital	-4m
Fixed Assets	10m
Current Assets	12m
Current Liabilities	11m

Clinton Cards Head Office
The Crystal Building Langston Road, Loughton, IG10 3TH
Tel: 020-8502 3711 **Fax:** 020-8502 0295
E-mail: enquiries@clintoncards.co.uk
Website: http://www.clintoncards.co.uk
Bank(s): Midland
Directors: P. Salador (Fin)
Managers: K. Woodbridge (Tech Serv Mgr), J. Robinson (Mktg Serv Mgr), K. Ashman (Personnel)
Ultimate Holding Company: CLINTON CARDS PLC
Immediate Holding Company: CLINTON CARDS PLC
Registration no: 00985739 **Date established:** 1970
Turnover: £250m - £500m **No.of Employees:** 1501 & over
Product Groups: 27

Date of Accounts	Jul 11	Aug 08	Aug 09
Sales Turnover	432m	465m	399m
Pre Tax Profit/Loss	-14m	-13m	24m
Working Capital	-32m	-52m	-45m
Fixed Assets	68m	131m	85m
Current Assets	83m	79m	65m
Current Liabilities	29m	33m	27m

Connaught Park Associates
16 York Hill, Loughton, IG10 1RL
Tel: 020-8502 2288
Directors: A. Montalto (Prop)
Immediate Holding Company: D T P ACQUISITIONS LTD
Registration no: 04439217 **Date established:** 2008
No.of Employees: 1 - 10 **Product Groups:** 35

D J Higgins Construction
1 Langston Road, Loughton, IG10 3SD
Tel: 020-8508 5555 **Fax:** 020-8502 2454
E-mail: info@higginsconstruction.co.uk
Website: http://www.higginsconstruction.co.uk
Directors: J. Marcus (Sales), P. Lewellen (Fin)
Managers: C. Chatfield, R. Dunmore
Ultimate Holding Company: HIGGINS GROUP PLC
Immediate Holding Company: HIGGINS HOMES PLC
Registration no: 00843093 **VAT No.:** GB 597 0743 03
Date established: 1965 **Turnover:** £20m - £50m
No.of Employees: 251 - 500 **Product Groups:** 52, 84

Date of Accounts	Jul 11	Jul 10	Jul 09
Sales Turnover	46m	29m	65m
Pre Tax Profit/Loss	1m	-3m	-4m
Working Capital	16m	15m	17m
Fixed Assets	7	8	9
Current Assets	60m	57m	56m
Current Liabilities	3m	691	5m

Gemini Office Solutions Ltd
306 East Wing Sterling House, Langston Road, Loughton, IG10 3TS
Tel: 020-3328 3400 **Fax:** 020-8502 0691
E-mail: info@geminioffice.co.uk
Website: http://www.geminioffice.co.uk
Directors: P. Sicklin (MD)
Registration no: 04565015 **Date established:** 2002
No.of Employees: 1 - 10 **Product Groups:** 44

Date of Accounts	Mar 10	Mar 09	Mar 08
Working Capital	99	134	94
Fixed Assets	12	8	11
Current Assets	509	569	644

Richard Hedin Ltd
Unit D14 Seedbed Centre Langston Road, Loughton, IG10 3TQ
Tel: 020-8787 7046 **Fax:** 020-8532 1171
E-mail: info@hedin.co.uk
Website: http://www.hedin.co.uk
Directors: R. Hedin (MD), T. Hedin (Co Sec)
Immediate Holding Company: RICHARD HEDIN LTD.
Registration no: 01533103 **VAT No.:** GB 626 2889 12
Date established: 1980 **Turnover:** £500,000 - £1m
No.of Employees: 1 - 10 **Product Groups:** 23, 33, 37, 40, 47, 66

Date of Accounts	Mar 11	Mar 10	Mar 09
Working Capital	201	181	219
Fixed Assets	18	23	6
Current Assets	391	346	420

Li-Lo Leisure Products Ltd
Sterling House Langston Road, Loughton, IG10 3TS
Tel: 020-8532 5800 **Fax:** 020-8532 5801
E-mail: liloleisure@btconnect.com
Website: http://www.liloleisure.com
Directors: D. Marren (Sales & Mktg), R. Maskell (Prop), T. Harden (Fin)
Ultimate Holding Company: R. MASKELL LIMITED
Immediate Holding Company: LI-LO LEISURE PRODUCTS LIMITED
Registration no: 01507411 **Date established:** 1980
Turnover: £20m - £50m **No.of Employees:** 21 - 50 **Product Groups:** 30

Date of Accounts	Dec 11	Dec 10	Dec 09
Sales Turnover	20m	25m	27m
Pre Tax Profit/Loss	-1m	531	5
Working Capital	3m	5m	4m
Fixed Assets	2m	2m	2m
Current Assets	11m	13m	13m
Current Liabilities	2m	2m	2m

Linens Direct
Langston Road, Loughton, IG10 3TQ
Tel: 020-8508 0707 **Fax:** 020-8532 1352
E-mail: customerservices@lduk.co.uk
Website: http://www.linensdirect.co.uk
Bank(s): Barclays
Directors: M. Zeff (Dir), S. Kaye (MD)
Managers: J. Carroll
Immediate Holding Company: LINENS DIRECT LIMITED
Registration no: 02717720 **VAT No.:** GB 609 9339 08
Date established: 1992 **Turnover:** £10m - £20m
No.of Employees: 101 - 250 **Product Groups:** 63

Date of Accounts	Jan 11	Jan 10	Jan 09
Sales Turnover	16m	16m	14m
Pre Tax Profit/Loss	160	703	263
Working Capital	716	692	484
Fixed Assets	3m	3m	2m
Current Assets	4m	4m	3m
Current Liabilities	2m	2m	1m

Mapra Technik Co.
Unit D13 The Seedbed Centre, Loughton, IG10 3TQ
Tel: 020-8508 4207 **Fax:** 020-8502 5107
E-mail: info@mapra.co.uk
Website: http://www.mapra.co.uk

Directors: R. Mendoza (Snr Part)
Turnover: £500,000 - £1m **No.of Employees:** 1 - 10 **Product Groups:** 38, 48, 65, 67, 85

Sitelink Communications Ltd

Ground Floor 7 Loughton Business Centre 5 Langston Road, Loughton, IG10 3FL
Tel: 020-8508 6688 **Fax:** 020-8508 0044
E-mail: sales@sitelink.co.uk
Website: http://www.sitelink.co.uk
Managers: I. Ross (Chief Mgr)
Immediate Holding Company: SITELINK COMMUNICATIONS LIMITED
Registration no: 01018478 **Date established:** 1971 **Turnover:** £1m - £2m
No.of Employees: 1 - 10 **Product Groups:** 29, 30, 37, 40, 44, 67, 79

Date of Accounts	Sep 11	Sep 10	Sep 09
Working Capital	641	414	658
Fixed Assets	497	738	1m
Current Assets	1m	1m	1m

Weyers Bros Ltd

Unit 1 Knight House Lenthall Road, Loughton, IG10 3UD
Tel: 020-8508 3886 **Fax:** 020-8508 7122
E-mail: john.weyers@weyersbros.co.uk
Directors: J. Weyers (MD)
Immediate Holding Company: WEYERS BROTHERS LIMITED
Registration no: 03869764 **VAT No.:** GB 744 4634 25
Date established: 1999 **Turnover:** Up to £250,000
No.of Employees: 1 - 10 **Product Groups:** 35

Date of Accounts	Nov 09	Nov 08	Nov 07
Working Capital	45	63	61
Fixed Assets	4	5	7
Current Assets	70	77	67

Maldon

A F Suter Ltd

1 Beckingham Business Park Beckingham Street, Tolleshunt Major, Maldon, CM9 8LZ
Tel: 01621-869600 **Fax:** 08707-773959
E-mail: afsuter@afsuter.com
Website: http://www.afsuter.com
Directors: S. Hall (MD)
Immediate Holding Company: TOLLESHUNT LIMITED
Registration no: 04296187 **VAT No.:** GB 696 5572 74
Date established: 1990 **Turnover:** £1m - £2m **No.of Employees:** 1 - 10
Product Groups: 31, 32, 66

Date of Accounts	Dec 11	Dec 10	Dec 09
Working Capital	-0	-538	-500
Fixed Assets	N/A	500	500
Current Assets	10	105	189
Current Liabilities	N/A	N/A	689

Advanced Infra Red Systems

3 Galliford Road Heybridge, Maldon, CM9 4XD
Tel: 01621-855000 **Fax:** 01621-853847
E-mail: info@h-v2000.co.uk
Website: http://www.ais.uk.com
Bank(s): Barclays, Chelmsford
Directors: T. Birkenshaw (MD)
Registration no: 00942208 **VAT No.:** GB 102 4481 15
Turnover: £500,000 - £1m **No.of Employees:** 21 - 50
Product Groups: 37, 40

Air Domestique Ltd

Unit 4b Benbridge Industrial Estate Holloway Road, Heybridge, Maldon, CM9 4ER
Tel: 01621-852994 **Fax:** 01621-850643
Directors: M. Bush (MD), S. Blyther (Fin)
Immediate Holding Company: AIR DOMESTIQUE LIMITED
Registration no: 01564359 **Date established:** 1981
Turnover: £500,000 - £1m **No.of Employees:** 1 - 10 **Product Groups:** 48

Date of Accounts	Jul 11	Jul 10	Jul 09
Working Capital	345	352	373
Fixed Assets	723	771	826
Current Assets	421	399	431

Anglia Forklifts

High Hall Oxley Hill, Tolleshunt D'Arcy, Maldon, CM9 8ES
Tel: 01621-817901 **Fax:** 01621-817901
Website: http://www.angliaforklifts.co.uk
Directors: S. Robertson (Ptnr)
Registration no: 06396379 **Date established:** 2007
No.of Employees: 1 - 10 **Product Groups:** 35, 39, 45

Anglia Valves LLP

Unit 12g West Station Industrial Estate West Station Yard Spital Road, Maldon, CM9 6TW
Tel: 01621-858861 **Fax:** 01621-855942
Website: http://www.angliavalves.co.uk
Directors: P. Fenner (Snr Part)
Registration no: 01725521 **VAT No.:** GB 396 8324 12
Turnover: Up to £250,000 **No.of Employees:** 1 - 10 **Product Groups:** 38, 66

Date of Accounts	Jul 07	Nov 06	Nov 05
Sales Turnover	155	352	369
Pre Tax Profit/Loss	50	49	47
Working Capital	50	149	124
Fixed Assets	N/A	2	2
Current Assets	113	186	152
Current Liabilities	62	38	29
ROCE% (Return on Capital Employed)	98.4	32.5	37.5
ROT% (Return on Turnover)	31.9	13.9	12.8

Autonnic Research Ltd

Woodrolfe Road Tollesbury, Maldon, CM9 8SE
Tel: 01621-869460 **Fax:** 01621-868815
E-mail: office@autonnic.com
Website: http://www.autonnic.com
Bank(s): HSBC Bank plc
Directors: C. Shelton (MD), R. Ward (Fin)
Immediate Holding Company: AUTONNIC RESEARCH LIMITED
Registration no: 01588602 **VAT No.:** GB 360 3374 72
Date established: 1981 **Turnover:** £250,000 - £500,000
No.of Employees: 11 - 20 **Product Groups:** 38

Date of Accounts	Sep 11	Sep 10	Sep 09
Working Capital	163	108	49
Fixed Assets	42	36	39
Current Assets	230	161	113

Blackman & White Ltd

Unit 8 The Street Industrial Estate Heybridge Street, Heybridge, Maldon, CM9 4XB
Tel: 01621-843404 **Fax:** 01621-842115
E-mail: sales@bwcutters.com
Website: http://www.bwcutters.com
Directors: A. White (MD), E. Ichikawa White (Co Sec)
Managers: T. Lloyd (Sales Prom Mgr)
Ultimate Holding Company: B W CUTTERS LIMITED
Immediate Holding Company: BLACKMAN & WHITE LIMITED
Registration no: 00866933 **VAT No.:** GB 246 1517 72
Date established: 1965 **No.of Employees:** 21 - 50 **Product Groups:** 23, 24, 27, 42, 43, 44, 46

Date of Accounts	Mar 11	Mar 10	Mar 09
Working Capital	617	370	143
Fixed Assets	356	297	332
Current Assets	1m	674	276

Block UK Ltd

Bentalls Shopping Centre Heybridge, Maldon, CM9 4GD
Tel: 01621-850666 **Fax:** 01621-850711
E-mail: info@blockuk.co.uk
Website: http://www.blockuk.co.uk
Managers: B. Liddle (Sales Prom Mgr)
Ultimate Holding Company: BLOCK TRANSFORMATOREN-ELEKTRONIK GMBH & CO(GERMANY)
Immediate Holding Company: BLOCK U.K. LIMITED
Registration no: 03235598 **Date established:** 1996 **Turnover:** £1m - £2m
No.of Employees: 1 - 10 **Product Groups:** 37, 38, 40, 44, 48, 67

Date of Accounts	Dec 11	Dec 10	Dec 09
Sales Turnover	5m	4m	3m
Pre Tax Profit/Loss	78	58	2
Working Capital	400	339	284
Fixed Assets	9	10	13
Current Assets	2m	1m	1m
Current Liabilities	169	135	99

Boddingtons Ltd

Blackwater Trading Estate The Causeway, Maldon, CM9 4GG
Tel: 01621-874200 **Fax:** 01621-874299
E-mail: john@boddingtons-ltd.com
Website: http://www.boddingtons-ltd.com
Bank(s): National Westminster Bank Plc
Directors: S. Revely (Fin), A. Butler (Tech Serv), M. Instone (Pers), S. Fairclough (Dir), J. Warner (Sales), J. Warner (MD), D. Fazel (Fab)
Managers: S. Ewles (Export Sales Mg), M. Instone, R. Jackson (Sales Prom Mgr), J. Rowlandson (Mktg Serv Mgr)
Immediate Holding Company: FIBERWEB GEOSYNTHETICS LIMITED
Registration no: 01589762 **VAT No.:** GB 214 6084 85
Date established: 1981 **Turnover:** £10m - £20m
No.of Employees: 51 - 100 **Product Groups:** 07, 29, 30, 35, 41, 49, 51

Date of Accounts	Jun 10	Jun 09	Jun 08
Sales Turnover	14m	12m	10m
Pre Tax Profit/Loss	817	705	344
Working Capital	508	357	-103
Fixed Assets	3m	3m	3m
Current Assets	5m	3m	3m
Current Liabilities	737	779	1m

Bollfilter UK Ltd

Unit 9 Station Way, Station Road Tolleshunt D'Arcy, Maldon, CM9 8TY
Tel: 01621-862180 **Fax:** 01621-869257
E-mail: sales@bollfilter.co.uk
Website: http://www.bollfilteruk.co.uk
Directors: J. Dow (MD)
Immediate Holding Company: Geedon Ltd
Registration no: 03880763 **Date established:** 1999
No.of Employees: 1 - 10 **Product Groups:** 38, 42

Date of Accounts	Dec 08	Dec 07	Dec 06
Working Capital	31	171	216
Fixed Assets	445	112	76
Current Assets	1209	826	664
Current Liabilities	1178	655	448
Total Share Capital	10	10	10

J R Bourne Powder Coatings Ltd

Beckingham Road Great Totham, Maldon, CM9 8EA
Tel: 01621-892972 **Fax:** 01621-893299
E-mail: sales@jrbourne.com
Website: http://www.jrbourne.co.uk
Directors: S. Bourne (MD)
Immediate Holding Company: J.R. BOURNE ENGINEERING LIMITED
Registration no: 01233817 **VAT No.:** GB 285 3504 49
Date established: 1975 **Turnover:** £500,000 - £1m
No.of Employees: 1 - 10 **Product Groups:** 26, 48

Date of Accounts	Jan 12	Jan 11	Jan 10
Working Capital	52	54	68
Fixed Assets	35	41	22
Current Assets	131	143	148

C M L Microcircuits UK Ltd

Oval Park Hatfield Road, Langford, Maldon, CM9 6WG
Tel: 01621-875500 **Fax:** 01621-875600
E-mail: mgurry@cmlmicro.com
Website: http://www.cmlmicro.com
Bank(s): Barclays, Colchester
Directors: N. Clark (Fin), M. Gurry (MD)
Managers: S. Pearce (Personnel), N. Ball, M. Freeman (Tech Serv Mgr), I. Ladkin (Purch Mgr), M. Lyman (Mktg Serv Mgr)
Ultimate Holding Company: CML MICROSYSTEMS PLC
Immediate Holding Company: CONSUMER MICROCIRCUITS LIMITED
Registration no: 02847062 **VAT No.:** GB 368 6007 36
Date established: 1993 **No.of Employees:** 51 - 100 **Product Groups:** 37

Calido Trading

Unit 4a Market Hill, Maldon, CM9 4PZ
Tel: 01621-842828 **Fax:** 01621-840064
E-mail: enquiries@calido.co.uk
Website: http://www.calido.co.uk
Directors: S. Perry (Co Sec)
Immediate Holding Company: CALIDO TRADING LIMITED
Registration no: 01490635 **VAT No.:** GB 250 1764 84
Date established: 1980 **Turnover:** £250,000 - £500,000
No.of Employees: 1 - 10 **Product Groups:** 33, 38

Date of Accounts	May 11	May 10	May 09
Working Capital	65	77	93
Fixed Assets	9	9	13
Current Assets	111	105	149

Calorex Heat Pumps Ltd

The Causeway Heybridge, Maldon, CM9 4XD
Tel: 01621-856611 **Fax:** 01621-850871
E-mail: sales@calorex.com
Website: http://www.calorex.com
Bank(s): Lloyds Bank plc
Directors: R. Carrington (MD)
Managers: A. Beaumont (Purch Mgr), C. Brown (Mktg Serv Mgr), L. Hawkins (Personnel)
Ultimate Holding Company: CALOREX LIMITED
Immediate Holding Company: CALOREX HEAT PUMPS LIMITED
Registration no: 02937462 **VAT No.:** GB 638 0859 12
Date established: 1994 **Turnover:** £10m - £20m
No.of Employees: 101 - 250 **Product Groups:** 07, 20, 23, 25, 30, 32, 37, 39, 40, 41, 42, 45, 66, 83

Date of Accounts	Mar 11	Mar 10	Mar 09
Sales Turnover	18m	14m	17m
Pre Tax Profit/Loss	1m	1m	2m
Working Capital	3m	4m	4m
Fixed Assets	392	214	293
Current Assets	8m	9m	8m
Current Liabilities	1m	757	760

Desch Plantpak Ltd

Burnham Road Mundon, Maldon, CM9 6NT
Tel: 01621-745500 **Fax:** 01621-745525
E-mail: sales@desch-plantpak.co.uk
Website: http://www.desch-plantpak.co.uk
Bank(s): National Westminster Bank Plc
Directors: A. Clay (Fin)
Managers: J. Gough (Mktg Serv Mgr), P. Steggles (Buyer), D. Branch (Tech Serv Mgr)
Ultimate Holding Company: DSG HOLDING LP (USA)
Immediate Holding Company: DESCH PLANTPAK LIMITED
Registration no: 00794214 **VAT No.:** GB 157 1326 74
Date established: 1964 **Turnover:** £10m - £20m
No.of Employees: 51 - 100 **Product Groups:** 30

Date of Accounts	Dec 11	Dec 10	Dec 09
Sales Turnover	14m	13m	12m
Pre Tax Profit/Loss	-499	-153	-870
Working Capital	6m	5m	4m
Fixed Assets	3m	3m	3m
Current Assets	9m	7m	6m
Current Liabilities	460	578	537

Ernest Doe & Sons Ltd

Ulting, Maldon, CM9 6QH
Tel: 01245-380311 **Fax:** 01245-381194
E-mail: info@ernestdoe.com
Website: http://www.ukgolfbuggies.com
Directors: A. Knight (Fin)
Managers: C. Mobbs (Chief Buyer), T. Thornton (Sales Prom Mgr), P. Scarfe (Sales Prom Mgr), P. Morris (Tech Serv Mgr)
Ultimate Holding Company: ERNEST DOE & SONS,LIMITED
Immediate Holding Company: ERNEST DOE INDUSTRIAL LIMITED
Registration no: 00776585 **Date established:** 1963
Turnover: £75m - £125m **No.of Employees:** 101 - 250
Product Groups: 07

Eltime Ltd

Hall Road Heybridge, Maldon, CM9 4NF
Tel: 01621-859500 **Fax:** 01621-855335
E-mail: sales@eltime.co.uk
Website: http://www.eltime.co.uk
Bank(s): The Royal Bank of Scotland
Directors: D. Hurst (MD), M. Hurst (Fin)
Managers: B. Keyes (Tech Serv Mgr)
Immediate Holding Company: ELTIME LIMITED
Registration no: 01446958 **VAT No.:** GB 341 6057 77
Date established: 1979 **Turnover:** £1m - £2m **No.of Employees:** 11 - 20
Product Groups: 37, 38, 49

Date of Accounts	Nov 11	Nov 10	Nov 09
Working Capital	257	139	281
Fixed Assets	2m	2m	2m
Current Assets	728	693	421

Essex Kilns Ltd

Woodrolfe Road Tollesbury, Maldon, CM9 8SE
Tel: 01621-869342 **Fax:** 01621-868522
E-mail: contact@essexkilns.co.uk
Website: http://www.essexkilns.co.uk
Directors: J. Phillips (MD), J. Phillips (Fin)
Immediate Holding Company: ESSEX KILNS LIMITED
Registration no: 02647872 **VAT No.:** GB 594 6886 66
Date established: 1991 **Turnover:** £500,000 - £1m
No.of Employees: 1 - 10 **Product Groups:** 40, 42, 46, 48

Date of Accounts	May 12	May 11	May 10
Working Capital	31	18	18
Fixed Assets	12	14	16
Current Assets	90	63	72

From Pen To Post

10 Hawthorn Road Tolleshunt Knights, Maldon, CM9 8WB
Tel: 01621-819207
E-mail: enquiries@frompentopost.com
Directors: C. Bunkle (Prop)
No.of Employees: 1 - 10 **Product Groups:** 28, 30, 35, 36

Gibbons Engineering Group Ltd

Woodrolfe Road Tollesbury, Maldon, CM9 8RY
Tel: 01621-868138 **Fax:** 01621-868188
E-mail: sales@gibbonsgroup.co.uk
Website: http://www.gibbonsgroup.co.uk
Directors: B. Horsfall (Dir)
Immediate Holding Company: GIBBONS ENGINEERING GROUP LTD
Registration no: 01361883 **Date established:** 1978 **Turnover:** £1m - £2m
No.of Employees: 11 - 20 **Product Groups:** 35, 37

Date of Accounts	Dec 11	Dec 10	Dec 09
Working Capital	868	789	669
Fixed Assets	542	487	503
Current Assets	1m	1m	951

I C S Triplex
10-14 Hall Road Heybridge, Maldon, CM9 4LA
Tel: 01621-854444 **Fax:** 01621-859221
E-mail: antonyp@icstriplex.com
Website: http://www.icstriplex.com
Bank(s): National Westminster Bank Plc
Directors: M. Snow (Sales), P. Mottershead (Grp Chief Exec), A. Parsell (Fin), C. Wheatley (Ch)
Managers: R. Cockmen (Mktg Serv Mgr), D. Bloomfield (I.T. Exec)
Ultimate Holding Company: FP053879
Immediate Holding Company: ICS TRIPLEX PLC
Registration no: 03249161 **VAT No.:** GB 463 4752 35
Date established: 1996 **Turnover:** £250,000 - £500,000
No.of Employees: 251 - 500 **Product Groups:** 38

Date of Accounts	Sep 08
Pre Tax Profit/Loss	1703
Working Capital	-5389
Fixed Assets	15012
Current Assets	167
Current Liabilities	5556
Total Share Capital	164
ROCE% (Return on Capital Employed)	17.7

J A P Contracts Ltd
The Old Dairy Broad Street Green Road, Great Totham, Maldon, CM9 8NX
Tel: 01621-855177 **Fax:** 01621-855080
E-mail: info@japcontracts.com
Website: http://www.japcontracts.com
Directors: A. Lawson (MD)
Immediate Holding Company: JAP CONTRACTS LIMITED
Registration no: 03060289 **Date established:** 1995 **Turnover:** £2m - £5m
No.of Employees: 1 - 10 **Product Groups:** 40, 41, 66

Date of Accounts	Mar 11
Working Capital	-63
Fixed Assets	392
Current Assets	17

Mantsbrite Ltd
19F Spital Road, Maldon, CM9 6DY
Tel: 01621-853003 **Fax:** 01621-850877
E-mail: sales@mantsbrite.com
Website: http://www.mantsbrite.com
Directors: D. Ash (MD)
Immediate Holding Company: MANTSBRITE LIMITED
Registration no: 00825352 **VAT No.:** 102 4148 25 **Date established:** 1964
No.of Employees: 1 - 10 **Product Groups:** 37, 39, 67, 84

Date of Accounts	Sep 11	Sep 10	Sep 09
Working Capital	246	243	242
Fixed Assets	N/A	N/A	3
Current Assets	349	338	318

Matrix Technology Services Ltd
Shipways North Street, Maldon, CM9 5HQ
Tel: 01621-841000 **Fax:** 01621-843849
E-mail: dave@matrix-ts.com
Website: http://www.matrix-ts.com
Directors: D. Lodge (MD)
Immediate Holding Company: MATRIX TECHNOLOGY SERVICES LIMITED
Registration no: 03309753 **Date established:** 1997
Turnover: £500,000 - £1m **No.of Employees:** 1 - 10 **Product Groups:** 37

Date of Accounts	May 11	May 10	May 09
Working Capital	12	24	16
Fixed Assets	5	5	7
Current Assets	55	82	62

Micom Engineering Ltd
Unit 7 The Street Industrial Estate Heybridge Street, Heybridge, Maldon, CM9 4XB
Tel: 01621-856324 **Fax:** 01621-858778
E-mail: paulatmicom@tiscali.co.uk
Bank(s): Barclays, Maldon
Directors: P. Webber (Fin), A. Webber (Fin)
Immediate Holding Company: MICOM ENGINEERING LIMITED
Registration no: 05308722 **VAT No.:** GB 102 6811 10
Date established: 2004 **Turnover:** £500,000 - £1m
No.of Employees: 11 - 20 **Product Groups:** 48

Date of Accounts	Mar 11	Mar 10	Mar 09
Working Capital	-25	-43	72
Fixed Assets	295	392	432
Current Assets	239	239	253

N B S Cryo Research
Woodrolfe Road Tollesbury, Maldon, CM9 8RY
Tel: 01621-868325 **Fax:** 01621-868729
Website: http://www.nbs.com
Directors: J. Orcutt (Dir)
Managers: K. Read (Mats Contrlr)
Ultimate Holding Company: EPPENDORF AG (GERMANY)
Immediate Holding Company: NEW BRUNSWICK SCIENTIFIC ENGLAND LIMITED
Registration no: 02959499 **Date established:** 1994
Turnover: £10m - £20m **No.of Employees:** 51 - 100 **Product Groups:** 36, 40

Date of Accounts	Dec 10	Dec 09	Dec 08
Sales Turnover	11m	8m	7m
Pre Tax Profit/Loss	3m	2m	2m
Working Capital	5m	4m	5m
Fixed Assets	1m	1m	1m
Current Assets	7m	5m	8m
Current Liabilities	2m	1m	1m

N D C Infra-Red Engineering Ltd
Quayside Industrial Estate, Maldon, CM9 5FA
Tel: 01621-852244 **Fax:** 01621-856180
E-mail: sales@ndcinfrared.co.uk
Website: http://www.ndc.com
Bank(s): National Westminster Bank Plc
Directors: B. Beadle (MD)
Managers: C. Macloughlin (Personnel), A. Brunt (Sales & Mktg Mg), C. Sweeney (Purch Mgr), D. Mitcham
Ultimate Holding Company: SPECTRIS PLC
Immediate Holding Company: NDC INFRARED ENGINEERING LIMITED
Registration no: 00630998 **VAT No.:** GB 102 3957 94
Date established: 1959 **Turnover:** £20m - £50m
No.of Employees: 51 - 100 **Product Groups:** 07, 20, 27, 31, 37, 38, 40, 41, 42, 44, 48, 67, 84, 85, 87

Date of Accounts	Dec 11	Dec 10	Dec 09
Sales Turnover	25m	20m	17m
Pre Tax Profit/Loss	7m	6m	5m
Working Capital	13m	7m	4m
Fixed Assets	289	1m	504
Current Assets	18m	10m	8m
Current Liabilities	2m	1m	3m

Ocean Express Ltd
Station House Station Road, Maldon, CM9 4LQ
Tel: 01621-878800 **Fax:** 01621-878888
E-mail: clive.lewis@vanguardlogistics.co.uk
Website: http://www.oceanexpress.co.uk
Bank(s): Lloyds TSB Bank plc
Directors: M. Gregson (Fin), M. Purcell (Dir), R. Clarke (MD), S. Holloway (Chief Op Offcr), S. Clayton (Dir)
Managers: J. Snowdon (I.T. Exec)
Immediate Holding Company: Oceanexpress Ltd
Registration no: 02193611 **VAT No.:** GB 466 1180 51
Date established: 1988 **Turnover:** £10m - £20m
No.of Employees: 21 - 50 **Product Groups:** 72, 74, 76

Date of Accounts	Dec 09	Dec 08	Dec 07
Sales Turnover	2m	12m	9m
Pre Tax Profit/Loss	29	1m	756
Working Capital	2m	3m	1m
Fixed Assets	285	471	715
Current Assets	3m	6m	4m
Current Liabilities	163	474	805

The P S L Group Ltd
Quayside Indl-Est, Maldon, CM9 5FA
Tel: 01621-854451 **Fax:** 01621-854452
E-mail: jason.mutton@pslgroup.net
Website: http://www.pslgroup.net
Directors: P. Dawson (Comm), J. Mutton (Dir), B. Benton (Fin), J. King (MD)
Managers: J. Mutton (Chief Mgr), C. Davies
Immediate Holding Company: THE PSL GROUP LIMITED
Registration no: 01794983 **Date established:** 1984
Turnover: £10m - £20m **No.of Employees:** 21 - 50 **Product Groups:** 23, 61, 76

Date of Accounts	Mar 11	Mar 10	Mar 09
Sales Turnover	20m	17m	17m
Pre Tax Profit/Loss	687	718	473
Working Capital	928	902	856
Fixed Assets	208	161	151
Current Assets	5m	4m	4m
Current Liabilities	556	475	352

Peter Feller
16 Downs Road, Maldon, CM9 5HG
Tel: 01621-854919
Directors: P. Feller (Prop)
Date established: 1967 **No.of Employees:** 1 - 10 **Product Groups:** 35, 36, 39

T A B Sheet Fabrications Ltd
Unit 3 Galliford Road Industrial Estate Heybridge, Maldon, CM9 4XD
Tel: 01621-858848 **Fax:** 01621-853847
E-mail: info@tabfab.co.uk
Website: http://www.tabfab.co.uk
Bank(s): Barclays, Chelmsford
Directors: T. Birkumshaw (MD), T. Birkumshaw (MD)
Managers: F. Wilson (Sales Admin)
Immediate Holding Company: T.A.B. SHEET FABRICATIONS LIMITED
Registration no: 02562335 **VAT No.:** GB 623 1209 83
Date established: 1990 **Turnover:** £500,000 - £1m
No.of Employees: 21 - 50 **Product Groups:** 30, 35, 36, 40, 45, 48

Date of Accounts	Mar 11	Mar 10	Mar 09
Working Capital	32	28	17
Fixed Assets	24	32	42
Current Assets	138	95	209

Terram Ltd
Blackwater Trading Estate The Causeway, Maldon, CM9 4GG
Tel: 01495-757722 **Fax:** 01495-762383
E-mail: kate.miles@terram.co.uk
Website: http://www.terram.com
Bank(s): Barclays
Directors: S. Sully (Dir), A. Holland (Fin)
Managers: C. Gore (Tech Serv Mgr), C. Roberts (Personnel), M. Lambley (Mktg Serv Mgr), M. Evans (Buyer), P. Langley (Mktg Serv Mgr)
Ultimate Holding Company: FIBERWEB PLC
Immediate Holding Company: TERRAM LIMITED
Registration no: 02254236 **Date established:** 1988
Turnover: £10m - £20m **No.of Employees:** 51 - 100 **Product Groups:** 23, 54

Date of Accounts	Dec 10	Dec 09	Dec 08
Sales Turnover	19m	18m	18m
Pre Tax Profit/Loss	-704	2m	1m
Working Capital	7m	7m	6m
Fixed Assets	886	1m	715
Current Assets	12m	12m	9m
Current Liabilities	853	2m	934

Thalest Ltd
Woodrolfe Road Tollesbury, Maldon, CM9 8SE
Tel: 01621-862583 **Fax:** 01621-862584
E-mail: admin@servowatch.co.uk
Website: http://www.servowatch.com
Directors: S. Smith (Dir)
Immediate Holding Company: THALEST LIMITED
Registration no: 01201246 **Date established:** 1975 **Turnover:** £2m - £5m
No.of Employees: 51 - 100 **Product Groups:** 35, 36, 39

Date of Accounts	May 11	May 10	May 09
Sales Turnover	4m	6m	6m
Pre Tax Profit/Loss	6	116	25
Working Capital	214	235	62
Fixed Assets	1m	1m	1m
Current Assets	2m	3m	3m
Current Liabilities	671	924	1m

Universal Services Sports Equipment Ltd
Beckingham Business Park Beckingham Street, Tolleshunt Major, Maldon, CM9 8LZ
Tel: 01621-868700 **Fax:** 01621-860697
E-mail: info@universalservicesuk.co.uk
Website: http://www.universalservicesuk.co.uk
Bank(s): HSBC
Managers: J. Heard (Sales Admin), J. Royce (Sales & Mktg Mg), J. Royce (Sales & Mktg Mg), M. Turner
Immediate Holding Company: UNIVERSAL SERVICES (SPORTS EQUIPMENT) LIMITED
Registration no: 05381217 **VAT No.:** GB 325 6565 48
Date established: 2005 **Turnover:** £2m - £5m **No.of Employees:** 51 - 100
Product Groups: 26, 49, 52

Vanguard Logistics Ltd
Station House, Maldon, CM9 4LQ
Tel: 01621-879200 **Fax:** 01708-555577
E-mail: ian.gill@vanguardlogistics.co.uk
Website: http://www.vls-global.com
Bank(s): Lloyds TSB Bank plc
Directors: I. Gill (MD), D. Hillman (Co Sec)
Managers: J. Hardy, N. Fost (Fin Mgr), P. Hutchinson (Tech Serv Mgr)
Ultimate Holding Company: O T S LOGISTICS GROUP LIMITED (CAYMAN ISLANDS)
Immediate Holding Company: VANGUARD LOGISTICS SERVICES LIMITED
Registration no: 03601330 **VAT No.:** GB 720 2340 90
Date established: 1998 **Turnover:** £20m - £50m
No.of Employees: 51 - 100 **Product Groups:** 72, 76

Date of Accounts	Dec 11	Dec 10	Dec 09
Sales Turnover	32m	25m	23m
Pre Tax Profit/Loss	289	492	679
Working Capital	122	-106	-467
Fixed Assets	515	560	560
Current Assets	5m	4m	4m
Current Liabilities	610	708	683

Wilks Rubber Plastics MFGS Co. Ltd
Woodrolfe Road Tollesbury, Maldon, CM9 8RY
Tel: 01621-869609 **Fax:** 01621-868863
E-mail: sales@wilks.co.uk
Website: http://www.wilks.co.uk
Directors: C. Berry (MD), S. Berry (MD)
Ultimate Holding Company: GIBBONS ENGINEERING GROUP LTD
Immediate Holding Company: WILKS (RUBBER PLASTICS) MFGS. CO. LIMITED
Registration no: 01215369 **VAT No.:** GB 103 8925 76
Date established: 1975 **Turnover:** £1m - £2m **No.of Employees:** 21 - 50
Product Groups: 29

Date of Accounts	Sep 11	Sep 10	Sep 09
Working Capital	322	294	227
Fixed Assets	217	230	240
Current Assets	589	642	560

Manningtree

Anglian Timber Ltd
The Sawmill Colchester Road, Wix, Manningtree, CO11 2RS
Tel: 01255-870881 **Fax:** 01255-870480
E-mail: sales@angliantimber.co.uk
Website: http://www.angliantimber.co.uk
Directors: Y. Jewell (Fin), R. Fennell (Dir)
Managers: P. Ling (Personnel)
Ultimate Holding Company: CASTLEWOOD HOLDINGS LIMITED
Immediate Holding Company: ANGLIAN TIMBER LIMITED
Registration no: 02229092 **Date established:** 1988 **Turnover:** £5m - £10m
No.of Employees: 21 - 50 **Product Groups:** 25, 35, 66

Date of Accounts	Feb 12	Feb 11	Feb 10
Sales Turnover	7m	6m	5m
Pre Tax Profit/Loss	220	212	21
Working Capital	1m	873	731
Fixed Assets	469	405	381
Current Assets	2m	2m	1m
Current Liabilities	139	104	58

E D M E Ltd
Edme House High Street, Mistley, Manningtree, CO11 1HG
Tel: 01206-393725 **Fax:** 01206-395471
E-mail: info@edme.com
Website: http://www.edme.com
Bank(s): Barclays, Norwich, Norfolk
Directors: A. Clark (Fin), J. Smith (Sales)
Managers: L. Smith (Mgr), C. Townes, I. Molfuld (Tech Serv Mgr)
Ultimate Holding Company: RAGLETH LIMITED
Immediate Holding Company: EDME LIMITED
Registration no: 00167031 **Date established:** 2020
Turnover: £10m - £20m **No.of Employees:** 51 - 100 **Product Groups:** 02, 07, 20, 61, 62

Date of Accounts	Dec 09	Dec 08
Working Capital	328	328
Fixed Assets	1	1
Current Assets	328	328

Manningtree Horsebox Hire & Horse Transport Ltd
63 Tile Barn Lane Lawford, Manningtree, CO11 2LT
Tel: 01206-230966 **Fax:** 01206-230966
E-mail: johndbooty28@hotmail.com
Website: http://www.essexequineselfdrive.co.uk
Directors: J. Booty (MD)
No.of Employees: 1 - 10 **Product Groups:** 25, 39, 41, 49, 72

Pultrex Ltd
18-20 Riverside Avenue West Lawford, Manningtree, CO11 1UN
Tel: 01206-395559 **Fax:** 01206-576554
E-mail: sales@pultrex.com
Website: http://www.pultrex.com
Bank(s): Barclays
Managers: K. Cannings (Sales Prom Mgr)
Ultimate Holding Company: DOUGLAS CURTIS MACHINE TOOLS (COLCHESTER) LIMITED
Immediate Holding Company: PULTREX LIMITED
Registration no: 04694438 **VAT No.:** GB 282 8070 49
Date established: 2003 **Turnover:** £1m - £2m **No.of Employees:** 21 - 50
Product Groups: 42

Date of Accounts	Jul 11	Jul 10	Jul 09
Working Capital	56	184	-46
Fixed Assets	263	215	227
Current Assets	1m	886	1m

S J H Row & Son Ltd
Unit 6 Riverside Avenue West Lawford, Manningtree, CO11 1UN
Tel: 01206-396688 **Fax:** 01206-393392
E-mail: peter@sjh-row.co.uk
Website: http://www.sjh-row.co.uk

Directors: P. Wakeling (MD)
Registration no: 00258190 **VAT No.:** GB 102 3513 33
Date established: 1880 **Turnover:** £1m - £2m **No.of Employees:** 1 - 10
Product Groups: 41, 67

Date of Accounts	Sep 08	Sep 07	Sep 06
Working Capital	66	111	48
Fixed Assets	38	55	60
Current Assets	248	210	167
Current Liabilities	182	99	119
Total Share Capital	121	121	15

Scanlift Ltd
Causeway End Industrial Estate Station Road, Lawford, Manningtree, CO11 2LH
Tel: 01206-396111 **Fax:** 01206-395870
E-mail: sales@scanlift.co.uk
Website: http://www.scanlift.co.uk
Directors: A. Harris (MD)
Immediate Holding Company: Badger Converters Ltd
Registration no: 02585509 **VAT No.:** GB 594 5436 05
No.of Employees: 1 - 10 **Product Groups:** 84

Sta Lok Terminals Ltd
The Forge The Heath, Mistley, Manningtree, CO11 2QH
Tel: 01206-391509 **Fax:** 01206-395286
E-mail: donna@stalok.com
Website: http://www.stalok.com
Bank(s): Lloyds TSB Bank plc
Directors: D. Ierston (Sales), D. Barfield (Dir)
Ultimate Holding Company: BARFIELD ENGINEERING COMPANY LIMITED
Immediate Holding Company: STA-LOK TERMINALS LIMITED
Registration no: 01751573 **VAT No.:** GB 390 5703 48
Date established: 1983 **Turnover:** £2m - £5m **No.of Employees:** 21 - 50
Product Groups: 23, 26, 33, 34, 35, 36, 37, 39, 41, 46, 48, 51, 66

Date of Accounts	Sep 11	Sep 10	Sep 09
Working Capital	897	880	865
Fixed Assets	306	393	342
Current Assets	1m	1m	1m

Ongar

Evolution Panels & Doors
1 High Laver Hall Cottages High Laver, Ongar, CM5 0DU
Tel: 01277-890616 **Fax:** 01277-890617
E-mail: sales@evolution-pd.com
Website: http://www.evolution-pd.com
Managers: S. Shadbolt (Mgr)
Registration no: 06275978 **Date established:** 2007 **Turnover:** £1m - £2m
No.of Employees: 1 - 10 **Product Groups:** 25

Gosport Engineering Company Ltd
Unit 3 Hallsford Bridge Industrial Estate Stondon Road, Ongar, CM5 9RB
Tel: 020-3179 1500 **Fax:** 020-3179 1501
E-mail: info@gosportengineering.co.uk
Website: http://www.gosportengineering.co.uk
Directors: R. Souster (MD)
Immediate Holding Company: GOSPORT ENGINEERING COMPANY LIMITED
Registration no: 00994246 **VAT No.:** GB 248 4876 17
Date established: 1970 **Turnover:** £1m - £2m **No.of Employees:** 21 - 50
Product Groups: 33, 35

Date of Accounts	Apr 12	Apr 11	Apr 10
Working Capital	264	352	280
Fixed Assets	961	1m	1m
Current Assets	410	573	615

Gustav Kaser Training International Ltd (Head Office)
Essex House 118 High Street, Ongar, CM5 9EB
Tel: 01277-365335 **Fax:** 01277-365277
E-mail: info@gustavkaeser.com
Website: http://www.gustavkaeser.com
Directors: T. Glover (MD)
Immediate Holding Company: K TRAINING KASER INTERNATIONAL LIMITED
Registration no: 01156474 **VAT No.:** GB 191 7175 47
Date established: 1974 **Turnover:** Up to £250,000
No.of Employees: 1 - 10 **Product Groups:** 80, 81, 86

Date of Accounts	Dec 10	Dec 09	Dec 08
Sales Turnover	N/A	172	151
Pre Tax Profit/Loss	N/A	-20	-26
Working Capital	-142	-118	-103
Fixed Assets	21	21	22
Current Assets	56	59	67
Current Liabilities	N/A	64	60

J H May Ltd
Hallsford Bridge Industrial Estate Stondon Road, Ongar, CM5 9RB
Tel: 01277-365500 **Fax:** 020-7739 8764
E-mail: tonym@jhmay.co.uk
Website: http://www.jhmay.com
Directors: A. May (MD)
Ultimate Holding Company: CROWNFIELD HOLDINGS LIMITED
Immediate Holding Company: J.H.MAY LIMITED
Registration no: 00577266 **VAT No.:** GB 233 4077 84
Date established: 1957 **Turnover:** Up to £250,000
No.of Employees: 1 - 10 **Product Groups:** 46, 49

Date of Accounts	Mar 11	Mar 10	Mar 09
Working Capital	-48	-48	-48
Fixed Assets	6	7	8
Current Assets	4	4	4

Thurston Engineering Ltd
Unit 4 Hallsford Industrial Estate, Ongar, CM5 9RB
Tel: 01277-362135 **Fax:** 01277-365076
E-mail: sales@thurstonengineering.co.uk
Website: http://www.thurstonengineering.co.uk
Directors: I. Terry (Dir), J. Terry (Co Sec)
Ultimate Holding Company: CROWNFIELD HOLDINGS LIMITED
Immediate Holding Company: THURSTON ENGINEERING LIMITED
Registration no: 03676570 **VAT No.:** GB 732 2761 47
Date established: 1998 **Turnover:** £500,000 - £1m
No.of Employees: 1 - 10 **Product Groups:** 48

Date of Accounts	Dec 11	Dec 10	Dec 09
Working Capital	-0	-16	-36
Fixed Assets	142	142	151
Current Assets	227	284	229

Purfleet

Barloworld Handling Ltd
Barlow House 2 Dolphin Way, Purfleet, RM19 1NZ
Tel: 01708-257300 **Fax:** 01727-869965
E-mail: info@handling.barloworld.co.uk
Website: http://www.barloworld.co.uk
Managers: T. Stroud (District Mgr)
Ultimate Holding Company: BARLOWORLD LIMITED (SOUTH AFRICA)
Immediate Holding Company: BARLOWORLD HANDLING LIMITED
Registration no: 00564646 **Date established:** 1956
Turnover: £75m - £125m **No.of Employees:** 21 - 50 **Product Groups:** 83

Date of Accounts	Sep 11	Sep 10	Sep 09
Sales Turnover	106m	96m	96m
Pre Tax Profit/Loss	-3m	-2m	-5m
Working Capital	-20m	10m	-18m
Fixed Assets	37m	55m	46m
Current Assets	33m	55m	23m
Current Liabilities	6m	6m	18m

Carpetright plc
Purfleet By Pass, Purfleet, RM19 1TT
Tel: 01708-802015 **Fax:** 01708-559361
E-mail: enquiries@carpetright.co.uk
Website: http://www.briggs.uk.com
Directors: S. Metcalf (Fin), P. Dregent (Co Sec), J. Kitching (MD), G. Weston (Dir), C. Sollesse (MD)
Immediate Holding Company: CARPETRIGHT PLC
Registration no: 02294875 **VAT No.:** GB 505 3507 75
Date established: 1988 **Turnover:** £500m - £1,000m
No.of Employees: 1 - 10 **Product Groups:** 63

Date of Accounts	Apr 11	Apr 12	May 09
Sales Turnover	487m	472m	483m
Pre Tax Profit/Loss	7m	14m	17m
Working Capital	209m	-48m	-40m
Fixed Assets	243m	205m	266m
Current Assets	80m	72m	95m
Current Liabilities	52m	52m	56m

Facelift Access Hire
Ensign Estate Botany Way, Purfleet, RM19 1TB
Tel: 01708-860830 **Fax:** 01753-650294
E-mail: jevers@facelift.co.uk
Website: http://www.facelift.co.uk
Managers: J. Evers (Depot Mgr)
Immediate Holding Company: HAULSAFE LIMITED
Registration no: OC338779 **Date established:** 2010
No.of Employees: 11 - 20 **Product Groups:** 45, 67, 83

French Connection Ltd
Unit B Dolphin Way, Purfleet, RM19 1NZ
Tel: 020-7036 7000
Website: http://www.frenchconnection.com
Directors: R. Grainger (Purch), R. Naysmith (Fin)
Managers: K. Felley (Sales Admin)
Ultimate Holding Company: FRENCH CONNECTION GROUP PLC
Immediate Holding Company: FRENCH CONNECTION LIMITED
Registration no: 01069342 **Date established:** 1972
No.of Employees: 101 - 250 **Product Groups:** 63

Date of Accounts	Jan 12	Jan 11	Jan 10
Sales Turnover	10m	10m	37m
Pre Tax Profit/Loss	-1m	23	-4m
Working Capital	42m	44m	41m
Fixed Assets	9	9	3m
Current Assets	44m	50m	93m
Current Liabilities	528	N/A	5m

Harveys Furnishing Ltd
Amberley House Dolphin Park, Dolphin Way, Purfleet, RM19 1NZ
Tel: 0844-8472626 **Fax:** 01708-521514
Website: http://www.harveysfurniture.co.uk
Bank(s): National Westminster Bank Plc
Directors: B. Hawkins (Dir), I. Topping (MD), M. Spicer (I.T. Dir), P. Burke (Sales), S. Tutt (Fin)
Managers: A. Hickford (Buyer), D. Hollis (Personnel), H. Vinken (Mktg Serv Mgr)
Ultimate Holding Company: Steinhoff UK Holdings Ltd
Immediate Holding Company: Steinhoff UK Retail Ltd
Registration no: 00281055 **VAT No.:** GB 506 3312 84
Turnover: £1m - £2m **No.of Employees:** 51 - 100 **Product Groups:** 61

Kerneos Ltd
Dolphin Way, Purfleet, RM19 1NZ
Tel: 01708-863333 **Fax:** 01708-861033
E-mail: a.beardmore@kerneos.com
Website: http://www.kerneosinc.com
Bank(s): Lloyds TSB Bank plc
Directors: P. Bottomley (Comm), P. Odendaal (Works), T. Newton (Mkt Research)
Managers: I. Adamson (Fin Mgr), S. Agassiz (Personnel)
Ultimate Holding Company: WENDEL INVESTISSEMENT SA (FRANCE)
Immediate Holding Company: KERNEOS LIMITED
Registration no: 01974484 **Date established:** 1985
Turnover: £20m - £50m **No.of Employees:** 51 - 100 **Product Groups:** 14, 33

Date of Accounts	Dec 11	Dec 10	Dec 09
Sales Turnover	43m	38m	32m
Pre Tax Profit/Loss	10m	7m	5m
Working Capital	2m	3m	4m
Fixed Assets	14m	14m	13m
Current Assets	15m	13m	15m
Current Liabilities	4m	2m	1m

Lakeside Karting
A1306 Arterial Road, Purfleet, RM19 1AE
Tel: 01708-863070 **Fax:** 01708-869450
E-mail: info@lakeside-karting.com
Website: http://www.go-karting.info
Directors: G. Murray (Co Sec), S. Wagstaff (Dir)
Ultimate Holding Company: LETSGOACTIVE LIMITED
Immediate Holding Company: LAKESIDE KARTING LIMITED
Registration no: 03584761 **Date established:** 1998 **Turnover:** £1m - £2m
No.of Employees: 1 - 10 **Product Groups:** 39

Date of Accounts	Jan 12	Jan 11	Jan 10
Working Capital	-151	-186	-155
Fixed Assets	371	399	437
Current Assets	87	58	74

Pruce Newman Pipework
London Road, Purfleet, RM19 1SD
Tel: 01708-891146
Website: http://www.prucenewman.co.uk
No.of Employees: 11 - 20 **Product Groups:** 35, 45

Tennants Distribution Ltd
Beacon Hill Industrial Estate Botany Way, Purfleet, RM19 1SR
Tel: 01708-860075 **Fax:** 01708-860074
E-mail: sales@tennantsdistribution.com
Website: http://www.tennantsdistribution.com
Bank(s): National Westminster Bank Plc
Managers: J. Swift (Chief Mgr)
Ultimate Holding Company: TENNANTS CONSOLIDATED LIMITED
Immediate Holding Company: TENNANTS DISTRIBUTION LIMITED
Registration no: 03133273 **Date established:** 1995
Turnover: £10m - £20m **No.of Employees:** 11 - 20 **Product Groups:** 31, 32, 38, 61

Date of Accounts	Dec 11	Dec 10	Dec 09
Sales Turnover	80m	69m	61m
Pre Tax Profit/Loss	2m	1m	1m
Working Capital	12m	11m	11m
Fixed Assets	7m	7m	6m
Current Assets	24m	24m	21m
Current Liabilities	2m	2m	1m

The Thurrock Hotel
Ship Lane, Purfleet, RM19 1YN
Tel: 01708-860222 **Fax:** 01708-866703
E-mail: reservations@thurrockhotel.co.uk
Website: http://www.thurrockhotel.co.uk
Directors: G. Hirani (Dir)
Registration no: 01857156 **VAT No.:** GB 731 3249 58
Turnover: £250,000 - £500,000 **No.of Employees:** 21 - 50
Product Groups: 69

Date of Accounts	Mar 08	Apr 07
Working Capital	246	381
Fixed Assets	1158	1082
Current Assets	502	691
Current Liabilities	256	310
Total Share Capital	1	1

Rainham

A C Structures
Unit 5a Albright Industrial Estate Ferry Lane, Rainham, RM13 9BU
Tel: 01708-521249 **Fax:** 01708-522388
E-mail: at@acstructures.com
Website: http://www.acstructures.com
Directors: A. Neale (Ptnr)
Date established: 1992 **No.of Employees:** 11 - 20 **Product Groups:** 35

Avilion
Unit 1 Gateway Xiii Industrial Estate Ferry Lane, Rainham, RM13 9JY
Tel: 01708-526361 **Fax:** 01708-550220
E-mail: steve.cole@avilion.co.uk
Website: http://www.perrinandrowe.com
Directors: S. Cole (Dir)
Managers: I. Walker (Fin Mgr), R. Eldridge (Tech Serv Mgr), D. Blayney (Personnel)
Ultimate Holding Company: TCL MANUFACTURING LIMITED
Immediate Holding Company: TCL MANUFACTURING LIMITED
Registration no: 02463775 **VAT No.:** 342 2790 65 **Date established:** 1990
Turnover: £10m - £20m **No.of Employees:** 101 - 250 **Product Groups:** 36

Date of Accounts	Dec 11	Dec 10	Dec 09
Sales Turnover	11m	15m	11m
Pre Tax Profit/Loss	-888	7m	-4m
Working Capital	611	1m	180
Fixed Assets	2m	2m	2m
Current Assets	4m	5m	4m
Current Liabilities	525	924	753

Bess Island Diesels
Albright Industrial Estate Ferry Lane, Rainham, RM13 9BU
Tel: 01708-550202
Directors: J. Foulger (Prop)
Date established: 1997 **No.of Employees:** 1 - 10 **Product Groups:** 40

F J Church Holdings Ltd
Centenary Works Manor Way, Rainham, RM13 8RH
Tel: 01708-522651 **Fax:** 01708-522786
E-mail: traders@fjchurch.co.uk
Website: http://www.fjchurch.co.uk
Bank(s): Barclays
Directors: P. Church (MD)
Managers: T. Guest (Sales Admin), S. Vivicanda (Chief Acct), A. Moran (Sales Prom Mgr)
Ultimate Holding Company: FJC HOLDINGS LIMITED
Immediate Holding Company: F.J. CHURCH & SONS LIMITED
Registration no: 00322723 **VAT No.:** GB 629 6020 42
Date established: 1937 **Turnover:** £125m - £250m
No.of Employees: 21 - 50 **Product Groups:** 34, 66

Date of Accounts	Mar 12	Mar 11	Mar 10
Sales Turnover	136m	150m	91m
Pre Tax Profit/Loss	5m	7m	198
Working Capital	15m	11m	7m
Fixed Assets	2m	2m	2m
Current Assets	22m	18m	14m
Current Liabilities	2m	2m	666

E-Freight Ltd
Freightmaster Estate Ferry Lane, Rainham, RM13 9BJ
Tel: 01708-555422
E-mail: annie@e-freight.net
Website: http://www.e-freight.net

see next page

E-Freight Ltd - Cont'd
Directors: A. Templeton (MD)
Immediate Holding Company: E-FREIGHT LIMITED
Registration no: 03933757 **Date established:** 2000 **Turnover:** £2m - £5m
No.of Employees: 11 - 20 **Product Groups:** 77

Date of Accounts	Apr 08	Apr 07	Apr 06
Working Capital	-92	-43	-10
Fixed Assets	483	327	299
Current Assets	682	702	672
Current Liabilities	774	745	682

F H Brundle
24-32 Ferry Lane Industrial Estate Lamson Road, Rainham, RM13 9YY
Tel: 01708-253545 **Fax:** 01708-253550
E-mail: sales@brundle.com
Website: http://www.fhbrundle.co.uk
Bank(s): National Westminster Bank Plc
Directors: M. Brundle (MD)
Immediate Holding Company: F H BRUNDLE
Registration no: 07168270 **Date established:** 2010
Turnover: £10m - £20m **No.of Employees:** 51 - 100 **Product Groups:** 30, 32, 34, 35, 36, 39, 46, 49, 66, 67

Fletcher Pallets Ltd
Freightmaster Estate Ferry Lane, Rainham, RM13 9BJ
Tel: 01708-553159 **Fax:** 01708-521796
E-mail: mail@fletcherpallets.com
Website: http://www.fletcherpallets.com
Directors: P. Fletcher (Fin)
Immediate Holding Company: FLETCHERS PALLETS LIMITED
Registration no: 03398519 **Date established:** 1997
No.of Employees: 11 - 20 **Product Groups:** 45, 48, 76

Date of Accounts	Aug 11	Aug 10	Aug 09
Working Capital	-13	-16	-12
Fixed Assets	64	36	32
Current Assets	116	89	103

Foreman Electrical Services
B6 Dovers Corner Industrial Estate New Road, Rainham, RM13 8QT
Tel: 01708-555381 **Fax:** 01708-525897
E-mail: foreman.electric@btconnect.com
Directors: R. Ship (Ptnr)
Registration no: 04739522 **No.of Employees:** 1 - 10 **Product Groups:** 37, 67

Griffiths Fabrications
Unit A10 Dovers Corner Industrial Estate New Road, Rainham, RM13 8QT
Tel: 01708-523797 **Fax:** 01708-522698
Directors: T. Griffiths (Prop)
No.of Employees: 1 - 10 **Product Groups:** 34, 35, 48

Homeserve Emergency Services
Unit 7a Orwell Close Fairview Industrial Estate, Marsh Way, Rainham, RM13 8UB
Tel: 01708-555088 **Fax:** 01708-554236
E-mail: phillip.bremner@evander.com
Website: http://www.homeserve.com
Bank(s): Lloyds TSB Bank plc
Directors: P. Milburn (MD)
Registration no: 01484358 **VAT No.:** GB 250 1814 95
No.of Employees: 11 - 20 **Product Groups:** 52

Hornett Bros & Co. Ltd
Ferry Lane, Rainham, RM13 9YH
Tel: 01708-556041 **Fax:** 01708-557546
E-mail: john@hornett-bros.co.uk
Website: http://www.hornett.net
Bank(s): HSBC Bank plc
Directors: D. Wellum (Tech Serv), J. Hornett (MD)
Immediate Holding Company: HORNETT BROS & CO,LIMITED
Registration no: 00520212 **VAT No.:** GB 311 7068 88
Date established: 1953 **Turnover:** £2m - £5m **No.of Employees:** 11 - 20
Product Groups: 31, 32

Date of Accounts	May 11	May 10	May 09
Working Capital	958	896	816
Fixed Assets	21	11	13
Current Assets	2m	2m	1m

Inmet Aluminium & Stainless Ltd
Unit D Boomes Industrial Estate New Road, Rainham, RM13 8BS
Tel: 01708-522673 **Fax:** 01708-555743
E-mail: inmet@netcomuk.co.uk
Website: http://www.inmet.co.uk
Directors: R. Greygoose (Sales)
Immediate Holding Company: INMET (ALUMINIUM & STAINLESS) LIMITED
Registration no: 01623788 **Date established:** 1982 **Turnover:** £1m - £2m
No.of Employees: 1 - 10 **Product Groups:** 34, 66

Date of Accounts	Jun 11	Jun 10	Jun 09
Working Capital	289	321	318
Fixed Assets	4	5	1
Current Assets	619	634	599

Keeble Recycling Ltd
Paper Recycling Centre Ferry Lane, Rainham, RM13 9DB
Tel: 01708-528000 **Fax:** 01708-521991
E-mail: recycle@kpr.co.uk
Website: http://www.keeblegroup.co.uk
Bank(s): HSBC Bank plc
Directors: D. Keeble (MD)
Immediate Holding Company: KEEBLE RECYCLING LTD.
Registration no: 00493526 **VAT No.:** GB 246 3909 45
Date established: 1951 **Turnover:** £2m - £5m **No.of Employees:** 11 - 20
Product Groups: 27, 80

Date of Accounts	Apr 11	Apr 10	Apr 09
Working Capital	605	445	260
Fixed Assets	2m	2m	2m
Current Assets	2m	1m	838

Metfab Steel Fabricators
8 Salamons Way, Rainham, RM13 9UL
Tel: 01708-526726 **Fax:** 01708-526667
E-mail: info@metfab.co.uk
Website: http://www.metfab.co.uk
Directors: P. Jarrett (Ptnr)
No.of Employees: 11 - 20 **Product Groups:** 35

Nestle Waters Powwow
21 Barlow Way, Rainham, RM13 8BT
Tel: 01708-526100 **Fax:** 01708-554655
Managers: P. Toomey (Mgr)
No.of Employees: 21 - 50 **Product Groups:** 40, 66

Penatube Ltd
Dovers Corner Industrial Estate New Road, Rainham, RM13 8QT
Tel: 01708-555595 **Fax:** 01708-526276
E-mail: sales@penatube.co.uk
Website: http://www.penatube.co.uk
Managers: G. Pearse (Prod Mgr)
Immediate Holding Company: PENATUBE LIMITED
Registration no: 00842233 **VAT No.:** GB 246 4201 84
Date established: 1965 **Turnover:** Up to £250,000
No.of Employees: 1 - 10 **Product Groups:** 30, 48, 66

Date of Accounts	Apr 12	Apr 11	Apr 10
Working Capital	35	28	26
Fixed Assets	69	78	76
Current Assets	105	97	90
Current Liabilities	53	51	N/A

Rainham Ductworks Ltd
Unit B10 Suttons Business Park New Road, Rainham, RM13 8DE
Tel: 01708-630222 **Fax:** 01708-630273
E-mail: stephen@rainhamductwork.co.uk
Directors: S. Smith (MD)
No.of Employees: 1 - 10 **Product Groups:** 37, 40, 48

Rainham Steel Company Ltd
Kathryn House Manor Way, Rainham, RM13 8RE
Tel: 01708-522311 **Fax:** 01708-559024
E-mail: kevin@rainham-steel.co.uk
Website: http://www.rainhamsteel.co.uk
Directors: W. Ives (MD)
Ultimate Holding Company: RAINHAM STEEL HOLDINGS LIMITED
Immediate Holding Company: RAINHAM STEEL COMPANY LIMITED
Registration no: 01093531 **VAT No.:** GB 247 2096 59
Date established: 1973 **Turnover:** £75m - £125m
No.of Employees: 101 - 250 **Product Groups:** 66

Date of Accounts	Mar 12	Mar 11	Mar 10
Sales Turnover	91m	86m	64m
Pre Tax Profit/Loss	3m	4m	-4m
Working Capital	21m	19m	20m
Fixed Assets	9m	9m	10m
Current Assets	50m	55m	38m
Current Liabilities	8m	19m	737

S G Magnets Ltd
85 Ferry Lane, Rainham, RM13 9YH
Tel: 01708-558411 **Fax:** 01708-554021
E-mail: sales@sgmagnets.com
Website: http://www.sgmagnets.com
Bank(s): H S B C, Poultry and Princes Street
Directors: J. Taylor (Tech Serv), J. Laing (Dir)
Managers: W. Harris (Purch Mgr), D. Lambert (Personnel), S. Hutcheon (Sales Prom Mgr), B. Mabbott (Comptroller)
Ultimate Holding Company: SG TECHNOLOGIES LIMITED
Immediate Holding Company: S.G. MAGNETS LIMITED
Registration no: 02163295 **VAT No.:** GB 475 2240 53
Date established: 1987 **Turnover:** £10m - £20m
No.of Employees: 101 - 250 **Product Groups:** 29, 34, 36, 37, 49

Date of Accounts	Mar 11	Mar 10	Mar 09
Sales Turnover	11m	9m	9m
Pre Tax Profit/Loss	2m	40	-1m
Working Capital	4m	3m	2m
Fixed Assets	4m	4m	4m
Current Assets	5m	4m	3m
Current Liabilities	489	354	210

Stellafoam Ltd
Blackwater Close, Rainham, RM13 8UA
Tel: 01708-522551 **Fax:** 01708-522162
E-mail: sales@stellafoam.co.uk
Website: http://www.stellafoam.co.uk
Bank(s): Barclays
Directors: D. Reed (MD)
Ultimate Holding Company: KATELLA PROPERTIES COMPANY LIMITED
Immediate Holding Company: STELLAFOAM LIMITED
Registration no: 00676869 **VAT No.:** GB 246 2455 63
Date established: 1960 **Turnover:** £2m - £5m **No.of Employees:** 11 - 20
Product Groups: 31

Date of Accounts	Dec 11	Dec 10	Dec 09
Sales Turnover	4m	4m	4m
Pre Tax Profit/Loss	43	-19	138
Working Capital	742	682	662
Fixed Assets	59	87	119
Current Assets	2m	2m	2m
Current Liabilities	148	558	372

Stewart Harvey & Woodbridge Ltd
22 Easter Industrial Park Ferry Lane, Rainham, RM13 9BP
Tel: 01708-253800 **Fax:** 020-8592 0827
E-mail: shw@shwlondon.co.uk
Website: http://www.shwlondon.co.uk
Bank(s): Barclays
Managers: P. West (Chief Mgr)
Ultimate Holding Company: DUNBAR WHARF HOLDINGS LIMITED
Immediate Holding Company: STEWART, HARVEY & WOODBRIDGE LIMITED
Registration no: 01004272 **VAT No.:** GB 246 2071 81
Date established: 1971 **Turnover:** £2m - £5m **No.of Employees:** 11 - 20
Product Groups: 72, 76

Date of Accounts	Dec 11	Dec 10	Dec 09
Sales Turnover	2m	3m	4m
Pre Tax Profit/Loss	80	-149	-276
Working Capital	807	721	806
Fixed Assets	46	80	149
Current Assets	1m	1m	1m
Current Liabilities	100	90	61

T P H Machine Tools Ltd
Unit 4 Blackwater Close Fairview Industrial Park, Rainham, RM13 8UA
Tel: 01708-523916 **Fax:** 01708-550042
E-mail: machines@tphmachinetools.co.uk
Website: http://www.tphmachinetools.co.uk
Directors: M. Thompson (Dir)
Ultimate Holding Company: HEADLAND HOLDINGS LIMITED
Immediate Holding Company: TPH MACHINE TOOLS LIMITED
Registration no: 06041293 **Date established:** 2007 **Turnover:** £5m - £10m
No.of Employees: 1 - 10 **Product Groups:** 46, 67

Date of Accounts	Jun 11	Jun 10	Jun 09
Working Capital	-2	109	96
Fixed Assets	14	15	19
Current Assets	591	746	683

Thermit Welding GB Ltd
87 Ferry Lane, Rainham, RM13 9YH
Tel: 01708-522626 **Fax:** 01708-553806
E-mail: richard@thermitwelding.co.uk
Website: http://www.thermit-welding.com
Bank(s): Deutsche, Bishopsgate
Directors: R. Johnson (MD), J. Leaning (Fin)
Managers: K. Hodges, R. Pearl (Purch Mgr), P. Daly
Ultimate Holding Company: GOLDSCHMIDT THERMIT GMBH (GERMANY)
Immediate Holding Company: THERMIT WELDING (GB) LIMITED
Registration no: 00616382 **VAT No.:** GB 246 6563 40
Date established: 1958 **Turnover:** £2m - £5m **No.of Employees:** 21 - 50
Product Groups: 45

Date of Accounts	Dec 11	Dec 10	Dec 09
Sales Turnover	4m	4m	5m
Pre Tax Profit/Loss	296	197	266
Working Capital	1m	942	2m
Fixed Assets	2m	2m	2m
Current Assets	2m	1m	2m
Current Liabilities	279	227	269

Tilda Ltd
Coldharbour Lane, Rainham, RM13 9YQ
Tel: 01708-717777 **Fax:** 01708-717700
E-mail: feedback@tilda.com
Website: http://www.tilda.com
Bank(s): Nat West
Directors: S. Thakrar (Dir)
Ultimate Holding Company: BRAUNSTONE PROPERTIES LIMITED
Immediate Holding Company: TILDA LIMITED
Registration no: 00990202 **VAT No.:** GB 222 7419 80
Date established: 1970 **Turnover:** £75m - £125m
No.of Employees: 101 - 250 **Product Groups:** 20

Date of Accounts	Dec 11	Dec 10	Dec 09
Sales Turnover	104m	103m	98m
Pre Tax Profit/Loss	1m	1m	-2m
Working Capital	1m	649	1m
Fixed Assets	20m	21m	22m
Current Assets	41m	40m	42m
Current Liabilities	19m	2m	3m

X R Fasteners Ltd
Unit 85 86 Imperial Trading Estate Lambs Lane North, Rainham, RM13 9XL
Tel: 01708-526274 **Fax:** 01708-525981
Directors: F. Pundu (Fin), C. Billings (MD)
Immediate Holding Company: X R FASTENERS LIMITED
Registration no: 02087956 **VAT No.:** GB 450 9432 53
Date established: 1987 **Turnover:** £250,000 - £500,000
No.of Employees: 11 - 20 **Product Groups:** 66

Date of Accounts	Mar 11	Mar 10	Mar 09
Working Capital	691	656	597
Fixed Assets	27	31	30
Current Assets	1m	924	879

Rayleigh

A G Fabrications Ltd
31 Imperial Park Industrial Estate Rawreth Lane, Rayleigh, SS6 9RS
Tel: 01268-785365 **Fax:** 01268-785227
E-mail: enquiries@agfabrications.co.uk
Website: http://www.agfabrications.co.uk
Directors: G. Chambers (Dir)
Immediate Holding Company: A.G. Fabrications Ltd
Registration no: 03061301 **Date established:** 1995
Turnover: Up to £250,000 **No.of Employees:** 1 - 10 **Product Groups:** 35, 37, 40, 44, 48, 66

Date of Accounts	Sep 09	Sep 08	Sep 07
Sales Turnover	187	161	148
Pre Tax Profit/Loss	27	17	25
Working Capital	37	35	35
Fixed Assets	1	2	2
Current Assets	96	84	89
Current Liabilities	33	24	32

Adform
Raytel House Brook Road, Rayleigh, SS6 7XH
Tel: 01268-775656 **Fax:** 01268-745001
E-mail: adform@dial.pipex.com
Website: http://www.adform.co.uk
Directors: R. Lawrence (Ch), E. Biddle (Co Sec), E. Biddle (Fin)
Managers: D. Fessey
Immediate Holding Company: ADFORM LIMITED
Registration no: 01203271 **VAT No.:** GB 394 9607 00
Date established: 1975 **Turnover:** £500,000 - £1m
No.of Employees: 1 - 10 **Product Groups:** 28, 80, 81

Date of Accounts	Jun 06	Jun 05	Jun 04
Working Capital	-78	-78	-78

M J Barham
London Road, Rayleigh, SS6 9ES
Tel: 01268-754500 **Fax:** 01268-754500
E-mail: mjbarham@blueyonder.co.uk
Directors: M. Barham (Prop)
Date established: 2000 **No.of Employees:** 1 - 10 **Product Groups:** 26, 35

Biffa Waste Services Ltd
Unit 12 Rawreth Industrial Estate, Rawreth Lane, Rayleigh, SS6 9RL
Tel: 01268-783069 **Fax:** 0871-7334341
E-mail: marketing@biffa.co.uk
Website: http://www.biffa.co.uk
Managers: K. Steward (District Mgr)
Registration no: 00946107 **No.of Employees:** 11 - 20
Product Groups: 32, 54

C W C Solutions Part of the CW Construction Group
Kingsleigh House 15-17 High Street, Rayleigh, SS6 7EW
Tel: 01268-745808 **Fax:** 01268-743803
E-mail: info@cw-construction.co.uk
Website: http://www.cw-construction.co.uk

Directors: C. Walsh (Prop)
Immediate Holding Company: THE ESSEX LASER LIPO CLINIC LTD
Registration no: 07090187 **Date established:** 2012
No.of Employees: 11 - 20 **Product Groups:** 80, 84, 85, 86, 87

Date of Accounts	May 11	Mar 12
Sales Turnover	131	104
Pre Tax Profit/Loss	45	-52
Working Capital	1	-43
Current Assets	16	53
Current Liabilities	15	15

Elmdale Welding & Engineering Supplies Ltd

23-27 Brook Road, Rayleigh, SS6 7XR
Tel: 01268-779011 **Fax:** 01268-745192
E-mail: sales@elmdale.co.uk
Website: http://www.elmdale.co.uk
Bank(s): National Westminster Bank Plc
Directors: P. Elmes (MD), P. Elms (MD), J. Elms (Co Sec)
Managers: A. Smith (Comptroller)
Immediate Holding Company: ELMDALE WELDING AND ENGINEERING SUPPLIES LIMITED
Registration no: 02018707 **VAT No.:** GB 250 3881 70
Date established: 1986 **Turnover:** £5m - £10m **No.of Employees:** 21 - 50
Product Groups: 24, 29, 30, 32, 33, 34, 35, 36, 38, 40, 46

Date of Accounts	Mar 11	Mar 10	Mar 09
Working Capital	526	463	436
Fixed Assets	150	185	172
Current Assets	1m	1m	1m

Fisco Tools Ltd

21 Brook Road, Rayleigh, SS6 7XD
Tel: 01268-747074 **Fax:** 01268-772936
E-mail: info@fisco.co.uk
Website: http://www.fisco.co.uk
Bank(s): National Westminster
Directors: P. Fisher (MD), L. Richardson (Fin), C. Murton (Mkt Research)
Managers: K. Tully (Personnel), I. Jarvis (Tech Serv Mgr), G. Beaden (Purch Mgr)
Ultimate Holding Company: INVESTMENT AB LATOUR (SWEDEN))
Immediate Holding Company: FISCO TOOLS LIMITED
Registration no: 00755735 **VAT No.:** GB 352 1395 69
Date established: 1963 **Turnover:** £5m - £10m
No.of Employees: 51 - 100 **Product Groups:** 36, 38, 49

Date of Accounts	Dec 11	Dec 10	Dec 09
Sales Turnover	6m	6m	5m
Pre Tax Profit/Loss	650	70	-441
Working Capital	3m	2m	2m
Fixed Assets	1m	1m	1m
Current Assets	3m	3m	3m
Current Liabilities	202	667	82

J Fuller & Sons Ltd

Unit 22 Imperial Park Rawreth Lane, Rayleigh, SS6 9RS
Tel: 01268-782368 **Fax:** 01268-782368
E-mail: sales@jfuller.co.uk
Website: http://www.jfullers.co.uk
Directors: R. Fuller (MD)
Immediate Holding Company: J. FULLER AND SONS LIMITED
Registration no: 00429840 **Date established:** 1947
No.of Employees: 1 - 10 **Product Groups:** 20, 40, 41

Date of Accounts	Mar 12	Mar 11	Mar 10
Working Capital	32	37	34
Fixed Assets	6	6	6
Current Assets	43	55	48

G H Catering Equipment Services

27 Imperial Park Rawreth Lane, Rayleigh, SS6 9RS
Tel: 01268-785990 **Fax:** 01268-785990
Website: http://www.gh-catering-equipment.co.uk
Directors: S. Hayward (MD)
Date established: 1987 **No.of Employees:** 1 - 10 **Product Groups:** 20, 40, 41

Date of Accounts	Jun 11	Jun 10	Jun 09
Working Capital	34	37	33
Fixed Assets	64	79	94
Current Assets	158	196	153

A P Hollings & Sons Ltd

14 Brook Road Industrial Estate Sirdar Road, Brook Road Industrial Estate, Rayleigh, SS6 7XF
Tel: 01268-770681 **Fax:** 01268-775144
E-mail: info@aphollings.co.uk
Website: http://www.aphollings.co.uk
Bank(s): National Westminster Bank Plc
Directors: A. Hollings (Dir)
Immediate Holding Company: A.P. HOLLINGS & SONS LIMITED
Registration no: 04691049 **VAT No.:** GB 250 4940 75
Date established: 2003 **Turnover:** £250,000 - £500,000
No.of Employees: 11 - 20 **Product Groups:** 25, 30, 48, 49, 84

Date of Accounts	Jun 11	Jun 10	Jun 09
Working Capital	62	37	25
Fixed Assets	88	101	115
Current Assets	299	310	326

M & W Grinding Services

Unit 10 Annwood Lodge Business Park Arterial Road, Rayleigh, SS6 7UA
Tel: 01268-590059 **Fax:** 01268-590058
E-mail: mwgrinding@btinternet.com
Website: http://www.mwgrinding.co.uk
Directors: C. Murrell (Ptnr)
Turnover: Up to £250,000 **No.of Employees:** 1 - 10 **Product Groups:** 46, 48

Monitor Audio Ltd

2 Brook Road Industrial Estate Brook Road, Brook Road Industrial Estate, Rayleigh, SS6 7XL
Tel: 01268-740580 **Fax:** 01268-740589
E-mail: info@monitoraudio.co.uk
Website: http://www.monitoraudio.com
Bank(s): Lloyds TSB
Directors: A. Flatt (Dir), P. Evans (Fin)
Managers: D. Rogers (Tech Serv Mgr), J. Legon
Immediate Holding Company: MONITOR AUDIO LIMITED
Registration no: 06018892 **VAT No.:** GB 214 8815 62
Date established: 2006 **Turnover:** £10m - £20m
No.of Employees: 21 - 50 **Product Groups:** 37

Date of Accounts	Sep 11	Sep 10	Sep 09
Sales Turnover	19m	18m	13m
Pre Tax Profit/Loss	2m	2m	-558
Working Capital	969	3m	2m
Fixed Assets	11m	11m	11m
Current Assets	9m	6m	4m
Current Liabilities	3m	446	110

Phase Ii Firearms

57 The Chase, Rayleigh, SS6 8QW
Tel: 01268-774606 **Fax:** 01702-300201
E-mail: sales@stalkingscotland.com
Website: http://www.stalkingscotland.com
Directors: S. Sweeting (Prop)
Date established: 1988 **No.of Employees:** 1 - 10 **Product Groups:** 36, 39, 40

Philpot Dairy Products Ltd

Philpot House Station Road, Rayleigh, SS6 7HH
Tel: 01268-775522 **Fax:** 01268-773848
E-mail: claud.bilbao@dairycrest.co.uk
Website: http://www.philpots.co.uk
Directors: R. Miller (Co Sec), C. Bilbao (Sales & Mktg)
Ultimate Holding Company: DAIRY CREST GROUP PLC
Immediate Holding Company: PHILPOT DAIRY PRODUCTS LIMITED
Registration no: 00879131 **Date established:** 1966
Turnover: £50m - £75m **No.of Employees:** 1 - 10 **Product Groups:** 20, 62

Date of Accounts	Mar 11	Mar 10	Mar 09
Sales Turnover	67m	37m	52m
Pre Tax Profit/Loss	527	312	501
Working Capital	1m	4m	4m
Fixed Assets	N/A	2	5
Current Assets	12m	6m	10m
Current Liabilities	339	166	567

Photomechanical Services Essex Ltd

Unit C Co-Ordinated Industrial Estate Claydons Lane, Rayleigh, SS6 7UP
Tel: 01268-741486 **Fax:** 01268-782538
E-mail: sales@photomechanical.co.uk
Website: http://www.photomechanical.co.uk
Bank(s): National Westminster Bank Plc
Directors: I. Paterson (MD)
Ultimate Holding Company: TRANSMITS HOPE LIMITED
Immediate Holding Company: PHOTOMECHANICAL SERVICES (ESSEX) LIMITED
Registration no: 01000305 **VAT No.:** GB 250 7555 63
Date established: 1971 **Turnover:** £1m - £2m **No.of Employees:** 11 - 20
Product Groups: 37

Date of Accounts	Dec 11	Dec 10	Dec 09
Working Capital	160	124	109
Fixed Assets	157	99	104
Current Assets	386	377	402

Professional Motorcycle Polishing

Lychgate Industrial Estate Arterial Road, Rayleigh, SS6 7TZ
Tel: 01268-775888 **Fax:** 01268-775888
E-mail: garymahan1965@yahoo.co.uk
Website: http://www.promopolishing.co.uk
Directors: G. Mahan (Prop)
No.of Employees: 1 - 10 **Product Groups:** 46, 48

Rayleigh Galvanizers Ltd

Unit 34 Rawreth Industrial Estate Rawreth Lane, Rayleigh, SS6 9RL
Tel: 01268-784456 **Fax:** 01268-784456
Directors: V. Buddin (Fin), D. Walsh (MD)
Immediate Holding Company: RAYLEIGH GALVANIZERS LIMITED
Registration no: 03900961 **Date established:** 1999
Turnover: Up to £250,000 **No.of Employees:** 1 - 10 **Product Groups:** 46, 48

Date of Accounts	Dec 06	Dec 05
Sales Turnover	127	89
Pre Tax Profit/Loss	15	4
Working Capital	-36	-44
Fixed Assets	58	53
Current Assets	24	18
Current Liabilities	61	62
ROCE% (Return on Capital Employed)	71.5	50.5
ROT% (Return on Turnover)	12.2	5.0

Rayleigh Instruments Ltd

Raytel House 19 Brook Road, Rayleigh, SS6 7XH
Tel: 01268-749300 **Fax:** 01268-749309
E-mail: sales@rayleigh.co.uk
Website: http://www.rayleigh.co.uk
Bank(s): Barclays
Directors: E. Biddle (Fin)
Managers: G. Lockhart (Sales & Mktg Mg), A. Rayleigh (Sales Prom Mgr), D. Coleman (Tech Serv Mgr)
Immediate Holding Company: RAYLEIGH INSTRUMENTS LIMITED
Registration no: 00808961 **VAT No.:** GB 394 9607 00
Date established: 1964 **No.of Employees:** 21 - 50 **Product Groups:** 37, 38, 49

Date of Accounts	Jun 11	Jun 10	Jun 09
Working Capital	561	766	690
Fixed Assets	5	14	23
Current Assets	2m	2m	1m

Raytel Security Systems Ltd

19 Brook Road, Rayleigh, SS6 7XH
Tel: 01268-749310 **Fax:** 01268-745001
E-mail: info@raytelsecurity.co.uk
Website: http://www.raytelsecurity.co.uk
Bank(s): Barclays
Directors: E. Biddle (Fin)
Immediate Holding Company: RAYTEL SECURITY SYSTEMS LIMITED
Registration no: 01280393 **VAT No.:** GB 394 9607 00
Date established: 1976 **No.of Employees:** 11 - 20 **Product Groups:** 36, 37, 40

Date of Accounts	Jun 11	Jun 10	Jun 09
Working Capital	269	254	246
Fixed Assets	N/A	1	4
Current Assets	744	660	846

S A A UK Ltd

70 Louis Dr, Rayleigh, SS6 9DX
Tel: 01268-786374
E-mail: saa.uk@btinternet.com
Website: http://www.saaelectrical.co.uk
Directors: S. Adams (Dir)
Immediate Holding Company: SAA UK LIMITED
Registration no: 06140115 **Date established:** 2007
No.of Employees: 1 - 10 **Product Groups:** 38, 85

Date of Accounts	Mar 12	Mar 11	Mar 10
Sales Turnover	141	155	131
Pre Tax Profit/Loss	57	70	55
Working Capital	31	28	21
Fixed Assets	5	6	5
Current Assets	58	68	48
Current Liabilities	25	26	21

Sam Headhunting Ltd

9 Quest End, Rayleigh, SS6 9JW
Tel: 01268-782250
E-mail: info-uk@samheadhunting.com
Website: http://www.samheadhunting.co.uk
Product Groups: 80

Date of Accounts	Dec 07	Dec 06	Dec 05
Sales Turnover	151	66	159
Pre Tax Profit/Loss	25	7	28
Working Capital	20	19	19
Current Assets	84	58	62
Current Liabilities	64	38	44
Total Share Capital	20	15	15
ROCE% (Return on Capital Employed)	126.1	39.0	149.2
ROT% (Return on Turnover)	16.8	11.4	17.8

Snooker Sports Manufacturing Ltd

Unit 21 Brook Road Industrial Centre, Brook Road Industrial Estate, Rayleigh, SS6 7XL
Tel: 01268-777293 **Fax:** 01268-777294
E-mail: sales@snookersports.com
Website: http://www.poolsnookertable.com
Directors: M. Sexton (Co Sec)
Ultimate Holding Company: INVESTMENT AB LATOUR (SWEDEN))
Immediate Holding Company: SNOOKER SPORTS (MANUFACTURING) LIMITED
Registration no: 01728301 **VAT No.:** GB 312 6134 03
Date established: 1983 **Turnover:** Up to £250,000
No.of Employees: 1 - 10 **Product Groups:** 49

Date of Accounts	Dec 11	Dec 10	Dec 09
Working Capital	-20	-25	-42
Fixed Assets	22	28	35
Current Assets	50	44	63

Thames Card Technology Ltd (Thames Group)

Thames House Arterial Road, Rayleigh, SS6 7UQ
Tel: 01268-775555 **Fax:** 01268-777660
E-mail: info@thamesgroup.co.uk
Website: http://www.thamescardtechnology.com
Directors: P. Underwood (Dir), T. Hood (Fin)
Managers: S. Peek (Tech Serv Mgr), N. Murphy (Purch Mgr), P. Robertson (Personnel)
Immediate Holding Company: THAMES CARD TECHNOLOGY LIMITED
Registration no: 02952822 **VAT No.:** GB 657 4028 27
Date established: 1994 **Turnover:** £10m - £20m
No.of Employees: 101 - 250 **Product Groups:** 23, 28, 48

Date of Accounts	May 09	Nov 11	Nov 10
Sales Turnover	17m	19m	18m
Pre Tax Profit/Loss	-2m	412	-91
Working Capital	5	278	348
Fixed Assets	3m	2m	2m
Current Assets	6m	7m	6m
Current Liabilities	388	1m	883

Toner Graphics Ltd

Hay Barn Studio Hullbridge Road, Rayleigh, SS6 9QG
Tel: 01268-780077 **Fax:** 01268-780177
E-mail: info@tonergraphics.co.uk
Website: http://www.tonergraphics.co.uk
Directors: J. Wood (Fin), P. Wood (MD)
Immediate Holding Company: TONER GRAPHICS LTD
Registration no: 04806681 **Date established:** 2003
Turnover: £500,000 - £1m **No.of Employees:** 1 - 10 **Product Groups:** 44, 48, 64

Date of Accounts	Jun 12	Jun 11	Jun 10
Working Capital	17	15	49
Fixed Assets	6	6	6
Current Assets	236	231	224

Tube Tech International Ltd

Unit 14 Rawreth Industrial Estate Rawreth Lane, Rayleigh, SS6 9RL
Tel: 01268-786999 **Fax:** 01268-786998
E-mail: info@tubetech.com
Website: http://www.tubetech.com
Directors: M. Byford (Dir), M. Watson (Dir)
Managers: R. Hayward (Tech Serv Mgr), S. Robinson (Mktg Serv Mgr)
Immediate Holding Company: TUBE TECH INTERNATIONAL LIMITED
Registration no: 02909304 **Date established:** 1994 **Turnover:** £2m - £5m
No.of Employees: 11 - 20 **Product Groups:** 54

Date of Accounts	Mar 11	Mar 10	Mar 09
Sales Turnover	N/A	N/A	2m
Pre Tax Profit/Loss	N/A	N/A	102
Working Capital	324	357	380
Fixed Assets	556	605	380
Current Assets	1m	743	702
Current Liabilities	N/A	N/A	53

J R Tyson & Sons Ltd

Unit 5 Rawreth Industrial Estate Rawreth Lane, Rayleigh, SS6 9RL
Tel: 01268-785881 **Fax:** 01268-782655
E-mail: john@jrtysonandsons.co.uk
Directors: J. Tyson (Dir)
Immediate Holding Company: J.R. TYSON (POWDER COATING) LIMITED
Registration no: 01608221 **Date established:** 1982
Turnover: £500,000 - £1m **No.of Employees:** 21 - 50 **Product Groups:** 48

Date of Accounts	Mar 11	Mar 10	Mar 09
Working Capital	86	96	146
Fixed Assets	107	120	131
Current Assets	144	138	190

United Engineering Services Ltd

Havana House Havana Drive, Rayleigh, SS6 9RQ
Tel: 01268-780886
Directors: F. Brest (Fin)
Managers: D. Smart (Mgr)
Immediate Holding Company: UNITED ENGINEERING SERVICES LIMITED
Registration no: 04763196 **Date established:** 2003
No.of Employees: 1 - 10 **Product Groups:** 40, 48, 54, 84

see next page

United Engineering Services Ltd - Cont'd

Date of Accounts	May 12	May 11	May 10
Working Capital	-56	-62	-47
Fixed Assets	13	17	14
Current Assets	107	187	174

Rochford

S J Adamson
94 Ashingdon Road, Rochford, SS4 1RE
Tel: 01702-544188
Directors: K. Adamson (Ptnr)
Date established: 1974 **No.of Employees:** 1 - 10 **Product Groups:** 26, 35

Albon Engineering & Manufacturing
Rochehall Way, Rochford, SS4 1JU
Tel: 01702-530500 **Fax:** 01702-547618
E-mail: reception@albonplc.com
Website: http://www.albonplc.com
Bank(s): Barclays, Westcliff
Directors: M. Albon (MD)
Managers: T. Dillon (Fin Mgr), I. Gurton (District Mgr), L. Emmett (Purch Mgr)
Immediate Holding Company: ALBON ENGINEERING AND MANUFACTURING PLC
Registration no: 01113447 **VAT No.:** GB 250 9196 55
Date established: 1973 **Turnover:** £50m - £75m
No.of Employees: 251 - 500 **Product Groups:** 30, 35, 39, 40, 46, 48, 68, 76

Date of Accounts	Dec 10	Dec 09	Dec 08
Sales Turnover	57m	34m	59m
Pre Tax Profit/Loss	1m	-6m	289
Working Capital	1m	-1m	-8m
Fixed Assets	38m	43m	48m
Current Assets	15m	9m	17m
Current Liabilities	2m	2m	2m

Charles Birch Essex Ltd
Units 7 & 8 Fleet Hall Road Purdeys Industrial Estate, Rochford, SS4 1NF
Tel: 01702-530656 **Fax:** 01702-531417
E-mail: mjackson@charlesbirch.com
Website: http://www.charlesbirch.com
Directors: M. Jackson (MD)
Ultimate Holding Company: CHARLES BIRCH LIMITED
Immediate Holding Company: CHARLES BIRCH (ESSEX) LIMITED
Registration no: 01184059 **Date established:** 1974 **Turnover:** £2m - £5m
No.of Employees: 11 - 20 **Product Groups:** 36, 43, 63

Date of Accounts	Jun 11	Jun 10	Jun 09
Sales Turnover	N/A	N/A	4m
Pre Tax Profit/Loss	N/A	N/A	374
Working Capital	3m	3m	2m
Fixed Assets	104	94	91
Current Assets	4m	3m	3m
Current Liabilities	N/A	N/A	196

Dee Jay Appliances
30 Rectory Avenue, Rochford, SS4 3AQ
Tel: 01702-540023 **Fax:** 0870-134 4608
E-mail: djappliances@hotmail.co.uk
Website: http://www.djappliances.co.uk
Directors: D. Pollington (Prop)
No.of Employees: 1 - 10 **Product Groups:** 40, 48, 69

Genesis Risk Solutions Ltd
2nd Floor Suite The Maltings Locks Hill, Rochford, SS4 1BB
Tel: 01702-209520 **Fax:** 01702-543728
E-mail: p.gibson@grslimited.co.uk
Website: http://www.grslimited.co.uk
Directors: G. Cheeseman (MD)
Immediate Holding Company: GENESIS RISK SOLUTIONS LIMITED
Registration no: 05638109 **Date established:** 2005
Turnover: £250,000 - £500,000 **No.of Employees:** 11 - 20
Product Groups: 82

Date of Accounts	Nov 11	Nov 10	Nov 09
Sales Turnover	N/A	792	792
Pre Tax Profit/Loss	N/A	N/A	157
Working Capital	171	98	-12
Fixed Assets	267	275	294
Current Assets	253	182	78
Current Liabilities	N/A	N/A	85

Hanningfield Process Systems Ltd
Unit 17 Rocheview Business Park Millhead Way, Purdeys Industrial Estate, Rochford, SS4 1LB
Tel: 01702-549777 **Fax:** 01702-549888
E-mail: info@hanningfield.com
Website: http://www.hanningfield.com
Directors: C. Ellis (MD)
Immediate Holding Company: HANNINGFIELD PROCESS SYSTEMS LIMITED
Registration no: 02791306 **Date established:** 1993
Turnover: £500,000 - £1m **No.of Employees:** 11 - 20
Product Groups: 29, 31, 36, 40, 41, 42, 45, 67

Date of Accounts	Aug 11	Aug 10	Aug 09
Working Capital	90	73	115
Fixed Assets	22	25	28
Current Assets	268	199	195
Current Liabilities	N/A	110	N/A

I M H Technologies Ltd
8 Roach View Boss Millhead Way, Purdeys Industrial Estate, Rochford, SS4 1LB
Tel: 01702-545429 **Fax:** 01702-545428
E-mail: sales@imh.co.uk
Website: http://www.imh.co.uk
Directors: I. Murdoch (MD)
Immediate Holding Company: IMH TECHNOLOGIES LIMITED
Registration no: 02880831 **VAT No.:** GB 629 0470 41
Date established: 1993 **Turnover:** £500,000 - £1m
No.of Employees: 1 - 10 **Product Groups:** 38

Date of Accounts	Dec 11	Dec 10	Dec 09
Working Capital	-10	-12	-7
Fixed Assets	11	12	17
Current Assets	96	65	178

Metroseal
Unit 30 Purdeys Industrial Estate Purdeys Way, Rochford, SS4 1ND
Tel: 01702-548800 **Fax:** 01702-549966
E-mail: sales@metroseal.co.uk
Website: http://www.metroseal.co.uk
Bank(s): National Westminster Bank Plc
Directors: M. Stevens (MD)
Immediate Holding Company: ACCRASYSTEM LTD
Registration no: 02127351 **VAT No.:** GB 506 1111 07
No.of Employees: 11 - 20 **Product Groups:** 29, 30, 31, 33, 39, 40, 63

P & A Hydraulics Ltd
Swains Industrial Estate Ashingdon Road, Rochford, SS4 1RG
Tel: 01702-549241 **Fax:** 01702-541080
E-mail: sales@pandahydraulics.co.uk
Website: http://www.pandahydraulicsltd.co.uk
Directors: I. Williams (Dir)
Immediate Holding Company: P & A HYDRAULICS LIMITED
Registration no: 01442819 **VAT No.:** GB 352 0001 24
Date established: 1979 **Turnover:** £500,000 - £1m
No.of Employees: 1 - 10 **Product Groups:** 48

Date of Accounts	Sep 11	Sep 10	Sep 09
Working Capital	-10	-6	-12
Fixed Assets	25	30	33
Current Assets	167	162	127

Period Stone
Rectory Cottage Hall Road, Rochford, SS4 1PD
Tel: 01702-546193
E-mail: periodstone@hotmail.co.uk
Website: http://www.periodstone.co.uk
Directors: N. Hedley (Ptnr)
Date established: 1961 **Turnover:** Up to £250,000
No.of Employees: 1 - 10 **Product Groups:** 33

Polair Ltd
17 Purdeys Industrial Estate Purdeys Way, Rochford, SS4 1ND
Tel: 01702-544141 **Fax:** 01702-544263
E-mail: enquiries@polairltd.co.uk
Website: http://www.polair.co.uk
Directors: S. Macmeikan (Dir)
Immediate Holding Company: POLAIR LIMITED
Registration no: 02578359 **Date established:** 1991
No.of Employees: 1 - 10 **Product Groups:** 20, 40, 41

Date of Accounts	May 09	May 08	May 07
Working Capital	-1	-2	5
Fixed Assets	6	7	8
Current Assets	82	106	105

Robinsons Quality Greenhouses
2 Alvina Cottages Hall Road, Rochford, SS4 1PQ
Tel: 01702-540700
Directors: P. Benson (Prop)
Date established: 1993 **No.of Employees:** 1 - 10 **Product Groups:** 26, 35

Scientific Electro Systems Ltd
Purdeys Industrial Estate 1 Rose Way, Rochford, SS4 1LY
Tel: 01702-530174 **Fax:** 01702-530200
E-mail: info@sesystems.co.uk
Website: http://www.sesystems.co.uk
Directors: D. Adams (Dir)
Immediate Holding Company: SCIENTIFIC ELECTRO SYSTEMS LIMITED
Registration no: 02072696 **Date established:** 1986
Turnover: £500,000 - £1m **No.of Employees:** 1 - 10 **Product Groups:** 85

Date of Accounts	Mar 11	Mar 10	Mar 09
Working Capital	-1	-5	10
Fixed Assets	98	103	98
Current Assets	90	59	69

Sirco Controls Ltd
Swaines Industrial Estate Ashingdon Road, Rochford, SS4 1RQ
Tel: 01702-545125 **Fax:** 01702-546873
E-mail: info@sirco-controls.co.uk
Website: http://www.sirco-controls.co.uk
Bank(s): Barclays
Directors: M. Norman (Fin)
Ultimate Holding Company: SIRCO PRODUCTS LTD (CANADA)
Immediate Holding Company: SIRCO CONTROLS LIMITED
Registration no: 00672489 **VAT No.:** GB 250 2302 20
Date established: 1960 **Turnover:** £500,000 - £1m
No.of Employees: 11 - 20 **Product Groups:** 37, 38, 40, 42

Date of Accounts	Feb 12	Feb 11	Feb 10
Working Capital	404	349	303
Fixed Assets	24	27	28
Current Assets	473	417	352

W Neal Services
29 Purdeys Industrial Estate Purdeys Way, Rochford, SS4 1ND
Tel: 01702-542554 **Fax:** 01702-542558
E-mail: sales@wnealservices.com
Website: http://www.wnealservices.com
Directors: W. Neal (Prop)
Registration no: 4851532 **Date established:** 1982
Turnover: £500,000 - £1m **No.of Employees:** 1 - 10 **Product Groups:** 46

Romford

Alex Electrical Ltd
191-193 North Street, Romford, RM1 1DU
Tel: 01708-744226 **Fax:** 01708-702002
E-mail: alexelectrical@btconnect.com
Directors: C. Mcbain (MD)
Immediate Holding Company: ALEX-ELECTRICAL LIMITED
Registration no: 00680352 **VAT No.:** GB 246 1524 75
Date established: 1961 **Turnover:** £500,000 - £1m
No.of Employees: 1 - 10 **Product Groups:** 52

Date of Accounts	Dec 10	Dec 09	Dec 08
Working Capital	93	110	155
Fixed Assets	7	8	12
Current Assets	146	171	218

Allen Ford
17 London Road, Romford, RM7 9QB
Tel: 01708-774747 **Fax:** 01708-774646
E-mail: ron.joseph@allen-ford.com
Website: http://www.allenford.com
Bank(s): Barclays
Directors: R. Joseph (Dir), R. Joseph (MD)
Immediate Holding Company: ALLEN FORD (UK) LIMITED
Registration no: 04782818 **VAT No.:** GB 542 5209 63
Date established: 2003 **Turnover:** £20m - £50m
No.of Employees: 21 - 50 **Product Groups:** 68

Andrew Mitchell Co. Ltd
Bates Business Centre, Church Road Harold Wood, The Old Brickworks, Romford, RM3 0JF
Tel: 01708-370800 **Fax:** 01708-377190
E-mail: sales@andrew-mitchell.co.uk
Website: http://www.andrew-mitchell.co.uk
Directors: K. Jesskyns (Dir)
Managers: D. Hall (Purch Mgr), J. Shearer (Computer Mgr), P. Fleming (District Mgr)
Immediate Holding Company: Andrew Mitchell Group P.L.C.
Registration no: SC003736 **Date established:** 2009
Turnover: £5m - £10m **No.of Employees:** 1 - 10 **Product Groups:** 23, 24, 35

Anvil Shutters Ltd
Ashetons Farm Tysea Hill, Stapleford Abbotts, Romford, RM4 1JU
Tel: 08451-212340
E-mail: sales@anvilshutters.co.uk
Website: http://www.anvilshutters.co.uk
Directors: S. Bass (MD)
Immediate Holding Company: ANVIL SHUTTERS LIMITED
Registration no: 07315516 **Date established:** 2010
Turnover: £500,000 - £1m **No.of Employees:** 1 - 10 **Product Groups:** 52, 80

Date of Accounts	Sep 11
Working Capital	-12
Fixed Assets	3
Current Assets	49

Atlas Dies
3 Northgate Industrial Park Collier Row Road, Romford, RM5 2BG
Tel: 020-8548 7230 **Fax:** 020-8548 7231
E-mail: sales@atlasdies.com
Website: http://www.atlas-dies.co.uk
Managers: R. Huxtable (Mgr)
Registration no: 04672739 **VAT No.:** GB 637 1876 14
Turnover: £1m - £2m **No.of Employees:** 11 - 20 **Product Groups:** 27, 66

Date of Accounts	Feb 08	Feb 11	Feb 10
Working Capital	249	121	95
Fixed Assets	226	53	109
Current Assets	509	378	320

Bar Contract Services Ltd
4b Bernard Road, Romford, RM7 0HX
Tel: 01708-743313 **Fax:** 01708-747520
E-mail: ron@barcontracts.freeserve.co.uk
Website: http://www.barcontracts.freeserve.co.uk
Directors: R. Holtom (Dir)
Date established: 1979 **No.of Employees:** 1 - 10 **Product Groups:** 52, 66, 84

Caricare Disability Equipment
The Stable Hammonds Farm Stapleford Road, Stapleford Tawney, Romford, RM4 1RR
Tel: 01708-688695 **Fax:** 01708-688601
E-mail: sales@caricare.co.uk
Website: http://www.caricare.co.uk
Managers: T. Coombs (Mgr)
Immediate Holding Company: A THOUSAND THREADS LIMITED
Date established: 2006 **No.of Employees:** 1 - 10 **Product Groups:** 38, 67

Date of Accounts	Jun 11	Jun 10	Jun 09
Working Capital	-14	-13	-6
Fixed Assets	3	4	2
Current Assets	16	12	16

Classic Gasket Ltd
895 High Road Chadwell Heath, Romford, RM6 4HL
Tel: 020-8590 6232 **Fax:** 020-8590 6568
Directors: T. Deykin (MD), L. Sharp (Co Sec)
Ultimate Holding Company: T.D. MANAGEMENT LIMITED
Immediate Holding Company: HAYNE INGLEBY,LIMITED
Registration no: 00466395 **VAT No.:** GB 185 6570 29
Date established: 1949 **Turnover:** £250,000 - £500,000
No.of Employees: 1 - 10 **Product Groups:** 27

Date of Accounts	Dec 11
Working Capital	24
Fixed Assets	4
Current Assets	186

Continental Disc UK Ltd
C The Business Centre Faringdon Avenue, Romford, RM3 8EN
Tel: 01708-386444 **Fax:** 01708-386486
E-mail: sales@contdisc.com
Website: http://www.contdisc.com
Directors: R. Doelling (Dir), G. Weber (Co Sec)
Managers: D. Butler (Mktg Serv Mgr), G. Ward (Sales Eng), T. Tokeley (Ops Mgr)
Immediate Holding Company: CONTINENTAL DISC UK LIMITED
Registration no: 02727841 **Date established:** 1992
No.of Employees: 1 - 10 **Product Groups:** 36, 38, 39, 40, 42

Date of Accounts	Dec 07	Dec 06	Dec 05
Working Capital	-800	-754	-702
Fixed Assets	10	6	9
Current Assets	344	339	476
Current Liabilities	1144	1094	1178

Designed Architectural Lighting Ltd
6 Conqueror Court Spilsby Road, Harold Hill, Romford, RM3 8SB
Tel: 01708-381999 **Fax:** 01708-381585
E-mail: sales@dal-uk.com
Website: http://www.dal-uk.com
Bank(s): National Westminster Bank Plc
Directors: C. Short (Dir), J. Dench (Fin)
Managers: W. Beaver (Purch Mgr)
Immediate Holding Company: DESIGNED ARCHITECTURAL LIGHTING CO. LIMITED

Registration no: 01748660 **VAT No.:** GB 403 8312 85
Date established: 1983 **Turnover:** £2m - £5m **No.of Employees:** 21 - 50
Product Groups: 67

Date of Accounts	Feb 08	Feb 11	Feb 10
Working Capital	58	46	36
Fixed Assets	55	58	72
Current Assets	1m	898	1m

Elektron Components Ltd

Melville Court Spilsby Road, Harold Hill, Romford, RM3 8SB
Tel: 01708-343800 **Fax:** 01708-376544
E-mail: johnwilson@bulgin.co.uk
Website: http://www.elektronplc.com
Bank(s): HSBC
Directors: I. Bye (Ch), J. Wilson (Grp Chief Exec), K. Daley (Dir), P. Burch (MD)
Managers: D. May (Eng Serv Mgr)
Ultimate Holding Company: ELEKTRON TECHNOLOGY PLC
Immediate Holding Company: ELEKTRON TECHNOLOGY UK LIMITED
Registration no: 04949934 **VAT No.:** GB 573 1726 36
Date established: 2003 **Turnover:** £20m - £50m
No.of Employees: 21 - 50 **Product Groups:** 30, 38

Date of Accounts	Jan 11	Jan 10	Jan 09
Sales Turnover	25m	18m	20m
Pre Tax Profit/Loss	3m	2m	-691
Working Capital	3m	1m	-195
Fixed Assets	691	505	629
Current Assets	11m	9m	7m
Current Liabilities	3m	2m	900

Elite Solutions

Unit 13 Ashton Gate Ashton Road, Romford, RM3 8UF
Tel: 01708-331100
Website: http://www.hsegroupuk.com
Directors: A. Howard (Fin)
Registration no: 05650076 **No.of Employees:** 21 - 50
Product Groups: 40, 66

Essex Gun

6 Eastbrook Drive, Romford, RM7 0YX
Tel: 020-8593 3502 **Fax:** 020-8924 0999
E-mail: info@essexgun.com
Website: http://www.essexgun.com
Directors: N. Jay (Prop)
Immediate Holding Company: ESSEX GUN LIMITED
Registration no: 04747191 **Date established:** 2003
No.of Employees: 1 - 10 **Product Groups:** 36, 39, 40

Fraser Ross Finance Ltd

185-187 High Road, Romford, RM6 6NA
Tel: 020-8597 8781 **Fax:** 020-8597 8673
E-mail: sales@alex-fraser.co.uk
Website: http://www.alex-fraser.co.uk
Directors: L. Heath (Dep Ch), I. Wilson (MD)
Managers: N. Chilvers (Sales Prom Mgr)
Immediate Holding Company: FRASER-ROSS FINANCE LIMITED
Registration no: 01163781 **Date established:** 1974
Turnover: Up to £250,000 **No.of Employees:** 1 - 10 **Product Groups:** 82

Date of Accounts	Sep 08	Sep 07	Sep 06
Sales Turnover	159	81	38
Pre Tax Profit/Loss	3	27	6
Working Capital	139	138	138
Current Assets	677	928	335
Current Liabilities	538	789	197
Total Share Capital	50	50	50
ROCE% (Return on Capital Employed)	2.0	19.8	4.0
ROT% (Return on Turnover)	1.8	34.0	14.4

G B S General Battery Supplies

Unit A 315 Collier Row Lane, Romford, RM5 3ND
Tel: 01708-769222 **Fax:** 01708-769282
E-mail: gbsbatteries@aol.com
Website: http://www.gbsbatteries.com
Directors: P. Abbott (Ptnr)
Registration no: 05697536 **Date established:** 2006 **Turnover:** £2m - £5m
No.of Employees: 1 - 10 **Product Groups:** 37

Gilt Edge Plastics Ltd

Unit 2 Elms Industrial Estate Church Road, Harold Wood, Romford, RM3 0JU
Tel: 01708-379005 **Fax:** 01708-379045
E-mail: sales@giltedgeplastics.co.uk
Website: http://www.giltedgeplastics.co.uk
Directors: M. Franklin (MD)
Immediate Holding Company: GILT EDGE PLASTICS LTD
Registration no: 04754291 **VAT No.:** GB 406 4461 70
Date established: 2003 **Turnover:** £500,000 - £1m
No.of Employees: 1 - 10 **Product Groups:** 28, 30, 48

Date of Accounts	Jun 12	Jun 11	Jun 10
Working Capital	524	429	345
Fixed Assets	212	194	225
Current Assets	752	666	601

Gold Trowel UK Ltd

Asheton Farm Stappleford Abbotts Stapleford Abbotts, Romford, RM4 1JU
Tel: 01708-344700 **Fax:** 01708-745935
E-mail: andymarshall@goldtrowel.co.uk
Website: http://www.goldtrowel.co.uk
Directors: A. Marshall (Dir)
Immediate Holding Company: GOLDTROWEL UK LIMITED
Registration no: 07435922 **Date established:** 2010
Turnover: Up to £250,000 **No.of Employees:** 1 - 10 **Product Groups:** 86, 87, 89

Gosnays Ltd

Eastern Avenue West, Romford, RM7 7NS
Tel: 01708-740668 **Fax:** 01708-733266
E-mail: sales@gosnays.co.uk
Website: http://www.gosnays.co.uk
Directors: A. Wilkes (Dir)
Immediate Holding Company: GOSNAY'S ENGINEERING COMPANY LIMITED
Registration no: 00710657 **Date established:** 1961
Turnover: £500,000 - £1m **No.of Employees:** 1 - 10 **Product Groups:** 48

Date of Accounts	Dec 11	Dec 10	Dec 09
Working Capital	423	438	454
Fixed Assets	88	66	39
Current Assets	503	513	533

Grangewood Plastic Packaging Ltd

Essex House Jutsums Lane, Romford, RM7 0ER
Tel: 01708-725911 **Fax:** 01708-728677
E-mail: gpp@btconnect.com
Website: http://www.grangewoodplastics.co.uk
Bank(s): Barclays, Romford
Directors: P. Bartholomew (Dir)
Immediate Holding Company: GRANGEWOOD PLASTIC PACKAGING LIMITED
Registration no: 00410048 **VAT No.:** GB 248 4373 43
Date established: 1946 **Turnover:** £2m - £5m **No.of Employees:** 11 - 20
Product Groups: 24, 27, 30, 31, 48, 66, 83

Date of Accounts	Jun 11	Jun 10	Jun 09
Working Capital	425	361	346
Fixed Assets	1m	1m	1m
Current Assets	1m	1m	1m

Harding Bros Electrical Ltd

50 Kenneth Road, Romford, RM6 6LL
Tel: 020-8597 5694 **Fax:** 020-8590 0852
E-mail: info@hardingbros.com
Website: http://www.hardingbros.com
Bank(s): National Westminster Bank Plc
Directors: V. Parker (Dir)
Immediate Holding Company: HARDING BROS. ELECTRICAL LIMITED
Registration no: 01237890 **VAT No.:** GB 247 9603 33
Date established: 1975 **Turnover:** £1m - £2m **No.of Employees:** 21 - 50
Product Groups: 52

Date of Accounts	Jan 12	Jan 11	Jan 10
Working Capital	149	154	229
Fixed Assets	185	180	186
Current Assets	287	275	336

Jewson Ltd

307-309 South Street, Romford, RM1 2BB
Tel: 01708-722433 **Fax:** 01708-732331
E-mail: mark.sanders@jewson.co.uk
Website: http://www.jewson.co.uk
Managers: M. Sanders (Mgr)
Ultimate Holding Company: COMPAGNIE DE SAINT GOBAIN (FRANCE)
Immediate Holding Company: JEWSON LIMITED
Registration no: 00348407 **VAT No.:** GB 394 1212 63
Date established: 1939 **No.of Employees:** 11 - 20 **Product Groups:** 66

Date of Accounts	Dec 11	Dec 10	Dec 09
Sales Turnover	1606m	1547m	1485m
Pre Tax Profit/Loss	18m	100m	45m
Working Capital	-345m	-250m	-349m
Fixed Assets	496m	387m	461m
Current Assets	657m	1005m	1320m
Current Liabilities	66m	120m	64m

Charles H Julian Ltd

Lambourne Hall Church Lane, Abridge, Romford, RM4 1AH
Tel: 01992-814242 **Fax:** 01992-813536
E-mail: recption@theparsonage.co.uk
Website: http://www.theparsonage.co.uk
Directors: I. Lockwood (MD)
Immediate Holding Company: CHARLES H JULIAN LIMITED
Registration no: SC158347 **VAT No.:** GB 662 9776 83
Date established: 1995 **Turnover:** £500,000 - £1m
No.of Employees: 1 - 10 **Product Groups:** 61

Date of Accounts	May 11	May 10	May 09
Working Capital	N/A	-1	-17
Fixed Assets	31	31	31
Current Assets	132	135	136

Kennett & Lindsell Ltd

Crow Lane, Romford, RM7 0ES
Tel: 01708-749732 **Fax:** 01708-733328
E-mail: sales@kennettlindsell.com
Website: http://www.kennettlindsell.com
Bank(s): Barclays
Directors: D. Lindsell (MD)
Immediate Holding Company: KENNETT & LINDSELL LIMITED
Registration no: 00551848 **VAT No.:** GB 246 1163 81
Date established: 1955 **Turnover:** £500,000 - £1m
No.of Employees: 11 - 20 **Product Groups:** 49

Date of Accounts	Jul 11	Jul 10	Jul 09
Sales Turnover	N/A	598	N/A
Pre Tax Profit/Loss	N/A	-46	N/A
Working Capital	99	107	128
Fixed Assets	361	366	380
Current Assets	276	261	220
Current Liabilities	N/A	88	N/A

La Roche

Unit 11-12 Danes Road, Romford, RM7 0HL
Tel: 01708-730488 **Fax:** 01708-749358
E-mail: email@la-roche.co.uk
Website: http://www.la-roche.co.uk
Directors: B. Wylie (Dir)
Immediate Holding Company: P.F. LA ROCHE & COMPANY LTD.
Registration no: 00845892 **VAT No.:** GB 506 5463 53
Date established: 1965 **Turnover:** £1m - £2m **No.of Employees:** 1 - 10
Product Groups: 37, 40, 45, 46, 47, 48, 67

Date of Accounts	Jun 11	Jun 10	Jun 09
Working Capital	8	27	85
Fixed Assets	498	511	522
Current Assets	556	591	673

Ladderfix Ltd

Fairholme Avenue, Romford, RM2 5UX
Tel: 01268-732607 **Fax:** 01708-475113
E-mail: sales@ladderfix.co.uk
Website: http://www.ladderfix.co.uk
Directors: E. Clarke (Dir)
Immediate Holding Company: LADDERFIX LIMITED
Registration no: 01765865 **Date established:** 1983
Turnover: £500,000 - £1m **No.of Employees:** 1 - 10 **Product Groups:** 30, 35

Date of Accounts	Oct 11	Oct 10	Oct 08
Working Capital	208	187	168
Fixed Assets	4	4	5
Current Assets	267	232	230

M & S Shipping International Ltd

Enterprise House 34 Faringdon Avenue, Romford, RM3 8SU
Tel: 01708-340034 **Fax:** 01708-373787
E-mail: logistics2000@msshipping.com
Website: http://www.msubm.co.uk
Directors: P. Latham (Grp Chief Exec), G. Gluck (MD)
Managers: J. Caxton-Idowu (I.T. Exec)
Immediate Holding Company: M & S SHIPPING (INTERNATIONAL) LIMITED
Registration no: 02855318 **VAT No.:** GB 627 7860 05
Date established: 1993 **Turnover:** £20m - £50m **No.of Employees:** 1 - 10
Product Groups: 72, 74, 76, 77

Date of Accounts	Dec 07
Sales Turnover	44626
Pre Tax Profit/Loss	1209
Working Capital	3496
Fixed Assets	78
Current Assets	7999
Current Liabilities	4504
Total Share Capital	700
ROCE% (Return on Capital Employed)	33.8

Meldrum Mailing Ltd

Units 1-2 Hainault Works Hainault Road, Little Heath, Romford, RM6 5NF
Tel: 020-8597 3218 **Fax:** 0845-644 5675
E-mail: info@meldrummailing.com
Website: http://www.meldrummailing.com
Bank(s): Midland
Directors: M. Wooldridge (MD)
Immediate Holding Company: MELDRUM MAILING LIMITED
Registration no: 01294370 **VAT No.:** 291 5175 49 **Date established:** 1977
Turnover: £500,000 - £1m **No.of Employees:** 11 - 20
Product Groups: 80, 81

Date of Accounts	Jan 11	Jan 10	Jan 09
Working Capital	-85	-51	32
Fixed Assets	76	87	118
Current Assets	76	112	155

Nectar Group Ltd

1 Ashton Gate Ashton Road, Romford, RM3 8UF
Tel: 01708-386555 **Fax:** 01708-386665
E-mail: guy@nectar.co.uk
Website: http://www.nectargroup.net
Directors: G. Wilkes (MD), K. Snow (Fin)
Ultimate Holding Company: NECTAR HOLDINGS LIMITED
Immediate Holding Company: NECTAR GROUP LIMITED
Registration no: 01459988 **VAT No.:** GB 597 3187 89
Date established: 1979 **Turnover:** £5m - £10m **No.of Employees:** 11 - 20
Product Groups: 39, 41, 45, 74, 76, 84

Date of Accounts	Dec 11	Dec 10	Dec 09
Sales Turnover	9m	7m	9m
Pre Tax Profit/Loss	1m	347	-266
Working Capital	2m	995	637
Fixed Assets	37	52	226
Current Assets	9m	7m	6m
Current Liabilities	2m	2m	1m

Neopost Ltd

Neopost House South Street, Romford, RM1 2AR
Tel: 01708-746000 **Fax:** 01992-760902
E-mail: sales@neopost.co.uk
Website: http://www.neopost.co.uk
Directors: M. Stone (MD)
Ultimate Holding Company: NEOPOST SA (FRANCE)
Immediate Holding Company: NEOPOST (HOLDINGS) LIMITED
Registration no: 02670823 **Date established:** 1991
Turnover: Up to £250,000 **No.of Employees:** 251 - 500
Product Groups: 38, 44

Date of Accounts	Jan 11	Jan 10	Jan 09
Pre Tax Profit/Loss	27m	47m	85m
Working Capital	-8m	-6m	-4m
Fixed Assets	62m	62m	62m
Current Assets	3m	6m	9m
Current Liabilities	24	72	94

Opus Windows

166 Collier Row Lane, Romford, RM5 3EA
Tel: 01708-723131 **Fax:** 01708-749994
E-mail: info@opus-windows.co.uk
Website: http://www.opus-windows.co.uk
Directors: G. Cresswell (Ptnr)
Registration no: 01718779 **Turnover:** £250,000 - £500,000
No.of Employees: 1 - 10 **Product Groups:** 30

O R S Scaffolding

22 Penzance Road, Romford, RM3 9NR
Tel: 0781-481 5077
E-mail: steve@orsscaffolding.co.uk
Website: http://www.orsscaffolding.co.uk
Directors: S. Gore (Dir)
Date established: 1992 **No.of Employees:** 1 - 10 **Product Groups:** 52, 83

Premier Lifts

Arundel Business Centre 49 Station Road, Harold Wood, Romford, RM3 0BS
Tel: 01708-373332 **Fax:** 01708-373766
E-mail: enquiries@premierlifts.co.uk
Website: http://www.premierlifts.co.uk
Directors: A. Larkin (Dir), J. Mitchell (Fin)
Immediate Holding Company: PREMIER LIFTS LIMITED
Registration no: 02182413 **Date established:** 1987
No.of Employees: 21 - 50 **Product Groups:** 35, 39, 45

Date of Accounts	Mar 11	Mar 10	Mar 09
Working Capital	341	352	354
Fixed Assets	58	50	58
Current Assets	508	560	765

R Bickley & Co.

13 Redcar Road, Romford, RM3 9PT
Tel: 07768-984720
Directors: G. Bickley (Prop)
Date established: 1966 **Turnover:** Up to £250,000
No.of Employees: 1 - 10 **Product Groups:** 52

Roding Armoury

Silver Street Abridge, Romford, RM4 1YA
Tel: 01992-813570 **Fax:** 01992-813005
Directors: J. Lane (Ptnr)
Date established: 1978 **No.of Employees:** 1 - 10 **Product Groups:** 36, 39, 40

S B Wholesale Co.
Tonbridge Works Tonbridge Road, Romford, RM3 8TS
Tel: 01708-346002 **Fax:** 01708-370853
E-mail: sales@sbwholesale.co.uk
Website: http://www.sbwholesale.co.uk
Directors: M. Saunders (Prop)
Date established: 1983 **No.of Employees:** 1 - 10 **Product Groups:** 35, 36

S R M Sound & Light Systems
17 Collier Row Lane, Romford, RM5 3BL
Tel: 01708-743795 **Fax:** 01708-743795
E-mail: dsmith70@ntlworld.com
Directors: D. Smith (Prop)
No.of Employees: 1 - 10 **Product Groups:** 37, 67

Security Shutters Ltd
Unit 2 Brooklands Approach, Romford, RM1 1DX
Tel: 01708-722334 **Fax:** 01708-750900
E-mail: john@securityshutters.entadsl.com
Website: http://www.securityshutters.com
Directors: J. Fagg (Dir)
Immediate Holding Company: SECURITY SHUTTERS LIMITED
Registration no: 03813124 **Date established:** 1999
No.of Employees: 1 - 10 **Product Groups:** 26, 35

Date of Accounts	May 11	May 10	May 09
Working Capital	41	-7	73
Fixed Assets	103	105	107
Current Assets	323	232	318

Sigma Glass Repair
28 Myrtle Road, Romford, RM3 8XS
Tel: 07956-862479 **Fax:** 01708-721313
E-mail: info@sigmaglassrepair.co.uk
Website: http://www.sigmaglassrepair.co.uk
Directors: M. Green (Prop)
Date established: 2000 **No.of Employees:** 1 - 10 **Product Groups:** 52

Silverhook Ltd
Silverhook House Bates Road, Romford, RM3 0JH
Tel: 01708-330500 **Fax:** 01708-340854
E-mail: 520@wipers.co.uk
Website: http://www.silverhook.co.uk
Directors: J. Iszatt (Fin), P. Iszatt (MD)
Managers: M. Iszatt (Tech Serv Mgr), R. Lewis (Sales Prom Mgr)
Immediate Holding Company: WARE MOTORAMA LIMITED
Registration no: 01382591 **Date established:** 1978
No.of Employees: 21 - 50 **Product Groups:** 31, 32, 37, 39, 40, 49, 61, 66, 68

Date of Accounts	May 12	May 11	May 10
Working Capital	769	794	-23
Fixed Assets	650	662	690
Current Assets	1m	1m	2m

Simply Umbrellas
17 Hampstead Gardens Chadwell Heath, Romford, RM6 4FE
Tel: 020-8598 2811
E-mail: gina@simplyumbrellas.co.uk
Website: http://www.simplyumbrellas.co.uk
Directors: G. Kemp (Prop)
No.of Employees: 1 - 10 **Product Groups:** 23, 24, 63

Solmedia Laboratory Supplies
6 The Parade Colchester Road, Romford, RM3 0AQ
Tel: 01708-343334 **Fax:** 01708-372785
E-mail: labsupplies@solmedialtd.com
Directors: D. Wallach (MD), N. Wallach (Sales & Mktg)
Registration no: 00292784 **VAT No.:** GB 248 1816 50
Date established: 1934 **Turnover:** £250,000 - £500,000
No.of Employees: 1 - 10 **Product Groups:** 30, 33, 38, 42, 63, 65, 67

Starna Industries Ltd
31-33 Station Road Chadwell Heath, Romford, RM6 4BL
Tel: 020-8599 5115 **Fax:** 020-8599 0707
E-mail: info@starnaindustries.co.uk
Website: http://www.starna.co.uk
Directors: A. Hulme (Dir), A. Hares (Fin)
Immediate Holding Company: STARNA INDUSTRIES LIMITED
Registration no: 02813452 **VAT No.:** 645 9133 24 **Date established:** 1993
Turnover: Up to £250,000 **No.of Employees:** 1 - 10 **Product Groups:** 40

Survey Express Services
Unit 3c Tonbridge Works Tonbridge Road, Romford, RM3 8TS
Tel: 01708-381525 **Fax:** 01708-381338
E-mail: romford@surveyexpress.co.uk
Website: http://www.surveyexpress.co.uk
Directors: P. Harden (Co Sec), S. Gennings (MD)
Ultimate Holding Company: WIMLONE LIMITED
Immediate Holding Company: SURVEY EXPRESS SERVICES (N.W.) LTD.
Registration no: 02353424 **Date established:** 1989
No.of Employees: 1 - 10 **Product Groups:** 38

Team Apogee
77 Cedar Road, Romford, RM7 7JS
Tel: 01708-762309 **Fax:** 01708-509712
E-mail: mail@teamapogee.com
Website: http://www.teamapogee.com
Directors: A. Pybus (MD)
Immediate Holding Company: TEAM APOGEE LIMITED
Registration no: 05038287 **Date established:** 2004
Turnover: Up to £250,000 **No.of Employees:** 1 - 10 **Product Groups:** 80

Date of Accounts	Jan 09	Jan 08	Jan 07
Pre Tax Profit/Loss	-10	-9	N/A
Working Capital	-35	-24	-22
Fixed Assets	1	1	1
Current Assets	-2	1	N/A

Vermikil Pest Control Services Ltd
PO Box 3049, Romford, RM3 7BQ
Tel: 0800-056 8834 **Fax:** 0800-056 8835
E-mail: contact@vermikil.com
Website: http://www.vermikil.com
Directors: T. Basri (MD)
Immediate Holding Company: VERMIKIL PEST CONTROL SERVICES LIMITED
Registration no: 05109906 **Date established:** 2004
No.of Employees: 1 - 10 **Product Groups:** 52

Date of Accounts	Mar 11	Mar 09	Mar 08
Working Capital	-9	-7	-6
Fixed Assets	9	8	7
Current Assets	28	26	25

Saffron Walden

Acrokool Ltd
1 Veerman Park Thaxted Road, Saffron Walden, CB10 2UP
Tel: 01799-513631 **Fax:** 01799-513635
E-mail: roger.moore@acrokool.com
Website: http://www.acrokool.com
Directors: R. Moore (MD)
Managers: D. Selek (I.T. Exec)
Immediate Holding Company: ACROKOOL LIMITED
Registration no: 01859195 **Date established:** 1984 **Turnover:** £1m - £2m
No.of Employees: 1 - 10 **Product Groups:** 33, 36, 40, 83

Date of Accounts	Sep 07	Sep 06	Sep 05
Working Capital	-30	19	53
Fixed Assets	466	475	485
Current Assets	410	346	340
Current Liabilities	439	326	287

Acrow Galvanising Ltd (Wedge Group Galvanizing)
Unit 4 Commercial Centre Ashdon Road, Saffron Walden, CB10 2NH
Tel: 01799-522219 **Fax:** 01799-522447
E-mail: nick.hasler@wedge-galv.co.uk
Website: http://www.wedge-galv.co.uk
Bank(s): Barclays
Directors: N. Hasler (MD)
Managers: J. Nicholsan (Sales Prom Mgr), S. Porter
Immediate Holding Company: B.E. WEDGE HOLDINGS LTD
Registration no: 01414982 **No.of Employees:** 21 - 50 **Product Groups:** 48

Audix Systems Ltd
Station Road Wendens Ambo, Saffron Walden, CB11 4LG
Tel: 01799-540888 **Fax:** 01799-541618
E-mail: sales@tepg.com
Website: http://www.tepg.com
Bank(s): Barclays
Directors: M. Stewart (Fin)
Managers: E. Moses (Sales Admin)
Immediate Holding Company: Thorn Security Ltd
Registration no: 00443219 **VAT No.:** GB 754 5301 40
Turnover: £2m - £5m **No.of Employees:** 51 - 100 **Product Groups:** 37

C P S International
78 High Street, Saffron Walden, CB10 1EE
Tel: 01223-890111 **Fax:** 01223-890222
E-mail: info@pack-track.com
Website: http://www.cps-int.com
Directors: A. Streeter (Dir), R. Ashton (Dir)
Managers: G. Hill (Research & Deve), K. Imai
Registration no: 02804691 **VAT No.:** GB 599 7448 55
Date established: 2003 **Turnover:** Up to £250,000
No.of Employees: 1 - 10 **Product Groups:** 84, 85

Date of Accounts	Mar 07	Sep 05
Fixed Assets	2	3
Current Assets	12	16
Current Liabilities	12	17

Cambridge Rapid Assembly Ltd
Unit 46 Shire Hill, Saffron Walden, CB11 3AQ
Tel: 01799-525982 **Fax:** 01799-521686
E-mail: jeremy@cambridgerapid.co.uk
Website: http://www.cambridgerapid.co.uk
Directors: E. Cornell (Fin)
Managers: R. Kidd (Prod Mgr)
Immediate Holding Company: CAMBRIDGE RAPID ASSEMBLY LIMITED
Registration no: 01694756 **VAT No.:** GB 453 3561 54
Date established: 1983 **Turnover:** £500,000 - £1m
No.of Employees: 1 - 10 **Product Groups:** 48

Date of Accounts	Mar 11	Mar 10	Mar 09
Working Capital	9	6	6
Fixed Assets	N/A	N/A	1
Current Assets	114	107	98

Camnet Data Communications Ltd
Bulse Grange Wendens Ambo, Saffron Walden, CB11 4JT
Tel: 0845-460 3602 **Fax:** 0800-007 3275
E-mail: james@camnet-communications.co.uk
Website: http://www.camnet-communications.co.uk
Directors: J. Whitby (Prop)
Registration no: 05286073 **No.of Employees:** 1 - 10 **Product Groups:** 37, 52, 67, 84

Diamond Engineering Ltd
Shire Hill, Saffron Walden, CB11 3AQ
Tel: 01799-523588 **Fax:** 01799-513381
E-mail: sales@diamond-engineering.co.uk
Website: http://www.diamond-engineering.co.uk
Directors: R. Hess (Dir)
Immediate Holding Company: DIAMOND ENGINEERING LTD
Registration no: 01474521 **Date established:** 1980 **Turnover:** £2m - £5m
No.of Employees: 11 - 20 **Product Groups:** 29, 30, 33, 34, 35, 36, 38, 40, 45, 46, 48, 84, 85

Date of Accounts	Dec 11	Dec 10	Dec 09
Working Capital	860	710	772
Fixed Assets	629	648	544
Current Assets	1m	857	970

European Emc Products Ltd
Unit 8 Saffron Business Centre Elizabeth Close, Saffron Walden, CB10 2NL
Tel: 01799-523073 **Fax:** 01799-521191
E-mail: info@euro-emc.co.uk
Website: http://www.euro-emc.co.uk
Directors: R. King (Fin), I. King (MD)
Immediate Holding Company: EUROPEAN EMC PRODUCTS LIMITED
Registration no: 03209118 **VAT No.:** GB 676 5479 78
Date established: 1996 **Turnover:** £5m - £10m **No.of Employees:** 1 - 10
Product Groups: 35, 37, 40, 85

Date of Accounts	Jun 11	Jun 10	Jun 09
Working Capital	-78	9	224
Fixed Assets	16	27	34
Current Assets	680	472	1m

European Technical Sales Ltd
Chroma House Shire Hill, Saffron Walden, CB11 3AQ
Tel: 01799-508076 **Fax:** 01799-508024
E-mail: etsltd@globalnet.co.uk
Website: http://www.eurotechspares.com
Directors: S. Pancewicz (Dir)
Immediate Holding Company: EUROPEAN TECHNICAL SALES LIMITED
Registration no: 02440665 **Date established:** 1989
No.of Employees: 1 - 10 **Product Groups:** 40, 41, 42, 44, 45, 46, 47, 67, 68, 84

Date of Accounts	Dec 11	Dec 10	Dec 09
Working Capital	55	51	46
Fixed Assets	N/A	1	2
Current Assets	208	151	183

High & Mighty Seating Ltd
40 Winstanley Road, Saffron Walden, CB11 3EQ
Tel: 0800-096 0414
E-mail: enquiries@highandmightyseating.com
Website: http://www.highandmightyseating.com
Directors: P. Boland (MD)
Turnover: £500,000 - £1m **No.of Employees:** 1 - 10 **Product Groups:** 26

Holroyd Components
Shire Hill, Saffron Walden, CB11 3AQ
Tel: 01799-523177 **Fax:** 01799-513714
E-mail: emily@holroydcomponents.com
Website: http://www.holroydcomponents.com
Bank(s): Lloyds TSB Bank plc
Directors: D. Taylor (MD), J. Taylor (Fin)
Managers: E. Gilson
Immediate Holding Company: HOLROYD COMPONENTS LIMITED
Registration no: 01083975 **VAT No.:** GB 213 7124 03
Date established: 1972 **Turnover:** £5m - £10m
No.of Employees: 51 - 100 **Product Groups:** 29, 33, 37, 40

Date of Accounts	Nov 11	Nov 10	Nov 09
Sales Turnover	9m	8m	N/A
Pre Tax Profit/Loss	1m	2m	N/A
Working Capital	3m	2m	3m
Fixed Assets	671	537	579
Current Assets	4m	4m	4m
Current Liabilities	960	1m	N/A

Lab Craft Ltd
Thunderley Hall Barns Thaxted Road, Wimbish, Saffron Walden, CB10 2UT
Tel: 01799-513434 **Fax:** 01799-513437
E-mail: sales@labcraft.co.uk
Website: http://www.labcraft.co.uk
Bank(s): National Westminster Bank Plc
Directors: N. Lescombe (MD), R. Akhtar (Fin)
Managers: L. Rybicki (Mktg Serv Mgr), D. Ayres (Purch Mgr)
Immediate Holding Company: LAB-CRAFT LIMITED
Registration no: 00561371 **VAT No.:** GB 246 3743 53
Date established: 1956 **Turnover:** £2m - £5m **No.of Employees:** 21 - 50
Product Groups: 37, 39

Date of Accounts	Sep 11	Sep 10	Sep 09
Working Capital	1m	1m	977
Fixed Assets	2m	1m	1m
Current Assets	2m	1m	1m

Norwood Group
Westbrook House Shire Hill, Saffron Walden, CB11 3AQ
Tel: 01799-504000
Directors: J. Temple (Ptnr)
Immediate Holding Company: R.B. RADLEY & COMPANY LIMITED
Date established: 1966 **No.of Employees:** 1 - 10 **Product Groups:** 35, 36

Date of Accounts	Dec 11	Dec 10	Dec 09
Working Capital	820	1m	912
Fixed Assets	846	241	239
Current Assets	2m	2m	2m

Pedley Furniture International Ltd
Shire Hill, Saffron Walden, CB11 3AL
Tel: 01799-522461 **Fax:** 01799-543403
E-mail: alan.pedley@pedley.com
Website: http://www.pedley.com
Bank(s): National Westminster
Directors: A. Pedley (Dir), A. Pedley (MD), M. Pedley (Ch)
Managers: D. Jamsma (Personnel)
Immediate Holding Company: PEDLEY FURNITURE INTERNATIONAL LIMITED
Registration no: 00596868 **VAT No.:** GB 424 8258 45
Date established: 1958 **Turnover:** £5m - £10m
No.of Employees: 51 - 100 **Product Groups:** 26, 49

Date of Accounts	Mar 09	Mar 08	Mar 07
Pre Tax Profit/Loss	-416	216	273
Working Capital	-386	118	1m
Fixed Assets	4m	4m	3m
Current Assets	2m	2m	3m
Current Liabilities	1m	950	1m

Plextek Ltd
London Road Great Chesterford, Saffron Walden, CB10 1NY
Tel: 01799-533200 **Fax:** 01799-533201
E-mail: post@plextek.com
Website: http://www.plextek.com
Bank(s): Barclays, Cambridge
Directors: S. Cassia (Sales & Mktg), D. Cox (Fin), C. Smithers (I.T. Dir), B. Garland (Tech Serv)
Managers: M. Brown (Buyer), J. Nicoll (Personnel)
Immediate Holding Company: PLEXTEK LIMITED
Registration no: 02305889 **Date established:** 1988
Turnover: £20m - £50m **No.of Employees:** 101 - 250
Product Groups: 44, 80, 85

Date of Accounts	Mar 11	Mar 10	Mar 09
Sales Turnover	29m	21m	31m
Pre Tax Profit/Loss	683	-1m	875
Working Capital	-3m	-2m	112
Fixed Assets	6m	5m	4m
Current Assets	5m	4m	6m
Current Liabilities	3m	2m	2m

Radleys
5 The Shires Shire Hill, Saffron Walden, CB11 3AZ
Tel: 01799-513320 **Fax:** 01799-513283
E-mail: sales@radleys.co.uk
Website: http://www.radleys.co.uk
Bank(s): Lloyds TSB Bank plc

Directors: J. Goodie (Fin)
Managers: H. Radley (Mktg Serv Mgr), S. Moorhouse, G. Cowell (Sales Prom Mgr)
Registration no: 00889911 **VAT No.:** GB 213 8100 12
Turnover: £1m - £2m **No.of Employees:** 21 - 50 **Product Groups:** 33, 38, 40, 42, 63, 66, 67

Ridgeons

Commercial Centre Ashdon Road, Saffron Walden, CB10 2NQ
Tel: 01799-583150 **Fax:** 01799-583039
E-mail: hguntrip@ridgeons.net
Website: http://www.ridgeons.co.uk
Managers: H. Guntrip (District Mgr), J. Dear (Tech Serv Mgr), B. Illsley
Ultimate Holding Company: RIDGEON GROUP LTD
Immediate Holding Company: RIDGEONS SUPPORT SERVICES LTD
Registration no: 00428870 **VAT No.:** GB 599 6045 82
Turnover: £2m - £5m **No.of Employees:** 101 - 250 **Product Groups:** 66

Date of Accounts	Dec 08	Dec 07
Sales Turnover	3711	3375
Pre Tax Profit/Loss	2114	2215
Working Capital	-17428	-19261
Fixed Assets	32771	32807
Current Assets	2318	123
Current Liabilities	19745	19385
Total Share Capital	20	20
ROCE% (Return on Capital Employed)	13.8	16.4
ROT% (Return on Turnover)	57.0	65.6

T C Fixings

Unit 39 Shirehill Industrial Estate, Saffron Walden, CB11 3AQ
Tel: 01799-520640 **Fax:** 01799-520744
E-mail: sales@tcfixings.co.uk
Website: http://www.tcfixings.co.uk
Directors: T. Collins (Dir)
Registration no: 00889911 **Date established:** 1966
No.of Employees: 1 - 10 **Product Groups:** 35

Team Consulting Ltd

Abbey Barns Ickleton, Saffron Walden, CB10 1SX
Tel: 01799-532700 **Fax:** 01799-532701
E-mail: info@team-consulting.com
Website: http://www.team-consulting.com
Bank(s): Lloyds TSB, Cambridge
Directors: C. Matthews (Dir)
Managers: N. Cooper, S. Palmer (Tech Serv Mgr), C. Corfield, C. Shaw
Ultimate Holding Company: TEAM HOLDINGS (UK) LIMITED
Immediate Holding Company: TEAM CONSULTING (UK) LIMITED
Registration no: 03023473 **VAT No.:** GB 676 5186 93
Date established: 1995 **Turnover:** £2m - £5m **No.of Employees:** 21 - 50
Product Groups: 85

The Telecottage

1 Haggers Close Great Chesterford, Saffron Walden, CB10 1QN
Tel: 0870-4441352 **Fax:** 0870-1313270
E-mail: info@telecottage.net
Website: http://www.telecottage.net
Managers: P. Hickmott (Mgr)
No.of Employees: 1 - 10 **Product Groups:** 37, 44, 67

Willis Toys Ltd

Church Lane Widdington, Saffron Walden, CB11 3SF
Tel: 01799-541850 **Fax:** 01799-541864
E-mail: tim@willistoys.co.uk
Website: http://www.willistoys.co.uk
Directors: T. Willis (MD)
Immediate Holding Company: WILLIS TOYS LIMITED
Registration no: 01121359 **VAT No.:** GB 214 5131 10
Date established: 1973 **Turnover:** Up to £250,000
No.of Employees: 1 - 10 **Product Groups:** 65

Date of Accounts	Jun 08	Jun 07	Jun 06
Sales Turnover	N/A	170	128
Pre Tax Profit/Loss	N/A	26	5
Working Capital	76	59	34
Fixed Assets	2	N/A	N/A
Current Assets	123	103	67
Current Liabilities	46	44	34
Total Share Capital	20	20	20
ROCE% (Return on Capital Employed)		43.1	14.8
ROT% (Return on Turnover)		15.1	3.9

Working Titles

2 The Boys British School East Street, Saffron Walden, CB10 1LS
Tel: 01799-525257 **Fax:** 020-8504 5588
E-mail: andy.sivell@workingtitles.com
Website: http://www.workingtitles.com
Directors: A. Sivell (Prop)
Immediate Holding Company: WORKING TITLES PUBLISHING LIMITED
Registration no: 03553875 **Date established:** 1998
Turnover: Up to £250,000 **No.of Employees:** 1 - 10 **Product Groups:** 28

Date of Accounts	Mar 11	Mar 10	Mar 09
Working Capital	-2	-2	11
Fixed Assets	2	2	3
Current Assets	4	4	26

South Ockendon

E B S Safety Netting

Bretts Farm Romford Road, Aveley, South Ockendon, RM15 4XD
Tel: 01708-860341 **Fax:** 01708-865701
E-mail: info@safety-netting.net
Website: http://www.safety-netting.net
Directors: M. Spiers (MD)
Registration no: 05229165 **VAT No.:** GB 291 6649 25
Date established: 1979 **Turnover:** £250,000 - £500,000
No.of Employees: 1 - 10 **Product Groups:** 23, 35, 52

Howard Tenens London Ltd

Tenens House South Ockenden Industrial Park, South Ockendon, RM15 6RL
Tel: 01708-854411 **Fax:** 01708-859485
E-mail: brian.chart@tenens.com
Website: http://www.tenens.com
Directors: B. Chart (Sales)
Managers: S. Coombes (Site Co-ord)
Ultimate Holding Company: HOWARD TENENS LIMITED
Immediate Holding Company: HOWARD TENENS (LONDON) LIMITED
Registration no: 03885123 **Date established:** 1999
Turnover: £20m - £50m **No.of Employees:** 251 - 500
Product Groups: 72, 77, 84

Date of Accounts	Sep 11	Sep 10	Sep 09
Sales Turnover	7m	9m	9m
Pre Tax Profit/Loss	50	-1	179
Working Capital	17	-117	318
Fixed Assets	342	450	16
Current Assets	2m	3m	2m
Current Liabilities	2m	2m	817

K P Event Catering Services

14 Rosie's Way Buckles Lane, South Ockendon, RM15 6RW
Tel: 01708-855998
E-mail: info@123kpc.co.uk
Website: http://www.123kpc.co.uk
Directors: P. Cooper (Prop)
Date established: 1986 **No.of Employees:** 21 - 50 **Product Groups:** 81

Labels Reloaded

6 Daiglen Drive, South Ockendon, RM15 5RN
Tel: 08452-261253
E-mail: sales@labelsreloaded.co.uk
Website: http://www.labelsreloaded.co.uk
Directors: R. Gunner (Prop)
Date established: 2004 **Turnover:** Up to £250,000
No.of Employees: 1 - 10 **Product Groups:** 27, 28, 30, 36, 37, 39, 42

Princia Shipping Ltd

Unit C1a Purfleet Industrial Park London Road, Aveley, South Ockendon, RM15 4YA
Tel: 01708-860848 **Fax:** 01708-867765
E-mail: princia@princia.fsnet.co.uk
Directors: K. McFarland (MD), K. McFarland (Dir)
Ultimate Holding Company: BUCKLE MANAGEMENT & HOLDINGS LIMITED
Immediate Holding Company: PRINCIA SHIPPING LIMITED
Registration no: 00950141 **Date established:** 1969
Turnover: £250,000 - £500,000 **No.of Employees:** 1 - 10
Product Groups: 76

Date of Accounts	Apr 11	Apr 10	Apr 09
Working Capital	261	281	282
Fixed Assets	1	5	8
Current Assets	358	336	360

Spectrum Engineering & Transmission Company Ltd

Unit 43 Purfleet Industrial Park London Road, Aveley, South Ockendon, RM15 4YA
Tel: 01708-861718 **Fax:** 01708-867540
E-mail: sales@spectrum-engineering.co.uk
Website: http://www.spectrum-engineering.co.uk
Directors: G. Caddy (MD), V. Caddy (Co Sec)
Immediate Holding Company: SPECTRUM ENGINEERING & TRANSMISSION COMPANY LIMITED
Registration no: 02676128 **VAT No.:** 436 4616 46 **Date established:** 1992
Turnover: £1m - £2m **No.of Employees:** 1 - 10 **Product Groups:** 30, 32, 33, 35

Date of Accounts	Mar 11	Mar 10	Mar 09
Working Capital	308	246	225
Fixed Assets	113	115	115
Current Assets	1m	999	721

Tudor Tea & Coffee

Unit 31-35 Thurrock Commercial Centre Juliet Way, Aveley, South Ockendon, RM15 4YD
Tel: 01708-866966 **Fax:** 01708-861709
E-mail: sales@tudorcoffee.co.uk
Website: http://www.tudorcoffee.co.uk
Directors: N. Klos (Prop)
Managers: R. Court (Warehouse Mgr), J. Alison
Immediate Holding Company: TUDOR TEA AND COFFEE LIMITED
Registration no: 03010729 **Date established:** 1995
No.of Employees: 11 - 20 **Product Groups:** 20, 27, 40, 49, 62, 63, 67, 69, 86

Southend On Sea

Akeron UK Ltd

15 Terminal Close Shoeburyness, Southend On Sea, SS3 9BN
Tel: 01702-297101 **Fax:** 01702-297101
E-mail: akeron@talktalkbusiness.net
Website: http://www.akeron.co.uk
Directors: J. Lemel (Fin), N. Lemel (MD)
Immediate Holding Company: AKERON (U.K.) LIMITED
Registration no: 00624709 **VAT No.:** GB 247 8638 19
Date established: 1959 **Turnover:** Up to £250,000
No.of Employees: 1 - 10 **Product Groups:** 23, 25, 30, 31, 32, 33, 34, 35, 36, 37, 38, 39, 46, 49, 66, 67

Date of Accounts	Jun 11	Jun 10	Jun 09
Sales Turnover	75	N/A	48
Pre Tax Profit/Loss	5	N/A	-4
Working Capital	22	21	11
Fixed Assets	59	59	59
Current Assets	37	30	27
Current Liabilities	2	N/A	1

Alljay Plastics Sheet Sales

321 Sutton Road, Southend On Sea, SS2 5PF
Tel: 01702-600320 **Fax:** 01702-600325
E-mail: alljayplastics@aol.com
Directors: J. Gooch (Ptnr)
Date established: 2002 **No.of Employees:** 1 - 10 **Product Groups:** 30, 39, 40

Alplus

Unit 1 Lancaster Business Park Aviation Way, Southend Airport, Southend On Sea, SS2 6UN
Tel: 01702-541000 **Fax:** 01702-541100
E-mail: bhood@alplus.com
Website: http://www.alplus.com
Bank(s): Barclays, Leigh-on-Sea
Directors: B. Hood (MD), T. Atkinson (Fin)
Managers: H. Davidson (Mktg Serv Mgr), A. Atkinson (Chief Mgr)
Immediate Holding Company: ALPLAS LIMITED
Registration no: 00851974 **VAT No.:** GB 251 2422 04
Date established: 1965 **Turnover:** £2m - £5m **No.of Employees:** 21 - 50
Product Groups: 27, 30, 35, 49, 81

Date of Accounts	Dec 11	Dec 10	Dec 09
Working Capital	2m	2m	2m
Fixed Assets	231	238	96
Current Assets	3m	2m	2m

Aquarium Masters

62 Barnstaple Road Office Only Thorpe Bay, Southend On Sea, SS1 3PA
Tel: 07767-612603
E-mail: info@aquariummasters.co.uk
Website: http://www.aquariummasters.co.uk
Directors: J. Marsden (Prop)
Managers: J. Marsden (Chief Mgr)
Date established: 2001 **No.of Employees:** 1 - 10 **Product Groups:** 62

Asbestos Environmental Services

12 Stock Road, Southend On Sea, SS2 5QF
Tel: 01702-611154 **Fax:** 01702-611391
E-mail: enquiries@aesltd.org
Website: http://www.aesltd.org
Managers: D. Deakin (Chief Mgr)
Immediate Holding Company: Asbestos Environmental Services Ltd
Registration no: 04328532 **Turnover:** £1m - £2m
No.of Employees: 1 - 10 **Product Groups:** 40, 85

Date of Accounts	Apr 08	Oct 06	Oct 05
Sales Turnover	N/A	1m	2m
Pre Tax Profit/Loss	N/A	-260	59
Working Capital	-123	-237	-16
Fixed Assets	136	120	147
Current Assets	457	337	543
Current Liabilities	580	574	559

B K Electronics

Unit 1-3-4-5 Comet Way, Southend On Sea, SS2 6TR
Tel: 01702-527572 **Fax:** 01702-420243
E-mail: sales@bkelec.com
Website: http://www.bkelec.com
Directors: B. Pearne (Ptnr)
Date established: 1979 **No.of Employees:** 1 - 10 **Product Groups:** 37

B P F Plastics

33 The Vintners Temple Farm Industrial Estate, Southend On Sea, SS2 5RZ
Tel: 01702-616224 **Fax:** 01702-616224
E-mail: brian@bpf6r.freeserve.co.uk
Website: http://www.bpf6r.freeserve.co.uk
Directors: B. Facey (Prop)
Turnover: Up to £250,000 **No.of Employees:** 1 - 10 **Product Groups:** 30, 42

Leigh Baxter Associates Ltd

17-18 Robert Leonard Industrial Estate Stock Road, Southend On Sea, SS2 5QD
Tel: 01702-460970 **Fax:** 01702-600544
E-mail: sales@leighbaxter.co.uk
Website: http://www.leighbaxter.co.uk
Directors: N. Mallard (Sales)
Immediate Holding Company: LEIGH BAXTER ASSOCIATES LIMITED
Registration no: 01328596 **VAT No.:** GB 328 4356 49
Date established: 1977 **Turnover:** £250,000 - £500,000
No.of Employees: 1 - 10 **Product Groups:** 24, 29, 30

Date of Accounts	Apr 11	Apr 10	Apr 09
Working Capital	113	128	137
Fixed Assets	16	14	18
Current Assets	282	270	260

Benson Lund Ltd (a division of Ipeco Holdings Ltd)

Aviation Way Southend Airport, Southend On Sea, SS2 6UN
Tel: 01702-547683 **Fax:** 01702-530884
E-mail: sales@ipeco.co.uk
Website: http://www.ipeco.co.uk
Bank(s): National Westminster Bank Plc
Directors: K. Ross (Fin)
Managers: G. Naylor (I.T. Exec), D. Highstead (Personnel), P. Hares (Purch Mgr)
Ultimate Holding Company: CASTLEDON LTD
Immediate Holding Company: BENSON LUND LIMITED
Registration no: 02007983 **VAT No.:** GB 250 3726 82
Date established: 1986 **Turnover:** £20m - £50m
No.of Employees: 21 - 50 **Product Groups:** 26, 39

Bright's Locksmiths Ltd

41 Alexandra Street, Southend On Sea, SS1 1BW
Tel: 01702-346274 **Fax:** 01702-391095
E-mail: brightslocksmith@btconnect.com
Website: http://www.brightslocksmithsltd.co.uk
Directors: S. Wakefield (Dir)
Immediate Holding Company: BRIGHTS LOCKSMITHS LIMITED
Registration no: 05028019 **Date established:** 2004
Turnover: Up to £250,000 **No.of Employees:** 1 - 10 **Product Groups:** 36, 49

Date of Accounts	Jun 11	Jun 10	Jun 09
Working Capital	-18	-18	-27
Fixed Assets	108	119	128
Current Assets	-18	85	74

Cadogan (A Subsidiary Of A. Oppenheimer & Co. Ltd)

20 Vanguard Way Shoeburyness, Southend On Sea, SS3 9RA
Tel: 01702-98888 **Fax:** 01702-294225
E-mail: cad@oppenheimers.co.uk
Website: http://www.oppenheimers.co.uk
Bank(s): Barclays
Directors: M. Adler (Ch)
Ultimate Holding Company: A.OPPENHEIMER & CO. LIMITED
Immediate Holding Company: CADOGAN INVESTMENTS LIMITED
Registration no: 00231744 **VAT No.:** GB 243 2555 77
Date established: 2028 **Turnover:** £1m - £2m **No.of Employees:** 11 - 20
Product Groups: 49

Date of Accounts	Feb 08	Feb 11	Feb 10
Working Capital	2	1	1
Current Assets	2	2	2
Current Liabilities	1	N/A	1

Chris Miller Limited
29 Holt Farm Way Rochford, Southend On Sea, SS4 1SB
Tel: 01702-540464 **Fax:** 01273-239218
E-mail: chris@designandillustration.co.uk
Website: http://www.designandillustration.co.uk
Directors: C. Millar (Prop), C. millert (Dir)
Registration no: 04896462 **Date established:** 2006
No.of Employees: 1 - 10 **Product Groups:** 44

D C Developments
13 Rosshill Industrial Park Sutton Road, Southend On Sea, SS2 5PZ
Tel: 01702-610964 **Fax:** 01702-610964
E-mail: dencornell@dcdevelopments.com
Website: http://www.dcdevelopments.com
Directors: D. Cornell (Prop)
Date established: 2001 **No.of Employees:** 1 - 10 **Product Groups:** 36, 37, 38

Eastern Security Ltd
172 North Avenue, Southend On Sea, SS2 4EU
Tel: 01702-467850 **Fax:** 01702-460178
Website: http://www.easternsec.co.uk
Directors: A. Lathem (Dir), R. Latham (MD)
Immediate Holding Company: EASTERN SECURITY LTD
Registration no: 04236821 **Date established:** 2001
No.of Employees: 1 - 10 **Product Groups:** 36, 40, 52, 67

Elite Digital Ltd
14 Rosshill Industrial Park Sutton Road, Southend On Sea, SS2 5PZ
Tel: 01702-600650 **Fax:** 01702-600630
E-mail: sales@elite-digital.co.uk
Website: http://www.elitedesignandprint.co.uk
Directors: J. Lawrence (Dir)
Date established: 2002 **No.of Employees:** 1 - 10 **Product Groups:** 23, 28, 44, 80, 81

Essex Injection Mouldings Ltd
Unit 15 Craftsman Square Temple Farm Industrial Estate, Southend On Sea, SS2 5RH
Tel: 01702-461160 **Fax:** 01702-600805
E-mail: ma@essexinjectionmouldings.co.uk
Website: http://www.essexinjectionmouldings.co.uk
Bank(s): Barclays, Rayleigh
Directors: P. Measures (MD), M. Edwards (Fin)
Immediate Holding Company: ESSEX INJECTION MOULDINGS LIMITED
Registration no: 02137067 **VAT No.:** GB 452 0991 50
Date established: 1987 **Turnover:** £1m - £2m **No.of Employees:** 21 - 50
Product Groups: 36, 48

Date of Accounts	Nov 11	Nov 10	Nov 09
Working Capital	59	-17	-106
Fixed Assets	146	122	125
Current Assets	449	460	288

Estuary Automation Ltd
40 Shoebury Avenue Shoeburyness, Southend On Sea, SS3 9BH
Tel: 01702-293901 **Fax:** 01702-297318
E-mail: estaut@netscapeonline.co.uk
Website: http://www.estuaryautomation.co.uk
Directors: D. Wall (MD)
Immediate Holding Company: ESTUARY AUTOMATION LIMITED
Registration no: 01001147 **Date established:** 1971
Turnover: Up to £250,000 **No.of Employees:** 1 - 10 **Product Groups:** 35, 42, 45, 46, 84

Date of Accounts	Jan 12	Jan 11	Jan 10
Sales Turnover	N/A	N/A	99
Pre Tax Profit/Loss	N/A	N/A	-22
Working Capital	39	6	N/A
Fixed Assets	41	43	45
Current Assets	92	73	45
Current Liabilities	N/A	N/A	37

Euro Group UK
7 Coopers Way Temple Farm Business Park, Southend On Sea, SS2 5TE
Tel: 01702-614444
E-mail: grahame@essexupholstery.com
Website: http://www.euro-group-uk.com
Directors: G. Jenkins (MD)
Registration no: 3670538 **Date established:** 1985 **Turnover:**
No.of Employees: 11 - 20 **Product Groups:** 26

Flying Toys Ltd
9 The Vanguards Vanguard Way Shoeburyness, Southend On Sea, SS3 9QJ
Tel: 01702-295110 **Fax:** 01702-294640
E-mail: sales@flyingtoys.com
Website: http://www.flyingtoys.com
Directors: D. Rawlins (Dir)
Immediate Holding Company: FLYING TOYS LIMITED
Registration no: 04820527 **VAT No.:** 311 6586 71 **Date established:** 2003
No.of Employees: 11 - 20 **Product Groups:** 49

Date of Accounts	Jul 12	Jul 11	Jul 10
Sales Turnover	800	445	544
Pre Tax Profit/Loss	54	-53	-87
Working Capital	85	73	98
Fixed Assets	34	37	40
Current Assets	355	153	164
Current Liabilities	90	8	5

Frith Flexible Packaging Ltd
1 The Forum Coopers Way, Temple Farm Industrial Estate, Southend On Sea, SS2 5TE
Tel: 01702-463566 **Fax:** 01702-616954
E-mail: davidw@macleansfoils.co.uk
Website: http://www.sfw.co.uk
Bank(s): HSBC Bank plc
Directors: D. Watson (MD)
Ultimate Holding Company: A M (HOLDINGS) LIMITED
Immediate Holding Company: FRITH'S FLEXIBLE PACKAGING LIMITED
Registration no: 00647804 **Date established:** 1960
Turnover: £500,000 - £1m **No.of Employees:** 21 - 50
Product Groups: 27, 28, 34

Date of Accounts	Feb 12	Feb 11	Feb 10
Sales Turnover	1m	844	882
Pre Tax Profit/Loss	80	3	-185
Working Capital	2m	2m	2m
Fixed Assets	421	442	520
Current Assets	3m	3m	3m
Current Liabilities	277	294	613

Gibli Com Ltd
Concord House Comet Way, Southend On Sea, SS2 6GD
Tel: 01702-425128 **Fax:** 07774-686428
E-mail: info@gibli.com
Website: http://gibli.com
Directors: C. Joynson (MD)
Immediate Holding Company: GIBLI.COM LTD
Registration no: 05366788 **Date established:** 2005
Turnover: Up to £250,000 **No.of Employees:** 1 - 10 **Product Groups:** 44

Date of Accounts	Feb 12	Feb 11	Feb 10
Working Capital	-39	-37	-32
Current Assets	2	2	2
Current Liabilities	N/A	N/A	1

Gifford Idustrial Finishers Ltd
1 The Vanguards Vanguard Way, Shoeburyness, Southend On Sea, SS3 9QJ
Tel: 01702-298954 **Fax:** 01702-298992
E-mail: dannygifford@fsmail.net
Website: http://www.haywardsfinishers.co.uk
Directors: D. Gifford (Prop)
Immediate Holding Company: HAYWARDS INDUSTRIAL FINISHERS LIMITED
Registration no: 06828201 **Date established:** 2009
No.of Employees: 1 - 10 **Product Groups:** 46, 48

Groms Garden Supplies Ltd
Unit 12 Parkside Centre Potters Way, Temple Farm Industrial Estate, Southend On Sea, SS2 5SJ
Tel: 01702-618556
E-mail: graham@groms-garden-supplies.co.uk
Website: http://www.groms-garden-supplies.co.uk
Managers: G. porteous (Chief Acct), T. Porteous ()
Registration no: 06718632 **Date established:** 2008
Turnover: Up to £250,000 **No.of Employees:** 1 - 10 **Product Groups:** 25

H F A Dolman
Rear of 34 Potters Way Temple Farm Industrial Estate, Southend On Sea, SS2 5SJ
Tel: 01702-461155 **Fax:** 01702-464177
E-mail: info@dolmangroup.co.uk
Website: http://www.dolmangroup.co.uk
Directors: K. Dolman (MD)
Registration no: 00579498 **VAT No.:** GB 250 3143 09
Turnover: £1m - £2m **No.of Employees:** 1 - 10 **Product Groups:** 51, 83

Adam Hall Ltd
3 The Cordwainers Temple Farm Industrial Estate, Southend On Sea, SS2 5RU
Tel: 01702-613922 **Fax:** 01702-617168
E-mail: sales@adamhall.co.uk
Website: http://www.adamhall.co.uk
Directors: A. Richardson (MD), I. Little (Fin)
Immediate Holding Company: ADAM HALL LTD.
Registration no: 01388340 **VAT No.:** GB 312 7525 80
Date established: 1978 **Turnover:** £2m - £5m **No.of Employees:** 1 - 10
Product Groups: 22, 25, 30, 35, 36, 37, 43, 49

Date of Accounts	Jun 12	Jun 11	Jun 10
Working Capital	417	1m	1m
Fixed Assets	4	15	54
Current Assets	547	1m	2m
Current Liabilities	N/A	N/A	298

Hellma UK Ltd
Cumberland House 24-28 Baxter Avenue, Southend On Sea, SS2 6HZ
Tel: 01702-333010 **Fax:** 01702-430652
E-mail: sales@hellma.co.uk
Website: http://www.hellma.co.uk
Directors: J. Grant (Dir)
Ultimate Holding Company: HELLMA HOLDING GMBH (GERMANY)
Immediate Holding Company: HELLMA UK LIMITED
Registration no: 00864109 **VAT No.:** GB 250 5988 42
Date established: 1965 **No.of Employees:** 1 - 10 **Product Groups:** 38

Date of Accounts	Dec 11	Dec 10	Dec 09
Working Capital	176	211	204
Fixed Assets	16	3	6
Current Assets	267	386	332

Herve Engineering Ltd
9 Towerfield Road Shoeburyness, Southend On Sea, SS3 9QE
Tel: 01702-293617 **Fax:** 01702-297410
E-mail: sales@herveengineering.com
Website: http://www.herveengineering.co.uk
Bank(s): Barclays, PO Box 1504 Southend, SS2 6XX
Directors: B. Herve (Co Sec), K. Herve (MD)
Ultimate Holding Company: L. HERVE LIMITED
Immediate Holding Company: HERVE ENGINEERING LIMITED
Registration no: 00162031 **VAT No.:** GB 730 6744 39
Date established: 2019 **Turnover:** £1m - £2m **No.of Employees:** 11 - 20
Product Groups: 35, 37, 46, 48

Date of Accounts	Dec 11	Dec 10	Dec 09
Sales Turnover	N/A	1m	788
Pre Tax Profit/Loss	N/A	116	-39
Working Capital	12	58	65
Fixed Assets	488	566	522
Current Assets	326	364	316
Current Liabilities	N/A	83	63

Hi-Tec Sports UK Ltd
Aviation Way, Southend On Sea, SS2 6GH
Tel: 01702-541741 **Fax:** 01702-547947
E-mail: mb@hitecsports.com
Website: http://www.hitecsports.com
Directors: I. Cameron (MD)
Ultimate Holding Company: SUNNINGDALE CORPORATION (BAHAMAS)
Immediate Holding Company: HI-TEC SPORTS PUBLIC LIMITED COMPANY
Registration no: 01159203 **Date established:** 1974
Turnover: £75m - £125m **No.of Employees:** 101 - 250
Product Groups: 22, 63

Date of Accounts	Dec 11	Dec 10	Dec 09
Sales Turnover	107m	106m	102m
Pre Tax Profit/Loss	-213	4m	3m
Working Capital	22m	15m	11m
Fixed Assets	2m	2m	2m
Current Assets	59m	61m	48m
Current Liabilities	8m	7m	10m

Hockley Enterprises Ltd
Grainger Road, Southend On Sea, SS2 5BZ
Tel: 01702-614067 **Fax:** 01702-462163
Website: http://www.hockleyelectroplaters.co.uk
Directors: L. Rainforth (MD)
Immediate Holding Company: HOCKLEY ENTERPRISES (ESSEX) LIMITED
Registration no: 01151428 **VAT No.:** GB 251 1467 84
Date established: 1973 **Turnover:** Up to £250,000
No.of Employees: 1 - 10 **Product Groups:** 48

Date of Accounts	Feb 11	Feb 10	Feb 09
Working Capital	60	70	69
Fixed Assets	5	7	27
Current Assets	102	106	108

A Howe Light Engineering
1 Priory Works Priory Cresent, Southend On Sea, SS2 6LD
Tel: 01702-611451 **Fax:** 01702-469078
E-mail: david.knight@steelfabricators1.co.uk
Website: http://www.steel-fabricators.co.uk
Directors: D. Knights (Snr Part)
Registration no: 05443507 **VAT No.:** GB 328 4585 34
Turnover: £250,000 - £500,000 **No.of Employees:** 1 - 10
Product Groups: 35, 48

I M S Ltd (South Essex Stockholders)
Metal Stock House Vanguard Way Shoeburyness, Southend On Sea, SS3 9RA
Tel: 01702-296955 **Fax:** 01702-296444
E-mail: sales@industrialmetal.co.uk
Website: http://www.industrialmetal.co.uk
Bank(s): National Westminster Bank Plc
Directors: G. Eyre (Pers), R. Rout (Dir)
Managers: N. Simpson (Fin Mgr), T. Gill (Tech Serv Mgr), P. Keogh (Sales & Mktg Mg)
Immediate Holding Company: IMS LIMITED
Registration no: 06677865 **VAT No.:** GB 251 3753 73
Date established: 2008 **Turnover:** £20m - £50m
No.of Employees: 101 - 250 **Product Groups:** 66

Ice Cool Refrigeration
26 Cranley Gardens Shoeburyness, Southend On Sea, SS3 9JP
Tel: 01702-291876 **Fax:** 01702-290503
E-mail: icecool_refrig@hotmail.com
Directors: S. Parker (Prop)
Date established: 1998 **No.of Employees:** 1 - 10 **Product Groups:** 36, 40

Inflite Southend Ltd
Aviation Way Southend Airport, Southend On Sea, SS2 6UN
Tel: 01702-542774 **Fax:** 01702-541534
E-mail: reception@inflite-southend.co.uk
Bank(s): Barclays Bank P.L.C., London
Directors: B. Peck (Dir)
Ultimate Holding Company: SWAN INVESTMENTS GROUP LIMITED
Immediate Holding Company: INFLITE (SOUTHEND) LIMITED
Registration no: 04356041 **VAT No.:** GB 760 2879 15
Date established: 2002 **Turnover:** £1m - £2m
No.of Employees: 101 - 250 **Product Groups:** 30, 31

Date of Accounts	Mar 11	Mar 10	Mar 09
Sales Turnover	7m	7m	6m
Pre Tax Profit/Loss	423	222	398
Working Capital	1m	935	806
Fixed Assets	422	410	387
Current Assets	3m	2m	3m
Current Liabilities	356	262	322

Ipe Co Holdings
Aviation Way Southend Airport, Southend On Sea, SS2 6UN
Tel: 01702-209258 **Fax:** 01702-542279
E-mail: sales@ipeco.co.uk
Website: http://www.ipeco.co.uk
Bank(s): National Westminster Bank Plc
Directors: K. Ross (Co Sec)
Managers: A. Elliott (Tech Serv Mgr), C. Martin (Purch Mgr)
Immediate Holding Company: CASTLEDON LTD
Registration no: 03384711 **VAT No.:** GB 250 3726 82
Date established: 1997 **Turnover:** £50m - £75m
No.of Employees: 501 - 1000 **Product Groups:** 68

Date of Accounts	Dec 11	Dec 10	Dec 09
Sales Turnover	55m	49m	56m
Pre Tax Profit/Loss	9m	979	4m
Working Capital	34m	28m	27m
Fixed Assets	12m	11m	12m
Current Assets	39m	32m	32m
Current Liabilities	2m	1m	2m

Jewson Ltd
Stock Road, Southend On Sea, SS2 5QB
Tel: 01702-612121 **Fax:** 01702-461604
Website: http://www.jewson.co.uk
Managers: G. Fenton (Mgr)
Ultimate Holding Company: COMPAGNIE DE SAINT GOBAIN (FRANCE)
Immediate Holding Company: JEWSON LIMITED
Registration no: 00348407 **Date established:** 1939
Turnover: Over £1,000m **No.of Employees:** 11 - 20 **Product Groups:** 66

Date of Accounts	Dec 11	Dec 10	Dec 09
Sales Turnover	1606m	1547m	1485m
Pre Tax Profit/Loss	18m	100m	45m
Working Capital	-345m	-250m	-349m
Fixed Assets	496m	387m	461m
Current Assets	657m	1005m	1320m
Current Liabilities	66m	120m	64m

Kestrel Printing Ltd
Journeymans Way Temple Farm Industrial Estate, Southend On Sea, SS2 5TF
Tel: 01702-444888 **Fax:** 01702-444880
E-mail: sales@kestrel-printing.co.uk
Website: http://www.kestrel-printing.co.uk
Directors: J. Galley (Dir)
Immediate Holding Company: KESTREL PRINTING LIMITED
Registration no: 00992784 **Date established:** 1970 **Turnover:** £1m - £2m
No.of Employees: 21 - 50 **Product Groups:** 28

Date of Accounts	Mar 11	Mar 10	Mar 09
Working Capital	-208	-245	-226
Fixed Assets	301	363	412
Current Assets	516	485	455

Keymed Ltd
Keymed House Stock Road, Southend On Sea, SS2 5QH
Tel: 01702-616333 **Fax:** 01702-465677
E-mail: keymed@keymed.co.uk
Website: http://www.keymed.co.uk
Bank(s): Barclays Lombard Street London
Directors: P. Hillman (Dir), M. Woodford (Grp MD), N. Williams (Dir)
Managers: H. Davis (Purch Mgr)
Ultimate Holding Company: OLYMPUS CORPORATION (JAPAN)
Immediate Holding Company: OLYMPUS KEYMED GROUP LIMITED
Registration no: 01210694 **VAT No.:** GB 250 3174 95
Date established: 1975 **Turnover:** £250m - £500m
No.of Employees: 501 - 1000 **Product Groups:** 38

Kingfisher Apparels Ltd
Robert Leonard Industrial Estate Southend Airport, Southend On Sea, SS2 6UN
Tel: 01702-548189 **Fax:** 01702-548183
E-mail: mgarbhe@yahoo.com
Website: http://www.ashdan.co.uk
Directors: M. Garbhe (MD)
Immediate Holding Company: KINGFISHER APPARELS LIMITED
Registration no: 02716631 **Date established:** 1992
Turnover: £250,000 - £500,000 **No.of Employees:** 1 - 10
Product Groups: 24, 63

Date of Accounts	Jun 11	Jun 10	Jun 09
Working Capital	-216	-178	-147
Fixed Assets	1	2	3
Current Assets	231	212	199

Kranzle UK Ltd
Unit 6 Cedar Park Stock Road, Southend On Sea, SS2 5QA
Tel: 01702-603462 **Fax:** 01702-603488
E-mail: sales@kranzle.co.uk
Website: http://www.kranzle.co.uk
Directors: G. Wilkinson (MD)
Immediate Holding Company: KRANZLE (UK) LIMITED
Registration no: 02083463 **Date established:** 1986
No.of Employees: 1 - 10 **Product Groups:** 40, 47, 48, 49

Date of Accounts	Dec 10	Dec 09	Dec 06
Working Capital	-55	-47	53
Fixed Assets	5	6	6
Current Assets	364	493	339

M & G Packaging
131 Johnstone Road, Southend On Sea, SS1 3NG
Tel: 01702-587580 **Fax:** 01702-588044
E-mail: gloriaandnick@talktalk.net
Website: http://www.onetel.co.uk
Directors: M. Goldring (MD)
Immediate Holding Company: M & G PACKAGING (ESSEX) LIMITED
Registration no: 01286716 **Date established:** 1976
No.of Employees: 1 - 10 **Product Groups:** 38, 42

Date of Accounts	Dec 10	Dec 09	Dec 07
Working Capital	1	N/A	2
Current Assets	4	4	5

Msca Ltd
20 Vanguard Way Shoeburyness, Southend On Sea, SS3 9RA
Tel: 01702-298901 **Fax:** 01702-382391
E-mail: adam@mscaltd.com
Directors: J. Harper (Dir & Co Sec), A. Harkness (Dir & Co Sec)
Immediate Holding Company: M S C A LIMITED
Registration no: 03072788 **Date established:** 1995
Turnover: £500,000 - £1m **No.of Employees:** 1 - 10 **Product Groups:** 23, 24

Date of Accounts	Sep 08	Sep 07	Sep 06
Working Capital	53	58	-14
Fixed Assets	1	1	46
Current Assets	195	126	20
Current Liabilities	142	68	34
Total Share Capital	1	1	1

NuTec Medical Ltd
285 Sutton Road, Southend On Sea, SS2 5PF
Tel: 01702-615665 **Fax:** 01702-615707
E-mail: info@nutec-medical.co.uk
Website: http://www.nutec-medical.co.uk
Directors: R. Moore (Dir), R. More (Dir), S. More (Dir)
Immediate Holding Company: NUTEC MEDICAL LIMITED
Registration no: 04134937 **Date established:** 2001
No.of Employees: 1 - 10 **Product Groups:** 38, 40

Date of Accounts	Dec 06	Dec 05
Working Capital	-233	-170
Fixed Assets	37	12
Current Assets	27	28
Current Liabilities	260	198
Total Share Capital	1	1

Oh So Bo Ho
100 Southchurch Road, Southend On Sea, SS1 2LX
Tel: 01702-469785 **Fax:** 01702-469785
E-mail: info@ohsoboho.com
Website: http://www.ohsoboho.com
Directors: M. Miller (Dir)
Date established: 1992 **No.of Employees:** 11 - 20 **Product Groups:** 38, 42

Olympus Keymed
Keymed House Stock Road, Southend On Sea, SS2 5QH
Tel: 01702-616333 **Fax:** 01702-465677
E-mail: info@olympus.co.uk
Website: http://www.olympus.co.uk
Bank(s): Barclays, Lombard Street, London
Directors: G. Walsh (Sales), J. Rowe (Fin), N. Williams (Dir)
Ultimate Holding Company: OLYMPUS CORPORATION (JAPAN)
Immediate Holding Company: OLYMPUS KEYMED GROUP LIMITED
Registration no: 01210694 **Date established:** 1975
Turnover: £250m - £500m **No.of Employees:** 501 - 1000
Product Groups: 37, 38

Date of Accounts	Mar 11	Mar 10	Mar 09
Sales Turnover	291m	289m	212m
Pre Tax Profit/Loss	32m	31m	37m
Working Capital	53m	-93m	45m
Fixed Assets	84m	149m	160m
Current Assets	135m	171m	126m
Current Liabilities	27m	49m	26m

Practical H R Ltd Health and Safety in the Office
34 Star Lane Industrial Estate Star Lane, Great Wakering, Southend On Sea, SS3 0PJ
Tel: 01702-216573 **Fax:** 01702-589161
E-mail: solutions@practical-hr.co.uk
Website: http://www.practical-hr.co.uk
Directors: P. Fisher (MD), P. Fisher (Fin)
Immediate Holding Company: PRACTICAL H.R. LIMITED
Registration no: 04430009 **Date established:** 2002
No.of Employees: 1 - 10 **Product Groups:** 44, 84

Date of Accounts	May 12	May 11	May 10
Working Capital	304	229	195
Fixed Assets	32	31	33
Current Assets	360	280	255

Profusion plc
4 T A H House Aviation Way, Southend Airport, Southend On Sea, SS2 6UN
Tel: 01702-543500 **Fax:** 01702-543700
E-mail: sales@profusionplc.com
Website: http://www.profusionplc.com
Directors: K. Persin (MD)
Managers: M. Persin (Chief Acct)
Immediate Holding Company: PROFUSION PLC
Registration no: 02343479 **VAT No.:** GB 545 8780 04
Date established: 1989 **Turnover:** £2m - £5m **No.of Employees:** 1 - 10
Product Groups: 37, 38

Date of Accounts	Dec 11	Dec 10	Dec 09
Sales Turnover	2m	2m	2m
Pre Tax Profit/Loss	195	190	-5
Working Capital	333	216	104
Fixed Assets	13	35	53
Current Assets	630	555	452
Current Liabilities	97	75	79

R B F Healthcare
55 Comet Way, Southend On Sea, SS2 6UW
Tel: 01702-527401 **Fax:** 01702-420240
E-mail: sales@rbf-products.co.uk
Website: http://www.rbfhealthcare.co.uk
Bank(s): HSBC, Stroud
Directors: D. Howard (Dir), D. Smith (Dir)
Managers: R. Tuscher (Purch Mgr), S. Hill (Sales Prom Mgr)
Ultimate Holding Company: RBF INDUSTRIES LIMITED
Immediate Holding Company: R.B.F.PRODUCTS LIMITED
Registration no: 00899823 **VAT No.:** GB 707 6460 32
Date established: 1967 **Turnover:** £2m - £5m **No.of Employees:** 21 - 50
Product Groups: 23, 24, 26, 30, 36, 67, 84

Date of Accounts	Mar 12	Mar 11
Working Capital	4	5
Fixed Assets	1	N/A
Current Assets	5	5
Current Liabilities	1	N/A

R F & Noise Components
Priory Works Priory Avenue, Southend On Sea, SS2 6LD
Tel: 05601-066930 **Fax:** 0870-340 2227
E-mail: sales@rfandnoisecomponents.co.uk
Website: http://www.rfandnoisecomponents.co.uk
Managers: G. Meredith (Mgr)
Immediate Holding Company: RF & NOISE COMPONENTS LTD
Registration no: 04652573 **Date established:** 2003
No.of Employees: 1 - 10 **Product Groups:** 37

Date of Accounts	Jan 12	Jan 11	Jan 10
Working Capital	97	125	144
Fixed Assets	14	17	12
Current Assets	115	151	180

Rayleigh Technical Design Ltd
9-10 Laurence Industrial Estate Eastwoodbury Lane, Southend On Sea, SS2 6RH
Tel: 01702-511678 **Fax:** 01702-527244
E-mail: ann@rayleightchdesign.co.uk
Website: http://www.rayleightechdesign.co.uk
Directors: K. Burgess (MD), K. Ralph (Tech Serv), C. Burgess (Fin)
Immediate Holding Company: RAYLEIGH TECHNICAL DESIGN LIMITED
Registration no: 01551887 **Date established:** 1981
Turnover: £500,000 - £1m **No.of Employees:** 1 - 10 **Product Groups:** 30, 48

Date of Accounts	Apr 08	Apr 07	Apr 06
Working Capital	18	5	4
Fixed Assets	93	116	128
Current Assets	299	332	249
Current Liabilities	281	328	246
Total Share Capital	1	1	1

Ruark Audio Ltd
59 Tailors Court, Southend On Sea, SS2 5TH
Tel: 01702-601410 **Fax:** 01702-601414
E-mail: info@ruark.co.uk
Website: http://www.ruarkaudio.com
Bank(s): HSBC
Directors: N. Adams (Fin)
Ultimate Holding Company: RUARK AUDIO LIMITED
Immediate Holding Company: RUARK ACOUSTICS LIMITED
Registration no: 02141374 **VAT No.:** GB 436 3832 45
Date established: 1987 **Turnover:** £1m - £2m **No.of Employees:** 11 - 20
Product Groups: 37

Date of Accounts	Dec 11	Dec 10	Dec 09
Working Capital	-255	-255	-252
Fixed Assets	105	105	105
Current Assets	1	3	14

Safety Unlimited
Unit 2 40 Comet Way, Southend On Sea, SS2 6XW
Tel: 01702-420000 **Fax:** 01702-528128
E-mail: sales@safetyunlimited.co.uk
Website: http://www.safetyunlimited.co.uk
Bank(s): Barclays
Directors: G. Wiley (Dir)
Ultimate Holding Company: Avonde Investments
Registration no: 01176243 **VAT No.:** GB 292 3690 37
Date established: 1974 **Turnover:** £1m - £2m **No.of Employees:** 11 - 20
Product Groups: 22, 24, 26, 29, 30, 32, 35, 36, 38, 40, 42, 45, 49, 54, 63, 77, 86

St Ann's Building Supplies
Unit 4 Bentalls Close, Southend On Sea, SS2 5PT
Tel: 01702-463363 **Fax:** 01702-469043
E-mail: sales@stannsbuildingsupplies.co.uk
Website: http://www.stannsbuildingsupplies.co.uk
Bank(s): Lloyds TSB Bank plc
Directors: M. Scanes (MD)
Immediate Holding Company: ST ANN'S MANUFACTURING COMPANY LIMITED
Registration no: 00098617 **Date established:** 2008 **Turnover:** £2m - £5m
No.of Employees: 11 - 20 **Product Groups:** 66, 67

Date of Accounts	Dec 11	Dec 10	Dec 09
Working Capital	773	879	932
Fixed Assets	327	344	376
Current Assets	926	1m	1m

Sign & Supply Wholesale
15 The Vanguards Vanguard Way, Shoeburyness, Southend On Sea, SS3 9QJ
Tel: 01702-294400
Website: http://www.signmakerswarehouse.com
Registration no: 04819789 **Date established:** 2003
No.of Employees: 1 - 10 **Product Groups:** 24, 32, 81

South Essex Fasteners Ltd
52 Tailors Court Temple Farm Industrial Estate, Southend On Sea, SS2 5SX
Tel: 01702-615326 **Fax:** 01702-461620
E-mail: roy@southessexfasteners.co.uk
Bank(s): National Westminster Bank Plc
Directors: R. Ricks (MD)
Immediate Holding Company: SOUTH ESSEX FASTENERS LIMITED
Registration no: 01164011 **Date established:** 1974 **Turnover:** £2m - £5m
No.of Employees: 11 - 20 **Product Groups:** 30, 34, 35, 36, 39, 66

Date of Accounts	Apr 12	Apr 11	Apr 10
Working Capital	243	189	142
Fixed Assets	59	49	51
Current Assets	674	630	573

Southend United Football Club Superstore
Roots Hall Victoria Avenue, Southend On Sea, SS2 6NQ
Tel: 01702-351117 **Fax:** 01702-330164
E-mail: info@soughendunited.co.uk
Website: http://www.shrimpers-clubshop.co.uk
Managers: J. Hilaire (Mgr)
Immediate Holding Company: SOUTHEND UNITED COMMUNITY & EDUCATIONAL TRUST
Registration no: 00089767 **Date established:** 2004
Turnover: £250,000 - £500,000 **No.of Employees:** 1 - 10
Product Groups: 87

Date of Accounts	Jul 11	Jul 10	Jul 09
Sales Turnover	301	483	344
Pre Tax Profit/Loss	-24	54	18
Working Capital	44	65	24
Fixed Assets	10	14	1
Current Assets	90	133	87
Current Liabilities	40	68	63

Southern Glass Windows & Conservatories Ltd
4-5 Fletchers Square Temple Farm Industrial Estate, Southend On Sea, SS2 5RN
Tel: 01702-618191 **Fax:** 01702-447014
E-mail: sales@southern-glass.co.uk
Website: http://www.southernglass.co.uk
Bank(s): Royal Bank of Scotland
Directors: K. Querney (Dir), K. Querney (Fin), D. Kemp (Fin), G. Edwards (MD)
Immediate Holding Company: SOUTHERN GLASS WINDOWS & CONSERVATORIES LIMITED
Registration no: 04338620 **VAT No.:** GB 583 2580 26
Date established: 2001 **Turnover:** £1m - £2m **No.of Employees:** 21 - 50
Product Groups: 35

Towerfield Plating Ltd
2 Towerfield Close Shoeburyness, Southend On Sea, SS3 9QP
Tel: 01702-294161 **Fax:** 01702-295743
E-mail: paul.macdonald@towerfieldplating.com
Managers: P. Macdonald (Mgr)
Immediate Holding Company: TOWERFIELD PLATING LIMITED
Registration no: 06526787 **VAT No.:** GB 250 7390 69
Date established: 2008 **Turnover:** £250,000 - £500,000
No.of Employees: 1 - 10 **Product Groups:** 48

Date of Accounts	Apr 11	Apr 10	Apr 09
Sales Turnover	1m	736	553
Pre Tax Profit/Loss	306	78	9
Working Capital	179	134	59
Fixed Assets	387	319	362
Current Assets	439	251	162
Current Liabilities	118	63	36

Tudor Forge
Rear of 40 Hamlet Road, Southend On Sea, SS1 1HH
Tel: 01702-348049 **Fax:** 01702-390664
E-mail: glen@tudorforge.co.uk
Directors: G. Taylor (Prop)
Date established: 1978 **No.of Employees:** 1 - 10 **Product Groups:** 26, 35

W K L Glass
High House Farm Barling Road, Barling Magna, Southend On Sea, SS3 0LZ
Tel: 01702-217539 **Fax:** 01702-217539
Directors: W. Esbrick (Ptnr), W. Esbrick (Prop)
Date established: 1996 **No.of Employees:** 1 - 10 **Product Groups:** 26, 35

Waverley Brownall Ltd
Unit 45 The Vintners Temple Farm Industrial Estate, Southend On Sea, SS2 5RZ
Tel: 01702-613883 **Fax:** 01702-613600
E-mail: sales@waverleybrownall.co.uk
Website: http://www.waverleybrownall.co.uk
Bank(s): Lloyds TSB Bank plc
Directors: J. Mcsweeny (MD), N. Douse (Sales), R. Sheriden (Dir)
Immediate Holding Company: WAVERLEY BROWNALL LIMITED
Registration no: 03837180 **Date established:** 1999 **Turnover:** £2m - £5m
No.of Employees: 21 - 50 **Product Groups:** 36

Date of Accounts	Mar 12	Mar 11	Mar 10
Working Capital	970	893	803
Fixed Assets	2m	1m	1m
Current Assets	1m	1m	1m

W & H Roads Ltd
25 Stock Road, Southend On Sea, SS2 5QG
Tel: 01702-469777 **Fax:** 01702-442017
E-mail: info@whroads.co.uk
Website: http://www.whroads.co.uk
Directors: P. Cook (Contracts)
Ultimate Holding Company: AWH HOLDINGS LIMITED
Immediate Holding Company: W.& H.(ROADS)LIMITED
Registration no: 00590714 **Date established:** 1957
No.of Employees: 21 - 50 **Product Groups:** 45, 51, 83, 84

Date of Accounts	Apr 11	Apr 10	Apr 09
Working Capital	24	-136	-182
Fixed Assets	721	736	720
Current Assets	1m	1m	1m

Worth & Co Blinds Ltd
Rear of 26-30 Christchurch Road, Southend On Sea, SS2 4JS
Tel: 01702-467581 **Fax:** 01702-467560
E-mail: sales@worthblinds.com
Website: http://www.worthblinds.com
Directors: M. Tomlin (Dir)
Immediate Holding Company: WORTH & CO BLINDS LIMITED
Registration no: 06282716 **Date established:** 2007
Turnover: £250,000 - £500,000 **No.of Employees:** 1 - 10
Product Groups: 35, 63, 66

Date of Accounts	Jun 11	Jun 10	Jun 09
Working Capital	-115	-126	-134
Fixed Assets	115	127	137
Current Assets	66	46	47

R G Wylie & Co. Ltd
Vanguard Way Shoeburyness, Southend On Sea, SS3 9QY
Tel: 01702-296751 **Fax:** 01702-297560
E-mail: rg.wylie@btconnect.com
Website: http://www.unitruck.co.uk
Directors: R. Wylie (MD)
Immediate Holding Company: R.G. WYLIE & CO. LIMITED
Registration no: 00966812 **VAT No.:** GB 250 6414 86
Date established: 1969 **Turnover:** £250,000 - £500,000
No.of Employees: 1 - 10 **Product Groups:** 30, 35

Date of Accounts	Mar 11	Mar 10	Mar 09
Working Capital	76	97	114
Fixed Assets	42	44	47
Current Assets	189	207	211

Southminster

Allen Bros Fittings Ltd
Hallmark Industrial Estate Hall Road, Southminster, CM0 7EH
Tel: 01621-774689 **Fax:** 01621-774536
E-mail: sales@allenbrothers.co.uk
Website: http://www.allenbrothers.co.uk
Bank(s): Barclays
Managers: R. Lyne (Sales Prom Mgr)
Immediate Holding Company: ALLEN & ASSOCIATES LTD
Registration no: 08004621 **Date established:** 2012
No.of Employees: 21 - 50 **Product Groups:** 39, 74

Date of Accounts	Oct 07	Oct 06	Oct 05
Working Capital	259	233	342
Fixed Assets	457	444	529
Current Assets	661	496	683
Current Liabilities	402	263	341
Total Share Capital	12	12	12

Dengie Crops Ltd
Hall Road Asheldham, Southminster, CM0 7JF
Tel: 01621-773883 **Fax:** 01621-773717
E-mail: chris.petts@dengie.com
Website: http://www.dengie.com
Bank(s): HSBC Bank plc
Directors: C. Petts (Co Sec)
Managers: D. Filce (Ops Mgr)
Immediate Holding Company: DENGIE CROPS LIMITED
Registration no: 02328408 **VAT No.:** GB 529 3547 25
Date established: 1988 **Turnover:** £10m - £20m
No.of Employees: 51 - 100 **Product Groups:** 62

Date of Accounts	Apr 11	Apr 10	Apr 09
Sales Turnover	14m	15m	15m
Pre Tax Profit/Loss	1m	1m	846
Working Capital	2m	2m	801
Fixed Assets	7m	7m	7m
Current Assets	7m	7m	6m
Current Liabilities	572	545	528

Europlaz Technologies Ltd
Unit 1-9 The Maltings Indl-Est Hall Road, Southminster, CM0 7EQ
Tel: 01621-773471 **Fax:** 01621-773792
E-mail: enquiries@europlaz.co.uk
Website: http://www.europlaz.co.uk
Bank(s): HSBC Bank plc
Directors: A. Hawkins (MD), E. O'Keeffe (Grp Chief Exec), L. Fenton (Dir), H. Hawkins (Dir)
Managers: E. Okeeles (Mgr)
Ultimate Holding Company: A.H. PRECISION PLASTICS HOLDINGS LTD
Immediate Holding Company: EUROPLAZ TECHNOLOGIES LTD
Registration no: 04046384 **VAT No.:** GB 683 2579 03
Date established: 2000 **Turnover:** £1m - £2m **No.of Employees:** 21 - 50
Product Groups: 30, 48

Date of Accounts	Dec 10	Dec 09	Dec 08
Working Capital	-60	-27	2
Fixed Assets	558	358	342
Current Assets	660	727	644

Vader Custom
Unit 8 The Maltings Industrial Estate Hall Road, Southminster, CM0 7EQ
Tel: 01621-773772 **Fax:** 01621- 773173
Directors: J. Rice (MD)
Date established: 2005 **No.of Employees:** 1 - 10 **Product Groups:** 35

Stanford Le Hope

A A Shutter Doors
82 Gardner Avenue Corringham, Stanford Le Hope, SS17 7SA
Tel: 01375-400542 **Fax:** 01375-644557
E-mail: aashutterdoors@yahoo.co.uk
Website: http://www.aashutterdoors.co.uk
Directors: T. Davey (Ptnr)
Date established: 2001 **No.of Employees:** 1 - 10 **Product Groups:** 26, 35

Lamberts Tool & Welding Supplies Ltd
Unit 1 The Manorway, Corringham, Stanford Le Hope, SS17 9LA
Tel: 01375-676667 **Fax:** 01375-679035
E-mail: simon@toolsandwelding.co.uk
Website: http://www.toolsandwelding.co.uk
Directors: S. Lambert (MD)
Immediate Holding Company: LAMBERTS TOOL & WELDING SUPPLIES LIMITED
Registration no: 04014500 **Date established:** 2000 **Turnover:** £1m - £2m
No.of Employees: 1 - 10 **Product Groups:** 46

Date of Accounts	Jun 11	Jun 10	Jun 09
Sales Turnover	N/A	2m	2m
Pre Tax Profit/Loss	N/A	75	10
Working Capital	109	28	46
Fixed Assets	69	74	87
Current Assets	565	355	416
Current Liabilities	N/A	72	57

Lenval Ltd
KT House Stanhope Industrial Park Wharf Road, Stanford Le Hope, SS17 0EH
Tel: 01375-640344 **Fax:** 01375-640331
E-mail: lenval@btconnect.com
Website: http://www.lenval.co.uk
Bank(s): National Westminster
Directors: K. Turp (MD), K. Turp (Fin)
Immediate Holding Company: LENVAL LIMITED
Registration no: 04544450 **VAT No.:** GB 583 1520 49
Date established: 2002 **Turnover:** £1m - £2m **No.of Employees:** 11 - 20
Product Groups: 54, 84

Date of Accounts	Mar 10	Mar 09	Jan 12
Sales Turnover	N/A	N/A	2m
Pre Tax Profit/Loss	N/A	N/A	207
Working Capital	-21	153	149
Fixed Assets	59	58	63
Current Assets	113	379	539
Current Liabilities	N/A	103	194

Light Plant
Mapledene Greathouse Chase High Road, Fobbing, Stanford Le Hope, SS17 9HU
Tel: 01375-644087 **Fax:** 01375-675114
E-mail: davelightplant@talktalk.net
Directors: D. Carpenter (Prop)
Date established: 1980 **No.of Employees:** 1 - 10 **Product Groups:** 35, 39, 45

Shea International Ltd
31 King Street, Stanford Le Hope, SS17 0HJ
Tel: 01375-642626 **Fax:** 01375-361304
E-mail: sheaint@btconnect.com
Directors: D. Shea (MD)
Immediate Holding Company: SHEA INTERNATIONAL LIMITED
Registration no: 01977167 **VAT No.:** 436 3591 41 **Date established:** 1986
Turnover: £1m - £2m **No.of Employees:** 1 - 10 **Product Groups:** 74, 75, 76

Date of Accounts	Dec 11	Dec 10	Dec 09
Sales Turnover	1m	1m	1m
Pre Tax Profit/Loss	5	34	11
Working Capital	211	208	183
Current Assets	278	256	252
Current Liabilities	19	25	28

Stansted

A E M Ltd
Unit 6001 Taylors End London Stansted Airport, Stansted, CM24 1RB
Tel: 01279-680030 **Fax:** 01279-688840
E-mail: aem@ametek.co.uk
Website: http://www.aem.co.uk
Bank(s): Lloyds TSB Bank plc
Directors: K. Sena (Co Sec)
Managers: A. France (Personnel), T. Suckling (Mktg Serv Mgr), J. Smith, P. Cook (Buyer), S. Leader
Ultimate Holding Company: AMETEK INC (USA)
Immediate Holding Company: AEM LIMITED
Registration no: 00620201 **VAT No.:** GB 571 9367 10
Date established: 1959 **Turnover:** £20m - £50m
No.of Employees: 101 - 250 **Product Groups:** 39

Date of Accounts	Dec 11	Dec 10	Dec 09
Sales Turnover	21m	20m	20m
Pre Tax Profit/Loss	3m	3m	3m
Working Capital	6m	6m	6m
Fixed Assets	11m	9m	9m
Current Assets	11m	10m	11m
Current Liabilities	1m	696	1m

Agar Scientific
Unit 7 M11 Business Link Parsonage Lane, Stansted, CM24 8GF
Tel: 01279-813519 **Fax:** 01279-815106
E-mail: sales@elektron-technology.com
Website: http://www.elektronplc.com
Bank(s): Lloyds TSB Bank plc
Directors: L. Hamon (Sales)
Managers: A. Price, A. Cutmore, A. Quaife
Ultimate Holding Company: ELEKTRON TECHNOLOGY PLC
Immediate Holding Company: BULGIN COMPONENTS PLC
Registration no: 02895884 **VAT No.:** GB 215 3207 76
Date established: 1994 **Turnover:** £2m - £5m **No.of Employees:** 21 - 50
Product Groups: 31, 38

Date of Accounts	Jan 11	Jan 10	Jan 09
Working Capital	2m	2m	2m
Current Assets	2m	2m	2m

Ardent Logistics
Unit 45a Parsonage Farm Forest Hall Road, Stansted, CM24 8TY
Tel: 01279-817001 **Fax:** 01279-817004
E-mail: ops@ardentlogistics.co.uk
Website: http://www.ardentlogistics.co.uk
Directors: R. Makepeace (Prop)
Managers: A. Gates (Ops Mgr)
Date established: 2001 **No.of Employees:** 11 - 20 **Product Groups:** 79

Federal Express Europe Inc
Stansted Airport Ltd Marketing Department London Stansted Airport, Stansted, CM24 1QX
Tel: 01279-680574 **Fax:** 01279-681930
E-mail: pmintram@fedex.com
Website: http://www.fedex.com
Bank(s): National Westminster Bank Plc
Directors: W. Martin (MD), N. Geens (Mkt Research)
Managers: N. Cobbe (Tech Serv Mgr)
Ultimate Holding Company: FEDERAL EXPRESS CORPORATION
Immediate Holding Company: FEDERAL EXPRESS EUROPE INC.
Registration no: FC015355 **Date established:** 1989 **Turnover:** £2m - £5m
No.of Employees: 251 - 500 **Product Groups:** 79

Inflite The Jet Centre Ltd
Hanger 173 First Avenue, London Stansted Airport, Stansted, CM24 1RY
Tel: 01279-831000 **Fax:** 01279-837900
E-mail: operations@inflite.co.uk
Website: http://www.inflite.co.uk
Directors: J. Milroy (Fin), S. Buckingham (Dir)
Managers: D. Mansell (Mgr)
Ultimate Holding Company: SWAN INVESTMENTS GROUP LIMITED
Immediate Holding Company: INFLITE LIMITED
Registration no: 02865494 **Date established:** 1993
Turnover: £50m - £75m **No.of Employees:** 51 - 100 **Product Groups:** 39

Date of Accounts	Mar 11	Mar 10	Mar 09
Sales Turnover	37m	51m	56m
Pre Tax Profit/Loss	-758	1m	4m
Working Capital	10m	10m	12m
Fixed Assets	9m	9m	7m
Current Assets	18m	19m	22m
Current Liabilities	4m	5m	4m

Pinewood Electronics Ltd
Pinewood House Riverside Business Park, Stansted, CM24 8ND
Tel: 01279-816666 **Fax:** 01279-816161
E-mail: sales@pinewood.gb.com
Website: http://www.pinewood.gb.com
Directors: D. Lacey (MD), G. Lacey (Fin)
Immediate Holding Company: PINEWOOD ELECTRONICS LIMITED
Registration no: 01742102 **VAT No.:** GB 386 0352 47
Date established: 1983 **Turnover:** £2m - £5m **No.of Employees:** 1 - 10
Product Groups: 35, 37, 38, 44

Date of Accounts	Jul 11	Jul 10	Jul 09
Working Capital	179	185	214
Fixed Assets	45	34	32
Current Assets	346	485	322

Stevens Security Ltd
7 Churchill Corner, Stansted, CM24 8UA
Tel: 01279-813345 **Fax:** 01279-813345
E-mail: info@stevens-security.co.uk
Website: http://www.stevens-security.co.uk
Directors: B. Wilkin (MD)
Immediate Holding Company: STEVENS SECURITY LIMITED
Registration no: 05354804 **Date established:** 2005
No.of Employees: 1 - 10 **Product Groups:** 36, 40, 52, 67

Date of Accounts	Apr 11	Apr 10	Apr 09
Working Capital	-12	-15	14
Fixed Assets	13	16	21
Current Assets	29	37	63

Titan Airways Ltd
Enterprise House Stanstead Airport Stanstead, London Stansted Airport, Stansted, CM24 1RN
Tel: 01279-680616 **Fax:** 01279-680110
E-mail: charter@titan-airways.co.uk
Website: http://www.titan-airways.com
Bank(s): National Westminster
Directors: S. Payne (Co Sec), G. Willson (MD), D. Macclinton (Co Sec), A. Kiernan (Comm)
Managers: S. Richmond (Personnel), P. Taylor (Tech Serv Mgr)
Ultimate Holding Company: HAGONDALE LIMITED
Immediate Holding Company: EXECAIR LIMITED
Registration no: 03205078 **VAT No.:** GB 466 1201 69
Date established: 1996 **Turnover:** £50m - £75m
No.of Employees: 101 - 250 **Product Groups:** 68, 75, 76

Date of Accounts	Mar 11	Mar 10	Mar 08
Working Capital	10	10	10
Current Assets	10	10	10

Thomas Watts Ltd
23-25 Lower Street, Stansted, CM24 8LN
Tel: 01279-817688 **Fax:** 01279-817699
E-mail: thomaswatts@btinternet.com
Website: http://www.thomaswatts.btinternet.co.uk
Directors: T. Watts (MD), P. Mortiboy (Dir)
Immediate Holding Company: THOMAS WATTS MACHINES AND CONTROLS LIMITED
Registration no: 04408020 **VAT No.:** GB 599 7722 61
Date established: 2002 **Turnover:** £250,000 - £500,000
No.of Employees: 1 - 10 **Product Groups:** 46, 84

Tilbury

A L M Training Services Ltd
The Riverside Business Centre Fort Road, Tilbury, RM18 7ND
Tel: 01375-489738 **Fax:** 01375-489 801
E-mail: info@almtrainingservices.co.uk
Website: http://www.almtrainingservices.co.uk
Directors: D. Coleman (MD)
Immediate Holding Company: ALM TRAINING SERVICES LIMITED
Registration no: 05419211 **Date established:** 2005
No.of Employees: 1 - 10 **Product Groups:** 45, 48, 67, 86

Date of Accounts	Apr 11	Apr 10	Apr 09
Working Capital	27	19	-1
Fixed Assets	8	1	1
Current Assets	100	72	55

Allied Mills

Sunblest Flour Mill Tilbury Docks, Tilbury, RM18 7JR
Tel: 01375-363100 **Fax:** 01375-850706
E-mail: customer.services@allied-mills.co.uk
Website: http://www.allied-mills.co.uk
Directors: S. Barton (MD)
Immediate Holding Company: ALLIED MILLS LIMITED
Registration no: 00037410 **Date established:** 1992
No.of Employees: 51 - 100 **Product Groups:** 41

Allport Ltd

Allport House Thurrock Park Way, Tilbury, RM18 7HZ
Tel: 01375-487800 **Fax:** 01375-487890
E-mail: info@allport.co.uk
Website: http://www.allport.co.uk
Bank(s): Barclays
Directors: D. Reagan (Dir)
Ultimate Holding Company: HUNDRED HONEST LIMITED (HONG KONG)
Immediate Holding Company: ALLPORT LIMITED
Registration no: 00772941 **VAT No.:** GB 226 8344 56
Date established: 1963 **No.of Employees:** 21 - 50 **Product Groups:** 72, 74, 76

Date of Accounts	Dec 11	Dec 10	Dec 09
Sales Turnover	236m	286m	192m
Pre Tax Profit/Loss	2m	-858	6m
Working Capital	5m	5m	3m
Fixed Assets	12m	12m	14m
Current Assets	60m	69m	47m
Current Liabilities	4m	13m	4m

C & H Hauliers Ltd

Broker House, Tilbury, RM18 7EH
Tel: 01375-842683 **Fax:** 01375-847095
E-mail: steve.mercer@charlesgeegroup.com
Website: http://www.charlesgeegroup.com
Bank(s): Royal Bank of Scotland plc, EC3
Directors: S. Mercer (MD)
Immediate Holding Company: CHARLES GEE & CO.
No.of Employees: 101 - 250 **Product Groups:** 72, 76

Date of Accounts	Mar 08	Mar 07	Mar 06
Sales Turnover	16328	16682	16258
Pre Tax Profit/Loss	-22	165	142
Working Capital	21	159	104
Fixed Assets	1958	1754	1823
Current Assets	2851	3096	3087
Current Liabilities	2830	2937	2983
Total Share Capital	226	226	226
ROCE% (Return on Capital Employed)	-1.1	8.6	7.4
ROT% (Return on Turnover)	-0.1	1.0	0.9

Cory Bros Shipping Ltd

Cory House, 21 Berth Tilbury Dock, Tilbury, RM18 7JT
Tel: 01375-488400 **Fax:** 01375-842854
E-mail: corythames@cory.co.uk
Website: http://www.cory.co.uk
Bank(s): National Westminster Bank Plc
Directors: I. Felixstowe (MD), K. Badderley (MD)
Immediate Holding Company: O'Connor & Mccann Ltd
Registration no: 04717201 **VAT No.:** GB 244 0497 69
Date established: 1993 **Turnover:** Up to £250,000
No.of Employees: 11 - 20 **Product Groups:** 76

Delphini Lifting & Securing Ltd

Unit 6 Tilbury Free Port, Tilbury, RM18 7HB
Tel: 01375-844394 **Fax:** 01375-843933
Website: http://www.delphini.org.uk
Directors: D. Cormack (MD), M. Hale (Fin)
Immediate Holding Company: DELPHINI LIMITED
Registration no: 04274476 **Date established:** 2001
No.of Employees: 11 - 20 **Product Groups:** 35, 39, 45

Date of Accounts	Dec 07	Dec 06	Dec 05
Working Capital	23	33	1
Fixed Assets	32	10	12
Current Assets	381	402	267
Current Liabilities	358	369	266

East Tilbury Saws

Unit 31 Readmans Industrial Estate Station Road, East Tilbury, Tilbury, RM18 8QR
Tel: 01375-855527 **Fax:** 01375-855527
E-mail: longhurstw@aol.com
Directors: C. Wakerly (Dir)
Registration no: 06956040 **Date established:** 2009
No.of Employees: 1 - 10 **Product Groups:** 46, 48

Essex Tube Windings Ltd

Macanie House Dock Road, Tilbury, RM18 7PT
Tel: 01375-851613 **Fax:** 01375-851717
E-mail: info@essextubes.com
Website: http://www.essextubes.com
Bank(s): National Westminster Bank Plc
Directors: K. Topliss (MD)
Immediate Holding Company: ESSEX TUBE WINDINGS LIMITED
Registration no: 02402078 **VAT No.:** GB 546 1794 22
Date established: 1989 **Turnover:** £1m - £2m **No.of Employees:** 11 - 20
Product Groups: 27, 66

Date of Accounts	Mar 12	Mar 11	Mar 10
Working Capital	316	302	318
Fixed Assets	79	100	95
Current Assets	594	569	575

Finnforest UK Ltd

46 Berth Tilbury Docks, Tilbury, RM18 7HS
Tel: 01375-856855 **Fax:** 01375-856264
E-mail: tom.tong@finnforest.com
Website: http://www.finnforest.co.uk
Directors: J. Tong (Sales), N. Wijesooriya (Fin), T. Tong (Mkt Research)
Managers: R. Ripley (Buyer), T. Chrisostomou (I.T. Exec), W. Dudding (Mktg Serv Mgr)
Ultimate Holding Company: METSALIITTO OSUUSKUNTA (FINLAND)
Immediate Holding Company: FINNFOREST UK LIMITED
Registration no: 03071064 **VAT No.:** GB 204 5133 13
Date established: 1995 **Turnover:** £125m - £250m
No.of Employees: 101 - 250 **Product Groups:** 25, 29, 66

Date of Accounts	Dec 09	Dec 08	Dec 07
Sales Turnover	218m	249m	278m
Pre Tax Profit/Loss	5m	3m	6m
Working Capital	40m	42m	28m
Fixed Assets	21m	23m	22m
Current Assets	63m	66m	72m
Current Liabilities	7m	12m	31m

K B R Foreign Exchange plc

Fort Road, Tilbury, RM18 7ND
Tel: 01375-489480 **Fax:** 01375-489488
E-mail: admin@kbrfx.com
Website: http://www.kbrfx.com
Directors: J. Bye (Prop), V. Rampersad (Ptnr)
Immediate Holding Company: KBR FOREIGN EXCHANGE PLC
Registration no: 05424125 **Date established:** 2005
Turnover: £50m - £75m **No.of Employees:** 1 - 10 **Product Groups:** 82

Date of Accounts	Apr 12	Apr 11	Apr 10
Sales Turnover	99m	75m	47m
Pre Tax Profit/Loss	247	68	-76
Working Capital	298	214	148
Fixed Assets	8	8	6
Current Assets	3m	3m	2m
Current Liabilities	64	11	13

P E P Ltd

Unit 23-24 Capstan Centre Thurrock Park Way, Tilbury, RM18 7HH
Tel: 01375-850300 **Fax:** 01375- 851099
E-mail: sales@pep.ltd.uk
Website: http://www.rentdisplayboards.co.uk
Directors: V. Wells (Fin)
Managers: D. Bridge
Immediate Holding Company: P E P LIMITED
Registration no: 01554118 **VAT No.:** GB 352 1505 88
Date established: 1981 **Turnover:** £250,000 - £500,000
No.of Employees: 1 - 10 **Product Groups:** 26, 30, 35, 49, 67, 81, 83

Date of Accounts	Mar 11	Mar 10	Mar 09
Working Capital	-19	-5	-3
Fixed Assets	30	35	42
Current Assets	12	21	19

Plastic Panel & Sheet Co.

Trafalgar House Princess Margaret Road, East Tilbury, Tilbury, RM18 8RH
Tel: 01375-850066 **Fax:** 01375-856800
E-mail: p.wicks@plasticpanelandsheetcompany.co.uk
Website: http://www.plastics.gb.com
Directors: P. Wicks (MD)
No.of Employees: 1 - 10 **Product Groups:** 30, 40, 66

Samskip

Europa House Tilbury Freeport, Tilbury, RM18 7HB
Tel: 01375-855003 **Fax:** 01375-855013
E-mail: tilbury@samskip.com
Website: http://www.samskip.com
Managers: J. Shaw (Mgr)
No.of Employees: 1 - 10 **Product Groups:** 76

Upminster

Continuous Piano Hinge Company Ltd

Unit 8-9 Hillview Southend Arterial Road, Upminster, RM14 1TE
Tel: 01277-213132 **Fax:** 01277-262555
E-mail: cphsales@aol.com
Website: http://www.continuoushinge.com
Directors: P. Quinlan (Prop)
Immediate Holding Company: CONTINUOUS PIANO HINGE COMPANY LIMITED
Registration no: 02839729 **VAT No.:** GB 627 4029 46
Date established: 1993 **Turnover:** £250,000 - £500,000
No.of Employees: 1 - 10 **Product Groups:** 35, 36, 49

Date of Accounts	Aug 11	Aug 10	Aug 09
Working Capital	49	65	89
Fixed Assets	4	13	25
Current Assets	67	79	105

H R Go Recruitment

62a Station Road, Upminster, RM14 2TD
Tel: 01708-250526 **Fax:** 01708-229335
E-mail: tjrout@psbrecruitment.co.uk
Website: http://www.hrgo.co.uk
Managers: A. Hegarty (District Mgr)
Immediate Holding Company: HR GO PLC
Registration no: 00924542 **Date established:** 1967
No.of Employees: 11 - 20 **Product Groups:** 80

The London Railing Company Ltd

Lower Dunton Road Bulphan, Upminster, RM14 3TD
Tel: 07581-365 471
E-mail: info@londonrailings.co.uk
Website: http://www.londonrailings.co.uk
Directors: S. Thorne (Prop)
Registration no: 07272513 **Date established:** 2004
No.of Employees: 1 - 10 **Product Groups:** 26, 35

Precision Lift Services Ltd

Unit 10 Upminster Trading Park Warley Street, Upminster, RM14 3PJ
Tel: 01708-250800 **Fax:** 01708-250400
E-mail: info@precisionlifts.co.uk
Website: http://www.precisionlifts.co.uk
Directors: C. Pace (Dir), V. Foley (Co Sec)
Ultimate Holding Company: P L S HOLDINGS LIMITED
Immediate Holding Company: PRECISION LIFT SERVICES LIMITED
Registration no: 03213600 **Date established:** 1996 **Turnover:** £5m - £10m
No.of Employees: 101 - 250 **Product Groups:** 35, 39, 45

Date of Accounts	Aug 10	Aug 09	Mar 11
Sales Turnover	9m	10m	5m
Pre Tax Profit/Loss	44	-104	311
Working Capital	647	607	745
Fixed Assets	50	51	69
Current Assets	3m	2m	3m
Current Liabilities	376	317	381

Regent Electrical Distributors

6 Upminster Trading Park Warley Street, Upminster, RM14 3PJ
Tel: 01708-227764 **Fax:** 01708-227663
Website: http://www.regentelectrical.com
Managers: R. Carr (District Mgr)
Ultimate Holding Company: ELECTRICAL WHOLESALE SYSTEMS LIMITED
Immediate Holding Company: REGENT ELECTRICAL SEVENOAKS LIMITED
Registration no: 05933557 **Date established:** 2006
No.of Employees: 1 - 10 **Product Groups:** 36, 40

Date of Accounts	Jun 11	Jun 10	Jun 09
Sales Turnover	629	605	539
Pre Tax Profit/Loss	-17	15	-42
Working Capital	242	248	202
Fixed Assets	3	8	18
Current Assets	243	253	204
Current Liabilities	1	6	2

Safer Cell Systems plc

Westbury Farm Sunnings Lane, Upminster, RM14 3NU
Tel: 0845-260 7233 **Fax:** 0871-250 2355
E-mail: info@safercell.co.uk
Website: http://www.safercell.co.uk
Product Groups: 26, 36

Date of Accounts	Jun 08	Jun 07	Jun 06
Sales Turnover	415	320	122
Pre Tax Profit/Loss	69	75	-88
Working Capital	111	64	31
Fixed Assets	35	26	7
Current Assets	365	259	61
Current Liabilities	254	195	30
Total Share Capital	50	50	50
ROCE% (Return on Capital Employed)	47.1	83.8	-230.4
ROT% (Return on Turnover)	16.5	23.6	-71.9

Safety Assured Ltd

Home Farm Fen Lane, North Ockendon, Upminster, RM14 3RD
Tel: 01708-855777 **Fax:** 01708-855125
E-mail: info@safetyassured.com
Website: http://www.safetyassured.com
Directors: S. Webb (MD)
Immediate Holding Company: SAFETY ASSURED LIMITED
Registration no: 04327961 **Date established:** 2001
No.of Employees: 1 - 10 **Product Groups:** 36, 67

Date of Accounts	Nov 11	Nov 10	Nov 09
Working Capital	31	61	52
Fixed Assets	8	11	8
Current Assets	74	113	99

Waltham Abbey

Abbey Lift Care Ltd

Ability House 121 Brooker Road, Waltham Abbey, EN9 1JH
Tel: 01992-655960 **Fax:** 01279-868899
E-mail: sales@abbeyliftcare.co.uk
Website: http://www.abbeyliftcare.co.uk
Directors: I. Hickson (MD), P. Gregory (Fin)
Ultimate Holding Company: GLEBE INVESTMENT LIMITED
Immediate Holding Company: ABBEY LIFTCARE LIMITED
Registration no: 02928817 **Date established:** 1994
No.of Employees: 21 - 50 **Product Groups:** 35, 39, 45

Date of Accounts	Aug 11	Aug 10	Aug 09
Working Capital	292	256	228
Fixed Assets	35	49	41
Current Assets	661	721	615

Bingham Appliances (I.B) Ltd

Unit 83 Hillgrove Business Park, Waltham Abbey, EN9 2HB
Tel: 01992-899158 **Fax:** 01992-899158
E-mail: sales@binghampluckers.com
Website: http://www.binghampluckers.com
Directors: M. McGeough (MD)
Date established: 2001 **No.of Employees:** 1 - 10 **Product Groups:** 20, 40, 41

Capital Refrigeration Services Ltd

16 Lea Road, Waltham Abbey, EN9 1AS
Tel: 01992-788844 **Fax:** 0870-850 1141
E-mail: info@capitalref.com
Website: http://www.capitalref.com
Directors: A. Hayes (MD), J. Hayes (Sales & Mktg)
Immediate Holding Company: CAPITAL REFRIGERATION LIMITED
Registration no: 06945358 **Date established:** 2009
No.of Employees: 21 - 50 **Product Groups:** 26, 37, 40, 41, 52, 63, 66, 67, 69

Cooper Lighting & Safety

Office 2 King Harold Court Sun Street, Waltham Abbey, EN9 1ER
Tel: 01992-787999 **Fax:** 01992-787222
Website: http://www.cooper-ls.com
Managers: K. Stubbs (Mgr)
No.of Employees: 1 - 10 **Product Groups:** 37, 67

Ctda Design Consultants

Unit 51 Hillgrove Business Park Nazeing Road, Nazeing, Waltham Abbey, EN9 2HB
Tel: 01992-890980 **Fax:** 01992-890830
E-mail: sales@ctda.co.uk
Website: http://www.ctda.co.uk
Directors: C. Thompson (MD), M. Thompson (MD), N. Thomson (MD)
Registration no: 01443364 **VAT No.:** GB 632 8075 67
No.of Employees: 1 - 10 **Product Groups:** 81

Curtis Metal Designs

Galley Hill Farm Galley Hill, Waltham Abbey, EN9 2AB
Tel: 01992-769324 **Fax:** 01992-769324
E-mail: bradley_curtis@hotmail.com
Website: http://www.metal-designs.co.uk
Directors: B. Curtis (MD)
Immediate Holding Company: CURTIS METAL DESIGNS LIMITED
Registration no: 06037718 **Date established:** 2006
No.of Employees: 1 - 10 **Product Groups:** 26, 35

Cushway Schmidt Ltd

180 Brooker Road, Waltham Abbey, EN9 1HT
Tel: 01992-713749 **Fax:** 01992-788367
E-mail: tonyhill@tonyhill.com
Website: http://www.cushways.co.uk

see next page

Cushway Schmidt Ltd - Cont'd
Directors: W. Mohammed (Fin)
Immediate Holding Company: CUSHWAY-SCHMIDT LIMITED
Registration no: 07201899 **Date established:** 2010
No.of Employees: 11 - 20 **Product Groups:** 46

Date of Accounts	May 11
Working Capital	128
Fixed Assets	95
Current Assets	393

Druce Grove Ltd
Unit 12 Abbey Mead Industrial Park Brooker Road, Waltham Abbey, EN9 1HU
Tel: 01992-650486 **Fax:** 01992-652226
E-mail: sales@drucegrove.co.uk
Website: http://www.drucegrove.co.uk
Directors: D. Kelly (MD)
Immediate Holding Company: Kelly Group Holdings Ltd
Registration no: 04474504 **No.of Employees:** 11 - 20
Product Groups: 35, 37, 38, 45

Date of Accounts	Jun 08	Jun 07	Jun 06
Working Capital	395	369	270
Current Assets	520	477	420
Current Liabilities	125	108	150

ETS Ltd (Environmental & Technical Services Ltd)
Unit 7 Millbrook Business Park Hoe Lane, Waltham Abbey, EN9 2RJ
Tel: 0870-870 6615 **Fax:** 0870-870 6616
E-mail: climatic@ets.co.uk
Website: http://www.ets.co.uk
Registration no: 01723607 **Turnover:** £1m - £2m
No.of Employees: 11 - 20 **Product Groups:** 38, 40, 54, 85

Flair Communications Ltd
Flair House 112 Brooker Road, Waltham Abbey, EN9 1JH
Tel: 01992-700511 **Fax:** 01992-700388
E-mail: info@flair-uk.com
Website: http://www.flair-uk.com
Directors: D. Hall (Dir)
Immediate Holding Company: FLAIR BUSINESS EQUIPMENT LIMITED
Registration no: 02808361 **Date established:** 1993
Turnover: £250,000 - £500,000 **No.of Employees:** 11 - 20
Product Groups: 37

Date of Accounts	Apr 11	Apr 10	Apr 09
Working Capital	443	583	619
Fixed Assets	15	15	22
Current Assets	553	704	827

G H Warner Footwear plc
Mercury House Lea Road, Waltham Abbey, EN9 1AT
Tel: 01992-769612 **Fax:** 01992-701123
E-mail: admin@mercuryhouse.com
Website: http://www.mercurysports.co.uk
Directors: M. Warner (Dir)
Ultimate Holding Company: WARNDELL INVESTMENTS P.L.C.
Immediate Holding Company: G.H. WARNER FOOTWEAR P.L.C.
Registration no: 01169658 **Date established:** 1974
Turnover: £10m - £20m **No.of Employees:** 21 - 50 **Product Groups:** 61

Date of Accounts	Dec 11	Dec 10	Dec 09
Sales Turnover	11m	14m	15m
Pre Tax Profit/Loss	11	31	-15
Working Capital	2m	2m	2m
Current Assets	5m	4m	6m
Current Liabilities	273	92	490

G I S
2325 Hillgrove Business Park Nazeing, Waltham Abbey, EN9 2HB
Tel: 01992-899199
E-mail: enquiries@g-i-s.co.uk
Website: http://www.g-i-s.co.uk
Directors: S. Georgio (MD)
Ultimate Holding Company: FORTUNA HOLDINGS LIMITED
Immediate Holding Company: G.I.S. INDUSTRIAL SUPPLY CO. LIMITED
Registration no: 01418337 **Date established:** 1979 **Turnover:** £2m - £5m
No.of Employees: 11 - 20 **Product Groups:** 22, 24, 36

Date of Accounts	Aug 10	Aug 09	Aug 08
Sales Turnover	3m	3m	3m
Pre Tax Profit/Loss	1	13	-41
Working Capital	258	253	237
Fixed Assets	34	39	44
Current Assets	887	768	714
Current Liabilities	92	99	82

G & S Sheet Metals Ltd
Unit A4 Lea Road, Waltham Abbey, EN9 1AE
Tel: 01992-713800 **Fax:** 01992-713800
Website: http://www.gssheetmet.plus.com
Directors: W. Stock (Fin), D. Young (MD)
Immediate Holding Company: G. & S. SHEET METALS LIMITED
Registration no: 01105224 **VAT No.:** GB 221 4881 80
Date established: 1973 **Turnover:** £250,000 - £500,000
No.of Employees: 1 - 10 **Product Groups:** 48

Date of Accounts	Apr 11	Apr 10	Apr 09
Working Capital	45	57	20
Fixed Assets	4	5	4
Current Assets	94	106	80

Group Components Ltd
The Potteries Woodgreen Road, Waltham Abbey, EN9 3TN
Tel: 01992-715900 **Fax:** 01992-711993
E-mail: sales@groupcomponents.co.uk
Directors: W. Dearman (Dir)
Immediate Holding Company: GROUP COMPONENTS LIMITED
Registration no: 01022034 **VAT No.:** GB 221 1754 05
Date established: 1971 **Turnover:** £500,000 - £1m
No.of Employees: 1 - 10 **Product Groups:** 35, 36, 37, 38, 45, 46

Date of Accounts	Aug 11	Aug 10	Aug 09
Working Capital	74	51	15
Fixed Assets	15	5	6
Current Assets	226	197	173

Hallmarks Fraulo Ltd
Units 55-56 Hillgrove Business Park Nazeing Road, Nazeing, Waltham Abbey, EN9 2HB
Tel: 01992-899025 **Fax:** 01992-899026
E-mail: info@hallmarkfraulo.co.uk
Website: http://www.hallmarkfraulo.co.uk
Directors: C. Pocock (MD)
Ultimate Holding Company: BAXTER & FRAULO LIMITED
Immediate Holding Company: HALLMARK FRAULO LIMITED
Registration no: 01680097 **Date established:** 1982 **Turnover:** £1m - £2m
No.of Employees: 1 - 10 **Product Groups:** 27, 29, 31, 32, 33, 66

Date of Accounts	Apr 12	Apr 11	Apr 10
Working Capital	240	230	208
Fixed Assets	22	27	18
Current Assets	396	405	369

Hilcrest Design Ltd
Lea Road, Waltham Abbey, EN9 1AJ
Tel: 01992-713005 **Fax:** 01992-710268
E-mail: sales@hilcrest.co.uk
Website: http://www.hilcrest.co.uk
Directors: S. Taylor (MD)
Immediate Holding Company: HILCREST DESIGN LIMITED
Registration no: 01279370 **Date established:** 1976
Turnover: £500,000 - £1m **No.of Employees:** 11 - 20
Product Groups: 29, 30

Date of Accounts	Sep 11	Sep 10	Sep 09
Working Capital	673	658	651
Fixed Assets	248	238	245
Current Assets	896	803	828

David Horner Associates Ltd
125 Brooker Road, Waltham Abbey, EN9 1JU
Tel: 01992-716063 **Fax:** 01992-764993
E-mail: chris@davidhorner.co.uk
Website: http://www.davidhorner.co.uk
Bank(s): Barclays
Directors: C. White (Sales), W. Holmes (Fab), A. Horner (Dir)
Managers: L. Hodge (Admin Off)
Immediate Holding Company: DAVID HORNER ASSOCIATES LIMITED
Registration no: 01084475 **VAT No.:** GB 221 1050 41
Date established: 1972 **Turnover:** £1m - £2m **No.of Employees:** 21 - 50
Product Groups: 23, 28

Date of Accounts	Aug 07	Aug 06
Working Capital	186	204
Fixed Assets	237	169
Current Assets	371	400
Current Liabilities	185	196
Total Share Capital	1	1

L F King & Son Ltd
60 North Street Nazeing, Waltham Abbey, EN9 2NW
Tel: 01992-892270 **Fax:** 01992-892967
E-mail: info@kingsboilerhire.com
Website: http://www.kingsboilerhire.com
Directors: H. King (Dir)
Immediate Holding Company: L.F.KING & SON LIMITED
Registration no: 00614730 **Date established:** 1958
Turnover: £500,000 - £1m **No.of Employees:** 1 - 10 **Product Groups:** 52

Date of Accounts	Sep 11	Sep 10	Sep 09
Working Capital	169	182	166
Fixed Assets	241	255	267
Current Assets	623	637	294

KX Network Solutions Ltd
Network House Hillgrove Business Park, Nazeing, Waltham Abbey, EN9 2HB
Tel: 01992-899899 **Fax:** 01992-899888
E-mail: enquiries@network-sol.com
Website: http://www.network-sol.com
Directors: D. Alexander (Fin), A. Head (MD), S. Wood (Dir & Buyer)
Managers: R. Hussain (I.T. Exec)
Immediate Holding Company: KX Investment Holdings Ltd
Registration no: 03279117 **Date established:** 1996
Turnover: £20m - £50m **No.of Employees:** 21 - 50 **Product Groups:** 44

Lignacite Ltd
Meadgate Works Meadgate Road, Nazeing, Waltham Abbey, EN9 2PD
Tel: 01992-464441 **Fax:** 01992-445713
E-mail: alan@lignacite.co.uk
Website: http://www.lignacite.co.uk
Directors: A. Eastwood (Dir)
Managers: P. Sharp (Sales Admin)
Immediate Holding Company: LIGNACITE LIMITED
Registration no: 00436709 **VAT No.:** GB 102 3711 29
Date established: 1947 **Turnover:** £2m - £5m **No.of Employees:** 21 - 50
Product Groups: 33

Date of Accounts	Dec 11	Dec 10	Dec 09
Sales Turnover	16m	14m	10m
Pre Tax Profit/Loss	434	-253	-730
Working Capital	2m	1m	771
Fixed Assets	10m	11m	11m
Current Assets	4m	4m	4m
Current Liabilities	395	444	305

Macclesfield Fire Protection Ltd
Unit 16 Hillgrove Business Park Nazeing Road, Nazeing, Waltham Abbey, EN9 2HB
Tel: 01625-613746 **Fax:** 01625-610405
Website: http://www.morganfire.co.uk
Directors: E. Doggart (Fin), P. Creasey (MD)
Registration no: 04717034 **No.of Employees:** 21 - 50
Product Groups: 38, 42

Metallon Ltd
Unit D Lea Road Trading Estate Lea Road, Waltham Abbey, EN9 1AE
Tel: 01992-715737 **Fax:** 01992-767607
E-mail: sales@metallon.co.uk
Website: http://www.metallon.co.uk
Directors: S. Tanfield (MD)
Immediate Holding Company: METALLON LIMITED
Registration no: 01909055 **VAT No.:** GB 427 1837 46
Date established: 1985 **Turnover:** £250,000 - £500,000
No.of Employees: 1 - 10 **Product Groups:** 26, 36, 49

Date of Accounts	Jul 11	Jul 10	Jul 09
Working Capital	N/A	-15	-8
Fixed Assets	26	31	35
Current Assets	67	82	64

Newmet Koch
Newmet House Rue De St. Lawrence, Waltham Abbey, EN9 1PF
Tel: 01992-703400 **Fax:** 01992-768393
Website: http://www.newmet.co.uk
Directors: R. Lindsay (Prop)
No.of Employees: 21 - 50 **Product Groups:** 31, 32

Newmetals & Chemicals Ltd (Newmet Koch, Newmet Composites, Surrey Electro-Shielding, Surrey Electro-Materials)
Newmet House Rue De St Lawrence, Waltham Abbey, EN9 1PF
Tel: 01992-711111 **Fax:** 01992-768393
E-mail: materials@newmet.com
Website: http://www.newmet.co.uk
Bank(s): Barclays, Lombard St, London
Directors: J. Lindsay (Dir)
Ultimate Holding Company: NEW METALS AND CHEMICALS (HOLDINGS) LIMITED
Immediate Holding Company: NEW METALS AND CHEMICALS LIMITED
Registration no: 00427388 **VAT No.:** GB 233 0013 33
Date established: 1947 **Turnover:** Up to £250,000
No.of Employees: 11 - 20 **Product Groups:** 31, 32, 34, 37, 66

Date of Accounts	May 11	May 10	May 09
Sales Turnover	3m	3m	3m
Pre Tax Profit/Loss	90	95	113
Working Capital	1m	1m	821
Fixed Assets	99	160	356
Current Assets	2m	2m	1m
Current Liabilities	278	300	232

Northgate Tubular Products Ltd
Woodgreen Road, Waltham Abbey, EN9 3SA
Tel: 01992-715797 **Fax:** 01992-650304
Directors: L. Holleyoake (Dir)
Immediate Holding Company: NORTHGATE TUBULAR PRODUCTS LIMITED
Registration no: 02978299 **Date established:** 1994
No.of Employees: 1 - 10 **Product Groups:** 46, 48

Date of Accounts	Feb 10	Feb 09	Feb 08
Working Capital	-48	-26	-29
Fixed Assets	74	32	32
Current Assets	22	65	24

Robert Lee Ltd
Lea Road, Waltham Abbey, EN9 1AS
Tel: 01992-703200 **Fax:** 0800-376 5556
E-mail: tjw@rlee.co.uk
Website: http://www.rlee.co.uk
Directors: T. Wayman (MD)
Managers: M. Earle (Mktg Serv Mgr), R. Ellender, A. Patterson (Personnel)
Ultimate Holding Company: MARCHASE LIMITED
Immediate Holding Company: ROBERT LEE DISTRIBUTION LIMITED
Registration no: 01812213 **Date established:** 1984
Turnover: £20m - £50m **No.of Employees:** 51 - 100 **Product Groups:** 30, 34, 66

Date of Accounts	Oct 11	Oct 10	Oct 09
Sales Turnover	27m	25m	23m
Pre Tax Profit/Loss	2m	1m	6m
Working Capital	8m	7m	6m
Fixed Assets	905	993	1m
Current Assets	12m	10m	9m
Current Liabilities	498	454	461

Safe Fire
Unit 16 Hillgrove Business Park Nazeing Road, Nazeing, Waltham Abbey, EN9 2HB
Tel: 01896-754353 **Fax:** 01896-757810
E-mail: pcreasey@morganfire.co.uk
Website: http://www.safe-fire.co.uk
Directors: J. McMenemy (Fin), P. Creasey (MD)
Immediate Holding Company: SAFE FIRE LIMITED
Registration no: SC257073 **Date established:** 2003
No.of Employees: 21 - 50 **Product Groups:** 38, 42

Date of Accounts	Jun 11	Jun 10	Jun 07
Working Capital	73	20	6
Fixed Assets	N/A	14	11
Current Assets	104	45	33

Wacker Neuson Ltd
Lea Road, Waltham Abbey, EN9 1AW
Tel: 01992-707200 **Fax:** 01495-718162
E-mail: theoffice@wackerneuson.com
Website: http://www.wackerneuson.com
Bank(s): Barclays
Directors: R. Harrison (MD)
Managers: J. Oakley (Comptroller), L. Hewitt (Tech Serv Mgr), P. Boehmer (Personnel)
Ultimate Holding Company: WACKER NEUSON SE (GERMANY)
Immediate Holding Company: WACKER NEUSON LIMITED
Registration no: 00721483 **VAT No.:** GB 220 8468 74
Date established: 1962 **Turnover:** £10m - £20m
No.of Employees: 21 - 50 **Product Groups:** 34

Date of Accounts	Dec 11	Dec 10	Dec 09
Sales Turnover	14m	13m	9m
Pre Tax Profit/Loss	292	222	-2m
Working Capital	3m	3m	2m
Fixed Assets	730	779	666
Current Assets	5m	5m	5m
Current Liabilities	575	674	1m

Walton On The Naze

A V I
7 Five Acres, Walton On The Naze, CO14 8RQ
Tel: 08456-026208 **Fax:** 07005-942838
E-mail: sales@aviltd.co.uk
Website: http://www.aviltd.co.uk
Directors: J. Mann (Dir)
Immediate Holding Company: AVI LIMITED
Registration no: 03918452 **Date established:** 2000
No.of Employees: 1 - 10 **Product Groups:** 37, 39, 80

Date of Accounts	Apr 11	Apr 10	Apr 09
Working Capital	22	27	34
Fixed Assets	38	45	17
Current Assets	79	82	68

French Marine Motors Ltd
Coles Lane, Walton on the Naze, CO14 8SL
Tel: 01255-850303 **Fax:** 01255-850303
E-mail: info@frenchmarine.com
Website: http://www.frenchmarine.com

Directors: C. French (MD)
Immediate Holding Company: FRENCH MARINE MOTORS LIMITED
Registration no: 01455234 **Date established:** 1979
No.of Employees: 11 - 20 **Product Groups:** 35, 36, 39

Date of Accounts	Oct 11	Oct 10	Oct 09
Working Capital	19	57	125
Fixed Assets	143	122	139
Current Assets	666	677	794

W S G Operating Co. Ltd
New Walton Pier Co Ltd, Walton on the Naze, CO14 8ES
Tel: 01255-670970 **Fax:** 01255-850383
E-mail: sales@wsgscales.com
Website: http://www.wsgscales.com
Directors: A. Loch (Fin), J. Sills (Dir)
Ultimate Holding Company: CP EQUITYCO LIMITED
Immediate Holding Company: W.S.G.OPERATING COMPANY LIMITED
Registration no: 00324991 **Date established:** 1937
Turnover: Up to £250,000 **No.of Employees:** 1 - 10 **Product Groups:** 38, 42

Date of Accounts	Dec 09	Dec 08	Dec 07
Sales Turnover	N/A	27	327
Pre Tax Profit/Loss	N/A	-291	11
Working Capital	522	522	405
Fixed Assets	N/A	N/A	354
Current Assets	522	522	688
Current Liabilities	N/A	N/A	16

Westcliff On Sea

D & J Export Ltd
33 Valkyrie Road, Westcliff On Sea, SS0 8BY
Tel: 01702-348340 **Fax:** 01702-331080
E-mail: sales@d-jexports.com
Website: http://www.d-jexports.com
Directors: J. Passley (Fin), D. Passley (MD)
Immediate Holding Company: D & J EXPORTS LIMITED
Registration no: 01753607 **Date established:** 1983
Turnover: £250,000 - £500,000 **No.of Employees:** 1 - 10
Product Groups: 23, 24, 25, 29, 30, 31, 32, 33, 34, 35, 36, 37, 38, 39, 40, 41, 42, 43, 44, 45, 46, 48, 49, 61, 67, 68, 71, 72, 84, 87

Date of Accounts	Aug 11	Aug 10	Aug 09
Working Capital	-48	-20	-5
Fixed Assets	4	4	5
Current Assets	1	24	22

Display Store
30 Hamlet Court Road, Westcliff On Sea, SS0 7LX
Tel: 01702-433505 **Fax:** 01702-347066
E-mail: info@displayteam.co.uk
Website: http://www.displayteam.co.uk
Directors: L. Carber (Ptnr)
No.of Employees: 1 - 10 **Product Groups:** 30, 49, 80

The Educators
8 Cliff Avenue, Westcliff On Sea, SS0 7AJ
Tel: 01702-348815 **Fax:** 01702-343046
E-mail: john_bridge@msn.com
Website: http://www.educators.co.uk
Directors: J. Bridge (Prop)
No.of Employees: 1 - 10 **Product Groups:** 44, 61, 69, 80, 81, 82, 84, 86, 89

Jewson Ltd
548-550 London Road, Westcliff On Sea, SS0 9HS
Tel: 01702-331131 **Fax:** 01702-331160
E-mail: chris.chapman@jewson.co.uk
Website: http://www.jewson.net
Managers: C. Chapman (District Mgr)
Ultimate Holding Company: COMPAGNIE DE SAINT GOBAIN (FRANCE)
Immediate Holding Company: JEWSON LIMITED
Registration no: 00348407 **Date established:** 1939 **Turnover:** £2m - £5m
No.of Employees: 11 - 20 **Product Groups:** 66

Date of Accounts	Dec 11	Dec 10	Dec 09
Sales Turnover	1606m	1547m	1485m
Pre Tax Profit/Loss	18m	100m	45m
Working Capital	-345m	-250m	-349m
Fixed Assets	496m	387m	461m
Current Assets	657m	1005m	1320m
Current Liabilities	66m	120m	64m

Maplin Electronics Ltd
233-237 London Road, Westcliff On Sea, SS0 7BP
Tel: 08432-277320 **Fax:** 01702-341013
E-mail: customercare@maplin.co.uk
Website: http://www.maplin.co.uk
Ultimate Holding Company: MONTAGU PRIVATE EQUITY LLP
Immediate Holding Company: MAPLIN ELECTRONICS LIMITED
Registration no: 01264385 **Date established:** 1976
Turnover: £125m - £250m **No.of Employees:** 1 - 10 **Product Groups:** 37, 61

Date of Accounts	Dec 11	Dec 08	Dec 09
Sales Turnover	205m	204m	204m
Pre Tax Profit/Loss	25m	32m	35m
Working Capital	118m	49m	75m
Fixed Assets	27m	28m	28m
Current Assets	207m	108m	142m
Current Liabilities	78m	51m	59m

Reeves Electrical Wholesalers
565 London Road, Westcliff On Sea, SS0 9PQ
Tel: 01702-339822 **Fax:** 01702-339806
Directors: P. Doman (Prop)
No.of Employees: 1 - 10 **Product Groups:** 36, 40

Rega Research Ltd
119 Park Street, Westcliff On Sea, SS0 7PD
Tel: 01702-333071 **Fax:** 01702-432427
E-mail: service@rega.co.uk
Website: http://www.rega.co.uk
Bank(s): Barclays
Directors: R. Gandy (Dir), K. Palmer (Co Sec)
Managers: P. Freeman (Mgr), M. Maskell (Sales Prom)
Immediate Holding Company: REGA RESEARCH LIMITED
Registration no: 01118303 **Date established:** 1973 **Turnover:** £1m - £2m
No.of Employees: 21 - 50 **Product Groups:** 37

Date of Accounts	Jun 11	Jun 10	Jun 09
Working Capital	2m	2m	2m
Fixed Assets	265	252	229
Current Assets	3m	3m	2m

Wickford

Airtech Analysis Ltd
Unit 6 Blenheim Court Hurricane Way, Wickford, SS11 8YT
Tel: 01268-562645 **Fax:** 01268-570198
E-mail: enquiries@airtechanalysisltd.com
Website: http://www.airtechanalysisltd.com
Directors: P. Abrey (MD), T. Abrey (Dir)
Immediate Holding Company: AIRTECH ANALYSIS LTD
Registration no: 02516089 **Date established:** 1990
Turnover: £250,000 - £500,000 **No.of Employees:** 21 - 50
Product Groups: 54, 85

Date of Accounts	Jun 11	Jun 10	Jun 09
Working Capital	-11	-40	-53
Fixed Assets	100	69	77
Current Assets	338	306	207

alligata.co.uk
Unit 3b Sopwith Crescent, Wickford Business Park, Wickford, SS11 8YU
Tel: 01268-768768 **Fax:** 01268-768764
E-mail: sales@alligata.co.uk
Website: http://www.alligata.co.uk
Date established: 1988 **No.of Employees:** 11 - 20 **Product Groups:** 30

Antislip Tapes Ltd
Unit 3b Sopwith Crescent Hurricane Way, Wickford, SS11 8YU
Tel: 01268-768768 **Fax:** 01268-768764
E-mail: graham@indigo.co
Website: http://www.indigoplc.com
Directors: G. Hamilton (Dir)
Immediate Holding Company: T & A TRADING LIMITED
Registration no: 04562556 **Date established:** 2002
No.of Employees: 11 - 20 **Product Groups:** 27, 32, 66

Date of Accounts	Oct 10	Oct 09	Oct 08
Working Capital	-2	-13	-29
Fixed Assets	8	12	17
Current Assets	74	86	147

B I S Door Systems Ltd
Unit 13-14 Hodgson Court Hodgson Way, Wickford, SS11 8XR
Tel: 01268-767566 **Fax:** 01268-560284
E-mail: sales@bis-doors.co.uk
Website: http://www.bis-doors.co.uk
Bank(s): Lloyds TSB Bank plc
Directors: L. Dando (MD)
Immediate Holding Company: B I S DOOR SYSTEMS LIMITED
Registration no: 03400080 **VAT No.:** GB 284 0988 22
Date established: 1997 **No.of Employees:** 21 - 50 **Product Groups:** 25, 30, 34, 35, 36, 39, 46, 48

Date of Accounts	Jul 11	Jul 10	Jul 09
Working Capital	4	9	24
Fixed Assets	88	93	112
Current Assets	198	146	143

B S C L Ltd
Unit 1 Bruce Grove, Wickford, SS11 8BP
Tel: 01268-578940 **Fax:** 01268-764058
E-mail: info@bscl.com
Website: http://www.bscl.com
Bank(s): Lloyds TSB Bank plc
Managers: S. Waughman (Serv Mgr)
Ultimate Holding Company: BSCL MANAGEMENT SERVICES LIMITED
Immediate Holding Company: BSCL LIMITED
Registration no: 02487238 **Date established:** 1990
No.of Employees: 21 - 50 **Product Groups:** 37, 44, 52

Date of Accounts	Mar 11	Mar 10	Mar 09
Sales Turnover	8m	7m	6m
Pre Tax Profit/Loss	63	39	8
Working Capital	420	377	249
Fixed Assets	39	47	55
Current Assets	2m	2m	1m
Current Liabilities	476	785	337

Bardon Concrete Ltd
Unit 7 Robert Way, Wickford, SS11 8DD
Tel: 01268-769696 **Fax:** 01268-769097
Website: http://www.bardonconcrete.co.uk
Directors: B. Fender (MD), J. Turner (MD)
Managers: N. Hope (Sales Off Mgr), H. Adams (Sales Admin), B. Fender (Chief Mgr)
Ultimate Holding Company: AGGREGATE INDUSTRIES HOLDINGS LIMITED
Immediate Holding Company: BARDON CONCRETE LIMITED
Registration no: 04553003 **VAT No.:** GB 388 7710 14
Date established: 2002 **Turnover:** £2m - £5m **No.of Employees:** 1 - 10
Product Groups: 14, 33

Brooke Air
J C House Hurricane Way, Wickford, SS11 8YB
Tel: 01268-572266 **Fax:** 01268-560606
E-mail: info@brookeair.co.uk
Website: http://www.brookeair.co.uk
Bank(s): National Westminster Bank Plc
Directors: N. Brooke Walder (Grp Chief Exec), C. Brooke-walder (MD)
Managers: W. Morrison (Purch Mgr)
Immediate Holding Company: BROOKE AIR HOLDINGS LIMITED
Registration no: 03713278 **VAT No.:** GB 250 4413 01
Date established: 1999 **Turnover:** £2m - £5m **No.of Employees:** 11 - 20
Product Groups: 35, 40

Date of Accounts	Jun 11	Jun 10	Jun 09
Working Capital	-5	-205	-403
Fixed Assets	1m	1m	1m

Columbia Staver Ltd
Unit A Russell Gardens, Wickford, SS11 8QR
Tel: 01268-733346 **Fax:** 01268-735893
E-mail: info@columbia-staver.co.uk
Website: http://www.columbia-staver.co.uk
Bank(s): Midland
Directors: A. Smith (MD)
Managers: T. Sampson (Tech Serv Mgr), H. Turrell (Chief Acct)
Immediate Holding Company: COLUMBIA-STAVER LIMITED
Registration no: 01158147 **VAT No.:** 208 1734 80 **Date established:** 1974
Turnover: £5m - £10m **No.of Employees:** 11 - 20 **Product Groups:** 37, 40, 48

Date of Accounts	Dec 11	Dec 10	Dec 09
Working Capital	1m	2m	1m
Fixed Assets	6	10	15
Current Assets	2m	3m	2m

Contract Welding
Russell Gardens, Wickford, SS11 8BH
Tel: 01268-766965 **Fax:** 01268-766927
E-mail: cws@netcomuk.co.uk
Website: http://www.contractwelding.co.uk
Bank(s): National Westminster Bank Plc
Directors: M. Gill (Dir)
Managers: D. Baillie (Consultant)
Ultimate Holding Company: KILN SUPPLY SERVICES LIMITED
Immediate Holding Company: WICKFORD VALETING CENTRE LTD
Registration no: 03396541 **VAT No.:** GB 507 1346 71
Date established: 2012 **Turnover:** £1m - £2m **No.of Employees:** 11 - 20
Product Groups: 34, 39, 48

Date of Accounts	Dec 10	Dec 09	Dec 08
Working Capital	-358	-328	-390
Fixed Assets	542	492	570
Current Assets	251	236	241

D P Energy Services Ltd
Unit 5-6 Heron Avenue, Wickford, SS11 8DL
Tel: 01268-560040 **Fax:** 01268-560261
E-mail: pw@drakepower.com
Website: http://www.drakepower.com
Bank(s): Barclays Bank PLC
Directors: P. Williams (MD)
Immediate Holding Company: D.P. ENERGY SERVICES LIMITED
Registration no: 05738994 **Date established:** 2006
Turnover: £500,000 - £1m **No.of Employees:** 11 - 20
Product Groups: 37, 38

Date of Accounts	Mar 11	Mar 10	Mar 09
Working Capital	15	28	-2
Fixed Assets	6	8	4
Current Assets	231	301	249

Dixons Surgical Instruments Ltd
1 Roman Court Hurricane Way, Wickford, SS11 8YB
Tel: 01268-764614 **Fax:** 01268-764615
E-mail: info@dixons-uk.com
Website: http://www.dixons-uk.com
Bank(s): Barclays
Directors: J. Dixon (MD), J. Dixons (MD), J. Dixon (Co Sec)
Immediate Holding Company: DIXON'S SURGICAL INSTRUMENTS LIMITED
Registration no: 00460740 **VAT No.:** GB 250 4492 76
Date established: 1948 **Turnover:** £1m - £2m **No.of Employees:** 11 - 20
Product Groups: 26, 38, 40, 41, 42

Date of Accounts	Dec 11	Dec 10	Dec 09
Working Capital	523	515	458
Fixed Assets	378	424	315
Current Assets	740	676	559

Effjey
Pilot Close 1 Fulmar Way, Wickford, SS11 8YW
Tel: 01268-733788 **Fax:** 01268-733477
E-mail: mail@effjey.co.uk
Website: http://www.effjey.co.uk
Managers: C. Hart (Mgr)
Immediate Holding Company: EFFJEY LIMITED
Registration no: 01273898 **VAT No.:** GB 231 4447 89
Date established: 1976 **Turnover:** £1m - £2m **No.of Employees:** 1 - 10
Product Groups: 48

Date of Accounts	Dec 11	Dec 10	Dec 09
Working Capital	76	47	32
Fixed Assets	21	28	37
Current Assets	247	171	193

Essex Fasteners
4 Byron Works Russell Gardens, Wickford, SS11 8QR
Tel: 01268-766122 **Fax:** 01268-560759
E-mail: info@orbitalhs.co.uk
Website: http://www.orbitalhs.co.uk
Directors: R. Thorogood (MD)
Date established: 1996 **No.of Employees:** 1 - 10 **Product Groups:** 35

Foundationwear Machinery Specialists Ltd
3 Orwell Court Hurricane Way, Wickford, SS11 8YJ
Tel: 01268-562022 **Fax:** 01268-562023
Website: http://www.lockstitch.com
Directors: C. Stratton (MD), S. Stratton (Fin)
Immediate Holding Company: FOUNDATIONWEAR MACHINERY SPECIALIST LIMITED
Registration no: 01091824 **Date established:** 1973
No.of Employees: 1 - 10 **Product Groups:** 43

Date of Accounts	Jan 11	Jan 10	Jan 09
Working Capital	94	94	102
Fixed Assets	16	17	23
Current Assets	117	124	134

Hadleigh Enterprises Ltd
Unit 11 Buckingham Square, Wickford, SS11 8YQ
Tel: 01268-572255 **Fax:** 01268-572121
E-mail: sales@hadleigh.u-net.com
Website: http://www.hadleigh.uk.com
Directors: D. Ogles (Dir)
Immediate Holding Company: HADLEIGH ENTERPRISES LIMITED
Registration no: 01035812 **VAT No.:** GB 250 4328 89
Date established: 1971 **Turnover:** £500,000 - £1m
No.of Employees: 1 - 10 **Product Groups:** 27

Date of Accounts	Apr 11	Apr 10	Apr 09
Working Capital	10	13	6
Fixed Assets	27	37	48
Current Assets	255	243	184

Hedinair Ovens Ltd
Unit 2-3 Enterprise Way, Wickford, SS11 8DH
Tel: 01268-761777 **Fax:** 01268-760210
E-mail: sales@hedinair.co.uk
Website: http://www.hedinair.co.uk

see next page

Hedinair Ovens Ltd - Cont'd
Directors: J. Nelson (MD), L. Nelson (MD)
Managers: D. Moon (Purch Mgr), I. Champness
Immediate Holding Company: HEDINAIR OVENS LIMITED
Registration no: 02878347 **VAT No.:** GB 542 3317 70
Date established: 1993 **Turnover:** £1m - £2m **No.of Employees:** 21 - 50
Product Groups: 40, 46, 48

Date of Accounts	Sep 11	Sep 10	Sep 09
Working Capital	76	59	26
Fixed Assets	12	5	10
Current Assets	674	452	338

Indigo
Unit 3b, Sopwith Crescent Wickford Business Park, Wickford, SS11 8YU
Tel: 01268-768768 **Fax:** 01268-768764
E-mail: sales@fantastick.co.uk
Website: http://www.indigo.co
Date established: 1992 **Turnover:** £250,000 - £500,000
No.of Employees: 21 - 50 **Product Groups:** 27, 42, 66

J C Vents Ltd (Louvre Division of Brooke-Air)
J C House Hurricane Way, Wickford, SS11 8YB
Tel: 01268-561122 **Fax:** 01268-560606
E-mail: info@brookeair.co.uk
Website: http://www.jcvents.co.uk
Bank(s): National Westminster Bank Plc
Directors: N. Brooke-Walder (MD)
Immediate Holding Company: J C V LIMITED
Registration no: 03758940 **VAT No.:** GB 352 0077 88
Date established: 1999 **Turnover:** £1m - £2m **No.of Employees:** 21 - 50
Product Groups: 35, 40, 48

Jeff Ayres & Associates
282 Southend Road, Wickford, SS11 8PS
Tel: 01268-730574
E-mail: jeff.ayres@btinternet.com
Website: http://www.jeffayres.co.uk
Directors: J. Ayres (Prop)
VAT No.: GB 924 7025 33 **Date established:** 2004
Turnover: Up to £250,000 **No.of Employees:** 1 - 10 **Product Groups:** 54, 80, 85, 86, 87

Lemon Groundworks
Russell Gardens, Wickford, SS11 8BH
Tel: 01268-571571 **Fax:** 01268-571555
E-mail: wickford@lemon-gs.co.uk
Website: http://www.lemon-gs.co.uk
Directors: J. Coleman (Fin), K. Childs (Prop)
Managers: H. Thompson (Sales & Mktg Mg), J. Jones (Sales & Mktg Mg), P. Pannell
Immediate Holding Company: LEMON STEEL SERVICES LIMITED
Registration no: 02615708 **Date established:** 1991 **Turnover:** £2m - £5m
No.of Employees: 11 - 20 **Product Groups:** 25, 27, 30, 31, 32, 34, 35, 37, 39, 45, 48, 66

Date of Accounts	Mar 12	Mar 11	Mar 10
Working Capital	842	858	849
Fixed Assets	129	125	125
Current Assets	1m	1m	1m

LJP UK Limited
14 Deirdre Close Innovation House, Wickford, SS12 0AZ
Tel: 01268-456804 **Fax:** 01268-456804
E-mail: sales@ljpuk.co.uk
Website: http://www.insta.de
Directors: L. Pyme (MD)
Registration no: 05567192 **No.of Employees:** 1 - 10 **Product Groups:** 37, 44, 67, 84

Matrix Catering Systems Ltd
Victoria Court Hurricane Way, Wickford, SS11 8YY
Tel: 01268-574001 **Fax:** 01268-574004
E-mail: info@matrixcatering.co.uk
Website: http://www.matrixcatering.co.uk
Directors: D. Pearce (Dir)
Immediate Holding Company: MATRIX CATERING SYSTEMS LTD.
Registration no: 02919108 **Date established:** 1994
No.of Employees: 1 - 10 **Product Groups:** 38, 42

Date of Accounts	Mar 12	Mar 11	Mar 10
Working Capital	38	23	83
Fixed Assets	188	189	191
Current Assets	217	217	252

Maywick Ltd
Unit 7 Hawk Hill Battlesbridge, Wickford, SS11 7RJ
Tel: 01268-573165 **Fax:** 01268-573085
E-mail: sales.maywick@btconnect.com
Website: http://www.maywick.co.uk
Directors: D. Bamber (MD)
Ultimate Holding Company: RED ONION LIMITED
Immediate Holding Company: MAYWICK LIMITED
Registration no: 00996871 **VAT No.:** GB 102 0667 21
Date established: 1970 **No.of Employees:** 1 - 10 **Product Groups:** 40, 42

Date of Accounts	Jun 11	Jun 10	Jun 09
Working Capital	422	339	329
Fixed Assets	40	4	8
Current Assets	480	420	387

Measuring Machines Ltd
9 Oban Court Hurricane Way, Wickford, SS11 8YB
Tel: 01268-560999 **Fax:** 01268-561222
E-mail: info@measuringmachines.co.uk
Website: http://www.measuringmachines.co.uk
Directors: A. Rogers (Dir)
Immediate Holding Company: MEASURING MACHINES LIMITED
Registration no: 00226734 **VAT No.:** GB 250 6532 80
Date established: 2027 **Turnover:** £1m - £2m **No.of Employees:** 1 - 10
Product Groups: 43

Date of Accounts	Dec 11	Dec 10	Dec 09
Working Capital	-4	-1	-1
Fixed Assets	2	2	3
Current Assets	25	35	36

Pioneer Tools Ltd
UNIT 12 FANTON HALL, Wickford, SS12 9JF
Tel: 01268-764734 **Fax:** 0870-7622512
Website: http://www.pioneertools.co.uk

Directors: D. Smith (Prop)
Registration no: 05017986 **Date established:** 2002
Turnover: £500,000 - £1m **No.of Employees:** 1 - 10 **Product Groups:** 37

Plastic Extruders Ltd
Russell Gardens, Wickford, SS11 8DN
Tel: 01268-571116 **Fax:** 01268-560027
E-mail: info@plastex.co.uk
Website: http://www.plastex.co.uk
Bank(s): Barclays
Directors: D. O'Sullivan (MD), P. O'Sullivan (Sales)
Managers: J. Azzoppard (Export Sales Mg), K. Rosser (Sales Prom Mgr)
Registration no: 00745566 **VAT No.:** GB 250 2879 62
Date established: 1962 **Turnover:** £5m - £10m
No.of Employees: 51 - 100 **Product Groups:** 23, 29, 30, 33, 35, 39, 40, 49

Date of Accounts	Apr 12	Apr 09	Apr 10
Sales Turnover	12m	8m	8m
Pre Tax Profit/Loss	1m	580	354
Working Capital	4m	3m	3m
Fixed Assets	5m	2m	2m
Current Assets	5m	4m	4m
Current Liabilities	782	456	388

Power Sonic Europe
3 Buckingham Square Hurricane Way, Wickford, SS11 8YQ
Tel: 01268-560686 **Fax:** 01268-560902
E-mail: sales@power-sonic.co.uk
Website: http://www.power-sonic.co.uk
Bank(s): National Westminster
Directors: R. Jefferys (MD)
Managers: S. Williams (Sales & Mktg Mg), S. Noyce
Ultimate Holding Company: POWER SONIC CORPORATION (USA)
Immediate Holding Company: POWER-SONIC EUROPE LIMITED
Registration no: 02014543 **VAT No.:** GB 436 4797 16
Date established: 1986 **Turnover:** £10m - £20m
No.of Employees: 11 - 20 **Product Groups:** 37

Date of Accounts	Dec 11	Dec 10	Dec 09
Sales Turnover	13m	12m	13m
Pre Tax Profit/Loss	1m	186	565
Working Capital	4m	3m	3m
Fixed Assets	512	532	522
Current Assets	6m	7m	6m
Current Liabilities	195	169	75

Rackmaster Ltd
Unit 5a Russell Court Russell Gardens, Wickford, SS11 8QU
Tel: 01268-730722 **Fax:** 01268-730723
Directors: P. Cubitt (MD)
Immediate Holding Company: RACKMASTER LIMITED
Registration no: 04467092 **Date established:** 2002
No.of Employees: 1 - 10 **Product Groups:** 20, 40, 41

Date of Accounts	Jul 11	Jul 10	Jul 09
Working Capital	-18	29	17
Fixed Assets	38	4	4
Current Assets	217	216	138

S B Z Corporation Ltd
Unit 13 Kendal Court Hurricane Way, Wickford, SS11 8YB
Tel: 01268-761504
E-mail: sales@sbzcorporation.com
Website: http://www.sbzcorporation.com
Directors: L. Holder (MD)
Immediate Holding Company: SBZ CORPORATION LIMITED
Registration no: 04823382 **Date established:** 2003
Turnover: £250,000 - £500,000 **No.of Employees:** 11 - 20
Product Groups: 87

Date of Accounts	Nov 11	Nov 10	Nov 09
Working Capital	380	172	102
Fixed Assets	479	133	98
Current Assets	4m	3m	2m

Saarlander UK Ltd
Unit 7 Wickford Enterprise Centre Enterprise Way, Wickford, SS11 8DH
Tel: 01268-561291 **Fax:** 01268-561292
E-mail: sales@saarlander.co.uk
Website: http://www.saarlander.co.uk
Directors: D. Wilson (Comm)
Immediate Holding Company: SAARLANDER (UK) LTD.
Registration no: 03326398 **Date established:** 1997 **Turnover:** £1m - £2m
No.of Employees: 1 - 10 **Product Groups:** 20, 21

Date of Accounts	Mar 11	Mar 10	Mar 09
Working Capital	41	-74	-28
Fixed Assets	2	2	3
Current Assets	116	118	183

Sax Paving
8 viking way, Wickford, SS11 7JA
Tel: 0800-0075250 **Fax:** 01268-768057
E-mail: niki.drury@tesco.net
Website: http://www.saxpaving.co.uk
Directors: N. drury (Dir)
Registration no: 6312218 **Date established:** 2000
Turnover: Up to £250,000 **No.of Employees:** 1 - 10 **Product Groups:** 52

Date of Accounts	Jul 08
Working Capital	-5
Fixed Assets	6
Current Assets	5
Current Liabilities	10

R D Simpson & Sons
Oak Villa Pound Lane, North Benfleet, Wickford, SS12 9JS
Tel: 01268-726628
E-mail: rdsimpson@dsl.pipex.com
Directors: R. Simpson (Prop)
Date established: 1984 **No.of Employees:** 1 - 10 **Product Groups:** 26, 35

Sorrells Wine Racks Ltd
Unit 14 Dollymans Farm Doublegate Lane, Rawreth, Wickford, SS11 8UD
Tel: 01268-570880 **Fax:** 01268-571035
E-mail: info@sorrells-wineracks.co.uk
Website: http://www.sorrells-winerack.co.uk
Directors: T. Lewis (Dir)
Immediate Holding Company: SORRELLS WINE RACKS LIMITED
Registration no: 04003226 **Date established:** 2000
No.of Employees: 11 - 20 **Product Groups:** 20, 40, 41

Date of Accounts	Jul 11	Jul 10	Jul 09
Working Capital	64	19	31
Fixed Assets	46	54	38
Current Assets	247	255	226

Steelcraft UK Ltd
Unit 6 Dollymans Farm Doublegate Lane, Rawreth, Wickford, SS11 8UD
Tel: 01268-560100 **Fax:** 01268-560102
E-mail: shaun@steelcraft-uk.com
Website: http://www.steelcraft-uk.com
Directors: S. Hannibal (Dir), P. Hannibal (Co Sec)
Immediate Holding Company: STEELCRAFT (UK) LTD
Registration no: 03819358 **Date established:** 1999
Turnover: £250,000 - £500,000 **No.of Employees:** 11 - 20
Product Groups: 35

Sytem Food Machinery Services
Unit 14 Clovelly Chelmsford Road, Rawreth, Wickford, SS11 8SY
Tel: 01268-561666 **Fax:** 01268-561667
E-mail: sytemfms@aol.com
Website: http://www.sytemfms.co.uk
Directors: S. Brown (Prop)
Date established: 1987 **No.of Employees:** 1 - 10 **Product Groups:** 20, 40, 41

Witham

A C S Fabrications
22-24 Crittall Road, Witham, CM8 3DR
Tel: 01376-513419 **Fax:** 01376-511615
Website: http://www.acsltdessex.co.uk
Directors: G. Vincent (MD), R. Vincent (MD)
Immediate Holding Company: ALUMINIUM COPPER & STAINLESS COMPANY LIMITED
Registration no: 00874594 **Date established:** 1966
Turnover: £250,000 - £500,000 **No.of Employees:** 1 - 10
Product Groups: 48

Date of Accounts	Mar 11	Mar 10	Mar 09
Sales Turnover	N/A	270	373
Pre Tax Profit/Loss	N/A	37	54
Working Capital	39	93	98
Fixed Assets	4	5	5
Current Assets	124	184	177
Current Liabilities	N/A	35	29

Acme Seals
Unit 22d Waterside Business Park Eastways, Witham, CM8 3YQ
Tel: 01376-521841 **Fax:** 01376-521617
E-mail: acme@acmeseals.co.uk
Website: http://www.acmeseals.com
Bank(s): National Westminster
Directors: J. Hedger (Dir)
Immediate Holding Company: ACME SEALS LIMITED
Registration no: 00235948 **VAT No.:** GB 248 0229 70
Date established: 2028 **Turnover:** £1m - £2m **No.of Employees:** 11 - 20
Product Groups: 30, 35, 36, 42, 49

Date of Accounts	Dec 11	Dec 10	Dec 09
Working Capital	4	45	19
Fixed Assets	99	64	76
Current Assets	350	330	338
Current Liabilities	110	20	N/A

Alexander Industrial Supplies
Unit D Eastways Motts Lane, Witham, CM8 3YQ
Tel: 01376-500303 **Fax:** 01376-502090
E-mail: sales@alexander-industrial.co.uk
Website: http://www.alexander-industrial.co.uk
Bank(s): National Westminster Bank Plc
Directors: J. Green (Co Sec)
Managers: R. Moore (Comm), C. Westrope
Ultimate Holding Company: FILTRONA PLC
Immediate Holding Company: ALEXANDER INDUSTRIAL SUPPLIES (ESSEX) LIMITED
Registration no: 01636696 **VAT No.:** GB 368 5845 01
Date established: 1982 **Turnover:** £1m - £2m **No.of Employees:** 11 - 20
Product Groups: 22, 24, 29, 30, 35, 36, 39, 40, 66

Date of Accounts	Dec 10	Dec 09	Dec 08
Sales Turnover	N/A	N/A	1m
Pre Tax Profit/Loss	N/A	N/A	138
Working Capital	302	N/A	302
Current Assets	313	N/A	322
Current Liabilities	N/A	N/A	20

Anglia Business Machines
26 Elm View Green Lanes, White Notley, Witham, CM8 1RB
Tel: 01376-511100
E-mail: info@abmsales.com
Website: http://www.angliabusinesssupplies.co.uk
Directors: J. Collins (Prop)
Date established: 1987 **No.of Employees:** 1 - 10 **Product Groups:** 44, 49, 64, 67

Anglia Rustguard Ltd
Unit 5 Swan Vale Industrial Estate Colchester Road, Witham, CM8 3DH
Tel: 01376-514152 **Fax:** 01376-512802
E-mail: angliarustguard@btconnect.com
Directors: J. Riley (MD)
Immediate Holding Company: ANGLIA RUSTGUARD LIMITED
Registration no: 01406427 **VAT No.:** GB 325 6324 70
Date established: 1978 **Turnover:** £250,000 - £500,000
No.of Employees: 1 - 10 **Product Groups:** 32, 48

Date of Accounts	Dec 11	Dec 10	Dec 09
Working Capital	10	82	122
Fixed Assets	69	74	84
Current Assets	76	126	189

Bluewater Forklift Whitham
170 Enterprise Court Eastways, Witham, CM8 3YS
Tel: 08700-771102
Website: http://www.bluewaterforklift.co.uk
Directors: R. Vost (MD)
Date established: 2005 **No.of Employees:** 1 - 10 **Product Groups:** 35, 39, 45

Brantham Engineering Ltd
3l Moss Road, Witham, CM8 3UQ
Tel: 01376-518384 **Fax:** 01376-518900
E-mail: mail@brantham.com
Website: http://www.brantham.com
Bank(s): Lloyds TSB Bank plc

Directors: A. Winch (Comm), D. Webb (Dir), S. Cruddace (Sales)
Managers: T. Mann (Chief Acct)
Ultimate Holding Company: Brantham (Holdings) Ltd
Immediate Holding Company: Brantham Ltd
Registration no: 01114549 **VAT No.:** GB 623 3616 60
Date established: 1994 **Turnover:** £10m - £20m
No.of Employees: 101 - 250 **Product Groups:** 37, 44, 48, 84

Date of Accounts	Dec 08	Dec 07	Dec 06
Sales Turnover	13m	14m	13m
Pre Tax Profit/Loss	340	350	30
Working Capital	2m	300	1m
Fixed Assets	470	580	750
Current Assets	5m	5m	6m
Current Liabilities	4m	4m	4m
Total Share Capital	30	30	30

Britannia Storage Systems Ltd
Unit E Eastways, Witham, CM8 3YQ
Tel: 01376-533820 **Fax:** 01376-500863
E-mail: enquiries@britannia-storage.co.uk
Website: http://www.britannia-storage.co.uk
Directors: J. Swampillai (Fin), P. Rimell (Dir), P. Rimmel (MD)
Managers: R. May (Mats Contrlr)
Immediate Holding Company: Britannia Storage Systems Ltd
Registration no: 01626141 **VAT No.:** GB 512 3807 74
Date established: 1982 **Turnover:** £2m - £5m **No.of Employees:** 11 - 20
Product Groups: 26, 30

Date of Accounts	Dec 09	Dec 08	Dec 07
Working Capital	235	399	145
Fixed Assets	721	615	562
Current Assets	598	1m	1m

Burlington
Eastways Park, Witham, CM8 3YE
Tel: 08456-384936
E-mail: sales@burlingtonbottling.com
Website: http://www.burlingtonbottling.com
Managers: J. Hayman, J. Williams, S. Strutt (Comptroller), S. Wilkinson, M. Mckee, M. Andrews
Ultimate Holding Company: HAYMAN LIMITED
Immediate Holding Company: THE BURLINGTON DRINKS COMPANY LIMITED
Registration no: 06310070 **Date established:** 2007
No.of Employees: 51 - 100 **Product Groups:** 21

Crittall Windows Ltd
Unit 4 Francis House Freebournes Road, Witham, CM8 3UN
Tel: 01376-530800 **Fax:** 01376-530801
E-mail: hq@crittall-windows.co.uk
Website: http://www.crittall-windows.co.uk
Bank(s): National Westminster Bank Plc
Directors: J. Pyatt (MD)
Ultimate Holding Company: CRITTALL HOLDINGS LIMITED
Immediate Holding Company: CRITTALL WINDOWS LIMITED
Registration no: 00200794 **VAT No.:** GB 665 7740 96
Date established: 2024 **Turnover:** £1m - £2m
No.of Employees: 101 - 250 **Product Groups:** 30, 35, 48

Date of Accounts	Dec 11	Dec 10	Dec 09
Sales Turnover	10m	11m	13m
Pre Tax Profit/Loss	-186	63	404
Working Capital	334	198	-166
Fixed Assets	596	675	744
Current Assets	3m	3m	3m
Current Liabilities	841	1m	1m

Dalebrook Supplies Ltd
1 Croft Way Eastways, Witham, CM8 2FB
Tel: 01376-510101 **Fax:** 01376-510153
E-mail: sales@dalebrook.com
Website: http://www.dalebrook.com
Bank(s): Barclays, London
Directors: G. Beresford (Co Sec)
Ultimate Holding Company: TEY HOLDINGS LIMITED
Immediate Holding Company: DALEBROOK SUPPLIES LIMITED
Registration no: 02770125 **VAT No.:** GB 608 0312 79
Date established: 1992 **Turnover:** £2m - £5m **No.of Employees:** 11 - 20
Product Groups: 25, 26, 30, 33, 36, 40, 41, 49, 61, 63, 67

Date of Accounts	Dec 11	Dec 10	Dec 09
Working Capital	1m	1m	2m
Fixed Assets	2m	2m	843
Current Assets	4m	3m	3m

Doel Engineering Ltd
5 Europa Park Croft Way, Witham, CM8 2FN
Tel: 01376-515515 **Fax:** 01376-500015
E-mail: mpullen@doelengineering.com
Website: http://www.doelengineering.com
Directors: M. Pullen (MD)
Immediate Holding Company: DOEL ENGINEERING LIMITED
Registration no: 01177646 **VAT No.:** GB 104 4515 12
Date established: 1974 **Turnover:** £500,000 - £1m
No.of Employees: 1 - 10 **Product Groups:** 42, 44, 67

Date of Accounts	Feb 12	Feb 11	Feb 10
Working Capital	176	170	-8
Fixed Assets	19	23	188
Current Assets	537	610	346
Current Liabilities	63	180	226

E A C Group Of Companies
Jubilee House Broadway, Silver End, Witham, CM8 3RQ
Tel: 01376-585855 **Fax:** 01376-587910
E-mail: mail@eacgroup.net
Website: http://www.eacgroup.net
Directors: P. Clark (Contracts)
Registration no: 02590576 **VAT No.:** GB 594 8014 16
Turnover: £500,000 - £1m **No.of Employees:** 1 - 10 **Product Groups:** 52

Halton Products Ltd
4 The Matchyns London Road, Rivenhall, Witham, CM8 3HA
Tel: 01376-507000 **Fax:** 01376-503060
E-mail: info.uk@halton.com
Website: http://www.halton.co.uk
Managers: M. Deeton
Ultimate Holding Company: OY HALTON GROUP LIMITED (FINLAND)
Immediate Holding Company: HALTON PRODUCTS LIMITED
Registration no: 02110581 **Date established:** 1987 **Turnover:** £5m - £10m
No.of Employees: 1 - 10 **Product Groups:** 35, 66

Date of Accounts	Dec 11	Dec 10	Dec 09
Working Capital	411	598	581
Fixed Assets	1	3	5
Current Assets	602	792	721

Interact Marketing Service (t/a Printwize)
9 Stepfield, Witham, CM8 3BN
Tel: 01376-500900 **Fax:** 01376-519192
E-mail: sales@printwize.co.uk
Website: http://www.printwize.co.uk
Bank(s): Lloyds TSB Bank plc
Directors: R. Wacey (Ch), R. Wacey (MD)
Immediate Holding Company: INTERACT MARKETING SERVICES LIMITED
Registration no: 01254713 **Date established:** 1976 **Turnover:** £1m - £2m
No.of Employees: 21 - 50 **Product Groups:** 28, 81

Date of Accounts	Mar 11	Mar 10	Mar 09
Working Capital	-603	-758	-709
Fixed Assets	2m	2m	2m
Current Assets	633	663	655

Kwikfast Power Tools & Fastners
3 Crittall Road, Witham, CM8 3DR
Tel: 01376-514131 **Fax:** 01376-520923
Website: http://www.kwikfastelectrical.co.uk
Directors: P. Dixon (MD)
Date established: 1993 **No.of Employees:** 1 - 10 **Product Groups:** 37

Masterframe Windows Ltd
4 Crittall Road, Witham, CM8 3DR
Tel: 01376-510410 **Fax:** 01376-510400
E-mail: sales@masterframe.co.uk
Website: http://www.masterframe.co.uk
Directors: A. Burgess (MD), C. Slade (Chief Op Offcr)
Managers: D. Gunn (Personnel), B. Game, S. Smith
Ultimate Holding Company: DUCHY INVESTMENTS LIMITED
Immediate Holding Company: MASTERFRAME WINDOWS LIMITED
Registration no: 02272659 **Date established:** 1988 **Turnover:** £2m - £5m
No.of Employees: 21 - 50 **Product Groups:** 25, 35

Date of Accounts	Sep 11	Sep 10	Sep 09
Working Capital	-56	173	225
Fixed Assets	90	39	34
Current Assets	1m	1m	1m

Orchards Project Consulting Ltd
10 Orchards, Witham, CM8 1DW
Tel: 07913-926208
E-mail: info@orchardspc.co.uk
Website: http://www.orchardspc.co.uk
Directors: J. Holroyd (Fin), G. Holroyd (Dir)
Registration no: 04375698 **Date established:** 2002
Turnover: Up to £250,000 **No.of Employees:** 1 - 10 **Product Groups:** 44

Date of Accounts	Feb 08	Feb 07	Feb 06
Sales Turnover	55	64	63
Pre Tax Profit/Loss	43	44	42
Working Capital	22	22	22
Fixed Assets	N/A	1	N/A
Current Assets	33	33	34
Current Liabilities	10	10	10

Panaf & Company
Unit 5 Swanbridge Industrial Park Black Croft Road, Witham, CM8 3YN
Tel: 01376-511550 **Fax:** 01376-515131
E-mail: info@panaf.co.uk
Website: http://www.lrspareparts.com
Directors: Z. Panjwani (MD)
Ultimate Holding Company: ARROW OUTER LTD
Registration no: 02096005 **VAT No.:** GB 452 0151 94
Turnover: £1m - £2m **No.of Employees:** 1 - 10 **Product Groups:** 40, 61

Perry Ellis Europe Ltd
Crittall Road, Witham, CM8 3DJ
Tel: 01376-502345 **Fax:** 01376-500733
E-mail: info@farah.co.uk
Website: http://www.perryellis.co.uk
Bank(s): Barclays, Witham
Directors: F. Hoffman (MD)
Managers: J. Reeve (Personnel), I. Fulcher (Tech Serv Mgr), B. Keasley (Comptroller), J. Collinson (Comptroller), M. McCann (Sales Prom Mgr)
Ultimate Holding Company: PERRY ELLIS INTERNAITONAL INC (USA)
Immediate Holding Company: PERRY ELLIS EUROPE RETAIL LIMITED
Registration no: 06552520 **VAT No.:** GB 232 8671 58
Date established: 2008 **Turnover:** £500,000 - £1m
No.of Employees: 101 - 250 **Product Groups:** 24

Date of Accounts	Jan 10	Jan 09	Jan 11
Sales Turnover	511	147	448
Pre Tax Profit/Loss	5	-5	N/A
Working Capital	1	-4	1
Current Assets	146	119	140
Current Liabilities	145	119	139

Persimmon Homes Ltd
10 Collingwood Road, Witham, CM8 2EA
Tel: 01376-518811 **Fax:** 01376-514027
Website: http://www.persimmonhomes.com
Bank(s): National Westminster Bank Plc
Directors: N. Sharpe (Sales), J. Fitzpatrick (Fin), G. Popele (Sales & Mktg), D. Jackson (MD)
Managers: S. Dawson (Buyer), S. Goodman (Sec)
Ultimate Holding Company: PERSIMMON PUBLIC LIMITED COMPANY
Immediate Holding Company: PERSIMMON HOMES LIMITED
Registration no: 04108747 **Date established:** 2000
Turnover: £20m - £50m **No.of Employees:** 21 - 50 **Product Groups:** 52, 80

Date of Accounts	Dec 11	Dec 10	Dec 09
Sales Turnover	1059m	1112m	1025m
Pre Tax Profit/Loss	76m	130m	591m
Working Capital	789m	740m	659m
Fixed Assets	433m	436m	466m
Current Assets	2309m	3954m	3494m
Current Liabilities	277m	697m	696m

Prime Appointments Ltd
Christmas House 98b Newland Street, Witham, CM8 1AH
Tel: 01376-502999 **Fax:** 01376-502846
E-mail: general@prime-appointments.co.uk
Website: http://www.prime-appointments.co.uk
Directors: R. Holmes (MD), C. Van Aalst (Fin), C. Vanaalst (Fin)
Immediate Holding Company: PRIME APPOINTMENTS LIMITED
Registration no: 02704145 **Date established:** 1992
Turnover: Up to £250,000 **No.of Employees:** 11 - 20 **Product Groups:** 80

Date of Accounts	Jan 12	Jan 11	Jan 10
Working Capital	76	31	87
Fixed Assets	14	14	21
Current Assets	521	425	451

Radio Data Technology Ltd
Unit 10 Taber Place Crittall Road, Witham, CM8 3YP
Tel: 01376-501255 **Fax:** 01376-501312
E-mail: sales@radiodata.co.uk
Website: http://www.radiodata.co.uk
Bank(s): Barclays, Colchester
Directors: A. Hall (Dir)
Ultimate Holding Company: CML MICROSYSTEMS PLC
Immediate Holding Company: RADIO DATA TECHNOLOGY LIMITED
Registration no: 01913610 **VAT No.:** GB 368 6007 36
Date established: 1985 **Turnover:** £500,000 - £1m
No.of Employees: 11 - 20 **Product Groups:** 37

Date of Accounts	Mar 12	Mar 11	Mar 10
Sales Turnover	759	769	722
Pre Tax Profit/Loss	-60	9	-11
Working Capital	421	889	868
Fixed Assets	22	27	35
Current Assets	524	1m	945
Current Liabilities	32	39	26

South East Galvanizers Ltd
Crittall Road, Witham, CM8 3DR
Tel: 01376-501501 **Fax:** 01376-513410
E-mail: south.east@wedge-galv.co.uk
Website: http://www.wedge-galv.co.uk
Directors: T. Beech (Sales), D. Lynam (Co Sec), J. Woolridge (MD)
Ultimate Holding Company: B.E. WEDGE HOLDINGS LIMITED
Immediate Holding Company: SOUTH EAST GALVANIZERS LIMITED
Registration no: 03228164 **Date established:** 1996 **Turnover:** £5m - £10m
No.of Employees: 21 - 50 **Product Groups:** 48

Date of Accounts	Mar 11	Mar 10	Mar 09
Pre Tax Profit/Loss	12	12	12
Current Assets	3	3	2
Current Liabilities	3	3	2

Teledyne Paradise Datacom Ltd
2-3 The Matchyns London Road, Rivenhall, Witham, CM8 3HA
Tel: 01376-515636 **Fax:** 01376-533764
E-mail: pmcconnell@paradise.co.uk
Website: http://www.paradisedata.com
Bank(s): Barclays, Swindon
Directors: P. Mcconnell (Develop)
Ultimate Holding Company: TELEDYNE TECHNOLOGIES INC (USA)
Immediate Holding Company: TELEDYNE PARADISE DATACOM LIMITED
Registration no: 02829165 **VAT No.:** GB 623 2255 71
Date established: 1993 **Turnover:** £1m - £2m **No.of Employees:** 11 - 20
Product Groups: 37, 38, 39, 44, 67

Date of Accounts	Dec 11	Dec 10	Mar 10
Sales Turnover	2m	1m	2m
Pre Tax Profit/Loss	379	187	387
Working Capital	1m	836	627
Fixed Assets	85	70	106
Current Assets	1m	1m	928
Current Liabilities	120	204	249

Time & Frequency Solutions Ltd
25 Eastways, Witham, CM8 3AL
Tel: 01376-514114 **Fax:** 01376-516116
E-mail: sales@timefreq.com
Website: http://www.timefreq.com
Directors: N. Pitman (MD)
Managers: D. Squires (Software Mgr), L. Mixture (Mgr)
Immediate Holding Company: TIME AND FREQUENCY SOLUTIONS LIMITED
Registration no: 02627556 **VAT No.:** GB 594 7347 91
Date established: 1991 **No.of Employees:** 11 - 20 **Product Groups:** 38, 44, 49, 65

Date of Accounts	May 11	May 10	May 09
Working Capital	568	1m	2m
Fixed Assets	14	18	22
Current Assets	972	1m	2m
Current Liabilities	N/A	2	2

Treif UK Ltd
4 Europa Park Croft Way, Witham, CM8 2FN
Tel: 01376-504060 **Fax:** 01376-504070
E-mail: info@treif.co.uk
Website: http://www.treif.co.uk
Directors: D. Henderson (I.T. Dir), M. Henderson (MD)
Ultimate Holding Company: CORDBRAY MANAGEMENT LTD
Immediate Holding Company: TREIF (UK) LIMITED
Registration no: 00590394 **VAT No.:** GB 246 4051 77
Date established: 1957 **Turnover:** £1m - £2m **No.of Employees:** 1 - 10
Product Groups: 41

Date of Accounts	Dec 09	Dec 08	Aug 11
Working Capital	36	106	15
Fixed Assets	477	494	29
Current Assets	465	494	363

Western Automation I V A C
5 Colemans Bridge, Witham, CM8 3HP
Tel: 01376-511808 **Fax:** 01376-500862
E-mail: sales@waivac.co.uk
Website: http://www.uk-electric.net
Managers: D. Hatton (Mgr)
Ultimate Holding Company: NEWBURY INVESTMENTS
Immediate Holding Company: UK ELECTRIC LTD
Registration no: 02742081 **VAT No.:** 614 8572 30 **Date established:** 1972
Turnover: £500,000 - £1m **No.of Employees:** 1 - 10 **Product Groups:** 30, 33, 36, 39, 40

Woodford Green

A N D Domestics
530 Chigwell Road, Woodford Green, IG8 8PA
Tel: 020-8505 5777
E-mail: info@andsalesrepairs.co.uk
Website: http://www.andsalesrepairs.co.uk
Directors: K. Holley (Prop)
Date established: 1979 **No.of Employees:** 1 - 10 **Product Groups:** 36, 40

Dataphone Communications Ltd

Riverside House Woodford Trading Estate Southend Road, Woodford Green, IG8 8HQ
Tel: 020-8550 8844
E-mail: chris@dataphone.co.uk
Website: http://www.dataphone.co.uk
Directors: C. Wilce (MD), G. Simia (Fin)
Managers: C. Jarvis (Sales Admin)
Immediate Holding Company: DATAPHONE COMMUNICATIONS LIMITED
Registration no: 02346987 **Date established:** 1989
No.of Employees: 21 - 50 **Product Groups:** 37, 48, 67, 84

Date of Accounts	Mar 11	Mar 10	Mar 09
Working Capital	560	439	272
Fixed Assets	84	80	127
Current Assets	703	616	504

Davenport Lift Control

3 Broadway Mews The Broadway, Woodford Green, IG8 0HQ
Tel: 020-8504 8286 **Fax:** 020-8504 8297
E-mail: info@davenportliftcontrol.com
Website: http://www.davenportliftcontrol.com
Directors: M. Gayford (Prop)
Immediate Holding Company: CITY & LONDON ESTATES LIMITED
Registration no: 06673762 **Date established:** 2008
No.of Employees: 1 - 10 **Product Groups:** 35, 39, 45

Date of Accounts	Aug 11	Aug 10	Aug 09
Current Assets	N/A	3	N/A

Designs With Iron

45 Broadmead Road, Woodford Green, IG8 0AT
Tel: 020-8505 0671
Directors: G. Gailer (Prop)
Date established: 2001 **No.of Employees:** 1 - 10 **Product Groups:** 26, 35

Fluorel Ltd

Riverside Works Broadmead Road, Woodford Green, IG8 8PQ
Tel: 020-8504 9691 **Fax:** 020-8506 1792
E-mail: djones@flourel.co.uk
Website: http://www.flourel.co.uk
Bank(s): Barclays
Directors: D. Jones (MD), L. Hawke (Ch)
Managers: M. Weller (Chief Mgr)
Immediate Holding Company: FLUOREL LIMITED
Registration no: 00444710 **VAT No.:** GB 246 1862 55
Date established: 1947 **Turnover:** £1m - £2m **No.of Employees:** 11 - 20
Product Groups: 37, 84

Date of Accounts	Oct 09	Oct 08	Oct 07
Working Capital	196	391	347
Fixed Assets	14	36	48
Current Assets	432	598	757

Holland Publishing Ltd

Unit 18 Bourne Court Unity Trading Estate, Woodford Green, IG8 8HD
Tel: 020-8551 7711 **Fax:** 020-8551 1266
E-mail: sales@holland-enterprises.co.uk
Website: http://www.holland-publishing.co.uk
Bank(s): Barclays
Directors: J. Holland (Dir)
Immediate Holding Company: HOLLAND PUBLISHING PLC
Registration no: 01502262 **Date established:** 1980 **Turnover:** £2m - £5m
No.of Employees: 11 - 20 **Product Groups:** 28, 49

Date of Accounts	Dec 11	Dec 10	Jun 09
Sales Turnover	3m	4m	3m
Pre Tax Profit/Loss	-160	-434	-109
Working Capital	937	1m	1m
Fixed Assets	537	558	565
Current Assets	2m	2m	2m
Current Liabilities	128	67	75

International Firearms

528 Chigwell Road, Woodford Green, IG8 8PA
Tel: 020-8504 9652
E-mail: info@internationalfirearms.co.uk
Website: http://www.internationalfirearms.co.uk
Directors: D. Bass (Prop)
Date established: 1987 **No.of Employees:** 1 - 10 **Product Groups:** 36, 39, 40

Pink Telecommunications Ltd

15 The Broadway, Woodford Green, IG8 0HL
Tel: 020-8506 6464 **Fax:** 020-8506 6400
E-mail: sales@pinktelecom.co.uk
Website: http://www.pinktelecom.co.uk
Directors: I. McNamara (Admin), P. Southgate (MD), S. Linehan (Fin)
Managers: B. Williams (Serv Mgr), S. Ives
Ultimate Holding Company: PINK HOLDINGS LIMITED
Immediate Holding Company: PINK TELECOMMUNICATIONS LIMITED
Registration no: 02434833 **VAT No.:** GB 524 9747 17
Date established: 1989 **Turnover:** £5m - £10m **No.of Employees:** 21 - 50
Product Groups: 37

Date of Accounts	Aug 11	Aug 10	Aug 09
Working Capital	28	23	31
Fixed Assets	3	2	1
Current Assets	50	43	47

Steelonthenet.com

22 Nesta Road, Woodford Green, IG8 9RG
Tel: 020-8504 2805
E-mail: info@steelonthenet.com
Website: http://www.steelonthenet.com
Directors: A. Kotas (Prop)
Immediate Holding Company: METALS CONSULTING INTERNATIONAL LIMITED
Registration no: 04938719 **Date established:** 2003
No.of Employees: 1 - 10 **Product Groups:** 85

Date of Accounts	Aug 12	Aug 11	Aug 10
Working Capital	-7	-11	-12
Fixed Assets	6	7	9
Current Assets	9	16	6

Yannedis

Unit 3 Southend Road, Woodford Green, IG8 8HF
Tel: 020-8550 8833 **Fax:** 020-8551 0026
E-mail: info@yannedis.com
Website: http://www.yannedis.com
Managers: G. Thomas (Sales Admin)
Ultimate Holding Company: GRAFTON GROUP PUBLIC LIMITED COMPANY
Immediate Holding Company: YANNEDIS LIMITED
Registration no: 03510389 **VAT No.:** GB 713 8278 28
Date established: 1998 **Turnover:** Up to £250,000
No.of Employees: 1 - 10 **Product Groups:** 26, 35, 36, 40, 49

Date of Accounts	Dec 10	Dec 09	Dec 08
Working Capital	68	68	68
Current Assets	68	68	68

GLOUCESTERSHIRE

Berkeley

The Brand In A Box
Damery Works Damery Lane, Woodford, Berkeley, GL13 9JR
Tel: 08452-011266 **Fax:** 0845-201 1265
E-mail: info@brandinabox.biz
Website: http://www.brandinabox.biz
Directors: R. Milton (Dir)
Immediate Holding Company: THE BRAND IN A BOX COMPANY LTD
Registration no: 05086588 **Date established:** 2004
No.of Employees: 1 - 10 **Product Groups:** 20

Date of Accounts	Mar 12	Mar 11	Mar 10
Working Capital	154	144	128
Current Assets	434	474	416

European Metals Recycling Ltd
The Docks Sharpness, Berkeley, GL13 9UX
Tel: 01453-512235 **Fax:** 01453-810322
Website: http://www.elrltd.com
Managers: T. Perry (Mgr)
Immediate Holding Company: EUROPEAN METAL RECYCLING LIMITED
Registration no: 02954623 **Date established:** 1994
Turnover: £10m - £20m **No.of Employees:** 11 - 20 **Product Groups:** 42, 66

Date of Accounts	Dec 11	Dec 10	Dec 09
Sales Turnover	3032m	2431m	1843m
Pre Tax Profit/Loss	116m	155m	91m
Working Capital	414m	371m	167m
Fixed Assets	518m	483m	480m
Current Assets	1027m	717m	557m
Current Liabilities	124m	118m	185m

Howard Tenens Sharpness Ltd
Burma Road Sharpness, Berkeley, GL13 9UQ
Tel: 01453-810580 **Fax:** 01453-810323
E-mail: mike.jones@tenens.com
Website: http://www.tenens.com
Managers: M. Jones (Chief Mgr)
Immediate Holding Company: HOWARD TENENS (SHARPNESS) LIMITED
Registration no: 03619410 **Date established:** 1998 **Turnover:** £2m - £5m
No.of Employees: 21 - 50 **Product Groups:** 72, 77, 84

Date of Accounts	Sep 11	Sep 10	Sep 09
Sales Turnover	2m	3m	3m
Pre Tax Profit/Loss	1m	1m	1m
Working Capital	3m	2m	950
Fixed Assets	8m	8m	8m
Current Assets	3m	3m	1m
Current Liabilities	768	978	458

Cheltenham

A C P Ltd
The Vineyards Gloucester Road, Cheltenham, GL51 8NH
Tel: 01242-512345 **Fax:** 01242-576633
E-mail: enquiries@adcoat.co.uk
Website: http://www.api-cop.com
Directors: M. Urquhart (Fin), N. Trilk (MD)
Managers: S. Jackson (Tech Serv Mgr), S. Hemsworth, L. Tremlett (Purch Mgr)
Ultimate Holding Company: BRIGHTBOROUGH CAPITAL LIMITED
Immediate Holding Company: ADVANCED COATED PRODUCTS LIMITED
Registration no: 00375718 **VAT No.:** GB 448 3124 53
Date established: 1942 **Turnover:** £10m - £20m
No.of Employees: 51 - 100 **Product Groups:** 27, 30, 66

Date of Accounts	Sep 11	Sep 10	Sep 09
Sales Turnover	19m	16m	13m
Pre Tax Profit/Loss	306	110	53
Working Capital	2m	2m	1m
Fixed Assets	440	379	420
Current Assets	7m	6m	5m
Current Liabilities	2m	2m	1m

Aapco Ltd
Alpha 8 Orchard Industrial Estate Toddington, Cheltenham, GL54 5EB
Tel: 01242-620062 **Fax:** 01242-620063
E-mail: stuartleonard1@virgin.net
Website: http://www.recap.co.uk
Directors: S. Leonard (MD)
Ultimate Holding Company: FOUR DIMENSION JOHNSON SECURITY UK LIMITED
Immediate Holding Company: FOUR DIMENSION JOHNSON SECURITY UK LIMITED
Registration no: 00934256 **Date established:** 1968
Turnover: £10m - £20m **No.of Employees:** 1 - 10 **Product Groups:** 26, 35

Aerials & Cable Equipment Distributors
343-345 High Street, Cheltenham, GL50 3HS
Tel: 01242-511511 **Fax:** 01242-221888
E-mail: sales@aceonline.co.uk
Website: http://www.aceonline.co.uk
Directors: R. Miller (MD)
Immediate Holding Company: AERIALS CABLE EQUIPMENT DISTRIBUTORS LIMITED
Registration no: 01710588 **VAT No.:** GB 391 9713 19
Date established: 1983 **Turnover:** £1m - £2m **No.of Employees:** 11 - 20
Product Groups: 37

Date of Accounts	Apr 12	Apr 11	Apr 10
Working Capital	467	481	500
Fixed Assets	5	9	6
Current Assets	853	945	1m

Airco Pneumatics
Malmesbury Road Kingsditch Trading Estate, Cheltenham, GL51 9PL
Tel: 01242-690480 **Fax:** 01242-690490
E-mail: info@directair.co.uk
Website: http://www.directair.co.uk
Bank(s): Lloyds TSB Bank plc
Directors: A. Dolby (MD)
Immediate Holding Company: SEVERNSIDE SAFETY SUPPLIES LIMITED
Registration no: 01568334 **VAT No.:** GB 348 1767 29
Date established: 1973 **Turnover:** £1m - £2m **No.of Employees:** 11 - 20
Product Groups: 18

Date of Accounts	Aug 09	Aug 08	Aug 07
Working Capital	159	124	81
Fixed Assets	21	37	50
Current Assets	457	355	298

Alan Dick UK Ltd
The Barlands London Road, Charlton Kings, Cheltenham, GL52 6UT
Tel: 01242-518500 **Fax:** 01242-510191
E-mail: contact@uk.alandickgroup.com
Website: http://www.alandick.com
Bank(s): National Westminster
Directors: P. Dost (Dir), W. Carruthers (Chief Op Offcr)
Ultimate Holding Company: ALAN DICK & COMPANY (HOLDINGS) LIMITED
Immediate Holding Company: ALAN DICK & COMPANY LIMITED
Registration no: 01007434 **VAT No.:** GB 274 1804 60
Date established: 1971 **Turnover:** £10m - £20m
No.of Employees: 101 - 250 **Product Groups:** 35, 37, 39, 84

Date of Accounts	Mar 10	Mar 09	Mar 08
Sales Turnover	20m	23m	23m
Pre Tax Profit/Loss	-1m	68	-5m
Working Capital	-5m	-4m	-18m
Fixed Assets	303	366	197
Current Assets	5m	7m	5m
Current Liabilities	3m	3m	4m

Frederick Allen Ltd
24 Winchcombe Street, Cheltenham, GL52 2LX
Tel: 01242-514869 **Fax:** 01242-514869
E-mail: enniskillen@allanarc.com
Website: http://www.allanarc.com
Directors: R. Jarvis (MD), T. Jarvis (Prop), S. Jarvis (Fin)
Managers: T. Jarvis (District Mgr)
Immediate Holding Company: R. JARVIS (JEWELLERS) LIMITED
Registration no: 00805210 **Date established:** 1964
Turnover: Up to £250,000 **No.of Employees:** 1 - 10 **Product Groups:** 65

Alutool Ltd
Unit 7 Bramery Business Park Alstone Lane, Cheltenham, GL51 8HE
Tel: 01242-231286 **Fax:** 01242-231289
E-mail: info@alutool.co.uk
Website: http://www.alutool.co.uk
Bank(s): National Westminster Bank Plc
Directors: R. Martin (Dir)
Ultimate Holding Company: AILSA INVESTMENTS LIMITED (ISLE OF MAN)
Immediate Holding Company: ALUTOOL (PREFORM DIE) CO. LIMITED
Registration no: 00931887 **VAT No.:** GB 276 6147 33
Date established: 1968 **Turnover:** £1m - £2m **No.of Employees:** 21 - 50
Product Groups: 34, 46

Date of Accounts	Aug 11	Aug 10	Aug 09
Working Capital	486	306	393
Fixed Assets	561	705	264
Current Assets	902	830	599

B J M Refrigeration
23 Valley Home Park Bamfurlong Lane, Cheltenham, GL51 6SL
Tel: 07966-130269
Directors: B. Miller (Prop)
Date established: 1998 **No.of Employees:** 1 - 10 **Product Groups:** 36, 40

B P E Solicitors LLP
St James House St James Square, Cheltenham, GL50 3PR
Tel: 01242-224433 **Fax:** 01242-574285
E-mail: john.workman@bpe.co.uk
Website: http://www.bpe.co.uk
Directors: J. Workman (Snr Part)
Managers: A. Coleman (Personnel)
Immediate Holding Company: BPE SOLICITORS LLP
Registration no: OC349012 **VAT No.:** GB 275 2424 59
Date established: 2009 **Turnover:** £2m - £5m **No.of Employees:** 51 - 100
Product Groups: 80

Date of Accounts	Sep 11	Sep 10	Sep 09
Working Capital	791	514	494
Fixed Assets	61	108	209
Current Assets	4m	3m	3m

Biolab UK Ltd
Unit 4 Andoversford Industrial Estate Andoversford, Cheltenham, GL54 4LB
Tel: 01242-820969 **Fax:** 01242-820180
E-mail: sales@biolabuk.com
Website: http://www.biolabuk.com
Bank(s): National Westminster Bank Plc
Directors: K. Buckman (Co Sec)
Managers: S. Groves
Ultimate Holding Company: CHEMTURA CORP (USA)
Immediate Holding Company: BIOLAB U.K. LIMITED
Registration no: 01972629 **VAT No.:** GB 109 9838 30
Date established: 1985 **Turnover:** £2m - £5m **No.of Employees:** 21 - 50
Product Groups: 32, 38, 52, 66

Date of Accounts	Dec 10	Dec 09	Dec 08
Sales Turnover	4m	5m	5m
Pre Tax Profit/Loss	-44	-131	3m
Working Capital	4m	4m	4m
Fixed Assets	1	28	65
Current Assets	5m	5m	6m
Current Liabilities	307	609	661

Bovis Homes Ltd
Cleeve Hall Cheltenham Road, Bishops Cleeve, Cheltenham, GL52 8GD
Tel: 01242-662400 **Fax:** 01242-662663
E-mail: david.ritchie@bovishomes.co.uk
Website: http://www.bovishomes.co.uk
Directors: S. Ray (Fin), M. Palmer (Co Sec), D. Ritchie (Grp Chief Exec), A. Jones (Tech Serv), B. Cummings (Sales & Mktg)
Managers: N. Brown, S. Smith (Mktg Serv Mgr), H. Clewes (Personnel)
Immediate Holding Company: BOVIS HOMES GROUP PLC
Registration no: 00306718 **VAT No.:** GB 286 2439 33
Date established: 1935 **Turnover:** £250m - £500m
No.of Employees: 501 - 1000 **Product Groups:** 52

Date of Accounts	Dec 11	Dec 10	Dec 09
Sales Turnover	365m	299m	282m
Pre Tax Profit/Loss	32m	19m	5m
Working Capital	723m	726m	687m
Fixed Assets	62m	63m	42m
Current Assets	931m	869m	777m
Current Liabilities	27m	142m	10m

Buck & Hickman Ltd
Unit R Kingsville Road Kingsditch Trading Estate, Cheltenham, GL51 9NX
Tel: 01242-519665 **Fax:** 01242-224097
E-mail: cheltenham@buckhickmaninone.co.uk
Website: http://www.buckandhickman.com
Managers: C. Carter (District Mgr)
Ultimate Holding Company: TRAVIS PERKINS PLC
Immediate Holding Company: BOSTON (2011) LIMITED
Registration no: 06028304 **Date established:** 2006
Turnover: £75m - £125m **No.of Employees:** 1 - 10 **Product Groups:** 24, 29, 30, 33, 36, 37, 41, 46

Date of Accounts	Dec 10	Mar 10	Mar 09
Working Capital	6m	6m	6m
Current Assets	27m	27m	27m

Business Air Centre
Gloucestershire Airport Staverton, Cheltenham, GL51 6SR
Tel: 01452-859500 **Fax:** 01452-715010
E-mail: charter@businessaircentre.co.uk
Website: http://www.businessaircentre.co.uk
Directors: S. Westlake (MD), M. Key (Sales & Mktg), P. Cassidy (Dir)
Managers: K. Welsh (Mktg Serv Mgr)
Ultimate Holding Company: EUROPEAN SKYTIME LIMITED
Immediate Holding Company: BUSINESS AIR CENTRE LIMITED
Registration no: 02401838 **VAT No.:** GB 532 4608 61
Date established: 1989 **Turnover:** £5m - £10m **No.of Employees:** 1 - 10
Product Groups: 68

Date of Accounts	Apr 11	Apr 10	Apr 09
Working Capital	20	20	-5
Current Assets	20	20	239

C B F
67 Hatherley Road, Cheltenham, GL51 6EG
Tel: 01242-237652 **Fax:** 01242-236186
E-mail: info@cbfnet.co.uk
Website: http://www.cbfnet.co.uk
Managers: L. Willett
Immediate Holding Company: CHELTENHAM BUSINESS FORMS LIMITED
Registration no: 02005932 **Date established:** 1986
Turnover: Up to £250,000 **No.of Employees:** 11 - 20 **Product Groups:** 27, 28

Date of Accounts	Mar 12	Mar 11	Mar 10
Working Capital	40	35	43
Fixed Assets	17	23	15
Current Assets	155	147	142

Chartus
5 Gratton Road, Cheltenham, GL50 2BT
Tel: 01242-701014 **Fax:** 01242-701014
E-mail: info@chartus.co.uk
Website: http://www.chartus.co.uk
Directors: R. Coburn (Prop)
Immediate Holding Company: CHARTUS LIMITED
Registration no: 05207279 **Date established:** 2004
Turnover: Up to £250,000 **No.of Employees:** 1 - 10 **Product Groups:** 44

Date of Accounts	Aug 11	Aug 10	Aug 09
Sales Turnover	N/A	N/A	23
Pre Tax Profit/Loss	N/A	N/A	3
Working Capital	13	10	5
Fixed Assets	1	1	1
Current Assets	45	30	8
Current Liabilities	N/A	N/A	2

Chelmix Concrete Ltd
Church Farm Leckhampton, Cheltenham, GL53 0QJ
Tel: 01242-224763 **Fax:** 01242-237727
E-mail: info@traditionallime.co.uk
Website: http://www.traditionallime.co.uk
Directors: J. Hicks (MD)
Ultimate Holding Company: LECKSMIX LIMITED
Immediate Holding Company: CHELMIX CONCRETE LIMITED
Registration no: 01784814 **VAT No.:** GB 276 7146 30
Date established: 1984 **Turnover:** £2m - £5m **No.of Employees:** 1 - 10
Product Groups: 33

Date of Accounts	Mar 11	Mar 10	Mar 09
Working Capital	723	716	722
Fixed Assets	172	185	192
Current Assets	933	928	935

Chelsea Building Society
Thirlestaine Hall Thirlestaine Road, Cheltenham, GL53 7AL
Tel: 01242-271271 **Fax:** 01242-571441
E-mail: peter.ford@thechelsea.co.uk
Website: http://www.thechelsea.co.uk
Directors: R. Hornbrook (MD), P. Ford (Co Sec)
Managers: R. Elliott (Personnel)
Ultimate Holding Company: 09000090
Immediate Holding Company: CHELSEA MORTGAGE SERVICES LIMITED
Registration no: 02443492 **Date established:** 1989
Turnover: Up to £250,000 **No.of Employees:** 501 - 1000
Product Groups: 82

Cheltenham Induction Heating Ltd
Saxon Way, Cheltenham, GL52 6RU
Tel: 01242-514042 **Fax:** 01242-224146
E-mail: mgrant@ambrell.com
Website: http://www.cihinduction.com
Bank(s): National Westminster Bank Plc
Managers: G. Dines (Sales & Mktg Mg), P. Lipscomb (Tech Serv Mgr)
Immediate Holding Company: AMBRELL LIMITED
Registration no: 05277750 **VAT No.:** GB 650 8024 57
Date established: 2004 **Turnover:** £1m - £2m **No.of Employees:** 11 - 20
Product Groups: 37, 40, 42, 45, 46, 47, 48, 66

Date of Accounts	Dec 10	Dec 09	Dec 08
Working Capital	-20	-66	186
Fixed Assets	97	122	150
Current Assets	684	663	788

Cleanacres Machinery Ltd
Hazleton, Cheltenham, GL54 4DX
Tel: 01451-860721 **Fax:** 01451-860139
E-mail: mark_curtoys@cleanacres.co.uk
Website: http://www.cleanacres.co.uk
Directors: J. Weston (MD)
Immediate Holding Company: CLEANACRES MACHINERY LIMITED
Registration no: 01384399 **Date established:** 1978 **Turnover:** £2m - £5m
No.of Employees: 1 - 10 **Product Groups:** 40

Date of Accounts	Dec 11	Dec 10	Dec 09
Working Capital	51	-22	-104
Fixed Assets	997	990	1m
Current Assets	412	443	401

Construction Leads
Eagle Tower Momtpellier Drive, Cheltenham, GL50 1TA
Tel: 01242-577277 **Fax:** 01242-527277
E-mail: ljespersen@camarguepr.com
Website: http://www.constructionleads.co.uk
Directors: M. Conway (MD), R. Aldridge (Fin)
Managers: A. Spears (I.T. Exec), L. Jespersen, D. Cox (Sales Admin)
Immediate Holding Company: Carmargue
Turnover: £2m - £5m **No.of Employees:** 21 - 50 **Product Groups:** 80

Cotswold Architectural Products
Manor Park Industrial Estate Manor Road, Swindon Village, Cheltenham, GL51 9SQ
Tel: 01242-233993 **Fax:** 01242-221146
E-mail: info@cotswold-windows.co.uk
Website: http://www.cotswold-windows.co.uk
Bank(s): Lloyds TSB
Directors: L. Mcdonough (Fin), I. Morgan (Sales)
Ultimate Holding Company: COTSWOLD HOLDINGS LIMITED
Immediate Holding Company: COTSWOLD ARCHITECTURAL PRODUCTS LIMITED
Registration no: 01160238 **VAT No.:** GB 576 3986 79
Date established: 1974 **Turnover:** £5m - £10m **No.of Employees:** 21 - 50
Product Groups: 36

Date of Accounts	Apr 12	Apr 11	Apr 10
Sales Turnover	7m	N/A	N/A
Pre Tax Profit/Loss	1m	N/A	N/A
Working Capital	3m	2m	2m
Fixed Assets	195	222	257
Current Assets	3m	3m	3m
Current Liabilities	538	N/A	N/A

D B Partners Ltd
Unit 26 Bamfurlong Industrial Park Staverton, Cheltenham, GL51 6SX
Tel: 01452-857111 **Fax:** 01452-857543
E-mail: anthony.watson@dbpartners.co.uk
Website: http://www.dbpartners.co.uk
Directors: A. Watson (MD), J. Watson (Co Sec)
Immediate Holding Company: DB PARTNERS LIMITED
Registration no: 01556381 **Date established:** 1981
No.of Employees: 11 - 20 **Product Groups:** 46, 48

Date of Accounts	Jun 09	Jun 08	Jun 07
Working Capital	104	113	59
Fixed Assets	80	88	86
Current Assets	336	375	312
Current Liabilities	N/A	N/A	58

Deburring Services
Cleeve Business Park Bishops Cleeve, Cheltenham, GL52 8TW
Tel: 01242-677007 **Fax:** 01242-677022
E-mail: john@deburring.co.uk
Website: http://www.deburring.co.uk
Bank(s): Lloyds TSB Bank plc
Directors: J. Wood (MD), M. Wood (Fin)
Ultimate Holding Company: DBSH LIMITED
Immediate Holding Company: DEBURRING SERVICES (CHELTENHAM) LIMITED
Registration no: 01373861 **Date established:** 1978 **Turnover:** £1m - £2m
No.of Employees: 11 - 20 **Product Groups:** 32, 33, 36, 46, 48

Date of Accounts	Dec 09	Dec 08	Dec 07
Working Capital	113	127	20
Fixed Assets	102	115	126
Current Assets	578	621	278
Current Liabilities	78	N/A	N/A

Derek Phippen
32 Christchurch Road, Cheltenham, GL50 2PL
Tel: 01242-522998
E-mail: info@ukdentallabs.com
Website: http://www.ukdentallabs.com
Directors: D. Phippen (Prop)
No.of Employees: 1 - 10 **Product Groups:** 37, 38, 88

Design Installation Service Electrical & Mechanical Ltd
42-44 Bath Road, Cheltenham, GL53 7HJ
Tel: 01242-533100 **Fax:** 01242-221187
E-mail: ccroome@dis-ltd.co.uk
Website: http://www.disgroup.co.uk
Directors: C. Croome (MD), P. Kerr (Fin)
Managers: D. Jenner (Sales Admin)
No.of Employees: 21 - 50 **Product Groups:** 40

Date of Accounts	Mar 08	Mar 07	Mar 06
Pre Tax Profit/Loss	469	381	281
Working Capital	1116	953	925
Fixed Assets	187	199	179
Current Assets	4809	3931	3833
Current Liabilities	3693	2978	2908
Total Share Capital	50	50	50
ROCE% (Return on Capital Employed)	36.0	33.1	25.4

Douglas Equipment
Douglas House Village Road, Cheltenham, GL51 0AB
Tel: 01242-527921 **Fax:** 01242-221198
E-mail: reception@douglas-equipment.com
Website: http://www.douglas-equipment.com
Bank(s): Lloyds TSB
Directors: R. Towill (Fin), M. Doane (Sales)
Managers: D. Dickerson, P. Edlin (Tech Serv Mgr), L. Nicholls, A. Cox (Personnel)
Ultimate Holding Company: AQUARIUS GROUP LTD (JERSEY)
Immediate Holding Company: DOUGLAS EQUIPMENT LIMITED
Registration no: 00697744 **VAT No.:** GB 800 4105 96
Date established: 1961 **Turnover:** £10m - £20m
No.of Employees: 101 - 250 **Product Groups:** 39, 67, 68

Date of Accounts	Mar 11	Mar 10	Mar 09
Sales Turnover	16m	13m	22m
Pre Tax Profit/Loss	258	-994	1m
Working Capital	5m	6m	7m
Fixed Assets	106	1m	2m
Current Assets	10m	9m	11m
Current Liabilities	1m	992	2m

Eden Halls Greenhouses Ltd
The Distribution Centre Stoke Road, Stoke Orchard, Cheltenham, GL52 7RS
Tel: 01242-676625 **Fax:** 01242-676626
E-mail: mail@eden-greenhouses.com
Website: http://www.edengreenhouses.com
Bank(s): Barclays
Directors: M. Koch Pedersen (Co Sec)
Managers: A. Pickwell (Sales Admin), A. Bowen-jones, M. Grancowski (Purch Mgr)
Ultimate Holding Company: JULIANA HOLDINGS A/S (DENMARK)
Immediate Holding Company: EDEN-HALLS GREENHOUSES LIMITED
Registration no: 01886856 **VAT No.:** GB 408 6748 28
Date established: 1985 **Turnover:** £5m - £10m **No.of Employees:** 21 - 50
Product Groups: 35

Date of Accounts	Dec 11	Dec 10	Dec 09
Sales Turnover	7m	9m	9m
Pre Tax Profit/Loss	-97	194	424
Working Capital	2m	2m	2m
Fixed Assets	2m	2m	2m
Current Assets	3m	3m	4m
Current Liabilities	182	283	338

Endsleigh Insurance Services Ltd
Shurdington Road Shurdington, Cheltenham, GL51 4UE
Tel: 01242-866866 **Fax:** 01242-866961
E-mail: matthew.byrne@endsleigh.co.uk
Website: http://www.endsleigh.co.uk
Managers: A. Reid (District Mgr)
Immediate Holding Company: Endsleigh Ltd
Registration no: 00856706 **Date established:** 1929
No.of Employees: 1 - 10 **Product Groups:** 82

Date of Accounts	Dec 07
Sales Turnover	61360
Pre Tax Profit/Loss	9690
Working Capital	22880
Fixed Assets	7700
Current Assets	86110
Current Liabilities	63230
Total Share Capital	2800
ROCE% (Return on Capital Employed)	31.7

Equestrian Needs
Cleeve Court Two Hedges Road, Bishops Cleeve, Cheltenham, GL52 8DU
Tel: 07969-798194
Website: http://www.equestrianneeds.com
Directors: G. Smith (Dir)
Immediate Holding Company: EQUESTRIAN NEEDS LTD
Registration no: 06680840 **Date established:** 2008
No.of Employees: 1 - 10 **Product Groups:** 24, 35, 49, 63

Date of Accounts	Jul 11	Jul 10	Jul 09
Working Capital	-4	-14	-16
Fixed Assets	4	6	7
Current Assets	10	12	1

Equipment For You
PO Box 6, Cheltenham, GL51 9NJ
Tel: 01242-241822 **Fax:** 01242-222994
E-mail: sales@3dsports.co.uk
Website: http://www.e4u.co.uk
Directors: D. Arthur (Grp Chief Exec)
Managers: P. Arthur (Sales Prom Mgr), R. Attwood (Mgr)
Ultimate Holding Company: Maschinenfabrik Gehring GmbH & Co.
Registration no: 01879464 **VAT No.:** GB 618 0745 41
No.of Employees: 1 - 10 **Product Groups:** 33, 36, 37, 39, 46

Fire Security Gloucester Co.
32 Prestbury Road, Cheltenham, GL52 2DA
Tel: 01242-523947
Directors: P. O'grady (Prop)
Date established: 1988 **No.of Employees:** 1 - 10 **Product Groups:** 38, 42

Focal Point Audio Visual Ltd
1-3 Kew Place, Cheltenham, GL53 7NQ
Tel: 01242-693118 **Fax:** 01242-693118
Directors: D. Smith (Prop)
Managers: D. Vincent (Chief Mgr)
Immediate Holding Company: Focal Point Audio Visual Ltd
Registration no: 04442885 **VAT No.:** GB 107 5356 80
Date established: 2002 **Turnover:** £500,000 - £1m
No.of Employees: 1 - 10 **Product Groups:** 38, 64, 81

Date of Accounts	Mar 06	Mar 05
Working Capital	35	63
Fixed Assets	3	5
Current Assets	92	120
Current Liabilities	57	56
Total Share Capital	5	5

Foxley Tagg Planning Ltd
Festival House Jessop Avenue, Cheltenham, GL50 3SH
Tel: 01242-222107 **Fax:** 01242-222112
E-mail: mail@ftplanning.co.uk
Website: http://www.foxleytaggplanning.co.uk
Directors: S. Tagg (MD)
Immediate Holding Company: FOXLEY TAGG PLANNING LIMITED
Registration no: 03952941 **Date established:** 2000
No.of Employees: 1 - 10 **Product Groups:** 84

Date of Accounts	Mar 11	Mar 10	Mar 09
Working Capital	401	351	355
Fixed Assets	95	90	92
Current Assets	455	395	428

G E Aviation
Cheltenham Road Bishops Cleeve, Cheltenham, GL52 8SF
Tel: 01242-673333 **Fax:** 01242-661661
Website: http://www.ge.com/aviation
Managers: M. Grunsa
Ultimate Holding Company: GENERAL ELECTRIC COMPANY (USA)
Immediate Holding Company: GE AVIATION SYSTEMS LIMITED
Registration no: 00745917 **Date established:** 1963
Turnover: £250m - £500m **No.of Employees:** 1501 & over
Product Groups: 39

Date of Accounts	Dec 11	Dec 10	Dec 09
Sales Turnover	487m	547m	571m
Pre Tax Profit/Loss	51m	23m	78m
Working Capital	186m	179m	138m
Fixed Assets	127m	168m	169m
Current Assets	373m	532m	458m
Current Liabilities	107m	110m	85m

Genhart Ltd
Unit 3 Malmesbury Road, Kingsditch Trading Estate, Cheltenham, GL51 9PL
Tel: 01242-241734 **Fax:** 01242-227500
E-mail: frank@genhart.co.uk
Website: http://www.genhart.co.uk
Bank(s): Lloyds TSB Bank plc
Directors: F. Clifford (MD), C. Thompson (Fin)
Immediate Holding Company: GENHART LIMITED
Registration no: 02593658 **VAT No.:** GB 326 2765 54
Date established: 1991 **Turnover:** £500,000 - £1m
No.of Employees: 11 - 20 **Product Groups:** 48

Date of Accounts	Apr 11	Apr 10	Apr 09
Working Capital	481	461	444
Fixed Assets	190	23	34
Current Assets	574	555	579

Glosfume Technologies
7 Isbourne Way Winchcombe, Cheltenham, GL54 5NS
Tel: 01242-609222 **Fax:** 01242-602755
E-mail: info@glosfume.com
Website: http://www.metcem.co.uk
Directors: B. Roberts (MD)
No.of Employees: 1 - 10 **Product Groups:** 32, 40, 41, 42

Gloucestershire Chamber of Commerce & Industry
Chargrove House Main Road Shurdington, Shurdington, Cheltenham, GL51 4GA
Tel: 01242-864164 **Fax:** 01242-864165
E-mail: kirsty.watts@glosccі.org
Website: http://www.glosccі.org
Directors: G. Day (Dir), J. Cripps (MD), M. Fabian (Co Sec)
Managers: K. Watts (Admin Off)
Immediate Holding Company: GLOUCESTERSHIRE CHAMBER OF COMMERCE AND INDUSTRY
Registration no: 02470772 **Date established:** 1990
Turnover: Up to £250,000 **No.of Employees:** 1 - 10 **Product Groups:** 87

Date of Accounts	Mar 08	Mar 07	Mar 06
Sales Turnover	127	128	81
Pre Tax Profit/Loss	2	9	-2
Working Capital	39	36	26
Fixed Assets	1	2	3
Current Assets	81	77	61
Current Liabilities	42	41	35
ROCE% (Return on Capital Employed)	4.0	24.2	-5.4
ROT% (Return on Turnover)	1.3	7.2	-1.9

Groves Batteries
Park Mews Works Lypiatt Street, Cheltenham, GL50 2UB
Tel: 01242-514940 **Fax:** 01242-256218
E-mail: groves.batteries@virgin.net
Website: http://www.grovesbatteries.co.uk
Directors: D. Groves (Dir), G. Groves (Fin)
Immediate Holding Company: GROVES BATTERIES LIMITED
Registration no: 05699836 **Date established:** 2006
Turnover: Up to £250,000 **No.of Employees:** 1 - 10 **Product Groups:** 37, 68

Date of Accounts	Mar 12	Mar 11	Mar 10
Working Capital	-6	19	57
Fixed Assets	169	175	188
Current Assets	188	141	149

Hollingsworth & Vose Co UK Ltd
Postlip Mills Winchcombe, Cheltenham, GL54 5BB
Tel: 01242-602227 **Fax:** 01242-604099
E-mail: info@hovo.com
Website: http://www.hovo.com
Directors: V. Hollingsworth (Dir), E. Swain (Fin)
Ultimate Holding Company: HOLLINGSWORTH AND VOSE COMPANY (USA)
Immediate Holding Company: HOLLINGSWORTH AND VOSE COMPANY (U.K.) LIMITED
Registration no: 01664523 **VAT No.:** GB 274 3704 54
Date established: 1982 **Turnover:** £20m - £50m **No.of Employees:** 1 - 10
Product Groups: 27

Date of Accounts	Dec 11	Dec 10	Dec 09
Sales Turnover	32m	35m	29m
Pre Tax Profit/Loss	2m	3m	3m
Working Capital	7m	10m	9m
Fixed Assets	14m	9m	9m
Current Assets	12m	17m	13m
Current Liabilities	2m	2m	2m

I P A Systems Ltd
The Priory 37 London Road, Cheltenham, GL52 6HA
Tel: 01242-573344 **Fax:** 01242-519364
E-mail: sales@ipasystems.co.uk
Website: http://www.ipasystems.co.uk
Managers: J. Mcelligott
Ultimate Holding Company: CROMAS TRADING INC (PANAMA)
Immediate Holding Company: IPA SYSTEMS LIMITED
Registration no: 01714750 **Date established:** 1983
Turnover: £500,000 - £1m **No.of Employees:** 1 - 10 **Product Groups:** 44

Date of Accounts	Mar 11	Mar 10	Mar 09
Sales Turnover	748	1m	1m
Pre Tax Profit/Loss	-21	-122	-45
Working Capital	109	-772	-668
Fixed Assets	86	89	88
Current Assets	330	437	557
Current Liabilities	156	1m	1m

Ian Greaves International Ltd
29 St Stephens Road, Cheltenham, GL51 3AB
Tel: 01242-244281
E-mail: ian@igint.co.uk
Website: http://www.igint.co.uk
Directors: I. Greaves (MD)
Immediate Holding Company: IAN GREAVES INTERNATIONAL LIMITED
Registration no: 04810976 **Date established:** 2003
No.of Employees: 1 - 10 **Product Groups:** 80

Date of Accounts	Nov 11	Nov 10	Nov 09
Working Capital	-46	-31	-53
Fixed Assets	47	52	53
Current Assets	48	96	80

Independent Tool Consultants Ltd
Unit 7 Bamfurlong Industrial Park, Staverton, Cheltenham, GL51 6SX
Tel: 01452-712519 **Fax:** 01452-714786
E-mail: sales@intoco.co.uk
Website: http://www.intoco.co.uk
Bank(s): National Westminster Bank Plc
Directors: G. Clarke (Sales), E. Berwick (Co Sec), A. Preece (MD)
Managers: M. Parker (I.T. Exec), R. McDonald (Works Gen Mgr), K. Carr (Sec)
Registration no: 01060362 **VAT No.:** GB 275 8043 41
Date established: 1972 **Turnover:** £2m - £5m **No.of Employees:** 21 - 50
Product Groups: 46

Date of Accounts	Mar 10	Mar 09	Mar 08
Sales Turnover	8m	11m	11m
Pre Tax Profit/Loss	225	971	5m
Working Capital	9m	9m	8m
Fixed Assets	3m	4m	5m
Current Assets	11m	12m	13m
Current Liabilities	387	252	605

J J Farm Services Ltd
Far Stanley Winchcombe, Cheltenham, GL54 5HF
Tel: 01242-620631 **Fax:** 01242-620423
E-mail: sales@jjfarm.co.uk
Website: http://www.jjfarm.co.uk
Directors: I. Jenkins (Fin), H. Jenkins (Co Sec), J. Jenkins (MD)
Managers: M. Jenkins (Mgr)
Immediate Holding Company: J. J. FARM SERVICES LIMITED
Registration no: 01467532 **Date established:** 1979 **Turnover:** £1m - £2m
No.of Employees: 11 - 20 **Product Groups:** 48

Date of Accounts	Jan 12	Jan 11	Jan 10
Working Capital	163	335	335
Fixed Assets	4m	4m	4m
Current Assets	1m	1m	1m

Johnson Security
Orchard Industrial Estate Toddington, Cheltenham, GL54 5EB
Tel: 01242-621362 **Fax:** 01242-621554
E-mail: sales@johnson-security.co.uk
Website: http://www.johnson-security.co.uk
Bank(s): Barclays
Directors: S. Reeves (Sales & Mktg), M. Usen (Plant)
Managers: A. Johnson (Tech Serv Mgr), M. Whiting (Purch Mgr)
Ultimate Holding Company: FOUR DIMENSION JOHNSON SECURITY UK LIMITED
Immediate Holding Company: JOHNSON SECURITY LIMITED
Registration no: 00934256 **VAT No.:** GB 274 2341 69
Date established: 1968 **Turnover:** £10m - £20m
No.of Employees: 51 - 100 **Product Groups:** 35, 36, 39, 40

Date of Accounts	Dec 10	Dec 09	Dec 08
Sales Turnover	10m	11m	16m
Pre Tax Profit/Loss	-2m	85	3m
Working Capital	2m	2m	2m
Fixed Assets	2m	3m	3m
Current Assets	4m	6m	8m
Current Liabilities	944	2m	1m

K T R Environmental Solutions Ltd
1 Close Barn Coberley Road, Coberley, Cheltenham, GL53 9QY
Tel: 01242-870134 **Fax:** 01242-870134
E-mail: pass.tony@gmail.com
Website: http://www.KTRworld.com
Directors: T. Pass (Prop)
Immediate Holding Company: KTR ENVIRONMENTAL SOLUTIONS LIMITED
Registration no: 04584498 **Date established:** 2002
No.of Employees: 1 - 10 **Product Groups:** 30, 35

Date of Accounts	Nov 11	Nov 10	Nov 08
Working Capital	-68	-68	-68
Current Assets	6	6	6
Current Liabilities	74	74	N/A

Nigel King
285 Old Bath Road, Cheltenham, GL53 9AJ
Tel: 01242-524274 **Fax:** 01242-524274
Directors: N. King (Prop)
Date established: 1979 **No.of Employees:** 1 - 10 **Product Groups:** 26, 35

Kohler Mira Ltd
Cromwell Road, Cheltenham, GL52 5EP
Tel: 08445-715000 **Fax:** 01242-724721
E-mail: dave_hill@mirashowers.com
Website: http://www.mirashowers.com
Bank(s): HSBC Bank plc
Directors: D. Hill (MD), G. Liddell (Fin), J. Curras (Tech Serv), T. Birch (Purch)
Managers: D. Brohn (Mktg Serv Mgr), P. Hollingsworth (Sales Prom Mgr), A. Cooper (Personnel)
Ultimate Holding Company: KOHLER CO (USA)
Immediate Holding Company: KOHLER MIRA LIMITED
Registration no: 00252115 **VAT No.:** GB 274 2126 73
Date established: 1930 **Turnover:** £75m - £125m
No.of Employees: 501 - 1000 **Product Groups:** 30, 36, 40

Date of Accounts	Dec 11	Dec 10	Dec 09
Sales Turnover	130m	124m	120m
Pre Tax Profit/Loss	15m	26m	25m
Working Capital	52m	60m	53m
Fixed Assets	33m	35m	33m
Current Assets	115m	143m	119m
Current Liabilities	15m	15m	13m

Kraft Foods UK Ltd
St George's House Bayshill Road, Cheltenham, GL50 3AE
Tel: 01242-236101 **Fax:** 01242-512084
E-mail: nbunker@krafteurope.com
Website: http://www.krafteurope.com
Bank(s): HSBC Bank plc
Directors: B. Carlisle (MD), C. Moore (Co Sec), J. Cook (Dir), N. Bunker (Dir), S. Colman (Dir)
Managers: J. Allan (Sales Prom Mgr)
Ultimate Holding Company: KRAFT FOODS INC (USA)
Immediate Holding Company: KRAFT FOODS UK LTD.
Registration no: 00203663 **VAT No.:** GB 366 2627 38
Date established: 2025 **Turnover:** £500m - £1,000m
No.of Employees: 251 - 500 **Product Groups:** 20

Date of Accounts	Dec 07	Dec 08	Dec 09
Sales Turnover	553m	539m	564m
Pre Tax Profit/Loss	36m	17m	10m
Working Capital	66m	90m	-10m
Fixed Assets	168m	130m	136m
Current Assets	218m	232m	162m
Current Liabilities	105m	92m	76m

Ladytone
23a Pittville Street, Cheltenham, GL52 2LN
Tel: 01242-226145
E-mail: ladytone@fitfaces.co.uk
Website: http://www.ladytone.co.uk
Directors: S. Powell (Prop), S. Carter (Prop), S. Carter (Grp Chief Exec)
Date established: 2005 **Turnover:** Up to £250,000
No.of Employees: 1 - 10 **Product Groups:** 89

Lamata Contract Furniture Ltd
The Barlands London Road, Charlton Kings, Cheltenham, GL52 6UT
Tel: 01242-524777 **Fax:** 01242-233031
E-mail: peter.whiteland@lamata.co.uk
Website: http://www.lamata.co.uk
Directors: A. Verbeeck (Fin), P. Whiteland (MD)
Ultimate Holding Company: LLOYDS BANKING GROUP PLC
Immediate Holding Company: LCF (LAMATA CONTRACT FURNITURE) LIMITED
Registration no: 03336770 **VAT No.:** GB 484 7344 15
Date established: 1997 **Turnover:** £1m - £2m **No.of Employees:** 1 - 10
Product Groups: 26, 29

Date of Accounts	Mar 10	Mar 09	Mar 08
Sales Turnover	N/A	1m	N/A
Pre Tax Profit/Loss	N/A	-142	N/A
Working Capital	181	156	-206
Fixed Assets	101	137	116
Current Assets	790	520	574
Current Liabilities	N/A	210	N/A

M A Design
Cheltenham Film Studios Hatherley Lane, Cheltenham, GL51 6PN
Tel: 01242-220320
E-mail: chris.davis@ma-design.biz
Website: http://www.ma-design.biz
Directors: C. Davis (Prop)
Immediate Holding Company: GUNPOWDER TREASON AND PLOT LIMITED
Registration no: 05983142 **Date established:** 2011
Turnover: Up to £250,000 **No.of Employees:** 1 - 10 **Product Groups:** 44, 81, 86

Date of Accounts	Jun 11
Working Capital	-2
Fixed Assets	1
Current Assets	4

M D G Crest Ltd
Malvern View Business Park Stella Way, Bishops Cleeve, Cheltenham, GL52 7DQ
Tel: 01242-675778 **Fax:** 01242-676999
Directors: D. Rawlings (MD)
Immediate Holding Company: M.D.G. CREST LIMITED
Registration no: 01404710 **Date established:** 1978
No.of Employees: 1 - 10 **Product Groups:** 46

Date of Accounts	Dec 11	Dec 10	Dec 09
Working Capital	-4	-25	-23
Fixed Assets	45	53	62
Current Assets	36	40	45

M J Services
31 Longlands Road Bishops Cleeve, Cheltenham, GL52 8JP
Tel: 01242-677624
Directors: M. Jenkins (Prop)
No.of Employees: 1 - 10 **Product Groups:** 26, 35

M P Filtri UK Ltd
Bourton Industrial Park Bourton-on-the-Water, Cheltenham, GL54 2HQ
Tel: 01451-822522 **Fax:** 01451-822282
E-mail: sales@mpfiltri.co.uk
Website: http://www.mpfiltri.com
Bank(s): Barclays, Gloucester
Directors: P. Keep (MD)
Managers: C. Roberts (Purch Mgr)
Ultimate Holding Company: M P FILTRI SPA (ITALY)
Immediate Holding Company: M P FILTRI (UK) LIMITED
Registration no: 02142443 **Date established:** 1987 **Turnover:** £2m - £5m
No.of Employees: 21 - 50 **Product Groups:** 35, 37, 38, 40, 42

Date of Accounts	Dec 11	Dec 10	Dec 09
Working Capital	1m	1m	937
Fixed Assets	412	330	360
Current Assets	3m	2m	2m

Mage Fasteners
7 Willow Court Bourton Industrial Park, Bourton-On-The-Water, Cheltenham, GL54 2HQ
Tel: 01451-822777 **Fax:** 01451-822771
E-mail: sales@magefasteners.co.uk
Website: http://www.magefasteners.co.uk
Managers: D. Lane (Prod Mgr)
Ultimate Holding Company: M P FILTRI SPA (ITALY)
Registration no: 02142443 **Date established:** 1987
No.of Employees: 11 - 20 **Product Groups:** 35

Magna Industrials Ltd
Rissington Business Park Upper Rissington, Cheltenham, GL54 2QB
Tel: 01451-821775 **Fax:** 01451-824159
E-mail: paul@magna-industrials.com
Website: http://www.magna-industrials.com
Directors: P. Harris (MD)
Immediate Holding Company: MAGNA INDUSTRIALS LIMITED
Registration no: 01703535 **VAT No.:** GB 115 9537 61
Date established: 1983 **Turnover:** £500,000 - £1m
No.of Employees: 1 - 10 **Product Groups:** 33, 42, 46

Date of Accounts	Apr 12	Apr 11	Apr 10
Working Capital	-38	14	17
Fixed Assets	249	202	219
Current Assets	219	251	187

Make Up Print Finishers Ltd
Willow Court Bourton Industrial Park Bourton-On-The-Water, Cheltenham, GL54 2HQ
Tel: 01451-822701
E-mail: pkeep@mpfiltri.co.uk
Website: http://www.mpfiltri.co.uk
Directors: J. Keep (MD)
Immediate Holding Company: MAKEUP PRINT FINISHERS LIMITED
Registration no: 04286021 **Date established:** 2001
No.of Employees: 1 - 10 **Product Groups:** 37, 38, 85

Maplin Electronics Ltd
Unit 2 Winchcombe Street, Cheltenham, GL52 2LZ
Tel: 01242-579036 **Fax:** 01242-579032
Website: http://www.maplin.co.uk
Managers: C. Stephenson (Mgr)
Ultimate Holding Company: MONTAGU PRIVATE EQUITY LLP
Immediate Holding Company: MAPLIN ELECTRONICS LIMITED
Registration no: 01264385 **Date established:** 1976
Turnover: £125m - £250m **No.of Employees:** 1 - 10 **Product Groups:** 37, 61

Date of Accounts	Dec 11	Dec 08	Dec 09
Sales Turnover	205m	204m	204m
Pre Tax Profit/Loss	25m	32m	35m
Working Capital	118m	49m	75m
Fixed Assets	27m	28m	28m
Current Assets	207m	108m	142m
Current Liabilities	78m	51m	59m

Mark's & Clerk LLP

27 Imperial Square, Cheltenham, GL50 1RQ
Tel: 01242-524520 **Fax:** 01242-579383
E-mail: cheltenham@marks-clerk.com
Website: http://www.marks-clerk.com
Directors: M. Brewer (Snr Part)
Immediate Holding Company: MARKS & CLERK LLP
Registration no: OC343273 **Date established:** 2009
Turnover: £250,000 - £500,000 **No.of Employees:** 1 - 10
Product Groups: 80

Date of Accounts	Jul 11	Jul 10	Jul 09
Sales Turnover	68m	61m	64m
Pre Tax Profit/Loss	16m	11m	11m
Working Capital	18m	15m	11m
Fixed Assets	10m	7m	9m
Current Assets	29m	25m	22m
Current Liabilities	4m	4m	4m

Masstock Arable UK Ltd

Station Road Andoversford, Cheltenham, GL54 4LZ
Tel: 0791-722 0868 **Fax:** 01242-820807
Website: http://www.masstock.co.uk
Directors: C. Bend (Dir)
Ultimate Holding Company: ARYZTA AG (SWITZERLAND)
Immediate Holding Company: MASSTOCK ARABLE (UK) LIMITED
Registration no: 02387531 **Date established:** 1989
Turnover: £250m - £500m **No.of Employees:** 11 - 20
Product Groups: 32, 85

Date of Accounts	Jul 11	Jul 10	Jul 09
Sales Turnover	333m	288m	284m
Pre Tax Profit/Loss	16m	17m	13m
Working Capital	-8m	13m	-3m
Fixed Assets	30m	24m	24m
Current Assets	139m	129m	97m
Current Liabilities	23m	22m	14m

Mayday Seals & Bearings

Units 3 & 4 The Runnings, Cheltenham, GL51 9NJ
Tel: 01242-241022 **Fax:** 01242-253214
E-mail: info@maydayseals.co.uk
Website: http://www.maydayseals.co.uk
Directors: C. Bridgen Page (Dir), C. Bridgen-Page (MD), P. Bridgen (Fin)
Immediate Holding Company: MAYDAY SEALS AND BEARINGS LIMITED
Registration no: 05997406 **Date established:** 2006
Turnover: Up to £250,000 **No.of Employees:** 11 - 20 **Product Groups:** 22, 25, 29, 30, 33, 34, 35, 36, 37, 39, 40, 45, 46, 61, 66

Date of Accounts	Mar 11	Mar 10	Mar 09
Working Capital	-38	-40	-29
Fixed Assets	56	61	65
Current Assets	29	32	33

Mil-Tek Direct

Gamma 3 Orchard Industrial Estate, Toddington, Cheltenham, GL54 5EB
Tel: 01242-620903 **Fax:** 01242-620873
E-mail: info@miltekdirect.com
Website: http://www.miltek-uk.co.uk
Directors: S. Taylor (MD)
Managers: C. Allsop (Sales Admin)
Immediate Holding Company: MIL-TEK (GB) LIMITED
Registration no: 05146245 **Date established:** 2004
No.of Employees: 21 - 50 **Product Groups:** 38, 42

Date of Accounts	Jun 11	Jun 10	Jun 09
Working Capital	-34	-39	-34
Fixed Assets	3	2	1
Current Assets	328	277	275

Minimoves

Unit 38 Lansdown Industrial Estate, Cheltenham, GL51 8PL
Tel: 01242-256858
E-mail: office@minimoves.co.uk
Website: http://www.minimoves.co.uk
Directors: R. Lane (Prop)
Date established: 2004 **Turnover:** Up to £250,000
No.of Employees: 1 - 10 **Product Groups:** 72

Mirror Technology Ltd

4 Redwood House Orchard Industrial Estate, Toddington, Cheltenham, GL54 5EB
Tel: 01242-621534 **Fax:** 01242-621529
E-mail: sales@mirrortechnology.co.uk
Website: http://www.mirrortechnology.co.uk
Bank(s): Lloyds, Tewkesbury
Directors: S. Finch (Co Sec), R. Chambers (MD)
Immediate Holding Company: MIRROR TECHNOLOGY LIMITED
Registration no: 00993071 **VAT No.:** GB 274 1400 84
Date established: 1970 **Turnover:** £500,000 - £1m
No.of Employees: 11 - 20 **Product Groups:** 33, 39

Date of Accounts	Mar 12	Mar 11	Mar 10
Sales Turnover	N/A	N/A	530
Pre Tax Profit/Loss	N/A	N/A	34
Working Capital	123	185	206
Fixed Assets	20	24	29
Current Assets	184	290	288
Current Liabilities	N/A	N/A	45

Modern Packaging UK Ltd

Unit 26 Lansdown Industrial Estate Gloucester Road, Cheltenham, GL51 8PL
Tel: 01242-262002 **Fax:** 01242-261919
E-mail: linda.c@modern-packaging.co.uk
Website: http://www.modern-packaging.co.uk
Directors: L. Cliffe (Fin), T. Woods (Snr Part)
Managers: A. Randell (Personnel), D. Bates (Tech Serv Mgr)
Immediate Holding Company: MODERN PACKAGING (UK) LIMITED
Registration no: 02553448 **Date established:** 1990 **Turnover:** £2m - £5m
No.of Employees: 21 - 50 **Product Groups:** 44

Date of Accounts	Nov 11	Nov 10	Nov 09
Working Capital	157	320	355
Fixed Assets	1m	258	371
Current Assets	2m	2m	1m

Montpellier Clocks

13 Rotunda Terrace Montpellier Street, Cheltenham, GL50 1SW
Tel: 01242-242178 **Fax:** 01242-242178
E-mail: info@montpellierclocks.com
Website: http://www.montpellierclocks.com
Directors: T. Birch (MD)
No.of Employees: 1 - 10 **Product Groups:** 38, 49, 65

Nixon Flowmeters Ltd

Unit 1-3 Badminton Close Leckhampton, Cheltenham, GL53 7BX
Tel: 01242-243006 **Fax:** 01242-222487
E-mail: mail@nixonflowmeters.co.uk
Website: http://www.nixonflowmeters.co.uk
Directors: D. Nixon (MD), K. Walker (Fin)
Immediate Holding Company: NIXON FLOWMETERS LIMITED
Registration no: 01184218 **VAT No.:** GB 276 3771 27
Date established: 1974 **No.of Employees:** 1 - 10 **Product Groups:** 38

Date of Accounts	Sep 11	Sep 10	Sep 09
Working Capital	156	134	131
Fixed Assets	33	37	34
Current Assets	296	288	265

Novellini UK Ltd

Orchard Industrial Estate Toddington, Cheltenham, GL54 5EB
Tel: 01242-621061 **Fax:** 01242-622151
E-mail: info-uk@novellini.com
Website: http://www.novellini.com
Directors: M. Novellini (Co Sec), S. West (Sales)
Managers: V. Hanson (Comptroller)
Ultimate Holding Company: NOVELLINI SPA (ITALY)
Immediate Holding Company: NOVELLINI BATHROOM PRODUCTS LIMITED
Registration no: 01958292 **VAT No.:** GB 419 2948 27
Date established: 1985 **Turnover:** £500,000 - £1m
No.of Employees: 21 - 50 **Product Groups:** 30

Noz-Alls Ltd

Unit 10 Knightsbridge Business Centre Knightsbridge Green, Knightsbridge, Cheltenham, GL51 9TA
Tel: 01242-681052 **Fax:** 01242-681053
E-mail: info@cheltenhamweldingsupplies.co.uk
Website: http://www.cheltenhamweldingsupplies.co.uk
Directors: T. Hill (MD)
Immediate Holding Company: NOZ-ALLS LIMITED
Registration no: 03225702 **Date established:** 1996
No.of Employees: 1 - 10 **Product Groups:** 46

Date of Accounts	Jun 11	Jun 10	Jun 09
Working Capital	106	88	54
Fixed Assets	10	6	8
Current Assets	179	222	176

Orchard Hire & Sales Ltd

Willow End Stoke Orchard Road, Bishops Cleeve, Cheltenham, GL52 7DG
Tel: 01242-677999 **Fax:** 01242-677355
E-mail: sales@orchardhireandsales.ltd.uk
Website: http://www.orchardhireandsales.ltd.uk
Managers: N. Finch (Mktg Serv Mgr)
Immediate Holding Company: ORCHARD HIRE AND SALES LTD
Registration no: 03679119 **Date established:** 1998
Turnover: £500,000 - £1m **No.of Employees:** 1 - 10 **Product Groups:** 83

Date of Accounts	Dec 11	Dec 10	Dec 09
Working Capital	282	209	168
Fixed Assets	102	115	96
Current Assets	360	263	206

Orthodynamics Ltd

Bourton Industrial Park Bourton-On-The-Water, Cheltenham, GL54 2HQ
Tel: 01202-481153 **Fax:** 01202-481150
E-mail: info@orthodynamics.co.uk
Website: http://www.orthodynamics.co.uk
Directors: D. Gates (Fin)
Managers: M. Cooper (Site Co-ord)
Ultimate Holding Company: RIVERSIDE EUROPE MEDICAL DEVICES LLC (DELAWARE)
Immediate Holding Company: ORTHODYNAMICS LIMITED
Registration no: 01982532 **Date established:** 1986 **Turnover:** £2m - £5m
No.of Employees: 1 - 10 **Product Groups:** 38

Date of Accounts	Mar 11	Mar 10	Mar 09
Sales Turnover	2m	2m	2m
Pre Tax Profit/Loss	704	424	406
Working Capital	1m	703	390
Fixed Assets	186	208	223
Current Assets	2m	996	849
Current Liabilities	234	140	255

Osprey Deep Clean Ltd

41 Central Way Cheltenham Trade Park, Cheltenham, GL51 8LX
Tel: 01242-513123 **Fax:** 01242-518666
E-mail: info@ospreydc.com
Website: http://www.ospreydc.com
Directors: A. Whiteley (Co Sec), T. Stucken (MD)
Ultimate Holding Company: PROVENTEC PLC
Immediate Holding Company: OSPREYDEEPCLEAN LIMITED
Registration no: 03119463 **Date established:** 1995 **Turnover:** £1m - £2m
No.of Employees: 11 - 20 **Product Groups:** 32, 40, 49, 63, 66

Date of Accounts	Mar 09	Mar 08	Sep 11
Sales Turnover	2m	2m	1m
Pre Tax Profit/Loss	-226	94	-3m
Working Capital	-261	129	-11
Fixed Assets	279	106	29
Current Assets	4m	3m	670
Current Liabilities	570	566	205

P F T Central

Laxton Meadow Farm Southam Road, Prestbury, Cheltenham, GL52 3NQ
Tel: 01242-236383 **Fax:** 01242-224794
E-mail: sales@pftcentral.co.uk
Website: http://www.pftcentral.co.uk
Product Groups: 17, 25, 27, 29, 30, 32, 33, 35, 36, 37, 38, 40, 41, 42, 45, 47, 52, 66, 67, 77, 83

P H I Group Ltd

Hadley House Bayshill Road, Cheltenham, GL50 3AW
Tel: 01242-707600 **Fax:** 08703-334121
E-mail: southern@phigroup.co.uk
Website: http://www.phigroup.co.uk
Bank(s): National Westminster
Managers: R. Torrington (Sales Prom Mgr), S. Tharia (Buyer), S. Keating (Tech Serv Mgr)
Ultimate Holding Company: KELLER GROUP PLC
Immediate Holding Company: PHI GROUP LIMITED
Registration no: 02827777 **VAT No.:** GB 535 6248 37
Date established: 1993 **Turnover:** £5m - £10m **No.of Employees:** 11 - 20
Product Groups: 33, 51

Date of Accounts	Dec 11	Dec 10	Dec 09
Sales Turnover	N/A	N/A	10m
Pre Tax Profit/Loss	N/A	N/A	340

Working Capital	1m	1m	1m
Fixed Assets	N/A	N/A	1
Current Assets	1m	1m	1m

PKL Healthcare Ltd

Stella Way Bishops Cleeve, Cheltenham, GL52 7DQ
Tel: 01242-663060 **Fax:** 01242-663088
E-mail: postbox@healthcarehire.co.uk
Website: http://www.healthcarehire.co.uk
Managers: K. Holmes (Chief Acct), S. Bailey (Mgr)
Immediate Holding Company: PKL Healthcare Ltd
Registration no: 06627288 **Date established:** 1996 **Turnover:** £5m - £10m
No.of Employees: 21 - 50 **Product Groups:** 33, 52

Date of Accounts	Dec 09	Oct 08
Sales Turnover	7m	N/A
Pre Tax Profit/Loss	3m	6m
Working Capital	-1m	-6m
Fixed Assets	17m	16m
Current Assets	2m	1m
Current Liabilities	3m	5m

Premiere Products Ltd

Oakley Gardens Bouncers Lane, Cheltenham, GL52 5JD
Tel: 01242-537150 **Fax:** 01242-528445
E-mail: custserv@premiereproducts.co.uk
Website: http://www.premiereproducts.co.uk
Directors: P. Hilltout (Ch & MD), R. Lawson-Lee (Co Sec), R. Cox (Fin), M. Hughes (Export), K. Day (Sales), P. Hilltout (Ch)
Managers: J. Davies (Sales Prom), R. Lawson Lee, S. Carling, R. Marquand, S. Whittaker (Sales Admin), N. Marquand, M. Raybould, J. Hopkinson, D. Berry
Immediate Holding Company: PREMIERE PRODUCTS LIMITED
Registration no: 00871272 **VAT No.:** GB 274 1767 40
Date established: 1966 **Turnover:** £10m - £20m
No.of Employees: 51 - 100 **Product Groups:** 24, 27, 29, 30, 31, 32, 36, 40, 45, 49, 63, 66

Date of Accounts	Dec 10	Jul 10	Jul 09
Working Capital	N/A	N/A	1
Current Assets	N/A	N/A	1

QualSoft House

88 Devon Avenue, Cheltenham, GL51 8BT
Tel: 020-7183 4966
E-mail: uk@qualsoftservices.com
Website: http://www.qualsoftservices.com/
Date established: 2004 **Turnover:** £2m - £5m **No.of Employees:** 51 - 100
Product Groups: 44

Quedron 2001 Ltd

Units 3-5 Runnings Road Kingsditch Industrial Estate, Cheltenham, GL51 9NU
Tel: 01242-241222 **Fax:** 01242-584934
E-mail: tim.hosken@quedron.co.uk
Website: http://www.quedron.co.uk
Directors: I. Hill (Co Sec)
Managers: T. Hosken (Mgr)
Date established: 1974 **No.of Employees:** 1 - 10 **Product Groups:** 26, 35

Date of Accounts	May 08	May 07	May 06
Sales Turnover	1384	N/A	N/A
Pre Tax Profit/Loss	117	659	441
Working Capital	1167	871	523
Fixed Assets	116	437	500
Current Assets	3992	2869	3494
Current Liabilities	2824	1998	2971
Total Share Capital	95	95	95
ROCE% (Return on Capital Employed)	9.1	50.4	43.1
ROT% (Return on Turnover)	8.4		

R & L Superfix

Unit 1 Mead Park Industrial Estate Mead Road, Cheltenham, GL53 7EF
Tel: 01242-224664 **Fax:** 01242-222977
Directors: D. Powell (MD)
Immediate Holding Company: R & L SUPERFIX LIMITED
Registration no: 05346093 **Date established:** 2005
No.of Employees: 1 - 10 **Product Groups:** 37

Date of Accounts	Mar 11	Mar 10	Mar 09
Working Capital	13	-49	-116
Fixed Assets	29	107	166
Current Assets	235	232	221
Current Liabilities	N/A	N/A	273

Race Furniture Ltd

Spartacus House Bourton Industrial Park, Bourton-On-The-Water, Cheltenham, GL54 2HQ
Tel: 01451-821446 **Fax:** 01451-821686
E-mail: enquiries@racefurniture.com
Website: http://www.racefurniture.com
Directors: I. Finlator (Fin)
Ultimate Holding Company: M P FILTRI SPA (ITALY)
Immediate Holding Company: RACE FURNITURE LIMITED
Registration no: 02454179 **Date established:** 1989
Turnover: Up to £250,000 **No.of Employees:** 11 - 20 **Product Groups:** 26

Date of Accounts	Dec 11	Dec 10	Dec 09
Sales Turnover	N/A	N/A	2m
Pre Tax Profit/Loss	N/A	N/A	160
Working Capital	199	47	248
Fixed Assets	349	407	441
Current Assets	475	433	696
Current Liabilities	N/A	N/A	93

Rhoda Precision Tooling Ltd

Unit 2 Lansdown Industrial Estate, Cheltenham, GL51 8PL
Tel: 01242-233791 **Fax:** 01242-226236
E-mail: neilcompton@rhodaprecision.wanadoo.co.uk
Website: http://www.rhodaprecision.co.uk
Directors: N. Compton (MD)
Immediate Holding Company: RHODA PRECISION TOOLING LIMITED
Registration no: 01388266 **VAT No.:** GB 302 4952 83
Date established: 1978 **Turnover:** Up to £250,000
No.of Employees: 1 - 10 **Product Groups:** 48

Date of Accounts	Sep 11	Sep 10	Sep 09
Working Capital	57	40	64
Fixed Assets	22	25	27
Current Assets	121	85	86

Rotastat

Unit 2 Manchester Park, Cheltenham, GL51 9EJ
Tel: 01242-521998 **Fax:** 01242-226217
E-mail: sales@rotastat.com
Website: http://www.rotastat.com
Bank(s): National Westminster Bank Plc

Directors: C. Knight (Prop)
Managers: S. O'Donnell (Systems Mgr), S. Campbell (Sales Prom Mgr), J. Chamberlain (Purch Mgr), V. Buckingham (Chief Acct)
VAT No.: GB 274 9045 38 **Date established:** 1972
Turnover: £500,000 - £1m **No.of Employees:** 21 - 50 **Product Groups:** 37

Sapa Profiles UK Ltd

Tewkesbury Road, Cheltenham, GL51 9DT
Tel: 01242-521641 **Fax:** 01242-513304
E-mail: kevin.donnelly@sapagroup.com
Website: http://www.sapagroup.com/uk/profiles
Bank(s): Barclays
Directors: K. Donnelly (Dir), J. Tate (Fin), D. Humphries (Sales)
Managers: J. Howson (Mktg Serv Mgr)
Ultimate Holding Company: ORKLA ASA (NORWAY)
Immediate Holding Company: SAPA PROFILES UK LIMITED
Registration no: 06249949 **VAT No.:** GB 551 5224 66
Date established: 2007 **Turnover:** £75m - £125m
No.of Employees: 251 - 500 **Product Groups:** 34, 35, 45, 46, 48, 66

Date of Accounts	Dec 11	Dec 10	Dec 09
Sales Turnover	99m	85m	70m
Pre Tax Profit/Loss	3m	2m	-58
Working Capital	17m	14m	13m
Fixed Assets	28m	25m	26m
Current Assets	38m	31m	25m
Current Liabilities	4m	2m	2m

Securistyle Ltd

Kingsmead Industrial Estate, Cheltenham, GL51 7RE
Tel: 01242-221200 **Fax:** 01242-520828
E-mail: paul_cook@securistyle.co.uk
Website: http://www.securistyle.co.uk
Bank(s): Bank of Scotland
Directors: P. Cook (MD), N. Thompson (Sales), C. Browning (MD), D. Walsh (Sales)
Managers: M. Williams (Purch Mgr)
Ultimate Holding Company: SECURISTYLE GROUP HOLDINGS LIMITED
Immediate Holding Company: SECURISTYLE LIMITED
Registration no: 01381767 **VAT No.:** GB 752 8872 91
Date established: 1978 **Turnover:** £20m - £50m
No.of Employees: 101 - 250 **Product Groups:** 35, 36

Date of Accounts	Dec 11	Dec 10	Dec 09
Sales Turnover	20m	22m	22m
Pre Tax Profit/Loss	2m	3m	3m
Working Capital	26m	24m	20m
Fixed Assets	2m	2m	2m
Current Assets	29m	38m	34m
Current Liabilities	639	507	676

Select Enclosures Ltd

Unit N Churchill Industrial Estate Churchill Road, Cheltenham, GL53 7FD
Tel: 01242-574709 **Fax:** 01242-572433
E-mail: sales@selectenclosures.co.uk
Website: http://www.selectenclosures.co.uk
Directors: C. Ryan (Dir), C. Ryan (MD)
Immediate Holding Company: SELECT ENCLOSURES LIMITED
Registration no: 03490347 **Date established:** 1998
Turnover: Up to £250,000 **No.of Employees:** 1 - 10 **Product Groups:** 26, 30, 35, 36, 37, 44, 66

Date of Accounts	Jan 08	Jan 07	Jan 06
Working Capital	-19	-32	-17
Fixed Assets	1	1	1
Current Assets	14	19	16
Current Liabilities	33	52	34

Senior Steel Ltd

Bamfurlong Industrial Park Staverton, Cheltenham, GL51 6SX
Tel: 01452-712843 **Fax:** 01452-856470
E-mail: info@seniorsteel.co.uk
Website: http://seniorsteel.co.uk
Bank(s): Barclays
Directors: J. Rowles (MD)
Ultimate Holding Company: L & J ROWLES LIMITED
Immediate Holding Company: SENIOR STEEL LIMITED
Registration no: 03770542 **VAT No.:** GB 275 3021 76
Date established: 1999 **Turnover:** £500,000 - £1m
No.of Employees: 11 - 20 **Product Groups:** 48

Date of Accounts	Jun 12	Jun 11	Jun 10
Working Capital	275	269	257
Fixed Assets	23	25	10
Current Assets	695	765	747

Severnside Recycling

Unit 6 Bamfurlong Industrial Park Staverton, Cheltenham, GL51 6SX
Tel: 01452-855767 **Fax:** 01452-713197
E-mail: justin@severnside.com
Website: http://www.severnside.com
Bank(s): National Westminster
Directors: G. West (Sales), J. Snow (I.T. Dir)
Managers: J. Powell (Mgr), J. Powell (Depot Mgr)
Immediate Holding Company: CENTRALWEDGE LIMITED
Registration no: 00489560 **VAT No.:** GB 479 5202 22
Date established: 1988 **Turnover:** £20m - £50m
No.of Employees: 21 - 50 **Product Groups:** 66

Shrinktek Polymers International Ltd

Herrick Way Staverton, Cheltenham, GL51 6TQ
Tel: 01452-714900 **Fax:** 01452-714959
E-mail: enquiries@shrinktek.co.uk
Website: http://www.shrinktek.co.uk
Directors: M. Haley (Dir), R. Haley (Fin)
Immediate Holding Company: SHRINKTEK POLYMERS INTERNATIONAL LIMITED
Registration no: 03572368 **VAT No.:** GB 484 7475 00
Date established: 1998 **No.of Employees:** 1 - 10 **Product Groups:** 30

Date of Accounts	Dec 11	Dec 10	Dec 09
Working Capital	370	347	302
Fixed Assets	51	71	104
Current Assets	648	598	462

Skyscan Aerial Photography

Oak House Toddington, Cheltenham, GL54 5BY
Tel: 01242-621357 **Fax:** 01242-621343
E-mail: info@skyscan.co.uk
Website: http://www.skyscan.co.uk
Managers: B. Marks (Mgr)
VAT No.: GB 408 3764 45 **Turnover:** Up to £250,000
No.of Employees: 1 - 10 **Product Groups:** 75, 81, 89

Smart Data Studio Ltd

Barn 3 Calcot, Cheltenham, GL54 3JZ
Tel: 05602-753 268 **Fax:** 01242-528999
E-mail: rmusker@smartdatastudio.com
Website: http://www.smartdatastudio.com
Directors: R. Musker (MD)
Immediate Holding Company: Smart Data Studio Ltd
Registration no: 05130158 **Date established:** 2003
No.of Employees: 1 - 10 **Product Groups:** 44

Date of Accounts	May 08	May 07	May 06
Working Capital	1	N/A	-6
Current Assets	11	22	10
Current Liabilities	10	22	16

Solo Interiors

5 Gravel Pit Lane Southam Road, Prestbury, Cheltenham, GL52 3NQ
Tel: 01242-220440 **Fax:** 01242-220441
E-mail: info@solointeriors.com
Website: http://solointeriors.com
Managers: P. Murphy (Mgr)
Immediate Holding Company: SOLO INTERIORS LIMITED
Registration no: 03578003 **Date established:** 1998
Turnover: £500,000 - £1m **No.of Employees:** 1 - 10 **Product Groups:** 24, 25, 26, 27, 30, 33, 35, 40, 41, 45, 52, 66

Date of Accounts	Jul 11	Jul 10	Jul 09
Working Capital	27	1	34
Fixed Assets	24	22	25
Current Assets	113	142	167

Spa Conservatory Company

Evesham Road Prestbury, Cheltenham, GL50 4SJ
Tel: 01242-676822 **Fax:** 01242-678570
E-mail: info@spaconservatoryvillages.co.uk
Website: http://www.spaconservatoryvillages.co.uk
Directors: P. Jarrett (Prop)
Immediate Holding Company: SPA CONSERVATORY COMPANY LIMITED
Registration no: 02675783 **Date established:** 1992
No.of Employees: 1 - 10 **Product Groups:** 25, 33, 35, 66

Spirax Sarco Ltd

132 St Georges Road, Cheltenham, GL50 3EN
Tel: 01242-583100 **Fax:** 01242-520498
Website: http://www.spiraxsarco.com
Directors: S. Thornley (Dir)
Immediate Holding Company: SPIRAX-SARCO LIMITED
Registration no: 00509018 **Date established:** 1952
Turnover: £75m - £125m **No.of Employees:** 1001 - 1500
Product Groups: 38, 48, 84

Spirax Sarco Ltd

Charlton House 15 Cirencester Road, Charlton Kings, Cheltenham, GL53 8ER
Tel: 01242-521361 **Fax:** 01242-520498
E-mail: markvernon@spiraxsarco.com
Website: http://www.spiraxsarco.com
Directors: D. Meredith (Fin), M. Vernon (Grp Chief Exec)
Ultimate Holding Company: SPIRAX-SARCO ENGINEERING PLC
Immediate Holding Company: SPIRAX-SARCO LIMITED
Registration no: 00509018 **Date established:** 1952
Turnover: £75m - £125m **No.of Employees:** 101 - 250
Product Groups: 35, 36, 39

Date of Accounts	Dec 11	Dec 10	Dec 09
Sales Turnover	124m	109m	103m
Pre Tax Profit/Loss	-463	5m	2m
Working Capital	-27m	-10m	4m
Fixed Assets	68m	60m	48m
Current Assets	63m	57m	47m
Current Liabilities	85m	5m	5m

Stewart & Allen Ltd

The Runnings, Cheltenham, GL51 9NW
Tel: 01242-523298 **Fax:** 01242-226416
E-mail: info@stewartallen.co.uk
Website: http://www.stewartallen.co.uk
Bank(s): Barclays
Managers: G. Chisholm (Chief Mgr)
Ultimate Holding Company: S.P. BROUGHTON & CO. LIMITED
Immediate Holding Company: STEWART & ALLEN LIMITED
Registration no: 01639991 **VAT No.:** GB 274 7955 09
Date established: 1982 **Turnover:** £500,000 - £1m
No.of Employees: 11 - 20 **Product Groups:** 26, 48

Date of Accounts	Dec 09	Dec 08	Dec 07
Sales Turnover	538	689	933
Pre Tax Profit/Loss	-33	-48	130
Working Capital	331	343	366
Fixed Assets	40	61	68
Current Assets	374	396	569
Current Liabilities	28	26	89

Stoate & Bishop Printers Ltd

Unit 1 Shaftesbury Industrial Estate The Runnings, Cheltenham, GL51 9NH
Tel: 01242-236741 **Fax:** 01242-222032
E-mail: sales@stoateandbishop.com
Website: http://www.stoateandbishop.com
Directors: T. Stoate (Fin)
Immediate Holding Company: STOATE AND BISHOP (PRINTERS) LIMITED
Registration no: 01022070 **Date established:** 1971
Turnover: Up to £250,000 **No.of Employees:** 11 - 20 **Product Groups:** 28

Date of Accounts	Nov 10	Nov 09	Nov 08
Working Capital	-372	-422	-247
Fixed Assets	773	1m	2m
Current Assets	177	304	252

Storacall Teleacoustics Ltd

6 Enterprise Way Cheltenham Trade Park, Cheltenham, GL51 8LZ
Tel: 01242-570995 **Fax:** 01242-226131
E-mail: sales@teleacoustics.co.uk
Website: http://www.teleacoustics.co.uk
Directors: R. Penney (Dir)
Immediate Holding Company: STORACALL (TELE ACOUSTICS) LIMITED
Registration no: 01292129 **Date established:** 1976
Turnover: £500,000 - £1m **No.of Employees:** 1 - 10 **Product Groups:** 35, 37, 38, 44, 80, 84, 86

Date of Accounts	Mar 11	Mar 10	Mar 09
Working Capital	322	309	240
Fixed Assets	2	6	9
Current Assets	425	554	454

Swan Portaforge Ltd

Unit 1-2 Gamma Orchard Industrial Estate, Toddington, Cheltenham, GL54 5EB
Tel: 01242-621590 **Fax:** 01242-621591
E-mail: info@gasforges.co.uk
Website: http://www.swan-portaforge.co.uk
Managers: R. Iles (Mgr)
Immediate Holding Company: SWAN PORTAFORGE LIMITED
Registration no: 07549175 **Date established:** 2011
Turnover: £500,000 - £1m **No.of Employees:** 1 - 10 **Product Groups:** 40, 46, 67

Date of Accounts	Mar 12
Working Capital	34
Fixed Assets	7
Current Assets	162

T W B Finishing Ltd

Tewkesbury Road, Cheltenham, GL51 9AJ
Tel: 01242-268000 **Fax:** 01242-268001
E-mail: sales@twbfinishing.co.uk
Website: http://www.twbfinishing.co.uk
Bank(s): Barclays
Directors: J. Bayston (MD), D. Fuller (Fin), C. Brooks (Chief Op Offcr)
Managers: K. Damsell (Sales Prom Mgr)
Ultimate Holding Company: BAYVEST LIMITED
Immediate Holding Company: TWB FINISHING LIMITED
Registration no: 00433954 **VAT No.:** GB 274 1998 21
Date established: 1947 **Turnover:** £1m - £2m **No.of Employees:** 21 - 50
Product Groups: 48

Date of Accounts	Mar 11	Mar 10	Mar 09
Working Capital	257	251	175
Fixed Assets	311	324	488
Current Assets	511	487	392

The Steeplechase Co Cheltenham Ltd

Prestbury Park Prestbury, Cheltenham, GL50 4SH
Tel: 01242-513014 **Fax:** 01242-224227
E-mail: cheltenham@jockeyclubracecourses.com
Website: http://www.cheltenham.co.uk
Bank(s): HSBC
Directors: S. Handley (Fin), D. Dommett (Tech Serv), E. Gillespie (MD)
Managers: I. Sedgwick, L. Bowles (Personnel), P. McNeile, C. Staddon
Ultimate Holding Company: THE JOCKEY CLUB (UK)
Immediate Holding Company: DEVON & EXETER STEEPLECHASES LIMITED
Registration no: 00575247 **Date established:** 1956 **Turnover:** £1m - £2m
No.of Employees: 51 - 100 **Product Groups:** 89

Date of Accounts	Dec 07	Dec 06	Dec 05
Sales Turnover	1m	2m	2m
Pre Tax Profit/Loss	-351	39	-13
Working Capital	254	-212	40
Fixed Assets	N/A	3m	3m
Current Assets	254	497	787
Current Liabilities	N/A	563	613

The Winnen Furnishing Company

35-39 Selkirk Street, Cheltenham, GL52 2HL
Tel: 01242-521661 **Fax:** 01242-222360
E-mail: info@winnens.co.uk
Website: http://www.winnens.co.uk
Directors: J. Newell (Prop)
Ultimate Holding Company: LILYFAST LTD
Registration no: 02889339 **Turnover:** £500,000 - £1m
No.of Employees: 1 - 10 **Product Groups:** 23, 25, 26, 29, 30, 31, 33, 35, 36, 37, 40, 43, 52, 63, 64, 66, 67, 84

Tombs & Bliss

Unit K Chosen View Road, Kingsditch Trading Estate, Cheltenham, GL51 9LT
Tel: 01242-525957 **Fax:** 01242-525957
Website: http://www.stonecot.demon.co.uk
Directors: S. Watson (Prop)
Immediate Holding Company: FRONTIER PRINT & DESIGN LIMITED
Registration no: 00953924 **Date established:** 1988
No.of Employees: 1 - 10 **Product Groups:** 46, 48

Date of Accounts	Mar 11	Mar 10	Mar 09
Working Capital	182	145	120
Fixed Assets	140	37	61
Current Assets	311	228	211

Torque Control Ltd

60 Alstone Lane, Cheltenham, GL51 8HE
Tel: 01242-261233 **Fax:** 01242-221115
E-mail: torquecontrolltd@btinternet.com
Website: http://www.torquecontrol.ltd.uk
Directors: S. Fellows (MD)
Immediate Holding Company: TORQUE CONTROL LIMITED
Registration no: 01604574 **VAT No.:** GB 477 7746 81
Date established: 1981 **Turnover:** £250,000 - £500,000
No.of Employees: 1 - 10 **Product Groups:** 35, 37, 40

Date of Accounts	Jul 11	Jul 10	Jul 09
Sales Turnover	N/A	N/A	329
Pre Tax Profit/Loss	N/A	N/A	-38
Working Capital	59	25	35
Fixed Assets	N/A	1	1
Current Assets	196	156	166
Current Liabilities	N/A	N/A	42

Tuftop

Unit R2 Bourton Link Bourton Industrial Park, Bourton-on-the-Water, Cheltenham, GL54 2HQ
Tel: 01451-824132 **Fax:** 01451-824282
E-mail: rob@tuftop.co.uk
Directors: R. Griffths (Ptnr)
Ultimate Holding Company: M P FILTRI SPA (ITALY)
Immediate Holding Company: M P FILTRI (UK) LIMITED
Registration no: 02142443 **VAT No.:** GB 619 7330 29
Date established: 1987 **Turnover:** £250,000 - £500,000
No.of Employees: 1 - 10 **Product Groups:** 33

Date of Accounts	Mar 11	Mar 10	Mar 09
Working Capital	5	-6	11
Fixed Assets	7	9	12
Current Assets	84	79	101

Ultra Dynamics Ltd

2 Upperfield Road Kingsditch Trading Estate, Cheltenham, GL51 9NY
Tel: 01242-707900 **Fax:** 01242-707901
E-mail: sales@ultrajet.co.uk
Website: http://www.ultradynamics.com

see next page

Ultra Dynamics Ltd - Cont'd

Bank(s): Barclays
Directors: A. Bathe (MD), M. Lane (Tech Serv)
Ultimate Holding Company: ULTRA DYNAMIC HOLDINGS LIMITED
Immediate Holding Company: ULTRA DYNAMICS LIMITED
Registration no: 03239600 **VAT No.:** GB 682 3569 07
Date established: 1996 **Turnover:** £5m - £10m **No.of Employees:** 21 - 50
Product Groups: 38, 39

Date of Accounts	Jul 11	Jul 10	Jul 09
Sales Turnover	7m	5m	6m
Pre Tax Profit/Loss	2m	735	916
Working Capital	4m	3m	2m
Fixed Assets	346	375	362
Current Assets	5m	4m	4m
Current Liabilities	327	659	710

Ultra Electronics

Upperfield Road Kingsditch Trading Estate, Cheltenham, GL51 9NY
Tel: 01242-221166 **Fax:** 01242-221167
E-mail: mark.doyle@ultra-electrics.com
Website: http://www.ultra-electronics.com
Bank(s): The Royal Bank of Scotland
Directors: D. Garbett-Edwards (Co Sec)
Ultimate Holding Company: ULTRA DYNAMIC HOLDINGS LIMITED
Immediate Holding Company: ULTRA DYNAMIC HOLDINGS LIMITED
Registration no: 03252068 **VAT No.:** GB 618 4577 16
Date established: 1996 **No.of Employees:** 251 - 500 **Product Groups:** 36, 37, 38, 39, 49, 68

Date of Accounts	Jul 11	Jul 10	Jul 09
Sales Turnover	7m	5m	6m
Pre Tax Profit/Loss	2m	735	916
Working Capital	4m	3m	2m
Fixed Assets	346	375	362
Current Assets	5m	4m	4m
Current Liabilities	327	659	710

Wave Seven Marine Ltd

Montpellier House Montpellier Drive, Cheltenham, GL50 1TY
Tel: 01242-541983 **Fax:** 0870-7120506
E-mail: sales@wseven.com
Website: http://www.wseven.com
Directors: R. Nadin (MD)
Turnover: £1m - £2m **No.of Employees:** 1 - 10 **Product Groups:** 39, 45, 68, 74

Date of Accounts	Mar 07	Mar 06
Working Capital	-92	-89
Fixed Assets	30	32
Current Assets	91	114
Current Liabilities	183	203

Woodward Diesel Systems

Hatherley Lane, Cheltenham, GL51 0EU
Tel: 01242-277000 **Fax:** 01242-277277
Website: http://www.woodward.com
Directors: R. Giavi (Tech Serv)
Turnover: £10m - £20m **No.of Employees:** 101 - 250 **Product Groups:** 40

Zurich Assurance

Bishops Cleeve, Cheltenham, GL52 8XX
Tel: 01242-221311 **Fax:** 01242-221554
Website: http://www.zurich.com
Directors: M. Cottell (Prop)
Ultimate Holding Company: ZURICH FINANCIAL SERVICES (SWITZERLAND)
Immediate Holding Company: ZURICH FINANCIAL SERVICES (UKISA) LIMITED
Registration no: 01860680 **VAT No.:** GB 243 6180 74
Date established: 1984 **No.of Employees:** 1 - 10 **Product Groups:** 82

Chipping Campden

Inverter Drive Supermarket Ltd

Unit 2 Battle Brook Drive, Chipping Campden, GL55 6JX
Tel: 01386-848830 **Fax:** 01386-848829
E-mail: enquiries@inverterdrive.com
Website: http://www.inverterdrive.com
Directors: S. Gibson (Mkt Research)
Immediate Holding Company: THE INVERTER DRIVE SUPERMARKET LIMITED
Registration no: 05913865 **Date established:** 2006
Turnover: £500,000 - £1m **No.of Employees:** 1 - 10 **Product Groups:** 37

Date of Accounts	Aug 11	Aug 10	Aug 09
Working Capital	41	80	57
Fixed Assets	7	3	4
Current Assets	380	180	119
Current Liabilities	N/A	9	23

Three Ways House Hotel

Chapel Lane Mickleton, Chipping Campden, GL55 6SB
Tel: 01386-438429 **Fax:** 01386-438118
E-mail: reception@puddingclub.com
Website: http://www.threewayshousehotel.com
Bank(s): Barclays
Directors: P. Henderson (Ptnr), S. Coombe (Prop)
Managers: C. Matthews (Hotel Mgr), J. Coombes (Sales & Mktg Mg), R. Righton (Personnel)
Immediate Holding Company: CLASSIC COUNTRY HOTELS LTD
Registration no: 03049751 **Turnover:** £1m - £2m
No.of Employees: 21 - 50 **Product Groups:** 69

P Yates

Haycroft Broadway Road, Mickleton, Chipping Campden, GL55 6PT
Tel: 01386-438267
Directors: P. Yates (Prop)
Date established: 1987 **No.of Employees:** 1 - 10 **Product Groups:** 41

Cinderford

A P D International Ltd

Crabtree Road Forest Vale Industrial Estate, Cinderford, GL14 2YQ
Tel: 01594-826363 **Fax:** 01594-827059
E-mail: apdi@netcomuk.co.uk
Website: http://www.apdiltd.com
Bank(s): Lloyds TSB Bank plc
Directors: P. Meak (MD)
Immediate Holding Company: APD INTERNATIONAL LIMITED
Registration no: 04358263 **Date established:** 2002 **Turnover:** £1m - £2m
No.of Employees: 11 - 20 **Product Groups:** 23, 32, 44, 67

Date of Accounts	Mar 12	Mar 11	Mar 10
Working Capital	3m	2m	616
Fixed Assets	28	33	25
Current Assets	3m	3m	3m

Biffa Waste Services Ltd

Valley Road, Cinderford, GL14 2NX
Tel: 01594-825803 **Fax:** 01594-825908
E-mail: martin.jones@biffa.co.uk
Website: http://www.biffa.co.uk
Managers: M. Jones (Depot Mgr)
Immediate Holding Company: BIFFA WASTE SERVICES LIMITED
Registration no: 00946107 **Date established:** 1969
Turnover: £20m - £50m **No.of Employees:** 51 - 100 **Product Groups:** 32, 54

Date of Accounts	Mar 08	Mar 09	Apr 10
Sales Turnover	555m	574m	492m
Pre Tax Profit/Loss	23m	50m	30m
Working Capital	229m	271m	293m
Fixed Assets	371m	360m	378m
Current Assets	409m	534m	609m
Current Liabilities	50m	100m	115m

Bituchem Group Ltd

Laymore Road Forest Vale Industrial Estate, Cinderford, GL14 2YH
Tel: 01594-826768 **Fax:** 01594-826948
E-mail: roger@bituchem.com
Website: http://www.bituchem.com
Directors: M. Paschali (Co Sec), R. Lord (Sales)
Ultimate Holding Company: BITUCHEM HOLDINGS LIMITED
Immediate Holding Company: BITUCHEM LIMITED
Registration no: 03026132 **Date established:** 1995
No.of Employees: 11 - 20 **Product Groups:** 17, 29, 30

Broadmoor Saw Mills

Whimsey Industrial Estate Whimsey, Cinderford, GL14 3JA
Tel: 01594-823725 **Fax:** 01594-826782
E-mail: nicholashyndman@xln.co.uk
Website: http://www.broadmoor-brickworks.co.uk
Directors: J. Tierney (Fin), N. Hyndman (Prop)
Immediate Holding Company: BROADMOOR SAWMILLS LIMITED
Registration no: 04666834 **VAT No.:** GB 391 9488 00
Date established: 2003 **Turnover:** £1m - £2m **No.of Employees:** 1 - 10
Product Groups: 33

Date of Accounts	Mar 11	Mar 09	Mar 08
Working Capital	-31	-25	-27
Fixed Assets	21	26	25
Current Assets	15	16	13

Cannop Foundry 1981 Ltd

Crabtree Road Forest Vale Industrial Estate, Cinderford, GL14 2YQ
Tel: 01594-822143 **Fax:** 01594-824200
E-mail: david.hall@cannop.co.uk
Website: http://www.cannop.co.uk
Bank(s): National Westminster Bank Plc
Directors: D. Hall (Dir), R. Meredith (Chief Op Offcr)
Managers: C. Lane (Sales Admin)
Immediate Holding Company: CANNOP FOUNDRY (1981) LIMITED
Registration no: 01531954 **VAT No.:** GB 359 0150 62
Date established: 1980 **Turnover:** £1m - £2m **No.of Employees:** 21 - 50
Product Groups: 34

Date of Accounts	Dec 11	Dec 10	Dec 09
Working Capital	-668	-295	-435
Fixed Assets	406	459	457
Current Assets	746	690	458

Coleford Brick & Tile

Hawkwell Green, Cinderford, GL14 3JJ
Tel: 01594-822160 **Fax:** 01594-826655
E-mail: sales@colefordbrick.co.uk
Website: http://www.colefordbrick.co.uk
Bank(s): Lloyds TSB Bank plc
Directors: H. Gilson (Dir), S. Evans (Co Sec)
Immediate Holding Company: CHARNWOOD BRICK HOLDINGS LTD
Registration no: 00208970 **VAT No.:** GB 115 1279 00
Date established: 1925 **Turnover:** £1m - £2m **No.of Employees:** 11 - 20
Product Groups: 33

Date of Accounts	Apr 03	Apr 02	Apr 01
Working Capital	25	-186	-203
Fixed Assets	N/A	185	182
Current Assets	181	491	383
Current Liabilities	156	677	586
Total Share Capital	20	20	20

E D M Sales & Service Engineering

Forest Vale Industrial Estate Birchwood Close, Cinderford, GL14 2YG
Tel: 01594-826779 **Fax:** 01594-826748
E-mail: paul@edm.co.uk
Website: http://www.edm.co.uk
Directors: P. Denton (Prop)
Ultimate Holding Company: TURNSHRED LTD
Date established: 1986 **Turnover:** £1m - £2m **No.of Employees:** 1 - 10
Product Groups: 36, 37, 42, 46, 48, 67

Farm Feed Systems Ltd

Foxes Bridge Road Forest Vale Industrial Estate, Cinderford, GL14 2PH
Tel: 01594-825106 **Fax:** 01594-824567
E-mail: sales@farmfeedsystems.co.uk
Website: http://www.farmfeedsystems.co.uk
Directors: P. Herbert (Prop)
Immediate Holding Company: FARM FEED SYSTEMS LIMITED
Registration no: 03811114 **Date established:** 1999
Turnover: £500,000 - £1m **No.of Employees:** 1 - 10 **Product Groups:** 41

Date of Accounts	Nov 11	Nov 10	Nov 09
Working Capital	57	21	4
Fixed Assets	80	92	96
Current Assets	116	79	63

Fordwater Pumping Supplies Ltd

Unit 2 Hollyhill Road Forest Vale Industrial Estate, Cinderford, GL14 2YA
Tel: 01594-826780 **Fax:** 01594-829426
E-mail: fordwater@hotmail.com
Website: http://www.fordwaterpumps.co.uk
Bank(s): HSBC Bank plc
Directors: B. Powell (Dir)
Immediate Holding Company: FORDWATER PUMPING SUPPLIES LIMITED
Registration no: 01311286 **VAT No.:** GB 113 4398 86
Date established: 1977 **Turnover:** £1m - £2m **No.of Employees:** 11 - 20
Product Groups: 35, 37, 39, 40, 41, 42, 45, 46, 48

Date of Accounts	Jun 12	Jun 11	Jun 10
Working Capital	42	51	65
Fixed Assets	345	351	358
Current Assets	284	263	244

House Of Flavours Ltd

Speculation Road Forest Vale Industrial Estate, Cinderford, GL14 2YD
Tel: 01594-822885 **Fax:** 01594-827050
E-mail: clivem@flavours.co.uk
Website: http://www.flavours.co.uk
Directors: L. Meek (Co Sec), A. Matthews (I.T. Dir), C. Matthews (MD)
Immediate Holding Company: HOUSE OF FLAVOURS LIMITED
Registration no: 02369108 **Date established:** 1989
No.of Employees: 11 - 20 **Product Groups:** 20, 31, 32, 41, 80, 85

Date of Accounts	Mar 12	Mar 11	Mar 10
Working Capital	104	24	4
Fixed Assets	95	55	63
Current Assets	680	492	515

J M Grail General Engineers Ltd

Newtown Road, Cinderford, GL14 3JE
Tel: 01594-822054 **Fax:** 01594-822054
E-mail: julian@grail.eu.com
Website: http://www.grail.eu.com
Bank(s): Lloyds TSB Bank plc
Directors: J. Grail (MD)
Immediate Holding Company: J.M. GRAIL (GENERAL ENGINEERS) LIMITED
Registration no: 01716637 **VAT No.:** GB 134 8344 69
Date established: 1983 **Turnover:** £1m - £2m **No.of Employees:** 21 - 50
Product Groups: 48, 84

Date of Accounts	Dec 11	Dec 10	Dec 09
Working Capital	328	277	296
Fixed Assets	270	287	299
Current Assets	522	422	447

Leoni-Temco Ltd

Whimsey Industrial Estate Whimsey, Cinderford, GL14 3HZ
Tel: 01594-820100 **Fax:** 01279-816270
E-mail: general@leonitemco.com
Website: http://www.leoni-special-conductors.com
Bank(s): Lloyds TSB Bank plc
Directors: R. Kuun (MD)
Ultimate Holding Company: LEONI AG (GERMANY)
Immediate Holding Company: LEONI TEMCO LIMITED
Registration no: 00434420 **VAT No.:** GB 406 1356 82
Date established: 1947 **Turnover:** £20m - £50m
No.of Employees: 51 - 100 **Product Groups:** 37, 44

Date of Accounts	Dec 11	Dec 10	Dec 09
Sales Turnover	23m	17m	11m
Pre Tax Profit/Loss	282	295	-291
Working Capital	-431	-926	-500
Fixed Assets	3m	3m	3m
Current Assets	6m	6m	4m
Current Liabilities	199	240	182

Mar Deb

2-4 Pavilion Business Park Speculation Road, Forest Vale Industrial Estate, Cinderford, GL14 2YD
Tel: 01594-826944 **Fax:** 01594-826637
E-mail: info@mardeb.co.uk
Website: http://www.mardeb.co.uk
Directors: P. Walker (Prop)
Turnover: £250,000 - £500,000 **No.of Employees:** 1 - 10
Product Groups: 25, 27, 28, 30, 31, 44, 45, 48, 66, 84, 85

Net International Ltd

Unit 1-4 Corinium Business Park Speculation Road, Forest Vale Industrial Estate, Cinderford, GL14 2YD
Tel: 01594-827200 **Fax:** 01594-827050
E-mail: sales@flavours.co.uk
Website: http://www.flavours.co.uk
Directors: M. Matthews (Co Sec), A. Matthews (I.T. Dir)
Immediate Holding Company: NET INTERNATIONAL LIMITED
Registration no: 02465593 **Date established:** 1990
No.of Employees: 1 - 10 **Product Groups:** 20, 31, 32, 41, 80, 85

Date of Accounts	Mar 12	Mar 11	Mar 10
Working Capital	177	177	178
Current Assets	273	293	353

Phoenix Electronics Ltd

Beech House Corinium Business Park Speculation Road, Forest Vale Industrial Estate, Cinderford, GL14 2YD
Tel: 01594-824421 **Fax:** 01594-824421
Directors: J. Deighton (Dir)
Immediate Holding Company: PHOENIX ELECTRONICS LIMITED
Registration no: 02926265 **Date established:** 1994
No.of Employees: 1 - 10 **Product Groups:** 36, 37

Rubbertech 2000 Ltd

Whimsey Trading Estate, Cinderford, GL14 3JA
Tel: 01594-826019 **Fax:** 01594-827259
E-mail: sales@rubbertech2000.co.uk
Website: http://www.rubbertech2000.co.uk
Bank(s): Barclays, Hereford
Directors: N. Hill (MD)
Managers: S. Turley (Accounts), S. Dawes (Works Gen Mgr), T. Smith (Sales Admin), S. Bryan (Sales Prom Mgr)
Registration no: 02034918 **VAT No.:** GB 448 3359 26
Date established: 1985 **Turnover:** £1m - £2m **No.of Employees:** 21 - 50
Product Groups: 29, 30, 37, 38, 40

Date of Accounts	Aug 08	Aug 07	Aug 06
Working Capital	610	681	727
Fixed Assets	25	33	42

Current Assets	1044	1025	1023
Current Liabilities	435	344	296

Tennants Inks & Coating Supplies Ltd
Eastern United Site, Cinderford, GL14 3AW
Tel: 01594-822375 **Fax:** 01594-826251
E-mail: brian.beddis@tg-tics.com
Website: http://www.tennantsinksandcoatings.co.uk
Managers: B. Beddis (Works Gen Mgr)
Immediate Holding Company: WHOOSHDA LIMITED
Registration no: 03381032 **Date established:** 1997 **Turnover:** £2m - £5m
No.of Employees: 1 - 10 **Product Groups:** 32

Cirencester

365 Environmental Services Ltd
Hangar G1 Kemble Airfield Kemble Enterprise Park, Kemble, Cirencester, GL7 6FD
Tel: 01793-706747 **Fax:** 01285-772328
E-mail: info@365es.co.uk
Website: http://www.365es.co.uk
Directors: J. Montgomerie (MD), N. Handover (Ch), A. Kerry (Develop)
Immediate Holding Company: 365 ENVIRONMENTAL SERVICES LIMITED
Registration no: 01135253 **VAT No.:** GB 286 2062 54
Date established: 1973 **Turnover:** £10m - £20m
No.of Employees: 51 - 100 **Product Groups:** 45

Date of Accounts	Mar 11	Sep 09	Sep 08
Sales Turnover	9m	8m	11m
Pre Tax Profit/Loss	-625	-524	339
Working Capital	-160	-544	-280
Fixed Assets	2m	3m	3m
Current Assets	2m	2m	3m
Current Liabilities	683	574	881

A R G Electrodesign Ltd
Querns Business Centre Whitworth Road, Cirencester, GL7 1RT
Tel: 01285-658501 **Fax:** 01285-885376
E-mail: info@arg.co.uk
Website: http://www.arg.co.uk
Directors: P. Gilchriest (Dir), N. Mactaggart (Co Sec)
Immediate Holding Company: A.R.G. ELECTRODESIGN LIMITED
Registration no: 01192394 **VAT No.:** GB 326 2059 77
Date established: 1974 **Turnover:** £1m - £2m **No.of Employees:** 1 - 10
Product Groups: 37, 38

Date of Accounts	Dec 11	Dec 10	Dec 09
Sales Turnover	546	1m	1m
Pre Tax Profit/Loss	-98	-62	-301
Working Capital	-16	54	20
Fixed Assets	22	51	97
Current Assets	244	375	374
Current Liabilities	130	171	319

B J C Europe
Unit 2 Beeches Workshops Beeches Road, Cirencester, GL7 1BN
Tel: 01285-643640
E-mail: info@bjc-europe.com
Website: http://www.bjc-europe.com
Directors: S. Sutton Cegarra (MD)
Date established: 2003 **No.of Employees:** 1 - 10 **Product Groups:** 44, 80

Date of Accounts	Dec 06	Dec 05
Sales Turnover	266	246
Pre Tax Profit/Loss	101	103
Working Capital	27	4
Fixed Assets	5	11
Current Assets	109	56
Current Liabilities	83	52
ROCE% (Return on Capital Employed)	323.6	720.9
ROT% (Return on Turnover)	38.0	42.0

Batten & Allen
2 Bridgend, Cirencester, GL7 1NQ
Tel: 01285-655220 **Fax:** 01285-652650
E-mail: sales@batten-allen.com
Website: http://www.batten-allen.com
Bank(s): Barclays
Directors: S. Batten (MD), A. Ody (Co Sec)
Managers: P. Allen (Purch Mgr), D. Wilson (Sales Prom Mgr), S. Smith (Tech Serv Mgr)
Ultimate Holding Company: BATTEN AND ALLEN LIMITED
Immediate Holding Company: PALMER PLATING LIMITED
Registration no: 01632233 **VAT No.:** 276 3489 20 **Date established:** 1982
Turnover: £10m - £20m **No.of Employees:** 51 - 100 **Product Groups:** 34, 37

Date of Accounts	May 10	May 09
Working Capital	48	48
Current Assets	48	48

Bison Plant Hire Ltd
Unit 12 Broadway Trading Estate, South Cerney, Cirencester, GL7 5UH
Tel: 01285-862222
Website: http://www.bisonplanthire.com
Directors: B. Smith (Dir)
Immediate Holding Company: BISON PLANT HIRE LTD
Registration no: 02290248 **Date established:** 1988
No.of Employees: 21 - 50 **Product Groups:** 45, 67, 83

Date of Accounts	Dec 11	Dec 10	Dec 09
Working Capital	-1	37	77
Fixed Assets	804	530	539
Current Assets	288	412	447

Bosch Rexroth Ltd
Broadway Lane South Cerney, Cirencester, GL7 5UH
Tel: 01285-863000 **Fax:** 01285-863003
E-mail: info@boschrexroth.co.uk
Website: http://www.boschrexroth.co.uk
Bank(s): Barclays, Milton Keynes
Directors: B. Hedges (Dir), J. Willmott (Fin), P. Bowden (Sales)
Managers: C. Hudson (Buyer), S. Rodigues (Tech Serv Mgr)
Ultimate Holding Company: ROBERT BOSCH GMBH (GERMANY)
Immediate Holding Company: BOSCH REXROTH LIMITED
Registration no: 00768471 **VAT No.:** GB 491 2899 06
Date established: 1963 **Turnover:** £5m - £10m
No.of Employees: 101 - 250 **Product Groups:** 37, 38

Date of Accounts	Dec 10	Dec 09	Dec 08
Sales Turnover	117m	77m	143m
Pre Tax Profit/Loss	4m	-6m	3m
Working Capital	17m	13m	-1m
Fixed Assets	13m	14m	18m
Current Assets	40m	28m	40m
Current Liabilities	6m	3m	3m

British Autogard Ltd
2 Wilkinson Road Love Lane Industrial Estate, Cirencester, GL7 1YT
Tel: 01285-640333 **Fax:** 01285-659476
E-mail: sales@autogard.co.uk
Website: http://www.autogard.co.uk
Bank(s): Barclays, Swindon
Managers: B. Howgego (Chief Mgr), P. Lewis (Comptroller), R. Hucker (Projects), J. Bishop (Buyer)
Ultimate Holding Company: REXNORD CORP (USA)
Immediate Holding Company: BRITISH AUTOGARD LIMITED
Registration no: 04380334 **VAT No.:** GB 348 1433 58
Date established: 2002 **Turnover:** £2m - £5m **No.of Employees:** 21 - 50
Product Groups: 35, 38, 39, 40, 41, 43, 45, 46

Date of Accounts	Mar 12	Jan 11	Jan 10
Sales Turnover	5m	4m	3m
Pre Tax Profit/Loss	532	413	87
Working Capital	154	119	214
Fixed Assets	239	189	196
Current Assets	2m	2m	2m
Current Liabilities	320	248	173

Colt Car Company Ltd
Watermoor, Cirencester, GL7 1LF
Tel: 01285-655777 **Fax:** 01285-658026
E-mail: enquiries@mitsubishi-cars.co.uk
Website: http://www.mitsubishi-cars.co.uk
Bank(s): HSBC, Cirencester
Directors: L. Bradley (MD), K. Tanaka (Fin), T. Marshall (Sales & Mktg)
Managers: J. Russell (Personnel), S. Smith (Tech Serv Mgr)
Ultimate Holding Company: MITSUBISHI CORP (JAPAN)
Immediate Holding Company: COLT CAR COMPANY LIMITED (THE)
Registration no: 01163954 **VAT No.:** GB 448 4291 29
Date established: 1974 **Turnover:** £250m - £500m
No.of Employees: 101 - 250 **Product Groups:** 68

Date of Accounts	Dec 09	Dec 08	Mar 12
Sales Turnover	276m	350m	292m
Pre Tax Profit/Loss	-2m	-6m	4m
Working Capital	25m	29m	30m
Fixed Assets	13m	11m	11m
Current Assets	115m	198m	119m
Current Liabilities	62m	144m	56m

Compuwrite Ltd
210 Stratton Heights, Cirencester, GL7 2RW
Tel: 01285-641611 **Fax:** 01285-641611
E-mail: edward@compuwrite.co.uk
Website: http://www.compuwrite.co.uk
Directors: S. Boswell (Fin), J. Boswell (MD)
Immediate Holding Company: COMPUWRITE LTD
Registration no: 03628154 **Date established:** 1998
Turnover: Up to £250,000 **No.of Employees:** 1 - 10 **Product Groups:** 80

Date of Accounts	Sep 11	Sep 10	Sep 09
Sales Turnover	63	46	N/A
Working Capital	22	10	14
Fixed Assets	9	12	12
Current Assets	27	21	21

Cotswold Shooting
80 Chesterton Lane, Cirencester, GL7 1YD
Tel: 01285-657527 **Fax:** 01285-652535
Website: http://www.cotswoldshooting.co.uk
Directors: P. Tupper (Prop), P. Carmody (Fin)
Immediate Holding Company: THE COTSWOLD SHOOTING CO. LIMITED
Registration no: 05519440 **Date established:** 2005
No.of Employees: 1 - 10 **Product Groups:** 36, 39, 40

David Smith Associates
Waterloo House 18 The Waterloo, Cirencester, GL7 2PY
Tel: 01285-657328 **Fax:** 01285-657328
E-mail: cirencester@dsagroup.co.uk
Website: http://www.dsagroup.co.uk
Managers: J. Mills (Mgr)
Immediate Holding Company: BAKER'S FARM LEISURE LIMITED
Date established: 1982 **No.of Employees:** 1 - 10 **Product Groups:** 35

Exhausts Tyres & Batteries
Love Lane, Cirencester, GL7 1YG
Tel: 01285-653428 **Fax:** 01285-653428
E-mail: enquiries@etbtyres.co.uk
Website: http://www.etbtyres.co.uk
Managers: S. Bond (Mgr)
Immediate Holding Company: HORIZON TELECOM UK LIMITED
Registration no: 01532384 **Date established:** 1997
No.of Employees: 1 - 10 **Product Groups:** 29, 68

Date of Accounts	Dec 11	Dec 10	Dec 09
Working Capital	106	157	145
Fixed Assets	136	60	73
Current Assets	589	692	575

G L Designs Ltd
5 Links View, Cirencester, GL7 2NF
Tel: 01285-650682 **Fax:** 01285-644891
E-mail: graeme@gldesigns.co.uk
Website: http://www.gldesigns.co.uk
Product Groups: 25, 35

Date of Accounts	Oct 06	Oct 05
Working Capital	4	12
Fixed Assets	1	1
Current Assets	36	36

Godwin Pumps Ltd
Quenington, Cirencester, GL7 5BX
Tel: 01285-750271 **Fax:** 01285-750352
E-mail: sales@godwinpumps.co.uk
Website: http://www.godwinpumps.co.uk
Bank(s): Lloyds TSB Bank plc
Directors: D. Braithwaite (I.T. Dir), J. Miller (MD), J. Paz (Ch), M. Stone (MD)
Ultimate Holding Company: GODWIN INTERNATIONAL INC (USA)
Immediate Holding Company: Godwin Holdings Ltd
Registration no: 00254887 **VAT No.:** GB 362 0233 93
Date established: 1931 **Turnover:** £20m - £50m
No.of Employees: 51 - 100 **Product Groups:** 39, 40, 42, 43, 45

Date of Accounts	Dec 09	Dec 08	Dec 07
Sales Turnover	18m	25m	22m
Pre Tax Profit/Loss	3m	5m	5m
Working Capital	8m	9m	8m
Fixed Assets	3m	3m	3m
Current Assets	13m	14m	13m
Current Liabilities	2m	3m	2m

Hardware.com
Trafalgar House Kemble Enterprise Park Kemble, Cirencester, GL7 6BQ
Tel: 01285-771633 **Fax:** 0870-242 9825
E-mail: info@hardware.com
Website: http://www.hardware.com
Managers: M. Cadbury (Mktg Serv Mgr)
Registration no: 04197529 **Date established:** 2001
Turnover: £20m - £50m **No.of Employees:** 1 - 10 **Product Groups:** 44

Helios Fabrications Ltd
Unit F Lakeside Business Park, South Cerney, Cirencester, GL7 5XL
Tel: 01285-869988 **Fax:** 01285-656217
Directors: H. Kilby (Dir)
Immediate Holding Company: HELIOS FABRICATIONS LIMITED
Registration no: 01358608 **VAT No.:** GB 302 4524 07
Date established: 1978 **Turnover:** Up to £250,000
No.of Employees: 1 - 10 **Product Groups:** 48

Date of Accounts	Apr 11	Apr 10	Apr 09
Working Capital	123	166	160
Fixed Assets	16	20	25
Current Assets	182	231	223

Hytek Europe
11 Elliott Road Love Lane Industrial Estate, Cirencester, GL7 1YS
Tel: 01285-659349 **Fax:** 01285-657915
E-mail: enquiries@hytekeurope.co.uk
Website: http://www.hytekeurope.co.uk
Directors: D. Barton (Grp Chief Exec), N. King (Tech Serv), B. Barton (Grp Chief Exec)
Managers: W. Barton (Accounts)
Registration no: 04909641 **VAT No.:** GB 576 3897 78
Date established: 2003 **Turnover:** £500,000 - £1m
No.of Employees: 1 - 10 **Product Groups:** 33, 36, 46

International Call Management Ltd
Bingham House 1 Dyer Street, Cirencester, GL7 2PP
Tel: 01285-627000 **Fax:** 01285-653023
E-mail: sales@icallmanagement.com
Website: http://www.icallmanagement.com
Directors: M. Tregoning (MD), M. Tregoning (Sales), C. McArthur (Dir), S. Tregoning (Fin)
Managers: R. March (Publicity)
Immediate Holding Company: INTERNATIONAL CALL MANAGEMENT LIMITED
Registration no: 03828439 **Date established:** 1999 **Turnover:** £2m - £5m
No.of Employees: 11 - 20 **Product Groups:** 81

Date of Accounts	Aug 08	Aug 07	Aug 06
Working Capital	-44	-61	-30
Fixed Assets	4	2	5
Current Assets	45	40	42
Current Liabilities	89	101	72

J N D Building Services Ltd
Unit 19 Cirencester Business Centre Elliott Road, Love Lane Industrial Estate, Cirencester, GL7 1YS
Tel: 01285-640287 **Fax:** 01285-653578
E-mail: sales@cotswoldbuildingplastics.co.uk
Website: http://www.cotswoldbuildingplastics.co.uk
Directors: A. Crozier (Dir)
Immediate Holding Company: JND BUILDING SERVICES LIMITED
Registration no: 04635761 **Date established:** 2003
Turnover: £500,000 - £1m **No.of Employees:** 11 - 20 **Product Groups:** 30

Date of Accounts	Mar 11	Mar 10	Mar 09
Working Capital	25	34	-7
Fixed Assets	79	19	10
Current Assets	649	407	406

Just Wholefoods Ltd
16 Elliott Road Love Lane Industrial Estate, Cirencester, GL7 1YS
Tel: 01285-651910 **Fax:** 01285-650266
E-mail: info@justwholefoods.co.uk
Website: http://www.justwholefoods.co.uk
Directors: J. White (Fin)
Immediate Holding Company: JUST WHOLEFOODS LTD.
Registration no: 03648498 **Date established:** 1998
No.of Employees: 1 - 10 **Product Groups:** 20

Kenson Network Engineering Ltd
Units 101-102 Cirencester Business Park Love Lane, Cirencester, GL7 1XD
Tel: 01285-647900 **Fax:** 01285-643686
E-mail: enquiries@kenson.co.uk
Website: http://www.kenson.co.uk
Directors: J. Woolford (Dir)
Ultimate Holding Company: NU HOLDINGS LTD
Immediate Holding Company: KENSON NETWORK ENGINEERING LIMITED
Registration no: 02631536 **Date established:** 1991 **Turnover:** £2m - £5m
No.of Employees: 1 - 10 **Product Groups:** 44

Date of Accounts	Mar 12	Mar 11	Mar 10
Sales Turnover	3m	3m	2m
Pre Tax Profit/Loss	334	267	216
Working Capital	429	246	422
Fixed Assets	9	4	4
Current Assets	2m	2m	2m
Current Liabilities	1m	1m	768

Roger Keylock
College Farm Cottage Tetbury Road, Cirencester, GL7 6PY
Tel: 01285-655542
Directors: R. Keylock (Prop)
Immediate Holding Company: MACE INVESTMENTS LIMITED
Registration no: 06858600 **Date established:** 2009
No.of Employees: 1 - 10 **Product Groups:** 35

Kingsbeech Ltd
Unit 5 Querns Business Centre, Cirencester, GL7 1RT
Tel: 01285-657756 **Fax:** 01285-652362
E-mail: sales@kingsbeech.co.uk
Website: http://www.kingsbeech.co.uk
Directors: A. Philips (MD)
Immediate Holding Company: KINGSBEECH LIMITED
Registration no: 02917460 **Date established:** 1994 **Turnover:** £1m - £2m
No.of Employees: 1 - 10 **Product Groups:** 30, 32, 33, 35, 37, 38, 39, 44, 46, 48, 66, 67, 68, 84

see next page

Kingsbeech Ltd - Cont'd

Date of Accounts	Aug 11	Aug 10	Aug 09
Working Capital	24	18	13
Fixed Assets	1	1	2
Current Assets	444	359	336

Learn H Q
The Scout Hall, Cirencester, GL7 1XW
Tel: 01285-659000
E-mail: info@learnhq.com
Website: http://www.learnhq.com
Managers: M. Poole (Sales Admin)
Immediate Holding Company: LEARN HQ LIMITED
Registration no: 05440762 **Date established:** 2005
Turnover: £250,000 - £500,000 **No.of Employees:** 1 - 10
Product Groups: 44, 80, 86

Date of Accounts	Dec 07	Dec 06	Dec 05
Working Capital	-17	-7	4
Fixed Assets	17	19	5
Current Assets	21	17	4

Making the Link
3 Maytree Close Coates, Cirencester, GL7 6NQ
Tel: 07812-596943
E-mail: info@makingthelink.co.uk
Website: http://www.makingthelink.co.uk
Directors: M. Ponting (Fin)
Immediate Holding Company: MAKING THE LINK LIMITED
Registration no: 06234575 **Date established:** 2007
No.of Employees: 1 - 10 **Product Groups:** 86

Date of Accounts	Apr 11	Apr 10	Apr 09
Working Capital	N/A	4	18
Current Assets	8	16	31

Mokveld UK Ltd
Unit 9, Suite 9 Cirencester Office Park, Tetbury Road, Cirencester, GL7 6JJ
Tel: 01285-700719 **Fax:** 01285-646320
E-mail: uk@mokveld.com
Website: http://www.mokveld.com
Managers: K. Elliott (District Mgr), R. Walker (Mgr)
Ultimate Holding Company: Mokveld Valves B.V.
Immediate Holding Company: Mokveld Holdings BV (NLD)
Registration no: 01276419 **Date established:** 1983 **Turnover:** £2m - £5m
No.of Employees: 1 - 10 **Product Groups:** 36, 37

Piller UK Ltd
Westgate Phoenix Way, Cirencester, GL7 1RY
Tel: 01285-657721 **Fax:** 01285-654823
E-mail: daniel.thomas@piller.com
Website: http://www.piller.com
Bank(s): National Westminster Bank Plc
Directors: K. Breen (MD), K. Chapman (Sales)
Managers: B. Rees (Chief Acct)
Ultimate Holding Company: LANGLEY HOLDINGS PLC
Immediate Holding Company: PILLER UK LIMITED
Registration no: 01234302 **Date established:** 1975
Turnover: £20m - £50m **No.of Employees:** 51 - 100 **Product Groups:** 37, 44

Date of Accounts	Dec 06
Sales Turnover	36m
Pre Tax Profit/Loss	9m
Working Capital	17m
Fixed Assets	531
Current Assets	26m
Current Liabilities	7m

Polar Cold Rooms Ltd
Unit 1c Foss Field Winstone, Cirencester, GL7 7JY
Tel: 01452-862300 **Fax:** 01452-862418
E-mail: info@polarcoldrooms.co.uk
Website: http://www.polarcoldrooms.co.uk
Directors: J. Manley (MD)
Immediate Holding Company: POLAR COLDROOMS LIMITED
Registration no: 05361617 **Date established:** 2005
No.of Employees: 1 - 10 **Product Groups:** 38, 40, 66, 83

Date of Accounts	Feb 11	Feb 10	Feb 09
Working Capital	-49	-40	-37
Fixed Assets	2	4	5
Current Assets	49	12	11

Rapid Racking Ltd
Kemble Enterprise Park Kemble, Cirencester, GL7 6BQ
Tel: 01285-686800 **Fax:** 01285-686968
E-mail: headoffice@rapidracking.com
Website: http://www.rapidracking.com
Directors: J. Troman (Fin)
Managers: K. Evans (Personnel), D. Grime, J. Bowley (Tech Serv Mgr), N. Cooper (Sales Prom Mgr), Y. Folliard (Mktg Serv Mgr)
Ultimate Holding Company: MANUTAN INTERNATIONAL SA (FRANCE)
Immediate Holding Company: RAPID RACKING LIMITED
Registration no: 01992143 **Date established:** 1986
Turnover: £10m - £20m **No.of Employees:** 51 - 100 **Product Groups:** 26, 39, 67, 85

Date of Accounts	Sep 11	Sep 10	Sep 09
Sales Turnover	17m	15m	15m
Pre Tax Profit/Loss	2m	2m	1m
Working Capital	14m	12m	11m
Fixed Assets	2m	2m	2m
Current Assets	20m	19m	17m
Current Liabilities	2m	2m	2m

Renubath Services Ltd
Unit 17g Village Farm, Preston, Cirencester, GL7 5PR
Tel: 01285-656624 **Fax:** 01285-652446
E-mail: info@renubath.co.uk
Website: http://www.renubath.co.uk
Directors: R. Adams (Dir), R. Gale (Jt MD), J. Milner (Co Sec), J. Milner (Fin)
Immediate Holding Company: RENUBATH SERVICES LIMITED
Registration no: 04259573 **VAT No.:** GB 575 9452 92
Date established: 2001 **Turnover:** £250,000 - £500,000
No.of Employees: 1 - 10 **Product Groups:** 32, 46

Date of Accounts	Jan 11	Jan 10	Jan 09
Working Capital	-10	3	7
Fixed Assets	138	148	158
Current Assets	47	52	65

St James' Place Partnership
St James's Place House 1 Tetbury Road, Cirencester, GL7 1FP
Tel: 01285-640302 **Fax:** 01285-640436
Website: http://www.sjp.co.uk
Directors: D. Bellamy (MD), M. Wilson (Ch), M. Lund (Grp Chief Exec), J. Newman (Sales), A. Batchelor (Sales)
Managers: D. Lamb, H. Gladman
Ultimate Holding Company: LLOYDS BANKING GROUP PLC
Immediate Holding Company: ST. JAMES'S PLACE PARTNERSHIP LIMITED
Registration no: 00425649 **VAT No.:** GB 243 4550 77
Date established: 1946 **Turnover:** £250m - £500m
No.of Employees: 1 - 10 **Product Groups:** 82

Date of Accounts	Dec 11	Dec 10	Dec 09
Sales Turnover	395m	359m	277m
Pre Tax Profit/Loss	4m	6m	-7m
Working Capital	29m	10m	6m
Current Assets	36m	18m	15m
Current Liabilities	2m	2m	4m

C Valenti
Studio 11 Brewery Workshop Cricklade Street, Cirencester, GL7 1JH
Tel: 01285-657622
E-mail: celestino2@btinternet.com
Directors: C. Valenti (Prop)
Date established: 1994 **No.of Employees:** 1 - 10 **Product Groups:** 35

Vygon UK Ltd
Bridge Road, Cirencester, GL7 1PT
Tel: 01285-657051 **Fax:** 01285-650293
E-mail: vygon@vygon.co.uk
Website: http://www.vygon.com
Bank(s): National Westminster
Directors: S. Power (Fin), L. Davies (MD)
Managers: H. Selby (Chief Mgr)
Immediate Holding Company: VYGON (U.K.) LIMITED
Registration no: 01131530 **VAT No.:** GB 484 9305 15
Date established: 1973 **Turnover:** £50m - £75m
No.of Employees: 51 - 100 **Product Groups:** 30, 38

Date of Accounts	Dec 09	Dec 08	Dec 07
Sales Turnover	53m	45m	41
Pre Tax Profit/Loss	9m	10m	11
Working Capital	20m	15m	17
Fixed Assets	3m	5m	5
Current Assets	24m	20m	23
Current Liabilities	3m	4m	5

Coleford

C U Phosco Lighting Ltd
Speech House Road Broadwell, Coleford, GL16 7EG
Tel: 01594-833369 **Fax:** 01594-836186
E-mail: d.blackett@cuphosco.co.uk
Website: http://www.cuphosco.co.uk
Managers: S. Brettle (Buyer), D. Blackett (Prod Mgr)
Ultimate Holding Company: C. U. PHOSCO LIGHTING LIMITED
Immediate Holding Company: C. U. PHOSCO LIGHTING LIMITED
Registration no: 05111041 **Date established:** 2004
No.of Employees: 21 - 50 **Product Groups:** 33, 34, 35, 66

Date of Accounts	Sep 11	Sep 10	Sep 09
Sales Turnover	16m	17m	16m
Pre Tax Profit/Loss	-479	255	70
Working Capital	2m	3m	2m
Fixed Assets	3m	3m	4m
Current Assets	7m	8m	7m
Current Liabilities	2m	2m	1m

Forest Of Dean District Council
High Street, Coleford, GL16 8HG
Tel: 01594-812388 **Fax:** 01594-812390
E-mail: council@fdean.gov.uk
Website: http://www.fdean.gov.uk
Managers: D. Broom, M. Thomas (Tech Serv Mgr), M. Butler, K. Gane (Personnel), P. Burrows (Comm)
VAT No.: GB 276 1971 29 **Turnover:** £1m - £2m
No.of Employees: 101 - 250 **Product Groups:** 80

Peter S Neale
Clays Road Sling, Coleford, GL16 8LJ
Tel: 01594-837309 **Fax:** 01594-835363
E-mail: psneale@peter-s-neale.demon.co.uk
Website: http://www.peter-s-neale.demon.co.uk
Directors: P. Neale (Prop)
Turnover: Up to £250,000 **No.of Employees:** 1 - 10 **Product Groups:** 35, 49

Newspace Containers Ltd
New Dunn Business Park Sling, Coleford, GL16 8JD
Tel: 01594-839243 **Fax:** 01594-839072
E-mail: info@newspacecontainers.co.uk
Website: http://www.newspacecontainers.co.uk
Directors: G. Thomas (MD), L. Francis (Sales), I. Frazer Holland (Fab), D. Francis (Sales & Mktg), I. Frazer-Holland (Dir)
Managers: M. Remnant
Immediate Holding Company: NEWSPACE CONTAINERS LIMITED
Registration no: 04099207 **Date established:** 2000 **Turnover:** £5m - £10m
No.of Employees: 51 - 100 **Product Groups:** 35, 42, 45

Date of Accounts	Jun 11	Jun 10	Jun 09
Sales Turnover	5m	4m	5m
Pre Tax Profit/Loss	410	15	307
Working Capital	1m	803	832
Fixed Assets	1m	1m	1m
Current Assets	2m	2m	2m
Current Liabilities	306	98	191

Plastotype
Crucible Close Mushet Industrial Park, Coleford, GL16 8RE
Tel: 01594-837474 **Fax:** 01594-837312
E-mail: info@plastotype.com
Website: http://www.plastotype.com
Directors: H. Pomeroy (Fin)
Immediate Holding Company: PLASTOTYPE LIMITED
Registration no: 06322374 **Date established:** 2007 **Turnover:** £2m - £5m
No.of Employees: 1 - 10 **Product Groups:** 28, 44

Date of Accounts	Jul 11	Jul 10	Jul 08
Working Capital	-0	-0	N/A
Current Assets	7	14	N/A
Current Liabilities	N/A	2	N/A

Polymer Products UK Ltd
Forest of Dean Business Estate 4 Stepbridge Road, Coleford, GL16 8PJ
Tel: 01594-833100 **Fax:** 01594-835666
E-mail: sales@polymerproducts.co.uk
Website: http://www.polymerproducts.co.uk
Directors: J. Hamilton (Co Sec), B. Hamilton (MD)
Immediate Holding Company: POLYMER PRODUCTS (U.K.) LIMITED
Registration no: 02831295 **Date established:** 1993
Turnover: £500,000 - £1m **No.of Employees:** 1 - 10 **Product Groups:** 29, 35, 39, 41, 68

Date of Accounts	Sep 11	Sep 10	Sep 09
Working Capital	1m	1m	929
Fixed Assets	538	498	494
Current Assets	1m	1m	1m

Watkins Hire Steam Boiler Hire Division Southern United Kingdom
New Dunn Business Park Sling, Coleford, GL16 8JD
Tel: 020-8667 0088 **Fax:** 01594-837463
E-mail: mark.hills@watkinshire.co.uk
Website: http://www.watkinshire.co.uk
Directors: P. Watkins (MD)
Immediate Holding Company: PROVINCIAL DEVELOPMENTS LIMITED
Registration no: 00517996 **VAT No.:** 762 7075 18 **Date established:** 1999
Turnover: £5m - £10m **No.of Employees:** 11 - 20 **Product Groups:** 40, 72, 83

Date of Accounts	Jul 10	Jul 09	Jul 08
Working Capital	-248	-127	-125
Fixed Assets	4m	4m	4m
Current Assets	26	44	24

Drybrook

Forest Profile Grinding
1 Oakland Road Harrow Hill, Drybrook, GL17 9JX
Tel: 01594-541698 **Fax:** 01594-541698
E-mail: forestprofilegrinding@hotmail.co.uk
Directors: A. Warren (Prop)
Date established: 2000 **No.of Employees:** 1 - 10 **Product Groups:** 46, 48

Dursley

Accura Surveys Ltd
Oakridge 40 Kingshill Road, Dursley, GL11 4EQ
Tel: 07704-887909
E-mail: info@accura-surveys.com
Website: http://www.accura-surveys.com
Registration no: 05453606 **Date established:** 2005
No.of Employees: 1 - 10 **Product Groups:** 37, 80, 84

Date of Accounts	Jun 10	Jun 09	Jun 08
Working Capital	18	22	16
Fixed Assets	4	5	6
Current Assets	38	41	32

Altrans Liquids Ltd
Sheephouse Farm Uley Road, Dursley, GL11 5AD
Tel: 01453-544940 **Fax:** 01453-546050
E-mail: info@altransliquids.co.uk
Website: http://www.altransliquids.co.uk
Directors: J. Dembrey (Dir), D. Dembrey (Co Sec)
Immediate Holding Company: ALTRANS LIQUIDS LIMITED
Registration no: 02251235 **Date established:** 1988 **Turnover:** £1m - £2m
No.of Employees: 1 - 10 **Product Groups:** 32, 39, 76, 77

Date of Accounts	Sep 11	Sep 10	Sep 09
Working Capital	-76	-106	-230
Fixed Assets	340	337	359
Current Assets	230	277	187

Amazing Tent Company Ltd
2 Blacknest Owlpen, Dursley, GL11 5BZ
Tel: 01453-861131
E-mail: accounts@amazingtent.co.uk
Website: http://www.amazingtent.co.uk
Directors: A. Haddrell (Fin)
No.of Employees: 1 - 10 **Product Groups:** 24, 47, 52, 83

AVL Contract Services Ltd
37 Box Road. Cam, Dursley, GL11 5DJ
Tel: 01453-890637
E-mail: enquiries@flowmeter-support.co.uk
Website: http://www.flowmeter-support.co.uk
Directors: A. Lane (Dir)
Registration no: 6163843 **Date established:** 2007
No.of Employees: 1 - 10 **Product Groups:** 67

Date of Accounts	Mar 09	Mar 08
Working Capital	1	N/A
Current Assets	16	26

Bridgeway Freighting
37 Silver Street, Dursley, GL11 4NA
Tel: 0845-2301600 **Fax:** 0845-2304618
E-mail: imd@bridgewayfreighting.co.uk
Website: http://www.bridgewayfreighting.co.uk
Directors: I. Davies (MD)
Managers: I. Davies
Registration no: 01797193 **VAT No.:** GB 402 4199 81
Date established: 1984 **Turnover:** £500,000 - £1m
No.of Employees: 1 - 10 **Product Groups:** 72, 76, 77, 84

Duo Tech UK Ltd
Goleen Far Green, Coaley, Dursley, GL11 5EL
Tel: 01453-861086 **Fax:** 01453-861086

Directors: G. Hanson (Fin)
Immediate Holding Company: DUO-TECH (UK) LIMITED
Registration no: 02700262 **Date established:** 1992
Turnover: Up to £250,000 **No.of Employees:** 1 - 10 **Product Groups:** 35, 39, 45

Date of Accounts	Mar 12	Mar 11	Mar 10
Sales Turnover	N/A	30	10
Pre Tax Profit/Loss	-5	-1	2
Working Capital	-4	1	2
Current Assets	9	16	15
Current Liabilities	3	2	1

Effortec Ltd

13 Station Road Cam, Dursley, GL11 5NS
Tel: 01453-546011 **Fax:** 01453-549222
E-mail: rtn@f4tec.co.uk
Website: http://www.f4tec.co.uk
Directors: R. Newman (MD)
Immediate Holding Company: EFFORTEC LIMITED
Registration no: 04046798 **VAT No.:** GB 762 2955 13
Date established: 2000 **No.of Employees:** 1 - 10 **Product Groups:** 26, 36, 39, 45, 66, 67

Date of Accounts	Dec 11	Dec 10	Dec 09
Working Capital	124	94	65
Fixed Assets	1	1	1
Current Assets	197	130	89

K H Williams Asbestos Management Solutions Ltd

51 Cam Green Cam, Dursley, GL11 5HL
Tel: 01453-549060 **Fax:** 0871-661 7645
E-mail: info@asbestosuk.net
Website: http://www.asbestosuk.net
Directors: K. Williams (MD), N. Williams (Fin)
Immediate Holding Company: ASBESTOS UK SURVEYS LIMITED
Registration no: 07921314 **Date established:** 2012
Turnover: Up to £250,000 **No.of Employees:** 1 - 10 **Product Groups:** 54

Date of Accounts	Mar 08	Mar 07	Mar 06
Working Capital	-7	-7	15
Fixed Assets	11	16	2
Current Assets	10	9	23
Current Liabilities	18	16	9

Lister Petter Ltd

Long Street, Dursley, GL11 4HS
Tel: 01453-544141 **Fax:** 01453-546732
E-mail: sales@lister-petter.co.uk
Website: http://www.lister-petter.co.uk
Bank(s): HSBC Bank plc, Birmingham
Directors: R. Grimes (Fin), P. Comer (MD), R. Sadhu (Sales)
Managers: H. Blackman (Comptroller), T. Skal (Purch Mgr), K. Fisher (Personnel), S. Clark (Tech Serv Mgr)
Ultimate Holding Company: LISTER PETTER INVESTMENT HOLDINGS LIMITED
Immediate Holding Company: LISTER PETTER LIMITED
Registration no: 04896960 **VAT No.:** GB 670 3147 520 001
Date established: 2003 **Turnover:** £20m - £50m
No.of Employees: 251 - 500 **Product Groups:** 37, 40

Date of Accounts	Mar 09	Mar 08	Apr 11
Sales Turnover	46m	48m	43m
Pre Tax Profit/Loss	495	420	-549
Working Capital	2m	2m	2m
Fixed Assets	1m	2m	843
Current Assets	20m	19m	25m
Current Liabilities	6m	6m	6m

Lister Shearing Equipment Ltd

Long Street, Dursley, GL11 4HR
Tel: 01453-544830 **Fax:** 01453-545110
E-mail: arnold.hennessy@lister-shearing.co.uk
Website: http://www.lister-shearing.co.uk
Bank(s): Lloyds
Directors: A. Williams (MD), R. Grimwood (Ch), M. Hemming (Fin)
Managers: G. Collis (Sales & Mktg Mg), A. Hennessy (Chief Mgr)
Immediate Holding Company: LISTER SHEARING EQUIPMENT LIMITED
Registration no: 03496830 **VAT No.:** 713 0133 94 **Date established:** 1998
Turnover: £2m - £5m **No.of Employees:** 21 - 50 **Product Groups:** 07, 36, 37, 41

Date of Accounts	Dec 11	Dec 10	Dec 09
Working Capital	2m	2m	2m
Fixed Assets	1m	757	446
Current Assets	3m	3m	2m
Current Liabilities	N/A	1	N/A

Manner UK Ltd

13 Station Road Cam, Dursley, GL11 5NS
Tel: 01453-546333 **Fax:** 01453-549222
E-mail: sales@manner.co.uk
Website: http://www.manner.co.uk
Directors: R. Newman (Fin)
Immediate Holding Company: MANNER (UK) LIMITED
Registration no: 02876887 **Date established:** 1993
Turnover: £250,000 - £500,000 **No.of Employees:** 1 - 10
Product Groups: 39, 66

Date of Accounts	Dec 06	Dec 05	Dec 04
Working Capital	151	103	79
Fixed Assets	11	12	11
Current Assets	259	198	170
Current Liabilities	38	27	26

Newsquest Media Ltd

Reliance House Long Street, Dursley, GL11 4LF
Tel: 01453-544000 **Fax:** 01453-540212
E-mail: reporters@dursleygazette.co.uk
Website: http://www.gazetteseries.co.uk
Bank(s): Lloyds TSB Bank plc
Directors: T. Sallis (Dir)
VAT No.: GB 188 4831 19 **Turnover:** £10m - £20m
No.of Employees: 21 - 50 **Product Groups:** 28

Reltech Ltd

Cam Mills Cam, Dursley, GL11 5PW
Tel: 01453-541200 **Fax:** 01453-545810
E-mail: sales@reltech.co.uk
Website: http://www.reltech.co.uk
Bank(s): Lloyds TSB Bank plc
Directors: P. Taylor (Co Sec), M. Ashley (MD)
Ultimate Holding Company: BRUMBY GROUP HOLDINGS LIMITED
Immediate Holding Company: RELTECH LIMITED
Registration no: 01187159 **VAT No.:** GB 286 1379 30
Date established: 1974 **Turnover:** £1m - £2m **No.of Employees:** 11 - 20
Product Groups: 37, 38, 85

Date of Accounts	Aug 11	Aug 10	Aug 09
Working Capital	183	174	172
Fixed Assets	34	32	41
Current Assets	406	363	430

Fairford

Betterhandy Ltd

Unit 2 Farhill Farm, Fairford, GL7 4PZ
Tel: 01285-713223 **Fax:** 01285-713222
E-mail: sales@betterhandy.co.uk
Website: http://www.betterhandy.co.uk
Directors: C. Dodwell (Fin)
Immediate Holding Company: BETTERHANDY LIMITED
Registration no: 02707228 **Date established:** 1992
No.of Employees: 1 - 10 **Product Groups:** 46

Date of Accounts	Apr 11	Apr 10	Apr 09
Working Capital	84	84	76
Fixed Assets	16	18	21
Current Assets	939	872	985

C J Griffin & Son

Springfields Kempsford, Fairford, GL7 4ET
Tel: 01285-810281
Directors: C. Griffin (Prop)
Date established: 1963 **No.of Employees:** 1 - 10 **Product Groups:** 41

Invertec Ltd

Whelford Road, Fairford, GL7 4DT
Tel: 01285-713550 **Fax:** 01285-713548
E-mail: sales@invertec.co.uk
Website: http://www.invertec.co.uk
Directors: P. Burnett (Fin), I. King (Sales), J. Ellison (Prop)
Managers: M. Skinner (Purch Mgr), M. Eden
Ultimate Holding Company: THE ELLISON COMPANY INC (USA)
Immediate Holding Company: INVERTEC LIMITED
Registration no: 02072273 **VAT No.:** GB 448 4849 04
Date established: 1986 **Turnover:** £5m - £10m
No.of Employees: 51 - 100 **Product Groups:** 37, 39

Date of Accounts	Dec 11	Dec 10	Dec 09
Sales Turnover	6m	5m	6m
Pre Tax Profit/Loss	259	1m	-255
Working Capital	2m	3m	1m
Fixed Assets	607	442	359
Current Assets	3m	3m	3m
Current Liabilities	257	256	223

Resintech Ltd

Unit 1-2 Horcott Industrial Estate Horcott Road, Fairford, GL7 4BX
Tel: 01285-712755 **Fax:** 01285-712999
E-mail: info@resintech.co.uk
Website: http://www.resintech.co.uk
Bank(s): National Westminster Bank Plc
Directors: A. Paton (MD), L. McMahon (Fin)
Immediate Holding Company: RESINTECH LIMITED
Registration no: 01918174 **VAT No.:** GB 435 3494 45
Date established: 1985 **Turnover:** £1m - £2m **No.of Employees:** 11 - 20
Product Groups: 31, 32, 37

Date of Accounts	Mar 11	Mar 10	Mar 09
Working Capital	230	108	76
Fixed Assets	48	63	85
Current Assets	355	288	241

Shoreheat Ltd

Quest House London Road, Fairford, GL7 4DS
Tel: 01285-713055 **Fax:** 01285-712937
E-mail: sueholton@progressgroup.co.uk
Website: http://www.progressgroup.co.uk
Bank(s): Barclays
Directors: G. Holton (MD)
Managers: G. Kemp (Tech Serv Mgr), L. Wood (Purch Mgr)
Ultimate Holding Company: GRAFTON GROUP PUBLIC LIMITED COMPANY
Immediate Holding Company: PROGRESS GROUP LIMITED
Registration no: 01403083 **VAT No.:** GB 793 9702 77
Date established: 1978 **Turnover:** £5m - £10m **No.of Employees:** 21 - 50
Product Groups: 40

Date of Accounts	Dec 11	Dec 10	Dec 09
Sales Turnover	5m	5m	4m
Pre Tax Profit/Loss	77	663	303
Working Capital	2m	2m	2m
Fixed Assets	854	851	889
Current Assets	4m	4m	3m
Current Liabilities	102	74	95

Gloucester

Abbey Surfacing

Parkend Farm Moreton Valence, Gloucester, GL2 7NG
Tel: 01452-720216 **Fax:** 01452-723038
E-mail: info@abbeysurfacing.co.uk
Website: http://www.abbeysurfacing.co.uk
Directors: F. Walters (Prop)
Turnover: £1m - £2m **No.of Employees:** 11 - 20 **Product Groups:** 31, 51, 84

Actemium

A Meteor Business Park Cheltenham Road East, Gloucester, GL2 9QL
Tel: 01452-713222 **Fax:** 01452-713444
E-mail: enquiries@actemium.co.uk
Website: http://www.actemium.com
Bank(s): Lloyds
Managers: R. Effandiarinia (District Mgr), R. Esfandiarinia (District Mgr)
Ultimate Holding Company: VINCI SA (FRANCE)
Immediate Holding Company: LEE BEESLEY HOLDINGS LIMITED
Registration no: 01234891 **Date established:** 1975 **Turnover:** £2m - £5m
No.of Employees: 21 - 50 **Product Groups:** 37

Advantage 1 Ltd

29 Brunswick Road, Gloucester, GL1 1JE
Tel: 01452-526688 **Fax:** 01452-524477
E-mail: info@advantage1.co.uk
Website: http://www.advantage1.co.uk
Directors: J. Haigh (MD)
Immediate Holding Company: ADVANTAGE 1 LIMITED
Registration no: 04114265 **Date established:** 2000
No.of Employees: 1 - 10 **Product Groups:** 80, 81

Date of Accounts	May 11	May 10	May 09
Working Capital	-17	-12	-9
Fixed Assets	44	14	18
Current Assets	285	183	176

Aircon World Ltd

1 Hucclecote Road Hucclecote, Gloucester, GL3 3TH
Tel: 01452-621521 **Fax:** 01452-621626
Website: http://www.airconworld.co.uk
Directors: S. Mercer (Co Sec)
Immediate Holding Company: Aircon World UK Ltd
Registration no: 03855536 **Date established:** 1999
No.of Employees: 1 - 10 **Product Groups:** 40, 66

Allcap Ltd

34 Bristol Road, Gloucester, GL1 5SD
Tel: 01452-525800 **Fax:** 01452-331125
E-mail: sales@allcap.co.uk
Website: http://www.allcap.co.uk
Bank(s): Lloyds TSB Bank plc
Directors: M. Roderick (MD)
Immediate Holding Company: JSM ETAPE (HOLDINGS) LIMITED
Registration no: 04886766 **VAT No.:** GB 408 3023 87
Date established: 2003 **Turnover:** £500,000 - £1m
No.of Employees: 21 - 50 **Product Groups:** 35, 66

Date of Accounts	Jun 11	Jun 10	Jun 09
Working Capital	-497	-496	-503
Fixed Assets	651	651	651
Current Assets	3	7	25

Anixter

Waterwells Drive Quedgeley, Gloucester, GL2 2FR
Tel: 01452-880500 **Fax:** 01444-870962
E-mail: floyd.thorpe@anixter.com
Website: http://www.anixter.com
Directors: L. Trinkoff (Fin)
Managers: F. Thorpe
Ultimate Holding Company: ANIXTER INTERNATIONAL INC (USA)
Immediate Holding Company: ANIXTER(U.K.)LIMITED
Registration no: 01017023 **VAT No.:** GB 705 3182 61
Date established: 1971 **Turnover:** Over £1,000m
No.of Employees: 101 - 250 **Product Groups:** 22, 29, 30, 31, 32, 33, 34, 35, 36, 37, 38, 39, 40, 43, 45, 66, 80

Date of Accounts	Dec 07	Jan 11	Jan 09
Pre Tax Profit/Loss	478	-239	662
Working Capital	16m	1m	1m
Fixed Assets	10m	10m	10m
Current Assets	21m	4m	4m
Current Liabilities	132	99	321

App UK Ltd

Unit 2 Cheltenham Road East, Gloucester, GL2 9QL
Tel: 01452-854445 **Fax:** 01452-854485
E-mail: salesuk@advancedpoly.com
Website: http://www.appuk.co.uk
Directors: K. Johnston (Sales)
Ultimate Holding Company: ADVANCED POLY-PACKAGING INC (USA)
Immediate Holding Company: APP (UK) LIMITED
Registration no: 04646615 **Date established:** 2003
No.of Employees: 1 - 10 **Product Groups:** 27, 30, 38, 42, 44, 66, 67

Date of Accounts	Jun 11	Jun 10	Jun 09
Working Capital	215	210	246
Fixed Assets	69	71	40
Current Assets	1m	562	577

Applied Rubber Linings Ltd

Unit 6 Chancel Close, Gloucester, GL4 3SN
Tel: 01452-381849 **Fax:** 01452-381845
E-mail: keith@applied-rubber.co.uk
Website: http://www.applied-rubber.co.uk
Bank(s): Barclays
Directors: K. Travell (MD)
Immediate Holding Company: APPLIED RUBBER LININGS LIMITED
Registration no: 02779065 **VAT No.:** GB 285 1645 41
Date established: 1993 **Turnover:** £1m - £2m **No.of Employees:** 11 - 20
Product Groups: 29, 35, 36, 41, 42, 46, 48

Date of Accounts	Sep 11	Sep 10	Sep 09
Working Capital	188	171	166
Fixed Assets	7	7	31
Current Assets	353	326	394

Arjo Med AB Ltd

St. Catherine Street, Gloucester, GL1 2SL
Tel: 01452-428200 **Fax:** 01452-428344
E-mail: uksales@arjo.co.uk
Website: http://www.arjo.com
Bank(s): Barclays Bank, Gloucester
Directors: B. Richardson (MD), P. Bacaer (MD), P. Vacher (MD), D. Telling (Co Sec)
Managers: A. Mason (Purch Mgr)
Ultimate Holding Company: GETINGE AB (SWEDEN)
Immediate Holding Company: JAMES INDUSTRIES LIMITED
Registration no: FC024121 **VAT No.:** GB 274 2276 54
Date established: 1978 **Turnover:** £20m - £50m
No.of Employees: 21 - 50 **Product Groups:** 26, 30, 36, 38

Date of Accounts	Dec 09	Dec 08	Dec 07
Pre Tax Profit/Loss	3	297	361
Working Capital	1m	1m	1m
Fixed Assets	784	784	784
Current Assets	2m	2m	8m

Avon Metals Ltd
Ashville Road, Gloucester, GL2 5DA
Tel: 01452-874500 **Fax:** 01452-300624
E-mail: enquiries@avonmetals.com
Website: http://www.avonmetals.com
Directors: J. Verdon (Dir), S. Munnoch (MD), S. Martin (Sales), R. Jones (Co Sec)
Ultimate Holding Company: THE REMET COMPANY LIMITED
Immediate Holding Company: AVON METALS LIMITED
Registration no: 04135396 **VAT No.:** GB 286 2325 48
Date established: 2001 **Turnover:** £50m - £75m
No.of Employees: 21 - 50 **Product Groups:** 31, 34, 66

Date of Accounts	Jun 11	Jun 10	Jun 09
Sales Turnover	59m	41m	29m
Pre Tax Profit/Loss	3m	2m	327
Working Capital	6m	3m	2m
Fixed Assets	522	417	358
Current Assets	17m	12m	6m
Current Liabilities	2m	812	622

Besarch Fabrications Ltd
Units 5-7 Frampton Industrial Estate Bridge Road, Frampton On Severn, Gloucester, GL2 7HE
Tel: 01452-742185 **Fax:** 01452-742186
E-mail: sales@besarch.co.uk
Website: http://www.besarch.co.uk
Directors: C. Morris (Dir)
Immediate Holding Company: BESARCH FABRICATIONS LIMITED
Registration no: 05836008 **Date established:** 2006
No.of Employees: 1 - 10 **Product Groups:** 30, 32, 42, 52

Date of Accounts	Jun 11	Jun 10	Jun 09
Working Capital	99	50	-29
Fixed Assets	44	36	77
Current Assets	408	320	278

Beta Marine Ltd
Unit 2 The Perry Centre Davy Way Waterwells Business Park, Quedgeley, Gloucester, GL2 2AD
Tel: 01452-723492 **Fax:** 01453-835284
E-mail: sales@betamarine.co.uk
Website: http://www.betamarine.co.uk
Directors: A. Winton (Co Sec), D. Morris (Tech Serv), J. Growcoot (Fin)
Managers: A. Growcoot, T. Fairclough (Purch Mgr)
Immediate Holding Company: BETA MARINE LIMITED
Registration no: 02114058 **Date established:** 1987 **Turnover:** £5m - £10m
No.of Employees: 21 - 50 **Product Groups:** 40

Date of Accounts	May 12	May 11	May 10
Sales Turnover	9m	8m	8m
Pre Tax Profit/Loss	328	327	337
Working Capital	797	784	730
Fixed Assets	1m	1m	1m
Current Assets	3m	2m	2m
Current Liabilities	420	400	372

Biffa Waste Services Ltd
Hempsted House 319 Bristol Road, Gloucester, GL2 5DN
Tel: 01452-521928 **Fax:** 01452-300045
E-mail: info@biffawasteservices.co.uk
Website: http://www.biffa.co.uk
Managers: M. Dwyer (Depot Mgr)
Immediate Holding Company: BIFFA WASTE SERVICES LIMITED
Registration no: 00946107 **Date established:** 1969
No.of Employees: 21 - 50 **Product Groups:** 54, 72, 83

Date of Accounts	Mar 08	Mar 09	Apr 10
Sales Turnover	555m	574m	492m
Pre Tax Profit/Loss	23m	50m	30m
Working Capital	229m	271m	293m
Fixed Assets	371m	360m	378m
Current Assets	409m	534m	609m
Current Liabilities	50m	100m	115m

Boiswood LLP
Unit A1 Spinnaker House Spinnaker Road, Hempsted, Gloucester, GL2 5FD
Tel: 01452-330011 **Fax:** 01452-330088
E-mail: info@boiswood.co.uk
Website: http://www.boiswood.co.uk
Directors: A. Kent (Ptnr)
Managers: S. Taylor (Fin Mgr)
Immediate Holding Company: BOISWOOD TECHNOLOGIES LIMITED
Registration no: 02390228 **VAT No.:** GB 532 1199 67
Date established: 1989 **Turnover:** £1m - £2m **No.of Employees:** 1 - 10
Product Groups: 30, 36

Date of Accounts	Dec 10	Dec 09	Dec 08
Working Capital	156	72	111
Fixed Assets	25	34	49
Current Assets	325	197	298

C R I Grinding Ltd
2a Goodridge Avenue, Gloucester, GL2 5EA
Tel: 01452-529475 **Fax:** 01452-306362
E-mail: cri.grinding@virgin.net
Directors: R. Koli (Co Sec), I. Koli (MD), R. Koli (Fin)
Immediate Holding Company: C.R.I. (GRINDING) LIMITED
Registration no: 01326664 **VAT No.:** GB 302 4327 49
Date established: 1977 **Turnover:** Up to £250,000
No.of Employees: 1 - 10 **Product Groups:** 48

Date of Accounts	Feb 08	Feb 07	Feb 06
Working Capital	32	31	22
Fixed Assets	1	1	3
Current Assets	42	41	36
Current Liabilities	11	10	14

Calton Site Safety
13 St Catherine Street, Gloucester, GL1 2BS
Tel: 01452-411445 **Fax:** 01452-310033
E-mail: sales@caltonsitesafety.com
Directors: D. Norton (Snr Part)
Immediate Holding Company: HOMESTYLE (SHEFFIELD) LIMITED
Date established: 2006 **Turnover:** Up to £250,000
No.of Employees: 1 - 10 **Product Groups:** 38, 39, 40, 49, 67

Certex UK Ltd
125 Business Park Llanthony Road, Gloucester, GL2 5JQ
Tel: 01452-526119 **Fax:** 01452-307632
E-mail: dclare@certex.co.uk
Website: http://www.certex.co.uk
Managers: D. Clare (Mgr)
Ultimate Holding Company: AXEL JOHNSON INTERNATIONAL AB (SWEDEN)
Immediate Holding Company: CERTEX (UK) LIMITED
Registration no: 00928803 **Date established:** 1968
No.of Employees: 11 - 20 **Product Groups:** 23, 30, 35, 83

Cheltenham & Gloucester plc
Barnett Way Barnwood, Gloucester, GL4 3RL
Tel: 01452-372372 **Fax:** 01452-373955
E-mail: info@chelglos.com
Website: http://www.cheltglos.co.uk
Bank(s): Cheltenham & Gloucester plc
Directors: C. Smyth (Co Sec), C. Smyth (Fin), J. Pain (MD)
Ultimate Holding Company: LLOYDS BANKING GROUP PLC
Immediate Holding Company: CHELTENHAM & GLOUCESTER PLC
Registration no: 02299428 **VAT No.:** GB 274 3042 74
Date established: 1988 **Turnover:** £250m - £500m
No.of Employees: 1501 & over **Product Groups:** 82

Date of Accounts	Dec 10	Dec 09	Dec 08
Sales Turnover	N/A	N/A	440m
Pre Tax Profit/Loss	94m	76m	98m
Working Capital	184m	N/A	53m
Fixed Assets	56m	64m	86m
Current Assets	369m	386m	410m
Current Liabilities	57m	318m	357m

C K F Systems Ltd
Unit 10 St Albans Road Empire Way, Gloucester, GL2 5FW
Tel: 01452-424565 **Fax:** 01452-423477
E-mail: info@ckf.co.uk
Website: http://www.ckf.co.uk
Bank(s): Barclays
Directors: K. Staines (Sales), P. Swift (Chief Op Offcr)
Managers: I. Oakey (Fin Mgr), D. Howell (Personnel), K. Bolton (Buyer)
Ultimate Holding Company: CKF HOLDINGS LIMITED
Immediate Holding Company: CKF SYSTEMS LIMITED
Registration no: 02267568 **VAT No.:** GB 484 7793 83
Date established: 1988 **Turnover:** £1m - £2m **No.of Employees:** 21 - 50
Product Groups: 37, 38, 41, 42, 45, 67, 84

Date of Accounts	Dec 11	Dec 10	Dec 09
Working Capital	938	746	618
Fixed Assets	103	125	64
Current Assets	2m	2m	2m

Climate World Ltd
New Chambers 9 Hucclecote Road, Gloucester, GL3 3TQ
Tel: 01452-612938 **Fax:** 01452-372112
E-mail: info@climateshop.com
Website: http://www.airconworld.co.uk
Directors: A. Murphy (MD)
Registration no: 05250612 **Product Groups:** 30, 39, 40, 66, 84

Compressor Systems West
Unit 720 Jupiter Court Cheltenham Road East, Gloucester, GL2 9QW
Tel: 01452-859944 **Fax:** 01452-857935
E-mail: gloucester@compressorsystems.co.uk
Website: http://www.compressorsystems.co.uk
Directors: L. Reynolds (Snr Part)
Immediate Holding Company: COMPRESSOR SYSTEMS (WEST) LTD
Registration no: 04097791 **Date established:** 1999
Turnover: £20m - £50m **No.of Employees:** 1 - 10 **Product Groups:** 40, 48, 84

Cordial A V
Unit 55 Morelands Trading Estate Bristol Road, Gloucester, GL1 5RZ
Tel: 08450-940361 **Fax:** 01452-616785
E-mail: timpellatt@blueyonder.co.uk
Website: http://www.cordialav.co.uk
Directors: T. Pellatt (Prop)
No.of Employees: 1 - 10 **Product Groups:** 37, 44, 89

Creatif Leven Displays Ltd
27 Morelands Trading Estate Bristol Road, Gloucester, GL1 5RZ
Tel: 01452-417832 **Fax:** 01452-302811
E-mail: sales@annequin.co.uk
Website: http://www.creatifleven.co.uk
Directors: A. Behiles (MD)
Immediate Holding Company: CRASHED MARKETING LTD
Date established: 2011 **No.of Employees:** 1 - 10 **Product Groups:** 49

Creepers BSP
21-23 Worcester Street, Gloucester, GL1 3AJ
Tel: 01452-330854 **Fax:** 01452-304695
E-mail: adrian@creepers.org.uk
Website: http://www.creepersbsp.co.uk
Directors: A. Creeper (Grp Chief Exec), A. Creeper (Prop)
Managers: A. Rudge (Mgr)
Registration no: 06259269 **Date established:** 2007
No.of Employees: 1 - 10 **Product Groups:** 30, 36

D S Smith Correx
7 Madleaze Trading Estate Madleaze Road, Gloucester, GL1 5SG
Tel: 01452-316500 **Fax:** 01452-300436
E-mail: sales@kayplast.com
Website: http://www.dssmithcorrex.com
Bank(s): National Westminster Bank Plc
Directors: M. Lightowler (MD), R. Sparey (Fab)
Managers: J. Waterhouse (Purch Mgr), M. Brind (Fin Mgr), R. Reed (Tech Serv Mgr), T. Dyer (Mktg Serv Mgr)
Immediate Holding Company: DS SMITH PLASTICS
Registration no: 01041480 **VAT No.:** GB 233 5046 90
Turnover: £10m - £20m **No.of Employees:** 51 - 100 **Product Groups:** 27, 30, 45, 66

R W Davis & Son Ltd
Junction Dry Dock Canal Bank, Saul, Gloucester, GL2 7LA
Tel: 01452-740233 **Fax:** 01452-741307
E-mail: sales@rwdavis.co.uk
Website: http://www.rwdavis.co.uk
Directors: P. Trotter (Dir)
Immediate Holding Company: R W DAVIS & SON LTD
Registration no: 04093532 **VAT No.:** GB 326 3861 53
Date established: 2000 **Turnover:** £250,000 - £500,000
No.of Employees: 1 - 10 **Product Groups:** 39

Date of Accounts	Apr 11	Apr 10	Apr 09
Working Capital	103	86	101
Fixed Assets	21	25	12
Current Assets	162	130	169

The Dent Clinic
Churchdown, Gloucester, GL3 1NB
Tel: 07976-277430
E-mail: info@thedentclinic.co.uk
Website: http://www.thedentclinic.co.uk
Directors: P. Morris (Prop)
Date established: 2002 **No.of Employees:** 1 - 10 **Product Groups:** 27, 37, 39

Design Installation Service Group
183 Westgate Street, Gloucester, GL1 2RN
Tel: 01452-314384 **Fax:** 01452-300195
Website: http://www.disgroup.com
Directors: R. Bell (Grp Chief Exec), C. Coombe (MD), C. Croom (MD), P. Kerr (Fin)
Managers: D. Dalgliesh (I.T. Exec), T. Hook, S. Davis (Chief Mgr)
Ultimate Holding Company: D.I.S. Ltd
Immediate Holding Company: Dis Holdings Ltd
Registration no: 00084512 **VAT No.:** GB 286 1359 36
Date established: 1841 **Turnover:** £2m - £5m **No.of Employees:** 21 - 50
Product Groups: 52

Date of Accounts	Mar 08	Mar 07	Mar 06
Working Capital	327	265	188
Fixed Assets	173	200	255
Current Assets	791	762	744
Current Liabilities	463	497	556
Total Share Capital	20	20	20

Earl & Thompson Marketing Ltd
1 Hucclecote Road Barnwood, Gloucester, GL3 3TH
Tel: 01452-627100 **Fax:** 01452-627101
E-mail: info@earl-thompson.co.uk
Website: http://www.earl-thompson.co.uk
Directors: S. Earl (MD), M. Earl (Fin)
Immediate Holding Company: EARL & THOMPSON MARKETING LIMITED
Registration no: 01770636 **VAT No.:** GB 484 6842 04
Date established: 1983 **Turnover:** £1m - £2m **No.of Employees:** 1 - 10
Product Groups: 81

Date of Accounts	Dec 07	Jun 11	Jun 10
Working Capital	142	172	174
Fixed Assets	21	26	21
Current Assets	335	310	365

ELG Haniel Metals Ltd
The Old Airfield Moreton Valence, Gloucester, GL2 7NG
Tel: 01452-883546 **Fax:** 01452-723461
E-mail: info@elg.co.uk
Website: http://www.elg.co.uk
Managers: A. Taylor (Sales Admin), M. Wort (Depot Mgr), M. Wort (Mgr)
Immediate Holding Company: E.L.G. HANIEL METALS LIMITED
Registration no: 01517971 **Date established:** 1980
No.of Employees: 1 - 10 **Product Groups:** 54, 66

Elite Extrusion Die Co. Ltd
Unit 6 Tuffley Industrial Estate, Gloucester, GL2 5YD
Tel: 01452-424455 **Fax:** 01452-300147
E-mail: sales@elite-extrusion-die.co.uk
Website: http://www.eliteextrusiondiecoltd.co.uk
Directors: S. Rogers (Asst MD), S. Rogers (Fin)
Immediate Holding Company: ELITE EXTRUSION DIE LIMITED
Registration no: 02079232 **Date established:** 1986
Turnover: £20m - £50m **No.of Employees:** 11 - 20 **Product Groups:** 46

Elmbridge Pump Co.
Shepherd Road, Gloucester, GL2 5EL
Tel: 01452-300110 **Fax:** 01452-303691
E-mail: sales@elmbridgepump.com
Website: http://www.elmbridgepump.com
Bank(s): Lloyds TSB Bank plc
Directors: R. Freeman (Ptnr)
Managers: L. Preston (Mktg Serv Mgr)
VAT No.: GB 650 9265 30 **Turnover:** £1m - £2m **No.of Employees:** 11 - 20
Product Groups: 39, 40

Epsilon Test Services
Epsilon House The Square Gloucester Business Park, Brockworth, Gloucester, GL3 4AD
Tel: 08452-336600 **Fax:** 0845-2336633
E-mail: t.beardsmore@epsilontest.com
Website: http://www.epsilontest.com
Bank(s): Lloyds TSB Bank plc
Directors: T. Beardsmore (MD)
Managers: D. Bakewell (Tech Serv Mgr), K. Maran (I.T. Exec), P. Woods (Mktg Serv Mgr), M. Cox (Personnel)
Registration no: 03141820 **VAT No.:** GB 618 1625 46
Turnover: £2m - £5m **No.of Employees:** 51 - 100 **Product Groups:** 38

Eriks (Gloucester Service Centre)
13 Eastville Close Eastern Avenue, Gloucester, GL4 3SJ
Tel: 01452-522265 **Fax:** 01452-306700
E-mail: gloucester@eriks.co.uk
Website: http://www.wyko.co.uk
Managers: G. Pitcock (Mgr)
Turnover: £250m - £500m **No.of Employees:** 1 - 10 **Product Groups:** 66

Eroga Die Co. Ltd
Unit 6 Eastbrook Road, Gloucester, GL4 3DB
Tel: 01452-524039 **Fax:** 01452-500615
E-mail: mail@erogadie.com
Website: http://www.erogadie.com
Bank(s): Barclays
Managers: A. Townsend (Prod Mgr), A. Blunt
Immediate Holding Company: EROGA DIE COMPANY LIMITED
Registration no: 00912136 **VAT No.:** GB 274 5810 45
Date established: 1967 **Turnover:** £500,000 - £1m
No.of Employees: 21 - 50 **Product Groups:** 46

Date of Accounts	Jul 11	Jul 10	Jul 09
Working Capital	909	804	785
Fixed Assets	2m	2m	2m
Current Assets	1m	1m	1m

European Metals Recycling Ltd
Byard Road, Gloucester, GL2 5DF
Tel: 01452-528354 **Fax:** 01452-419442
Website: http://www.elrltd.com
Managers: P. Maguire (Mgr)
Immediate Holding Company: EUROPEAN METAL RECYCLING LIMITED
Registration no: 02954623 **Date established:** 1994
Turnover: £10m - £20m **No.of Employees:** 1 - 10 **Product Groups:** 42, 66

Date of Accounts	Dec 11	Dec 10	Dec 09
Sales Turnover	3032m	2431m	1843m
Pre Tax Profit/Loss	116m	155m	91m
Working Capital	414m	371m	167m
Fixed Assets	518m	483m	480m
Current Assets	1027m	717m	557m
Current Liabilities	124m	118m	185m

Fabric Architecture

Unit B4 Nexus Gloucester Business Park Hurricane Road, Brockworth, Gloucester, GL3 4AG
Tel: 01452-612800 **Fax:** 01452-621200
E-mail: info@fabricarchitecture.com
Website: http://www.fabricarchitecture.com
Directors: N. Browne (Ptnr), D. Drew (MD)
Managers: J. Smith (Commun Mgr)
Immediate Holding Company: FABRIC ARCHITECTURE LIMITED
Registration no: 04119655 **Date established:** 2000
No.of Employees: 21 - 50 **Product Groups:** 23, 24, 35, 40, 49, 63, 65

Date of Accounts	Mar 11	Mar 10	Mar 09
Working Capital	412	-643	-1m
Fixed Assets	21	1m	1m
Current Assets	966	1m	798

Fast Tools Ltd

Llanthony Road Hempsted, Gloucester, GL2 5HL
Tel: 01452-529671 **Fax:** 01452-307992
E-mail: sales@fasttoolsltd.co.uk
Website: http://www.fasttoolsltd.co.uk
Bank(s): National Westminster Bank Plc
Directors: J. Wadley (MD)
Immediate Holding Company: FAST TOOLS (HOLDINGS) LIMITED
Registration no: 03051380 **VAT No.:** GB 274 1034 83
Date established: 1995 **Turnover:** £1m - £2m **No.of Employees:** 11 - 20
Product Groups: 67

Date of Accounts	Aug 11	Aug 10	Aug 09
Working Capital	-168	-172	-174
Fixed Assets	184	142	144
Current Assets	N/A	1	1

Food Equipment Europe Ltd

The Luther Challis Business Centre Barnwood Road, Gloucester, GL4 3HX
Tel: 01452-535154 **Fax:** 01452-535176
Website: http://www.foodequipmenteurope.co.uk
Directors: H. Griffiths (MD)
Immediate Holding Company: FOOD EQUIPMENT EUROPE LIMITED
Registration no: 03799628 **Date established:** 1999
Turnover: Up to £250,000 **No.of Employees:** 1 - 10 **Product Groups:** 20, 40, 41

Date of Accounts	Jul 11	Jul 10	Jul 09
Working Capital	38	22	16
Fixed Assets	18	22	10
Current Assets	182	169	144

Fosteco Ltd

Unit 810 Jupiter Court Cheltenham Road East, Gloucester, GL2 9QW
Tel: 01452-857800 **Fax:** 01452-857600
E-mail: sales@fosteco.co.uk
Website: http://www.fosteco.co.uk
Directors: G. Foster (Dir)
Immediate Holding Company: FOSTECO LIMITED
Registration no: 03340065 **VAT No.:** GB 535 5471 39
Date established: 1997 **Turnover:** £20m - £50m **No.of Employees:** 1 - 10
Product Groups: 30, 37

FRITZ & MACZIOL

Studio 15, Kestrel Court Waterwells Business Park, Quedgeley, Gloucester, GL2 2AT
Tel: 01452-849099
E-mail: abrown@fumgroup.com
Website: http://www.fumgroup.com
Product Groups: 38, 44, 54, 80, 84

G R Lane Health Products Ltd

Sisson Road, Gloucester, GL2 0GR
Tel: 01452-524012 **Fax:** 01452-300105
E-mail: info@laneshealth.com
Website: http://www.laneshealth.com
Bank(s): Handelsbanken AB, Swindon
Directors: G. Latham (MD), P. Whatley (Fin)
Managers: J. Oakley, J. Groves, B. Hares (Personnel), J. Powell, L. Jeans (Chief Buyer)
Ultimate Holding Company: G.R. LANE HOLDINGS LIMITED
Immediate Holding Company: G.R. LANE HOLDINGS LIMITED
Registration no: 00601878 **Date established:** 1958
Turnover: £20m - £50m **No.of Employees:** 101 - 250
Product Groups: 02, 20, 31, 61, 63

Date of Accounts	Jul 11	Jul 10	Jul 09
Sales Turnover	23m	22m	22m
Pre Tax Profit/Loss	2m	2m	2m
Working Capital	4m	4m	5m
Fixed Assets	14m	14m	14m
Current Assets	9m	8m	9m
Current Liabilities	2m	1m	2m

Garden Concepts Ltd

15 Bentley Close Quedgeley, Gloucester, GL2 4SH
Tel: 01452-729150 **Fax:** 01452-729150
E-mail: tim@gardenconceptsltd.co.uk
Website: http://www.gardenconceptsltd.co.uk
Directors: D. Williams (Fin), T. Williams (MD)
Immediate Holding Company: EXCLUSIVELY KIDS LTD
Registration no: 04874062 **Date established:** 2012
No.of Employees: 1 - 10 **Product Groups:** 41

Date of Accounts	Aug 07	Aug 06
Working Capital	-9	-5
Fixed Assets	19	25
Current Assets	1	5
Current Liabilities	11	10

Gardiner Bros & Co.

Unit F-G Quedgeley West Business Park Bristol Road, Hardwicke, Gloucester, GL2 4PH
Tel: 01452-727300 **Fax:** 01452-307220
E-mail: sales@gardinerbros.co.uk
Website: http://www.gardinerbros.co.uk
Directors: P. Gardiner (MD)
Managers: M. Holloway (Tech Serv Mgr), H. Paget, G. Restall (Comptroller), H. Knight (Personnel)
Immediate Holding Company: GARDINER BROS. AND COMPANY (LEATHERS) LIMITED
Registration no: 00534801 **Date established:** 1954 **Turnover:** £5m - £10m
No.of Employees: 51 - 100 **Product Groups:** 22, 63

Date of Accounts	Dec 11	Dec 10	Dec 09
Sales Turnover	7m	7m	N/A
Pre Tax Profit/Loss	97	92	N/A
Working Capital	1m	1m	967
Fixed Assets	1m	1m	1m
Current Assets	4m	4m	3m
Current Liabilities	1m	1m	N/A

Glevum Security

16 Wheatstone Court Davy Way Waterwells Business Park, Quedgeley, Gloucester, GL2 2AQ
Tel: 01452-729713 **Fax:** 0870-774 5546
E-mail: info@glevum-security.co.uk
Website: http://www.glevum-security.co.uk
Directors: M. Baker (Dir)
Immediate Holding Company: GLEVUM SECURITY LTD.
Registration no: 03938360 **Date established:** 2000
No.of Employees: 51 - 100 **Product Groups:** 81, 86

Date of Accounts	Mar 12	Mar 11	Mar 10
Working Capital	-42	-1	21
Fixed Assets	50	49	53
Current Assets	539	489	267

Gloucester City Council (Economic Development - Housing and Regeneration Dept)

North Warehouse The Docks, Gloucester, GL1 2EP
Tel: 01452-396396 **Fax:** 01452-396140
E-mail: julian.wain@gloucester.gov.uk
Website: http://www.gloucester.gov.uk
Directors: J. Wain (Grp Chief Exec)
Immediate Holding Company: GL1 SPORTS LTD
Registration no: 04396593 **Date established:** 2002
Turnover: Up to £250,000 **No.of Employees:** 501 - 1000
Product Groups: 87

Date of Accounts	Mar 10	Mar 09	Mar 07
Sales Turnover	N/A	N/A	224
Pre Tax Profit/Loss	N/A	N/A	27
Working Capital	N/A	N/A	65
Current Assets	N/A	N/A	116
Current Liabilities	N/A	N/A	51

Gloucester Heat Treatment Ltd

Unit 7 Venture Business Centre Madleaze Road, Gloucester, GL1 5SJ
Tel: 01452-526434 **Fax:** 01452-303680
E-mail: kevin@ghtl.co.uk
Website: http://www.ghtl.co.uk
Bank(s): Lloyds TSB Bank plc
Directors: S. Wells (MD)
Immediate Holding Company: GLOUCESTER HEAT TREATMENT SPECIALISTS LIMITED
Registration no: 01747021 **VAT No.:** GB 618 2722 43
Date established: 1983 **Turnover:** £1m - £2m **No.of Employees:** 11 - 20
Product Groups: 48

Date of Accounts	Mar 12	Mar 11	Mar 10
Working Capital	-14	-9	-11
Fixed Assets	370	379	389
Current Assets	6	11	8

Gis Healthcare Gloucestershire County Council

Sudmeadow Road Hempsted, Gloucester, GL2 5HS
Tel: 01452-520438 **Fax:** 01452-300850
Managers: B. Dobbs (Purch Mgr), C. Shellam (Chief Mgr)
Date established: 1990 **No.of Employees:** 21 - 50 **Product Groups:** 38, 67

Goodridge Engineering Ltd

Goodridge Avenue, Gloucester, GL2 5EG
Tel: 01452-527457 **Fax:** 01452-300280
E-mail: sales@goodridgeengineering.co.uk
Website: http://www.goodridgeengineering.co.uk
Directors: N. Mckay (Prop)
Immediate Holding Company: GOODRIDGE ENGINEERING LTD
Registration no: 03005000 **VAT No.:** GB 618 4489 13
Date established: 1994 **Turnover:** £500,000 - £1m
No.of Employees: 11 - 20 **Product Groups:** 40

Date of Accounts	Mar 12	Mar 11	Jun 10
Working Capital	10	84	75
Fixed Assets	120	78	85
Current Assets	325	290	263

Graham

Unit 7 Woodrow Way, Gloucester, GL2 5DX
Tel: 01452-521501 **Fax:** 01452-306910
Website: http://www.graham-group.co.uk
Managers: A. Dee (District Mgr)
Immediate Holding Company: GRAHAM GROUP LTD
Registration no: 00066738 **Turnover:** £75m - £125m
No.of Employees: 1 - 10 **Product Groups:** 66

Great British Card Company plc

Waterwells Drive Quedgeley, Gloucester, GL2 2PH
Tel: 01452-888999 **Fax:** 01452-888912
E-mail: enquiries@paperhouse.co.uk
Website: http://www.paperhouse.co.uk
Directors: C. Wilcox (Comm)
Ultimate Holding Company: THE GREAT BRITISH CARD COMPANY PLC
Immediate Holding Company: THE PAPER HOUSE GROUP LIMITED
Registration no: 03149450 **Date established:** 1996
Turnover: £10m - £20m **No.of Employees:** 21 - 50 **Product Groups:** 27

Helipebs Controls Ltd

Premier Works Sisson Road, Gloucester, GL2 0RE
Tel: 01452-423201 **Fax:** 01452-307665
E-mail: sales@helipebs.co.uk
Website: http://www.helipebs-controls.co.uk
Bank(s): Lloyds TSB Bank plc
Directors: R. Tyler (Fin), J. Harris (Fin), G. Davis (MD)
Managers: S. Codd (Tech Serv Mgr), A. Hodges, H. Anderton (Sales & Mktg Mg)
Ultimate Holding Company: HELIPEBS (HOLDINGS) LIMITED
Immediate Holding Company: HELIPEBS (HOLDINGS) LIMITED
Registration no: 00182954 **VAT No.:** GB 274 4768 23
Date established: 2022 **Turnover:** £5m - £10m **No.of Employees:** 21 - 50
Product Groups: 42

Date of Accounts	Mar 12	Mar 11	Mar 10
Sales Turnover	5m	7m	8m
Pre Tax Profit/Loss	112	272	326
Working Capital	2m	2m	2m
Fixed Assets	609	625	665
Current Assets	3m	3m	3m
Current Liabilities	310	400	310

High Tech Fabrications Ltd

Unit 1 & 2 Crown Estate Sudmeadow Road, Gloucester, GL2 5HG
Tel: 01452-304466 **Fax:** 01452-306622
E-mail: sales@hightechfabrications.co.uk
Website: http://www.hightechfabrications.co.uk
Directors: P. Lynch (MD)
Ultimate Holding Company: P & R SYNERGY HOLDINGS LIMITED
Immediate Holding Company: HIGH TECH FABRICATIONS LIMITED
Registration no: 04247418 **Date established:** 2001
No.of Employees: 11 - 20 **Product Groups:** 30, 35, 36, 37, 40, 42, 46, 48, 66, 84

Date of Accounts	Jul 11	Jul 10	Jul 09
Working Capital	1m	1m	999
Fixed Assets	135	107	38
Current Assets	2m	2m	2m

Hoerbiger-Origa Ltd

Unit 12 Brunel Court Waterwells Business Park, Quedgeley, Gloucester, GL2 2AL
Tel: 01452-887880 **Fax:** 0870-0600656
E-mail: info-hogb-marketing@hoerbiger.com
Website: http://www.parker.com
Managers: M. Sutherland (Purch Mgr), R. Barnes (Mgr)
Ultimate Holding Company: Hoerbiger Division Int (Austria)
Immediate Holding Company: Origa Holding AG (CHE)
Registration no: 01562979 **Turnover:** £5m - £10m
No.of Employees: 11 - 20 **Product Groups:** 30, 36, 37, 38, 39, 40, 48

Date of Accounts	Dec 07	Dec 06	Dec 05
Sales Turnover	2853	2786	3087
Pre Tax Profit/Loss	269	326	-248
Working Capital	434	401	403
Fixed Assets	55	61	80
Current Assets	790	741	720
Current Liabilities	356	340	317
Total Share Capital	500	500	500
ROCE% (Return on Capital Employed)	55.0	70.6	-51.4
ROT% (Return on Turnover)	9.4	11.7	-8.0

Hofbauer (UK) Ltd

St Albans Road Empire Way, Gloucester, GL2 5FW
Tel: 01452-309782 **Fax:** 01452-309884
E-mail: cases@hofbauer.co.uk
Website: http://www.hofbauer.co.uk
Directors: T. Murray (Dir), J. Murray (Dir), P. Hofbauer (MD)
Managers: J. Clift (Accounts), T. Murray (Mktg Serv Mgr)
Registration no: 02007260 **VAT No.:** GB 435 4676 34
Date established: 1986 **Turnover:** £1m - £2m **No.of Employees:** 1 - 10
Product Groups: 22, 27, 30, 35, 38, 39, 44, 45, 49, 63, 66

Date of Accounts	Dec 09	Dec 08	Dec 07
Working Capital	-4	147	103
Fixed Assets	301	308	316
Current Assets	444	503	565

Hooper Knight Workplace Equipment LLP

Units A1 & A2 Goodridge Avenue, Gloucester, GL2 5EA
Tel: 01452-502888 **Fax:** 01452-502960
E-mail: ian@hooperknight.com
Website: http://www.hooperknight.com
Directors: I. Jones (Ptnr)
Registration no: 02007260 **VAT No.:** GB 133 5212 52
Date established: 1986 **Turnover:** £500,000 - £1m
No.of Employees: 1 - 10 **Product Groups:** 26, 32, 36, 40, 41, 46, 47, 66

Hydraproducts Ltd

Unit 5 Tuffley Trading Estate Pearce Way, Gloucester, GL2 5YD
Tel: 01452-523352 **Fax:** 01452-523353
E-mail: benlee@hydraproducts.co.uk
Website: http://www.hydraproducts.co.uk
Directors: B. Lee (Dir)
Immediate Holding Company: HYDRAPRODUCTS LIMITED
Registration no: 04578558 **Date established:** 2002
Turnover: £250,000 - £500,000 **No.of Employees:** 1 - 10
Product Groups: 40, 45

Date of Accounts	Oct 11	Oct 10	Oct 09
Working Capital	256	219	131
Fixed Assets	12	19	18
Current Assets	405	391	214

Hydraulic Equipment Supermarkets Ltd

Dowco House Innsworth Technology Park Innsworth Lane, Gloucester, GL3 1DL
Tel: 01452-730774 **Fax:** 01452-731637
E-mail: admin@grouphes.com
Website: http://www.grouphes.com
Bank(s): HSBC, Cheltenham
Directors: S. Diesel (MD)
Managers: M. Tatlow (Tech Serv Mgr), S. Alexander
Ultimate Holding Company: GROUP HES (HOLDINGS) LIMITED
Immediate Holding Company: HYDRAULIC EQUIPMENT SUPERMARKETS LIMITED
Registration no: 00866291 **VAT No.:** GB 275 1357 53
Date established: 1965 **Turnover:** £5m - £10m **No.of Employees:** 21 - 50
Product Groups: 22, 25, 29, 30, 33, 35, 36, 37, 38, 39, 40, 42, 46, 47, 48, 67

Date of Accounts	Jun 10	Jun 09
Working Capital	10	10
Current Assets	10	10

Ink Cottage

135 Eastgate Street, Gloucester, GL1 1QB
Tel: 01452-380000 **Fax:** 01452-386000
E-mail: customerservices@inkcottage.com
Website: http://www.inkcottage.com
Directors: Y. Addam (MD)
Registration no: 05866340 **No.of Employees:** 1 - 10 **Product Groups:** 27, 44, 67

Invista

Ermin Street Brockworth, Gloucester, GL3 4HP
Tel: 01452-633000 **Fax:** 01452-633082
Website: http://www.invista.com

see next page

Invista - Cont'd

Managers: S. Johnson (Mgr)
Ultimate Holding Company: DU PONT, (USA)
Registration no: 00565289 **No.of Employees:** 251 - 500
Product Groups: 23

Iswise

43 Apperley Park Apperley, Gloucester, GL19 4EB
Tel: 01452-780762 **Fax:** 01452-780910
E-mail: ian@iswise.co.uk
Website: http://www.iswise.co.uk
Directors: I. Wiseman (Snr Part), A. Wiseman (Ptnr)
Turnover: Up to £250,000 **No.of Employees:** 1 - 10 **Product Groups:** 84

J H P Training Ltd

2nd Floor Eastgate House 121-131 Eastgate Street, Gloucester, GL1 1PX
Tel: 01452-381883 **Fax:** 01452-381688
E-mail: dee.northedge@jhpemployability.com
Website: http://www.jhptraining.com
Managers: D. Northedge (Mgr)
Immediate Holding Company: JHP TRAINING LIMITED
Registration no: 03247918 **Date established:** 1996
Turnover: £50m - £75m **No.of Employees:** 11 - 20 **Product Groups:** 86

John Deere Credit

J D C House Meteor Court Barnett Way, Barnwood, Gloucester, GL4 3GG
Tel: 01452-372255 **Fax:** 01452-376066
E-mail: sales@johndeerecredit.co.uk
Website: http://www.johndeerecredit.co.uk
Managers: S. Tittings (Chief Mgr), S. Gittings
Ultimate Holding Company: NATIONAL WESTMINSTER BANK P.L.C.
Immediate Holding Company: LOMBARD P.L.C.
Registration no: 00436088 **Date established:** 1997
No.of Employees: 11 - 20 **Product Groups:** 82

King Builders Gloucester Ltd

Unit 3 Tuffley Trading Estate 20 Pearce Way, Gloucester, GL2 5YD
Tel: 01452-526631 **Fax:** 01452-527638
E-mail: info@kingbuildersglosltd.co.uk
Website: http://www.kingbuildersglosltd.co.uk
Directors: M. Corbally (Dir)
Immediate Holding Company: KING BUILDERS (GLOUCESTER) LIMITED
Registration no: 01487839 **Date established:** 1980 **Turnover:** £2m - £5m
No.of Employees: 1 - 10 **Product Groups:** 51, 52

Date of Accounts	Sep 11	Sep 10	Sep 09
Sales Turnover	2m	4m	3m
Pre Tax Profit/Loss	-240	253	244
Working Capital	675	926	702
Fixed Assets	50	74	94
Current Assets	2m	2m	3m
Current Liabilities	59	188	225

Kingsley Welding Alloys Ltd

Nortons Piece Bristol Road, Hardwicke, Gloucester, GL2 4RF
Tel: 01452-720210 **Fax:** 01452-723224
Directors: M. Cruse (MD)
Immediate Holding Company: KINGSLEY WELDING ALLOYS LIMITED
Registration no: 04381961 **Date established:** 2002
No.of Employees: 1 - 10 **Product Groups:** 46

Date of Accounts	Mar 11	Mar 10	Mar 09
Working Capital	67	65	37
Fixed Assets	37	40	34
Current Assets	156	177	153

Leeways Packaging Services Ltd

Lobstock Churcham, Gloucester, GL2 8AN
Tel: 01452-750487 **Fax:** 01452-750653
E-mail: info@leeways.co.uk
Website: http://www.leeways.co.uk
Bank(s): National Westminster Bank Plc
Directors: P. Scott (Sales), L. Walding (Co Sec), A. Walding (MD)
Managers: T. Coull (Fin Mgr), N. Townsend, P. Redington (Mktg Serv Mgr), A. Walding (Tech Serv Mgr)
Ultimate Holding Company: LEEWAYS HOLDINGS LIMITED
Immediate Holding Company: LEEWAYS PACKAGING SERVICES LIMITED
Registration no: 01030853 **VAT No.:** GB 666 9875 57
Date established: 1971 **Turnover:** £5m - £10m
No.of Employees: 51 - 100 **Product Groups:** 30, 42, 48

Date of Accounts	Jun 11	Jun 10	Jun 08
Sales Turnover	10m	9m	N/A
Pre Tax Profit/Loss	-10	424	213
Working Capital	1m	1m	809
Fixed Assets	3m	1m	1m
Current Assets	5m	5m	3m
Current Liabilities	1m	1m	281

Levolux A T Ltd

Levolux House 24 Eastville Close Eastern Avenue, Gloucester, GL4 3SJ
Tel: 01452-500007 **Fax:** 01452-527496
E-mail: sales@levoluxat.co.uk
Website: http://www.levolux.co.uk
Bank(s): Bank of Scotland
Directors: A. Harris (Sales), S. Johnson (MD), N. Marriott (Pers), P. Stern (Fin)
Managers: A. James (Tech Serv Mgr), R. Atherton (Buyer), C. Phippen (Mktg Serv Mgr)
Ultimate Holding Company: THE ALUMASC GROUP PLC
Immediate Holding Company: LEVOLUX A.T. LIMITED
Registration no: 02678660 **VAT No.:** GB 576 2973 93
Date established: 1992 **Turnover:** £5m - £10m
No.of Employees: 51 - 100 **Product Groups:** 35

Date of Accounts	Jun 11	Jun 10	Jun 09
Sales Turnover	9m	10m	14m
Pre Tax Profit/Loss	224	2m	3m
Working Capital	4m	4m	4m
Fixed Assets	133	176	158
Current Assets	7m	6m	6m
Current Liabilities	308	788	779

Lilleshall Steel Services Ltd

Steel House 1 Bristol Road, Gloucester, GL1 5TF
Tel: 01452-526821 **Fax:** 01452-300430
E-mail: sales@lilleshall-steel.co.uk
Website: http://www.lilleshall-steel.co.uk
Bank(s): Midland, Bradford
Directors: N. Farth (MD)
Ultimate Holding Company: BARRETT STEEL LIMITED
Immediate Holding Company: LILLESHALL STEEL SERVICES LIMITED
Registration no: 02760565 **VAT No.:** GB 647 1757 14
Date established: 1992 **Turnover:** £5m - £10m **No.of Employees:** 21 - 50
Product Groups: 34, 35

Date of Accounts	Sep 08
Working Capital	1
Current Assets	1

M & W Toyota Handling

The Luther Challis Business Centre Barnwood Road, Gloucester, GL4 3HX
Tel: 01452-523490 **Fax:** 01452-523491
Website: http://www.toyotahandling.co.uk
Immediate Holding Company: ADVANCED CONSERVATORIES LIMITED
Date established: 2003 **No.of Employees:** 51 - 100 **Product Groups:** 35, 39, 45

Marshall Langston Ltd

Marlan House Lower Tuffley Lane, Gloucester, GL2 5DT
Tel: 01452-529717 **Fax:** 01452-309994
E-mail: kevin.langston@marshalllangston.co.uk
Website: http://www.marshalllangston.co.uk
Directors: K. Langston (Dir)
Immediate Holding Company: MARSHALL LANGSTON LIMITED
Registration no: 00871097 **VAT No.:** GB 274 4687 23
Date established: 1966 **Turnover:** £500,000 - £1m
No.of Employees: 1 - 10 **Product Groups:** 27

Date of Accounts	Mar 12	Mar 11	Mar 10
Working Capital	54	59	105
Fixed Assets	339	344	361
Current Assets	199	192	199

Mecelec Design Ltd

Unit 1-2 Brearley Court Baird Road Quedgeley, Gloucester, GL2 2AF
Tel: 01452-880990 **Fax:** 01452-382888
E-mail: sch@mecdes.co.uk
Website: http://www.mecdes.co.uk
Directors: S. Hacker (MD)
Immediate Holding Company: MECELEC DESIGN LIMITED
Registration no: 02410618 **Date established:** 1989
No.of Employees: 21 - 50 **Product Groups:** 38, 40, 46

Date of Accounts	May 11	May 10	May 09
Working Capital	34	70	176
Fixed Assets	28	41	58
Current Assets	453	385	491

Merbro Welding

Unit 7a Shepherd Road, Gloucester, GL2 5EL
Tel: 01452-419156 **Fax:** 01452-419156
Directors: D. Mace (Prop)
Date established: 1967 **No.of Employees:** 1 - 10 **Product Groups:** 35

Messier Dowty Ltd

Cheltenham Road East, Gloucester, GL2 9QH
Tel: 01452-712424 **Fax:** 01452-713821
E-mail: neville.kite@messier-dowty.com
Website: http://www.messier-dowty.com
Directors: N. Kite (Fin)
Managers: J. Morgan, P. Thomas (Purch Mgr), P. Hull (Mktg Serv Mgr), R. McGlothlen
Ultimate Holding Company: SAFRAN SA (FRANCE)
Immediate Holding Company: MESSIER-DOWTY LIMITED
Registration no: 03548809 **VAT No.:** GB 650 8767 11
Date established: 1998 **Turnover:** £250m - £500m
No.of Employees: 501 - 1000 **Product Groups:** 39

Date of Accounts	Dec 11	Dec 10	Dec 09
Sales Turnover	337m	345m	295m
Pre Tax Profit/Loss	9m	22m	-6m
Working Capital	49m	42m	1m
Fixed Assets	82m	89m	160m
Current Assets	181m	166m	193m
Current Liabilities	29m	16m	41m

Messier Services Ltd

Meteor Business Park Cheltenham Road East, Gloucester, GL2 9QL
Tel: 01452-716500 **Fax:** 01452-716500
E-mail: repair@messierservices.co.uk
Website: http://www.messierservices.com
Bank(s): National Westminster Bank Plc
Directors: P. Clifford (Chief Op Offcr), T. Rice (MD)
Managers: Z. Townsend (Mgr)
Ultimate Holding Company: SAFRAN SA (FRANCE)
Registration no: 03528628 **VAT No.:** GB 713 0687 51
Date established: 1998 **Turnover:** £20m - £50m
No.of Employees: 101 - 250 **Product Groups:** 39

Date of Accounts	Dec 09	Dec 08	Dec 07
Sales Turnover	39m	30m	25m
Pre Tax Profit/Loss	5m	1m	2m
Working Capital	-3m	-4m	2m
Fixed Assets	18m	17m	11m
Current Assets	20m	19m	16m
Current Liabilities	13m	12m	5m

Mozley

370 Bristol Road, Gloucester, GL2 5DH
Tel: 01452-833800 **Fax:** 01209-211068
E-mail: asbl@axsia.com
Website: http://www.axsia.com
Bank(s): National Westminster Bank Plc
Directors: D. Cash (Sales & Mktg), D. Hope (Fin), I. Harding (Chief Op Offcr), R. Keating (Eng Serv)
Managers: G. Childs (Mgr), P. Salter (Mgr)
Immediate Holding Company: Axsia Group Limited
Registration no: 00961792 **VAT No.:** GB 212 1438 16
Turnover: £10m - £20m **No.of Employees:** 11 - 20 **Product Groups:** 13, 36, 39, 40, 42, 45, 48

NATIONAL TEST SERVICES

The White House Hempsted Lane, Hempsted, GLOUCESTER, GL2 5JA
Tel: 01452-505066 **Fax:** 01452-505664
E-mail: sales@nts.uk.net
Website: http://www.nts.uk.net
Turnover: £250,000 - £500,000 **No.of Employees:** 11 - 20
Product Groups: 38, 85

Nicks Co Timber Ltd

Canada Wharf Bristol Road, Gloucester, GL1 5TE
Tel: 01452-300159 **Fax:** 01452-386016
E-mail: phil@glostimber.co.uk
Website: http://www.directdiy.co.uk
Bank(s): HSBC Bank plc
Directors: R. McCormick (Co Sec), P. Mccormick (MD), N. Buckley Ryan (MD)
Immediate Holding Company: GLOUCESTER TIMBER COMPANY LIMITED
Registration no: 02632621 **VAT No.:** GB 274 6465 31
Date established: 1991 **Turnover:** £5m - £10m **No.of Employees:** 21 - 50
Product Groups: 08, 25, 32, 35, 48, 52, 61, 66, 84, 87

Date of Accounts	Jan 10	Jan 06	Jan 05
Sales Turnover	N/A	86	104
Pre Tax Profit/Loss	N/A	2	-10
Working Capital	-73	-66	-69
Fixed Assets	1	4	5
Current Assets	45	40	23
Current Liabilities	N/A	75	20

Oceaneering Ltd

Unit 3b Bristol Road, Gloucester, GL2 5HE
Tel: 01452-304694 **Fax:** 01452-416656
E-mail: ahutchinson@oceaneering.com
Website: http://www.oceaneering.com
Managers: A. Hutchinson
Registration no: 01023217 **Turnover:** Up to £250,000
No.of Employees: 1 - 10 **Product Groups:** 37, 38, 44, 48, 51, 85

Original Style

117 Bristol Road, Gloucester, GL1 5SW
Tel: 01452-308060 **Fax:** 01452-308317
Website: http://www.originalstyle.com
Directors: G. Brook (MD)
No.of Employees: 251 - 500 **Product Groups:** 33, 35

Parmley Graham Ltd

Secunda Way Hempsted, Gloucester, GL2 5GA
Tel: 01452-416585 **Fax:** 01452-307143
E-mail: gloucester@parmley-graham.co.uk
Website: http://www.parmley-graham.co.uk
Managers: S. Hodges (District Mgr)
Immediate Holding Company: PARMLEY GRAHAM LIMITED
Registration no: 00172842 **Date established:** 2021
No.of Employees: 1 - 10 **Product Groups:** 37, 40

Date of Accounts	Dec 11	Dec 10	Dec 09
Sales Turnover	34m	33m	26m
Pre Tax Profit/Loss	1m	910	353
Working Capital	4m	4m	3m
Fixed Assets	1m	1m	1m
Current Assets	10m	9m	7m
Current Liabilities	1m	900	415

Permali Gloucester Ltd

Bristol Road, Gloucester, GL1 5TT
Tel: 01452-528282 **Fax:** 01452-507409
E-mail: sales@permali.co.uk
Website: http://www.permali-gloucester.co.uk
Bank(s): Lloyds TSB
Directors: N. Baird (Sales), G. King (Dir)
Managers: S. Farmer, P. Mitchell (Purch Mgr), S. Minchew (Comptroller), C. Smith
Immediate Holding Company: PERMALI GLOUCESTER LIMITED
Registration no: 03546214 **VAT No.:** GB 682 4422 32
Date established: 1998 **Turnover:** £5m - £10m
No.of Employees: 51 - 100 **Product Groups:** 30, 31

Date of Accounts	May 11	May 10	May 09
Sales Turnover	10m	20m	14m
Pre Tax Profit/Loss	197	3m	2m
Working Capital	5m	5m	4m
Fixed Assets	2m	2m	2m
Current Assets	7m	9m	7m
Current Liabilities	502	2m	991

Poeton Gloucester (Coating Technology Worldwide)

Southbrook Road Eastern Avenue, Gloucester, GL4 3DN
Tel: 01452-300500 **Fax:** 01452-500400
E-mail: sales@poeton.co.uk
Website: http://www.poeton.co.uk
Bank(s): Barclays, Bristol
Directors: A. Poeton (Ch), D. Bignell (Fin)
Managers: N. Morris (Purch Mgr)
Ultimate Holding Company: A.T. POETON & SON LIMITED
Immediate Holding Company: POETON HOLDINGS LIMITED
Registration no: 04036407 **VAT No.:** GB 435 4192 56
Date established: 2000 **Turnover:** £5m - £10m
No.of Employees: 51 - 100 **Product Groups:** 30, 32, 46, 48

Date of Accounts	Dec 11	Dec 10	Dec 09
Sales Turnover	6m	6m	6m
Pre Tax Profit/Loss	608	195	256
Working Capital	963	740	565
Fixed Assets	2m	2m	2m
Current Assets	2m	1m	1m
Current Liabilities	532	366	354

Prima Dental Group Ltd

Statesman House Stephenson Drive Quedgeley, Gloucester, GL2 2AG
Tel: 01452-307171 **Fax:** 01452-307187
E-mail: admin@primadentalgroup.com
Website: http://www.sswhite.com
Bank(s): Barclays
Managers: A. John (Chief Mgr), A. John (Chief Mgr)
Ultimate Holding Company: A D BURS LIMITED
Immediate Holding Company: SSW REALISATIONS
Registration no: 02036605 **VAT No.:** GB 618 1005 76
Date established: 1986 **Turnover:** £5m - £10m
No.of Employees: 51 - 100 **Product Groups:** 31

Date of Accounts	Dec 11	Dec 10	Dec 09
Sales Turnover	9m	9m	8m
Pre Tax Profit/Loss	928	762	939
Working Capital	3m	2m	3m
Fixed Assets	7m	8m	4m
Current Assets	5m	4m	5m
Current Liabilities	672	1m	720

Pro Door Ltd

Unit R3 Innsworth Technology Park Innsworth Lane, Gloucester, GL3 1DL
Tel: 01452-739191 **Fax:** 01452-739190
E-mail: linda.prodoor@virgin.net
Website: http://www.pro-door.co.uk
Directors: L. Jenkins (Fin)
Immediate Holding Company: PRO-DOOR LIMITED
Registration no: 03801177 **Date established:** 1999
No.of Employees: 1 - 10 **Product Groups:** 26, 35

Date of Accounts	Jul 12	Jul 11	Jul 10
Working Capital	243	187	159
Fixed Assets	3	5	3
Current Assets	422	335	336

Procut Diamond Tools

Unit F6 Innsworth Technology Park Innsworth Lane, Gloucester, GL3 1DL
Tel: 01452-730260 **Fax:** 01452-730260
E-mail: sales@procutdiamondtools.com
Website: http://www.procutdiamondtools.com
Directors: L. Cox (Fin), P. Cox (MD)
Immediate Holding Company: Procut Superabrasives Ltd
Registration no: 04279239 **Date established:** 2001
No.of Employees: 1 - 10 **Product Groups:** 46

Date of Accounts	Mar 08	Mar 07	Mar 06
Working Capital	-5	7	-4
Fixed Assets	24	29	38
Current Assets	46	55	45
Current Liabilities	52	48	48

Prospect Training & Recruitment

Unit C4 Brunel Court Quedgeley, Gloucester, GL2 2AL
Tel: 01452-886888 **Fax:** 01452-886776
E-mail: enquiries@trainandrecruit.com
Website: http://www.trainandrecruit.com
Managers: D. Evans (Mgr), A. Devlin (Fin Mgr)
Immediate Holding Company: CRYPTEK HOLDCO UK LIMITED
Registration no: 06426627 **Date established:** 2007
No.of Employees: 11 - 20 **Product Groups:** 35, 39, 45

Date of Accounts	May 11	May 10	Jul 09
Pre Tax Profit/Loss	N/A	489	N/A
Working Capital	N/A	N/A	-489
Fixed Assets	2m	2m	2m

R & R Manufacturing

The Gate House Calton Road, Gloucester, GL1 5DT
Tel: 01452-416060 **Fax:** 01452-416060
Website: http://www.randrgroup.co.uk
No.of Employees: 1 - 10 **Product Groups:** 35, 37

Rapid Rail GB Ltd (Worldwide Installation Specialists)

Empire Way, Gloucester, GL2 5HY
Tel: 01452-383001 **Fax:** 01452-301301
E-mail: info@rapidrail.co.uk
Website: http://www.rapidrail.co.uk
Directors: L. Benson Ansell (Dir)
Managers: C. Turner (Comptroller), S. Cottam, L. Davies (Sales Admin), S. Durstan (Personnel)
Immediate Holding Company: RAPID RAIL LIMITED
Registration no: 02784855 **Date established:** 1993 **Turnover:** £2m - £5m
No.of Employees: 11 - 20 **Product Groups:** 30, 32, 35, 36, 37, 39, 40, 45, 48

Date of Accounts	Mar 09	Mar 08	Mar 07
Working Capital	130	382	523
Fixed Assets	188	221	70
Current Assets	2m	3m	1m

Rem Systems Ltd

Unit 24-26 Sabre Close Quedgeley, Gloucester, GL2 4NZ
Tel: 01452-314100 **Fax:** 01452-314101
E-mail: jryland@remsystems.co.uk
Website: http://www.remsystems.co.uk
Directors: J. Ryland (Jt MD), J. Ryland (MD), P. Ryland (Jt MD), P. Ryland (Fin)
Immediate Holding Company: REM SYSTEMS LIMITED
Registration no: 03426205 **VAT No.:** GB 391 9475 09
Date established: 1997 **Turnover:** £1m - £2m **No.of Employees:** 1 - 10
Product Groups: 46

Date of Accounts	Sep 10	Sep 09	Sep 08
Working Capital	255	239	294
Fixed Assets	50	53	59
Current Assets	474	449	772

Roechling Engineering Plastics Ltd

Waterwells Drive Waterwells Business Park, Quedgeley, Gloucester, GL2 2AA
Tel: 01452-727900 **Fax:** 01452-728056
E-mail: m.knowles@roechling.co.uk
Website: http://www.roechling.co.uk
Bank(s): HSBC Bank plc
Directors: M. Knowles (MD)
Ultimate Holding Company: ROCHLING ENGINEERING PLASTICS HAREN KG
Immediate Holding Company: ROCHLING ENGINEERING PLASTICS (UK) LIMITED
Registration no: 01947990 **VAT No.:** GB 419 2970 34
Date established: 1985 **Turnover:** £5m - £10m **No.of Employees:** 21 - 50
Product Groups: 25, 30, 31, 48, 66

Date of Accounts	Dec 11	Dec 10	Dec 09
Sales Turnover	8m	8m	6m
Pre Tax Profit/Loss	506	557	258
Working Capital	2m	2m	2m
Fixed Assets	2m	2m	2m
Current Assets	4m	4m	3m
Current Liabilities	460	579	312

Ryan Jayberg

Unit 18 Highnam Business Centre Newent Road, Highnam, Gloucester, GL2 8DN
Tel: 01452-414118 **Fax:** 01452-414119
E-mail: enquiries@ryan-jayberg.co.uk
Website: http://www.ryan-jayberg.co.uk
Directors: C. Green (Chief Op Offcr)
No.of Employees: 1 - 10 **Product Groups:** 40, 66

Safpro Industrial Supply Co.

Unit 4-5 Ashville Industrial Estate Ashville Road, Gloucester, GL2 5EU
Tel: 01452-529050 **Fax:** 01452-311221
E-mail: sales@safpro.co.uk
Website: http://www.safpro.co.uk
Directors: A. Simmonds (Snr Part), G. Simmonds (Ptnr), R. Simmonds (Ptnr), R. Jones (Ptnr)
VAT No.: GB 275 5809 18 **Date established:** 1975 **Turnover:** £2m - £5m
No.of Employees: 21 - 50 **Product Groups:** 24

Saint-Gobain Abrasives Ltd

Anson Business Park Cheltenham Road East, Gloucester, GL2 9QN
Tel: 01452-858700 **Fax:** 01452-858800
E-mail: sales.gloucester.uk@saint-gobain.com
Website: http://www.saint-gobain.com
Directors: S. Johnson (Dir)
Managers: K. Swiford (I.T. Exec), S. Wardrop (Plant), J. Cooke (Sales Prom Mgr)
Immediate Holding Company: Saint-Gobain Ltd
Registration no: 02943990 **Date established:** 1893 **Turnover:** £5m - £10m
No.of Employees: 21 - 50 **Product Groups:** 33

Sapa Components Pressweld

Spinnaker Park Spinnaker Road, Hempsted, Gloucester, GL2 5DG
Tel: 01452-502502 **Fax:** 01452-503503
E-mail: sales@pressweld.co.uk
Website: http://www.sapagroup.com
Bank(s): Royal Bank of Scotland
Directors: G. Ryske (Co Sec), H. Gronningsaeter (Dir)
Ultimate Holding Company: ORKLA ASA (NORWAY)
Immediate Holding Company: SAPA COMPONENTS UK LIMITED
Registration no: 06249930 **VAT No.:** GB 274 3174 57
Date established: 2007 **Turnover:** £10m - £20m
No.of Employees: 101 - 250 **Product Groups:** 35, 36, 39, 48

Date of Accounts	Dec 10	Dec 09	Dec 08
Sales Turnover	18m	6m	8m
Pre Tax Profit/Loss	-2m	-1m	-266
Working Capital	9m	2m	1m
Fixed Assets	9m	5m	5m
Current Assets	17m	3m	3m
Current Liabilities	3m	579	426

Service Aluminium Company Ltd

Eastbrook Road, Gloucester, GL4 3DB
Tel: 01452-423541 **Fax:** 01452-501643
E-mail: office@serval.co.uk
Website: http://www.serval.co.uk
Bank(s): Lloyds
Directors: A. Castle (Tech Serv), I. Avent (MD), T. Avent (Co Sec)
Immediate Holding Company: SERVICE ALUMINIUM COMPANY LIMITED
Registration no: 01033720 **Date established:** 1971 **Turnover:** £1m - £2m
No.of Employees: 11 - 20 **Product Groups:** 34

Date of Accounts	Dec 11	Dec 10	Dec 09
Working Capital	43	112	208
Fixed Assets	390	400	443
Current Assets	451	437	450

Severn Glocon Ltd

Olympus Park Quedgeley, Gloucester, GL2 4NF
Tel: 08452-232040 **Fax:** 0845-223 2041
E-mail: reception@severnglocon.co.uk
Website: http://www.severnglocon.com
Bank(s): Barclays, Clifton
Directors: M. Critchley (MD), R. Baker (Sales), M. Millington (Fin)
Managers: N. Clarke (Sales & Mktg Mg), S. Brown (Tech Serv Mgr), J. Clarke (Purch Mgr), N. Huldert (Personnel)
Ultimate Holding Company: SEVERN GLOCON GROUP PLC
Immediate Holding Company: SEVERN GLOCON LIMITED
Registration no: 00688539 **VAT No.:** GB 242 3380 87
Date established: 1961 **Turnover:** £50m - £75m
No.of Employees: 101 - 250 **Product Groups:** 36, 38, 40

Date of Accounts	Dec 11	Dec 10	Dec 09
Sales Turnover	50m	36m	23m
Pre Tax Profit/Loss	6m	5m	6m
Working Capital	6m	4m	-1m
Fixed Assets	6m	5m	4m
Current Assets	34m	20m	11m
Current Liabilities	7m	3m	3m

Shading Systems Ltd

Unit F5 Innsworth Technology Park Innsworth Lane, Gloucester, GL3 1DL
Tel: 01452-536000 **Fax:** 01452-731901
E-mail: info@shadings.co.uk
Website: http://www.shadings.co.uk
Directors: P. Woodman (MD), R. Woodman (Fin)
Immediate Holding Company: SHADING SYSTEMS LIMITED
Registration no: 02689314 **VAT No.:** GB 576 3546 10
Date established: 1992 **Turnover:** £250,000 - £500,000
No.of Employees: 1 - 10 **Product Groups:** 24, 30, 35, 36

Date of Accounts	Mar 08	Mar 07	Mar 06
Working Capital	15	4	-19
Fixed Assets	7	11	18
Current Assets	48	53	50
Current Liabilities	32	49	68
Total Share Capital	10	10	10

Shelving & Partitioning Systems Ltd

35 Pinewood Road, Gloucester, GL2 4RY
Tel: 01452-541044 **Fax:** 01452-541045
E-mail: sales@shelvingpartitioning.co.uk
Website: http://www.shelvingpartitioning.co.uk
Directors: T. Cannon (MD)
Immediate Holding Company: SHELVING AND PARTITIONING SYSTEMS LIMITED
Registration no: 03316625 **Date established:** 1997
No.of Employees: 1 - 10 **Product Groups:** 35, 42, 45

Date of Accounts	Mar 11	Mar 10	Mar 09
Working Capital	144	177	156
Fixed Assets	17	22	21
Current Assets	194	212	221

Sign Werx

Brunel Court Waterwells Business Park, Quedgeley, Gloucester, GL2 2AL
Tel: 01452-729909 **Fax:** 01452-729925
E-mail: rob.whitney@signwerx.co.uk
Website: http://www.signwerx.co.uk
Managers: F. Smith (Mgr)
Immediate Holding Company: CRYPTEK HOLDCO UK LIMITED
Registration no: 06962026 **Date established:** 2007
No.of Employees: 1 - 10 **Product Groups:** 24, 63

Date of Accounts	May 11	May 10	Jul 09
Pre Tax Profit/Loss	N/A	489	N/A
Working Capital	N/A	N/A	-489
Fixed Assets	2m	2m	2m

Horace Sinclair & Son Ltd

123 Pearce Way, Gloucester, GL2 5YD
Tel: 01452-503662 **Fax:** 01452-311084
E-mail: sinclairedm@btconnect.com
Directors: P. Sinclair (MD)
Immediate Holding Company: HORACE SINCLAIR & SON LIMITED
Registration no: 01587724 **Date established:** 1981
No.of Employees: 1 - 10 **Product Groups:** 46

Date of Accounts	Dec 11	Dec 10	Dec 09
Working Capital	-1	-2	2
Fixed Assets	1	2	2
Current Assets	26	23	34

Sinclair Optical Services Ltd

Unit 3-8 Corse Industrial Estate Gloucester Road, Corse, Gloucester, GL19 3RD
Tel: 01452-840771 **Fax:** 01452-840315
E-mail: nigelcorbett@sinclairoptical.co.uk
Website: http://www.sinclairoptical.co.uk
Directors: N. Corbett (Dir), J. Smith (Fin)
Managers: J. Ursell (Mktg Serv Mgr)
Immediate Holding Company: SINCLAIR OPTICAL SERVICES COMPANY LIMITED
Registration no: 01760801 **Date established:** 1983 **Turnover:** £5m - £10m
No.of Employees: 21 - 50 **Product Groups:** 37, 38, 65

Date of Accounts	Dec 11	Dec 10	Dec 09
Sales Turnover	5m	6m	6m
Pre Tax Profit/Loss	426	229	172
Working Capital	554	2m	2m
Fixed Assets	358	493	551
Current Assets	2m	2m	2m
Current Liabilities	2m	561	531

Springfast Ltd

Southbrook House Southbrook Road, Gloucester, GL4 3YY
Tel: 01452-416688 **Fax:** 01452-308723
E-mail: enquiries@springfast.co.uk
Website: http://www.springfast.co.uk
Directors: D. Rees (Prop)
Immediate Holding Company: SPRINGFAST LIMITED
Registration no: 01455685 **VAT No.:** GB 326 3699 36
Date established: 1979 **Turnover:** £2m - £5m **No.of Employees:** 1 - 10
Product Groups: 35, 36, 48, 66

Date of Accounts	Oct 11	Oct 10	Oct 09
Working Capital	1m	1m	1m
Fixed Assets	585	632	571
Current Assets	2m	2m	2m

Target Catering Equipment

Unit 1 Ashville Trading Estate, Gloucester, GL2 5EU
Tel: 01452-410447 **Fax:** 01452-410471
E-mail: sales@targetcatering.co.uk
Website: http://www.targetcatering.co.uk
Directors: D. Pedrette (MD)
Immediate Holding Company: PEDRETTE ENGINEERING LIMITED
Registration no: 02284651 **Date established:** 1988
Turnover: £500,000 - £1m **No.of Employees:** 1 - 10 **Product Groups:** 26, 40, 52, 63, 66, 67, 69

Date of Accounts	Dec 11	Dec 10	Dec 09
Working Capital	-252	-253	-227
Fixed Assets	136	176	180
Current Assets	144	120	115

The Safety Knife Co. Ltd

Olympus Park Quedgeley, Gloucester, GL2 4NF
Tel: 08452-232050 **Fax:** 0845-223 2051
E-mail: sales@safetyknife.net
Website: http://www.safetyknife.net
Managers: D. Harris (Chief Mgr)
Immediate Holding Company: THE SAFETY KNIFE CO. LTD.
Registration no: 02827044 **Date established:** 1993
No.of Employees: 1 - 10 **Product Groups:** 38, 42

Date of Accounts	Dec 11	Dec 10	Dec 09
Working Capital	156	68	36
Fixed Assets	22	32	21
Current Assets	410	330	297

Thermo Radiometrie Ltd

Shepherd Road, Gloucester, GL2 5HF
Tel: 01452-337800 **Fax:** 01452-415156
Website: http://www.radiometrie.com
Bank(s): Barclays, 54 Lombard St, London EC3V 9EX
Directors: N. Ward (Fin), K. Quinn (MD)
Managers: D. Avery (Quality Control), R. Jurga (I.T. Exec)
Ultimate Holding Company: THERMO FISHER SCIENTIFIC INC (USA)
Immediate Holding Company: THERMO RADIOMETRIE LIMITED
Registration no: 01018174 **VAT No.:** GB 286 1997 04
Date established: 1971 **Turnover:** £2m - £5m **No.of Employees:** 51 - 100
Product Groups: 37, 38

Date of Accounts	Dec 10	Dec 09	Dec 08
Sales Turnover	5m	4m	5m
Pre Tax Profit/Loss	722	1m	344
Working Capital	11m	11m	10m
Fixed Assets	134	195	251
Current Assets	13m	11m	10m
Current Liabilities	874	587	229

Twyver Switchgear

Unit 9 Chancel Close, Gloucester, GL4 3SN
Tel: 01452-525096 **Fax:** 01452-356555
E-mail: sales@twyverswitchgear.co.uk
Website: http://www.twyverswitchgear.co.uk
Bank(s): Barclays, Queens Square, Wolverhamptom
Directors: S. Baker (Fin)
Managers: C. Smith (Mgr)
Ultimate Holding Company: VINCI SA (FRANCE)
Immediate Holding Company: TWYVER LIMITED
Registration no: 01559207 **VAT No.:** GB 545 1884 27
Date established: 1981 **Turnover:** £1m - £2m **No.of Employees:** 21 - 50
Product Groups: 37

Date of Accounts	Dec 08
Working Capital	1
Current Assets	1

Ultra Electronics Ltd
Anson Business Park Cheltenham Road East, Gloucester, GL2 9QU
Tel: 01452-714382 **Fax:** 01452-715252
E-mail: sales@uews.co.uk
Website: http://www.hippag.com
Bank(s): Royal Bank of Scotland, London
Managers: V. Bussell
Ultimate Holding Company: ULTRA ELECTRONICS HOLDINGS PLC
Immediate Holding Company: ULTRA ELECTRONICS LIMITED
Registration no: 02830644 **VAT No.:** GB 618 4576 18
Date established: 1993 **Turnover:** £2m - £5m **No.of Employees:** 51 - 100
Product Groups: 39

Date of Accounts	Dec 11	Dec 10	Dec 09
Sales Turnover	379m	313m	286m
Pre Tax Profit/Loss	59m	19m	24m
Working Capital	37m	-27m	15m
Fixed Assets	70m	76m	73m
Current Assets	208m	135m	160m
Current Liabilities	79m	68m	58m

Wenzel UK Ltd
29 Brunel Court Stephensons Court, Quedgeley, Gloucester, GL2 2AL
Tel: 01452-728298 **Fax:** 01452-728288
E-mail: info@uk.wenzel-cmm.com
Website: http://www.wenzel-cmm.co.uk
Directors: M. Hawkins (MD)
Ultimate Holding Company: WENZEL GROUP GMBH & CO KG (GERMANY)
Immediate Holding Company: WENZEL UK LIMITED
Registration no: 02931730 **Date established:** 1994 **Turnover:** £1m - £2m
No.of Employees: 1 - 10 **Product Groups:** 85

Date of Accounts	Dec 11	Dec 10	Dec 09
Working Capital	-594	-419	-111
Fixed Assets	43	37	44
Current Assets	611	660	648

T H White Ltd
Ross Road Huntley, Gloucester, GL19 3EX
Tel: 01452-830303 **Fax:** 01452-830984
Website: http://www.thwhite.co.uk
Managers: P. Leeming (Mgr)
Ultimate Holding Company: T. H. WHITE HOLDINGS LIMITED
Immediate Holding Company: T. H. WHITE LIMITED
Registration no: 00519868 **Date established:** 1953 **Turnover:** £1m - £2m
No.of Employees: 11 - 20 **Product Groups:** 41

Date of Accounts	Dec 11	Dec 10	Dec 09
Sales Turnover	96m	86m	81m
Pre Tax Profit/Loss	1m	697	1m
Working Capital	9m	9m	9m
Fixed Assets	2m	2m	2m
Current Assets	27m	22m	21m
Current Liabilities	7m	8m	4m

Williams Metal Polishers
5 Highfield Business Park Tewkesbury Road, Deerhurst, Gloucester, GL19 4BP
Tel: 01684-291564 **Fax:** 01684-291564
Website: http://www.osb.co.uk
Directors: A. Williams (Prop)
Date established: 1987 **No.of Employees:** 1 - 10 **Product Groups:** 46, 48

Window Widget
Unit C Quedgeley West Business Park Bristol Road, Hardwicke, Gloucester, GL2 4PA
Tel: 01452-300912 **Fax:** 01452-300912
E-mail: wendy@windowwidgets.co.uk
Website: http://www.windowwidgets.co.uk
Directors: W. Gill (Dir)
No.of Employees: 11 - 20 **Product Groups:** 46

Date of Accounts	May 08	May 07	May 06
Working Capital	-88	127	197
Fixed Assets	297	297	110
Current Assets	N/A	180	773
Current Liabilities	88	53	576

Lechlade

Cotswold Woollen Weavers
Filkins, Lechlade, GL7 3JJ
Tel: 01367-860660 **Fax:** 01367-860661
E-mail: info@naturalbest.co.uk
Website: http://www.naturalbest.co.uk
Directors: R. Martin (Dir)
VAT No.: GB 348 6466 18 **No.of Employees:** 21 - 50 **Product Groups:** 23

Longhope

Richard Read Transport Ltd
The Transport Depot Monmouth Road, Longhope, GL17 0QG
Tel: 01452-830456 **Fax:** 01452-831422
E-mail: brenda.herring@richardreadcommercials.co.uk
Website: http://www.richardreadtransport.co.uk
Bank(s): National Westminster, Gloucester
Directors: K. Read (Fin), M. Read (Co Sec), B. Herring (Dir)
Managers: J. Garner (Chief Mgr), S. Brackston (Buyer)
Immediate Holding Company: RICHARD READ HOLDINGS LIMITED
Registration no: 06181300 **VAT No.:** GB 274 2095 58
Date established: 2007 **Turnover:** £2m - £5m **No.of Employees:** 51 - 100
Product Groups: 72

Date of Accounts	Apr 12	Apr 11	Apr 10
Sales Turnover	4m	4m	4m
Pre Tax Profit/Loss	93	-6	-5
Working Capital	-102	-325	-539
Fixed Assets	4m	4m	4m
Current Assets	968	985	1m
Current Liabilities	412	342	345

Lydbrook

Lydwood Glos Ltd
Lower Lydbrook, Lydbrook, GL17 9NB
Tel: 01594-860374 **Fax:** 01594-861312
E-mail: nick@lydwood.co.uk
Website: http://www.lydwood.co.uk
Directors: N. Jones (MD)
Managers: J. Addis (Admin Off)
Immediate Holding Company: LYDWOOD (GLOS) LIMITED
Registration no: 00815004 **VAT No.:** GB 275 0823 55
Date established: 1964 **Turnover:** £1m - £2m **No.of Employees:** 1 - 10
Product Groups: 25, 63

Date of Accounts	Jul 11	Jul 10	Jul 09
Working Capital	291	272	246
Fixed Assets	177	182	194
Current Assets	372	358	323

Y-Ryte Ltd
2 Prides Place School Road Central Lydbrook, Lydbrook, GL17 9PP
Tel: 0117-230 1423 **Fax:** 0117-370 1004
E-mail: sales@y-ryte.co.uk
Website: http://www.y-ryte.co.uk
Directors: R. Thory (Prop)
Immediate Holding Company: Y-RYTE LIMITED
Registration no: 02650744 **Date established:** 1991
No.of Employees: 1 - 10 **Product Groups:** 49, 64

Date of Accounts	Oct 11	Oct 10	Oct 09
Sales Turnover	N/A	N/A	20
Pre Tax Profit/Loss	N/A	N/A	-9
Working Capital	-28	-32	-39
Fixed Assets	1	3	12
Current Assets	6	4	4
Current Liabilities	N/A	N/A	1

Lydney

Albany Pumps
Church Road, Lydney, GL15 5EQ
Tel: 01594-842275 **Fax:** 01594-842574
E-mail: sales@albany-pumps.co.uk
Website: http://www.albany-pumps.co.uk
Bank(s): Royal Bank of Scotland, London
Directors: M. Cowmeadow (Dir), M. Swaffield (MD)
Managers: G. Maxsted (Sales Prom Mgr), L. Taylor (Buyer)
Immediate Holding Company: ALBANY ENGINEERING COMPANY LIMITED(THE)
Registration no: 00313089 **VAT No.:** GB 274 1342 72
Date established: 1936 **Turnover:** £2m - £5m **No.of Employees:** 51 - 100
Product Groups: 29, 33, 36, 37, 39, 40, 45, 48

Date of Accounts	Mar 12	Mar 11	Mar 10
Sales Turnover	4m	4m	4m
Pre Tax Profit/Loss	198	139	96
Working Capital	2m	2m	2m
Fixed Assets	190	323	381
Current Assets	3m	2m	2m
Current Liabilities	376	567	336

Beads Findings 'N' Things
Unit 8 Princess Royal Industrial Estate Whitecroft, Lydney, GL15 4SU
Tel: 01594-564634 **Fax:** 01594-564634
E-mail: sales@bfnt.co.uk
Website: http://www.bfnt.co.uk
Directors: S. James (Prop)
Date established: 2007 **No.of Employees:** 1 - 10 **Product Groups:** 02, 22, 33, 35, 49, 64, 65

Celtic Communications Europe Ltd
The Oaks Allaston Road, Lydney, GL15 5SS
Tel: 01594-842584
E-mail: paul.chesters@celticcommunication.com
Website: http://www.celticcommunication.com
Directors: P. Chesters (Prop)
Immediate Holding Company: CELTIC COMMUNICATIONS EUROPE LIMITED
Registration no: 04412877 **Date established:** 2002
No.of Employees: 1 - 10 **Product Groups:** 86

Date of Accounts	Mar 08	Mar 07	Mar 06
Working Capital	-47	-91	-81
Fixed Assets	38	53	69
Current Assets	1	2	1

Double E International LLC
8 The Marina Harbour Road, Lydney, GL15 5ET
Tel: 01594-844455 **Fax:** 01594-844466
E-mail: mktg@doubleeusa.com
Website: http://www.doubleeusa.com
Directors: M. Fortin (Pres)
Immediate Holding Company: DOUBLE E INTERNATIONAL LLC
Registration no: FC020416 **Date established:** 1997
Turnover: £10m - £20m **No.of Employees:** 1 - 10 **Product Groups:** 29, 39, 43

Exhaust Tyres & Batteries Ltd
Hams Road, Lydney, GL15 5PE
Tel: 01594-842385 **Fax:** 01594-842385
Managers: D. Roberts (Mgr)
Immediate Holding Company: EXHAUST TYRES AND BATTERIES (WORCESTER) LIMITED
Registration no: 01532384 **Date established:** 1980
No.of Employees: 1 - 10 **Product Groups:** 29, 68

Date of Accounts	Jan 11	Jan 10	Jan 09
Sales Turnover	21m	18m	16m
Pre Tax Profit/Loss	1m	1m	871
Working Capital	406	1m	853
Fixed Assets	5m	4m	4m
Current Assets	6m	5m	4m
Current Liabilities	922	718	635

Forest Of Dean Metal Finishers
Unit 114 Lydney Industrial Estate Harbour Road, Lydney, GL15 4EJ
Tel: 01594-843288 **Fax:** 01594-844865
Directors: E. Potter (Prop)
Registration no: 01687650 **Date established:** 1982
No.of Employees: 1 - 10 **Product Groups:** 46, 48

Forest Of Dean Stone Firms Ltd
Cannop Road Parkend, Lydney, GL15 4JS
Tel: 01594-562304 **Fax:** 01594-564184
E-mail: info@fodstone.co.uk
Website: http://www.fodstone.co.uk
Directors: M. Scott Russell (MD), N. Horton (MD)
Ultimate Holding Company: FOREST OF DEAN STONE FIRMS LIMITED
Immediate Holding Company: LIGHTENING SOLUTIONS LIMITED
Registration no: 00179968 **Date established:** 2022
Turnover: £250,000 - £500,000 **No.of Employees:** 21 - 50
Product Groups: 14, 33, 66

Date of Accounts	Jun 08
Working Capital	215
Current Assets	339

Mabey Bridge Ltd
Harbour Road Trading Estate, Lydney, GL15 4EJ
Tel: 01594-844377 **Fax:** 01594-843040
E-mail: mail@mabeybridge.co.uk
Website: http://www.mabeybridge.co.uk
Directors: M. Morgan (Fin), P. Brookes (Works), T. Broke (Dir)
Managers: K. Jones, L. Isaac (Personnel)
Ultimate Holding Company: MABEY HOLDINGS LIMITED
Immediate Holding Company: MABEY BRIDGE LIMITED
Registration no: 04300396 **Date established:** 2001
Turnover: £50m - £75m **No.of Employees:** 101 - 250 **Product Groups:** 35

Date of Accounts	Sep 11	Sep 10	Sep 09
Sales Turnover	65m	56m	N/A
Pre Tax Profit/Loss	3m	-1m	N/A
Working Capital	48m	40m	N/A
Fixed Assets	52m	47m	18m
Current Assets	59m	54m	N/A
Current Liabilities	6m	8m	N/A

Milbury Systems Ltd
Milbury Precast Lydney Industrial Estate, Harbour Road, Lydney, GL15 4EJ
Tel: 01594-847500 **Fax:** 01594-847501
E-mail: sales@milbury.com
Website: http://www.milbury.com
Bank(s): Lloyds
Directors: I. Barton (Co Sec), R. Honey (MD), S. Pearson (Jt MD), S. Pugh (Jt MD)
Immediate Holding Company: Eleco plc
Registration no: 03242959 **VAT No.:** GB 321 0083 23
Turnover: £5m - £10m **No.of Employees:** 11 - 20 **Product Groups:** 38, 42, 77

Date of Accounts	Jun 08	Dec 06	Dec 05
Sales Turnover	13915	N/A	N/A
Pre Tax Profit/Loss	1027	N/A	N/A
Working Capital	1129	969	652
Fixed Assets	895	570	452
Current Assets	3711	2328	1844
Current Liabilities	2583	1359	1193
Total Share Capital	10	10	10
ROCE% (Return on Capital Employed)	50.7		
ROT% (Return on Turnover)	7.4		

Watts Industrial Tyres plc
Church Road, Lydney, GL15 5EN
Tel: 01594-847100 **Fax:** 01594-842429
E-mail: info@interfit-uk.com
Website: http://www.industrialtyre.com
Directors: D. Rothwell (Co Sec), J. Mindermann (MD)
Managers: J. Pick (Mktg Serv Mgr)
Ultimate Holding Company: TRELLEBORG AB (SWEDEN)
Immediate Holding Company: TRELLEBORG INDUSTRIAL TYRES UK LIMITED
Registration no: 01434811 **Date established:** 1979 **Turnover:** £5m - £10m
No.of Employees: 51 - 100 **Product Groups:** 29, 39, 68

Date of Accounts	Dec 10	Dec 09	Dec 08
Sales Turnover	9m	7m	12m
Pre Tax Profit/Loss	804	489	914
Working Capital	4m	3m	3m
Fixed Assets	596	583	608
Current Assets	6m	5m	8m
Current Liabilities	233	121	238

Watts Urethane Products Ltd
Church Road, Lydney, GL15 5EN
Tel: 01594-847150 **Fax:** 01594-843586
E-mail: sales@wattspu.co.uk
Website: http://www.wattsurethane.com
Bank(s): National Westminster
Directors: J. Thurston (Ch), S. Mason (Fin), M. Fuller (Fin)
Ultimate Holding Company: WATTS OF LYDNEY GROUP LIMITED
Immediate Holding Company: WATTS URETHANE PRODUCTS LIMITED
Registration no: 00543805 **VAT No.:** GB 274 9312 41
Date established: 1955 **Turnover:** £2m - £5m **No.of Employees:** 21 - 50
Product Groups: 29

Date of Accounts	Dec 11	Dec 10	Dec 09
Sales Turnover	3m	4m	5m
Pre Tax Profit/Loss	7	72	80
Working Capital	161	160	106
Fixed Assets	174	168	155
Current Assets	2m	2m	2m
Current Liabilities	210	221	304

Mitcheldean

Cooper Security
Security House Vantage Point Business Village, Mitcheldean, GL17 0SZ
Tel: 01594-545400 **Fax:** 01594-545401
E-mail: sales@coopersecurity.co.uk
Website: http://www.coopersecurity.co.uk
Directors: T. Helz (Fin), P. Maxwell (Fin)
Managers: C. Robinson, S. Kendell (Buyer)
Immediate Holding Company: CLASSIC STEEL STOCKHOLDING LIMITED
Date established: 1997 **No.of Employees:** 51 - 100 **Product Groups:** 40, 66, 67

G & E Industrial Paint Finishers
Ladygrove Business Park Gloucester Road, Mitcheldean, GL17 0DS
Tel: 01452-831088 **Fax:** 01452-831088
Directors: G. Gardner (Prop)
Date established: 1989 **No.of Employees:** 1 - 10 **Product Groups:** 46, 48

Machines4sale
Knockalls Farm, Mitcheldean, GL17 0DP
Tel: 01594-542578
E-mail: team@machines4sale.com
Website: http://www.machines4sale.com
Directors: M. Mortimer (Ptnr)
Date established: 2007 **Turnover:** Up to £250,000
No.of Employees: 1 - 10 **Product Groups:** 67

Mechtech Valves Services
The Stenders, Mitcheldean, GL17 0ZE
Tel: 01594-541717 **Fax:** 01594-541716
Website: http://www.mechtechvalveservices.com
Directors: K. Roberts (Ptnr)
Immediate Holding Company: MVS (EXPORT) LTD
Registration no: 02098031 **Date established:** 2010
Turnover: £500,000 - £1m **No.of Employees:** 1 - 10 **Product Groups:** 36, 37, 38

Medekit
Building 8 Vantage Point Business Village, Mitcheldean, GL17 0DD
Tel: 01594-545100 **Fax:** 01594-545101
E-mail: phil.hughes@medikit.com
Website: http://www.medikit.com
Directors: M. Jaques (MD)
Managers: P. Hughes (Chief Mgr), L. Evans (Mgr), J. Ackroyd (Mktg Serv Mgr), L. Elsmore (Accounts), L. Powell (Chief Mgr)
Immediate Holding Company: MEDEKIT.COM LIMITED
Registration no: 03971430 **Date established:** 2000 **Turnover:** £1m - £2m
No.of Employees: 1 - 10 **Product Groups:** 61

Metric Co UK Ltd
6 Ladygrove Business Park Gloucester Road, Mitcheldean, GL17 0DS
Tel: 01452-830390 **Fax:** 01452-830690
E-mail: sales@metric-company.co.uk
Website: http://www.metric-company.co.uk
Directors: V. Budhia (MD)
Immediate Holding Company: METRIC COMPANY (UK) LIMITED
Registration no: 04576873 **Date established:** 2002
No.of Employees: 1 - 10 **Product Groups:** 38, 42

Date of Accounts	Oct 11	Oct 10	Oct 09
Working Capital	2	5	-1
Fixed Assets	1	1	2
Current Assets	34	25	15

Motor Transmission & Pumps Services
7 Ladygrove Business Park Gloucester Road, Mitcheldean, GL17 0DS
Tel: 01452-831019 **Fax:** 01452-831017
E-mail: info@mtpservices.co.uk
Website: http://www.mtpservices.co.uk
Directors: P. Starkey (Prop)
Date established: 1987 **No.of Employees:** 1 - 10 **Product Groups:** 35, 37, 40, 48, 67

Toolite Co.
Building 3 Unit 2 The Mews, Mitcheldean, GL17 0SL
Tel: 01594-544521 **Fax:** 01594-542552
E-mail: sales@toolite.org.uk
Website: http://www.toolite.org.uk
Directors: R. David (Prop)
VAT No.: GB 484 9137 10 **Date established:** 1986
Turnover: £500,000 - £1m **No.of Employees:** 1 - 10 **Product Groups:** 35

Moreton In Marsh

The Cotswold Casements
Cotswold Business Village London Road, Moreton In Marsh, GL56 0JQ
Tel: 01608-650568 **Fax:** 01608-651699
E-mail: info@cotswold-casements.co.uk
Website: http://www.cotswold-casements.co.uk
Bank(s): H S B C
Managers: T. Woskett (Chief Mgr)
Immediate Holding Company: COTSWOLD COFFEE COMPANY LTD
Registration no: 02821800 **VAT No.:** GB 662 8441 22
Date established: 1888 **Turnover:** £2m - £5m **No.of Employees:** 21 - 50
Product Groups: 35

Cotswold Seeds Ltd
Cotswold Business Village London Road, Moreton In Marsh, GL56 0JQ
Tel: 01608-652552 **Fax:** 01608-652256
E-mail: info@cotswoldseeds.com
Website: http://www.cotswoldseeds.com
Directors: I. Wilkinson (MD), C. Wilkinson (Fin)
Immediate Holding Company: COTSWOLD SEEDS LIMITED
Registration no: 01163604 **Date established:** 1974 **Turnover:** £1m - £2m
No.of Employees: 1 - 10 **Product Groups:** 02

Date of Accounts	Dec 11	Dec 10	Dec 09
Working Capital	957	638	329
Fixed Assets	420	381	378
Current Assets	1m	827	505

Cronexrabo Ltd
Unit 61 Northwick Business Centre Northwick Park, Blockley, Moreton In Marsh, GL56 9RF
Tel: 01386-700193 **Fax:** 01386-701069
E-mail: info@cronex.co.uk
Website: http://www.crabo.co.uk
Bank(s): Barclays
Directors: S. Frechette (MD)
Immediate Holding Company: CRONEXRABO LIMITED
Registration no: 01617553 **VAT No.:** 369 4527 14 **Date established:** 1982
Turnover: £500,000 - £1m **No.of Employees:** 11 - 20 **Product Groups:** 66

Date of Accounts	Apr 11	Apr 10	Apr 09
Working Capital	347	234	286
Fixed Assets	82	110	104
Current Assets	1m	851	771

Freezteq Products Ltd
88 Northwick Business Centre Blockley, Moreton In Marsh, GL56 9RF
Tel: 01386-701050 **Fax:** 01386-700007
E-mail: norman@freezteq.co.uk
Website: http://www.freezteq.co.uk
Directors: P. Fawdry (Fin)
Immediate Holding Company: FREEZTEQ PRODUCTS LIMITED
Registration no: 02796701 **VAT No.:** GB 630 6726 49
Date established: 1993 **Turnover:** Up to £250,000
No.of Employees: 1 - 10 **Product Groups:** 23

Date of Accounts	Oct 11	Oct 10	Oct 09
Working Capital	-5	-3	2
Fixed Assets	4	5	6
Current Assets	13	20	7

The Grtass Seed Store
Hill Farm Buildings Main Road, Oddington, Moreton In Marsh, GL56 0XW
Tel: 01451-830839
E-mail: info@thegrassseedstore.co.uk
Website: http://www.thegrassseedstore.co.uk
Directors: P. Lane (MD)
Immediate Holding Company: THE GRASS SEED STORE LTD
Registration no: 06448824 **Date established:** 2007
No.of Employees: 1 - 10 **Product Groups:** 02

Isl Cone Values Technology
Wolford Lodge Great Wolford Road, Moreton In Marsh, GL56 0PE
Tel: 01608-652123 **Fax:** 08704-602236
E-mail: info@conevalve.com
Website: http://www.conevalve.com
Directors: I. Semenenko (MD), L. Holmes (Fin)
Immediate Holding Company: IVAN SEMENENKO LIMITED
Registration no: 03079197 **Date established:** 1995
Turnover: Up to £250,000 **No.of Employees:** 1 - 10 **Product Groups:** 29, 41, 42, 46

Date of Accounts	Aug 11	Aug 10	Aug 09
Sales Turnover	142	57	64
Pre Tax Profit/Loss	53	12	-403
Working Capital	189	136	122
Fixed Assets	1	2	2
Current Assets	191	141	124
Current Liabilities	1	1	1

Kalend Ltd
Draycott Business Village Draycott Industrial Estate, Draycott, Moreton In Marsh, GL56 9JY
Tel: 01386-700075 **Fax:** 01386-701796
E-mail: enquiries@kalend.co.uk
Website: http://www.kalend.co.uk
Directors: E. Hardwick (Fin), D. Hardwick (MD)
Registration no: 03358761 **No.of Employees:** 1 - 10 **Product Groups:** 28, 49, 64, 65

Matcon Ltd
Matcon House London Road, Moreton In Marsh, GL56 0HJ
Tel: 01608-651666 **Fax:** 01608-651635
E-mail: charles.lee@matcon-cone.com
Website: http://www.matcon.com
Bank(s): Lloyds, 130 High Street, Cheltenham
Directors: J. Thompson (Co Sec), C. Lee (MD), P. Cooper (Dir), J. Aird (Ch)
Managers: J. Powell (Purch Mgr), K. Bridger (Mktg Serv Mgr), G. Blockson (Fin Mgr), T. Parsloe, S. Gibson (Mktg Serv Mgr), J. Thompson (Accounts)
Immediate Holding Company: MATCON GROUP LIMITED
Registration no: 02939693 **VAT No.:** GB 589 4920 79
Date established: 1994 **Turnover:** £10m - £20m
No.of Employees: 101 - 250 **Product Groups:** 27, 30, 36, 42, 45

Date of Accounts	Dec 07	Dec 06	Dec 05
Sales Turnover	14193	12910	12520
Pre Tax Profit/Loss	381	106	-178
Working Capital	712	487	518
Fixed Assets	1091	1106	1143
Current Assets	5355	4152	3771
Current Liabilities	4643	3665	3253
Total Share Capital	1485	1485	1485
ROCE% (Return on Capital Employed)	21.1	6.7	-10.7
ROT% (Return on Turnover)	2.7	0.8	-1.4

Monroe Brothers Ltd
PO Box 12, Moreton In Marsh, GL56 9YX
Tel: 01386-701777 **Fax:** 01386-701888
E-mail: alexia@monroebrothers.co.uk
Website: http://www.monroebrothers.co.uk
Directors: A. Monroe (Dir), C. Monroe (MD)
Immediate Holding Company: MONROE BROTHERS LTD.
Registration no: 03293973 **Date established:** 1996
Turnover: £250,000 - £500,000 **No.of Employees:** 1 - 10
Product Groups: 36, 38, 52, 84

Date of Accounts	Dec 10	Dec 08	Dec 07
Working Capital	27	14	-0
Fixed Assets	1	1	2
Current Assets	38	33	26

Northcot Brick
Station Road Blockley, Moreton In Marsh, GL56 9LH
Tel: 01386-700551 **Fax:** 01386-700852
E-mail: sales@northcotbrick.co.uk
Website: http://www.northcotbrick.co.uk
Bank(s): Barclays
Managers: D. Moss (Works Gen Mgr)
Ultimate Holding Company: E H SMITH HOLDINGS LTD
Immediate Holding Company: WESTHAVEN INVESTMENTS LTD
Registration no: 00494330 **Date established:** 1952 **Turnover:** £2m - £5m
No.of Employees: 21 - 50 **Product Groups:** 33

Northwick Fabrications
57 Northwick Business Centre Northwick Park, Blockley, Moreton In Marsh, GL56 9RF
Tel: 01386-700960 **Fax:** 01386-700960
Directors: T. Wilson (Prop)
Date established: 1974 **No.of Employees:** 1 - 10 **Product Groups:** 35, 42, 45

Spartal Ltd
Unit 69 Northwick Business Centre Northwick Park, Blockley, Moreton In Marsh, GL56 9RF
Tel: 01386-700898 **Fax:** 01386-701122
E-mail: richardevans@spartal.co.uk
Website: http://www.spartal.co.uk
Directors: R. Evans (Dir), S. Phillips (Sales)
Managers: J. Aubrey (Prod Mgr)
Ultimate Holding Company: SPARTAL HOLDINGS LIMITED
Immediate Holding Company: SPARTAL LIMITED
Registration no: 01551538 **Date established:** 1981
Turnover: £500,000 - £1m **No.of Employees:** 11 - 20
Product Groups: 30, 34, 35, 36, 40

Date of Accounts	Mar 12	Mar 11	Mar 10
Working Capital	231	207	191
Fixed Assets	39	37	35
Current Assets	616	612	551

Watsonian Squire Ltd
70 Northwick Business Centre Blockley, Moreton In Marsh, GL56 9RF
Tel: 01386-700907 **Fax:** 01386-700738
E-mail: sales@watsonian-squire.com
Website: http://www.watsonian-squire.com
Bank(s): Barclays Bank
Managers: R. Jones (Chief Mgr)
Immediate Holding Company: WATSONIAN SQUIRE LIMITED
Registration no: 02319399 **VAT No.:** 488 1034 36 **Date established:** 1988
Turnover: £1m - £2m **No.of Employees:** 11 - 20 **Product Groups:** 39, 40, 68

Date of Accounts	Mar 11	Mar 10	Mar 09
Sales Turnover	2m	2m	2m
Pre Tax Profit/Loss	-24	57	49
Working Capital	470	486	440
Fixed Assets	9	18	11
Current Assets	918	929	812
Current Liabilities	158	165	148

Newent

Andrew Marsham & Co.
Hill Cottage Cliffords Mesne, Newent, GL18 1JN
Tel: 01531-820330 **Fax:** 01531-822056
E-mail: andrewmarcham@btconnect.com
Directors: A. Marcham (Prop)
No.of Employees: 1 - 10 **Product Groups:** 35

Chainings Ltd
Pomona Works Newent Business Park, Newent, GL18 1DZ
Tel: 01531-822244 **Fax:** 01531-821555
E-mail: info@chainings.com
Website: http://www.chainings.com
Directors: P. Wattam (MD)
Immediate Holding Company: CHAININGS LIMITED
Registration no: 01769983 **Date established:** 1983
Turnover: £500,000 - £1m **No.of Employees:** 1 - 10 **Product Groups:** 23, 36, 39, 40, 42, 45

Date of Accounts	Feb 12	Feb 11	Feb 10
Working Capital	514	317	285
Fixed Assets	64	78	82
Current Assets	718	467	365

D F Cook Construction
Three Ashes Lane, Newent, GL18 1DF
Tel: 01531-828484 **Fax:** 01531-822609
E-mail: duncan@dfcook.co.uk
Website: http://www.dfcook.co.uk
Directors: D. Cook (Prop)
Date established: 2002 **No.of Employees:** 1 - 10 **Product Groups:** 35

Euroquip Newent Ltd
Strawberry Hill Business Park Strawberry Hill, Newent, GL18 1LH
Tel: 01531-820986 **Fax:** 01531-822025
E-mail: sales@euroquip.net
Website: http://www.euroquip.net
Managers: A. Beard (Mgr)
Immediate Holding Company: EUROQUIP NEWENT LTD
Registration no: 06126114 **Date established:** 2007
Turnover: £250,000 - £500,000 **No.of Employees:** 11 - 20
Product Groups: 39, 42, 45

Date of Accounts	Mar 11	Mar 10	Mar 09
Working Capital	-37	35	16
Fixed Assets	88	100	110
Current Assets	100	120	126

Ladder & Fencing Industries Newent Ltd
Horse Fair Lane, Newent, GL18 1RP
Tel: 01531-820541 **Fax:** 01531-821161
E-mail: david.walker@lfi-ladders.co.uk
Website: http://www.lfi-ladders.co.uk
Bank(s): Lloyds TSB Bank plc
Directors: B. Pinchin (Fin), D. Walker (Dir)
Managers: P. Dunphy, A. Roberts
Ultimate Holding Company: ROWAN (216) LIMITED
Immediate Holding Company: LADDER AND FENCING INDUSTRIES(NEWENT)LIMITED
Registration no: 00588937 **VAT No.:** GB 274 7976 01
Date established: 1957 **Turnover:** £2m - £5m **No.of Employees:** 21 - 50
Product Groups: 25, 30, 35, 39, 40, 45, 66

Date of Accounts	Jan 12	Jan 11	Jan 10
Working Capital	2m	2m	3m
Fixed Assets	2m	2m	2m
Current Assets	3m	3m	4m

Stonehouse

Auwell Electronics Ltd
Unit 16-17 Oldends Industrial Estate, Oldends, Stonehouse, GL10 3RQ
Tel: 01453-791111 **Fax:** 01453-791313
E-mail: susant@auwell.co.uk
Website: http://www.auwell.co.uk
Directors: S. Base (Dir), S. Twissell (Dir)
Immediate Holding Company: AUWELL ELECTRONICS LIMITED
Registration no: 01332531 **Date established:** 1977 **Turnover:** £1m - £2m
No.of Employees: 21 - 50 **Product Groups:** 27, 37, 48, 84

Date of Accounts	Mar 12	Mar 11	Mar 10
Working Capital	151	135	118
Fixed Assets	67	77	91
Current Assets	280	289	280

B I D Technology Ltd
Red Lodge Bonds Mill Bristol Road, Stonehouse, GL10 3RF
Tel: 01453-829595 **Fax:** 01225-851226
E-mail: jobs@bidtechnology.ltd.uk
Website: http://www.bidtechnology.ltd.uk
Directors: P. Clark (Dir)
Ultimate Holding Company: BAY GROUP LTD (BERMUDA)
Immediate Holding Company: B.I.D. TECHNOLOGY LIMITED
Registration no: 02916597 **VAT No.:** GB 639 4495 95
Date established: 1994 **Turnover:** £1m - £2m **No.of Employees:** 1 - 10
Product Groups: 80

Date of Accounts	Apr 11	Apr 10	Apr 09
Working Capital	-8	3	-3
Fixed Assets	1	2	4
Current Assets	14	59	143

C & G Services Ltd
Unit 201 Sperry Way, Stonehouse, GL10 3UT
Tel: 01453-826781 **Fax:** 01453-792123
E-mail: bob.oldmeadow@cgserv.com
Website: http://www.gettrained.co.uk
Directors: J. Oldmeadow (Fin), R. Oldmeadow (MD)
Immediate Holding Company: C & G SERVICES (EUROPE) LIMITED
Registration no: 03555819 **Date established:** 1998
Turnover: £500,000 - £1m **No.of Employees:** 21 - 50
Product Groups: 34, 38, 45, 52, 86

Date of Accounts	Apr 11	Apr 10	Apr 09
Working Capital	384	385	292
Fixed Assets	795	801	821
Current Assets	676	654	606

C T L Manufacturing
Brunel Court Stroudwater Business Park, Stonehouse, GL10 3SW
Tel: 01453-794100 **Fax:** 01453-825424
Website: http://www.abacus.co.uk
Directors: S. Fox (MD)
Managers: K. Wilcocks (Sales & Mktg Mg), R. Auty (Personnel)
Ultimate Holding Company: ASTRAZENECA PLC
Immediate Holding Company: ABACUS POLAR HOLDINGS LTD
Registration no: 01480123 **Date established:** 1980
Turnover: £20m - £50m **No.of Employees:** 1 - 10 **Product Groups:** 67

Cee Vee
Unit 27 Upper Mills Trading Estate, Stonehouse, GL10 2BJ
Tel: 01453-821666 **Fax:** 01453-822298
E-mail: sales@cee-vee.co.uk
Website: http://www.cee-vee.co.uk
Directors: J. Apperly (MD), A. Parnell (Fin)
Immediate Holding Company: CEE VEE LIMITED
Registration no: 03659315 **Date established:** 1998
No.of Employees: 1 - 10 **Product Groups:** 29, 30, 33, 36, 38, 40, 67

Date of Accounts	Mar 12	Mar 11	Mar 10
Working Capital	80	77	71
Fixed Assets	2	2	3
Current Assets	188	151	142

Ceramet Plasma Coatings Ltd
Ryeford Industrial Estate Ryeford, Stonehouse, GL10 2LA
Tel: 01453-828416 **Fax:** 01453-823068
E-mail: sales@ceramet.co.uk
Website: http://www.ceramet.co.uk
Bank(s): Lloyds TSB Bank plc
Directors: B. Anderson (MD), D. Sleight (Dir), J. Grime (Co Sec), B. Anderson (Dir)
Managers: R. Bryan ()
Ultimate Holding Company: BODYCOTE PLC
Immediate Holding Company: CERAMET PLASMA COATINGS LIMITED
Registration no: 01904701 **Date established:** 1985 **Turnover:** £1m - £2m
No.of Employees: 11 - 20 **Product Groups:** 48

Date of Accounts	Dec 09	Dec 07	Dec 06
Sales Turnover	N/A	N/A	1m
Pre Tax Profit/Loss	N/A	N/A	701
Working Capital	2	2m	2m
Current Assets	2	2m	2m

Circonix (a division of Auwell Electronics Ltd)
Unit 16-17 Oldends Lane, Industrial Estate, Stonehouse, GL10 3RQ
Tel: 01453-791111 **Fax:** 01453-791313
E-mail: enquiries@auwell.co.uk
Website: http://www.auwell.co.uk
Bank(s): HSBC Bank plc
Directors: S. Jarvis (Fab), S. Base (Ch)
Managers: S. Twissell (Accounts)
Immediate Holding Company: Auwell Electronics Ltd
Registration no: 01415881 **Turnover:** £1m - £2m
No.of Employees: 21 - 50 **Product Groups:** 37, 38, 44, 84

Date of Accounts	Mar 04	Mar 03	Mar 02
Working Capital	5	5	5
Current Assets	5	5	5

Coburn Fasteners Ltd
Unit 3 Springfield Business Centre Brunel Way, Stroudwater Business Park, Stonehouse, GL10 3SX
Tel: 01453-828515 **Fax:** 01453-791040
E-mail: andy@coburnfasteners.co.uk
Website: http://www.coburnfasteners.co.uk
Directors: A. Coburn (MD)
Immediate Holding Company: COBURN FASTENERS LIMITED
Registration no: 05218232 **VAT No.:** GB 448 3568 17
Date established: 2004 **Turnover:** Up to £250,000
No.of Employees: 1 - 10 **Product Groups:** 66

Date of Accounts	Dec 11	Dec 10	Dec 09
Working Capital	275	220	184
Fixed Assets	12	13	13
Current Assets	501	365	264

Cotswold Property Management Services Ltd
Bonds Mill Bristol Road, Stonehouse, GL10 3RF
Tel: 01453-825694 **Fax:** 01453-827359
E-mail: admin@cpmsltd.co.uk
Website: http://www.cpmsltd.co.uk
Directors: E. Mcdougall (MD), R. McDougall (Co Sec)
Immediate Holding Company: COTSWOLD PROPERTY MANAGEMENT SERVICES LIMITED
Registration no: 04855944 **Date established:** 2003
Turnover: Up to £250,000 **No.of Employees:** 1 - 10 **Product Groups:** 80

Date of Accounts	Aug 11	Aug 10	Aug 09
Sales Turnover	N/A	N/A	160
Pre Tax Profit/Loss	N/A	N/A	47
Working Capital	1	-5	-0
Fixed Assets	11	15	8
Current Assets	34	34	30
Current Liabilities	N/A	N/A	26

D K M Sheet Metal Co. Ltd
Unit 9 Oldends Industrial Estate Oldends, Stonehouse, GL10 3RQ
Tel: 01453-827661 **Fax:** 01453-824094
E-mail: mnorton@dkmsheetmetal.freeserve.co.uk
Website: http://www.dkmsheetmetal.co.uk
Bank(s): HSBC Bank plc
Directors: S. Hearn (MD)
Ultimate Holding Company: DKM SHEET METAL HOLDINGS LIMITED
Immediate Holding Company: DKM SHEET METAL COMPANY LIMITED
Registration no: 01872575 **VAT No.:** GB 326 2594 55
Date established: 1984 **Turnover:** £250,000 - £500,000
No.of Employees: 21 - 50 **Product Groups:** 48

Date of Accounts	Jan 12	Jan 11	Jan 10
Working Capital	312	216	254
Fixed Assets	264	357	147
Current Assets	779	645	536

Delphi Diesel Systems
Brunel Way Stroudwater Business Park, Stonehouse, GL10 3SX
Tel: 01453-828282 **Fax:** 01453-794302
E-mail: marketing@delphi.com
Website: http://www.delphi.com
Bank(s): Barclays, Newcastle, Staffs
Managers: M. Dillon (Sales & Mktg Mg), N. Mann (Personnel), S. Lacy (Plant), S. Knight (Buyer)
Immediate Holding Company: LIGHTSPEED CONSTRUCTION LIMITED
Registration no: 03292083 **Date established:** 2011
No.of Employees: 501 - 1000 **Product Groups:** 39

Date of Accounts	Jan 11	Jan 10	Jan 09
Working Capital	82	70	69
Fixed Assets	17	18	22
Current Assets	176	138	158

Designex Cabinets Ltd
Unit 2 Severn Vale Building Lower Mills Road, Bridgend, Stonehouse, GL10 2BB
Tel: 01453-826868 **Fax:** 01453-826868
E-mail: sales@designex-cabinets.co.uk
Website: http://www.designex-cabinets.co.uk
Directors: B. Newman (Fin), T. Farr (Dir)
Immediate Holding Company: DESIGNEX CABINETS LIMITED
Registration no: 04486763 **VAT No.:** GB 794 0641 13
Date established: 2002 **Turnover:** £250,000 - £500,000
No.of Employees: 1 - 10 **Product Groups:** 26, 49, 61, 67

Date of Accounts	Jun 11	Jun 10	Jun 09
Working Capital	25	24	16
Fixed Assets	4	3	4
Current Assets	50	44	35

Gloucester Composites
Fox House Stonedale Road, Stonehouse, GL10 3SA
Tel: 01453-791616 **Fax:** 01453-791516
E-mail: purchaseadmin@gloucestercomposites.com
Website: http://www.gloucestercomposites.com
Directors: B. Hesketh (Co Sec), P. Lawrence (Dir)
Managers: B. Ellis (Prod Mgr), B. Hale (Reg Mgr)
Ultimate Holding Company: ACSTK HOLDINGS
Immediate Holding Company: GLOUCESTER COMPOSITES LIMITED
Registration no: 02868648 **Date established:** 1993
No.of Employees: 21 - 50 **Product Groups:** 30, 31, 33, 35, 37, 39, 42, 66

Date of Accounts	Dec 11	Dec 10	Dec 09
Pre Tax Profit/Loss	N/A	N/A	30
Working Capital	2m	3m	2m
Fixed Assets	730	835	943
Current Assets	4m	4m	3m
Current Liabilities	N/A	N/A	191

Handling Techniques Ltd
Unit 30-31upper Mills Trading Estate Bristol Road, Stonehouse, GL10 2BJ
Tel: 01453-826290 **Fax:** 01453-823994
E-mail: sales@handlingtechniques.co.uk
Website: http://www.handlingtechniques.co.uk
Directors: D. Howell (MD)
Immediate Holding Company: HANDLING TECHNIQUES LIMITED
Registration no: 01190841 **VAT No.:** 366 2181 52 **Date established:** 1974
Turnover: £250,000 - £500,000 **No.of Employees:** 1 - 10
Product Groups: 45, 84

Date of Accounts	Jun 11	Jun 10	Jun 09
Working Capital	77	99	129
Fixed Assets	46	48	52
Current Assets	583	436	430

International Intelligence Limited Intelligent (UK Holdings) Limited
Eastington Bridge, Stonehouse, GL10 3SQ
Tel: 01453-791444 **Fax:** 01453-791550
E-mail: bomberg@int-int.co.uk
Website: http://www.int-int.co.uk
Directors: R. Attwater (Dir)
Managers: A. Bomberg (Ops Mgr)
Registration no: 04483341 **Turnover:** £2m - £5m
No.of Employees: 11 - 20 **Product Groups:** 80, 81, 82

Date of Accounts	Jun 08	Jun 07	Jun 06
Sales Turnover	171	89	54
Pre Tax Profit/Loss	-1	-1	-23
Working Capital	-27	-15	-8
Fixed Assets	15	5	5
Current Assets	7	8	14
Current Liabilities	34	23	23
ROCE% (Return on Capital Employed)	10.9	14.3	600.0
ROT% (Return on Turnover)	-0.7	-1.7	-42.9

Lady Clare Ltd
Oldends Lane Industrial Estate Oldends, Stonehouse, GL10 3RQ
Tel: 01453-824482 **Fax:** 01453-827855
E-mail: info@lady-clare.com
Website: http://www.lady-clare.com
Bank(s): Lloyds TSB Bank plc
Directors: S. Moreland (MD)
Ultimate Holding Company: MORELAND (HOLDINGS) LIMITED
Immediate Holding Company: LADY CLARE LIMITED
Registration no: 00408870 **VAT No.:** GB 114 1300 41
Date established: 1946 **Turnover:** £1m - £2m **No.of Employees:** 11 - 20
Product Groups: 24, 25, 30

Date of Accounts	Dec 11	Dec 10	Dec 09
Working Capital	285	325	392
Fixed Assets	31	36	27
Current Assets	483	548	555

R McMahon Engineering Ltd
Unit 5 Oldends Industrial Estate Oldends, Stonehouse, GL10 3RQ
Tel: 01453-828666 **Fax:** 01453-828360
E-mail: info@mcmahon-engineering.com
Website: http://www.mcmahon-engineering.co.uk
Directors: C. Tennant (Fin), H. Tennant (MD)
Immediate Holding Company: R. MCMAHON ENGINEERING LIMITED
Registration no: 01169977 **VAT No.:** GB 276 3460 44
Date established: 1974 **Turnover:** £500,000 - £1m
No.of Employees: 1 - 10 **Product Groups:** 38, 80

Date of Accounts	May 12	May 11	May 10
Working Capital	-65	-88	-96
Fixed Assets	121	140	164
Current Assets	76	59	56

N O V Downhole
Oldends Industrial Estate Oldends, Stonehouse, GL10 3RQ
Tel: 01453-853000 **Fax:** 01453-825833
Website: http://www.nov.com
Directors: G. Richie (Fin)
Managers: A. Jenning (I.T. Exec), S. Coulter (Personnel), P. Smith (Tech Serv Mgr), J. Shipman (Purch Mgr), F. Hampton (Chief Mgr)
Ultimate Holding Company: GRANT PRIDECO INC (USA)
Immediate Holding Company: REEDHYCALOG UK LIMITED
Registration no: FC020107 **Date established:** 1997
Turnover: £125m - £250m **No.of Employees:** 251 - 500
Product Groups: 36

On 3 Ltd
Unit 3 Quedgeley Trading Estate East, Haresfield, Stonehouse, GL10 3EX
Tel: 08450-612333 **Fax:** 08450-612334
E-mail: info@onthree.co.uk
Website: http://www.onthree.co.uk
Directors: K. Scammell (Fin)
Immediate Holding Company: ON3 LIMITED
Registration no: 04653288 **Date established:** 2003
No.of Employees: 1 - 10 **Product Groups:** 35, 39, 45

Date of Accounts	Jan 11	Jan 10	Jan 09
Working Capital	-28	-30	-37
Fixed Assets	81	73	118
Current Assets	115	130	195

Roots Systems Ltd
Upper Mills Trading Estate Bristol Road, Stonehouse, GL10 2BJ
Tel: 01453-826581 **Fax:** 01453-826122
E-mail: info@roots-blowers.com
Website: http://www.roots-blowers.com
Bank(s): Barclays, Newton Abbott
Directors: G. Hook (MD)
Managers: N. Dolphin (Sales Prom Mgr)
Ultimate Holding Company: ROTOLOK (HOLDINGS) LIMITED
Immediate Holding Company: ROOTS SYSTEMS LIMITED
Registration no: 01676736 **VAT No.:** GB 408 4798 23
Date established: 1982 **Turnover:** £2m - £5m **No.of Employees:** 21 - 50
Product Groups: 40

Date of Accounts	May 11	May 10	May 09
Working Capital	2m	2m	2m
Fixed Assets	442	485	524
Current Assets	4m	3m	3m

Rospen Industries
Unit 15 Oldends Industrial Estate Oldends, Stonehouse, GL10 3RQ
Tel: 01453-825212 **Fax:** 01453-828279
E-mail: enquiries@rospen.com
Website: http://www.rospen.com
Bank(s): The Royal Bank of Scotland
Directors: T. Mcgeever (MD)
Immediate Holding Company: ROSPEN INDUSTRIES LIMITED
Registration no: 05841106 **VAT No.:** GB 359 2554 28
Date established: 2006 **Turnover:** £2m - £5m **No.of Employees:** 21 - 50
Product Groups: 37, 38, 46

Sharetree Ltd
Unit 3 Meadow Mill Eastington Trading Estate Churchend, Eastington, Stonehouse, GL10 3RZ
Tel: 01453-828642 **Fax:** 01453-828076
E-mail: sales@sharetree.co.uk
Website: http://www.sharetree.com
Directors: M. Coleman (MD)
Immediate Holding Company: SHARETREE LIMITED
Registration no: 05133619 **VAT No.:** GB 821 8207 48
Date established: 2004 **Turnover:** £2m - £5m **No.of Employees:** 1 - 10
Product Groups: 37, 38, 83, 84, 85

Date of Accounts	May 12	May 11	May 10
Working Capital	256	176	86
Fixed Assets	47	52	81
Current Assets	564	433	347

Stonehouse Paper & Bag Mills Ltd
Lower Mills, Stonehouse, GL10 2BD
Tel: 01453-822173 **Fax:** 01453-822174
E-mail: stonehousepaper@aol.com
Website: http://www.spbm.com
Directors: J. Daniels (Dir)
Immediate Holding Company: STONEHOUSE PAPER & BAG MILLS LIMITED
Registration no: 00182580 **VAT No.:** GB 274 8728 15 0000
Date established: 2022 **Turnover:** £1m - £2m **No.of Employees:** 11 - 20
Product Groups: 24, 27, 28, 42, 48

Date of Accounts	Mar 12	Mar 11	Mar 10
Working Capital	521	594	515
Fixed Assets	332	359	425
Current Assets	726	817	673

Storage & Interior Services Ltd
Unit 12 Springfield Business Centre Brunel Way, Stroudwater Business Park, Stonehouse, GL10 3SX
Tel: 01453-827210 **Fax:** 01453-822209
E-mail: tonygover@storage-interior.co.uk
Website: http://www.storage-interior.co.uk

Directors: A. Gover (Dir)
Immediate Holding Company: STORAGE & INTERIOR SERVICES LIMITED
Registration no: 02884394 **Date established:** 1994
No.of Employees: 1 - 10 **Product Groups:** 35, 42, 45

Stroud Sewing Services
Unit 44 Upper Mills Trading Estate, Stonehouse, GL10 2BJ
Tel: 01453-791487 **Fax:** 01453-791487
E-mail: john.dymond@tiscali.co.uk
Website: http://www.stroudsewingservices.co.uk
Directors: J. Dymond (Ptnr)
Turnover: £250,000 - £500,000 **No.of Employees:** 1 - 10
Product Groups: 24

Swift Fasteners Ltd
Unit 20 Oldends Industrial Estate Oldends, Stonehouse, GL10 3RQ
Tel: 01453-825222 **Fax:** 01453-827824
E-mail: sales@swift-fasteners-ltd.co.uk
Website: http://www.swift-fasteners-ltd.co.uk
Directors: J. Brackstone (Fin)
Immediate Holding Company: SWIFT FASTENERS LIMITED
Registration no: 01616423 **Date established:** 1982 **Turnover:** £1m - £2m
No.of Employees: 1 - 10 **Product Groups:** 35

Date of Accounts	Jan 11	Jan 10	Jan 09
Working Capital	-18	41	-22
Fixed Assets	64	76	92
Current Assets	160	255	213

Utility Detection Specialists
Whispers St Cyrils Road, Stonehouse, GL10 2QG
Tel: 01453-885981 **Fax:** 01453-885981
E-mail: nigel@utilitydetection.freeserve.co.uk
No.of Employees: 1 - 10 **Product Groups:** 38, 80, 81

Valvelink UK Ltd
17 Cotswold Green, Stonehouse, GL10 2ES
Tel: 01453-822222 **Fax:** 01453- 821111
E-mail: mw@valvelinkuk.freeserve.co.uk
Website: http://www.valvelinkuk.freeserve.co.uk
Directors: M. Weldt (MD), S. Weldt (Fin)
Immediate Holding Company: VALVELINK (UK) LTD.
Registration no: 03605027 **Date established:** 1998
No.of Employees: 1 - 10 **Product Groups:** 36, 37, 38

Date of Accounts	Mar 08	Mar 07	Mar 06
Working Capital	61	47	41
Fixed Assets	1	2	2
Current Assets	128	105	107
Current Liabilities	67	58	66

Vital Signs Ltd (Visual Technology)
Unit 2 Oldends Industrial Estate, Oldends, Stonehouse, GL10 3RQ
Tel: 01453-822286 **Fax:** 01453-828126
E-mail: info@vitalsigns.co.uk
Website: http://www.vitalsigns.co.uk
Bank(s): Royal Bank of Scotland
Directors: K. Hanman (MD)
Ultimate Holding Company: GENERAL ELECTRIC COMPANY (USA)
Immediate Holding Company: VITAL SIGNS LIMITED
Registration no: 02717063 **VAT No.:** GB 701 1827 75
Date established: 1992 **Turnover:** £250,000 - £500,000
No.of Employees: 11 - 20 **Product Groups:** 26, 28, 30, 48, 49, 52

Date of Accounts	Dec 11	Dec 10	Dec 09
Sales Turnover	N/A	3m	6m
Pre Tax Profit/Loss	25	2m	903
Working Capital	550	10m	8m
Current Assets	550	10m	9m
Current Liabilities	N/A	283	578

Warlord Contract Carpets Ltd
Stanley Mills, Stonehouse, GL10 3HQ
Tel: 01453-821800 **Fax:** 01453-791167
E-mail: sales@warlordcarpets.co.uk
Website: http://www.warlordcarpets.co.uk
Directors: R. Carr (Dir), N. Stroud (Tech Serv), M. Holroyd (Fab), J. May (Ch)
Immediate Holding Company: Peter Griffiths (Stanley Mills) Ltd
Registration no: 02539133 **VAT No.:** GB 484 7373 08
Date established: 1990 **Turnover:** £2m - £5m **No.of Employees:** 1 - 10
Product Groups: 23, 63

Date of Accounts	Mar 06	Mar 05	Mar 04
Working Capital	181	181	21
Fixed Assets	N/A	N/A	21
Current Assets	181	181	786

A & D Webb Metal Polishing Specialists
3 Standard Works Orchard Place, Stonehouse, GL10 2PL
Tel: 01453-825573 **Fax:** 01453-825573
E-mail: travis@adwebbmetalpolishers.com
Website: http://www.adwebbmetalpolishers.com
Directors: T. Noblet (Dir)
Date established: 1979 **Turnover:** Up to £250,000
No.of Employees: 1 - 10 **Product Groups:** 48

Stroud

A & K Metal Polishing
Bourne Mills London Road, Brimscombe, Stroud, GL5 2TA
Tel: 01453-883747 **Fax:** 01453-883747
Directors: A. Dick (Prop)
Date established: 1979 **Turnover:** Up to £250,000
No.of Employees: 1 - 10 **Product Groups:** 48

Aquamat 4 Seasons
Unit 8g Chalford Industrial Estate Chalford, Stroud, GL6 8NT
Tel: 01453-884411 **Fax:** 01453-884499
E-mail: sales@aquamatcovers.co.uk
Website: http://www.aquamat4seasons.co.uk
Directors: M. Goodall (Dir)
Immediate Holding Company: AQUATECH UK LTD
Registration no: 03122880 **VAT No.:** GB 641 9832 22
Date established: 1995 **Turnover:** £500,000 - £1m
No.of Employees: 1 - 10 **Product Groups:** 30, 42

Date of Accounts	Jan 06
Working Capital	-113
Current Assets	6
Current Liabilities	118
Total Share Capital	5

Architectural & Allied Model Makers
Edge Hill St Marys, Chalford, Stroud, GL6 8QB
Tel: 01453-887788 **Fax:** 01453-887788
E-mail: coxrac@aol.com
Website: http://www.aamodelmakers.com
Directors: R. Cox (Prop)
No.of Employees: 1 - 10 **Product Groups:** 49, 84

Avon Scientific
Unit 101 Aston Down Frampton Mansell, Stroud, GL6 8GA
Tel: 01285-760199 **Fax:** 08452-301207
E-mail: sales@avonsci.co.uk
Website: http://www.avonsci.co.uk
Directors: S. Blundell (Dir)
Registration no: 03000797 **Turnover:** £500,000 - £1m
No.of Employees: 1 - 10 **Product Groups:** 30

Date of Accounts	Jan 09	Jan 08	Jan 07
Sales Turnover	N/A	N/A	712
Pre Tax Profit/Loss	N/A	N/A	78
Working Capital	-1	10	-9
Fixed Assets	24	26	26
Current Assets	146	198	133
Current Liabilities	147	188	142
Total Share Capital	1	1	1
ROCE% (Return on Capital Employed)			466.8
ROT% (Return on Turnover)			11.0

B P I Recycle Products
Unit N Bath Road Trading Estate, Lightpill, Stroud, GL5 3QF
Tel: 01453-751471 **Fax:** 01453-752843
E-mail: miketyre@bpipoly.com
Website: http://www.bpipoly.com
Bank(s): Clydesdale Bank PLC
Directors: M. Tyre (Dir), A. Thorburn (Fin)
Managers: D. Chapman (I.T. Exec), N. Jones (Personnel)
Immediate Holding Company: BRITISH POLYTHENE INDUSTRIES P.L.C.
Registration no: 00350729 **No.of Employees:** 51 - 100
Product Groups: 30

Bond Fabrications
Unit E1 Bath Road Trading Estate, Lightpill, Stroud, GL5 3QF
Tel: 01453-767171 **Fax:** 01453-767177
E-mail: enquiries@bondfabrications.co.uk
Website: http://www.bondfabrications.co.uk
Directors: N. Acland (Prop)
No.of Employees: 1 - 10 **Product Groups:** 24, 35, 49

Bottle Green Drinks Co.
Frogmarsh Mill South Woodchester, Stroud, GL5 5ET
Tel: 01453-872882 **Fax:** 01453-872188
E-mail: simonspeers@bottlegreen.co.uk
Website: http://www.bottlegreen.co.uk
Directors: N. Clay (Fin), N. Briggs Evison (Co Sec), N. Clay (Fin), S. Speers (Dir)
Managers: M. Langley (Mktg Serv Mgr)
Immediate Holding Company: CAUSEWAY SHELF COMPANY (NO.3) LIMITED
Registration no: 06043801 **Date established:** 2007 **Turnover:** £5m - £10m
No.of Employees: 21 - 50 **Product Groups:** 20, 21, 62, 84

Brimscombe Platers Ltd
Lower Mills Brimscombe, Stroud, GL5 2SD
Tel: 01453-883352 **Fax:** 01453-883352
Directors: J. Bishop (Fin), K. Bishop (MD)
Immediate Holding Company: BRIMSCOMBE PLATERS LIMITED
Registration no: 03648489 **Date established:** 1998
No.of Employees: 1 - 10 **Product Groups:** 46, 48

Date of Accounts	Aug 11	Aug 10	Aug 09
Working Capital	78	76	57
Fixed Assets	29	27	16
Current Assets	118	116	102

Burkert Controlmatics Ltd
Fluid Control Centre Brimscombe Port Business Park, Brimscombe, Stroud, GL5 2QQ
Tel: 01453-731353 **Fax:** 01453-731343
E-mail: sales.uk@burkert.com
Website: http://www.burkert.co.uk
Bank(s): Barclays, Stroud
Directors: D. Leonard (Co Sec)
Managers: P. Trevitt (Chief Mgr)
Ultimate Holding Company: BURKERT CONTROMATIC AG (SWITZERLAND)
Immediate Holding Company: BURKERT CONTROMATIC LIMITED
Registration no: 00831741 **VAT No.:** GB 274 1309 70
Date established: 1964 **Turnover:** £2m - £5m **No.of Employees:** 21 - 50
Product Groups: 36, 38, 39, 40, 46, 84

Date of Accounts	Dec 11	Dec 10	Dec 09
Pre Tax Profit/Loss	N/A	N/A	-257
Working Capital	2m	2m	1m
Fixed Assets	98	104	82
Current Assets	3m	3m	2m
Current Liabilities	N/A	N/A	331

C Burr
unit 10 Hope Mills Business Centre, Brimscombe, Stroud, GL5 2SE.
Tel: 01453-889 683 **Fax:** 020-7358 5225
E-mail: info@coryburr.com
Website: http://www.coryburr.com
Managers: C. Burr (Sales Admin)
Turnover: Up to £250,000 **No.of Employees:** 1 - 10 **Product Groups:** 35, 44, 48, 66

Cantilever Bar Systems Ltd
The Chapel London Road, Brimscombe, Stroud, GL5 2SA
Tel: 01453-732040 **Fax:** 01453-886906
E-mail: caroline.craven@cantileverbars.com
Website: http://www.cantileverbars.com
Directors: S. Knowles (Fin), C. Craven (MD)
Immediate Holding Company: CANTILEVER BAR SYSTEMS LIMITED
Registration no: 02622453 **Date established:** 1991 **Turnover:** £1m - £2m
No.of Employees: 1 - 10 **Product Groups:** 26, 40, 41, 52, 67, 69

Date of Accounts	Jun 11	Jun 10	Jun 09
Working Capital	271	232	54
Fixed Assets	81	94	88
Current Assets	642	779	413

Chalford Building Supplies Ltd
Belvedere Mill Chalford Industrial Estate, Chalford, Stroud, GL6 8NT
Tel: 01453-732600 **Fax:** 01453-884776
E-mail: sales@chalfordbuilding.co.uk
Website: http://www.chalford.oxfree.com
Bank(s): Bank of Wales PLC
Directors: M. Creed (Dir)
Managers: C. Hope (Comptroller)
Immediate Holding Company: CHALFORD BUILDING SUPPLIES LIMITED
Registration no: 01162203 **VAT No.:** GB 276 3361 46
Date established: 1974 **Turnover:** £1m - £2m **No.of Employees:** 21 - 50
Product Groups: 39, 66

Date of Accounts	Apr 11	Apr 10	Apr 09
Working Capital	575	497	408
Fixed Assets	1m	2m	2m
Current Assets	1m	1m	870

Cristie Software
New Mill Chestnut Lane, Stroud, GL5 3EH
Tel: 01453-847000 **Fax:** 01453-847001
E-mail: sales@cristie.com
Website: http://www.cristie.com
Bank(s): Bank of Scotland
Directors: B. Smith (Sales), I. Cameron (MD)
Managers: N. Schofield (Mktg Serv Mgr)
Immediate Holding Company: CRISTIE DATA LIMITED
Registration no: 03457111 **VAT No.:** GB 709 4289 14
Date established: 1997 **Turnover:** £2m - £5m **No.of Employees:** 51 - 100
Product Groups: 44

Date of Accounts	Dec 11	Dec 10	Dec 09
Sales Turnover	5m	4m	4m
Pre Tax Profit/Loss	190	202	167
Working Capital	575	448	950
Fixed Assets	40	74	78
Current Assets	2m	1m	2m
Current Liabilities	434	326	328

Cumberland Europe Ltd
Daniels Industrial Estate 104 Bath Road, Stroud, GL5 3TJ
Tel: 01453-768980 **Fax:** 01453-768990
E-mail: europeansales@cumberland-plastics.com
Website: http://www.cumberland-plastics.com
Directors: M. Santoni (Co Sec)
Immediate Holding Company: CUMBERLAND EUROPE LIMITED
Registration no: 03821314 **VAT No.:** GB 741 7953 12
Date established: 1999 **Turnover:** £1m - £2m **No.of Employees:** 1 - 10
Product Groups: 42

Date of Accounts	Dec 11	Dec 10	Dec 09
Working Capital	-2m	-2m	-1m
Fixed Assets	N/A	N/A	1
Current Assets	376	850	599

D M Foundries Ltd
Stafford Mill London Road, Thrupp, Stroud, GL5 2AZ
Tel: 01453-763325 **Fax:** 01453-753253
E-mail: info@dmfoundries.plus.com
Website: http://www.dmfoundries.co.uk
Bank(s): National Westminster Bank Plc
Directors: P. Morris (Ptnr), A. Morris (MD)
Immediate Holding Company: D.M. FOUNDRIES LIMITED
Registration no: 01625660 **VAT No.:** GB 535 6362 39
Date established: 1982 **Turnover:** £1m - £2m **No.of Employees:** 21 - 50
Product Groups: 34, 48, 66

Date of Accounts	Dec 11	Dec 10	Dec 09
Working Capital	352	415	412
Fixed Assets	327	334	338
Current Assets	488	515	506

Danarm Machinery Ltd
Unit 1 Gigg Mill Old Bristol Road, Nailsworth, Stroud, GL6 0JP
Tel: 01453-835577 **Fax:** 01453-765553
E-mail: info@danarm.com
Website: http://www.danarm.com
Directors: K. Blanch (MD)
Immediate Holding Company: DANARM MACHINERY LIMITED
Registration no: 03883770 **VAT No.:** GB 576 2398 04
Date established: 1999 **Turnover:** £1m - £2m **No.of Employees:** 1 - 10
Product Groups: 41, 61

Date of Accounts	Dec 11	Mar 10	Dec 09
Working Capital	415	423	415
Fixed Assets	N/A	N/A	2
Current Assets	438	437	469

Dietary Needs Direct
2 Bedford Street, Stroud, GL5 1AY
Tel: 01453-790999 **Fax:** 01453-751 402
E-mail: info@dietaryneedsdirect.co.uk
Website: http://www.dietaryneedsdirect.co.uk
Managers: R. Hill (Mgr)
Date established: 2001 **Turnover:** Up to £250,000
No.of Employees: 1 - 10 **Product Groups:** 20

Diptech UK Ltd
Cotswold Villa All Saints Road, Stroud, GL5 1TT
Tel: 01453-752597 **Fax:** 01453-752654
E-mail: info@diptech.co.uk
Website: http://www.diptech.co.uk
Directors: B. Harrison (Dir)
Immediate Holding Company: DIPTECH (UK) LIMITED
Registration no: 02687096 **VAT No.:** GB 576 3492 07
Date established: 1992 **Turnover:** £500,000 - £1m
No.of Employees: 1 - 10 **Product Groups:** 29, 42, 43, 46, 66

Date of Accounts	Mar 11	Mar 10	Mar 09
Working Capital	-17	-16	-24
Fixed Assets	1	1	1
Current Assets	10	9	3

Exled Ltd
Phoenix Mill Phoenix Works London Road, Stroud, GL5 2BU
Tel: 01453-756361
E-mail: sales@exled.co.uk
Website: http://www.led-lightbulbs.co.uk
Directors: A. Jones (Fin), M. Renecle (MD)
Immediate Holding Company: EXLED LIMITED
Registration no: 05265846 **Date established:** 2004
No.of Employees: 11 - 20 **Product Groups:** 37, 67

Date of Accounts	Mar 11	Mar 10	Mar 09
Working Capital	426	335	247
Fixed Assets	21	20	25

see next page

Exled Ltd - *Cont'd*

Current Assets	578	493	384

1st Fire Solutions Ltd 0

PO Box 231, Stroud, GL6 6ZQ
Tel: 0800-781 0019
E-mail: info@1stfiresolutions.co.uk
Website: http://www.1stfiresolutions.co.uk
Directors: S. Price (Fin), J. Price (MD)
Immediate Holding Company: 1ST FIRE SOLUTIONS LTD
Registration no: 04870853 **Date established:** 2003
No.of Employees: 1 - 10 **Product Groups:** 40, 49, 52, 67, 86

Date of Accounts	Sep 11	Sep 10	Sep 09
Working Capital	19	15	11
Fixed Assets	9	12	3
Current Assets	41	44	38

Fluid Transfer Internatonal Ltd

Nailsworth Mills Estate Avening Road, Nailsworth, Stroud, GL6 0BS
Tel: 01453-833381 **Fax:** 01453-833529
E-mail: sales@fluid-transfer.co.uk
Website: http://www.fluid-transfer.co.uk
Bank(s): Barclays
Directors: C. Bignell (Fin), J. Little (MD)
Ultimate Holding Company: STURROCK AND ROBSON INTERNATIONAL BV (THE NETHERLANDS)
Immediate Holding Company: FLUID TRANSFER INTERNATIONAL LIMITED
Registration no: 03658293 **VAT No.:** GB 713 6603 53
Date established: 1998 **Turnover:** £10m - £20m
No.of Employees: 51 - 100 **Product Groups:** 36, 39, 40

Date of Accounts	Jun 12	Jun 11	Jun 10
Sales Turnover	10m	10m	20m
Pre Tax Profit/Loss	575	259	2m
Working Capital	2m	3m	6m
Fixed Assets	783	184	242
Current Assets	6m	5m	11m
Current Liabilities	2m	1m	3m

Footprint Wireless Ltd

4 Wheelwrights Corner Cossack Square, Nailsworth, Stroud, GL6 0DB
Tel: 01666-505123 **Fax:** 01666-505126
E-mail: sales@footprintwireless.co.uk
Website: http://www.footprintwireless.co.uk
Directors: P. Stroud (MD), S. Lemar (Dir)
Immediate Holding Company: FOOTPRINT WIRELESS LIMITED
Registration no: 05842860 **Date established:** 2006
Turnover: £500,000 - £1m **No.of Employees:** 1 - 10 **Product Groups:** 37, 44, 84

Genesis Plastics

Unit 21b Stafford Mill London Road, Thrupp, Stroud, GL5 2AZ
Tel: 01453-751000 **Fax:** 01453-755556
Directors: C. Russell (Prop)
Immediate Holding Company: GENESIS PLASTICS LIMITED
Registration no: 02933275 **Date established:** 1994
Turnover: Up to £250,000 **No.of Employees:** 1 - 10 **Product Groups:** 30, 42

Date of Accounts	May 11	May 10	May 09
Working Capital	42	27	20
Fixed Assets	60	46	69
Current Assets	95	73	59

Hampton Colours Ltd

Toadsmoor Mills Brimscombe, Stroud, GL5 2UH
Tel: 01453-731555 **Fax:** 01453-731234
E-mail: sales@hamptoncolours.co.uk
Website: http://www.hamptoncolours.co.uk
Bank(s): HSBC Bank plc
Directors: C. Hampton (MD)
Immediate Holding Company: HAMPTON COLOURS LIMITED
Registration no: 01180128 **VAT No.:** GB 276 3673 27
Date established: 1974 **Turnover:** £1m - £2m **No.of Employees:** 11 - 20
Product Groups: 32

Date of Accounts	Sep 11	Sep 10	Sep 09
Working Capital	151	85	94
Fixed Assets	402	408	406
Current Assets	452	348	338

Heber Ltd

Belvedere Mill Chalford, Stroud, GL6 8NT
Tel: 01453-886000 **Fax:** 01453-885013
E-mail: les.ashton-smith@heber.co.uk
Website: http://www.heber.co.uk
Directors: L. Ashton Smith (MD), L. Ashton-Smith (MD)
Managers: R. Horne (Sales & Mktg Mg), J. Langley (Comptroller), R. Pullinger (Purch Mgr), B. Thompson (Tech Serv Mgr)
Immediate Holding Company: HEBER LIMITED
Registration no: 01744505 **VAT No.:** GB 392 0922 49
Date established: 1983 **Turnover:** £2m - £5m **No.of Employees:** 21 - 50
Product Groups: 37, 38, 40, 44, 45, 67, 84

Date of Accounts	Mar 12	Mar 11	Mar 10
Working Capital	2m	2m	2m
Fixed Assets	32	52	56
Current Assets	3m	3m	2m

Heyes Engineering

Unit 4a Lightpill Trading Estate 117 Bath Road, Stroud, GL5 3JW
Tel: 01453-750491 **Fax:** 01453-750491
E-mail: heyeseng@stroud50.fsnet.co.uk
Website: http://www.stroud50.fsnet.co.uk
Directors: G. Anderson (Prop)
Turnover: £250,000 - £500,000 **No.of Employees:** 1 - 10
Product Groups: 30

Himag Solutions

3 Stroud Enterprise Centre Lightpill, Stroud, GL5 3NL
Tel: 01453-750011 **Fax:** 01453-768823
E-mail: laura.atkinson@himag.co.uk
Website: http://www.himag.co.uk
Directors: L. Atkinson (Fin)
No.of Employees: 11 - 20 **Product Groups:** 37, 46, 67

The History Press

The Mill Brimscombe Port, Brimscombe, Stroud, GL5 2QG
Tel: 01453-883300 **Fax:** 01453-883233
E-mail: sbiles@thehistorypress.co.uk
Website: http://www.thehistorypress.co.uk
Directors: G. Swain (Fin)
Managers: S. Biles, J. Kinnear (Sales Prom Mgr), N. Carter (Personnel), R. Seaman
Immediate Holding Company: HAYENS PUBLISHING
Registration no: 01394835 **VAT No.:** GB 653 3262 352 79
Date established: 1978 **Turnover:** £5m - £10m **No.of Employees:** 21 - 50
Product Groups: 28

Howdon Power Transmission Ltd

Paganhill Lane, Stroud, GL5 4JT
Tel: 01453-750814 **Fax:** 01453-765320
E-mail: heath.pinkney@howdon.co.uk
Website: http://www.howdon.co.uk
Directors: H. Pinkney (Sales), L. Pinkney (Co Sec)
Immediate Holding Company: HOWDON POWER TRANSMISSION LIMITED
Registration no: 01316321 **VAT No.:** GB 298 4367 03
Date established: 1977 **Turnover:** £500,000 - £1m
No.of Employees: 1 - 10 **Product Groups:** 29, 35, 39, 40, 41, 43, 45, 46, 67

Date of Accounts	Apr 11	Apr 10	Apr 09
Working Capital	193	157	115
Fixed Assets	8	2	4
Current Assets	359	250	234

Intertech Process Machinery Ltd

Unit 1-3 Phoenix Trading Estate London Road, Thrupp, Stroud, GL5 2BX
Tel: 01453-882585 **Fax:** 01453-882676
Directors: T. Preece (MD)
Immediate Holding Company: INTERTECH PROCESS MACHINERY LIMITED
Registration no: 02658232 **Date established:** 1991
No.of Employees: 1 - 10 **Product Groups:** 20, 40, 41

Date of Accounts	Apr 11	Apr 10	Apr 09
Working Capital	-6	-6	-26
Fixed Assets	6	6	9
Current Assets	N/A	144	84

J V Hydraulics Ltd

1 Stroud Enterprise Centre Lightpill, Stroud, GL5 3NL
Tel: 01453-767729 **Fax:** 01453-767099
E-mail: sales@jvhydraulics.co.uk
Website: http://www.jvhydraulics.co.uk
Directors: R. Lang (MD)
Immediate Holding Company: J.V. HYDRAULICS LIMITED
Registration no: 04178487 **Date established:** 2001
No.of Employees: 1 - 10 **Product Groups:** 30, 35, 36, 37, 38, 40, 42, 46, 47, 67

Date of Accounts	Mar 11	Mar 10	Mar 09
Working Capital	62	220	253
Fixed Assets	8	15	22
Current Assets	277	326	354

Jewson Ltd

Fromeside Industrial Estate Wallbridge, Stroud, GL5 3JX
Tel: 01453-762444 **Fax:** 01453-756708
E-mail: barry.hilliker@jewson.co.uk
Website: http://www.jewson.co.uk
Managers: B. Hilliker (Mgr)
Ultimate Holding Company: COMPAGNIE DE SAINT GOBAIN (FRANCE)
Immediate Holding Company: JEWSON LIMITED
Registration no: 00348407 **Date established:** 1939 **Turnover:** £2m - £5m
No.of Employees: 11 - 20 **Product Groups:** 66

Date of Accounts	Dec 11	Dec 10	Dec 09
Sales Turnover	1606m	1547m	1485m
Pre Tax Profit/Loss	18m	100m	45m
Working Capital	-345m	-250m	-349m
Fixed Assets	496m	387m	461m
Current Assets	657m	1005m	1320m
Current Liabilities	66m	120m	64m

The Keyboard Company UK Ltd

8 Canal Iron Works Hope Mill Lane London Road, Brimscombe, Stroud, GL5 2SH
Tel: 01453-884938 **Fax:** 07000-500515
E-mail: sales@keyboardco.com
Website: http://www.keyboardco.com
Directors: B. Whiting (MD)
Immediate Holding Company: THE KEYBOARD COMPANY (UK) LIMITED
Registration no: 03446142 **Date established:** 1997
Turnover: £500,000 - £1m **No.of Employees:** 1 - 10 **Product Groups:** 37, 44, 67

Date of Accounts	Dec 10	Dec 09	Dec 08
Working Capital	561	487	439
Fixed Assets	9	12	7
Current Assets	677	602	544

L B Bentley Ltd

Kingfisher Business Park London Road, Thrupp, Stroud, GL5 2BY
Tel: 01453-733060 **Fax:** 01453-761505
E-mail: bernard.bentley@lb-bentley.com
Website: http://www.lb-bentley.com
Bank(s): National Westminster, Stroud
Directors: B. Bentley (Grp Chief Exec)
Immediate Holding Company: L.B. BENTLEY LIMITED
Registration no: 01059801 **VAT No.:** GB 274 2991 30
Date established: 1972 **Turnover:** £10m - £20m
No.of Employees: 101 - 250 **Product Groups:** 33, 36, 40, 42

Date of Accounts	Apr 11	Apr 10	Apr 09
Sales Turnover	10m	16m	12m
Pre Tax Profit/Loss	424	2m	-398
Working Capital	2m	2m	246
Fixed Assets	1m	1m	1m
Current Assets	6m	5m	6m
Current Liabilities	2m	2m	2m

Lounge Design Limited

25 Bluebell Rise Chalford, Stroud, GL6 8NP
Tel: 01453-731664
E-mail: relax@loungedesign.co.uk
Website: http://www.loungedesign.co.uk
Directors: A. Vines (Dir), Q. Lin (Sales)
Registration no: 6684114 **Date established:** 2006
Turnover: Up to £250,000 **No.of Employees:** 1 - 10 **Product Groups:** 64, 81

Machine Covers Ltd

Stancombe Works Bisley, Stroud, GL6 7NQ
Tel: 01452-770166 **Fax:** 01452-770188
E-mail: info@machinecovers.co.uk
Website: http://www.machinecovers.co.uk
Directors: G. Powles (MD), R. Cratchley (Dir)
Ultimate Holding Company: MACHINE COVERS LIMITED
Immediate Holding Company: SEVERN VALLEY ENTERPRISES LIMITED
Registration no: 00097187 **Date established:** 2008
Turnover: £500,000 - £1m **No.of Employees:** 21 - 50 **Product Groups:** 46

Date of Accounts	Mar 11	Mar 10	Mar 09
Working Capital	27	11	-10
Fixed Assets	N/A	15	27
Current Assets	30	109	111

Mikris Finishers

Lower Dudbridge House Selsley Hill, Dudbridge, Stroud, GL5 3HF
Tel: 01453-763873 **Fax:** 01453-763873
Website: http://www.mikrisfinishers.com
Directors: C. Buckle (Prop)
Immediate Holding Company: MIKRIS FINISHERS LIMITED
Registration no: 07788665 **Date established:** 2011
No.of Employees: 1 - 10 **Product Groups:** 46, 48

Milliken Woollen Speciality Products

Lodgemore Mills, Stroud, GL5 3EJ
Tel: 01453-764456 **Fax:** 01453-752919
E-mail: davidwsp.smith@milliken.com
Website: http://www.milliken-wsp.co.uk
Bank(s): Barclays
Directors: M. Woodworth (Fin), R. Milliken (Dir), A. Allen (Dir)
Managers: D. Smith (Mgr)
Immediate Holding Company: LUDUS CAPITAL LIMITED
Registration no: 00172105 **VAT No.:** GB 145 9283 45
Date established: 2011 **No.of Employees:** 101 - 250 **Product Groups:** 23, 63

Paul Norman Plastics Ltd

Unit S5 Inchbrook Trading Estate Bath Road, Woodchester, Stroud, GL5 5EY
Tel: 01453-833388 **Fax:** 01453-834055
E-mail: info@pnplastics.co.uk
Website: http://www.pnplastics.co.uk
Bank(s): Yorkshire Bank PLC
Directors: P. Norman (MD), E. Crowley (Sales)
Immediate Holding Company: PAUL NORMAN PLASTICS LIMITED
Registration no: 01722616 **VAT No.:** GB 392 0513 66
Date established: 1983 **Turnover:** £1m - £2m **No.of Employees:** 21 - 50
Product Groups: 30, 42

Date of Accounts	Aug 11	Aug 10	Aug 09
Working Capital	17	-17	-2
Fixed Assets	87	109	110
Current Assets	186	185	127

Nortim Tools Ltd

5 New Mills Industrial Estate Libbys Drive, Stroud, GL5 1RN
Tel: 01453-759613 **Fax:** 01453-753803
E-mail: global@nortim.co.uk
Website: http://www.nortim.co.uk
Directors: P. Carpenter (Fin), T. Powell (MD)
Immediate Holding Company: NORTIM TOOLS LIMITED
Registration no: 01020543 **Date established:** 1971
No.of Employees: 1 - 10 **Product Groups:** 46

Date of Accounts	Oct 11	Oct 10	Oct 09
Working Capital	83	59	25
Fixed Assets	95	41	51
Current Assets	177	146	69

Olympic Industries Ltd

Val D'Or Works Knapp Lane, Brimscombe, Stroud, GL5 2TQ
Tel: 01453-883164 **Fax:** 01453-886719
E-mail: sales@olympicvarnish.co.uk
Website: http://www.olympicvarnish.co.uk
Directors: B. Petyan (Fin), W. Petyan (MD)
Managers: S. Gasperovitz (Personnel)
Immediate Holding Company: OLYMPIC VARNISH COMPANY LIMITED
Registration no: 00343387 **Date established:** 1938 **Turnover:** £2m - £5m
No.of Employees: 21 - 50 **Product Groups:** 27

Date of Accounts	Jun 11	Jun 10	Jun 09
Sales Turnover	4m	4m	5m
Pre Tax Profit/Loss	78	91	202
Working Capital	3m	3m	3m
Fixed Assets	1m	1m	1m
Current Assets	4m	3m	3m
Current Liabilities	200	162	201

Omnitrack Ltd

Ball Unit House Station Road Industrial Estate Station Road, Woodchester, Stroud, GL5 5EQ
Tel: 01453-873345 **Fax:** 01453-878500
E-mail: info@omnitrack.co.uk
Website: http://www.omnitrack.co.uk
Bank(s): Bank of Scotland
Directors: J. Cabrini-Dale (Dir), K. Dale (Fin)
Ultimate Holding Company: Autoset (Production) Ltd
Immediate Holding Company: OMNITRACK NORTH AMERICA LIMITED
Registration no: 06991283 **VAT No.:** GB 736 4628 15
Date established: 2009 **Turnover:** £500,000 - £1m
No.of Employees: 11 - 20 **Product Groups:** 35, 39, 41, 45, 46, 49, 67

Date of Accounts	Feb 11	Feb 10
Working Capital	5	3
Current Assets	34	7

P H M Plant Services Ltd

117 Bath Road, Stroud, GL5 3JW
Tel: 01453-763532 **Fax:** 01453-755083
E-mail: andy@phmplant.plus.com
Website: http://www.phmplant.co.uk
Directors: A. Farthing (MD)
Immediate Holding Company: P.H.M. PLANT SERVICES LIMITED
Registration no: 01297884 **Date established:** 1977
Turnover: £500,000 - £1m **No.of Employees:** 1 - 10 **Product Groups:** 37

Date of Accounts	Feb 11	Feb 10	Feb 09
Working Capital	52	52	46
Fixed Assets	80	75	71
Current Assets	251	252	243

Prima Medical Ltd

Mill 16 Bath Road Trading Estate, Lightpill, Stroud, GL5 3QF
Tel: 01453-752626 **Fax:** 01453-756750
E-mail: sales@prima-medical.com
Website: http://www.prima-medical.com
Directors: G. Brooke (MD), A. Young (Fin)
Immediate Holding Company: PRIMA MEDICAL LIMITED
Registration no: 04831749 **Date established:** 2003
No.of Employees: 1 - 10 **Product Groups:** 37, 38, 67

Date of Accounts	Jul 11	Jul 10	Jul 09
Working Capital	293	195	205
Fixed Assets	9	15	29
Current Assets	680	558	578

ReetPetite
Suite M1 Stag House Gydynap Lane, Inchbrook, Stroud, GL5 5EZ
Tel: 01453-833823
E-mail: sales@reetpetite.biz
Website: http://www.reetpetite.biz
Directors: R. Armitage (Prop)
Immediate Holding Company: B.S.M.A.
Date established: 1995 **No.of Employees:** 1 - 10 **Product Groups:** 23, 24

Rollercoaster Records Ltd
Rock House St Marys Chalford, Stroud, GL6 8PU
Tel: 01453-886252 **Fax:** 01453-885361
E-mail: john@rollercoasterrecords.com
Website: http://www.rollercoasterrecords.com
Directors: J. Beecher (Dir)
Immediate Holding Company: ROLLERCOASTER RECORDS LTD
Registration no: 05310556 **VAT No.:** GB 217 6161 75
Date established: 2004 **Turnover:** £250,000 - £500,000
No.of Employees: 1 - 10 **Product Groups:** 61

Date of Accounts	Dec 10	Dec 07	Dec 06
Working Capital	43	84	95
Fixed Assets	5	8	9
Current Assets	107	98	117

S T B Engineering Ltd
Toadsmoor Road Brimscombe, Stroud, GL5 2UF
Tel: 01453-885353 **Fax:** 01453-886824
E-mail: sales@stbengineering.com
Website: http://www.stbengineering.com
Directors: H. Dickinson (Ch)
Ultimate Holding Company: WILLHELM LIMITED
Immediate Holding Company: S.T.B. ENGINEERING LIMITED
Registration no: 00958390 **Date established:** 1969
No.of Employees: 11 - 20 **Product Groups:** 35, 42, 45

Date of Accounts	Sep 11	Sep 10	Sep 09
Working Capital	397	429	388
Fixed Assets	36	41	53
Current Assets	738	893	1m

Scorpion Tooling Services
Unit 7 & 9 Libbys Drive, Stroud, GL5 1RN
Tel: 01453-751511 **Fax:** 01453-766676
E-mail: chris@scorpiontooling.co.uk
Website: http://www.scorpiontooling.co.uk
Directors: C. Wands (Prop)
Immediate Holding Company: SCORPION TOOLING UK LIMITED
Registration no: 05945178 **Date established:** 2006
No.of Employees: 1 - 10 **Product Groups:** 46

Date of Accounts	Mar 12	Mar 11	Mar 10
Working Capital	1	-23	6
Fixed Assets	251	208	116
Current Assets	133	97	89

Severn Electrical Wholesale Ltd
Fromeside Industrial Estate Newtons Way, Wallbridge, Stroud, GL5 3JX
Tel: 01453-768888
E-mail: severnelectrical@lineone.net
Website: http://www.lampsatstroud.co.uk
Directors: D. Maltby (MD)
Immediate Holding Company: SEVERN ELECTRICAL WHOLESALE LIMITED
Registration no: 02065142 **Date established:** 1986
No.of Employees: 1 - 10 **Product Groups:** 37, 67

Date of Accounts	Mar 12	Mar 11	Mar 10
Working Capital	34	86	87
Fixed Assets	N/A	N/A	1
Current Assets	130	167	167

South West Battery Charging Systems
Oakley House Church Road, North Woodchester, Stroud, GL5 5PQ
Tel: 01453-872865 **Fax:** 01453-872065
E-mail: info@swbattery.co.uk
Website: http://www.swbattery.co.uk
Bank(s): Lloyds TSB Bank plc
Directors: A. Fiddler (Tech Serv), G. Bastin (Prop)
Immediate Holding Company: L
VAT No.: GB 666 5120 33 **Date established:** 1977
Turnover: £500,000 - £1m **No.of Employees:** 21 - 50 **Product Groups:** 37

Sprayco Industrial Finishers
Unit D4 Bath Road Trading Estate Lightpill, Stroud, GL5 3QF
Tel: 01453-755025 **Fax:** 01453-755025
Directors: A. Biddlecombe (MD), C. Koutsoupas (Fin)
Immediate Holding Company: SPRAYCO INDUSTRIAL FINISHERS LIMITED
Registration no: 04564311 **Date established:** 2002
No.of Employees: 1 - 10 **Product Groups:** 46, 48

Date of Accounts	Mar 11	Mar 10	Mar 09
Working Capital	33	42	52
Fixed Assets	20	26	13
Current Assets	76	74	98

Staitech Ltd
PO Box 152, Stroud, GL6 8YT
Tel: 01453-882736 **Fax:** 01453-882744
E-mail: info@staitech.com
Website: http://www.staitech.com
Directors: A. Ferguson (MD), J. Ferguson (Fin)
Immediate Holding Company: STAITECH LIMITED
Registration no: 03406904 **Date established:** 1997
Turnover: £500,000 - £1m **No.of Employees:** 1 - 10 **Product Groups:** 36, 37, 38

Date of Accounts	Jul 11	Jul 10	Jul 09
Sales Turnover	N/A	773	854
Pre Tax Profit/Loss	N/A	92	106
Working Capital	311	178	216
Fixed Assets	156	116	76
Current Assets	511	359	309
Current Liabilities	N/A	62	56

Stroud College Of Further Education
Stratford Road, Stroud, GL5 4AH
Tel: 01453-763424 **Fax:** 01453-753543
E-mail: berihare@stroudcol.ac.uk
Website: http://www.stroud.ac.uk
Managers: B. Hare
Date established: 1960 **No.of Employees:** 101 - 250 **Product Groups:** 86

Stroud Instruments Ltd
36-40 Slad Road, Stroud, GL5 1QW
Tel: 01453-765433 **Fax:** 01453-764256
E-mail: sales@sil.co.uk
Website: http://www.sil.co.uk
Directors: R. Davis (Dir), G. Davis (MD)
Immediate Holding Company: STROUD INSTRUMENTS LIMITED
Registration no: 01008238 **VAT No.:** GB 275 4663 31
Date established: 1971 **Turnover:** £500,000 - £1m
No.of Employees: 1 - 10 **Product Groups:** 37, 38

Date of Accounts	Jul 11	Jul 10	Jul 09
Working Capital	13	12	14
Fixed Assets	426	428	428
Current Assets	87	41	37

Stroud Metal Co. Ltd
Dudbridge, Stroud, GL5 3EZ
Tel: 01453-763331 **Fax:** 01453-753804
E-mail: enquiries@stroudmetal.co.uk
Website: http://www.stroudmetal.co.uk
Bank(s): Lloyds TSB Bank plc
Directors: M. Large (MD), M. Large (MD), R. Harmer (Fin)
Managers: B. Williams (Mktg Serv Mgr), S. Heaney (Buyer)
Ultimate Holding Company: DUDBRIDGE ESTATES,LIMITED(THE)
Immediate Holding Company: STROUD METAL COMPANY LIMITED
Registration no: 00216529 **VAT No.:** GB 275 1889 20
Date established: 2026 **Turnover:** £2m - £5m **No.of Employees:** 21 - 50
Product Groups: 35, 48

Date of Accounts	Sep 11	Sep 10	Sep 09
Pre Tax Profit/Loss	N/A	N/A	-640
Working Capital	3m	3m	3m
Fixed Assets	1m	1m	1m
Current Assets	4m	4m	4m

Tecmaco International Ltd
Unit C5 Phoenix Trading Estate London Road, Thrupp, Stroud, GL5 2BX
Tel: 01453-731737 **Fax:** 01453-731747
E-mail: sales@trampoilskimmers.co.uk
Website: http://www.trampoilskimmers.co.uk
Directors: S. Mcallister (MD)
Immediate Holding Company: TECMACO INTERNATIONAL LIMITED
Registration no: 00989402 **VAT No.:** GB 448 3822 37
Date established: 1970 **Turnover:** £250,000 - £500,000
No.of Employees: 1 - 10 **Product Groups:** 30, 35

Date of Accounts	Jun 12	Jun 11	Jun 10
Working Capital	179	113	58
Fixed Assets	8	N/A	1
Current Assets	330	216	164

Howard Tenens Associates Ltd
Kingfisher Business Park London Road, Thrupp, Stroud, GL5 2BY
Tel: 01453-885087 **Fax:** 01453-886145
E-mail: peter.morris@tenens.com
Website: http://www.tenens.com
Bank(s): Barclays, Oxford
Directors: J. Beecham (Fin), P. Morris (MD)
Managers: B. Morris
Ultimate Holding Company: HOWARD TENENS LIMITED
Immediate Holding Company: TENENS ASSOCIATES LIMITED
Registration no: 01707348 **VAT No.:** GB 391 9766 95
Date established: 1983 **Turnover:** £2m - £5m **No.of Employees:** 21 - 50
Product Groups: 72, 77, 84

Date of Accounts	Sep 10	Sep 09	Sep 08
Sales Turnover	N/A	4m	7m
Pre Tax Profit/Loss	N/A	159	2m
Working Capital	13m	13m	3m
Fixed Assets	5	5	24m
Current Assets	13m	13m	7m
Current Liabilities	N/A	N/A	1m

West Country Metal Polishers
Unit D5 Bath Road Trading Estate, Lightpill, Stroud, GL5 3QF
Tel: 01453-759737 **Fax:** 01453-759737
Directors: A. Nobes (Dir), K. Nobes (Fin)
Immediate Holding Company: WEST COUNTRY METAL POLISHERS LTD
Registration no: 05857318 **Date established:** 2003
No.of Employees: 1 - 10 **Product Groups:** 46, 48

Western Patterns
The Clock House Stafford Mil London Road Thrupp, Stroud, GL5 2AZ
Tel: 01453-766095 **Fax:** 01453-753830
E-mail: tony@westernpatterns.co.uk
Website: http://www.westernpatterns.net
Directors: T. Nash (Prop)
Immediate Holding Company: D.M. FOUNDRIES LIMITED
Date established: 1982 **No.of Employees:** 1 - 10 **Product Groups:** 30, 34, 44, 46, 47, 48, 84

Date of Accounts	Dec 11	Dec 10	Dec 09
Working Capital	352	415	412
Fixed Assets	327	334	338
Current Assets	488	515	506

Wyatt Engineering Fuel Services
Unit 20a Merretts Mill Industrial Estate Woodchester, Stroud, GL5 5EX
Tel: 01453-835484
Website: http://www.wyattfuelengineers.com
Directors: R. Wyatt (Ptnr), R. Cotterell (Ptnr)
No.of Employees: 1 - 10 **Product Groups:** 36, 52, 84

Tetbury

Autonumis
Cirencester Road, Tetbury, GL8 8SA
Tel: 01666-502641 **Fax:** 01666-504397
E-mail: info@autonumis.co.uk
Website: http://www.autonumis.co.uk
Bank(s): Barclays, Bristol
Directors: D. Seymour (MD)
Managers: G. King (Tech Serv Mgr), P. Jones (Fin Mgr)
Ultimate Holding Company: MAGNUM GROUP LIMITED
Immediate Holding Company: MAGNUM GROUP PENSION TRUSTEE LIMITED
Registration no: 02195301 **Date established:** 1987 **Turnover:** £5m - £10m
No.of Employees: 21 - 50 **Product Groups:** 40, 49

Date of Accounts	Mar 11	Mar 10	Mar 09
Sales Turnover	5m	5m	6m
Pre Tax Profit/Loss	-86	13	-98
Working Capital	87	-42	16
Fixed Assets	3m	3m	3m
Current Assets	1m	1m	1m
Current Liabilities	354	402	248

Beta Plastics Ltd
Unit 4f Tetbury Industrial Estate, Tetbury, GL8 8EZ
Tel: 01666-503001
Directors: B. Reay (Prop)
Immediate Holding Company: DELTA PRECISION LIMITED
Registration no: 05253517 **Date established:** 2004
No.of Employees: 1 - 10 **Product Groups:** 29, 30, 67

Date of Accounts	Dec 11	Dec 10	Dec 09
Working Capital	474	470	419
Fixed Assets	104	41	48
Current Assets	577	566	531

Foster & Brown Research
Stonecroft Hampton Street, Tetbury, GL8 8JP
Tel: 01666-504301 **Fax:** 01666-504301
E-mail: paulinef6@aol.com
Website: http://www.fabresearch.com
Directors: P. Foster (Prop)
Date established: 2001 **Turnover:** Up to £250,000
No.of Employees: 1 - 10 **Product Groups:** 81, 85

Melcourt Industries
Boldridge Brake Long Newnton, Tetbury, GL8 8RT
Tel: 01666-502711 **Fax:** 01666-504398
E-mail: mail@melcourt.co.uk
Website: http://www.melcourt.co.uk
Directors: P. Watson (Co Sec), A. Chalmers (Dir)
Immediate Holding Company: MELCOURT INDUSTRIES LIMITED
Registration no: 01734220 **VAT No.:** GB 393 9260 18
Date established: 1983 **Turnover:** £250,000 - £500,000
No.of Employees: 1 - 10 **Product Groups:** 25, 32, 66

Date of Accounts	Oct 11	Oct 10	Oct 09
Working Capital	590	520	457
Fixed Assets	516	558	473
Current Assets	2m	1m	939

Timberpride Ltd
Quercus Road, Tetbury, GL8 8GX
Tel: 01666-504436 **Fax:** 01666-505207
E-mail: info@timberpride.co.uk
Website: http://www.timberpride.co.uk
Directors: V. Golesworthy (Dir)
Immediate Holding Company: TIMBERPRIDE LIMITED
Registration no: 03624722 **Date established:** 1998
No.of Employees: 1 - 10 **Product Groups:** 08, 25, 48, 66

Date of Accounts	Sep 11	Sep 10	Sep 09
Working Capital	-87	-99	-149
Fixed Assets	174	190	190
Current Assets	147	227	204

Velton Industries Ltd
PO Box 9, Tetbury, GL8 8TW
Tel: 01666-502112
Directors: T. Billington (Fin), D. Billington (MD)
Immediate Holding Company: VELTON INDUSTRIES LIMITED
Registration no: 01705895 **Date established:** 1983
No.of Employees: 1 - 10 **Product Groups:** 35

Date of Accounts	Jun 11	Jun 10	Jun 08
Working Capital	-129	-120	-103
Fixed Assets	1	1	2
Current Assets	10	10	12

T H White Ltd
Sherston Works Knockdown, Tetbury, GL8 8QY
Tel: 01454-238181 **Fax:** 01454-238772
E-mail: head_office@thwhite.co.uk
Website: http://www.thwhite.co.uk
Directors: P. Smith (Dir)
Managers: V. Webb
Ultimate Holding Company: T. H. WHITE HOLDINGS LIMITED
Immediate Holding Company: T. H. WHITE LIMITED
Registration no: 00519868 **Date established:** 1953
No.of Employees: 21 - 50 **Product Groups:** 41

Date of Accounts	Dec 11	Dec 10	Dec 09
Sales Turnover	96m	86m	81m
Pre Tax Profit/Loss	1m	697	1m
Working Capital	9m	9m	9m
Fixed Assets	2m	2m	2m
Current Assets	27m	22m	21m
Current Liabilities	7m	8m	4m

Tewkesbury

Adglow Ltd
Ledbury House Alexandra Way, Ashchurch, Tewkesbury, GL20 8NB
Tel: 01684-272900 **Fax:** 01684-850729
E-mail: dainge@adinstall.co.uk
Website: http://www.adglow.co.uk
Directors: J. Howell (Fin), D. Ainge (MD)
Managers: G. Ainge, D. Clark (Mktg Serv Mgr), B. Sheppard (Personnel)
Ultimate Holding Company: RDG HOLDINGS LIMITED
Immediate Holding Company: ADGLOW LIMITED
Registration no: 00579219 **VAT No.:** GB 393 9276 03
Date established: 1957 **Turnover:** £5m - £10m
No.of Employees: 51 - 100 **Product Groups:** 81

Date of Accounts	Mar 12	Mar 11	Mar 10
Sales Turnover	6m	6m	7m
Pre Tax Profit/Loss	155	-511	-896
Working Capital	234	-1m	-872
Fixed Assets	57	66	141
Current Assets	2m	1m	1m
Current Liabilities	1m	2m	2m

Allen Vanguard Ltd (formerly P.W. Allen)

Unit 700 Allen House Ashchurch Business Centre Alexandra Way, Ashchurch, Tewkesbury, GL20 8TD
Tel: 01684-851100 **Fax:** 01684-851101
E-mail: tom.maher@allenvanguard.com
Website: http://www.allenvanguard.com
Directors: E. Preston (Fin), N. Walsh (Pers)
Managers: T. Maher (Chief Mgr), M. Fadra, R. John
Ultimate Holding Company: ALLEN-VANGUARD CORPORATION (CANADA)
Immediate Holding Company: ALLEN-VANGUARD LTD
Registration no: 01230899 **VAT No.:** GB 354 2996 26
Date established: 1975 **Turnover:** £20m - £50m
No.of Employees: 101 - 250 **Product Groups:** 33, 36, 37, 40, 45, 86

Date of Accounts	Dec 11	Dec 10	Dec 09
Sales Turnover	32m	32m	25m
Pre Tax Profit/Loss	2m	4m	-5m
Working Capital	4m	2m	-3m
Fixed Assets	693	1m	1m
Current Assets	17m	16m	16m
Current Liabilities	10m	1m	1m

Ash Photography Ltd

Church Farm Ashchurch Road, Ashchurch, Tewkesbury, GL20 8JU
Tel: 01684-291200 **Fax:** 01684-291201
E-mail: info@ashphotography.co.uk
Website: http://www.ashphotography.co.uk
Directors: J. Ash (MD)
Immediate Holding Company: ASH PHOTOGRAPHY LIMITED
Registration no: 02712818 **Date established:** 1992
Turnover: £250,000 - £500,000 **No.of Employees:** 1 - 10
Product Groups: 81

Date of Accounts	May 11	May 10	May 09
Working Capital	117	14	-104
Fixed Assets	45	70	61
Current Assets	172	75	47

B G Technical Mouldings Ltd

Fiddington, Tewkesbury, GL20 7BJ
Tel: 01684-299290 **Fax:** 01684-850198
E-mail: sales@bgtechnical.co.uk
Website: http://www.british-gaskets.co.uk
Bank(s): Barclays
Directors: T. Brown (Dir)
Managers: K. Gilmore (Sales Prom Mgr), M. Gardiner, H. Williams (Personnel)
Immediate Holding Company: D & R BULL LIMITED
Registration no: 01378916 **VAT No.:** GB 299 1860 06
Date established: 1978 **Turnover:** £2m - £5m **No.of Employees:** 21 - 50
Product Groups: 29

Date of Accounts	May 11	May 10	May 09
Working Capital	-200	-200	-200
Fixed Assets	439	439	439

B S Elastomers

Sigma Close Shannon Way, Ashchurch, Tewkesbury, GL20 8ND
Tel: 01684-292724 **Fax:** 01684-292619
E-mail: neil.bayliss@bselastomers.com
Website: http://www.bselastomers.com
Directors: N. Bayliss (MD)
Immediate Holding Company: VERTON 2011 LTD
Registration no: 07411387 **Date established:** 2010
Turnover: £50m - £75m **No.of Employees:** 1 - 10 **Product Groups:** 29, 30

C B Agricultural Repairs

10 Pyke Road, Tewkesbury, GL20 8DX
Tel: 01684-292635
Directors: C. Bedwell (Prop)
Date established: 1987 **No.of Employees:** 1 - 10 **Product Groups:** 41

Charlton Networks

Canterbury Business Centre Ashchurch Road, Tewkesbury, GL20 8BT
Tel: 01684-856830 **Fax:** 01684-856849
E-mail: enquiries@charltonnetworks.co.uk
Website: http://www.charltonnetworks.co.uk
Directors: R. Perry (MD)
Immediate Holding Company: CHARLTON NETWORKS LIMITED
Registration no: 03288824 **Date established:** 1996
Turnover: £500,000 - £1m **No.of Employees:** 11 - 20
Product Groups: 44, 48, 52, 67, 80, 84

Date of Accounts	Dec 11	Dec 10	Dec 09
Working Capital	33	2	3
Fixed Assets	91	111	106
Current Assets	142	174	154

The Cotswold Forge

Unit 5 Fiddington House Farm Fiddington, Tewkesbury, GL20 7BJ
Tel: 01684-276870 **Fax:** 01242-242754
Website: http://www.thecottswoldforge.com
Directors: G. Clarke (Prop)
Immediate Holding Company: AGRISERVICES (GLOSHIRE) LIMITED
Registration no: 07428594 **Date established:** 1985
No.of Employees: 1 - 10 **Product Groups:** 35, 48, 84

Davis Scientific Treatments Ltd

Delta Drive, Tewkesbury, GL20 8HB
Tel: 01684-296601 **Fax:** 01684-274239
E-mail: davis.scientific@btconnect.com
Directors: G. Davis (MD), P. Davis (Fin)
Immediate Holding Company: DAVIS SCIENTIFIC TREATMENTS LIMITED
Registration no: 01816932 **VAT No.:** GB 419 1342 68
Date established: 1984 **Turnover:** £250,000 - £500,000
No.of Employees: 1 - 10 **Product Groups:** 48

Date of Accounts	Mar 11	Mar 10	Mar 09
Working Capital	45	49	91
Fixed Assets	20	26	32
Current Assets	70	74	120

Dax International Ltd '

Unit E4 Green Lane Business Park Green Lane, Tewkesbury, GL20 8SJ
Tel: 01684-276688 **Fax:** 01684-276699
E-mail: sales@daxinternational.co.uk
Website: http://www.daxinternational.co.uk
Directors: G. Buck (Fin), A. Buck (MD)
Immediate Holding Company: DAX INTERNATIONAL LIMITED
Registration no: 03931554 **Date established:** 2000
No.of Employees: 1 - 10 **Product Groups:** 37

Date of Accounts	Mar 11	Mar 10	Mar 09
Working Capital	139	161	159
Fixed Assets	31	39	50
Current Assets	480	346	390

E M S Satcom

Newtown Trading Estate Green Lane, Tewkesbury, GL20 8HD
Tel: 01684-290020 **Fax:** 01684-295535
E-mail: holmes.j@ems-t.com
Website: http://www.emsaviation.com
Directors: I. Jenkins (Co Sec), J. Holmes (Dir)
Managers: K. Meriday (Fin Mgr)
Ultimate Holding Company: EMS TECHNOLOGIES INC (USA)
Immediate Holding Company: EMS SATCOM UK, LTD.
Registration no: 03164520 **Date established:** 1996 **Turnover:** £2m - £5m
No.of Employees: 21 - 50 **Product Groups:** 37, 79

Date of Accounts	Dec 10	Dec 09	Dec 08
Sales Turnover	4m	3m	3m
Pre Tax Profit/Loss	393	335	523
Working Capital	758	279	-371
Fixed Assets	608	731	984
Current Assets	2m	885	1m
Current Liabilities	280	219	224

Eastbrook Company

Plot 7100 Severn Drive, Tewkesbury Business Park, Tewkesbury, GL20 8TX
Tel: 01684-298106 **Fax:** 01684-298109
Managers: B. Derrick (Chief Mgr)
Ultimate Holding Company: ORKLA ASA (NORWAY)
Immediate Holding Company: SAPA BUILDING SYSTEMS LIMITED
Date established: 1971 **No.of Employees:** 51 - 100 **Product Groups:** 30, 36, 66

Exceptional Thinking LLP

10 Orchard Road Alderton, Tewkesbury, GL20 8NS
Tel: 0845-644 9371 **Fax:** 0870-751 8215
E-mail: info@exceptionalthinking.co.uk
Website: http://www.exceptionalthinking.co.uk
Directors: N. Dowling (Dir)
Immediate Holding Company: EXCEPTIONAL THINKING LLP
Registration no: OC319247 **Date established:** 2006
No.of Employees: 1 - 10 **Product Groups:** 80

Date of Accounts	Mar 12	Mar 11	Mar 10
Working Capital	1	-0	4
Fixed Assets	8	11	4
Current Assets	14	9	12

Fensell Fabrications Ltd (Fensell Properties Ltd)

Oak Lodge Fiddington, Tewkesbury, GL20 7BJ
Tel: 01684-273091 **Fax:** 01684-273090
E-mail: simonbillinghurst@yahoo.com
Website: http://www.fensell.co.uk
Directors: H. Billinghurst (Co Sec), S. Billinghurst (Dir)
Immediate Holding Company: FENSELL PROPERTIES LIMITED
Registration no: 00875812 **Date established:** 1966
Turnover: £500,000 - £1m **No.of Employees:** 1 - 10 **Product Groups:** 27, 34, 35, 66

Date of Accounts	Mar 11	Mar 10	Mar 09
Working Capital	120	41	41
Fixed Assets	451	394	398
Current Assets	173	70	69

Group 4 Total Security Ltd

Alexandra Way Ashchurch, Tewkesbury, GL20 8NB
Tel: 08704-117700 **Fax:** 01684-295574
E-mail: enquires@group4.com
Website: http://www.group4.co.uk
Bank(s): National Westminster Bank Plc
Directors: V. Patel (Co Sec), G. Grosso (Dir)
Ultimate Holding Company: G4S PLC
Immediate Holding Company: GROUP 4 TOTAL SECURITY LIMITED
Registration no: 02380900 **VAT No.:** GB 274 1901 62
Date established: 1989 **Turnover:** £20m - £50m
No.of Employees: 1501 & over **Product Groups:** 40, 44, 52, 67, 80, 81, 82, 86, 87

Date of Accounts	Dec 11	Dec 10	Dec 09
Sales Turnover	137m	131m	128m
Pre Tax Profit/Loss	5m	8m	5m
Working Capital	57m	90m	98m
Fixed Assets	1m	11m	1m
Current Assets	157m	143m	188m
Current Liabilities	14m	16m	17m

Gullivers Sports Travel

Fiddington Manor Fiddington, Tewkesbury, GL20 7BJ
Tel: 01684-293175 **Fax:** 01684-297926
E-mail: pscholfield@gulliversports.co.uk
Website: http://www.gulliverstravel.co.uk
Directors: D. Hall (Dir), D. Morris (Fin), N. Magnay (MD)
Managers: A. Strahan (Chief Mgr), P. Schofield (Tech Serv Mgr), R. Bressington (Mktg Serv Mgr)
Ultimate Holding Company: BIBBY LINE GROUP LIMITED
Immediate Holding Company: BEAVER BUREAU LIMITED
Registration no: 02746479 **Date established:** 1983
Turnover: £20m - £50m **No.of Employees:** 21 - 50 **Product Groups:** 61, 72, 74, 84

Date of Accounts	Jun 08	Jun 09	Jun 10
Sales Turnover	633	867	854
Pre Tax Profit/Loss	-21	79	64
Working Capital	334	211	262
Fixed Assets	4	3	2
Current Assets	380	357	350
Current Liabilities	44	68	76

Inducto Heat Tewkesbury Ltd

Unit 20 Cotteswold Dairy Estate Northway Lane, Tewkesbury, GL20 8JE
Tel: 01684-293473 **Fax:** 01684-850442
E-mail: sales@inducto-heat.co.uk
Website: http://www.inducto-heat.co.uk
Directors: S. Kingsford (Fin), R. Reynolds (MD)
Immediate Holding Company: INDUCTOHEAT (TEWKESBURY) LTD
Registration no: 05184711 **VAT No.:** GB 274 4531 54
Date established: 2004 **Turnover:** Up to £250,000
No.of Employees: 1 - 10 **Product Groups:** 48

Date of Accounts	Aug 11	Aug 10	Aug 09
Sales Turnover	N/A	121	144
Pre Tax Profit/Loss	N/A	14	29
Working Capital	-9	-13	-13
Fixed Assets	17	17	21
Current Assets	45	26	26
Current Liabilities	N/A	35	13

Kemper Rhodes UK

Basepoint Business Centre Oakfield Close, Tewkesbury, GL20 8SD
Tel: 01684-854455 **Fax:** 01684-854456
E-mail: sales@kemper-rhodes.co.uk
Website: http://www.kemper-rhodes.co.uk
Turnover: £2m - £5m **Product Groups:** 34, 35, 36, 37, 40, 48, 66

L-3 T R L Technology

Shannon Way Ashchurch, Tewkesbury, GL20 8ND
Tel: 01684-278700 **Fax:** 01684-850406
E-mail: p_mckee@trltech.co.uk
Website: http://www.l-3comm.com
Bank(s): Barclays
Managers: C. Hill
Ultimate Holding Company: L-3 COMMUNICATIONS HOLDINGS INC (USA)
Immediate Holding Company: TRL TECHNOLOGY LIMITED
Registration no: 01705039 **VAT No.:** GB 487 9279 69
Date established: 1983 **Turnover:** £50m - £75m
No.of Employees: 251 - 500 **Product Groups:** 37

Date of Accounts	Dec 11	Dec 10	Dec 09
Sales Turnover	58m	69m	60m
Pre Tax Profit/Loss	10m	10m	9m
Working Capital	21m	20m	12m
Fixed Assets	3m	3m	5m
Current Assets	37m	40m	49m
Current Liabilities	13m	17m	18m

Lakes Bathrooms Ltd

Alexandra Way Ashchurch, Tewkesbury, GL20 8NB
Tel: 01684-853870 **Fax:** 01684-276979
E-mail: info@lakesbathrooms.co.uk
Website: http://www.lakesbathrooms.co.uk
Bank(s): HSBC Bank plc
Directors: C. Organ (Sales & Mktg), R. Ashmeade (Fin), R. Craddock (MD)
Immediate Holding Company: PROVEX PRODUCTS LIMITED
Registration no: 05969283 **VAT No.:** GB 810 9314 55
Date established: 2006 **Turnover:** £10m - £20m
No.of Employees: 21 - 50 **Product Groups:** 33, 36, 66

M X Group Ltd

Alpha Close, Tewkesbury, GL20 8JF
Tel: 01684-293311 **Fax:** 01684-293900
E-mail: sales@mx-group.com
Website: http://www.mx-group.com
Directors: B. Robinson (MD), R. Johnson (Sales)
Managers: A. Pratt
Immediate Holding Company: MX GROUP LTD.
Registration no: 06047438 **Date established:** 2007
No.of Employees: 101 - 250 **Product Groups:** 25, 30, 37

Date of Accounts	Mar 10	Mar 09	Mar 08
Working Capital	-58	13	-2
Fixed Assets	9	8	N/A
Current Assets	14	63	3

Marleton Cross Ltd (Part of The M X Group)

Alpha Close, Tewkesbury, GL20 8JF
Tel: 01684-293311 **Fax:** 01684-293900
E-mail: enquiries@mx-group.com
Website: http://www.mx-group.com
Bank(s): Yorkshire
Directors: L. Jakeman (Fin), R. Johnson (Sales)
Managers: A. Platt (Purch Mgr)
Immediate Holding Company: MARLETON CROSS LIMITED
Registration no: 01215692 **VAT No.:** GB 228 6970 29
Date established: 1975 **Turnover:** £20m - £50m
No.of Employees: 101 - 250 **Product Groups:** 26, 29, 36

Date of Accounts	Aug 11	Aug 10	Aug 09
Sales Turnover	20m	20m	16m
Pre Tax Profit/Loss	1m	637	354
Working Capital	2m	2m	1m
Fixed Assets	2m	2m	1m
Current Assets	7m	6m	6m
Current Liabilities	2m	2m	2m

Masterline Walker Ltd

Severn Drive Tewkesbury Business Park, Tewkesbury, GL20 8SF
Tel: 01684-299000 **Fax:** 01684-292557
E-mail: sales@masterline.co.uk
Website: http://www.thenumberone.co.uk
Managers: S. Taylor (Comptroller)
Immediate Holding Company: MASTERLINE WALKER LIMITED
Registration no: 00985755 **VAT No.:** GB 274 2749 37
Date established: 1970 **Turnover:** £1m - £2m **No.of Employees:** 1 - 10
Product Groups: 49

Date of Accounts	Aug 09	Aug 08	Sep 11
Working Capital	314	-48	649
Fixed Assets	976	993	942
Current Assets	843	947	1m

Mecwash Systems Ltd

64 Hundred Severn Drive Tewkesbury Business Park, Tewkesbury, GL20 8SF
Tel: 01684-271600 **Fax:** 01684-271601
E-mail: enquiries@mecwash.co.uk
Website: http://www.mecwash.co.uk
Directors: J. Pattison (MD)
Ultimate Holding Company: VENTUREPORT LIMITED
Immediate Holding Company: MECWASH SYSTEMS LIMITED
Registration no: 02878493 **Date established:** 1993
No.of Employees: 21 - 50 **Product Groups:** 46, 47

Date of Accounts	Dec 11	Dec 10	Dec 09
Working Capital	986	748	675
Fixed Assets	368	381	395
Current Assets	2m	2m	1m

P & D Engineering Bredon

Fleet Lane Bredon, Tewkesbury, GL20 7EF
Tel: 01684-772912 **Fax:** 01684-772309
E-mail: sales@pandd.co.uk
Website: http://www.panddengineering.com

Directors: M. Pullan (Prop)
Immediate Holding Company: P & D ENGINEERING (BREDON) LIMITED
Registration no: 05522146 **Date established:** 2005
No.of Employees: 1 - 10 **Product Groups:** 41

Date of Accounts	Oct 11	Oct 10	Oct 09
Working Capital	271	264	134
Fixed Assets	83	85	82
Current Assets	1m	654	521

Patrico Ltd

Northway Lodge Northway Lane, Tewkesbury, GL20 8JG
Tel: 01684-299212 **Fax:** 01684-850210
E-mail: sales@patrico.co.uk
Website: http://www.patrico.co.uk
Directors: J. Herbert (Dir), R. Lanchbury (Dir)
Immediate Holding Company: PATRICO LIMITED
Registration no: 01724354 **Date established:** 1983 **Turnover:** £1m - £2m
No.of Employees: 21 - 50 **Product Groups:** 38, 42

Date of Accounts	Jun 12	Jun 11	Jun 10
Working Capital	378	320	263
Fixed Assets	2m	2m	2m
Current Assets	1m	1m	1m

Peter Gillard Company Ltd

Alexandra Way Ashchurch, Tewkesbury, GL20 8NB
Tel: 01684-290243 **Fax:** 01684-290330
E-mail: sales@wecut.eu
Website: http://www.wecut.eu
Bank(s): National Westminster Bank Plc
Directors: C. Gillard (MD)
Immediate Holding Company: PETER GILLARD & CO. LIMITED
Registration no: 01034752 **VAT No.:** GB 207 7061 81
Date established: 1971 **Turnover:** £1m - £2m **No.of Employees:** 11 - 20
Product Groups: 42

Date of Accounts	Mar 12	Mar 11	Mar 10
Working Capital	52	43	13
Fixed Assets	480	445	465
Current Assets	611	720	308

Philips Healthcare

102-103 Church Street, Tewkesbury, GL20 5AB
Tel: 01684-274774 **Fax:** 01684-274754
Directors: S. Wills (Sales)
No.of Employees: 1 - 10 **Product Groups:** 38, 67

Quintech Computer Systems Ltd

Ashton Road Beckford, Tewkesbury, GL20 7AU
Tel: 01386-883800 **Fax:** 01386-883801
E-mail: info@quintech.co.uk
Website: http://www.quintech.co.uk
Directors: C. Poulton (MD), D. Beck Johnson (Sales), D. Beck-Johnson (Sales & Mktg), J. Turner (Fin)
Managers: S. Mabery (Purch Mgr)
Immediate Holding Company: Quintech Holdings Ltd
Registration no: 05264585 **Date established:** 2004 **Turnover:** £1m - £2m
No.of Employees: 11 - 20 **Product Groups:** 44, 67, 86

Sapa Building Systems

Alexandra Way Ashchurch, Tewkesbury, GL20 8NB
Tel: 01684-853500 **Fax:** 01684-853500
E-mail: info.buildingsystems.uk@sapagroup.com
Website: http://www.sapabuildingsystems.co.uk
Directors: D. Ashby (Dir), N. Sissons (Dir), N. Sissons (MD)
Ultimate Holding Company: ORKLA ASA (NORWAY)
Immediate Holding Company: SAPA BUILDING SYSTEMS LIMITED
Registration no: 01029071 **Date established:** 1971
Turnover: £20m - £50m **No.of Employees:** 101 - 250
Product Groups: 35, 36, 37, 39

Date of Accounts	Dec 09	Dec 08	Dec 07
Sales Turnover	31m	35m	33m
Pre Tax Profit/Loss	947	744	2m
Working Capital	9m	7m	6m
Fixed Assets	4m	4m	4m
Current Assets	14m	12m	12m
Current Liabilities	1m	2m	1m

Satamatics Ltd

Miller Court Severn Drive, Tewkesbury Business Park, Tewkesbury, GL20 8DN
Tel: 01684-278610 **Fax:** 01684-278611
E-mail: info@emsglobaltracking.com
Website: http://www.emsglobaltracking.com
Bank(s): National Westminster Bank Plc
Managers: D. Koutrouki (Mgr)
Ultimate Holding Company: HONEYWELL INTERNATIONAL INC (USA)
Immediate Holding Company: SATAMATICS GLOBAL LIMITED
Registration no: 05753389 **VAT No.:** GB 826 9740 92
Date established: 2006 **Turnover:** £10m - £20m
No.of Employees: 21 - 50 **Product Groups:** 37, 38, 39, 40, 44, 67, 79, 81, 85

Date of Accounts	Sep 07
Sales Turnover	16m
Pre Tax Profit/Loss	-2m
Working Capital	-635
Fixed Assets	179
Current Assets	3m
Current Liabilities	2m

Smart Stabilizer Systems

Ashchurch Business Centre Alexandra Way, Ashchurch, Tewkesbury, GL20 8TD
Tel: 01684-853860 **Fax:** 01684-853861
E-mail: dsmith@transnorm.co.uk
Website: http://www.precisiondrilling.com
Bank(s): Fenska handling Bank
Managers: S. Hall, P. Dunthorne (Purch Mgr)
Ultimate Holding Company: HARALD QUANT HOLDINGS GMBH (GERMANY)
Immediate Holding Company: TRANSNORM SYSTEM LIMITED
Registration no: 01728413 **VAT No.:** GB 409 7608 33
Date established: 1983 **Turnover:** £2m - £5m **No.of Employees:** 51 - 100
Product Groups: 45

Date of Accounts	Dec 10	Dec 09	Dec 08
Sales Turnover	2m	3m	3m
Pre Tax Profit/Loss	40	29	23
Working Capital	834	807	773
Fixed Assets	49	61	71
Current Assets	1m	2m	2m
Current Liabilities	398	553	659

Smartline International Ltd

22 The Sandfield Northway, Tewkesbury, GL20 8RU
Tel: 0870-143 0025 **Fax:** 01684-297662
E-mail: sales@smartline.co.uk
Website: http://www.smart-survey.co.uk
Directors: G. Naser (MD)
Immediate Holding Company: SMARTLINE INTERNATIONAL LIMITED
Registration no: 04885155 **Date established:** 2003
No.of Employees: 1 - 10 **Product Groups:** 44

Date of Accounts	Mar 12	Mar 11	Mar 10
Working Capital	20	70	39
Fixed Assets	13	10	5
Current Assets	65	111	68

Stanway Screens Ltd

Oil Croft Orchard Main Road, Bredon, Tewkesbury, GL20 7LX
Tel: 01684-772378 **Fax:** 01684-772013
E-mail: marcus.priest@stanwayscreens.co.uk
Bank(s): National Westminster Bank Plc
Directors: S. Priest (Comm), M. Priest (MD), T. Priest (Fin)
Immediate Holding Company: STANWAY SCREENS LIMITED
Registration no: 00488564 **VAT No.:** GB 274 1976 31
Date established: 1950 **Turnover:** £1m - £2m **No.of Employees:** 21 - 50
Product Groups: 30, 39

Date of Accounts	Nov 11	Nov 10	Nov 09
Working Capital	295	99	33
Fixed Assets	922	980	944
Current Assets	1m	980	1m

Status Instruments Ltd

Green Lane Business Park Green Lane, Tewkesbury, GL20 8DE
Tel: 01684-296818 **Fax:** 01684-293746
E-mail: sales@status.co.uk
Website: http://www.status.co.uk
Bank(s): Barclay Bank, Haverhill
Directors: L. Evans (Fin), I. Pullin (MD)
Ultimate Holding Company: STATUS HOLDINGS LIMITED
Immediate Holding Company: STATUS INSTRUMENTS LIMITED
Registration no: 01675034 **Date established:** 1982 **Turnover:** £2m - £5m
No.of Employees: 21 - 50 **Product Groups:** 37, 38, 67, 68, 85

Date of Accounts	Mar 12	Mar 11	Mar 10
Working Capital	880	850	786
Fixed Assets	26	34	21
Current Assets	1m	1m	958

Tewkesbury Diamond Chrome Plating Co. Ltd

Northway Lane, Tewkesbury, GL20 8HA
Tel: 01684-292132 **Fax:** 01684-290592
E-mail: sales@tdcp.co.uk
Website: http://www.tdcp.co.uk
Directors: R. Guy (Co Sec), D. Curry (MD)
Immediate Holding Company: TEWKESBURY (DIAMOND CHROME) PLATING CO. LIMITED
Registration no: 04012467 **Date established:** 2000
No.of Employees: 11 - 20 **Product Groups:** 48

Date of Accounts	Jun 12	Jun 11	Jun 10
Working Capital	15	-9	-28
Fixed Assets	531	540	930
Current Assets	215	171	184

Tewkesbury Saw Co. Ltd

Newtown Trading Estate, Tewkesbury, GL20 8JG
Tel: 01684-293092 **Fax:** 01684-850628
E-mail: sales@tewkesburysaw.co.uk
Website: http://www.tewkesburysaw.co.uk
Bank(s): National Westminster
Directors: B. Keen (MD)
Immediate Holding Company: TEWKESBURY SAW COMPANY LIMITED
Registration no: 01176919 **VAT No.:** GB 327 0240 94
Date established: 1974 **Turnover:** £1m - £2m **No.of Employees:** 11 - 20
Product Groups: 36, 37

Date of Accounts	Dec 11	Dec 10	Dec 09
Working Capital	18	21	18
Fixed Assets	53	54	54
Current Assets	299	296	269

Trelleborg Sealing Solutions

International Drive Tewkesbury Business Park, Tewkesbury, GL20 8UQ
Tel: 01684-857600 **Fax:** 01686-624875
E-mail: james.douglas@trelleborg.com
Website: http://www.trelleborg.com
Directors: J. Douglas (MD)
Ultimate Holding Company: TRELLEBORG AB (SWEDEN)
Immediate Holding Company: TRELLEBORG SEALING SOLUTIONS UK LIMITED
Registration no: 00446036 **Date established:** 1947
Turnover: £75m - £125m **No.of Employees:** 51 - 100
Product Groups: 30, 39, 66

Date of Accounts	Dec 11	Dec 10	Dec 09
Sales Turnover	95m	87m	70m
Pre Tax Profit/Loss	18m	14m	2m
Working Capital	38m	52m	41m
Fixed Assets	20m	21m	23m
Current Assets	61m	69m	70m
Current Liabilities	16m	11m	10m

Trio Motion Technology Ltd

Shannon Way Ashchurch, Tewkesbury, GL20 8ND
Tel: 01684-292333 **Fax:** 01684-297929
E-mail: sales@triomotion.com
Website: http://www.triomotion.com
Bank(s): Barclays, Cheltenham
Directors: C. Backhouse (Co Sec), S. Crampton (MD)
Immediate Holding Company: TRIO MOTION TECHNOLOGY LIMITED
Registration no: 02169624 **VAT No.:** GB 493 8071 18
Date established: 1987 **Turnover:** £2m - £5m **No.of Employees:** 11 - 20
Product Groups: 37, 45

Date of Accounts	Dec 11	Dec 10	Dec 09
Working Capital	2m	1m	942
Fixed Assets	635	629	653
Current Assets	2m	2m	1m

Tungum Ltd

Unit 1 Ashchurch Parkway, Tewkesbury, GL20 8TU
Tel: 01684-271290 **Fax:** 01684-291714
E-mail: sales@tungum.com
Website: http://www.tungum.com
Directors: S. Hammond (Sales & Mktg), I. Johnstone (MD), J. Zbihlyj (Chief Op Offcr)
Managers: S. Bywater (Personnel)
Ultimate Holding Company: TUNGUM HOLDINGS LIMITED
Immediate Holding Company: TUNGUM LIMITED
Registration no: 00282202 **VAT No.:** GB 274 6616 36
Date established: 1933 **Turnover:** £2m - £5m **No.of Employees:** 1 - 10
Product Groups: 30, 36, 38, 40, 48

Date of Accounts	Dec 11	Dec 10	Dec 09
Working Capital	568	841	566
Fixed Assets	292	364	428
Current Assets	698	991	1m

Wam Engineering

Unit 13 Alexandra Way, Ashchurch, Tewkesbury, GL20 8NB
Tel: 01684-299100 **Fax:** 01684-299104
E-mail: fabrizio@wameng.com
Website: http://www.wamgroup.com
Directors: F. Vanghi (MD), M. Marchesini (Co Sec)
Immediate Holding Company: WAM ENGINEERING LIMITED
Registration no: 02199494 **VAT No.:** GB 488 2003 42
Date established: 1987 **Turnover:** £2m - £5m **No.of Employees:** 1 - 10
Product Groups: 36, 38, 40, 41, 42, 45

Date of Accounts	Dec 11	Dec 10	Dec 09
Working Capital	467	492	518
Fixed Assets	15	32	21
Current Assets	1m	1m	1m

Warren Engineering

B4-B5 Unit Northway Trading Estate Northway Lane, Tewkesbury, GL20 8JH
Tel: 01684-298000 **Fax:** 01684-295981
E-mail: warrenengineering@aol.com
Directors: S. Warren (Prop)
Registration no: 04962381 **VAT No.:** GB 348 1133 70
Date established: 1982 **Turnover:** £500,000 - £1m
No.of Employees: 1 - 10 **Product Groups:** 48

Westbury On Severn

Severn Valley Woodworks Ltd

Calders Yard Church Lane, Northwood Green, Westbury On Severn, GL14 1ND
Tel: 01452-760994 **Fax:** 01452-760993
E-mail: office@svw2000.co.uk
Website: http://www.svw2000.co.uk
Bank(s): Lloyds TSB Bank plc
Directors: A. Jenkins (MD), D. Twigg (Sales & Mktg), S. Brown (Dir)
Immediate Holding Company: SEVERN VALLEY WOODWORKS LIMITED
Registration no: 02021938 **VAT No.:** GB 274 7980 10
Date established: 1986 **Turnover:** £5m - £10m
No.of Employees: 51 - 100 **Product Groups:** 25, 45, 76

Date of Accounts	Oct 11	Oct 10	Oct 09
Sales Turnover	10m	9m	8m
Pre Tax Profit/Loss	183	128	92
Working Capital	447	398	392
Fixed Assets	1m	1m	1m
Current Assets	3m	3m	2m
Current Liabilities	1m	1m	997

Wotton Under Edge

AG Smith Agricultural Engineering

Millmans Farm Southend, Wotton Under Edge, GL12 7PD
Tel: 01453-544955 **Fax:** 01453-544955
Directors: A. Smith (Prop)
No.of Employees: 1 - 10 **Product Groups:** 35, 41

Alderely Systems Ltd

Kingfisher House Arnoldsfield Trading Estate The Downs, Wickwar, Wotton Under Edge, GL12 8JB
Tel: 01454-294556 **Fax:** 01454-292117
E-mail: sales@alderley.com
Website: http://www.alderley.com
Directors: G. Christou (MD), P. Slatter (Dir), L. Reed (Co Sec), S. Young (Sales & Mktg), N. Hull (MD), A. Shepherd (Grp Chief Exec), J. McAleese (MD)
Managers: D. Lloyd (Tech Sales Mgr), K. Coggins (Personnel), A. Cappi (I.T. Exec), S. Franklin (Fin Mgr), K. Bell, K. Lockyer (Sales Prom Mgr)
Immediate Holding Company: ALDERLEY METERING SYSTEMS LTD
Registration no: 02122431 **Date established:** 1987
Turnover: £20m - £50m **No.of Employees:** 51 - 100 **Product Groups:** 38, 40, 84

Heritage Wine Co. Ltd

The Old Brewery 61 Station Road, Wickwar, Wotton Under Edge, GL12 8NB
Tel: 01454-294099 **Fax:** 08707-408041
E-mail: contact@heritagewine.co.uk
Website: http://www.heritagewine.co.uk
Directors: G. Adams (MD), C. Adams (Dir), G. Adams (MD)
Ultimate Holding Company: SUNCOOL LIMITED
Immediate Holding Company: HERITAGE WINE COMPANY LIMITED
Registration no: 01117280 **Date established:** 1973 **Turnover:** £5m - £10m
No.of Employees: 21 - 50 **Product Groups:** 21

Date of Accounts	May 09	May 08	Jun 11
Working Capital	393	397	426
Fixed Assets	48	69	71
Current Assets	1m	1m	1m

Majorlift Hydraulic Equipment Ltd

Arnolds Field Estate Wickwar, Wotton Under Edge, GL12 8JD
Tel: 01454-299299 **Fax:** 01454-294003
E-mail: info@majorlift.com
Website: http://www.majorlift.co.uk
Directors: L. Abel Smith (MD)
Immediate Holding Company: Majorlift Holdings Ltd
Registration no: 01358382 **Date established:** 1978 **Turnover:** £2m - £5m
No.of Employees: 21 - 50 **Product Groups:** 35, 39, 45

Date of Accounts	Mar 08	Mar 07	Mar 06
Sales Turnover	N/A	2980	3047
Pre Tax Profit/Loss	N/A	283	317

see next page

Majorlift Hydraulic Equipment Ltd - Cont'd

Working Capital	1655	1618	1483
Fixed Assets	553	466	487
Current Assets	2552	2500	2205
Current Liabilities	897	882	722
Total Share Capital	30	30	30
ROCE% (Return on Capital Employed)		13.6	16.1
ROT% (Return on Turnover)		9.5	10.4

Orchestra Wotton Group Ltd

Walk Mills Kingswood, Wotton Under Edge, GL12 8JT
Tel: 01453-843621 **Fax:** 01453-845019
E-mail: enquiries@orchestragroup.co.uk
Website: http://www.orchestragroup.co.uk
Bank(s): Lloyds TSB
Directors: B. Dickson (Dir), M. Cartwright (MD), B. Dickerson (MD)
Immediate Holding Company: ORCHESTRA WOTTON LIMITED
Registration no: 00369034 **VAT No.:** GB 681 7094 14
Date established: 1941 **Turnover:** £5m - £10m
No.of Employees: 51 - 100 **Product Groups:** 27, 28

Date of Accounts	Dec 09	Dec 08	Dec 07
Sales Turnover	10m	10m	11m
Pre Tax Profit/Loss	-174	2m	1m
Working Capital	105	3m	1m
Fixed Assets	1m	817	1m
Current Assets	3m	6m	4m
Current Liabilities	1m	1m	921

Power A Door

Unit B Old Cider Mill Estate Station Road, Wickwar, Wotton Under Edge, GL12 8NB
Tel: 08452-262733 **Fax:** 08452-262744
E-mail: robertwilliams@poweradoor.co.uk
Website: http://www.poweradoor.co.uk
Directors: A. Steven (Prop)
Immediate Holding Company: E C P DESIGN LIMITED
Registration no: 01313934 **Date established:** 1977
No.of Employees: 1 - 10 **Product Groups:** 26, 35

Date of Accounts	Dec 11	Dec 10	Dec 09
Working Capital	573	485	376
Fixed Assets	35	62	57
Current Assets	878	741	634

Renishaw plc

New Mills, Wotton Under Edge, GL12 8JR
Tel: 01453-524524 **Fax:** 01453-524901
E-mail: uk@renishaw.com
Website: http://www.renishaw.com
Bank(s): Lloyds TSB Bank plc
Directors: T. Garthwaite (Fin)
Managers: A. Roberts
Ultimate Holding Company: RENISHAW P L C
Immediate Holding Company: RENISHAW P L C
Registration no: 01106260 **VAT No.:** GB 422 9005 81
Date established: 1973 **Turnover:** £125m - £250m
No.of Employees: 501 - 1000 **Product Groups:** 38, 46

Date of Accounts	Jun 11	Jun 10	Jun 09
Sales Turnover	289m	182m	171m
Pre Tax Profit/Loss	82m	27m	5m
Working Capital	110m	86m	58m
Fixed Assets	161m	110m	127m
Current Assets	157m	116m	80m
Current Liabilities	33m	19m	21m

Teague Precision Chokes Ltd

Larkspur Cottage Tortworth, Wotton Under Edge, GL12 8HF
Tel: 01454-260226 **Fax:** 01454-261663
E-mail: nigelteague@tiscali.co.uk
Website: http://www.teagueprecisionchokesltd.co.uk
Directors: N. Teague (MD), J. Price (Fin)
Immediate Holding Company: TEAGUE PRECISION CHOKES LIMITED
Registration no: 04484322 **Date established:** 2002
Turnover: £250,000 - £500,000 **No.of Employees:** 1 - 10
Product Groups: 36, 39, 40

Date of Accounts	Sep 11	Sep 10	Sep 09
Working Capital	172	229	169
Fixed Assets	55	68	72
Current Assets	210	307	231
Current Liabilities	24	45	42

HAMPSHIRE

Aldershot

Adventure Laif Signs Ltd
Evelyn Woods Road Tournai House, Aldershot, GU11 2LL
Tel: 01252-326555
E-mail: sales@lifesignsgroup.co.uk
Website: http://www.lifesignsgroup.co.uk
No.of Employees: 1 - 10 **Product Groups:** 30, 38, 84, 86

Aldershot Car Spares
Hollybush Lane, Aldershot, GU11 2PX
Tel: 01252-311117 **Fax:** 01252-311117
E-mail: enquiries@aldershotcarspares.com
Website: http://www.aldershotcarspares.com
Directors: G. Boulden (Prop)
Immediate Holding Company: CENTRAL LINEMARKINGS LIMITED
Registration no: 03473544 **Date established:** 1997
No.of Employees: 11 - 20 **Product Groups:** 40, 68

Date of Accounts	Feb 08	Feb 11	Feb 10
Working Capital	353	292	275
Fixed Assets	15	6	10
Current Assets	492	416	354

B T U Europe Ltd
Unit 13 LDL Business Centre Station Road West, Ash Vale, Aldershot, GU12 5RT
Tel: 01252-549848 **Fax:** 01252-660011
E-mail: sales@btu.com
Website: http://www.btu.com
Directors: T. Kealy (Dir)
Ultimate Holding Company: BTU INTERNATIONAL INC (USA)
Immediate Holding Company: BTU EUROPE LIMITED
Registration no: 01587124 **VAT No.:** GB 188 1345 43
Date established: 1981 **Turnover:** £1m - £2m **No.of Employees:** 1 - 10
Product Groups: 40, 46

Date of Accounts	Dec 11	Dec 10	Dec 09
Sales Turnover	1m	1m	1m
Pre Tax Profit/Loss	-129	-445	-603
Working Capital	-94	34	480
Current Assets	367	514	936
Current Liabilities	261	262	179

Beacon Packaging
Unit 4 Blackwater Park, Aldershot, GU12 4PQ
Tel: 01252-353333 **Fax:** 01420-592010
E-mail: sales@beaconpack.co.uk
Website: http://www.beaconpack.co.uk
Bank(s): National Westminster Bank Plc
Directors: G. Rimmer (Co Sec), F. Singer (Fin), F. Eliet (MD)
Managers: N. Bainbridge (Tech Serv Mgr), S. Bainbridge (Buyer)
Immediate Holding Company: MIRAMAR INVESTMENTS LTD
Registration no: 02549984 **VAT No.:** GB 568 3081 23
Date established: 1990 **Turnover:** £5m - £10m
No.of Employees: 51 - 100 **Product Groups:** 27, 85

C Brewer & Sons
122 North Lane, Aldershot, GU12 4QN
Tel: 01252-328316 **Fax:** 01252-317609
Website: http://www.brewers.com
Managers: S. Gilbert (Mgr)
Immediate Holding Company: C.BREWER & SONS LIMITED
Registration no: 00203852 **VAT No.:** GB 190 1565 70
Date established: 1925 **Turnover:** £50m - £75m **No.of Employees:** 1 - 10
Product Groups: 23, 25, 27, 30, 32, 61

C S C
Royal Pavillion Wellesley Road, Aldershot, GU11 1PZ
Tel: 01252-534000 **Fax:** 01252-534100
E-mail: guy.hains@csc.com
Website: http://www.csc.com
Directors: G. Haines (Pres), J. Hobson (Pers)
Managers: A. Bowland
Ultimate Holding Company: COMPUTER SCIENCES CORP (USA)
Immediate Holding Company: COMPUTER SCIENCES UK LIMITED
Registration no: 02594248 **VAT No.:** GB 584 6865 81
Date established: 1991 **Turnover:** Over £1,000m
No.of Employees: 1501 & over **Product Groups:** 44

Date of Accounts	Mar 08	Apr 09	Apr 10
Sales Turnover	1044m	1125m	N/A
Pre Tax Profit/Loss	71m	117m	N/A
Working Capital	-25m	252m	-756
Fixed Assets	353m	314m	240m
Current Assets	937m	1250m	10m
Current Liabilities	505m	537m	N/A

Cameron Forecourt
3 Redan Hill Estate Redan Road, Aldershot, GU12 4SJ
Tel: 01252-361730 **Fax:** 01252-331318
E-mail: info@cameron-forecourt.co.uk
Website: http://www.cameron-forecourt.co.uk
Directors: B. Jenner (MD), K. Jenner (Fin)
Managers: G. Webb (Chief Mgr)
No.of Employees: 21 - 50 **Product Groups:** 40

Capital Hair & Beauty
2 Northtown Trading Estate 122-128 North Lane, Aldershot, GU12 4UB
Tel: 01252-325609 **Fax:** 01252-343669
E-mail: aldershot@capitalhairandbeauty.co.uk
Website: http://www.capitalhairandbeauty.co.uk
Managers: D. Asher (Mgr)
Immediate Holding Company: CAPITAL (HAIR AND BEAUTY) LIMITED
Registration no: 00530201 **Date established:** 1954
No.of Employees: 1 - 10 **Product Groups:** 32, 40, 63, 67

Date of Accounts	Dec 11	Dec 10	Dec 09
Sales Turnover	32m	28m	24m
Pre Tax Profit/Loss	4m	749	2m
Working Capital	7m	4m	3m
Fixed Assets	3m	3m	2m
Current Assets	13m	8m	7m
Current Liabilities	4m	3m	3m

Carlo Gavazzi UK Ltd
7 Springlakes Industrial Estate Deadbrook Lane, Aldershot, GU12 4UH
Tel: 01252-339600 **Fax:** 01252-326799
E-mail: info@carlogavazzi.com
Website: http://www.carlogavazzi.com
Bank(s): National Westminster Bank Plc
Directors: A. Hickman (Dir)
Ultimate Holding Company: CARLO GAVAZZI HOLDING AG (SWITZERLAND)
Immediate Holding Company: CARLO GAVAZZI UK LIMITED
Registration no: 01540907 **Date established:** 1981 **Turnover:** £2m - £5m
No.of Employees: 11 - 20 **Product Groups:** 37, 38, 39, 42, 49

Date of Accounts	Mar 12	Mar 11	Mar 10
Sales Turnover	4m	3m	2m
Pre Tax Profit/Loss	357	112	113
Working Capital	537	152	38
Fixed Assets	45	54	56
Current Assets	1m	1m	914
Current Liabilities	318	261	151

Colourways Print & Embroidery
135 High Street, Aldershot, GU11 1TT
Tel: 01252-344944 **Fax:** 01252-344858
E-mail: service@colourwaysuk.co.uk
Website: http://www.colourwaysuk.co.uk
Directors: D. Coulter (Ptnr)
Immediate Holding Company: INTRAFLAG LIMITED
Registration no: 01805425 **Date established:** 1984
Turnover: Up to £250,000 **No.of Employees:** 1 - 10 **Product Groups:** 24, 49, 63, 65

Compact Sweepers Limited Worldwide
Woodlands Woollards Road, Ash Vale, Aldershot, GU12 5DS
Tel: 01252-660438 **Fax:** 01252-324724
E-mail: sales@compactsweepers.com
Website: http://www.compactsweepers.com
Product Groups: 40, 45, 49, 83

Date of Accounts	Aug 09	Aug 08	Aug 07
Working Capital	64	138	126
Fixed Assets	9	7	8
Current Assets	128	192	188

Corewire Ltd
Station Road West Ash Vale, Aldershot, GU12 5LZ
Tel: 01252-517766 **Fax:** 01252-515833
E-mail: alisdair@corewire.com
Website: http://www.corewire.com
Bank(s): Royal Bank of Scotland, Farnborough
Directors: A. Boag (MD), I. Welch (Fin)
Ultimate Holding Company: BLACKWATER HOLDINGS LTD
Immediate Holding Company: COREWIRE LIMITED
Registration no: 01236964 **VAT No.:** GB 358 7715 11
Date established: 1975 **Turnover:** £10m - £20m
No.of Employees: 51 - 100 **Product Groups:** 35

Date of Accounts	Sep 11	Sep 10	Sep 09
Pre Tax Profit/Loss	1m	496	-135
Working Capital	2m	1m	776
Fixed Assets	2m	2m	2m
Current Assets	8m	6m	5m
Current Liabilities	617	404	100

Crystal Finishes Ltd
Blackwater Way, Aldershot, GU12 4DP
Tel: 01252-325999 **Fax:** 01252-330256
Directors: D. Pike (MD), B. Arnold (Fin)
Immediate Holding Company: CRYSTAL FINISHES LIMITED
Registration no: 01784217 **VAT No.:** 641 3749 39 **Date established:** 1984
Turnover: Up to £250,000 **No.of Employees:** 1 - 10 **Product Groups:** 28, 48

Date of Accounts	Apr 11	Apr 10	Apr 09
Sales Turnover	209	200	245
Pre Tax Profit/Loss	21	-31	-39
Working Capital	-21	-31	11
Fixed Assets	209	215	221
Current Assets	41	42	68
Current Liabilities	15	18	13

Dymet Alloys (Division of Corewire Ltd)
Station Road West Ash Vale, Aldershot, GU12 5LZ
Tel: 01252-517651 **Fax:** 01252-522517
E-mail: info@corewire.com
Website: http://www.corewire.com
Bank(s): The Royal Bank Of Scotland, Farnborough
Directors: A. Boag (MD)
Ultimate Holding Company: BLACKWATER HOLDINGS LTD
Immediate Holding Company: DYMET ALLOYS LIMITED
Registration no: 00513090 **Date established:** 1952 **Turnover:** £1m - £2m
No.of Employees: 21 - 50 **Product Groups:** 31, 33, 34, 35, 36, 38, 45, 46, 48

Elgamec Ltd
Unit 10-11 Enterprise Industrial Estate Station Road West, Ash Vale, Aldershot, GU12 5QJ
Tel: 01252-518177 **Fax:** 01252-541331
E-mail: info@elgamec.com
Website: http://www.elgamec.com
Directors: N. Clinch (Dir)
Immediate Holding Company: ELGAMEC LIMITED
Registration no: 01361541 **Date established:** 1978
Turnover: Up to £250,000 **No.of Employees:** 1 - 10 **Product Groups:** 33, 35, 45, 48, 52

Date of Accounts	Mar 11	Mar 10	Mar 09
Working Capital	33	9	25
Fixed Assets	11	14	9
Current Assets	128	71	66

Ergomounts Ltd
Unit 10 Pegasus Court North Lane, Aldershot, GU12 4QP
Tel: 01252-333326
E-mail: sales@ergomounts.co.uk
Website: http://www.ergomounts.co.uk
Managers: M. Connor (Sales Prom Mgr)
Immediate Holding Company: ERGO MOUNTS LIMITED
Registration no: 05251741 **Date established:** 2004
No.of Employees: 1 - 10 **Product Groups:** 37, 44

Date of Accounts	Oct 11	Oct 10	Oct 09
Working Capital	1m	937	733
Fixed Assets	407	400	410
Current Assets	1m	1m	1m

Farleygreene (Sieving & Mixing Technology for Powders or Liquids)
Unit 8 Alpha Centre Alpha Road, Aldershot, GU12 4RG
Tel: 01252-322233 **Fax:** 01252-325111
E-mail: info@farleygreene.com
Website: http://www.farleygreene.com
Directors: S. Hare (Fin)
Immediate Holding Company: FARLEYGREENE LIMITED
Registration no: 01243329 **Date established:** 1976
No.of Employees: 1 - 10 **Product Groups:** 29, 30, 32, 33, 35, 36, 37, 38, 40, 41, 42, 43, 44, 45, 46, 47, 67, 84

Date of Accounts	Jun 11	Jun 10	Jun 09
Working Capital	184	41	7
Fixed Assets	33	15	14
Current Assets	370	232	144

Fletchers Packaging Ltd
Unit 4 Blackwater Park, Aldershot, GU12 4PQ
Tel: 020-8684 4201 **Fax:** 020-8681 5453
E-mail: gillian@beaconpack.co.uk
Website: http://www.youngsley-packaging.co.uk
Bank(s): Natwest
Directors: F. Eliet (MD), G. Rimmer (Fin)
Managers: S. Bainbridge (Sales Off Mgr)
Ultimate Holding Company: Miramar Investments Ltd
Immediate Holding Company: FLETCHERS PACKAGING LIMITED
Registration no: 00435584 **VAT No.:** GB 494 5631 15
Date established: 1947 **Turnover:** £1m - £2m **No.of Employees:** 51 - 100
Product Groups: 27, 30

Gang-Nail
Christy Estate Ivy Road, Aldershot, GU12 4XG
Tel: 01252-334691 **Fax:** 01252-334562
E-mail: info@gangnail.co.uk
Website: http://www.gangnail.co.uk
Bank(s): Barclays
Managers: P. Baron (Chief Mgr), S. Cunningham (Tech Serv Mgr), J. Ruddle (Mktg Serv Mgr), J. McGuire (Works Gen Mgr)
Ultimate Holding Company: ELECO PUBLIC LIMITED COMPANY
Immediate Holding Company: ELECO (GNS) LIMITED
Registration no: 00863156 **Date established:** 1965 **Turnover:** £5m - £10m
No.of Employees: 51 - 100 **Product Groups:** 25, 32, 33, 34, 35, 52, 66

Date of Accounts	Dec 11	Jun 10	Jun 09
Sales Turnover	8m	5m	6m
Pre Tax Profit/Loss	-510	-245	-472
Working Capital	2m	2m	3m
Fixed Assets	18	341	373
Current Assets	3m	4m	4m
Current Liabilities	690	622	557

Good Containers Suppliers
The Firs White Lane, Ash Green, Aldershot, GU12 6HN
Tel: 01252-317351 **Fax:** 01252-333134
Directors: D. Stephens (Prop), D. Stevens (Prop)
Date established: 2000 **No.of Employees:** 1 - 10 **Product Groups:** 38, 42

Greywell Holland & Watts
1 Paragon Court Tongham Road, Aldershot, GU12 4AA
Tel: 01252-344200 **Fax:** 01252-343466
E-mail: sales@hollandandwatts.com
Website: http://www.hollandandwatts.com
Directors: C. Holland (Dir)
Immediate Holding Company: HOLLAND & WATTS LIMITED
Registration no: 03902328 **Date established:** 2000
Turnover: £500,000 - £1m **No.of Employees:** 1 - 10 **Product Groups:** 28

Date of Accounts	Mar 09	Mar 08	Mar 07
Sales Turnover	N/A	N/A	815
Pre Tax Profit/Loss	N/A	N/A	-44
Working Capital	77	148	58
Fixed Assets	37	42	188
Current Assets	405	471	337
Current Liabilities	N/A	N/A	74

Hogan Company
Hippodrome House Birchett Road, Aldershot, GU11 1LZ
Tel: 01252-325700
E-mail: mail@ehogans.com
Website: http://www.ehogans.com
Directors: N. Hogan (MD)
Immediate Holding Company: HOGAN & CO., (INVESTIGATIONS & SECURITY) LIMITED
Registration no: 02045318 **Date established:** 1986 **Turnover:** £1m - £2m
No.of Employees: 1 - 10 **Product Groups:** 81

Date of Accounts	Mar 12	Mar 11	Mar 10
Working Capital	812	815	722
Fixed Assets	1	20	44
Current Assets	921	937	848

Ideas Furnace Ltd
Tournai Hall Evelyn Woods Road, Aldershot, GU11 2LL
Tel: 08456-188291
E-mail: info@ideas-furnace.com
Website: http://www.ideas-furnace.com
Managers: P. Butcher (Accounts)
Registration no: 06329644 **Date established:** 2007
No.of Employees: 1 - 10 **Product Groups:** 44

Johnson Controls Ltd
Royal Pavilion Wellesley Road, Aldershot, GU11 1PZ
Tel: 01252-346300 **Fax:** 01252-346301
Website: http://www.jci.com
Bank(s): National Westminster
Managers: A. Osborn (Fin Mgr), A. Bird (Sales Admin)
Ultimate Holding Company: JOHNSON CONTROLS INC (USA)
Immediate Holding Company: JOHNSON CONTROLS LIMITED
Registration no: 00661449 **Date established:** 1960
Turnover: Over £1,000m **No.of Employees:** 51 - 100 **Product Groups:** 38

Date of Accounts	Sep 11	Sep 10	Sep 09
Sales Turnover	644m	612m	542m
Pre Tax Profit/Loss	8m	4m	3m
Working Capital	-228m	-195m	-239m
Fixed Assets	429m	317m	326m
Current Assets	220m	239m	167m
Current Liabilities	261m	265m	262m

Johnston Sweepers Ltd
Lysons Avenue Ash Vale, Aldershot, GU12 5QF
Tel: 01252-513351 **Fax:** 01252-546241
E-mail: ashvale@johnstonsweepers.com
Website: http://www.johnstonsweepers.com
Managers: J. Smizth (Mgr)
Ultimate Holding Company: BUCHER INDUSTRIES AG (SWITZERLAND)
Immediate Holding Company: JOHNSTON SWEEPERS LIMITED
Registration no: 00199841 **Date established:** 2024
Turnover: £50m - £75m **No.of Employees:** 11 - 20 **Product Groups:** 39, 40, 45

Date of Accounts	Dec 11	Dec 10	Dec 09
Sales Turnover	56m	52m	58m
Pre Tax Profit/Loss	10m	9m	4m
Working Capital	9m	8m	12m
Fixed Assets	17m	17m	13m
Current Assets	26m	20m	24m
Current Liabilities	5m	5m	6m

Kenure Developments Ltd
2-3 Springlakes Estate Deadbrook Lane, Aldershot, GU12 4UH
Tel: 01252-338554 **Fax:** 01252-329105
E-mail: sales@kenure.co.uk
Website: http://www.kenure.co.uk
Directors: A. Blackburn (Fin)
Managers: D. Carroway (Sales & Mktg Mg), S. Browning (Purch Mgr), S. Hockey (Personnel)
Immediate Holding Company: KENURE DEVELOPMENTS LIMITED
Registration no: 02265402 **VAT No.:** GB 498 0282 5
Date established: 1988 **Turnover:** £2m - £5m **No.of Employees:** 21 - 50
Product Groups: 34, 37, 38, 39, 47, 48, 84, 85

Date of Accounts	Jun 11	Jun 10	Jun 09
Sales Turnover	4m	3m	3m
Pre Tax Profit/Loss	697	134	63
Working Capital	2m	1m	1m
Fixed Assets	409	301	428
Current Assets	2m	2m	2m
Current Liabilities	229	443	328

Link-Up Ltd
Unit 5 Holder Road, Aldershot, GU12 4RH
Tel: 0845-3032930 **Fax:** 0845-3032931
E-mail: sales@linkupltd.com
Website: http://www.linkupltd.com
Directors: D. Clifford (MD), L. Clifford (Dir)
Immediate Holding Company: Link-Up Ltd
Registration no: 02900927 **VAT No.:** GB 641 2074 73
Date established: 1994 **Turnover:** Up to £250,000
No.of Employees: 1 - 10 **Product Groups:** 22, 23, 24, 25, 27, 28, 30, 32, 33, 35, 36, 37, 38, 44, 49, 63, 64, 65, 81

Mclennan Servo Supplies Ltd
Lynchford Road Ash Vale, Aldershot, GU12 5PQ
Tel: 08707-700700 **Fax:** 0870-770 0699
E-mail: sales@mclennan.co.uk
Website: http://www.mclennan.co.uk
Bank(s): Lloyds TSB Bank plc
Managers: G. Wingate
Immediate Holding Company: MCLENNAN SERVO SUPPLIES LIMITED
Registration no: 01260586 **VAT No.:** GB 200 8261 13
Date established: 1976 **Turnover:** £2m - £5m **No.of Employees:** 11 - 20
Product Groups: 37, 38

Date of Accounts	Sep 11	Sep 10	Sep 09
Working Capital	1m	1m	1m
Fixed Assets	90	73	78
Current Assets	2m	1m	1m

Mann Mcgowan Fabrications Ltd
4 The Brook Trading Estate Deadbrook Lane, Aldershot, GU12 4XB
Tel: 01252-333601 **Fax:** 01252-322724
E-mail: sales@mannmcgowan.co.uk
Website: http://www.mannmcgowan.co.uk
Bank(s): Barclays
Directors: K. Hulin (MD)
Immediate Holding Company: MANN MCGOWAN FABRICATIONS LIMITED
Registration no: 01212744 **VAT No.:** GB 213 1820 13
Date established: 1975 **No.of Employees:** 21 - 50 **Product Groups:** 30, 32, 33, 40

Date of Accounts	Dec 11	Dec 10	Dec 09
Working Capital	54	191	232
Fixed Assets	74	84	95
Current Assets	494	489	369

Mantek Manufacturing Ltd
11 Holder Road, Aldershot, GU12 4RH
Tel: 01252-343335 **Fax:** 01252-343570
E-mail: sales@mantek.co.uk
Website: http://www.mantek.co.uk
Bank(s): National Westminster Bank Plc
Directors: C. Mandell (MD)
Immediate Holding Company: MANTEK MANUFACTURING LIMITED
Registration no: 01621351 **VAT No.:** GB 358 8507 13
Date established: 1982 **Turnover:** £1m - £2m **No.of Employees:** 11 - 20
Product Groups: 22, 23, 25, 27, 29, 30, 32, 33, 35, 36, 37, 39, 40, 49, 68

Date of Accounts	Mar 11	Mar 10	Mar 09
Working Capital	169	163	194
Fixed Assets	378	371	338
Current Assets	339	357	315

Marksman Industrial Ltd
130b North Lane, Aldershot, GU12 4QN
Tel: 01252-345455 **Fax:** 01252-345455
E-mail: info@marksman-ind.com
Website: http://www.marksman-ind.com
Directors: M. Green (MD)
Immediate Holding Company: MARKSMAN INDUSTRIAL LIMITED
Registration no: 05127937 **Date established:** 2004
No.of Employees: 1 - 10 **Product Groups:** 30, 33, 35

Date of Accounts	May 11	May 09	May 08
Working Capital	-2	1	7
Fixed Assets	3	3	3
Current Assets	74	110	56

Mastiff Electronic Systems Ltd
8 Holder Road, Aldershot, GU12 4RH
Tel: 01252-342200 **Fax:** 01252-342400
E-mail: enquiries@mastiff.co.uk
Website: http://www.mastiff.co.uk
Directors: T. Oram (Dir)
Immediate Holding Company: MASTIFF ELECTRONIC SYSTEMS LIMITED
Registration no: 00969947 **VAT No.:** GB 10 1822 27
Date established: 1970 **Turnover:** Up to £250,000
No.of Employees: 1 - 10 **Product Groups:** 36, 40

Date of Accounts	Dec 11	Dec 10	Dec 09
Sales Turnover	157	225	271
Pre Tax Profit/Loss	-131	-118	-124
Working Capital	-39	-29	12
Fixed Assets	11	18	27
Current Assets	37	61	128
Current Liabilities	15	21	24

Merrychef Ltd
Station Road West Ash Vale, Aldershot, GU12 5XA
Tel: 01252-371000 **Fax:** 01252-371007
E-mail: bob.arthey@merrychef.com
Website: http://www.merrychef.com
Directors: B. Arthey (Fin), G. Veal (Dir), K. Blades (Fin)
Ultimate Holding Company: THE MANITOWOC CO INC(USA)
Immediate Holding Company: MERRYCHEF LIMITED
Registration no: 00487712 **Date established:** 1950
Turnover: £10m - £20m **No.of Employees:** 101 - 250
Product Groups: 40, 42, 46

Date of Accounts	Dec 10	Dec 09	Dec 08
Sales Turnover	25m	20m	22m
Pre Tax Profit/Loss	-3m	44	-36
Working Capital	6m	8m	8m
Fixed Assets	N/A	1m	2m
Current Assets	6m	13m	12m
Current Liabilities	N/A	823	1m

Modular Hydraulic Systems Ltd
9 Redan Hill Estate Redan Road, Aldershot, GU12 4SJ
Tel: 01252-333883 **Fax:** 01252-343615
E-mail: allan@mhs.co.uk
Website: http://www.mhs.co.uk
Directors: A. Dudman (MD)
Immediate Holding Company: MODULAR HYDRAULIC SYSTEMS LIMITED
Registration no: 01398055 **Date established:** 1978
Turnover: £500,000 - £1m **No.of Employees:** 1 - 10 **Product Groups:** 38, 40, 67

Date of Accounts	Oct 11	Oct 10	Oct 09
Sales Turnover	N/A	N/A	796
Pre Tax Profit/Loss	N/A	N/A	-1
Working Capital	-40	-23	-68
Fixed Assets	4	4	4
Current Assets	478	408	359
Current Liabilities	N/A	N/A	221

Nendle Acoustics Ltd
153 High Street, Aldershot, GU11 1TT
Tel: 01252-344222 **Fax:** 01252-333782
E-mail: enquiries@nendle.co.uk
Website: http://www.nendle.co.uk
Directors: J. Williams (Tech Serv)
Immediate Holding Company: NENDLE ACOUSTICS COMPANY (SOUTHERN) LIMITED
Registration no: 05669328 **Date established:** 2006 **Turnover:** £1m - £2m
No.of Employees: 1 - 10 **Product Groups:** 38, 52

Date of Accounts	Jan 11	Jan 10	Jan 09
Working Capital	90	127	112
Fixed Assets	7	9	8
Current Assets	182	258	246

Perei Group Ltd
Sunbury House 4 Christy Estate Ivy Road, Aldershot, GU12 4TX
Tel: 01252-350833 **Fax:** 01252-350875
E-mail: sales@perei.co.uk
Website: http://www.perei.co.uk
Bank(s): Barclays
Directors: R. Perei (Dir), W. Perei (Fin)
Managers: G. Pennels (Buyer)
Ultimate Holding Company: DELTRONIC LIMITED
Immediate Holding Company: PEREI GROUP LIMITED
Registration no: 00761224 **VAT No.:** GB 293 5530 43
Date established: 1963 **Turnover:** £10m - £20m
No.of Employees: 51 - 100 **Product Groups:** 39

Date of Accounts	Jun 11	Jun 10	Jun 09
Sales Turnover	12m	12m	8m
Pre Tax Profit/Loss	666	491	73
Working Capital	2m	2m	3m
Fixed Assets	2m	2m	2m
Current Assets	4m	5m	5m
Current Liabilities	767	2m	912

Pest Help Ltd
Unit 1 Fairfax Industrial Estate Eastern Road, Aldershot, GU12 4TU
Tel: 023-9217 8584 **Fax:** 0114-276 6556
E-mail: sales@pesthelp.co.uk
Website: http://www.pesthelp.co.uk
Directors: D. Brooks (Dir)
Immediate Holding Company: PESTHELP (UK) LTD
Registration no: 08028422 **Date established:** 2012
Turnover: Up to £250,000 **No.of Employees:** 1 - 10 **Product Groups:** 07, 40, 52, 66

Date of Accounts	Mar 07	Mar 06
Working Capital	-19	-16
Current Assets	8	N/A
Current Liabilities	26	16

Pro Tech Precision Ltd
Station Road West Ash Vale, Aldershot, GU12 5QD
Tel: 01252-516242 **Fax:** 01252-524025
E-mail: kwise@pro-techprecision.com
Website: http://www.pro-techprecision.com
Directors: K. Wise (MD)
Immediate Holding Company: PRO-TECH PRECISION LIMITED
Registration no: 00647721 **Date established:** 1960 **Turnover:** £5m - £10m
No.of Employees: 11 - 20 **Product Groups:** 48

Date of Accounts	Jun 11	Jun 10	Jun 09
Working Capital	121	268	289
Fixed Assets	273	347	91
Current Assets	369	449	404

Protec Metal Work Ltd
7 H T H Complex Blackwater Way, Aldershot, GU12 4DN
Tel: 01252-310443 **Fax:** 01252-341787
E-mail: protecmetal@btconnect.com
Website: http://www.protecmetalwork.com
Directors: E. Foster (Dir), P. Foster (Jt MD)
Managers: J. Foster (Accounts)
Registration no: 01370304 **VAT No.:** GB 296 3028 42
Date established: 1978 **Turnover:** £250,000 - £500,000
No.of Employees: 1 - 10 **Product Groups:** 48

Date of Accounts	May 08	May 07	May 06
Working Capital	26	24	7
Fixed Assets	11	13	14
Current Assets	119	74	53
Current Liabilities	92	50	46
Total Share Capital	1	1	1

Quality Irrigation Ltd
309 Vale Road Ash Vale, Aldershot, GU12 5LN
Tel: 01252-328017 **Fax:** 01252-328017
E-mail: alanaustin@qualityirrigation.co.uk
Website: http://www.qualityirrigation.co.uk

Directors: D. Austin (Fin)
Immediate Holding Company: QUALITY IRRIGATION LIMITED
Registration no: 02413255 **Date established:** 1989
Turnover: Up to £250,000 **No.of Employees:** 1 - 10 **Product Groups:** 51, 67, 84

Date of Accounts	Dec 11	Dec 10	Dec 09
Sales Turnover	N/A	134	N/A
Pre Tax Profit/Loss	N/A	8	N/A
Working Capital	-11	2	N/A
Fixed Assets	13	8	N/A
Current Assets	9	30	15
Current Liabilities	N/A	12	N/A

Rhodes Packaging Ltd
9a Holder Road, Aldershot, GU12 4RH
Tel: 01252-320672 **Fax:** 01252-313660
E-mail: sales@rhodespackaging.co.uk
Website: http://www.rhodespackaging.co.uk
Directors: C. Rhodes (Dir)
Immediate Holding Company: RHODES PACKAGING LIMITED
Registration no: 07414186 **Date established:** 2010
Turnover: £250m - £500m **No.of Employees:** 1 - 10 **Product Groups:** 25, 27, 30

Date of Accounts	Nov 11
Working Capital	33
Current Assets	246

Richard Thorpe Fire Safety Services & Citadel Security
235 Ash Road, Aldershot, GU12 4DD
Tel: 01252-316330 **Fax:** 01483-235569
E-mail: info@richardthorpefire.co.uk
Website: http://www.richardthorpefire.co.uk
Directors: R. Thorpe (Prop)
Date established: 1980 **No.of Employees:** 1 - 10 **Product Groups:** 38, 42

Season Master
Unit 13 Redan Hill Estate Redan Road, Aldershot, GU12 4SJ
Tel: 01252-319670 **Fax:** 01252-341983
E-mail: info@seasonmaster.com
Website: http://www.seasonmaster.com
Directors: A. Fletcher (Prop)
Turnover: £500,000 - £1m **No.of Employees:** 1 - 10 **Product Groups:** 30, 33, 40, 52, 66

Securikey Ltd
Unit 5 Springlakes Estate Deadbrook Lane, Aldershot, GU12 4UH
Tel: 01252-311888 **Fax:** 01252-343950
E-mail: enquiries@securikey.co.uk
Website: http://www.securikey.co.uk
Bank(s): Barclays
Directors: L. Scott (Fin)
Ultimate Holding Company: HARBOUR SECURITY PRODUCTS LIMITED
Immediate Holding Company: SECURIKEY LIMITED
Registration no: 04137284 **VAT No.:** GB 212 3330 26
Date established: 2001 **Turnover:** £2m - £5m **No.of Employees:** 11 - 20
Product Groups: 33, 35, 36, 40, 52

Date of Accounts	Sep 11	Sep 10	Sep 09
Working Capital	917	876	830
Fixed Assets	52	45	52
Current Assets	2m	2m	2m

Streamlined Propeller Repairs
Unit 17 Cavendish Mews, Aldershot, GU11 3EH
Tel: 01252-316412 **Fax:** 01252-316412
E-mail: streamlined@ukgateway.net
Website: http://www.streamlinedpropellers.co.uk
Directors: G. Beard (Ptnr)
Turnover: Up to £250,000 **No.of Employees:** 1 - 10 **Product Groups:** 39, 84

Technical Lapping Co. Ltd
138 North Lane, Aldershot, GU12 4QN
Tel: 01252-327733 **Fax:** 01252-332241
E-mail: info@technicallapping.com
Website: http://www.technicallapping.com
Directors: M. Ridgers (MD)
Immediate Holding Company: TECHNICAL LAPPING COMPANY LIMITED
Registration no: 00953545 **VAT No.:** GB 211 8665 73
Date established: 1969 **No.of Employees:** 1 - 10 **Product Groups:** 48

Date of Accounts	Jun 12	Jun 11	Jun 10
Working Capital	134	144	72
Fixed Assets	11	6	6
Current Assets	251	278	130

Tritools
15 Albert Road, Aldershot, GU11 1SZ
Tel: 01252-310429 **Fax:** 01252-324428
Directors: J. Dixon (Prop)
Immediate Holding Company: TRITOOLS LIMITED
Registration no: 05175941 **VAT No.:** GB 189 3958 91
Date established: 2004 **Turnover:** £250,000 - £500,000
No.of Employees: 1 - 10 **Product Groups:** 46, 48

Date of Accounts	Jul 10	Jul 09	Jul 08
Sales Turnover	246	296	N/A
Pre Tax Profit/Loss	77	115	N/A
Working Capital	38	52	23
Fixed Assets	28	38	53
Current Assets	151	184	119
Current Liabilities	22	40	N/A

T-Thermal Division Of Selas-Linde
Unit 1 Blackwater Park, Aldershot, GU12 4PQ
Tel: 01252-321811 **Fax:** 01252-321355
E-mail: nary.mistry@sl-t-thermal.com
Website: http://www.sl-t-thermal.com
Managers: N. Mistry (Chief Mgr)
Immediate Holding Company: LINDE
Registration no: 02537470 **Date established:** 1990
Turnover: £50m - £75m **No.of Employees:** 1 - 10 **Product Groups:** 54

Wel Medical Services
Southern House Sebastopol Road, Aldershot, GU11 1SG
Tel: 01252-344007 **Fax:** 01252-344004
E-mail: info@welmedical.com
Website: http://www.welmedical.com
Directors: I. Pearse (Dir)
Immediate Holding Company: WEL MEDICAL LTD
Registration no: 05714397 **Date established:** 2006
Turnover: £500,000 - £1m **No.of Employees:** 1 - 10 **Product Groups:** 38

Youngsley Packaging
Unit 4 Blackwater Park, Aldershot, GU12 4PQ
Tel: 01420-592025 **Fax:** 01420-592045
E-mail: jim@youngsley-packaging.co.uk
Website: http://www.beaconhispeed.co.uk
Directors: F. Eliet (MD)
Managers: J. Scott (Mgr)
Immediate Holding Company: CERATECH ELECTRONICS LIMITED
Registration no: 02944509 **Date established:** 1994 **Turnover:** £1m - £2m
No.of Employees: 11 - 20 **Product Groups:** 38, 42

Alresford

Calltec Services
Winton Farm Petersfield Road, Monkwood, Alresford, SO24 0HB
Tel: 01962-772217 **Fax:** 01962-772217
Directors: J. Collins (MD), M. Collins (Co Sec)
Immediate Holding Company: CALLTEC SERVICES LIMITED
Registration no: 04882632 **Date established:** 2003
No.of Employees: 1 - 10 **Product Groups:** 20, 40, 41

Date of Accounts	Jan 11	Jan 10	Jan 09
Working Capital	-19	-28	-18
Fixed Assets	8	10	19
Current Assets	16	21	25
Current Liabilities	N/A	N/A	5

Carvill Design International
The Old Granary Western Court, Bishop's Sutton, Alresford, SO24 0AA
Tel: 01962-737913 **Fax:** 01962-738825
Managers: S. Carvill (Mgr)
Immediate Holding Company: REMOTE SENSING APPLICATIONS CONSULTANTS LIMITED
Date established: 1996 **No.of Employees:** 1 - 10 **Product Groups:** 37, 67

Date of Accounts	Mar 11	Mar 10	Mar 09
Working Capital	493	486	468
Fixed Assets	84	110	71
Current Assets	787	611	686

Ceejay Systems Ltd
The Dean, Alresford, SO24 9BN
Tel: 01962-733088 **Fax:** 01962-732833
E-mail: chris@ceejaysystems.com
Website: http://www.ceejaysystems.com
Directors: C. Jones (Dir)
Ultimate Holding Company: CEEJAY HOLDINGS LIMITED
Immediate Holding Company: CEEJAY SYSTEMS (S.V.) LIMITED
Registration no: 02941843 **Date established:** 1994
No.of Employees: 21 - 50 **Product Groups:** 42, 45

Date of Accounts	Apr 12	Apr 11	Apr 10
Working Capital	736	638	629
Fixed Assets	35	56	44
Current Assets	1m	860	942

D N A UK Ltd
Bighton Hill Ropley, Alresford, SO24 9SQ
Tel: 01962-772666 **Fax:** 01962-772660
E-mail: info@dnacap.com
Website: http://www.dnacap.com
Directors: J. Reeve (MD)
Immediate Holding Company: DNA (UK) LIMITED
Registration no: 02493821 **Date established:** 1990 **Turnover:** £2m - £5m
No.of Employees: 1 - 10 **Product Groups:** 35, 37

Date of Accounts	Dec 11	Dec 10	Dec 09
Working Capital	140	184	174
Current Assets	241	304	339

Griffin Glasshouses Ltd
Unit 3 Dean Farm Buildings Bighton Hill, Ropley, Alresford, SO24 9SQ
Tel: 01962-772512 **Fax:** 01962-773119
E-mail: linda@griffinglasshouses.com
Website: http://www.griffinglasshouses.com
Directors: L. Lane (MD)
Immediate Holding Company: GRIFFIN GLASSHOUSES LIMITED
Registration no: 01786962 **Date established:** 1984
No.of Employees: 1 - 10 **Product Groups:** 25, 35

Date of Accounts	May 11	May 10	May 09
Working Capital	-22	-43	-27
Fixed Assets	20	27	37
Current Assets	80	50	39

Huxley Golf
The Dean, Alresford, SO24 9BL
Tel: 01962-733222 **Fax:** 01962-734702
E-mail: sales@huxleygolf.co.uk
Website: http://www.huxleygolf.com
Directors: P. Huxley (Dir)
Immediate Holding Company: HUXLEY (UK) LIMITED
Registration no: 02829270 **Date established:** 1993
No.of Employees: 1 - 10 **Product Groups:** 41

Date of Accounts	Jul 11	Jul 10	Jul 09
Working Capital	220	226	287
Fixed Assets	2m	2m	2m
Current Assets	433	404	476

Impact Sewing Machinery Ltd
Barton Lodge Upper Wield, Alresford, SO24 9RN
Tel: 01420-564433 **Fax:** 01420-564433
E-mail: taitnick@aol.com
Website: http://www.impact.co.uk
Directors: N. Tait (Fin)
Immediate Holding Company: IMPACT SEWING MACHINERY LIMITED
Registration no: 02941002 **Date established:** 1994
No.of Employees: 1 - 10 **Product Groups:** 43

Date of Accounts	Jun 11	Jun 10	Jun 09
Working Capital	-8	-13	-7
Fixed Assets	7	13	17
Current Assets	55	60	65

In2Connect UK Ltd
PO Box 66, Alresford, SO24 0WX
Tel: 01962-773004 **Fax:** 01962-773104
E-mail: sales@in2connect.uk.com
Website: http://www.in2connect.uk.com
Bank(s): National Westminster Bank Plc
Directors: B. Hart (Dir)
Immediate Holding Company: IN2CONNECT UK LTD
Registration no: 04423574 **VAT No.:** GB 736 9209 10
Date established: 2002 **No.of Employees:** 11 - 20 **Product Groups:** 37

Date of Accounts	Mar 11	Mar 10	Mar 09
Sales Turnover	N/A	N/A	262
Pre Tax Profit/Loss	N/A	N/A	23
Working Capital	-40	-81	-80
Fixed Assets	33	63	94
Current Assets	235	182	191
Current Liabilities	N/A	N/A	18

Mcgregor Polytunnels Ltd
Winton Farm Petersfield Road, Monkwood, Alresford, SO24 0HB
Tel: 01962-772368 **Fax:** 01962-772471
E-mail: sales@mcgregorpolytunnels.co.uk
Website: http://www.mcgregorpolytunnels.co.uk
Directors: M. Mcgregor (MD)
Immediate Holding Company: MCGREGOR POLYTUNNELS LIMITED
Registration no: 01466493 **Date established:** 1979
No.of Employees: 11 - 20 **Product Groups:** 26, 35

Date of Accounts	Dec 11	Dec 10	Dec 09
Working Capital	228	168	138
Fixed Assets	50	49	61
Current Assets	532	396	347

Pica Design Ltd
Legendary House 4a Broad Street, Alresford, SO24 9AQ
Tel: 01962-779667 **Fax:** 01962-735355
E-mail: r.clark@picadesign.co.uk
Website: http://www.picadesign.co.uk
Directors: R. Clark (Prop)
Immediate Holding Company: PICA DESIGN LIMITED
Registration no: 02060840 **Date established:** 1986 **Turnover:** £1m - £2m
No.of Employees: 1 - 10 **Product Groups:** 80, 81

Date of Accounts	Sep 11	Sep 10	Sep 09
Working Capital	7	5	11
Fixed Assets	2	6	7
Current Assets	18	57	71

R & R Attachments Ltd
1 Yew Tree Cottage Wood Lane, Bramdean, Alresford, SO24 0JW
Tel: 01962-771837 **Fax:** 01962-771837
E-mail: reldisney@fsmail.net
Website: http://www.randrattachments.co.uk
Directors: A. Disney (Co Sec)
Registration no: 02304776 **Date established:** 1988
No.of Employees: 1 - 10 **Product Groups:** 45

Date of Accounts	Dec 06	Dec 05
Working Capital	-63	-99
Fixed Assets	10	13
Current Assets	31	36
Current Liabilities	94	135
Total Share Capital	50	50

Rod Brown Engineering Ltd
58 The Dean, Alresford, SO24 9BD
Tel: 01962-735220 **Fax:** 01962-735239
E-mail: info@rodbrowneng.co.uk
Website: http://www.rodbrowneng.co.uk
Directors: R. Brown (MD)
Immediate Holding Company: ROD BROWN ENGINEERING LIMITED
Registration no: 02144217 **VAT No.:** GB 344 8014 67
Date established: 1987 **Turnover:** £500,000 - £1m
No.of Employees: 1 - 10 **Product Groups:** 42, 45

Date of Accounts	Mar 12	Mar 11	Mar 10
Working Capital	45	38	28
Fixed Assets	N/A	N/A	1
Current Assets	89	49	60

Robin Sharp Agricultural Engineers
The Dean, Alresford, SO24 9BH
Tel: 01962-734400 **Fax:** 01962-734873
E-mail: robinsharp67@tiscali.co.uk
Directors: R. Sharp (Prop)
Date established: 1979 **No.of Employees:** 1 - 10 **Product Groups:** 41

Warwick Bros Alresford Ltd
The Dean, Alresford, SO24 9BN
Tel: 01962-732681 **Fax:** 01962-735385
E-mail: chris@warwicktrailers.co.uk
Website: http://www.warwicktrailers.co.uk
Bank(s): Barclays
Directors: L. Jones (Co Sec), C. Jones (MD), C. Jones (MD)
Managers: N. Bell (Sales Admin)
Ultimate Holding Company: CEEJAY HOLDINGS LIMITED
Immediate Holding Company: WARWICK BROS.(ALRESFORD)LIMITED
Registration no: 00604875 **VAT No.:** GB 188 6766 91
Date established: 1958 **No.of Employees:** 21 - 50 **Product Groups:** 41

Date of Accounts	Apr 12	Apr 11	Apr 10
Working Capital	1m	986	1m
Fixed Assets	50	58	47
Current Assets	2m	2m	2m

Weld Shop & Fabrications Ltd
Barton House Upper Wield, Alresford, SO24 9RN
Tel: 01420-561715 **Fax:** 01420-561716
Directors: M. Barrett (MD)
Immediate Holding Company: WELDSHOP & FABRICATION LIMITED
Registration no: 03276551 **Date established:** 1996
No.of Employees: 1 - 10 **Product Groups:** 35

Date of Accounts	Nov 11	Nov 10	Nov 09
Working Capital	-52	-4	119
Fixed Assets	27	24	25
Current Assets	206	216	320

E Williams Plating Hampshire Ltd
The Dean, Alresford, SO24 9BQ
Tel: 01962-733199 **Fax:** 01962-735146
E-mail: enquiries@ewp-hants.co.uk
Website: http://www.ewp-hants.co.uk

see next page

E Williams Plating Hampshire Ltd - Cont'd

Directors: T. Brierley (Dir), G. Wyeth (MD)
Immediate Holding Company: E WILLIAMS PLATING LIMITED
Registration no: 05756618 **VAT No.:** GB 212 0643 20
Date established: 2006 **Turnover:** £500,000 - £1m
No.of Employees: 1 - 10 **Product Groups:** 48

Date of Accounts	Mar 11	Mar 10	Mar 09
Working Capital	120	59	8
Fixed Assets	45	51	111
Current Assets	228	154	147

Winchester Consulting Ltd

Manor Barn Kilmeston, Alresford, SO24 0NL
Tel: 01962-771149 **Fax:** 01962-771199
E-mail: info@wincon.co.uk
Website: http://www.wincon.co.uk
Directors: C. Jarman (MD)
Immediate Holding Company: WINCHESTER CONSULTING LIMITED
Registration no: 04210584 **Date established:** 2001
Turnover: £500,000 - £1m **No.of Employees:** 1 - 10 **Product Groups:** 80

Date of Accounts	May 11	May 10	May 09
Working Capital	18	43	35
Fixed Assets	3	4	4
Current Assets	122	153	221

Alton

Advanced Medical Supplies Ltd

Chartwell House Business Centre, Wilsom Road, Alton, GU34 2PP
Tel: 01420-86756 **Fax:** 01635-297546
E-mail: sales@ams-med.com
Website: http://www.ams-med.com
Directors: J. Young (MD)
Managers: C. Newman (Mgr)
Registration no: NI063798 **Turnover:** £500,000 - £1m
No.of Employees: 1 - 10 **Product Groups:** 38, 42, 48

The Aerogen Co. Ltd

Unit 3 Alton Business Centre, Alton, GU34 2YU
Tel: 01420-83744 **Fax:** 01420-80032
E-mail: info@aerogen.co.uk
Website: http://www.aerogen.co.uk
Managers: M. Martin (Fin Mgr)
Immediate Holding Company: AEROGEN HOLDINGS LIMITED
Registration no: 06663202 **Date established:** 2008 **Turnover:** £2m - £5m
No.of Employees: 1 - 10 **Product Groups:** 40, 46

Date of Accounts	Dec 10	Dec 09	Dec 08
Working Capital	165	76	1
Fixed Assets	581	404	N/A
Current Assets	220	97	1

Alresford Marquees Hire Ltd

Ashdell Farm Headmoor Lane, Four Marks, Alton, GU34 3ES
Tel: 01420-587444 **Fax:** 01420-587444
E-mail: info@hiremarquee.co.uk
Website: http://www.hiremarquee.co.uk
Directors: N. Merrix (Dir)
Immediate Holding Company: ALRESFORD MARQUEE HIRE LIMITED
Registration no: 03120185 **Date established:** 1995
Turnover: Up to £250,000 **No.of Employees:** 1 - 10 **Product Groups:** 24, 81, 83, 89

Date of Accounts	Dec 11	Dec 10	Dec 09
Working Capital	-92	-77	-64
Fixed Assets	116	118	89
Current Assets	63	45	55

Anderson Bradshaw

Unit 2-3 Woodlea Park Station Approach, Four Marks, Alton, GU34 5AZ
Tel: 01420-562645 **Fax:** 01420-561696
E-mail: sales@andersonbradshaw.co.uk
Website: http://www.andersonbradshaw.co.uk
Directors: G. Johnson (Dir)
No.of Employees: 1 - 10 **Product Groups:** 26, 61, 63

Astech Electronics Ltd

Forge Industrial Estate The Street, Binsted, Alton, GU34 4PF
Tel: 01420-22689 **Fax:** 01420-22636
E-mail: sales@astechelectronics.com
Website: http://www.astechelectronics.co.uk
Directors: K. Baker (MD), S. Cooke (Tech Serv)
Immediate Holding Company: ASTECH ELECTRONICS LIMITED
Registration no: 01164924 **Date established:** 1973
Turnover: £500,000 - £1m **No.of Employees:** 1 - 10 **Product Groups:** 37, 47

Date of Accounts	Dec 11	Dec 10	Dec 09
Working Capital	169	174	50
Current Assets	179	471	183

Avacs Ltd

2 The Kerridge Industrial Estate Station Road, Alton, GU34 2PT
Tel: 01420-80808
E-mail: admin@avacs.co.uk
Website: http://www.avacs.co.uk
Directors: G. Osgood (MD)
Immediate Holding Company: AVACS LIMITED
Registration no: 03542004 **Date established:** 1998
Turnover: Up to £250,000 **No.of Employees:** 1 - 10 **Product Groups:** 39, 40, 68

Aviation Parts Supplies

Lasham Airfield The Avenue, Lasham, Alton, GU34 5SS
Tel: 01256-381919 **Fax:** 01256-381645
E-mail: bhoward@apsparts.co.uk
Website: http://www.aircraftpartsmart.com
Directors: R. Howard (MD)
Immediate Holding Company: THE GLIDING HERITAGE CENTRE
Registration no: 03043423 **Date established:** 2012
Turnover: Up to £250,000 **No.of Employees:** 1 - 10 **Product Groups:** 39, 68

Awltech Plastic Fabrication Sales Ltd

4 The Omni Business Centre Omega Park, Alton, GU34 2QD
Tel: 01420-525222 **Fax:** 01420-525226
E-mail: info@awltech.co.uk
Website: http://www.awltech.co.uk
Directors: A. Gleeson (Dir)
Immediate Holding Company: AWLTECH PFE LIMITED
Date established: 2006 **No.of Employees:** 1 - 10 **Product Groups:** 40, 42, 48

Date of Accounts	Mar 09	Mar 08	Mar 07
Working Capital	-48	-52	N/A
Fixed Assets	59	61	N/A
Current Assets	80	103	N/A

Bachy Soletanche Ltd

Unit 2 Prospect Place Mill Lane, Alton, GU34 2SX
Tel: 01420-594700 **Fax:** 01483-417021
E-mail: chris.merridew@bacsol.co.uk
Website: http://www.bacsol.co.uk
Bank(s): Barclays, Ascot
Directors: C. Merridew (Dir), G. Trafford (Co Sec)
Immediate Holding Company: BACHY SOLETANCHE LIMITED
Registration no: 00752082 **VAT No.:** GB 413 9272 59
Date established: 1963 **Turnover:** £20m - £50m
No.of Employees: 21 - 50 **Product Groups:** 51

Date of Accounts	Dec 10	Dec 09	Dec 08
Sales Turnover	43m	76m	87m
Pre Tax Profit/Loss	899	-348	4m
Working Capital	10m	11m	10m
Fixed Assets	9m	12m	13m
Current Assets	55m	62m	62m
Current Liabilities	22m	21m	22m

Beckworth Technical Plating Ltd

16 Caker Stream Road, Alton, GU34 2QF
Tel: 01420-80880 **Fax:** 01420-80881
E-mail: admin@beckworth.net
Website: http://www.beckworth.net
Bank(s): HSBC Bank plc
Directors: N. Dent (Dir), R. Jones (Co Sec)
Managers: M. Gray (Tech Serv Mgr)
Immediate Holding Company: BECKWORTH TECHNICAL PLATING LIMITED
Registration no: 02158584 **Date established:** 1987 **Turnover:** £1m - £2m
No.of Employees: 11 - 20 **Product Groups:** 48

Date of Accounts	Dec 09	Dec 08	Dec 07
Sales Turnover	N/A	N/A	1m
Pre Tax Profit/Loss	N/A	N/A	70
Working Capital	64	147	101
Fixed Assets	120	133	167
Current Assets	183	259	295
Current Liabilities	N/A	N/A	49

Britannia Architectural Metalwork Ltd

The Old Coach House Draymans Way, Alton, GU34 1AY
Tel: 01420-84427 **Fax:** 01420-89056
E-mail: info@britannia.uk.com
Website: http://www.britannia.uk.com
Directors: A. Cohen (MD), C. Wigzell (Fin)
Immediate Holding Company: BRITANNIA ARCHITECTURAL METALWORK LIMITED
Registration no: 01655393 **Date established:** 1982
No.of Employees: 1 - 10 **Product Groups:** 26, 35

Date of Accounts	Dec 11	Dec 10	Dec 09
Working Capital	20	55	30
Fixed Assets	37	39	45
Current Assets	66	105	106

Ceratech Electronics Ltd

1 Omega Park, Alton, GU34 2QE
Tel: 01420-85470 **Fax:** 01420-83545
E-mail: sales@ceratech.co.uk
Website: http://www.ceratech.co.uk
Directors: J. Hodge (Fin), G. Hobbs (Dir)
Immediate Holding Company: CERATECH ELECTRONICS LIMITED
Registration no: 02944509 **VAT No.:** GB 631 8508 43
Date established: 1994 **Turnover:** £1m - £2m **No.of Employees:** 1 - 10
Product Groups: 37, 44

Date of Accounts	Dec 11	Dec 10	Dec 09
Working Capital	-225	-131	40
Fixed Assets	53	38	50
Current Assets	416	432	384

Compsoft plc

Delta House 7 Oriel Business Park Omega Park, Alton, GU34 2YT
Tel: 08453-707274 **Fax:** 01420-81444
E-mail: info@compsoft.co.uk
Website: http://www.compsoft.co.uk
Directors: P. Lenton (MD), D. Melhuish Hancock (Co Sec)
Ultimate Holding Company: COMPSOFT (HOLDINGS) LIMITED
Immediate Holding Company: COMPSOFT (UK) LTD
Registration no: 04193333 **Date established:** 2001 **Turnover:** £1m - £2m
No.of Employees: 21 - 50 **Product Groups:** 44, 84

Date of Accounts	Oct 11	Oct 10	Oct 09
Fixed Assets	868	868	868

Conquip Industrial Ltd

Waterbrook Estate Waterbrook Road, Alton, GU34 2UD
Tel: 01420-592900 **Fax:** 01420-592901
Website: http://www.conquipindustrial.com
Directors: A. Critchley (MD), A. Critchley (Co Sec)
Managers: R. James
Immediate Holding Company: CONQUIP INDUSTRIAL
Registration no: 04791365 **Date established:** 2003
No.of Employees: 21 - 50 **Product Groups:** 35, 39, 45

D & G Moulding Ltd

Unit 8 The Omni Business Centre Omega Park, Alton, GU34 2QD
Tel: 01420-549347
E-mail: sales@dgmouldingltd.com
Website: http://www.dgmouldingltd.com
Directors: D. Ivey (MD)
Immediate Holding Company: D & G MOULDING LTD.
Registration no: 03831026 **Date established:** 1999
No.of Employees: 1 - 10 **Product Groups:** 30, 42

Date of Accounts	Aug 11	Aug 10	Aug 09
Working Capital	4	-11	-12
Fixed Assets	42	53	62
Current Assets	45	72	41

De Maeyer International

Pyramid House 59 Winchester Road, Four Marks, Alton, GU34 5HR
Tel: 01420-562776 **Fax:** 01420-562874
E-mail: admin@demaeyer.co.uk
Website: http://www.demaeyerltd.com
Directors: C. Jokield (Prop)
Immediate Holding Company: PREMIER HEALTH & FITNESS LIMITED
Registration no: 04618647 **VAT No.:** GB 568 4342 16
Date established: 2002 **Turnover:** Up to £250,000
No.of Employees: 1 - 10 **Product Groups:** 30, 33

Designer Marine Ltd

Lavenham Adams Lane, Selborne, Alton, GU34 3LJ
Tel: 01420-511493 **Fax:** 07714-234994
E-mail: sales@designermarine.com
Website: http://www.designermarine.com
Registration no: 07151382 **Product Groups:** 35, 66

Dorwin Ltd

Unit 1 Grove Park Mill Lane, Alton, GU34 2QG
Tel: 01420-84217 **Fax:** 01420-541648
E-mail: reception@dorwin.co.uk
Website: http://www.dorwin.co.uk
Bank(s): Lloyds TSB Bank plc
Directors: C. Stokes (Mkt Research), D. Harrison (MD)
Managers: J. Sills (Fin Mgr), R. Bedford (Personnel)
Ultimate Holding Company: DORWIN HOLDINGS LIMITED
Immediate Holding Company: DORWIN LIMITED
Registration no: 01143161 **VAT No.:** GB 189 6285 04
Date established: 1973 **Turnover:** £5m - £10m
No.of Employees: 51 - 100 **Product Groups:** 30

Date of Accounts	Mar 11	Mar 10	Mar 09
Sales Turnover	10m	9m	N/A
Pre Tax Profit/Loss	570	677	725
Working Capital	961	2m	1m
Fixed Assets	123	145	148
Current Assets	4m	4m	3m
Current Liabilities	2m	2m	888

Engelmann & Buckham Ltd

Access House 16a Lenten Street, Alton, GU34 1HG
Tel: 01420-824210 **Fax:** 01420-89193
E-mail: sales@buckham.co.uk
Website: http://www.buckham.co.uk
Directors: G. Lennon (Fin), M. Henderson (MD)
Ultimate Holding Company: ENGELMANN & BUCKHAM (HOLDINGS) LIMITED
Immediate Holding Company: ENGELMANN & BUCKHAM LTD
Registration no: 00487221 **Date established:** 1950
No.of Employees: 1 - 10 **Product Groups:** 40, 41

Date of Accounts	Oct 11	Oct 10	Oct 09
Working Capital	140	97	97
Fixed Assets	29	26	26
Current Assets	709	1m	1m

Experience

15-17 Market Square, Alton, GU34 1HD
Tel: 01420-87688
E-mail: cliffferne@experience.unioffice.co.uk
Website: http://www.experiencethedifference.co.uk
Directors: C. Ferne (Prop)
Managers: C. Ferne (Chief Mgr)
Immediate Holding Company: PARKER STAG MORTGAGE SOLUTIONS LTD
Registration no: 03884072 **Date established:** 1980
No.of Employees: 1 - 10 **Product Groups:** 61

Fernplas

2 Newman Lane, Alton, GU34 2QR
Tel: 08456-804068 **Fax:** 01420-87389
E-mail: paul.crisp@fernhoward.com
Website: http://www.fernplas.com
Bank(s): Lloyds
Directors: P. Crisp (MD), T. Detrafford (Fin)
Managers: I. Bryan (Mktg Serv Mgr), M. Jones (Tech Serv Mgr)
Ultimate Holding Company: FERN-HOWARD LIMITED
Immediate Holding Company: ICARUS HOUSEWARES LIMITED
Registration no: 02871194 **Date established:** 2000 **Turnover:** £2m - £5m
No.of Employees: 21 - 50 **Product Groups:** 48

Date of Accounts	Dec 11	Dec 10	Dec 09
Sales Turnover	9m	8m	7m
Pre Tax Profit/Loss	3	200	209
Working Capital	497	483	702
Fixed Assets	1m	2m	324
Current Assets	3m	3m	3m
Current Liabilities	1m	2m	2m

Gardner Denver Ltd

Unit 1 Waterbrook Estate, Alton, GU34 2UD
Tel: 01420-567424 **Fax:** 01420-544183
E-mail: info.alton@gardnerdenver.com
Website: http://www.gd-alton.co.uk
Bank(s): Barclays
Directors: G. Davenport (Dir), P. Brookson (Fin)
Managers: J. Mason (Mktg Serv Mgr), S. Nicholson (Mgr), J. Watson (Mgr)
Ultimate Holding Company: GARDNER DENVER INC (USA)
Immediate Holding Company: GARDNER DENVER LTD
Registration no: 03047245 **VAT No.:** GB 303 8155 83
Date established: 1995 **Turnover:** £10m - £20m
No.of Employees: 21 - 50 **Product Groups:** 40, 42, 48

Date of Accounts	Dec 11	Dec 10	Dec 09
Sales Turnover	136m	136m	67m
Pre Tax Profit/Loss	8m	2m	-668
Working Capital	-11m	-23m	26m
Fixed Assets	86m	92m	101m
Current Assets	45m	44m	63m
Current Liabilities	11m	6m	10m

Mike Garwood Ltd

Shelleys Barn Shelleys Lane, East Worldham, Alton, GU34 3AQ
Tel: 01420-84458 **Fax:** 01420-88594
E-mail: m.garwood@mikegarwoodltd.co.uk
Website: http://www.mikegarwoodltd.co.uk
Directors: M. Garwood (Dir)
Immediate Holding Company: MIKE GARWOOD LTD
Registration no: 05156943 **Date established:** 2004
No.of Employees: 11 - 20 **Product Groups:** 39, 41, 48, 67

Date of Accounts	Mar 11	Mar 10	Mar 09
Working Capital	574	587	585
Fixed Assets	91	104	104
Current Assets	1m	1m	1m

Grovewood Machines Ltd
Unit 3 Caker Stream Road, Alton, GU34 2QA
Tel: 01420-83940 **Fax:** 01256- 358777
E-mail: info@grovewoodmachines.co.uk
Website: http://www.grovewoodmachines.co.uk
Directors: N. Groves (Dir), P. Taylor (Co Sec)
Immediate Holding Company: PROWOOD MACHINERY LTD
Registration no: 04693443 **Date established:** 2003
No.of Employees: 1 - 10 **Product Groups:** 46

Date of Accounts	Mar 10	Mar 09	Mar 08
Working Capital	-7	-11	-0
Fixed Assets	20	29	15
Current Assets	102	81	95

Hamilton Hall Consultants Ltd
4 The Windmills St Marys Close, Alton, GU34 1EF
Tel: 01420-548548 **Fax:** 01420-548549
E-mail: tom.hall@hamiltonhall.co.uk
Website: http://www.hamiltonhall.co.uk
Directors: T. Hall (MD)
Immediate Holding Company: HAMILTON HALL CONSULTANTS LIMITED
Registration no: 01747241 **VAT No.:** GB 362 8193 39
Date established: 1983 **Turnover:** £1m - £2m **No.of Employees:** 1 - 10
Product Groups: 44, 84

Date of Accounts	Sep 10	Sep 09	Sep 08
Working Capital	-69	68	170
Fixed Assets	237	242	245
Current Assets	122	235	393

Hi-Store
Station Approach Four Marks, Alton, GU34 5HN
Tel: 01420-562522 **Fax:** 01420-564420
E-mail: info@hi-store.com
Website: http://www.hi-store.com
Bank(s): The Royal Bank of Scotland
Directors: A. Butler (Dir), J. Nurpuri (Co Sec), J. Youle (Sales)
Immediate Holding Company: HI-STORE LIMITED
Registration no: 02613326 **VAT No.:** GB 568 4063 20
Date established: 1991 **Turnover:** £2m - £5m **No.of Employees:** 21 - 50
Product Groups: 26, 35

House Of Dorchester
Unit 10 Alton Business Centre Omega Park, Alton, GU34 2YU
Tel: 01420-84181 **Fax:** 01420- 543047
E-mail: info@hodchoc.com
Website: http://www.hodchoc.com
Bank(s): HSBC Bank plc
Directors: R. Young (Fin)
Managers: K. Ebbs (Mktg Serv Mgr), W. Bills (Purch Mgr)
Immediate Holding Company: HOUSE OF DORCHESTER LIMITED
Registration no: 04499810 **Date established:** 2002 **Turnover:** £5m - £10m
No.of Employees: 11 - 20 **Product Groups:** 20

Date of Accounts	Dec 11	Dec 10	Dec 09
Sales Turnover	5m	6m	6m
Pre Tax Profit/Loss	-62	289	202
Working Capital	285	665	638
Fixed Assets	2m	2m	2m
Current Assets	1m	2m	2m
Current Liabilities	305	593	517

Hubertis Limited
12 High Street, Alton, GU34 1TJ
Tel: 01420-80900 **Fax:** 01420-80997
E-mail: sales@hubertis.co.uk
Website: http://www.hubertis.co.uk
Directors: D. Tinson (Prop)
Date established: 2004 **No.of Employees:** 1 - 10 **Product Groups:** 36, 39, 40

Date of Accounts	Jul 05	Jul 04
Working Capital	-22	-20
Fixed Assets	9	3
Current Assets	175	61
Current Liabilities	198	80

Ist Ltd
Station Road, Alton, GU34 2PZ
Tel: 01420-541600 **Fax:** 01420-541700
E-mail: info@istcourt.com
Website: http://www.istimaging.com
Bank(s): HSBC Bank plc
Directors: E. Baber (Fin), D. Lambert (Dir), A. Sibley (MD), B. Johnson (Comm), K. Neal (Sales & Mktg)
Immediate Holding Company: I.S.T. (New York)
Registration no: 01884217 **Date established:** 2001
Turnover: £250,000 - £500,000 **No.of Employees:** 51 - 100
Product Groups: 37, 38, 40, 45, 52

Date of Accounts	Dec 07	Mar 07	Mar 06
Working Capital	1	12	12
Fixed Assets	N/A	39	39
Current Assets	2	12	12
Current Liabilities	1	N/A	N/A
Total Share Capital	38	38	38

Katko UK Ltd
Unit 1 Blacknest Business Park Blacknest Road, Blacknest, Alton, GU34 4PX
Tel: 01420-520530 **Fax:** 01420-520560
E-mail: sales@katko.co.uk
Website: http://www.katko.co.uk
Directors: K. McCarthy (MD)
Registration no: 03773351 **VAT No.:** GB 733 3433 53
Date established: 1999 **No.of Employees:** 1 - 10 **Product Groups:** 37

Date of Accounts	Dec 09	Dec 08	Dec 07
Working Capital	N/A	37	35
Current Assets	147	220	149

Laleham Healthcare Ltd
Sycamore Park Mill Lane, Alton, GU34 2PR
Tel: 01420-566500 **Fax:** 01420-566566
E-mail: reception@laleham-healthcare.com
Website: http://www.laleham-healthcare.com
Bank(s): HSBC Bank plc
Directors: M. Crawley (I.T. Dir)
Ultimate Holding Company: DCC PUBLIC LIMITED COMPANY
Immediate Holding Company: LALEHAM HEALTHCARE LIMITED
Registration no: 00997221 **VAT No.:** GB 329 9927 01
Date established: 1970 **Turnover:** £20m - £50m
No.of Employees: 101 - 250 **Product Groups:** 31, 32, 48

Date of Accounts	Mar 11	Mar 10	Mar 09
Sales Turnover	34m	28m	28m
Pre Tax Profit/Loss	2m	1m	307
Working Capital	2m	1m	178
Fixed Assets	6m	6m	6m
Current Assets	11m	8m	6m
Current Liabilities	3m	2m	2m

Lockmasters Mobile Safes & Locks
Keys House Vyne Close, Alton, GU34 2EH
Tel: 01420-542448 **Fax:** 01420-542448
E-mail: enquiries@lock-masters.co.uk
Website: http://www.lock-masters.co.uk
Managers: S. Silver (Personnel)
Immediate Holding Company: LOCKMASTERS MOBILE LIMITED
Registration no: 02666344 **VAT No.:** GB 568 7452 91
Date established: 1991 **Turnover:** £250,000 - £500,000
No.of Employees: 1 - 10 **Product Groups:** 36, 52

M B Components Ltd
43 Wellhouse Road Beech, Alton, GU34 4AQ
Tel: 01420-542500 **Fax:** 01420-542700
E-mail: sales@mbcomponents.co.uk
Website: http://www.mbcomponents.co.uk
Directors: S. Bailey (Fin)
Immediate Holding Company: MB COMPONENTS LIMITED
Registration no: 02757759 **VAT No.:** GB 614 5911 49
Date established: 1992 **Turnover:** £500,000 - £1m
No.of Employees: 1 - 10 **Product Groups:** 37

Date of Accounts	Mar 11	Mar 10	Mar 08
Working Capital	12	19	25
Fixed Assets	1	N/A	N/A
Current Assets	25	28	31

Mintech Semiconductors Ltd
2,Oriel Court Omega Park, Alton, GU34 2YT
Tel: 01420-594 180 **Fax:** 01420-891 51
E-mail: sales@mintech.co.uk
Website: http://www.mintech.co.uk
Directors: G. White (MD), A. Taylor (Dir), F. Rogers (Dir)
Managers: M. Nicols (Ops Mgr), J. Johnson (Sales Prom Mgr), S. Kick (I.T. Exec), J. Hawes
Immediate Holding Company: Ms Acquisition Co Ltd
Registration no: 04140225 **Date established:** 1984 **Turnover:** £5m - £10m
No.of Employees: 21 - 50 **Product Groups:** 37, 67, 85

Date of Accounts	Dec 09	Dec 08	Dec 07
Sales Turnover	6m	6m	6m
Pre Tax Profit/Loss	5m	943	963
Working Capital	4m	3m	2m
Fixed Assets	4m	882	988
Current Assets	7m	5m	5m
Current Liabilities	639	229	833

Nylon Fasteners Ltd
Unit 14 Hazel Road, Alton, GU34 5EY
Tel: 01256-533088 **Fax:** 01256-651143
E-mail: sales@nyfast.co.uk
Website: http://www.nyfast.co.uk
Directors: M. Birkmyre (MD)
Managers: M. Birkmyre (Chief Mgr)
Immediate Holding Company: NYLON FASTENERS LIMITED
Registration no: 06789432 **Date established:** 2009
Turnover: £250,000 - £500,000 **No.of Employees:** 1 - 10
Product Groups: 30, 35, 39

Date of Accounts	Mar 11	Mar 10
Working Capital	7	-9
Fixed Assets	6	9
Current Assets	124	52

Ortho Europe Ltd
Mill Lane, Alton, GU34 2PX
Tel: 01420-83294 **Fax:** 01420-80068
E-mail: info@ortho-europe.co.uk
Website: http://www.ortho-europe.co.uk
Bank(s): HSBC Bank plc
Directors: M. O'byrne (Dir), K. Bell (Sales)
Managers: S. Giles (Purch Mgr)
Immediate Holding Company: VESSA LIMITED
Registration no: 03271539 **VAT No.:** GB 684 7749 70
Date established: 1996 **Turnover:** £2m - £5m **No.of Employees:** 21 - 50
Product Groups: 38

Date of Accounts	Oct 11	Oct 10	Oct 09
Working Capital	80	80	80
Current Assets	80	80	80

Oxford Electronics Ltd
59 Winchester Road Four Marks, Alton, GU34 5HR
Tel: 01420-561200 **Fax:** 01420-561300
E-mail: sales@oxford-electronics.com
Website: http://www.oxford-electronics.com
Directors: M. Johnson (Dir)
Immediate Holding Company: OXFORD ELECTRONICS LIMITED
Registration no: 02699274 **Date established:** 1992
No.of Employees: 1 - 10 **Product Groups:** 33

Date of Accounts	Oct 11	Oct 10	Oct 09
Working Capital	89	95	120
Fixed Assets	5	7	9
Current Assets	115	209	149

P D M Neptec Ltd
4-6 Alton Business Centre Omega Park, Alton, GU34 2YU
Tel: 01420-85848 **Fax:** 01420-84288
E-mail: petrd@pdmneptec.com
Website: http://www.pdmneptec.com
Bank(s): Lloyds TSB Bank plc
Directors: I. Doble (MD), W. Oxley (Dir), C. Hunter (Co Sec)
Ultimate Holding Company: TELEDYNE IMPULSE-PDM HOLDINGS LTD.
Immediate Holding Company: TELEDYNE IMPULSE-PDM LTD.
Registration no: 01804527 **VAT No.:** GB 413 1098 89
Date established: 1984 **Turnover:** £2m - £5m **No.of Employees:** 21 - 50
Product Groups: 37

Date of Accounts	Mar 12	Mar 11	Mar 10
Sales Turnover	6m	5m	4m
Pre Tax Profit/Loss	799	807	473
Working Capital	1m	1m	912
Fixed Assets	47	63	79
Current Assets	3m	2m	1m
Current Liabilities	536	295	131

Pneuform Machines
Unit 16 19c Caker Stream Road, Alton, GU34 2QF
Tel: 01420-86987 **Fax:** 01420-87003
E-mail: pneuform@pneuform.com
Website: http://www.pneuform.com
Directors: D. Williams (Co Sec), M. Williams (Co Sec), T. Clark (MD)
Managers: T. Clarke (Mgr)
Immediate Holding Company: PNEUFORM MACHINES LIMITED
Registration no: 03623837 **VAT No.:** GB 709 1806 35
Date established: 1998 **Turnover:** £2m - £5m **No.of Employees:** 1 - 10
Product Groups: 46, 48

Date of Accounts	Aug 10	Aug 09	Aug 08
Working Capital	119	111	54
Fixed Assets	2	6	11
Current Assets	141	181	125

Printed Motor Works Ltd
Newman Lane, Alton, GU34 2QW
Tel: 01420-594140 **Fax:** 01420-83930
E-mail: sales@printedmotorworks.com
Website: http://www.printedmotorworks.com
Managers: S. Peaty (Mgr)
Immediate Holding Company: PRINTED MOTOR WORKS LIMITED
Registration no: 06838137 **Date established:** 2009 **Turnover:** £2m - £5m
No.of Employees: 21 - 50 **Product Groups:** 37, 45

Date of Accounts	Dec 11	Dec 10	Dec 09
Working Capital	593	413	316
Fixed Assets	23	32	44
Current Assets	917	636	499

Professional Database Solutions
8a Hartley Park Farm Business Centre Selborne Road, Alton, GU34 3HD
Tel: 01420-511668 **Fax:** 01420-511511
E-mail: info@pdbsolutions.co.uk
Website: http://www.pdbsolutions.co.uk
Directors: T. Gordon Jones (Prop)
Managers: T. Gordon-Jones
Immediate Holding Company: PROFESSIONAL DATABASE SOLUTIONS LIMITED
Registration no: 05147329 **Date established:** 2004
No.of Employees: 1 - 10 **Product Groups:** 44, 81

Date of Accounts	Jun 09	Jun 08	Jun 07
Working Capital	14	-1	-1
Fixed Assets	1	2	2
Current Assets	54	29	36

Rediweld Rubber & Plastics Ltd
6-10 Newman Lane, Alton, GU34 2QR
Tel: 01420-543007 **Fax:** 01420-544090
E-mail: info@rediweld.co.uk
Website: http://www.rediweld.co.uk
Bank(s): HSBC Bank plc
Directors: R. McDougall (Dir), R. Marsh (MD), D. How (Ch)
Managers: P. Gill (Quality Control), J. Holder (Sales Prom), K. Banfill (Prod Mgr), D. Bigg (Prod Mgr), P. Norman (Mgr), A. Bunkle (Mgr), J. Holder (Mgr)
Ultimate Holding Company: REDIWELD HOLDINGS LIMITED
Immediate Holding Company: REDIWELD RUBBER & PLASTICS LIMITED
Registration no: 01885505 **VAT No.:** GB 568 5590 89
Date established: 1985 **Turnover:** £2m - £5m **No.of Employees:** 21 - 50
Product Groups: 29, 30, 31, 35, 39, 42, 48, 63

Date of Accounts	Dec 11	Dec 10	Dec 09
Working Capital	1m	1m	1m
Fixed Assets	469	463	402
Current Assets	2m	2m	1m

Se Acoustics Ltd
The Well House Lower Noar Hill Farm, Selborne, Alton, GU34 3LW
Tel: 01420-511374
E-mail: lynn.lipscombe@seacoustics.com
Directors: L. Lipscombe (Prop)
Immediate Holding Company: SEACOUSTICS LIMITED
Registration no: 02184469 **Date established:** 1987
Turnover: Up to £250,000 **No.of Employees:** 1 - 10 **Product Groups:** 37, 38, 39

Date of Accounts	Mar 11	Mar 10	Mar 09
Sales Turnover	N/A	N/A	13
Working Capital	-15	-15	-23
Fixed Assets	2	4	4
Current Assets	30	30	18
Current Liabilities	N/A	32	N/A

Southern Temperature Sensors Ltd
Unit 6 Weyside Park, Newman Lane, Alton, GU34 2PJ
Tel: 01420-541422 **Fax:** 01420-541433
E-mail: sales@southerntemp.co.uk
Website: http://www.southerntemp.co.uk
Directors: D. Skinner (MD)
Managers: D. Skinner (Sales Prom Mgr)
Registration no: 03938539 **VAT No.:** GB 733 6232 48
Date established: 2000 **Turnover:** £1m - £2m **No.of Employees:** 1 - 10
Product Groups: 36, 37, 38, 44, 85

Date of Accounts	Mar 10	Mar 09	Mar 08
Working Capital	60	68	80
Fixed Assets	17	11	14
Current Assets	299	326	316

Specialised Welding Products Ltd
Unit 1 Farringdon Industrial Estate Gosport Road, Farringdon, Alton, GU34 3DD
Tel: 01420-588180 **Fax:** 01420-588184
E-mail: sales@swp.uk.net
Website: http://www.specialisedwelding.co.uk
Directors: J. Packer (MD)
Managers: T. Moors (Comptroller), N. Packer (Personnel)
Ultimate Holding Company: NEW SWP LIMITED
Immediate Holding Company: SPECIALISED WELDING PRODUCTS LIMITED
Registration no: 02573967 **Date established:** 1991 **Turnover:** £5m - £10m
No.of Employees: 21 - 50 **Product Groups:** 46

Date of Accounts	Mar 11	Mar 10	Mar 09
Sales Turnover	8m	7m	7m
Pre Tax Profit/Loss	182	474	299
Working Capital	2m	2m	2m
Fixed Assets	102	124	65
Current Assets	4m	4m	3m
Current Liabilities	2m	2m	331

T P S Fronius
1 The Omni Business Centre Omega Park, Alton, GU34 2QD
Tel: 01420-546855 **Fax:** 01420-546856
E-mail: briand@tps-fronius.co.uk
Website: http://www.tps-fronius.co.uk

see next page

T P S Fronius - Cont'd

Managers: K. Palmer (Mgr)
Registration no: SC053928 **Date established:** 1973 **Turnover:** £2m - £5m
No.of Employees: 1 - 10 **Product Groups:** 35, 36, 37, 42, 45, 46, 48, 67, 83, 84

Tectonics Ltd

Caker Stream Road, Alton, GU34 2QA
Tel: 01420-83910 **Fax:** 01420- 541196
E-mail: s.taylor@tectonicsltd.co.uk
Website: http://www.tectonicsltd.co.uk
Bank(s): Lloyds Bank
Directors: S. Taylor (Co Sec)
Managers: D. Stewart (Personnel), A. Shannon (Tech Serv Mgr), S. Warner (Purch Mgr)
Ultimate Holding Company: OSBORNE MANUFACTURING LIMITED
Immediate Holding Company: TECTONICS LIMITED
Registration no: 01474876 **Date established:** 1980 **Turnover:** £2m - £5m
No.of Employees: 21 - 50 **Product Groups:** 25

Date of Accounts	Dec 11	Dec 10	Dec 09
Working Capital	3	431	491
Fixed Assets	226	285	356
Current Assets	321	511	699

Turbex Ltd

Unit 1 Riverwey Industrial Park Newman Lane, Alton, GU34 2QL
Tel: 01420-544909 **Fax:** 01420-542264
E-mail: sales@turbex.co.uk
Website: http://www.turbex.co.uk
Directors: J. Huntingdon (Dir)
Ultimate Holding Company: GEO. KINGSBURY HOLDINGS LIMITED
Immediate Holding Company: TURBEX LIMITED
Registration no: 01574489 **Date established:** 1981 **Turnover:** £1m - £2m
No.of Employees: 1 - 10 **Product Groups:** 37, 39, 41, 42, 44, 46

Date of Accounts	Dec 11	Dec 10	Dec 09
Sales Turnover	2m	2m	2m
Pre Tax Profit/Loss	186	64	-90
Working Capital	674	533	471
Fixed Assets	6	9	22
Current Assets	1m	1m	813
Current Liabilities	303	408	176

Vixen Software Solutions Ltd

Market House 21 Lenten Street, Alton, GU34 1HG
Tel: 01420-89898 **Fax:** 01420-541223
E-mail: marketing@vixensoft.co.uk
Website: http://www.vixensoft.co.uk
Turnover: £5m - £10m **No.of Employees:** 51 - 100 **Product Groups:** 37, 44, 80, 84

Date of Accounts	Dec 07	Dec 06	Dec 05
Working Capital	930	909	981
Fixed Assets	51	66	126
Current Assets	1547	1429	1564
Current Liabilities	617	520	583
Total Share Capital	1	1	1

Andover

Adept Power Solutions Ltd

Unit 1 Viscount Court, Andover, SP10 5NW
Tel: 01264-351415 **Fax:** 01264-351217
E-mail: sales@adeptpower.co.uk
Website: http://www.adeptpower.co.uk
Directors: J. Mackay (Fin), I. Mackay (MD)
Immediate Holding Company: ADEPT POWER SOLUTIONS LTD
Registration no: 04718081 **Date established:** 2003 **Turnover:** £2m - £5m
No.of Employees: 11 - 20 **Product Groups:** 37

Date of Accounts	May 11	May 10	May 09
Working Capital	276	249	223
Fixed Assets	108	104	136
Current Assets	675	632	555

Advance Generators

7 Ox Drove Picket Piece, Andover, SP11 6ND
Tel: 01264-369295 **Fax:** 01264-369313
E-mail: dieselgenerators@aol.com
Website: http://www.advancegenerators.com
Directors: S. Beale (Prop)
No.of Employees: 1 - 10 **Product Groups:** 37, 52

Alexander's Appliances Direct

Alexander House North Acre, Longparish, Andover, SP11 6QX
Tel: 01264-333388 **Fax:** 01264-720007
E-mail: sales@alexanders-direct.co.uk
Website: http://www.alexanders-direct.co.uk
Directors: M. Alexander (Prop)
No.of Employees: 1 - 10 **Product Groups:** 20, 40, 41

Andover Punch Press Ltd

35 Shaw Close, Andover, SP10 3BT
Tel: 07850-706539 **Fax:** 01264-395516
E-mail: ralph@hartley-engineering.co.uk
Website: http://www.hartley-engineering.co.uk
Directors: A. Williams (Fin), R. Williams (MD)
Immediate Holding Company: ANDOVER PUNCH PRESS LIMITED
Registration no: 02870718 **Date established:** 1993
No.of Employees: 1 - 10 **Product Groups:** 46

Date of Accounts	Mar 11	Mar 10	Mar 09
Working Capital	-11	-8	-13
Fixed Assets	5	5	6
Current Assets	17	12	8

Ashdale Engineering

Mitchell Close, Andover, SP10 3TJ
Tel: 01264-355642 **Fax:** 01264-333641
E-mail: jason.stepney@ashdale.uk.net
Website: http://www.ashdaleengineering.co.uk
Directors: D. Bell (Dir), J. Stepney (Dir), H. Lockie (Co Sec)
Immediate Holding Company: ASHDALE ENGINEERING (HAMPSHIRE) LIMITED
Registration no: 02903513 **Date established:** 1994 **Turnover:** £2m - £5m
No.of Employees: 21 - 50 **Product Groups:** 48

Date of Accounts	Jul 11	Jul 10	Jul 09
Working Capital	90	129	74
Fixed Assets	650	629	674
Current Assets	662	546	615

Atlantic Zeiser Ltd

53 Central Way, Andover, SP10 5AN
Tel: 01264-324222 **Fax:** 01264-324333
E-mail: lewin@atlanticzeiser.com
Website: http://www.atlanticzeiseruk.com
Directors: R. Lewin (Fin), B. Lewin (MD), R. Lewin (MD)
Managers: G. Harris (Tech Serv Mgr)
Ultimate Holding Company: ORELL FUSSLI HOLDING AG (SWITZERLAND)
Immediate Holding Company: ATLANTIC ZEISER LIMITED
Registration no: 01707841 **Date established:** 1983 **Turnover:** £2m - £5m
No.of Employees: 21 - 50 **Product Groups:** 32, 44

Date of Accounts	Dec 11	Dec 10	Dec 09
Sales Turnover	3m	4m	4m
Pre Tax Profit/Loss	302	425	469
Working Capital	3m	4m	4m
Fixed Assets	214	249	293
Current Assets	3m	4m	5m
Current Liabilities	191	292	742

Aztec Flooring Services Ltd

Unit 1-3 Focus 303 Business Centre Focus Way, Andover, SP10 5NY
Tel: 01264-848071 **Fax:** 01264-848072
E-mail: enquires@aztecflooringservices.co.uk
Website: http://www.aztecflooringservices.co.uk
Directors: J. Fleming (MD)
Immediate Holding Company: AZTEC FLOORING SERVICES LIMITED
Registration no: 05731258 **Date established:** 2006
Turnover: Up to £250,000 **No.of Employees:** 11 - 20 **Product Groups:** 23, 25, 29, 30, 33, 49, 52, 66

Date of Accounts	Mar 10	Mar 09	Mar 08
Working Capital	-6	51	20
Fixed Assets	38	13	16
Current Assets	261	227	87

B D C Systems

Prospect Farm Monxton, Andover, SP11 7DA
Tel: 01264-710900 **Fax:** 01264-710987
E-mail: info@bdcsystems.com
Website: http://www.bdcsystems.com
Directors: A. Head (MD)
Immediate Holding Company: B D C SYSTEMS LIMITED
Registration no: 02898684 **Date established:** 1994 **Turnover:** £1m - £2m
No.of Employees: 1 - 10 **Product Groups:** 33, 41, 62

Date of Accounts	Dec 11	Dec 10	Dec 09
Working Capital	675	429	245
Fixed Assets	54	15	18
Current Assets	1m	1m	835

Bespoke Access Systems

17 Brackenbury, Andover, SP10 3XJ
Tel: 01264-351727 **Fax:** 01264-400068
E-mail: phil-partidge@bespokeaccess.com
Website: http://www.bespokeaccess.com
Directors: P. Partridge (Prop), P. Partidge (Prop)
Turnover: Up to £250,000 **No.of Employees:** 1 - 10 **Product Groups:** 35

Boyriven

The Fairground Fairview Road, Weyhill, Andover, SP11 0ST
Tel: 01264-771414 **Fax:** 01264-771444
E-mail: marc.duncan@boyriven.co.uk
Website: http://www.boyriven.co.uk
Directors: P. Espinasse (Dir), J. Brambley (Co Sec)
Immediate Holding Company: BOYRIVEN LIMITED
Registration no: 00257380 **VAT No.:** GB 505 3351 80
Date established: 1931 **Turnover:** £2m - £5m **No.of Employees:** 1 - 10
Product Groups: 23, 39

Date of Accounts	Jun 11	Jun 10	Jun 09
Working Capital	196	276	306
Fixed Assets	1m	1m	1m
Current Assets	777	778	744

Brass Construction

Unit 10 Walworth Enterprise Centre Duke Close West Way, Andover, SP10 5AP
Tel: 01264-355968
Directors: N. Bond (Prop)
Date established: 1986 **No.of Employees:** 1 - 10 **Product Groups:** 35

Britax Excelsior Ltd

1 Churchill Way West, Andover, SP10 3UW
Tel: 01264-333343 **Fax:** 01264-334146
E-mail: sales_marketing_email@britax.com
Website: http://www.britax.co.uk
Bank(s): Barclays
Directors: K. Shean (Fin), J. Huxably (Chief Op Offcr), I. Watson (MD)
Managers: M. Turner (Sales & Mktg Mg), A. Williams (Personnel)
Ultimate Holding Company: BRITAX CHILDCARE HOLDINGS LIMITED
Immediate Holding Company: BRITAX EXCELSIOR LIMITED
Registration no: 00294545 **Date established:** 1934
Turnover: £500,000 - £1m **No.of Employees:** 101 - 250
Product Groups: 26

Date of Accounts	Dec 11	Dec 10	Dec 09
Sales Turnover	32m	36m	33
Pre Tax Profit/Loss	3m	13m	2
Working Capital	16m	16m	4
Fixed Assets	5m	4m	4
Current Assets	25m	23m	11
Current Liabilities	4m	2m	3

Brooks Crownhill Patternmakers Ltd

Unit 4 North Way, Andover, SP10 5AZ
Tel: 01264-366500 **Fax:** 01264-332145
E-mail: info@bcplimited.co.uk
Website: http://www.bcplimited.co.uk
Bank(s): HSBC Bank plc
Directors: S. Coggins (Dir)
Immediate Holding Company: BROOKS, CROWNHILL PATTERNMAKERS LIMITED
Registration no: 00711971 **VAT No.:** GB 222 3238 07
Date established: 1962 **Turnover:** £2m - £5m **No.of Employees:** 51 - 100
Product Groups: 34, 48

Date of Accounts	Apr 11	Apr 10	Apr 09
Working Capital	1m	1m	1m
Fixed Assets	564	691	724
Current Assets	3m	2m	2m

Calibration Dynamics

7 Regents Court South Way, Andover, SP10 5NX
Tel: 01264-339030 **Fax:** 01264-339040
E-mail: sales@calibrationdynamics.com
Website: http://www.calibrationdynamics.com
Directors: K. Crowhurst (Fin)
Managers: P. Crowhurst (Chief Mgr)
Immediate Holding Company: CALIBRATION DYNAMICS LIMITED
Registration no: 05406638 **Date established:** 2005 **Turnover:**
No.of Employees: 1 - 10 **Product Groups:** 37, 38, 40, 44, 85

Date of Accounts	Dec 11	Mar 11	Mar 10
Working Capital	1	176	109
Fixed Assets	N/A	34	24
Current Assets	1	342	332

Chimflue Ltd

Unit 4-5 Viscount Court, Andover, SP10 5NW
Tel: 01264-332878 **Fax:** 01264-366647
E-mail: sales@chimflue.co.uk
Website: http://www.chimflue.co.uk
Bank(s): Barclays
Directors: S. Ford (Co Sec), S. Ford (MD)
Immediate Holding Company: CHIMFLUE LIMITED
Registration no: 02271512 **VAT No.:** GB 504 3415 86
Date established: 1988 **Turnover:** £1m - £2m **No.of Employees:** 11 - 20
Product Groups: 24, 33, 40, 52

Date of Accounts	Jul 11	Jul 10	Jul 09
Working Capital	97	-34	-50
Fixed Assets	169	121	159
Current Assets	619	455	438

Coldseal Packaging Limited

3 Winchester Street, Andover, SP10 2EA
Tel: 01264-335334 **Fax:** 01264-335355
Website: http://www.angusandwright.com
Directors: J. Wright (Dir)
Registration no: 04011777 **Date established:** 1989
No.of Employees: 1 - 10 **Product Groups:** 38, 42

Control Techniques Dynamics Ltd

South Way, Andover, SP10 5AB
Tel: 01264-387600 **Fax:** 01264-356561
E-mail: khedges@ctdynamics.com
Website: http://www.ctdynamics.com
Directors: K. Hedges (MD), P. Turtle (Fin)
Managers: R. Turpin, A. Snowden (Personnel)
Ultimate Holding Company: EMERSON ELECTRIC CO INC (USA)
Immediate Holding Company: CONTROL TECHNIQUES DYNAMICS LIMITED
Registration no: 00741360 **VAT No.:** GB 541 7000 85
Date established: 1962 **Turnover:** £10m - £20m
No.of Employees: 101 - 250 **Product Groups:** 37, 38

Date of Accounts	Sep 11	Sep 10	Sep 09
Sales Turnover	13m	10m	9m
Pre Tax Profit/Loss	3m	2m	2m
Working Capital	14m	13m	11m
Fixed Assets	2m	2m	2m
Current Assets	17m	14m	12m
Current Liabilities	584	233	497

Custom Moulds & Moulding Ltd

Unit 1-2 Ludgershall Business Park, Ludgershall, Andover, SP11 9TX
Tel: 01264-790077 **Fax:** 01264-790353
E-mail: sales@custommouldings.co.uk
Website: http://www.custommouldings.co.uk
Bank(s): Barclays, Andover
Managers: C. Hammett (Admin Off)
Registration no: 03566942 **VAT No.:** GB 723 3349 49
Turnover: £500,000 - £1m **No.of Employees:** 11 - 20
Product Groups: 30, 48

Darren Howard Ornamental Fabrication

The Old Dairy Cottonworth, Andover, SP11 7JX
Tel: 01264-861010
E-mail: djhwelding@aol.com
Website: http://www.darrenhowardornamentalfabrication.com
Directors: D. Howarth (Prop)
No.of Employees: 1 - 10 **Product Groups:** 26, 35, 49

Deublin Ltd

Sopwith Park Royce Close, Andover, SP10 3TS
Tel: 01264-333355 **Fax:** 01264-333304
E-mail: info@deublin.co.uk
Website: http://www.deublin.co.uk
Directors: S. Bryant (Fin), D. Ralph (MD)
Ultimate Holding Company: DEUBLIN CO (USA)
Immediate Holding Company: DEUBLIN LIMITED
Registration no: 01088395 **Date established:** 1972 **Turnover:** £2m - £5m
No.of Employees: 1 - 10 **Product Groups:** 36

Date of Accounts	Dec 11	Dec 10	Dec 09
Sales Turnover	2m	2m	2m
Pre Tax Profit/Loss	268	275	-28
Working Capital	581	685	481
Fixed Assets	87	85	95
Current Assets	929	1m	838
Current Liabilities	214	206	104

Diagraph Products

Unit 9 Brunel Gate West Portway Industrial Estate, Andover, SP10 3SL
Tel: 01264-357511 **Fax:** 01264-355964
E-mail: denewth@loveshaw_europe.co.uk
Website: http://www.diagraohproducts.co.uk
Date established: 1960 **Turnover:** £250,000 - £500,000
No.of Employees: 11 - 20 **Product Groups:** 27, 32

Easab Cutting Systems

Unit 2-3 Crown Way, Andover, SP10 5LU
Tel: 01264-332233 **Fax:** 01264-332074
Website: http://www.easab.co.uk
Bank(s): HSBC Bank plc
Directors: D. Gibson (Fin)
Managers: I. Kirkpatrick (Mgr)
Ultimate Holding Company: CHARTER LIMITED
Immediate Holding Company: ESAB AUTOMATION LIMITED
Registration no: 01730600 **VAT No.:** GB 373 8128 37
Date established: 1983 **Turnover:** £5m - £10m **No.of Employees:** 11 - 20
Product Groups: 46

Enham Charity Shop
13 Newbury Road Enham Alamein, Andover, SP11 6HQ
Tel: 01264-359391 **Fax:** 01264-333638
E-mail: richard.ashdown@enham.co.uk
Website: http://www.gordonsfinefoods.com
Managers: M. Sanders (District Mgr)
Immediate Holding Company: ENHAM
Registration no: 04228452 **VAT No.:** GB 198 9781 73
Date established: 1921 **Turnover:** £10m - £20m **No.of Employees:** 1 - 10
Product Groups: 32

Halesway Ltd
36 East Street, Andover, SP10 1ES
Tel: 01264-339955 **Fax:** 01264-339424
E-mail: liz.rawlingson@halesway.co.uk
Website: http://www.halesway.co.uk
Directors: L. Rawlingson (MD)
Immediate Holding Company: HALESWAY LIMITED
Registration no: 02818414 **Date established:** 1993
No.of Employees: 21 - 50 **Product Groups:** 81

Date of Accounts	May 11	May 10	May 09
Working Capital	229	248	275
Fixed Assets	53	53	38
Current Assets	566	665	617

I Candy Design Ltd
Russell House 40 East Street, Andover, SP10 1ES
Tel: 01264-356256 **Fax:** 0560-1141938
E-mail: info@icandydesign.com
Website: http://www.icandydesign.com
Directors: M. Mcintrye (MD), M. Mcintyre (MD)
Immediate Holding Company: Icandy Design Ltd
Registration no: 04734339 **Date established:** 2003
No.of Employees: 1 - 10 **Product Groups:** 81

Date of Accounts	Apr 09	Apr 08	Apr 07
Working Capital	12	11	9
Fixed Assets	4	6	3
Current Assets	61	51	48

Input Joinery
The Fairground Fairview Road Weyhill, Andover, SP11 0ST
Tel: 01264-771900 **Fax:** 01264-771901
E-mail: info@inputjoinery.co.uk
Website: http://www.inputjoinery.co.uk
Directors: M. Fisher (Sales), G. Ruddick (MD)
Managers: K. Stephens (Buyer), D. Rice (Tech Serv Mgr), C. Pattern, R. Ruddick (Personnel)
Immediate Holding Company: INPUT JOINERY LIMITED
Registration no: 01410695 **Date established:** 1979
No.of Employees: 51 - 100 **Product Groups:** 25, 35, 52, 66

Date of Accounts	Mar 12	Mar 11	Mar 10
Working Capital	-589	-540	-550
Fixed Assets	2m	2m	2m
Current Assets	519	626	529

Inseto UK Ltd
Unit 25 Focus 303 Business Centre Focus Way, Andover, SP10 5NY
Tel: 01264-334505 **Fax:** 01264-334449
E-mail: sales@inseto.co.uk
Website: http://www.inseto.co.uk
Directors: A. Brown (MD), M. Brown (Sales & Mktg), P. Brown (Co Sec)
Immediate Holding Company: INSETO (UK) LIMITED
Registration no: 02096377 **Date established:** 1987
No.of Employees: 1 - 10 **Product Groups:** 32, 33, 47, 49, 66

Date of Accounts	Dec 11	Dec 10	Dec 09
Working Capital	304	279	255
Fixed Assets	67	57	48
Current Assets	656	676	624

Jewson Ltd
12 Junction Road, Andover, SP10 3RB
Tel: 01264-324071 **Fax:** 01264-333734
Website: http://www.jewson.co.uk
Managers: P. Gilbert (District Mgr)
Ultimate Holding Company: Saint-Gobain Ltd
Immediate Holding Company: Saint-Gobain Building Distribution Ltd
Registration no: 00348407 **No.of Employees:** 1 - 10 **Product Groups:** 66

K A Machine Tools
27 Highlands Road, Andover, SP10 2PX
Tel: 01264-355108 **Fax:** 01264-355108
E-mail: kamachinetools@tiscali.co.uk
Directors: K. Lockie (Snr Part)
Date established: 1988 **No.of Employees:** 1 - 10 **Product Groups:** 46

Kone Cranes
Unit 2 Viscount Court, Andover, SP10 5NW
Tel: 01264-364499 **Fax:** 01273-483288
E-mail: sales@mts-gb.co.uk
Website: http://www.koneycranes.com
Managers: B. Street (District Mgr), D. Stoodley
Immediate Holding Company: MACHINE TOOL SERVICES (G.B.) LIMITED
Registration no: 01782417 **Date established:** 1984
Turnover: £250,000 - £500,000 **No.of Employees:** 1 - 10
Product Groups: 46

Date of Accounts	Jan 08
Working Capital	159
Fixed Assets	16
Current Assets	235
Current Liabilities	76
Total Share Capital	1

Lloyds Konecranes Ltd
Unit 2 Viscount Court, Andover, SP10 5NW
Tel: 01264-364499 **Fax:** 01264-366063
E-mail: bob.street@konecranes.com
Website: http://www.konecranes.co.uk
Managers: B. Street (District Mgr)
Immediate Holding Company: Kci Holding UK Ltd
Registration no: 00969869 **No.of Employees:** 1 - 10 **Product Groups:** 35, 39, 45

L E D Synergy Ltd
1 Knights Court Magellan Close, Andover, SP10 5NT
Tel: 01264-303030 **Fax:** 01264-400900
E-mail: sales@ledsynergy.co.uk
Website: http://www.ledsynergy.co.uk
Directors: J. Harwood (MD)
Immediate Holding Company: LEDSYNERGY LTD
Registration no: 05203189 **Date established:** 2004
No.of Employees: 1 - 10 **Product Groups:** 37, 40, 49

Date of Accounts	Aug 08	Mar 11	Mar 10
Working Capital	N/A	-3	-0
Fixed Assets	N/A	23	24
Current Assets	N/A	214	91

Lansdowne Cartmel Ltd
3e West Way, Andover, SP10 5AS
Tel: 01264-353234 **Fax:** 01264-359025
E-mail: lansdownecartmel@aol.com
Bank(s): Barclays
Directors: R. Woods (Dir), R. Woods (MD)
Immediate Holding Company: LANSDOWNE-CARTMEL LTD
Registration no: 01467766 **Date established:** 1979
Turnover: £250,000 - £500,000 **No.of Employees:** 11 - 20
Product Groups: 48

Date of Accounts	Feb 07	Feb 06
Sales Turnover	273	290
Pre Tax Profit/Loss	5	6
Working Capital	19	19
Fixed Assets	29	37
Current Assets	84	89
Current Liabilities	65	70
ROCE% (Return on Capital Employed)	10.6	10.9
ROT% (Return on Turnover)	1.9	2.1

Lenham Storage Southern Ltd
Fyfield Road Weyhill, Andover, SP11 8DL
Tel: 01264-772166 **Fax:** 01264-773431
E-mail: geoff.bourner@lenham.com
Website: http://www.lenhamstorage.co.uk
Bank(s): Barclays
Directors: A. Burgess (Fin), G. Bourner (Dir)
Managers: C. Tolhurst (Tech Serv Mgr), S. Hall (Sales & Mktg Mg), D. Close (Personnel)
Immediate Holding Company: LENHAM STORAGE (SOUTHERN) LIMITED
Registration no: 00874230 **VAT No.:** GB 199 3786 87
Date established: 1966 **Turnover:** £5m - £10m
No.of Employees: 51 - 100 **Product Groups:** 72, 76, 77

Date of Accounts	Aug 11	Aug 10	Aug 09
Sales Turnover	6m	5m	5m
Pre Tax Profit/Loss	38	43	49
Working Capital	-39	-115	-238
Fixed Assets	2m	2m	2m
Current Assets	2m	1m	863
Current Liabilities	704	635	573

Linnet Technology Ltd
3 Darby Gate West Portway, Andover, SP10 3LF
Tel: 01264-366812 **Fax:** 01264-366778
E-mail: sales@linnet-tec.co.uk
Website: http://www.linnet-tec.co.uk
Bank(s): Clydesdale Bank PLC
Managers: C. Quiggley (Reg Mgr)
Ultimate Holding Company: LINNET HOLDINGS LIMITED
Immediate Holding Company: LINNET TECHNOLOGY LIMITED
Registration no: SC168688 **Date established:** 1996 **Turnover:** £1m - £2m
No.of Employees: 11 - 20 **Product Groups:** 37, 51

Date of Accounts	Oct 11	Oct 10	Oct 09
Working Capital	768	627	570
Fixed Assets	91	140	146
Current Assets	1m	1m	1m

The Locksmith
Shaw Close, Andover, SP10 3BT
Tel: 01264-357163 **Fax:** 01264-357163
Website: http://www.thelocksmithofandover.co.uk
Directors: I. Whincup (Prop)
No.of Employees: 1 - 10 **Product Groups:** 36, 37, 52

J M Loveridge
6a Kingsway, Andover, SP10 5LQ
Tel: 023-8022 2008 **Fax:** 023-8022 2117
E-mail: admin@jmloveridge.com
Website: http://www.jmloveridge.com
Managers: Knight (Ops Mgr)
Registration no: 00388090 **Turnover:** £5m - £10m
No.of Employees: 1 - 10 **Product Groups:** 31

Loveshaw Europe
Unit 9 Brunel Gate West Portway Industrial Estate, Andover, SP10 3SL
Tel: 01264-357511 **Fax:** 01264-355964
E-mail: sales@loveshaw-europe.co.uk
Website: http://www.loveshaw.co.uk
Directors: K. Green (MD)
Managers: A. Warren (), K. Greene (Mgr), C. Hinkin (Publicity)
Ultimate Holding Company: ILLINOIS TOOL WORKS
Immediate Holding Company: LOVESHAW CORP. (USA)
Registration no: 00559693 **VAT No.:** GB 189 8583 83
Turnover: £1m - £2m **No.of Employees:** 11 - 20 **Product Groups:** 42, 44

Material Handling Solutions
F The Alexander Bell Centre Hopkinson Way, Andover, SP10 3UR
Tel: 01264-332323 **Fax:** 01264-332343
E-mail: info@mhsltd.co.uk
Website: http://www.mhsltd.co.uk
Directors: A. Dymond (Ptnr)
Immediate Holding Company: MATERIALS HANDLING SOLUTIONS UK LIMITED
Registration no: 03790566 **Date established:** 1999
No.of Employees: 1 - 10 **Product Groups:** 38, 42

Date of Accounts	Jun 11	Jun 10	Jun 09
Working Capital	110	131	257
Fixed Assets	10	13	17
Current Assets	133	144	260

Merlin Power Management
29 North Way Walworth Industrial Estate Walworth Industrial Estate, Andover, SP10 5BE
Tel: 01264-349349 **Fax:** 08700-623350
Website: http://www.merlinpower.co.uk
Directors: R. Meek (Snr Part)
Ultimate Holding Company: SCIENTIFIC MANAGEMENT ASSOCIATES (AUSTRALIA) PTY LTD
Immediate Holding Company: BROOKS, CROWNHILL PATTERNMAKERS LIMITED
Registration no: 01082025 **Date established:** 1962
No.of Employees: 1 - 10 **Product Groups:** 37, 40

Mitutoyo UK Ltd
Joule Road West Point Business Park, Andover, SP10 3UX
Tel: 01264-353123 **Fax:** 01264-354883
E-mail: sales@mitutoyo.co.uk
Website: http://www.mitutoyo.co.uk
Directors: M. Smith (Co Sec), M. Weeks (Dir)
Managers: G. Horne, S. McDonald
Ultimate Holding Company: MITUTOYO CORPORATION (JAPAN).
Immediate Holding Company: MITUTOYO (U.K.) LIMITED
Registration no: 01439214 **Date established:** 1979
Turnover: £10m - £20m **No.of Employees:** 21 - 50 **Product Groups:** 38

Date of Accounts	Dec 11	Dec 10	Dec 09
Sales Turnover	22m	15m	16m
Pre Tax Profit/Loss	1m	242	411
Working Capital	7m	12m	13m
Fixed Assets	4m	4m	5m
Current Assets	10m	15m	16m
Current Liabilities	2m	1m	1m

Moto-Lita Ltd
Thruxton, Andover, SP11 8PW
Tel: 01264-772811 **Fax:** 01264-773102
E-mail: info@moto-lita.co.uk
Website: http://www.moto-lita.co.uk
Directors: K. Tester (Dir)
Immediate Holding Company: MOTO-LITA LIMITED
Registration no: 00821489 **Date established:** 1964
No.of Employees: 11 - 20 **Product Groups:** 39

Date of Accounts	Apr 12	Apr 11	Apr 10
Working Capital	381	336	363
Fixed Assets	16	14	11
Current Assets	533	523	520

MRT Castings Ltd
South Way Walworth Estate, Andover, SP10 5JT
Tel: 01264-324021 **Fax:** 01264-333773
E-mail: phil@mrt-castings.co.uk
Website: http://www.mrt-castings.co.uk
Bank(s): HSBC Bank plc
Directors: P. Rawnson (MD), C. Rawnson (Sales)
Managers: P. Davies (Purch Mgr), R. Baker
Registration no: 03150165 **VAT No.:** GB 199 1318 33
Date established: 1947 **Turnover:** £2m - £5m **No.of Employees:** 21 - 50
Product Groups: 34, 48

Date of Accounts	Mar 12	Mar 11	Mar 10
Sales Turnover	4m	4m	3m
Pre Tax Profit/Loss	147	166	-32
Working Capital	399	389	275
Fixed Assets	1m	848	788
Current Assets	1m	1m	810
Current Liabilities	254	255	125

Muirhead Aerospace
East Portway, Andover, SP10 3LU
Tel: 01264-349600 **Fax:** 01264-336444
E-mail: martin.webb@ametek.co.uk
Website: http://www.muirheadaerospace.com
Bank(s): Barclays Bank
Managers: M. Webb (Eng Serv Mgr)
Immediate Holding Company: LAURUS BRANDS LIMITED
Registration no: 04212526 **VAT No.:** GB 740 5949 19
Date established: 2008 **Turnover:** £2m - £5m **No.of Employees:** 51 - 100
Product Groups: 37

Date of Accounts	Aug 11	Aug 10	Aug 09
Working Capital	-19	-18	-1
Fixed Assets	8	5	8
Current Assets	29	40	74
Current Liabilities	N/A	N/A	10

Office Depot UK
Guilbert House Greenwich Way, Andover, SP10 4JZ
Tel: 08444-120042 **Fax:** 08704-114735
E-mail: john.moore@officedepot.com
Website: http://www.officedepot.co.uk
Bank(s): Lloyds TSB
Directors: S. Derbyshire (Sales), J. Hills (Co Sec), T. Bennett (Sales), M. Horn (Fin), J. O'Keeffe (Mkt Research), J. Moore (MD)
Managers: S. Flynn, M. Johnson (Tech Serv Mgr), A. Parry (I.T. Exec), J. Scorer (Mktg Serv Mgr)
Ultimate Holding Company: OFFICE DEPOT INC (USA)
Immediate Holding Company: OFFICE DEPOT UK LIMITED
Registration no: 02654682 **VAT No.:** GB 673 4785 94
Date established: 1991 **Turnover:** £250m - £500m
No.of Employees: 1001 - 1500 **Product Groups:** 64

Date of Accounts	Dec 11	Dec 08	Dec 09
Sales Turnover	298m	305m	278m
Pre Tax Profit/Loss	1m	20m	-11m
Working Capital	3m	22m	15m
Fixed Assets	31m	29m	27m
Current Assets	140m	156m	137m
Current Liabilities	8m	9m	8m

P J P Supplies
128 Weyhill Road, Andover, SP10 3BE
Tel: 01264-324375
Directors: P. Perren (Prop)
Date established: 1982 **No.of Employees:** 1 - 10 **Product Groups:** 35

PDL Gates and Automation
17, Batchelors Barn Road, Andover, SP10 1HR
Tel: 023-8030 8927
E-mail: sales@pdlgates.co.uk
Website: http://www.pdlgatesandautomation.co.uk
Managers: P. Lockington (Chief Acct)
Date established: 2005 **Turnover:** Up to £250,000
No.of Employees: 1 - 10 **Product Groups:** 25

Pitkin
Healey House Dene Road, Andover, SP10 2AA
Tel: 01264-409200 **Fax:** 01264-334110
E-mail: sales@tempus-publishing.com
Website: http://www.pitkin-guides.com

see next page

Pitkin - Cont'd

Managers: S. Swalwell (Mgr)
Immediate Holding Company: OLIVER & SANDERS LTD
Registration no: 04025279 **VAT No.:** GB 501 9020 00
Date established: 2000 **Turnover:** £2m - £5m **No.of Employees:** 1 - 10
Product Groups: 28

Date of Accounts	Dec 11	Dec 10	Dec 09
Working Capital	114	62	39
Fixed Assets	148	182	142
Current Assets	235	167	107

Plimto Ltd

Thruxton Airport Thruxton, Andover, SP11 8PW
Tel: 01264-773173 **Fax:** 01264-772936
E-mail: sales@plimtosolder.com
Website: http://www.plimtosolder.com
Directors: N. Foster (Dir)
Immediate Holding Company: PLIMTO LIMITED
Registration no: 01221036 **VAT No.:** GB 200 6293 10
Date established: 1975 **Turnover:** £250,000 - £500,000
No.of Employees: 1 - 10 **Product Groups:** 32, 34

Date of Accounts	Jul 11	Jul 10	Jul 09
Working Capital	26	21	34
Fixed Assets	5	6	7
Current Assets	70	63	63

Point 2 Point Andover Ltd

Unit 2 Balksbury Hill Industrial Estate Balksbury Hill, Upper Clatford, Andover, SP11 7LW
Tel: 01264-333000 **Fax:** 01264-332820
E-mail: charlesconnaught@point2pointandover.co.uk
Website: http://www.point2point.co.uk
Directors: E. Malden (MD), P. Malden (Fin)
Immediate Holding Company: POINT 2 POINT (ANDOVER) LIMITED
Registration no: 03440035 **Date established:** 1997
Turnover: £500,000 - £1m **No.of Employees:** 1 - 10 **Product Groups:** 79

Date of Accounts	Jul 11	Jul 10	Jul 09
Working Capital	139	120	122
Fixed Assets	66	21	43
Current Assets	193	159	145

Powerbox Group Ltd

4-5 Knights Court Magellan Close, Andover, SP10 5NT
Tel: 01264-384460 **Fax:** 01264-334337
E-mail: patricia.mitter@powerbox.se
Website: http://www.powerbox.co.uk
Bank(s): National Westminster
Directors: P. Mitter (Fin), S. Pitcher (Sales)
Ultimate Holding Company: POWERBOX INTERNATIONAL AB (SWEDEN)
Immediate Holding Company: POWERBOX LIMITED
Registration no: 02332220 **VAT No.:** GB 541 7091 56
Date established: 1989 **Turnover:** £1m - £2m **No.of Employees:** 11 - 20
Product Groups: 37, 38

Date of Accounts	Dec 11	Dec 10	Dec 09
Sales Turnover	2m	901	1m
Pre Tax Profit/Loss	81	-8	1
Working Capital	590	551	577
Fixed Assets	207	197	169
Current Assets	2m	1m	749
Current Liabilities	472	145	94

Precision Varionics Ltd

307 The Commercial Centre Picket Piece, Andover, SP11 6RU
Tel: 01264-334522 **Fax:** 01264-334422
E-mail: sales@varionics.co.uk
Website: http://www.varionics.co.uk
Directors: J. Heiron (MD)
Immediate Holding Company: PRECISION VARIONICS LIMITED
Registration no: 01356807 **VAT No.:** GB 302 4433 10
Date established: 1978 **Turnover:** Up to £250,000
No.of Employees: 1 - 10 **Product Groups:** 37, 38

Date of Accounts	Mar 11	Mar 10	Mar 09
Working Capital	36	38	42
Current Assets	40	43	51

Preformed Line Products GB Ltd

East Portway, Andover, SP10 3LH
Tel: 01264-366234 **Fax:** 01264-356714
E-mail: sales@preformed.com
Website: http://www.preformed.com
Bank(s): Barclays, Andover
Directors: G. Mason (Fin), R. Ruhlman (Pres)
Ultimate Holding Company: PREFORMED LINE PRODUCTS COMPANY (USA)
Immediate Holding Company: PREFORMED LINE PRODUCTS (GREAT BRITAIN) LIMITED
Registration no: 00578922 **VAT No.:** GB 199 4109 27
Date established: 1957 **Turnover:** £5m - £10m
No.of Employees: 51 - 100 **Product Groups:** 35, 37

Date of Accounts	Dec 11	Dec 10	Dec 09
Sales Turnover	10m	8m	8m
Pre Tax Profit/Loss	1m	594	788
Working Capital	4m	3m	3m
Fixed Assets	815	847	816
Current Assets	5m	4m	3m
Current Liabilities	587	386	493

M Price Ltd

D The Alexander Bell Centre Hopkinson Way, Andover, SP10 3UR
Tel: 01264-333452 **Fax:** 01264-338070
E-mail: c.chapman@mprice.co.uk
Website: http://www.mprice.co.uk
Directors: C. Chapman (MD)
Immediate Holding Company: M.PRICE LIMITED
Registration no: 00604114 **Date established:** 1958
No.of Employees: 11 - 20 **Product Groups:** 46

Date of Accounts	Apr 11	Apr 10	Apr 09
Sales Turnover	28m	20m	27m
Pre Tax Profit/Loss	1m	1m	1m
Working Capital	2m	2m	3m
Fixed Assets	998	925	696
Current Assets	11m	9m	10m
Current Liabilities	3m	3m	2m

Primary Business Support

Lower Farm Foxcotte, Andover, SP10 4AA
Tel: 01264-324403
E-mail: peter.bird@primarybs.co.uk
Website: http://www.primarybs.co.uk
Directors: P. Bird (Prop)
Turnover: Up to £250,000 **No.of Employees:** 1 - 10 **Product Groups:** 81

Puma Products Ltd

Unit 6 Viscount Court, Andover, SP10 5NW
Tel: 01264-333305 **Fax:** 01264-333310
E-mail: sales@pumaproducts.co.uk
Website: http://www.pumaproducts.co.uk
Directors: P. Newton (Dir)
Immediate Holding Company: PUMA PRODUCTS LIMITED
Registration no: 03230570 **VAT No.:** GB 362 7640 45
Date established: 1996 **Turnover:** £500,000 - £1m
No.of Employees: 1 - 10 **Product Groups:** 40

Date of Accounts	Sep 11	Sep 10	Sep 09
Working Capital	108	79	36
Fixed Assets	13	15	17
Current Assets	293	227	112

Pumpsets Ltd

Unit 2 North Way, Andover, SP10 5AZ
Tel: 01264-332004 **Fax:** 01264-355399
E-mail: enquiries@pumpsets.com
Website: http://www.pumpsets.com
Directors: M. Waters (Dir)
Managers: M. Walters (Sales Prom Mgr)
Immediate Holding Company: PUMPSETS LTD.
Registration no: 02920603 **VAT No.:** GB 631 8491 34
Date established: 1994 **Turnover:** £500,000 - £1m
No.of Employees: 1 - 10 **Product Groups:** 37, 40, 67

Date of Accounts	Sep 11	Sep 10	Sep 09
Sales Turnover	941	978	842
Pre Tax Profit/Loss	5	6	25
Working Capital	92	94	86
Fixed Assets	12	6	9
Current Assets	434	347	293
Current Liabilities	158	134	122

R. Twining & Co. Ltd

South Way, Andover, SP10 5AQ
Tel: 0845-6019612 **Fax:** 01264-337177
E-mail: info@twinings.com
Website: http://www.twinings.com
Directors: G. Maccallum (Dir), R. Tavener (Grp Chief Exec)
Managers: M. Battison
Ultimate Holding Company: Associated British Foods
Registration no: 00525071 **VAT No.:** GB 730 1685 54
Turnover: Over £1,000m **No.of Employees:** 1 - 10 **Product Groups:** 20, 62

S S I Schaefer Ltd

83-84 Livingstone Road Walworth Industrial Estate, Andover, SP10 5QZ
Tel: 01264-386600 **Fax:** 01264-386611
E-mail: solutions@ssi-schaefer.co.uk
Website: http://www.ssi-schaefer.co.uk
Bank(s): HSBC
Directors: J. Vos (MD), A. Zwaan (Sales)
Managers: D. Griffiths, V. Higginson, S. Shah (Comptroller), A. Baker (Buyer)
Ultimate Holding Company: SSI SCHAEFER HOLDING INTERNATIONAL GMBH
Immediate Holding Company: SSI SCHAEFER LTD
Registration no: 00676451 **VAT No.:** GB 198 9763 75
Date established: 1960 **Turnover:** £50m - £75m
No.of Employees: 51 - 100 **Product Groups:** 26, 30, 35

Date of Accounts	Dec 11	Dec 10	Dec 09
Sales Turnover	62m	34m	58m
Pre Tax Profit/Loss	-129	-240	104
Working Capital	2m	2m	2m
Fixed Assets	3m	3m	4m
Current Assets	21m	7m	14m
Current Liabilities	8m	872	2m

Scorpion Power Systems

Shenton House Walworth Road, Walworth Business Park, Andover, SP10 5LH
Tel: 0844-8884445 **Fax:** 0844-8884446
E-mail: info@shentongroup.co.uk
Website: http://www.shentongroup.co.uk
Bank(s): Lloyds TSB Bank plc
Directors: R. Meek (Snr Part)
Managers: D. Barry (Chief Mgr)
Registration no: 01082025 **VAT No.:** GB 362 5368 45
Date established: 1972 **Turnover:** £2m - £5m **No.of Employees:** 21 - 50
Product Groups: 37

Sealock Ltd

Scott Close, Andover, SP10 5NU
Tel: 01264-358185 **Fax:** 01264-332203
E-mail: info@sealock.co.uk
Website: http://www.sealock.co.uk
Bank(s): HSBC
Directors: R. Ladd (Fin), P. Young (Dir), B. Young (Co Sec), C. Young (MD)
Immediate Holding Company: SEALOCK LIMITED
Registration no: 01725851 **VAT No.:** GB 384 2369 32
Date established: 1983 **Turnover:** £2m - £5m **No.of Employees:** 11 - 20
Product Groups: 32

Date of Accounts	Sep 11	Sep 10	Sep 09
Sales Turnover	5m	4m	4m
Pre Tax Profit/Loss	302	318	194
Working Capital	646	578	525
Fixed Assets	1m	1m	1m
Current Assets	2m	2m	1m
Current Liabilities	261	245	115

Stannah

Watt Close, Andover, SP10 3SD
Tel: 01264-332244 **Fax:** 01264-353943
Website: http://www.stannah.com
Bank(s): National Westminster
Directors: D. Walton (MD), J. Stannah (MD)
Ultimate Holding Company: STANNAH LIFTS HOLDINGS LIMITED
Immediate Holding Company: STANNAH MANAGEMENT SERVICES LIMITED
Registration no: 02483693 **Date established:** 1990
Turnover: £125m - £250m **No.of Employees:** 501 - 1000
Product Groups: 45

Date of Accounts	Dec 11	Dec 10	Dec 09
Sales Turnover	74m	71m	68m
Pre Tax Profit/Loss	7m	6m	6m
Working Capital	15m	14m	14m
Fixed Assets	5m	5m	6m
Current Assets	21m	21m	20m
Current Liabilities	3m	3m	2m

Stannah Lifts Ltd

Anton Mill Anton Mill Lane, Andover, SP10 2NX
Tel: 01264-339090 **Fax:** 01264-337942
E-mail: alastair_stannah@stannah.co.uk
Website: http://www.stannahlifts.co.uk
Directors: A. Stannah (Dir), D. Coveney (Fin), D. Greaves (Co Sec)
Managers: C. Vos (Personnel), K. Saville (Purch Mgr), L. Wilson (Tech Serv Mgr), L. Carruthers, J. Monro (Mktg Serv Mgr)
Ultimate Holding Company: STANNAH LIFTS HOLDINGS LIMITED
Immediate Holding Company: STANNAH LIFTS LIMITED
Registration no: 01189836 **Date established:** 1974
Turnover: £10m - £20m **No.of Employees:** 101 - 250
Product Groups: 35, 39, 45

Date of Accounts	Dec 11	Dec 10	Dec 09
Sales Turnover	15m	15m	16m
Pre Tax Profit/Loss	-2m	-2m	-1m
Working Capital	2m	3m	3m
Fixed Assets	489	567	662
Current Assets	5m	6m	6m
Current Liabilities	2m	2m	2m

Stannah Management Services Ltd

Watt Close East Portway, Andover, SP10 3SD
Tel: 01264-364311 **Fax:** 01264-353943
E-mail: jon_stannah@stannah.co.uk
Website: http://www.stannah.co.uk
Bank(s): National Westminster Bank Plc
Directors: A. Stannah (Dir), A. Stannah (Ch), B. Stannah (Dir), D. Walton (Dir), I. Ash (Fin), J. Stannah (Dir), J. Stannah (Ptnr), D. Greaves (Co Sec)
Managers: T. Kaye (Sales Prom Mgr)
Ultimate Holding Company: STANNAH LIFTS HOLDINGS LIMITED
Immediate Holding Company: STANNAH MANAGEMENT SERVICES LIMITED
Registration no: 02483693 **VAT No.:** GB 236 7783 28
Date established: 1990 **Turnover:** £125m - £250m
No.of Employees: 501 - 1000 **Product Groups:** 39, 45, 48

Date of Accounts	Dec 10	Dec 09	Dec 08
Sales Turnover	6m	6m	462
Pre Tax Profit/Loss	156	199	132
Working Capital	309	1m	1m
Fixed Assets	929	773	759
Current Assets	21m	18m	5m
Current Liabilities	2m	2m	2m

Stannah Microlifts Ltd

Caxton Close, Andover, SP10 3QN
Tel: 01264-351922 **Fax:** 01264-333465
E-mail: graham_mears@stannah.co.uk
Website: http://www.stannah.co.uk
Bank(s): Natwest
Directors: D. Coveney (Co Sec), D. Greaves (Co Sec), P. Stannah (MD)
Managers: T. Howell (Purch Mgr), M. Chapman (Chief Mgr), A. Porter (Tech Serv Mgr), J. Henslowe (Personnel)
Ultimate Holding Company: STANNAH LIFTS HOLDINGS LIMITED
Immediate Holding Company: STANNAH MICROLIFTS LIMITED
Registration no: 00964804 **VAT No.:** GB 236 7783 28
Date established: 1969 **Turnover:** £2m - £5m **No.of Employees:** 21 - 50
Product Groups: 45

Date of Accounts	Dec 11	Dec 10	Dec 09
Working Capital	434	435	386
Fixed Assets	150	142	105
Current Assets	2m	2m	1m
Current Liabilities	372	N/A	N/A

Stortext Ltd

Hikenield House Icknield Way, Andover, SP10 5AH
Tel: 01264-360900 **Fax:** 01264-360901
E-mail: richard.butler@stortextfm.com
Website: http://www.stortextfm.com
Directors: J. Williams (Fin), M. Iveson (Sales)
Managers: R. Butler
Registration no: 01984079 **VAT No.:** GB 829 6761 81
Turnover: £2m - £5m **No.of Employees:** 21 - 50 **Product Groups:** 44, 80, 81

The Swimming Pool & Allied Trades Association Ltd

4 Eastgate House 5-7 East Street, Andover, SP10 1EP
Tel: 01264-356210 **Fax:** 01264-332628
E-mail: admin@sparta.co.uk
Website: http://www.sparta.co.uk
Directors: C. Hayes (MD)
Immediate Holding Company: THE SWIMMING POOL AND ALLIED TRADES ASSOCIATION LIMITED
Registration no: 04112055 **VAT No.:** GB 218 6581 47
Date established: 2000 **Turnover:** Up to £250,000
No.of Employees: 1 - 10 **Product Groups:** 80

Date of Accounts	Mar 12	Mar 11	Mar 10
Sales Turnover	226	218	195
Pre Tax Profit/Loss	-2	8	4
Working Capital	40	42	34
Current Assets	66	66	94
Current Liabilities	21	23	21

Taylors Embroidery

Unit 115 The Commercial Centre Picket Piece, Andover, SP11 6RU
Tel: 01264-324383 **Fax:** 01264-333491
E-mail: info@taylorsembroidery.co.uk
Website: http://www.taylorsembroidery.co.uk
Directors: J. Barton (Snr Part)
Date established: 1983 **No.of Employees:** 11 - 20 **Product Groups:** 24

Howard Tenens Andover Ltd

Unit 2c Macadam Way West Portway, Andover, SP10 3LF
Tel: 01264-324449 **Fax:** 01264-332253
E-mail: enquiries@tenens.com
Website: http://www.tenens.com
Bank(s): Barclays, Oxford
Directors: R. Brown (Fin)
Managers: T. Fryer (Sales Admin)
Ultimate Holding Company: HOWARD TENENS LIMITED
Immediate Holding Company: HOWARD TENENS (ANDOVER) LIMITED
Registration no: 02160206 **VAT No.:** GB 391 9766 95
Date established: 1987 **Turnover:** £10m - £20m
No.of Employees: 101 - 250 **Product Groups:** 72, 77, 84

Date of Accounts	Sep 11	Sep 10	Sep 09
Sales Turnover	13m	13m	11m
Pre Tax Profit/Loss	793	1m	879
Working Capital	354	-332	-634
Fixed Assets	4m	4m	4m
Current Assets	3m	3m	2m
Current Liabilities	3m	3m	2m

3form Design

Unit 63 Basepoint Business & Innovation Centre Caxton Close, Andover, SP10 3FG
Tel: 01264-326306 **Fax:** 01264-326308
E-mail: web@3formdesign.com
Website: http://www.3formdesign.com
Directors: A. Miller (Snr Part)
Date established: 1999 **Turnover:** £250,000 - £500,000
No.of Employees: 1 - 10 **Product Groups:** 80, 84

Titan

West Portway, Andover, SP10 3LF
Tel: 01264-357666 **Fax:** 01264-366446
E-mail: darren.crane@titanpc.co.uk
Website: http://www.titanpc.co.uk
Directors: P. Johnstone (Fin)
Managers: A. Thomson (), D. Vincent (Buyer), N. Baldwin (I.T. Exec), C. Porter (Accounts)
Immediate Holding Company: BP ROLLS SIGNS & GRAPHICS LIMITED
Registration no: 03733291 **Date established:** 1999
Turnover: £250,000 - £500,000 **No.of Employees:** 1 - 10
Product Groups: 30, 33, 42

Date of Accounts	Dec 06	Dec 05	Dec 04
Pre Tax Profit/Loss	N/A	N/A	-1
Working Capital	771	4911	4911
Current Assets	4911	4911	4911
Current Liabilities	4139	N/A	N/A

Transplus Delivery Services

Unit 4 Stephenson Close, Andover, SP10 3RU
Tel: 01264-350700 **Fax:** 01264-366400
E-mail: roger@transplus.co.uk
Website: http://www.transplus.co.uk
Directors: R. Smith (Fin)
Immediate Holding Company: TRANSPLUS LIMITED
Registration no: 03427971 **Date established:** 1997
No.of Employees: 1 - 10 **Product Groups:** 77

Date of Accounts	Sep 11	Sep 10	Sep 09
Working Capital	272	288	292
Fixed Assets	36	39	43
Current Assets	754	741	634

Traxsys

East Portway, Andover, SP10 3LU
Tel: 01264-349640 **Fax:** 01425-463111
E-mail: leigh.smith@ametek.co.uk
Website: http://www.traxsys.com
Directors: J. Randall (MD), J. Randle (Dir), L. Smith (MD)
Immediate Holding Company: LAURUS BRANDS LIMITED
Registration no: 04067603 **Date established:** 2008 **Turnover:** £2m - £5m
No.of Employees: 21 - 50 **Product Groups:** 37, 44, 67

Vernham Labels Ltd

Unit 6 Mayfield Avenue Industrial Park Fyfield Road Weyhill, Andover, SP11 8HU
Tel: 01264-773501 **Fax:** 01264-773065
E-mail: mail@vernhamlabels.co.uk
Website: http://www.vernhamlabels.co.uk
Directors: S. Bishop (MD)
Immediate Holding Company: VERNHAM LABELS LIMITED
Registration no: 03850924 **Date established:** 1999
Turnover: £500,000 - £1m **No.of Employees:** 1 - 10 **Product Groups:** 27, 30

Date of Accounts	Jan 12	Jan 11	Jan 10
Working Capital	81	57	9
Fixed Assets	163	185	214
Current Assets	143	159	156

Vision Assurance Systems

Basepoint Business & Innovation Centre Caxton Close, East Portway Ind Est, Andover, SP10 3FG
Tel: 01264-326309 **Fax:** 01264-326327
E-mail: sales@visionassurancesystems.com
Website: http://www.visionassurancesystems.com
Directors: P. Raynsford (MD)
Immediate Holding Company: Vacuumatic Colchester Ltd
Registration no: 05669215 **VAT No.:** GB 637 0368 37
Date established: 2002 **Turnover:** £250,000 - £500,000
No.of Employees: 1 - 10 **Product Groups:** 38, 44

Willings Services Ltd

Kenyons Yard Weyhill Road, Andover, SP10 3NP
Tel: 01264-334786 **Fax:** 01264-351933
E-mail: info@willings.co.uk
Website: http://www.willings.co.uk
Directors: C. Hussey (Prop)
Immediate Holding Company: WILLINGS SERVICES LIMITED
Registration no: 03308490 **Date established:** 1997
No.of Employees: 11 - 20 **Product Groups:** 38, 42

Date of Accounts	Dec 11	Dec 10	Dec 09
Working Capital	272	235	248
Fixed Assets	58	53	59
Current Assets	405	432	372

Basingstoke

A C Plastic Industries Ltd

Unit J Loddon Business Centre Roentgen Road, Basingstoke, RG24 8NG
Tel: 01256-329334 **Fax:** 01256-817862
E-mail: sales@ac-plastics.com
Website: http://www.ac-plastics.com
Directors: N. Hudec (Fin)
Managers: M. Oshea (Sales Prom Mgr)
Ultimate Holding Company: ACSTK HOLDINGS
Immediate Holding Company: A.C. PLASTIC INDUSTRIES LIMITED
Registration no: 05300925 **VAT No.:** GB 217 9508 48
Date established: 2004 **Turnover:** £1m - £2m **No.of Employees:** 1 - 10
Product Groups: 30

Date of Accounts	Dec 11	Dec 10	Dec 09
Working Capital	-158	-165	-141
Fixed Assets	45	51	46
Current Assets	791	491	418

Activator UK Ltd

Vickers House Priestley Road, Basingstoke, RG24 9NP
Tel: 0845-4565960
E-mail: sales@activator-uk.net
Website: http://www.activator-uk.com
Directors: P. Moss (Sales)
Registration no: 03576971 **Date established:** 1998
Turnover: Up to £250,000 **No.of Employees:** 1 - 10 **Product Groups:** 37, 44, 79

Date of Accounts	Dec 08	Dec 07	Dec 06
Sales Turnover	N/A	N/A	171
Pre Tax Profit/Loss	N/A	N/A	-40
Working Capital	-11	-21	-7
Fixed Assets	7	6	7
Current Assets	48	31	33
Current Liabilities	59	52	39

Advanced Engineering

Guardian House Stroudley Road, Basingstoke, RG24 8NL
Tel: 01256-460300 **Fax:** 01256-462266
E-mail: sales@advancedengineering.co.uk
Website: http://www.advancedengineering.co.uk
Bank(s): Barclays
Directors: C. Pratt (Tech Serv), B. Lea (Co Sec)
Ultimate Holding Company: STERLING LTD
Immediate Holding Company: ADVANCED ENGINEERING LTD
Registration no: 01645348 **VAT No.:** GB 358 9070 21
Date established: 1982 **Turnover:** £1m - £2m **No.of Employees:** 11 - 20
Product Groups: 39, 40, 42, 52, 84

Date of Accounts	Feb 08	Feb 11	Feb 10
Working Capital	68	372	404
Fixed Assets	405	197	94
Current Assets	941	1m	1m

Alberto-Culver Co. (UK) Ltd

Lime Tree Way Hampshire International Business Park, Chineham, Basingstoke, RG24 8ER
Tel: 01256-705000 **Fax:** 01256-705001
Website: http://www.alberto.co.uk
Directors: G. Fish (Dep Pres), L. Lavin (Pres)
Ultimate Holding Company: Alberto-Culver International Inc.
Immediate Holding Company: Alberto Culver Group Ltd
Registration no: 02064021 **VAT No.:** 235 5050 87 **Date established:** 1994
Turnover: £75m - £125m **No.of Employees:** 501 - 1000
Product Groups: 32

Ampex Great Britain Ltd

5 Elmwood Chineham Business Park, Basingstoke, RG24 8WG
Tel: 01256-814410 **Fax:** 01256-814474
E-mail: sales@ampexgb.co.uk
Website: http://www.ampexdata.com
Directors: M. Brake (Fin), W. Bjorklund (MD)
Managers: K. Russ (Sales & Mktg Mg)
Ultimate Holding Company: AMPEX CORP (USA)
Immediate Holding Company: Ampex Corporation (U.S.A.)
Registration no: 02987174 **VAT No.:** GB 641 4023 80
Date established: 1994 **Turnover:** £250,000 - £500,000
No.of Employees: 1 - 10 **Product Groups:** 37, 44

Date of Accounts	Dec 07	Dec 06	Dec 05
Sales Turnover	583	600	666
Pre Tax Profit/Loss	-17	-14	-76
Working Capital	-215	-163	-149
Fixed Assets	34	N/A	N/A
Current Assets	233	302	281
Current Liabilities	448	465	430
Total Share Capital	100	100	100
ROCE% (Return on Capital Employed)	9.7	8.8	51.4
ROT% (Return on Turnover)	-3.0	-2.4	-11.5

Amphenol-Tuchel Great Britain

14 Plover Close Kempshott, Basingstoke, RG22 5PQ
Tel: 01256-330749 **Fax:** 01256-330749
Website: http://www.amphenol.info/en/index.shtml
Product Groups: 37, 39, 47

Anglian Pharma

Units 3 & 4 Quidhampton Business Units Polhampton Lane, Overton, Basingstoke, RG25 3ED
Tel: 01256-772742 **Fax:** 01256-772745
E-mail: mail@anglianpharma.com
Website: http://www.anglianpharma.com
Bank(s): Barclays
Managers: C. Weaver (Mgr)
Ultimate Holding Company: CRESCENT PHARMACEUTICALS LIMITED
Immediate Holding Company: ANGLIAN PHARMA SALES & MARKETING LIMITED
Registration no: 03940020 **Date established:** 2000
Turnover: £500,000 - £1m **No.of Employees:** 11 - 20
Product Groups: 31, 32, 63

Date of Accounts	Dec 11	Dec 10	Dec 09
Sales Turnover	N/A	N/A	2m
Pre Tax Profit/Loss	N/A	N/A	6
Working Capital	110	-68	185
Fixed Assets	27	111	128
Current Assets	628	675	702
Current Liabilities	N/A	N/A	20

Aqua Nouveau Ltd

Unit 20 Basingstoke Enterprise Centre West Ham Lane, Basingstoke, RG22 6NQ
Tel: 01256-844044 **Fax:** 01256-844045
E-mail: alan.matthews@aqua-nouveau.co.uk
Website: http://www.aquanouveau.co.uk
Directors: A. Matthews (Dir)
Immediate Holding Company: AQUANOUVEAU LIMITED
Registration no: 02190047 **Date established:** 1987
No.of Employees: 11 - 20 **Product Groups:** 38, 42

Date of Accounts	Dec 10	Dec 09	Dec 08
Working Capital	-102	-179	-228
Fixed Assets	7	8	10
Current Assets	152	62	85

Ashford Hill Roofing Co

Head Office Hart House Priestley Road, Basingstoke, RG24 9PU
Tel: 01256-811910
E-mail: nigelappleton@ashfordhillroofing.co.uk
Website: http://www.ashfordhillroofing.co.uk
Directors: N. Appleton (Dir)
Immediate Holding Company: WEBFORCES LTD
Registration no: 06291159 **Date established:** 2004
No.of Employees: 1 - 10 **Product Groups:** 26, 35

Axa Wealth

Winterthur Way, Basingstoke, RG21 6SZ
Tel: 01256-470707 **Fax:** 08453-012940
E-mail: mike.kellard@winterthur-life.co.uk
Website: http://www.axawealth.co.uk
Bank(s): Barclays, London
Directors: B. Hooper (Dir), J. Small (Co Sec), D. Griffiths (Ch), M. Kellard (Grp Chief Exec)
Managers: J. Hare, D. Deadman (Purch Mgr), G. Boutle
Immediate Holding Company: WINTERTHUR LIFE UK HOLDINGS LIMITED
Registration no: 03223752 **Date established:** 1996
Turnover: £10m - £20m **No.of Employees:** 501 - 1000
Product Groups: 82

Date of Accounts	Dec 11	Dec 10	Dec 09
Sales Turnover	28m	14m	710
Pre Tax Profit/Loss	-24m	-4m	6
Working Capital	18m	25m	1m
Current Assets	26m	26m	1m
Current Liabilities	2m	345	56

Balfour Beatty Living Places Balfour Beatty Group

Pavilion B Ashwood Park Ashwood Way, Basingstoke, RG23 8BG
Tel: 01256-400400 **Fax:** 01256-400401
E-mail: foundations@stent.co.uk
Website: http://www.bblivingplaces.com
Bank(s): Barclays
Directors: J. Jackson (MD), J. Brown (Pers)
Managers: L. Lamerton (Commun Mgr), J. Wilkinson, N. Gibbons (Tech Serv Mgr)
Ultimate Holding Company: BALFOUR BEATTY PLC
Immediate Holding Company: BALFOUR BEATTY LIVING PLACES LIMITED
Registration no: 02067112 **VAT No.:** GB 217 9672 35
Date established: 1986 **Turnover:** Over £1,000m
No.of Employees: 101 - 250 **Product Groups:** 33, 34, 45, 51, 66

Basingstoke Bolt & Tool

Armstrong Road, Basingstoke, RG24 8NU
Tel: 01256-329781 **Fax:** 01256-817150
E-mail: sales@basingstokeboltandtool.co.uk
Directors: S. Mann (Prop)
Immediate Holding Company: BOLT & TOOL SUPPLIES LIMITED
Registration no: 06749436 **VAT No.:** GB 200 3616 27
Date established: 2008 **Turnover:** £250,000 - £500,000
No.of Employees: 1 - 10 **Product Groups:** 30, 31, 32, 33, 35, 36, 37, 38, 46, 48, 66

Date of Accounts	Nov 10	Nov 09
Working Capital	-55	-10
Fixed Assets	14	18
Current Assets	85	90

Basingstoke & Deane Borough Council

Civic Offices London Road, Basingstoke, RG21 4AH
Tel: 01256-844844 **Fax:** 01256-845200
E-mail: customer.service@basingstoke.gov.uk
Website: http://www.basingstoke.gov.uk
Directors: T. Curtis (Grp Chief Exec)
Managers: J. Welch (I.T. Exec), L. George
Immediate Holding Company: THE MAKING
Registration no: 04482627 **Date established:** 2002
Turnover: Up to £250,000 **No.of Employees:** 251 - 500
Product Groups: 80, 87

Date of Accounts	Mar 11	Mar 10	Mar 09
Sales Turnover	177	163	190
Pre Tax Profit/Loss	-23	-40	-35
Working Capital	135	156	196
Fixed Assets	2	4	3
Current Assets	165	176	225
Current Liabilities	30	20	24

Bayham Ltd

Rutherford Road, Basingstoke, RG24 8PG
Tel: 01256-464911 **Fax:** 01256-464366
E-mail: chris@bayham.demon.co.uk
Website: http://www.tankgauges.co.uk
Bank(s): HSBC Bank plc
Directors: C. Balment (MD), S. Clements (Co Sec)
Ultimate Holding Company: BAYHAM HOLDINGS LIMITED
Immediate Holding Company: RANGER INSTRUMENT COMPANY LIMITED(THE)
Registration no: 00762552 **VAT No.:** GB 198 9641 89
Date established: 1963 **Turnover:** £250,000 - £500,000
No.of Employees: 21 - 50 **Product Groups:** 38

Date of Accounts	Apr 11	Apr 10	Apr 09
Sales Turnover	N/A	301	389
Pre Tax Profit/Loss	N/A	11	11
Working Capital	223	122	114
Current Assets	337	145	147
Current Liabilities	N/A	8	7

Benteler Distribution

Daneshill Indl-Est Armstrong Road, Basingstoke, RG24 8NU
Tel: 01256-811121 **Fax:** 01256-842310
E-mail: south@benteler-distribution.co.uk
Website: http://www.benteler-distribution.co.uk
Managers: D. Guest (I.T. Exec), R. Haith (Reg Sales Mgr), R. Hughes (Reg Sales Mgr)
Immediate Holding Company: TWO GUYS BATHROOMS LIMITED
Registration no: 00456349 **Date established:** 2008
Turnover: £10m - £20m **No.of Employees:** 21 - 50 **Product Groups:** 36

Date of Accounts	Jul 10	Jul 09
Working Capital	-58	-32
Fixed Assets	65	51
Current Assets	77	69

Biomerieux UK Ltd
Grafton Way, Basingstoke, RG22 6HY
Tel: 01256-461881 **Fax:** 01256-816863
E-mail: ukmarketing@biomerieux.com
Website: http://www.biomerieux.com
Bank(s): Lloyds TSB Bank plc
Directors: I. Chemarin (Fin)
Ultimate Holding Company: MERIEUX ALLIANCE (FRANCE)
Immediate Holding Company: BIOMERIEUX UK LIMITED
Registration no: 01061914 **Date established:** 1972
Turnover: £20m - £50m **No.of Employees:** 21 - 50 **Product Groups:** 31

Date of Accounts	Dec 11	Dec 10	Dec 09
Sales Turnover	39m	35m	37m
Pre Tax Profit/Loss	1m	363	3m
Working Capital	738	1m	2m
Fixed Assets	7m	6m	6m
Current Assets	11m	10m	9m
Current Liabilities	2m	2m	N/A

Chas A Blatchford & Sons Ltd
Lister Road, Basingstoke, RG22 4AH
Tel: 01256-316600 **Fax:** 01256-329256
E-mail: blatchfordb@blatchford.co.uk
Website: http://www.blatchford.co.uk
Bank(s): Barclays
Directors: M. Weston (Fin), B. Blatchford (MD)
Managers: D. Naidoo (Tech Serv Mgr), S. Kerry, J. Eggerton (Personnel)
Immediate Holding Company: CHAS.A.BLATCHFORD & SONS,LIMITED
Registration no: 00162114 **VAT No.:** GB 198 9476 78
Date established: 2019 **Turnover:** £20m - £50m
No.of Employees: 251 - 500 **Product Groups:** 38

Date of Accounts	Mar 11	Mar 10	Mar 09
Sales Turnover	45m	39m	34m
Pre Tax Profit/Loss	2m	2m	2m
Working Capital	8m	7m	5m
Fixed Assets	6m	5m	5m
Current Assets	13m	12m	10m
Current Liabilities	3m	3m	2m

Brickell Swimming Pools
84a Oakley Lane Oakley, Basingstoke, RG23 7JU
Tel: 01256-780567 **Fax:** 01256-782385
E-mail: info@brickellpools.co.uk
Website: http://www.brickellpools.co.uk
Directors: B. Brickell (Prop), D. Brickell (Fin)
Ultimate Holding Company: FREDERICK BRICKELL AND SONS LIMITED
Immediate Holding Company: BRICKELL SWIMMING POOLS LIMITED
Registration no: 00781508 **VAT No.:** GB 199 0341 43
Date established: 1963 **No.of Employees:** 1 - 10 **Product Groups:** 52

Buhrs UK Ltd
Ashwood Park Ashwood Way, Basingstoke, RG22 6NQ
Tel: 01256-329191 **Fax:** 01256-843245
E-mail: sale@computermail.co.uk
Website: http://www.computermail.co.uk
Directors: T. Eden (MD)
Managers: C. Rees (Sales Prom Mgr), J. Connel (Contrlr)
Immediate Holding Company: Mayplace Holdings P.L.C.
Registration no: 05762863 **Turnover:** £5m - £10m
No.of Employees: 1 - 10 **Product Groups:** 67

Date of Accounts	Dec 07	Dec 06
Working Capital	198	150
Fixed Assets	40	31
Current Assets	2931	2524
Current Liabilities	2733	2373
Total Share Capital	600	350

Bunzl Catering Supplies Ltd
K60 Lister Road, Basingstoke, RG22 4AS
Tel: 08453-017607 **Fax:** 01256-383540
E-mail: basingstoke@bunzl.co.uk
Website: http://www.bunzlcatering.co.uk
Managers: M. Cook (Mgr)
Ultimate Holding Company: BUNZL PUBLIC LIMITED COMPANY
Immediate Holding Company: CENTRAL CATERING SUPPLIES LIMITED
Registration no: 03888254 **Date established:** 1999 **Turnover:** £5m - £10m
No.of Employees: 51 - 100 **Product Groups:** 20

Camrose Air Conditioning Ltd
Unit D4 Brunswick Place, Basingstoke, RG21 3NN
Tel: 01256-466657 **Fax:** 01256-322801
E-mail: peter@camroseair.co.uk
Website: http://www.camroseair.co.uk
Directors: D. Shirley (MD)
Immediate Holding Company: CAMROSE AIR CONDITIONING LIMITED
Registration no: 01831846 **Date established:** 1984
Turnover: £500,000 - £1m **No.of Employees:** 1 - 10 **Product Groups:** 37, 38, 40, 52, 66, 84

Date of Accounts	Feb 10	Feb 09	Feb 08
Working Capital	6	20	17
Fixed Assets	5	7	13
Current Assets	71	76	122

Canadean Ltd
Unit 9-12 Faraday Court Rankine Road, Basingstoke, RG24 8PF
Tel: 01256-394200 **Fax:** 01256-394201
E-mail: marketing@canadean.com
Website: http://www.canadean.com
Directors: J. Gordon Stewart (Co Sec), R. Moore (Fin), A. Dixon (Sales)
Managers: G. Bever (Tech Serv Mgr), L. Garforth (Personnel)
Ultimate Holding Company: PROGRESSIVE DIGITAL MEDIA GROUP PLC
Immediate Holding Company: CANADEAN LIMITED
Registration no: 01078157 **Date established:** 1972 **Turnover:** £5m - £10m
No.of Employees: 51 - 100 **Product Groups:** 85

Date of Accounts	Dec 11	Dec 10	Dec 09
Sales Turnover	8m	7m	6m
Pre Tax Profit/Loss	2m	-948	83
Working Capital	937	-426	562
Fixed Assets	704	435	412
Current Assets	4m	3m	2m
Current Liabilities	3m	3m	1m

J & J Carter Ltd
8 Lion Court, Basingstoke, RG24 8QU
Tel: 01256-811455 **Fax:** 01256-811458
E-mail: john.carter@jjcarter.com
Website: http://www.jjcarter.com
Directors: R. Carter (Dir), C. Carter (Dir), J. Carter (MD)
Managers: A. Robinson (Sales Prom Mgr)
Immediate Holding Company: J. & J. CARTER LIMITED
Registration no: 02214348 **Date established:** 1988 **Turnover:** £1m - £2m
No.of Employees: 11 - 20 **Product Groups:** 23, 24, 30, 35, 36, 48, 49, 83

Cold Kit Ltd
Unit 3 Stewart Road, Basingstoke, RG24 8NF
Tel: 01256-811400 **Fax:** 01256-810200
E-mail: ccook@coldkit.com
Website: http://www.coldkit.com
Directors: W. Quail (MD)
Immediate Holding Company: COLDKIT (UK) LIMITED
Registration no: 05387304 **Date established:** 2005 **Turnover:** £1m - £2m
No.of Employees: 1 - 10 **Product Groups:** 26, 40, 42, 48, 67

Date of Accounts	Dec 11	Dec 10	Dec 09
Sales Turnover	N/A	2m	N/A
Working Capital	288	682	-261
Fixed Assets	39	8	8
Current Assets	2m	1m	1m

Computer 2000
Hampshire House Wade Road, Basingstoke, RG24 8NE
Tel: 08718-803000 **Fax:** 0870-060 7998
Website: http://www.computer2000.co.uk
Directors: A. Gass (MD), J. Doughty (Sales), F. Cooke (Mkt Research)
Ultimate Holding Company: TECH DATA CORP (USA)
Immediate Holding Company: COMPUTER 2000 DISTRIBUTION LIMITED
Registration no: 01691472 **Date established:** 1983
Turnover: Over £1,000m **No.of Employees:** 251 - 500
Product Groups: 44

Date of Accounts	Jan 11	Jan 10	Jan 09
Sales Turnover	1243m	1082m	1022m
Pre Tax Profit/Loss	16m	11m	9m
Working Capital	72m	58m	73m
Fixed Assets	4m	6m	6m
Current Assets	336m	301m	228m
Current Liabilities	19m	15m	21m

Crouzet Ltd
8 Crockford Lane Chineham Business Park, Chineham, Basingstoke, RG24 8WD
Tel: 01256-318900 **Fax:** 01256-318901
E-mail: info@crouzet.co.uk
Website: http://www.crouzet.com
Directors: J. Tichler (Fin)
Managers: V. Noens (Personnel)
Ultimate Holding Company: SCHNEIDER ELECTRIC SA (FRANCE)
Immediate Holding Company: CROUZET LIMITED
Registration no: 00689946 **Date established:** 1961 **Turnover:** £5m - £10m
No.of Employees: 1 - 10 **Product Groups:** 37, 38, 39, 40, 44, 46, 49

Date of Accounts	Dec 11	Dec 10	Dec 09
Sales Turnover	6m	6m	6m
Pre Tax Profit/Loss	796	1m	1m
Working Capital	2m	1m	1m
Fixed Assets	15	4	7
Current Assets	3m	3m	3m
Current Liabilities	496	584	684

Crown Lift Trucks Ltd
Rutherford Road, Basingstoke, RG24 8PD
Tel: 0845-850 9276 **Fax:** 0845-850 9277
E-mail: basingstoke@crown.com
Website: http://www.crown.com
Bank(s): Barclays
Directors: D. Kerr (Dep Pres), J. Dicke Ii (Dir), J. Jones (Co Sec), S. Emery (Sales), N. Dessaint (Fin)
Managers: S. Lightford
Ultimate Holding Company: CROWN EQUIPMENT CORPORATION (USA)
Immediate Holding Company: CROWN LIFT TRUCKS LIMITED
Registration no: 02319386 **Date established:** 1988
Turnover: £10m - £20m **No.of Employees:** 101 - 250
Product Groups: 38, 40, 45, 48, 67, 84

Date of Accounts	Mar 10	Mar 09	Mar 08
Sales Turnover	19m	25m	26m
Pre Tax Profit/Loss	-1m	-863	-839
Working Capital	-498	3m	-1m
Fixed Assets	2m	2m	2m
Current Assets	8m	9m	11m
Current Liabilities	2m	3m	2m

D M S Fabrications
The Station Station Hill, Overton, Basingstoke, RG25 3JH
Tel: 01256-771844 **Fax:** 01256-771625
Directors: M. Spence (Prop)
Immediate Holding Company: DMS FABRICATIONS LTD
Registration no: 05916284 **Date established:** 2006
Turnover: £250,000 - £500,000 **No.of Employees:** 1 - 10
Product Groups: 35

Date of Accounts	Mar 11	Mar 10	Mar 09
Sales Turnover	N/A	N/A	372
Pre Tax Profit/Loss	N/A	N/A	-0
Working Capital	37	16	17
Fixed Assets	50	47	57
Current Assets	140	93	68
Current Liabilities	N/A	N/A	11

Data Translation
Unit 2 Prisma Park Berrington Way, Basingstoke, RG24 8GT
Tel: 01256-333330 **Fax:** 01256-333388
E-mail: sales@datatranslation.co.uk
Website: http://www.datatranslation.co.uk
Directors: A. Molinari (Dir), E. Harpin (Fin)
Ultimate Holding Company: DATA TRANSLATION INCORPORATION (USA)
Immediate Holding Company: DATA TRANSLATION LIMITED
Registration no: 02985167 **VAT No.:** GB 641 4057 63
Date established: 1994 **Turnover:** £2m - £5m **No.of Employees:** 1 - 10
Product Groups: 38, 44, 80

Date of Accounts	Nov 11	Nov 10	Nov 09
Pre Tax Profit/Loss	N/A	N/A	-30
Working Capital	-2	-1	-1
Current Assets	1	1	2
Current Liabilities	N/A	N/A	3

De La Rue plc (Cash Systems Division)
De Lane Rue House Jays Close, Basingstoke, RG22 4BS
Tel: 01256-605000 **Fax:** 01256-605336
E-mail: jean.hermans@uk.delarue.com
Website: http://www.delarue.com
Directors: J. Hermans (Co Sec)
Ultimate Holding Company: DE LA RUE PLC
Immediate Holding Company: DE LA RUE OVERSEAS LIMITED
Registration no: 00355881 **Date established:** 1939
Turnover: £250m - £500m **No.of Employees:** 251 - 500
Product Groups: 44

Date of Accounts	Mar 08	Mar 11	Mar 10
Working Capital	159m	159m	159m
Current Assets	161m	161m	161m

Devlin Electronics Ltd
Unit D1 Grafton Way, Basingstoke, RG22 6HZ
Tel: 01256-467367 **Fax:** 01256-840048
E-mail: sales@devlin.co.uk
Website: http://www.devlin.co.uk
Bank(s): Barclays
Directors: M. Baker (Prop)
Immediate Holding Company: DEL REALISATIONS LIMITED
Registration no: 04067603 **VAT No.:** GB 200 8583 88
Date established: 2000 **Turnover:** £2m - £5m **No.of Employees:** 21 - 50
Product Groups: 37, 38, 39, 44, 67

Date of Accounts	Dec 09	Dec 08	Dec 07
Sales Turnover	N/A	5m	5m
Pre Tax Profit/Loss	N/A	-139	-147
Working Capital	547	183	286
Fixed Assets	455	566	693
Current Assets	2m	2m	2m
Current Liabilities	N/A	453	473

A N Dunning Metal Polishing
Station Yard Andover Road, Oakley, Basingstoke, RG23 7HA
Tel: 07909-151826 **Fax:** 01256-781665
E-mail: tdunning@hotmail.co.uk
Directors: A. Dunnings (Prop)
Date established: 1979 **No.of Employees:** 1 - 10 **Product Groups:** 46, 48

E C Electronics Ltd
4 Newton Court Rankine Road, Basingstoke, RG24 8GF
Tel: 01256-461894 **Fax:** 01256-843393
E-mail: info@ecelectronics.co.uk
Website: http://www.ecelectronics.co.uk
Directors: W. Green (Comm), E. Clarke (Co Sec), A. Mount (Chief Op Offcr), P. Simmonds (MD)
Immediate Holding Company: E C ELECTRONICS LIMITED
Registration no: 03573232 **Date established:** 1998 **Turnover:** £2m - £5m
No.of Employees: 21 - 50 **Product Groups:** 37, 39, 40, 41, 44, 46, 47

Date of Accounts	Jun 12	Jun 11	Jun 10
Working Capital	515	382	417
Fixed Assets	320	356	323
Current Assets	2m	1m	1m

Evalve Ltd
Unit Dberrington Way, Basingstoke, RG24 8GZ
Tel: 01256-479 000 **Fax:** 01256-478 727
E-mail: sales@evalve.co.uk
Website: http://www.evalve.co.uk
Directors: P. Burch (Prop)
Immediate Holding Company: Evalve (Southern) Ltd
Registration no: 04279473 **Date established:** 2004
No.of Employees: 1 - 10 **Product Groups:** 36, 37, 38

Date of Accounts	Aug 09	Aug 08	Aug 07
Working Capital	7	-1	-36
Fixed Assets	120	87	105
Current Assets	872	778	357

Fax 2 Mail Ltd
Vickers House Priestley Road, Basingstoke, RG24 9NP
Tel: 0870-1141000 **Fax:** 0870-1142000
E-mail: info@fax2mail.co.uk
Website: http://www.fax2mail.co.uk
Directors: G. Ward (Dir)
Registration no: 05208977 **No.of Employees:** 1 - 10 **Product Groups:** 81

Founders Total Spectrum Ltd
11 Intec 2 Wade Road, Basingstoke, RG24 8NE
Tel: 01256-814114 **Fax:** 01256-814115
E-mail: sales@totalspectrum.co.uk
Website: http://www.totalspectrum.co.uk
Directors: M. Norsworthy (MD)
Immediate Holding Company: FOUNDERS - TOTAL SPECTRUM LTD
Registration no: 02922266 **Date established:** 1994 **Turnover:** £2m - £5m
No.of Employees: 1 - 10 **Product Groups:** 38, 42

Date of Accounts	Apr 06
Working Capital	-98
Fixed Assets	75
Current Assets	1594
Current Liabilities	1692
Total Share Capital	1

Fyffes Group Ltd
Houndmills Road, Basingstoke, RG21 6XL
Tel: 01256-383200 **Fax:** 01256-383259
E-mail: c.bos@fyffes.com
Website: http://www.fyffes.com
Bank(s): Barclays, Pall Mall
Directors: C. Bos (MD), W. Faulkner (Pers)
Managers: T. Napier (Comptroller)
Ultimate Holding Company: FYFFES PUBLIC LIMITED COMPANY
Immediate Holding Company: FYFFES GROUP LIMITED
Registration no: 00070123 **Date established:** 2001
Turnover: £125m - £250m **No.of Employees:** 251 - 500
Product Groups: 62

Date of Accounts	Dec 11	Dec 10	Dec 09
Sales Turnover	244m	217m	243m
Pre Tax Profit/Loss	11m	612	-3m
Working Capital	10m	241	-8m
Fixed Assets	30m	31m	35m
Current Assets	59m	57m	52m
Current Liabilities	4m	3m	4m

G T K UK Ltd
Unit C2 Bond Close, Basingstoke, RG24 8PZ
Tel: 01256-472000 **Fax:** 01256-473000
E-mail: sales@gtk.co.uk
Website: http://www.gtk.co.uk
Directors: J. Morath (MD), S. Robinson (Fin)
Managers: P. Matters (Cust Serv Mgr), M. Sansum (Chief Buyer), M. Titchbon

Immediate Holding Company: G.T.K. (U.K.) LTD.
Registration no: 02460213 **VAT No.:** GB 529 1550 46
Date established: 1990 **Turnover:** £5m - £10m **No.of Employees:** 21 - 50
Product Groups: 37

Date of Accounts	Jul 11	Jul 10	Jul 09
Sales Turnover	8m	7m	N/A
Pre Tax Profit/Loss	207	138	N/A
Working Capital	562	170	-11
Fixed Assets	150	438	409
Current Assets	4m	3m	2m
Current Liabilities	431	318	N/A

Goodall Barnard Construction Ltd

Kestrel Court Vyne Road Sherborne St John, Basingstoke, RG24 9HJ
Tel: 01256-851155 **Fax:** 01256-851234
E-mail: davidwhitmarsh@goodall-barnard.co.uk
Website: http://www.goodall-barnard.co.uk
Directors: D. Whitmarsh (Dir)
Immediate Holding Company: GOODALL BARNARD HOLDINGS LIMITED
Registration no: 01860487 **VAT No.:** GB 641 8140 56
Date established: 1984 **Turnover:** £1m - £2m **No.of Employees:** 1 - 10
Product Groups: 52

Date of Accounts	Dec 11	Dec 10	Dec 09
Working Capital	805	1m	721
Fixed Assets	860	860	861
Current Assets	834	1m	773

GoodLifeGateway

30 Belle Vue Road Old Basing, Basingstoke, RG24 7JU
Tel: 07798-638892
E-mail: gwen@goodlifegateway.com
Website: http://www.goodlifegateway.com
No.of Employees: 1 - 10 **Product Groups:** 28, 32, 63, 81, 89

Gordian Strapping Ltd

Brunel Road, Basingstoke, RG21 6XX
Tel: 01256-394400 **Fax:** 01256-394429
E-mail: sales@gordianstrapping.com
Website: http://www.gordianstrapping.com
Bank(s): HSBC Bank plc, Basingstoke Branch, Hampshire
Directors: P. Marsh (Fin), A. Lea (MD), J. Phillips (Sales)
Ultimate Holding Company: STRAPACK CORPORATION (JAPAN)
Immediate Holding Company: GORDIAN STRAPPING LIMITED
Registration no: 00331258 **Date established:** 1937 **Turnover:** £5m - £10m
No.of Employees: 11 - 20 **Product Groups:** 29, 30, 34, 42

Date of Accounts	Dec 11	Dec 10	Dec 09
Sales Turnover	7m	6m	6m
Pre Tax Profit/Loss	215	134	42
Working Capital	3m	2m	2m
Fixed Assets	469	632	656
Current Assets	4m	3m	3m
Current Liabilities	614	561	632

Goyen Controls Co UK

Unit 3b Beechwood Lime Tree Way Chineham Business Park, Chineham, Basingstoke, RG24 8WA
Tel: 01256-817800 **Fax:** 01256-843164
E-mail: asimpson@tyco-environmental.co.uk
Website: http://www.cleanairsystems.com
Directors: C. Howes (Fin)
Managers: A. Simpson
Ultimate Holding Company: TYCO INTERNATIONAL LTD.
Immediate Holding Company: GOYEN CONTROLS CO UK LIMITED
Registration no: 04444736 **VAT No.:** GB 222 2632 08
Date established: 2002 **Turnover:** £2m - £5m **No.of Employees:** 1 - 10
Product Groups: 36, 39

G T X Europe Ltd

Unit 8 Cedarwood Crockford Lane Chineham, Chineham, Basingstoke, RG24 8WD
Tel: 01256-814444 **Fax:** 01256-324634
E-mail: info@gtx.co.uk
Website: http://www.gtx.com
Directors: B. Brown (MD)
Ultimate Holding Company: GTX CORP (USA)
Immediate Holding Company: GTX EUROPE LIMITED
Registration no: 02156326 **Date established:** 1987
Turnover: £250,000 - £500,000 **No.of Employees:** 1 - 10
Product Groups: 37, 44

Date of Accounts	Mar 11	Mar 10	Mar 09
Sales Turnover	382	362	342
Pre Tax Profit/Loss	84	77	-18
Working Capital	-56	-70	-56
Fixed Assets	1	2	2
Current Assets	161	93	124
Current Liabilities	169	154	163

H C R Ltd

Copenhagen Court 32 New Street, Basingstoke, RG21 7DT
Tel: 01256-812700 **Fax:** 01256-333420
E-mail: info@hcr.co.uk
Website: http://www.hcr.co.uk
Directors: A. Smith (Chief Op Offcr)
Ultimate Holding Company: HCR GROUP HOLDINGS LIMITED
Immediate Holding Company: HCR LIMITED
Registration no: 02046903 **Date established:** 1986 **Turnover:** £5m - £10m
No.of Employees: 101 - 250 **Product Groups:** 80

Date of Accounts	Sep 08	Sep 07	Sep 06
Pre Tax Profit/Loss	201	244	142
Working Capital	-586	-867	-1m
Fixed Assets	1m	2m	2m
Current Assets	4m	4m	7m
Current Liabilities	4m	4m	7m

Hire Intelligence

Unit 45 Basepoint Enterprise Centre Stroudly Road, Basingstoke, RG24 8UP
Tel: 0845-223 9215
E-mail: enquiries@hire-intelligence-basingstoke.co.uk
Website: http://www.hire-intelligence-basingstoke.co.uk
Product Groups: 67, 81, 83

Holloid Plastics

Stephenson Road, Basingstoke, RG21 6XR
Tel: 01256-334700 **Fax:** 01425-616374
E-mail: admin@holloid-plastics.co.uk
Website: http://www.a-tec.co.uk
Bank(s): Lloyds,TSB
Directors: H. Spreckelfen (Ch)
Immediate Holding Company: A-TEC PLASTICS LIMITED
Registration no: 03219477 **VAT No.:** GB 199 2305 37
Date established: 1996 **No.of Employees:** 21 - 50 **Product Groups:** 30, 66

Date of Accounts	Jul 11	Jul 10	Jul 09
Working Capital	2	157	92
Fixed Assets	3	35	39
Current Assets	246	350	185

Honeywell Aerospace Ltd Aerospace Electronic Systems UK Service Centre

Edison Road, Basingstoke, RG21 6QD
Tel: 01256-722200 **Fax:** 01256-722201
E-mail: adrian.paul@honeywell.com
Website: http://www.honeywelluk.com
Bank(s): Citibank International plc
Directors: A. Paul (Dir)
Managers: S. Beck (Personnel), S. Thornton (Fin Mgr)
Ultimate Holding Company: HONEYWELL INTERNATIONAL INC (USA)
Immediate Holding Company: HONEYWELL AVIONICS SYSTEMS LIMITED
Registration no: 02160822 **VAT No.:** GB 223 4728 76
Date established: 1987 **Turnover:** Up to £250,000
No.of Employees: 51 - 100 **Product Groups:** 37, 38, 39

Date of Accounts	Dec 11	Dec 10	Dec 09
Sales Turnover	124	113	114
Pre Tax Profit/Loss	7m	8m	7m
Working Capital	45m	38m	120m
Current Assets	136m	128m	124m

I T T Ltd

Viables Industrial Estate Jays Close, Basingstoke, RG22 4BA
Tel: 01256-311200 **Fax:** 01256-322356
E-mail: info@i-t-t.com
Website: http://www.ittind.com
Bank(s): National Westminster
Directors: D. Charnell (Fin)
Managers: R. Patel (Mgr)
Ultimate Holding Company: ITT CORPORATION (USA)
Immediate Holding Company: ITT LIMITED
Registration no: 00132076 **Date established:** 2013
Turnover: £20m - £50m **No.of Employees:** 101 - 250 **Product Groups:** 37

Date of Accounts	Dec 10	Dec 09	Dec 08
Working Capital	421	421	421
Current Assets	421	421	421

I T W Nexus Europe (Division of ITW)

Unit 12 Bilton Industrial Estate, Bilton Road, Basingstoke, RG24 8NJ
Tel: 01256-317663 **Fax:** 01256-317682
E-mail: mike@itwnexes.co.uk
Website: http://www.itwnexus.com
Managers: M. Ridler (Comm)
Ultimate Holding Company: ITW Corporate Chicago
Immediate Holding Company: ITW Espana
Registration no: 00559693 **VAT No.:** GB 533 3509 62
Turnover: £10m - £20m **No.of Employees:** 1 - 10 **Product Groups:** 30, 39, 40, 68

Icn Pharmaceuticals Ltd

Cedarwood Crockford Lane Chineham Business Park, Chineham, Basingstoke, RG24 8WD
Tel: 01256-707744 **Fax:** 01256-707334
E-mail: sales@valeant.com
Website: http://www.icnpharm.com
Directors: A. Gilroy (Dir), M. Solarz (Fin)
Managers: A. Gilroy (Mktg Serv Mgr), C. Terry (Chief Mgr), D. Cherroni (I.T. Exec), W. Pincombe (Personnel)
Ultimate Holding Company: ICN Pharmaceuticals Inc. (USA)
Immediate Holding Company: I C N Pharmaceuticals Ltd
Registration no: SC043236 **Turnover:** £5m - £10m
No.of Employees: 1 - 10 **Product Groups:** 31

Index

Unit D The Loddon Centre Wade Road, Basingstoke, RG24 8FL
Tel: 01256-843844 **Fax:** 01256-843367
E-mail: sales@indexplastics.co.uk
Website: http://www.indexplastics.co.uk
Directors: A. Cecil (Dir)
Ultimate Holding Company: Minigrip Belgium SA (Belgium)
Immediate Holding Company: INDEX PLASTICS LIMITED
Registration no: 02674498 **VAT No.:** GB 570 0747 51
Date established: 1991 **Turnover:** £1m - £2m **No.of Employees:** 1 - 10
Product Groups: 30, 35, 49, 66, 81

Date of Accounts	Dec 11	May 11	May 10
Working Capital	168	54	55
Fixed Assets	79	96	118
Current Assets	509	443	415

Inductotherm Heating & Welding Technologies Ltd

Thermatool House Crockford Lane, Chineham, Basingstoke, RG24 8NA
Tel: 01256-335533 **Fax:** 01256-467224
E-mail: info@inductothermhw.co.uk
Website: http://www.thermatool-europe.com
Bank(s): Lloyds TSB Bank plc
Directors: W. Albert (MD)
Managers: H. Willacy (Tech Serv Mgr), S. Margetts (Personnel), A. Malik (Fin Mgr), D. Gardiner (Sales & Mktg Mg)
Ultimate Holding Company: ROWAN TECHNOLOGIES INC (USA)
Immediate Holding Company: INDUCTOTHERM HEATING & WELDING LIMITED
Registration no: 01013852 **VAT No.:** GB 185 5197 30
Date established: 1971 **Turnover:** £20m - £50m
No.of Employees: 51 - 100 **Product Groups:** 37, 40, 42, 46, 47, 48

Date of Accounts	Dec 11	Dec 10	Dec 09
Sales Turnover	23m	14m	14m
Pre Tax Profit/Loss	2m	249	2m
Working Capital	6m	7m	7m
Fixed Assets	2m	2m	3m
Current Assets	13m	13m	10m
Current Liabilities	5m	5m	2m

Inspek Services

Unit 41 Basepoint Enterprise Centre Stroudley Road, Basingstoke, RG24 8UP
Tel: 01256-406644 **Fax:** 01256-406643
E-mail: paul@inspekservices.co.uk
Website: http://www.inspekservices.co.uk
Directors: P. Clowes (Prop)
Immediate Holding Company: CRSU LTD
Date established: 2010 **No.of Employees:** 1 - 10 **Product Groups:** 38, 51, 80, 84, 85

Date of Accounts	Dec 11	Dec 10	Dec 09
Working Capital	162	152	143
Fixed Assets	5	3	5
Current Assets	1m	726	1m

J D S U UK Ltd

Spinnaker House Lime Tree Way, Chineham, Basingstoke, RG24 8GG
Tel: 01256-891400 **Fax:** 01256-891439
E-mail: sales.uk@jdsu.com
Website: http://www.jdsu.com
Directors: A. Paulley (Dir)
Managers: P. Browne (Tech Serv Mgr), A. Palmer (Personnel)
Ultimate Holding Company: JDS UNIPHASE CORP (USA)
Immediate Holding Company: JDSU UK LIMITED
Registration no: 00887400 **Date established:** 1966
Turnover: £20m - £50m **No.of Employees:** 21 - 50 **Product Groups:** 38, 44

Date of Accounts	Jun 08	Jun 09	Jul 10
Sales Turnover	14m	17m	24m
Pre Tax Profit/Loss	365	52	1m
Working Capital	13m	14m	16m
Fixed Assets	2m	2m	2m
Current Assets	24m	16m	25m
Current Liabilities	5m	2m	5m

Jewson Ltd

Bell Road, Basingstoke, RG24 8PY
Tel: 01256-841464 **Fax:** 01256-842287
Website: http://www.jewson.co.uk
Directors: P. Hindle (MD)
Managers: A. Meharg (District Mgr)
Ultimate Holding Company: COMPAGNIE DE SAINT GOBAIN (FRANCE)
Immediate Holding Company: JEWSON LIMITED
Registration no: 00348407 **Date established:** 1939 **Turnover:** £2m - £5m
No.of Employees: 21 - 50 **Product Groups:** 66

Date of Accounts	Dec 11	Dec 10	Dec 09
Sales Turnover	1606m	1547m	1485m
Pre Tax Profit/Loss	18m	100m	45m
Working Capital	-345m	-250m	-349m
Fixed Assets	496m	387m	461m
Current Assets	657m	1005m	1320m
Current Liabilities	66m	120m	64m

Kew Technik Ltd

Rankine Road, Basingstoke, RG24 8PP
Tel: 01256-864100 **Fax:** 01256-864164
E-mail: richardp@kewt.co.uk
Website: http://www.kewt.co.uk
Bank(s): The Royal Bank of Scotland
Directors: D. Harris (Grp Chief Exec), M. Rooney (Fin), M. Rooney (Co Sec), L. Lawner (Dir), R. Penney (MD), D. Harris (Dir)
Managers: L. Lurner (Mktg Serv Mgr)
Immediate Holding Company: RIPLEY ENGINEERING LIMITED
Registration no: 02184550 **Date established:** 1962 **Turnover:** £2m - £5m
No.of Employees: 21 - 50 **Product Groups:** 22, 35, 36, 37, 44, 45

Date of Accounts	Mar 11	Mar 10	Mar 09
Sales Turnover	N/A	2m	N/A
Pre Tax Profit/Loss	N/A	-433	-289
Working Capital	586	794	2m
Fixed Assets	548	681	896
Current Assets	1m	1m	2m
Current Liabilities	N/A	194	145

Key Training Ltd

Network House Basing View, Basingstoke, RG21 4HG
Tel: 01256-841111 **Fax:** 01256-330015
E-mail: sales@keytraining.co.uk
Website: http://www.keytraining.co.uk
Bank(s): HSBC, Basingstoke
Directors: A. Kennealy (Co Sec), A. Dunsire (Fin)
Ultimate Holding Company: KEY TRAINING INVESTMENTS LIMITED
Immediate Holding Company: KEY TRAINING LIMITED
Registration no: 01325577 **VAT No.:** GB 641 8536 31
Date established: 1977 **Turnover:** £2m - £5m **No.of Employees:** 11 - 20
Product Groups: 86

Date of Accounts	Dec 11	Jul 10	Jul 09
Working Capital	677	561	451
Fixed Assets	147	103	90
Current Assets	2m	1m	1m
Current Liabilities	N/A	587	N/A

Kulite Sensors Ltd

Kulite House Stroudley Road, Basingstoke, RG24 8UG
Tel: 01256-461646 **Fax:** 01256-479510
E-mail: info@kulite.com
Website: http://www.kulite.com
Directors: M. Eckstein (Fin)
Managers: D. Copley (Sales Prom Mgr)
Ultimate Holding Company: KULITE SEMICONDUCTOR (INT) LTD (BRITISH VIRGIN ISLES)
Immediate Holding Company: KULITE SENSORS LIMITED
Registration no: 01158138 **VAT No.:** GB 200 3189 20
Date established: 1974 **Turnover:** £2m - £5m **No.of Employees:** 1 - 10
Product Groups: 37, 38

Date of Accounts	Dec 11	Dec 10	Dec 09
Working Capital	153	-22	-55
Fixed Assets	385	434	412
Current Assets	892	708	763

L G Motion Ltd

Unit 1 Telford Road Houndmills Estate, Basingstoke, RG21 6YU
Tel: 01256-365600 **Fax:** 01256-365645
E-mail: info@lg-motion.co.uk
Website: http://www.lg-motion.co.uk
Turnover: £500,000 - £1m **No.of Employees:** 1 - 10 **Product Groups:** 37, 38, 45

Date of Accounts	Mar 11	Mar 10	Mar 09
Working Capital	129	126	133
Fixed Assets	46	36	30
Current Assets	283	219	214

Lada Engineering Services Ltd

Unit 1 Vickers Business Centre, Basingstoke, RG24 9RA
Tel: 01256-460737 **Fax:** 01256-353130
E-mail: info@ladaengineering.co.uk
Website: http://www.ladaengineering.co.uk
Directors: A. Saitch (Dir)
Managers: M. Donald, T. Hatchett, A. Saitch (Fin Mgr), T. Fry (Tech Serv Mgr)

see next page

Lada Engineering Services Ltd - *Cont'd*

Immediate Holding Company: LADA ENGINEERING SERVICES LIMITED
Registration no: 03920816 **Date established:** 2000
Turnover: £500,000 - £1m **No.of Employees:** 51 - 100
Product Groups: 48

Date of Accounts	Dec 09	Mar 11	Jun 09
Working Capital	643	803	717
Fixed Assets	1m	1m	N/A
Current Assets	2m	2m	731

Lancer Labels Ltd

Unit 26a Basepoint Enterprise Centre Stroudley Road, Basingstoke, RG24 8UP
Tel: 08458-330854 **Fax:** 028-704586883
E-mail: info@lancerlabels.co.uk
Website: http://www.lancerlabels.co.uk
Directors: M. Roberts (Dir)
Immediate Holding Company: LANCER LABELS LIMITED
Registration no: 05692935 **Date established:** 2006
Turnover: Up to £250,000 **No.of Employees:** 1 - 10 **Product Groups:** 27, 30, 44

Date of Accounts	Mar 12	Mar 11	Mar 10
Working Capital	8	11	12
Fixed Assets	1	1	1
Current Assets	23	24	31

Lansing Linde Ltd

Kingsclere Road, Basingstoke, RG21 2XJ
Tel: 01256-342000 **Fax:** 01256-342921
E-mail: enquiries@linde-mh.co.uk
Website: http://www.linde-mh.co.uk
Bank(s): Barclays, 23 St. James's Street, London SW1
Directors: K. Mcdonagh (MD)
Ultimate Holding Company: SUPERLIFT HOLDINGS SARL (LUXEMBOURG)
Immediate Holding Company: LANSING LINDE SEVERNSIDE LIMITED
Registration no: 02951636 **Date established:** 1994
Turnover: £10m - £20m **No.of Employees:** 101 - 250
Product Groups: 39, 40, 45, 67, 71, 74, 83, 84

Luxonic Lighting plc

17 Priestley Road, Basingstoke, RG24 9JP
Tel: 01256-363090 **Fax:** 01256-842349
E-mail: info@luxonic.co.uk
Website: http://www.luxonic.co.uk
Directors: G. Goodman (Pers), J. Goodman (Fin), N. Shelton (Comm), N. Tavare (MD)
Managers: A. Shivers, P. Messer (Tech Serv Mgr)
Immediate Holding Company: LUXONIC LIGHTING PLC
Registration no: 02024289 **VAT No.:** GB 507 1266 62
Date established: 1986 **Turnover:** £10m - £20m
No.of Employees: 101 - 250 **Product Groups:** 37

Date of Accounts	Aug 11	Aug 10	Aug 09
Sales Turnover	10m	10m	8m
Pre Tax Profit/Loss	165	498	160
Working Capital	37	122	-9
Fixed Assets	3m	2m	2m
Current Assets	3m	3m	3m
Current Liabilities	2m	1m	1m

M V T S Technologies

Waterside Frog Lane, Mapledurwell, Basingstoke, RG25 2JR
Tel: 01256-638450
Directors: N. Donovon (MD)
Immediate Holding Company: MVTS TECHNOLOGIES (EUROPE) LTD.
Registration no: 05287198 **Date established:** 2004 **Turnover:** £2m - £5m
No.of Employees: 1 - 10 **Product Groups:** 37, 38, 47

Date of Accounts	Dec 11	Dec 10	Dec 09
Sales Turnover	N/A	N/A	3m
Pre Tax Profit/Loss	N/A	N/A	60
Working Capital	362	250	151
Fixed Assets	55	88	117
Current Assets	1m	1m	468
Current Liabilities	N/A	N/A	101

Markwins International Ltd

Unit 4 Elmwood Crockford Lane Chineham, Chineham, Basingstoke, RG24 8WG
Tel: 01256-374010 **Fax:** 01256-375469
E-mail: anew@markwins.uk.com
Website: http://www.markwins.com
Managers: A. New
Ultimate Holding Company: MARKWINS INTERNATIONAL CORPORATION (USA)
Immediate Holding Company: MARKWINS INTERNATIONAL CORPORATION LIMITED
Registration no: 03922404 **Date established:** 2000 **Turnover:** £5m - £10m
No.of Employees: 1 - 10 **Product Groups:** 32, 63

Date of Accounts	Dec 11	Dec 10	Dec 09
Sales Turnover	8m	8m	6m
Pre Tax Profit/Loss	578	32	-1m
Working Capital	-461	-1m	-1m
Fixed Assets	2	5	44
Current Assets	3m	5m	3m
Current Liabilities	272	733	723

Mars Drinks

Armstrong Road Daneshill Industrial Estate, Basingstoke, RG24 8NU
Tel: 01256-471500 **Fax:** 01256-487000
E-mail: marsdrinks.co.uk@euffem.com
Website: http://www.marsdrinks.co.uk
Bank(s): Lloyds TSB Bank plc
Managers: A. Mullins (Mktg Serv Mgr), K. Mroncz (Cust Serv Mgr)
Immediate Holding Company: TWO GUYS BATHROOMS LIMITED
Registration no: 06649987 **Date established:** 2008
No.of Employees: 251 - 500 **Product Groups:** 49

Date of Accounts	Jul 10	Jul 09	Jan 12
Working Capital	-58	-32	-38
Fixed Assets	65	51	49
Current Assets	77	69	43

Mass Systems UK Ltd

33 Primrose Gardens Hatch Warren, Basingstoke, RG22 4UZ
Tel: 01256-355517
E-mail: kevin.stacey@mass.demon.co.uk
Website: http://www.mass.demon.co.uk/
Directors: K. Stacey (Dir)
Immediate Holding Company: MASS SYSTEMS UK LIMITED
Registration no: 04682912 **Date established:** 2003
No.of Employees: 1 - 10 **Product Groups:** 35, 39, 45

Date of Accounts	Mar 12	Mar 11	Mar 10
Working Capital	31	30	17
Current Assets	39	45	37

Metrix Electronics

Precision Enterprise House Rankine Road Daneshill West, Basingstoke, RG24 8PP
Tel: 01256-864150 **Fax:** 01256-864154
E-mail: p.rummer@metrix-electronics.com
Website: http://www.metrix-electronics.com
Directors: M. Rummer (Fin), P. Rummer (Dir)
Immediate Holding Company: METRIX ELECTRONICS LIMITED
Registration no: 03846687 **VAT No.:** GB 668 0032 43
Date established: 1999 **No.of Employees:** 1 - 10 **Product Groups:** 28, 37, 38, 67

Date of Accounts	Mar 10	Mar 09	Mar 08
Working Capital	117	145	141
Fixed Assets	23	N/A	7
Current Assets	182	216	233

Micro Peripherals Ltd

Unit 1 Elmwood Crockford Lane Chineham, Chineham, Basingstoke, RG24 8WG
Tel: 01256-707070 **Fax:** 01256-707505
E-mail: sales@micro-p.com
Website: http://www.micro-p.com
Bank(s): National Westminster
Directors: J. Chibnall (Tech Serv), P. Bryan (Sales), S. Townsley (Fin), N. Foster (Pers), G. O'keeffe (Dir), M. Kahr (Dir)
Managers: J. Noakes (Mktg Serv Mgr)
Ultimate Holding Company: DCC PUBLIC LIMITED COMPANY
Immediate Holding Company: MICRO P LIMITED
Registration no: 01511931 **VAT No.:** GB 314 7105 90
Date established: 1980 **Turnover:** £500m - £1,000m
No.of Employees: 101 - 250 **Product Groups:** 44

Date of Accounts	Mar 11	Mar 10	Mar 09
Sales Turnover	548m	476m	383m
Pre Tax Profit/Loss	5m	7m	2m
Working Capital	19m	29m	26m
Fixed Assets	32m	11m	12m
Current Assets	196m	182m	129m
Current Liabilities	14m	18m	9m

Middlesex Group Ltd

Telford Road Houndmills Industrial Estate, Basingstoke, RG21 6YU
Tel: 01256-353711 **Fax:** 01256-842613
E-mail: sales@middlesex.co.uk
Website: http://www.middlesex.co.uk
Bank(s): HSBC
Directors: L. Foulds (MD), P. Foulds (Grp Chief Exec)
Managers: B. Kinge (I.T. Exec), S. Miller (Purch Mgr)
Registration no: 00723314 **VAT No.:** GB 212 6191 04
Date established: 1945 **Turnover:** £5m - £10m
No.of Employees: 101 - 250 **Product Groups:** 34, 35, 36, 38, 48, 61, 68, 80, 85

Date of Accounts	Mar 08	Mar 07	Mar 06
Sales Turnover	9546	8063	8675
Pre Tax Profit/Loss	424	115	29
Working Capital	532	236	253
Fixed Assets	4011	3802	3734
Current Assets	5015	4281	4131
Current Liabilities	4482	4045	3878
Total Share Capital	101	101	101
ROCE% (Return on Capital Employed)	9.3	2.8	0.7
ROT% (Return on Turnover)	4.4	1.4	0.3

Minitec UK Ltd

Unit 1 Telford Road, Basingstoke, RG21 6YU
Tel: 01256-365605 **Fax:** 01256-365606
E-mail: info@minitec.co.uk
Website: http://www.minitec.co.uk
Directors: G. Livingstone (MD)
Immediate Holding Company: MINITEC UK LIMITED
Registration no: 05366075 **Date established:** 2005
No.of Employees: 11 - 20 **Product Groups:** 35, 38, 40, 45, 47

Date of Accounts	Mar 12	Mar 11	Mar 10
Working Capital	-50	-192	-162
Fixed Assets	80	50	4
Current Assets	879	752	433

Motorola Ltd (Radio Network Solutions Group)

Viables Industrial Estate Jays Close, Basingstoke, RG22 4PD
Tel: 01256-358211 **Fax:** 01256-469838
E-mail: graeme.hobbs@mot.com
Website: http://www.motorola.com
Bank(s): First National City, Strand, London
Directors: T. Vasylevska (Fin), G. Hobbs (Dir), T. Wilson (Co Sec)
Ultimate Holding Company: MOTOROLA INC (USA)
Immediate Holding Company: MOTOROLA SOLUTIONS UK LIMITED
Registration no: 00912182 **VAT No.:** GB 260 3112 13
Date established: 1967 **Turnover:** £250m - £500m
No.of Employees: 1501 & over **Product Groups:** 37, 38

Date of Accounts	Dec 11	Dec 10	Dec 09
Sales Turnover	311m	562m	613m
Pre Tax Profit/Loss	15m	111m	-3m
Working Capital	148m	295m	264m
Fixed Assets	18m	27m	32m
Current Assets	253m	437m	531m
Current Liabilities	65m	90m	137m

Oxoid Holdings Ltd

Wade Road Kingsland Industrial Park, Basingstoke, RG24 8PW
Tel: 01256-841144 **Fax:** 01256-463388
E-mail: oxoid@oxoid.com
Website: http://www.oxoid.com
Directors: R. Best (Gen Sec), P. Roberts (Dep Pres), N. Ward (Co Sec), T. Floyd (Grp Chief Exec), A. Ball (Dep Pres), M. Hosgson (Dep Pres), J. Coley (Dir)
Managers: R. Marsh (Sales Prom Mgr), M. Gilly (Sales Prom Mgr), M. Cunningham (Mktg Serv Mgr), K. Stamp (Buyer), A. Clark (I.T. Exec), J. Broughall
Immediate Holding Company: OXOID HOLDINGS LIMITED
Registration no: 03291574 **VAT No.:** GB 567 7750 77
Date established: 1996 **Turnover:** £75m - £125m
No.of Employees: 1 - 10 **Product Groups:** 31, 42

Pandatel Ag

Lutyens Close Grove House, Lychpit, Basingstoke, RG24 8AG
Tel: 01256-316571 **Fax:** 01252-693093
E-mail: sales@pandatel.com
Website: http://www.pandatel.com
Managers: G. Windsor (Nat Sales Mgr)
Immediate Holding Company: MARK TWO LIMITED
Registration no: 04306582 **Date established:** 2000
Turnover: Up to £250,000 **No.of Employees:** 1 - 10 **Product Groups:** 37, 38, 44, 67

Peek Traffic Ltd

Hazelwood House Lime Tree Way, Chineham, Basingstoke, RG24 8WZ
Tel: 01256-891800 **Fax:** 01256-891871
E-mail: bryan.east@peek-traffic.co.uk
Website: http://www.peek.co.uk
Bank(s): Barclays
Directors: B. East (Fin)
Ultimate Holding Company: IMTECH NV (NETHERLANDS)
Immediate Holding Company: PEEK TRAFFIC LIMITED
Registration no: 01490333 **VAT No.:** GB 568 3350 22
Date established: 1980 **Turnover:** £50m - £75m
No.of Employees: 251 - 500 **Product Groups:** 37, 38, 39, 44, 51

Date of Accounts	Dec 11	Dec 10	Dec 09
Sales Turnover	63m	63m	58m
Pre Tax Profit/Loss	6m	6m	2m
Working Capital	17m	14m	7m
Fixed Assets	2m	2m	6m
Current Assets	29m	27m	16m
Current Liabilities	9m	9m	4m

Planet Leisure UK

The LNS Building Unit 4 Crockford Lane, Chineham, Basingstoke, RG24 8NA
Tel: 01256-841950 **Fax:** 01256-818255
E-mail: adam@planetleisureuk.co.uk
Website: http://www.planetleisureuk.co.uk
Managers: A. Littleford (Sales Prom Mgr)
Immediate Holding Company: PLANET LEISURE UK LTD
Registration no: 05056908 **Date established:** 2004
No.of Employees: 1 - 10 **Product Groups:** 24, 35

Date of Accounts	Jun 08	Jun 07	Jun 06
Working Capital	1	9	8
Current Assets	106	250	62
Current Liabilities	15	N/A	N/A

Portals

Overton Mill Overton, Basingstoke, RG25 3JG
Tel: 01256-770770 **Fax:** 01256-770937
E-mail: sales.portals@delarue.co.uk
Website: http://www.delarue.com
Bank(s): The Royal Bank of Scotland
Directors: M. Wilkinson (Comm), J. Hussey (MD)
Managers: A. Day (Personnel), G. Chambers (Purch Mgr), J. Winchcombe (Sales & Mktg Mg)
Ultimate Holding Company: De La Rue plc
Immediate Holding Company: Portals Group Ltd
Registration no: 00813378 **VAT No.:** GB 238 9404 40
Turnover: £50m - £75m **No.of Employees:** 501 - 1000
Product Groups: 27

Pritchard Tyrite

Crockford Lane Chineham, Basingstoke, RG24 8NA
Tel: 01256-400600 **Fax:** 01256-400622
E-mail: sales@pritchard-tyrite.co.uk
Website: http://www.pritchard-tyrite.co.uk
Directors: M. Calhoun (MD), R. Cakaett (Sales)
Managers: L. Saunders (I.T. Exec)
Immediate Holding Company: Pritchard Tyrite Ltd
Registration no: 06521940 **Date established:** 2008 **Turnover:** £5m - £10m
No.of Employees: 1 - 10 **Product Groups:** 24, 35

Date of Accounts	Dec 09	Dec 08
Working Capital	449	404
Fixed Assets	23	34
Current Assets	650	1m

Protect Doors Ltd

Vickers House Vickers Business Centre Priestley Road, Basingstoke, RG24 9NP
Tel: 01256-814000 **Fax:** 01256-814443
E-mail: sales@protectdoors.co.uk
Website: http://www.protectdoors.co.uk
Directors: M. Annetts (MD)
Immediate Holding Company: PROTECT DOORS LIMITED
Registration no: 02957268 **Date established:** 1994
No.of Employees: 1 - 10 **Product Groups:** 26, 35

Date of Accounts	Oct 11	Oct 10	Oct 09
Working Capital	-13	-37	-7
Fixed Assets	5	8	5
Current Assets	96	73	110
Current Liabilities	N/A	3	N/A

Qualitasse Ltd

Unit 4 Kempshott Park Industrial Estate Longwood Copse Lane, Beggarwood, Basingstoke, RG23 7LP
Tel: 01256-396300 **Fax:** 01256-396301
Website: http://www.qualitasse.co.uk
Directors: C. Layton (Co Sec)
Immediate Holding Company: QUALITASSE LIMITED
Registration no: 02166525 **Date established:** 1987
No.of Employees: 21 - 50 **Product Groups:** 38, 42

Date of Accounts	Dec 07	Dec 06	Dec 05
Working Capital	300	412	379
Fixed Assets	42	83	186
Current Assets	644	915	974
Current Liabilities	344	503	595

R F I Global Services

Pavilion 1 Ashwood Park Ashwood Way, Basingstoke, RG23 8BG
Tel: 01256-312000 **Fax:** 01256-851192
E-mail: sales@rfi-global.com
Website: http://www.rfi-global.com
Managers: J. Rose, P. Williamson (Tech Serv Mgr), H. Webber (Personnel)
Ultimate Holding Company: UL INTERNATIONAL (UK) LIMITED
Immediate Holding Company: RFI GLOBAL SERVICES LTD
Registration no: 02117901 **Date established:** 1987 **Turnover:** £2m - £5m
No.of Employees: 51 - 100 **Product Groups:** 37, 38

Date of Accounts	Dec 11	Dec 10	Mar 10
Sales Turnover	8m	5m	7m
Pre Tax Profit/Loss	-254	-1m	-769

Working Capital	475	265	-2m
Fixed Assets	4m	2m	2m
Current Assets	4m	2m	2m
Current Liabilities	3m	1m	1m

Reed Accountancy Personnel Ltd

27 Wote Street, Basingstoke, RG21 7NE
Tel: 01256-460399 **Fax:** 01256-842189
E-mail: rapbasingstoke@reed.co.uk
Website: http://www.reed.co.uk
Managers: R. Bass (District Mgr)
Immediate Holding Company: WOTE ST EMPLOYMENT BUREAU LIMITED
Registration no: 00973629 **Date established:** 2003
Turnover: £75m - £125m **No.of Employees:** 1 - 10 **Product Groups:** 80

Date of Accounts	Jul 11	Jul 10	Jul 09
Working Capital	76	96	91
Fixed Assets	37	40	44
Current Assets	116	143	131

Reed Employment Ltd

27-29 Wote Street, Basingstoke, RG21 7NE
Tel: 01256-463385 **Fax:** 01256-842386
E-mail: neil.hardy@reed.co.uk
Website: http://www.reed.co.uk
Managers: N. Hardy (Mgr)
Ultimate Holding Company: REED GLOBAL LTD (MALTA)
Immediate Holding Company: REED EMPLOYMENT LIMITED
Registration no: 00669854 **Date established:** 1960
Turnover: £75m - £125m **No.of Employees:** 1 - 10 **Product Groups:** 80

Date of Accounts	Jun 11	Jun 10	Dec 07
Sales Turnover	618	450	287m
Pre Tax Profit/Loss	-2m	310	8m
Working Capital	23m	28m	28m
Fixed Assets	31	36	5m
Current Assets	28m	30m	74m
Current Liabilities	37	29	21m

Rotair Systems Ltd

23 Whitestones Hatch Warren, Basingstoke, RG22 4QX
Tel: 01256-326377 **Fax:** 01256-321519
E-mail: info@rotairsystems.co.uk
Website: http://www.rotairsystems.com
Directors: M. Ward (MD)
Registration no: 05100315 **Date established:** 2004
Turnover: Up to £250,000 **No.of Employees:** 1 - 10 **Product Groups:** 35, 39, 45

Date of Accounts	Mar 08	Mar 07	Mar 06
Sales Turnover	127	73	141
Pre Tax Profit/Loss	N/A	-2	10
Working Capital	31	32	36
Fixed Assets	9	2	1
Current Assets	45	41	44
Current Liabilities	14	9	8
ROCE% (Return on Capital Employed)		-5.1	26.8
ROT% (Return on Turnover)		-2.5	7.0

Royce Communications Ltd

1 Joule Road, Basingstoke, RG21 6XH
Tel: 01256-814814 **Fax:** 01256-810940
E-mail: info@roycecomms.com
Website: http://www.roycecomms.com
Bank(s): Lloyds TSB Bracknell
Directors: B. Mitchell (MD)
Immediate Holding Company: ROYCE COMMUNICATIONS LIMITED
Registration no: 02236752 **VAT No.:** GB 529 0159 49
Date established: 1988 **Turnover:** £2m - £5m **No.of Employees:** 11 - 20
Product Groups: 44

Date of Accounts	Mar 12	Mar 11	Mar 10
Working Capital	620	497	358
Fixed Assets	78	86	101
Current Assets	1m	1m	921

Sarena

15 Century House Vickers Business Centre, Basingstoke, RG24 9NP
Tel: 01634-370887 **Fax:** 01634-370915
E-mail: info@sarena.co.uk
Website: http://www.sarena.co.uk
Directors: E. Parkinson (MD)
Immediate Holding Company: SARENA PROPERTIES LIMITED
Registration no: 00598713 **Date established:** 1958
No.of Employees: 1 - 10 **Product Groups:** 30

Date of Accounts	Oct 10	Oct 09	Apr 08
Working Capital	2m	2m	2m
Fixed Assets	695	866	929
Current Assets	2m	2m	2m

Sauter Automations

Inova House Crockford Lane Hampshire Int Business Park, Chineham, Basingstoke, RG24 8WH
Tel: 01256-374400 **Fax:** 01256-374455
E-mail: info@uk.sauter-bc.com
Website: http://www.sauterautomation.co.uk
Bank(s): Barclays
Directors: J. Buckley (Fin)
Managers: A. Costello (Purch Mgr)
Ultimate Holding Company: FR SAUTER AG BASLE (SWITZERLAND)
Immediate Holding Company: SAUTER AUTOMATION LIMITED
Registration no: 01292827 **Date established:** 1976 **Turnover:** £5m - £10m
No.of Employees: 51 - 100 **Product Groups:** 36, 38, 39, 48, 49

Date of Accounts	Dec 11	Dec 10	Dec 09
Sales Turnover	9m	10m	10m
Pre Tax Profit/Loss	629	1m	695
Working Capital	3m	3m	2m
Fixed Assets	925	969	1m
Current Assets	5m	5m	5m
Current Liabilities	943	2m	2m

Sematron UK Ltd

Sandpiper House Aviary Court Wade Road, Basingstoke, RG24 8GX
Tel: 01256-812222 **Fax:** 01256-812666
E-mail: sales@sematron.com
Website: http://www.sematron.com
Bank(s): Lloyds TSB
Directors: J. Obrien (MD), K. Hall (Mkt Research)
Managers: H. Wakelen
Immediate Holding Company: EUSYS LTD.
Registration no: 03000026 **VAT No.:** GB 537 4464 13
Date established: 1994 **Turnover:** £10m - £20m
No.of Employees: 21 - 50 **Product Groups:** 39

Date of Accounts	Dec 10	Dec 09	Dec 08
Working Capital	1	1	1
Current Assets	1	1	1

Sherwood Interim Management Ltd

5 Bayley House Sherborne Road, Basingstoke, RG21 5AB
Tel: 01256-812472
E-mail: steve@sherwoodinterim.co.uk
Website: http://www.sherwoodinterim.co.uk
Directors: S. Sherwood (Dir)
Immediate Holding Company: SHERWOOD INTERIM MANAGEMENT LTD
Registration no: 06609116 **Date established:** 2008
Turnover: Up to £250,000 **No.of Employees:** 1 - 10 **Product Groups:** 80, 82, 88

Snamprogetti Ltd

Snamprogetti House Basingview, Basingstoke, RG21 4YY
Tel: 01256-461211 **Fax:** 01256-482211
E-mail: alake@snampro.co.uk
Website: http://www.snampro.co.uk
Bank(s): Banca Commerciale Italiana, London
Directors: A. Lake (Co Sec), F. Guarrvella (MD)
Managers: A. Evans (Develop Mgr), P. Bealing (I.T. Exec)
Ultimate Holding Company: ENI SPA (ITALY)
Immediate Holding Company: SNAMPROGETTI LIMITED
Registration no: 01154614 **VAT No.:** GB 244 5811 64
Date established: 1974 **Turnover:** £20m - £50m
No.of Employees: 101 - 250 **Product Groups:** 52, 84

Date of Accounts	Dec 11	Dec 10	Dec 09
Sales Turnover	21m	25m	30m
Pre Tax Profit/Loss	6m	5m	4m
Working Capital	6m	22m	23m
Fixed Assets	N/A	5m	5m
Current Assets	11m	34m	35m
Current Liabilities	4m	9m	9m

Sony Professional Services

Viables Industrial Estate Jays Close, Basingstoke, RG22 4SB
Tel: 01256-355011 **Fax:** 01256-474585
E-mail: naomi.climber@sonycom.com
Website: http://www.sonybiz.net
Bank(s): National Westminster
Managers: N. Climer
Ultimate Holding Company: SONY CORPORATION OF JAPAN
Immediate Holding Company: SONY UNITED KINGDOM LTD
Registration no: 02422874 **VAT No.:** GB 636 1100 80
Turnover: £250m - £500m **No.of Employees:** 251 - 500
Product Groups: 37

Spafax International Ltd (Head Office)

Kingsland Industrial Park Stroudley Road, Basingstoke, RG24 8UG
Tel: 01256-814400 **Fax:** 01256-814141
E-mail: sales@spafaxmirrors.com
Website: http://www.spafaxmirrors.com
Directors: F. Norman (Fin), T. Norman (Prop)
Immediate Holding Company: SPAFAX INTERNATIONAL LIMITED
Registration no: 01419291 **VAT No.:** GB 543 4811 51
Date established: 1979 **Turnover:** £500,000 - £1m
No.of Employees: 1 - 10 **Product Groups:** 39

Date of Accounts	Mar 11	Mar 10	Mar 09
Working Capital	169	155	139
Fixed Assets	390	382	366
Current Assets	730	427	425

Spectracom Ltd

Unit 6a Beechwood Lime Tree Way Chineham Business Park, Chineham, Basingstoke, RG24 8WA
Tel: 01256-303630 **Fax:** 01256-322695
E-mail: sales@spectracom.co.uk
Website: http://www.spectracomcoldcorp.com
Managers: J. Westwood (Chief Eng)
Immediate Holding Company: ALTARIA SOLUTIONS LTD
Registration no: 00985985 **VAT No.:** GB 199 4633 10
Date established: 1970 **Turnover:** £1m - £2m **No.of Employees:** 1 - 10
Product Groups: 38, 49

Date of Accounts	Dec 08	Dec 07	Dec 06
Working Capital	323	389	434
Fixed Assets	2	45	48
Current Assets	592	454	610
Current Liabilities	268	65	176
Total Share Capital	2	2	2

Sterling Lift Products

23 The Beresford Centre Wade Road, Basingstoke, RG24 8FA
Tel: 01256-869773 **Fax:** 01256-869774
E-mail: info@sterlinglifts.co.uk
Website: http://www.sterlinglift.co.uk
Directors: G. Taylor (Dir)
Immediate Holding Company: STERLING LIFT PRODUCTS LIMITED
Registration no: 04980917 **Date established:** 2003
No.of Employees: 1 - 10 **Product Groups:** 35, 39, 45

Tallygenicom

Rutherford Road, Basingstoke, RG24 8PD
Tel: 0870-8722888
E-mail: sales@tallygenicom.co.uk
Website: http://www.tally.co.uk
Bank(s): Barclays, 32 Bridge Street, Banbury, Oxon
Directors: R. Edwards (MD), R. Gardiner (Fin), R. Edwardes (MD)
Managers: G. Hunter (Sales Prom Mgr), J. Spreadborough (Sales Prom Mgr), S. Lakhani (Comptroller)
Immediate Holding Company: TALLYGENICOM LIMITED
Registration no: 00820842 **VAT No.:** GB 199 6679 73
Date established: 1964 **Turnover:** £20m - £50m
No.of Employees: 51 - 100 **Product Groups:** 44

Testbourne

Unit 2 The Hatch Industrial Park Greywell Road, Mapledurwell, Basingstoke, RG24 7NG
Tel: 01256-467055 **Fax:** 01256-842929
E-mail: info@testbourne.co.uk
Website: http://www.testbourne.com
Directors: G. Mihill (Ch)
Registration no: 01413864 **Turnover:** £1m - £2m
No.of Employees: 11 - 20 **Product Groups:** 40, 42

Date of Accounts	Mar 08
Working Capital	305
Fixed Assets	29

Current Assets	522
Current Liabilities	218
Total Share Capital	1

Thales Missile Electronics

Basing View Mountbatten House, Basingstoke, RG21 4HJ
Tel: 01256-387200 **Fax:** 01256-387650
Website: http://www.thales-group.co.uk
Directors: M. Greenwood (Mkt Research), J. Pernotte (Dir), P. Shore (Fin), M. Seabrook (Co Sec), G. McDonald (Comm), D. Barnes (Dir)
Ultimate Holding Company: Thales Holdings UK plc
Immediate Holding Company: Thales UK Ltd
Registration no: 03004769 **Date established:** 1994
Turnover: £20m - £50m **No.of Employees:** 501 - 1000
Product Groups: 32, 39

Date of Accounts	Dec 07	Dec 06	Dec 05
Sales Turnover	29196	43328	41407
Pre Tax Profit/Loss	1755	3721	4590
Working Capital	11802	14813	13895
Fixed Assets	4587	2369	3005
Current Assets	28893	28622	31065
Current Liabilities	17091	13809	17170
ROCE% (Return on Capital Employed)	10.7	21.7	27.2
ROT% (Return on Turnover)	6.0	8.6	11.1

Thin Metal Films Ltd

Stroudley Road, Basingstoke, RG24 8UG
Tel: 01256-840830 **Fax:** 01256-840443
E-mail: sales@tmf.uk.com
Website: http://www.tmf.uk.com
Directors: T. Walker (MD)
Immediate Holding Company: THIN METAL FILMS LIMITED
Registration no: 05783983 **Date established:** 2006
No.of Employees: 1 - 10 **Product Groups:** 33, 48

Date of Accounts	Sep 11	Jun 10	Jun 09
Working Capital	16	14	-7
Fixed Assets	23	20	25
Current Assets	103	70	72

Tiltmans

43a Reading Road Chineham, Basingstoke, RG24 8LT
Tel: 01256-321059 **Fax:** 01256-818768
Directors: F. Tiltman (Prop)
Date established: 1964 **No.of Employees:** 1 - 10 **Product Groups:** 37

Travis Perkins plc

Roentgen Road Daneshill East Industrial Estate, Basingstoke, RG24 8NT
Tel: 01256-841551 **Fax:** 01256-842214
E-mail: andrewwoods@travisperkins.co.uk
Website: http://www.travisperkins.co.uk
Managers: A. Woods (Mgr)
Immediate Holding Company: TRAVIS PERKINS PLC
Registration no: 00824821 **Date established:** 1964 **Turnover:** £1m - £2m
No.of Employees: 1 - 10 **Product Groups:** 66

Date of Accounts	Dec 11	Dec 10	Dec 09
Sales Turnover	4779m	3153m	2931m
Pre Tax Profit/Loss	270m	197m	213m
Working Capital	133m	159m	248m
Fixed Assets	2771m	2749m	2108m
Current Assets	1421m	1329m	1035m
Current Liabilities	473m	412m	109m

Tritec Systems Ltd

Riverview House London Road, Old Basing, Basingstoke, RG24 7JL
Tel: 01256-477778 **Fax:** 01256-477776
E-mail: sales@tritec.co.uk
Website: http://www.tritec.co.uk
Bank(s): Barclays, Basingstoke
Directors: G. Haines (MD)
Immediate Holding Company: TRITEC SYSTEMS LIMITED
Registration no: 02636961 **VAT No.:** GB 641 9976 95
Date established: 1991 **Turnover:** £2m - £5m **No.of Employees:** 11 - 20
Product Groups: 38, 39, 44

Date of Accounts	Sep 11	Sep 10	Sep 09
Working Capital	249	232	227
Fixed Assets	570	582	596
Current Assets	610	548	677
Current Liabilities	223	N/A	N/A

Urbis Lighting Ltd

Unit 1-5 Telford Road, Basingstoke, RG21 6YW
Tel: 01256-354446 **Fax:** 01256-841314
E-mail: sales@urbislighting.com
Website: http://www.urbislighting.com
Bank(s): National Westminster
Directors: I. Pratt (MD)
Ultimate Holding Company: SCHREDER SA (BELGIUM)
Immediate Holding Company: URBIS LIGHTING LIMITED
Registration no: 01095726 **Date established:** 1973
Turnover: £20m - £50m **No.of Employees:** 101 - 250
Product Groups: 26, 37

Date of Accounts	Dec 11	Dec 10	Dec 09
Sales Turnover	32m	33m	29m
Pre Tax Profit/Loss	443	2m	539
Working Capital	5m	5m	5m
Fixed Assets	2m	2m	2m
Current Assets	11m	13m	10m
Current Liabilities	2m	3m	2m

Vectair Systems Ltd

Unit 3 Trident Centre Armstrong Road, Basingstoke, RG24 8NU
Tel: 01256-319500 **Fax:** 01256-319510
E-mail: info@vectair.co.uk
Website: http://www.vectair.co.uk
Bank(s): Lloyds TSB Bank plc
Directors: J. Ovenden (Sales), C. Davies (Fin)
Managers: C. Defrancisci, D. Thompson (Buyer), L. Goldsmith (Mktg Serv Mgr)
Ultimate Holding Company: VECTAIR HOLDINGS LIMITED
Immediate Holding Company: VECTAIR SYSTEMS LIMITED
Registration no: 02245377 **VAT No.:** GB 510 5027 05
Date established: 1988 **Turnover:** £5m - £10m **No.of Employees:** 21 - 50
Product Groups: 66

Date of Accounts	Oct 11	Oct 10	Oct 09
Sales Turnover	8m	8m	8m
Pre Tax Profit/Loss	661	621	601
Working Capital	3m	2m	1m
Fixed Assets	432	409	464
Current Assets	5m	4m	4m
Current Liabilities	1m	2m	1m

Vickers Metal Finishers
Unit 9 Vickers Business Centre, Basingstoke, RG24 9NP
Tel: 07999-279262 **Fax:** 01256-353130
E-mail: vickers@technicalwebservices.com
Website: http://www.vickersmetalfinishers.co.uk
Directors: T. Hitchings (Prop)
Date established: 2007 **No.of Employees:** 1 - 10 **Product Groups:** 48, 52

Virtual Techie
20 Marshcourt Lychpit, Basingstoke, RG24 8UY
Tel: 08454-639304
E-mail: ian@virtualtechie.co.uk
Website: http://www.virtualtechie.co.uk
Directors: I. Elvar (Prop)
Date established: 2007 **No.of Employees:** 1 - 10 **Product Groups:** 44, 67

Vishay Measurements Group UK Ltd
1 Cartel Units Stroudley Road, Basingstoke, RG24 8FW
Tel: 01256-462131 **Fax:** 01256-471441
E-mail: info@measurementsgroup.co.uk
Website: http://www.vishaypg.co.uk
Bank(s): Bank of Wales PLC
Directors: J. Goodson (Dir), L. Bell (Co Sec)
Managers: B. Becker (Personnel), G. Redshaw (Comptroller), S. Hollocks (Tech Serv Mgr)
Ultimate Holding Company: VISHAY INTERTECHNOLOGY INC (USA)
Immediate Holding Company: VISHAY MEASUREMENTS GROUP UK LIMITED
Registration no: 02593388 **VAT No.:** GB 615 6429 39
Date established: 1991 **Turnover:** £10m - £20m
No.of Employees: 51 - 100 **Product Groups:** 38

Date of Accounts	Dec 11	Dec 10	Dec 09
Sales Turnover	16m	15m	13m
Pre Tax Profit/Loss	399	652	12
Working Capital	6m	6m	6m
Fixed Assets	1m	2m	1m
Current Assets	8m	8m	8m
Current Liabilities	326	446	88

W S P Group
Mountbatten House Basing View, Basingstoke, RG21 4HJ
Tel: 01256-318800 **Fax:** 01256-318700
E-mail: peter.day@wspgroup.com
Website: http://www.wspgroup.com
Bank(s): Barclays, 8-9 Hanover Sq, London, W1A 4ZW
Directors: P. Day (Dir), S. Jordan (Fin)
Managers: B. Albats, P. Pawson, S. Hunt (Mktg Serv Mgr)
Ultimate Holding Company: MONDRAGON COOPERATIVE CORP(SPAIN)
Immediate Holding Company: WSP CIVILS LIMITED
Registration no: 02430067 **Date established:** 1989
Turnover: £20m - £50m **No.of Employees:** 101 - 250 **Product Groups:** 84

Date of Accounts	Dec 07	Dec 06	Dec 05
Sales Turnover	42252	38042	38052
Pre Tax Profit/Loss	3454	1762	797
Working Capital	4809	2876	2031
Fixed Assets	243	338	849
Current Assets	14944	13619	12319
Current Liabilities	10135	10743	10288
Total Share Capital	550	550	550
ROCE% (Return on Capital Employed)	68.4	54.8	27.7
ROT% (Return on Turnover)	8.2	4.6	2.1

Wella UK
Wella Road, Basingstoke, RG22 4AF
Tel: 01256-490500 **Fax:** 01256-329384
E-mail: info@wella.co.uk
Website: http://www.wella.co.uk
Bank(s): HSBC Bank plc
Directors: A. Kirkby (MD), E. Parkinson (Dir), P. Batten (Non Exec), R. Bartlett (Sales), R. Sykes (Fin)
Managers: C. Weller (Purch Mgr), S. Lowe (Sales Prom Mgr), C. Martin (Chief Mgr)
Ultimate Holding Company: PROCTER & GAMBLE COMPANY (USA)
Immediate Holding Company: WELLA (UK) HOLDINGS LIMITED
Registration no: 02906614 **Date established:** 1994 **Turnover:** £2m - £5m
No.of Employees: 21 - 50 **Product Groups:** 32, 40

Date of Accounts	Jun 11	Jun 10	Jun 09
Sales Turnover	3m	3m	4m
Pre Tax Profit/Loss	162	-4m	184
Working Capital	-406	-598	-1m
Fixed Assets	230m	31m	35m
Current Assets	3m	2m	2m
Current Liabilities	381	195	289

Western House
Armstrong Road, Basingstoke, RG24 8QE
Tel: 01256-462341 **Fax:** 01256-840585
E-mail: sales@western-house.com
Website: http://www.western-house.com
Directors: G. South (Ch), J. Edmunds (Dir), K. Johnson (Fin)
Ultimate Holding Company: WESTERN GROUP (HOLDINGS) LIMITED
Immediate Holding Company: WESTERN HOUSE LIMITED
Registration no: 00474735 **VAT No.:** GB 235 5005 92
Date established: 1949 **Turnover:** £5m - £10m **No.of Employees:** 1 - 10
Product Groups: 33, 49, 65

Date of Accounts	Mar 12	Mar 11	Mar 10
Working Capital	852	781	847
Fixed Assets	37	52	66
Current Assets	1m	2m	2m

Wicks & Wilson Ltd
Morse Road, Basingstoke, RG22 6PQ
Tel: 01256-842211 **Fax:** 01256-840997
E-mail: sales@wwl.co.uk
Website: http://www.wwl.co.uk
Bank(s): HSBC
Directors: I. McMinn (Sales & Mktg), R. Randall (Fin)
Immediate Holding Company: WICKS AND WILSON LIMITED
Registration no: 01148362 **VAT No.:** GB 240 8839 51
Date established: 1973 **No.of Employees:** 21 - 50 **Product Groups:** 38, 44, 65

Date of Accounts	Dec 11	Dec 10	Dec 09
Working Capital	726	775	833
Fixed Assets	11	18	27
Current Assets	874	965	1m

Yamaichi Electronics
4 Woodlands Business Village Coronation Road, Basingstoke, RG21 4JX
Tel: 01256-463131 **Fax:** 01256-463132
E-mail: sales.uk@yamaichi.de
Website: http://www.yamaichi.de
Managers: S. Denny (Reg Mgr)
Immediate Holding Company: YAMAICHI ELECTRONICS GREAT BRITAIN LTD
Registration no: 03764371 **Date established:** 1999
Turnover: £250,000 - £500,000 **No.of Employees:** 1 - 10
Product Groups: 37, 67

Date of Accounts	Mar 08	Mar 07	Mar 06
Sales Turnover	471	487	574
Pre Tax Profit/Loss	43	44	52
Working Capital	160	128	102
Fixed Assets	10	15	12
Current Assets	192	182	154
Current Liabilities	32	54	52
Total Share Capital	1	1	1
ROCE% (Return on Capital Employed)	25.2	31.0	45.8
ROT% (Return on Turnover)	9.1	9.1	9.1

Bordon

Adelco Screen Process Ltd
Unit 18 Highview Business Centre High Street, Bordon, GU35 0AX
Tel: 01420-488388 **Fax:** 01420-476445
E-mail: sales@adelco.co.uk
Website: http://www.adelco.co.uk
Directors: M. Smith (Sales)
Immediate Holding Company: ADELCO SCREEN PROCESS LIMITED
Registration no: 01069153 **VAT No.:** GB 189 0868 10
Date established: 1972 **Turnover:** £1m - £2m **No.of Employees:** 1 - 10
Product Groups: 32, 44

Date of Accounts	Aug 11	Aug 10	Aug 09
Working Capital	246	152	202
Fixed Assets	15	17	11
Current Assets	540	355	374

Anopol South Ltd
Old Station Way Bordon Trading Estate, Bordon, GU35 9HH
Tel: 01420-488753 **Fax:** 01420-488239
E-mail: stevejarvis@anopol.co.uk
Website: http://www.anopol.co.uk
Directors: T. Mustill (MD)
Ultimate Holding Company: ANOPOL LIMITED
Immediate Holding Company: ANOPOL (SOUTH) LIMITED
Registration no: 02325889 **Date established:** 1988 **Turnover:** £1m - £2m
No.of Employees: 11 - 20 **Product Groups:** 34, 48

Date of Accounts	Dec 11	Dec 10	Dec 09
Working Capital	-216	-295	-370
Fixed Assets	75	95	119
Current Assets	167	167	113

Auto Leads Ltd
25 Woolmer Way, Bordon, GU35 9QE
Tel: 01420-476767 **Fax:** 01420-477137
E-mail: info@armourauto.com
Website: http://www.autoleads.co.uk
Directors: R. Tirelli (Sales), D. Tolson (Dir)
Managers: S. Jones (District Mgr)
Ultimate Holding Company: ARMOUR GROUP PLC
Immediate Holding Company: AUTOLEADS LIMITED
Registration no: 00769094 **Date established:** 1963
No.of Employees: 101 - 250 **Product Groups:** 35, 37, 67

Blackburne & Haynes
Meadow Cottage Churt Road, Headley, Bordon, GU35 8SS
Tel: 01428-712155 **Fax:** 01428-714001
Directors: P. Haynes (Ptnr)
Turnover: £250,000 - £500,000 **No.of Employees:** 1 - 10
Product Groups: 61, 62

Capso Ltd
Unit 1 Highland Farm Lindford, Bordon, GU35 0JX
Tel: 01420-476677 **Fax:** 01420-476677
E-mail: kalbabur@aol.com
Website: http://www.capso.com
Directors: K. Babur (MD)
Immediate Holding Company: CAPSO LIMITED
Registration no: 06523049 **Date established:** 2008
No.of Employees: 1 - 10 **Product Groups:** 36, 40

Date of Accounts	Mar 11	Mar 10	Mar 09
Working Capital	-47	10	7
Fixed Assets	7	10	15
Current Assets	121	141	145

Celab Ltd
25 Woolmer Way, Bordon, GU35 9QE
Tel: 01420-477011 **Fax:** 01420-472034
E-mail: roger.mier@murata-ps.com
Website: http://www.celab.co.uk
Bank(s): HSBC Farnham, Surrey
Directors: J. Hatcher (Fin), J. Wood (MD), R. Mier (Fin), S. Pellet (Sales)
Managers: B. Mier (Tech Serv Mgr), J. Edwards (Purch Mgr)
Ultimate Holding Company: MURATA MANUFACTURING CO LTD (JAPAN)
Immediate Holding Company: MURATA POWER SOLUTIONS (CELAB) LIMITED
Registration no: 01000030 **VAT No.:** GB 582 5030 52
Date established: 1971 **Turnover:** £5m - £10m
No.of Employees: 51 - 100 **Product Groups:** 37

Date of Accounts	Mar 12	Mar 11	Mar 10
Sales Turnover	8m	7m	6m
Pre Tax Profit/Loss	2m	1m	1m
Working Capital	7m	5m	4m
Fixed Assets	562	549	215
Current Assets	9m	9m	8m
Current Liabilities	2m	4m	3m

Europharma Machinery Ltd
12 Highview High Street, Bordon, GU35 0AX
Tel: 01420-473344 **Fax:** 01420-488030
E-mail: admin@europharma.co.uk
Website: http://www.europharma.co.uk
Directors: S. Waterhouse (MD)
Immediate Holding Company: EURO-PHARMA MACHINERY LIMITED
Registration no: 02550154 **Date established:** 1990
No.of Employees: 1 - 10 **Product Groups:** 38, 42

Date of Accounts	Dec 11	Dec 10	Dec 09
Working Capital	638	108	206
Fixed Assets	672	629	637
Current Assets	2m	2m	2m

Fern-Howard Ltd
Unit 1 Bordon Trading Estate Old Station Way, Bordon, GU35 9HH
Tel: 01420-470400 **Fax:** 01420-489536
E-mail: peter.scott@fernhoward.com
Website: http://www.fernhoward.com
Directors: P. Scott (MD), S. Waite (Dir), S. Weight (Comm), S. Waite (Fin)
Managers: B. Horne (Comptroller), P. Bennett (Purch Mgr), G. Hall (Quality Control), M. Jones (I.T. Exec), H. Mathews (Sales Prom Mgr), J. Wraith (Sales Prom Mgr), S. Good (Sales Prom Mgr), S. Good (Sales Admin)
Immediate Holding Company: FERN-HOWARD LIMITED
Registration no: 03202749 **VAT No.:** GB 679 5345 81
Date established: 1996 **Turnover:** £5m - £10m
No.of Employees: 51 - 100 **Product Groups:** 37, 38

Date of Accounts	Dec 08	Dec 07	Dec 06
Pre Tax Profit/Loss	191	161	76
Working Capital	305	279	225
Fixed Assets	485	576	667
Current Assets	2621	2551	2615
Current Liabilities	2316	2272	2390
Total Share Capital	710	70	70
ROCE% (Return on Capital Employed)	24.2	18.8	8.6

Goldburn Finishers Ltd
Unit 1-2 Broxhead Industrial Estate Broxhead Farm Road, Lindford, Bordon, GU35 0JX
Tel: 01420-477696 **Fax:** 01420-478151
E-mail: goldburn.finish@btconnect.com
Website: http://www.goldburnfinishers.co.uk
Directors: K. Way (Dir)
Immediate Holding Company: GOLDBURN FINISHERS LIMITED
Registration no: 01749851 **Date established:** 1983
No.of Employees: 1 - 10 **Product Groups:** 46, 48

Date of Accounts	Mar 11	Mar 10	Mar 09
Working Capital	5	-4	20
Fixed Assets	15	22	24
Current Assets	113	130	128

Kea Flex Mouldings Ltd
53 Woolmer Way, Bordon, GU35 9QE
Tel: 01420-473645 **Fax:** 01420-487498
E-mail: andrew.tuffield@jameswalker.biz
Website: http://www.jameswalker.biz/keaflex
Bank(s): Midland Bank
Directors: A. Tuffield (MD)
Ultimate Holding Company: JAMES WALKER GROUP LIMITED
Immediate Holding Company: KEA-FLEX MOULDINGS LIMITED
Registration no: 00598173 **VAT No.:** GB 189 5357 10
Date established: 1958 **Turnover:** £2m - £5m **No.of Employees:** 21 - 50
Product Groups: 29, 36

Date of Accounts	Mar 12	Mar 11	Mar 10
Working Capital	364	449	759
Fixed Assets	227	245	202
Current Assets	866	809	1m

Liss Fabrications
Unit 2 Main Road Kingsley, Bordon, GU35 9LW
Tel: 01420-476466 **Fax:** 01420-476466
Directors: D. Rudd (Prop)
Date established: 1999 **No.of Employees:** 1 - 10 **Product Groups:** 35

Loadwise International Ltd (A division of Hawkley Group)
50 Woolmer Way, Bordon, GU35 9QF
Tel: 01420-476500 **Fax:** 01420-479090
E-mail: sales@loadwise.co.uk
Website: http://www.loadwise.co.uk
Managers: K. Grant (Chief Mgr)
Immediate Holding Company: Hawkley Group Ltd
Registration no: 01877012 **Date established:** 1985
No.of Employees: 1 - 10 **Product Groups:** 38, 45, 67

Plasplant Ltd
Oakhanger Farm Oakhanger Road, Oakhanger, Bordon, GU35 9JA
Tel: 01420-473013 **Fax:** 01420-475152
E-mail: sales@plasplant.com
Website: http://www.plasplant.com
Directors: R. Simpson (Fin), K. Simpson (Tech Serv)
Immediate Holding Company: PLASPLANT LIMITED
Registration no: 01366725 **VAT No.:** GB 199 4544 09
Date established: 1978 **Turnover:** £250,000 - £500,000
No.of Employees: 1 - 10 **Product Groups:** 42

Date of Accounts	Mar 12	Mar 11	Mar 10
Working Capital	53	26	9
Fixed Assets	1	1	1
Current Assets	107	70	59

Seismic Sewage Systems Ltd
134 Chalet Hill, Bordon, GU35 0DF
Tel: 01420-488383 **Fax:** 01420-488384
Directors: R. Cordina (Dir)
Immediate Holding Company: SEISMIC SEWAGE SYSTEMS LIMITED
Registration no: 07094970 **Date established:** 2009
No.of Employees: 1 - 10 **Product Groups:** 80

Date of Accounts	Apr 12	Apr 11
Working Capital	-6	4
Fixed Assets	1	N/A
Current Assets	9	17

Silex Ltd
Units 4 & 5 Broxhead Trading Estate Broxhead Farm Road, Lindford, Bordon, GU35 0JX
Tel: 01420-487130 **Fax:** 01420-489274
E-mail: info@silex.co.uk
Website: http://www.silex.co.uk
Bank(s): National Westminster Bank Plc
Directors: N. Soudah (Fin)
Immediate Holding Company: SILEX LIMITED
Registration no: 01951973 **VAT No.:** GB 432 3498 55
Date established: 1985 **Turnover:** £2m - £5m **No.of Employees:** 21 - 50
Product Groups: 29, 30, 31, 32, 36, 42, 48, 49, 61, 63, 66

Date of Accounts	Oct 11	Oct 10	Oct 09
Working Capital	730	539	421
Fixed Assets	184	158	181
Current Assets	2m	1m	977

Brockenhurst

David Bradley Engineering Ltd
Hollybush Farmhouse Lymington Road, Brockenhurst, SO42 7UF
Tel: 01590-622440
Directors: D. Bradley (Prop)
Immediate Holding Company: DAVID BRADLEY ENGINEERING LIMITED
Registration no: 04938835 **Date established:** 2003
Turnover: £500,000 - £1m **No.of Employees:** 1 - 10 **Product Groups:** 37, 38

Eastleigh

A G Bathspray
14 Highcliffe Drive, Eastleigh, SO50 4RB
Tel: 023-8036 0161 **Fax:** 023-8061 9626
E-mail: info@agbathspray.co.uk
Website: http://www.agbathspray.co.uk
Directors: A. Gregory (Prop)
Immediate Holding Company: GREGORY BATHSPRAY LIMITED
Registration no: 04605791 **Date established:** 2002
No.of Employees: 1 - 10 **Product Groups:** 52

Date of Accounts	Mar 10	Mar 09	Mar 08
Working Capital	N/A	1	5
Current Assets	1	2	6

Abbey Air Systems Ltd
Unit 4d Barton Park Chickenhall Lane, Eastleigh, SO50 6RR
Tel: 023-8061 1311 **Fax:** 023-8061 1600
E-mail: cyril@abbeyairsystems.co.uk
Website: http://www.abbeyairsystems.co.uk
Directors: C. Line (MD), V. Roles (Fin)
Managers: K. Sessions (Purch Mgr), V. Rones (Fin Mgr), D. Line (Mgr)
Immediate Holding Company: ABBEY AIR SYSTEMS LIMITED
Registration no: 01916149 **VAT No.:** GB 411 6947 57
Date established: 1985 **No.of Employees:** 11 - 20 **Product Groups:** 52

Date of Accounts	May 10	May 09	May 08
Working Capital	-2	20	-6
Fixed Assets	15	23	32
Current Assets	137	169	355

Advanced Semiconductor Europe Ltd
Unit 17 Hathaway Close, Eastleigh, SO50 4SR
Tel: 023-8065 3457 **Fax:** 0870-042 0841
E-mail: jgibson@asieurope.net
Website: http://www.asieurope.net
Managers: M. Tandon (Sales Admin)
Ultimate Holding Company: ADVANCED SEMI CONDUCTOR INC (USA)
Immediate Holding Company: ADVANCED SEMICONDUCTOR (EUROPE) LTD
Registration no: 02662708 **Date established:** 1991 **Turnover:** £1m - £2m
No.of Employees: 1 - 10 **Product Groups:** 37, 67

Date of Accounts	Dec 11	Dec 10	Dec 09
Working Capital	561	338	265
Fixed Assets	N/A	13	15
Current Assets	1m	2m	1m

Aeromatic Fielder Ltd
15 Chandlers Ford Chandler's Ford, Eastleigh, SO53 4ZD
Tel: 023-8026 7131 **Fax:** 023-8025 3381
E-mail: sales-uk@aeromatic-fielder.com
Website: http://www.gea-ps.com
Bank(s): Danske Bank
Directors: R. Young (Dir)
Managers: P. Dodwell (Tech Serv Mgr), R. Gay (Fin Mgr), S. Gray, J. Freeman (Personnel), S. Gibson
Ultimate Holding Company: MG AG (GERMANY)
Immediate Holding Company: GEA PT HOLDINGS LTD
Registration no: 00930232 **VAT No.:** GB 188 1153 52
Date established: 1960 **No.of Employees:** 51 - 100 **Product Groups:** 42

Date of Accounts	Dec 07
Sales Turnover	34770
Pre Tax Profit/Loss	-210
Working Capital	-3730
Fixed Assets	3290
Current Assets	20510
Current Liabilities	24240
Total Share Capital	180
ROCE% (Return on Capital Employed)	47.7

Ahmad Tea Ltd
Unit C Winchester Road Chandler's Ford, Eastleigh, SO53 2PZ
Tel: 023-8027 8900 **Fax:** 023-8025 5867
E-mail: info@ahmadtea.com
Website: http://www.ahmadtea.com
Bank(s): Barclays
Directors: E. Afshar (Fin)
Managers: A. Afshar (Buyer), F. Hicks (Tech Serv Mgr), G. Cook, N. Afshar (Mktg Serv Mgr)
Immediate Holding Company: AHMAD TEA LIMITED
Registration no: 02019274 **Date established:** 1986
Turnover: £20m - £50m **No.of Employees:** 51 - 100 **Product Groups:** 20

Date of Accounts	Dec 11	Dec 10	Dec 09
Sales Turnover	23m	22m	18m
Pre Tax Profit/Loss	1m	806	807
Working Capital	2m	2m	2m
Fixed Assets	8m	7m	6m
Current Assets	8m	7m	6m
Current Liabilities	550	449	669

Arco Chandlers Ford
PO Box 151, Eastleigh, SO53 4ZS
Tel: 023-8027 0000 **Fax:** 023-8027 0077
E-mail: jeremy.shelton@arco.co.uk
Website: http://www.arco.co.uk
Managers: J. Shelton (District Mgr)
Immediate Holding Company: ARCO GROUP
Registration no: 06765870 **Date established:** 2008
Turnover: £75m - £125m **No.of Employees:** 11 - 20 **Product Groups:** 24, 29, 30

B & Q Head Office Customer Service Line
Head Office 1 Hampshire Corporate Park Templars Way, Chandler's Ford, Eastleigh, SO53 3YX
Tel: 08456-096688 **Fax:** 023-8025 7480
E-mail: customerservicedepartment@b-and-q.co.uk
Website: http://www.diy.com
Directors: J. Skelton (Fin)
Managers: T. O'connell, T. Martin (Mktg Serv Mgr)
Ultimate Holding Company: KINGFISHER PLC
Immediate Holding Company: B & Q PLC
Registration no: 00973387 **Date established:** 1970
Turnover: Over £1,000m **No.of Employees:** 1501 & over
Product Groups: 61

Date of Accounts	Jan 09	Jan 10	Jan 11
Sales Turnover	3683m	3792m	3712m
Pre Tax Profit/Loss	114m	400m	145m
Working Capital	2467m	2926m	2986m
Fixed Assets	867m	728m	699m
Current Assets	3306m	3882m	3977m
Current Liabilities	447m	404m	438m

Bettavend Ltd
5 Speedwell Close Chandlers Ford Industrial Estate, Chandler's Ford, Eastleigh, SO53 4BT
Tel: 023-8025 5222 **Fax:** 023-8027 6644
E-mail: office@bettavend.co.uk
Website: http://www.betttavend.co.uk
Directors: J. Ferguson (MD)
Immediate Holding Company: BETTAVEND LIMITED
Registration no: 02169453 **Date established:** 1987
Turnover: Up to £250,000 **No.of Employees:** 21 - 50 **Product Groups:** 49, 61, 62

Date of Accounts	Mar 12	Mar 11	Mar 10
Working Capital	113	36	-45
Fixed Assets	438	468	476
Current Assets	463	393	349

Bounce UK
77 Stranding Street, Eastleigh, SO50 5GR
Tel: 0800-448 8240
E-mail: p.shelton-smith@virgin.net
Website: http://www.bounceuk.biz
Directors: P. Shelton-Smith (Prop)
Turnover: Up to £250,000 **No.of Employees:** 1 - 10 **Product Groups:** 24, 49, 66, 83

Brookwood Barn Company
25 Compton Close, Eastleigh, SO50 4RE
Tel: 08448-004202 **Fax:** 0844-800 4203
E-mail: sales@oakbarns.com
Website: http://www.oakbarns.com
Directors: S. Holly (Prop)
Date established: 2006 **No.of Employees:** 1 - 10 **Product Groups:** 25, 52

C Brewer & Sons
Brickfield Lane Chandler's Ford, Eastleigh, SO53 4DP
Tel: 023-8026 7242 **Fax:** 023-8026 9006
E-mail: southampton@brewers.co.uk
Website: http://www.brewers.co.uk
Bank(s): Barclays
Managers: D. Powell (Mgr)
Immediate Holding Company: POPPIES PRE-SCHOOL EDUCATION LLP
Registration no: 00203852 **VAT No.:** GB 191 1565 70
Date established: 2007 **Turnover:** £10m - £20m
No.of Employees: 21 - 50 **Product Groups:** 27, 66

Date of Accounts	Jul 11	Jul 10	Jul 09
Sales Turnover	17m	14m	19m
Pre Tax Profit/Loss	2m	353	3m
Working Capital	22m	15m	12m
Fixed Assets	867	848	736
Current Assets	27m	20m	17m
Current Liabilities	409	146	521

Campbell Coutts Ltd
Unit 7 Tower Industrial Estate, Eastleigh, SO50 6NZ
Tel: 023-8061 3700 **Fax:** 023-8061 3355
E-mail: sales@flocking.biz
Website: http://www.flocking.biz
Directors: A. Campbell (MD)
Immediate Holding Company: CAMPBELL COUTTS LIMITED
Registration no: 02709880 **Date established:** 1992
Turnover: £500,000 - £1m **No.of Employees:** 1 - 10 **Product Groups:** 43, 48

Date of Accounts	Apr 11	Apr 10	Apr 09
Sales Turnover	542	697	N/A
Working Capital	94	136	135
Fixed Assets	32	26	30
Current Assets	197	247	195

P G Carmichael
Plot B Toynbee Road, Eastleigh, SO50 9DH
Tel: 023-8061 5900 **Fax:** 023-8026 6480
E-mail: sales@classicgaragedoors.co.uk
Website: http://www.classicgaragedoors.co.uk
Directors: P. Carmichael (Prop)
Date established: 1983 **No.of Employees:** 1 - 10 **Product Groups:** 35

Charntec Electronics Ltd
PO Box 477, Eastleigh, SO5 0AR
Tel: 01962-735718 **Fax:** 01962-736756
E-mail: info@charntecelectronics.co.uk
Website: http://www.charntecelectronics.co.uk
Directors: P. Chandler (Dir), R. Quaife (MD)
Immediate Holding Company: CHARNTEC ELECTRONICS LIMITED
Registration no: 01438222 **Date established:** 1979 **Turnover:** £1m - £2m
No.of Employees: 1 - 10 **Product Groups:** 38

Date of Accounts	Jul 11	Jul 10	Jul 08
Working Capital	6	9	N/A
Fixed Assets	5	2	3
Current Assets	21	28	20

Citadel Security Ltd
73 Park Road Chandler's Ford, Eastleigh, SO53 2EL
Tel: 023-8025 3100 **Fax:** 01483-235569
E-mail: info@citadelsecurity.org.uk
Website: http://www.citadelsecurity.org.uk
Directors: K. Downer (I.T. Dir)
Immediate Holding Company: CITADEL SECURITY LTD
Registration no: 06914192 **Date established:** 2009
No.of Employees: 1 - 10 **Product Groups:** 38, 42

Date of Accounts	May 11
Working Capital	-1
Fixed Assets	2
Current Assets	4

Coilmaster Ltd
Unit 30 Swift Farm Estate Hensting Lane, Fishers Pond, Eastleigh, SO50 7HH
Tel: 023-8069 5524 **Fax:** 023-8069 5525
E-mail: coilmaster@ic24.net
Website: http://www.coilmasterltd.co.uk
Product Groups: 35, 36, 40, 46, 84

Date of Accounts	Jul 07	Jul 06
Working Capital	89	92
Fixed Assets	19	26
Current Assets	109	112
Current Liabilities	20	20
Total Share Capital	1	1

Cooper Vision
Erith House Warrior Close, Chandler's Ford, Eastleigh, SO53 4TE
Tel: 01489-883000
E-mail: info@coopervision.co.uk
Website: http://www.coopervision.co.uk
Directors: A. Cedrick (MD)
No.of Employees: 1 - 10 **Product Groups:** 37, 38, 65

Dasic Marine Ltd
Unit N & M Eagle Close Chandlers Ford Industrial Estate, Chandler's Ford, Eastleigh, SO53 4NF
Tel: 023-8025 2264 **Fax:** 023-8026 6233
E-mail: enquiries@dasic-marine.co.uk
Website: http://www.dasic-marine.co.uk
Directors: A. Murray (MD)
Immediate Holding Company: DASIC MARINE LIMITED
Registration no: 00914692 **Date established:** 1967
No.of Employees: 11 - 20 **Product Groups:** 38, 42

Date of Accounts	Apr 12	Apr 11	Apr 10
Working Capital	826	887	820
Fixed Assets	110	64	61
Current Assets	1m	1m	1m

Derica Intermouldal Ltd
8 West Links Tollgate, Chandler's Ford, Eastleigh, SO53 3TG
Tel: 023-8062 3300 **Fax:** 023-8062 0144
Website: http://www.derica.com
Managers: T. Porter (Accounts), T. Porter (Sales Prom Mgr)
Turnover: Over £1,000m **No.of Employees:** 1 - 10 **Product Groups:** 76

Draper Tools Ltd
Hursley Road Chandler's Ford, Eastleigh, SO53 1YF
Tel: 023-8026 6355 **Fax:** 023-8026 0784
E-mail: sales@drapertools.com
Website: http://www.drapertools.com
Directors: P. Denney (Fin), G. Wade (MD), C. Richardson (Mkt Research), A. Cole (Purch)
Managers: C. Richmond (Tech Serv Mgr)
Ultimate Holding Company: DRAPER TOOL GROUP LIMITED(THE)
Immediate Holding Company: DRAPER TOOLS LIMITED
Registration no: 00570630 **Date established:** 1956
Turnover: £50m - £75m **No.of Employees:** 251 - 500
Product Groups: 36, 37, 41

Date of Accounts	Aug 11	Aug 10	Aug 09
Sales Turnover	55m	53m	52m
Pre Tax Profit/Loss	5m	4m	6m
Working Capital	41m	38m	36m
Fixed Assets	28m	28m	44m
Current Assets	47m	44m	40m
Current Liabilities	4m	3m	3m

Eastleigh College
Chestnut Avenue, Eastleigh, SO50 5FS
Tel: 023-8091 1000 **Fax:** 023-8032 2131
E-mail: rjarvis@eastleigh.ac.uk
Website: http://www.eastleigh.ac.uk
Directors: A. Lau Walker (Grp Chief Exec), T. Lauwalker (Prop)
Immediate Holding Company: EASTLEIGH COLLEGE LIMITED
Registration no: 02912213 **Date established:** 1994
Turnover: Up to £250,000 **No.of Employees:** 501 - 1000
Product Groups: 86

Date of Accounts	Jul 11	Jul 10	Jul 09
Sales Turnover	10	10	7
Pre Tax Profit/Loss	10	10	7
Current Assets	10	11	7

Elliotts
Unit 8 Goodwood Road, Eastleigh, SO50 4NT
Tel: 023-8062 3960 **Fax:** 023-8062 3965
E-mail: donnac@elliott-brothers.co.uk
Website: http://www.elliotts.uk.com
Managers: D. Cross
No.of Employees: 11 - 20 **Product Groups:** 33, 66

Exfo Europe Ltd
Unit A1 Omega Enterprise Park Electron Way Chandler's Ford, Eastleigh, SO53 4SE
Tel: 023-8024 6800 **Fax:** 023-8024 6801
E-mail: colin.jones@exfo.com
Website: http://www.exfo.com
Managers: C. Jones
Ultimate Holding Company: EXFO ELECTRO OPTICAL ENGINEERING INC (CANADA)
Immediate Holding Company: EXFO EUROPE LIMITED
Registration no: 02316168 **Date established:** 1988
No.of Employees: 21 - 50 **Product Groups:** 37, 67, 79

Date of Accounts	Aug 11	Aug 10	Aug 09
Sales Turnover	45m	36m	29m
Pre Tax Profit/Loss	1m	659	147

see next page

***Exfo Europe Ltd** - Cont'd*

Working Capital	4m	2m	2m
Fixed Assets	162	218	207
Current Assets	11m	8m	6m
Current Liabilities	2m	2m	1m

Fortis UK Ltd

Fortis House Tollgate, Chandler's Ford, Eastleigh, SO53 3YA
Tel: 023-8064 4455 **Fax:** 023-8064 1146
Website: http://www.fortisinsurance.co.uk
Bank(s): National Westminster Bank Plc
Directors: J. Grosvenor (I.T. Dir), R. Smith (Fin), P. Robinson (Snr Part), B. Smith (MD), R. Smith (Co Sec), A. Sendall (Cust Serv), M. Cranston (Fin)
Managers: J. Buchanan (Sales & Mktg Mg), J. Watson (Personnel), T. Skinner, C. Dobson (Mktg Serv Mgr), W. Baker
Immediate Holding Company: AGEAS (UK) LIMITED
Registration no: 01093301 **VAT No.:** GB 411 5162 01
Date established: 1973 **Turnover:** £125m - £250m
No.of Employees: 501 - 1000 **Product Groups:** 82

Date of Accounts	Dec 10	Dec 09	Dec 08
Pre Tax Profit/Loss	4m	8m	29m
Working Capital	-52m	17m	-40m
Fixed Assets	438m	119m	121m
Current Assets	35m	28m	26m
Current Liabilities	7m	11m	66m

Hales Waste Control Ltd Southampton Customer Centre

10 Brambridge, Eastleigh, SO50 6HZ
Tel: 01962-711990 **Fax:** 023-8033 8499
E-mail: salesdepartment@biffa.co.uk
Website: http://www.biffa.co.uk
Managers: T. Munn (Mgr), T. Munn (Depot Mgr)
Ultimate Holding Company: Wasteinvestments LLP
Immediate Holding Company: HALES WASTE CONTROL LIMITED
Registration no: 04602277 **Date established:** 2002
No.of Employees: 1 - 10 **Product Groups:** 54

Hemco Power & Control Systems Ltd

Unit 33 Parham Drive Boyatt Wood, Eastleigh, SO50 4NU
Tel: 023-8061 8833 **Fax:** 023-8061 4313
E-mail: sales@hemco.co.uk
Website: http://www.hemco.co.uk
Directors: A. Ansell (Dir)
Immediate Holding Company: HEMCO POWER & CONTROL SYSTEMS LTD.
Registration no: 00758547 **Date established:** 1963
Turnover: £250,000 - £500,000 **No.of Employees:** 11 - 20
Product Groups: 38, 80

Date of Accounts	Aug 11	Aug 10	Aug 09
Working Capital	95	163	210
Fixed Assets	28	18	23
Current Assets	211	252	298

I G T Industries Ltd

Woodside Road, Eastleigh, SO50 4ET
Tel: 023-8061 0818 **Fax:** 023-8061 0828
E-mail: sales@igt-industries.com
Website: http://www.igt-industries.com
Bank(s): National Westminster Bank Plc
Directors: N. Giles (MD), V. Light (Tech Serv), D. McLaughlan (Sales), R. Hide (Co Sec)
Managers: T. Moss (Sales Prom Mgr), M. Flanders (Purch Mgr)
Immediate Holding Company: STADIUM IGT LIMITED
Registration no: 02164435 **VAT No.:** GB 458 7196 01
Date established: 1987 **Turnover:** £2m - £5m **No.of Employees:** 51 - 100
Product Groups: 30, 37, 38, 44

Date of Accounts	Oct 11	Oct 10	Oct 09
Sales Turnover	N/A	N/A	4m
Pre Tax Profit/Loss	N/A	N/A	580
Working Capital	243	153	145
Fixed Assets	193	222	144
Current Assets	2m	2m	1m
Current Liabilities	538	580	633

Industrial Door Services Ltd

Unit K Eagle Close, Chandler's Ford, Eastleigh, SO53 4NF
Tel: 023-8025 5255 **Fax:** 01489-780906
E-mail: sales@indoorserv.co.uk
Website: http://www.indoorserv.co.uk
Directors: C. Chalker (Fin)
Managers: D. Pearce (Chief Mgr)
Immediate Holding Company: INDUSTRIAL DOOR SERVICES LIMITED
Registration no: 03139260 **Date established:** 1995
No.of Employees: 1 - 10 **Product Groups:** 35, 39, 48

Date of Accounts	Apr 12	Apr 11	Apr 10
Working Capital	111	52	61
Fixed Assets	671	681	698
Current Assets	637	494	567

Klinger

Unit 16 Parham Drive, Eastleigh, SO50 4NU
Tel: 023-8061 1855 **Fax:** 023-8061 0360
E-mail: info@klingeruk.co.uk
Website: http://www.klinger.co.uk
Managers: M. Stickley (Mgr)
Turnover: £500,000 - £1m **No.of Employees:** 1 - 10 **Product Groups:** 22, 23, 24, 25, 27, 29, 30, 32, 33, 34, 36, 40

Lambert Brothers Holdings Ltd

Woodside Avenue Boyatt Wood Industrial Estate, Eastleigh, SO50 4ZR
Tel: 023-8061 7331 **Fax:** 023-8062 9261
E-mail: robert.trotter@lambros.co.uk
Website: http://www.lambertbrothers.co.uk
Directors: R. Trotter (Dir)
Immediate Holding Company: LAMBERT BROTHERS HOLDINGS LIMITED
Registration no: 02195321 **VAT No.:** GB 522 4630 75
Date established: 1987 **Turnover:** £500,000 - £1m
No.of Employees: 1 - 10 **Product Groups:** 72, 77

Date of Accounts	May 11	May 10	May 09
Sales Turnover	580	358	437
Pre Tax Profit/Loss	224	487	162
Working Capital	166	192	2m
Fixed Assets	5m	5m	5m
Current Assets	2m	2m	3m
Current Liabilities	131	1m	680

M S L Oilfield Services LTD

14 Brickfield Lane Chandler's Ford, Eastleigh, SO53 4DP
Tel: 023-8027 5100 **Fax:** 023-8027 5200
E-mail: mc@msluk.net
Website: http://www.msluk.net
Directors: M. Clark (MD), M. Hudson (Fin)
Immediate Holding Company: MONITORING SERVICES (U.K.) LIMITED
Registration no: 03634432 **VAT No.:** GB 723 2444 60
Date established: 1998 **Turnover:** £10m - £20m **No.of Employees:** 1 - 10
Product Groups: 37, 38, 39, 45, 51, 67, 85

Date of Accounts	Jan 11	Jan 10	Jan 09
Working Capital	-217	-249	-254
Current Assets	1	1	N/A

Mobility Plus Eastleigh Ltd

Unit 3 6a Wells Place, Eastleigh, SO50 5PP
Tel: 023-8061 3789 **Fax:** 023-8061 3799
Directors: P. Streams (MD)
Immediate Holding Company: MOBILITYPLUS EASTLEIGH LTD
Registration no: 06825914 **Date established:** 2009
No.of Employees: 1 - 10 **Product Groups:** 26, 38, 39

Date of Accounts	Feb 11	Feb 10
Working Capital	5	3
Fixed Assets	10	12
Current Assets	51	30

Paul Murray plc

School Lane Chandler's Ford, Eastleigh, SO53 4YN
Tel: 023-8046 0600 **Fax:** 023-8046 0601
E-mail: nhayton@paulmurrayplc.co.uk
Website: http://www.murrayshealthandbeauty.com
Bank(s): Barclays.
Directors: S. Coatham (Fin), N. Hayton (Sales), N. Hayton (Sales), T. Pickford (Purch)
Immediate Holding Company: PAUL MURRAY PLC
Registration no: 01172728 **VAT No.:** GB 189 6029 22
Date established: 1974 **Turnover:** £10m - £20m
No.of Employees: 51 - 100 **Product Groups:** 61

Date of Accounts	Dec 11	Dec 10	Dec 09
Sales Turnover	12m	10m	8m
Pre Tax Profit/Loss	560	301	125
Working Capital	2m	2m	1m
Fixed Assets	2m	2m	2m
Current Assets	5m	4m	4m
Current Liabilities	875	542	318

Nor-Cote International Ltd

Unit 8 Eagle Close Chandler's Ford, Eastleigh, SO53 4NF
Tel: 023-8027 0542 **Fax:** 023-8027 0543
E-mail: sales@norcote.com
Website: http://www.norcote.com
Directors: M. Bain (Dir)
Immediate Holding Company: NOR-COTE INTERNATIONAL LIMITED
Registration no: 02878763 **VAT No.:** GB 467 9692 75
Date established: 1993 **Turnover:** £500,000 - £1m
No.of Employees: 1 - 10 **Product Groups:** 32

Date of Accounts	Aug 11	Aug 10	Aug 09
Sales Turnover	N/A	783	817
Pre Tax Profit/Loss	N/A	-9	-50
Working Capital	389	331	336
Fixed Assets	24	26	29
Current Assets	468	438	454
Current Liabilities	N/A	24	25

O K International Ltd

Eagle Close Chandler's Ford, Eastleigh, SO53 4NF
Tel: 023-8027 4677 **Fax:** 023-8048 9109
E-mail: info@okinternational.com
Website: http://www.okinternational.com
Bank(s): HSBC Bank plc
Directors: C. Shaw (Co Sec)
Managers: A. Vincent (Warehouse Mgr), G. Williams (Ops Mgr), M. Griffin (Fin Mgr), N. Morrin (Sales & Mktg Mg)
Ultimate Holding Company: DOVER CORPORATION (U.S.A.)
Immediate Holding Company: OK INTERNATIONAL LIMITED
Registration no: 01346318 **Date established:** 1977
Turnover: £10m - £20m **No.of Employees:** 21 - 50 **Product Groups:** 40, 46, 47

Date of Accounts	Dec 11	Dec 10	Dec 09
Sales Turnover	11m	10m	8m
Pre Tax Profit/Loss	2m	2m	-181
Working Capital	8m	7m	6m
Fixed Assets	74	105	70
Current Assets	9m	8m	7m
Current Liabilities	787	814	374

P & M Packing

Unit 2 Tower Industrial Estate Tower Lane, Eastleigh, SO50 6NZ
Tel: 023-8062 3770 **Fax:** 023-8049 0444
E-mail: andy@pmpacking.com
Website: http://www.pmpacking.com
Managers: A. Jones (Mgr)
Ultimate Holding Company: CONSTANTINE GROUP PLC
Immediate Holding Company: PETERS & MAY (PACKING) LIMITED
Registration no: 02887465 **Date established:** 1994
Turnover: Up to £250,000 **No.of Employees:** 1 - 10 **Product Groups:** 76

Date of Accounts	Aug 11	Aug 10	Aug 09
Working Capital	6	6	6
Current Assets	6	6	6

John Pipe International

Mayflower Close Chandler's Ford, Eastleigh, SO53 4AR
Tel: 023-8036 0100 **Fax:** 023-8027 3080
E-mail: jon.bradley@johnpipe.co.uk
Website: http://www.johnpipe.co.uk
Directors: J. Bradley (Dir)
Ultimate Holding Company: ORBIS BUSINESS INTERNATIONAL LIMITED
Immediate Holding Company: KIRKSTYLE DEVELOPMENT LIMITED
Registration no: 00710494 **Date established:** 1954
Turnover: £250,000 - £500,000 **No.of Employees:** 1 - 10
Product Groups: 48, 76, 84

Date of Accounts	Mar 12	Mar 11	Mar 10
Working Capital	-1	-1	-1
Current Liabilities	1	1	1

Pipestock.Com

Highland House Mayflower Close Chandler's Ford, Eastleigh, SO53 4AR
Tel: 08456-341053 **Fax:** 0845-634 1056
E-mail: info@pipestock.com
Website: http://www.pipestock.com
Managers: D. Ashworth (Chief Mgr)
Immediate Holding Company: PIPE STOCK LIMITED
Registration no: 05075646 **Date established:** 2004
Turnover: £500,000 - £1m **No.of Employees:** 11 - 20 **Product Groups:** 30

Date of Accounts	Mar 11	Mar 10	Mar 09
Working Capital	113	83	87
Fixed Assets	9	34	44
Current Assets	525	303	298

Premier Foods Group

Toynbee Road, Eastleigh, SO50 9YU
Tel: 08707-288888 **Fax:** 023-8064 1612
Website: http://www.premierfoods.co.uk
Bank(s): Barclays
Managers: C. Vitty (Mgr), R. Curtis (Comptroller)
Ultimate Holding Company: PREMIER FOODS PLC
Immediate Holding Company: BRITISH BAKERIES LIMITED
Registration no: 00241018 **Date established:** 1929
Turnover: £20m - £50m **No.of Employees:** 251 - 500 **Product Groups:** 20

Saint Gobain Abrasives Ltd

Millbrook Close Chandler's Ford, Eastleigh, SO53 4BZ
Tel: 023-8025 4777 **Fax:** 023-8025 5930
E-mail: terry.hughes@saint-gobain.com
Website: http://www.saint-gobain.com
Bank(s): National Westminster Bank Plc
Directors: D. Lees (Co Sec), R. Poole (MD), T. Hughes (MD)
Managers: R. Myzkowski (I.T. Exec)
Ultimate Holding Company: Saint-Gobain Ltd
Immediate Holding Company: Saint-Gobain Ltd
Registration no: 02943990 **VAT No.:** GB 188 2317 43
No.of Employees: 21 - 50 **Product Groups:** 33, 36, 47

Scott Drummond Ltd

3 City Grove Trading Estate Woodside Road, Eastleigh, SO50 4ET
Tel: 023-8061 3536 **Fax:** 023-8062 0353
E-mail: accounts@electrofreeze.co.uk
Website: http://www.electrofreeze.co.uk
Directors: J. King (Dir)
Immediate Holding Company: SCOTT - DRUMMOND LIMITED
Registration no: 01317360 **Date established:** 1977
No.of Employees: 11 - 20 **Product Groups:** 20, 40, 41

Date of Accounts	Sep 11	Sep 10	Sep 09
Working Capital	168	127	134
Fixed Assets	44	79	91
Current Assets	430	407	381

Selwood Ltd

Bournemouth Rd Chandlers Ford, Eastleigh, SO53 3ZL
Tel: 023-8025 0137 **Fax:** 023-8027 1012
E-mail: tony.killick@selwoodpumps.com
Website: http://www.selwoodpumps.com
Bank(s): National Westminster Bank Plc
Directors: M. Page (Dir)
Managers: T. Killick (Chief Mgr)
Ultimate Holding Company: Selwood Group Ltd
Registration no: 00494547 **VAT No.:** GB 188 7246 15
Date established: 1946 **Turnover:** £50m - £75m **Product Groups:** 40, 42

Date of Accounts	Dec 11	Dec 10	Dec 09
Sales Turnover	46m	39m	38m
Pre Tax Profit/Loss	4m	2m	554
Working Capital	3m	1m	2m
Fixed Assets	52m	51m	52m
Current Assets	13m	12m	10m
Current Liabilities	4m	3m	3m

Solent Powder Finishers Ltd

3 Brookwood Industrial Estate Brookwood Avenue, Eastleigh, SO50 9EY
Tel: 023-8064 2632 **Fax:** 023-8064 2631
E-mail: enquiries@s-p-f.co.uk
Website: http://www.s-p-f.co.uk
Bank(s): Lloyds TSB Bank plc
Directors: G. Sumner (MD)
Immediate Holding Company: SOLENT POWDER FINISHERS LIMITED
Registration no: 01661984 **VAT No.:** GB 382 5039 50
Date established: 1982 **Turnover:** £250,000 - £500,000
No.of Employees: 11 - 20 **Product Groups:** 48

Date of Accounts	Dec 11	Dec 10	Dec 09
Working Capital	96	83	73
Fixed Assets	40	35	32
Current Assets	246	185	191

South Midlands Communications Ltd

South Midlands House School Close, Chandler's Ford, Eastleigh, SO53 4BY
Tel: 023-8024 6200 **Fax:** 023-8024 6206
E-mail: sales@smc-comms.com
Website: http://www.smc-comms.com
Bank(s): Barclays, Southampton
Directors: S. Brown (Non Exec), D. Gardner (Co Sec), J. Lightfoot (MD)
Managers: N. Deadill (Tech Serv Mgr), T. Haughton (Purch Mgr), S. Deabill (Admin Off)
Immediate Holding Company: SOUTH MIDLANDS COMMUNICATIONS LIMITED
Registration no: 00603500 **VAT No.:** GB 329 9048 29
Date established: 1958 **Turnover:** £5m - £10m
No.of Employees: 51 - 100 **Product Groups:** 35, 37, 48

Date of Accounts	Jun 11	Jun 10	Jun 09
Sales Turnover	5m	11m	9m
Pre Tax Profit/Loss	189	307	283
Working Capital	3m	3m	3m
Fixed Assets	3m	3m	3m
Current Assets	6m	5m	5m
Current Liabilities	711	1m	2m

Stewart Signs Ltd

Trafalgar Close Chandler's Ford, Eastleigh, SO53 4BW
Tel: 023-8025 4781 **Fax:** 023-8026 0760
E-mail: sales@stewartsigns.co.uk
Website: http://www.stewartsigns.co.uk
Directors: S. Cripps (Dir)
Immediate Holding Company: STEWART SIGNS LIMITED
Registration no: 00782263 **VAT No.:** GB 188 7627 03
Date established: 1963 **Turnover:** £2m - £5m **No.of Employees:** 51 - 100
Product Groups: 30

Date of Accounts	Apr 12	Apr 11	Apr 10
Sales Turnover	N/A	N/A	4m
Pre Tax Profit/Loss	N/A	N/A	-255

Working Capital	2m	2m	1m
Fixed Assets	176	203	288
Current Assets	3m	3m	3m
Current Liabilities	N/A	N/A	826

Superior Fascias
99 Leigh Road, Eastleigh, SO50 9DR
Tel: 023-8178 0141 **Fax:** 07005-964609
E-mail: info@superiorfascias.co.uk
Website: http://www.superiorfascias.co.uk
Directors: J. Spencer (Ptnr), N. Munton (MD)
Registration no: 03862804 **No.of Employees:** 1 - 10 **Product Groups:** 30, 52, 63, 66, 67

Tecton Ltd
Fishers Court Main Road Fishers Pond, Eastleigh, SO50 7HG
Tel: 023-8069 5858 **Fax:** 023-8069 5702
E-mail: chrishall@tecton.co.uk
Website: http://www.tecton.co.uk
Directors: C. Hall (MD)
Immediate Holding Company: TECTON LIMITED
Registration no: 02193340 **VAT No.:** 458 7966 75 **Date established:** 1987
Turnover: £250,000 - £500,000 **No.of Employees:** 11 - 20
Product Groups: 37

Date of Accounts	Dec 11	Dec 10	Dec 09
Working Capital	2m	2m	1m
Fixed Assets	7	9	14
Current Assets	3m	3m	3m

The Nuance Group UK Ltd
84-98 Southampton Road, Eastleigh, SO50 5ZF
Tel: 023-8067 3000 **Fax:** 023-8067 3199
Website: http://www.nuancegroup.com
Directors: C. Stegemann (Fin)
Ultimate Holding Company: THE NUANCE GROUP AG (SWITZERLAND)
Immediate Holding Company: THE NUANCE GROUP (UK) LIMITED
Registration no: 01131604 **VAT No.:** GB 188 0436 45
Date established: 1973 **Turnover:** £50m - £75m
No.of Employees: 251 - 500 **Product Groups:** 74

Date of Accounts	Dec 11	Dec 10	Dec 09
Sales Turnover	65m	67m	74m
Pre Tax Profit/Loss	3m	11m	-801
Working Capital	12m	9m	-4m
Fixed Assets	4m	5m	6m
Current Assets	19m	24m	25m
Current Liabilities	3m	4m	5m

Tower Machine Tools Ltd
Mayflower Close Chandler's Ford, Eastleigh, SO53 4AR
Tel: 023-8026 0266 **Fax:** 023-8026 1012
E-mail: info@towermachinetools.co.uk
Website: http://www.towermachinetools.co.uk
Directors: J. Spencer (MD), S. Noakes (Fin)
Ultimate Holding Company: TOWER STEEL (HOLDINGS) LIMITED
Immediate Holding Company: TOWER MACHINE TOOLS LIMITED
Registration no: 01246818 **VAT No.:** GB 241 5603 89
Date established: 1976 **Turnover:** £2m - £5m **No.of Employees:** 1 - 10
Product Groups: 46, 67

Date of Accounts	Dec 11	Dec 10	Dec 09
Working Capital	128	125	129
Fixed Assets	199	216	179
Current Assets	311	308	254

U M C International
Warrior Close Chandler's Ford, Eastleigh, SO53 4TE
Tel: 023-8026 9866 **Fax:** 023-8025 3198
E-mail: alan.trevarthen@umc-int.com
Website: http://www.umc.co.uk
Bank(s): Barclays, Lymington
Directors: P. Naylor (Fin), J. Jackson (I.T. Dir), A. Trevarthen (MD)
Managers: R. Burgess, A. Reed (Fin Mgr)
Immediate Holding Company: U.M.C. INTERNATIONAL PLC
Registration no: 01069620 **VAT No.:** GB 189 0482 32
Date established: 1972 **Turnover:** £5m - £10m **No.of Employees:** 11 - 20
Product Groups: 39

Date of Accounts	Dec 11	Dec 10	Dec 09
Sales Turnover	9m	9m	9m
Pre Tax Profit/Loss	353	45	930
Working Capital	2m	1m	1m
Fixed Assets	13	639	613
Current Assets	2m	2m	2m
Current Liabilities	238	539	669

Ubichem plc
Mayflower Close Chandler's Ford, Eastleigh, SO53 4AR
Tel: 023-8026 3030 **Fax:** 023-8026 3012
E-mail: sales@ubichem.com
Website: http://www.ubichem.com
Bank(s): Barclays
Directors: B. Headicar (Co Sec)
Managers: A. Hiscock (Tech Serv Mgr), T. Wilton (Sales Prom Mgr), D. Cable (Comptroller), H. Harrison (Purch Mgr)
Immediate Holding Company: UBICHEM PLC
Registration no: 01363294 **VAT No.:** GB 522 4803 70
Date established: 1978 **Turnover:** £5m - £10m **No.of Employees:** 11 - 20
Product Groups: 31

Date of Accounts	Dec 10	Dec 09	Dec 08
Sales Turnover	8m	6m	9m
Pre Tax Profit/Loss	-299	-925	617
Working Capital	739	857	2m
Fixed Assets	4m	4m	4m
Current Assets	3m	3m	4m
Current Liabilities	432	308	622

V E S Ltd
Unit 3 Eagle Close, Chandler's Ford, Eastleigh, SO53 4NF
Tel: 08448-156060 **Fax:** 023-8026 1204
E-mail: vesltd@ves.co.uk
Website: http://www.ves.co.uk
Bank(s): HSBC
Directors: S. Birks (Sales), J. Peters (MD), K. White (Fin)
Managers: F. Gillgower, R. Redfern (Personnel), P. Tarrant, A. Gale
Immediate Holding Company: VES LIMITED
Registration no: 02359866 **VAT No.:** GB 314 5332 89
Date established: 1989 **Turnover:** £5m - £10m
No.of Employees: 101 - 250 **Product Groups:** 40

Wessex Galvanisers Ltd
Tower Industrial Estate Tower Lane, Eastleigh, SO50 6NZ
Tel: 023-8062 9952 **Fax:** 023-8065 0289
E-mail: wessex@wedge-galv.co.uk
Website: http://www.wedge-galv.co.uk
Directors: D. Lynam (Co Sec), T. Beech (Sales)
Ultimate Holding Company: B.E. WEDGE HOLDINGS LIMITED
Immediate Holding Company: WESSEX GALVANIZERS LIMITED
Registration no: 02414902 **Date established:** 1989
No.of Employees: 1 - 10 **Product Groups:** 48

Date of Accounts	Mar 11	Mar 10	Mar 09
Pre Tax Profit/Loss	12	12	12
Current Assets	3	3	3
Current Liabilities	3	3	2

Woodside Metal Polishing
4 Allington Manor Business Centre Allington Lane, Fair Oak, Eastleigh, SO50 7DE
Tel: 023-8069 5505 **Fax:** 023-8069 5505
Directors: G. Cox (Dir), P. Cox (Fin)
Immediate Holding Company: WOODSIDE METAL POLISHING LIMITED
Registration no: 05269043 **Date established:** 2004
No.of Employees: 1 - 10 **Product Groups:** 46, 48

Date of Accounts	Dec 10	Dec 09	Dec 07
Working Capital	8	12	11
Fixed Assets	1	1	2
Current Assets	22	23	19

H Young Transport Ltd
Tower Industrial Estate Tower Lane, Eastleigh, SO50 6NZ
Tel: 023-8061 0611 **Fax:** 023-8061 2711
E-mail: contact@hyoung-transport.co.uk
Website: http://www.hyoung-transport.co.uk
Bank(s): Barclays, Southampton
Directors: R. Webster (Dir)
Managers: D. Moss (Chief Mgr), M. Jackson (Tech Serv Mgr), P. Limburn (Sales & Mktg Mg)
Ultimate Holding Company: H YOUNG LOGISTICS LIMITED
Immediate Holding Company: H. YOUNG (PROPERTIES) LIMITED
Registration no: 00886597 **VAT No.:** GB 188 6706 12
Date established: 1966 **Turnover:** £5m - £10m
No.of Employees: 101 - 250 **Product Groups:** 72

Date of Accounts	Oct 11	Oct 10	Oct 09
Working Capital	-245	-182	-193
Fixed Assets	4m	4m	4m
Current Assets	90	178	137

Emsworth

Artec Engineering Ltd
8 Seagull Lane, Emsworth, PO10 7QH
Tel: 01243-375555 **Fax:** 01243-379282
E-mail: artec@lineone.net
Website: http://www.artecengineering.co.uk
Bank(s): Barclays
Directors: C. Kemp (Fin), P. Kemp (MD)
Immediate Holding Company: ARTEC ENGINEERING LIMITED
Registration no: 00812221 **VAT No.:** GB 107 3025 16
Date established: 1964 **Turnover:** £1m - £2m **No.of Employees:** 11 - 20
Product Groups: 48

Date of Accounts	Mar 11	Mar 10	Mar 09
Working Capital	64	41	35
Fixed Assets	48	54	66
Current Assets	401	463	368

BLT&C Ltd
604 Southleigh Road, Emsworth, PO10 7TA
Tel: 07753-662602
E-mail: keith.sparrow@bltandc.co.uk
Website: http://bltandc.co.uk
Directors: K. Sparrow (Dir)
Registration no: 03899129 **Date established:** 2001
Turnover: Up to £250,000 **No.of Employees:** 1 - 10 **Product Groups:** 44, 61, 80, 86

Bean Glass Houses Ltd
Foxton Cemetery Lane, Emsworth, PO10 8QB
Tel: 01243-376159 **Fax:** 01243-376159
E-mail: beanglasshouses@tesco.net
Directors: K. Bean (Fin), B. Bean (MD)
Immediate Holding Company: BEAN GLASSHOUSES LTD
Registration no: 04147736 **Date established:** 2001
No.of Employees: 1 - 10 **Product Groups:** 26, 35

Date of Accounts	Dec 11	Dec 10	Dec 09
Working Capital	16	24	29
Fixed Assets	12	17	22
Current Assets	28	50	38

Cutler Marine
Thornham Lane, Emsworth, PO10 8DD
Tel: 01243-375014 **Fax:** 01243-375292
E-mail: john@cutlermarine.com
Website: http://www.cutlermarine.com
Directors: J. Cutler (Prop)
Immediate Holding Company: MULTIHULL WORLD BROKERAGE LIMITED
Registration no: 01999564 **Date established:** 1986
No.of Employees: 1 - 10 **Product Groups:** 35, 36, 39

Date of Accounts	Jun 11	Jun 10	Jun 09
Working Capital	166	121	179
Fixed Assets	4	5	7
Current Assets	265	258	307

Emsworth Yacht Harbour Ltd
Thorney Road, Emsworth, PO10 8BP
Tel: 01243-377727 **Fax:** 01243-373432
E-mail: info@emsworth-marina.co.uk
Website: http://www.emsworth-marina.co.uk
Directors: A. Wakelin (MD)
Ultimate Holding Company: Tarquin Industrial Holdings Ltd
Immediate Holding Company: EMSWORTH YACHT HARBOUR LIMITED
Registration no: 00839408 **VAT No.:** GB 643 2940 42
Date established: 1965 **Turnover:** Up to £250,000
No.of Employees: 1 - 10 **Product Groups:** 71

Date of Accounts	Mar 12	Mar 11	Mar 10
Working Capital	-284	-104	-1m
Fixed Assets	705	718	791
Current Assets	276	281	502

Hyspeed C N C Ltd
Clovelly Road Southbourne, Emsworth, PO10 8PE
Tel: 01243-377751 **Fax:** 01243-377754
E-mail: info@hyspeed.co.uk
Website: http://www.hyspeed.co.uk
Directors: A. Kwiatkowski (Co Sec), G. Francis (MD)
Ultimate Holding Company: UNIVERSAL STEELS AND ALUMINIUM GROUP LIMITED
Immediate Holding Company: HYSPEED (CNC) LIMITED
Registration no: 02866048 **Date established:** 1993 **Turnover:** £1m - £2m
No.of Employees: 21 - 50 **Product Groups:** 33, 46, 48

Date of Accounts	Mar 11	Mar 10	Mar 09
Sales Turnover	2m	2m	4m
Pre Tax Profit/Loss	31	94	1m
Working Capital	507	436	290
Fixed Assets	866	921	1m
Current Assets	1m	762	777
Current Liabilities	94	167	398

J S G Engineering
Units 3-4 Wren Centre Westbourne Road, Emsworth, PO10 7SU
Tel: 01243-379698 **Fax:** 01243-379857
E-mail: jim@jsgeng.fsnet.co.uk
Directors: J. Carpenter (Prop)
VAT No.: GB 582 8296 96 **Turnover:** £250,000 - £500,000
No.of Employees: 1 - 10 **Product Groups:** 48

Microsec Computer Systems
3b The Old Flour Mill Queen Street, Emsworth, PO10 7BT
Tel: 01243-370073 **Fax:** 01243-379997
E-mail: james@microsec.co.uk
Website: http://www.microsec.co.uk
Bank(s): National Westminster
Directors: J. Lavery (Dir), J. Lavery (MD), V. Russell (MD)
Immediate Holding Company: MICROSEC LIMITED
Registration no: 01462783 **VAT No.:** GB 459 5710 17
Date established: 1979 **No.of Employees:** 11 - 20 **Product Groups:** 44, 85

Date of Accounts	Mar 11	Mar 10	Mar 09
Working Capital	125	213	180
Fixed Assets	108	110	107
Current Assets	215	305	252

Morgan Contract Furniture Ltd
Clovelly Road Southbourne, Emsworth, PO10 8PQ
Tel: 01243-371111 **Fax:** 01243-378796
E-mail: info@morganfurniture.co.uk
Website: http://www.morganfurniture.co.uk
Bank(s): Royal Bank of Scotland
Directors: R. Fitch (Dir), R. McMahon (MD)
Managers: M. Shawyer (Buyer)
Immediate Holding Company: MORGAN CONTRACT FURNITURE LIMITED
Registration no: 02985988 **VAT No.:** GB 615 1318 73
Date established: 1994 **Turnover:** £2m - £5m **No.of Employees:** 51 - 100
Product Groups: 26

Date of Accounts	Jun 11	Jun 10	Jun 09
Working Capital	353	162	165
Fixed Assets	210	206	267
Current Assets	1m	842	627

Oyster Marketing & Design Ltd
The Studio 12a North Street, Emsworth, PO10 7DQ
Tel: 01243-389713 **Fax:** 01243-389714
E-mail: sales@oysterdesign.co.uk
Website: http://www.oysterdesign.co.uk
Directors: M. Blatch (Fin)
Immediate Holding Company: OYSTER MARKETING AND DESIGN LIMITED
Registration no: 03912515 **VAT No.:** GB 750 2596 34
Date established: 2000 **Turnover:** £250,000 - £500,000
No.of Employees: 1 - 10 **Product Groups:** 81

Date of Accounts	Jan 12	Jan 11	Jan 10
Working Capital	-13	-6	-5
Fixed Assets	6	8	6
Current Assets	83	75	106

Polytronics Design Ltd
The Old Flour Mill Queen Street, Emsworth, PO10 7BT
Tel: 01243-372207 **Fax:** 01243-379383
E-mail: info@polytronics.co.uk
Website: http://www.polytronics.co.uk
Directors: N. Nelson (Fin)
Immediate Holding Company: POLYTRONICS DESIGN LIMITED
Registration no: 02298023 **VAT No.:** GB 430 6765 55
Date established: 1988 **Turnover:** £500,000 - £1m
No.of Employees: 1 - 10 **Product Groups:** 44, 84, 85

Date of Accounts	Nov 11	Nov 10	Nov 09
Working Capital	178	380	227
Fixed Assets	9	11	12
Current Assets	230	570	342

Ian Porter Sales Ltd
Unit 1b Emsworth Yacht Harbour Thorney Road, Emsworth, PO10 8BP
Tel: 01243-377522
E-mail: sales@porters.org.uk
Website: http://www.porters.org.uk
Directors: I. Porter (Prop)
Immediate Holding Company: IAN PORTER SALES LIMITED
Registration no: 06136936 **VAT No.:** 684 6635 90 **Date established:** 2007
Turnover: £500,000 - £1m **No.of Employees:** 1 - 10 **Product Groups:** 39

Date of Accounts	Feb 12	Feb 11	Feb 09
Working Capital	8	7	11
Fixed Assets	N/A	1	N/A
Current Assets	50	7	59

Reedway Precision Ltd
Park Road, Emsworth, PO10 8QJ
Tel: 01243-376777 **Fax:** 01243-376776
E-mail: sales@reedway.co.uk
Website: http://www.reedway.co.uk
Bank(s): National Westminster

see next page

Reedway Precision Ltd - Cont'd

Directors: M. Treadwell (MD)
Immediate Holding Company: REEDWAY PRECISION LIMITED
Registration no: 02198228 **VAT No.:** GB 108 7022 93
Date established: 1987 **Turnover:** £500,000 - £1m
No.of Employees: 11 - 20 **Product Groups:** 42, 46

Date of Accounts	May 11	May 10	May 09
Working Capital	90	11	40
Fixed Assets	831	890	958
Current Assets	264	171	170

Sequel Glitter Fabrics Ltd

A Chartwell Building Manor Road, Emsworth, PO10 8NX
Tel: 01243-377821 **Fax:** 01243-374052
E-mail: sequelglitter@yahoo.com
Website: http://www.sequelglitterfabrics.co.uk
Bank(s): Barclays
Directors: S. Hewitt (Fin)
Registration no: 02405440 **VAT No.:** GB 543 9803 25
Date established: 1989 **Turnover:** £2m - £5m **No.of Employees:** 11 - 20
Product Groups: 22, 23, 35, 36

Date of Accounts	Dec 07	Dec 06	Dec 05
Sales Turnover	N/A	2766	N/A
Pre Tax Profit/Loss	N/A	304	N/A
Working Capital	268	162	152
Fixed Assets	83	88	92
Current Assets	807	982	620
Current Liabilities	539	821	469
ROCE% (Return on Capital Employed)		121.9	
ROT% (Return on Turnover)		11.0	

Straightpoint UK Ltd

Clovelly Road Southbourne, Emsworth, PO10 8PE
Tel: 01243-378921 **Fax:** 01243-377745
E-mail: sales@straightpoint.com
Website: http://www.straightpoint.com
Bank(s): Barclays
Directors: D. Ayling (MD)
Managers: P. Moody (Sales & Mktg Mg), T. Lowe (Sales Admin)
Registration no: 04031406 **Turnover:** £500,000 - £1m
No.of Employees: 11 - 20 **Product Groups:** 37, 38, 39, 48, 67

Date of Accounts	Jul 10	Jul 09	Jul 08
Working Capital	89	178	181
Fixed Assets	354	224	15
Current Assets	373	352	308

West Sussex Signs

Clovelly Road Southbourne, Emsworth, PO10 8PF
Tel: 01243-377702 **Fax:** 01243-376454
E-mail: info@westsussexsigns.com
Website: http://www.westsussexsigns.co.uk
Managers: G. Turpin (Mgr)
Immediate Holding Company: HYSPEED GROUP LIMITED
Registration no: 02866048 **Date established:** 1993 **Turnover:** £2m - £5m
No.of Employees: 1 - 10 **Product Groups:** 30, 39, 40

Westbournes Steel & Pipe

1 Clovelly Road Southbourne, Emsworth, PO10 8PE
Tel: 01243-376751 **Fax:** 01243-376613
Directors: D. Sawkins (MD)
Date established: 1985 **No.of Employees:** 1 - 10 **Product Groups:** 26, 35

Fareham

Absolute Calibration Ltd

14 Murrills Estate Portchester, Fareham, PO16 9RD
Tel: 023-9232 1712 **Fax:** 023-9221 0034
E-mail: calit@absolute-cal.co.uk
Website: http://www.absolute-cal.co.uk
Bank(s): Barclays
Directors: T. Reid (Sales), G. Mills (I.T. Dir), D. Abbott (MD)
Registration no: 03493012 **VAT No.:** GB 711 7601 64
Turnover: £1m - £2m **No.of Employees:** 21 - 50 **Product Groups:** 37, 38, 39, 44, 67, 85, 86

Date of Accounts	Dec 11	Dec 10	Dec 09
Working Capital	71	82	47
Fixed Assets	281	255	268
Current Assets	309	306	276

Ajay Solutions LLP

52 Cowes Court Frogmore, Fareham, PO14 3DA
Tel: 0845-055 8964
E-mail: jodey@ajaysolutions.co.uk
Website: http://www.ajaysolutions.co.uk
Directors: J. Grist (Dir)
Immediate Holding Company: AJAY SOLUTIONS LLP
Registration no: OC329243 **Date established:** 2007
Turnover: Up to £250,000 **No.of Employees:** 1 - 10 **Product Groups:** 37, 44, 79

Date of Accounts	Jun 11	Jun 10	Jun 09
Sales Turnover	N/A	2	2
Pre Tax Profit/Loss	-1	1	1
Working Capital	-9	-7	-7
Fixed Assets	6	6	6
Current Assets	1	N/A	N/A
Current Liabilities	N/A	7	7

Anderton Structural Repair Service

Unit 10 Axis Park Newgate Lane, Fareham, PO14 1JE
Tel: 01329-285892 **Fax:** 01329-285842
E-mail: vic.anderton@orange.net
Website: http://www.andertonstructural.co.uk
Directors: V. Anderton (Prop)
Immediate Holding Company: ANDERTON STRUCTURAL REPAIR SERVICES LTD
Registration no: 05580110 **Date established:** 2005
No.of Employees: 1 - 10 **Product Groups:** 35

Aspen International Ltd

11 Apple Industrial Estate Whittle Avenue, Fareham, PO15 5SX
Tel: 01489-573888 **Fax:** 01489-584485
E-mail: sales@aspen-international.com
Website: http://www.aspen-international.com
Directors: A. Spencer (MD)
Immediate Holding Company: ASPEN INTERNATIONAL LIMITED
Registration no: 02009376 **Date established:** 1986
No.of Employees: 1 - 10 **Product Groups:** 22, 23, 24, 29, 30, 36, 37, 38, 40

Date of Accounts	Mar 12	Mar 11	Mar 10
Working Capital	384	401	388
Fixed Assets	9	16	13
Current Assets	420	462	440

Astroflame Fire Seals Ltd

Unit 8 The I O Centre Stephenson Road, Fareham, PO15 5RU
Tel: 01329-844500 **Fax:** 01329-844600
E-mail: sales@astroflame.com
Website: http://www.astroflame.com
Directors: P. Kieser (MD)
Immediate Holding Company: ASTROFLAME (FIRESEALS) LIMITED
Registration no: 02981298 **Date established:** 1994
No.of Employees: 1 - 10 **Product Groups:** 30, 32, 33, 36, 39, 40

Date of Accounts	Mar 11	Mar 10	Mar 09
Working Capital	691	313	199
Fixed Assets	1m	2m	1m
Current Assets	2m	1m	993

Automated Cutting Services Ltd

18 Mitchell Close, Fareham, PO15 5SE
Tel: 01489-579144 **Fax:** 01489-575325
E-mail: info@automatedcutting.co.uk
Website: http://www.automatedcutting.co.uk
Directors: S. Verner (Fin)
Immediate Holding Company: AUTOMATED CUTTING SERVICES LIMITED
Registration no: 02307350 **Date established:** 1988
No.of Employees: 1 - 10 **Product Groups:** 24, 27, 45, 48

Date of Accounts	Mar 12	Mar 11	Mar 10
Working Capital	12	26	47
Fixed Assets	19	25	33
Current Assets	48	75	96

B M T Reliability Consultants Ltd

12 Little Park Farm Road, Fareham, PO15 5SU
Tel: 01489-553100 **Fax:** 01489-553101
E-mail: messages@bmtrcl.com
Website: http://www.bmtrcl.com
Directors: M. Long (Co Sec), T. Collins (Mkt Research)
Ultimate Holding Company: BMT GROUP LIMITED
Immediate Holding Company: BMT RELIABILITY CONSULTANTS LIMITED
Registration no: 01636835 **Date established:** 1982 **Turnover:** £2m - £5m
No.of Employees: 21 - 50 **Product Groups:** 44, 84, 86

Date of Accounts	Sep 11	Sep 10	Sep 09
Sales Turnover	3m	3m	3m
Pre Tax Profit/Loss	10	105	138
Working Capital	460	580	850
Fixed Assets	8	8	N/A
Current Assets	1m	1m	1m
Current Liabilities	367	473	310

Barnbrook Systems Ltd

25 Fareham Park Road, Fareham, PO15 6LD
Tel: 01329-847722 **Fax:** 01329-844132
E-mail: sales@barnbrook.co.uk
Website: http://www.barnbrook.co.uk
Bank(s): Barclays, Fareham
Directors: A. Barnett (MD)
Managers: J. Whittingham, J. Moore (Comptroller)
Immediate Holding Company: BARNBROOK SYSTEMS LIMITED
Registration no: 01362146 **VAT No.:** GB 109 0480 92
Date established: 1978 **Turnover:** £1m - £2m **No.of Employees:** 21 - 50
Product Groups: 37, 38

Date of Accounts	Jun 11	Jun 10	Jun 09
Working Capital	1m	961	964
Fixed Assets	60	58	73
Current Assets	1m	1m	1m

Beryl Whitehurst

26-27 High Street, Fareham, PO16 7AE
Tel: 01329-281314
Directors: B. Whitehurst (Prop)
No.of Employees: 1 - 10 **Product Groups:** 37, 67

Building Monitoring Services

Royal House 3 Kingdom Close, Fareham, PO15 5TJ
Tel: 01489-557777 **Fax:** 01489-576910
E-mail: info@bms-ltd.co.uk
Website: http://www.buildingmonitoringservices.co.uk
Managers: D. Eddy (Sales Admin)
Immediate Holding Company: BUILDING MONITORING SERVICES LIMITED
Registration no: 03085722 **Date established:** 1995
Turnover: £250,000 - £500,000 **No.of Employees:** 1 - 10
Product Groups: 84

Date of Accounts	Dec 11	Dec 10	Dec 09
Working Capital	4	-20	-10
Fixed Assets	115	153	117
Current Assets	381	358	322

Claremont Business Environment

Design Studio 2 Quay Side Commerce Centre Lower Quay, Fareham, PO16 0XR
Tel: 01329-220123 **Fax:** 01329-221322
E-mail: graham.smith@claremontgi.com
Website: http://www.claremont-europe.com
Bank(s): National Westminster Bank Plc
Directors: C. Airey (I.T. Dir), A. Mallone (Pers), T. Frankland (Sales), M. Gardner (MD), G. Smith (Dir)
Managers: C. Airey (I.T. Exec), G. Smith (Mgr), A. Clarke (Mktg Serv Mgr)
Immediate Holding Company: DEEP BLUE FINANCIAL LIMITED
Registration no: 03816301 **Date established:** 1999
Turnover: £20m - £50m **No.of Employees:** 101 - 250
Product Groups: 52, 84

Clivet UK

Unit 4 Kingdom Close Segenworth East, Fareham, PO15 5TJ
Tel: 01489-572238 **Fax:** 01489-573033
E-mail: l.joy@clivet-uk.co.uk
Website: http://www.clivet.com
Directors: J. Sheril (Fin), L. Joy (MD), S. Mills (Pers)
Managers: D. Airey
Ultimate Holding Company: CLIVET SPA (ITALY)
Immediate Holding Company: CLIVET UK LIMITED
Registration no: 04285855 **Date established:** 2001 **Turnover:** £2m - £5m
No.of Employees: 11 - 20 **Product Groups:** 66

Date of Accounts	Dec 11	Dec 10	Dec 09
Working Capital	685	650	500
Fixed Assets	6	10	23
Current Assets	1m	1m	1m

Coilmech Transformer Manufacturers

1 Barratt Industrial Park Whittle Avenue, Fareham, PO15 5SL
Tel: 01489-885309 **Fax:** 01489-885309
Directors: T. Masters (Ptnr)
Immediate Holding Company: COILMECH LTD
Registration no: 06201666 **VAT No.:** GB 522 2192 83
Date established: 2007 **Turnover:** £250,000 - £500,000
No.of Employees: 1 - 10 **Product Groups:** 37

Coote Vibratory Co. Ltd

10 The Apex Centre Speedfields Park, Fareham, PO14 1TP
Tel: 01329-287841 **Fax:** 01329-827451
E-mail: andrew@coote-vibratory.co.uk
Website: http://www.coote-vibratory.co.uk
Directors: A. Coote (Dir)
Immediate Holding Company: COOTE VIBRATORY CO. LIMITED
Registration no: 00922275 **VAT No.:** GB 107 3412 09
Date established: 1967 **Turnover:** £250,000 - £500,000
No.of Employees: 1 - 10 **Product Groups:** 42, 45

Date of Accounts	Nov 11	Nov 10	Nov 09
Working Capital	19	5	-8
Fixed Assets	11	9	10
Current Assets	111	85	102

Covidien UK Ltd

4500 Park Way, Fareham, PO15 7NY
Tel: 01329-224000 **Fax:** 01329-220213
E-mail: dave.cox@emea.tycohealthcare.com
Website: http://www.covidien.com
Bank(s): National Westminster Bank Plc
Directors: G. Smith (Tech Serv), D. Reynold (Fin), D. Reynolds (Fin)
Immediate Holding Company: COVIDIEN HEALTHCARE HOLDING UK LIMITED
Registration no: 06927127 **VAT No.:** GB 754 9442 02
Date established: 2009 **Turnover:** £5m - £10m
No.of Employees: 101 - 250 **Product Groups:** 38

Date of Accounts	Sep 11	Sep 10
Pre Tax Profit/Loss	-38	-2m
Working Capital	-1	-596
Fixed Assets	91m	N/A
Current Assets	1	1m

Craft Packs

Unit 3 Axis Park Fort Fareham Industrial Site, Fareham, PO14 1FD
Tel: 01329-238282 **Fax:** 01329-234550
E-mail: sales@craftpacks.co.uk
Website: http://www.craftpacks.co.uk
Directors: V. Wyatt (Snr Part)
Date established: 2005 **No.of Employees:** 1 - 10 **Product Groups:** 33, 38, 49, 64

D Q Global

Unit E2 Fareham Heights, Fareham, PO16 8XT
Tel: 023-9298 8303 **Fax:** 023-9298 8302
E-mail: sales@dqglobal.com
Website: http://www.dqglobal.com
Managers: M. Doyle
Immediate Holding Company: DQ GLOBAL LTD
Registration no: 04995571 **Date established:** 2003
No.of Employees: 1 - 10 **Product Groups:** 44

D W Engineering Services Karcher Agent

34 Earls Road, Fareham, PO16 0RT
Tel: 01329-233147
E-mail: enquiries@dwengineeringservices.co.uk
Website: http://www.dwengineeringservices.co.uk
Directors: D. Wheaton (Prop)
Turnover: Up to £250,000 **No.of Employees:** 1 - 10 **Product Groups:** 40, 44, 52

Data Card Ltd

Forum 3 Parkway, Whiteley, Fareham, PO15 7FH
Tel: 01489-555600 **Fax:** 01489-555601
E-mail: jim_runcie@datacard.com
Website: http://www.datacard.co.uk
Bank(s): National Westminster Bank Plc
Directors: A. Hoskins (Fin), J. Runcie (MD)
Managers: C. Holmes (Personnel)
Ultimate Holding Company: DATACARD CORPORATION (USA)
Immediate Holding Company: DATA CARD INTERNATIONAL LIMITED
Registration no: 00987011 **Date established:** 1970
Turnover: £10m - £20m **No.of Employees:** 51 - 100 **Product Groups:** 30, 44, 81

Date of Accounts	Mar 11	Mar 10	Mar 09
Sales Turnover	15m	18m	21m
Pre Tax Profit/Loss	257	-219	2m
Working Capital	5m	5m	11m
Fixed Assets	776	519	483
Current Assets	9m	9m	15m
Current Liabilities	3m	3m	3m

Dawmec Ltd

Unit 1 Salterns Lane, Fareham, PO16 0SU
Tel: 01329-242000 **Fax:** 01329-821226
E-mail: sales@dawmec.co.uk
Website: http://www.searle.co.uk
Directors: R. Marsden (MD)
Ultimate Holding Company: GEA GROUP AG (GERMANY)
Immediate Holding Company: DAWMEC LIMITED
Registration no: 01824257 **Date established:** 1984 **Turnover:** £2m - £5m
No.of Employees: 1 - 10 **Product Groups:** 40

Date of Accounts	Dec 10	Dec 09	Dec 08
Sales Turnover	5m	4m	3m
Pre Tax Profit/Loss	153	236	-937
Working Capital	533	163	-15
Current Assets	3m	2m	2m
Current Liabilities	121	207	82

Dougland Support Services Ltd
Little Park Farm 11 Little Park Farm Road, Fareham, PO15 5SN
Tel: 01489-574234 **Fax:** 01489-576104
E-mail: info@dougland.co.uk
Website: http://www.dougland.co.uk
Directors: B. Richards (MD), S. Conroy (Sales & Mktg), C. Dickens (Chief Op Offcr)
Managers: R. Smith
Ultimate Holding Company: DOUGLAND HOLDINGS LIMITED
Immediate Holding Company: DOUGLAND SUPPORT SERVICES LTD
Registration no: 02323704 **Date established:** 1988
Turnover: £10m - £20m **No.of Employees:** 11 - 20 **Product Groups:** 52

Date of Accounts	Jul 11	Jul 10	Jul 09
Sales Turnover	13m	13m	16m
Pre Tax Profit/Loss	594	910	117
Working Capital	-6	129	-562
Fixed Assets	1m	1m	1m
Current Assets	3m	2m	3m
Current Liabilities	2m	1m	2m

Drain Centre a division of Wolseley UK
248 Gosport Road, Fareham, PO16 0SS
Tel: 01329-232129 **Fax:** 01329-822368
E-mail: customerservices@wolseley.co.uk
Website: http://www.draincentre.co.uk
Managers: P. Mazgay (District Mgr)
Ultimate Holding Company: GLYNWED INTERNATIONAL
Immediate Holding Company: GLYNWED PIPE SYSTEMS
Registration no: 00636445 **Turnover:** £500m - £1,000m
No.of Employees: 1 - 10 **Product Groups:** 30, 36, 39, 40, 42, 48, 66

Eaton Aerospace Ltd
Abbey Park Southampton Road, Titchfield, Fareham, PO14 4QA
Tel: 01329-853000 **Fax:** 01202-880096
Website: http://www.cobham.com
Directors: J. Nightingale (Co Sec), M. Vincent (Dir)
Ultimate Holding Company: COBHAM PLC
Immediate Holding Company: FLIGHT REFUELLING LIMITED
Registration no: 00293529 **Date established:** 1934
Turnover: £75m - £125m **No.of Employees:** 501 - 1000
Product Groups: 32, 36, 37, 39

Date of Accounts	Dec 11	Dec 10	Dec 09
Sales Turnover	104m	94m	71m
Pre Tax Profit/Loss	14m	18m	4m
Working Capital	79m	62m	79m
Fixed Assets	28m	29m	21m
Current Assets	140m	117m	137m
Current Liabilities	21m	17m	18m

Elan Digital Systems Ltd
Elan House Little Park Farm Road, Fareham, PO15 5SJ
Tel: 01489-579799 **Fax:** 01489-577516
E-mail: melanie.howard@elandigitalsystems.com
Website: http://www.elandigitalsystems.com
Bank(s): Lloyds TSB Bank plc
Directors: A. Bible (MD), M. Howard (Fin), J. Barnard (MD), A. Bible (Ch)
Managers: R. Hall (Sales Prom), F. Davids (Accounts), C. Hadingham (Mktg Serv Mgr), D. Ockwell (Purch Mgr), T. Olech (I.T. Exec)
Ultimate Holding Company: ELAN TRADING LIMITED
Immediate Holding Company: ELAN DIGITAL SYSTEMS LIMITED
Registration no: 01283654 **Date established:** 1976 **Turnover:** £2m - £5m
No.of Employees: 21 - 50 **Product Groups:** 44, 67

Date of Accounts	Nov 10	Nov 09	Nov 08
Working Capital	369	836	1m
Fixed Assets	18	31	34
Current Assets	813	948	2m

Elite Engineering Ltd
1 Davis Way, Fareham, PO14 1JF
Tel: 01329-231435 **Fax:** 01329-822759
E-mail: johnp@eliteeng.com
Website: http://www.elite-eng.co.uk
Bank(s): National Westminster
Directors: J. Pendry (MD), M. Pendry (Fin)
Managers: C. O'Keef (Sales Prom Mgr)
Immediate Holding Company: ELITE ENGINEERING LIMITED
Registration no: 00834906 **VAT No.:** GB 619 9262 10
Date established: 1965 **Turnover:** £2m - £5m **No.of Employees:** 11 - 20
Product Groups: 37, 48

Date of Accounts	Aug 11	Aug 10	Aug 09
Working Capital	285	258	317
Fixed Assets	585	550	546
Current Assets	383	373	397

Elta Fans Ltd
17 Barnes Wallis Road, Fareham, PO15 5ST
Tel: 01489-583044 **Fax:** 01489-566555
E-mail: mailbox@eltafans.co.uk
Website: http://www.eltafans.com
Bank(s): Barclays
Directors: D. Buxton (Fin)
Ultimate Holding Company: ELTA GROUP LIMITED
Immediate Holding Company: ELTA FANS LIMITED
Registration no: 00820750 **VAT No.:** GB 212 1228 27
Date established: 1964 **Turnover:** £2m - £5m **No.of Employees:** 51 - 100
Product Groups: 40

Date of Accounts	Mar 11	Mar 10	Mar 09
Sales Turnover	16m	14m	16m
Pre Tax Profit/Loss	1m	1m	2m
Working Capital	3m	5m	5m
Fixed Assets	3m	3m	3m
Current Assets	8m	8m	7m
Current Liabilities	356	457	606

Environmental Treatment Concept Ltd
7 Funtley Court 19 Funtley Hill, Fareham, PO16 7UY
Tel: 01329-836960 **Fax:** 01329-835406
E-mail: sales@electronicdescaler.com
Website: http://www.electronicdescaler.com
Directors: S. Thompson (MD), B. Thompson (Co Sec)
Immediate Holding Company: ENVIRONMENTAL TREATMENT CONCEPTS LIMITED
Registration no: 02999601 **Date established:** 1994
Turnover: £500,000 - £1m **No.of Employees:** 11 - 20
Product Groups: 37, 40

Date of Accounts	Jun 11	Jun 10	Jun 09
Sales Turnover	N/A	N/A	696
Pre Tax Profit/Loss	N/A	N/A	58
Working Capital	311	326	281
Fixed Assets	25	30	27
Current Assets	374	425	371
Current Liabilities	N/A	N/A	24

Fleinns Medicare Ltd
Dean Farm Estate Wickham Road, Fareham Common, Fareham, PO17 5BN
Tel: 01329-823258 **Fax:** 023-8065 0230
Directors: M. Finn (MD)
Immediate Holding Company: FLEINNS MEDICARE LIMITED
Registration no: 02572898 **Date established:** 1991
No.of Employees: 11 - 20 **Product Groups:** 38, 67

Date of Accounts	Sep 10	Sep 09	Sep 08
Working Capital	224	237	227
Fixed Assets	5	6	12
Current Assets	396	318	372

Fontware Ltd
25 Barnes Wallis Road, Fareham, PO15 5TT
Tel: 01489-505075 **Fax:** 0870-051 5816
E-mail: kevin@fontware.com
Website: http://www.fontware.com
Directors: K. Coolbear (Dir)
Immediate Holding Company: FONTWARE LIMITED
Registration no: 03432815 **VAT No.:** GB 699 4400 90
Date established: 1997 **Turnover:** £500,000 - £1m
No.of Employees: 1 - 10 **Product Groups:** 44

Date of Accounts	Sep 11	Sep 10	Sep 09
Working Capital	-26	-63	-96
Fixed Assets	196	211	222
Current Assets	170	131	106

G S B Specialized Fabrications
Castle Trading Estate, Fareham, PO16 9SF
Tel: 023-9221 0787 **Fax:** 023-9220 1252
Directors: S. Bendell (Prop)
Immediate Holding Company: G S B FABRICATIONS LIMITED
Registration no: 04078471 **Date established:** 2000
No.of Employees: 1 - 10 **Product Groups:** 35

Date of Accounts	Mar 12	Mar 11	Mar 10
Working Capital	-5	3	-6
Fixed Assets	6	7	6
Current Assets	80	107	89

Geest Line
3700 Parkway Whiteley, Fareham, PO15 7AL
Tel: 01489-873550 **Fax:** 01489-873551
E-mail: sales@geest-bananas.co.uk
Website: http://www.geestline.com
Bank(s): Barclays
Directors: B. Cornbert (MD), T. Murphy (Fin)
Managers: C. Roberts (Comptroller)
Immediate Holding Company: GEEST LINE LIMITED
Registration no: 00266840 **Date established:** 1932
Turnover: £20m - £50m **No.of Employees:** 51 - 100 **Product Groups:** 02, 81

Date of Accounts	Jan 10	Dec 08	Dec 07
Sales Turnover	50m	43m	36m
Pre Tax Profit/Loss	-4m	3m	2m
Working Capital	58m	59m	57m
Fixed Assets	3m	2m	2m
Current Assets	72m	71m	65m
Current Liabilities	12m	9m	6m

Gill Engineering Ltd
111 Wickham Road, Fareham, PO16 7HZ
Tel: 01329-221341 **Fax:** 01329-221388
E-mail: gill@ltds.fslife.co.uk
Website: http://www.ltds.fslife.co.uk
Directors: R. Gill (MD)
Immediate Holding Company: GILL ENGINEERING LIMITED
Registration no: 01866004 **VAT No.:** GB 108 7650 46
Date established: 1984 **Turnover:** £500,000 - £1m
No.of Employees: 1 - 10 **Product Groups:** 40, 46, 48

Date of Accounts	Dec 11	Dec 10	Dec 09
Working Capital	403	411	432
Fixed Assets	526	569	613
Current Assets	456	440	462

H P Hydraulics Ltd
Unit 2 Davis Way, Fareham, PO14 1JF
Tel: 01329-828877 **Fax:** 01329-822277
E-mail: denise@hphydraulics.uk.net
Website: http://www.hydraulicengineeringuk.com
Directors: N. Howes (Dir)
Managers: A. Jefferies
Registration no: 03025390 **Turnover:** £500,000 - £1m
No.of Employees: 1 - 10 **Product Groups:** 35, 39, 40, 45, 48, 67

Date of Accounts	Jun 11	Jun 10	Jun 09
Working Capital	348	280	264
Fixed Assets	46	27	42
Current Assets	644	578	489

Hampshire Sewing Machines
122-124 West Street, Fareham, PO16 0EP
Tel: 01329-280499 **Fax:** 01329-280499
E-mail: support@hampshiresewingmachines.com
Website: http://www.hampshiresewingmachines.com
Directors: P. Catchpole (Prop), P. Catchpole (MD)
Managers: S. Catchpole
No.of Employees: 1 - 10 **Product Groups:** 35, 37, 43, 48

Industrial Boilerhouse Supplies Ltd
Unit 34 Brunel Way Segensworth East, Fareham, PO15 5SF
Tel: 01489-570737 **Fax:** 01489-570767
E-mail: info@ibhs.co.uk
Website: http://www.ibhs.co.uk
Directors: D. Holland (MD)
Immediate Holding Company: INDUSTRIAL BOILERHOUSE SUPPLIES LIMITED
Registration no: 02803457 **Date established:** 1993
No.of Employees: 11 - 20 **Product Groups:** 18, 27, 29, 30, 31, 32, 33, 34, 35, 36, 37, 38, 39, 40, 41, 42, 45, 46, 48, 49, 66, 67

Date of Accounts	Dec 11	Dec 10	Dec 09
Working Capital	1m	990	798
Fixed Assets	43	40	32
Current Assets	2m	2m	1m

Innovation Mouldings
Unit C Site 6 Fort Fareham Industrial Site, Fareham, PO14 1AH
Tel: 01329-234848 **Fax:** 01329-234848
E-mail: innovationmouldings@tiscali.co.uk
Directors: A. Crook (Ptnr)
Immediate Holding Company: THE CERTUS PARTNERSHIP LLP
Date established: 2003 **Turnover:** £1m - £2m **No.of Employees:** 11 - 20
Product Groups: 30, 33

Date of Accounts	Apr 11	Apr 10	Apr 09
Working Capital	50	52	-3
Fixed Assets	3	1	195
Current Assets	108	123	96

Intamet Ltd
Unit 11 The I O Centre Stephenson Road, Fareham, PO15 5RU
Tel: 01329-843355 **Fax:** 01329-847799
E-mail: sales@intamet.co.uk
Website: http://www.intamet.co.uk
Directors: G. Rowe (MD), N. Rowe (Fin)
Immediate Holding Company: INTAMET LIMITED
Registration no: 03488193 **VAT No.:** GB 704 5627 45
Date established: 1998 **Turnover:** £2m - £5m **No.of Employees:** 1 - 10
Product Groups: 34, 35, 36, 66

Date of Accounts	Apr 12	Apr 11	Apr 10
Working Capital	878	948	833
Fixed Assets	143	149	63
Current Assets	2m	2m	1m

Intereurope Ltd
21-23 East Street, Fareham, PO16 0BZ
Tel: 01329-823047 **Fax:** 01329-822058
Website: http://www.intereurope.com
Bank(s): National Westminster Bank Plc & HSBC Bank plc
Directors: R. Rubio (MD), D. Immanuel (Fin)
Ultimate Holding Company: RIDGMOUNT HOLDINGS LIMITED
Immediate Holding Company: INTEREUROPE LIMITED
Registration no: 01010935 **VAT No.:** GB 199 2836 38
Date established: 1971 **Turnover:** £10m - £20m
No.of Employees: 21 - 50 **Product Groups:** 37, 44, 48, 67, 80

Date of Accounts	Jun 11	Jun 10	Jun 09
Working Capital	2m	2m	2m
Fixed Assets	928	949	966
Current Assets	3m	2m	3m

Kayospruce Ltd
2 Cockerell Close, Fareham, PO15 5SR
Tel: 01489-581696 **Fax:** 01489-573489
E-mail: kayospruce@sailcloth.co.uk
Website: http://www.kayospruce.com
Bank(s): Lloyds
Directors: I. Dawson (MD)
Managers: J. Parry
Immediate Holding Company: KAYOSPRUCE LIMITED
Registration no: 01709530 **VAT No.:** 380 9825 21 **Date established:** 1983
Turnover: £2m - £5m **No.of Employees:** 21 - 50 **Product Groups:** 22, 23, 24, 27, 30, 35, 36, 39, 49, 63, 66, 83

Date of Accounts	Nov 11	Nov 10	Nov 09
Working Capital	1m	1m	1m
Fixed Assets	176	180	168
Current Assets	2m	2m	2m

Kern Ltd
Unit 5 Concorde Close, Fareham, PO15 5RT
Tel: 01489-564141 **Fax:** 01489-565009
E-mail: info@kern.co.uk
Website: http://www.kern.co.uk
Directors: U. Kern (Comm)
Ultimate Holding Company: KERN AG (SWITZERLAND)
Immediate Holding Company: KERN LIMITED
Registration no: 01727919 **VAT No.:** GB 341 3590 74
Date established: 1983 **Turnover:** £5m - £10m **No.of Employees:** 21 - 50
Product Groups: 37, 44, 61, 79, 81, 84

Date of Accounts	Dec 11	Dec 10	Dec 09
Sales Turnover	9m	8m	8m
Pre Tax Profit/Loss	-470	-873	-770
Working Capital	3m	3m	3m
Fixed Assets	204	229	256
Current Assets	6m	7m	7m
Current Liabilities	1m	2m	1m

Kooltech Ltd
9 Standard Way, Fareham, PO16 8XB
Tel: 01329-231166
Website: http://www.kooltech.co.uk
Managers: D. Brown (Mgr)
Immediate Holding Company: KOOLTECH LIMITED
Registration no: SC293806 **Date established:** 2005
Turnover: £5m - £10m **No.of Employees:** 11 - 20 **Product Groups:** 40, 66

Date of Accounts	Oct 11	Oct 10	Oct 09
Sales Turnover	22m	21m	22m
Pre Tax Profit/Loss	252	214	97
Working Capital	885	644	440
Fixed Assets	878	1m	1m
Current Assets	8m	8m	9m
Current Liabilities	787	831	576

Lightdome Road Products
4 Fielder Drive, Fareham, PO14 1JE
Tel: 01329-284780 **Fax:** 01329-829485
E-mail: sales@lightdome.co.uk
Website: http://www.lightdome.co.uk
Directors: S. Vine (Comm)
Ultimate Holding Company: INDUSTRIAL RUBBER LIMITED
Immediate Holding Company: LIGHT-DOME ROAD MARKER INSERTS LIMITED
Registration no: 02999953 **Date established:** 1994
No.of Employees: 1 - 10 **Product Groups:** 29, 33, 39, 51

Date of Accounts	Sep 10	Sep 09	Sep 02
Working Capital	238	238	462
Current Assets	238	238	462

London Emblem Plc "All About Badges"
Unit 9 Apex Centre Speedfields Park, Newgate Lane, Fareham, PO14 1TP
Tel: 01329-822900 **Fax:** 01329-829000
E-mail: suem@londonemblem.com
Website: http://www.allaboutbadges.com

see next page

London Emblem Plc "All About Badges" - *Cont'd*
Directors: S. Morse (Sales), D. Bane (Dir)
Managers: D. Daw (Sales Off Mgr)
Ultimate Holding Company: London Emblem PLC
Registration no: 04696549 **VAT No.:** GB 812 0562 69
Turnover: £1m - £2m **No.of Employees:** 1 - 10 **Product Groups:** 23, 30, 35, 42, 46, 49, 67

Lynq Ltd
5 The Potteries Wickham Road, Fareham, PO16 7ET
Tel: 01329-800000 **Fax:** 023-9227 1009
E-mail: sales@lynq.co.uk
Website: http://www.lynq.co.uk
Bank(s): Bank of Scotland
Managers: J. Grima (Sales Prom Mgr)
Immediate Holding Company: LYNQ LIMITED
Registration no: 01541402 **VAT No.:** GB 322 0824 01
Date established: 1981 **Turnover:** £1m - £2m **No.of Employees:** 11 - 20
Product Groups: 44

Date of Accounts	Apr 11	Apr 10	Apr 09
Working Capital	303	131	86
Fixed Assets	33	81	86
Current Assets	518	280	227

Meggitt Avionics
7 Whittle Avenue, Fareham, PO15 5SH
Tel: 01489-483300 **Fax:** 01489-564092
E-mail: richard.greaves@meggitt.com
Website: http://www.meggitt-avionics.co.uk
Directors: R. Greaves (MD), S. Watson (Fin), S. Watson (Fin)
Managers: C. Butler (Mktg Serv Mgr), J. Morgan (Comm), A. Hughes (I.T. Exec), R. Tobin
Ultimate Holding Company: MEGGITT P.L.C.
Immediate Holding Company: MEGGITT UK LTD
Registration no: 00629814 **VAT No.:** GB 452 4031 84
Date established: 1947 **Turnover:** £20m - £50m
No.of Employees: 251 - 500 **Product Groups:** 39

O K W Enclosures Ltd
15 Brunel Way, Fareham, PO15 5TX
Tel: 01489-583858 **Fax:** 01489-583836
E-mail: sales@okw.co.uk
Website: http://www.okw.co.uk
Bank(s): HSBC Bank plc
Directors: R. Cox (Dir), M. Hedges (MD), M. Hedges (Co Sec)
Ultimate Holding Company: Odenwalder Kunststoffwerke GmbH & Co. (Germany)
Immediate Holding Company: OKW ENCLOSURES LIMITED
Registration no: 02125249 **Date established:** 1987 **Turnover:** £1m - £2m
No.of Employees: 11 - 20 **Product Groups:** 26, 30, 35, 37

Date of Accounts	Apr 12	Apr 11	Apr 10
Working Capital	332	236	227
Fixed Assets	2m	2m	2m
Current Assets	1m	922	852

PCI Membranes
Unit H Victory Park Solent Way, Whiteley, Fareham, PO15 7FN
Tel: 01256-303800 **Fax:** 01256-303801
E-mail: pcimembranes@itt.com
Website: http://www.pcimembranes.com
Bank(s): National Westminster Bank Plc
Managers: D. Reed (), I. Sadler (Sales Prom Mgr)
Ultimate Holding Company: ITT Corporation
VAT No.: GB 803 9247 38 **Turnover:** £2m - £5m **No.of Employees:** 21 - 50
Product Groups: 41, 42

Pains Wessex Ltd
Chemring House 1500 Parkway, Whiteley, Fareham, PO15 7AF
Tel: 01489-884130 **Fax:** 01489-884131
E-mail: info@chemringmarine.com
Website: http://www.pwss.com
Bank(s): National Westminster, Portsmouth
Directors: P. Cutler (Tech Serv), R. Hill (MD), M. Aslett (MD), J. Heeley (MD)
Ultimate Holding Company: CHEMRING GROUP PLC
Immediate Holding Company: PAINS WESSEX LIMITED
Registration no: 01975276 **VAT No.:** GB 188 7079 08
Date established: 1986 **Turnover:** £20m - £50m
No.of Employees: 11 - 20 **Product Groups:** 32, 36, 37, 39

Palmer & Harvey Ltd
11 Barnes Wallis Road, Fareham, PO15 5TT
Tel: 01489-555800 **Fax:** 01489-555883
E-mail: graham.barton@palmerharvey.co.uk
Website: http://www.palmerharvey.co.uk
Bank(s): National Westminster
Directors: G. Barton (Dir)
Ultimate Holding Company: PALMER & HARVEY (HOLDINGS) PLC
Immediate Holding Company: PALMER & HARVEY LIMITED
Registration no: 02815232 **VAT No.:** GB 188 7246 15
Date established: 1993 **Turnover:** £50m - £75m
No.of Employees: 251 - 500 **Product Groups:** 52

Date of Accounts	Apr 12	Apr 11
Working Capital	N/A	7m
Current Assets	N/A	7m

Panda Diesel Injection
4 Bridge Industries, Fareham, PO16 8SX
Tel: 01329-310099 **Fax:** 01329-232822
Directors: M. Barfoot (Prop)
Date established: 1973 **No.of Employees:** 1 - 10 **Product Groups:** 40

Pennant Information Services Ltd
Units 4 & 5 Dartmouth Buildings Fort Fareham Industrial Estate, Newgate Lane, Fareham, PO14 1AH
Tel: 01329-226300 **Fax:** 01329-226301
E-mail: sales@pennantplc.co.uk
Website: http://www.pennantplc.co.uk
Directors: C. Mair (Sales & Mktg)
Ultimate Holding Company: O M I International P.L.C.
Registration no: 03782911 **Date established:** 1948 **Turnover:** £5m - £10m
No.of Employees: 51 - 100 **Product Groups:** 44, 84

Phoenix Systems UK Ltd
48 Standard Way, Fareham, PO16 8XQ
Tel: 01329-230530 **Fax:** 0845-658 6222
E-mail: sales@phoenixsystemsuk.com
Website: http://www.phoenixsystemsuk.com
Directors: N. Hobden (Fin), S. Jacobs (Dir), S. Jacobs (MD)
Managers: S. Miandashti
Immediate Holding Company: PHOENIX SYSTEMS UK LIMITED
Registration no: 04356233 **Date established:** 2002 **Turnover:** £1m - £2m
No.of Employees: 21 - 50 **Product Groups:** 32, 37, 40, 48, 67

Date of Accounts	Feb 12	Feb 11	Feb 10
Working Capital	216	154	133
Fixed Assets	135	170	220
Current Assets	2m	2m	1m
Current Liabilities	974	N/A	N/A

Pipe Center
Unit D3 Premier Business Centre Speedfields Park, Fareham, PO14 1TY
Tel: 01329-237215 **Fax:** 01329-823641
E-mail: k73.fareham@wolseley.co.uk
Website: http://www.pipecenter.co.uk
Managers: M. Streeter (Mgr)
Immediate Holding Company: GREEN MAGNET LIMITED
Registration no: 03244411 **Date established:** 2008
No.of Employees: 1 - 10 **Product Groups:** 30, 34, 35, 36, 40

Date of Accounts	Jun 11	Jun 10	Jun 09
Sales Turnover	87m	96m	96m
Pre Tax Profit/Loss	-2m	5m	5m
Working Capital	-2m	1m	4m
Fixed Assets	36m	34m	26m
Current Assets	34m	33m	45m
Current Liabilities	9m	7m	9m

Portsdown Engineering Sales
69 Hill Road, Portchester, Fareham, PO16 8JZ
Tel: 023-9221 4879 **Fax:** 01329-232244
E-mail: portsdown1@googlemail.com
Website: http://www.portsdownengineering.co.uk
Directors: W. Williamson (MD)
Immediate Holding Company: Portsdown Engineering Ltd
Registration no: 06623789 **VAT No.:** GB 108 8641 60
Date established: 2008 **Turnover:** £500,000 - £1m
No.of Employees: 1 - 10 **Product Groups:** 42, 45

Prosig Ltd
44a High Street, Fareham, PO16 7BQ
Tel: 01329-239925 **Fax:** 01329-239159
E-mail: chris.mason@prosig.com
Website: http://www.prosig.com
Bank(s): Lloyds TSB Bank plc
Directors: C. Mason (Dir)
Immediate Holding Company: PROSIG LIMITED
Registration no: 01336698 **VAT No.:** GB 293 6561 27
Date established: 1977 **Turnover:** £2m - £5m **No.of Employees:** 11 - 20
Product Groups: 44

Date of Accounts	Oct 11	Oct 10	Oct 09
Working Capital	730	647	469
Fixed Assets	1m	1m	1m
Current Assets	1m	975	803

R J C Refrigeration
Unit 4 The I O Centre Stephenson Road, Fareham, PO15 5RU
Tel: 01329-847358 **Fax:** 03129-847658
E-mail: ryan.goodyear@rjcltd.com
Website: http://www.rjcltd.com
Directors: R. Cawte (MD)
Immediate Holding Company: R.J.C. REFRIGERATION & AIR CONDITIONING LTD
Registration no: 03438130 **Date established:** 1997 **Turnover:** £1m - £2m
No.of Employees: 21 - 50 **Product Groups:** 29, 36, 38, 39, 40, 52, 66, 83, 84

Date of Accounts	Sep 11	Sep 10	Sep 09
Working Capital	49	334	383
Fixed Assets	227	276	329
Current Assets	1m	1m	931

Robinson Read Ltd
3600 Parkway Whiteley, Fareham, PO15 7AN
Tel: 01489-579911 **Fax:** 01489-579933
E-mail: sales@robinsonreade.co.uk
Website: http://www.robinsonread.com
Directors: J. Burmingham (Dir), J. Earley (Fin)
Immediate Holding Company: ROBINSON READE LIMITED
Registration no: 05185152 **Date established:** 2004
No.of Employees: 1 - 10 **Product Groups:** 80

Date of Accounts	Jul 11	Jul 10	Jul 09
Working Capital	30	53	56
Fixed Assets	8	9	5
Current Assets	72	97	87

Searle Manufacturing
20 Davies Way, Fareham, PO14 1AR
Tel: 01329-822222 **Fax:** 01329-821238
E-mail: sales@searle.co.uk
Website: http://www.searle.co.uk
Bank(s): Lloyds TSB Bank plc
Directors: N. Stephenson (Fin), M. Reed (Dir), D. Gillett (MD), J. Williams (Co Sec)
Managers: A. Hamilton (Buyer), J. Christopher (Mktg Serv Mgr), S. Armitage (Sales Prom Mgr)
Ultimate Holding Company: GEA GROUP AG (GERMANY)
Immediate Holding Company: BLISS & CO. LIMITED
Registration no: 00139788 **Date established:** 2002
No.of Employees: 251 - 500 **Product Groups:** 36, 38, 40

Date of Accounts	Dec 10	Dec 09	Dec 08
Sales Turnover	N/A	N/A	38
Pre Tax Profit/Loss	1m	1m	35
Working Capital	2m	2m	2m
Fixed Assets	750	750	750
Current Assets	2m	2m	2m

Selectron Ltd
1 Davis Way, Fareham, PO14 1JF
Tel: 01329-230525 **Fax:** 01329-822759
E-mail: sales@solectron-ltd.co.uk
Website: http://www.elite-eng.co.uk
Directors: M. Pendry (Dir)
Managers: C. O'Keefe (Sales Prom Mgr)
Ultimate Holding Company: ELITE ENGINEERING LIMITED
Immediate Holding Company: SOLECTRON LIMITED
Registration no: 01884386 **Date established:** 1985 **Turnover:** £1m - £2m
No.of Employees: 21 - 50 **Product Groups:** 37, 48

Date of Accounts	Aug 11	Aug 10	Aug 09
Working Capital	27	25	22
Fixed Assets	N/A	4	8
Current Assets	36	43	30

Solent Roof Trusses Ltd Gang-Nail Systems Ltd
2 Crompton Way Segensworth West, Fareham, PO15 5SS
Tel: 01489-578344 **Fax:** 01489-579485
Website: http://www.solentrooftrusses.com
Directors: K. Kian (Fin)
Immediate Holding Company: SOLENT TRUSSES LIMITED
Registration no: 02852716 **Date established:** 1993
No.of Employees: 1 - 10 **Product Groups:** 35, 66

Date of Accounts	Feb 08	Feb 11	Feb 10
Working Capital	680	605	611
Fixed Assets	263	248	257
Current Assets	706	632	638

Solent Welding & Fabrication Ltd
1 Shogun House Newgate Lane Industrial Estate, Fareham, PO14 1JF
Tel: 01329-823535
E-mail: solent@live.co.uk
Directors: T. Barker (Dir)
Immediate Holding Company: SOLENT WELDING & FABRICATION LIMITED
Registration no: 06733471 **Date established:** 2008
No.of Employees: 1 - 10 **Product Groups:** 35

Date of Accounts	Oct 11	Oct 10	Oct 09
Working Capital	-3	N/A	-4
Fixed Assets	4	N/A	N/A
Current Assets	44	50	32

Southern Belting Ltd
Unit 4-5 Pennant Park Standard Way, Fareham, PO16 8XU
Tel: 01329-822929 **Fax:** 01329-825445
E-mail: sales@southern-belting.co.uk
Website: http://www.southern-belting.co.uk
Directors: G. Bishop (Dir)
Immediate Holding Company: SOUTHERN BELTING LIMITED
Registration no: 00939044 **Date established:** 1968 **Turnover:** £2m - £5m
No.of Employees: 11 - 20 **Product Groups:** 22, 23, 29, 30, 32, 33, 35, 39, 40

Date of Accounts	Sep 11	Sep 10	Sep 09
Working Capital	649	674	701
Fixed Assets	46	46	69
Current Assets	744	755	780

Synergy Connections Ltd
189-199 West Street, Fareham, PO16 0EN
Tel: 01329-229300 **Fax:** 01329-229301
E-mail: enquiries@synergyconnections.co.uk
Website: http://www.synergyconnections.co.uk
Directors: G. Curran (MD)
Immediate Holding Company: SYNERGY CONNECTIONS LIMITED
Registration no: 03495785 **Date established:** 1998
Turnover: £500,000 - £1m **No.of Employees:** 21 - 50
Product Groups: 61, 80, 81

Date of Accounts	Dec 09	Dec 08	Dec 07
Working Capital	159	-2	-44
Fixed Assets	60	69	77
Current Assets	159	267	147

T U V Product Service
Octagon House Concorde Way, Fareham, PO15 5RL
Tel: 01489-558100 **Fax:** 01489-558101
E-mail: info@tuvps.co.uk
Website: http://www.tuvps.co.uk
Directors: C. Ormerod (Co Sec), J. Evans (Dir)
Ultimate Holding Company: TUV SUDDEUTSCHLAND AG (GERMANY)
Immediate Holding Company: TUV SUD SERVICES (UK) LIMITED
Registration no: 00560225 **Date established:** 1956
Turnover: £10m - £20m **No.of Employees:** 101 - 250
Product Groups: 37, 48, 51, 54, 84, 85, 88

Date of Accounts	Dec 11	Dec 10	Dec 09
Sales Turnover	16m	12m	11m
Pre Tax Profit/Loss	1m	795	677
Working Capital	-2m	-899	N/A
Fixed Assets	10m	11m	8m
Current Assets	5m	5m	3m
Current Liabilities	1m	1m	997

Talana Plastics Holdings Ltd
28 Standard Way Fareham Industrial Park, Fareham, PO16 8XG
Tel: 01329-822940 **Fax:** 01329-231034
E-mail: enquiries@talanaplastics.com
Website: http://www.talanaplastics.com
Directors: I. Hunter (Dir)
Ultimate Holding Company: HWH HOLDINGS LIMITED
Immediate Holding Company: HWH HOLDINGS LIMITED
Registration no: 06812549 **VAT No.:** GB 459 6603 13
Date established: 2009 **Turnover:** £2m - £5m **No.of Employees:** 1 - 10
Product Groups: 30

Date of Accounts	Oct 11	Oct 10	Oct 09
Working Capital	6	6	N/A
Current Assets	9	9	N/A

Telsis Ltd
16-18 Barnes Wallis Road, Fareham, PO15 5TT
Tel: 01489-760000 **Fax:** 01489-885826
E-mail: info@telsis.com
Website: http://www.telsis.com
Bank(s): Lloyds
Directors: R. Webb (Dir)
Managers: S. Claxton (Buyer), N. Bath
Ultimate Holding Company: TELSIS GROUP LIMITED
Immediate Holding Company: TELSIS LIMITED
Registration no: 02556809 **Date established:** 1990 **Turnover:** £2m - £5m
No.of Employees: 51 - 100 **Product Groups:** 37, 44, 67

Date of Accounts	Dec 11	Dec 10	Dec 09
Sales Turnover	2m	4m	3m
Pre Tax Profit/Loss	-975	-1m	-4m
Working Capital	-3m	-3m	-2m
Fixed Assets	4m	4m	583
Current Assets	3m	5m	4m
Current Liabilities	702	1m	696

Timberwise UK Ltd
19 Eagle Close, Fareham, PO16 8QX
Tel: 01329-826737 **Fax:** 01329-510186
E-mail: fareham@timberwise.co.uk
Website: http://www.timberwise.co.uk

Ultimate Holding Company: TIMBERWISE HOLDINGS LIMITED
Immediate Holding Company: TIMBERWISE (UK) LIMITED
Registration no: 03230356 **Date established:** 1996
No.of Employees: 1 - 10 **Product Groups:** 07, 32, 52

Date of Accounts	Dec 11	Dec 10	Dec 09
Sales Turnover	N/A	N/A	5m
Pre Tax Profit/Loss	N/A	N/A	214
Working Capital	397	343	326
Fixed Assets	265	291	301
Current Assets	1m	1m	1m
Current Liabilities	N/A	N/A	585

Turbocam Europe Ltd

Unit 1 155 Highlands Road, Fareham, PO15 6JR
Tel: 01329-845800 **Fax:** 01329-846000
E-mail: uk@turbocam.com
Website: http://www.turbocam.com
Bank(s): Barclays
Directors: R. Taylor (MD), A. Taylor (Co Sec)
Immediate Holding Company: TURBOCAM EUROPE LIMITED
Registration no: 02548769 **VAT No.:** GB 571 8772 06
Date established: 1990 **Turnover:** £2m - £5m **No.of Employees:** 21 - 50
Product Groups: 39, 40, 45, 48, 49

Date of Accounts	Mar 11	Mar 10	Mar 09
Working Capital	-40	-7	-96
Fixed Assets	1m	1m	1m
Current Assets	957	1m	825

Turbomeca Ltd

Concorde Way, Fareham, PO15 5RL
Tel: 01489-564848 **Fax:** 01489-563905
E-mail: michael.risdon@microturbo.co.uk
Website: http://www.microturbo.co.uk
Bank(s): HSBC
Directors: M. Risdon (Fin)
Ultimate Holding Company: SAFRAN SA (FRANCE)
Immediate Holding Company: TURBOMECA UK LIMITED
Registration no: 01148466 **VAT No.:** GB 108 4823 74
Date established: 1973 **Turnover:** £50m - £75m
No.of Employees: 101 - 250 **Product Groups:** 37, 39

Date of Accounts	Dec 08
Sales Turnover	59m
Pre Tax Profit/Loss	3m
Working Capital	8m
Fixed Assets	9m
Current Assets	37m
Current Liabilities	9m

Valvestock Pipe Center

Shogun House 2 Fielder Drive, Fareham, PO14 1JG
Tel: 01329-283425 **Fax:** 01329-822741
E-mail: enquiries@valvestock.co.uk
Website: http://www.valvestock.co.uk
Bank(s): HSBC Bank plc
Managers: M. Sampson
Immediate Holding Company: WOLSELEY CENTERS LTD
Registration no: 636445 **VAT No.:** GB 100 5835 13 **Date established:** 1974
Turnover: £5m - £10m **No.of Employees:** 21 - 50 **Product Groups:** 35, 36, 38, 40

W R Refrigeration Ltd

Unit H2 Knowle Village Business Park Mayles Lane, Knowle, Fareham, PO17 5DY
Tel: 01329-834029 **Fax:** 01329-836886
Bank(s): Midland
Managers: R. Craigie
Ultimate Holding Company: HUURRE GROUP OY (FINLAND)
Immediate Holding Company: WR REFRIGERATION LIMITED
Registration no: 00594746 **Date established:** 1957
No.of Employees: 11 - 20 **Product Groups:** 84

Date of Accounts	Dec 11	Dec 10	Dec 09
Sales Turnover	45m	44m	57m
Pre Tax Profit/Loss	412	-2m	1m
Working Capital	29m	21m	23m
Fixed Assets	3m	4m	3m
Current Assets	52m	45m	36m
Current Liabilities	4m	2m	2m

Walcon Marine Ltd

Cockerell Close Segensworth West, Fareham, PO15 5SR
Tel: 01489-579977 **Fax:** 01489-579988
E-mail: sales@walconmarine.com
Website: http://www.walconmarine.com
Bank(s): National Westminster
Directors: J. Walters (MD)
Immediate Holding Company: WALCON LIMITED
Registration no: 00764785 **VAT No.:** GB 522 4934 55
Date established: 1963 **Turnover:** £10m - £20m
No.of Employees: 21 - 50 **Product Groups:** 51, 84

Date of Accounts	Apr 11	Apr 10	Apr 09
Sales Turnover	15m	9m	13m
Pre Tax Profit/Loss	254	506	181
Working Capital	622	579	244
Fixed Assets	4m	4m	5m
Current Assets	4m	3m	4m
Current Liabilities	946	1m	1m

Wickham Laboratories Ltd

Winchester Road Wickham, Fareham, PO17 5EU
Tel: 01329-832511 **Fax:** 01329-834262
E-mail: mail@wickhamlabs.co.uk
Website: http://www.wickhamlabs.co.uk
Directors: C. Bishop (Tech Serv), W. Cartmell (MD)
Immediate Holding Company: WICKHAM LABORATORIES LIMITED
Registration no: 00752951 **VAT No.:** GB 109 0902 07
Date established: 1963 **Turnover:** £1m - £2m **No.of Employees:** 1 - 10
Product Groups: 80, 84, 85, 88

Date of Accounts	Mar 11	Mar 10	Mar 09
Working Capital	-1m	460	404
Fixed Assets	3m	1m	1m
Current Assets	1m	948	1m
Current Liabilities	938	N/A	N/A

Xylem

Unit 11 Fulcrum 2 Solent Way, Whiteley, Fareham, PO15 7FN
Tel: 01489-563470 **Fax:** 01489-563471
E-mail: info@totton-pumps.com
Website: http://www.itt.com

Managers: P. Wright (Mgr)
Immediate Holding Company: BEECHBROOK PROPERTIES LIMITED
Registration no: 00814151 **Date established:** 1999
No.of Employees: 11 - 20 **Product Groups:** 40, 46

Date of Accounts	May 11	May 10	May 09
Working Capital	-83	-80	-92
Fixed Assets	439	437	437
Current Assets	61	61	62

Farnborough

A V M Ltd

6 Hawley Lane Industrial Estate Hawley Lane, Farnborough, GU14 8EH
Tel: 01252-510363 **Fax:** 01252-519874
E-mail: sales@avmltd.co.uk
Website: http://www.avmltd.co.uk
Bank(s): Midland
Directors: R. Allpress (Fin), M. Nisbet (MD)
Immediate Holding Company: AVM LIMITED
Registration no: 05659631 **VAT No.:** GB 211 4678 84
Date established: 2005 **Turnover:** £2m - £5m **No.of Employees:** 11 - 20
Product Groups: 83

Date of Accounts	Jun 11	Jun 10	Jun 09
Sales Turnover	36m	35m	39m
Pre Tax Profit/Loss	388	197	-313
Working Capital	-511	-2m	-775
Fixed Assets	9m	8m	9m
Current Assets	10m	6m	8m
Current Liabilities	5m	3m	4m

Airside GSE

Shieling House 30 Invincible Road Industrial Estate, Farnborough, GU14 7QU
Tel: 01252-372555 **Fax:** 01252-517512
E-mail: airsideairporteq@btconnect.com
Website: http://www.airsidegseltd.com
Directors: M. Cardy (Dir)
Immediate Holding Company: AIRSIDE GSE LIMITED
Registration no: 04804481 **Date established:** 2003
No.of Employees: 1 - 10 **Product Groups:** 39, 45, 67

Date of Accounts	Mar 12	Mar 11	Mar 10
Working Capital	148	54	66
Fixed Assets	18	20	11
Current Assets	397	142	128

Analytical Technologies Ltd

Lynchford House Lynchford Lane, Farnborough, GU14 6JB
Tel: 01252-514711 **Fax:** 01252-511855
E-mail: analyticaltechnologies@aol.com
Directors: J. Watcham (MD), J. Elliott (Fin)
Managers: C. Plows (Sales & Mktg Mg)
Ultimate Holding Company: FP010633
Immediate Holding Company: ANALYTICAL TECHNOLOGIES LIMITED
Registration no: 03162350 **Date established:** 1996 **Turnover:** £1m - £2m
No.of Employees: 1 - 10 **Product Groups:** 28, 31, 38, 42

Atex Equipment

17 Hercules Way, Farnborough, GU14 6UU
Tel: 01252-510550 **Fax:** 01252-373596
E-mail: info@atexequipment.com
Website: http://www.atexequipment.com
Directors: R. Hunt (MD)
Ultimate Holding Company: AATTITUDE LTD
Immediate Holding Company: ATEX EQUIPMENT LTD
Registration no: 03709011 **Date established:** 1999
No.of Employees: 1 - 10 **Product Groups:** 37, 40, 48, 52, 85

Date of Accounts	Jul 11	Jul 10	Jul 09
Working Capital	136	92	50
Fixed Assets	8	13	7
Current Assets	252	428	136

Autodesk Ltd

1 Columbus Drive Southwood Business Park, Farnborough, GU14 0NZ
Tel: 01252-456600 **Fax:** 01252-456601
E-mail: info@autodesk.com
Website: http://www.autodesk.com
Directors: J. O Donnell (Co Sec)
Managers: M. Gall (Mktg Serv Mgr), D. Bourne (Sales Admin), D. Chilvers (Personnel)
Ultimate Holding Company: AUTODESK INC (USA)
Immediate Holding Company: AUTODESK LIMITED
Registration no: 01839239 **Date established:** 1984
Turnover: £20m - £50m **No.of Employees:** 101 - 250 **Product Groups:** 44

Date of Accounts	Jan 11	Jan 10	Jan 09
Sales Turnover	35m	31m	37m
Pre Tax Profit/Loss	3m	2m	875
Working Capital	12m	8m	8m
Fixed Assets	8m	8m	8m
Current Assets	19m	12m	13m
Current Liabilities	6m	4m	5m

Canada Wood UK

PO Box 9, Farnborough, GU14 6WE
Tel: 01252-522545 **Fax:** 01252-522546
E-mail: office@canadawooduk.org
Website: http://www.canadawood.info
Directors: J. Park (Ch)
Turnover: £250,000 - £500,000 **No.of Employees:** 1 - 10
Product Groups: 08, 25

Cove Industrial Enterprises Ltd

18 Invincible Road Invinciblerial Road Industrial Estate, Farnborough, GU14 7QU
Tel: 01252-512919 **Fax:** 01252-543384
E-mail: info@cove-industries.co.uk
Website: http://www.cove-industries.co.uk
Bank(s): Barclays Bank Richmond
Directors: P. Gower (MD)
Managers: P. Spencer (Purch Mgr), D. Iles (Mgr)
Immediate Holding Company: COVE BROADCAST LIMITED
Registration no: 05446835 **VAT No.:** GB 492 9503 16
Date established: 2005 **Turnover:** £1m - £2m **No.of Employees:** 21 - 50
Product Groups: 30, 37, 39, 42, 46, 48, 66

Data Techniques

7 Farnborough Business Centre Eelmoor Road, Farnborough, GU14 7XA
Tel: 01252-375566 **Fax:** 01252-375577
E-mail: info@datatechniques.co.uk
Website: http://www.datatechniques.co.uk
Directors: I. Everett (Dir)
Managers: R. Sankey (Tech Serv Mgr)
No.of Employees: 21 - 50 **Product Groups:** 37, 44, 52, 80

E P C

43 Alexandra Road, Farnborough, GU14 6BS
Tel: 01252-547939 **Fax:** 01252-377588
Directors: P. Norfolk (Prop)
No.of Employees: 1 - 10 **Product Groups:** 29, 39, 67

Engelbert Strauss

1 Apollo Rise Southwood Business Park, Farnborough, GU14 0GT
Tel: 0800-294 9000 **Fax:** 0800-197 4444
E-mail: sales@engelbert-strauss.co.uk
Website: http://www.engelbert-strauss.co.uk
Managers: M. Koegler (Mgr)
Ultimate Holding Company: LABORATOIRES DE BIOLOGIE VEGETALE YVES ROCHER SA (FRA.)
Immediate Holding Company: YVES ROCHER (LONDON) LIMITED
Registration no: 04508746 **Date established:** 1974 **Turnover:**
No.of Employees: 11 - 20 **Product Groups:** 22, 24, 31, 36, 40

Date of Accounts	Dec 11	Dec 10	Dec 09
Sales Turnover	3m	3m	3m
Pre Tax Profit/Loss	263	251	-327
Working Capital	-7m	-7m	-8m
Current Assets	540	616	880
Current Liabilities	113	96	82

Ester Line Advanced Cencus

124 Victoria Road, Farnborough, GU14 7PW
Tel: 01252-544433 **Fax:** 01252-371316
E-mail: info@esterline.com
Website: http://www.esterline.com
Bank(s): Bank of Scotland
Directors: L. Hart (Pers), C. Buckley (Co Sec), C. Lewis (Sales), C. Lewis (Sales)
Managers: S. Wood (Tech Serv Mgr), S. Wood, N. Clark (Purch Mgr), S. Prevett, P. Ravenhill, L. Hart (Personnel)
Ultimate Holding Company: SCHLUMBERGER LTD (NETHERLANDS ANTILLES)
Immediate Holding Company: SCHLUMBERGER FLOW MEASUREMENT LIMITED
Registration no: 02852989 **VAT No.:** GB 554 0821 551 1
Date established: 1945 **Turnover:** £20m - £50m
No.of Employees: 101 - 250 **Product Groups:** 37, 38, 39, 40, 68, 84, 85

Date of Accounts	Dec 91	Dec 90
Current Assets	185	185

Executive Freight Services

7 Arrow Industrial Estate Eelmoor Road, Farnborough, GU14 7QH
Tel: 01252-513300 **Fax:** 01252-378918
E-mail: sales@executivefreightservices.co.uk
Website: http://www.executivefreightservices.co.uk
Directors: R. Mitchell (Dir)
Immediate Holding Company: EXECUTIVE FREIGHT SERVICES LIMITED
Registration no: 05215325 **Date established:** 2004
Turnover: £500,000 - £1m **No.of Employees:** 1 - 10 **Product Groups:** 61, 67, 72, 74, 76

Date of Accounts	Aug 11	Aug 10	Aug 09
Working Capital	50	26	-1
Fixed Assets	23	14	18
Current Assets	467	343	284

Farnborough Aircraft Interiors

Farnborough Airport, Farnborough, GU14 6XA
Tel: 01252-377234 **Fax:** 01252-511190
E-mail: info@aircraftinteriors.co.uk
Website: http://www.aircraftinteriors.co.uk
Directors: H. Macrae (MD)
Ultimate Holding Company: TAG GROUP LIMITED (JERSEY)
Immediate Holding Company: TAG FARNBOROUGH (HOLDINGS) LIMITED
Registration no: 03460142 **Date established:** 1998
Turnover: £125m - £250m **No.of Employees:** 1 - 10 **Product Groups:** 26, 39

Date of Accounts	Dec 11	Dec 10	Dec 09
Sales Turnover	47m	40m	34m
Pre Tax Profit/Loss	10m	7m	7m
Working Capital	-4m	4m	2m
Fixed Assets	115m	102m	79m
Current Assets	13m	13m	13m
Current Liabilities	9m	6m	3m

The G I Group

222 Farnborough Road, Farnborough, GU14 7JT
Tel: 01252-522299 **Fax:** 01252-375548
E-mail: farnborough@right4staff.com
Website: http://www.right4staff.com
Managers: N. Brightwell (Mgr)
Ultimate Holding Company: RIGHT4STAFF HOLDINGS LTD
Immediate Holding Company: RIGHT4STAFF LIMITED
Registration no: 01949160 **VAT No.:** GB 413 6615 70
Date established: 1985 **Turnover:** £5m - £10m **No.of Employees:** 1 - 10
Product Groups: 80

Date of Accounts	Dec 07	Dec 06	Dec 05
Sales Turnover	99733	85773	74267
Pre Tax Profit/Loss	3575	3216	2454
Working Capital	9441	6581	4324
Fixed Assets	3975	4298	4329
Current Assets	24192	17704	14085
Current Liabilities	14751	11123	9761
Total Share Capital	20	20	20
ROCE% (Return on Capital Employed)	26.6	29.6	28.4
ROT% (Return on Turnover)	3.6	3.7	3.3

Infinity Motorcycles Ltd

153 Lynchford Road, Farnborough, GU14 6HG
Tel: 01252-400400 **Fax:** 01252-400001
E-mail: farnborough@infinitymotorcycles.com
Website: http://www.infinitymotorcycles.com
Managers: N. Armstrong (Mgr)
Registration no: 03778646 **VAT No.:** GB 211 9998 41
Turnover: £20m - £50m **No.of Employees:** 11 - 20 **Product Groups:** 39

see next page

***Infinity Motorcycles Ltd** - Cont'd*

Date of Accounts	Oct 05
Sales Turnover	18320
Pre Tax Profit/Loss	-206
Working Capital	1791
Fixed Assets	575
Current Assets	5273
Current Liabilities	3482
Total Share Capital	201
ROCE% (Return on Capital Employed)	-8.7

J I S

18 Farnborough Road, Farnborough, GU14 6AY
Tel: 01252-377077 **Fax:** 01252-377228
E-mail: admin@jiselectronics.com
Website: http://www.jiselectronics.com
Directors: J. Simmonds (MD)
Ultimate Holding Company: ENDECOTTS INTERNATIONAL LIMITED
Immediate Holding Company: CRAWFORD, HANSFORD & KIMBER LIMITED
Registration no: 00732310 **VAT No.:** GB 211 3393 08
Date established: 1962 **Turnover:** £500,000 - £1m
No.of Employees: 1 - 10 **Product Groups:** 37, 38, 46, 84

Date of Accounts	Dec 08	Dec 07	Dec 06
Working Capital	111	137	231
Fixed Assets	11	13	14
Current Assets	233	255	349
Current Liabilities	80	48	27

Kerry Commercial Services

22 Hercules Way, Farnborough, GU14 6UU
Tel: 01252-546477
Website: http://www.kerrycommercial.co.uk
Directors: C. Peach (Dir)
Managers: S. Moulding (Ops Mgr)
Immediate Holding Company: KERRY COMMERCIAL SERVICES LIMITED
Registration no: 02578138 **Date established:** 1991
No.of Employees: 21 - 50 **Product Groups:** 46, 48, 67

Date of Accounts	Jun 07	Jun 06
Working Capital	-49	-153
Fixed Assets	327	270
Current Assets	663	449
Current Liabilities	712	602

Knowledge Software Ltd

62 Fernhill Road, Farnborough, GU14 9RZ
Tel: 01252-520667 **Fax:** 01252-377226
Website: http://www.knosof.co.uk
Directors: R. Hallas (Fin), D. Williams (Dir)
Immediate Holding Company: KNOWLEDGE SOFTWARE LIMITED
Registration no: 01721575 **Date established:** 1983
Turnover: Up to £250,000 **No.of Employees:** 1 - 10 **Product Groups:** 44

Date of Accounts	Jun 11	Jun 10	Jun 09
Working Capital	789	759	742
Fixed Assets	2	2	2
Current Assets	1m	1m	1m

M T H Ltd

Unit 14 Farnborough Business Centre Eelmoor Road, Farnborough, GU14 7XA
Tel: 01252-519251 **Fax:** 01252-524494
E-mail: info@mthltd.co.uk
Website: http://www.nildram.co.uk
Directors: J. Green (MD), S. Green (Co Sec)
Immediate Holding Company: MTH LIMITED
Registration no: 02490159 **VAT No.:** GB 572 4038 48
Date established: 1990 **Turnover:** £250,000 - £500,000
No.of Employees: 1 - 10 **Product Groups:** 44, 85

Date of Accounts	May 11	May 10	May 09
Working Capital	239	238	241
Fixed Assets	1	1	2
Current Assets	533	380	422

Neil Foundations Systems Ltd

Stake Works Invincible Road, Farnborough, GU14 7QT
Tel: 01252-550222 **Fax:** 01252-550223
E-mail: piling@neilfoundations.co.uk
Website: http://www.neilfoundations.co.uk
Directors: N. Miller (MD)
Immediate Holding Company: NEIL FOUNDATIONS SYSTEMS LIMITED
Registration no: 05040021 **Date established:** 2004
Turnover: £500,000 - £1m **No.of Employees:** 21 - 50 **Product Groups:** 66

Date of Accounts	Mar 11	Mar 10	Mar 09
Working Capital	369	298	276
Fixed Assets	533	367	371
Current Assets	1m	919	750

Next Control Systems Ltd

6 Farnborough Business Centre Eelmoor Road, Farnborough, GU14 7XA
Tel: 01252-406398 **Fax:** 01252-406401
E-mail: tim.bartholomew@nextcontrols.com
Website: http://www.nextcontrols.com
Directors: T. Bartholomew (MD), N. Segal (Co Sec)
Managers: R. Ifill (Tech Serv Mgr), S. Sims (Personnel)
Immediate Holding Company: NEXT CONTROL SYSTEMS LIMITED
Registration no: 02540171 **Date established:** 1990 **Turnover:** £5m - £10m
No.of Employees: 21 - 50 **Product Groups:** 38

Date of Accounts	Dec 11	Dec 10	Dec 09
Sales Turnover	6m	5m	5m
Pre Tax Profit/Loss	555	305	96
Working Capital	1m	1m	846
Fixed Assets	214	140	159
Current Assets	3m	2m	2m
Current Liabilities	810	740	520

Plastic Box Web Design

Shieling House Invincible Road, Farnborough, GU14 7QU
Tel: 01252-758329 **Fax:** 01252-560064
E-mail: sales@plasticbox.co.uk
Website: http://www.plasticbox.co.uk
Directors: G. Harris (Prop)
Registration no: 06448297 **Date established:** 2008 **Turnover:** £2m - £5m
No.of Employees: 1 - 10 **Product Groups:** 44

PORTALP Automatic Doors Metro Doors Limited

Unit 16 Invincible Road Industrial Estate, Farnborough, GU14 7QU
Tel: 0845-603 1137 **Fax:** 0845-450 6356
E-mail: sales@metro-doors.com
Website: http://www.portalp.com
Directors: K. Howlett (Dir)
No.of Employees: 11 - 20 **Product Groups:** 35, 36, 37, 45, 66

Power Stax plc

Unit B5 Armstrong Mall, Southwood Business Park, Farnborough, GU14 0NR
Tel: 01252-407800 **Fax:** 01252-407810
E-mail: sales@powerstaxplc.com
Website: http://www.powerstaxplc.com
Bank(s): HSBC Bank plc
Directors: T. Worley (Grp Chief Exec), E. Barnes (Co Sec)
Immediate Holding Company: POWERSTAX PUBLIC LIMITED COMPANY
Registration no: 02688692 **VAT No.:** GB 591 8522 15
Date established: 1992 **Turnover:** Over £1,000m
No.of Employees: 11 - 20 **Product Groups:** 37

Date of Accounts	Dec 11	Dec 10	Dec 09
Sales Turnover	2715m	4m	4m
Pre Tax Profit/Loss	-341m	426	265
Working Capital	924m	1m	810
Fixed Assets	17m	12	21
Current Assets	1343m	2m	2m
Current Liabilities	162m	164	406

Qinetiq

Cody Technology Park Ively Road, Farnborough, GU14 0LX
Tel: 01252-392000 **Fax:** 01252-393399
E-mail: marketing@qinetiq.com
Website: http://www.qinetiq.com
Managers: G. Love (Comptroller), L. Quinn
Ultimate Holding Company: QINETIQ GROUP PLC
Immediate Holding Company: QINETIQ UK LIMITED
Registration no: 06764256 **Date established:** 2008
Turnover: £500,000 - £1m **No.of Employees:** 1501 & over
Product Groups: 20, 22, 24, 28, 29, 31, 32, 33, 35, 36, 37, 38, 39, 40, 42, 44, 45, 52, 54, 67, 75, 79, 80, 81, 84, 85, 86, 87

Date of Accounts	Mar 12	Mar 11	Mar 10
Sales Turnover	618m	664m	772m
Pre Tax Profit/Loss	277m	-40m	-19m
Working Capital	118m	287m	309m
Fixed Assets	338m	360m	387m
Current Assets	487m	608m	587m
Current Liabilities	348m	295m	239m

St Bernard Composites Ltd

21 Invincible Road Industrial Estate, Farnborough, GU14 7QU
Tel: 01252-304000 **Fax:** 01252-304001
E-mail: jmerritt@stbernard.co.uk
Website: http://www.stbernard.co.uk
Bank(s): National Westminster
Directors: C. Webborn (MD), D. Kempster (Co Sec), J. Merritt (Dir)
Managers: A. Butterfield (Sales Admin), R. Gray (I.T. Exec)
Immediate Holding Company: ST BERNARD COMPOSITES LIMITED
Registration no: 00706645 **VAT No.:** GB 211 7433 02
Date established: 1961 **Turnover:** £20m - £50m
No.of Employees: 101 - 250 **Product Groups:** 30, 33, 34

Date of Accounts	Dec 09	Dec 08	Dec 07
Sales Turnover	22m	23m	17m
Pre Tax Profit/Loss	4m	-4m	1m
Working Capital	5m	2m	6m
Fixed Assets	6m	7m	7m
Current Assets	13m	15m	10m
Current Liabilities	4m	8m	1m

Steadman Machine Tools

78 Avenue Road, Farnborough, GU14 7BG
Tel: 01252-378338
E-mail: mike@smts.co.uk
Website: http://www.smts.co.uk
Directors: M. Steadman (Prop)
Immediate Holding Company: STEADMAN MACHINE TOOLS SERVICES LIMITED
Registration no: 04362513 **Date established:** 2002
No.of Employees: 1 - 10 **Product Groups:** 46

Date of Accounts	Jun 12	Jun 11	Jun 10
Working Capital	-10	-2	43
Fixed Assets	22	27	N/A
Current Assets	130	161	112

Turnaround 360

G1300 Lane S 112 Hawley Lane, Farnborough, GU14 8JE
Tel: 07973-430950
E-mail: turnaro360@aol.com
Website: http://www.turnaround360.co.uk
Directors: R. Binyon (Prop)
Date established: 2000 **Turnover:** £250,000 - £500,000
No.of Employees: 1 - 10 **Product Groups:** 37, 38, 67, 83

Visual Communications

209 Lynchford Road, Farnborough, GU14 6HF
Tel: 01252-540044 **Fax:** 01252-516616
E-mail: sales@vis-com.net
Website: http://www.vis-com.net
Managers: S. Leah (Design Mgr)
Immediate Holding Company: EXECULENCE LIMITED
Registration no: 05701919 **Date established:** 2005
No.of Employees: 1 - 10 **Product Groups:** 52

Date of Accounts	Mar 11	Mar 10	Mar 09
Working Capital	134	88	56
Current Assets	169	110	86

West Heath Garage Farnborough Ltd

11 Minley Road, Farnborough, GU14 9RR
Tel: 01252-541294 **Fax:** 01252-375642
E-mail: sales@westheath.co.uk
Website: http://www.westheath.co.uk
Bank(s): Lloyds TSB Bank plc
Directors: M. Nicholson (Fin)
Managers: M. Reynolds (Sales Prom Mgr)
Immediate Holding Company: WEST HEATH GARAGE (FARNBOROUGH) LIMITED
Registration no: 00706981 **VAT No.:** GB 610 4427 83
Date established: 1961 **No.of Employees:** 11 - 20 **Product Groups:** 39, 68

Date of Accounts	Dec 11	Dec 10	Dec 09
Working Capital	140	148	149
Fixed Assets	12	16	21
Current Assets	358	370	412

Fleet

2012 Marine Restoration 2012 Marine

58 Wakefords Park Church Crookham, Fleet, GU52 8EY
Tel: 0791-948 8550
E-mail: enquiries@2012marine.com
Website: http://www.2012marinerestoration.com
Directors: G. Marsden (Prop)
No.of Employees: 1 - 10 **Product Groups:** 40, 48, 68

Cat Pumps UK Ltd

Fleet Business Park Sandy Lane, Church Crookham, Fleet, GU52 8BF
Tel: 01252-622031 **Fax:** 01252-626655
E-mail: sales@catpumps.co.uk
Website: http://www.catpumps.co.uk
Bank(s): Lloyds TSB Bank plc
Managers: B. Hubbard (Chief Mgr)
Ultimate Holding Company: DIVERSIFIED DYNAMICS CORPORATION (USA)
Immediate Holding Company: CAT PUMPS (U.K.) LIMITED
Registration no: 01217723 **VAT No.:** GB 189 7609 96
Date established: 1975 **Turnover:** £2m - £5m **No.of Employees:** 11 - 20
Product Groups: 39, 40, 46, 67

Date of Accounts	Nov 11	Nov 10	Nov 09
Working Capital	2m	2m	3m
Fixed Assets	557	563	584
Current Assets	2m	2m	3m

Del Industrial Fastenings Ltd

Unit 9 Elvetham Bridge, Fleet, GU51 1AE
Tel: 01252-627229 **Fax:** 01252-811741
E-mail: info@delindustrial.co.uk
Website: http://www.delindustrial.co.uk
Directors: S. Harris (MD), S. Harris (Fin)
Immediate Holding Company: DEL INDUSTRIAL FASTENINGS LIMITED
Registration no: 01170596 **VAT No.:** GB 213 0258 17
Date established: 1974 **Turnover:** £500,000 - £1m
No.of Employees: 1 - 10 **Product Groups:** 35, 66

Date of Accounts	Mar 12	Mar 11	Mar 10
Working Capital	5	6	5
Fixed Assets	4	6	8
Current Assets	49	37	29

Jewson Ltd

128 Clarence Road, Fleet, GU51 3RS
Tel: 01252-613555 **Fax:** 01252-811593
Website: http://www.jewson.co.uk
Directors: P. Daley (Prop)
Ultimate Holding Company: COMPAGNIE DE SAINT GOBAIN (FRANCE)
Immediate Holding Company: JEWSON LIMITED
Registration no: 00348407 **VAT No.:** GB 497 7184 83
Date established: 1939 **No.of Employees:** 1 - 10 **Product Groups:** 66

Date of Accounts	Dec 11	Dec 10	Dec 09
Sales Turnover	1606m	1547m	1485m
Pre Tax Profit/Loss	18m	100m	45m
Working Capital	-345m	-250m	-349m
Fixed Assets	496m	387m	461m
Current Assets	657m	1005m	1320m
Current Liabilities	66m	120m	64m

The Logic Group

Logic House Waterfront Business Park, Fleet, GU51 3SB
Tel: 01252-776755 **Fax:** 01252-776758
E-mail: info@the-logic-group.com
Website: http://www.the-logic-group.com
Managers: A. Jones
Ultimate Holding Company: THE LOGIC GROUP HOLDINGS LIMITED
Immediate Holding Company: THE LOGIC GROUP ENTERPRISES LIMITED
Registration no: 02609323 **Date established:** 1991
Turnover: £10m - £20m **No.of Employees:** 101 - 250
Product Groups: 44, 79

Date of Accounts	Sep 11	Sep 10	Sep 09
Sales Turnover	19m	19m	19m
Pre Tax Profit/Loss	313	-1m	-1m
Working Capital	-793	-3m	-2m
Fixed Assets	987	866	1m
Current Assets	7m	5m	5m
Current Liabilities	6m	6m	6m

Moorepay Ltd

Palmerston House 111-113 Fleet Road, Fleet, GU51 3PD
Tel: 0845-1844615 **Fax:** 0845-2701150
E-mail: sales@moorepay.co.uk
Website: http://www.moorepay.co.uk
Bank(s): Barclays, New Malden
Directors: A. Cumbers (Sales & Mktg), D. Meades (Fin), K. Mason (MD)
Ultimate Holding Company: Northgate Information Solutions Ltd
Immediate Holding Company: Rebus HR Management Ltd
Registration no: 00891686 **Turnover:** £75m - £125m
No.of Employees: 101 - 250 **Product Groups:** 44

Murata Electronics Ltd

Oak House Ancells Road, Fleet, GU51 2QW
Tel: 01252-811666 **Fax:** 01252-811777
E-mail: enquiry@murata.co.uk
Website: http://www.murata.co.uk
Bank(s): Barclays, Aldershot
Directors: C. Griffiths (Co Sec)
Managers: P. Wellford
Ultimate Holding Company: MURATA MANUFACTURING CO LTD (JAPAN)
Immediate Holding Company: MURATA ELECTRONICS (UK) LIMITED
Registration no: 01640046 **VAT No.:** GB 370 0462 83
Date established: 1982 **Turnover:** £20m - £50m
No.of Employees: 21 - 50 **Product Groups:** 37

Date of Accounts	Mar 12	Mar 11	Mar 10
Sales Turnover	4m	39m	25m
Pre Tax Profit/Loss	3m	4m	2m
Working Capital	10m	32m	28m
Fixed Assets	2m	2m	2m
Current Assets	10m	35m	30m
Current Liabilities	762	1m	799

Nacco Material Handling Group (Head Office)
Flagship House Reading Road North, Fleet, GU51 4WD
Tel: 01252-810261 **Fax:** 01252-770702
E-mail: sales@hyster.co.uk
Website: http://www.nacco.com
Bank(s): National Westminster Bank Plc
Managers: M. Tomkins (I.T. Exec)
Ultimate Holding Company: NACCO INDUSTRIES INC (USA)
Immediate Holding Company: NACCO MATERIALS HANDLING GROUP (UK) PENSION CO., LTD
Registration no: 03288052 **Date established:** 1996
Turnover: £500m - £1,000m **No.of Employees:** 51 - 100
Product Groups: 45, 74

Production Techniques Ltd
13 Kings Road, Fleet, GU51 3AU
Tel: 01252-616575 **Fax:** 01252-615818
E-mail: sales@production-techniques.com
Website: http://www.production-techniques.com
Directors: C. Brand (MD)
Immediate Holding Company: PRODUCTION TECHNIQUES LIMITED
Registration no: 00892277 **VAT No.:** GB 188 5861 05
Date established: 1966 **Turnover:** Up to £250,000
No.of Employees: 1 - 10 **Product Groups:** 30, 31, 38, 40, 48

Date of Accounts	Feb 08	Feb 11	Feb 10
Sales Turnover	193	N/A	N/A
Pre Tax Profit/Loss	-60	N/A	N/A
Working Capital	82	115	79
Fixed Assets	126	116	118
Current Assets	102	126	107
Current Liabilities	9	N/A	N/A

J Robinson Engineering Ltd
12 Clarence Road, Fleet, GU51 3RZ
Tel: 01252-621312 **Fax:** 01252-819100
E-mail: jim@jrobinsoneng.fsnet.co.uk
Website: http://www.jrobinsonengineering.co.uk
Directors: S. Robinson (Fin), J. Robinson (Prop), J. Robinson (MD)
Immediate Holding Company: J. ROBINSON ENGINEERING LIMITED
Registration no: 05390009 **VAT No.:** GB 572 7374 17
Date established: 2005 **Turnover:** Up to £250,000
No.of Employees: 1 - 10 **Product Groups:** 37, 67

Date of Accounts	Apr 10	Apr 09	Apr 08
Sales Turnover	129	204	188
Pre Tax Profit/Loss	-1	21	16
Working Capital	-29	-34	-40
Fixed Assets	91	98	104
Current Assets	31	57	47
Current Liabilities	6	11	6

Rohde & Schwarz UK Ltd
Ancells Business Park, Fleet, GU51 2UZ
Tel: 01252-818888 **Fax:** 01252-811447
E-mail: frank.mackel@rohde-schwarz.com
Website: http://www.rohde-schwarz.com
Bank(s): HSBC Bank plc
Directors: F. Mackel (MD)
Ultimate Holding Company: ROHDE & SCHWARTZ CO KG (GERMANY)
Immediate Holding Company: ROHDE & SCHWARZ U.K. LIMITED
Registration no: 00539607 **VAT No.:** GB 215 9451 63
Date established: 1954 **Turnover:** £20m - £50m
No.of Employees: 51 - 100 **Product Groups:** 37, 38, 84

Date of Accounts	Jun 12	Jun 11	Jun 10
Sales Turnover	35m	34m	30m
Pre Tax Profit/Loss	3m	3m	3m
Working Capital	26m	25m	26m
Fixed Assets	412	318	234
Current Assets	33m	35m	33m
Current Liabilities	2m	3m	2m

Seco Engineering Co. Ltd
32 Reading Road South, Fleet, GU52 7QL
Tel: 01252-622333 **Fax:** 01252-623888
E-mail: m.appleton@secoeng.co.uk
Website: http://www.secoeng.co.uk
Directors: M. Appleton (MD)
Immediate Holding Company: S.E.C.O. ENGINEERING COMPANY LIMITED
Registration no: 01004704 **VAT No.:** GB 199 7713 94
Date established: 1971 **Turnover:** £250,000 - £500,000
No.of Employees: 1 - 10 **Product Groups:** 37, 40, 46

Date of Accounts	Aug 11	Aug 10	Aug 09
Sales Turnover	280	220	197
Pre Tax Profit/Loss	1	36	-27
Working Capital	58	67	29
Fixed Assets	7	7	9
Current Assets	102	98	61
Current Liabilities	11	6	3

Smiths
4a Crookham Road, Fleet, GU51 5DR
Tel: 01252-622300 **Fax:** 01252-811115
E-mail: services@smithsfleet.co.uk
Website: http://www.smiths-fleet.co.uk
Directors: J. Smith (MD)
Immediate Holding Company: SMITHS OF FLEET LIMITED
Registration no: 02628607 **VAT No.:** GB 641 3364 59
Date established: 1991 **Turnover:** £250,000 - £500,000
No.of Employees: 1 - 10 **Product Groups:** 39

Date of Accounts	Aug 11	Aug 10	Aug 09
Working Capital	-11	-17	-11
Fixed Assets	3	4	3
Current Assets	37	32	26

Synektics Ltd
60 Alton Road, Fleet, GU51 3HW
Tel: 01252-815281 **Fax:** 01252-624433
E-mail: info@synektics.co.uk
Website: http://www.synektics.co.uk
Directors: C. Veness (Dir)
Immediate Holding Company: SCREENSCENE (2000) LIMITED
Registration no: 01147011 **Date established:** 1973
No.of Employees: 1 - 10 **Product Groups:** 24, 25, 35, 36, 40, 63, 66

Date of Accounts	Mar 12	Mar 11	Mar 09
Working Capital	26	17	13
Fixed Assets	1	8	10
Current Assets	35	44	38

Talk Allergy
PO Box 403, Fleet, GU51 9AD
Tel: 01252-642153
E-mail: gwen@talkhealthgroup.com
Website: http://www.talkallergy.com
Product Groups: 31, 32

Talk Eczema
PO Box 403, Fleet, GU51 9AD
Tel: 01252-642153
E-mail: gwen@talkhealthgroup.com
Website: http://www.talkeczema.com
Product Groups: 31, 32

Talk Psoriasis
PO Box 403, Fleet, GU51 9AD
Tel: 01252-642153
E-mail: gwen@talkhealthgroup.com
Website: http://www.talkpsoriasis.com
Product Groups: 31, 32

Wanner International Ltd
8-9 Fleet Business Park Sandy Lane, Church Crookham, Fleet, GU52 8BF
Tel: 01252-816847 **Fax:** 01252-629242
E-mail: dheath@wannerint.com
Website: http://www.hydra-cell.com
Directors: P. Davis (MD)
Ultimate Holding Company: WEC INC (USA)
Immediate Holding Company: WANNER INTERNATIONAL LIMITED
Registration no: 01784976 **Date established:** 1984
No.of Employees: 1 - 10 **Product Groups:** 40

Date of Accounts	Dec 11	Dec 10	Dec 09
Working Capital	1m	1m	922
Fixed Assets	1m	1m	1m
Current Assets	2m	2m	1m

Yale
Flagship House, Fleet, GU51 4WD
Tel: 01252-770700 **Fax:** 01252-770791
Website: http://www.nmhg.com
Managers: S. Ridgway (Publicity)
Ultimate Holding Company: FP001348
Immediate Holding Company: YALE MATERIALS HANDLING UK LIMITED
Registration no: 01228726 **Date established:** 1975
Turnover: £10m - £20m **No.of Employees:** 51 - 100 **Product Groups:** 45

Fordingbridge

Allsopp Helikites Ltd
South End Damerham, Fordingbridge, SP6 3HW
Tel: 01725-518750 **Fax:** 01725-518786
E-mail: allsopp@helikites.com
Website: http://www.allsopphelikites.com
Directors: G. Allsopp (Fin), D. Allsopp (MD)
Immediate Holding Company: ALLSOPP HELIKITES LIMITED
Registration no: 03466204 **Date established:** 1997
Turnover: Up to £250,000 **No.of Employees:** 1 - 10 **Product Groups:** 41, 52

Date of Accounts	Dec 09	Dec 08	Dec 07
Working Capital	18	43	32
Fixed Assets	11	13	15
Current Assets	107	84	60

David Cutler Associates
2 Home Farm Cottages Upper Street, Breamore, Fordingbridge, SP6 2DD
Tel: 07766-005576 **Fax:** 07766-005576
E-mail: info@dca-architectural.co.uk
Website: http://www.dca-architectural.co.uk
Directors: D. Cutler (Prop)
Date established: 1990 **No.of Employees:** 1 - 10 **Product Groups:** 84

Dean & Tranter
Rockbourne Road Sandleheath, Fordingbridge, SP6 1RA
Tel: 01425-654011 **Fax:** 01425-654141
E-mail: office@deantranter.co.uk
Website: http://www.deantranter.co.uk
Directors: A. Allwood (MD)
Immediate Holding Company: DEAN AND TRANTER LIMITED
Registration no: 00172132 **VAT No.:** GB 185 8007 46
Date established: 2020 **Turnover:** £1m - £2m **No.of Employees:** 1 - 10
Product Groups: 30, 33, 34, 35

Date of Accounts	Mar 11	Mar 10	Mar 09
Working Capital	28	66	47
Fixed Assets	442	465	422
Current Assets	744	648	834

Incare International Ltd
Little Brook Farm Ringwood Road, North Gorley, Fordingbridge, SP6 2PD
Tel: 01425-479932 **Fax:** 01425-471146
E-mail: freight@incare.co.uk
Website: http://www.incare.co.uk
Directors: L. Toomer (Dir)
Immediate Holding Company: INCARE INTERNATIONAL LIMITED
Registration no: 01762892 **VAT No.:** GB 392 9003 44
Date established: 1983 **Turnover:** £1m - £2m **No.of Employees:** 1 - 10
Product Groups: 76

Date of Accounts	May 11	May 10	May 09
Working Capital	-55	-135	-164
Fixed Assets	55	35	24
Current Assets	142	170	112

James Allied Engineering Ltd
West Park Drive Damerham, Fordingbridge, SP6 3HJ
Tel: 01725-518493 **Fax:** 01725-518652
Directors: J. O'sullivan (MD)
Immediate Holding Company: JAMES ALLIED ENGINEERING LIMITED
Registration no: 05126244 **Date established:** 2004
No.of Employees: 1 - 10 **Product Groups:** 41

Date of Accounts	Mar 12	Mar 11	Mar 10
Working Capital	3	-5	-7
Fixed Assets	5	7	9
Current Assets	51	19	16

New Forest Saw Co.
Courtwood Farm Sandleheath, Fordingbridge, SP6 1QD
Tel: 01425-657720 **Fax:** 01425-657720
Directors: P. Blake (Prop)
Date established: 1989 **No.of Employees:** 1 - 10 **Product Groups:** 46, 48

Pharmaq Ltd
Unit 15 Sandleheath Industrial Estate Old Brickyard Road Sandleheath, Fordingbridge, SP6 1PA
Tel: 01425-656081 **Fax:** 01425-655309
E-mail: ben.north@pharmaq.no
Website: http://www.pharmaq.no
Directors: B. North (MD)
Immediate Holding Company: PHARMAQ LTD
Registration no: 02024398 **Date established:** 1986 **Turnover:** £5m - £10m
No.of Employees: 11 - 20 **Product Groups:** 09

Date of Accounts	Dec 11	Dec 10	Dec 09
Sales Turnover	7m	10m	10m
Pre Tax Profit/Loss	298	450	419
Working Capital	2m	2m	2m
Fixed Assets	168	81	78
Current Assets	3m	3m	2m
Current Liabilities	226	194	217

R N C Fabrications
Unit 18 Sandleheath Industrial Estate Old Brickyard Road, Sandleheath, Fordingbridge, SP6 1PA
Tel: 01425-652156 **Fax:** 01425-653399
E-mail: richard@rncfabrications.co.uk
Website: http://www.rncfabrications.co.uk
Directors: R. Crossley (MD)
Turnover: £1m - £2m **No.of Employees:** 1 - 10 **Product Groups:** 48

Gosport

Acrol UK Ltd
The Sanderson Centre Lees Lane, Gosport, PO12 3UL
Tel: 023-9250 2999 **Fax:** 023-9250 2999
Website: http://www.acrolltd.co.uk
Directors: M. French (MD), R. French (Fin)
Immediate Holding Company: ACROL UK LIMITED
Registration no: 04265231 **Date established:** 2001
Turnover: Up to £250,000 **No.of Employees:** 1 - 10 **Product Groups:** 38, 42

Date of Accounts	Aug 11	Aug 10	Aug 09
Working Capital	N/A	-1	-2
Fixed Assets	N/A	1	2
Current Assets	77	62	62

Advanced Marine Innovation Technology Subsea Ltd
Unit 9, Gosport Business Centre Aerodrome Road, Gosport, PO13 0FQ
Tel: 01329-848670 **Fax:** 01329-848672
E-mail: martinrq@advancedmarineinnovation.com
Website: http://www.advancedmarineinnovation.com
No.of Employees: 1 - 10 **Product Groups:** 29, 32, 36, 37, 38, 39, 40, 45, 49, 51, 67, 68, 84, 85, 87

Date of Accounts	Jun 11	Jun 10	Jun 09
Working Capital	289	205	128
Fixed Assets	2	2	2
Current Assets	345	307	170

Alverstoke Precision Tools Ltd
82-84 Clayhall Road, Gosport, PO12 2AJ
Tel: 023-9258 2407 **Fax:** 023-9258 6254
E-mail: enquiries@aptuk.com
Website: http://www.aptuk.com
Bank(s): Lloyds TSB Bank plc
Directors: S. Millerchip (Dir)
Immediate Holding Company: ALVERSTOKE PRECISION TOOLS LIMITED
Registration no: 01232161 **Date established:** 1975
Turnover: £500,000 - £1m **No.of Employees:** 11 - 20
Product Groups: 46, 48

Date of Accounts	Nov 11	Nov 10	Nov 09
Working Capital	186	232	189
Fixed Assets	6	11	23
Current Assets	228	298	213

Amark Safety Markings
28 HARTINGTON ROAD, GOSPORT, PO12 3AG
Tel: 07841-160636 **Fax:** 023-9279 0110
E-mail: rjwright2005@yahoo.co.uk
Website: http://www.amarksafetymarkings.co.uk
Directors: R. Wright (Prop)
Date established: 2004 **No.of Employees:** 1 - 10 **Product Groups:** 32, 51, 52, 84

Anubis Label Technology Ltd
The Sanderson Centre Lees Lane, Gosport, PO12 3UL
Tel: 023-9251 1234 **Fax:** 023-9251 3322
E-mail: sales@anubislabels.com
Website: http://www.anubislabels.com
Directors: R. Keene (MD)
Managers: R. Keene (Sales Prom Mgr)
Registration no: 04065502 **Turnover:** £500,000 - £1m
No.of Employees: 1 - 10 **Product Groups:** 22, 23, 27, 28, 30, 33, 35, 44, 49

Date of Accounts	Sep 11	Sep 10	Sep 09
Sales Turnover	639	N/A	N/A
Pre Tax Profit/Loss	250	N/A	N/A
Working Capital	409	354	237
Fixed Assets	25	32	42
Current Assets	500	470	352
Current Liabilities	77	N/A	N/A

C P G Logistics Ltd
Unit 900 166 Fareham Road, Gosport, PO13 0FW
Tel: 01329-245600 **Fax:** 01329-245666
E-mail: sales@cpg-logistics.com
Website: http://www.cpg-logistics.com
Bank(s): Bank of Scotland
Directors: L. Goddard (Sales & Mktg), I. Brown (Tech Serv), D. Jones (Chief Op Offcr)

see next page

***C P G Logistics Ltd** - Cont'd*

Managers: A. Brown (Comptroller)
Ultimate Holding Company: CPG HOLDINGS LIMITED
Immediate Holding Company: CPG LOGISTICS LIMITED
Registration no: 02597908 **Date established:** 1991
Turnover: £10m - £20m **No.of Employees:** 101 - 250
Product Groups: 72, 76, 77, 84

Date of Accounts	Mar 11	Mar 10	Mar 09
Sales Turnover	13m	13m	N/A
Pre Tax Profit/Loss	315	485	-64
Working Capital	-440	-1m	-985
Fixed Assets	4m	4m	4m
Current Assets	3m	3m	3m
Current Liabilities	700	731	655

Christian Software Engineering Ltd
Room 1a 18 Hambrook Road, Gosport, PO12 3JH
Tel: 023-9235 0694
E-mail: enquire@chrissofteng.co.uk
Website: http://www.chrissofteng.co.uk
Directors: E. Christian (Co Sec), A. Christian (Dir)
Registration no: 02452540 **Date established:** 1989
Turnover: Up to £250,000 **No.of Employees:** 1 - 10 **Product Groups:** 44

Date of Accounts	Oct 05
Working Capital	-1
Fixed Assets	2
Current Assets	4
Current Liabilities	6

Crewsaver Ltd
Clarence Square Mumby Road, Gosport, PO12 1AQ
Tel: 023-9252 8621 **Fax:** 023-9251 0905
E-mail: info@crewsaver.co.uk
Website: http://www.crewsaver.co.uk
Bank(s): National Westminster
Directors: F. Wood (Dir), D. Ellis (Sales & Mktg)
Managers: L. Searle (Comptroller), J. Thomas (Personnel)
Immediate Holding Company: CREWSAVER LIMITED
Registration no: 00593296 **VAT No.:** GB 503 7790 46
Date established: 1957 **Turnover:** £5m - £10m
No.of Employees: 51 - 100 **Product Groups:** 30, 39, 40

D S Smith Recycling PLC
Cranbourne Road, Gosport, PO12 1RL
Tel: 023-9258 2327 **Fax:** 023-9251 1637
E-mail: enquiries@severnside-paper.co.uk
Website: http://www.severnside.com
Bank(s): National Westminster
Managers: D. Stuart (Mgr)
Immediate Holding Company: LIMBURN BOILER & HEATING SERVICES LIMITED
Registration no: 00489560 **VAT No.:** GB 479 5202 22
Date established: 2001 **Turnover:** £20m - £50m
No.of Employees: 11 - 20 **Product Groups:** 66

Date of Accounts	Mar 12	Mar 11	Mar 10
Working Capital	932	829	556
Fixed Assets	58	71	86
Current Assets	1m	2m	809
Current Liabilities	N/A	330	157

Frenstar
Unit 160 Ordnance Business Park Aerodrome Road, Gosport, PO13 0FG
Tel: 01329-233445 **Fax:** 01329-233450
E-mail: info@frenstar.co.uk
Website: http://www.frenstar.co.uk
Directors: D. Moir (Dir)
Immediate Holding Company: FRENSTAR LIMITED
Registration no: 01325773 **Date established:** 1977
Turnover: £500,000 - £1m **No.of Employees:** 1 - 10 **Product Groups:** 29, 30, 36, 39, 40, 63, 66, 67

Date of Accounts	Mar 12	Mar 11	Mar 10
Working Capital	1m	853	383
Fixed Assets	252	229	256
Current Assets	2m	1m	1m

George Kingsbury Ltd
Quay Lane Hardway, Gosport, PO12 4LB
Tel: 023-9258 0371 **Fax:** 023-9250 1741
E-mail: richard.kingsbury@gkholdings.com
Website: http://www.gkholdings.com
Directors: R. Kingsbury (Dir), D. Mcgrath (Fin)
Immediate Holding Company: GEORGE KINGSBURY HOLDINGS
Registration no: 02609431 **Turnover:** £2m - £5m
No.of Employees: 11 - 20 **Product Groups:** 38, 46, 48, 67, 84

Date of Accounts	Dec 10	Dec 09	Dec 08
Sales Turnover	8m	4m	6m
Pre Tax Profit/Loss	525	-573	-1m
Working Capital	2m	1m	379
Fixed Assets	49	43	241
Current Assets	4m	5m	7m
Current Liabilities	974	392	348

Go Business Communications Ltd
Regents Trade Park Barwell Lane, Gosport, PO13 0EQ
Tel: 01329-823825 **Fax:** 01329-235040
E-mail: norman@portsmouthcomms.co.uk
Website: http://www.portsmouthcomms.co.uk
Directors: S. Burton (Fin), C. Burton (Dir)
Immediate Holding Company: SILVER LINING CONVERGENCE LTD
Registration no: 06212357 **Date established:** 2007
Turnover: £500,000 - £1m **No.of Employees:** 1 - 10 **Product Groups:** 38, 52, 67, 84

Date of Accounts	Apr 12	Apr 11	Apr 10
Working Capital	125	65	-25
Fixed Assets	50	78	61
Current Assets	877	576	199

Gosport Business Centre
Aerodrome Road, Gosport, PO13 0FQ
Tel: 01329-848700 **Fax:** 01329-848701
E-mail: gosport@basepoint.co.uk
Website: http://www.basepoint.co.uk
Managers: A. Weston (District Mgr)
Immediate Holding Company: GO LIGHT LIMITED
Registration no: 06023756 **Date established:** 2012
Turnover: Up to £250,000 **No.of Employees:** 1 - 10 **Product Groups:** 80

Date of Accounts	Mar 11	Mar 10	Mar 09
Working Capital	-46	-18	-27
Fixed Assets	16	20	25
Current Assets	65	64	24

Gosport Marina
Mumby Road, Gosport, PO12 1AH
Tel: 023-9252 4811 **Fax:** 023-9258 9541
E-mail: gosport@premiermarinas.com
Website: http://www.premiermarinas.com
Managers: W. Barker (Mgr)
Immediate Holding Company: PREMIER MARINAS (GOSPORT) LIMITED
Registration no: 02973858 **Date established:** 2003 **Turnover:** £1m - £2m
No.of Employees: 1 - 10 **Product Groups:** 71

Huhtamaki UK Ltd
Grange Road, Gosport, PO13 9UP
Tel: 023-9258 4234 **Fax:** 023-9251 2330
E-mail: sales@gb.huhtamaki.com
Website: http://www.huhtamaki.com
Directors: J. Young (Sales & Mktg), R. Mason (MD), G. Wilkins (Co Sec)
Managers: V. Daal (Personnel), J. Frost (Tech Serv Mgr), J. Cadman (Purch Mgr)
Ultimate Holding Company: HUHTAMAKI VAN LEER OYJ (FINLAND)
Immediate Holding Company: HUHTAMAKI LIMITED
Registration no: 01871645 **Date established:** 1984
Turnover: £75m - £125m **No.of Employees:** 251 - 500
Product Groups: 22, 24, 26, 27, 29, 30, 31, 32, 34, 35, 38, 42, 49, 63, 66, 67, 69, 84, 85

Date of Accounts	Dec 11	Dec 10	Dec 09
Pre Tax Profit/Loss	6m	10m	-12m
Working Capital	4m	-3m	-7m
Fixed Assets	5m	5m	N/A
Current Assets	16m	14m	10m
Current Liabilities	39	277	264

Leadatom Europe Ltd
1 Shamrock Enterprise Centre Wingate Road, Gosport, PO12 4DP
Tel: 023-9252 3973 **Fax:** 023-9252 3973
E-mail: sales@leadatom.co.uk
Website: http://www.leadatom.co.uk
Directors: B. Hale (Dir)
Immediate Holding Company: LEADATOM EUROPE LIMITED
Registration no: 02267626 **Date established:** 1988
No.of Employees: 1 - 10 **Product Groups:** 34, 37, 66

Date of Accounts	Jun 11	Jun 10	Jun 09
Working Capital	-1	N/A	1
Fixed Assets	4	4	5
Current Assets	35	30	29

Miltools Engineering Supplies
The Sanderson Centre Lees Lane, Gosport, PO12 3UL
Tel: 023-9252 6551 **Fax:** 023-9252 2559
Directors: R. Milton (Prop)
Immediate Holding Company: MULTISEAL LTD
Registration no: 03699934 **Date established:** 1999
Turnover: Up to £250,000 **No.of Employees:** 1 - 10 **Product Groups:** 36, 66

Plasticoat GB Ltd
Shamrock Enterprise Centre Wingate Road, Gosport, PO12 4DP
Tel: 023-9252 1321 **Fax:** 023-9250 1793
E-mail: enquiries@plasticoat.co.uk
Website: http://www.plasticoat.co.uk
Directors: C. Stoppani (Dir), E. Stoppani (Fin)
Immediate Holding Company: PLASTICOAT GB LIMITED
Registration no: 03575142 **Date established:** 1998
No.of Employees: 1 - 10 **Product Groups:** 46, 48

Date of Accounts	Aug 11	Aug 10	Aug 09
Working Capital	9	-27	9
Fixed Assets	29	31	28
Current Assets	92	63	94
Current Liabilities	15	20	11

Resin Technical Systems (a division of R.M.P Plastics Ltd)
Fort Brockhurst Industrial Estate Alphage Road, Gosport, PO12 4DU
Tel: 023-9258 5899 **Fax:** 023-9251 0306
E-mail: sales@resintek.co.uk
Website: http://www.resintek.co.uk
Directors: A. Porter (Dir), D. Grant (Dir), R. Porter (Dir), R. Porter (Ch)
Managers: C. Utterson (Purch Mgr)
Ultimate Holding Company: R M P Plastics Ltd
Registration no: 01714218 **Date established:** 1998 **Turnover:** £1m - £2m
No.of Employees: 11 - 20 **Product Groups:** 30, 31, 32, 37, 42, 66

Date of Accounts	Apr 08	Apr 07	Apr 06
Working Capital	390	378	319
Fixed Assets	28	22	25
Current Assets	604	598	537
Current Liabilities	214	220	218
Total Share Capital	3	3	3

Rotomarine Boat Equipment
Haslar Marina Haslar Road, Gosport, PO12 1NU
Tel: 023-9258 3633 **Fax:** 023-9258 3634
E-mail: info@rotostay.co.uk
Website: http://www.rotostay.co.uk
Directors: S. Cochrane (Co Sec), I. Cochran (MD), I. Cochrane (MD), I. Cockron (MD)
Managers: R. Wilson (Sales Prom Mgr)
Immediate Holding Company: ROTOMARINE LIMITED
Registration no: 01063779 **VAT No.:** GB 193 2539 48
Date established: 1972 **Turnover:** Up to £250,000
No.of Employees: 1 - 10 **Product Groups:** 39, 74

Date of Accounts	Dec 09	Dec 08	Dec 07
Sales Turnover	103	117	99
Working Capital	-32	-29	-31
Fixed Assets	4	5	6
Current Assets	28	35	36

S T S Defence Ltd
Mumby Road, Gosport, PO12 1AF
Tel: 023-9258 4222 **Fax:** 023-9252 9598
E-mail: sales@sts-defence.com
Website: http://www.sts-defence.com
Managers: J. Thompkinson (I.T. Exec), J. Thompkinson (Tech Serv Mgr), P. Withers (Sales & Mktg Mg), S. Denness (Purch Mgr), K. Chamberlin (Personnel)
Ultimate Holding Company: KEY TECHNOLOGIES PLC
Immediate Holding Company: STS DEFENCE LIMITED
Registration no: 03193298 **Date established:** 1996
No.of Employees: 101 - 250 **Product Groups:** 35

Date of Accounts	Jun 11	Jun 10	Jun 09
Sales Turnover	12m	12m	10m
Pre Tax Profit/Loss	2m	2m	2m
Working Capital	5m	4m	2m
Fixed Assets	480	343	284
Current Assets	9m	6m	6m
Current Liabilities	1m	2m	2m

Scruse & Crossland Ltd
2 Wingate Road, Gosport, PO12 4DR
Tel: 023-9250 2403 **Fax:** 023-9251 1728
E-mail: sales@scruse.co.uk
Website: http://www.scruse.co.uk
Bank(s): Gosport
Directors: N. Scruse (Fin), N. Scruse (MD)
Managers: D. Fletcher (Workshop), P. Gravestock (Sales Admin)
Immediate Holding Company: SCRUSE & CROSSLAND LIMITED
Registration no: 02877694 **VAT No.:** GB 108 0434 08
Date established: 1993 **Turnover:** £500,000 - £1m
No.of Employees: 11 - 20 **Product Groups:** 48

Date of Accounts	Feb 07	Feb 06
Working Capital	10	-26
Fixed Assets	306	311
Current Assets	187	192
Current Liabilities	177	218
Total Share Capital	1	1

Seaway Marine
Haslar Road, Gosport, PO12 1NU
Tel: 023-9260 2722 **Fax:** 023-9252 3335
Website: http://www.seawaymarine.co.uk
Managers: R. Delahunty (Mgr)
No.of Employees: 1 - 10 **Product Groups:** 35, 36, 39

Selden Mast Ltd
Lederle Lane, Gosport, PO13 0FZ
Tel: 01329-504000 **Fax:** 01329-504049
E-mail: info@seldenmast.co.uk
Website: http://www.seldenmast.com
Directors: S. Norbury (MD)
Ultimate Holding Company: FURLEX AB (SWEDEN)
Immediate Holding Company: SELDEN MASTS LIMITED
Registration no: 00952439 **VAT No.:** GB 188 2682 20
Date established: 1969 **Turnover:** £2m - £5m **No.of Employees:** 21 - 50
Product Groups: 35, 39

Date of Accounts	Dec 11	Dec 10	Dec 09
Working Capital	605	447	364
Fixed Assets	4m	4m	4m
Current Assets	2m	2m	2m

David Sharp Ltd
The Sanderson Centre Lees Lane, Gosport, PO12 3UL
Tel: 023-9260 1318 **Fax:** 0845-833 5103
E-mail: sales@davidsharp.co.uk
Website: http://www.davidsharp.co.uk
Directors: D. Bunce (Dir)
Immediate Holding Company: DAVID SHARP LIMITED
Registration no: 05997694 **VAT No.:** GB 118 7925 44
Date established: 2006 **No.of Employees:** 1 - 10 **Product Groups:** 84

Date of Accounts	Mar 11	Mar 10	Nov 08
Working Capital	27	8	5
Fixed Assets	1	N/A	N/A
Current Assets	49	29	41

Smurfit Kappa Gosport
Fort Brockhurst Industrial Estate Wingate Road, Gosport, PO12 4DR
Tel: 023-9258 4511 **Fax:** 023-9250 3161
E-mail: paul.gatt@smurfitkappa.co.uk
Website: http://www.smurfitkappa.co.uk
Managers: P. Gatt (Mgr), G. Male (Buyer), D. Edwards (Fin Mgr)
No.of Employees: 21 - 50 **Product Groups:** 27

Technical Services
Unit 5 Quay Lane, Hardway, Gosport, PO12 4LJ
Tel: 023-9258 8059 **Fax:** 023-9258 9556
E-mail: enquiries@techsoundsystems.co.uk
Website: http://www.techsoundsystems.co.uk
Directors: J. Kemp (Prop)
Date established: 1986 **No.of Employees:** 1 - 10 **Product Groups:** 37, 67, 83

Havant

Acorn Engineering
6 Kingscroft Court Ridgway, Havant, PO9 1LS
Tel: 023-9249 2040 **Fax:** 023-9247 0377
E-mail: mail@acorn-engineering.co.uk
Website: http://www.acorn-engineering.co.uk
Directors: N. Van Der Lugt (MD)
Immediate Holding Company: ACORN ENGINEERING (HOLBEACH) LIMITED
Registration no: 05573284 **Date established:** 2005
Turnover: £500,000 - £1m **No.of Employees:** 1 - 10 **Product Groups:** 48

Date of Accounts	Oct 11	Oct 10	Oct 09
Working Capital	-46	-44	-34
Fixed Assets	115	121	130
Current Assets	53	78	71

Apollo Fire Detectors Ltd (A Halma Group Company)
36 Brookside Road, Havant, PO9 1JR
Tel: 023-9249 2412 **Fax:** 023-9249 2754
E-mail: marketing@apollo-fire.co.uk
Website: http://www.apollo-fire.co.uk
Bank(s): National Westminster
Directors: R. Bramham (Mkt Research), T. Preston (Fin), T. Preston (Co Sec)
Managers: L. Truong
Ultimate Holding Company: HALMA PUBLIC LIMITED COMPANY
Immediate Holding Company: APOLLO FIRE DETECTORS LIMITED
Registration no: 01483208 **Date established:** 1980
Turnover: £50m - £75m **No.of Employees:** 251 - 500 **Product Groups:** 38

Date of Accounts	Mar 12	Mar 09	Apr 10
Sales Turnover	63m	60m	58m
Pre Tax Profit/Loss	14m	10m	11m

Working Capital	19m	12m	14m
Fixed Assets	9m	10m	10m
Current Assets	28m	24m	24m
Current Liabilities	1m	1m	2m

Asahi Thermofil UK Ltd

28 New Lane, Havant, PO9 2NQ
Tel: 023-9248 6350 **Fax:** 023-9247 2388
Website: http://www.thermofil.co.uk
Directors: J. Gilder (MD), P. Claydon (Fin)
Ultimate Holding Company: SUMIKA POLYMER COMPOUNDS (EUROPE) LTD
Immediate Holding Company: SUMIKA POLYMER COMPOUNDS (UK) LTD
Registration no: 02594313 **Date established:** 1991
Turnover: £20m - £50m **No.of Employees:** 101 - 250
Product Groups: 30, 48

Date of Accounts	Dec 11	Dec 10	Dec 09
Sales Turnover	39m	32m	25m
Pre Tax Profit/Loss	-1m	-836	-984
Working Capital	-4m	-2m	216
Fixed Assets	9m	9m	8m
Current Assets	13m	14m	11m
Current Liabilities	10m	6m	5m

Bedhampton Piano Shop Ltd

90 Bedhampton Road, Havant, PO9 3EZ
Tel: 023-9248 4802 **Fax:** 0800-298 5087
E-mail: sales@bpspianos.com
Website: http://www.bedhamptonpianoshop.co.uk
Directors: G. Nicholls (Fin), G. Nicholls (MD)
Immediate Holding Company: BEDHAMPTON PIANOSHOP LIMITED
Registration no: 04167613 **Date established:** 2001
Turnover: Up to £250,000 **No.of Employees:** 1 - 10 **Product Groups:** 49

Date of Accounts	Mar 11	Mar 10	Mar 09
Working Capital	17	15	2
Fixed Assets	1	1	1
Current Assets	29	36	26

Butterick Co. Ltd

38 New Lane, Havant, PO9 2ND
Tel: 023-9248 6221 **Fax:** 023-9247 5383
E-mail: sales@butterick-vogue.co.uk
Website: http://www.sewdirect.com
Bank(s): Lloyds TSB Bank plc
Directors: I. Scorer (Sales), K. Jones (MD)
Ultimate Holding Company: MP HOLDINGS INC (USA)
Immediate Holding Company: BUTTERICK GROUP LIMITED
Registration no: 02190449 **VAT No.:** GB 582 9067 09
Date established: 1987 **Turnover:** £2m - £5m **No.of Employees:** 21 - 50
Product Groups: 28

Date of Accounts	Dec 11	Dec 10	Dec 09
Working Capital	-2m	-2m	-2m
Fixed Assets	4m	4m	4m
Current Assets	128	128	256

Colt Service Ltd

New Lane, Havant, PO9 2LY
Tel: 023-9245 5411 **Fax:** 023-9249 2067
Website: http://www.coltgroup.com
Directors: M. Ward Penny (Dir), P. Winfield (Co Sec), J. Humphrey (MD)
Ultimate Holding Company: COLT INVESTMENTS LIMITED
Immediate Holding Company: COLT SERVICE LIMITED
Registration no: 00442015 **Date established:** 1947 **Turnover:** £5m - £10m
No.of Employees: 21 - 50 **Product Groups:** 40, 66

Date of Accounts	Dec 10	Dec 09	Dec 08
Sales Turnover	6m	5m	5m
Pre Tax Profit/Loss	870	625	829
Working Capital	2m	2m	1m
Fixed Assets	5	3	4
Current Assets	3m	2m	2m
Current Liabilities	509	362	364

Covelward Ltd (t/a Road Runner Despatch)

19 South Street, Havant, PO9 1BU
Tel: 023-9249 2492 **Fax:** 023-9249 2493
E-mail: rob@roadrunnerdispatch.co.uk
Website: http://www.roadrunnerdispatch.co.uk
Directors: K. Edwards (MD), T. Cowper (Fin)
Immediate Holding Company: COVELWARD LIMITED
Registration no: 01340877 **VAT No.:** GB 321 6239 85
Date established: 1977 **No.of Employees:** 1 - 10 **Product Groups:** 79

Date of Accounts	Mar 11	Mar 10	Mar 09
Working Capital	49	80	65
Fixed Assets	21	8	8
Current Assets	109	122	113

Deep Sea Seals Ltd

4 Marples Way, Havant, PO9 1NX
Tel: 023-9249 2123 **Fax:** 023-9249 2470
E-mail: robert.burford@deepseaseals.com
Website: http://www.wartsila.com
Directors: J. Cousins (MD), R. Burford (MD), T. Eaves (Co Sec)
Ultimate Holding Company: TI Group P.L.C.
Immediate Holding Company: WARTSILA UK LIMITED
Registration no: 01004816 **Date established:** 1971
Turnover: £75m - £125m **No.of Employees:** 101 - 250
Product Groups: 39

E M P Tooling Services Ltd

9 Brockhampton Lane, Havant, PO9 1LU
Tel: 023-9249 2626 **Fax:** 023-9249 2582
E-mail: info@e-m-p.biz
Website: http://www.e-m-p.biz
Bank(s): Lloyds TSB Bank plc
Directors: P. Barker (Dir)
Immediate Holding Company: EMP TOOLING SERVICES LIMITED
Registration no: 04778951 **Date established:** 2003
Turnover: £500,000 - £1m **No.of Employees:** 11 - 20
Product Groups: 42, 48

Date of Accounts	May 11	May 10	May 09
Working Capital	67	106	44
Fixed Assets	495	466	425
Current Assets	195	276	202

Eaton Hydraulics

46 New Lane, Havant, PO9 2NB
Tel: 023-9248 6451 **Fax:** 023-9248 7110
E-mail: barryking@eaton.com
Website: http://www.eaton.com
Managers: M. Foreman (Plant), P. Hine (Comptroller), B. Byrne (Purch Mgr), B. King (Mktg Serv Mgr)
Ultimate Holding Company: EATON CORPORATION (USA)
Immediate Holding Company: EATON PENSION PLAN TRUSTEE LIMITED
Registration no: 02554378 **Date established:** 1990
Turnover: Over £1,000m **No.of Employees:** 101 - 250
Product Groups: 36, 38, 40

Five Star Units (Slopekarn Ltd)

60-62 Bedhampton Road, Havant, PO9 3EY
Tel: 023-9248 6101 **Fax:** 023-9247 6666
E-mail: sales@fivestarunits.co.uk
Website: http://www.engineandgearbox.co.uk
Directors: A. Vine (Prop)
Immediate Holding Company: KWIK CLUTCH LIMITED
Registration no: 04208736 **Date established:** 2006
Turnover: Up to £250,000 **No.of Employees:** 1 - 10 **Product Groups:** 35, 40, 68

Itk Services

6 Fern Drive, Havant, PO9 2YH
Tel: 08450-580657
E-mail: info@itkservices.co.uk
Website: http://www.itkservices.co.uk
Directors: A. Drain (Prop)
Immediate Holding Company: F.D. CARPENTRY LTD
Registration no: 06170542 **Date established:** 2007
No.of Employees: 1 - 10 **Product Groups:** 49, 80

Date of Accounts	Mar 12	Mar 11	Mar 10
Working Capital	22	24	18
Fixed Assets	6	8	10
Current Assets	26	25	21

Kenwood Ltd

1-3 Kenwood Business Park New Lane, Havant, PO9 2NH
Tel: 023-9247 6000 **Fax:** 023-9239 2400
E-mail: info@kenwood.co.uk
Website: http://www.kenwood.co.uk
Bank(s): Barclays
Directors: F. De' Longhi (Dir), I. Fry (Fin), R. Kirk (Dir)
Ultimate Holding Company: DELONGHI SPA (ITALY)
Immediate Holding Company: KENWOOD LIMITED
Registration no: 00872044 **VAT No.:** GB 486 9897 49
Date established: 1966 **Turnover:** £250m - £500m
No.of Employees: 101 - 250 **Product Groups:** 40

Date of Accounts	Dec 11	Dec 10	Dec 09
Sales Turnover	298m	297m	240m
Pre Tax Profit/Loss	15m	20m	15m
Working Capital	37m	47m	36m
Fixed Assets	12m	11m	8m
Current Assets	111m	125m	103m
Current Liabilities	22m	30m	28m

Kier Southern

St Andrews House West Street, Havant, PO9 1LB
Tel: 023-9248 4343 **Fax:** 023-9245 5414
E-mail: lisa.haywood@kier.co.uk
Website: http://www.kier.co.uk
Directors: G. Willoughby (MD), M. Orr (Dir)
Managers: C. Capelan (Purch Mgr), L. Halford (I.T. Exec), G. Harrison, A. Lamb (Comm)
Ultimate Holding Company: KIER REGIONAL LTD
Immediate Holding Company: KIER GROUP
Registration no: 02099533 **VAT No.:** GB 530 9576 35
Turnover: £20m - £50m **No.of Employees:** 21 - 50 **Product Groups:** 51, 66, 84

Lewmar Ltd

South Moore Lane, Havant, PO9 1JJ
Tel: 023-9247 1841 **Fax:** 023-9248 5770
E-mail: reception@lewmar.com
Website: http://www.lewmar.com
Managers: M. Johnston (Mgr)
Ultimate Holding Company: LEWMAR MARINE LIMITED
Immediate Holding Company: LEWMAR LIMITED
Registration no: 00620277 **VAT No.:** GB 381 0064 82
Date established: 1959 **Turnover:** £20m - £50m **No.of Employees:** 1 - 10
Product Groups: 39, 45, 68

Date of Accounts	Dec 11	Dec 10	Dec 09
Sales Turnover	35m	33m	45m
Pre Tax Profit/Loss	2m	1m	-9m
Working Capital	-2m	-3m	-6m
Fixed Assets	2m	2m	3m
Current Assets	14m	15m	15m
Current Liabilities	2m	2m	2m

Northshore Composites Ltd

Brockhampton Road, Havant, PO9 1JU
Tel: 023-9247 1428 **Fax:** 023-9245 2228
E-mail: lester.abbott@northshore.co.uk
Website: http://www.northshore-composites.co.uk
Directors: L. Legon (Co Sec), B. Mabb (MD), B. Moffat (Ch), J. Course (MD), L. Abbott (Ch), L. Abbott (MD)
Managers: D. Palmer (Chief Mgr), M. Taylor (I.T. Exec)
Ultimate Holding Company: SUNCHALK LIMITED
Immediate Holding Company: NORTHSHORE COMPOSITES LIMITED
Registration no: 01373288 **Date established:** 1978 **Turnover:** £1m - £2m
No.of Employees: 21 - 50 **Product Groups:** 30, 48

Date of Accounts	Dec 10	Dec 09	Dec 08
Working Capital	115	144	111
Fixed Assets	29	38	5
Current Assets	474	402	398

Owen Advertising Ltd

Hall Place South Street, Havant, PO9 1DA
Tel: 023-9247 6431 **Fax:** 023-9245 3262
E-mail: advertising@theowenagency.co.uk
Website: http://www.theowenagency.co.uk
Directors: D. Newnham (MD)
Immediate Holding Company: OWEN ADVERTISING LIMITED
Registration no: 01252009 **Date established:** 1976
No.of Employees: 1 - 10 **Product Groups:** 81

Date of Accounts	Feb 11	Feb 10	Feb 09
Working Capital	39	35	32
Current Assets	171	226	166

Portsmouth Water Company

West Street, Havant, PO9 1LG
Tel: 023-9249 9666 **Fax:** 023-9245 3632
E-mail: customers@portsmouthwater.co.uk
Website: http://www.portsmouthwater.co.uk
Bank(s): Natwest
Directors: N. Smith (MD), N. Roadnight (MD)
Managers: P. Mosley (Tech Serv Mgr), H. Fancourt (Purch Mgr), I. Limb (Personnel)
Ultimate Holding Company: SOUTH DOWNS CAPITAL LIMITED
Immediate Holding Company: PORTSMOUTH WATER LIMITED
Registration no: 02536455 **VAT No.:** GB 615 3758 35
Date established: 1990 **Turnover:** £20m - £50m
No.of Employees: 101 - 250 **Product Groups:** 18, 51, 84

Date of Accounts	Mar 11	Mar 10	Mar 09
Sales Turnover	36m	37m	35m
Pre Tax Profit/Loss	868	8m	6m
Working Capital	-10m	-13m	-10m
Fixed Assets	176m	165m	163m
Current Assets	7m	7m	7m
Current Liabilities	10m	11m	10m

Premier Sheet Metal & Engineering Co. Ltd

4 Premier Building Brockhampton Road, Havant, PO9 1JU
Tel: 023-9247 2633 **Fax:** 023-9249 8210
E-mail: sales@premiersheetmetal.co.uk
Website: http://www.premiersheetmetal.co.uk
Directors: S. Boyd Brown (Fin), J. Boyd Brown (Dir), J. Boyd-Brown (MD)
Immediate Holding Company: PREMIER SHEET METAL AND ENGINEERING COMPANY LIMITED
Registration no: 01039641 **VAT No.:** GB 107 3616 90
Date established: 1972 **Turnover:** £250,000 - £500,000
No.of Employees: 1 - 10 **Product Groups:** 48

Date of Accounts	Jan 08	Jan 07	Jan 06
Working Capital	22	10	-6
Fixed Assets	11	4	4
Current Assets	129	111	106
Current Liabilities	107	101	112
Total Share Capital	1	1	1

R M Rotary Services Ltd

New Lane, Havant, PO9 2LT
Tel: 023-9249 2360 **Fax:** 023-9249 2544
E-mail: sales@rmrotary.co.uk
Website: http://www.rmrotary.co.uk
Bank(s): Abbey National
Directors: M. Waterhouse (Co Sec), J. Brown (Sales)
Immediate Holding Company: R.M. (ROTARY) SERVICES LIMITED
Registration no: 01986291 **VAT No.:** GB 109 1727 79
Date established: 1986 **Turnover:** £1m - £2m **No.of Employees:** 11 - 20
Product Groups: 44

Date of Accounts	Sep 11	Sep 10	Sep 09
Working Capital	281	272	274
Fixed Assets	321	330	337
Current Assets	376	363	349

Rowland Way Ltd

Southmoor Lane, Havant, PO9 1JW
Tel: 023-9245 3879 **Fax:** 023-9245 5593
E-mail: rowlandwayltd@netscapeonline.co.uk
Website: http://www.rowlandwayltd.com
Directors: C. Ashton (Fin), G. Short (MD)
Immediate Holding Company: ROWLAND WAY LIMITED
Registration no: 01174654 **Date established:** 1974
No.of Employees: 21 - 50 **Product Groups:** 46, 48

Date of Accounts	Mar 12	Mar 11	Mar 10
Working Capital	120	120	105
Fixed Assets	1	4	7
Current Assets	170	171	146

Sargrove Automation

The Chestnuts 11 Eastern Road, Havant, PO9 2JE
Tel: 023-9247 7244 **Fax:** 023-9247 1981
E-mail: sargrove@btinternet.com
Directors: M. Vick (Prop)
VAT No.: GB 503 8878 27 **Date established:** 1986
Turnover: Up to £250,000 **No.of Employees:** 1 - 10 **Product Groups:** 84

Technical Architectural Lighting UK Ltd

8 Havant Business Centre Harts Farm Way, Havant, PO9 1HU
Tel: 023-9244 0555 **Fax:** 023-9247 3099
E-mail: sales@tallighting.com
Website: http://www.tal.be
Directors: R. Cutting (MD), S. Cutting (Co Sec)
Immediate Holding Company: TECHNICAL ARCHITECTURAL LIGHTING (UK) LIMITED
Registration no: 05051429 **Date established:** 2004
Turnover: Up to £250,000 **No.of Employees:** 1 - 10 **Product Groups:** 37, 67

Date of Accounts	May 11	May 10	May 08
Sales Turnover	237	287	N/A
Pre Tax Profit/Loss	-6	-3	N/A
Working Capital	-168	-164	-88
Fixed Assets	2	3	2
Current Assets	149	119	131
Current Liabilities	57	62	N/A

Town & Country Covers Ltd

Unit 7 6 Larchwood Avenue, Havant, PO9 3BE
Tel: 023-9247 4711 **Fax:** 023-9247 4722
E-mail: info@townandcountrycovers.com
Website: http://www.townandcountrycovers.com
Directors: P. Newman (MD)
Immediate Holding Company: TOWN & COUNTRY COVERS LIMITED
Registration no: 05049328 **Date established:** 2004 **Turnover:** £1m - £2m
No.of Employees: 11 - 20 **Product Groups:** 68

Date of Accounts	Mar 11	Mar 10	Mar 09
Working Capital	539	513	432
Fixed Assets	71	56	57
Current Assets	764	583	550

W A S P Ltd (Wessex Advanced Switching Products Ltd)

Alexandria Park 1 Penner Road, Havant, PO9 1QY
Tel: 023-9245 7000 **Fax:** 023-9247 3918
E-mail: sales@wasp-ltd.co.uk
Website: http://www.waspswitches.co.uk
Bank(s): Bank of Scotland

see next page

W A S P Ltd (Wessex Advanced Switching Products Ltd) - Cont'd

Directors: J. Martyn (Co Sec)
Managers: S. Austin (Sales Off Mgr), S. Nash (Mats Contrlr), M. Porter (Tech Serv Mgr)
Immediate Holding Company: W.A.S.P. LIMITED
Registration no: 01720998 **Date established:** 1983 **Turnover:** £2m - £5m
No.of Employees: 51 - 100 **Product Groups:** 29, 37, 44

Date of Accounts	Apr 11	Apr 10	Apr 09
Working Capital	79	200	238
Fixed Assets	56	65	91
Current Assets	203	323	445

Xyratex Technology Limited

Langstone Technology Park Langstone Road, Havant, PO9 1SA
Tel: 023-9249 6000 **Fax:** 023-9245 3654
E-mail: info@uk.xyratex.com
Website: http://www.xyratex.com
Directors: J. Easson (MD), R. Pearce (Co Sec)
Managers: G. Yarnall (Sales & Mktg Mg), M. Blunt (Mktg Serv Mgr)
Ultimate Holding Company: XYRATEX LTD (BERMUDA)
Immediate Holding Company: Xyratex Technology Ltd
Registration no: 02857496 **Date established:** 1993 **Turnover:** £2m - £5m
No.of Employees: 501 - 1000 **Product Groups:** 44, 84

Date of Accounts	Nov 06
Pre Tax Profit/Loss	21290
Working Capital	27480
Current Assets	27480
Total Share Capital	390

Hayling Island

Hawk Marine Products

Mill Rythe Lane, Hayling Island, PO11 0QG
Tel: 023-9246 3864 **Fax:** 023-9246 7204
E-mail: sales@hawkmouldings.co.uk
Website: http://www.hawkmarineproducts.com
Directors: R. Search (Prop)
Immediate Holding Company: HAWK MARINE PRODUCTS LIMITED
Registration no: 05815745 **VAT No.:** GB 107 6471 75
Date established: 2006 **Turnover:** £250,000 - £500,000
No.of Employees: 1 - 10 **Product Groups:** 30, 48

Date of Accounts	Oct 11	Oct 10	May 08
Working Capital	-32	-33	N/A
Fixed Assets	18	23	N/A
Current Assets	67	74	N/A

Marine Propulsion Services Limited

254a Havant Road, Hayling Island, PO11 0LW
Tel: 023-9246 1694 **Fax:** 023-9246 7824
E-mail: info@marinepropulsion.co.uk
Website: http://www.marinepropulsion.co.uk
Directors: L. Judge (Ptnr)
Registration no: 01973318 **Date established:** 1983
No.of Employees: 1 - 10 **Product Groups:** 35, 36, 39

Pullingers Furnishers Ltd

108-110 Elm Grove, Hayling Island, PO11 9EN
Tel: 023-9246 3922 **Fax:** 023-9246 1123
E-mail: sales@pullingers.net
Website: http://www.pullingers.net
Bank(s): National Westminster
Directors: I. Currie (Fin), B. Smith (Co Sec)
Managers: E. Shepherd (Chief Mgr), S. Beale
Immediate Holding Company: PULLINGERS (FURNISHERS) LIMITED
Registration no: 00621265 **Date established:** 1959 **Turnover:** £1m - £2m
No.of Employees: 11 - 20 **Product Groups:** 61

Date of Accounts	Mar 12	Mar 11	Mar 10
Working Capital	285	328	391
Fixed Assets	2m	2m	2m
Current Assets	832	846	1m

Seaboard Ltd

Quayside Marine Walk, Hayling Island, PO11 9PQ
Tel: 023-9246 2295 **Fax:** 023-9246 2295
Website: http://www.workboathire.com
Directors: M. Walton (Dir)
Immediate Holding Company: SEABOARD LIMITED
Registration no: 03906318 **Date established:** 2000
No.of Employees: 1 - 10 **Product Groups:** 35, 36, 39

Date of Accounts	Jan 08	Jan 07	Jan 06
Working Capital	-85	-60	-55
Fixed Assets	N/A	3	25
Current Assets	2	3	7
Current Liabilities	87	63	62
Total Share Capital	1	1	1

Hook

A P T Systems

Unit 1 Westfields Coopers Hill, Eversley, Hook, RG27 0QA
Tel: 01252-877704 **Fax:** 01252-877705
E-mail: info@timefore.co.uk
Website: http://www.timefore.co.uk
Directors: N. Hinchliffe (Prop)
No.of Employees: 1 - 10 **Product Groups:** 29

B M W Financial Services Group

Europa House Berkeley Way, Hook, RG27 9XA
Tel: 08705-050150 **Fax:** 01256-749010
E-mail: customer.service@bmwfin.com
Website: http://www.bmw.co.uk
Directors: G. Lorenz (Dir), M. Ferriss (Co Sec)
Ultimate Holding Company: BAYERISCHE MOTOREN WERKE AG (GERMANY)
Immediate Holding Company: BMW FINANCIAL SERVICES (GB) LIMITED
Registration no: 01288537 **Date established:** 1976
Turnover: £250m - £500m **No.of Employees:** 251 - 500
Product Groups: 82

Date of Accounts	Dec 11	Dec 10	Dec 09
Sales Turnover	374m	383m	364m
Pre Tax Profit/Loss	145m	130m	52m
Working Capital	-258m	-173m	-222m
Fixed Assets	2432m	2133m	2063m
Current Assets	1824m	1743m	1688m
Current Liabilities	310m	333m	395m

Bliss Sound Direct UK Ltd

Old Police Cottage Gaston Lane, South Warnborough, Hook, RG29 1RH
Tel: 01256-862733 **Fax:** 01256- 862889
E-mail: donhockman@blisssound.com
Website: http://www.blisssound.com
Directors: D. Hockman (MD)
Immediate Holding Company: BLISS SOUND DIRECT (UK) LTD
Registration no: 04428517 **VAT No.:** GB 784 1783 92
Date established: 2002 **Turnover:** Up to £250,000
No.of Employees: 1 - 10 **Product Groups:** 49

Date of Accounts	Jul 09	Jul 08	Jul 07
Sales Turnover	121	434	611
Pre Tax Profit/Loss	-26	22	33
Working Capital	17	66	110
Fixed Assets	1	1	3
Current Assets	30	102	170
Current Liabilities	2	14	19

C K Gas Products

Unit 3 Murrell Green Business Park London Road, Hook, RG27 9GR
Tel: 01256-766633 **Fax:** 01270-258880
E-mail: sales@ckgas.com
Website: http://www.ckgas.com
Directors: W. Pepper (Prop)
Registration no: 02550018 **VAT No.:** GB 592 0711 46
Turnover: £500,000 - £1m **No.of Employees:** 1 - 10 **Product Groups:** 31, 36, 37, 38, 42

Date of Accounts	Oct 07	Oct 06	Oct 05
Working Capital	145	54	-16
Fixed Assets	138	154	156
Current Assets	538	464	368
Current Liabilities	393	410	384

Coveford Data Systems Ltd

Old Bank House 59 High Street Odiham, Hook, RG29 1LF
Tel: 01256-704333 **Fax:** 07031-159754
E-mail: brian.bidston@coveford.com
Website: http://www.coveford.com
Directors: B. Bidston (Prop), B. Bidston (Dir), S. Talbot-Walsh (I.T. Dir)
Managers: M. Wilson (Personnel)
Ultimate Holding Company: COVEFORD LIMITED
Immediate Holding Company: COVEFORD LIMITED
Registration no: 03026024 **VAT No.:** GB 664 6111 41
Date established: 1995 **Turnover:** £250,000 - £500,000
No.of Employees: 1 - 10 **Product Groups:** 44, 84

Date of Accounts	Jul 11	Jul 10	Jul 09
Sales Turnover	48	47	256
Pre Tax Profit/Loss	15	-83	325
Working Capital	168	105	96
Fixed Assets	1m	1m	1m
Current Assets	168	106	130
Current Liabilities	N/A	2	33

E E F Ltd

Station Road, Hook, RG27 9TL
Tel: 01256-763969 **Fax:** 01256-768530
E-mail: schicken@eef.org.uk
Website: http://www.eef.org.uk
Bank(s): Lloyds TSB Bank plc
Directors: S. Chicken (Dir)
Managers: L. Murfitt (Personnel), M. Wilson, D. Douglas (Mktg Serv Mgr)
Immediate Holding Company: EEF LIMITED
Registration no: 05950172 **Date established:** 2006 **Turnover:** £1m - £2m
No.of Employees: 51 - 100 **Product Groups:** 54, 80, 81, 84, 85, 86, 87

Date of Accounts	Dec 11	Dec 10	Dec 09
Sales Turnover	35m	36m	47m
Pre Tax Profit/Loss	2m	-2m	-7m
Working Capital	-331	-2m	-517
Fixed Assets	49m	49m	50m
Current Assets	9m	7m	8m
Current Liabilities	8m	6m	5m

Elvetham Hotel Ltd

Elvetham, Hook, RG27 8AR
Tel: 01252-844871 **Fax:** 01252-844161
E-mail: enquiries@elvethamhotel.co.uk
Website: http://www.elvethamhotel.co.uk
Bank(s): Barclays, London
Directors: P. Warden (MD), S. Scarr (Fin), S. Scarr (Fin)
Managers: L. Taylor, A. Bushnell (I.T. Exec), A. Bushnell (Tech Serv Mgr), B. Cotton (Mktg Serv Mgr), L. Ralph
Immediate Holding Company: KAYE ENTERPRISES LTD
VAT No.: GB 199 1292 25 **Turnover:** £1m - £2m
No.of Employees: 51 - 100 **Product Groups:** 69, 81

Date of Accounts	Jan 08	Jan 07	Jan 06
Working Capital	-241	-261	-113
Fixed Assets	451	471	571
Current Assets	776	537	423
Current Liabilities	1017	799	537

Favio Ltd

29 Bell Meadow Road, Hook, RG27 9HL
Tel: 01256-760732 **Fax:** 01256-760732
E-mail: support@favio.co.uk
Website: http://www.favio.co.uk
Directors: N. Perrins (Dir)
Immediate Holding Company: FAVIO LTD
Registration no: 04722963 **Date established:** 2003
No.of Employees: 1 - 10 **Product Groups:** 44

Date of Accounts	Apr 11	Apr 10	Apr 09
Working Capital	5	N/A	-1
Fixed Assets	1	N/A	N/A
Current Assets	40	37	30
Current Liabilities	N/A	N/A	28

First Drinks Brands Ltd

Form 1 17 Bartley Wood Business Park, Hook, RG27 9XA
Tel: 01256-748100 **Fax:** 023-8031 6202
E-mail: enquiries@firstdrinks.co.uk
Website: http://www.firstdrinks.co.uk
Managers: G. Hayes (Projects)
Ultimate Holding Company: WILLIAM GRANT & SONS HOLDINGS LIMITED
Immediate Holding Company: FIRST DRINKS BRANDS LIMITED
Registration no: 02288241 **VAT No.:** GB 643 3943 31
Date established: 1988 **Turnover:** £50m - £75m
No.of Employees: 101 - 250 **Product Groups:** 62

Date of Accounts	Dec 11	Dec 10	Dec 09
Sales Turnover	126m	122m	97m
Pre Tax Profit/Loss	479	521	500
Working Capital	-939	-1m	252
Fixed Assets	1m	2m	142
Current Assets	132m	120m	118m
Current Liabilities	50m	43m	37m

High Pressure Hire Ltd

Unit 8 Tylney Park Drive Rotherwick, Hook, RG27 9AY
Tel: 01256-763440 **Fax:** 01256-760748
E-mail: info@highpressurehire.co.uk
Website: http://www.highpressurehire.co.uk
Directors: H. Gould (Fin), M. Lane (Dir)
Immediate Holding Company: HIGH PRESSURE HIRE LIMITED
Registration no: 02420842 **VAT No.:** GB 537 5275 27
Date established: 1989 **Turnover:** £250,000 - £500,000
No.of Employees: 1 - 10 **Product Groups:** 29, 30, 36, 39, 40, 45, 46, 48, 52, 68

Date of Accounts	Apr 11	Apr 10	Apr 09
Working Capital	-7	-3	2
Fixed Assets	117	122	98
Current Assets	80	84	120

J D Engineering

Albion Forge Dunleys Hill, North Warnborough, Hook, RG29 1DX
Tel: 01256-702477 **Fax:** 01256-702477
Website: http://www.albiongatesandrailings.co.uk
Directors: J. Sherwood (Prop)
Registration no: 03443519 **Date established:** 1997
No.of Employees: 1 - 10 **Product Groups:** 26, 35, 46

K3 Panacea

Bartley House Station Road, Hook, RG27 9JF
Tel: 01256-744000 **Fax:** 01256-769388
E-mail: enquiries@k3panacea.co.uk
Website: http://www.k3panacea.co.uk
Bank(s): Lloyds
Directors: A. Fox (Fin)
Ultimate Holding Company: K3 BUSINESS TECHNOLOGY GROUP PLC
Immediate Holding Company: K3 PANACEA LIMITED
Registration no: 02052916 **Date established:** 1986
Turnover: £10m - £20m **No.of Employees:** 11 - 20 **Product Groups:** 44

Date of Accounts	Dec 09	Dec 08	Dec 07
Sales Turnover	9m	10m	11m
Pre Tax Profit/Loss	-148	287	753
Working Capital	1m	2m	1m
Fixed Assets	376	385	515
Current Assets	6m	8m	7m
Current Liabilities	4m	3m	3m

Kistler Instruments Ltd

Unit 13 Murrell Green Business Park London Road, Hook, RG27 9GR
Tel: 01256-741550 **Fax:** 01256-741551
E-mail: sales.uk@kistler.com
Website: http://www.kistler.com
Directors: J. Vaughan (MD)
Immediate Holding Company: KISTLER INSTRUMENTS LIMITED
Registration no: 01106319 **Date established:** 1973 **Turnover:** £2m - £5m
No.of Employees: 1 - 10 **Product Groups:** 37, 38

Date of Accounts	Dec 11	Dec 10	Dec 09
Working Capital	583	500	432
Fixed Assets	54	85	98
Current Assets	2m	2m	1m

Lyons Sleeman Hoare Ltd

Nero Brewery Cricket Green, Hartley Wintney, Hook, RG27 8QA
Tel: 01252-844144 **Fax:** 01252-844800
E-mail: enquiries@lsharch.co.uk
Website: http://www.lsharch.co.uk
Bank(s): Royal Bank of Scotland P.L.C.
Directors: M. Lyons (Ch), N. Ralls (MD), A. Falkiner (Fin)
Managers: S. Spencer (Personnel), J. Hudson (Tech Serv Mgr)
Immediate Holding Company: LYONS + SLEEMAN + HOARE LIMITED
Registration no: 06950454 **VAT No.:** GB 239 6627 29
Date established: 2009 **Turnover:** £2m - £5m **No.of Employees:** 21 - 50
Product Groups: 84

Date of Accounts	Mar 12	Mar 11	Mar 10
Working Capital	691	226	92
Fixed Assets	88	64	83
Current Assets	2m	1m	1m

M & G Steel Fabrications Ltd

B1 Reading Road Rotherwick, Hook, RG27 9DA
Tel: 01256-764457 **Fax:** 01256-764458
E-mail: mark@mg-steel.co.uk
Website: http://www.mg-steel.com
Directors: M. Guzam (MD)
Immediate Holding Company: M & G STEEL FABRICATIONS LIMITED
Registration no: 03190427 **Date established:** 1996
No.of Employees: 1 - 10 **Product Groups:** 35, 40, 48

Date of Accounts	Mar 12	Mar 11	Mar 10
Working Capital	13	-10	-4
Fixed Assets	17	12	15
Current Assets	188	212	178

Micro Movements Ltd

Eversley Centre, Hook, RG27 0NB
Tel: 0118-973 0200 **Fax:** 0118-932 8872
E-mail: georgewilliams@micromovements.co.uk
Website: http://www.daqsys.com
Directors: A. Smith (MD), G. Gibbons (Co Sec), G. Williams (Dir)
Ultimate Holding Company: APPLIED DYNAMIC SYSTEMS LIMITED
Immediate Holding Company: MICRO MOVEMENTS LIMITED
Registration no: 02900700 **VAT No.:** GB 641 2392 59
Date established: 1994 **Turnover:** £500,000 - £1m
No.of Employees: 1 - 10 **Product Groups:** 37, 38, 44

Date of Accounts	Dec 11	Dec 10	Dec 09
Working Capital	136	106	162
Fixed Assets	N/A	N/A	1
Current Assets	291	244	256

Neale Consulting Engineers Ltd
Highfield Pilcot Hill, Dogmersfield, Hook, RG27 8SX
Tel: 01252-629199 **Fax:** 01252-815625
E-mail: mike@chalkdell.com
Website: http://www.tribology.co.uk
Directors: M. Neale (MD)
Immediate Holding Company: NEALE CONSULTING ENGINEERS LTD.
Registration no: 01238569 **VAT No.:** GB 189 9225 07
Date established: 1975 **Turnover:** £250,000 - £500,000
No.of Employees: 1 - 10 **Product Groups:** 35, 37, 80, 81, 84, 85, 86

Date of Accounts	Sep 11	Sep 10	Sep 09
Working Capital	80	101	125
Fixed Assets	1	1	1
Current Assets	141	158	166

Paella Co. Ltd
Lodge Farm Hook Road North Warnborough, Hook, RG29 1HA
Tel: 01256-702020 **Fax:** 01256-703086
E-mail: info@thepaellacompany.co.uk
Website: http://www.thepaellacompany.co.uk
Directors: K. White (MD)
Ultimate Holding Company: MAVUNO HOLDINGS (UK) LIMITED
Immediate Holding Company: WHITEWATER POTATOES LIMITED
Date established: 1987 **No.of Employees:** 1 - 10 **Product Groups:** 40, 67, 83

Date of Accounts	Jun 11	Jun 10	Jun 09
Working Capital	-374	-524	-2m
Fixed Assets	8m	8m	8m
Current Assets	3m	2m	1m

Protus Electronics Ltd
Millford House New Mill Lane, Eversley, Hook, RG27 0RA
Tel: 0118-973 0255 **Fax:** 0118-973 0070
E-mail: peterwhoward@btopenworld.com
Directors: P. Howard (Jt MD), P. Howard (MD), E. Ireland (Dir), E. Ireland (Fin)
Immediate Holding Company: PROTUS ELECTRONICS LIMITED
Registration no: 01610875 **VAT No.:** GB 314 2892 66
Date established: 1982 **Turnover:** £250,000 - £500,000
No.of Employees: 1 - 10 **Product Groups:** 37, 44

Date of Accounts	Feb 08	Feb 11	Feb 10
Working Capital	-10	35	-14
Fixed Assets	1	N/A	1
Current Assets	17	35	15

Wellhouse Storage
Well, Hook, RG29 1TL
Tel: 01256-862059 **Fax:** 01256-862115
Directors: W. Lowe (Dir)
Immediate Holding Company: D.S. JACKSON CONSTRUCTION LIMITED
Registration no: 06851015 **Date established:** 2007
No.of Employees: 1 - 10 **Product Groups:** 71

Serco Defence
Bartley Wood Business Park Bartley Way, Hook, RG27 9XA
Tel: 01256-745900 **Fax:** 01256-745995
E-mail: steve.clarke@serco.com
Website: http://www.serco.com
Bank(s): National Westminster
Directors: R. Bond (Mkt Research), S. Cuthill (MD), D. Merritt (Co Sec)
Managers: D. Burke
Ultimate Holding Company: SERCO GROUP P.L.C.
Immediate Holding Company: SERCO LTD
Registration no: 00427272 **VAT No.:** GB 207 5233 88
Date established: 1981 **Turnover:** £75m - £125m
No.of Employees: 1501 & over **Product Groups:** 71, 84, 85

Sorbican Distribution
27 Priory Lane Hartley Wintney, Hook, RG27 8EX
Tel: 01256-762435
E-mail: enquiries@sorbican.com
Website: http://www.sorbican.com
Directors: D. Lee (Prop)
No.of Employees: 1 - 10 **Product Groups:** 32, 46, 52, 54, 66, 74

STI Alliance
Osborn Way, Hook, RG27 9HX
Tel: 01256-768070 **Fax:** 01256-746746
E-mail: enquire@sti-limited.com
Website: http://www.sti-alliance.com
Managers: G. Allen (Eng)
Date established: 2006 **No.of Employees:** 251 - 500 **Product Groups:** 37, 38, 44, 67, 81, 84

Twin Industries International Ltd
1 Hartley Mews High Street, Hartley Wintney, Hook, RG27 8NX
Tel: 01252-845521 **Fax:** 01252-845523
E-mail: julie.outhwaite@twin-industries.co.uk
Website: http://www.twin-industries.co.uk
Directors: J. Outhwaite (MD)
Immediate Holding Company: TWIN INDUSTRIES AGENCIES LIMITED
Registration no: 01105961 **Date established:** 1973
No.of Employees: 1 - 10 **Product Groups:** 39, 40, 48, 66, 83

Date of Accounts	Apr 12	Apr 11	Apr 10
Working Capital	81	84	141
Fixed Assets	940	941	941
Current Assets	87	89	145

Warner Lewis
7 Murrell Green Business Park London Road, Hook, RG27 9GR
Tel: 01256-768811 **Fax:** 01256-768818
E-mail: sales@warnerlewis.co.uk
Website: http://www.warnerlewis.de
Directors: M. Hoye (MD), R. Hooton (Fin)
Managers: R. Hooton (Mgr)
Date established: 1989 **No.of Employees:** 1 - 10 **Product Groups:** 38, 42

Whitehead Incorporating County Keys Ltd
County Keys High Street Hartley Wintney, Hook, RG27 8NY
Tel: 01252-843000 **Fax:** 01252-843033
E-mail: info@countykeys.co.uk
Website: http://www.countykeys.co.uk
Directors: J. Derham (Dir), A. Hudson (Dir)
Managers: J. Watson (Sales Prom Mgr), R. Harvey (Mgr)
Immediate Holding Company: COUNTY KEYS LIMITED
Registration no: 04205403 **Date established:** 2001
Turnover: Up to £250,000 **No.of Employees:** 1 - 10 **Product Groups:** 80

Date of Accounts	Mar 10	Mar 08	Mar 07
Sales Turnover	N/A	96	89
Pre Tax Profit/Loss	N/A	10	-14
Working Capital	6	-20	-31
Fixed Assets	7	8	10
Current Assets	38	45	123
Current Liabilities	N/A	65	154

Windsor Workforce
Suite 3 The Centre Reading Road, Eversley, Hook, RG27 0NB
Tel: 0118-973 7963 **Fax:** 0845-257 3208
E-mail: claire.davis@windsorworkforce.com
Website: http://www.windsorworkforce.com
Managers: K. Robertson (Sales Prom Mgr)
Immediate Holding Company: DIVERSE PERSONAL TRAINING LIMITED
Registration no: SC294844 **Date established:** 2009
No.of Employees: 1 - 10 **Product Groups:** 80

Lee On The Solent

Britten Norman
Chark Lane Broom Way, Lee On The Solent, PO13 9YA
Tel: 020-3371 4000 **Fax:** 020-3371 4001
E-mail: enquiries@britten-norman.com
Website: http://www.britten-norman.com
Bank(s): Barclays, Ilford
Directors: I. Wilson (Dir), R. Wilson (Tech Serv), R. Standley (Dir), W. Hynett (Grp Chief Exec)
Managers: P. Bartlett, J. Pidgeon (Purch Mgr), D. Tomlinson (Import Mgr), B. Jacobs (Security), A. Smart (Inspect Mgr), A. Roxburgh (Eng Serv Mgr), M. Dore (Drawing Office), D. Wyckmans (Plant)
Ultimate Holding Company: B-N GROUP LIMITED
Immediate Holding Company: BRITTEN-NORMAN LIMITED
Registration no: 06929455 **VAT No.:** GB 109 1742 83
Date established: 2009 **Turnover:** £10m - £20m
No.of Employees: 101 - 250 **Product Groups:** 39, 84

Date of Accounts	Feb 12	Feb 11	Feb 10
Working Capital	-27	-36	16
Fixed Assets	13	16	2
Current Assets	72	66	100

Liphook

Allianz Engineering
Haslemere Road, Liphook, GU30 7UN
Tel: 01428-722407 **Fax:** 01428-724824
E-mail: alan.harris@allianzcornhillengineering.co.uk
Website: http://www.allianz.co.uk
Directors: A. Torrance (MD), E. Hutchins (Fin)
Managers: C. Price (Mktg Serv Mgr)
Ultimate Holding Company: ALLIANZ A.G.
Immediate Holding Company: CORNHILL INSURANCE P.L.C.
No.of Employees: 101 - 250 **Product Groups:** 82

Christian Faversham
Falkners Rectory Lane, Bramshott, Liphook, GU30 7QZ
Tel: 01428-725731
E-mail: peter-stuart@btinternet.com
Website: http://www.outside-catering-hire.co.uk
Directors: P. Stuart (Dir)
No.of Employees: 21 - 50 **Product Groups:** 24, 26, 27, 30, 36, 40, 49, 63, 83, 89

Inwood Stoves & Fireplaces
6 The Square, Liphook, GU30 7AH
Tel: 01428-725441 **Fax:** 01428-725441
E-mail: inwoodstoves@googlemail.com
Website: http://www.inwoodstoves.co.uk
Directors: R. Green (Prop)
Date established: 1992 **No.of Employees:** 1 - 10 **Product Groups:** 40

P R Fabrications
Unit 3 & 4 North Lodge Farm Hollycombe, Liphook, GU30 7LP
Tel: 01428-722766 **Fax:** 01428-722229
Directors: K. Pearson (Prop)
Date established: 2000 **No.of Employees:** 1 - 10 **Product Groups:** 35

Wendage Pollution Control Ltd
Rangeways Farm Conford, Liphook, GU30 7QP
Tel: 01428-751296 **Fax:** 01428-751541
E-mail: info@wpc.uk.net
Website: http://www.wpc.uk.net
Directors: M. Mansfield (MD)
Ultimate Holding Company: WENDAGE LIMITED
Immediate Holding Company: WENDAGE POLLUTION CONTROL LIMITED
Registration no: 01507590 **Date established:** 1980
No.of Employees: 1 - 10 **Product Groups:** 30, 31, 32, 33, 34, 37, 38, 40, 42, 48, 51, 52, 54, 66, 67, 83, 84, 85

Date of Accounts	Jun 11	Jun 10	Jun 09
Working Capital	109	109	155
Fixed Assets	66	73	66
Current Assets	447	449	542

Liss

Edwards Fordham & Leslie
4 School Lane, Liss, GU33 7EB
Tel: 01730-892494 **Fax:** 01730-892494
E-mail: ad.edwards@ntlworld.com
Directors: A. Edwards (Prop)
Date established: 1993 **No.of Employees:** 1 - 10 **Product Groups:** 35

English Fireplaces
Unit 6 The Brows Industrial Estate Farnham Road, Liss, GU33 6JG
Tel: 01730-897600 **Fax:** 01730-897609
E-mail: info@englishfireplaces.co.uk
Website: http://www.englishfireplaces.co.uk
Directors: M. Johnson (Prop)
Immediate Holding Company: ELIFAR PRIMARY CARE LIMITED
Date established: 2010 **Turnover:** £1m - £2m **No.of Employees:** 1 - 10
Product Groups: 35, 49, 66

Morgan Automation
Rake Heath House Hill Brow, Liss, GU33 7NT
Tel: 01730-895900 **Fax:** 01730-895922
E-mail: sales@morgan-automation.com
Website: http://www.morgan-automation.com
Bank(s): National Westminster
Directors: S. Clarke (Comm), B. Westwater (Mkt Research), H. Clarke (Tech Serv)
Immediate Holding Company: MORGAN INNOVATION & TECHNOLOGY LTD
Registration no: 02174066 **VAT No.:** GB 474 3269 34
Date established: 1987 **No.of Employees:** 11 - 20 **Product Groups:** 37

Date of Accounts	Dec 07	Dec 06	Dec 05
Working Capital	-147	130	-163
Fixed Assets	369	59	50
Current Assets	321	494	204
Current Liabilities	468	364	368
Total Share Capital	1	1	1

Tritech Computer Services Ltd
Suite 4 Hillbrow House Linden Drive, Liss, GU33 7RJ
Tel: 01730-893789 **Fax:** 01730-894589
E-mail: info@tritech.org.uk
Website: http://www.tritech.org.uk
Directors: J. Tabor (Fin), P. Douglass (MD)
Immediate Holding Company: TRITECH COMPUTER SERVICES LIMITED
Registration no: 00970805 **Date established:** 1970
Turnover: Up to £250,000 **No.of Employees:** 1 - 10 **Product Groups:** 44, 84

Date of Accounts	Jun 11	Jun 10	Jun 09
Sales Turnover	122	140	190
Pre Tax Profit/Loss	13	14	21
Working Capital	54	50	49
Fixed Assets	166	170	174
Current Assets	124	129	162
Current Liabilities	66	76	109

Lymington

Cooling & Heating Solutions Ltd
Marlwood House Silver Street, Sway, Lymington, SO41 6DG
Tel: 01590-682579 **Fax:** 01590-682900
E-mail: sales@coolingandheatingsolutions.com
Website: http://www.coolingandheatingsolutions.com
Directors: G. Jordan (MD), A. Wilson (Fin)
Immediate Holding Company: COOLING & HEATING SOLUTIONS LIMITED
Registration no: 03284618 **Date established:** 1996
No.of Employees: 1 - 10 **Product Groups:** 83

Date of Accounts	Apr 11	Apr 10	Apr 09
Working Capital	861	641	394
Fixed Assets	236	297	409
Current Assets	1m	885	635

D F Webber & Harrison Ltd
Unit 270 Ricardo Way, Lymington, SO41 8JU
Tel: 01590-689009 **Fax:** 01590-689006
E-mail: allanwebber@btconnect.com
Website: http://www.webberfurniture.co.uk
Directors: A. Webber (MD)
Immediate Holding Company: D. F. WEBBER & HARRISON LIMITED
Registration no: 02145407 **Date established:** 1987
Turnover: £500,000 - £1m **No.of Employees:** 1 - 10 **Product Groups:** 26

Date of Accounts	Sep 11	Sep 10	Sep 09
Working Capital	911	928	948
Fixed Assets	438	468	487
Current Assets	1m	1m	1m

Fischer Instrumentation GB Ltd
Gordleton Industrial Park Pennington, Lymington, SO41 8JD
Tel: 01590-684100 **Fax:** 01590-684110
E-mail: mail@fischergb.co.uk
Website: http://www.fischergb.co.uk
Bank(s): Lloyds TSB Bank plc
Managers: P. Ho (Chief Mgr)
Ultimate Holding Company: HELMUT FISCHER & CO GMBH (GERMANY)
Immediate Holding Company: FISCHER MAINTENANCE LIMITED
Registration no: 02834973 **Date established:** 1993
Turnover: £20m - £50m **No.of Employees:** 11 - 20 **Product Groups:** 37, 38

Date of Accounts	Dec 11	Dec 10	Dec 09
Working Capital	N/A	44	109
Current Assets	52	47	111

Gill Instruments Ltd
Saltmarsh Park 67 Gosport Street, Lymington, SO41 9EG
Tel: 01590-613500 **Fax:** 01590-613501
E-mail: gill@gill.co.uk
Website: http://www.gill.co.uk
Directors: L. Gill (Dir), M. Creagh (Dir)
Managers: G. White (Tech Serv Mgr), G. Oliver (Personnel), C. Stock (Sales Prom Mgr), A. Lamb (Chief Buyer), M. Rees (Mktg Serv Mgr)
Immediate Holding Company: GILL INSTRUMENTS LIMITED
Registration no: 02281574 **Date established:** 1988 **Turnover:** £5m - £10m
No.of Employees: 51 - 100 **Product Groups:** 37, 38, 39

Date of Accounts	Oct 11	Oct 10	Oct 09
Sales Turnover	8m	7m	6m
Pre Tax Profit/Loss	2m	2m	1m
Working Capital	3m	2m	2m
Fixed Assets	1m	1m	1m
Current Assets	4m	3m	3m
Current Liabilities	529	633	413

Gill Technology Ltd
Saltmarsh Park 67 Gosport Street, Lymington, SO41 9EG
Tel: 01590-613400 **Fax:** 01590-613401
E-mail: info@gilltechnology.com
Website: http://www.gilltechnology.co.uk
Directors: S. Whale (MD), M. Gill (MD), L. Gill (Dir)
Registration no: 03154453 **No.of Employees:** 11 - 20
Product Groups: 38, 39, 67, 84, 85

International Waxes
Limestones Victoria Road, Milford On Sea, Lymington, SO41 0NL
Tel: 01590-641542 **Fax:** 01590-641299
E-mail: peter@rigidaxuk.com
Directors: P. Linnington (MD)
No.of Employees: 1 - 10 **Product Groups:**

Jewson Ltd
Gosport Street, Lymington, SO41 9BE
Tel: 01590-675055 **Fax:** 01590-678138
E-mail: paul.baker@jewson.co.uk
Website: http://www.jewson.co.uk
Managers: P. Baker (Mgr)
Ultimate Holding Company: COMPAGNIE DE SAINT GOBAIN (FRANCE)
Immediate Holding Company: JEWSON LIMITED
Registration no: 00348407 **Date established:** 1939
Turnover: £500m - £1,000m **No.of Employees:** 1 - 10
Product Groups: 66

Date of Accounts	Dec 11	Dec 10	Dec 09
Sales Turnover	1606m	1547m	1485m
Pre Tax Profit/Loss	18m	100m	45m
Working Capital	-345m	-250m	-349m
Fixed Assets	496m	387m	461m
Current Assets	657m	1005m	1320m
Current Liabilities	66m	120m	64m

John D Wood & Co.
53 High Street, Lymington, SO41 9ZB
Tel: 01590-690195 **Fax:** 01590-672460
E-mail: kallen@johndwood.co.uk
Website: http://www.johndwood.co.uk/
Managers: K. Allen (Mgr)
Immediate Holding Company: JOHN D WOOD & CO. (RESIDENTIAL & AGRICULTURAL) LIMITED
Registration no: 02349482 **Date established:** 1989 **Turnover:** £5m - £10m
No.of Employees: 1 - 10 **Product Groups:** 80

Ohmex Ltd
9 Gordleton Industrial Estate Hannah Way, Pennington, Lymington, SO41 8JD
Tel: 01590-681584
E-mail: sales@ohmex.com
Website: http://www.ohmex.com
Directors: L. Read (Fin), E. Read (Dir)
Immediate Holding Company: OHMEX LIMITED
Registration no: 03964735 **Date established:** 2000
No.of Employees: 1 - 10 **Product Groups:** 37, 38, 39

Date of Accounts	Sep 11	Sep 10	Sep 09
Working Capital	397	352	287
Fixed Assets	N/A	1	1
Current Assets	469	434	396
Current Liabilities	N/A	75	N/A

Poseidon Aquatic Resource Management Ltd
Windrush Warborne Lane, Portmore, Lymington, SO41 5RJ
Tel: 01590-610168
E-mail: tim@consult-poseidon.com
Website: http://www.consult-poseidon.com
Directors: T. Huntington (Dir)
Immediate Holding Company: POSEIDON AQUATIC RESOURCE MANAGEMENT LTD.
Registration no: 04297215 **Date established:** 2001
Turnover: Up to £250,000 **No.of Employees:** 1 - 10 **Product Groups:** 54, 84, 85

Date of Accounts	Sep 11	Sep 10	Sep 09
Working Capital	11	11	10
Current Assets	248	294	157
Current Liabilities	N/A	163	53

Precise Plastics Ltd
Beck Farm St Leonards Road, East End, Lymington, SO41 5SR
Tel: 01590-626233
Immediate Holding Company: PRECISE PLASTICS LIMITED
Registration no: 02466579 **Date established:** 1990 **Turnover:** £1m - £2m
No.of Employees: 1 - 10 **Product Groups:** 30, 31, 85

Date of Accounts	Mar 12	Mar 11	Mar 10
Sales Turnover	N/A	900	921
Pre Tax Profit/Loss	N/A	237	263
Working Capital	160	64	-22
Fixed Assets	577	374	412
Current Assets	344	288	159
Current Liabilities	N/A	65	78

Retrodata
St Andrews New Street, Lymington, SO41 9BQ
Tel: 01590-673808
E-mail: info@retrodata.co.uk
Website: http://www.retrodata.co.uk
Directors: D. Clarke (Snr Part)
Immediate Holding Company: RETRODATA LLP
Registration no: OC355361 **Date established:** 2010
Turnover: Up to £250,000 **No.of Employees:** 1 - 10 **Product Groups:** 44

S I S Chemicals Ltd
22 Whitefield Road Pennington, Lymington, SO41 8GN
Tel: 01425-621021 **Fax:** 01425-618191
E-mail: sales@sischem.co.uk
Website: http://www.sischem.co.uk
Directors: B. Eaton (Sales), G. Lavis (Dir), M. Lavis (MD), P. Cunliffe (Fin)
Managers: C. Rogers (Admin Off)
Immediate Holding Company: Sis Chemicals Ltd
Registration no: 02061653 **VAT No.:** GB 235 5872 65
Date established: 2007 **Turnover:** £2m - £5m **No.of Employees:** 1 - 10
Product Groups: 66

Date of Accounts	Dec 07	Dec 06	Dec 05
Sales Turnover	3814	3707	3577
Pre Tax Profit/Loss	29	13	-29
Working Capital	-59	-89	-114
Fixed Assets	503	518	538
Current Assets	838	794	781
Current Liabilities	897	883	896
Total Share Capital	119	119	119
ROCE% (Return on Capital Employed)	6.6	3.0	-6.9
ROT% (Return on Turnover)	0.8	0.4	-0.8

Stainless Steve Engineering
Mount Pleasant Lane, Lymington, SO41 8LS
Tel: 01590-674988 **Fax:** 01590-674988
Website: http://www.stainless-steve.co.uk
Directors: S. Batchelor (Prop)
Immediate Holding Company: C - PRO HOLDINGS LIMITED
Registration no: 04729572 **Date established:** 2009
Turnover: Up to £250,000 **No.of Employees:** 1 - 10 **Product Groups:** 35, 36, 39

Date of Accounts	Mar 11	Mar 10	Mar 07
Working Capital	-797	-800	141
Fixed Assets	1m	1m	1m
Current Assets	55	128	182

Lyndhurst

Diak Technical Export Ltd
PO Box 45, Lyndhurst, SO40 3GN
Tel: 01794-518808 **Fax:** 01794-519960
E-mail: candy.battiscombe@diak.com
Website: http://www.diak.com
Directors: C. Battiscombe (Co Sec)
Immediate Holding Company: DIAK TECHNICAL EXPORT LTD
Registration no: 01415104 **VAT No.:** GB 631 5692 39
Date established: 1979 **Turnover:** £2m - £5m **No.of Employees:** 1 - 10
Product Groups: 61

Date of Accounts	Dec 10	Dec 09	Dec 08
Working Capital	234	186	238
Fixed Assets	71	68	66
Current Assets	245	208	600

New Milton

Apollo Blinds Ltd
Unit 8 Elm Court 27 Old Milton Road, New Milton, BH25 6DY
Tel: 01425-623624 **Fax:** 01425-629709
E-mail: apolloblinds1@btconnect.com
Website: http://www.apollo-blinds.co.uk
Directors: D. Taylor (Prop)
Immediate Holding Company: APOLLO BLINDS LIMITED
Registration no: 04500306 **Date established:** 2002
No.of Employees: 1 - 10 **Product Groups:** 25, 36, 63, 66

Date of Accounts	Jul 12	Jul 11	Jul 10
Working Capital	N/A	-2	-4
Fixed Assets	N/A	4	5
Current Assets	4	21	10

A-Tec Plastics
6 Queensway, New Milton, BH25 5NN
Tel: 01425-638433 **Fax:** 01425-616374
E-mail: sales@atec.co.uk
Website: http://www.a-tec.co.uk
Directors: R. George (Prop), R. George (Prop), W. Cawthorne (Fin)
Managers: M. Verity (I.T. Exec), W. Corthorn (Accounts)
Immediate Holding Company: A-Tec Plastics Ltd
Registration no: 03219477 **VAT No.:** GB 679 5073 88
Date established: 1996 **Turnover:** £500,000 - £1m
No.of Employees: 11 - 20 **Product Groups:** 30

Date of Accounts	Jul 08	Jul 07	Jul 06
Sales Turnover	840	660	584
Pre Tax Profit/Loss	139	51	40
Working Capital	87	24	13
Fixed Assets	27	27	32
Current Assets	247	171	198
Current Liabilities	160	147	185
ROCE% (Return on Capital Employed)	121.5	99.4	89.0
ROT% (Return on Turnover)	16.6	7.7	6.9

Cannon Technologies Ltd
13 Queensway Stem Lane Industrial Estate, New Milton, BH25 5NU
Tel: 01425-638148 **Fax:** 01425-619276
E-mail: matt.goulding@cannontech.co.uk
Website: http://www.cannontech.co.uk
Directors: E. Reddicliffe (Ch)
Managers: V. Newton (Mktg Serv Mgr), R. Shivas, D. Nicholason
Ultimate Holding Company: CANNON TECHNOLOGIES GROUP LIMITED
Immediate Holding Company: CANNON TECHNOLOGIES EUROPE LTD
Registration no: 02794047 **Date established:** 1993 **Turnover:** £5m - £10m
No.of Employees: 101 - 250 **Product Groups:** 30, 37

Date of Accounts	Jun 11	Jun 10	Jun 09
Pre Tax Profit/Loss	N/A	N/A	-0
Fixed Assets	1	1	1

Cirrus Communications Ltd
Oregon House 19 Queensway, New Milton, BH25 5NN
Tel: 01425-626300 **Fax:** 01425-626345
E-mail: enquiries@cirruscom.co.uk
Website: http://www.cirruscom.co.uk
Directors: A. Davey (MD), C. Underhill (Fin)
Ultimate Holding Company: EURO INVESTMENTS OVERSEAS INC (BRITISH VIRGIN ISLANDS)
Immediate Holding Company: CIRRUS COMMUNICATION SYSTEMS LIMITED
Registration no: 01444995 **Date established:** 1979
Turnover: £10m - £20m **No.of Employees:** 251 - 500
Product Groups: 40, 52, 88

Date of Accounts	Dec 11	Dec 10	Dec 09
Sales Turnover	12m	12m	14m
Pre Tax Profit/Loss	-1m	-1m	-808
Working Capital	172	-1m	-302
Fixed Assets	339	442	613
Current Assets	8m	4m	6m
Current Liabilities	2m	1m	2m

Delta Rubber Ltd
Unit 13g Queensway, New Milton, BH25 5NN
Tel: 01425-621900 **Fax:** 01425-621202
E-mail: deltasales@deltarubber.co.uk
Website: http://www.deltarubber.co.uk
Directors: J. Fisher (Dir)
Immediate Holding Company: DELTA RUBBER LIMITED
Registration no: 06033135 **Date established:** 2006
Turnover: Up to £250,000 **No.of Employees:** 1 - 10 **Product Groups:** 29, 66

Date of Accounts	Mar 11	Mar 10	Mar 09
Working Capital	31	19	41
Fixed Assets	2	4	2
Current Assets	128	101	80

Deval Ltd
Unit 6 Hamilton Way, New Milton, BH25 6TQ
Tel: 01425-620772 **Fax:** 01425-638431
E-mail: sales@deval-ltd.co.uk
Website: http://www.deval-ltd.co.uk
Managers: R. Croad (Chief Acct), T. Dawe (Chief Mgr)
Immediate Holding Company: DEVAL LIMITED
Registration no: 02029956 **Date established:** 1986
Turnover: £500,000 - £1m **No.of Employees:** 11 - 20 **Product Groups:** 37

Date of Accounts	Dec 11	Dec 10	Dec 09
Working Capital	375	345	321
Fixed Assets	55	42	41
Current Assets	457	461	393

E & P Plastics Ltd
Gore Road Industrial Estate, New Milton, BH25 6TB
Tel: 01425-611026 **Fax:** 01425-615500
E-mail: david.gower@epplastics.co.uk
Directors: D. Gower (MD), R. Atkins (Ch)
Immediate Holding Company: E & P PLASTICS LIMITED
Registration no: 01817907 **VAT No.:** GB 188 3806 23
Date established: 1984 **Turnover:** £500,000 - £1m
No.of Employees: 1 - 10 **Product Groups:** 30

Date of Accounts	Oct 10	Oct 09	Oct 08
Working Capital	152	196	226
Fixed Assets	240	246	244
Current Assets	236	265	331

Jewson Ltd
Wick Ii Industrial Estate Gore Road, New Milton, BH25 6TJ
Tel: 01425-619202 **Fax:** 01425-638957
Website: http://www.jewson.co.uk
Managers: J. Coleman (Mgr)
Ultimate Holding Company: COMPAGNIE DE SAINT GOBAIN (FRANCE)
Immediate Holding Company: JEWSON LIMITED
Registration no: 00348407 **Date established:** 1939
Turnover: £500m - £1,000m **No.of Employees:** 11 - 20
Product Groups: 66

Date of Accounts	Dec 11	Dec 10	Dec 09
Sales Turnover	1606m	1547m	1485m
Pre Tax Profit/Loss	18m	100m	45m
Working Capital	-345m	-250m	-349m
Fixed Assets	496m	387m	461m
Current Assets	657m	1005m	1320m
Current Liabilities	66m	120m	64m

L & J Marine
Unit 17-18 Hamilton Way, New Milton, BH25 6TQ
Tel: 01425-613746 **Fax:** 01425-638029
Website: http://www.landjmarine.com
Directors: D. Keeling (Dir)
No.of Employees: 1 - 10 **Product Groups:** 35, 36, 39

Mccarthy & Stone Construction Services Ltd
3 Queensway, New Milton, BH25 5PB
Tel: 01425-638855 **Fax:** 01425-638343
E-mail: geoff.hatt@mccarthyandstone.co.uk
Managers: G. Hatt (Chief Mgr)
Registration no: 00770529 **VAT No.:** GB 370 0308 93
No.of Employees: 1 - 10 **Product Groups:** 37, 39, 45

R.H.H. Franks (New Milton) Ltd
Gore Road Industrial Estate, New Milton, BH25 6SA
Tel: 01425-614730 **Fax:** 01425-616472
E-mail: iann@rhhfranks.co.uk
Website: http://www.rhhfranks.com
Bank(s): National Westminster Bank Plc
Directors: J. House (Dir), P. Dawkins (Ch)
Managers: P. Smith (I.T. Exec)
Immediate Holding Company: R.H.H. Franks (New Milton) Ltd
Registration no: 00690175 **VAT No.:** GB 188 6969 77
Date established: 1999 **Turnover:** £2m - £5m **No.of Employees:** 21 - 50
Product Groups: 33, 34, 36, 39, 48

Southern Springs & Pressings Ltd
Stem Lane, New Milton, BH25 5NE
Tel: 01425-611517 **Fax:** 01425-638142
E-mail: enquiries@southernsprings.co.uk
Website: http://www.southernsprings.co.uk
Bank(s): National Westminster
Directors: D. Banks Fear (MD)
Managers: S. Blunt, P. Banks Fear (Mktg Serv Mgr)
Immediate Holding Company: SOUTHERN SPRINGS AND PRESSINGS LIMITED
Registration no: 00452833 **Date established:** 1948 **Turnover:** £1m - £2m
No.of Employees: 21 - 50 **Product Groups:** 35, 46

Date of Accounts	Mar 12	Mar 11	Mar 10
Working Capital	294	270	217
Fixed Assets	99	116	154
Current Assets	565	504	426

Petersfield

Adaptsys Ltd
Unit 1 Rotherbrook Court Bedford Road, Petersfield, GU32 3QG
Tel: 01730-262444 **Fax:** 01730-262333
Website: http://www.adaptsys.com
Directors: C. Bennetts (Dir)
Immediate Holding Company: ADAPTSYS LIMITED
Registration no: 04784200 **Date established:** 2003
No.of Employees: 1 - 10 **Product Groups:** 37, 46, 85

Date of Accounts	Jun 11	Jun 10	Jun 09
Working Capital	-14	-10	26
Fixed Assets	113	141	185

Current Assets	464	268	207

Avialec International Ltd
Unit 1 Petersfield Business Park, Petersfield, GU32 3QA
Tel: 01730-264825 **Fax:** 01730-264496
E-mail: sales@avialec.co.uk
Website: http://www.avialec.co.uk
Directors: B. Prescott (Dir), E. Green (Mkt Research), R. Holton (Dir)
Managers: K. Wells (Develop Mgr)
Immediate Holding Company: KIRKHILL AIRCRAFT PARTS CO. UK LTD
Registration no: 01726275 **VAT No.:** GB 382 6731 33
Date established: 1983 **Turnover:** £2m - £5m **No.of Employees:** 21 - 50
Product Groups: 67

Date of Accounts	Mar 11	Mar 10	Mar 09
Sales Turnover	6m	5m	3m
Pre Tax Profit/Loss	-3	-150	-1
Working Capital	327	328	452
Fixed Assets	250	251	226
Current Assets	3m	2m	3m
Current Liabilities	146	573	823

C T Tooling Ltd
Unit H Nyewood Industries Nyewood, Petersfield, GU31 5HA
Tel: 01730-821002 **Fax:** 01730-821622
E-mail: sales@cellulardevelopments.co.uk
Website: http://www.cttooling.co.uk
Directors: C. Forster (Fin), T. Forster (MD)
Immediate Holding Company: C T TOOLING LIMITED
Registration no: 02884696 **Date established:** 1994
Turnover: Up to £250,000 **No.of Employees:** 1 - 10 **Product Groups:** 48

Date of Accounts	Oct 11	Oct 10	Oct 09
Working Capital	87	128	53
Fixed Assets	16	29	42
Current Assets	131	159	74

Channel Safety Systems Ltd
Petersfield Business Park Bedford Road, Petersfield, GU32 3QA
Tel: 08458-847000 **Fax:** 01730-266699
E-mail: sales@channelsafety.co.uk
Website: http://www.channelsafety.co.uk
Bank(s): Lloyd TSB
Directors: B. Channon (Fin), R. Collier (Sales), P. Mazalon (MD), I. Morrison (Comm)
Managers: J. Taylor (Personnel), L. Owen (Prod Mgr), E. Smith (Sales & Mktg Mg), A. Kind (Sales Prom Mgr), C. Ellis (Personnel)
Ultimate Holding Company: CHANNEL SAFETY SYSTEMS GROUP LIMITED
Immediate Holding Company: CHANNEL SAFETY SYSTEMS LIMITED
Registration no: 03853978 **VAT No.:** GB 369 9420 07
Date established: 1999 **Turnover:** £5m - £10m **No.of Employees:** 21 - 50
Product Groups: 28, 80, 81

Date of Accounts	Oct 11	Oct 10	Oct 09
Sales Turnover	9m	9m	8m
Pre Tax Profit/Loss	138	413	180
Working Capital	259	-214	-396
Fixed Assets	789	1m	1m
Current Assets	3m	3m	2m
Current Liabilities	767	813	2m

J B Corrie & Co. Ltd
Frenchmans Road, Petersfield, GU32 3AP
Tel: 01730-237100 **Fax:** 01730-264915
E-mail: admin@jbcorrie.co.uk
Website: http://www.jbcorrie.co.uk
Bank(s): HSBC
Directors: H. Kennedy (MD), M. Hickman (Sales)
Immediate Holding Company: J.B.CORRIE AND COMPANY LIMITED
Registration no: 00208517 **VAT No.:** GB 192 6798 10
Date established: 2025 **Turnover:** £10m - £20m
No.of Employees: 51 - 100 **Product Groups:** 35, 49, 52, 66

Date of Accounts	Dec 11	Dec 10	Dec 09
Sales Turnover	8m	12m	10m
Pre Tax Profit/Loss	-264	290	103
Working Capital	2m	3m	3m
Fixed Assets	3m	2m	2m
Current Assets	3m	5m	6m
Current Liabilities	648	1m	2m

E X P D
2 Viceroy Court Bedford Road, Petersfield, GU32 3LJ
Tel: 01730-231975 **Fax:** 01730-231445
E-mail: enquiries@expd.co.uk
Website: http://www.expd.co.uk
Directors: M. Fenton (Co Sec), R. Fenton (MD), A. Harris (Sales), N. Tillyard (I.T. Dir)
Immediate Holding Company: EXPERT PERIPHERAL DESIGNS LIMITED
Registration no: 02757251 **Date established:** 1992 **Turnover:** £2m - £5m
No.of Employees: 1 - 10 **Product Groups:** 44, 67

Date of Accounts	Oct 11	Oct 10	Oct 09
Working Capital	399	386	347
Fixed Assets	76	35	60
Current Assets	721	706	643

Elemental Technology Ltd
Top Floor 70b Station Road, Petersfield, GU32 3HZ
Tel: 01730-269857 **Fax:** 0870-706 5719
E-mail: enquiries@etluk.com
Website: http://www.etluk.com
Directors: G. Whiting (Dir), J. Harfield (Fin)
Immediate Holding Company: ELEMENTAL TECHNOLOGY LIMITED
Registration no: 03114511 **Date established:** 1995
Turnover: Up to £250,000 **No.of Employees:** 1 - 10 **Product Groups:** 44

Date of Accounts	Dec 11	Dec 10	Dec 09
Working Capital	55	49	30
Fixed Assets	1	1	1
Current Assets	69	57	31

G T 85 Ltd
Leith House Petersfield Road, South Harting, Petersfield, GU31 5PH
Tel: 01730-825151 **Fax:** 01730-825151
E-mail: sales@gt85.co.uk
Website: http://www.gt85.co.uk
Directors: J. Self (Dir), J. Suntees Chapman (Co Sec)
Immediate Holding Company: GT 85 Ltd
Registration no: 02303768 **Date established:** 1988
Turnover: Up to £250,000 **No.of Employees:** 21 - 50 **Product Groups:** 39, 68

Date of Accounts	Jul 08	Jul 07	Jul 06
Working Capital	93	82	78
Fixed Assets	22	30	40
Current Assets	395	331	285
Current Liabilities	302	249	207

I D Data
The New Mint House Bedford Road, Petersfield, GU32 3AL
Tel: 01730-235700 **Fax:** 01730-268680
E-mail: enquiries@iddata.com
Website: http://www.iddata.com
Bank(s): National Westminster Bank Plc
Directors: J. Cooke (Develop), P. Cox (Grp Chief Exec), M. Griffin (Prop)
Managers: K. McCullen (Sales Admin), S. Mitchell (Comptroller), C. Brown (), B. Ocrien (I.T. Exec), M. Haldane (Ops Mgr)
Immediate Holding Company: ID DATA GROUP PLC
Registration no: 01385703 **VAT No.:** GB 493 6101 45
Date established: 2001 **No.of Employees:** 51 - 100 **Product Groups:** 28, 44, 48

I H S Mccloskey
Unit 6 Rotherbrook Court Bedford Road, Petersfield, GU32 3QG
Tel: 01730-265095
E-mail: gerard.mccloskey@mccloskeycoal.com
Website: http://www.mccloskeycoal.com
Directors: D. McNee (Fin), G. McCloskey (Dir)
No.of Employees: 21 - 50 **Product Groups:** 11, 36, 84

John Jenkins & Sons Ltd
Nyewood, Petersfield, GU31 5HZ
Tel: 01730-821811 **Fax:** 01730-821698
E-mail: office@johnjenkins.co.uk
Website: http://www.williamyeowardcrystal.com
Bank(s): National Westminster Bank Plc
Directors: D. Lynch (Mkt Research), P. Bramfitt (Dir)
Immediate Holding Company: JOHN JENKINS & SONS LIMITED
Registration no: 00576342 **Date established:** 1956 **Turnover:** £2m - £5m
No.of Employees: 51 - 100 **Product Groups:** 33, 61, 63

Date of Accounts	Mar 11	Mar 10	Mar 09
Sales Turnover	4m	4m	N/A
Pre Tax Profit/Loss	50	52	55
Working Capital	2m	2m	2m
Fixed Assets	2m	2m	2m
Current Assets	3m	3m	3m
Current Liabilities	197	336	303

M C I
Durford Mill, Petersfield, GU31 5AZ
Tel: 01730-821969 **Fax:** 0870-442 9940
E-mail: sales@mci-group.com
Website: http://www.mci-group.com
Managers: D. Clarke (Tech Serv Mgr), G. Wilcox (Mktg Serv Mgr), M. Wheeler, J. Jenkins (Chief Mgr), S. Way (Personnel), V. Owens (Sales Prom Mgr)
Ultimate Holding Company: MCI EVENT HOLDINGS SA (SWITZERLAND)
Immediate Holding Company: MCI UK LIMITED
Registration no: 01332326 **Date established:** 1977
Turnover: £10m - £20m **No.of Employees:** 51 - 100 **Product Groups:** 49

Date of Accounts	Dec 11	Dec 10	Dec 09
Sales Turnover	11m	10m	9m
Pre Tax Profit/Loss	136	76	263
Working Capital	58	70	169
Fixed Assets	2m	2m	2m
Current Assets	2m	4m	3m
Current Liabilities	1m	4m	3m

Parkwood Arts Ltd
Froxfield, Petersfield, GU32 1DJ
Tel: 01730-266151 **Fax:** 01730-265866
E-mail: info@parkwood-arts.co.uk
Website: http://www.parkwood-arts.co.uk
Directors: S. Wade (Fin), W. Peters (MD)
Immediate Holding Company: PARKWOOD ARTS LIMITED
Registration no: 00841110 **Date established:** 1965
Turnover: £500,000 - £1m **No.of Employees:** 1 - 10 **Product Groups:** 25

Date of Accounts	Mar 11	Mar 10	Mar 09
Working Capital	-30	9	76
Fixed Assets	88	101	120
Current Assets	130	122	131

John Rutter
28 Penns Road, Petersfield, GU32 2EN
Tel: 01730-263352 **Fax:** 01730-263352
Directors: J. Rutter (Prop)
Date established: 1969 **No.of Employees:** 1 - 10 **Product Groups:** 41

S E S Controls Ltd
Greenforde Farm Stoner Hill Road, Froxfield, Petersfield, GU32 1DY
Tel: 01730-266222 **Fax:** 01730-264355
E-mail: sales@sescontrols.co.uk
Website: http://www.sescontrols.co.uk
Directors: N. Rogers (MD)
Immediate Holding Company: SES CONTROLS LTD
Registration no: 01352963 **VAT No.:** GB 194 1959 25
Date established: 1978 **No.of Employees:** 11 - 20 **Product Groups:** 38

Date of Accounts	Mar 12	Mar 11	Mar 10
Working Capital	704	465	354
Fixed Assets	31	20	21
Current Assets	1m	849	637

Sentinal Equipment Ltd T/A Amey Plastics
Unit 6 Amey Industrial Estate, Petersfield, GU32 3AN
Tel: 01730-266525 **Fax:** 01730-268454
E-mail: info@amey-plastics.co.uk
Website: http://www.ameyplastics.co.uk
Directors: K. Scott (MD)
Immediate Holding Company: ROOKERY AND ORCHARD FARMS LIMITED
Registration no: 02515067 **VAT No.:** GB 582 5339 22
Date established: 1990 **Turnover:** £500,000 - £1m
No.of Employees: 1 - 10 **Product Groups:** 30, 42

Date of Accounts	Aug 11	Aug 10	Aug 09
Working Capital	917	933	644
Fixed Assets	2m	2m	2m
Current Assets	930	1m	709

Southern Inflatables UK Ltd
Greenforde Farm Stoner Hill Road, Froxfield, Petersfield, GU32 1DY
Tel: 01730-827027 **Fax:** 01730-827028
E-mail: enquiries@southerninflatables.net
Website: http://www.southerninflatables.net
Directors: A. Weal (MD)
Immediate Holding Company: SOUTHERN INFLATABLES UK LIMITED
Registration no: 02951117 **Date established:** 1994
No.of Employees: 1 - 10 **Product Groups:** 24, 29, 30, 83

Date of Accounts	Aug 11	Aug 10	Aug 09
Working Capital	6	17	-6
Fixed Assets	16	21	23
Current Assets	47	86	41

Alex Zdankowicz Ceramic Design
Unit 1 Durleigh Marsh Farm, Petersfield, GU31 5AX
Tel: 07791-725826
E-mail: info@alexzdankowicz.co.uk
Website: http://www.alexzdankowicz.co.uk
Directors: A. Zdankowicz (Prop)
No.of Employees: 1 - 10 **Product Groups:** 33

Portsmouth

Accuracy International Ltd
PO Box 81, Portsmouth, PO3 5SJ
Tel: 023-9267 1225 **Fax:** 023-9269 1852
E-mail: ai@accuracyinternational.org
Website: http://www.accuracyinternational.com/
Bank(s): The Bank of Scotland
Directors: M. Kay (Dir)
Managers: P. Bagshaw (Gen Contact)
Immediate Holding Company: Accuracy Group Ltd
Registration no: 05375397 **VAT No.:** GB 430 6893 46
Date established: 1978 **Turnover:** £2m - £5m **No.of Employees:** 21 - 50
Product Groups: 36, 67

Alto Handling Ltd
6b Fitzherbert Spur Farlington, Portsmouth, PO6 1TT
Tel: 023-9221 0490 **Fax:** 023-9221 0814
E-mail: colin@altohandling.co.uk
Website: http://www.altohandling.co.uk
Directors: C. Ivory (MD)
Immediate Holding Company: ALTO HANDLING LIMITED
Registration no: 03788891 **Date established:** 1999
No.of Employees: 1 - 10 **Product Groups:** 35, 39, 45

Date of Accounts	Aug 11	Aug 10	Aug 09
Working Capital	-10	-44	201
Fixed Assets	423	329	46
Current Assets	218	133	382

Amberley Security
185-187 Copnor Road, Portsmouth, PO3 5BT
Tel: 023-9266 0730 **Fax:** 023-9265 0349
E-mail: info@amberley-security.co.uk
Website: http://www.amberley-security.co.uk
Directors: J. Andrews (Dir)
Immediate Holding Company: AMBERLEY STORES LIMITED
Registration no: 00714933 **VAT No.:** GB 107 3530 03
Date established: 1962 **Turnover:** £250,000 - £500,000
No.of Employees: 1 - 10 **Product Groups:** 52, 66

Date of Accounts	Feb 08	Feb 11	Feb 10
Working Capital	15	-22	-10
Fixed Assets	64	52	55
Current Assets	61	34	38

Amdale Ltd
6-7 Culverin Square Limberline Road, Hilsea, Portsmouth, PO3 5BU
Tel: 023-9266 0726 **Fax:** 023-9265 5177
E-mail: martin.koerner@amdale.co.uk
Website: http://www.amdale.co.uk
Bank(s): National Westminster Bank Plc
Directors: M. Koerner (Dir), D. Koerner (Co Sec)
Immediate Holding Company: AMDALE LIMITED
Registration no: 02263063 **Date established:** 1988 **Turnover:** £1m - £2m
No.of Employees: 21 - 50 **Product Groups:** 35, 37, 38, 48, 84

Date of Accounts	Apr 11	Apr 10	Apr 09
Working Capital	-16	-84	-1
Fixed Assets	1m	980	1m
Current Assets	556	343	445

Andrews Sykes
Southampton Road, Portsmouth, PO6 4RJ
Tel: 023-9237 6425 **Fax:** 023-9237 7022
E-mail: info@andrews-sykes.com
Website: http://www.andrews-sykes.com
Managers: S. Burne (Mgr)
Immediate Holding Company: ANDREWS SYKES GROUP PLC
Registration no: 02985657 **VAT No.:** GB 100 4295 24
Turnover: £5m - £10m **No.of Employees:** 1 - 10 **Product Groups:** 40

Anglepoise Ltd
A10 Railway Triangle Walton Road, Portsmouth, PO6 1TN
Tel: 023-9222 4450 **Fax:** 023-9238 5445
E-mail: info@anglepoise.co.uk
Website: http://www.anglepoise.com
Directors: M. Chivers (Chief Op Offcr)
Ultimate Holding Company: ANGLEPOISE HOLDINGS LIMITED
Immediate Holding Company: ANGLEPOISE LIMITED
Registration no: 05045384 **VAT No.:** GB 112 8321 10
Date established: 2004 **Turnover:** £250,000 - £500,000
No.of Employees: 1 - 10 **Product Groups:** 30, 37, 67

Date of Accounts	Apr 11	Apr 10	Apr 09
Working Capital	358	149	-275
Fixed Assets	187	239	257
Current Assets	845	749	691

Architectural Systems Technology Ltd
Units 4-5 84 Court Lane, Portsmouth, PO6 2LR
Tel: 023-9221 4414 **Fax:** 023-9237 6600
E-mail: sales@ast-ltd.net
Website: http://www.astlimited.co.uk
Directors: S. Baxter (MD)
Immediate Holding Company: ARCHITECTURAL SYSTEMS TECHNOLOGY LIMITED
Registration no: 03662833 **Date established:** 1998
No.of Employees: 11 - 20 **Product Groups:** 35, 38, 48, 52

Date of Accounts	Dec 11	Dec 10	Dec 09
Working Capital	125	106	100
Fixed Assets	55	17	22

see next page

***Architectural Systems Technology Ltd** - Cont'd*

Current Assets	267	204	144

ArtChroma

PO Box 627, Portsmouth, PO6 2WZ
Tel: 07779-325222
E-mail: info@artchroma.com
Website: http://www.artchroma.com
Directors: R. Clarke (Prop)
No.of Employees: 1 - 10 **Product Groups:** 28, 44, 64, 81

Barnes Engineering

10 Mitchell Way, Portsmouth, PO3 5PR
Tel: 023-9265 3337 **Fax:** 023-9267 7332
E-mail: ian@barnesengineering.org
Directors: I. Barnes (MD)
Ultimate Holding Company: BARNES ENGINEERING (HOLDINGS) LIMITED
Immediate Holding Company: BARNES ENGINEERING LTD.
Registration no: 03729927 **Date established:** 1999
Turnover: Up to £250,000 **No.of Employees:** 1 - 10 **Product Groups:** 46, 48

Date of Accounts	Mar 12	Mar 11	Mar 10
Working Capital	257	224	202
Fixed Assets	15	18	23
Current Assets	322	279	242

Brittany Ferries

Wharf Road, Portsmouth, PO2 8RU
Tel: 08712-441402 **Fax:** 023-9289 2204
Website: http://www.brittanyferries.com
Managers: S. Tucwell (Mgr)
Ultimate Holding Company: B.A.I. S.A. ROSCOFF (FRANCE)
Immediate Holding Company: B.A.I. (UK) LTD
Registration no: 01080495 **Turnover:** £1m - £2m
No.of Employees: 101 - 250 **Product Groups:** 74

C Brewer & Sons

Albany House Waterworks Road, Portsmouth, PO6 1RD
Tel: 023-9221 0121 **Fax:** 023-9232 4853
E-mail: portsmouth@brewers.co.uk
Website: http://www.brewers.co.uk
Managers: L. Woods (Mgr)
Immediate Holding Company: C.BREWER & SONS LIMITED
Registration no: 00203852 **VAT No.:** GB 202 1565 70
Date established: 1925 **No.of Employees:** 11 - 20 **Product Groups:** 61

City Technology Ltd

City Technology Centre Walton Road, Portsmouth, PO6 1SZ
Tel: 023-9232 5511 **Fax:** 023-9238 6611
E-mail: antony.cowburn@citytech.com
Website: http://www.citytech.com
Directors: A. Cowburn (Dir)
Managers: C. Brown (Fin Mgr), J. Lowes (Personnel), C. Hardiman (Mktg Serv Mgr), D. Hall (Purch Mgr)
Ultimate Holding Company: HONEYWELL INTERNATIONAL INC (USA)
Immediate Holding Company: CITY TECHNOLOGY LIMITED
Registration no: 01326515 **VAT No.:** GB 314 7680 56
Date established: 1977 **Turnover:** £10m - £20m
No.of Employees: 251 - 500 **Product Groups:** 37, 38, 39, 40, 41

Date of Accounts	Dec 11	Dec 10	Dec 09
Sales Turnover	14m	10m	10m
Pre Tax Profit/Loss	2m	842	754
Working Capital	57m	54m	53m
Fixed Assets	2m	2m	3m
Current Assets	63m	62m	60m
Current Liabilities	429	766	959

Computer Room Consultants

8 Carbis Way Port Solent, Portsmouth, PO6 4TW
Tel: 023-9222 0699
E-mail: doug.latta@computerroomconsultants.co.uk
Website: http://www.computerroomconsultants.co.uk
Directors: D. Latta (Prop)
Date established: 2007 **No.of Employees:** 1 - 10 **Product Groups:** 84

Cope Allmann Jay Care

The Triangle Walton Road, Portsmouth, PO6 1TS
Tel: 023-9237 0102 **Fax:** 023-9238 0314
E-mail: info@cajaycare.com
Website: http://www.cajaycare.com
Directors: I. Winkfield (Prop)
Ultimate Holding Company: C A PORTSMOUTH LIMITED
Immediate Holding Company: COPE ALLMAN JAYCARE LIMITED
Registration no: 00598957 **Date established:** 1958
Turnover: £10m - £20m **No.of Employees:** 101 - 250
Product Groups: 30, 66

Date of Accounts	Dec 09	Dec 08	Dec 07
Sales Turnover	24m	24m	12m
Pre Tax Profit/Loss	1m	289	51
Working Capital	3m	3m	3m
Fixed Assets	3m	3m	2m
Current Assets	8m	9m	5m
Current Liabilities	2m	2m	503

Copy That

Spur Road Cosham, Portsmouth, PO6 3DY
Tel: 023-9237 5737
E-mail: bob@copythat.biz
Website: http://www.copythat.biz
Directors: B. Bruce (Prop)
No.of Employees: 1 - 10 **Product Groups:** 24, 27, 28, 49, 64

Credit Card Sentinel UK Ltd

Sentinel House Airspeed Road, Portsmouth, PO3 5RF
Tel: 0800-414717 **Fax:** 023-9267 7450
Website: http://www.sentinelgold.com
Directors: D. Palmer (MD)
Ultimate Holding Company: CUC INTERNATIONAL INC. (USA)
Immediate Holding Company: C.U.C. INTERNATIONAL
Registration no: 01761354 **No.of Employees:** 101 - 250
Product Groups: 82

Date of Accounts	Dec 08	Dec 07	Dec 06
Working Capital	469	469	469
Current Assets	469	469	469
Total Share Capital	469	469	469

Custom Metal Polishers Limited

Unit 24Gunners Buildings Limberline Road, Portsmouth, PO3 5BJ
Tel: 023-9269 9441 **Fax:** 023-9266 8803
E-mail: enquiries@custommetalpolishers.co.uk
Website: http://www.custommetalpolishers.co.uk
Directors: B. Shipman (Prop)
Registration no: 06551034 **Date established:** 2005
No.of Employees: 1 - 10 **Product Groups:** 46, 48

Dalkia

Portsmouth Technopole Kingston Crescent, Portsmouth, PO2 8FA
Tel: 023-9265 8233 **Fax:** 023-9262 9656
E-mail: enquiries@dalkia.co.uk
Website: http://www.dalkia.co.uk
Directors: P. Stevens (Fin)
Managers: G. Berthier, S. Fulcher (Tech Serv Mgr), K. Lusher (Personnel), S. Kelly, N. Burchett
Immediate Holding Company: SHORETECH SOLUTIONS LIMITED
Registration no: NF002924 **VAT No.:** GB 468 8788 61
Date established: 2011 **No.of Employees:** 11 - 20 **Product Groups:** 40, 48, 52, 80, 84

Davtrend Ltd

7a Fitzherbert Spur Farlington, Portsmouth, PO6 1TT
Tel: 023-9237 2004 **Fax:** 023-9232 6307
E-mail: sales@davtrend.co.uk
Website: http://www.davtrend.co.uk
Bank(s): National Westminster Bank Plc
Directors: D. Valentine (MD)
Managers: R. Valentine (Sales Prom Mgr)
Registration no: 01502449 **VAT No.:** GB 339 1509 52
Date established: 1980 **Turnover:** £1m - £2m **No.of Employees:** 11 - 20
Product Groups: 37

Date of Accounts	Oct 09	Oct 08	Oct 07
Working Capital	-20	48	48
Fixed Assets	249	255	247
Current Assets	84	158	187

Direct Catering Equipment Ltd

414 Havant Road Farlington, Portsmouth, PO6 1NF
Tel: 023-9232 4444 **Fax:** 023-9237 5389
E-mail: directcatering@ntlworld.com
Website: http://www.directcatering.mfbiz.com
Immediate Holding Company: DIRECT CATERING EQUIPMENT LIMITED
Registration no: 03071911 **Date established:** 1995
No.of Employees: 1 - 10 **Product Groups:** 40, 48, 63

Date of Accounts	Jun 11	Jun 10	Jun 09
Working Capital	-6	-9	-8
Fixed Assets	11	13	12
Current Assets	45	18	41

E M J Management Ltd

Aspen House Airport Service Road, Portsmouth, PO3 5RA
Tel: 023-9243 4650 **Fax:** 023-9243 4681
E-mail: sales@emjltd.com
Website: http://www.emjltd.com
Directors: A. Eggett (Dir)
Immediate Holding Company: E.M.J. MANAGEMENT LIMITED
Registration no: 03217564 **Date established:** 1996
Turnover: £500,000 - £1m **No.of Employees:** 1 - 10 **Product Groups:** 22, 23, 24, 26, 29, 30, 32, 35, 36, 37, 38, 39, 40, 49, 63, 66, 67, 68, 86

Date of Accounts	Aug 11	Aug 10	Aug 09
Working Capital	8	19	-4
Fixed Assets	14	17	20
Current Assets	468	351	308

E N L

Units 6-8 Victory Trading Estate Kiln Road, Portsmouth, PO3 5LP
Tel: 023-9266 8517 **Fax:** 023-9267 3378
E-mail: rg@enl.co.uk
Website: http://www.enl.co.uk
Directors: R. Gamble (MD)
Managers: K. Osbourne (Ops Mgr), R. Stephenson (Tech Serv Mgr)
Immediate Holding Company: ENL LIMITED
Registration no: 00612062 **Date established:** 1958 **Turnover:** £5m - £10m
No.of Employees: 51 - 100 **Product Groups:** 30, 48

Date of Accounts	Dec 11	Dec 10	Sep 09
Working Capital	834	862	857
Fixed Assets	889	440	515
Current Assets	3m	2m	2m
Current Liabilities	958	N/A	N/A

Elan-Dragonair Ltd

162 Southampton Road, Portsmouth, PO6 4RY
Tel: 023-9237 6451 **Fax:** 023-9237 0411
E-mail: david@elan-dragonair.co.uk
Website: http://www.elandragonair.co.uk
Directors: C. Holmes (Fin), D. Payne (MD)
Immediate Holding Company: ELAN-DRAGONAIR LIMITED
Registration no: 03659544 **Date established:** 1998
No.of Employees: 1 - 10 **Product Groups:** 35, 36, 40, 48

Date of Accounts	Mar 11	Mar 10	Mar 09
Working Capital	11	13	23
Fixed Assets	3	5	6
Current Assets	37	53	51

Elfords Sheds

Unit 16 Limberline Spur, Portsmouth, PO3 5HJ
Tel: 023-9266 4811 **Fax:** 023-9266 4811
E-mail: info@elfords.co.uk
Website: http://www.elfords.co.uk
Directors: D. Woodgate (Dir)
No.of Employees: 1 - 10 **Product Groups:** 25, 33, 35, 66

Elite Energy - The Specialist Energy Consultancy

1St Floor Arundel House 42 Arundel Street, Portsmouth, PO1 1NL
Tel: 023-9366 0106
E-mail: portsmouth@eliteenergy.org.uk
Website: http://www.eliteenergy.org.uk
Directors: C. Evans (Dir)
Registration no: 04225982 **Date established:** 2001
Turnover: £500,000 - £1m **No.of Employees:** 1 - 10 **Product Groups:** 80

Export Africa

1 Terminus Industrial Estate Durham Street, Portsmouth, PO1 1NR
Tel: 023-9282 3590 **Fax:** 023-9281 2038
E-mail: info@rundleholdings.co.uk
Website: http://www.rundleholdings.co.uk
Directors: R. Rundle (Dir)
Immediate Holding Company: RUNDLE HOLDINGS LTD
Registration no: 01661042 **VAT No.:** GB 359 5968 83
Turnover: £500,000 - £1m **No.of Employees:** 1 - 10 **Product Groups:** 61

Freight Transport Ltd

Unit C3-C5 Railway Triangle Walton Road, Portsmouth, PO6 1TW
Tel: 023-9232 4213 **Fax:** 023-9221 0324
E-mail: enquiries@freighttransport.co.uk
Website: http://www.freighttransport.co.uk
Bank(s): Lloyds TSB Bank plc
Managers: S. Butt (Sales Admin)
Immediate Holding Company: FREIGHT TRANSPORT LIMITED
Registration no: 02286068 **VAT No.:** GB 238 5748 28
Date established: 1988 **Turnover:** £2m - £5m **No.of Employees:** 21 - 50
Product Groups: 76

Date of Accounts	Apr 11	Apr 10	Apr 09
Working Capital	861	595	468
Fixed Assets	535	348	172
Current Assets	3m	3m	2m

Furneaux Riddall & Co. Ltd

Alchorne Place, Portsmouth, PO3 5PA
Tel: 023-9266 8621 **Fax:** 023-9269 0521
E-mail: sales@furneauxriddall.com
Website: http://www.furneauxriddall.com
Directors: G. Weston (MD), J. Coates (Fin)
Immediate Holding Company: FURNEAUX RIDDALL & CO.LIMITED
Registration no: 00591120 **VAT No.:** GB 107 4600 03
Date established: 1957 **Turnover:** £1m - £2m **No.of Employees:** 1 - 10
Product Groups: 37

Date of Accounts	Sep 11	Sep 10	Sep 09
Working Capital	72	63	72
Fixed Assets	177	183	189
Current Assets	312	315	314

G K N Aerospace Ltd

Airport Service Road, Portsmouth, PO3 5PE
Tel: 01983-283000 **Fax:** 023-9267 0899
E-mail: neil.house@gknaerospace.com
Website: http://www.gknaerospace.com
Bank(s): Barclays, Birmingham
Directors: G. Chipchase (Co Sec)
Managers: N. House (Sales Admin)
Ultimate Holding Company: GKN PLC
Immediate Holding Company: F.P.T. INDUSTRIES LIMITED
Registration no: 00355317 **Date established:** 1939
Turnover: £10m - £20m **No.of Employees:** 101 - 250
Product Groups: 29, 30, 32, 39

Date of Accounts	Dec 06	Dec 05
Working Capital	7055	7055
Current Assets	7055	7055
Total Share Capital	202	202

Gosport Metal Treatments Ltd

249 New Road, Portsmouth, PO2 7QY
Tel: 023-9269 3744 **Fax:** 023-9267 3352
E-mail: info@gmt-ltd.u-net.com
Bank(s): Lloyds TSB Bank plc
Directors: B. Morgan (MD)
Managers: S. Morgan (Mgr)
Ultimate Holding Company: GOSPORT HOLDINGS LIMITED
Immediate Holding Company: GOSPORT METAL TREATMENTS LIMITED
Registration no: 00926988 **VAT No.:** GB 107 4271 93
Date established: 1968 **Turnover:** £500,000 - £1m
No.of Employees: 11 - 20 **Product Groups:** 48

Date of Accounts	Dec 10	Dec 09	Dec 08
Working Capital	2m	1m	2m
Fixed Assets	546	991	324
Current Assets	2m	2m	2m

Graham

Nevil Shute Road, Portsmouth, PO3 5RX
Tel: 023-9265 4853 **Fax:** 023-9269 3123
Website: http://www.graham-group.co.uk
Bank(s): HSBC Bank plc
Managers: J. Doyle (Mgr)
Immediate Holding Company: GRAHAM BUILDERS MERCHANTS LIMITED
Registration no: 00066738 **VAT No.:** 394 1212 63 **Date established:** 2000
Turnover: £250,000 - £500,000 **No.of Employees:** 21 - 50
Product Groups: 66

H Fisher Ltd

9-10 Highbury Buildings Portsmouth Road, Cosham, Portsmouth, PO6 2SN
Tel: 023-9237 2111 **Fax:** 023-9238 0243
E-mail: sales@hfishertools.co.uk
Website: http://www.hfishertools.co.uk
Directors: N. Fisher (MD)
Immediate Holding Company: H.FISHER DISTRIBUTORS AND FACTORS(FAREHAM)LIMITED
Registration no: 00666803 **VAT No.:** GB 107 5625 79
Date established: 1960 **Turnover:** Up to £250,000
No.of Employees: 1 - 10 **Product Groups:** 23, 29, 30, 35, 36, 37, 39, 41, 63, 67

Date of Accounts	Apr 12	Apr 11	Apr 10
Working Capital	171	164	166
Fixed Assets	2	4	7
Current Assets	217	222	225

Hargreaves Promotions

Aspen House Airport Service Road, Portsmouth, PO3 5RA
Tel: 023-9282 2436 **Fax:** 023-9282 2177
E-mail: sales@hargreavespromotions.co.uk
Website: http://www.hargreavespromotions.co.uk
Directors: S. Linn (Sales & Mktg)
Immediate Holding Company: TECHSTITCH LIMITED
Registration no: 02841259 **VAT No.:** GB 750 1851 49
Date established: 2001 **Turnover:** £2m - £5m **No.of Employees:** 1 - 10
Product Groups: 23, 24, 65

Date of Accounts	Aug 11	Aug 10	Aug 09
Working Capital	-43	-13	4
Fixed Assets	115	58	64
Current Assets	133	16	47

Hendy Ford Cosham (Hendy Power)

Southampton Road, Portsmouth, PO6 4RW
Tel: 023-9232 2900 **Fax:** 023-9232 2922
E-mail: accounts@hendy-group.com
Website: http://www.hendygroup.com
Bank(s): Lloyds TSB Bank plc

Directors: N. Hendy (Ch), C. Moir (Fin), C. Hendy (Dir)
Managers: S. Nicholas (Tech Serv Mgr), N. Dawes (Purch Mgr), A. Stephenson, M. Weatherston (Mktg Serv Mgr)
Ultimate Holding Company: HENDY INVESTMENTS LIMITED
Immediate Holding Company: HENDY HOLDINGS LIMITED
Registration no: 00056988 **VAT No.:** GB 568 7215 08
Date established: 1998 **No.of Employees:** 101 - 250 **Product Groups:** 40

Date of Accounts	Dec 11	Dec 10	Dec 09
Sales Turnover	251m	246m	221m
Pre Tax Profit/Loss	437	-753	-132
Working Capital	-9m	-11m	-11m
Fixed Assets	34m	37m	41m
Current Assets	39m	58m	45m
Current Liabilities	11m	10m	10m

Henleycraft Ltd

Claybank Road, Portsmouth, PO3 5NH
Tel: 023-9266 3209 **Fax:** 023-9265 0652
E-mail: d.james@henleycraft.co.uk
Website: http://www.henleycraft.co.uk
Directors: D. James (MD)
Immediate Holding Company: HENLEYCRAFT LIMITED
Registration no: 00648083 **Date established:** 1960
Turnover: Up to £250,000 **No.of Employees:** 1 - 10 **Product Groups:** 30

Date of Accounts	May 11	May 10	May 09
Working Capital	275	284	251
Fixed Assets	48	48	50
Current Assets	332	351	307

I B M UK Ltd

PO Box 41, Portsmouth, PO6 3AU
Tel: 01962-815000 **Fax:** 0870-542 6329
E-mail: goldservice@uk.ibm.com
Website: http://www.ibm.com
Managers: S. Leonard (Chief Mgr)
Ultimate Holding Company: INTERNATIONAL BUSINESS MACHINES CORP (USA)
Immediate Holding Company: IBM LIMITED
Registration no: 01503908 **VAT No.:** GB 463 2923 44
Date established: 1980 **Turnover:** Over £1,000m
No.of Employees: 1001 - 1500 **Product Groups:** 24, 26, 28, 33, 37, 38, 39, 44, 45, 61, 67, 74, 80, 85, 86

I T W Switches & Switch Panel Ltd

Norway Road Hilsea, Portsmouth, PO3 5HT
Tel: 023-9269 4971 **Fax:** 023-9265 6278
E-mail: info@itwswitches.co.uk
Website: http://www.itwswitches.com
Bank(s): National Westminster Bank Plc
Managers: C. Nightingale (Comm), K. Carruthers, N. Dalmutt-rudd (Tech Serv Mgr), S. Meacher (Buyer), S. Efford (Chief Mgr), E. Burt (Comptroller)
Immediate Holding Company: CONCEPT FOODS LIMITED
Registration no: 00559693 **Date established:** 1999 **Turnover:** £5m - £10m
No.of Employees: 51 - 100 **Product Groups:** 30, 34, 35, 36, 37, 38, 39, 40, 44, 46, 47, 49, 65, 67, 68

Date of Accounts	Dec 11	Dec 10	Dec 09
Working Capital	185	154	105
Fixed Assets	11	24	46
Current Assets	604	618	482

Kelectronic

1 Waterworks Road, Portsmouth, PO6 1NG
Tel: 07889-422842 **Fax:** 023-9237 2077
E-mail: kkeirle@aol.com
Website: http://www.kelectronic.co.uk
Directors: K. Keirle (Prop)
Turnover: Up to £250,000 **No.of Employees:** 1 - 10 **Product Groups:** 48

L B L Finishers

Gunstore Road, Portsmouth, PO3 5HL
Tel: 023-9269 2020 **Fax:** 023-9267 0379
E-mail: sales@tomburn.co.uk
Website: http://www.tomburn.co.uk
Directors: J. Tomlinson (Dir)
Ultimate Holding Company: TOMBURN LIMITED
Immediate Holding Company: LBL FINISHERS LIMITED
Registration no: 03153422 **Date established:** 1996
No.of Employees: 21 - 50 **Product Groups:** 46

M L UK Ltd

Kettering Terrace Mile End, Portsmouth, PO2 7QH
Tel: 023-9281 9114 **Fax:** 023-9282 3386
E-mail: mick@mluk.co.uk
Website: http://www.mluk.co.uk
Bank(s): Natwest
Directors: M. Hobson (Dir), M. Liney (MD)
Immediate Holding Company: M L (UK) LIMITED
Registration no: 04547232 **VAT No.:** GB 823 8506 40
Date established: 2002 **Turnover:** £1m - £2m **No.of Employees:** 11 - 20
Product Groups: 48, 51

Date of Accounts	Dec 11	Dec 10	Dec 09
Working Capital	371	390	309
Fixed Assets	192	182	196
Current Assets	545	579	470

Macro Developments

2 Limberline Industrial Estate Limberline Spur, Portsmouth, PO3 5HJ
Tel: 023-9269 6615 **Fax:** 023-9267 3651
E-mail: info@macrodevelopments.co.uk
Website: http://www.macrodevelopments.co.uk
Directors: L. Willett (Co Sec)
Immediate Holding Company: MACRO DEVELOPMENTS (PORTSMOUTH) LIMITED
Registration no: 01401035 **VAT No.:** GB 321 7135 92
Date established: 1978 **Turnover:** £250,000 - £500,000
No.of Employees: 1 - 10 **Product Groups:** 48

Date of Accounts	Dec 11	Dec 10	Dec 09
Working Capital	82	91	100
Fixed Assets	14	7	11
Current Assets	165	163	140

Maplin Electronics Ltd

98-100 Kingston Road, Portsmouth, PO2 7PA
Tel: 08432-277313 **Fax:** 023-9265 4334
E-mail: customercare@maplin.co.uk
Website: http://www.maplin.co.uk
Managers: T. Rolf (Mgr)
Ultimate Holding Company: MONTAGU PRIVATE EQUITY LLP
Immediate Holding Company: MAPLIN ELECTRONICS LIMITED
Registration no: 01264385 **Date established:** 1976
Turnover: £125m - £250m **No.of Employees:** 1 - 10 **Product Groups:** 37, 61

Date of Accounts	Dec 11	Dec 08	Dec 09
Sales Turnover	205m	204m	204m
Pre Tax Profit/Loss	25m	32m	35m
Working Capital	118m	49m	75m
Fixed Assets	27m	28m	28m
Current Assets	207m	108m	142m
Current Liabilities	78m	51m	59m

Metatec Metaflux Ltd

Fitzherbert Road, Portsmouth, PO6 1RU
Tel: 023-9238 1382 **Fax:** 023-9238 0888
E-mail: metatec.sales@btconnect.com
Website: http://www.metatec.co.uk
Directors: P. White (Fin), B. White (MD)
Immediate Holding Company: METATEC LIMITED
Registration no: 01606662 **Date established:** 1982 **Turnover:** £1m - £2m
No.of Employees: 1 - 10 **Product Groups:** 52

Date of Accounts	Mar 12	Mar 11	Mar 10
Working Capital	23	47	48
Fixed Assets	36	43	59
Current Assets	260	241	238

Motor Homing

38 Second Avenue Farlington, Portsmouth, PO6 1JS
Tel: 023-9238 5022 **Fax:** 023-9238 5022
E-mail: kenayling@motorhoming.com
Website: http://www.motorhoming.com
Directors: K. Ayling (MD)
Turnover: Up to £250,000 **No.of Employees:** 1 - 10 **Product Groups:** 28, 39, 61, 68, 79, 80, 81

Motortech Marine Engineering

4-5 The Slipway Marina Keep, Port Solent, Portsmouth, PO6 4TR
Tel: 023-9220 1171 **Fax:** 023-9220 1172
E-mail: portsmouth@motortechmarine.co.uk
Website: http://www.motortechmarine.co.uk
Managers: T. Matthews (Chief Mgr)
Immediate Holding Company: ADJ (SUSSEX) LTD
Registration no: 02633341 **No.of Employees:** 1 - 10 **Product Groups:** 35, 36, 39

Date of Accounts	Jun 07
Working Capital	62
Fixed Assets	88
Current Assets	293
Current Liabilities	231
Total Share Capital	120

Nevada Music

12 Fitzherbert Spur Farlington, Portsmouth, PO6 1TT
Tel: 023-9220 5100 **Fax:** 023-9220 5101
E-mail: music@nevada.co.uk
Website: http://www.nevadamusic.co.uk
Directors: M. Devereaux (MD)
Immediate Holding Company: NEVADA MUSIC LIMITED
Registration no: 06430151 **Date established:** 2007
No.of Employees: 1 - 10 **Product Groups:** 37, 49, 65

Nightsearcher Ltd

Unit 4 Applied House Fitzherbert Spur, Farlington, Portsmouth, PO6 1TT
Tel: 023-9238 9774 **Fax:** 023-9238 9788
E-mail: sales@nightsearcher.co.uk
Website: http://www.nightsearcher.co.uk
Directors: C. Ford (MD)
Managers: R. Fuller (Develop Mgr)
Immediate Holding Company: NIGHTSEARCHER LIMITED
Registration no: 04661749 **Date established:** 2003
Turnover: Up to £250,000 **No.of Employees:** 11 - 20 **Product Groups:** 37

Date of Accounts	May 11	May 10	May 09
Working Capital	265	297	336
Fixed Assets	113	100	125
Current Assets	1m	938	966
Current Liabilities	162	N/A	107

Pall Europe Corporate Services

Europa House Havant Street, Portsmouth, PO1 3PD
Tel: 023-9230 3303 **Fax:** 023-9230 2506
E-mail: info@pall.com
Website: http://www.pall.com
Directors: H. Chapman (MD), N. Macdonald (Dir)
Ultimate Holding Company: PALL CORPORATION (USA)
Immediate Holding Company: PALL EUROPE LIMITED
Registration no: 07211681 **Date established:** 2010
Turnover: £125m - £250m **No.of Employees:** 1 - 10 **Product Groups:** 34, 35, 36, 37, 38, 40, 46

Date of Accounts	Jul 11
Sales Turnover	205m
Pre Tax Profit/Loss	13m
Working Capital	327
Fixed Assets	16m
Current Assets	72m
Current Liabilities	18m

Pall Industrial Hydraulics Redruth

Havant Street, Portsmouth, PO1 3PD
Tel: 023-9230 3303 **Fax:** 023-9230 2506
E-mail: info@pall.com
Website: http://www.pall.com
Managers: M. Fitzgerald (District Mgr)
Immediate Holding Company: H & A WASTE SERVICES LIMITED
Registration no: 03405502 **Date established:** 2001
No.of Employees: 101 - 250 **Product Groups:** 38, 42

Portchester Micro Tools

Bilton Way, Portsmouth, PO3 5FH
Tel: 023-9265 8000 **Fax:** 023-9265 8001
E-mail: info@pmtltd.co.uk
Website: http://www.pmtltd.co.uk
Bank(s): HSBC Bank plc
Directors: A. Wragg (Fin)
Managers: T. Rudkin
Ultimate Holding Company: P.M.T. (METAL CRAFT) LIMITED
Immediate Holding Company: PORTCHESTER MICROTOOLS LIMITED
Registration no: 00724391 **VAT No.:** GB 107 3947 67
Date established: 1962 **Turnover:** £2m - £5m
No.of Employees: 1501 & over **Product Groups:** 35, 36, 38, 39, 40, 44, 45, 46, 48, 49, 84

Date of Accounts	Apr 12	Apr 11	Apr 10
Working Capital	48	95	121
Fixed Assets	24	34	44
Current Assets	74	136	158

Portsmouth Fibreglass Centre

Unit 3 Marshlands Spur, Portsmouth, PO6 1TL
Tel: 023-9238 5075 **Fax:** 023-9238 5064
E-mail: nick@fibreglass-centre.co.uk
Website: http://www.fibreglass-centre.co.uk
Directors: N. Williams (Ptnr)
Date established: 1992 **Turnover:** Up to £250,000
No.of Employees: 1 - 10 **Product Groups:** 30

Portsmouth Gun Centre

295 London Road North End, Portsmouth, PO2 9HF
Tel: 023-9266 0574 **Fax:** 023-9264 4666
Website: http://www.portsmouthguncentre.com
Directors: S. Crabtree (Dir), S. Crabtree (Fin)
Immediate Holding Company: PORTSMOUTH GUN CENTRE LIMITED
Registration no: 04614035 **Date established:** 2002
No.of Employees: 1 - 10 **Product Groups:** 36, 39, 40

Date of Accounts	Jan 12	Jan 11	Jan 10
Working Capital	87	64	64
Fixed Assets	41	40	37
Current Assets	182	158	142

Portsmouth Publishing & Printing Ltd

The News Centre Hilsea, Portsmouth, PO2 9SX
Tel: 023-9266 4488 **Fax:** 023-9267 7777
E-mail: newsdesk@thenews.co.uk
Website: http://www.portsmouth.co.uk
Bank(s): Lloyds Ltd
Directors: C. Fisher (Fin), G. Fearon (Dir)
Ultimate Holding Company: JOHNSTON PRESS PLC
Immediate Holding Company: PORTSMOUTH PUBLISHING AND PRINTING LIMITED
Registration no: 01248289 **VAT No.:** GB 466 4183 30
Date established: 1976 **Turnover:** £5m - £10m
No.of Employees: 101 - 250 **Product Groups:** 28

Date of Accounts	Dec 11	Dec 08	Jan 10
Sales Turnover	7m	11m	10m
Working Capital	25m	25m	25m
Current Assets	25m	25m	25m

Quality Mouldings

3 Culverin Square Limberline Road, Hilsea, Portsmouth, PO3 5BU
Tel: 023-9267 9704 **Fax:** 023-9267 8531
E-mail: d_barclay@btconnect.com
Bank(s): Lloyds
Directors: D. Barclay (Ptnr)
VAT No.: GB 474 2577 24 **Date established:** 1987 **Turnover:** £1m - £2m
No.of Employees: 11 - 20 **Product Groups:** 30

R & M Marine

East Street Camber Quay Old Portsmouth, Portsmouth, PO1 2JJ
Tel: 023-9273 7555
E-mail: info@rm-marine.co.uk
Website: http://www.rm-marine.co.uk
Directors: R. Irwin (Dir)
No.of Employees: 1 - 10 **Product Groups:** 35, 36, 39

Radiator Show Room

326 London Road, Portsmouth, PO2 9JT
Tel: 023-9269 6622 **Fax:** 08451-274125
E-mail: enquiries@radiatorshowroom.co.uk
Website: http://www.radiatorshowroom.co.uk
Directors: S. Voros (Prop)
No.of Employees: 1 - 10 **Product Groups:** 26, 30, 32, 34, 36, 37, 39, 40, 47, 48, 66

Rapid Weldings & Industrial Supplies Ltd

Unit 2d Hamilton Road, Cosham, Portsmouth, PO6 4QE
Tel: 023-9221 4214 **Fax:** 023-9220 1505
E-mail: sales@rapidwelding.co.uk
Website: http://www.rapidwelding.co.uk
Bank(s): Nat West
Directors: R. Edwards (MD)
Managers: D. Austin (Tech Serv Mgr)
Immediate Holding Company: RAPID WELDING AND INDUSTRIAL SUPPLIES LIMITED
Registration no: 02431802 **VAT No.:** GB 054 4027 46
Date established: 1989 **Turnover:** £2m - £5m **No.of Employees:** 21 - 50
Product Groups: 34, 35, 38

Date of Accounts	Mar 12	Mar 11	Mar 10
Working Capital	124	82	29
Fixed Assets	144	182	121
Current Assets	968	917	859

Resmar Ltd

Fitzherbert Road, Portsmouth, PO6 1RU
Tel: 023-9221 5700 **Fax:** 023-9237 6744
E-mail: sales@resmar.co.uk
Website: http://www.resmar.co.uk
Directors: D. Hawkins (Dir), R. Barcoe (MD)
Registration no: 03742894 **Date established:** 1987 **Turnover:** £1m - £2m
No.of Employees: 1 - 10 **Product Groups:** 38, 40

Date of Accounts	Jun 08	Jun 07	Jun 06
Sales Turnover	2813	N/A	N/A
Pre Tax Profit/Loss	79	N/A	N/A
Working Capital	-90	-130	-136
Fixed Assets	144	150	170
Current Assets	830	648	707
Current Liabilities	920	778	843
Total Share Capital	1	1	1
ROCE% (Return on Capital Employed)	144.9		
ROT% (Return on Turnover)	2.8		

Righton Ltd
Unit 5-6 The Nelson Centre Portfield Road, Portsmouth, PO3 5SF
Tel: 023-9262 3070 **Fax:** 023-9267 7502
E-mail: ian.board@righton.co.uk
Website: http://www.righton.co.uk
Managers: I. Board (District Mgr)
Ultimate Holding Company: HENLEY MANAGEMENT COMPANY (USA)
Immediate Holding Company: RIGHTON LIMITED
Registration no: 00143411 **VAT No.:** GB 655 1301 62
Date established: 2016 **Turnover:** £5m - £10m **No.of Employees:** 21 - 50
Product Groups: 34, 66

Date of Accounts	Dec 11	Dec 10	Dec 09
Sales Turnover	71m	74m	50m
Pre Tax Profit/Loss	943	1m	-632
Working Capital	11m	7m	6m
Fixed Assets	1m	2m	2m
Current Assets	31m	30m	27m
Current Liabilities	2m	4m	2m

Rolls Royce Marine Electrical Systems Ltd
Northarbour Road, Portsmouth, PO6 3TL
Tel: 023-9231 0000 **Fax:** 023-9231 0001
Website: http://www.rolls-royce.com
Bank(s): National Westminster Bank Plc
Managers: M. Townend
Ultimate Holding Company: ROLLS-ROYCE GROUP PLC
Immediate Holding Company: ROLLS-ROYCE MARINE ELECTRICAL SYSTEMS LIMITED
Registration no: 02766255 **VAT No.:** GB 600 6962 58
Date established: 1992 **Turnover:** £10m - £20m
No.of Employees: 101 - 250 **Product Groups:** 36, 38, 39, 49

Date of Accounts	Dec 11	Dec 10	Dec 09
Sales Turnover	14m	14m	15m
Pre Tax Profit/Loss	505	2m	865
Working Capital	8m	8m	6m
Fixed Assets	113	216	309
Current Assets	14m	14m	12m
Current Liabilities	3m	3m	4m

S K Interiors Ltd
202 Havant Road Drayton, Portsmouth, PO6 2EH
Tel: 023-9232 4393 **Fax:** 023-9237 7027
E-mail: info@skinteriors.co.uk
Website: http://www.skinteriors.co.uk
Directors: T. Kilford (Fin), S. Kilford (MD)
Immediate Holding Company: S.K. INTERIORS LIMITED
Registration no: 03707008 **Date established:** 1999
Turnover: £500,000 - £1m **No.of Employees:** 1 - 10 **Product Groups:** 24, 25, 26, 30, 33, 35, 40, 48, 52, 66, 67, 84

Date of Accounts	Jun 11	Jun 10	Jun 09
Working Capital	42	92	47
Current Assets	143	166	139

Saacke Combustion Services Ltd
Marshlands Spur, Portsmouth, PO6 1RX
Tel: 023-9238 3111 **Fax:** 023-9232 7120
E-mail: m.cook@saacke.co.uk
Website: http://www.saacke.co.uk
Bank(s): National Westminster Bank Plc
Directors: D. Golden (MD), M. Cook (Dir)
Managers: J. Franklin (Purch Mgr), B. Hense, A. Rowsell
Ultimate Holding Company: SAACKE KG (GERMANY)
Immediate Holding Company: SAACKE LIMITED
Registration no: 00655236 **VAT No.:** GB 107 4529 80
Date established: 1960 **Turnover:** £5m - £10m
No.of Employees: 101 - 250 **Product Groups:** 38, 40, 45

Date of Accounts	Dec 08	Dec 07	Dec 06
Sales Turnover	10m	10m	10m
Pre Tax Profit/Loss	-367	-373	48
Working Capital	2m	2m	3m
Fixed Assets	230	338	442
Current Assets	5m	5m	6m
Current Liabilities	2m	2m	1m

Securitas Mobile
Trafalgar Wharf Hamilton Road, Cosham, Portsmouth, PO6 4PX
Tel: 023-9237 2502 **Fax:** 023-9237 0054
E-mail: info@securitas.com
Website: http://www.securitas.com
Managers: J. Hatch (District Mgr)
Date established: 2000 **Turnover:** £500,000 - £1m
No.of Employees: 11 - 20 **Product Groups:** 81

Date of Accounts	Dec 10	Dec 09	Dec 08
Sales Turnover	N/A	2m	849
Pre Tax Profit/Loss	20	-991	-1m
Working Capital	-3m	-3m	-2m
Fixed Assets	N/A	683	494
Current Assets	N/A	539	890
Current Liabilities	N/A	110	131

Select Cables Ltd
Painter Close, Portsmouth, PO3 5RS
Tel: 023-9265 2552 **Fax:** 023-9265 5277
E-mail: sales@selectcables.com
Website: http://www.selectcables.com
Directors: G. Scott (Dir)
Immediate Holding Company: SELECT CABLES LIMITED
Registration no: 02817924 **Date established:** 1993 **Turnover:** £2m - £5m
No.of Employees: 21 - 50 **Product Groups:** 37, 38, 39, 44, 67

Date of Accounts	Nov 11	Nov 10	Nov 09
Working Capital	2m	1m	2m
Fixed Assets	45	47	65
Current Assets	3m	2m	2m

Selex Galileo Ltd
Nevil Shute Road, Portsmouth, PO3 5RT
Tel: 023-9265 0595 **Fax:** 023-9267 0639
E-mail: sales.marketing@baesystems.com
Website: http://www.selexgalileo.com
Directors: A. Holding (Co Sec)
Managers: M. Jennison (Mgr)
Ultimate Holding Company: BAE SYSTEMS PLC
Immediate Holding Company: BAE SYSTEMS ELECTRONICS LIMITED
Registration no: 00053403 **Date established:** 1997
Turnover: £250m - £500m **No.of Employees:** 21 - 50
Product Groups: 33, 37, 38, 39, 40

Date of Accounts	Dec 11	Dec 10	Dec 09
Sales Turnover	281m	469m	375m
Pre Tax Profit/Loss	63m	-8m	12m
Working Capital	97m	707m	647m
Fixed Assets	773m	776m	835m
Current Assets	1524m	1454m	1382m
Current Liabilities	24m	110m	158m

Signs Express Ltd
Unit G3 Railway Triangle Industrial Estate Walton Road, Portsmouth, PO6 1TQ
Tel: 023-9238 3821 **Fax:** 023-9238 3822
E-mail: portsmouth@signsexpress.co.uk
Website: http://www.signsexpress.co.uk
Directors: J. Cardy (Dir)
Immediate Holding Company: SIGNS EXPRESS LIMITED
Registration no: 02375913 **Date established:** 1989
No.of Employees: 1 - 10 **Product Groups:** 30, 37, 40, 49

Date of Accounts	May 11	May 10	May 09
Working Capital	2m	1m	988
Fixed Assets	112	87	105
Current Assets	2m	2m	1m

Soumac Assembly Services
Unit 1 Victory Trading Estate Kiln Road, Portsmouth, PO3 5LP
Tel: 023-9267 9200 **Fax:** 023-9267 9499
E-mail: mike@soumac.co.uk
Website: http://www.soumac.co.uk
Directors: M. Souter (MD), S. Woods (Dir)
Managers: J. Merritt
Immediate Holding Company: CENTRALFLOW SYSTEMS LIMITED
Registration no: 05180403 **Date established:** 2004
No.of Employees: 11 - 20 **Product Groups:** 37, 38, 39, 40, 41, 42, 43, 44, 45

Date of Accounts	Dec 11	Dec 10	Dec 09
Working Capital	157	124	142
Fixed Assets	25	22	21
Current Assets	186	127	158

Starfish Ltd
6 St Georges Business Centre St Georges Square, Portsmouth, PO1 3EY
Tel: 023-9242 8176 **Fax:** 023-9277 9803
E-mail: info@starfishdesign.co.uk
Website: http://www.starfishdesign.co.uk
Directors: J. Scrivener (MD)
Immediate Holding Company: STARFISH LIMITED
Registration no: 04882830 **Date established:** 2003
No.of Employees: 1 - 10 **Product Groups:** 81

Date of Accounts	Aug 11	Aug 10	Aug 08
Sales Turnover	122	132	136
Pre Tax Profit/Loss	N/A	N/A	100
Working Capital	-11	-8	-6
Fixed Assets	11	9	9
Current Assets	60	48	59
Current Liabilities	N/A	N/A	66

Technograph Microcircuits Ltd
Railway Triangle Industrial Estate Walton Road, Portsmouth, PO6 1TN
Tel: 023-9232 1654 **Fax:** 023-9237 5353
E-mail: sales@technographmicro.com
Website: http://www.technographmicro.com
Directors: B. Batesford (MD), S. Edwards (Sales)
Immediate Holding Company: TECHNOGRAPH MICROCIRCUITS LIMITED
Registration no: 02174118 **VAT No.:** GB 444 5592 34
Date established: 1987 **Turnover:** £5m - £10m **No.of Employees:** 21 - 50
Product Groups: 37

Date of Accounts	Dec 09	Dec 08	Jan 12
Working Capital	1m	1m	1m
Fixed Assets	29	71	5
Current Assets	1m	1m	2m

Tri Pack Supplies Ltd
10b Fitzherbert Spur Farlington, Portsmouth, PO6 1TT
Tel: 023-9232 6696 **Fax:** 023-9221 4447
E-mail: sales@tripack.co.uk
Website: http://www.tripack.co.uk
Directors: S. Daburn (Dir)
Immediate Holding Company: TRI PACK SUPPLIES LTD
Registration no: 03132717 **Date established:** 1995
No.of Employees: 1 - 10 **Product Groups:** 22, 24, 25, 27, 28, 29, 30, 31, 32, 33, 34, 35, 36, 37, 38, 39, 40, 41, 42, 43, 44, 45, 46, 47, 48, 49, 61, 63, 65, 66, 67, 68, 72, 80, 81, 82, 83, 86, 89

Date of Accounts	Dec 11	Dec 10	Dec 09
Working Capital	542	423	324
Fixed Assets	633	664	755
Current Assets	1m	917	842

Warings Contractors Ltd
Gatcombe House Copnor Road, Portsmouth, PO2 0TU
Tel: 023-9269 4900 **Fax:** 023-9269 4948
E-mail: jouyp@waringsgroup.com
Website: http://www.waringsgroup.com
Bank(s): Lloyds
Directors: A. Durkin (Fin), P. Jouy (MD), H. Southwell (Pers)
Managers: C. Jones (Purch Mgr), P. Wood (Mktg Serv Mgr)
Ultimate Holding Company: BOUYGUES S.A. (FRANCE)
Immediate Holding Company: WARINGS CONSTRUCTION GROUP HOLDINGS LIMITED
Registration no: 03458583 **VAT No.:** GB 380 9154 42
Date established: 1997 **Turnover:** £75m - £125m
No.of Employees: 101 - 250 **Product Groups:** 51

Date of Accounts	Dec 11	Dec 10	Dec 09
Pre Tax Profit/Loss	N/A	N/A	-3
Working Capital	-4m	-4m	N/A
Fixed Assets	7m	7m	7m
Current Assets	15	15	15
Current Liabilities	4m	N/A	N/A

Wellman Defence Ltd
Dolphin House Williams Road, Portsmouth, PO3 5FP
Tel: 023-9266 4911 **Fax:** 023-9269 7864
E-mail: enquiries@wellmandefence.co.uk
Website: http://www.wellmandefence.co.uk
Bank(s): Barclays, 15 Colmore Road, Birmingham B3 2EP
Directors: S. Cassidy (Dir)
Managers: S. Morgans (Comptroller)
Ultimate Holding Company: WELLMAN TECHNOLOGIES INTERNATIONAL LIMITED
Immediate Holding Company: WELLMAN DEFENCE LIMITED
Registration no: 08035560 **VAT No.:** GB 239 9422 32
Date established: 2012 **Turnover:** £5m - £10m
No.of Employees: 51 - 100 **Product Groups:** 31, 39, 40, 42

Date of Accounts	Dec 11	Dec 10	Dec 09
Sales Turnover	10m	9m	11m
Pre Tax Profit/Loss	2m	2m	1m
Working Capital	-4m	3m	3m
Fixed Assets	5m	74	96
Current Assets	3m	8m	9m
Current Liabilities	5m	4m	5m

Westminster Business Machines Ltd (WBM)
7 Highbury Buildings
Portsmouth Road
Cosham, Portsmouth, PO6 2SN
02392-381121
michelle@w-b-m.co.uk
Website: http://www.w-b-m.co.uk
Directors: A. Brown (MD)
Product Groups: 27, 28, 44, 49

Wightlink Group Ltd
PO Box 59, Portsmouth, PO1 2JE
Tel: 08713-761000 **Fax:** 023-9285 5432
E-mail: info@wightlink.co.uk
Website: http://www.wightlink.co.uk
Directors: A. Willson (MD), J. Pascoe (Fin)
Managers: I. Winn (Sales Prom Mgr), R. Sandford, J. Saville (Mktg Serv Mgr)
Ultimate Holding Company: MACQUARIE EUROPEAN INFRASTRUCTURE FUND LP (GUERNSEY)
Immediate Holding Company: WIGHTLINK GROUP LIMITED
Registration no: 03043379 **Date established:** 1995
Turnover: Up to £250,000 **No.of Employees:** 21 - 50 **Product Groups:** 74

Ringwood

Automated Control Services
Unit 16 Hightown Industrial Estate Crow Arch Lane, Ringwood, BH24 1ND
Tel: 01425-461008 **Fax:** 01425-461009
E-mail: sales@automatedcontrolservices.co.uk
Website: http://www.automatedcontrolservices.co.uk
Directors: A. Wiseman (Dir)
Immediate Holding Company: AUTOMATED CONTROL SERVICES LTD
Registration no: 03671960 **Date established:** 1998
No.of Employees: 1 - 10 **Product Groups:** 26, 35

Date of Accounts	Jan 12	Jan 11	Jan 10
Sales Turnover	8m	7m	6m
Pre Tax Profit/Loss	519	354	-39
Working Capital	2m	2m	2m
Fixed Assets	870	728	434
Current Assets	3m	3m	3m
Current Liabilities	1m	965	967

Coolmation Ltd
Unit 7 Millstream Trading Estate Christchurch Road, Ringwood, BH24 3SD
Tel: 0800-731 5466 **Fax:** 01425-470745
E-mail: enquiries@coolmation.co.uk
Website: http://www.coolmation.co.uk
Bank(s): Barclays
Directors: C. Newman (Fin), G. Franklin (Ch)
Managers: K. McDermott (Personnel)
Immediate Holding Company: COOLMATION LIMITED
Registration no: 01744381 **VAT No.:** GB 392 7371 25
Date established: 1983 **Turnover:** £5m - £10m **No.of Employees:** 21 - 50
Product Groups: 39, 40, 41, 42, 44, 49, 52, 66, 83, 84, 87

Date of Accounts	Jan 12	Jan 11	Jan 10
Sales Turnover	8m	7m	6m
Pre Tax Profit/Loss	519	354	-39
Working Capital	2m	2m	2m
Fixed Assets	870	728	434
Current Assets	3m	3m	3m
Current Liabilities	1m	965	967

Corrugated Plastic Products Ltd
21 Hightown Industrial Estate Crow Arch Lane, Ringwood, BH24 1ND
Tel: 01425-470249 **Fax:** 01425-480090
E-mail: sales@cppltd.com
Website: http://www.cppltd.com
Directors: P. Farrington (MD)
Immediate Holding Company: CORRUGATED PLASTIC PRODUCTS LIMITED
Registration no: 01492161 **VAT No.:** GB 323 6568 54
Date established: 1980 **Turnover:** £2m - £5m **No.of Employees:** 1 - 10
Product Groups: 30, 66

Date of Accounts	Sep 11	Sep 10	Sep 09
Working Capital	131	122	112
Fixed Assets	13	16	11
Current Assets	489	496	615

D J M Video
41 Quomp, Ringwood, BH24 1NT
Tel: 01425-475415 **Fax:** 01425-475415
E-mail: martyn@djm.co.uk
Website: http://www.djm.co.uk
Directors: D. Maidman (Prop)
No.of Employees: 1 - 10 **Product Groups:** 28, 37, 44

Dean & Dyball Civil Engineering Ltd
Endeavour House Crowe Arch Lane, Ringwood, BH24 1PN
Tel: 01425-470000 **Fax:** 01425-472724
E-mail: guy@deandyball.co.uk
Website: http://www.deandyball.co.uk
Bank(s): Lloyds
Directors: M. Hirst (Ch), P. Morris (Fin), P. Morris (Co Sec), H. Macaulay (MD), H. Flint (Fin), G. Hardacre (Dir), C. Howarth (MD), A. Dyball (Grp Chief Exec), A. Crawford (Dir), D. Swan (Mkt Research)
Managers: K. Barker, T. Murley (Personnel), J. Taylor (Mktg Serv Mgr), M. Haines (Mktg Serv Mgr), M. Christopher (I.T. Exec), J. Powis (Chief Buyer)
Ultimate Holding Company: BALFOUR BEATTY PLC
Immediate Holding Company: DEAN & DYBALL WORKFORCE LIMITED
Registration no: 01239585 **VAT No.:** GB 355 6392 32
Date established: 1976 **Turnover:** Up to £250,000
No.of Employees: 21 - 50 **Product Groups:** 51, 52, 84

Date of Accounts	Dec 10	Dec 09	Dec 08
Sales Turnover	63m	86m	275m
Pre Tax Profit/Loss	-2m	1m	-22m

Working Capital	3m	-8m	-9m
Fixed Assets	2m	3m	4m
Current Assets	26m	23m	44m
Current Liabilities	1m	4m	11m

Handling Aids Ltd
Crowe Arch Lane, Ringwood, BH24 1PB
Tel: 01425-472263 **Fax:** 01425-471248
E-mail: darren.hill@handlingaidstrailers.co.uk
Website: http://www.handlingaidstrailers.co.uk
Bank(s): Barclays
Directors: D. Hill (MD)
Immediate Holding Company: HANDLING AIDS LIMITED
Registration no: 00593775 **VAT No.:** GB 185 6887 00
Date established: 1957 **Turnover:** £500,000 - £1m
No.of Employees: 11 - 20 **Product Groups:** 39, 40, 41, 45, 84

Date of Accounts	Jan 11	Jan 10	Jan 09
Working Capital	15	12	21
Fixed Assets	N/A	5	10
Current Assets	17	99	135

Henderson Bearings
Crow Arch Lane, Ringwood, BH24 1NZ
Tel: 01425-477787 **Fax:** 01425-478883
E-mail: sales@hendersonbearings.com
Website: http://www.hendersonbearings.com
Managers: P. Humphreys (Mgr)
Immediate Holding Company: RONALD V.HENDERSON (BEARINGS)
Registration no: 00632031 **VAT No.:** GB 468 3308 29
Date established: 1959 **Turnover:** £2m - £5m **No.of Employees:** 11 - 20
Product Groups: 30, 33, 34, 35, 39, 45, 48

Date of Accounts	Oct 02
Sales Turnover	2m
Pre Tax Profit/Loss	133
Working Capital	1m
Fixed Assets	573
Current Assets	2m
Current Liabilities	276

Horn Cutting Tools Ltd
32 New Street, Ringwood, BH24 3AD
Tel: 01425-481800 **Fax:** 01425-481888
E-mail: info@phorn.co.uk
Website: http://www.phorn.co.uk
Managers: A. Channell (Tech Serv Mgr), M. Green (Chief Mgr)
Immediate Holding Company: HORN CUTTING TOOLS LIMITED
Registration no: 06427770 **Date established:** 2007
No.of Employees: 21 - 50 **Product Groups:** 46

Date of Accounts	Dec 11	Dec 10	Dec 09
Sales Turnover	8m	6m	4m
Pre Tax Profit/Loss	989	445	-450
Working Capital	416	12	-174
Fixed Assets	284	355	222
Current Assets	5m	4m	3m
Current Liabilities	552	415	210

Innov8 Events limited
DMC House Pullman Business Park, Pullman Way, Ringwood, BH24 1HD
Tel: 0871-4269988 **Fax:** 0871-426 9989
E-mail: info@innov8-events.com
Website: http://www.innov8-events.com
Managers: J. Cleaver (Mgr)
Registration no: 05970374 **Date established:** 2006
No.of Employees: 1 - 10 **Product Groups:** 89

Date of Accounts	Dec 07
Working Capital	-13
Fixed Assets	14
Current Assets	19
Current Liabilities	32

Lambert & Wiltshire Gunsmiths Ltd
16 Market Place, Ringwood, BH24 1AW
Tel: 01425-473223 **Fax:** 01425-473221
E-mail: sales@lambertandwiltshire.com
Directors: P. Fullwood (Prop), R. Mileham (Fin)
Immediate Holding Company: LAMBERT AND WILTSHIRE GUNSMITHS LIMITED
Registration no: 03096947 **Date established:** 1995
Turnover: £500,000 - £1m **No.of Employees:** 1 - 10 **Product Groups:** 36, 39, 40

Date of Accounts	Jan 12	Jan 11	Jan 09
Sales Turnover	N/A	N/A	689
Pre Tax Profit/Loss	N/A	N/A	3
Working Capital	92	99	104
Fixed Assets	8	10	14
Current Assets	187	192	184
Current Liabilities	N/A	N/A	26

Landscape Irrigation Systems
River View Salisbury Road, Ringwood, BH24 1AS
Tel: 01425-473790 **Fax:** 01425-471157
E-mail: office@landscape-irrigation.co.uk
Website: http://www.landscape-irrigation.co.uk
Directors: E. Powell (Prop)
Date established: 1990 **No.of Employees:** 1 - 10 **Product Groups:** 41, 51, 67

Multi Fuel Heating Centre
209 Ringwood Road St Leonards, Ringwood, BH24 2QA
Tel: 01202-890321 **Fax:** 01202-890420
E-mail: info@multifuelheating.co.uk
Website: http://www.multifuelheating.co.uk
Directors: G. Humber (Prop)
Date established: 1979 **No.of Employees:** 1 - 10 **Product Groups:** 40

Multi Signs
Hightown Industrial Estate Crow Arch Lane, Ringwood, BH24 1ND
Tel: 01425-471537
E-mail: les@multi-signs.co.uk
Website: http://www.multi-signs.co.uk
Directors: L. Hole (Prop)
No.of Employees: 1 - 10 **Product Groups:** 30, 40, 49

New Forest Precision Ltd
3 Parkside, Ringwood, BH24 3SG
Tel: 01425-479007 **Fax:** 01425-480231
E-mail: sales@n-f-p.co.uk
Website: http://www.n-f-p.co.uk
Bank(s): National Westminster Bank Plc
Directors: G. Clark (MD), P. Cosser (Dir), M. Wood (Fin)
Immediate Holding Company: NEW FOREST PRECISION LIMITED
Registration no: 01327215 **VAT No.:** GB 323 4047 92
Date established: 1977 **Turnover:** £1m - £2m **No.of Employees:** 11 - 20
Product Groups: 48

Date of Accounts	Oct 11	Oct 10	Oct 09
Working Capital	199	253	360
Fixed Assets	155	169	197
Current Assets	323	399	503

Scott Marketing
2 Doughty Building Crow Arch Lane, Ringwood, BH24 1NZ
Tel: 01425-477951 **Fax:** 01425-478969
E-mail: enquiries@scottmarketing.com
Website: http://www.scottmarketing.com
Directors: D. Scott (MD)
Registration no: 04629696 **VAT No.:** GB 392 7809 10
No.of Employees: 1 - 10 **Product Groups:** 61, 81, 86

Testing, Regulatory & Compliance
Holly Grove Farm Verwood Road, Ashley, Ringwood, BH24 2DB
Tel: 01425-479979 **Fax:** 01425-480637
E-mail: info@tracglobal.com
Website: http://www.tracglobal.com
Bank(s): National Westminster Bank Plc
Directors: M. Wood (MD), N. Adams (Dir), B. Bodeker (Fin)
Ultimate Holding Company: Bioquell plc
Immediate Holding Company: Trac Environmental & Analysis Ltd
Registration no: 01914948 **Turnover:** £1m - £2m
No.of Employees: 11 - 20 **Product Groups:** 85

Date of Accounts	Dec 07	Dec 06
Sales Turnover	1137	1216
Pre Tax Profit/Loss	4	186
Working Capital	93	85
Fixed Assets	427	412
Current Assets	335	410
Current Liabilities	242	325
Total Share Capital	2	2
ROCE% (Return on Capital Employed)	0.8	37.4
ROT% (Return on Turnover)	0.4	15.3

Romsey

Advance Jetters Ltd
Hill View Road Michelmersh, Romsey, SO51 0NN
Tel: 01794-367458 **Fax:** 01794-367833
E-mail: sales@advancejetters.co.uk
Website: http://www.water-jetting.co.uk
Directors: L. Moss (Dir), R. Flux (MD)
Managers: S. Flux (Sales Admin)
Registration no: 06750963 **Turnover:** £1m - £2m
No.of Employees: 1 - 10 **Product Groups:** 39, 40

Anker Machinery Company Ltd
Church Walk House Farley Lane, Braishfield, Romsey, SO51 0QL
Tel: 01794-367722 **Fax:** 01794-369119
E-mail: info@ankermachinery.co.uk
Directors: S. Rawson-Smith (Co Sec)
Immediate Holding Company: ANKER MACHINERY COMPANY LIMITED
Registration no: 02884705 **Date established:** 1994
Turnover: £500,000 - £1m **No.of Employees:** 1 - 10 **Product Groups:** 41

Date of Accounts	Mar 11	Mar 10	Mar 09
Working Capital	31	51	62
Fixed Assets	17	27	37
Current Assets	52	67	76

B & G Ltd
2 Premier Way, Romsey, SO51 9DH
Tel: 01794-518448 **Fax:** 01794-518077
E-mail: info@navico.com
Website: http://www.navico.com
Bank(s): Royal Bank of Scotland
Directors: P. Mackison (I.T. Dir), R. Acland (Ch)
Managers: T. Coletta (Purch Mgr), R. Yatman (Mktg Serv Mgr), R. Northover (Mgr), J. Totczyk (Prod Mgr), J. Scollard, G. Pollard (Sales Prom Mgr), D. Hamer (Comptroller)
Immediate Holding Company: BG LTD
Registration no: 03896442 **Date established:** 1999 **Turnover:** £5m - £10m
No.of Employees: 21 - 50 **Product Groups:** 37, 38, 39, 49

B K P Group Waste & Recycling Ltd
Unit 8 Casbrook Park Bunny Lane, Timsbury, Romsey, SO51 0PG
Tel: 01794-368288 **Fax:** 01794-367799
E-mail: sales@bkpgroup.com
Website: http://www.bkpgroup.com
Directors: N. Healey (Prop)
Immediate Holding Company: BKP WASTE & RECYCLING LTD
Registration no: 06777950 **Date established:** 2008
No.of Employees: 21 - 50 **Product Groups:** 32, 42, 54, 83

Date of Accounts	Mar 12	Mar 11	Mar 10
Working Capital	-144	-509	-285
Fixed Assets	297	214	336
Current Assets	732	264	506

B R C Southampton
2 Belbins Business Park Cupernham Lane, Romsey, SO51 7JF
Tel: 01794-521158 **Fax:** 01794-521154
E-mail: sales@brc.ltd.uk
Website: http://www.selsa.com
Managers: P. Trussler (Mgr)
Registration no: 03271267 **No.of Employees:** 11 - 20
Product Groups: 34, 35, 66

Business Analysis Ltd
Units 11-12 Shorts Farm Scallows Lane, Sherfield English, Romsey, SO51 6DX
Tel: 01794-325120 **Fax:** 01794-322743
E-mail: alan@business-analysis.co.uk
Website: http://www.business-analysis.co.uk
Registration no: 01399592 **Turnover:** £500,000 - £1m
No.of Employees: 1 - 10 **Product Groups:** 44, 80, 82

Date of Accounts	Dec 07	Dec 06	Dec 05
Sales Turnover	N/A	336	421
Pre Tax Profit/Loss	N/A	-16	17
Working Capital	4	-7	4
Fixed Assets	12	16	21
Current Assets	160	153	141
Current Liabilities	157	160	137
ROCE% (Return on Capital Employed)		-179.8	67.8
ROT% (Return on Turnover)		-4.9	4.0

C P V Ltd
Woodington Mill East Wellow, Romsey, SO51 6DQ
Tel: 01794-322884 **Fax:** 01794-322885
E-mail: sales@cpv.co.uk
Website: http://www.cpv.co.uk
Bank(s): Royal Bank of Scotland, Farnborough
Directors: M. Wettall (MD)
Ultimate Holding Company: BLACKWATER HOLDINGS LTD
Immediate Holding Company: CPV LTD
Registration no: 00468471 **VAT No.:** GB 358 7714 13
Date established: 1949 **Turnover:** £5m - £10m **No.of Employees:** 21 - 50
Product Groups: 30, 36, 37, 40, 41, 42, 48, 52, 66

Date of Accounts	Sep 11	Sep 10	Sep 09
Working Capital	3m	3m	3m
Fixed Assets	1m	1m	1m
Current Assets	4m	3m	3m

D M S Technologies Ltd
Belbins Business Park Cupernham Lane, Romsey, SO51 7JF
Tel: 01794-525400 **Fax:** 01794-525450
E-mail: info@dmstech.co.uk
Website: http://www.dmstech.co.uk
Directors: P. Edwards (Sales), C. Bumstead (Fin)
Managers: D. Claxton (Mktg Serv Mgr), M. Heritage (Purch Mgr), H. Monroe (Mktg Serv Mgr)
Ultimate Holding Company: KIRKPACE LIMITED
Immediate Holding Company: DMS TECHNOLOGIES LTD
Registration no: 02215145 **Date established:** 1988 **Turnover:** £5m - £10m
No.of Employees: 21 - 50 **Product Groups:** 37, 39, 67

Dasic International Ltd
Winchester Hill, Romsey, SO51 7YD
Tel: 01794-512419 **Fax:** 01794-522346
E-mail: info@dasicinter.com
Website: http://www.dasicinternational.com
Bank(s): Lloyds
Directors: J. Belk (MD)
Immediate Holding Company: DASIC INTERNATIONAL LIMITED
Registration no: 02005284 **VAT No.:** GB 188 5232 36
Date established: 1986 **No.of Employees:** 11 - 20 **Product Groups:** 32, 66

Date of Accounts	Dec 11	Dec 10	Dec 09
Working Capital	1m	1m	1m
Fixed Assets	737	754	757
Current Assets	2m	1m	1m

Dawnthrive
Unit 7 Westlink Belbins Business Park Cupernham Lane, Romsey, SO51 7AA
Tel: 01794-830352 **Fax:** 01794-523539
E-mail: david@dawnthrive.com
Website: http://www.dawnthrive.com
Directors: D. Coombs (MD)
Immediate Holding Company: DAWNTHRIVE LIMITED
Registration no: 02026081 **Date established:** 1986
Turnover: £500,000 - £1m **No.of Employees:** 11 - 20 **Product Groups:** 80

Date of Accounts	Aug 11	Aug 10	Aug 09
Working Capital	250	256	257
Fixed Assets	23	19	10
Current Assets	250	528	641

Fans & Spares Ltd
Unit 32 Romsey Industrial Estate Greatbridge Road, Romsey, SO51 0HR
Tel: 01794-830399 **Fax:** 01794-830336
E-mail: coev@systemair.co.uk
Website: http://www.fansandspares.co.uk
Managers: C. Evans (Mgr)
Immediate Holding Company: FANS & SPARES LTD
Registration no: 07240936 **VAT No.:** GB 300 0687 11
Date established: 2010 **Turnover:** £10m - £20m **No.of Employees:** 1 - 10
Product Groups: 39, 40, 48, 52

Femcare Nikomed Ltd
Stuart Court Salisbury Road, Romsey, SO51 6DJ
Tel: 01794-525100 **Fax:** 01794-525101
E-mail: enquiries@femcare-nikomed.co.uk
Website: http://www.femcare-nikomed.co.uk
Bank(s): Lloyds TSB Bank plc
Directors: A. Mcquilkin (Dir), J. Willis (Co Sec)
Ultimate Holding Company: FEMCARE GROUP LIMITED
Immediate Holding Company: FEMCARE - NIKOMED LIMITED
Registration no: 02301779 **VAT No.:** GB 385 1367 35
Date established: 1988 **Turnover:** £5m - £10m **No.of Employees:** 11 - 20
Product Groups: 30, 38

Date of Accounts	Dec 11	Mar 11	Mar 10
Sales Turnover	7m	9m	7m
Pre Tax Profit/Loss	3m	3m	-522
Working Capital	3m	1m	-1m
Fixed Assets	5m	5m	6m
Current Assets	16m	16m	13m
Current Liabilities	1m	4m	3m

Fluid Film Devices Ltd
8 Greatbridge Business Park Budds Lane, Romsey, SO51 0HA
Tel: 01794-514551 **Fax:** 01794-524116
E-mail: info@fluidfilmdevices.co.uk
Website: http://www.fluidfilmdevices.co.uk
Directors: P. Humby (Dir)
Immediate Holding Company: FLUID FILM DEVICES LIMITED
Registration no: 01911658 **VAT No.:** GB 458 5708 10
Date established: 1985 **Turnover:** £250,000 - £500,000
No.of Employees: 1 - 10 **Product Groups:** 35

Date of Accounts	Mar 12	Mar 11	Mar 10
Working Capital	-17	-1	9
Fixed Assets	45	52	52
Current Assets	29	48	50

Greaves Best Design Ltd
Unit 26 Home Farm Business Park East Tytherley Road, Lockerley, Romsey, SO51 0JT
Tel: 01794-342341 **Fax:** 01794-342349
E-mail: enquiries@greavesbest.com
Website: http://www.greavesbest.com

see next page

***Greaves Best Design Ltd** - Cont'd*

Directors: J. Greaves (Ptnr)
Immediate Holding Company: GBD UK LIMITED
Registration no: 05835309 **Date established:** 2006
Turnover: £250,000 - £500,000 **No.of Employees:** 1 - 10
Product Groups: 51, 81

Date of Accounts	Jun 11	Jun 10	Jun 08
Working Capital	-42	-16	3
Fixed Assets	2	3	2
Current Assets	55	65	52
Current Liabilities	97	N/A	18

H Kuhnke Ltd

21 Abbey Enterprise Centre Premier Way, Romsey, SO51 9AQ
Tel: 01794-514445 **Fax:** 01794-513514
E-mail: sales@kuhnke.co.uk
Website: http://www.kuhnke.co.uk
Directors: P. Wiggins (MD)
Immediate Holding Company: H. KUHNKE LIMITED
Registration no: 00665193 **VAT No.:** GB 207 7664 51
Date established: 1960 **Turnover:** £500,000 - £1m
No.of Employees: 1 - 10 **Product Groups:** 37, 38, 40, 46, 49

Date of Accounts	Dec 11	Dec 10	Dec 09
Working Capital	252	167	119
Fixed Assets	10	7	9
Current Assets	350	346	245

Haworth Castings Ltd

Budds Lane Industrial Estate, Romsey, SO51 0HA
Tel: 01794-512685 **Fax:** 01794-830086
E-mail: admin@haworthcastings.co.uk
Website: http://www.haworthcastings.co.uk
Directors: D. Haworth (Fin), A. Haworth (MD)
Managers: P. Bonham (Sales Prom Mgr), M. Hancock (Sales Admin)
Ultimate Holding Company: HAWORTH ROMSEY LIMITED
Immediate Holding Company: HAWORTH CASTINGS LIMITED
Registration no: 00897489 **Date established:** 1967 **Turnover:** £2m - £5m
No.of Employees: 11 - 20 **Product Groups:** 34

Date of Accounts	Jan 12	Jan 11	Jan 10
Working Capital	862	1m	1m
Fixed Assets	667	417	357
Current Assets	1m	2m	2m

Image Computer Systems Ltd

Frenches Farm The Frenches, East Wellow, Romsey, SO51 6FE
Tel: 01794-323981 **Fax:** 01202-897682
E-mail: sales@image-cs.co.uk
Website: http://www.image-cs.co.uk
Directors: J. Poole (Ch), L. Hartley (Dir)
Managers: A. Lockett (Mktg Serv Mgr)
Immediate Holding Company: IMAGE COMPUTER SYSTEMS LIMITED
Registration no: 01553871 **VAT No.:** GB 323 5886 45
Date established: 1981 **Turnover:** £250,000 - £500,000
No.of Employees: 1 - 10 **Product Groups:** 44

Date of Accounts	Dec 11	Dec 10	Dec 09
Working Capital	249	293	251
Fixed Assets	12	10	11
Current Assets	457	325	290

Ironart The Forge

6 Portersbridge Street, Romsey, SO51 8DJ
Tel: 01794-522284 **Fax:** 01794-522284
E-mail: timironart@aol.com
Website: http://www.iron-art.com
Directors: T. Hirst (Prop)
Date established: 1976 **No.of Employees:** 1 - 10 **Product Groups:** 26, 35

Jena UK Ltd

Unit 17 Romsey Industrial Estate, Romsey, SO51 0HR
Tel: 01794-519220 **Fax:** 01794-519188
E-mail: sales@jena-uk.com
Website: http://www.jena-uk.com
Directors: D. Smith (Dir)
Managers: P. Griffiths (Buyer), P. Stokes (Sales Prom Mgr)
Immediate Holding Company: JENA (UK) LIMITED
Registration no: 01097456 **VAT No.:** GB 568 6057 05
Date established: 1973 **Turnover:** £10m - £20m
No.of Employees: 21 - 50 **Product Groups:** 30

Date of Accounts	Dec 11	Dec 10	Dec 09
Sales Turnover	19m	17m	18m
Pre Tax Profit/Loss	438	634	443
Working Capital	2m	2m	1m
Fixed Assets	2m	2m	2m
Current Assets	7m	6m	7m
Current Liabilities	917	880	1m

Maloto Property Consultants Ltd

Fernacre Business Park Budds Lane, Romsey, SO51 0HA
Tel: 01794-324320 **Fax:** 01794-324330
E-mail: jo@maloto.com
Website: http://www.malotopc.com
Directors: M. Davis (Dir)
Immediate Holding Company: MALOTO PROPERTY CONSULTANTS LIMITED
Registration no: 05814519 **Date established:** 2006
Turnover: Up to £250,000 **No.of Employees:** 1 - 10 **Product Groups:** 80

Date of Accounts	May 11	May 10	May 09
Working Capital	26	34	-1
Fixed Assets	1	1	1
Current Assets	129	78	45

Merryhill Envirotec Ltd

Merryhill House Budds Lane, Romsey, SO51 0HA
Tel: 01794-515848 **Fax:** 01794-525386
E-mail: paul.fox@merryhill-idm.co.uk
Website: http://www.merryhillenvirotec.com
Bank(s): Barclays, Park Gate, Southampton
Directors: P. Fox (Dir)
Managers: I. Afzal
Immediate Holding Company: RESTART LIMITED
Registration no: 02772898 **Date established:** 1992 **Turnover:** £2m - £5m
No.of Employees: 21 - 50 **Product Groups:** 52, 54

Date of Accounts	Nov 11	Nov 10	Nov 09
Working Capital	-31	-30	-30

Navico UK (Marine Division UK)

Navico Premier Way, Romsey, SO51 9DH
Tel: 01794-510010 **Fax:** 01794-510006
E-mail: paul.griffiths@navico.com
Website: http://www.navico.com
Bank(s): Den Norske Bank, London
Directors: D. Hamer (Fin)
Managers: P. Griffiths
Immediate Holding Company: NAVICO UK LIMITED
Registration no: 00565631 **VAT No.:** GB 684 5086 05
Date established: 1956 **Turnover:** £5m - £10m **No.of Employees:** 21 - 50
Product Groups: 37, 39

Date of Accounts	Dec 11	Dec 10	Dec 09
Sales Turnover	5m	5m	8m
Pre Tax Profit/Loss	180	184	185
Working Capital	2m	2m	2m
Fixed Assets	135	216	296
Current Assets	3m	3m	2m
Current Liabilities	229	299	N/A

New Glass Structures Ltd

Bidey House The Hundred, Romsey, SO51 8GD
Tel: 01794-516501
E-mail: info@newglassstructures.co.uk
Website: http://www.newglassstructures.co.uk
Directors: T. Silley (Fin)
Ultimate Holding Company: NGS HOLDINGS LIMITED
Immediate Holding Company: NEW GLASS STRUCTURES LIMITED
Registration no: 05842483 **Date established:** 2006
No.of Employees: 1 - 10 **Product Groups:** 35, 36

Date of Accounts	Dec 09	Dec 08	Dec 07
Working Capital	-324	-208	-22
Fixed Assets	2	2	3
Current Assets	189	12	75

PWM Distribution

Wild Cherry saunders lane, awbridge, Romsey, SO51 0GP
Tel: 01794-830 841 **Fax:** 0844-7790347
E-mail: enquiries@pwm-distribution.com
Website: http://www.pwm-distribution.com
Directors: S. Kelly (Dir)
Registration no: 07011866 **Date established:** 1997
Turnover: Up to £250,000 **No.of Employees:** 1 - 10 **Product Groups:** 40, 52

Rentajet Group Ltd

Paultons Park Ower, Romsey, SO51 6AL
Tel: 023-8081 2921 **Fax:** 023-8081 4016
E-mail: rentajet@rentajet.co.uk
Website: http://www.rentajet.co.uk
Directors: J. Twigg (Fin)
Immediate Holding Company: RENTAJET GROUP LIMITED
Registration no: 01788078 **Date established:** 1984 **Turnover:** £1m - £2m
No.of Employees: 11 - 20 **Product Groups:** 39, 40, 45, 46, 51, 52, 54

Date of Accounts	Jan 12	Jan 11	Jan 10
Working Capital	-36	-136	-175
Fixed Assets	377	353	481
Current Assets	280	232	196

Roke Manor Research Ltd

Old Salisbury Lane, Romsey, SO51 0ZN
Tel: 01794-833000 **Fax:** 01794-833433
E-mail: info@roke.co.uk
Website: http://www.roke.co.uk
Directors: D. Smith (MD)
Ultimate Holding Company: CHEMRING GROUP PLC
Immediate Holding Company: ROKE MANOR RESEARCH LIMITED
Registration no: 00267550 **VAT No.:** GB 566 4727 08
Date established: 1932 **Turnover:** £20m - £50m
No.of Employees: 251 - 500 **Product Groups:** 37, 38, 44, 79, 85

Date of Accounts	Oct 11	Sep 10	Sep 09
Sales Turnover	50m	47m	45m
Pre Tax Profit/Loss	3m	3m	3m
Working Capital	7m	4m	19m
Fixed Assets	17m	15m	14m
Current Assets	15m	19m	28m
Current Liabilities	4m	11m	5m

S C H Bearings & Power Transmission

Unit 2 & 3 Greatbridge Business Park Budds Lane, Romsey, SO51 0HA
Tel: 01794-830377 **Fax:** 01794- 830366
E-mail: info@gsl.eu.com
Website: http://www.schgroup.com
Directors: T. Smith (MD), R. Bush (Dir), A. Smith (MD), A. Smith (Co Sec)
Managers: P. Rusbridge (Warehouse Mgr), J. King (Mgr)
Immediate Holding Company: SCH GROUP LTD
Registration no: 01824411 **VAT No.:** GB 382 8751 17
Turnover: £2m - £5m **No.of Employees:** 1 - 10 **Product Groups:** 22, 23, 29, 30, 32, 33, 35, 39, 44, 45, 48

Safe Air Products

Farley Lane Braishfield, Romsey, SO51 0QL
Tel: 01794-367360 **Fax:** 01794-367361
Website: http://www.air-fire-control.co.uk
Managers: C. Deacon (Chief Mgr)
Immediate Holding Company: LIVIN LTD
Date established: 2009 **No.of Employees:** 1 - 10 **Product Groups:** 29, 30, 35, 37, 38, 39, 40, 44, 46, 66

Date of Accounts	Nov 11	Nov 10
Working Capital	18	10
Fixed Assets	9	6
Current Assets	85	75

Sam Electronics

Unit 51 Abbey Enterprise Centre Premier Way, Romsey, SO51 9DF
Tel: 01794-518718 **Fax:** 01794-518711
Website: http://www.sam-electronics.co.uk
Directors: J. Gibson (MD)
Ultimate Holding Company: L-3 Communications Holdings Inc (USA)
Registration no: 01368289 **Date established:** 1978 **Turnover:** £1m - £2m
No.of Employees: 1 - 10 **Product Groups:** 37

Southern Stainless

Unit 3 Budds Lane, Romsey, SO51 0HA
Tel: 01794-830085 **Fax:** 01794-830923
E-mail: info@southernpolishers.co.uk
Website: http://www.southernpolishers.co.uk
Directors: B. Rhone (Fin), V. Rhone (Dir)
Immediate Holding Company: SOUTHERN POLISHING SERVICES LIMITED
Registration no: 02345895 **Date established:** 1989
No.of Employees: 1 - 10 **Product Groups:** 46, 48

Date of Accounts	Mar 11	Mar 10	Mar 09
Working Capital	-22	-16	-14
Fixed Assets	23	26	30
Current Assets	47	57	54

Space Way Self

Premier House The Premier Centre, Romsey, SO51 9DG
Tel: 01794-835600 **Fax:** 01794-835601
E-mail: sales@spaceway.co.uk
Website: http://www.spaceway.co.uk
Bank(s): National Westminster Bank Plc
Directors: M. Jeary (MD)
Immediate Holding Company: SPACEWAY SOUTH LIMITED
Registration no: 02561649 **VAT No.:** GB 568 3285 07
Date established: 1990 **Turnover:** £5m - £10m **No.of Employees:** 11 - 20
Product Groups: 26, 35

Date of Accounts	Mar 08
Working Capital	470
Fixed Assets	373
Current Assets	2296
Current Liabilities	1826
Total Share Capital	5

spaces bespoke joinery

The Old Poultry Shed, Upper Slackstead Farm Farley Lane, Braishfield, Romsey, SO51 0QL
Tel: 01794-874520
E-mail: info@spacesltd.co.uk
Website: http://www.spacesltd.co.uk
Directors: S. Gardiner (Dir)
Date established: 2003 **No.of Employees:** 1 - 10 **Product Groups:** 25

Talley Medical

Talley Group Ltd Premier Way Abbey Park Industrial Estate, Romsey, SO51 9DQ
Tel: 01794-503500 **Fax:** 01794-503555
E-mail: sales@talleygroup.com
Website: http://www.talleygroup.com
Bank(s): Barclays
Directors: K. Mearns (Chief Op Offcr), M. Webb (Fin)
Managers: I. Monckton (Personnel), J. Ramage (Tech Serv Mgr), M. Winkwor (Purch Mgr)
Registration no: 00520386 **VAT No.:** GB 505 3742 65
Turnover: £5m - £10m **No.of Employees:** 101 - 250 **Product Groups:** 26

Veltrucks Fork Lift Trucks Ltd

Unit 22 Wynford Farm Industrial Estate Belbins, Romsey, SO51 0PW
Tel: 01794-367036
E-mail: vel.trucks@tiscali.co.uk
Website: http://www.veltrucks.fsworld.co.uk
Directors: J. Vella (Dir)
Date established: 2003 **No.of Employees:** 1 - 10 **Product Groups:** 35, 39, 45

Vermont Systems Ltd

B P C House Unit 12 Romsey Industrial Estate Greatbridge Road, Romsey, SO51 0HR
Tel: 01794-521201 **Fax:** 01794-514721
E-mail: info@vermont.co.uk
Website: http://www.vermont.co.uk
Directors: C. Ward (MD), O. Mackley (Fin)
Immediate Holding Company: VERMONT SYSTEMS LTD
Registration no: 03466232 **Date established:** 1997
Turnover: £250,000 - £500,000 **No.of Employees:** 11 - 20
Product Groups: 44

Date of Accounts	Dec 11	Dec 10	Dec 09
Working Capital	4	6	2
Fixed Assets	31	29	33
Current Assets	72	108	112

Wessex Resins & Adhesives Ltd

Cupernham Lane, Romsey, SO51 7LF
Tel: 01794-521111 **Fax:** 08707-701032
E-mail: info@wessex-resins.com
Website: http://www.wessex-resins.com
Bank(s): Lloyds TSB Bank plc
Directors: S. Keating (Co Sec), I. Oliver (Sales)
Managers: H. Cook
Immediate Holding Company: WESSEX RESINS & ADHESIVES LIMITED
Registration no: 01607313 **VAT No.:** GB 369 9084 94
Date established: 1982 **Turnover:** £2m - £5m **No.of Employees:** 21 - 50
Product Groups: 31, 32

Date of Accounts	Dec 11	Dec 10	Dec 09
Working Capital	983	963	904
Fixed Assets	327	328	325
Current Assets	1m	1m	1m

Wessex Translations

500 The Grange Romsey Road, Michelmersh, Romsey, SO51 0AE
Tel: 08701-669300 **Fax:** 01794-830145
E-mail: sales@wt-lm.com
Website: http://www.wt-lm.com
Bank(s): Barclays
Directors: P. Stewart (Ptnr)
Immediate Holding Company: WESSEX LANGUAGE PARTNERS LTD
Registration no: 04167127 **VAT No.:** GB 329 9351 28
Date established: 1972 **Turnover:** £1m - £2m **No.of Employees:** 11 - 20
Product Groups: 80

Southampton

A I M Group plc

16 Carlton Cresent, Southampton, SO15 2ES
Tel: 023-8033 5111 **Fax:** 023-8022 9733
E-mail: jeffrey.smith@aimaviation.com
Website: http://www.aimaviation.com
Directors: S. Winship (Co Sec), J. Smith (MD)
Managers: R. Green
Immediate Holding Company: AIM GROUP PLC
Registration no: 00972433 **Date established:** 1970
Turnover: £20m - £50m **No.of Employees:** 1 - 10 **Product Groups:** 39

Date of Accounts	Dec 11	Dec 10	Apr 10
Sales Turnover	40m	33m	96m
Pre Tax Profit/Loss	5m	32m	9m
Working Capital	66m	62m	24m
Fixed Assets	6m	4m	13m
Current Assets	69m	65m	50m
Current Liabilities	2m	2m	7m

A J Mobility
Trinity Industrial Estate Millbrook Road West, Southampton, SO15 0LA
Tel: 023-8070 5000 **Fax:** 023-8070 3269
Website: http://www.ajmobility.co.uk
Directors: A. Bass (MD)
Ultimate Holding Company: A J Holdings Ltd
Immediate Holding Company: A J Mobility Ltd
Registration no: 03485122 **No.of Employees:** 1 - 10 **Product Groups:** 38, 67

A1 Powder Coatings Ltd
Unit 5 Beta Buildings Willments Industrial Estate Hazel Road, Southampton, SO19 7HS
Tel: 023-8044 6874 **Fax:** 023-8044 6879
E-mail: admin@a1powdercoatings.co.uk
Website: http://www.a1powdercoatings.co.uk
Directors: G. Willis (Fin), M. Willis (MD)
Immediate Holding Company: A1 POWDER COATINGS LIMITED
Registration no: 04637974 **Date established:** 2003
Turnover: Up to £250,000 **No.of Employees:** 11 - 20 **Product Groups:** 46

Date of Accounts	Sep 11	Sep 10	Sep 09
Working Capital	128	149	101
Fixed Assets	92	99	108
Current Assets	228	260	194

Aalco
Test Lane, Southampton, SO16 9TA
Tel: 023-8087 5200 **Fax:** 023-8087 5275
E-mail: southampton@aalco.co.uk
Website: http://www.aalco.co.uk
Directors: D. Parker (Reg)
Managers: P. Barnes (Chief Acct), S. Barron (Chief Mgr), G. Barlow, G. Ford (Purch Mgr)
Immediate Holding Company: AAL & CO. LTD
Registration no: 05762562 **Date established:** 2006
Turnover: £20m - £50m **No.of Employees:** 51 - 100 **Product Groups:** 34, 36

Abbey Polythene
Unit 10 Bury Farm Curbridge, Botley, Southampton, SO30 2HB
Tel: 01489-790666 **Fax:** 01489-788819
E-mail: sales@abbeypolythene.co.uk
Website: http://www.abbeypolythene.co.uk
Directors: J. Waight (Prop)
Date established: 1993 **No.of Employees:** 1 - 10 **Product Groups:** 30

Abbirko UK Ltd
Unit 3-4 Manor Park Industrial Estate Station Road South, Totton, Southampton, SO40 9HP
Tel: 023-8066 8833 **Fax:** 023-8066 7777
E-mail: sales@abbirko.co.uk
Website: http://www.abbirko.co.uk
Directors: J. Wirdnam (MD)
Immediate Holding Company: ABBIRKO UK LIMITED
Registration no: 03091987 **VAT No.:** GB 661 0242 74
Date established: 1995 **Turnover:** £500,000 - £1m
No.of Employees: 1 - 10 **Product Groups:** 32, 37, 38

Date of Accounts	Dec 11	Dec 10	Dec 09
Working Capital	278	220	158
Fixed Assets	11	22	37
Current Assets	417	396	338

Action Optics
16 Butts Ash Gardens Hythe, Southampton, SO45 3BL
Tel: 023-8084 2801 **Fax:** 023-8084 2801
E-mail: richard@actionoptics.co.uk
Website: http://www.actionoptics.co.uk
Directors: R. Biggs (Prop)
Turnover: Up to £250,000 **No.of Employees:** 1 - 10 **Product Groups:** 38, 48

Advanced Water Softeners Ltd
144 Cranbourne Park Hedge End, Southampton, SO30 0NZ
Tel: 01489-798868 **Fax:** 01489-798868
Directors: L. Thorpe (Fin), M. Smith (MD)
Immediate Holding Company: ADVANCED WATER SOFTENERS LIMITED
Registration no: 04739672 **Date established:** 2003
No.of Employees: 1 - 10 **Product Groups:** 38, 42

Date of Accounts	Apr 12	Apr 11	Apr 10
Working Capital	-4	-6	-8
Fixed Assets	4	1	2
Current Assets	3	8	1

Ainsworth Acoustics, Thermal & Building Insulation
Old Grange Farm Bursledon, Southampton, SO31 8GD
Tel: 01489-885565 **Fax:** 01489-885258
E-mail: enquiries@ainsworth-insulation.co.uk
Website: http://www.ainsworth-insulation.co.uk
Bank(s): Barclays, Park Gate
Directors: D. Cresswell (MD), D. Rickard (Dir)
Registration no: 00851776 **VAT No.:** GB 339 1457 45
Turnover: £2m - £5m **No.of Employees:** 11 - 20 **Product Groups:** 14, 33

Date of Accounts	Dec 11	Dec 10	Dec 09
Working Capital	143	135	193
Fixed Assets	34	19	25
Current Assets	476	242	204
Current Liabilities	241	N/A	N/A

Alden Sheet Metal Fabrications Ltd
Peel Street, Southampton, SO14 5QU
Tel: 023-8021 1707 **Fax:** 023-8033 4494
E-mail: info@aldensheetmetal.co.uk
Website: http://www.aldensheetmetal.co.uk
Directors: D. Spender (Fin), S. Spender (Dir)
Immediate Holding Company: ALDEN SHEETMETAL FABRICATIONS LIMITED
Registration no: 01822240 **VAT No.:** GB 411 7162 88
Date established: 1984 **Turnover:** £250,000 - £500,000
No.of Employees: 1 - 10 **Product Groups:** 48

Date of Accounts	Jul 11	Jul 10	Jul 09
Working Capital	118	113	102
Fixed Assets	26	25	31
Current Assets	199	192	152

Alpha Systems Consultants Ltd
5 Lindal Court Allen Road Hedge End, Hedge End, Southampton, SO30 4FD
Tel: 01489-781802 **Fax:** 08707-620864
E-mail: sales@alpha-sys-consult.co.uk
Website: http://www.alpha-sys-consult.co.uk
Directors: R. Goddard (MD), R. Goddard (Fin)
Immediate Holding Company: ALPHA SYSTEMS CONSULTANTS LTD
Registration no: 04475345 **Date established:** 2002
Turnover: Up to £250,000 **No.of Employees:** 1 - 10 **Product Groups:** 44

Date of Accounts	Mar 11	Mar 10	Mar 08
Working Capital	-1	4	1
Fixed Assets	N/A	N/A	8
Current Assets	1	5	1

Amari Metals Ltd
Test Lane, Southampton, SO16 9TA
Tel: 023-8087 5330 **Fax:** 023-8087 5275
E-mail: helpdesk@amari-metals.com
Website: http://www.amari-aerospace.com
Managers: G. Barlow (Tech Serv Mgr), G. Barlow (I.T. Exec)
Ultimate Holding Company: HENLEY MANAGEMENT COMPANY (USA)
Immediate Holding Company: AMARI METALS LIMITED
Registration no: 02023155 **Date established:** 1986
No.of Employees: 21 - 50 **Product Groups:** 34, 39, 48, 68, 84

Date of Accounts	Dec 11	Dec 10	Dec 09
Sales Turnover	591m	527m	408m
Pre Tax Profit/Loss	13m	15m	3m
Working Capital	99m	47m	36m
Fixed Assets	15m	19m	21m
Current Assets	227m	206m	169m
Current Liabilities	21m	24m	14m

Amsam Holdings Ltd
Forest Brook Lodge Beechwood Road Bartley, Southampton, SO40 2LP
Tel: 023-8081 4433 **Fax:** 023-8081 1090
E-mail: lflack@amsam.co.uk
Website: http://www.amsam.co.uk
Directors: L. Flack (Dir)
Ultimate Holding Company: AMSAM (SOUTHAMPTON) LIMITED
Immediate Holding Company: AMSAM HOLDINGS LIMITED
Registration no: 04125034 **Date established:** 2000
No.of Employees: 1 - 10 **Product Groups:** 08, 25, 39, 51, 66, 82, 84

Date of Accounts	Dec 05	Mar 11	Mar 10
Working Capital	-5	52	59
Fixed Assets	N/A	3	5
Current Assets	53	68	129

Andywrap Film
PO Box 62, Southampton, SO30 3ZJ
Tel: 023-8047 7007 **Fax:** 023-8047 7886
E-mail: sales@andywrap.co.uk
Website: http://www.andywrapfilm.com
Managers: D. Mckezie-Philips (Mgr)
Immediate Holding Company: ANDYWRAP EUROFILM LTD
Registration no: 02714674 **No.of Employees:** 1 - 10 **Product Groups:** 30

Aon Ltd
Capital House Houndwell Place, Southampton, SO14 1HU
Tel: 023-8060 7500 **Fax:** 023-8063 1055
E-mail: andrew.wren@aon.co.uk
Website: http://www.aon.co.uk
Managers: A. Wren
Ultimate Holding Company: C D I CORPORATION (USA)
Immediate Holding Company: A1 VENTURES LIMITED
Registration no: 04578543 **Date established:** 2002 **Turnover:** £2m - £5m
No.of Employees: 1 - 10 **Product Groups:** 82

APAS Engineering Ltd
4 Shamrock Quay William Street, Southampton, SO14 5QL
Tel: 023-8063 2558 **Fax:** 023-8022 9281
E-mail: sales@seastream.com
Website: http://www.seastream.com
Directors: A. Rose (MD)
Immediate Holding Company: APAS ENGINEERING LIMITED
Registration no: 01608647 **VAT No.:** GB 369 7387 76
Date established: 1982 **No.of Employees:** 1 - 10 **Product Groups:** 40

Date of Accounts	Apr 11	Apr 10	Apr 09
Working Capital	-45	-41	-24
Fixed Assets	7	4	5
Current Assets	27	30	36

Argonaut Powder Coating Ltd
13 Nutwood Way Totton, Southampton, SO40 3SZ
Tel: 023-8087 3455 **Fax:** 023-8087 2255
E-mail: info@argonaut-uk.com
Website: http://www.argonaut-uk.com
Bank(s): Lloyds TSB Bank plc
Directors: B. Wingrove (Sales), P. Farrell (Co Sec)
Immediate Holding Company: ARGONAUT POWDER COATING LIMITED
Registration no: 02269746 **VAT No.:** GB 490 8289 09
Date established: 1988 **Turnover:** £500,000 - £1m
No.of Employees: 21 - 50 **Product Groups:** 48

Date of Accounts	Jun 11	Jun 10	Jun 09
Working Capital	1m	865	1m
Fixed Assets	333	340	438
Current Assets	3m	3m	3m

S W Asgood Engineering Ltd
Unit A1 Empress Park Empress Road, Southampton, SO14 0JX
Tel: 023-8022 3880 **Fax:** 023-8033 5131
E-mail: su.waterman@swasgood.co.uk
Directors: R. Waterman (MD)
Ultimate Holding Company: S W ASGOOD HOLDINGS LIMITED
Immediate Holding Company: S.W. ASGOOD ENG. LIMITED
Registration no: 01332899 **VAT No.:** GB 293 6890 08
Date established: 1977 **Turnover:** £500,000 - £1m
No.of Employees: 1 - 10 **Product Groups:** 48

Date of Accounts	Feb 12	Feb 11	Feb 10
Working Capital	195	244	197
Fixed Assets	115	104	107
Current Assets	275	375	273

Associated Pallets Ltd
Eling Wharf Totton, Southampton, SO40 4TE
Tel: 023-8066 7999 **Fax:** 023-8066 3362
E-mail: info@associated-pallets.co.uk
Website: http://www.associated-pallets.co.uk
Directors: J. Shawyer (Dir)
Immediate Holding Company: ASSOCIATED PALLETS LIMITED
Registration no: 02679001 **Date established:** 1992
No.of Employees: 11 - 20 **Product Groups:** 25

Date of Accounts	Apr 11	Apr 10	Apr 09
Working Capital	188	170	185
Fixed Assets	108	126	162
Current Assets	472	408	367

Auto & Marine Services
20a High Street Botley, Southampton, SO30 2EA
Tel: 01489-785009 **Fax:** 01489-785009
Directors: T. Hobbs (MD)
Date established: 1986 **No.of Employees:** 1 - 10 **Product Groups:** 35, 36, 39

Autopaint
Portsmouth Road Bursledon, Southampton, SO31 8EQ
Tel: 023-8040 6136 **Fax:** 023-8040 6137
Directors: D. Oakley (Prop)
Registration no: 01234333 **Date established:** 1975
No.of Employees: 1 - 10 **Product Groups:** 38, 42

Azdec Ltd
32 Gladstone Road, Southampton, SO19 8GT
Tel: 023-8044 4393 **Fax:** 023-8043 2071
E-mail: cheryldomone@azdec.com
Website: http://www.azdec.com
Directors: A. Domone (MD), C. Domone (Fin)
Ultimate Holding Company: LINK MICROTEK LIMITED
Immediate Holding Company: AZDEC LIMITED
Registration no: 01961200 **VAT No.:** GB 411 6735 72
Date established: 1985 **Turnover:** £500,000 - £1m
No.of Employees: 1 - 10 **Product Groups:** 37, 39, 44, 84

Date of Accounts	Jun 11	Jun 10	Feb 09
Working Capital	67	159	257
Fixed Assets	N/A	5	7
Current Assets	67	627	512

B B M S Swanwick Ltd
Eastlands Coal Park Lane, Swanwick, Southampton, SO31 7GW
Tel: 01489-580250 **Fax:** 01489-580251
Website: http://www.bbmsltd.co.uk
Directors: P. Brackenbury (Dir)
Immediate Holding Company: BBMS (SWANWICK) LIMITED
Registration no: 06439467 **Date established:** 2007
No.of Employees: 1 - 10 **Product Groups:** 35, 36, 39

Date of Accounts	Dec 10	Dec 09	Dec 08
Working Capital	-11	-10	-13
Fixed Assets	7	11	14
Current Assets	79	60	48

B M T Nigel Gee Ltd
Building 14 Shamrock Quay William Street, Southampton, SO14 5QL
Tel: 023-8022 6655 **Fax:** 023-8022 8855
E-mail: jbonafoux@ngal.co.uk
Website: http://www.ngal.co.uk
Bank(s): National Westminster Bank Plc
Directors: J. Bonafoux (MD), M. Willbourn (Mkt Research)
Ultimate Holding Company: BMT GROUP LIMITED
Immediate Holding Company: BMT NIGEL GEE LIMITED
Registration no: 02718748 **VAT No.:** GB 568 6868 65
Date established: 1992 **Turnover:** £2m - £5m **No.of Employees:** 21 - 50
Product Groups: 84

Date of Accounts	Sep 11	Sep 10	Sep 09
Sales Turnover	3m	3m	4m
Pre Tax Profit/Loss	-164	120	-165
Working Capital	395	553	367
Fixed Assets	26	27	87
Current Assets	1m	1m	999
Current Liabilities	552	380	343

B S A Tube Runner
Speedwell House West Quay Road, Southampton, SO15 1GY
Tel: 023-8036 6410 **Fax:** 01280-709674
E-mail: sales@tuberunner.co.uk
Website: http://www.tuberunner.co.uk
Managers: S. Wilson (Chief Mgr)
Ultimate Holding Company: BSA-REGAL GROUP LIMITED
Immediate Holding Company: BSA TUBE RUNNER LIMITED
Registration no: 01479878 **VAT No.:** GB 319 9753 15
Date established: 1980 **Turnover:** £500,000 - £1m
No.of Employees: 1 - 10 **Product Groups:** 40, 42, 46, 48

Date of Accounts	Mar 11	Mar 10	Mar 09
Sales Turnover	625	629	711
Pre Tax Profit/Loss	20	70	108
Working Capital	-15	12	104
Fixed Assets	28	1	1
Current Assets	402	472	452
Current Liabilities	11	14	15

B V M Ltd
Hobb Lane Hedge End, Southampton, SO30 0GH
Tel: 01489-780144 **Fax:** 01489-783589
E-mail: info@bvmltd.co.uk
Website: http://www.bvm-store.com
Directors: D. Smith (Dir)
Immediate Holding Company: B.V.M. LIMITED
Registration no: 02328010 **VAT No.:** GB 522 2630 85
Date established: 1988 **Turnover:** £2m - £5m **No.of Employees:** 11 - 20
Product Groups: 37, 38, 39, 44

Date of Accounts	Apr 11	Apr 10	Apr 09
Working Capital	323	360	398
Fixed Assets	14	24	15
Current Assets	760	793	938

Bainbridge Aqua-Marine
Unit 8 Flanders Industrial Park Flanders Road Hedge End, Southampton, SO30 2FZ
Tel: 01489-776000 **Fax:** 01489-776005
E-mail: info@bainbridgeint.co.uk
Website: http://www.bainbridgemarine.co.uk
Bank(s): The Royal Bank of Scotland
Directors: J. O'connor (Dir)
Managers: G. Coventry (Sales Prom Mgr), N. Irvine (Mktg Serv Mgr), P. Brown (Purch Mgr), J. Keith (Fin Mgr), L. Crowhurst (Tech Serv Mgr)
Immediate Holding Company: BAINBRIDGE MARINE LIMITED
Registration no: 05673886 **Date established:** 2006 **Turnover:** £5m - £10m
No.of Employees: 21 - 50 **Product Groups:** 30, 35, 74

Banair Electronic Engineers
48 Ivy Road, Southampton, SO17 2JN
Tel: 023-8032 4334 **Fax:** 023-8032 4332
E-mail: nhaynesa@banair.co.uk
Website: http://www.banair.co.uk
Directors: N. Haynes (Dir), S. Thomas (Fin)
Immediate Holding Company: BANAIR LIMITED
Registration no: 02481859 **VAT No.:** GB 474 3185 36
Date established: 1990 **Turnover:** £250,000 - £500,000
No.of Employees: 1 - 10 **Product Groups:** 38, 84

Bandai UK Ltd
Jellicoe House Grange Drive, Hedge End, Southampton, SO30 2AF
Tel: 01489-790944 **Fax:** 01489-790643
E-mail: info@bandai.co.uk
Website: http://www.bandai.co.uk
Bank(s): Barclays
Directors: D. Jones (Mkt Research), S. Fettes (Fin)
Ultimate Holding Company: NAMCO BANDAI HOLDINGS INC (JAPAN)
Immediate Holding Company: BANDAI UK LIMITED
Registration no: 01632311 **VAT No.:** GB 358 8954 85
Date established: 1982 **Turnover:** £20m - £50m
No.of Employees: 11 - 20 **Product Groups:** 49, 61

Date of Accounts	Dec 10	Dec 09	Dec 08
Sales Turnover	23m	40m	39m
Pre Tax Profit/Loss	2m	8m	10m
Working Capital	40m	42m	41m
Fixed Assets	733	776	787
Current Assets	45m	53m	54m
Current Liabilities	3m	4m	6m

Banks Sails Ltd
372 Brook Lane Sarisbury Green, Southampton, SO31 7ZA
Tel: 01489-582444 **Fax:** 01489-589789
E-mail: enquiries@banks.co.uk
Website: http://www.banks.co.uk
Bank(s): HSBC Bank plc
Directors: D. Banks (MD)
Immediate Holding Company: BRUCE BANKS SAILS LIMITED
Registration no: 01134188 **VAT No.:** GB 108 4162 92
Date established: 1973 **Turnover:** £1m - £2m **No.of Employees:** 21 - 50
Product Groups: 24

Date of Accounts	Oct 11	Oct 10	Oct 09
Working Capital	36	-6	-24
Fixed Assets	23	25	22
Current Assets	555	570	579

Bassaire Ltd
Duncan Road Park Gate, Southampton, SO31 1ZS
Tel: 01489-885111 **Fax:** 01489-885211
E-mail: neil.thomas@bassaire.co.uk
Website: http://www.bassaire.co.uk
Directors: N. Thomas (Dir)
Ultimate Holding Company: BASSAIRE HOLDINGS LIMITED
Immediate Holding Company: BASSAIRE LIMITED
Registration no: 02107555 **VAT No.:** GB 458 6195 08
Date established: 1987 **Turnover:** £2m - £5m **No.of Employees:** 1 - 10
Product Groups: 38, 40, 42

Date of Accounts	May 11	May 10	May 09
Working Capital	724	810	862
Fixed Assets	84	51	72
Current Assets	3m	2m	2m

Bengco Marine Engineers
Unit 5.1 Hamblepoint Marina School Lane, Hamble, Southampton, SO31 4JD
Tel: 023-8045 7595
E-mail: sales@bengco.co.uk
Website: http://www.bengco.co.uk
Directors: J. Ross (Prop)
Immediate Holding Company: MARINE COMMUNICATION AND ELECTRONICS LIMITED
Registration no: 02208567 **Date established:** 1987
No.of Employees: 1 - 10 **Product Groups:** 35, 36, 39

Date of Accounts	Mar 11	Mar 10	Mar 09
Working Capital	53	69	85
Fixed Assets	6	6	7
Current Assets	292	282	271

David Bowler & Sons Ltd
Hardley Industrial Estate Hardley, Hythe, Southampton, SO45 3YQ
Tel: 023-8084 3109 **Fax:** 023-8084 0034
E-mail: bowler.group@virgin.net
Website: http://www.metal-presswork.com
Directors: R. Bowler (Dir)
Immediate Holding Company: DAVID BOWLER & SONS LIMITED
Registration no: 00841081 **Date established:** 1965 **Turnover:** £2m - £5m
No.of Employees: 11 - 20 **Product Groups:** 48

Date of Accounts	Apr 11	Apr 10	Apr 09
Working Capital	-205	-213	-230
Fixed Assets	2m	2m	2m
Current Assets	493	341	329

BSA Rational Automation Ltd
Speedwell House West Quay Road, Southampton, SO15 1GY
Tel: 023-8036 6407 **Fax:** 023-8036 6301
E-mail: david.bennett@bsa-regal.co.uk
Website: http://www.bsa-regal.co.uk
Directors: D. Bennett (MD), C. Bennett (Dir)
Ultimate Holding Company: BSA-REGAL GROUP LIMITED
Immediate Holding Company: BSA RATIONAL AUTOMATION LIMITED
Registration no: 00577151 **Date established:** 1957
Turnover: Up to £250,000 **No.of Employees:** 1 - 10 **Product Groups:** 20, 40, 41

Date of Accounts	Mar 11	Mar 10	Mar 09
Sales Turnover	2m	1m	1m
Pre Tax Profit/Loss	117	-6	162
Working Capital	50	14	72
Fixed Assets	94	116	145
Current Assets	481	519	442
Current Liabilities	64	41	53

Buck & Hickman Ltd
Unit 3 City Industrial Park Southern Road, Southampton, SO15 1HG
Tel: 023-8071 5300 **Fax:** 023-8074 2301
E-mail: southampton@buckandhickman.com
Website: http://www.buckandhickman.com
Managers: S. Warick (District Mgr)
Ultimate Holding Company: TRAVIS PERKINS PLC
Immediate Holding Company: BOSTON (2011) LIMITED
Registration no: 06028304 **Date established:** 2006
Turnover: £20m - £50m **No.of Employees:** 11 - 20 **Product Groups:** 24, 29, 30, 33, 36, 37, 41, 46

Date of Accounts	Dec 10	Mar 10	Mar 09
Working Capital	6m	6m	6m
Current Assets	27m	27m	27m

C & C Rewinds
7 Test Valley Business Centre Test Lane, Southampton, SO16 9JW
Tel: 023-8086 3079 **Fax:** 023-8066 0317
E-mail: info@candc-rewinds.com
Website: http://www.candc-rewinds.com
Directors: C. Clarke (Dir)
Immediate Holding Company: C & C REWINDS LIMITED
Registration no: 05527610 **Date established:** 2005
Turnover: Up to £250,000 **No.of Employees:** 1 - 10 **Product Groups:** 37, 48

Date of Accounts	Mar 12	Mar 11	Mar 10
Working Capital	-3	-1	-6
Fixed Assets	18	2	7
Current Assets	29	30	29

C J R Propulsion Ltd
72 Quayside Road, Southampton, SO18 1AD
Tel: 023-8063 9366 **Fax:** 023-8021 1832
E-mail: info@cjrprop.com
Website: http://www.cjrprop.com
Bank(s): Natwest
Directors: M. Russell (MD)
Immediate Holding Company: CJR PROPULSION LIMITED
Registration no: 02526127 **VAT No.:** GB 584 2053 43
Date established: 1990 **No.of Employees:** 21 - 50 **Product Groups:** 39

Date of Accounts	May 11	May 10	May 09
Working Capital	-334	-341	-221
Fixed Assets	2m	3m	3m
Current Assets	1m	1m	1m

C L C Contractors Ltd
Northbrook Industrial Estate Vincent Avenue, Southampton, SO16 6PQ
Tel: 023-8070 1111 **Fax:** 023-8070 1171
E-mail: pia@clcgroup.com
Website: http://www.clcgroup.com
Bank(s): Barclays
Directors: M. White (Co Sec), N. Hilton (Sales & Mktg), N. Hilton (Sales), P. Armitage (I.T. Dir), P. Armitage Snr. (MD), P. Armitage (MD)
Ultimate Holding Company: CLC Group Ltd
Immediate Holding Company: C.L.C. CONTRACTORS LIMITED
Registration no: 01230435 **Date established:** 1975
Turnover: £50m - £75m **No.of Employees:** 501 - 1000
Product Groups: 33, 39, 52

Date of Accounts	Dec 09	Dec 08	Dec 07
Sales Turnover	60m	69m	55m
Pre Tax Profit/Loss	3m	2m	2m
Working Capital	12m	11m	11m
Current Assets	19m	17m	17m
Current Liabilities	3m	2m	2m

C M Beasy Ltd
Ashurst Lodge Ashurst, Southampton, SO40 7AA
Tel: 023-8029 3223 **Fax:** 023-8029 2853
E-mail: info@beasy.com
Website: http://www.beasy.com
Directors: C. Brebbia (Co Sec)
Ultimate Holding Company: COMPUTATIONAL MECHANICS INTERNATIONAL LIMITED
Immediate Holding Company: CM BEASY LIMITED
Registration no: 01865517 **Date established:** 1984
Turnover: £500,000 - £1m **No.of Employees:** 1 - 10 **Product Groups:** 44

Date of Accounts	Mar 12	Mar 11	Mar 10
Working Capital	60	29	7
Fixed Assets	9	6	4
Current Assets	180	162	168

C P L Petroleum Ltd
Oil Depot Belvidere Road, Southampton, SO14 5AF
Tel: 023-8022 9477 **Fax:** 023-8033 9043
E-mail: southhampton@cplpetroleum.co.uk
Website: http://www.cplpetroleum.co.uk
Managers: C. Bull (Depot Mgr)
Ultimate Holding Company: CPL INDUSTRIES HOLDINGS LIMITED
Immediate Holding Company: CPL PETROLEUM LIMITED
Registration no: 03003860 **Date established:** 1994
Turnover: £500m - £1,000m **No.of Employees:** 11 - 20
Product Groups: 66

Date of Accounts	Mar 12	Mar 11	Mar 10
Pre Tax Profit/Loss	N/A	878	904
Working Capital	31	30m	30m
Fixed Assets	26	26m	26m
Current Assets	57	56m	56m
Current Liabilities	26	246	253

Cadogan Travel Ltd
Cadogan House 37 Commercial Road, Southampton, SO15 1GG
Tel: 023-8082 8313 **Fax:** 023-8022 8601
E-mail: moreinfo@cadoganholidays.com
Website: http://www.cadogantravel.com
Directors: S. Reynolds (Co Sec), C. Attwood (Dir), G. David (MD), J. Gaggero (MD)
Managers: D. Connelly (Sales & Mktg Mg)
Ultimate Holding Company: JARGO HOLDINGS LIMITED (GUERNSEY)
Immediate Holding Company: CADOGAN HOLIDAYS LIMITED
Registration no: 01031864 **Date established:** 1971
Turnover: £10m - £20m **No.of Employees:** 51 - 100 **Product Groups:** 69

Capital Hair & Beauty
Unit 4 Southern Trade Park Belgrave Road, Southampton, SO17 3ES
Tel: 023-8055 3380 **Fax:** 023-8055 3320
E-mail: soton@capitalhairandbeauty.co.uk
Website: http://www.capitalhairandbeauty.co.uk
Managers: K. Humphries (Mgr)
Immediate Holding Company: CAPITAL (HAIR AND BEAUTY) LIMITED
Registration no: 00530201 **Date established:** 1954
No.of Employees: 1 - 10 **Product Groups:** 32, 40, 63, 67

Date of Accounts	Dec 11	Dec 10	Dec 09
Sales Turnover	32m	28m	24m
Pre Tax Profit/Loss	4m	749	2m
Working Capital	7m	4m	3m
Fixed Assets	3m	3m	2m
Current Assets	13m	8m	7m
Current Liabilities	4m	3m	3m

CDS UK
4 Ash Walk Alresford, Southampton, SO24 9JP
Tel: 07866-781379 **Fax:** 01962-734228
E-mail: patrick@cdsuk.biz
Website: http://www.cdsuk.biz
Directors: P. Davies (Dir)
Registration no: 07535806 **Date established:** 2009
Turnover: Up to £250,000 **No.of Employees:** 1 - 10 **Product Groups:** 67

Cemex UK Ltd
Marine Parade, Southampton, SO14 5JF
Tel: 08451-551820 **Fax:** 023-8033 4528
E-mail: john.miller@cemex.co.uk
Website: http://www.cemex.co.uk
Managers: J. Hopkins (District Mgr)
Ultimate Holding Company: CEMEX S A B DE CV (MEXICO)
Immediate Holding Company: CEMEX UK
Registration no: 05196131 **Date established:** 2004
No.of Employees: 1 - 10 **Product Groups:** 51

Date of Accounts	Dec 10	Dec 09	Dec 08
Pre Tax Profit/Loss	-64m	612m	-101m
Working Capital	-2m	-3m	-452m
Fixed Assets	2432m	2432m	1721m
Current Assets	N/A	218	11m
Current Liabilities	2m	3m	10m

Central Point Services
20 Goodwood Gardens Calmore, Totton, Southampton, SO40 2GF
Tel: 023-8013 5693 **Fax:** 023-8067 5919
E-mail: centralpoint@btinternet.com
Directors: A. Hulme (Dir)
Immediate Holding Company: CENTRAL POINT SERVICES LIMITED
Registration no: 06343228 **Date established:** 2007
No.of Employees: 1 - 10 **Product Groups:** 25

Date of Accounts	Mar 12	Mar 11	Mar 10
Working Capital	71	59	57
Fixed Assets	11	15	16
Current Assets	118	105	112

Chilworth Manor Ltd
Chilworth, Southampton, SO16 7JF
Tel: 023-8076 7333 **Fax:** 023-8070 1743
E-mail: general@chilworth-manor.co.uk
Website: http://www.chilworth-manor.co.uk
Managers: S. Mairriott (Chief Mgr)
Ultimate Holding Company: LA RUCHE HOLDINGS LIMITED
Immediate Holding Company: CHILWORTH MANOR LIMITED
Registration no: 02328662 **Date established:** 1988 **Turnover:** £2m - £5m
No.of Employees: 1 - 10 **Product Groups:** 69

Date of Accounts	Jul 11	Jul 10	Jul 09
Sales Turnover	4m	4m	4m
Pre Tax Profit/Loss	-3m	32	-59
Working Capital	-613	-458	-223
Fixed Assets	4m	10m	12m
Current Assets	520	525	822
Current Liabilities	478	335	372

Chilworth Technology
Beta House Enterprise Road Chilworth Science Park, Chilworth, Southampton, SO16 7NS
Tel: 023-8076 0722 **Fax:** 01242-251388
E-mail: info@chilworth.co.uk
Website: http://www.chilworth.co.uk
Directors: P. Cartwright (Dir)
Managers: M. Rodgers (Personnel)
Ultimate Holding Company: CHILWORTH HOLDINGS LIMITED
Immediate Holding Company: CHILWORTH TECHNOLOGY LIMITED
Registration no: 02000153 **Date established:** 1986
No.of Employees: 21 - 50 **Product Groups:** 38, 54, 84, 85

Date of Accounts	Dec 11	Dec 10	Dec 09
Sales Turnover	5m	5m	N/A
Pre Tax Profit/Loss	1m	1m	N/A
Working Capital	2m	1m	603
Fixed Assets	334	405	366
Current Assets	2m	2m	1m
Current Liabilities	228	450	N/A

Chloride
Unit C George Curl Way, Southampton, SO18 2RY
Tel: 023-8061 0311 **Fax:** 023-8061 0852
E-mail: martin.coulthard@chloridepower.com
Website: http://www.emerson.com
Bank(s): HSBC Bank plc
Directors: J. Messent (Co Sec)
Managers: M. Coulthard
Ultimate Holding Company: EMERSON ELECTRIC CO INC (USA)
Immediate Holding Company: CHLORIDE ELECTRONICS LIMITED
Registration no: 00913511 **Date established:** 1967
Turnover: £75m - £125m **No.of Employees:** 51 - 100 **Product Groups:** 37

Date of Accounts	Mar 10	Mar 09	Mar 08
Sales Turnover	61m	57m	56m
Pre Tax Profit/Loss	9m	10m	8m
Working Capital	18m	21m	15m
Fixed Assets	15m	5m	3m
Current Assets	52m	43m	34m
Current Liabilities	10m	10m	7m

CIBA Vision (UK) Ltd
Flanders Road Hedge End, Southampton, SO30 2LG
Tel: 01489-785580 **Fax:** 01489-786802
E-mail: parkwest.reception@cibavision.com
Website: http://www.cibavision.com
Directors: H. Barnes (MD), H. Barns (MD), R. Brazier (Fin)
Managers: K. Keymist (Personnel), J. Harvey (I.T. Exec)
Ultimate Holding Company: NOVARTIS AG (SWITZERLAND)
Registration no: 00809238 **Date established:** 1964
Turnover: £75m - £125m **Product Groups:** 38

Date of Accounts	Dec 09	Dec 08	Dec 07
Sales Turnover	87m	86m	84m
Pre Tax Profit/Loss	642	4m	8m
Working Capital	3m	8m	10m
Fixed Assets	1m	220	453
Current Assets	23m	29m	31m
Current Liabilities	17m	19m	7m

Clarke Lane Engineering Ltd
101-121 Belgrave Road, Southampton, SO17 3AN
Tel: 023-8067 1564 **Fax:** 023-8067 6774
E-mail: info@clarke-lane.co.uk
Website: http://www.clarke-lane.co.uk
Directors: R. Clarke (Prop)
Immediate Holding Company: CLARKE LANE ENGINEERING LIMITED
Registration no: 03156241 **VAT No.:** GB 412 0684 87
Date established: 1996 **Turnover:** £500,000 - £1m
No.of Employees: 11 - 20 **Product Groups:** 48

Cognis Performance Chemicals Ltd
Hardley Hythe, Southampton, SO45 3ZG
Tel: 023-8089 4666 **Fax:** 023-8024 3113
Website: http://www.cognis.com
Directors: N. Liptrot (Co Sec), N. Littop (Dir), P. Allen (Dir), S. Catchpole (MD)
Ultimate Holding Company: COGNIS GMBH (GERMANY)
Immediate Holding Company: COGNIS PERFORMANCE CHEMICALS UK LIMITED
Registration no: 03823580 **Date established:** 1999
Turnover: £75m - £125m **No.of Employees:** 11 - 20 **Product Groups:** 31, 32

Date of Accounts	Dec 10	Dec 09	Dec 08
Working Capital	2m	2m	2m
Current Assets	2m	2m	2m

Composite Mouldings Group
Unit 5a East Street Marchwood Industrial Park, Marchwood, Southampton, SO40 4BX
Tel: 023-8066 0770 **Fax:** 023-8066 3022
E-mail: tommi@cm.com
Website: http://www.compositemouldings.com
Directors: E. Buckley (Co Sec)
No.of Employees: 11 - 20 **Product Groups:** 30, 31, 84

Alexander Comrie & Sons Ltd
Unit 8 Second Avenue, Southampton, SO15 0LP
Tel: 023-8070 2911 **Fax:** 023-8070 2617
Directors: A. Comrie (Prop)
Immediate Holding Company: ALEXANDER COMRIE AND SONS LIMITED
Registration no: 01282009 **VAT No.:** GB 293 5150 53
Date established: 1976 **Turnover:** Up to £250,000
No.of Employees: 1 - 10 **Product Groups:** 29, 30, 33, 36, 68

Date of Accounts	Mar 11	Mar 10	Mar 09
Working Capital	-65	-60	-56
Fixed Assets	46	47	50
Current Assets	9	12	19

Coopervision Manufacturing Ltd
Unit 6 Ensign Way Hamble, Southampton, SO31 4RF
Tel: 023-8060 5200 **Fax:** 023-8060 5299
E-mail: asedgwick@coopervision.co.uk
Website: http://www.coopervision.co.uk
Directors: A. Edwards (Co Sec), A. Sedgwick (MD)
Ultimate Holding Company: THE COOPER COMPANIES INC (USA)
Immediate Holding Company: COOPERVISION LIMITED
Registration no: 03685161 **Date established:** 1998
Turnover: £75m - £125m **No.of Employees:** 1 - 10 **Product Groups:** 37, 38, 65

Date of Accounts	Oct 10	Oct 09	Oct 08
Sales Turnover	93m	85m	74m
Pre Tax Profit/Loss	2m	1m	6m
Working Capital	41m	39m	38m
Fixed Assets	3	18	33
Current Assets	56m	57m	49m
Current Liabilities	2m	2m	802

Corrotherm International
Unit 31 South Hampshire Industrial Park, Totton, Southampton, SO40 3SA
Tel: 023-8074 8100 **Fax:** 023-8074 8114
E-mail: sales@corrotherm.co.uk
Website: http://www.corrotherm.co.uk
Bank(s): NatWest
Directors: J. Ward (MD)
Registration no: 03143112 **VAT No.:** GB 673 8307 13
Turnover: £5m - £10m **No.of Employees:** 11 - 20 **Product Groups:** 34, 36

Date of Accounts	Apr 08
Working Capital	976
Fixed Assets	46
Current Assets	2321
Current Liabilities	1345
Total Share Capital	1

Corrpro Companies Europe
4 Mill Court The Sawmills, Durley, Southampton, SO32 2EJ
Tel: 01489-861980 **Fax:** 01489-861981
E-mail: mmoffat@insituform.com
Website: http://www.corrpro.co.uk
Bank(s): National Westminster Bank Plc
Directors: M. Moffat (Mkt Research), K. Chandler (Fin)
Managers: A. Gillespie (Chief Acct)
Ultimate Holding Company: CORRPRO COMPANIES INC
Immediate Holding Company: WILSON WALTON GROUP
Registration no: 00944432 **VAT No.:** GB 409 2514 63
Date established: 2001 **Turnover:** £2m - £5m **No.of Employees:** 11 - 20
Product Groups: 37

Date of Accounts	Dec 10	Dec 09	Mar 09
Sales Turnover	8m	6m	10m
Pre Tax Profit/Loss	439	301	563
Working Capital	2m	2m	2m
Fixed Assets	444	345	376
Current Assets	3m	3m	4m
Current Liabilities	129	182	271

Cory Logistics Ltd
Room 8-13, Currie House Herbert Walker Avenue, Western Docks, Southampton, SO15 1HJ
Tel: 023-8022 7338 **Fax:** 023-8023 7479
E-mail: corysoton@cory.co.uk
Website: http://www.cory.co.uk
Directors: J. Bottomley (MD), A. Williamson (Dir), D. Henderson (Dir), J. Dawson (Dir), L. Lawns (MD), R. Alexander (Dir)
Managers: A. Forest (Sales & Mktg Mgr)
Registration no: 05105859 **Date established:** 1946
Turnover: £250,000 - £500,000 **No.of Employees:** 1 - 10
Product Groups: 39, 40, 44, 45, 72, 74, 76, 82, 84

Country Craftsman Ironwork Ltd
Unit 1a Ashley Cresent, Southampton, SO19 9NA
Tel: 023-8042 2440 **Fax:** 023-8043 8777
Directors: R. Fuller (MD), H. Fuller (Fin)
Immediate Holding Company: COUNTRY CRAFTSMAN IRONWORK LIMITED
Registration no: 01877728 **Date established:** 1985
Turnover: Up to £250,000 **No.of Employees:** 1 - 10 **Product Groups:** 26, 35

Date of Accounts	Apr 10	Apr 09	Apr 08
Working Capital	-7	-7	-2
Fixed Assets	8	9	6
Current Assets	29	40	64

Crest Installation & Maintenance Ltd
3 Saribsury Buildings Bridge Road, Sarisbury Green, Southampton, SO31 7EH
Tel: 01489-564880
E-mail: sales@crest.freeserve.co.uk
Website: http://www.crest.freeserve.co.uk
Directors: K. Martin (MD), J. Martin (Fin)
Immediate Holding Company: CREST INSTALLATIONS & MAINTENANCE LIMITED
Registration no: 03244643 **Date established:** 1996
No.of Employees: 1 - 10 **Product Groups:** 40

Curtis Holt Southampton Ltd
Westwood Business Park Nutwood Way, Totton, Southampton, SO40 3WW
Tel: 023-8086 1991 **Fax:** 023-8066 4555
E-mail: sales@tallbank.com
Website: http://www.tallbank.com
Bank(s): HSBC, London
Directors: P. Corby (I.T. Dir), S. Morris (Co Sec), J. Twallin (Ch)
Immediate Holding Company: CURTIS HOLT (SOUTHAMPTON) LIMITED
Registration no: 00433740 **VAT No.:** GB 202 9347 83
Date established: 1947 **Turnover:** £20m - £50m
No.of Employees: 101 - 250 **Product Groups:** 35, 37

Custom Covers 1984 Ltd
Quayside Road, Southampton, SO18 1AD
Tel: 023-8033 5744 **Fax:** 023-8022 5581
E-mail: sales@customcovers.co.uk
Website: http://www.customcovers.co.uk
Bank(s): HSBC Bank plc
Directors: D. Sanders (Dir)
Managers: A. Guest (Comptroller), V. Coutts (Sales Prom Mgr)
Ultimate Holding Company: CUSTOM COVERS HOLDINGS LIMITED
Immediate Holding Company: CUSTOM COVERS (1984) LIMITED
Registration no: 01710336 **VAT No.:** GB 382 7951 14
Date established: 1983 **Turnover:** £5m - £10m
No.of Employees: 51 - 100 **Product Groups:** 24

Date of Accounts	Nov 11	Nov 10	Nov 09
Sales Turnover	6m	6m	5m
Pre Tax Profit/Loss	489	542	367
Working Capital	757	780	643
Fixed Assets	1m	1m	1m
Current Assets	2m	2m	1m
Current Liabilities	535	585	395

D P World
Berth 204-206 Prince Charles Container Port Western Docks, Southampton, SO15 1DA
Tel: 023-8070 1701 **Fax:** 023-8052 8285
E-mail: admin@sct.uk.com
Website: http://www.sct.uk.com
Directors: N. Loader (Fin), R. Woods (MD)
Ultimate Holding Company: DUBAI WORLD CORPORATION (DUBAI)
Immediate Holding Company: SOUTHAMPTON CONTAINER TERMINALS LIMITED
Registration no: 01960484 **Date established:** 1985
Turnover: £75m - £125m **No.of Employees:** 501 - 1000
Product Groups: 71

Date of Accounts	Dec 11	Dec 10	Dec 09
Sales Turnover	100m	97m	90m
Pre Tax Profit/Loss	10m	280	-8m
Working Capital	13m	21m	26m
Fixed Assets	100m	98m	97m
Current Assets	33m	40m	45m
Current Liabilities	14m	12m	12m

Davies Turner & Co. Ltd
184 Portswood Road, Southampton, SO17 2NJ
Tel: 023-8055 5955 **Fax:** 023-8055 5644
E-mail: southampton@daviesturner.co.uk
Website: http://www.daviesturner.co.uk
Managers: P. Cooper (Mgr)
Ultimate Holding Company: DAVIES TURNER HOLDINGS PLC
Immediate Holding Company: DAVIES TURNER & CO. LIMITED
Registration no: 04345197 **Date established:** 2001
Turnover: £50m - £75m **No.of Employees:** 1 - 10 **Product Groups:** 72, 74, 76, 82

Date of Accounts	Mar 12	Mar 11	Mar 10
Sales Turnover	97m	100m	84m
Pre Tax Profit/Loss	2m	2m	1m
Working Capital	3m	8m	7m
Fixed Assets	2m	1m	2m
Current Assets	20m	24m	22m
Current Liabilities	3m	4m	3m

Deecee Upholstrey & Interiors
502 Portswood Road, Southampton, SO17 3SP
Tel: 023-8055 5888 **Fax:** 023-8067 6761
E-mail: sales@deeceeupholstery.co.uk
Website: http://www.deeceeupholstery.co.uk
Directors: D. Caplen (Ptnr)
Date established: 1979 **No.of Employees:** 1 - 10 **Product Groups:** 24, 26

Denholm Shipping Company Ltd
Liner House Test Road, Eastern Docks, Southampton, SO14 3GE
Tel: 023-8071 3100 **Fax:** 023-8071 3129
E-mail: finadmin@denshipsouth.co.uk
Website: http://www.denholm-group.co.uk
Ultimate Holding Company: J. & J. DENHOLM LIMITED
Immediate Holding Company: DENHOLM SHIPPING COMPANY LIMITED
Registration no: 00709942 **Date established:** 1961
Turnover: £20m - £50m **No.of Employees:** 11 - 20 **Product Groups:** 72, 74

Di -Pak Packaging Services
9 Belgrave Industrial Estate Belgrave Road, Southampton, SO17 3EA
Tel: 023-8055 5986 **Fax:** 08709-089394
E-mail: marketing@dipakpackaging.co.uk
Website: http://www.di-pakpackaging.co.uk
Directors: J. Foster (Ptnr)
Date established: 1979 **No.of Employees:** 1 - 10 **Product Groups:** 38, 42

Diametric Technical
Lake House Waltham Business Park Brickyard Road, Swanmore, Southampton, SO32 2SA
Tel: 01489-899555 **Fax:** 01489-860180
E-mail: sales@diametric.gb.com
Website: http://www.diametric.gb.com
Bank(s): National Westminster Bank Plc
Directors: G. Steele (Sales)
Ultimate Holding Company: DIAMETRIC SERVICES LTD
Immediate Holding Company: DIAMETRIC TECHNICAL LIMITED
Registration no: 01193047 **Date established:** 1974 **Turnover:** £2m - £5m
No.of Employees: 11 - 20 **Product Groups:** 35, 49

Date of Accounts	Dec 11	Dec 10	Dec 09
Working Capital	933	838	678
Fixed Assets	202	207	227
Current Assets	2m	1m	1m

Display Wizard Ltd
Unit 5 Avon Building Wallops Wood Farm, Droxford, Southampton, SO32 3QY
Tel: 01489-878200 **Fax:** 01489-878201
E-mail: info@displaywizard.co.uk
Website: http://www.displaywizard.co.uk
Directors: S. Hiscutt (Dir), S. Hiscutt (Ptnr)
Immediate Holding Company: DISPLAY WIZARD LIMITED
Registration no: 05054229 **Date established:** 2004
No.of Employees: 1 - 10 **Product Groups:** 26, 30, 35, 49, 52, 81, 83, 84

Dowding & Mills Engineering Services Ltd
William Street, Southampton, SO14 5QH
Tel: 023-8023 4999 **Fax:** 023-8023 4312
E-mail: engineering.southampton-mechanical@dowdingandmills.com
Website: http://www.dowdingandmills.com
Managers: B. Rogers (District Mgr), C. Mudd (District Mgr), W. Harton (Mktg Serv Mgr), A. Phillips (Sales Admin)
Ultimate Holding Company: Castle Support Services plc
Immediate Holding Company: EBBTIDE MARINE LIMITED
Registration no: SC028056 **Date established:** 2008 **Turnover:** £2m - £5m
No.of Employees: 11 - 20 **Product Groups:** 37

Dresser
Unit 1 Yeoman Industrial Park Test Lane, Nursling, Southampton, SO16 9JX
Tel: 023-8087 5600 **Fax:** 023-8087 5601
E-mail: riosales@dresser.com
Website: http://www.dresser.com
Managers: N. Barker (Sales Prom Mgr)
Immediate Holding Company: Dresser Industries Inc
Registration no: 00196631 **VAT No.:** GB 582 2898 01
Turnover: £2m - £5m **No.of Employees:** 11 - 20 **Product Groups:** 36, 38, 40, 45

Duroy Ltd
Willments Industrial Estate Hazel Road, Southampton, SO19 7HS
Tel: 023-8043 5800 **Fax:** 023-8043 5807
E-mail: j.duff@duroy.co.uk
Website: http://www.duroy.co.uk
Directors: J. Duff (Dir), A. Gonzalez (Fin)
Immediate Holding Company: DUROY LIMITED
Registration no: 04671262 **VAT No.:** GB 109 0359 91
Date established: 2003 **Turnover:** £500,000 - £1m
No.of Employees: 1 - 10 **Product Groups:** 30

Date of Accounts	Mar 11	Mar 10	Mar 09
Working Capital	31	27	20
Fixed Assets	26	21	24
Current Assets	110	109	107

Dynamic Load Monitoring
3 Bridgers Farm Nursling Street, Nursling, Southampton, SO16 0YA
Tel: 023-8074 1700 **Fax:** 023-8074 1701
E-mail: martin@dlm-uk.com
Website: http://www.dlm-uk.com
Directors: M. Halford (MD)
Immediate Holding Company: DYNAMIC LOAD MONITORING (UK) LIMITED
Registration no: 02924110 **Date established:** 1994
Turnover: £500,000 - £1m **No.of Employees:** 11 - 20
Product Groups: 38, 39, 45, 85

Date of Accounts	Sep 11	Sep 10	Sep 09
Working Capital	107	58	38
Fixed Assets	15	10	12
Current Assets	305	189	96

Elford Sheds
The Yard Botley Road, North Baddesley, Southampton, SO52 9DP
Tel: 0800-644 6334 **Fax:** 023-8066 3013
E-mail: info@elfordsheds.co.uk
Website: http://www.elfordsheds.co.uk
Directors: J. Sleet (Prop)
Immediate Holding Company: GODWIN FENCING SPECIALISTS LIMITED
Registration no: 07384902 **Date established:** 2009
Turnover: £500,000 - £1m **No.of Employees:** 1 - 10 **Product Groups:** 25

Date of Accounts	Dec 11	Dec 10
Working Capital	-32	-9
Fixed Assets	15	19
Current Assets	19	30

Elliott Brothers Ltd
Millbank Wharf Millbank Street, Northam, Southampton, SO14 5AG
Tel: 023-8022 6852 **Fax:** 023-8063 8780
E-mail: info@elliott-brothers.co.uk
Website: http://www.elliotts.uk.com
Directors: P. Cleary (Sales), T. Adams (Comm)
Managers: A. Heddell, D. Cross
Ultimate Holding Company: ELLIOTT BROTHERS (BUILDERS MERCHANTS) LIMITED
Immediate Holding Company: ELLIOTT BROTHERS LIMITED
Registration no: 02511005 **Date established:** 1990
Turnover: £20m - £50m **No.of Employees:** 101 - 250
Product Groups: 33, 66

see next page

Elliott Brothers Ltd - *Cont'd*

Date of Accounts	Dec 11	Dec 10	Dec 09
Sales Turnover	40m	38m	37m
Pre Tax Profit/Loss	438	341	138
Working Capital	9m	9m	8m
Fixed Assets	2m	2m	2m
Current Assets	16m	16m	14m
Current Liabilities	1m	4m	1m

Elvstrom Sails Ltd

Unit 2 Hys, Hamble, Southampton, SO31 4NN
Tel: 023-8045 0430 **Fax:** 023-8045 2465
E-mail: sales@sobstad.co.uk
Website: http://www.elvstromsails.co.uk
Managers: J. White (Sales Prom Mgr)
Ultimate Holding Company: ELVSTROM SAILS A/S (DENMARK)
Immediate Holding Company: ELVSTROM SAILS UK LIMITED
Registration no: 01136087 **VAT No.:** GB 108 3292 84
Date established: 1973 **No.of Employees:** 1 - 10 **Product Groups:** 63

Date of Accounts	Sep 11	Sep 10	Sep 09
Working Capital	-101	27	-471
Fixed Assets	8	13	32
Current Assets	40	93	128

Enecon UK

Newport Bridge Road, Bursledon, Southampton, SO31 8AL
Tel: 023-8040 5254 **Fax:** 023-8040 5254
E-mail: info@enecon.co.uk
Website: http://www.enecon.co.uk
Directors: G. Wilson (Dir)
Immediate Holding Company: TRYTON DESIGNS LIMITED
Registration no: 03614200 **Date established:** 1998
Turnover: Up to £250,000 **No.of Employees:** 1 - 10 **Product Groups:** 46, 48

Date of Accounts	Aug 11	Aug 10	Aug 09
Sales Turnover	72	N/A	N/A
Pre Tax Profit/Loss	6	N/A	N/A
Working Capital	-8	4	6
Fixed Assets	9	11	12
Current Assets	11	81	69
Current Liabilities	9	N/A	N/A

e-Plenish.com

5A Herald Industrial Estate Botley Road, Hedge End, Southampton, SO30 2JW
Tel: 01489-774 498 **Fax:** 01489-774 499
E-mail: info@e-plenish.com
Website: http://www.e-plenish.com
Date established: 2006 **No.of Employees:** 21 - 50 **Product Groups:** 67

Eriks Industrial Services (Southampton Electro Mechanical)

144 Commercial Road Totton, Southampton, SO40 3AA
Tel: 023-8086 2125 **Fax:** 023-8086 6355
E-mail: paul.witts@eriks.co.uk
Website: http://www.eriks.co.uk
Managers: A. Prior
Turnover: £250m - £500m **No.of Employees:** 11 - 20 **Product Groups:** 35

European Marine & Machinery Agencies Ltd

Nutsey House Nutsey Lane, Totton, Southampton, SO40 3NB
Tel: 023-8058 0020 **Fax:** 023-8058 0021
E-mail: sales@europeanmarine.co.uk
Website: http://www.europeanmarine.co.uk
Directors: M. Sayer (Dir)
Ultimate Holding Company: FOSNA HOLDINGS LIMITED
Immediate Holding Company: EUROPEAN MARINE & MACHINERY AGENCIES LIMITED
Registration no: 05854645 **VAT No.:** GB 293 5535 33
Date established: 2006 **Turnover:** £250,000 - £500,000
No.of Employees: 1 - 10 **Product Groups:** 35, 39

European Metals Recycling Ltd

Princes Street, Southampton, SO14 5AP
Tel: 023-8033 6288 **Fax:** 023-8033 5884
Website: http://www.emrltd.com
Managers: T. Porter (Mgr)
Immediate Holding Company: EUROPEAN METAL RECYCLING LIMITED
Registration no: 02954623 **Date established:** 1994
No.of Employees: 21 - 50 **Product Groups:** 42, 66

Date of Accounts	Dec 11	Dec 10	Dec 09
Sales Turnover	3032m	2431m	1843m
Pre Tax Profit/Loss	116m	155m	91m
Working Capital	414m	371m	167m
Fixed Assets	518m	483m	480m
Current Assets	1027m	717m	557m
Current Liabilities	124m	118m	185m

F C M Electrical & Mechanical Ltd

Merlin Quay Hazel Road, Southampton, SO19 7GB
Tel: 023-8043 4466 **Fax:** 023-8043 4477
E-mail: richardrhodes@fcm-facilities.co.uk
Website: http://www.fcm-group.co.uk
Directors: R. Rhodes (MD), R. Rhodes (Dir)
Immediate Holding Company: FCM ELECTRICAL AND MECHANICAL LTD
Registration no: 06782585 **Date established:** 2009
Turnover: Up to £250,000 **No.of Employees:** 11 - 20 **Product Groups:** 52

Date of Accounts	Jan 10
Current Assets	5

F H Brundle

Third Avenue, Southampton, SO15 0JX
Tel: 023-8070 3333 **Fax:** 023-8070 5555
E-mail: sales@brundle.co.uk
Website: http://www.brundle.co.uk
Managers: J. Bryers (Mgr)
Immediate Holding Company: F H BRUNDLE
Registration no: 07168270 **Date established:** 2010
Turnover: £10m - £20m **No.of Employees:** 21 - 50 **Product Groups:** 30, 32, 34, 35, 36, 39, 46, 49, 66

Fibercore Ltd

Fibercore House University Parkway, Chilworth, Southampton, SO16 7QQ
Tel: 023-8076 9893 **Fax:** 023-8076 9895
E-mail: info@fibrecore.com
Website: http://www.fibrecore.com
Bank(s): National Westminster Bank Plc
Directors: A. De Waele (Fin)
Ultimate Holding Company: H.I.G. EUROPE - FIBERCORE BIDCO LIMITED
Immediate Holding Company: FIBERCORE LIMITED
Registration no: 02795233 **VAT No.:** GB 631 5748 38
Date established: 1993 **Turnover:** £10m - £20m
No.of Employees: 11 - 20 **Product Groups:** 33, 37

Date of Accounts	Jul 08	Jul 09
Sales Turnover	9m	9m
Pre Tax Profit/Loss	1m	1m
Working Capital	1m	3m
Fixed Assets	5m	5m
Current Assets	8m	5m
Current Liabilities	358	171

Film Technik

8 The Crosshouse Centre Crosshouse Road, Southampton, SO14 5GZ
Tel: 023-8038 6713 **Fax:** 023-8023 0549
E-mail: sales@filmtechnik.co.uk
Website: http://www.filmtechnik.co.uk
Directors: T. O'neill (MD)
No.of Employees: 1 - 10 **Product Groups:** 23, 28, 32

Fork Lightning

135a Ringwood Road Totton, Southampton, SO40 8DX
Tel: 023-8066 0783 **Fax:** 023-8057 2731
Directors: S. O'donnell (Prop)
Date established: 1994 **No.of Employees:** 1 - 10 **Product Groups:** 35, 39, 45

Formerton Sheet Sales Ltd

Unit 5 Lower William Street, Southampton, SO14 5QE
Tel: 023-8033 2761 **Fax:** 023-8022 5148
E-mail: sales@formertonsheetsales.co.uk
Website: http://www.polycarbonateonline.co.uk
Bank(s): Lloyds TSB Bank plc
Managers: M. Sheridan (District Mgr)
Ultimate Holding Company: SIG PLC
Immediate Holding Company: FORMERTON SHEET SALES LIMITED
Registration no: 01767482 **VAT No.:** GB 329 9189 11
Date established: 1983 **Turnover:** £2m - £5m **No.of Employees:** 11 - 20
Product Groups: 30

G A Wedderburn Co. Ltd

56 Shirley Road, Southampton, SO15 3UH
Tel: 023-8022 7645 **Fax:** 023-8022 7537
E-mail: info@wedderburn.co.uk
Website: http://www.wedderburn.co.uk
Directors: C. Barker (MD), P. Wedderburn (MD)
Managers: T. Smith (Buyer), M. Farnell (Tech Serv Mgr)
Immediate Holding Company: G.A.WEDDERBURN & CO.LIMITED
Registration no: 00272418 **Date established:** 1933
Turnover: £250,000 - £500,000 **No.of Employees:** 21 - 50
Product Groups: 38, 44

Date of Accounts	Dec 11	Mar 11	Mar 10
Working Capital	372	636	636
Fixed Assets	71	73	98
Current Assets	708	2m	2m

Geco Lift Trucks Ltd

Lower William Street Northam, Southampton, SO14 5QE
Tel: 023-8022 5535 **Fax:** 023-8063 4590
Website: http://www.gecolifttrucks.co.uk
Managers: M. Richardson (Mgr)
Immediate Holding Company: GECO LIFT TRUCKS LIMITED
Registration no: 00862595 **Date established:** 1965
No.of Employees: 1 - 10 **Product Groups:** 35, 39, 45

Date of Accounts	Mar 11	Mar 10	Mar 09
Working Capital	608	811	889
Fixed Assets	344	346	366
Current Assets	634	831	913

Gemini Travel Southampton Ltd

North Road Marchwood Industrial Park, Marchwood, Southampton, SO40 4BL
Tel: 023-8066 0066 **Fax:** 023-8087 1308
E-mail: kenhatch@btconnect.com
Website: http://www.btconect.com
Directors: M. Bennett (MD)
Managers: N. Smith (Mgr)
Immediate Holding Company: GEMINI TRAVEL SOUTHAMPTON LTD
Registration no: 05066697 **Date established:** 2004
Turnover: £250,000 - £500,000 **No.of Employees:** 21 - 50
Product Groups: 72

Date of Accounts	Mar 11	Mar 10	Mar 09
Sales Turnover	419	472	466
Pre Tax Profit/Loss	50	67	28
Working Capital	-50	-51	-56
Fixed Assets	139	166	189
Current Assets	52	53	48
Current Liabilities	21	24	18

Gifford

Carlton House Ringwood Road, Woodlands, Southampton, SO40 7HT
Tel: 023-8081 7500 **Fax:** 023-8081 7600
E-mail: debbie.montgomery@gifford.uk.com
Website: http://www.gifford.co.uk
Directors: G. Clark (Grp Chief Exec), D. Montgomery (Fin)
Ultimate Holding Company: GIFFORD LLP
Immediate Holding Company: GIFFORD SERVICES LIMITED
Registration no: 02973958 **Date established:** 1994 **Turnover:** £2m - £5m
No.of Employees: 501 - 1000 **Product Groups:** 35, 51, 54, 81, 84, 85, 86

Date of Accounts	Dec 09	Dec 08	Dec 07
Sales Turnover	42m	50m	42m
Pre Tax Profit/Loss	3m	4m	4m
Working Capital	4m	5m	5m
Fixed Assets	6m	6m	5m
Current Assets	14m	15m	16m
Current Liabilities	6m	5m	5m

Glen Dimplex UK Ltd

Millbrook House Grange Drive, Hedge End, Southampton, SO30 2DF
Tel: 08456-005111 **Fax:** 0870-727 0109
E-mail: enquiries@dimplex.co.uk
Website: http://www.dimplex.co.uk
Bank(s): National Westminster Bank Plc
Directors: L. George (Fin), S. O'Driscoll (Grp Chief Exec)
Ultimate Holding Company: GLEN DIMPLEX (ROI)
Immediate Holding Company: GDC GROUP LIMITED
Registration no: 01313016 **VAT No.:** GB 287 1315 50
Date established: 1977 **Turnover:** £75m - £125m
No.of Employees: 101 - 250 **Product Groups:** 40

Date of Accounts	Mar 11	Mar 10	Mar 09
Sales Turnover	85m	77m	74m
Pre Tax Profit/Loss	399	2m	5m
Working Capital	18m	19m	16m
Fixed Assets	15m	15m	15m
Current Assets	36m	30m	27m
Current Liabilities	10m	8m	9m

Graham

Unit 1 South Hampshire Industrial Park Totton, Southampton, SO40 3SA
Tel: 023-8086 2909 **Fax:** 023-8086 2562
E-mail: russell.kennell@graham-group.co.uk
Website: http://www.graham-group.co.uk
Managers: R. Kennell (Mgr)
Immediate Holding Company: DAVID GRAHAM VEHICLE REPAIRS LTD
Registration no: SC254141 **Date established:** 2004
Turnover: £10m - £20m **No.of Employees:** 1 - 10 **Product Groups:** 66

Gresham Computer Services

Sopwish House Brook Avenue, Warsash, Southampton, SO31 9HP
Tel: 01489-555500 **Fax:** 01489-555560
E-mail: info@gresham-computing.com
Website: http://www.gresham-computing.com
Bank(s): Lloyds TSB Bank plc
Directors: R. Grubb (Co Sec)
Managers: C. Errington
Immediate Holding Company: GRESHAM COMPUTING PLC.
Registration no: 01072032 **Date established:** 1972
Turnover: £10m - £20m **No.of Employees:** 21 - 50 **Product Groups:** 44

Date of Accounts	Dec 11	Dec 10	Dec 09
Sales Turnover	12m	9m	10m
Pre Tax Profit/Loss	1m	271	-8m
Working Capital	2m	1m	-319
Fixed Assets	4m	2m	2m
Current Assets	7m	7m	4m
Current Liabilities	4m	4m	3m

M D Guy & Son Verwood Ltd

Unit 2 Northbrook Industrial Estate Vinvent Avenue, Southampton, SO16 6PQ
Tel: 023-8070 1111 **Fax:** 023-8070 1171
E-mail: info@mdguys.co.uk
Website: http://www.mdguys.co.uk
Bank(s): HSBC
Directors: A. Wells (MD), M. Guy (Dir), M. White (Co Sec), P. Armitage (Dir), P. Armitage (MD), S. Guy (Dir)
Ultimate Holding Company: CLC Group Ltd
Immediate Holding Company: M.D. GUY & SON (VERWOOD) LIMITED
Registration no: 01829468 **VAT No.:** GB 393 0303 71
Date established: 1984 **Turnover:** £2m - £5m **No.of Employees:** 21 - 50
Product Groups: 52

Date of Accounts	Dec 07	Dec 06	Dec 05
Working Capital	377	280	216
Fixed Assets	25	22	21
Current Assets	801	903	678
Current Liabilities	424	623	463

H I E Plumbing Direct

Unit 8 Claylands Park Claylands Road, Bishops Waltham, Southampton, SO32 1QD
Tel: 01489-894456 **Fax:** 01489-899943
E-mail: info@h-i-e.co.uk
Website: http://www.h-i-e.co.uk
No.of Employees: 1 - 10 **Product Groups:** 30, 36, 40

Hampshire Chamber Of Commerce

Bugle House 53 Bugle Street, Southampton, SO14 2LF
Tel: 023-8022 3541 **Fax:** 023-8022 7426
E-mail: info@hampshirechamber.co.uk
Website: http://www.hampshirechamber.co.uk
Bank(s): Lloyds
Directors: L. Hall (Co Sec), J. Chestnutt (Grp Chief Exec)
Managers: L. Gourley
Immediate Holding Company: HAMPSHIRE ENTERPRISE LTD
Registration no: 00009806 **VAT No.:** GB 188 0556 35
Date established: 1975 **Turnover:** £500,000 - £1m
No.of Employees: 21 - 50 **Product Groups:** 87

Date of Accounts	Mar 11	Feb 08	Feb 10
Sales Turnover	778	702	656
Pre Tax Profit/Loss	25	10	5
Working Capital	-140	-127	-87
Fixed Assets	667	605	589
Current Assets	530	100	107
Current Liabilities	519	203	180

Hampshire Electroplating Co. Ltd

69-75 Empress Road, Southampton, SO14 0JW
Tel: 023-8022 5639 **Fax:** 023-8063 9874
E-mail: info@hepcoltd.co.uk
Website: http://www.hepcoltd.co.uk
Directors: N. Arnold (Dir)
Immediate Holding Company: HAMPSHIRE ELECTRO PLATING CO. LIMITED
Registration no: 00410782 **VAT No.:** GB 188 2692 17
Date established: 1946 **Turnover:** £1m - £2m **No.of Employees:** 11 - 20
Product Groups: 48

Date of Accounts	May 11	May 10	May 09
Working Capital	87	170	255
Fixed Assets	43	48	59
Current Assets	304	363	437

Hampshire Hose Services Ltd

1 The Crosshouse Centre Crosshouse Road, Southampton, SO14 5GZ
Tel: 023-8033 5588 **Fax:** 023-8063 1509
E-mail: sales@hampshirehose.co.uk
Website: http://www.hampshirehose.co.uk
Directors: P. Reynolds (MD)
Immediate Holding Company: HAMPSHIRE HOSE SERVICES LIMITED
Registration no: 01812034 **Date established:** 1984 **Turnover:** £1m - £2m
No.of Employees: 11 - 20 **Product Groups:** 22, 23, 29, 30, 33, 35, 36, 37, 38, 39, 40, 41, 42, 45, 46, 63, 66, 84

Date of Accounts	Aug 11	Aug 10	Aug 09
Working Capital	949	800	629
Fixed Assets	434	447	470

Current Assets	1m	1m	898

Hampshire Press
Unit 4-5 Dukes Road, Southampton, SO14 0SQ
Tel: 023-8001 1911 **Fax:** 023-8058 1970
E-mail: enquiries@hampshirepress.co.uk
Website: http://www.hampshirepress.co.uk
Directors: C. Swanbrow (Dir)
Immediate Holding Company: HAMPSHIRE PRESS LIMITED
Registration no: 06591944 **Date established:** 2008
Turnover: £250,000 - £500,000 **No.of Employees:** 1 - 10
Product Groups: 28

Date of Accounts	May 11	May 10	May 09
Working Capital	105	-7	-46
Fixed Assets	42	31	38
Current Assets	129	137	82

Hants & Dorset Trim Ltd
Quayside House William Street, Southampton, SO14 5QH
Tel: 023-8064 4200 **Fax:** 023-8064 7802
E-mail: dclack@hdtrim.co.uk
Website: http://www.hantsanddorsettrims.co.uk
Directors: A. Carter (MD), M. Dolphin (Fin)
Ultimate Holding Company: The Go-Ahead Group plc
Immediate Holding Company: Go South Coast Ltd
Registration no: 02017829 **Date established:** 2008
Turnover: £250m - £500m **No.of Employees:** 21 - 50
Product Groups: 42, 45

Harris Transport Ltd
Unit 17 Eling Wharf Totton, Southampton, SO40 4TE
Tel: 023-8087 3774 **Fax:** 01709-555977
E-mail: traffic@harristransport.co.uk
Website: http://www.harristransport.co.uk
Directors: D. Harris (MD), P. Harris (Fin)
Managers: C. Rollett (Sales & Mktg Mg)
Immediate Holding Company: HARRIS TRANSPORT LIMITED
Registration no: 02598552 **Date established:** 1991
Turnover: Up to £250,000 **No.of Employees:** 51 - 100
Product Groups: 77

Date of Accounts	Jun 12	Jun 11	Jun 10
Sales Turnover	8m	N/A	N/A
Pre Tax Profit/Loss	118	N/A	N/A
Working Capital	117	-49	-293
Fixed Assets	865	782	1m
Current Assets	2m	2m	1m
Current Liabilities	71	N/A	N/A

Hendy Ford Southampton
360-364 Shirley Road, Southampton, SO15 3UF
Tel: 023-8070 1700 **Fax:** 023-8070 2437
E-mail: paul@hendy.co.uk
Website: http://www.hendy-group.com
Bank(s): Lloyds
Directors: T. Mynott (Dir), B. Hendy (Ch), B. Hendy (Dir), I. Jones (Dir), J. Weatherstone (Mkt Research), M. Nicholas (I.T. Dir), N. Hendy (Ch), N. Hendy (Dir), P. Hendy (Dir), P. Hill (Sales), S. Hendy (Dir), T. J. (Dir)
Immediate Holding Company: HENDY HOLDINGS LIMITED
Registration no: 00056988 **VAT No.:** GB 568 7215 08
Date established: 1998 **Turnover:** £125m - £250m
No.of Employees: 21 - 50 **Product Groups:** 68, 82

Highview Salt Supplies
Highview New Road, Meonstoke, Southampton, SO32 3NN
Tel: 01489-877175
Website: http://www.highviewsaltsupplies.co.uk
Directors: R. Baker (Prop)
Date established: 2003 **No.of Employees:** 1 - 10 **Product Groups:** 38, 42

Hill & Son
Bottings Industrial Estate Curdridge, Southampton, SO30 2GE
Tel: 01489-782343 **Fax:** 01489-782913
Directors: C. Hill (Prop)
Immediate Holding Company: HILL & SONS(BOTLEY & DENMEAD)LIMITED
Registration no: 00403721 **VAT No.:** GB 108 4617 77
Date established: 1946 **Turnover:** £250,000 - £500,000
No.of Employees: 1 - 10 **Product Groups:** 72, 77, 82

Date of Accounts	Jun 11	Jun 10	Jun 09
Working Capital	-39	-22	-100
Fixed Assets	994	1m	1m
Current Assets	23	60	59

Hobbs The Printers Ltd
Brunel Road Totton, Southampton, SO40 3WX
Tel: 023-8066 4800 **Fax:** 023-8066 4801
E-mail: info@hobbs.uk.com
Website: http://www.hobbs.uk.com
Directors: T. Ozanne (Sales & Mktg), D. Hobbs (MD)
Managers: M. Whiteside (Chief Acct), R. Dix (Personnel)
Ultimate Holding Company: P C HOLDINGS (SOUTHAMPTON) LIMITED
Immediate Holding Company: HOBBS THE PRINTERS LIMITED
Registration no: 00422132 **Date established:** 1946
Turnover: £10m - £20m **No.of Employees:** 101 - 250
Product Groups: 27, 28

Date of Accounts	Jul 11	Jul 10	Jul 09
Sales Turnover	11m	10m	11m
Pre Tax Profit/Loss	248	449	352
Working Capital	2m	6m	5m
Fixed Assets	3m	2m	3m
Current Assets	3m	7m	6m
Current Liabilities	440	679	486

Htec Ltd
Unit H George Curl Way, Southampton, SO18 2RX
Tel: 023-8068 9200 **Fax:** 023-8068 9201
E-mail: sales@htec.co.uk
Website: http://www.htec.co.uk
Bank(s): National Westminster Bank Plc
Directors: R. Smeeton (Fin)
Managers: S. Mccleod, S. Mcleod
Ultimate Holding Company: UNIVERSE GROUP PLC
Immediate Holding Company: HTEC LIMITED
Registration no: 01486255 **VAT No.:** GB 522 3860 63
Date established: 1980 **Turnover:** £10m - £20m
No.of Employees: 101 - 250 **Product Groups:** 37, 44, 84

Date of Accounts	Dec 11	Dec 10	Dec 09
Sales Turnover	12m	11m	12m
Pre Tax Profit/Loss	261	458	147

Working Capital	5m	4m	4m
Fixed Assets	2m	3m	3m
Current Assets	8m	8m	9m
Current Liabilities	3m	3m	4m

Kelvin Hughes Ltd
Kilgraston House 11-13 Southampton Street, Southampton, SO15 2ED
Tel: 023-8063 4911 **Fax:** 023-8033 0014
E-mail: southampton@kelvinhughes.co.uk
Website: http://www.bookharbour.com
Managers: M. Kerr (Mgr)
Ultimate Holding Company: ECI PARTNERS LLP
Immediate Holding Company: KELVIN HUGHES LIMITED
Registration no: 01030135 **Date established:** 1971
No.of Employees: 1 - 10 **Product Groups:** 28, 39, 44

Date of Accounts	Jul 11	Jul 10	Jul 09
Sales Turnover	57m	54m	59m
Pre Tax Profit/Loss	6m	3m	1m
Working Capital	14m	8m	6m
Fixed Assets	11m	11m	11m
Current Assets	43m	33m	29m
Current Liabilities	1m	3m	2m

P D Hunt Ltd
Lynwood Grange Winsor Road, Winsor, Southampton, SO40 2HE
Tel: 023-8081 4348 **Fax:** 023-8081 2911
Directors: P. Hunt (MD)
Immediate Holding Company: P.D. HUNT LIMITED
Registration no: 01256633 **Date established:** 1976 **Turnover:** £2m - £5m
No.of Employees: 1 - 10 **Product Groups:** 52

Date of Accounts	Jun 11	Jun 10	Jun 09
Working Capital	505	804	975
Fixed Assets	71	100	122
Current Assets	934	1m	1m

Hurst UK Ltd
Medina Chambers Town Quay, Southampton, SO14 2AQ
Tel: 020-7588 9978 **Fax:** 020-7588 9977
E-mail: info@hurstuk.com
Website: http://www.hurstuk.com
Managers: C. Huntingdon (Sales Prom Mgr), T. Hale (Mktg Serv Mgr)
Ultimate Holding Company: PowerTronic Drive Systems Ltd
Registration no: 04638677 **Turnover:** Up to £250,000
No.of Employees: 1 - 10 **Product Groups:** 35, 37

Hyde Sails Ltd
PO Box 441, Southampton, SO31 0AA
Tel: 0845-5438945 **Fax:** 0800-3899254
E-mail: sales@hydesails.co.uk
Website: http://www.hydesails.com
Directors: R. Franks (Sales & Mktg), B. Twogood (Co Sec), N. Humphrey (Sales & Mktg), A. Hyde (Ch)
Managers: S. Dixon (Personnel), H. Solana (Buyer)
Immediate Holding Company: HYDE SAILS LIMITED
Registration no: 01530833 **VAT No.:** GB 368 7828 88
Date established: 1980 **Turnover:** £2m - £5m **No.of Employees:** 1 - 10
Product Groups: 24

Date of Accounts	Mar 10	Mar 09	Sep 07
Pre Tax Profit/Loss	N/A	-201	N/A
Working Capital	593	697	899
Fixed Assets	93	67	75
Current Assets	2m	2m	2m
Current Liabilities	N/A	203	N/A

Hydralon Coatings Ltd
Britannia Road Northam, Southampton, SO14 5RH
Tel: 023-8022 5573 **Fax:** 023-8033 2145
E-mail: info@hydralon.com
Website: http://www.hydralon.com
Bank(s): Barclays, Ocean Village
Directors: C. Baker (Dir), D. Watts (Tech Serv)
Managers: M. Higham (Comptroller)
Immediate Holding Company: Hydralon Ltd
Registration no: 00551768 **Date established:** 1955 **Turnover:** £2m - £5m
No.of Employees: 11 - 20 **Product Groups:** 33, 48

Date of Accounts	Apr 07	Apr 06	Apr 05
Working Capital	-410	-287	164
Fixed Assets	1m	1m	908
Current Assets	384	332	417

Hygromatik
PO Box 1399, Southampton, SO18 9AA
Tel: 023-8044 3127 **Fax:** 0870-167 0346
E-mail: sales@hygromatik.co.uk
Website: http://www.hygromatik.com
Managers: A. Chessun
Turnover: £1m - £2m **No.of Employees:** 1 - 10 **Product Groups:** 66

Hyphose Ltd
Unit 1 Trinity Industrial Estate Millbrook Road West, Southampton, SO15 0LA
Tel: 023-8051 2555 **Fax:** 023-8051 2999
E-mail: sales@hyphose.com
Website: http://www.hyphose.com
Managers: S. Whitehead (District Mgr)
Immediate Holding Company: HYPHOSE LIMITED
Registration no: 01472439 **VAT No.:** GB 323 5820 75
Date established: 1980 **Turnover:** £2m - £5m **No.of Employees:** 1 - 10
Product Groups: 29, 30, 36, 42

Date of Accounts	Mar 12	Mar 11	Mar 10
Working Capital	269	270	368
Fixed Assets	1m	948	908
Current Assets	2m	2m	2m

I C S Cool Energy Ltd
I C S House Unit 19-22 Calmore Industrial Esate, Totton, Southampton, SO40 3RY
Tel: 023-8052 7300 **Fax:** 01425-639041
E-mail: info@icstemp.com
Website: http://www.icstemp.com
Directors: R. Wilson (MD), S. West (Fin)
Managers: W. Hinchcliffe (Personnel), A. Clark (Purch Mgr), S. Wilders (Grp Mktg Mgr), T. Rice (Tech Serv Mgr)
Ultimate Holding Company: ICS GROUP HOLDINGS LIMITED
Immediate Holding Company: ICS COOL ENERGY LIMITED
Registration no: 05509182 **Date established:** 2005
No.of Employees: 51 - 100 **Product Groups:** 38, 40, 41, 42, 45

Date of Accounts	Dec 11	Dec 10	Dec 09
Sales Turnover	21m	20m	17m
Pre Tax Profit/Loss	2m	2m	2m

Working Capital	4m	2m	1m
Fixed Assets	248	388	616
Current Assets	10m	10m	8m
Current Liabilities	3m	3m	2m

I C S Robotics & Automation Ltd
Unit 6 Manor Park Industrial Estate Station Road South, Totton, Southampton, SO40 9HP
Tel: 023-8066 7661 **Fax:** 023-8066 7881
E-mail: martin.templeman@ics-robotics.co.uk
Website: http://www.ics-robotics.co.uk
Bank(s): Lloyds TSB Bank plc
Directors: M. Templeman (MD), M. Templeman (Dir), B. Templeman (Dir), B. Templeman (Fin)
Immediate Holding Company: ICS ROBOTICS AND AUTOMATION LIMITED
Registration no: 02354143 **VAT No.:** GB 522 3927 57
Date established: 1989 **Turnover:** £1m - £2m **No.of Employees:** 11 - 20
Product Groups: 37, 45, 48, 84

Date of Accounts	Dec 07	Dec 06	Dec 05
Working Capital	240	150	51
Fixed Assets	87	75	15
Current Assets	486	332	187
Current Liabilities	246	182	137
Total Share Capital	1	1	1

ICS Temperature Control Ltd
ICS House Stephenson Road, Calmore Industrial Estate, Totton, Southampton, SO40 3RY
Tel: 023-8052 7300 **Fax:** 023-8042 8366
E-mail: sales@icstemp.com
Website: http://www.icstemp.com
Product Groups: 38, 40, 41, 42, 45

ICS Tricool Thermal
ICS House Stephenson Road, Calmore Industrial Estate, Totton, Southampton, SO40 3RY
Tel: 023-8052 7300 **Fax:** 023-8042 8366
E-mail: sales@icstemp.com
Website: http://www.icstemp.com
Product Groups: 38, 40, 41, 42, 45

Index Fabrications Southampton Ltd
Rochester Street, Southampton, SO14 5QW
Tel: 023-8063 1484 **Fax:** 023-8063 1484
E-mail: indexfabs@aol.com
Directors: I. Swaffield (MD), K. Swaffield (Fin)
Immediate Holding Company: INDEX FABRICATIONS (SOUTHAMPTON) LIMITED
Registration no: 01022587 **VAT No.:** GB 188 6542 16
Date established: 1971 **Turnover:** Up to £250,000
No.of Employees: 1 - 10 **Product Groups:** 48

Date of Accounts	Oct 11	Oct 10	Oct 09
Working Capital	59	65	68
Fixed Assets	41	42	43
Current Assets	150	126	135
Current Liabilities	18	N/A	N/A

Inmar Automation Ltd
Test House 118 Ringwood Road, Totton, Southampton, SO40 8DS
Tel: 023-8086 4179 **Fax:** 023-8086 1613
E-mail: sales@inmar.co.uk
Website: http://www.inmar.co.uk
Directors: J. Whiting (Fin)
Immediate Holding Company: INMAR AUTOMATION LIMITED
Registration no: 01246028 **Date established:** 1976
Turnover: £250,000 - £500,000 **No.of Employees:** 1 - 10
Product Groups: 84

Date of Accounts	Oct 11	Oct 10	Oct 09
Working Capital	22	16	1
Fixed Assets	35	46	46
Current Assets	89	70	62

J K Controls Ltd
9 Ashlett Close Fawley, Southampton, SO45 1DR
Tel: 023-8089 2021 **Fax:** 023-8089 7950
E-mail: sales@jkcontrols.co.uk
Website: http://www.jkcontrols.co.uk
Directors: K. Rider (Dir)
Immediate Holding Company: J K CONTROLS LIMITED
Registration no: 03073964 **Date established:** 1995
Turnover: £250,000 - £500,000 **No.of Employees:** 1 - 10
Product Groups: 18, 28, 36, 37, 38, 39, 40, 41, 42, 44, 45, 46, 48, 52, 67, 84, 85

Date of Accounts	Sep 11	Sep 10	Sep 09
Working Capital	147	229	143
Fixed Assets	148	65	64
Current Assets	228	320	221

J & S Laser Profile Ltd
Unit 30 South Hampshire Industrial Park Totton, Southampton, SO40 3SA
Tel: 023-8087 2827 **Fax:** 023-8086 0033
E-mail: info@jslaserprofiles.com
Website: http://www.jslaserprofiles.com
Directors: M. Stancombe (Ptnr)
Immediate Holding Company: J & S LASER PROFILES LIMITED
Registration no: 03045472 **Date established:** 1995
No.of Employees: 11 - 20 **Product Groups:** 35

Date of Accounts	Oct 11	Oct 10	Oct 09
Working Capital	444	322	60
Fixed Assets	155	180	226
Current Assets	699	553	442

J & S Sheet Metal Products
Unit 30 South Hampshire Industrial Park, Totton, Southampton, SO40 3SA
Tel: 023-8087 2827 **Fax:** 023-8086 0033
E-mail: sales@jssheetmeta1.com
Website: http://www.jssheetmetal.com
Directors: A. Stancombe (Prop)
No.of Employees: 1 - 10 **Product Groups:** 34, 48

Jayco UK Ltd
10 Old Bridge Close Bursledon, Southampton, SO31 8AX
Tel: 023-8040 2025 **Fax:** 023-8040 5812
E-mail: info@jayco-uk.com
Website: http://www.jayco-uk.com

see next page

***Jayco UK Ltd** - Cont'd*
Directors: P. Cooney (Prop)
Immediate Holding Company: JAYCO (UK) LTD
Registration no: 05733216 **Date established:** 2006
No.of Employees: 1 - 10 **Product Groups:** 24, 29

Date of Accounts	Mar 11	Mar 10	Mar 09
Working Capital	251	56	-138
Fixed Assets	455	487	518
Current Assets	881	774	643

Jewson Ltd
Nutsey Lane Totton, Southampton, SO40 3NB
Tel: 023-8066 5656 **Fax:** 023-8087 3917
E-mail: john.herring@jewson.co.uk
Website: http://www.jewson.co.uk
Managers: J. Herring (Mgr)
Ultimate Holding Company: COMPAGNIE DE SAINT GOBAIN (FRANCE)
Immediate Holding Company: JEWSON LIMITED
Registration no: 00348407 **VAT No.:** GB 497 7184 83
Date established: 1939 **Turnover:** £125m - £250m
No.of Employees: 1 - 10 **Product Groups:** 66

Date of Accounts	Dec 11	Dec 10	Dec 09
Sales Turnover	1606m	1547m	1485m
Pre Tax Profit/Loss	18m	100m	45m
Working Capital	-345m	-250m	-349m
Fixed Assets	496m	387m	461m
Current Assets	657m	1005m	1320m
Current Liabilities	66m	120m	64m

John Penny Restoration Ltd
Unit 10 City Industrial Park Southern Road, Southampton, SO15 1HA
Tel: 023-8023 2066 **Fax:** 023-8021 2129
Directors: J. Penny (MD)
Immediate Holding Company: JOHN PENNY RESTORATION LIMITED
Registration no: 04647188 **Date established:** 2003
No.of Employees: 1 - 10 **Product Groups:** 35, 36

Date of Accounts	Jan 12	Jan 11	Jan 10
Working Capital	86	67	49
Fixed Assets	8	5	7
Current Assets	222	200	168

Jonathan Jones Electrical Services
Solent Business Centre 303 Millbrook Road West, Southampton, SO15 0HW
Tel: 023-8077 2288 **Fax:** 023-8077 1666
E-mail: info@jjes.co.uk
Website: http://www.jjes.co.uk
Directors: J. Jones (Prop)
Registration no: 04432762 **Date established:** 2002
Turnover: £250,000 - £500,000 **No.of Employees:** 1 - 10
Product Groups: 52

Just Lasers Plus
Blackdown Farm Offices Blackdown Lane, Upham, Southampton, SO32 1HS
Tel: 01962-777859 **Fax:** 01962-777660
E-mail: promotion@justlasersplus.co.uk
Website: http://www.lasersplus.co.uk
Managers: I. Norris (Mgr)
Date established: 2001 **Turnover:** £250,000 - £500,000
No.of Employees: 1 - 10 **Product Groups:** 35, 44, 64, 67

K & G Metalcraft
17a Bury Farm Curbridge, Botley, Southampton, SO30 2HB
Tel: 01489-795427 **Fax:** 01489-795427
Directors: K. Henry (Prop)
Date established: 1996 **No.of Employees:** 1 - 10 **Product Groups:** 35

Kempsafe Ltd
Kemps Quay Industrial Park Quayside Road Bitterne Manor, Southampton, SO18 1BZ
Tel: 023-8022 7582 **Fax:** 023-8022 6002
E-mail: sales@kempsafe.com
Website: http://www.kempsafe.com
Bank(s): National Westminster Bank Plc
Directors: C. Stapley (MD), F. Coulter (Co Sec)
Managers: C. Howells (Tech Serv Mgr)
Immediate Holding Company: KEMPSAFE LIMITED
Registration no: 00623350 **VAT No.:** GB 188 6119 27
Date established: 1959 **Turnover:** £1m - £2m **No.of Employees:** 11 - 20
Product Groups: 40

Date of Accounts	Mar 12	Mar 11	Mar 10
Working Capital	304	257	263
Fixed Assets	49	52	56
Current Assets	626	754	894

Kendata Peripherals Ltd
Nutsey Lane Totton, Southampton, SO40 3NB
Tel: 023-8086 9922 **Fax:** 023-8086 0800
E-mail: sales@kendata.com
Website: http://www.kenda.co.uk
Bank(s): HSBC Bank plc
Directors: W. Clarke (MD)
Ultimate Holding Company: Kenda Group
Immediate Holding Company: Kenda Electronic Systems Ltd
Registration no: 01416919 **VAT No.:** GB 329 6802 36
Date established: 1976 **Turnover:** £1m - £2m **No.of Employees:** 11 - 20
Product Groups: 44

KES Power & Light Ltd
Stanton Road, Southampton, SO15 4HU
Tel: 023-8070 4703 **Fax:** 023-8070 1430
E-mail: sales@kes.co.uk
Website: http://www.kes.co.uk
Bank(s): National Westminster Bank Plc
Directors: B. Hamilton (Dir), G. Sparks (MD), G. Sparkes (Dir)
Managers: J. Robinson (Buyer), D. Maycock (Chief Acct), M. Whalley (Sales Prom Mgr), R. Hayward
Immediate Holding Company: K.E.S. (U.K.) Ltd
Registration no: 02587961 **Date established:** 1991 **Turnover:** £2m - £5m
No.of Employees: 21 - 50 **Product Groups:** 37

H Kimber Friction Ltd
Printing Trades House Bond Street, Southampton, SO14 5QA
Tel: 023-8022 6577 **Fax:** 023-8063 1154
E-mail: hkimber.kflh@autonetplus.co.uk
Website: http://www.kimbercarparts.co.uk
Bank(s): National Westminster Bank Plc
Directors: A. Kimber (MD)
Immediate Holding Company: H. KIMBER (FRICTION) LIMITED
Registration no: 00823338 **VAT No.:** GB 188 1002 73
Date established: 1964 **Turnover:** £1m - £2m **No.of Employees:** 21 - 50
Product Groups: 35, 39

Date of Accounts	Dec 11	Dec 10	Sep 09
Working Capital	600	834	806
Fixed Assets	185	159	415
Current Assets	1m	1m	1m

Kinetico UK Ltd
Bridge House Park Gate Business Centre Chandlers Way, Park Gate, Southampton, SO31 1FQ
Tel: 01489-566970 **Fax:** 01489-566976
E-mail: info@kinetico.co.uk
Website: http://www.kinetico.co.uk
Directors: J. Bisset (Dir), D. Goddard (Dir), I. Goddard (Dir)
Ultimate Holding Company: AXEL JOHNSON INC (USA)
Immediate Holding Company: KINETICO UK LIMITED
Registration no: 02473777 **Date established:** 1990 **Turnover:** £2m - £5m
No.of Employees: 11 - 20 **Product Groups:** 30, 36, 40, 42

Date of Accounts	Dec 11	Dec 10	Dec 09
Working Capital	1m	1m	888
Fixed Assets	77	96	71
Current Assets	2m	2m	1m

L C Kittow Ltd
34 Spear Road, Southampton, SO14 6UH
Tel: 023-8032 2650 **Fax:** 023-8032 2651
E-mail: info@lckittow.com
Directors: K. Kittow (MD), N. Kittow (Dir), S. Hargreaves (Co Sec)
Immediate Holding Company: L.C. KITTOW & CO.LIMITED
Registration no: 00855404 **Date established:** 1965
Turnover: £250,000 - £500,000 **No.of Employees:** 1 - 10
Product Groups: 35, 37, 39

Date of Accounts	Jun 08	Jun 07	Jun 06
Working Capital	-11	-9	20
Fixed Assets	35	37	26
Current Assets	83	60	86
Current Liabilities	94	69	66
Total Share Capital	5	5	5

Lawson H I S
Unit 1 Itchen House 184 Empress Road, Southampton, SO14 0JY
Tel: 023-8072 4775 **Fax:** 023-8072 4779
E-mail: r.brown@lawson-his.co.uk
Website: http://www.lawson-his.co.uk
Bank(s): National Westminster Bank Plc
Managers: R. Brown (I.T. Exec)
Immediate Holding Company: LAWSON H.I.S. LIMITED
Registration no: 00380831 **Date established:** 1943 **Turnover:** £2m - £5m
No.of Employees: 21 - 50 **Product Groups:** 24, 35, 63

Date of Accounts	Jan 12	Jan 11	Jan 10
Working Capital	362	221	171
Fixed Assets	109	123	62
Current Assets	2m	2m	1m

Liftability Ltd
Unit 16 Ensign Way Hamble, Southampton, SO31 4RF
Tel: 023-8045 8444 **Fax:** 023-8045 5584
E-mail: admin@liftabilityltd.com
Website: http://www.liftabilityltd.com
Directors: M. Murley (MD), A. Fenwick (Sales & Mktg)
Immediate Holding Company: LIFTABILITY LIMITED
Registration no: 03782380 **Date established:** 1999
No.of Employees: 11 - 20 **Product Groups:** 35, 39, 45

Date of Accounts	Jun 12	Jun 11	Jun 10
Working Capital	251	291	244
Fixed Assets	73	17	38
Current Assets	462	556	587
Current Liabilities	N/A	N/A	2

Lightning Electrical Construction Ltd
Lec House Ringwood Road, Woodlands, Southampton, SO40 7GX
Tel: 023-8086 5890 **Fax:** 023-8086 6876
E-mail: general@lightninggroup.co.uk
Website: http://www.lightninggroup.co.uk
Bank(s): HSBC
Directors: M. Harkins (Co Sec)
Immediate Holding Company: LIGHTNING ELECTRICAL CONSTRUCTION LIMITED
Registration no: 02107966 **VAT No.:** GB 658 8262 90
Date established: 1987 **Turnover:** £10m - £20m
No.of Employees: 101 - 250 **Product Groups:** 52

Date of Accounts	Oct 10	Oct 09	Oct 08
Pre Tax Profit/Loss	N/A	N/A	1m
Working Capital	2m	1m	1m
Fixed Assets	84	94	61
Current Assets	3m	3m	5m
Current Liabilities	N/A	N/A	2m

Lynden Micros Ltd
Unit 4 Copse Business Centre Hounsdown Business Park Bulls Copse Road, Totton, Southampton, SO40 9LR
Tel: 023-8066 3200 **Fax:** 023-8086 4659
E-mail: j.futter@lynden.co.uk
Website: http://www.lynden.co.uk
Directors: J. Futter (MD)
Immediate Holding Company: LYNDEN MICROS LIMITED
Registration no: 01397234 **VAT No.:** GB 225 1686 69
Date established: 1978 **Turnover:** Up to £250,000
No.of Employees: 1 - 10 **Product Groups:** 37

Date of Accounts	Oct 11	Oct 10	Oct 09
Sales Turnover	162	124	200
Pre Tax Profit/Loss	10	-24	21
Working Capital	9	2	51
Fixed Assets	6	6	7
Current Assets	63	47	91
Current Liabilities	4	3	12

Lyndhurst Plastic Fabrication
Unit A Liners Industrial Estate Pitt Road, Southampton, SO15 3FQ
Tel: 023-8021 2170 **Fax:** 023-8021 2173
E-mail: lpf.uk@tiscali.co.uk
Website: http://www.lyndhurstplasticfabrication.com
Directors: P. Lightfoot (Prop)
Immediate Holding Company: ANDREOU ENTERPRISES LTD
Date established: 2011 **No.of Employees:** 1 - 10 **Product Groups:** 30, 48, 49, 66, 84

Date of Accounts	Feb 12
Working Capital	1
Fixed Assets	5
Current Assets	1

M G H Interiors
111 Mousehole Lane, Southampton, SO18 4TA
Tel: 023-8067 2245
E-mail: sales@southamptonceilings.co.uk
Website: http://www.ceilingsdryliningpartitions.co.uk
Directors: M. Galysa (Dir)
Immediate Holding Company: MGH INTERIORS LIMITED
Registration no: 06411093 **Date established:** 2007 **Turnover:**
No.of Employees: 1 - 10 **Product Groups:** 25, 30, 33, 35, 52

Date of Accounts	Apr 11	Apr 10	Apr 09
Working Capital	19	-5	-4
Fixed Assets	6	6	10
Current Assets	25	-5	N/A

M Squared Instrumentation
Unit 36d New Forest Enterprise Centre Chapel Lane, Totton, Southampton, SO40 9LA
Tel: 023-8086 8393 **Fax:** 023-8066 7720
E-mail: sales@msquaredinst.co.uk
Website: http://www.msquaredinst.co.uk
Directors: M. Miller (Prop)
VAT No.: 568 3462 11 **Date established:** 1992 **Turnover:** Up to £250,000
No.of Employees: 1 - 10 **Product Groups:** 37, 38

Mac Signs
49 Long Lane Holbury, Southampton, SO45 2LG
Tel: 023-8089 2228 **Fax:** 023-8089 9268
E-mail: info@mac-signs.co.uk
Website: http://www.mac-signs.co.uk
Directors: N. Mcmorran (Prop)
Immediate Holding Company: MAC SIGNS UK LTD
Registration no: 06336676 **Date established:** 2007
No.of Employees: 1 - 10 **Product Groups:** 30, 39, 40

Mach Engineering Ltd
4 Bury Farm Curbridge, Botley, Southampton, SO30 2HB
Tel: 01489-790791 **Fax:** 01489-790117
E-mail: m.ward@traffordhall.com
Website: http://www.mach-eng.co.uk
Directors: M. Ward (MD), R. Ward (Co Sec)
Immediate Holding Company: MACH LTD
Registration no: 02845199 **Date established:** 1993
No.of Employees: 1 - 10 **Product Groups:** 48

Machine Mart Ltd
516-518 Portswood Road, Southampton, SO17 3SP
Tel: 023-8055 7788 **Fax:** 023-8067 8824
Website: http://www.machinemart.co.uk
Managers: L. Sinkinson (Asst Gen Mgr)
Immediate Holding Company: MACHINE MART LIMITED
Registration no: 01555925 **Date established:** 1981
Turnover: £50m - £75m **No.of Employees:** 1 - 10 **Product Groups:** 40

Date of Accounts	May 11	May 10	May 09
Sales Turnover	67m	64m	56m
Pre Tax Profit/Loss	11m	11m	9m
Working Capital	61m	53m	27m
Fixed Assets	4m	5m	5m
Current Assets	68m	59m	51m
Current Liabilities	3m	3m	21m

Magenta Chemicals
Golf Course Road, Southampton, SO16 7LE
Tel: 023-8076 8842 **Fax:** 023-8076 6460
E-mail: magentachemicals@btclick.com
Directors: M. Shepherd (MD), G. Shepherd (Fin)
Immediate Holding Company: MAGENTA CHEMICALS LIMITED
Registration no: 03611806 **Date established:** 1998
No.of Employees: 1 - 10 **Product Groups:** 31, 61, 66

Date of Accounts	Sep 11	Sep 10	Sep 09
Working Capital	47	44	49
Current Assets	126	119	91

Majortek Components Ltd
Netley Firs Kanes Hill, Southampton, SO19 6AJ
Tel: 023-8040 5276 **Fax:** 023-8040 2873
E-mail: sales@majortek.co.uk
Website: http://www.majortek.co.uk
Directors: M. Renshaw (Fin)
Immediate Holding Company: MAJORTEK COMPONENTS LIMITED
Registration no: 02654801 **Date established:** 1991
Turnover: £500,000 - £1m **No.of Employees:** 1 - 10 **Product Groups:** 37

Date of Accounts	Sep 11	Sep 10	Sep 08
Working Capital	-7	9	-4
Fixed Assets	8	11	5
Current Assets	56	64	51

Mansell Construction Services Ltd
Roman House Salisbury Road, Totton, Southampton, SO40 3XF
Tel: 023-8058 0400 **Fax:** 023-8058 0401
E-mail: southampton@mansell.plc.uk
Website: http://www.mansell.plc.uk
Directors: B. Kingwill (MD)
Managers: A. Jackson (Buyer)
Ultimate Holding Company: BALFOUR BEATTY PLC
Immediate Holding Company: MANSELL CONSTRUCTION SERVICES LIMITED
Registration no: 01197246 **Date established:** 1975
Turnover: £20m - £50m **No.of Employees:** 101 - 250 **Product Groups:** 52

Date of Accounts	Dec 11	Dec 10	Dec 09
Sales Turnover	868m	772m	859m
Pre Tax Profit/Loss	14m	15m	20m
Working Capital	86m	85m	102m
Fixed Assets	37m	38m	32m
Current Assets	379m	383m	366m
Current Liabilities	232m	258m	248m

Maplin Electronics Ltd
10 - 11 East Bargate, Southampton, SO14 2DL
Tel: 08432-277365
E-mail: customercare@maplin.co.uk
Website: http://www.maplin.co.uk

Managers: M. Hayes (Mgr)
Ultimate Holding Company: MONTAGU PRIVATE EQUITY LLP
Immediate Holding Company: MAPLIN ELECTRONICS LIMITED
Registration no: 01264385 **Date established:** 1976
Turnover: £125m - £250m **No.of Employees:** 21 - 50
Product Groups: 37, 61

Date of Accounts	Dec 11	Dec 08	Dec 09
Sales Turnover	205m	204m	204m
Pre Tax Profit/Loss	25m	32m	35m
Working Capital	118m	49m	75m
Fixed Assets	27m	28m	28m
Current Assets	207m	108m	142m
Current Liabilities	78m	51m	59m

Maplin Electronics Ltd

46-48 Bevois Valley Road, Southampton, SO14 0JR
Tel: 08432-277302 **Fax:** 023-8033 9150
E-mail: customercare@maplin.co.uk
Website: http://www.maplin.co.uk
Managers: M. Lyons (Mgr)
Ultimate Holding Company: MONTAGU PRIVATE EQUITY LLP
Immediate Holding Company: MAPLIN ELECTRONICS LIMITED
Registration no: 01264385 **Date established:** 1976
Turnover: £125m - £250m **No.of Employees:** 1 - 10 **Product Groups:** 37, 61

Date of Accounts	Dec 11	Dec 08	Dec 09
Sales Turnover	205m	204m	204m
Pre Tax Profit/Loss	25m	32m	35m
Working Capital	118m	49m	75m
Fixed Assets	27m	28m	28m
Current Assets	207m	108m	142m
Current Liabilities	78m	51m	59m

Marathon Microfilming Ltd

St Marys Place, Southampton, SO14 3HY
Tel: 023-8022 0481 **Fax:** 023-8023 0452
E-mail: info@marathonmicro.com
Website: http://www.marathonmicro.com
Directors: K. Cantwell (MD)
Immediate Holding Company: MARATHON MICROFILMING LIMITED
Registration no: 01659256 **Date established:** 1982
Turnover: £500m - £1,000m **No.of Employees:** 11 - 20
Product Groups: 38, 81

Date of Accounts	Jun 11	Jun 10	Jun 09
Working Capital	6	-65	-42
Fixed Assets	25	35	47
Current Assets	209	118	129

Marine Electronic Systems

Unit 14 Westwood Court Brunel Road, Totton, Southampton, SO40 3WX
Tel: 023-8066 3316 **Fax:** 023-8066 3241
E-mail: mike@mesuk.com
Website: http://www.mesuk.com
Bank(s): The Royal Bank of Scotland
Directors: M. Whitlock (MD)
Ultimate Holding Company: J.M. WHITLOCK LIMITED
Immediate Holding Company: MARINE ELECTRONIC SYSTEMS LIMITED
Registration no: 01316635 **VAT No.:** GB 293 5749 14
Date established: 1977 **Turnover:** £1m - £2m **No.of Employees:** 11 - 20
Product Groups: 37

Date of Accounts	Mar 11	Mar 10	Mar 09
Working Capital	1m	304	478
Fixed Assets	14	13	16
Current Assets	2m	1m	1m

Marquis Motorhomes

Winchester Road Upham, Southampton, SO32 1HA
Tel: 01489-860666 **Fax:** 01489-860752
E-mail: sales@marquismotorhomes.co.uk
Website: http://www.marquismotorhomes.co.uk
Bank(s): Barclays
Directors: T. Willoughby (Fin), M. Crouch (MD), A. Buckwell (Sales)
Managers: A. Brand (Mktg Serv Mgr)
Registration no: 01415591 **VAT No.:** GB 631 8627 35
Turnover: £10m - £20m **No.of Employees:** 21 - 50 **Product Groups:** 39

Martin's Rubber Co. Ltd

Orchard Place, Southampton, SO14 3PE
Tel: 023-8022 6330 **Fax:** 023-8063 1577
E-mail: sales@martins-rubber.co.uk
Website: http://www.martins-rubber.co.uk
Directors: P. Hooper (Dir), S. Williamson (Mkt Research)
Managers: R. Doyle (Personnel), S. Bowring, P. Elliott (Purch Mgr), P. Hardy (Sales Prom Mgr), T. Hunt, T. Hunt (Tech Serv Mgr), C. Ford, K. Folland
Ultimate Holding Company: MARTIN'S GROUP LIMITED
Immediate Holding Company: MARTINS RUBBER COMPANY LIMITED
Registration no: 00275978 **Date established:** 1933 **Turnover:** £2m - £5m
No.of Employees: 21 - 50 **Product Groups:** 25, 29, 30, 33, 36, 40, 42, 63, 66

Date of Accounts	Mar 12	Mar 11	Mar 10
Working Capital	448	159	20
Fixed Assets	196	86	94
Current Assets	894	686	522

Mechtech Valve Services

33 Pennycress Locks Heath, Southampton, SO31 6SY
Tel: 01489-609609 **Fax:** 01489- 609610
Website: http://www.mechtechvalveservices.com
Managers: L. Davies (Mgr)
Date established: 1998 **No.of Employees:** 1 - 10 **Product Groups:** 36, 37, 38

Mitchells Worktops

Third Avenue, Southampton, SO15 0LD
Tel: 023-8077 1004 **Fax:** 023-8070 4736
E-mail: sales@mitchellsworktops.co.uk
Website: http://www.mitchellsworktops.co.uk
Bank(s): Barclays
Directors: A. Mitchell (MD), S. Mitchell (Fin)
Immediate Holding Company: MITCHELLS (MILLBROOK) LIMITED
Registration no: 00440743 **VAT No.:** GB 188 2126 50
Date established: 1947 **Turnover:** Up to £250,000
No.of Employees: 11 - 20 **Product Groups:** 26, 48

Date of Accounts	Sep 11	Sep 10	Sep 09
Working Capital	1m	1m	929
Fixed Assets	93	84	112
Current Assets	2m	1m	1m

Moore Blatch

11 The Avenue, Southampton, SO17 1XF
Tel: 023-8071 8000 **Fax:** 023-8033 2205
E-mail: david.thompson@mooreblatch.com
Website: http://www.mooreblatch.com
Directors: D. Thompson (MD)
Immediate Holding Company: MOORE BLATCH LIMITED
Registration no: 02693831 **Date established:** 1992 **Turnover:** £5m - £10m
No.of Employees: 51 - 100 **Product Groups:** 80

Multilift Sales

24 Clifton Road Regents Park, Southampton, SO15 4GX
Tel: 023-8077 2325 **Fax:** 023-8032 0732
E-mail: info@multiliftsales.co.uk
Website: http://www.multiliftsales.co.uk
Directors: P. Harvey (Prop)
Date established: 1999 **No.of Employees:** 1 - 10 **Product Groups:** 35, 39, 45

Navimo UK Ltd

Hamilton Business Park Botley Road, Hedge End, Southampton, SO30 2HE
Tel: 01489-778850 **Fax:** 0870-751 1950
E-mail: stephen.pusey@navimo.co.uk
Website: http://www.plastimo.com
Bank(s): Lloyds
Directors: P. Callus (MD), A. Lesaffre (Dir)
Managers: S. Pusey (Comptroller)
Ultimate Holding Company: FINANCIERE NAVIMO SA (FRANCE)
Immediate Holding Company: NAVIMO UK LIMITED
Registration no: 01255245 **VAT No.:** GB 189 9394 81
Date established: 1976 **Turnover:** £5m - £10m **No.of Employees:** 21 - 50
Product Groups: 35, 68, 74

Date of Accounts	Sep 10	Sep 09	Sep 08
Sales Turnover	9m	9m	10m
Pre Tax Profit/Loss	-312	-2m	-953
Working Capital	-554	422	2m
Fixed Assets	25	20	672
Current Assets	2m	3m	4m
Current Liabilities	196	204	307

Neatafan

Solent Industrial Estate Hedge End, Southampton, SO30 2FX
Tel: 01489-783783 **Fax:** 01489-788048
E-mail: sales@neatafan.co.uk
Website: http://www.neatafan.co.uk
Directors: K. Shafford (Sales), P. Daw (MD)
Immediate Holding Company: NEATAFAN LIMITED
Registration no: 01742171 **Date established:** 1983 **Turnover:** £1m - £2m
No.of Employees: 11 - 20 **Product Groups:** 37, 38, 40

Date of Accounts	Sep 11	Sep 10	Sep 09
Working Capital	90	55	176
Fixed Assets	42	47	38
Current Assets	391	399	533

New Air Southern Ltd

Compass Point Ensign Way, Hamble, Southampton, SO31 4RA
Tel: 023-8060 5960 **Fax:** 023-8060 5968
E-mail: info@newair.co.uk
Website: http://www.newair.co.uk
Directors: G. Hancock (MD)
Immediate Holding Company: NEW AIR SOUTHERN LIMITED
Registration no: 01393494 **Date established:** 1978
Turnover: £500,000 - £1m **No.of Employees:** 11 - 20
Product Groups: 40, 52, 66, 83, 84

Date of Accounts	Oct 11	Oct 10	Oct 09
Working Capital	243	221	206
Fixed Assets	309	313	326
Current Assets	384	398	360

Newsquest (Southern)

Test Lane, Southampton, SO16 9JX
Tel: 023-8048 4777 **Fax:** 023-8042 4775
E-mail: newsdesk@dailyecho.co.uk
Website: http://www.dailyecho.co.uk
Bank(s): Lloyds TSB Bank plc
Directors: S. Dunn (MD)
Registration no: 00001350 **VAT No.:** GB 568 3960 92
Turnover: £75m - £125m **No.of Employees:** 101 - 250
Product Groups: 28

Norbert Dentressangle

1b Mauretania Road Nursling, Southampton, SO16 0YS
Tel: 023-8073 0330 **Fax:** 023-8073 8219
E-mail: rowan.fisher@norbert-dentressangle.com
Website: http://www.norbert-dentressangle.com
Managers: R. Fisher
Registration no: SC007173 **No.of Employees:** 51 - 100
Product Groups: 39, 72, 84

O T Systems

74 Larkspur Gardens Old Manor Park, Holbury, Southampton, SO45 2QH
Tel: 023-8089 4545 **Fax:** 023-8089 4545
E-mail: ccb@bctalk.net
Website: http://www.anglefire.com/ok4/otsystems/
Directors: C. Babbs (Prop)
Date established: 1996 **No.of Employees:** 1 - 10 **Product Groups:** 35, 37, 40, 45, 66

Osprey Computer Services Ltd

Unit 40 New Forest Enterprise Centre Chapel Lane, Totton, Southampton, SO40 9LA
Tel: 01794-517979 **Fax:** 01794-517116
E-mail: info@ospreysoftware.co.uk
Website: http://www.ospreycomputerservices.co.uk
Directors: G. Gaunt (Dir)
Immediate Holding Company: OSPREY COMPUTER SERVICES LIMITED
Registration no: 01227255 **Date established:** 1975
Turnover: £250,000 - £500,000 **No.of Employees:** 21 - 50
Product Groups: 44

Date of Accounts	Dec 11	Dec 10	Dec 09
Sales Turnover	N/A	295	280
Pre Tax Profit/Loss	N/A	-17	-40
Working Capital	23	47	55
Fixed Assets	507	474	483
Current Assets	88	64	65
Current Liabilities	N/A	12	2

P E I Genesis UK Ltd

George Curl Way, Southampton, SO18 2RZ
Tel: 08448-716060 **Fax:** 0844-871 6070
E-mail: doug.mercer@peigenesis.co.uk
Website: http://www.peigenesis.co.uk
Managers: T. Houghton (Mgr)
Ultimate Holding Company: PEI GENESIS INC (USA)
Immediate Holding Company: PEI-GENESIS (U.K.) LIMITED
Registration no: 03290190 **Date established:** 1996
Turnover: £10m - £20m **No.of Employees:** 51 - 100 **Product Groups:** 35, 37, 39, 40, 67, 68

Date of Accounts	Aug 11	Aug 10	Aug 09
Sales Turnover	29m	25m	19m
Pre Tax Profit/Loss	1m	158	-1m
Working Capital	2m	320	36
Fixed Assets	1m	1m	1m
Current Assets	11m	9m	6m
Current Liabilities	1m	1m	640

Parmley Graham Ltd

218-220 Barnes Lane Sarisbury Green, Southampton, SO31 7BG
Tel: 01489-570270 **Fax:** 01489-570370
E-mail: soton@parmley-graham.co.uk
Website: http://www.parmley-graham.co.uk
Managers: N. Perry (District Mgr)
Immediate Holding Company: PARMLEY GRAHAM LIMITED
Registration no: 00172842 **VAT No.:** GB 176 7008 54
Date established: 2021 **Turnover:** £2m - £5m **No.of Employees:** 1 - 10
Product Groups: 52

Date of Accounts	Dec 11	Dec 10	Dec 09
Sales Turnover	34m	33m	26m
Pre Tax Profit/Loss	1m	910	353
Working Capital	4m	4m	3m
Fixed Assets	1m	1m	1m
Current Assets	10m	9m	7m
Current Liabilities	1m	900	415

Pfeifer Rope & Tackle Ltd

Unit C2 Marchwood Industrial Park, Marchwood, Southampton, SO40 4BL
Tel: 023-8066 5470 **Fax:** 023-8066 5471
E-mail: sales@ropeandtackle.com
Website: http://www.ropeandtackle.com
Managers: A. Trippick (Chief Mgr), S. Jones (Fin Mgr)
Ultimate Holding Company: PFEIFER HOLDING GMBH & CO KG (GERMANY)
Immediate Holding Company: PFEIFER ROPE AND TACKLE LIMITED
Registration no: 01487274 **Date established:** 1980 **Turnover:** £2m - £5m
No.of Employees: 11 - 20 **Product Groups:** 35, 39, 45

Date of Accounts	Dec 11	Dec 10	Dec 09
Sales Turnover	4m	3m	4m
Pre Tax Profit/Loss	216	133	156
Working Capital	188	155	96
Fixed Assets	66	74	47
Current Assets	1m	1m	1m
Current Liabilities	455	393	545

Phase 3 Plastics

2-4 William Street, Southampton, SO14 5QH
Tel: 023-8022 9844 **Fax:** 023-8023 2928
E-mail: sales@phase3plastics.co.uk
Website: http://www.phase3plastics.co.uk
Directors: P. Lucas (Fin), T. Lucas (MD)
Immediate Holding Company: PHASE 3 PLASTICS LIMITED
Registration no: 01291927 **VAT No.:** GB 293 6033 52
Date established: 1976 **Turnover:** £1m - £2m **No.of Employees:** 11 - 20
Product Groups: 30, 31, 48, 49, 66, 84

Date of Accounts	Jul 11	Jul 10	Jul 09
Working Capital	169	172	71
Fixed Assets	456	473	489
Current Assets	421	427	269

C Phillips

Ridge Farm 323 Woodlands Road, Woodlands, Southampton, SO40 7GE
Tel: 023-8029 3993 **Fax:** 023-8029 3992
Website: http://www.colin-phillips.co.uk
Directors: C. Phillips (Prop)
Date established: 1999 **No.of Employees:** 1 - 10 **Product Groups:** 26, 35

Phoenix Fire Extinguishing Services Ltd

32 Bullar Road, Southampton, SO18 1GS
Tel: 023-8055 8638 **Fax:** 023-8034 9121
Directors: R. Gleeson (MD), J. Gleeson (Fin)
Immediate Holding Company: PHOENIX FIRE EXTINGUISHER SERVICES LIMITED
Registration no: 04776642 **Date established:** 2003
No.of Employees: 1 - 10 **Product Groups:** 38, 42

Date of Accounts	May 11	May 10	May 09
Working Capital	-19	-4	3
Fixed Assets	18	23	21
Current Assets	25	31	25

Pipeline & Construction Supplies Ltd

Unit 2e North Road Marchwood Industrial Park, Marchwood, Southampton, SO40 4BL
Tel: 023-8042 8284 **Fax:** 023-8042 8285
E-mail: admin@pcs-southampton.co.uk
Website: http://www.pcs-southampton.co.uk
Directors: G. Noakes (MD)
Immediate Holding Company: PIPELINE AND CONSTRUCTION SUPPLIES LIMITED
Registration no: 01491599 **VAT No.:** GB 329 0549 52
Date established: 1980 **Turnover:** £2m - £5m **No.of Employees:** 1 - 10
Product Groups: 36

Date of Accounts	Jun 12	Jun 11	Jun 10
Working Capital	629	547	401
Fixed Assets	33	50	46
Current Assets	1m	1m	990

Polimeri Europa Ltd

Cadland Road Hythe, Southampton, SO45 3YY
Tel: 023-8089 4919 **Fax:** 023-8088 3306
E-mail: james.macdonald@polimerieuropa.com
Website: http://www.enichem.it
Bank(s): National Westminster Bank Plc

see next page

***Polimeri Europa Ltd** - Cont'd*

Directors: J. Macdonald (Dir)
Ultimate Holding Company: ENI SPA (ITALY)
Immediate Holding Company: POLIMERI EUROPA UK LIMITED
Registration no: 00557780 **Date established:** 1955
Turnover: £250m - £500m **No.of Employees:** 251 - 500
Product Groups: 31, 32, 63, 66

Date of Accounts	Dec 11	Dec 10	Dec 09
Sales Turnover	270m	218m	163m
Pre Tax Profit/Loss	21m	13m	-2m
Working Capital	19m	12m	6m
Fixed Assets	19m	17m	19m
Current Assets	108m	72m	72m
Current Liabilities	5m	34m	961

Polycast Ltd

Clocktower Buildings Shore Road, Warsash, Southampton, SO31 9GQ
Tel: 01489-885560 **Fax:** 01489-885608
E-mail: sales@polycast.co.uk
Website: http://www.polycast.co.uk
Bank(s): HSBC Bank plc
Directors: G. Harris (Sales), I. Haddon (Fin), D. Sadler (Tech Serv)
Immediate Holding Company: POLYCAST LIMITED
Registration no: 01851411 **VAT No.:** GB 411 4167 93
Date established: 1984 **Turnover:** £1m - £2m **No.of Employees:** 21 - 50
Product Groups: 34, 66

Date of Accounts	Mar 11	Mar 10	Mar 09
Working Capital	315	282	402
Fixed Assets	123	161	209
Current Assets	1m	910	1m

Portmere Rubber Ltd

Victoria Street Northam, Southampton, SO14 5QZ
Tel: 023-8022 3628 **Fax:** 023-8022 3250
E-mail: sales@portmererubber.co.uk
Website: http://www.portmererubber.co.uk
Bank(s): The Royal Bank of Scotland
Directors: K. Fisher (MD)
Immediate Holding Company: PORTMERE RUBBER LIMITED
Registration no: 01237764 **Date established:** 1975 **Turnover:** £1m - £2m
No.of Employees: 11 - 20 **Product Groups:** 29, 49, 63

Date of Accounts	Sep 11	Sep 10	Sep 09
Working Capital	224	181	126
Fixed Assets	64	62	46
Current Assets	502	407	417
Current Liabilities	19	33	41

Power Accountax - Accountants For Contractors In Southampton

8c High Street, Southampton, SO14 2DH
Tel: 08444-150944 **Fax:** 0844-415 0925
E-mail: services@poweraccountax.co.uk
Website: http://www.poweraccountax.co.uk
Managers: O. Kohli
Immediate Holding Company: POWER ACCOUNT LIMITED
Registration no: 04342341 **Date established:** 2001
Turnover: Up to £250,000 **No.of Employees:** 1 - 10 **Product Groups:** 80

Date of Accounts	Mar 11	Mar 10	Mar 09
Working Capital	82	86	85
Fixed Assets	1	N/A	N/A
Current Assets	161	151	134

Precise Electro Plating Works Ltd

Pitt Road, Southampton, SO15 3FQ
Tel: 023-8022 8014 **Fax:** 023-8022 8114
Directors: A. Samways (MD)
Immediate Holding Company: PRECISE ELECTRO-PLATING WORKS LIMITED
Registration no: 00611593 **VAT No.:** GB 188 1598 14
Date established: 1958 **Turnover:** £250,000 - £500,000
No.of Employees: 1 - 10 **Product Groups:** 48

Date of Accounts	Dec 11	Dec 10	Dec 09
Working Capital	270	280	277
Fixed Assets	31	36	41
Current Assets	344	345	316

Pro-Fix Access

Pylands Lane Bursledon, Southampton, SO31 1BH
Tel: 023-8040 4411 **Fax:** 023-8040 4422
E-mail: info@profixaccess.co.uk
Website: http://www.profixaccess.co.uk
Directors: S. Lewis (Fin), A. Harris (Dir)
Immediate Holding Company: PRO-FIX ACCESS LIMITED
Registration no: 03192365 **Date established:** 1996 **Turnover:** £1m - £2m
No.of Employees: 1 - 10 **Product Groups:** 35

Date of Accounts	Mar 11	Mar 10	Mar 09
Working Capital	58	49	151
Fixed Assets	76	49	57
Current Assets	109	170	201

Progressive Product Developments Ltd

24 Beacon Bottom Park Gate, Southampton, SO31 7GQ
Tel: 01489-576787 **Fax:** 01489-578463
E-mail: sales@ppd-ltd.com
Website: http://www.ppd-ltd.com
Directors: W. Carr (MD)
Immediate Holding Company: PROGRESSIVE PRODUCT DEVELOPMENTS LTD.
Registration no: 02244254 **Date established:** 1988
No.of Employees: 1 - 10 **Product Groups:** 30, 33, 36, 40, 42, 67

Date of Accounts	Mar 12	Mar 11	Mar 10
Working Capital	76	76	79
Fixed Assets	1	6	12
Current Assets	112	102	124

R.B.Scientific

PO Box 5, Southampton, SO30 2WG
Tel: 023-8040 6787 **Fax:** 023-8040 6787
E-mail: sales@rbscientific.co.uk
Website: http://www.rbscientific.co.uk
Directors: R. Bowen (Prop)
No.of Employees: 1 - 10 **Product Groups:** 26, 38, 40, 42, 67

R K Marine

Hamble River Boat Yard Bridge Road, Swanwick, Southampton, SO31 7EB
Tel: 01489-583572 **Fax:** 01489-583172
E-mail: info@rkmarine.co.uk
Website: http://www.rkmarine.co.uk
Bank(s): Nat West
Directors: N. Kimish (Prop)
Immediate Holding Company: R. K. MARINE LIMITED
Registration no: 02226134 **VAT No.:** GB 458 9853 78
Date established: 1988 **Turnover:** £1m - £2m **No.of Employees:** 11 - 20
Product Groups: 84

Date of Accounts	Nov 11	Nov 10	Nov 09
Working Capital	2m	2m	2m
Fixed Assets	232	167	119
Current Assets	2m	2m	2m

R & M Electrical Group Ltd

Unit 1 Central Trading Estate Marine Parade, Southampton, SO14 5JP
Tel: 023-8023 1800 **Fax:** 01425-471012
E-mail: sales@rm-electrical.com
Website: http://www.rm-electrical.com
Managers: M. Shortridge (District Mgr)
Immediate Holding Company: R & M ELECTRICAL GROUP LIMITED
Registration no: 02218034 **Date established:** 1988
No.of Employees: 11 - 20 **Product Groups:** 51, 52, 67, 84

Date of Accounts	Apr 12	Apr 11	Apr 10
Sales Turnover	62m	48m	38m
Pre Tax Profit/Loss	2m	753	557
Working Capital	3m	2m	2m
Fixed Assets	4m	2m	2m
Current Assets	14m	12m	10m
Current Liabilities	3m	2m	2m

R S Components Ltd - Trade Counter

Unit 6 Flanders Industrial Park, Hedge End, Southampton, SO30 2FZ
Tel: 01489-789890 **Fax:** 01489-780567
E-mail: rsint@rs-components.com
Website: http://www.rswww.com
Managers: B. Percy (Mgr)
Immediate Holding Company: RS COMPONENTS LIMITED
Registration no: 01002091 **Date established:** 1971
Turnover: £250m - £500m **No.of Employees:** 1 - 10 **Product Groups:** 67

Red Funnel Ferries Ltd

12 Bugle Street, Southampton, SO14 2JY
Tel: 08704-448898 **Fax:** 0844-844 2698
E-mail: post@redfunnel.co.uk
Website: http://www.redfunnel.co.uk
Bank(s): Lloyds
Directors: S. Anderson (Pers)
Ultimate Holding Company: PRUDENTIAL PUBLIC LIMITED COMPANY
Immediate Holding Company: RED FUNNEL FERRIES LIMITED
Registration no: 04281782 **VAT No.:** GB 188 2184 36
Date established: 2001 **Turnover:** £20m - £50m
No.of Employees: 251 - 500 **Product Groups:** 74

Date of Accounts	Dec 09	Dec 08
Working Capital	-13	-13
Fixed Assets	72m	72m
Current Assets	11m	11m

Reed Insurance

9 High Street, Southampton, SO14 2DH
Tel: 023-8023 4346 **Fax:** 023-8063 1897
E-mail: nicola@reed.co.uk
Website: http://www.reedglobal.com
Directors: C. Lloyd (MD)
Managers: A. Montgomerie (Mgr), G. Sofokleous (District Mgr), N. Halle (District Mgr)
Immediate Holding Company: L&E Title Group Ltd
Registration no: 04459633 **No.of Employees:** 1 - 10 **Product Groups:** 80

Reed Specialist Recruitment

51-67 Commercial Road, Southampton, SO15 1GG
Tel: 023-8063 1896 **Fax:** 023-8063 1897
E-mail: southampton.employment@reed.co.uk
Website: http://www.reed.co.uk
Managers: J. Mason (Comm)
Ultimate Holding Company: REED GLOBAL LTD (MALTA)
Immediate Holding Company: REED EMPLOYMENT LIMITED
Registration no: 00669854 **Date established:** 1960
Turnover: £250m - £500m **No.of Employees:** 1 - 10 **Product Groups:** 80

Date of Accounts	Jun 11	Jun 10	Dec 07
Sales Turnover	618	450	287m
Pre Tax Profit/Loss	-2m	310	8m
Working Capital	23m	28m	28m
Fixed Assets	31	36	5m
Current Assets	28m	30m	74m
Current Liabilities	37	29	21m

Rigmasters UK Ltd

Unit 14 City Commerce Centre Marsh Lane, Southampton, SO14 3EW
Tel: 023-8051 1929 **Fax:** 023-8077 2510
E-mail: info@rigmasters.co.uk
Website: http://www.rigmasters.co.uk
Directors: J. Mieth (Prop)
Immediate Holding Company: RIGMASTERS (UK) LIMITED
Registration no: 06193021 **Date established:** 2007
No.of Employees: 1 - 10 **Product Groups:** 23, 49

Date of Accounts	Mar 11	Mar 10	Mar 09
Sales Turnover	N/A	102	128
Pre Tax Profit/Loss	N/A	25	41
Working Capital	41	30	20
Fixed Assets	5	6	8
Current Assets	66	59	52
Current Liabilities	N/A	22	23

Robert Half Ltd

Oceana House 39-49 Commercial Road, Southampton, SO15 1GA
Tel: 023-8071 8900 **Fax:** 01202-786550
E-mail: sales@accounttemps.net
Website: http://www.roberthalf.co.uk
Managers: R. Blythin (District Mgr)
Ultimate Holding Company: ROBERT HALF INTERNATIONAL INC (USA)
Immediate Holding Company: ROBERT HALF LIMITED
Registration no: 02087139 **VAT No.:** GB 355 7994 96
Date established: 1987 **Turnover:** Up to £250,000
No.of Employees: 11 - 20 **Product Groups:** 80

Date of Accounts	Dec 11	Dec 10	Dec 09
Sales Turnover	96m	91m	94m
Pre Tax Profit/Loss	-857	-896	1m
Working Capital	13m	14m	13m
Fixed Assets	2m	1m	1m
Current Assets	30m	27m	25m
Current Liabilities	9m	9m	8m

S & S Diesel Services

Winchester Road Waltham Chase, Southampton, SO32 2LL
Tel: 01489-895244 **Fax:** 01489-894647
E-mail: info@ss-diesel-services.co.uk
Website: http://www.ss-diesel-services.co.uk
Directors: C. Smith (Fin)
Immediate Holding Company: S & S DIESEL SERVICES LTD
Registration no: 06364496 **Date established:** 2007
No.of Employees: 1 - 10 **Product Groups:** 40

Date of Accounts	Sep 11	Sep 10	Sep 09
Working Capital	20	16	-3
Fixed Assets	83	50	57
Current Assets	132	116	107

S S F Design

44 Botley Gardens, Southampton, SO19 0SW
Tel: 023-8040 4818
E-mail: info@ssfdesign.com
Website: http://www.SSFdesign.com
Directors: S. Brown (Prop), S. Felton (Dir)
Date established: 2006 **Turnover:** Up to £250,000
No.of Employees: 1 - 10 **Product Groups:** 24, 44

Sadler Energy & Environmental Services Ltd

Suite 3 Kingfisher House, North Baddesley, Southampton, SO52 9LP
Tel: 023-8073 0311 **Fax:** 023-8000 0311
E-mail: enquiries@sadlerenergy.co.uk
Website: http://www.sadlerenergy.co.uk
Directors: N. Sadler (Dir)
Immediate Holding Company: SADLER ENERGY AND ENVIRONMENTAL SERVICES LIMITED
Registration no: 06548294 **Date established:** 2008
Turnover: Up to £250,000 **No.of Employees:** 1 - 10 **Product Groups:** 84

Date of Accounts	Mar 11	Mar 10	Mar 09
Working Capital	5	8	2
Fixed Assets	9	9	9
Current Assets	58	33	25

St. Clare Engineering Ltd (Grab-O-Matic)

Unit 4 Trinity Industrial Est Millbrook Road West, Southampton, SO15 0LA
Tel: 023-8051 0770 **Fax:** 023-8051 0772
Website: http://www.stclare-engineering.co.uk
Managers: M. Bow, A. Bow
Registration no: 00619491 **VAT No.:** GB 736 9267 93
Date established: 1958 **Turnover:** £250,000 - £500,000
No.of Employees: 1 - 10 **Product Groups:** 35, 38, 43, 45, 61, 67, 83, 84

Date of Accounts	Dec 08	Dec 07	Dec 06
Working Capital	91	73	46
Fixed Assets	1	1	3
Current Assets	143	141	113
Current Liabilities	52	68	66
Total Share Capital	2	2	2

St Cross Electronics Ltd

14 Mount Pleasant Industrial Estate Mount Pleasant Road, Southampton, SO14 0SP
Tel: 023-8022 7636 **Fax:** 023-8033 1769
E-mail: sales@st-cross-electronics.co.uk
Website: http://www.st-cross-electronics.co.uk
Directors: D. Ward (MD)
Managers: K. Brooks (Purch Mgr), S. Lacey (Comptroller)
Ultimate Holding Company: ST. CROSS HOLDINGS LIMITED
Immediate Holding Company: ST. CROSS ELECTRONICS LIMITED
Registration no: 01810453 **VAT No.:** GB 330 1581 01
Date established: 1984 **Turnover:** £1m - £2m **No.of Employees:** 21 - 50
Product Groups: 37

Date of Accounts	Dec 11	Dec 10	Dec 09
Working Capital	129	231	223
Fixed Assets	37	32	18
Current Assets	577	507	381

Sallco Tools Ltd

3-4 Baddesley Park Industrial Estate Botley Road, North Baddesley, Southampton, SO52 9NW
Tel: 023-8073 7355 **Fax:** 023-8073 8647
E-mail: sales@sallcotools.co.uk
Website: http://www.sallcotools.co.uk
Directors: E. Clark (Fin), S. Nolan (MD)
Immediate Holding Company: SALLCO TOOLS LIMITED
Registration no: 03102495 **Date established:** 1995
No.of Employees: 1 - 10 **Product Groups:** 37

Date of Accounts	Sep 11	Sep 10	Sep 09
Working Capital	-5	5	8
Fixed Assets	12	16	21
Current Assets	212	239	222

Sea Power Ltd

Hamble Point Marina School Lane, Hamble, Southampton, SO31 4JD
Tel: 023-8045 4333 **Fax:** 023-8045 4333
E-mail: info@seapower.ltd.uk
Website: http://www.seapower.ltd.uk
Managers: J. Phillips (Mgr)
Immediate Holding Company: SEA POWER LIMITED
Registration no: 02764754 **Date established:** 1992
Turnover: £250,000 - £500,000 **No.of Employees:** 1 - 10
Product Groups: 35, 36, 39

Date of Accounts	Jan 12	Jan 11	Jan 10
Sales Turnover	N/A	N/A	318
Pre Tax Profit/Loss	N/A	N/A	35
Working Capital	264	243	236
Fixed Assets	N/A	N/A	3
Current Assets	364	265	265
Current Liabilities	N/A	N/A	19

Sea Start Ltd

Unit 13 Hamble Point Marina School Lane, Hamble, Southampton, SO31 4JD
Tel: 023-8045 8000 **Fax:** 023-8045 2666
E-mail: sales@seastart.co.uk
Website: http://www.seastart.co.uk
Directors: N. Eales (MD), R. Curry (Co Sec)
Immediate Holding Company: SEA START LIMITED
Registration no: 03822209 **Date established:** 1999
No.of Employees: 1 - 10 **Product Groups:** 35, 36, 39

Date of Accounts	Oct 11	Oct 10	Oct 09
Working Capital	-16	-14	-43
Fixed Assets	190	190	195
Current Assets	114	116	76

Seatallan Ltd
Unit 1 Calcot Calcot Lane, Curdridge, Southampton, SO32 2BN
Tel: 01489-790049 **Fax:** 01489-790040
E-mail: enquiries@seatallan.com
Website: http://www.seatallan.com
Directors: R. Muttitt (MD)
Immediate Holding Company: SEATALLAN ENGINEERING LTD
Registration no: 04153925 **Date established:** 2001
Turnover: Up to £250,000 **No.of Employees:** 1 - 10 **Product Groups:** 38, 44

Date of Accounts	Mar 11	Mar 10	Mar 09
Working Capital	-22	-27	-14
Fixed Assets	67	81	97
Current Assets	76	72	69
Current Liabilities	N/A	17	12

Sensus UK Systems
International House George Curl Way, Southampton, SO18 2RZ
Tel: 01794-526100 **Fax:** 01794-526101
E-mail: jamie.longman@sensus.com
Website: http://www.sensus.com
Managers: J. Longman (Chief Mgr)
Immediate Holding Company: COURIER FREIGHT LOGISTICS LTD
Registration no: 02621960 **Date established:** 2009
Turnover: £10m - £20m **No.of Employees:** 1 - 10 **Product Groups:** 38

Date of Accounts	Mar 11
Working Capital	-40
Fixed Assets	3
Current Assets	3

Series 4 Ltd
9 Westwood Court Caomoor Industrial Estate, Totton, Southampton, SO40 3WX
Tel: 023-8086 6377 **Fax:** 023-8086 6323
E-mail: info@series4.co.uk
Website: http://www.series4.co.uk
Directors: N. Mcclure (Fin)
Immediate Holding Company: SERIES 4 LIMITED
Registration no: 02292503 **VAT No.:** GB 504 4674 57
Date established: 1988 **Turnover:** £1m - £2m **No.of Employees:** 1 - 10
Product Groups: 61, 67

Date of Accounts	Dec 10	Dec 09	Dec 08
Working Capital	336	398	510
Fixed Assets	441	462	424
Current Assets	444	467	648

Sholing Ornamental Ironwork
5 Drove Road, Southampton, SO19 8GL
Tel: 023-8077 5550 **Fax:** 023-8077 5550
Directors: W. Knott (Prop)
Date established: 1974 **No.of Employees:** 1 - 10 **Product Groups:** 26, 35

Shoreheat Ltd
2c Herald Industrial Estate Hedge End, Southampton, SO30 2JW
Tel: 01489-781456 **Fax:** 01489-785939
Website: http://www.shoreheat.co.uk
Managers: J. Saunders
Ultimate Holding Company: PROGRESS GROUP LIMITED
Immediate Holding Company: SHOREHEAT LIMITED
Registration no: 01566154 **VAT No.:** GB 484 6088 12
Date established: 1981 **Turnover:** £5m - £10m **No.of Employees:** 1 - 10
Product Groups: 36, 38, 40

Date of Accounts	Dec 10	Dec 09	Dec 08
Sales Turnover	17m	13m	14m
Pre Tax Profit/Loss	540	327	393
Working Capital	2m	2m	2m
Fixed Assets	461	505	481
Current Assets	6m	6m	5m
Current Liabilities	480	388	504

Simplefit Ltd
Marchwood Industrial Estate 4w Normandy Way, Marchwood, Southampton, SO40 4PB
Tel: 023-8066 3210 **Fax:** 023-8066 3086
E-mail: ian.macdonald@simplefit.co.uk
Website: http://www.simplefit.co.uk
Bank(s): Barclays Bank
Directors: K. Jay (Fin), J. Macdonald (MD)
Managers: M. Lysandrides (Sales & Mktg Mg), R. Gibbens
Immediate Holding Company: SIMPLEFIT LIMITED
Registration no: 01359731 **VAT No.:** GB 329 7653 22
Date established: 1978 **Turnover:** £2m - £5m **No.of Employees:** 51 - 100
Product Groups: 33, 34, 35, 36, 40, 46, 48, 84

Date of Accounts	Apr 12	Apr 11	Apr 10
Working Capital	433	305	288
Fixed Assets	383	441	513
Current Assets	967	887	820

Snows Business Forms Ltd
Manor House Avenue, Southampton, SO15 0DF
Tel: 023-8077 7711 **Fax:** 08456-344330
E-mail: sales@snowsbf.co.uk
Website: http://www.snowsbf.co.uk
Bank(s): Barclays
Directors: L. Cutts (Fin), M. Middleton (Sales), P. Wheeler (Fin)
Managers: A. Osbourne (Tech Serv Mgr), A. Rawling
Ultimate Holding Company: BONDCO 667 LIMITED
Immediate Holding Company: SNOWS BUSINESS FORMS LIMITED
Registration no: 01700975 **VAT No.:** GB 382 6080 48
Date established: 1983 **Turnover:** £2m - £5m **No.of Employees:** 51 - 100
Product Groups: 27

Date of Accounts	Oct 11	Oct 10	Oct 09
Sales Turnover	5m	5m	5m
Pre Tax Profit/Loss	55	41	-145
Working Capital	2m	2m	2m
Fixed Assets	962	951	1m
Current Assets	3m	3m	3m
Current Liabilities	160	164	142

Solent Bearings
20-21 Test Valley Business Centre Test Lane, Southampton, SO16 9JW
Tel: 023-8066 7100 **Fax:** 023-8066 7015
E-mail: sales@solent-bearings.co.uk
Website: http://www.solent-bearings.co.uk
Directors: A. Brown (Prop)
No.of Employees: 1 - 10 **Product Groups:** 35, 39, 66

Solent Sound & Fire Systems Ltd
7 Mitchell Point Ensign Way, Hamble, Southampton, SO31 4RF
Tel: 023-8045 6700 **Fax:** 023-8045 6789
E-mail: sales@solentsound.com
Website: http://www.solentsound.com
Directors: A. Belair (Dir)
Immediate Holding Company: SOLENT SOUND & FIRE SYSTEMS LTD
Registration no: 08032249 **VAT No.:** GB 631 8876 14
Date established: 2012 **No.of Employees:** 1 - 10 **Product Groups:** 37

Date of Accounts	Dec 09	Dec 08	Dec 07
Working Capital	44	60	36
Fixed Assets	29	23	15
Current Assets	138	148	104

South Coast Port Services Ltd
Canute Chambers Ocean Way, Southampton, SO14 3TU
Tel: 023-8023 7051 **Fax:** 023-8023 7648
E-mail: meadley@scps.sagehoust.co.uk
Website: http://www.scps.sagehost.co.uk
Bank(s): Lloyds, Southampton
Directors: M. Eardley (Fin), S. Pearce (Fin)
Managers: S. McCabe (Personnel)
Ultimate Holding Company: CANUTE MANAGEMENT SERVICES LIMITED
Immediate Holding Company: SOUTH COAST PORT SERVICES LIMITED
Registration no: 03847838 **VAT No.:** GB 744 9907 88
Date established: 1999 **Turnover:** £10m - £20m
No.of Employees: 251 - 500 **Product Groups:** 71

Date of Accounts	Dec 11	Dec 10	Dec 09
Sales Turnover	N/A	N/A	14m
Pre Tax Profit/Loss	29	-14	-0
Working Capital	32	-9	18
Fixed Assets	3	4	6
Current Assets	951	981	760
Current Liabilities	895	958	728

Southampton Rubber Stamp Co.
PO Box 271, Southampton, SO45 5XP
Tel: 023-8087 9759 **Fax:** 023-8086 9998
E-mail: sales@southamptonrubberstamp.com
Website: http://www.southamptonrubberstamp.com
Directors: B. Moseley (Prop)
No.of Employees: 1 - 10 **Product Groups:** 30, 49, 64

Southern Calibration Laboratories Ltd
7 Solent Industrial Estate Shamblehurst Lane, Hedge End, Southampton, SO30 2FX
Tel: 01489-790296 **Fax:** 01489-790294
E-mail: info@southcal.co.uk
Website: http://www.southcal.co.uk
Directors: S. Sparks (Dir)
Immediate Holding Company: SOUTHERN CALIBRATION LABORATORIES LIMITED
Registration no: 02483176 **Date established:** 1990
Turnover: £500,000 - £1m **No.of Employees:** 11 - 20 **Product Groups:** 85

Date of Accounts	Apr 12	Apr 11	Apr 10
Working Capital	169	129	118
Fixed Assets	43	31	26
Current Assets	255	202	180
Current Liabilities	57	N/A	N/A

Southern Sheet Metal Ltd
Bury Farm Curbridge Botley, Southampton, SO30 2HB
Tel: 01489-789143 **Fax:** 01489-789069
Website: http://www.southernsheetmetal.co.uk
Directors: M. Sollis (MD)
Immediate Holding Company: SOUTHERN SHEET METAL LIMITED
Registration no: 02085566 **VAT No.:** GB 458 8006 27
Date established: 1986 **Turnover:** £250,000 - £500,000
No.of Employees: 1 - 10 **Product Groups:** 48

Date of Accounts	Dec 11	Dec 10	Dec 09
Working Capital	76	83	80
Fixed Assets	14	15	17
Current Assets	126	155	175

Spar-Tec Engineering Ltd
Port Hamble Satchell Lane, Hamble, Southampton, SO31 4NN
Tel: 023-8045 7444 **Fax:** 023-8045 7444
E-mail: info@spartecengineering.com
Website: http://www.spartecengineering.com
Directors: P. Butt (MD)
Ultimate Holding Company: ANCASTA GROUP LIMITED
Immediate Holding Company: SPAR-TEC ENGINEERING LIMITED
Registration no: 04520401 **Date established:** 2002
No.of Employees: 1 - 10 **Product Groups:** 35

Date of Accounts	Mar 12	Mar 11	Mar 10
Working Capital	2	-8	17
Fixed Assets	19	23	22
Current Assets	73	58	82

Sparkford Chemicals
58 The Avenue, Southampton, SO17 1XS
Tel: 023-8022 8747 **Fax:** 023-8021 0240
E-mail: info@sparkford.co.uk
Website: http://www.sparkford.co.uk
Directors: S. Gibbons (Dir)
Immediate Holding Company: SPARKFORD CHEMICALS LIMITED
Registration no: 00883126 **Date established:** 1966 **Turnover:** £5m - £10m
No.of Employees: 1 - 10 **Product Groups:** 31, 66

Date of Accounts	Jul 11	Jul 10	Jul 09
Working Capital	780	706	608
Fixed Assets	61	50	66
Current Assets	2m	1m	1m

Speedy Lifting Ltd
Unit 10 Central Trading Estate Marine Parade, Southampton, SO14 5JP
Tel: 023-8082 9522 **Fax:** 023-8063 1712
E-mail: southampton-lifting@speedydepos.co.uk
Website: http://www.speedyhire.com
Managers: S. Pearson (Mgr)
Ultimate Holding Company: SPEEDY HIRE PLC
Immediate Holding Company: SPEEDY LIFTING LIMITED
Registration no: 04529136 **Date established:** 2002
No.of Employees: 11 - 20 **Product Groups:** 35, 37, 38, 39, 45, 48, 83

Date of Accounts	Mar 12	Mar 11	Mar 10
Sales Turnover	N/A	N/A	21m
Pre Tax Profit/Loss	N/A	N/A	4m
Working Capital	20m	20m	20m
Current Assets	20m	20m	21m

Stadium Crayons Ltd
Unit 1-5 Muira Off William Street, Southampton, SO14 5QH
Tel: 023-8022 6765 **Fax:** 023-8063 0304
E-mail: sales@stadiumcrayons.co.uk
Website: http://www.stadiumcrayons.co.uk
Bank(s): Lloyds, High St
Managers: T. Maidment (Mgr)
Immediate Holding Company: STADIUM CRAYONS LTD
Registration no: 06771292 **VAT No.:** GB 188 5859 89
Date established: 2008 **Turnover:** £1m - £2m **No.of Employees:** 11 - 20
Product Groups: 49

Date of Accounts	Dec 11	Dec 10	Dec 09
Working Capital	146	20	21
Fixed Assets	7	11	13
Current Assets	245	105	91

Stanelco R F Technologies
Marchwood Industrial Park Marchwood, Southampton, SO40 4PB
Tel: 023-8086 7100 **Fax:** 023-8086 7070
E-mail: info@stanelco.co.uk
Website: http://www.stanelcoplc.com
Directors: P. Mines (Grp Chief Exec)
Ultimate Holding Company: BIOME TECHNOLOGIES PLC
Immediate Holding Company: STANELCO RF TECHNOLOGIES LIMITED
Registration no: 03338752 **Date established:** 1997 **Turnover:** £2m - £5m
No.of Employees: 1 - 10 **Product Groups:** 48

Date of Accounts	Dec 11	Dec 10	Dec 09
Sales Turnover	3m	2m	1m
Pre Tax Profit/Loss	582	411	32
Working Capital	-11m	-12m	-12m
Fixed Assets	515	580	545
Current Assets	1m	2m	1m
Current Liabilities	212	438	12m

Stephens & Stuart Engineering Co. Ltd
Rockingham Works Nutwood Way Totton, Southampton, SO40 3SZ
Tel: 023-8086 3666 **Fax:** 023-8086 3777
E-mail: info@saseng.co.uk
Website: http://www.saseng.co.uk
Directors: L. Wolhom (Dir)
Immediate Holding Company: STEPHENS AND STUARTS ENGINEERING COMPANY LIMITED
Registration no: 01360450 **Date established:** 1978
No.of Employees: 11 - 20 **Product Groups:** 35

Date of Accounts	Dec 11	Dec 10	Dec 09
Working Capital	1m	824	752
Fixed Assets	235	204	183
Current Assets	2m	1m	1m

Sterling Business Ltd
C/o Strategy Matrix Offices, Tradeteam Building, Nutsey Lane Calmore Industrial Estate, Totton, Southampton, SO40 3NB
Tel: 0845-226 0387 **Fax:** 0870-4602981
E-mail: paul@sterlingbusiness.co.uk
Website: http://www.sterlingbusiness.co.uk
Directors: P. Haley (MD)
Registration no: 04408667 **VAT No.:** GB 784 3810 08
Date established: 1902 **Turnover:** Up to £250,000
No.of Employees: 1 - 10 **Product Groups:** 80, 81

Stylefine Clentech Ltd
Unit 117 Solent Business Centre 343 Millbrook Road West, Southampton, SO15 0HW
Tel: 023-8077 0551 **Fax:** 023-8070 1284
Website: http://www.stylefine.co.uk
Directors: P. Argyle (Comm)
Immediate Holding Company: STYLEFINE CLENTECH LIMITED
Registration no: 01644778 **Date established:** 1982
No.of Employees: 1 - 10 **Product Groups:** 46, 48

Date of Accounts	Dec 07	Dec 06	Dec 05
Working Capital	-296	-126	44
Fixed Assets	155	203	264
Current Assets	891	843	748
Current Liabilities	1188	968	704
Total Share Capital	5	5	5

Sub Aqua Products Ltd
Lycroft Farm 8 Upper Swanmore, Swanmore, Southampton, SO32 2QQ
Tel: 01489-878055 **Fax:** 01489-878002
E-mail: info@subaqua-products.com
Website: http://www.subaqua-products.com
Directors: M. Hall (Dir)
Immediate Holding Company: SUB-AQUA PRODUCTS (UK) LIMITED
Registration no: 04881440 **Date established:** 2003
Turnover: £250,000 - £500,000 **No.of Employees:** 1 - 10
Product Groups: 24, 40, 49

Date of Accounts	Oct 11	Oct 10	Oct 08
Working Capital	28	26	31
Fixed Assets	1	N/A	1
Current Assets	72	64	71

Swiftfix Fasteners & Fixing Devices
Unit 8 Mill View Barn Grange Road, Bursledon, Southampton, SO31 8GD
Tel: 023-8044 6644 **Fax:** 023-8049 1842
E-mail: sales@swiftfix.co.uk
Website: http://www.swiftfix.co.uk
Directors: S. Harris (Prop)
No.of Employees: 1 - 10 **Product Groups:** 33, 35, 36

System Insight
PO Box 150, Southampton, SO32 2PN
Tel: 01329-835500 **Fax:** 01329-835501
E-mail: info@systeminsight.co.uk
Website: http://www.systeminsight.co.uk
Directors: S. Morley (Prop)
Immediate Holding Company: SYSTEM INSIGHT LIMITED
Registration no: 08047310 **VAT No.:** GB 540 3269 67
Date established: 2012 **Turnover:** £500,000 - £1m
No.of Employees: 1 - 10 **Product Groups:** 27, 38, 81

T W Metals Ltd
Nursling Industrial Estate Majestic Road, Nursling, Southampton, SO16 0AF
Tel: 023-8073 9333 **Fax:** 023-8073 9601
E-mail: paul.sandcraft@twmetals.co.uk
Website: http://www.twmetals.co.uk
Bank(s): Lloyds TSB Bank plc
Directors: C. Lewis (Fin), L. Brown (Co Sec)
Managers: M. Griffiths (Purch Mgr), R. McDonald (Personnel), P. Sandcraft, P. Orton (Tech Serv Mgr)

see next page

T W Metals Ltd - Cont'd

Ultimate Holding Company: O'NEAL STEEL INC (USA)
Immediate Holding Company: TW METALS LIMITED
Registration no: 00961098 **VAT No.:** GB 188 2846 16
Date established: 1969 **Turnover:** £20m - £50m
No.of Employees: 101 - 250 **Product Groups:** 34, 36

Date of Accounts	Dec 11	Dec 10	Dec 09
Sales Turnover	57m	47m	44m
Pre Tax Profit/Loss	5m	3m	2m
Working Capital	21m	22m	19m
Fixed Assets	8m	9m	9m
Current Assets	34m	33m	26m
Current Liabilities	5m	2m	1m

Technic Electric Ltd

Unit 5 Lulworth Business Centre Nutwood Way, Totton, Southampton, SO40 3WW
Tel: 023-8066 7486 **Fax:** 023-8066 3830
E-mail: sales@technic.co.uk
Website: http://www.technic.co.uk
Directors: S. Thomas (Dir), S. Thomas (MD), L. Thomas (MD)
Immediate Holding Company: TECHNIC ELECTRIC LIMITED
Registration no: 02284350 **VAT No.:** 522 0490 85 **Date established:** 1988
Turnover: £1m - £2m **No.of Employees:** 1 - 10 **Product Groups:** 37, 44, 47

Date of Accounts	Aug 10	Aug 09	Aug 08
Sales Turnover	N/A	N/A	1m
Pre Tax Profit/Loss	N/A	N/A	-58
Working Capital	-40	-30	-0
Fixed Assets	41	55	78
Current Assets	429	322	371
Current Liabilities	N/A	N/A	195

Technix Rubber & Plastics Ltd

Unit 1 362 Spring Road, Southampton, SO19 2PB
Tel: 023-8043 0040 **Fax:** 01489-798866
E-mail: sales@technix-rubber.com
Website: http://www.technix-rubber.com
Directors: J. Keith (Fin), R. Lynch (Dir)
Managers: B. Upson (Sales Prom Mgr)
Immediate Holding Company: TECHNIX RUBBER & PLASTICS LIMITED
Registration no: 02336704 **Date established:** 1989
Turnover: £500,000 - £1m **No.of Employees:** 1 - 10 **Product Groups:** 29

Date of Accounts	Jun 11	Jun 10	Jun 09
Working Capital	-95	81	3
Fixed Assets	428	54	83
Current Assets	1m	1m	945

Testbank Ship Repair

Western Avenue Western Docks, Southampton, SO15 0HH
Tel: 023-8078 7878 **Fax:** 023-8078 7826
E-mail: k.ryan@testbank.co.uk
Website: http://www.testbank.co.uk
Bank(s): National Westminster Bank Plc
Directors: K. Ryan (Fin)
Managers: A. Farwell (Buyer), P. Watts (Sales & Mktg Mg)
Ultimate Holding Company: TESTBANK HOLDINGS LIMITED
Immediate Holding Company: TESTBANK SHIP REPAIR LIMITED
Registration no: 01758534 **VAT No.:** GB 665 0685 16
Date established: 1983 **Turnover:** £2m - £5m **No.of Employees:** 21 - 50
Product Groups: 39, 84

Date of Accounts	Dec 11	Dec 10	Dec 09
Working Capital	818	1m	915
Fixed Assets	231	169	193
Current Assets	3m	2m	2m
Current Liabilities	N/A	54	N/A

The Environ & Process Engineering Group Ltd

Monza House Unit 4, Southampton, SO15 0LD
Tel: 023-8070 3344 **Fax:** 023-8070 2679
E-mail: leepickering@workingenvironments.co.uk
Website: http://www.workingenvironment.co.uk
Bank(s): Barclays
Directors: L. Pickering (MD)
Immediate Holding Company: THE ENVIRONMENTAL & PROCESS ENGINEERING GROUP LIMITED
Registration no: 05702342 **Date established:** 2006
Turnover: £20m - £50m **No.of Employees:** 51 - 100 **Product Groups:** 52

Date of Accounts	Sep 11	Sep 10	Sep 09
Sales Turnover	47m	39m	37m
Pre Tax Profit/Loss	937	1m	2m
Working Capital	-3m	-4m	-3m
Fixed Assets	5m	5m	5m
Current Assets	11m	8m	7m
Current Liabilities	3m	4m	3m

Toricourt Ltd

Unit 4 Stanton Buildings Stanton Road, Southampton, SO15 4HU
Tel: 01794-518594 **Fax:** 08452-871894
E-mail: info@spectruminteriors.co.uk
Website: http://www.spectrumcoatings.co.uk
Directors: J. Whitmarsh (MD)
Immediate Holding Company: TORICOURT LIMITED
Registration no: 02837079 **Date established:** 1993
Turnover: £250,000 - £500,000 **No.of Employees:** 1 - 10
Product Groups: 48

Date of Accounts	Nov 11	Nov 10	Nov 09
Working Capital	-58	-61	-84
Fixed Assets	12	9	11
Current Assets	49	68	43

Torqueflow-Sydex Ltd

International House George Curl Way, Southampton, SO18 2RZ
Tel: 08452-302006 **Fax:** 0845-2991971
E-mail: dlee@torqueflow-sydex.com
Website: http://www.torqueflow-sydex.com
Directors: D. Lee (MD)
Immediate Holding Company: TORQUEFLOW-SYDEX LIMITED
Registration no: 06052671 **Date established:** 2007
No.of Employees: 1 - 10 **Product Groups:** 40

Date of Accounts	Jan 08
Working Capital	-6
Fixed Assets	1
Current Assets	30
Current Liabilities	36

Trant Construction Ltd

Rushington Business Park Rushington House Chapel Lane, Totton, Southampton, SO40 9LT
Tel: 023-8066 5544 **Fax:** 023-8066 5500
E-mail: holdings@trant.co.uk
Website: http://www.trant.co.uk
Bank(s): National Westminster, Southampton
Directors: R. Horgan (Fin), R. Horgan (Fin)
Managers: R. Trant (Tech Serv Mgr), N. Pullen (Sales & Mktg Mg), M. Collins (Personnel), M. Habgood (Purch Mgr)
Ultimate Holding Company: TRANT HOLDINGS LTD
Immediate Holding Company: TRANT CONSTRUCTION LIMITED
Registration no: 00769274 **VAT No.:** GB 411 6861 67
Date established: 1963 **Turnover:** £75m - £125m
No.of Employees: 501 - 1000 **Product Groups:** 51

Date of Accounts	Dec 11	Dec 10	Dec 09
Sales Turnover	78m	56m	66m
Pre Tax Profit/Loss	1m	1m	487
Working Capital	7m	7m	6m
Fixed Assets	3m	2m	2m
Current Assets	25m	25m	20m
Current Liabilities	5m	5m	4m

Trestan Finishers Ltd

Unit B 26 Hazel Road, Southampton, SO19 7GA
Tel: 023-8043 3081 **Fax:** 023-8043 2196
E-mail: info@trestanfinishers.co.uk
Website: http://www.trestanfinishers.com
Directors: A. Blandford (Dir), J. Sillence (Co Sec)
Immediate Holding Company: TRESTAN FINISHERS LIMITED
Registration no: 01348891 **VAT No.:** GB 293 6834 18
Date established: 1978 **Turnover:** £250,000 - £500,000
No.of Employees: 1 - 10 **Product Groups:** 48

Date of Accounts	Mar 12	Mar 11	Mar 10
Working Capital	28	17	11
Fixed Assets	40	37	39
Current Assets	84	84	65

Tricool Thermal

Ics House, Stephenson Road Calmore Industrial Estate, Totton, Southampton, SO40 3RY
Tel: 023-8052 7300 **Fax:** 023-8042 8366
E-mail: info@icstemp.com
Website: http://www.tricool.com
Bank(s): Lloyds TSB
Directors: B. Hall (Dir), M. Storey (Chief Op Offcr), P. Wilson (MD), R. Dewane (Dir)
Managers: D. Palmer, R. Stocker (Product), V. Evans
Ultimate Holding Company: ICS Group
Registration no: 06669159 **Date established:** 1978 **Turnover:** £5m - £10m
No.of Employees: 51 - 100 **Product Groups:** 38, 40, 41, 42, 45

Trowtronics UK Ltd

Unit 41 South Hampshire Industrial Park Totton, Southampton, SO40 3SA
Tel: 023-8066 0055 **Fax:** 023-8066 0012
E-mail: mike@trowtronics.com
Website: http://www.trowtronics.com
Directors: M. Curtis (MD)
Immediate Holding Company: TROWTRONICS (UK) LIMITED
Registration no: 02977201 **VAT No.:** GB 631 9462 36
Date established: 1994 **Turnover:** £500,000 - £1m
No.of Employees: 1 - 10 **Product Groups:** 37

Date of Accounts	Mar 11	Mar 10	Mar 09
Working Capital	19	62	51
Fixed Assets	47	52	61
Current Assets	182	209	226

Truvox International Ltd

Third Avenue Millbrook, Southampton, SO15 0LE
Tel: 023-8070 2200 **Fax:** 023-8070 5001
E-mail: sales@truvox.com
Website: http://www.truvox.com
Bank(s): HSBC Bank plc
Directors: D. Overell (MD)
Managers: N. Dowse (Mktg Serv Mgr)
Ultimate Holding Company: TACONY INC (USA)
Immediate Holding Company: TRUVOX INTERNATIONAL LIMITED
Registration no: 00731273 **VAT No.:** GB 290 8195 34
Date established: 1962 **Turnover:** £5m - £10m **No.of Employees:** 21 - 50
Product Groups: 40

Date of Accounts	Dec 11	Dec 10	Dec 09
Sales Turnover	6m	6m	6m
Pre Tax Profit/Loss	79	28	-164
Working Capital	2m	2m	2m
Fixed Assets	159	173	150
Current Assets	3m	3m	3m
Current Liabilities	221	169	217

U T I Worldwide Ltd

Overline House Blechynden Terrace, Southampton, SO15 1GW
Tel: 023-8022 8351 **Fax:** 023-8021 9089
E-mail: ianmoran@go2uti.com
Website: http://www.go2uti.com
Bank(s): Barclays
Managers: C. Palford (Mgr)
Ultimate Holding Company: UTI WORLDWIDE INC (BRITISH VIRGIN ISLANDS)
Immediate Holding Company: UTI WORLDWIDE (UK) LIMITED
Registration no: 02402322 **Date established:** 1989
Turnover: £20m - £50m **No.of Employees:** 11 - 20 **Product Groups:** 76

Date of Accounts	Jan 12	Jan 11	Jan 10
Sales Turnover	135m	95m	75m
Pre Tax Profit/Loss	-816	-3m	-3m
Working Capital	-972	-325	-1m
Fixed Assets	878	849	2m
Current Assets	15m	20m	16m
Current Liabilities	5m	4m	3m

Under Cover

7-9 Vincent Grove, Southampton, SO15 5HW
Tel: 023-8070 4044 **Fax:** 023-8051 2213
E-mail: under_cover@btconnect.com
Website: http://www.undercoversouthampton.co.uk
Directors: J. Hines (Prop)
Turnover: Up to £250,000 **No.of Employees:** 1 - 10 **Product Groups:** 22, 23, 24, 30, 39, 48, 49, 66

V1 Creative Media Ltd

2 Highview Way Midanbury, Southampton, SO18 4FG
Tel: 023-8067 1352 **Fax:** 0870-762 6063
E-mail: thorhayton@v1creativemedia.co.uk
Website: http://www.v1creativemedia.com
Directors: G. Gilbert (Fin), T. Hayton (Dir)
Immediate Holding Company: V1 CREATIVE MEDIA LIMITED
Registration no: 04958861 **Date established:** 2003
No.of Employees: 1 - 10 **Product Groups:** 44

Date of Accounts	Nov 11	Nov 10	Nov 09
Working Capital	5	-1	-2
Fixed Assets	1	1	2
Current Assets	29	23	23

V T Group

VT House Grange Drive, Hedge End, Southampton, SO30 2DQ
Tel: 023-8083 9001 **Fax:** 023-8042 6010
E-mail: jeffriesmichael@vtplc.com
Website: http://www.vtplc.com
Directors: C. Cundy (Fin), C. Rickard (Fin), M. Jefferys (Ch), M. Jeffries (Ch), P. Lester (Grp Chief Exec)
Immediate Holding Company: BABCOCK SOUTHERN HOLDINGS LIMITED
Registration no: 01915771 **Date established:** 1985
Turnover: Over £1,000m **No.of Employees:** 1 - 10 **Product Groups:** 39, 84

Viking Life Saving Equipment Ltd

Hamble Court Business Park Hamble Lane, Hamble, Southampton, SO31 4QL
Tel: 023-8045 4184 **Fax:** 023-8045 4284
E-mail: viking-uk@viking-life.com
Website: http://www.viking-life.com
Managers: B. Durant (Chief Mgr)
Immediate Holding Company: VIKING LIFE-SAVING EQUIPMENT LIMITED
Registration no: 01350590 **VAT No.:** GB 249 8435 21
Date established: 1978 **Turnover:** £500,000 - £1m
No.of Employees: 11 - 20 **Product Groups:** 20, 23, 24, 29, 32, 36, 37, 38, 39, 40, 42, 45, 67, 74

Date of Accounts	Dec 11	Dec 10	Dec 09
Sales Turnover	N/A	N/A	5m
Pre Tax Profit/Loss	N/A	N/A	557
Working Capital	1m	585	971
Fixed Assets	991	900	626
Current Assets	2m	2m	1m
Current Liabilities	N/A	N/A	171

Vital Workplace

Trinder House Free Street, Bishops Waltham, Southampton, SO32 1EE
Tel: 023-8076 4514 **Fax:** 023-8070 5380
E-mail: sales@vitalworkplace.com
Website: http://www.vitalworkplace.co.uk
Directors: R. Dennis (Prop)
Immediate Holding Company: BUSHVELDT MEATS LTD
Date established: 2007 **No.of Employees:** 1 - 10 **Product Groups:** 26

Date of Accounts	Jun 11
Working Capital	6
Current Assets	13

W H Rowe & Son Property Ltd

Quayside Engineering Works Quayside Road, Southampton, SO18 1DH
Tel: 023-8022 5636 **Fax:** 023-8022 5146
E-mail: sales@whrowe.com
Website: http://www.whrowe.com
Directors: S. Rowe (MD), I. Fowler (Co Sec)
Immediate Holding Company: W.H. ROWE & SON PROPERTY LIMITED
Registration no: 00339798 **VAT No.:** GB 189 9594 73
Date established: 1938 **Turnover:** £2m - £5m **No.of Employees:** 1 - 10
Product Groups: 34

Date of Accounts	Apr 11	Apr 10	Apr 09
Working Capital	77	77	75
Fixed Assets	270	270	270
Current Assets	79	79	81

Waltham Shutter Door Services Ltd

1 Albany Drive Bishops Waltham, Southampton, SO32 1GE
Tel: 01489-895151 **Fax:** 01489-895151
E-mail: john@wsds.uk.com
Website: http://www.wsds.uk.com
Directors: J. Hadlow (Prop)
Immediate Holding Company: WALTHAM SHUTTER DOOR SERVICES LIMITED
Registration no: 06845492 **Date established:** 2009
Turnover: £250,000 - £500,000 **No.of Employees:** 1 - 10
Product Groups: 26, 35

Date of Accounts	Mar 11	Mar 10
Working Capital	-18	-2
Fixed Assets	19	2
Current Assets	24	39

Waters Marine

Building 5 Shamrock Quay William Street, Southampton, SO14 5QL
Tel: 023-8022 0144 **Fax:** 023-8022 0144
Directors: R. Waters (Prop)
Ultimate Holding Company: MARK ELECTRONICS LIMITED
Immediate Holding Company: GREENHAM MARINE LIMITED
Registration no: 03360337 **Date established:** 1964
No.of Employees: 1 - 10 **Product Groups:** 35, 36, 39

Date of Accounts	Nov 08	Nov 07	Nov 06
Working Capital	122	122	122
Current Assets	122	122	122

Waterside Laboratories Ltd

Unit 39 South Hampshire Industrial Park Totton, Southampton, SO40 3SA
Tel: 0870-7513922 **Fax:** 0870-7513937
Immediate Holding Company: WATERSIDE LABORATORIES LIMITED
Registration no: 01792032 **Date established:** 1984
No.of Employees: 21 - 50 **Product Groups:** 37, 38, 65

J M Watson & Associates Ltd

Avalon House Waltham Business Park Brickyard Road, Swanmore, Southampton, SO32 2SA
Tel: 01489-891875 **Fax:** 01489-894631
E-mail: jmw@jmwatson.co.uk
Website: http://www.jmwatson.co.uk

Directors: M. Watson (Fin), J. Watson (MD)
Immediate Holding Company: J.M. WATSON & ASSOCIATES LIMITED
Registration no: 03626605 **VAT No.:** GB 631 5477 43
Date established: 1998 **Turnover:** Up to £250,000
No.of Employees: 1 - 10 **Product Groups:** 80, 86

Date of Accounts	Jan 12	Jan 11	Jan 10
Working Capital	-22	-9	-11
Fixed Assets	9	N/A	N/A
Current Assets	13	14	14

Watts Industrial Tyres plc
1 Shield Industrial Park Manor House Avenue, Southampton, SO15 0LF
Tel: 023-8078 0078 **Fax:** 023-8051 2218
E-mail: nicolasharris@watts-tyres.co.uk
Website: http://www.southampton.com
Directors: S. Collins (MD), R. Nailer (Sales)
Managers: N. Harris (District Mgr), N. Harris (Mgr), P. Hudson (Sales Prom Mgr), R. Bampton (Mgr)
Ultimate Holding Company: TRELLEBORG AB (SWEDEN)
Immediate Holding Company: WATTS INDUSTRIAL TYRES LIMITED
Registration no: 01434811 **Date established:** 1979
No.of Employees: 1 - 10 **Product Groups:** 29, 45, 67, 68

Date of Accounts	Dec 10	Dec 09	Dec 08
Sales Turnover	9m	7m	12m
Pre Tax Profit/Loss	804	489	914
Working Capital	4m	3m	3m
Fixed Assets	596	583	608
Current Assets	6m	5m	8m
Current Liabilities	233	121	238

Weightwash Ltd
Unit 8 Lulworth Business Centre Nutwood Way, Totton, Southampton, SO40 3WW
Tel: 023-8021 1343 **Fax:** 023-8087 0795
E-mail: info@weightwash.co.uk
Website: http://www.weightwash.co.uk
Directors: C. Wellsted (Fin)
Immediate Holding Company: WEIGHTWASH LIMITED
Registration no: 00890555 **Date established:** 1966
No.of Employees: 1 - 10 **Product Groups:** 23

Date of Accounts	Dec 11	Dec 10	Dec 09
Working Capital	78	36	23
Fixed Assets	198	145	143
Current Assets	262	156	138
Current Liabilities	N/A	N/A	72

Wessex Institute
Lyndhurst Road Ashurst Lodge, Ashurst, Southampton, SO40 7AA
Tel: 023-8029 3223 **Fax:** 023-8029 2853
E-mail: carlos@wessex.ac.uk
Website: http://www.wessex.ac.uk
Bank(s): Lloyds TSB
Directors: C. Brebbia (Ch)
Managers: B. Blain
VAT No.: GB 329 9443 23 **Turnover:** £1m - £2m **No.of Employees:** 21 - 50
Product Groups: 44, 81, 86

White & Co Plc
Bottings Industrial Estate Hillsons Road, Curdridge, Southampton, SO30 2DY
Tel: 01489-788118 **Fax:** 01489-774977
E-mail: southampton@whiteandcompany.co.uk
Website: http://www.whiteandcompany.co.uk
Directors: D. Pateman (Fin), I. Palmer (Grp Chief Exec)
Managers: D. Mussel (Purch Mgr)
Ultimate Holding Company: WHITPORT LIMITED
Immediate Holding Company: WHITE & CO PLC
Registration no: 00052204 **Date established:** 1997
Turnover: £20m - £50m **No.of Employees:** 21 - 50 **Product Groups:** 76

Date of Accounts	Jan 12	Jan 11	Jan 10
Sales Turnover	23m	19m	18m
Pre Tax Profit/Loss	-586	-344	-776
Working Capital	676	875	367
Fixed Assets	6m	6m	6m
Current Assets	4m	5m	3m
Current Liabilities	2m	2m	2m

Williams & Co Southampton Ltd
Victoria Street, Southampton, SO14 5QZ
Tel: 023-8022 0897 **Fax:** 023-8063 8930
E-mail: sales@williams-eng.co.uk
Website: http://www.williams-eng.co.uk
Bank(s): Lloyds TSB Bank plc
Directors: D. Fripp (MD)
Immediate Holding Company: WILLIAMS & CO (SOUTHAMPTON) LIMITED
Registration no: 00296591 **VAT No.:** GB 188 4841 16
Date established: 1935 **Turnover:** £1m - £2m **No.of Employees:** 11 - 20
Product Groups: 48, 85

Date of Accounts	May 11	May 10	May 09
Working Capital	257	265	177
Fixed Assets	483	444	486
Current Assets	569	532	486

Winchcombe Power Tools
299 Wimpson Lane, Southampton, SO16 4PY
Tel: 023-8039 9957 **Fax:** 023-8078 1719
Directors: D. Winchcombe (Prop)
Date established: 1986 **No.of Employees:** 1 - 10 **Product Groups:** 37

Windsor Kitchens
39 Martley Gardens Hedge End, Southampton, SO30 2XB
Tel: 01489-795489
E-mail: sales@windsorkitchens.com
Website: http://www.windsorkitchens.co.uk
Directors: M. Pettyfer (Prop)
Turnover: Up to £250,000 **No.of Employees:** 1 - 10 **Product Groups:** 25, 30, 52

Workhorse Communications
Shedfield Grange Sandy Lane, Shedfield, Southampton, SO32 2HQ
Tel: 01329-833865 **Fax:** 01329-832543
E-mail: markphillimore@btconnect.com
Directors: M. Phillimore (Dir)
Registration no: 02239594 **VAT No.:** GB 412 0647 93
Date established: 1986 **Turnover:** Up to £250,000
No.of Employees: 1 - 10 **Product Groups:** 81

Yacht Tec Ltd
1 Hamble Court Business Park Hamble Lane, Hamble, Southampton, SO31 4QJ
Tel: 023-8045 7854 **Fax:** 023-8045 7954
E-mail: info@yachttec.co.uk
Website: http://www.yachttec.co.uk
Directors: P. Morrill (MD)
Immediate Holding Company: YACHT TEC LIMITED
Registration no: 03434041 **Date established:** 1997
No.of Employees: 1 - 10 **Product Groups:** 35, 36, 39

Date of Accounts	Sep 11	Sep 10	Sep 09
Working Capital	57	149	-11
Fixed Assets	12	17	23
Current Assets	409	554	738

Southsea

Affordable Automation & Controls Ltd
54 Middlesex Road Portsmouth, Southsea, PO4 8EG
Tel: 023-9278 0136
E-mail: r@aac-ltd.co.uk
Website: http://www.aachampshire.co.uk
Directors: T. Wiltshire (MD), L. Smith (MD)
No.of Employees: 1 - 10 **Product Groups:** 26, 35

Harrison Industrial Ltd
3 Rodney Road, Southsea, PO4 8SY
Tel: 023-9275 1687 **Fax:** 023-9281 8564
E-mail: aharrison@harrisonindustrial.com
Website: http://www.harrisonindustrial.co.uk
Bank(s): National Westminster Bank Plc
Directors: N. Harrison (MD)
Managers: D. Bookham (Admin Off)
Ultimate Holding Company: WONELL HOLDINGS LIMITED
Immediate Holding Company: HARRISON INDUSTRIAL LIMITED
Registration no: 01854671 **VAT No.:** GB 381 0158 73
Date established: 1984 **Turnover:** £1m - £2m **No.of Employees:** 21 - 50
Product Groups: 48

Date of Accounts	Nov 11	Nov 10	Nov 09
Working Capital	173	90	88
Fixed Assets	105	97	102
Current Assets	813	777	673

Hilsea Engineering Ltd
3 St Georges Industrial Estate Rodney Road, Southsea, PO4 8SS
Tel: 023-9273 1676 **Fax:** 023-9282 7801
E-mail: hilseaeng@fsbdial.co.uk
Website: http://www.hilseaengineering.co.uk
Directors: K. Edmundson (MD), P. Kilshaun (Prop)
Immediate Holding Company: HILSEA ENGINEERING LIMITED
Registration no: 05454339 **VAT No.:** GB 109 2485 72
Date established: 2005 **Turnover:** £10m - £20m **No.of Employees:** 1 - 10
Product Groups: 48

Home Tanning Ltd
PO Box 697, Southsea, PO4 9WZ
Tel: 08707-120582 **Fax:** 08707-120581
E-mail: info@hometanning.co.uk
Website: http://www.hometanning.co.uk
Directors: C. Harwood (Fin), R. Hepworth (MD)
No.of Employees: 1 - 10 **Product Groups:** 32, 37

Date of Accounts	Apr 07	Apr 06
Working Capital	-4	-7
Fixed Assets	5	5
Current Assets	15	6
Current Liabilities	19	13

Jewson Ltd
105-119 Blackfriars Road, Southsea, PO5 4LW
Tel: 023-9282 3321 **Fax:** 023-9229 1705
E-mail: nigel.hanlon@jewson.co.uk
Website: http://www.jewson.co.uk
Managers: N. Hanlon (District Mgr)
Ultimate Holding Company: COMPAGNIE DE SAINT GOBAIN (FRANCE)
Immediate Holding Company: JEWSON LIMITED
Registration no: 00348407 **Date established:** 1939 **Turnover:** £2m - £5m
No.of Employees: 11 - 20 **Product Groups:** 66

Date of Accounts	Dec 11	Dec 10	Dec 09
Sales Turnover	1606m	1547m	1485m
Pre Tax Profit/Loss	18m	100m	45m
Working Capital	-345m	-250m	-349m
Fixed Assets	496m	387m	461m
Current Assets	657m	1005m	1320m
Current Liabilities	66m	120m	64m

Mig Tig Arc Welding Supplies
261-263 Milton Road, Southsea, PO4 8PQ
Tel: 023-9229 5612 **Fax:** 023-9229 5612
E-mail: migtigarc@lineone.net
Website: http://www.migtigarc.co.uk
Directors: G. Smith (Prop)
Immediate Holding Company: MIGTIGARC LIMITED
Registration no: 05306353 **Date established:** 2004
No.of Employees: 1 - 10 **Product Groups:** 46

Red Wasp Marketing Ltd
Top Floor Unit B Froddington House Northumberland Road, Southsea, PO5 1DS
Tel: 023-9289 3900
E-mail: info@red-wasp.co.uk
Website: http://www.red-wasp.co.uk
Directors: R. Keyes (MD)
Immediate Holding Company: RED WASP MARKETING LIMITED
Registration no: 05932700 **Date established:** 2006 **Turnover:** £1m - £2m
No.of Employees: 1 - 10 **Product Groups:** 81

Date of Accounts	Dec 10	Dec 09	Sep 08
Working Capital	-36	-5	-14
Fixed Assets	10	16	17
Current Assets	48	57	64

Phillip Sanderson Chartered Engineer
10 Exeter Road, Southsea, PO4 9PZ
Tel: 023-9273 1256 **Fax:** 023-9242 9313
E-mail: phill@consulting-structural-engineer.co.uk
Website: http://www.consulting-structural-engineer.co.uk
Directors: P. Sanderson (Prop)
Date established: 1994 **No.of Employees:** 1 - 10 **Product Groups:** 35

Trident Blinds Ltd
199 Milton Road, Southsea, PO4 8PH
Tel: 023-9275 6011 **Fax:** 023-9287 1296
E-mail: sales@tridentblinds.com
Website: http://www.tridentblinds.co.uk
Managers: E. White (Mgr)
Ultimate Holding Company: STAGG HOLDINGS LIMITED
Immediate Holding Company: TRIDENT BLINDS LIMITED
Registration no: 03548070 **Date established:** 1998
No.of Employees: 1 - 10 **Product Groups:** 23, 66

Date of Accounts	Jun 10	Jun 09	Jun 08
Working Capital	-65	7	-72
Fixed Assets	80	91	106
Current Assets	735	576	457

Stockbridge

Coprisystems
Broughton Down Nether Wallop, Stockbridge, SO20 8DS
Tel: 01794-301000 **Fax:** 01794-301342
E-mail: info@coprisystems.com
Website: http://www.coprisystems.com
Directors: L. Colenso (Fin)
Managers: V. Holmes (Sales Admin)
Registration no: 01636032 **No.of Employees:** 1 - 10 **Product Groups:** 30, 35, 77

Date of Accounts	Jun 08	Jun 07
Sales Turnover	1622	N/A
Pre Tax Profit/Loss	275	N/A
Working Capital	258	57
Fixed Assets	168	150
Current Assets	808	667
Current Liabilities	550	611
ROCE% (Return on Capital Employed)	64.5	
ROT% (Return on Turnover)	16.9	

Kiwi Fencing Ltd
Meon Hill Farm House, Stockbridge, SO20 6HS
Tel: 01264-810564 **Fax:** 01264-810242
E-mail: kiwifence@aol.com
Website: http://www.kiwifence.co.uk
Directors: A. Murphy (Fin), V. Murphy (MD)
Immediate Holding Company: KIWI FENCING LIMITED
Registration no: 04959194 **Date established:** 2003
No.of Employees: 1 - 10 **Product Groups:** 25, 35, 49, 52

Date of Accounts	Mar 12	Mar 11	Mar 10
Working Capital	-24	-28	-25
Fixed Assets	64	57	72
Current Assets	24	17	26

R O - D O R Ltd
Stevens Drove Houghton, Stockbridge, SO20 6LP
Tel: 01794-388080 **Fax:** 01794-388090
E-mail: mikegregory@ro-dor.co.uk
Website: http://www.ro-dor.co.uk
Directors: M. Gregory (MD)
Immediate Holding Company: RO-DOR LIMITED
Registration no: 01895877 **Date established:** 1985
No.of Employees: 11 - 20 **Product Groups:** 26, 35

Date of Accounts	Mar 11	Mar 10	Mar 09
Working Capital	407	399	397
Fixed Assets	56	79	91
Current Assets	530	519	500

Watson & Haig Installations Ltd
Martins Lane Chilbolton, Stockbridge, SO20 6BL
Tel: 01264-861188 **Fax:** 01264-861188
E-mail: watson_haig@hotmail.com
Website: http://www.watson-haig.com
Directors: P. Bryant (Dir)
Immediate Holding Company: WATSON & HAIG INSTALLATIONS LIMITED
Registration no: 04629928 **Date established:** 2003
Turnover: £10m - £20m **No.of Employees:** 1 - 10 **Product Groups:** 41

Date of Accounts	Jan 12	Jan 11	Jan 10
Working Capital	377	333	300
Fixed Assets	6	7	8
Current Assets	794	507	441

Tadley

E & K Automation
25 Campbell Court Business Park Bramley, Tadley, RG26 5EG
Tel: 01256-880228 **Fax:** 01256-880338
E-mail: info.uk@ek-automation.com
Website: http://www.ek-automation.com
Directors: P. Holdcroft (MD)
Ultimate Holding Company: EILERS & KIRF GMBH, GERMANY
Registration no: 01487293 **VAT No.:** GB 348 2596 25
Date established: 1980 **Turnover:** £1m - £2m **No.of Employees:** 1 - 10
Product Groups: 45

Enterprise Security Distribution
14 Campbell Court Bramley, Tadley, RG26 5EG
Tel: 01256-886123 **Fax:** 01256-886124
Website: http://www.esdsec.com
Managers: M. Borehm (Mgr)
Immediate Holding Company: ENTERPRISE SECURITY DISTRIBUTION LIMITED
Registration no: 02760626 **Date established:** 1992
No.of Employees: 1 - 10 **Product Groups:** 37, 38, 40

Date of Accounts	Nov 11	Nov 10	Nov 09
Sales Turnover	4m	3m	3m
Pre Tax Profit/Loss	138	93	120
Working Capital	878	845	834
Fixed Assets	21	10	18
Current Assets	3m	2m	2m
Current Liabilities	75	77	81

G & D Steel Fabrications Ltd
Unit 7 Witch Lane Farm Deans Lane, Charter Alley, Tadley, RG26 5SE
Tel: 01256-851752 **Fax:** 01256-851753
E-mail: neal@gdsteel.co.uk
Directors: N. Collins (MD)
Immediate Holding Company: G & D STEEL AND FABRICATIONS LIMITED
Registration no: 03384361 **Date established:** 1997
No.of Employees: 1 - 10 **Product Groups:** 35

Date of Accounts	Jun 11	Jun 10	Jun 09
Working Capital	58	52	38
Fixed Assets	51	24	29
Current Assets	168	178	105
Current Liabilities	36	N/A	N/A

Glassman Europe Ltd
21 Campbell Court Campbell Rd, Bramley, Tadley, RG26 5EG
Tel: 01256-883007 **Fax:** 01256-883017
E-mail: sales@glassmaneurope.co.uk
Website: http://www.glassmaneurope.co.uk
Managers: J. Belden, S. Glassman, P. James (Chief Mgr)
Ultimate Holding Company: Glassman High Voltage Inc
Registration no: 02379302 **Date established:** 1989 **Turnover:** £2m - £5m
No.of Employees: 1 - 10 **Product Groups:** 37, 38

Date of Accounts	Dec 10	Dec 09	Dec 08
Working Capital	1m	1m	2m
Fixed Assets	6	5	6
Current Assets	2m	2m	2m

John Stacey & Sons Ltd
Stacey Industrial Park Silchester Road, Tadley, RG26 3PZ
Tel: 0118-981 3531 **Fax:** 0118-981 3458
E-mail: info@john-stacey.co.uk
Website: http://www.john-stacey.co.uk
Directors: G. Stacey (MD), N. Stacey (Grp Chief Exec), K. Brown (Co Sec)
Managers: T. McGoldrick, S. Stacey, S. Fetchett (Mgr), P. Osborne (Tech Serv Mgr), G. Baker, D. Stanton, D. Saul, C. Stone (Mktg Serv Mgr), C. Slone
Immediate Holding Company: JOHN STACEY & SONS LIMITED
Registration no: 00805205 **Date established:** 1964
Turnover: £10m - £20m **No.of Employees:** 51 - 100 **Product Groups:** 48, 51, 54, 83

Date of Accounts	May 11	May 10	May 09
Pre Tax Profit/Loss	-0	-0	-0
Working Capital	33	33	33
Current Assets	34	46	46
Current Liabilities	N/A	1	1

Oakside Classic Clocks
1 Heath Road Pamber Heath, Tadley, RG26 3DR
Tel: 0118-970 1377 **Fax:** 0118-970 1506
E-mail: frank@classic-clocks.co.uk
Website: http://www.classic-clocks.co.uk
Directors: F. Redmile (Ptnr)
Turnover: Up to £250,000 **No.of Employees:** 1 - 10 **Product Groups:** 40, 49, 65

Rosonica Ltd
PO BOX 7361, Tadley, RG26 9BZ
Tel: 023-9315 0016 **Fax:** 023-9315 0017
E-mail: contact@rosonica.com
Website: http://rosonica.com
Managers: L. Osborne (Comm), J. Radford (Eng Serv Mgr)
Registration no: 6610045 **Date established:** 2008
No.of Employees: 1 - 10 **Product Groups:** 37

Sandford Springs Golf Club
Wolverton, Tadley, RG26 5RT
Tel: 01635-296800 **Fax:** 01635-296801
E-mail: info@sandfordspringsgolf.co.uk
Website: http://www.sandfordspringsgolf.co.uk
Directors: B. Cox (Co Sec)
Managers: A. Wild (Chief Mgr)
Ultimate Holding Company: LEADERBOARD GOLF HOLDINGS LIMITED
Immediate Holding Company: SANDFORD SPRINGS LIMITED
Registration no: 02533899 **Date established:** 1990 **Turnover:** £1m - £2m
No.of Employees: 21 - 50 **Product Groups:** 89

Date of Accounts	Dec 11	Dec 10	Dec 09
Working Capital	2m	-891	-866
Fixed Assets	580	4m	4m
Current Assets	4m	174	142

Sherborne Metal Masters Ltd
Ash Lane Little London, Tadley, RG26 5EL
Tel: 01256-880096 **Fax:** 01256-880096
Directors: M. Mosdell (MD)
Immediate Holding Company: SHERBORNE METAL MASTERS LIMITED
Registration no: 04504165 **VAT No.:** GB 537 7540 24
Date established: 2002 **Turnover:** £250,000 - £500,000
No.of Employees: 1 - 10 **Product Groups:** 35, 36, 40, 48

Date of Accounts	Aug 11	Aug 10	Aug 09
Working Capital	13	8	18
Fixed Assets	6	7	9
Current Assets	90	62	51

Waterlooville

A & A Packaging
Westfield Industrial Estate Portsmouth Road, Horndean, Waterlooville, PO8 9JX
Tel: 023-9259 7792 **Fax:** 023-9259 0049
E-mail: sales@aandapackaging.co.uk
Directors: S. Knight (MD)
Turnover: £1m - £2m **No.of Employees:** 11 - 20 **Product Groups:** 23, 25, 26, 27, 29, 30, 32, 33, 35, 42, 43, 66

Arcadia Heating Ltd
53 Chalton Lane, Waterlooville, PO8 0PP
Tel: 023-9257 1417 **Fax:** 023-9257 1422
Directors: W. Barnard (Prop)
No.of Employees: 1 - 10 **Product Groups:** 37, 45, 48

Archfact Ltd
10 Pipers Wood Industrial Park Waterberry Drive, Waterlooville, PO7 7XU
Tel: 023-9224 0700 **Fax:** 023-9223 0157
E-mail: info@archfact.com
Website: http://www.archfact.co.uk
Directors: S. Mcgrath (MD)
Ultimate Holding Company: A.I.M.S. PRECISION LTD.
Immediate Holding Company: ARCHFACT LIMITED
Registration no: 01959065 **VAT No.:** GB 446 8024 44
Date established: 1985 **Turnover:** £500,000 - £1m
No.of Employees: 11 - 20 **Product Groups:** 48

Date of Accounts	Dec 11	Dec 10	Dec 09
Working Capital	214	190	188
Fixed Assets	8	10	14
Current Assets	270	212	263

Barlow Sheet Metal Ltd
2b Wessex Gate Industrial Estate, Waterlooville, PO8 9LP
Tel: 023-9259 9551 **Fax:** 023-9259 9043
E-mail: sales@barlowsheetmetal.com
Website: http://www.barlowsheetmetal.com
Directors: A. Barlow (Co Sec), S. Barlow (MD)
Immediate Holding Company: BARLOW SHEET METAL LIMITED
Registration no: 01182261 **Date established:** 1974 **Turnover:** £1m - £2m
No.of Employees: 21 - 50 **Product Groups:** 26, 35, 37, 44, 48, 66, 84

Date of Accounts	Sep 11	Sep 10	Sep 09
Working Capital	1m	1m	2m
Fixed Assets	278	230	249
Current Assets	2m	2m	2m

Bigneat Ltd
4-5 Pipers Wood Industrial Park Waterberry Drive, Waterlooville, PO7 7XU
Tel: 023-9226 6400 **Fax:** 023-9226 3373
E-mail: info@bigneat.com
Website: http://www.bigneat.com
Directors: R. Monks (MD)
Managers: R. Rees (Comptroller), E. O'Flynn (Purch Mgr)
Ultimate Holding Company: SOLENT STEEL ENGINEERING LIMITED
Immediate Holding Company: BIGNEAT LIMITED
Registration no: 01137691 **VAT No.:** GB 108 4492 71
Date established: 1973 **Turnover:** Up to £250,000
No.of Employees: 21 - 50 **Product Groups:** 26, 67

Date of Accounts	Oct 11	Oct 10	Oct 09
Working Capital	3m	3m	3m
Fixed Assets	110	93	114
Current Assets	4m	4m	4m

British Engineering Productions Ltd
19 Arnside Road, Waterlooville, PO7 7UP
Tel: 023-9226 8733 **Fax:** 023-9225 1104
E-mail: steveb@bep-manifolds.com
Website: http://www.bep-manifolds.co.uk
Bank(s): Barclays
Directors: S. Bryant (Dir)
Ultimate Holding Company: THE WEST GROUP (FLUID POWER) LIMITED
Immediate Holding Company: BRITISH ENGINEERING PRODUCTIONS (PORTSMOUTH) LIMITED
Registration no: 00404394 **Date established:** 1946 **Turnover:** £2m - £5m
No.of Employees: 11 - 20 **Product Groups:** 40, 41, 45, 46

Date of Accounts	Aug 11	Aug 10	Aug 09
Working Capital	-1m	-1m	-961
Fixed Assets	870	968	1m
Current Assets	792	702	595

C P L Circuits Ltd
Unit 8-14 Highcroft Industrial Estate Enterprise Road, Waterlooville, PO8 0BT
Tel: 023-9259 9333 **Fax:** 023-9259 3127
E-mail: cpl@dsl.pipex.com
Bank(s): National Westminster Bank Plc
Directors: P. Holmes (MD)
Immediate Holding Company: CPL CIRCUITS LIMITED
Registration no: 03174939 **VAT No.:** GB 108 7365 63
Date established: 1996 **Turnover:** £500,000 - £1m
No.of Employees: 11 - 20 **Product Groups:** 37

Date of Accounts	Mar 11	Mar 10	Mar 09
Working Capital	76	81	106
Fixed Assets	41	52	75
Current Assets	172	163	192

Christie Intruder Alarms Ltd
212-218 London Road, Waterlooville, PO7 7AJ
Tel: 023-9226 5111 **Fax:** 023-9226 5112
E-mail: enquiries@ciaalarms.co.uk
Website: http://www.ciaalarms.co.uk
Directors: D. Rayner (Fin), S. Kimber (MD)
Managers: A. Jenkins, C. Langdown (Chief Mgr), P. Childs (Sales Prom Mgr), F. Whittaker (Personnel), G. Gardner (Mktg Serv Mgr)
Immediate Holding Company: MOSSHAVEN LIMITED
Registration no: 01036542 **Date established:** 1971
No.of Employees: 101 - 250 **Product Groups:** 37, 38, 52

Date of Accounts	Dec 09	Dec 08	Sep 11
Working Capital	381	6	1
Fixed Assets	441	509	N/A
Current Assets	2m	2m	1

Chubb Electronic Security Ltd
84-86 Jubilee Road, Waterlooville, PO7 7RE
Tel: 08448-791753 **Fax:** 023-9226 2124
E-mail: waterlooville.security@chubb.co.uk
Website: http://www.chubb.uk.com
Managers: K. O'Neil (District Mgr)
Immediate Holding Company: CHUBB GROUP SECURITY LTD
Registration no: 00524469 **No.of Employees:** 11 - 20 **Product Groups:** 81

Circuit Engineering Marketing Company Ltd
1-2 Silverthorne Way, Waterlooville, PO7 7XB
Tel: 023-9226 2120 **Fax:** 023-9226 2089
E-mail: ken.bishop@cemco.com
Website: http://www.cemco.com
Bank(s): Lloyds TSB Bank plc
Directors: K. Bishop (Tech Serv)
Immediate Holding Company: CIRCUIT ENGINEERING MARKETING COMPANY LIMITED
Registration no: 01500012 **VAT No.:** GB 321 9673 54
Date established: 1980 **Turnover:** £1m - £2m **No.of Employees:** 11 - 20
Product Groups: 46, 47

Date of Accounts	Dec 11	Dec 10	Dec 09
Working Capital	2m	1m	831
Fixed Assets	873	16	20
Current Assets	3m	2m	1m
Current Liabilities	40	N/A	N/A

Cobham Micromill Products Ltd
Leydene House Waterberry Drive, Waterlooville, PO7 7XX
Tel: 023-9236 6600 **Fax:** 023-9236 6673
E-mail: sales@micromill.com
Website: http://www.cobham.com
Directors: R. Sherwood (Fin), P. Long (Fin), P. Holland (Dir)
Ultimate Holding Company: COBHAM PLC
Immediate Holding Company: COBHAM TCS LIMITED
Registration no: 01456922 **Date established:** 1979
Turnover: £10m - £20m **No.of Employees:** 51 - 100 **Product Groups:** 40, 84

Date of Accounts	Dec 10	Dec 09	Dec 08
Sales Turnover	11m	10m	9m
Pre Tax Profit/Loss	-1m	898	-110
Working Capital	3m	3m	2m
Fixed Assets	201	247	395
Current Assets	8m	5m	4m
Current Liabilities	1m	1m	788

C R M Saw & Tool Co
17 Arnside Road, Waterlooville, PO7 7UP
Tel: 023-9226 3202 **Fax:** 023-9226 5565
E-mail: kevin@crmsaw.co.uk
Website: http://www.crmsaw.co.uk
Bank(s): Lloyds TSB Bank plc
Directors: R. Parsley (Ch), R. Dent (MD), K. Proctor (Sales), K. Parsley (MD)
Managers: S. Thomas (Accounts)
Immediate Holding Company: CRM. SAW COMPANY LIMITED
Registration no: 00933497 **VAT No.:** GB 107 3935 74
Date established: 1968 **Turnover:** £1m - £2m **No.of Employees:** 11 - 20
Product Groups: 36, 37, 47, 48

Date of Accounts	Dec 10	Dec 09	Dec 08
Working Capital	-126	-35	-45
Fixed Assets	32	42	62
Current Assets	136	205	226

Datum Smart Card Shop Ltd
Hook Cottage Blendworth, Waterlooville, PO8 0AH
Tel: 023-9224 1154 **Fax:** 023-9224 1156
E-mail: sales@datum-automation.com
Website: http://www.datum-designs.eu
Directors: A. Sills (Dir)
Immediate Holding Company: JAMES MOTORCYCLES LIMITED
Registration no: 01687705 **Date established:** 2012
Turnover: £500,000 - £1m **No.of Employees:** 1 - 10 **Product Groups:** 37

Date of Accounts	Dec 05
Working Capital	567
Fixed Assets	119
Current Assets	1221
Current Liabilities	655
Total Share Capital	1

Fineline Environmental Ltd
1 Lovage Way, Waterlooville, PO8 0JG
Tel: 01237-441772 **Fax:** 01237-441851
E-mail: info@finelineonline.co.uk
Website: http://www.finelineonline.co.uk
Directors: D. Walker (Prop), S. Walker (Dir)
Registration no: 06806596 **Date established:** 2002
Turnover: Over £1,000m **No.of Employees:** 1 - 10 **Product Groups:** 52, 85

Flowseal Ltd
34h Aston Road, Waterlooville, PO7 7XQ
Tel: 023-9226 5031 **Fax:** 023-9224 0382
E-mail: sales@flowseal.co.uk
Website: http://www.flowseal.co.uk
Directors: J. Hollingshead (MD), L. Pratt (Fin)
Immediate Holding Company: FLOWSEAL LIMITED
Registration no: 01195021 **Date established:** 1974
Turnover: £250,000 - £500,000 **No.of Employees:** 1 - 10
Product Groups: 29, 31, 36, 66, 68

Date of Accounts	Dec 11	Dec 10	Dec 09
Working Capital	46	45	50
Fixed Assets	1	3	4
Current Assets	69	63	66

Format Fabrications
4 Enterprise Industrial Estate Enterprise Road, Waterlooville, PO8 0BB
Tel: 023-9257 1181 **Fax:** 023-9257 1181
Directors: M. Brace (Prop)
Date established: 1992 **No.of Employees:** 1 - 10 **Product Groups:** 35

Garage Doors 4 U
A 4 Highfield Parade, Waterlooville, PO7 7QH
Tel: 023-9224 1848 **Fax:** 023-9224 1858
E-mail: garagedy@aol.com
Website: http://www.garagedoors4u.co.uk
Directors: D. Greig (Prop)
Immediate Holding Company: GARAGEDOORS4U.COM LIMITED
Date established: 2000 **No.of Employees:** 1 - 10 **Product Groups:** 25, 30, 35

Date of Accounts	May 11	May 10	May 09
Working Capital	3	2	1
Current Assets	11	12	15

Goss & Crested China Ltd
62 Murray Road Horndean, Waterlooville, PO8 9JL
Tel: 023-9259 7440 **Fax:** 023-9259 1975
E-mail: info@gosschinaclub.co.uk
Website: http://www.gosschinaclub.co.uk
Directors: W. Pine (Fin), L. Pine (MD)
Immediate Holding Company: GOSS & CRESTED CHINA LIMITED
Registration no: 01193051 **Date established:** 1974
Turnover: Up to £250,000 **No.of Employees:** 1 - 10 **Product Groups:** 33

Date of Accounts	Mar 11	Mar 10	Mar 09
Working Capital	-42	-15	12
Fixed Assets	2	2	2
Current Assets	20	49	81

A Healey Office Equipment Ltd
The Meadows 2 Waterberry Drive, Waterlooville, PO7 7XX
Tel: 023-9226 9711 **Fax:** 023-9226 9722
E-mail: linda.healey@ahealey.co.uk
Website: http://www.ahealey.co.uk
Bank(s): National Westminster Bank Plc
Directors: L. Healey (Fin), A. Healey (MD)
Immediate Holding Company: A. HEALEY OFFICE EQUIPMENT LIMITED
Registration no: 01284811 **Date established:** 1976 **Turnover:** £2m - £5m
No.of Employees: 21 - 50 **Product Groups:** 28, 64, 67

Date of Accounts	Mar 10	Mar 09	Mar 08
Sales Turnover	N/A	N/A	3m
Pre Tax Profit/Loss	N/A	N/A	71
Working Capital	351	343	254
Fixed Assets	571	586	612
Current Assets	851	678	721
Current Liabilities	N/A	N/A	118

I C E E Manage Services Ltd
20 Arnside Road, Waterlooville, PO7 7UP
Tel: 023-9223 0604 **Fax:** 023-9223 0605
E-mail: paul.harris@icee.co.uk
Website: http://www.icee.co.uk
Directors: P. Harris (Prop)
Immediate Holding Company: I.C.E.E. LTD
Registration no: 01922470 **Date established:** 1985
No.of Employees: 21 - 50 **Product Groups:** 37, 48

Date of Accounts	Sep 06	Sep 05	Sep 04
Pre Tax Profit/Loss	47	-820	-336
Working Capital	-41	109	-378
Fixed Assets	494	263	426
Current Assets	1693	1371	2679
Current Liabilities	1734	1262	3057
ROCE% (Return on Capital Employed)	10.4	-220.6	-700.0

Jasun Envirocare PLC
5 Stratfield Park Elettra Avenue, Waterlooville, PO7 7XN
Tel: 023-9264 4700 **Fax:** 023-9264 4677
E-mail: sales@envirocare-services.com
Website: http://www.envirocare-services.com
Directors: R. Wilson (Dir)
Ultimate Holding Company: JASUN ENVIROCARE PLC
Immediate Holding Company: ENVIROCARE SERVICES LIMITED
Registration no: 02464800 **VAT No.:** GB 544 1270 68
Date established: 1990 **Turnover:** £2m - £5m **No.of Employees:** 1 - 10
Product Groups: 33, 35, 40, 42, 48

Date of Accounts	Mar 11	Mar 10	Mar 09
Sales Turnover	2m	N/A	N/A
Pre Tax Profit/Loss	311	N/A	N/A
Working Capital	647	275	154
Fixed Assets	N/A	210	221
Current Assets	647	772	670

Johnson Controls Ltd
2-3 The Briars Waterberry Drive, Waterlooville, PO7 7YH
Tel: 023-9223 0500 **Fax:** 023-9223 0501
Website: http://www.jci.com
Bank(s): Lloyds TSB Bank plc
Managers: C. Bullock (Mgr)
Ultimate Holding Company: JOHNSON CONTROLS INC (USA)
Immediate Holding Company: JOHNSON CONTROLS LIMITED
Registration no: 00661449 **Date established:** 1960
Turnover: £500m - £1,000m **No.of Employees:** 101 - 250
Product Groups: 36, 37, 38, 39, 40, 66

Date of Accounts	Sep 11	Sep 10	Sep 09
Sales Turnover	644m	612m	542m
Pre Tax Profit/Loss	8m	4m	3m
Working Capital	-228m	-195m	-239m
Fixed Assets	429m	317m	326m
Current Assets	220m	239m	167m
Current Liabilities	261m	265m	262m

Key 2 Plastics Ltd
Unit C4 Hazleton Interchange Lakesmere Road, Horndean, Waterlooville, PO8 9JU
Tel: 023-9257 2591 **Fax:** 023-9238 6858
E-mail: info@key2uk.com
Website: http://www.key2uk.com
Directors: M. Keating (MD)
Ultimate Holding Company: KEY2 GROUP (HOLDINGS) LIMITED
Immediate Holding Company: KEY2 PLASTICS LIMITED
Registration no: 04472140 **Date established:** 2002
No.of Employees: 21 - 50 **Product Groups:** 27, 28, 30, 35, 37, 39, 40, 45, 48, 49, 67, 68, 84

Date of Accounts	Jul 11	Jul 10	Jul 09
Working Capital	140	169	182
Fixed Assets	364	335	275
Current Assets	405	464	503

Mainance Engineering Ltd
7a Arnside Road, Waterlooville, PO7 7UP
Tel: 023-9225 7222 **Fax:** 023-9225 4270
E-mail: mainance@dsl.pipex.com
Directors: T. Dollery (Dir)
Ultimate Holding Company: TMS HOLDINGS LIMITED
Immediate Holding Company: MAINANCE ENGINEERING LIMITED
Registration no: 04280769 **VAT No.:** GB 615 1887 34
Date established: 2001 **No.of Employees:** 1 - 10 **Product Groups:** 37

Date of Accounts	Sep 11	Sep 10	Sep 09
Working Capital	-50	-41	-6
Fixed Assets	4	5	5
Current Assets	86	95	102

Metal Art Design Co
Four Acres Forest Road, Denmead, Waterlooville, PO7 6UF
Tel: 023-9225 9911 **Fax:** 023-9225 9911
Directors: B. Charlesworth (Dir), B. Charleswoth (Dir)
Immediate Holding Company: ACE GAS & HEATING (UK) LTD
Registration no: 06948564 **Date established:** 2009
No.of Employees: 1 - 10 **Product Groups:** 26, 35

Photon Power Technology Ltd
Suite 8 Brambles Business Centre, Hussar Court, Waterlooville, PO7 7SG
Tel: 023-9226 4890 **Fax:** 0845-8338923
E-mail: info@photonpower.co.uk
Website: http://www.photonpower.co.uk
Directors: P. Revell (MD)
Registration no: 5717348 **Date established:** 2006
No.of Employees: 1 - 10 **Product Groups:** 37, 44

Quicks Archery
18-22 Stakes Hill Road, Waterlooville, PO7 7JF
Tel: 023-9225 4114 **Fax:** 023-9225 1519
E-mail: quicks@quicks.com
Website: http://www.quicksarchery.co.uk
Bank(s): Lloyds, Waterloovile
Directors: T. Bishop (MD)
Managers: E. Power, L. Mactherson (Buyer), K. Longmore (Chief Acct)
Registration no: 01141200 **VAT No.:** GB 108 4829 62
Turnover: £2m - £5m **No.of Employees:** 21 - 50 **Product Groups:** 23, 35, 36, 49, 63

Rimor Ltd
Denmead Industrial Estate Forest Road, Denmead, Waterlooville, PO7 6TJ
Tel: 023-9226 4063 **Fax:** 023-9226 1611
E-mail: excellence@rimor.co.uk
Website: http://www.rimor.co.uk
Directors: P. Mason (MD), G. Musson (Fin), R. Greenway (Sales)
Managers: J. Wheeler (Personnel), P. Matthews, B. Matthews (Personnel), A. Claire (Buyer), P. Matthews
Immediate Holding Company: RIMOR LIMITED
Registration no: 02987112 **Date established:** 1994
Turnover: £10m - £20m **No.of Employees:** 51 - 100 **Product Groups:** 48

Date of Accounts	Dec 11	Dec 10	Dec 09
Sales Turnover	12m	10m	8m
Pre Tax Profit/Loss	670	309	-124
Working Capital	3m	2m	1m
Fixed Assets	3m	3m	3m
Current Assets	5m	4m	3m
Current Liabilities	965	869	751

SGMR Market Research Ltd
114 Valley Park Drive, Waterlooville, PO8 0PT
Tel: 07766-086042
E-mail: sueatagmr@aol.com
Directors: S. Garrett (Dir)
No.of Employees: 1 - 10 **Product Groups:** 81

Southern Mower Services Sales & Repairs Ltd
4 Hillside Industrial Estate London Road, Horndean, Waterlooville, PO8 0BL
Tel: 023-9259 2954 **Fax:** 023-9259 4537
E-mail: southernmowers@yahoo.co.uk
Directors: L. Flynn (MD)
Registration no: 04795671 **No.of Employees:** 1 - 10 **Product Groups:** 37, 41, 67

Southern Sealed Units & Glass Ltd
21 Arnside Road, Waterlooville, PO7 7UU
Tel: 023-9223 1251 **Fax:** 023-9223 1394
E-mail: sales@removalgroup.com
Website: http://www.ssu-ltd.co.uk
Directors: K. Morton (Co Sec), K. Morton (Fin), N. Cartmell (MD)
Immediate Holding Company: SOUTHERN SEALED UNITS AND GLASS LIMITED
Registration no: 02681410 **Date established:** 1992
No.of Employees: 11 - 20 **Product Groups:** 46

Date of Accounts	Jan 08	Jan 07	Jan 06
Working Capital	-64	-74	-38
Fixed Assets	784	120	157
Current Assets	260	267	272
Current Liabilities	324	341	311

Sunlight Plastics Ltd
15-16 Aston Road, Waterlooville, PO7 7XG
Tel: 023-9225 9500 **Fax:** 023-9225 9400
E-mail: sales@sunlightplastics.co.uk
Website: http://www.sunlightplastics.co.uk
Directors: S. Hogg (Dir)
Immediate Holding Company: SUNLIGHT PLASTICS LIMITED
Registration no: 02600517 **Date established:** 1991
No.of Employees: 11 - 20 **Product Groups:** 30, 48, 66

Date of Accounts	Oct 11	Oct 10	Oct 09
Working Capital	-18	-16	-23
Fixed Assets	36	47	60
Current Assets	205	210	194

Thomas Sanderson Ltd
Tileasy House Waterberry Drive, Waterlooville, PO7 7UW
Tel: 023-9223 2600 **Fax:** 023-9223 2700
E-mail: curleyj@thomas-sanderson.co.uk
Website: http://www.thomas-sanderson.co.uk
Directors: J. Curley (Fin)
Managers: N. Thomas (Mktg Serv Mgr), L. Johnston (Personnel), J. Baker, D. Oakley (Tech Serv Mgr)
Ultimate Holding Company: HUNTER DOUGLAS NV (NETHERLANDS ANTILLES)
Immediate Holding Company: THOMAS SANDERSON LIMITED
Registration no: 04626841 **Date established:** 2003
Turnover: £20m - £50m **No.of Employees:** 251 - 500
Product Groups: 24, 25, 27, 36, 39, 46

Date of Accounts	Dec 11	Dec 10	Dec 09
Sales Turnover	38m	37m	36m
Pre Tax Profit/Loss	3m	3m	2m
Working Capital	543	-2m	-601
Fixed Assets	38m	38m	38m
Current Assets	10m	8m	9m
Current Liabilities	5m	5m	5m

Tyre-Finder I T B UK
3 Inhurst Avenue, Waterlooville, PO7 7QS
Tel: 08452-301966 **Fax:** 0845-230 1966
E-mail: info@tyre-finder.co.uk
Website: http://www.tyre-finder.co.uk
Directors: M. Powell (Prop)
No.of Employees: 1 - 10 **Product Groups:** 29, 67, 68

The West Group Ltd
29 Aston Road, Waterlooville, PO7 7XJ
Tel: 023-9226 6366 **Fax:** 023-9224 0323
E-mail: sales@westgroup.co.uk
Website: http://www.westgroup.co.uk
Bank(s): Barclays
Directors: D. Osborne (Sales), J. Dunning (Dir), P. Brown (Co Sec)
Ultimate Holding Company: THE WEST GROUP (FLUID POWER) LIMITED
Immediate Holding Company: THE WEST GROUP LIMITED
Registration no: 01273971 **Date established:** 1976 **Turnover:** £2m - £5m
No.of Employees: 21 - 50 **Product Groups:** 23, 29, 38, 40

Date of Accounts	Aug 11	Aug 10	Aug 09
Working Capital	532	273	256
Fixed Assets	555	586	618
Current Assets	2m	2m	870

Western Laboratory Solutions
Safeguard House Hazleton Interchange, Horndean, Waterlooville, PO8 9JU
Tel: 08448-936500 **Fax:** 0844-893 6540
E-mail: sales@consumables-uk.com
Website: http://www.wls.co.uk
Bank(s): The Royal Bank of Scotland
Directors: R. Hall (MD)
Managers: J. Hall, P. Neal (Fin Mgr)
Ultimate Holding Company: CONSUMABLES CORPORATE GROUP LIMITED
Immediate Holding Company: WESTERN HEALTHCARE SOLUTIONS LIMITED
Registration no: 07122491 **VAT No.:** GB 370 8099 44
Date established: 2010 **Turnover:** £250,000 - £500,000
No.of Employees: 11 - 20 **Product Groups:** 33, 42, 63, 67

Date of Accounts	Oct 07	Oct 06	Oct 05
Working Capital	148	140	193
Fixed Assets	46	65	52
Current Assets	816	741	912
Current Liabilities	668	601	719
Total Share Capital	20	20	20

William Teknix
113 London Road Horndean, Waterlooville, PO8 0BJ
Tel: 023-9259 2500 **Fax:** 023-9259 4081
E-mail: ian@teknix.me.uk
Directors: I. Williams (Prop)
Immediate Holding Company: L & C WILLIAMS LIMITED
Registration no: 07278743 **Date established:** 2010
Turnover: Up to £250,000 **No.of Employees:** 1 - 10 **Product Groups:** 45

Date of Accounts	Mar 12	Mar 11
Working Capital	-4	-5
Fixed Assets	5	5
Current Assets	10	6

Woodleigh Power Equipment Ltd
Unit 20 Highcroft Industrial Estate Enterprise Rd, Horndean, Waterlooville, PO8 0BT
Tel: 023-9257 1360 **Fax:** 023-9259 2056
E-mail: enquiries@woodleighpower.co.uk
Website: http://www.woodleighpower.co.uk
Registration no: 02021798 **VAT No.:** GB 411 9516 69
Date established: 1985 **No.of Employees:** 1 - 10 **Product Groups:** 40, 41, 48, 68

Date of Accounts	May 12	May 11	May 10
Working Capital	30	25	8
Fixed Assets	6	5	7
Current Assets	154	185	141
Current Liabilities	N/A	N/A	57

Zones4U Ltd
Westfield Industrial Estate Horndean, Waterlooville, PO8 9JX
Tel: 0870-7122200 **Fax:** 0870-712 2201
E-mail: sales@mainzone.co.uk
Website: http://www.mainzone.co.uk
Directors: R. Hart (Fin)
Registration no: 05405894 **Date established:** 1996 **Turnover:** £5m - £10m
No.of Employees: 21 - 50 **Product Groups:** 44

Date of Accounts	Sep 07	Sep 06
Working Capital	-12	9
Current Assets	27	29
Current Liabilities	39	20

Whitchurch

Adept Precision Sheet Metal Ltd
Ardglen Trading Estate, Whitchurch, RG28 7BB
Tel: 01256-893177 **Fax:** 01256-893904
E-mail: info@adept-sheetmetal.co.uk
Website: http://www.adept-sheetmetal.co.uk
Directors: C. Adams (MD)
Immediate Holding Company: ADEPT PRECISION SHEETMETAL LIMITED
Registration no: 01994050 **VAT No.:** GB 438 2248 47
Date established: 1986 **Turnover:** £1m - £2m **No.of Employees:** 1 - 10
Product Groups: 48

Date of Accounts	Jul 11	Jul 10	Jul 09
Working Capital	-86	-104	-95
Fixed Assets	244	290	316
Current Assets	212	295	342
Current Liabilities	N/A	N/A	34

Albright International Ltd
Units A-E Evingar Trading Estate Ardglen Road, Whitchurch, RG28 7BB
Tel: 01256-893060 **Fax:** 01256-893562
E-mail: dianeg@albrightinternational.com
Website: http://www.albrightinternational.com
Directors: N. Bedgood (Dir), L. Bedggood (Dir)
Managers: S. Procter (Personnel), R. Hunt (Comptroller), R. Belbin (Purch Mgr), I. Fenton (Tech Serv Mgr)
Ultimate Holding Company: LEA REDWAY LIMITED
Immediate Holding Company: ALBRIGHT INTERNATIONAL LIMITED
Registration no: 01278761 **Date established:** 1976
Turnover: £20m - £50m **No.of Employees:** 101 - 250
Product Groups: 36, 37

Date of Accounts	Sep 11	Sep 10	Sep 09
Sales Turnover	31m	22m	17m
Pre Tax Profit/Loss	-2	671	-324
Working Capital	12m	14m	13m
Fixed Assets	7m	6m	5m
Current Assets	18m	17m	15m
Current Liabilities	725	681	695

All Solutions Products Ltd
4 Skylark Rise, Whitchurch, RG28 7SY
Tel: 01256-893863 **Fax:** 01256-893863
E-mail: sales@allsolutionproducts.com
Website: http://www.allsolutionproducts.com

see next page

All Solutions Products Ltd - Cont'd

Directors: N. Saunders (Dir), N. Saunders (MD)
Immediate Holding Company: ALL SOLUTION PRODUCTS LIMITED
Registration no: 04882493 **Date established:** 2003
Turnover: £250,000 - £500,000 **No.of Employees:** 1 - 10
Product Groups: 46

Date of Accounts	Sep 11	Sep 10	Sep 09
Working Capital	-9	-13	-4
Fixed Assets	2	N/A	N/A
Current Assets	21	15	9

J J Systems Ltd

PO Box 7304, Whitchurch, RG28 7YP
Tel: 01256-895111 **Fax:** 01256-896100
E-mail: info@jj-systems.co.uk
Website: http://www.jj-systems.co.uk
Directors: S. James (Fin)
Immediate Holding Company: J.J. SYSTEMS LIMITED
Registration no: 03026663 **Date established:** 1995
Turnover: Up to £250,000 **No.of Employees:** 1 - 10 **Product Groups:** 37, 38, 44

Date of Accounts	Dec 11	Dec 10	Dec 09
Working Capital	34	28	30
Fixed Assets	6	2	3
Current Assets	70	63	36

Reeling Systems Ltd

Unit A3 Pegasus Court Ardglen Road, Whitchurch, RG28 7BP
Tel: 01256-896517 **Fax:** 01256-895624
E-mail: martin.campbell@reelingsystems.co.uk
Directors: J. Campbell (Fin), M. Campbell (MD)
Immediate Holding Company: REELING SYSTEMS LIMITED
Registration no: 02512106 **Date established:** 1990
No.of Employees: 1 - 10 **Product Groups:** 38, 42

Date of Accounts	Dec 11	Dec 10	Dec 09
Working Capital	758	831	651
Fixed Assets	226	269	218
Current Assets	796	978	721

Urethane Industrial Products Ltd

Evingar Industrial Estate Ardglen Road, Whitchurch, RG28 7BB
Tel: 01256-892830 **Fax:** 01256-896899
E-mail: sales@uipltd.com
Website: http://www.uipltd.com
Bank(s): National Westminster
Directors: J. Seaman (Fin)
Immediate Holding Company: URETHANE INDUSTRIAL PRODUCTS LIMITED
Registration no: 01750774 **VAT No.:** GB 787 4440 89
Date established: 1983 **Turnover:** £2m - £5m **No.of Employees:** 21 - 50
Product Groups: 29, 31

Date of Accounts	Mar 11	Mar 10	Mar 09
Working Capital	280	277	314
Fixed Assets	35	26	42
Current Assets	612	558	513
Current Liabilities	N/A	N/A	2

Winchester

Arup Acoustics

8 St Thomas Street, Winchester, SO23 9HE
Tel: 01962-829900 **Fax:** 01962-867270
E-mail: rob.harris@arup.com
Website: http://www.arup.com
Directors: R. Harris (Dir)
Ultimate Holding Company: OVE ARUP PARTNERSHIP
Registration no: 01312453 **Turnover:** £2m - £5m
No.of Employees: 11 - 20 **Product Groups:** 54

AvexiA Ltd

58 Church Street Micheldever, Winchester, SO21 3DB
Tel: 01962-774762
E-mail: graham.salvage@avexia.co.uk
Website: http://www.avexia.co.uk
Directors: G. Salvage (MD)
Immediate Holding Company: AVEXIA LIMITED
Registration no: 06622264 **Date established:** 2008
No.of Employees: 1 - 10 **Product Groups:** 37

Date of Accounts	Mar 11	Mar 10	Mar 09
Working Capital	156	74	78
Fixed Assets	12	1	2
Current Assets	580	97	127

B E Chaplin Gunmakers Ltd

6 Southgate Street, Winchester, SO23 9EF
Tel: 01962-840055 **Fax:** 01962-851146
E-mail: info@bechaplin.co.uk
Website: http://www.bechaplin.co.uk
Directors: S. Hart (Co Sec)
Ultimate Holding Company: BURDEN AND HART LIMITED
Immediate Holding Company: B.E. CHAPLIN (GUNMAKERS) LIMITED
Registration no: 00937572 **Date established:** 1968
No.of Employees: 1 - 10 **Product Groups:** 36, 39, 40

Date of Accounts	May 11	May 10	May 09
Working Capital	65	96	84
Fixed Assets	10	13	16
Current Assets	151	165	161

Chaplin Farrant Wiltshire Ltd

69 High Street, Winchester, SO23 9DA
Tel: 01962-862234 **Fax:** 01962-840506
E-mail: info@cfw-architects.com
Website: http://www.cfw-architects.com
Directors: M. Wiltshire (MD)
Immediate Holding Company: CHAPLIN, FARRANT, WILTSHIRE LIMITED
Registration no: 01089784 **Date established:** 1973 **Turnover:** £5m - £10m
No.of Employees: 1 - 10 **Product Groups:** 54, 84

Date of Accounts	Apr 11	Apr 10	Apr 09
Working Capital	40	47	17
Fixed Assets	11	13	16
Current Assets	120	122	79

County Windows Winchester Ltd

Glassworks Easton Lane, Winchester, SO23 7RU
Tel: 01962-840780 **Fax:** 01926-841532
E-mail: ian@county-glass.co.uk
Website: http://www.county-glass.co.uk
Managers: A. Fosberry (Mktg Serv Mgr)
Ultimate Holding Company: COUNTY GLASS LIMITED
Immediate Holding Company: COUNTY WINDOWS (WINCHESTER) LIMITED
Registration no: 02327567 **Date established:** 1988
Turnover: £500,000 - £1m **No.of Employees:** 51 - 100
Product Groups: 30, 35, 36

Date of Accounts	Mar 11	Mar 10	Mar 09
Working Capital	-209	-229	-195
Fixed Assets	65	82	73
Current Assets	189	78	92

Denplan Ltd

Denplan Court Victoria Road, Winchester, SO23 7RG
Tel: 01962-828000 **Fax:** 01962-840846
E-mail: denplan@denplan.co.uk
Website: http://www.denplan.co.uk
Directors: S. Cross (Fin), S. Gates (MD)
Managers: P. Metcalfe, S. Ellis (Personnel), A. Brown
Ultimate Holding Company: SIMPLYHEALTH GROUP LIMITED
Immediate Holding Company: DENPLAN LIMITED
Registration no: 01981238 **Date established:** 1986
Turnover: £20m - £50m **No.of Employees:** 251 - 500
Product Groups: 63, 88

Date of Accounts	Dec 11	Dec 10	Dec 09
Sales Turnover	39m	35m	37m
Pre Tax Profit/Loss	11m	12m	12m
Working Capital	378	15m	13m
Fixed Assets	886	1m	1m
Current Assets	18m	41m	36m
Current Liabilities	16m	25m	23m

Domain Attraction Ltd (Domain Attraction Ltd)

19 Nations Hill, Winchester, SO23 7QY
Tel: 01962-883754
E-mail: info@jobsinsearch.com
Website: http://www.domainattraction.co.uk
Directors: M. Taylor (MD), J. Taylor (Fin)
Immediate Holding Company: DOMAIN ATTRACTION LIMITED
Registration no: 03788387 **Date established:** 1999
No.of Employees: 1 - 10 **Product Groups:** 80

Date of Accounts	Mar 11	Mar 10	Mar 09
Working Capital	47	63	10
Fixed Assets	2	2	1
Current Assets	82	119	20
Current Liabilities	N/A	N/A	10

Elliotts Tool Warehouse (Elliot Brothers)

Unit 10 Winchester Trade Park Easton Lane, Winchester, SO23 7FA
Tel: 01962-827610 **Fax:** 01962-827611
E-mail: winchester@elliott-brothers.co.uk
Website: http://www.elliotts4tools.com
Managers: T. Tugwell
Ultimate Holding Company: ELLIOTT BROTHERS (BUILDERS MERCHANTS) LIMITED
Immediate Holding Company: ELLIOTT BROTHERS LIMITED
Registration no: 02511005 **Date established:** 1990
Turnover: £250,000 - £500,000 **No.of Employees:** 1 - 10
Product Groups: 36, 37, 40, 41, 46, 67

Date of Accounts	Dec 10	Dec 09	Dec 08
Sales Turnover	38m	37m	44m
Pre Tax Profit/Loss	341	138	1m
Working Capital	9m	8m	8m
Fixed Assets	2m	2m	2m
Current Assets	16m	14m	15m
Current Liabilities	4m	1m	4m

Forest Traffic Services Ltd

FTS House Moorside Road, Winchester, SO23 7RX
Tel: 01962-855351
E-mail: winchester@forestsupportservices.co.uk
Website: http://www.forestsupportservices.co.uk
Managers: D. Thorn (Mgr)
Ultimate Holding Company: FOREST SUPPORT SERVICES LTD
Immediate Holding Company: FOREST TRAFFIC SERVICES LIMITED
Registration no: 01664145 **Date established:** 1982 **Turnover:** £5m - £10m
No.of Employees: 51 - 100 **Product Groups:** 30, 39, 44

Date of Accounts	Mar 12	Mar 11	Mar 10
Sales Turnover	13m	11m	9m
Pre Tax Profit/Loss	487	402	124
Working Capital	197	-118	-703
Fixed Assets	717	641	975
Current Assets	4m	3m	2m
Current Liabilities	2m	1m	550

Garbuiodickinson

Moorside Road, Winchester, SO23 7SS
Tel: 01962-842222 **Fax:** 01962-840567
E-mail: sales@garbuiodickinson.eu
Website: http://www.garbuiodickinson.eu
Bank(s): Barclays
Directors: P. North (Grp Sales), D. Heath (MD)
Managers: K. Rowlands (Tech Serv Mgr), G. Szentesi (Comptroller), C. Zych (Mktg Serv Mgr), R. Davis (Purch Mgr)
Ultimate Holding Company: FINTREVI SRL (ITALY)
Immediate Holding Company: DICKINSON LEGG LIMITED
Registration no: 01488755 **VAT No.:** GB 329 9571 14
Date established: 1980 **Turnover:** £20m - £50m
No.of Employees: 101 - 250 **Product Groups:** 41

Date of Accounts	Oct 11	Oct 10	Oct 09
Sales Turnover	30m	28m	46m
Pre Tax Profit/Loss	3m	2m	3m
Working Capital	9m	7m	5m
Fixed Assets	2m	2m	3m
Current Assets	17m	15m	14m
Current Liabilities	5m	4m	4m

Gradko International Ltd

77 Wales Street, Winchester, SO23 0RH
Tel: 01962-860331 **Fax:** 01962-841339
E-mail: admin@gradko.co.uk
Website: http://www.gradko.co.uk
Directors: C. Wallage (Dir)
Managers: C. Gardner (I.T. Exec)
Immediate Holding Company: GRADKO INTERNATIONAL LIMITED
Registration no: 01148546 **VAT No.:** GB 329 9426 23
Date established: 1973 **Turnover:** £500,000 - £1m
No.of Employees: 11 - 20 **Product Groups:** 30

Date of Accounts	Oct 11	Oct 10	Oct 09
Working Capital	860	746	842
Fixed Assets	330	409	292
Current Assets	1m	1m	1m

Hampshire Windscreens

5 Southbrook Cottages Micheldever, Winchester, SO21 3DJ
Tel: 01962-774156 **Fax:** 01962-774566
E-mail: info@hampshirewindscreens.co.uk
Website: http://www.hampshirewindscreens.co.uk
Directors: B. Davison (Prop)
No.of Employees: 1 - 10 **Product Groups:** 39

Helga Chapman

20 Staple Gardens, Winchester, SO23 8SR
Tel: 01962-622500 **Fax:** 01722-782513
E-mail: info@chapmanmolony.com
Website: http://www.chapmanmolony.com
Directors: H. Chapman (Prop)
Managers: N. Heron (Sec), R. Lane (I.T. Exec), V. Dalton (Accounts)
Ultimate Holding Company: ADVANTIP LIMITED
Immediate Holding Company: CHAPMAN IP LIMITED
Registration no: 04465454 **Date established:** 2002
Turnover: Up to £250,000 **No.of Employees:** 11 - 20 **Product Groups:** 80

Date of Accounts	Jun 11	Jun 10	Jun 09
Working Capital	177	187	148
Fixed Assets	49	59	74
Current Assets	702	708	639

I A C Company Ltd

Winnall Industrial Estate Moorside Road, Winchester, SO23 7RX
Tel: 01962-873000 **Fax:** 01962-873111
E-mail: info@iacl.co.uk
Website: http://www.iacl.co.uk
Bank(s): HSBC
Directors: B. Quarendon (MD)
Ultimate Holding Company: INTERNATIONAL MEZZANINE INVESTMENTS N.V (NETHERLAND
Immediate Holding Company: INDUSTRIAL ACOUSTICS COMPANY LIMITED
Registration no: 00606877 **VAT No.:** GB 448 8703 12
Date established: 1958 **Turnover:** £50m - £75m
No.of Employees: 101 - 250 **Product Groups:** 26, 28, 29, 30, 31, 32, 33, 35, 37, 38, 39, 40, 44, 46, 48, 49, 54, 66, 83, 84, 85, 86, 89

Date of Accounts	Dec 11	Dec 10	Dec 09
Sales Turnover	78m	63m	60m
Pre Tax Profit/Loss	5m	3m	3m
Working Capital	13m	10m	8m
Fixed Assets	6m	6m	6m
Current Assets	43m	38m	30m
Current Liabilities	12m	15m	12m

Jewson Ltd

Moorside Road, Winchester, SO23 7SQ
Tel: 01962-861672 **Fax:** 01962-842578
Website: http://www.jewson.co.uk
Managers: K. Ashby (District Mgr)
Ultimate Holding Company: COMPAGNIE DE SAINT GOBAIN (FRANCE)
Immediate Holding Company: JEWSON LIMITED
Registration no: 00348407 **VAT No.:** GB 497 7184 83
Date established: 1939 **Turnover:** £2m - £5m **No.of Employees:** 11 - 20
Product Groups: 66

Date of Accounts	Dec 11	Dec 10	Dec 09
Sales Turnover	1606m	1547m	1485m
Pre Tax Profit/Loss	18m	100m	45m
Working Capital	-345m	-250m	-349m
Fixed Assets	496m	387m	461m
Current Assets	657m	1005m	1320m
Current Liabilities	66m	120m	64m

Kings Worthy Foundry Co. Ltd

London Road, Winchester, SO23 7QG
Tel: 01962-883776 **Fax:** 01962-882925
E-mail: kwf@fsbdial.co.uk
Website: http://www.kingsworthyfoundry.co.uk
Directors: B. Peake (MD), S. Peake (Dir)
Managers: A. Pearson (Chief Mgr)
Immediate Holding Company: KINGSWORTHY FOUNDRY COMPANY LIMITED
Registration no: 00401133 **VAT No.:** GB 188 5183 23
Date established: 1945 **Turnover:** £500,000 - £1m
No.of Employees: 1 - 10 **Product Groups:** 26, 36

Date of Accounts	Mar 08	Mar 07	Mar 06
Working Capital	962	918	894
Fixed Assets	454	452	435
Current Assets	1055	1025	1018
Current Liabilities	93	107	124
Total Share Capital	5	5	5

Merlin Accessories

Unit G Nickel Close Winnall Trading Estate, Winchester, SO23 7RJ
Tel: 01962-842400 **Fax:** 01962-842420
E-mail: sales@merlinaccessories.com
Directors: M. Carey (Fin)
Immediate Holding Company: MERLIN ACCESSORIES LIMITED
Registration no: 01448569 **VAT No.:** 329 8288 14 **Date established:** 1979
Turnover: £1m - £2m **No.of Employees:** 1 - 10 **Product Groups:** 35, 37

Date of Accounts	Nov 11	Nov 10	Nov 09
Working Capital	252	254	255
Fixed Assets	57	30	45
Current Assets	534	544	560

Mitchell Bridges

London Road Kings Worthy, Winchester, SO23 7QN
Tel: 01962-885040 **Fax:** 01962-882305
E-mail: info@mitchellbridges.com
Website: http://www.mitchellbridges.com
Directors: C. Mitchell (Dir)
Immediate Holding Company: MITCHELL BRIDGES LIMITED
Registration no: 02084498 **Date established:** 1986
Turnover: £250,000 - £500,000 **No.of Employees:** 1 - 10
Product Groups: 35, 40, 67, 83

Date of Accounts	May 12	May 11	May 10
Working Capital	332	351	138
Fixed Assets	297	331	438

Current Assets	504	578	347

Nomax Ltd
22 Hyde Street, Winchester, SO23 7DR
Tel: 01962-840850 **Fax:** 01962-841512
E-mail: quote@nomax.co.uk
Website: http://www.nomax.co.uk
Directors: C. Bogan (MD)
Immediate Holding Company: NOMAX LIMITED
Registration no: 02143972 **VAT No.:** GB 458 6535 10
Date established: 1987 **Turnover:** £500,000 - £1m
No.of Employees: 1 - 10 **Product Groups:** 66

Date of Accounts	Jun 11	Jun 10	Jun 09
Working Capital	910	963	888
Fixed Assets	16	22	25
Current Assets	1m	1m	1m

Oakes Brothers
Cowdown Farm Micheldever, Winchester, SO21 3DN
Tel: 01962-794100 **Fax:** 01962-794118
E-mail: edmundl@oakesbros.co.uk
Website: http://www.oakesbros.co.uk
Directors: E. Lindley (MD)
Ultimate Holding Company: ARMOX TRUST (NEVIS)
Immediate Holding Company: OAKES BROS. LIMITED
Registration no: 00395809 **Date established:** 1945
Turnover: £20m - £50m **No.of Employees:** 21 - 50 **Product Groups:** 41

Date of Accounts	Dec 11	Dec 10	Dec 09
Sales Turnover	22m	22m	23m
Pre Tax Profit/Loss	381	232	262
Working Capital	2m	3m	3m
Fixed Assets	539	559	600
Current Assets	7m	5m	7m
Current Liabilities	3m	1m	1m

Permabond Engineering Adhesives Ltd
Wessex Business Park Wessex Way, Colden Common, Winchester, SO21 1WP
Tel: 01962-711661 **Fax:** 01962-711662
E-mail: daniella.davidson@permabond.com
Website: http://www.permabond.com
Managers: D. Davidson
Immediate Holding Company: PERMABOND ENGINEERING ADHESIVES LIMITED
Registration no: 04908229 **Date established:** 2003 **Turnover:** £1m - £2m
No.of Employees: 1 - 10 **Product Groups:** 32, 37, 42, 66, 85

Date of Accounts	Dec 11	Dec 10	Dec 09
Working Capital	789	345	-50
Fixed Assets	676	700	731
Current Assets	2m	1m	1m

Personal Home Finders
63 High Street, Winchester, SO23 9BX
Tel: 01962-878887 **Fax:** 01962-844789
E-mail: post@personal-homefinders.com
Website: http://www.personal-homefinders.com
Directors: P. Cole (Dir)
Immediate Holding Company: PERSONAL HOMEFINDERS LIMITED
Registration no: 02179894 **VAT No.:** GB 522 0674 75
Date established: 1987 **Turnover:** Up to £250,000
No.of Employees: 1 - 10 **Product Groups:** 80

Date of Accounts	Sep 11	Sep 10	Sep 09
Working Capital	-55	124	123
Fixed Assets	267	11	7
Current Assets	1m	887	656

PrintSafe Ltd
Unit 2 Old Dairy Buildings Lower Norton Farm, Sutton Scotney, Winchester, SO21 3NE
Tel: 01962-761 761 **Fax:** 01962-761762
E-mail: sales@printsafe.co.uk
Website: http://www.printsafe.co.uk
Directors: N. Turner (Dir)
Registration no: 05841037 **Turnover:** £2m - £5m
No.of Employees: 1 - 10 **Product Groups:** 28, 44

Date of Accounts	Jun 08	Jun 07
Working Capital	114	55
Fixed Assets	5	3
Current Assets	208	191
Current Liabilities	94	137

Redwood Health Therapies
11 Bridge Street, Winchester, SO23 0HL
Tel: 01962-844032
E-mail: info@redwoodhealth.co.uk
Website: http://www.redwoodhealth.co.uk
Directors: T. Millineer (MD), T. Millinder (Prop)
Immediate Holding Company: TRADE EXCHANGE NETWORK (SOUTH EAST) LTD
Registration no: 05841658 **Date established:** 2012
No.of Employees: 21 - 50 **Product Groups:** 88

Date of Accounts	Jun 10	Jun 09	Jun 08
Working Capital	-11	-5	-5
Fixed Assets	17	14	8
Current Assets	-11	15	13

Scientific Instrument Centre Ltd
Unit 4 Leylands Park Nobs Crook, Colden Common, Winchester, SO21 1TH
Tel: 023-8069 6092 **Fax:** 023-8069 5026
E-mail: sales@sic.uk.com
Website: http://www.sic.uk.com
Directors: M. Preston (MD)
Immediate Holding Company: SCIENTIFIC INSTRUMENT CENTRE LIMITED(THE)
Registration no: 00435060 **Date established:** 1947 **Turnover:** £1m - £2m
No.of Employees: 1 - 10 **Product Groups:** 61

Date of Accounts	Dec 11	Dec 10	Dec 09
Working Capital	310	326	317
Fixed Assets	39	42	24
Current Assets	410	444	442

Shape Rubber Co.
Unit 1 Beeches Crawley, Winchester, SO21 2QD
Tel: 01962-882877 **Fax:** 01962-883605
E-mail: sales@shaperubber.com
Website: http://www.shaperubber.com
Directors: J. Townson (Prop)
Turnover: £500,000 - £1m **No.of Employees:** 1 - 10 **Product Groups:** 29, 30, 49

Southern Power Tools & Abrasives Ltd
Unit A Nickel Close, Winchester, SO23 7RJ
Tel: 01962-856022 **Fax:** 01962-842395
E-mail: info@spta.co.uk
Directors: P. Bartlett (MD), J. Bartlett (Fin)
Immediate Holding Company: SOUTHERN POWER TOOLS AND ABRASIVES LIMITED
Registration no: 01498438 **Date established:** 1980
No.of Employees: 1 - 10 **Product Groups:** 37

Date of Accounts	Dec 07	Mar 11	Mar 10
Working Capital	27	29	30
Fixed Assets	12	8	12
Current Assets	254	260	361

Steel Services Winchester Ltd
Foundry Yard London Road, Kings Worthy, Winchester, SO23 7QA
Tel: 01962-884588 **Fax:** 01962-889366
E-mail: sswinchester@btconnect.com
Website: http://www.steel-serviceswinchester.co.uk
Directors: P. Thompson (Prop)
Immediate Holding Company: STEEL SERVICES (WINCHESTER) LIMITED
Registration no: 03294230 **Date established:** 1996 **Turnover:** £5m - £10m
No.of Employees: 1 - 10 **Product Groups:** 26, 35

Date of Accounts	Jan 12	Jan 11	Jan 10
Working Capital	-12	-19	-12
Fixed Assets	13	17	22
Current Assets	25	19	26

Storck Travel Retail Ltd
Moorside Road, Winchester, SO23 7SA
Tel: 01962-830990 **Fax:** 01962-841547
E-mail: lara.candido@uk.storck.com
Website: http://www.storck-tr.com
Managers: E. Sopf (Mktg Serv Mgr)
Ultimate Holding Company: AUGUST STORCK KG (GERMANY)
Immediate Holding Company: STORCK TRAVEL RETAIL LIMITED
Registration no: 02269670 **VAT No.:** GB 382 6250 49
Date established: 1988 **Turnover:** £500,000 - £1m
No.of Employees: 1 - 10 **Product Groups:** 20

Date of Accounts	Dec 11	Dec 10	Dec 09
Sales Turnover	738	571	571
Pre Tax Profit/Loss	35	-12	8
Working Capital	193	153	163
Fixed Assets	N/A	15	15
Current Assets	625	395	338
Current Liabilities	N/A	98	94

Paul Tanner Associates
8 Upper High Street, Winchester, SO23 8UT
Tel: 01962-859800 **Fax:** 01962-856452
E-mail: admin@paultannerassociates.co.uk
Website: http://www.paul-tanner.com
Directors: P. Tanner (Prop)
Immediate Holding Company: CANDOVER GREEN LIMITED
Date established: 2008 **No.of Employees:** 1 - 10 **Product Groups:** 35

Date of Accounts	Mar 12	Mar 11	Sep 09
Working Capital	5	3	N/A
Fixed Assets	46	48	N/A
Current Assets	37	32	N/A

Trion The Division Of Ruskin Air Management Ltd
Unit 1a The Cavendish Centre Winnall Close, Winchester, SO23 0LB
Tel: 01962-840465 **Fax:** 01962-828619
E-mail: kbristow@airsysco.com
Website: http://www.trion.co.uk
Directors: K. Bristow (Sales)
Immediate Holding Company: EVERYCARE (CENTRAL HANTS) LTD
Registration no: 01401364 **Date established:** 2010 **Turnover:** £1m - £2m
No.of Employees: 1 - 10 **Product Groups:** 40, 52

Date of Accounts	Dec 10	Dec 09	Dec 08
Working Capital	-0	-3	63
Fixed Assets	3	4	26
Current Assets	81	79	156

Trussbuilt UK Ltd
Winnall Valley Road, Winchester, SO23 0LD
Tel: 01962-840330 **Fax:** 01962-840334
E-mail: trussbuilt@aol.com
Directors: A. Dadgostar (MD)
Immediate Holding Company: TRUSSBUILT (UK) LIMITED
Registration no: 03833001 **VAT No.:** GB 643 3822 43
Date established: 1999 **Turnover:** £500,000 - £1m
No.of Employees: 1 - 10 **Product Groups:** 25

Date of Accounts	Jan 12	Jan 11	Jan 10
Working Capital	69	59	112
Fixed Assets	109	119	47
Current Assets	140	134	174

W M Group
18 City Business Centre Hyde Street, Winchester, SO23 7TA
Tel: 01962-841250 **Fax:** 01962-870558
E-mail: hello@thewm-group.com
Website: http://www.thewm-group.com
Directors: A. Ayling (Co Sec)
Immediate Holding Company: WM TRAINING LIMITED
Registration no: 03065128 **VAT No.:** 522 1205 08 **Date established:** 1995
Turnover: £500,000 - £1m **No.of Employees:** 1 - 10 **Product Groups:** 81

Whitwam Ltd
2 Moorside Business Park Moorside Road, Winchester, SO23 7RX
Tel: 01962-870408 **Fax:** 01962-850820
E-mail: hire@whitwam.ltd.uk
Website: http://www.whitwam.ltd.uk
Directors: D. Harding (Dir)
Immediate Holding Company: WHITWAM HOLDINGS LIMITED
Registration no: 01392822 **Date established:** 1978
No.of Employees: 1 - 10 **Product Groups:** 37, 67, 83

Date of Accounts	Dec 11	Dec 10	Dec 09
Working Capital	239	241	228
Fixed Assets	828	830	839
Current Assets	609	469	537

Winchester Joinery & Flooring Ltd
Mooreside Road, Winchester, SO23 7SB
Tel: 01962-868650 **Fax:** 01962-852666
E-mail: info@wjaf.co.uk
Website: http://www.wjaf.co.uk
Directors: A. Foster (MD)
Immediate Holding Company: WINCHESTER JOINERY LIMITED
Registration no: 02903054 **Date established:** 1994
No.of Employees: 11 - 20 **Product Groups:** 25, 52, 66

Date of Accounts	Feb 08	Feb 09	Feb 07
Working Capital	56	51	2
Fixed Assets	145	133	97
Current Assets	482	570	359

Yateley

ABUS Crane Systems Ltd
Unit 1 1 Business Village, Yateley, GU46 6GA
Tel: 01252-749000 **Fax:** 01252-749001
E-mail: info@abuscranes.co.uk
Website: http://www.abuscranes.co.uk
Bank(s): HSBC Bank plc
Directors: C. Kauferstein (MD)
Managers: D. Edwards (Sales Admin)
Ultimate Holding Company: ABUS GRUNDSTUCKSVERWALTUNG GMBH & CO KG (GERMANY)
Immediate Holding Company: ABUS CRANE SYSTEMS LIMITED
Registration no: 02591463 **VAT No.:** GB 572 7340 34
Date established: 1991 **No.of Employees:** 21 - 50 **Product Groups:** 35, 39, 45, 48, 67, 84, 85

Date of Accounts	Dec 11	Dec 10	Dec 09
Working Capital	542	516	440
Fixed Assets	945	927	948
Current Assets	1m	3m	2m

Alecto Solutions Ltd
1 Ilex Close, Yateley, GU46 6JP
Tel: 0845-026 1493 **Fax:** 0845-026 1494
E-mail: enquiries@alectosolutions.co.uk
Website: http://www.alectosolutions.co.uk
Directors: Z. Wagstaff (Fin)
Immediate Holding Company: ALECTO SOLUTIONS LIMITED
Registration no: 06585115 **Date established:** 2008
Turnover: Up to £250,000 **No.of Employees:** 1 - 10 **Product Groups:** 37, 44, 48, 52

Date of Accounts	May 11	May 10
Working Capital	4	-2
Fixed Assets	1	2
Current Assets	11	5

Artisan Resourcing
The Studio 24 Pond Croft, Yateley, GU46 7UR
Tel: 01252-890030 **Fax:** 01252-890031
E-mail: brian@artisanuk.co.uk
Website: http://www.artisanuk.co.uk
Directors: B. Coultrip (Dir), S. Coultrip (Fin)
Managers: B. Coultrip (Ops Mgr)
Immediate Holding Company: Artisan Resourcing Ltd
Registration no: 04827706 **Date established:** 2003
Turnover: Up to £250,000 **No.of Employees:** 1 - 10 **Product Groups:** 80

Date of Accounts	Dec 07	Dec 06	Dec 05
Sales Turnover	N/A	191	N/A
Pre Tax Profit/Loss	N/A	37	N/A
Working Capital	-17	6	-5
Fixed Assets	1	2	3
Current Assets	121	71	5
Current Liabilities	138	65	10
ROCE% (Return on Capital Employed)		464.4	
ROT% (Return on Turnover)		19.1	

Byron Creative Organisation
6-7 Aragon Road Blackbushe Business Park, Yateley, GU46 6GA
Tel: 01252-879427 **Fax:** 01252-860052
E-mail: info@byroncreative.com
Website: http://www.byroncreative.com
Directors: M. Treverton (Ptnr)
No.of Employees: 1 - 10 **Product Groups:** 44, 81

Camberley Signs
Unit B2 Galway Road Blackbushe Business Park, Yateley, GU46 6GE
Tel: 01252-872888 **Fax:** 01252-873332
E-mail: info@camberleysigns.co.uk
Website: http://www.camberleysigns.co.uk
Directors: M. Love (Prop), M. Love (Prop), W. Love (Co Sec)
Registration no: 03717241 **No.of Employees:** 21 - 50
Product Groups: 24, 26, 30, 39

Connections UK
28 Hall Farm Cresent, Yateley, GU46 6HT
Tel: 01252-877552 **Fax:** 01252-877552
Directors: R. Bosworth (Prop)
Date established: 1993 **No.of Employees:** 1 - 10 **Product Groups:** 46

Dakat Ltd
Maple Cottage Beaver Lane, Yateley, GU46 6XJ
Tel: 01252-872256 **Fax:** 01252-872256
E-mail: gellicott@yahoo.com
Website: http://www.dakat.co.uk
Directors: E. Ellicott (Fin)
Immediate Holding Company: DAKAT LIMITED
Registration no: 03793543 **Date established:** 1999
Turnover: Up to £250,000 **No.of Employees:** 1 - 10 **Product Groups:** 38, 54

Date of Accounts	Jun 11	Jun 10	Jun 08
Working Capital	44	25	10
Fixed Assets	3	4	4
Current Assets	59	61	33

Innotech Controls UK Ltd
18 Henley Gardens, Yateley, GU46 6LG
Tel: 01252-669317 **Fax:** 01252-877644
E-mail: sales@innotechcontrolsuk.com
Website: http://www.innotechcontrolsuk.com
Directors: K. Taylor (MD)
Immediate Holding Company: INNOVATION CONTROL LIMITED
Registration no: 03355982 **Date established:** 1997
Turnover: £250,000 - £500,000 **No.of Employees:** 1 - 10
Product Groups: 38

see next page

***Innotech Controls UK Ltd** - Cont'd*

Date of Accounts	May 11	May 10	May 09
Working Capital	62	24	57
Fixed Assets	11	15	3
Current Assets	259	275	197

Linatex Ltd

Wilkinson House Galway Road Blackbushe Business Park, Yateley, GU46 6GE
Tel: 01252-743000 **Fax:** 01252-743030
E-mail: helen.kenward@linatex.com
Website: http://www.linatex.com
Bank(s): Barclays
Directors: B. Cook (Dir), H. Kenward (Co Sec)
Managers: S. Barber
Ultimate Holding Company: WEIR GROUP PLC(THE)
Immediate Holding Company: LINATEX LIMITED
Registration no: 00246713 **Date established:** 1930
Turnover: £10m - £20m **No.of Employees:** 51 - 100 **Product Groups:** 14, 23, 29, 36, 40, 42, 45, 66

Date of Accounts	Dec 09	Dec 08	Dec 07
Sales Turnover	11m	16m	14m
Pre Tax Profit/Loss	1m	-893	310
Working Capital	-777	-2m	-1m
Fixed Assets	5m	6m	6m
Current Assets	6m	7m	5m
Current Liabilities	947	2m	1m

Origyn NLP Training

99 Reading Road, Yateley, GU46 7LR
Tel: 01252-861351
E-mail: info@origyn.co.uk
Website: http://www.origyn.co.uk
Directors: R. Ballentine (Prop)
Turnover: Up to £250,000 **No.of Employees:** 1 - 10 **Product Groups:** 26, 38, 63, 86

Sonardyne International Ltd

Ocean House Blackbush Business Park, Yateley, GU46 6GD
Tel: 01252-872288 **Fax:** 01252-876100
E-mail: sales@sonardyne.co.uk
Website: http://www.sonardyne.com
Bank(s): Lloyds TSB
Directors: J. Partridge (MD), R. Balloch (Sales)
Managers: C. Brannan (Personnel)
Ultimate Holding Company: SONARDYNE GROUP LIMITED
Immediate Holding Company: SONARDYNE GROUP LIMITED
Registration no: 01968550 **VAT No.:** GB 591 6950 04
Date established: 1985 **Turnover:** £20m - £50m
No.of Employees: 101 - 250 **Product Groups:** 37, 38, 67, 84

Date of Accounts	Mar 11	Mar 10	Mar 09
Sales Turnover	37m	33m	48m
Pre Tax Profit/Loss	7m	4m	14m
Working Capital	35m	31m	29m
Fixed Assets	10m	9m	10m
Current Assets	43m	37m	42m
Current Liabilities	7m	5m	11m

HEREFORDSHIRE

Bromyard

Harris Bros
Upper House Farm Edwyn Ralph, Bromyard, HR7 4LU
Tel: 01885-488532 **Fax:** 01885-483999
E-mail: harris_bros@hotmail.com
Directors: R. Harris (MD), I. Harris (Dir)
Date established: 1993 **No.of Employees:** 51 - 100 **Product Groups:** 35, 39, 45

Holden Vintage & Classic Ltd
Linton Trading Estate, Bromyard, HR7 4QT
Tel: 01885-488000 **Fax:** 01885-488889
E-mail: sales@holden.co.uk
Website: http://www.holden.co.uk
Directors: J. Parker (MD)
Immediate Holding Company: HOLDEN VINTAGE & CLASSIC LIMITED
Registration no: 02295151 **VAT No.:** GB 488 0473 15
Date established: 1988 **Turnover:** £1m - £2m **No.of Employees:** 1 - 10
Product Groups: 68

Date of Accounts	Dec 11	Dec 10	Dec 09
Sales Turnover	1m	1m	995
Pre Tax Profit/Loss	41	17	13
Working Capital	141	133	144
Fixed Assets	67	55	57
Current Assets	328	307	315
Current Liabilities	27	17	17

Micron Sprayers Ltd
Bromyard Industrial Estate, Bromyard, HR7 4HS
Tel: 01885-482397 **Fax:** 01885-483043
E-mail: john.clayton@micron.co.uk
Website: http://www.micron.co.uk
Bank(s): Lloyds TSB Bank plc
Directors: T. Bals (Ch), J. Clayton (Tech Serv), D. Spackman (Fin)
Managers: A. Landey (Mktg Serv Mgr), S. Page-jones (Prod Mgr)
Ultimate Holding Company: MICRON SPRAYERS LIMITED
Immediate Holding Company: CDA LIMITED
Registration no: 01335361 **VAT No.:** GB 135 5341 84
Date established: 1977 **Turnover:** £2m - £5m **No.of Employees:** 21 - 50
Product Groups: 39, 41, 75

Polytec Holden Ltd
Porthouse Industrial Estate, Bromyard, HR7 4NS
Tel: 01885-483000 **Fax:** 01885-483057
E-mail: reception@polytec-group.com
Website: http://www.polytec-group.com
Bank(s): National Westminster Bank Plc
Directors: M. Collinson (Dir), N. Munster (MD)
Ultimate Holding Company: POLYTEC HOLDING AG (AUSTRIA)
Immediate Holding Company: POLYTEC CAR STYLING BROMYARD LIMITED
Registration no: 04026072 **VAT No.:** GB 672 8636 00
Date established: 2000 **Turnover:** £20m - £50m
No.of Employees: 251 - 500 **Product Groups:** 30, 39

Date of Accounts	Apr 11	Apr 10	Apr 04
Working Capital	5	5	5
Current Assets	5	5	5

S S M International
Tedstone Wafre, Bromyard, HR7 4PY
Tel: 01886-853646 **Fax:** 01886-853539
E-mail: sales@ssminternational.com
Website: http://www.ssminternational.com
Directors: D. Parsons (Prop)
Date established: 1968 **No.of Employees:** 1 - 10 **Product Groups:** 36, 39, 40

C T Watkins
Panniers Lane Hereford Road, Bromyard, HR7 4QU
Tel: 01885-482100 **Fax:** 01885-482100
Directors: C. Watkins (Prop)
Date established: 1995 **No.of Employees:** 1 - 10 **Product Groups:** 41

Wicks & Martin Ltd
Station Road, Bromyard, HR7 4HT
Tel: 01885-483636 **Fax:** 01885-483692
E-mail: mike@wicksandmartin.co.uk
Website: http://www.wicksandmartin.co.uk
Directors: D. Young (Fin), G. Williams (Chief Op Offcr)
Immediate Holding Company: WICKS & MARTIN LIMITED
Registration no: 01042507 **VAT No.:** GB 136 0880 73
Date established: 1972 **Turnover:** £500,000 - £1m
No.of Employees: 1 - 10 **Product Groups:** 35

Date of Accounts	Mar 11	Mar 10	Mar 09
Working Capital	82	65	95
Fixed Assets	56	53	53
Current Assets	164	150	140

Hereford

A K Industries Ltd
Unit 1-2 Foxwood Court, Rotherwas Industrial Estate, Hereford, HR2 6JQ
Tel: 01432-375100 **Fax:** 01432-263532
E-mail: sales@aki.co.uk
Website: http://www.aki.co.uk
Directors: A. Green (MD)
Managers: N. Thompson (Buyer), G. Wallace (Tech Serv Mgr), A. Green
Immediate Holding Company: A K INDUSTRIES LIMITED
Registration no: 03121038 **Date established:** 1995
No.of Employees: 51 - 100 **Product Groups:** 30

Date of Accounts	Mar 11	Mar 10	Mar 09
Pre Tax Profit/Loss	N/A	N/A	56
Working Capital	1m	1m	1m
Fixed Assets	439	443	508
Current Assets	3m	2m	2m
Current Liabilities	N/A	N/A	391

Aconbury Sprouts Ltd
Unit 4 Westwood Industrial Estate Ewyas Harold, Hereford, HR2 0EL
Tel: 01981-241155 **Fax:** 01981-241386
E-mail: info@aconbury.co.uk
Website: http://www.aconbury.co.uk
Directors: J. Hardy (MD)
Managers: A. Kura, R. Peacock (Mktg Serv Mgr)
Immediate Holding Company: ACONBURY SPROUTS LIMITED
Registration no: 05954402 **Date established:** 2006
Turnover: Up to £250,000 **No.of Employees:** 11 - 20 **Product Groups:** 02, 62

Date of Accounts	Oct 11	Oct 10	Oct 09
Working Capital	-65	-40	-130
Fixed Assets	293	327	355
Current Assets	110	166	182

Ascari Cafe
11-14 West Street, Hereford, HR4 0BX
Tel: 01432-265147 **Fax:** 01432-356602
E-mail: info@cafe-ascari.net
Website: http://www.cafe-ascari.net
Directors: N. Vaughan (Prop)
Immediate Holding Company: CAFE ASCARI LIMITED
Registration no: 05057598 **Date established:** 2004
No.of Employees: 21 - 50 **Product Groups:** 40, 63, 69, 83

Axon Enterprises Ltd
8a St Martins Street, Hereford, HR2 7RE
Tel: 01432-359906 **Fax:** 01432-352436
E-mail: sales@axon-enterprises.co.uk
Website: http://www.axon-enterprises.co.uk
Directors: P. Emberton (MD)
Managers: D. Phillips (Chief Acct)
Ultimate Holding Company: PSD HOLDINGS LIMITED
Immediate Holding Company: AXON ENTERPRISES LIMITED
Registration no: 02311866 **Date established:** 1988 **Turnover:** £5m - £10m
No.of Employees: 11 - 20 **Product Groups:** 26, 32, 35, 36, 40, 41, 42, 45, 49, 63, 66, 67

Date of Accounts	Mar 11	Mar 10	Mar 09
Sales Turnover	5m	5m	4m
Pre Tax Profit/Loss	247	287	267
Working Capital	2m	2m	1m
Fixed Assets	7	8	11
Current Assets	3m	3m	3m
Current Liabilities	372	521	587

Baugh & Weedon Ltd
Beech Business Park Tillington Road, Hereford, HR4 9QJ
Tel: 01432-267671 **Fax:** 01432-359017
E-mail: sales@bandwndt.co.uk
Website: http://www.bandwndt.co.uk
Bank(s): Lloyds TSB Bank plc
Directors: J. Minton (Co Sec)
Managers: J. Bone (Chief Mgr)
Ultimate Holding Company: MINTON,TREHARNE & DAVIES LIMITED
Immediate Holding Company: BAUGH & WEEDON LIMITED
Registration no: 00918792 **VAT No.:** GB 133 5258 83
Date established: 1967 **Turnover:** £1m - £2m **No.of Employees:** 11 - 20
Product Groups: 37, 38

Date of Accounts	Dec 08	Dec 07	Mar 11
Working Capital	19	1	-2
Fixed Assets	444	455	425
Current Assets	217	205	203

Bearings Belts & Sprockets Hereford Ltd
4-5 Cattle Market, Hereford, HR4 9HX
Tel: 01432-357318 **Fax:** 01432-340438
E-mail: bbs@ukonline.co.uk
Website: http://www.bbsdirect.com
Directors: C. Davies (MD), T. Davies (Dir)
Immediate Holding Company: BEARINGS BELTS AND SPROCKETS (HEREFORD) LIMITED
Registration no: 02414053 **Date established:** 1989
No.of Employees: 1 - 10 **Product Groups:** 35, 39, 66

Blue Sail Consulting Ltd
Park House Wormelow, Hereford, HR2 8EQ
Tel: 01981-540934
E-mail: contact@bluesail.com
Website: http://www.bluesail.com
Directors: L. Easton (Dir)
Immediate Holding Company: BLUE SAIL CONSULTING LIMITED
Registration no: 06021556 **Date established:** 2006
Turnover: £250,000 - £500,000 **No.of Employees:** 1 - 10
Product Groups: 84

Date of Accounts	Mar 12	Mar 11	Mar 10
Working Capital	29	17	18
Current Assets	78	63	148

Bodycote Hip Ltd
College Road, Hereford, HR1 1JR
Tel: 01432-263377 **Fax:** 01432-263388
E-mail: david.chapman@bodycote.com
Website: http://www.bodycote.com
Managers: D. Chapman (Mgr)
Ultimate Holding Company: BODYCOTE PLC
Immediate Holding Company: BODYCOTE H.I.P. LIMITED
Registration no: 01276450 **Date established:** 1976 **Turnover:** £5m - £10m
No.of Employees: 21 - 50 **Product Groups:** 46, 48

Date of Accounts	Dec 11	Dec 10	Dec 09
Sales Turnover	5m	5m	7m
Pre Tax Profit/Loss	1m	417	1m
Working Capital	2m	3m	242
Fixed Assets	9m	10m	11m
Current Assets	4m	4m	3m
Current Liabilities	1m	1m	2m

Border Craft Workshop Ltd
Unit 1 The Old Forge Peterchurch, Hereford, HR2 0SD
Tel: 01981-550251 **Fax:** 01981-550552
E-mail: sales@bordercraft.co.uk
Website: http://www.bordercraft.co.uk
Directors: D. Hodgson (Grp Chief Exec)
Date established: 1972 **No.of Employees:** 1 - 10 **Product Groups:** 26

Date of Accounts	Mar 08	Mar 07	Mar 06
Working Capital	-21	-39	-48
Fixed Assets	107	114	109
Current Assets	68	74	68
Current Liabilities	89	113	116

Cash Generator Ltd
47 Eign Gate, Hereford, HR4 0AB
Tel: 01432-263060 **Fax:** 01432-261329
Website: http://www.cashgenerator.co.uk
Directors: D. Elwood (Prop)
Ultimate Holding Company: CNG FINANCIAL CORP (USA)
Immediate Holding Company: CASH GENERATOR LIMITED
Registration no: 02258951 **Date established:** 1988
No.of Employees: 1 - 10 **Product Groups:** 36, 40

Date of Accounts	Dec 11	Jan 10	Jan 09
Sales Turnover	19m	12m	N/A
Pre Tax Profit/Loss	-669	1m	-319
Working Capital	7m	2m	2m
Fixed Assets	3m	1m	1m
Current Assets	10m	4m	4m
Current Liabilities	1m	2m	1m

Cookmate Kitchen Shop
43 Widemarsh Street, Hereford, HR4 9EA
Tel: 01432-275013 **Fax:** 01432-275013
E-mail: enquiries@cookmate.co.uk
Website: http://www.cookmate.co.uk
Directors: A. Mcelhayer (Prop)
No.of Employees: 1 - 10 **Product Groups:** 36, 40, 67

Environmental Management Solutions Ltd
Sigeric Business Park Holme Lacy Road, Hereford, HR2 6BQ
Tel: 01432-263333 **Fax:** 01432-263355
E-mail: emsinfo@ems-asbestos.co.uk
Website: http://www.ems-asbestos.co.uk
Directors: J. Perkins-Best (Dir)
Immediate Holding Company: ENVIRONMENTAL MANAGEMENT SOLUTIONS LIMITED
Registration no: 04855462 **Date established:** 2003
No.of Employees: 1 - 10 **Product Groups:** 31, 54, 85

Date of Accounts	Aug 11	Aug 10	Aug 09
Working Capital	-5	-0	23
Fixed Assets	10	8	7
Current Assets	112	101	117

Franklin Hodge Industries Ltd
Jubilee Building Faraday Road, Westfields Trading Estate, Hereford, HR4 9NS
Tel: 01432-269605 **Fax:** 01432-277454
E-mail: sales@franklinhodge.com
Website: http://www.franklinhodge.com
Managers: N. Snee (Chief Mgr), R. Davies (Contracts Mgr), B. Makin (Sales Prom Mgr)
Ultimate Holding Company: Carter Thermal Industries Ltd
Registration no: 01101574 **VAT No.:** GB 163 2707 94
Date established: 1973 **Turnover:** £5m - £10m **No.of Employees:** 21 - 50
Product Groups: 35, 38, 48, 77

Freedom Mobility Equipment NRG STAR GROUP
Fayre Acres Roman Road, Hereford, HR4 9QW
Tel: 0800-0126024 **Fax:** 01568-797578
E-mail: info@freedommobilityequipment.com
Website: http://www.24nrghealthcare.co.uk
No.of Employees: 1 - 10 **Product Groups:** 30, 39, 67, 86

Gelpack Excelsior Ltd
Westfields Trading Estate, Hereford, HR4 9NT
Tel: 01432-267391 **Fax:** 01432-264809
E-mail: info@gelpack.co.uk
Website: http://www.gelpack.co.uk
Directors: S. Ratcliffe (Fin)
Ultimate Holding Company: AZALEE MANAGEMENT CORPORATION (PANAMA)
Immediate Holding Company: GELPACK EXCELSIOR LIMITED
Registration no: 02222284 **Date established:** 1988
Turnover: £20m - £50m **No.of Employees:** 101 - 250 **Product Groups:** 30

Date of Accounts	Dec 11	Dec 10	Dec 09
Sales Turnover	30m	27m	24m
Pre Tax Profit/Loss	466	449	580
Working Capital	3m	2m	2m
Fixed Assets	3m	3m	3m
Current Assets	9m	9m	8m
Current Liabilities	3m	3m	2m

Halco Europe Ltd
6 Beacon Road Rotherwas Industrial Estate, Hereford, HR2 6JF
Tel: 08452-417526 **Fax:** 0845-241 7528
E-mail: sales@halcotapes.co.uk
Website: http://www.halcoeurope.com
Directors: G. Haughton (Dir)
Immediate Holding Company: HALCO EUROPE LIMITED
Registration no: 07879791 **Date established:** 2011
Turnover: £500,000 - £1m **No.of Employees:** 11 - 20
Product Groups: 27, 30, 35, 66

M J Hamer
Redway Ullingswick, Hereford, HR1 3JQ
Tel: 01432-820287 **Fax:** 01432-820287
Directors: M. Hamer (Prop)
Date established: 1954 **No.of Employees:** 1 - 10 **Product Groups:** 35

Hay & Brecon Farmers Ltd
New Port Street Hay-On-Wye, Hereford, HR3 5BZ
Tel: 01497-820516 **Fax:** 01497-821007
E-mail: sales@hayandbrecon.com
Website: http://www.hayandbrecon.com
Directors: N. Terkins (Grp Chief Exec)
Registration no: 0007128R **Turnover:** £10m - £20m
No.of Employees: 21 - 50 **Product Groups:** 25, 26, 35, 41, 63, 65, 66

Hereford Casks Ltd
Glebe Farm Business Park Stoke Edith, Hereford, HR1 4HG
Tel: 01432-890602 **Fax:** 01432-890792
E-mail: cstrangehcasks@yahoo.co.uk
Website: http://www.herefordcasks.co.uk
Directors: A. Strange (Fin), C. Strange (MD)
Immediate Holding Company: HEREFORD CASKS LIMITED
Registration no: 04648899 **Date established:** 2003
No.of Employees: 1 - 10 **Product Groups:** 20, 40, 41

Date of Accounts	Mar 12	Mar 11	Mar 10
Working Capital	129	90	69
Fixed Assets	51	66	36
Current Assets	233	207	153

Hereford Galvanizers Ltd
Westfields Trading Estate, Hereford, HR4 9NS
Tel: 01432-267664 **Fax:** 01432-352735
E-mail: michelle.jackson@hereford.galvanizers.co.uk
Website: http://www.galvanizers.co.uk
Bank(s): Lloyds TSB Bank plc
Directors: M. Jackson (Fin)
Managers: D. Howle (Personnel), M. Holmes (Purch Mgr), P. Shipley (Sales & Mktg Mg)
Immediate Holding Company: HEREFORD GALVANIZERS LIMITED
Registration no: 00817600 **VAT No.:** GB 133 5027 05
Date established: 1964 **Turnover:** £5m - £10m
No.of Employees: 51 - 100 **Product Groups:** 48

Date of Accounts	Mar 11	Mar 10	Mar 09
Sales Turnover	5m	5m	6m
Pre Tax Profit/Loss	106	344	817
Working Capital	463	612	715
Fixed Assets	2m	2m	2m
Current Assets	2m	2m	1m
Current Liabilities	282	302	411

Hereford Glass Fibre Co.
Unit 2 Tarsmill Court Rotherwas Industrial Estate, Hereford, HR2 6JZ
Tel: 01432-357111 **Fax:** 01432-357178
E-mail: info@hgfcomposites.co.uk
Website: http://www.hgfcomposites.co.uk
Directors: D. Muir (Prop)
Date established: 1986 **No.of Employees:** 1 - 10 **Product Groups:** 30, 33, 49, 66

Hereford Metal Finishers Ltd
Unit 10 Oakleys Yard, Rotherwas Industrial Estate, Hereford, HR2 6LR
Tel: 01432-357630 **Fax:** 01432-357630
Directors: M. Wear (MD), J. Wear (Fin)
Immediate Holding Company: HEREFORD METAL FINISHERS LIMITED
Registration no: 01146028 **VAT No.:** GB 136 9616 45
Date established: 1973 **Turnover:** Up to £250,000
No.of Employees: 1 - 10 **Product Groups:** 48

Date of Accounts	Nov 11	Nov 10	Nov 09
Working Capital	-6	-3	-8
Fixed Assets	28	10	12
Current Assets	29	14	12

John E Hitchings Hereford Ltd
Twyford Road Rotherwas Industrial Estate, Hereford, HR2 6JR
Tel: 01432-272584 **Fax:** 01432- 353072
E-mail: enquiries@hitchingsofhereford.co.uk
Website: http://www.hitchingsofhereford.co.uk
Directors: B. Hitchings (Fin)
Immediate Holding Company: JOHN E.HITCHINGS(HEREFORD)LIMITED
Registration no: 00649819 **VAT No.:** GB 134 3319 93
Date established: 1960 **No.of Employees:** 1 - 10 **Product Groups:** 41

Date of Accounts	Apr 10	Apr 09	Apr 08
Working Capital	214	205	175
Fixed Assets	44	48	50
Current Assets	441	412	402

HR4 Ltd
Unit 6-7 Ravenswood Court, Rotherwas Industrial Estate, Hereford, HR2 6JX
Tel: 01432-353555 **Fax:** 01432-353797
E-mail: info@hr4.co.uk
Website: http://www.hr4.co.uk
Directors: R. Peacock (Dir)
Immediate Holding Company: HR4 LIMITED
Registration no: 03575295 **Date established:** 1998
No.of Employees: 11 - 20 **Product Groups:** 80, 86

Date of Accounts	Jun 11	Jun 10	Jun 09
Working Capital	25	223	275
Fixed Assets	13	24	36
Current Assets	62	310	348

I A Technology Ltd
Units 11-16 Burcott Business Park Burcott Road, Hereford, HR4 9JQ
Tel: 01432-342377 **Fax:** 01432-352721
E-mail: sales@iatechnology.co.uk
Website: http://www.iatechnology.co.uk
Bank(s): Lloyds TSB Bank plc
Directors: D. Williams (MD), S. Cook (Comm)
Managers: Y. King (Purch Mgr), R. Slade (Sales Prom Mgr), A. Collins, H. Williams (Personnel)
Ultimate Holding Company: IA TECHNOLOGY HOLDINGS LIMITED
Immediate Holding Company: IA TECHNOLOGY HOLDINGS LIMITED
Registration no: 04962763 **VAT No.:** GB 315 2334 94
Date established: 2003 **Turnover:** £1m - £2m **No.of Employees:** 21 - 50
Product Groups: 37, 44, 84

Date of Accounts	Dec 11	Dec 10	Dec 09
Working Capital	-298	-298	-298
Fixed Assets	332	332	332
Current Liabilities	N/A	298	298

Incotest
Holmer Road, Hereford, HR4 9SL
Tel: 01432-352230 **Fax:** 01432-352230
E-mail: info@incotest.co.uk
Website: http://www.incotest.co.uk
Bank(s): HSBC Bank plc
Managers: S. Smith (Purch Mgr), R. Hunt (Personnel), J. Briggs, C. Adams (Tech Serv Mgr), H. Smith (Mgr)
Ultimate Holding Company: PRECISION CASTPARTS CORP (USA)
Immediate Holding Company: SPECIAL METALS WIGGIN TRUSTEES LIMITED
Registration no: 03072597 **Date established:** 1996
Turnover: Up to £250,000 **No.of Employees:** 51 - 100
Product Groups: 38, 67, 85

Ingrams Servequip Ltd
Carpigiani House Coldnose Road, Rotherwas Industrial Estate, Hereford, HR2 6JL
Tel: 01432-351009 **Fax:** 01432-271910
E-mail: sales@ingrams-hfd.com
Website: http://www.carpigiani.co.uk
Directors: J. Miller (Fin), R. Cumbo (Dir)
Registration no: 03245764 **Date established:** 2000
No.of Employees: 1 - 10 **Product Groups:** 20, 40, 41

Instrumentation & Control Services
Unit 3 The Old Forge Peterchurch, Hereford, HR2 0SD
Tel: 01981-550011 **Fax:** 01981-550955
E-mail: nigel@ics-hereford.co.uk
Website: http://www.ics-hereford.co.uk
Directors: J. Watson (Fin), N. Birch (MD)
Immediate Holding Company: INSTRUMENTATION & CONTROL SERVICES (HEREFORD) LIMITED
Registration no: 01049597 **VAT No.:** GB 136 1861 72
Date established: 1972 **No.of Employees:** 1 - 10 **Product Groups:** 37, 38

Date of Accounts	Dec 11	Dec 10	Dec 09
Working Capital	184	192	161
Fixed Assets	22	30	39
Current Assets	219	251	204

Robert Jackson-Wardle
The Courtyard Bodenham, Hereford, HR1 3JX
Tel: 01568-797611 **Fax:** 01568-797630
E-mail: rwardle1@btconnect.com
Website: http://www.robertjacksonwardle.com
Directors: N. Jackson Wardle (Ptnr)
Immediate Holding Company: FREEDOM CONSULTING LIMITED
Date established: 2005 **No.of Employees:** 1 - 10 **Product Groups:** 46

Date of Accounts	Dec 11	Dec 10	Dec 09
Working Capital	23	20	18
Fixed Assets	1	1	2
Current Assets	31	25	24
Current Liabilities	8	5	5

Jewson Ltd
Canal Road, Hereford, HR1 2EB
Tel: 01432-272276 **Fax:** 01432-354097
E-mail: richardm.roberts@jewson.co.uk
Website: http://www.jewson.co.uk
Managers: R. Roberts (Mgr)
Ultimate Holding Company: COMPAGNIE DE SAINT GOBAIN (FRANCE)
Immediate Holding Company: JEWSON LIMITED
Registration no: 00348407 **Date established:** 1939
No.of Employees: 21 - 50 **Product Groups:** 66

Date of Accounts	Dec 11	Dec 10	Dec 09
Sales Turnover	1606m	1547m	1485m
Pre Tax Profit/Loss	18m	100m	45m
Working Capital	-345m	-250m	-349m
Fixed Assets	496m	387m	461m
Current Assets	657m	1005m	1320m
Current Liabilities	66m	120m	64m

M W Circuit Design
Unit 2a Folbigg Court Ramsden Road, Rotherwas Industrial Estate, Hereford, HR2 6LR
Tel: 01432-264238
Website: http://www.mwcircuitdesigns.co.uk
Directors: M. Watkins (MD)
No.of Employees: 1 - 10 **Product Groups:** 37, 44, 84

Magna Electronics Ltd
9 Harrow Road, Hereford, HR4 0EH
Tel: 01432-353434 **Fax:** 01432-278749
E-mail: sales@magna-electronics.co.uk
Website: http://www.magna-electronics.co.uk
Bank(s): Barclays
Directors: J. Davey (Fin), M. Herbert (Dir)
Immediate Holding Company: MAGNA ELECTRONICS LIMITED
Registration no: 03800101 **VAT No.:** GB 736 8583 88
Date established: 1999 **Turnover:** £1m - £2m **No.of Employees:** 21 - 50
Product Groups: 37, 84

Date of Accounts	Aug 11	Aug 10	Aug 09
Working Capital	-27	-41	N/A
Fixed Assets	70	91	103
Current Assets	189	144	132

Marshfield Cross Keys Ltd
Unit 4a Bridge Business Centre Burcott Road, Hereford, HR4 9LW
Tel: 01432-820101 **Fax:** 01432-820101
E-mail: enquiry@marshfieldcrosskeys.co.uk
Website: http://www.marshfieldcrosskeys.co.uk
Directors: P. Beale (Dir)
Immediate Holding Company: MARSHFIELD CROSS KEYS LTD
Registration no: 05885280 **Date established:** 2006
No.of Employees: 1 - 10 **Product Groups:** 35, 84

Date of Accounts	Mar 11	Mar 10	Mar 09
Working Capital	-48	-58	-51
Fixed Assets	89	80	57
Current Assets	170	86	8

M C Mayglothling
240 Kings Acre Road, Hereford, HR4 0SD
Tel: 01432-278709
Directors: M. Mayglothlin (Prop)
Date established: 1959 **No.of Employees:** 1 - 10 **Product Groups:** 26, 35

Mercian Lifting Gear UK Ltd
Netherwood Road Rotherwas Industrial Estate, Hereford, HR2 6JU
Tel: 01432-355272 **Fax:** 01432-354592
E-mail: andrew@mercian.co.uk
Website: http://www.mercian.co.uk
Bank(s): Midland
Directors: A. Davies (MD)
Immediate Holding Company: MERCIAN LIFTING GEAR (UK) LIMITED
Registration no: 02774600 **VAT No.:** GB 594 2500 37
Date established: 1992 **Turnover:** £1m - £2m **No.of Employees:** 11 - 20
Product Groups: 48

Date of Accounts	Feb 12	Feb 11	Feb 10
Working Capital	167	122	250
Fixed Assets	61	76	133
Current Assets	332	269	391

Steve Methven
Lower Tomlinsfield St Weonards, Hereford, HR2 8QE
Tel: 01981-580400 **Fax:** 01981-580574
Directors: S. Methven (Prop)
Date established: 1976 **No.of Employees:** 1 - 10 **Product Groups:** 41

Moudmasters UK Ltd
Netherwood Road Rotherwas Industrial Estate, Hereford, HR2 6JU
Tel: 01432-265768 **Fax:** 01432-263782
E-mail: office@moldmasters.co.uk
Website: http://www.pmssystems.com
Bank(s): Barclays
Directors: I. Nunn (Ptnr)
Ultimate Holding Company: 1003059 ONTARIO LTD (CANADA)
Immediate Holding Company: MOLD MASTERS (UK) LIMITED
Registration no: 01912861 **VAT No.:** GB 425 5381 55
Date established: 1985 **Turnover:** £1m - £2m **No.of Employees:** 21 - 50
Product Groups: 38, 42

Date of Accounts	Dec 11	Dec 10	Dec 09
Sales Turnover	5m	1m	1m
Pre Tax Profit/Loss	220	-483	-231
Working Capital	240	2m	-1m
Fixed Assets	3m	2m	2m
Current Assets	3m	2m	521
Current Liabilities	593	52	35

P R P Polymer Engineering
Unit 7-10 Tarsmill Court, Rotherwas Industrial Estate, Hereford, HR2 6JZ
Tel: 01432-357686 **Fax:** 01432-352702
E-mail: info@prp.co.uk
Website: http://www.prp.co.uk
Bank(s): HSBC Bank plc

Directors: D. Wilkins (MD)
Ultimate Holding Company: REEVITE INDUSTRIAL MOULDINGS LTD
VAT No.: GB 489 0030 43 **Turnover:** £1m - £2m **No.of Employees:** 11 - 20
Product Groups: 29

Painter Bros Ltd
Holmer Road, Hereford, HR4 9SW
Tel: 01432-374400 **Fax:** 01432-374427
E-mail: enquiries@painterbrothers.com
Website: http://www.painterbrothers.com
Bank(s): Natwest
Directors: D. Goldsmith (MD), T. Stinton (Dir)
Ultimate Holding Company: BALFOUR BEATTY PLC
Immediate Holding Company: PAINTER BROTHERS LIMITED
Registration no: 00238081 **VAT No.:** GB 217 9672 35
Date established: 2029 **Turnover:** £5m - £10m **No.of Employees:** 21 - 50
Product Groups: 35

Date of Accounts	Dec 11	Dec 10	Dec 09
Working Capital	585	585	585
Current Assets	585	585	585

Pallisers Of Hereford Ltd
Acorns Park Yarkhill, Hereford, HR1 3SX
Tel: 01432-890300 **Fax:** 01432-890301
E-mail: sales@pallisers.co.uk
Website: http://www.pallisers.co.uk
Directors: R. Palliser (Fin)
Immediate Holding Company: PALLISERS OF HEREFORD LTD.
Registration no: 02850220 **Date established:** 1993
No.of Employees: 21 - 50 **Product Groups:** 41

Date of Accounts	Dec 11	Dec 10	Dec 09
Working Capital	397	426	489
Fixed Assets	151	160	155
Current Assets	2m	2m	2m

Paul Barber Registered Gunsmith
The Coach House Moccas, Hereford, HR2 9LE
Tel: 01981-500634 **Fax:** 01981-500651
E-mail: enquiry@paulbarber.co.uk
Website: http://www.paulbarber.co.uk
Directors: P. Barber (Prop)
Date established: 1995 **No.of Employees:** 1 - 10 **Product Groups:** 36, 39, 40

Allan Pearce
Tarrington, Hereford, HR1 4JQ
Tel: 01531-670766
E-mail: allan.pearce@lowerhazlefarm.co.uk
Directors: A. Pearce (Prop)
No.of Employees: 1 - 10 **Product Groups:** 35

Pol Roger Ltd
4 Coningsby Street, Hereford, HR1 2DY
Tel: 01432-262800 **Fax:** 01432-262806
E-mail: polroger@polroger.co.uk
Website: http://polroger.co.uk
Directors: N. James (MD), I. Mills (Co Sec)
Ultimate Holding Company: POL ROGER & COMPANY SA (FRANCE)
Immediate Holding Company: POL ROGER LIMITED
Registration no: 02516334 **Date established:** 1990 **Turnover:** £5m - £10m
No.of Employees: 11 - 20 **Product Groups:** 21, 62

Date of Accounts	Dec 11	Dec 10	Dec 09
Sales Turnover	10m	9m	9m
Pre Tax Profit/Loss	158	35	116
Working Capital	2m	2m	2m
Fixed Assets	89	76	92
Current Assets	4m	4m	4m
Current Liabilities	464	366	393

Primasil Silicones Ltd
Kington Road Weobly, Weobley, Hereford, HR4 8QU
Tel: 01544-312600 **Fax:** 01544-318940
E-mail: enquiries@primasil.com
Website: http://www.primasil.com
Bank(s): HSBC Bank plc
Directors: A. Wadley (Fin)
Managers: M. Wheeler (Tech Serv Mgr), A. Frost (Personnel), P. Sharples, M. Hurn (Sales Prom Mgr)
Immediate Holding Company: CHASE PRODUCTS LIMITED
Registration no: 02105252 **VAT No.:** GB 378 9761 77
Date established: 1987 **Turnover:** £5m - £10m
No.of Employees: 51 - 100 **Product Groups:** 29, 63

Date of Accounts	Apr 11	Apr 10	Apr 09
Sales Turnover	9m	9m	8m
Pre Tax Profit/Loss	40	296	-127
Working Capital	-860	-828	-73
Fixed Assets	3m	3m	3m
Current Assets	3m	3m	2m
Current Liabilities	417	438	326

Raytech International Ltd
Coldnose Road Rotherwas Industrial Estate, Hereford, HR2 6JL
Tel: 01432-340833 **Fax:** 01432-340844
E-mail: sales@raytech.uk.com
Website: http://www.raytechinternational.com
Directors: P. Rayfield (MD)
Immediate Holding Company: RAYTECH INTERNATIONAL LTD
Registration no: 03242683 **VAT No.:** GB 641 3088 57
Date established: 1996 **Turnover:** £500,000 - £1m
No.of Employees: 1 - 10 **Product Groups:** 37

Date of Accounts	Aug 11	Aug 10	Aug 09
Working Capital	-142	-120	-101
Fixed Assets	223	214	221
Current Assets	200	190	206

Rebus Badges & Regalia Ltd
Clayfields Bodenham, Hereford, HR1 3LG
Tel: 01568-797401 **Fax:** 01568-600481
E-mail: sales@e-badges.co.uk
Website: http://www.e-badges.co.uk
Directors: P. Hamblin (Dir)
Registration no: 02206232 **VAT No.:** GB 594 0402 47
Turnover: Up to £250,000 **No.of Employees:** 1 - 10 **Product Groups:** 49

San Electroheat
Po Box 259, Hereford, HR1 9AU
Tel: 01432-851999 **Fax:** 01432-851299
E-mail: san@san-as.com
Website: http://www.san-as.com

Managers: J. Comerford (Accounts), H. Comerford (Sales Prom Mgr)
Turnover: £250m - £500m **No.of Employees:** 1 - 10 **Product Groups:** 37, 38, 39, 40, 42, 43, 46

Sanders Polyfilms Ltd
Westfields Trading Estate, Hereford, HR4 9NS
Tel: 01432-277558 **Fax:** 01432-279898
E-mail: sales@polyfilms.co.uk
Website: http://www.theshrinkfilmcompany.com
Bank(s): National Westminster
Directors: S. Mohan (Comm), E. Fairclough (Co Sec), B. Davies (Fin), A. Aftalion (MD)
Managers: M. Andrews (Sales Prom Mgr), M. Floyd (Tech Serv Mgr), J. Davies (Personnel)
Ultimate Holding Company: SANDERS POLYFILMS LIMITED
Immediate Holding Company: COFLEX FILMS LIMITED
Registration no: 03557284 **VAT No.:** GB 549 6778 74
Date established: 1998 **Turnover:** £500,000 - £1m
No.of Employees: 51 - 100 **Product Groups:** 30

Date of Accounts	Dec 10	Dec 09	Dec 08
Sales Turnover	N/A	825	7m
Pre Tax Profit/Loss	N/A	45	225
Working Capital	32	32	14
Fixed Assets	N/A	N/A	566
Current Assets	32	32	1m
Current Liabilities	N/A	N/A	665

Saturn Graphics UK
Old School House Glasbury, Hereford, HR3 5NL
Tel: 01497-847086
E-mail: sales@saturngraphicsuk.com
Website: http://www.saturngraphicsuk.com
Directors: P. Knowles (Prop)
Date established: 2007 **No.of Employees:** 1 - 10 **Product Groups:** 52

T D G Ltd
Pippins Fold Westhide, Hereford, HR1 3RF
Tel: 01432-820546 **Fax:** 01432-820514
E-mail: tdg.recycling@btinternet.com
Directors: S. Lambert (Dir)
Ultimate Holding Company: NORBERT DENTRESSANGLE SA (FRANCE)
Immediate Holding Company: TDG LIMITED
Registration no: 00469605 **Date established:** 1949
Turnover: £500,000 - £1m **No.of Employees:** 1 - 10 **Product Groups:** 30

Date of Accounts	Dec 11	Dec 10	Dec 09
Sales Turnover	N/A	678m	662m
Pre Tax Profit/Loss	35m	26m	13m
Working Capital	-42m	15m	5m
Fixed Assets	138m	227m	271m
Current Assets	230m	158m	174m
Current Liabilities	N/A	77m	100m

T R P Sealing Systems Ltd
24 Netherwood Road Rotherwas Industrial Estate, Hereford, HR2 6JU
Tel: 01432-279366 **Fax:** 01432-273017
E-mail: admin@trpsealing.com
Website: http://www.trpsealing.com
Bank(s): National Westminster Bank Plc
Directors: S. Children (MD), R. Children (Co Sec)
Managers: S. Royal (Comm), A. Hironok (Purch Mgr), G. Children
Immediate Holding Company: TRP SEALING SYSTEMS LIMITED
Registration no: 01588087 **VAT No.:** GB 359 0731 42
Date established: 1981 **Turnover:** £20m - £50m
No.of Employees: 251 - 500 **Product Groups:** 27, 29, 30, 33, 36, 38, 39, 40, 41, 66

Date of Accounts	Apr 11	Apr 10	Apr 09
Sales Turnover	21m	14m	18m
Pre Tax Profit/Loss	1m	530	299
Working Capital	940	482	831
Fixed Assets	4m	4m	3m
Current Assets	9m	6m	5m
Current Liabilities	1m	688	1m

The Design I V Partnership
PO Box 194 Peterchurch, Hereford, HR2 0YG
Tel: 01981-550400 **Fax:** 08705-165061
E-mail: info@design-iv.com
Website: http://www.design-iv.com
Directors: M. Curtis (Ptnr)
Ultimate Holding Company: Boothroyd Dewhurst, Inc.
VAT No.: GB 615 6818 28 **Turnover:** £2m - £5m **No.of Employees:** 1 - 10
Product Groups: 44

Votex Hereford Ltd
Redhill Depot Redhill, Hereford, HR2 8BH
Tel: 01432-274361 **Fax:** 01432-352743
E-mail: sales@votex.co.uk
Website: http://www.votex.co.uk
Directors: G. Rivers (Sales)
Immediate Holding Company: VOTEX HEREFORD LIMITED
Registration no: 01975787 **Date established:** 1986
No.of Employees: 1 - 10 **Product Groups:** 41

Date of Accounts	Dec 11	Dec 10	Dec 09
Working Capital	3	25	7
Fixed Assets	158	180	201
Current Assets	392	387	311

Worcester Electrical Distributors Ltd
Unit 12 Grandstand Business Centre Westfields Trading Estate, Hereford, HR4 9NS
Tel: 01432-265500 **Fax:** 01432-268866
E-mail: hereford@worcesterelectrical.co.uk
Website: http://www.worcesterelectrical.co.uk
Managers: I. Butler (District Mgr)
Immediate Holding Company: WORCESTER ELECTRICAL DISTRIBUTORS LIMITED
Registration no: 02203536 **Date established:** 1987
No.of Employees: 1 - 10 **Product Groups:** 37, 38, 67

Date of Accounts	Mar 12	Mar 11	Mar 10
Sales Turnover	13m	11m	8m
Pre Tax Profit/Loss	583	252	-153
Working Capital	436	76	-192
Fixed Assets	249	231	307
Current Assets	5m	4m	3m
Current Liabilities	1m	192	1m

Wyevale Garden Centres Ltd
Kings Acre Road, Hereford, HR4 0SE
Tel: 01432-266261 **Fax:** 01432-341863
E-mail: hereford@thegardencentregroup.co.uk
Website: http://www.wyevale.co.uk

Managers: S. Lowden
Ultimate Holding Company: THE GARDEN CENTRE GROUP LIMITED
Immediate Holding Company: THE GARDEN CENTRE GROUP HOLDINGS LIMITED
Registration no: 01972554 **Date established:** 1985
No.of Employees: 1 - 10 **Product Groups:** 33, 61

Date of Accounts	Dec 07	Dec 08	Dec 09
Sales Turnover	N/A	N/A	64m
Pre Tax Profit/Loss	-3m	45	133m
Working Capital	-240m	-243m	-183m
Fixed Assets	365m	365m	473m
Current Assets	894	15m	963
Current Liabilities	4m	3m	2m

Kington

Briliant Polishes
2-4b Arrow Court Industrial Estate Hergest, Kington, HR5 3ER
Tel: 07789-286821
E-mail: sales@briliant.biz
Website: http://www.briliant.biz
Directors: P. lewin (MD)
Date established: 2002 **Turnover:** £250,000 - £500,000
No.of Employees: 21 - 50 **Product Groups:** 32

Hilson Wire Products Ltd
Nextend Farm Lyonshall, Kington, HR5 3HZ
Tel: 01544-340608
Directors: I. Hilditch (Dir)
Ultimate Holding Company: ETL SYSTEMS LIMITED
Immediate Holding Company: ETL PROPERTIES LTD
Registration no: 04981422 **Date established:** 2003
No.of Employees: 1 - 10 **Product Groups:** 35

T J & S Croose Contracting Ltd
Grove Farm Huntington, Kington, HR5 3PJ
Tel: 01544-370285 **Fax:** 01544-370285
Directors: S. Croose (MD)
Immediate Holding Company: T J & S CROOSE CONTRACTING LIMITED
Registration no: 04835889 **Date established:** 2003
Turnover: Up to £250,000 **No.of Employees:** 1 - 10 **Product Groups:** 35

Date of Accounts	Mar 11	Mar 10	Mar 08
Sales Turnover	N/A	N/A	30
Pre Tax Profit/Loss	N/A	N/A	2
Working Capital	40	31	24
Fixed Assets	9	4	8
Current Assets	48	37	26
Current Liabilities	N/A	N/A	2

Ledbury

Amcor Flexibles
Lower Road Trading Estate, Ledbury, HR8 2DJ
Tel: 01531-638638 **Fax:** 01531-635716
E-mail: guy.woolley@amcor.com
Website: http://www.amcor.com
Bank(s): National Westminster
Directors: B. Fox (Fin)
Managers: E. Blackwell (Personnel), G. Woolley (Chief Mgr), S. Rogers (Fin Mgr), A. Risbey (Personnel)
Immediate Holding Company: LEDBURY EXHAUST & MOT TEST CENTRE LIMITED
Registration no: 06378434 **Date established:** 2012
Turnover: £125m - £250m **No.of Employees:** 251 - 500
Product Groups: 30, 31

Bavenhill Mechanics Company Ltd
Preston Cross, Ledbury, HR8 2LJ
Tel: 01531-660258 **Fax:** 01531-660610
E-mail: robertchapman@bavenhill.co.uk
Directors: R. Chapman (MD)
Immediate Holding Company: BAVENHILL MECHANICS COMPANY LIMITED
Registration no: 00489320 **Date established:** 1950
No.of Employees: 1 - 10 **Product Groups:** 41

Date of Accounts	Dec 11	Dec 10	Dec 09
Working Capital	-105	-96	-65
Fixed Assets	7	9	11
Current Assets	243	259	237

Can Closure Sales
7a Lower Road, Ledbury, HR8 2DH
Tel: 01531-631668 **Fax:** 01534-631669
E-mail: canclosure@btinternet.com
Website: http://www.canclosures.co.uk
Directors: J. Webster (Fin), B. Webster (MD)
Immediate Holding Company: CAN CLOSURE SALES LIMITED
Registration no: 03862476 **Date established:** 1999
Turnover: Up to £250,000 **No.of Employees:** 1 - 10 **Product Groups:** 38, 42

Date of Accounts	Oct 11	Oct 10	Oct 09
Working Capital	-74	-62	-57
Fixed Assets	28	31	34
Current Assets	105	112	139

Carey Gunmakers Ltd
88 The Homend, Ledbury, HR8 1BX
Tel: 01531-632838 **Fax:** 01531-632838
Directors: M. Carey (MD)
Immediate Holding Company: CAREY (GUNMAKERS) LIMITED
Registration no: 00776709 **Date established:** 1963
No.of Employees: 1 - 10 **Product Groups:** 36, 39, 40

Date of Accounts	Dec 11	Dec 10	Dec 09
Working Capital	206	196	198
Fixed Assets	21	23	27
Current Assets	643	654	633

P Evans
Unit 12 Bromyard Road Industrial Estate, Ledbury, HR8 1NS
Tel: 01531-634177 **Fax:** 01531-634177

see next page

P Evans - Cont'd
Directors: P. Evans (Prop)
Date established: 1987 **No.of Employees:** 1 - 10 **Product Groups:** 38, 42

Hamster Baskets
Aylhill Aylton, Ledbury, HR8 2QJ
Tel: 01531-670209 **Fax:** 01531-670630
E-mail: richard@hamsterbaskets.co.uk
Website: http://www.hamsterbaskets.co.uk
Directors: R. Lucy (Prop)
VAT No.: GB 134 3118 06 **Turnover:** £250,000 - £500,000
No.of Employees: 1 - 10 **Product Groups:** 35, 36, 49

Helping Hand Co.
Unit 9 Bromyard Road Industrial Estate, Ledbury, HR8 1NS
Tel: 01531-635388 **Fax:** 01531-638059
E-mail: sales@helpinghand.co.uk
Website: http://www.thehelpinghand.co.uk
Bank(s): National Westminster Bank Plc
Directors: G. James (Prop)
Managers: A. Wilson (Sales & Mktg Mg), C. Price (Tech Serv Mgr), M. Bennett (Comptroller), W. Howes (Personnel), W. Howes (Personnel), A. Welson (Sales & Mktg Mg)
Immediate Holding Company: THE HELPING HAND COMPANY (LEDBURY) LIMITED
Registration no: 02172956 **VAT No.:** GB 477 7948 69
Date established: 1987 **Turnover:** £10m - £20m
No.of Employees: 101 - 250 **Product Groups:** 36

Date of Accounts	Jun 11	Jun 10	Jun 09
Sales Turnover	10m	10m	10m
Pre Tax Profit/Loss	773	475	502
Working Capital	2m	956	841
Fixed Assets	2m	2m	2m
Current Assets	3m	3m	3m
Current Liabilities	867	779	895

Intime Engineering Ltd
Lower Road Trading Estate, Ledbury, HR8 2DH
Tel: 01531-634300 **Fax:** 01531-635197
E-mail: colin@intime-eng.com
Website: http://www.intime-eng.com
Bank(s): Lloyds TSB Bank plc
Directors: C. Selwyn (MD)
Ultimate Holding Company: COLJEN LIMITED
Immediate Holding Company: INTIME ENGINEERING (LEDBURY) LIMITED
Registration no: 01567739 **VAT No.:** GB 282 6869 12
Date established: 1981 **Turnover:** £1m - £2m **No.of Employees:** 11 - 20
Product Groups: 48

Date of Accounts	Jul 12	Jul 11	Jul 10
Working Capital	385	114	23
Fixed Assets	770	327	204
Current Assets	848	413	290

P & O Craft
Unit 2 Bankside Industrial Estate Little Marcle Road, Ledbury, HR8 2DR
Tel: 01531-632873
E-mail: dave@pocraft.co.uk
Website: http://www.daveprestonartistblacksmith.co.uk
Directors: D. Preston (Prop)
Date established: 1988 **No.of Employees:** 1 - 10 **Product Groups:** 26, 35

Puresep Holdings Ltd (Puresep Filtration Technologies Ltd) (Pursep Water Technologies Ltd)
Unit 14a Bromyard Road Trading Estate, Ledbury, HR8 1NS
Tel: 01531-636328 **Fax:** 01531-634012
E-mail: jcolins@puresep.com
Website: http://www.puresep.com
Directors: V. Payne (MD)
Ultimate Holding Company: Q HOLDINGS LIMITED
Immediate Holding Company: AMPLIO FILTRATION HOLDINGS LIMITED
Registration no: 04996871 **Date established:** 2003 **Turnover:** £5m - £10m
No.of Employees: 1 - 10 **Product Groups:** 23, 41

Date of Accounts	Mar 12	Mar 11	Mar 10
Working Capital	212	137	84
Fixed Assets	712	746	742
Current Assets	883	892	846

S E S Glos Ltd
Unit 19a Lower Road Trading Estate, Ledbury, HR8 2DJ
Tel: 01531-637206 **Fax:** 01531-631152
E-mail: service@sparcerosion.biz
Website: http://www.sparcerosion.biz
Directors: C. Skuse (MD)
Immediate Holding Company: SES (GLOS) LIMITED
Registration no: 04524458 **VAT No.:** 800 4355 73 **Date established:** 2002
Turnover: Up to £250,000 **No.of Employees:** 1 - 10 **Product Groups:** 46, 48

Date of Accounts	Dec 11	Dec 10	Dec 09
Working Capital	47	83	119
Fixed Assets	1	1	1
Current Assets	68	99	130

H Weston & Sons Ltd
The Bounds Much Marcle, Ledbury, HR8 2NQ
Tel: 01531-660233 **Fax:** 01531-660619
E-mail: enquiries@westons-cider.co.uk
Website: http://www.westonscider.co.uk
Directors: H. Thomas (MD)
Immediate Holding Company: H.WESTON & SONS LIMITED
Registration no: 00672234 **VAT No.:** GB 133 5767 62
Date established: 1960 **Turnover:** £20m - £50m
No.of Employees: 101 - 250 **Product Groups:** 21

Date of Accounts	Mar 11	Mar 10	Mar 09
Sales Turnover	38m	33m	27m
Pre Tax Profit/Loss	4m	5m	3m
Working Capital	6m	5m	4m
Fixed Assets	15m	14m	15m
Current Assets	15m	12m	10m
Current Liabilities	4m	3m	2m

Leominster

Amtex
Kingsland, Leominster, HR6 9QT
Tel: 01568-720302
E-mail: info@amtexltd.co.uk
Website: http://www.amtexltd.co.uk
Registration no: 02994251 **Date established:** 1994
Turnover: Up to £250,000 **No.of Employees:** 1 - 10 **Product Groups:** 36, 40

R J Barrington Ltd
Clinton Road, Leominster, HR6 0RJ
Tel: 01568-612101 **Fax:** 01568-612501
E-mail: sales@rjbarringtonltd.co.uk
Website: http://www.rjbarringtonltd.co.uk
Bank(s): Trustee savings
Directors: R. Barrington (MD), J. Lily (Dir)
Managers: M. Lily (Chief Acct)
Immediate Holding Company: R.J. BARRINGTON LIMITED
Registration no: 02153766 **VAT No.:** GB 315 2494 72
Date established: 1987 **Turnover:** £1m - £2m **No.of Employees:** 11 - 20
Product Groups: 48

Date of Accounts	Jun 11	Jun 10	Jun 09
Working Capital	943	848	1m
Fixed Assets	582	619	278
Current Assets	1m	1m	2m

Bayliss
Martins Nest Pudleston, Leominster, HR6 0QY
Tel: 01568-760245 **Fax:** 01568-760245
E-mail: peterbayliss@supanet.com
Directors: P. Bayliss (Prop)
Date established: 1990 **No.of Employees:** 1 - 10 **Product Groups:** 41

Border Oak Design & Construction Ltd
Kingsland Sawmills Kingsland, Leominster, HR6 9SF
Tel: 01568-708752 **Fax:** 01568-708295
E-mail: sales@borderoak.com
Website: http://www.borderoak.com
Bank(s): Barclays Bank, Hereford
Directors: J. Green (MD), J. Greene (Fin)
Managers: S. Robinson, M. Albright (Mktg Serv Mgr), B. Radnor (Fin Mgr)
Immediate Holding Company: BORDER OAK DESIGN & CONSTRUCTION LIMITED
Registration no: 01657744 **VAT No.:** GB 359 1967 08
Date established: 1982 **Turnover:** £5m - £10m
No.of Employees: 51 - 100 **Product Groups:** 25

Date of Accounts	Jun 11	Jun 10	Jun 09
Sales Turnover	9m	8m	10m
Pre Tax Profit/Loss	449	519	1m
Working Capital	874	956	2m
Fixed Assets	111	97	772
Current Assets	3m	3m	4m
Current Liabilities	1m	1m	1m

bpi.agri
Worcester Road, Leominster, HR6 0QA
Tel: 01568-617220 **Fax:** 01568-611435
E-mail: sales@bpiagri.com
Website: http://www.bpiagri.com
Bank(s): Cydesdale Bank P.L.C, 100 West Black St, Greenock PA15 1XR
Directors: B. Buckley (Sales), A. Brown (Fin), C. McLapchie (Ch), D. Pendlebury (MD), T. Sole (Chief Op Offcr)
Managers: R. Griffiths (Purch Mgr)
Ultimate Holding Company: British Polythene Industries PLC
Immediate Holding Company: The Low & Bonar Group
VAT No.: GB 134 4364 83 **Turnover:** £20m - £50m
No.of Employees: 101 - 250 **Product Groups:** 30, 66

Morris Corfield & Co. Ltd
Westington Works Hatfield, Leominster, HR6 0SJ
Tel: 01885-488884 **Fax:** 01885-483888
Website: http://www.morriscorfield.co.uk
Directors: O. Morris (Dir)
Immediate Holding Company: MORRIS, CORFIELD & CO HOLDINGS LTD
Registration no: 00647325 **Date established:** 1960
Turnover: £20m - £50m **No.of Employees:** 1 - 10 **Product Groups:** 41

Date of Accounts	Nov 10	Nov 09	Nov 08
Sales Turnover	23m	20m	18m
Pre Tax Profit/Loss	514	395	225
Working Capital	3m	3m	2m
Fixed Assets	2m	2m	2m
Current Assets	7m	5m	5m
Current Liabilities	524	410	187

Eagle Tools & Fixings
The Willows Eardisland, Leominster, HR6 9BN
Tel: 01544-388830 **Fax:** 01544-388830
Directors: M. Connop (Prop)
Date established: 1987 **No.of Employees:** 1 - 10 **Product Groups:** 35

Forbes Group
Glendower Road, Leominster, HR6 0RL
Tel: 01568-616638 **Fax:** 01568-616639
E-mail: info@forbesgroup.eu
Website: http://www.forbesgroup.eu
Bank(s): Barclays
Directors: P. Graville (MD), D. Lloyd (Fin), V. Graville (Fin)
Managers: C. Graville (Mktg Serv Mgr)
Immediate Holding Company: FORBES GROUP LIMITED
Registration no: 01591882 **VAT No.:** GB 681 9779 69
Date established: 1981 **Turnover:** Up to £250,000
No.of Employees: 21 - 50 **Product Groups:** 26

Date of Accounts	Dec 11	Dec 10	Dec 09
Working Capital	316	317	507
Fixed Assets	294	313	320
Current Assets	828	848	923

H.R. Smith Group of Companies
Street Court Kingsland, Leominster, HR6 9QA
Tel: 01568-708744 **Fax:** 01568-708713
E-mail: sales@hr-smith.com
Website: http://www.hr-smith.com
Directors: R. Smith (MD), S. Smith (Dir)
Immediate Holding Company: H.R. Smith (Technical Developments) Ltd
Registration no: 00878510 **Date established:** 1976 **Turnover:** £2m - £5m
No.of Employees: 1 - 10 **Product Groups:** 37, 39, 67

Andrew D Hill
The Old Blacksmith Shop Docklow, Leominster, HR6 0RX
Tel: 01568-760389 **Fax:** 01568-760389
E-mail: andrew@adhill.org
Directors: A. Hill (Prop)
Date established: 1992 **No.of Employees:** 1 - 10 **Product Groups:** 41

Horse Boutique
North Road Kingsland, Leominster, HR6 9SA
Tel: 01568-708280 **Fax:** 01568-708101
E-mail: enquiries@horseboutique.co.uk
Website: http://www.horseboutique.co.uk
Directors: M. Burley (Prop)
No.of Employees: 1 - 10 **Product Groups:** 20, 22, 24, 41, 49, 63, 65

H.R. Smith Technical Development Ltd
Street Court Kingsland, Leominster, HR6 9QA
Tel: 01568-708744 **Fax:** 01568-708713
E-mail: sales@hr-smith.com
Website: http://www.hr-smith.com
Directors: S. Smith (Comm), R. Smith (MD)
Immediate Holding Company: H.R. Smith (Technical Developments) Ltd
Registration no: 00878510 **Date established:** 1966
Turnover: £500,000 - £1m **No.of Employees:** 1 - 10 **Product Groups:** 37

Jewson Ltd (t/a Graham)
The Tanyard Bridge Street, Leominster, HR6 8DZ
Tel: 01568-615261 **Fax:** 01568-616092
E-mail: graham.rushton@jewson.co.uk
Website: http://www.jewson.co.uk
Managers: G. Rushton (District Mgr)
Ultimate Holding Company: COMPAGNIE DE SAINT GOBAIN (FRANCE)
Immediate Holding Company: JEWSON LIMITED
Registration no: 00348407 **VAT No.:** GB 394 1212 63
Date established: 1939 **Turnover:** £2m - £5m **No.of Employees:** 1 - 10
Product Groups: 66

Date of Accounts	Dec 11	Dec 10	Dec 09
Sales Turnover	1606m	1547m	1485m
Pre Tax Profit/Loss	18m	100m	45m
Working Capital	-345m	-250m	-349m
Fixed Assets	496m	387m	461m
Current Assets	657m	1005m	1320m
Current Liabilities	66m	120m	64m

Kingspan Insulation Ltd
Torvale Industrial Estate Pembridge, Leominster, HR6 9LA
Tel: 08708-508555 **Fax:** 08708-508666
E-mail: johntreanor@kingspan.com
Website: http://www.insulation.kingspan.com
Directors: C. Guest (Sales), J. Treanor (Fin), M. Rochefort (I.T. Dir), P. Wilson (MD)
Managers: C. Young (Sales Prom Mgr)
Ultimate Holding Company: KINGSPAN GROUP PUBLIC LIMITED COMPANY
Immediate Holding Company: KINGSPAN INSULATION LIMITED
Registration no: 01882722 **Date established:** 1985
Turnover: £75m - £125m **No.of Employees:** 251 - 500
Product Groups: 67

Date of Accounts	Dec 10	Dec 09	Dec 08
Sales Turnover	113m	106m	132m
Pre Tax Profit/Loss	10m	8m	7m
Working Capital	-22m	-36m	-51m
Fixed Assets	64m	70m	77m
Current Assets	72m	51m	33m
Current Liabilities	11m	13m	16m

Leominster Gun Room
49 Etnam Street, Leominster, HR6 8AE
Tel: 01568-615652 **Fax:** 01568-615652
Directors: M. Pierce (Ptnr)
Date established: 1956 **No.of Employees:** 1 - 10 **Product Groups:** 36, 39, 40

Premier Manufacturing Ltd
The Old Cinema Shobdon, Leominster, HR6 9NR
Tel: 01568-709297 **Fax:** 01568-709283
E-mail: info@premier-mobiles.com
Website: http://www.premier-manufacturing.co.uk
Directors: M. Williams (MD)
Immediate Holding Company: PREMIER MOBILES (UK) LIMITED
Registration no: 03853767 **Date established:** 1999
Turnover: £500,000 - £1m **No.of Employees:** 1 - 10 **Product Groups:** 37

Date of Accounts	Oct 10	Oct 09	Oct 08
Working Capital	24	28	12
Fixed Assets	4	4	4
Current Assets	290	307	375

Q-Par Angus Ltd
Barons Cross Laboratories Barons Cross Road, Barons Cross, Leominster, HR6 8RS
Tel: 01568-612138 **Fax:** 01568-616373
E-mail: sales@q-par.com
Website: http://www.q-par.com
Bank(s): Lloyds TSB Bank plc
Directors: R. Holliday (MD), J. Holliday (Fin)
Managers: P. Sherman (Tech Serv Mgr), R. Lowther (Sales & Mktg Mg), C. Bean (Purch Mgr)
Immediate Holding Company: Q-PAR ANGUS LIMITED
Registration no: 01826221 **VAT No.:** GB 412 7815 63
Date established: 1984 **Turnover:** £500,000 - £1m
No.of Employees: 21 - 50 **Product Groups:** 37

Date of Accounts	May 11	May 10	May 09
Working Capital	532	539	347
Fixed Assets	255	298	353
Current Assets	1m	1m	1m

Shopmobility
6 Morris Mews, Leominster, HR6 8LZ
Tel: 01568-616755
Managers: K. Harmer (Mgr)
Date established: 1998 **No.of Employees:** 1 - 10 **Product Groups:** 38, 67

Supercraft Structrual Ltd
Shobdon Airfield Shobdon, Leominster, HR6 9NR
Tel: 01568-708456 **Fax:** 01568-708212
E-mail: info@supercraftltd.co.uk
Website: http://www.supercraftltd.co.uk
Directors: M. Pugh (MD), S. Williams (Fin)
Immediate Holding Company: SUPERCRAFT STRUCTURES LIMITED
Registration no: 01896897 **Date established:** 1985
Turnover: Up to £250,000 **No.of Employees:** 21 - 50 **Product Groups:** 35

Date of Accounts	Apr 11	Apr 10	Apr 09
Working Capital	209	388	-70
Fixed Assets	185	210	218
Current Assets	662	678	651

Teme Valley Tractors Ltd
Castle Works Wigmore, Leominster, HR6 9UJ
Tel: 01568-770208 **Fax:** 01568-770207
E-mail: brian.smart@madasafish.com
Website: http://www.temevalleytractors.co.uk
Directors: B. Smart (Dir)
Immediate Holding Company: TEME VALLEY TRACTORS LIMITED
Registration no: 01717662 **Date established:** 1983
No.of Employees: 1 - 10 **Product Groups:** 41

Date of Accounts	Dec 11	Dec 10	Dec 09
Sales Turnover	903	869	845
Pre Tax Profit/Loss	150	135	132
Working Capital	1m	1m	1m
Fixed Assets	87	97	118
Current Assets	3m	3m	3m
Current Liabilities	156	185	169

Ross On Wye

A B T Products Ltd
Ashburton Industrial Estate, Ross On Wye, HR9 7BW
Tel: 01989-563656 **Fax:** 01989-566824
E-mail: nigel.mummery@abtproducts.com
Website: http://www.abtproducts.com
Bank(s): HSBC Bank plc
Directors: M. Hignett (MD), E. Mummery (Fin)
Ultimate Holding Company: NAM ENG LIMITED
Immediate Holding Company: A.B.T.PRODUCTS LIMITED
Registration no: 01021755 **VAT No.:** GB 134 0168 08
Date established: 1971 **Turnover:** £2m - £5m **No.of Employees:** 51 - 100
Product Groups: 39, 45

Date of Accounts	Dec 11	Dec 10	Dec 09
Sales Turnover	N/A	N/A	4m
Pre Tax Profit/Loss	N/A	N/A	2
Working Capital	868	714	522
Fixed Assets	123	153	212
Current Assets	2m	2m	1m
Current Liabilities	N/A	N/A	213

Accredited Marketing Ltd
25 Watling Street, Ross On Wye, HR9 5UF
Tel: 01989-762243
E-mail: cgreenman@accreditedmarketing.com
Website: http://www.accreditedmarketing.com
Directors: C. Greenman (Prop)
Immediate Holding Company: ACCREDITED MARKETING LIMITED
Registration no: 05576833 **Date established:** 2005
Turnover: Up to £250,000 **No.of Employees:** 1 - 10 **Product Groups:** 81

Date of Accounts	Mar 11	Mar 10	Mar 09
Sales Turnover	34	19	21
Pre Tax Profit/Loss	10	3	-8
Working Capital	3	-1	-3
Current Assets	5	4	4
Current Liabilities	2	4	6

C J G
Box Bush Farm Oxenhall Lane, Gorsley, Ross On Wye, HR9 7BJ
Tel: 01989-720788 **Fax:** 01989-720788
E-mail: c.garlick@cjgcatering.co.uk
Website: http://www.cjgcatering.co.uk
Directors: C. Garlick (Prop)
Turnover: Up to £250,000 **No.of Employees:** 1 - 10 **Product Groups:** 37, 40, 49, 69

Dayla Liquid Packing Ltd
Netherton Road Overross Industrial Estate, Ross On Wye, HR9 7QQ
Tel: 01989-760400 **Fax:** 01989-760414
E-mail: dayla@dayla.co.uk
Website: http://www.dayla.co.uk
Bank(s): Lloyds TSB Bank plc
Managers: K. Wigmore, S. Hardy (Ops Mgr), J. Fitzpatrick (Sales Prom Mgr), L. Crowdace (Purch Mgr)
Ultimate Holding Company: NICHOLS PLC
Immediate Holding Company: DAYLA LIQUID PACKING LIMITED
Registration no: 00603111 **VAT No.:** GB 134 6529 67
Date established: 1958 **Turnover:** £5m - £10m **No.of Employees:** 21 - 50
Product Groups: 30, 42, 48

Date of Accounts	Dec 11	Dec 10	Dec 09
Sales Turnover	11m	10m	13m
Pre Tax Profit/Loss	-195	578	535
Working Capital	903	1m	883
Fixed Assets	529	617	632
Current Assets	3m	3m	3m
Current Liabilities	238	575	818

The Haigh Group Ltd
Alton Road, Ross On Wye, HR9 5NG
Tel: 01989-763131 **Fax:** 01989- 766360
E-mail: info@haigh.co.uk
Website: http://www.haigh.co.uk
Directors: P. Shepherd (Dir), M. Freeman (Co Sec)
Ultimate Holding Company: KWIGO LIMITED
Immediate Holding Company: HAIGH GROUP LIMITED(THE)
Registration no: 00639089 **VAT No.:** GB 134 1449 90
Date established: 1959 **Turnover:** £500,000 - £1m
No.of Employees: 1 - 10 **Product Groups:** 36, 38, 40, 42

Date of Accounts	Apr 11	Apr 10	Apr 09
Sales Turnover	648	648	8m
Pre Tax Profit/Loss	877	430	160
Working Capital	832	142	2m
Fixed Assets	3m	3m	872
Current Assets	1m	268	3m
Current Liabilities	127	103	1m

Alan Keef Ltd
Lea Line Lea, Ross On Wye, HR9 7LQ
Tel: 01989-750757 **Fax:** 01989-750780
E-mail: sales@alankeef.co.uk
Website: http://www.alankeef.co.uk
Bank(s): Barclays
Directors: P. Keef (MD), A. Basey (Co Sec)
Immediate Holding Company: ALAN KEEF LIMITED
Registration no: 01232542 **VAT No.:** GB 195 8508 17
Date established: 1975 **Turnover:** £500,000 - £1m
No.of Employees: 11 - 20 **Product Groups:** 39, 48, 49, 65

Date of Accounts	Nov 11	Nov 10	Nov 09
Working Capital	-59	-116	-363
Fixed Assets	26	27	161
Current Assets	281	275	231

A J Lowther & Son Ltd
Whitchurch, Ross On Wye, HR9 6DF
Tel: 01600-890482 **Fax:** 01600-890930
E-mail: info@ajlowther.co.uk
Website: http://www.ajlowther.co.uk
Directors: T. Faulkner (MD), M. Bailey (Fin), A. Lowther (MD)
Managers: R. Smith (Est), A. Rollings (Chief Buyer)
Ultimate Holding Company: LOWTHER HOLDINGS LIMITED
Immediate Holding Company: A.J. LOWTHER & SON LTD
Registration no: 00841528 **Date established:** 1965
Turnover: £10m - £20m **No.of Employees:** 51 - 100 **Product Groups:** 35

Date of Accounts	Jun 12	Jun 11	Jun 10
Sales Turnover	13m	14m	14m
Pre Tax Profit/Loss	315	305	428
Working Capital	615	600	557
Fixed Assets	508	470	455
Current Assets	5m	5m	6m
Current Liabilities	1m	1m	4m

Micross Electronics Ltd
Units 4-5 Great Western Court, Ashburton Industrial Estate, Ross On Wye, HR9 7XP
Tel: 01989-768080 **Fax:** 01989-768163
E-mail: sales@micross.co.uk
Website: http://www.micross.co.uk
Directors: J. Nelson (Co Sec)
Immediate Holding Company: MICROSS ELECTRONICS LIMITED
Registration no: 01510533 **VAT No.:** GB 337 9567 10
Date established: 1980 **Turnover:** £500,000 - £1m
No.of Employees: 1 - 10 **Product Groups:** 38, 44

Date of Accounts	Aug 11	Aug 10	Aug 09
Working Capital	143	83	109
Fixed Assets	20	22	25
Current Assets	206	126	157

Muddy Boots Software Ltd
Phocle Green, Ross On Wye, HR9 7XU
Tel: 01989-780540 **Fax:** 01989-780436
E-mail: sales@muddyboots.com
Website: http://www.muddyboots.com
Directors: J. Goulding (Sales), R. Fleming (Co Sec)
Registration no: 03134834 **Date established:** 1995
No.of Employees: 11 - 20 **Product Groups:** 44

Date of Accounts	Dec 09	Dec 08	Dec 07
Working Capital	-127	-147	-47
Fixed Assets	171	136	69
Current Assets	813	651	583

Perriflex Products Ltd
Unit 4b Alton Road Industrial Estate, Ross On Wye, HR9 5NB
Tel: 01989-763510 **Fax:** 01989-566884
E-mail: i.perry@perriflex.co.uk
Website: http://www.perriflex.co.uk
Directors: I. Perry (MD), D. Rendell (Co Sec)
Immediate Holding Company: PERRIFLEX PRODUCTS LIMITED
Registration no: 01032443 **Date established:** 1971
Turnover: £500,000 - £1m **No.of Employees:** 1 - 10 **Product Groups:** 23, 25, 27, 29, 32, 33, 36, 49

Date of Accounts	Dec 11	Dec 10	Dec 09
Working Capital	-107	-127	-137
Fixed Assets	4	5	5
Current Assets	29	28	24

Rehau Ltd
Hill Court Walford, Ross On Wye, HR9 5QN
Tel: 01989-762600 **Fax:** 01989-762601
E-mail: enquiries@rehau.com
Website: http://www.rehau.com
Bank(s): Barclays
Directors: P. O'Gallagher (Fin), C. Ware (Pers)
Managers: S. Williams (Tech Serv Mgr), I. Smith (Mktg Serv Mgr), M. Hitchen
Ultimate Holding Company: WAGNER HOLDING AG (SWITZERLAND)
Immediate Holding Company: REHAU LIMITED
Registration no: 00722004 **Date established:** 1962
Turnover: £75m - £125m **No.of Employees:** 101 - 250
Product Groups: 29, 30, 31, 48, 66

Date of Accounts	Dec 11	Dec 10	Dec 09
Sales Turnover	84m	89m	89m
Pre Tax Profit/Loss	-249	-3m	-1m
Working Capital	17m	15m	17m
Fixed Assets	20m	22m	25m
Current Assets	24m	25m	27m
Current Liabilities	3m	3m	N/A

Roe
Enterprise Centre Alton Road Industrial Estate, Ross On Wye, HR9 5NB
Tel: 01989-567474 **Fax:** 01989-762206
E-mail: rcs@jack-roe.co.uk
Website: http://www.jack-roe.co.uk
Directors: B. Roe (MD)
Managers: S. Caffelle (Sales & Mktg Mg), J. Roe (Personnel), N. Clarke (I.T. Exec)
Immediate Holding Company: INNOVA SYSTEMS LIMITED
Date established: 2002 **No.of Employees:** 11 - 20 **Product Groups:** 44

Date of Accounts	Mar 11	Mar 10	Mar 09
Sales Turnover	115	169	185
Pre Tax Profit/Loss	-1	66	72
Working Capital	8	15	13
Fixed Assets	3	5	6
Current Assets	78	127	121
Current Liabilities	69	110	106

Ross Farm Machinery Ltd
8-9 Alton Road, Ross On Wye, HR9 5NB
Tel: 01989-768811 **Fax:** 01989-768465
E-mail: postroom@rossfarm.co.uk
Website: http://www.rossfarm.co.uk
Directors: A. Stuffins (Fin), P. Stuffins (Fin), R. Brett (Mkt Research)
Managers: T. Farr (Parts Mgr)
Immediate Holding Company: ROSS FARM MACHINERY LIMITED
Registration no: 01348974 **Date established:** 1978
Turnover: £20m - £50m **No.of Employees:** 21 - 50 **Product Groups:** 48, 51, 83

Date of Accounts	May 11	May 10	May 09
Sales Turnover	22m	22m	23m
Pre Tax Profit/Loss	166	116	275
Working Capital	2m	2m	2m
Fixed Assets	267	260	293
Current Assets	7m	6m	6m
Current Liabilities	2m	644	555

Routing West Ltd
Unit 1 The Walled Garden Coughton, Ross On Wye, HR9 5ST
Tel: 01989-566390 **Fax:** 01989-763528
Website: http://www.routingwest.co.uk
Directors: D. Sandford (MD), P. Sandford (Fin)
Immediate Holding Company: ROUTING WEST LIMITED
Registration no: 04863608 **Date established:** 2003
No.of Employees: 1 - 10 **Product Groups:** 46

Date of Accounts	Aug 11	Aug 10	Aug 09
Working Capital	69	63	69
Fixed Assets	2	3	4
Current Assets	116	112	117

Salvagnini UK Ltd
Alton House Alton Business Park Alton Road, Ross On Wye, HR9 5BP
Tel: 01989-767032 **Fax:** 01989-563829
E-mail: gary.powell@salvagnini.co.uk
Website: http://www.salvagnini.co.uk
Directors: C. Avery (Fin), G. Powell (MD)
Ultimate Holding Company: SALVAGNINI BV (NETHERLANDS)
Immediate Holding Company: SALVAGNINI UK & IRELAND LIMITED
Registration no: 03385506 **Date established:** 1997 **Turnover:** £1m - £2m
No.of Employees: 11 - 20 **Product Groups:** 34, 39, 40, 46, 48, 67

Date of Accounts	Apr 12	Apr 11	Apr 10
Working Capital	203	76	-17
Fixed Assets	375	414	402
Current Assets	735	651	587

Spurside Saw Works
The Workshop The Downs, Ross On Wye, HR9 7TJ
Tel: 01989-562943 **Fax:** 01989-567360
Directors: S. Hunt (Prop)
Date established: 1963 **No.of Employees:** 1 - 10 **Product Groups:** 36

T P Jordeson & Co. Ltd
Gloucester House 35 Old Gloucester Road, Ross On Wye, HR9 5PB
Tel: 01989-567000 **Fax:** 01989-567020
E-mail: mark@jordeson.co.uk
Website: http://www.jordeson.co.uk
Directors: J. Briggs (MD), M. Briggs (MD), E. Briggs (Co Sec)
Immediate Holding Company: T P JORDESON & COMPANY LIMITED
Registration no: 02382646 **Date established:** 1989
No.of Employees: 1 - 10 **Product Groups:** 66

Date of Accounts	Dec 07	Dec 06	Dec 05
Working Capital	367	275	238
Fixed Assets	18	18	21
Current Assets	2418	2397	1655
Current Liabilities	2051	2122	1417
Total Share Capital	13	13	13

Trucut Bandsaw Blades
The Workshop The Downs, Ross On Wye, HR9 7TJ
Tel: 01989-769371 **Fax:** 01989-567360
E-mail: spursidesawworks@internet.com
Website: http://www.trucutbandsaw.co.uk
Directors: J. Hunt (Prop)
Date established: 1996 **No.of Employees:** 1 - 10 **Product Groups:** 36

U Pack Ltd
Peterstow, Ross On Wye, HR9 6LB
Tel: 01989-563684 **Fax:** 01989-569267
E-mail: info@u-pack.com
Website: http://www.u-pack.com
Directors: R. Gardiner (MD)
Immediate Holding Company: U-PACK INTERNATIONAL LTD.
Registration no: 06965427 **Date established:** 2009
No.of Employees: 1 - 10 **Product Groups:** 38, 42

Date of Accounts	Jul 11
Working Capital	10m
Current Assets	10m

Wye Valley Precision Engineering Holdings Ltd
Station Approach Station Street, Ross On Wye, HR9 7AQ
Tel: 01989-763519 **Fax:** 01989-766662
E-mail: sales@wye-valley.co.uk
Website: http://www.wye-valley.co.uk
Bank(s): Lloyds TSB Bank plc
Directors: P. Nelson (MD), R. Nelson (Ch)
Immediate Holding Company: WYE VALLEY PRECISION ENGINEERING (HOLDINGS) LIMITED
Registration no: 00728245 **VAT No.:** GB 135 8933 44
Date established: 1962 **Turnover:** £2m - £5m **No.of Employees:** 21 - 50
Product Groups: 29

Date of Accounts	Dec 11	Dec 10	Dec 09
Working Capital	2m	2m	2m
Fixed Assets	279	197	206
Current Assets	2m	2m	2m

HERTFORDSHIRE

Baldock

A B L Circuits Ltd
Icknield Way, Baldock, SG7 5BB
Tel: 01462-894312 **Fax:** 01462-491125
E-mail: sales@ablcircuits.co.uk
Website: http://www.ablcircuits.co.uk
Directors: M. Leverett (MD)
Managers: C. Lewis (Prod Mgr)
Ultimate Holding Company: N
Registration no: 04207139 **Date established:** 1983
Turnover: £500,000 - £1m **No.of Employees:** 1 - 10 **Product Groups:** 37, 44, 47, 67, 84

Date of Accounts	Aug 11	Aug 10	Aug 09
Working Capital	79	10	42
Fixed Assets	51	80	95
Current Assets	229	200	173

A1 Magnetics Ltd
Unit 1, Royston Road, Baldock, SG7 6PA
Tel: 01462-499644 **Fax:** 01462-499648
E-mail: sales@a1magnetics.co.uk
Website: http://www.a1magnetics.co.uk
Directors: C. Sterling (MD), C. Stirling (MD)
Registration no: 04523715 **VAT No.:** GB 573 1925 30
Date established: 2002 **Turnover:** £500,000 - £1m
No.of Employees: 1 - 10 **Product Groups:** 29, 30, 34, 37, 44, 46

Assembly Solutions
Unit 8 Bondor Business Centre London Road, Baldock, SG7 6HP
Tel: 01462-896990 **Fax:** 01462-681788
E-mail: sales@assemblysol.co.uk
Website: http://www.assemblysol.co.uk
Directors: M. Davis (MD), L. Davis (Fin)
Immediate Holding Company: ASSEMBLY SOLUTIONS (UK) LIMITED
Registration no: 03303637 **Date established:** 1997
No.of Employees: 1 - 10 **Product Groups:** 37, 39, 41, 48, 68

Date of Accounts	Dec 09	Dec 08	Dec 07
Working Capital	-9	-12	3
Fixed Assets	17	20	23
Current Assets	65	37	110

Connah Sewing Services
15 Whitehorse Street, Baldock, SG7 6QB
Tel: 01462-893339 **Fax:** 01462-893339
E-mail: connahsewing@aol.com
Directors: T. Connah (Prop)
Date established: 2002 **No.of Employees:** 1 - 10 **Product Groups:** 43

Digiverse Ltd
The Chequers 28 Whitehorse Street, Baldock, SG7 6QQ
Tel: 01462-639816 **Fax:** 01462-895777
E-mail: sales@digiverse.co.uk
Website: http://www.digiverse.co.uk
Managers: J. Mortimer (Sales Prom Mgr)
Immediate Holding Company: DIGIVERSE LIMITED
Registration no: 03768158 **Date established:** 1999
Turnover: Up to £250,000 **No.of Employees:** 1 - 10 **Product Groups:** 28

Date of Accounts	May 11	May 10	May 09
Working Capital	45	44	39
Fixed Assets	N/A	1	N/A
Current Assets	66	87	81

E M S Lifts
Marquis Business Centre Royston Road, Baldock, SG7 6XL
Tel: 01462-499700
E-mail: info@emslifts.co.uk
Directors: J. Muir (Dir)
Immediate Holding Company: EMS LIFTS LIMITED
Registration no: 06427222 **Date established:** 2007
No.of Employees: 21 - 50 **Product Groups:** 26, 45

Date of Accounts	Dec 11	Dec 10	Dec 09
Working Capital	243	90	176
Fixed Assets	467	483	396
Current Assets	559	325	276
Current Liabilities	N/A	150	N/A

Floyd Automatic Tooling Ltd
Unit 17 Bondor Business Centre London Road, Baldock, SG7 6HP
Tel: 01462-491919 **Fax:** 01462-490835
E-mail: sales@floydautomatic.co.uk
Website: http://www.floydautomatic.co.uk
Directors: R. Floyd (MD)
Immediate Holding Company: FLOYD AUTOMATIC TOOLING LIMITED
Registration no: 02556559 **Date established:** 1990
No.of Employees: 1 - 10 **Product Groups:** 36, 46

Date of Accounts	Dec 11	Dec 10	Dec 09
Working Capital	160	131	113
Fixed Assets	71	5	8
Current Assets	563	507	502

Gearing Scientific Ltd
4 Springhead Ashwell, Baldock, SG7 5LL
Tel: 01462-742007 **Fax:** 01462-742565
E-mail: info@gearingscientific.net
Website: http://www.gearingscientific.com
Directors: J. Gearing (Fin)
Immediate Holding Company: GEARING SCIENTIFIC LIMITED
Registration no: 04306142 **VAT No.:** GB 637 0945 25
Date established: 2001 **Turnover:** £250,000 - £500,000
No.of Employees: 1 - 10 **Product Groups:** 38, 84, 85

Date of Accounts	Nov 11	Nov 10	Nov 09
Working Capital	-1	20	27
Fixed Assets	114	96	44
Current Assets	26	76	45

I D Products Ltd
West End Ashwell, Baldock, SG7 5PL
Tel: 01462-742305 **Fax:** 01462-742171
E-mail: info@id-products.co.uk
Website: http://www.id-products.co.uk
Directors: A. Smith (Sales)
Immediate Holding Company: I.D.PRODUCTS LIMITED
Registration no: 00636257 **Date established:** 1959
Turnover: £250,000 - £500,000 **No.of Employees:** 11 - 20
Product Groups: 48

Date of Accounts	Apr 11	Apr 10	Apr 09
Working Capital	22	51	63
Fixed Assets	48	54	63
Current Assets	175	184	116

J Cooke Engineering Ltd
Ashwell Street Ashwell, Baldock, SG7 5QT
Tel: 01462-742888 **Fax:** 01462-742188
E-mail: sales@jcooke.co.uk
Website: http://www.jcooke.co.uk
Directors: J. Cooke (MD)
Immediate Holding Company: J. COOKE ENGINEERING LIMITED
Registration no: 01137205 **VAT No.:** GB 198 3370 27
Date established: 1973 **Turnover:** £2m - £5m **No.of Employees:** 21 - 50
Product Groups: 30, 35

Date of Accounts	Dec 11	Dec 10	Dec 09
Working Capital	236	338	257
Fixed Assets	571	504	563
Current Assets	891	1m	832

L & C Precision Engineering Ltd
Unit 14 Baldock Industrial Estate London Road, Baldock, SG7 6NG
Tel: 01462-893108 **Fax:** 01462-490055
E-mail: lcprecision@btconnect.com
Website: http://www.l-cprecision-eng.co.uk
Directors: P. Thornton (Dir)
Immediate Holding Company: L&C PRECISION ENGINEERING LIMITED
Registration no: 04045797 **VAT No.:** GB 197 1145 50
Date established: 2000 **Turnover:** £500,000 - £1m
No.of Employees: 1 - 10 **Product Groups:** 46, 48

Date of Accounts	Mar 12	Mar 11	Mar 10
Working Capital	578	466	352
Fixed Assets	109	128	147
Current Assets	730	704	525

Patterson
Unit 17 Baldock Industrial Estate London Road, Baldock, SG7 6NG
Tel: 01462-893022 **Fax:** 01462-490076
Directors: B. Randhawa (Prop)
Registration no: 05353943 **VAT No.:** GB 198 1896 96
Date established: 2005 **No.of Employees:** 1 - 10 **Product Groups:** 48

Tele Sheds
Unit 1 Newnham Road, Newnham, Baldock, SG7 5LA
Tel: 01704-571215
E-mail: sales@telesheds.co.uk
Website: http://www.telesheds.co.uk
Directors: K. Summan (Dir)
No.of Employees: 1 - 10 **Product Groups:** 25, 35, 41, 66

The Lamp Company Ltd
4 Ashville Trading Estate Royston Road, Baldock, SG7 6NN
Tel: 01462-490066 **Fax:** 01462-491166
E-mail: sales@lampco.co.uk
Website: http://www.lampco.co.uk
Bank(s): Lloyds TSB Bank plc
Directors: I. Fursland (Dir)
Immediate Holding Company: THE LAMP COMPANY LIMITED
Registration no: 02838626 **VAT No.:** GB 538 5876 92
Date established: 1993 **Turnover:** £2m - £5m **No.of Employees:** 21 - 50
Product Groups: 36, 37, 39, 40, 48, 52, 63, 67

Date of Accounts	Jun 11	Jun 10	Jun 09
Working Capital	-135	-110	-246
Fixed Assets	677	719	752
Current Assets	748	771	610

Tilt Measurement Ltd
Horizon House Baldock Industrial Estate London Road, Baldock, SG7 6NG
Tel: 01462-894566 **Fax:** 01462-895990
E-mail: info@tilt-measurement.com
Website: http://www.tilt-measurement.com
Directors: A. Shaw (MD), Y. Whyte (Fin)
Immediate Holding Company: TILT MEASUREMENT LIMITED
Registration no: 01198538 **VAT No.:** GB 198 6980 82
Date established: 1975 **Turnover:** Up to £250,000
No.of Employees: 1 - 10 **Product Groups:** 38, 39

Date of Accounts	Dec 11	Dec 10	Dec 09
Sales Turnover	N/A	74	11
Pre Tax Profit/Loss	N/A	N/A	-61
Working Capital	-7	-3	-1
Fixed Assets	64	66	67
Current Assets	47	63	54
Current Liabilities	N/A	N/A	53

Universal Manufacturing Supplies
25 Whitehorse Street, Baldock, SG7 6QB
Tel: 01462-743966 **Fax:** 01462-892277
Directors: E. Sore (Prop)
Date established: 1989 **No.of Employees:** 1 - 10 **Product Groups:** 35

Widenoble Services Ltd
Tower House Unit 25 Baldock Industrial Estate London Road, Baldock, SG7 6NG
Tel: 01462-895431 **Fax:** 01462-895096
E-mail: laurie@widenoble.co.uk
Website: http://www.widenoble.co.uk
Directors: L. Fox (Dir)
Immediate Holding Company: WIDENOBLE SERVICES LIMITED
Registration no: 02791386 **VAT No.:** GB 632 2088 63
Date established: 1993 **Turnover:** £250,000 - £500,000
No.of Employees: 1 - 10 **Product Groups:** 48

Date of Accounts	Mar 11	Mar 10	Mar 09
Working Capital	62	10	119
Fixed Assets	305	313	325
Current Assets	150	106	192

Barnet

Architectural Window Films
45-47 Lancaster Road, Barnet, EN4 8AR
Tel: 08450-261125 **Fax:** 08450-261126
E-mail: solutions@architecturalwindowfilms.com
Directors: R. Walton (Prop)
Immediate Holding Company: STENNOR LIMITED
Date established: 2012 **Turnover:** £500,000 - £1m
No.of Employees: 1 - 10 **Product Groups:** 30

B E M
3 5 & 7 Henry Road, Barnet, EN4 8BL
Tel: 020-8449 4600 **Fax:** 020-8441 4738
E-mail: bemelectrical@aol.com
Website: http://www.bem-elec.co.uk
Directors: B. Howe (Prop)
Date established: 1977 **No.of Employees:** 1 - 10 **Product Groups:** 67

Barnet Service & Tuning Centre
1 Motorway Margaret Road, Barnet, EN4 8DW
Tel: 020-8441 6667 **Fax:** 020-8441 7516
E-mail: bstc@scimitarmotorservices.co.uk
Website: http://www.scimitarmotorservices.co.uk

Directors: M. Sargeant (Dir)
Date established: 1990 **Turnover:** £1m - £2m **No.of Employees:** 1 - 10
Product Groups: 39, 48, 72, 85

Capulet World
2 East Barnet Road, Barnet, EN4 8RW
Tel: 08700-603190 **Fax:** 08700-603190
E-mail: sales@capuletworld.com
Website: http://www.capuletworld.com
Directors: M. Thoraval (Prop)
Immediate Holding Company: CAPULET LIMITED
Registration no: 05911654 **Date established:** 2006
Turnover: Up to £250,000 **No.of Employees:** 1 - 10 **Product Groups:** 22, 24, 25, 63

Enable Access
16 Plantagenet Road, Barnet, EN5 5JG
Tel: 020-8275 0375 **Fax:** 020-8449 0326
E-mail: sales@enable-access.com
Website: http://www.enable-access.com
Managers: H. Morrish (Sales Admin)
Immediate Holding Company: VILLAGE MILL
Turnover: £1m - £2m **No.of Employees:** 1 - 10 **Product Groups:** 35, 39, 40, 45

Enterpride P.L.C.
1A Chalk Lane Cockfosters, Barnet, EN4 9JQ
Tel: 020-8370 0800 **Fax:** 020-8370 0888
Website: http://www.enterprise.plc.uk
Bank(s): Lloyds
Directors: J. Flood (MD)
Immediate Holding Company: Thames Water Services Ltd
Registration no: 02518607 **No.of Employees:** 101 - 250
Product Groups: 51

Eurocoin Ltd
Fortune House Moxon Street, Barnet, EN5 5TS
Tel: 020-8275 3000 **Fax:** 020-8275 3030
E-mail: reception@eurocoin.co.uk
Website: http://www.eurocoin.co.uk
Directors: N. Veitch (Fin), S. Smith (Dir)
Managers: C. Veitch (Purch Mgr), N. Davies (Tech Serv Mgr), G. Lewis (Personnel)
Ultimate Holding Company: VEITCH FAMILY HOLDINGS LIMITED
Immediate Holding Company: EUROCOIN LIMITED
Registration no: 01135951 **Date established:** 1973
Turnover: £10m - £20m **No.of Employees:** 21 - 50 **Product Groups:** 44

Date of Accounts	Dec 11	Dec 10	Dec 09
Sales Turnover	21m	17m	14m
Pre Tax Profit/Loss	524	363	279
Working Capital	2m	2m	1m
Fixed Assets	126	129	100
Current Assets	7m	6m	5m
Current Liabilities	707	588	457

Family Pet Services
88 Victoria Road New Barnet, Barnet, EN4 9PB
Tel: 020-8441 8361
E-mail: orders@familypetservices.co.uk
Website: http://www.familypetservices.co.uk
Managers: G. Mccombie (Chief Acct)
Date established: 1998 **No.of Employees:** 1 - 10 **Product Groups:** 07, 49, 62, 84

Dermot Gallagher Graphics
91 Margaret Road, Barnet, EN4 9RA
Tel: 020-8440 8938
E-mail: dermotgal@aol.com
Website: http://www.dgg.uk.com
Directors: D. Gallagher (Prop)
Date established: 1978 **Turnover:** Up to £250,000
No.of Employees: 1 - 10 **Product Groups:** 81

Gunshop
15 Cat Hill, Barnet, EN4 8HG
Tel: 020-8440 2974
E-mail: joe@gunshop-eb.co.uk
Website: http://www.gunshop-eb.co.uk
Directors: J. Beatham (Prop)
Registration no: 01892410 **Date established:** 1985
Turnover: £250,000 - £500,000 **No.of Employees:** 1 - 10
Product Groups: 36, 39, 40

Interior Property Solutions
Unit 17 Wrotham Business Park Wrotham Park, Barnet, EN5 4SZ
Tel: 020-8275 1095 **Fax:** 020-8449 0521
E-mail: contact@ips-interiors.co.uk
Website: http://www.ips-interiors.co.uk
Managers: M. Richardson (Sales Prom Mgr)
Immediate Holding Company: RED 7 PROPERTY LIMITED
Registration no: 06864677 **VAT No.:** GB 594 9317 90
Date established: 2008 **No.of Employees:** 1 - 10 **Product Groups:** 52

Johnson Sewing Machines
106 Woodville Road, Barnet, EN5 5NJ
Tel: 020-8441 7603
Directors: S. Crabb (Prop)
Date established: 1992 **No.of Employees:** 1 - 10 **Product Groups:** 43

Lighting & Gift Centre Ltd
269 East Barnet Road, Barnet, EN4 8SX
Tel: 020-8440 6610 **Fax:** 020-8440 6610
E-mail: thelightingcentre@btinternet.com
Website: http://www.theinternetlightingshop.co.uk
Directors: J. Muslin (Fin), J. Muslin (MD)
Immediate Holding Company: LIGHTING & GIFTS CENTRE LIMITED (THE)
Registration no: 00997685 **Date established:** 1970
No.of Employees: 1 - 10 **Product Groups:** 37

Date of Accounts	Mar 11	Mar 10	Mar 09
Working Capital	12	7	11
Fixed Assets	2	2	3
Current Assets	30	22	29

Lloyds TSB Bank plc
113-115 Cockfosters Road, Barnet, EN4 0DA
Tel: 08453-000000 **Fax:** 020-8447 2601
E-mail: firstname.lastname@ltsbasset.co.uk
Website: http://www.lloydstsb.com
Directors: J. Oliver (Dir), S. Green (Dir)
Managers: I. Durston (Sales Prom Mgr)
Ultimate Holding Company: LLOYDS BANKING GROUP PLC
Immediate Holding Company: LLOYDS TSB BANK PLC
Registration no: 00002065 **Date established:** 1965
Turnover: £75m - £125m **No.of Employees:** 1 - 10 **Product Groups:** 68

Date of Accounts	Dec 11	Dec 10	Dec 09
Pre Tax Profit/Loss	-1531m	725m	-4378m
Fixed Assets	134798m	281068m	34831m
Current Assets	53568m	27664m	38149m
Current Liabilities	896283m	929612m	403643m

Madgecourt Curtains
Cockfosters Parade Cockfosters Road, Barnet, EN4 0BX
Tel: 020-8447 0220 **Fax:** 020-8447 0330
E-mail: info@madgecourt.com
Website: http://www.madgecourt.com
Directors: A. Hamalis (Fin), M. Hamalis (MD)
Immediate Holding Company: MADGECOURT LIMITED
Registration no: 01585418 **VAT No.:** GB 355 1782 44
Date established: 1981 **Turnover:** £2m - £5m **No.of Employees:** 1 - 10
Product Groups: 23, 61

Date of Accounts	Oct 11	Oct 10	Oct 09
Working Capital	-927	-147	-148
Fixed Assets	2m	1m	1m
Current Assets	50	61	57

Malone Associates
59a High Street, Barnet, EN5 5UR
Tel: 020-8364 8688 **Fax:** 020-8364 9556
E-mail: maloneassoc@aol.com
Website: http://www.malones.co.uk
Directors: B. Malone (Prop)
Immediate Holding Company: ALAN COX ASSOCIATES LIMITED
Registration no: 06563552 **Date established:** 2008
No.of Employees: 1 - 10 **Product Groups:** 35

Date of Accounts	Jun 11	Jun 10	Jun 09
Working Capital	-202	-245	-270
Fixed Assets	263	304	347
Current Assets	456	33	34

Microscopes Plus Ltd
PO Box 3378, Barnet, EN5 9BL
Tel: 08452-724007
E-mail: info@microscopesplus.co.uk
Website: http://www.microscopesplus.co.uk
Directors: T. Meyers (Dir)
Immediate Holding Company: MICROSCOPES PLUS LIMITED
Registration no: 02929803 **Date established:** 1994
Turnover: £250,000 - £500,000 **No.of Employees:** 1 - 10
Product Groups: 38

Date of Accounts	Jun 11	Jun 10	Jun 06
Working Capital	-102	-103	-51
Current Assets	24	17	31

Newman Labelling Systems Ltd
Newman House Queens Road, Barnet, EN5 4DL
Tel: 020-8440 0044 **Fax:** 020-8449 2890
E-mail: sales@newman.co.uk
Website: http://www.newman.co.uk
Bank(s): Barclays, Pall Mall East, London SW1
Directors: J. Clayton (MD)
Ultimate Holding Company: NUFREND LIMITED
Immediate Holding Company: NEWMAN LABELLING SYSTEMS LIMITED
Registration no: 02745532 **Date established:** 1992 **Turnover:** £5m - £10m
No.of Employees: 21 - 50 **Product Groups:** 42

Date of Accounts	Mar 09	Mar 08	Sep 11
Working Capital	1m	1m	711
Fixed Assets	65	100	11
Current Assets	2m	2m	2m

Northgate Solar Controls
PO Box 200, Barnet, EN4 9EW
Tel: 020-8441 4545 **Fax:** 020-8441 4888
E-mail: enquiries@northgateuk.com
Website: http://www.northgateuk.com
Managers: C. Roberts
Turnover: £250,000 - £500,000 **No.of Employees:** 1 - 10
Product Groups: 30

Oakfield Foods Ltd
Kingmaker House Station Road, New Barnet, Barnet, EN5 1NZ
Tel: 020-8441 8211 **Fax:** 020-8440 1359
E-mail: miles@oakfieldfood.co.uk
Website: http://www.oakfieldfoods.co.uk
Directors: M. Levy (MD), D. Burr (Fin)
Ultimate Holding Company: OAKFIELD (FOODS) LIMITED
Immediate Holding Company: OAKFIELD (FOODS) LIMITED
Registration no: 02103137 **Date established:** 1987
Turnover: £75m - £125m **No.of Employees:** 21 - 50 **Product Groups:** 62

Date of Accounts	Dec 11	Dec 10	Dec 09
Sales Turnover	115m	98m	120m
Pre Tax Profit/Loss	2m	4m	3m
Working Capital	14m	15m	13m
Fixed Assets	2m	684	889
Current Assets	32m	27m	29m
Current Liabilities	5m	5m	6m

Paperun Group Of Companies
1 East Barnet Road, Barnet, EN4 8RR
Tel: 020-8447 4141 **Fax:** 020-8447 4241
E-mail: paperun@paper4u.com
Website: http://www.paperun.com
Bank(s): Natwest
Directors: D. Osborne (Co Sec), G. Brady (MD)
Ultimate Holding Company: PALACE HOLDINGS LIMITED
Immediate Holding Company: PAPERUN LIMITED
Registration no: 01299881 **VAT No.:** GB 235 8648 35
Date established: 1977 **Turnover:** £2m - £5m **No.of Employees:** 11 - 20
Product Groups: 66

Date of Accounts	Oct 11	Oct 10	Oct 09
Working Capital	96	98	90
Fixed Assets	48	35	46
Current Assets	2m	2m	1m

Prestige Healthcare London Ltd
5-7 Church Hill Road East Barnet, Barnet, EN4 8SY
Tel: 020-8364 8800 **Fax:** 020-8441 9123
E-mail: enquiries@prestigehealthcare.co.uk
Website: http://www.prestige.co.uk
Directors: R. Affutu Nartey (MD)
Managers: G. Stott, J. Robinson
Immediate Holding Company: PRESTIGE HEALTHCARE (LONDON) LIMITED
Registration no: 04266554 **Date established:** 2001
No.of Employees: 11 - 20 **Product Groups:** 22, 24

Date of Accounts	Jul 11	Jul 10	Jul 09
Working Capital	-2	40	136
Fixed Assets	37	7	9
Current Assets	167	311	709

Romco Equipment Ltd
Meadow Works Great North Road, Barnet, EN5 1AU
Tel: 020-8449 9515 **Fax:** 020-8449 6021
Directors: G. Morris (MD), S. Morris (Fin)
Immediate Holding Company: ROMCO EQUIPMENT LIMITED
Registration no: 01824710 **Date established:** 1984
No.of Employees: 1 - 10 **Product Groups:** 41

Date of Accounts	Mar 12	Jun 11	Jun 10
Working Capital	22	4	10
Fixed Assets	N/A	6	5
Current Assets	29	51	23
Current Liabilities	N/A	40	N/A

S M L Ltd
2 Red Rose Trading Estate Lancaster Road, Barnet, EN4 8BZ
Tel: 020-8447 1199 **Fax:** 020-8447 0880
E-mail: paulcarroll@sml.ltd.uk
Website: http://www.sml.ltd.uk
Directors: P. Carroll (MD), A. Carroll (Fin)
Immediate Holding Company: SML LIMITED
Registration no: 01747352 **VAT No.:** GB 396 4365 11
Date established: 1983 **No.of Employees:** 1 - 10 **Product Groups:** 38, 48, 85

Date of Accounts	Mar 11	Mar 10	Mar 09
Working Capital	690	467	626
Fixed Assets	57	72	95
Current Assets	890	650	972

Stock Films (Window Films to the Trade)
PO Box 11, Barnet, EN5 4DE
Tel: 020-8441 0449 **Fax:** 020-8441 4888
E-mail: sales@stockfilms.co.uk
Website: http://www.stockfilms.co.uk
Bank(s): Barclays, Whetstone
Directors: R. Walton (Dir)
No.of Employees: 11 - 20 **Product Groups:** 30

Berkhamsted

Advisorz Ltd
271 High Street, Berkhamsted, HP4 1AA
Tel: 07956-531699 **Fax:** 01442-877769
E-mail: enquiries@advisorz.co.uk
Website: http://www.advisorz.co.uk
Directors: I. Walker (MD), I. Walker (Prop)
Managers: J. Field
Immediate Holding Company: ADVISORZ LIMITED
Registration no: 06763329 **Date established:** 2008
Turnover: Up to £250,000 **No.of Employees:** 1 - 10 **Product Groups:** 61

Date of Accounts	Nov 10	Nov 09
Sales Turnover	199	11
Pre Tax Profit/Loss	102	5
Working Capital	42	1
Fixed Assets	3	3
Current Assets	94	26
Current Liabilities	46	17

Ashridge Business School
Ashridge, Berkhamsted, HP4 1NS
Tel: 01442-843491 **Fax:** 01442-841260
E-mail: contact@ashridge.org.uk
Website: http://www.ashridge.org.uk
Bank(s): Lloyds TSB Bank plc
Directors: T. Hamer (Pers), K. Peters (Grp Chief Exec)
Managers: M. Woodland (Tech Serv Mgr), P. Stanbury (Fin Mgr), C. Long
Ultimate Holding Company: ASHRIDGE (BONAR LAW MEMORIAL) TRUST
Immediate Holding Company: ASHRIDGE EXECUTIVE & ORGANISATION DEVELOPMENT LIMITED
Registration no: 01784086 **Date established:** 1984 **Turnover:** £5m - £10m
No.of Employees: 251 - 500 **Product Groups:** 80

Date of Accounts	Dec 11	Dec 10	Dec 09
Sales Turnover	9m	9m	8m
Working Capital	10	10	10
Current Assets	2m	3m	2m
Current Liabilities	1m	2m	1m

British & Continental Traders Ltd
Oxford House North Bridge Road, Berkhamsted, HP4 1EH
Tel: 01442-877415 **Fax:** 01442-872782
E-mail: sales@b-ct.co.uk
Website: http://www.b-ct.co.uk
Directors: M. Ginger (Dir), R. Odell (MD)
Managers: M. Williams (Accounts)
Immediate Holding Company: BRITISH & CONTINENTAL TRADERS LIMITED
Registration no: 00148054 **Date established:** 2017
Turnover: £250,000 - £500,000 **No.of Employees:** 1 - 10
Product Groups: 30, 33, 34, 35, 36, 38, 40, 42, 45, 46, 48, 67

Date of Accounts	Mar 11	Mar 10	Mar 09
Sales Turnover	N/A	380	N/A
Pre Tax Profit/Loss	N/A	49	N/A
Working Capital	233	200	186
Fixed Assets	N/A	N/A	1
Current Assets	318	272	298
Current Liabilities	N/A	30	N/A

Carapax Ltd
29 South Park Gardens, Berkhamsted, HP4 1JA
Tel: 01442-870399
Website: http://www.carapax.co.uk
Directors: M. Parsons (Prop)
Registration no: 03447156 **Date established:** 1997
No.of Employees: 11 - 20 **Product Groups:** 30, 39, 45

De Soutter Medical Ltd
1a Riverpark Billet Lane, Berkhamsted, HP4 1HL
Tel: 01442-860300 **Fax:** 01442-860333
E-mail: richard.bromage@de-souttermedical.com
Website: http://www.de-soutter.com
Bank(s): HSBC
Directors: R. Bromage (Fin), A. Wansbrough (Comm), C. De Soutter (MD)
Immediate Holding Company: DE SOUTTER MEDICAL LIMITED
Registration no: 03164365 **VAT No.:** GB 541 2983 44
Date established: 1996 **Turnover:** £10m - £20m
No.of Employees: 51 - 100 **Product Groups:** 38

Date of Accounts	May 10	May 09	May 08
Sales Turnover	17m	16m	N/A
Pre Tax Profit/Loss	4m	5m	4m
Working Capital	4m	4m	4m
Fixed Assets	396	371	405
Current Assets	6m	7m	7m
Current Liabilities	1m	2m	1m

Delta Press Ltd
Cameron House North Bridge Road, Berkhamsted, HP4 1EH
Tel: 01442-877794 **Fax:** 01442-877828
E-mail: deltap98@aol.com
Website: http://www.deltapressbooks.co.uk
Directors: F. Hymas (Fin), L. Cameron (MD)
Managers: D. Robinson (Sec)
Immediate Holding Company: DELTA PRESS LIMITED
Registration no: 01968841 **Date established:** 1985 **Turnover:** £2m - £5m
No.of Employees: 1 - 10 **Product Groups:** 28, 64

Date of Accounts	Mar 11	Mar 10	Mar 09
Working Capital	-36	-36	-36
Current Assets	2	2	2
Current Liabilities	38	N/A	38

Flowsource
Bank Mill Wharf Bank Mill Lane, Berkhamsted, HP4 2NT
Tel: 01442-865111 **Fax:** 01442-865222
E-mail: info@flowsource.co.uk
Website: http://www.flowsource.co.uk
Directors: S. Squires (Prop)
Turnover: £500,000 - £1m **No.of Employees:** 1 - 10 **Product Groups:** 36, 41, 42, 48, 67, 84

Focom Ltd
Greene Field Road, Berkhamsted, HP4 2XD
Tel: 01442-200000 **Fax:** 01442-200020
E-mail: sarah.glavin@focom.com
Website: http://www.focom.com
Managers: S. Glavin
Immediate Holding Company: FOCOM LIMITED
Registration no: 03206269 **Date established:** 1996
No.of Employees: 11 - 20 **Product Groups:** 37, 44

Date of Accounts	Oct 11	Oct 10	Oct 09
Working Capital	-59	-71	-88
Fixed Assets	4	3	3
Current Assets	23	44	45

G & E Automatic Equipment Ltd
North Bridge Road, Berkhamsted, HP4 1GE
Tel: 01442-872323 **Fax:** 01442-866900
E-mail: sales@geautomatic.co.uk
Website: http://www.geautomatic.co.uk
Directors: V. Ditchburn (Dir)
Ultimate Holding Company: G.& E.AUTOMATIC EQUIPMENT LIMITED
Immediate Holding Company: PEKO EQUIPMENT LIMITED
Registration no: 01908936 **VAT No.:** GB 448 6142 36
Date established: 1985 **Turnover:** Up to £250,000
No.of Employees: 1 - 10 **Product Groups:** 40

Igloo RPO Ltd
The Dower House 108 High Street, Berkhamsted, HP4 2BL
Tel: 0844-3570189
E-mail: info@igloorpo.com
Website: http://www.igloorpo.com
Directors: L. Whitehead (Comm), K. Mead (Chief Op Offcr)
Registration no: 06490097 **Date established:** 2007
No.of Employees: 11 - 20 **Product Groups:** 80, 81

Landlink Ltd
North Bridge Road, Berkhamsted, HP4 1EF
Tel: 01442-879777 **Fax:** 01442-877720
E-mail: info@landlinkltd.co.uk
Website: http://www.landlinkltd.co.uk
Directors: N. Keeler (Dir)
Immediate Holding Company: LANDLINK LTD
Registration no: 01668360 **VAT No.:** GB 527 1270 64
Date established: 1982 **Turnover:** £500,000 - £1m
No.of Employees: 1 - 10 **Product Groups:** 80

Date of Accounts	Mar 11	Mar 10	Mar 09
Sales Turnover	940	3m	3m
Pre Tax Profit/Loss	169	449	-1m
Working Capital	3m	2m	3m
Fixed Assets	4m	4m	3m
Current Assets	4m	5m	5m
Current Liabilities	1m	1m	236

Magnet Applications Ltd
North Bridge Road, Berkhamsted, HP4 1EH
Tel: 01442-875081 **Fax:** 01442-875009
E-mail: sales@magnetuk.com
Website: http://www.magnetapplications.com
Bank(s): Lloyds TSB Bank plc
Directors: C. Danes (Fin), R. Steff (MD)
Managers: J. Tompkins (Sales Prom Mgr), T. Heffernan (Sales Prom Mgr)
Ultimate Holding Company: BUNTING MAGNETICS CO (USA)
Immediate Holding Company: MAGNET APPLICATIONS LIMITED
Registration no: 00790396 **VAT No.:** GB 727 5589 92
Date established: 1964 **Turnover:** £5m - £10m **No.of Employees:** 21 - 50
Product Groups: 27, 29, 30, 32, 34, 35, 36, 37, 38, 49

Date of Accounts	Dec 10	Dec 09	May 09
Sales Turnover	N/A	N/A	3m
Pre Tax Profit/Loss	N/A	N/A	39
Working Capital	272	N/A	432
Fixed Assets	66	N/A	52
Current Assets	951	1	889
Current Liabilities	N/A	N/A	131

Matrix Handling Ltd
Haresfoot Farm Haresfoot Park, Berkhamsted, HP4 2SU
Tel: 01442-875021 **Fax:** 01442-878895
E-mail: info@matrixhandling.com
Website: http://www.matrixhandling.com
Directors: G. Lake (MD), D. Lake (Fin)
Immediate Holding Company: MATRIX HANDLING LIMITED
Registration no: 03045779 **Date established:** 1995
Turnover: £500,000 - £1m **No.of Employees:** 1 - 10 **Product Groups:** 35, 39, 45

Date of Accounts	Apr 11	Apr 10	Apr 09
Working Capital	-1	21	26
Fixed Assets	14	13	7
Current Assets	115	55	133
Current Liabilities	20	N/A	N/A

Mobile Expertise Ltd
Unit B Wooland Works Water End Road, Potten End, Berkhamsted, HP4 2SH
Tel: 01442-874604 **Fax:** 01442-500577
E-mail: sales@mobile-expertise.co.uk
Website: http://www.mobile-expertise.co.uk
Registration no: 05425840 **Date established:** 2005 **Turnover:** £1m - £2m
No.of Employees: 11 - 20 **Product Groups:** 37

Mount Lighting
York House North Bridge Road, Berkhamsted, HP4 1TA
Tel: 01442-865388 **Fax:** 01442-879074
Website: http://www.mountlighting.co.uk
Directors: Y. Tuffin (Ptnr)
No.of Employees: 1 - 10 **Product Groups:** 37, 67

Office Furniture Company Ltd
North Bridge Road, Berkhamsted, HP4 1EH
Tel: 01442-874597 **Fax:** 01442-874495
E-mail: enquiries@ofcuk.com
Website: http://www.ofcuk.com
Directors: A. Deacon (MD)
Immediate Holding Company: TV OVER LAN LIMITED
Registration no: 04582184 **Date established:** 2010 **Turnover:** £2m - £5m
No.of Employees: 11 - 20 **Product Groups:** 26, 30, 37, 49, 52, 61, 67, 72

Date of Accounts	Mar 12
Working Capital	-30
Current Assets	1m
Current Liabilities	2

P & R Finishing
1 Site 2 North Bridge Road, Berkhamsted, HP4 1EH
Tel: 01442-873962 **Fax:** 01442-873962
Directors: C. Jerome (Fin)
Immediate Holding Company: P & R FINISHING LIMITED
Registration no: 02622727 **VAT No.:** GB 596 1060 32
Date established: 1991 **Turnover:** Up to £250,000
No.of Employees: 1 - 10 **Product Groups:** 48

Date of Accounts	Jan 12	Jan 11	Jan 10
Working Capital	42	58	52
Fixed Assets	22	12	16
Current Assets	102	106	83

Phillips Plastics Ltd
North Bridge Road, Berkhamsted, HP4 1EH
Tel: 0845-4567 007 **Fax:** 0845-4567706
E-mail: sales@phillipsplastics.co.uk
Website: http://www.phillipsplastics.co.uk
Directors: P. Phillips (Dir)
Managers: D. Tatum (Personnel)
Immediate Holding Company: Phillips Presentation Products Ltd
Registration no: 01794730 **VAT No.:** GB 441 9042 67
Date established: 1984 **No.of Employees:** 11 - 20 **Product Groups:** 28, 30, 49

Date of Accounts	Dec 09	Dec 08	Dec 07
Working Capital	478	512	340
Fixed Assets	32	47	96
Current Assets	781	896	686
Current Liabilities	N/A	148	112

Prologic Computer Consultants Ltd
Redwood House Rectory Lane, Berkhamsted, HP4 2DH
Tel: 01442-876277 **Fax:** 01442-877245
E-mail: info@prologic.com
Website: http://www.prologic.com
Bank(s): Lloyds TSB
Directors: S. Jackson (MD), T. Fischer (MD), M. Tourlamain (Dir), C. Brown (Dir)
Managers: F. Roberts (Mktg Serv Mgr)
Ultimate Holding Company: PROLOGIC LIMITED
Immediate Holding Company: PROLOGIC COMPUTER CONSULTANTS LIMITED
Registration no: 01829656 **Date established:** 1984
Turnover: £10m - £20m **No.of Employees:** 51 - 100 **Product Groups:** 28, 44

Date of Accounts	Mar 11	Mar 10	Mar 09
Pre Tax Profit/Loss	-858	N/A	N/A
Working Capital	N/A	858	858
Current Assets	N/A	858	858

R M Sealers Ltd
Valley Farm Hemel Hempstead Road, Dagnall, Berkhamsted, HP4 1QR
Tel: 01442-843387 **Fax:** 01442-843387
E-mail: rmtool@hotmail.com
Website: http://www.rmtool.co.uk
No.of Employees: 1 - 10 **Product Groups:** 30, 40, 42, 46, 48, 67, 85

Date of Accounts	Aug 07	Aug 06
Working Capital	32	14
Current Assets	52	30

Sensonics Ltd
North Bridge Road, Berkhamsted, HP4 1EF
Tel: 01442-876833 **Fax:** 01442-876477
E-mail: sales@sensonics.co.uk
Website: http://www.sensonics.co.uk
Bank(s): Barclays, Watford
Directors: D. Sipos (Fin), N. Thompson (MD)
Immediate Holding Company: SENSONICS LIMITED
Registration no: 03346114 **VAT No.:** GB 669 3001 33
Date established: 1997 **Turnover:** £1m - £2m **No.of Employees:** 21 - 50
Product Groups: 37, 38, 39, 45, 67, 84

Date of Accounts	Apr 12	Apr 11	Apr 10
Working Capital	278	254	204
Fixed Assets	65	46	61
Current Assets	739	941	561

Tradelinens Ltd
Mile Barn Farm Hemel Hempstead Road, Dagnall, Berkhamsted, HP4 1QR
Tel: 01442-843769 **Fax:** 01442-843769
E-mail: sales@tradelinens.co.uk
Website: http://www.tradelinens.co.uk
Directors: R. Lancaster Gaye (MD)
Immediate Holding Company: TRADELINENS LIMITED
Registration no: 05065746 **Date established:** 2004
No.of Employees: 1 - 10 **Product Groups:** 23, 24, 63

Date of Accounts	Apr 11	Apr 10	Apr 09
Working Capital	51	55	75
Fixed Assets	10	4	4
Current Assets	469	330	290

Bishops Stortford

A K Rubber & Industrial Supplies Ltd
18 Twyford Business Centre London Road, Bishops Stortford, CM23 3YT
Tel: 01279-719000 **Fax:** 01279-719001
E-mail: sales@akrubber.co.uk
Website: http://www.akrubber.co.uk
Directors: K. Atkinson (Fin), A. Atkinson (MD)
Immediate Holding Company: A.K. RUBBER & INDUSTRIAL SUPPLIES LIMITED
Registration no: 02282814 **VAT No.:** GB 493 2221 55
Date established: 1988 **Turnover:** £1m - £2m **No.of Employees:** 1 - 10
Product Groups: 29, 30, 31, 32, 39, 42, 49, 63

Date of Accounts	Jan 12	Jan 11	Jan 10
Working Capital	50	19	-21
Fixed Assets	50	61	61
Current Assets	388	341	255

Alcohols Ltd
Charringtons House The Causeway, Bishops Stortford, CM23 2ER
Tel: 01279-658464 **Fax:** 01279-757613
E-mail: info@alcohols.co.uk
Website: http://www.alcohols.co.uk
Bank(s): National Westminster Bank Plc
Directors: B. Ling (Fin)
Managers: S. Read (Mgr), S. Read (Sales Admin)
Ultimate Holding Company: W.H.PALMER & CO.(INDUSTRIES)LIMITED
Immediate Holding Company: ALCOHOLS LIMITED
Registration no: 00547325 **VAT No.:** GB 232 3604 01
Date established: 1955 **Turnover:** £20m - £50m
No.of Employees: 11 - 20 **Product Groups:** 21, 31, 32, 62

Date of Accounts	Dec 11	Dec 10	Dec 09
Sales Turnover	22m	20m	19m
Pre Tax Profit/Loss	874	694	782
Working Capital	4m	4m	4m
Fixed Assets	1m	1m	1m
Current Assets	8m	7m	7m
Current Liabilities	2m	1m	963

B J Ashpole Ltd
Southmill Road, Bishops Stortford, CM23 3DJ
Tel: 01279-653211 **Fax:** 01279-651694
E-mail: bernard@ashpoles.co.uk
Website: http://www.ashpole.com
Directors: B. Ashpole (Prop)
Immediate Holding Company: B.J.ASHPOLE LIMITED
Registration no: 00597472 **VAT No.:** GB 213 6575 72
Date established: 1958 **Turnover:** £250,000 - £500,000
No.of Employees: 1 - 10 **Product Groups:** 68

Date of Accounts	Dec 11	Dec 10	Dec 09
Working Capital	102	87	85
Fixed Assets	36	38	33
Current Assets	230	199	180

Grant Barnett & Co. Ltd
Waterfront House 55 South Street, Bishops Stortford, CM23 3AL
Tel: 01279-758075 **Fax:** 01279-758095
E-mail: enquiries@grantbarnett.com
Website: http://www.grantbarnett.com
Directors: P. Hewitt (MD), P. Thomas (Sales)
Ultimate Holding Company: GRANT, BARNETT HOLDINGS LIMITED
Immediate Holding Company: GRANT, BARNETT HOLDINGS LIMITED
Registration no: 04108513 **VAT No.:** GB 248 0958 35
Date established: 2000 **Turnover:** £10m - £20m
No.of Employees: 21 - 50 **Product Groups:** 24

Date of Accounts	Dec 11	Dec 10	Dec 09
Sales Turnover	8m	10m	9m
Pre Tax Profit/Loss	276	438	388
Working Capital	1m	1m	1m
Fixed Assets	638	650	722
Current Assets	3m	4m	3m
Current Liabilities	416	849	344

Belcom Cables Ltd
Warish Hall Takeley, Bishops Stortford, CM22 6NZ
Tel: 01279-871150 **Fax:** 01279-871129
E-mail: sales@belcom.co.uk
Website: http://www.belcom.co.uk
Bank(s): HSBC
Directors: M. Hayton (MD), K. Ewing (Dir)
Managers: D. Trott (Mgr)
Registration no: 03276772 **VAT No.:** GB 700 4623 82
Date established: 1992 **Turnover:** £2m - £5m **No.of Employees:** 11 - 20
Product Groups: 30, 35, 37, 39, 44, 67

Date of Accounts	Oct 11	Oct 10	Oct 09
Working Capital	301	259	185
Fixed Assets	157	117	81
Current Assets	2m	1m	881

C M Z Machinery Ltd
Fullers End Elsenham, Bishops Stortford, CM22 6DU
Tel: 01279-814491 **Fax:** 01279-814541
E-mail: info@cmzweb.co.uk
Website: http://www.cmzweb.co.uk
Managers: J. Perryman (Sales Prom Mgr)
Immediate Holding Company: CMZ (MACHINERY) LIMITED
Registration no: 02777500 **VAT No.:** GB 573 3570 31
Date established: 1993 **No.of Employees:** 1 - 10 **Product Groups:** 46

Date of Accounts	Dec 11	Dec 10	Dec 09
Working Capital	97	101	103
Fixed Assets	6	7	8

Current Assets	158	189	217

C P L Aromas Ltd

Barrington Hall Dunmow Road, Hatfield Broad Oak, Bishops Stortford, CM22 7LE
Tel: 01279-717200 **Fax:** 01279-718527
E-mail: chrissy.marshall@cplaromas.com
Website: http://www.cplaromas.com
Bank(s): Hambro
Directors: C. Marshall (MD)
Managers: F. Pickthall
Ultimate Holding Company: CPL AROMAS (HOLDINGS) LIMITED
Immediate Holding Company: CPL AROMAS LIMITED
Registration no: 01031292 **Date established:** 1971
Turnover: £50m - £75m **No.of Employees:** 21 - 50 **Product Groups:** 20, 32

Date of Accounts	Mar 11	Mar 10	Mar 09
Sales Turnover	55m	47m	41m
Pre Tax Profit/Loss	6m	6m	2m
Working Capital	27m	23m	21m
Fixed Assets	8m	9m	6m
Current Assets	39m	36m	30m
Current Liabilities	6m	7m	4m

Capital Engineering Personnel Ltd

2nd Floors Millars Three Southmill Road, Bishops Stortford, CM23 3DH
Tel: 01279-508632 **Fax:** 01279-758903
E-mail: admin@cap-recuirt.co.uk
Website: http://www.capital-group.uk.com
Directors: M. Trott (Contracts)
Ultimate Holding Company: CAPITAL ENGINEERING GROUP HOLDINGS LTD
Immediate Holding Company: CAPITAL ENGINEERING PERSONNEL LIMITED
Registration no: 01005235 **Date established:** 1971
Turnover: £20m - £50m **No.of Employees:** 1 - 10 **Product Groups:** 80

Date of Accounts	Mar 11	Mar 10	Mar 09
Sales Turnover	10m	8m	6m
Pre Tax Profit/Loss	-141	-298	-76
Working Capital	3m	2m	2m
Fixed Assets	6	12	24
Current Assets	3m	3m	2m
Current Liabilities	203	173	85

Carolina Blinds

24 Leigh Drive Elsenham, Bishops Stortford, CM22 6BY
Tel: 01279-816580 **Fax:** 01279-817132
E-mail: info@carolina-blinds.co.uk
Website: http://www.carolina-blinds.co.uk
Directors: J. Bowles (Fin), B. Bowles (MD)
Immediate Holding Company: THE CAROLINA BLIND COMPANY LIMITED
Registration no: 04693159 **Date established:** 2003
Turnover: Up to £250,000 **No.of Employees:** 1 - 10 **Product Groups:** 24, 35, 63, 66

Computerised Engineering Co.

Unit 2a High Pastures Stortford Road, Hatfield Heath, Bishops Stortford, CM22 7DL
Tel: 01279-739455 **Fax:** 01279-739454
E-mail: mail@computerisedengineering.com
Website: http://www.computerisedengineering.com
Directors: J. Constable-Knight (Prop)
Turnover: Up to £250,000 **No.of Employees:** 1 - 10 **Product Groups:** 48, 84

Cuisine Royale

Hadham Road, Bishops Stortford, CM23 1JH
Tel: 01279-467586 **Fax:** 01279-755022
E-mail: sales@cuisineroyale.co.uk
Website: http://www.cuisineroyale.co.uk
Managers: L. Wallis (Mgr)
Date established: 2001 **No.of Employees:** 1 - 10 **Product Groups:** 20, 30, 41

Cullen Metcalfe & Co. Ltd

Southmill Road, Bishops Stortford, CM23 3DH
Tel: 01279-505533 **Fax:** 01279-504697
E-mail: sales@cullenmetcalfe.com
Website: http://www.cullenmetcalfe.com
Directors: J. Inch (Mkt Research), M. Mahaffy (Fin)
Immediate Holding Company: CULLEN.METCALFE & CO.LIMITED
Registration no: 00952195 **VAT No.:** GB 524 7630 48
Date established: 1969 **Turnover:** £500,000 - £1m
No.of Employees: 1 - 10 **Product Groups:** 27, 29, 36, 39, 61, 74, 84

Date of Accounts	Dec 11	Dec 10	Dec 09
Working Capital	30	22	16
Fixed Assets	5	5	3
Current Assets	61	95	73

Dab Pumps Ltd

4 Stortford Hall Industrial Park Dunmow Road, Bishops Stortford, CM23 5GZ
Tel: 01279-652776 **Fax:** 01279-655147
E-mail: info@dabpumps.com
Website: http://www.dabpumps.com
Bank(s): National Westminster Bank Plc
Managers: S. Gristwoods (Fin Mgr)
Ultimate Holding Company: GRUNDFOS AS (DENMARK)
Immediate Holding Company: DAB PUMPS LIMITED
Registration no: 01365973 **Date established:** 1978 **Turnover:** £2m - £5m
No.of Employees: 11 - 20 **Product Groups:** 39, 40, 45

Date of Accounts	Dec 11	Dec 10	Dec 09
Working Capital	869	539	589
Fixed Assets	116	116	17
Current Assets	2m	2m	2m

E L Component Ltd

Unit 5 Southmill Trading Centre, Bishops Stortford, CM23 3DY
Tel: 01279-503173 **Fax:** 01279-654441
E-mail: sales@elcomponent.co.uk
Website: http://www.elcomponent.co.uk
Managers: D. Burton (Sales Admin)
Immediate Holding Company: ELCOMPONENT LIMITED
Registration no: 01963289 **VAT No.:** GB 424 8123 68
Date established: 1985 **Turnover:** £500,000 - £1m
No.of Employees: 1 - 10 **Product Groups:** 38, 67

Date of Accounts	Dec 11	Dec 10	Dec 09
Working Capital	433	334	254
Fixed Assets	28	98	162
Current Assets	803	738	610

Falkland Islands Company Ltd

Kenburgh Court 131-137 South Street, Bishops Stortford, CM23 3HX
Tel: 01279-461630 **Fax:** 01279-461631
E-mail: admin@fihplc.com
Website: http://www.fihplc.com
Directors: J. Foster (MD)
Ultimate Holding Company: FALKLAND ISLANDS HOLDINGS PLC
Immediate Holding Company: FALKLAND ISLANDS HOLDINGS PLC
Registration no: 03416346 **Date established:** 1997
Turnover: £20m - £50m **No.of Employees:** 1 - 10 **Product Groups:** 76

Date of Accounts	Mar 12	Mar 11	Mar 10
Sales Turnover	34m	32m	29m
Pre Tax Profit/Loss	3m	2m	6m
Working Capital	3m	4m	3m
Fixed Assets	37m	34m	39m
Current Assets	14m	14m	13m
Current Liabilities	4m	4m	3m

FindTheNeedle.co.uk (Alpha-Publishing)

Alpha House, Bishops Stortford, CM23 5SB
Tel: 01279-306159 **Fax:** 01279-306186
E-mail: contactus@findtheneedle.co.uk
Website: http://www.findtheneedle.co.uk
Directors: E. Lancaster (MD)
No.of Employees: 11 - 20 **Product Groups:** 28

Forefront Signs Ltd

Unit 8 Southmill Trading Centre, Bishops Stortford, CM23 3DY
Tel: 01279-757751 **Fax:** 01279-757751
E-mail: info@forefrontsigns.co.uk
Website: http://www.forefrontsigns.co.uk
Directors: L. Richards (Prop)
Immediate Holding Company: FOREFRONT SIGNS LIMITED
Registration no: 05950414 **Date established:** 2006
No.of Employees: 1 - 10 **Product Groups:** 28, 30, 49, 67

Date of Accounts	Sep 11	Sep 10	Sep 09
Working Capital	-4	-7	-6
Fixed Assets	15	19	16
Current Assets	53	48	38

Foster Schoolwear

Unit 41 Golds Nurseries Business Park Jenkins Drive, Elsenham, Bishops Stortford, CM22 6JX
Tel: 01279-815596 **Fax:** 01279-815526
E-mail: info@fostersschoolwear.co.uk
Website: http://www.greatforschool.co.uk
Directors: I. Foster (MD)
Immediate Holding Company: FOSTER GROUP (UK) LIMITED
Registration no: 03575771 **Date established:** 1998
Turnover: £500,000 - £1m **No.of Employees:** 1 - 10 **Product Groups:** 49

Date of Accounts	May 09	May 08	May 07
Working Capital	37	33	-5
Fixed Assets	15	16	18
Current Assets	207	161	138
Current Liabilities	170	128	143
Total Share Capital	45	45	45

Globe Tooling Co.

24-25 Raynham Road, Bishops Stortford, CM23 5PD
Tel: 01279-656047 **Fax:** 01279-504711
E-mail: sales@globetooling.co.uk
Website: http://www.globetooling.co.uk
Directors: J. Worby (Ptnr)
Registration no: 04407525 **Date established:** 2002
No.of Employees: 1 - 10 **Product Groups:** 36

Grosvenor Technology Ltd

Millars Three Southmill Road, Bishops Stortford, CM23 3DH
Tel: 01279-838000 **Fax:** 01279-504776
E-mail: customerservices@gtl.biz
Website: http://www.grosvenortechnology.com
Directors: B. Beecraft (Fin)
Managers: J. Simms (Sales Admin), I. Summers (Purch Mgr), S. Woolhead (Tech Serv Mgr)
Ultimate Holding Company: NEWMARK SECURITY PLC
Immediate Holding Company: GROSVENOR TECHNOLOGY LIMITED
Registration no: 02412554 **VAT No.:** GB 538 2323 51
Date established: 1989 **Turnover:** £5m - £10m **No.of Employees:** 11 - 20
Product Groups: 40, 44, 81

Date of Accounts	Apr 12	Apr 11	Apr 10
Sales Turnover	6m	6m	6m
Pre Tax Profit/Loss	117	566	1m
Working Capital	-596	-188	14
Fixed Assets	5m	4m	4m
Current Assets	3m	3m	3m
Current Liabilities	852	1m	890

H S Services

Green Gables Dell Lane, Little Hallingbury, Bishops Stortford, CM22 7SH
Tel: 01279-658154 **Fax:** 01279-723112
E-mail: sales@hs-services.co.uk
Website: http://www.hs-services.co.uk
Directors: N. Bennett (Prop)
No.of Employees: 1 - 10 **Product Groups:** 45

Harlow Agricultural Merchants Ltd

Latchmore Bank Little Hallingbury, Bishops Stortford, CM22 7PJ
Tel: 01279-658313 **Fax:** 01279-755395
E-mail: ron@harlow-ag.co.uk
Website: http://www.harlow-ag.co.uk
Bank(s): Barclays
Directors: R. Gilder (Dir)
Immediate Holding Company: HARLOW AGRICULTURAL MERCHANTS LIMITED
Registration no: 01520770 **VAT No.:** GB 215 7417 73
Date established: 1980 **Turnover:** £50m - £75m
No.of Employees: 21 - 50 **Product Groups:** 61, 62

Date of Accounts	Jan 12	Jan 11	Jan 10
Sales Turnover	68m	60m	50m
Pre Tax Profit/Loss	2m	1m	377
Working Capital	3m	3m	2m
Fixed Assets	5m	5m	5m
Current Assets	12m	13m	11m
Current Liabilities	2m	2m	2m

Hayter Ltd

Spellbrook Lane West Spellbrook, Bishops Stortford, CM23 4BU
Tel: 01279-723444 **Fax:** 01279-723821
E-mail: sales@hayter.co.uk
Website: http://www.hayter.co.uk
Bank(s): H S B C
Managers: J. Dommett (Mktg Serv Mgr), T. O'Riordan (Purch Mgr), M. Chinnery (Personnel), A. Goodge (Tech Serv Mgr), V. Hoskin, R. Das
Ultimate Holding Company: TORO COMPANY (USA)
Immediate Holding Company: HAYTER LIMITED
Registration no: 05286686 **VAT No.:** GB 573 0876 22
Date established: 2004 **Turnover:** £10m - £20m
No.of Employees: 101 - 250 **Product Groups:** 41

Date of Accounts	Oct 11	Oct 10	Oct 09
Sales Turnover	20m	20m	20m
Pre Tax Profit/Loss	-1m	-105	-2m
Working Capital	2m	3m	5m
Fixed Assets	5m	5m	5m
Current Assets	8m	9m	9m
Current Liabilities	819	547	849

Hytek GB Ltd

Delta House Green Street, Elsenham, Bishops Stortford, CM22 6DS
Tel: 01279-815600 **Fax:** 01279-812978
E-mail: info@hytekgb.com
Website: http://www.hytekgb.com
Bank(s): Lloyds TSB Bank plc
Directors: A. Seal (Sales), F. Trewick (Chief Op Offcr), K. Arnold (MD)
Managers: T. Holyomes (Tech Serv Mgr)
Ultimate Holding Company: FLOWMAX HOLDINGS LIMITED (BVI)
Immediate Holding Company: HYTEK (GB) LIMITED
Registration no: 01915382 **VAT No.:** GB 420 2122 27
Date established: 1985 **Turnover:** £2m - £5m **No.of Employees:** 21 - 50
Product Groups: 30, 36, 39, 40

Date of Accounts	Apr 12	Apr 11	Apr 10
Working Capital	826	309	296
Fixed Assets	2m	1m	1m
Current Assets	2m	2m	2m
Current Liabilities	522	565	539

Interagro UK Ltd

Sworder's Barn North Street, Bishops Stortford, CM23 2LD
Tel: 01279-501995 **Fax:** 01279-501996
E-mail: info@interagro.co.uk
Website: http://www.interagro.co.uk
Directors: J. Underhill (Fin), M. Roche (MD)
Managers: A. Nicholson (I.T. Exec)
Registration no: 02849808 **Turnover:** £1m - £2m
No.of Employees: 1 - 10 **Product Groups:** 32

Date of Accounts	Jun 08
Working Capital	246
Fixed Assets	144
Current Assets	1891
Current Liabilities	1645
Total Share Capital	30

Little Hallingbury Church Of England Primary School

Wright's Green Lane Little Hallingbury, Bishops Stortford, CM22 7RE
Tel: 01279-723382 **Fax:** 01279-721286
E-mail: admin@littlehallingbury.essex.sch.uk
Website: http://www.littlehallingburychool.co.uk
Managers: B. Coates
Date established: 2000 **No.of Employees:** 21 - 50 **Product Groups:** 25, 35, 39

M H C Events Ltd

Sheering Hall Bambers Green, Takeley, Bishops Stortford, CM22 6PD
Tel: 0800-7348368
E-mail: info@mhcevents.co.uk
Website: http://www.mhcevents.co.uk
Directors: S. Moore (MD), S. Moore (Prop)
Immediate Holding Company: MHC EVENTS LIMITED
Registration no: 05741400 **Date established:** 2006
Turnover: Up to £250,000 **No.of Employees:** 1 - 10 **Product Groups:** 24, 63, 66, 83

Medisafe UK Ltd

Twyford Road, Bishops Stortford, CM23 3LJ
Tel: 01279-461641 **Fax:** 01279-461643
E-mail: info@medisafeinternational.com
Website: http://www.medisafeinternational.com
Directors: D. Smith (MD), L. Dawson (MD)
Managers: K. Edmondson (I.T. Exec), E. Prior (Buyer), M. Johnson (Sales Prom Mgr)
Immediate Holding Company: MEDISAFE UK LIMITED
Registration no: 02533282 **Date established:** 1990
Turnover: £10m - £20m **No.of Employees:** 1 - 10 **Product Groups:** 37, 42, 46

Date of Accounts	Aug 11	Aug 10	Aug 09
Sales Turnover	12m	10m	9m
Pre Tax Profit/Loss	97	1m	820
Working Capital	720	935	598
Fixed Assets	2m	2m	2m
Current Assets	5m	4m	3m
Current Liabilities	1m	1m	709

Minitran Ltd

5 Myson Way Raynham Close, Bishops Stortford, CM23 5JZ
Tel: 01279-757775 **Fax:** 01279-653535
E-mail: sales@minitran.co.uk
Website: http://www.minitran.co.uk
Directors: S. Garfield (Fin), S. Minns (Dir)
Immediate Holding Company: MINITRAN LIMITED
Registration no: 02298136 **Date established:** 1988
No.of Employees: 11 - 20 **Product Groups:** 29, 30, 35, 36

Date of Accounts	May 12	May 11	May 10
Working Capital	540	498	449
Fixed Assets	14	25	49
Current Assets	2m	2m	2m

Molton Brown

Green Street Elsenham, Bishops Stortford, CM22 6DS
Tel: 01279-648700 **Fax:** 01279-813924
E-mail: jimhigginson@moltonbrown.com
Website: http://www.moltonbrown.co.uk
Directors: C. Whinney (Fin)
Managers: T. Taank, J. Higginson
Immediate Holding Company: MOLTON BROWN LIMITED
Registration no: 02414997 **Date established:** 1989
No.of Employees: 101 - 250 **Product Groups:** 32, 63

P D S Design Solutions Ltd

2 The Staddles Little Hallingbury, Bishops Stortford, CM22 7SW
Tel: 01279-219175 **Fax:** 01279-219175
E-mail: sales@whatpowersupply.com
Website: http://www.whatpowersupply.com
Directors: C. Watkins (Dir)
Immediate Holding Company: PDS DESIGN SOLUTIONS LIMITED
Registration no: 03465624 **Date established:** 1997
Turnover: £500,000 - £1m **No.of Employees:** 1 - 10 **Product Groups:** 37, 44

Date of Accounts	Aug 11	Aug 10	Aug 09
Working Capital	-28	-31	-16
Fixed Assets	2	2	2
Current Assets	77	56	30

Peshawear UK Ltd

Millars 3 Southmill Road, Bishops Stortford, CM23 3DH
Tel: 01279-306257 **Fax:** 020-8654 9524
E-mail: david@peshawear-bs.com
Website: http://www.peshawear.co.uk
Managers: J. Worrall (Mgr)
Immediate Holding Company: KAVATINA LIMITED
Registration no: 01009049 **Date established:** 1971
Turnover: £250,000 - £500,000 **No.of Employees:** 1 - 10
Product Groups: 24

Date of Accounts	Mar 10	Mar 09	Mar 08
Sales Turnover	N/A	N/A	4m
Pre Tax Profit/Loss	N/A	N/A	380
Working Capital	3m	3m	3m
Fixed Assets	5	4	17
Current Assets	3m	3m	3m
Current Liabilities	N/A	N/A	189

Planet Scuba

Unit 2 The Links Raynham Road, Bishops Stortford, CM23 5NZ
Tel: 01279-466011
E-mail: info@planetscuba.co.uk
Website: http://www.planetscuba.co.uk
Directors: S. Manton (Dir)
No.of Employees: 1 - 10 **Product Groups:** 51

Powersem Ltd

Dawill Lower Road, Little Hallingbury, Bishops Stortford, CM22 7RA
Tel: 01279-726911 **Fax:** 01279-600589
E-mail: pb@pbentley.com
Website: http://www.pbentley.com
Directors: P. Bentley (MD)
Ultimate Holding Company: A B L (Aluminium Components) Ltd
Registration no: 03079963 **VAT No.:** 666 0981 06
Turnover: Up to £250,000 **No.of Employees:** 1 - 10 **Product Groups:** 37

Date of Accounts	Aug 07	Aug 06	Aug 05
Sales Turnover	14	11	11
Pre Tax Profit/Loss	1	1	N/A
Working Capital	3	2	1
Current Assets	5	3	3
Current Liabilities	2	2	2
ROCE% (Return on Capital Employed)	118.8	42.0	
ROT% (Return on Turnover)	28.3	6.5	

Prophotonix Ltd

Pierce Williams Sparrow Lane, Hatfield Broad Oak, Bishops Stortford, CM22 7BA
Tel: 01279-717170 **Fax:** 01279-717171
E-mail: jlane@prophotonix.com
Website: http://www.prophotonix.com
Directors: D. McGuinness (Sales & Mktg), J. Lane (MD)
Managers: P. Gottlieb (Tech Serv Mgr), S. Hutchins (Purch Mgr), T. Lea (Fin Mgr)
Ultimate Holding Company: STOCKER YALE INC (USA)
Immediate Holding Company: PROPHOTONIX LIMITED
Registration no: 03110900 **Date established:** 1995 **Turnover:** £5m - £10m
No.of Employees: 21 - 50 **Product Groups:** 37

Date of Accounts	Dec 11	Dec 10	Dec 09
Sales Turnover	5m	5m	4m
Pre Tax Profit/Loss	204	318	-540
Working Capital	548	316	33
Fixed Assets	171	222	257
Current Assets	2m	2m	2m
Current Liabilities	525	554	456

R D M Test Equipment Ltd

Unit 39 Golds Nurseries Business Park Jenkins Drive Elsenham, Bishops Stortford, CM22 6JX
Tel: 01279-817171 **Fax:** 01279-815743
E-mail: info@rdmtest.com
Website: http://www.rdmtest.com
Directors: D. Murrell (MD)
Immediate Holding Company: RDM TEST EQUIPMENT LIMITED
Registration no: 02073214 **Date established:** 1986 **Turnover:** £1m - £2m
No.of Employees: 1 - 10 **Product Groups:** 38, 42, 48

Date of Accounts	Mar 11	Mar 10	Mar 09
Working Capital	21	50	38
Fixed Assets	15	20	9
Current Assets	292	350	240
Current Liabilities	143	N/A	N/A

Seltek Consultants

25a Hockerill Street, Bishops Stortford, CM23 2DH
Tel: 01279-657716 **Fax:** 01279-651119
E-mail: sales@seltekconsultants.co.uk
Website: http://www.seltekconsultants.co.uk
Directors: G. Buncombe (MD), R. Lock (Fin)
Immediate Holding Company: SELTEK CONSULTANTS LIMITED
Registration no: 04474708 **VAT No.:** GB 573 2095 40
Date established: 2002 **Turnover:** £1m - £2m **No.of Employees:** 1 - 10
Product Groups: 80

Date of Accounts	Aug 11	Aug 10	Aug 09
Working Capital	218	260	256
Fixed Assets	74	131	197
Current Assets	292	320	306

Southwoodford Electronics Ltd

Southmill Trading Centre Southmill Road, Bishops Stortford, CM23 3DY
Tel: 01279-659509 **Fax:** 01279-758299
E-mail: sales@sweconnect.com
Website: http://www.sweconnect.com
Managers: B. Johnstone (Chief Mgr), G. Aisabley, J. Grier King (Mktg Serv Mgr)
Ultimate Holding Company: ELCOMPONENT LIMITED
Immediate Holding Company: SOUTH WOODFORD ELECTRONICS LIMITED
Registration no: 01203430 **VAT No.:** GB 247 8300 56
Date established: 1975 **Turnover:** £2m - £5m **No.of Employees:** 11 - 20
Product Groups: 35, 37

Date of Accounts	Dec 11	Dec 10	Dec 09
Working Capital	172	141	109
Fixed Assets	2	4	5
Current Assets	322	333	262

Springwell Forge

The Forge Cambridge Road, Ugley, Bishops Stortford, CM22 6HY
Tel: 01799-543270
Directors: D. Gowlett (Prop)
Date established: 1989 **No.of Employees:** 1 - 10 **Product Groups:** 26, 35

Thyssen Lift & Escalators Ltd

Unit 3 Myson Way Raynham Close, Bishops Stortford, CM23 5JZ
Tel: 01279-713777 **Fax:** 01245-478063
E-mail: new.projects@tke-uk-thyssenkrupp.com
Website: http://www.thyssenkruppelevator.co.uk
Managers: K. Rollings (District Mgr)
Ultimate Holding Company: THYSSEN KRUPP AG (GERMANY)
Immediate Holding Company: THYSSENKRUPP ELEVATOR UK LIMITED
Registration no: 00688790 **Date established:** 1961
No.of Employees: 1 - 10 **Product Groups:** 35, 39, 45

Date of Accounts	Sep 10	Sep 09	Sep 08
Sales Turnover	66m	94m	97m
Pre Tax Profit/Loss	-23m	-10m	-3m
Working Capital	6m	11m	14m
Fixed Assets	1m	2m	2m
Current Assets	31m	55m	57m
Current Liabilities	21m	10m	12m

Wentmore Shipping & Haulage Ltd

The Lodge Barrington Hall Dunmow Road, Hatfield Broad Oak, Bishops Stortford, CM22 7JL
Tel: 01279-718711 **Fax:** 01279-718510
E-mail: wentmore@globalnet.co.uk
Directors: P. Bradley (Fin), N. Walker (MD)
Ultimate Holding Company: WENTMORE HOLDINGS LIMITED
Immediate Holding Company: WENTMORE SHIPPING AND HAULAGE LIMITED
Registration no: 01084607 **Date established:** 1972
Turnover: £250,000 - £500,000 **No.of Employees:** 1 - 10
Product Groups: 76

Date of Accounts	Jan 11	Jan 09	Jan 08
Working Capital	-25	-27	-22
Fixed Assets	2	21	25
Current Assets	20	19	24

Woods Radio Frequency Services Ltd

Bullocks Farm Bullocks Lane, Takeley, Bishops Stortford, CM22 6TA
Tel: 01279-870432 **Fax:** 01279-871689
E-mail: jimw@woods-rf.co.uk
Website: http://www.woods-rf.co.uk
Managers: J. Woods (Mgr)
Immediate Holding Company: WOODS RADIO FREQUENCY TECHNOLOGY LTD
Date established: 2003 **No.of Employees:** 1 - 10 **Product Groups:** 46

Date of Accounts	Mar 11	Mar 10	Mar 09
Working Capital	-12	-3	-3
Fixed Assets	13	6	2
Current Assets	12	7	1

www.caelectrocomps.co.uk

36 Park Lane, Bishops Stortford, CM23 3NH
Tel: 01279-656051 **Fax:** 01279-656051
E-mail: chris@caelectrocomps.co.uk
Website: http://www.caelectrocomps.co.uk
Directors: C. Cutting (MD)
Turnover: Up to £250,000 **No.of Employees:** 1 - 10 **Product Groups:** 35, 37, 38

Borehamwood

Adecco UK Ltd

44 Shenley Road, Borehamwood, WD6 1DR
Tel: 020-8953 6700 **Fax:** 020- 82074686
E-mail: 1493.borehamwood@adecco.co.uk
Website: http://www.adecco.co.uk
Managers: S. Hook (District Mgr)
Ultimate Holding Company: ADECCO SA (SWITZERLAND)
Immediate Holding Company: ADECCO UK LIMITED
Registration no: 00593232 **Date established:** 1957
Turnover: £500m - £1,000m **No.of Employees:** 1 - 10
Product Groups: 80

Date of Accounts	Dec 11	Dec 10	Dec 09
Sales Turnover	357m	343m	414m
Pre Tax Profit/Loss	-672	-5m	-3m
Working Capital	37m	35m	35m
Fixed Assets	6m	7m	11m
Current Assets	299m	149m	131m
Current Liabilities	34m	29m	38m

Ardan Exhibitions

North Medburn Farm Watling Street Elstree, Borehamwood, WD6 3AA
Tel: 020-8207 4957 **Fax:** 020-8207 3040
E-mail: b-jones@ardan.co.uk
Website: http://www.ardan.co.uk
Directors: K. Daniels (Dir)
Immediate Holding Company: SOUTH MEDBURN FARM LIMITED
Registration no: 01073051 **Date established:** 1983
Turnover: £500,000 - £1m **No.of Employees:** 1 - 10 **Product Groups:** 81

Date of Accounts	Dec 10	Dec 09	Dec 08
Sales Turnover	500	564	568
Pre Tax Profit/Loss	-642	-582	-509
Working Capital	2m	1m	1m
Fixed Assets	3m	2m	2m
Current Assets	2m	1m	2m
Current Liabilities	215	180	154

Babcock Wanson UK Ltd

7 Elstree Way, Borehamwood, WD6 1SA
Tel: 020-8953 7111 **Fax:** 020-8207 5177
E-mail: info@babcock-wanson.co.uk
Website: http://www.babcock-wanson.co.uk
Bank(s): Barclays
Directors: C. Horsley (MD)
Managers: G. Bolton (Purch Mgr), R. Hogg (Fin Mgr)
Ultimate Holding Company: C N I M (FRANCE)
Immediate Holding Company: BABCOCK WANSON UK LIMITED
Registration no: 00573874 **Date established:** 1956 **Turnover:** £5m - £10m
No.of Employees: 51 - 100 **Product Groups:** 32, 39, 40, 66

Date of Accounts	Dec 11	Dec 10	Dec 09
Sales Turnover	8m	8m	7m
Pre Tax Profit/Loss	525	349	156
Working Capital	3m	3m	3m
Fixed Assets	3m	3m	3m
Current Assets	6m	5m	5m
Current Liabilities	1m	1m	1m

Bellwinch Homes 1992 Ltd

1 Oaks Court Warwick Road Herts, Borehamwood, WD6 1GS
Tel: 020-8953 0782 **Fax:** 020-8905 1499
E-mail: bellwinchsales@bellwinchhomes.co.uk
Website: http://www.bellwinchhomes.co.uk
Directors: R. Gregory (Ch), R. Page (MD), R. Peach (MD), R. King (Ch), R. Jones (Fin), S. White (Fin)
Managers: J. McCormack (Sales & Mktg Mg)
Immediate Holding Company: BELLWINCH HOMES 1992 LIMITED
Registration no: 01545789 **VAT No.:** GB 424 1411 01
Date established: 1981 **Turnover:** £20m - £50m **No.of Employees:** 1 - 10
Product Groups: 52

Blitz Communications Ltd

100 Centennial Avenue Centennial Park, Elstree, Borehamwood, WD6 3SA
Tel: 020-8327 1000 **Fax:** 0870-162 1111
E-mail: enquiries@blitzcommunications.co.uk
Website: http://www.blitzcommunications.co.uk
Bank(s): Lloyds TSB Bank plc
Directors: A. Makanji (Fin)
Managers: M. Shayler (Tech Serv Mgr), D. Watchorn (Ops Mgr)
Ultimate Holding Company: BLITZ COMMUNICATIONS GROUP LIMITED
Immediate Holding Company: BLITZ COMMUNICATIONS LIMITED
Registration no: 02595358 **Date established:** 1991
Turnover: £10m - £20m **No.of Employees:** 51 - 100 **Product Groups:** 37, 38, 81

Date of Accounts	Dec 11	Dec 10	Dec 09
Sales Turnover	11m	10m	10m
Pre Tax Profit/Loss	1m	298	-778
Working Capital	6m	5m	4m
Fixed Assets	4m	4m	4m
Current Assets	8m	7m	8m
Current Liabilities	2m	2m	2m

Computer People

Adecco House Elstree Way, Borehamwood, WD6 1HY
Tel: 020-8307 6000 **Fax:** 01727-841356
Website: http://www.computerpeople.co.uk
Directors: P. Searle (Grp Chief Exec), P. Searle (Dir)
Managers: D. Rabone (Contracts Mgr), J. Selby (Chief Mgr), R. Core (District Mgr), S. Copperwhite ()
Immediate Holding Company: KPG COMPUTER HOLDINGS LIMITED
Registration no: 02378928 **Date established:** 1989
Turnover: £125m - £250m **No.of Employees:** 21 - 50 **Product Groups:** 80

Donatantonio

Lupa House York Way, Borehamwood, WD6 1PX
Tel: 020-8236 2222 **Fax:** 020-8236 2288
E-mail: lupa@donatantonio.com
Website: http://www.donatantonio.com
Directors: M. Mandavia (Dir), S. Bell (Grp Chief Exec)
Managers: R. Edlin, W. Biszta (Purch Mgr)
Ultimate Holding Company: DONATANTONIO GROUP LIMITED
Immediate Holding Company: DONATANTONIO (2005) LIMITED
Registration no: 00576736 **Date established:** 1957
Turnover: £10m - £20m **No.of Employees:** 21 - 50 **Product Groups:** 20, 62

Date of Accounts	Jan 11	Jan 10	Jan 09
Working Capital	4m	4m	4m
Current Assets	4m	4m	4m

Equanet Ltd

Horizon One Studio Way, Borehamwood, WD6 5WH
Tel: 020-8327 5000 **Fax:** 020-8953 7617
E-mail: sales@microwarehouse.co.uk
Website: http://www.equanet.co.uk
Bank(s): National Westminster Bank Plc
Directors: M. Stevens (Co Sec), J. Sheahan (MD), D. Page (Dir), P. Holt (Fin)
Managers: M. Atkins
Immediate Holding Company: MICROWAREHOUSE LTD
Registration no: NI074065 **VAT No.:** GB 227 0792 63
Date established: 2009 **Turnover:** £75m - £125m
No.of Employees: 101 - 250 **Product Groups:** 26, 44

Date of Accounts	Apr 07	Apr 06
Pre Tax Profit/Loss	330	N/A
Working Capital	13890	13570
Current Assets	13890	13570
Total Share Capital	17850	17850

Flowline Manufacturing Ltd

Elstree Business Centre Elstree Way, Borehamwood, WD6 1RX
Tel: 020-8207 6565 **Fax:** 020-8207 3082
E-mail: mark.davis@flowline.co.uk
Website: http://www.flowline.co.uk
Directors: M. Davis (MD), M. Davis (Sales)
Managers: L. Austin (Mgr)
Immediate Holding Company: FLOWLINE MANUFACTURING LIMITED
Registration no: 01999031 **VAT No.:** GB 454 2137 72
Date established: 1986 **Turnover:** £2m - £5m **No.of Employees:** 1 - 10
Product Groups: 38

Date of Accounts	Dec 07	Dec 06	Dec 05
Working Capital	61	78	56
Fixed Assets	13	34	22
Current Assets	261	430	275
Current Liabilities	200	352	219
Total Share Capital	10	10	10

Fujitsu General UK Co. Ltd

330 Centennial Avenue Centennial Park, Elstree, Borehamwood, WD6 3TJ
Tel: 020-8238 7810 **Fax:** 020-8731 3469
E-mail: h.shimanoe@fujitsu-general.com
Website: http://www.fujitsu-general.com

Managers: A. Gaffar (Fin Mgr)
Ultimate Holding Company: FUJITSU GENERAL LTD (JAPAN)
Immediate Holding Company: FUJITSU GENERAL (U.K.) CO. LIMITED
Registration no: 01322291 **VAT No.:** GB 312 4414 07
Date established: 1977 **Turnover:** £75m - £125m
No.of Employees: 1 - 10 **Product Groups:** 40, 52

Date of Accounts	Mar 12	Mar 11	Mar 10
Sales Turnover	1	13	25
Pre Tax Profit/Loss	955	-807	-1m
Working Capital	-4m	-5m	-4m
Fixed Assets	5m	5m	5m
Current Assets	2m	3m	4m
Current Liabilities	226	268	175

George Supplies
201 Shenley Road, Borehamwood, WD6 1AT
Tel: 020-8207 6464 **Fax:** 020-8207 6464
Website: http://www.george-supplies.co.uk
Directors: E. Boxley (Prop)
Date established: 2004 **No.of Employees:** 1 - 10 **Product Groups:** 37

Gilberts Food Equipment Ltd
Gilbert House 1 Warwick Place Warwick Road, Borehamwood, WD6 1UA
Tel: 020-8731 3700 **Fax:** 0845-230 0682
E-mail: sales@topgourmet.co.uk
Website: http://www.gilberts-foodequipment.com
Directors: A. Moorfoot (Fin), R. Gilbert (MD)
Ultimate Holding Company: GILBERTS FOOD EQUIPMENT LIMITED
Immediate Holding Company: ABSOLUT FORM LIMITED
Registration no: 04279866 **Date established:** 2001
No.of Employees: 21 - 50 **Product Groups:** 20, 24, 30, 36, 37, 40, 41, 49, 63, 67

Date of Accounts	Apr 11	Apr 10	Apr 08
Working Capital	-4	-4	-4
Current Assets	N/A	N/A	19
Current Liabilities	4	4	N/A

Gospel Restoration Ltd
124 Manor Way, Borehamwood, WD6 1QX
Tel: 020-8536 0300
E-mail: edgospel@aol.com
Website: http://www.gospelstainedglass.co.uk
Directors: E. Willis (Dir)
Immediate Holding Company: GOSPEL RESTORATION LIMITED
Registration no: 07546242 **VAT No.:** GB 417 5284 48
Date established: 2011 **No.of Employees:** 1 - 10 **Product Groups:** 28, 33, 35, 48, 52

Date of Accounts	Sep 10	Sep 09	Sep 08
Working Capital	9	-1	N/A
Fixed Assets	34	44	N/A
Current Assets	46	51	N/A
Current Liabilities	16	16	N/A

H E L
Unit 9-10 Capital Business Park Manor Way, Borehamwood, WD6 1GW
Tel: 020-8736 0640 **Fax:** 020-8736 0641
E-mail: info@helgroup.com
Website: http://www.helgroup.com
Directors: J. Singh (MD)
Managers: D. Ames (Mgr), M. Addy (Comptroller)
Ultimate Holding Company: HEL LIMITED
Immediate Holding Company: HAZARD EVALUATION LABORATORY (CONSULTANTS) LTD
Registration no: 03067250 **Date established:** 1995
No.of Employees: 21 - 50 **Product Groups:** 38, 42, 67, 85

Date of Accounts	Jun 11	Jun 10	Jun 09
Working Capital	95	95	95
Current Assets	95	95	95

Harvard plc
Harvard House The Waterfront Elstree Road, Elstree, Borehamwood, WD6 3BS
Tel: 020-8238 7650 **Fax:** 020-8953 8465
E-mail: ashleym@albaplc.com
Website: http://www.harvardplc.com
Directors: R. Thompson (Fin)
Managers: S. Miller, M. Jenkins, M. Ashley
Ultimate Holding Company: HARVARD INTERNATIONAL LIMITED
Immediate Holding Company: HARVARD HOLDINGS LIMITED
Registration no: 02235123 **Date established:** 1988
Turnover: £75m - £125m **No.of Employees:** 21 - 50 **Product Groups:** 84

Date of Accounts	Mar 12	Mar 11	Mar 10
Pre Tax Profit/Loss	-2m	N/A	-223
Working Capital	-2m	-2m	-2m
Fixed Assets	N/A	2m	2m
Current Assets	33m	32m	32m
Current Liabilities	5	5	5

Andrew Isaacs Machinery International Ltd
The Kinetic Centre Theobald Street, Borehamwood, WD6 4PJ
Tel: 020-8387 5434 **Fax:** 020-8387 5409
E-mail: info@isaacsmachinery.com
Website: http://www.isaacsmachinery.com
Directors: D. Pound (Fin), A. Isaacs (MD)
Immediate Holding Company: ANDREW ISAACS MACHINERY INTERNATIONAL LTD.
Registration no: 03827678 **Date established:** 1999
No.of Employees: 1 - 10 **Product Groups:** 29, 34, 42, 46, 48

Date of Accounts	Dec 11	Dec 10	Dec 07
Working Capital	669	590	506
Fixed Assets	12	16	2
Current Assets	909	780	757

Kennedy Occupational Health
The Kinetic Centre Theobald Street, Borehamwood, WD6 4PJ
Tel: 020-8387 4050
E-mail: imp@kennedyoh.co.uk
Directors: F. Kennedy (Prop)
Immediate Holding Company: FITZROY PROPERTY SERVICES LIMITED
Registration no: 06771879 **Date established:** 2011
Turnover: Up to £250,000 **No.of Employees:** 1 - 10 **Product Groups:** 84

Masters Pharmaceuticals Ltd
380 Centennial Park Centennial Avenue, Elstree, Borehamwood, WD6 3TJ
Tel: 020-8327 0900 **Fax:** 020-8327 0901
E-mail: info@mastersglobal.com
Website: http://www.mastersglobal.com
Directors: S. Clarke (Fin)
Managers: H. Campbell (Mktg Serv Mgr), D. Moran
Immediate Holding Company: MASTERS PHARMACEUTICALS LIMITED
Registration no: 01856573 **Date established:** 1984
Turnover: £10m - £20m **No.of Employees:** 21 - 50 **Product Groups:** 61

Date of Accounts	Dec 11	Dec 10	Dec 09
Sales Turnover	19m	19m	11m
Pre Tax Profit/Loss	-1m	-116	166
Working Capital	2m	2m	91
Fixed Assets	1m	1m	186
Current Assets	5m	4m	3m
Current Liabilities	411	508	532

Pelham Leather Goods Ltd
110 Centennial Park Centennial Avenue, Elstree, Borehamwood, WD6 3SB
Tel: 020-8731 3500 **Fax:** 020-8731 3501
E-mail: sales@pelhamgroup.co.uk
Website: http://www.delsey.com
Directors: S. Spitz (MD), N. Crossick (Sales), J. Kraines (Chief Op Offcr), G. Sarang (Co Sec)
Managers: S. Williams (Mktg Serv Mgr), M. Crowe, V. Vekaria (Personnel)
Ultimate Holding Company: PELHAM LEATHER GOODS LIMITED
Immediate Holding Company: DELSEY LUGGAGE LIMITED
Registration no: 01393318 **Date established:** 1978
Turnover: £500,000 - £1m **No.of Employees:** 21 - 50
Product Groups: 22, 63

Date of Accounts	Jan 12	Jan 11	Jan 10
Sales Turnover	920	1m	2m
Pre Tax Profit/Loss	35	-144	-50
Working Capital	N/A	-959	-822
Fixed Assets	N/A	8	16
Current Assets	N/A	289	329
Current Liabilities	N/A	164	106

Pizza Hut UK Ltd
Building One Imperial Place Elstree Way, Borehamwood, WD6 1JN
Tel: 020-8732 9000 **Fax:** 020-8732 9001
Website: http://www.pizzahut.co.uk
Directors: H. Birts (Fin), J. Hofma (Dir), R. Sen (Purch), S. Ash (Tech Serv), T. Ashby (Co Sec), J. Little (Pers)
Managers: C. Wells
Ultimate Holding Company: YUM! BRANDS INC (USA)
Immediate Holding Company: PIZZA HUT (U.K.) LIMITED
Registration no: 01072921 **VAT No.:** GB 454 1466 52
Date established: 1972 **Turnover:** £250m - £500m
No.of Employees: 1501 & over **Product Groups:** 69

Date of Accounts	Nov 08	Nov 09	Nov 10
Sales Turnover	356m	365m	346m
Pre Tax Profit/Loss	-13m	-12m	-22m
Working Capital	-91m	-65m	-74m
Fixed Assets	118m	106m	93m
Current Assets	17m	20m	19m
Current Liabilities	44m	33m	31m

Pooleys Flight Equipment
Elstree Aerodrome Elstree, Borehamwood, WD6 3AW
Tel: 020-8953 4870 **Fax:** 020-8953 2512
E-mail: sales@pooleys.com
Website: http://www.pooleys.com
Directors: R. Pooley (Grp Chief Exec)
Immediate Holding Company: FIRECREST AVIATION LIMITED
Registration no: 01893988 **VAT No.:** GB 674 7970 78
Date established: 1985 **Turnover:** Up to £250,000
No.of Employees: 1 - 10 **Product Groups:** 67

Date of Accounts	Dec 10	Dec 09	Dec 08
Working Capital	-44	-34	-31
Fixed Assets	2	3	4
Current Assets	36	22	35

Reggiani Lighting Ltd
12 Chester Road, Borehamwood, WD6 1LT
Tel: 020-8236 3000 **Fax:** 020-8236 3099
E-mail: point@reggiani.net
Website: http://www.reggiani.net
Directors: R. Martelo (Design), A. Merola (Sales), L. Moffat (Fin), A. Hill (MD)
Managers: N. Turrell (Tech Serv Mgr)
Ultimate Holding Company: REGGIANI SPA ILLIMUNAZIONE (ITALY)
Immediate Holding Company: GILTLAND LIMITED
Registration no: 01883783 **Date established:** 1985 **Turnover:** £5m - £10m
No.of Employees: 21 - 50 **Product Groups:** 37

Date of Accounts	Dec 11	Dec 10	Dec 09
Pre Tax Profit/Loss	-9	-9	-9
Working Capital	-124	-124	-124
Fixed Assets	123	132	141
Current Liabilities	124	124	124

Scandanavian Tobacco
250 Centennial Park Centennial Avenue, Elstree, Borehamwood, WD6 3TH
Tel: 020-8731 3400 **Fax:** 020-8207 7977
E-mail: info@st.dk
Website: http://www.st-group.com
Directors: N. Lambert (Fin), H. Williams (MD), A. Graham (Mkt Research), A. Williams (Sales)
Managers: N. Raynor (Tech Serv Mgr)
Date established: 1989 **No.of Employees:** 11 - 20 **Product Groups:** 20

Secomak Holdings Ltd (Halma Group)
Unit 330 Centennial Park, Elstree, Borehamwood, WD6 3TJ
Tel: 020-8732 1300 **Fax:** 020-8732 1301
E-mail: info@secomak.com
Website: http://www.secomak.com
Bank(s): Barclays
Directors: J. Moore (Fin)
Managers: N. McKenna (Sales Off Mgr), D. Joshua (Personnel), J. Middleton (Mktg Serv Mgr), J. Birbeck (Ops Mgr)
Immediate Holding Company: SECOMAK HOLDINGS LIMITED
Registration no: 05528682 **VAT No.:** GB 226 7786 29
Date established: 2005 **Turnover:** Up to £250,000
No.of Employees: 21 - 50 **Product Groups:** 30, 32, 33, 38, 40, 41, 42, 43, 44, 45, 46, 47, 84

Date of Accounts	Mar 12	Mar 11	Mar 10
Working Capital	-874	-874	-1m
Fixed Assets	2m	2m	2m
Current Assets	N/A	10	2

Tormo Ltd
7 Devonshire Business Park Chester Road, Borehamwood, WD6 1NA
Tel: 020-8207 5777 **Fax:** 020-8207 5888
E-mail: dave.rutter@tormo.co.uk
Website: http://www.tormo.co.uk
Directors: D. Rutter (MD), J. Fredenham (Fin)
Immediate Holding Company: TORMO LIMITED
Registration no: 00369405 **VAT No.:** GB 229 3742 51
Date established: 1941 **Turnover:** £2m - £5m **No.of Employees:** 1 - 10
Product Groups: 35, 49, 66

Date of Accounts	Mar 11	Mar 10	Mar 09
Working Capital	1m	1m	959
Fixed Assets	476	466	483
Current Assets	2m	1m	1m

G R Wallis
25 Well End Road, Borehamwood, WD6 5NZ
Tel: 020-8953 5305 **Fax:** 020-8953 8111
E-mail: graham@hartwellsuk.com
Website: http://www.hartwellsuk.com
Directors: G. Wallis (Prop)
Date established: 1998 **No.of Employees:** 1 - 10 **Product Groups:** 38, 42

Waters
730-740 Centennial Park Centennial Way, Elstree, Borehamwood, WD6 3SZ
Tel: 020-8238 6100 **Fax:** 020-8207 7070
E-mail: uk@waters.com
Website: http://www.waters.com
Bank(s): Barclays, Crawley
Directors: A. Ayash (Dir)
Ultimate Holding Company: WATERS
Registration no: 03162904 **VAT No.:** GB 659 7606 83
Turnover: £125m - £250m **No.of Employees:** 21 - 50 **Product Groups:** 38

White Ellerton Products
9 Warwick Road, Borehamwood, WD6 1US
Tel: 020-8236 0444 **Fax:** 020-8207 6766
E-mail: wep.uk@virgin.net
Website: http://www.whiteellerton.co.uk
Directors: G. Handley (MD)
Immediate Holding Company: WHITE ELLERTON PRODUCTS LIMITED
Registration no: 00912310 **VAT No.:** GB 229 8717 25
Date established: 1967 **Turnover:** £500,000 - £1m
No.of Employees: 1 - 10 **Product Groups:** 26, 30

Date of Accounts	Sep 11	Sep 10	Sep 09
Working Capital	-48	-20	22
Fixed Assets	260	273	270
Current Assets	97	108	101

Broxbourne

Broxbourne Solutions
5 St. Catherines Road, Broxbourne, EN10 7LG
Tel: 01992-448588 **Fax:** 01992-448588
E-mail: info@broxbourne-solutions.co.uk
Website: http://www.broxbourne-solutions.co.uk
Directors: J. Ross (Dir), S. Jackson (Fin)
Immediate Holding Company: Broxbourne Solutions Ltd
Registration no: 04372517 **Date established:** 2002
Turnover: Up to £250,000 **No.of Employees:** 1 - 10 **Product Groups:** 44, 80

Date of Accounts	Mar 10	Mar 09	Mar 08
Working Capital	-6	-4	-1
Fixed Assets	1	1	1
Current Assets	9	17	13

Cashback Vat Reclaim UK Ltd
Cottage Beaumont Road, Broxbourne, EN10 7QJ
Tel: 01992-464279 **Fax:** 01992-44 2229
E-mail: constantine@cashbackuk.co.uk
Website: http://www.cashbackvatreclaim.com
Directors: C. Malekkou (MD)
Immediate Holding Company: CASHBACK VAT RECLAIM UK LTD
Registration no: 06796202 **Date established:** 2009
No.of Employees: 1 - 10 **Product Groups:** 80

Date of Accounts	Jun 11	Jun 10
Working Capital	-18	-13
Fixed Assets	13	20
Current Assets	53	113

Mcdowall Welding Services Ltd
Lee Valley Forge Wharf Road, Broxbourne, EN10 6HF
Tel: 01992-442896 **Fax:** 01992-442896
E-mail: elaine_mcdowall@hotmail.com
Directors: E. McDowall (Fin), L. Mcdowall (MD)
Immediate Holding Company: MCDOWALL WELDING SERVICES LIMITED
Registration no: 04731659 **Date established:** 2003
Turnover: Up to £250,000 **No.of Employees:** 1 - 10 **Product Groups:** 26, 35

Date of Accounts	Apr 11	Apr 10	Apr 09
Sales Turnover	156	138	173
Pre Tax Profit/Loss	21	18	32
Working Capital	2	-0	1
Fixed Assets	5	7	4
Current Assets	39	36	47
Current Liabilities	32	9	10

Nazeing Glassworks Ltd
Nazeing New Road, Broxbourne, EN10 6SU
Tel: 01992-464485 **Fax:** 01992-450966
E-mail: sales@nazeing-glass.com
Website: http://www.nazeing-glass.com
Bank(s): Barclays, Cheshunt
Directors: J. Doyle (Dir), S. Pollock Hill (MD), S. Pollock-Hill (MD)
Ultimate Holding Company: NAZEING GLASS INVESTMENTS LIMITED
Immediate Holding Company: NAZEING GLASS WORKS LIMITED
Registration no: 00253535 **Date established:** 1931 **Turnover:** £1m - £2m
No.of Employees: 21 - 50 **Product Groups:** 28, 33

Date of Accounts	Mar 12	Mar 11	Mar 10
Working Capital	346	365	536
Fixed Assets	38	44	44
Current Assets	537	519	671

Quantum Binders Ltd
Unit 6 Meridian Building Nazeing Glassworks Estate Nazeing New Road, Broxbourne, EN10 6SX
Tel: 01992-479900 **Fax:** 01992-479911
E-mail: sales@quantumbinders.co.uk
Website: http://www.quantumbinders.co.uk

see next page

Quantum Binders Ltd - Cont'd

Directors: P. Webb (Fin), T. Redgrave (MD)
Immediate Holding Company: QUANTUM BINDERS LIMITED
Registration no: 03118831 **Date established:** 1995
Turnover: £500,000 - £1m **No.of Employees:** 1 - 10 **Product Groups:** 20, 27, 28, 30, 49, 64

Date of Accounts	Oct 11	Oct 10	Oct 09
Working Capital	-13	-6	-3
Fixed Assets	14	13	11
Current Assets	126	130	107

Team Overseas Ltd

Meridan Building Nazeing New Road, Broxbourne, EN10 6SX
Tel: 01992-464462 **Fax:** 01992-464643
E-mail: sales@teamoverseas.com
Website: http://www.teamoverseas.com
Directors: L. Powell (Sales), J. Gayler (MD)
Managers: C. Hammond (Sales Prom)
Immediate Holding Company: TEAM OVERSEAS LIMITED
Registration no: 03119064 **VAT No.:** GB 668 2110 39
Date established: 1995 **Turnover:** £1m - £2m **No.of Employees:** 1 - 10
Product Groups: 23, 24, 30, 31, 32, 33, 34, 35, 36, 37, 38, 39, 40, 41, 44, 45, 46, 47, 66, 67, 68, 83

Date of Accounts	Oct 10	Mar 10	Mar 09
Working Capital	43	184	160
Fixed Assets	1	2	3
Current Assets	408	687	683

Towers Thompson Ltd

Turnford Place Great Cambridge Road, Turnford, Broxbourne, EN10 6NH
Tel: 01992-456456 **Fax:** 01992-473600
E-mail: enquiry@towers-thompson.co.uk
Website: http://www.towers-thompson.co.uk
Bank(s): Barclays
Directors: T. Goddard (Fin)
Ultimate Holding Company: TOWERS THOMPSON HOLDINGS LIMITED
Immediate Holding Company: TOWERS & CO.,LIMITED
Registration no: 00058397 **VAT No.:** GB 524 6660 44
Date established: 1998 **Turnover:** £75m - £125m
No.of Employees: 21 - 50 **Product Groups:** 62

Date of Accounts	Dec 11	Dec 10	Dec 09
Sales Turnover	123m	119m	114m
Pre Tax Profit/Loss	-1m	-986	267
Working Capital	6m	8m	9m
Fixed Assets	7m	5m	5m
Current Assets	35m	31m	30m
Current Liabilities	3m	4m	3m

Buntingford

Alpha Springs Ltd

Unit 3 Firs Park Watermill Industrial Estate, Buntingford, SG9 9JS
Tel: 01763-274909 **Fax:** 01763-274910
E-mail: info@alphasprings.co.uk
Website: http://www.alphasprings.co.uk
Directors: M. Aldred (Co Sec), P. Pearce (Dir)
Registration no: 36622749 **VAT No.:** GB 720 1880 63
Turnover: £250,000 - £500,000 **No.of Employees:** 1 - 10
Product Groups: 35, 36, 38, 39, 49, 66, 68, 85

Date of Accounts	Dec 10	Dec 09	Dec 08
Working Capital	-77	-76	-105
Fixed Assets	80	74	98
Current Assets	133	103	125

Amwell Systems Ltd

Buntingford Business Park Baldock Road, Buntingford, SG9 9ER
Tel: 01763-276200 **Fax:** 01763-276222
E-mail: contact@amswell_systems.com
Website: http://www.amwell-systems.com
Directors: V. Charles (MD)
Managers: A. Owens (Comptroller), T. Wallbridge (Tech Serv Mgr), R. Darlow (Purch Mgr), R. Borthwick (Personnel)
Ultimate Holding Company: INTERCEDE HOLDCO LIMITED
Immediate Holding Company: AMWELL SYSTEMS LIMITED
Registration no: 02611422 **Date established:** 1991
Turnover: £10m - £20m **No.of Employees:** 21 - 50 **Product Groups:** 25

Date of Accounts	Dec 11	Dec 10	Dec 09
Sales Turnover	11m	14m	15m
Pre Tax Profit/Loss	-10m	-453	858
Working Capital	8m	9m	9m
Fixed Assets	175	283	639
Current Assets	10m	11m	12m
Current Liabilities	1m	1m	936

Environmental Projects UK Ltd

Honeywood Light Industrial Estate Throcking Road, Cottered, Buntingford, SG9 9RB
Tel: 01763-281400 **Fax:** 01763-281500
E-mail: info@epuk-ltd.com
Website: http://www.epuk-ltd.com
Directors: J. Berdicchio (Dir)
Immediate Holding Company: ENVIRONMENTAL PROJECTS UK LIMITED
Registration no: 05419871 **Date established:** 2005
Turnover: Up to £250,000 **No.of Employees:** 11 - 20 **Product Groups:** 32, 52, 83, 84

Date of Accounts	Apr 10	Apr 09	Apr 08
Working Capital	-34	3	-15
Fixed Assets	26	37	47
Current Assets	57	75	106

First Class Business Solutions Ltd

Unit 43-45 Park Farm Industrial Estate Ermine Street, Buntingford, SG9 9AZ
Tel: 01763-273731 **Fax:** 01763-273833
E-mail: sales@fcbs.co.uk
Website: http://www.fcbs.co.uk
Directors: A. Baxter (MD), N. Baxter (Fin)
Immediate Holding Company: FIRST CLASS BUSINESS SOLUTIONS LIMITED
Registration no: 02979465 **Date established:** 1994
No.of Employees: 21 - 50 **Product Groups:** 44

Date of Accounts	Jan 11	Jan 10	Jan 09
Working Capital	95	42	-27
Fixed Assets	239	237	276
Current Assets	1m	1m	1m

Grannatech Ltd

The Close Hare Street, Buntingford, SG9 0AE
Tel: 01763-289009 **Fax:** 01763-289011
E-mail: sales@grannatech.co.uk
Website: http://www.grannatech.co.uk
Directors: J. Medlicott (Dir)
Immediate Holding Company: GRANNATECH LIMITED
Registration no: 03943047 **Date established:** 2000
Turnover: Up to £250,000 **No.of Employees:** 1 - 10 **Product Groups:** 37

Date of Accounts	Aug 11	Aug 10	Aug 09
Working Capital	1	N/A	N/A
Current Assets	59	73	30

J K M Scaffolding Ltd

Unit 1b Firs Watermill Industrial Estate Aspenden Road, Buntingford, SG9 9JS
Tel: 01763-273323 **Fax:** 01763-273324
E-mail: timcave@jkmscaffolding.co.uk
Website: http://www.jkmscaffolding.co.uk
Directors: T. Cave (Dir)
Immediate Holding Company: J.K.M. SCAFFOLDING LIMITED
Registration no: 04316498 **Date established:** 2001
No.of Employees: 1 - 10 **Product Groups:** 25, 35, 52, 66, 83

Meura Brewery Equipment Ltd

Unit 1 Park Farm Industrial Estate Ermine Street, Buntingford, SG9 9AZ
Tel: 01763-272680 **Fax:** 01763-272321
E-mail: david.clifford@meura.co.uk
Website: http://www.meura.com
Directors: D. Clifford (MD)
Immediate Holding Company: MEURA (BREWERY EQUIPMENT) LIMITED
Registration no: 01330508 **Date established:** 1977 **Turnover:** £2m - £5m
No.of Employees: 1 - 10 **Product Groups:** 35, 41, 42

Date of Accounts	Dec 11	Dec 10	Dec 09
Working Capital	453	359	345
Fixed Assets	19	33	19
Current Assets	2m	716	1m

R & G Mouldings

Watermill Industrial Estate, Buntingford, SG9 9JS
Tel: 01763-271065 **Fax:** 01763-273309
E-mail: r.reason@rgmouldings.co.uk
Website: http://www.rgmouldings.co.uk
Directors: R. Reason (Ptnr)
Registration no: 03365893 **VAT No.:** GB 336 5893 23
No.of Employees: 1 - 10 **Product Groups:** 48

Robert J Turner & Co.

Roe Green Sandon, Buntingford, SG9 0QE
Tel: 01763-288371 **Fax:** 01763-288440
E-mail: sales@robertjturner.co.uk
Website: http://www.robertjturner.co.uk
Directors: J. Turner (Prop)
VAT No.: GB 197 8556 91 **Date established:** 1970
Turnover: Up to £250,000 **No.of Employees:** 1 - 10 **Product Groups:** 25, 52, 66

Systems Services

Little Thatches Rushden, Buntingford, SG9 0SH
Tel: 01763-288165
E-mail: john.lever@btinternet.com
Website: http://www.datarecoveruk.co.uk
Directors: J. Lever (Prop)
Turnover: Up to £250,000 **No.of Employees:** 1 - 10 **Product Groups:** 44

T & C Services

Little Meadow Baldock Road, Buntingford, SG9 9RH
Tel: 01763-281644 **Fax:** 01763-281646
E-mail: info@recovery-equipment.co.uk
Website: http://www.recovery-equipment.co.uk
Directors: C. Smith (Prop)
Date established: 1990 **No.of Employees:** 1 - 10 **Product Groups:** 35, 39, 45

Wellglaze Ltd

Watermill Industrial Estate, Buntingford, SG9 9JS
Tel: 01763-271811 **Fax:** 01763-273108
E-mail: sales@welglaze.co.uk
Website: http://www.welguard.co.uk
Bank(s): Barclays
Directors: T. Clarke (MD), T. Clarke (Dir)
Immediate Holding Company: CLICKONCONSERVATORIES.COM LIMITED
Registration no: 04419520 **VAT No.:** 393 2576 26 **Date established:** 2002
Turnover: £2m - £5m **No.of Employees:** 21 - 50 **Product Groups:** 30, 35

Bushey

Citizen Machinery UK Ltd

1 Park Avenue, Bushey, WD23 2DA
Tel: 01923-691500 **Fax:** 01923-691599
E-mail: sales@citizenmachinery.co.uk
Website: http://www.citizenmachinery.co.uk
Bank(s): Barclays
Directors: A. Pearce (Fin), D. Wilkins (Sales), G. Bryant (Dir)
Managers: T. Punel (Tech Serv Mgr)
Ultimate Holding Company: CITIZEN HOLDINGS CO LIMITED (JAPAN)
Immediate Holding Company: CITIZEN MACHINERY UK LTD
Registration no: 01174902 **VAT No.:** GB 241 0582 96
Date established: 1974 **Turnover:** £10m - £20m
No.of Employees: 21 - 50 **Product Groups:** 46, 47

Date of Accounts	Dec 11	Dec 10	Dec 09
Sales Turnover	33m	17m	4m
Pre Tax Profit/Loss	2m	1m	-711
Working Capital	3m	3m	2m
Fixed Assets	2m	2m	2m
Current Assets	14m	12m	4m
Current Liabilities	4m	3m	2m

Medipin Ltd

24 Chiltern Avenue, Bushey, WD23 4QB
Tel: 020-8950 8773
E-mail: bljcbs@aol.com
Website: http://www.medipin.net
Directors: H. Caron Jacobs (Co Sec)
Immediate Holding Company: MEDIPIN LIMITED
Registration no: 04990972 **Date established:** 2003
No.of Employees: 1 - 10 **Product Groups:** 67

Date of Accounts	Mar 11	Mar 10	Mar 09
Working Capital	-8	-7	-5
Fixed Assets	7	8	8
Current Assets	3	2	6
Current Liabilities	10	N/A	N/A

Newlyn Forge

70 Bushey Hall Road, Bushey, WD23 2EQ
Tel: 01923-251660 **Fax:** 01923-251660
E-mail: newlynforge@uwclub.net
Website: http://www.newlynforge.co.uk
Directors: S. Rook (Prop)
Date established: 1986 **No.of Employees:** 1 - 10 **Product Groups:** 26, 35

Readymade Companies Worldwide.com

Overseas House 66-68 High Road, Bushey Heath, Bushey, WD23 1GG
Tel: 020-8421 7475 **Fax:** 020-8421 9883
E-mail: info@readymadecompaniesworldwide.com
Website: http://www.readymadecompaniesworldwide.com
Managers: T. Quinton (Mktg Serv Mgr)
Registration no: 06433633 **Date established:** 2008
Turnover: Up to £250,000 **No.of Employees:** 1 - 10 **Product Groups:** 61

Riley Larkin Partnership

Hadleigh House 96 High Street, Bushey, WD23 3HB
Tel: 020-8421 8670 **Fax:** 020-8421 8671
E-mail: mark@rileylarkin.co.uk
Website: http://www.rileylarkin.co.uk
Directors: M. Riley (Ptnr)
Immediate Holding Company: RILEY LARKIN LTD
Registration no: 04375930 **Date established:** 2002
No.of Employees: 1 - 10 **Product Groups:** 35

Date of Accounts	Mar 11	Mar 10	Mar 09
Working Capital	414	379	662
Fixed Assets	24	36	203
Current Assets	749	740	959

Smiths Detection

459 Park Avenue, Bushey, WD23 2BW
Tel: 01923-658000 **Fax:** 01923-240285
E-mail: m.maginnis@smithdetection.com
Website: http://www.smithsdetection.com
Bank(s): Barclays, Cambridge
Directors: K. Sutterby (Chief Op Offcr)
Managers: R. Wilson (Site Co-ord), J. Poppin
Ultimate Holding Company: SMITHS INDUSTRIES
Registration no: 00480992 **VAT No.:** GB 393 2419 42
Date established: 1950 **Turnover:** £20m - £50m
No.of Employees: 251 - 500 **Product Groups:** 38, 39, 40, 85

Harpenden

Access UK Ltd

3 Marlborough Park Southdown Road, Harpenden, AL5 1NL
Tel: 01582-465100 **Fax:** 01582-465199
E-mail: info@armstrong-consultants.com
Website: http://www.theaccessgroup.com
Managers: C. White (Mktg Serv Mgr)
Immediate Holding Company: ACCOUNTING TECHNOLOGY LIMITED
Registration no: 03028490 **Date established:** 1995
Turnover: £10m - £20m **No.of Employees:** 1 - 10 **Product Groups:** 44

Date of Accounts	Mar 11	Mar 10	Mar 09
Sales Turnover	N/A	N/A	520
Pre Tax Profit/Loss	N/A	N/A	-21
Working Capital	51	58	32
Fixed Assets	7	9	9
Current Assets	144	151	123
Current Liabilities	N/A	N/A	34

Beacon Private Trust

Ellerd House Amenbury Lane, Harpenden, AL5 2EJ
Tel: 01582-761125 **Fax:** 01582-761126
E-mail: beacon@beacon-ifa.co.uk
Website: http://www.beacon-ifa.com
Directors: A. Davis (Dir)
Immediate Holding Company: NORTH TAWTON POTTERY LLP
Registration no: 01983121 **VAT No.:** GB 197 5448 12
Date established: 2007 **Turnover:** Up to £250,000
No.of Employees: 1 - 10 **Product Groups:** 80, 82

Date of Accounts	Feb 11	Feb 10	Feb 09
Working Capital	5	-31	-26
Fixed Assets	2	3	3
Current Assets	30	8	6

C H S Powersystems Ltd

3 Batford Mill Industrial Estate Lower Luton Road, Harpenden, AL5 5BZ
Tel: 01582-766008 **Fax:** 01582-461386
E-mail: mailbox@chsswitchgear.co.uk
Website: http://www.powersystems.co.uk
Bank(s): Barclays
Directors: G. Boost (MD), J. Stocking (Fin)
Immediate Holding Company: C H S SWITCHGEAR LIMITED
Registration no: 01096933 **VAT No.:** GB 198 1632 33
Date established: 1973 **Turnover:** £1m - £2m **No.of Employees:** 11 - 20
Product Groups: 37, 38, 48

Date of Accounts	Mar 10	Mar 09	Mar 08
Working Capital	-36	26	51
Fixed Assets	48	57	24
Current Assets	337	494	514

Cooper Printing Machinery Ltd

42 Coldharbour Lane, Harpenden, AL5 4UN
Tel: 01582-764431 **Fax:** 01582-768608
E-mail: sales@cooperprint.co.uk
Website: http://www.cooperprint.co.uk
Directors: C. Cooper (MD), J. Cooper (Fin)
Immediate Holding Company: COOPER PRINTING MACHINERY LIMITED
Registration no: 03596239 **Date established:** 1998 **Turnover:** £2m - £5m
No.of Employees: 1 - 10 **Product Groups:** 28, 29, 32, 44

Date of Accounts	Dec 11	Dec 10	Dec 09
Working Capital	-3	-12	-7
Fixed Assets	16	14	16

Current Assets	50	40	80

Dark Matter Composites Ltd

Unit 20 Thrales End Farm, Harpenden, AL5 3NS
Tel: 01582-469069 **Fax:** 01582-469069
E-mail: info@darkmattercomposites.co.uk
Website: http://www.darkmattercomposites.co.uk
Directors: R. Hansen (MD)
Registration no: 5395870 **Date established:** 2005
Turnover: Up to £250,000 **No.of Employees:** 1 - 10 **Product Groups:** 30, 33, 84

Date of Accounts	Oct 09	Oct 08	Oct 07
Working Capital	8	5	-6
Fixed Assets	43	14	8
Current Assets	35	46	22

Dor-2-Dor.Com

41 Hollybush Lane, Harpenden, AL5 4AY
Tel: 08443-571152 **Fax:** 01582-462727
E-mail: sales@dor2dor.com
Website: http://www.dor2dor.com
Directors: J. Frankling (Fin)
Immediate Holding Company: DOR-2-DOR LIMITED
Registration no: 02984550 **Date established:** 1994
Turnover: £500,000 - £1m **No.of Employees:** 1 - 10 **Product Groups:** 81

Fobbed Off

Riverside House 42 Coldharbour Lane, Harpenden, AL5 4UN
Tel: 01582-768295 **Fax:** 01582-768295
E-mail: nick@ncooper45.freeserve.co.uk
Website: http://www.fobbedoff.co.uk
Directors: N. Cooper (Prop)
Immediate Holding Company: COOPER PRINTING MACHINERY LIMITED
Date established: 1998 **Turnover:** Up to £250,000
No.of Employees: 1 - 10 **Product Groups:** 24, 27, 28, 30

Date of Accounts	Dec 10	Dec 09	Dec 08
Working Capital	-12	-7	7
Fixed Assets	14	16	18
Current Assets	40	80	83

G A B Designs

29 Coldharbour Lane, Harpenden, AL5 4NQ
Tel: 01582-769049 **Fax:** 01582-769049
E-mail: gabdes@talktalk.net
Website: http://www.gabdesigns.co.uk
Directors: G. Butler (Prop)
Date established: 1992 **No.of Employees:** 1 - 10 **Product Groups:** 84

J M S Plant Hire

32 Coldharbour Lane, Harpenden, AL5 4UN
Tel: 01582-467000 **Fax:** 01582-467999
E-mail: sales@jms-planthire.co.uk
Website: http://www.jms-planthire.co.uk
Directors: M. Jackson (Prop)
Managers: J. Lynn (Sales Off Mgr)
No.of Employees: 21 - 50 **Product Groups:** 35, 36, 40, 42, 46, 66, 83

Jarvis Group Ltd

Unit 1 Waterside Station Road, Harpenden, AL5 4US
Tel: 01582-761211 **Fax:** 01582-764100
E-mail: mpeters@jarvisgroupltd.co.uk
Website: http://www.jarvisgroupltd.co.uk
Directors: M. Peters (Dir)
Ultimate Holding Company: JARVIS GROUP LIMITED
Immediate Holding Company: JARVIS COMMERCIAL LIMITED
Registration no: 00401234 **Date established:** 1945
Turnover: £250,000 - £500,000 **No.of Employees:** 51 - 100
Product Groups: 51, 52

Date of Accounts	Apr 11	Apr 10	Apr 09
Sales Turnover	308	383	849
Pre Tax Profit/Loss	-78	-45	-410
Working Capital	604	682	727
Fixed Assets	15	15	15
Current Assets	1m	2m	2m
Current Liabilities	676	881	968

London Letter File Company Ltd

Tenet House 7 Mons Close, Harpenden, AL5 1TD
Tel: 01582-460547 **Fax:** 01582-460482
E-mail: sales@londonletterfile.com
Website: http://www.londonletterfile.com
Directors: G. Crowther (MD)
Immediate Holding Company: LONDON LETTER FILE COMPANY LIMITED
Registration no: 00224226 **VAT No.:** GB 232 6788 47
Date established: 2027 **Turnover:** £500,000 - £1m
No.of Employees: 1 - 10 **Product Groups:** 22, 27, 28, 30, 49, 64

Date of Accounts	Mar 12	Mar 11	Mar 10
Working Capital	1	1	2
Fixed Assets	1	2	2
Current Assets	22	27	25

Prayon UK plc

Rivers Lodge West Common, Harpenden, AL5 2JD
Tel: 01582-769999 **Fax:** 01582-769989
E-mail: info@prayon.co.uk
Website: http://www.prayon.com
Directors: P. Holdon (Dir), P. Schils (Co Sec)
Managers: P. Holden (Mgr)
Ultimate Holding Company: PRAYON SA (BELGIUM)
Immediate Holding Company: PRAYON (UK) PUBLIC LIMITED COMPANY
Registration no: 01283674 **VAT No.:** GB 284 0688 34
Date established: 1976 **Turnover:** £500,000 - £1m
No.of Employees: 1 - 10 **Product Groups:** 31, 32

Date of Accounts	Dec 11	Dec 10	Dec 09
Sales Turnover	986	890	880
Pre Tax Profit/Loss	297	129	211
Working Capital	413	597	1m
Fixed Assets	12	9	9
Current Assets	508	739	1m
Current Liabilities	84	135	55

Q H I Group Ltd

9-10 Allied Business Centre Coldharbour Lane, Harpenden, AL5 4UT
Tel: 01582-461123 **Fax:** 01582-461117
E-mail: info@qhigroup.com
Website: http://www.qhigroup.com
Directors: R. Kennedy (Dir)
Immediate Holding Company: QHI GROUP LIMITED
Registration no: 02171982 **VAT No.:** GB 490 5395 25
Date established: 1987 **Turnover:** £1m - £2m **No.of Employees:** 21 - 50
Product Groups: 31, 37, 38, 39, 40

Date of Accounts	Mar 11	Mar 10	Mar 09
Working Capital	3m	2m	2m
Fixed Assets	346	337	280
Current Assets	4m	3m	3m

R T I UK Ltd (t/a Calder Equipment)

Batford Mill Lower Luton Road, Harpenden, AL5 5BZ
Tel: 01582-764331 **Fax:** 01582-761526
E-mail: inbox@rtiuk.co.uk
Website: http://www.rtiuk.co.uk
Bank(s): Barclays
Managers: R. Hills (Prod Mgr), D. McClennan, M. Mcmannon (Ops Mgr)
Immediate Holding Company: RTI (UK) LIMITED
Registration no: 00686484 **VAT No.:** 222 8054 89 **Date established:** 1961
Turnover: £500,000 - £1m **No.of Employees:** 11 - 20 **Product Groups:** 65

Russell Plastics

Progress House 37 Grove Avenue, Harpenden, AL5 1EY
Tel: 01582-762868 **Fax:** 01582-461086
E-mail: sales@russellplastics.co.uk
Website: http://www.russellplastics.co.uk
Directors: I. Russell (Dir), K. McCaw (Co Sec)
Registration no: 01639185 **VAT No.:** GB 367 0467 38
Date established: 1982 **Turnover:** £500,000 - £1m
No.of Employees: 1 - 10 **Product Groups:** 30, 66

S B Electronic Systems Ltd

Arden Grove, Harpenden, AL5 4SL
Tel: 01582-769991 **Fax:** 01582-461705
E-mail: sales@telepen.co.uk
Website: http://www.telepen.co.uk
Bank(s): Barclays
Directors: P. Burchett (MD)
Immediate Holding Company: S. B. ELECTRONIC SYSTEMS LIMITED
Registration no: 00920069 **VAT No.:** GB 198 3121 48
Date established: 1967 **Turnover:** £1m - £2m **No.of Employees:** 11 - 20
Product Groups: 44

Date of Accounts	Mar 12	Mar 11	Mar 10
Working Capital	286	361	269
Fixed Assets	89	52	64
Current Assets	870	1m	875

Stanley Handling Ltd

48 Coldharbour Lane, Harpenden, AL5 4UR
Tel: 01582-767711 **Fax:** 01582-765994
E-mail: sales@stanleyhandling.co.uk
Website: http://www.stanleyhandling.co.uk
Bank(s): HSBC Bank plc
Directors: R. Stanley (MD), M. Stanley (Dir)
Managers: P. Wallis (Comm)
Ultimate Holding Company: NORMAN STANLEY (MECHANICAL HANDLING) LIMITED
Immediate Holding Company: STANLEY HANDLING LIMITED
Registration no: 00967713 **VAT No.:** GB 336 8696 10
Date established: 1969 **Turnover:** £2m - £5m **No.of Employees:** 11 - 20
Product Groups: 26, 45

Date of Accounts	Apr 11	Apr 10	Apr 09
Working Capital	-30	16	73
Fixed Assets	60	71	90
Current Assets	611	482	572

Star Cargo plc

Star Cargo House Thompsons Close, Harpenden, AL5 4SB
Tel: 01582-469933 **Fax:** 01582-461643
E-mail: sales@sealane.co.uk
Website: http://www.starcargo.co.uk
Bank(s): Nat West
Directors: R. Edgell (Fin)
Managers: D. Wild, J. Reidy (Tech Serv Mgr)
Immediate Holding Company: STAR CARGO PLC
Registration no: 01870657 **Date established:** 1984
Turnover: £50m - £75m **No.of Employees:** 21 - 50 **Product Groups:** 76

Date of Accounts	Sep 11	Sep 10	Sep 09
Sales Turnover	72m	60m	50m
Pre Tax Profit/Loss	3m	3m	3m
Working Capital	4m	3m	4m
Fixed Assets	6m	4m	4m
Current Assets	18m	16m	14m
Current Liabilities	6m	5m	3m

Storax Ltd (t/a Storax Interiors)

Interior House 40 Coldharbour Lane, Harpenden, AL5 4UN
Tel: 01582-766766 **Fax:** 01582-768612
E-mail: sales@storax.co.uk
Website: http://www.storax.co.uk
Directors: I. Young (MD)
Ultimate Holding Company: STORAX HOLDINGS LIMITED
Immediate Holding Company: STORAX LIMITED
Registration no: 02990344 **VAT No.:** GB 640 0934 56
Date established: 1994 **Turnover:** £1m - £2m **No.of Employees:** 1 - 10
Product Groups: 26, 35, 36, 52

Date of Accounts	Mar 12	Mar 11	Mar 10
Working Capital	298	330	356
Fixed Assets	7	8	8
Current Assets	741	901	939

Strutt & Parker LLP

49 High Street, Harpenden, AL5 2SJ
Tel: 01582-764343 **Fax:** 01582-461630
E-mail: harpenden@strutandparker.com
Website: http://www.struttandparker.com
Managers: T. Pearse (Mgr)
Immediate Holding Company: STRUTT & PARKER LLP
Registration no: OC334522 **Date established:** 2008
No.of Employees: 1 - 10 **Product Groups:** 80

Date of Accounts	Apr 11	Apr 10	Apr 09
Sales Turnover	79m	74m	65m
Pre Tax Profit/Loss	14m	13m	3m
Working Capital	18m	14m	3m
Fixed Assets	24m	25m	28m
Current Assets	34m	29m	17m
Current Liabilities	15m	12m	9m

Surface Engineering Ltd

F Lea Industrial Estate Ox Lane, Harpenden, AL5 4PS
Tel: 01582-761919 **Fax:** 01582-761967
E-mail: sales@surface-engineering.co.uk
Website: http://www.surface-engineering.co.uk
Directors: N. Mian (Dir)
Immediate Holding Company: SURFACE ENGINEERING LIMITED
Registration no: 02487123 **Date established:** 1990
No.of Employees: 1 - 10 **Product Groups:** 46, 48

Date of Accounts	Mar 08	Mar 07	Mar 06
Sales Turnover	N/A	N/A	75
Pre Tax Profit/Loss	N/A	N/A	-2
Working Capital	4	10	10
Fixed Assets	1	1	1
Current Assets	11	20	18
Current Liabilities	8	10	8
Total Share Capital	4	4	4
ROCE% (Return on Capital Employed)			-14.1
ROT% (Return on Turnover)			-2.0

Total Soft Water

54 Westfield Road, Harpenden, AL5 4HW
Tel: 01582-461313 **Fax:** 01582-461313
E-mail: info@totalsoftwater.com
Website: http://www.totalsoftwater.com
Managers: P. Riley (Mgr)
Date established: 2003 **No.of Employees:** 1 - 10 **Product Groups:** 38, 42

Hatfield

Association For Science Education

College Lane, Hatfield, AL10 9AA
Tel: 01707-283000 **Fax:** 01707-266532
E-mail: info@ase.org.uk
Website: http://www.ase.org.uk
Directors: A. Smith (Grp Chief Exec)
Immediate Holding Company: SCIENCE EDUCATION SERVICES LTD
Registration no: 03960436 **Turnover:** £2m - £5m
No.of Employees: 11 - 20 **Product Groups:** 86

Biffa Waste Services Ltd

Travellers Close North Mymms, Hatfield, AL9 7JL
Tel: 01727-868231 **Fax:** 01727-850381
E-mail: salesdepartment@biffa.co.uk
Website: http://www.biffa.co.uk
Managers: A. Highland (Mgr)
Immediate Holding Company: BIFFA WASTE SERVICES LIMITED
Registration no: 00946107 **Date established:** 1969
No.of Employees: 11 - 20 **Product Groups:** 54, 72, 83

Date of Accounts	Mar 08	Mar 09	Apr 10
Sales Turnover	555m	574m	492m
Pre Tax Profit/Loss	23m	50m	30m
Working Capital	229m	271m	293m
Fixed Assets	371m	360m	378m
Current Assets	409m	534m	609m
Current Liabilities	50m	100m	115m

British Nursing Association

The Colonnades Beaconsfield Close, Hatfield, AL10 8HU
Tel: 01707-263544 **Fax:** 01707-272250
E-mail: info@bna.co.uk
Website: http://www.nestorplc.co.uk
Directors: A. Wilson (MD), S. Booty (Grp Chief Exec), A. Beevor (Ch)
Ultimate Holding Company: NESTOR HEALTHCARE GROUP LIMITED
Immediate Holding Company: BRITISH NURSING ASSOCIATION HEALTHCARE SERVICES LIMITED
Registration no: 03751985 **VAT No.:** GB 235 4135 84
Date established: 1999 **Turnover:** £250m - £500m
No.of Employees: 251 - 500 **Product Groups:** 80

Bromwall Ltd

6-7 A Salisbury Square, Hatfield, AL9 5AD
Tel: 01707-883377 **Fax:** 01707-883088
E-mail: info@bromwall.co.uk
Website: http://www.bromwall.co.uk
Directors: R. Walton (Dir)
Immediate Holding Company: BROMWALL LIMITED
Registration no: 01174715 **Date established:** 1974
No.of Employees: 1 - 10 **Product Groups:** 81, 82

Date of Accounts	Jun 11	Jun 10	Jun 09
Working Capital	89	65	90
Fixed Assets	70	40	16
Current Assets	381	385	405

Brown & Newirth Ltd

Elma House Beaconsfield Close, Hatfield, AL10 8YG
Tel: 01707-255000 **Fax:** 01707-255055
E-mail: sales@brownandnewirth.com
Website: http://www.brownandnewirth.com
Bank(s): National Westminster Bank Plc
Directors: J. Ball (MD)
Managers: A. Anderson (Comptroller)
Ultimate Holding Company: ABBEYCREST PLC
Immediate Holding Company: BRNE REALISATIONS LIMITED
Registration no: 00910429 **VAT No.:** GB 232 1042 27
Date established: 1967 **Turnover:** £10m - £20m
No.of Employees: 51 - 100 **Product Groups:** 49

Date of Accounts	Feb 08	Feb 11	Feb 10
Sales Turnover	13m	12m	12m
Pre Tax Profit/Loss	1m	-238	538
Working Capital	6m	6m	6m
Fixed Assets	735	1m	1m
Current Assets	15m	9m	12m
Current Liabilities	2m	748	538

Business Link East

Maclaurin Building 4 Bishops Square Business Park, Hatfield, AL10 9NE
Tel: 08457-171615 **Fax:** 01245-241500
E-mail: p.smith@businesslinkeast.org.uk
Website: http://www.businesslink.gov.uk
Directors: W. Mossman (Co Sec), A. Puddefoot (Fin), P. Smith (Grp Chief Exec)

see next page

***Business Link East** - Cont'd*
Managers: S. McAteer
Immediate Holding Company: STARSHAKE LTD
Registration no: 03334568 **Date established:** 2011
Turnover: Up to £250,000 **No.of Employees:** 51 - 100
Product Groups: 80, 81

C M D Ceilings Ltd
1 Fiddle Bridge Lane, Hatfield, AL10 0SP
Tel: 01707-264315
E-mail: info@cmdsuspendedceilings-hatfield.co.uk
Website: http://www.cmdsuspendedceilings-hatfield.co.uk
Directors: C. Aldrige (Dir)
Immediate Holding Company: CMD CEILINGS LIMITED
Registration no: 04949097 **Date established:** 2003
No.of Employees: 1 - 10 **Product Groups:** 30, 35, 52

Date of Accounts	Oct 11	Oct 10	Oct 09
Working Capital	-5	3	4
Fixed Assets	59	65	63
Current Assets	66	65	66

Cimtech
College Lane, Hatfield, AL10 9AB
Tel: 01707-281060 **Fax:** 01707-281061
E-mail: hendleyanthony@cimtech.co.uk
Website: http://www.cimtech.co.uk
Directors: A. Hendley (Dir), P. Waters (Co Sec)
Ultimate Holding Company: UNIVERSITY OF HERTFORDSHIRE
Immediate Holding Company: CIMTECH LIMITED
Registration no: 02342651 **VAT No.:** GB 539 9596 72
Date established: 1989 **Turnover:** £500,000 - £1m
No.of Employees: 1 - 10 **Product Groups:** 28, 86

Date of Accounts	Jul 11	Jul 10	Jul 09
Sales Turnover	N/A	673	782
Pre Tax Profit/Loss	-0	2	1
Working Capital	12	15	13
Current Assets	12	146	182
Current Liabilities	N/A	18	68

Computer Aided Business Systems Ltd
8 Forum Place Fiddlebridge Lane, Hatfield, AL10 0RN
Tel: 01707-258338 **Fax:** 01707-258339
E-mail: info@cabs-cad.com
Website: http://www.cabs-cad.com
Directors: M. Hall (MD), G. Haynes (Fin)
Immediate Holding Company: COMPUTER AIDED BUSINESS SYSTEMS LIMITED
Registration no: 03523862 **Date established:** 1998 **Turnover:** £2m - £5m
No.of Employees: 1 - 10 **Product Groups:** 25, 38, 44, 47, 52, 84, 86, 89

Date of Accounts	Dec 11	Dec 10	Dec 09
Working Capital	112	137	102
Fixed Assets	9	11	8
Current Assets	276	347	303

Connexions UK plc
Unit 3 Travellers Close Welham Green, North Mymms, Hatfield, AL9 7JL
Tel: 01707-272091 **Fax:** 01707-269444
E-mail: sales@cxcxcx.com
Website: http://www.cxcxcx.com
Bank(s): Barclays
Directors: L. Edwards (Dir), M. Goodwin (Co Sec), S. McCarroll (MD)
Managers: D. Carp (Tech Serv Mgr)
Immediate Holding Company: CONNEXIONS (UK) PUBLIC LIMITED COMPANY
Registration no: 01719521 **VAT No.:** GB 396 3077 21
Date established: 1983 **Turnover:** £5m - £10m **No.of Employees:** 11 - 20
Product Groups: 44

Date of Accounts	Sep 11	Sep 10	Sep 09
Sales Turnover	7m	8m	3m
Pre Tax Profit/Loss	-151	658	-265
Working Capital	1m	2m	3m
Fixed Assets	6m	6m	6m
Current Assets	4m	5m	4m
Current Liabilities	1m	1m	424

Datex Ohmeda Ltd
71 Great North Road, Hatfield, AL9 5EN
Tel: 01707-263570 **Fax:** 01707-260065
Website: http://www.gemedical.com
Bank(s): HSBC Bank plc
Directors: C. Hughes (MD)
Managers: I. Harper (Sales Prom Mgr), J. Mansfield (Purch Mgr), R. Gilder, T. Clouff (Mktg Serv Mgr), T. Defendi (Buyer)
Registration no: 03385644 **No.of Employees:** 101 - 250
Product Groups: 38

Denso International UK Ltd
1 Bishop Square, Hatfield, AL10 9NE
Tel: 01707-282400 **Fax:** 01707-282450
E-mail: g.livingstone@denso-sales.co.uk
Website: http://www.denso-europe.com
Directors: G. Livingstone (Fin)
Ultimate Holding Company: DENSO CORPORATION (JAPAN)
Immediate Holding Company: DENSO INTERNATIONAL UK LTD
Registration no: 02490566 **VAT No.:** GB 406 3518 72
Date established: 1990 **Turnover:** £250m - £500m
No.of Employees: 101 - 250 **Product Groups:** 39

Date of Accounts	Mar 12	Mar 11	Mar 10
Pre Tax Profit/Loss	-77m	15m	-10m
Working Capital	48m	41m	41m
Fixed Assets	87m	94m	81m
Current Assets	93m	144m	110m
Current Liabilities	1m	3m	8

Design Rationale Ltd
4 Bury Road, Hatfield, AL10 8BJ
Tel: 01707-272771 **Fax:** 01707-275772
E-mail: info@designrationale.co.uk
Website: http://www.designrationale.co.uk
Directors: J. Morgan (Dir), J. Morgan (Fin)
Managers: B. Cooper (Design Mgr)
Immediate Holding Company: DESIGN RATIONALE LIMITED
Registration no: 02692834 **Date established:** 1992 **Turnover:** £2m - £5m
No.of Employees: 21 - 50 **Product Groups:** 26, 35

Date of Accounts	Aug 11	Aug 10	Aug 09
Sales Turnover	N/A	N/A	5m
Pre Tax Profit/Loss	N/A	N/A	267
Working Capital	-134	-100	-2
Fixed Assets	196	219	102
Current Assets	877	764	1m
Current Liabilities	N/A	N/A	208

Diffusion Alloys Ltd
160-162 Great North Road, Hatfield, AL9 5JW
Tel: 01707-266111 **Fax:** 01707-276669
E-mail: enquiries@diffusion-alloys.com
Website: http://www.diffusionalloys.co.uk
Directors: S. Walters (Fin)
Ultimate Holding Company: CHROME-ALLOYING CO.LIMITED(THE)
Immediate Holding Company: DIFFUSION ALLOYS LIMITED
Registration no: 01613918 **Date established:** 1982 **Turnover:** £5m - £10m
No.of Employees: 51 - 100 **Product Groups:** 48

Date of Accounts	Mar 11	Mar 10	Mar 09
Sales Turnover	7m	9m	10m
Pre Tax Profit/Loss	-336	179	483
Working Capital	509	655	581
Fixed Assets	950	1m	1m
Current Assets	2m	2m	3m
Current Liabilities	412	543	789

Hallett Silbermann Ltd
Travellers Lane North Mymms, Hatfield, AL9 7HF
Tel: 01707-268255 **Fax:** 01707-272638
E-mail: enquiries@hallettsilbermann.com
Website: http://www.hallettsilbermann.com
Bank(s): Bank Leumi le Israel BM & National Westminster Bank plc
Directors: M. Hart (Fin), N. Brockless (MD), J. Hugill (Sales)
Ultimate Holding Company: BRENT GROUP LIMITED
Immediate Holding Company: HALLETT SILBERMANN LIMITED
Registration no: 00414851 **VAT No.:** GB 222 6819 69
Date established: 1946 **Turnover:** £2m - £5m **No.of Employees:** 21 - 50
Product Groups: 72, 76

Date of Accounts	Dec 11	Dec 10	Dec 09
Sales Turnover	N/A	4m	3m
Pre Tax Profit/Loss	N/A	1	-177
Working Capital	-178	-123	-253
Fixed Assets	1m	1m	1m
Current Assets	880	836	975
Current Liabilities	N/A	289	185

Henkel Ltd
Apollo Court Bishops Square Business Park, Hatfield, AL10 9EY
Tel: 01707-635000 **Fax:** 01707-635099
E-mail: info@lincolnshire.gov.uk
Website: http://www.henkel.co.uk
Directors: D. Graham (Fin)
Ultimate Holding Company: HENKEL AG & CO. KGAA (GERMANY)
Immediate Holding Company: HENKEL LIMITED
Registration no: 00215496 **Date established:** 2026
Turnover: £250m - £500m **No.of Employees:** 251 - 500
Product Groups: 27, 30, 32, 33, 49, 66

Date of Accounts	Dec 11	Dec 10	Dec 09
Sales Turnover	300m	278m	275m
Pre Tax Profit/Loss	10m	168	2m
Working Capital	28m	17m	-1m
Fixed Assets	129m	144m	164m
Current Assets	136m	141m	165m
Current Liabilities	16m	17m	17m

The Herts Meter Co. Ltd
Unit 10 Bury Road, Hatfield, AL10 8BJ
Tel: 01707-270404 **Fax:** 01707-270152
E-mail: info@hertsmeter.com
Website: http://www.hertsmeter.com
Directors: R. Longcroft (Dir)
Registration no: 01964915 **VAT No.:** GB 440 7731 608
Turnover: £1m - £2m **No.of Employees:** 1 - 10 **Product Groups:** 38

International Greetings plc
Belgrave House Hatfield Business Park Frobisher Way, Hatfield, AL10 9TQ
Tel: 01707-630630 **Fax:** 01707-630660
E-mail: mail@intg.co.uk
Website: http://www.internationalgreetings.co.uk
Directors: A. Lawrinson (Fin)
Ultimate Holding Company: INTERNATIONAL GREETINGS PLC
Immediate Holding Company: INTERNATIONAL GREETINGS PLC
Registration no: 01401155 **Date established:** 1978
Turnover: £125m - £250m **No.of Employees:** 11 - 20 **Product Groups:** 27

Date of Accounts	Mar 12	Mar 11	Mar 10
Sales Turnover	221m	217m	200m
Pre Tax Profit/Loss	3m	4m	525
Working Capital	20m	-4m	-11m
Fixed Assets	69m	70m	71m
Current Assets	67m	69m	68m
Current Liabilities	13m	40m	55m

Intrad Ltd
St Albans Road West, Hatfield, AL10 0TF
Tel: 01707-266726 **Fax:** 01707-263614
E-mail: sales@intrad.co.uk
Website: http://www.intrad.co.uk
Directors: P. Clark (MD)
Immediate Holding Company: INTRAD LIMITED
Registration no: 00791410 **Date established:** 1964 **Turnover:** £2m - £5m
No.of Employees: 11 - 20 **Product Groups:** 26, 36

Date of Accounts	Dec 11	Dec 10	Dec 09
Working Capital	327	452	431
Fixed Assets	62	81	99
Current Assets	828	891	794

Jumbo Games Ltd
Hatfield Park, Hatfield, AL9 5NB
Tel: 01707-289289 **Fax:** 01707-275086
E-mail: gray.richmond@jumbo.eu
Website: http://www.jumbo.eu
Directors: G. Richmond (Dir)
Managers: K. Oliver (Mktg Serv Mgr), V. Allen, C. Schwertheim (Fin Mgr)
Ultimate Holding Company: M & R DE MONCHY NV (NETHERLANDS)
Immediate Holding Company: FALCON GAMES LIMITED
Registration no: 02282970 **Date established:** 1988 **Turnover:** £5m - £10m
No.of Employees: 1 - 10 **Product Groups:** 49

Date of Accounts	Jun 11	Jun 10	Jun 09
Working Capital	799	799	799
Current Assets	799	799	799

Live Software Solutions
17 The Broadway, Hatfield, AL9 5HZ
Tel: 0844-8474424
E-mail: contact@lss.co.uk
Website: http://www.lss.co.uk
Directors: J. Boother (MD)
Managers: T. Boother (Develop Mgr), T. Boother (Mgr)
Immediate Holding Company: LIVE SOFTWARE SOLUTIONS LIMITED
Registration no: 05198199 **Date established:** 2004
No.of Employees: 1 - 10 **Product Groups:** 44

Date of Accounts	Aug 09	Aug 08	Aug 07
Working Capital	-38	78	50
Fixed Assets	9	16	10
Current Assets	18	134	91

London Polyester
134 Great North Road, Hatfield, AL9 5JN
Tel: 01707-265055 **Fax:** 01707-265098
E-mail: info@londonpolyester.co.uk
Website: http://www.londonpolyester.co.uk
Directors: J. Pountain (Prop)
Registration no: 00456551 **Date established:** 1994
Turnover: £500,000 - £1m **No.of Employees:** 1 - 10 **Product Groups:** 23

M J P Ltd
9 Alpha Business Park Travellers Close, North Mymms, Hatfield, AL9 7NT
Tel: 01707-261179 **Fax:** 01707-272470
E-mail: mike.player@virgin.net
Directors: M. Player (MD)
Immediate Holding Company: M.J.P. LIMITED
Registration no: 01867900 **Date established:** 1984
Turnover: Up to £250,000 **No.of Employees:** 1 - 10 **Product Groups:** 24, 30, 33, 34, 35, 36, 38, 46

Date of Accounts	Dec 11	Dec 10	Dec 09
Working Capital	34	28	28
Fixed Assets	111	112	114
Current Assets	103	106	78

Mollart Universal Joints Ltd (a division of Davall Gears)
Davall House, Travellers Lane Welam Green, Hatfield, AL9 7JB
Tel: 01707-283193 **Fax:** 01707-283111
E-mail: info@mollarts.com
Website: http://www.mollarts.com
Bank(s): Barclays, 160 Piccadilly, London
Managers: D. Crompton (Chief Mgr), M. Liddle (Accounts)
Immediate Holding Company: T I Group PLC
Registration no: 05939858 **Turnover:** £2m - £5m
No.of Employees: 11 - 20 **Product Groups:** 35

Mulmar Foodservice Solutions
Inspiration House 152 Great North Road, Hatfield, AL9 5JN
Tel: 08456-885282 **Fax:** 0844-826 3155
E-mail: martin@mulmar.com
Website: http://www.mulmar.co.uk
Directors: M. Canning (Co Sec)
Managers: M. Barnett (Ops Mgr)
Immediate Holding Company: MULMAR FOODSERVICE SOLUTIONS LTD
Registration no: 05227999 **Date established:** 2004
Turnover: Up to £250,000 **No.of Employees:** 21 - 50 **Product Groups:** 67

Nestor Healthcare Ltd
Beaconsfield Court Beaconsfield Road, Hatfield, AL10 8HU
Tel: 01707-255635 **Fax:** 01707-272250
E-mail: info@nestor-healthcare.co.uk
Website: http://www.nestorplc.co.uk
Bank(s): National Westminster Bank Plc
Directors: D. Collison (Co Sec), C. Thomas (Co Sec), P. Chamberlain (MD), S. Booty (Chief Op Offcr)
Managers: A. Pleavin (Mktg Serv Mgr)
Ultimate Holding Company: ACROMAS HOLDINGS LIMITED
Immediate Holding Company: NESTOR HEALTHCARE LIMITED
Registration no: 00839132 **Date established:** 1965
Turnover: £125m - £250m **No.of Employees:** 51 - 100
Product Groups: 80

Date of Accounts	Dec 10	Dec 09	Dec 08
Pre Tax Profit/Loss	-6	-6	-6
Working Capital	2m	2m	2m
Current Assets	2m	2m	2m

No Climb Products Ltd
Eddison House 163 Dixons Hill Road, North Mymms, Hatfield, AL9 7JE
Tel: 01707-282760 **Fax:** 01707-282777
E-mail: m.rossiter@noclimb.com
Website: http://www.detectortesters.com
Bank(s): National Westminster Bank Plc
Directors: S. Pepper (I.T. Dir), F. Maine (Chief Op Offcr), W. Rossiter (MD)
Managers: S. Pepper (I.T. Exec), P. Bartlam (Sales Eng)
Immediate Holding Company: NO CLIMB PRODUCTS LIMITED
Registration no: 00839470 **VAT No.:** GB 421 4499 61
Date established: 1965 **Turnover:** £1m - £2m **No.of Employees:** 51 - 100
Product Groups: 40, 67

Date of Accounts	Mar 11	Mar 10	Mar 09
Sales Turnover	7m	N/A	N/A
Pre Tax Profit/Loss	711	N/A	151
Working Capital	3m	3m	2m
Fixed Assets	325	217	271
Current Assets	5m	4m	3m
Current Liabilities	1m	N/A	417

Power Units Hatfield
16-17 Bury Road, Hatfield, AL10 8BJ
Tel: 01707-264310 **Fax:** 01707-262557
E-mail: neil.willmott@hotmail.co.uk
Directors: N. Willmott (Prop)
No.of Employees: 1 - 10 **Product Groups:** 39, 40, 68

Renz UK Ltd
Hill End Farm, Hatfield, AL9 5PQ
Tel: 01707-270001 **Fax:** 01707-271769
E-mail: iainbullock@renz.co.uk
Website: http://www.renzuk.com
Directors: I. Bullock (MD)
Ultimate Holding Company: CHR. RENZ GMBH & CO (GERMANY)
Immediate Holding Company: RENZ (UK) LTD
Registration no: 02679014 **Date established:** 1992 **Turnover:** £2m - £5m
No.of Employees: 11 - 20 **Product Groups:** 44

Date of Accounts	Dec 11	Dec 10	Dec 09
Working Capital	388	357	368
Fixed Assets	43	35	41
Current Assets	1m	1m	990

Shindengen
Marquis House 68 Great North Road, Hatfield, AL9 5ER
Tel: 01707-252550 **Fax:** 01707-252551
E-mail: info@shindengen.co.uk
Website: http://www.shindengen.co.uk
Directors: M. Fukunaga (MD)
Ultimate Holding Company: SHINDENGEN ELECTRIC MANUFACTURING CO LTD
Immediate Holding Company: SHINDENGEN UK LIMITED
Registration no: 01458574 **VAT No.:** GB 344 4203 84
Date established: 1979 **Turnover:** £5m - £10m **No.of Employees:** 1 - 10
Product Groups: 37, 38

Date of Accounts	Dec 08	Dec 07	Dec 06
Sales Turnover	9204	12495	12399
Pre Tax Profit/Loss	-136	90	890
Working Capital	1377	1583	1746
Fixed Assets	69	92	48
Current Assets	3945	5653	5646
Current Liabilities	2567	4070	3900
Total Share Capital	142	142	142
ROCE% (Return on Capital Employed)	-9.4	5.4	49.6
ROT% (Return on Turnover)	-1.5	0.7	7.2

Spire Peugeot Ltd
Harpsfield Broadway Comet Way, Hatfield, AL10 9TF
Tel: 01707-264521 **Fax:** 01707-251139
E-mail: peugeot@waters.co.uk
Website: http://www.spirepeugeot.co.uk
Bank(s): National Westminster, St Albans Business Centre
Managers: C. Thompson
Immediate Holding Company: WATERS RETAIL LIMITED
Registration no: 03716100 **VAT No.:** GB 727 9469 82
Date established: 1999 **Turnover:** £10m - £20m
No.of Employees: 51 - 100 **Product Groups:** 39, 68

Statebrook Ltd
Brent House Travellers Lane Welham Green, North Mymms, Hatfield, AL9 7HF
Tel: 01707-282300 **Fax:** 020-8907 7669
E-mail: davidsilbermann@brentgroup.com
Directors: D. Silbermann (MD)
Ultimate Holding Company: BRENT GROUP LIMITED
Immediate Holding Company: STATEBROOK LIMITED
Registration no: 00950333 **Date established:** 1969
Turnover: £250,000 - £500,000 **No.of Employees:** 1 - 10
Product Groups: 28, 38, 44, 61, 80, 82

Date of Accounts	Dec 11	Dec 10	Dec 09
Sales Turnover	N/A	372	357
Pre Tax Profit/Loss	N/A	120	135
Working Capital	-2m	-2m	-2m
Fixed Assets	6m	6m	6m
Current Assets	428	258	254
Current Liabilities	N/A	2m	126

Tail Lift Services
9 The I O Centre Hearle Way, Hatfield, AL10 9EW
Tel: 01707-267007 **Fax:** 01707-259007
E-mail: hatfield@tail-lift-services.co.uk
Website: http://www.tailliftservices.co.uk
Directors: S. Bosley (Prop)
No.of Employees: 1 - 10 **Product Groups:** 35, 39, 45

T-Mobile UK
Building 3 T-Mobile Campus Hatfield Business Park Mosquito Way, Hatfield, AL10 9BW
Tel: 01707-315988 **Fax:** 01707-319001
Website: http://www.t-mobile.co.uk
Directors: J. Hyde (MD), J. Blendis (Dep Pres), J. Blendis (Co Sec), H. Jones (MD), B. McBride (MD), S. Ainslie (Sales & Mktg)
Ultimate Holding Company: DEUTSCHE TELEKOM AKTIENGESELLSCHAFT (GERMANY)
Immediate Holding Company: T-MOBILE (UK) RETAIL LIMITED
Registration no: 02757677 **Date established:** 1992
Turnover: £20m - £50m **No.of Employees:** 1 - 10 **Product Groups:** 37

Tool Venture Ltd Astra Ltd
Unit 4 Hearle Way Hatfield Business Park, Hatfield, AL10 9EW
Tel: 0845-680 0112 **Fax:** 0845-680 0114
E-mail: sales@toolventure.co.uk
Website: http://www.ToolVenture.co.uk
Registration no: 06138208 **Product Groups:** 24, 63

Tradewings Worldwide Ltd
18 Wood Vale, Hatfield, AL10 8TT
Tel: 07961-119985 **Fax:** 020-3163 0707
E-mail: sales@tradewingsworldwide.co.uk
Website: http://www.tradewingsworldwide.co.uk
Directors: M. Patel (Fin)
Immediate Holding Company: TRADEWINGS WORLDWIDE LTD
Registration no: 06623915 **Date established:** 2008
Turnover: £250,000 - £500,000 **No.of Employees:** 1 - 10
Product Groups: 24, 30, 67

Date of Accounts	Jun 11	Jun 10	Jun 09
Working Capital	24	15	10
Current Assets	69	50	35

Tuchkin Enterprises Ltd
PO Box 88, Hatfield, AL9 5JS
Tel: 01707-278436 **Fax:** 01707-269347
E-mail: tuchkin@ntlworld.com
Directors: A. Datta (MD)
Immediate Holding Company: TUCHKIN ENTERPRISES LIMITED
Registration no: 01870235 **VAT No.:** GB 421 3518 88
Date established: 1984 **Turnover:** £500,000 - £1m
No.of Employees: 1 - 10 **Product Groups:** 17, 33

Date of Accounts	Mar 11	Mar 10	Mar 09
Working Capital	-2	1	3
Fixed Assets	1	1	2
Current Assets	105	101	108

Wyvern Scaffolding
37 Wellfield Road, Hatfield, AL10 0BY
Tel: 01707-251591 **Fax:** 01707-276879
E-mail: wyvernscaff@aol.com
Directors: S. Williams (Prop)
Date established: 1989 **No.of Employees:** 1 - 10 **Product Groups:** 52

Hemel Hempstead

A D Services
18 Malmes Croft, Hemel Hempstead, HP3 8QX
Tel: 01442-215885
E-mail: andydraper7@msn.com
Website: http://www.powered-stairclimber.org.uk
Directors: A. Draper (Prop)
No.of Employees: 1 - 10 **Product Groups:** 45, 67, 68, 86

A E Butler & Partners Ltd
13a Marlowes, Hemel Hempstead, HP1 1LA
Tel: 01442-233638 **Fax:** 01442-234364
E-mail: jim@aebutler-partners.co.uk
Website: http://www.aebutler-partners.co.uk
Directors: J. Butler (Comm)
Immediate Holding Company: A.E. BUTLER & PARTNERS LIMITED
Registration no: 03699330 **Date established:** 1999
No.of Employees: 1 - 10 **Product Groups:** 35

Date of Accounts	Jan 11	Jan 10	Jan 09
Working Capital	-36	-21	1
Fixed Assets	1	1	1
Current Assets	24	32	33

Acoustical Investigation & Research Organisation Ltd
Duxons Turn, Hemel Hempstead, HP2 4SB
Tel: 01442-247146 **Fax:** 01442-256749
E-mail: aero@bcs.org.uk
Website: http://www.airo.co.uk
Bank(s): HSBC Bank plc
Directors: A. Jones (MD), R. Harding (Fin)
Immediate Holding Company: ACOUSTICAL INVESTIGATION & RESEARCH ORGANISATION LIMITED
Registration no: 00603110 **VAT No.:** GB 232 1957 75
Date established: 1958 **Turnover:** £500,000 - £1m
No.of Employees: 11 - 20 **Product Groups:** 54, 85

Date of Accounts	Dec 11	Dec 10	Dec 09
Working Capital	336	387	451
Fixed Assets	71	81	94
Current Assets	360	419	487

Adaptainer Ltd
Long Meadow Flaunden Lane, Bovingdon, Hemel Hempstead, HP3 0PA
Tel: 01442-834566 **Fax:** 01442-834335
E-mail: office@adaptainer.co.uk
Website: http://www.adaptainer.co.uk
Directors: C. Walker (Dir), J. Walker (Co Sec)
Immediate Holding Company: ADAPTAINER LIMITED
Registration no: 02360563 **VAT No.:** GB 505 5666 45
Date established: 1989 **No.of Employees:** 1 - 10 **Product Groups:** 72, 76, 82

Date of Accounts	Dec 11	Dec 10	Dec 09
Working Capital	416	298	269
Fixed Assets	N/A	170	174
Current Assets	2m	1m	1m

Adex Interiors For Industry Ltd
5 Avebury Court, Hemel Hempstead, HP2 7TA
Tel: 01442-232327 **Fax:** 01442-262713
E-mail: info@adex.co.uk
Website: http://www.adex.co.uk
Directors: J. Latimer (MD), P. Atherton (Co Sec)
Ultimate Holding Company: HOWARD SANDCLIFFE INVESTMENTS 3 LIMITED
Immediate Holding Company: ADEX INTERIORS FOR INDUSTRY LTD
Registration no: 01425629 **Date established:** 1979 **Turnover:** £2m - £5m
No.of Employees: 1 - 10 **Product Groups:** 30, 35

Date of Accounts	Jan 11	Jan 10	Jan 09
Sales Turnover	4m	5m	6m
Pre Tax Profit/Loss	287	491	582
Working Capital	2m	1m	1m
Fixed Assets	14	18	24
Current Assets	3m	3m	2m
Current Liabilities	566	320	533

Aerotest Ltd
Unit 5 Sovereign Park Cleveland Way, Hemel Hempstead Industrial Estate, Hemel Hempstead, HP2 7DA
Tel: 01442-235557 **Fax:** 01442-235547
E-mail: info@aerotest.com
Website: http://www.aerotest.com
Directors: A. Hines (Comm)
Immediate Holding Company: AEROTEST LIMITED
Registration no: 02540429 **Date established:** 1990 **Turnover:** £5m - £10m
No.of Employees: 1 - 10 **Product Groups:** 38

Date of Accounts	Dec 10	Dec 09	Dec 08
Working Capital	176	226	596
Fixed Assets	109	124	130
Current Assets	837	2m	2m

Air B P Ltd
Breakspear Way, Hemel Hempstead, HP2 4UL
Tel: 01442-223344 **Fax:** 01442-225951
E-mail: info@airbp.com
Website: http://www.airbpaviation.com
Bank(s): National Westminster Bank Plc
Managers: I. Harrison, P. Ambury
Ultimate Holding Company: BP P.L.C.
Immediate Holding Company: AIR BP LIMITED
Registration no: 01150609 **VAT No.:** GB 243 5105 93
Date established: 1973 **Turnover:** £20m - £50m
No.of Employees: 51 - 100 **Product Groups:** 31, 39, 80, 84

Airmasters 88
Marchmont Farm Link Road, Hemel Hempstead, HP2 6JH
Tel: 01442-266831 **Fax:** 01442-266831
Directors: D. Wellham (Prop)
Date established: 1988 **No.of Employees:** 1 - 10 **Product Groups:** 36, 39, 40

Amir Power Transmission Ltd
Amir House Maxted Road, Hemel Hempstead Industrial Estate, Hemel Hempstead, HP2 7DX
Tel: 01442-212671 **Fax:** 01442-246640
E-mail: saeed.khodadoost@amirpower.co.uk
Website: http://www.amirpower.co.uk
Directors: S. Khodadoost (Dir)
Managers: I. Milsted (Sales Prom Mgr)
Immediate Holding Company: AMIR POWER TRANSMISSION LIMITED
Registration no: 01741522 **Date established:** 1983 **Turnover:** £2m - £5m
No.of Employees: 1 - 10 **Product Groups:** 35, 37, 38, 39

Date of Accounts	Dec 11	Dec 10	Dec 09
Sales Turnover	N/A	4m	3m
Pre Tax Profit/Loss	N/A	-18	115
Working Capital	663	538	610
Fixed Assets	180	187	194
Current Assets	2m	1m	1m
Current Liabilities	N/A	139	125

ATA Engineering Processes
88 House Unit B Boundary Way, Hemel Hempstead Industrial Estate, Hemel Hempstead, HP2 7SS
Tel: 01442-264411 **Fax:** 01442-231383
E-mail: sales@ataeng.com
Website: http://www.ataeng.com
Directors: T. Stafford (MD), C. Spicer (Dir), M. Amos (Dir)
Managers: M. Whitbread (Mgr), M. Whitbread (Sales Prom Mgr)
Immediate Holding Company: A.T.A. (ENGINEERING PROCESSES)
Registration no: 00755893 **VAT No.:** GB 207 5606 75
Date established: 1963 **Turnover:** £1m - £2m **No.of Employees:** 1 - 10
Product Groups: 31, 33, 35, 36, 37, 46

Date of Accounts	Mar 92	Mar 91
Working Capital	238	105
Fixed Assets	60	56
Current Assets	1m	1m

Atlas Copco Compressors Ltd
Swallowdale Lane Hemel Hempstead Indl-Est, Hemel Hempstead, HP2 7EA
Tel: 01442-261201 **Fax:** 01543-676501
E-mail: kevin.prince@uk.atlascopco.com
Website: http://www.atlascopco.co.uk
Directors: K. Prince (MD), L. van Diggele (Dir)
Managers: S. Matthews (Serv Mgr)
Immediate Holding Company: MOBILE TELEMETRY DESIGNS LTD
Registration no: 00159809 **Date established:** 2011 **Turnover:** £2m - £5m
No.of Employees: 251 - 500 **Product Groups:** 40

Date of Accounts	Jun 11	Jun 10	Jun 07
Working Capital	22	14	3
Current Assets	52	35	3

Atlas Copco Compressors Ltd
PO Box 79 Swallowdale Lane, Hemel Hempstead, HP2 7HA
Tel: 0800-181085 **Fax:** 01442-234791
E-mail: gbainfo@atlascopco.com
Website: http://www.atlascopco.com
Bank(s): Barclays
Directors: A. Bongaerts (Co Sec), G. Follens (Dir)
Managers: A. Walker (Serv Mgr), C. Robinson (Maint), J. Forman (Mktg Serv Mgr), S. Matthews (Reg Mgr), L. Hughes (Personnel)
Ultimate Holding Company: Atlas Copco Ab (Sweden)
Immediate Holding Company: ATLAS COPCO LIMITED
Registration no: 00159809 **VAT No.:** GB 207 5463 71
Date established: 2019 **Turnover:** £50m - £75m
No.of Employees: 251 - 500 **Product Groups:** 30, 31, 34, 38, 39, 40, 42, 48, 67, 68, 83

Date of Accounts	Dec 09	Dec 08	Dec 07
Sales Turnover	56m	71m	77m
Pre Tax Profit/Loss	-2m	753	992
Working Capital	-6m	-4m	-4m
Fixed Assets	6m	5m	5m
Current Assets	16m	25m	27m
Current Liabilities	7m	10m	9m

Atlas Copco Tools Ltd
Swallowdale Lane Hemel Hempstead Industrial Estate, Hemel Hempstead, HP2 7EA
Tel: 01442-261202 **Fax:** 01442-240596
E-mail: toolsuk._info@atlascopco.com
Website: http://www.atlascopco.com
Directors: F. Moller (Dir)
Managers: N. Smith (Chief Mgr)
Ultimate Holding Company: ATLAS COPCO AB (SWEDEN)
Immediate Holding Company: ATLAS COPCO TOOLS LIMITED
Registration no: 02550981 **Date established:** 1990
Turnover: £10m - £20m **No.of Employees:** 1 - 10 **Product Groups:** 36, 37

Date of Accounts	Dec 09	Dec 08	Dec 07
Sales Turnover	11m	15m	13m
Pre Tax Profit/Loss	536	355	132
Working Capital	463	99	-99
Fixed Assets	55	101	104
Current Assets	3m	5m	5m
Current Liabilities	1m	2m	1m

Azteq Solutions Ltd
Azteq House Maxted Corner Maxted Road, Hemel Hempstead Industrial Estate, Hemel Hempstead, HP2 7RA
Tel: 01442-244444 **Fax:** 01442-244443
E-mail: info@azteqsolutions.com
Website: http://www.azteq.com
Directors: G. Smith (MD)
Immediate Holding Company: AZTEQ SOLUTIONS LIMITED
Registration no: 04385339 **Date established:** 2002 **Turnover:** £2m - £5m
No.of Employees: 11 - 20 **Product Groups:** 44, 52

Date of Accounts	Mar 11	Mar 10	Mar 09
Working Capital	89	150	114
Fixed Assets	27	24	57
Current Assets	408	371	398

B A M Construction UK Ltd
Breakspear Park Breakspear Way, Hemel Hempstead, HP2 4FL
Tel: 01442-238300 **Fax:** 01442-238301
E-mail: aneill@bam.co.uk
Website: http://www.bam.co.uk
Directors: A. Neill (Pers), A. Singh (Chief Op Offcr), C. Gilmore (Mkt Research)

see next page

B A M Construction UK Ltd - Cont'd

Managers: G. Jones
Ultimate Holding Company: ROYAL BAM GROUP NV (NETHERLANDS)
Immediate Holding Company: BAM CONSTRUCT UK LIMITED
Registration no: 03311781 **VAT No.:** GB 226 5868 37
Date established: 1997 **Turnover:** £500m - £1,000m
No.of Employees: 101 - 250 **Product Groups:** 52

Date of Accounts	Dec 11	Dec 10	Dec 09
Sales Turnover	946m	1037m	1134m
Pre Tax Profit/Loss	12m	17m	20m
Working Capital	200m	183m	188m
Fixed Assets	6m	8m	11m
Current Assets	546m	593m	588m
Current Liabilities	281m	323m	304m

B W Grinding Services

15 Bourne End Lane, Hemel Hempstead, HP1 2RL
Tel: 01442-872819 **Fax:** 01442-872819
Directors: B. Wallis (Prop)
Date established: 1986 **No.of Employees:** 1 - 10 **Product Groups:** 46

Bio-Rad Laboratories Ltd

Bio-Rad House Maylands Avenue, Hemel Hempstead, HP2 7TD
Tel: 020-8328 2000 **Fax:** 020-8328 2500
E-mail: norman_schwartz@bio-rad.com
Website: http://www.bio-rad.com
Bank(s): Barclays
Directors: D. Forrester (Grp Chief Exec), N. Schwartz (MD)
Ultimate Holding Company: BIO-RAD LABORATORIES INC (USA)
Immediate Holding Company: BIO-METRICS (U.K.) LIMITED
Registration no: 02483713 **VAT No.:** GB 196 7282 16
Date established: 1990 **Turnover:** £50m - £75m
No.of Employees: 101 - 250 **Product Groups:** 31, 38, 42

Date of Accounts	Dec 10	Dec 09	Dec 08
Working Capital	10	10	-1m
Fixed Assets	10m	4m	4m
Current Assets	125	125	25
Current Liabilities	N/A	15	N/A

Bodet UK Ltd

4 Sovereign Park Cleveland Way, Hemel Hempstead Industrial Estate, Hemel Hempstead, HP2 7DA
Tel: 01442-418800 **Fax:** 01442-234345
E-mail: enquiries@bodet.com
Website: http://www.bodet.co.uk
Bank(s): Barclays
Directors: M. Clavereau (MD)
Ultimate Holding Company: BODET SA (FRANCE)
Immediate Holding Company: BODET LIMITED
Registration no: 02485024 **VAT No.:** GB 540 1950 70
Date established: 1990 **Turnover:** £1m - £2m **No.of Employees:** 11 - 20
Product Groups: 48, 49, 67

Date of Accounts	Dec 11	Dec 10	Dec 09
Working Capital	209	278	305
Fixed Assets	11	15	22
Current Assets	594	706	748

Bourne Leisure

1 Park Lane, Hemel Hempstead, HP2 4YL
Tel: 01442-230300 **Fax:** 01442-230368
E-mail: jane.bentall@bourneleisuregroup.co.uk
Website: http://www.haven.com
Directors: J. Bentall (Fin)
Ultimate Holding Company: BOURNE LEISURE HOLDINGS LIMITED
Immediate Holding Company: BOURNE HOLIDAYS LIMITED
Registration no: 01854900 **Date established:** 1984
Turnover: £75m - £125m **No.of Employees:** 501 - 1000
Product Groups: 69

Date of Accounts	Dec 11	Dec 10	Dec 09
Sales Turnover	109m	110m	111m
Pre Tax Profit/Loss	6m	8m	7m
Working Capital	-73m	-74m	-73m
Fixed Assets	147m	148m	146m
Current Assets	21m	17m	27m
Current Liabilities	13m	12m	13m

Bovingdon Brickworks Ltd

Leyhill Road Bovingdon, Hemel Hempstead, HP3 0NW
Tel: 01442-833176 **Fax:** 01442-834539
E-mail: info@bovingdonbricks.co.uk
Website: http://www.bovingdonbricks.co.uk
Bank(s): Barclays, Acocks Green, Birmingham B27 6AB
Managers: K. Lin (Admin Off)
Ultimate Holding Company: E H SMITH HOLDINGS LTD
Immediate Holding Company: BOVINGDON BRICKWORKS LIMITED
Registration no: 00642656 **Date established:** 1959 **Turnover:** £1m - £2m
No.of Employees: 21 - 50 **Product Groups:** 33

Date of Accounts	Jun 11	Jun 10	Jun 09
Working Capital	73	307	618
Fixed Assets	731	675	653
Current Assets	2m	2m	2m

BSI

Kitemark House Maylands Avenue, Hemel Hempstead Industrial Estate, Hemel Hempstead, HP2 4SQ
Tel: 08450-765600 **Fax:** 01442-278630
E-mail: info@bsi.org.uk
Website: http://www.bsi.org.uk
Managers: K. Convey (Mgr)
Ultimate Holding Company: BRITISH STANDARDS INSTITUTION
No.of Employees: 251 - 500 **Product Groups:** 85, 87

Chiltern Blast Cleaning Ltd

Runways Farm Upper Bourne End Lane, Hemel Hempstead, HP1 2RR
Tel: 01442-832262 **Fax:** 01442-833386
E-mail: chiltblast@hotmail.com
Website: http://www.blast-clean.co.uk
Directors: M. Humphreys (Dir), S. Humphreys (Fin)
Immediate Holding Company: CHILTERN BLAST CLEANING LIMITED
Registration no: 05526600 **Date established:** 2005
No.of Employees: 1 - 10 **Product Groups:** 48

Date of Accounts	Nov 11	Nov 10	Nov 09
Working Capital	45	39	-37
Fixed Assets	207	239	274
Current Assets	98	114	167

City Self Drive

Swallowdale Lane Hemel Hempstead Industrial Estate, Hemel Hempstead, HP2 7EA
Tel: 01442-419300 **Fax:** 01442-419201
E-mail: info@citygroup.com
Website: http://www.citygroupuk.co.uk
Directors: A. Hall (Grp Chief Exec), A. Hoare (MD), F. Price (Sales), M. Gooden (MD), P. Porter (Fin), T. Harris (MD)
Managers: D. Fisk (Sales Prom Mgr), S. Savage (I.T. Exec)
Ultimate Holding Company: City Lights Group
Immediate Holding Company: BEE CARBON FREE LTD
Registration no: 03049323 **VAT No.:** GB 640 0783 60
Date established: 2008 **Turnover:** £2m - £5m **No.of Employees:** 1 - 10
Product Groups: 35, 48, 84

Citysprint UK Ltd

Unit 3 Sovereign Park Cleveland Way, Hemel Hempstead Industrial Estate, Hemel Hempstead, HP2 7DA
Tel: 01442-231231 **Fax:** 01442-256663
E-mail: hemel@citysprint.co.uk
Website: http://www.citysprint.co.uk
Managers: B. Lett (District Mgr)
Ultimate Holding Company: CITYSPRINT (UK) GROUP LIMITED
Immediate Holding Company: CITYSPRINT (UK) LIMITED
Registration no: 04327611 **Date established:** 2001
Turnover: Up to £250,000 **No.of Employees:** 1 - 10 **Product Groups:** 79

Date of Accounts	Dec 11	Dec 10	Dec 09
Sales Turnover	74m	61m	47m
Pre Tax Profit/Loss	4m	4m	3m
Working Capital	3m	4m	3m
Fixed Assets	14m	6m	5m
Current Assets	16m	17m	15m
Current Liabilities	6m	5m	4m

Colaingrove Ltd

Normandy Court 1 Wolsey Road, Hemel Hempstead, HP2 4TU
Tel: 01442-269251 **Fax:** 01442-219031
Directors: D. King (Co Sec)
Ultimate Holding Company: BOURNE LEISURE HOLDINGS LIMITED
Immediate Holding Company: COLAINGROVE LIMITED
Registration no: 01188281 **Date established:** 1974
Turnover: £75m - £125m **No.of Employees:** 1 - 10 **Product Groups:** 69

Date of Accounts	Dec 11	Dec 10	Dec 09
Pre Tax Profit/Loss	23m	21m	12m
Working Capital	2m	2m	2m
Fixed Assets	890	890	890
Current Assets	2m	2m	2m

D P C Engineering

Unit 30 Bourne End Mills Upper Bourne End Lane, Hemel Hempstead, HP1 2UJ
Tel: 01442-871871 **Fax:** 01442-871871
E-mail: dave@dpcengineering.co.uk
Directors: D. Clout (Prop)
Date established: 1979 **No.of Employees:** 1 - 10 **Product Groups:** 35

Dixons Retail

Maylands Avenue Hemel Hempstead Industrial Estate, Hemel Hempstead, HP2 7TG
Tel: 08448-002030 **Fax:** 01442-233218
E-mail: john.browett@dsgiplc.com
Website: http://www.dixons.co.uk
Directors: H. Singer (Fin), S. Hyndman (Pers), A. Silver (Mkt Research)
Managers: J. Browett, P. Greenwood (Tech Serv Mgr), S. Mayes (Purch Mgr), V. Stevenson
Immediate Holding Company: DIXONS RETAIL PLC
Registration no: 03847921 **Date established:** 1999
Turnover: Over £1,000m **No.of Employees:** 501 - 1000
Product Groups: 33, 35, 40, 44, 48, 63, 66

Date of Accounts	Apr 11	Apr 12	May 09
Sales Turnover	8342m	8193m	8365m
Pre Tax Profit/Loss	-224m	-119m	-140m
Working Capital	-182m	-290m	-349m
Fixed Assets	1884m	1502m	1956m
Current Assets	1693m	1545m	1703m
Current Liabilities	812m	692m	1056m

Drager Ltd

2 The Willows Mark Road, Hemel Hempstead Industrial Estate, Hemel Hempstead, HP2 7BN
Tel: 01442-213542 **Fax:** 01442-240327
Website: http://www.draeger.co.uk
Directors: A. Goswell (Pers)
Managers: L. Beard (Personnel), M. Bedford (Fin Mgr), P. Biddulph (Mgr), R. Clark (Chief Mgr)
Immediate Holding Company: DRAEGER MEDICAL UK LIMITED
Registration no: 04310199 **Date established:** 2001
Turnover: £20m - £50m **No.of Employees:** 51 - 100 **Product Groups:** 38, 67

E H Smith Builders Merchants

Leyhill Road Bovingdon, Hemel Hempstead, HP3 0NW
Tel: 01442-833888 **Fax:** 01442-834110
E-mail: south@ehsmith.co.uk
Website: http://www.ehsmith.co.uk
Bank(s): Barclays, Acocks Green
Directors: D. Ensell (Co Sec)
Managers: K. Doherty (District Mgr), C. Miller, M. Tyler (Sales Prom Mgr), P. Ling (I.T. Exec), J. Rich (Comm)
Ultimate Holding Company: E H SMITH HOLDINGS LTD
Immediate Holding Company: E H SMITH (BUILDERS MERCHANTS) LIMITED
Registration no: 00800907 **Date established:** 1964
Turnover: £10m - £20m **No.of Employees:** 21 - 50 **Product Groups:** 66

Date of Accounts	Jun 11	Jun 10	Jun 09
Sales Turnover	95m	80m	82m
Pre Tax Profit/Loss	218	-795	-2m
Working Capital	10m	9m	10m
Fixed Assets	9m	10m	10m
Current Assets	26m	21m	20m
Current Liabilities	1m	977	1m

Edincare Pumps

8 Heron Business Park Eastman Way, Hemel Hempstead Industrial Estate, Hemel Hempstead, HP2 7FW
Tel: 01442-211554 **Fax:** 01442-211553
E-mail: info@edincare.com
Website: http://www.edincare.com
Directors: R. Collis (Prop)
Registration no: 02812959 **Turnover:** £500,000 - £1m
No.of Employees: 11 - 20 **Product Groups:** 34, 36, 37, 38, 40, 42, 45, 48, 51, 54, 66, 67, 85

Electron Beam Services (E B Services)

Unit 15 Avebury Court, Hemel Hempstead, HP2 7TA
Tel: 01442-236390 **Fax:** 01442-243060
E-mail: info@ebservices.co.uk
Website: http://www.electronbeamservices.co.uk
Directors: K. Osborn (Fin), R. Edmonds (Dir)
Immediate Holding Company: ELECTRON BEAM SERVICES LIMITED
Registration no: 03333898 **VAT No.:** GB 540 3424 81
Date established: 1997 **Turnover:** £250,000 - £500,000
No.of Employees: 1 - 10 **Product Groups:** 48

Date of Accounts	Apr 11	Apr 10	Apr 09
Working Capital	270	301	249
Fixed Assets	195	208	227
Current Assets	317	368	318

Eltek UK Ltd

Eltek House Maxted Road, Hemel Hempstead Industrial Estate, Hemel Hempstead, HP2 7DX
Tel: 01442-219355 **Fax:** 01442-245894
E-mail: jason.butcher@eltek.com
Website: http://www.eltek.com
Bank(s): Lloyds TSB Bank plc
Managers: J. Butcher (Serv Mgr)
Ultimate Holding Company: ELTEK AS (NORWAY)
Immediate Holding Company: ELTEK POWER (UK) LTD
Registration no: 01755876 **VAT No.:** GB 348 9035 30
Date established: 1983 **Turnover:** £10m - £20m
No.of Employees: 21 - 50 **Product Groups:** 37, 38

Date of Accounts	Dec 11	Dec 10	Dec 09
Sales Turnover	13m	13m	15m
Pre Tax Profit/Loss	878	1m	1m
Working Capital	3m	3m	2m
Fixed Assets	13	46	82
Current Assets	5m	6m	5m
Current Liabilities	2m	1m	1m

Epson

100 The Campus Maylands Avenue, Hemel Hempstead, HP2 7TJ
Tel: 08702-416900 **Fax:** 01422-227227
E-mail: retailpos@epson.co.uk
Website: http://www.epson.co.uk
Bank(s): Barclays
Directors: E. Ide (MD), M. Taylor (Pers)
Managers: S. Cullen (Sales Admin), C. Marsh (), M. Taylor (Personnel)
Ultimate Holding Company: SEIKO EPSON CORP (JAPAN)
Immediate Holding Company: EPSON (U.K.) LIMITED
Registration no: 01461516 **Date established:** 1979
Turnover: £125m - £250m **No.of Employees:** 101 - 250
Product Groups: 44

Date of Accounts	Oct 11	Oct 10	Oct 09
Sales Turnover	16	9	9
Pre Tax Profit/Loss	-60	-69	-59
Working Capital	193	249	314
Fixed Assets	174	178	183
Current Assets	468	460	1m
Current Liabilities	3	2	2

F F E I Ltd

Graphics House Boundary Way, Hemel Hempstead, HP2 7SU
Tel: 01442-213440 **Fax:** 01733-462359
E-mail: sales@ffei.co.uk
Website: http://www.ffei.co.uk
Directors: A. Cook (MD)
Ultimate Holding Company: FFEI HOLDINGS LIMITED
Immediate Holding Company: FFEI LIMITED
Registration no: 03244452 **Date established:** 1996
Turnover: £10m - £20m **No.of Employees:** 101 - 250 **Product Groups:** 44

Date of Accounts	Mar 12	Mar 11	Mar 10
Sales Turnover	18m	18m	17m
Pre Tax Profit/Loss	1m	770	4m
Working Capital	11m	9m	9m
Fixed Assets	803	989	1m
Current Assets	15m	13m	13m
Current Liabilities	2m	2m	2m

Fenton Packaging

27 Mark Road Hemel Hempstead Industrial Estate, Hemel Hempstead, HP2 7BN
Tel: 01442-241112 **Fax:** 01442-213605
E-mail: bobclarke@fentonpackaging.co.uk
Website: http://www.fentonpackaging.co.uk
Directors: R. Clarke (MD)
No.of Employees: 11 - 20 **Product Groups:** 24, 30

Fullbrook Systems Ltd

Unit 4 Bourne End Mills Upper Bourne End Lane, Hemel Hempstead, HP1 2UJ
Tel: 01442-876777 **Fax:** 01442-877144
E-mail: carlton@fullbrook.com
Website: http://www.fullbrook.com
Directors: C. Humphreys (MD)
Immediate Holding Company: FULLBROOK SYSTEMS LIMITED
Registration no: 01671421 **Date established:** 1982
Turnover: £500,000 - £1m **No.of Employees:** 1 - 10 **Product Groups:** 37, 38, 40, 41, 42, 47, 67

Date of Accounts	Mar 12	Mar 11	Mar 10
Working Capital	340	283	171
Fixed Assets	11	14	4
Current Assets	617	487	462

Furnell Transport Ltd

Enterprise House Maxted Road, Hemel Hempstead Industrial Estate, Hemel Hempstead, HP2 7BT
Tel: 01442-212744 **Fax:** 01442-255244
E-mail: sales@furnell.com
Website: http://www.furnell.com
Directors: D. Furnell (MD), I. Kidd (Fin), J. Kidd (Fin), Z. Thole (MD), A. Furnell (Mkt Research)
Managers: M. Dawson (Sales Prom Mgr)
Immediate Holding Company: FURNELL TRANSPORT LIMITED
Registration no: 02662213 **Date established:** 1991 **Turnover:** £1m - £2m
No.of Employees: 21 - 50 **Product Groups:** 72, 77, 79

GB Kent & Sons plc
London Road, Hemel Hempstead, HP3 9SA
Tel: 01442-251531 **Fax:** 01442-231672
E-mail: info@kentbrushes.com
Website: http://www.kentbrushes.com
Bank(s): Barclays
Directors: A. Cosby (MD), L. Kern (Fin), M. Cosby (Mkt Research)
Managers: S. Davis (Tech Serv Mgr)
Ultimate Holding Company: COSBY BRUSHES (CHRH) LTD.
Immediate Holding Company: G.B. KENT & SONS PLC
Registration no: 00066471 **VAT No.:** GB 238 7893 09
Date established: 2000 **Turnover:** £2m - £5m **No.of Employees:** 21 - 50
Product Groups: 49

Date of Accounts	Dec 11	Dec 10	Dec 09
Sales Turnover	5m	3m	3m
Pre Tax Profit/Loss	442	117	-278
Working Capital	1m	1m	981
Fixed Assets	1m	1m	1m
Current Assets	2m	2m	2m
Current Liabilities	435	411	379

Greensheilds J C B Ltd
78a Maxted Road Hemel Hempstead Industrial Estate, Hemel Hempstead, HP2 7DX
Tel: 01442-418700
E-mail: jmiller@gjcb.co.uk
Website: http://www.greensheildsjcb.com
Directors: C. Bean (Fin)
Immediate Holding Company: AMIR POWER TRANSMISSION LIMITED
Date established: 1983 **No.of Employees:** 11 - 20 **Product Groups:** 42, 45

Date of Accounts	Dec 11	Dec 10	Dec 09
Sales Turnover	N/A	4m	3m
Pre Tax Profit/Loss	N/A	-18	115
Working Capital	663	538	610
Fixed Assets	180	187	194
Current Assets	2m	1m	1m
Current Liabilities	N/A	139	125

Hammond & Co. Ltd
Finway Road Hemel Hempstead Industrial Estate, Hemel Hempstead, HP2 7PT
Tel: 01442-212211 **Fax:** 01442-252003
E-mail: sales@hammco.com
Website: http://www.hammco.com
Bank(s): HSBC Bank plc
Directors: D. Hammond (MD)
Immediate Holding Company: HAMMOND & COMPANY LTD.
Registration no: 00779611 **VAT No.:** GB 207 9253 62
Date established: 1963 **Turnover:** £1m - £2m **No.of Employees:** 11 - 20
Product Groups: 46

Date of Accounts	Nov 11	Nov 10	Nov 09
Working Capital	451	452	504
Fixed Assets	333	347	384
Current Assets	638	616	622

Htspe Ltd
Thamesfield House Boundary Way, Hemel Hempstead Industrial Estate, Hemel Hempstead, HP2 7SR
Tel: 01442-202400 **Fax:** 01442-219886
E-mail: chris.lockett@htspe.com
Website: http://www.htspe.com
Directors: D. Timmins (Grp Chief Exec), C. Lockett (Dir)
Managers: C. Fittus (Personnel), C. Hutton (Tech Serv Mgr)
Immediate Holding Company: HTSPE LIMITED
Registration no: 06407873 **Date established:** 2007
Turnover: £20m - £50m **No.of Employees:** 51 - 100 **Product Groups:** 80, 81, 86

Date of Accounts	Mar 12	Mar 11	Mar 10
Sales Turnover	41m	35m	30m
Pre Tax Profit/Loss	2m	2m	1m
Working Capital	3m	2m	2m
Fixed Assets	261	302	332
Current Assets	10m	10m	10m
Current Liabilities	5m	5m	5m

Hydraulic Component & Systems Ltd
Unit 14 Sovereign Park Cleveland Way, Hemel Hempstead Industrial Estate, Hemel Hempstead, HP2 7DA
Tel: 01442-240202 **Fax:** 01442-243133
E-mail: hydcompdrf@hotmail.com
Website: http://www.hydrauliccompsyst.co.uk
Directors: D. Fawcett (MD)
Immediate Holding Company: HYDRAULIC COMPONENTS & SYSTEMS LIMITED
Registration no: 01770108 **Date established:** 1983
Turnover: £250,000 - £500,000 **No.of Employees:** 1 - 10
Product Groups: 37, 38, 40, 67

Date of Accounts	Dec 11	Dec 10	Dec 09
Working Capital	-3	-3	-4
Fixed Assets	3	3	4
Current Assets	25	30	30

International Trade Shows Link Ltd
Ramsay House Piccotts End Lane, Hemel Hempstead, HP2 6JH
Tel: 01442-230033 **Fax:** 01442-230012
E-mail: info@itsluk.com
Website: http://www.itsl.com
Directors: J. Maddocks Born (MD)
Immediate Holding Company: INTERNATIONAL TRADE SHOWS LINK LIMITED
Registration no: 03330710 **VAT No.:** GB 690 2728 23
Date established: 1997 **No.of Employees:** 1 - 10 **Product Groups:** 69, 81, 83

Date of Accounts	Dec 07	Dec 06	Dec 05
Working Capital	21	-89	118
Fixed Assets	9	17	17
Current Assets	124	45	196

Jarman Iron Gates
44 High Street Bovingdon, Hemel Hempstead, HP3 0HJ
Tel: 01442-831477 **Fax:** 01442-832141
Website: http://www.jarmanirongates.co.uk
Directors: M. Jarman (Ptnr)
Date established: 1989 **No.of Employees:** 1 - 10 **Product Groups:** 26, 35

Kcom
Technology House Maylands Avenue, Hemel Hempstead Industrial Estate, Hemel Hempstead, HP2 7DF
Tel: 01442-883300 **Fax:** 01442-883315
E-mail: contactus@kcom.com
Website: http://www.affiniti.co.uk
Directors: P. Renicci (MD), P. Halls (Sales)
Ultimate Holding Company: KCOM GROUP PLC
Immediate Holding Company: OMNETICA LTD
Registration no: 01136753 **No.of Employees:** 101 - 250
Product Groups: 37, 38, 44, 48, 52, 79, 80, 81, 84, 86

Kingston Communications
Technology House Hemel Hempstead Industrial Est, Hemel Hempstead, HP2 7DS
Tel: 01908-442000 **Fax:** 01442-883315
E-mail: me@kcom.com
Website: http://www.kingstoncommunications.co.uk
Directors: D. Branton (Tech Serv), R. Griffiths (Sales & Mktg), S. Royce (Fin)
Managers: G. Pyrah (Purch Mgr), H. Roberts (Personnel)
Ultimate Holding Company: SIEMENS AG
Immediate Holding Company: SIEMENS HOLDINGS P.L.C.
Registration no: 03317871 **Turnover:** £125m - £250m
No.of Employees: 51 - 100 **Product Groups:** 67, 80, 81

Date of Accounts	Mar 07	Mar 06
Sales Turnover	135600	135900
Pre Tax Profit/Loss	4470	-5910
Working Capital	38070	490
Fixed Assets	N/A	41740
Current Assets	38070	50340
Current Liabilities	N/A	49850
Total Share Capital	22590	22590
ROCE% (Return on Capital Employed)		-14.0
ROT% (Return on Turnover)	3.3	-4.3

Kodak Ltd (Kodak Graphic Communication)
Hemel One Boundary Way, Hemel Hempstead, HP2 7YU
Tel: 01442-261122 **Fax:** 01442-240609
Website: http://www.kodak.co.uk
Directors: D. Lambert (Fin), D. Wigfield (MD), P. Holloway (Mkt Research), P. Clough (Co Sec), R. Wildman (Dir)
Managers: N. Yeomans (Sales Prom Mgr), F. Stickley (Sales Admin)
Ultimate Holding Company: EASTMAN KODAK COMPANY (USA)
Immediate Holding Company: KODAK LIMITED
Registration no: 00059535 **Date established:** 1998
Turnover: £75m - £125m **No.of Employees:** 101 - 250
Product Groups: 28, 44

Date of Accounts	Dec 07	Dec 06	Dec 05
Pre Tax Profit/Loss	-253	-3433	3318
Working Capital	27286	27539	30972
Current Assets	28285	28534	31967
Current Liabilities	999	995	995
Total Share Capital	25487	25487	25487
ROCE% (Return on Capital Employed)	-0.9	-12.5	10.7

Masco Print Developments Ltd
Stags End Cottage Barn Gaddesden Row, Hemel Hempstead, HP2 6HN
Tel: 01582-791190 **Fax:** 01582-791199
E-mail: info@mascoprint.co.uk
Website: http://www.mascoprint.co.uk
Directors: Y. Mason (Fin)
Immediate Holding Company: MASCOPRINT DEVELOPMENTS LIMITED
Registration no: 01040660 **VAT No.:** GB 196 9926 85
Date established: 1972 **No.of Employees:** 1 - 10 **Product Groups:** 28, 43, 44

Date of Accounts	Jun 11	Jun 10	Jun 09
Working Capital	35	34	18
Fixed Assets	4	13	21
Current Assets	144	161	140

Maxon C I C Europe Ltd
Maxon House Cleveland Road, Hemel Hempstead Industrial Estate, Hemel Hempstead, HP2 7EY
Tel: 01442-267777 **Fax:** 01442-215515
E-mail: sales@maxoncic.co.uk
Website: http://www.maxoncic.co.uk
Managers: H. Crowhurst (Chief Mgr)
Immediate Holding Company: MAXON CIC EUROPE LIMITED
Registration no: 05416627 **VAT No.:** 467 2323 44 **Date established:** 2005
Turnover: £10m - £20m **No.of Employees:** 1 - 10 **Product Groups:** 37, 44

Date of Accounts	Dec 11	Dec 10	Dec 09
Working Capital	-2m	-2m	-2m
Fixed Assets	2	1	16
Current Assets	480	607	979

Microlin Cooper Ltd
9 Heron Business Park Eastman Way, Hemel Hempstead Industrial Estate, Hemel Hempstead, HP2 7FW
Tel: 01442-248797 **Fax:** 01442-252912
E-mail: microlina@msn.com
Website: http://www.microlincooper.co.uk
Directors: D. Pinter (Ch)
Immediate Holding Company: MICROLIN COOPER LTD
Registration no: 03623411 **Date established:** 1998 **Turnover:** £1m - £2m
No.of Employees: 1 - 10 **Product Groups:** 24

Date of Accounts	Aug 11	Aug 10	Aug 09
Working Capital	-249	-278	-300
Fixed Assets	705	688	694
Current Assets	1m	1m	1m

Muraspec
74-78 Wood Lane End, Hemel Hempstead, HP2 4RF
Tel: 01442-268890 **Fax:** 0870-532 9020
E-mail: trashid@muraspec.com
Website: http://www.muraspec.com
Bank(s): Barclays
Directors: T. Rashid (MD)
Managers: N. Morgan (Purch Mgr), H. Skinkys, V. Smith (Personnel), F. McGuckian (Tech Serv Mgr)
Ultimate Holding Company: MURASPEC LIMITED
Immediate Holding Company: MURASPEC DECORATIVE SOLUTIONS LIMITED
Registration no: 03564408 **VAT No.:** 419 0876 36 **Date established:** 1998
Turnover: £20m - £50m **No.of Employees:** 51 - 100 **Product Groups:** 23

Date of Accounts	Nov 11	Nov 10	Nov 09
Sales Turnover	52m	46m	42m
Pre Tax Profit/Loss	603	-2m	2m
Working Capital	2m	1m	716
Fixed Assets	5m	5m	8m
Current Assets	18m	18m	23m
Current Liabilities	3m	3m	3m

N A C D Ltd
Unit 8 Heron Business Park Eastman Way, Hemel Hempstead Industrial Estate, Hemel Hempstead, HP2 7FW
Tel: 01442-211848 **Fax:** 01442-212776
E-mail: info@nacd.co.uk
Website: http://www.nacd.co.uk
Bank(s): HSBC Bank plc
Directors: A. Davies (Fin), R. Collis (MD)
Immediate Holding Company: N.A.C.D. LIMITED
Registration no: 03212230 **VAT No.:** GB 695 1188 04
Date established: 1996 **Turnover:** £2m - £5m **No.of Employees:** 21 - 50
Product Groups: 40

Date of Accounts	Dec 11	Dec 10	Dec 09
Sales Turnover	N/A	3m	N/A
Pre Tax Profit/Loss	N/A	49	N/A
Working Capital	12	-17	-152
Fixed Assets	133	114	342
Current Assets	2m	1m	1m
Current Liabilities	N/A	707	N/A

N G K Spark Plugs UK Ltd
Maylands Avenue Hemel Hempstead Industrial Estate, Hemel Hempstead, HP2 4SD
Tel: 01442-281000 **Fax:** 01442-281001
E-mail: enquiries@ngk.co.uk
Website: http://www.ngkntk.co.uk
Bank(s): HSBC Bank Plc
Directors: B. Childs (Dir), C. Whiddington (Co Sec)
Managers: K. Wall (Fin Mgr)
Ultimate Holding Company: N G K SPARK PLUG CO LTD (JAPAN)
Immediate Holding Company: NGK SPARK PLUGS (UK) LIMITED
Registration no: 01212088 **VAT No.:** GB 214 8259 66
Date established: 1975 **Turnover:** £50m - £75m
No.of Employees: 51 - 100 **Product Groups:** 29, 33, 37, 38, 39, 40, 42, 68

Date of Accounts	Dec 11	Dec 10	Dec 09
Sales Turnover	75m	65m	52m
Pre Tax Profit/Loss	4m	5m	4m
Working Capital	19m	20m	20m
Fixed Assets	3m	3m	3m
Current Assets	38m	38m	34m
Current Liabilities	3m	4m	3m

Nine Shipton
1 Frogmore Road Industrial Estate Frogmore Road, Hemel Hempstead, HP3 9TG
Tel: 01442-345600 **Fax:** 01442-345612
Website: http://www.shipton.co.uk
Bank(s): HSBC Bank plc
Directors: A. Turner (Dir)
Ultimate Holding Company: GEBRUEDER ROECHLING (GERMANY)
Immediate Holding Company: COMMUNIO GROUP LIMITED
Registration no: 01397417 **Date established:** 1981 **Turnover:** £2m - £5m
No.of Employees: 21 - 50 **Product Groups:** 37, 80

Northgate & Arinso
2 Peoplebuilding Estate Maylands Avenue, Hemel Hempstead Industrial Estate, Hemel Hempstead, HP2 4NW
Tel: 01442-232434 **Fax:** 01442-256454
E-mail: solutions@northgate-is.com
Website: http://www.northgate-hrs.com
Directors: D. Knight (Dir)
Ultimate Holding Company: NIS HOLDINGS SARL (LUXEMBOURG)
Immediate Holding Company: NORTHGATEARINSO UK LIMITED
Registration no: 01587537 **VAT No.:** GB 207 5885 45
Date established: 1981 **Turnover:** £125m - £250m
No.of Employees: 1 - 10 **Product Groups:** 44

Date of Accounts	Apr 11	Apr 10	Apr 09
Sales Turnover	127m	128m	125m
Pre Tax Profit/Loss	15m	8m	-4m
Working Capital	-99m	-79m	-68m
Fixed Assets	160m	169m	180m
Current Assets	51m	192m	217m
Current Liabilities	40m	38m	46m

P C D Products LLP
Cleveland Road Hemel Hempstead Industrial Estate, Hemel Hempstead, HP2 7EY
Tel: 01442-248565 **Fax:** 01442-241033
E-mail: d.stoneham@pcdproducts.co.uk
Website: http://www.pcdproducts.com
Bank(s): Lloyds TSB
Directors: D. Stoneham (MD)
Managers: Z. Cutts, N. Miller (Prod Mgr)
Ultimate Holding Company: EVER 2420 LIMITED
Immediate Holding Company: PCD PRODUCTS LLP
Registration no: OC323544 **VAT No.:** GB 349 1898 08
Date established: 2006 **Turnover:** £1m - £2m **No.of Employees:** 21 - 50
Product Groups: 26, 35

Date of Accounts	Mar 11	Mar 10	Mar 09
Working Capital	329	290	-352
Fixed Assets	420	492	595
Current Assets	1m	1m	942

Red Sky I T Ltd
Viking House Swallowdale Lane, Hemel Hempstead, HP2 7EA
Tel: 020-3002 8600 **Fax:** 020-3070 0925
E-mail: enquiry@redskyit.com
Website: http://www.redskyit.com
Managers: B. Sheerin (Chief Mgr)
Registration no: 03045231 **No.of Employees:** 21 - 50 **Product Groups:** 84

Redsky It (Formerly Ramesys Construction Services)
Viking House Swallowdale Lane, Hemel Hempstead, HP2 7EA
Tel: 020-3002 8600 **Fax:** 020-3070 0925
E-mail: construction.webenquiry@redskyit.com
Website: http://www.redskyit.com
Directors: M. Aspinwall (MD)
Registration no: 01510606 **Date established:** 1980
Turnover: £20m - £50m **No.of Employees:** 51 - 100 **Product Groups:** 30, 37, 44, 49, 67, 79, 80, 81, 84, 86, 87

S P B Metal Works
Unit 32a, Bourne End Mills Industrial Estate Bourne End, Hemel Hempstead, HP1 2UJ
Tel: 01442-878165 **Fax:** 01442-878444
E-mail: enquiries@spbmetalworks.co.uk
Website: http://www.spbmetalworks.co.uk

see next page

S P B Metal Works - Cont'd
Directors: M. Perry (Dir), R. Perry (Dir)
Immediate Holding Company: S.P.B. Metal Works Ltd
Registration no: 01316473 **VAT No.:** GB 301 6191 04
Date established: 1977 **Turnover:** £250,000 - £500,000
No.of Employees: 1 - 10 **Product Groups:** 48

Date of Accounts	Jun 10	Jun 09	Jun 08
Sales Turnover	269	289	361
Pre Tax Profit/Loss	8	30	70
Working Capital	47	73	98
Fixed Assets	9	10	11
Current Assets	98	116	158
Current Liabilities	8	13	24

Satellite Television Contractors
106 London Road, Hemel Hempstead, HP3 9SD
Tel: 01442-252051 **Fax:** 01442-321839
E-mail: theresa.gee@stcltd.co.uk
Website: http://www.stcltd.co.uk
Directors: T. Gee (Fin)
Immediate Holding Company: SATELLITE TELEVISION CONTRACTORS LIMITED
Registration no: 02335874 **Date established:** 1989
Turnover: £250,000 - £500,000 **No.of Employees:** 1 - 10
Product Groups: 37

Date of Accounts	Mar 11	Mar 10	Mar 08
Working Capital	-47	-28	44
Fixed Assets	38	54	90
Current Assets	17	14	119

Schroff UK Ltd
Grovelands Business Centre Boundary Way, Hemel Hempstead Indl-Est, Hemel Hempstead, HP2 7TE
Tel: 01442-240471 **Fax:** 01442-213508
E-mail: schroff.uk@pentair.com
Website: http://www.schroff.co.uk
Bank(s): National Westminster Bank Plc
Managers: A. McLean-Hall (Sales Prom Mgr), K. Reynolds (Mktg Serv Mgr)
Ultimate Holding Company: PENTAIR INC (USA)
Immediate Holding Company: SCHROFF UK LIMITED
Registration no: 00558343 **Date established:** 1962
Turnover: £10m - £20m **No.of Employees:** 21 - 50 **Product Groups:** 26, 30, 37, 40

Date of Accounts	Dec 11	Dec 10	Dec 09
Sales Turnover	12m	12m	10m
Pre Tax Profit/Loss	1m	921	361
Working Capital	3m	2m	2m
Fixed Assets	249	17	31
Current Assets	5m	5m	4m
Current Liabilities	829	1m	528

Season Master Double Glazing Ltd
10 Maxted Road Hemel Hempstead Industrial Estate, Hemel Hempstead, HP2 7DX
Tel: 01442-240487 **Fax:** 01442-211311
E-mail: seasonmaster@aol.com
Directors: T. Britten (MD)
Immediate Holding Company: SEASON MASTER DOUBLE GLAZING LIMITED
Registration no: 01206591 **Date established:** 1975
No.of Employees: 1 - 10 **Product Groups:** 26, 35

Date of Accounts	Apr 12	Apr 11	Apr 10
Working Capital	551	448	546
Fixed Assets	229	200	198
Current Assets	973	922	913
Current Liabilities	N/A	N/A	175

Smiths Coffee Co. Ltd
Arabica House Ebberns Road, Hemel Hempstead, HP3 9RD
Tel: 01442-234257 **Fax:** 01422-248614
E-mail: sales@smiths-coffee.demon.co.uk
Website: http://www.smithscoffee.co.uk
Directors: C. Smith (MD), M. Ashby (Dir)
Managers: M. Jones (Mktg Serv Mgr)
Immediate Holding Company: SMITH'S COFFEE COMPANY LIMITED
Registration no: 03560937 **Date established:** 1998 **Turnover:** £1m - £2m
No.of Employees: 11 - 20 **Product Groups:** 20, 40, 62

Date of Accounts	Jun 12	Jun 11	Jun 10
Working Capital	193	90	-4
Fixed Assets	131	115	142
Current Assets	699	638	704

Stabilag E S H Ltd
Lower Gade Farm Dagnall Road Great Gaddesden, Hemel Hempstead, HP1 3BP
Tel: 01442-843843 **Fax:** 0870-990 6762
E-mail: sales@stabilag.com
Website: http://www.stabilag.com
Directors: R. Bull (MD)
Immediate Holding Company: STABILAG (E. S. H.) LIMITED
Registration no: 01066020 **VAT No.:** GB 208 2104 11
Date established: 1972 **Turnover:** £500,000 - £1m
No.of Employees: 1 - 10 **Product Groups:** 37, 39, 40, 42, 52, 66, 80

Date of Accounts	Aug 11	Aug 10	Aug 09
Working Capital	21	42	44
Fixed Assets	3	4	5
Current Assets	71	88	72

Starlec Electrical Wholesaler
Unit 10 Saracen Industrial Area Mark Road, Hemel Hempstead Industrial Estate, Hemel Hempstead, HP2 7BJ
Tel: 01442-412200 **Fax:** 01442-412201
E-mail: info@starlec.co.uk
Website: http://www.starlec.co.uk
Managers: F. East (District Mgr)
Immediate Holding Company: STARLEC LIMITED
Registration no: 04142289 **Date established:** 2001
No.of Employees: 11 - 20 **Product Groups:** 36, 40

Date of Accounts	Aug 10	Aug 09	Aug 08
Working Capital	28	-51	35
Fixed Assets	69	77	89
Current Assets	600	731	697

Steel Wire Rope Ltd
3 Eastman Way Hemel Hempstead Industrial Estate, Hemel Hempstead, HP2 7DU
Tel: 0800-455555 **Fax:** 01442-259918
E-mail: sales@steelwirerope.com
Website: http://www.swrgroup.com
Bank(s): Barclays
Directors: J. Lee (MD), J. Bates (Prop)
Managers: P. Kehoe (Sales Admin), S. Wood (Sales Prom Mgr)
Immediate Holding Company: SWR LIMITED
Registration no: 02260632 **VAT No.:** GB 541 1159 78
Date established: 1988 **Turnover:** £2m - £5m **No.of Employees:** 21 - 50
Product Groups: 35

Date of Accounts	Sep 11	Sep 10	Sep 09
Working Capital	665	582	517
Fixed Assets	159	133	145
Current Assets	2m	1m	1m

Sunnen Products Ltd
Unit 1b Centro 1 Maxted Road, Hemel Hempstead Industrial Estate, Hemel Hempstead, HP2 7EF
Tel: 01442-393939 **Fax:** 01442-391212
E-mail: hemel@sunnen.co.uk
Website: http://www.sunnen.com
Directors: Y. Palmer (Co Sec)
Ultimate Holding Company: SUNNEN PRODUCTS CO INC (USA)
Immediate Holding Company: SUNNEN PRODUCTS LIMITED
Registration no: 02890320 **Date established:** 1994
Turnover: £10m - £20m **No.of Employees:** 11 - 20 **Product Groups:** 46

Date of Accounts	Dec 11	Dec 10	Dec 09
Sales Turnover	20m	15m	14m
Pre Tax Profit/Loss	667	-845	-82
Working Capital	4m	4m	8m
Fixed Assets	1m	2m	1m
Current Assets	13m	11m	11m
Current Liabilities	3m	1m	2m

Texcel Division (a division of Crosslink Business Services Ltd)
8 Avebury Court Mark Road, Hemel Hempstead, HP2 7TA
Tel: 01442-231700 **Fax:** 01442-261918
E-mail: info@texcel.uk.com
Website: http://www.texcel.uk.com
Directors: M. Tullberg (MD), P. Tullberg (Fin)
Immediate Holding Company: TEXCEL LIMITED
Registration no: 00980943 **VAT No.:** GB 290 7787 14
Date established: 1970 **Turnover:** £500,000 - £1m
No.of Employees: 1 - 10 **Product Groups:** 30, 35, 36, 37, 38, 40, 67

Thermo Fisher Scientific
Boundary Park Stafford House Hemel Hempstead Industrial Estate, Hemel Hempstead, HP2 7GE
Tel: 01442-233555 **Fax:** 01442-233667
Website: http://www.thermofisher.com
Bank(s): Barclays
Managers: A. Penble (Buyer), H. Mayo, A. Whitehouse (Fin Mgr), B. Adamson, J. Mole, J. Goulding
Immediate Holding Company: PRESTIGIOUS DEVELOPMENT SERVICES LTD
Registration no: 00886408 **VAT No.:** GB 687 9263 68
Date established: 2004 **Turnover:** £10m - £20m
No.of Employees: 51 - 100 **Product Groups:** 44

Date of Accounts	Dec 11	Dec 10	Dec 09
Sales Turnover	21m	18m	14m
Pre Tax Profit/Loss	337	238	106
Working Capital	2m	1m	1m
Fixed Assets	503	544	531
Current Assets	8m	5m	5m
Current Liabilities	439	516	483

Toshiba Tec Europe Ltd
Campus 300 Spring Way, Hemel Hempstead, HP2 7GG
Tel: 08708-907200 **Fax:** 0870-890 7350
E-mail: info@toshibatec-eu.co.uk
Website: http://www.toshibatec-eu.co.uk
Bank(s): National Westminster
Directors: J. Hillier (Fin)
Managers: B. Vickers (Sales & Mktg Mg), N. Wright (Personnel), C. Daily, C. Dailey, D. Jevans
Ultimate Holding Company: TOSHIBA GROUP
Registration no: FC022693 **VAT No.:** GB 318 0292 76
Date established: 1980 **Turnover:** £10m - £20m
No.of Employees: 51 - 100 **Product Groups:** 28, 44

Trademark Interiors Ltd
8 March Monte Gate, Hemel Hempstead, HP2 7BF
Tel: 01442-260022 **Fax:** 01442-232244
E-mail: barrycollins@tmark.co.uk
Website: http://www.tmark.co.uk
Directors: B. Collins (MD)
Immediate Holding Company: TRADEMARK INTERIORS LIMITED
Registration no: 03234748 **VAT No.:** GB 684 9061 01
Date established: 1996 **Turnover:** £2m - £5m **No.of Employees:** 1 - 10
Product Groups: 26, 49, 67

Date of Accounts	Dec 10	Dec 09	Dec 08
Working Capital	25	1	57
Fixed Assets	10	19	36
Current Assets	190	266	265

Twinmar Ltd
Maxted Road Hemel Hempstead Industrial Estate, Hemel Hempstead, HP2 7DX
Tel: 01442-241431 **Fax:** 01442-230760
E-mail: enquiries@twinmar.co.uk
Website: http://www.soletrader.co.uk
Directors: S. Bordon (Ch), C. Collins (MD), D. Bordon (Dir)
Managers: D. Hoyle (Buyer), H. Tout (Personnel), E. Powell
Immediate Holding Company: TWINMAR LIMITED
Registration no: 00763926 **Date established:** 1963
Turnover: £20m - £50m **No.of Employees:** 11 - 20 **Product Groups:** 63

Date of Accounts	Jun 08	Jun 09	Jun 10
Sales Turnover	35m	34m	32m
Pre Tax Profit/Loss	1m	1m	1m
Working Capital	21m	21m	21m
Fixed Assets	2m	1m	1m
Current Assets	23m	23m	23m
Current Liabilities	1m	1m	1m

Utopia Signs Ltd
77 London Road, Hemel Hempstead, HP3 9SP
Tel: 01442-264600 **Fax:** 01442-233566
E-mail: sales@utopiasigns.co.uk
Website: http://www.utopiasigns.com
Directors: L. Palmer Thompson (MD)
Immediate Holding Company: UTOPIA SIGNS LIMITED
Registration no: 03126848 **Date established:** 1995
No.of Employees: 1 - 10 **Product Groups:** 30, 37, 40, 49

Date of Accounts	Mar 12	Mar 11	Mar 10
Working Capital	-1	-2	-8
Fixed Assets	8	9	10
Current Assets	23	38	30

Vidlink International Ltd
27 Maylands Avenue Hemel Hempstead Industrial Estate, Hemel Hempstead, HP2 7DE
Tel: 01442-431300 **Fax:** 01494-791127
E-mail: sales@vislink.com
Website: http://www.vidlink.com
Bank(s): Barclays
Directors: H. Jones (Pers), S. Rudd (MD)
Managers: J. Darby (Chief Buyer), M. Anderson, J. Walton (Personnel), B. Mann (Tech Serv Mgr)
Ultimate Holding Company: Vislink PLC
Immediate Holding Company: Vislink plc
Registration no: 01910243 **VAT No.:** GB 540 2640 80
Date established: 1972 **Turnover:** £10m - £20m
No.of Employees: 51 - 100 **Product Groups:** 37, 38

Date of Accounts	Dec 11	Dec 10	Dec 09
Sales Turnover	2m	2m	5m
Pre Tax Profit/Loss	-54	74	-130
Working Capital	6m	6m	6m
Fixed Assets	9	10	15
Current Assets	7m	7m	7m
Current Liabilities	387	176	524

W F Electrical
Cleveland Way Hemel Hempstead Industrial Estate, Hemel Hempstead, HP2 7DL
Tel: 01442-212811 **Fax:** 01442-265460
E-mail: wf@wf-online.com
Website: http://www.wf-online.com
Managers: N. Dilloway (District Mgr)
Ultimate Holding Company: RAY INVESTMENT SARL (LUXEMBOURG)
Immediate Holding Company: WF ELECTRICAL LIMITED
Registration no: 00085004 **VAT No.:** 466 6077 19 **Date established:** 2005
Turnover: £2m - £5m **No.of Employees:** 1 - 10 **Product Groups:** 77

Date of Accounts	Dec 11	Dec 10	Dec 09
Pre Tax Profit/Loss	N/A	-1	2
Working Capital	25m	25m	25m
Current Assets	38m	38m	38m

Welfare Paint Finishers
21 Mark Road Hemel Hempstead Industrial Estate, Hemel Hempstead, HP2 7BN
Tel: 01442-235585 **Fax:** 01442- 251735
Directors: T. Welfare (Prop)
Immediate Holding Company: R.B. FINISHERS LTD
Registration no: 05664902 **Date established:** 1994
No.of Employees: 1 - 10 **Product Groups:** 46, 48

Xara Ltd
Gaddesden Place Great Gaddesden, Hemel Hempstead, HP2 6EX
Tel: 01442-350000 **Fax:** 01442-350010
E-mail: sales@xara.com
Website: http://www.xara.com
Bank(s): National Westminster Bank Plc
Directors: C. Moir (MD)
Ultimate Holding Company: MAGIX AG (GERMANY)
Immediate Holding Company: XARA LIMITED
Registration no: 02034831 **VAT No.:** GB 640 2223 88
Date established: 1986 **Turnover:** Up to £250,000
No.of Employees: 21 - 50 **Product Groups:** 44

Hertford

Air Energy Ltd
Unit 6 Mead Lane Fountain Drive, Hertford, SG13 7UB
Tel: 01992-586666 **Fax:** 01992-586677
E-mail: sales@air-energy.co.uk
Website: http://air-energy.co.uk
Directors: W. Chaudry (MD)
Immediate Holding Company: AIR ENERGY LIMITED
Registration no: 04403261 **Date established:** 2002
No.of Employees: 1 - 10 **Product Groups:** 18, 30, 31, 32, 33, 34, 35, 36, 37, 38, 39, 40, 42, 45, 48, 67, 68, 83

Date of Accounts	Mar 12	Mar 11	Mar 10
Working Capital	60	65	44
Fixed Assets	24	18	14
Current Assets	219	212	185

Allaway Acoustics Ltd
1 Queens Road, Hertford, SG14 1EN
Tel: 01992-550825 **Fax:** 01992-554982
E-mail: enquiries@allawayacoustics.co.uk
Website: http://www.allawayacoustics.co.uk
Bank(s): Barclays, Thetford
Directors: C. Dye (Co Sec), J. Grieves (Dir)
Managers: C. Chen (Tech Serv Mgr)
Ultimate Holding Company: ALLAWAY GROUP LIMITED
Immediate Holding Company: ALLAWAY ACOUSTICS LIMITED
Registration no: 00958950 **VAT No.:** GB 229 2245 70
Date established: 1969 **Turnover:** £5m - £10m **No.of Employees:** 11 - 20
Product Groups: 54

Date of Accounts	Jun 11	Jun 10	Jun 09
Sales Turnover	9m	11m	N/A
Pre Tax Profit/Loss	85	1m	N/A
Working Capital	555	657	701
Fixed Assets	302	198	128
Current Assets	3m	5m	3m
Current Liabilities	252	568	N/A

Alpha Ironwork Ltd
Broom Hall Farm House Watton at Stone, Hertford, SG14 2RN
Tel: 01920-830673
Directors: W. Burt (Fin)
Immediate Holding Company: ALPHA IRONWORK LIMITED
Registration no: 05662930 **Date established:** 2005
No.of Employees: 1 - 10 **Product Groups:** 26, 35

Date of Accounts	Dec 10	Dec 09	Dec 07
Working Capital	-90	-89	-92
Fixed Assets	1	10	34
Current Assets	2	2	6

Ammeraal Beltech Ltd
John Tate Road Foxholes Business Park, Hertford, SG13 7QE
Tel: 01992-500550 **Fax:** 01992-553010
E-mail: south@ammeraalbeltech.co.uk
Website: http://www.ammeraalbeltech.com
Bank(s): National Westminster Bank Plc
Directors: M. Weller (Dir), S. Farley (Co Sec)
Managers: D. Melton
Ultimate Holding Company: GAMMA HOLDING NV (NETHERLANDS)
Immediate Holding Company: AMMERAAL BELTECH LIMITED
Registration no: 01163300 **Date established:** 1974
Turnover: £10m - £20m **No.of Employees:** 21 - 50 **Product Groups:** 30, 45

Date of Accounts	Dec 11	Dec 10	Dec 09
Sales Turnover	17m	15m	12m
Pre Tax Profit/Loss	2m	1m	652
Working Capital	819	941	108
Fixed Assets	2m	2m	2m
Current Assets	8m	6m	5m
Current Liabilities	3m	2m	2m

Stephen Austin
Caxton Hill, Hertford, SG13 7LU
Tel: 01992-584955 **Fax:** 01992-500021
E-mail: info@stephenaustin.co.uk
Website: http://www.stephenaustin.co.uk
Bank(s): Midland, Hertford
Directors: I. Angus (Co Sec), R. Fowler (MD)
Managers: P. Halton (Tech Serv Mgr), C. Turner (Personnel)
Ultimate Holding Company: JACOB & JOHNSON LIMITED
Immediate Holding Company: STEPHEN AUSTIN & SONS LIMITED
Registration no: 04381773 **Date established:** 2002
Turnover: £10m - £20m **No.of Employees:** 51 - 100 **Product Groups:** 28

Date of Accounts	Sep 11	Sep 10	Sep 09
Sales Turnover	14m	14m	13m
Pre Tax Profit/Loss	486	904	968
Working Capital	5m	5m	5m
Fixed Assets	2m	2m	3m
Current Assets	9m	9m	9m
Current Liabilities	1m	1m	1m

Bycon Ltd
141 London Rd Hertford Heath, Hertford, SG13 7RH
Tel: 07745-466608
E-mail: enquiries@bycon.co.uk
Website: http://www.bycon.co.uk
Managers: B. Yeamans (Trng Mgr)
Registration no: 03362225 **Turnover:** Up to £250,000
No.of Employees: 1 - 10 **Product Groups:** 86

Date of Accounts	Sep 09	Sep 08	Sep 07
Working Capital	-0	-0	-1
Current Assets	N/A	1	1

C & D Fork Truck Ltd
Drapers Yard Warrenwood Industrial Estate, Stapleford, Hertford, SG14 3NU
Tel: 01992-503463 **Fax:** 01992-501584
Website: http://www.cdforktruckservices.co.uk
Managers: R. Cook (Mgr)
Date established: 1991 **Turnover:** £250,000 - £500,000
No.of Employees: 1 - 10 **Product Groups:** 45, 48, 67

Colar Engineering
Unit 6 Marshgate Drive, Hertford, SG13 7AQ
Tel: 01992-552809
Managers: N. Dosh (Mgr)
Date established: 1978 **No.of Employees:** 1 - 10 **Product Groups:** 35

G W Cowler Precision Engineers
16 Merchant Drive Mead Lane, Hertford, SG13 7AY
Tel: 01992-501494 **Fax:** 01992-501495
E-mail: sales@gwcowler.demon.co.uk
Website: http://www.gwcowler.co.uk
Bank(s): Barclays
Directors: G. Cowler (Ch)
VAT No.: GB 370 4671 54 **Turnover:** £500,000 - £1m
No.of Employees: 11 - 20 **Product Groups:** 35, 46, 48

Crossbrook Furniture Ltd
8 Marshgate Industrial Estate 20 Marshgate Drive, Hertford, SG13 7AJ
Tel: 01992-557000 **Fax:** 01992-501666
E-mail: sales@crossbrook.co.uk
Website: http://www.crossbrook.co.uk
Bank(s): HSBC Bank plc
Directors: M. Mitchell (MD), P. Archer (Dir)
Managers: F. Akinsanmi
Immediate Holding Company: CROSSBROOK FURNITURE LIMITED
Registration no: 00955665 **Date established:** 1969 **Turnover:** £2m - £5m
No.of Employees: 21 - 50 **Product Groups:** 26, 67

Date of Accounts	May 11	May 10	May 09
Working Capital	243	216	244
Fixed Assets	104	126	148
Current Assets	1m	1m	949

Daleba Electronics
49 Tamworth Road, Hertford, SG13 7DJ
Tel: 01992-582232 **Fax:** 01992-582222
E-mail: sales@daleba.co.uk
Website: http://www.daleba.co.uk
Directors: J. McNamee (Comm), A. Grisbrooke (MD)
Managers: C. Wall (Sales Prom Mgr)
Ultimate Holding Company: TAPPENDEN & CO. LIMITED
Immediate Holding Company: DALEBA ELECTRONICS LIMITED
Registration no: 00748985 **VAT No.:** GB 213 5270 02
Date established: 1963 **Turnover:** £5m - £10m
No.of Employees: 51 - 100 **Product Groups:** 37, 84

Date of Accounts	Sep 11	Sep 10	Sep 09
Sales Turnover	8m	8m	8m
Pre Tax Profit/Loss	24	-100	-118
Working Capital	1m	1m	1m
Fixed Assets	90	100	89
Current Assets	3m	4m	3m
Current Liabilities	310	787	247

Data Room Supplies
Conbar House Mead Lane, Hertford, SG13 7AP
Tel: 01992-558737 **Fax:** 01992- 558714
E-mail: info@dataroomdirect.com
Website: http://www.dataroomdirect.com
Directors: C. Coates (Prop)
Immediate Holding Company: DATA ROOM SUPPLIES LIMITED
Registration no: 05206150 **Date established:** 2004
Turnover: £500,000 - £1m **No.of Employees:** 1 - 10 **Product Groups:** 33, 37, 67

Date of Accounts	Dec 11	Dec 08	Oct 10
Sales Turnover	N/A	161	634
Pre Tax Profit/Loss	N/A	8	31
Working Capital	27	19	36
Fixed Assets	3	N/A	N/A
Current Assets	142	24	57
Current Liabilities	N/A	5	21

Distinctly Different Days Ltd
38 Newland Gardens, Hertford, SG13 7WN
Tel: 01992-581751 **Fax:** 01992-583713
E-mail: info@distinctlydifferentdays.co.uk
Website: http://www.distinctlydifferentdays.co.uk
Directors: L. Winterton (Fin), M. Winterton (MD)
Immediate Holding Company: DISTINCTLY DIFFERENT DESIGNS LIMITED
Registration no: 03095505 **Date established:** 1995
Turnover: Up to £250,000 **No.of Employees:** 1 - 10 **Product Groups:** 89

Date of Accounts	Mar 12	Mar 11	Mar 10
Working Capital	N/A	-1	-1
Fixed Assets	1	1	2
Current Assets	141	110	132

E M E Electronic & Mechanical Engineering Ltd
25 The Mead Business Centre Mead Lane, Hertford, SG13 7BJ
Tel: 01992-552151
E-mail: sales@emeltd.com
Website: http://www.emeltd.com
Directors: L. Potucek (MD)
Immediate Holding Company: EME (ELECTRONIC & MECHANICAL ENGINEERING) LIMITED
Registration no: 01172103 **VAT No.:** GB 221 7863 67
Date established: 1974 **Turnover:** £500,000 - £1m
No.of Employees: 1 - 10 **Product Groups:** 84

Date of Accounts	Oct 10	Oct 09	Oct 08
Working Capital	71	43	34
Fixed Assets	N/A	2	2
Current Assets	143	138	162

Enspire Health
10 Harforde Court John Tate Road, Hertford, SG13 7NW
Tel: 01992-526300 **Fax:** 01992-526320
Website: http://www.enspirehealth.com
Bank(s): Lloyds, Coventry
Directors: S. Mills (Dir)
Ultimate Holding Company: NSPIRE HEALTH LLC (USA)
Immediate Holding Company: NSPIRE HEALTH LTD
Registration no: 00734155 **Date established:** 1962 **Turnover:** £2m - £5m
No.of Employees: 11 - 20 **Product Groups:** 38

Date of Accounts	Dec 11	Dec 10	Dec 09
Sales Turnover	3m	3m	3m
Pre Tax Profit/Loss	-22	-292	73
Working Capital	833	825	1m
Fixed Assets	54	84	140
Current Assets	1m	2m	2m
Current Liabilities	435	518	469

Fluorocarbon Co. Ltd
Caxton Hill, Hertford, SG13 7NH
Tel: 01992-550731 **Fax:** 01992-584697
E-mail: info@fluorocarbon.co.uk
Website: http://www.fluorocarbon.co.uk
Bank(s): Lloyds TSB Bank plc
Directors: T. Wells (Dir), J. Cumins (Fin)
Managers: V. Gooding (Personnel), E. Collinson (Purch Mgr), R. Ballago (Export Sales Mg)
Ultimate Holding Company: FLUOROCARBON GROUP LIMITED
Immediate Holding Company: FLUOROCARBON HOLDINGS LIMITED
Registration no: 01171574 **Date established:** 1974
Turnover: £20m - £50m **No.of Employees:** 251 - 500
Product Groups: 29, 30, 36

Date of Accounts	Aug 11	Aug 10	Aug 09
Pre Tax Profit/Loss	N/A	N/A	3m
Working Capital	N/A	N/A	538
Fixed Assets	8m	7m	10m
Current Assets	N/A	N/A	538

Forgetrack Ltd
Thistle House St Andrews Street, Hertford, SG14 1JA
Tel: 01992-500900 **Fax:** 01992-589495
E-mail: sales@forgetrack.co.uk
Website: http://www.forgetrack.co.uk
Directors: C. Loxley-Ford (Dir), L. Croucher (Co Sec)
Immediate Holding Company: FORGETRACK LIMITED
Registration no: 02281356 **VAT No.:** GB 493 3630 33
Date established: 1988 **Turnover:** £500,000 - £1m
No.of Employees: 11 - 20 **Product Groups:** 44, 80

Date of Accounts	Dec 11	Dec 10	Dec 07
Working Capital	123	184	539
Fixed Assets	18	13	33
Current Assets	483	492	868

Fullpoint Ltd
Brickendon Bury Brickendon, Hertford, SG13 8NP
Tel: 01992-501777 **Fax:** 01992-504859
E-mail: info@fullpoint.co.uk
Website: http://www.fullpoint.co.uk
Bank(s): Lloyds TSB
Directors: L. Coffey (Fin), A. Coffey (MD)
Ultimate Holding Company: FULLPOINT HOLDINGS LIMITED
Immediate Holding Company: FULLPOINT LIMITED
Registration no: 02945091 **VAT No.:** 424 7744 41 **Date established:** 1994
Turnover: £500,000 - £1m **No.of Employees:** 11 - 20
Product Groups: 28, 80, 81

Date of Accounts	Aug 11	Aug 10	Aug 09
Working Capital	37	14	N/A
Fixed Assets	81	42	42
Current Assets	1m	1m	848

Fumair Ltd
Unit 21 Mead Business Centre, Hertford, SG13 7BJ
Tel: 01992-589115 **Fax:** 01992-584905
E-mail: sales@fumair.co.uk
Website: http://www.fumair.co.uk
Directors: P. Clarke (MD)
Immediate Holding Company: FUMAIR LIMITED
Registration no: 01169821 **VAT No.:** GB 336 5881 30
Date established: 1974 **Turnover:** £500,000 - £1m
No.of Employees: 1 - 10 **Product Groups:** 40, 42, 54

Date of Accounts	Sep 11	Sep 10	Sep 09
Working Capital	80	21	17
Fixed Assets	38	45	49
Current Assets	327	235	262

Gates Of Hertford
Gascoyne Way, Hertford, SG13 8EL
Tel: 01992-821000 **Fax:** 01992-822049
E-mail: enquiries@gates.co.uk
Website: http://www.gates.co.uk
Bank(s): HSBC Bank plc
Managers: M. Lowden (Chief Mgr)
Immediate Holding Company: FRANK G. GATES LTD
Registration no: 00245843 **VAT No.:** GB 246 1372 72
No.of Employees: 11 - 20 **Product Groups:** 39, 68, 72

Harris Performance Products Ltd
Unit 4 A&B Fountain Drive, Hertford, SG13 7UB
Tel: 01992-532500 **Fax:** 01992-587052
E-mail: steve.h@harris-performance.com
Website: http://www.harris-performance.com
Bank(s): National Westminster Bank Plc
Directors: S. Harris (MD)
Immediate Holding Company: HARRIS PERFORMANCE PRODUCTS LIMITED
Registration no: 01306748 **VAT No.:** GB 215 1685 78
Date established: 1977 **Turnover:** £1m - £2m **No.of Employees:** 21 - 50
Product Groups: 39, 68

Date of Accounts	Apr 11	Apr 10	Apr 09
Sales Turnover	2m	2m	3m
Pre Tax Profit/Loss	20	-66	101
Working Capital	-87	-104	-28
Fixed Assets	121	179	234
Current Assets	848	771	1m
Current Liabilities	347	241	317

Huco Dynatork
5-8 Merchant Drive, Hertford, SG13 7BL
Tel: 01992-509888 **Fax:** 01992-509890
E-mail: sales@huco.com
Website: http://www.huco.com
Bank(s): Bank of Scotland, The Mound, Edinburgh EH1 1YZ
Directors: C. Christenson (Dir)
Ultimate Holding Company: ALTRA HOLDINGS INC (USA)
Immediate Holding Company: HUCO ENGINEERING INDUSTRIES LIMITED
Registration no: 00836225 **VAT No.:** GB 751 0959 28
Date established: 1965 **Turnover:** £5m - £10m
No.of Employees: 51 - 100 **Product Groups:** 29, 30, 35, 38, 40, 45, 46, 66

Date of Accounts	Dec 11	Dec 10	Dec 09
Sales Turnover	6m	5m	4m
Pre Tax Profit/Loss	455	227	-356
Working Capital	2m	2m	2m
Fixed Assets	890	959	877
Current Assets	4m	4m	4m
Current Liabilities	128	241	175

In Case Solutions
Nevis House Rush Green, Hertford, SG13 7SD
Tel: 01920-464333 **Fax:** 020-8441 3432
E-mail: roy@incasesolutions.co.uk
Website: http://www.incasesolutions.co.uk
Bank(s): Barclays Bank
Directors: J. Galea (Ptnr)
Immediate Holding Company: IN CASE SOLUTIONS LIMITED
Registration no: 04374314 **Date established:** 2002
Turnover: Up to £250,000 **No.of Employees:** 11 - 20 **Product Groups:** 22, 25, 26, 30, 35, 38, 44, 45, 49, 66, 67

Date of Accounts	Jul 11	Jul 10	Jul 09
Sales Turnover	N/A	N/A	1m
Pre Tax Profit/Loss	N/A	N/A	19

Insight Visual Systems Ltd
1a Foxholes Avenue, Hertford, SG13 7JG
Tel: 01992-505177 **Fax:** 01992-505178
E-mail: sales@insight-visual.co.uk
Website: http://www.insight-visual.co.uk
Directors: M. Mcgill (Dir), J. McGill (Fin)
Immediate Holding Company: INSIGHT VISUAL SYSTEMS LIMITED
Registration no: 02617208 **Date established:** 1991
No.of Employees: 1 - 10 **Product Groups:** 37, 83

Date of Accounts	Mar 11	Mar 10	Mar 09
Working Capital	67	181	195
Fixed Assets	437	466	489
Current Assets	229	299	307

L D Engineering Ltd
Great Northern Works Hartham Lane, Hertford, SG14 1QW
Tel: 01992-584049 **Fax:** 01992-584927
E-mail: contracts@ldengineering.co.uk
Website: http://www.ldengineeringltd.com
Bank(s): National Westminster Bank Plc
Directors: T. Hutchison (MD)
Immediate Holding Company: L.D. ENGINEERING LIMITED
Registration no: 02367135 **VAT No.:** GB 532 2265 75
Date established: 1989 **Turnover:** £1m - £2m **No.of Employees:** 11 - 20
Product Groups: 35, 48

Date of Accounts	Apr 11	Apr 10	Apr 09
Working Capital	47	89	91
Fixed Assets	11	22	34
Current Assets	154	179	191

Ma Granite & Marble Works Ltd
Unit 6 Warrenwood Industrial Estate Stapleford, Hertford, SG14 3NU
Tel: 01992-558320 **Fax:** 01992-558970
E-mail: info@magranite.co.uk
Website: http://www.magraniteandmarble.co.uk
Directors: M. Adams (Dir)
Immediate Holding Company: M A GRANITE & MARBLE WORKS LIMITED
Registration no: 05336813 **Date established:** 2005
No.of Employees: 1 - 10 **Product Groups:** 14, 26, 33, 52, 63, 66

Date of Accounts	Jan 12	Jan 11	Jan 10
Working Capital	-30	-23	-23
Fixed Assets	30	28	31

see next page

Ma Granite & Marble Works Ltd - Cont'd

Current Assets	26	22	18
Current Liabilities	18	N/A	N/A

Mer Products Ltd
12 Centrus Mead Lane, Hertford, SG13 7GX
Tel: 01992-512698 **Fax:** 020-8401 0003
E-mail: sales@merproducts.com
Website: http://www.merproducts.com
Managers: S. Povey (Mgr)
Ultimate Holding Company: SURFACE SOLUTIONS INTERNATIONAL LIMITED
Immediate Holding Company: MER PRODUCTS LIMITED
Registration no: 06776882 **VAT No.:** GB 407 5566 45
Date established: 2008 **Turnover:** £1m - £2m **No.of Employees:** 1 - 10
Product Groups: 32, 49

Mode Lighting
Chelsing House Mead Lane, Hertford, SG13 7AW
Tel: 01992-554566 **Fax:** 01992-553644
E-mail: sales@modelighting.com
Website: http://www.modelighting.com
Directors: A. Morris (MD)
Ultimate Holding Company: TAPPENDEN & CO. LIMITED
Immediate Holding Company: MODE LIGHTING (UK) LIMITED
Registration no: 02137393 **VAT No.:** GB 214 8630 74
Date established: 1987 **Turnover:** £5m - £10m **No.of Employees:** 21 - 50
Product Groups: 37

Date of Accounts	Sep 11	Sep 10	Sep 09
Sales Turnover	7m	6m	6m
Pre Tax Profit/Loss	234	200	63
Working Capital	3m	2m	2m
Fixed Assets	150	176	207
Current Assets	4m	4m	4m
Current Liabilities	530	364	344

Neptune Engineering
2 Merchant Drive Mead Lane, Hertford, SG13 7BH
Tel: 01992-587889 **Fax:** 01992-554478
E-mail: sales@neptune-eng.demon.co.uk
Website: http://www.neptune-eng.co.uk
Directors: A. Statham (MD)
Immediate Holding Company: NEPTUNE ENGINEERING CO.LIMITED
Registration no: 00995083 **VAT No.:** GB 213 6966 57
Date established: 1970 **Turnover:** £250,000 - £500,000
No.of Employees: 1 - 10 **Product Groups:** 30, 48

Date of Accounts	Jan 12	Jan 11	Jan 10
Working Capital	5	-40	-20
Fixed Assets	101	61	42
Current Assets	148	116	37

Norbury Fencing & Building Supplies Ltd
28 Marshgate Drive, Hertford, SG13 7AJ
Tel: 01992-554327 **Fax:** 01992-505978
E-mail: steven608@btinternet.com
Website: http://www.norburyfencing.co.uk
Bank(s): Lloyds
Directors: S. Alan (MD)
Immediate Holding Company: NORBURY FENCING AND BUILDING MATERIALS LIMITED
Registration no: 02915524 **VAT No.:** GB 632 3964 36
Date established: 1994 **Turnover:** £1m - £2m **No.of Employees:** 11 - 20
Product Groups: 25

Date of Accounts	Sep 11	Sep 10	Sep 09
Working Capital	121	115	138
Fixed Assets	69	88	26
Current Assets	724	733	673

P D Models Ltd
2-3 Priory Wharf, Hertford, SG14 1RJ
Tel: 01992-550535 **Fax:** 01992-550584
E-mail: jan@pdmodels.demon.co.uk
Website: http://www.pdmodels.co.uk
Directors: P. Durbin (Prop)
Immediate Holding Company: PD MODELS LIMITED
Registration no: 05173856 **VAT No.:** GB 215 3891 65
Date established: 2004 **Turnover:** £250,000 - £500,000
No.of Employees: 1 - 10 **Product Groups:** 49

Date of Accounts	Dec 11	Dec 10	Dec 09
Working Capital	56	96	109
Fixed Assets	14	18	22
Current Assets	89	151	182

P J Pipe & Valve Co. Ltd T/A P J Valves
10 Merchant Drive Mead Lane, Hertford, SG13 7BH
Tel: 01992-587878 **Fax:** 01992-550132
E-mail: sales@pjvalves.co.uk
Website: http://www.pjvalves.co.uk
Bank(s): HSBC
Directors: J. Boddy (Co Sec), C. Gordon (Ch), C. Rosser (Mkt Research), D. Munro (Ch), D. Munro (MD), S. Parrish (Sales)
Immediate Holding Company: P.J. PIPE & VALVE CO. LIMITED
Registration no: 01271151 **VAT No.:** GB 215 0354 09
Date established: 1976 **Turnover:** £2m - £5m **No.of Employees:** 21 - 50
Product Groups: 36

Date of Accounts	Dec 10	Dec 09	Dec 08
Sales Turnover	4m	9m	N/A
Pre Tax Profit/Loss	955	2m	N/A
Working Capital	2m	2m	2m
Fixed Assets	156	161	153
Current Assets	2m	6m	5m
Current Liabilities	446	962	N/A

Period Style Lighting
Foxholes Farm London Road, Hertford, SG13 7NT
Tel: 01992-554943 **Fax:** 01992-554943
E-mail: sales@periodstylelighting.co.uk
Website: http://www.periodstylelighting.co.uk
Directors: G. Day (Dir)
No.of Employees: 1 - 10 **Product Groups:** 22, 24, 27, 30, 33, 35, 36, 37, 84

Date of Accounts	Jul 07
Working Capital	-61
Fixed Assets	68
Current Assets	19
Current Liabilities	80

Power Valves International Ltd
14 Centrus Mead Lane, Hertford, SG13 7GX
Tel: 01992-538022 **Fax:** 01992-538033
E-mail: power.valves@btconnect.com
Website: http://www.powervalvesinternational.com
Directors: L. McDonald (Fin), J. Cullip (MD)
Immediate Holding Company: POWER VALVES INTERNATIONAL LIMITED
Registration no: 04006484 **Date established:** 2000
No.of Employees: 1 - 10 **Product Groups:** 36, 37, 38

Date of Accounts	Nov 11	Nov 10	Nov 09
Working Capital	412	275	169
Fixed Assets	51	38	31
Current Assets	1m	956	808
Current Liabilities	100	N/A	N/A

Qualiturn Products Ltd
18 Merchant Drive Mead Lane, Hertford, SG13 7AY
Tel: 01992-584499 **Fax:** 01992-551726
E-mail: info@qualiturn.co.uk
Website: http://www.qualiturn.co.uk
Bank(s): National Westminster Bank Plc
Directors: B. Groom (Ch), N. Groom (MD), L. Aldridge (Co Sec), M. Groom (Co Sec)
Immediate Holding Company: QUALITURN PRODUCTS LIMITED
Registration no: 01157257 **VAT No.:** GB 214 5439 79
Date established: 1974 **Turnover:** £1m - £2m **No.of Employees:** 21 - 50
Product Groups: 35, 48

Date of Accounts	Dec 11	Dec 10	Dec 09
Working Capital	349	209	41
Fixed Assets	1m	1m	984
Current Assets	1m	841	540

Quality Assured Industrial Services Ltd
Riverside Works Chambers Street, Hertford, SG14 1PL
Tel: 01992-553363 **Fax:** 01992-553035
E-mail: sales@qaisl.co.uk
Website: http://www.qaisl.co.uk
Directors: P. Carter (Dir)
Immediate Holding Company: PRESSURE SYSTEMS INSPECTION LIMITED
Registration no: 02458239 **Date established:** 1990 **Turnover:** £2m - £5m
No.of Employees: 1 - 10 **Product Groups:** 26, 35, 38, 40

Date of Accounts	Mar 09	Mar 08	Sep 11
Working Capital	8	10	1
Current Assets	564	553	364
Current Liabilities	N/A	N/A	363

Regency Preservation
Conbar House Mead Lane, Hertford, SG13 7AP
Tel: 01992-509201 **Fax:** 01992-552277
E-mail: regencydamp@googlemail.com
Website: http://www.regencypreservation.com
Directors: S. England (Dir)
Immediate Holding Company: REGENCY PRESERVATION LIMITED
Registration no: 03147417 **Date established:** 1996
No.of Employees: 1 - 10 **Product Groups:** 25, 40, 52, 66

Round Window Media
13 Riversmeet, Hertford, SG14 1LF
Tel: 07976-388414 **Fax:** 01992-586859
E-mail: info@roundwindowmedia.com
Website: http://www.roundwindowmedia.com
Directors: D. Martin (Fin)
Immediate Holding Company: ROUND WINDOW MEDIA LTD
Registration no: 06084315 **Date established:** 2007
Turnover: Up to £250,000 **No.of Employees:** 1 - 10 **Product Groups:** 44

Date of Accounts	Feb 12	Feb 11	Feb 10
Sales Turnover	N/A	N/A	68
Working Capital	9	13	19
Current Assets	9	13	19

Rubber Consultants (MRPRA)
Brickendonbury Brickendon, Hertford, SG13 8NL
Tel: 01992-554657 **Fax:** 01992-504248
E-mail: general@tarrc.co.uk
Website: http://www.tarrc.co.uk
Bank(s): Barclays
Directors: S. Cook (MD)
Managers: D. Newton (Tech Serv Mgr), A. Green (Personnel), C. Langham, K. Lawson (Mktg Serv Mgr), Z. Bakar (Fin Mgr)
Immediate Holding Company: TUN ABDUL RAZAK RESEARCH CENTRE
Registration no: 00336256 **VAT No.:** GB 197 3292 27
Date established: 1938 **Turnover:** £2m - £5m **No.of Employees:** 51 - 100
Product Groups: 80, 81, 85

Date of Accounts	Dec 11	Dec 10	Dec 09
Sales Turnover	5m	4m	5m
Pre Tax Profit/Loss	-47	-1m	-42
Working Capital	2m	2m	3m
Fixed Assets	2m	2m	2m
Current Assets	2m	2m	3m
Current Liabilities	180	272	193

Sealine Business Products
27 Postwood Green Hertford Heath, Hertford, SG13 7QJ
Tel: 01992-558001 **Fax:** 01992-304569
E-mail: sales@sealinemediastorage.com
Website: http://www.sealinemediastorage.com
Directors: M. White (Dir)
Immediate Holding Company: SEALINE BUSINESS PRODUCTS LIMITED
Registration no: 01478559 **Date established:** 1980
No.of Employees: 1 - 10 **Product Groups:** 35, 42, 45

Date of Accounts	Dec 11	Dec 10	Dec 09
Working Capital	-50	-30	-44
Fixed Assets	14	18	22
Current Assets	4	11	31
Current Liabilities	N/A	N/A	7

Semikron UK Ltd Semikron International GmbH
9 Harforde Court John Tate Road, Hertford, SG13 7NW
Tel: 01992-584677 **Fax:** 01992-554942
E-mail: p.newman@semikron.com
Website: http://www.semikron.com
Bank(s): Midland, Fore Street
Directors: K. Peers (Fin), P. Newman (MD)
Managers: A. Triggs (Comptroller), A. Cross (Develop Mgr)
Ultimate Holding Company: SEMIKRON INTERNATIONAL DR FRITZ MARTIN GMBH (GERMANY)
Immediate Holding Company: SEMIKRON LIMITED
Registration no: 03380812 **Date established:** 1997
Turnover: £20m - £50m **No.of Employees:** 11 - 20 **Product Groups:** 37

Date of Accounts	Dec 11	Dec 10	Dec 09
Sales Turnover	27m	25m	17m
Pre Tax Profit/Loss	567	2m	833
Working Capital	2m	2m	1m
Fixed Assets	60	69	81
Current Assets	7m	11m	4m
Current Liabilities	990	2m	562

Space Labs Healthcare
1-2 Harforde Court John Tate Road, Hertford, SG13 7NW
Tel: 01992-507700 **Fax:** 01992-501213
E-mail: uksales@spacelabshealthcare.com
Website: http://www.spacelabshealthcare.com
Directors: K. Lassila (Fin), R. Lines (Fin)
Managers: S. Rayner (Personnel), D. Sexton (Tech Serv Mgr), G. Barnes (Mktg Serv Mgr), M. Barkham
Immediate Holding Company: BLEASE MEDICAL HOLDINGS LTD
Registration no: 00570647 **Turnover:** £10m - £20m
No.of Employees: 21 - 50 **Product Groups:** 31, 67

Train 4 Work Ltd
Pimlico House Gascoyne Way, Hertford, SG13 8EA
Tel: 01992-507494 **Fax:** 01992-507471
E-mail: info@train4.uk.com
Website: http://www.train4.uk.com
Directors: M. Mayhew (MD)
Immediate Holding Company: TRAIN 4 WORK LIMITED
Registration no: 06426336 **Date established:** 2007
Turnover: Up to £250,000 **No.of Employees:** 1 - 10 **Product Groups:** 86

Date of Accounts	Mar 09	Sep 10
Working Capital	-18	8
Fixed Assets	17	9
Current Assets	129	92

Hitchin

A S M Engineering Ltd
74 Wilbury Way, Hitchin, SG4 0TP
Tel: 01462-477360 **Fax:** 01582-454772
E-mail: office@asmeng.co.uk
Website: http://www.asmeng.co.uk
Bank(s): National Westminster Bank Plc
Directors: A. McKenna (Fin), R. Head (MD)
Managers: S. Patel (Mktg Serv Mgr)
Immediate Holding Company: A.S.M. ENGINEERING LIMITED
Registration no: 01522080 **VAT No.:** GB 341 4402 96
Date established: 1980 **Turnover:** £2m - £5m **No.of Employees:** 21 - 50
Product Groups: 52

Date of Accounts	Mar 11	Mar 10	Mar 09
Sales Turnover	12m	11m	15m
Pre Tax Profit/Loss	247	594	2m
Working Capital	797	617	2m
Fixed Assets	272	252	297
Current Assets	3m	3m	5m
Current Liabilities	505	517	1m

Access Academy
32 Bucklersbury, Hitchin, SG5 1BG
Tel: 01462-433221 **Fax:** 05600-750095
E-mail: sales@accessacademy.co.uk
Website: http://www.accessacademy.co.uk
Directors: C. Greenchild (MD)
Immediate Holding Company: ACCESSACADEMY LIMITED
Registration no: 04737179 **Date established:** 2003
No.of Employees: 1 - 10 **Product Groups:** 86

Date of Accounts	Dec 09	Dec 08	Dec 07
Working Capital	-27	-129	-98
Fixed Assets	25	41	43
Current Assets	164	76	27

BEKA Associates Ltd
Old Charlton Road, Hitchin, SG5 2DA
Tel: 01462-438301 **Fax:** 01462-453971
E-mail: accounts@beka.co.uk
Website: http://www.beka.co.uk
Bank(s): National Westminster Bank Plc
Directors: B. Brough (MD), B. Brough (Dir), D. Turner (Sales)
Managers: A. Clarke (Tech Serv Mgr), M. Revell (Purch Mgr), S. Hammond (Mgr)
Immediate Holding Company: BEKA ASSOCIATES LIMITED
Registration no: 01847014 **VAT No.:** GB 396 7959 64
Date established: 1984 **Turnover:** £2m - £5m **No.of Employees:** 21 - 50
Product Groups: 37, 38, 40, 49

Date of Accounts	May 12	May 11	May 10
Working Capital	4m	3m	3m
Fixed Assets	322	366	304
Current Assets	4m	4m	4m

Belmont Engineering Co. Ltd
Unit 2 Bilton Road, Hitchin, SG4 0SB
Tel: 01462-451497 **Fax:** 01462-451688
E-mail: mail@belmont-engineering.com
Website: http://www.belmont-engineering.com
Bank(s): National Westminster
Directors: A. Nash (MD)
Registration no: 02486532 **VAT No.:** GB 197 3764 12
Date established: 1990 **Turnover:** £500,000 - £1m
No.of Employees: 11 - 20 **Product Groups:** 35, 42, 46, 47, 48, 85

Date of Accounts	Mar 08	Mar 07	Mar 06
Working Capital	-38	-14	-41
Fixed Assets	530	450	480
Current Assets	327	319	209
Current Liabilities	365	333	250
Total Share Capital	10	10	10

Jas Bowman & Sons Ltd
Arlesey Road Ickleford, Hitchin, SG5 3UN
Tel: 01462-422722 **Fax:** 01462-420897
E-mail: rorybowman@bowmaningredients.co.uk
Website: http://www.bowmaningredients.co.uk
Bank(s): Barclays

Directors: M. Isaacson (Comm), S. Fox (Fin)
Managers: R. Bowman
Immediate Holding Company: JAS BOWMAN & SONS LIMITED
Registration no: 00189717 **VAT No.:** GB 335 1407 84
Date established: 2023 **Turnover:** £50m - £75m
No.of Employees: 101 - 250 **Product Groups:** 20

Date of Accounts	Apr 08	Apr 09	May 10
Sales Turnover	49m	63m	62m
Pre Tax Profit/Loss	804	2m	4m
Working Capital	4m	4m	6m
Fixed Assets	13m	16m	16m
Current Assets	14m	14m	15m
Current Liabilities	2m	2m	1m

C2 RF Solutions

C2 Knowl Piece Wilbury Way, Hitchin, SG4 0TY
Tel: 01462-423449 **Fax:** 01462-423552
Website: http://www.c2rf.com
Directors: D. Patrick (Prop)
No.of Employees: 1 - 10 **Product Groups:** 37, 84

Chenery Funeral Services Ltd

44 Bedford Road, Hitchin, SG5 2TY
Tel: 01462-434375 **Fax:** 01462-459025
E-mail: dawncavanagh@cheneryfunerals.co.uk
Website: http://www.cheneryfunerals.co.uk
Directors: D. Cavanagh (Dir)
Immediate Holding Company: CHENERY FUNERAL SERVICES LIMITED
Registration no: 00276803 **Date established:** 1933
Turnover: Up to £250,000 **No.of Employees:** 1 - 10 **Product Groups:** 35, 39, 45

Date of Accounts	May 11	May 10	May 09
Sales Turnover	222	238	215
Working Capital	-31	-33	-35
Fixed Assets	31	33	35
Current Assets	70	64	142
Current Liabilities	15	12	9

Constant Power Services Ltd

Unit 3 Trust Industrial Estate, Hitchin, SG4 0UZ
Tel: 01462-422955 **Fax:** 01462-422754
E-mail: info@constantpowerservices.com
Website: http://www.constantpowerservices.com
Bank(s): National Westminster
Managers: S. Penhall, M. Pearce (Sales & Mktg Mg), C. Dewhurst
Ultimate Holding Company: RIELLO ELETTRONICA SPA (ITALY)
Immediate Holding Company: CONSTANT POWER SERVICES LIMITED
Registration no: 05893658 **VAT No.:** GB 491 3830 37
Date established: 2006 **Turnover:** £5m - £10m **No.of Employees:** 21 - 50
Product Groups: 37, 44, 67

Date of Accounts	Dec 11	Dec 10	Dec 09
Working Capital	931	341	10
Fixed Assets	3m	3m	4m
Current Assets	3m	2m	3m

Custom Antenna Systems Ltd

10-12 Wallace Way, Hitchin, SG4 0SE
Tel: 01462-454331 **Fax:** 01462-423484
E-mail: admin@custom-antennas.co.uk
Website: http://www.custom-antennas.co.uk
Bank(s): National Westminster Bank Plc
Directors: K. Debenish (Fin)
Immediate Holding Company: CUSTOM ANTENNA SYSTEMS LIMITED
Registration no: 03533954 **VAT No.:** GB 504 6323 76
Date established: 1998 **Turnover:** £500,000 - £1m
No.of Employees: 21 - 50 **Product Groups:** 35, 37, 84

Date of Accounts	Mar 11	Mar 10	Mar 09
Working Capital	859	645	597
Fixed Assets	238	216	84
Current Assets	1m	1m	914

Danfood Technology Ltd

6 Enterprise Park Kimpton, Hitchin, SG4 8HP
Tel: 01438-833000 **Fax:** 01438-833030
E-mail: sales@danfood.co.uk
Website: http://www.danfood.co.uk
Directors: F. Muller (Dir)
Immediate Holding Company: DANFOOD TECHNOLOGY LIMITED
Registration no: 02760283 **Date established:** 1992
No.of Employees: 1 - 10 **Product Groups:** 20, 40, 41

Date of Accounts	Dec 11	Dec 10	Dec 09
Working Capital	407	393	361
Fixed Assets	8	9	10
Current Assets	778	639	721

Dapro Ltd

Wilbury Meadows Wilbury Way, Hitchin, SG4 0TY
Tel: 01462-432021
E-mail: daprosonics@talktalk.net
Directors: D. Allen (MD), M. Allen (Fin)
Immediate Holding Company: DAPRO LIMITED
Registration no: 01636122 **Date established:** 1982
Turnover: Up to £250,000 **No.of Employees:** 1 - 10 **Product Groups:** 48

Date of Accounts	Mar 11	Mar 10	Mar 09
Sales Turnover	19	17	19
Pre Tax Profit/Loss	6	6	7
Working Capital	-1	-0	1
Fixed Assets	8	N/A	N/A
Current Assets	5	3	5
Current Liabilities	4	3	4

Dowding & Mills Engineering Services Ltd

60 Wilbury Way, Hitchin, SG4 0TA
Tel: 01462-421234 **Fax:** 01462-420012
E-mail: calibration.hitchin@dowdingandmills.com
Website: http://www.dowdingandmills.com
Bank(s): HSBC, Birmingham
Directors: B. Epton (Mkt Research), G. Hartley (MD)
Managers: B. Epton (Sales Prom Mgr), M. Hume (Chief Mgr), K. Ward (Chief Mgr), K. Wards (District Mgr)
Ultimate Holding Company: Castle Support Services plc
Immediate Holding Company: Dowding & Mills plc
Registration no: SC028056 **VAT No.:** GB 109 5683 53
Date established: 1976 **Turnover:** £5m - £10m **No.of Employees:** 21 - 50
Product Groups: 44, 48, 85

Exposure TV

Date Centre Cooks Way, Hitchin, SG4 0JE
Tel: 08456-121123
E-mail: jon@exposuretv.com
Website: http://www.exposuretv.com
Directors: J. Harwood (Dir)
Immediate Holding Company: Exposure Tv Ltd
Registration no: 05320492 **Date established:** 2004
No.of Employees: 1 - 10 **Product Groups:** 37, 81, 83

Ferex Ltd

Unit 22 Cam Centre Wilbury Way, Hitchin, SG4 0TW
Tel: 01462-420666 **Fax:** 01462-420779
E-mail: sales@euraqua.co.uk
Website: http://www.euraqua.co.uk
Bank(s): Barclays
Managers: A. Moorlidge (Chief Mgr)
Immediate Holding Company: FEREX LIMITED
Registration no: 01834894 **VAT No.:** GB 396 2660 19
Date established: 1984 **Turnover:** £2m - £5m **No.of Employees:** 11 - 20
Product Groups: 32, 42, 54

Date of Accounts	Dec 11	Dec 10	Dec 09
Working Capital	552	530	516
Fixed Assets	14	20	29
Current Assets	945	886	903

Fire Fighting Enterprises

9 Hunting Gate, Hitchin, SG4 0TJ
Tel: 01462-444740 **Fax:** 0845-402 4201
E-mail: info@ffeuk.com
Website: http://www.ffeuk.com
Bank(s): Bank of Scotland
Directors: I. Steel (MD), D. Smoley (Fin)
Managers: J. O'Connell (Purch Mgr), T. Kirk
Ultimate Holding Company: HALMA PUBLIC LIMITED COMPANY
Immediate Holding Company: FIRE FIGHTING ENTERPRISES LIMITED
Registration no: 01192710 **VAT No.:** GB 700 1840 89
Date established: 1974 **Turnover:** £5m - £10m **No.of Employees:** 21 - 50
Product Groups: 40

Date of Accounts	Mar 12	Mar 09	Apr 10
Sales Turnover	9m	7m	7m
Pre Tax Profit/Loss	3m	2m	2m
Working Capital	2m	1m	2m
Fixed Assets	2m	2m	1m
Current Assets	4m	3m	4m
Current Liabilities	498	448	821

H R J Law

7-8 Portmill Lane, Hitchin, SG5 1AS
Tel: 01462-628888 **Fax:** 01462-631233
E-mail: enquiries@hrjlaw.co.uk
Website: http://www.hrjlaw.co.uk
Bank(s): National Westminster Bank Plc
Directors: G. Kennedy (Dir)
Managers: D. Howard, C. Alderson, D. Small
Immediate Holding Company: HRJ LAW LLP
Registration no: OC338662 **VAT No.:** GB 196 4597 06
Date established: 2008 **Turnover:** £1m - £2m **No.of Employees:** 21 - 50
Product Groups: 80

Date of Accounts	Mar 11	Mar 10
Working Capital	282	359
Fixed Assets	89	144
Current Assets	882	895

Hermitage Sheet Metal Ltd

25 Knowl Piece Wilbury Way, Hitchin, SG4 0TY
Tel: 01462-422421 **Fax:** 01462-422026
E-mail: info@hermitagesm.co.uk
Website: http://www.hermitagesm.co.uk
Bank(s): HSBC
Directors: D. Spencer (MD), L. Spencer (Co Sec)
Immediate Holding Company: HERMITAGE S.M.LIMITED
Registration no: 01033757 **Date established:** 1971 **Turnover:** £1m - £2m
No.of Employees: 11 - 20 **Product Groups:** 48

Date of Accounts	Dec 11	Dec 10	Dec 09
Working Capital	-120	-92	-60
Fixed Assets	291	292	294
Current Assets	66	92	85

Hunting Gate Developments Ltd

2 Hunting Gate, Hitchin, SG4 0TJ
Tel: 01462-434444 **Fax:** 01462-435905
E-mail: rtimlett@hunting-gate.co.uk
Website: http://www.hunting-gate.co.uk
Managers: R. Timlett (Sales Admin)
Ultimate Holding Company: HUNTING GATE GROUP LIMITED
Immediate Holding Company: HUNTING GATE DEVELOPMENTS LIMITED
Registration no: 01167451 **VAT No.:** GB 197 9040 24
Date established: 1974 **Turnover:** Up to £250,000
No.of Employees: 1 - 10 **Product Groups:** 80

Date of Accounts	Dec 11	Dec 10	Dec 09
Sales Turnover	1	N/A	N/A
Pre Tax Profit/Loss	-135	-50	32
Working Capital	1m	1m	1m
Current Assets	1m	1m	1m
Current Liabilities	29	26	28

Insoll Components Ltd

39 Wilbury Way, Hitchin, SG4 0TW
Tel: 01462-450741 **Fax:** 01462-421162
E-mail: sales@insoll.com
Website: http://www.insoll.com
Bank(s): HSBC
Directors: M. Fryer (MD), R. Stark (MD)
Managers: B. Travis (Mktg Serv Mgr)
Immediate Holding Company: INSOLL COMPONENTS LIMITED
Registration no: 03508514 **Date established:** 1998 **Turnover:** £1m - £2m
No.of Employees: 21 - 50 **Product Groups:** 30, 84

Date of Accounts	Nov 11	Nov 10	Nov 09
Working Capital	335	228	151
Fixed Assets	269	205	190
Current Assets	710	526	366

Intelligent Comfort Group Ltd

Suite 3-4a Bancroft Business Centre 35 Bancroft, Hitchin, SG5 1LA
Tel: 01462-435700 **Fax:** 01462-435444
E-mail: sales@icglimited.co.uk
Website: http://www.icglimited.co.uk
Directors: M. Pike (Chief Op Offcr)
Immediate Holding Company: INTELLIGENT COMFORT GROUP LIMITED
Registration no: 05297087 **Date established:** 2004
No.of Employees: 1 - 10 **Product Groups:** 40, 66

Date of Accounts	Mar 11	Mar 10	Mar 09
Working Capital	596	633	498
Fixed Assets	20	19	18
Current Assets	2m	2m	3m

Intra Ltd

27 Wilbury Way, Hitchin, SG4 0TS
Tel: 01462-424800 **Fax:** 01462-453667
E-mail: info@intra-corp.co.uk
Website: http://www.intra-corp.co.uk
Bank(s): Lloyds TSB Bank plc
Directors: B. Grabinski (Dir)
Managers: A. Cornish, M. Foster
Immediate Holding Company: INTRA LIMITED
Registration no: 05264494 **VAT No.:** GB 211 6864 77
Date established: 2004 **Turnover:** £5m - £10m **No.of Employees:** 21 - 50
Product Groups: 37, 38, 44, 46, 67, 84

Date of Accounts	Dec 11	Jan 11	Jan 10
Sales Turnover	8m	6m	7m
Pre Tax Profit/Loss	614	26	-28
Working Capital	2m	2m	2m
Fixed Assets	21	7	15
Current Assets	5m	3m	3m
Current Liabilities	998	1m	971

D Jenkins Photography Ltd

158 High Street Codicote, Hitchin, SG4 8UB
Tel: 01438-820530
E-mail: djenkins@ndirect.co.uk
Website: http://www.dj-photo.com
Directors: H. Jenkins (Fin), D. Jenkins (MD)
Immediate Holding Company: D JENKINS PHOTOGRAPHY LIMITED
Registration no: 04654562 **Date established:** 2003
No.of Employees: 1 - 10 **Product Groups:** 81

Date of Accounts	Feb 12	Feb 08	Feb 11
Working Capital	22	-0	6
Fixed Assets	21	11	18
Current Assets	48	26	28

Koolway Auto Air Conditioning

45 Bury Mead Road, Hitchin, SG5 1RX
Tel: 01462-453640 **Fax:** 01462-422661
Website: http://www.koolway-aircon.co.uk
Directors: M. Huthwaite (Prop)
Immediate Holding Company: WILMOND LIMITED
VAT No.: GB 197 5846 00 **Date established:** 2002
Turnover: £500,000 - £1m **No.of Employees:** 1 - 10 **Product Groups:** 39, 40

Date of Accounts	Aug 11	Aug 10	Aug 08
Working Capital	-75	-62	-52
Fixed Assets	227	227	228
Current Assets	16	8	7
Current Liabilities	23	N/A	23

Kopak Rubber & Plastics Ltd (Head Office)

Unit 19 The Cam Centre, Hitchin, SG4 0TW
Tel: 01462-452487 **Fax:** 01462-452249
E-mail: peter.estwick@kopak.co.uk
Website: http://www.kopak.co.uk
Directors: P. Estwick (Dir)
Immediate Holding Company: KOPAK RUBBER AND PLASTICS LIMITED
Registration no: 04377411 **Date established:** 2002 **Turnover:** £1m - £2m
No.of Employees: 1 - 10 **Product Groups:** 29, 63

Date of Accounts	Apr 11	Apr 10	Apr 09
Working Capital	84	11	-36
Fixed Assets	267	327	250
Current Assets	338	130	33

M S Air Movement

Unit 2a Hexton Manor Stables Hexton, Hitchin, SG5 3JH
Tel: 01582-883662 **Fax:** 01582-881009
E-mail: info@msairmovement.co.uk
Website: http://www.msairmovement.co.uk
Directors: B. Rennie (Prop)
Immediate Holding Company: M.S. AIR MOVEMENT LIMITED
Registration no: 05912890 **Date established:** 2006
No.of Employees: 1 - 10 **Product Groups:** 52

Date of Accounts	Aug 11	Aug 10	Aug 09
Working Capital	-0	-1	-0
Fixed Assets	1	1	N/A
Current Assets	72	108	51

Manufacturing Support & Design Ltd

25a Knowl Piece Wilbury Way, Hitchin, SG4 0TY
Tel: 01462-421400 **Fax:** 01462-423300
Website: http://www.msd-ltd.org
Directors: G. Bardell (Sales), M. Godbold (MD)
Immediate Holding Company: MANUFACTURING SUPPORT AND DESIGN LIMITED
Registration no: 03930035 **Date established:** 2000
No.of Employees: 1 - 10 **Product Groups:** 45

Date of Accounts	Mar 11	Mar 10	Mar 09
Working Capital	208	147	160
Fixed Assets	8	5	6
Current Assets	314	193	225

Marcon Diamond Products Ltd

Marcon House 131 High Street, Codicote, Hitchin, SG4 8UB
Tel: 01438-820581 **Fax:** 01438-821352
Directors: L. Peake (Dir)
Immediate Holding Company: MARCON DIAMOND PRODUCTS LIMITED
Registration no: 01799190 **VAT No.:** GB 396 8845 74
Date established: 1984 **Turnover:** £500,000 - £1m
No.of Employees: 1 - 10 **Product Groups:** 33, 36

Date of Accounts	Mar 11	Mar 10	Mar 09
Working Capital	66	69	81
Fixed Assets	114	114	115
Current Assets	126	124	123

Planet Furniture

The Crocodile House 9 Bridge Street, Hitchin, SG5 2DE
Tel: 01462-452233 **Fax:** 01462-452200
E-mail: info@planetfurniture.co.uk
Website: http://www.planetfurniture.co.uk
Directors: R. Milligan (Dir)
Immediate Holding Company: PLANET FURNITURE LTD
Registration no: 04489009 **Date established:** 2002
No.of Employees: 1 - 10 **Product Groups:** 26, 36, 67

Plasmech Packaging Ltd

Unit 27 Cam Centre Wilbury Way, Hitchin, SG4 0TW
Tel: 01462-432525 **Fax:** 01462-432124
E-mail: keith@wirelesslans.co.uk
Website: http://www.plasmechpackaging.co.uk
Bank(s): HSBC Bank plc
Directors: K. Bartlett (MD), K. Emmerson (Fin)
Immediate Holding Company: PLASMECH PACKAGING LIMITED
Registration no: 03458871 **VAT No.:** GB 440 7923 51
Date established: 1997 **Turnover:** £1m - £2m **No.of Employees:** 11 - 20
Product Groups: 30, 66

Date of Accounts	Mar 12	Mar 11	Mar 10
Working Capital	1m	1m	778
Fixed Assets	169	201	213
Current Assets	2m	2m	1m

Plasmoulds Ltd

44 Wilbury Way, Hitchin, SG4 0UB
Tel: 01462-456441 **Fax:** 01462-420904
E-mail: sales@plasmoulds.com
Website: http://www.plasmoulds.com
Bank(s): Lloyds TSB Bank plc
Directors: B. Underwood (Dir)
Managers: E. Barton (Chief Acct)
Immediate Holding Company: PLASMOULDS LIMITED
Registration no: 00415868 **Date established:** 1946 **Turnover:** £2m - £5m
No.of Employees: 11 - 20 **Product Groups:** 34, 35, 44, 47, 48

Date of Accounts	Aug 11	Aug 10	Aug 09
Working Capital	123	118	124
Fixed Assets	505	519	534
Current Assets	724	723	613

Prism Protection

28 Church Street, Hitchin, SG5 3LH
Tel: 01462-712899 **Fax:** 01462-712889
E-mail: enquiries@prism-protection.co.uk
Website: http://www.prism-protection.co.uk
Product Groups: 30, 33, 35, 36, 66

Promain UK Ltd

Unit 1 North Road Bury Mead Road, Hitchin, SG5 1RT
Tel: 0845-890 3434 **Fax:** 01464-421337
E-mail: info@promain.co.uk
Website: http://www.promain.co.uk
Directors: C. Barry (Co Sec)
Immediate Holding Company: PROMAIN (UK) LIMITED
Registration no: 05271223 **Date established:** 2004
No.of Employees: 1 - 10 **Product Groups:** 30, 31, 48

Date of Accounts	Oct 11	Oct 10	Oct 09
Working Capital	127	75	60
Fixed Assets	45	68	49
Current Assets	294	233	205

Publicity Plastics Ltd

73a High Street Stotfold, Hitchin, SG5 4LD
Tel: 01462-733939 **Fax:** 01462-733929
Website: http://www.publicity-plastics.com
Directors: A. Mahoney (Dir), B. Cobb (MD)
Immediate Holding Company: PUBLICITY PLASTICS LIMITED
Registration no: 06601477 **Date established:** 2008
Turnover: Up to £250,000 **No.of Employees:** 1 - 10 **Product Groups:** 22, 30, 32, 44

Date of Accounts	May 11	May 10	May 09
Working Capital	-89	-88	-59
Fixed Assets	12	21	19
Current Assets	71	81	44
Current Liabilities	56	N/A	N/A

Quinata Ltd

26 High Street Graveley, Hitchin, SG4 7LA
Tel: 01438-361547 **Fax:** 01438-362058
E-mail: info@quinata.co.uk
Website: http://www.quinata.co.uk
Directors: S. Jarvis (MD)
Immediate Holding Company: QUINATA LIMITED
Registration no: 04455651 **Date established:** 2002
No.of Employees: 1 - 10 **Product Groups:** 44, 81

Date of Accounts	Jun 11	Jun 10	Jun 05
Working Capital	-68	-41	-18
Fixed Assets	1	N/A	1
Current Assets	12	4	5

R & A Coatings Ltd

Unit 24-25 Wilbury Way, Hitchin, SG4 0TW
Tel: 01462-636123 **Fax:** 01462-636234
Directors: R. Essence (MD)
Immediate Holding Company: R & A COATING LIMITED
Registration no: 03112099 **Date established:** 1995
No.of Employees: 1 - 10 **Product Groups:** 46, 48

Date of Accounts	Nov 11	Nov 10	Nov 09
Working Capital	-24	-4	-43
Fixed Assets	119	126	132
Current Assets	36	44	26

William Ransom plc

51 Bury Mead Road, Hitchin, SG5 1RT
Tel: 01462-437615 **Fax:** 01462-420528
E-mail: iharrison@williamransom.com
Website: http://www.williamransom.com
Bank(s): Barclays
Directors: M. Bath (Sales), R. Howard (Fin), T. Dye (Grp Chief Exec), I. Harrison (Grp Chief Exec)
Managers: K. Dorsett (Personnel), M. Lightowl (Mktg Serv Mgr), R. Babb (I.T. Exec), S. Sowerby (Chief Mgr)
Immediate Holding Company: WILLIAM RANSOM & SON HOLDINGS PLC
Registration no: 00126138 **VAT No.:** GB 196 3363 36
Date established: 2010 **Turnover:** £20m - £50m
No.of Employees: 21 - 50 **Product Groups:** 31

Regal Sterling Blinds

Unit 14 Churchgate Hitchin Market, Hitchin, SG5 1DN
Tel: 01438-238650
E-mail: sales@regalsterling.com
Website: http://www.regalsterling.com
Directors: G. Simpson (Dir)
No.of Employees: 1 - 10 **Product Groups:** 24, 63, 66

Robric Engineering Ltd

Baldock Road Stotfold, Hitchin, SG5 4NZ
Tel: 01462-732143 **Fax:** 01462-735273
Directors: R. Goodman (Dir)
Immediate Holding Company: ROBRIC ENGINEERING LIMITED
Registration no: 05027071 **Date established:** 2004
Turnover: Up to £250,000 **No.of Employees:** 1 - 10 **Product Groups:** 48

Date of Accounts	Jan 12	Jan 11	Jan 10
Working Capital	-30	-40	-41
Fixed Assets	60	60	60
Current Assets	39	23	27

Rococo Style Ltd

80-81 Walsworth Road, Hitchin, SG4 9SX
Tel: 01462-435393 **Fax:** 01462-452773
E-mail: des.rococo@virgin.net
Website: http://rococostyleschoolwear.co.uk
Directors: D. Robinson (Dir)
Immediate Holding Company: ROCOCO STYLE LIMITED
Registration no: 02819704 **Date established:** 1993 **Turnover:** £2m - £5m
No.of Employees: 1 - 10 **Product Groups:** 24

Date of Accounts	May 12	May 11	May 10
Working Capital	76	63	56
Fixed Assets	1	1	N/A
Current Assets	136	118	109

Royde & Tucker Ltd

Unit 6 Bilton Road Cadwell Lane, Hitchin, SG4 0SB
Tel: 01462-444444 **Fax:** 01462-444433
E-mail: sales@ratman.co.uk
Website: http://www.ratman.co.uk
Directors: S. Gardiner (Sales), S. Jenkins (Dir)
Managers: D. Whitehead (Purch Mgr), R. Hughes (Personnel)
Ultimate Holding Company: ROYDE & TUCKER HOLDINGS LIMITED
Immediate Holding Company: ROYDE & TUCKER LIMITED
Registration no: 00531276 **Date established:** 1954 **Turnover:** £5m - £10m
No.of Employees: 21 - 50 **Product Groups:** 30, 36, 38

Date of Accounts	Mar 12	Mar 11	Mar 10
Sales Turnover	5m	5m	6m
Pre Tax Profit/Loss	180	43	1m
Working Capital	2m	2m	2m
Fixed Assets	1m	1m	1m
Current Assets	3m	3m	3m
Current Liabilities	383	297	582

Seneca Services Ltd

Royal Oak Lane Pirton, Hitchin, SG5 3QT
Tel: 01462-711174 **Fax:** 08717-128683
E-mail: info@seneca-services.co.uk
Website: http://www.seneca-services.co.uk
Directors: F. Turner (Dir)
Immediate Holding Company: SENECA SERVICES LIMITED
Registration no: 05178898 **Date established:** 2004
Turnover: Up to £250,000 **No.of Employees:** 1 - 10 **Product Groups:** 80

Date of Accounts	Jul 11	Jul 10	Jul 09
Working Capital	-3	16	13
Fixed Assets	4	5	7
Current Assets	37	24	23
Current Liabilities	41	N/A	N/A

Sewerin Ltd

Walsworth Road, Hitchin, SG4 9SP
Tel: 01462-634363
E-mail: info@sewerin.co.uk
Website: http://www.sewerin.co.uk
Directors: G. Martin (Dir)
Immediate Holding Company: SEWERIN LIMITED
Registration no: 05698627 **Date established:** 2006
No.of Employees: 1 - 10 **Product Groups:** 38, 52

Date of Accounts	Dec 11	Dec 10	Dec 09
Working Capital	221	35	-6
Current Assets	588	256	160

Stevenage Machine Tools Ltd

Unit 12 Ironcroft Industrial Estate 18 Baldock Road, Stotfold, Hitchin, SG5 4NZ
Tel: 01462-731691 **Fax:** 01462-835214
Directors: D. Fenner (MD)
Immediate Holding Company: STEVENAGE MACHINE TOOLS LIMITED
Registration no: 00490021 **Date established:** 1950
Turnover: £500,000 - £1m **No.of Employees:** 1 - 10 **Product Groups:** 66

Date of Accounts	Mar 11	Mar 10	Mar 09
Working Capital	29	31	69
Fixed Assets	3	3	4
Current Assets	122	127	191

Stringer & Co. (Scales) Ltd

Unit 5 Kimpton Enterprise Park Claggy Road, Kimpton, Hitchin, SG4 8HP
Tel: 01438-832052 **Fax:** 01438-833614
E-mail: info@stringerscales.co.uk
Website: http://www.stringerscales.co.uk
Directors: G. Stringer (MD)
No.of Employees: 1 - 10 **Product Groups:** 38, 42

Date of Accounts	Dec 07	Dec 06	Dec 05
Sales Turnover	899	913	933
Pre Tax Profit/Loss	71	30	56
Working Capital	476	468	452
Fixed Assets	261	488	136
Current Assets	650	600	622
Current Liabilities	174	132	171
Total Share Capital	19	29	29
ROCE% (Return on Capital Employed)	9.7	3.1	9.6
ROT% (Return on Turnover)	7.9	3.2	6.0

Systemware Europe Ltd

Unit 2-5 A R C Progress Mill Lane, Stotfold, Hitchin, SG5 4NY
Tel: 01462-734777 **Fax:** 01462-734777
E-mail: enquiries@sysware-europe.com
Website: http://www.sysware-europe.com
Directors: K. Hughs (Fin), L. Matthews (Dir)
Immediate Holding Company: SYSTEMWARE EUROPE LIMITED
Registration no: 03916672 **Date established:** 2000 **Turnover:** £1m - £2m
No.of Employees: 1 - 10 **Product Groups:** 37, 38, 39, 84

Date of Accounts	Dec 11	Dec 10	Dec 09
Sales Turnover	N/A	2m	1m
Pre Tax Profit/Loss	N/A	91	-66
Working Capital	417	452	403
Fixed Assets	2	8	11
Current Assets	654	730	795
Current Liabilities	N/A	53	112

T T M Consultancy Services Ltd

The Foundry St Ippolyts, Hitchin, SG4 7NX
Tel: 01438-750085 **Fax:** 01462-422282
E-mail: traffic@ttm-ltd.co.uk
Website: http://www.ttm-ltd.co.uk
Managers: T. Reid (Mgr)
Immediate Holding Company: TTM CONSULTANCY SERVICES LIMITED
Registration no: 03451626 **VAT No.:** GB 704 2899 27
Date established: 1997 **Turnover:** £250,000 - £500,000
No.of Employees: 1 - 10 **Product Groups:** 39, 40

Date of Accounts	Oct 11	Oct 10	Oct 09
Working Capital	64	86	119
Fixed Assets	24	30	30
Current Assets	131	131	162

Test Solutions Ltd

58 Wilbury Way, Hitchin, SG4 0TP
Tel: 0845-8696200 **Fax:** 0845-8690915
E-mail: sales@testsolutions.biz
Website: http://www.testsolutions.biz
Bank(s): Bank of Scotland
Directors: M. El Faham (Dir), M. El-Faham (Fin), R. West (Dir), T. Lyons (Tech Serv)
Managers: S. Yeomans (Sales Off Mgr)
Immediate Holding Company: T.S.L. Holdings Ltd
Registration no: 02026990 **VAT No.:** 641 6631 47 **Date established:** 1986
Turnover: £2m - £5m **No.of Employees:** 11 - 20 **Product Groups:** 38, 44, 84

Date of Accounts	Dec 07	Dec 06
Sales Turnover	2307	2323
Pre Tax Profit/Loss	71	-77
Working Capital	-285	-341
Fixed Assets	513	461
Current Assets	462	241
Current Liabilities	747	583
Total Share Capital	381	381
ROCE% (Return on Capital Employed)	31.3	-63.9
ROT% (Return on Turnover)	3.1	-3.3

Thomas Brooker & Sons Ltd

Unit 7 Bilton Road, Hitchin, SG4 0SB
Tel: 01462-434501 **Fax:** 01462-421803
E-mail: industrial@tbrooker.co.uk
Website: http://www.tbrooker.co.uk
Bank(s): National Westminster
Directors: A. Brooker (MD), D. Brooker (Sales & Mktg)
Managers: I. Tweed (Ops Mgr), L. Cooke
Immediate Holding Company: THOMAS BROOKER & SONS LIMITED
Registration no: 00101749 **VAT No.:** GB 196 2292 38
Date established: 2009 **Turnover:** £2m - £5m **No.of Employees:** 51 - 100
Product Groups: 66

Date of Accounts	Sep 11	Sep 10	Sep 09
Sales Turnover	4m	5m	5m
Pre Tax Profit/Loss	11	-117	92
Working Capital	2m	2m	2m
Fixed Assets	7m	7m	7m
Current Assets	2m	2m	2m
Current Liabilities	154	107	136

Timberworks UK Ltd

Priors End Priors Hill, Pirton, Hitchin, SG5 3QA
Tel: 01462-713682 **Fax:** 01462-713682
E-mail: info@timberworksuk.com
Website: http://www.timberworksuk.com
Directors: R. Graham (Fin)
Immediate Holding Company: TIMBERWORKS UK LTD
Registration no: 06485691 **Date established:** 2008
No.of Employees: 1 - 10 **Product Groups:** 52

Date of Accounts	Jun 11	Jun 10	Jun 09
Working Capital	-1	31	3
Fixed Assets	20	8	8
Current Assets	36	33	10

United Paper Products Ltd

Unit 7 -11 Bury Mead Road, Hitchin, SG5 1RT
Tel: 01462-456001 **Fax:** 01462-456005
E-mail: yildirim@unitedpaperproducts.co.uk
Website: http://www.unitedpaperproducts.co.uk
Directors: A. Gondas (Fin), K. Gondas (MD)
Managers: G. SHAHID (Sales Prom Mgr)
Immediate Holding Company: UNITED PAPER PRODUCTS LIMITED
Registration no: 04344285 **Date established:** 2001 **Turnover:** £1m - £2m
No.of Employees: 21 - 50 **Product Groups:** 66

Date of Accounts	Dec 10	Dec 09	Dec 08
Working Capital	531	345	157
Fixed Assets	219	274	258
Current Assets	985	857	723

Valeport Services Ltd

12a Arlesey Road Stotfold Stotfold, Hitchin, SG5 4HA
Tel: 01462-735359
E-mail: info@valeportservices.com
Website: http://www.valeportservices.com
Directors: A. Thaker (Fin), A. Thaker (MD)
Immediate Holding Company: VALEPORT (SERVICES) LIMITED
Registration no: 04688365 **Date established:** 2003
Turnover: Up to £250,000 **No.of Employees:** 1 - 10 **Product Groups:** 46

Date of Accounts	Mar 12	Mar 11	Mar 10
Sales Turnover	30	27	36
Pre Tax Profit/Loss	1	-2	-0
Working Capital	3	5	9
Fixed Assets	17	18	20
Current Assets	16	20	19
Current Liabilities	1	1	1

Viking Johnson

46-48 Wilbury Way, Hitchin, SG4 0UD
Tel: 01462-443322 **Fax:** 01462-443311
E-mail: sales@vikingjohnson.com
Website: http://www.vikingjohnson.com
Directors: M. Hopes (Mkt Research), T. Feeney (Dir), T. Seeney (Dir)
Managers: L. Collen, M. Sanders (Tech Serv Mgr), M. Comley (Purch Mgr)
Ultimate Holding Company: A CRANE CO. COMPANY
Registration no: 00098677 **Turnover:** £2m - £5m
No.of Employees: 251 - 500 **Product Groups:** 33, 36

Welwyn Machinery Ltd
116 High Street Kimpton, Hitchin, SG4 8QP
Tel: 01438-832123 **Fax:** 01438-833792
E-mail: eck@which.net
Directors: M. Bode (Fin), H. Eck (MD)
Immediate Holding Company: WELWYN MACHINERY LIMITED
Registration no: 03739276 **Date established:** 1999
Turnover: Up to £250,000 **No.of Employees:** 1 - 10 **Product Groups:** 46

Date of Accounts	Mar 11	Mar 10	Mar 09
Sales Turnover	43	91	N/A
Working Capital	41	47	44
Fixed Assets	1	1	1
Current Assets	41	73	67

Wilmott Dixon Construction
Willmott Dixon House Park Street, Hitchin, SG4 9AH
Tel: 01462-442200 **Fax:** 01462-442204
E-mail: jan.dear@willmottdixon.co.uk
Website: http://www.willmottdixon.co.uk
Directors: C. Tredgett (MD)
Immediate Holding Company: WILLMOTT DIXON CONSTRUCTION LIMITED
Registration no: 00768173 **Date established:** 1963
Turnover: £500m - £1,000m **No.of Employees:** 101 - 250
Product Groups: 52

Woodside Welding & Fabrications Ltd
196 Cambridge Road, Hitchin, SG4 0JW
Tel: 01462-621996
Directors: J. Woods (MD), E. Woods (Fin)
Immediate Holding Company: WOODSIDE WELDING & FABRICATIONS LIMITED
Registration no: 04819044 **Date established:** 2003
Turnover: Up to £250,000 **No.of Employees:** 1 - 10 **Product Groups:** 35, 48, 52

Date of Accounts	Mar 11	Mar 10	Mar 09
Sales Turnover	85	91	48
Pre Tax Profit/Loss	5	7	1
Working Capital	1	3	11
Fixed Assets	3	5	7
Current Assets	25	41	27
Current Liabilities	14	23	2

Wrought Iron Designs
Clouds Hill Farm Offley, Hitchin, SG5 3BZ
Tel: 01462-768206 **Fax:** 01462- 768206
Directors: A. Eagling (Prop)
Immediate Holding Company: THE PRINTED WORD UK LIMITED
Registration no: 02844000 **Date established:** 1993
No.of Employees: 1 - 10 **Product Groups:** 26, 35

Date of Accounts	Dec 11	Dec 10	Dec 09
Working Capital	2	3	3
Current Assets	2	4	4
Current Liabilities	N/A	1	N/A

Hoddesdon

A D C Gas Analysis Ltd
Hoddesdon Industrial Centre Pindar Road, Hoddesdon, EN11 0FF
Tel: 01992-478600 **Fax:** 01992-478938
E-mail: sales@adc-analysers.com
Website: http://www.adc-analysers.com
Directors: D. Booth (Sales)
Immediate Holding Company: ADC GAS ANALYSIS LIMITED
Registration no: 03482018 **Date established:** 1997
No.of Employees: 1 - 10 **Product Groups:** 38, 42

Date of Accounts	Dec 11	Dec 10	Dec 09
Working Capital	42	48	123
Fixed Assets	5	8	6
Current Assets	205	264	326

Addressing & Mailing Solutions
1 Optima Business Park Pindar Road, Hoddesdon, EN11 0DQ
Tel: 01992-460111 **Fax:** 01992-449111
E-mail: sales@ams-gb.com
Website: http://www.ams-gb.com
Directors: K. Mcpheat (MD)
Immediate Holding Company: ADDRESSING & MAILING SOLUTIONS LIMITED
Registration no: 04702481 **Date established:** 2003
No.of Employees: 11 - 20 **Product Groups:** 27, 28, 30, 37, 42, 44, 46, 66, 67, 81

Date of Accounts	Dec 11	Dec 10	Dec 09
Working Capital	423	336	345
Fixed Assets	74	111	148
Current Assets	1m	1m	968

Andrena Direct Furniture
Auction House Geddings Road, Hoddesdon, EN11 0NT
Tel: 01992-451722 **Fax:** 01992-466024
E-mail: enquiries@andrena.co.uk
Website: http://www.andrena.co.uk
Bank(s): Barclays
Directors: G. Anderson (Dir), M. Anderson (Dir)
Managers: E. Anderson (Asst Gen Mgr)
Immediate Holding Company: ANDRENA FURNITURE LTD
Registration no: 01574169 **VAT No.:** GB 214 4058 96
Date established: 1981 **Turnover:** £1m - £2m **No.of Employees:** 21 - 50
Product Groups: 26

Date of Accounts	Mar 12	Mar 11	Mar 10
Working Capital	-24	6	26
Fixed Assets	925	923	946
Current Assets	294	269	249

Ansmann Energy UK Ltd
Units 19-20 Maple Park, Hoddesdon, EN11 0EX
Tel: 08706-092233 **Fax:** 0870-609 2234
E-mail: info@ansmann.co.uk
Website: http://www.ansmann.de/cms/index.php?l=en
Directors: L. Ward (Prop), K. Scheuermann (Co Sec), G. Thomasson (Comm), G. Schifferdecker (Sales), E. Ansmann (Legal), P. Channell (MD)
Managers: S. Polley (Tech Serv Mgr), P. Turnell (Ops Mgr), M. Gardner (Comptroller), D. Sergeant (Reg Sales Mgr)
Immediate Holding Company: ANSMANN ENERGY (UK) LIMITED
Registration no: 04078195 **Date established:** 2000
Turnover: £20m - £50m **No.of Employees:** 1 - 10 **Product Groups:** 37, 38, 44, 48, 67

Date of Accounts	Dec 09	Dec 08	Dec 07
Working Capital	345	323	252
Fixed Assets	995	1m	1m
Current Assets	1m	1m	835

Autonic Engineering Co. Ltd
Salisbury Road, Hoddesdon, EN11 0HU
Tel: 01992-471101 **Fax:** 01992-471102
E-mail: enquiries@autonic.co.uk
Website: http://www.autonic.co.uk
Directors: D. Lee (MD)
Immediate Holding Company: AUTONIC ENGINEERING CO. LIMITED
Registration no: 01857838 **Date established:** 1984
Turnover: £500,000 - £1m **No.of Employees:** 1 - 10 **Product Groups:** 35, 48

Date of Accounts	Nov 11	Nov 10	Nov 09
Sales Turnover	542	570	445
Pre Tax Profit/Loss	146	72	86
Working Capital	753	735	811
Fixed Assets	151	150	168
Current Assets	829	857	871
Current Liabilities	54	100	41

Capital Hair & Beauty
Unit E Nicholson Court, Hoddesdon, EN11 0NE
Tel: 01992-440866 **Fax:** 01992-470681
E-mail: laural@capitalhb.co.uk
Website: http://www.capitalhairandbeauty.co.uk
Managers: L. Wildash (Mgr)
Immediate Holding Company: CAPITAL (HAIR AND BEAUTY) LIMITED
Registration no: 00530201 **Date established:** 1954
No.of Employees: 1 - 10 **Product Groups:** 32, 40, 63, 67

Date of Accounts	Dec 11	Dec 10	Dec 09
Sales Turnover	32m	28m	24m
Pre Tax Profit/Loss	4m	749	2m
Working Capital	7m	4m	3m
Fixed Assets	3m	3m	2m
Current Assets	13m	8m	7m
Current Liabilities	4m	3m	3m

Cert Group Of Companies plc
Riverside House Charlton Mead Lane, Hoddesdon, EN11 0DJ
Tel: 01992-822922 **Fax:** 01992-440753
E-mail: nigel.jagger@cert.co.uk
Website: http://www.cert.co.uk
Directors: G. Taylor (Fin), J. Stanton (Grp Chief Exec), M. Lainas (Develop), N. Jagger (Dir), V. O'brien (Co Sec)
Immediate Holding Company: CERT OCTAVIAN PLC
Registration no: 01974240 **Date established:** 1985
Turnover: £20m - £50m **No.of Employees:** 501 - 1000
Product Groups: 72

Clivnars Ltd
Pindar Road, Hoddesdon, EN11 0EA
Tel: 01992-467710 **Fax:** 01992-467866
E-mail: sales@clivnars.co.uk
Website: http://www.clivnars.co.uk
Bank(s): Lloyds TSB Bank plc
Directors: K. Squires (MD)
Managers: J. Dansie (Buyer), R. Gibbs (Tech Serv Mgr), J. Millar (Personnel)
Immediate Holding Company: CLIVNARS LIMITED
Registration no: 00900892 **Date established:** 1967 **Turnover:** £2m - £5m
No.of Employees: 21 - 50 **Product Groups:** 30, 35

Date of Accounts	May 11	May 10	May 09
Working Capital	1m	905	678
Fixed Assets	2m	2m	2m
Current Assets	2m	2m	2m

Cobury
Pindar Road, Hoddesdon, EN11 0DH
Tel: 01992-465221 **Fax:** 01992-465342
E-mail: info@gibbsscrap.co.uk
Website: http://www.cobury.co.uk
Managers: L. Carrington (Mgr)
Ultimate Holding Company: ROBERT GIBBS (CONTRACTING) COMPANY LIMITED
Immediate Holding Company: COBURY LIMITED
Registration no: 00798045 **VAT No.:** GB 220 4334 18
Date established: 1964 **Turnover:** Up to £250,000
No.of Employees: 1 - 10 **Product Groups:** 66

Date of Accounts	Oct 11	Oct 10	Oct 09
Sales Turnover	104	104	104
Pre Tax Profit/Loss	-3	99	97
Working Capital	66	79	2m
Fixed Assets	410	350	465
Current Assets	184	116	2m
Current Liabilities	55	37	35

Cortland Fibron B X Ltd
Unit C R D Park Stephenson Close, Hoddesdon, EN11 0BW
Tel: 01992-471444 **Fax:** 01992-471555
E-mail: nmcadam@cortlandfibron.co.uk
Website: http://www.cortlandcompany.com
Bank(s): HSBC, Ware
Directors: D. Hislop (Sales), N. Mcadam (MD)
Managers: A. Finch (Fin Mgr), E. Verdult
Ultimate Holding Company: ACTUANT CORP (USA)
Immediate Holding Company: CORTLAND FIBRON BX LIMITED
Registration no: 02094347 **Date established:** 1987
Turnover: £10m - £20m **No.of Employees:** 51 - 100 **Product Groups:** 29, 37, 45

Date of Accounts	Aug 11	Aug 10	Aug 09
Sales Turnover	15m	10m	20m
Pre Tax Profit/Loss	2m	1m	-118
Working Capital	7m	5m	5m
Fixed Assets	5m	5m	4m
Current Assets	13m	8m	9m
Current Liabilities	2m	962	1m

Croft Diamond Tools Uk91 Ltd
Unit 12 Plumpton House, Hoddesdon, EN11 0LB
Tel: 01992-447700 **Fax:** 01992-447519
E-mail: rosecroft@btconnect.com
Directors: W. Parker (Prop)
Ultimate Holding Company: TECKWELL LTD
Immediate Holding Company: CROFT DIAMOND TOOLS (U.K. 91) LIMITED
Registration no: 02656254 **Date established:** 1991
Turnover: Up to £250,000 **No.of Employees:** 1 - 10 **Product Groups:** 33, 36

Date of Accounts	Oct 11	Oct 10	Oct 09
Working Capital	22	58	54
Fixed Assets	3	3	3
Current Assets	51	97	93

Cyber Science Corporation Ltd
Rawdon House High Street, Hoddesdon, EN11 8BD
Tel: 01992-441111 **Fax:** 01992-442740
E-mail: info@cyberscience.com
Website: http://www.cyberscience.com
Directors: L. Konopinski (Dir), S. Foden (Chief Op Offcr)
Immediate Holding Company: CYBERSCIENCE PLC
Registration no: 01345830 **Date established:** 1977 **Turnover:** £5m - £10m
No.of Employees: 21 - 50 **Product Groups:** 44, 81

Date of Accounts	Dec 11	Dec 10	Dec 09
Sales Turnover	7m	7m	6m
Pre Tax Profit/Loss	2m	3m	2m
Working Capital	3m	3m	3m
Fixed Assets	6m	6m	5m
Current Assets	7m	7m	6m
Current Liabilities	5m	3m	3m

Demco Europe Ltd
Grange House 2 Geddings Road, Hoddesdon, EN11 0NT
Tel: 01992-454500 **Fax:** 01992-448989
E-mail: d.southern@demcoeurope.eu
Website: http://www.demcoeurope.eu
Directors: D. Southern (MD)
Ultimate Holding Company: WALL FAMILY ENTERPRISE INC (UNITED STATES OF AMERICA)
Immediate Holding Company: DEMCO EUROPE LIMITED
Registration no: 02067190 **Date established:** 1986
Turnover: £10m - £20m **No.of Employees:** 51 - 100 **Product Groups:** 26, 67

Date of Accounts	Dec 11	Dec 10	Dec 09
Sales Turnover	16m	13m	16m
Pre Tax Profit/Loss	335	43	326
Working Capital	3m	3m	3m
Fixed Assets	1m	1m	1m
Current Assets	8m	6m	6m
Current Liabilities	2m	832	1m

E.S.C
Pindar Road, Hoddesdon, EN11 0DL
Tel: 01992-462307 **Fax:** 01992-443237
E-mail: sales@escutters.co.uk
Website: http://www.escutters.co.uk
Directors: A. Walker (Prop)
Immediate Holding Company: ESCUT LTD.
Registration no: 00755015 **Date established:** 1963
No.of Employees: 1 - 10 **Product Groups:** 48

Date of Accounts	Mar 12	Mar 11	Mar 10
Working Capital	136	135	72
Fixed Assets	33	18	6
Current Assets	200	178	108

Elaflex Ltd
Riverside House Plumpton Road, Hoddesdon, EN11 0PA
Tel: 01992-452950 **Fax:** 01992-452911
E-mail: sales@elaflex.co.uk
Website: http://www.elaflex.co.uk
Managers: G. Clements (Sales Prom Mgr)
Ultimate Holding Company: PERMEX LIMITED
Immediate Holding Company: ELAFLEX LIMITED
Registration no: 02137286 **Date established:** 1987 **Turnover:** £2m - £5m
No.of Employees: 11 - 20 **Product Groups:** 29, 35, 36, 39

Date of Accounts	Jun 11	Jun 10	Jun 09
Working Capital	828	805	1m
Fixed Assets	N/A	1	3
Current Assets	2m	2m	2m

Greenweld
Co Permex Ltd Riverside House, Hoddesdon, EN11 0PA
Tel: 01992-452980 **Fax:** 01992-452981
E-mail: sales@greenweld.co.uk
Website: http://www.greenweld.co.uk
Directors: P. Knight (Dir), C. Knight (MD)
Registration no: 00728777 **Date established:** 1962
Turnover: Up to £250,000 **No.of Employees:** 1 - 10 **Product Groups:** 37, 61, 81

E J Herok Ltd
Charlton Mead Lane, Hoddesdon, EN11 0DJ
Tel: 01992-462943 **Fax:** 01992-464792
E-mail: info@herok.com
Website: http://www.herok.com
Managers: C. Gardiner (Chief Mgr)
Immediate Holding Company: E.J. HEROK LIMITED
Registration no: 00882057 **VAT No.:** GB 213 4181 06
Date established: 1966 **Turnover:** £500,000 - £1m
No.of Employees: 1 - 10 **Product Groups:** 26

Date of Accounts	Sep 11	Sep 10	Sep 09
Working Capital	80	153	159
Fixed Assets	44	55	69
Current Assets	266	266	282

Heward & Dean
Unit N4 R D Park Essex Road, Hoddesdon, EN11 0FB
Tel: 01992-467557 **Fax:** 01992-467477
E-mail: sales@hewardanddean.com
Website: http://www.hewardanddean.com
Managers: D. Shah (Mgr)
Immediate Holding Company: HEWARD & DEAN (BD) LIMITED
Registration no: 04185075 **VAT No.:** GB 554 1333 63
Date established: 2001 **Turnover:** £1m - £2m **No.of Employees:** 1 - 10
Product Groups: 35, 36, 37, 66

Date of Accounts	Aug 11	Aug 10	Aug 09
Working Capital	-129	-184	-186
Fixed Assets	198	190	197
Current Assets	511	489	428

Humphrey & Stretton plc

Stretton House 20 Pindar Road, Hoddesdon, EN11 0EU
Tel: 01992-462965 **Fax:** 01992-463996
E-mail: david.humphrey@humphreystretton.com
Website: http://www.humphreystretton.com
Bank(s): Barclays
Directors: D. Humphrey (Dir)
Ultimate Holding Company: HUMPHREY & STRETTON GROUP PLC
Immediate Holding Company: HUMPHREY & STRETTON PLC
Registration no: 00689414 **Date established:** 1961 **Turnover:** £2m - £5m
No.of Employees: 11 - 20 **Product Groups:** 25, 36

Date of Accounts	Jun 11	Jun 10	Jun 09
Sales Turnover	2m	2m	2m
Pre Tax Profit/Loss	N/A	-62	-68
Working Capital	-67	-71	-7
Fixed Assets	147	170	187
Current Assets	604	575	539
Current Liabilities	131	104	60

ITT Industries Jabsco Pumps

Bingley Road, Hoddesdon, EN11 0BU
Tel: 01992-450145 **Fax:** 01992-467132
E-mail: enquiries.emea@itt.com
Website: http://www.jabsco.co.uk
Directors: M. Gill (MD)
Managers: K. Church (Mktg Serv Mgr), J. Monday (Comptroller), S. McNamee (I.T. Exec), A. Clark (Personnel)
Ultimate Holding Company: ITT INDUSTRIES
Immediate Holding Company: ITT INDUSTRIES LTD
Registration no: 00568129 **Date established:** 1941
Turnover: £50m - £75m **No.of Employees:** 101 - 250
Product Groups: 39, 40, 41, 46, 67, 68

K K S Stainless Steel Co. Ltd

Charlton Mead Lane, Hoddesdon, EN11 0DJ
Tel: 01992-445222 **Fax:** 01992-446887
E-mail: sales@kksstainless.co.uk
Website: http://www.kksstainless.co.uk
Bank(s): HSBC Bank plc
Managers: T. Raby (Comm)
Immediate Holding Company: K.K.S. (STAINLESS STEEL) CO. LIMITED
Registration no: 05504949 **VAT No.:** GB 220 7657 76
Date established: 2005 **Turnover:** £2m - £5m **No.of Employees:** 11 - 20
Product Groups: 66

Kemlows Diecasting Products Ltd

Charlton Mead Lane, Hoddesdon, EN11 0HB
Tel: 01992-460671 **Fax:** 01992-446889
E-mail: carm.teoli@kemlows.co.uk
Website: http://www.kemlows.co.uk
Bank(s): Barclays
Directors: C. Teoli (I.T. Dir), C. Teoli (MD)
Managers: D. Reade, R. Bateman (Chief Acct)
Ultimate Holding Company: CT ACQUISITIONS LIMITED
Immediate Holding Company: KEMLOWS DIE CASTING PRODUCTS LIMITED
Registration no: 01327424 **VAT No.:** GB 215 2358 88
Date established: 1977 **Turnover:** £2m - £5m **No.of Employees:** 21 - 50
Product Groups: 34, 46, 48

Date of Accounts	Dec 11	Dec 10	Dec 09
Working Capital	2m	812	257
Fixed Assets	538	471	412
Current Assets	2m	2m	846

Mercantile Met Tech Ltd

Plumpton House Plumpton Road, Hoddesdon, EN11 0LB
Tel: 01992-445709 **Fax:** 01992-467217
E-mail: info@mercantilemettech.co.uk
Website: http://www.mercantilemettech.co.uk
Bank(s): Lloyds TSB Bank plc
Directors: C. Martin (Dir)
Immediate Holding Company: MERCANTILE MET TECH LIMITED
Registration no: 04842326 **VAT No.:** GB 424 7487 35
Date established: 2003 **Turnover:** £1m - £2m **No.of Employees:** 21 - 50
Product Groups: 48

Date of Accounts	Oct 11	Oct 10	Oct 09
Working Capital	59	59	28
Current Assets	71	131	72

Metra Non Ferrous Metals

Unit N7rd Park Essex Road, Hoddesdon, EN11 0FB
Tel: 01992-460455 **Fax:** 01992-451207
E-mail: enquiries@metra-metals.co.uk
Website: http://www.metra-metals.co.uk
Directors: J. Johnson (Fin), T. Goodey (MD), T. Goody (MD)
Ultimate Holding Company: GRILLO WERKE AG(GERMANY)
Immediate Holding Company: METRA NON-FERROUS METALS LIMITED
Registration no: 01131700 **Date established:** 1973
Turnover: £10m - £20m **No.of Employees:** 1 - 10 **Product Groups:** 34, 35

Date of Accounts	Sep 11	Sep 10	Sep 09
Sales Turnover	10m	8m	8m
Pre Tax Profit/Loss	920	913	825
Working Capital	3m	3m	3m
Fixed Assets	2m	2m	2m
Current Assets	5m	4m	4m
Current Liabilities	819	677	675

Permex Ltd

Riverside House Plumpton Road, Hoddesdon, EN11 0PA
Tel: 01992-452900 **Fax:** 01992-452911
E-mail: sales@permex.co.uk
Website: http://www.permex.co.uk
Directors: C. Knight (MD)
Immediate Holding Company: PERMEX LIMITED
Registration no: 00728777 **Date established:** 1962
No.of Employees: 1 - 10 **Product Groups:** 36, 38, 39, 40, 42, 45, 46

Date of Accounts	Jun 11	Jun 10	Jun 09
Working Capital	659	708	283
Fixed Assets	837	843	837
Current Assets	2m	1m	849

Phoenix Surgical Instruments Ltd

14b Pindar Road, Hoddesdon, EN11 0BZ
Tel: 01992-479444 **Fax:** 01992-478878
E-mail: info@phoenixsurgical.co.uk
Website: http://www.phoenixsurgical.com
Directors: N. Mitchinson (Dir), P. Gannaway (Dir), J. Twigger (Fin)
Ultimate Holding Company: PHOENIX SURGICAL HOLDINGS LIMITED
Immediate Holding Company: PHOENIX SURGICAL INSTRUMENTS LIMITED

Registration no: 01642571 **Date established:** 1982
No.of Employees: 21 - 50 **Product Groups:** 38, 67

Date of Accounts	Jun 12	Jun 11	Jun 10
Working Capital	379	310	303
Fixed Assets	330	325	353
Current Assets	879	1000	1m

Power Plex Technologies

Unit 36 Hoddesdon Industrial Centre Pindar Road, Hoddesdon, EN11 0FF
Tel: 01992-478254 **Fax:** 01992-479557
Directors: L. Geary (Ptnr)
Immediate Holding Company: POWER-PLEX TECHNOLOGIES (UK) LIMITED
Registration no: 03777461 **Date established:** 1999
No.of Employees: 1 - 10 **Product Groups:** 37, 38, 67

Premier Engineering

Unit 14 Hoddesdon Industrial Centre Pindar Road, Hoddesdon, EN11 0DD
Tel: 01992-304300 **Fax:** 01992-304307
E-mail: ian.willmot@iwilimited.co.uk
Website: http://www.iwilimited.co.uk
Directors: D. Coffey (MD), I. Willmot (Dir), M. Willmot (Fin)
Immediate Holding Company: PREMIER ENGINEERING LIMITED
Registration no: 02892038 **VAT No.:** GB 650 6533 46
Date established: 1994 **Turnover:** £500,000 - £1m
No.of Employees: 1 - 10 **Product Groups:** 37, 44, 67

Prestige Formal Wear Ltd

102 High Street, Hoddesdon, EN11 8HD
Tel: 01992-444217 **Fax:** 01992-444636
E-mail: contactus@prestigeformalwear.co.uk
Website: http://www.prestigeformalwear.co.uk
Directors: E. Harrington (Dir)
Immediate Holding Company: THE PRESTIGE FORMAL WEAR CO. LTD.
Registration no: 05499423 **Date established:** 2005
Turnover: Up to £250,000 **No.of Employees:** 1 - 10 **Product Groups:** 22, 24, 63, 66

Date of Accounts	Nov 11	Nov 10	Nov 07
Working Capital	-19	-18	-51
Fixed Assets	23	29	51
Current Assets	106	102	58

R C J Metal Finishers Ltd

3 Pindar Road, Hoddesdon, EN11 0BZ
Tel: 01992-467931 **Fax:** 01992-471547
E-mail: john@rcjmf.co.uk
Website: http://www.chromeplaters.co.uk
Bank(s): National Westminster
Directors: E. Mayhew (Fin)
Immediate Holding Company: R.C.J. (METAL FINISHERS) LIMITED
Registration no: 01618137 **VAT No.:** GB 370 3855 49
Date established: 1982 **Turnover:** £500,000 - £1m
No.of Employees: 11 - 20 **Product Groups:** 48

Date of Accounts	May 11	May 10	May 09
Working Capital	9	15	38
Fixed Assets	60	55	57
Current Assets	262	305	313

Rawmec Eec

Rawmec Industrial Park Plumpton Road, Hoddesdon, EN11 0EE
Tel: 01992-471796 **Fax:** 01992-471797
E-mail: rawmec@btconnect.com
Website: http://www.rawmec.com
Directors: M. Cook (Prop)
Immediate Holding Company: RAWMEC (EEC) LIMITED
Registration no: 02562936 **Date established:** 1990 **Turnover:** £2m - £5m
No.of Employees: 1 - 10 **Product Groups:** 38, 40, 42, 48

Date of Accounts	Mar 11	Mar 10	Mar 09
Working Capital	74	60	10
Fixed Assets	36	38	42
Current Assets	187	176	178

Riverdale Mahoney

Unit 5 Pindar Works Pindar Road, Hoddesdon, EN11 0BZ
Tel: 01992-447481 **Fax:** 01992-583988
E-mail: enquiries@riverdalemahoney.co.uk
Directors: E. Porch (Fin)
Immediate Holding Company: RIVERDALE MAHONEY LIMITED
Registration no: 02327241 **VAT No.:** GB 370 9628 30
Date established: 1988 **Turnover:** £500,000 - £1m
No.of Employees: 1 - 10 **Product Groups:** 46, 48

Date of Accounts	Mar 11	Mar 10	Mar 09
Sales Turnover	N/A	N/A	733
Pre Tax Profit/Loss	N/A	N/A	46
Working Capital	593	564	531
Current Assets	754	686	621
Current Liabilities	N/A	N/A	35

Smart Inc UK Ltd

Cavendish House Plumpton Road, Hoddesdon, EN11 0EP
Tel: 01992-410960 **Fax:** 08715-227416
E-mail: info@smart-inc.co.uk
Website: http://www.smart-inc.co.uk
Directors: H. Smart (Fin), P. Smart (MD)
Immediate Holding Company: SMART INC UK LTD
Registration no: 03965858 **Date established:** 2000
Turnover: £250,000 - £500,000 **No.of Employees:** 1 - 10
Product Groups: 28

Date of Accounts	Jul 11	Jul 10	Jul 09
Sales Turnover	468	275	N/A
Working Capital	11	-12	-1
Fixed Assets	10	12	16
Current Assets	71	44	99

Speakerbus

Fourways House Ware Road, Hoddesdon, EN11 9RS
Tel: 01992-706500 **Fax:** 01992-706501
E-mail: info@speakerbus.co.uk
Website: http://www.speakerbus.co.uk
Directors: A. Wodhams (MD)
Ultimate Holding Company: SPEAKERBUS GROUP PLC
Immediate Holding Company: SPEAKERBUS LIMITED
Registration no: 02110131 **VAT No.:** GB 787 4433 86
Date established: 1987 **Turnover:** £10m - £20m
No.of Employees: 21 - 50 **Product Groups:** 37

Date of Accounts	May 11	May 10	May 09
Sales Turnover	10m	8m	7m
Pre Tax Profit/Loss	33	43	23
Working Capital	2m	2m	1m
Fixed Assets	80	130	231
Current Assets	5m	4m	4m
Current Liabilities	2m	2m	2m

Stronghold International Ltd

Unit A Nicholson Court, Hoddesdon, EN11 0NE
Tel: 01992-479470 **Fax:** 01992-479471
E-mail: sales@stronghold.co.uk
Website: http://www.stronghold.co.uk
Directors: A. Westwood (MD), L. Rowell (Co Sec)
Managers: E. Lawler (Fin Mgr), B. Watts (Sales Prom Mgr), D. Innocent, R. Sands (Purch Mgr)
Immediate Holding Company: STRONGHOLD INTERNATIONAL LIMITED
Registration no: 00867533 **VAT No.:** GB 220 7066 02
Date established: 1965 **Turnover:** £2m - £5m **No.of Employees:** 21 - 50
Product Groups: 23, 24

Date of Accounts	Jun 12	Jun 11	Jun 10
Working Capital	67	-61	-140
Fixed Assets	1m	1m	1m
Current Assets	1m	1m	1m

Tunewell Transformers

2 Maple Park Essex Road, Hoddesdon, EN11 0EX
Tel: 01992-801300 **Fax:** 01992-801301
E-mail: i.turner@tunewell.com
Website: http://www.tunewell.com
Directors: H. Turner (Fin), I. Turner (Dir), J. Turner (Ch), I. Turner (MD)
Managers: P. Hammond (Buyer), P. Rimmer (Research & Deve), G. McGovern (I.T. Exec)
Registration no: 00581930 **VAT No.:** GB 220 7635 86
Turnover: £1m - £2m **No.of Employees:** 1 - 10 **Product Groups:** 37

Date of Accounts	Mar 08	Mar 07	Mar 06
Working Capital	-58	-68	-55
Fixed Assets	474	485	496
Current Assets	307	326	289
Current Liabilities	365	394	343
Total Share Capital	22	22	22

Volkerhighways Ltd

Hertford Road, Hoddesdon, EN11 9BX
Tel: 01992-305000 **Fax:** 01992-446862
E-mail: enquiries@volkerfitzpatrick.co.uk
Website: http://www.volkerhighways.co.uk
Bank(s): Bank of Scotland
Directors: P. Hyde (Dir), A. Foster (Co Sec)
Ultimate Holding Company: STORM INVESTMENTS BV (THE NETHERLANDS)
Immediate Holding Company: VOLKERHIGHWAYS LIMITED
Registration no: 00638559 **VAT No.:** GB 424 8943 30
Date established: 1959 **Turnover:** £125m - £250m
No.of Employees: 21 - 50 **Product Groups:** 51

Date of Accounts	Dec 11	Dec 10	Dec 09
Sales Turnover	468m	397m	350m
Pre Tax Profit/Loss	9m	11m	19m
Working Capital	24m	18m	14m
Fixed Assets	17m	15m	16m
Current Assets	117m	117m	99m
Current Liabilities	29m	29m	24m

W S M Ltd

6 Hazlemere Estate Charlton Mead Lane, Hoddesdon, EN11 0DJ
Tel: 01992-479449 **Fax:** 01992-469604
E-mail: info@wsmltd.com
Website: http://www.wsmltd.com
Directors: D. Marven (MD)
Immediate Holding Company: W.S.M. LIMITED
Registration no: 03116541 **Date established:** 1995
Turnover: Up to £250,000 **No.of Employees:** 11 - 20 **Product Groups:** 40, 66

Date of Accounts	Dec 11	Dec 10	Dec 09
Working Capital	-3	-3	-3
Current Assets	2	2	2

D W Windsor Ltd

Pindar Road, Hoddesdon, EN11 0DX
Tel: 01992-474600 **Fax:** 01992-474601
E-mail: terrydean@dwwindsor.co.uk
Website: http://www.dwwindsor.co.uk
Bank(s): National Westminster Bank Plc
Directors: T. Dean (MD), R. Wood (Co Sec), J. Green (Grp Chief Exec), M. Richards (Tech Serv)
Managers: G. Clark (Mktg Serv Mgr), T. Hughes (I.T. Exec)
Ultimate Holding Company: D W GROUP HOLDINGS LIMITED
Immediate Holding Company: D.W. WINDSOR LIMITED
Registration no: 01309755 **VAT No.:** GB 214 9465 58
Date established: 1977 **Turnover:** £5m - £10m
No.of Employees: 51 - 100 **Product Groups:** 26, 34, 37

Date of Accounts	Sep 11	Sep 10	Sep 09
Sales Turnover	7m	7m	8m
Pre Tax Profit/Loss	318	316	309
Working Capital	3m	3m	3m
Fixed Assets	848	802	664
Current Assets	5m	5m	5m
Current Liabilities	612	519	470

Kings Langley

Chiltern Demolition Ltd

Unit 3 Langley Wharf Railway Terrace, Kings Langley, WD4 8JE
Tel: 01923-265917 **Fax:** 01923-271164
E-mail: enquiries@chilterndemolition.co.uk
Website: http://www.chilterndemolition.co.uk
Directors: J. Tagg (Dir)
Immediate Holding Company: CHILTERN DEMOLITION LIMITED
Registration no: 03465052 **Date established:** 1997
No.of Employees: 11 - 20 **Product Groups:** 51

Date of Accounts	Nov 11	Nov 10	Nov 09
Working Capital	129	13	23
Fixed Assets	162	173	157
Current Assets	487	520	249

Terence Fidler

65 High Street, Kings Langley, WD4 9HU
Tel: 01923-291554 **Fax:** 01923-291553
E-mail: info@tfpengineers.co.uk

Directors: J. Fidler (MD)
Registration no: 05825204 **Date established:** 2006
Turnover: £250,000 - £500,000 **No.of Employees:** 1 - 10
Product Groups: 35

Flexelec UK Ltd

Unit 11 Kings Park Industrial Estate Primrose Hill, Kings Langley, WD4 8ST
Tel: 01923-274477 **Fax:** 01923-270264
E-mail: sales@omerin.co.uk
Website: http://www.flexelec.com
Managers: N. Lecointe (Chief Mgr)
Ultimate Holding Company: OMERIN CABLES SAS (FRANCE)
Immediate Holding Company: FLEXELEC (UK) LIMITED
Registration no: 01126791 **VAT No.:** GB 225 3698 52
Date established: 1973 **Turnover:** £1m - £2m **No.of Employees:** 1 - 10
Product Groups: 37, 40, 63, 66

Date of Accounts	Dec 11	Dec 10	Dec 09
Sales Turnover	965	767	673
Pre Tax Profit/Loss	218	164	71
Working Capital	278	313	361
Fixed Assets	8	13	13
Current Assets	551	477	486
Current Liabilities	107	77	42

G P S Document Management (Watford Office)

24 Watford Road, Kings Langley, WD4 8EA
Tel: 01923-274670 **Fax:** 01923-244475
E-mail: info@gpsdm.co.uk
Website: http://www.gpsdm.co.uk
Bank(s): HSBC, Walsall
Directors: R. Smith (Prop), R. Ward (Fin)
Ultimate Holding Company: G.P. GROUP OF COMPANIES LTD
Immediate Holding Company: G.P. GROUP OF COMPANIES LIMITED
Registration no: 01633340 **VAT No.:** GB 369 7145 13
Date established: 1982 **Turnover:** £1m - £2m **No.of Employees:** 11 - 20
Product Groups: 27, 28, 81

Date of Accounts	Aug 11	Aug 10	Aug 09
Working Capital	3	2	44
Fixed Assets	82	80	29
Current Assets	411	382	466

I F A M UK Ltd

3 Monaco Works Station Road, Kings Langley, WD4 8LQ
Tel: 01923-263333 **Fax:** 01923-270913
E-mail: info@ifam.co.uk
Website: http://www.ifam.co.uk
Directors: S. Lopez De Silanes (Fin)
Managers: S. Lopez (Chief Mgr)
Immediate Holding Company: IFAM (UK) LIMITED
Registration no: 02604256 **VAT No.:** GB 579 3445 95
Date established: 1991 **No.of Employees:** 1 - 10 **Product Groups:** 35, 36

Date of Accounts	Dec 11	Dec 10	Dec 09
Working Capital	104	103	50
Fixed Assets	64	66	72
Current Assets	146	137	149

I P S Fencing

65 Toms Lane, Kings Langley, WD4 8NJ
Tel: 01923-264831 **Fax:** 01923-261459
E-mail: emma@ipsfencing.com
Website: http://www.ipsfencing.com
Directors: E. Salo (Prop)
Registration no: 01057389 **VAT No.:** GB 924 5338 22
Date established: 1972 **Turnover:** £1m - £2m **No.of Employees:** 1 - 10
Product Groups: 25

K J T Plastics Ltd

Unit 4-5 Happy Valley Industrial Estate Primrose Hill, Kings Langley, WD4 8HD
Tel: 01923-267913 **Fax:** 01923-261853
E-mail: enquiry@kjtplastics.co.uk
Website: http://www.kjtplastics.co.uk
Bank(s): Barclays
Directors: M. Thody (MD), A. Thody (Fin)
Managers: R. Hornsby (Tech Serv Mgr)
Immediate Holding Company: K.J.T. PLASTICS LIMITED
Registration no: 00944434 **VAT No.:** GB 354 1666 52
Date established: 1968 **Turnover:** £500,000 - £1m
No.of Employees: 11 - 20 **Product Groups:** 30

Date of Accounts	Feb 11	Feb 10	Feb 09
Working Capital	-268	-307	-74
Fixed Assets	783	388	439
Current Assets	205	299	304

London Fluid Systems Technology

Unit 2 Kingley Park Station Road, Kings Langley, WD4 8GW
Tel: 01923-272000 **Fax:** 020-8200 9819
E-mail: info@london.swagelok.com
Website: http://www.swagelok.com/london
Bank(s): Bank of Scotland
Managers: S. Starkes (Mgr)
Immediate Holding Company: LONDON FLUID SYSTEM TECHNOLOGIES LIMITED
Registration no: 04025463 **VAT No.:** GB 757 0690 10
Date established: 2000 **Turnover:** £2m - £5m **No.of Employees:** 21 - 50
Product Groups: 29, 30, 36, 38, 39, 66

Date of Accounts	Dec 11	Dec 10	Dec 09
Sales Turnover	14m	12m	10m
Pre Tax Profit/Loss	196	-791	392
Working Capital	1m	3m	3m
Fixed Assets	2m	2m	3m
Current Assets	4m	4m	4m
Current Liabilities	299	412	184

Manufacturers Supplies Acton Ltd

2 Langley Wharf Railway Terrace, Kings Langley, WD4 8JE
Tel: 01923-260845 **Fax:** 01923-260847
E-mail: manusupplies@aol.com
Website: http://www.manufacturerssupplies.co.uk
Directors: P. Bayley (Dir)
Immediate Holding Company: MANUFACTURERS SUPPLIES (ACTON) LIMITED
Registration no: 00664198 **VAT No.:** GB 222 3800 08
Date established: 1960 **Turnover:** £500,000 - £1m
No.of Employees: 1 - 10 **Product Groups:** 22, 24

Date of Accounts	Mar 11	Mar 10	Mar 09
Working Capital	-135	-138	-104
Fixed Assets	110	112	113
Current Assets	68	78	67

Programmed Cleaning & Support Services Ltd

Unit 1 Chipperfield Business Centre Tower Hill, Chipperfield, Kings Langley, WD4 9LH
Tel: 01442-833141 **Fax:** 01442-834955
E-mail: admin@pcss.org.uk
Website: http://www.pcss.org.uk
Directors: P. Green (MD)
Managers: E. Smith (Sales Admin)
Immediate Holding Company: PROGRAMMED CLEANING & SUPPORT SERVICES LTD
Registration no: 04925072 **Date established:** 2003 **Turnover:** £2m - £5m
No.of Employees: 251 - 500 **Product Groups:** 52

Date of Accounts	Jul 12	Jul 11	Jul 10
Working Capital	169	86	99
Fixed Assets	162	194	217
Current Assets	416	415	357

Rosedale Sheet Metal Engineering

6 Langley Wharf Railway Terrace, Kings Langley, WD4 8JE
Tel: 01923-260835 **Fax:** 01923-261728
Directors: P. Redmond (MD), P. Redman (MD)
Registration no: 02331409 **VAT No.:** GB 225 1139 01
Date established: 1978 **Turnover:** £250,000 - £500,000
No.of Employees: 1 - 10 **Product Groups:** 48

Spacemaster Watford

128 Wharf Way Hunton Bridge, Kings Langley, WD4 8FN
Tel: 01923-772800 **Fax:** 01923-776659
E-mail: info@spacemasterwatford.co.uk
Website: http://www.spacemasterwatford.co.uk
Directors: D. Viccars (Prop)
Registration no: 05936025 **Date established:** 2006
No.of Employees: 1 - 10 **Product Groups:** 35, 36

Knebworth

Environmental Technology

Entech House London Road, Woolmer Green, Knebworth, SG3 6JR
Tel: 01438-812812 **Fax:** 01438-814224
E-mail: entech.admin@etl-entech.co.uk
Website: http://www.etl-entech.co.uk
Bank(s): HBSC
Directors: B. Bailey (Dir), J. Bailey (Fin)
Ultimate Holding Company: ENVIRONMENTAL TECHNOLOGY HOLDINGS LIMITED
Immediate Holding Company: ENVIRONMENTAL TECHNOLOGY LIMITED
Registration no: 00950152 **VAT No.:** GB 676 6990 65
Date established: 1969 **Turnover:** £5m - £10m **No.of Employees:** 21 - 50
Product Groups: 35

Date of Accounts	Oct 11	Oct 10	Oct 09
Working Capital	363	504	924
Current Assets	1m	1m	1m

Nobilla Machine Tools

The Barns Deards End Lane, Knebworth, SG3 6NL
Tel: 01438-812409 **Fax:** 01438-815233
E-mail: john@nobilla.co.uk
Website: http://www.nobilla.co.uk
Directors: J. Allibon (Prop)
Immediate Holding Company: NOBILLA MACHINE TOOLS LIMITED
Registration no: 06317102 **Date established:** 2007
No.of Employees: 1 - 10 **Product Groups:** 36, 37, 38, 43, 45, 46, 47, 48, 67

Date of Accounts	Jul 11	Jul 10
Working Capital	-25	-33
Fixed Assets	19	34
Current Assets	120	134

Letchworth Garden City

Adept Scientific plc

18 Amor Way, Letchworth Garden City, SG6 1ZA
Tel: 01462-480055 **Fax:** 01462-480213
E-mail: info@adeptscience.co.uk
Website: http://www.adeptscience.co.uk
Bank(s): HSBC Bank plc
Directors: M. Willis (Fin)
Managers: A. French (Mktg Serv Mgr), A. Brown (Personnel), N. Broughall (Tech Serv Mgr), M. Pisapia (Nat Sales Mgr)
Immediate Holding Company: ADEPT SCIENTIFIC PUBLIC LIMITED COMPANY
Registration no: 01865488 **VAT No.:** GB 418 9633 23
Date established: 1984 **Turnover:** £5m - £10m
No.of Employees: 51 - 100 **Product Groups:** 44

Date of Accounts	Oct 11	Oct 10	Oct 09
Sales Turnover	6m	6m	6m
Pre Tax Profit/Loss	140	117	96
Working Capital	-148	-234	-364
Fixed Assets	110	114	120
Current Assets	1m	1m	1m
Current Liabilities	419	445	719

Alsamex Products Ltd

1 Protea Way Pixmore Avenue, Letchworth Garden City, SG6 1JT
Tel: 01462-672951 **Fax:** 01462-480660
E-mail: enquiries@alsamex.co.uk
Website: http://www.alsamex.co.uk
Bank(s): Barclays Peterborough
Directors: M. Middleton (Fin), D. Ratcliffe (Ch)
Immediate Holding Company: ALSAMEX PRODUCTS LIMITED
Registration no: 00590205 **VAT No.:** GB 196 2308 49
Date established: 1957 **No.of Employees:** 11 - 20 **Product Groups:** 27, 30, 84

Date of Accounts	Nov 11	Nov 10	Nov 09
Working Capital	52	8	172
Fixed Assets	455	437	339
Current Assets	657	587	680

Altro

Works Road, Letchworth Garden City, SG6 1NW
Tel: 01462-480480 **Fax:** 01462-707504
E-mail: enquiries@altro.co.uk
Website: http://www.altro.com
Directors: R. Kahn (Grp Chief Exec), D. Kahn (Grp Chief Exec)
Managers: L. Belotto (Sales Prom Mgr), A. Houston (I.T. Exec), J. Austin (Mktg Serv Mgr), I. Crawforth (Purch Mgr)
Ultimate Holding Company: 01493087
Immediate Holding Company: ALTRO LIMITED
Registration no: 00154159 **VAT No.:** GB 213 2283 08
Date established: 1919 **Turnover:** £75m - £125m
No.of Employees: 1 - 10 **Product Groups:** 29, 52

Apex Security Engineering Ltd

Flint Road, Letchworth Garden City, SG6 1HJ
Tel: 01462-673431 **Fax:** 01462-671518
E-mail: sales@apexsecurityfurniture.com
Website: http://www.apexsecurityfurniture.com
Bank(s): National Westminster Bank Plc
Directors: J. Muncey (Fin), B. Butterfield (Fin), K. Woods (MD)
Managers: J. Prendergast, R. Prendergast (Purch Mgr)
Immediate Holding Company: APEX SECURITY ENGINEERING LIMITED
Registration no: 02727620 **VAT No.:** GB 456 0571 48
Date established: 1992 **Turnover:** £1m - £2m **No.of Employees:** 21 - 50
Product Groups: 48

Date of Accounts	Dec 11	Dec 10	Dec 09
Working Capital	726	636	445
Fixed Assets	113	130	136
Current Assets	2m	1m	1m

Apogee International Ltd

172 Kristiansand Way, Letchworth Garden City, SG61TY
Tel: 0871-226 1830 **Fax:** 0871-2530320
E-mail: david@apogee-international.co.uk
Website: http://www.apogee-international.co.uk
Directors: D. Wood (Co Sec)
Registration no: 02987245 **Date established:** 1994
No.of Employees: 1 - 10 **Product Groups:** 38, 42

Date of Accounts	Dec 07	Dec 06	Dec 05
Working Capital	173	175	167
Fixed Assets	2	2	3
Current Assets	329	311	261
Current Liabilities	156	137	94
Total Share Capital	1	1	1

Arenastock Ltd

11-14 Campus 5, Letchworth Garden City, SG6 2JF
Tel: 01462-481184 **Fax:** 01462-480868
E-mail: sales@arenastock.co.uk
Website: http://www.arenastock.co.uk
Bank(s): HSBC Bank plc
Directors: B. Knight (Co Sec), D. Pearson (MD)
Ultimate Holding Company: KNIGHT STRIP METALS LIMITED
Immediate Holding Company: ARENASTOCK LIMITED
Registration no: 02260485 **VAT No.:** GB 780 3621 35
Date established: 1988 **Turnover:** £2m - £5m **No.of Employees:** 11 - 20
Product Groups: 34

Date of Accounts	May 11	May 10	May 09
Working Capital	33	15	30
Fixed Assets	114	108	130
Current Assets	860	643	617

Askit Consultancy & Training

23 Norton Way North, Letchworth Garden City, SG6 1BX
Tel: 01462-483818
E-mail: admin@askit.co.uk
Website: http://www.askit.co.uk
Directors: C. Vickers (Ptnr)
Date established: 1990 **No.of Employees:** 1 - 10 **Product Groups:** 80

Autoglym

Works Road, Letchworth Garden City, SG6 1LU
Tel: 01462-677766 **Fax:** 01462-677712
E-mail: info@autoglym.com
Website: http://www.autoglym.com
Bank(s): Barclays
Directors: E. Boyle (Fin), N. Gaskin (Sales & Mktg)
Managers: P. Caller, P. Gibson (Buyer), O. James (Mktg Serv Mgr), J. Potter (Personnel)
Ultimate Holding Company: ALTRO GROUP PLC(THE)
Immediate Holding Company: AUTOGLYM LIMITED
Registration no: 01480449 **Date established:** 1980 **Turnover:** £5m - £10m
No.of Employees: 51 - 100 **Product Groups:** 32, 68

Barron Mccann Technology Ltd

Bemac House Fifth Avenue, Letchworth Garden City, SG6 2HF
Tel: 01462-482333 **Fax:** 01462-482112
E-mail: info@bemac.com
Website: http://www.bemac.com
Bank(s): Barclays
Directors: P. Alderson (MD), T. Stokes (Co Sec)
Immediate Holding Company: BARRON MCCANN LIMITED
Registration no: 01071331 **Date established:** 1972
Turnover: £10m - £20m **No.of Employees:** 21 - 50 **Product Groups:** 40, 44

Date of Accounts	Mar 11	Mar 10	Mar 09
Sales Turnover	15m	15m	14m
Pre Tax Profit/Loss	1m	1m	1m
Working Capital	3m	3m	2m
Fixed Assets	6m	6m	6m
Current Assets	8m	9m	7m
Current Liabilities	3m	3m	3m

Barton Jones Packaging Ltd

Unit 3 Dunhams Court Dunhams Lane, Letchworth Garden City, SG6 1WB
Tel: 01462-680888 **Fax:** 01462-481125
E-mail: sales@bartonjonespackaging.co.uk
Website: http://www.bartonjonespackaging.co.uk
Directors: A. Spark-Hall (MD)
Immediate Holding Company: BARTON JONES PACKAGING LIMITED
Registration no: 02847255 **VAT No.:** GB 608 6320 50
Date established: 1993 **Turnover:** £500m - £1,000m
No.of Employees: 1 - 10 **Product Groups:** 27, 30

Date of Accounts	Sep 11	Sep 10	Sep 09
Working Capital	55	48	49
Fixed Assets	21	26	21
Current Assets	407	346	298

Bier Group Ltd
Dorchester House Station Parade, Letchworth Garden City, SG6 3AW
Tel: 01462-681558 **Fax:** 01462-682384
Directors: B. Evans (Fin)
Immediate Holding Company: BIER GROUP LIMITED
Registration no: 00770563 **Date established:** 1963 **Turnover:** £2m - £5m
No.of Employees: 1 - 10 **Product Groups:** 61

Date of Accounts	Jun 11	Jun 10	Jun 09
Working Capital	16	16	15
Fixed Assets	108	108	108
Current Assets	16	16	15

Blackmore Cutters
670 Saunders Close Green Lane, Letchworth Garden City, SG6 1PF
Tel: 01462-685819 **Fax:** 01462-679550
E-mail: johnb@blackmore-cutters.co.uk
Website: http://www.blackmorecutters.co.uk
Directors: C. Morton (Prop)
Date established: 1983 **No.of Employees:** 1 - 10 **Product Groups:** 44

Bridger T D Ltd (a division of T.D. Bridger Ltd)
Avenue One, Letchworth Garden City, SG6 2WP
Tel: 01462-636465 **Fax:** 01462-636433
E-mail: sales@bridger.co.uk
Website: http://www.bridger.co.uk
Bank(s): Barclays, London
Directors: P. Nash (Sales & Mktg), L. Bridger (Fin)
Immediate Holding Company: T D BRIDGER LIMITED
Registration no: 00366193 **VAT No.:** GB 196 2240 57
Date established: 1941 **Turnover:** £2m - £5m **No.of Employees:** 51 - 100
Product Groups: 27, 30, 34

Date of Accounts	Mar 11	Mar 10	Mar 09
Working Capital	59	-161	-159
Fixed Assets	2m	2m	3m
Current Assets	1m	833	651

Brightwater Engineering
Unit 2 The Business Centre Avenue One, Letchworth Garden City, SG6 2HB
Tel: 01462-485005 **Fax:** 01462-485003
E-mail: peter.gaynor@brightwater.uk.com
Website: http://www.brightwater.co.uk
Bank(s): Lloyds
Directors: P. Gaynor (Co Sec)
Ultimate Holding Company: F.L.I. INTERNATIONAL LIMITED
Immediate Holding Company: F.L.I. WATER AND ENERGY LIMITED
Registration no: 02438143 **VAT No.:** GB 563 3171 52
Date established: 1989 **No.of Employees:** 11 - 20 **Product Groups:** 42, 52

Date of Accounts	Dec 11	Dec 10	Dec 09
Working Capital	825	830	1m
Fixed Assets	69	81	160
Current Assets	3m	2m	2m
Current Liabilities	971	323	349

Cedesa Ltd
Chater Lea Building Icknield Way, Letchworth Garden City, SG6 1WT
Tel: 01462-480764 **Fax:** 01462-480765
E-mail: norman.wildon@cedesa.co.uk
Website: http://www.cedesa.co.uk
Bank(s): Barclays
Directors: N. Wildon (Dir), N. Wildon (MD)
Managers: S. Mason (Sales Admin)
Immediate Holding Company: CEDESA LIMITED
Registration no: 02255194 **VAT No.:** GB 491 1384 44
Date established: 1988 **Turnover:** £2m - £5m **No.of Employees:** 21 - 50
Product Groups: 32, 48

Date of Accounts	Dec 11	Dec 10	Dec 09
Working Capital	317	282	256
Fixed Assets	43	65	37
Current Assets	2m	1m	951

Centurion DIY Conservatories Llp
Unit 1 City Business Centre Works Road, Letchworth Garden City, SG6 1FH
Tel: 0800-389 7261 **Fax:** 01462-489 908
E-mail: info@centuriondiyconservatories.com
Website: http://www.centuriondiyconservatories.com
Directors: S. Randall (Dir)
Immediate Holding Company: CRAWFORD PARCELS LIMITED
Date established: 2006 **Turnover:** £500,000 - £1m
No.of Employees: 1 - 10 **Product Groups:** 30, 33

Chasestead Ltd
Icknield Way East, Letchworth Garden City, SG6 1JX
Tel: 01462-480048 **Fax:** 01462-682778
E-mail: mail@chasestead.co.uk
Website: http://www.chasestead.co.uk
Bank(s): Lloyds TSB Bank plc
Directors: L. Primett (Fin), R. Wilson (MD)
Immediate Holding Company: CHASESTEAD LIMITED
Registration no: 00764976 **VAT No.:** GB 290 7471 41
Date established: 1963 **No.of Employees:** 21 - 50 **Product Groups:** 35, 39, 46, 48, 84

Date of Accounts	Aug 11	Aug 10	Aug 09
Working Capital	845	415	52
Fixed Assets	258	228	283
Current Assets	2m	1m	868
Current Liabilities	N/A	298	433

Chilfen Joinery Ltd
Unit 1 Flint Road, Letchworth Garden City, SG6 1HJ
Tel: 01462-705390 **Fax:** 01462-674327
E-mail: info@chilfen.co.uk
Website: http://www.chilfen.co.uk
Directors: M. Dear (MD), M. Childs (Dir)
Managers: D. Sagnella, M. Logan (Buyer)
Ultimate Holding Company: WILTONSIGN PROPERTIES LIMITED
Immediate Holding Company: CHILFEN JOINERY LIMITED
Registration no: 01925576 **VAT No.:** GB 196 3202 60
Date established: 1985 **Turnover:** £2m - £5m **No.of Employees:** 51 - 100
Product Groups: 25, 26, 49, 52, 76

Date of Accounts	Feb 12	Feb 11	Feb 10
Working Capital	536	391	421
Fixed Assets	200	234	208
Current Assets	1m	1m	976

Chiltern Plastics Ltd
Unit 31 Jubilee Trade Centre Jubilee Road, Letchworth Garden City, SG6 1SP
Tel: 01462-676262 **Fax:** 01462-481075
E-mail: info@nissenpackaging.co.uk
Website: http://www.nissenpackaging.co.uk
Bank(s): Hitchin
Directors: C. Shipway (Fin)
Immediate Holding Company: NISSEN PACKAGING LIMITED
Registration no: 02646557 **VAT No.:** GB 283 6596 15
Date established: 1991 **Turnover:** £500,000 - £1m
No.of Employees: 11 - 20 **Product Groups:** 30

Date of Accounts	Mar 11	Mar 10	Mar 09
Working Capital	127	122	144
Fixed Assets	184	197	214
Current Assets	315	281	234

Cleghorn Waring & Co Pumps Ltd
Icknield Way, Letchworth Garden City, SG6 1EZ
Tel: 01462-480380 **Fax:** 01462-482422
E-mail: mail@cleghorn.co.uk
Website: http://www.cleghorn.co.uk
Bank(s): National Westminster Bank Plc
Managers: R. Gayton (Chief Mgr)
Ultimate Holding Company: ITT INDUSTRIES
Immediate Holding Company: ITT JABSCO LTD
Registration no: 00853597 **VAT No.:** GB 196 2108 57
Date established: 1954 **No.of Employees:** 21 - 50 **Product Groups:** 39, 40, 41

Date of Accounts	Dec 07	Dec 06	Dec 05
Sales Turnover	5970	5153	4537
Pre Tax Profit/Loss	363	522	158
Working Capital	1395	1020	661
Fixed Assets	N/A	121	116
Current Assets	1395	1867	1270
Current Liabilities	N/A	847	609
Total Share Capital	42	42	42
ROCE% (Return on Capital Employed)		45.7	20.3
ROT% (Return on Turnover)	6.1	10.1	3.5

Cutler & Woolf Steel Ltd
Unit 32 Jubilee Trade Centre, Letchworth Garden City, SG6 1SP
Tel: 01462-480420 **Fax:** 01462-480430
E-mail: sales@cutlerandwoolf.co.uk
Website: http://www.cutlerandwoolf.co.uk
Directors: S. Catlin (Dir)
Ultimate Holding Company: COIL SLITTING LETCHWORTH LIMITED
Immediate Holding Company: CUTLER & WOOLF (STEEL) LIMITED
Registration no: 00985842 **Date established:** 1970
No.of Employees: 1 - 10 **Product Groups:** 34, 48, 66

Date of Accounts	Jan 12	Jan 11	Jan 10
Working Capital	98	112	115
Fixed Assets	57	55	21
Current Assets	1m	954	713

D B C Tools Ltd
Unit 3 Trade Centre Jubilee Road, Letchworth Garden City, SG6 1SP
Tel: 01462-679905 **Fax:** 01462-480219
E-mail: sales@dbctools.co.uk
Website: http://www.dbctools.co.uk
Directors: D. Carter (MD), M. Carter (Fin)
Immediate Holding Company: D.B.C. TOOLS LIMITED
Registration no: 01026008 **VAT No.:** GB 196 5776 01
Date established: 1971 **Turnover:** £500,000 - £1m
No.of Employees: 11 - 20 **Product Groups:** 48, 67

Date of Accounts	Sep 11	Sep 10	Sep 09
Working Capital	-93	-85	-21
Fixed Assets	391	403	419
Current Assets	112	93	112

Davies Industrial Supplies
Flint Road, Letchworth Garden City, SG6 1HJ
Tel: 01462-678111 **Fax:** 01462-673963
E-mail: sales@davies.co.uk
Website: http://www.davies.co.uk
Directors: S. Davies (Dir), T. Davies (Mkt Research)
Registration no: 01214715 **VAT No.:** GB 283 7730 32
Date established: 1967 **Turnover:** £1m - £2m **No.of Employees:** 1 - 10
Product Groups: 27

Dorchester House Business Centre (Bond Focus Ltd)
Station Road, Letchworth Garden City, SG6 3AW
Tel: 01462-478900 **Fax:** 01462-482616
E-mail: irene@dorchesterhouse.co.uk
Website: http://www.dorchesterhouse.co.uk
Managers: I. Busherway (Mgr)
Ultimate Holding Company: BIER GROUP LIMITED
Immediate Holding Company: TISHRI SOLOMON KING & COMPANY LIMITED
Registration no: 04933459 **Date established:** 2012
Turnover: £250,000 - £500,000 **No.of Employees:** 1 - 10
Product Groups: 80

Drax (UK) Ltd
Pixmore Centre Pixmore Avenue, Letchworth Garden City, SG6 1JG
Tel: 0845-459 2300 **Fax:** 0845-4592400
E-mail: info@draxuk.com
Website: http://www.draxuk.com
Directors: A. Cother (Sales)
Registration no: 04164079 **Date established:** 1996
No.of Employees: 1 - 10 **Product Groups:** 84

Date of Accounts	Mar 10	Mar 09	Mar 08
Working Capital	400	137	240
Fixed Assets	18	12	21
Current Assets	936	665	872

E B W Machine Service Ltd
12 Furmston Court, Letchworth Garden City, SG6 1UJ
Tel: 01462-670683 **Fax:** 01462-483156
Directors: T. Brockington (MD)
Immediate Holding Company: E.B.W. MACHINE SERVICE LIMITED
Registration no: 03212598 **Date established:** 1996
No.of Employees: 1 - 10 **Product Groups:** 46

Date of Accounts	Jun 11	Jun 10	Jun 09
Working Capital	27	25	28
Fixed Assets	N/A	N/A	1
Current Assets	62	58	57

Eagle Controls International Ltd
PO Box 42, Letchworth Garden City, SG6 1HQ
Tel: 01462-670566 **Fax:** 01462-673992
E-mail: info@eaglecontrols.co.uk
Website: http://www.eaglecontrols.co.uk
Directors: C. Parfitt (MD)
Immediate Holding Company: EAGLE CONTROLS INTERNATIONAL LIMITED
Registration no: 01173167 **VAT No.:** GB 214 5976 53
Date established: 1974 **Turnover:** £500,000 - £1m
No.of Employees: 1 - 10 **Product Groups:** 37, 38, 49

Date of Accounts	Dec 11	Dec 10	Dec 09
Working Capital	12	52	29
Fixed Assets	23	30	1
Current Assets	84	93	51

Electrox
Avenue One, Letchworth Garden City, SG6 2HB
Tel: 01462-472400 **Fax:** 01462-472444
E-mail: sales@electrox.com
Website: http://www.electrox.com
Bank(s): National Westminster Bank Plc
Directors: A. Myers (Co Sec)
Managers: P. Mincher (Chief Mgr)
Ultimate Holding Company: BT GROUP PLC
Immediate Holding Company: BASILICA COMPUTING LIMITED
Registration no: 01466005 **Date established:** 1991
No.of Employees: 21 - 50 **Product Groups:** 37, 38, 42, 44, 46, 47

Date of Accounts	Jun 11	Jun 10	Jun 09
Working Capital	63	28	-10
Fixed Assets	2m	2m	2m
Current Assets	181	134	129

Essential Water Services Ltd
Unit 4 Oakfield Business Corner Works Road, Letchworth Garden City, SG6 1FB
Tel: 01462-675769 **Fax:** 01462-675769
E-mail: info@essentialwaterservices.co.uk
Website: http://www.essentialwaterservices.co.uk
Directors: J. Kitchener (Dir)
Immediate Holding Company: ESSENTIAL WATER SERVICES LIMITED
Registration no: 04661727 **Date established:** 2003
No.of Employees: 11 - 20 **Product Groups:** 22, 24, 29, 30, 40, 63

Date of Accounts	Feb 12	Feb 11	Feb 10
Working Capital	-23	-120	2
Fixed Assets	65	229	233
Current Assets	1m	1m	405

Euro Circuit Boards Ltd
Spiggie Briar Patch Lane, Letchworth Garden City, SG6 3LY
Tel: 01462-480707 **Fax:** 01462-480978
E-mail: sales@eurocircuitboards.co.uk
Website: http://www.eurocircuitboards.co.uk
Directors: V. Smith (MD)
Immediate Holding Company: EURO CIRCUIT BOARDS LIMITED
Registration no: 04011224 **VAT No.:** GB 789 0666 71
Date established: 2000 **Turnover:** £250,000 - £500,000
No.of Employees: 1 - 10 **Product Groups:** 37

Date of Accounts	Dec 11	Dec 10	Dec 09
Working Capital	16	13	12
Current Assets	47	33	45
Current Liabilities	N/A	N/A	3

F B Chain Ltd
616 Jubilee Trading Estate Jubilee Road, Letchworth Garden City, SG6 1NE
Tel: 01462-670844 **Fax:** 01462-480745
E-mail: sales@fbchain.com
Website: http://www.fbchain.com
Bank(s): National Westminster Bank Plc
Directors: P. Church (MD)
Ultimate Holding Company: ADDTECH AB (PUBL.) (SWEDEN)
Immediate Holding Company: FB CHAIN LIMITED
Registration no: 01958761 **VAT No.:** GB 426 6958 15
Date established: 1985 **Turnover:** £2m - £5m **No.of Employees:** 21 - 50
Product Groups: 35, 45

Date of Accounts	Mar 11	Mar 10	Mar 09
Sales Turnover	2m	1m	2m
Pre Tax Profit/Loss	94	-281	10
Working Capital	449	369	540
Fixed Assets	25	37	63
Current Assets	1m	676	798
Current Liabilities	227	117	105

Fbh-Fichet Ltd (formerly Fichet (UK) Ltd)
7-8 Amor Way, Letchworth Garden City, SG6 1UG
Tel: 01462-472900 **Fax:** 01462-472901
E-mail: sales@fbh-fichet.com
Website: http://www.fbh-fichet.com
Bank(s): Barclays, London
Directors: A. Mackey (MD), J. Finn (Dir), J. Waker (Fin)
Managers: I. Cocker (Sales & Mktg Mg), R. Clowser (I.T. Exec)
Ultimate Holding Company: FIMAK GROUP LIMITED
Immediate Holding Company: FBH-FICHET LIMITED
Registration no: 00962212 **VAT No.:** GB 235 7650 53
Date established: 1969 **Turnover:** £1m - £2m **No.of Employees:** 11 - 20
Product Groups: 36

Date of Accounts	Dec 10	Dec 09	Dec 08
Working Capital	353	442	459
Fixed Assets	57	45	52
Current Assets	656	979	1m

F G H Controls Ltd
Blackhorse Road, Letchworth Garden City, SG6 1HN
Tel: 01462-686677 **Fax:** 01462-480633
E-mail: sales@fgh.co.uk
Website: http://www.fgh.co.uk
Bank(s): Barclays
Directors: C. Green (MD)
Managers: S. Herbert (Tech Serv Mgr), V. Noble (Chief Acct)
Ultimate Holding Company: SUPERTECH HOLDINGS INC (USA)
Immediate Holding Company: FGH CONTROLS LIMITED
Registration no: 01298491 **VAT No.:** GB 563 4971 15
Date established: 1977 **Turnover:** £1m - £2m **No.of Employees:** 21 - 50
Product Groups: 38, 44

Date of Accounts	Sep 11	Sep 10	Sep 09
Working Capital	196	301	560
Fixed Assets	207	227	178
Current Assets	2m	1m	983

H & V Controls Ltd

Blackhorse Road, Letchworth Garden City, SG6 1HD
Tel: 01462-674201 **Fax:** 01462-480226
E-mail: john.miller@hav.co.uk
Website: http://www.hav.co.uk
Bank(s): Lloyds TSB Bank plc
Directors: S. Westbrook (Fin)
Managers: J. Miller (District Mgr)
Ultimate Holding Company: NEWBURY INVESTMENTS BV (NETHERLANDS)
Immediate Holding Company: H & V CONTROLS LIMITED
Registration no: 01037303 **VAT No.:** GB 288 0653 29
Date established: 1972 **No.of Employees:** 11 - 20 **Product Groups:** 36, 37, 38, 40, 49

Date of Accounts	Dec 10	Dec 09	Dec 08
Working Capital	-20	-20	-20
Fixed Assets	20	20	20

Helmet Integrated Systems Ltd

Unit 3 Focus 4 Fourth Avenue, Letchworth Garden City, SG6 2TU
Tel: 01462-478000 **Fax:** 01462-478010
E-mail: sales@helmets.co.uk
Website: http://www.helmets.co.uk
Bank(s): Midland, Harpenden
Directors: C. Watson (Fin), I. Hoyle (MD)
Ultimate Holding Company: MIDDLEMACE LIMITED
Immediate Holding Company: HELMET INTEGRATED SYSTEMS LIMITED
Registration no: 02766754 **VAT No.:** GB 404 0831 95
Date established: 1992 **Turnover:** £10m - £20m
No.of Employees: 21 - 50 **Product Groups:** 24, 40

Date of Accounts	Oct 11	Oct 10	Oct 09
Sales Turnover	13m	12m	12m
Pre Tax Profit/Loss	934	682	301
Working Capital	2m	601	-151
Fixed Assets	2m	2m	2m
Current Assets	5m	6m	5m
Current Liabilities	906	829	390

Hiflex Doors

Unit 16 Such Close, Letchworth Garden City, SG6 1JF
Tel: 01462-620250 **Fax:** 01462-620330
Directors: A. Hoiles (Prop)
Date established: 1980 **No.of Employees:** 1 - 10 **Product Groups:** 26, 35

Johnson Apparelmaster

15 Pixmore Avenue, Letchworth Garden City, SG6 1JW
Tel: 01462-686355 **Fax:** 01462-671006
E-mail: sales@apparelmaster.co.uk
Website: http://www.johnsonplc.com
Bank(s): National Westminster Bank Plc
Managers: J. Annand (Chief Mgr)
Immediate Holding Company: JOHNSON GROUP CLEANERS P.L.C.
Registration no: 00464645 **Date established:** 1999
No.of Employees: 51 - 100 **Product Groups:** 83

L P C Plating Services Ltd

2 Castings House Birds Hill, Letchworth Garden City, SG6 1PH
Tel: 01462-684161 **Fax:** 01462-481572
E-mail: shaun.lpcplating@btconnect.com
Website: http://www.lpcplating.co.uk
Directors: A. Foster (Dir)
Immediate Holding Company: L P C PLATING SERVICES LIMITED
Registration no: 04355747 **Date established:** 2002
No.of Employees: 1 - 10 **Product Groups:** 48

Date of Accounts	Mar 11	Mar 10	Mar 09
Working Capital	-33	-68	-80
Fixed Assets	34	41	55
Current Assets	216	182	158

Letchworth Garden City Heritage Foundation

Suite 401 Spirella Buildings Bridge Road, Letchworth Garden City, SG6 4ET
Tel: 01462-476007 **Fax:** 01462-476050
E-mail: info@letchworth.com
Website: http://www.lgchf.com
Bank(s): HSBC
Directors: S. Kenny (Dir), S. Kenney (Dir & Gen Mgr), J. Lewis (Dir), I. Webb (Dir), H. Patterson (Co Sec), A. Howard (Mkt Research)
Managers: T. Roberts (I.T. Exec)
Immediate Holding Company: MULTIPLE SCLEROSIS TRUST
Registration no: 09000252 **Date established:** 2001 **Turnover:** £1m - £2m
No.of Employees: 101 - 250 **Product Groups:** 80

Date of Accounts	Sep 08	Sep 07	Sep 06
Sales Turnover	1401	1169	1150
Pre Tax Profit/Loss	33	-65	-17
Working Capital	811	780	866
Fixed Assets	187	185	164
Current Assets	1510	1170	1291
Current Liabilities	699	390	425
Total Share Capital	1100	1100	1100
ROCE% (Return on Capital Employed)	3.3	-6.7	-1.7
ROT% (Return on Turnover)	2.4	-5.6	-1.5

Letchworth self storage limited

1 Works Road Corner of Pixmore Ave, Letchworth Garden City, SG6 1FR
Tel: 01462-674666
E-mail: info@thesecure-store.com
Website: http://www.thesecure-store.com
Directors: M. Jefferys (Develop)
Registration no: 06320605 **Date established:** 2008
No.of Employees: 1 - 10 **Product Groups:** 72, 77

Lloyds & Co Letchworth Ltd

Birds Hill, Letchworth Garden City, SG6 1JE
Tel: 01462-683031 **Fax:** 01462-481964
E-mail: sales@lloydsandco.com
Website: http://www.lloydsandco.com
Bank(s): Barclays
Directors: C. Nottingham (MD)
Immediate Holding Company: LLOYDS & COMPANY LETCHWORTH LIMITED
Registration no: 00172097 **VAT No.:** GB 196 7110 45
Date established: 2020 **Turnover:** £1m - £2m **No.of Employees:** 11 - 20
Product Groups: 67

Date of Accounts	Sep 11	Sep 10	Sep 09
Sales Turnover	N/A	N/A	1m
Pre Tax Profit/Loss	N/A	N/A	50
Working Capital	151	192	68
Fixed Assets	58	74	100
Current Assets	622	755	777
Current Liabilities	N/A	N/A	104

Meridian Technical Recruitment Ltd

Broadway, Letchworth Garden City, SG6 3PQ
Tel: 01462-481499 **Fax:** 01462-481500
E-mail: simon@meridianrecruitment.fsnet.co.uk
Directors: P. Muncey (Fin)
Immediate Holding Company: MERIDIAN TECHNICAL RECRUITMENT LIMITED
Registration no: 02800862 **Date established:** 1993
Turnover: £500,000 - £1m **No.of Employees:** 1 - 10 **Product Groups:** 80

Date of Accounts	Mar 12	Mar 11	Mar 10
Working Capital	3m	2m	2m
Fixed Assets	1	N/A	N/A
Current Assets	3m	3m	2m

Mho Trak Ltd

Blackhorse Road, Letchworth Garden City, SG6 1HB
Tel: 01462-480123 **Fax:** 01462-480246
E-mail: stevesmith@mhotrak.com
Website: http://www.mhotrak.com
Bank(s): Barclays
Directors: S. Smith (MD)
Managers: B. Williams (Quality Control), M. Bowen (Prod Mgr)
Ultimate Holding Company: BRIMAIR LIMITED
Immediate Holding Company: MHO TRAK LIMITED
Registration no: 01902540 **Date established:** 1985
Turnover: £500,000 - £1m **No.of Employees:** 21 - 50 **Product Groups:** 37

Date of Accounts	Nov 09	Nov 08	Nov 07
Working Capital	-36	-20	104
Fixed Assets	155	230	284
Current Assets	440	640	758

Millgar Engineering Ltd

Unit 15 Jubilee Trading Estate, Letchworth Garden City, SG6 1SP
Tel: 01462-678245 **Fax:** 01462-675150
E-mail: info@millgar.co.uk
Website: http://www.millgar.co.uk
Directors: G. Mills (Fin)
Immediate Holding Company: MILLGAR ENGINEERING LTD
Registration no: 04928189 **Date established:** 2003
No.of Employees: 1 - 10 **Product Groups:** 30, 34, 35, 42, 46, 48

Date of Accounts	Oct 11	Oct 10	Oct 09
Working Capital	107	103	72
Fixed Assets	26	27	36
Current Assets	180	168	141

Mondside Ltd

Unit 22 Jubilee Trade Centre Jubilee Road, Letchworth Garden City, SG6 1SP
Tel: 01462-682875 **Fax:** 01462-686698
E-mail: mail@monside.com
Website: http://www.mondside.com
Directors: D. Banks (MD), R. Banks (Fin)
Managers: C. Banks (Sales Prom Mgr)
Immediate Holding Company: MONDSIDE LIMITED
Registration no: 01660886 **Date established:** 1982 **Turnover:** £1m - £2m
No.of Employees: 1 - 10 **Product Groups:** 30

Date of Accounts	Mar 10	Mar 09	Mar 08
Working Capital	443	471	461
Fixed Assets	7	13	25
Current Assets	579	596	650

Ogle Models & Prototypes Ltd

Birds Hill, Letchworth Garden City, SG6 1JA
Tel: 01462-682661 **Fax:** 01462-680131
E-mail: sales@oglemodels.com
Website: http://www.oglemodels.com
Bank(s): Barclays
Directors: L. Martin (MD)
Immediate Holding Company: OGLE MODELS AND PROTOTYPES LIMITED
Registration no: 01357897 **VAT No.:** GB 301 8791 67
Date established: 1978 **Turnover:** £2m - £5m **No.of Employees:** 11 - 20
Product Groups: 28, 48, 49, 81, 84, 85

Date of Accounts	Mar 11	Mar 10	Mar 09
Working Capital	618	454	422
Fixed Assets	812	911	981
Current Assets	1m	892	791

P M P K9 Services

37 Whitehicks, Letchworth Garden City, SG6 4QA
Tel: 0800-3283013
E-mail: info@pmpk9services.co.uk
Website: http://www.pmpk9services.co.uk
Managers: J. O'Leary (Nat Sales Mgr)
Date established: 2000 **No.of Employees:** 1 - 10 **Product Groups:** 81

P T F E Tubes Ltd

Unit 663 Saunders Close Green Lane, Letchworth Garden City, SG6 1PF
Tel: 01462-631562 **Fax:** 01462-631563
E-mail: sales@ptfetubes.co.uk
Website: http://www.ptfetubes.co.uk
Directors: D. Bates (Dir)
Immediate Holding Company: PTFE TUBES LIMITED
Registration no: 04438760 **Date established:** 2002
Turnover: Up to £250,000 **No.of Employees:** 1 - 10 **Product Groups:** 30, 31, 42, 48, 66

Date of Accounts	Mar 11	Mar 10	Mar 09
Working Capital	-19	-18	-7
Fixed Assets	6	9	12
Current Assets	41	30	30

Peak Production Equipment Ltd

Peak House Works Road, Letchworth Garden City, SG6 1GB
Tel: 01462-475600 **Fax:** 01462-480294
E-mail: f.nuttall@thepeakgroup.com
Website: http://www.thepeakgroup.com
Bank(s): Midland
Directors: F. Nuttall (MD)
Managers: K. Thompson (Buyer)
Immediate Holding Company: PEAK PRODUCTION EQUIPMENT LIMITED
Registration no: 01815079 **VAT No.:** 409 5553 42 **Date established:** 1984
Turnover: £1m - £2m **No.of Employees:** 21 - 50 **Product Groups:** 38

Date of Accounts	Aug 11	Aug 10	Aug 09
Working Capital	427	450	305
Fixed Assets	157	86	156
Current Assets	1m	1m	1m

Phillips Welding & Fabrication

Unit 8 Such Close, Letchworth Garden City, SG6 1JF
Tel: 01462-671856 **Fax:** 01462-480873
Directors: B. Phillips (MD)
Immediate Holding Company: PHILLIPS WELDING & FABRICATION LIMITED
Registration no: 08113378 **Date established:** 2012
No.of Employees: 1 - 10 **Product Groups:** 35

R A Rodriguez UK Ltd

28 Campus Five, Letchworth Garden City, SG6 2JF
Tel: 01462-670044 **Fax:** 01462-670880
E-mail: info@raruk.com
Website: http://www.rarodriguez.co.uk
Bank(s): Barclays, Letchworth
Directors: P. Wiliamson (MD)
Ultimate Holding Company: R A RODRIGUEZ INTERNATIONAL INC (USA)
Immediate Holding Company: R.A.RODRIGUEZ (U.K.) LIMITED
Registration no: 00934271 **VAT No.:** GB 229 7521 47
Date established: 1968 **Turnover:** £2m - £5m **No.of Employees:** 11 - 20
Product Groups: 35, 45, 46

Date of Accounts	Dec 11	Dec 10	Dec 09
Working Capital	2m	2m	2m
Fixed Assets	162	114	120
Current Assets	3m	3m	3m

Rainbow Engineering Services

Unit 17 Shaftesbury Industrial Centre Icknield Way, Letchworth Garden City, SG6 1RR
Tel: 01462-480442 **Fax:** 01462-480449
E-mail: sales@rainbow-dukane.com
Website: http://www.rainbow-dukane.com
Directors: A. Profit (MD)
Immediate Holding Company: RAINBOW ENGINEERING SERVICES LIMITED
Registration no: 07192414 **VAT No.:** GB 432 2630 86
Date established: 2010 **Turnover:** £1m - £2m **No.of Employees:** 1 - 10
Product Groups: 42, 48

Red & Blue Ltd

1 Avenue One, Letchworth Garden City, SG6 2HB
Tel: 08706-007780 **Fax:** 01462-708266
E-mail: simon.hunt@redandblue.co.uk
Website: http://www.redandblue.co.uk
Directors: S. Hunt (Sales), S. Hunt (Dir)
Ultimate Holding Company: BT GROUP PLC
Immediate Holding Company: RED AND BLUE LIMITED
Registration no: 03906957 **Date established:** 2000 **Turnover:** £2m - £5m
No.of Employees: 1 - 10 **Product Groups:** 80

Date of Accounts	Aug 08	Aug 07	Mar 10
Sales Turnover	2m	2m	3m
Pre Tax Profit/Loss	221	138	48
Working Capital	366	238	386
Fixed Assets	28	N/A	18
Current Assets	695	365	474
Current Liabilities	123	61	26

Rocket Radio

Unit 1 Business Centre West Avenue One, Letchworth Garden City, SG6 2HB
Tel: 01462-675481 **Fax:** 01462-675481
E-mail: sales@rocketradio.net
Website: http://www.rocketradio.net
Directors: M. Russell (Prop), M. Rusell (Prop)
No.of Employees: 1 - 10 **Product Groups:** 37

Sabre Plastic Tooling & Mouldings

5 Jubilee Trade Centre Jubilee Road, Letchworth Garden City, SG6 1SP
Tel: 01462-484648 **Fax:** 01462-480068
E-mail: sales@sabre-tooling.com
Website: http://www.sabre-tooling.com
Directors: R. Stimson (MD)
Date established: 1995 **No.of Employees:** 11 - 20 **Product Groups:** 30, 37, 38, 42, 45, 46, 48, 67, 84

Date of Accounts	Oct 07	Oct 06	Oct 05
Sales Turnover	N/A	532	589
Pre Tax Profit/Loss	N/A	65	21
Working Capital	51	67	65
Fixed Assets	197	153	172
Current Assets	125	154	137
Current Liabilities	74	87	72
ROCE% (Return on Capital Employed)		29.5	9.0
ROT% (Return on Turnover)		12.2	3.6

Schottlander Dental Equipment Supplies (t/a Schottlander)

Fifth Avenue, Letchworth Garden City, SG6 2WD
Tel: 01462-480848 **Fax:** 01462-482802
E-mail: sales@schottlander.co.uk
Website: http://www.schottlander.com
Bank(s): HSBC Bank plc
Directors: B. Schottlander (Dir), P. Peacock (Fin)
Managers: J. Spiter (Sales Prom Mgr), J. Spicer (Sales & Mktg Mg), T. Maciver (Systems Mgr), L. Coulson Rutter (Mktg Serv Mgr), V. Maciver (Purch Mgr)
Immediate Holding Company: SCHOTTLANDER LIMITED
Registration no: 02633400 **VAT No.:** GB 232 2688 71
Date established: 1991 **Turnover:** £5m - £10m
No.of Employees: 51 - 100 **Product Groups:** 31, 38

The Secure-Store

1 Works Road Corner of Pixmore Avenue, Letchworth Garden City, SG6 1FR
Tel: 01462-674666
E-mail: letchworthstorage@yahoo.co.uk
Website: http://www.thesecure-store.com
Directors: M. Jefferys (Dir)
Immediate Holding Company: WONDERLAND DAY NURSERY LIMITED
Date established: 1995 **No.of Employees:** 1 - 10 **Product Groups:** 72, 77

Date of Accounts	Dec 11	Dec 10	Dec 09
Working Capital	60	30	24
Fixed Assets	N/A	N/A	2
Current Assets	168	170	88

Stevenage Sheet Metal Co. Ltd

Unit 1 Jubilee Trade Centre Jubilee Road, Letchworth Garden City, SG6 1SP
Tel: 01462-674794 **Fax:** 01462-481132
E-mail: sales@stevenagesheetmetal.com
Website: http://www.stevenagesheetmetal.com
Directors: G. Byatt (MD)
Managers: S. Kelly (Chief Mgr), J. Kandola (Buyer)
Immediate Holding Company: STEVENAGE SHEET METAL CO. LIMITED
Registration no: 02782093 **Date established:** 1993 **Turnover:** £1m - £2m
No.of Employees: 21 - 50 **Product Groups:** 25, 30, 34, 35, 36, 37, 38, 39, 45, 48

Date of Accounts	Jan 11	Jan 10	Jan 09
Working Capital	252	127	-83
Fixed Assets	2m	2m	1m
Current Assets	1m	1m	1m

Stoddard Manufacturing Co. Ltd

Blackhorse Road, Letchworth Garden City, SG6 1HB
Tel: 01462-686221 **Fax:** 01462-480711
E-mail: admin@stoddard.co.uk
Website: http://www.stoddard.co.uk
Bank(s): Barclays
Directors: M. Stoddard (Dir), S. Stoddard (Co Sec)
Managers: A. Riederer (Sales & Mktg Mg), M. Gage (Purch Mgr)
Immediate Holding Company: STODDARD MANUFACTURING COMPANY LIMITED
Registration no: 00668352 **VAT No.:** GB 197 3971 07
Date established: 1960 **Turnover:** £2m - £5m **No.of Employees:** 21 - 50
Product Groups: 36, 38, 49

Date of Accounts	Aug 11	Aug 10	Aug 09
Working Capital	157	-67	393
Fixed Assets	2m	1m	734
Current Assets	2m	1m	1m

T P S Visual Communications Ltd

Unit 39 Jubilee Trade Centre Jubilee Road, Letchworth Garden City, SG6 1SP
Tel: 01462-682203 **Fax:** 01462-686862
E-mail: info@tpsvisual.com
Website: http://www.tpsdisplay.com
Directors: M. Adams (MD)
Managers: C. Gates (Sales Prom Mgr)
Immediate Holding Company: TPS VISUAL COMMUNICATIONS LIMITED
Registration no: 01723618 **VAT No.:** GB 382 2874 31
Date established: 1983 **No.of Employees:** 21 - 50 **Product Groups:** 28, 37, 49

Date of Accounts	May 12	May 11	May 10
Working Capital	590	206	71
Fixed Assets	437	222	254
Current Assets	2m	2m	1m
Current Liabilities	400	N/A	N/A

Taktec Ltd

158 Kristiansand Way, Letchworth Garden City, SG6 1TY
Tel: 01462-486985 **Fax:** 01462-486985
Directors: P. Liversidge (MD), S. Liversidge (Fin)
Immediate Holding Company: TAKTEC LIMITED
Registration no: 03238658 **Date established:** 1996
No.of Employees: 1 - 10 **Product Groups:** 46

Date of Accounts	Aug 11	Aug 09	Aug 08
Working Capital	4	10	10
Current Assets	48	46	47

Valeters Pride

Unit 7 Green Lane 3 Industrial Estate, Off Green Lane, Letchworth Garden City, SG6 1HP
Tel: 01462-338785
E-mail: valeterspride@hotmail.com
Website: http://www.valeterspride.co.uk
Product Groups: 32, 39, 68

Weldability S I F

1 The Orbital Centre Icknield Way, Letchworth Garden City, SG6 1ET
Tel: 01462-482200 **Fax:** 01462-482202
E-mail: reception@weldability-sif.com
Website: http://www.wholeweld.co.uk
Bank(s): National Westminster Bank Plc
Directors: J. Hawkins (Co Sec)
Immediate Holding Company: WHOLESALE WELDING SUPPLIES LIMITED
Registration no: 01684362 **VAT No.:** GB 638 0191 44
Date established: 1982 **No.of Employees:** 11 - 20 **Product Groups:** 32, 34, 35

Date of Accounts	Mar 11	Mar 10	Mar 09
Working Capital	2m	1m	1m
Fixed Assets	3m	2m	3m
Current Assets	3m	3m	2m

Weldspeed Ltd

Unit 1-2 The Orbital Centre Icknield Way, Letchworth Garden City, SG6 1ET
Tel: 01462-481616 **Fax:** 01462-482202
E-mail: info@weldability-sif.com
Website: http://www.weldability-sif.com
Directors: G. Hawkins (Dir)
Immediate Holding Company: WELDSPEED LIMITED
Registration no: 02211472 **Date established:** 1988 **Turnover:** £1m - £2m
No.of Employees: 21 - 50 **Product Groups:** 24, 30, 32, 33, 34, 35, 36, 37, 38, 40, 45, 46

Wholesale Welding Supplies Ltd

1 The Orbital Centre Icknield Way, Letchworth Garden City, SG6 1ET
Tel: 01462-482200 **Fax:** 01462-482202
E-mail: adrian.hawkins@wholeweld.co.uk
Website: http://www.wholeweld.co.uk
Directors: A. Hawkins (MD), J. Hawkins (Fin)
Managers: G. Hawkins (I.T. Exec), K. Mullan (Chief Mgr), J. Williams (Sales Prom Mgr)
Immediate Holding Company: WHOLESALE WELDING SUPPLIES LIMITED
Registration no: 01684362 **VAT No.:** GB 382 1727 49
Date established: 1982 **Turnover:** £2m - £5m **No.of Employees:** 11 - 20
Product Groups: 24, 30, 32, 33, 34, 35, 36, 37, 38, 40, 45, 46

Date of Accounts	Mar 10	Mar 09	Mar 08
Working Capital	1m	1m	845
Fixed Assets	2m	3m	3m
Current Assets	3m	2m	3m

Potters Bar

Abbey Developments Ltd

Abbey House 2 Southgate Road, Potters Bar, EN6 5DU
Tel: 01707-651266 **Fax:** 01707-646836
E-mail: william.callinan@abbeydev.co.uk
Website: http://www.abbeynewhomes.co.uk
Directors: B. Callinan (Sales), D. Dawson (Fin), W. Callinan (Dir)
Managers: R. Lea (Tech Serv Mgr), N. Phipps (Personnel)
Ultimate Holding Company: ABBEY PUBLIC LIMITED COMPANY
Immediate Holding Company: ABBEY DEVELOPMENTS LIMITED
Registration no: 00348843 **Date established:** 1939
Turnover: £20m - £50m **No.of Employees:** 21 - 50 **Product Groups:** 80

Date of Accounts	Apr 12	Apr 11	Apr 10
Sales Turnover	55m	48m	66m
Pre Tax Profit/Loss	8m	8m	7m
Working Capital	52m	49m	45m
Fixed Assets	23m	19m	17m
Current Assets	94m	92m	90m
Current Liabilities	16m	14m	16m

All 4 Kids

14 The Service Road, Potters Bar, EN6 1QA
Tel: 01707-659383 **Fax:** 01707-665809
E-mail: information@all4kidsuk.com
Website: http://www.all4kidsuk.com
Directors: J. Woodhouse (Ptnr)
Immediate Holding Company: ALL4KIDSUK LIMITED
Registration no: 04321784 **Date established:** 2001
Turnover: Up to £250,000 **No.of Employees:** 1 - 10 **Product Groups:** 22, 24, 26, 61, 63

Date of Accounts	Dec 10	Dec 09	Dec 08
Sales Turnover	N/A	128	149
Pre Tax Profit/Loss	N/A	12	44
Working Capital	75	101	100
Fixed Assets	20	9	1
Current Assets	79	108	113
Current Liabilities	4	6	14

A.J. Binns Ltd

Harvest House Cranbourne Road, Potters Bar, EN6 3JF
Tel: 01707-855555 **Fax:** 01707-857565
E-mail: enq@ajbinns.com
Website: http://www.ajbinns.com
Bank(s): National Westminster Bank Plc
Directors: J. Binns (MD), J. Sander (Dir), V. Parker (Co Sec)
Managers: J. Cairns (Chief Mgr), E. Nicholls (Purch Mgr)
Registration no: 00331839 **VAT No.:** GB 220 3374 11
Turnover: £500,000 - £1m **No.of Employees:** 11 - 20 **Product Groups:** 26

Date of Accounts	Apr 08	Apr 07	Apr 06
Working Capital	436	369	354
Fixed Assets	34	42	52
Current Assets	665	555	608
Current Liabilities	229	186	254
Total Share Capital	10	10	10

Binns Fencing Ltd

Harvest House 2 Cranborne Industrial Estate Cranborne Road, Potters Bar, EN6 3JF
Tel: 01707-855555 **Fax:** 01707-857565
E-mail: contracts@binns-fencing.com
Website: http://www.binns-fencing.com
Bank(s): National Westminster Bank Plc
Directors: A. Binn (MD), V. Parker (Co Sec), A. Binns (MD)
Managers: P. May (Comptroller)
Immediate Holding Company: BINNS FENCING LIMITED
Registration no: 00489736 **VAT No.:** GB 220 3728 02
Date established: 1950 **Turnover:** £5m - £10m **No.of Employees:** 21 - 50
Product Groups: 35, 49, 52

Date of Accounts	Apr 12	Apr 11	Apr 10
Sales Turnover	8m	7m	10m
Pre Tax Profit/Loss	120	-432	51
Working Capital	2m	2m	3m
Fixed Assets	2m	3m	3m
Current Assets	3m	3m	5m
Current Liabilities	413	278	568

D Brash & Sons Ltd

5 Summit Centre Summit Road, Potters Bar, EN6 3QW
Tel: 01707-652212 **Fax:** 01707-649806
E-mail: sales@dbrash.co.uk
Website: http://www.dbrash.co.uk
Directors: D. Christie (MD)
Immediate Holding Company: D. BRASH & SONS LIMITED
Registration no: SC056784 **Date established:** 1974
No.of Employees: 1 - 10 **Product Groups:** 38, 42

Date of Accounts	Dec 11	Dec 10	Dec 09
Working Capital	3m	3m	3m
Fixed Assets	2m	2m	2m
Current Assets	4m	4m	3m

Canada Life Group Services UK Ltd

Canada Life Place High Street, Potters Bar, EN6 5BA
Tel: 01707-651122 **Fax:** 01707-646088
E-mail: customer.services@canadalife.co.uk
Website: http://www.CANADALIFE.CO.UK
Bank(s): Lloyds TSB Bank plc
Directors: I. Gilmore (Ch & MD), I. Gilmour (Dir), W. Richards (Dir)
Ultimate Holding Company: POWER CORPORATION OF CANADA
Immediate Holding Company: CANADA LIFE GROUP SERVICES (U.K.) LIMITED
Registration no: 02259495 **VAT No.:** GB 231 5055 04
Date established: 1988 **Turnover:** £250,000 - £500,000
No.of Employees: 501 - 1000 **Product Groups:** 82

Date of Accounts	Dec 09	Dec 08	Dec 07
Sales Turnover	344	407	449
Pre Tax Profit/Loss	23	64	57
Working Capital	940	1m	1m
Current Assets	1m	1m	1m
Current Liabilities	75	102	100

E Break Ltd

Unit 5 Station Close, Potters Bar, EN6 1TL
Tel: 08707-461888 **Fax:** 08707-461899
E-mail: barry@incupplus.com
Website: http://www.incupplus.com
Directors: B. Marks (Dir), N. Marks (Co Sec)
Ultimate Holding Company: IN CUP PLUS PLC
Immediate Holding Company: E BREAK LTD
Registration no: 04139847 **Date established:** 2001
Turnover: Up to £250,000 **No.of Employees:** 11 - 20 **Product Groups:** 49

Date of Accounts	Dec 11	Dec 10	Dec 09
Sales Turnover	239	354	586
Pre Tax Profit/Loss	39	-4	-25
Working Capital	-211	45	61
Fixed Assets	7	12	18
Current Assets	119	130	158
Current Liabilities	7	26	31

Everyvalve Ltd

19 Station Close, Potters Bar, EN6 1TL
Tel: 01707-642018 **Fax:** 01707-646340
E-mail: sales@everyvalve.com
Website: http://www.everyvalve.com
Directors: C. Townsend (Dir)
Managers: C. Townsend (Sales Prom Mgr)
Registration no: 04688071 **VAT No.:** GB 386 9261 05
Date established: 1983 **Turnover:** £1m - £2m **No.of Employees:** 1 - 10
Product Groups: 29, 30, 33, 34, 36, 37, 38, 39, 40, 41, 66, 67

Date of Accounts	Aug 11	Aug 10	Aug 09
Working Capital	564	498	436
Fixed Assets	88	120	149
Current Assets	705	650	586

FOCUS Eap

1st Floor The Podium Metropolitan House Darkes Lane, Potters Bar, EN6 1AG
Tel: 01707-661300 **Fax:** 01707-661242
E-mail: info@focuseap.co.uk
Website: http://www.focuseap.co.uk
Bank(s): National Westminster Bank Plc
Directors: E. Marshall (Co Sec), M. Bryan (Dir)
Ultimate Holding Company: UNITEDHEALTH GROUP INC (USA)
Immediate Holding Company: FOCUS EAP LIMITED
Registration no: 03504168 **VAT No.:** GB 710 3790 61
Date established: 1998 **Turnover:** £250,000 - £500,000
No.of Employees: 21 - 50 **Product Groups:** 80

Date of Accounts	Dec 11	Dec 10	Dec 09
Sales Turnover	134	322	862
Pre Tax Profit/Loss	14	-5	90
Working Capital	188	172	172
Fixed Assets	N/A	2	7
Current Assets	348	401	434
Current Liabilities	N/A	30	98

G E T

Key Point 3-17 High Street, Potters Bar, EN6 5AJ
Tel: 01707-601601 **Fax:** 01707-601708
E-mail: sales@getplc.com
Website: http://www.getplc.com
Directors: L. Joseph (Grp Chief Exec), N. Williams (Co Sec), P. Tuhrim (Fin)
Ultimate Holding Company: SCHNEIDER ELECTRIC SA (FRANCE)
Immediate Holding Company: Get Group plc
Registration no: 01311353 **VAT No.:** GB 245 0799 47
Date established: 1977 **Turnover:** £50m - £75m
No.of Employees: 11 - 20 **Product Groups:** 37, 67

ILS Lift Services Ltd (Industrial Lift Services)

Unit 7 Summit Centre, Summit Road, Potters Bar, EN6 3QW
Tel: 01707-649609 **Fax:** 01707-660553
E-mail: enquiries@ils-crown.co.uk
Website: http://www.ils-crown.co.uk
Product Groups: 45, 48, 67, 84, 85

Knight Precision Wire Ltd

Hadley Works Cranborne Rd, Potters Bar, EN6 3JL
Tel: 01707-645261 **Fax:** 01707-649225
E-mail: kpw.sales@knight-group.co.uk
Website: http://www.knight-precision-wire.co.uk
Bank(s): HSBC Bank plc
Directors: A. Ferguson (Dir), C. Knight (Dir), B. Knight (Ch)
Registration no: 04549481 **VAT No.:** GB 806 3869 11
Turnover: £1m - £2m **No.of Employees:** 11 - 20 **Product Groups:** 34, 35, 37

Date of Accounts	Mar 11	Mar 10	Mar 09
Working Capital	728	824	715
Fixed Assets	373	366	408
Current Assets	2m	1m	1m

Knight Strip Metals Ltd

Linkside Summit Road Cranborne Road, Potters Bar, EN6 3JB
Tel: 01707-650251 **Fax:** 01707-651238
E-mail: sales@knight-group.co.uk
Website: http://www.knight-group.co.uk
Directors: M. Wilkshire (Fin), M. Wilson (Sales), D. Pearce (Dir)
Managers: G. Manning (Personnel), D. Smith (Tech Serv Mgr), J. Needs (Purch Mgr)
Immediate Holding Company: KNIGHT STRIP METALS LIMITED
Registration no: 00382978 **VAT No.:** GB 780 3621 35
Date established: 1943 **Turnover:** £10m - £20m **No.of Employees:** 1 - 10
Product Groups: 34, 35, 46

Date of Accounts	May 11	May 10	May 09
Sales Turnover	20m	15m	13m
Pre Tax Profit/Loss	944	534	19
Working Capital	8m	7m	7m
Fixed Assets	977	918	704
Current Assets	12m	10m	8m
Current Liabilities	1m	731	305

Omega Resistance Wire Ltd

Hadley Works Cranborne Road, Potters Bar, EN6 3JL
Tel: 01707-620111 **Fax:** 01707-649225
E-mail: sales@omega-wire.com
Website: http://www.omega-wire.com
Bank(s): HSBC
Directors: A. Ferguson (MD), R. Smeaton (Sales)
Registration no: 04549481 **VAT No.:** GB 806 3869 11
Turnover: £1m - £2m **No.of Employees:** 11 - 20 **Product Groups:** 34, 35, 36, 37

Plandent

Summit House Cranborne Road, Potters Bar, EN6 3EE
Tel: 01707-822400 **Fax:** 01438-758905
Website: http://www.claudiusash.co.uk
Bank(s): Bank of Scotland Edinburgh

Directors: K. Abrahams (MD)
Managers: D. Davis
Ultimate Holding Company: PLANMECA OY (FINLAND)
Immediate Holding Company: PLANDENT LIMITED
Registration no: 00443223 VAT No.: GB 421 4121 13
Date established: 1947 Turnover: £2m - £5m
No.of Employees: 101 - 250 Product Groups: 26, 31, 33, 63, 67

Date of Accounts	Jan 11	Jan 10	Jan 09
Sales Turnover	17m	22m	24m
Pre Tax Profit/Loss	-2m	-1m	-989
Working Capital	3m	4m	2m
Fixed Assets	1m	1m	1m
Current Assets	7m	9m	8m
Current Liabilities	1m	1m	2m

The Power Service Ltd
Unit 4 Reliant House Oakmere Mews, Potters Bar, EN6 5DT
Tel: 01707-654600 Fax: 01707-647119
E-mail: info@thepowerservice.co.uk
Website: http://www.thepowerservice.co.uk
Directors: M. Peart (Fin), S. Peart (Dir)
Immediate Holding Company: THE POWER SERVICE LIMITED
Registration no: 03661656 Date established: 1998
No.of Employees: 1 - 10 Product Groups: 38, 67, 85

Date of Accounts	Jan 11	Jan 10	Jan 09
Working Capital	-7	6	12
Fixed Assets	8	2	N/A
Current Assets	52	42	42

Sir William Burnett & Co Timber Ltd
Nelson House Sopers Road, Cuffley, Potters Bar, EN6 4SE
Tel: 01707-875211 Fax: 01707- 873503
E-mail: sales@swb.co.uk
Website: http://www.swb.co.uk
Bank(s): National Westminster
Directors: C. Dossetter (MD), R. Harrison (Fin), A. Nicolas (Co Sec)
Immediate Holding Company: SIR WILLIAM BURNETT AND COMPANY LIMITED
Registration no: 00277459 VAT No.: GB 248 0220 88
Date established: 1933 Turnover: £10m - £20m
No.of Employees: 11 - 20 Product Groups: 08

Date of Accounts	Dec 10	Dec 09	Dec 08
Working Capital	119	2m	2m
Fixed Assets	2m	176	176
Current Assets	119	2m	2m

Soundcraft Harman International
Cranborne House Cranborne Industrial Estate Cranborne Road, Potters Bar, EN6 3JN
Tel: 01707-665000 Fax: 01707-660482
E-mail: keith.watson@harman.com
Website: http://www.soundcraft.com
Bank(s): HSBC Bank plc
Directors: V. Cowley (Fin), R. Sales (Fin), A. Trott (MD)
Managers: I. Riley (Purch Mgr), H. Chisholme (Personnel), H. Chisholme (Personnel), P. Wright (I.T. Exec), I. Riley (Purch Mgr), J. Ridel (Sales Prom Mgr), D. Neal, D. Neal (Mktg Serv Mgr), J. Ridel (Sales Prom Mgr)
Immediate Holding Company: THE HILLBURY PRESS LIMITED
Registration no: 04722374 VAT No.: GB 491 9810 13
Date established: 2003 Turnover: £20m - £50m
No.of Employees: 101 - 250 Product Groups: 37

Date of Accounts	Mar 11	Mar 10	Mar 09
Working Capital	46	45	55
Fixed Assets	2	4	5
Current Assets	73	72	108

Sterling Springs Ltd
Cranborne Industrial Estate Cranborne Road, Potters Bar, EN6 3JB
Tel: 01707-650191 Fax: 01707-649677
E-mail: mike.thompson@knight-group.co.uk
Website: http://www.sterling-springs.co.uk
Directors: M. Thompson (Dir), B. Knight (Fin)
Ultimate Holding Company: KNUWAY INVESTMENTS LIMITED
Immediate Holding Company: STERLING SPRINGS LIMITED
Registration no: 00530688 VAT No.: GB 805 3145 59
Date established: 1954 Turnover: £500,000 - £1m
No.of Employees: 1 - 10 Product Groups: 35, 37, 49

Date of Accounts	May 11	May 10	May 09
Working Capital	635	633	633
Fixed Assets	12	14	12
Current Assets	745	781	834

System Uvex Ltd
Unit 3 Summit Centre Summit Road, Potters Bar, EN6 3QW
Tel: 01707-642358 Fax: 01707-645785
E-mail: info@systemuvex.co.uk
Website: http://www.systemuvex.co.uk
Directors: D. Withers (Dir)
Ultimate Holding Company: SYSTEM UVEX LIMITED
Immediate Holding Company: UVEX WORLD SYSTEMS LIMITED
Registration no: 02167816 Date established: 1987
Turnover: £500,000 - £1m No.of Employees: 1 - 10 Product Groups: 42

Therapy Equipment Ltd
1 Cranborne Industrial Estate Cranborne Road, Potters Bar, EN6 3JN
Tel: 01707-652270 Fax: 01707-652622
E-mail: sales@therapyequipment.co.uk
Website: http://www.therapyequipment.co.uk
Directors: S. Munn (Dir)
Managers: S. Munn (Chief Mgr)
Immediate Holding Company: THERAPY EQUIPMENT LIMITED
Registration no: 01733885 Date established: 1983 Turnover: £2m - £5m
No.of Employees: 21 - 50 Product Groups: 38

Date of Accounts	Sep 11	Sep 10	Sep 09
Working Capital	2m	2m	2m
Fixed Assets	435	500	534
Current Assets	2m	2m	2m

Tilgear
Bridge House Station Road, Potters Bar, EN6 4TG
Tel: 01707-873434 Fax: 01707-870383
E-mail: andrew@tilgear.info
Directors: A. Tilbrook (Ptnr), R. Tilbrook (Snr Part)
Managers: J. Byne (Buyer)
VAT No.: GB 220 9790 64 Date established: 1965
No.of Employees: 11 - 20 Product Groups: 67

Total Polyfilm
9a Cranborne Industrial Estate Cranborne Road, Potters Bar, EN6 3JN
Tel: 01707-650771 Fax: 01707-646736
E-mail: sales@totalpolyfilm.com
Website: http://www.totalpolyfilm.com
Bank(s): The Royal Bank of Scotland
Managers: J. Hammond (Sales Prom Mgr), M. Hussein (Chief Mgr)
Immediate Holding Company: 800 LIMITED
Registration no: 05070981 VAT No.: GB 629 9040 21
Date established: 2004 Turnover: £50m - £75m
No.of Employees: 21 - 50 Product Groups: 27, 30

Date of Accounts	Mar 11	Mar 10	Mar 09
Working Capital	46	45	55
Fixed Assets	2	4	5
Current Assets	73	72	108

Radlett

Jinlogic Ltd
14 Scrubbitts Square, Radlett, WD7 8JR
Tel: 01923-855306
E-mail: enquiries@jinlogic.com
Website: http://www.jinlogic.com
Directors: B. Poon (Dir)
Immediate Holding Company: JINLOGIC LIMITED
Registration no: 04877854 Date established: 2003
Turnover: £250,000 - £500,000 No.of Employees: 1 - 10
Product Groups: 30, 37, 48, 66

Date of Accounts	Jun 11	Jun 10	Jun 09
Working Capital	3	4	5
Fixed Assets	1	1	1
Current Assets	27	16	27

Kauser International Trading Ltd
PO Box 85, Radlett, WD7 7ZN
Tel: 01727-874088 Fax: 01727-874088
E-mail: info@kauserinternational.com
Website: http://www.kauserinternational.com
Directors: C. Kamruddin (Fin), H. Kamruddin (Dir)
Immediate Holding Company: KAUSER INTERNATIONAL TRADING LIMITED
Registration no: 03293664 Date established: 1996 Turnover: £1m - £2m
No.of Employees: 1 - 10 Product Groups: 38

Date of Accounts	Dec 11	Dec 10	Dec 09
Working Capital	-71	-55	-19
Fixed Assets	5	6	6
Current Assets	11	8	10

Primos Steel Fabrication
Purfley Farm London Road, Shenley, Radlett, WD7 9EN
Tel: 01923-853613 Fax: 01923-853696
Directors: T. Violante (Prop)
Immediate Holding Company: JOHN E. GRIGGS & SONS LIMITED
Registration no: 01074092 Date established: 1972
No.of Employees: 1 - 10 Product Groups: 35

Date of Accounts	Mar 11	Mar 10	Mar 09
Working Capital	63	65	342
Fixed Assets	885	844	515
Current Assets	331	255	583

Radlett Valve & Engineering Co. Ltd
38 Watling Street, Radlett, WD7 7NN
Tel: 01923-852131 Fax: 01923-854484
E-mail: sales@radlettvalve.co.uk
Website: http://www.radlettvalve.co.uk
Directors: J. Jarrett (MD), C. Jarrett (Fin)
Immediate Holding Company: RADLETT VALVE & ENGINEERING CO. LIMITED
Registration no: 01402236 VAT No.: GB 322 4332 02
Date established: 1978 Turnover: £500,000 - £1m
No.of Employees: 1 - 10 Product Groups: 36, 39

Date of Accounts	Nov 11	Nov 10	Nov 09
Working Capital	135	120	115
Fixed Assets	2	1	1
Current Assets	190	205	186

Rickmansworth

Ambassador Lift Co.
50 Shepherds Way, Rickmansworth, WD3 7NL
Tel: 01923-772817 Fax: 01923-772817
E-mail: mike@ambassadorlifts.com
Website: http://www.ambassadorlifts.co.uk
Directors: M. Bardawil (Prop)
Immediate Holding Company: AMBASSADOR LIFT COMPANY LIMITED
Registration no: 07193068 Date established: 2010
No.of Employees: 1 - 10 Product Groups: 35, 39, 45

Date of Accounts	Jun 11
Working Capital	-79
Fixed Assets	138
Current Assets	154

Burkard Manufacturing Company Ltd
Woodcock Hill Estate, Rickmansworth, WD3 1PJ
Tel: 01923-773134 Fax: 01923-774790
E-mail: sales@burkard.co.uk
Website: http://www.burkard.co.uk
Directors: G. Wili (MD), S. Wili (Co Sec)
Immediate Holding Company: BURKARD MANUFACTURING COMPANY LIMITED
Registration no: 00621017 Date established: 1959 Turnover: £2m - £5m
No.of Employees: 11 - 20 Product Groups: 38

Date of Accounts	Mar 11	Mar 10	Mar 09
Working Capital	274	238	218
Fixed Assets	66	75	88
Current Assets	352	298	270

Cattle Information Services
Scotsbridge House Scots Hill, Croxley Green, Rickmansworth, WD3 3BB
Tel: 01923-695319 Fax: 01923-770003
E-mail: info@thecis.co.uk
Website: http://www.thecis.co.uk
Managers: J. Holmes (Sales Admin)
Immediate Holding Company: IMC VISION LIMITED
Registration no: SC144462 Date established: 1994
Turnover: £5m - £10m No.of Employees: 11 - 20 Product Groups: 07

Date of Accounts	Dec 97	Dec 96	Dec 10
Working Capital	-0	-0	-0
Current Assets	N/A	46	N/A

Cementation Skanska
Maple Cross House Denham Way, Maple Cross, Rickmansworth, WD3 9SW
Tel: 01923-423100 Fax: 01302-821111
E-mail: cementation.foundations@skanska.co.uk
Website: http://www.skanska.co.uk
Managers: R. Mcintyer (Mgr)
Ultimate Holding Company: SKANSKA AB (SWEDEN)
Immediate Holding Company: CEMENTATION SKANSKA LIMITED
Registration no: 00937574 Date established: 1968
Turnover: £20m - £50m No.of Employees: 21 - 50 Product Groups: 51

Date of Accounts	Dec 11	Dec 10
Pre Tax Profit/Loss	-3m	-1m
Working Capital	-194	4m
Fixed Assets	2m	310
Current Assets	35m	4m
Current Liabilities	15m	N/A

Corero Systems Ltd
Mondas House 169 High Street, Rickmansworth, WD3 1AY
Tel: 01923-897333 Fax: 01923-897323
E-mail: info@corero.com
Website: http://www.corero.com
Directors: B. Snowe (Dir), D. Swallow (Co Sec)
Managers: M. Stringer (Tech Serv Mgr), R. Alleyne (Fin Mgr), J. Holt (Personnel)
Ultimate Holding Company: CORERO NETWORK SECURITY PLC
Immediate Holding Company: CORERO BUSINESS SYSTEMS LIMITED
Registration no: 02666282 VAT No.: GB 635 9395 05
Date established: 1991 Turnover: £2m - £5m No.of Employees: 51 - 100
Product Groups: 44

Date of Accounts	Dec 11	Dec 10	Dec 09
Sales Turnover	4m	4m	5m
Pre Tax Profit/Loss	1m	3m	305
Working Capital	-1m	-631	-509
Fixed Assets	918	41	90
Current Assets	1m	2m	2m
Current Liabilities	3m	2m	2m

Country Pursuits
1a Grove Road Mill End, Rickmansworth, WD3 8EB
Tel: 01923-772916 Fax: 01923-711476
E-mail: leslie.yeoward@country-pursuits.co.uk
Website: http://www.country-pursuits.co.uk
Directors: T. Stanton (Prop)
Date established: 1995 No.of Employees: 1 - 10 Product Groups: 36, 39, 40

Engineering & Development Consultants Ltd
Keruing Cedar Chess Hill, Loudwater, Rickmansworth, WD3 4HU
Tel: 01923-776567 Fax: 01923-721438
E-mail: gmcrook@lineone.net
Directors: D. Crook (Fin), G. Crook (MD)
Immediate Holding Company: ENGINEERING AND DEVELOPMENT CONSULTANTS LIMITED
Registration no: 00816436 Date established: 1964
Turnover: Up to £250,000 No.of Employees: 1 - 10 Product Groups: 80

Date of Accounts	Sep 11	Sep 10	Sep 09
Working Capital	-177	-162	-155
Fixed Assets	1	1	1
Current Assets	139	125	102

Excel Packaging & Insulation Company Ltd
Unit 9 Woodcock Hill Estate Harefield Road, Rickmansworth, WD3 1PQ
Tel: 01923-770247 Fax: 01923-770248
E-mail: enquiries@excelpackaging.co.uk
Website: http://www.excelpackaging.co.uk
Bank(s): Lloyds TSB Bank plc
Directors: G. Woolley (MD)
Immediate Holding Company: EXCEL PACKAGING & INSULATION CO. LIMITED
Registration no: 02887148 VAT No.: GB 629 5788 82
Date established: 1994 Turnover: £1m - £2m No.of Employees: 11 - 20
Product Groups: 23, 25, 27, 29, 30, 31, 37, 40, 49, 66, 76, 84, 85

Date of Accounts	Jan 12	Jan 11	Jan 10
Working Capital	519	426	365
Fixed Assets	96	95	78
Current Assets	802	751	637

Fidelity Information Services
Trinity Court Church Street, Rickmansworth, WD3 1RT
Tel: 01923-710123 Fax: 01923-713188
E-mail: emea.marketing@fisglobal.com
Website: http://www.fisglobal.com
Directors: M. Davey (MD)
Managers: E. Reid, R. Guess (Sales Admin)
Ultimate Holding Company: ADVANCED LIGHTING TECHNOLOGIES INC (USA)
Immediate Holding Company: VENTURE LIGHTING EUROPE LIMITED
Registration no: 02225203 Date established: 1997
Turnover: £10m - £20m No.of Employees: 51 - 100 Product Groups: 84

Date of Accounts	Mar 12	Jun 11	Jun 10
Sales Turnover	22m	28m	24m
Pre Tax Profit/Loss	635	1m	-375
Working Capital	11m	11m	10m
Fixed Assets	359	403	502
Current Assets	18m	16m	15m
Current Liabilities	1m	1m	1m

John Heyer Paper Ltd
14 Langwood House 63-81 High Street, Rickmansworth, WD3 1EQ
Tel: 01923-713870 Fax: 0870-242 1114
E-mail: sales@johnheyerpaper.co.uk
Website: http://www.johnheyerpaper.co.uk
Directors: K. Paw (Fin)
Managers: T. Elson
Immediate Holding Company: JOHN HEYER PAPER LIMITED
Registration no: 00579939 Date established: 1957 Turnover: £2m - £5m
No.of Employees: 1 - 10 Product Groups: 66

see next page

John Heyer Paper Ltd - Cont'd

Date of Accounts	Dec 07	Jun 11	Jun 10
Sales Turnover	14m	4m	3m
Pre Tax Profit/Loss	217	-375	-109
Working Capital	1m	1m	2m
Fixed Assets	34	19	31
Current Assets	5m	2m	2m
Current Liabilities	939	351	227

Jetter Conversions

Red Lion Lane Sarratt, Rickmansworth, WD3 6BN
Tel: 01923-270273 **Fax:** 01923-270361
Directors: J. Cook (Prop)
Immediate Holding Company: JETTER CONVERSIONS LTD
Registration no: 05277048 **Date established:** 2004
No.of Employees: 1 - 10 **Product Groups:** 45

Date of Accounts	Dec 11	Dec 10	Dec 09
Working Capital	27	35	35
Fixed Assets	61	80	101
Current Assets	27	96	93

Kier Construction Southern Ltd

Maple Lodge Close Maple Cross, Rickmansworth, WD3 9SN
Tel: 01923-721277 **Fax:** 01923-771600
Website: http://www.keir.co.uk
Directors: P. Durigan (Dir), P. Durigan (MD), S. Atkinson (Ch)
Managers: G. Prior (Mktg Serv Mgr), J. Simpson (Buyer), L. Baxter (I.T. Exec), M. Doyle (Mgr)
Ultimate Holding Company: Kier Group PLC
Registration no: 02099533 **Turnover:** £20m - £50m
No.of Employees: 51 - 100 **Product Groups:** 51, 52

Logax Ltd

PO Box 26, Rickmansworth, WD3 3HW
Tel: 01923-223660 **Fax:** 01923-252601
E-mail: info@logax.com
Website: http://www.logax.com
Directors: T. Corbishley (MD)
Immediate Holding Company: LOGAX LIMITED
Registration no: 02096939 **VAT No.:** GB 467 2873 09
Date established: 1987 **Turnover:** £250,000 - £500,000
No.of Employees: 1 - 10 **Product Groups:** 28, 30

Date of Accounts	Mar 12	Mar 11	Mar 10
Working Capital	27	41	69
Fixed Assets	50	54	47
Current Assets	84	100	129

Miton Systems

49 Dove Park Chorleywood, Rickmansworth, WD3 5NY
Tel: 01923-286501
E-mail: info@miton.co.uk
Website: http://www.miton.co.uk
Directors: A. Mountifield (Dir), M. Quelch (Fin)
Immediate Holding Company: MITON SYSTEMS LIMITED
Registration no: 05060224 **Date established:** 2004
Turnover: Up to £250,000 **No.of Employees:** 1 - 10 **Product Groups:** 44, 81

Date of Accounts	Mar 11	Mar 10	Mar 09
Sales Turnover	243	185	155
Pre Tax Profit/Loss	-7	5	20
Working Capital	16	22	20
Fixed Assets	2	3	N/A
Current Assets	17	31	38
Current Liabilities	N/A	N/A	17

Nestle Waters UK Ltd

Trinity Court Church Street, Rickmansworth, WD3 1LD
Tel: 01923-897700 **Fax:** 01923-897608
E-mail: enquiries@waters.nestle.com
Website: http://www.buxtonwater.co.uk
Bank(s): HSBC, Belgravia
Directors: P. Sangiorgi (MD)
Managers: J. Beadle (Buyer)
Ultimate Holding Company: NESTLE SA (SWITZERLAND)
Immediate Holding Company: NESTL++ WATERS GB LIMITED
Registration no: 02069102 **Date established:** 1986 **Turnover:** £2m - £5m
No.of Employees: 51 - 100 **Product Groups:** 21

Date of Accounts	Dec 11	Dec 10	Dec 09
Sales Turnover	N/A	N/A	3m
Pre Tax Profit/Loss	N/A	N/A	-446
Working Capital	14m	14m	14m
Current Assets	14m	14m	14m

R B J Reinforced Plastics

Unit 1 Woodcock Hill Industrial Estate Harefield Road, Rickmansworth, WD3 1PE
Tel: 01923-778853 **Fax:** 01923-896080
E-mail: laurence@rbjplastics.com
Website: http://www.rbjplastics.com
Bank(s): National Westminster Bank Plc
Directors: K. Maguire (Fin), L. Maguire (MD)
Ultimate Holding Company: G.R.P. COMPONENTS LIMITED
Immediate Holding Company: G.R.P. COMPONENTS LIMITED
Registration no: 01394754 **VAT No.:** GB 382 3567 35
Date established: 1978 **Turnover:** £1m - £2m **No.of Employees:** 11 - 20
Product Groups: 30

Date of Accounts	Jan 08
Working Capital	-27
Fixed Assets	28
Current Liabilities	27

Renault UK Ltd

Rivers Office Park Denham Way, Maple Cross, Rickmansworth, WD3 9YS
Tel: 01923-895000 **Fax:** 01923-895101
E-mail: customer.services@renault.co.uk
Website: http://www.renault.co.uk
Bank(s): Societe Generale, London
Directors: J. Llobet (Dir), P. Lane (Co Sec)
Ultimate Holding Company: RENAULT GROUP SA (FRANCE)
Immediate Holding Company: RENAULT U.K. LIMITED
Registration no: 00082932 **Date established:** 2004
Turnover: Over £1,000m **No.of Employees:** 251 - 500
Product Groups: 39

Date of Accounts	Dec 11	Dec 10	Dec 09
Sales Turnover	1089m	1328m	873m
Pre Tax Profit/Loss	-8m	4m	1m
Working Capital	46m	56m	53m
Fixed Assets	3m	4m	4m
Current Assets	202m	264m	201m
Current Liabilities	106m	150m	91m

Senior plc

59-61 High Street, Rickmansworth, WD3 1RH
Tel: 01923-775547 **Fax:** 01923-896027
E-mail: info@seniorplc.com
Website: http://www.seniorplc.com
Bank(s): HSBC
Directors: A. Bodenham (Fin)
Managers: M. Rollins, S. Nicholls
Ultimate Holding Company: SENIOR PLC
Immediate Holding Company: SENIOR ENGINEERING INVESTMENTS LIMITED
Registration no: 00938893 **VAT No.:** GB 531 3292 73
Date established: 1968 **Turnover:** £250m - £500m
No.of Employees: 11 - 20 **Product Groups:** 82, 84

Date of Accounts	Dec 11	Dec 10	Dec 09
Pre Tax Profit/Loss	389m	1m	50m
Working Capital	-72m	-130m	-101m
Fixed Assets	657m	304m	304m
Current Assets	288m	83m	101m
Current Liabilities	513	310	3m

Skanska Construction Company

Maple Cross House Denham Way, Maple Cross, Rickmansworth, WD3 9SW
Tel: 01923-776666 **Fax:** 01923-423940
E-mail: skanska@skanska.co.uk
Website: http://www.kvaerner.com
Directors: D. Fisson (Pres), S. Morton (Dir), S. Leven (Fin)
Ultimate Holding Company: SKANSKA AB (SWEDEN)
Immediate Holding Company: SKANSKA CONSTRUCTION COMPANY LIMITED
Registration no: 06264171 **Date established:** 2007
Turnover: £500m - £1,000m **No.of Employees:** 1 - 10
Product Groups: 84

Date of Accounts	Dec 10
Pre Tax Profit/Loss	-1m
Working Capital	4m
Fixed Assets	310
Current Assets	4m

The Austin Company Of UK Ltd

Cardinal Point Park Road, Rickmansworth, WD3 1RE
Tel: 01923-432658 **Fax:** 01923-432795
E-mail: enquiries@austin.co.uk
Website: http://www.austin.co.uk
Bank(s): National Westminster Bank Plc
Directors: P. Davda (MD)
Managers: S. Taylor, B. Pond (Comptroller)
Immediate Holding Company: AUSTIN (GB) LIMITED
Registration no: 05655408 **VAT No.:** GB 226 6563 54
Date established: 2005 **Turnover:** £5m - £10m **No.of Employees:** 21 - 50
Product Groups: 52, 84

Date of Accounts	Nov 11	Nov 10	Nov 09
Sales Turnover	10m	8m	20m
Pre Tax Profit/Loss	-1m	170	3m
Working Capital	4m	5m	5m
Fixed Assets	43	39	29
Current Assets	8m	7m	10m
Current Liabilities	2m	564	3m

Unisys Ltd

Hertford Place Denham Way, Maple Cross, Rickmansworth, WD3 9AB
Tel: 01895-237137 **Fax:** 01895-862092
E-mail: sales@unisys.com
Website: http://www.unisys.com
Directors: N. Fraser (MD)
Ultimate Holding Company: UNISYS CORP (USA)
Immediate Holding Company: UNISYS LIMITED
Registration no: 00103709 **Date established:** 2009
Turnover: Up to £250,000 **No.of Employees:** 1501 & over
Product Groups: 37, 44

Date of Accounts	Dec 11	Dec 10	Dec 09
Sales Turnover	154m	159m	181
Pre Tax Profit/Loss	19m	-50m	-3
Working Capital	211m	110m	115
Fixed Assets	31m	32m	34
Current Assets	268m	220m	220
Current Liabilities	44m	41m	46

Vocalink Ltd

Drake House Three Rivers Court Homestead, Rickmansworth, WD3 1FX
Tel: 08700-100699
Website: http://www.vocalink.com
Bank(s): National Westminster Bank Plc
Managers: D. Lanbard, R. Hillier (Comptroller), P. Stoddart (Sales & Mktg Mg), L. Wittett (Sales Admin), N. Kosanovic (Purch Mgr)
Ultimate Holding Company: VOCALINK HOLDINGS LIMITED
Immediate Holding Company: VOCALINK LIMITED
Registration no: 06119048 **VAT No.:** GB 226 6112 87
Date established: 2007 **Turnover:** £125m - £250m
No.of Employees: 251 - 500 **Product Groups:** 87

Date of Accounts	Dec 11	Dec 10	Dec 09
Sales Turnover	153m	165m	165m
Pre Tax Profit/Loss	31m	-24m	-4m
Working Capital	12m	-10m	-24m
Fixed Assets	73m	69m	95m
Current Assets	58m	39m	35m
Current Liabilities	36m	34m	23m

Royston

A M J Maters Partnership Ltd

12 Barley Road Great Chishill, Royston, SG8 8SA
Tel: 01763-838164 **Fax:** 01763-838871
E-mail: sales@maters.co.uk
Website: http://www.maters.co.uk
Directors: W. Maters (MD), S. Maters (Fin)
Immediate Holding Company: A.M.J. MATERS LIMITED
Registration no: 01504306 **VAT No.:** GB 370 4321 81
Date established: 1980 **Turnover:** £1m - £2m **No.of Employees:** 1 - 10
Product Groups: 42, 45

ACO Electronics Ltd

Unit 3 Manor Farm Business Park Shingay cum Wendy, Royston, SG8 0HW
Tel: 01223-208222 **Fax:** 01223-208150
E-mail: sales@acoelectronics.com
Website: http://www.acoelectronics.com
Directors: P. Williams (Fin)
Immediate Holding Company: ACO ELECTRONICS LIMITED
Registration no: 02086981 **VAT No.:** GB 446 2290 53
Date established: 1987 **Turnover:** £250,000 - £500,000
No.of Employees: 1 - 10 **Product Groups:** 32, 37, 38, 44

Date of Accounts	Oct 11	Oct 10	Oct 09
Working Capital	58	94	85
Fixed Assets	32	35	37
Current Assets	147	312	168

Ampac Security Products Ltd

Saxon Way Melbourn, Royston, SG8 6DN
Tel: 01763-261900 **Fax:** 01763-261234
E-mail: jason.rowley@ampaconline.com
Directors: J. Rowley (Dir), A. Burt (Fin)
Managers: D. Pilkington (Buyer), F. Cassidy (Mktg Serv Mgr), S. Hopkins (Personnel), B. Mynott (Tech Serv Mgr)
Immediate Holding Company: AMPAC SECURITY PRODUCTS, LTD.
Registration no: 05990845 **Date established:** 2006 **Turnover:** £5m - £10m
No.of Employees: 51 - 100 **Product Groups:** 24, 27, 30, 36, 44, 81

Date of Accounts	Dec 11	Dec 10	Dec 09
Sales Turnover	12m	10m	11m
Pre Tax Profit/Loss	1m	618	342
Working Capital	2m	3m	2m
Fixed Assets	975	1m	1m
Current Assets	4m	3m	4m
Current Liabilities	722	614	496

Asterand plc

2A Orchard Road, Royston, SG8 5HD
Tel: 01763-211600 **Fax:** 01763-211555
E-mail: jack.davis@asterand.com
Website: http://www.pharmagene.com
Directors: J. Davis (Dir)
Immediate Holding Company: BIOSEEK PLC
Registration no: 03355618 **Date established:** 1997
Turnover: £20m - £50m **No.of Employees:** 21 - 50 **Product Groups:** 31

Date of Accounts	Dec 08
Sales Turnover	15m
Pre Tax Profit/Loss	4m
Working Capital	11m
Fixed Assets	1m
Current Assets	15m
Current Liabilities	4m

B A S

Priory Arcade 25 Kneesworth Street, Royston, SG8 5AB
Tel: 01763-244755 **Fax:** 01763-244755
Managers: I. Morris (Mgr)
Immediate Holding Company: BIGGLESWADE AUTO SUPPLIES LIMITED
Registration no: 01628541 **VAT No.:** GB 336 0159 55
Date established: 1982 **Turnover:** Up to £250,000
No.of Employees: 1 - 10 **Product Groups:** 39

Date of Accounts	Dec 11	Dec 10	Dec 09
Sales Turnover	161	172	N/A
Pre Tax Profit/Loss	-20	-7	N/A
Working Capital	-68	-48	-42
Fixed Assets	1	1	2
Current Assets	24	27	24
Current Liabilities	6	5	N/A

B H M Plastics Ltd

The Station High Street, Meldreth, Royston, SG8 6JR
Tel: 01763-260452 **Fax:** 01763-261152
E-mail: bhm.plastics@virgin.net
Website: http://www.bhmplasticsltd.co.uk
Directors: V. Clarke (Dir)
Immediate Holding Company: B.H.M.PLASTICS LTD
Registration no: 01185390 **VAT No.:** GB 301 8015 14
Date established: 1974 **Turnover:** £250,000 - £500,000
No.of Employees: 1 - 10 **Product Groups:** 30, 42

Date of Accounts	Mar 12	Mar 11	Mar 10
Working Capital	-3	7	10
Fixed Assets	31	39	40
Current Assets	2	16	22

Bluedelta

Unit 2 Saxon Way Melbourn, Royston, SG8 6DN
Tel: 01763-263120 **Fax:** 01763-261958
E-mail: info@bluedelta.co.uk
Website: http://www.bluedelta.co.uk
Directors: C. Skelton (Prop)
Immediate Holding Company: AIRVISION ENGINEERING LIMITED
Registration no: 01222411 **Date established:** 1975
Turnover: £250,000 - £500,000 **No.of Employees:** 1 - 10
Product Groups: 37, 44

Cambridge Manufacturing Services

3 Hale Close Melbourn, Royston, SG8 6ET
Tel: 01763-260070 **Fax:** 01763-260070
E-mail: cammas_uk@yahoo.co.uk
Directors: M. Sherwen (Prop)
Turnover: Up to £250,000 **No.of Employees:** 1 - 10 **Product Groups:** 33

Cambridge Vibration Maintenance Services Ltd

Millside The Moor, Melbourn, Royston, SG8 6ED
Tel: 01763-262112 **Fax:** 01763-263335
E-mail: sales@cvmsl.co.uk
Website: http://www.cvmsl.co.uk
Bank(s): Lloyds
Directors: G. Parrish (Dir)
Managers: P. Collyer (Admin Off)
Registration no: 04304007 **VAT No.:** GB 388 7019 10
Turnover: £500,000 - £1m **No.of Employees:** 11 - 20 **Product Groups:** 85

Date of Accounts	Mar 08	Mar 07	Mar 06
Sales Turnover	1421	1158	969
Pre Tax Profit/Loss	-8	86	46
Working Capital	161	238	151
Fixed Assets	11	23	45
Current Assets	462	486	367
Current Liabilities	301	249	216
Total Share Capital	38	118	118
ROCE% (Return on Capital Employed)	-4.8	32.9	23.3
ROT% (Return on Turnover)	-0.6	7.4	4.7

Conqueror Industries Ltd
Unit 3-4 & 789 South Close, Royston, SG8 5UH
Tel: 01763-249535 **Fax:** 01763-247276
E-mail: info@c-i-ltd.co.uk
Website: http://www.c-i-ltd.co.uk
Directors: P. Ireland (Comm), J. Ireland (MD)
Managers: M. Cummins (Purch Mgr)
Immediate Holding Company: CONQUEROR INDUSTRIES LIMITED
Registration no: 02666823 **VAT No.:** GB 599 4966 48
Date established: 1991 **Turnover:** £1m - £2m **No.of Employees:** 21 - 50
Product Groups: 37, 48

Date of Accounts	May 12	May 11	May 10
Working Capital	139	86	52
Fixed Assets	45	114	183
Current Assets	524	496	482

Cosmark Ltd
4 Station Road Shepreth, Royston, SG8 6PZ
Tel: 01763-262677 **Fax:** 01763-262676
E-mail: cosmark@intracel.co.uk
Website: http://www.intracel.co.uk
Directors: H. Sethi (Fin), M. Conway (Dir)
Registration no: 04042627 **VAT No.:** GB 215 1850 89
Turnover: £500,000 - £1m **No.of Employees:** 1 - 10 **Product Groups:** 42

Episys Group Ltd
Newark Close York Way, Royston, SG8 5HL
Tel: 01763-248866 **Fax:** 01763-246000
E-mail: reception@episys.com
Website: http://www.episys.com
Directors: J. Herron (Fin)
Managers: A. Page (Mktg Serv Mgr), C. St Clair (Sales Prom Mgr), D. Buchanan, S. Turner (Tech Serv Mgr)
Immediate Holding Company: EPISYS GROUP LIMITED
Registration no: 03200863 **Date established:** 1996 **Turnover:** £2m - £5m
No.of Employees: 21 - 50 **Product Groups:** 27, 28, 42, 44

Date of Accounts	Mar 11	Feb 08	Feb 10
Sales Turnover	5m	6m	6m
Pre Tax Profit/Loss	3	-234	6
Working Capital	601	324	127
Fixed Assets	1m	1m	1m
Current Assets	3m	2m	2m
Current Liabilities	1m	771	901

Fibre-Tech Industries LLP
Unit 12 Saxon Way Melbourn, Royston, SG8 6DN
Tel: 01763-269600 **Fax:** 01763-260632
E-mail: david.smith@rbfindustries.co.uk
Website: http://www.fibre-tech.net
Directors: D. Smith (Dir), D. Howard (Dir)
Ultimate Holding Company: R B F Industries Ltd
Immediate Holding Company: R B F Industries Ltd
Registration no: 01907211 **Date established:** 1985 **Product Groups:** 33, 34, 39, 40, 45, 48, 68, 84, 85

1st Webbing
Greys Therfield Road, Royston, SG8 9NW
Tel: 01763-245721 **Fax:** 01763-245511
E-mail: sales@1stwebbing.com
Website: http://www.1stwebbing.com
Directors: T. Stokes (MD)
Immediate Holding Company: GREEN GLOBE CONSULTANCY LIMITED
Registration no: 02506215 **Date established:** 1990
No.of Employees: 1 - 10 **Product Groups:** 23, 33, 39, 40

Date of Accounts	Sep 11	Sep 10	Sep 09
Working Capital	-0	-0	-0

Gilbros Ltd
The Fox The Green, Steeple Morden, Royston, SG8 0NB
Tel: 01763-853322 **Fax:** 01462-484048
E-mail: clivegilley@hotmail.com
Website: http://www.gilbros.com
Directors: M. Gilley (Co Sec), C. Gilley (MD)
Immediate Holding Company: GILBROS LIMITED
Registration no: 03991028 **VAT No.:** GB 196 2421 53
Date established: 2000 **Turnover:** £1m - £2m **No.of Employees:** 1 - 10
Product Groups: 52

Date of Accounts	Oct 11	Oct 10	Oct 09
Working Capital	-23	-23	-22
Fixed Assets	N/A	2	5
Current Assets	26	10	21

Grant Instruments Cambridge Ltd
29 Station Road Shepreth, Royston, SG8 6GB
Tel: 01763-260811 **Fax:** 01763-262410
E-mail: ludo.chapman@grant.co.uk
Website: http://www.grantinstruments.com
Directors: N. Tiley (Fin), N. Neal (Sales & Mktg), L. Chapman (Dir), N. Tiley (Fin)
Managers: E. Hewson, J. Bemrose, S. Standing, S. Fisher (Tech Serv Mgr)
Immediate Holding Company: GRANT INSTRUMENTS (CAMBRIDGE) LIMITED
Registration no: 00658133 **Date established:** 1960 **Turnover:** £5m - £10m
No.of Employees: 51 - 100 **Product Groups:** 38, 44

Date of Accounts	May 11	May 10	May 09
Sales Turnover	8m	8m	8m
Pre Tax Profit/Loss	-2	1m	769
Working Capital	3m	3m	3m
Fixed Assets	3m	3m	3m
Current Assets	4m	4m	3m
Current Liabilities	369	419	228

Heasell Electro Mechanical Services
11-13 Baldock Street, Royston, SG8 5AY
Tel: 01763-243369 **Fax:** 01763-248108
E-mail: sales@heasell.net
Website: http://www.heasell.net
Directors: G. Abrams (Prop)
Immediate Holding Company: JAZZ COMPUTER SUPPLIES LIMITED
Registration no: 03057118 **VAT No.:** GB 197 0006 69
Date established: 1995 **Turnover:** £1m - £2m **No.of Employees:** 21 - 50
Product Groups: 35, 37, 40, 48, 54, 67

Date of Accounts	Apr 11	Apr 10	Apr 09
Working Capital	-4	-11	-11
Fixed Assets	1	1	1
Current Assets	12	16	19

High Style Furnishings
Saxon Way Melbourn, Royston, SG8 6DN
Tel: 01763-261837 **Fax:** 01763-262489
E-mail: enquiries@highstyle.co.uk
Website: http://www.highstyle.co.uk
Bank(s): HSBC Bank plc
Directors: R. Willcox (MD), W. Willcox (MD), S. Willcox (Fin), G. Kidd (Co Sec)
Managers: T. Parry (Sales Prom Mgr)
Ultimate Holding Company: AIRVISION ENGINEERING LIMITED
Immediate Holding Company: A.V. ENGINEERING SERVICES LIMITED
Registration no: 00636892 **VAT No.:** GB 213 4168 95
Date established: 1975 **Turnover:** £2m - £5m **No.of Employees:** 51 - 100
Product Groups: 23, 63

Date of Accounts	Jun 11	Jun 10	Jun 09
Working Capital	115	112	119
Fixed Assets	28	22	28
Current Assets	251	207	211

Iaws Fertilisers Ltd
Freeman Court 1-3 Jarman Way, Royston, SG8 5HW
Tel: 01763-255500 **Fax:** 01763-244240
Website: http://www.aryzta.com
Bank(s): National Westminster Bank Plc
Directors: M. Pater (Sales), M. Pratt (Dir), M. Redden (Co Sec), P. Lynch (Dir)
Ultimate Holding Company: IAWS Group P.L.C.
Immediate Holding Company: Origin Enterprises UK Ltd
Registration no: 02465499 **VAT No.:** GB 631 6107 71
Turnover: £10m - £20m **No.of Employees:** 101 - 250 **Product Groups:** 66

Intracel Ltd
4 Station Road Shepreth, Royston, SG8 6PZ
Tel: 01763-262680 **Fax:** 01763-262676
E-mail: tim@intracel.co.uk
Website: http://www.intracel.co.uk
Directors: P. Scott (Fin), T. Scott (MD)
Immediate Holding Company: INTRACEL LIMITED
Registration no: 01990562 **Date established:** 1986
Turnover: £500,000 - £1m **No.of Employees:** 1 - 10 **Product Groups:** 37, 38

Date of Accounts	Dec 04	May 11	May 10
Pre Tax Profit/Loss	1	N/A	N/A
Working Capital	1	N/A	N/A
Fixed Assets	2	N/A	N/A
Current Assets	1	N/A	N/A

Ion Science Ltd
The Way Fowlmere, Royston, SG8 7UJ
Tel: 01763-208503 **Fax:** 01763-208814
E-mail: info@ionscience.com
Website: http://www.ionscience.com
Bank(s): Barclays
Directors: D. Johns (MD)
Managers: M. Reynolds (Personnel), S. Hunt, S. Holson (Mktg Serv Mgr)
Immediate Holding Company: ION SCIENCE LIMITED
Registration no: 02359038 **VAT No.:** GB 532 2024 00
Date established: 1989 **Turnover:** £1m - £2m **No.of Employees:** 21 - 50
Product Groups: 38, 40, 42, 45, 67, 84, 85

Date of Accounts	Dec 11	Dec 10	Dec 09
Working Capital	1m	857	863
Fixed Assets	937	954	994
Current Assets	2m	2m	2m

J R Technology
30a Barrington Road Shepreth, Royston, SG8 6QE
Tel: 01763-260721 **Fax:** 01763-260809
E-mail: enquiries@jrtech.co.uk
Website: http://www.jrtech.co.uk
Directors: P. Rogger (MD), J. Rogger (Fin)
Immediate Holding Company: JR TECHNOLOGY LIMITED
Registration no: 01755342 **VAT No.:** GB 432 1991 59
Date established: 1983 **Turnover:** £500,000 - £1m
No.of Employees: 1 - 10 **Product Groups:** 30, 31, 37, 39

Date of Accounts	Apr 11	Apr 10	Apr 09
Working Capital	104	108	94
Fixed Assets	3	3	4
Current Assets	153	137	125

L D S Test & Measurment Ltd
Jarman Way, Royston, SG8 5BQ
Tel: 01763-242424 **Fax:** 01763-249711
E-mail: sales@lds-group.com
Website: http://www.lds-group.com
Directors: D. Read (Pres)
Ultimate Holding Company: SPECTRIS PLC
Immediate Holding Company: BRUEL & KJAER VTS LIMITED
Registration no: 01539186 **VAT No.:** GB 220 5558 88
Date established: 1981 **Turnover:** £20m - £50m **No.of Employees:** 1 - 10
Product Groups: 37, 38

Date of Accounts	Dec 11	Dec 10	Dec 09
Sales Turnover	18m	19m	19m
Pre Tax Profit/Loss	-435	1m	1m
Working Capital	24m	24m	22m
Fixed Assets	2m	2m	2m
Current Assets	27m	27m	27m
Current Liabilities	1m	1m	2m

Leardock Ltd
Newark Close, Royston, SG8 5HL
Tel: 01763-247458 **Fax:** 01763-249217
E-mail: jeffery.david@leardock.com
Website: http://www.leardock.com
Directors: D. Jeffery (Dir), F. Tansley (MD)
Immediate Holding Company: LEARDOCK LIMITED
Registration no: 00757708 **Date established:** 1963
No.of Employees: 11 - 20 **Product Groups:** 35, 36, 46, 48

Date of Accounts	Apr 11	Apr 10	Apr 09
Working Capital	45	8	-25
Fixed Assets	431	452	404
Current Assets	565	378	293

Machine Tools Maintenance Cambridge Ltd
94 Ermine Way Arrington, Royston, SG8 0AH
Tel: 01223-208223 **Fax:** 01223-208223
E-mail: ronfyson@o2.co.uk
Website: http://www.machine-tools-maintance.co.uk
Directors: R. Fyson (MD)
Immediate Holding Company: MACHINE TOOL MAINTENANCE (CAMBRIDGE) LIMITED
Registration no: 03981972 **Date established:** 2000
No.of Employees: 1 - 10 **Product Groups:** 46

Date of Accounts	Jul 11	Jul 10	Jul 09
Working Capital	12	-2	-1
Fixed Assets	10	15	17
Current Assets	26	17	17

Mettler-Toledo Safeline X-Ray Ltd
Greenfield, Royston, SG8 5HN
Tel: 01763-257900 **Fax:** 01763-257909
E-mail: safelineavs@cs.com
Bank(s): Barclays
Directors: D. Richardson (MD)
Ultimate Holding Company: METTLER TOLEDO INTERNATIONAL INC (USA)
Immediate Holding Company: METTLER-TOLEDO SAFELINE X-RAY LIMITED
Registration no: 04082763 **VAT No.:** GB 573 1890 32
Date established: 2000 **Turnover:** £10m - £20m
No.of Employees: 11 - 20 **Product Groups:** 37

Date of Accounts	Dec 11	Dec 10	Dec 09
Sales Turnover	21m	15m	13m
Pre Tax Profit/Loss	5m	3m	3m
Working Capital	7m	3m	753
Fixed Assets	5m	5m	5m
Current Assets	11m	6m	3m
Current Liabilities	2m	1m	1m

Morley Manufacturing
Unit 3 Church Street Whaddon, Royston, SG8 5RU
Tel: 01223-207814
Website: http://www.morleymanufacturing.co.uk
Directors: P. Morley (Prop)
Date established: 1985 **No.of Employees:** 1 - 10 **Product Groups:** 26, 35

Omya UK Ltd
75 Station Road Steeple Morden, Royston, SG8 0NX
Tel: 01763-852181 **Fax:** 01763-852186
E-mail: graham.skelham@omya.com
Website: http://www.omya.co.uk
Bank(s): National Westminster Bank Plc
Managers: G. Skelham (Mgr)
Ultimate Holding Company: OMYA AG (SWITZERLAND)
Immediate Holding Company: OMYA UK LIMITED
Registration no: 00436591 **VAT No.:** GB 356 7319 31
Date established: 1947 **Turnover:** £2m - £5m **No.of Employees:** 11 - 20
Product Groups: 14

Date of Accounts	Dec 11	Dec 10	Dec 09
Sales Turnover	109m	102m	86m
Pre Tax Profit/Loss	-422	146	-766
Working Capital	24m	23m	17m
Fixed Assets	63m	63m	62m
Current Assets	40m	38m	36m
Current Liabilities	15m	15m	17m

P A Consulting Group
Back Lane Melbourn, Royston, SG8 6DP
Tel: 01763-261222 **Fax:** 01763-260023
E-mail: info@paconsulting.com
Website: http://www.paconsulting.com
Directors: J. Buckley (MD)
Immediate Holding Company: PA CONSULTING GROUP LIMITED
Registration no: 06555894 **VAT No.:** GB 238 5350 57
Date established: 2008 **Turnover:** £125m - £250m
No.of Employees: 501 - 1000 **Product Groups:** 85

Date of Accounts	Dec 11	Dec 10	Dec 09
Sales Turnover	336m	328m	370m
Pre Tax Profit/Loss	27m	31m	55m
Working Capital	179m	190m	191m
Fixed Assets	45m	44m	52m
Current Assets	279m	284m	335m
Current Liabilities	97m	90m	143m

Pelmark Ltd
Barley Road Flint Cross, Heydon, Royston, SG8 7PU
Tel: 01763-208020 **Fax:** 01763-208021
E-mail: danny@pelmark.co.uk
Website: http://www.pelmark.com
Directors: J. Ridge (Co Sec), D. Marsh (Dir), D. Marsh (MD)
Managers: D. Cooper (I.T. Exec), M. Woodbridge (Mktg Serv Mgr), G. Bishop (Export Sales Mg), D. Goodwin (Sales Prom Mgr)
Immediate Holding Company: PELMARK INTERNATIONAL LIMITED
Registration no: 06956239 **Date established:** 2009
Turnover: £10m - £20m **No.of Employees:** 21 - 50 **Product Groups:** 81

Date of Accounts	Dec 10
Working Capital	285
Fixed Assets	33
Current Assets	954

Prototype Projects Ltd
Unit 1 Greenfield, Royston, SG8 5HN
Tel: 01763-249760 **Fax:** 01763-249382
E-mail: sales@prototypeprojects.com
Website: http://www.prototypeprojects.com
Directors: A. Pringle (MD)
Immediate Holding Company: PROTOTYPE PROJECTS LIMITED
Registration no: 03926132 **Date established:** 2000
No.of Employees: 11 - 20 **Product Groups:** 34, 38, 42, 47, 48, 84

Date of Accounts	Feb 12	Feb 11	Feb 10
Working Capital	399	261	35
Fixed Assets	243	216	125
Current Assets	649	455	114

R K Printcoat
Abington Road Litlington, Royston, SG8 0QZ
Tel: 01763-852187 **Fax:** 01763-852502
E-mail: sales@rkprint.com
Website: http://www.rkprint.com
Bank(s): Lloyds TSB Bank plc
Directors: T. Kerchiss (MD)
Immediate Holding Company: R.K. PRINT-COAT INSTRUMENTS LIMITED
Registration no: 00775106 **VAT No.:** GB 288 0063 50
Date established: 1963 **Turnover:** £2m - £5m **No.of Employees:** 21 - 50
Product Groups: 42, 44

Date of Accounts	Apr 11	Apr 10	Apr 09
Working Capital	656	392	997
Fixed Assets	664	681	721
Current Assets	2m	2m	2m

RailMeasurement Ltd

Barrington Road, Royston, SG8 5QP
Tel: 01223-208791 **Fax:** 01223-208795
E-mail: enquiries@railmeasurement.com
Website: http://www.railmeasurement.com
Directors: M. Saxon (Dir)
No.of Employees: 1 - 10 **Product Groups:** 45

Rooster Books Ltd (t/a Solutions for Business)

The Old Police Station Priory Lane, Royston, SG8 9DU
Tel: 01763-242717 **Fax:** 01763-243332
E-mail: mailbox@solutions-for-business.co.uk
Website: http://www.largeprintbookshop.co.uk
Directors: G. Garfit (MD), J. Garfit (Dir)
Ultimate Holding Company: Rooster Books Ltd
Registration no: 01367626 **VAT No.:** GB 432 2294 76
Date established: 1978 **Turnover:** Up to £250,000
No.of Employees: 1 - 10 **Product Groups:** 80

Date of Accounts	Jun 06
Sales Turnover	140
Pre Tax Profit/Loss	-21
Working Capital	-80
Fixed Assets	118
Current Assets	34
Current Liabilities	113
Total Share Capital	30
ROCE% (Return on Capital Employed)	-53.4

Royston Labels Ltd

Unit 18 Orchard Road, Royston, SG8 5HD
Tel: 01763-212020 **Fax:** 01763-248004
E-mail: enquiries@roystonlabels.co.uk
Website: http://www.roystonlabels.co.uk
Bank(s): HSBC
Directors: P. Clayton (MD)
Immediate Holding Company: ROYSTON LABELS LIMITED
Registration no: 03027229 **Date established:** 1995 **Turnover:** £1m - £2m
No.of Employees: 21 - 50 **Product Groups:** 27, 28

Date of Accounts	Apr 11	Apr 10	Apr 09
Working Capital	1m	2m	2m
Fixed Assets	2m	1m	2m
Current Assets	4m	3m	3m

Seppi

28 High Street Meldreth, Royston, SG8 6JU
Tel: 01763-260326 **Fax:** 01763-260035
E-mail: gareth@seppities.co.uk
Website: http://www.seppities.co.uk
Directors: G. Chapman (Prop)
Turnover: Up to £250,000 **No.of Employees:** 1 - 10 **Product Groups:** 24

Star Instruments Ltd

Barkway, Royston, SG8 8EH
Tel: 01763-848886 **Fax:** 01763-848881
E-mail: sales@star-instruments.co.uk
Website: http://www.star-instruments.co.uk
Directors: S. Boniface (Tech Serv), S. Donnelly (MD), S. Donnoly (MD), R. Castle (Fin)
Immediate Holding Company: STAR INSTRUMENTS (N.I.) LIMITED
Registration no: 00881910 **VAT No.:** GB 251 7688 38
Date established: 1966 **Turnover:** £2m - £5m **No.of Employees:** 1 - 10
Product Groups: 38, 40

Tapbio Systems

Grantham Close, Royston, SG8 5WY
Tel: 01763-227200 **Fax:** 01763-227201
E-mail: info@tapbiosystems.com
Website: http://www.tapbiosystems.com
Directors: D. Parnell (Dir), D. Newble (Fin)
Ultimate Holding Company: TAP BIOSYSTEMS GROUP PLC
Immediate Holding Company: TAP BIOSYSTEMS GROUP PLC
Registration no: 03596119 **Date established:** 1998
Turnover: £10m - £20m **No.of Employees:** 101 - 250
Product Groups: 38, 42

Date of Accounts	Mar 12	Apr 09	Apr 10
Sales Turnover	20m	17m	16m
Pre Tax Profit/Loss	1m	210	585
Working Capital	3m	925	1m
Fixed Assets	4m	1m	2m
Current Assets	9m	6m	7m
Current Liabilities	4m	4m	5m

Tru-Lon Printed Circuits Ltd

Newark Close, Royston, SG8 5HL
Tel: 01763-248922 **Fax:** 01763-249281
E-mail: rob@tru-lon.co.uk
Website: http://www.tru-lon.co.uk
Bank(s): Barclays
Directors: B. Savill (MD)
Managers: B. Jones, D. Braithwaite (Tech Sales Mgr), S. Payne (Admin Off), T. Gee (Tech Supp Mgr), Brown (Mgr), R. Brown (Mgr), S. Williams (Sales Prom Mgr)
Ultimate Holding Company: GALLUS HOLDING AG (SWITZERLAND)
Immediate Holding Company: NIGHTINGALE PRESS LIMITED
Registration no: 02673749 **VAT No.:** GB 215 7944 50
Date established: 1972 **Turnover:** £10m - £20m
No.of Employees: 21 - 50 **Product Groups:** 37

Unispare Domestic Appliances

11 Melbourn Street, Royston, SG8 7BP
Tel: 01763-247333 **Fax:** 01763-245988
Directors: R. Fulker (Prop)
No.of Employees: 1 - 10 **Product Groups:** 27

Walters & Walters Ltd

Unit 16 Orchard Road, Royston, SG8 5HA
Tel: 01763-245445 **Fax:** 01763-249810
E-mail: sales@waltersandwalters.co.uk
Website: http://www.industrial-markers.co.uk
Directors: M. Tribble (MD), L. Tribble (Fin)
Immediate Holding Company: WALTERS AND WALTERS LIMITED
Registration no: 00548442 **VAT No.:** GB 432 2398 66
Date established: 1955 **Turnover:** £250,000 - £500,000
No.of Employees: 1 - 10 **Product Groups:** 14, 17, 29, 32, 38, 49

Date of Accounts	Apr 11	Apr 10	Apr 09
Working Capital	19	-3	-0
Fixed Assets	179	184	187
Current Assets	78	67	75

Welding Alloys Ltd

The Way Fowlmere, Royston, SG8 7QS
Tel: 01763-207500 **Fax:** 01763-207501
E-mail: richard.hancox@welding-alloys.com
Website: http://www.welding-alloys.com
Directors: R. Hancox (Fin)
Managers: C. Ndungu (Purch Mgr), J. Everest, F. Fezzardi (Mktg Serv Mgr), L. Dalgaard (Personnel)
Immediate Holding Company: WELDING ALLOYS LIMITED
Registration no: 00793416 **VAT No.:** GB 213 8172 84
Date established: 1964 **Turnover:** £10m - £20m
No.of Employees: 51 - 100 **Product Groups:** 34, 35, 45, 46

Date of Accounts	Dec 10	Dec 09	Dec 08
Sales Turnover	13m	11m	9m
Pre Tax Profit/Loss	46	26	422
Working Capital	2m	2m	3m
Fixed Assets	4m	4m	5m
Current Assets	9m	7m	9m
Current Liabilities	993	370	776

Sawbridgeworth

Action Handling Equipment Ltd

Maltings Industrial Estate Station Road, Sawbridgeworth, CM21 9JY
Tel: 01279-724989 **Fax:** 01279-600224
E-mail: sales@actionhandling.co.uk
Website: http://www.actionhandling.co.uk
Directors: S. Phillips (Dir)
Immediate Holding Company: ACTION HANDLING EQUIPMENT LIMITED
Registration no: 00985730 **VAT No.:** GB 214 9913 57
Date established: 1970 **Turnover:** £1m - £2m **No.of Employees:** 11 - 20
Product Groups: 26, 27, 29, 35, 36, 39, 40, 42, 45, 84

Date of Accounts	Jul 11	Jul 10	Jul 09
Working Capital	4	-15	-23
Fixed Assets	329	314	325
Current Assets	289	279	251

Brilliant Ltd

Drake House 2 Duckling Lane, Sawbridgeworth, CM21 9QA
Tel: 01279-725358
E-mail: craig@brilliant.ltd.uk
Website: http://www.brilliant.ltd.uk
Directors: C. Mckenzie (MD), C. McKenzie (Fin)
Immediate Holding Company: BRILLIANT LIMITED
Registration no: 05292936 **Date established:** 2004
No.of Employees: 1 - 10 **Product Groups:** 44

Date of Accounts	Dec 11	Dec 10	Dec 09
Working Capital	55	56	49
Fixed Assets	4	5	5
Current Assets	107	99	71

Robson Scientific

4c Clarklands Industrial Estate Parsonage Lane, Sawbridgeworth, CM21 0NG
Tel: 01279-724324 **Fax:** 01279-600306
E-mail: sales@robsonscientific.co.uk
Website: http://www.robsonscientific.co.uk
Directors: P. Hollington (Prop)
VAT No.: GB 493 2318 40 **Date established:** 1988
Turnover: £500,000 - £1m **No.of Employees:** 1 - 10 **Product Groups:** 17, 31, 33, 37, 38, 40

St Albans

A G S Acrylics Ltd

15 Stanmore Chase, St Albans, AL4 0EZ
Tel: 01727-865050 **Fax:** 01727-865058
E-mail: sales@agsacrylics.co.uk
Website: http://www.agsacrylics.co.uk
Directors: C. Waugh (Dir)
Immediate Holding Company: A G S ACRYLICS LTD
Registration no: 03924353 **Date established:** 2000
No.of Employees: 1 - 10 **Product Groups:** 30, 49

Date of Accounts	Feb 12	Feb 11	Feb 10
Working Capital	22	18	15
Fixed Assets	9	12	15
Current Assets	122	253	249

Acugrip Ltd

Unit 7 Executive Park Hatfield Road, St Albans, AL1 4TA
Tel: 01727-845225 **Fax:** 01727-845345
E-mail: mail@acugrip.co.uk
Website: http://www.acugrip.co.uk
Directors: I. Potter (MD)
Immediate Holding Company: ACUGRIP LIMITED
Registration no: 04406823 **VAT No.:** GB 600 4054 06
Date established: 2002 **Turnover:** £250,000 - £500,000
No.of Employees: 1 - 10 **Product Groups:** 35, 36, 38, 45, 46, 47, 48

Date of Accounts	Mar 11	Mar 10	Mar 09
Sales Turnover	455	247	426
Pre Tax Profit/Loss	165	35	106
Working Capital	80	6	53
Fixed Assets	20	30	40
Current Assets	224	121	242
Current Liabilities	98	98	167

Arbor Flooring

56 Royston Road, St Albans, AL1 5NG
Tel: 01727-854678 **Fax:** 01727-854678
E-mail: mail@arborflooring.co.uk
Website: http://www.arborflooring.co.uk
Directors: J. Little (Prop)
Immediate Holding Company: JON LITTLE LTD
Registration no: 6441309 **Date established:** 2007
Turnover: Up to £250,000 **No.of Employees:** 1 - 10 **Product Groups:** 25

Date of Accounts	Nov 11	Nov 10	Nov 09
Working Capital	-12	-10	-7
Fixed Assets	13	10	10
Current Assets	29	8	6

Arc International Overseas Holdings Ltd

Verulam Point Station Way, St Albans, AL1 5HE
Tel: 01727-891400 **Fax:** 01727-891401
E-mail: info@arc.com
Website: http://www.arc.com
Directors: C. Rendell (Co Sec), C. Schlachte (Grp Chief Exec)
Immediate Holding Company: ARC INTERNATIONAL OVERSEAS HOLDINGS LTD
Registration no: 03923324 **Date established:** 2000
Turnover: £10m - £20m **No.of Employees:** 1 - 10 **Product Groups:** 37

Date of Accounts	Dec 07	Dec 06	Dec 05
Pre Tax Profit/Loss	-5	N/A	-3667
Working Capital	55	83	83
Fixed Assets	2711	2688	2688
Current Assets	55	90	90
Current Liabilities	N/A	7	7
Total Share Capital	520	520	520
ROCE% (Return on Capital Employed)			-132.3

Assign I T

4 Brick Knoll Park Ashley Road, St Albans, AL1 5UG
Tel: 01727-843888 **Fax:** 01727-839999
E-mail: helpdesk@assign-it.co.uk
Website: http://www.assign-it.co.uk
Directors: C. Delcore (Prop)
Immediate Holding Company: ASSIGN-IT LIMITED
Registration no: 04289206 **Date established:** 2001
No.of Employees: 1 - 10 **Product Groups:** 44, 80, 86

Date of Accounts	Sep 11	Sep 10	Sep 09
Working Capital	47	47	35
Fixed Assets	69	78	4
Current Assets	180	172	113

Aston Taylor

Unit 4 Salar House 61 Campfield Road, St Albans, AL1 5HT
Tel: 01727-773580 **Fax:** 01727-773588
E-mail: atm@astontaylor.com
Website: http://www.astontaylor.com
Directors: K. Canning (Sales), V. Chuntz (MD)
Immediate Holding Company: ASTON TAYLOR LIMITED
Registration no: 03748088 **Date established:** 1999
No.of Employees: 21 - 50 **Product Groups:** 80

Date of Accounts	Sep 11	Sep 10	Sep 09
Working Capital	322	306	250
Fixed Assets	2	8	54
Current Assets	453	415	365

Ateis UK Subsidiary of Ateis International S.A

102 Victoria Street, St Albans, AL1 3TG
Tel: 08456-521511 **Fax:** 08456-522 527
E-mail: infoplease@ateis.co.uk
Website: http://www.ateis.co.uk
Directors: N. Voce (Prop)
No.of Employees: 1 - 10 **Product Groups:** 37, 40, 67

Austin Trueman Associates

8 Spicer Street, St Albans, AL3 4PQ
Tel: 01727-858752 **Fax:** 01727-852376
E-mail: sales@austintrueman.co.uk
Website: http://www.austintrueman.co.uk
Directors: A. Trueman (Prop), B. Thompson (Fin)
Immediate Holding Company: AUSTIN TRUEMAN LIMITED
Registration no: 03631873 **VAT No.:** GB 600 5477 70
Date established: 1998 **Turnover:** Up to £250,000
No.of Employees: 1 - 10 **Product Groups:** 84

Date of Accounts	Oct 11	Oct 10	Oct 03
Working Capital	N/A	N/A	-32
Fixed Assets	N/A	N/A	32

Barcodemania.Com

Ver House London Road, Markyate, St Albans, AL3 8JP
Tel: 08455-085608 **Fax:** 0845-337 0260
E-mail: sales@barcodemania.com
Website: http://www.barcodemania.com
Directors: P. Cunningham (MD)
Immediate Holding Company: REPARATION CUSTOMER AND LEGAL SERVICES LTD
Registration no: 05488939 **Date established:** 2006
Turnover: £500,000 - £1m **No.of Employees:** 1 - 10 **Product Groups:** 44, 67

Date of Accounts	Mar 09	Mar 08	Mar 07
Working Capital	6	4	8
Fixed Assets	2	7	7
Current Assets	57	42	31

Blacks Of Sopwell Ltd

North Barn D New Barnes Mill, St Albans, AL1 2HA
Tel: 01727-856053 **Fax:** 01727-836448
E-mail: info@blacksofsopwell.com
Website: http://www.blacksofsopwell.com
Directors: I. Black (Dir)
Immediate Holding Company: BLACKS OF SOPWELL LIMITED
Registration no: 05475004 **Date established:** 2005
Turnover: £250,000 - £500,000 **No.of Employees:** 1 - 10
Product Groups: 26

Date of Accounts	Mar 11	Mar 10	Mar 09
Sales Turnover	434	377	328
Pre Tax Profit/Loss	49	34	21
Working Capital	4	5	-2
Fixed Assets	1	1	3
Current Assets	98	109	80
Current Liabilities	60	73	61

Blue Arrow Personnel Services Ltd

154 Hatfield Road, St Albans, AL1 4JA
Tel: 01727-841433 **Fax:** 01727-844241
E-mail: info@bluearrow.co.uk
Website: http://www.bluearrow.co.uk
Managers: J. Wandrow (Mgr)
Immediate Holding Company: SALES SERVICES LTD
Registration no: 06746393 **Date established:** 1984
Turnover: £75m - £125m **No.of Employees:** 1 - 10 **Product Groups:** 80, 86

Broadband Technology 2000 Ltd

Unit 4 Woodland Court Soothouse Spring, St Albans, AL3 6NR
Tel: 01727-791000 **Fax:** 01727-791001
E-mail: sales@broadband.uk.com
Website: http://www.broadband.uk.com
Directors: S. Bembenek (Ch), T. Cullen (MD)
Managers: C. Newman (Sales Prom Mgr), J. Simpson (Admin Off)
Registration no: 03062369 **VAT No.:** GB 604 1280 85
Date established: 1995 **Turnover:** £5m - £10m **No.of Employees:** 1 - 10
Product Groups: 07, 37, 38, 39, 40, 44, 47, 49, 67, 84

Date of Accounts	Mar 08	Mar 07	Mar 06
Working Capital	194	252	330
Fixed Assets	53	48	50
Current Assets	535	556	671
Current Liabilities	340	304	341
Total Share Capital	21	21	21

Brook Street plc

Clarence House 134 Hatfield Road, St Albans, AL1 4JB
Tel: 01727-813004 **Fax:** 01727-846654
E-mail: info@brookstreet.com
Website: http://www.brookstreet.co.uk
Directors: J. McDonald (Fin), M. Brennan (Tech Serv), R. Napper (Pers), E. Bannerman (Sales & Mktg)
Ultimate Holding Company: MANPOWER INC (USA)
Immediate Holding Company: BROOK STREET (UK) LIMITED
Registration no: 00459637 **Date established:** 1948
No.of Employees: 51 - 100 **Product Groups:** 80, 87

Date of Accounts	Dec 11	Dec 10	Dec 09
Sales Turnover	150m	150m	140m
Pre Tax Profit/Loss	-5m	-1m	-3m
Working Capital	40m	42m	42m
Fixed Assets	2m	3m	4m
Current Assets	58m	59m	58m
Current Liabilities	9m	9m	8m

Broomhills Shooting Ground UK

Windmill Road Markyate, St Albans, AL3 8LP
Tel: 01582-842280 **Fax:** 01582- 842318
Website: http://www.broomhills.co.uk
Directors: M. Duglan (Fin), A. Brown (MD)
Registration no: 05240201 **Date established:** 2004
Turnover: Up to £250,000 **No.of Employees:** 1 - 10 **Product Groups:** 36, 39, 40

Buttle plc

Soothouse Spring, St Albans, AL3 6NX
Tel: 01727-834242 **Fax:** 01727-834248
E-mail: peter.buttle@buttle.co.uk
Website: http://www.buttle.co.uk
Bank(s): Barclays
Directors: M. Prescott (Pers), P. Buttle (Fin)
Managers: L. Letts (Tech Serv Mgr), S. Buttle (Sales Prom Mgr)
Immediate Holding Company: BUTTLE PLC.
Registration no: 02657821 **VAT No.:** GB 433 0944 67
Date established: 1991 **Turnover:** £5m - £10m
No.of Employees: 51 - 100 **Product Groups:** 66

Date of Accounts	Dec 11	Dec 10	Dec 09
Sales Turnover	8m	7m	7m
Pre Tax Profit/Loss	-176	-359	67
Working Capital	389	560	914
Fixed Assets	110	153	136
Current Assets	1m	2m	2m
Current Liabilities	462	416	258

C D Kenworthy

56 Albert Street, St Albans, AL1 1RU
Tel: 01727-858788
Directors: C. Kenworthy (Prop)
No.of Employees: 1 - 10 **Product Groups:** 24, 26

Cars For Stars St Albans

The Victoria Suite 36 Marlborough Road, St Albans, AL1 3XQ
Tel: 08455-003030 **Fax:** 01604-810381
E-mail: info@carsforstars-stalbans.co.uk
Website: http://www.carsforstars-stalbans.co.uk
Managers: A. Drummond (Mgr)
Registration no: 04668387 **Date established:** 2003
No.of Employees: 1 - 10 **Product Groups:** 72

Clean Room Installation Services Ltd

9 The Metro Centre Ronsons Way, St Albans, AL4 9QT
Tel: 01727-840594 **Fax:** 01727-843368
E-mail: cleanrooms@stodec.co.uk
Website: http://www.cleanroominstallations.com
Directors: M. Daldry (MD)
Immediate Holding Company: Stodec Systems Ltd
Registration no: 02712045 **VAT No.:** GB 639 8229 96
Turnover: £1m - £2m **No.of Employees:** 1 - 10 **Product Groups:** 30, 40, 52

Date of Accounts	May 10	May 09	May 08
Working Capital	-277	-191	-152
Current Assets	19	29	47

Collins Plant Hire

3 Brinsmead Frogmore, St Albans, AL2 2LS
Tel: 01727-873797 **Fax:** 01727-874681
E-mail: info@collinsplanthire.com
Website: http://www.collinsplanthire.com
Directors: J. Collins (Prop)
No.of Employees: 1 - 10 **Product Groups:** 52, 83

Computer Two Thousand Ltd

Eclipse Court Half Moon Yard, 14b Chequer Street, St Albans, AL1 3YD
Tel: 01727-868176 **Fax:** 01727-831202
E-mail: mail@2000group.co.uk
Website: http://www.2000group.co.uk
Directors: P. Sambrook (MD), N. Clark (Sales), P. Sambrook (MD)
Ultimate Holding Company: 2000 Group P.L.C.
Registration no: 01437372 **VAT No.:** GB 626 3798 10
Turnover: £10m - £20m **No.of Employees:** 1 - 10 **Product Groups:** 80

Coral Press Office Products Ltd

115 Hatfield Road, St Albans, AL1 4JS
Tel: 01727-844131 **Fax:** 01727-851331
E-mail: sales@coralpress.co.uk
Website: http://www.coralpress.co.uk

Directors: P. Yapp (MD)
Immediate Holding Company: EVERYDAYS A CELEBRATION LIMITED
Registration no: 05300409 **VAT No.:** GB 336 9633 29
Date established: 2011 **Turnover:** Up to £250,000
No.of Employees: 1 - 10 **Product Groups:** 27, 44

Date of Accounts	Apr 08
Sales Turnover	69
Pre Tax Profit/Loss	-12
Working Capital	6
Fixed Assets	4
Current Assets	14
Current Liabilities	8
ROCE% (Return on Capital Employed)	-117.1

Crohn's & Colitis UK

4 Beaumont House Beaumont Works Sutton Road, St Albans, AL1 5HH
Tel: 01727-830038 **Fax:** 01727-862550
E-mail: enquiries@crohnsandcolitis.org.uk
Website: http://www.crohnsandcolitis.org.uk
Managers: R. Driscoll
Immediate Holding Company: THE NATIONAL ASSOCIATION FOR COLITIS AND CROHN'S DISEASE
Registration no: 05973370 **Date established:** 2006 **Turnover:** £2m - £5m
No.of Employees: 21 - 50 **Product Groups:** 85, 87

Date of Accounts	Dec 07
Sales Turnover	1853
Pre Tax Profit/Loss	-80
Working Capital	2422
Fixed Assets	122
Current Assets	3198
Current Liabilities	776
ROCE% (Return on Capital Employed)	-3.1

Datalogic Automation

Datalogic House Dunstable Road, Redbourn, St Albans, AL3 7PR
Tel: 01582-464900 **Fax:** 01582-464999
E-mail: info@datalogic.com
Website: http://www.datalogic.com
Directors: S. Clapham (Dir)
Immediate Holding Company: DATALOGIC REAL ESTATE UK LIMITED
Registration no: 01683412 **VAT No.:** GB 382 3644 43
Date established: 1982 **Turnover:** £1m - £2m **No.of Employees:** 1 - 10
Product Groups: 44

Date of Accounts	Dec 11	Dec 10	Dec 09
Working Capital	2m	2m	2m
Fixed Assets	2m	2m	2m
Current Assets	2m	2m	2m

Dewars Forktrucks

Tollgate Farm Tollgate Road, Colney Heath, St Albans, AL4 0NY
Tel: 01727-821460 **Fax:** 01727-821465
E-mail: dewarsforktrucks@aol.com
Website: http://www.dewarsforktrucks.com
Directors: W. Dewar (Prop)
Immediate Holding Company: DEWARS FORK TRUCKS LIMITED
Registration no: 05052043 **Date established:** 2004
No.of Employees: 1 - 10 **Product Groups:** 35, 39, 45

Date of Accounts	Jul 11	Jul 10	Jul 09
Working Capital	-10	-24	-23
Fixed Assets	4	6	9
Current Assets	132	75	74

Edding UK Ltd

Edding House Merlin Centre Acrewood Way, St Albans, AL4 0JY
Tel: 01727-846688 **Fax:** 01727-839970
E-mail: info@edding.co.uk
Website: http://www.edding.co.uk
Bank(s): HSBC Bank plc
Directors: B. Hall (MD), I. Finn (Fin)
Ultimate Holding Company: EDDING AKTIENGESELLSCHAFT (GERMANY)
Immediate Holding Company: EDDING (U.K.) LIMITED
Registration no: 01249697 **Date established:** 1976 **Turnover:** £5m - £10m
No.of Employees: 11 - 20 **Product Groups:** 38, 49

Date of Accounts	Dec 11	Dec 10	Dec 09
Sales Turnover	6m	5m	5m
Pre Tax Profit/Loss	109	-97	-244
Working Capital	748	650	742
Fixed Assets	26	15	18
Current Assets	2m	2m	2m
Current Liabilities	369	399	220

Embassy Machinery Ltd

104 High Street London Colney, St Albans, AL2 1QL
Tel: 01727-823461 **Fax:** 01727-826822
E-mail: info@embassy-mach.co.uk
Website: http://www.embassy-mach.co.uk
Bank(s): Barclays
Directors: M. Ayres (Co Sec), N. Pistol (Dir)
Immediate Holding Company: EMBASSY MACHINERY LIMITED
Registration no: 00922106 **VAT No.:** GB 490 5938 13
Date established: 1967 **Turnover:** £5m - £10m **No.of Employees:** 11 - 20
Product Groups: 46

Date of Accounts	Aug 11	Aug 10	Aug 09
Working Capital	80	79	61
Current Assets	369	430	434

Enterprise A B Ltd

The Old Pump House 1a Stonecross, St Albans, AL1 4AA
Tel: 01727-751445 **Fax:** 01727-759507
E-mail: sales@eab.co.uk
Website: http://www.eab.co.uk
Directors: A. Bottin (MD), C. Bottin (Fin)
Immediate Holding Company: ENTERPRISE AB LIMITED
Registration no: 03944489 **Date established:** 2000
Turnover: Up to £250,000 **No.of Employees:** 1 - 10 **Product Groups:** 44, 79

Date of Accounts	Mar 11	Mar 10	Mar 09
Sales Turnover	N/A	50	N/A
Pre Tax Profit/Loss	N/A	11	N/A
Working Capital	-25	-24	-29
Fixed Assets	3	2	2
Current Assets	8	4	7
Current Liabilities	N/A	15	N/A

Epl Skylift

Watling Street Flamstead, St Albans, AL3 8HB
Tel: 01582-843202 **Fax:** 01582-843208
E-mail: marketing@nationwideaccess.co.uk
Website: http://www.nationwideplatforms.co.uk

Directors: H. Walters (Mkt Research)
Managers: W. Taylor (Mgr), J. Brown (Depot Mgr)
Ultimate Holding Company: LAVENDON GROUP PLC
Registration no: 02266921 **Date established:** 2001
Turnover: £20m - £50m **No.of Employees:** 21 - 50 **Product Groups:** 45, 83

Date of Accounts	Dec 10	Dec 09	Dec 08
Sales Turnover	93m	87m	81m
Pre Tax Profit/Loss	13m	-4m	1m
Working Capital	-96m	-103m	-106m
Fixed Assets	134m	157m	175m
Current Assets	65m	61m	136m
Current Liabilities	19m	16m	20m

Flexible & Specialist Cables FS Cables, FSC Global, FSC Global Ltd

Alban Point Alban Park Hatfield Road, St Albans, AL4 0JX
Tel: 01727-840841 **Fax:** 01727-840842
E-mail: sales@fscables.com
Website: http://www.fscables.com
Directors: J. Herbert (Sales), K. Maltman (Pers), D. Keene (Fin)
Immediate Holding Company: FSC UK LIMITED
Registration no: 06723859 **Date established:** 2008
No.of Employees: 21 - 50 **Product Groups:** 35, 36, 37, 39, 44, 45, 67

FOCUS International Ltd

109 Ashley Road, St Albans, AL1 5UB
Tel: 01727-883555 **Fax:** 01727-883550
E-mail: reception@focus-south.net
Website: http://www.focusg.co.uk
Directors: M. Schaffer (Fin), J. Moore (Dir)
Managers: D. Khwaja (Tech Serv Mgr)
Ultimate Holding Company: PENTLAND GROUP PLC
Immediate Holding Company: FOCUS INTERNATIONAL LIMITED
Registration no: 01461548 **Date established:** 1979
Turnover: £20m - £50m **No.of Employees:** 21 - 50 **Product Groups:** 24

Date of Accounts	Jan 12	Jan 11	Jan 10
Sales Turnover	28m	31m	24m
Pre Tax Profit/Loss	912	6m	2m
Working Capital	836	17m	13m
Fixed Assets	578	645	725
Current Assets	10m	24m	22m
Current Liabilities	1m	4m	3m

FSC Global Ltd

Abbey House Wellington Road, London Colney, St Albans, AL2 1EY
Tel: 01727-821822 **Fax:** 01727-744099
E-mail: sales@fscglobal.com
Website: http://www.fsc-global.com
Directors: D. Keene (Fin), G. Clements (Sales), J. Herbert (Dir)
Registration no: 04326243 **VAT No.:** GB 505 8219 55
Date established: 2008 **No.of Employees:** 1 - 10 **Product Groups:** 37, 44, 67

Date of Accounts	Oct 08	Oct 07	Oct 06
Working Capital	789	636	491
Fixed Assets	19	7	3
Current Assets	1252	1083	594
Current Liabilities	463	448	103
Total Share Capital	1	1	1

Furniture Fittings

111 Sandpit Lane, St Albans, AL4 0BP
Tel: 01727-863221 **Fax:** 01727-862617
E-mail: jandp@parisi1.orangehome.co.uk
Directors: J. Parisi (Prop)
Date established: 1988 **No.of Employees:** 1 - 10 **Product Groups:** 35, 36

G D Golding Ltd

220 Hatfield Road, St Albans, AL1 4LW
Tel: 01727-841321 **Fax:** 01727-831462
E-mail: goldings@tailors.co.uk
Website: http://www.tailors.co.uk
Bank(s): Barclays Bank P.L.C.,
Directors: G. Golding (MD)
Immediate Holding Company: G.D. GOLDING (TAILORS) LIMITED
Registration no: 01336299 **VAT No.:** GB 322 3250 09
Date established: 1977 **Turnover:** £500,000 - £1m
No.of Employees: 11 - 20 **Product Groups:** 24

Date of Accounts	Dec 10	Dec 09	Dec 08
Sales Turnover	899	1m	1m
Pre Tax Profit/Loss	104	185	207
Working Capital	223	195	148
Fixed Assets	35	52	72
Current Assets	424	445	534
Current Liabilities	129	159	110

G E Inspection Technologies

129-135 Camp Road, St Albans, AL1 5HL
Tel: 01727-795500 **Fax:** 01727-795400
E-mail: sales.uk@ge.com
Website: http://www.geinspectiontechnologies.com
Bank(s): Barclays, London
Directors: P. Wise (Dir), J. Twydle (Sales)
Managers: M. Skilling (Chief Mgr)
Immediate Holding Company: General Electric
Registration no: 03645466 **VAT No.:** GB 196 4267 27
Date established: 1971 **No.of Employees:** 21 - 50 **Product Groups:** 38, 48

Date of Accounts	Dec 09	Dec 08	Dec 07
Sales Turnover	10m	10m	11m
Pre Tax Profit/Loss	-737	220	346
Working Capital	-5m	-5m	-6m
Fixed Assets	5m	6m	6m
Current Assets	11m	10m	9m
Current Liabilities	1m	1m	817

Geesink Norba (Service & Spares Department)

Acrewood Way, St Albans, AL4 0JT
Tel: 01727-739000 **Fax:** 01727-739029
E-mail: kelvin.foster@geesinknorba.com
Website: http://www.geesinknorba.com
Managers: K. Foster
Registration no: 00306452 **No.of Employees:** 11 - 20
Product Groups: 36, 39, 44, 46, 48, 54

Bill Gilbert Meat Marketing
19 De Tany Court, St Albans, AL1 1TT
Tel: 01727-811331 **Fax:** 01727-851694
E-mail: enquiries@bgmeatmarketing.com
Website: http://www.bgmeatmarketing.com
Directors: B. Gilbert (Snr Part)
Date established: 1986 **Turnover:** £10m - £20m **No.of Employees:** 1 - 10
Product Groups: 20, 81

H T C Fastenings Ltd
Lyon Way Hatfield Road, St Albans, AL4 0LR
Tel: 01727-832131 **Fax:** 01727-843234
E-mail: slobban@htbrigham.co.uk
Website: http://www.hertstools.co.uk
Directors: D. Lobban (MD), S. Lobban (Comm), J. Taylor-Lavallee (Fin)
Managers: P. Grimbal (Sales Prom Mgr)
Immediate Holding Company: H. T. C. FASTENINGS LIMITED
Registration no: 01253974 **Date established:** 1976
Turnover: £500,000 - £1m **No.of Employees:** 1 - 10 **Product Groups:** 35, 66

Date of Accounts	May 08	May 07
Working Capital	843	905
Fixed Assets	95	65
Current Assets	1181	1293
Current Liabilities	338	387

Hardy Sheet Metal Ltd
Beech Farm Coopers Green Lane, St Albans, AL4 9HW
Tel: 01727-837833 **Fax:** 01727-837833
Directors: D. Hardy (MD)
VAT No.: GB 467 2257 31 **Date established:** 1995
Turnover: Up to £250,000 **No.of Employees:** 1 - 10 **Product Groups:** 48

Herts Tool Company
Lyon Way, St Albans, AL4 0LR
Tel: 01727-832131
E-mail: info@hertstools.co.uk
Website: http://www.hertstools.co.uk
Directors: S. Lobban (Prop)
No.of Employees: 1 - 10 **Product Groups:** 37, 41, 83

Icon P.L.C.
Albright House 156 St Albans Road, St Albans, AL4 9LP
Tel: 01727-730000 **Fax:** 01727-730001
E-mail: enquiries@icon-plc.co.uk
Website: http://www.icon-plc.co.uk
Directors: A. Coster (Dir)
Immediate Holding Company: Independent Computers Owners Network plc
Registration no: 02732784 **Date established:** 1992
No.of Employees: 1 - 10 **Product Groups:** 80

Date of Accounts	Aug 08
Pre Tax Profit/Loss	81
Working Capital	2120
Current Assets	2143
Current Liabilities	23
Total Share Capital	1200
ROCE% (Return on Capital Employed)	3.8

Indisplay Ltd
Ventura Park Old Parkbury Lane, Colney Street, St Albans, AL2 2DB
Tel: 01923-851580 **Fax:** 01923-854681
E-mail: sales@jmtindisplay.co.uk
Website: http://www.jmtindisplay.co.uk
Bank(s): Barclays, Aylesbury, Bucks
Directors: G. Shepheard (Co Sec), R. Groombridge (Ch), R. Sharp (MD), T. Barnard (MD)
Managers: S. Wilson (Ops Mgr), J. Power (Sales Off Mgr)
Immediate Holding Company: INDISPLAY INTERNATIONAL LIMITED
Registration no: 02434524 **VAT No.:** GB 541 2226 84
Date established: 1989 **Turnover:** £2m - £5m **No.of Employees:** 21 - 50
Product Groups: 26, 30, 35, 49, 81, 83

Date of Accounts	Dec 11	Dec 10	Dec 09
Working Capital	124	124	124
Fixed Assets	30	30	30
Current Assets	124	124	124

Intelligent People Ltd
Suite 8 Phoenix House Campfield Road, St Albans, AL1 5FL
Tel: 01727-736690 **Fax:** 01727-859 517
E-mail: info@intelligentpeople.co.uk
Website: http://www.intelligentpeople.co.uk
Directors: D. Bates (Dir)
Immediate Holding Company: INTELLIGENT PEOPLE LIMITED
Registration no: 04352450 **Date established:** 2002 **Turnover:** £1m - £2m
No.of Employees: 1 - 10 **Product Groups:** 80

Date of Accounts	Jan 12	Jan 11	Jan 10
Working Capital	234	221	208
Fixed Assets	19	18	22
Current Assets	372	373	295

International Labmate Ltd
Oak Court Business Centre Sandridge Park Porters Wood, Porters Wood, St Albans, AL3 6PH
Tel: 01727-855574 **Fax:** 01727-841694
E-mail: info@intlabmate.com
Website: http://www.labmate-online.com
Bank(s): Barclays
Directors: M. Patterson (MD), J. Page (Fin)
Managers: T. Akhtar (Tech Serv Mgr)
Ultimate Holding Company: INTERNATIONAL LABMATE LIMITED
Immediate Holding Company: LABMATE LIMITED
Registration no: 05814323 **VAT No.:** GB 600 7516 76
Date established: 2006 **Turnover:** £2m - £5m **No.of Employees:** 21 - 50
Product Groups: 28

Date of Accounts	May 08	Jun 11	Jun 10
Sales Turnover	2m	N/A	N/A
Pre Tax Profit/Loss	72	N/A	N/A
Working Capital	9	1m	1m
Fixed Assets	1m	N/A	N/A
Current Assets	156	1m	1m
Current Liabilities	3	N/A	N/A

J & P Windows
Hicks Road Markyate, St Albans, AL3 8LG
Tel: 01582-849303 **Fax:** 01582-849304
E-mail: enquiries@jandpwindows.com
Website: http://www.jandpwindows.com
Directors: A. Harris (Prop)
Immediate Holding Company: J & P WINDOWS LIMITED
Registration no: 06673420 **Date established:** 2008
No.of Employees: 1 - 10 **Product Groups:** 30, 66

Date of Accounts	Dec 11	Dec 10	Dec 09
Working Capital	-5	10	-16
Fixed Assets	10	12	16
Current Assets	135	213	94

Kenburn Waste Management
Kenburn House Porters Wood, St Albans, AL3 6HX
Tel: 01727-844988 **Fax:** 01727-844778
E-mail: info@kenburn.co.uk
Website: http://www.kenburn.co.uk
Directors: E. Bolt (Fin)
Ultimate Holding Company: MAMMON'S FUGLEMEN LIMITED
Immediate Holding Company: KENBURN WASTE MANAGEMENT LIMITED
Registration no: 02132685 **Date established:** 1987
No.of Employees: 21 - 50 **Product Groups:** 42, 45, 46, 48, 54

Date of Accounts	Sep 11	Sep 10	Sep 09
Working Capital	72	71	45
Fixed Assets	17	25	32
Current Assets	551	675	644

Kestronics Ltd
Unit 26 North Orbital Commercial Park Napsbury Lane, St Albans, AL1 1XB
Tel: 01727-812222 **Fax:** 01727-811920
E-mail: sales@kestronics.co.uk
Website: http://www.kestronics.com
Directors: P. Holm (Dir)
Immediate Holding Company: KESTRONICS LIMITED
Registration no: 02337714 **VAT No.:** GB 371 0160 14
Date established: 1989 **Turnover:** £5m - £10m **No.of Employees:** 1 - 10
Product Groups: 44, 67

Date of Accounts	Apr 11	Apr 10	Apr 09
Working Capital	221	239	271
Fixed Assets	162	173	210
Current Assets	809	693	906

Kilburn & Strode
Blenheim Gate 22-24 Upper Marlborough Road, St Albans, AL1 3AL
Tel: 020-7539 4200 **Fax:** 020-7539 4299
E-mail: ks@kstrode.co.uk
Website: http://www.kstrode.co.uk
Directors: N. Jennings (Ptnr)
Managers: B. Henry (Tech Serv Mgr), D. Bowman (Personnel)
Immediate Holding Company: KILBURN & STRODE LLP
Registration no: OC342299 **Date established:** 2008
Turnover: £20m - £50m **No.of Employees:** 11 - 20 **Product Groups:** 80

Date of Accounts	Mar 11	Mar 10	Mar 09
Sales Turnover	28m	25m	25m
Pre Tax Profit/Loss	7m	6m	6m
Working Capital	7m	6m	5m
Fixed Assets	242	341	329
Current Assets	9m	8m	7m
Current Liabilities	869	772	926

Masterbill Micro Systems Ltd
Units 2-3 Woodland Court Soothouse Spring, St Albans, AL3 6NR
Tel: 01727-855563 **Fax:** 01727-854624
E-mail: sales@masterbill.com
Website: http://www.masterbill.com
Directors: D. Rinter (Dir), A. Lovett (Fin)
Ultimate Holding Company: WOODLAND SOFTWARE SOLUTIONS LIMITED
Immediate Holding Company: MASTERBILL MICRO SYSTEMS LIMITED
Registration no: 01605823 **Date established:** 1981
Turnover: £250,000 - £500,000 **No.of Employees:** 1 - 10
Product Groups: 44

Date of Accounts	Sep 11	Sep 10	Sep 09
Working Capital	80	87	75
Fixed Assets	3	3	4
Current Assets	178	218	179

M B Honing Services
77 Maynard Drive, St Albans, AL1 2JX
Tel: 0781-216 0353 **Fax:** 01923-246 856
E-mail: mbhoningservices@googlemail.com
Directors: M. Broadbent (Dir)
Turnover: Up to £250,000 **No.of Employees:** 1 - 10 **Product Groups:** 36, 48

Metalwood Fencing Ltd
Soothouse Spring, St Albans, AL3 6PG
Tel: 01727-861141 **Fax:** 01727-846018
E-mail: info@metalwoodfencinguk.co.uk
Website: http://www.metalwoodfencing.com
Directors: J. Hutton (Co Sec)
Ultimate Holding Company: METALWOOD FENCING LIMITED
Immediate Holding Company: METALWOOD FENCING (CONTRACTS) LIMITED
Registration no: 02217664 **Date established:** 1988 **Turnover:** £2m - £5m
No.of Employees: 21 - 50 **Product Groups:** 25, 30, 35, 36, 40, 41, 52, 66

Date of Accounts	Mar 11	Mar 10	Mar 09
Working Capital	-52	-61	-48
Fixed Assets	312	314	316
Current Assets	75	65	78
Current Liabilities	117	N/A	N/A

Millers Ltd
Albert Bygrave Centre North Orbital Road, St Albans, AL2 1DN
Tel: 01727-824277 **Fax:** 01727-824277
E-mail: millerslimited@aol.com
Website: http://www.millersgardenbuildings.com
Managers: C. Whitaker (Mgr), C. Whittaker (District Mgr)
Immediate Holding Company: MILLERS LIMITED
Registration no: 02884602 **Date established:** 1994
No.of Employees: 1 - 10 **Product Groups:** 25, 33, 35, 66

Minerva Football Company Ltd
Unit 10 Metro Centre Ronsons Way, Sandridge, St Albans, AL4 9QT
Tel: 01727-845550 **Fax:** 01727-841555
E-mail: sales@minervafootballs.co.uk
Website: http://www.htsports.co.uk
Directors: J. Metselaar (MD), R. Metselaar (Dir)
Immediate Holding Company: MINERVA FOOTBALL COMPANY LIMITED
Registration no: 00556262 **Date established:** 1955
Turnover: Up to £250,000 **No.of Employees:** 1 - 10 **Product Groups:** 49

Date of Accounts	Nov 10	Nov 09	Nov 08
Working Capital	1	6	5
Fixed Assets	246	248	250
Current Assets	37	36	45

Murco Petroleum Ltd
4 Beaconsfield Road, St Albans, AL1 3RH
Tel: 01727-892400 **Fax:** 01727-892544
E-mail: murco_uk@murphyoilcorp.com
Website: http://www.murco.co.uk
Bank(s): National Westminster
Directors: P. Haylock (Co Sec), S. Rhodes (Fin)
Managers: S. Hogg
Ultimate Holding Company: MURPHY OIL CORPORATION (USA)
Immediate Holding Company: MURCO PETROLEUM LIMITED
Registration no: 00677691 **VAT No.:** GB 229 7543 37
Date established: 1960 **Turnover:** Over £1,000m
No.of Employees: 101 - 250 **Product Groups:** 66

Date of Accounts	Dec 11	Dec 10	Dec 09
Sales Turnover	3894m	2049m	1810m
Pre Tax Profit/Loss	15m	-35m	62m
Working Capital	92m	95m	70m
Fixed Assets	309m	322m	302m
Current Assets	599m	509m	376m
Current Liabilities	109m	117m	109m

Nagra Kudelski GB Ltd
Unit 3u St Albans Enterprise Centre Long Spring, Porters Wood, St Albans, AL3 6EN
Tel: 01727-810002 **Fax:** 01727-837677
Managers: J. Rudling (Chief Mgr)
Ultimate Holding Company: KUDELSKI S A (SWITZERLAND)
Immediate Holding Company: NAGRA KUDELSKI (GB) LIMITED
Registration no: 02706854 **Date established:** 1992 **Turnover:** £1m - £2m
No.of Employees: 1 - 10 **Product Groups:** 37, 38

Date of Accounts	Dec 10	Dec 09	Dec 08
Sales Turnover	2m	2m	2m
Pre Tax Profit/Loss	-498	7	-751
Working Capital	-2m	-1m	-1m
Fixed Assets	1	31	64
Current Assets	553	468	572
Current Liabilities	87	128	146

Nationwide Trust Ltd
Nationwide House 20 Lower Dagnall Street, St Albans, AL3 4RR
Tel: 01727-832241 **Fax:** 01727-795102
E-mail: martin.gahbauer@nationwide.co.uk
Website: http://www.nationwide.co.uk
Directors: B. Cornfield (Fin), B. Smith (Purch), D. Townsley (Sales & Mktg), K. Whiteford (Fin), P. Vinall (Co Sec), R. Heaf (Dir)
Managers: L. Rix (Mgr), R. Adcock (Comptroller), P. Whiteford (Comptroller)
Immediate Holding Company: NATIONWIDE BUILDING SOCIETY
Registration no: 01060355 **Date established:** 1972
Turnover: £250m - £500m **No.of Employees:** 101 - 250
Product Groups: 82

Date of Accounts	Mar 08	Mar 07	Mar 06
Pre Tax Profit/Loss	1700	-3000	20200
Working Capital	-16580	-195510	-219370
Fixed Assets	925190	1177m	1292m
Current Assets	412580	465880	480390
Current Liabilities	429160	661390	699760
Total Share Capital	6850	6850	730
ROCE% (Return on Capital Employed)	0.2	-0.3	1.9

New Brunswick Scientific UK Ltd
17 Alban Park Hatfield Road, St Albans, AL4 0JJ
Tel: 01727-853855 **Fax:** 01727-835666
E-mail: sales@nbsuk.co.uk
Website: http://www.nbsuk.co.uk
Directors: L. Helling (Chief Op Offcr)
Managers: P. Gold (Chief Mgr)
Immediate Holding Company: NEW BRUNSWICK SCIENTIFIC (UK) LIMITED
Registration no: 02098107 **VAT No.:** 540 1204 08 **Date established:** 1987
Turnover: £20m - £50m **No.of Employees:** 1 - 10 **Product Groups:** 38, 42

Date of Accounts	Dec 07	Dec 06	Dec 05
Sales Turnover	5612	4884	4722
Pre Tax Profit/Loss	420	210	263
Working Capital	4027	3745	3657
Fixed Assets	11	14	20
Current Assets	4537	4111	4001
Current Liabilities	510	366	344
Total Share Capital	5077	5077	5077
ROCE% (Return on Capital Employed)	10.4	5.6	7.2
ROT% (Return on Turnover)	7.5	4.3	5.6

Noshe Engineering Ltd
Beech Farm Coopers Green Lane, St Albans, AL4 9HW
Tel: 01727-837146 **Fax:** 01727-854144
E-mail: john.auld@noshe.co.uk
Website: http://www.noshe.co.uk
Directors: J. Auld (Dir)
Immediate Holding Company: NOSHE ENGINEERING LIMITED
Registration no: 02061811 **Date established:** 1986
No.of Employees: 1 - 10 **Product Groups:** 38, 42

Date of Accounts	Oct 11	Oct 10	Oct 09
Working Capital	27	-4	32
Fixed Assets	8	6	7
Current Assets	89	37	113

P R D
23 Marlborough Gate, St Albans, AL1 3TX
Tel: 01727-841455 **Fax:** 01727-847846
E-mail: cerys@prd.co.uk
Website: http://www.prd.co.uk
Directors: S. Blinkhorn (MD)
Immediate Holding Company: PSYCHOMETRIC RESEARCH & DEVELOPMENT LIMITED
Registration no: 01909571 **VAT No.:** GB 426 5690 36
Date established: 1985 **Turnover:** £500,000 - £1m
No.of Employees: 1 - 10 **Product Groups:** 80

Date of Accounts	Aug 11	Aug 10	Aug 09
Working Capital	27	57	26
Fixed Assets	2	3	3
Current Assets	67	62	31

Park Street Test Centre
Paynes Yard Park Street Lane, Park Street, St Albans, AL2 2NE
Tel: 01727-873814 **Fax:** 01727-875449
E-mail: parkstreetguns@talk21.com
Website: http://www.gunshot.co.uk

Directors: B. Lawrence (Ptnr)
Date established: 1981 **No.of Employees:** 1 - 10 **Product Groups:** 22, 23, 27, 32, 36, 67

Peek Traffic Ltd

Unit 5 Handley Page Way, Colney Street, St Albans, AL2 2DQ
Tel: 01923-289300 **Fax:** 01923-858453
E-mail: sales@peek-traffic.co.uk
Website: http://www.peek-traffic.co.uk
Directors: C. Parratt (Fin)
Ultimate Holding Company: IMTECH NV (NETHERLANDS)
Immediate Holding Company: PEEK TRAFFIC LIMITED
Registration no: 01490333 **Date established:** 1980
Turnover: £125m - £250m **No.of Employees:** 21 - 50
Product Groups: 37, 38, 39, 44, 51

Date of Accounts	Dec 11	Dec 10	Dec 09
Sales Turnover	63m	63m	58m
Pre Tax Profit/Loss	6m	6m	2m
Working Capital	17m	14m	7m
Fixed Assets	2m	2m	6m
Current Assets	29m	27m	16m
Current Liabilities	9m	9m	4m

Maurice Phillips

1 Old Parkbury Lane Colney Street, St Albans, AL2 2EB
Tel: 01923-289289 **Fax:** 01923-289200
E-mail: joannerobbins@mauricephillips.co.uk
Website: http://www.maurice-phillips.co.uk
Directors: B. Hendon (Jt MD), F. Pritchard (Dir), I. Phillips (MD), S. Molloy (Fin)
Ultimate Holding Company: SENZA GROUP LIMITED
Immediate Holding Company: MPL HOME LIMITED
Registration no: 00402965 **VAT No.:** GB 243 5130 94
Date established: 1946 **Turnover:** £10m - £20m
No.of Employees: 21 - 50 **Product Groups:** 24, 63

Date of Accounts	Dec 10	Dec 09	Dec 08
Sales Turnover	14m	17m	24m
Pre Tax Profit/Loss	36	-126	-489
Working Capital	1m	1m	1m
Fixed Assets	156	187	219
Current Assets	6m	5m	7m
Current Liabilities	1m	741	1m

Precision Data Prep Services

8 Thorpefield Close, St Albans, AL4 9TJ
Tel: 08450-039029
E-mail: nigel.seager@dataprep.co.uk
Website: http://www.dataprep.co.uk
Directors: N. Seager (Dir)
Immediate Holding Company: COSMOS SYSTEMS AND PROGRAMMERS LIMITED
Registration no: 00993264 **VAT No.:** GB 196 5969 87
Date established: 1970 **Turnover:** Up to £250,000
No.of Employees: 1 - 10 **Product Groups:** 44

Date of Accounts	Mar 11	Mar 10	Mar 09
Sales Turnover	N/A	N/A	54
Pre Tax Profit/Loss	N/A	N/A	31
Working Capital	44	46	35
Fixed Assets	N/A	1	1
Current Assets	62	67	72
Current Liabilities	9	20	9

Premier Deep Hole Drilling Ltd

Wellington Road London Colney, St Albans, AL2 1EY
Tel: 01727-825031 **Fax:** 01727-826819
E-mail: s.grant@premier-drilling.co.uk
Website: http://www.premier-drilling.co.uk
Bank(s): Bank of Scotland
Directors: S. Grant (Fin), S. Grant (MD)
Managers: P. Norris (Tech Serv Mgr)
Immediate Holding Company: PREMIER DEEP HOLE DRILLING LIMITED
Registration no: 01215178 **VAT No.:** GB 231 3727 88
Date established: 1975 **Turnover:** £2m - £5m **No.of Employees:** 21 - 50
Product Groups: 35, 48

Date of Accounts	Dec 11	Dec 10	Dec 09
Working Capital	410	371	256
Fixed Assets	685	644	726
Current Assets	2m	2m	968

Quadragraphics Ltd

Pickford Road Off Sutton Road, St Albans, AL1 5JH
Tel: 01727-856365 **Fax:** 01727-847911
E-mail: paulhooker@quadragraphics.co.uk
Website: http://www.quadragraphics.co.uk
Directors: P. Hooker (MD)
Immediate Holding Company: QUADRAGRAPHICS LIMITED
Registration no: 01263233 **Date established:** 1976
No.of Employees: 1 - 10 **Product Groups:** 28

Date of Accounts	Oct 11	Oct 10	Oct 09
Working Capital	24	22	30
Fixed Assets	2	2	2
Current Assets	34	26	36

Quester Assessment Systems Ltd

Thanet House Sleapshyde, Smallford, St Albans, AL4 0SE
Tel: 01727-826183
E-mail: crawford@quester.uk.com
Website: http://www.quester.uk.com
Directors: V. Crawford (Dir)
Immediate Holding Company: QUESTER ASSESSMENT SYSTEMS LIMITED
Registration no: 02318407 **Date established:** 1988
Turnover: Up to £250,000 **No.of Employees:** 1 - 10 **Product Groups:** 80

Date of Accounts	Mar 11	Mar 10	Mar 09
Working Capital	-0	-3	-3
Fixed Assets	N/A	N/A	3
Current Assets	1	1	1

R L Polk UK Ltd

26-30 Upper Marlborough Road, St Albans, AL1 3UU
Tel: 01727-845558 **Fax:** 01727-734700
E-mail: info@polk.co.uk
Website: http://www.polk.com
Bank(s): HSBC, Corn St, Bristol
Directors: M. Froemgen (Sales)
Ultimate Holding Company: R L POLK & COMPANY (USA)
Immediate Holding Company: R. L. POLK UK LTD
Registration no: 03086027 **VAT No.:** GB 674 4594 95
Date established: 1995 **Turnover:** £2m - £5m **No.of Employees:** 21 - 50
Product Groups: 86

Date of Accounts	Mar 11	Mar 10	Mar 09
Sales Turnover	5m	5m	5m
Pre Tax Profit/Loss	-552	-2m	-2m
Working Capital	2m	920	56
Fixed Assets	3m	3m	4m
Current Assets	3m	2m	2m
Current Liabilities	908	642	695

Screwfast Foundations Ltd

Unit 7c Smallford Works Smallford Lane, Smallford, St Albans, AL4 0SA
Tel: 01727-821282 **Fax:** 01727-828098
E-mail: info@screwfast.com
Website: http://www.aardvarksi.com
Directors: M. Lawrence (Fin)
Managers: A. Collins (Sales & Mktg Mg), L. Wakeling (Sales Admin)
Immediate Holding Company: AARDVARK SITE INVESTIGATIONS LIMITED
Registration no: 03615308 **VAT No.:** GB 741 0325 76
Date established: 1998 **Turnover:** £10m - £20m **No.of Employees:** 1 - 10
Product Groups: 33, 34, 35, 45, 51, 66, 84

Date of Accounts	May 11	May 10	May 09
Sales Turnover	N/A	13m	8m
Pre Tax Profit/Loss	N/A	343	494
Working Capital	756	846	837
Fixed Assets	282	398	267
Current Assets	3m	5m	2m
Current Liabilities	N/A	492	333

Security Unlimited Ltd

1 Flint Cottages Inglewood Gardens North Orbital Road, St Albans, AL2 2EX
Tel: 01727-810418
E-mail: vince@securityun-limited.com
Website: http://www.securityunlimited.co.uk
Directors: V. Cook (MD)
Immediate Holding Company: SECURITY UN LIMITED
Registration no: 04890512 **Date established:** 2003
No.of Employees: 1 - 10 **Product Groups:** 81

Date of Accounts	Sep 11	Sep 10	Sep 09
Working Capital	-47	-58	-44
Fixed Assets	2	2	3
Current Assets	24	6	15

Sensors UK Ltd

135a Hatfield Road, St Albans, AL1 4JX
Tel: 01727-859373 **Fax:** 01727-844272
E-mail: sales@sensorsuk.com
Website: http://www.sensorsuk.com
Directors: D. White (MD)
Immediate Holding Company: SENSORS UK LIMITED
Registration no: 03870982 **VAT No.:** GB 198 6313 24
Date established: 1999 **Turnover:** £500,000 - £1m
No.of Employees: 1 - 10 **Product Groups:** 38

Date of Accounts	Jan 12	Jan 11	Jan 10
Working Capital	132	97	56
Fixed Assets	114	105	106
Current Assets	214	173	234
Current Liabilities	31	30	39

Sick UK Ltd

39 Hedley Road, St Albans, AL1 5BN
Tel: 01727-831121 **Fax:** 01727-856767
E-mail: info@sick.co.uk
Website: http://www.sick.co.uk
Bank(s): Deutsche
Directors: D. Nauth (Pers), A. Reeves (MD)
Managers: D. Benbow (Tech Serv Mgr), A. Hornby (Mktg Serv Mgr)
Ultimate Holding Company: SICK AG (GERMANY)
Immediate Holding Company: SICK (UK) LTD.
Registration no: 01147832 **VAT No.:** GB 198 3620 30
Date established: 1973 **Turnover:** £20m - £50m
No.of Employees: 21 - 50 **Product Groups:** 37, 38, 40, 44, 45, 46

Date of Accounts	Dec 11	Dec 10	Dec 09
Sales Turnover	23m	20m	16m
Pre Tax Profit/Loss	3m	2m	2m
Working Capital	4m	4m	3m
Fixed Assets	726	744	796
Current Assets	7m	7m	6m
Current Liabilities	2m	2m	1m

Simply Sites Ltd

35 High Street Sandridge, St Albans, AL4 9DD
Tel: 01727-893888 **Fax:** 01727-893777
E-mail: kevin@simplysites.net
Website: http://www.simplysites.net
Directors: K. Wong (Grp Chief Exec), K. Moyles (MD)
Managers: K. Ooyles (Mgr)
Immediate Holding Company: SIMPLY SITES LIMITED
Registration no: 04024109 **Date established:** 2000
Turnover: Up to £250,000 **No.of Employees:** 1 - 10 **Product Groups:** 44

Date of Accounts	Mar 09	Mar 08	Mar 07
Working Capital	-11	2	-3
Fixed Assets	6	7	3
Current Assets	15	18	9

John Smith

84 Oakwood Drive, St Albans, AL4 0XA
Tel: 01727-862052
E-mail: jeansmith_59@hotmail.com
Directors: J. Smith (Prop)
Date established: 1992 **No.of Employees:** 1 - 10 **Product Groups:** 36, 40

Stephen Webster Plastics

2 Brick Knoll Park Ashley Road, St Albans, AL1 5UG
Tel: 01727-863138 **Fax:** 01727-844291
E-mail: sales@stephen-webster.co.uk
Website: http://www.stephen-webster.co.uk
Directors: D. Williams (MD), R. Howard (Fin)
Ultimate Holding Company: BLACKFRIARS CORP (USA)
Immediate Holding Company: STEPHEN WEBSTER PLASTICS LIMITED
Registration no: 01435830 **VAT No.:** GB 334 1980 60
Date established: 1979 **Turnover:** £2m - £5m **No.of Employees:** 1 - 10
Product Groups: 30

Date of Accounts	Dec 11	Dec 10
Working Capital	10	10
Current Assets	10	10

Thornycroft Ltd

Thornycroft House 107 Holywell Hill, St Albans, AL1 1HQ
Tel: 01727-840011 **Fax:** 01727-855030
E-mail: info@thornycroft.co.uk
Website: http://www.thornycroft.co.uk
Directors: A. Walsh (Ch & MD), E. Budgen (Fin), M. Lodge (Co Sec), S. Walsh (Dir)
Managers: P. Stone
Registration no: 00549179 **VAT No.:** GB 223 3173 03
Date established: 1955 **Turnover:** £20m - £50m **No.of Employees:** 1 - 10
Product Groups: 20, 62

Date of Accounts	Mar 09	Mar 08	Mar 07
Sales Turnover	26m	24m	22m
Pre Tax Profit/Loss	649	2m	22
Working Capital	3m	N/A	3m
Fixed Assets	1m	N/A	761
Current Assets	11m	N/A	7m
Current Liabilities	1m	N/A	401

Viglen Technology Ltd

7 Handley Page Way Colney Street Colney Street, St Albans, AL2 2DQ
Tel: 01727-201800 **Fax:** 01727-201888
E-mail: customercare@viglen.co.uk
Website: http://www.viglen.co.uk
Directors: M. Ray (Fin)
Managers: G. Pendelton (Mktg Serv Mgr), H. Morris, M. Bailey (Nat Sales Mgr), P. Armstrong, J. Doornveld (Personnel)
Ultimate Holding Company: AMSPROP LONDON LIMITED
Immediate Holding Company: VIGLEN TECHNOLOGY LIMITED
Registration no: 04495621 **VAT No.:** GB 674 9503 02
Date established: 2002 **Turnover:** £50m - £75m
No.of Employees: 101 - 250 **Product Groups:** 67

Date of Accounts	Sep 11	Sep 10	Sep 09
Sales Turnover	63m	69m	54m
Pre Tax Profit/Loss	2m	510	861
Working Capital	10m	8m	8m
Fixed Assets	3m	3m	3m
Current Assets	23m	23m	21m
Current Liabilities	5m	5m	5m

Walton Engineering Co. Ltd

61 London Road, St Albans, AL1 1LJ
Tel: 01727-855616 **Fax:** 01727-841145
E-mail: pkemp@waltonengineering.co.uk
Website: http://www.waltonengineering.co.uk
Bank(s): HSBC, St Albans
Directors: P. Kemp (MD)
Immediate Holding Company: WALTON ENGINEERING CO.LIMITED
Registration no: 00377353 **VAT No.:** GB 238 4545 47
Date established: 1942 **Turnover:** £500,000 - £1m
No.of Employees: 11 - 20 **Product Groups:** 36, 38

Date of Accounts	Oct 11	Oct 10	Oct 09
Working Capital	260	214	197
Fixed Assets	125	93	92
Current Assets	415	421	355

Stevenage

A C I Ltd (ACI Firepipe)

Unit 7 Chells Enterprise Village Chells Way, Stevenage, SG2 0LQ
Tel: 01438-368888 **Fax:** 01438-728855
E-mail: sales@acionline.co.uk
Website: http://www.acionline.co.uk
Directors: D. Mitchell (Dir)
Immediate Holding Company: ACI LIMITED
Registration no: 06165168 **Date established:** 2007
No.of Employees: 1 - 10 **Product Groups:** 30, 38, 39, 40, 52, 84

Date of Accounts	Mar 08	Mar 07	Mar 06
Working Capital	35	7	8
Fixed Assets	25	31	30
Current Assets	171	114	98
Current Liabilities	136	107	90

A V C Europe Ltd

Bessemer Drive, Stevenage, SG1 2DT
Tel: 08702-430555 **Fax:** 01438-341301
E-mail: reception@avcgroup.co.uk
Website: http://www.avcgroup.co.uk
Directors: S. Dance (Tech Serv), M. Every (Dir)
Ultimate Holding Company: AVC GLOBAL SERVICES GROUP PLC
Immediate Holding Company: AVC (EUROPE) LIMITED
Registration no: 03028485 **Date established:** 1995 **Turnover:** £5m - £10m
No.of Employees: 1 - 10 **Product Groups:** 37, 44

Date of Accounts	Jan 11	Jan 10	Jan 09
Sales Turnover	7m	9m	14m
Pre Tax Profit/Loss	218	268	564
Working Capital	3m	2m	3m
Fixed Assets	595	716	976
Current Assets	5m	7m	22m
Current Liabilities	1m	1m	1m

Abbey Steel & Shearing Co. Ltd

5 Cartwright Road, Stevenage, SG1 4QJ
Tel: 01438-741888 **Fax:** 01438-740980
E-mail: sales@abbeysteel.co.uk
Website: http://www.abbeysteel.co.uk
Bank(s): HSBC, Luton
Directors: J. Cooper (Fin), P. Cooper (MD)
Ultimate Holding Company: BONDREALM LIMITED
Immediate Holding Company: ABBEY STEEL AND SHEARING COMPANY LIMITED
Registration no: 01570148 **Date established:** 1981 **Turnover:** £2m - £5m
No.of Employees: 11 - 20 **Product Groups:** 34, 48, 51

Date of Accounts	Mar 11	Mar 10	Mar 09
Working Capital	657	600	569
Fixed Assets	28	31	33
Current Assets	2m	2m	1m

Aeroflex Ltd

Six Hills Way, Stevenage, SG1 2AN
Tel: 01438-742200 **Fax:** 01438-727601
E-mail: derek.smith@aeroflex.com
Website: http://www.aeroflex.com
Bank(s): National Westminster Bank Plc
Directors: D. Smith (Fin)
Immediate Holding Company: AEROFLEX UK LIMITED
Registration no: 04626614 **Date established:** 2003
Turnover: £50m - £75m **No.of Employees:** 251 - 500
Product Groups: 37, 38, 44, 85

Allan Dyson Asbestos Services Ltd

Cagex House Leyden Road, Stevenage, SG1 2BP
Tel: 01438-360656 **Fax:** 01438-721973
E-mail: mailbox@allandyson-asbestos.co.uk
Website: http://www.allandyson-asbestos.co.uk
Directors: A. Dyson (MD)
Immediate Holding Company: ALLAN DYSON ASBESTOS SERVICES LIMITED
Registration no: 03227042 **Date established:** 1996 **Turnover:** £1m - £2m
No.of Employees: 11 - 20 **Product Groups:** 33, 40, 54, 80

Date of Accounts	Sep 11	Sep 10	Sep 09
Working Capital	280	188	216
Fixed Assets	79	82	75
Current Assets	623	468	534

Allstat Ltd

Unit 10 Bowmans Trading Estate Bessemer Drive, Stevenage, SG1 2DL
Tel: 01438-759084 **Fax:** 01438-740958
E-mail: info@allstat.co.uk
Website: http://www.allstat.co.uk
Bank(s): The Royal Bank of Scotland
Directors: P. Tingle (MD)
Ultimate Holding Company: ALL HOLDINGS LIMITED
Immediate Holding Company: ALLSTAT LIMITED
Registration no: 00926448 **VAT No.:** GB 213 3324 15
Date established: 1968 **Turnover:** £1m - £2m **No.of Employees:** 11 - 20
Product Groups: 27

Date of Accounts	Dec 10	Dec 09	Dec 08
Working Capital	40	59	44
Fixed Assets	169	161	167
Current Assets	500	521	475

Alroy Sheet Metal Ltd

Gunnels Wood Road, Stevenage, SG1 2BL
Tel: 01438-355687 **Fax:** 01438-367608
E-mail: info@alroys.com
Website: http://www.alroys.com
Directors: D. Grist (MD), L. Grist (Fin)
Immediate Holding Company: ALROY SHEET METALS LIMITED
Registration no: 00693133 **VAT No.:** GB 196 4841 21
Date established: 1961 **Turnover:** £1m - £2m **No.of Employees:** 1 - 10
Product Groups: 48

Date of Accounts	Mar 12	Sep 11	Sep 10
Working Capital	57	73	-103
Fixed Assets	100	107	124
Current Assets	149	140	162

Arista Tubes Ltd

Unit 6 Meadway Technology Park, Rutherford Close, Stevenage, SG1 2EF
Tel: 01438-342200 **Fax:** 01438-316424
E-mail: evelyn.tweedlie@arista-tubes.com
Website: http://www.arista-tubes.com
Bank(s): Lloyds TSB Bank plc
Directors: E. Tweedlie (Sales & Mktg)
Managers: R. Mason (Buyer)
Registration no: 03582296 **VAT No.:** GB 720 2344 82
No.of Employees: 101 - 250 **Product Groups:** 30, 31, 48, 66

Date of Accounts	Dec 07	Dec 06	Dec 05
Sales Turnover	14390	13981	11830
Pre Tax Profit/Loss	-1492	-443	-671
Working Capital	-329	-762	-521
Fixed Assets	879	2755	2253
Current Assets	6919	5010	3966
Current Liabilities	7248	5772	4487
Total Share Capital	917	917	100
ROCE% (Return on Capital Employed)	-271.3	-22.2	-38.7
ROT% (Return on Turnover)	-10.4	-3.2	-5.7

B J C Communication Contracts Ltd

212 Mendip Way, Stevenage, SG1 6GB
Tel: 07879-605543 **Fax:** 0844-587 5728
E-mail: mail@bjccommunications.co.uk
Website: http://www.bjccommunications.co.uk
Directors: B. Edger (MD), D. Edgar (Dir)
Registration no: 02572615 **Turnover:** Up to £250,000
No.of Employees: 1 - 10 **Product Groups:** 40

Date of Accounts	Jan 11	Jan 10	Jan 09
Working Capital	-16	-19	-6
Fixed Assets	4	5	7
Current Assets	34	27	41

B M W Group Ltd

Gunnels Wood Road, Stevenage, SG1 2BH
Tel: 01438-760200 **Fax:** 01438-317789
E-mail: info@mfk.co.uk
Website: http://www.mfk.co.uk
Directors: F. Gypps (MD), N. Dartnall (Sales)
Immediate Holding Company: LAZERBUILT LIMITED
Date established: 1981 **Turnover:** £2m - £5m **No.of Employees:** 1 - 10
Product Groups: 28

I A Barnes & Co. Ltd

Unit 21 Gunnels Wood Park Gunnels Wood Road, Stevenage, SG1 2BH
Tel: 01438-354972 **Fax:** 01438-741530
E-mail: nicola@iabco.co.uk
Website: http://www.iabco.co.uk
Directors: M. Barnes (Dir)
Ultimate Holding Company: I A BARNES HOLDINGS LIMITED
Immediate Holding Company: I.A. BARNES & CO., LIMITED
Registration no: 01654903 **VAT No.:** GB 366 0700 64
Date established: 1982 **Turnover:** £1m - £2m **No.of Employees:** 1 - 10
Product Groups: 35

Date of Accounts	Sep 11	Sep 10	Sep 09
Working Capital	120	106	88
Fixed Assets	33	11	15
Current Assets	1m	1m	1m

Blythewood Plant Hire Ltd

Wedgewood Gate Industrial Estate Wedgewood Way, Stevenage, SG1 4SU
Tel: 01438-311222 **Fax:** 01438-367000
E-mail: hiredesk@blythewood-plant.co.uk
Website: http://www.blythewood-plant.co.uk
Managers: H. South (Depot Mgr)
Ultimate Holding Company: DOYLE PLC
Immediate Holding Company: BPH REALISATIONS LIMITED
Registration no: 01518966 **Date established:** 1980
Turnover: £500,000 - £1m **No.of Employees:** 1 - 10 **Product Groups:** 45, 67, 83

Date of Accounts	Mar 12	Mar 11	Mar 10
Working Capital	-20	-9	-14
Fixed Assets	8	1	4
Current Assets	1	N/A	N/A

J E Buckle Engineers Ltd

High Street Cromer, Stevenage, SG2 7QA
Tel: 01438-861257 **Fax:** 01438-861783
E-mail: gary.buckle@jebuckle.co.uk
Website: http://www.jebuckle.co.uk
Directors: G. Buckle (MD)
Immediate Holding Company: J. E. BUCKLE (ENGINEERS) LIMITED
Registration no: 01369618 **Date established:** 1978
Turnover: £10m - £20m **No.of Employees:** 11 - 20 **Product Groups:** 22, 24, 37, 39, 41, 45, 48, 63, 67, 68, 72, 76, 83

Date of Accounts	May 11	May 10	May 09
Sales Turnover	10m	8m	N/A
Pre Tax Profit/Loss	343	245	N/A
Working Capital	986	820	800
Fixed Assets	647	619	472
Current Assets	4m	3m	3m
Current Liabilities	373	227	N/A

Campbell Collins

Carlton House Boulton Road, Stevenage, SG1 4QX
Tel: 01438-369466 **Fax:** 01438-316465
E-mail: sales@camcol.co.uk
Website: http://www.camcol.co.uk
Directors: I. Campbell (Prop)
Managers: K. Sweetlove (Mgr)
Immediate Holding Company: CAMPBELL COLLINS LIMITED
Registration no: 01498963 **VAT No.:** GB 491 1580 44
Date established: 1980 **Turnover:** £2m - £5m **No.of Employees:** 11 - 20
Product Groups: 30, 33, 37, 38, 39, 44, 67

Date of Accounts	Jul 11	Jul 10	Jul 09
Working Capital	69	48	51
Fixed Assets	42	11	14
Current Assets	678	577	703

Catomance Technologies Ltd

4 Caxton Place, Stevenage, SG1 2UF
Tel: 01438-360747
E-mail: michael.woods@catomance.co.uk
Website: http://www.catomance.co.uk
Directors: M. Woods (Dir)
Immediate Holding Company: HAYESSHELF NUMBER 1 LIMITED
Registration no: 03984360 **Date established:** 2000
No.of Employees: 1 - 10 **Product Groups:** 22, 32

Comark Ltd

Comark House Gunnels Wood Park Gunnels Wood Road, Stevenage, SG1 2TA
Tel: 01438-367367 **Fax:** 01438- 367400
E-mail: nigelfearn@comarkltd.com
Website: http://www.comarkltd.com
Bank(s): HSBC Bank plc & Bank of Scotland
Directors: D. Tunley (Co Sec), N. Fearn (MD), D. Tunley (Fin)
Managers: A. Butler (Mktg Serv Mgr), M. Dawkes (I.T. Exec)
Ultimate Holding Company: DANAHER CORPORATION (DELAWARE U.S.A)
Immediate Holding Company: COMARK LIMITED
Registration no: 02929930 **Date established:** 1994
Turnover: £500,000 - £1m **No.of Employees:** 51 - 100
Product Groups: 38

Date of Accounts	Dec 10	Dec 09	Dec 08
Sales Turnover	828	5m	5m
Pre Tax Profit/Loss	941	-137	-8
Working Capital	4m	3m	5m
Fixed Assets	N/A	12	23
Current Assets	4m	3m	6m
Current Liabilities	148	412	546

Coster Aerosols

Babbage Road, Stevenage, SG1 2EQ
Tel: 01438-367763 **Fax:** 01438-728305
E-mail: info@coster.com
Website: http://www.coster.co.uk
Bank(s): National Westminster Bank Plc
Directors: K. Holloway (Dir), D. Goch (MD)
Managers: M. Barnes, P. Latter
Immediate Holding Company: COSTER AEROSOLS LIMITED
Registration no: 00897588 **VAT No.:** GB 197 7870 90
Date established: 1967 **Turnover:** £10m - £20m
No.of Employees: 21 - 50 **Product Groups:** 30, 31, 32, 36, 38, 40, 42, 49

Date of Accounts	Dec 11	Dec 10	Dec 09
Sales Turnover	17m	19m	14m
Pre Tax Profit/Loss	408	844	799
Working Capital	4m	4m	4m
Fixed Assets	2m	2m	2m
Current Assets	8m	7m	7m
Current Liabilities	585	595	880

Custom Electronic Design Services Ltd

Allied House Boulton Road, Stevenage, SG1 4QX
Tel: 01438-743855 **Fax:** 01438-743832
E-mail: info@custom-electronic.co.uk
Website: http://www.custom-electronic.co.uk
Directors: D. Broom (MD)
Immediate Holding Company: CUSTOM ELECTRONIC DESIGN SERVICES LIMITED
Registration no: 02255034 **VAT No.:** 491 1839 29 **Date established:** 1988
Turnover: £500,000 - £1m **No.of Employees:** 1 - 10 **Product Groups:** 44, 84

Date of Accounts	Jul 11	Jul 10	Jul 09
Working Capital	-10	-10	2
Fixed Assets	8	10	12
Current Assets	65	24	41

Definitive Special Projects Ltd

High Tree Farm Wood End Ardeley, Ardeley, Stevenage, SG2 7BB
Tel: 01438-869005 **Fax:** 01438-869006
E-mail: steve@laserlightshows.co.uk
Website: http://www.laserlightshows.co.uk
Directors: S. Hitchins (MD)
Immediate Holding Company: DEFINITIVE SPECIAL PROJECTS LIMITED
Registration no: 02742484 **VAT No.:** UK 720 1137 92
Date established: 1992 **Turnover:** £250,000 - £500,000
No.of Employees: 1 - 10 **Product Groups:** 32, 37, 52, 83, 89

Date of Accounts	Aug 11	Aug 10	Aug 09
Working Capital	40	10	9
Fixed Assets	75	96	61
Current Assets	60	26	39
Current Liabilities	20	16	N/A

Du Pont UK Ltd

Wedgewood Way, Stevenage, SG1 4QN
Tel: 01438-734000 **Fax:** 01438-734836
Website: http://www.dupont.co.uk
Bank(s): Morgan Guaranty Trust Company of New York, 33 Lombard Street, EC3
Directors: P. Horry (Dir), R. Doig (MD)
Managers: A. Jordan
Ultimate Holding Company: EI DU PONT DE NEMOURS & CO (USA)
Immediate Holding Company: DU PONT (U.K.) LIMITED
Registration no: 04556216 **VAT No.:** GB 243 1152 07
Date established: 2002 **Turnover:** £250m - £500m
No.of Employees: 101 - 250 **Product Groups:** 23, 31

Date of Accounts	Dec 11	Dec 10	Dec 09
Sales Turnover	314m	302m	240m
Pre Tax Profit/Loss	35m	46m	40m
Working Capital	87m	100m	80m
Fixed Assets	132m	132m	126m
Current Assets	132m	158m	131m
Current Liabilities	13m	21m	19m

Enfield Electrical Supplies Ltd

Leyden Road, Stevenage, SG1 2BP
Tel: 01438-316144 **Fax:** 01438-364946
E-mail: info@leydenelectrical.co.uk
Website: http://www.leydenelectrical.co.uk
Directors: S. Tanna (MD)
Immediate Holding Company: ENFIELD ELECTRICAL SUPPLIES LIMITED
Registration no: 00934651 **VAT No.:** GB 196 6583 07
Date established: 1968 **No.of Employees:** 1 - 10 **Product Groups:** 25, 27, 29, 30, 33, 35, 37, 38, 67

Date of Accounts	Jun 11	Jun 10	Jun 09
Working Capital	630	783	878
Fixed Assets	801	830	851
Current Assets	1m	2m	1m
Current Liabilities	146	N/A	N/A

Eriks UK Ltd (Stevenage Service Centre)

8 Hyatt Trading Estate Babbage Road, Stevenage, SG1 2EQ
Tel: 01438-728801 **Fax:** 01438-367455
E-mail: kevin.miles@eriks.co.uk
Website: http://www.eriks.co.uk
Managers: K. Miles (District Mgr)
Immediate Holding Company: COSTER AEROSOLS LIMITED
Registration no: 00917112 **Date established:** 1967
No.of Employees: 1 - 10 **Product Groups:** 66

Date of Accounts	Apr 11	Apr 10	Apr 09
Working Capital	9	38	100
Fixed Assets	1	2	2
Current Assets	28	42	130

Ets-Lindgren Ltd

4 Eastman Way, Stevenage, SG1 4SZ
Tel: 01438-730700 **Fax:** 01438-730750
E-mail: info@ets-lindgren.com
Website: http://www.ets-lindgren.com
Bank(s): Barclays
Directors: T. Hawkes (Fin)
Ultimate Holding Company: ESCO TECHNOLOGIES INC (USA)
Immediate Holding Company: ETS LINDGREN LIMITED
Registration no: 00895272 **VAT No.:** GB 417 3775 39
Date established: 1967 **Turnover:** £2m - £5m **No.of Employees:** 21 - 50
Product Groups: 37, 38, 40

Date of Accounts	Sep 11	Sep 10	Sep 09
Sales Turnover	N/A	5m	4m
Pre Tax Profit/Loss	N/A	376	21
Working Capital	3m	2m	2m
Fixed Assets	186	192	212
Current Assets	4m	3m	3m
Current Liabilities	N/A	368	506

Fira International (Furniture Industry Research Association)

Maxwell Road, Stevenage, SG1 2EW
Tel: 01438-777700 **Fax:** 01438-777800
E-mail: info@fira.co.uk
Website: http://www.fira.co.uk
Bank(s): Lloyds TSB Bank plc
Managers: P. Reynolds
Immediate Holding Company: BM TRADA GROUP LTD
Registration no: 03181481 **VAT No.:** GB 669 0833 03
Turnover: £2m - £5m **No.of Employees:** 51 - 100 **Product Groups:** 38, 80, 85

Date of Accounts	Dec 07	Dec 06	Dec 05
Sales Turnover	5073	4146	3546
Pre Tax Profit/Loss	179	-24	-385
Working Capital	-177	-391	-468
Fixed Assets	232	211	195
Current Assets	1880	965	687
Current Liabilities	2058	1356	1154
Total Share Capital	100	N/A	N/A
ROCE% (Return on Capital Employed)	329.2	13.5	141.2
ROT% (Return on Turnover)	3.5	-0.6	-10.9

Flair Electronics Ltd

Brittania House 24-26 Boulton Road, Stevenage, SG1 4QX
Tel: 01438-727391 **Fax:** 01438-740232
E-mail: sales@flairelectronics.co.uk
Website: http://www.flairelectronics.co.uk
Directors: P. Hickton (MD), C. Hickton (Fin)
Immediate Holding Company: FLAIR ELECTRONIC SYSTEMS LIMITED
Registration no: 01353631 **Date established:** 1978 **Turnover:** £1m - £2m
No.of Employees: 21 - 50 **Product Groups:** 37

Date of Accounts	Apr 11	Apr 10	Apr 09
Working Capital	138	83	92
Fixed Assets	175	212	197
Current Assets	435	365	324

G & Y Services Stocktakers & Valuers

44 Hazelmere Road, Stevenage, SG2 8SF
Tel: 01438-355049 **Fax:** 01438-355049
E-mail: info@stocktaker.co.uk
Website: http://www.stocktaker.co.uk
Directors: P. Gandy (Prop)
Date established: 1972 **No.of Employees:** 1 - 10 **Product Groups:**

Gotec Trading Ltd
Boulton Road, Stevenage, SG1 4QL
Tel: 01438-740400 **Fax:** 01438-740005
Website: http://www.gotectrading.com
Directors: L. Gonnermann (Dir)
Immediate Holding Company: GOTEC TRADING LIMITED
Registration no: 01374951 **VAT No.:** GB 231 9235 79
Date established: 1978 **Turnover:** £250,000 - £500,000
No.of Employees: 1 - 10 **Product Groups:** 24, 38

Date of Accounts	Dec 11	Dec 10	Dec 09
Working Capital	38	79	118
Fixed Assets	6	7	8
Current Assets	66	107	147

Haesler Machine Tools
19 Whitney Drive, Stevenage, SG1 4BE
Tel: 01438-350835 **Fax:** 01438-229482
E-mail: ben.haesler@ntlworld.com
Directors: B. Haesler (Prop), B. Haesler (MD)
VAT No.: GB 632 3200 90 **Turnover:** £1m - £2m **No.of Employees:** 1 - 10
Product Groups: 36, 46

Harkness Screens Ltd
Unit A Norton Road, Stevenage, SG1 2BB
Tel: 01438-725200 **Fax:** 01438-344400
E-mail: arobinson@harkness-screens.com
Website: http://www.harkness-screens.com
Bank(s): Bank of Scotland
Directors: A. Robinson (MD), D. Lightley (Co Sec)
Ultimate Holding Company: ALLEN MCGUIRE & PARTNERS LIMITED
Immediate Holding Company: HARKNESS SCREENS (UK) LIMITED
Registration no: 02576490 **VAT No.:** GB 707 0120 86
Date established: 1991 **Turnover:** £2m - £5m **No.of Employees:** 21 - 50
Product Groups: 38

Date of Accounts	Sep 11	Sep 10	Sep 09
Working Capital	4m	3m	2m
Fixed Assets	135	162	99
Current Assets	6m	5m	5m
Current Liabilities	670	2m	2m

Nick Harris Specialist Mouldings
11 Braemar Close, Stevenage, SG2 8TA
Tel: 01438-228848 **Fax:** 01438-222992
E-mail: nick.harris47@ntlworld.com
Website: http://www.nickharris-specialistmouldings.co.uk
Directors: N. Harris (Prop)
No.of Employees: 1 - 10 **Product Groups:** 30, 32, 66

Harris Regrinds
Cromer House Caxton Way, Stevenage, SG1 2DF
Tel: 01438-311233 **Fax:** 01438-740794
Directors: F. Harris (Prop)
Immediate Holding Company: POPWORKS LIMITED
Registration no: 02143993 **Date established:** 2005
No.of Employees: 1 - 10 **Product Groups:** 46

Hi Fi Industrial Film Ltd
Wedgewood Way, Stevenage, SG1 4SX
Tel: 01438-314354 **Fax:** 01438-743183
E-mail: info@hififilm.com
Website: http://www.hififilm.com
Directors: D. Wodcke (MD), S. Stockbridge (Fin)
Ultimate Holding Company: MAAS DRIEHOEK BV (NETHERLANDS)
Immediate Holding Company: HIFI INDUSTRIAL FILM LIMITED
Registration no: 01869458 **Date established:** 1984 **Turnover:** £5m - £10m
No.of Employees: 21 - 50 **Product Groups:** 30, 37, 44

Date of Accounts	Dec 11	Dec 10	Dec 09
Sales Turnover	8m	7m	5m
Pre Tax Profit/Loss	377	131	139
Working Capital	3m	3m	3m
Fixed Assets	642	582	604
Current Assets	4m	3m	3m
Current Liabilities	243	169	105

Hydrophilm Ltd
7 Wedgewood Court Wedgewood Way, Stevenage, SG1 4QR
Tel: 01438-728700 **Fax:** 01438-728007
E-mail: sales@hydrophilm.com
Website: http://www.hydrophilm.com
Directors: L. Turner (Co Sec), J. Heys (MD)
Immediate Holding Company: THORPES ADVERTISING LIMITED
Registration no: 03362358 **Date established:** 2011
No.of Employees: 1 - 10 **Product Groups:** 46, 48

Initial Cleaning Services
P Gunnels Wood Park Gunnels Wood Road, Stevenage, SG1 2BH
Tel: 01438-728311 **Fax:** 01438-318477
E-mail: contactus@intialcleaning.co.uk
Website: http://www.initialcleaning.co.uk
Directors: M. Dring (Dir), A. Wrightson (Div)
Managers: P. Yeoman (Admin Off)
Ultimate Holding Company: Rentokil Initial plc
Immediate Holding Company: Bet UK Ltd
Registration no: 02329448 **VAT No.:** GB 625 9496 02
No.of Employees: 1 - 10 **Product Groups:** 52

Institution Of Engineering & Technology
Michael Faraday House Six Hills Way, Stevenage, SG1 2AY
Tel: 01438-313311 **Fax:** 01438-313465
E-mail: postmaster@theiet.org
Website: http://www.theiet.org
Directors: K. Woodward (Sales & Mktg), C. Oxland (Co Sec), A. Dowd (Dir), E. Almond (Fin)
Managers: R. Best, M. McAleer (Personnel)
Immediate Holding Company: THE INSTITUTION OF ENGINEERING AND TECHNOLOGY BENEVOLENT FUND
Registration no: 00441284 **Date established:** 1947 **Turnover:** £1m - £2m
No.of Employees: 21 - 50 **Product Groups:** 87

Date of Accounts	Jun 11	Jun 10	Jun 09
Sales Turnover	1m	2m	2m
Pre Tax Profit/Loss	3m	2m	-2m
Working Capital	1m	1m	1m
Fixed Assets	19m	16m	13m
Current Assets	1m	1m	2m
Current Liabilities	167	166	304

Intrinsica Networks Ltd
Business & Technology Centre Bessemer Drive, Stevenage, SG1 2DX
Tel: 01438-745000 **Fax:** 01438-745111
E-mail: enquiries@intrinsica.co.uk
Website: http://www.intrinsica.co.uk
Directors: J. Caser (Ch), J. Owen (Grp Chief Exec), J. Owen (Dir)
Managers: B. Hall (Sales Prom Mgr), D. Jappey (I.T. Exec), G. Owen (Sales Prom Mgr)
Immediate Holding Company: INTRINSICA NETWORKS LIMITED
Registration no: 02629643 **VAT No.:** GB 578 2181 17
Date established: 1991 **Turnover:** £1m - £2m **No.of Employees:** 1 - 10
Product Groups: 44

Date of Accounts	Jul 09	Jul 08	Sep 11
Working Capital	246	233	56
Fixed Assets	1	6	5
Current Assets	450	446	171
Current Liabilities	178	157	N/A

J M J Precision Sheet Metal Ltd
11 Boulton Road, Stevenage, SG1 4QX
Tel: 01438-360711 **Fax:** 01438-360721
E-mail: sales@jmjltd.co.uk
Website: http://www.jmjltd.co.uk
Directors: J. Carr (MD)
Ultimate Holding Company: JMJ HOLDINGS LIMITED (BVI)
Immediate Holding Company: J.M.J. PRECISION SHEET METAL LIMITED
Registration no: 04691025 **Date established:** 2003
Turnover: £250,000 - £500,000 **No.of Employees:** 11 - 20
Product Groups: 48

Date of Accounts	Mar 12	Mar 11	Mar 10
Working Capital	181	168	18
Fixed Assets	375	196	47
Current Assets	555	510	329

Just Sunglasses
Énergie Fitness Club North Road, Stevenage, SG1 4BB
Tel: 01438-318100
E-mail: sales@just-sunglasses.co.uk
Website: http://www.just-sunglasses.co.uk/
Product Groups: 38, 40, 63

Kalstan Engineering Ltd
Cavendish Road, Stevenage, SG1 2ET
Tel: 01438-745588 **Fax:** 01438-360579
E-mail: sjkalmar@kalstanengineering.co.uk
Website: http://www.kalstanengineering.co.uk
Directors: S. Kalmar (Dir)
Immediate Holding Company: KALSTAN ENGINEERING LIMITED
Registration no: 01497440 **VAT No.:** GB 335 1909 60
Date established: 1980 **Turnover:** £5m - £10m **No.of Employees:** 1 - 10
Product Groups: 30, 35, 48

Date of Accounts	Nov 11	Nov 10	Nov 09
Working Capital	-40	-30	-74
Fixed Assets	247	182	167
Current Assets	67	83	56

LeoTel Software Systems Ltd
Lines House 78 High Street, Stevenage, SG1 3DW
Tel: 01438-220200 **Fax:** 01438-233777
E-mail: info@leotel-software.co.uk
Website: http://www.leotel-software.co.uk
Directors: J. Bridson (MD)
Managers: H. Sarling
Immediate Holding Company: LEOTEL SOFTWARE SYSTEMS LIMITED
Registration no: 04493471 **VAT No.:** GB 801 8956 21
Date established: 2002 **Turnover:** £250,000 - £500,000
No.of Employees: 1 - 10 **Product Groups:** 44

Date of Accounts	Dec 11	Dec 10	Dec 09
Working Capital	432	373	331
Fixed Assets	5	7	8
Current Assets	592	589	565

Lime Technical Recruitment
Lime House 102 High Street, Stevenage, SG1 3DW
Tel: 01438-362088
E-mail: info@lime-tr.co.uk
Website: http://www.lime-tr.co.uk
Directors: S. Balstone (Ptnr)
Date established: 2010 **Turnover:** **No.of Employees:** Unknown
Product Groups: 80

M B D A
Six Hills Way, Stevenage, SG1 2DA
Tel: 01438-752000 **Fax:** 01438-753377
E-mail: precision.solutions@mbda-systems.com
Website: http://www.mbda.net
Directors: C. Evans (Fin)
Ultimate Holding Company: MBDA SAS (FRANCE)
Immediate Holding Company: MBDA UK LIMITED
Registration no: 03144919 **Date established:** 1996
Turnover: £500m - £1,000m **No.of Employees:** 1501 & over
Product Groups: 37, 38, 44, 48, 54, 67, 84, 85

Date of Accounts	Dec 11	Dec 10	Dec 09
Sales Turnover	512m	490m	721m
Pre Tax Profit/Loss	52m	-6m	27m
Working Capital	-270m	-292m	-300m
Fixed Assets	634m	577m	617m
Current Assets	364m	443m	522m
Current Liabilities	500m	630m	661m

M D Plating Ltd
Unit 21 Wedgewood Gate Industrial Estate Wedgewood Way, Stevenage, SG1 4SU
Tel: 01438-350527
Directors: J. Vieira (Dir)
Immediate Holding Company: M D PLATING LIMITED
Registration no: 01898720 **Date established:** 1985
No.of Employees: 1 - 10 **Product Groups:** 46, 48

Date of Accounts	Aug 11	Aug 10	Aug 09
Working Capital	-5	N/A	4
Fixed Assets	7	3	4
Current Assets	34	21	15

Maplin Electronics Ltd
14-16 Park Place, Stevenage, SG1 1DP
Tel: 08432-277328 **Fax:** 01438-353695
E-mail: customercare@maplin.co.uk
Website: http://www.maplin.co.uk
Managers: J. Green (Mgr)
Ultimate Holding Company: MONTAGU PRIVATE EQUITY LLP
Immediate Holding Company: MAPLIN ELECTRONICS LIMITED
Registration no: 01264385 **Date established:** 1976
Turnover: £125m - £250m **No.of Employees:** 1 - 10 **Product Groups:** 37, 61

Date of Accounts	Dec 11	Dec 08	Dec 09
Sales Turnover	205m	204m	204m
Pre Tax Profit/Loss	25m	32m	35m
Working Capital	118m	49m	75m
Fixed Assets	27m	28m	28m
Current Assets	207m	108m	142m
Current Liabilities	78m	51m	59m

Morrison Utility Services Ltd
Morrison House Primett Road, Stevenage, SG1 3EE
Tel: 01438-743744 **Fax:** 01438-369687
E-mail: charles.morrison@morrisonus.com
Website: http://www.morrisonus.com
Managers: K. Shires (Personnel), C. Morrison
Ultimate Holding Company: MORRISON UTILITY SERVICES GROUP LIMITED
Immediate Holding Company: MORRISON UTILITY SERVICES LIMITED
Registration no: 04530602 **VAT No.:** GB 297 2809 13
Date established: 2002 **Turnover:** £500m - £1,000m
No.of Employees: 21 - 50 **Product Groups:** 51, 52

Date of Accounts	Mar 12	Mar 11	Mar 10
Sales Turnover	545m	494m	480m
Pre Tax Profit/Loss	18m	18m	15m
Working Capital	75m	60m	48m
Fixed Assets	11m	15m	14m
Current Assets	188m	163m	137m
Current Liabilities	39m	32m	29m

Phosphor Technology Ltd
Norton Road, Stevenage, SG1 2BB
Tel: 01438-364343 **Fax:** 01438-364344
E-mail: gsorce@phosphor-technology.com
Website: http://www.phosphor-technology.com
Directors: G. Sorce (MD)
Ultimate Holding Company: BITHERSTONE SERVICES LIMITED
Immediate Holding Company: PHOSPHOR TECHNOLOGY LIMITED
Registration no: 02281612 **VAT No.:** GB 524 8319 43
Date established: 1988 **Turnover:** £500,000 - £1m
No.of Employees: 11 - 20 **Product Groups:** 32

Date of Accounts	Mar 12	Mar 11	Mar 10
Working Capital	1m	869	674
Fixed Assets	283	268	322
Current Assets	1m	1m	847

Plaspro & Company
Southgate House Southgate, Stevenage, SG1 1HG
Tel: 01438-726269 **Fax:** 01438-726267
E-mail: roger@plaspro.co.uk
Website: http://www.plaspro.co.uk
Directors: R. Whitten (MD)
Immediate Holding Company: PLASPRO & COMPANY LIMITED
Registration no: 01612385 **Date established:** 1982
Turnover: £500,000 - £1m **No.of Employees:** 1 - 10 **Product Groups:** 30, 31

Date of Accounts	Jun 11	Jun 10	Jun 09
Working Capital	48	57	84
Fixed Assets	14	17	18
Current Assets	379	423	346

Precision Optical Engineering A Business Centre of MBDA UK Ltd
Pb75A Mbda, Six Hills Way, Stevenage, SG1 2DA
Tel: 01438-754477 **Fax:** 01438-751198
E-mail: sales@p-oe.co.uk
Website: http://www.p-oe.co.uk
Bank(s): HSBC Bank plc
Managers: G. Old, R. Addison (Sales & Mktg Mg), D. Adams (Purch Mgr), J. Myler (Chief Mgr)
Ultimate Holding Company: MBDA UK Ltd
Registration no: 03144919 **VAT No.:** GB 641 4071 69
Turnover: £2m - £5m **No.of Employees:** 11 - 20 **Product Groups:** 37, 38, 48, 65, 85

Propak Sheet Metal Ltd
Unit 1 Gunnels Wood Park Gunnels Wood Road, Stevenage, SG1 2BH
Tel: 01438-728885 **Fax:** 01438-740298
E-mail: kevin@protak.co.uk
Website: http://www.propak.co.uk
Bank(s): Lloyds, Stevenage
Directors: A. Hughes (Sales), B. Bennett (MD), K. Baker (Fin)
Managers: B. Usher (Tech Serv Mgr), M. Bennett (Purch Mgr)
Immediate Holding Company: PROPAK SHEET METAL LIMITED
Registration no: 01328169 **VAT No.:** GB 322 2446 94
Date established: 1977 **Turnover:** £5m - £10m
No.of Employees: 51 - 100 **Product Groups:** 48

Date of Accounts	Aug 11	Aug 10	Aug 09
Sales Turnover	9m	8m	7m
Pre Tax Profit/Loss	388	948	113
Working Capital	3m	3m	3m
Fixed Assets	850	563	698
Current Assets	4m	4m	3m
Current Liabilities	253	539	243

Q E S Ltd
4 Chells Enterprise Village Chells Way, Stevenage, SG2 0LQ
Tel: 01438-749849 **Fax:** 01438-318420
E-mail: sales@qesltd.co.uk
Website: http://www.qesltd.co.uk
Directors: P. Marshall (Dir)
Immediate Holding Company: Q.E.S. LIMITED
Registration no: 02555706 **Date established:** 1990
Turnover: £500,000 - £1m **No.of Employees:** 1 - 10 **Product Groups:** 37, 44

Date of Accounts	Mar 12	Mar 11	Mar 10
Working Capital	65	64	89
Current Assets	91	91	117

Reed Specialist
20 The Forum, Stevenage, SG1 1EH
Tel: 01438-750649 **Fax:** 01438-750683
Website: http://www.reed.co.uk

see next page

***Reed Specialist** - Cont'd*
Directors: J. Reed (MD)
Managers: E. Wallis (District Mgr), J. Schneider (District Mgr), M. Doocey (Asst Gen Mgr)
Immediate Holding Company: REED EMPLOYMENT LIMITED
Registration no: 00669854 **Date established:** 1960
Turnover: £75m - £125m **No.of Employees:** 1 - 10 **Product Groups:** 80

The Retail Doctor
PO Box 463, Stevenage, SO30 2NF
Tel: 0845-1162138
E-mail: enquiries@theretaildoctor.co.uk
Website: http://www.theretaildoctor.co.uk
Directors: G. Thomas (Develop)
Date established: 2003 **Turnover:** Up to £250,000
No.of Employees: 1 - 10 **Product Groups:** 44

Ridgemond Training
Q3 Building Caxton Way, Stevenage, SG1 2DF
Tel: 01438-842200 **Fax:** 01438-842250
E-mail: enquiries@ridgemondtraining.org.uk
Website: http://www.ridgemondtraining.co.uk
Directors: S. McQueen (Fin), L. Collins (Co Sec)
Managers: C. Collins, L. Penman (Personnel), L. Andrew (Fin Mgr), M. Gittings (Mktg Serv Mgr)
Immediate Holding Company: RIDGEMOND TRAINING LTD.
Registration no: 01731533 **VAT No.:** GB 396 7146 08
Date established: 1983 **Turnover:** £1m - £2m **No.of Employees:** 51 - 100
Product Groups: 80, 86

Date of Accounts	Mar 11	Mar 10	Mar 09
Sales Turnover	2m	N/A	2m
Pre Tax Profit/Loss	-229	N/A	-78
Working Capital	-113	106	167
Fixed Assets	51	61	87
Current Assets	375	441	463
Current Liabilities	420	N/A	149

Safeway Lifting
9 Corton Close, Stevenage, SG1 2LB
Tel: 01438-724663 **Fax:** 01438-724663
Directors: K. Hemmings (Prop)
Date established: 1990 **No.of Employees:** 1 - 10 **Product Groups:** 35, 39, 45

Sodexho Ltd
Solar House Stevenage Leisure Park, Stevenage, SG1 2UA
Tel: 01438-341400 **Fax:** 01438-341541
E-mail: ian.anderson@sodexho-uk.com
Website: http://www.sodexho.com
Bank(s): Midland
Directors: G. John (Co Sec)
Managers: S. Kennoy (Mgr)
Ultimate Holding Company: SODEXO SA (FRANCE)
Immediate Holding Company: SODEXO LIMITED
Registration no: 00842846 **Date established:** 1965
Turnover: £500m - £1,000m **No.of Employees:** 1501 & over
Product Groups: 20, 61, 69

Date of Accounts	Aug 11	Aug 10	Aug 09
Sales Turnover	951m	971m	1011m
Pre Tax Profit/Loss	67m	61m	106m
Working Capital	95m	96m	55m
Fixed Assets	70m	56m	58m
Current Assets	322m	307m	305m
Current Liabilities	141m	125m	117m

Spies Hecker UK
Wedgewood Way, Stevenage, SG1 4QN
Tel: 01438-734705 **Fax:** 01438-734730
E-mail: contact-sh-gb@gbr.spieshecker.com
Website: http://www.spieshecker.co.uk
Managers: A. Cashel (Mktg Serv Mgr)
Ultimate Holding Company: E.I. du Pont De Nemours and Company
Immediate Holding Company: Du Pont Performance Coatings
Registration no: 02110814 **VAT No.:** GB 246 6685 26
Turnover: £10m - £20m **No.of Employees:** 51 - 100 **Product Groups:** 32

Stevenage Glass Co. Ltd
Cavendish Road, Stevenage, SG1 2EU
Tel: 01438-369311 **Fax:** 01438-740741
E-mail: stevenage.glass@lineone.net
Website: http://www.stevenage-glass.co.uk
Bank(s): HSBC
Directors: J. King (Fin), King (Dir), K. King (MD), S. Broom (Sales)
Managers: P. Williams (Personnel)
Immediate Holding Company: STEVENAGE GLASS COMPANY LIMITED
Registration no: 00874868 **VAT No.:** GB 197 3141 48
Date established: 1966 **Turnover:** £1m - £2m **No.of Employees:** 21 - 50
Product Groups: 33, 52

Date of Accounts	Mar 12	Mar 11	Mar 10
Working Capital	147	293	347
Fixed Assets	1m	986	1m
Current Assets	677	699	690

Stevenage Knitting Co. Ltd
Sish Lane, Stevenage, SG1 3LS
Tel: 01438-353240 **Fax:** 01438-748364
E-mail: stevenageknitting@hotmail.co.uk
Bank(s): National Westminster
Directors: P. Pinkstone (MD)
Immediate Holding Company: STEVENAGE KNITTING COMPANY LIMITED(THE)
Registration no: 00313978 **VAT No.:** GB 196 6557 08
Date established: 1936 **Turnover:** £500,000 - £1m
No.of Employees: 11 - 20 **Product Groups:** 24

Date of Accounts	Dec 09	Dec 08	Dec 07
Working Capital	87	167	167
Fixed Assets	255	317	313
Current Assets	166	243	250

Tristar UK Ltd
2 The Glebe, Stevenage, SG2 0DJ
Tel: 01438-221009 **Fax:** 01438-745511
E-mail: tristar_uk@hotmail.com
Website: http://www.tristar-uk.com
Directors: P. Kotecha (Dir)
Immediate Holding Company: TRISTAR (UK) LTD.
Registration no: 02912530 **Date established:** 1994
Turnover: £500,000 - £1m **No.of Employees:** 1 - 10 **Product Groups:** 38, 42

Date of Accounts	Dec 11	Dec 10	Dec 09
Sales Turnover	N/A	N/A	812
Pre Tax Profit/Loss	N/A	N/A	-14
Working Capital	33	37	26
Fixed Assets	3	4	2
Current Assets	363	422	376
Current Liabilities	N/A	N/A	145

U L O Optics Ltd
2 Caxton Place Caxton Way, Stevenage, SG1 2UG
Tel: 01438-767500 **Fax:** 01438-767555
E-mail: sales@ulooptics.com
Website: http://www.ulooptics.com
Directors: P. Maclennan (Sales), J. Barton (MD)
Managers: C. Coolbear (Chief Acct)
Immediate Holding Company: ULO OPTICS LIMITED
Registration no: 01682587 **VAT No.:** GB 370 9328 42
Date established: 1982 **No.of Employees:** 21 - 50 **Product Groups:** 33, 38, 48, 65

Date of Accounts	Dec 11	Dec 10	Dec 09
Working Capital	536	547	612
Fixed Assets	312	361	356
Current Assets	1m	1m	1m

Veale Associates Ltd
16 North Road, Stevenage, SG1 4AL
Tel: 01438-747666 **Fax:** 01438-742500
E-mail: va@vealea.com
Website: http://www.vealea.com
Directors: E. Veale (MD)
Managers: W. Douglas
Immediate Holding Company: VEALE ASSOCIATES LIMITED
Registration no: 01159968 **VAT No.:** GB 230 8496 62
Date established: 1974 **No.of Employees:** 1 - 10 **Product Groups:** 40, 54, 84, 85

Date of Accounts	Apr 11	Apr 10	Apr 09
Working Capital	219	190	211
Fixed Assets	55	71	77
Current Assets	326	217	395

Walters Associates (this entry will not appear in the book)
1 School Lane Aston, Stevenage, SG2 7HA
Tel: 01438-880484 **Fax:** 01438-880543
E-mail: pete@wavelength.co.uk
Website: http://www.wavelength.co.uk
Directors: P. Walters (Prop)
Immediate Holding Company: 3ARC CARESYSTEMS LIMITED
Registration no: 05754303 **Date established:** 2011
Turnover: £250,000 - £500,000 **No.of Employees:** 1 - 10
Product Groups: 44, 81, 84

Date of Accounts	Mar 11	Mar 10	Mar 09
Working Capital	-57	-57	-33
Fixed Assets	26	29	1
Current Assets	27	8	11

Webbs Spare Parts
129c High Street, Stevenage, SG1 3HS
Tel: 01438-312669 **Fax:** 01438-729867
E-mail: web21.stevenage@autonetplus.co.uk
Website: http://www.bennetts.com
Directors: M. Major (Co Sec)
Managers: I. Wilkinson (Mgr)
VAT No.: GB 344 4261 70 **Date established:** 1954 **Turnover:** £1m - £2m
No.of Employees: 1 - 10 **Product Groups:** 68

Date of Accounts	Dec 07	Dec 06	Dec 05
Working Capital	205	210	213
Fixed Assets	657	657	626
Current Assets	219	226	228
Current Liabilities	15	16	16
Total Share Capital	1	1	1

Welding Tool Supplies Ltd
Cromer House Caxton Way, Stevenage, SG1 2DF
Tel: 01438-726991 **Fax:** 01438-350022
E-mail: sales@weldingtools.co.uk
Website: http://www.wts.demon.co.uk
Directors: G. Argent (MD)
Immediate Holding Company: WELDING TOOL SUPPLIES LIMITED
Registration no: 02618852 **Date established:** 1991
Turnover: Up to £250,000 **No.of Employees:** 1 - 10 **Product Groups:** 46

Date of Accounts	Apr 11	Apr 10	Apr 09
Sales Turnover	N/A	218	175
Pre Tax Profit/Loss	N/A	45	35
Working Capital	-11	-12	-1
Fixed Assets	13	12	2
Current Assets	39	64	68
Current Liabilities	N/A	11	N/A

Whitehot Creative
Southgate House Southgate, Stevenage, SG1 1HG
Tel: 0845-2015160
E-mail: info@whitehot-creative.co.uk
Website: http://www.whitehot-creative.co.uk
Directors: T. Earl (Sales), L. Earle (Prop)
Immediate Holding Company: WESTAWAY HEIGHTS (PILTON) MANAGEMENT LIMITED
Registration no: 02098111 **Date established:** 2004
Turnover: £250,000 - £500,000 **No.of Employees:** 1 - 10
Product Groups: 81

Willian Design Ltd
15 Leyden Road, Stevenage, SG1 2BW
Tel: 01438-742100 **Fax:** 01438-742121
E-mail: sales@willian.com
Website: http://www.willian.com
Directors: J. Lee (MD)
Immediate Holding Company: WILLIAN DESIGN LIMITED
Registration no: 01312907 **VAT No.:** GB 301 7306 08
Date established: 1977 **Turnover:** £2m - £5m **No.of Employees:** 1 - 10
Product Groups: 84

Date of Accounts	May 11	May 10	May 09
Working Capital	653	658	465
Fixed Assets	7	8	11
Current Assets	704	759	536

Tring

4b Martin Vest Ltd
Unit 3 Icknield Way Industrial Estate Icknield Way, Tring, HP23 4JX
Tel: 01442-892080 **Fax:** 0845-1662869
E-mail: info@4bmartinvest.co.uk
Website: http://www.4bmartinvest.co.uk
Directors: P. Bridson (MD), S. Bridson (Sales), S. Bridson (MD), D. Bridson (Dir), D. Bridson (Co Sec)
Managers: A. Hart (Prod Mgr), M. Bridson
Immediate Holding Company: 4B MARTINVEST LIMITED
Registration no: 01695586 **Date established:** 1983 **Turnover:** £1m - £2m
No.of Employees: 1 - 10 **Product Groups:** 44

Date of Accounts	Apr 08	Apr 07	Apr 06
Working Capital	-369	-208	-225
Fixed Assets	164	23	29
Current Assets	49	89	61
Current Liabilities	417	298	287
Total Share Capital	4	4	4

G E C Anderson Ltd
Oakengrove Shire Lane, Hastoe, Tring, HP23 6LY
Tel: 01442-826999 **Fax:** 01442-825999
E-mail: info@gecanderson.co.uk
Website: http://www.gecanderson.co.uk
Directors: M. Tye (Dir)
Immediate Holding Company: G.E.C. ANDERSON LIMITED
Registration no: 00743152 **VAT No.:** GB 196 4094 32
Date established: 1962 **Turnover:** £1m - £2m **No.of Employees:** 1 - 10
Product Groups: 26, 36

Date of Accounts	Mar 11	Mar 10	Mar 09
Working Capital	19	21	33
Fixed Assets	10	10	12
Current Assets	162	171	185

Brunel Design
Unit 40 Brook Street, Tring, HP23 5EF
Tel: 01442-827119 **Fax:** 01442-827119
E-mail: brunnel.design@talktalkbuisness.net
Directors: R. Sprat (Prop)
No.of Employees: 1 - 10 **Product Groups:** 35

Champneys
Wigginton, Tring, HP23 6HY
Tel: 01442-291000 **Fax:** 01442-291001
E-mail: grant.noble@champneys.co.uk
Website: http://www.champneys.co.uk
Directors: S. Perdew (MD)
Managers: A. Wikman (Co-Ordinator), G. Noble (Chief Mgr)
Immediate Holding Company: CHAMPNEYS AT TRING HEALTHSHARE CLUB LIMITED
Registration no: 02780877 **Date established:** 1993
No.of Employees: 251 - 500 **Product Groups:** 69

Company Fusion Ltd
Tring House 77-81 High Street, Tring, HP23 4AB
Tel: 020-7993 3368
E-mail: recruitment@companyfusion.com
Website: http://www.companyfusion.com
Managers: G. Hart
Immediate Holding Company: COMPANY FUSION LIMITED
Registration no: 05651649 **Date established:** 2005
No.of Employees: 11 - 20 **Product Groups:** 80

Date of Accounts	Dec 10	Dec 09	Dec 08
Working Capital	-245	-202	-42
Fixed Assets	2	12	26
Current Assets	70	24	63

Controls Testing Equipment Ltd
Icknield Way Industrial Estate Icknield Way, Tring, HP23 4JX
Tel: 01442-828311 **Fax:** 01442-828466
E-mail: sales@controlstesting.co.uk
Website: http://www.controlstesting.co.uk
Directors: F. Galli (Dir)
Ultimate Holding Company: ALBA SRL
Immediate Holding Company: CONTROLS TESTING EQUIPMENT LIMITED
Registration no: 01753477 **Date established:** 1983 **Turnover:** £2m - £5m
No.of Employees: 1 - 10 **Product Groups:** 38, 85

Date of Accounts	Dec 11	Dec 10	Dec 09
Sales Turnover	3m	3m	4m
Pre Tax Profit/Loss	255	439	-174
Working Capital	430	488	170
Fixed Assets	37	41	42
Current Assets	2m	2m	1m
Current Liabilities	232	414	321

Cowroast Marine Engineering
Cow Roast, Tring, HP23 5RE
Tel: 01442-825522 **Fax:** 01442-825522
Website: http://www.cowroastmarina.co.uk
Directors: D. Killick (Prop)
Date established: 2003 **No.of Employees:** 1 - 10 **Product Groups:** 35, 36, 39

Dean & Associates
93 Western Road, Tring, HP23 4BN
Tel: 01442-824242 **Fax:** 01442-891172
E-mail: sales@deanandassociates.co.uk
Website: http://www.deanandassociates.co.uk
Directors: M. Dean (Ptnr)
Immediate Holding Company: EAS DISTRIBUTORS (UK) LIMITED
Registration no: 06567475 **Date established:** 1991 **Turnover:** £2m - £5m
No.of Employees: 1 - 10 **Product Groups:** 30

Date of Accounts	Nov 11	Nov 10	Nov 09
Working Capital	33	51	61
Fixed Assets	108	106	113
Current Assets	57	81	84

Falcon Copiers plc
Icknield Industrial Estate Icknield Way, Tring, HP23 4JZ
Tel: 01442-822229 **Fax:** 01442-828811
E-mail: general@falconcopiers.co.uk
Website: http://www.falconcopiers.co.uk

Directors: R. Guttfield (Fin), R. Kedgley (Dir), R. Duttfield (MD)
Managers: V. Mehpa (Tech Serv Mgr)
Immediate Holding Company: FALCON COPIERS PLC
Registration no: 02818404 **Date established:** 1993 **Turnover:** £5m - £10m
No.of Employees: 21 - 50 **Product Groups:** 32, 44, 83

Date of Accounts	Sep 11	Sep 10	Sep 09
Sales Turnover	7m	7m	5m
Pre Tax Profit/Loss	398	280	318
Working Capital	821	1m	589
Fixed Assets	2m	964	2m
Current Assets	2m	3m	2m
Current Liabilities	952	1m	740

Grass Roots

Tring Business Centre Icknield Way Industrial Estate, Tring, HP23 4RN
Tel: 01442-829400 **Fax:** 01442-829405
E-mail: david.evans@grg.com
Website: http://www.grg.com
Directors: D. Evans (Ch), D. Evans (Prop), N. Egerton King (Fin), R. Burrage (MD), R. Burridge (MD), J. White (Dir)
Managers: N. Wake (Mktg Serv Mgr)
Ultimate Holding Company: THE GRASS ROOTS GROUP PLC
Immediate Holding Company: THE GRASS ROOTS GROUP UK LIMITED
Registration no: 01724108 **Date established:** 2001
Turnover: £250m - £500m **No.of Employees:** 1 - 10 **Product Groups:** 44, 49, 69, 80, 81, 86, 89

H E Stringer Ltd

Icknield Way Industrial Estate Icknield Way, Tring, HP23 4JZ
Tel: 01442-822621 **Fax:** 01442-822727
E-mail: info@stringer-flavour.com
Website: http://www.stringer-flavour.com
Bank(s): Barclays
Directors: H. Williams (MD)
Immediate Holding Company: H.E.STRINGER LIMITED
Registration no: 00556211 **VAT No.:** GB 196 7294 09
Date established: 1955 **Turnover:** £1m - £2m **No.of Employees:** 11 - 20
Product Groups: 20, 31, 66

Date of Accounts	Jul 11	Jul 10	Jul 09
Sales Turnover	N/A	N/A	2m
Pre Tax Profit/Loss	N/A	N/A	1m
Working Capital	1m	1m	2m
Fixed Assets	2m	2m	2m
Current Assets	1m	2m	2m
Current Liabilities	N/A	N/A	47

King Acre Paving & Fencing Centre

Bulbourne Road, Tring, HP23 5HF
Tel: 01442-828022 **Fax:** 01442-891749
Website: http://www.kingacretring.com
Managers: P. Manship (District Mgr)
No.of Employees: 1 - 10 **Product Groups:** 36

Kuhrt Leach LLP

81-82 Akeman Street, Tring, HP23 6AF
Tel: 01442-822880 **Fax:** 01442-381669
E-mail: contact@kuhrtleach.com
Website: http://www.kuhrtleach.com
Directors: R. Leach (Ptnr)
Immediate Holding Company: KUHRT LEACH LLP
Registration no: OC336527 **Date established:** 2008
Turnover: Up to £250,000 **No.of Employees:** 1 - 10 **Product Groups:** 80

Date of Accounts	Apr 11	Apr 10	Apr 09
Working Capital	27	26	14
Fixed Assets	1	2	2
Current Assets	69	34	15

Nikon Metrology UK Ltd

Unit 5 Icknield Way Industrial Estate Icknield Way, Tring, HP23 4JX
Tel: 01442-828700 **Fax:** 01442-828118
E-mail: sales@nikonmetrology.com
Website: http://www.nikonmetrology.com
Directors: C. Stevens (Fin)
Ultimate Holding Company: NIKON CORP (JAPAN)
Immediate Holding Company: X-TEK SYSTEMS LIMITED
Registration no: 01981536 **Date established:** 1986
Turnover: £10m - £20m **No.of Employees:** 51 - 100 **Product Groups:** 37, 38, 47, 85

Date of Accounts	Dec 09	Dec 08	Dec 07
Sales Turnover	4m	11m	7m
Pre Tax Profit/Loss	-1m	-549	-808
Working Capital	-3m	-2m	-35
Fixed Assets	795	1m	2m
Current Assets	14m	9m	4m
Current Liabilities	390	592	2m

Noble Foods Ltd

Bridgeway House Icknield Way Industrial Estate Icknield Way, Tring, HP23 4JX
Tel: 01442-891811 **Fax:** 01442-891880
E-mail: peterd@deansfoods.co.uk
Website: http://www.noblefoods.co.uk
Bank(s): Barclays
Directors: C. Willcox (Fin), G. Cooper (Sales), P. Dean (Ch), P. Challands (Mkt Research)
Ultimate Holding Company: NOBLE FOODS GROUP LIMITED
Immediate Holding Company: DEANS FARM LTD
Registration no: 02642686 **Date established:** 1991
Turnover: £250m - £500m **No.of Employees:** 1501 & over
Product Groups: 20

Date of Accounts	Sep 08
Working Capital	56
Current Assets	56

Proactive Test Solutions Ltd

15a The Old Silk Mill Brook Street, Tring, HP23 5ES
Tel: 01442-825547
E-mail: info@proactivetest.com
Website: http://www.proactivetest.co.uk
Directors: J. Hurley (Prop)
Immediate Holding Company: PROACTIVE TEST SOLUTIONS LIMITED
Registration no: 04809795 **Date established:** 2003
Turnover: £250,000 - £500,000 **No.of Employees:** 1 - 10
Product Groups: 85

Date of Accounts	Jun 11	Jun 10	Jun 08
Working Capital	-3	-4	-3
Current Assets	28	22	11

Stokvis Tapes UK Ltd

Unit 8 Tring Industrial Estate Icknield Way, Tring, HP23 4JX
Tel: 01442-821700 **Fax:** 01442-248871
E-mail: info@stokvistapes.co.uk
Website: http://www.stokvistapes.co.uk
Bank(s): ABN Ambro Bank N.V.
Directors: J. Hartman (MD)
Managers: A. Craig (Purch Mgr), S. Farmer (Comptroller)
Immediate Holding Company: STOKVIS TAPES GROUP BV
Registration no: 02500193 **VAT No.:** GB 198 3249 22
Turnover: £2m - £5m **No.of Employees:** 21 - 50 **Product Groups:** 23, 27, 30, 42, 66, 68

Date of Accounts	Nov 08	Dec 07	Dec 06
Sales Turnover	4229	2933	2953
Pre Tax Profit/Loss	-143	65	-46
Working Capital	-1499	-898	-1151
Fixed Assets	1562	1804	2007
Current Assets	1312	1512	953
Current Liabilities	2811	2410	2104
Total Share Capital	100	100	100
ROCE% (Return on Capital Employed)	-227.0	7.2	-5.4
ROT% (Return on Turnover)	-3.4	2.2	-1.6

Waltham Cross

Allied Meat Importers

Windsor House Britannia Road, Waltham Cross, EN8 7NX
Tel: 01992-807950 **Fax:** 01992-807951
E-mail: amiuk@alliedmeats.com
Website: http://www.alliedmeats.com
Managers: M. Shuttle (Chief Mgr)
Ultimate Holding Company: BOTSWANA MEAT COMMISSION (BOTSWANA)
Immediate Holding Company: ALLIED MEAT IMPORTERS (UK) LIMITED
Registration no: 00877969 **Date established:** 1966
Turnover: £500,000 - £1m **No.of Employees:** 11 - 20
Product Groups: 20, 40, 41, 61, 62

Bandapac Packaging Materials

9 Fieldings Road Cheshunt, Waltham Cross, EN8 9TL
Tel: 01992-622799 **Fax:** 01992-628873
E-mail: info@bandapac.com
Directors: K. Price (Prop)
Turnover: Up to £250,000 **No.of Employees:** 1 - 10 **Product Groups:** 23, 27, 30, 34, 35, 42

Biffa Waste Services Ltd

New Ford Road, Waltham Cross, EN8 7PG
Tel: 01992-709380 **Fax:** 01992-709390
E-mail: marketing@biffa.co.uk
Website: http://www.biffa.co.uk
Managers: R. Shoots (Mgr)
Ultimate Holding Company: PIRIN HOLDINGS LIMITED
Immediate Holding Company: BIFFA WASTE SERVICES LIMITED
Registration no: 00946107 **Date established:** 1969
Turnover: £10m - £20m **No.of Employees:** 21 - 50 **Product Groups:** 54, 83

Date of Accounts	Mar 08	Mar 09	Apr 10
Sales Turnover	555m	574m	492m
Pre Tax Profit/Loss	23m	50m	30m
Working Capital	229m	271m	293m
Fixed Assets	371m	360m	378m
Current Assets	409m	534m	609m
Current Liabilities	50m	100m	115m

Car Spares Ltd

Delamare Road Cheshunt, Waltham Cross, EN8 9AP
Tel: 01992-639844 **Fax:** 01992-623871
E-mail: sales@carspares.co.uk
Website: http://www.carspares.co.uk
Bank(s): Barclays
Directors: G. Aylott (Dir)
Immediate Holding Company: CAR SPARES (CHESHUNT) LIMITED
Registration no: 03910096 **VAT No.:** GB 220 3792 90
Date established: 2000 **Turnover:** £2m - £5m **No.of Employees:** 21 - 50
Product Groups: 68

Date of Accounts	Mar 12	Mar 11	Mar 10
Working Capital	241	215	226
Fixed Assets	136	118	174
Current Assets	1m	1m	1m

Claude Lyons Ltd

Brook Road, Waltham Cross, EN8 7LR
Tel: 01992-768888 **Fax:** 01992-788000
E-mail: sales@claudelyons.co.uk
Website: http://www.claudelyons.co.uk
Bank(s): National Westminster Bank Plc
Directors: M. Ward (Tech Serv), J. McIlfatrick (MD), J. Mcilfatrick (MD)
Immediate Holding Company: CLAUDE LYONS LIMITED
Registration no: 00222791 **VAT No.:** GB 213 5042 15
Date established: 2027 **Turnover:** £2m - £5m **No.of Employees:** 21 - 50
Product Groups: 37, 38, 44, 67

Date of Accounts	Jun 11	Jun 10	Jun 09
Sales Turnover	3m	3m	4m
Pre Tax Profit/Loss	-123	-81	454
Working Capital	2m	2m	2m
Fixed Assets	556	585	599
Current Assets	3m	3m	3m
Current Liabilities	294	399	735

D R Coe Ltd

5 Delamare Road Cheshunt, Waltham Cross, EN8 9SU
Tel: 01992-624330 **Fax:** 01992- 624330
E-mail: darren@drcoe.co.uk
Directors: J. Drabwell (MD)
Immediate Holding Company: D.R. COE LTD
Registration no: 00968995 **Date established:** 1969
No.of Employees: 1 - 10 **Product Groups:** 26, 35

D O I Group

Unit 3 New Ford Road, Waltham Cross, EN8 7PG
Tel: 01992-788582 **Fax:** 01992-650284
E-mail: interiors@doi.co.uk
Website: http://www.doi.co.uk
Directors: S. Bates (MD)
Registration no: 03367842 **Date established:** 1990 **Turnover:** £2m - £5m
No.of Employees: 11 - 20 **Product Groups:** 52

Date of Accounts	Sep 08	Sep 07
Working Capital	714	758
Fixed Assets	530	549
Current Assets	1066	1102
Current Liabilities	352	344
Total Share Capital	10	10

Durkan Ltd

Durkan House 212-224 High Street, Waltham Cross, EN8 7DR
Tel: 01992-781400 **Fax:** 01992-781500
E-mail: info@durkan.co.uk
Website: http://www.durkan.co.uk
Bank(s): Bank of Ireland
Directors: P. McGowan (I.T. Dir), D. Nathan (Sales & Mktg), D. Durkan (Grp Chief Exec), A. Fraher (Fin), A. Fraher (Fin)
Managers: P. Rend (Tech Serv Mgr), C. Riviere (Develop Mgr), S. Cooksley (Buyer), R. Craft (Personnel), S. Cooksley (Buyer)
Ultimate Holding Company: DURKAN HOLDINGS LIMITED
Immediate Holding Company: DURKAN LIMITED
Registration no: 00997195 **VAT No.:** GB 350 7675 45
Date established: 1970 **Turnover:** £20m - £50m
No.of Employees: 251 - 500 **Product Groups:** 52

Date of Accounts	Jan 12	Jan 11	Jan 10
Sales Turnover	126m	115m	157m
Pre Tax Profit/Loss	2m	8m	4m
Working Capital	28m	27m	20m
Fixed Assets	175	201	208
Current Assets	63m	61m	60m
Current Liabilities	31m	4m	11m

E S A B Group UK Ltd

Hanover House Britannia Road Queens Gate, Waltham Cross, EN8 7TF
Tel: 01992-768515 **Fax:** 01992-715803
E-mail: info@esab.co.uk
Website: http://www.esab.co.uk
Bank(s): Lloyds TSB Bank plc
Directors: D. Gibson (Fin), G. Kisby (Sales)
Ultimate Holding Company: CHARTER INTERNATIONAL PLC (JERSEY)
Immediate Holding Company: ESAB GROUP (UK) LTD
Registration no: 00275947 **VAT No.:** GB 373 8128 37
Date established: 1933 **Turnover:** £20m - £50m
No.of Employees: 51 - 100 **Product Groups:** 35, 83

Date of Accounts	Dec 10	Dec 09	Dec 08
Sales Turnover	33m	31m	35m
Pre Tax Profit/Loss	2m	-920	4m
Working Capital	72m	40m	43m
Fixed Assets	169	226	330
Current Assets	88m	56m	58m
Current Liabilities	3m	4m	3m

EasyBuild (Construction Software) Ltd

Durkan House 214-224 High Street, Waltham Cross, EN8 7DR
Tel: 01992-781699 **Fax:** 01992-781500
E-mail: enquiries@easybuilduk.com
Website: http://www.easybuilduk.com
Product Groups: 44, 80

Date of Accounts	Jan 08	Jan 07	Jan 06
Sales Turnover	212	33	35
Pre Tax Profit/Loss	5	1	14
Working Capital	16	14	13
Fixed Assets	3	N/A	N/A
Current Assets	95	49	34
Current Liabilities	79	34	21
ROCE% (Return on Capital Employed)	27.2	8.7	107.7
ROT% (Return on Turnover)	2.3	3.8	41.1

Efav Group UK Ltd

Hanover House Britannia Road Queens Gate, Waltham Cross, EN8 7TF
Tel: 01992-710000 **Fax:** 01992-715803
E-mail: info@murexwelding.co.uk
Website: http://www.esab.co.uk
Directors: D. Gibson (Fin), P. Dodd (Dir)
Immediate Holding Company: TELFORD HOMES (PROPERTIES) LIMITED
Registration no: OC347105 **Date established:** 2008
No.of Employees: 101 - 250 **Product Groups:** 46

Fourway Communication Ltd

Delamare Road Cheshunt, Waltham Cross, EN8 9SH
Tel: 01992-629182 **Fax:** 01992-639227
E-mail: enquiries@fourway.co.uk
Website: http://www.fourway.co.uk
Bank(s): National Westminster Bank Plc
Directors: L. Snell (Dir)
Ultimate Holding Company: THE FOURWAY GROUP LIMITED
Immediate Holding Company: FOURWAY COMMUNICATION LIMITED
Registration no: 00714431 **VAT No.:** GB 220 5065 14
Date established: 1962 **No.of Employees:** 11 - 20 **Product Groups:** 37, 40, 48, 52

Date of Accounts	Mar 11	Mar 10	Mar 09
Working Capital	3m	2m	2m
Fixed Assets	194	49	60
Current Assets	4m	4m	3m

Gates Of Waltham Cross

Britannia Road Waltham Cross, Waltham Cross, EN8 7NZ
Tel: 01992-712323 **Fax:** 01992-760257
E-mail: enquiries@gates.co.uk
Website: http://www.gates.co.uk
Managers: A. Earle (Serv Mgr), A. Camp (Mktg Serv Mgr)
No.of Employees: 11 - 20 **Product Groups:** 68

H D Collins Ltd

Precise Works Delamare Road, Cheshunt, Waltham Cross, EN8 9TB
Tel: 01992-426600 **Fax:** 01992-426605
E-mail: enquiry@hdcollins.ltd.uk
Website: http://www.hdcollins.ltd.uk
Bank(s): Barclays, Cheshunt, Herts
Directors: D. Collins (MD)
Immediate Holding Company: H.D.COLLINS LIMITED
Registration no: 00659223 **VAT No.:** GB 220 3189 06
Date established: 1960 **Turnover:** £1m - £2m **No.of Employees:** 11 - 20
Product Groups: 30, 35, 37, 46, 48

Date of Accounts	Apr 11	Apr 10	Apr 09
Working Capital	-263	-277	-279
Fixed Assets	473	487	503
Current Assets	157	206	216

Hitashi Kokusai
Windsor House Britannia Road, Waltham Cross, EN8 7NX
Tel: 08451-212177 **Fax:** 08451-212180
E-mail: p.roache@hitachi-keu.com
Website: http://www.hitachi-keu.com
Managers: P. Roach (Chief Mgr)
Ultimate Holding Company: HITACHI DENSHI LTD (JAPAN)
Registration no: 00945097 **Turnover:** £2m - £5m
No.of Employees: 1 - 10 **Product Groups:** 37, 38, 44, 47

Imperial Cleaning
Unit 7 Springwood Cheshunt, Waltham Cross, EN7 6AZ
Tel: 01992-628342 **Fax:** 01992-628342
E-mail: imperialenquiries@btinternet.com
Website: http://www.imperialcleaning.co.uk
Directors: G. Starkey (Dir)
No.of Employees: 1 - 10 **Product Groups:** 25, 32, 52

J P M Contractors Ltd
St James Road Goffs Oak, Waltham Cross, EN7 6TR
Tel: 08456-009187 **Fax:** 0845-600 9189
E-mail: jp@plant-hire-london.co.uk
Website: http://www.plant-hire-london.co.uk
Directors: J. Hill (Fin), J. Mccabe (MD)
Immediate Holding Company: J.P.M. CONTRACTORS LIMITED
Registration no: 03910982 **Date established:** 2000
No.of Employees: 1 - 10 **Product Groups:** 41, 45, 83

Date of Accounts	Apr 11	Apr 10	Apr 09
Working Capital	-39	-65	10
Fixed Assets	638	642	568
Current Assets	86	109	134

Last Bros Tabs Direct Ltd
Delamare Road Cheshunt, Waltham Cross, EN8 9TE
Tel: 01992-638283 **Fax:** 01992-638286
E-mail: enquiries@lastbros.co.uk
Website: http://www.lastbros.co.uk
Directors: P. Last (Dir), S. Last (Co Sec)
Managers: M. Hutchinson, P. Brand (Buyer)
Immediate Holding Company: LAST BROS LIMITED
Registration no: 00483868 **Date established:** 1950
Turnover: Up to £250,000 **No.of Employees:** 21 - 50 **Product Groups:** 23, 28

Date of Accounts	Jul 11	Jul 10	Jul 09
Working Capital	722	738	740
Fixed Assets	1m	1m	1m
Current Assets	852	883	885

Leach Lewis Ltd
Victoria House Britannia Road, Waltham Cross, EN8 7NU
Tel: 01992-704100 **Fax:** 01992-704170
E-mail: sales@leachlewis.co.uk
Website: http://www.leachlewis.co.uk
Bank(s): Barclays
Directors: P. Whittal (MD)
Managers: C. Morton (Personnel), N. Leach
Immediate Holding Company: LEACH-LEWIS LIMITED
Registration no: 00902091 **VAT No.:** GB 226 9170 58
Date established: 1967 **Turnover:** £20m - £50m
No.of Employees: 51 - 100 **Product Groups:** 66, 67

Date of Accounts	Mar 11	Mar 10	Mar 09
Sales Turnover	44m	26m	37m
Pre Tax Profit/Loss	-2m	-1m	-100
Working Capital	-3m	-1m	-529
Fixed Assets	4m	5m	4m
Current Assets	11m	10m	8m
Current Liabilities	2m	1m	2m

Lyons Instruments
Brook Road, Waltham Cross, EN8 7LR
Tel: 01992-768888 **Fax:** 01992-788000
E-mail: li@claudelyons.co.uk
Website: http://www.claudelyons.co.uk
Directors: I. Rowley (Dir), W. Lyons (Ch)
Managers: I. Reeves (Sales Prom Mgr)
Ultimate Holding Company: Claude Lyons Ltd
Registration no: 00933687 **Turnover:** £250,000 - £500,000
No.of Employees: 1 - 10 **Product Groups:** 37, 38

Motivair Compressors Ltd
Crompton Court Attwood Road, Waltham Cross, EN8 7NU
Tel: 01992-704300 **Fax:** 01992-704170
E-mail: enquiries@leachlewis.co.uk
Website: http://www.motivair.co.uk
Bank(s): Barclays
Directors: M. Brown (Fin), C. Rhodes (MD), C. Watkins (Sales)
Managers: G. Ford (Personnel), D. Munn, D. Cashmore (Mktg Serv Mgr)
Ultimate Holding Company: LEACH-LEWIS LIMITED
Immediate Holding Company: MOTIVAIR COMPRESSORS LIMITED
Registration no: 00918800 **VAT No.:** GB 222 3483 91
Date established: 1967 **Turnover:** £10m - £20m
No.of Employees: 51 - 100 **Product Groups:** 30, 31, 33, 35, 36, 37, 38, 39, 40, 42, 44, 45, 46, 47, 48, 61, 67, 83, 84, 85, 87

Date of Accounts	Mar 11	Mar 10	Mar 09
Sales Turnover	11m	6m	6m
Pre Tax Profit/Loss	-934	-67	1m
Working Capital	-584	236	50
Fixed Assets	2m	2m	2m
Current Assets	3m	3m	3m
Current Liabilities	759	561	346

Murex Welding Products Ltd
Hanover House Queensgate, Britania Road, Waltham Cross, EN8 7TF
Tel: 01992-710000 **Fax:** 01992-716486
E-mail: info@murexwelding.co.uk
Website: http://www.murexwelding.co.uk
Bank(s): HSBC Bank plc
Managers: J. Boot (Publicity)
Ultimate Holding Company: ESAB Group (Sweden)
Registration no: 01698860 **Turnover:** £20m - £50m
No.of Employees: 51 - 100 **Product Groups:** 35, 46

Ponders End Cash & Carry Ltd
Cardin House Beatty Road, Waltham Cross, EN8 7UD
Tel: 01992-650700 **Fax:** 01992-650800
Directors: F. Cole (Fin), J. Bourn (Dir)
Immediate Holding Company: PONDERS END CASH AND CARRY LIMITED
Registration no: 02542588 **Date established:** 1990
Turnover: £500,000 - £1m **No.of Employees:** 1 - 10 **Product Groups:** 24

Date of Accounts	Jun 08	Jun 07
Sales Turnover	1125	1206
Working Capital	-13	-18
Fixed Assets	13	18
Current Assets	422	1252
Current Liabilities	436	1270

Rowan Cable Products Ltd
Rowan House Delamare Road, Cheshunt, Waltham Cross, EN8 9SP
Tel: 01992-627377 **Fax:** 01992-628111
E-mail: sales@rowancable.co.uk
Website: http://www.rowancable.co.uk
Bank(s): Barclays
Directors: P. Latta (Grp Chief Exec), C. Pocock (Prop), J. Lingwood (Dir)
Managers: P. Deadman (Sales Prom), J. Lingwood (Export Sales Mg), C. Nicoletti (Mgr), P. Deadman (Sales Prom Mgr)
Registration no: 02732860 **VAT No.:** GB 587 2834 94
Date established: 1992 **Turnover:** £1m - £2m **No.of Employees:** 11 - 20
Product Groups: 23, 29, 30, 33, 34, 35, 36, 37, 39, 66, 67

Date of Accounts	Jun 11	Jun 10	Jun 09
Working Capital	858	760	701
Fixed Assets	274	284	284
Current Assets	1m	969	852

Townsend Material Handling Ltd
5 Meux Close Cheshunt, Waltham Cross, EN7 5DQ
Tel: 01992-630434 **Fax:** 01992-628393
E-mail: info@t_m_h.co.uk
Directors: J. Townsend (MD), T. Townsend (Fin)
Immediate Holding Company: TOWNSEND MATERIAL HANDLING LIMITED
Registration no: 03570847 **Date established:** 1998
No.of Employees: 1 - 10 **Product Groups:** 35, 39, 45

Date of Accounts	May 11	May 10	May 09
Working Capital	-2	-12	-15
Fixed Assets	27	11	15
Current Assets	27	26	26

Ware

A J Engineering
Unit 4b Swains Mill Crane Mead, Ware, SG12 9PY
Tel: 01920-465442
Directors: A. Crouch (Prop)
Registration no: 06887505 **Date established:** 2009
No.of Employees: 1 - 10 **Product Groups:** 37, 48, 67

Abbott Tool & Die Co.
Unit 4 Leeside Works Lawrence Avenue, Stanstead Abbotts, Ware, SG12 8DL
Tel: 01920-870203 **Fax:** 01920-870597
E-mail: abbott.tools@btconnect.com
Directors: M. Jacobson (Prop)
Date established: 1980 **No.of Employees:** 1 - 10 **Product Groups:** 46

Astute Electronics Ltd
Church House Church Street, Ware, SG12 9EN
Tel: 01920-484838 **Fax:** 01920-486399
E-mail: sales@astute.co.uk
Website: http://www.astute.co.uk
Bank(s): National Westminster Bank Plc
Directors: I. Fantham (Fin)
Managers: J. McArthy (Sales Prom Mgr)
Immediate Holding Company: ASTUTE ELECTRONICS LIMITED
Registration no: 02326213 **VAT No.:** GB 506 4207 76
Date established: 1988 **Turnover:** £20m - £50m
No.of Employees: 51 - 100 **Product Groups:** 33, 35, 37, 38, 39, 40, 42, 67

Date of Accounts	Dec 11	Dec 10	Dec 09
Sales Turnover	34m	31m	24m
Pre Tax Profit/Loss	907	713	324
Working Capital	2m	2m	1m
Fixed Assets	1m	2m	2m
Current Assets	14m	10m	7m
Current Liabilities	2m	2m	858

B M G Industries Ltd
Unit 2 Amwell Lane Stanstead Abbotts, Ware, SG12 8EB
Tel: 01920-870240 **Fax:** 01920-870652
E-mail: bmgprint@aol.com
Website: http://www.bmg.uk.net
Directors: J. Rayfield (MD)
Immediate Holding Company: BMG INDUSTRIES LIMITED
Registration no: 01335658 **Date established:** 1977
Turnover: £250,000 - £500,000 **No.of Employees:** 1 - 10
Product Groups: 23

Date of Accounts	Oct 11	Oct 10	Oct 09
Working Capital	-15	-22	-26
Fixed Assets	20	26	31
Current Assets	170	159	133

Birch Engineering Ltd
Unit 2 Furlong Way Great Amwell, Ware, SG12 9BE
Tel: 01920-485525 **Fax:** 01920-485530
E-mail: john@birchengineering.com
Website: http://www.birchengineering.com
Managers: J. Proctor (Chief Mgr)
Immediate Holding Company: BIRCH ENGINEERING (CUFFLEY) LIMITED
Registration no: 01072962 **VAT No.:** GB 229 3327 63
Date established: 1972 **Turnover:** £500,000 - £1m
No.of Employees: 1 - 10 **Product Groups:** 35, 45, 46, 48

Date of Accounts	Aug 11	Aug 10	Aug 09
Working Capital	184	220	176
Fixed Assets	88	54	55
Current Assets	351	385	272

Cintel International Ltd
Watton Road, Ware, SG12 0AE
Tel: 01920-463939 **Fax:** 01920-460803
E-mail: sales@cintel.co.uk
Website: http://www.cintel.co.uk
Bank(s): Bank of Scotland
Directors: P. Giles (Dir)
Managers: K. Bishop (Sales & Mktg Mg)
Ultimate Holding Company: P H GILES & CO LIMITED
Immediate Holding Company: CINTEL INTERNATIONAL LIMITED
Registration no: 04053340 **VAT No.:** GB 688 6626 67
Date established: 2000 **Turnover:** £2m - £5m **No.of Employees:** 11 - 20
Product Groups: 37

Date of Accounts	Dec 10	Dec 09	Dec 08
Sales Turnover	3m	4m	5m
Pre Tax Profit/Loss	-548	271	196
Working Capital	1m	2m	1m
Fixed Assets	134	33	28
Current Assets	2m	3m	3m
Current Liabilities	746	563	835

D & C Lifts
The Maltings Roydon Road, Stanstead Abbotts, Ware, SG12 8UU
Tel: 01992-764200 **Fax:** 01920-872609
Managers: C. Berry (Mgr)
Date established: 1998 **No.of Employees:** 1 - 10 **Product Groups:** 35, 39, 45

Electronic & General Services Ltd
3 Hitchs Yard Church Street, Ware, SG12 9ES
Tel: 01920-468991 **Fax:** 01920-469938
E-mail: info@egs.co.uk
Website: http://www.egs.co.uk
Directors: M. Mehmet (MD), M. Denman (MD)
Immediate Holding Company: ELECTRONIC & GENERAL SERVICES LIMITED
Registration no: 01277366 **Date established:** 1976 **Turnover:** £1m - £2m
No.of Employees: 11 - 20 **Product Groups:** 44, 67

Date of Accounts	Oct 10	Oct 09	Oct 08
Working Capital	16	153	252
Fixed Assets	8	32	36
Current Assets	353	324	567

Energy I C T
Leeside Works Lawrence Avenue, Stanstead Abbotts, Ware, SG12 8DL
Tel: 01920-871094 **Fax:** 01920-871853
E-mail: info@energyict.com
Website: http://www.energyict.com
Managers: J. Wilkinson (Sales Admin)
Ultimate Holding Company: REMBRANDT HOLDINGS SA (LUXEMBOURG)
Immediate Holding Company: ENERGY ICT LIMITED
Registration no: 01230591 **Date established:** 1975
Turnover: £250,000 - £500,000 **No.of Employees:** 21 - 50
Product Groups: 37, 38, 44, 84

Date of Accounts	Dec 11	Dec 10	Dec 09
Working Capital	2m	2m	840
Fixed Assets	8	11	20
Current Assets	3m	3m	1m

European Flavours & Fragrances plc
9 Peerglow Estate Marsh Lane, Ware, SG12 9QL
Tel: 01920-485485 **Fax:** 01920-485100
E-mail: clive.kersey@eff-ware.com
Website: http://www.eff-ware.com
Directors: C. Kersey (MD), G. Kersey (Purch), M. Clift (Sales)
Managers: J. Blackman (Chief Acct)
Immediate Holding Company: EUROPEAN FLAVOURS & FRAGRANCES PLC
Registration no: 01551982 **Date established:** 1981
Turnover: £10m - £20m **No.of Employees:** 21 - 50 **Product Groups:** 20, 31, 32, 63

Date of Accounts	Mar 12	Mar 11	Mar 10
Sales Turnover	12m	11m	9m
Pre Tax Profit/Loss	324	530	338
Working Capital	2m	2m	1m
Fixed Assets	1m	1m	1m
Current Assets	5m	5m	4m
Current Liabilities	932	1m	1m

French & Jupps
The Maltings Roydon Road, Stanstead Abbotts, Ware, SG12 8HG
Tel: 01920-870015 **Fax:** 01920-871001
E-mail: david.jupp@frenchandjupps.co.uk
Website: http://www.frenchandjupps.co.uk
Bank(s): Lloyds TSB Bank plc
Directors: D. Jupp (MD)
Immediate Holding Company: FRENCH & JUPPS LIMITED
Registration no: 00165116 **VAT No.:** GB 213 2098 03
Date established: 2020 **Turnover:** £1m - £2m **No.of Employees:** 11 - 20
Product Groups: 41

Date of Accounts	Sep 11	Sep 10	Sep 09
Working Capital	2m	2m	1m
Fixed Assets	5m	5m	5m
Current Assets	2m	2m	2m

Gibbs Sandtech Ltd (t/a Tregarne)
Station Road Braughing, Ware, SG11 2PB
Tel: 01920-822404 **Fax:** 01920-822909
E-mail: info@gibbsfinishing.com
Website: http://www.gibbsfinishing.com
Directors: A. Gibbs (Dir)
Immediate Holding Company: GIBBS-SANDTECH LIMITED
Registration no: 04229844 **VAT No.:** GB 522 5788 35
Date established: 2001 **Turnover:** £250,000 - £500,000
No.of Employees: 1 - 10 **Product Groups:** 47

Date of Accounts	Jul 11	Jul 10	Jul 09
Working Capital	205	180	203
Fixed Assets	47	14	37
Current Assets	372	348	447

Hertford Controls Ltd
Ermine Point 14 Gentlemens Field, Ware, SG12 0EF
Tel: 01920-467578 **Fax:** 01920-487037
E-mail: sales@hertfordcontrols.co.uk
Website: http://www.hertfordcontrols.co.uk
Directors: C. Jowitt (Dir)
Immediate Holding Company: HERTFORD CONTROLS LIMITED
Registration no: 02763826 **Date established:** 1992
No.of Employees: 1 - 10 **Product Groups:** 67

Date of Accounts	Dec 11	Dec 10	Dec 09
Working Capital	90	199	261
Fixed Assets	165	166	174
Current Assets	166	310	389

Howe Green Ltd
Marsh Lane, Ware, SG12 9QQ
Tel: 01920-463230 **Fax:** 01920-463231
E-mail: info@howegreen.co.uk
Website: http://www.howegreen.co.uk
Directors: P. Centa (MD)
Immediate Holding Company: Howe Green Ltd
Registration no: 01707882 **Date established:** 1983 **Turnover:** £2m - £5m
No.of Employees: 11 - 20 **Product Groups:** 35

Date of Accounts	Aug 08	Aug 07	Aug 06
Working Capital	885	741	487
Fixed Assets	575	713	293
Current Assets	1380	1508	713
Current Liabilities	495	767	226
Total Share Capital	1	1	1

Investalist Ltd
Dimmings Cottage Chapmore End, Ware, SG12 0HG
Tel: 0870-9109400
E-mail: admin@investalist.co.uk
Website: http://www.investalist.co.uk
Directors: A. Stefanczyk (Develop)
Registration no: 5465744 **Date established:** 2004 **Turnover:** £1m - £2m
No.of Employees: 1 - 10 **Product Groups:** 80

G & A Kirsten Ltd
11 Amwell End, Ware, SG12 9HP
Tel: 01920-487300 **Fax:** 01920-487304
E-mail: gakirsten@btclick.com
Website: http://www.kirsten-group.com
Directors: F. Kirsten (Fin)
Immediate Holding Company: G. & A. KIRSTEN LIMITED
Registration no: 00900431 **VAT No.:** GB 220 8424 94
Date established: 1967 **Turnover:** £500,000 - £1m
No.of Employees: 1 - 10 **Product Groups:** 30, 35, 49

Date of Accounts	Jun 11	Jun 09	Jun 08
Working Capital	-397	-413	-419
Fixed Assets	2	2	3
Current Assets	27	34	35
Current Liabilities	424	N/A	N/A

L A Packing Company Ltd (A10 Timber Co.)
Barwick Ford, Ware, SG11 1DA
Tel: 01279-842819 **Fax:** 01279-842798
E-mail: sales@lapacking.co.uk
Website: http://www.lapacking.co.uk
Directors: A. Hemming (Jt MD), K. Kersey (Co Sec), K. Hemming (Dir), D. Silver (Dir)
Managers: D. Silver (Transport)
Immediate Holding Company: L.A. PACKING COMPANY LIMITED
Registration no: 01160213 **VAT No.:** GB 215 1700 11
Date established: 1974 **Turnover:** £1m - £2m **No.of Employees:** 1 - 10
Product Groups: 25, 35, 45, 76

Date of Accounts	Dec 10	Apr 10	Apr 09
Working Capital	85	10	138
Fixed Assets	627	642	627
Current Assets	447	437	592

M B O UK Ltd
Mill End Standon, Ware, SG11 1LR
Tel: 01920-823999 **Fax:** 01920-823631
E-mail: info@mbouk.co.uk
Website: http://www.mbouk.co.uk
Managers: F. Nimoo (Mgr)
Immediate Holding Company: M.B.O. (UK) LIMITED
Registration no: 02191558 **Date established:** 1987
Turnover: £500,000 - £1m **No.of Employees:** 1 - 10 **Product Groups:** 32, 34

Date of Accounts	Feb 12	Feb 11	Feb 10
Sales Turnover	685	620	423
Working Capital	223	151	83
Fixed Assets	4	5	4
Current Assets	479	399	306

M J D Labelling & Presentation Systems
28 Millers Lane Stanstead Abbotts, Ware, SG12 8AF
Tel: 01920-872992 **Fax:** 01920-872992
E-mail: mike-davis@mjdlabelling.co.uk
Website: http://www.mjdlabelling.co.uk
Directors: M. Davis (Ptnr)
Date established: 1989 **No.of Employees:** 1 - 10 **Product Groups:** 38, 42

Macro Engineering Ltd
6 Gentlemens Field Westmill Road, Ware, SG12 0EF
Tel: 01920-487711 **Fax:** 01920-468880
E-mail: t.ruddy@macroengineering.co.uk
Website: http://www.macroengineering.co.uk
Directors: T. Ruddy (Dir)
Immediate Holding Company: MACRO ENGINEERING LIMITED
Registration no: 01499788 **VAT No.:** GB 327 9198 22
Date established: 1980 **Turnover:** £250,000 - £500,000
No.of Employees: 1 - 10 **Product Groups:** 67

Date of Accounts	Mar 12	Mar 11	Mar 10
Working Capital	369	367	-227
Fixed Assets	301	309	851
Current Assets	663	647	99

Mode Lighting UK Ltd
The Maltings 63 High Street, Ware, SG12 9AD
Tel: 01920-462121 **Fax:** 01920-466882
E-mail: sales@modelighting.com
Website: http://www.modelighting.com
Directors: G. Brown (Mkt Research), J. King (Sales), B. Gilbert (Pers), R. Gambles (Co Sec)
Ultimate Holding Company: TAPPENDEN & CO. LIMITED
Immediate Holding Company: MODE LIGHTING (UK) LIMITED
Registration no: 02137393 **VAT No.:** GB 573 1217 57
Date established: 1987 **Turnover:** £5m - £10m **No.of Employees:** 21 - 50
Product Groups: 37

Date of Accounts	Sep 11	Sep 10	Sep 09
Sales Turnover	7m	6m	6m
Pre Tax Profit/Loss	234	200	63
Working Capital	3m	2m	2m
Fixed Assets	150	176	207
Current Assets	4m	4m	4m
Current Liabilities	530	364	344

Oakley Coach Builders
High Cross, Ware, SG11 1AD
Tel: 01920-466781 **Fax:** 01920-467895
E-mail: sales@oakleyhorseboxes.co.uk
Website: http://www.oakleyhorseboxes.co.uk
Bank(s): HSBC Bank plc
Directors: B. Oakley (Prop)
Managers: A. Oakley (Chief Mgr), J. Bennett (Sales Prom Mgr), K. Holden
Turnover: £2m - £5m **No.of Employees:** 101 - 250 **Product Groups:** 39

Oceanic Resources International
Ground Floor Oceanic House Star Street, Ware, SG12 7AA
Tel: 01920-468811 **Fax:** 01920-468833
E-mail: info@oceanicresources.com
Website: http://www.oceanicresources.com
Directors: M. Murphy (Fin)
Immediate Holding Company: OCEANIC RESOURCES INTERNATIONAL LTD
Registration no: 03192467 **Date established:** 1996
Turnover: £250,000 - £500,000 **No.of Employees:** 11 - 20
Product Groups: 80

Date of Accounts	Apr 11	Apr 10	Apr 08
Working Capital	-86	-93	-5
Fixed Assets	355	356	316
Current Assets	122	70	133

R F I Screening (Experts in Shot Blasting & Thermal Spray technologies)
3a Station Road Braughing, Ware, SG11 2PB
Tel: 01920-822730 **Fax:** 01920-821475
E-mail: info@rfiscreening.co.uk
Website: http://www.rfiscreening.co.uk
Directors: S. Noble (MD)
Turnover: £250,000 - £500,000 **No.of Employees:** 1 - 10
Product Groups: 14, 29, 32, 46, 48, 52

Rapier Design Ltd
Rapier House Crane Mead, Ware, SG12 9PW
Tel: 08709-007782 **Fax:** 0870-900 7783
E-mail: contact@rapiergroup.com
Website: http://www.rapiergroup.com
Bank(s): Coutts & Co
Managers: C. Whittaker
Ultimate Holding Company: RAPIER DESIGN GROUP LIMITED
Immediate Holding Company: RAPIER DESIGN LTD
Registration no: 02245988 **VAT No.:** GB 523 4238 69
Date established: 1988 **Turnover:** £5m - £10m **No.of Employees:** 21 - 50
Product Groups: 81

Date of Accounts	Dec 11	Dec 10	Mar 10
Sales Turnover	9m	8m	N/A
Pre Tax Profit/Loss	262	333	568
Working Capital	854	2m	2m
Fixed Assets	1m	517	558
Current Assets	7m	5m	9m
Current Liabilities	5m	3m	6m

Spirex Metal Products Ltd
Marsh Lane, Ware, SG12 9QQ
Tel: 01920-460516 **Fax:** 01920-487028
E-mail: info@spirex.co.uk
Website: http://www.spirex.co.uk
Bank(s): Barclays, Cheshunt
Directors: R. Scorah (MD), J. Scorah (Fin)
Immediate Holding Company: SPIREX METAL PRODUCTS LIMITED
Registration no: 00982832 **VAT No.:** GB 214 0706 10
Date established: 1970 **No.of Employees:** 11 - 20 **Product Groups:** 26, 34, 35, 36, 38, 45, 46, 48

Date of Accounts	Jun 11	Jun 10	Jun 09
Working Capital	89	95	116
Fixed Assets	440	460	480
Current Assets	166	150	180

Two County Business Services
Unit 108 The Maltings Roydon Road, Stanstead Abbotts, Ware, SG12 8HG
Tel: 01920-877888 **Fax:** 01920-877800
E-mail: sales@acecomputers.co.uk
Website: http://www.2counties.co.uk
Directors: R. Wilkie (Dir), R. Wilkie (Prop)
Immediate Holding Company: AILSA HOUSE MANAGEMENT COMPANY LIMITED
Date established: 2005 **Turnover:** £250,000 - £500,000
No.of Employees: 1 - 10 **Product Groups:** 44

Date of Accounts	Sep 10	Sep 09
Working Capital	11	12
Fixed Assets	1	1
Current Assets	14	17

Weblight Ltd
Netherfield Lane Stanstead Abbotts, Ware, SG12 8HE
Tel: 01920-872287 **Fax:** 01506-465524
E-mail: info@weblight.co.uk
Website: http://www.weblight.co.uk
Bank(s): National Westminster
Directors: M. Thompson (MD)
Ultimate Holding Company: D W GROUP HOLDINGS LIMITED
Immediate Holding Company: WEBLIGHT PROJECTS LIMITED
Registration no: 00912376 **Date established:** 1967
Turnover: £10m - £20m **No.of Employees:** 11 - 20 **Product Groups:** 52, 85

Date of Accounts	Sep 11	Sep 10	Sep 09
Sales Turnover	14m	11m	11m
Pre Tax Profit/Loss	507	353	304
Working Capital	6m	5m	5m
Fixed Assets	250	219	126
Current Assets	9m	8m	8m
Current Liabilities	2m	2m	2m

Whitby Tool & Engineering
3 Meridian Way Stanstead Abbotts, Ware, SG12 8DW
Tel: 01920-871122
E-mail: jon@whitby-tool.co.uk
Website: http://www.whitby-tool.co.uk
Directors: J. Whitby (Prop)
Immediate Holding Company: WHITBY TOOL & ENGINEERING CO. LIMITED(THE)
Registration no: 00546248 **Date established:** 1955
No.of Employees: 1 - 10 **Product Groups:** 37, 40, 84

Date of Accounts	Mar 11	Mar 10	Mar 09
Working Capital	188	174	290
Fixed Assets	156	157	2

Current Assets	218	227	369

Wholeserve Southern Ltd
The Old Wood Yard Marsh Lane, Ware, SG12 9QQ
Tel: 01920-486853
E-mail: wholeserve1@btconnect.com
Website: http://www.wholeserverecyclingltd.co.uk
Directors: T. Perry (Dir)
Immediate Holding Company: SPIREX METAL PRODUCTS LIMITED
Registration no: 06956308 **Date established:** 1970
No.of Employees: 1 - 10 **Product Groups:** 45, 48, 54, 76

Date of Accounts	Jun 11	Jun 10	Jun 09
Working Capital	426	332	272
Fixed Assets	84	105	131
Current Assets	544	426	351

Wood Bros Furniture Ltd
London Road, Ware, SG12 9QH
Tel: 08451-303303 **Fax:** 01920-464388
E-mail: sales@oldcharm.co.uk
Website: http://www.oldcharm.co.uk
Directors: H. House (Dir), H. House (Ch), P. Stavrinides (Co Sec), P. Sheffield (Grp Chief Exec)
Managers: J. Beadle (Buyer), G. Kroll (Sales Prom Mgr)
Ultimate Holding Company: OLD ENGLISH (FURNITURE) LIMITED
Immediate Holding Company: WOOD BROS (FURNITURE) LIMITED
Registration no: 00493172 **Date established:** 1951 **Turnover:** £5m - £10m
No.of Employees: 21 - 50 **Product Groups:** 26

Date of Accounts	Mar 11	Mar 08	Mar 09
Sales Turnover	N/A	5m	N/A
Pre Tax Profit/Loss	N/A	-2m	N/A
Working Capital	1m	326	1m
Fixed Assets	131	274	165
Current Assets	1m	2m	1m
Current Liabilities	N/A	566	N/A

Watford

A C L Engineering Ltd
Anglia House Sandown Road Industrial Estate, Watford, WD24 7UA
Tel: 01923-249444 **Fax:** 01923-242368
E-mail: sales@aclengineering.co.uk
Website: http://www.aclengineering.co.uk
Bank(s): HSBC Bank plc
Directors: J. Doherty (Dir), S. Smithard (Co Sec), C. Russell (Dir)
Immediate Holding Company: A.C.L. ENGINEERING LIMITED
Registration no: 01476789 **VAT No.:** GB 344 2186 68
Date established: 1980 **Turnover:** £2m - £5m **No.of Employees:** 21 - 50
Product Groups: 33, 40, 42, 48, 52, 54, 83, 84

Date of Accounts	Jan 12	Jan 11	Jan 10
Working Capital	534	483	459
Fixed Assets	271	318	297
Current Assets	2m	2m	1m

Abbey Pynford plc
Second Floor Hille House 132 St Albans Road, Watford, WD24 4AQ
Tel: 01923-211160 **Fax:** 01923-234434
E-mail: vicki.highcock@abbeypynford.co.uk
Website: http://www.abbeypynford.co.uk
Directors: P. Kiss (Ch & MD)
Managers: V. Highcock (Mgr), S. Howe (Gen Contact)
Immediate Holding Company: ABBEY PYNFORD HOLDINGS LIMITED
Registration no: 05027756 **Date established:** 2004
Turnover: £10m - £20m **No.of Employees:** 1 - 10 **Product Groups:** 52

Abloy UK
Abloy House Hatters Lane, Watford, WD18 8QY
Tel: 01923-255066 **Fax:** 01923-230281
E-mail: rrice@abloysecurity.co.uk
Website: http://www.abloy.co.uk
Directors: R. Rice (MD)
Managers: K. Cartmell (I.T. Exec), M. Parker (I.T. Exec)
Ultimate Holding Company: Assa Abloy AB (Sweden)
Immediate Holding Company: ABLOY SECURITY LIMITED
Registration no: 02078532 **Date established:** 1986
No.of Employees: 21 - 50 **Product Groups:** 36

Date of Accounts	Dec 09	Dec 08	Dec 07
Working Capital	N/A	673	673
Current Assets	N/A	673	673

Abrasive Blades Ltd
4 Greenhill Crescent Watford Business Park, Watford, WD18 8RE
Tel: 01923-223248 **Fax:** 01923-210234
E-mail: general@abrasive-blades.co.uk
Website: http://www.abrasive-blades.co.uk
Bank(s): Barclays
Directors: A. Phillips (Co Sec), R. Sneesby (MD)
Immediate Holding Company: ABRASIVE BLADES LIMITED
Registration no: 00478958 **Date established:** 1950 **Turnover:** £2m - £5m
No.of Employees: 51 - 100 **Product Groups:** 33

Date of Accounts	Mar 11	Mar 10	Mar 09
Working Capital	405	67	73
Fixed Assets	573	582	593
Current Assets	732	503	616

Acrylic Design UK Ltd
Unit 3a-3b Shakespeare Industrial Estate Shakespeare Street, Watford, WD24 5RS
Tel: 01923-241122 **Fax:** 01923-241144
E-mail: sales@acrylicdesign.co.uk
Website: http://www.acrylicdesign.co.uk
Directors: N. Jennings (Fin)
Managers: P. Beaumont (Mgr)
Immediate Holding Company: ACRYLIC DESIGN UK LIMITED
Registration no: 04658580 **Date established:** 2003
Turnover: Up to £250,000 **No.of Employees:** 21 - 50 **Product Groups:** 26, 49

Date of Accounts	May 11	May 10	May 09
Working Capital	236	442	422
Fixed Assets	88	104	89
Current Assets	719	722	674

Adwel International Ltd
Park House, Greenhill CrescentWatford Business Park, Watford, WD18 8PH
Tel: 01923-254433 **Fax:** 01923-218278
E-mail: info@adwel.co.uk
Website: http://www.irispower.com
Bank(s): Royal Bank of Canada, London EC4V 4DE
Directors: B. Haddock (Co Sec), D. Burtonshaw (Div), M. Flamini (Dir)
Managers: A. Mohan, S. Bermingham (Mktg Serv Mgr)
Ultimate Holding Company: Black & McDonald Ltd
Registration no: FC020182 **VAT No.:** GB 663 5042 45
Date established: 1986 **Turnover:** £5m - £10m
No.of Employees: 501 - 1000 **Product Groups:** 36, 37, 38, 85

Antalis Morton Ltd
3 Imperial Park Imperial Way, Watford, WD24 4PP
Tel: 08706-073114 **Fax:** 08706-073168
E-mail: sham.ahmed@antalis-mcnaughton.co.uk
Website: http://www.antalis-mcnaughton.co.uk
Bank(s): National Westminster Bank Plc
Managers: D. Waring (Sales Prom Mgr), S. Ahmed (Sales Prom Mgr)
Immediate Holding Company: ANTALIS LIMITED
Registration no: NF003153 **Date established:** 1994
Turnover: £20m - £50m **No.of Employees:** 11 - 20 **Product Groups:** 27, 66

Date of Accounts	Dec 11	Dec 10	Dec 09
Sales Turnover	451m	393m	256m
Pre Tax Profit/Loss	-1m	-6m	-11m
Working Capital	40m	44m	-21m
Fixed Assets	525	8m	37m
Current Assets	140m	161m	121m
Current Liabilities	14m	11m	43m

Anthan Engineering Ltd
PO BOX N0.39, Watford, WD19 4EZ
Tel: 01923-249474 **Fax:** 01923-249477
E-mail: anthan@anthan.co.uk
Website: http://www.anthan.co.uk
Registration no: 02845559 **Turnover:** £500,000 - £1m
No.of Employees: 1 - 10 **Product Groups:** 23, 66

Arco
16 Colonial Way, Watford, WD24 4YT
Tel: 01923-202090 **Fax:** 01923-202010
E-mail: john.dean@arco.co.uk
Website: http://www.arco.co.uk
Bank(s): HSBC Bank plc
Managers: J. Dean (District Mgr), M. Bond (Fin Mgr)
Immediate Holding Company: ARCO GROUP HUMBERSIDE
Registration no: 00486220 **VAT No.:** GB 166 9115 46
Turnover: £2m - £5m **No.of Employees:** 11 - 20 **Product Groups:** 24, 67

Arkady Feed UK Ltd
5 Hercules Way Leavesden, Watford, WD25 7GS
Tel: 01923-279000
E-mail: whiteheadm@toepfer.com
Website: http://www.toepfer.com
Directors: M. Whitehead (MD), P. Briggs (Fin)
Managers: C. Hunt (Personnel)
Ultimate Holding Company: ARCHER DANIELS MIDLAND COMPANY INC (USA)
Immediate Holding Company: ARKADY FEED (U.K.) LIMITED
Registration no: 00904957 **Date established:** 1967
Turnover: £250m - £500m **No.of Employees:** 21 - 50 **Product Groups:** 61

Date of Accounts	Dec 11	Dec 10	Nov 09
Sales Turnover	353m	314m	301m
Pre Tax Profit/Loss	4m	6m	13m
Working Capital	20m	18m	13m
Fixed Assets	1m	1m	2m
Current Assets	52m	54m	37m
Current Liabilities	2m	3m	3m

Axia Computer Systems Ltd
111 St Albans Road, Watford, WD17 1UH
Tel: 01923-333111 **Fax:** 01923-213141
E-mail: sales@axia.co.uk
Website: http://www.axia.co.uk
Directors: A. Ali (Sales)
Immediate Holding Company: AXIA COMPUTER SYSTEMS LIMITED
Registration no: 02969346 **Date established:** 1994 **Turnover:** £2m - £5m
No.of Employees: 11 - 20 **Product Groups:** 44

Date of Accounts	Nov 11	Nov 10	Nov 09
Working Capital	56	45	17
Fixed Assets	134	148	166
Current Assets	450	430	315

B N International
Metro Centre Dwight Road, Watford, WD18 9YD
Tel: 01923-219132 **Fax:** 01923-219134
Website: http://www.bnint.nl
Directors: J. Krenning (Fin), J. Petersen (MD), R. Eve (Mkt Research)
Managers: B. Mustill (Ops Mgr)
Immediate Holding Company: BN INTERNATIONAL
Registration no: FC008120 **Date established:** 1974
Turnover: £50m - £75m **No.of Employees:** 251 - 500
Product Groups: 22, 23, 67

B & S Polishing
72 Sydney Road, Watford, WD18 7QX
Tel: 01923-211116 **Fax:** 01923-255183
E-mail: bspolishing@btconnect.com
Directors: S. Murphy (Prop)
Date established: 1985 **No.of Employees:** 1 - 10 **Product Groups:** 46, 48

Baker Engineering Co.
Unit 11 Paramount Industrial Estate Sandown Road, Watford, WD24 7XA
Tel: 01923-229309 **Fax:** 01923-801182
E-mail: raybaker@bakereng.co.uk
Website: http://www.bakereng.co.uk
Directors: R. Baker (Prop)
Turnover: £250,000 - £500,000 **No.of Employees:** 1 - 10
Product Groups: 48

Barr Mason Ltd
10 Greycaine Road, Watford, WD24 7GG
Tel: 01923-212 400 **Fax:** 01923-817024
E-mail: sales@barrmason.co.uk
Website: http://www.barr-mason.co.uk
Directors: S. Hogg (Dir)
Managers: V. Gleeson (Personnel)
Immediate Holding Company: Barr, Mason Ltd
Registration no: 00454143 **VAT No.:** GB 196 2770 28
Date established: 1948 **Turnover:** £2m - £5m **No.of Employees:** 21 - 50
Product Groups: 30

Date of Accounts	Sep 09	Sep 08	Sep 07
Working Capital	23	120	128
Fixed Assets	927	979	1m
Current Assets	327	402	400

Becker Sliding Partitions Ltd
Wemco House 477 Whippendell Road, Watford, WD18 7QY
Tel: 01923-236906 **Fax:** 01923-236906
E-mail: g-browne@becker.uk.com
Website: http://www.becker.uk.com
Directors: G. Browne (Dir)
Immediate Holding Company: BECKER (SLIDING PARTITIONS) LIMITED
Registration no: 02010956 **VAT No.:** GB 449 3255 32
Date established: 1986 **Turnover:** £1m - £2m **No.of Employees:** 1 - 10
Product Groups: 25

Date of Accounts	Jun 11	Jun 10	Jun 09
Working Capital	1m	1m	1m
Fixed Assets	33	27	34
Current Assets	1m	1m	1m

C P Holdings Ltd
CP House Otterspool Way, Watford, WD25 8HL
Tel: 01923-250500 **Fax:** 01923-221628
E-mail: someone@cpholdingsltd.com
Website: http://www.cpholdingsltd.com
Directors: P. Filer (Fin), R. Levy (Dir)
Managers: F. Temple (Sales & Mktg Mg)
Ultimate Holding Company: CP HOLDINGS LIMITED
Immediate Holding Company: CP HOLDINGS LIMITED
Registration no: 00580471 **VAT No.:** GB 229 8269 26
Date established: 1957 **Turnover:** £250m - £500m
No.of Employees: 21 - 50 **Product Groups:** 51, 80

Date of Accounts	Dec 11	Dec 10	Dec 09
Sales Turnover	431m	386m	417m
Pre Tax Profit/Loss	6m	9m	22m
Working Capital	41m	66m	28m
Fixed Assets	399m	413m	458m
Current Assets	225m	217m	215m
Current Liabilities	46m	54m	52m

Casewise Ltd
64 Clarendon Road, Watford, WD17 1DA
Tel: 01923-830300
E-mail: mike.hodes@casewise.com
Website: http://www.casewise.com
Directors: M. Hodes (Fin)
Managers: M. Senatore (Sales & Mktg Mg), I. Hancock
Ultimate Holding Company: CASEWISE SYSTEMS LIMITED
Immediate Holding Company: CASEWISE LIMITED
Registration no: 03280714 **Date established:** 1996 **Turnover:** £5m - £10m
No.of Employees: 21 - 50 **Product Groups:** 44

Date of Accounts	Dec 10	Dec 09	Dec 08
Working Capital	1m	1m	1m
Current Assets	2m	2m	2m

Compucorp Ltd
Gresham House 53 Clarendon Road, Watford, WD17 1LA
Tel: 01923-220121
E-mail: info@compucorp.co.uk
Website: http://www.compucorp.co.uk
Bank(s): Lloyds TSB Bank plc
Directors: J. Novick (MD)
Immediate Holding Company: COMPUCORP LIMITED
Registration no: 01303299 **VAT No.:** GB 231 6002 20
Date established: 1977 **Turnover:** £500,000 - £1m
No.of Employees: 11 - 20 **Product Groups:** 44

Date of Accounts	Mar 11	Mar 10	Mar 09
Working Capital	54	77	122
Fixed Assets	10	9	12
Current Assets	142	212	254

Cooper Controls Ltd
20 Greenhill Crescent, Watford, WD18 8JA
Tel: 01923-495495 **Fax:** 01923-800190
E-mail: charlie.madsen@cooperindustries.com
Website: http://www.coopercontrols.co.uk/cortina
Bank(s): Barclay
Managers: C. Madsen (Mktg Serv Mgr)
Ultimate Holding Company: COOPER INDUSTRIES PUBLIC LIMITED COMPANY
Immediate Holding Company: COOPER CONTROLS LIMITED
Registration no: 05029521 **VAT No.:** GB 366 9098 04
Date established: 2004 **Turnover:** £2m - £5m **No.of Employees:** 21 - 50
Product Groups: 37, 46

Date of Accounts	Dec 11	Dec 10	Dec 09
Sales Turnover	13m	13m	13m
Pre Tax Profit/Loss	-241	833	556
Working Capital	1m	2m	781
Fixed Assets	1m	1m	1m
Current Assets	7m	10m	8m
Current Liabilities	373	866	709

Costco Wholesale UK Ltd
Hartspring Lane, Watford, WD25 8JS
Tel: 01923-699805 **Fax:** 01923-801125
Website: http://www.costco.com
Bank(s): HSBC Bank plc
Directors: S. Pappas (MD), M. Chauhan (Fin)
Ultimate Holding Company: COSTCO WHOLESALE CORP (USA)
Immediate Holding Company: COSTCO WHOLESALE UK LIMITED
Registration no: 02635489 **VAT No.:** GB 650 1862 52
Date established: 1991 **Turnover:** Over £1,000m
No.of Employees: 1501 & over **Product Groups:** 61

Date of Accounts	Aug 08	Aug 09	Aug 10
Sales Turnover	1274m	1405m	1438m
Pre Tax Profit/Loss	26m	22m	21m
Working Capital	-1m	10m	30m
Fixed Assets	311m	322m	321m
Current Assets	143m	157m	192m
Current Liabilities	65m	74m	83m

Custom Hose & Fitting Ltd
194 Queens Road, Watford, WD17 2NT
Tel: 01923-225534 **Fax:** 01923-818714
E-mail: enquiries@customhose.co.uk
Website: http://www.customhose.co.uk
Directors: M. Gibson (MD), J. Gibson (Fin)
Date established: 1991 **No.of Employees:** 1 - 10 **Product Groups:** 29, 30, 35, 36

D D D Ltd
94 Rickmansworth Road, Watford, WD18 7JJ
Tel: 01923-229251 **Fax:** 01923-220728
Website: http://www.dddgroup.co.uk
Directors: D. Rainsford (Dir), M. Birkett (Non Exec), N. Freer (Grp Chief Exec), N. Halsby (Ch)
Immediate Holding Company: D.D.D. Ltd
Registration no: 00122029 **Date established:** 1912
Turnover: £20m - £50m **No.of Employees:** 101 - 250
Product Groups: 31, 61, 69

Date of Accounts	Dec 09	Dec 08	Dec 07
Sales Turnover	33m	29m	25m
Pre Tax Profit/Loss	2m	116	1m
Working Capital	3m	3m	2m
Fixed Assets	4m	4m	5m
Current Assets	16m	13m	10m
Current Liabilities	6m	5m	4m

Davin Optronics Ltd
Instrument House 15 Greycaine Road, Watford, WD24 7GW
Tel: 01923-206800 **Fax:** 01923-234220
E-mail: sales@davinoptronics.com
Website: http://www.davinoptronics.com
Directors: R. Parsons (MD)
Ultimate Holding Company: OPTRONIC INVESTMENTS LTD.
Immediate Holding Company: DAVIN OPTRONICS LIMITED
Registration no: 01152753 **VAT No.:** GB 544 4995 09
Date established: 1973 **Turnover:** £5m - £10m
No.of Employees: 51 - 100 **Product Groups:** 38, 48

Date of Accounts	Sep 11	Sep 10	Sep 09
Working Capital	348	1m	1m
Fixed Assets	282	219	368
Current Assets	2m	2m	2m

Digital Applications International Ltd
York House 4 Wolsey Business Park, Watford, WD18 9BL
Tel: 01923-815400 **Fax:** 01923-818034
E-mail: enquiries@dai.co.uk
Website: http://www.dai.co.uk
Directors: J. Millard (Dir)
Immediate Holding Company: DIGITAL APPLICATIONS INTERNATIONAL LIMITED
Registration no: 01008089 **Date established:** 1971
No.of Employees: 21 - 50 **Product Groups:** 44, 84

Date of Accounts	Nov 11	Nov 10	Nov 09
Sales Turnover	16m	12m	13m
Pre Tax Profit/Loss	3m	2m	2m
Working Capital	8m	6m	8m
Fixed Assets	6m	6m	4m
Current Assets	11m	8m	11m
Current Liabilities	3m	2m	3m

Electro Replacement Ltd
Unit 1 Moor Park Industrial Centre Tolpits Lane, Watford, WD18 9EU
Tel: 01923-255344 **Fax:** 01923-255829
E-mail: info@apt-erlltd.co.uk
Website: http://www.apt-erlltd.co.uk
Directors: L. Schonthal (MD)
Managers: G. Stockinger (Tech Serv Mgr)
Ultimate Holding Company: PETER SCHONTHAL AGENCIES LIMITED
Immediate Holding Company: ELECTRO-REPLACEMENT LIMITED
Registration no: 01013271 **Date established:** 1971 **Turnover:** £1m - £2m
No.of Employees: 1 - 10 **Product Groups:** 36, 37, 40, 67

Date of Accounts	Dec 11	Jun 10	Jun 09
Working Capital	954	1m	1m
Fixed Assets	80	97	89
Current Assets	1m	1m	1m

Europa Ltd
Unit 35 Moor Park Industrial Centre Tolpits Lane, Watford, WD18 9SP
Tel: 01923-212700 **Fax:** 01923-212727
E-mail: sales@europaconservatories.co.uk
Website: http://www.europaconservatories.co.uk
Directors: G. Upton (Dir)
Immediate Holding Company: EUROPA OUTDOOR LIVING LTD
Registration no: 07925975 **Date established:** 2012
No.of Employees: 11 - 20 **Product Groups:** 35

Fibrerod Pultrusions
Wemco House 477 Whippendell Road, Watford, WD18 7PS
Tel: 01923-221255 **Fax:** 01923-221255
E-mail: jamie@fibrerodpultrusions.co.uk
Website: http://www.fibrerodpultrusions.co.uk
Managers: J. Holland (Mgr)
Immediate Holding Company: FIBREROD PULTRUSIONS LIMITED
Registration no: 06434744 **Date established:** 2007
Turnover: £250,000 - £500,000 **No.of Employees:** 1 - 10
Product Groups: 30

Date of Accounts	May 11	May 10	May 09
Working Capital	22	-89	N/A
Fixed Assets	81	89	N/A
Current Assets	83	45	N/A

Thomas Fox & Co. Ltd
3 Rhodes Way, Watford, WD24 4YA
Tel: 01923-811700 **Fax:** 01923-811710
E-mail: peter.cooper@thomasfox.co.uk
Website: http://www.thomasfox.co.uk
Bank(s): HSBC Bank plc
Directors: B. Rutter (MD), P. Cooper (Dir), P. Rutter (Dir), C. Rutter (Dir), O. Martin (Co Sec)
Immediate Holding Company: THOMAS FOX & COMPANY LIMITED
Registration no: 00200011 **VAT No.:** GB 233 0244 14
Date established: 2024 **Turnover:** £2m - £5m **No.of Employees:** 51 - 100
Product Groups: 36, 49, 72

Gate Machinery International Ltd
Unit B Penfold Works Imperial Way, Watford, WD24 4YY
Tel: 01923-211000 **Fax:** 01923-682875
E-mail: sales@gatemachinery.com
Website: http://www.gatemachinery.com

Directors: A. Fidelia (MD)
Immediate Holding Company: GATE MACHINERY INTERNATIONAL LIMITED
Registration no: 02798858 **VAT No.:** GB 629 5212 38
Date established: 1993 **Turnover:** £1m - £2m **No.of Employees:** 1 - 10
Product Groups: 67

Date of Accounts	Mar 11	Mar 10	Mar 09
Working Capital	188	188	207
Fixed Assets	1	2	3
Current Assets	448	547	522

G B G Structural Services (a division G B G Geotechnics Ltd)

Bucknalls Lane, Watford, WD25 9XX
Tel: 01923-678800 **Fax:** 01923-678500
E-mail: works@gbg.co.uk
Website: http://www.gbg.co.uk
Managers: D. Wilson
Immediate Holding Company: CODE FOR SUSTAINABLE BUILDINGS LIMITED
Registration no: 01573939 **VAT No.:** GB 396 4022 41
Date established: 1994 **Turnover:** Up to £250,000
No.of Employees: 1 - 10 **Product Groups:** 85

Date of Accounts	Dec 11	Dec 10	Dec 09
Working Capital	88	87	83
Fixed Assets	12	14	22
Current Assets	539	361	344

Glasses on Spec Ltd

Unit 7 Olds Close, Watford, WD18 9RU
Tel: 08712-003720 **Fax:** 01923-710175
E-mail: info@glassesonspec.co.uk
Website: http://www.glassesonspec.co.uk
Directors: W. Luff (Dir)
No.of Employees: 1 - 10 **Product Groups:** 38

Goran Plastics Ltd

5 Caxton Way, Watford, WD18 8UA
Tel: 01923-255700 **Fax:** 01923-255698
E-mail: sales@goran.co.uk
Website: http://www.goran.co.uk
Directors: P. Cox (Fin), C. King (MD)
Immediate Holding Company: GORAN PLASTICS LIMITED
Registration no: 03651053 **Date established:** 1998 **Turnover:** £1m - £2m
No.of Employees: 11 - 20 **Product Groups:** 42

Date of Accounts	Dec 11	Dec 10	Dec 09
Working Capital	-210	-210	-161
Fixed Assets	674	729	784
Current Assets	696	707	778

H R S Heat Exchanges Ltd

HRS House 1012 Caxton Way, Watford, WD18 8UA
Tel: 01923-232335 **Fax:** 01923-230266
E-mail: mail@hrs.co.uk
Website: http://www.hrs.co.uk
Bank(s): The Royal Bank of Scotland
Directors: R. Twydle (Fin), S. Pither (MD)
Immediate Holding Company: HRS INVESTMENTS LIMITED
Registration no: 03737053 **Date established:** 1999
Turnover: Up to £250,000 **No.of Employees:** 21 - 50 **Product Groups:** 40, 42, 48

Date of Accounts	Dec 10	Dec 09	Dec 08
Sales Turnover	179	N/A	N/A
Pre Tax Profit/Loss	-24	N/A	N/A
Working Capital	434	229	22
Fixed Assets	1m	849	873
Current Assets	1m	-43	268
Current Liabilities	177	N/A	N/A

H T C Group Ltd

6 Station Road, Watford, WD17 1EQ
Tel: 01923-652500 **Fax:** 01923-652515
E-mail: trish@htc.co.uk
Website: http://www.htc.co.uk
Directors: P. Demirag (MD)
Immediate Holding Company: HTC GROUP LIMITED
Registration no: 01742433 **Date established:** 1983
Turnover: Up to £250,000 **No.of Employees:** 1 - 10 **Product Groups:** 61

Date of Accounts	May 11	May 10	May 09
Working Capital	991	896	913
Fixed Assets	13	9	18
Current Assets	2m	2m	2m

Hamerville Magazines Ltd

Regal House Regal Way, Watford, WD24 4YF
Tel: 01923-237799 **Fax:** 01923-246901
E-mail: office@hamerville.co.uk
Website: http://www.hamerville.co.uk
Bank(s): National Westminster Bank Plc
Directors: B. Shannon (MD), S. Shannon (Fin)
Immediate Holding Company: HAMERVILLE MEDIA GROUP LIMITED
Registration no: 00903957 **Date established:** 1967 **Turnover:** £5m - £10m
No.of Employees: 51 - 100 **Product Groups:** 28

Date of Accounts	Oct 11	Oct 10	Oct 09
Sales Turnover	10m	9m	8m
Pre Tax Profit/Loss	473	244	-218
Working Capital	2m	2m	2m
Fixed Assets	2m	804	820
Current Assets	3m	4m	3m
Current Liabilities	873	583	502

Hilton Hotel

Maple Court Reeds Cresent, Watford, WD24 4QQ
Tel: 020-7850 4000 **Fax:** 01923-434001
Website: http://www.hilton.com
Directors: M. Way (Fin), D. Taljaard (Dir), J. Farrow (Dir), D. Jarvis (Dir), D. Andrew (Dir), J. Bamsey (Dir)
Immediate Holding Company: HILTON UK HOTELS LIMITED
Registration no: 00081009 **Date established:** 2004 **Turnover:** £5m - £10m
No.of Employees: 1 - 10 **Product Groups:** 69

Hire Technicians Group Ltd

Chalk Hill House 8 Chalk Hill, Watford, WD19 4BH
Tel: 01923-252230 **Fax:** 01923-238799
E-mail: sales@hiretech.biz
Website: http://www.hiretech.biz
Directors: C. Hedger (Tech Serv), J. Rogers (MD), M. Rogers (MD)
Managers: B. Coshall (Buyer), B. Dewrance (Personnel), C. Baker (Sales Prom)
Immediate Holding Company: Hire Technicians Group Ltd
Registration no: 01294951 **VAT No.:** GB 196 4006 55
Date established: 1977 **Turnover:** £2m - £5m **No.of Employees:** 1 - 10
Product Groups: 36, 37, 83

Date of Accounts	Apr 08	Apr 07	Apr 06
Sales Turnover	N/A	N/A	2223
Pre Tax Profit/Loss	N/A	N/A	-375
Working Capital	637	485	561
Fixed Assets	153	237	364
Current Assets	1196	1147	1350
Current Liabilities	559	661	788
Total Share Capital	72	72	72
ROCE% (Return on Capital Employed)			-40.6
ROT% (Return on Turnover)			-16.9

House Of Colour Ltd

Unit 2 Building 6 Hatters Lane, Watford, WD18 8YH
Tel: 0800-318526 **Fax:** 01923-218823
E-mail: info@houseofcolour.co.uk
Website: http://www.houseofcolour.co.uk
Directors: H. Venables (MD)
Ultimate Holding Company: FESTIVAL ROAD LIMITED
Immediate Holding Company: HOUSE OF COLOUR LIMITED
Registration no: 01972801 **Date established:** 1985
Turnover: £500,000 - £1m **No.of Employees:** 1 - 10 **Product Groups:** 80

Date of Accounts	Apr 11	Apr 10	Apr 09
Working Capital	100	100	113
Fixed Assets	1	3	6
Current Assets	206	216	216

Industrial Finishers Watford Ltd

6 Greenhill Crescent, Watford, WD18 8RF
Tel: 01923-225388 **Fax:** 01923-227943
E-mail: info@industrial-finishers.com
Website: http://www.industrial-finishers.com
Directors: W. Holdham (MD)
Managers: L. Barringer (Works Gen Mgr), J. Laland (Mktg Serv Mgr), S. Brook (Mktg Serv Mgr)
Immediate Holding Company: INDUSTRIAL FINISHERS (WATFORD) LIMITED
Registration no: 00762523 **VAT No.:** GB 196 2401 59
Date established: 1963 **Turnover:** Up to £250,000
No.of Employees: 1 - 10 **Product Groups:** 48

Iveco Trucks Ltd International Operations

Iveco House Station Road, Watford, WD17 1SR
Tel: 01923-246400 **Fax:** 01923-240574
E-mail: fuller@iveco.com
Website: http://www.iveco.com
Directors: L. Sra (Dir), S. Cribbin (Fin), S. Beeton (Sales)
Managers: R. Barker (Purch Mgr)
Ultimate Holding Company: FIAT SPA (ITALY)
Immediate Holding Company: IVECO LIMITED
Registration no: 01975271 **VAT No.:** GB 579 4529 84
Date established: 1986 **Turnover:** £250m - £500m
No.of Employees: 101 - 250 **Product Groups:** 36, 39, 40, 67, 68, 72

Date of Accounts	Dec 11	Dec 10	Dec 09
Sales Turnover	273m	214m	190m
Pre Tax Profit/Loss	6m	517	292
Working Capital	125m	121m	131m
Fixed Assets	4m	3m	4m
Current Assets	254m	206m	229m
Current Liabilities	68m	53m	59m

J D Cables Ltd

Unit 14 The Metro Centre Dwight Road, Watford, WD18 9SS
Tel: 01923-222600 **Fax:** 01923-222608
E-mail: sales@jdcables.com
Website: http://www.jdcables.com
Directors: G. Cole (Fin), J. Duffy (MD)
Immediate Holding Company: J.D. CABLES LIMITED
Registration no: 03060902 **VAT No.:** GB 645 1286 39
Date established: 1995 **Turnover:** £1m - £2m **No.of Employees:** 1 - 10
Product Groups: 37, 48, 67

Date of Accounts	May 12	May 11	May 10
Working Capital	13	3	-7
Fixed Assets	8	10	10
Current Assets	272	239	280

J D Wetherspoon plc

Wetherspoon House Reeds Crescent, Watford, WD24 4QL
Tel: 01923-477777 **Fax:** 01923-219810
E-mail: sales@jdwetherspoon.co.uk
Website: http://www.jdwetherspoon.co.uk
Directors: T. Martin (Ch)
Immediate Holding Company: J D WETHERSPOON PLC
Registration no: 01709784 **Date established:** 1983
Turnover: Over £1,000m **No.of Employees:** 101 - 250
Product Groups: 62, 69

Date of Accounts	Jul 08	Jul 09	Jul 10
Sales Turnover	908m	955m	996m
Pre Tax Profit/Loss	54m	45m	60m
Working Capital	-81m	-199m	-111m
Fixed Assets	805m	797m	845m
Current Assets	46m	59m	66m
Current Liabilities	76m	82m	86m

Kromachem Ltd

Unit 10-11 Moor Park Industrial Centre Tolpits Lane, Watford, WD18 9ER
Tel: 01923-223368 **Fax:** 01923-239308
E-mail: info@kromachem.com
Website: http://www.kromachem.com
Directors: E. Kensbock (Grp MD), S. Kensbock (MD)
Managers: R. Elliott (Chief Mgr)
Ultimate Holding Company: KROMACHEM HOLDINGS LIMITED
Immediate Holding Company: KROMACHEM HOLDINGS LIMITED
Registration no: 02448159 **VAT No.:** GB 541 2850 63
Date established: 1989 **Turnover:** £10m - £20m **No.of Employees:** 1 - 10
Product Groups: 31, 32, 34

Date of Accounts	Dec 11	Dec 10	Dec 09
Sales Turnover	16m	15m	13m
Pre Tax Profit/Loss	2m	1m	1m
Working Capital	5m	3m	3m
Fixed Assets	2m	2m	1m
Current Assets	7m	7m	6m
Current Liabilities	817	1m	949

F H Lambert Ltd

Rembrandt House King Georges Avenue, Watford, WD18 7PW
Tel: 01923-229444 **Fax:** 01923-255717
E-mail: jamie@fhlambert.com
Website: http://www.fhlambert.com
Bank(s): The Royal Bank of Scotland
Directors: P. Mitchell (Dir), F. Lambert (MD), F. Lambert (Dir), J. Lambert (Dir), S. Lambert (Dir)
Managers: S. Farmer (Sec)
Immediate Holding Company: F.H. LAMBERT LIMITED
Registration no: 00968050 **VAT No.:** GB 196 8561 07
Date established: 1969 **Turnover:** £500,000 - £1m
No.of Employees: 11 - 20 **Product Groups:** 48

Date of Accounts	Jul 09	Jul 08	Jul 07
Working Capital	636	669	359
Fixed Assets	8	21	62
Current Assets	862	889	472

Leonhard Kurz UK Ltd

Garnet Close, Watford, WD24 7JW
Tel: 01923-249988 **Fax:** 01923-252516
E-mail: andrew.ferrar@kurz.co.uk
Website: http://www.kurz.de
Bank(s): Barclays, Watford
Directors: A. Ferrar (MD)
Managers: R. O'Brien (Sales Prom Mgr), A. McNally (Comptroller)
Ultimate Holding Company: FP010267
Immediate Holding Company: LEONHARD KURZ (U.K.) LIMITED
Registration no: 01344994 **VAT No.:** GB 301 7808 81
Date established: 1977 **Turnover:** £10m - £20m
No.of Employees: 21 - 50 **Product Groups:** 34

Loading Bay Specialists Ltd

4 Garnet Close, Watford, WD24 7JX
Tel: 01923-208888 **Fax:** 01923-208899
E-mail: info@saralbs.co.uk
Website: http://www.saralbs.co.uk
Bank(s): Barclays
Directors: A. Thomson (Dir), L. Hales (Fin), R. Seidler (MD), U. Schubert (Ch)
Managers: D. Quelch, E. Wilks (Admin Off), L. Hales (Comptroller), A. Georgio (Mgr), E. Wilkes (Ops Mgr), J. Sartin (Admin Off)
Ultimate Holding Company: DOOR AND DOOR COMPONENTS LTD (BVI)
Immediate Holding Company: LOADING BAY SPECIALISTS LIMITED
Registration no: 01699363 **Date established:** 1983 **Turnover:** £5m - £10m
No.of Employees: 21 - 50 **Product Groups:** 48, 83

Lumitron Lighting Services Ltd

Unit 31 The Metro Centre Dwight Road, Watford, WD18 9UD
Tel: 01923-226222 **Fax:** 01923-211300
E-mail: sales@lumitron.co.uk
Website: http://www.lumitron.co.uk
Managers: T. Purcell (Chief Mgr)
Immediate Holding Company: LUMITRON LIGHTING (SERVICES) LIMITED
Registration no: 04654341 **VAT No.:** GB 681 6571 11
Date established: 2003 **Turnover:** £1m - £2m **No.of Employees:** 1 - 10
Product Groups: 37

Date of Accounts	Jan 12	Jan 11	Jan 10
Working Capital	88	82	N/A
Current Assets	198	130	N/A

M J S Packaging Machines

176 Hillcroft Crescent, Watford, WD19 4NZ
Tel: 0783-144 3868 **Fax:** 01923-448640
E-mail: sales@mjspack.co.uk
Website: http://www.mjspack.co.uk
Directors: M. Smyth (MD)
Immediate Holding Company: MJS PACKAGING SERVICES LTD
Registration no: 07086936 **Date established:** 2009
Turnover: Up to £250,000 **No.of Employees:** 1 - 10 **Product Groups:** 20, 27, 30, 34, 37, 38, 39, 40, 41, 42, 43, 44, 45, 46, 48, 49, 66, 67, 76, 83, 84

Date of Accounts	Mar 11
Sales Turnover	117
Pre Tax Profit/Loss	26
Working Capital	15
Current Assets	35
Current Liabilities	11

M T R Ltd

58 Cross Road Bushey, Watford, WD19 4DQ
Tel: 01923-234050 **Fax:** 01923-255746
E-mail: support@mtraudio.com
Website: http://www.mtraudio.com
Directors: A. Reeves (MD)
Immediate Holding Company: M.T.R. LIMITED
Registration no: 01600746 **VAT No.:** GB 366 9549 94
Date established: 1981 **Turnover:** £2m - £5m **No.of Employees:** 1 - 10
Product Groups: 37

Date of Accounts	Dec 11	Dec 10	Dec 09
Working Capital	2	-0	-0
Current Assets	37	46	53

Majestic Wine Warehouse

Otterspool Way, Watford, WD25 8WW
Tel: 01923-298200 **Fax:** 01923-819105
E-mail: info@majestic.co.uk
Website: http://www.majestic.co.uk
Directors: J. Apthorp (Purch), S. Gibbs (Pers), S. Lewis (Dir), J. Bendon (Tech Serv), N. Alldritt (Fin)
Immediate Holding Company: MAJESTIC WINE PLC
Registration no: 02281640 **VAT No.:** GB 563 0589 32
Date established: 1988 **Turnover:** £250m - £500m
No.of Employees: 501 - 1000 **Product Groups:** 62, 84

Date of Accounts	Mar 09	Mar 10	Mar 11
Sales Turnover	202m	233m	257m
Pre Tax Profit/Loss	7m	16m	20m
Working Capital	-3m	-659	7m
Fixed Assets	59m	62m	75m
Current Assets	53m	55m	64m
Current Liabilities	11m	15m	20m

Maplin Electronics Ltd

138 High Street, Watford, WD17 2EN
Tel: 08432-277323 **Fax:** 01923-246854
E-mail: customercare@maplin.co.uk
Website: http://www.maplin.co.uk

see next page

Maplin Electronics Ltd - Cont'd
Managers: R. Stanworth (Mgr)
Ultimate Holding Company: MONTAGU PRIVATE EQUITY LLP
Immediate Holding Company: MAPLIN ELECTRONICS LIMITED
Registration no: 01264385 **Date established:** 1976
Turnover: £125m - £250m **No.of Employees:** 1 - 10 **Product Groups:** 37, 61

Date of Accounts	Dec 11	Dec 08	Dec 09
Sales Turnover	205m	204m	204m
Pre Tax Profit/Loss	25m	32m	35m
Working Capital	118m	49m	75m
Fixed Assets	27m	28m	28m
Current Assets	207m	108m	142m
Current Liabilities	78m	51m	59m

Marata Vision
20 Greenhill Crescent, Watford, WD18 8JA
Tel: 01923-495595 **Fax:** 01923-495599
E-mail: info@marata.co.uk
Website: http://www.marata.co.uk
Directors: S. Sparrow (MD)
Turnover: £500,000 - £1m **No.of Employees:** 21 - 50
Product Groups: 37, 67

Martindale Electrics Ltd
Metrohm House Penfold Trading Estate, Watford, WD24 4YY
Tel: 01923-441717 **Fax:** 01923-446900
E-mail: sales@martindale-electric.co.uk
Website: http://www.martindale-electric.co.uk
Directors: P. Ohara (Co Sec), P. O'hara (MD)
Ultimate Holding Company: INSTROTECH LIMITED
Immediate Holding Company: MARTINDALE ELECTRIC COMPANY LIMITED
Registration no: 03387451 **Date established:** 1997
No.of Employees: 21 - 50 **Product Groups:** 36, 40

Date of Accounts	Dec 11	Dec 10	Dec 09
Working Capital	754	672	739
Fixed Assets	68	90	66
Current Assets	2m	1m	1m

Mercseller.com
35 Cecil Street, Watford, WD24 5AS
Tel: 01923-463620
E-mail: mercseller.com@gmail.com
Website: http://www.merccseller.com
Directors: R. Selwyn Barnett (Prop)
Turnover: Up to £250,000 **No.of Employees:** 1 - 10 **Product Groups:** 37, 39, 68

Millipore UK Ltd
Suite 3-5 Building 6 Crossley Green Business Park Hatters Lane, Watford, WD18 8YH
Tel: 08709-004645 **Fax:** 0870-900 4646
E-mail: csr_uk@millipore.com
Website: http://www.millipore.com
Bank(s): Barclays, Rickmansworth
Directors: A. Packard (Co Sec), G. Young (Dir)
Managers: S. Damary (Mktg Serv Mgr), C. Szarka (Mktg Serv Mgr), S. Evans (Sales Prom Mgr), O. Wyatt (Cust Serv Mgr)
Ultimate Holding Company: MILLIPORE CORP (USA)
Immediate Holding Company: MILLIPORE (U.K.) LIMITED
Registration no: 04130249 **Date established:** 2000
Turnover: £10m - £20m **No.of Employees:** 51 - 100 **Product Groups:** 38, 42

Date of Accounts	Dec 11	Dec 10	Dec 09
Sales Turnover	82m	84m	73m
Pre Tax Profit/Loss	-3m	4m	9m
Working Capital	-313m	-315m	-316m
Fixed Assets	361m	365m	366m
Current Assets	77m	70m	54m
Current Liabilities	6m	5m	3m

Monster Play Systems
Unit 1a Sandown Road Industrial Estate, Watford, WD24 7UB
Tel: 01923-236627 **Fax:** 01923-818339
E-mail: sales@monsterplay.co.uk
Website: http://www.monsterplay.co.uk
Bank(s): Lloyds TSB Bank plc
Directors: P. Quinn (MD), M. Quinn (Co Sec)
Immediate Holding Company: MONSTER PLAY SYSTEMS LIMITED
Registration no: 01600784 **VAT No.:** GB 367 0017 69
Date established: 1981 **No.of Employees:** 21 - 50 **Product Groups:** 48

Date of Accounts	Sep 11	Sep 10	Sep 09
Working Capital	-46	62	125
Fixed Assets	188	150	97
Current Assets	1m	951	785

Mothercare plc
Cherry Tree Road, Watford, WD24 6SH
Tel: 01923-241000 **Fax:** 01923-240944
Website: http://www.mothercare.com
Directors: C. Timey (Pers), A. James (Mkt Research), S. Glew (Fin), B. Gordan (MD)
Managers: K. O'Brien (I.T. Exec), S. Morgan (Buyer), J. Kerr (Tech Serv Mgr), T. Holdway
Immediate Holding Company: MOTHERCARE PLC.
Registration no: 01950509 **Date established:** 1985 **Turnover:** £2m - £5m
No.of Employees: 501 - 1000 **Product Groups:** 24

Musonic UK Ltd
Unit 271b The Wenta Business Centre Colne Way, Watford, WD24 7ND
Tel: 020-8950 5151 **Fax:** 020-8950 5391
E-mail: info@musonic.co.uk
Website: http://www.musonic.co.uk
Directors: M. Blank (Dir)
Immediate Holding Company: MUSONIC (U.K.) LIMITED
Registration no: 01318480 **VAT No.:** GB 301 6450 06
Date established: 1977 **Turnover:** Up to £250,000
No.of Employees: 1 - 10 **Product Groups:** 37

Date of Accounts	Jun 11	Jun 10	Jun 09
Working Capital	15	15	16
Fixed Assets	1	1	N/A
Current Assets	85	74	86

Neogene LLP
14 Caxton Way, Watford, WD18 8UJ
Tel: 01923-213737 **Fax:** 01923-213617
E-mail: mail@neogenepaints.co.uk
Website: http://www.neogenepaints.co.uk
Bank(s): National Westminster Bank Plc
Directors: N. Brampton (Ptnr), P. Brown (I.T. Dir)
Immediate Holding Company: NEOGENE PAINTS LIMITED
Registration no: 00285972 **VAT No.:** GB 289 0245 73
Date established: 1934 **Turnover:** £2m - £5m **No.of Employees:** 11 - 20
Product Groups: 32

Date of Accounts	Mar 11	Mar 10	Mar 09
Working Capital	2m	1m	1m
Fixed Assets	436	49	62
Current Assets	2m	2m	2m

Nicenstripy (Watford & St Albans)
Unit 46 Berry Avenue, Watford, WD24 6RY
Tel: 01923-352671 **Fax:** 01923-462153
E-mail: c.french@nicenstripy.com
Website: http://www.nicenstripy.com
Directors: C. French (Dir)
Registration no: 06330380 **Date established:** 2007
Turnover: Up to £250,000 **No.of Employees:** 1 - 10 **Product Groups:** 07

Nitto Kohki Europe Co. Ltd
Unit 21 Empire Centre Imperial Way, Watford, WD24 4TS
Tel: 01923-239351 **Fax:** 01923-248815
E-mail: info@nitto-europe.com
Website: http://www.nitto-europe.com
Directors: M. Ogue (MD)
Ultimate Holding Company: NITTO KOHKI CO. LTD (JAPAN)
Immediate Holding Company: NITTO KOHKI EUROPE CO. LIMITED
Registration no: 01413144 **VAT No.:** GB 242 8055 73
Date established: 1979 **Turnover:** £2m - £5m **No.of Employees:** 1 - 10
Product Groups: 30, 36, 37, 40, 42, 45

Date of Accounts	Dec 11	Dec 10	Dec 09
Sales Turnover	13m	12m	10m
Pre Tax Profit/Loss	841	720	-93
Working Capital	8m	8m	8m
Fixed Assets	2m	2m	2m
Current Assets	10m	10m	9m
Current Liabilities	980	625	331

J R Nobbs & Sons Ltd (t/a I M P Engineering)
Unit 3 15-19 Greenhill Crescent, Watford, WD18 8PH
Tel: 01923-234176 **Fax:** 01923-211146
E-mail: sales@imp-engineering.co.uk
Website: http://www.imp-engineering.co.uk
Directors: N. Roper (Fab)
Immediate Holding Company: J.R. NOBBS & SONS LIMITED
Registration no: 01320033 **VAT No.:** GB 301 6464 92
Date established: 1977 **Turnover:** £500,000 - £1m
No.of Employees: 1 - 10 **Product Groups:** 48

Date of Accounts	Jul 12	Jul 11	Jul 10
Sales Turnover	379	N/A	N/A
Working Capital	81	69	61
Fixed Assets	27	33	39
Current Assets	190	155	106

Not Just Taps
CP House Otterspool Way, Watford, WD25 8JJ
Tel: 08456-017097
E-mail: salesinfo@notjusttaps.co.uk
Website: http://www.notjusttaps.co.uk
Directors: D. Aaronson (Ptnr), D. Aaronson (Dir)
Immediate Holding Company: R. & W. ESTATES (BUXTON) LIMITED
Date established: 1972 **Turnover:** £250,000 - £500,000
No.of Employees: 1 - 10 **Product Groups:** 30

Date of Accounts	Dec 10	Dec 09	Dec 08
Sales Turnover	2m	2m	99
Pre Tax Profit/Loss	-216	-125	-106
Working Capital	-4m	-1m	-1m
Fixed Assets	4m	4m	4m
Current Assets	257	260	639
Current Liabilities	2m	1m	1m

Optelec Ltd
2 Millfield House Woodshots Meadow, Watford, WD18 8YX
Tel: 01923-231313 **Fax:** 01923-231385
E-mail: info@optelec.co.uk
Website: http://www.optelec.co.uk
Directors: P. Fletcher (MD)
Immediate Holding Company: OPTELEC LIMITED
Registration no: 01970594 **Date established:** 1985
No.of Employees: 1 - 10 **Product Groups:** 38, 67

Date of Accounts	Dec 11	Dec 10	Dec 09
Working Capital	-122	-168	-180
Fixed Assets	14	23	8
Current Assets	679	707	696

PNMsoft
38 Clarendon road, Watford, WD17 1JJ
Tel: 01923-813420
E-mail: info@pnmsoft.com
Website: http://www.pnmsoft.com
Directors: G. Horvitz (Grp Chief Exec)
Date established: 1996 **Turnover:** £20m - £50m
No.of Employees: 101 - 250 **Product Groups:** 80

Polaron Cortina Ltd
20 Greenhill Crescent, Watford, WD18 8JA
Tel: 01923-495495 **Fax:** 01923-228796
E-mail: rkay@polaron.co.uk
Website: http://www.coopercontrols.co.uk/cortina
Bank(s): Bank Leumi le Israel BM
Directors: R. Kay (Dir), M. Payne (Sales), J. Stelzer (MD), C. Madson (Sales & Mktg), T. Helz (Co Sec)
Managers: L. Madlani (Purch Mgr)
Ultimate Holding Company: 05029521
Immediate Holding Company: COOPER CONTROLS (WATFORD) LIMITED
Registration no: 00739673 **VAT No.:** GB 366 9098 04
Date established: 1962 **Turnover:** £10m - £20m
No.of Employees: 51 - 100 **Product Groups:** 37, 38, 39, 46, 49

Pure Klenz
Greenhill House 26 Greenhill Crescent, Watford, WD18 8JA
Tel: 01923-274635
E-mail: pureklenz@btconnect.com
Website: http://www.pureklenz.co.uk
Directors: E. O'connor (Prop)
Immediate Holding Company: COMAERO FASTENERS LIMITED
Registration no: 03060902 **Date established:** 2001
No.of Employees: 1 - 10 **Product Groups:** 24, 63

Date of Accounts	Apr 11	Apr 10	Apr 09
Working Capital	13	17	-2
Fixed Assets	4	5	7
Current Assets	161	139	153

Ralco Tubings Ltd
Unit 14-15 Fisher Industrial Estate Wiggenhall Road, Watford, WD18 0FN
Tel: 01923-212777 **Fax:** 01923-212606
E-mail: sales@ralco-tubings.co.uk
Website: http://www.ralco-tubings.co.uk
Directors: C. O'dell (Fin)
Immediate Holding Company: RALCO TUBINGS LIMITED
Registration no: 01078991 **Date established:** 1972
Turnover: £500,000 - £1m **No.of Employees:** 1 - 10 **Product Groups:** 29, 30, 35

Date of Accounts	Jun 11	Jun 10	Jun 09
Working Capital	-2	21	13
Fixed Assets	84	73	105
Current Assets	336	337	279

Ram Power Ltd (Hydraulic Equipment Manufacturers)
16 Greenhill Crescent, Watford, WD18 8SE
Tel: 01923-231661 **Fax:** 01923-246856
E-mail: enquiries@rampower.co.uk
Website: http://www.rampower.co.uk
Bank(s): Barclays, 11 Bank Court, Hemel Hempstead
Directors: C. Jarman (Fin), A. Kirchin (MD), D. Goss (I.T. Dir)
Immediate Holding Company: RAM POWER LIMITED
Registration no: 01156821 **VAT No.:** GB 198 3708 16
Date established: 1974 **Turnover:** £1m - £2m **No.of Employees:** 11 - 20
Product Groups: 40, 46, 84

Date of Accounts	Mar 12	Mar 11	Mar 10
Working Capital	730	663	558
Fixed Assets	33	45	56
Current Assets	966	894	878

Reed Accountancy
68 High Street, Watford, WD17 2BS
Tel: 01923-471100 **Fax:** 01923-471105
E-mail: watford.employment@reed.co.uk
Website: http://www.reed.co.uk
Managers: L. Brown (Mgr)
Registration no: 00973629 **No.of Employees:** 1 - 10 **Product Groups:** 80

Rhodia Ltd
Oak House Reeds Crescent, Watford, WD24 4QP
Tel: 01923-485868 **Fax:** 01923-211580
E-mail: info@rhodia.com
Website: http://www.rhodia.com
Directors: B. Tyler (MD), R. Tyler (MD), A. Johnson (Purch)
Managers: B. Miles
Ultimate Holding Company: RHODIA SA (FRANCE)
Immediate Holding Company: RHODIA LIMITED
Registration no: 00213674 **Date established:** 1926
Turnover: £125m - £250m **No.of Employees:** 11 - 20
Product Groups: 32, 87

Date of Accounts	Dec 10	Dec 09	Dec 08
Pre Tax Profit/Loss	3m	4m	9m
Working Capital	149m	147m	143m
Fixed Assets	1m	1m	1m
Current Assets	160m	348m	340m
Current Liabilities	230	230	230

Sanyo Sales & Marketing Europe GmbH
Sanyo House 18 Colonial Way, Watford, WD24 4PT
Tel: 01923-246363 **Fax:** 01923-477450
E-mail: b.lakin@sanyo.co.uk
Website: http://www.uk.sanyo.com
Bank(s): HSBC
Directors: B. Lakin (Fin)
Ultimate Holding Company: PANASONIC CORPORATION (JAPAN)
Immediate Holding Company: SANYO EUROPE LTD
Registration no: 00956870 **Date established:** 1969
Turnover: £50m - £75m **No.of Employees:** 51 - 100 **Product Groups:** 37, 40

Date of Accounts	Mar 11	Mar 10	Mar 09
Sales Turnover	N/A	50m	76m
Pre Tax Profit/Loss	-62m	-12m	-10m
Working Capital	2m	2m	-15m
Fixed Assets	14m	77m	77m
Current Assets	6m	4m	27m
Current Liabilities	756	1m	4m

Science Engineering & Manufacturing Technologies
14 Upton Road, Watford, WD18 0JT
Tel: 01923-238441 **Fax:** 01923-256086
E-mail: pwhiteman@semta.org.uk
Website: http://www.semta.org.uk
Directors: P. Whiteman (Grp Chief Exec), S. Ball (Fin)
Managers: N. White
Immediate Holding Company: SCIENCE, ENGINEERING AND MANUFACTURING TECHNOLOGIES ALLIANCE
Registration no: 02324869 **Date established:** 1988
Turnover: £10m - £20m **No.of Employees:** 51 - 100 **Product Groups:** 86

Date of Accounts	Mar 11	Mar 10	Mar 09
Sales Turnover	15m	20m	21m
Pre Tax Profit/Loss	-3m	7m	-7m
Working Capital	-3m	-3m	-397
Fixed Assets	30m	33m	24m
Current Assets	4m	4m	8m
Current Liabilities	5m	5m	7m

Signs Express
Unit 21 Metro Centre Dwight Road Tolpits Lane, Watford, WD18 9SS
Tel: 01923-257580 **Fax:** 01923-802510
E-mail: watford@signsexpress.co.uk
Website: http://www.signsexpress.co.uk
Directors: J. Patel (MD)
Immediate Holding Company: SIGNS EXPRESS LTD
Registration no: 02375913 **Date established:** 2007
No.of Employees: 1 - 10 **Product Groups:** 49

Soundcheck Ltd
6 Woodshots Meadow, Watford, WD18 8YS
Tel: 0844-5678969 **Fax:** 08707-285269
E-mail: mail@soundcheckltd.co.uk
Website: http://www.soundcheckltd.co.uk

Managers: G. Backhoust (Mgr)
Immediate Holding Company: SOUNDCHECK LIMITED
Registration no: 03078877 **VAT No.:** 667 7134 06 **Date established:** 1995
No.of Employees: 1 - 10 **Product Groups:** 37, 38, 52, 61, 65, 67, 81, 83, 84, 89

Date of Accounts	Jul 07	Jul 06
Working Capital	-14	-10
Fixed Assets	100	99
Current Assets	72	46
Current Liabilities	86	57

South Midland Steel Ltd

PO Box 41, Watford, WD19 4SD
Tel: 01923-252089 **Fax:** 01923-250525
E-mail: smsteel@freeuk.com
Website: http://www.smsteel.sagehost.co.uk
Directors: G. Attewill (Dir)
Immediate Holding Company: SOUTH MIDLAND STEEL LIMITED
Registration no: 02390282 **VAT No.:** GB 366 9026 29
Date established: 1989 **Turnover:** £250,000 - £500,000
No.of Employees: 1 - 10 **Product Groups:** 66

Date of Accounts	May 11	May 10	May 09
Working Capital	133	113	106
Fixed Assets	2	3	3
Current Assets	325	230	236

Splendour Snacks

1a Clive Way, Watford, WD24 4PX
Tel: 01923-253290 **Fax:** 01923-253290
Website: http://www.splendoursnacks.com
Directors: B. Cox (Ptnr)
Date established: 1981 **Turnover:** Up to £250,000
No.of Employees: 1 - 10 **Product Groups:** 62

Star Computer Group plc

Building 3 Hatters Lane, Watford, WD18 8YG
Tel: 01923-246414 **Fax:** 01923-254301
E-mail: sales@starplc.com
Website: http://www.starplc.com
Bank(s): Bank of Scotland, London
Directors: D. Evans (Fin), D. Evans (Co Sec), R. Blechner (Dir)
Managers: J. Baer (Personnel), J. Camp (Sales Prom Mgr), S. Downing (I.T. Exec), S. Edwards (Purch Mgr), J. Baer (Personnel), A. Khan (Tech Serv Mgr)
Immediate Holding Company: STAR COMPUTER GROUP LIMITED
Registration no: 04432362 **VAT No.:** GB 245 9142 55
Date established: 2002 **Turnover:** £5m - £10m
No.of Employees: 51 - 100 **Product Groups:** 44

Date of Accounts	Jun 11	Jun 10	Jun 09
Sales Turnover	N/A	N/A	5m
Pre Tax Profit/Loss	17	17	311
Working Capital	N/A	N/A	746
Fixed Assets	3m	3m	52
Current Assets	3	N/A	2m
Current Liabilities	N/A	N/A	927

T S Technology

7 Langwood 87 Langley Road, Watford, WD17 4PW
Tel: 01923-221155 **Fax:** 01923-218625
E-mail: sales@tstechnology.co.uk
Website: http://www.tstechnology.co.uk
Directors: A. Smith (Prop)
Immediate Holding Company: UNDISCOVERED ALPS LIMITED
VAT No.: GB 579 2574 89 **Date established:** 2005
Turnover: £500,000 - £1m **No.of Employees:** 1 - 10 **Product Groups:** 40, 46, 47

Date of Accounts	Mar 10	Mar 09	Mar 08
Working Capital	1	-12	-10
Fixed Assets	2	3	2
Current Assets	48	16	6

Tad Communications Ltd

Unit 3 Peerglow Industrial Estate Olds Approach, Watford, WD18 9SR
Tel: 01923-712430 **Fax:** 08458-694493
E-mail: sales@tadcomms.com
Website: http://www.tadcomms.co.uk
Directors: T. Duerden (MD)
Immediate Holding Company: T.A.D. COMMUNICATIONS LTD
Registration no: 03429988 **Date established:** 1997
No.of Employees: 1 - 10 **Product Groups:** 35, 36, 37, 38, 39, 40, 41, 42, 68

Date of Accounts	Dec 11	Dec 10	Dec 09
Working Capital	262	70	73
Fixed Assets	20	28	32
Current Assets	532	225	245

Techna International

Unit 1 Metro Centre Dwight Road, Watford, WD18 9HG
Tel: 01923-222227 **Fax:** 01923-219700
E-mail: john@techna.co.uk
Website: http://www.techna.co.uk
Bank(s): Barclays
Directors: A. Mestitz (Fin), J. Mestitz (MD)
Immediate Holding Company: TECHNA INTERNATIONAL LIMITED
Registration no: 00577868 **VAT No.:** GB 222 4101 29
Date established: 1957 **Turnover:** £1m - £2m **No.of Employees:** 11 - 20
Product Groups: 37

Date of Accounts	Sep 11	Sep 10	Sep 09
Working Capital	124	264	200
Fixed Assets	1m	694	688
Current Assets	780	994	716

Testrade Ltd

Unit 22 Olds Close, Watford, WD18 9RU
Tel: 01923-720222 **Fax:** 01923-720444
E-mail: sales@testrade.co.uk
Directors: G. Long (MD)
Immediate Holding Company: TESTRADE LIMITED
Registration no: 01011406 **VAT No.:** GB 223 2759 75
Date established: 1971 **Turnover:** £1m - £2m **No.of Employees:** 1 - 10
Product Groups: 32, 34, 37

Date of Accounts	Oct 11	Oct 10	Oct 09
Sales Turnover	N/A	1m	1m
Pre Tax Profit/Loss	N/A	18	43
Working Capital	370	324	311
Fixed Assets	11	7	5
Current Assets	558	517	521
Current Liabilities	N/A	35	37

The Zerny Engineering Co. Ltd

Unit 13-14 Olds Close, Watford, WD18 9RU
Tel: 01923-774777 **Fax:** 01923-774777
Directors: J. Wells (Fin), J. Zerny (MD)
Immediate Holding Company: ZERNY ENGINEERING COMPANY LIMITED(THE)
Registration no: 00430290 **VAT No.:** GB 197 2039 44
Date established: 1947 **Turnover:** Up to £250,000
No.of Employees: 1 - 10 **Product Groups:** 35

Date of Accounts	Apr 11	Apr 10	Apr 09
Sales Turnover	71	83	74
Pre Tax Profit/Loss	56	26	60
Working Capital	590	570	585
Fixed Assets	835	837	838
Current Assets	639	614	634
Current Liabilities	46	38	36

Thomas & Vines Ltd

Unit 5-6 Sutherland Court Moor Park Industrial Centre Tolpits Lane, Watford, WD18 9SP
Tel: 01923-775111 **Fax:** 01923-771452
E-mail: orders@flocking.co.uk
Website: http://www.flocking.co.uk
Directors: R. Thomas (MD)
Immediate Holding Company: THOMAS & VINES LTD
Registration no: 02048835 **VAT No.:** GB 449 4626 18
Date established: 1986 **Turnover:** Up to £250,000
No.of Employees: 1 - 10 **Product Groups:** 28, 29, 30, 48, 66

Date of Accounts	Mar 11	Mar 10	Mar 09
Working Capital	46	50	54
Fixed Assets	N/A	2	2
Current Assets	96	105	88

Tower Systems Ltd

Unit 4b Sandown Road Industrial Estate, Watford, WD24 7UB
Tel: 01923-238603 **Fax:** 01923-239093
E-mail: info@towersystems.co.uk
Website: http://www.towersystems.co.uk
Directors: J. Williams (MD)
Immediate Holding Company: TOWER SYSTEMS LIMITED
Registration no: 02971924 **Date established:** 1994
No.of Employees: 11 - 20 **Product Groups:** 40, 48, 51, 52, 84

Date of Accounts	Dec 11	Dec 10	Dec 09
Working Capital	149	136	174
Fixed Assets	264	263	270
Current Assets	641	724	798

Trend Machinery & Cutting Tools Ltd

Unit 6 Odhams Trading Estate St Albans Road, Watford, WD24 7TR
Tel: 01923-249911 **Fax:** 01923-236879
E-mail: sales@trendm.co.uk
Website: http://www.trend-uk.com
Bank(s): National Westminster Bank Plc
Directors: J. Willcocks (MD), P. Bailey (Mkt Research)
Managers: M. Tideswell (Sales Prom Mgr), J. Hughes (Export Sales Mg)
Immediate Holding Company: TREND MACHINERY & CUTTING TOOLS LIMITED
Registration no: 01338493 **Date established:** 1977
Turnover: £10m - £20m **No.of Employees:** 51 - 100 **Product Groups:** 36, 37, 47

Date of Accounts	Dec 11	Dec 10	Dec 09
Sales Turnover	12m	12m	11m
Pre Tax Profit/Loss	245	39	29
Working Capital	2m	2m	2m
Fixed Assets	273	146	106
Current Assets	6m	6m	6m
Current Liabilities	1m	798	860

T F Tull Ltd

Unit D Caxton Court Caxton Way, Watford, WD18 8RH
Tel: 01923-235288 **Fax:** 01923-247040
E-mail: enquiries@tftull.co.uk
Website: http://www.tftull.co.uk
Bank(s): Lloyds, Rickmansworth
Directors: P. O'grady (MD), R. Evans (Dir)
Managers: I. Link (Tech Serv Mgr)
Immediate Holding Company: T.F. TULL LIMITED
Registration no: 01026256 **VAT No.:** 196 9708 95 **Date established:** 1971
Turnover: £5m - £10m **No.of Employees:** 21 - 50 **Product Groups:** 35, 37

Date of Accounts	Oct 11	Oct 10	Oct 09
Sales Turnover	N/A	N/A	6m
Pre Tax Profit/Loss	N/A	N/A	308
Working Capital	665	202	225
Fixed Assets	146	163	143
Current Assets	1m	2m	2m
Current Liabilities	1	N/A	689

UK Lift

1 Millfield House Woodshots Meadow, Watford, WD18 8YX
Tel: 01923-656200 **Fax:** 01923- 221231
E-mail: info@uk-lift.co.uk
Website: http://www.uk-lift.co.uk
Bank(s): Barclays
Directors: I. Green (Ch)
Managers: D. McDonald (Mgr)
Immediate Holding Company: UK LIFT (HOLDINGS) LTD
Registration no: 04748753 **VAT No.:** GB 579 2684 82
Date established: 2003 **Turnover:** £10m - £20m
No.of Employees: 101 - 250 **Product Groups:** 45, 48

V B Johnson LLP

St Johns House 304-310 St Albans Road, Watford, WD24 6PW
Tel: 01923-227236 **Fax:** 01923-231134
E-mail: watford@vbjohnson.co.uk
Website: http://www.vbjohnson.co.uk
Directors: G. Hadden (Ptnr)
Immediate Holding Company: V B JOHNSON LLP
Registration no: OC306567 **Date established:** 2004
Turnover: £500,000 - £1m **No.of Employees:** 1 - 10 **Product Groups:** 80, 84

Date of Accounts	Mar 11	Mar 10	Mar 09
Sales Turnover	N/A	N/A	840
Pre Tax Profit/Loss	N/A	N/A	157
Working Capital	354	230	249
Fixed Assets	385	397	464
Current Assets	571	432	501
Current Liabilities	N/A	N/A	146

Vinci plc

Astral House Imperial Way, Watford, WD24 4WW
Tel: 01923-233433 **Fax:** 01923-256481
Website: http://www.vinci.plc.uk
Bank(s): National Westminster Bank Plc
Directors: A. Comba (Dir), C. Cocking (Dir)
Ultimate Holding Company: VINCI SA (FRANCE)
Immediate Holding Company: VINCI CONSTRUCTION UK LIMITED
Registration no: 02295904 **VAT No.:** GB 165 1030 03
Date established: 1988 **Turnover:** Over £1,000m
No.of Employees: 101 - 250 **Product Groups:** 35, 51, 84, 85

Date of Accounts	Dec 11	Dec 10	Dec 09
Sales Turnover	1113m	1025m	1163m
Pre Tax Profit/Loss	20m	39m	15m
Working Capital	-87m	-90m	-110m
Fixed Assets	192m	175m	173m
Current Assets	676m	607m	441m
Current Liabilities	689m	403m	343m

Vinci Facilities

Lucidus Building 41-43 Clarendon Road, Watford, WD17 1TR
Tel: 01923-478400 **Fax:** 01325-385500
E-mail: info@vincifacilities.com
Website: http://www.vincicontruction.co.uk
Directors: A. Comba (Co Sec), C. Brennan (Fin)
Managers: J. Olson (Mgr), P. McGee, C. Jellicoe (Personnel), T. Parfitt (Tech Serv Mgr)
Ultimate Holding Company: VINCI SA (FRANCE)
Immediate Holding Company: TAYLOR WOODROW CONSTRUCTION UN
Registration no: 03213873 **Date established:** 1996
Turnover: £125m - £250m **No.of Employees:** 51 - 100
Product Groups: 51

Date of Accounts	Dec 11	Dec 10	Dec 09
Sales Turnover	223m	265m	471m
Pre Tax Profit/Loss	19m	32m	11m
Working Capital	43m	26m	2m
Fixed Assets	10m	11m	9m
Current Assets	162m	168m	183m
Current Liabilities	74m	88m	95m

Vitalighting Ltd

Unit 5b Hille Business Centre 132a St Albans Road, Watford, WD24 4AE
Tel: 01923-256700 **Fax:** 01923-897741
E-mail: sales@vitalighting.com
Website: http://www.vitalighting.com
Directors: M. Green (Sales), P. Halford (Co Sec), S. Green (Fin)
Immediate Holding Company: VITALIGHTING LIMITED
Registration no: 02266727 **Date established:** 1988
Turnover: £250,000 - £500,000 **No.of Employees:** 1 - 10
Product Groups: 37

Date of Accounts	Mar 08	Mar 07	Mar 06
Sales Turnover	N/A	283	210
Pre Tax Profit/Loss	N/A	45	19
Working Capital	46	36	15
Fixed Assets	97	106	112
Current Assets	88	100	72
Current Liabilities	42	64	57
ROCE% (Return on Capital Employed)		31.3	15.1
ROT% (Return on Turnover)		15.7	9.1

Watford Coatings Ltd

Park House Greenhill CR, Watford, WD18 8QU
Tel: 01923-235640 **Fax:** 01923- 449229
E-mail: richard@watfordcoatings.co.uk
Website: http://www.watfordcoatings.co.uk
Managers: R. Stock (Mgr)
Immediate Holding Company: WATFORD COATINGS LIMITED
Registration no: 06563879 **VAT No.:** GB 649 1973 93
Date established: 2008 **Turnover:** £500,000 - £1m
No.of Employees: 1 - 10 **Product Groups:** 48

Date of Accounts	Mar 11	Mar 10	Mar 09
Working Capital	-14	-5	-4
Fixed Assets	27	19	24
Current Assets	72	79	57

Watford & West Herts Chamber Of Commerce

Unit 47 The Business Centre Colne Way, Watford, WD24 7NF
Tel: 01923-442442 **Fax:** 01923-445050
E-mail: r@watford-chamber.co.uk
Website: http://www.watfordchamber.co.uk
Directors: R. Gagan (Grp Chief Exec), L. Marshall (Co Sec), J. Lennarddo (I.T. Dir)
Immediate Holding Company: WATFORD CHAMBER OF COMMERCE AND INDUSTRY(THE)
Registration no: 02055398 **Date established:** 1986
Turnover: Up to £250,000 **No.of Employees:** 1 - 10 **Product Groups:** 87

Wembley Sign Writers

40 Highlands, Watford, WD19 4LY
Tel: 01923-350039
E-mail: sales@harrowsigns.com
Website: http://www.harrowsigns.com
Managers: J. Rand (Mgr)
Immediate Holding Company: WATFORD SIGNS LIMITED
Registration no: 07101261 **Date established:** 2010
No.of Employees: 1 - 10 **Product Groups:** 49

Whippendell Electrical Ltd

477-479 Whippendell Road, Watford, WD18 7PU
Tel: 01923-228201 **Fax:** 01923-228007
E-mail: sales@whippendell-marine.co.uk
Website: http://www.whippendell.co.uk
Bank(s): TSB, Brighton Branch
Directors: J. Swabey (Mkt Research), D. Swabey (MD), B. Swabey (Co Sec)
Managers: J. Basinski, N. Lampadas (Sales Prom Mgr)
Immediate Holding Company: WHIPPENDELL ELECTRICAL LIMITED
Registration no: 00578012 **Date established:** 1957 **Turnover:** £1m - £2m
No.of Employees: 21 - 50 **Product Groups:** 37

Date of Accounts	Dec 11	Dec 10	Dec 09
Sales Turnover	2m	2m	2m
Pre Tax Profit/Loss	-109	-26	12
Working Capital	2m	2m	2m
Fixed Assets	644	665	694
Current Assets	2m	2m	2m
Current Liabilities	167	186	186

Woodman Hill Ltd

Chiltern Estate Imperial Way, Watford, WD24 4YX
Tel: 01923-233977 **Fax:** 01923-235941
E-mail: sales@woodmanhill.co.uk
Website: http://www.woodmanhill.co.uk
Directors: C. Randall (Fin)
Ultimate Holding Company: J. V. BARRETT & CO. LIMITED
Immediate Holding Company: WOODMAN HILL LIMITED
Registration no: 03544384 **VAT No.:** GB 196 3668 14
Date established: 1998 **Turnover:** £1m - £2m **No.of Employees:** 1 - 10
Product Groups: 76

Date of Accounts	Dec 11	Dec 10	Dec 09
Sales Turnover	2m	2m	2m
Pre Tax Profit/Loss	91	111	92
Working Capital	207	187	179
Fixed Assets	116	137	143
Current Assets	258	233	245
Current Liabilities	28	46	61

Welwyn

Adolph Numerical Controls

Arema Farm Danesbury Lane, Welwyn, AL6 9SG
Tel: 01438-718882 **Fax:** 01438-718884
E-mail: info@adolph-numerical.co.uk
Website: http://www.adolph-numerical.co.uk
Directors: E. Adolph (Dir)
Immediate Holding Company: ADOLPH NUMERICAL CONTROLS LIMITED
Registration no: 01223158 **VAT No.:** GB 247 8807 22
Date established: 1975 **Turnover:** Up to £250,000
No.of Employees: 1 - 10 **Product Groups:** 37, 38, 45, 46

Date of Accounts	Mar 11	Mar 10	Mar 09
Sales Turnover	N/A	34	72
Pre Tax Profit/Loss	N/A	5	-8
Working Capital	33	11	7
Fixed Assets	1	1	1
Current Assets	58	49	51
Current Liabilities	N/A	10	10

Incinco

113-115 Codicote Road, Welwyn, AL6 9TY
Tel: 01438-821000 **Fax:** 01438-820888
E-mail: enquiries@incinco.com
Website: http://www.incinco.com
Directors: M. Moynihan (Dir)
Ultimate Holding Company: INCINCO HOLDINGS
Immediate Holding Company: PHOTOSWAPSHOP LIMITED
Registration no: 05565907 **VAT No.:** GB 716 1660 48
Date established: 2005 **Turnover:** £2m - £5m **No.of Employees:** 1 - 10
Product Groups: 40, 42, 52

Date of Accounts	Dec 07	Dec 06	Dec 05
Working Capital	135	46	89
Fixed Assets	3	3	2
Current Assets	691	380	396
Current Liabilities	556	335	307

Knebworth Fire Protection

18 Danesbury Park Caravan Site Danesbury Park Road, Welwyn, AL6 9SP
Tel: 01438-712642
Directors: D. Sendall (Ptnr)
Date established: 1994 **No.of Employees:** 1 - 10 **Product Groups:** 38, 42

Spectral Dynamics

The Fulling Mill Fulling Mill Lane, Welwyn, AL6 9NP
Tel: 01438-716626 **Fax:** 01438-716628
E-mail: itraffford@spectraldynamics.co.uk
Website: http://www.spectraldynamics.com
Directors: I. Trafford (Chief Op Offcr)
Ultimate Holding Company: SPECTRAL DYNAMICS INC (USA)
Immediate Holding Company: SPECTRAL DYNAMICS (UK) LIMITED
Registration no: 03028241 **Date established:** 1995 **Turnover:** £1m - £2m
No.of Employees: 1 - 10 **Product Groups:** 37, 38, 44

Date of Accounts	Sep 11	Sep 10	Sep 09
Working Capital	-22	-16	1
Current Assets	118	46	59

Tonibell Southern Counties Ltd

113-115 Codicote Road, Welwyn, AL6 9TY
Tel: 01438-821200
Directors: P. Cook (Prop)
Immediate Holding Company: PHOTOSWAPSHOP LIMITED
Registration no: 05565907 **Date established:** 2005
No.of Employees: 1 - 10 **Product Groups:** 20, 40, 41

Welwyn Garden City

Aurora

6 Little Burrow, Welwyn Garden City, AL7 4SW
Tel: 01707-351820 **Fax:** 01707-351821
E-mail: info@aurora.eu.com
Website: http://www.aurora.eu.com
Managers: J. Kirsop (Warehouse Mgr)
No.of Employees: 11 - 20 **Product Groups:** 37, 52

Avdel UK Ltd

2 Swiftfields Watchmead Industrial Estate, Welwyn Garden City, AL7 1LY
Tel: 01707-292000 **Fax:** 01707-292199
E-mail: salesavdel@acument.com
Website: http://www.avdel-global.com
Bank(s): HSBC Bank plc
Managers: A. Blackwell (Personnel), A. Cooke (Mktg Serv Mgr), C. Hellmund (Sales Prom Mgr), D. Hopper (Comm), M. Guy (Tech Serv Mgr), R. Huntington (Fin Mgr), A. Pejkovski
Ultimate Holding Company: PLATINUM EQUITY LLC (USA)
Immediate Holding Company: AVDEL UK LIMITED
Registration no: 00315076 **VAT No.:** GB 196 2502 53
Date established: 1936 **Turnover:** £20m - £50m
No.of Employees: 51 - 100 **Product Groups:** 35, 36, 37, 39, 40

Date of Accounts	Dec 11	Dec 10	Dec 09
Sales Turnover	52m	43m	30m
Pre Tax Profit/Loss	7m	30m	-541
Working Capital	33m	27m	-2m
Fixed Assets	16m	17m	6m
Current Assets	46m	42m	18m
Current Liabilities	2m	3m	3m

Brig Ayd Controls

56a Bridge Road East, Welwyn Garden City, AL7 1BS
Tel: 01707-322322 **Fax:** 01707-394149
E-mail: sales@brig-aydcontrols.co.uk
Website: http://www.brig-aydcontrols.co.uk
Directors: O. Briggs (MD)
No.of Employees: 1 - 10 **Product Groups:** 38, 67

British Lead

Peartree Lane, Welwyn Garden City, AL7 3UB
Tel: 01707-324595 **Fax:** 01707-328941
E-mail: sales@britishlead.co.uk
Website: http://www.britishlead.co.uk
Bank(s): Lloyds TSB Bank plc
Managers: N. Edwards (Fin Mgr), D. Murray (Sales Off Mgr)
Ultimate Holding Company: ECO-BAT TECHNOLOGIES P.L.C.
Immediate Holding Company: H.J. ENTHOVEN LTD
Registration no: 02821551 **VAT No.:** GB 598 6365 70
Turnover: £20m - £50m **No.of Employees:** 51 - 100 **Product Groups:** 34, 35

Carl Zeiss Ltd

15 Woodfield Road, Welwyn Garden City, AL7 1JQ
Tel: 01707-871200 **Fax:** 01707-330237
E-mail: info@zeiss.co.uk
Website: http://www.zeiss.co.uk
Directors: D. Kurz (Dir), J. Barker (Fin), J. Cockerill (Dir), P. Adderley (MD)
Managers: D. Stewart (Serv Mgr), R. Kollmorgen (Personnel), A. Lambert (Mktg Serv Mgr), D. Kent (I.T. Exec), L. Jarmain, E. McGuigan (Sales Prom Mgr), S. Brannon (Serv Mgr), T. Reev (I.T. Exec), L. Jarmain
Ultimate Holding Company: FP001130
Immediate Holding Company: CARL ZEISS LTD
Registration no: 00542141 **Date established:** 1954
Turnover: £20m - £50m **No.of Employees:** 51 - 100 **Product Groups:** 30, 33, 38, 65, 67

Date of Accounts	Sep 08	Sep 07
Sales Turnover	30960	30620
Pre Tax Profit/Loss	4110	4190
Working Capital	5260	4330
Fixed Assets	3930	4870
Current Assets	13790	12830
Current Liabilities	8530	8500
Total Share Capital	1570	1570
ROCE% (Return on Capital Employed)	44.7	45.5
ROT% (Return on Turnover)	13.3	13.7

Central Compressor Services Ltd

38 Burrowfield, Welwyn Garden City, AL7 4SR
Tel: 01707-390888 **Fax:** 01707-390548
E-mail: enquiries@ccslimited.com
Website: http://www.ccslimited.com
Directors: M. Free (Dir)
Immediate Holding Company: CENTRAL COMPRESSOR SERVICES LIMITED
Registration no: SC132910 **Date established:** 1991
No.of Employees: 1 - 10 **Product Groups:** 39, 40

Date of Accounts	Dec 11	Dec 10	Dec 09
Working Capital	257	250	204
Fixed Assets	10	9	22
Current Assets	502	400	329

Clamcleats Ltd

Clamcleats Building Watchmead, Welwyn Garden City, AL7 1AP
Tel: 01707-330101 **Fax:** 020-8801 9907
E-mail: sales@clamcleat.com
Website: http://www.clamcleats.com
Bank(s): HSBC Bank plc
Directors: D. Emery (Dir)
Immediate Holding Company: SEVARG ENGINEERING LIMITED
Registration no: 01273776 **Date established:** 1976
Turnover: £500,000 - £1m **No.of Employees:** 21 - 50
Product Groups: 30, 35, 39, 48, 65, 74

Date of Accounts	Oct 08	Oct 07	Apr 11
Sales Turnover	231	287	N/A
Pre Tax Profit/Loss	13	24	N/A
Working Capital	95	86	-12
Fixed Assets	43	51	N/A
Current Assets	120	105	2
Current Liabilities	7	9	N/A

D B C Food Service Ltd

Denmark House Parkway, Welwyn Garden City, AL8 6JN
Tel: 01707-323421 **Fax:** 01707-372199
E-mail: info@dbcfoodservice.co.uk
Website: http://www.dbcfoodservice.co.uk
Directors: S. Heal (Comm), C. Horne (MD), C. Horn (MD), C. Jakobsen (Ch)
Managers: B. Metcalf (Buyer), P. Rawling (Personnel), D. Bryant-Pugh (Mktg Serv Mgr), C. Threadgold (Buyer), A. Allan (I.T. Exec)
Ultimate Holding Company: WPD HOLDINGS LIMITED
Immediate Holding Company: DBC FOODSERVICE LIMITED
Registration no: 00160100 **Date established:** 2019 **Turnover:** £5m - £10m
No.of Employees: 21 - 50 **Product Groups:** 20, 27, 34, 62, 63, 66

Date of Accounts	Mar 08	Mar 09	Mar 10
Sales Turnover	247m	270m	273m
Pre Tax Profit/Loss	668	2m	1m
Working Capital	-3m	824	9m
Fixed Assets	17m	11m	10m
Current Assets	44m	51m	57m
Current Liabilities	4m	5m	3m

D P T Wear Ltd

30 Watchmead, Welwyn Garden City, AL7 1LT
Tel: 01707-373838 **Fax:** 01707-332288
E-mail: info@dptwear.com
Website: http://www.dptwear.com
Directors: J. Pestell (Fin), V. Matthews (Pers), A. Oliver (MD)
Managers: M. Gordon (Chief Mgr), M. Coates (I.T. Exec), J. Pestell (Fin Mgr), M. Coates (Tech Serv Mgr)
Immediate Holding Company: THE MALTINGS STUDIOS LIMITED
Registration no: 02281590 **Date established:** 1999
Turnover: £500,000 - £1m **No.of Employees:** 21 - 50
Product Groups: 24, 32, 77, 84

Date of Accounts	May 07	May 06
Sales Turnover	44890	43349
Pre Tax Profit/Loss	14	-103
Working Capital	-662	-762
Fixed Assets	1069	1424
Current Assets	8340	8578
Current Liabilities	9002	9340
Total Share Capital	10	10
ROCE% (Return on Capital Employed)	3.4	-15.5
ROT% (Return on Turnover)	0.0	-0.2

Easthill Faraday

Unit 1 Martinfield Business Centre Martinfield, Welwyn Garden City, AL7 1HG
Tel: 01707-377355 **Fax:** 01707-377358
E-mail: chriss@easthill.co.uk
Website: http://www.easthill.co.uk
Bank(s): HSBC Bank plc
Directors: C. Letherby (Fin), C. Sadler (Dir)
Immediate Holding Company: EASTHILL LIMITED
Registration no: 02743575 **VAT No.:** GB 579 4293 87
Date established: 1992 **Turnover:** £10m - £20m
No.of Employees: 11 - 20 **Product Groups:** 35, 37, 52

Date of Accounts	Sep 09	Sep 08	Sep 07
Working Capital	209	329	294
Fixed Assets	25	33	33
Current Assets	839	1m	705

Elder Engineering Herts

City Park Watchmead, Welwyn Garden City, AL7 1LT
Tel: 01707-325513 **Fax:** 01707-375121
E-mail: sales@elderengineering.co.uk
Website: http://www.elderengineering.co.uk
Bank(s): National Westminster
Directors: T. Flain (Dir)
Managers: T. Worsley (Chief Mgr)
Immediate Holding Company: ELDER ENGINEERING (HERTS) LIMITED
Registration no: 01473439 **VAT No.:** 335 0600 95 **Date established:** 1980
Turnover: £1m - £2m **No.of Employees:** 21 - 50 **Product Groups:** 30, 42, 48, 66

Date of Accounts	Apr 12	Apr 11	Apr 10
Working Capital	801	639	520
Fixed Assets	87	114	179
Current Assets	1m	996	782

Ensign Plastic Moulders Ltd

8 Woodfield Road, Welwyn Garden City, AL7 1JQ
Tel: 01707-886795 **Fax:** 01707-882566
E-mail: ensignplastic.moulders@ntlbusiness.com
Website: http://www.ensignplastic.com
Directors: V. Lewis (Dir)
Immediate Holding Company: ENSIGN PLASTIC MOULDERS LIMITED
Registration no: 01524738 **VAT No.:** GB 335 2333 82
Date established: 1980 **Turnover:** £250,000 - £500,000
No.of Employees: 1 - 10 **Product Groups:** 30

Date of Accounts	Mar 11	Mar 10	Mar 09
Working Capital	65	106	171
Fixed Assets	N/A	3	5
Current Assets	83	127	198

Exclusive Ranges Ltd

1 Sutherland Court Brownfields, Welwyn Garden City, AL7 1BJ
Tel: 01707-361770 **Fax:** 01707-361777
E-mail: sales@exclusiveranges.co.uk
Website: http://www.exclusiveranges.co.uk
Directors: G. Burke (Fin), T. Burke (MD)
Ultimate Holding Company: EXCLUSIVE RANGES DOMESTIC LIMITED
Immediate Holding Company: EXCLUSIVE RANGES LIMITED
Registration no: 03194723 **Date established:** 1996
No.of Employees: 1 - 10 **Product Groups:** 26, 40, 52, 63, 67

Date of Accounts	Jun 11	Jun 10	Jun 09
Working Capital	17	-12	21
Fixed Assets	43	46	62
Current Assets	590	769	766

Robert P D Frost & Co. Ltd

45 Burrowfield, Welwyn Garden City, AL7 4SS
Tel: 01707-331188 **Fax:** 01707-393714
E-mail: sales@rpdfrost.co.uk
Website: http://www.rpdfrost.co.uk
Bank(s): Barclays
Directors: W. Drymoni (MD)
Immediate Holding Company: ROBERT P.D. FROST & CO. LIMITED
Registration no: 03493495 **VAT No.:** GB 197 9012 29
Date established: 1998 **Turnover:** £250,000 - £500,000
No.of Employees: 11 - 20 **Product Groups:** 30

Date of Accounts	May 12	May 11	May 10
Working Capital	133	113	83
Fixed Assets	54	56	66
Current Assets	226	206	156

Geemarc Telecom S A

5 Swallow Court, Welwyn Garden City, AL7 1SB
Tel: 01707-372372 **Fax:** 01707-372529
E-mail: sales@geemarc.com
Website: http://www.geemarc.com
Managers: C. Sutherland (Sales Admin)
Ultimate Holding Company: CANTRUST (CI) LTD (CHANNEL ISLANDS)
Immediate Holding Company: GEEMARC TELECOM S.A.
Registration no: FC027879 **Date established:** 2007
Turnover: £10m - £20m **No.of Employees:** 11 - 20 **Product Groups:** 37

Date of Accounts	Mar 11	Mar 05	Mar 04
Working Capital	N/A	N/A	-1
Fixed Assets	N/A	N/A	5
Current Assets	N/A	N/A	-10
Current Liabilities	N/A	N/A	9

Gilbertson & Page Ltd

45-55 Brownfields, Welwyn Garden City, AL7 1AN
Tel: 01707-367900 **Fax:** 01707-339221
E-mail: info@gilpa.co.uk
Website: http://www.gilpa.co.uk
Bank(s): Barclays
Directors: A. Booth (Fin), R. Ware (MD), K. Wong (Fin), A. Dale (Chief Op Offcr)
Managers: M. Moss (Personnel), D. Watson (Nat Sales Mgr)
Immediate Holding Company: GILBERTSON & PAGE,LIMITED
Registration no: 00055762 **Date established:** 1998
Turnover: £10m - £20m **No.of Employees:** 21 - 50 **Product Groups:** 20, 62

Date of Accounts	Dec 11	Dec 10	Dec 09
Sales Turnover	14m	12m	11m
Pre Tax Profit/Loss	322	616	237

Working Capital	1m	1m	961
Fixed Assets	6m	6m	6m
Current Assets	3m	3m	3m
Current Liabilities	461	630	643

Glasson Metalworks Ltd

Stanboroughbury Farm Great North Road, Welwyn Garden City, AL8 7TD
Tel: 01707-262662 **Fax:** 01707-262663
E-mail: info@glassonmetalworks.co.uk
Website: http://www.glassonmetalworks.co.uk
Directors: J. Glasson (Dir)
Immediate Holding Company: GLASSON METALWORKS LIMITED
Registration no: 04913155 **VAT No.:** GB 440 7258 60
Date established: 2003 **Turnover:** Up to £250,000
No.of Employees: 1 - 10 **Product Groups:** 35, 66

Date of Accounts	Apr 11	Apr 10	Apr 09
Working Capital	-10	-36	-48
Fixed Assets	29	31	38
Current Assets	70	71	65

Hamamatsu Photonics UK Ltd

2 Howard Court 10 Tewin Road, Welwyn Garden City, AL7 1BW
Tel: 01707-294888 **Fax:** 01707-325777
E-mail: info@hamamatsu.co.uk
Website: http://www.hamamatsu.co.uk
Bank(s): National Westminster Bank Plc
Directors: C. Singh (Fin), A. Tsujimura (MD)
Managers: R. Clemence (Tech Serv Mgr), J. Brown (Comm), M. Fetta
Ultimate Holding Company: HAMAMATSU PHOTONICS KK (JAPAN)
Immediate Holding Company: HAMAMATSU PHOTONICS UK LIMITED
Registration no: 02228744 **Date established:** 1988
Turnover: £20m - £50m **No.of Employees:** 21 - 50 **Product Groups:** 37, 38

Date of Accounts	Sep 11	Sep 10	Sep 09
Sales Turnover	26m	19m	16m
Pre Tax Profit/Loss	3m	2m	941
Working Capital	4m	4m	3m
Fixed Assets	2m	2m	2m
Current Assets	10m	9m	6m
Current Liabilities	642	910	610

Henleys Medical Supplies Ltd

39 Brownfields, Welwyn Garden City, AL7 1AN
Tel: 01707-333164 **Fax:** 01707-334795
E-mail: info@henleysmed.com
Website: http://www.henleysmed.com
Bank(s): Barclays, Pall Mall Corporate Banking Group, 50 Pall Mall, London, SW1A 1QB
Directors: G. Mizon (Fin), D. Henley (Dir)
Managers: C. Cooper (Mktg Serv Mgr)
Immediate Holding Company: HENLEYS MEDICAL SUPPLIES LIMITED
Registration no: 00452882 **Date established:** 1948 **Turnover:** £2m - £5m
No.of Employees: 21 - 50 **Product Groups:** 38

Date of Accounts	Mar 11	Mar 10	Mar 09
Sales Turnover	5m	5m	5m
Pre Tax Profit/Loss	44	262	-141
Working Capital	1m	1m	1m
Fixed Assets	1m	1m	2m
Current Assets	2m	2m	2m
Current Liabilities	346	307	269

Hertfordshire Highways

Highways House 41-45 Broadwater Road, Welwyn Garden City, AL7 3AX
Tel: 01707-356200 **Fax:** 01707-356380
E-mail: vince.gilbert@hertshighways.org.uk
Website: http://www.mouchel.com
Managers: V. Gilbert (Mgr)
Immediate Holding Company: HIGHWAYS (UK) LIMITED
Registration no: 07502103 **Date established:** 2011
Turnover: £10m - £20m **No.of Employees:** 251 - 500 **Product Groups:** 84

Date of Accounts	Mar 12
Working Capital	23
Fixed Assets	1
Current Assets	211

Hopespare Ltd

2 East Burrowfield, Welwyn Garden City, AL7 4TB
Tel: 01707-321212 **Fax:** 01707-371717
E-mail: sales@hopespare.com
Website: http://www.hopespare.com
Managers: D. Eley (Mgr)
Immediate Holding Company: HOPESPARE LIMITED
Registration no: 02016031 **VAT No.:** GB 231 3011 34
Date established: 1986 **Turnover:** £500,000 - £1m
No.of Employees: 1 - 10 **Product Groups:** 30, 36

Date of Accounts	May 11	May 10	May 09
Working Capital	243	297	230
Fixed Assets	169	117	77
Current Assets	1m	1m	1m

Howards Gate Ltd

15 The Old Drive, Welwyn Garden City, AL8 6TB
Tel: 01707-392552 **Fax:** 01707-391380
E-mail: info@howardsgate.co.uk
Website: http://www.howardsgate.co.uk
Directors: S. Hollis (MD)
Immediate Holding Company: HOWARDSGATE LLP
Registration no: OC300986 **Date established:** 2001
Turnover: Up to £250,000 **No.of Employees:** 1 - 10 **Product Groups:** 44, 80, 81

Date of Accounts	Mar 11	Mar 10	Mar 06
Working Capital	42	46	157
Fixed Assets	9	11	14
Current Assets	53	70	172

i3Q Systems Limited

Unit 6, Mundells Court, Welwyn Garden City, AL7 1EN
Tel: 01438-518700 **Fax:** 01438-518749
E-mail: business@i3q.com
Website: http://www.i3q.com
Managers: C. Clark (Chief Acct)
Registration no: 04116351 **Date established:** 2000
No.of Employees: 1 - 10 **Product Groups:** 44

Date of Accounts	Jul 08	Jul 07	Jul 06
Sales Turnover	2057	1548	937
Pre Tax Profit/Loss	122	35	31

Working Capital	626	339	167
Fixed Assets	2	3	2
Current Assets	1387	813	509
Current Liabilities	761	474	341
ROCE% (Return on Capital Employed)	19.5	10.2	18.5
ROT% (Return on Turnover)	6.0	2.2	3.3

J & P Services

61 Cole Green Lane, Welwyn Garden City, AL7 3PP
Tel: 01707-324438 **Fax:** 01707-375266
Directors: S. Long (Ptnr)
Date established: 1970 **No.of Employees:** 1 - 10 **Product Groups:** 20, 40, 49

Jeol UK Ltd

Silver Court Watchmead, Welwyn Garden City, AL7 1LT
Tel: 01707-377117 **Fax:** 01707-373254
E-mail: uk.sales@jeoluk.com
Website: http://www.jeoluk.com
Bank(s): Mitsubishi
Directors: Y. Masumoto (MD), A. Fusc (Fin), Y. Matsumoto (MD)
Immediate Holding Company: JEOL LTD (JAPAN)
Registration no: 00939456 **Turnover:** £10m - £20m
No.of Employees: 21 - 50 **Product Groups:** 38, 47

John Doyle Construction plc

John Doyle House 2-3 Little Burrow, Welwyn Garden City, AL7 4SP
Tel: 01707-329481 **Fax:** 01707-328213
E-mail: ian.carr@doyleplc.co.uk
Website: http://www.john-doyle.co.uk
Bank(s): National Westminster Bank Plc
Directors: P. Merton (MD), I. Carr (Fin), S. Stefanue (Grp Chief Exec)
Managers: K. Chandler (Mktg Serv Mgr), I. Marquis (Purch Mgr), J. Brown (I.T. Exec)
Ultimate Holding Company: DOYLE PLC
Immediate Holding Company: JOHN DOYLE CONSTRUCTION LIMITED
Registration no: 00893735 **VAT No.:** GB 455 9299 96
Date established: 1966 **Turnover:** £20m - £50m
No.of Employees: 21 - 50 **Product Groups:** 51

Date of Accounts	Dec 10	Dec 09	Dec 08
Sales Turnover	28m	47m	64m
Pre Tax Profit/Loss	-3m	524	2m
Working Capital	-327	2m	2m
Fixed Assets	682	853	522
Current Assets	16m	17m	20m
Current Liabilities	1m	4m	3m

Lemsford Metal Products 1982 Ltd

24 Hyde Way, Welwyn Garden City, AL7 3UQ
Tel: 01707-323725 **Fax:** 01707-373059
E-mail: sales@lemsford.co.uk
Website: http://www.lemsford.co.uk
Directors: P. Davis (MD)
Immediate Holding Company: LEMSFORD METAL PRODUCTS (1982) LIMITED
Registration no: 01622858 **Date established:** 1982
Turnover: £500,000 - £1m **No.of Employees:** 11 - 20 **Product Groups:** 48

Date of Accounts	Jun 11	Jun 10	Jun 09
Working Capital	350	303	303
Fixed Assets	1m	1m	1m
Current Assets	633	509	517

Miniplas Ltd

3-5 West Burrowfield, Welwyn Garden City, AL7 4TW
Tel: 01707-332801 **Fax:** 01707-371574
E-mail: info@miniplas.co.uk
Website: http://www.miniplas.co.uk
Directors: J. Henderson (Fin)
Immediate Holding Company: MINI-PLAS LIMITED
Registration no: 01114056 **Date established:** 1973
Turnover: Up to £250,000 **No.of Employees:** 1 - 10 **Product Groups:** 30

Date of Accounts	May 11	May 10	May 09
Working Capital	70	106	132
Fixed Assets	14	16	15
Current Assets	398	436	319

N B Metals Ltd

Unit 10 Blenhiem Court Brownfields, Welwyn Garden City, AL7 1AD
Tel: 01707-324472 **Fax:** 01707-324473
E-mail: info@nbmetals.co.uk
Website: http://www.nbmetals.co.uk
Directors: G. Hurrell (MD), G. Hurrell (Dir), G. Major (Fin)
Managers: N. Glaister
Immediate Holding Company: N.B. METALS LIMITED
Registration no: 02610330 **Date established:** 1991 **Turnover:** £5m - £10m
No.of Employees: 21 - 50 **Product Groups:** 34, 36, 46, 48, 66

Date of Accounts	Mar 11	Sep 09	Sep 08
Sales Turnover	N/A	6m	9m
Pre Tax Profit/Loss	N/A	-382	369
Working Capital	-118	-146	12
Fixed Assets	211	324	678
Current Assets	2m	2m	3m
Current Liabilities	N/A	295	416

Omega Citylifts Ltd

Unit 7 Bridge Gate Centre Martinfield, Welwyn Garden City, AL7 1JG
Tel: 01707-334962 **Fax:** 01925-210112
E-mail: sales@omegacitylifts.co.uk
Website: http://www.omegacitylifts.co.uk
Directors: M. Fuller (Dir)
Ultimate Holding Company: GALLEY BRIDGE (HOLDINGS) LIMITED
Immediate Holding Company: OMEGA CITYLIFTS LIMITED
Registration no: 05061402 **Date established:** 2004
No.of Employees: 21 - 50 **Product Groups:** 35, 39, 45

Date of Accounts	Dec 11	Dec 10	Dec 09
Working Capital	228	155	57
Fixed Assets	225	209	214
Current Assets	1m	1m	670

Omega Group Management Services Ltd

Trevelyan House 7 Church Road, Welwyn Garden City, AL8 6NT
Tel: 01707-373330 **Fax:** 01707-373345
E-mail: enquiries@omegagroup.co.uk
Website: http://www.omegagroup.co.uk
Directors: J. Cartwright (Co Sec), T. Evans (Fin)
Managers: J. Warby (Buyer)
Ultimate Holding Company: GARDEN HOLDINGS LTD (CAYMAN ISLANDS)
Immediate Holding Company: OMEGA GROUP MANAGEMENT SERVICES LIMITED

Registration no: 01472693 **Date established:** 1980
Turnover: £500,000 - £1m **No.of Employees:** 1 - 10 **Product Groups:** 68, 80

Date of Accounts	Dec 11	Dec 10	Dec 09
Sales Turnover	711	781	769
Pre Tax Profit/Loss	24	14	-15
Working Capital	378	345	345
Fixed Assets	13	27	16
Current Assets	5m	5m	5m
Current Liabilities	135	120	89

Omniledger Ltd

5 Bridge Gate Centre Martinfield, Welwyn Garden City, AL7 1JG
Tel: 01707-324201 **Fax:** 01707-375572
E-mail: sales@omniledger.co.uk
Website: http://www.omniledger.co.uk
Directors: R. Blyth (MD)
Immediate Holding Company: OMNILEDGER LIMITED
Registration no: 01648566 **VAT No.:** GB 382 4418 47
Date established: 1982 **Turnover:** £500,000 - £1m
No.of Employees: 1 - 10 **Product Groups:** 28, 44

Date of Accounts	Jun 11	Jun 10	Jun 09
Working Capital	248	269	280
Fixed Assets	71	47	28
Current Assets	878	780	713

Pakex UK plc

1 Prime Point Bessemer Road, Welwyn Garden City, AL7 1FE
Tel: 01707-384858 **Fax:** 01707-332838
E-mail: sales@pakexuk.com
Website: http://www.pakexuk.com
Directors: D. Russell (MD)
Immediate Holding Company: PAKEX (UK) PLC
Registration no: 03083059 **VAT No.:** GB 587 2381 08
Date established: 1995 **Turnover:** £2m - £5m **No.of Employees:** 11 - 20
Product Groups: 27, 30

Date of Accounts	Dec 11	Dec 10	Dec 09
Sales Turnover	5m	5m	5m
Pre Tax Profit/Loss	518	433	568
Working Capital	17	336	-5
Fixed Assets	1m	1m	1m
Current Assets	2m	2m	1m
Current Liabilities	555	442	330

Prompt Fire Protection

Unit 25 Peartree Farm Peartree Lane, Welwyn Garden City, AL7 3UW
Tel: 01707-339358 **Fax:** 01707-690122
Website: http://www.promptfireprotection.co.uk
Directors: S. Green (Prop)
Date established: 1983 **No.of Employees:** 1 - 10 **Product Groups:** 38, 42

Ratcliff Palfinger

Bessemer Road, Welwyn Garden City, AL7 1ET
Tel: 01707-325571 **Fax:** 01707-327752
E-mail: reception@ratcliffpalfinger.co.uk
Website: http://www.ratcliffpalfinger.co.uk
Bank(s): National Westminster Bank Plc
Directors: P. Addis (MD)
Ultimate Holding Company: PALFINGER AG (AUSTRIA)
Immediate Holding Company: RATCLIFF PALFINGER LIMITED
Registration no: 01019643 **Date established:** 1971
Turnover: £10m - £20m **No.of Employees:** 101 - 250 **Product Groups:** 45

Date of Accounts	Dec 11	Dec 10	Dec 09
Sales Turnover	15m	12m	11m
Pre Tax Profit/Loss	-780	-393	-609
Working Capital	-614	1m	1m
Fixed Assets	1m	508	528
Current Assets	6m	5m	4m
Current Liabilities	1m	643	635

Reed

31a Howardsgate, Welwyn Garden City, AL8 6AP
Tel: 01707-373133 **Fax:** 01707-376549
Website: http://www.reed.co.uk
Managers: J. Bennett (District Mgr)
Ultimate Holding Company: REED GLOBAL LTD (MALTA)
Immediate Holding Company: REED EMPLOYMENT LIMITED
Registration no: 00669854 **Date established:** 1960
Turnover: £75m - £125m **No.of Employees:** 1 - 10 **Product Groups:** 80

Date of Accounts	Jun 11	Jun 10	Dec 07
Sales Turnover	618	450	287m
Pre Tax Profit/Loss	-2m	310	8m
Working Capital	23m	28m	28m
Fixed Assets	31	36	5m
Current Assets	28m	30m	74m
Current Liabilities	37	29	21m

Rogar Packaging

9-12 Tewin Court, Welwyn Garden City, AL7 1AU
Tel: 01707-371251 **Fax:** 01707-334838
E-mail: sales@rogar.co.uk
Website: http://www.rogar.co.uk
Directors: S. Lester (Dir), R. Lester (MD), R. Lester (Fin), S. Lester (MD)
Managers: G. Lester (Sales Prom)
Ultimate Holding Company: 03399929
Immediate Holding Company: ROGAR PRODUCTS LIMITED
Registration no: 01590121 **Date established:** 1981
Turnover: £500,000 - £1m **No.of Employees:** 1 - 10 **Product Groups:** 27, 30, 45

Date of Accounts	Mar 09	Mar 08	Mar 07
Working Capital	-66	-377	-297
Fixed Assets	65	90	163
Current Assets	514	803	1m

S K Sales Ltd

11 Little Mundells, Welwyn Garden City, AL7 1EW
Tel: 01707-395442 **Fax:** 01707-395443
Website: http://www.sksales.co.uk
Managers: R. Murphy (Mgr)
Immediate Holding Company: S.K.(SALES) LIMITED
Registration no: 02809456 **Date established:** 1993
No.of Employees: 1 - 10 **Product Groups:** 37, 40, 48

Date of Accounts	Apr 12	Apr 11	Apr 10
Sales Turnover	17m	15m	14m
Pre Tax Profit/Loss	1m	722	511
Working Capital	3m	3m	2m
Fixed Assets	2m	2m	2m
Current Assets	8m	7m	6m
Current Liabilities	737	590	599

Saville Audio Visual

Saville Vupoint 2 Blenheim Court Brownfields, Welwyn Garden City, AL7 1AD
Tel: 01707-378770 **Fax:** 01707-378771
E-mail: adam.pike@saville-av.com
Website: http://www.saville-av.com
Managers: A. Pike (Mgr)
Ultimate Holding Company: SEA HOLDINGS LIMITED
Immediate Holding Company: THE SAVILLE GROUP LIMITED
Registration no: 02170847 **VAT No.:** GB 640 2284 68
Date established: 1987 **Turnover:** £1m - £2m **No.of Employees:** 1 - 10
Product Groups: 28, 30, 37, 38

Date of Accounts	Dec 11	Dec 10	Dec 09
Sales Turnover	26m	25m	25m
Pre Tax Profit/Loss	3	84	88
Working Capital	1m	1m	684
Fixed Assets	1m	1m	1m
Current Assets	6m	7m	6m
Current Liabilities	3m	3m	2m

Sevarg Engineering Ltd

Clamcleats Building Watchmead, Welwyn Garden City, AL7 1AP
Tel: 01707-330101 **Fax:** 020-8801 9907
E-mail: sales@clamcleat.com
Website: http://www.sevargclara.net
Directors: D. Emery (Dir), G. Ewing (Sales), R. Simmonds (Sales & Mktg), V. Simmonds (Dir)
Immediate Holding Company: SEVARG ENGINEERING LIMITED
Registration no: 01273776 **Date established:** 1976
Turnover: Up to £250,000 **No.of Employees:** 1 - 10 **Product Groups:** 38

Date of Accounts	Oct 08	Oct 07	Apr 11
Sales Turnover	231	287	N/A
Pre Tax Profit/Loss	13	24	N/A
Working Capital	95	86	-12
Fixed Assets	43	51	N/A
Current Assets	120	105	2
Current Liabilities	7	9	N/A

Silverstream Engineering Ltd

58a Bridge Road East, Welwyn Garden City, AL7 1JU
Tel: 01707-322552 **Fax:** 01707-334124
E-mail: info@silverpowerflush.com
Website: http://www.silverpowerflush.com
Directors: J. Burrows (Dir)
Immediate Holding Company: SILVERSTREAM ENGINEERING LIMITED
Registration no: 03221591 **Date established:** 1996
Turnover: Up to £250,000 **No.of Employees:** 1 - 10 **Product Groups:** 27, 29, 48

Date of Accounts	Dec 11	Dec 10	Dec 09
Working Capital	-10	-2	1
Fixed Assets	303	304	304
Current Assets	16	17	28

Swift Aerospace Services Ltd

Unit B City Park Watchmead, Welwyn Garden City, AL7 1LT
Tel: 01707-294400 **Fax:** 01707-294409
E-mail: rgerber@swiftaero.com
Website: http://www.swiftaero.com
Directors: R. Gerber (MD)
Immediate Holding Company: SWIFT AEROSPACE SERVICES LIMITED
Registration no: 02724904 **Date established:** 1992 **Turnover:** £5m - £10m
No.of Employees: 21 - 50 **Product Groups:** 35, 39

Date of Accounts	Jun 11	Jun 10	Jun 09
Working Capital	2m	2m	934
Fixed Assets	169	202	256
Current Assets	3m	3m	3m

T M Robotics (Europe) Ltd

Unit 2 Bridge Gate Centre, Martinfield, Welwyn Garden City, AL7 1JG
Tel: 01707-290370 **Fax:** 01707-376662
E-mail: sales@tmrobotics.co.uk
Website: http://www.tmrobotics.co.uk
Bank(s): HSBC
Directors: N. Smith (Dir)
Managers: H. Keeble (Sales Admin)
Registration no: 03946170 **VAT No.:** GB 752 5039 39
Date established: 2000 **Product Groups:** 45, 84

Date of Accounts	Mar 11	Mar 10	Mar 09
Working Capital	143	161	191
Fixed Assets	9	11	14
Current Assets	1m	784	1m

Welwyn Tool Group Ltd

9 Blenheim Court 9 Blenheim Court, Welwyn Garden City, AL7 1AD
Tel: 01707-331111 **Fax:** 01707-372175
E-mail: info@welwyntoolgroup.co.uk
Website: http://www.welwyntoolgroup.co.uk
Directors: C. Day (MD)
Immediate Holding Company: WELWYN TOOL GROUP LIMITED
Registration no: 05515557 **VAT No.:** GB 196 8401 29
Date established: 2005 **Turnover:** Up to £250,000
No.of Employees: 1 - 10 **Product Groups:** 40

Date of Accounts	Mar 11	Mar 10	Mar 09
Working Capital	304	316	349
Fixed Assets	28	37	49
Current Assets	676	595	712

Martin Woolman Ltd

Unit 12 Martinfield Business Centre Martinfield, Welwyn Garden City, AL7 1HG
Tel: 01707-373181 **Fax:** 01707-373174
E-mail: info@martinwoolman.co.uk
Website: http://www.martinwoolman.co.uk
Bank(s): HSBC
Directors: L. Knight (Fin)
Immediate Holding Company: MARTIN-WOOLMAN LIMITED
Registration no: 01035308 **VAT No.:** GB 197 1406 48
Date established: 1971 **Turnover:** £1m - £2m **No.of Employees:** 11 - 20
Product Groups: 37

Date of Accounts	Mar 11	Mar 10	Mar 09
Sales Turnover	1m	835	1m
Pre Tax Profit/Loss	133	63	49
Working Capital	215	186	142
Fixed Assets	31	32	43
Current Assets	414	350	297
Current Liabilities	53	32	32

NORTH HUMBERSIDE

Beverley

Bea Fastening Systems Ltd
Behrens House Plaxton Bridge Road, Woodmansey, Beverley, HU17 0RT
Tel: 01482-889911 **Fax:** 01482-871804
E-mail: sales@uk.bea-group.com
Website: http://www.bea-group.com
Bank(s): The Royal Bank of Scotland
Directors: J. Mercer (MD), M. Philpot (Fin)
Managers: S. Carruthers (Mktg Serv Mgr), P. Shepherd (Sales Prom Mgr), D. Belcher (Buyer)
Ultimate Holding Company: JOH FRIEDRICK BEHRENS AG (GERMANY)
Immediate Holding Company: BEA FASTENING SYSTEMS LIMITED
Registration no: 01055930 **Date established:** 1972 **Turnover:** £5m - £10m
No.of Employees: 21 - 50 **Product Groups:** 32, 35, 36, 37, 40, 42, 47, 49, 61, 66, 67

Date of Accounts	Dec 11	Dec 10	Dec 09
Sales Turnover	6m	6m	5m
Pre Tax Profit/Loss	236	210	855
Working Capital	1m	1m	1m
Fixed Assets	268	260	237
Current Assets	2m	2m	2m
Current Liabilities	271	219	167

Beverley Veneers Ltd
Grovehill Road, Beverley, HU17 0JJ
Tel: 01482-882537 **Fax:** 01482-869520
E-mail: info@beverleyveneers.com
Bank(s): Barclays
Directors: W. Dunlop (MD)
Ultimate Holding Company: YEW HOLDINGS LIMITED
Immediate Holding Company: BEVERLEY VENEERS LIMITED
Registration no: 01632099 **VAT No.:** GB 433 6531 62
Date established: 1982 **Turnover:** £2m - £5m **No.of Employees:** 11 - 20
Product Groups: 25

Date of Accounts	Jul 11	Jul 10	Jul 09
Sales Turnover	N/A	3m	N/A
Pre Tax Profit/Loss	N/A	163	N/A
Working Capital	1m	1m	893
Fixed Assets	1m	2m	2m
Current Assets	2m	2m	1m
Current Liabilities	N/A	107	N/A

Dr Reddy's Laboratories UK Ltd
Riverview Road, Beverley, HU17 0LD
Tel: 01482-860228 **Fax:** 01482-872042
Website: http://www.drreddys.com
Ultimate Holding Company: DR REDDY'S LABORATORIES LTD (INDIA)
Immediate Holding Company: DR REDDY'S LABORATORIES (UK) LIMITED
Registration no: 01729064 **VAT No.:** GB 500 6541 90
Date established: 1983 **Turnover:** £20m - £50m
No.of Employees: 51 - 100 **Product Groups:** 63

Date of Accounts	Mar 11	Mar 10	Mar 09
Sales Turnover	33m	26m	26m
Pre Tax Profit/Loss	3m	683	66
Working Capital	2m	-192	-462
Fixed Assets	4m	3m	3m
Current Assets	12m	11m	9m
Current Liabilities	3m	10m	2m

Julian Graves Ltd
22 Toll Gavel, Beverley, HU17 9AR
Tel: 01482-880866 **Fax:** 01482-880866
E-mail: customercare@juliangraves.co.uk
Website: http://www.juliangraves.co.uk
Managers: J. Allison
Ultimate Holding Company: THE CARLYLE GROUP LLC (USA)
Immediate Holding Company: JULIAN GRAVES LIMITED
Registration no: 02109178 **Date established:** 1987
No.of Employees: 1 - 10 **Product Groups:** 31, 32

Date of Accounts	Mar 08	Mar 07	Sep 10
Sales Turnover	70m	62m	64m
Pre Tax Profit/Loss	-2m	700	3m
Working Capital	-10m	-1m	-6m
Fixed Assets	14m	13m	3m
Current Assets	15m	19m	12m
Current Liabilities	3m	2m	3m

Harborlite Ltd
Westwood, Beverley, HU17 8RQ
Tel: 01482-645265 **Fax:** 01482-641176
E-mail: enquiries@worldminerals.com
Website: http://www.worldminerals.com
Directors: P. Woodward (Dir), A. Turkington (Dir), H. Trehair Davies (Co Sec)
Ultimate Holding Company: IMERYS SA (FRANCE)
Immediate Holding Company: WORLD MINERALS (UK) LIMITED
Registration no: 02749713 **Date established:** 1992 **Turnover:** £2m - £5m
No.of Employees: 1 - 10 **Product Groups:** 38, 42

Date of Accounts	Dec 10	Dec 09	Dec 08
Sales Turnover	N/A	3m	3m
Pre Tax Profit/Loss	N/A	380	172
Working Capital	2m	2m	1m
Fixed Assets	N/A	3	3
Current Assets	2m	2m	2m
Current Liabilities	N/A	56	78

Hodgson Sealants Ltd
Belprin Road, Beverley, HU17 0LN
Tel: 01482-868321 **Fax:** 01482-870729
E-mail: sales@hodgsonsealants.com
Website: http://www.hodgsonsealants.com
Bank(s): Lloyds TSB Bank plc
Directors: R. Hodgson (Fin)
Managers: R. Best (Mktg Serv Mgr), K. Nickolay (Sales Prom Mgr), L. Russell
Ultimate Holding Company: HODGSON SEALANTS (HOLDINGS) LIMITED
Immediate Holding Company: HODGSON SEALANTS LIMITED
Registration no: 02799221 **VAT No.:** GB 282 3456 52
Date established: 1993 **Turnover:** £10m - £20m
No.of Employees: 21 - 50 **Product Groups:** 30, 32, 33, 66

Date of Accounts	Mar 12	Mar 11	Mar 10
Sales Turnover	16m	18m	15m
Pre Tax Profit/Loss	363	657	369
Working Capital	N/A	1m	1m
Fixed Assets	N/A	3m	3m
Current Assets	3m	7m	5m
Current Liabilities	3m	4m	2m

Jewson Ltd
36 Flemingate, Beverley, HU17 0NU
Tel: 01482-860888 **Fax:** 01482-872634
E-mail: steve.gamble@jewson.co.uk
Website: http://www.jewson.co.uk
Managers: S. Gamble (District Mgr)
Ultimate Holding Company: COMPAGNIE DE SAINT GOBAIN (FRANCE)
Immediate Holding Company: JEWSON LIMITED
Registration no: 00348407 **VAT No.:** GB 394 1212 63
Date established: 1939 **Turnover:** £500,000 - £1m
No.of Employees: 1 - 10 **Product Groups:** 66, 67

Date of Accounts	Dec 11	Dec 10	Dec 09
Sales Turnover	1606m	1547m	1485m
Pre Tax Profit/Loss	18m	100m	45m
Working Capital	-345m	-250m	-349m
Fixed Assets	496m	387m	461m
Current Assets	657m	1005m	1320m
Current Liabilities	66m	120m	64m

Krehalon UK Ltd
Tokenspire Business Park Hull Road, Woodmansey, Beverley, HU17 0TB
Tel: 01482-865277 **Fax:** 01482-865280
E-mail: info@krehalonuk.co.uk
Website: http://www.krehalonuk.co.uk
Directors: S. Hinchley (MD), V. Aspill (Fin)
Managers: L. Benson, A. Thompson, P. Spink
Ultimate Holding Company: KUREHA CORPORATION (JAPAN)
Immediate Holding Company: KREHALON UK LIMITED
Registration no: 01663266 **Date established:** 1982 **Turnover:** £5m - £10m
No.of Employees: 11 - 20 **Product Groups:** 38, 42

Date of Accounts	Dec 11	Dec 10	Dec 09
Sales Turnover	9m	7m	6m
Pre Tax Profit/Loss	495	361	236
Working Capital	598	380	144
Fixed Assets	273	115	91
Current Assets	4m	3m	2m
Current Liabilities	839	756	444

P Marin
Low Works Grovehill Road, Beverley, HU17 0JJ
Tel: 01482-870370
Directors: P. Marin (Prop)
Ultimate Holding Company: YEW HOLDINGS LIMITED
Immediate Holding Company: A.HAXBY & SONS (FILEY) LIMITED
Registration no: 02808343 **Date established:** 1949
No.of Employees: 1 - 10 **Product Groups:** 35

Nicky Dunning Mill Garage
Walkington, Beverley, HU17 8RT
Tel: 01482-868365 **Fax:** 01482-865232
E-mail: nicky@nickydunning.co.uk
Website: http://www.nickydunning.co.uk
Directors: N. Dunning (Prop)
Date established: 1968 **No.of Employees:** 1 - 10 **Product Groups:** 41

Nottingham Industrial Flooring Ltd
Unit 2 Beckside Court Annie Reed Road, Beverley, HU17 0LF
Tel: 01482-856162 **Fax:** 01482-856168
E-mail: paul@nifl.co.uk
Website: http://www.nisl.co.uk
Directors: P. Scott (Sales), S. Scott (Sales)
Immediate Holding Company: NOTTINGHAM INDUSTRIAL FLOORING LIMITED
Registration no: 03529930 **Date established:** 1998 **Turnover:** £1m - £2m
No.of Employees: 1 - 10 **Product Groups:** 52

Date of Accounts	Jul 11	Jul 10	Jul 09
Working Capital	238	187	300
Fixed Assets	21	28	37
Current Assets	352	261	429

Ormston Technology Ltd
St Nicholas Road, Beverley, HU17 0EH
Tel: 01482-677655 **Fax:** 01346-513112
E-mail: francis@ormtec.co.uk
Website: http://www.ormtec.co.uk
Directors: T. Pybus (MD), T. Pybuf (MD), F. West (Tech Serv)
Managers: D. Shandley (Sales Prom Mgr), S. Mason (Sales Admin), L. Middleton (I.T. Exec), J. Pickles (Mktg Serv Mgr), I. Mitchell (Tech Serv Mgr)
Immediate Holding Company: ORMSTON TECHNOLOGY LIMITED
Registration no: 02189974 **Date established:** 1987 **Turnover:** £1m - £2m
No.of Employees: 1 - 10 **Product Groups:** 37, 84

Date of Accounts	Dec 10	Dec 09	Dec 08
Working Capital	-95	3	13
Fixed Assets	51	59	70
Current Assets	285	359	411

P J Heaven
PO Box 164, Beverley, HU17 7AP
Tel: 01482-860777 **Fax:** 01482-860777
E-mail: sales@pjheaven.co.uk
Website: http://www.pjheaven.co.uk
Directors: B. Mar (Prop)
Date established: 1991 **No.of Employees:** 1 - 10 **Product Groups:** 24, 63

Riders Paradise Ltd
Unit 7a Tokenspire Business Park, Woodmansey, Beverley, HU17 0TB
Tel: 01482-870604
E-mail: info@ridersparadise.co.uk
Website: http://www.ridersparadise.co.uk
Directors: S. Walsh (Prop)
Immediate Holding Company: RIDERS PARADISE LIMITED
Registration no: 06688810 **Date established:** 2008
No.of Employees: 1 - 10 **Product Groups:** 24, 49, 63

Scope Engineers Ltd
Unit 4 Beverley Business Centre St. Nicholas Road, Beverley, HU17 0QT
Tel: 01482-882590 **Fax:** 01482-867309
E-mail: info@scopeuk.fsnet.co.uk
Website: http://www.scopeuk.co.uk
Directors: P. Barratt (MD)
Managers: D. Barratt (Sales & Mktg Mg), T. Bennett
Registration no: 00981504 **VAT No.:** GB 168 1743 45
Turnover: Up to £250,000 **No.of Employees:** 1 - 10 **Product Groups:** 48

Date of Accounts	Sep 09	Sep 08	Sep 07
Working Capital	-12	-13	-17
Fixed Assets	16	21	26
Current Assets	38	42	45

C Swift
Eske Lane Nurseries Eske Lane, Tickton, Beverley, HU17 9SG
Tel: 01964-541444 **Fax:** 01964-541444
Directors: C. Swift (Prop)
Date established: 2000 **No.of Employees:** 1 - 10 **Product Groups:** 41

Yorkshire Accountancy Ltd

Unit C Annie Reed Court Annie Reed Road, Beverley, HU17 0LF
Tel: 01482-845750 **Fax:** 01482-846380
E-mail: n.robinson@yorkshireaccountancy.co.uk
Website: http://www.yorkshireaccountancy.co.uk
Directors: N. King (MD)
Immediate Holding Company: YORKSHIRE ACCOUNTANCY LIMITED
Registration no: 05460543 **Date established:** 2005
Turnover: Up to £250,000 **No.of Employees:** 1 - 10 **Product Groups:** 80

Date of Accounts	May 11	May 10	May 09
Working Capital	-237	-85	-185
Fixed Assets	373	202	250
Current Assets	131	124	110

Bridlington

A B Graphics International Ltd

Carnaby Industrial Estate Lancaster Road, Carnaby, Bridlington, YO15 3QY
Tel: 01262-671138 **Fax:** 01262-606359
E-mail: info@abgint.com
Website: http://www.abgint.com
Bank(s): Yorkshire Bank
Directors: C. Burton (Dir), M. Reader (Fin)
Ultimate Holding Company: O F AHLMARK AND COMPANY AB - SWEDEN
Immediate Holding Company: INTERNATIONAL GRAPHIC MATERIALS LIMITED
Registration no: 00992129 **VAT No.:** GB 390 2247 63
Date established: 1970 **Turnover:** £10m - £20m
No.of Employees: 51 - 100 **Product Groups:** 44

Bemptons Agricultural Services Ltd

The Garage 51 High Street, Bempton, Bridlington, YO15 1HB
Tel: 01262-850383 **Fax:** 01262-851165
E-mail: info@stgowan.co.uk
Website: http://www.stgowan.co.uk
Managers: S. Gowan
Immediate Holding Company: BEMPTON AGRICULTURAL SERVICES LTD
Registration no: 06954387 **Date established:** 2009
No.of Employees: 1 - 10 **Product Groups:** 41

Date of Accounts	Jul 11	Jul 10
Working Capital	9	2
Fixed Assets	6	9
Current Assets	60	93

Britax P M G Ltd

Bessingby Industrial Estate, Bridlington, YO16 4SJ
Tel: 01262-670161 **Fax:** 01262-605666
E-mail: info@britax-pmg.com
Website: http://www.britax-pmg.com
Bank(s): Barclays, Birmingham
Directors: M. Rayner (MD)
Ultimate Holding Company: PSE NEWCO LIMITED
Immediate Holding Company: BRITAX PMG LIMITED
Registration no: 00406476 **Date established:** 1946
Turnover: £20m - £50m **No.of Employees:** 101 - 250
Product Groups: 29, 39

Date of Accounts	Dec 11	Dec 10	Jun 10
Sales Turnover	27m	10m	19m
Pre Tax Profit/Loss	1m	828	951
Working Capital	-2m	8m	8m
Fixed Assets	2m	2m	2m
Current Assets	13m	15m	16m
Current Liabilities	4m	3m	3m

Carnaby Caravans Ltd

Carnaby Industrial Estate Lancaster Road, Carnaby, Bridlington, YO15 3QY
Tel: 01262-679971 **Fax:** 01262-670315
E-mail: info@carnabycaravans.com
Website: http://www.carnabycaravans.com
Bank(s): Bank of Scotland, Hull
Directors: A. Mccarthy (Ptnr), R. Austin (MD), S. Matson (Fin)
Ultimate Holding Company: CARNABY GROUP HOLDINGS LIMITED
Immediate Holding Company: CARNABY CARAVANS LIMITED
Registration no: 01239687 **VAT No.:** GB 282 3417 62
Date established: 1976 **Turnover:** £10m - £20m
No.of Employees: 51 - 100 **Product Groups:** 39

Date of Accounts	Oct 11	Oct 10	Oct 09
Sales Turnover	14m	16m	13m
Pre Tax Profit/Loss	1m	2m	1m
Working Capital	4m	3m	4m
Fixed Assets	240	239	114
Current Assets	7m	7m	7m
Current Liabilities	273	351	359

Coastal Stairlifts & Mobility

Field House Bessingby, Bridlington, YO16 4UH
Tel: 01262-601395 **Fax:** 01262-601395
Directors: J. Perrow (Prop)
Registration no: 03723486 **Date established:** 1999
No.of Employees: 1 - 10 **Product Groups:** 35, 39, 45

Graham

Bessingby Industrial Estate, Bridlington, YO16 4SJ
Tel: 01262-677441 **Fax:** 01262-606822
E-mail: gordoncree@graham-group.co.uk
Website: http://www.graham-group.co.uk
Managers: D. Vincent (Mgr)
Immediate Holding Company: LUXIHOMES LIMITED
Registration no: 02079462 **VAT No.:** GB 394 1212 63
Date established: 1986 **Turnover:** £20m - £50m
No.of Employees: 21 - 50 **Product Groups:** 35, 52

Date of Accounts	Sep 11	Sep 10	Sep 09
Sales Turnover	N/A	N/A	3m
Pre Tax Profit/Loss	N/A	N/A	131
Working Capital	-9	-170	-42
Fixed Assets	1m	1m	1m
Current Assets	754	297	346
Current Liabilities	N/A	N/A	150

Greenstik Ltd

Unit 9 Carnaby Industrial Estate Lancaster Road, Carnaby, Bridlington, YO15 3QY
Tel: 01262-602222 **Fax:** 01262-677007
E-mail: sales@greenstik.co.uk
Website: http://www.greenstik.co.uk
Directors: G. Dunn (MD)
Ultimate Holding Company: GREENSTIK CONVERTERS LIMITED
Immediate Holding Company: GREENSTIK LIMITED
Registration no: 04104521 **Date established:** 2000
Turnover: Up to £250,000 **No.of Employees:** 11 - 20 **Product Groups:** 27, 66

Date of Accounts	Dec 09	Dec 08	Jun 12
Working Capital	847	870	1m
Fixed Assets	397	423	56
Current Assets	2m	2m	2m

J E Hill

Danes Dyke Flamborough, Bridlington, YO15 1AA
Tel: 07866-919579 **Fax:** 01262-850899
Directors: J. Hills (Ptnr)
Date established: 1967 **No.of Employees:** 1 - 10 **Product Groups:** 26, 35

Inventair Ltd

Carnaby Industrial Estate Lancaster Road, Carnaby, Bridlington, YO15 3QY
Tel: 01262-400919 **Fax:** 01262-401358
E-mail: david@inventair.co.uk
Website: http://www.inventair.co.uk
Directors: D. Seed (MD)
Immediate Holding Company: INVENTAIR LIMITED
Registration no: 04121169 **VAT No.:** GB 601 8253 71
Date established: 2000 **Turnover:** £10m - £20m **No.of Employees:** 1 - 10
Product Groups: 48, 52

Date of Accounts	Mar 12	Mar 11	Mar 10
Working Capital	335	286	317
Fixed Assets	68	76	84
Current Assets	912	773	784

Kozee Komforts

Komfort House Boundary Road Bessingby Industrial Estate, Bridlington, YO16 4SD
Tel: 01262-409200 **Fax:** 01262-602102
E-mail: sales@kozeekomforts.co.uk
Website: http://www.kozeekomforts.co.uk
Directors: P. Ward (MD)
Registration no: 03818270 **Turnover:** £500,000 - £1m
No.of Employees: 11 - 20 **Product Groups:** 24

Lightspeed Entertainments

108 Quay Road, Bridlington, YO16 4JB
Tel: 07831-192740 **Fax:** 01262-679735
E-mail: sales@lightspeed-entertainments.com
Website: http://www.lightspeed-entertainments.com
Directors: G. Cooper (Prop)
No.of Employees: 1 - 10 **Product Groups:** 37, 48

Mixerman

28 Marshall Avenue, Bridlington, YO15 2DS
Tel: 01262-674111
E-mail: info@mixerman.co.uk
Website: http://www.mixerman.co.uk
Directors: A. Winter (Prop)
Date established: 2006 **Turnover:** Up to £250,000
No.of Employees: 1 - 10 **Product Groups:** 29, 37, 63

Peter Haddock Ltd

Pinfold Lane Industrial Estate, Bridlington, YO16 6BT
Tel: 01262-678121 **Fax:** 01262-400043
E-mail: rodney.noon@phpublishing.co.uk
Website: http://www.phpublishing.co.uk
Bank(s): Yorkshire Bank Bridlington
Directors: R. Noon (MD), P. Hornby (Co Sec), C. Meah (Comm)
Managers: S. Cuthbert (Tech Serv Mgr), J. Hickey (Ops Mgr), S. Russell (Chief Mgr)
Ultimate Holding Company: PETER HADDOCK LIMITED
Immediate Holding Company: PETER HADDOCK PUBLISHING LTD.
Registration no: 04534681 **Date established:** 2002 **Turnover:** £5m - £10m
No.of Employees: 21 - 50 **Product Groups:** 28

Premier Hazard Ltd

Bessingby Industrial Estate, Bridlington, YO16 4SJ
Tel: 01262-670161 **Fax:** 0113-239 1131
E-mail: info@premierhazard.co.uk
Website: http://www.premierhazard.co.uk
Managers: A. Yasin (Tech Serv Mgr), B. Driscoll (Chief Mgr), B. Kirbitson (Buyer)
Ultimate Holding Company: PSE NEWCO LIMITED
Immediate Holding Company: PREMIER HAZARD LIMITED
Registration no: 01725643 **VAT No.:** 387 9234 02 **Date established:** 1983
Turnover: £5m - £10m **No.of Employees:** 51 - 100 **Product Groups:** 39

Date of Accounts	Dec 11	Dec 10	Jun 10
Sales Turnover	6m	3m	6m
Pre Tax Profit/Loss	259	64	453
Working Capital	118	3m	2m
Fixed Assets	149	111	150
Current Assets	2m	4m	4m
Current Liabilities	866	532	557

Stera Tape Ltd

Carnaby Industrial Estate Lancaster Road, Carnaby, Bridlington, YO15 3QY
Tel: 01262-603721 **Fax:** 01262-400028
E-mail: sales@steratape.co.uk
Website: http://www.steratape.com
Bank(s): Yorkshire Bank
Directors: S. Dawson (Pers), B. Dhillon (MD)
Managers: S. Metcalfe (Buyer), R. Milburn (Fin Mgr), K. Mayer (Comm)
Ultimate Holding Company: FILTRONA PLC
Immediate Holding Company: STERA TAPE LIMITED
Registration no: 02390276 **Date established:** 1989 **Turnover:** £5m - £10m
No.of Employees: 21 - 50 **Product Groups:** 23, 27, 30, 32

Date of Accounts	Dec 11	Dec 10	Apr 10
Sales Turnover	7m	4m	N/A
Pre Tax Profit/Loss	794	-425	N/A
Working Capital	1m	1m	2m
Fixed Assets	952	567	697
Current Assets	3m	2m	3m
Current Liabilities	738	470	N/A

Transglobal Engineering Ltd

124 Quay Road, Bridlington, YO16 4JB
Tel: 01262-672602
Website: http://www.transtool.co.uk
Directors: L. Topham (Dir)
Ultimate Holding Company: BECK HOLDINGS LIMITED
Immediate Holding Company: TRANS-GLOBAL ENGINEERING LIMITED
Registration no: 02996578 **Date established:** 1994
No.of Employees: 21 - 50 **Product Groups:** 37, 52

Date of Accounts	Dec 11	Dec 10	Dec 09
Working Capital	853	734	567
Fixed Assets	2	4	5
Current Assets	1m	1m	878

Brough

Britspace Modular Buildings Ltd

Unicorn House Broad Lane, Gilberdyke, Brough, HU15 2TS
Tel: 01430-444400 **Fax:** 01430-444401
E-mail: dharris@britspace.com
Website: http://www.britspace.com
Bank(s): Barclays
Directors: T. Jackson (Fin), S. Wood (Comm), G. Townend (Sales & Mktg), A. Horncastle (Comm), D. Harris (MD)
Managers: S. Stanley (Personnel), S. Stanley, P. Taylor (Prod Mgr), M. Wright (Buyer), M. Roberts (Comm), M. Wright (Purch Mgr), A. Haley (I.T. Exec), C. Mainard (Est)
Ultimate Holding Company: 06993030
Immediate Holding Company: BRITSPACE MODULAR BUILDINGS LIMITED
Registration no: 04503758 **VAT No.:** GB 551 9457 23
Date established: 2002 **Turnover:** £20m - £50m
No.of Employees: 101 - 250 **Product Groups:** 25, 35

Date of Accounts	Mar 10	Mar 09	Mar 08
Sales Turnover	31m	27m	28m
Pre Tax Profit/Loss	925	1m	3m
Working Capital	8m	7m	6m
Fixed Assets	630	758	962
Current Assets	18m	16m	17m
Current Liabilities	9m	5m	7m

Business Solutions

10 Westbrook CR Gilberdyke, Brough, HU15 2TR
Tel: 01430-473150
Website: http://www.deal.bedfordshire.gov.uk
Directors: M. Lees (Prop)
Date established: 2002 **No.of Employees:** 1 - 10 **Product Groups:** 35

Crystal Heart Salad Co. Ltd

Eastrington Road Sandholme, Brough, HU15 2XS
Tel: 01430-440110 **Fax:** 01430-440315
E-mail: jamesbean@crystalheartsalad.co.uk
Website: http://www.crystalheartsalad.co.uk
Directors: A. Bunting (Co Sec), J. Bean (MD)
Immediate Holding Company: CRYSTAL HEART SALAD COMPANY LIMITED
Registration no: 01023813 **Date established:** 1971
No.of Employees: 11 - 20 **Product Groups:** 26, 35

Date of Accounts	Dec 11	Dec 10	Dec 09
Working Capital	-100	9	-177
Fixed Assets	472	495	573
Current Assets	202	162	89

Factory Fit UK Ltd

108 Main Road Newport, Brough, HU15 2RG
Tel: 01430-449000 **Fax:** 01430-449999
E-mail: info@factory-fit.com
Website: http://www.factory-fit.com
Managers: L. Armstrong (Fin Mgr)
Immediate Holding Company: FACTORY-FIT (UK) LIMITED
Registration no: 02842261 **Date established:** 1993 **Turnover:** £1m - £2m
No.of Employees: 1 - 10 **Product Groups:** 24, 25, 26, 35

Date of Accounts	Dec 11	Dec 10	Dec 09
Working Capital	74	50	-14
Fixed Assets	7	5	35
Current Assets	228	208	158

Humber Growers Ltd

Common Lane Welton, Brough, HU15 1UT
Tel: 01482-667151 **Fax:** 01482-667678
E-mail: sales@humbervhb.com
Website: http://www.humbergrowers.co.uk
Directors: N. Gibbons (Fin), P. Cooper (Comm), R. Sayer (Prop)
Managers: J. Ward
Ultimate Holding Company: HUMBER DEVELOPMENTS LIMITED
Immediate Holding Company: HUMBER GROWERS LIMITED
Registration no: 00940258 **Date established:** 1968 **Turnover:** £5m - £10m
No.of Employees: 1 - 10 **Product Groups:** 02

Date of Accounts	Dec 11	Dec 10	Dec 09
Sales Turnover	6m	8m	33m
Pre Tax Profit/Loss	468	17m	2m
Working Capital	7m	6m	-482
Fixed Assets	5m	5m	6m
Current Assets	9m	10m	8m
Current Liabilities	1m	2m	6m

Keltic Seal Solutions

Broad Lane Gilberdyke, Brough, HU15 2TB
Tel: 01430-441520 **Fax:** 01430-441904
E-mail: sales@trugroup.co.uk
Website: http://www.trugroup.co.uk
Bank(s): HSBC Bank plc
Directors: M. Mell (Fin), K. Mell (MD)
Immediate Holding Company: N.J.R. ENTERPRISES LIMITED
Registration no: 03097023 **VAT No.:** GB 168 0579 37
Date established: 2009 **Turnover:** £1m - £2m **No.of Employees:** 11 - 20
Product Groups: 30

Date of Accounts	Dec 11	Dec 10	Dec 09
Working Capital	-45	-115	-75
Fixed Assets	77	78	95
Current Assets	488	469	473

Smith & Nephew Extruded Films Ltd
Gateway To Humberside Trading Estate Gilberdyke, Brough, HU15 2TD
Tel: 01430-440757 **Fax:** 01430-440211
E-mail: karl.douglas@smith-nephew.com
Website: http://www.snef.co.uk
Directors: P. Webster (Fin)
Managers: K. Douglas (Chief Mgr), J. Marshall, J. Telford
Ultimate Holding Company: SMITH & NEPHEW PLC
Immediate Holding Company: SMITH & NEPHEW EXTRUDED FILMS LIMITED
Registration no: 00592411 **Date established:** 1957 **Turnover:** £1m - £2m
No.of Employees: 51 - 100 **Product Groups:** 23, 30, 35

Trims & Things
258 Main Road Newport, Brough, HU15 2RH
Tel: 01430-440309 **Fax:** 01430-448278
E-mail: sales@fascias-soffits-guttering.co.uk
Website: http://www.fascias-soffits-guttering.co.uk
Directors: J. Gough (Prop)
No.of Employees: 1 - 10 **Product Groups:** 30, 66, 67

Vuba Industrial Supplies
37 Robin Close, Brough, HU15 1RY
Tel: 01482-665050 **Fax:** 01482-424081
E-mail: info@vuba-group.co.uk
Website: http://www.vubasupplies.co.uk
Directors: S. Scott (Dir)
Date established: 2008 **Turnover:** £500,000 - £1m
No.of Employees: 1 - 10 **Product Groups:** 32, 33, 51

Cottingham

JJQuilling
Skidby, Cottingham, HU16 5UA
Tel: 01482-843721
Website: http://www.jjquilling.co.uk
Directors: P. Jenkins (MD), J. Jenkins (Prop)
No.of Employees: 1 - 10 **Product Groups:** 27, 36, 64, 66

The Swift Group
Dunswell Road, Cottingham, HU16 4JX
Tel: 01482-847332 **Fax:** 01482-876335
E-mail: enquiry@swiftleisure.co.uk
Website: http://www.swiftgroup.co.uk
Bank(s): HSBC Bank plc
Directors: N. Page (Sales)
Ultimate Holding Company: KESTREL INDUSTRIES LIMITED
Immediate Holding Company: SWIFT GROUP LIMITED
Registration no: 00832994 **VAT No.:** GB 501 0617 10
Date established: 1965 **Turnover:** £125m - £250m
No.of Employees: 501 - 1000 **Product Groups:** 39

Date of Accounts	Aug 11	Aug 10	Aug 09
Sales Turnover	196m	192m	137m
Pre Tax Profit/Loss	10m	11m	556
Working Capital	29m	21m	17m
Fixed Assets	3m	3m	4m
Current Assets	60m	46m	38m
Current Liabilities	6m	5m	4m

Driffield

Aesthetic Frames & Pictures
33 Northfield Crescent, Driffield, YO25 5ES
Tel: 01377-256243
E-mail: contact@pictureframing-uk.com
Website: http://www.pictureframing-uk.com
Directors: M. Egleton (MD)
No.of Employees: 1 - 10 **Product Groups:** 25, 26, 36, 49

Bankside Patterson Ltd
Catwick Lane Brandesburton, Driffield, YO25 8RW
Tel: 01964-545454 **Fax:** 01964-545459
E-mail: sales@bankside-patterson.com
Website: http://www.banksidepatterson.com
Bank(s): HSBC Bank plc
Directors: C. Adams (MD)
Managers: M. Westoby (Tech Serv Mgr), H. Macintosh
Immediate Holding Company: BANKSIDE PATTERSON LIMITED
Registration no: 00619346 **Date established:** 1959
Turnover: £10m - £20m **No.of Employees:** 51 - 100 **Product Groups:** 35, 39

Date of Accounts	Aug 11	Aug 10	Aug 09
Sales Turnover	14m	16m	12m
Pre Tax Profit/Loss	-553	711	313
Working Capital	1m	2m	1m
Fixed Assets	4m	4m	4m
Current Assets	5m	5m	5m
Current Liabilities	243	579	416

Cranswick Mill Division B O C M Pauls
Cranswick Industrial Estate Beverley Road, Cranswick, Driffield, YO25 9PF
Tel: 01377-270649 **Fax:** 01377-270994
E-mail: m.davey@cranswick.co.uk
Website: http://www.cranswickmill.co.uk
Directors: M. Davey (Fin), B. Mayne (Grp Chief Exec)
Immediate Holding Company: CRANSWICK PLC
Registration no: 01074383 **VAT No.:** GB 433 5957 33
Date established: 1972 **Turnover:** £500m - £1,000m
No.of Employees: 1 - 10 **Product Groups:** 20

Date of Accounts	Mar 12	Mar 11	Mar 10
Sales Turnover	821m	758m	740m
Pre Tax Profit/Loss	48m	47m	44m
Working Capital	46m	21m	23m
Fixed Assets	255m	262m	236m
Current Assets	145m	116m	126m
Current Liabilities	35m	34m	36m

Dewhirst Group Ltd
Dewhirst House Westgate, Driffield, YO25 6TH
Tel: 01377-252561 **Fax:** 01377-253814
E-mail: enquiries@dewhirst.co.uk
Website: http://www.dewhirst.com
Bank(s): HSBC Bank plc
Directors: C. Wilde (Co Sec), D. Witt (Grp Chief Exec)
Ultimate Holding Company: DRIFFORD LIMITED
Immediate Holding Company: DEWHIRST GROUP LIMITED
Registration no: 01063766 **Date established:** 1972
No.of Employees: 21 - 50 **Product Groups:** 63

Date of Accounts	Jan 10	Jan 11	Jan 12
Pre Tax Profit/Loss	-74	1m	1m
Working Capital	-2m	-897	352
Fixed Assets	40m	40m	40m
Current Assets	30m	31m	31m
Current Liabilities	39	39	39

Easterby Trailers Ltd
Cottam Grange Cottam, Driffield, YO25 3BY
Tel: 01377-267415 **Fax:** 01377-267416
E-mail: info@easterbytrailers.co.uk
Website: http://www.easterbytrailers.co.uk
Directors: E. Johnson (Fin), P. Easterby (MD)
Immediate Holding Company: EASTERBY TRAILERS LIMITED
Registration no: 03132676 **Date established:** 1995
Turnover: £500,000 - £1m **No.of Employees:** 1 - 10 **Product Groups:** 39

Date of Accounts	Dec 11	Dec 10	Dec 09
Working Capital	46	44	40
Fixed Assets	50	53	58
Current Assets	347	353	327

Graham
41 Eastgate South, Driffield, YO25 6LW
Tel: 01377-253861 **Fax:** 01377-241597
E-mail: philip.hewittson@graham-group.co.uk
Website: http://www.graham-group.co.uk
Managers: B. Watson (District Mgr)
Ultimate Holding Company: SAINT-GOBAIN PLC
Immediate Holding Company: GRAHAM GROUP LTD
Registration no: 00066738 **Turnover:** £10m - £20m
No.of Employees: 1 - 10 **Product Groups:** 66

J S R Farming Group
Southburn Offices Southburn, Driffield, YO25 9ED
Tel: 01377-229264 **Fax:** 01377-229253
E-mail: info@jsr.co.uk
Website: http://www.jsr.co.uk
Directors: T. Rymer (Grp Chief Exec)
Ultimate Holding Company: J.S.R. FARMS LIMITED
Immediate Holding Company: SWAYTHORPE GROWERS LIMITED
Registration no: 03902341 **Date established:** 1996
No.of Employees: 21 - 50 **Product Groups:** 67, 80

Date of Accounts	Apr 11	Apr 10	Apr 09
Working Capital	246	223	196
Fixed Assets	4	9	14
Current Assets	318	327	302

J B Filters Ltd
Unit 99 Kellythorpe Industrial Estate Kellythorpe, Driffield, YO25 9DJ
Tel: 01377-240158 **Fax:** 01377-256283
Directors: M. Bell (Dir)
Immediate Holding Company: J B FILTERS LIMITED
Registration no: 06438394 **Date established:** 2007
No.of Employees: 1 - 10 **Product Groups:** 38, 42

Date of Accounts	Dec 11	Dec 10	Dec 09
Working Capital	-90	-57	-32
Fixed Assets	36	43	38
Current Assets	94	116	94

Jefferson Electrical Ltd
25 Eastgate South, Driffield, YO25 6LW
Tel: 01377-253100 **Fax:** 01377-241955
E-mail: jeffersonelectrical@fsmail.net
Directors: A. Kilbington (MD)
Immediate Holding Company: JEFFERSON ELECTRICAL LIMITED
Registration no: 04396996 **Date established:** 2002
Turnover: £250,000 - £500,000 **No.of Employees:** 1 - 10
Product Groups: 48, 52

Date of Accounts	Dec 11	Dec 10	Dec 09
Working Capital	62	47	33
Fixed Assets	5	6	8
Current Assets	146	131	130

Jewson Ltd
Kelleythorpe Industrial Estate Kellythorpe, Driffield, YO25 9DJ
Tel: 01377-256581 **Fax:** 01377-241489
Website: http://www.jewson.co.uk
Directors: P. Hindle (MD)
Managers: P. Hunt (District Mgr)
Ultimate Holding Company: COMPAGNIE DE SAINT GOBAIN (FRANCE)
Immediate Holding Company: JEWSON LIMITED
Registration no: 00348407 **VAT No.:** GB 497 7184 33
Date established: 1939 **Turnover:** £2m - £5m **No.of Employees:** 11 - 20
Product Groups: 66

Date of Accounts	Dec 11	Dec 10	Dec 09
Sales Turnover	1606m	1547m	1485m
Pre Tax Profit/Loss	18m	100m	45m
Working Capital	-345m	-250m	-349m
Fixed Assets	496m	387m	461m
Current Assets	657m	1005m	1320m
Current Liabilities	66m	120m	64m

Main Line Optical Connections Ltd
Kellythorpe Industrial Estate Kellythorpe, Driffield, YO25 9DJ
Tel: 01377-257752 **Fax:** 01377-256702
E-mail: sales@opticalconnections.co.uk
Website: http://www.mainline-opticalconnections.co.uk
Directors: P. Christian (MD)
Ultimate Holding Company: MAIN LINE OPTICAL LIMITED
Immediate Holding Company: MAIN LINE OPTICAL CONNECTIONS LIMITED
Registration no: 05321231 **Date established:** 2004
Turnover: £250,000 - £500,000 **No.of Employees:** 1 - 10
Product Groups: 38, 47, 67

Date of Accounts	Dec 11	Dec 10	Dec 09
Working Capital	102	137	113
Fixed Assets	64	13	23
Current Assets	557	570	457

Porterfield Iron Work Ltd
New Holland Cottage Kilham Road, Langtoft, Driffield, YO25 3TU
Tel: 01377-267472 **Fax:** 01377-267695
E-mail: stuart-porter@talktalkbusiness.net
Website: http://www.porterfield-ironwork.com
Directors: S. Porter (MD), Z. Porter (Fin)
Immediate Holding Company: PORTERFIELD IRONWORK LIMITED
Registration no: 04767470 **Date established:** 2003
No.of Employees: 1 - 10 **Product Groups:** 26, 35

Date of Accounts	Mar 08	Mar 07	Mar 06
Working Capital	-5	-4	7
Fixed Assets	7	8	9
Current Assets	7	6	10
Current Liabilities	12	9	4

Premier Interlink Waco UK Ltd (Waco UK Ltd)
Catfoss Airfield Brandesburton, Driffield, YO25 8EJ
Tel: 01964-545000 **Fax:** 01964-544377
E-mail: jenny.oconnor@waco.co.uk
Website: http://www.waco.co.uk
Directors: E. Dafa (MD)
Ultimate Holding Company: WACO INTERNATIONAL LTD (SOUTH AFRICA)
Immediate Holding Company: USHER AND ROOMS LTD
Registration no: 02420029 **Date established:** 2006
Turnover: Up to £250,000 **No.of Employees:** 101 - 250
Product Groups: 25, 35

Date of Accounts	Mar 11	Mar 10	Mar 09
Sales Turnover	160	117	207
Pre Tax Profit/Loss	39	10	16
Working Capital	4	-14	-24
Fixed Assets	11	17	28
Current Assets	49	35	18
Current Liabilities	20	13	6

Richardson Ford Ltd
Westgate, Driffield, YO25 6SY
Tel: 01377-252166 **Fax:** 01377-252887
E-mail: info@richardson-ford.co.uk
Website: http://www.richardson-ford.co.uk
Directors: T. Richardson (MD)
Managers: A. O'Connor (Chief Acct)
Ultimate Holding Company: RICHARDSONS (HOLDINGS) LIMITED
Immediate Holding Company: RICHARDSONS LIMITED
Registration no: 00280806 **VAT No.:** GB 167 4854 27
Date established: 1933 **Turnover:** £10m - £20m
No.of Employees: 51 - 100 **Product Groups:** 68

Date of Accounts	Dec 11	Dec 10	Dec 09
Sales Turnover	10m	11m	11m
Pre Tax Profit/Loss	23	58	113
Working Capital	640	608	560
Fixed Assets	2m	2m	2m
Current Assets	2m	3m	3m
Current Liabilities	167	172	207

Wilfred Scruton Ltd
Providence Foundry Foxholes, Driffield, YO25 3QQ
Tel: 01262-470221 **Fax:** 01262-470335
E-mail: info@wilfredscruton.co.uk
Website: http://www.wilfredscruton.co.uk
Directors: C. Scruton (MD), I. Scruton (MD), P. Scruton (Dir)
Managers: A. Adkins (Stores Mgr)
Registration no: 00496990 **Date established:** 1951
Turnover: £10m - £20m **No.of Employees:** 21 - 50 **Product Groups:** 67

Date of Accounts	Dec 07	Dec 06	Dec 05
Sales Turnover	11981	9434	8583
Pre Tax Profit/Loss	119	23	-23
Working Capital	692	703	719
Fixed Assets	542	493	512
Current Assets	3218	3210	2944
Current Liabilities	2526	2506	2225
Total Share Capital	18	18	18
ROCE% (Return on Capital Employed)	9.7	1.9	-1.8
ROT% (Return on Turnover)	1.0	0.2	-0.3

R Whitfield
Manorfield Fridaythorpe, Driffield, YO25 9RT
Tel: 01377-288263 **Fax:** 01377-288437
E-mail: gwhitfield72@gmail.com
Directors: G. Whitfield (Ptnr)
Date established: 1967 **No.of Employees:** 1 - 10 **Product Groups:** 41

Mike Whitley Leather Goods
St Marys Chapel Lane Back Street, Langtoft, Driffield, YO25 3TD
Tel: 01377-267426 **Fax:** 01377-267477
E-mail: casework@langtoft.net
Website: http://www.cambraicovers.com
Directors: M. Whitley (Prop)
Date established: 1979 **Turnover:** Up to £250,000
No.of Employees: 1 - 10 **Product Groups:** 22, 23, 24, 38, 49, 66

Yorkshire Marine Containers Ltd
Moorgate Farm Catfoss Airfield, Brandesburton, Driffield, YO25 8EJ
Tel: 01964-542146 **Fax:** 01482-870319
Directors: D. O'sullivan (Co Sec)
Ultimate Holding Company: FP008858
Immediate Holding Company: YORKSHIRE MARINE CONTAINERS LIMITED
Registration no: 00971789 **Date established:** 1970
No.of Employees: 101 - 250 **Product Groups:** 35, 42, 45

Goole

Arc Labels Ltd
Unit 5 The Maltings Industrial Estate Doncaster Road, Whitley Bridge, Goole, DN14 0HH
Tel: 01977-663063 **Fax:** 01977-663064
E-mail: sales@arclabels.com
Website: http://www.arclabels.com
Directors: A. Ford (Dir)
Immediate Holding Company: ARC LABELS LIMITED
Registration no: 01711137 **Date established:** 1983 **Turnover:** £1m - £2m
No.of Employees: 1 - 10 **Product Groups:** 27, 28, 30, 35, 49

Date of Accounts	Apr 12	Apr 11	Apr 10
Working Capital	34	31	14
Fixed Assets	213	224	233
Current Assets	152	160	164

Bankside

White Rose Park Larsen Road, Goole, DN14 6XF
Tel: 01405-768137 **Fax:** 01405-720913
E-mail: traffic@banksidedistribution.biz
Website: http://www.bankside.com
Directors: S. Butterworth (Prop)
Managers: B. McKinnon (Mgr), C. Moss (Transport), R. Barrass (Sales Admin)
Immediate Holding Company: BANKSIDE CONVERTERS LIMITED
Registration no: 01788159 **Date established:** 1984
No.of Employees: 21 - 50 **Product Groups:** 77

Date of Accounts	Apr 12	Apr 11	Apr 10
Working Capital	30	-39	-17
Fixed Assets	52	67	18
Current Assets	217	161	211
Current Liabilities	N/A	N/A	50

C N M Online Ltd

Unit 1 The Maltings Industrial Estate Doncaster Road Whitley Bridge, Goole, DN14 0HH
Tel: 01977-663331 **Fax:** 01977-663306
E-mail: web@s163416436.websitehome.co.uk
Website: http://www.cnmonline.co.uk
Managers: G. Jones (Sales Admin)
Immediate Holding Company: CNM ONLINE LIMITED
Registration no: 05950980 **Date established:** 2006
No.of Employees: 11 - 20 **Product Groups:** 61, 66

Date of Accounts	Sep 11	Sep 10	Sep 09
Working Capital	-76	-91	-115
Fixed Assets	185	194	194
Current Assets	344	281	336

Charles Products

13 Windermere Drive, Goole, DN14 6JW
Tel: 01405-720281 **Fax:** 01405-761883
E-mail: info@charlesproducts.co.uk
Website: http://www.charlesproducts.co.uk
Directors: K. Charles (Ptnr)
Immediate Holding Company: STONELUX LTD
Registration no: 04829872 **Date established:** 2003
No.of Employees: 1 - 10 **Product Groups:** 66

Date of Accounts	Dec 11	Dec 10	Dec 07
Working Capital	-0	-0	-0

Croda International plc

Cowick Hall Snaith, Goole, DN14 9AA
Tel: 01405-860551 **Fax:** 01405-860205
E-mail: enquiries@croda.com
Website: http://www.croda.com
Bank(s): National Westminster Bank Plc
Directors: S. Smith (Tech Serv), S. Christie (Fin), S. Brooke (Pers)
Managers: S. Arnott, A. Butterfield, C. Nottingham
Ultimate Holding Company: CRODA INTERNATIONAL PUBLIC LIMITED COMPANY
Immediate Holding Company: CRODA LIMITED
Registration no: 00446902 **Date established:** 1947
Turnover: £50m - £75m **No.of Employees:** 101 - 250
Product Groups: 31, 32, 66

Roger Fell Ltd

Northside Industrial Park Whitley Bridge, Goole, DN14 0GH
Tel: 01977-662211 **Fax:** 01977-662334
E-mail: tim.fell@fellscarpets.co.uk
Website: http://www.fellscarpets.co.uk
Bank(s): National Westminster
Directors: C. Cummings (Sales), P. Stringer (Co Sec), T. White (Sales), T. Fell (MD)
Managers: G. Stirr
Immediate Holding Company: ROGER FELL LIMITED
Registration no: 01347186 **VAT No.:** GB 183 0211 02
Date established: 1978 **Turnover:** £5m - £10m **No.of Employees:** 21 - 50
Product Groups: 23

Date of Accounts	Apr 12	Apr 11	Apr 10
Sales Turnover	N/A	N/A	6m
Pre Tax Profit/Loss	N/A	N/A	6
Working Capital	878	844	797
Fixed Assets	627	641	691
Current Assets	2m	2m	2m
Current Liabilities	N/A	N/A	296

Filplastic UK Ltd

High Street Eastrington, Goole, DN14 7PW
Tel: 01430-410450 **Fax:** 01430-410449
E-mail: sales@filplastic.com
Website: http://www.filplastic.co.uk
Bank(s): Barclays Bank plc
Managers: A. Sirth (Mktg Serv Mgr), J. Beighton (Sales Admin)
Immediate Holding Company: FILPLASTIC (UK) LIMITED
Registration no: 02822285 **VAT No.:** GB 624 5590 36
Date established: 1993 **No.of Employees:** 11 - 20 **Product Groups:** 26, 39, 52, 67

Date of Accounts	May 11	May 10	May 09
Working Capital	47	-9	-38
Fixed Assets	187	166	163
Current Assets	1m	742	942

Fluid Pumps Ltd

Unit 2 The Grange Rawcliffe Road, Goole, DN14 6TY
Tel: 01405-780660 **Fax:** 01482- 866472
E-mail: leebarker@fluidpumps.co.uk
Website: http://www.fluidpumps.co.uk
Directors: A. dixon (Dir), L. barker (Dir), L. Barker (Fin)
Immediate Holding Company: FLUID PUMPS LIMITED
Registration no: 04799134 **Date established:** 2003 **Turnover:** £1m - £2m
No.of Employees: 1 - 10 **Product Groups:** 30, 40

Date of Accounts	Jun 11	Jun 10	Jun 09
Working Capital	183	106	76
Fixed Assets	52	60	64
Current Assets	405	321	207

G R M Engineering & Contract Services Ltd

Selby Road Snaith, Goole, DN14 9HP
Tel: 01405-861720 **Fax:** 01405-861991
E-mail: dave.grm@btconnect.com
Website: http://www.grmengineering.co.uk
Bank(s): National Westminster Bank Plc
Directors: D. Harrison (Dir), R. Owens (Sales)
Ultimate Holding Company: GRM MANAGEMENT LIMITED
Immediate Holding Company: G.R.M. ENGINEERING & CONTRACT SERVICES LIMITED
Registration no: 01321655 **VAT No.:** GB 298 1283 24
Date established: 1977 **Turnover:** £500,000 - £1m
No.of Employees: 11 - 20 **Product Groups:** 48

Date of Accounts	Jul 11	Jul 10	Jul 09
Working Capital	436	448	480
Fixed Assets	137	113	108
Current Assets	654	584	683

H C K Group Ltd

Unit A1 Larsen Road, Goole, DN14 6XF
Tel: 08454-026503 **Fax:** 08454-026505
Website: http://www.chef-king.co.uk
Directors: G. Gofforth (MD)
Immediate Holding Company: HCK GROUP LIMITED
Registration no: 03592899 **Date established:** 1998
No.of Employees: 21 - 50 **Product Groups:** 20, 40, 41

Date of Accounts	Apr 09	Apr 08	Apr 07
Sales Turnover	9m	N/A	N/A
Pre Tax Profit/Loss	209	N/A	N/A
Working Capital	1m	435	367
Fixed Assets	216	684	720
Current Assets	4m	1m	1m
Current Liabilities	735	N/A	N/A

Pete Harris Wrought Iron & Metal Craft

47 George Street Snaith, Goole, DN14 9HZ
Tel: 01405-860083
Directors: P. Harris (Prop)
Date established: 1982 **No.of Employees:** 1 - 10 **Product Groups:** 26, 35

Hornitex

A W Nielsen Road, Goole, DN14 6TG
Tel: 01482-644671
Website: http://www.hornitex.com
No.of Employees: 1 - 10 **Product Groups:** 25, 30, 52

Humberside Communication Equipment

The Grange, Goole, DN14 6TY
Tel: 01405-769031 **Fax:** 01405-720047
Directors: J. Sellers (Fin)
Immediate Holding Company: HUMBERSIDE COMMUNICATION EQUIPMENT LIMITED
Registration no: 01320576 **Date established:** 1977
Turnover: £250,000 - £500,000 **No.of Employees:** 1 - 10
Product Groups: 37

Date of Accounts	Dec 11	Dec 10	Dec 09
Working Capital	229	361	557
Fixed Assets	4m	4m	4m
Current Assets	650	666	1m

Jewson Ltd

Unit C3-C4 Larsen Road, Goole, DN14 6XF
Tel: 01405-763068 **Fax:** 01405-763448
Website: http://www.jewson.co.uk
Directors: P. Hindle (MD)
Managers: M. Coates (District Mgr)
Ultimate Holding Company: COMPAGNIE DE SAINT GOBAIN (FRANCE)
Immediate Holding Company: JEWSON LIMITED
Registration no: 00348407 **VAT No.:** GB 497 7184 83
Date established: 1939 **Turnover:** £75m - £125m
No.of Employees: 11 - 20 **Product Groups:** 66

Date of Accounts	Dec 11	Dec 10	Dec 09
Sales Turnover	1606m	1547m	1485m
Pre Tax Profit/Loss	18m	100m	45m
Working Capital	-345m	-250m	-349m
Fixed Assets	496m	387m	461m
Current Assets	657m	1005m	1320m
Current Liabilities	66m	120m	64m

Marine & Industrial Transmissions Ltd

80 Weeland Road Hensall, Goole, DN14 0QE
Tel: 01977-661467 **Fax:** 01977-662099
E-mail: g.clarke@mitgroup.co.uk
Website: http://www.mitgroup.co.uk
Managers: G. Clarke (Mgr)
Immediate Holding Company: MARINE AND INDUSTRIAL TRANSMISSIONS LIMITED
Registration no: 01183364 **Date established:** 1974
No.of Employees: 11 - 20 **Product Groups:** 35, 36, 39, 45

Date of Accounts	Apr 11	Apr 10	Apr 09
Sales Turnover	8m	9m	12m
Pre Tax Profit/Loss	316	1m	1m
Working Capital	2m	2m	3m
Fixed Assets	391	297	274
Current Assets	5m	4m	5m
Current Liabilities	542	687	752

P W M (Sales) Ltd

Gowdall Lane Pollington, Goole, DN14 0AU
Tel: 01405-862688 **Fax:** 01405-862622
E-mail: info@pwm-sales.co.uk
Website: http://www.pwm-sales.co.uk
Directors: P. Welburn (Dir)
Immediate Holding Company: PWM (Sales) Ltd
Registration no: 03003088 **Date established:** 1994
Turnover: £500,000 - £1m **No.of Employees:** 1 - 10 **Product Groups:** 29, 32, 40, 41, 44, 45, 47, 52, 54, 66, 67, 83

Date of Accounts	Jan 10	Jan 09	Jan 08
Working Capital	136	116	102
Fixed Assets	68	60	71
Current Assets	225	218	191

Pipe Major David Waterton-Anderson KSG

Stapleton Lodge High Street, Carlton, Goole, DN14 9LU
Tel: 01405-860165 **Fax:** 01405-860165
E-mail: dwa@pipingscot.co.uk
Website: http://www.pipingscot.com
Directors: D. Waterton-Anderson (Prop), D. Waterton Anderson Ksg (Prop)
No.of Employees: 1 - 10 **Product Groups:** 89

Power-Rite UK Ltd

The Gate House Claypit Lane, Carlton, Goole, DN14 9PR
Tel: 0844-800 8472 **Fax:** 01405-869686
E-mail: shaun@power-rite.co.uk
Website: http://www.power-rite.co.uk
Directors: S. Hymes (Co Sec), S. Davey (Dir)
Immediate Holding Company: POWER-RITE (UK) LIMITED
Registration no: 05148895 **Date established:** 2004 **Turnover:** £1m - £2m
No.of Employees: 1 - 10 **Product Groups:** 83

Date of Accounts	Jul 11	Jul 10	Jul 09
Working Capital	-113	-367	-209
Fixed Assets	575	705	828
Current Assets	356	285	236

Repair Protection & Maintenance Ltd

Roall Lane Kellington, Goole, DN14 0NY
Tel: 01977-663111 **Fax:** 01977-663222
E-mail: dan@rpmltd.co.uk
Website: http://www.rpmltd.co.uk
Directors: D. Macdonald (MD), P. Hodgson (Dir)
Managers: G. Roberts (Sales Eng)
Registration no: 03298689 **Date established:** 1997 **Turnover:** £1m - £2m
No.of Employees: 11 - 20 **Product Groups:** 30, 31, 32, 33, 34, 51

Date of Accounts	Jun 11	Jun 10	Jun 09
Working Capital	129	20	167
Fixed Assets	67	83	52
Current Assets	259	165	438

Tarmac Ltd (Traffic Management)

Roall Lane Roall, Goole, DN14 0NA
Tel: 01977-662633 **Fax:** 01977- 662638
E-mail: info@tarmac-central.co.uk
Website: http://www.tarmac.co.uk
Managers: C. Wright (Chief Mgr), E. Garrett (Fin Mgr)
Ultimate Holding Company: ANGLO AMERICAN PLC
Immediate Holding Company: TARMAC LIMITED
Registration no: 00453791 **Date established:** 1948
No.of Employees: 21 - 50 **Product Groups:** 33

Date of Accounts	Dec 11	Dec 10	Dec 09
Sales Turnover	1081m	1069m	1247m
Pre Tax Profit/Loss	-20m	75m	-47m
Working Capital	-86m	-24m	25m
Fixed Assets	1199m	1244m	1391m
Current Assets	329m	321m	431m
Current Liabilities	99m	93m	168m

Technikraft Ltd

Britannia Road, Goole, DN14 6ET
Tel: 01405-768815
E-mail: sales@technikraft.co.uk
Website: http://www.technikraft.co.uk
Directors: M. Gibson (Ptnr)
Immediate Holding Company: TECHNIKRAFT LIMITED
Registration no: 02124501 **Date established:** 1987
No.of Employees: 21 - 50 **Product Groups:** 32

Date of Accounts	Nov 11	Nov 10	Nov 09
Working Capital	857	770	879
Fixed Assets	193	205	170
Current Assets	2m	2m	2m

Timloc Building Products

Rawcliffe Road, Goole, DN14 6UQ
Tel: 01405-765567 **Fax:** 01405-720479
E-mail: sales@timloc.co.uk
Website: http://www.timloc.co.uk
Directors: A. Magson (Co Sec), M. Leaf (MD), D. Coleman (Fin), D. Bean (Sales)
Managers: A. McHale (Buyer), C. Langley (Mktg Serv Mgr)
Ultimate Holding Company: THE ALUMASC GROUP PLC
Immediate Holding Company: TIMLOC BUILDING PRODUCTS LIMITED
Registration no: 00930724 **VAT No.:** GB 809 4429 16
Date established: 1968 **Turnover:** £2m - £5m **No.of Employees:** 51 - 100
Product Groups: 30, 33, 35, 40, 66

Tunstall Healthcare UK Ltd

Whitley Lodge Whitley Bridge, Whitley, Goole, DN14 0HR
Tel: 01977-661234 **Fax:** 01977-662570
E-mail: enquiries@tunstall.co.uk
Website: http://www.tunstall.co.uk
Bank(s): National Westminster
Directors: G. Baldwin (Grp Chief Exec), S. Essam (Pers), R. Rawcliffe (Sales), N. Duffy (Fin), J. Cain (Tech Serv), A. Rogan (Grp Mktg)
Managers: A. Allen, K. Dyson
Ultimate Holding Company: TUNSTALL HEALTHCARE GROUP LIMITED
Immediate Holding Company: TUNSTALL GROUP LIMITED
Registration no: 00580348 **Date established:** 1957
Turnover: £75m - £125m **No.of Employees:** 501 - 1000
Product Groups: 37, 40

Date of Accounts	Sep 11	Sep 10	Sep 09
Sales Turnover	104m	104m	99m
Pre Tax Profit/Loss	34m	31m	26m
Working Capital	107m	87m	65m
Fixed Assets	17m	13m	13m
Current Assets	207m	181m	149m
Current Liabilities	23m	95m	20m

Hessle

939 Design LImited

The Studio 10 The Circle, Hessle, HU13 0QJ
Tel: 01482-627939
E-mail: mike@939design.com
Website: http://www.939design.com/
Registration no: 05673513 **Date established:** 2006
Turnover: Up to £250,000 **No.of Employees:** 1 - 10 **Product Groups:** 44

Date of Accounts	Dec 08	Dec 07	Dec 06
Working Capital	-2	-1	-1
Fixed Assets	6	6	1
Current Assets	39	32	12
Current Liabilities	41	33	13

ADT Fire & Security plc

Security House 3-4 Priory Park Saxon Way, Hessle, HU13 9PB
Tel: 0800-542 3108 **Fax:** 01482-579601
E-mail: sales@adt.co.uk
Website: http://www.adt.co.uk
Managers: B. Flynn (Mgr), I. Stones (Sales Prom Mgr), S. Foster (Mgr)
Immediate Holding Company: ADT FIRE AND SECURITY PLC
Registration no: 01161045 **Date established:** 1974
No.of Employees: 51 - 100 **Product Groups:** 37, 38, 39, 40, 47, 52, 81

Aalco
Saxon Way Priory Park West, Hessle, HU13 9PB
Tel: 01482-626262 **Fax:** 01482-626263
E-mail: hull@aalco.co.uk
Website: http://www.aalco.co.uk
Bank(s): National Westminster Bank Plc
Directors: P. Marritt (MD), W. Taylor (Fin)
Managers: D. James (Quality Control)
Immediate Holding Company: STRAIT DEVELOPMENTS LIMITED
Registration no: 02880621 **Date established:** 2004
Turnover: £250,000 - £500,000 **No.of Employees:** 21 - 50
Product Groups: 34, 35, 36, 66

Date of Accounts	Dec 11	Dec 10	Dec 09
Sales Turnover	8m	6m	16m
Pre Tax Profit/Loss	-3m	-1m	-6m
Working Capital	-3m	-1m	-5m
Fixed Assets	33	1m	1m
Current Assets	5m	4m	5m
Current Liabilities	5m	3m	6m

Afos Ltd
Kingston House Saxon Way Priory Park, Hessle, HU13 9PB
Tel: 01482-372100 **Fax:** 01482-372150
E-mail: peter.martin@afosgroup.com
Website: http://www.afosgroup.com
Bank(s): Lloyds TSB Bank plc
Directors: M. Sutton (MD), L. Featherstone (Co Sec)
Managers: N. Allwood (Tech Serv Mgr), S. Higson (Mktg Serv Mgr)
Immediate Holding Company: AFOS LIMITED
Registration no: 05874829 **Date established:** 2006 **Turnover:** £2m - £5m
No.of Employees: 11 - 20 **Product Groups:** 26, 40, 41, 48

Date of Accounts	Dec 11	Dec 10	Dec 09
Sales Turnover	3m	3m	3m
Pre Tax Profit/Loss	117	110	195
Working Capital	183	52	-42
Fixed Assets	223	238	203
Current Assets	1m	1m	930
Current Liabilities	546	151	140

Anlaby Wrought Iron
77 Swanland Road, Hessle, HU13 0NN
Tel: 01482-647038 **Fax:** 01482-647038
E-mail: kenlol@freeuk.com
Directors: K. Dunn (Prop)
Date established: 2006 **No.of Employees:** 1 - 10 **Product Groups:** 26, 35

Citech Energy Recovery Systems UK Ltd
Salisbury House Saxon Way, Hessle, HU13 9PB
Tel: 01482-719746 **Fax:** 01482-719740
E-mail: info@citech.co.uk
Website: http://www.citech.co.uk
Directors: Z. Sedek (MD)
Managers: S. Wati (Fin Mgr), J. Purdy (Personnel), D. Binns (Sales & Mktg Mg)
Ultimate Holding Company: TANJUNG CITECH UK LIMITED
Immediate Holding Company: CITECH ENERGY RECOVERY SYSTEMS UK LIMITED
Registration no: 06674030 **Date established:** 2008 **Turnover:** £5m - £10m
No.of Employees: 1 - 10 **Product Groups:** 40, 42, 67

Date of Accounts	Dec 11	Dec 10	Dec 09
Sales Turnover	8m	6m	16m
Pre Tax Profit/Loss	-3m	-1m	-6m
Working Capital	-3m	-1m	-5m
Fixed Assets	33	1m	1m
Current Assets	5m	4m	5m
Current Liabilities	5m	3m	6m

Fenner plc
Hesslewood Office Park Ferriby Road, Hessle, HU13 0PW
Tel: 01482-626500 **Fax:** 01482-626502
E-mail: mark.abrahams@fenner-group.com
Website: http://www.fenner.com
Bank(s): Barclays, Trinity House
Directors: D. Bradbury (Co Sec), N. Hobson (Grp Chief Exec), R. Perry (Fin)
Managers: A. Fussey (Tech Serv Mgr)
Immediate Holding Company: FENNER PLC
Registration no: 00329377 **VAT No.:** GB 167 2713 55
Date established: 1937 **Turnover:** £500m - £1,000m
No.of Employees: 21 - 50 **Product Groups:** 45

Date of Accounts	Aug 11	Aug 10	Aug 09
Sales Turnover	718m	553m	499m
Pre Tax Profit/Loss	70m	37m	6m
Working Capital	132m	61m	45m
Fixed Assets	441m	404m	389m
Current Assets	326m	215m	181m
Current Liabilities	92m	70m	67m

Identify UK Ltd
Prestongate, Hessle, HU13 0RD
Tel: 01482-222070 **Fax:** 01482-327214
E-mail: douglas@rfidsystems.co.uk
Website: http://www.rfidsystems.co.uk
Directors: I. Hazeel (Fin)
Immediate Holding Company: IDENTIFY UK LIMITED
Registration no: 03603023 **Date established:** 1998
No.of Employees: 1 - 10 **Product Groups:** 37

Date of Accounts	Dec 11	Dec 10	Dec 09
Working Capital	-119	-97	-193
Fixed Assets	11	12	16
Current Assets	187	138	146

Impact Fork Trucks Ltd
Saxon Way Priory Park, Hessle, HU13 9PB
Tel: 01482-329824 **Fax:** 01469-578450
E-mail: steven.kent@impact-handling.com
Website: http://www.impact-handling.com
Directors: A. Sperrin (Fin)
Managers: S. Kent (Ops Mgr)
Ultimate Holding Company: EQSTRA HOLDINGS LTD (SOUTH AFRICA)
Immediate Holding Company: IMPACT FORK TRUCKS LIMITED
Registration no: 02550150 **Date established:** 1990
No.of Employees: 11 - 20 **Product Groups:** 35, 39, 45

Date of Accounts	Jun 11	Jun 10	Jun 09
Sales Turnover	26m	26m	32m
Pre Tax Profit/Loss	820	293	-3m
Working Capital	-21m	-3m	-13m
Fixed Assets	27m	24m	28m
Current Assets	8m	8m	10m
Current Liabilities	25m	3m	4m

Intrasource Ltd
Redcliff Court Redcliff Road, Hessle, HU13 0EY
Tel: 01482-628800 **Fax:** 01482-628801
E-mail: enquiry@intrasource.co.uk
Website: http://www.intrasource.co.uk
Directors: C. Jacques (MD), D. Hurt (MD), C. Emmerson (Chief Op Offcr)
Registration no: 03916612 **No.of Employees:** 51 - 100
Product Groups: 44

Date of Accounts	Jan 10	Jan 09	Jan 08
Working Capital	40	50	64
Fixed Assets	24	10	14
Current Assets	347	348	470

J L Seaton (t/a Seatons)
First Floor 7 Waterside Business Park Livingstone Road, Hessle, HU13 0EG
Tel: 01482-579700 **Fax:** 01482-647313
E-mail: enquiries@seatons-uk.co.uk
Website: http://www.croda.com/seatons
Bank(s): National Westminster Bank Plc
Directors: M. Coverdale (MD)
Ultimate Holding Company: CRODA INTERNATIONAL PLC
Immediate Holding Company: TWS WELLNESS LTD
Registration no: 02554548 **VAT No.:** GB 167 6797 03
Date established: 2012 **No.of Employees:** 11 - 20 **Product Groups:** 20, 31, 32, 48, 63, 66

L G S A Marine
Dunston House Livingstone Road, Hessle, HU13 0EG
Tel: 01482-629993 **Fax:** 01482-640918
E-mail: hull@lgsasurvey.co.uk
Website: http://www.lgsamarine.co.uk
Managers: D. Fenner (Mgr)
Immediate Holding Company: NET EXPECTATIONS LIMITED
Registration no: 03151141 **VAT No.:** GB 164 6020 84
Date established: 2006 **No.of Employees:** 1 - 10 **Product Groups:** 74

Date of Accounts	Mar 12	Mar 11	Mar 10
Working Capital	96	83	75
Fixed Assets	15	13	16
Current Assets	370	285	224
Current Liabilities	N/A	N/A	98

Andrew Marr International Ltd
Livingstone Road, Hessle, HU13 0EE
Tel: 01482-642304 **Fax:** 01482-642303
E-mail: info@marce.co.uk
Website: http://www.marce.co.uk
Directors: C. Burt (Co Sec), M. Moore (MD)
Managers: P. Farrar (Comptroller)
Immediate Holding Company: ANDREW MARR INTERNATIONAL LIMITED
Registration no: 02011550 **Date established:** 1986
Turnover: £250m - £500m **No.of Employees:** 21 - 50 **Product Groups:** 62

Date of Accounts	Mar 11	Mar 10	Mar 09
Sales Turnover	450m	334m	344m
Pre Tax Profit/Loss	13m	9m	11m
Working Capital	29m	33m	31m
Fixed Assets	35m	26m	27m
Current Assets	80m	65m	66m
Current Liabilities	N/A	14m	18m

J Marr Seafoods Ltd
Livingstone Road, Hessle, HU13 0EE
Tel: 01482-642302 **Fax:** 01482-642303
E-mail: seafoods@marsea.co.uk
Website: http://www.marsea.co.uk
Directors: M. Moore (MD)
Managers: S. Morris
Ultimate Holding Company: ANDREW MARR INTERNATIONAL LIMITED
Immediate Holding Company: J. MARR SEAFOODS (HOLDINGS) LIMITED
Registration no: 00656332 **Date established:** 1960
Turnover: £125m - £250m **No.of Employees:** 21 - 50 **Product Groups:** 62

Date of Accounts	Mar 11	Mar 10	Mar 08
Working Capital	40	40	40
Current Assets	40	40	40

Neill & Brown Global Logistics Group Ltd
Overseas House Waterside Business Park, Hessle, HU13 0AW
Tel: 01482-644287 **Fax:** 01482-644284
E-mail: info@neillbrown.com
Website: http://www.neillbrown.com
Bank(s): Yorkshire Bank PLC
Directors: P. Brown (Dir), P. Brown (Prop), P. Whinham (Dir), G. Atkinson (Dir)
Immediate Holding Company: NEILL & BROWN GLOBAL LOGISTICS GROUP LIMITED
Registration no: 02253582 **VAT No.:** GB 167 9696 91
Date established: 1988 **Turnover:** £10m - £20m
No.of Employees: 51 - 100 **Product Groups:** 76, 84

Date of Accounts	Apr 11	Apr 10	Apr 09
Sales Turnover	16m	14m	14m
Pre Tax Profit/Loss	1m	731	696
Working Capital	1m	1m	624
Fixed Assets	2m	2m	3m
Current Assets	5m	5m	4m
Current Liabilities	2m	1m	1m

Hull

3g Foodservice Ltd
30 West Dock Street, Hull, HU3 4HL
Tel: 01482-593700 **Fax:** 01482-324550
E-mail: info@3gfoodservice.co.uk
Website: http://www.3gfoodservice.co.uk
Managers: R. Milburn (Fin Mgr)
Ultimate Holding Company: F. Smales & Son Ltd
Immediate Holding Company: 3G FOOD SERVICE (ANDOVER) LIMITED
Registration no: 01604106 **Date established:** 1981
Turnover: £20m - £50m **No.of Employees:** 11 - 20 **Product Groups:** 09, 20, 62, 69

A P D Communications Ltd
1e Newlands Centre Inglemire Lane, Hull, HU6 7TQ
Tel: 01482-808300 **Fax:** 01482-803901
E-mail: sales@apdcomms.co.uk
Website: http://www.apdcomms.com
Bank(s): National Westminster Bank Plc
Directors: R. Brown (Fin), P. Sinnett (Co Sec)
Managers: M. Hughes (Mktg Serv Mgr), A. McArthy (Purch Mgr), S. Hancock (Tech Serv Mgr), S. Lazenby (Personnel)
Ultimate Holding Company: LYNX GROUP LIMITED
Immediate Holding Company: APD COMMUNICATIONS LIMITED
Registration no: 01847526 **VAT No.:** GB 686 4276 90
Date established: 1984 **Turnover:** £5m - £10m
No.of Employees: 101 - 250 **Product Groups:** 44

Date of Accounts	Sep 11	Sep 10	Sep 09
Sales Turnover	9m	11m	10m
Pre Tax Profit/Loss	-132	1m	121
Working Capital	454	3m	2m
Fixed Assets	226	213	140
Current Assets	4m	5m	4m
Current Liabilities	3m	2m	2m

Aarhuskarlshamn Hull Ltd
Aarhus Karlshamn King George Dock, Hull, HU9 5PX
Tel: 01482-701271 **Fax:** 01482-709447
E-mail: john.hart@aak.com
Website: http://www.aak.com
Directors: D. Taylor (Fin)
Managers: D. Milns, J. Murdoch (Sales & Mktg Mg), J. Hart (Factory Mgr), D. Cockerill (Tech Serv Mgr), L. Bales (Personnel)
Ultimate Holding Company: AARHUSKARLSHAMN AB (SWEDEN)
Immediate Holding Company: AARHUSKARLSHAMN HULL LIMITED
Registration no: 02193829 **VAT No.:** GB 598 8679 37
Date established: 1987 **Turnover:** £20m - £50m
No.of Employees: 251 - 500 **Product Groups:** 20

Date of Accounts	Dec 11	Dec 10	Dec 09
Pre Tax Profit/Loss	2	17	-21
Working Capital	8m	8m	8m
Fixed Assets	282	282	277
Current Assets	9m	9m	9m
Current Liabilities	6	47	11

Abnormal Load Services part of ALS (Freight Management Group) Ltd
1501 Hedon Road, Hull, HU9 5NX
Tel: 01482-796214 **Fax:** 01482-707650
E-mail: info@als-europe.com
Website: http://www.abnormal-loads.com
Managers: P. Tuton (Tech Serv Mgr), J. Watson (Sales Admin), A. Civil (Chief Mgr), M. Hussey (Mktg Serv Mgr), M. Peacock (Fin Mgr)
Ultimate Holding Company: A.L.S. (FREIGHT MANAGEMENT GROUP) LIMITED
Immediate Holding Company: ABNORMAL LOAD SERVICES (INTERNATIONAL) LIMITED
Registration no: 01465007 **Date established:** 1979
Turnover: £10m - £20m **No.of Employees:** 21 - 50 **Product Groups:** 39, 45, 61, 72, 74, 75, 76, 77, 80, 84

Date of Accounts	Dec 11	Dec 10	Dec 09
Sales Turnover	15m	13m	15m
Pre Tax Profit/Loss	115	11	49
Working Capital	116	13	-33
Fixed Assets	45	67	104
Current Assets	3m	3m	3m
Current Liabilities	335	146	715

Adaptable Fork Lift Services Ltd
33 Copenhagen Road, Hull, HU7 0XQ
Tel: 01482-830308 **Fax:** 01482-825440
E-mail: chris@adaptableforklifts.co.uk
Website: http://www.adaptableforklifts.co.uk
Directors: C. Moulds (MD), J. Moulds (Fin)
Immediate Holding Company: ADAPTABLE FORKLIFT SERVICES LIMITED
Registration no: 03307316 **Date established:** 1997
No.of Employees: 1 - 10 **Product Groups:** 35, 39, 45

Date of Accounts	Apr 12	Apr 11	Apr 10
Working Capital	134	90	89
Fixed Assets	261	275	239
Current Assets	304	216	206

Adfil Ltd
Unit 28 Bergen Way, Hull, HU7 0YQ
Tel: 01482-863777 **Fax:** 01482-872800
E-mail: info@adfil.co.uk
Website: http://www.adfil.co.uk
Directors: D. Carter (Fin)
Managers: E. Lewis (Admin Off)
Registration no: 02272096 **VAT No.:** 500 7313 01 **Date established:** 1988
Turnover: £1m - £2m **No.of Employees:** 11 - 20 **Product Groups:** 23

Aerotech Engineering Ltd
Unit 40 Louis Pearlman Centre Goulton Street, Hull, HU3 4DL
Tel: 01482-586300 **Fax:** 01482-586303
E-mail: john@aerotecheng.com
Website: http://www.aerotecheng.com
Directors: J. Cudbertson (MD), J. Hasinski (I.T. Dir)
Registration no: 03025658 **Date established:** 2001
No.of Employees: 1 - 10 **Product Groups:** 33, 42, 45, 66, 67

Date of Accounts	Feb 10	Feb 09	Feb 08
Working Capital	11	8	11
Current Assets	44	54	53

Akzo Nobel Packaging Coatings Ltd
Rotterdam Road, Hull, HU7 0XX
Tel: 01482-825101 **Fax:** 01482-838231
E-mail: alvin.wilson@akzonobel.com
Website: http://www.akzonobel.com
Bank(s): Lloyds TSB Bank plc
Directors: N. Paton (Co Sec)
Managers: A. Wilson (Works Gen Mgr)
Ultimate Holding Company: AKZO NOBEL NV (NETHERLANDS)
Immediate Holding Company: AKZO NOBEL PACKAGING COATINGS LIMITED
Registration no: 00059837 **Date established:** 1998 **Turnover:** £5m - £10m
No.of Employees: 51 - 100 **Product Groups:** 32

Date of Accounts	Dec 11	Dec 10	Dec 09
Sales Turnover	103m	77m	68m
Pre Tax Profit/Loss	11m	21m	15m
Working Capital	25m	21m	18m
Fixed Assets	18m	14m	11m
Current Assets	51m	51m	48m
Current Liabilities	10m	13m	10m

Andritz Seed & Bio Fuel Ltd

Stockholm Road, Hull, HU7 0XL
Tel: 01482-825119 **Fax:** 01482-839806
Website: http://www.andritz.com
Bank(s): Lloyds
Directors: D. Pattersfield (MD)
Managers: D. Tattersfield (Chief Mgr)
Immediate Holding Company: ANDRITZ FEED & BIOFUEL LIMITED
Registration no: 04122501 **VAT No.:** GB 766 9366 70
Date established: 2000 **Turnover:** £2m - £5m **No.of Employees:** 21 - 50
Product Groups: 45

Date of Accounts	Dec 11	Dec 10	Dec 09
Sales Turnover	5m	5m	5m
Pre Tax Profit/Loss	321	437	399
Working Capital	1m	2m	2m
Fixed Assets	302	291	305
Current Assets	3m	3m	3m
Current Liabilities	276	307	317

Apollo Plastics

62 St James Street, Hull, HU3 2DH
Tel: 01482-325394 **Fax:** 01482-229826
E-mail: info@apolloplasticshull.co.uk
Website: http://www.apolloplasticshull.co.uk
Directors: R. White (MD)
Immediate Holding Company: HEYDAY INDUSTRIAL LTD
Registration no: 01375330 **VAT No.:** GB 317 5144 72
Date established: 1978 **Turnover:** £500,000 - £1m
No.of Employees: 1 - 10 **Product Groups:** 30

Apple International Ltd

Unit 23 Gothenburg Way, Hull, HU7 0YG
Tel: 01482-824200 **Fax:** 01482-824196
E-mail: info@appleint.co.uk
Website: http://www.appleint.co.uk
Bank(s): Barclays
Directors: A. Towle (Sales), S. Smith (MD), L. Smith (Co Sec)
Managers: A. Fraser (Tech Serv Mgr), J. Ellerington
Immediate Holding Company: APPLE INTERNATIONAL LIMITED
Registration no: 06527927 **VAT No.:** GB 375 4930 26
Date established: 2008 **Turnover:** £2m - £5m **No.of Employees:** 21 - 50
Product Groups: 40, 41, 42, 45, 67

Date of Accounts	May 11	May 10	May 09
Working Capital	-38	-124	-13
Fixed Assets	98	119	141
Current Assets	608	635	464

Arco Ltd

PO Box 21, Hull, HU1 2SH
Tel: 01482-222522 **Fax:** 01924-280262
E-mail: arco.central@arco.co.uk
Website: http://www.arco.co.uk
Directors: K. Quinn (Mkt Research), T. Martin (MD)
Ultimate Holding Company: ARCO LIMITED
Immediate Holding Company: ARCO (G.B.) LIMITED
Registration no: 01967332 **Date established:** 1985
Turnover: £10m - £20m **No.of Employees:** 501 - 1000
Product Groups: 24, 29, 30

Date of Accounts	Jun 11	Jun 10	Jun 09
Sales Turnover	229m	216m	214m
Pre Tax Profit/Loss	98	6m	260
Working Capital	32m	27m	29m
Fixed Assets	19m	21m	23m
Current Assets	82m	67m	62m
Current Liabilities	12m	13m	8m

Armstong Precision Components Ltd

Unit 28-29 Stoneferry Park Foster Street, Hull, HU8 8BT
Tel: 01482-325425 **Fax:** 01482-327229
E-mail: leigh.burgoyne@apc-caparo.com
Website: http://www.apc-caparo.com
Bank(s): Barclays, Birmingham
Directors: L. Burgoyne (MD), J. Bastow (Fin)
Managers: C. Hodges (Sales Prom Mgr), K. Robinson (Sales Admin)
Immediate Holding Company: RCT GROUP LIMITED
Registration no: 05839696 **VAT No.:** GB 245 2598 470 088
Date established: 2002 **Turnover:** £2m - £5m **No.of Employees:** 21 - 50
Product Groups: 35

Date of Accounts	Aug 11	Aug 10	Aug 09
Working Capital	-73	-71	-65
Fixed Assets	97	87	115
Current Assets	15	18	29

Assco Humber

11 Nelson Street, Hull, HU1 1XE
Tel: 01482-324336 **Fax:** 01482-212064
E-mail: admin@assco.co.uk
Website: http://www.assco.co.uk
Directors: G. Markwell (Co Sec), M. Straw (Dir), S. Pullen (MD)
Registration no: 01231388 **VAT No.:** GB 282 3528 53
Turnover: £500,000 - £1m **No.of Employees:** 1 - 10 **Product Groups:** 39, 45, 74, 76

Atkinson & Prickett (a division of Thomas E. Kettlewell & Sons Ltd)

PO Box 35, Hull, HU1 1RJ
Tel: 01482-324191 **Fax:** 01482-224914
E-mail: hull@kettlewell.com
Website: http://www.kettlewell.com
Directors: T. Kettlewell (Dir)
Registration no: 00229063 **VAT No.:** GB 166 8879 94
Date established: 1928 **Turnover:** £5m - £10m **No.of Employees:** 1 - 10
Product Groups: 76

Attric Ltd

Sovereign House Craven Street South, Hull, HU9 1AP
Tel: 01482-324558 **Fax:** 01482-216045
E-mail: sales@attric.co.uk
Website: http://www.attric.co.uk
Directors: D. Risebury (MD)
Managers: I. Oliver (Mgr), D. Risebury (Mgr), A. Long (I.T. Exec)
Ultimate Holding Company: LIST GROUP PLC
Immediate Holding Company: ATTRIC LTD
Registration no: 06134174 **Date established:** 2007
No.of Employees: 21 - 50 **Product Groups:** 80

Date of Accounts	Apr 11	Apr 10	Apr 09
Sales Turnover	6m	6m	6m
Pre Tax Profit/Loss	173	143	55

Working Capital	787	544	455
Fixed Assets	255	635	656
Current Assets	2m	2m	2m
Current Liabilities	508	407	400

Axesrus Ltd

Mollison Road, Hull, HU4 7HH
Tel: 01482-647630
E-mail: sales@axesrus.com
Website: http://www.axesrus.com
Directors: J. Jackson (Fin), A. Jackson (Ptnr)
Immediate Holding Company: AXESRUS LIMITED
Registration no: 05272347 **Date established:** 2004
No.of Employees: 1 - 10 **Product Groups:** 49

Date of Accounts	Oct 11	Oct 10	Oct 09
Working Capital	264	342	268
Fixed Assets	101	1	N/A
Current Assets	327	407	337

B & A Tool Hire

D Therm Road, Hull, HU8 7BF
Tel: 01482-594413 **Fax:** 01482-594417
E-mail: dave.artley@bandascaffolding.co.uk
Website: http://www.bandascaffolding.co.uk
Directors: D. Artley (MD)
Immediate Holding Company: VIC COUPLAND LIMITED
Registration no: 01623817 **Date established:** 1937
No.of Employees: 1 - 10 **Product Groups:** 46

Date of Accounts	Apr 12	Apr 11	Apr 10
Working Capital	486	369	414
Fixed Assets	280	290	264
Current Assets	965	717	715

B M H Feedgear

Gothenburg Way Sutton Fields Industrial Estate, Hull, HU7 0YG
Tel: 01482-831736 **Fax:** 01482-878363
E-mail: d.broughton@bmhfeedgear.co.uk
Website: http://www.bmhfeedgear.co.uk
Directors: D. Broughton (Ptnr)
No.of Employees: 1 - 10 **Product Groups:** 38, 42

Barek Lift Trucks Ltd

Marvel Street, Hull, HU9 1DS
Tel: 01482-218151 **Fax:** 01482-324142
E-mail: mleek@barek.fsbusiness.co.uk
Website: http://www.barek.fsbusiness.co.uk
Directors: M. Leek (MD), J. Chapman (Fin)
Immediate Holding Company: BAREK LIFT TRUCKS LIMITED
Registration no: 03214102 **Date established:** 1996
No.of Employees: 1 - 10 **Product Groups:** 35, 39, 45

Date of Accounts	Aug 11	Aug 10	Aug 09
Working Capital	342	296	184
Fixed Assets	464	479	565
Current Assets	342	397	326

Becker UK Ltd

Link 63 Liverpool Street, Hull, HU3 4XS
Tel: 01482-835280 **Fax:** 01482-831275
E-mail: sales@becker.co.uk
Website: http://www.becker-international.com
Bank(s): Barclays
Directors: N. Hughes (Dir)
Ultimate Holding Company: GEBR BECKER GMBH & CO (GERMANY)
Immediate Holding Company: BECKER U K LIMITED
Registration no: 01688038 **VAT No.:** GB 317 2014 03
Date established: 1982 **Turnover:** £2m - £5m **No.of Employees:** 11 - 20
Product Groups: 40

Date of Accounts	Dec 11	Dec 10	Dec 09
Working Capital	2m	1m	1m
Fixed Assets	206	193	124
Current Assets	2m	2m	2m

Bemrosebooth Paragon Ltd

Stockholm Road, Hull, HU7 0XY
Tel: 01482-826343 **Fax:** 01482-826667
E-mail: contact@bemrosebooth.co.uk
Website: http://www.bemrosebooth.com
Bank(s): HSBC Bank plc
Directors: A. Lindsey (MD)
Ultimate Holding Company: BEMROSE BOOTH INVESTMENT COMPANY LIMITED
Immediate Holding Company: BEMROSEBOOTH LIMITED
Registration no: 03978232 **VAT No.:** GB 558 4401 33
Date established: 2000 **Turnover:** £50m - £75m
No.of Employees: 51 - 100 **Product Groups:** 28

Date of Accounts	Dec 05	Dec 06	Dec 07
Sales Turnover	61m	62m	57m
Pre Tax Profit/Loss	-1m	-696	-1m
Working Capital	5m	4m	3m
Fixed Assets	15m	14m	12m
Current Assets	23m	23m	24m
Current Liabilities	8m	7m	6m

Bericap UK Ltd

Sutton Fields Industrial Estate Oslo Road, Hull, HU7 0YN
Tel: 01482-826666 **Fax:** 01482-832839
E-mail: info@bericap.com
Website: http://www.bericap.com
Bank(s): National Westminster Bank Plc
Directors: M. Wilkinson (Sales), A. Rascoe (Pers), P. Shearman (Fin), P. Evans (Dir)
Managers: J. Dixon (Purch Mgr)
Immediate Holding Company: BERICAP U.K. LIMITED.
Registration no: 02566980 **VAT No.:** GB 167 3334 58
Date established: 1990 **Turnover:** £20m - £50m
No.of Employees: 101 - 250 **Product Groups:** 30, 35

Date of Accounts	Dec 11	Dec 10	Dec 09
Sales Turnover	31m	24m	21m
Pre Tax Profit/Loss	2m	1m	1m
Working Capital	374	-2m	1m
Fixed Assets	14m	16m	9m
Current Assets	10m	7m	7m
Current Liabilities	1m	1m	1m

Bonus Plug In Systems

Unit 1 Connaught Road Kingswood, Hull, HU7 3AP
Tel: 01482-313700 **Fax:** 01482-588753
Website: http://www.bonuspluginsystems.co.uk
Bank(s): National Westminster Bank Plc & Barclays Bank PLC
Directors: S. Bonus (Ch), S. Boanas (MD)
Managers: G. Atkins (Purch Mgr), G. Sanderson (Sales Prom Mgr), I. Norton (Buyer)
Ultimate Holding Company: SGS INTERNATIONAL INC (USA)
Immediate Holding Company: SGS PACKAGING EUROPE LIMITED
Registration no: 00631503 **VAT No.:** GB 347 7884 01
Date established: 1959 **Turnover:** £10m - £20m
No.of Employees: 21 - 50 **Product Groups:** 39, 67

Braham & Dixon Ltd

88 Hodgson Street, Hull, HU8 7JB
Tel: 01482-328202 **Fax:** 01482-211865
E-mail: info@bd-eng.co.uk
Website: http://www.bd-eng.co.uk
Bank(s): HSBC Bank plc
Directors: E. Mudd (MD)
Immediate Holding Company: BRAHAM AND DIXON (1985) LIMITED
Registration no: 01670782 **Date established:** 1982
Turnover: £500,000 - £1m **No.of Employees:** 11 - 20
Product Groups: 45, 84

Date of Accounts	Apr 11	Apr 10	Apr 09
Working Capital	247	273	272
Fixed Assets	232	245	260
Current Assets	474	473	446

Broady Flow Controller Ltd

English Street, Hull, HU3 2DU
Tel: 01482-619600 **Fax:** 01482-619700
E-mail: sales@broady.co.uk
Website: http://www.broady.co.uk
Directors: R. Moulds (MD), A. Robinson (Purch)
Managers: D. Jude, P. Derrick (Tech Serv Mgr)
Immediate Holding Company: BROADY FLOW CONTROL LIMITED
Registration no: 03959530 **Date established:** 2000 **Turnover:** £5m - £10m
No.of Employees: 51 - 100 **Product Groups:** 35, 36, 39, 40

Date of Accounts	Dec 11	Dec 10	Mar 10
Sales Turnover	9m	6m	10m
Pre Tax Profit/Loss	2m	764	2m
Working Capital	3m	4m	4m
Fixed Assets	629	626	867
Current Assets	6m	6m	6m
Current Liabilities	669	1m	1m

Burnand X H Ltd

66 Gillett Street, Hull, HU3 4JF
Tel: 01482-219596 **Fax:** 01482-826414
E-mail: hull@bxh.co.uk
Website: http://www.bxh.co.uk
Managers: A. Dalton (District Mgr)
Ultimate Holding Company: SCX LIMITED
Immediate Holding Company: BURNAND XH LIMITED
Registration no: 00680355 **Date established:** 1961
No.of Employees: 1 - 10 **Product Groups:** 36, 40

Date of Accounts	Mar 11	Mar 10	Mar 09
Sales Turnover	3m	3m	4m
Pre Tax Profit/Loss	1m	55	124
Working Capital	1m	-154	-214
Fixed Assets	182	203	223
Current Assets	2m	1m	1m
Current Liabilities	53	82	88

N R Burnett Ltd

West Carr Lane, Hull, HU7 0AW
Tel: 01482-838800 **Fax:** 01482-822110
E-mail: sales@nrburnett.co.uk
Website: http://www.nrburnett.co.uk
Directors: M. Fennell (MD), P. Burnett (Fin)
Immediate Holding Company: N.R. BURNETT (HOLDINGS) LIMITED
Registration no: 01783043 **VAT No.:** GB 599 2173 93
Date established: 1984 **No.of Employees:** 21 - 50 **Product Groups:** 08, 25

Date of Accounts	Sep 11	Sep 10	Sep 09
Working Capital	2m	2m	2m
Fixed Assets	2m	2m	2m
Current Assets	2m	2m	2m

C B North Ltd

65 Hedon Road, Hull, HU9 1LW
Tel: 01482-329847 **Fax:** 01482-215048
E-mail: info@cbnorth.co.uk
Website: http://www.cbnorth.co.uk
Bank(s): Barclays
Directors: A. North (Dir), R. North (Dir)
Immediate Holding Company: C.B.NORTH LIMITED
Registration no: 00327340 **Date established:** 1937 **Turnover:** £2m - £5m
No.of Employees: 21 - 50 **Product Groups:** 66

Date of Accounts	Sep 11	Sep 10	Sep 09
Working Capital	41	76	85
Fixed Assets	1m	1m	1m
Current Assets	799	732	599

C Jackson & Sons Ltd

633-653 Hedon Road, Hull, HU9 5LU
Tel: 01482-328472 **Fax:** 01482-384494
E-mail: office@cjackson.co.uk
Website: http://www.cjackson.co.uk
Directors: A. Jackson (MD)
Immediate Holding Company: C. JACKSON & SONS LIMITED
Registration no: 02800735 **Date established:** 1993 **Turnover:** £2m - £5m
No.of Employees: 21 - 50 **Product Groups:** 05, 25, 27, 32, 33, 35, 36, 38, 39, 41, 45, 47, 48, 52, 61, 66, 67, 68, 74, 76, 84, 87

Date of Accounts	Mar 11	Mar 10	Mar 09
Working Capital	579	782	794
Fixed Assets	1m	1m	1m
Current Assets	1m	1m	938

C & N Door Systems Ltd

Unit B 43 Gillett Street, Hull, HU3 4JF
Tel: 01482-666662 **Fax:** 01482-666662
E-mail: info@candndoorsystems.co.uk
Website: http://www.candndoorsystems.co.uk
Directors: N. Kinroy (MD)
Immediate Holding Company: C & N DOOR SYSTEMS LIMITED
Registration no: 05344554 **Date established:** 2005
No.of Employees: 1 - 10 **Product Groups:** 26, 35

Date of Accounts	Mar 11	Mar 10	Mar 09
Working Capital	6	13	28
Fixed Assets	17	17	12
Current Assets	61	69	108

Cablepoint Ltd
Amsterdam Road, Hull, HU7 0XF
Tel: 01482-837400 **Fax:** 01482-839651
E-mail: marketing@cablepoint.co.uk
Website: http://www.cablepoint.co.uk
Bank(s): National Westminster Bank Plc
Managers: A. De Kok (Chief Acct), D. Crow (Purch Mgr), A. Dekok (Chief Mgr)
Immediate Holding Company: CABLEPOINT LIMITED
Registration no: 02099359 **VAT No.:** GB 552 2025 89
Date established: 1987 **Turnover:** £2m - £5m **No.of Employees:** 51 - 100
Product Groups: 35, 37, 44

Date of Accounts	Dec 11	Dec 10	Dec 09
Working Capital	194	184	83
Fixed Assets	510	507	639
Current Assets	915	2m	941

Carafax Ltd
Rotterdam Road, Hull, HU7 0XD
Tel: 01482-825941 **Fax:** 01482-878357
E-mail: derek.waldren@carafax.co.uk
Website: http://www.carafax.co.uk
Directors: C. Burton (Dir)
Immediate Holding Company: CARAFAX LIMITED
Registration no: 01874815 **VAT No.:** GB 390 4492 40
Date established: 1984 **Turnover:** £5m - £10m **No.of Employees:** 11 - 20
Product Groups: 24, 30, 36, 37, 39

Date of Accounts	Aug 11	Aug 10	Aug 09
Sales Turnover	7m	7m	4m
Pre Tax Profit/Loss	249	402	-11
Working Capital	3m	2m	3m
Fixed Assets	360	383	377
Current Assets	4m	3m	4m
Current Liabilities	259	233	146

Carbide UK Ltd
8 Park Street, Hull, HU3 2JF
Tel: 01482-227234 **Fax:** 01482-212902
E-mail: carbideuk@carbideuk.com
Website: http://www.carbideuk.com
Bank(s): Barclays
Directors: L. Witherwick (Dir)
Managers: A. Cross (Chief Mgr)
Immediate Holding Company: CARBIDE (UK) LIMITED
Registration no: 01862499 **VAT No.:** GB 390 4180 59
Date established: 1984 **Turnover:** £2m - £5m **No.of Employees:** 11 - 20
Product Groups: 47

Date of Accounts	Dec 11	Dec 10	Dec 09
Working Capital	27	23	40
Fixed Assets	250	199	211
Current Assets	562	671	582

Chaucer Foods Ltd
Unit 26 Freightliner Road Brighton Street Industrial Estate, Hull, HU3 4UN
Tel: 01482-588088 **Fax:** 01482-588082
E-mail: customerservices@chaucerfoods.com
Website: http://www.chaucerfoods.com
Bank(s): National Westminster Bank Plc
Directors: D. Manning (Ch), P. Sibbald (Purch)
Managers: G. Walsh (Sales Prom Mgr), M. Moore (Comptroller)
Ultimate Holding Company: BROOMCO (3554) LIMITED
Immediate Holding Company: CHAUCER FOODS LIMITED
Registration no: 01620320 **VAT No.:** GB 430 8679 38
Date established: 1982 **Turnover:** £20m - £50m
No.of Employees: 101 - 250 **Product Groups:** 20, 62

Date of Accounts	Dec 11	Dec 10	Dec 09
Sales Turnover	33m	27m	34m
Pre Tax Profit/Loss	542	3m	5m
Working Capital	-673	-1m	8m
Fixed Assets	11m	11m	11m
Current Assets	23m	36m	45m
Current Liabilities	23m	1m	1m

Cobus Communications
22 Strickland Street, Hull, HU3 4AQ
Tel: 01482-225666 **Fax:** 01482-225111
E-mail: enquiries@cobus.co.uk
Website: http://www.cobus.co.uk
Directors: M. Smith (Dir), M. O'Grady (Dir)
Managers: V. O'Grady (Mktg Serv Mgr), J. Easby
Immediate Holding Company: COBUS LTD
Registration no: 04575004 **Date established:** 2002
Turnover: £500,000 - £1m **No.of Employees:** 21 - 50
Product Groups: 37, 38, 44, 52, 79, 84

Date of Accounts	Jan 11	Jan 10	Jan 09
Working Capital	-29	40	27
Fixed Assets	53	37	59
Current Assets	163	245	171

College For International Cooperation & Development
Winestead Hall Winestead, Hull, HU12 0NP
Tel: 01964-631824 **Fax:** 01964-631695
E-mail: karenb@cicd-volunteerinafrica.org
Website: http://www.cicd-volunteerinafrica.org
Directors: K. Barsoe (Co Sec)
Immediate Holding Company: COLLEGE FOR INTERNATIONAL COOPERATION AND DEVELOPMENT
Registration no: 03390280 **Date established:** 1997
No.of Employees: 11 - 20 **Product Groups:** 63, 86

Date of Accounts	Dec 11	Dec 10	Dec 09
Working Capital	-418	-341	-288
Fixed Assets	358	251	268
Current Assets	55	66	45

Comet Group Ltd
George House George Street, Hull, HU1 3AU
Tel: 08712-009009 **Fax:** 023-8065 1401
Website: http://www.comet.co.uk
Directors: I. Edwards (Dir), H. Harvey (MD)
Managers: P. Kirby (Mgr)
Ultimate Holding Company: DARTY PLC
Immediate Holding Company: COMET GROUP LIMITED
Registration no: 00278576 **VAT No.:** GB 232 5555 75
Date established: 1933 **Turnover:** Over £1,000m
No.of Employees: 21 - 50 **Product Groups:** 61

Date of Accounts	Apr 11	Apr 10	Apr 09
Sales Turnover	1478m	1586m	1594m
Pre Tax Profit/Loss	-40m	-3m	-8m
Working Capital	4m	36m	31m
Fixed Assets	99m	98m	111m
Current Assets	293m	302m	291m
Current Liabilities	99m	102m	98m

Computype
Connaught Road Kingswood, Hull, HU7 3AP
Tel: 01482-835366 **Fax:** 01482-822441
E-mail: john.newton@compu-inc.co.uk
Website: http://www.computype.com
Bank(s): The Royal Bank of Scotland
Directors: J. Newton (Dir), S. Richardson (Fin)
Managers: H. Moore (Personnel), L. Clancy (Mktg Serv Mgr), A. Preen (Buyer)
Ultimate Holding Company: SDL PLC
Immediate Holding Company: COMPUTYPE LIMITED
Registration no: 01270901 **Date established:** 1976 **Turnover:** £5m - £10m
No.of Employees: 21 - 50 **Product Groups:** 27, 28

Date of Accounts	Dec 11	Dec 10	Dec 09
Pre Tax Profit/Loss	-1	-3	12

Conceptus UK Ltd
Unit 3 Caughey Street, Hull, HU2 8TH
Tel: 01482-330750 **Fax:** 01482-330753
E-mail: design@conceptus.karoo.co.uk
Website: http://www.conceptus.co.uk
Directors: M. Wilson (MD)
Immediate Holding Company: CONCEPTUS UK LIMITED
Registration no: 03951356 **Date established:** 2000
No.of Employees: 21 - 50 **Product Groups:** 26, 35

Date of Accounts	Mar 12	Mar 11	Mar 10
Working Capital	255	241	256
Fixed Assets	81	97	84
Current Assets	474	546	326

Ron Cook Engineers
48-50 Oxford Street, Hull, HU2 0QP
Tel: 01482-327187 **Fax:** 01482-213658
Directors: A. Cook (Ptnr)
VAT No.: GB 167 9765 01 **Date established:** 1972
Turnover: £500,000 - £1m **No.of Employees:** 1 - 10 **Product Groups:** 48

B Cooke & Son Ltd
58-59 Market Place, Hull, HU1 1RH
Tel: 01482-223454 **Fax:** 01482-219793
E-mail: priyanka@cooke.karoo.co.uk
Website: http://www.bcookeandson.co.uk
Directors: P. Perera (MD)
Immediate Holding Company: B.COOKE & SON,LIMITED
Registration no: 00224604 **Date established:** 2027
Turnover: £500,000 - £1m **No.of Employees:** 1 - 10 **Product Groups:** 38, 64

Date of Accounts	Mar 11	Mar 10	Mar 09
Working Capital	484	432	442
Fixed Assets	2	3	2
Current Assets	622	497	471

Cory Bros Shipping Ltd
The Deep Business Centre Tower Street, Hull, HU1 4BG
Tel: 01482-382841 **Fax:** 01482-382841
E-mail: coreyhull@corey.co.uk
Website: http://www.cory.co.uk
Directors: M. Harrison (Dir)
Managers: J. Gledhill (Mgr)
Immediate Holding Company: GORMAN CORY SHIPPING AGENCY LIMITED
Registration no: 05653202 **VAT No.:** GB 244 0497 69
Date established: 2005 **No.of Employees:** 1 - 10 **Product Groups:** 74, 76

Co-Var Ltd
Ellenshaw Works Lockwood Street, Hull, HU2 0HN
Tel: 01482-328053 **Fax:** 01482-219266
E-mail: info@coo-var.co.uk
Website: http://www.coo-var.co.uk
Bank(s): HSBC Bank plc
Directors: J. Mackrill (Prop)
Ultimate Holding Company: TEAL & MACKRILL LIMITED
Immediate Holding Company: COO-VAR LIMITED
Registration no: 00446603 **Date established:** 1947
No.of Employees: 51 - 100 **Product Groups:** 32, 48

Date of Accounts	Dec 11	Dec 10	Dec 09
Working Capital	16	16	16
Current Assets	16	16	16

Cranswick Country Foods plc
14 Staithes Road Preston, Hull, HU12 8TB
Tel: 01482-891001 **Fax:** 01482-890080
E-mail: sales@cranswick.co.uk
Website: http://www.cranswick.co.uk
Directors: A. Couch (MD), G. Keyworth (Sales), M. Windeatt (Fin)
Ultimate Holding Company: CRANSWICK PLC
Immediate Holding Company: CRANSWICK COUNTRY FOODS PLC
Registration no: 01803402 **Date established:** 1984
Turnover: £500m - £1,000m **No.of Employees:** 501 - 1000
Product Groups: 20

Date of Accounts	Mar 12	Mar 11	Mar 10
Sales Turnover	566m	512m	464m
Pre Tax Profit/Loss	24m	23m	26m
Working Capital	22m	21m	26m
Fixed Assets	121m	105m	89m
Current Assets	112m	88m	85m
Current Liabilities	20m	14m	11m

Crating Solutions
Unit 6 Dairycoates Industrial Estate Wiltshire Road, Hull, HU4 6PA
Tel: 01482-470490 **Fax:** 01482-441433
E-mail: sales@cratingsolutions.co.uk
Website: http://www.cratingsolutions.co.uk
Directors: M. Jones (MD)
Immediate Holding Company: HIDER FOOD IMPORTS LIMITED
Registration no: 06246494 **Date established:** 1965
No.of Employees: 1 - 10 **Product Groups:** 25, 66

Date of Accounts	Nov 11	Nov 10	Nov 09
Working Capital	-103	-8	21
Fixed Assets	396	138	51
Current Assets	466	180	168

Croda Chemicals Europe Ltd
Oak Road, Hull, HU6 7PH
Tel: 01482-443181 **Fax:** 01482-341792
Website: http://www.croda.com
Directors: B. Jones (Fin), J. Ainger (Co Sec)
Managers: G. Parkinson, P. Walker (Purch Mgr)
Immediate Holding Company: CRODA INTERNATIONAL P.L.C.
Registration no: 00117512 **VAT No.:** GB 168 6045 44
Date established: 1911 **Turnover:** £5m - £10m
No.of Employees: 101 - 250 **Product Groups:** 31, 32

Danfast Ltd
English Street, Hull, HU3 2DZ
Tel: 01482-599300 **Fax:** 01482-599321
E-mail: enquiries@danfast.co.uk
Website: http://www.danfast.co.uk
Bank(s): HSBC Bank plc
Directors: M. Lenney (MD), L. Sumpton (Fin)
Ultimate Holding Company: DANBY HOLDINGS LIMITED
Immediate Holding Company: DANFAST LIMITED
Registration no: 01764887 **Date established:** 1983 **Turnover:** £5m - £10m
No.of Employees: 21 - 50 **Product Groups:** 31, 32, 35, 39, 40

Date of Accounts	Apr 11	Apr 10	Apr 09
Working Capital	137	31	21
Fixed Assets	105	99	119
Current Assets	2m	2m	1m

Dearing Plastics Ltd
Unit 12 National Avenue, Hull, HU5 4HT
Tel: 01482-348588 **Fax:** 01482-470255
E-mail: sales@dearingplastics.com
Website: http://www.dearingplastics.com
Directors: A. Dearing (Prop), A. Dearing (MD)
Immediate Holding Company: DEARING PLASTICS LIMITED
Registration no: 03559498 **VAT No.:** GB 433 6189 47
Date established: 1998 **Turnover:** £500,000 - £1m
No.of Employees: 11 - 20 **Product Groups:** 30, 66

Date of Accounts	Jun 08	Jun 07	Jun 06
Working Capital	74	69	69
Fixed Assets	40	57	61
Current Assets	407	308	276
Current Liabilities	333	239	208

Deborah Services Ltd
312 Wincolmlee, Hull, HU2 0QE
Tel: 01482-225322 **Fax:** 01482-219096
Website: http://www.deborahservices.co.uk
Managers: C. Bartle (Mgr)
Immediate Holding Company: DEBORAH SERVICES LIMITED
Registration no: 04013621 **Date established:** 2000
No.of Employees: 1 - 10 **Product Groups:** 35, 66, 83, 86

Date of Accounts	Apr 11	Apr 10	Apr 09
Sales Turnover	81m	70m	88m
Pre Tax Profit/Loss	3m	71	2m
Working Capital	5m	8m	8m
Fixed Assets	25m	14m	16m
Current Assets	25m	25m	26m
Current Liabilities	10m	8m	8m

Denholm Barwil Ltd
The Deep Business Centre Tower Street, Hull, HU1 4BG
Tel: 01482-385260 **Fax:** 01482-385278
E-mail: enquiries@denholm-barwil.com
Website: http://www.denholm-barwil.com
Managers: S. Ellerton (Mgr)
Immediate Holding Company: I AM YOUR LIMITED
Registration no: SC032785 **Date established:** 2006
No.of Employees: 1 - 10 **Product Groups:** 72, 74

Date of Accounts	Dec 11	Dec 10	Dec 09
Sales Turnover	7m	8m	9m
Pre Tax Profit/Loss	283	372	406
Working Capital	72	-6	-176
Fixed Assets	312	399	613
Current Assets	6m	7m	5m
Current Liabilities	1m	2m	2m

Direct Gaskets Ltd
Unit 2 Lee Smith Street, Hull, HU9 1SD
Tel: 01482-219655 **Fax:** 01482-321162
E-mail: info@direct-gaskets.co.uk
Website: http://www.direct-gaskets.co.uk
Directors: L. Weichardt (MD)
Immediate Holding Company: DIRECT GASKETS LIMITED
Registration no: 02835648 **Date established:** 1993
No.of Employees: 1 - 10 **Product Groups:** 38, 42

Date of Accounts	Apr 11	Apr 10	Apr 09
Working Capital	-19	-4	-7
Fixed Assets	26	16	22
Current Assets	68	66	49

Donaldson Filter Components Ltd
Oslo Road, Hull, HU7 0YN
Tel: 01482-835213 **Fax:** 01482-835411
E-mail: john.mearns@donaldson.com
Website: http://www.donaldson.com
Bank(s): National Westminster Bank Plc
Directors: D. Jowett (Dir)
Managers: J. Mearns (Plant)
Ultimate Holding Company: DONALDSON CO INC (USA)
Immediate Holding Company: DONALDSON FILTER COMPONENTS LIMITED
Registration no: 01222246 **Date established:** 1975
Turnover: £75m - £125m **No.of Employees:** 101 - 250
Product Groups: 33, 34, 35, 37, 40

Date of Accounts	Jul 11	Jul 10	Jul 09
Sales Turnover	76m	59m	70m
Pre Tax Profit/Loss	4m	4m	3m
Working Capital	16m	12m	12m
Fixed Assets	4m	4m	5m
Current Assets	24m	19m	21m
Current Liabilities	1m	792	2m

Duncans Gunmakers Ltd
200 Willerby Road, Hull, HU5 5JW
Tel: 01482-328150 **Fax:** 01482-225612
E-mail: sales@duncansgunmakers.co.uk
Website: http://www.duncansgunmakers.co.uk

see next page

Duncans Gunmakers Ltd - *Cont'd*

Directors: W. Featherby (Fin)
Immediate Holding Company: DUNCANS (GUNMAKERS) LIMITED
Registration no: 00419861 **Date established:** 1946
Turnover: Up to £250,000 **No.of Employees:** 1 - 10 **Product Groups:** 36, 39, 40

Date of Accounts	Apr 12	Apr 11	Apr 10
Sales Turnover	N/A	N/A	203
Pre Tax Profit/Loss	N/A	N/A	2
Working Capital	1	13	10
Fixed Assets	14	2	2
Current Assets	120	131	132
Current Liabilities	N/A	N/A	10

East Riding Training Solutions Limited

Unit 4 & 9 South Boulevard Factory Estate Hessle Road, Hull, HU3 4AY
Tel: 01482-222585
E-mail: ken@erts.org.uk
Website: http://www.erts.org.uk
Registration no: 05921383 **Turnover:** Up to £250,000
No.of Employees: 1 - 10 **Product Groups:** 38, 86

East Yorkshire Motor Services Ltd

252 Anlaby Road, Hull, HU3 2RS
Tel: 01482-327142 **Fax:** 01482-212040
E-mail: helpdesk@eyms.co.uk
Website: http://www.eyms.co.uk
Directors: P. Shipp (Ch)
Managers: M. Kerwin (Sales Prom), D. Stockdale (I.T. Exec), D. Wilmott (Mgr)
Immediate Holding Company: EAST YORKSHIRE MOTOR SERVICES LIMITED
Registration no: 00216628 **Date established:** 2026
Turnover: £20m - £50m **No.of Employees:** 1 - 10 **Product Groups:** 72

Date of Accounts	Dec 09	Dec 08	Dec 07
Sales Turnover	30m	30m	28m
Pre Tax Profit/Loss	586	684	909
Working Capital	-814	-447	-402
Fixed Assets	25m	22m	20m
Current Assets	6m	5m	5m
Current Liabilities	2m	2m	2m

Energas Head Office

Westmoreland Street, Hull, HU2 0HX
Tel: 01482-329333 **Fax:** 01482-212335
E-mail: sales@energas.co.uk
Website: http://www.energas.co.uk
Bank(s): Lloyds
Directors: M. Robinson (Prop)
Immediate Holding Company: ENERGAS LIMITED
Registration no: 01603643 **Date established:** 1981
Turnover: £20m - £50m **No.of Employees:** 21 - 50 **Product Groups:** 31, 46, 67

Date of Accounts	Sep 11	Sep 10	Sep 09
Sales Turnover	22m	18m	18m
Pre Tax Profit/Loss	5m	3m	5m
Working Capital	5m	10m	10m
Fixed Assets	9m	9m	10m
Current Assets	7m	12m	13m
Current Liabilities	1m	638	2m

Engineering & Welding Supplies Ltd

Westmoreland Street, Hull, HU2 0HX
Tel: 01482-329333 **Fax:** 01482-212335
E-mail: info@engweld.co.uk
Website: http://www.engweld.co.uk
Bank(s): Lloyds TSB Bank plc
Directors: M. Robinson (MD), P. Brown (Co Sec), M. Wright (Co Sec)
Managers: M. Wright
Immediate Holding Company: ENGINEERING AND WELDING SUPPLIES LIMITED
Registration no: 00815796 **VAT No.:** GB 167 8304 42
Date established: 1964 **Turnover:** £10m - £20m
No.of Employees: 21 - 50 **Product Groups:** 66, 67

Date of Accounts	Sep 11	Sep 10	Sep 09
Sales Turnover	18m	15m	14m
Pre Tax Profit/Loss	2m	1m	1m
Working Capital	8m	7m	6m
Fixed Assets	3m	3m	3m
Current Assets	10m	9m	8m
Current Liabilities	627	423	470

Envirohold Ltd

Viking Close Willerby, Hull, HU10 6DZ
Tel: 01482-651090 **Fax:** 01482-651002
E-mail: michael.roberts@envirohold.com
Website: http://www.envirohold.com
Directors: D. Lewis (MD), M. Roberts (MD)
Managers: L. McKenzie (Sales & Mktg Mg), D. Dixon (Accounts), D. Thompson (Ops Mgr)
Ultimate Holding Company: BRAMROW LIMITED
Immediate Holding Company: ENVIROHOLD LIMITED
Registration no: 01664962 **VAT No.:** GB 450 6354 62
Date established: 1982 **Turnover:** £250,000 - £500,000
No.of Employees: 1 - 10 **Product Groups:** 30, 33, 35, 36

Date of Accounts	Dec 10	Dec 09	Dec 08
Sales Turnover	396	568	N/A
Pre Tax Profit/Loss	208	420	-177
Working Capital	925	716	293
Fixed Assets	39	40	43
Current Assets	3m	3m	2m
Current Liabilities	60	44	53

Eriks Industrial Services (Hull Service Centre)

Unit 3 Rugby Business Park Rugby Street, Hull, HU3 4RB
Tel: 01482-327906 **Fax:** 01482-588067
E-mail: hull@eriks.co.uk
Website: http://www.eriks.co.uk
Managers: Y. Pritchit (District Mgr), Y. Pritchett (Mgr)
Registration no: 03142338 **Turnover:** £250m - £500m
No.of Employees: 1 - 10 **Product Groups:** 22

Euro Info Centre Humber

Brynmor Jones Library University of Hull Cottingham Road, Hull, HU6 7RX
Tel: 01482-465935
E-mail: euro-info-centre@hull.ac.uk
Website: http://www.hull.ac.uk/euroinfo

Immediate Holding Company: NEW LIFE DISTRIBUTION LIMITED
Registration no: 04050741 **Date established:** 2010
No.of Employees: 1 - 10 **Product Groups:** 86

Europa Industrial Supplies UK Ltd

5 Factory Estate Wharram Street, Hull, HU2 0JP
Tel: 01482-338435 **Fax:** 01482-338438
E-mail: sales@eisabrasives.co.uk
Website: http://www.eisabrasives.co.uk
Directors: A. Bourne (Fin), J. Soulsby (Dir), J. Soulsby (MD), R. Soulsby (Dir)
Immediate Holding Company: EUROPA INDUSTRIAL SUPPLIES (UK) LIMITED
Registration no: 04332872 **Date established:** 2001
No.of Employees: 1 - 10 **Product Groups:** 33

Date of Accounts	May 08	May 07	May 06
Working Capital	97	90	70
Fixed Assets	80	84	93
Current Assets	180	196	160
Current Liabilities	83	105	90
Total Share Capital	251	251	251

Ever Cal

Citadel Trading Park Citadel Way, Hull, HU9 1TQ
Tel: 01482-610601 **Fax:** 01482-610602
E-mail: sales@ever-cal.com
Website: http://www.ever-cal.com
Managers: S. Wilkinson (Chief Mgr)
Ultimate Holding Company: SGS INTERNATIONAL INC (USA)
Immediate Holding Company: SGS PACKAGING EUROPE LIMITED
Registration no: 00631503 **Date established:** 1959
Turnover: £10m - £20m **No.of Employees:** 1 - 10 **Product Groups:** 38, 39, 67, 85

Date of Accounts	Dec 11	Dec 10	Dec 09
Sales Turnover	25m	17m	13m
Pre Tax Profit/Loss	2m	1m	347
Working Capital	4m	3m	4m
Fixed Assets	3m	2m	2m
Current Assets	14m	11m	9m
Current Liabilities	7m	1m	4m

Fabricast Multi Metals Ltd

Main Street, Hull, HU2 0LF
Tel: 01482-327944 **Fax:** 01482-216670
E-mail: sales@fabricast.co.uk
Website: http://www.fabricast.co.uk
Bank(s): National Westminster Bank Plc
Directors: S. Hilton (MD), C. Hilton (Co Sec)
Ultimate Holding Company: CKM HOLDINGS LIMITED
Immediate Holding Company: FABRICAST GROUP LIMITED
Registration no: 01997780 **Date established:** 1986 **Turnover:** £2m - £5m
No.of Employees: 11 - 20 **Product Groups:** 66

Date of Accounts	Dec 11	Dec 10	Dec 09
Working Capital	694	648	611
Fixed Assets	8	17	35
Current Assets	1m	1m	989

Fairburns Group Ltd

73-79 Clarence Street, Hull, HU9 1DH
Tel: 01482-323352 **Fax:** 01482-229873
E-mail: glen@fairburn.karoo.co.uk
Website: http://www.fairburns.co.uk
Bank(s): National Westminster Bank Plc
Directors: A. Ward (Fin), P. Fairburn (MD)
Ultimate Holding Company: FAIRBURNS HOLDINGS LIMITED
Immediate Holding Company: FAIRBURNS GROUP LIMITED
Registration no: 00534394 **VAT No.:** GB 167 6630 39
Date established: 1954 **Turnover:** £500,000 - £1m
No.of Employees: 101 - 250 **Product Groups:** 84

Date of Accounts	Mar 11	Mar 10	Mar 09
Pre Tax Profit/Loss	N/A	N/A	48
Working Capital	752	725	586
Fixed Assets	150	154	206
Current Assets	2m	2m	2m
Current Liabilities	N/A	N/A	512

Fenner Dunlop Europe

Marfleet, Hull, HU9 5RA
Tel: 01482-781234 **Fax:** 01482-785438
E-mail: jim.jones@fennerdunlop.com
Website: http://www.fennerdunlopeurope.com
Bank(s): Barclays
Directors: G. Griffiths (Sales), G. Oxley (Mkt Research), J. Jones (Sales), J. Pratt (MD)
Managers: S. Bean (Purch Mgr), P. Cooke (), R. Perry (Comptroller), D. Quigley (Personnel)
Immediate Holding Company: Fenner P.L.C.
Registration no: 00527331 **Turnover:** £10m - £20m
No.of Employees: 101 - 250 **Product Groups:** 29, 30

Flowstar UK Ltd

1 Gillett Street, Hull, HU3 4JA
Tel: 01482-210484 **Fax:** 01482-586064
E-mail: sales@flowstar.co.uk
Website: http://www.flowstar.co.uk
Directors: C. Turner (Dir), R. Stephenson (Sales)
Immediate Holding Company: FLOWSTAR (U.K.) LIMITED
Registration no: 01384915 **Date established:** 1978
No.of Employees: 1 - 10 **Product Groups:** 37, 66

Date of Accounts	Mar 12	Mar 11	Mar 10
Working Capital	664	533	627
Fixed Assets	38	53	17
Current Assets	2m	978	939

Forge Forgings Ltd

11 Hedon Road, Hull, HU9 1LL
Tel: 01482-323089 **Fax:** 01482-324735
E-mail: info@wp-forging.co.uk
Website: http://www.wp-forging.co.uk
Bank(s): HSBC, 55 Whitefriargate
Directors: P. Waterman (Fin)
Managers: J. Braithwaite (Admin Off)
Immediate Holding Company: W & P Forging Ltd
Registration no: 04445938 **Date established:** 2002 **Turnover:** £2m - £5m
No.of Employees: 21 - 50 **Product Groups:** 48

Fortrace Ltd

Valletta House Valletta Street, Hull, HU9 5NP
Tel: 01482-703672
E-mail: spalmer@fortrace.com
Website: http://www.fortrace.com
Directors: S. Palmer (MD)
Managers: D. Applin (Fin Mgr), L. Redfern (Purch Mgr)
Ultimate Holding Company: HALLMARK GROUP PRODUCTS LIMITED
Immediate Holding Company: FORTRACE LIMITED
Registration no: 02556377 **Date established:** 1990
No.of Employees: 21 - 50 **Product Groups:** 30

Date of Accounts	Aug 11	Aug 10	Aug 09
Working Capital	480	524	484
Fixed Assets	61	34	78
Current Assets	717	733	679

Fred Balls Ltd

Unit 3 Bontoft Avenue, Hull, HU5 4HF
Tel: 01482-445447 **Fax:** 01482-492162
E-mail: sales@fredballs.co.uk
Website: http://www.fredballs.co.uk
Directors: R. Parkin (MD)
Ultimate Holding Company: FRED BALLS FASTENINGS LIMITED
Immediate Holding Company: FRED BALLS FASTENINGS LIMITED
Registration no: 06651402 **VAT No.:** GB 598 8477 49
Date established: 2008 **Turnover:** £2m - £5m **No.of Employees:** 1 - 10
Product Groups: 35, 66

Date of Accounts	Mar 11	Mar 10	Mar 09
Working Capital	-98	-70	-47
Fixed Assets	652	652	652
Current Liabilities	N/A	N/A	47

Frige Spares Wholesale

Unit X5 South Orbital Trading Park Hedon Road, Hull, HU9 1NJ
Tel: 01482-219888 **Fax:** 01482-320043
E-mail: pf@nrw.uk.com
Website: http://www.nrw.uk.com
Directors: P. Fisher (Prop)
Registration no: 03284427 **No.of Employees:** 1 - 10 **Product Groups:** 40, 63

Future Fixings Ltd

Unit 13 Acorn Industrial Estate Bontoft Avenue, Hull, HU5 4HF
Tel: 01482-345181 **Fax:** 01482-345133
Website: http://www.futurefixings.co.uk
Directors: P. Bahn (MD), G. Bahn (Fin)
Immediate Holding Company: FUTURE FIXINGS LIMITED
Registration no: 03543643 **Date established:** 1998
Turnover: £250,000 - £500,000 **No.of Employees:** 1 - 10
Product Groups: 23, 26, 40

Date of Accounts	Apr 11	Apr 10	Apr 09
Working Capital	2	13	20
Fixed Assets	N/A	1	4
Current Assets	88	100	150

G F Smith

Lockwood Street, Hull, HU2 0HL
Tel: 01482-323503 **Fax:** 01482-223174
E-mail: info@gfsmith.com
Website: http://www.gfsmith.com
Bank(s): National Westminster Bank Plc
Directors: P. Alexander (MD), G. Cheeky (Fin)
Managers: B. Grabbe (Tech Serv Mgr)
Immediate Holding Company: G.F.SMITH & SON(LONDON),LIMITED
Registration no: 00490873 **VAT No.:** GB 167 7800 35
Date established: 1951 **Turnover:** £20m - £50m
No.of Employees: 101 - 250 **Product Groups:** 27

Date of Accounts	Oct 11	Oct 10	Oct 09
Sales Turnover	24m	21m	19m
Pre Tax Profit/Loss	594	435	146
Working Capital	9m	9m	9m
Fixed Assets	1m	1m	1m
Current Assets	13m	13m	11m
Current Liabilities	2m	2m	887

G&S Engineering

2 Madeley Street, Hull, HU3 2AH
Tel: 01482-210336 **Fax:** 01482-793297
E-mail: info@gandsengineering.co.uk
Website: http://www.gandsengineering.co.uk
Directors: K. Siddle (Prop), T. Greendale (Prop)
Date established: 2008 **No.of Employees:** 1 - 10 **Product Groups:** 48

Gardiner Security Ltd

Unit 10 Unit Factory Estate Hawthorn Avenue, Hull, HU3 5JB
Tel: 01482-585005 **Fax:** 01482-585006
E-mail: chris.morley@adiglobal.com
Website: http://www.gardinersecurity.co.uk
Managers: C. Morley (Mgr)
Immediate Holding Company: GARDINER SECURITY LIMITED
Registration no: 04124719 **Date established:** 2000
No.of Employees: 1 - 10 **Product Groups:** 37, 40

Glenair Services

Hessle Road, Hull, HU3 4AA
Tel: 01482-223313 **Fax:** 01482-229962
E-mail: info@glenair.uk.com
Website: http://www.glenair.uk.com
Bank(s): Natwest
Directors: G. Hood (MD)
Managers: M. Eyles (Sales Admin)
Immediate Holding Company: GLENAIR SERVICES LIMITED
Registration no: 06952911 **VAT No.:** GB 500 9299 56
Date established: 2009 **Turnover:** £1m - £2m **No.of Employees:** 11 - 20
Product Groups: 40

Date of Accounts	Mar 12	Mar 11	Mar 10
Working Capital	143	106	50
Fixed Assets	64	49	42
Current Assets	610	426	178

H B Draughting

Unit 14 266-290 Wincolmlee, Hull, HU2 0PZ
Tel: 01482-322995 **Fax:** 01482-226511
Directors: C. Harvatt (MD)
Immediate Holding Company: HB DRAUGHTING LIMITED
Registration no: 04359814 **Date established:** 2002
No.of Employees: 1 - 10 **Product Groups:** 35

Date of Accounts	Jan 12	Jan 11	Jan 10
Working Capital	21	17	4
Fixed Assets	1	N/A	N/A
Current Assets	38	32	12

H Gostelow Terapin Sales
21-22 Francis Street, Hull, HU2 8DT
Tel: 01482-323459 **Fax:** 01482-586325
E-mail: tim@gostelow.karoo.co.uk
Directors: L. Gostelow (Fin), D. Ricks (Dir)
Immediate Holding Company: GOSTELOW ADVERTISING LIMITED
Registration no: 04573227 **Date established:** 2002
Turnover: £250,000 - £500,000 **No.of Employees:** 1 - 10
Product Groups: 22, 66

Date of Accounts	Mar 12	Mar 11	Mar 10
Working Capital	7	11	14
Current Assets	15	22	28

H M C Dismantling & Demolition
The Station Station Road, Patrington, Hull, HU12 0NE
Tel: 01964-630519 **Fax:** 01964-631118
E-mail: info@expotrak.co.uk
Website: http://www.expotrak.co.uk
Directors: A. Hupper (MD)
Immediate Holding Company: SEATHORN CONSTRUCTION SERVICES LIMITED
Registration no: 01908395 **Date established:** 1985
No.of Employees: 11 - 20 **Product Groups:** 36, 48, 51

Date of Accounts	Dec 11	Dec 10	Dec 09
Working Capital	50	50	50
Fixed Assets	29	30	31
Current Assets	80	80	82

Hall Construction Group Ltd
Clay Street, Hull, HU8 8HE
Tel: 01482-329204 **Fax:** 01482-587722
E-mail: enquiries@hallgroup.co.uk
Website: http://www.hallgroup.co.uk
Bank(s): Barclays
Directors: M. Bowers (Fin), N. Symmonds (Comm), M. Hall (MD)
Immediate Holding Company: HALL CONSTRUCTION GROUP LIMITED
Registration no: 00458044 **VAT No.:** GB 166 8058 37
Date established: 1948 **Turnover:** £10m - £20m
No.of Employees: 101 - 250 **Product Groups:** 51, 52

Date of Accounts	Sep 11	Sep 10	Sep 09
Sales Turnover	16m	18m	19m
Pre Tax Profit/Loss	12	-47	15
Working Capital	1m	1m	1m
Fixed Assets	3m	3m	3m
Current Assets	5m	5m	4m
Current Liabilities	804	558	884

Harlequin Metalworx
Ropery Street, Hull, HU3 2BU
Tel: 01482-217730 **Fax:** 01482-217730
Directors: J. Shields (Prop)
Immediate Holding Company: SINCLAIR ELECTRICAL SERVICES LTD
Registration no: 05600630 **Date established:** 2005
No.of Employees: 11 - 20 **Product Groups:** 35

Date of Accounts	Jan 11	Jan 10	Apr 09
Working Capital	-43	-37	-22
Fixed Assets	111	89	94
Current Assets	16	21	34

Hepworths Shipyard Ltd
Main Street Paull, Hull, HU12 8AN
Tel: 01482-338817 **Fax:** 01482-338820
E-mail: john.rix@holyhead.co.uk
Website: http://www.holyhead.co.uk
Bank(s): National Westminster Bank Plc
Directors: J. Rix (MD)
Ultimate Holding Company: J.R. RIX & SONS LIMITED
Immediate Holding Company: HEPWORTH SHIPYARD LIMITED
Registration no: 01342877 **Date established:** 1977 **Turnover:** £2m - £5m
No.of Employees: 11 - 20 **Product Groups:** 39

Date of Accounts	Dec 11	Dec 10	Dec 09
Sales Turnover	3m	4m	3m
Pre Tax Profit/Loss	-801	96	118
Working Capital	-464	122	252
Current Assets	5m	1m	2m
Current Liabilities	19	43	39

Holliday Pigments Ltd
Morley Street, Hull, HU8 8DN
Tel: 01482-329875 **Fax:** 01484-329791
E-mail: sales@holliday-pigments.com
Website: http://www.holliday-pigments.com
Directors: R. Atkinson (Co Sec), R. Rae (Grp Chief Exec)
Managers: P. Wilson (Personnel), I. Wilkinson (I.T. Exec), S. Bell (Sales Prom Mgr), S. Cox (Purch Mgr), J. Holudridge (Mktg Serv Mgr)
Ultimate Holding Company: Yule Catto & Co plc
Immediate Holding Company: Yule Catto International Ltd
Registration no: 00107845 **Turnover:** Up to £250,000
No.of Employees: 101 - 250 **Product Groups:** 32

Date of Accounts	Dec 07
Sales Turnover	11200
Pre Tax Profit/Loss	-8070
Working Capital	-11930
Fixed Assets	600
Current Assets	-5060
Current Liabilities	6870
Total Share Capital	590

Hull Resin Floors Ltd
44 Summergangs Road, Hull, HU8 8LP
Tel: 01482-703081
E-mail: ian@hullresinfloors.co.uk
Website: http://www.hullresinfloors.co.uk
Directors: I. Roper (MD)
Immediate Holding Company: HULL RESIN FLOORS LIMITED
Registration no: 05776499 **Date established:** 2006
No.of Employees: 1 - 10 **Product Groups:** 29, 30, 52

Date of Accounts	Jan 11	Jan 10	Jan 09
Working Capital	50	20	3
Fixed Assets	17	7	9
Current Assets	145	46	16

Humber Electrical Engineering Co. Ltd
45 Portland Place, Hull, HU2 8QP
Tel: 01482-323042 **Fax:** 01482-326811
E-mail: info@humberelectrical.com
Website: http://www.humberelectrical.com
Managers: D. Thompson (Tech Sales Mgr)
Immediate Holding Company: HUMBER ELECTRICAL ENGINEERING COMPANY LIMITED(THE)
Registration no: 00208127 **Date established:** 2025
Turnover: £10m - £20m **No.of Employees:** 101 - 250
Product Groups: 37, 39, 84

Date of Accounts	Dec 11	Dec 10	Dec 09
Sales Turnover	7m	14m	12m
Pre Tax Profit/Loss	132	128	69
Working Capital	2m	1m	1m
Fixed Assets	1m	1m	1m
Current Assets	3m	7m	10m
Current Liabilities	793	5m	7m

Humber Fabrications Hull Ltd
99 Wincolmlee, Hull, HU2 8AH
Tel: 01482-226100 **Fax:** 01482-215884
E-mail: sales@humberboats.co.uk
Website: http://www.ribworld.co.uk
Directors: A. Roffee (Dir), P. Roffee (Fin)
Immediate Holding Company: HUMBER FABRICATIONS (HULL) LIMITED
Registration no: 02803785 **Date established:** 1993
No.of Employees: 11 - 20 **Product Groups:** 29, 30, 49

Date of Accounts	Aug 11	Aug 10	Aug 09
Working Capital	362	383	366
Fixed Assets	405	425	444
Current Assets	459	494	467

Humber Galvanising Ltd
J Citadel Trading Park Citadel Way, Hull, HU9 1TQ
Tel: 01482-322466 **Fax:** 01482-227201
E-mail: info@wedge-galv.co.uk
Website: http://www.wedge-galv.co.uk
Managers: R. Speake (Chief Mgr)
Ultimate Holding Company: B.E. WEDGE HOLDINGS LIMITED
Immediate Holding Company: HUMBER GALVANIZING LIMITED
Registration no: 03011476 **Date established:** 1995 **Turnover:** £1m - £2m
No.of Employees: 21 - 50 **Product Groups:** 48

Date of Accounts	Mar 11	Mar 10	Mar 09
Pre Tax Profit/Loss	12	12	12
Current Assets	3	3	2
Current Liabilities	3	3	2

Humberside Food Machinery Ltd
Spyvee Street, Hull, HU8 7JJ
Tel: 01482-211956 **Fax:** 01482-211957
E-mail: dave@humbfood.co.uk
Website: http://www.humbfood.co.uk
Directors: G. Mckie (MD), R. Pyrah (Dir), G. McKay (MD), B. Pyrah (Dir)
Managers: S. Stokes (Sec)
Immediate Holding Company: HUMBERSIDE FOOD MACHINERY LIMITED
Registration no: 01430822 **Date established:** 1979
Turnover: £500,000 - £1m **No.of Employees:** 1 - 10 **Product Groups:** 40, 66

Date of Accounts	May 11	Mar 10	Mar 09
Working Capital	-35	51	72
Fixed Assets	100	100	104
Current Assets	22	84	114

Humberside Offshore Training Association Ltd
Malmo Road, Hull, HU7 0YF
Tel: 01482-820567 **Fax:** 01482-823202
E-mail: bookings@hota.org
Website: http://www.hota.org
Bank(s): Natwest
Managers: L. Ellis (Chief Mgr)
Immediate Holding Company: HUMBERSIDE OFFSHORE TRAINING ASSOCIATION
Registration no: 02190605 **Date established:** 1987
Turnover: £500,000 - £1m **No.of Employees:** 21 - 50 **Product Groups:** 86

Date of Accounts	Dec 11	Dec 10	Dec 09
Working Capital	1m	1m	807
Fixed Assets	913	834	851
Current Assets	1m	1m	1m

Hurst Plastics Ltd
Unit I Kingston International Business Park Somerden Road, Hull, HU9 5PE
Tel: 01482-790790 **Fax:** 01482-790690
E-mail: info@hurst-plastics.co.uk
Website: http://www.hurst-plastics.co.uk
Managers: L. Dennison
Ultimate Holding Company: HURST GROUP (NORTHERN) LIMITED
Immediate Holding Company: HURST PLASTICS LIMITED
Registration no: 03034235 **Date established:** 1995 **Turnover:** £5m - £10m
No.of Employees: 101 - 250 **Product Groups:** 25, 30, 33, 35

Date of Accounts	Mar 11	Mar 10	Mar 09
Sales Turnover	9m	9m	9m
Pre Tax Profit/Loss	-538	-580	-977
Working Capital	-325	115	573
Fixed Assets	89	187	367
Current Assets	2m	1m	3m
Current Liabilities	836	57	118

I T @ Spectrum Ltd
1 Trinity Street, Hull, HU3 1JR
Tel: 01482-586732 **Fax:** 01482-211428
E-mail: smonkman@itatspectrum.co.uk
Website: http://www.itatspectrum.co.uk
Directors: E. Cavill (Dir)
Managers: M. Richardson (Publicity), S. Kemp (Personnel)
Immediate Holding Company: Dellstrong Ltd
Registration no: 01875120 **Date established:** 1983
No.of Employees: 21 - 50 **Product Groups:** 44

Date of Accounts	Apr 08	Apr 07
Working Capital	559	570
Fixed Assets	193	218
Current Assets	1905	2239
Current Liabilities	1346	1669
Total Share Capital	1	1

Ideal Heating
National Avenue, Hull, HU5 4JN
Tel: 01482-492251 **Fax:** 01482-448858
E-mail: enquires@idealboilers.com
Website: http://www.idealheating.com
Bank(s): HSBC, London
Directors: R. Young (Purch), M. Buttree (Fin)
Managers: D. Skalli (Personnel), W. Olston, C. Young (Mktg Serv Mgr), C. Hussey (Tech Serv Mgr)
Ultimate Holding Company: 06953890
Immediate Holding Company: IDEAL BOILERS LIMITED
Registration no: 00322137 **Date established:** 1936
Turnover: £75m - £125m **No.of Employees:** 501 - 1000
Product Groups: 40, 46

Ideal Standard Ltd
National Avenue, Hull, HU5 4HF
Tel: 01482-346461 **Fax:** 01482-445886
E-mail: webmaster@ideal-standard.co.uk
Website: http://www.idealstandard.co.uk
Bank(s): Lloyds TSB Bank plc
Directors: K. Boad (MD)
Ultimate Holding Company: BAIN CAPITAL PARTNERS LLC (USA)
Immediate Holding Company: IDEAL STANDARD (UK) LIMITED
Registration no: 00091891 **VAT No.:** GB 166 9210 52
Date established: 2007 **Turnover:** £125m - £250m
No.of Employees: 251 - 500 **Product Groups:** 25, 30, 33, 36, 63, 66

Date of Accounts	Dec 11	Dec 10	Dec 09
Sales Turnover	141m	149m	155m
Pre Tax Profit/Loss	2m	5m	9m
Working Capital	50m	50m	47m
Fixed Assets	37m	37m	27m
Current Assets	98m	88m	80m
Current Liabilities	27m	25m	27m

Industrial Racking Supplies Ltd
Unit 2 Aqua Park Reservoir Road, Hull, HU6 7QD
Tel: 01482-441122 **Fax:** 01482-342620
E-mail: sales@racking-uk.net
Website: http://www.racking-uk.net
Directors: R. Bradley (MD), D. Palmer (Co Sec)
Immediate Holding Company: INDUSTRIAL RACKING SUPPLIES LIMITED
Registration no: 06818726 **Date established:** 2009
No.of Employees: 1 - 10 **Product Groups:** 35

Date of Accounts	Mar 12	Mar 11	Mar 10
Working Capital	-17	-34	-53
Fixed Assets	47	59	87
Current Assets	486	321	310

Inotec UK Ltd
Unit 1 Viking Close, Willerby, Hull, HU10 6DZ
Tel: 01482-654466 **Fax:** 01482-655004
E-mail: info@inotecbsl.com
Website: http://www.inotec.info
Managers: D. Stocker (Mgr)
Immediate Holding Company: INOTEC BARCODE SECURITY LIMITED
Registration no: 03780640 **Date established:** 1999 **Turnover:** £1m - £2m
No.of Employees: 1 - 10 **Product Groups:** 27, 30, 35, 49

Date of Accounts	Dec 11	Dec 10	Dec 09
Working Capital	243	126	123
Fixed Assets	54	57	67
Current Assets	522	535	519

Instruments & Controls Hull
Faraday Works Crowle Street, Hull, HU9 1RH
Tel: 01482-225607 **Fax:** 01482-217122
E-mail: sales@instco.co.uk
Website: http://www.instco.co.uk
Directors: M. Miller (MD)
Managers: D. Green (Serv Mgr), G. Gorford (Sales Prom Mgr)
Ultimate Holding Company: KIRKBY LINDSEY ELECTRICAL ENGINEERING LIMITED
Immediate Holding Company: KIRKBY LINDSEY ELECTRICAL COMPANY LIMITED
Registration no: 00416451 **VAT No.:** GB 167 5887 07
Date established: 1946 **Turnover:** £500,000 - £1m
No.of Employees: 21 - 50 **Product Groups:** 37, 38

Iris Group
Victoria House 36 Derringham Street, Hull, HU3 1EL
Tel: 01482-326971 **Fax:** 01482-228465
E-mail: richard.bearpark@aim.co.uk
Website: http://www.iris.co.uk
Bank(s): Bank Of Scotland, Newcastle Upon Tyne
Directors: R. Bearpark (Prop)
Ultimate Holding Company: AIM HOLDINGS GROUP
Immediate Holding Company: AIM HOLDINGS LTD
Registration no: 02120855 **Turnover:** £5m - £10m
No.of Employees: 21 - 50 **Product Groups:** 44, 81

J & C R Wood Ltd
66 Clough Road, Hull, HU5 1SR
Tel: 01482-345067 **Fax:** 01482-441141
E-mail: info@jandcrwood.co.uk
Website: http://www.metalcraft.co.uk
Bank(s): Barclays
Directors: B. Wood (Dir), I. Wood (Dir)
Immediate Holding Company: J & C R WOOD LIMITED
Registration no: 07573833 **Date established:** 2011
No.of Employees: 21 - 50 **Product Groups:** 35, 45, 49

J H P Training Ltd
Unit 10 Bridge View Park Henry Boot Way, Hull, HU4 7DW
Tel: 01482-224340 **Fax:** 01482-587992
E-mail: hull.business.centre@jhp-group.com
Website: http://www.jhptraining.com
Managers: A. Hadfield (Mgr)
Immediate Holding Company: JHP TRAINING LIMITED
Registration no: 03247918 **Date established:** 1996
No.of Employees: 21 - 50 **Product Groups:** 86

William Jackson & Son Recreation Club Ltd
40 Derringham Street, Hull, HU3 1EW
Tel: 01482-224939 **Fax:** 01482-588237
E-mail: info@wjs.co.uk
Website: http://www.crippslaw.com
Directors: P. Farnsworth (Jt MD), N. Oughtred (Dir), N. Oughtred (Co Sec), N. Dawson (Fin), R. Holt (Co Sec), C. Oughdred (MD), C. Oughtred (Ch & MD), M. Oughtred (Dir)
Managers: T. Maplethorpe (Sales Prom Mgr), A. Wheelwright, J. Taylor (I.T. Exec)
Immediate Holding Company: WILLIAM JACKSON & SON RECREATION CLUB LIMITED
Registration no: 01785391 **VAT No.:** GB 166 8600 44
Date established: 1984 **Turnover:** £125m - £250m
No.of Employees: 1 - 10 **Product Groups:** 20

Jewson Ltd
Clough Road, Hull, HU5 1SW
Tel: 01482-449444 **Fax:** 01482-449429
E-mail: gavin.waugh@jewson.co.uk
Website: http://www.jewson.co.uk
Managers: G. Waugh (Mgr)
Ultimate Holding Company: COMPAGNIE DE SAINT GOBAIN (FRANCE)
Immediate Holding Company: JEWSON LIMITED
Registration no: 00348407 **VAT No.:** GB 497 7184 33
Date established: 1939 **Turnover:** Up to £250,000
No.of Employees: 1 - 10 **Product Groups:** 66

Date of Accounts	Dec 11	Dec 10	Dec 09
Sales Turnover	1606m	1547m	1485m
Pre Tax Profit/Loss	18m	100m	45m
Working Capital	-345m	-250m	-349m
Fixed Assets	496m	387m	461m
Current Assets	657m	1005m	1320m
Current Liabilities	66m	120m	64m

Jewson Ltd
Rotterdam Road, Hull, HU7 0XU
Tel: 01482-826123 **Fax:** 01482-371412
Website: http://www.jewson.co.uk
Managers: M. Nelson (Mgr)
Ultimate Holding Company: COMPAGNIE DE SAINT GOBAIN (FRANCE)
Immediate Holding Company: JEWSON LIMITED
Registration no: 00348407 **VAT No.:** GB 497 7184 33
Date established: 1939 **No.of Employees:** 21 - 50 **Product Groups:** 66

Date of Accounts	Dec 11	Dec 10	Dec 09
Sales Turnover	1606m	1547m	1485m
Pre Tax Profit/Loss	18m	100m	45m
Working Capital	-345m	-250m	-349m
Fixed Assets	496m	387m	461m
Current Assets	657m	1005m	1320m
Current Liabilities	66m	120m	64m

John Habblett
Townside Lodge Ryehill, Hull, HU12 9NH
Tel: 01964-622131
Directors: J. Habblett (Prop)
Date established: 1982 **No.of Employees:** 1 - 10 **Product Groups:** 41

Johnsons Sheetmetal Works Ltd
18 Madeley Street, Hull, HU3 2AH
Tel: 01482-323019 **Fax:** 01482-588754
Directors: J. Tanfield (MD)
Immediate Holding Company: JOHNSONS SHEETMETAL WORKS LIMITED
Registration no: 00303404 **VAT No.:** GB 167 1830 56
Date established: 1935 **Turnover:** Up to £250,000
No.of Employees: 1 - 10 **Product Groups:** 48

Date of Accounts	Jun 12	Jun 11	Jun 10
Working Capital	165	157	147
Fixed Assets	69	72	82
Current Assets	292	241	207

Jordans Ltd
45-52 Witham, Hull, HU9 1BS
Tel: 01482-222500 **Fax:** 01482-338580
E-mail: pjh@rix.co.uk
Website: http://www.jordanscars.co.uk
Bank(s): National Westminster Bank Plc
Directors: P. Hasnip (MD)
Ultimate Holding Company: J.R. RIX & SONS LIMITED
Immediate Holding Company: JORDAN & COMPANY (HULL) LIMITED
Registration no: 00858063 **VAT No.:** GB 500 7123 06
Date established: 1965 **Turnover:** £10m - £20m
No.of Employees: 51 - 100 **Product Groups:** 39, 68

Date of Accounts	Dec 11	Dec 10	Dec 09
Sales Turnover	12m	13m	16m
Pre Tax Profit/Loss	82	52	30
Working Capital	480	424	378
Current Assets	1m	2m	2m
Current Liabilities	34	36	32

Justinor Products Ltd
St Johns Business Park St Johns Grove, Hull, HU9 3RL
Tel: 01482-799321 **Fax:** 01482-799470
E-mail: sales@justinor.co.uk
Website: http://www.justinor.co.uk
Directors: J. Wood (I.T. Dir), J. Wood (MD), N. Wood (MD), N. Wood (Fin)
Managers: S. Wood (Sales Prom Mgr), C. McKay (Sales Prom Mgr)
Immediate Holding Company: JUSTINOR PRODUCTS LIMITED
Registration no: 01910809 **VAT No.:** GB 317 3881 48
Date established: 1985 **Turnover:** £500,000 - £1m
No.of Employees: 11 - 20 **Product Groups:** 27

Date of Accounts	Mar 10	Mar 09	Mar 08
Working Capital	-126	-117	-48
Fixed Assets	404	468	464
Current Assets	168	193	290

Ken Rooms Ltd
Cumberland Street, Hull, HU2 0PU
Tel: 01482-320129 **Fax:** 01482-586040
E-mail: barry.white@ken-rooms.co.uk
Website: http://www.ken-rooms.co.uk
Bank(s): Yorkshire Bank PLC
Directors: B. White (MD)
Immediate Holding Company: KEN ROOMS LIMITED
Registration no: 00653880 **VAT No.:** GB 167 4793 15
Date established: 1960 **Turnover:** £500,000 - £1m
No.of Employees: 11 - 20 **Product Groups:** 35

Date of Accounts	Mar 11	Mar 10	Mar 09
Working Capital	56	56	31
Fixed Assets	N/A	N/A	79
Current Assets	56	56	388

Kinetic Laboratories Ltd
Unit 7-9 Wiltshire Road, Hull, HU4 6PA
Tel: 01482-829292 **Fax:** 01482-837997
E-mail: sales@kineticlaboratories.co.uk
Website: http://www.kineticlaboratories.co.uk
Directors: A. Hird (MD)
Immediate Holding Company: KINETIC LABORATORIES LIMITED
Registration no: 05115409 **Date established:** 2004
Turnover: Up to £250,000 **No.of Employees:** 1 - 10 **Product Groups:** 26, 40, 42, 67

Date of Accounts	Apr 11	Apr 10	Apr 09
Working Capital	202	76	51
Fixed Assets	4	5	8
Current Assets	414	134	211

Kingston Carton Co. Ltd
Cumberland Street, Hull, HU2 0PS
Tel: 01482-329886 **Fax:** 01482-226785
E-mail: info@kingstoncarton.co.uk
Website: http://www.kingstoncarton.co.uk
Bank(s): Barclays
Directors: A. Buitendam (MD), R. Wilkinson (Fin)
Managers: P. Metcalfe (Tech Serv Mgr)
Immediate Holding Company: KINGSTON CARTON COMPANY LIMITED(THE)
Registration no: 00146383 **VAT No.:** GB 167 4081 56
Date established: 2017 **Turnover:** £5m - £10m
No.of Employees: 51 - 100 **Product Groups:** 27

Date of Accounts	Jun 11	Jun 10	Jun 09
Sales Turnover	8m	7m	6m
Pre Tax Profit/Loss	979	888	698
Working Capital	4m	4m	3m
Fixed Assets	4m	4m	3m
Current Assets	5m	5m	4m
Current Liabilities	907	685	571

Kingston Communications
Telephone House 37 Carr Lane, Hull, HU1 3RE
Tel: 0800-915 5777 **Fax:** 01482-320652
E-mail: bill.halbert@kcom.com
Website: http://www.kcom.co.uk
Directors: M. Conway (Dir)
Managers: B. Halbert, D. Branton, P. Simpson (Comptroller), S. Kemp (Mktg Serv Mgr), C. Stephenson, M. Upfield (Purch Mgr)
Ultimate Holding Company: KCOM GROUP PUBLIC LIMITED COMPANY
Immediate Holding Company: KINGSTON COMMUNICATIONS LIMITED
Registration no: 03317871 **Date established:** 1997
Turnover: £75m - £125m **No.of Employees:** 101 - 250
Product Groups: 28, 37, 39

Date of Accounts	Mar 11	Mar 10	Mar 09
Sales Turnover	113m	246m	245m
Pre Tax Profit/Loss	43m	33m	20m
Working Capital	129m	-18m	-7m
Fixed Assets	76m	170m	170m
Current Assets	166m	74m	74m
Current Liabilities	26m	61m	50m

Kingston Craftsmen Timber Engineering Ltd
Cannon Street, Hull, HU2 0AB
Tel: 01482-225171 **Fax:** 01482-217032
E-mail: sales@kingston-craftsmen.co.uk
Website: http://www.kingston-craftsmen.co.uk
Directors: B. Boyce (Dir)
Managers: J. Barlow (Tech Serv Mgr)
Ultimate Holding Company: ROBERT SANDERSON & SONS (HOLDINGS) LIMITED
Immediate Holding Company: KINGSTON CRAFTSMEN STRUCTURAL TIMBER ENGINEERING LIMITED
Registration no: 02601099 **Date established:** 1991 **Turnover:** £2m - £5m
No.of Employees: 11 - 20 **Product Groups:** 52, 66

Date of Accounts	Feb 12	Feb 11	Feb 10
Working Capital	153	292	419
Fixed Assets	25	28	31
Current Assets	232	554	729

Kingston Engineering Hull Ltd
Pennington Street, Hull, HU8 7LD
Tel: 01482-325676 **Fax:** 01482-216438
E-mail: sales@kingston-engineering.co.uk
Website: http://www.kingston-engineering.co.uk
Bank(s): Barclays
Directors: J. Harrison (Dir), G. Hickson (Fin)
Immediate Holding Company: KINGSTON ENGINEERING CO. (HULL) LIMITED
Registration no: 01690570 **VAT No.:** GB 390 1077 67
Date established: 1983 **No.of Employees:** 21 - 50 **Product Groups:** 35, 46, 48

Date of Accounts	Mar 12	Mar 11	Mar 10
Working Capital	259	282	359
Fixed Assets	469	476	506
Current Assets	855	784	721

Kingston Marine Services
Victoria Works Swann Street, Hull, HU2 0PH
Tel: 01482-620046 **Fax:** 01482-229100
E-mail: enquiries@kingston-marine.com
Website: http://www.kingston-marine.com
Directors: C. Hall (MD), C. Halls (Prop)
Ultimate Holding Company: L. G. PROUT & SONS LIMITED
Immediate Holding Company: GEMMELL & PROUT MARINE LIMITED
Registration no: 02920502 **Date established:** 1994
No.of Employees: 11 - 20 **Product Groups:** 35, 36, 39

Date of Accounts	Nov 11	Nov 10	Nov 09
Working Capital	-163	17	120
Fixed Assets	229	73	54
Current Assets	518	353	255

Kingstonian Paints Ltd
Sculcoates Lane, Hull, HU5 1DR
Tel: 01482-342216 **Fax:** 01482-493096
E-mail: info@kpaints.co.uk
Website: http://www.kpaints.co.uk
Directors: E. Lorimer (Fin), J. Lorrimer (Fin)
Managers: K. Lorimer (Sales Prom Mgr)
Immediate Holding Company: KINGSTONIAN PAINTS LIMITED
Registration no: 02774039 **VAT No.:** GB 167 2938 31
Date established: 1992 **Turnover:** £1m - £2m **No.of Employees:** 1 - 10
Product Groups: 31, 32

Date of Accounts	Dec 09	Dec 08	Dec 07
Working Capital	-110	-73	-47
Fixed Assets	142	155	126
Current Assets	149	131	131
Current Liabilities	N/A	N/A	54

Laminated Supplies Ltd
Valletta House Valletta Street, Hull, HU9 5NP
Tel: 01482-781111 **Fax:** 01482-701185
E-mail: info@hallmarkpanels.com
Website: http://www.hallmarkpanels.com
Bank(s): HSBC Bank plc
Directors: B. Frisby (Fin), B. Sonley (Dir)
Managers: D. Applin (Sales Admin), L. Redfern (Purch Mgr)
Ultimate Holding Company: HALLMARK GROUP PRODUCTS LIMITED
Immediate Holding Company: LAMINATED SUPPLIES LIMITED
Registration no: 00791635 **VAT No.:** GB 551 8216 50
Date established: 1964 **Turnover:** £5m - £10m
No.of Employees: 101 - 250 **Product Groups:** 35, 37

Date of Accounts	Aug 11	Aug 10	Aug 09
Working Capital	860	872	867
Fixed Assets	52	68	85
Current Assets	3m	3m	3m

Lasercroft Ltd
9 Hedon Road, Hull, HU9 1LL
Tel: 01482-229119 **Fax:** 01482-223077
E-mail: info@lasercroft.com
Website: http://www.lasercroft.com
Bank(s): HSBC
Directors: M. Crowhurst (Fin), S. Whitaker (Sales)
Immediate Holding Company: LASERCROFT LIMITED
Registration no: 02613181 **Date established:** 1991 **Turnover:** £2m - £5m
No.of Employees: 11 - 20 **Product Groups:** 52

Date of Accounts	Mar 12	Mar 11	Apr 10
Working Capital	226	83	63
Fixed Assets	27	25	10
Current Assets	497	399	401

Len Beck
443 Endike Lane, Hull, HU6 8AG
Tel: 01482-852131 **Fax:** 01482-805850
E-mail: lenbeck@lenbeck.karoo.co.uk
Website: http://www.lenbeck.co.uk
Directors: R. Dawes (Sales), C. Beck (MD)
Immediate Holding Company: LEN BECK & SON LIMITED
Registration no: 01180983 **VAT No.:** GB 166 9663 15
Date established: 1974 **Turnover:** Up to £250,000
No.of Employees: 1 - 10 **Product Groups:** 24

Date of Accounts	Aug 11	Aug 10	Aug 08
Working Capital	-1	2	10
Fixed Assets	62	62	63
Current Assets	70	79	94

Linertech Ltd
127 Hedon Road, Hull, HU9 1ND
Tel: 01482-223428 **Fax:** 01482-227186
E-mail: hull@interbulkgroup.com
Website: http://www.linertech.co.uk
Bank(s): Yorkshire
Directors: M. Lewis (MD), N. Barnet (MD), P. Orvis (Dir)
Managers: G. Dawson (Personnel), M. Shaw (I.T. Exec)
Ultimate Holding Company: Interbulk UK Holdings Ltd
Immediate Holding Company: Ubc Ltd
Registration no: 02490240 **VAT No.:** GB 345 6343 36
Date established: 1990 **Turnover:** Up to £250,000
No.of Employees: 21 - 50 **Product Groups:** 30

Date of Accounts	Sep 07	Sep 06	Sep 05
Sales Turnover	7570	8515	7995
Pre Tax Profit/Loss	-597	174	83
Working Capital	-771	-273	-162
Fixed Assets	200	319	419
Current Assets	4588	5143	4835
Current Liabilities	5359	5416	4997
Total Share Capital	359	359	359
ROCE% (Return on Capital Employed)	104.6	378.3	32.3
ROT% (Return on Turnover)	-7.9	2.0	1.0

Logan Teleflex UK Ltd (a member of Daifuku Group)
Sutton Road Kingston Upon Hull, Hull, HU7 0DR
Tel: 01482-785600 **Fax:** 01482-785699
E-mail: marketing@loganteleflex.com
Website: http://www.loganteleflex.com
Bank(s): Barclays
Directors: M. Jeffrey (MD)
Managers: K. Booker (Personnel), G. Alden (Comptroller), T. Morley (Tech Serv Mgr), I. Buffey (Purch Mgr)
Ultimate Holding Company: DAIFUKU COMPANY LIMITED (JAPAN)
Immediate Holding Company: LOGAN TELEFLEX (UK) LIMITED
Registration no: 03116545 **Date established:** 1995
Turnover: £20m - £50m **No.of Employees:** 101 - 250
Product Groups: 38, 44, 45

Date of Accounts	Dec 11	Dec 10	Dec 09
Sales Turnover	32m	24m	17m
Pre Tax Profit/Loss	-2m	-2m	-104
Working Capital	4m	-2m	207
Fixed Assets	2m	2m	2m
Current Assets	12m	13m	11m
Current Liabilities	1m	7m	5m

M A B Systems
Bontoft Avenue, Hull, HU5 4HF
Tel: 01482-342299 **Fax:** 01482-449872
E-mail: info@mab-systems.co.uk
Website: http://www.mab-systems.co.uk
Directors: M. Armstrong (MD)
Immediate Holding Company: NORMANDY CARAVANS LIMITED
Registration no: 01411151 **Date established:** 2003
Turnover: £20m - £50m **No.of Employees:** 21 - 50 **Product Groups:** 49, 89

Date of Accounts	May 11	May 10	May 09
Working Capital	97	105	91
Fixed Assets	2	3	6
Current Assets	183	229	201

Robert Mcbride Ltd
West Carr Lane, Hull, HU7 0BU
Tel: 01482-836222 **Fax:** 01482-839856
Website: http://www.mcbride.co.uk
Directors: C. Barnet (Co Sec)
Ultimate Holding Company: MCBRIDE PLC
Immediate Holding Company: ROBERT MCBRIDE LTD
Registration no: 00220175 **Date established:** 2027
No.of Employees: 251 - 500 **Product Groups:** 35, 45

Date of Accounts	Jun 11	Jun 10	Jun 09
Sales Turnover	311m	320m	305m
Pre Tax Profit/Loss	-5m	10m	4m
Working Capital	-21m	-13m	-18m
Fixed Assets	81m	90m	93m
Current Assets	88m	76m	74m
Current Liabilities	20m	22m	21m

Mail News Media
Blundells Corner Beverley Road, Hull, HU3 1XS
Tel: 01482-327111 **Fax:** 01482-872170
Website: http://www.thisishull.co.uk
Bank(s): National Westminster Bank Plc
Managers: D. Oakley (Tech Serv Mgr), S. Morgan, M. Lewis, R. Austin (Mktg Serv Mgr), R. Jenkinson
Immediate Holding Company: MAIL NEWS & MEDIA LIMITED
Registration no: 00249958 **VAT No.:** GB 167 1489 39
Date established: 1930 **Turnover:** £10m - £20m
No.of Employees: 101 - 250 **Product Groups:** 28

Majestic Gates
Unit 5 Temple Street, Hull, HU5 1AD
Tel: 01482-441466 **Fax:** 01482-441466
E-mail: mail@majesticgates.com
Website: http://www.majesticgates.com
Directors: H. Towle (Prop)
No.of Employees: 1 - 10 **Product Groups:** 26, 35

Mancells Marfleet Ltd
Erimus Works Valletta Street, Hull, HU9 5NU
Tel: 01482-375231 **Fax:** 01482-706545
E-mail: james.barrett@mancells.co.uk
Website: http://www.struthers-carter.co.uk
Bank(s): HSBC
Directors: F. Radford (MD), J. Barrett (Dir), J. Davidson (Purch), A. Durham (Co Sec)
Managers: S. Smith (Sales Admin)
Ultimate Holding Company: 02755663
Immediate Holding Company: MANCELLS (MARFLEET) LIMITED
Registration no: 01982674 **VAT No.:** GB 433 6640 57
Date established: 1986 **Turnover:** £2m - £5m **No.of Employees:** 11 - 20
Product Groups: 66

Date of Accounts	Sep 07	Sep 06
Sales Turnover	2170	N/A
Working Capital	158250	158250
Current Assets	158250	158250
Total Share Capital	140000	140000

Maplin Electronics Ltd
Unit 2 Myton Street, Hull, HU1 2PS
Tel: 08432-277357 **Fax:** 01482-587935
E-mail: customercare@maplin.co.uk
Website: http://www.maplin.co.uk
Managers: P. Coulson (Mgr)
Ultimate Holding Company: MONTAGU PRIVATE EQUITY LLP
Immediate Holding Company: MAPLIN ELECTRONICS LIMITED
Registration no: 01264385 **Date established:** 1976
Turnover: £125m - £250m **No.of Employees:** 1 - 10 **Product Groups:** 37, 61

Date of Accounts	Dec 11	Dec 08	Dec 09
Sales Turnover	205m	204m	204m
Pre Tax Profit/Loss	25m	32m	35m
Working Capital	118m	49m	75m
Fixed Assets	27m	28m	28m
Current Assets	207m	108m	142m
Current Liabilities	78m	51m	59m

Mark C Brown Ltd
PO Box 69, Hull, HU2 8HS
Tel: 01482-323464 **Fax:** 01482-214999
E-mail: info@markcbrown.co.uk
Website: http://www.markcbrown.co.uk
Bank(s): HSBC Bank plc
Directors: K. Mistry (MD)
Immediate Holding Company: MARK C. BROWN LIMITED
Registration no: 03175098 **VAT No.:** GB 647 5837 93
Date established: 1996 **Turnover:** £2m - £5m **No.of Employees:** 11 - 20
Product Groups: 67

Date of Accounts	Mar 12	Mar 11	Mar 10
Sales Turnover	2m	2m	1m
Pre Tax Profit/Loss	N/A	-69	-301
Working Capital	273	99	-92
Fixed Assets	188	65	115
Current Assets	1m	882	716
Current Liabilities	210	124	396

Mauri Products Ltd
Stockholm Road Sutton Fields Industrial Estate, Hull, HU7 0XW
Tel: 01482-833133 **Fax:** 01482-838460
E-mail: abmaurihullreception@abmauri.com
Website: http://www.abfoods.com
Directors: A. Pollard (MD)
Ultimate Holding Company: WITTINGTON INVESTMENTS LIMITED
Immediate Holding Company: MAURI PRODUCTS LIMITED
Registration no: 01413180 **Date established:** 1979
Turnover: £10m - £20m **No.of Employees:** 51 - 100 **Product Groups:** 20, 41, 42, 62

Date of Accounts	Aug 08	Aug 09	Aug 10
Sales Turnover	17m	19m	20m
Pre Tax Profit/Loss	3m	795	2m
Working Capital	7m	5m	5m
Fixed Assets	10m	10m	11m
Current Assets	11m	7m	9m
Current Liabilities	2m	585	1m

Metal Coating Services Ltd
Hamburg Road Off Rotterdam Road, Hull, HU7 0XD
Tel: 01482-820202 **Fax:** 01482-820150
E-mail: gareth@metalcoatingservices.com
Website: http://www.metalcoatingservices.com
Directors: G. Deakin (MD)
Immediate Holding Company: METAL COATING SERVICES LIMITED
Registration no: 01670248 **VAT No.:** GB 390 3058 61
Date established: 1982 **Turnover:** £250,000 - £500,000
No.of Employees: 1 - 10 **Product Groups:** 48

Date of Accounts	Mar 11	Mar 10	Mar 09
Working Capital	-20	-36	-17
Fixed Assets	36	46	61
Current Assets	138	92	82

MH Group Ltd
M.H. House Madeley Street, Hull, HU3 2AH
Tel: 01482-300665 **Fax:** 01482-300665
E-mail: sales@mhindustrial.co.uk
Website: http://www.mhindustrial.co.uk
Directors: K. Mulgrow (MD), R. Leivers (Sales & Mktg)
Managers: J. Dickenson (Admin Off)
Registration no: 01633761 **Turnover:** £250,000 - £500,000
No.of Employees: 21 - 50 **Product Groups:** 45, 84

Millership Engineering
Unit 40 254-260 Wincolmlee, Hull, HU2 0PZ
Tel: 01482-218603 **Fax:** 01482-784890
Website: http://www.paneltex.co.uk
Directors: I. Winn (MD)
Immediate Holding Company: MILLERSHIP ENGINEERING LIMITED
Registration no: 06042933 **Date established:** 2007
Turnover: Up to £250,000 **No.of Employees:** 1 - 10 **Product Groups:** 38, 42

Date of Accounts	Mar 11	Mar 10	Mar 09
Sales Turnover	N/A	89	21
Pre Tax Profit/Loss	N/A	2	3
Working Capital	-12	-11	N/A
Fixed Assets	1	1	N/A
Current Assets	16	4	9
Current Liabilities	N/A	11	N/A

Modern Metal Finishes Ltd
Ellifoot Lane Burstwick, Hull, HU12 9EF
Tel: 01964-671040 **Fax:** 01964-671040
E-mail: admin@mmfgold.co.uk
Website: http://www.mmfgold.co.uk
Directors: P. Crombie (MD), S. Crombie (Fin)
Immediate Holding Company: MODERN METAL FINISHES LIMITED
Registration no: 01485210 **VAT No.:** GB 347 7688 01
Date established: 1980 **Turnover:** £500,000 - £1m
No.of Employees: 1 - 10 **Product Groups:** 48

Date of Accounts	Sep 11	Sep 10	Sep 09
Working Capital	118	116	97
Fixed Assets	28	30	43
Current Assets	156	116	97

N T Foster
1 Northcroft Drive, Hull, HU8 9UL
Tel: 01482-701066 **Fax:** 01482-701066
Website: http://www.ntfdesigns.fsnet.co.uk
Directors: N. Foster (Prop)
Date established: 1989 **No.of Employees:** 1 - 10 **Product Groups:** 35

N B M Timber Products Ltd
Sitwell Street, Hull, HU8 7BG
Tel: 01482-323904 **Fax:** 01482-224198
E-mail: info@nbm-timberproducts.co.uk
Website: http://www.nbm-timberproducts.co.uk
Directors: G. Nelson (Ch), L. Nelson (Fin)
Immediate Holding Company: N.B.M.TIMBER PRODUCTS LIMITED
Registration no: 00327516 **Date established:** 1937 **Turnover:** £2m - £5m
No.of Employees: 21 - 50 **Product Groups:** 25

Date of Accounts	Apr 12	Apr 11	Apr 10
Working Capital	240	317	329
Fixed Assets	478	375	385
Current Assets	888	941	958

North Sea Ventilation Ltd
West Carr Lane, Hull, HU7 0BW
Tel: 01482-834050 **Fax:** 01482-834060
E-mail: enquiries@nsv.co.uk
Website: http://www.nsv.co.uk
Directors: A. Griegg (Co Sec), P. Hart (Dir)
Managers: J. Parker (Chief Acct)
Ultimate Holding Company: HASTIE GROUP LIMITED (AUSTRALIA)
Immediate Holding Company: NS VENTILATION REALISATIONS 2012 LIMITED
Registration no: 02736872 **Date established:** 1992 **Turnover:** £5m - £10m
No.of Employees: 51 - 100 **Product Groups:** 66, 84

Date of Accounts	Jun 11	Jun 10	Jun 09
Sales Turnover	9m	8m	12m
Pre Tax Profit/Loss	15	-494	862
Working Capital	2m	1m	1m
Fixed Assets	239	322	308
Current Assets	5m	3m	5m
Current Liabilities	374	228	563

Northfield Agricultural Services Ltd
Withernsea Road Halsham, Hull, HU12 0BT
Tel: 01964-614233 **Fax:** 01964-613227
E-mail: enquiries@northfieldagric.com
Website: http://www.northfieldagric.com
Directors: R. Cross (Sales), G. Cross (MD)
Immediate Holding Company: NORTHFIELD AGRICULTURAL SERVICES LIMITED
Registration no: 01279171 **Date established:** 1976
No.of Employees: 11 - 20 **Product Groups:** 41

Date of Accounts	Dec 11	Dec 10	Dec 09
Working Capital	430	516	488
Fixed Assets	438	455	501
Current Assets	2m	2m	2m

Andrew J Oliver
Redroofs Main Road, Sproatley, Hull, HU11 4PJ
Tel: 01482-814867
Directors: A. Oliver (Prop)
Date established: 1990 **No.of Employees:** 1 - 10 **Product Groups:** 41

One Stop Sealing Ltd
41-47 Scarborough Street, Hull, HU3 4TG
Tel: 01482-216660
E-mail: sales@onestopsealing.co.uk
Directors: K. Deacon (Dir)
Immediate Holding Company: ONE STOP SEALING LIMITED
Registration no: 05119240 **Date established:** 2004
No.of Employees: 1 - 10 **Product Groups:** 36, 40

Date of Accounts	May 12	May 11	May 10
Working Capital	-28	-18	6
Fixed Assets	71	70	61
Current Assets	159	183	171

Orvec International Ltd
Malmo Road, Hull, HU7 0YF
Tel: 01482-625333 **Fax:** 01482-625325
E-mail: service@orvec.com
Website: http://www.orvec.com
Bank(s): Barclays, Hull
Directors: K. Stamp (MD), B. Meddings (Fin)
Managers: M. Turner (Tech Serv Mgr), D. Arksey
Ultimate Holding Company: PHIPPS & COMPANY LIMITED
Immediate Holding Company: ORVEC INTERNATIONAL LIMITED
Registration no: 01168299 **VAT No.:** GB 168 7516 26
Date established: 1974 **Turnover:** £5m - £10m **No.of Employees:** 21 - 50
Product Groups: 39

Date of Accounts	Mar 11	Mar 10	Mar 09
Sales Turnover	9m	10m	N/A
Pre Tax Profit/Loss	94	454	1m
Working Capital	2m	2m	2m
Fixed Assets	2m	2m	2m
Current Assets	4m	4m	4m
Current Liabilities	356	463	400

P A Fabrications
Unit C5 South Orbital Trading Park Hedon Road, Hull, HU9 1NJ
Tel: 01482-322132 **Fax:** 01482-322132
E-mail: peteratkin@peteratkin.karoo.co.uk
Directors: J. Atkin (Fin), P. Atkin (MD)
Immediate Holding Company: PA FABRICATIONS LIMITED
Registration no: 04499479 **Date established:** 2002
No.of Employees: 1 - 10 **Product Groups:** 26, 35

Date of Accounts	Jul 12	Jul 11	Jul 10
Working Capital	-27	-28	-16
Fixed Assets	2	2	3
Current Assets	8	5	12

Paneltex Ltd
Kingston International Business Park Somerden Road, Hull, HU9 5PE
Tel: 01482-787236 **Fax:** 01482-787238
E-mail: sales@paneltex.co.uk
Website: http://www.paneltex.co.uk
Managers: P. Wilson (Buyer), K. Drake (Chief Acct), J. Berridge, A. Lacy (Sales Prom Mgr)
Ultimate Holding Company: PANELTEX LIMITED
Immediate Holding Company: CSC (SPECIALISED VEHICLES) LIMITED
Registration no: 03067528 **VAT No.:** 766 9139 81 **Date established:** 1995
Turnover: £10m - £20m **No.of Employees:** 101 - 250
Product Groups: 39, 40

Date of Accounts	Jun 11	Jun 10	Jun 09
Sales Turnover	19m	15m	12m
Pre Tax Profit/Loss	197	263	-344
Working Capital	2m	2m	1m
Fixed Assets	2m	2m	2m
Current Assets	7m	6m	4m
Current Liabilities	917	725	424

Paragon Precision Ltd
Harpings Road National Avenue, Hull, HU5 4JF
Tel: 01482-497777
E-mail: info@paragonprecision.co.uk
Website: http://www.paragonprecision.co.uk
Directors: M. Wear (MD)
Ultimate Holding Company: PARAGON ASSET MANAGEMENT LTD
Immediate Holding Company: PARAGON PRECISION LIMITED
Registration no: 02147813 **Date established:** 1987 **Turnover:** £1m - £2m
No.of Employees: 21 - 50 **Product Groups:** 48

Date of Accounts	Mar 11	Mar 10	Mar 09
Working Capital	464	438	120
Fixed Assets	987	1m	1m
Current Assets	1m	2m	1m

Paragon Precision Ltd (Toolmaking Division)
321 National Avenue, Hull, HU5 4JB
Tel: 01482-497777 **Fax:** 01482-497788
E-mail: info@paragonprecision.co.uk
Website: http://www.paragon-tools.co.uk
Bank(s): Barclays
Directors: C. Canty (Ch)
Managers: M. Wear (Chief Mgr), K. Thompson (Purch Mgr), L. Blanchard
Registration no: 00852618 **Date established:** 1969 **Turnover:** £1m - £2m
No.of Employees: 21 - 50 **Product Groups:** 36, 46, 47, 48

Peter Hird & Sons Ltd
English Street, Hull, HU3 2BT
Tel: 01482-227333 **Fax:** 01482-587710
E-mail: peterj@peter-hird.co.uk
Website: http://www.peter-hird.co.uk
Bank(s): National Westminster Bank Plc
Directors: R. Blanchard (Fin), P. Hird (MD), P. Hird (Prop)
Managers: P. Hird (Mgr)
Immediate Holding Company: PETER HIRD AND SONS LIMITED
Registration no: 01678881 **VAT No.:** GB 347 8749 02
Date established: 1982 **Turnover:** £1m - £2m **No.of Employees:** 21 - 50
Product Groups: 72

Date of Accounts	Mar 11	Mar 10	Mar 09
Working Capital	-1m	-717	-385
Fixed Assets	4m	4m	4m
Current Assets	971	845	1m

Pipe Center
Leads Road, Hull, HU7 0BY
Tel: 01482-838880 **Fax:** 01482-878827
E-mail: phill.richardson@wolseley.co.uk
Website: http://www.wolseley.co.uk
Managers: P. Richardson (District Mgr)
Ultimate Holding Company: WOLSELEY P.L.C.
Immediate Holding Company: WOLSELEY CENTERS LTD
Registration no: 00636445 **Turnover:** £2m - £5m
No.of Employees: 1 - 10 **Product Groups:** 30, 34, 35, 36, 40

Date of Accounts	Jun 11	Jun 10	Jun 09
Sales Turnover	87m	96m	96m
Pre Tax Profit/Loss	-2m	5m	5m
Working Capital	-2m	1m	4m
Fixed Assets	36m	34m	26m
Current Assets	34m	33m	45m
Current Liabilities	9m	7m	9m

Pittaway Sempol Ltd
106-114 Flinton Street, Hull, HU3 4NA
Tel: 01482-329007 **Fax:** 01482-213053
E-mail: graeme.pittaway@ilumitex.co.uk
Website: http://www.ilumitex.co.uk

see next page

Pittaway Sempol Ltd - Cont'd
Directors: G. Pittaway (Fin)
Immediate Holding Company: PITTAWAY SEMPOL LIMITED
Registration no: 03853571 **VAT No.:** GB 316 9186 42
Date established: 1999 **Turnover:** £500,000 - £1m
No.of Employees: 1 - 10 **Product Groups:** 32

Date of Accounts	Nov 11	Nov 10	Nov 09
Working Capital	62	61	56
Fixed Assets	8	13	19
Current Assets	110	110	113

Plastic Engineering Products Ltd
A3 Citadel Trading Park Citadel Way, Hull, HU9 1TQ
Tel: 01482-585222 **Fax:** 01482-215485
E-mail: tim@plasticproducts.karoo.co.uk
Directors: C. Richards (Dir), T. Caley (Fin)
Immediate Holding Company: PLASTIC ENGINEERING PRODUCTS LTD
Registration no: 04384949 **Date established:** 2002
No.of Employees: 1 - 10 **Product Groups:** 30

Date of Accounts	Mar 11	Mar 10	Mar 09
Working Capital	142	129	120
Fixed Assets	12	16	21
Current Assets	175	164	156

Prentice & Jackson
Bontoft Avenue, Hull, HU5 4HF
Tel: 01482-781910 **Fax:** 01482-781920
E-mail: info@pjpallets.co.uk
Website: http://www.pjpallets.co.uk
Managers: G. Prentice (Mgr)
Immediate Holding Company: PRENTICE & JACKSON LIMITED
Registration no: 04719466 **Date established:** 2003
Turnover: £20m - £50m **No.of Employees:** 11 - 20 **Product Groups:** 45, 48

Date of Accounts	Mar 11	Mar 10	Mar 09
Working Capital	93	90	90
Fixed Assets	29	27	27
Current Assets	254	217	228

Prospect Training Organisations Ltd
Kingston House Myton Street, Hull, HU1 2PS
Tel: 01482-606242 **Fax:** 01482-609941
E-mail: kingston@prospect-training.co.uk
Website: http://www.prospect-training.co.uk
Bank(s): HSBC
Directors: P. Stephenson (MD)
Immediate Holding Company: PROSPECT TRAINING ORGANISATIONS LIMITED
Registration no: 02225542 **VAT No.:** GB 500 9494 58
Date established: 1988 **Turnover:** Up to £250,000
No.of Employees: 21 - 50 **Product Groups:** 86, 87

Date of Accounts	Mar 11	Mar 10	Mar 09
Working Capital	448	445	365
Fixed Assets	111	126	103
Current Assets	516	516	434

Quay Plastics
Unit 7 Central Park Cornwall Street, Hull, HU8 8AF
Tel: 01482-329037 **Fax:** 01482-221825
E-mail: hull@quayplastics.co.uk
Website: http://www.quayplastics.co.uk
Managers: B. Walsh (Depot Mgr)
Ultimate Holding Company: EPWIN GROUP LIMITED
Immediate Holding Company: QUAY PLASTICS LIMITED
Registration no: 00982490 **Date established:** 1970
No.of Employees: 1 - 10 **Product Groups:** 25, 30, 32

Quibell & Son Holdings Ltd
Stepney Lane, Hull, HU5 1LJ
Tel: 01482-342177 **Fax:** 01482-440296
E-mail: j-stephenson@quibell.co.uk
Website: http://www.quibell.co.uk
Bank(s): Barclays
Directors: J. Stephenson (Ch & MD), J. Stephenson (Dir), P. Alexander (Co Sec), P. O'Brien (Jt MD), R. Brown (Dir)
Managers: A. Thorpe (Buyer), D. Barnes (Consultant), M. Hoe (I.T. Exec)
Immediate Holding Company: QUIBELL AND SON (HOLDINGS) LIMITED
Registration no: 00078400 **VAT No.:** GB 298 1308 34
Date established: 2003 **Turnover:** £10m - £20m
No.of Employees: 101 - 250 **Product Groups:** 52

Date of Accounts	Jan 08	Jan 07	Jan 06
Sales Turnover	18206	14637	20414
Pre Tax Profit/Loss	233	86	143
Working Capital	510	408	406
Fixed Assets	786	718	706
Current Assets	5439	3249	4316
Current Liabilities	4928	2841	3910
Total Share Capital	29	29	29
ROCE% (Return on Capital Employed)	18.0	7.6	12.9
ROT% (Return on Turnover)	1.3	0.6	0.7

R L M Packaging Ltd
Dairycoates Industrial Estate Wiltshire Road, Hull, HU4 6PA
Tel: 01482-505585 **Fax:** 01482-568115
E-mail: info@rlm-packaging.co.uk
Website: http://www.rlm-packaging.co.uk
Managers: R. Knott (Sales Prom Mgr)
Immediate Holding Company: RLM PACKAGING LIMITED
Registration no: 00684471 **Date established:** 1961
No.of Employees: 21 - 50 **Product Groups:** 38, 42

Date of Accounts	May 11	May 10	May 09
Working Capital	706	548	409
Fixed Assets	245	261	506
Current Assets	1m	1m	910

Reality Solutions Ltd
1 Global Business Park, Hull, HU7 0AE
Tel: 01482-828000 **Fax:** 01482-832869
E-mail: sales@realitysolutions.co.uk
Website: http://www.realitysolutions.co.uk
Directors: A. Burnett (MD)
Immediate Holding Company: REALITY SOLUTIONS (TRADING) LTD
Registration no: 07956068 **Date established:** 2012
No.of Employees: 11 - 20 **Product Groups:** 44, 52

Reckitt Benckiser Health Care UK Ltd
Dansom Lane, Hull, HU8 7DS
Tel: 01482-326151 **Fax:** 01482-582532
E-mail: info@reckittbenckiser.com
Website: http://www.reckittbenckifer.com
Bank(s): HSBC
Directors: P. Fryer (Dir)
Ultimate Holding Company: RECKITT BENCKISER GROUP PLC
Immediate Holding Company: RECKITT BENCKISER HEALTHCARE (UK) LIMITED
Registration no: 00261312 **Date established:** 1931
Turnover: £125m - £250m **No.of Employees:** 501 - 1000
Product Groups: 31

Date of Accounts	Dec 10	Dec 09	Dec 08
Sales Turnover	828m	600m	476m
Pre Tax Profit/Loss	319m	302m	152m
Working Capital	-854m	-1033m	-1368m
Fixed Assets	2601m	1674m	1692m
Current Assets	801m	442m	499m
Current Liabilities	237m	102m	64m

Red Box Supplies
Unit 19d Bergen Way, Hull, HU7 0YQ
Tel: 01482-321713 **Fax:** 01482-321714
E-mail: sales@redboxsupplies.co.uk
Website: http://www.redboxsupplies.co.uk
Directors: L. Palmer (Ptnr)
Immediate Holding Company: RED BOX SUPPLIES LLP
Registration no: OC361437 **Date established:** 2011
Turnover: £500,000 - £1m **No.of Employees:** 1 - 10 **Product Groups:** 23, 29, 30, 35, 45

Red Frog Design Ltd
9 Grammar School Yard Fish Street, Hull, HU1 1SE
Tel: 01482-224425 **Fax:** 01482-224425
E-mail: sales@theredfrog.com
Website: http://www.theredfrog.com
Directors: A. Jenneson (Dir)
Immediate Holding Company: RED FROG DESIGN LIMITED
Registration no: 06464536 **Date established:** 2008
No.of Employees: 1 - 10 **Product Groups:** 38, 44

Date of Accounts	Mar 12	Mar 11	Mar 10
Working Capital	43	31	25
Fixed Assets	2	4	1
Current Assets	249	58	70

Rivetts Of London Ltd
138-140 Beverley Road, Hull, HU3 1UX
Tel: 01482-585569 **Fax:** 01482-325836
Website: http://www.rivetts.co.uk
Managers: A. Gaze (Mgr)
Registration no: 00482701 **Date established:** 1950
No.of Employees: 1 - 10 **Product Groups:** 22, 24, 39, 40

Rix Petroleum Hull Ltd
Witham House 45 Spyvee Street, Hull, HU8 7JR
Tel: 01482-224422 **Fax:** 01482-338591
E-mail: sales@rix.co.uk
Website: http://www.rix.co.uk
Bank(s): National Westminster
Directors: D. Evans (Fin), J. Rix (Dir)
Managers: K. Taylor (Tech Serv Mgr), J. Drury (Personnel), J. Brook (Mktg Serv Mgr)
Ultimate Holding Company: J.R. RIX & SONS LIMITED
Immediate Holding Company: J.R. RIX & SONS LIMITED
Registration no: 00577587 **Date established:** 1957
Turnover: £250m - £500m **No.of Employees:** 21 - 50 **Product Groups:** 31

Date of Accounts	Dec 11	Dec 10	Dec 09
Sales Turnover	425m	350m	267m
Pre Tax Profit/Loss	2m	5m	4m
Working Capital	5m	9m	12m
Fixed Assets	46m	40m	34m
Current Assets	49m	41m	36m
Current Liabilities	3m	4m	3m

Rollits LLP
Wilberforce Court High Street, Hull, HU1 1YJ
Tel: 01482-323239 **Fax:** 01482-326239
E-mail: info@rollits.com
Website: http://www.rollits.co.uk
Directors: M. Wasling (Tech Serv), S. Trynka (Snr Part), C. Field (Fin), P. Coyle (Mkt Research)
Managers: L. Cook (Sales Admin)
Immediate Holding Company: ROLLITS LIMITED
Registration no: 02354479 **Date established:** 1989
Turnover: £500,000 - £1m **No.of Employees:** 51 - 100
Product Groups: 80

Date of Accounts	Apr 11
Working Capital	80
Current Assets	102

C Rosingdale & Son
English Close, Hull, HU3 2DR
Tel: 01482-329641 **Fax:** 01482-218269
Directors: K. Kidd (Prop)
Date established: 1906 **No.of Employees:** 1 - 10 **Product Groups:** 35, 36

Roundbrand Ltd
187 Askew Avenue, Hull, HU4 6NN
Tel: 01482-573573 **Fax:** 01482-569569
Directors: J. Hilton (Dir)
Ultimate Holding Company: ARMTHORPE GLASS LIMITED
Immediate Holding Company: ROUNDBRAND LIMITED
Registration no: 02105739 **Date established:** 1987 **Turnover:** £5m - £10m
No.of Employees: 1 - 10 **Product Groups:** 25, 30

Date of Accounts	Nov 11	Nov 10	Nov 09
Sales Turnover	5m	5m	6m
Pre Tax Profit/Loss	63	33	220
Working Capital	-135	-81	-135
Fixed Assets	5m	5m	5m
Current Assets	875	821	1m
Current Liabilities	248	314	332

Sally
Harbour Deck Princes Quay, Hull, HU1 2PQ
Tel: 01482-620044
Managers: D. Thompson (Mgr)
Date established: 2003 **No.of Employees:** 1 - 10 **Product Groups:** 30, 36, 40

Samskip MCL Ltd
Queen Elizabeth Dock, Hull, HU9 5PB
Tel: 01482-707075 **Fax:** 01482-719090
E-mail: hull@samkskip.com
Website: http://www.samskip.com
Directors: J. Nielsen (MD)
Product Groups: 76

Sangwin Ltd
Dansom Lane South, Hull, HU8 7LN
Tel: 01482-329921 **Fax:** 01482-215353
E-mail: info@sangwin.co.uk
Website: http://www.sangwin.co.uk
Directors: D. Spurgeon (Fin), N. Sangwin (Mkt Research), N. Sangwin (MD)
Managers: J. Daine (Chief Buyer), R. Tolson (Chief Acct)
Ultimate Holding Company: SANGWIN HOLDINGS LIMITED
Immediate Holding Company: SANGWIN,LIMITED
Registration no: 00180028 **Date established:** 2022 **Turnover:** £5m - £10m
No.of Employees: 101 - 250 **Product Groups:** 51, 52

Date of Accounts	Feb 12	Feb 11	Feb 10
Sales Turnover	8m	9m	7m
Pre Tax Profit/Loss	-340	-689	28
Working Capital	-317	-2	642
Fixed Assets	25	54	87
Current Assets	2m	3m	2m
Current Liabilities	319	264	280

F R Scott Ltd
Canning Street, Hull, HU2 8QS
Tel: 01482-324731 **Fax:** 01482-214290
E-mail: sales@frscott.co.uk
Website: http://www.frscott.co.uk
Bank(s): HSBC Bank plc
Directors: R. Scott (MD)
Managers: P. Clark (Sales Prom Mgr)
Immediate Holding Company: F.R. SCOTT LIMITED
Registration no: 00399387 **VAT No.:** GB 167 5602 49
Date established: 1945 **Turnover:** £2m - £5m **No.of Employees:** 21 - 50
Product Groups: 35, 52

Date of Accounts	Sep 11	Sep 10	Sep 09
Working Capital	2m	1m	1m
Fixed Assets	177	186	222
Current Assets	2m	2m	2m

Screencraft Publicity Ltd
Reservoir Road, Hull, HU6 7QD
Tel: 01482-499999 **Fax:** 01482-499994
E-mail: info@screencraft-display.co.uk
Website: http://www.screencraft-display.co.uk
Directors: M. Thistleton (MD), S. Gorbutt (Co Sec)
Immediate Holding Company: SCREENCRAFT PUBLICITY (HULL) LIMITED
Registration no: 00647644 **Date established:** 1960
Turnover: £500,000 - £1m **No.of Employees:** 11 - 20 **Product Groups:** 49

Date of Accounts	Jan 12	Jan 11	Jan 10
Working Capital	254	264	333
Fixed Assets	807	876	933
Current Assets	462	537	790

Selkirk Mechanical Handling
Dairycoates Industrial Estate Wiltshire Road, Hull, HU4 6PA
Tel: 01482-502010
E-mail: gary@selkirk-mh.co.uk
Website: http://www.selkirk-mh.co.uk
Directors: G. Selkirk (Dir), S. Lunt (Fin)
Immediate Holding Company: SELKIRK MECHANICAL HANDLING LIMITED
Registration no: 03250162 **Date established:** 1996
No.of Employees: 11 - 20 **Product Groups:** 35, 39, 45

Date of Accounts	Sep 11	Sep 10	Sep 09
Working Capital	-165	-115	-135
Fixed Assets	1m	1m	1m
Current Assets	316	396	356

Seven Sea's Ltd
Hedon Road, Hull, HU9 5NJ
Tel: 01482-375234 **Fax:** 01482-374345
E-mail: sevenseaspressoffice@virgohealth.com
Website: http://www.sseas.com
Bank(s): National Westminster Bank Plc
Directors: J. Redman (MD)
Ultimate Holding Company: MERCK KGaA (GERMANY)
Immediate Holding Company: BRITISH COD LIVER OILS LIMITED
Registration no: 00535007 **VAT No.:** GB 167 4271 51
Date established: 1954 **Turnover:** £50m - £75m
No.of Employees: 251 - 500 **Product Groups:** 31

Shipham Valves (Flow Group Ltd)
Hawthorn Avenue, Hull, HU3 5JX
Tel: 01482-323163 **Fax:** 01482-224057
E-mail: info@shipham-valves.com
Website: http://www.shipham-valves.com
Bank(s): Barclays, Walsall
Directors: S. Worsley (Fin), J. Wall (Prop), T. Fairhurst (Sales & Mktg)
Managers: M. May (Tech Serv Mgr), M. Lawson (Purch Mgr)
Ultimate Holding Company: WARTSILA VALVES LIMITED
Immediate Holding Company: SHIPHAM VALVES LIMITED
Registration no: 00676667 **VAT No.:** GB 599 1955 68
Date established: 1960 **Turnover:** £5m - £10m
No.of Employees: 51 - 100 **Product Groups:** 36, 39, 40, 48

Date of Accounts	Oct 07
Working Capital	530
Current Assets	530

Edwin Snowden & Co. Ltd
173 Fountain Road, Hull, HU2 0LJ
Tel: 01482-320143 **Fax:** 01482-225589
E-mail: info@edwin-snowden.co.uk
Website: http://www.edwin-snowden.co.uk
Bank(s): National Westminster Bank Plc
Directors: G. Barrick (MD)
Immediate Holding Company: EDWIN SNOWDEN & CO. LIMITED
Registration no: 02429891 **VAT No.:** GB 551 7129 50
Date established: 1989 **Turnover:** £500,000 - £1m
No.of Employees: 11 - 20 **Product Groups:** 35, 39, 48

Date of Accounts	Mar 11	Mar 10	Mar 09
Working Capital	274	262	327
Fixed Assets	41	60	77
Current Assets	537	397	420

Sondia Lighting Ltd
45 Portland Place, Hull, HU2 8QP
Tel: 01482-223353 **Fax:** 01482-225681
E-mail: sales@sondialighting.com
Website: http://www.sondialighting.co.uk
Bank(s): Midland

Directors: E. Shuttleworth (Dir), G. Taylor (Div)
Managers: C. Blacker (Purch Mgr), P. Hunt (Sales Prom Mgr)
Immediate Holding Company: Humber Electrical Engineering Company Limited(The)
Registration no: 00786062 **VAT No.:** GB 166 9832 18
Date established: 1963 **No.of Employees:** 51 - 100 **Product Groups:** 37

Sovereign Signs Ltd
Strata House 300 Hawthorn Avenue, Hull, HU3 5LL
Tel: 01482-618234 **Fax:** 01482-380530
E-mail: ianj@sovsigns.co.uk
Website: http://www.sovsigns.co.uk
Directors: I. Jones (MD)
Managers: S. Henderson
Ultimate Holding Company: STRATA HOLDINGS LIMITED
Immediate Holding Company: SOVEREIGN SIGNS LTD
Registration no: 02264929 **Date established:** 1988 **Turnover:** £2m - £5m
No.of Employees: 21 - 50 **Product Groups:** 27, 30, 33, 35, 37

Date of Accounts	Jun 11	Jun 10	Jun 09
Working Capital	600	645	595
Fixed Assets	20	32	73
Current Assets	769	854	891

Springfield Solutions Ltd
Unit 1-5 Acorn Industrial Estate Thomas Street, Hull, HU9 1EH
Tel: 01482-484700
E-mail: info@fortdearborn.com
Website: http://www.springfieldsolutions.co.uk
Directors: A. Dass (Dir)
Ultimate Holding Company: SPRINGFIELD LABELS LIMITED
Immediate Holding Company: SPRINGFIELD SOLUTIONS LIMITED
Registration no: 01331331 **VAT No.:** GB 721 4098 55
Date established: 1977 **Turnover:** £5m - £10m **No.of Employees:** 1 - 10
Product Groups: 27, 28, 30

Date of Accounts	Dec 11	Dec 10	Dec 09
Working Capital	1m	1m	1m
Fixed Assets	526	575	379
Current Assets	3m	3m	3m

Stagecoach Ltd
Foster Street, Hull, HU8 8BT
Tel: 01482-222333 **Fax:** 01482-217623
E-mail: hull@stagecoachbus.com
Website: http://www.stagecoachbus.com/hull
Bank(s): Royal Bank of Scotland
Managers: T. Fieldsend (Mgr)
Ultimate Holding Company: STAGECOACH GROUP PLC
Immediate Holding Company: STAGECOACH LIMITED
Registration no: 03092390 **Date established:** 1995 **Turnover:** £5m - £10m
No.of Employees: 101 - 250 **Product Groups:** 72

Date of Accounts	Apr 11	Apr 10	Apr 09
Working Capital	-64	-40	-41
Fixed Assets	36	40	42
Current Assets	983	1m	745

Stenhouse Equipment Safety Co. Ltd
Seco Works Cannon Street, Hull, HU2 0AE
Tel: 01482-329045 **Fax:** 01482-226774
E-mail: info@stenhouse-safety.co.uk
Website: http://www.stenhouse-safety.co.uk
Directors: J. Todd (MD)
Immediate Holding Company: STENHOUSE EQUIPMENT (SAFETY) LIMITED
Registration no: 01242837 **VAT No.:** GB 433 5486 46
Date established: 1976 **Turnover:** £500,000 - £1m
No.of Employees: 1 - 10 **Product Groups:** 23, 24, 35, 39, 40, 45, 67

Date of Accounts	Feb 12	Feb 11	Feb 10
Working Capital	326	206	162
Fixed Assets	79	113	120
Current Assets	418	269	229

Stonegate Floor Preparation Equipment
5-7 Westmoreland Street, Hull, HU2 0DJ
Tel: 01482-620400
E-mail: info@stonegate.org.uk
Website: http://www.stonegatetooling.com
Directors: G. Hazel (Ptnr)
Immediate Holding Company: STONEGATE PRECISION TOOLING LIMITED
Registration no: 07876144 **Date established:** 2011
No.of Employees: 11 - 20 **Product Groups:** 40, 45, 52

Struthers & Carter Ltd
Erimus Works Valletta Street, Hull, HU9 5NU
Tel: 01482-375231 **Fax:** 01482-708926
E-mail: sales@struthers-carter.co.uk
Website: http://www.struthers-carter.co.uk
Bank(s): National Westminster Bank Plc
Managers: S. Dykes (District Mgr)
Ultimate Holding Company: BARRETT STEEL LIMITED
Immediate Holding Company: STRUTHERS & CARTER LIMITED
Registration no: 00349307 **VAT No.:** GB 166 8568 14
Date established: 1939 **Turnover:** £10m - £20m
No.of Employees: 11 - 20 **Product Groups:** 82

Date of Accounts	Sep 09	Sep 08
Working Capital	158	158m
Current Assets	158	158m

Sumitomo Drive Technologies S M Cyclo UK Ltd
Unit 29 Bergen Way, Hull, HU7 0YQ
Tel: 01482-790340 **Fax:** 01482-790321
E-mail: marketing@sumitomoeurope.com
Website: http://www.sumitomodriveeurope.com
Managers: S. Brown (Chief Mgr)
Ultimate Holding Company: SUMITOMO HEAVY INDUSTRIES LTD (JAPAN)
Immediate Holding Company: SM-CYCLO UK LIMITED
Registration no: 03270912 **VAT No.:** GB 167 2713 55
Date established: 1996 **Turnover:** £5m - £10m **No.of Employees:** 11 - 20
Product Groups: 25, 35, 39

Date of Accounts	Dec 11	Dec 10	Dec 09
Sales Turnover	8m	6m	4m
Pre Tax Profit/Loss	937	316	241
Working Capital	1m	729	628
Fixed Assets	11	N/A	14
Current Assets	4m	3m	2m
Current Liabilities	412	270	185

T T S Communications Ltd
Telecom House 277 Anlaby Road, Hull, HU3 2SE
Tel: 01482-755001 **Fax:** 01482-381909
E-mail: sales@ttscomms.co.uk
Website: http://www.ttscomms.co.uk
Directors: T. Wildbore (MD)
Immediate Holding Company: T.T.S. COMMUNICATIONS LIMITED
Registration no: 03845270 **Date established:** 1999
No.of Employees: 1 - 10 **Product Groups:** 37, 79, 84

Date of Accounts	Sep 11	Sep 10	Sep 09
Working Capital	30	35	15
Fixed Assets	168	162	163
Current Assets	101	91	66
Current Liabilities	N/A	46	N/A

Teal & Mackrill Ltd
Lockwood Street, Hull, HU2 0HN
Tel: 01482-320194 **Fax:** 01482-219266
E-mail: info@teamac.co.uk
Website: http://www.teamac.co.uk
Bank(s): HSBC
Directors: S. Moore (Fin), G. Mackrill (MD)
Immediate Holding Company: TEAL & MACKRILL LIMITED
Registration no: 00126674 **Date established:** 2013 **Turnover:** £2m - £5m
No.of Employees: 51 - 100 **Product Groups:** 32

Date of Accounts	Dec 11	Dec 10	Dec 09
Working Capital	440	421	478
Fixed Assets	358	366	437
Current Assets	2m	1m	1m

Tecnica Services Ltd
Unit 13 National Industrial Estate Bontoft Avenue, Hull, HU5 4HF
Tel: 01482-848829
E-mail: sales@tecnicaservices.co.uk
Website: http://www.tecnicaservices.co.uk
Directors: S. Blanchard (MD)
Immediate Holding Company: TECNICA SERVICES LIMITED
Registration no: 04920821 **Date established:** 2003
No.of Employees: 1 - 10 **Product Groups:** 25

Date of Accounts	Oct 11	Oct 10	Oct 09
Working Capital	-2	-19	-17
Fixed Assets	11	13	15
Current Assets	22	9	2

Terminic UK Ltd
Crown House 94-96 Alexandra Road, Hull, HU5 2NX
Tel: 01482-348834 **Fax:** 01482-443445
E-mail: sales@terminic.co.uk
Website: http://www.terminic.co.uk
Directors: P. Smith (Dir)
Immediate Holding Company: TERMINIC U.K. LIMITED
Registration no: 03901834 **Date established:** 2000
No.of Employees: 1 - 10 **Product Groups:** 28

Date of Accounts	Dec 11	Dec 10	Dec 09
Working Capital	198	97	9
Fixed Assets	2	2	8
Current Assets	298	337	351

Thermica Ltd
Themework House Vulcan Street Clough Road, Hull, HU6 7PS
Tel: 01482-348771 **Fax:** 01482-444626
E-mail: kerry@thermica.co.uk
Website: http://www.thermica.co.uk
Directors: J. Van Nes (MD), K. Grovener (MD), K. Grover (MD), P. Vaness (Ch)
Managers: K. Barnes (Sales Admin)
Ultimate Holding Company: Nestaan Group, Tholen, Netherlands
Registration no: 02080727 **VAT No.:** GB 475 4351 34
Date established: 1986 **Turnover:** £1m - £2m **No.of Employees:** 1 - 10
Product Groups: 32, 33, 40

Date of Accounts	Dec 09	Dec 08	Dec 07
Working Capital	186	289	227
Fixed Assets	345	377	414
Current Assets	281	351	289

Tool Shop Direct
UNIT 5 THE SHINE KNOWLEDGE & INNOVATION PARK, ST MARKS STREET, Hull, HU8 7FB
Tel: 01482-499955 **Fax:** 01482-440887
E-mail: sales@toolshopdirect.co.uk
Website: http://www.toolshopdirect.co.uk
Directors: J. Dean (Dir)
Immediate Holding Company: Jetstone Construction Ltd
Registration no: 06675028 **Date established:** 2008
No.of Employees: 11 - 20 **Product Groups:** 37

Toolnweld
Main Street, Hull, HU2 0HX
Tel: 0800-9155092
E-mail: sales@toolnweld.com
Website: http://www.toolnweld.com/
Managers: P. Thompson (Publicity)
Date established: 2006 **Turnover:** Up to £250,000
No.of Employees: 21 - 50 **Product Groups:** 32

Tooltek Supplies Ltd
Spyvee Street, Hull, HU8 7JJ
Tel: 01482-229628 **Fax:** 01482-229630
E-mail: sales@tooltek.co.uk
Website: http://www.tooltek.co.uk
Directors: D. Peach (MD)
Immediate Holding Company: TOOLTEK SUPPLIES LIMITED
Registration no: 02401883 **Date established:** 1989
Turnover: £500,000 - £1m **No.of Employees:** 1 - 10 **Product Groups:** 30, 32, 33, 35

Date of Accounts	Nov 11	Nov 10	Nov 09
Working Capital	11	-4	-5
Fixed Assets	153	131	131
Current Assets	221	171	171

Traditional Games Co.
Matrich House Hatfield Hi-Tech Park Goulton Street, Hull, HU3 4DD
Tel: 01482-327019 **Fax:** 01482-210490
E-mail: info@sac-games.com
Website: http://www.sac-games.com
Directors: M. Lee (MD)
Immediate Holding Company: THE TRADITIONAL GAMES COMPANY LTD
Registration no: 05115745 **Turnover:** £500,000 - £1m
No.of Employees: 1 - 10 **Product Groups:** 49

Date of Accounts	Jun 07	Jun 06
Working Capital	-35	-65
Fixed Assets	17	22
Current Assets	155	143
Current Liabilities	190	208
Total Share Capital	1	1

Tranfield Of Cumbria Ltd Vion Foods
Liverpool Street, Hull, HU3 4HW
Tel: 01482-326234 **Fax:** 01482-210375
E-mail: kelly.wood@vionfood.com
Managers: M. Wiltshire (Fin Mgr), K. Wood (Fin Mgr), A. Adams (Personnel)
Ultimate Holding Company: THE GLOBAL GROUP PLC
Registration no: 01666877 **No.of Employees:** 21 - 50 **Product Groups:** 20

Neville Tucker
Rotterdam Road, Hull, HU7 0XD
Tel: 01482-834900 **Fax:** 01482-879852
E-mail: info@ntuckerheating.co.uk
Website: http://www.ntuckerheating.co.uk
Directors: R. Abbott (MD), A. Garten (Ptnr)
Managers: I. Jeffrey (Buyer), K. McManus
Immediate Holding Company: NEVILLE TUCKER HEATING LIMITED
Registration no: 03695967 **VAT No.:** GB 598 8674 47
Date established: 1999 **Turnover:** £20m - £50m
No.of Employees: 101 - 250 **Product Groups:** 52, 67

Date of Accounts	Jan 12	Jan 11	Jan 10
Sales Turnover	22m	15m	19m
Pre Tax Profit/Loss	262	23	268
Working Capital	2m	1m	952
Fixed Assets	569	825	1m
Current Assets	6m	4m	3m
Current Liabilities	664	546	1m

Turbo Systems Ltd
1 Gillett Street, Hull, HU3 4JA
Tel: 01482-325651 **Fax:** 01483-300078
E-mail: vdavies@turbo-systems.com
Website: http://www.turbo-systems.com
Bank(s): Bank of Scotland, London
Directors: S. Weaver (Fin), V. Davies (Tech Serv), C. Guest (Sales), A. Lang (MD)
Managers: J. Wilks (Purch Mgr)
Ultimate Holding Company: TURBO SYSTEMS LIMITED
Immediate Holding Company: FP PACKAGING MACHINERY LIMITED
Registration no: 01431792 **Date established:** 1979
Turnover: £250,000 - £500,000 **No.of Employees:** 21 - 50
Product Groups: 41, 42

Date of Accounts	Aug 08	Aug 07	Mar 11
Sales Turnover	335	124	N/A
Pre Tax Profit/Loss	-86	-146	N/A
Working Capital	-793	-716	-157
Fixed Assets	N/A	9	N/A
Current Assets	3	115	N/A
Current Liabilities	794	629	157

U C M Magnesia Ltd
Hull Road Saltend, Hull, HU12 8ED
Tel: 01482-899141 **Fax:** 01482-890196
E-mail: hull@ucm-magnesia.com
Website: http://www.ucm-magnesia.com
Directors: H. Trahair Davies (Co Sec)
Managers: D. Selkirk (Sales & Mktg Mg), P. Anderson, P. Bettles (Prod Mgr), R. Jackson (Chief Acct)
Ultimate Holding Company: IMERYS SA (FRANCE)
Immediate Holding Company: UCM MAGNESIA LIMITED
Registration no: 02765383 **VAT No.:** 642 8946 06 **Date established:** 1992
Turnover: £5m - £10m **No.of Employees:** 21 - 50 **Product Groups:** 33

Date of Accounts	Dec 11	Dec 10	Dec 09
Sales Turnover	9m	9m	7m
Pre Tax Profit/Loss	-182	319	-210
Working Capital	-3m	-3m	-2m
Fixed Assets	2m	2m	2m
Current Assets	5m	6m	4m
Current Liabilities	821	89	60

Valeway Technology Ltd
Unit 4 Shine Knowledge & Innovation Park St Mark Street, Hull, HU8 7FB
Tel: 01482-319700 **Fax:** 01482-319701
E-mail: sales@valewaytechnology.com
Website: http://www.valewaytechnology.com
Directors: P. Moss (MD)
Ultimate Holding Company: MWS GROUP LTD
Immediate Holding Company: VALEWAY TECHNOLOGY LIMITED
Registration no: 05702444 **Date established:** 2006
No.of Employees: 11 - 20 **Product Groups:** 37, 61, 63, 83

Date of Accounts	May 11	May 10	May 09
Working Capital	255	5	N/A
Fixed Assets	1m	1m	798
Current Assets	255	5	1
Current Liabilities	N/A	N/A	1

Vanguard Precision Machinist
Unit A Acorn Industrial Estate Strawberry Street, Hull, HU9 1EN
Tel: 01482-224226 **Fax:** 01482-328129
E-mail: pete.weath@vigin.net
Directors: P. Weatherill (MD)
Date established: 1999 **No.of Employees:** 1 - 10 **Product Groups:** 36

Ventex Ltd
Strickland Street, Hull, HU3 4AD
Tel: 01482-221157
No.of Employees: 51 - 100 **Product Groups:** 40, 66

Veolia Environmental Services Ltd
Thomas House Staithes Road, Hedon, Hull, HU12 8DX
Tel: 01482-894380 **Fax:** 01482-891167
Website: http://www.onyx.co.uk
Managers: P. Collins (Mgr)
Immediate Holding Company: P. BARKER PROPERTIES LIMITED
Registration no: 04282598 **Date established:** 2001 **Turnover:** £2m - £5m
No.of Employees: 1 - 10 **Product Groups:** 34, 40, 42, 54, 84

Date of Accounts	Mar 12	Mar 11	Mar 10
Working Capital	-119	-64	-89
Fixed Assets	2m	2m	2m
Current Assets	75	94	131

WHW Plastics Ltd

Therm Rd Cleveland St, Hull, HU8 7BF
Tel: 01482-329154 **Fax:** 01482-217140
E-mail: mike@whwplastics.com
Website: http://www.whwplastics.com
Bank(s): National Westminster Bank Plc
Directors: M. Wright (MD), A. Wright (Dir), C. Clinton (Dir), P. Wright (Dir)
Managers: M. Wright (Sales Admin)
Ultimate Holding Company: WHW Plastics
Registration no: 06942043 **VAT No.:** GB 282 2227 72
Date established: 1960 **Turnover:** £1m - £2m **No.of Employees:** 11 - 20
Product Groups: 24, 31, 32, 38, 40, 42, 67

Date of Accounts	Sep 11	Sep 10
Working Capital	230	21
Fixed Assets	107	57
Current Assets	860	718

Waterloo Motor Trade Ltd

Main Street, Hull, HU2 0JX
Tel: 01482-328308 **Fax:** 01482-212398
E-mail: info@waterloo-mt.co.uk
Website: http://www.waterloo-mt.co.uk
Bank(s): National Westminster
Directors: C. Munday (Fin), J. Munday (MD)
Managers: A. Simpson
Ultimate Holding Company: WATERLOO (MOTOR TRADE) LIMITED
Registration no: 00396347 **VAT No.:** GB 166 8237 37
Date established: 1945 **Turnover:** £1m - £2m **No.of Employees:** 21 - 50
Product Groups: 39

Date of Accounts	Jun 11	Jun 10	Jun 09
Working Capital	390	439	428
Fixed Assets	104	110	117
Current Assets	837	806	809

White & Farrell Ltd

Caroline Street, Hull, HU2 8ED
Tel: 01482-329997 **Fax:** 01482-325956
E-mail: info@whiteandfarrell.co.uk
Website: http://www.whiteandfarrell.co.uk
Bank(s): Bank of Scotland
Directors: C. Sendall (MD), S. Dennis (MD)
Immediate Holding Company: WHITE & FARRELL, LIMITED
Registration no: 00206102 **Date established:** 2025 **Turnover:** £1m - £2m
No.of Employees: 21 - 50 **Product Groups:** 27, 28

Date of Accounts	Jun 12	Jun 11	Jun 10
Working Capital	27	40	87
Fixed Assets	341	364	408
Current Assets	366	389	425

Willerby Holiday Homes Ltd

Imperial House 1251 Hedon Road, Hull, HU9 5NA
Tel: 01482-707808 **Fax:** 01482-711482
E-mail: info@willerby.com
Website: http://www.willerby.com
Directors: P. White (Sales), B. Murphy (Dir)
Managers: W. Dennitt (Purch Mgr)
Ultimate Holding Company: SCAID INVESTMENTS LIMITED
Immediate Holding Company: WILLERBY HOLIDAY HOMES LTD.
Registration no: 00387583 **Date established:** 1944
Turnover: £75m - £125m **No.of Employees:** 501 - 1000
Product Groups: 82

Date of Accounts	Sep 08	Oct 09	Oct 10
Sales Turnover	120m	99m	135m
Pre Tax Profit/Loss	11m	7m	18m
Working Capital	49m	55m	68m
Fixed Assets	3m	2m	2m
Current Assets	63m	77m	88m
Current Liabilities	3m	3m	5m

Winch Systems Ltd

Craven House Craven Street South, Hull, HU9 1AP
Tel: 01482-620991 **Fax:** 08700-567721
E-mail: sales@winchsystems.co.uk
Website: http://www.winchsystems.co.uk
Directors: N. Giblin (MD), J. Giblin (Fin), M. Findlow (Sales)
Immediate Holding Company: WINCH SYSTEMS LIMITED
Registration no: 03509897 **Date established:** 1998
Turnover: £500,000 - £1m **No.of Employees:** 1 - 10 **Product Groups:** 35, 39, 45

Date of Accounts	Mar 11	Mar 10	Mar 09
Sales Turnover	N/A	830	N/A
Working Capital	516	558	599
Fixed Assets	83	79	61
Current Assets	858	887	977

A & E Woodward Ltd

North Bridge Works Lime Street, Hull, HU8 7AB
Tel: 01482-329185 **Fax:** 01482-216619
E-mail: sales@a-ewoodwardltd.karoo.co.uk
Website: http://www.aewoodward.co.uk
Directors: D. Woodward (Dir)
Immediate Holding Company: A & E WOODWARD LIMITED
Registration no: 02885881 **VAT No.:** GB 599 2262 94
Date established: 1994 **Turnover:** £500,000 - £1m
No.of Employees: 1 - 10 **Product Groups:** 29, 39, 40

Date of Accounts	Feb 12	Feb 11	Feb 10
Working Capital	66	81	72
Fixed Assets	37	25	30
Current Assets	283	322	308

North Ferriby

Advertising Gift Connect Ltd

PO Box 328, North Ferriby, HU14 3UX
Tel: 01482-221209 **Fax:** 01482-224324
E-mail: sales@ad-gift.co.uk
Website: http://www.ad-gift.co.uk
Directors: E. Harrison (Dir)
Immediate Holding Company: ADVERTISING GIFT CONNECT LIMITED
Registration no: 06080774 **Date established:** 2007
Turnover: £250,000 - £500,000 **No.of Employees:** 1 - 10
Product Groups: 24, 44, 49, 81

Date of Accounts	Jul 11	Jul 10	Jul 09
Working Capital	-3	-8	-9
Fixed Assets	1	1	2
Current Assets	15	15	7

Gardner Aerospace

Unit 3a Gibson Lane, Melton, North Ferriby, HU14 3LH
Tel: 01482-633144 **Fax:** 01482-633180
E-mail: info@gardner-aerospace.com
Website: http://www.gardner-aerospace.com
Bank(s): Barclays
Directors: K. Lee (Dir)
Immediate Holding Company: GARDNER AEROSPACE
Registration no: 00644243 **VAT No.:** GB 239 9422 32
Date established: 2005 **Turnover:** £2m - £5m **No.of Employees:** 11 - 20
Product Groups: 34, 39

Date of Accounts	Aug 11	Aug 10	Aug 09
Sales Turnover	2m	2m	3m
Pre Tax Profit/Loss	-114	-320	138
Working Capital	-126	299	448
Fixed Assets	2m	844	1m
Current Assets	824	663	980
Current Liabilities	130	138	115

House Of Townend

Wyke Way Melton West Business Park East, North Ferriby, HU14 3BQ
Tel: 01482-638888 **Fax:** 01482-587042
E-mail: info@houseoftownend.co.uk
Website: http://www.houseoftownend.com
Directors: A. Whitehead (Sales)
Ultimate Holding Company: J.TOWNEND & SONS(HULL)LIMITED
Immediate Holding Company: HOUSE OF TOWNEND LIMITED
Registration no: 00723084 **Date established:** 1962
No.of Employees: 1 - 10 **Product Groups:** 21, 62

Date of Accounts	Apr 12	Apr 11	Apr 10
Sales Turnover	13m	13m	13m
Pre Tax Profit/Loss	-66	41	41
Working Capital	319	486	737
Fixed Assets	629	526	236
Current Assets	5m	5m	5m
Current Liabilities	943	733	619

SOUTH HUMBERSIDE

Barnetby

Greenhouse Repairs
3 Railway Street Barnetby Le Wold, Barnetby, DN38 6DH
Tel: 08454-631845 **Fax:** 0845-686 0773
E-mail: sales@greenhouserepairs.com
Website: http://www.greenhouserepairs.com
Directors: C. Van Eijk (Prop)
Registration no: 05225835 **Date established:** 2004
Turnover: £250,000 - £500,000 **No.of Employees:** 1 - 10
Product Groups: 25, 30, 33, 35, 40, 52, 84

Barrow Upon Humber

Geomatix Ltd
Inglenook Cottage Westoby Lane, Barrow Upon Humber, DN19 7DJ
Tel: 01469-532481
E-mail: set@geomatix.net
Website: http://www.geomatix.net
Directors: S. Taylor (Co Sec)
Immediate Holding Company: GEOMATIX LIMITED
Registration no: 02895577 **Date established:** 1994
Turnover: £250,000 - £500,000 **No.of Employees:** 1 - 10
Product Groups: 39, 84, 85

Date of Accounts	Feb 08	Feb 11	Feb 10
Working Capital	16	N/A	-11
Fixed Assets	3	2	2
Current Assets	31	18	6

Barton Upon Humber

Birse Group Services Ltd
Humber Road, Barton Upon Humber, DN18 5BW
Tel: 01652-633222 **Fax:** 01652-633360
E-mail: john.ruane@birse.co.uk
Website: http://www.birsecl.co.uk
Bank(s): HSBC Bank plc
Directors: A. Church (Co Sec), M. Budden (Dir)
Managers: A. Dawson (Comptroller)
Ultimate Holding Company: BALFOUR BEATTY PLC
Immediate Holding Company: BIRSE DEVELOPMENTS LIMITED
Registration no: 03173974 **VAT No.:** GB 613 6806 47
Date established: 1996 **Turnover:** £1m - £2m **No.of Employees:** 21 - 50
Product Groups: 84

Date of Accounts	Dec 10	Dec 09	Dec 08
Working Capital	-479	-479	-479

Braun International Ltd
19 Pasture Road Barton On Humber, Barton Upon Humber, DN18 5HN
Tel: 01652-632273 **Fax:** 01652-633399
E-mail: barry@braunmedical.co.uk
Website: http://www.brauninternational.com
Directors: T. Shepherd (Fin), B. Shepherd (MD)
Immediate Holding Company: BRAUN INTERNATIONAL LIMITED
Registration no: 03085847 **VAT No.:** GB 220 9793 58
Date established: 1995 **Turnover:** £250,000 - £500,000
No.of Employees: 1 - 10 **Product Groups:** 38

Date of Accounts	Jul 09	Jul 08
Working Capital	-15	-15
Current Liabilities	N/A	15

Pinewrap Ltd
Humber Road, Barton Upon Humber, DN18 5BN
Tel: 08703-607070 **Fax:** 08703-608080
Website: http://www.pinewrap.com
Directors: D. Mash (Fin)
Immediate Holding Company: PINEWRAP LIMITED
Registration no: 03326867 **Date established:** 1997
No.of Employees: 21 - 50 **Product Groups:** 25, 33, 40

Date of Accounts	Jul 11	Jul 09	Jul 08
Working Capital	-15	N/A	N/A
Current Assets	53	N/A	N/A

Pro-Optocam Ltd
Unit 14 Fathom Works - The Ropewalk Maltkiln Road, Barton Upon Humber, DN18 5JT
Tel: 01652-660888 **Fax:** 01652-660888
E-mail: enquiries@optocam.co.uk
Website: http://www.infra-led.co.uk
Directors: J. Franks (Dir)
Immediate Holding Company: PRO-OPTOCAM LIMITED
Registration no: 04299048 **Date established:** 2001
Turnover: £500,000 - £1m **No.of Employees:** 1 - 10 **Product Groups:** 37, 38

Date of Accounts	Sep 11	Sep 10	Sep 09
Working Capital	N/A	-1	3
Fixed Assets	2	3	3
Current Assets	10	12	13

T C Power Ltd
Stanley House Falkland Way, Barton Upon Humber, DN18 5RL
Tel: 01652-631000 **Fax:** 01652-631099
E-mail: reception@tcpower.co.uk
Website: http://www.tcpower.co.uk
Directors: S. Elliott (MD), S. Dent (Co Sec)
Immediate Holding Company: TC POWER LIMITED
Registration no: 04182459 **Date established:** 2001
Turnover: Up to £250,000 **No.of Employees:** 21 - 50 **Product Groups:** 35, 36, 39

Date of Accounts	Mar 09	Mar 08	Mar 07
Pre Tax Profit/Loss	N/A	109	N/A
Working Capital	522	216	140
Fixed Assets	1m	1m	1m
Current Assets	3m	3m	1m
Current Liabilities	N/A	443	N/A

Weir Engineering Services
Humber Road, Barton Upon Humber, DN18 5BN
Tel: 01652-632702 **Fax:** 01652-633112
E-mail: neil.mackmin@weirpowerindustrial.com
Website: http://www.weirpowerindustrial.com
Bank(s): Royal Bank of Scotland, Glasgow
Directors: N. Mackmin (Chief Op Offcr)
Managers: D. Blackwood (Fin Mgr), J. Fillingham, P. Wakefield
Ultimate Holding Company: CLYDE BLOWERS CAPITAL FUND II LP (SCOTLAND)
Immediate Holding Company: CLYDE UNION LIMITED
Registration no: SC317760 **VAT No.:** GB 128 1650 80
Date established: 2007 **Turnover:** £5m - £10m **No.of Employees:** 21 - 50
Product Groups: 39, 40, 45, 48

Date of Accounts	Dec 10	Dec 09	Dec 08
Sales Turnover	123m	107m	84m
Pre Tax Profit/Loss	8m	3m	-9m
Working Capital	18m	3m	-463
Fixed Assets	49m	41m	39m
Current Assets	97m	54m	40m
Current Liabilities	31m	31m	29m

Weldtite Products Ltd
Unit 9 Harrier Road, Humber Bridge Industrial Estate, Barton Upon Humber, DN18 5RP
Tel: 01652-660000 **Fax:** 01652-660066
E-mail: sales@weldtite.co.uk
Website: http://www.weldtite.co.uk
Bank(s): Nat west
Directors: D. Baggs (Dir)
Managers: D. Taylor (Fin Mgr)
Ultimate Holding Company: C.B. BAGGS GROUP LIMITED
Immediate Holding Company: WELDTITE PRODUCTS LIMITED
Registration no: 02558918 **Date established:** 1990 **Turnover:** £2m - £5m
No.of Employees: 21 - 50 **Product Groups:** 68

Date of Accounts	Dec 11	Dec 10	Dec 09
Working Capital	963	883	814
Fixed Assets	100	71	63
Current Assets	2m	2m	2m

William Blyth Ltd
Far Ings Road, Barton Upon Humber, DN18 5AZ
Tel: 01652-637222 **Fax:** 01652-660966
E-mail: g-harrison@williamblyth.co.uk
Website: http://www.williamblyth.co.uk
Bank(s): Barkleys
Directors: G. Harrison (MD)
Immediate Holding Company: WILLIAM BLYTH LIMITED
Registration no: 05754770 **VAT No.:** 127 9846 29 **Date established:** 2006
Turnover: £250,000 - £500,000 **No.of Employees:** 11 - 20
Product Groups: 33

Brigg

D D M Agriculture
Eastfield Albert Street, Brigg, DN20 8HS
Tel: 01652-653669 **Fax:** 01652-653311
E-mail: tony.dale@ddmagriculture.co.uk
Website: http://www.ddmagriculture.co.uk
Directors: A. Dale (Dir)
Immediate Holding Company: DDM AGRICULTURE LIMITED
Registration no: 03740827 **Date established:** 1999 **Turnover:** £5m - £10m
No.of Employees: 1 - 10 **Product Groups:** 80

Date of Accounts	Jun 11	Jun 10	Jun 09
Working Capital	91	-72	224
Fixed Assets	96	93	94
Current Assets	203	137	348

E H Advertising Ltd
Castlethorpe Court Castlethorpe, Brigg, DN20 9LG
Tel: 01652-650100 **Fax:** 01652-650035
E-mail: eh.advertising@virgin.net
Website: http://www.ehadvertisingltd.co.uk
Directors: M. McGlone (MD)
Immediate Holding Company: E.H. ADVERTISING LIMITED
Registration no: 01751681 **VAT No.:** GB 364 6733 31
Date established: 1983 **Turnover:** £1m - £2m **No.of Employees:** 1 - 10
Product Groups: 33, 49, 64, 65, 81

Date of Accounts	Mar 12	Mar 11	Mar 10
Working Capital	7	7	-0
Fixed Assets	10	11	13
Current Assets	52	80	88

Falcon Cycles Ltd
PO Box 3, Brigg, DN20 8PB
Tel: 01652-656000 **Fax:** 01652-650040
E-mail: info@falconcycles.co.uk
Website: http://www.falconcycles.co.uk
Bank(s): Barclays, Manchester
Directors: J. Shears (Fin), S. Bell (MD)
Ultimate Holding Company: TANDEM GROUP PLC
Immediate Holding Company: TANDEM GROUP CYCLES LIMITED
Registration no: 01704676 **VAT No.:** GB 167 9381 19
Date established: 1983 **Turnover:** £20m - £50m
No.of Employees: 21 - 50 **Product Groups:** 39

Date of Accounts	Dec 11	Jan 11	Jan 10
Sales Turnover	18m	20m	16m
Pre Tax Profit/Loss	402	-263	197
Working Capital	-2m	-3m	-2m
Fixed Assets	535	606	183
Current Assets	9m	10m	6m
Current Liabilities	3m	2m	2m

Farm Star Ltd
Bridge Street, Brigg, DN20 8NF
Tel: 01652-654944 **Fax:** 01652-655171
E-mail: clive.parker@farmstar.co.uk
Website: http://www.farmstar.co.uk
Managers: C. Parker (Mgr)
Immediate Holding Company: FARMSTAR LIMITED
Registration no: 02262473 **Date established:** 1988
No.of Employees: 11 - 20 **Product Groups:** 41

Date of Accounts	Jun 12	Jun 11	Jun 10
Sales Turnover	26m	23m	21m
Pre Tax Profit/Loss	504	402	379
Working Capital	617	876	465
Fixed Assets	4m	4m	4m
Current Assets	8m	8m	7m
Current Liabilities	313	266	324

Lincolnshire Motors Ltd
Unit 2 Atherton Way, Brigg, DN20 8AR
Tel: 01652-657671 **Fax:** 01652-658616
E-mail: astevens@lincsmotors.co.uk
Website: http://www.lincsmotors.co.uk
Managers: A. Stevens (Mgr)
Immediate Holding Company: LINCOLNSHIRE MOTORS LIMITED
Registration no: 02579212 **Date established:** 1991
No.of Employees: 1 - 10 **Product Groups:** 41

Date of Accounts	Feb 12	Feb 11	Feb 10
Sales Turnover	N/A	7m	7m
Pre Tax Profit/Loss	N/A	79	80

see next page

Lincolnshire Motors Ltd - Cont'd

Working Capital	485	634	632
Fixed Assets	752	719	726
Current Assets	2m	2m	3m
Current Liabilities	N/A	289	322

Frazer Melton

18 Redcombe Lane, Brigg, DN20 8AU
Tel: 07771-948899
E-mail: helpdesk@osict.co.uk
Website: http://www.osict.co.uk/frazer.html
Directors: F. Melton (MD)
Turnover: Up to £250,000 **No.of Employees:** 1 - 10 **Product Groups:** 79, 81

Peacock & Binnington

Old Foundry, Brigg, DN20 8NR
Tel: 01652-600200 **Fax:** 01652-657532
E-mail: enquire@peacock.co.uk
Website: http://www.peacock.co.uk
Directors: G. Main (MD), G. Wright (Fin)
Managers: S. Bradford (Buyer)
Ultimate Holding Company: PEACOCK & BINNINGTON HOLDINGS LIMITED
Immediate Holding Company: PEACOCK & BINNINGTON
Registration no: 00328944 **Date established:** 1937
Turnover: £20m - £50m **No.of Employees:** 21 - 50 **Product Groups:** 41

Date of Accounts	Dec 11	Dec 10	Dec 09
Sales Turnover	36m	35m	34m
Pre Tax Profit/Loss	361	202	267
Working Capital	2m	2m	1m
Fixed Assets	2m	1m	1m
Current Assets	8m	8m	7m
Current Liabilities	653	231	599

Red Apple Cleaning Ltd

2 Wrawby Road, Brigg, DN20 8DL
Tel: 01652-653704 **Fax:** 01652-657777
E-mail: sales@redapplecleaning.co.uk
Website: http://www.redapplecleaning.co.uk
Directors: S. Cogan (Dir)
Immediate Holding Company: RED APPLE CLEANING LIMITED
Registration no: 06559601 **Date established:** 2008
Turnover: Up to £250,000 **No.of Employees:** 11 - 20 **Product Groups:** 32, 40, 49, 52

Date of Accounts	Apr 11	Apr 10	Apr 09
Working Capital	26	44	12
Fixed Assets	10	N/A	N/A
Current Assets	51	68	15

Vindotco UK Ltd

11a Elwes Street, Brigg, DN20 8LB
Tel: 01652-652444 **Fax:** 01652-652808
E-mail: vindotco@compuserve.com
Website: http://www.vindotco.co.uk
Directors: A. Corcoran (Co Sec), M. Donald (MD)
Immediate Holding Company: VIN-DOTCO (U.K.) LIMITED
Registration no: 01895347 **VAT No.:** GB 365 0002 94
Date established: 1985 **Turnover:** £250,000 - £500,000
No.of Employees: 1 - 10 **Product Groups:** 66

Date of Accounts	Apr 11	Apr 10	Apr 09
Working Capital	-137	-138	-142
Fixed Assets	2	N/A	N/A
Current Assets	116	155	94

Cleethorpes

Advance Mobility Ltd

135 Grimsby Road, Cleethorpes, DN35 7DG
Tel: 01472-240404 **Fax:** 01472- 242223
Directors: P. Tolson (Sales)
Immediate Holding Company: ADVANCE MOBILITY LIMITED
Registration no: 03013495 **Date established:** 1995
No.of Employees: 1 - 10 **Product Groups:** 24, 26, 39

Arne Fabrications

Rear of 1 Elm Road, Cleethorpes, DN35 8HN
Tel: 01472-699784 **Fax:** 01472-699784
E-mail: sales@arnefabs.co.uk
Website: http://www.arnefabs.co.uk
Directors: S. Vick (Prop)
Immediate Holding Company: CLEETHORPES BOWLING CLUB LIMITED(THE)
Registration no: 00100500 **Date established:** 2008
Turnover: Up to £250,000 **No.of Employees:** 1 - 10 **Product Groups:** 35

Date of Accounts	Nov 11	Nov 10	Nov 09
Sales Turnover	N/A	49	54
Pre Tax Profit/Loss	N/A	-0	1
Working Capital	9	-39	-39
Fixed Assets	15	40	39
Current Assets	11	N/A	N/A
Current Liabilities	N/A	2	2

Dixon Industrial Spraying Services Ltd

46 Berkeley Road, Cleethorpes, DN35 0NX
Tel: 01472-811136
E-mail: keithrobertdixon@hotmail.com
Directors: K. Dixon (Fin)
Registration no: 04043597 **Date established:** 2000
No.of Employees: 1 - 10 **Product Groups:** 46, 48

Date of Accounts	Jul 07	Jul 06	Jul 05
Working Capital	-1	2	3
Fixed Assets	2	2	1
Current Assets	N/A	3	5
Current Liabilities	1	1	2

Humberside Instruments Ltd

15 Barkhouse Lane, Cleethorpes, DN35 8RA
Tel: 01472-691157 **Fax:** 01472-692585
E-mail: sales@humbersideinstruments.co.uk
Website: http://www.humbersideinstruments.co.uk
Directors: M. Egarr (MD)
Immediate Holding Company: HUMBERSIDE INSTRUMENTS LIMITED
Registration no: 01855594 **Date established:** 1984
Turnover: £250,000 - £500,000 **No.of Employees:** 1 - 10
Product Groups: 49, 84

Date of Accounts	Oct 11	Oct 10	Oct 09
Working Capital	15	24	1
Fixed Assets	12	2	4
Current Assets	83	111	73

Grimsby

A B C Polishing & Engineering Supplies Picador Engineering

103 Louth Road Holton-Le-Clay, Grimsby, DN36 5AD
Tel: 01472-824520 **Fax:** 01472-824520
E-mail: sales@abcpolishing.co.uk
Website: http://www.abcpolishing.co.uk
Directors: A. Brook (Prop)
Date established: 1928 **Turnover:** £250,000 - £500,000
No.of Employees: 1 - 10 **Product Groups:** 30, 35, 36, 39, 45

A C S & T

Estate Road 2 South Humberside Industrial Estate, Grimsby, DN31 2TG
Tel: 01472-358207 **Fax:** 01472-240269
E-mail: malcolm.johnstone@acst.co.uk
Website: http://www.acstlogistics.co.uk
Bank(s): HSBC Bank plc
Directors: M. Johnstone (MD), S. Tomlinson (Fin)
Managers: A. Beasley (Tech Serv Mgr), R. Lightwood (Personnel)
Immediate Holding Company: LIMANDA LIMITED
Registration no: 00553154 **VAT No.:** GB 365 8312 45
Date established: 2007 **Turnover:** £20m - £50m
No.of Employees: 51 - 100 **Product Groups:** 77, 84

A P T Marine Engineering Company Ltd

Unit 3 South Humberside Industrial Estate, Grimsby, DN31 2TB
Tel: 01472-362550
E-mail: anthony.tofton2@btopenworld.com
Website: http://www.aptengineering.co.uk
Directors: J. Tofton (MD), A. Tofton (MD)
Immediate Holding Company: A.P.T. MARINE ENGINEERING LIMITED
Registration no: 02090925 **Date established:** 1987
Turnover: £250,000 - £500,000 **No.of Employees:** 11 - 20
Product Groups: 35, 36, 39

Date of Accounts	Dec 11	Dec 10	Dec 09
Working Capital	254	144	170
Fixed Assets	63	70	94
Current Assets	512	194	240

Asd Metal Services (a division of ASD P.L.C.)

Estate Road Number 5 South Humberside Industrial Estate, Grimsby, DN31 2TX
Tel: 01472-353851 **Fax:** 01472-240028
E-mail: grimsby@asdmetalservices.co.uk
Website: http://www.asdmetalservices.co.uk
Bank(s): Barclays
Managers: S. Makin (Chief Mgr)
Immediate Holding Company: KLOCKNER & CO
VAT No.: GB 176 2423 63 **Turnover:** £2m - £5m **No.of Employees:** 11 - 20
Product Groups: 66

ABEKO (UK) Ltd

Viking Haven Inghams Road, Tetney, Grimsby, DN36 5LW
Tel: 01472-210054 **Fax:** 01472-210484
E-mail: enquiries@abeko.uk.com
Website: http://www.abeko.uk.com
Bank(s): Bank of Scotland
Directors: C. Koster (Dir), M. Cleve (MD)
Managers: J. Cleve (Mgr), M. Cleve (Purch Mgr)
Registration no: 03722954 **VAT No.:** GB 727 9309 07
Date established: 1999 **Turnover:** £2m - £5m **No.of Employees:** 11 - 20
Product Groups: 34, 39, 41, 42, 45, 46, 51, 68, 74, 83, 84

Date of Accounts	Apr 08	Apr 07	Apr 06
Working Capital	61	24	34
Fixed Assets	44	23	9
Current Assets	1074	551	168
Current Liabilities	1013	527	134

Auto Trail V R Ltd

Trigano House Genesis Way, Grimsby, DN37 9TU
Tel: 01472-571000 **Fax:** 01472-571001
E-mail: sales@auto-trail.co.uk
Website: http://www.auto-trail.co.uk
Directors: S. Devoy (Fin), D. Turpin (Sales)
Managers: L. Turpin (Sales Admin), E. Turpin (Personnel), S. Ellis (Purch Mgr)
Ultimate Holding Company: TRIGANO SA (FRANCE)
Immediate Holding Company: AUTO-TRAIL V.R. LIMITED
Registration no: 03533638 **Date established:** 1998
Turnover: £20m - £50m **No.of Employees:** 51 - 100 **Product Groups:** 72

Date of Accounts	Aug 11	Aug 10	Aug 09
Sales Turnover	45m	39m	37m
Pre Tax Profit/Loss	6m	4m	-1m
Working Capital	9m	6m	9m
Fixed Assets	677	849	1m
Current Assets	16m	14m	11m
Current Liabilities	641	2m	401

Biffa Waste Services Ltd

Pyewipe Gilbey Road, Grimsby, DN31 2SJ
Tel: 01472-268130 **Fax:** 01472-251697
E-mail: grimsby@biffa.co.uk
Website: http://www.biffa.co.uk
Directors: M. Bettington (MD)
Managers: I. Shortland (Mgr)
Immediate Holding Company: BIFFA WASTE SERVICES LIMITED
Registration no: 00946107 **Date established:** 1969
Turnover: £20m - £50m **No.of Employees:** 1 - 10 **Product Groups:** 54

Date of Accounts	Mar 08	Mar 09	Apr 10
Sales Turnover	555m	574m	492m
Pre Tax Profit/Loss	23m	50m	30m
Working Capital	229m	271m	293m
Fixed Assets	371m	360m	378m
Current Assets	409m	534m	609m
Current Liabilities	50m	100m	115m

Compton Buildings Ltd

Estate Road 3 South Humberside Industrial Estate, Grimsby, DN31 2TB
Tel: 01472-241775 **Fax:** 01472-241775
Managers: K. Allen (Mgr), K. Allen (District Mgr)
Immediate Holding Company: COMPTON BUILDINGS LIMITED
Registration no: 07171283 **Date established:** 2010
No.of Employees: 1 - 10 **Product Groups:** 25, 33, 35, 66

Cameron

45 High Street Limber, Grimsby, DN37 8JL
Tel: 01469-569857 **Fax:** 01469- 569857
Website: http://www.ccvalve.com
Managers: N. Hunton
Date established: 2002 **No.of Employees:** 1 - 10 **Product Groups:** 36, 37, 38

Cosalt International Ltd

Wickham Road, Grimsby, DN31 3SL
Tel: 01472-504300 **Fax:** 01472-504200
E-mail: neil.carrick@cosalt.com
Website: http://www.cosalt.com
Bank(s): National Westminster
Directors: D. Robinson (Co Sec), W. Phillips (MD), S. Wood (MD), N. Carrick (Dir), M. Short (Dir), A. Robson (Co Sec)
Managers: A. Cromar (Export Sales Mg), G. Oxley (I.T. Exec)
Ultimate Holding Company: COSALT PUBLIC LIMITED COMPANY
Immediate Holding Company: SURVITEC SERVICE & DISTRIBUTION LIMITED
Registration no: 00553893 **VAT No.:** GB 455 4353 44
Date established: 1955 **Turnover:** £20m - £50m
No.of Employees: 21 - 50 **Product Groups:** 22, 24, 63

Date of Accounts	Oct 10	Oct 07	Oct 08
Sales Turnover	42m	50m	55m
Pre Tax Profit/Loss	2m	-2m	5m
Working Capital	2m	-5m	995
Fixed Assets	5m	4m	3m
Current Assets	25m	27m	38m
Current Liabilities	2m	4m	3m

Cray Valley Ltd

Laporte Road Stallingborough, Grimsby, DN41 8DR
Tel: 01469-572464 **Fax:** 01469-572988
E-mail: info@crayvalley.com
Website: http://www.crayvalley.com
Directors: D. Vincent (MD), P. Chausserie Lapree (Fin)
Managers: R. Roberts, R. Aitken (Tech Serv Mgr), L. Fowler, R. Hodges
Ultimate Holding Company: TOTAL SAFETY INC (USA)
Immediate Holding Company: CCP COMPOSITES UK LTD
Registration no: 00342856 **VAT No.:** GB 542 8230 57
Date established: 1938 **Turnover:** £50m - £75m
No.of Employees: 51 - 100 **Product Groups:** 30, 31, 32, 66

Date of Accounts	Dec 11	Dec 10	Dec 09
Sales Turnover	51m	64m	65m
Pre Tax Profit/Loss	-1m	4m	4m
Working Capital	12m	16m	16m
Fixed Assets	19m	30m	26m
Current Assets	16m	24m	24m
Current Liabilities	1m	3m	4m

Dunlop Oil & Marine Ltd

Moody Lane, Grimsby, DN31 2SY
Tel: 01472-359281 **Fax:** 01472-362948
E-mail: michael.sloan@dunoil.com
Website: http://www.dunlop-oil-marine.co.uk
Bank(s): Barclays
Directors: M. Sloan (Fin)
Managers: J. Cunliffe (Sales & Mktg Mg), M. Carn (Personnel), R. Critten, J. Mitchell (Tech Serv Mgr)
Ultimate Holding Company: CONTINENTAL AG (GERMANY)
Immediate Holding Company: DUNLOP OIL & MARINE LIMITED
Registration no: 03471656 **VAT No.:** GB 746 1747 15
Date established: 1997 **Turnover:** £20m - £50m
No.of Employees: 101 - 250 **Product Groups:** 23, 29

Date of Accounts	Dec 10	Dec 09	Dec 08
Sales Turnover	43m	45m	35m
Pre Tax Profit/Loss	-7m	7m	10m
Working Capital	3m	-4m	6m
Fixed Assets	19m	20m	22m
Current Assets	18m	17m	18m
Current Liabilities	2m	1m	6m

E Bacon & Co. Ltd

Hutton Road, Grimsby, DN31 3PS
Tel: 01472-351313 **Fax:** 01472-250987
E-mail: info@baconengineering.com
Website: http://www.baconengineering.com
Bank(s): Yorkshire Bank PLC
Directors: J. Owen (Co Sec), R. Bacon (MD)
Immediate Holding Company: E.BACON & CO.,LIMITED
Registration no: 00178235 **VAT No.:** GB 127 7150 76
Date established: 2021 **Turnover:** £250,000 - £500,000
No.of Employees: 11 - 20 **Product Groups:** 48

Date of Accounts	Dec 11	Dec 10	Dec 09
Working Capital	130	68	78
Fixed Assets	33	35	38
Current Assets	236	138	149

Engineering & Welding Supplies Ltd

Adam Smith Street, Grimsby, DN31 1SJ
Tel: 01472-353596 **Fax:** 01472-241991
E-mail: sales@engweld.co.uk
Website: http://www.engweld.co.uk
Bank(s): Lloyds TSB Bank plc
Managers: A. Lait (Mgr)
Ultimate Holding Company: RAMSDEN HOLDINGS LIMITED
Immediate Holding Company: ENGINEERING AND WELDING SUPPLIES LIMITED
Registration no: 00815796 **VAT No.:** GB 167 8304 42
Date established: 1964 **No.of Employees:** 11 - 20 **Product Groups:** 67, 84

Date of Accounts	Sep 11	Sep 10	Sep 09
Sales Turnover	18m	15m	14m
Pre Tax Profit/Loss	2m	1m	1m
Working Capital	8m	7m	6m
Fixed Assets	3m	3m	3m
Current Assets	10m	9m	8m
Current Liabilities	627	423	470

Eriks UK (Grimsby Service Centre)
Unit 3-6 Europarc Peryton Way, Grimsby, DN37 9TL
Tel: 01472-242642 **Fax:** 01472-251273
E-mail: grimsby@eriks.co.uk
Website: http://www.eriks.co.uk
Managers: M. Ingall (Mgr)
Registration no: 03142338 **Turnover:** £250m - £500m
No.of Employees: 11 - 20 **Product Groups:** 66

Fabrenco Ltd
Wilton Road Humberston, Grimsby, DN36 4AW
Tel: 01472-814845 **Fax:** 01472-210412
E-mail: mikep@fabrenco.co.uk
Website: http://www.fabrenco.co.uk
Directors: M. Payne (Fin), R. Mayfield (Dir), S. Dixon (Sales)
Immediate Holding Company: FABRENCO LIMITED
Registration no: 01847216 **VAT No.:** GB 364 8698 94
Date established: 1984 **Turnover:** £500,000 - £1m
No.of Employees: 21 - 50 **Product Groups:** 48

Date of Accounts	Aug 09	Aug 08	Aug 07
Working Capital	-201	-121	-64
Fixed Assets	463	450	464
Current Assets	698	955	671

Fabriform Engineering
Dixon Close Humberston Road, Tetney, Grimsby, DN36 5PE
Tel: 08452-414852 **Fax:** 01472-816862
E-mail: fabriform@btconnect.com
Website: http://www.fabriform.co.uk
Directors: A. Turner (Dir)
Managers: C. Norvock (Mgr), F. Fiello (Mgr)
Immediate Holding Company: FABRIFORM ENGINEERING LIMITED
Registration no: 04453376 **VAT No.:** GB 796 7255 68
Date established: 2002 **Turnover:** £1m - £2m **No.of Employees:** 11 - 20
Product Groups: 26, 30, 34, 35, 38, 39, 41, 42, 43, 45, 46, 48, 80, 84

Date of Accounts	May 11	May 10	May 09
Working Capital	-51	-43	-2
Fixed Assets	54	71	71
Current Assets	53	44	111

Fabweld Grimsby Ltd
Rear of 193 Alexandra Road, Grimsby, DN31 1SE
Tel: 01472-241906 **Fax:** 01472-241906
Directors: D. Clark (Dir)
Immediate Holding Company: FABWELD GRIMSBY LIMITED
Registration no: 06775069 **Date established:** 2008
No.of Employees: 1 - 10 **Product Groups:** 26, 35

Date of Accounts	Dec 11	Dec 10	Dec 09
Working Capital	-24	-26	-27
Fixed Assets	24	26	27
Current Assets	42	33	24

Ian Flockton Developments Ltd
Estate Road 1 South Humberside Industrial Estate, Grimsby, DN31 2TB
Tel: 01472-359634 **Fax:** 01472-241392
E-mail: info@ianflockton.co.uk
Website: http://www.ianflockton.co.uk
Directors: C. Flockton (Dir)
Immediate Holding Company: IAN FLOCKTON DEVELOPMENTS LIMITED
Registration no: 00963155 **Date established:** 1969 **Turnover:** £1m - £2m
No.of Employees: 21 - 50 **Product Groups:** 30

Date of Accounts	Mar 09	Mar 08	Mar 07
Working Capital	125	115	116
Fixed Assets	291	278	287
Current Assets	728	558	573

Floor Heating Online
Unit 2 400 Cromwell Road, Grimsby, DN31 2BN
Tel: 01472-346809 **Fax:** 01472-346796
E-mail: sales@floorheatingonline.com
Website: http://www.floorheatingonline.com
Directors: S. Dixon (Dir)
Immediate Holding Company: FLOOR HEATING ONLINE LTD
Registration no: 05938171 **Date established:** 2001
No.of Employees: 1 - 10 **Product Groups:** 66

Front Line Extrusions Ltd
Estate Road 1 South Humberside Industrial Estate, Grimsby, DN31 2TB
Tel: 01472-347139 **Fax:** 01472-240226
E-mail: sales@frontlineprofile.com
Website: http://www.frontlineprofile.com
Directors: I. Potter (Fin)
Managers: J. Nurish (Sales Prom Mgr), K. Martin (Chief Mgr), C. Wild (Sales Prom Mgr), M. Fisher (Chief Mgr), R. Bishop (Chief Mgr)
Immediate Holding Company: FRONT LINE EXTRUSIONS LIMITED
Registration no: 01845096 **VAT No.:** GB 697 7141 06
Date established: 1984 **Turnover:** £2m - £5m **No.of Employees:** 51 - 100
Product Groups: 30

Date of Accounts	Dec 07	Dec 06	Dec 05
Sales Turnover	4382	N/A	4416
Pre Tax Profit/Loss	297	257	139
Working Capital	262	594	127
Fixed Assets	2751	1771	2140
Current Assets	2013	1731	1238
Current Liabilities	1750	1137	1111
Total Share Capital	18	18	18
ROCE% (Return on Capital Employed)	9.9	10.9	6.1
ROT% (Return on Turnover)	6.8		3.2

Grimsby Telegraph
Telegraph House 80 Cleethorpe Road, Grimsby, DN31 3EH
Tel: 01472-360360 **Fax:** 01472-372257
E-mail: mark.price@gsmg.co.uk
Website: http://www.thisisgrimsby.co.uk
Directors: H. Telegraph (Mkt Research), M. Price (MD)
Managers: J. Whattan (Tech Serv Mgr), J. Braithwaite (Mktg Serv Mgr)
Immediate Holding Company: COMMUNITY PRESS OFFICE LTD.
Registration no: 05510365 **Date established:** 2005
Turnover: £10m - £20m **No.of Employees:** 101 - 250 **Product Groups:** 28

Date of Accounts	Mar 11	Mar 10	Mar 09
Working Capital	42	77	69
Fixed Assets	6	11	14
Current Assets	72	122	89

Guntools Shop
90 Eleanor Street, Grimsby, DN32 8AL
Tel: 01472-343052 **Fax:** 01472-314630
Directors: A. Fox (Prop)
Date established: 1979 **No.of Employees:** 1 - 10 **Product Groups:** 36, 39, 40

Handtrans Road Haulage Services
North Moss Lane Industrial Estate Kiln Lane, Stallingborough, Grimsby, DN41 8DW
Tel: 01469-578000 **Fax:** 01469-578100
E-mail: alanbroughton@handtrans.com
Website: http://www.handtrans.com
Directors: S. Hand (Dir)
Immediate Holding Company: HANDTRANS LIMITED
Registration no: 03663630 **Date established:** 1998
No.of Employees: 11 - 20 **Product Groups:** 77

Date of Accounts	Dec 11	Dec 10	Dec 09
Working Capital	312	336	240
Fixed Assets	613	632	829
Current Assets	730	696	602

Humberside Wrappings Ltd
186 King Edward Street, Grimsby, DN31 3JP
Tel: 01472-343810 **Fax:** 01472-242072
E-mail: david@humbersidewrappings.co.uk
Website: http://www.humbersidewrappings.co.uk
Directors: D. Moore (MD)
Immediate Holding Company: HUMBERSIDE WRAPPINGS LIMITED
Registration no: 00777349 **Date established:** 1963
No.of Employees: 1 - 10 **Product Groups:** 38, 42

Date of Accounts	Oct 11	Oct 10	Oct 09
Working Capital	59	105	117
Fixed Assets	10	13	17
Current Assets	201	222	196

Icelandic UK Ltd
4 Origin Way Europarc, Grimsby, DN37 9TZ
Tel: 01472-582900 **Fax:** 01472-582920
E-mail: mgeirsson@icelandic.is
Website: http://www.icelandic.is
Directors: M. Geirsson (MD)
Ultimate Holding Company: ICELANDIC GROUP PLC (ICELAND)
Immediate Holding Company: ICELANDIC UK LIMITED
Registration no: 03184635 **VAT No.:** GB 613 6839 32
Date established: 1996 **No.of Employees:** 11 - 20 **Product Groups:** 09, 20

Immingham Port Storage Ltd
Netherlands Way Stallingborough, Grimsby, DN41 8DF
Tel: 01469-576363 **Fax:** 01469-571934
E-mail: peterdibdin@tpdibdin.com
Website: http://www.irtltd.co.uk
Directors: P. Dibdin (Ch), T. Dibdin (Dir), I. Davey (Fin)
Managers: J. Dibdin (Chief Acct)
Immediate Holding Company: IMMINGHAM PORT STORAGE LIMITED
Registration no: 01335908 **Date established:** 1977 **Turnover:** £1m - £2m
No.of Employees: 1 - 10 **Product Groups:** 76

Date of Accounts	Mar 08	Mar 07
Working Capital	-103	-237
Fixed Assets	23	63
Current Assets	240	104
Current Liabilities	343	341
Total Share Capital	10	10

J James
Somersby Street, Grimsby, DN31 1TT
Tel: 01472-344691
Directors: M. Oldham (Prop)
Date established: 1970 **No.of Employees:** 1 - 10 **Product Groups:** 35

Jewson Ltd
Pyewipe Road, Grimsby, DN31 2QN
Tel: 01472-350205 **Fax:** 01472-351971
E-mail: cliff.loveday@jewson.co.uk
Website: http://www.jewson.co.uk
Bank(s): Barclays
Managers: C. Loveday (District Mgr)
Ultimate Holding Company: COMPAGNIE DE SAINT GOBAIN (FRANCE)
Immediate Holding Company: JEWSON LIMITED
Registration no: 00348407 **VAT No.:** GB 497 7184 83
Date established: 1939 **No.of Employees:** 11 - 20 **Product Groups:** 66

Date of Accounts	Dec 11	Dec 10	Dec 09
Sales Turnover	1606m	1547m	1485m
Pre Tax Profit/Loss	18m	100m	45m
Working Capital	-345m	-250m	-349m
Fixed Assets	496m	387m	461m
Current Assets	657m	1005m	1320m
Current Liabilities	66m	120m	64m

Jewson Ltd
Wilton Road Humberston, Grimsby, DN36 4AN
Tel: 01472-813611 **Fax:** 01472-210382
Website: http://www.jewson.co.uk
Directors: P. Hindle (MD)
Managers: K. Tillison (District Mgr)
Immediate Holding Company: Saint Gobain
Registration no: 00348407 **VAT No.:** GB 497 7184 83
No.of Employees: 11 - 20 **Product Groups:** 66

L M S Ltd
Top Farm House Duckthorpe Lane, Marshchapel, Grimsby, DN36 5TL
Tel: 01472-388882 **Fax:** 01472-388441
E-mail: davidjchubb@aol.com
Directors: D. Chubb (MD)
Immediate Holding Company: L.M.S. LIMITED
Registration no: 01459110 **Date established:** 1979
No.of Employees: 1 - 10 **Product Groups:** 20, 35, 39, 40, 41, 45

Date of Accounts	Dec 11	Dec 10	Dec 09
Working Capital	288	282	295
Fixed Assets	91	90	99
Current Assets	360	344	329
Current Liabilities	N/A	23	13

Lindum BMS Grimsby
1 Alexandra Road, Grimsby, DN31 1RD
Tel: 01472-355171 **Fax:** 01472-236667
E-mail: ew@lindumgroup.co.uk
Directors: D. Chambers (Ch), T. Wright (Dir), B. Nixon (Tech Serv), K. Damarell (MD)
Managers: I. Hind (Design Mgr), M. Glover (I.T. Exec), S. Porter (Mgr), M. Watson (Comm), S. Coyne, G. Sarjantson (Admin Off)
Immediate Holding Company: LINDUM GROUP LTD
Registration no: 03490743 **VAT No.:** GB 613 9922 30
Turnover: £20m - £50m **No.of Employees:** 1 - 10 **Product Groups:** 81, 84

Lynx Polythene Ltd
Estate Road 7 South Humberside Industrial Estate, Grimsby, DN31 2TP
Tel: 01472-886287 **Fax:** 01472-884524
E-mail: sales@lynxpolythene.com
Website: http://www.lynxpolythene.com
Directors: A. Male (Dir), A. Juul (Fin)
Immediate Holding Company: LYNX POLYTHENE LIMITED
Registration no: 06697391 **Date established:** 2008 **Turnover:** £1m - £2m
No.of Employees: 1 - 10 **Product Groups:** 38, 42

Date of Accounts	Oct 11	Oct 10	Oct 09
Working Capital	-10	-25	-14
Fixed Assets	69	50	32
Current Assets	299	225	177
Current Liabilities	N/A	43	42

M P F Labelling Systems Ltd
Jasmin House Ayscough Street, Grimsby, DN31 1TG
Tel: 01472-240291 **Fax:** 01472-240291
Directors: V. Power (Dir)
Ultimate Holding Company: TENEO (UK) LIMITED
Immediate Holding Company: MPF LABELLING SYSTEMS LIMITED
Registration no: 04339561 **Date established:** 2001
No.of Employees: 1 - 10 **Product Groups:** 38, 42

Date of Accounts	Mar 12	Mar 11	Mar 09
Working Capital	4	4	21
Current Assets	5	26	32
Current Liabilities	1	N/A	N/A

Maplin Electronics Ltd
Unit 3 Victoria Street North, Grimsby, DN31 1TY
Tel: 08432-277329 **Fax:** 01472-356393
E-mail: customercare@maplin.co.uk
Website: http://www.maplin.co.uk
Managers: M. Mennell (Mgr)
Ultimate Holding Company: MONTAGU PRIVATE EQUITY LLP
Immediate Holding Company: MAPLIN ELECTRONICS LIMITED
Registration no: 01264385 **Date established:** 1976
Turnover: £125m - £250m **No.of Employees:** 1 - 10 **Product Groups:** 37, 61

Date of Accounts	Dec 11	Dec 08	Dec 09
Sales Turnover	205m	204m	204m
Pre Tax Profit/Loss	25m	32m	35m
Working Capital	118m	49m	75m
Fixed Assets	27m	28m	28m
Current Assets	207m	108m	142m
Current Liabilities	78m	51m	59m

Mariner Packaging Co. Ltd
King Edward Street, Grimsby, DN31 3JU
Tel: 01472-242244 **Fax:** 01472-242288
E-mail: sales@easy-grow.co.uk
Directors: S. Kettleborough (Fin), S. Atkinson (MD)
Immediate Holding Company: MARINER PACKAGING CO LIMITED
Registration no: 04880022 **Date established:** 2003
No.of Employees: 11 - 20 **Product Groups:** 38, 42

Date of Accounts	Aug 11	Aug 10	Aug 09
Working Capital	747	643	431
Fixed Assets	90	47	56
Current Assets	1m	1m	836

Metropes Metals Ltd
Estate Road 3 South Humberside Industrial Estate, Grimsby, DN31 2TB
Tel: 01472-342440 **Fax:** 01472-267815
Directors: S. Craig (Co Sec), J. West (Dir)
Immediate Holding Company: METROPES (METALS) LIMITED
Registration no: 00879837 **VAT No.:** GB 128 3176 72
Date established: 1966 **Turnover:** £250,000 - £500,000
No.of Employees: 1 - 10 **Product Groups:** 66

Date of Accounts	Mar 11	Mar 10	Mar 09
Working Capital	37	20	16
Fixed Assets	187	130	126
Current Assets	108	64	52

Nergeco UK Ltd
Estate Road 2 South Humberside Industrial Estate, Grimsby, DN31 2TG
Tel: 01472-354296 **Fax:** 01472-360409
E-mail: elizabeth.skelton@nergeco.co.uk
Managers: E. Skelton (Mgr)
Immediate Holding Company: NERGECO LIMITED
Registration no: 04419450 **Date established:** 2002
No.of Employees: 1 - 10 **Product Groups:** 26, 35

Norbert Dentressangle
Ladysmith Road, Grimsby, DN32 9SL
Tel: 01472-327200 **Fax:** 01472-327210
Website: http://www.salvesen.co.uk
Managers: S. Walker Smith (Chief Mgr)
Immediate Holding Company: CHRISTIAN SALVESEN P.L.C.
Registration no: SC007173 **Turnover:** £125m - £250m
No.of Employees: 101 - 250 **Product Groups:** 39, 72, 84

Olympus Welding & Industrial Supplies
Unit 35-38 Grimsby Business Centre King Edward Street, Grimsby, DN31 3JH
Tel: 01472-353373 **Fax:** 01472-352612
E-mail: info@olympuswelding.co.uk
Website: http://www.olympuswelding.co.uk
Directors: S. Mclean (Fin)
Date established: 1998 **No.of Employees:** 1 - 10 **Product Groups:** 46

P M C Safety Netting Ltd
Unit 3 Appian Way, Grimsby, DN31 2UT
Tel: 01472-267733 **Fax:** 01472-350921
E-mail: enquiries@pmcsafety.net
Website: http://www.pmcsafety.net
Directors: M. Atkinson (Fin), P. Cullen (MD)
Managers: G. Collins (Personnel)
Immediate Holding Company: PMC SAFETY NETTING LIMITED
Registration no: 04477935 **Date established:** 2002
Turnover: Over £1,000m **No.of Employees:** 21 - 50 **Product Groups:** 23, 35, 40, 67, 86

Date of Accounts	Oct 11	Oct 10	Oct 09
Working Capital	220	192	153
Fixed Assets	14	18	25
Current Assets	1m	1m	1m

Renco Nets Ltd
King Edward Street, Grimsby, DN31 3LA
Tel: 01472-241289 **Fax:** 01472-250680
E-mail: netting@renco.co.uk
Website: http://www.renco.co.uk
Directors: R. Jorgensen (MD), I. Jorgensen (Fin)
Immediate Holding Company: RENCO NETS LIMITED
Registration no: 03449127 **Date established:** 1997
Turnover: £500,000 - £1m **No.of Employees:** 1 - 10 **Product Groups:** 23, 26, 41, 49, 63

Date of Accounts	Feb 12	Feb 08	Feb 11
Working Capital	136	130	135
Fixed Assets	38	47	34
Current Assets	390	260	398

Right Action Ltd
PO Box 283, Grimsby, DN31 9FH
Tel: 01472-358222 **Fax:** 01472-358666
E-mail: mail@rightaction.co.uk
Website: http://www.rightaction.co.uk
Directors: M. Norris (Fin)
Immediate Holding Company: RIGHTACTION LIMITED
Registration no: 01991648 **Date established:** 1986
No.of Employees: 1 - 10 **Product Groups:** 38, 42

Date of Accounts	Apr 12	Apr 11	Apr 10
Working Capital	18	14	5
Fixed Assets	2	2	4
Current Assets	31	29	25

Rob Joynson Management Solutions Ltd
Norman Cottage Church Lane Marshchapel, Grimsby, DN36 5TW
Tel: 01472-596929
E-mail: rob@robjoynson.com
Website: http://www.robjoynson.com
Directors: R. Joynson (MD), B. Joynson (Co Sec)
Registration no: 05210414 **Date established:** 2004
No.of Employees: 1 - 10 **Product Groups:** 80

Date of Accounts	Sep 07	Sep 06
Working Capital	-12	-13
Fixed Assets	1	2
Current Assets	2	N/A
Current Liabilities	13	13

S P C International Food Ltd
35 Pinfold Lane, Grimsby, DN33 2EW
Tel: 01472-505080 **Fax:** 01472-505088
E-mail: sales@spcfood.co.uk
Website: http://www.spcfood.co.uk
Directors: G. Mason (MD)
Immediate Holding Company: SPC INTERNATIONAL (FOOD) LIMITED
Registration no: 03902162 **Date established:** 2000
No.of Employees: 1 - 10 **Product Groups:** 20, 40, 41

Date of Accounts	Mar 12	Mar 11	Mar 10
Working Capital	161	174	15
Fixed Assets	8	5	5
Current Assets	246	307	71

Samskip
Trondheim Way Redwood Park Estate, Stallingborough, Grimsby, DN41 8TH
Tel: 01469-575403 **Fax:** 01469-574102
E-mail: samskipltd@samskip.is
Website: http://www.samskip.is
Bank(s): National Westminster Bank Plc
Directors: A. Gislason (Dir), S. Dwyer (Fin)
Ultimate Holding Company: SAMSKIP HF (ICELAND)
Immediate Holding Company: SAMSKIP LIMITED
Registration no: 03014549 **Date established:** 1995 **Turnover:** £2m - £5m
No.of Employees: 21 - 50 **Product Groups:** 76

Date of Accounts	Dec 11	Dec 10	Dec 09
Sales Turnover	3m	5m	6m
Pre Tax Profit/Loss	170	-199	50
Working Capital	509	343	223
Fixed Assets	15	20	138
Current Assets	1m	982	1m
Current Liabilities	318	312	512

Signs Express
Venture Business Park Gilbey Road, Grimsby, DN31 2UW
Tel: 01472-343551 **Fax:** 01472-352212
E-mail: grimsby@signsexpress.co.uk
Website: http://www.signsexpress.co.uk
Directors: K. Beavis (MD)
Immediate Holding Company: SUSSEX TIMBER PRODUCTS LIMITED
Registration no: 02375913 **Date established:** 1996
No.of Employees: 11 - 20 **Product Groups:** 28, 30, 37, 40

Speedy Lifting
Unit 2 Adam Smith Street, Grimsby, DN31 1SJ
Tel: 01472-362685 **Fax:** 01472-342612
E-mail: 0806.grimsby@speedyhire.com
Website: http://www.speedyhire.com
Managers: A. Banaster (Chief Mgr), A. Banister (Mgr), A. Banster (Chief Mgr)
Ultimate Holding Company: L.G.H. Group Ltd
Immediate Holding Company: Speedy Hire plc
Registration no: 00927680 **Turnover:** £20m - £50m
No.of Employees: 1 - 10 **Product Groups:** 35, 37, 38, 39, 45, 48, 83

Springboard Recruitment
23 Osborne Street, Grimsby, DN31 1EY
Tel: 01472-362363 **Fax:** 01472-359040
E-mail: stuart@springboardrecruitment.co.uk
Website: http://www.springboardrecruitment.co.uk
Directors: S. Maxell (Dir)
Managers: S. Maxwell (Mgr)
Immediate Holding Company: SPRINGBOARD RECRUITMENT LIMITED
Registration no: 04929279 **Date established:** 2003
No.of Employees: 1 - 10 **Product Groups:** 80, 87

Date of Accounts	Jul 10	Jan 09	Jan 08
Working Capital	7	-2	-4
Fixed Assets	4	3	5
Current Assets	101	47	31

Stage One Costume Hire
133 Corporation Road, Grimsby, DN31 1UR
Tel: 01472-230196
Directors: S. Grommett (Prop)
Date established: 1997 **No.of Employees:** 1 - 10 **Product Groups:** 26, 35

Styropack
Fiskerton Way, Grimsby, DN37 9SZ
Tel: 01472-241424 **Fax:** 01472-250602
E-mail: grimsby@styropack.co.uk
Website: http://www.styropack.co.uk
Managers: P. Barnstable
Ultimate Holding Company: SYNBRA GROUP BV (NETHERLANDS)
Immediate Holding Company: OMERTA (GB) LTD
Registration no: SC041753 **VAT No.:** GB 265 4621 54
Date established: 2004 **Turnover:** Up to £250,000
No.of Employees: 1 - 10 **Product Groups:** 30

Date of Accounts	Dec 10	Dec 09	Dec 08
Sales Turnover	13m	14m	16m
Pre Tax Profit/Loss	-44	-728	-3m
Working Capital	-2m	-2m	-2m
Fixed Assets	5m	6m	7m
Current Assets	4m	4m	4m
Current Liabilities	1m	1m	1m

John Sutcliffe & Son Grimsby Ltd
Alexandra Chambers Flour Square, Grimsby, DN31 3LS
Tel: 01472-359101 **Fax:** 01472-241936
E-mail: agency@jsutcliffe.co.uk
Website: http://www.sutcliffe-shipping.com
Bank(s): National Westminster
Directors: R. Carter (Fin)
Ultimate Holding Company: JOHN SUTCLIFFE & SON (HOLDINGS) LIMITED
Immediate Holding Company: JOHN SUTCLIFFE & SON (HOLDINGS) LIMITED
Registration no: 01797046 **VAT No.:** GB 546 5975 95
Date established: 1984 **Turnover:** £10m - £20m
No.of Employees: 11 - 20 **Product Groups:** 76

Date of Accounts	Mar 11	Mar 10	Mar 09
Working Capital	-438	-459	-472
Fixed Assets	838	855	873
Current Assets	71	66	73

Sylvester Keal Ltd
Westside Business Park Estate Road No 2 South Humberside Business Park, Grimsby, DN31 2TG
Tel: 01472-352033 **Fax:** 01472-359356
E-mail: sales@sylvesterkeal.co.uk
Website: http://www.sylvesterkeal.co.uk
Directors: M. Keal (MD)
Immediate Holding Company: SYLVESTER KEAL LIMITED
Registration no: 03857573 **Date established:** 1999
No.of Employees: 21 - 50 **Product Groups:** 20, 40, 41

Date of Accounts	Dec 11	Dec 10	Dec 09
Working Capital	59	11	28
Fixed Assets	99	91	113
Current Assets	441	341	335

T H Brown Employment Services Ltd
Estate Road 1 South Humberside Industrial Estate, Grimsby, DN31 2TB
Tel: 01472-240824 **Fax:** 01472-360112
E-mail: p.marchant@thbrown.co.uk
Website: http://www.thbrown.com
Managers: P. Marchant (Mgr)
Immediate Holding Company: T.H. BROWN LIMITED
Registration no: 00608768 **Date established:** 1958 **Turnover:** £5m - £10m
No.of Employees: 1 - 10 **Product Groups:** 72

Date of Accounts	Jul 11	Jul 10	Jul 09
Working Capital	-58	63	205
Fixed Assets	311	395	426
Current Assets	398	478	714

Technical Absorbents
1 Moody Lane Great Coates, Grimsby, DN31 2SS
Tel: 01472-244053 **Fax:** 01472-244266
E-mail: sales@techabsorbents.com
Website: http://www.techabsorbents.com
Directors: M. Forman (Fin)
Managers: M. Riley (Comptroller), N. Matthews (Personnel), P. Cooper (Tech Serv Mgr), M. Baker, A. Owen, D. Hill (Sales Prom Mgr), A. Bemrose (Mktg Serv Mgr)
Immediate Holding Company: TECHNICAL ABSORBENTS LIMITED
Registration no: 02806731 **Date established:** 1993 **Turnover:** £5m - £10m
No.of Employees: 21 - 50 **Product Groups:** 23, 24, 27, 30, 32, 37

Date of Accounts	Dec 11	Dec 10	Dec 09
Sales Turnover	N/A	8m	7m
Pre Tax Profit/Loss	N/A	105	527
Working Capital	-7m	N/A	-121
Fixed Assets	N/A	N/A	5m
Current Assets	N/A	N/A	2m
Current Liabilities	N/A	N/A	246

Thermal Reflections Ltd
Unit 1-2 400 Cromwell Road, Grimsby, DN31 2BN
Tel: 01472-346795 **Fax:** 01472-346796
E-mail: sales@thermalreflections.co.uk
Website: http://www.thermalreflections.co.uk
Directors: S. Dixon (MD)
Immediate Holding Company: THERMAL REFLECTIONS LIMITED
Registration no: 03840230 **Date established:** 1999
No.of Employees: 1 - 10 **Product Groups:** 29, 30, 37, 40, 48, 52, 67

Date of Accounts	Oct 11	Oct 10	Oct 09
Working Capital	-42	-16	-26
Fixed Assets	20	26	35
Current Assets	134	143	149

Total Signs & Graphics Ltd
Unit 7-8 Birchin Way, Grimsby, DN31 2SG
Tel: 01472-350606
E-mail: info@totalsigns.eu
Website: http://www.totalsigns.eu
Managers: K. Tully (Ops Mgr)
Immediate Holding Company: TOTAL SIGNS AND GRAPHICS LIMITED
Registration no: 05710936 **Date established:** 2006
No.of Employees: 1 - 10 **Product Groups:** 23, 30, 40, 80

Date of Accounts	May 11	May 10	May 09
Working Capital	-10	32	25
Fixed Assets	56	17	23
Current Assets	125	127	93

Travis Perkins plc
Rowlandson Street Riby Square, Grimsby, DN31 3LL
Tel: 01472-345471 **Fax:** 01472-242760
E-mail: richard.lenthall@travisperkins.co.uk
Website: http://www.travisperkins.co.uk
Managers: R. Lenthall (Depot Mgr)
Immediate Holding Company: TRAVIS PERKINS PLC
Registration no: 00824821 **Date established:** 1964 **Turnover:** £2m - £5m
No.of Employees: 1 - 10 **Product Groups:** 66

Date of Accounts	Dec 11	Dec 10	Dec 09
Sales Turnover	4779m	3153m	2931m
Pre Tax Profit/Loss	270m	197m	213m
Working Capital	133m	159m	248m
Fixed Assets	2771m	2749m	2108m
Current Assets	1421m	1329m	1035m
Current Liabilities	473m	412m	109m

United Fish Industries UK Ltd
Gilbey Road, Grimsby, DN31 2SL
Tel: 01472-263333 **Fax:** 01472-263451
Website: http://www.iaws.ie
Bank(s): National Westminster
Managers: M. Haryscovan (Chief Mgr), M. Haryskowian (Mgr), T. Parker (Sales Prom Mgr)
Ultimate Holding Company: WELCON INVEST AS (NORWAY)
Immediate Holding Company: UNITED FISH INDUSTRIES (UK) LIMITED
Registration no: 02746845 **Date established:** 1992
Turnover: £20m - £50m **No.of Employees:** 21 - 50 **Product Groups:** 20

Date of Accounts	Dec 11	Dec 10	Dec 09
Sales Turnover	32m	31m	41m
Pre Tax Profit/Loss	4m	3m	4m
Working Capital	4m	4m	4m
Fixed Assets	6m	6m	6m
Current Assets	7m	8m	10m
Current Liabilities	2m	3m	5m

E A West
Pyewipe, Grimsby, DN31 2SW
Tel: 01472-232000 **Fax:** 01472-232020
E-mail: hmats_uk@huntsman.com
Website: http://www.huntsman.com
Bank(s): Lloyds TSB Bank plc
Managers: B. Jacks (Mgr)
Ultimate Holding Company: HUNTSMAN CORP
Immediate Holding Company: R.P.M. INDUSTRIAL SERVICES LIMITED
Registration no: 00082532 **Date established:** 1972 **Turnover:** £2m - £5m
No.of Employees: 11 - 20 **Product Groups:** 31, 32

Date of Accounts	Mar 12	Mar 11	Mar 10
Working Capital	820	578	64
Fixed Assets	307	250	123
Current Assets	1m	914	390

M J Wilson Group Ltd
Charlton Street, Grimsby, DN31 1SQ
Tel: 01472-361425 **Fax:** 01472-340172
E-mail: sales@mjwilsongroup.com
Website: http://www.mjwilsongroup.com
Bank(s): National Westminster Bank Plc
Directors: R. Beveridge (Sales)
Managers: A. Deakin (District Mgr)
Immediate Holding Company: M J WILSON GROUP LIMITED
Registration no: 01044427 **VAT No.:** GB 364 3846 33
Date established: 1972 **Turnover:** £1m - £2m **No.of Employees:** 11 - 20
Product Groups: 30, 34, 36, 37, 38, 39, 66

Date of Accounts	Feb 08	Feb 11	Feb 10
Working Capital	746	-65	4m
Fixed Assets	6m	2m	2m
Current Assets	2m	2m	6m

Yara UK Ltd
Harvest House Origin Way, Europarc, Grimsby, DN37 9TZ
Tel: 01472-889250 **Fax:** 01284-850322
Website: http://www.yara.com
Directors: B. Lamaisom (MD)
Ultimate Holding Company: YARA INTERNATIONAL ASA (NORWAY)
Immediate Holding Company: YARA CHAFER LIMITED
Registration no: 04975912 **Date established:** 2003
No.of Employees: 51 - 100 **Product Groups:** 66

Yearsley Group Ltd
Tower Primary Distribution Centre Marsden Road, Grimsby, DN31 3FS
Tel: 01472-252100 **Fax:** 01472-268628
E-mail: chris.herbert@yearsley.co.uk
Website: http://www.yearsleygroup.co.uk
Managers: C. Herbert (Chief Mgr)
Ultimate Holding Company: PROLOGIS
Registration no: 07137981 **Date established:** 1910
Turnover: £75m - £125m **No.of Employees:** 1 - 10 **Product Groups:** 72

Youngs Seafood
Ross House Wickham Road, Grimsby, DN31 3SW
Tel: 01472-585858
E-mail: askus@youngsseafood.co.uk
Website: http://www.youngsseafood.co.uk
Managers: S. Howard (Buyer), P. Millstead
Ultimate Holding Company: FINDUS UK GROUP LIMITED
Immediate Holding Company: YOUNG'S SEAFOOD LIMITED
Registration no: 03751665 **VAT No.:** GB 716 5297 21
Date established: 1999 **Turnover:** £250m - £500m
No.of Employees: 1501 & over **Product Groups:** 20, 62

Date of Accounts	Dec 10	Dec 09	Sep 07
Sales Turnover	343m	476m	354m
Pre Tax Profit/Loss	495	-23m	-11m
Working Capital	-63m	-2m	985
Fixed Assets	39m	2m	45m
Current Assets	159m	N/A	82m
Current Liabilities	106m	N/A	45m

Immingham

C A S Filtration Media Specialists
Eastfield Road South Killingholme, Immingham, DN40 3NF
Tel: 01469-574715 **Fax:** 01469-571644
E-mail: info@casfiltration.com
Website: http://www.casfiltration.com
Directors: G. Bourkes (Dir)
Immediate Holding Company: C.A.S. FILTRATION LIMITED
Registration no: 03673132 **Date established:** 1998
Turnover: £500,000 - £1m **No.of Employees:** 1 - 10 **Product Groups:** 11, 14, 17, 18, 31, 32, 42

Date of Accounts	Dec 11	Dec 10	Mar 10
Working Capital	147	135	123
Current Assets	402	459	408

C P L Petroleum

Manby Road, Immingham, DN40 2LL
Tel: 01472-350421 **Fax:** 01472-250690
E-mail: grimsby@cplpetroleum.co.uk
Website: http://www.cplpetroleum.co.uk
Managers: S. Loughran (Mgr)
Ultimate Holding Company: CPL INDUSTRIES HOLDINGS LIMITED
Immediate Holding Company: CPL PETROLEUM LIMITED
Registration no: 03003860 **Date established:** 1994 **Turnover:** £1m - £2m
No.of Employees: 21 - 50 **Product Groups:** 66

Date of Accounts	Mar 12	Mar 11	Mar 10
Pre Tax Profit/Loss	N/A	878	904
Working Capital	31	30m	30m
Fixed Assets	26	26m	26m
Current Assets	57	56m	56m
Current Liabilities	26	246	253

Endotec Ltd

Unit D Hall Park Road, Immingham, DN40 2LT
Tel: 01469-577655 **Fax:** 01469-577668
E-mail: enquiries@endotec.co.uk
Website: http://www.endotec.co.uk
Directors: S. Doe (MD)
Immediate Holding Company: ENDOTEC LIMITED
Registration no: 04192916 **Date established:** 2001
No.of Employees: 21 - 50 **Product Groups:** 29, 30, 31, 33, 34, 35, 36, 37, 38, 39, 40, 41, 45, 46, 48, 49, 66, 67, 68, 80

Date of Accounts	Dec 10	Dec 09	Nov 09
Working Capital	-336	76	76
Fixed Assets	437	42	42
Current Assets	214	197	197

Exxtor Shipping Services Ltd

PO Box 40, Immingham, DN40 3EG
Tel: 01469-551308 **Fax:** 01469-571012
E-mail: jbh@exxtor.com
Website: http://www.abpconnect.com
Bank(s): National Westminster Bank Plc
Directors: J. Baker (Dir), P. Allen (MD)
Managers: J. Power (Export Sales Mg), N. Ingram (Mgr)
Immediate Holding Company: ABP Associated British Parts
Registration no: 00516824 **VAT No.:** GB 232 4251 13
No.of Employees: 21 - 50 **Product Groups:** 76

Date of Accounts	Dec 06	Dec 05
Working Capital	11210	11210
Current Assets	11210	11210
Total Share Capital	5000	5000

Fabricom Oil Gas & Power Ltd

Kings Road, Immingham, DN40 1FN
Tel: 01469-576411 **Fax:** 01469-571533
E-mail: s.gaughan@fabricom.co.uk
Website: http://www.fabricom-gdfsuez.co.uk
Bank(s): Barclays
Directors: N. Carlton (MD), R. Webster (Fin)
Managers: Y. Day (Personnel), G. Haley (Tech Serv Mgr), J. Davidson (Purch Mgr)
Immediate Holding Company: FABRICOM OIL, GAS AND POWER LIMITED
Registration no: 01189290 **VAT No.:** GB 129 6068 54
Date established: 1974 **Turnover:** £20m - £50m
No.of Employees: 101 - 250 **Product Groups:** 48

Date of Accounts	Dec 11	Dec 10	Dec 09
Sales Turnover	36m	28m	56m
Pre Tax Profit/Loss	-721	-1m	1m
Working Capital	6m	6m	7m
Fixed Assets	4m	4m	5m
Current Assets	17m	12m	15m
Current Liabilities	7m	3m	5m

Fussey Piling Ltd

Lancaster Approach North Killingholme, Immingham, DN40 3JZ
Tel: 01469-540644 **Fax:** 01469-540849
E-mail: yvonne@fusseyengineering.com
Website: http://www.fusseyengineering.com
Bank(s): Lloyds TSB
Directors: Y. Mager (Fin)
Immediate Holding Company: FUSSEY PILING LTD
Registration no: 01796291 **VAT No.:** GB 310 9580 74
Date established: 1984 **Turnover:** £5m - £10m **No.of Employees:** 21 - 50
Product Groups: 35, 51

Date of Accounts	Aug 11	Aug 10	Aug 09
Sales Turnover	6m	6m	5m
Pre Tax Profit/Loss	220	148	44
Working Capital	2m	2m	2m
Fixed Assets	1m	1m	1m
Current Assets	3m	3m	3m
Current Liabilities	184	136	123

Humber Inspection Services Ltd

Rivardy Manby Road, Immingham, DN40 2LG
Tel: 01469-577774 **Fax:** 01469-577400
E-mail: alan@humberinspection.co.uk
Website: http://www.humberinspectionservices.co.uk
Directors: A. Wilson (Dir)
Immediate Holding Company: HUMBER INSPECTION SERVICES LIMITED
Registration no: 02968016 **Date established:** 1994 **Turnover:** £1m - £2m
No.of Employees: 1 - 10 **Product Groups:** 66, 74, 85

Date of Accounts	Oct 11	Oct 10	Oct 09
Working Capital	205	136	144
Fixed Assets	117	115	71
Current Assets	1m	538	265

Jewson Ltd

Middleplatt Road, Immingham, DN40 1AH
Tel: 01469-571471 **Fax:** 01469-572870
Website: http://www.jewson.co.uk
Managers: M. Thomas (Mgr)
Ultimate Holding Company: COMPAGNIE DE SAINT GOBAIN (FRANCE)
Immediate Holding Company: JEWSON LIMITED
Registration no: 00348407 **Date established:** 1939
Turnover: £500m - £1,000m **No.of Employees:** 1 - 10
Product Groups: 66

Date of Accounts	Dec 11	Dec 10	Dec 09
Sales Turnover	1606m	1547m	1485m
Pre Tax Profit/Loss	18m	100m	45m
Working Capital	-345m	-250m	-349m
Fixed Assets	496m	387m	461m
Current Assets	657m	1005m	1320m
Current Liabilities	66m	120m	64m

Kempton Security Ltd

3 School Road South Killingholme, Immingham, DN40 3HS
Tel: 01469-541739
E-mail: mark@kemptonsecurity.co.uk
Website: http://www.kemptonsecurity.co.uk
Directors: M. Elliott (MD)
Immediate Holding Company: KEMPTON SECURITY LIMITED
Registration no: 06931111 **Date established:** 2009
No.of Employees: 1 - 10 **Product Groups:** 36, 40, 67

Date of Accounts	Mar 11
Working Capital	-1
Fixed Assets	4
Current Assets	16

Lectec Services Ltd (Electrical & Instrumentation Division)

Manby Road, Immingham, DN40 2LG
Tel: 01469-574262 **Fax:** 01469-571051
E-mail: admin@lectec.co.uk
Website: http://www.lectec.co.uk
Directors: L. Foundation (MD), G. Wood (Fin)
Managers: B. O'Hare (Purch Mgr), K. Booth (Personnel)
Ultimate Holding Company: ENGENDA GROUP LIMITED
Immediate Holding Company: ENGENDA LIMITED
Registration no: 01316156 **VAT No.:** GB 288 6735 94
Date established: 1977 **Turnover:** £5m - £10m
No.of Employees: 51 - 100 **Product Groups:** 52

Date of Accounts	May 11	May 10	May 09
Sales Turnover	8m	10m	N/A
Pre Tax Profit/Loss	-1	490	1m
Working Capital	2m	2m	2m
Fixed Assets	131	141	216
Current Assets	4m	4m	3m
Current Liabilities	913	888	631

Northrop Grumman Sperry Marine

Unit 2 East Riverside Immingham Dock, Immingham, DN40 2QJ
Tel: 01469-576122 **Fax:** 01469-571695
E-mail: william.lampton@sperry.ngc.com
Website: http://www.sperry-marine.com
Managers: W. Lambton (Mgr)
Registration no: 05259312 **Date established:** 2004
No.of Employees: 1 - 10 **Product Groups:** 35, 36, 39

Oceaneering

Unit 3 Queens Road, Immingham, DN40 1QR
Tel: 01469-577088 **Fax:** 01469-572641
E-mail: info@oceaneering.com
Website: http://www.oceaneering.com
Managers: K. Fellows (District Mgr)
Turnover: £2m - £5m **No.of Employees:** 1 - 10 **Product Groups:** 37, 38, 44, 48, 51, 85

On Line Design & Engineering Ltd

Online House Pelham Road, Immingham, DN40 1AB
Tel: 01469-577695 **Fax:** 01469-578216
E-mail: info@oldesign.co.uk
Website: http://www.oldesign.co.uk
Bank(s): Barclays
Directors: S. Laird (Fin)
Managers: R. Horrex (Personnel)
Immediate Holding Company: ON-LINE DESIGN & ENGINEERING LIMITED
Registration no: 01612986 **VAT No.:** GB 364 3722 51
Date established: 1982 **Turnover:** £20m - £50m
No.of Employees: 51 - 100 **Product Groups:** 84

Date of Accounts	Mar 12	Mar 11	Mar 10
Sales Turnover	35m	30m	24m
Pre Tax Profit/Loss	3m	2m	2m
Working Capital	4m	3m	2m
Fixed Assets	1m	1m	892
Current Assets	9m	9m	6m
Current Liabilities	3m	3m	2m

Scanlift UK Ltd

4a Manby Road, Immingham, DN40 2LH
Tel: 01469-571243 **Fax:** 01469-571729
Directors: R. Graves (Fin), S. Graves (MD)
Immediate Holding Company: SCANLIFT UK LIMITED
Registration no: 04070913 **Date established:** 2000
No.of Employees: 1 - 10 **Product Groups:** 35, 39, 45

Date of Accounts	Sep 11	Sep 10	Sep 09
Working Capital	194	91	40
Fixed Assets	62	6	8
Current Assets	322	257	224

Svitzer Humber Ltd

Triton House Immingham Dock, Immingham, DN40 2LZ
Tel: 01469-571115 **Fax:** 01469- 571616
E-mail: jacqueline.readman@svitzer.com
Website: http://www.svitzer.com
Directors: J. Readman (Dir), J. Curry (Dir), D. Noakes (Co Sec)
Ultimate Holding Company: AP MOLLER MAERSK A/S (DENMARK)
Immediate Holding Company: SVITZER HUMBER LIMITED
Registration no: 00524008 **VAT No.:** GB 526 1995 26
Date established: 1953 **Turnover:** £10m - £20m
No.of Employees: 51 - 100 **Product Groups:** 71, 74

Date of Accounts	Dec 10	Dec 09	Dec 08
Sales Turnover	16m	19	20m
Pre Tax Profit/Loss	-6m	-7	-5m
Working Capital	-6m	N/A	-3m
Fixed Assets	23m	N/A	31m
Current Assets	9m	N/A	7m
Current Liabilities	1m	13	2m

Malcolm West Immingham Ltd

Victoria House Immingham Dock, Immingham, DN40 2LZ
Tel: 01469-575558 **Fax:** 01469-571113
E-mail: andy@malcolmwest.co.uk
Website: http://www.malcolmwest-mitsubishi.co.uk
Managers: A. Kinnard (Mgr)
Immediate Holding Company: PORT EQUIPMENT ENGINEERING LIMITED
Registration no: 05259312 **Date established:** 2004
No.of Employees: 11 - 20 **Product Groups:** 35, 39, 45

Date of Accounts	Oct 11	Oct 10	Oct 09
Working Capital	26	1	10
Fixed Assets	15	20	13
Current Assets	144	126	169

Yara UK lt Ltd Fertilizers

Immingham Dock, Immingham, DN40 2NS
Tel: 01469-571136 **Fax:** 01469-571624
E-mail: yarauk.info@yara.com
Website: http://www.yara.com
Directors: D. Spindler (MD)
Immediate Holding Company: YARA LIMITED
Registration no: 05039958 **VAT No.:** GB 638 3726 19
Date established: 2004 **Turnover:** £250m - £500m
No.of Employees: 1 - 10 **Product Groups:** 32

Scunthorpe

Access Panel Co. Ltd

Winterton Road, Scunthorpe, DN15 0BA
Tel: 01724-853090 **Fax:** 08702-012311
E-mail: sales@accesspanels.co.uk
Website: http://www.accesspanels.co.uk
Directors: M. Stapleton (Fin), S. Crabtree (Dir)
Managers: J. Brummell (Mgr)
Immediate Holding Company: THE ACCESS PANEL COMPANY LTD
Registration no: 04004043 **Date established:** 2000
No.of Employees: 11 - 20 **Product Groups:** 30, 35, 39

Date of Accounts	May 11	May 10	May 09
Working Capital	346	56	265
Fixed Assets	801	584	577
Current Assets	751	750	706

Adams Hydraulics

Unit 1-4 Phoenix Court Atkinsons Way, Foxhills Industrial Estate, Scunthorpe, DN15 8QJ
Tel: 01724-845778 **Fax:** 01724-271285
Website: http://www.adamshydraulics.co.uk
Managers: C. Schofield (Mgr)
Ultimate Holding Company: MONDI PLC
Immediate Holding Company: WHEATLEY PACKAGING LIMITED
Date established: 1997 **No.of Employees:** 11 - 20 **Product Groups:** 30, 40, 67

Andrews Sykes

Snowdonia Avenue, Scunthorpe, DN15 8NL
Tel: 01482-224803 **Fax:** 01482-281237
E-mail: scunthorpe@andrews-sykes.com
Website: http://www.andrews-sykes.com
Managers: I. Short (Depot Mgr)
Immediate Holding Company: ANDREWS SYKES GROUP PLC
Registration no: 02985657 **VAT No.:** GB 100 4295 24
Date established: 1987 **Turnover:** £5m - £10m **No.of Employees:** 1 - 10
Product Groups: 40

Avnet Abacus

Deltron Emcon House Hargreaves Way, Sawcliffe Industrial Park, Scunthorpe, DN15 8RF
Tel: 01724-281770 **Fax:** 01724-281650
E-mail: scunthorpe@avnet.eu
Website: http://www.abacus.co.uk
Managers: D. Myers (Sales Prom Mgr), N. Copely (Chief Mgr)
Date established: 1995 **Turnover:** £75m - £125m
No.of Employees: 1 - 10 **Product Groups:** 37

B O M Agri Equipment

South Grange Carr Dyke Road, Burringham, Scunthorpe, DN17 3AB
Tel: 01724-783887 **Fax:** 01724-784242
E-mail: bomagri@btinternet.com
Website: http://www.bomagri.com
Directors: C. Thompson (Prop)
No.of Employees: 1 - 10 **Product Groups:** 41

B S Supplies

20 Midland Road, Scunthorpe, DN16 1DQ
Tel: 01724-278733 **Fax:** 01724-278744
E-mail: leegnorris@hotmail.com
Website: http://www.barclay.net
Directors: L. Norris (MD)
Immediate Holding Company: BCS PRODUCTS LIMITED
Registration no: 04246694 **Date established:** 2001
No.of Employees: 1 - 10 **Product Groups:** 34, 66

Date of Accounts	Apr 12	Apr 11	Apr 10
Working Capital	91	76	63
Fixed Assets	245	240	255
Current Assets	929	808	875

Boulting Group Ltd

Suite 4 Woodfield House Berkeley Business Centre Doncaster Road, Scunthorpe, DN15 7DQ
Tel: 01724-860346 **Fax:** 01724-281385
E-mail: markstanford@boulting.co.uk
Website: http://www.boulting.co.uk
Managers: W. Monks (Reg Mgr)
Immediate Holding Company: BOULTING GROUP LIMITED
Registration no: 02950900 **Date established:** 1994
Turnover: £20m - £50m **No.of Employees:** 1 - 10 **Product Groups:** 52

Date of Accounts	Oct 11	Oct 10	Oct 09
Sales Turnover	95m	98m	95m
Pre Tax Profit/Loss	765	1m	2m
Working Capital	6m	6m	7m
Fixed Assets	5m	5m	4m
Current Assets	29m	27m	21m
Current Liabilities	11m	10m	9m

T Brighton Valves Ltd

Woodhouse Road, Scunthorpe, DN16 1BD
Tel: 01724-855388 **Fax:** 01724-870528
E-mail: enquiries@tbrightonvalves.co.uk
Website: http://www.tbrightonvalves.co.uk
Directors: A. Short (Fin)
Managers: M. Storey (Mgr)
Ultimate Holding Company: STOCKS GROUP LIMITED
Immediate Holding Company: T BRIGHTON ENGINEERING SERVICES LIMITED

see next page

T Brighton Valves Ltd - Cont'd

Registration no: 04772400 **Date established:** 2003
No.of Employees: 1 - 10 **Product Groups:** 36, 37, 38

Date of Accounts	Mar 12	Mar 11	Mar 10
Working Capital	54	61	89
Fixed Assets	16	18	N/A
Current Assets	99	131	251

Civil and Marine Ltd

Brigg Road, Scunthorpe, DN16 1AW
Tel: 01724-282211 **Fax:** 01724-280338
E-mail: webenquiry@applebygroup.co.uk
Website: http://www.heidelbergcement.com
Bank(s): Bank of Scotland
Directors: R. Sindell (MD), J. Marrison (Dir)
Managers: T. Clark (Admin Off), I. Dalgairns (I.T. Exec), M. Johnson
Ultimate Holding Company: North East Slag Cement Ltd
Immediate Holding Company: Appleby Group Ltd
Registration no: 02301423 **VAT No.:** 127 8030 81 **Date established:** 1961
Turnover: £5m - £10m **No.of Employees:** 51 - 100 **Product Groups:** 30, 33, 66

Clugston Distribution Services Ltd

Brigg Road, Scunthorpe, DN16 1BB
Tel: 01724-281281 **Fax:** 01724-270240
E-mail: andrew.hansed@clugston.co.uk
Website: http://www.clugston.co.uk
Managers: D. Heath (Chief Mgr)
Ultimate Holding Company: CLUGSTON GROUP LIMITED
Immediate Holding Company: CLUGSTON DISTRIBUTION SERVICES LIMITED
Registration no: 05517733 **VAT No.:** GB 317 1629 68
Date established: 2005 **Turnover:** Up to £250,000
No.of Employees: 101 - 250 **Product Groups:** 72

Date of Accounts	Jan 12	Jan 11	Jan 09
Sales Turnover	10m	10m	14m
Pre Tax Profit/Loss	-669	-351	532
Working Capital	-373	-140	-516
Fixed Assets	3m	3m	3m
Current Assets	3m	2m	2m
Current Liabilities	243	319	364

Clugston Group Ltd

St Vincent House Normanby Road, Scunthorpe, DN15 8QT
Tel: 01724-843491 **Fax:** 01724-281714
E-mail: sales@clugston.co.uk
Website: http://www.clugston.co.uk
Directors: M. Bales (Fin), S. Martin (Grp Chief Exec)
Managers: C. Gibson (Personnel)
Ultimate Holding Company: CLUGSTON GROUP LIMITED
Immediate Holding Company: CLUGSTON GROUP LIMITED
Registration no: 00333188 **Date established:** 1937
Turnover: £75m - £125m **No.of Employees:** 51 - 100
Product Groups: 51, 52, 84

Date of Accounts	Jan 12	Jan 11	Jan 09
Sales Turnover	84m	65m	142m
Pre Tax Profit/Loss	2m	-4m	3m
Working Capital	1m	894	3m
Fixed Assets	15m	15m	16m
Current Assets	32m	15m	29m
Current Liabilities	16m	3m	9m

Corus Cogier

Hebden Road, Scunthorpe, DN15 8DT
Tel: 01724-862131 **Fax:** 01724-295243
E-mail: pat.marshall@coruscogifer.com
Website: http://www.coruscogifer.com
Bank(s): HSBC Bank plc
Directors: I. Lindsay (MD)
Managers: D. Walters (Develop Mgr), P. Marshall (Ops Mgr), L. Smith (Personnel)
Immediate Holding Company: CORUS COGIFER SWITCHES AND CROSSINGS LIMITED
Registration no: 04114382 **Date established:** 2000
Turnover: £10m - £20m **No.of Employees:** 51 - 100 **Product Groups:** 39, 51

Date of Accounts	Dec 11	Dec 10	Dec 09
Sales Turnover	13m	16m	20m
Pre Tax Profit/Loss	2m	2m	2m
Working Capital	5m	6m	6m
Fixed Assets	2m	2m	2m
Current Assets	9m	10m	11m
Current Liabilities	3m	2m	3m

Crawfords Shooting Supplies

27 Hebden Road, Scunthorpe, DN15 8DT
Tel: 08700-660325 **Fax:** 01724-846001
Directors: G. Allison (MD), P. Allison (Fin)
Immediate Holding Company: CRAWFORDS SHOOTING SUPPLIES LIMITED
Registration no: 04675501 **Date established:** 2003
Turnover: £250,000 - £500,000 **No.of Employees:** 1 - 10
Product Groups: 36, 39, 40

Date of Accounts	Mar 11	Mar 10	Mar 09
Working Capital	13	14	14
Fixed Assets	8	5	15
Current Assets	47	32	38

Cross-Guard

8 Dunlop Way Queensway Industrial Estate, Scunthorpe, DN16 3RN
Tel: 01724-277999
E-mail: becky.vanwyk@bradburyuk.com
Website: http://www.bradburyuk.com
Directors: B. Vanwyk (Sales), D. Banford (Fab), P. Neville-jones (Sales)
Managers: A. Wan (Tech Serv Mgr), J. Watt, A. Gipps (Mktg Serv Mgr)
No.of Employees: 21 - 50 **Product Groups:** 35, 38

Energy Services Management Ltd

Woodford House Moorwell Business Park Moorwell Road, Scunthorpe, DN17 2RU
Tel: 01724-847325 **Fax:** 01724-846982
E-mail: info@e-s-m.co.uk
Website: http://www.e-s-m.co.uk
Bank(s): HSBC Bank plc
Directors: R. Banford (MD)
Managers: L. Bamford (Develop Mgr)
Immediate Holding Company: ESM POWER LIMITED
Registration no: 04611637 **VAT No.:** GB 780 6895 80
Date established: 2002 **No.of Employees:** 11 - 20 **Product Groups:** 37, 38, 84

Date of Accounts	Apr 11	Apr 10	Apr 09
Working Capital	142	82	82
Fixed Assets	79	8	10
Current Assets	354	175	152

T & J Fletcher

91-93 North Street Winterton, Scunthorpe, DN15 9QW
Tel: 01724-732217 **Fax:** 01724-732242
E-mail: franfletcher@live.co.uk
Website: http://www.windowworld.org.uk
Directors: M. Fletcher (Fin), R. Fletcher (MD)
Immediate Holding Company: T & J FLETCHER LTD
Registration no: 04708520 **Date established:** 2003
No.of Employees: 1 - 10 **Product Groups:** 41

Date of Accounts	Mar 12	Mar 11	Mar 10
Working Capital	-14	-15	-12
Fixed Assets	20	23	22
Current Assets	76	71	90

Flixborough Wharf Ltd

Trent Port House Stather Road, Flixborough, Scunthorpe, DN15 8RS
Tel: 01724-867691 **Fax:** 01724-851207
E-mail: info@flixboroughwharf.co.uk
Website: http://www.rms-humber.co.uk
Bank(s): National Westminster Bank Plc
Directors: D. Johnson (Fin), G. Evison (MD), P. Crossland (Mkt Research)
Managers: M. Smith (Tech Serv Mgr)
Ultimate Holding Company: RMS GROUP HOLDINGS LIMITED
Immediate Holding Company: GUNNESS WHARF LIMITED
Registration no: 00317586 **Date established:** 1936 **Turnover:** £2m - £5m
No.of Employees: 251 - 500 **Product Groups:** 74, 77, 84

Date of Accounts	Dec 11	Dec 10	Dec 09
Sales Turnover	4m	4m	3m
Pre Tax Profit/Loss	-223	-11	-292
Working Capital	768	887	825
Fixed Assets	2m	2m	2m
Current Assets	2m	2m	2m
Current Liabilities	340	537	375

Furmanite Ltd

Sunningdale House Sunningdale Road, Scunthorpe, DN17 2TY
Tel: 01724-849904 **Fax:** 01724-861033
Website: http://www.furmanite.com
Directors: A. Ruffle (Fin), P. Brown (MD)
Ultimate Holding Company: FURMANITE CORPORATION (USA)
Immediate Holding Company: FURMANITE LIMITED
Registration no: 02530049 **VAT No.:** GB 364 4112 73
Date established: 1990 **No.of Employees:** 11 - 20 **Product Groups:** 36

Date of Accounts	Dec 11	Dec 10	Dec 09
Sales Turnover	42m	37m	39m
Pre Tax Profit/Loss	3m	1m	2m
Working Capital	14m	17m	16m
Fixed Assets	5m	6m	9m
Current Assets	19m	23m	21m
Current Liabilities	3m	3m	3m

G W F Engineering Ltd

Woodhouse Road, Scunthorpe, DN16 1BD
Tel: 01724-868646 **Fax:** 01724-867747
E-mail: info@gwf.co.uk
Website: http://www.gwf.co.uk
Bank(s): Lloyds TSB Bank plc
Directors: C. Leaning (MD), G. Franklin (Co Sec)
Managers: J. Johnstone
Immediate Holding Company: GWF ENGINEERING LIMITED
Registration no: 04239645 **Date established:** 2001
No.of Employees: 21 - 50 **Product Groups:** 48

Date of Accounts	Dec 11	Dec 10	Dec 09
Working Capital	104	11	-130
Fixed Assets	348	449	509
Current Assets	761	767	474

G W S Engineers Ltd

First Avenue Flixborough Industrial Estate, Flixborough, Scunthorpe, DN15 8SE
Tel: 01724-856665 **Fax:** 01724-280805
E-mail: mail@gws-engineers.co.uk
Website: http://www.gws-engineers.co.uk
Directors: S. Stones (Dir)
Immediate Holding Company: GWS ENGINEERS LIMITED
Registration no: 01360021 **Date established:** 1978
Turnover: £500,000 - £1m **No.of Employees:** 1 - 10 **Product Groups:** 40, 42, 84

Date of Accounts	Feb 11	Feb 10	Feb 09
Working Capital	1m	1m	928
Fixed Assets	961	868	865
Current Assets	1m	1m	1m

G W Trading Ltd

Colin Road, Scunthorpe, DN16 1TT
Tel: 01724-281222 **Fax:** 01724-292704
E-mail: ibar@tayto.com
Website: http://www.golden-wonder.co.uk
Directors: S. Alan (Mkt Research), T. Fowler (Co Sec), S. Hutchinson (Grp Chief Exec), N. Smith (Grp Chief Exec)
Managers: W. Cummins (Personnel), W. Cummings (Mgr), W. Cummins, A. Patterson (Eng Serv Mgr), S. Hardacre (Mgr), I. Barnes (Chief Mgr), D. Brown (Transport), S. Hardaker (Comptroller)
Ultimate Holding Company: MANDERLEY FOOD GROUP LIMITED
Immediate Holding Company: GW TRADING LIMITED
Registration no: 05695113 **VAT No.:** GB 638 6535 08
Date established: 2006 **Turnover:** £20m - £50m
No.of Employees: 251 - 500 **Product Groups:** 20

Date of Accounts	Jul 08	Jul 09	Jul 10
Sales Turnover	39m	33m	29m
Pre Tax Profit/Loss	209	-1m	363
Working Capital	1m	6m	6m
Fixed Assets	886	N/A	N/A
Current Assets	12m	6m	7m
Current Liabilities	2m	241	235

Georgian Bar

Lake Enterprise Park Birkdale Road, Scunthorpe, DN17 2AU
Tel: 01724-858686 **Fax:** 01724-858597
E-mail: palongden@aol.com
Website: http://www.georgianbarsystem.com
Directors: P. Longden (MD)
Date established: 2002 **No.of Employees:** 1 - 10 **Product Groups:** 30

Date of Accounts	Sep 07	Sep 06	Sep 05
Working Capital	-179	-267	-255
Fixed Assets	24	29	31
Current Assets	219	130	69
Current Liabilities	398	396	324

Gunness Wharf Traffic Office

Trent Port House Stather Road, Flixborough, Scunthorpe, DN15 8RS
Tel: 01724-877899 **Fax:** 01724-851207
E-mail: traffic@flixboroughwharf.co.uk
Website: http://www.flixboroughwharf.co.uk
Managers: P. Readhead (Transport)
Immediate Holding Company: GWS ENGINEERS LIMITED
Registration no: 01762380 **VAT No.:** GB 128 2710 83
Date established: 1978 **No.of Employees:** 1 - 10 **Product Groups:** 72, 76

Guns & Tackle

251 Ashby High Street, Scunthorpe, DN16 2SQ
Tel: 01724-865445 **Fax:** 01724-865445
Directors: J. Bowden (Prop)
Date established: 1959 **No.of Employees:** 1 - 10 **Product Groups:** 36, 39, 40

Hanson Support Services Ltd

Scotter Road, Scunthorpe, DN17 2BU
Tel: 01724-867595 **Fax:** 01724-282411
E-mail: answers@hanserve.com
Website: http://www.hanserve.com
Directors: J. McDonald (Prop)
Immediate Holding Company: Hanson Resource Management Ltd
Registration no: 00735742 **No.of Employees:** 501 - 1000
Product Groups: 34, 66

Humberside Lifting Services Ltd

Unit 3 Ealand Industrial Estate Wharf Road, Ealand, Scunthorpe, DN17 4JW
Tel: 01724-711043 **Fax:** 01522-520344
E-mail: sales@lifting-safety.co.uk
Website: http://www.lifting-safety.co.uk
Directors: M. Armstrong (MD)
Ultimate Holding Company: RYANBRIDGE LIMITED
Immediate Holding Company: HUMBERSIDE LIFTING SERVICES LTD
Registration no: 07124195 **Date established:** 2010
Turnover: £500,000 - £1m **No.of Employees:** 1 - 10 **Product Groups:** 23, 25, 27, 30, 33, 35, 36, 37, 38, 39, 40, 41, 43, 44, 45, 46, 47, 48, 54, 63, 66, 67, 83, 84

Date of Accounts	Jan 12	Jan 11
Sales Turnover	245	284
Pre Tax Profit/Loss	-46	-121
Working Capital	-168	-121
Current Assets	97	105
Current Liabilities	37	15

Jewson Ltd

Rowland Road, Scunthorpe, DN16 1TL
Tel: 01724-844771 **Fax:** 01724-280811
Website: http://www.jewson.co.uk
Managers: B. Cartwright (Mgr)
Ultimate Holding Company: COMPAGNIE DE SAINT GOBAIN (FRANCE)
Immediate Holding Company: JEWSON LIMITED
Registration no: 00348407 **VAT No.:** GB 497 7184 83
Date established: 1939 **No.of Employees:** 1 - 10 **Product Groups:** 66

Date of Accounts	Dec 11	Dec 10	Dec 09
Sales Turnover	1606m	1547m	1485m
Pre Tax Profit/Loss	18m	100m	45m
Working Capital	-345m	-250m	-349m
Fixed Assets	496m	387m	461m
Current Assets	657m	1005m	1320m
Current Liabilities	66m	120m	64m

K B Dale Ltd

18 Warren Road, Scunthorpe, DN15 6XH
Tel: 01724-855645 **Fax:** 01724-278278
E-mail: info@daleuk.co.uk
Website: http://www.daleuk.co.uk
Directors: K. Dale (Prop)
Immediate Holding Company: K.B. DALE LIMITED
Registration no: 02644741 **Date established:** 1991
No.of Employees: 1 - 10 **Product Groups:** 23, 31, 52, 66

Date of Accounts	Nov 11	Nov 10	Nov 09
Working Capital	271	260	281
Fixed Assets	27	33	41
Current Assets	374	381	390

Karden Pipework Limited

21A Hebden Road Berkely Industrial Estate, Scunthorpe, DN15 8DT
Tel: 01724-277686 **Fax:** 01724-277300
E-mail: enquiries@kardenpipework.co.uk
Website: http://www.kardenpipework.co.uk
Bank(s): Royal Bank of Scotland
Directors: D. Lake (MD)
Managers: P. Herrick (Purch Mgr)
Registration no: 02962152 **VAT No.:** GB 616 9814 15
Date established: 1994 **Turnover:** £1m - £2m **No.of Employees:** 20
Product Groups: 35, 45, 48, 51, 52, 54, 84

Date of Accounts	Dec 11	Dec 10	Dec 09
Working Capital	71	63	52
Fixed Assets	16	9	7
Current Assets	322	307	365

Kestrel B C E Ltd

Billet Lane, Scunthorpe, DN15 9YH
Tel: 01724-400440 **Fax:** 01724-280241
E-mail: enquiries@kbp.co.uk
Website: http://www.kestrelbce.co.uk
Directors: C. Martin (Fin), P. Copestick (Chief Op Offcr)
Managers: K. Carter (Mktg Serv Mgr), K. Fleming (Buyer), S. Allen (Mktg Serv Mgr)
Ultimate Holding Company: LATIUM BUILDING PRODUCTS LIMITED
Immediate Holding Company: KESTREL-BCE LIMITED
Registration no: 05600098 **VAT No.:** GB 119 7195 49
Date established: 2005 **Turnover:** £20m - £50m
No.of Employees: 101 - 250 **Product Groups:** 30, 66

Date of Accounts	Dec 11	Oct 10	Oct 09
Sales Turnover	29m	25m	25m
Pre Tax Profit/Loss	-521	532	669
Working Capital	6m	9m	7m
Fixed Assets	2m	2m	2m
Current Assets	17m	20m	19m
Current Liabilities	3m	2m	2m

M A Hydraulics Ltd
11 Exmoor Avenue, Scunthorpe, DN15 8NJ
Tel: 01724-279508 **Fax:** 01724-279509
E-mail: sales@mahydraulics.co.uk
Website: http://www.mahydraulics.co.uk
Directors: R. Allery (MD)
Immediate Holding Company: M. A. HYDRAULICS LIMITED
Registration no: 03626039 **Date established:** 1998
Turnover: £500,000 - £1m **No.of Employees:** 1 - 10 **Product Groups:** 22, 38, 39, 40, 45, 67

Date of Accounts	Dec 11	Dec 10	Dec 09
Working Capital	350	311	224
Fixed Assets	20	21	26
Current Assets	669	613	524

Minelco Ltd
Third Avenue Flixborough, Scunthorpe, DN15 8SF
Tel: 01724-277411 **Fax:** 01724-866405
E-mail: ra-boulton@minelco.com
Website: http://www.minelco.com
Directors: S. Franey (Comm), R. Boulton (MD)
Managers: J. Potts (Fin Mgr), K. Walker (Personnel), T. Harding (Purch Mgr), G. Pennant
Ultimate Holding Company: LKAB (SWEDEN)
Immediate Holding Company: QUAY MINERALS LIMITED
Registration no: 02732626 **Date established:** 1992
Turnover: £20m - £50m **No.of Employees:** 51 - 100 **Product Groups:** 12, 14, 17, 31, 33

Date of Accounts	Dec 10	Dec 09	Dec 04
Working Capital	1m	1m	1m
Current Assets	1m	1m	1m

Moulded Foams
Unit 5-7 Menasha Way Queensway Industrial Estate, Scunthorpe, DN16 3RT
Tel: 01724-868153 **Fax:** 01724-270021
E-mail: ns@mouldedfoams.com
Website: http://www.mouldedfoams.com
Managers: D. Davies (Site Co-ord), N. Smith
Immediate Holding Company: TRENT REFRACTORIES LIMITED
Registration no: 00342627 **VAT No.:** GB 377 5307 28
Date established: 1989 **Turnover:** £2m - £5m **No.of Employees:** 21 - 50
Product Groups: 27, 30, 48, 76, 84

Date of Accounts	Jun 11	Jun 10	Jun 09
Working Capital	1m	947	856
Fixed Assets	229	223	215
Current Assets	2m	2m	1m

N S D Ltd
South Park Road, Scunthorpe, DN17 2BY
Tel: 01724-810000 **Fax:** 01724-819981
E-mail: robertleech@nsd.ltd.uk
Website: http://www.nsd.ltd.uk
Bank(s): Lloyds TSB
Directors: A. Levison (Dir), M. Lambert (Sales), P. Hart (MD), R. Leech (Dir)
Managers: H. Brown (I.T. Exec)
Immediate Holding Company: N.S.D. LIMITED
Registration no: 01924617 **VAT No.:** GB 429 7204 43
Date established: 1985 **Turnover:** £20m - £50m
No.of Employees: 101 - 250 **Product Groups:** 66

Date of Accounts	Dec 09	Dec 08	Dec 07
Sales Turnover	38m	79m	64m
Pre Tax Profit/Loss	-7m	2m	2m
Working Capital	-1m	5m	3m
Fixed Assets	6m	6m	6m
Current Assets	17m	46m	33m
Current Liabilities	10m	9m	9m

Nisa
Waldo Way, Scunthorpe, DN15 9GE
Tel: 01724-282028 **Fax:** 01724-278727
E-mail: info@nisaretail.com
Website: http://www.nisaretail.com
Bank(s): Barclays.
Directors: N. Turton (Grp Chief Exec), S. Webster (Fin), W. Swallow (Tech Serv)
Managers: M. Plaskitt, D. Droddle (Personnel), J. Sharpe
Immediate Holding Company: NISA LIMITED
Registration no: 01679354 **VAT No.:** GB 308 0829 66
Date established: 1982 **Turnover:** £250m - £500m
No.of Employees: 251 - 500 **Product Groups:** 61

North Lincolnshire Credit Union
162 High Street, Scunthorpe, DN15 6EH
Tel: 01724-868888 **Fax:** 01724-868888
E-mail: simon.green@northlincs.gov.uk
Website: http://www.northlincs.gov.uk
Directors: K. Foster (Dir)
Immediate Holding Company: NORTH LINCOLNSHIRE COUNCIL
Date established: 1996 **Turnover:** Up to £250,000
No.of Employees: 1 - 10 **Product Groups:** 80, 87

Petrochem UK Ltd
Grove Farm Grove Wharf, Gunness, Scunthorpe, DN15 8TZ
Tel: 01724-782322 **Fax:** 01724-784214
E-mail: sales@petrochemcarless.com
Website: http://www.petrochemcarless.com
Immediate Holding Company: Petrochem Carless Holdings Ltd
Registration no: 01601509 **Date established:** 1981
No.of Employees: 21 - 50 **Product Groups:** 31, 32, 66

Pollock Engineering
7c 27 Birkdale Road, Scunthorpe, DN17 2AU
Tel: 01724-845714 **Fax:** 01724-845714
Directors: M. Pollock (Prop)
No.of Employees: 1 - 10 **Product Groups:** 35

Premier Sealant Systems
Mercia Way Foxhills Industrial Estate, Scunthorpe, DN15 8RE
Tel: 01724-864100 **Fax:** 01724-860116
E-mail: alan.thomas@premseal.co.uk
Website: http://www.premseal.co.uk
Directors: J. Burns (MD), P. Duffy (Ptnr)
Managers: K. Darlow (Purch Mgr), A. Thomas (Sales Prom Mgr)
Immediate Holding Company: PREMIER SEALANT SYSTEMS LIMITED
Registration no: 03000843 **Date established:** 1994 **Turnover:** £2m - £5m
No.of Employees: 11 - 20 **Product Groups:** 27, 29, 30, 31, 32, 33, 34, 35, 52, 66

Date of Accounts	Dec 08	Jul 11	Jul 10
Working Capital	-223	31	166
Fixed Assets	405	96	54
Current Assets	1m	1m	1m

Rubie Gates
Unit 4 Bedford Park Banbury Road, Scunthorpe, DN16 1UN
Tel: 01724-281200 **Fax:** 01724-281200
Directors: R. Rubie (Prop)
Registration no: 04370037 **Date established:** 2002
No.of Employees: 1 - 10 **Product Groups:** 26, 35

Russell Ductile Castings Ltd
Trent Foundary Dawes Lane, Scunthorpe, DN15 6UW
Tel: 01724-862152 **Fax:** 01724-280461
E-mail: general@russellductile.co.uk
Website: http://www.ductile.co.uk
Bank(s): The Royal Bank of Scotland
Directors: C. Hammond (MD)
Managers: A. Lacey (Personnel), M. Taylor (Fin Mgr), M. McGough (Tech Serv Mgr), S. Wadsworth (Develop Mgr), T. Palmer (Sales Prom Mgr), L. Longland
Ultimate Holding Company: CHAMBERLIN PLC
Immediate Holding Company: DUCTILE CASTINGS LIMITED
Registration no: 01814643 **VAT No.:** GB 538 6867 88
Date established: 1984 **Turnover:** £10m - £20m
No.of Employees: 51 - 100 **Product Groups:** 34

Date of Accounts	Mar 09
Working Capital	4m
Current Assets	4m

Scunthorpe Sheet Metal Co
Grange Lane North, Scunthorpe, DN16 1BN
Tel: 01724-866100 **Fax:** 01724-282245
Directors: K. Walker (Prop)
Managers: R. Bromby (Sales Prom Mgr)
Immediate Holding Company: SCUNTHORPE SHEET METAL (2010) LIMITED
Registration no: 02417807 **VAT No.:** 128 4022 94 **Date established:** 2010
Turnover: £250,000 - £500,000 **No.of Employees:** 1 - 10
Product Groups: 48

Date of Accounts	Jul 11
Working Capital	17
Fixed Assets	26
Current Assets	39

Simon Engineering
Sixth Avenue Flixborough Industrial Estate, Flixborough, Scunthorpe, DN15 8SH
Tel: 01724-282937 **Fax:** 01724-278811
E-mail: info@simon-engineering.co.uk
Website: http://www.simon-engineering.co.uk
Directors: S. Hague (Comm)
Immediate Holding Company: S.J. HAGUE LIMITED
Registration no: 04092237 **Date established:** 2000
No.of Employees: 11 - 20 **Product Groups:** 35, 42, 45

Date of Accounts	Oct 11	Oct 10	Oct 09
Working Capital	995	999	956
Fixed Assets	36	58	71
Current Assets	1m	1m	1m

Solutions 4 Plastic
Triangle West End, Garthorpe, Scunthorpe, DN17 4RX
Tel: 01724-798717 **Fax:** 01724-798717
E-mail: solutions4.plastic@virgin.net
Website: http://www.solutions4plastic.co.uk
Directors: K. Whitchurch (Fin)
Immediate Holding Company: SOLUTIONS 4 PLASTIC LIMITED
Registration no: 06371649 **Date established:** 2007
Turnover: Up to £250,000 **No.of Employees:** 1 - 10 **Product Groups:** 29, 30, 31, 32, 84

Date of Accounts	Sep 11	Sep 10	Sep 09
Working Capital	49	19	19
Fixed Assets	15	13	15
Current Assets	92	41	52

T Freemantle Ltd
13 Atkinson Way Foxhills Industrial Estate, Scunthorpe, DN15 8QJ
Tel: 01724-276908 **Fax:** 01724-276909
E-mail: sales@tfreemantle.com
Website: http://www.tfreemantle.com
Directors: L. Freemantle (MD)
Immediate Holding Company: T.Freemantle Ltd
Registration no: 03147425 **Date established:** 1994 **Turnover:** £2m - £5m
No.of Employees: 21 - 50 **Product Groups:** 20, 27, 30, 33, 38, 41, 42, 44, 48, 67, 83, 84

Date of Accounts	Mar 12	Mar 11	Mar 10
Sales Turnover	3m	3m	2m
Pre Tax Profit/Loss	278	341	146
Working Capital	2m	1m	1m
Fixed Assets	329	334	330
Current Assets	2m	2m	2m
Current Liabilities	361	394	152

Terebro Plant & Machinery Hire
Terebro House Brigg Road, Scunthorpe, DN16 1AP
Tel: 01724-855501 **Fax:** 01724-855502
E-mail: adam.clarke@terebro.net
Website: http://www.terebo.net
Directors: A. Clarke (MD), J. Priestley (Dir)
Ultimate Holding Company: 02703484
Immediate Holding Company: TEREBRO LTD
Registration no: 04250478 **VAT No.:** GB 785 4295 84
Date established: 2001 **Turnover:** £500,000 - £1m
No.of Employees: 1 - 10 **Product Groups:** 22, 23, 24, 27, 29, 30, 37, 38, 39, 40, 45, 46, 48, 49, 51, 63, 67, 83, 84

Date of Accounts	Dec 07	Dec 06	Dec 05
Working Capital	-313	111	51
Fixed Assets	883	345	222
Current Assets	254	299	174
Current Liabilities	568	187	123

Trent Lifting Ltd
Brigg Road, Scunthorpe, DN16 1AP
Tel: 01724-280064 **Fax:** 01724-289988
E-mail: sales@trentlifting.co.uk
Website: http://www.trentlifting.co.uk
Managers: D. Sanderson (Mgr)
Ultimate Holding Company: STOCKS GROUP LIMITED
Immediate Holding Company: TRENT LIFTING LIMITED
Registration no: 06750266 **Date established:** 2008
No.of Employees: 1 - 10 **Product Groups:** 35, 39, 45

Date of Accounts	Mar 12	Mar 11	Mar 10
Working Capital	-98	-128	-139
Fixed Assets	62	66	69
Current Assets	234	193	134

Trevafield Fasteners
South Park Road, Scunthorpe, DN17 2BY
Tel: 01724-845017 **Fax:** 01724-280528
E-mail: sales@trevafield.co.uk
Website: http://www.trevafield.co.uk
Directors: J. Robinson (Dir), M. Robinson (Dir), R. Blythe (MD), S. Robinson (MD)
Immediate Holding Company: TREVAFIELD LIMITED
Registration no: 01268442 **Date established:** 1976
Turnover: £50m - £75m **No.of Employees:** 21 - 50 **Product Groups:** 35, 66

Date of Accounts	Mar 10	Mar 09	Mar 08
Working Capital	196	280	311
Fixed Assets	837	471	506
Current Assets	833	850	1m

Vessey Neil Storage Tanks Ltd
Flixborough Industrial Estate Flixborough, Scunthorpe, DN15 8SH
Tel: 01724-850224 **Fax:** 01724-289317
E-mail: n-vessey@neilvessey.com
Website: http://www.neilvessey.com
Directors: N. Vessey (Prop)
Immediate Holding Company: NEIL VESSEY (STORAGE TANKS) LIMITED
Registration no: 01315076 **VAT No.:** GB 298 1271 31
Date established: 1977 **No.of Employees:** 1 - 10 **Product Groups:** 30, 35, 37, 39, 41, 42, 45, 67, 76

Date of Accounts	Oct 11	Oct 10	Oct 09
Working Capital	31	36	174
Fixed Assets	326	330	1
Current Assets	267	350	448

Ulceby

A.C.T
Concorde House Limber Road Kirmington, Ulceby, DN39 6YP
Tel: 01652-682202
E-mail: sjh@act-it.co.uk
Website: http://www.act-it.co.uk
Directors: S. Bailey (MD)
Immediate Holding Company: ACT HALO LIMITED
Registration no: 06885730 **Date established:** 2009
Turnover: Up to £250,000 **No.of Employees:** 1 - 10 **Product Groups:** 44, 79

Date of Accounts	Sep 08	Sep 07	Sep 06
Working Capital	-2	-24	-43
Fixed Assets	19	19	16
Current Assets	158	58	11

Bytron
Concorde House Kirmington, Ulceby, DN39 6YP
Tel: 01652-688626 **Fax:** 01652-680788
E-mail: info@bytron.com
Website: http://www.bryton.com
Directors: S. Bailey (Dir), I. Harris (Fin)
Immediate Holding Company: BYTRON LIMITED
Registration no: 01817829 **VAT No.:** GB 364 8180 36
Date established: 1984 **Turnover:** £500,000 - £1m
No.of Employees: 1 - 10 **Product Groups:** 44

Date of Accounts	Sep 10	Sep 09	Sep 08
Working Capital	241	187	80
Fixed Assets	91	96	139
Current Assets	441	672	575

H L Display Ltd Head Office
Fosse House Schipol Way Kirmington, Ulceby, DN39 6GB
Tel: 01652-682140 **Fax:** 01652-688663
E-mail: info@hl-display.com
Website: http://www.hldisplay.com
Directors: D. Hill (MD), I. McKinnon (Fin)
Ultimate Holding Company: H L DISPLAY AB (SWEDEN)
Immediate Holding Company: HL DISPLAY (UK) LIMITED
Registration no: 02187037 **Date established:** 1987
Turnover: £10m - £20m **No.of Employees:** 1 - 10 **Product Groups:** 26, 30, 37, 38, 39, 44, 49, 67

Date of Accounts	Dec 11	Dec 10	Dec 09
Sales Turnover	10m	10m	8m
Pre Tax Profit/Loss	1m	955	922
Working Capital	2m	2m	1m
Fixed Assets	17	24	27
Current Assets	5m	6m	5m
Current Liabilities	981	596	535

Tanks 'R' Us Ltd
Main Street Thornton Curtis, Ulceby, DN39 6XW
Tel: 01469-531229 **Fax:** 01469-530611
E-mail: sales@tanksrus.co.uk
Website: http://www.tanksrus.co.uk
Directors: B. Chapman (MD)
Immediate Holding Company: W.H. DALE LIMITED
Registration no: 01907223 **Date established:** 1985
No.of Employees: 1 - 10 **Product Groups:** 30, 35, 37, 39, 42, 48, 84

Date of Accounts	Apr 11	Apr 10	Apr 09
Working Capital	88	33	65
Fixed Assets	194	160	123
Current Assets	681	290	374

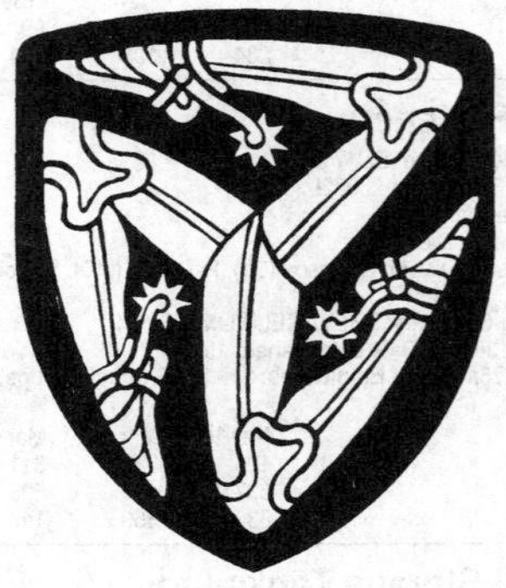

ISLE OF MAN

Isle Of Man

ADT Fire & Security plc (Branch Office)
Unit 33 Spring Valley Industrial Estate Douglas, Isle Of Man, IM2 2QT
Tel: 01624-676573 **Fax:** 01624-627938
E-mail: j-surridge@adt.co.uk
Website: http://www.adt.co.uk
Managers: A. Edwards (Sales Prom Mgr), P. Tipples (Ops Mgr)
Ultimate Holding Company: TYCO INTERNATIONAL LIMITED (SWITZERLAND)
Immediate Holding Company: ADT FIRE AND SECURITY PLC
Registration no: 01161045 **VAT No.:** GB 000 2705 49
Date established: 1974 **No.of Employees:** 1 - 10 **Product Groups:** 40, 44

Date of Accounts	Sep 11	Sep 08	Sep 09
Sales Turnover	363m	414m	384m
Pre Tax Profit/Loss	18m	4m	10m
Working Capital	450m	618m	561m
Fixed Assets	120m	193m	171m
Current Assets	710m	765m	722m
Current Liabilities	81m	57m	42m

Auldyn Construction Ltd
Unit 15e Tromode Estate Tromode, Douglas, Isle of Man, IM4 4RG
Tel: 01624-662466 **Fax:** 01624-663636
E-mail: reception@auldyn-construction.com
Website: http://www.auldyn-construction.com
Directors: G. Walker (MD)
Managers: C. Brew (Chief Acct)
Date established: 2001 **No.of Employees:** 51 - 100 **Product Groups:** 51, 52

Banana Computers Ltd
River Lodge Milntown Lezayre Road, Ramsey, Isle of Man, IM8 2TG
Tel: 01624-815400 **Fax:** 01624-811570
E-mail: sales@bananacomputers.com
Website: http://www.bananacomputers.com
Directors: G. Wilson (MD)
Immediate Holding Company: BANANA COMPUTERS LIMITED
Registration no: 04501721 **Date established:** 2002 **Turnover:** £1m - £2m
No.of Employees: 1 - 10 **Product Groups:** 67

Date of Accounts	Aug 06
Working Capital	1
Current Assets	1

Bottomline Ltd
Unit 8 Middle River Industrial Estate, Douglas, Isle Of Man, IM2 1AL
Tel: 01624-671671 **Fax:** 01624-628169
E-mail: dean@bottomline.im
Website: http://www.bottomline.im
Directors: D. Bolton (MD)
No.of Employees: 1 - 10 **Product Groups:** 35, 36, 39

D L P
Snugborough Trading Estate Union Mills, Isle of Man, IM4 4LH
Tel: 01624-691620 **Fax:** 01624-620112
E-mail: lisa@dlplimited.com
Website: http://www.dlplimited.com
Directors: N. Parson (MD)
Managers: L. Frost, S. Noon (Personnel), C. Spencer (Buyer)
No.of Employees: 51 - 100 **Product Groups:** 38, 67

Diesel Fuel Injection Services
Killane Nurseries Killane, Ballaugh, Isle Of Man, IM7 5BB
Tel: 01624-897410
Directors: W. Denney (Prop)
Date established: 2004 **No.of Employees:** 1 - 10 **Product Groups:** 40

Ebis Engineering & Plastics
Hills Meadow Douglas, Isle of Man, IM1 5EB
Tel: 01624-660971 **Fax:** 01624-660972
E-mail: ebis@manx.net
Website: http://www.manx.net
Directors: B. Irvine (Dir)
Registration no: 0108276C **Turnover:** Up to £250,000
No.of Employees: 1 - 10 **Product Groups:** 48

Eclipse Nursecall Systems Ltd
The Mount Mount Gawne Road, Port St Mary, Isle Of Man, IM9 5LX
Tel: 01624-832821 **Fax:** 01624-836279
E-mail: sales@nursecall.co.uk
Website: http://www.nursecall.co.uk
Directors: C. Parish (Dir)
Registration no: IM030689 **VAT No.:** GB 001 3031 65
Turnover: £1m - £2m **No.of Employees:** 1 - 10 **Product Groups:** 40

Good Health
Shop F Church Road Port Erin, Isle of Man, IM9 6AH
Tel: 01624-832865
E-mail: thegoodhealthstore@manx.net
Directors: M. Wade (Prop)
No.of Employees: 1 - 10 **Product Groups:** 31, 32

Island Seafare
Lime Street Port St Mary, Isle of Man, IM9 5EF
Tel: 07624-495930 **Fax:** 01624-835550
E-mail: enquiries@islandseafare.co.uk
Website: http://www.islandseafare.co.uk
Directors: T. Croft (Prop)
Registration no: 0052952C **Date established:** 1991
Turnover: Up to £250,000 **No.of Employees:** 11 - 20 **Product Groups:** 20

Isle Of Man Steam Packet Company Ltd
Imperial Buildings Douglas, Isle Of Man, IM1 2BY
Tel: 01624-645645 **Fax:** 01624-645608
E-mail: wayne.lisy@steam-packet.com
Website: http://www.steam-packet.com
Directors: D. Jude (Fin)
Managers: D. Jude (Comptroller), P. Watterson (Tech Serv Mgr), E. Docherty (Personnel), R. Kaley (Mktg Serv Mgr)
Immediate Holding Company: ISLE OF MAN STEAM PACKET COMPANY,LIMITED (THE)
Registration no: FC006682 **Date established:** 1985
Turnover: £50m - £75m **No.of Employees:** 251 - 500 **Product Groups:** 74

Date of Accounts	Dec 10	Dec 09	Dec 08
Sales Turnover	52m	57m	54m
Pre Tax Profit/Loss	14m	15m	10m
Working Capital	55m	40m	23m
Fixed Assets	34m	35m	40m
Current Assets	74m	74m	70m
Current Liabilities	N/A	N/A	7m

K & S Structural Steel
Old Brick Works Mines Road, Foxdale, Isle of Man, IM4 3EX
Tel: 01624-801182 **Fax:** 01624-801183
Website: http://www.manx.net
No.of Employees: 1 - 10 **Product Groups:** 40, 48, 79

Liftmann
Valley Crest Main Road, Santon, Isle of Man, IM4 1EJ
Tel: 01624-822568 **Fax:** 01624-823860
E-mail: rach@liftmann.com
Website: http://www.liftmann.com
Directors: R. Corlett (Prop)
Date established: 2004 **No.of Employees:** 1 - 10 **Product Groups:** 35, 39, 45

Manx Independent Carriers
Union Mills, Isle of Man, IM4 4LG
Tel: 01624-692100 **Fax:** 01624-610987
E-mail: sales@mic.co.im
Website: http://www.mic.co.im
Directors: M. Coleman (MD)
Managers: A. Morgan
Registration no: 10936 **Date established:** 1985 **Turnover:** £10m - £20m
No.of Employees: 51 - 100 **Product Groups:** 72

Marine & General Transport & Warehousing Ltd
M & G House Douglas Head Industrial Estate, Douglas, Isle of Man, IM1 5BF
Tel: 01624-623841 **Fax:** 01624-623004
E-mail: geoff.briers@mcb.co.im
Website: http://www.mcb.co.im
Directors: G. Briers (Dir)
Date established: 2002 **No.of Employees:** 1 - 10 **Product Groups:** 44, 72, 74, 84

Matty P Services
67 Cronk Grianagh Douglas, Isle of Man, IM4 4RN
Tel: 07624-496608
Directors: M. Talbot (Prop)
No.of Employees: 1 - 10 **Product Groups:** 41

Mill Shop Ltd
Tynwald Mills St Johns, Isle of Man, IM4 3AD
Tel: 01624-801213 **Fax:** 01624-801893
E-mail: info@themillshop.co.im
Website: http://www.themillshop.co.im
Bank(s): Isle of Man Bank
Directors: S. Bradley (MD), S. Bradley (MD)
Ultimate Holding Company: TYNWALD MILLS (I.O.M.) LTD
Registration no: 00006053 **Date established:** 1997 **Turnover:** £2m - £5m
No.of Employees: 51 - 100 **Product Groups:** 23, 24

Palace Hotel & Casino
Palace Buildings Central Promenade, Douglas, Isle Of Man, IM2 4NA
Tel: 01624-662662 **Fax:** 01624-625535
E-mail: info@palacehotel.co.im
Website: http://www.seftongroup.co.im
Bank(s): Isle of Man
Managers: R. McCauley (Sales & Mktg Mg), G. Kerruish (Personnel), P. Forrest (Chief Mgr)
VAT No.: GB 001 2017 64 **No.of Employees:** 101 - 250
Product Groups: 69, 89

Progress Shaving Brush Vulfix Ltd
Unit 24 Spring Valley Industrial Estate, Douglas, Isle Of Man, IM2 2QR
Tel: 01624-676030 **Fax:** 01624-662056
E-mail: enquiries@progress-vulfix.com
Website: http://www.vulfixoldoriginal.com
Directors: M. Watterson (MD)
Registration no: 00001342 **VAT No.:** GB 000 0061 77
Turnover: £500,000 - £1m **No.of Employees:** 1 - 10 **Product Groups:** 32, 33, 49

Ronaldsway Aircraft
Ballasalla, Isle of Man, IM9 2RY
Tel: 01624-820555 **Fax:** 01624-820550
E-mail: leah.marsden@rlc-group.com
Website: http://www.ronaldsway-aircraft.com
Bank(s): Isle of Man Bank
Directors: D. Nutton (Grp Chief Exec), C. Horley (Tech Serv), S. Comer (Fin)
Managers: D. Cowley, L. Howes (Personnel)
Ultimate Holding Company: RLC ENGINEERING GROUP LTD
Immediate Holding Company: RONALDSWAY AIRCRAFT (HOLDINGS) LTD
Registration no: 00001253 **VAT No.:** GB 000 0527 57
Date established: 1991 **Turnover:** £10m - £20m
No.of Employees: 101 - 250 **Product Groups:** 39, 48

Saws & Cutters Sharpening Service
Kirk Michael, Isle Of Man, IM6 1ET
Tel: 07624-492242
Directors: G. Hughes (Prop)
No.of Employees: 1 - 10 **Product Groups:** 36

T C Components
Castletown Windmill 1 Arbory Road, Castletown, Isle of Man, IM9 1HA
Tel: 01624-829689 **Fax:** 01624-829686
E-mail: tcatiom@hotmail.com
Directors: T. Critchlow (Prop)
VAT No.: GB 001 8766 90 **Turnover:** £500,000 - £1m
No.of Employees: 1 - 10 **Product Groups:** 37

Tower Insurance
PO Box 27, Isle Of Man, IM99 1BF
Tel: 01624-645900 **Fax:** 01624-663864
E-mail: tower.insurance@uk.rsagroup.com
Website: http://www.twrgrp.com
Bank(s): Isle of Man Bank
Managers: N. Holker
Immediate Holding Company: ROYAL & SUN ALLIANCE
No.of Employees: 21 - 50 **Product Groups:** 82

Unique Fire Protection
Unit 26 Snugborough Trading Estate Union Mills, Isle of Man, IM4 4LH
Tel: 01624-623592 **Fax:** 01624-679470
Website: http://www.mcb.net
Directors: K. Midghill (Prop)
Date established: 1973 **No.of Employees:** 1 - 10 **Product Groups:** 38, 42

ISLE OF WIGHT

Cowes

Bodywise Ltd
Unit 8 Enterprise Way, Cowes, PO31 8AP
Tel: 01983-248888 **Fax:** 01983-248899
E-mail: sales@bodywise.biz
Website: http://www.bodywise.biz
Managers: R. Sheppard (Chief Mgr)
Immediate Holding Company: BODYWISE LIMITED
Registration no: 01490051 **VAT No.:** GB 714 7448 28
Date established: 1980 **Turnover:** £250,000 - £500,000
No.of Employees: 1 - 10 **Product Groups:** 32, 42, 63

Date of Accounts	Mar 12	Mar 11	Mar 10
Working Capital	430	284	249
Fixed Assets	628	635	616
Current Assets	538	366	323
Current Liabilities	N/A	N/A	47

Comar Systems Ltd
Unit 7 Medina Court Arctic Road, Cowes, PO31 7XD
Tel: 01983-282400
E-mail: info@comarsystems.com
Website: http://www.comarsystems.com
Directors: P. Cotton (MD)
Immediate Holding Company: COMAR SYSTEMS LTD.
Registration no: 01175310 **Date established:** 1974
No.of Employees: 1 - 10 **Product Groups:** 37, 39

Date of Accounts	Sep 11	Sep 10	Sep 09
Working Capital	228	165	160
Fixed Assets	16	19	23
Current Assets	324	206	208

Isle Of Wight Tourist Guide
5 Cotton Close, Cowes, PO31 7UG
Tel: 01983-292746 **Fax:** 01983-280005
E-mail: info@isleofwighttouristguide.com
Website: http://www.isleofwighttouristguide.com
Directors: M. ager (Dir), V. Tice (Fin)
Immediate Holding Company: Islandwide Leisure Ltd
Registration no: 05890181 **Date established:** 2006
No.of Employees: 1 - 10 **Product Groups:** 84

Date of Accounts	Jul 08	Jul 07
Working Capital	5	11
Fixed Assets	11	14
Current Assets	9	12
Current Liabilities	4	1

Clare Lallow Ltd
3 Medina Road, Cowes, PO31 7BU
Tel: 01983-292112 **Fax:** 01983-281180
E-mail: lallows@lallowsboatyard.com
Website: http://www.lallowsboatyard.com
Bank(s): Lloyds TSB Bank plc
Directors: L. Boarer (MD)
Immediate Holding Company: CLARE LALLOW LIMITED
Registration no: 04719417 **Date established:** 2003
Turnover: £500,000 - £1m **No.of Employees:** 11 - 20
Product Groups: 25, 39

Date of Accounts	Mar 11	Mar 10	Mar 09
Working Capital	10	-42	-41
Fixed Assets	57	67	91
Current Assets	186	268	275

Powerplus Marine Services
Thetis Wharf Medina Road, Cowes, PO31 7BX
Tel: 01983-290421
E-mail: sales@rhpmarine.co.uk
Website: http://www.powerplusmarine.co.uk
Directors: R. Pierrepont (Prop)
Immediate Holding Company: RHP MARINE LIMITED
Date established: 2004 **No.of Employees:** 1 - 10 **Product Groups:** 35, 36, 39

Date of Accounts	Mar 11	Mar 10	Mar 09
Working Capital	-80	-59	-14
Fixed Assets	73	83	89
Current Assets	100	144	152

Ratsey & Lapthorn Ltd
42 Medina Road, Cowes, PO31 7BY
Tel: 01983-294051 **Fax:** 01983-294053
E-mail: ratseysails@ratsey.com
Website: http://www.ratsey.com
Directors: A. Cassell (Dir)
Immediate Holding Company: R & L (UK) LTD.
Registration no: 03651495 **VAT No.:** GB 411 3198 87
Date established: 1998 **Turnover:** Up to £250,000
No.of Employees: 1 - 10 **Product Groups:** 23, 24

Date of Accounts	Sep 11	Sep 10	Sep 09
Pre Tax Profit/Loss	-3	-4	-4
Working Capital	4	5	-106
Fixed Assets	8	9	13
Current Assets	5	5	6
Current Liabilities	1	N/A	N/A

T A Reader Transport Ltd
Prospect Road, Cowes, PO31 7AD
Tel: 01983-281138 **Fax:** 01983-281178
Website: http://www.tareadertransport.co.uk
Managers: J. Foreman (Chief Mgr)
Immediate Holding Company: BUTTERFLY PARAGLIDING LIMITED
Registration no: 04022235 **Date established:** 2000
No.of Employees: 11 - 20 **Product Groups:** 20, 40, 41

Date of Accounts	Apr 12	Apr 11
Working Capital	1	1
Current Assets	1	1

Readers Trading Ltd
79 Place Road, Cowes, PO31 7AF
Tel: 01983-292131 **Fax:** 01983-296042
E-mail: michael.reader@readersgroup.com
Website: http://www.readersgroup.com
Directors: M. Reader (Dir), C. Cutler (Dir), M. Reader (MD)
Managers: L. Reader (I.T. Exec), T. Snudden (Chief Acct)
Immediate Holding Company: READERS (ISLE OF WIGHT) LIMITED
Registration no: 02027823 **VAT No.:** GB 458 6330 28
Date established: 1986 **Turnover:** £20m - £50m **No.of Employees:** 1 - 10
Product Groups: 30, 33, 37

Date of Accounts	Mar 11	Mar 10	Mar 09
Working Capital	-2	-2	-2
Current Liabilities	2	2	2

Richard Newnham Project Management Services
4 Princes Esplanade, Cowes, PO31 8LE
Tel: 01983-290168 **Fax:** 01983-281882
E-mail: ricnewnham@onwhite.net
Website: http://www.richardnewnham.co.uk
Directors: R. Newnham (MD)
Immediate Holding Company: PROJECT MANAGEMENT SERVICES (SOUTH COAST) LIMITED
Registration no: 05807631 **Date established:** 2006
Turnover: Up to £250,000 **No.of Employees:** 1 - 10 **Product Groups:** 80

Date of Accounts	May 11	May 10
Working Capital	-1	7
Fixed Assets	13	9
Current Assets	38	22

Seatek Engineering
46 Cross Street, Cowes, PO31 7TD
Tel: 01983-281158 **Fax:** 01983-281158
Directors: P. Dunstan (Ptnr)
Date established: 1992 **No.of Employees:** 1 - 10 **Product Groups:** 35, 36, 39

Spencer Rigging Ltd
Empire Buildings St Marys Road, Cowes, PO31 7SX
Tel: 01983-292022 **Fax:** 01983-291589
E-mail: mark@spencerrigging.co.uk
Website: http://www.spencerrigging.co.uk
Bank(s): National Westminster Bank Plc
Directors: M. Spencer (MD)
Ultimate Holding Company: SPENCER (ISLE OF WIGHT) LIMITED
Immediate Holding Company: SPENCER RIGGING LIMITED
Registration no: 01614521 **VAT No.:** GB 107 6092 87
Date established: 1982 **Turnover:** £1m - £2m **No.of Employees:** 11 - 20
Product Groups: 39

Date of Accounts	Jan 11	Jan 10	Jan 09
Working Capital	535	913	872
Fixed Assets	624	630	667
Current Assets	855	979	1m

Spinlock Ltd
41 Birmingham Road, Cowes, PO31 7BH
Tel: 01983-295555 **Fax:** 01983-295542
E-mail: info@spinlock.co.uk
Website: http://www.spinlock.co.uk
Bank(s): Lloyds, Newport
Directors: C. Hill (MD), R. Hogg (MD)
Managers: J. Hall (Mktg Serv Mgr), C. Senior (Ops Mgr), J. Wells
Immediate Holding Company: SPINLOCK LIMITED
Registration no: 00943480 **VAT No.:** GB 226 7542 57
Date established: 1968 **Turnover:** £1m - £2m **No.of Employees:** 21 - 50
Product Groups: 39

Date of Accounts	Jul 11	Jul 10	Jul 09
Working Capital	2m	2m	2m
Fixed Assets	488	504	297
Current Assets	2m	2m	2m

Strainstall
8-10 Mariners Way, Cowes, PO31 8PD
Tel: 01983-203600 **Fax:** 01983-291335
E-mail: enquiries@strainstall.com
Website: http://www.strainstallloadcells.com
Bank(s): Bank of Scotland
Directors: K. Lucas (Fin)
Managers: D. Hume (Purch Mgr), H. Cornish (Grp Mktg Mgr)
Ultimate Holding Company: JAMES FISHER AND SONS PUBLIC LIMITED COMPANY
Immediate Holding Company: STRAINSTALL GROUP LIMITED
Registration no: 04038899 **VAT No.:** GB 760 1924 41
Date established: 2000 **Turnover:** £500,000 - £1m
No.of Employees: 21 - 50 **Product Groups:** 37, 38, 39, 45, 84, 85

Date of Accounts	Dec 11	Dec 10	Dec 09
Sales Turnover	784	613	609
Pre Tax Profit/Loss	4m	4m	2m
Working Capital	3m	-8m	-8m
Fixed Assets	10m	10m	10m
Current Assets	5m	2m	512
Current Liabilities	130	135	241

D G Wroath Marine Electrical
7 Cowes Yacht Haven High Street, Cowes, PO31 7AY
Tel: 01983-281467 **Fax:** 01983-296742
E-mail: davidwroath@aol.com
Directors: D. Wroath (MD)
Date established: 1990 **No.of Employees:** 1 - 10 **Product Groups:** 35, 36, 39

East Cowes

Datum Electronics Ltd
Needles Building Trinity Wharf, East Cowes, PO32 6RF
Tel: 01983-282834 **Fax:** 01983-282835
E-mail: web@datum-electronics.co.uk
Website: http://www.datum-electronics.co.uk
Directors: R. Habens (Fin)
Immediate Holding Company: DATUM ELECTRONICS LTD
Registration no: 03087255 **Date established:** 1995 **Turnover:** £1m - £2m
No.of Employees: 11 - 20 **Product Groups:** 37, 38

Date of Accounts	Mar 11	Mar 10	Mar 09
Working Capital	241	155	106
Fixed Assets	36	37	46
Current Assets	437	295	214

South Coast Cooling Ltd
88 Upper Yarborough Road, East Cowes, PO32 6EE
Tel: 01983-293302
E-mail: sales@southcoastcooling.co.uk
Website: http://www.southcoastcooling.co.uk
Directors: C. Howard (Fin), P. Howard (Dir)
Immediate Holding Company: SOUTH COAST COOLING LIMITED
Registration no: 06456423 **Date established:** 2007
Turnover: Up to £250,000 **No.of Employees:** 1 - 10 **Product Groups:** 52

Date of Accounts	Dec 11	Dec 10	Dec 09
Working Capital	-10	-0	7
Fixed Assets	12	6	7
Current Assets	29	19	15

Vikoma International Ltd
Kingston Road, East Cowes, PO32 6JS
Tel: 01983-200570 **Fax:** 023-8021 1644
E-mail: sales@vikoma.com
Website: http://www.vikoma.com
Bank(s): H S B C

see next page

Vikoma International Ltd - Cont'd
Directors: D. Healy (MD), M. Hammond (Fin)
Managers: M. Haymer (Buyer), H. Farrant (Personnel)
Ultimate Holding Company: ENERGY ENVIRONMENTAL LIMITED
Immediate Holding Company: VIKOMA INTERNATIONAL LIMITED
Registration no: 03015615 **VAT No.:** GB 349 1177 44
Date established: 1995 **Turnover:** £10m - £20m
No.of Employees: 51 - 100 **Product Groups:** 29, 30, 32, 36, 38, 39, 42, 45, 46, 54, 74

Date of Accounts	Mar 12	Mar 11	Mar 10
Sales Turnover	10m	15m	9m
Pre Tax Profit/Loss	-66	2m	669
Working Capital	4m	4m	3m
Fixed Assets	2m	3m	3m
Current Assets	7m	7m	6m
Current Liabilities	2m	2m	2m

Freshwater

Intermedia Sales Europe Ltd
Afton Road, Freshwater, PO40 9UH
Tel: 01983-753161 **Fax:** 01983-754683
E-mail: admin@mediamec.net
Website: http://www.mediamec.net
Managers: R. Stanner (Mgr)
Date established: 2004 **No.of Employees:** 1 - 10 **Product Groups:** 38, 42

Newport

Biffa Waste Services Ltd
45 Manners View, Newport, PO30 5FA
Tel: 01983-821041 **Fax:** 01983-822784
E-mail: marketing@biffa.co.uk
Website: http://www.biffa.co.uk
Managers: M. Allen (Mgr)
Immediate Holding Company: BIFFA WASTE SERVICES LIMITED
Registration no: 00946107 **Date established:** 1969
Turnover: Up to £250,000 **No.of Employees:** 21 - 50 **Product Groups:** 32, 54

Date of Accounts	Mar 08	Mar 09	Apr 10
Sales Turnover	555m	574m	492m
Pre Tax Profit/Loss	23m	50m	30m
Working Capital	229m	271m	293m
Fixed Assets	371m	360m	378m
Current Assets	409m	534m	609m
Current Liabilities	50m	100m	115m

Chamber Of Commerce Tourism & Industry
Mill Court Furrlongs, Newport, PO30 2AA
Tel: 01983-520777 **Fax:** 01983-554555
E-mail: chamber@iwchamber.co.uk
Website: http://www.iwchamber.co.uk
Directors: K. Smith (Grp Chief Exec)
Immediate Holding Company: ISLE OF WIGHT CHAMBER OF COMMERCE
Registration no: 01150487 **VAT No.:** GB 643 3343 55
Date established: 1973 **Turnover:** £500,000 - £1m
No.of Employees: 11 - 20 **Product Groups:** 80, 81

Date of Accounts	Mar 12	Mar 11	Mar 10
Sales Turnover	657	821	912
Pre Tax Profit/Loss	N/A	11	60
Working Capital	250	244	234
Fixed Assets	26	32	34
Current Assets	429	508	606
Current Liabilities	149	227	320

Countrywide Fleet Services
114 Carisbrooke Road, Newport, PO30 1DF
Tel: 01983-532123 **Fax:** 0870-608 0859
E-mail: sales@countrywide-fleet.co.uk
Website: http://www.countrywide-fleet.co.uk
Directors: J. Cooper (Prop)
Immediate Holding Company: COUNTRYWIDE FLEET SERVICES (UK) LIMITED
Registration no: 04500619 **VAT No.:** GB 669 1882 82
Date established: 2002 **Turnover:** Up to £250,000
No.of Employees: 1 - 10 **Product Groups:** 82

Date of Accounts	Aug 05	Aug 04	Aug 03
Sales Turnover	93	98	N/A
Pre Tax Profit/Loss	78	65	N/A
Working Capital	-29	-29	N/A
Fixed Assets	1	2	N/A
Current Assets	33	6	N/A
Current Liabilities	52	32	N/A

Gurit UK Ltd
St Cross Business Park, Newport, PO30 5WU
Tel: 01983-828000 **Fax:** 01983-828100
E-mail: graham.harvey@gurit.com
Website: http://www.gurit.com
Bank(s): Lloyds TSB Bank plc
Directors: G. Harvey (Dir)
Managers: A. Pordage (Fin Mgr)
Ultimate Holding Company: GURIT HOLDING AG (SWITZERLAND)
Immediate Holding Company: STRUCTURAL POLYMER (HOLDINGS) LIMITED
Registration no: 02339945 **Date established:** 1989
Turnover: £50m - £75m **No.of Employees:** 251 - 500
Product Groups: 23, 30, 31, 32, 33, 48, 66, 84

Date of Accounts	Dec 11	Dec 10	Dec 08
Pre Tax Profit/Loss	2m	-4m	127
Working Capital	3m	3m	7m
Fixed Assets	4m	4m	12m
Current Assets	3m	3m	7m
Current Liabilities	6	6	17

I T S Tools Ltd
Dodnor Lane Industrial Estate, Newport, PO30 5XA
Tel: 01983-526344 **Fax:** 01983-821547
E-mail: itstools@tiscali.co.uk
Website: http://www.thetoolman.co.uk
Managers: M. Mahoney (Mgr)
Immediate Holding Company: I.T.S. TOOLS LIMITED
Registration no: 01245101 **Date established:** 1976
No.of Employees: 11 - 20 **Product Groups:** 40, 41, 47, 83

Date of Accounts	Sep 11	Sep 10	Sep 09
Working Capital	351	344	369
Fixed Assets	99	109	127
Current Assets	613	529	523

I C R Touch LLP
26 Daish Way Dodnor Industrial Estate, Newport, PO30 5XB
Tel: 08446-931119 **Fax:** 01983-821682
E-mail: sales@icrtouch.com
Website: http://www.icrtouch.com
Directors: C. Ringer (Dir)
Immediate Holding Company: ICRTOUCH LLP
Registration no: OC320451 **Date established:** 2006
Turnover: £500,000 - £1m **No.of Employees:** 11 - 20 **Product Groups:** 44

Date of Accounts	Mar 11	Mar 10	Mar 09
Working Capital	377	426	309
Fixed Assets	21	23	27
Current Assets	463	471	398

Island Waste Services Ltd
Forest Park Forest Road, Newport, PO30 5YS
Tel: 01983-821234 **Fax:** 01983-825664
E-mail: islandwaste@biffa.co.uk
Website: http://www.islandwaste.co.uk
Directors: T. Lowth (Fin)
Managers: S. Crook (Chief Mgr)
Ultimate Holding Company: WASTEINVESTMENTS LLP
Immediate Holding Company: ISLAND WASTE SERVICES LIMITED
Registration no: 01552791 **Date established:** 1981
No.of Employees: 101 - 250 **Product Groups:** 32, 54

Date of Accounts	Mar 08	Mar 09	Apr 10
Sales Turnover	11m	12m	12m
Pre Tax Profit/Loss	592	1m	1m
Working Capital	-4m	-3m	-1m
Fixed Assets	7m	6m	6m
Current Assets	2m	2m	2m
Current Liabilities	803	971	2m

Isle Of Wight County Press Ltd
Brannon House 123 Pyle Street, Newport, PO30 1ST
Tel: 01983-521333 **Fax:** 01983-527204
E-mail: adman@iwcpress.demon.co.uk
Website: http://www.iwcp.co.uk
Directors: E. Munder (Fin), R. Freeman (MD), R. Freeman (MD)
Managers: Y. Linton, F. Jupe (Mktg Serv Mgr), B. Castle (Tech Serv Mgr), D. Thornton
Ultimate Holding Company: ISLE OF WIGHT COUNTY PRESS GROUP LIMITED
Immediate Holding Company: ISLE OF WIGHT COUNTY PRESS LIMITED
Registration no: 01342243 **Date established:** 1977 **Turnover:** £2m - £5m
No.of Employees: 51 - 100 **Product Groups:** 64

Date of Accounts	Jun 11	Jun 10	Jun 09
Sales Turnover	4m	4m	4m
Pre Tax Profit/Loss	105	217	164
Working Capital	-48	-115	-24
Fixed Assets	246	283	220
Current Assets	1m	1m	1m
Current Liabilities	285	277	243

L C M Systems Ltd
Unit 15 Barry Way, Newport, PO30 5GY
Tel: 01983-249264 **Fax:** 01983-249266
E-mail: info@lcmsystems.com
Website: http://www.lcmsystems.com
Bank(s): National Westminster Bank Plc
Managers: P. Dearling (Sales Prom Mgr)
Ultimate Holding Company: LCM (HOLDINGS) LIMITED
Immediate Holding Company: L.C.M. SYSTEMS LIMITED
Registration no: 02057541 **VAT No.:** GB 785 3956 71
Date established: 1986 **Turnover:** £1m - £2m **No.of Employees:** 11 - 20
Product Groups: 37, 38, 39, 45, 48, 67, 84

Date of Accounts	Nov 11	Nov 10	Nov 09
Working Capital	640	606	452
Fixed Assets	413	257	262
Current Assets	990	818	663

Maplin Electronics Ltd
Coppins Bridge Retail Park, Newport, PO30 2TA
Tel: 08432-277368
E-mail: sales@maplin.co.uk
Website: http://www.maplin.co.uk
Managers: C. Starky (Mgr)
Ultimate Holding Company: MONTAGU PRIVATE EQUITY LLP
Immediate Holding Company: MAPLIN ELECTRONICS LIMITED
Registration no: 01264385 **Date established:** 1976
Turnover: £125m - £250m **No.of Employees:** 1 - 10 **Product Groups:** 37, 61

Date of Accounts	Dec 11	Dec 08	Dec 09
Sales Turnover	205m	204m	204m
Pre Tax Profit/Loss	25m	32m	35m
Working Capital	118m	49m	75m
Fixed Assets	27m	28m	28m
Current Assets	207m	108m	142m
Current Liabilities	78m	51m	59m

Marghams Stores Ltd
47a Crocker Street, Newport, PO30 5DB
Tel: 01983-522282 **Fax:** 01983-822871
E-mail: marghams.stores@btopenworld.com
Website: http://www.marghams.co.uk
Directors: I. Margham (Dir)
Immediate Holding Company: MARGHAMS STORES LIMITED
Registration no: 03783649 **Date established:** 1999
No.of Employees: 1 - 10 **Product Groups:** 38, 42

Date of Accounts	Mar 09	Mar 08	Sep 11
Working Capital	22	72	-20
Fixed Assets	9	12	6
Current Assets	167	219	152

Newey & Eyre Ltd
62 Manners View Link Road, Newport, PO30 5FA
Tel: 01983-523481 **Fax:** 01983-520723
Website: http://www.neweysonline.co.uk
Bank(s): Barclays
Managers: N. Witlock (Mgr)
Immediate Holding Company: NEWEY & EYRE LIMITED
Registration no: 00216596 **VAT No.:** 614 2136 80 **Date established:** 2026
Turnover: £75m - £125m **No.of Employees:** 21 - 50 **Product Groups:** 37, 67

Date of Accounts	Dec 11	Dec 10	Dec 09
Pre Tax Profit/Loss	N/A	N/A	387
Working Capital	15m	15m	15m
Fixed Assets	265	265	265
Current Assets	15m	15m	15m

P B Structures Steel Erectors Roof Cladding
87 Noke Common, Newport, PO30 5TY
Tel: 01983-825672
Directors: P. Bennett (Prop)
Registration no: 03073702 **Date established:** 1995
No.of Employees: 1 - 10 **Product Groups:** 35

Rainbow Trading Post
21a Horsebridge Hill, Newport, PO30 5TJ
Tel: 01983-533129 **Fax:** 01983-533129
Website: http://www.rainbow.co.uk
Directors: J. Eveleigh (Ptnr)
No.of Employees: 1 - 10 **Product Groups:** 37, 39, 63

Ralphs Health Foods
73 St James Street, Newport, PO30 1LQ
Tel: 01983-522353 **Fax:** 01983-522353
Directors: E. McCombe (Prop)
Date established: 1918 **Turnover:** Up to £250,000
No.of Employees: 1 - 10 **Product Groups:** 31, 32

Solent Blasters
Unit 3-5 Bowcombe Meadows Business Park Bowcombe Road, Newport, PO30 3HZ
Tel: 01983-530070 **Fax:** 01983-530070
E-mail: paulgti6@hotmail.com
Website: http://www.solentblasters.com
Directors: P. Atkins (Ptnr)
Registration no: 00960730 **Date established:** 1969
No.of Employees: 1 - 10 **Product Groups:** 46, 48

The Southern Vectis Omnibus Co. Ltd
Nelson Road, Newport, PO30 1RD
Tel: 01983-827000 **Fax:** 01983-524961
E-mail: talk2us@islandbuses.info
Website: http://www.irelandbuses.info
Bank(s): National Westminster
Directors: M. Morgan-Huws (Div)
Immediate Holding Company: SOUTHERN VECTIS LIMITED
Registration no: 02005917 **VAT No.:** GB 412 0986 71
Date established: 1986 **Turnover:** £20m - £50m
No.of Employees: 21 - 50 **Product Groups:** 72

Date of Accounts	Jun 07
Working Capital	2180
Current Assets	2180
Total Share Capital	1980

T R S Fleet Management
23 St Thomas Square, Newport, PO30 1SG
Tel: 08454-504810 **Fax:** 08454-504801
E-mail: trsfleet@yahoo.co.uk
Directors: T. O'connor (MD)
No.of Employees: 1 - 10 **Product Groups:** 68

Vectis Optical Laboratories Ltd
81a High Street, Newport, PO30 1BG
Tel: 01983-525272 **Fax:** 01983-525272
Directors: M. Bridger (Dir)
Immediate Holding Company: VECTIS OPTICAL LABORATORIES LIMITED
Registration no: 00873289 **VAT No.:** GB 108 1105 22
Date established: 1966 **Turnover:** £250,000 - £500,000
No.of Employees: 1 - 10 **Product Groups:** 45

Date of Accounts	Mar 12	Mar 11	Mar 10
Working Capital	102	118	145
Fixed Assets	105	108	100
Current Assets	134	154	178

W Hurst & Sons I W Ltd
33 Holyrood Street, Newport, PO30 5AX
Tel: 01983-523636 **Fax:** 01983-825334
E-mail: shop@hurst-iw.co.uk
Website: http://www.tryhurstfirst.co.uk
Bank(s): Lloyds TSB
Directors: D. Bowley (MD)
Managers: I. Carpenter (Mgr), P. Lewis (Buyer)
Immediate Holding Company: W.HURST & SON.(I.W.)LIMITED
Registration no: 00693444 **VAT No.:** 107 3598 66 **Date established:** 1961
Turnover: £2m - £5m **No.of Employees:** 51 - 100 **Product Groups:** 61

Date of Accounts	May 11	May 10	May 09
Sales Turnover	5m	5m	5m
Pre Tax Profit/Loss	303	289	204
Working Capital	2m	2m	2m
Fixed Assets	5m	4m	4m
Current Assets	3m	3m	3m
Current Liabilities	277	255	140

Weldwise Welding Equipment
Bernard Way, Newport, PO30 5YL
Tel: 01983-822711 **Fax:** 01983-528311
Website: http://www.idml.com
Directors: T. Philips (Ptnr)
Date established: 1981 **No.of Employees:** 1 - 10 **Product Groups:** 46

Date of Accounts	Jul 11	Jul 10	Jul 09
Working Capital	-37	-32	-28
Fixed Assets	8	10	10
Current Assets	5	8	3

Wight Materials Handling Ltd
Unit 13 Barry Way, Newport, PO30 5GY
Tel: 01983-532163 **Fax:** 01983-754203
E-mail: kevin@wightforklifttrucks.com
Website: http://www.wighthandling.co.uk
Directors: K. Sykes (MD)
Immediate Holding Company: WIGHT MATERIALS HANDLING LIMITED
Registration no: 06541519 **Date established:** 2008
No.of Employees: 1 - 10 **Product Groups:** 35, 39, 45

Date of Accounts	Mar 12	Mar 11	Mar 10
Working Capital	85	58	-2
Fixed Assets	57	48	38
Current Assets	242	235	127

Zeta Dynamics Ltd

Zeta House Daish Way, Newport, PO30 5XJ
Tel: 01983-527725 **Fax:** 01483-417105
E-mail: admin@opusmaxim.com
Website: http://www.opusmaxim.com
Directors: D. Connolly (Dir)
Immediate Holding Company: ZETA DYNAMICS LIMITED
Registration no: 05967976 **Date established:** 2006
Turnover: £500,000 - £1m **No.of Employees:** 11 - 20 **Product Groups:** 80

Ryde

AWI Ltd

AWI Ltd Cothey Way, Ryde, PO33 1QT
Tel: 01983-817220 **Fax:** 01983-616295
E-mail: paulw@awilmicrowaves.com
Website: http://www.awilmicrowaves.com
Directors: P. Wicks (Prop)
Ultimate Holding Company: NEUTRIK AG (LIECHTENSTEIN)
Immediate Holding Company: A.W.I. LIMITED
Registration no: 02048227 **VAT No.:** GB 446 7500 43
Date established: 1986 **Turnover:** £1m - £2m **No.of Employees:** 1 - 10
Product Groups: 37

Date of Accounts	Sep 09	Sep 08	Sep 07
Working Capital	17	300	291
Fixed Assets	1m	1m	1m
Current Assets	418	627	620

Cemoc Ltd

Cemoc House Rectory Drive, Wootton Bridge, Ryde, PO33 4QQ
Tel: 01983-884321
E-mail: info@cemoc.co.uk
Website: http://www.cemoc.com
Directors: R. Doran (Co Sec)
Immediate Holding Company: CEMOC LIMITED
Registration no: 01610723 **VAT No.:** GB 339 3554 37
Date established: 1982 **Turnover:** £500,000 - £1m
No.of Employees: 11 - 20 **Product Groups:** 80

Date of Accounts	May 12	May 11	May 10
Working Capital	115	89	81
Fixed Assets	13	11	12
Current Assets	199	188	182

Clark Mast Systems Ltd

Ringwood Road Binstead, Ryde, PO33 3PA
Tel: 01983-563691 **Fax:** 01983-811157
E-mail: info@clarkmasts.com
Website: http://www.clarkmasts.co.uk
Bank(s): National Westminster Bank Plc
Directors: S. Bennett (Sales)
Managers: N. Glasgow (Buyer), D. Blackwell (Fin Mgr)
Ultimate Holding Company: BENNETT TELEMAT LIMITED
Immediate Holding Company: EVERGREEN HOLDINGS LIMITED
Registration no: 00531509 **VAT No.:** GB 109 2321 05
Date established: 1954 **No.of Employees:** 51 - 100 **Product Groups:** 35, 39

Date of Accounts	Jun 11	Jun 10	Jun 09
Working Capital	2m	2m	2m
Fixed Assets	927	799	814
Current Assets	2m	2m	2m

Pascall Electronics Ltd

Westridge Business Park Cothey Way, Ryde, PO33 1QT
Tel: 01983-817300 **Fax:** 01983-564708
E-mail: info@pascall.co.uk
Website: http://www.pascall.co.uk
Directors: A. Maclachlan (Sales & Mktg), G. Higgins (Fin), C. Oliva (MD)
Managers: C. Wheeler (Sales Prom Mgr), E. Crab (Personnel), O. Paul (Tech Serv Mgr), A. Baskill
Ultimate Holding Company: EMRISE CORPORATION (USA)
Immediate Holding Company: PASCALL ELECTRONICS LIMITED
Registration no: 01316674 **VAT No.:** GB 448 7051 34
Date established: 1977 **Turnover:** £5m - £10m
No.of Employees: 101 - 250 **Product Groups:** 37, 67

Date of Accounts	Dec 11	Dec 10	Dec 09
Sales Turnover	10m	8m	9m
Pre Tax Profit/Loss	981	542	508
Working Capital	2m	2m	2m
Fixed Assets	377	387	435
Current Assets	5m	4m	6m
Current Liabilities	1m	752	711

Right Wire Ltd

11 Hornbeam Square, Ryde, PO33 1RF
Tel: 01983-868188
E-mail: info@rightwire.co.uk
Website: http://www.rightwire.co.uk
Immediate Holding Company: RIGHT WIRE LIMITED
Registration no: 05564429 **Date established:** 2005
No.of Employees: 1 - 10 **Product Groups:** 35, 37, 52

Date of Accounts	Mar 11	Mar 10	Mar 09
Working Capital	15	27	-2
Fixed Assets	2	2	2
Current Assets	46	70	50

Sound & Light Co

86 Marlborough Road, Ryde, PO33 1AN
Tel: 01983-563555 **Fax:** 01983- 563777
E-mail: sales@sound-light-company.co.uk
Website: http://www.sound-light-company.co.uk
Directors: P. Humber (Fin)
Immediate Holding Company: THE SOUND & LIGHT COMPANY LIMITED
Registration no: 04767377 **Date established:** 2003
No.of Employees: 1 - 10 **Product Groups:** 37, 52

Trucast Ltd

Marlborough Road, Ryde, PO33 1AD
Tel: 01983-567611 **Fax:** 01983-567618
E-mail: dtinker@doncasters.com
Website: http://www.doncasters.com
Bank(s): Lloyds TSB Bank plc
Directors: C. Thomas (MD), D. Tinker (Fin)
Ultimate Holding Company: DUBAI HOLDING LLC (DUBAI)
Immediate Holding Company: TRUCAST LIMITED
Registration no: 04110903 **VAT No.:** GB 107 3688 65
Date established: 2000 **Turnover:** £20m - £50m
No.of Employees: 251 - 500 **Product Groups:** 34, 39, 40

Date of Accounts	Dec 10	Dec 09	Dec 08
Sales Turnover	46m	19m	48m
Pre Tax Profit/Loss	6m	794	5m
Working Capital	51m	45m	42m
Fixed Assets	3m	4m	4m
Current Assets	58m	49m	48m
Current Liabilities	1m	233	2m

Sandown

W Stay & Son Ltd

Quay Lane Farm Quay Lane, Brading, Sandown, PO36 0AT
Tel: 01983-407077 **Fax:** 01983-408656
E-mail: blacksmithwill@fsmail.net
Website: http://www.wstayandson.com
Directors: T. Stay (Dir)
Immediate Holding Company: W.STAY & SON LIMITED
Registration no: 04842876 **Date established:** 2003
No.of Employees: 1 - 10 **Product Groups:** 26, 35

Date of Accounts	Jul 11	Jul 10	Jul 09
Working Capital	25	62	69
Fixed Assets	58	68	77
Current Assets	69	130	168

Tencate Advanced Armour

Isle of Wight Airport Scotchells Brook Lane, Sandown, PO36 0JP
Tel: 01983-406711 **Fax:** 01983-404211
E-mail: sales@tencate.com
Website: http://www.tencateadvancedarmour.com
Directors: J. Diffey (Chief Op Offcr)
No.of Employees: 11 - 20 **Product Groups:** 30, 31

Waveguide Service

33 Carter Street, Sandown, PO36 8DQ
Tel: 01983-404342 **Fax:** 01983-404342
E-mail: waveguide@madasafish.com
Directors: J. Garrod (Prop)
Date established: 1981 **No.of Employees:** 1 - 10 **Product Groups:** 36, 40

Wight Fire Co. Ltd

16 Faulkner Lane, Sandown, PO36 9AZ
Tel: 01983-407155 **Fax:** 01983-408167
E-mail: sales@wightfire.co.uk
Website: http://www.wightfire.co.uk
Directors: S. Winter (Dir)
Date established: 1981 **No.of Employees:** 11 - 20 **Product Groups:** 38, 42

Shanklin

Wessex Fire & Safety Ltd

8 St Martins Avenue, Shanklin, PO37 6HB
Tel: 01983-862765 **Fax:** 01983-867326
E-mail: sales@wessexfire.com
Website: http://www.wessexfire.com
Directors: M. Leaver (Dir)
Immediate Holding Company: WESSEX FIRE AND SAFETY LIMITED
Registration no: 02689434 **Date established:** 1992
Turnover: Up to £250,000 **No.of Employees:** 1 - 10 **Product Groups:** 38, 42

Date of Accounts	Mar 11	Mar 10	Mar 09
Working Capital	-35	-22	-32
Fixed Assets	12	15	15
Current Assets	39	36	22

Ventnor

Island Getaways

Champion House Highwood Lane, Rookley, Ventnor, PO38 3NN
Tel: 01983-721111 **Fax:** 08718-710072
Website: http://www.islandgetaways.co.uk
Directors: M. Nolan (Fin), C. Nolan (MD)
Immediate Holding Company: ISLAND GETAWAYS LTD
Registration no: 01949619 **Date established:** 1985 **Turnover:** £2m - £5m
No.of Employees: 1 - 10 **Product Groups:** 69, 72

Date of Accounts	Dec 11	Dec 10	Oct 09
Sales Turnover	3m	2m	4m
Pre Tax Profit/Loss	312	172	606
Working Capital	-300	-620	-500
Fixed Assets	4m	4m	4m
Current Assets	49	24	390
Current Liabilities	91	330	227

Islandwide Garage Doors

The Garage Door Centre Old Station Road, Ventnor, PO38 1DX
Tel: 01983-856856 **Fax:** 01983-856856
E-mail: islandwidegaragedoors@yahoo.co.uk
Website: http://www.iwgd.co.uk
Directors: M. Gallop (MD)
Registration no: 03648436 **Date established:** 1998
No.of Employees: 1 - 10 **Product Groups:** 35, 36, 37, 39, 66

Michael J Long

The Green Patch Shanklin Road, Sandford, Ventnor, PO38 3EU
Tel: 01983-840782 **Fax:** 01983-840782
Directors: M. Long (Prop)
Date established: 2000 **No.of Employees:** 1 - 10 **Product Groups:** 35

S Peachey

Highwood Farm Main Road, Rookley, Ventnor, PO38 3NH
Tel: 01983-721333 **Fax:** 01983-721588
Directors: S. Peachey (Prop)
Date established: 1994 **No.of Employees:** 1 - 10 **Product Groups:** 41

Toogood Plastics

Pritchetts Way Rookley, Ventnor, PO38 3LT
Tel: 01983-721511 **Fax:** 01983-721522
Managers: K. Lapworth (Mgr)
Immediate Holding Company: ROOKLEY SCRAP LTD
Registration no: 05525920 **Date established:** 2012
Turnover: Up to £250,000 **No.of Employees:** 1 - 10 **Product Groups:** 08, 25, 35

Wight Aerials

Caxton House Old Station Road, Ventnor, PO38 1DX
Tel: 01983-852968
E-mail: sales@wightaerials.com
Website: http://www.wightaerials.com
Directors: M. Downes (Prop)
Date established: 2004 **No.of Employees:** 1 - 10 **Product Groups:** 26, 37, 39, 67

Isles Of Scilly

Nike Engineering Ltd

Units 8 9 & 10 Porthmellon St Mary's, Isles Of Scilly, TR21 0JY
Tel: 01720-422991 **Fax:** 01720-422505
E-mail: nike_engineering@btopenworld.com
Managers: N. Bromham (Mgr)
Immediate Holding Company: NIKE ENGINEERING LIMITED
Registration no: 04948289 **Date established:** 2003
No.of Employees: 1 - 10 **Product Groups:** 35, 36, 39

Southard Engineering LLP

Thorofare St Mary's, Isles Of Scilly, TR21 0LN
Tel: 01720-422539 **Fax:** 01720-422539
E-mail: southardllp@tiscali.co.uk
Directors: C. Jenkins (Ptnr)
Immediate Holding Company: SOUTH'ARD ENGINEERING LLP
Registration no: OC313422 **Date established:** 2005
No.of Employees: 1 - 10 **Product Groups:** 35, 36, 39

Date of Accounts	**Feb 08**	**Feb 11**	**Feb 10**
Working Capital	-42	59	46
Fixed Assets	52	42	45
Current Assets	161	77	71

Steamship Chandlers & Marine Engineers

Hugh Street St Mary's, Isles Of Scilly, TR21 0LJ
Tel: 01720-422710 **Fax:** 01720-422192
Managers: J. Wright (Mgr)
No.of Employees: 1 - 10 **Product Groups:** 35, 36, 39

KENT

Ashford

2 D Engineering Ltd
Court Reed Farm Sandy Lane, Great Chart, Ashford, TN26 1JN
Tel: 01233-820080 **Fax:** 01233-820994
E-mail: sales@2d-engineering.com
Website: http://www.2d-engineering.com
Directors: P. Daniels (Fin), K. Daniels (MD)
Immediate Holding Company: 2D ENGINEERING LIMITED
Registration no: 02678155 **VAT No.:** GB 583 8221 24
Date established: 1992 **Turnover:** £250,000 - £500,000
No.of Employees: 1 - 10 **Product Groups:** 48

Date of Accounts	Dec 11	Dec 10	Dec 09
Working Capital	-92	-161	-139
Fixed Assets	341	232	252
Current Assets	193	121	109
Current Liabilities	224	188	180

A E R UK Ltd
47-49 Whitfield Road, Ashford, TN23 7TS
Tel: 01233-632777 **Fax:** 01233-661673
E-mail: ian.curd@aer.co.uk
Website: http://www.aer.co.uk
Managers: I. Curd (Sales Prom Mgr)
Ultimate Holding Company: C-SCOPE INTERNATIONAL HOLDINGS LIMITED
Immediate Holding Company: AER (UK) LTD
Registration no: 07578184 **Date established:** 2011 **Turnover:** £1m - £2m
No.of Employees: 1 - 10 **Product Groups:** 36, 38, 39, 40, 41, 42, 43, 45, 46, 48, 67

Date of Accounts	Dec 09	Dec 08	Dec 07
Sales Turnover	767	910	989
Pre Tax Profit/Loss	85	80	55
Working Capital	-16	-33	-41
Fixed Assets	26	34	42
Current Assets	277	224	290
Current Liabilities	213	149	317

Aden Electronics Holdings Ltd
21 Ellingham Industrial Centre Ellingham Way, Ashford, TN23 6NF
Tel: 01233-664445 **Fax:** 01233-664626
E-mail: info@adenelectronics.co.uk
Website: http://www.adenelectronics.co.uk
Directors: D. Butcher (MD), A. Godden (Fin)
Immediate Holding Company: ADEN ELECTRONICS (HOLDINGS) LIMITED
Registration no: 03371479 **Date established:** 1997
Turnover: £250,000 - £500,000 **No.of Employees:** 1 - 10
Product Groups: 37, 39

Date of Accounts	Jun 11	Jun 10	Jun 09
Working Capital	106	120	138
Current Assets	111	120	155

Andrews Sykes Hire Ltd
5 Chunnel Estate Victoria Road, Ashford, TN23 7HJ
Tel: 01233-624461 **Fax:** 01233-647380
E-mail: bob.young@andrews-sykes.com
Website: http://www.andrews-sykes.com
Managers: R. Young (District Mgr)
Immediate Holding Company: ANDREWS SYKES HIRE LIMITED
Registration no: 02985657 **VAT No.:** GB 100 4295 24
Date established: 1994 **Turnover:** £5m - £10m **No.of Employees:** 1 - 10
Product Groups: 40

Date of Accounts	Dec 11	Dec 10	Dec 09
Sales Turnover	35m	36m	34m
Pre Tax Profit/Loss	10m	10m	8m
Working Capital	8m	6m	2m
Fixed Assets	7m	7m	9m
Current Assets	33m	35m	35m
Current Liabilities	7m	7m	5m

Ashford Guns & Tackle
Brundett House Tannery Lane, Ashford, TN23 1PN
Tel: 01233-622444 **Fax:** 01233-664489
E-mail: sheep@k-w-g.co.uk
Website: http://www.kentwoolgrowers.co.uk
Managers: K. Husk (Mgr)
No.of Employees: 1 - 10 **Product Groups:** 36, 39, 40

Ashford Woodturners
Old Saw Mill Hothfield, Ashford, TN26 1EN
Tel: 01233-623090 **Fax:** 01233-643423
E-mail: ashford.woodturners@btinternet.com
Directors: M. Wood (Prop)
VAT No.: GB 397 8835 71 **Date established:** 1983
Turnover: £250,000 - £500,000 **No.of Employees:** 1 - 10
Product Groups: 25

Bond Agency
87 Ellingham Industrial Centre Ellingham Way, Ashford, TN23 6JZ
Tel: 01233-647878 **Fax:** 01233-646487
E-mail: clive@cards4magic.co.uk
Website: http://www.cards4magic.co.uk
Directors: C. Leewarden (Ptnr)
No.of Employees: 1 - 10 **Product Groups:** 49

Bradleys
Wotton Road, Ashford, TN23 6LL
Tel: 01233-622224 **Fax:** 01233-623424
E-mail: info@bradleysfoods.co.uk
Website: http://www.bradleysfoods.co.uk
Directors: G. Linkins (MD)
Immediate Holding Company: KOMPLEAT PHARMACEUTICALS LIMITED
Registration no: 03682747 **Date established:** 2010
No.of Employees: 11 - 20 **Product Groups:** 20, 40, 41

D C Brown & Son
Eastmead Trading Estate, Ashford, TN23 7RX
Tel: 01233-636108
E-mail: dcbfabrications@tiscali.co.uk
Website: http://www.dc-brown.co.uk
Directors: M. Brown (Prop)
Immediate Holding Company: FRIZBEE LTD
Registration no: 04703320 **Date established:** 2003
Turnover: Up to £250,000 **No.of Employees:** 1 - 10 **Product Groups:** 35

Car Treat Mobile Car Valeting
137 Faversham Road Kennington, Ashford, TN24 9DE
Tel: 07771-556305
E-mail: jonathan4reeves@uk2.net
Website: http://www.cartreat.co.uk
Directors: J. Reeves (Prop)
Date established: 2000 **No.of Employees:** 1 - 10 **Product Groups:** 32, 39, 68

Century Street & Leisure Ltd
Unit 1-2 Paddock Farm Bethersden Road, Hothfield, Ashford, TN26 1EP
Tel: 01233-661210 **Fax:** 01233-620889
E-mail: info@centurystreet.com
Website: http://www.centurystreet.com
Directors: D. Jones (Co Sec)
Registration no: 03426423 **Date established:** 1997
Turnover: Up to £250,000 **No.of Employees:** 1 - 10 **Product Groups:** 26, 35

Date of Accounts	Aug 08	Aug 07	Aug 06
Working Capital	3	6	3
Fixed Assets	2	5	8
Current Assets	98	52	53
Current Liabilities	94	46	50
Total Share Capital	1	1	1

Channel Commercials plc
Cobbswood Industrial Estate Brunswick Road, Ashford, TN23 1EH
Tel: 01233-629272 **Fax:** 01233-636322
E-mail: info@ccplc.co.uk
Website: http://www.channelcommercials.co.uk
Directors: M. Macintyre (MD), M. Macintyre (MD), P. Taylor (Sales), R. Ades (Sales)
Ultimate Holding Company: CHANNEL COMMERCIALS HOLDINGS LIMITED
Immediate Holding Company: CHANNEL COMMERCIALS PLC
Registration no: 02143098 **Date established:** 1987
Turnover: £20m - £50m **No.of Employees:** 101 - 250 **Product Groups:** 39

Date of Accounts	Nov 08	Nov 09	Nov 10
Sales Turnover	37m	23m	23m
Pre Tax Profit/Loss	426	186	379
Working Capital	39	120	573
Fixed Assets	3m	2m	2m
Current Assets	9m	7m	7m
Current Liabilities	1m	2m	2m

Commidea Ltd
100 Eureka Park Upper Pemberton Kennington, Ashford, TN25 4AZ
Tel: 08444-828200 **Fax:** 0844-482 8210
E-mail: enquiries@commidea.com
Website: http://www.commidea.com
Directors: I. Rutland (MD), M. Hardman (Tech Serv)
Managers: J. Woods, S. Taylor (Fin Mgr), D. Nelson (Personnel)
Immediate Holding Company: VERIFONE SERVICES UK & IRELAND LIMITED
Registration no: 02747866 **Date established:** 1992
Turnover: £10m - £20m **No.of Employees:** 101 - 250
Product Groups: 44, 67

Date of Accounts	Dec 11	Dec 10	Dec 09
Sales Turnover	23m	20m	14m
Pre Tax Profit/Loss	2m	2m	667
Working Capital	1m	790	1m
Fixed Assets	11m	9m	7m
Current Assets	11m	8m	8m
Current Liabilities	5m	5m	3m

Corralls C P L Petroleum Products Ltd
1 The Boulevard Orbital Park, Ashford, TN24 0GA
Tel: 01227-830221 **Fax:** 01227-831975
E-mail: bridge@cplpetroleum.co.uk
Website: http://www.cplpetroleum.co.uk
Managers: G. Langston (Mgr)
Ultimate Holding Company: B.P. DIRECT MAIL COMPANY LIMITED
Immediate Holding Company: ORBITAL PRINT LIMITED
Registration no: 03003860 **VAT No.:** GB 721 5764 39
Date established: 1998 **No.of Employees:** 1 - 10 **Product Groups:** 66

Date of Accounts	Aug 08	Mar 11	Mar 10
Pre Tax Profit/Loss	N/A	1m	N/A
Working Capital	412	37	37
Fixed Assets	75	34	75
Current Assets	479	37	37

Coty UK Ltd
Bradfield Road Eureka Science Park, Ashford, TN25 4AQ
Tel: 01233-625076 **Fax:** 01233-628974
E-mail: gabrielle_gavin@cotyinc.com
Website: http://www.coty.com
Managers: G. Gavin (Purch Mgr)
Ultimate Holding Company: DONATA HOLDING SE
Immediate Holding Company: COTY BRANDS GROUP LIMITED
Registration no: 02254150 **Date established:** 1988
Turnover: £20m - £50m **No.of Employees:** 251 - 500 **Product Groups:** 63

Date of Accounts	Jun 11	Jun 10	Jun 09
Working Capital	-5m	-5m	-5m
Fixed Assets	52m	52m	52m
Current Assets	17m	17m	17m

Countrywide Photographic
102 Herbert Road Willesborough, Ashford, TN24 0DL
Tel: 01233-666868
E-mail: martin@countrywidephotographic.co.uk
Website: http://www.countrywidephotographic.co.uk
Directors: M. Apps (Prop), T. Hollands (Ptnr), M. Apps (Ptnr)
Turnover: Up to £250,000 **No.of Employees:** 1 - 10 **Product Groups:** 75, 81

C-Scope International Ltd
Kingsnorth Technology Estate Wotton Road, Ashford, TN23 6LN
Tel: 01233-629181 **Fax:** 01233-645897
E-mail: info@cscope.co.uk
Website: http://www.cscope.co.uk
Bank(s): National Westminster, Tunbridge Wells
Directors: G. Smith (Fin), M. Fry (MD)
Managers: C. Crook (Tech Serv Mgr), D. Galloway (Purch Mgr), J. Fry (Mktg Serv Mgr)
Ultimate Holding Company: C-SCOPE INTERNATIONAL HOLDINGS LIMITED
Immediate Holding Company: C-SCOPE INTERNATIONAL HOLDINGS LIMITED
Registration no: 01873847 **VAT No.:** GB 624 6885 12
Date established: 1984 **Turnover:** £5m - £10m **No.of Employees:** 21 - 50
Product Groups: 38, 52

Date of Accounts	Mar 11	Mar 10	Mar 09
Sales Turnover	6m	6m	391
Pre Tax Profit/Loss	215	-202	280
Working Capital	2m	2m	-157
Fixed Assets	478	575	6m
Current Assets	3m	3m	6
Current Liabilities	257	254	29

D A D UK
Unit 12-15 Wotton Trading Estate, Ashford, TN23 6LL
Tel: 01233-630406 **Fax:** 01233-630708
E-mail: info@dadgroup.co.uk
Website: http://www.dadgroup.co.uk

see next page

***D A D UK** - Cont'd*

Managers: E. Charbonnel (Mgr)
Date established: 1872 **Turnover:** **No.of Employees:** 1 - 10
Product Groups: 35, 36

Destra Engineering Ltd

5 St Georges Business Centre Cobbswood Industrial Estate, Ashford, TN23 1EL
Tel: 01233-638996 **Fax:** 01233-610752
E-mail: enquiries@destra.co.uk
Website: http://www.destra.co.uk
Bank(s): National Westminster Bank Plc
Directors: S. Williams (Fin)
Immediate Holding Company: DESTRA ENGINEERING LIMITED
Registration no: 01723115 **VAT No.:** GB 332 8287 51
Date established: 1983 **Turnover:** £250,000 - £500,000
No.of Employees: 11 - 20 **Product Groups:** 30

Date of Accounts	Aug 11	Aug 10	Aug 09
Working Capital	149	107	98
Fixed Assets	202	212	223
Current Assets	269	167	146

Directline Structures Ltd

Orbital House Moat Way, Orbital Park, Ashford, TN24 0TT
Tel: 01233-504770 **Fax:** 01233-501821
E-mail: info@directlinestructures.co.uk
Website: http://www.directlinestructures.co.uk
Directors: D. Murray (Admin)
Immediate Holding Company: Directline Holdings Ltd
Registration no: 02344297 **Date established:** 1989 **Turnover:** £2m - £5m
No.of Employees: 11 - 20 **Product Groups:** 35, 52

Date of Accounts	Nov 08	Nov 07	Nov 06
Working Capital	246	261	308
Fixed Assets	66	63	53
Current Assets	1034	1419	627
Current Liabilities	788	1158	319

Dog World Ltd

Somerfield House Wotton Road, Ashford, TN23 6LW
Tel: 01233-621877 **Fax:** 01233-645669
E-mail: info@dogworld.co.uk
Website: http://www.dogworld.co.uk
Bank(s): Barclays
Directors: S. Baillie (MD)
Managers: E. Dyckhoff, C. Owers (Fin Mgr)
Ultimate Holding Company: DW MEDIA HOLDINGS LIMITED
Immediate Holding Company: DOG WORLD,LIMITED(THE)
Registration no: 00178331 **Date established:** 2021 **Turnover:** £2m - £5m
No.of Employees: 21 - 50 **Product Groups:** 28

Date of Accounts	Mar 12	Mar 11	Mar 10
Working Capital	-36	96	161
Fixed Assets	49	60	51
Current Assets	262	361	465

Dowding & Mills Engineering Services Ltd

6 Wyvern Way Henwood Industrial Estate, Ashford, TN24 8DW
Tel: 01233-623183 **Fax:** 01233-625591
E-mail: engineering.ashford@dowdingandmills.com
Website: http://www.dowdingandmills.com
Bank(s): HSBC Bank plc
Managers: I. Ledgerton (District Mgr)
Ultimate Holding Company: CASTLE SUPPORT SERVICES PLC
Immediate Holding Company: DOWDING & MILLS PLC
Registration no: SC028056 **Turnover:** Up to £250,000
No.of Employees: 11 - 20 **Product Groups:** 37, 44, 45, 48, 84, 85

Emetco Lighting Ltd

81 Ellingham Industrial Centre Ellingham Way, Ashford, TN23 6JZ
Tel: 01233-663333 **Fax:** 01233-663366
E-mail: sales@emetco.co.uk
Website: http://www.emetco.co.uk
Directors: J. Bolton (Fin), N. Bolton (MD)
Immediate Holding Company: EMETCO LIGHTING LIMITED
Registration no: 03599390 **VAT No.:** GB 201 3118 37
Date established: 1998 **Turnover:** £250,000 - £500,000
No.of Employees: 1 - 10 **Product Groups:** 37, 38

Date of Accounts	Jul 11	Jul 10	Jul 09
Working Capital	19	24	23
Fixed Assets	1	2	1
Current Assets	54	62	63

Emmerich Berlon Ltd

Kingsnorth Industrial Estate Wotton Road, Ashford, TN23 6JY
Tel: 01233-622684 **Fax:** 01233-645801
E-mail: enquiries@emir.co.uk
Website: http://www.emir.co.uk
Bank(s): HSBC, Ashford
Directors: S. Rowe (MD)
Managers: E. Neil (Sales Admin)
Ultimate Holding Company: EMMERICH HOLDINGS LIMITED
Immediate Holding Company: EMMERICH (BERLON) LIMITED
Registration no: 02706079 **Date established:** 1992 **Turnover:** £1m - £2m
No.of Employees: 21 - 50 **Product Groups:** 25, 36, 43, 48

Date of Accounts	Jun 11	Jun 10	Jun 09
Working Capital	491	498	565
Fixed Assets	279	305	140
Current Assets	671	853	922

Envirogard Specialist Hires Ltd

Units 5 & 6 Wembdon Farm Bower Road, Smeeth, Ashford, TN25 6SZ
Tel: 01303-814930 **Fax:** 01233-720846
E-mail: accounts@envirogard.co.uk
Website: http://www.envirogard.co.uk
Directors: J. Henderson (Dir)
Immediate Holding Company: ARTISAN WELDING SERVICES LIMITED
Registration no: 02347451 **Date established:** 2012
No.of Employees: 1 - 10 **Product Groups:** 83

Facts International Ltd

Fact Centre 3 Henwood, Henwood Industrial Estate, Ashford, TN24 8FL
Tel: 01233-637000 **Fax:** 01233-626950
E-mail: crispin@facts.uk.com
Website: http://www.facts.co.uk
Bank(s): Lloyds TSB Bank plc
Managers: E. Kettle (Mktg Serv Mgr), C. Beale, S. Wood, C. Carter (Fin Mgr), K. Meyers (Personnel)
Ultimate Holding Company: CHIME COMMUNICATIONS PLC
Immediate Holding Company: FACTS INTERNATIONAL LIMITED
Registration no: 06064157 **VAT No.:** GB 414 2970 64
Date established: 2007 **Turnover:** £2m - £5m **No.of Employees:** 51 - 100
Product Groups: 81

Date of Accounts	Dec 11	Dec 10	Dec 09
Sales Turnover	7m	6m	4m
Pre Tax Profit/Loss	1m	1m	378
Working Capital	-53	713	-115
Fixed Assets	1000	1m	955
Current Assets	2m	4m	3m
Current Liabilities	1m	1m	1m

Farmura Ltd

Stone Hill Stone Hill Road, Egerton, Ashford, TN27 9DU
Tel: 01233-756241 **Fax:** 01233-756419
E-mail: info@farmura.com
Website: http://www.farmura.com
Directors: J. Harmer (Sales)
Immediate Holding Company: FARMURA LIMITED
Registration no: 01035479 **VAT No.:** GB 263 3427 67
Date established: 1971 **Turnover:** £500,000 - £1m
No.of Employees: 1 - 10 **Product Groups:** 32

Date of Accounts	Dec 10	Dec 09	Dec 08
Working Capital	177	83	68
Fixed Assets	68	74	84
Current Assets	671	542	455

Fotoflite

2 Norfolk Drive Leacon Road, Ashford, TN23 4FB
Tel: 01233-635556 **Fax:** 01233-635557
E-mail: p.neumann@fotoflite.com
Website: http://www.fotoflite.com
Directors: P. Neumann (Dir)
Immediate Holding Company: ANDREWS PROFESSIONAL COLOUR LABORATORIES
Registration no: 02426349 **VAT No.:** GB 201 6661 01
Date established: 1989 **No.of Employees:** 1 - 10 **Product Groups:** 75

Date of Accounts	Dec 07	Dec 06	Dec 05
Working Capital	-109	-136	-110
Fixed Assets	561	605	667
Current Assets	89	113	142
Current Liabilities	198	249	252
Total Share Capital	11	11	11

Stewart Fraser Ltd

Henwood Industrial Estate, Ashford, TN24 8DR
Tel: 01233-265911 **Fax:** 01233- 633149
E-mail: cbrimson@stewartfraser.com
Website: http://www.stewartfraser.com
Bank(s): Midland
Directors: C. Brimson (MD), C. Croucher (Fin)
Immediate Holding Company: STEWART FRASER LIMITED
Registration no: 00392490 **VAT No.:** GB 201 1703 36
Date established: 1945 **Turnover:** £5m - £10m
No.of Employees: 51 - 100 **Product Groups:** 26, 34, 35, 52

Date of Accounts	Mar 11	Mar 10	Mar 09
Sales Turnover	6m	5m	6m
Pre Tax Profit/Loss	32	-77	49
Working Capital	829	865	954
Fixed Assets	2m	2m	2m
Current Assets	2m	2m	2m
Current Liabilities	290	338	294

Geerings Of Ashford Ltd

Cobbs Wood House Chart Road, Ashford, TN23 1EP
Tel: 01233-633366 **Fax:** 01233-663357
E-mail: info@geerings.co.uk
Website: http://www.geerings.co.uk
Directors: R. Geering (Ch), W. Geering (MD)
Managers: P. Hollander (Fin Mgr)
Immediate Holding Company: GEERINGS OF ASHFORD LIMITED
Registration no: 00297673 **Date established:** 1935 **Turnover:** £5m - £10m
No.of Employees: 51 - 100 **Product Groups:** 23, 24, 32, 49, 63, 66, 67

Date of Accounts	Mar 11	Mar 10	Mar 08
Sales Turnover	7m	7m	N/A
Pre Tax Profit/Loss	-40	448	61
Working Capital	2m	3m	4m
Fixed Assets	4m	4m	2m
Current Assets	4m	4m	6m
Current Liabilities	688	865	874

Graham

Unit E1-E2 Beaver Industrial Estate Beaver Road, Ashford, TN23 7SH
Tel: 01233-623355 **Fax:** 01233-628787
E-mail: gordoncree@graham-group.co.uk
Website: http://www.graham-group.co.uk
Managers: M. Barrett (District Mgr)
Ultimate Holding Company: SAINT-GOBAIN PLC
Immediate Holding Company: FRIZBEE LTD
Registration no: 04703320 **Date established:** 2003
Turnover: Up to £250,000 **No.of Employees:** 1 - 10 **Product Groups:** 40, 52, 66

Hardigg UK Ltd

Unit 4 Brookfield Industrial Estate, Ashford, TN23 4TU
Tel: 01233-895895 **Fax:** 01233-895899
E-mail: info@peli.com
Website: http://www.peli.com
Directors: J. Blackman (Fin)
Managers: M. Heydon
Immediate Holding Company: HARDIGG UK LIMITED
Registration no: 03874419 **Date established:** 1999
No.of Employees: 21 - 50 **Product Groups:** 30, 33, 38

Date of Accounts	Dec 11	Dec 10	Dec 09
Sales Turnover	5m	4m	N/A
Pre Tax Profit/Loss	161	298	N/A
Working Capital	1m	1m	1m
Fixed Assets	85	95	137
Current Assets	2m	2m	2m
Current Liabilities	147	172	N/A

Headley Brothers Ltd

The Invicta Press Queens Road, Ashford, TN24 8HH
Tel: 01233-623131 **Fax:** 01233-612345
E-mail: sales@headley.co.uk
Website: http://www.headley.co.uk
Bank(s): Lloyds TSB Bank plc
Directors: R. Pitt (Dir), S. Bingham (Fin)
Managers: J. Duggan (Tech Serv Mgr), J. Inshaw (Mktg Serv Mgr), A. Owden (Works Gen Mgr)
Ultimate Holding Company: HEADLEY BROTHERS (HOLDINGS) LIMITED
Immediate Holding Company: HEADLEY BROTHERS LIMITED
Registration no: 00491836 **VAT No.:** GB 792 4285 01
Date established: 1951 **Turnover:** £10m - £20m
No.of Employees: 251 - 500 **Product Groups:** 28

Date of Accounts	Oct 11	Oct 08	Oct 09
Sales Turnover	20m	21m	20m
Pre Tax Profit/Loss	-122	584	55
Working Capital	760	432	67
Fixed Assets	6m	6m	7m
Current Assets	6m	5m	6m
Current Liabilities	787	407	462

Houchin Aerospace Ltd

Hilton Road, Ashford, TN23 1DZ
Tel: 01233-623211 **Fax:** 01223-638403
E-mail: enquiries@houchin.co.uk
Website: http://www.houchin.co.uk
Bank(s): HSBC Bank plc
Managers: S. Fraser (Chief Mgr)
Ultimate Holding Company: ILLINOIS TOOL WORKS INC (USA)
Immediate Holding Company: HOUCHIN AEROSPACE
Registration no: 00255879 **VAT No.:** GB 624 8169 28
Date established: 1931 **Turnover:** £10m - £20m
No.of Employees: 101 - 250 **Product Groups:** 37, 39

Hypocell Ltd

Unit 4 Longscorner Farm Bethersden, Ashford, TN26 3HD
Tel: 01233-627209 **Fax:** 01233-629846
E-mail: generalenquiries@hypocell.co.uk
Website: http://www.hypocell.org
Directors: L. Chittinden (Dir)
Immediate Holding Company: HYPOCELL LIMITED
Registration no: 01366066 **VAT No.:** GB 205 2911 00
Date established: 1978 **Turnover:** £500,000 - £1m
No.of Employees: 1 - 10 **Product Groups:** 30, 42

Date of Accounts	Nov 11	Nov 10	Nov 09
Working Capital	11	15	N/A
Fixed Assets	3	4	5
Current Assets	58	55	29
Current Liabilities	N/A	N/A	13

Hy-Tex UK Ltd

Aldington Mill Mill Lane, Aldington, Ashford, TN25 7AJ
Tel: 01233-720097 **Fax:** 01233-720098
E-mail: info@hy-tex.co.uk
Website: http://www.hy-tex.co.uk
Directors: S. Hyder (Co Sec), M. Hyder (MD), D. Poole (Sales)
Immediate Holding Company: HY-TEX (U.K.) LIMITED
Registration no: 02597134 **Date established:** 1991
No.of Employees: 1 - 10 **Product Groups:** 23, 38, 67, 84

Date of Accounts	Sep 10	Sep 09	Sep 08
Working Capital	273	121	300
Fixed Assets	136	256	34
Current Assets	389	357	555

Imperial Welding Supplies Challock Ltd

4 Faversham Road Challock, Ashford, TN25 4BQ
Tel: 01233-740435 **Fax:** 01233-740623
Directors: A. Seager (Dir)
Immediate Holding Company: IMPERIAL WELDING SUPPLIES (CHALLOCK) LIMITED
Registration no: 02758431 **Date established:** 1992
No.of Employees: 1 - 10 **Product Groups:** 46

Date of Accounts	Oct 11	Oct 10	Oct 08
Working Capital	-1	-1	-1
Fixed Assets	N/A	1	1
Current Assets	18	11	13

Integrated Technologies Ltd

Ellingham Industrial Centre Ellingham Way, Ashford, TN23 6NF
Tel: 01233-638383 **Fax:** 01233-639401
E-mail: thc@itl.co.uk
Website: http://www.itl.co.uk
Directors: G. Smith (Dir), T. Cole (MD)
Managers: T. Wilson (Chief Acct)
Ultimate Holding Company: LE PORT-NOIR S.A. (SWITZERLAND)
Immediate Holding Company: INTEGRATED TECHNOLOGIES LIMITED
Registration no: 01300238 **VAT No.:** GB 572 0385 47
Date established: 1977 **Turnover:** £5m - £10m
No.of Employees: 51 - 100 **Product Groups:** 37, 42

Date of Accounts	Apr 11	Apr 10	Apr 09
Sales Turnover	5m	7m	16m
Pre Tax Profit/Loss	297	431	2m
Working Capital	5m	5m	5m
Fixed Assets	620	392	444
Current Assets	6m	6m	6m
Current Liabilities	694	476	1m

Jacksons Fine Fencing Ltd

Stowting Common Stowting, Ashford, TN25 6BN
Tel: 01233-750393 **Fax:** 01233-750403
E-mail: info@jacksons-fencing.co.uk
Website: http://www.jacksons-fencing.co.uk
Directors: R. Jackson (MD), N. Jordan (Fin), P. Jackson (Sales)
Managers: L. Reid, R. Parsons (Tech Serv Mgr), L. Tomlin (Mktg Serv Mgr)
Immediate Holding Company: H S JACKSON & SON (FENCING) LIMITED
Registration no: 00910291 **VAT No.:** GB 201 1048 42
Date established: 1967 **Turnover:** £10m - £20m
No.of Employees: 101 - 250 **Product Groups:** 25, 35, 66

Date of Accounts	Sep 11	Sep 10	Sep 09
Sales Turnover	22m	19m	20m
Pre Tax Profit/Loss	377	182	367
Working Capital	7m	7m	7m
Fixed Assets	2m	2m	3m
Current Assets	11m	10m	10m
Current Liabilities	1m	1m	985

Jewson Ltd

Carlton Road, Ashford, TN23 1DP
Tel: 01233-610828 **Fax:** 01233-629492
Website: http://www.jewson.co.uk
Managers: R. Greenfield (Chief Mgr)
Ultimate Holding Company: COMPAGNIE DE SAINT GOBAIN (FRANCE)
Immediate Holding Company: JEWSON LIMITED
Registration no: 00348407 **Date established:** 1939
Turnover: £500m - £1,000m **No.of Employees:** 1 - 10
Product Groups: 66

Date of Accounts	Dec 11	Dec 10	Dec 09
Sales Turnover	1606m	1547m	1485m
Pre Tax Profit/Loss	18m	100m	45m

Working Capital	-345m	-250m	-349m
Fixed Assets	496m	387m	461m
Current Assets	657m	1005m	1320m
Current Liabilities	66m	120m	64m

Kent Leisure Buildings

Hythe Road Willesborough, Ashford, TN24 0NE
Tel: 01233-501150 **Fax:** 01233-501150
Website: http://www.kentconservatories.co.uk
Managers: R. Summers (Mgr)
Immediate Holding Company: ROMACK CONSTRUCTION LTD
Registration no: 03106194 **Date established:** 1995
Turnover: £250,000 - £500,000 **No.of Employees:** 1 - 10
Product Groups: 25, 33, 35, 66

Date of Accounts	Dec 11
Working Capital	-17
Fixed Assets	21
Current Assets	58

Kent Metal Spinners

Unit E Chilmington Works Chilmington Green, Great Chart, Ashford, TN23 3DR
Tel: 01233-610404 **Fax:** 01233-647344
E-mail: clive@kentmetalspinners.co.uk
Website: http://www.kentmetalspinners.co.uk
Directors: C. Chadwick (MD)
Immediate Holding Company: A.D. MOORE METAL SPINNING LIMITED
Registration no: 03834757 **VAT No.:** GB 811 5199 43
Date established: 1999 **Turnover:** Up to £250,000
No.of Employees: 1 - 10 **Product Groups:** 48

Kent Pharmaceuticals Ltd

Wotton Road, Ashford, TN23 6LL
Tel: 01233-638614 **Fax:** 01233-646899
E-mail: oneilld@kentpharm.co.uk
Website: http://www.kentpharm.co.uk
Directors: D. O'Neill (Dir), A. Amos (Gen Sec), M. Overy (Dir)
Managers: J. Clark (Mktg Serv Mgr), J. Hennessy (Develop Mgr), J. Haylott (Sales Prom Mgr)
Ultimate Holding Company: KENT PHARMACEUTICALS (HOLDINGS) LIMITED
Immediate Holding Company: OPD CARTONS LIMITED
Registration no: 01994709 **VAT No.:** GB 509 7133 46
Date established: 1986 **Turnover:** £20m - £50m
No.of Employees: 51 - 100 **Product Groups:** 63

Date of Accounts	Aug 09	Aug 08	Aug 07
Sales Turnover	37m	N/A	N/A
Pre Tax Profit/Loss	3m	N/A	N/A
Working Capital	3m	648	675
Fixed Assets	292	235	N/A
Current Assets	17m	9m	710
Current Liabilities	5m	N/A	N/A

Kingfisher Blinds

4 Cradlebridge Drive Willesborough, Ashford, TN24 0RN
Tel: 01233-642971 **Fax:** 01233-640913
E-mail: sales@kingfisherblinds.com
Website: http://www.kingfisherblinds.com
Directors: V. King (Prop)
Immediate Holding Company: Kingfisher Blinds (Bath) Ltd
Registration no: 04609463 **Turnover:** Up to £250,000
No.of Employees: 1 - 10 **Product Groups:** 24

Knapp Hicks & Partners

Kingston House The Long Barrow, Ashford, TN24 0GP
Tel: 01233-502255 **Fax:** 01233-502288
E-mail: pregardso@knapphicks.co.uk
Website: http://www.knapphicks.co.uk
Managers: J. Moss (Sales Admin)
Ultimate Holding Company: SOUTH EAST HEALTH MEDICAL LIMITED
Immediate Holding Company: SOUTH EAST HEALTH PLUS LIMITED
Registration no: 02886020 **Date established:** 2007 **Turnover:** £1m - £2m
No.of Employees: 11 - 20 **Product Groups:** 35

Date of Accounts	Mar 11	Mar 10	Mar 09
Sales Turnover	2m	312	N/A
Pre Tax Profit/Loss	-324	-262	N/A
Working Capital	306	122	N/A
Fixed Assets	341	187	N/A
Current Assets	733	213	N/A
Current Liabilities	61	32	N/A

L A E Valeo Ltd

Unit 4 Wissenden Corner Wissenden Lane, Bethersden, Ashford, TN26 3EL
Tel: 01233-822580 **Fax:** 01233-820701
E-mail: sales@laeltd.co.uk
Website: http://www.laeltd.co.uk
Directors: P. Seabourne (MD)
Registration no: 00820939 **Turnover:** £1m - £2m
No.of Employees: 1 - 10 **Product Groups:** 31, 33, 35, 37, 39, 40, 41, 67, 68

Letraset Ltd

Kingsnorth Industrial Estate Wotton Road, Ashford, TN23 6FL
Tel: 01233-624421 **Fax:** 01233-658877
E-mail: enquiries@letraset.com
Website: http://www.letraset.com
Bank(s): Barclays, London
Directors: S. Hodges (Mkt Research), S. Baldock (Fin), M. Gibson (MD)
Managers: J. Neville (Purch Mgr)
Ultimate Holding Company: LETRASET LIMITED
Immediate Holding Company: CREATIVE OPPORTUNITIES LIMITED
Registration no: 04597597 **VAT No.:** GB 624 5152 60
Date established: 2002 **Turnover:** Up to £250,000
No.of Employees: 21 - 50 **Product Groups:** 64

Date of Accounts	Dec 11	Dec 10	May 10
Sales Turnover	165	96	165
Pre Tax Profit/Loss	-160	84	145
Working Capital	-33	-21	-15
Fixed Assets	348	669	680
Current Liabilities	33	21	15

Loadtec Engineered Systems

The Stables Smeeth, Ashford, TN25 6SP
Tel: 01303-813030 **Fax:** 01303-814040
E-mail: sales@loadtec.co.uk
Website: http://www.loadtec.co.uk
Directors: S. Keeler (Co Sec)
Immediate Holding Company: THE CALDECOTT FOUNDATION LIMITED
Registration no: 03291720 **Date established:** 1946
No.of Employees: 1 - 10 **Product Groups:** 74

Date of Accounts	Jul 09	Jul 08
Sales Turnover	40	43
Pre Tax Profit/Loss	24	27
Current Assets	11	6
Current Liabilities	11	6

A A Lock Transport Headcorn Ltd

Biddenden Road Headcorn, Ashford, TN27 9LW
Tel: 01622-890002 **Fax:** 01622-891413
Website: http://www.aalocktransport.co.uk
Bank(s): National Westminster Bank Plc
Directors: A. Lock (MD), A. Lock (Dir)
Immediate Holding Company: A.A. LOCK TRANSPORT (HEADCORN) LIMITED
Registration no: 01161351 **VAT No.:** GB 204 4581 88
Date established: 1974 **Turnover:** £2m - £5m **No.of Employees:** 21 - 50
Product Groups: 72

Date of Accounts	Mar 11	Mar 10	Mar 09
Working Capital	3m	3m	3m
Fixed Assets	1m	2m	2m
Current Assets	3m	3m	3m

Luminate Design

Zealds House Church Street, Ashford, TN25 5BL
Tel: 01233-660481 **Fax:** 07092-389684
E-mail: info@luminatedesign.co.uk
Website: http://www.luminatedesign.co.uk
Directors: Z. Rushforth (Dir), R. Oates (Ptnr)
No.of Employees: 1 - 10 **Product Groups:** 44, 49

M J Allen Group Of Companies

Cobbs Wood Industrial Estate Hilton Road, Ashford, TN23 1EW
Tel: 01233-622214 **Fax:** 01233-643534
E-mail: sales@mjallen.co.uk
Website: http://www.mjallen.co.uk
Bank(s): National Westminster Bank Plc
Directors: A. Gibson (Fin), G. Ealham (Sales), T. Allen (MD)
Managers: A. Johnson (Tech Serv Mgr), P. Carter (Purch Mgr), M. Sinclair
Ultimate Holding Company: M.J. ALLEN HOLDINGS LIMITED
Immediate Holding Company: M.J. ALLEN (NON-FERROUS FOUNDERS) LIMITED
Registration no: 00878983 **VAT No.:** GB 201 1387 20
Date established: 1966 **Turnover:** £2m - £5m **No.of Employees:** 51 - 100
Product Groups: 35, 46, 48, 67

Date of Accounts	Sep 11	Sep 10	Sep 09
Sales Turnover	3m	1m	2m
Pre Tax Profit/Loss	-15	3m	-326
Working Capital	454	416	-2m
Fixed Assets	112	165	218
Current Assets	642	612	712
Current Liabilities	45	40	24

Mirror Image Metal Polishing

79 Bridge Street Wye, Ashford, TN25 5ED
Tel: 01233-182542 **Fax:** 01233-812542
Directors: M. Nance (Prop)
Immediate Holding Company: MIRROR IMAGE METAL POLISHING LIMITED
Registration no: 07674911 **Date established:** 2011
No.of Employees: 1 - 10 **Product Groups:** 46, 48

Orbital Response

The Boulevard Orbital Park, Ashford, TN24 0GA
Tel: 01233-500800 **Fax:** 01233-500400
E-mail: mail@omsg.co.uk
Website: http://www.orbitalresponse.co.uk
Managers: C. Gray (Mktg Serv Mgr), N. Williams (Mgr)
Ultimate Holding Company: B.P. DIRECT MAIL COMPANY LIMITED
Immediate Holding Company: ORBITAL MARKETING LIMITED
Registration no: 04526029 **Date established:** 2002
Turnover: £20m - £50m **No.of Employees:** 251 - 500
Product Groups: 80, 81

Date of Accounts	Mar 11	Mar 10	Mar 09
Sales Turnover	24m	25m	21m
Pre Tax Profit/Loss	1m	1m	1m
Working Capital	1m	2m	852
Fixed Assets	6m	5m	8m
Current Assets	8m	8m	8m
Current Liabilities	4m	4m	4m

Paramount Plating Ltd

South Stour Avenue, Ashford, TN23 7RS
Tel: 01233-626748 **Fax:** 01233-641787
E-mail: home.supplies@virgin.net
Website: http://www.paramountplating.co.uk
Directors: J. Norman (Works)
Immediate Holding Company: PARAMOUNT PLATING LIMITED
Registration no: 00906007 **Date established:** 1967
Turnover: £500,000 - £1m **No.of Employees:** 1 - 10 **Product Groups:** 48

Date of Accounts	Jan 12	Jan 11	Jan 10
Working Capital	15	25	54
Fixed Assets	64	63	70
Current Assets	126	187	150

Pipe Center

Unit 9 Brunswick Industrial Centre Cobbswood Industrial Esta Brunswick Road, Ashford, TN23 1ED
Tel: 01233-631940 **Fax:** 01233-642456
Website: http://www.wolseley.co.uk
Managers: C. Rodway (District Mgr)
No.of Employees: 1 - 10 **Product Groups:** 40, 48

Date of Accounts	Jun 11	Jun 10	Jun 09
Sales Turnover	87m	96m	96m
Pre Tax Profit/Loss	-2m	5m	5m
Working Capital	-2m	1m	4m
Fixed Assets	36m	34m	26m
Current Assets	34m	33m	45m
Current Liabilities	9m	7m	9m

Plastek Mailing Services Ltd

Willow Court Bilsington Road, Ruckinge, Ashford, TN26 2PB
Tel: 01233-730200 **Fax:** 01233-730975
E-mail: sales@plas-tek.co.uk
Website: http://www.plas-tek.co.uk
Directors: L. Day (Dir)
Immediate Holding Company: PLAS-TEK MAILING SERVICES LIMITED
Registration no: 01997918 **Date established:** 1986
No.of Employees: 1 - 10 **Product Groups:** 38, 42

Date of Accounts	Mar 11	Mar 10	Mar 09
Working Capital	-72	-18	159
Fixed Assets	91	115	78
Current Assets	75	105	374

Plasticom Ltd

Hilton Road, Ashford, TN23 1EW
Tel: 01233-621601 **Fax:** 01233-622169
E-mail: user@plasticomgroup.com
Website: http://www.plasticom.softnet.co.uk
Bank(s): National Westminster Bank Plc
Directors: S. Simmonds (Fin), E. Simmonds (MD)
Ultimate Holding Company: PLASTICOM LTD.
Immediate Holding Company: ASHFORD MOULDINGS LIMITED
Registration no: 00965699 **VAT No.:** GB 201 1576 17
Date established: 1969 **Turnover:** £1m - £2m **No.of Employees:** 21 - 50
Product Groups: 30

Date of Accounts	Sep 11	Sep 10	Sep 09
Working Capital	341	374	422
Fixed Assets	945	959	1m
Current Assets	554	624	760

Premier Coatings Ltd

Marley Farm Headcorn Road, Smarden, Ashford, TN27 8PJ
Tel: 01233-770663 **Fax:** 01233-770633
E-mail: tcapps@denso.net
Website: http://www.premiercoatings.com
Bank(s): Bank of Scotland
Directors: S. Ahearne (Co Sec), T. Capps (MD)
Ultimate Holding Company: WINN & COALES INTERNATIONAL LIMITED
Immediate Holding Company: PREMIER COATINGS LIMITED
Registration no: 01636433 **Date established:** 1982 **Turnover:** £2m - £5m
No.of Employees: 11 - 20 **Product Groups:** 31

Date of Accounts	Jun 11	Jun 10	Jun 09
Sales Turnover	5m	4m	3m
Pre Tax Profit/Loss	264	390	150
Working Capital	529	822	524
Fixed Assets	144	183	163
Current Assets	2m	2m	1m
Current Liabilities	87	231	74

Pressure Welding Machines Ltd

Belmont Farm Business Centre Snoad Hill, Bethersden, Ashford, TN26 3DY
Tel: 01233-820817 **Fax:** 01233-820591
E-mail: sales@pwmltd.co.uk
Website: http://www.pwmltd.co.uk
Directors: S. Mepsted (MD), T. Sherwen (Fin)
Ultimate Holding Company: GLADETREE LIMITED
Immediate Holding Company: PRESSURE WELDING MACHINES LIMITED
Registration no: 01814478 **VAT No.:** GB 003 7445 11
Date established: 1984 **Turnover:** £1m - £2m **No.of Employees:** 1 - 10
Product Groups: 46

Date of Accounts	Jul 11	Jul 10	Jul 09
Working Capital	859	792	767
Fixed Assets	17	23	18
Current Assets	1m	1m	1m

Raker Freight

100 Ellingham Industrial Centre Ellingham Way, Ashford, TN23 6LZ
Tel: 01233-651660 **Fax:** 01233-651661
E-mail: val.kerly@rakerfreight.co.uk
Website: http://www.rakerfreight.co.uk
Managers: V. Kerly (Mgr)
Registration no: 01759344 **Date established:** 2003 **Turnover:** £1m - £2m
No.of Employees: 1 - 10 **Product Groups:** 76

Reeves Water Services

Brushwood Villa School Road, Bethersden, Ashford, TN26 3AH
Tel: 01233-820284 **Fax:** 01233-822179
E-mail: info@reeveswater.co.uk
Website: http://www.reeveswater.co.uk
Directors: R. Reeves (Prop)
Date established: 1988 **Turnover:** Up to £250,000
No.of Employees: 1 - 10 **Product Groups:** 18

Russell Laboratories Ltd

Kingsnorth Industrial Estate Wotton Road, Ashford, TN23 6LN
Tel: 01233-635241 **Fax:** 01233-610960
E-mail: ray@russell-labs.co.uk
Website: http://www.russell-laboratories.co.uk
Managers: R. Elbourn (Mgr)
Immediate Holding Company: RUSSELL LABORATORIES LIMITED
Registration no: 06599885 **Date established:** 2008
No.of Employees: 21 - 50 **Product Groups:** 46, 48

Date of Accounts	Mar 12	Mar 11	Mar 10
Working Capital	-721	-640	-557
Fixed Assets	1m	978	738
Current Assets	308	312	312

Sauflon Pharmaceuticals

Units 3-11 Mace Industrial Estate Mace Lane, Ashford, TN24 8EP
Tel: 01233-646599 **Fax:** 01233-646614
Website: http://www.sauflon.co.uk
Managers: S. Keeka, R. Bonsier (Purch Mgr)
No.of Employees: 101 - 250 **Product Groups:** 37, 38, 65

Selvin Fluid Power Ltd

Selvin Wood Ashford Road, Hamstreet, Ashford, TN26 2EW
Tel: 01233-730830 **Fax:** 01233-730890
E-mail: sales@selvinfluidpower.com
Website: http://www.selvinfluidpower.com
Directors: R. Ward (MD)
Immediate Holding Company: SELVIN FLUID POWER LIMITED
Registration no: 02678173 **Date established:** 1992
Turnover: Up to £250,000 **No.of Employees:** 1 - 10 **Product Groups:** 40, 46

Date of Accounts	Mar 11	Mar 10	Mar 09
Working Capital	13	-1	N/A
Fixed Assets	12	17	7
Current Assets	58	63	65

Silver Steel Fabrication

Fridd Farm Bethersden, Ashford, TN26 3DX
Tel: 01233-822252 **Fax:** 01233-822252
E-mail: silversteel@tiscali.co.uk
Directors: T. Given (MD)
No.of Employees: 1 - 10 **Product Groups:** 35

Skinner Sheds Ltd
Hamstreet Garden Centre Marsh Road, Hamstreet, Ashford, TN26 2QP
Tel: 01424-716716
E-mail: info@skinners-sheds.com
Website: http://www.skinners-sheds.com
No.of Employees: 1 - 10 **Product Groups:** 08, 25, 35, 49, 66

Smith's Medical
1500 Eureka Park Lower Pemberton, Kennington, Ashford, TN25 4BF
Tel: 01233-722100 **Fax:** 01923-231595
E-mail: matthew.sassone@smiths-medical.com
Website: http://www.smiths-medical.com
Bank(s): Barclays, Bury
Directors: M. Sassone (MD), M. Sassone (MD), S. Wilde (Pers), S. Eggleston (Fin)
Managers: J. Clease (Mgr), K. Jayne (Mktg Serv Mgr)
Ultimate Holding Company: SMITHS GROUP PLC
Immediate Holding Company: SMITHS MEDICAL GROUP LIMITED
Registration no: 05137144 **VAT No.:** GB 375 4901 33
Date established: 2004 **Turnover:** £125m - £250m
No.of Employees: 101 - 250 **Product Groups:** 30, 38

Date of Accounts	Jul 11	Jul 10	Jul 09
Pre Tax Profit/Loss	59m	86m	37m
Working Capital	618m	608m	614m
Fixed Assets	384m	383m	366m
Current Assets	974m	964m	1011m
Current Liabilities	512	518	6m

South East Gates Ltd
134 Grasmere Road Kennington, Ashford, TN24 9BQ
Tel: 01233-661785 **Fax:** 01233-661785
E-mail: garywestseg@aol.com
Website: http://www.seg.com
Directors: N. West (Fin)
Immediate Holding Company: SOUTH EAST GATES LIMITED
Registration no: 03696292 **Date established:** 1999
No.of Employees: 1 - 10 **Product Groups:** 26, 35

Date of Accounts	Mar 12	Mar 11	Mar 10
Working Capital	25	23	25
Fixed Assets	N/A	4	18
Current Assets	102	85	80

Structura UK Ltd
6 The Glenmore Centre Moat Way, Sevington, Ashford, TN24 0TL
Tel: 01233-501 504 **Fax:** 01233-503 372
Website: http://www.structura.co.uk
Directors: P. Mackett (Dir)
Immediate Holding Company: Structura (U.K.) Ltd
Registration no: 02499497 **No.of Employees:** 1 - 10 **Product Groups:** 26, 35

Sunray Engineering Ltd
Wotton Road, Ashford, TN23 6LL
Tel: 01233-639039 **Fax:** 01233-625137
E-mail: sales@sunraydoors.co.uk
Website: http://www.sunraydoors.co.uk
Bank(s): HSBC
Directors: D. Evans (MD)
Managers: J. Vogle (Tech Serv Mgr), A. Singh (Chief Acct)
Immediate Holding Company: SUNRAY ENGINEERING LIMITED
Registration no: 01480389 **VAT No.:** 530 8510 70 **Date established:** 1980
Turnover: £250,000 - £500,000 **No.of Employees:** 21 - 50
Product Groups: 35, 36

Date of Accounts	Jul 11	Jul 10	Jul 09
Working Capital	266	196	317
Fixed Assets	580	414	462
Current Assets	927	899	2m

Task Masters UK Ltd
International House Dover Place, Ashford, TN23 1HU
Tel: 01233-631300 **Fax:** 01233-631230
E-mail: info@taskmasters-uk.com
Website: http://www.taskmasters-uk.com
Managers: V. Gillings (Admin Off)
Immediate Holding Company: TASK MASTERS (UK) LIMITED
Registration no: 03774242 **Date established:** 1999
Turnover: £250,000 - £500,000 **No.of Employees:** 1 - 10
Product Groups: 52, 84

Date of Accounts	Sep 11	Sep 10	Sep 09
Working Capital	41	38	35
Fixed Assets	11	13	15
Current Assets	110	38	125

Topper International
Kingsnorth Industrial Estate Wotton Road, Ashford, TN23 6LN
Tel: 01233-629186 **Fax:** 01233-645897
E-mail: martin.fry@toppersailboats.com
Website: http://www.toppersailboats.co.uk
Bank(s): National Westminster, Tunbridge Wells
Directors: M. Fry (MD)
Ultimate Holding Company: C-SCOPE INTERNATIONAL HOLDINGS LIMITED
Immediate Holding Company: TOPPER INTERNATIONAL LIMITED
Registration no: 02242893 **VAT No.:** 624 6885 12 **Date established:** 1988
No.of Employees: 21 - 50 **Product Groups:** 39, 45, 74

Date of Accounts	Mar 11	Mar 10	Mar 09
Working Capital	888	690	919
Fixed Assets	92	122	122
Current Assets	1m	1m	1m

U C D Ltd
Unit 1 Sheerland Farm Pluckley, Ashford, TN27 0PN
Tel: 01233-840296 **Fax:** 01233-840113
E-mail: sales@ucd.uk.com
Website: http://www.theancillariesstore.co.uk
Directors: J. Tombs (MD)
Immediate Holding Company: S.W.HIGHWOOD(PLUCKLEY)LIMITED
Registration no: 04210182 **Date established:** 1952
Turnover: £500,000 - £1m **No.of Employees:** 1 - 10 **Product Groups:** 20, 62, 67

Date of Accounts	Jun 11	Jun 10	Jun 09
Working Capital	-42	-12	-178
Fixed Assets	630	558	520
Current Assets	489	396	312

Universal Filling Machine Co. Ltd
Pound Lane Kingsnorth, Ashford, TN23 3JE
Tel: 01233-643666
E-mail: mail@universalfilling.com
Website: http://www.universalfilling.com
Directors: A. Morrison (Dir)
Ultimate Holding Company: L.O.G.G. HOLDINGS LIMITED
Immediate Holding Company: ASHFORD PACKAGING EQUIPMENT LIMITED
Registration no: 01272348 **Date established:** 1976
Turnover: £500,000 - £1m **No.of Employees:** 11 - 20
Product Groups: 38, 42

Date of Accounts	Dec 11	Dec 10	Dec 09
Pre Tax Profit/Loss	N/A	N/A	-0
Working Capital	N/A	-0	N/A
Fixed Assets	913	913	913
Current Assets	1	N/A	N/A

Verdict Gauge Ltd (a member of the M.J. Allen Group of Companies)
Hilton Road, Ashford, TN23 1EW
Tel: 01233-631554 **Fax:** 01233-631888
E-mail: sales@mjallen.co.uk
Website: http://www.mjallen.co.uk
Bank(s): National Westminster Bank Plc
Directors: A. Gibson (Co Sec), T. Allen (MD)
Ultimate Holding Company: M.J. ALLEN HOLDINGS LIMITED
Immediate Holding Company: VERDICT GAUGE LIMITED
Registration no: 01363601 **Date established:** 1978
Turnover: £250,000 - £500,000 **No.of Employees:** 51 - 100
Product Groups: 38, 48

Date of Accounts	Sep 11	Sep 10	Sep 09
Sales Turnover	253	204	209
Pre Tax Profit/Loss	-4	223	-57
Working Capital	190	11	-215
Fixed Assets	6	3	5
Current Assets	222	272	268
Current Liabilities	6	3	4

Windsor Food Machinery Ltd
Mountain Farm Marsh Road, Hamstreet, Ashford, TN26 2JD
Tel: 01233-733737 **Fax:** 01233-733392
E-mail: sales@windsorfoodmachinery.com
Website: http://www.windsorfoodmachinery.com
Directors: T. Stuart (Dir)
Immediate Holding Company: WINDSOR FOOD MACHINERY LIMITED
Registration no: 05766547 **Date established:** 2006 **Turnover:** £2m - £5m
No.of Employees: 11 - 20 **Product Groups:** 20, 40, 41

Date of Accounts	Mar 12	Mar 11	Mar 10
Sales Turnover	N/A	N/A	3m
Pre Tax Profit/Loss	N/A	N/A	341
Working Capital	60	-264	-242
Fixed Assets	531	566	584
Current Assets	1m	1m	1m
Current Liabilities	N/A	N/A	229

Xcel Power Systems Ltd
Brunswick Road, Ashford, TN23 1EH
Tel: 01233-623404 **Fax:** 01233-641777
E-mail: sales@xcelpower.com
Website: http://www.fpdsavills.co.uk
Bank(s): Lloyds TSB Bank plc
Directors: R. Moon (Fin), R. Weller (MD)
Managers: D. Stringer (Chief Buyer), H. Biajanza (Tech Serv Mgr)
Ultimate Holding Company: EMRISE CORPORATION (USA)
Immediate Holding Company: XCEL POWER SYSTEMS LTD.
Registration no: 00575679 **VAT No.:** GB 571 9287 08
Date established: 1956 **Turnover:** £2m - £5m **No.of Employees:** 21 - 50
Product Groups: 37

Date of Accounts	Dec 11	Dec 10	Dec 09
Sales Turnover	4m	4m	5m
Pre Tax Profit/Loss	37	141	1m
Working Capital	4m	4m	4m
Fixed Assets	108	104	170
Current Assets	5m	5m	5m
Current Liabilities	472	355	674

Aylesford

Act Communications Ltd
1b Quarry Wood Industrial Estate Mills Road, Aylesford, ME20 7NA
Tel: 01622-790888 **Fax:** 01622-790887
E-mail: info@act-comm.com
Website: http://www.act-comm.com
Directors: M. Peach (Dir)
Immediate Holding Company: A.C.T. COMMUNICATIONS LIMITED
Registration no: 02865752 **Date established:** 1993 **Turnover:** £5m - £10m
No.of Employees: 21 - 50 **Product Groups:** 37

Date of Accounts	Mar 12	Mar 11	Mar 10
Working Capital	72	63	115
Fixed Assets	97	104	114
Current Assets	624	610	704

Astran Cargo Services
519 New Hythe Lane Larkfield, Aylesford, ME20 6SB
Tel: 01622-716441 **Fax:** 01622-791854
E-mail: sales@astran-cargo.com
Website: http://www.astran-cargo.com
Directors: K. Letham (MD)
Immediate Holding Company: ASTRAN CARGO SERVICES LIMITED
Registration no: 05215087 **VAT No.:** GB 619 0089 43
Date established: 2004 **Turnover:** £2m - £5m **No.of Employees:** 1 - 10
Product Groups: 72, 76

Date of Accounts	Oct 11	Oct 10	Oct 09
Working Capital	181	172	150
Fixed Assets	1	1	1
Current Assets	540	662	875

Aylesford Fire Protection
5 Elm Walk, Aylesford, ME20 7LR
Tel: 01622-710978 **Fax:** 01622-710978
E-mail: info@aylesfordfire.co.uk
Website: http://aylesfordfire.co.uk
Directors: L. Graham (Prop)
Date established: 1995 **No.of Employees:** 1 - 10 **Product Groups:** 38, 42

Aylesford Newsprint Ltd
Newsprint House Bellingham Way, Aylesford, ME20 7DL
Tel: 01622-796000 **Fax:** 01622-796001
E-mail: reception@aylnews.com
Website: http://www.aylesford-newsprint.co.uk
Directors: R. Boast (Sales), R. Hampton (Ch), O. Terland (Dir), M. Lunabba (Dir), M. Lunabba (MD), H. Eriksson (Dir), D. Charlesworth (Co Sec), A. McKendrick (Grp Chief Exec), A. Trahar (Dir), I. Broxup (Fin), R. Hampton (Dir)
Managers: T. Feneren, M. Atkinson (Personnel), C. Gardener (Purch Mgr)
Ultimate Holding Company: AYLESFORD NEWSPRINT HOLDINGS LIMITED
Immediate Holding Company: AYLESFORD NEWSPRINT HOLDINGS LIMITED
Registration no: 02816412 **VAT No.:** GB 619 3027 50
Date established: 1993 **Turnover:** £125m - £250m
No.of Employees: 251 - 500 **Product Groups:** 27, 28

Date of Accounts	Dec 10	Dec 09	Dec 08
Sales Turnover	135m	155m	154m
Pre Tax Profit/Loss	-29m	5m	-8m
Working Capital	-9m	8m	-1m
Fixed Assets	127m	141m	155m
Current Assets	37m	39m	44m
Current Liabilities	43m	25m	23m

Brett Concrete
Brett House St Michaels Close, Aylesford, ME20 7XE
Tel: 01622-793800 **Fax:** 01622-793890
E-mail: brettcl@brett-concrete.co.uk
Website: http://www.brett.co.uk
Bank(s): Lloyds TSB Bank plc
Directors: C. Chapman (MD)
Immediate Holding Company: ROBERT BRETT & SONS,LIMITED
Registration no: 00641279 **Turnover:** £10m - £20m
No.of Employees: 11 - 20 **Product Groups:** 52

Date of Accounts	Dec 07	Dec 06	Dec 05
Sales Turnover	41108	32616	30472
Pre Tax Profit/Loss	-790	-1200	-1929
Working Capital	2640	1820	711
Fixed Assets	9957	9911	9321
Current Assets	9865	10982	6100
Current Liabilities	7225	9162	5389
Total Share Capital	90	90	90
ROCE% (Return on Capital Employed)	-6.3	-10.2	-19.2
ROT% (Return on Turnover)	-1.9	-3.7	-6.3

C T L Audio Visual Services Ltd
Unit 2 Britannia Business Park, Quarry Wood, Aylesford, ME20 7NT
Tel: 01622-719151 **Fax:** 01622-716425
E-mail: sales@ctlav.co.uk
Website: http://www.ctlav.co.uk
Bank(s): National Westminster Bank Plc
Directors: R. Owen (MD)
Immediate Holding Company: CTL AUDIOVISUAL SERVICES LIMITED
Registration no: 03409936 **Date established:** 1997 **Turnover:** £1m - £2m
No.of Employees: 11 - 20 **Product Groups:** 84

Date of Accounts	May 11	May 10	May 09
Sales Turnover	N/A	N/A	1m
Pre Tax Profit/Loss	N/A	N/A	18
Working Capital	49	46	43
Fixed Assets	29	39	53
Current Assets	406	299	231
Current Liabilities	N/A	N/A	38

DHL Global Mail UK Ltd
Mills Road Quarry Wood, Aylesford, ME20 7WZ
Tel: 01622-792111 **Fax:** 01622-792333
Website: http://www.mercury-international.com
Directors: C. Davey (Dir), M. Siviter (MD)
Managers: S. Brooks (Develop Mgr)
Immediate Holding Company: Msas Global Logistics Ltd
Registration no: 02110134 **Date established:** 1996
Turnover: £20m - £50m **No.of Employees:** 501 - 1000
Product Groups: 81

F G F Ltd
Unit 1a-1b Larkfield Mill Bellingham Way, Larkfield, Aylesford, ME20 6SQ
Tel: 01622-716100 **Fax:** 01622-714180
E-mail: colin.fordham@fgflimited.co.uk
Website: http://www.fgflimited.co.uk
Bank(s): Barclays Charlton
Managers: C. Fordham (Mgr)
Immediate Holding Company: F.G.F. LIMITED
Registration no: 00530903 **VAT No.:** GB 113 0698 94
Date established: 1954 **Turnover:** £2m - £5m **No.of Employees:** 11 - 20
Product Groups: 23, 33, 36, 66

Date of Accounts	Apr 11	Apr 10	Apr 09
Sales Turnover	24m	30m	39m
Pre Tax Profit/Loss	-2m	-4m	-2m
Working Capital	699	3m	4m
Fixed Assets	2m	2m	2m
Current Assets	8m	9m	11m
Current Liabilities	657	804	624

Goldstar
Unit 6 Britannia Business Park Mills Road Quarrywood, Quarry Wood, Aylesford, ME20 7NT
Tel: 01622-717332 **Fax:** 01622-715508
E-mail: sales@goldstaruk.com
Website: http://www.goldstaruk.com
Directors: G. Bastone (Prop)
Immediate Holding Company: M G A CORPORATION LIMITED
Registration no: 03327407 **Date established:** 1997
Turnover: £250,000 - £500,000 **No.of Employees:** 1 - 10
Product Groups: 23, 24, 28

Headline Filters Ltd
Mill Hall Business Estate Mill Hall, Aylesford, ME20 7JZ
Tel: 01622-718927 **Fax:** 01622-882448
E-mail: info@headlinefilters.com
Website: http://www.headlinefilters.com
Bank(s): HSBC Bank plc
Managers: R. Adams (Admin Off), G. King
Immediate Holding Company: HEADLINE FILTERS LIMITED
Registration no: 01994218 **Date established:** 1986 **Turnover:** £2m - £5m
No.of Employees: 21 - 50 **Product Groups:** 33, 34, 40, 42

Date of Accounts	Jun 11	Jun 10	Jun 09
Working Capital	-12	25	191
Fixed Assets	595	586	391
Current Assets	585	679	517

Arthur Heath & Co. Ltd
Hall Road, Aylesford, ME20 7QZ
Tel: 01622-717507 **Fax:** 01622-710551
E-mail: sales@arthurheath.co.uk
Website: http://www.arthurheatheducation.co.uk

Directors: J. Webb (Co Sec), T. Bishop (MD)
Immediate Holding Company: ARTHUR HEATH & CO.,LIMITED
Registration no: 00181634 **Date established:** 2022
No.of Employees: 1 - 10 **Product Groups:** 25, 49

Date of Accounts	Sep 11	Sep 10	Sep 09
Working Capital	540	601	492
Fixed Assets	212	219	235
Current Assets	791	745	548

Intermedical UK Ltd

Unit 6 Mill Hall Business Estate Mill Hall, Aylesford, ME20 7JZ
Tel: 01732-522444 **Fax:** 01732-872883
E-mail: derek.curtis@intermedical.co.uk
Website: http://www.intermedical.co.uk
Directors: S. Curtis (Fin), D. Curtis (MD)
Immediate Holding Company: INTERMEDICAL (UK) LTD
Registration no: 03456073 **VAT No.:** GB 707 2721 50
Date established: 1997 **Turnover:** £250,000 - £500,000
No.of Employees: 1 - 10 **Product Groups:** 31, 37, 38

Date of Accounts	Apr 11	Apr 10	Apr 09
Working Capital	69	104	64
Fixed Assets	14	13	17
Current Assets	326	254	272

International Decorative Surfaces

Unit 11 Wood Close Quarry Wood, Aylesford, ME20 7UB
Tel: 01622-711400 **Fax:** 01622-717770
Website: http://www.idsurfaces.co.uk
Managers: B. Carmichael (Mgr)
Immediate Holding Company: MEYER FOREST PRODUCTS LTD
Registration no: 00070341 **Turnover:** £2m - £5m
No.of Employees: 21 - 50 **Product Groups:** 26

Keemlaw Ltd

Unit 4 Super Abbey Estate Off Beddow Way, Aylesford, ME20 7BH
Tel: 01622-717177 **Fax:** 01622-790348
E-mail: info@keemlaw.co.uk
Website: http://www.keemlaw.co.uk
Directors: D. Law (Dir)
Immediate Holding Company: KEEMLAW LIMITED
Registration no: 02661484 **Date established:** 1991
No.of Employees: 11 - 20 **Product Groups:** 20, 24, 27, 30, 32, 33, 35, 36, 37, 38, 40, 41, 42, 44, 45, 48, 63, 64, 66, 67, 83

Date of Accounts	Dec 11	Dec 10	Dec 09
Sales Turnover	1m	N/A	N/A
Pre Tax Profit/Loss	110	N/A	N/A
Working Capital	156	106	196
Fixed Assets	174	186	92
Current Assets	419	423	314
Current Liabilities	167	N/A	N/A

Kent Frozen Foods Ltd

Priory Park Mills Road, Aylesford, ME20 7PP
Tel: 01622-612400 **Fax:** 01622-612401
E-mail: caroline.harrison@kff.co.uk
Website: http://www.kfs.co.uk
Directors: P. Clarke (Asst MD), C. Harrison (Fin)
Managers: B. Burdett (Reg Sales Mgr), S. Clarke
Immediate Holding Company: KENT FROZEN FOODS LIMITED
Registration no: 00723950 **Date established:** 1962
Turnover: £20m - £50m **No.of Employees:** 101 - 250
Product Groups: 20, 62, 69

Date of Accounts	Dec 11	Dec 10	Dec 09
Sales Turnover	36m	34m	34m
Pre Tax Profit/Loss	439	557	671
Working Capital	3m	2m	2m
Fixed Assets	6m	7m	7m
Current Assets	7m	6m	6m
Current Liabilities	1m	1m	1m

Kent Messenger Group Ltd

Messenger House New Hythe Lane, Larkfield, Aylesford, ME20 6SG
Tel: 01622-717880 **Fax:** 01622-719637
E-mail: mphippen@thekmgroup.co.uk
Website: http://www.kentonline.co.uk
Bank(s): Lloyds TSB Bank plc
Directors: R. Elliot (MD), R. Elliott (Fin)
Managers: E. Underdown, B. Clarke (Tech Serv Mgr), S. Hampton (Mktg Serv Mgr), A. Watts (Personnel)
Immediate Holding Company: KENT MESSENGER LIMITED
Registration no: 00505554 **Date established:** 1952
Turnover: £20m - £50m **No.of Employees:** 51 - 100 **Product Groups:** 28

Date of Accounts	Dec 11	Jan 09	Jan 10
Sales Turnover	19m	35m	23m
Pre Tax Profit/Loss	-835	-4m	-9m
Working Capital	-1m	-2m	-3m
Fixed Assets	13m	22m	16m
Current Assets	3m	5m	3m
Current Liabilities	1m	1m	2m

L C Designs Ltd

London House Larkfield, Aylesford, ME20 6SE
Tel: 01622-716000 **Fax:** 01622-791119
E-mail: raycarr@lc-designs.co.uk
Website: http://www.lcdesigns.com
Bank(s): HSBC London
Directors: R. Carr (Sales), K. Pestell (Dir)
Ultimate Holding Company: LONDON CLOCK HOLDING COMPANY LIMITED(THE)
Immediate Holding Company: LC DESIGNS CO. LIMITED
Registration no: 00360505 **Date established:** 1940 **Turnover:** £5m - £10m
No.of Employees: 21 - 50 **Product Groups:** 25, 65

Date of Accounts	Mar 11	Mar 10	Mar 09
Sales Turnover	8m	9m	N/A
Pre Tax Profit/Loss	29	7	18
Working Capital	7m	7m	7m
Fixed Assets	2m	2m	2m
Current Assets	8m	8m	9m
Current Liabilities	809	1m	2m

Leay Ltd

Unit 1-3 Lake Road Quarry Wood, Aylesford, ME20 7TQ
Tel: 01622-882345 **Fax:** 01622-882208
E-mail: enquiries@leay.com
Website: http://www.leay.com
Directors: J. Hodges (MD), K. Hirani (Dir)
Managers: D. Pettett (Buyer)
Immediate Holding Company: LEAY LIMITED
Registration no: 00327747 **Date established:** 1937
No.of Employees: 21 - 50 **Product Groups:** 35

Date of Accounts	Mar 11	Mar 10	Mar 09
Working Capital	2m	2m	2m
Fixed Assets	344	396	485
Current Assets	3m	3m	3m

Loomis UK Ltd

34 Lake Road Quarry Wood, Aylesford, ME20 7TQ
Tel: 01622-719242 **Fax:** 01622-710478
E-mail: wayne.moule@loomis.co.uk
Website: http://www.loomis.co.uk
Bank(s): Barclays
Managers: M. Hobson, R. Balls (Mgr)
Ultimate Holding Company: SECURITAS AB (SWEDEN)
Immediate Holding Company: LOOMIS UK LIMITED
Registration no: 03200432 **Date established:** 1996
No.of Employees: 21 - 50 **Product Groups:** 36, 81

Date of Accounts	Dec 11	Dec 10	Dec 09
Sales Turnover	109	105m	109m
Pre Tax Profit/Loss	7	2m	-419
Working Capital	3	5m	9m
Fixed Assets	47	42m	41m
Current Assets	29	28m	23m
Current Liabilities	14	17m	12m

Loxton Installation Ltd

14 Mill Hall Estate, Aylesford, ME20 7JZ
Tel: 01622-716131 **Fax:** 01622-719217
E-mail: info@loxtons.com
Website: http://www.loxtons.com
Directors: I. Wright (Fin)
Managers: A. Wilson (Buyer)
Immediate Holding Company: LOXTON INSTALLATIONS LIMITED
Registration no: 01275429 **Date established:** 1976 **Turnover:** £1m - £2m
No.of Employees: 21 - 50 **Product Groups:** 37, 52, 67

Date of Accounts	Mar 11	Mar 10	Mar 09
Sales Turnover	2m	2m	2m
Pre Tax Profit/Loss	117	231	44
Working Capital	34	24	-7
Fixed Assets	1	24	57
Current Assets	492	415	547
Current Liabilities	264	256	266

M C Group Ltd

Beddow Way Forstal Road, Aylesford, ME20 7BT
Tel: 01622-710811 **Fax:** 01622-710430
E-mail: peter.booth@mcgroupltd.co.uk
Website: http://www.mcgroupltd.co.uk
Bank(s): National Westminster
Directors: A. Dawson (Ch), H. Moon (Sales), J. Harman (Chief Op Offcr), N. Riley (Mkt Research), P. Booth (Co Sec), P. Booth (Fin), S. Dawson (Sales), S. Dawson (MD)
Ultimate Holding Company: MC Group Ltd
Immediate Holding Company: M C GROUP LIMITED
Registration no: 02035458 **VAT No.:** GB 522 8290 53
Date established: 1986 **Turnover:** £50m - £75m
No.of Employees: 251 - 500 **Product Groups:** 72, 82

Date of Accounts	Dec 09	Dec 08	Dec 07
Sales Turnover	53m	68m	63m
Pre Tax Profit/Loss	1m	2m	2m
Working Capital	-6m	-6m	-6m
Fixed Assets	39m	39m	34m
Current Assets	10m	14m	15m
Current Liabilities	3m	4m	4m

Main Aim Binding

15 Lake Road Quarry Wood, Aylesford, ME20 7TQ
Tel: 01622-791200 **Fax:** 01622-791300
Directors: K. Buckley (Sales)
Immediate Holding Company: MAIN AIM BINDING LIMITED
Registration no: 02896382 **Date established:** 1994
No.of Employees: 1 - 10 **Product Groups:** 28, 30

Date of Accounts	Aug 11	Aug 09	Aug 08
Working Capital	N/A	72	139
Fixed Assets	N/A	9	6
Current Assets	N/A	124	265

Parker Merchanting Ltd

Larkfield Trading Estate New Hythe Lane, Larkfield, Aylesford, ME20 6XQ
Tel: 08451-202454 **Fax:** 01622-719222
E-mail: info.parker@hagemeyer.co.uk
Website: http://www.parker-direct.com
Managers: M. Hodges (Mgr)
Ultimate Holding Company: RAY INVESTMENT SARL (LUXEMBOURG)
Immediate Holding Company: PARKER MERCHANTING LIMITED
Registration no: 00224779 **VAT No.:** GB 614 2136 80
Date established: 2027 **Turnover:** £75m - £125m
No.of Employees: 1 - 10 **Product Groups:** 22, 23, 24, 29, 30, 33, 37, 39, 40, 45, 63, 66, 68

Date of Accounts	Dec 10	Dec 09	Dec 08
Working Capital	51	51	51
Current Assets	51	51	51

R F Bright Enterprises Ltd

Unit 6 Access 4.20 New Hythe Business Park Bellingham Way, Aylesford, ME20 7HP
Tel: 01622-717141 **Fax:** 01622-717163
E-mail: enquiries@rfbright.co.uk
Website: http://www.rfbright.co.uk
Managers: J. Deacon (Comm)
Immediate Holding Company: R.F. BRIGHT ENTERPRISES LIMITED
Registration no: 00947136 **VAT No.:** GB 203 4119 18
Date established: 1969 **Turnover:** £500,000 - £1m
No.of Employees: 1 - 10 **Product Groups:** 30, 31, 42

Date of Accounts	Dec 11	Dec 10	Dec 09
Working Capital	-253	-249	-73
Fixed Assets	527	530	400
Current Assets	120	108	345

Royal British Legion Poppy Appeal

Royal British Legion Village, Aylesford, ME20 7NX
Tel: 01622-717172 **Fax:** 01622-719360
E-mail: enquries@rbli.co.uk
Website: http://www.rbli.co.uk
Bank(s): Barclays, Maidstone
Managers: N. Buckley (Mgr)
Immediate Holding Company: ROYAL BRITISH LEGION INDUSTRIES LTD.
Registration no: 07052659 **Date established:** 2019
No.of Employees: 21 - 50 **Product Groups:** 37, 39, 45

Date of Accounts	Mar 12	Mar 11	Mar 10
Sales Turnover	12m	18m	19m
Pre Tax Profit/Loss	-2m	-54	2m
Working Capital	472	633	433
Fixed Assets	21m	22m	22m
Current Assets	3m	4m	4m
Current Liabilities	1m	2m	3m

S C A Containerboard

East Mill, Aylesford, ME20 7PA
Tel: 01622-883661 **Fax:** 01622-883660
E-mail: scacontainerboard.uk@sca.com
Website: http://www.scacontainerboard.com
Directors: N. Massart (Sales), J. Resimont (MD)
Immediate Holding Company: SCA Packaging Ltd
Registration no: 00053913 **Turnover:** £125m - £250m
No.of Employees: 1 - 10 **Product Groups:** 27

Sasco Sauces Ltd

Unit 2 St Michaels Close, Aylesford, ME20 7BU
Tel: 01622-714940 **Fax:** 01622-719422
E-mail: garysauces@aol.com
Website: http://www.sascosauces.co.uk
Directors: G. Spicer (MD)
Immediate Holding Company: SASCO SAUCES LIMITED
Registration no: 04614082 **Date established:** 2002
No.of Employees: 1 - 10 **Product Groups:** 20

Date of Accounts	Apr 11	Apr 10	Apr 09
Sales Turnover	11m	11m	492
Pre Tax Profit/Loss	331	-115	1m
Working Capital	-238	-667	-989
Fixed Assets	4m	4m	5m
Current Assets	2m	2m	3
Current Liabilities	1m	2m	250

Southern Vision Technology Ltd

242 Bull Lane Eccles, Aylesford, ME20 7HF
Tel: 01622-791800 **Fax:** 01622-791800
E-mail: info@southernvisiontechnology.com
Website: http://www.southernvisiontechnology.com
Directors: C. Hills (Dir)
Immediate Holding Company: SOUTHERN VISION TECHNOLOGY LTD
Registration no: 05511881 **Date established:** 2005
No.of Employees: 1 - 10 **Product Groups:** 36, 37, 40, 52

Date of Accounts	Aug 11	Aug 10	Aug 09
Working Capital	36	228	166
Fixed Assets	45	29	16
Current Assets	328	443	329

Travis Perkins plc

Forstal Road, Aylesford, ME20 7AG
Tel: 01622-710111 **Fax:** 01622-715692
E-mail: aylesford@travisperkins.co.uk
Website: http://www.travisperkins.co.uk
Bank(s): National Westminster, Maidstone
Managers: V. Murdoch (District Mgr)
Immediate Holding Company: TRAVIS PERKINS PLC
Registration no: 00824821 **Date established:** 1964
Turnover: £250m - £500m **No.of Employees:** 21 - 50 **Product Groups:** 66

W M Lillico & Son Ltd

The Forstall Beddow Way, Aylesford, ME20 7BT
Tel: 01622-718062 **Fax:** 01622-882475
E-mail: post@lillico.co.uk
Website: http://www.lillico.co.uk
Directors: D. Chapman (Co Sec), M. Booth (MD)
Managers: J. Scott (Chief Mgr), R. Steel
Ultimate Holding Company: WM. LILLICO & SON (HOLDINGS) LIMITED
Immediate Holding Company: WM.LILLICO & SON LIMITED
Registration no: 00332458 **VAT No.:** GB 218 3752 61
Date established: 1937 **Turnover:** £10m - £20m
No.of Employees: 51 - 100 **Product Groups:** 32, 62

Date of Accounts	Mar 11	Mar 10	Mar 09
Sales Turnover	19m	21m	23m
Pre Tax Profit/Loss	-21	191	396
Working Capital	3m	3m	2m
Fixed Assets	341	1m	1m
Current Assets	5m	5m	5m
Current Liabilities	101	110	137

Waterloo Air Products

111 Mills Road Quarry Wood, Aylesford, ME20 7NB
Tel: 01622-717861 **Fax:** 01622-718863
E-mail: sales@waterloo.co.uk
Website: http://www.waterloo.co.uk
Bank(s): National Westminster Bank Plc
Directors: K. Searles (Fin), A. Smith (Sales & Mktg), J. Stolworthy (Fin)
Managers: J. Froggett (Purch Mgr), D. Martin, N. Bailey (Contracts Mgr)
Ultimate Holding Company: WATERLOO GROUP LIMITED
Immediate Holding Company: WATERLOO GROUP LIMITED
Registration no: 04934917 **Date established:** 2003
Turnover: £10m - £20m **No.of Employees:** 51 - 100 **Product Groups:** 35, 39, 40, 42, 52

Date of Accounts	Dec 10	Dec 09	Dec 08
Sales Turnover	11m	13m	14m
Pre Tax Profit/Loss	-714	71	82
Working Capital	-596	-489	-508
Fixed Assets	3m	3m	4m
Current Assets	3m	3m	4m
Current Liabilities	1m	938	3m

Beckenham

Accesscaff International Ltd

37 Croydon Road, Beckenham, BR3 4AB
Tel: 08448-487784 **Fax:** 0844-848 7785
E-mail: mraccess@mraccessuk.com
Website: http://www.accesscaffinternational.com
Directors: G. Pilott (Dir)
Immediate Holding Company: ACCESSCAFF INTERNATIONAL LTD
Registration no: 03004123 **Date established:** 1995
No.of Employees: 1 - 10 **Product Groups:** 25, 30, 35, 36, 39, 52, 66, 83

Date of Accounts	Dec 11	Dec 10	Dec 09
Working Capital	562	455	329
Fixed Assets	183	182	184
Current Assets	677	577	467

Aldous & Stamp Ltd

90 Avenue Road, Beckenham, BR3 4SA
Tel: 020-8659 1833 **Fax:** 020-8676 9676
E-mail: sales@aldous-stamp.co.uk
Website: http://www.aldous-stamp.co.uk
Managers: B. Bennett (Chief Mgr)
Immediate Holding Company: ALDOUS & STAMP LIMITED
Registration no: 00935497 **VAT No.:** GB 427 0343 76
Date established: 1968 **No.of Employees:** 1 - 10 **Product Groups:** 32, 38, 42

Date of Accounts	Sep 11	Sep 10	Sep 09
Working Capital	374	288	164
Fixed Assets	405	368	376
Current Assets	539	445	218

Bondaglass Voss Ltd

158 Ravenscroft Road, Beckenham, BR3 4TW
Tel: 020-8778 0071 **Fax:** 020-8659 5297
E-mail: bondaglass@btconnect.com
Directors: P. Owen (Dir), A. Swaby (Co Sec)
Immediate Holding Company: BONDAGLASS VOSS LIMITED
Registration no: 01063923 **VAT No.:** GB 205 5484 75
Date established: 1972 **Turnover:** £1m - £2m **No.of Employees:** 1 - 10
Product Groups: 32

Date of Accounts	Jul 11	Jul 10	Jul 09
Sales Turnover	N/A	N/A	2m
Pre Tax Profit/Loss	N/A	N/A	23
Working Capital	86	185	185
Fixed Assets	456	456	465
Current Assets	628	550	626
Current Liabilities	N/A	204	70

C B D Research Ltd

PO Box 524, Beckenham, BR3 9HU
Tel: 020-8650 7745 **Fax:** 020-8650 0768
E-mail: shirley.henderson@cbdresearch.com
Website: http://www.cbdresearch.com
Directors: A. Henderson (MD)
Immediate Holding Company: C.B.D.RESEARCH LIMITED
Registration no: 00700855 **VAT No.:** GB 205 4233 08
Date established: 1961 **No.of Employees:** 1 - 10 **Product Groups:** 28

Date of Accounts	Oct 11	Oct 10	Oct 09
Working Capital	-163	-115	6
Fixed Assets	131	136	141
Current Assets	26	24	109

Croft Structural Engineers Ltd

132 Mackenzie Road, Beckenham, BR3 4SD
Tel: 020-8684 4744
E-mail: ctomlin@croftse.co.uk
Website: http://www.croftse.co.uk
Directors: J. Casey (Fin), C. Tomlin (MD)
Immediate Holding Company: CROFT STRUCTURAL ENGINEERS LIMITED
Registration no: 05143436 **Date established:** 2004
No.of Employees: 1 - 10 **Product Groups:** 35

Date of Accounts	Aug 11	Aug 10	Aug 09
Working Capital	127	70	43
Fixed Assets	6	4	4
Current Assets	200	116	73

Dixon Glass Ltd

127-129 Avenue Road, Beckenham, BR3 4RX
Tel: 020-8778 6458 **Fax:** 020-8778 1270
E-mail: info@dixonglass.co.uk
Website: http://www.dixonglass.co.uk
Directors: R. Bramley (Dir), G. Bramley (Fin)
Immediate Holding Company: DIXON GLASS LIMITED
Registration no: 04526840 **Date established:** 2002
No.of Employees: 1 - 10 **Product Groups:** 28, 30, 33, 37, 38, 40, 42, 45, 48, 49, 63, 66

Date of Accounts	Dec 11	Dec 10	Dec 09
Working Capital	203	194	156
Fixed Assets	23	1	1
Current Assets	224	231	197

European Springs & Pressings Ltd

Chaffinch Business Park Croydon Road, Beckenham, BR3 4DW
Tel: 020-8663 1800 **Fax:** 020-8663 1900
E-mail: sales@europeansprings.com
Website: http://www.europeansprings.com
Bank(s): Barclays
Directors: K. Lindback (Dir), M. Gibbs (Co Sec)
Ultimate Holding Company: ESP HOLDINGS (UK) LIMITED
Immediate Holding Company: EUROPEAN SPRINGS AND PRESSINGS LIMITED
Registration no: 00548932 **Date established:** 1955
Turnover: £10m - £20m **No.of Employees:** 101 - 250 **Product Groups:** 35

Date of Accounts	Dec 11	Dec 10	Dec 09
Sales Turnover	11m	11m	7m
Pre Tax Profit/Loss	2m	2m	746
Working Capital	2m	2m	2m
Fixed Assets	2m	1m	982
Current Assets	4m	4m	3m
Current Liabilities	754	754	588

Fontus Ltd

Greenways, Beckenham, BR3 3NQ
Tel: 020-8650 1837
E-mail: info@fontus.co.uk
Website: http://www.fontus.co.uk
Directors: S. Leather (Fin), H. Leather (MD)
Immediate Holding Company: FONTUS LTD.
Registration no: 04385494 **Date established:** 2002
Turnover: Up to £250,000 **No.of Employees:** 1 - 10 **Product Groups:** 41

Date of Accounts	Mar 11	Mar 10	Mar 09
Sales Turnover	66	69	64
Pre Tax Profit/Loss	31	22	18
Working Capital	-0	-1	N/A
Fixed Assets	1	2	2
Current Assets	8	6	5
Current Liabilities	8	6	5

G K A Rubber & Plastics Ltd

Unit 2 Gardener Industrial Estate Kent House Lane, Beckenham, BR3 1QZ
Tel: 020-8659 1331 **Fax:** 020-8659 4823
E-mail: ken@gkarubberandplastics.co.uk
Website: http://www.gkarubberandplastics.co.uk
Bank(s): Lloyds TSB Bank plc
Directors: E. Bard (Dir)
Immediate Holding Company: GKA RUBBER & PLASTICS LIMITED
Registration no: 05351499 **VAT No.:** GB 583 9054 12
Date established: 2005 **Turnover:** £500,000 - £1m
No.of Employees: 11 - 20 **Product Groups:** 27, 29, 48

Date of Accounts	Dec 10	Dec 09	Dec 08
Working Capital	17	21	43
Current Assets	173	135	134

I S G Steel Stockholders Ltd

Unit 5 Laker Industrial Estate Kent House Lane, Beckenham, BR3 1JT
Tel: 020-8778 8881 **Fax:** 020-8659 1643
E-mail: info@isg-steel.co.uk
Website: http://www.isg-steel.co.uk
Bank(s): HSBC Bank plc
Directors: S. Brown (Co Sec), S. Loots (MD)
Managers: M. Hutchinson (Sales Prom Mgr), N. Buss (Purch Mgr)
Ultimate Holding Company: I S & G (HOLDINGS) LIMITED
Immediate Holding Company: I. S. & G. STEEL STOCKHOLDERS LIMITED
Registration no: 00251016 **VAT No.:** GB 205 6860 68
Date established: 1930 **Turnover:** £2m - £5m **No.of Employees:** 21 - 50
Product Groups: 34

Date of Accounts	Mar 11	Mar 10	Mar 09
Sales Turnover	9m	8m	12m
Pre Tax Profit/Loss	298	-236	132
Working Capital	2m	1m	1m
Fixed Assets	358	302	378
Current Assets	4m	4m	4m
Current Liabilities	462	1m	1m

Ic2 CCTV & Security Specialists UK Ltd

Bromley Business Services Provident House Burrell Row High Street, Beckenham, BR3 1AT
Tel: 020-8249 6495 **Fax:** 020-8249 6496
E-mail: info@ic2cctv.com
Website: http://www.ic2cctv.com
Directors: A. Whelan (MD)
Immediate Holding Company: IC2 CCTV SECURITY SPECIALISTS UK LTD
Registration no: 04227542 **Date established:** 2001
No.of Employees: 11 - 20 **Product Groups:** 35, 52, 67, 81

Date of Accounts	May 11	May 10	May 09
Working Capital	81	85	51
Fixed Assets	25	10	20
Current Assets	663	408	499

Loft Ladders (t/a Loft Ladders)

Unit C2 83 Copers Cope Road, Beckenham, BR3 1NR
Tel: 020-8663 1973 **Fax:** 020-8663 1974
E-mail: loftladders@dsl.pipex.com
Website: http://www.loftladdersltd.co.uk
Directors: B. Hemmings (Dir), R. Hemmings (Dir)
Immediate Holding Company: PREFERGRANT SERVICES LIMITED
Registration no: 02783210 **Date established:** 1993
Turnover: £250,000 - £500,000 **No.of Employees:** 1 - 10
Product Groups: 35

Date of Accounts	Jan 11	Jan 10	Jan 08
Working Capital	32	43	-13
Fixed Assets	2	4	7
Current Assets	71	59	51

Natural Stone Care Ltd

50 Burnhill Road, Beckenham, BR3 3LA
Tel: 020-8249 6063 **Fax:** 020-8249 6006
E-mail: jeff@naturalstonecare.co.uk
Website: http://www.naturalstonecare.co.uk
Directors: D. McGregor (Fin), J. McGregor (MD)
Immediate Holding Company: NATURAL STONE CARE LIMITED
Registration no: 04547208 **Date established:** 2002
Turnover: £250,000 - £500,000 **No.of Employees:** 1 - 10
Product Groups: 52, 80

Date of Accounts	Mar 12	Mar 11	Mar 10
Sales Turnover	N/A	N/A	279
Pre Tax Profit/Loss	N/A	N/A	57
Working Capital	556	546	60
Fixed Assets	31	32	7
Current Assets	637	917	128
Current Liabilities	N/A	N/A	59

Paul Owen Associates Ltd

Burnhill Business Centre 50 Burnhill Road, Beckenham, BR3 3LA
Tel: 020-8249 6066 **Fax:** 020-8658 4580
E-mail: s.williams@paulowen.co.uk
Website: http://www.paulowen.co.uk
Directors: P. Owen (Ptnr)
Registration no: 01357305 **Date established:** 1978
No.of Employees: 1 - 10 **Product Groups:** 35

Principal Catering Consultants Ltd

321 Upper Elmers End Road, Beckenham, BR3 3QP
Tel: 020-8663 6686 **Fax:** 020-8663 0383
E-mail: catering@pc-fare.co.uk
Website: http://www.fare-catering.com
Directors: J. Durden (MD)
Managers: G. Fisher
Immediate Holding Company: PRINCIPAL CATERING CONSULTANTS LIMITED
Registration no: 02419830 **Date established:** 1989 **Turnover:** £5m - £10m
No.of Employees: 1 - 10 **Product Groups:** 69

Date of Accounts	Aug 11	Aug 10	Aug 09
Sales Turnover	7m	7m	8m
Pre Tax Profit/Loss	279	240	394
Working Capital	721	622	606
Fixed Assets	85	114	104
Current Assets	1m	1m	1m
Current Liabilities	393	305	356

Pump Technical Services

Unit 2b Beco Works Kent House Lane, Beckenham, BR3 1LA
Tel: 020-8778 4271 **Fax:** 020-8659 3576
E-mail: sales@pts-jung.co.uk
Website: http://www.pts-jung.co.uk
Bank(s): National Westminster
Directors: C. Kavanagh (Fin)
Immediate Holding Company: PUMP TECHNICAL SALES LIMITED
Registration no: 02468274 **VAT No.:** GB 299 5017 19
Date established: 1990 **Turnover:** £1m - £2m **No.of Employees:** 11 - 20
Product Groups: 40

Date of Accounts	May 12	May 11	May 10
Working Capital	-0	-0	-0
Current Assets	1	1	1
Current Liabilities	1	N/A	N/A

Quicks Ltd

7 Gardner Industrial Estate Kent House Lane, Beckenham, BR3 1JR
Tel: 020-8659 1931 **Fax:** 020-8676 8939
E-mail: ian@quicks.biz
Website: http://www.quicks.biz
Directors: I. Quick (MD), I. Quick (Dir)
Ultimate Holding Company: QUICKS HOLDINGS LIMITED
Immediate Holding Company: QUICKS LIMITED
Registration no: 01067334 **Date established:** 1972
No.of Employees: 11 - 20 **Product Groups:** 27, 28, 35, 64

Sonique Ltd

Burnhill Business Centre 50 Burnhill Road, Beckenham, BR3 3LA
Tel: 020-8249 6091 **Fax:** 020-8249 6031
E-mail: info@soniqueltd.com
Website: http://www.allmediadirect.co.uk
Directors: C. Ryan (MD), L. Williams (MD), N. Griffiths (Design), S. Williams (Fin)
Immediate Holding Company: ALL MEDIA DIRECT LIMITED
Registration no: 04151557 **Date established:** 2001
Turnover: Up to £250,000 **No.of Employees:** 1 - 10 **Product Groups:** 81, 89

Date of Accounts	Nov 06
Sales Turnover	94
Pre Tax Profit/Loss	15
Working Capital	-1
Fixed Assets	14
Current Assets	6
Current Liabilities	7
ROCE% (Return on Capital Employed)	112.6

Peter Steele

24 White Oak Drive, Beckenham, BR3 6QE
Tel: 020-8650 3798
Directors: P. Steele (Prop)
Date established: 1987 **No.of Employees:** 1 - 10 **Product Groups:** 35

Straight Curve

Burnhill House 50 Burnhill Road, Beckenham, BR3 3LA
Tel: 020-8249 6073
E-mail: info@straightcurve.co.uk
Website: http://www.straightcurve.co.uk
Directors: J. Santilli (Dir)
Immediate Holding Company: SANDERSTEAD HEIGHTS RTM COMPANY LIMITED
Registration no: 06368472 **Date established:** 2011
No.of Employees: 1 - 10 **Product Groups:** 37, 44, 67, 89

Date of Accounts	Dec 11
Sales Turnover	6

Symon Communications

Ironstone House Burrell Row, Beckenham, BR3 1AT
Tel: 020-8650 8805 **Fax:** 020-8249 6446
E-mail: info@symon.com
Website: http://www.symon.co.uk
Directors: W. Cole (Co Sec)
Ultimate Holding Company: SYMON COMMUNICATIONS INC (USA)
Immediate Holding Company: SYMON COMMUNICATIONS, LTD.
Registration no: 03917701 **Date established:** 2000 **Turnover:** £5m - £10m
No.of Employees: 1 - 10 **Product Groups:** 37, 52

Date of Accounts	Jan 12	Jan 11	Jan 10
Sales Turnover	7m	N/A	5m
Pre Tax Profit/Loss	1m	N/A	176
Working Capital	962	-948	828
Fixed Assets	852	877	849
Current Assets	3m	N/A	2m
Current Liabilities	2m	N/A	1m

The Lift Company

Burnhill Business Centre 50 Burnhill Road, Beckenham, BR3 3LA
Tel: 020-8653 7771 **Fax:** 020-8653 7775
E-mail: theliftco@blueyonder.co.uk
Website: http://www.theliftco.org.uk
Directors: J. Kavanagh (MD)
Immediate Holding Company: SANDERSTEAD HEIGHTS RTM COMPANY LIMITED
Registration no: 06368472 **Date established:** 2011
Turnover: Up to £250,000 **No.of Employees:** 11 - 20 **Product Groups:** 35, 39, 45

Date of Accounts	Dec 11
Sales Turnover	6

H S Walsh & Sons Ltd

243 Beckenham Road, Beckenham, BR3 4TS
Tel: 020-8778 7061 **Fax:** 020-8676 8669
E-mail: desmond@hswalsh.com
Website: http://www.hswalsh.com
Bank(s): National Westminster Bank Plc
Directors: D. Walsh (MD), M. Eyers (Dir)
Managers: D. Crisp (I.T. Exec)
Immediate Holding Company: H S WALSH & SONS LIMITED
Registration no: 03553069 **VAT No.:** GB 205 4651 87
Date established: 1998 **Turnover:** £2m - £5m **No.of Employees:** 21 - 50
Product Groups: 47

Date of Accounts	Jun 08	Jun 07	Jun 06
Working Capital	702	685	644
Fixed Assets	43	53	63
Current Assets	1291	1318	1127
Current Liabilities	590	633	483
Total Share Capital	76	76	76

Belvedere

A Latter & Co. Ltd

River Wharf Mulberry Way, Belvedere, DA17 6AR
Tel: 020-8310 0123 **Fax:** 020-8310 0868
E-mail: admin@alatter.co.uk
Website: http://www.alatter.co.uk
Bank(s): National Westminster Bank Plc

Directors: F. Barr (Dir), M. Daniel (Fin)
Ultimate Holding Company: A LATTER & COMPANY (MANCHESTER) LIMITED
Immediate Holding Company: A LATTER & COMPANY LIMITED
Registration no: 00299058 Date established: 1935 Turnover: £2m - £5m
No.of Employees: 11 - 20 Product Groups: 27, 28, 30, 45

Date of Accounts	Dec 11	Dec 10	Dec 09
Working Capital	59	43	22
Fixed Assets	50	65	78
Current Assets	744	630	591

Durable Contracts Ltd
Crabtree Manorway South, Belvedere, DA17 6AW
Tel: 020-8311 1211 Fax: 020-8310 7893
E-mail: sales@durable-online.com
Website: http://www.durable-online.com
Directors: B. Perdeaux (Dir)
Immediate Holding Company: DURABLE CONTRACTS LIMITED
Registration no: 06053929 Date established: 2007
Turnover: Over £1,000m No.of Employees: 1 - 10 Product Groups: 52

Interserve Project Service Ltd
Crabtree Manorway South, Belvedere, DA17 6BH
Tel: 020-8311 5500 Fax: 020-8311 1701
E-mail: belbedere.office@interserveprojects.com
Website: http://www.interserve.com
Managers: W. Howell (Mgr)
Ultimate Holding Company: INTERSERVE PLC
Immediate Holding Company: INTERSERVE GROUP HOLDINGS LTD
Registration no: 00303359 Turnover: £500m - £1,000m
No.of Employees: 11 - 20 Product Groups: 51, 52

R E Knight Ltd
Fishers Way, Belvedere, DA17 6BS
Tel: 020-8310 8900 Fax: 020-8311 4530
E-mail: enquiries@reknight.co.uk
Website: http://www.reknight.co.uk
Bank(s): Barclays, London
Directors: J. Knight (Dir), R. Knight (MD), D. Knight (MD), J. Knight (Fin)
Managers: D. Knight (Chief Mgr)
Immediate Holding Company: R.E.KNIGHT LIMITED
Registration no: 00984509 VAT No.: GB 205 7769 49
Date established: 1970 Turnover: £500,000 - £1m
No.of Employees: 21 - 50 Product Groups: 30, 46, 48

Date of Accounts	Aug 11	Aug 10	Aug 09
Working Capital	75	75	60
Fixed Assets	95	108	121
Current Assets	113	121	147

Seropa Ltd
Crabtree Manorway South, Belvedere, DA17 6BJ
Tel: 020-8311 9069 Fax: 020-8311 8656
E-mail: admin@seropa.co.uk
Website: http://www.seropa.co.uk
Directors: T. Seguss (Dir)
Immediate Holding Company: SEROPA LIMITED
Registration no: 03731421 Date established: 1999
Turnover: £500,000 - £1m No.of Employees: 1 - 10 Product Groups: 20, 40, 41

Date of Accounts	Mar 11	Mar 10	Mar 09
Sales Turnover	564	512	478
Pre Tax Profit/Loss	143	83	7
Working Capital	21	-4	18
Fixed Assets	1	1	2
Current Assets	175	137	152
Current Liabilities	90	106	75

Vencel Resil Ltd
Infinity House Anderson Way, Belvedere, DA17 6BG
Tel: 020-8320 9100 Fax: 020-8320 9110
E-mail: admin@vencel.co.uk
Website: http://www.vencel.co.uk
Bank(s): National Westminster Bank Plc
Directors: J. Verstegen (Dir), K. Hutchins (Fin)
Managers: J. Crisfield (Tech Serv Mgr)
Immediate Holding Company: Synbra UK Ltd
Registration no: 01073622 VAT No.: GB 680 7189 27
Date established: 1980 Turnover: £10m - £20m
No.of Employees: 21 - 50 Product Groups: 30

Welding Erection Services Ltd
6 Capital Industrial Estate Crabtree Manorway South, Belvedere, DA17 6BJ
Tel: 020-8310 7666 Fax: 020-8310 7667
E-mail: admin@wefltdsouthern.com
Website: http://www.wesltdsouthern.com
Directors: C. Riley (MD), R. Riley (Fin)
Immediate Holding Company: WELDING ERECTION SERVICES (SOUTHERN) LTD.
Registration no: 03294728 Date established: 1996
No.of Employees: 11 - 20 Product Groups: 35

Date of Accounts	Dec 11	Dec 10	Dec 09
Working Capital	260	238	596
Fixed Assets	570	564	227
Current Assets	281	261	773

Bexley

Airflow Industries Ltd
Old Bexley Business Park Bourne Road, Bexley, DA5 1LR
Tel: 01322-529402 Fax: 020-8294 1887
E-mail: airflo@btinternet.com
Directors: T. Richards (Fin), A. Mccloat (Sales)
Immediate Holding Company: AIRFLO INDUSTRIES LIMITED
Registration no: 03650724 Date established: 1998
No.of Employees: 1 - 10 Product Groups: 38, 42

Date of Accounts	Sep 11	Sep 10	Sep 09
Working Capital	469	492	524
Fixed Assets	1	2	2
Current Assets	572	645	623

Chartwell Design Services
1 Chalet Close, Bexley, DA5 2EZ
Tel: 01322-557761 Fax: 01322-557761
Directors: A. Carter (Prop)
Date established: 1972 No.of Employees: 1 - 10 Product Groups: 35

Forest Laboratories UK Ltd
Bourne Road, Bexley, DA5 1NX
Tel: 01322-550550 Fax: 01322-559100
E-mail: alivingstone@forest-labs.co.uk
Website: http://www.forestlabs.com
Bank(s): Barclays
Directors: A. Livingstone (Co Sec), A. Livingstone (Fin)
Managers: B. Stagg (Export Sales Mg), D. Liman (I.T. Exec), J. Lovely (Tech Serv Mgr), J. Ridley (Chief Acct)
Ultimate Holding Company: FOREST LABORATORIES INC (USA)
Immediate Holding Company: FOREST LABORATORIES UK LIMITED
Registration no: 00532832 VAT No.: GB 299 5752 86
Date established: 1954 Turnover: £20m - £50m
No.of Employees: 101 - 250 Product Groups: 31

Date of Accounts	Mar 08	Mar 07	Mar 06
Sales Turnover	25338	25660	24790
Pre Tax Profit/Loss	-216	-2140	-1289
Working Capital	1303	923	3194
Fixed Assets	4171	5192	5628
Current Assets	14192	12614	15304
Current Liabilities	12889	11691	12110
Total Share Capital	535	535	535
ROCE% (Return on Capital Employed)	-4.0	-35.0	-14.6
ROT% (Return on Turnover)	-0.9	-8.3	-5.2

Geoffrey Waldmeyer Associates Ltd
Vale Mascal Court 132 North Cray Road, Bexley, DA5 3NB
Tel: 01322-522133
E-mail: sales@security-labels.co.uk
Website: http://www.security-labels.co.uk
Directors: S. Wilton (Dir)
Immediate Holding Company: GEOFFREY WALDMEYER ASSOCIATES LIMITED
Registration no: 01985620 Date established: 1986
No.of Employees: 1 - 10 Product Groups: 29, 30, 36

Date of Accounts	Mar 11	Mar 10	Mar 09
Working Capital	-2	19	45
Fixed Assets	6	1	1
Current Assets	43	79	83

Modern Screws Ltd
5 Dartford Road, Bexley, DA5 2BH
Tel: 01322-553224 Fax: 01322-555093
E-mail: sales@modern-screws.co.uk
Website: http://www.modern-screws.co.uk
Directors: R. Martingell (Fin), T. Martingell (MD)
Immediate Holding Company: MODERN SCREWS LIMITED
Registration no: 06431427 VAT No.: GB 249 1119 66
Date established: 2007 Turnover: Up to £250,000
No.of Employees: 1 - 10 Product Groups: 35, 66

Date of Accounts	Jan 12	Jan 11	Jan 10
Working Capital	-10	99	94
Fixed Assets	12	17	22
Current Assets	144	128	117

Starguard Services
46 Blendon Drive, Bexley, DA5 3AB
Tel: 020-8303 6807 Fax: 020-8304 6139
Directors: A. Hyde (Prop)
Date established: 1983 No.of Employees: 1 - 10 Product Groups: 37, 40, 48

T C S Computer Services Ltd
The Brewhouse 19 Old Bexley Business Park Bourne Road, Bexley, DA5 1LR
Tel: 01322-559840 Fax: 01322-550010
E-mail: info@tcscs.co.uk
Website: http://www.tcscs.co.uk
Directors: G. Jackson (Co Sec), R. Gent (MD)
Immediate Holding Company: TCS COMPUTER SERVICES LIMITED
Registration no: 00309737 VAT No.: GB 205 4522 01
Date established: 1936 Turnover: £500,000 - £1m
No.of Employees: 1 - 10 Product Groups: 44

Date of Accounts	Feb 12	Feb 11	Feb 10
Working Capital	-56	-100	-73
Fixed Assets	8	6	5
Current Assets	91	63	70

Titan Elevators Ltd
West Lodge 167 Blendon Road, Bexley, DA5 1BT
Tel: 020-8303 0033 Fax: 020-8303 0022
E-mail: sales@titanelevators.co.uk
Website: http://www.titanelevators.co.uk
Directors: M. Dykes (Fin)
Immediate Holding Company: TITAN ELEVATORS LIMITED
Registration no: 03398412 Date established: 1997
No.of Employees: 51 - 100 Product Groups: 35, 39, 45

Date of Accounts	Mar 11	Mar 10	Mar 09
Working Capital	473	505	335
Fixed Assets	151	151	128
Current Assets	2m	1m	1m
Current Liabilities	N/A	N/A	905

Bexleyheath

Charter Building Services Ltd
158 Mayplace Road East, Bexleyheath, DA7 6EJ
Tel: 01322-558011 Fax: 01322-520282
E-mail: mail@charter.uk.com
Website: http://www.charter.uk.com
Directors: R. Saddington (MD)
Immediate Holding Company: CHARTER BUILDING SERVICES LIMITED
Registration no: 02701061 Date established: 1992
Turnover: £500,000 - £1m No.of Employees: 1 - 10 Product Groups: 39, 45

Date of Accounts	Mar 11	Mar 10	Mar 09
Working Capital	12	N/A	19
Fixed Assets	10	10	5
Current Assets	182	143	128

Diving Unlimited
The Dive Centre 56 Lessness Avenue, Bexleyheath, DA7 5SJ
Tel: 020-8311 0201 Fax: 01322-431254
E-mail: info@divingunlimited.co.uk
Website: http://www.divingunlimited.co.uk

Directors: P. Pain (Prop)
No.of Employees: 11 - 20 Product Groups: 40, 74, 89

Wontner Smith Stocktakers & Gaugers Ltd
9 Sringfield Road, Bexleyheath, DA7 6DX
Tel: 01322-523186
E-mail: anthonylast@btconnect.com
Website: http://wontnersmith.co.uk
Directors: A. Last (Prop)
Immediate Holding Company: WONTNER SMITH (STOCKTAKERS & GAUGERS) LIMITED
Registration no: 00058412 Date established: 1998
Turnover: Up to £250,000 No.of Employees: 1 - 10 Product Groups: 80

Date of Accounts	Mar 11	Mar 10	Mar 09
Sales Turnover	N/A	16	14
Pre Tax Profit/Loss	N/A	-1	-1
Working Capital	-5	-4	-5
Current Liabilities	N/A	5	5

The Woolwich
Corporate Headquarters Watling Street, Bexleyheath, DA6 7RR
Tel: 0870-1660060 Fax: 01322-271117
E-mail: customer.services@woolwich.co.uk
Website: http://www.woolwich.co.uk
Bank(s): Woolwich
Directors: B. Kelsall (Mkt Research), M. Richardson (Sales)
Managers: A. Boxall (Mktg Serv Mgr)
Ultimate Holding Company: Barclays plc
Immediate Holding Company: Barclays Bank plc
Registration no: 03295699 Date established: 1993
Turnover: Over £1,000m No.of Employees: 501 - 1000
Product Groups: 82

Xtreme Vortex
Chessington Avenue, Bexleyheath, DA7 5NP
Tel: 07739-560990
E-mail: mail@xtremevortex.co.uk
Website: http://www.xtremevortex.co.uk
Directors: A. Green (Prop)
Date established: 2006 Turnover: Up to £250,000
No.of Employees: 1 - 10 Product Groups: 87

Birchington

Fordhay Office Interiors Ltd
Ford Hay House 8 Shakespeare Road, Birchington, CT7 9ES
Tel: 08452-303133 Fax: 01843-848027
E-mail: simon@fordhay.co.uk
Website: http://www.fordhay.co.uk
Directors: S. Coleman (Contracts)
No.of Employees: 11 - 20 Product Groups: 25, 30, 33, 35, 40, 52

Multiglow Fires
Coastways Garage Canterbury Road, St Nicholas At Wade, Birchington, CT7 0PQ
Tel: 01843-847575 Fax: 01843- 848300
E-mail: steve.lebaigue@multiglow.com
Website: http://www.multiglow.com
Directors: S. Lebaigue (Ptnr), S. Le Baigue (Prop)
No.of Employees: 11 - 20 Product Groups: 40

Premier Signs
Unit 17 Hedgend Industrial Estate Shuart Lane, St Nicholas At Wade, Birchington, CT7 0NB
Tel: 01843-843895 Fax: 01843-843895
Website: http://www.premiersigns-kent.co.uk
Directors: I. Pettman (Prop)
Date established: 2006 No.of Employees: 1 - 10 Product Groups: 30, 39, 40

Broadstairs

All About Asbestos Ltd
177 Percy Avenue, Broadstairs, CT10 3LF
Tel: 01843-600765 Fax: 01843-600765
E-mail: info@allaboutasbestos.co.uk
Website: http://www.allaboutasbestos.co.uk
Directors: D. Jack (Dir)
Immediate Holding Company: ALL ABOUT ASBESTOS LIMITED
Registration no: 05405688 Date established: 2005
No.of Employees: 1 - 10 Product Groups: 84

Date of Accounts	May 11	May 10	May 09
Working Capital	48	70	13
Fixed Assets	23	16	29
Current Assets	139	132	56

Bell R & Co.
Unit 10 Anson Close, Pysons Road Industrial Estate, Broadstairs, CT10 2YB
Tel: 01843-602548 Fax: 01843-602549
E-mail: rtbellcoltd@btconnect.com
Website: http://www.rtbellcoltd.co.uk
Managers: A. Frost (Mgr)
Immediate Holding Company: R T BELL & CO (BROADSTAIRS) LIMITED
Registration no: 05290058 Date established: 2004
Turnover: £250,000 - £500,000 No.of Employees: 1 - 10
Product Groups: 25, 45

Date of Accounts	Sep 07
Working Capital	-36
Fixed Assets	43
Current Assets	124
Current Liabilities	160

Blaze Neon Ltd
Patricia Way Pysons Road Industrial Estate, Broadstairs, CT10 2XZ
Tel: 01843-601075 Fax: 01843-867924
E-mail: chrisa@blazeneon.com
Website: http://www.blazeneon.com
Bank(s): National Westminster Bank Plc
Directors: J. Boraston (Fin), C. Abbott (Sales & Mktg), C. Knight (MD)
Managers: D. Johnson (Buyer), I. Banks (Tech Serv Mgr), S. Dawkins (Personnel)

see next page

Blaze Neon Ltd - Cont'd

Ultimate Holding Company: BLAZE SIGNS HOLDINGS LIMITED
Immediate Holding Company: BLAZE NEON LIMITED
Registration no: 01524697 **Date established:** 1980
Turnover: £10m - £20m **No.of Employees:** 101 - 250
Product Groups: 30, 37

Date of Accounts	Mar 12	Mar 11	Mar 10
Sales Turnover	15m	15m	11m
Pre Tax Profit/Loss	1m	1m	85
Working Capital	3m	3m	3m
Fixed Assets	3m	2m	2m
Current Assets	6m	7m	5m
Current Liabilities	708	952	537

Denture Clinic

110 High Street, Broadstairs, CT10 1JB
Tel: 01843-600789
E-mail: mikepond@aol.com
Website: http://www.the-denture-clinic.com
Directors: M. Pond (Ptnr)
Immediate Holding Company: M & J AESTHETICS LIMITED
Date established: 2009 **No.of Employees:** 1 - 10 **Product Groups:** 32, 38, 88

Date of Accounts	Mar 11	Mar 10
Sales Turnover	261	235
Pre Tax Profit/Loss	74	88
Working Capital	-37	-33
Fixed Assets	50	46
Current Assets	14	29
Current Liabilities	43	56

Elgate Products Ltd

Patricia Way 1 Pysons Road Industrial Estate, Pysons Road Industrial Estate, Broadstairs, CT10 2LF
Tel: 01843-609200 **Fax:** 01843-866234
E-mail: sales@elgate.co.uk
Website: http://www.elgate.co.uk
Directors: J. Elliott (Dir), W. Venables (Fin), G. Askew (Sales)
Managers: J. Crisp (Personnel)
Immediate Holding Company: ELGATE PRODUCTS LIMITED
Registration no: 01013962 **Date established:** 1971 **Turnover:** £5m - £10m
No.of Employees: 21 - 50 **Product Groups:** 65

Date of Accounts	Dec 11	Dec 10	Dec 09
Sales Turnover	9m	7m	7m
Pre Tax Profit/Loss	353	399	342
Working Capital	2m	1m	2m
Fixed Assets	2m	2m	2m
Current Assets	4m	4m	3m
Current Liabilities	795	830	765

Fujifilm Sericol Ltd

Patricia Way Pysons Road Industrial Estate, Broadstairs, CT10 2LE
Tel: 01843-866668 **Fax:** 01843-872184
E-mail: human.resources@sericol.com
Website: http://www.sericol.co.uk
Bank(s): National Westminster
Directors: R. Wiles (Co Sec), M. Frier (Pers)
Managers: R. Marsh (Purch Mgr), P. Scott (Tech Serv Mgr)
Ultimate Holding Company: FUJIFILM HOLDINGS CORPORATION (JAPAN)
Immediate Holding Company: SERICOL LIMITED
Registration no: 00840375 **VAT No.:** GB 243 5105 93
Date established: 1965 **Turnover:** Up to £250,000
No.of Employees: 251 - 500 **Product Groups:** 32

Date of Accounts	Mar 12	Mar 11	Mar 10
Sales Turnover	20	22	18
Pre Tax Profit/Loss	54	56	52
Working Capital	5m	5m	5m
Current Assets	5m	5m	5m

Herbs Gardens & Health

27 Northdown Road 27 Northdown Road St Peter's, Broadstairs, CT10 2UW
Tel: 01843-600201 **Fax:** 01843-863134
E-mail: info@herbsgardenshealth.com
Website: http://www.herbsgardenshealth.co.uk
Directors: J. Brazil (Prop)
Date established: 2001 **No.of Employees:** 1 - 10 **Product Groups:** 20

D C Homewood Ltd

Unit 2 Oakwood Industrial Estate Dane Valley Road, Broadstairs, CT10 3JL
Tel: 01843-873400 **Fax:** 01843-873402
E-mail: donna@dchomewood.co.uk
Website: http://www.lightingworld.co.uk
Bank(s): Midland
Directors: D. Homewood (Dir)
Managers: M. Kinsella (Mgr)
Immediate Holding Company: D. C. HOMEWOOD LIMITED
Registration no: 01013066 **VAT No.:** GB 202 8205 11
Date established: 1971 **Turnover:** £2m - £5m **No.of Employees:** 11 - 20
Product Groups: 77

Date of Accounts	Mar 11	Mar 10	Mar 09
Working Capital	204	217	169
Fixed Assets	60	34	37
Current Assets	594	556	659
Current Liabilities	N/A	58	N/A

In Signs

The Old Council Yard Dane Valley Road, St Peters, Broadstairs, CT10 3JJ
Tel: 01843-871321 **Fax:** 01843-871321
E-mail: insigns@tiscali.co.uk
Directors: E. Cartland (Prop)
Immediate Holding Company: SATEFORGE LIMITED
Registration no: 04934833 **Date established:** 1977
No.of Employees: 1 - 10 **Product Groups:** 30, 39, 40

Instro Precision Ltd

Unit 15 Pysons Road Industrial Estate Hornet Close, Pysons Road Industrial Estate, Broadstairs, CT10 2YD
Tel: 01843-604455 **Fax:** 01843-861032
E-mail: admin@instro.com
Website: http://www.instro.com
Bank(s): Lloyds TSB Bank plc
Directors: C. Morcom (MD), I. Mitchell (Sales), M. Smith (Comm)
Ultimate Holding Company: S REISMAN LIMITED (ISRAEL)
Immediate Holding Company: INSTRO PRECISION LIMITED
Registration no: 00794972 **Date established:** 1964 **Turnover:** £5m - £10m
No.of Employees: 51 - 100 **Product Groups:** 37, 38, 39, 42, 44, 67

Date of Accounts	Dec 11	Dec 10	Dec 09
Sales Turnover	10m	10m	9m
Pre Tax Profit/Loss	508	22	1m
Working Capital	4m	4m	4m
Fixed Assets	720	841	971
Current Assets	7m	6m	5m
Current Liabilities	769	1m	1m

Inter Resources Europe Ltd

PO Box 153, Broadstairs, CT10 2GT
Tel: 01843-600232 **Fax:** 01843-600232
Website: http://www.stoprust.co.uk
Directors: J. Britton (Dir), J. Glynn (Fin)
Immediate Holding Company: DEEPWATER EU LTD
Registration no: 03757813 **Date established:** 1999
Turnover: £10m - £20m **No.of Employees:** 1 - 10 **Product Groups:** 46, 48

Date of Accounts	Dec 11	Dec 10	Dec 09
Sales Turnover	1m	10m	725
Pre Tax Profit/Loss	9	-51	233
Working Capital	-8	16	-53
Fixed Assets	101	74	18
Current Assets	1m	557	296
Current Liabilities	118	458	52

Medusa

95 Albion Road, Broadstairs, CT10 2UT
Tel: 01843-602500
Directors: L. Davies (Prop)
No.of Employees: 1 - 10 **Product Groups:** 30, 36, 40

Postsafe Ltd

Unit B3 Millennium Way, Broadstairs, CT10 2LA
Tel: 01843-860212 **Fax:** 01843-864393
E-mail: sales@plasticenvelopes.co.uk
Website: http://www.plasticenvelopes.co.uk
Managers: J. Pullman (Chief Mgr)
Immediate Holding Company: POSTSAFE LIMITED
Registration no: 01382347 **Date established:** 1978
No.of Employees: 11 - 20 **Product Groups:** 27, 30, 64, 66

Date of Accounts	Sep 11	Sep 10	Sep 09
Sales Turnover	2m	2m	2m
Pre Tax Profit/Loss	121	67	-53
Working Capital	403	253	131
Fixed Assets	86	153	238
Current Assets	641	540	495
Current Liabilities	83	64	71

Siegrist-Orel Ltd

Hornet Close Pysons Road Industrial Estate, Broadstairs, CT10 2LQ
Tel: 01843-865241 **Fax:** 01843-867180
E-mail: info@siegrist-orel.co.uk
Website: http://www.siegrist-orel.co.uk
Bank(s): National Westminster Bank Plc
Directors: M. Daniell (MD)
Immediate Holding Company: SIEGRIST - OREL LIMITED
Registration no: 00412829 **VAT No.:** GB 201 7143 18
Date established: 1946 **Turnover:** £1m - £2m **No.of Employees:** 21 - 50
Product Groups: 27, 29, 30, 31, 35, 37, 39, 47, 48

Date of Accounts	Apr 11	Apr 10	Apr 09
Working Capital	699	666	638
Fixed Assets	256	236	261
Current Assets	902	869	810

Silent Gliss Ltd

Pyramid Business Park Poorhole Lane, Broadstairs, CT10 2PT
Tel: 01843-863571 **Fax:** 01843-864503
E-mail: info@silentgliss.co.uk
Website: http://www.silentgliss.co.uk
Bank(s): National Westminster Bank Plc
Directors: P. Broennimann (Sales), J. Laslett (Fin)
Managers: M. Wilson, T. Campbell (Tech Serv Mgr), B. Brown (Personnel), S. Shervill (Mktg Serv Mgr), P. Head
Ultimate Holding Company: SILENT GLISS HOLDINGS A G (SWITZERLAND)
Immediate Holding Company: SILENT GLISS LIMITED
Registration no: 00532505 **Date established:** 1954
No.of Employees: 101 - 250 **Product Groups:** 24, 25, 36

Date of Accounts	Dec 11	Dec 10	Dec 09
Pre Tax Profit/Loss	2m	2m	1m
Working Capital	2m	3m	4m
Fixed Assets	5m	5m	5m
Current Assets	6m	6m	6m
Current Liabilities	1m	1m	709

Survey & Test

5 Stone Gardens, Broadstairs, CT10 1EA
Tel: 01843-865269 **Fax:** 01843-865269
E-mail: sales@surveyandtest.com
Website: http://www.surveyandtest.com
Directors: S. Rayfield (Prop)
No.of Employees: 1 - 10 **Product Groups:** 38, 67, 85

Wavelength Electronics Ltd

Kent Innovation Centre Millennium Way Thanet Reach Business Park, Broadstairs, CT10 2QQ
Tel: 01843-609380 **Fax:** 01843-609384
E-mail: sales@wavelengthelectronics.co.uk
Website: http://www.wavelengthelectronics.co.uk
Directors: P. Glover (MD)
Immediate Holding Company: WAVELENGTH ELECTRONICS LIMITED
Registration no: 02755004 **Date established:** 1992
Turnover: £250,000 - £500,000 **No.of Employees:** 1 - 10
Product Groups: 33, 37, 38, 67

Date of Accounts	Dec 11	Dec 10	Dec 09
Working Capital	137	121	140
Fixed Assets	1	2	1
Current Assets	165	198	187

Wilverley Ltd

14 Gladstone Road, Broadstairs, CT10 2HZ
Tel: 01843-603462 **Fax:** 01344-989215
E-mail: mail@wilverley.com
Website: http://www.wilverley.com
Directors: E. Durrant (Prop)
Immediate Holding Company: WILVERLEY FURNITURE LIMITED
Registration no: 06532723 **Date established:** 2008
No.of Employees: 1 - 10 **Product Groups:** 26

Date of Accounts	Mar 11	Mar 10
Working Capital	255	138
Fixed Assets	9	11
Current Assets	269	164

Bromley

Astaroth Solutions

Exchange Apartments Sparkes Close, Bromley, BR2 9EX
Tel: 08458-686914
E-mail: sales@astarothsolutions.com
Website: http://www.astarothsolutions.com
Directors: D. Tremain (Ptnr)
Date established: 2006 **Turnover:** Up to £250,000
No.of Employees: 1 - 10 **Product Groups:** 44

B C R Publishing Ltd

3 Cobden Court Wimpole Close, Bromley, BR2 9JF
Tel: 020-8466 6987 **Fax:** 020-8466 0654
E-mail: mb@bcrpub.co.uk
Website: http://www.bcrpub.co.uk
Directors: M. Bickers (MD)
Immediate Holding Company: BCR PUBLISHING LTD.
Registration no: 03505649 **Date established:** 1998
Turnover: Up to £250,000 **No.of Employees:** 1 - 10 **Product Groups:** 28

Date of Accounts	Apr 11	Apr 10	Apr 09
Working Capital	162	96	94
Fixed Assets	1	2	1
Current Assets	200	126	142

Beulah Packaging Cards Ltd

25 Scotts Road, Bromley, BR1 3QD
Tel: 020-8466 8610 **Fax:** 020-8466 8612
E-mail: mark@beulahpackaging.co.uk
Website: http://www.beulahpackaging.co.uk
Directors: D. Hammond (MD), M. Tanner (MD)
Managers: M. Tanner (I.T. Exec)
Immediate Holding Company: BEULAH PACKAGING CARDS LIMITED
Registration no: SC067666 **Date established:** 1979
Turnover: £500,000 - £1m **No.of Employees:** 1 - 10 **Product Groups:** 27

Date of Accounts	Mar 08	Mar 07	Mar 06
Sales Turnover	N/A	N/A	997
Pre Tax Profit/Loss	N/A	N/A	77
Working Capital	-96	-78	74
Fixed Assets	53	131	161
Current Assets	106	164	307
Current Liabilities	202	241	233
ROCE% (Return on Capital Employed)			32.8
ROT% (Return on Turnover)			7.7

Bromley Brush Co Kent Ltd

1 Pembroke Road, Bromley, BR1 2TJ
Tel: 020-8464 1707 **Fax:** 020-8313 3494
Website: http://www.bromleybrush.co.uk
Directors: T. Robinson (Fin), D. Robinson (MD)
Immediate Holding Company: BROMLEY BRUSH COMPANY (KENT) LIMITED(THE)
Registration no: 00687618 **VAT No.:** GB 205 3074 07
Date established: 1961 **Turnover:** £1m - £2m **No.of Employees:** 1 - 10
Product Groups: 24, 49, 63

Date of Accounts	Mar 12	Mar 11	Mar 10
Working Capital	174	172	170
Fixed Assets	37	40	53
Current Assets	320	316	321

Bromley Gas Service

4 Malling Way, Bromley, BR2 7PJ
Tel: 020-8462 9706
E-mail: sales@bromleygas.co.uk
Website: http://www.bromleygas.co.uk
Directors: M. McCusker (Prop)
Date established: 2002 **Turnover:** Up to £250,000
No.of Employees: 1 - 10 **Product Groups:** 40, 48, 52

Martin Bunzl Ltd

27 London Road, Bromley, BR1 1DF
Tel: 020-8464 4141 **Fax:** 020-8460 2035
E-mail: pferrier@martinbunzl.co.uk
Website: http://www.martinbunzl.co.uk
Directors: P. Ferrier (Fin), D. Bunzl (Dir), M. Bunzl (MD)
Managers: A. Bahra (Export Sales Mg)
Ultimate Holding Company: MARTIN BUNZL INTERNATIONAL LIMITED
Immediate Holding Company: MARTIN BUNZL MARKETING LIMITED
Registration no: 00876306 **VAT No.:** GB 378 4245 23
Date established: 1966 **Turnover:** £10m - £20m **No.of Employees:** 1 - 10
Product Groups: 87

Date of Accounts	Mar 11	Mar 10	Mar 08
Working Capital	818	783	707
Current Assets	828	803	754

C W Gosling Ltd

69a Albert Road, Bromley, BR2 9PZ
Tel: 020-8460 8844 **Fax:** 020-8313 0263
Directors: B. Gosling (MD)
Immediate Holding Company: C.W.GOSLING LIMITED
Registration no: 00388371 **VAT No.:** GB 205 3136 11
Date established: 1944 **Turnover:** £1m - £2m **No.of Employees:** 1 - 10
Product Groups: 52

Date of Accounts	Jun 11	Jun 10	Jun 09
Working Capital	-152	-102	-33
Fixed Assets	1m	1m	860
Current Assets	42	48	73

Carbolic Soap Co. Ltd

Piells Court Yard Bourne Road, Bromley, BR2 9NS
Tel: 020-8460 9999
E-mail: sales@carbolicsoap.com
Website: http://www.carbolicsoaps.com
Directors: J. Martin (MD)
Immediate Holding Company: CARBOLIC SOAP COMPANY LTD
Registration no: 05590365 **Date established:** 2005
No.of Employees: 1 - 10 **Product Groups:** 32

Date of Accounts	Dec 11	Oct 08	Mar 11
Working Capital	6	3	-0
Fixed Assets	4	7	5
Current Assets	29	31	21

Cobra Fabrication

To The Rear of 10 Station Road, Shortlands, Bromley, BR2 0EY
Tel: 020-8313 1642 **Fax:** 020- 84640961
E-mail: bryan@cobrafabrication.co.uk

Managers: P. Froggatt (Mgr)
No.of Employees: 1 - 10 **Product Groups:** 34, 35, 48

Date of Accounts	Sep 06	Sep 05
Working Capital	87	13
Fixed Assets	14	13
Current Assets	170	75
Current Liabilities	83	62
Total Share Capital	1	1

Colland Lift Company

217 Southlands Road, Bromley, BR2 9QZ
Tel: 020-8290 6195 **Fax:** 020-8249 2128
Website: http://www.liftengineers.com
Directors: A. Collins (Ptnr)
Date established: 1989 **No.of Employees:** 1 - 10 **Product Groups:** 35, 39, 45

Cosmos Holidays plc

Wren Court 17 London Road, Bromley, BR1 1DE
Tel: 020-8464 3444 **Fax:** 020-8290 0714
E-mail: rfrancis@cosmos.co.uk
Website: http://www.cosmos.co.uk
Bank(s): National Westminster Bank Plc
Directors: R. Francis (Fin)
Ultimate Holding Company: AMERALD INVESTMENTS NV (NETHERLAND ANTILLES)
Immediate Holding Company: COSMOS HOLIDAYS LIMITED
Registration no: 02098654 **VAT No.:** GB 668 0236 27
Date established: 1987 **Turnover:** £125m - £250m
No.of Employees: 101 - 250 **Product Groups:** 69

Date of Accounts	Oct 11	Oct 10	Oct 09
Sales Turnover	162m	154m	168m
Pre Tax Profit/Loss	2m	18m	-33m
Working Capital	5m	3m	-20m
Fixed Assets	1m	2m	2m
Current Assets	50m	47m	39m
Current Liabilities	31m	27m	46m

Elevators Ltd

Clarindon Business Centre 21-23 Elmfield Road, Bromley, BR1 1LT
Tel: 020-8315 6738 **Fax:** 020-8315 6739
E-mail: rich@elevatorsltd.co.uk
Website: http://www.elevatorsltd.co.uk
Directors: R. Cohen (Dir)
Immediate Holding Company: ELEVATORS LTD
Registration no: 04463335 **Date established:** 2002
Turnover: £500,000 - £1m **No.of Employees:** 1 - 10 **Product Groups:** 39, 45, 48, 67

Date of Accounts	Jun 11	Jun 10	Jun 09
Sales Turnover	N/A	587	834
Pre Tax Profit/Loss	N/A	117	132
Working Capital	16	22	19
Fixed Assets	16	20	24
Current Assets	94	156	180
Current Liabilities	N/A	102	116

Functional Art Ltd Use your art

127 Homesdale Road, Bromley, BR2 9LE
Tel: 07818-423001
E-mail: info@functional-art.co.uk
Website: http://www.functional-art.co.uk
Registration no: 06477887 **Product Groups:** 32, 36, 65

Geologistics Ltd

Royal Court 81 Tweedy Road, Bromley, BR1 1TW
Tel: 020-8460 5050 **Fax:** 020-8461 8884
E-mail: prandall@geo-logistics.com
Website: http://www.geo-logistics.com
Bank(s): Barclays
Directors: G. Papageorghiou (Fin)
Managers: P. Randall (District Mgr), A. Watts, C. Wheelden, M. Tindall, S. Finch, L. Phillips
Ultimate Holding Company: Geologistics Corp.
Registration no: 00112456 **VAT No.:** GB 243 5125 87
Date established: 1849 **Turnover:** Up to £250,000
No.of Employees: 51 - 100 **Product Groups:** 72, 75, 76, 77

Group Sigma Ltd

143 Westmoreland Road, Bromley, BR2 0TY
Tel: 020-8460 9191 **Fax:** 020-8460 3969
E-mail: info@groupsigma.com
Website: http://www.groupsigma.com
Directors: S. Barns (Fin), M. Safey (MD)
Immediate Holding Company: SIGMA LTD
Registration no: 04573475 **Date established:** 2002
Turnover: £250,000 - £500,000 **No.of Employees:** 1 - 10
Product Groups: 81

Date of Accounts	Oct 10	Oct 09	Oct 08
Pre Tax Profit/Loss	N/A	N/A	-0
Working Capital	N/A	N/A	36
Current Assets	N/A	N/A	36
Current Liabilities	N/A	N/A	1

H M T Rubbaglas Ltd

2a Newman Road, Bromley, BR1 1RJ
Tel: 020-8464 7888 **Fax:** 020-8464 7788
E-mail: info@hmttank.com
Website: http://www.hmttank.com
Bank(s): Barclays P.L.C.
Directors: S. Wong (Co Sec)
Managers: D. Cheeseman
Ultimate Holding Company: HMTBP HOLDINGS INC (USA)
Immediate Holding Company: HMT RUBBAGLAS LIMITED
Registration no: 04149257 **VAT No.:** GB 236 2650 72
Date established: 2001 **Turnover:** £10m - £20m
No.of Employees: 11 - 20 **Product Groups:** 36

Date of Accounts	Dec 11	Dec 10	Dec 09
Sales Turnover	16m	11m	10m
Pre Tax Profit/Loss	224	287	875
Working Capital	3m	4m	4m
Fixed Assets	2m	34	41
Current Assets	8m	9m	8m
Current Liabilities	2m	2m	3m

Harry Taylor Of Ashton Ltd

Kitsons Works Aylesbury Road, Bromley, BR2 0QZ
Tel: 020-8464 0915 **Fax:** 020-8464 0916
E-mail: info@harrytaylor.co.uk
Website: http://www.harrytaylor.co.uk
Directors: J. Howard (MD)
Managers: J. Jenkins (Sales Prom Mgr)
Immediate Holding Company: HARRY TAYLOR OF ASHTON LIMITED
Registration no: 00742009 **Date established:** 1962 **Turnover:** £1m - £2m
No.of Employees: 21 - 50 **Product Groups:** 40, 66

Date of Accounts	Mar 11	Mar 10	Mar 09
Working Capital	382	412	279
Fixed Assets	4m	4m	4m
Current Assets	806	896	729

Hinges & Brackets

18 London Road, Bromley, BR1 3QR
Tel: 020-8466 9992 **Fax:** 020-8460 2203
E-mail: info@hingesandbrackets.com
Website: http://www.hingesandbrackets.co.uk
Managers: V. Patel (Mgr)
Date established: 1985 **No.of Employees:** 1 - 10 **Product Groups:** 35, 36

Kent Catering Services

Unit T The Enterprise Centre 27 Hastings Road, Bromley, BR2 8NA
Tel: 020-8462 9911 **Fax:** 020- 84629922
E-mail: info@kentcatering.com
Website: http://www.kentcatering.com
Directors: D. Clarke (Prop)
Date established: 1994 **No.of Employees:** 11 - 20 **Product Groups:** 20, 40, 41

Law & Accountancy Agency Services Ltd

42-44 Prospect Place, Bromley, BR2 9HN
Tel: 020-7250 1410 **Fax:** 020-7250 1973
E-mail: paul.payne@lawact.co.uk
Website: http://www.lawact.co.uk
Directors: B. Griffin (MD), P. Payne (Dir), P. Payne (MD)
Immediate Holding Company: LAW & ACCOUNTANCY (AGENCY SERVICES) LIMITED
Registration no: 01469987 **Date established:** 1979 **Turnover:** £1m - £2m
No.of Employees: 1 - 10 **Product Groups:** 80

Date of Accounts	Aug 10	Aug 09	Aug 08
Working Capital	304	305	357
Fixed Assets	509	529	557
Current Assets	427	400	494

Niche Lifts Ltd

27 London Road, Bromley, BR1 1DG
Tel: 020-8295 2852 **Fax:** 020-8467 1044
E-mail: info@nichelifts.com
Website: http://www.nichelifts.com
Directors: T. Pamment (MD)
Ultimate Holding Company: MOCAD LIMITED
Immediate Holding Company: NICHE LIFTS LTD
Registration no: 04948731 **Date established:** 2003
No.of Employees: 1 - 10 **Product Groups:** 35, 39, 45

Date of Accounts	Mar 12	Mar 11	Mar 10
Working Capital	128	50	22
Fixed Assets	5	6	9
Current Assets	380	201	267

Patron Lifts

47a College Road, Bromley, BR1 3PU
Tel: 020-8466 8499 **Fax:** 020-8466 8405
E-mail: sales@patronlifts.com
Website: http://www.patronlifts.com
Directors: S. Hull (MD)
Immediate Holding Company: PATRON LIFTS LIMITED
Registration no: 03102514 **Date established:** 1995
No.of Employees: 1 - 10 **Product Groups:** 35, 39, 45

Date of Accounts	Dec 11	Dec 10	Dec 09
Working Capital	198	159	31
Fixed Assets	8	11	9
Current Assets	492	752	711

Pritchitts

21-23 Elmfield Road, Bromley, BR1 1LT
Tel: 020-8290 7020 **Fax:** 020-8290 7030
E-mail: info@pritchitts.com
Website: http://www.pritchitts.com
Managers: S. Muschamp
Immediate Holding Company: MOBILE 5 LIMITED
Registration no: 05359513 **Date established:** 2005
Turnover: £500,000 - £1m **No.of Employees:** 21 - 50
Product Groups: 20, 62, 67

Date of Accounts	Mar 11	Mar 10	Mar 09
Sales Turnover	N/A	N/A	520
Pre Tax Profit/Loss	N/A	N/A	62
Working Capital	113	48	3
Fixed Assets	19	14	9
Current Assets	211	208	49

Reed Accountancy Personnel Ltd

28 High Street, Bromley, BR1 1EA
Tel: 020-8290 6688 **Fax:** 020-8464 6696
E-mail: rapbromley@reed.co.uk
Website: http://www.reed.co.uk
Managers: A. Goodfellow (Mgr), A. Goodfellow (District Mgr), S. Wall (Chief Mgr)
Immediate Holding Company: Reed Personnel Services Ltd
Registration no: 00973629 **Turnover:** £125m - £250m
No.of Employees: 1 - 10 **Product Groups:** 80

Reed Employment Ltd

12 Elmfield Road, Bromley, BR1 1LR
Tel: 020-8315 4600 **Fax:** 020-8315 4601
E-mail: simon.dudley@reedglobal.com
Website: http://www.reed.co.uk
Managers: R. Griffiths (Mgr)
Ultimate Holding Company: REED GLOBAL LTD (MALTA)
Immediate Holding Company: REED EMPLOYMENT LIMITED
Registration no: 00669854 **Date established:** 1960
Turnover: £250m - £500m **No.of Employees:** 1 - 10 **Product Groups:** 80

Date of Accounts	Jun 11	Jun 10	Dec 07
Sales Turnover	618	450	287m
Pre Tax Profit/Loss	-2m	310	8m
Working Capital	23m	28m	28m
Fixed Assets	31	36	5m
Current Assets	28m	30m	74m
Current Liabilities	37	29	21m

Russell & Bromley Ltd

24-54 Farwig Lane, Bromley, BR1 3RB
Tel: 020-8460 1122 **Fax:** 020-8460 4424
E-mail: roger.bromley@russellandbromley.co.uk
Website: http://www.russellandbromley.co.uk
Directors: R. Bromley (Dir)
Managers: J. Brown (Personnel), B. Reagan, E. Allingham, S. Graham (Tech Serv Mgr)
Immediate Holding Company: RUSSELL & BROMLEY LIMITED
Registration no: 00512958 **Date established:** 1952
Turnover: £75m - £125m **No.of Employees:** 51 - 100
Product Groups: 22, 63

Date of Accounts	Dec 11	Dec 10	Dec 09
Sales Turnover	101m	96m	88m
Pre Tax Profit/Loss	21m	19m	14m
Working Capital	26m	26m	26m
Fixed Assets	28m	27m	26m
Current Assets	38m	38m	37m
Current Liabilities	10m	10m	8m

Shaw Security

5a The Gable Beaconsfield Road, Bromley, BR1 2BL
Tel: 020-8313 3535
E-mail: ian@shawsecurity.co.uk
Website: http://www.shawsecurity.co.uk
Directors: I. Shaw (Prop)
Turnover: Up to £250,000 **No.of Employees:** 1 - 10 **Product Groups:** 35, 36, 66

Skills Workshop Ltd

168 Ravensbourne Avenue, Bromley, BR2 0AY
Tel: 020-8460 3557
E-mail: skillsworkshop@hotmail.co.uk
Website: http://www.skillsworkshop.net
Directors: M. Wood (MD)
Managers: M. Wood (Consultant)
Immediate Holding Company: SKILLS WORKSHOP LIMITED
Registration no: 04592281 **Date established:** 2002
Turnover: Up to £250,000 **No.of Employees:** 1 - 10 **Product Groups:** 86

Date of Accounts	Mar 10	Mar 09	Mar 07
Working Capital	12	16	12
Fixed Assets	N/A	N/A	3
Current Assets	50	40	28

Stephen Whitby Plumbing & Heating

99 College Road, Bromley, BR1 3QG
Tel: 020-8460 8627
E-mail: info@plumber-bromley.co.uk
Website: http://www.plumber-bromley.co.uk
Directors: S. Whitby (Prop)
No.of Employees: 1 - 10 **Product Groups:** 40, 52, 66

Michael Stevens & Partners Ltd

Invicta Works Elliott Road, Bromley, BR2 9NT
Tel: 020-8460 7299 **Fax:** 020-8460 0499
E-mail: penelope.stevens@michael-stevens.com
Website: http://www.michael-stevens.com
Directors: P. Stevens (Fin), M. Stevens (Ch)
Managers: S. Adamson (Asst Gen Mgr)
Immediate Holding Company: CHROMATEC VIDEO PRODUCTS LIMITED
Registration no: 02064683 **Date established:** 1986 **Turnover:** £1m - £2m
No.of Employees: 1 - 10 **Product Groups:** 38, 40

Date of Accounts	Nov 07	Nov 06	Nov 05
Working Capital	130	231	283
Fixed Assets	88	88	68
Current Assets	322	348	416
Current Liabilities	193	117	133
Total Share Capital	1	1	1

Tool Room

25 Widmore Road, Bromley, BR1 1RW
Tel: 020-8466 6040 **Fax:** 020- 84669070
Managers: J. Weller (Mgr)
Date established: 1988 **No.of Employees:** 1 - 10 **Product Groups:** 37

Union Transport Group plc

Imperial House 21-25 North Street, Bromley, BR1 1SJ
Tel: 020-8290 1234 **Fax:** 020-8402 7770
E-mail: paul.watkins@uniontransport.co.uk
Website: http://www.uniontransport.co.uk
Bank(s): Barclays
Directors: P. Watkins (Co Sec)
Immediate Holding Company: UNION TRANSPORT GROUP PLC
Registration no: 00417277 **VAT No.:** GB 512 8825 47
Date established: 1946 **Turnover:** £20m - £50m
No.of Employees: 11 - 20 **Product Groups:** 39, 74, 76

Date of Accounts	Sep 11	Sep 10	Sep 09
Sales Turnover	21m	17m	18m
Pre Tax Profit/Loss	-2m	-1m	-5m
Working Capital	-15m	-10m	-5m
Fixed Assets	19m	16m	11m
Current Assets	3m	3m	3m
Current Liabilities	2m	1m	223

Canterbury

A D M Computing

Chaucer Road, Canterbury, CT1 1HH
Tel: 01227-473530 **Fax:** 01227-473509
E-mail: adrian@adm-computing.co.uk
Website: http://www.admcomputing.co.uk
Directors: A. Bryant (Prop)
Managers: M. Knibbs, L. Sinclair (Personnel), J. Simmons (Purch Mgr), A. Noronha (Fin Mgr)
Immediate Holding Company: KENT TECHNICAL SERVICES LTD
Registration no: 06770432 **Date established:** 2008 **Turnover:** £2m - £5m
No.of Employees: 21 - 50 **Product Groups:** 44

Date of Accounts	Dec 11	Dec 10	Dec 09
Working Capital	58	53	46
Current Assets	71	68	97

Accappella
Nightingale Farm Whiteacre Lane, Waltham, Canterbury, CT4 5SR
Tel: 0770-8925412
E-mail: emma@accappellastudio.co.uk
Website: http://www.accappellastudio.co.uk
Directors: E. Scott (Prop)
Managers: J. Pattison (Designer)
No.of Employees: 1 - 10 **Product Groups:** 26, 28

Arjo Wiggins Chartham Ltd
The Mill Station Road, Chartham, Canterbury, CT4 7JA
Tel: 01227-813500 **Fax:** 01227-738883
E-mail: mark.hobday@arjowiggins.com
Website: http://www.arjowiggins-tracingpapers.com
Bank(s): Lloyds TSB Bank plc
Managers: I. Castle, J. Marshall (Personnel), G. Howard (Purch Mgr), C. Payne (Purch Mgr), J. Marshall (Personnel), J. Barclay (Sales & Mktg Mg), I. Castle, C. Higginbottom (Tech Serv Mgr), C. Higenbottam, M. Hobday (Mgr)
Ultimate Holding Company: SEQUANA SA (FRANCE)
Immediate Holding Company: ARJOWIGGINS CHARTHAM LIMITED
Registration no: 04915241 **VAT No.:** GB 238 5870 31
Date established: 2003 **Turnover:** Over £1,000m
No.of Employees: 101 - 250 **Product Groups:** 27

Date of Accounts	Dec 11	Dec 10	Dec 09
Sales Turnover	17m	18m	15m
Pre Tax Profit/Loss	-3m	432	-684
Working Capital	-3m	-1m	-2m
Fixed Assets	6m	8m	8m
Current Assets	4m	5m	5m
Current Liabilities	976	1m	1m

Blighline Ltd
Unit 5-10 Sparrow Way Lakesview International Business Park, Hersden, Canterbury, CT3 4JQ
Tel: 01227-712000 **Fax:** 01227-719000
E-mail: roy.corker@blighline.co.uk
Website: http://www.blighline.co.uk
Directors: A. Richardson (Fin), L. Crush (I.T. Dir), M. Thomas (Purch), R. Corker (Fin), S. Sparrow (MD)
Immediate Holding Company: BLIGHLINE LIMITED
Registration no: 01005112 **Date established:** 1971
Turnover: £20m - £50m **No.of Employees:** 1 - 10 **Product Groups:** 26, 40, 52

Date of Accounts	Dec 08	Dec 07	Dec 06
Sales Turnover	30m	38m	31m
Pre Tax Profit/Loss	-483	-862	2m
Working Capital	-2m	-626	441
Fixed Assets	7m	7m	7m
Current Assets	7m	10m	9m
Current Liabilities	835	655	1m

Brett Specialised Aggregates
Sturry Quarry Fordwich Road, Sturry, Canterbury, CT2 0BW
Tel: 08456-080572 **Fax:** 08456-080573
E-mail: sales@brett-specialised-aggregates.co.uk
Website: http://www.brett.co.uk
Managers: R. Hardes (Mgr)
Ultimate Holding Company: ROBERT BRETT & SONS LTD
Immediate Holding Company: BRETT AGGREGATES LTD
Registration no: 00000316 **VAT No.:** GB 201 1388 18
Turnover: £2m - £5m **No.of Employees:** 1 - 10 **Product Groups:** 14, 33

Brinkman Engineering
3 Wingham Industrial Estate Goodnestone Road, Wingham, Canterbury, CT3 1AR
Tel: 01227-721040 **Fax:** 01227-728094
E-mail: enquiries@brinkmanengineering.co.uk
Website: http://www.brinkmanengineering.co.uk
Directors: A. Brinkman (Prop)
Registration no: 03801137 **Date established:** 1999
Turnover: Up to £250,000 **No.of Employees:** 1 - 10 **Product Groups:** 41

C Brewer & Sons
Maynard Road Wincheap Industrial Estate, Canterbury, CT1 3RJ
Tel: 01227-863800 **Fax:** 01227-863801
E-mail: decorating@brewers.co.uk
Website: http://www.brewers.co.uk
Managers: B. Hughes (District Mgr), M. Bragg (Mgr)
Immediate Holding Company: C.BREWER & SONS LIMITED
Registration no: 00203852 **VAT No.:** GB 197 1565 70
Date established: 1925 **Turnover:** £50m - £75m
No.of Employees: 11 - 20 **Product Groups:** 61

Canterbury Cathedral Shop
25 Burgate, Canterbury, CT1 2HA
Tel: 01227-865300 **Fax:** 01227-865333
E-mail: enquiries@cathedral-enterprises.co.uk
Website: http://www.cathedral-enterprises.co.uk
Directors: B. Meardon (Co Sec)
Managers: C. Needham (Chief Mgr)
Immediate Holding Company: CANTERBURY CATHEDRAL TRUST FUND
Registration no: 05588837 **Date established:** 2005 **Turnover:** £1m - £2m
No.of Employees: 21 - 50 **Product Groups:** 65

Date of Accounts	Mar 11	Mar 10	Mar 09
Sales Turnover	2m	2m	2m
Pre Tax Profit/Loss	531	85	-220
Working Capital	233	202	117
Fixed Assets	500	N/A	N/A
Current Assets	272	297	192
Current Liabilities	39	90	74

Canterbury Christ Church University College
North Holmes Road, Canterbury, CT1 1QU
Tel: 01227-767700 **Fax:** 01227-470442
E-mail: robin.baker@canterbury.ac.uk
Website: http://www.canterbury.ac.uk
Managers: R. Higgins, R. Baker, D. Leah, I. Ellery (Tech Serv Mgr)
Immediate Holding Company: CANTERBURY CHRIST CHURCH UNIVERSITY
Registration no: 04793659 **Date established:** 2003
Turnover: £75m - £125m **No.of Employees:** 1001 - 1500
Product Groups: 86

Date of Accounts	Jul 11	Jul 10	Jul 09
Sales Turnover	119m	113m	103m
Pre Tax Profit/Loss	9m	5m	4m
Working Capital	-2m	-11m	-16m
Fixed Assets	129m	116m	106m
Current Assets	29m	17m	17m
Current Liabilities	18m	20m	26m

Claremont & May
Unit 11 Claremont Way Lakesview International Business Park, Hersden, Canterbury, CT3 4JG
Tel: 08707-569999 **Fax:** 0870-410 2550
E-mail: info@claremontandmay.com
Website: http://www.claremontandmay.com
Bank(s): HSBC Bank plc
Directors: S. Khan (Prop), S. Khan (MD)
Managers: M. Harding (Export Sales Mg)
Immediate Holding Company: S K BRAND MANAGEMENT LIMITED
Registration no: 06828350 **VAT No.:** GB 571 9317 25
Date established: 2009 **No.of Employees:** 11 - 20 **Product Groups:** 24, 26, 31, 32, 33, 35, 36, 63

Crossley & Davis
The Coach House 7 Mill Road, Sturry, Canterbury, CT2 0AJ
Tel: 01227-712714 **Fax:** 01227-712721
E-mail: finance@crossleydavis.com
Website: http://www.crossleydavis.com
Directors: M. Marsh (Prop)
Immediate Holding Company: CROSSLEY + DAVIS LIMITED
Registration no: 02846688 **Date established:** 1993
Turnover: £250,000 - £500,000 **No.of Employees:** 1 - 10
Product Groups: 80

Date of Accounts	Jul 11	Jul 10	Jul 09
Working Capital	338	299	37
Fixed Assets	13	13	260
Current Assets	517	482	129

Elite Blinds
38 The Hill Littlebourne, Canterbury, CT3 1TA
Tel: 01227-720881 **Fax:** 01227-720902
E-mail: info@elite-blinds.co.uk
Website: http://www.kentblinds.co.uk
Directors: D. Lester (Ptnr)
No.of Employees: 1 - 10 **Product Groups:** 35, 63, 66

A Gomez Ltd
Cold Harbour Lane Patrixbourne, Canterbury, CT4 5HL
Tel: 01227-832121 **Fax:** 01227-831894
E-mail: sales@agomez.co.uk
Website: http://www.agomez.co.uk
Directors: I. Sullivan (Dir)
Immediate Holding Company: A GOMEZ LIMITED
Registration no: 02446884 **VAT No.:** GB 239 1127 74
Date established: 1989 **Turnover:** £75m - £125m
No.of Employees: 251 - 500 **Product Groups:** 62

Date of Accounts	Sep 11	Sep 10	Sep 09
Sales Turnover	109m	87m	90m
Pre Tax Profit/Loss	5m	2m	2m
Working Capital	2m	409	469
Fixed Assets	9m	9m	10m
Current Assets	17m	11m	11m
Current Liabilities	2m	2m	1m

Graham
Roper Road, Canterbury, CT2 7RJ
Tel: 01227-451274 **Fax:** 01227-763594
Website: http://www.graham-group.co.uk
Managers: C. Standdard (Mgr)
Ultimate Holding Company: SAINT-GOBAIN PLC
Immediate Holding Company: GRAHAM GROUP LTD
Registration no: 00066738 **Turnover:** £250,000 - £500,000
No.of Employees: 1 - 10 **Product Groups:** 40, 52

Inca Geometric Ltd
Bolts Hill Chartham, Canterbury, CT4 7JZ
Tel: 01227-738565 **Fax:** 01227-730915
E-mail: sales@inca-ltd.demon.co.uk
Website: http://www.incageometric.com
Directors: A. Cain (Fin), M. Cain (Dir)
Immediate Holding Company: INCA GEOMETRIC LIMITED
Registration no: 01731487 **Date established:** 1983
Turnover: £500,000 - £1m **No.of Employees:** 21 - 50
Product Groups: 38, 46

Date of Accounts	Jun 11	Jun 10	Jun 09
Working Capital	239	267	363
Fixed Assets	787	761	573
Current Assets	434	424	480

Invicta Paints
59-61 Sturry Road, Canterbury, CT1 1DR
Tel: 01227-866146 **Fax:** 01227-864718
E-mail: geoff.nickols@invictamotors.com
Website: http://www.invictamotors.co.uk
Managers: G. Nickols (Mgr)
Registration no: 02953829 **VAT No.:** GB 218 1290 83
Turnover: £2m - £5m **No.of Employees:** 1 - 10 **Product Groups:** 68

Jewson Ltd
Riverdale Road, Canterbury, CT1 1TG
Tel: 01227-761171 **Fax:** 01227-450322
Website: http://www.jewson.co.uk
Directors: P. Hindle (Grp Chief Exec)
Managers: A. King (District Mgr)
Ultimate Holding Company: COMPAGNIE DE SAINT GOBAIN (FRANCE)
Immediate Holding Company: JEWSON LIMITED
Registration no: 00348407 **VAT No.:** GB 497 7184 83
Date established: 1939 **Turnover:** £500,000 - £1m
No.of Employees: 11 - 20 **Product Groups:** 66

Date of Accounts	Dec 11	Dec 10	Dec 09
Sales Turnover	1606m	1547m	1485m
Pre Tax Profit/Loss	18m	100m	45m
Working Capital	-345m	-250m	-349m
Fixed Assets	496m	387m	461m
Current Assets	657m	1005m	1320m
Current Liabilities	66m	120m	64m

Ken Kimble Reactor Vessel Ltd
Unit 85 Thomas Way Lakesview International Business Park, Hersden, Canterbury, CT3 4NH
Tel: 01227-710274 **Fax:** 01732-885840
E-mail: general@kenkimble.co.uk
Website: http://www.kenkimble.com
Directors: A. Kimble (MD)
Immediate Holding Company: KEN KIMBLE (REACTOR VESSELS) LIMITED
Registration no: 01266476 **VAT No.:** GB 207 4839 57
Date established: 1976 **Turnover:** £1m - £2m **No.of Employees:** 1 - 10
Product Groups: 33, 35, 38, 40, 42

Date of Accounts	Jun 11	Jun 10	Jun 09
Sales Turnover	1m	597	592
Pre Tax Profit/Loss	95	21	-99
Working Capital	323	240	214
Fixed Assets	84	97	81
Current Assets	405	317	328
Current Liabilities	56	22	17

Kingsmead Associates
Goose Farm Shalloak Road, Broad Oak, Canterbury, CT2 0QE
Tel: 01227-713386 **Fax:** 01227-713386
Directors: M. Hargreaves (Prop)
Date established: 1994 **No.of Employees:** 1 - 10 **Product Groups:** 26, 35

Lambak Engineering
6 Broadlands Indl-Est Blean Common, Blean, Canterbury, CT2 9JQ
Tel: 01227-768285
Directors: K. Lamb (Ptnr)
Date established: 1988 **No.of Employees:** 1 - 10 **Product Groups:** 35

M A R C Co GB Ltd
Rear of Gardeners Paradise Stodmarsh Road, Canterbury, CT3 4AP
Tel: 01227-459999 **Fax:** 01227-459990
E-mail: info@marcltd.com
Website: http://www.marcltd.com
Directors: C. Hanks (Dir)
Immediate Holding Company: M.A.R.C. (CO. GB) LIMITED
Registration no: 03226364 **Date established:** 1996
No.of Employees: 1 - 10 **Product Groups:** 13, 18, 24, 25, 26, 33, 36, 39, 40, 67

Date of Accounts	Jul 12	Jul 11	Jul 10
Working Capital	73	126	250
Fixed Assets	32	36	32
Current Assets	90	240	421

Ovenden Earthmoving Company Ltd
Wellhead Farm Wingham Well, Canterbury, CT3 1NS
Tel: 01227-720777 **Fax:** 01227-728332
E-mail: info@ovenden.biz
Website: http://www.ovenden.biz
Product Groups: 31, 33, 42, 45, 51, 52

Date of Accounts	Mar 11	Mar 10	Mar 09
Sales Turnover	8m	7m	N/A
Pre Tax Profit/Loss	458	135	553
Working Capital	-1m	-1m	-1m
Fixed Assets	5m	4m	5m
Current Assets	2m	1m	1m
Current Liabilities	844	309	379

P A V Products Ltd
Canterbury Industrial Park Island Road, Hersden, Canterbury, CT3 4HQ
Tel: 01227-712329 **Fax:** 01227-712911
Directors: P. Vango (MD)
Immediate Holding Company: PAV PRODUCTS LTD
Registration no: 01727954 **Date established:** 1983
Turnover: Up to £250,000 **No.of Employees:** 1 - 10 **Product Groups:** 48

Date of Accounts	Aug 11	Aug 09	Aug 08
Working Capital	379	393	378
Fixed Assets	153	154	160
Current Assets	432	476	461

Paint Pig & PXL Pig
22 Island Road Sturry, Canterbury, CT2 0ED
Tel: 01227-710305
E-mail: chris@pxlpig.com
Website: http://www.paintpig.co.uk
Directors: C. Taylor (Prop)
Registration no: 06525491 **Date established:** 2006
Turnover: Up to £250,000 **No.of Employees:** 1 - 10 **Product Groups:** 81, 84

Preco Europe Inc
81-82 Castle Street, Canterbury, CT1 2QD
Tel: 01227-473900 **Fax:** 01227-473901
E-mail: sales@precoindustries.com
Website: http://www.precoinc.com
Directors: M. Regan (MD)
Immediate Holding Company: PRECO EUROPE, INC.
Registration no: FC019669 **Date established:** 1996
Turnover: Up to £250,000 **No.of Employees:** 1 - 10 **Product Groups:** 46

Date of Accounts	Dec 09	Dec 08	Dec 05
Sales Turnover	226	319	280
Pre Tax Profit/Loss	28	11	4
Working Capital	30	1	-99
Fixed Assets	3	5	1
Current Assets	33	25	56
Current Liabilities	2	23	153

Robins Paper Bag Co. Ltd
Unit 6A Thomas Way, Lakesview International Business Park, Hersden, Canterbury, CT3 4JZ
Tel: 01227-714933 **Fax:** 01227-719750
E-mail: info@robinspkg.co.uk
Website: http://www.robinspkg.co.uk
Bank(s): Nat West
Directors: P. Robins (MD)
Managers: D. Amos (Purch Mgr), S. Cuming (Sales Prom Mgr), K. Williams (Accounts), T. Maidment (Mktg Serv Mgr)
Registration no: 00683597 **VAT No.:** GB 201 0205 57
Date established: 1930 **Turnover:** £500,000 - £1m
No.of Employees: 11 - 20 **Product Groups:** 22, 24, 27, 28, 30, 40, 66

Date of Accounts	Mar 12	Mar 11	Mar 10
Working Capital	336	290	214
Fixed Assets	124	119	121
Current Assets	563	517	408

S J L Fabrications
Unit 5 Wingham Industrial Estate Goodnestone Road, Wingham, Canterbury, CT3 1AR
Tel: 01227-720886 **Fax:** 01227-721133
E-mail: enquiries@sjlfabs.co.uk
Website: http://www.sjlfabs.co.uk

Directors: S. Sandford (Ptnr)
Immediate Holding Company: WINGHAM TIMBER & MOULDINGS LIMITED
Registration no: 06602625 **Date established:** 1981
No.of Employees: 1 - 10 **Product Groups:** 35

Date of Accounts	May 11	May 10	May 09
Working Capital	265	179	290
Fixed Assets	141	172	170
Current Assets	938	834	795
Current Liabilities	259	242	187

Showan Hydraulics
Unit 5 Aylesham Industrial Estate Aylesham, Canterbury, CT3 3EP
Tel: 01227-832000 **Fax:** 01227-831000
E-mail: sales@showan.com
Website: http://www.showan.com
Directors: J. Showan (Prop)
Turnover: £500,000 - £1m **No.of Employees:** 1 - 10 **Product Groups:** 28, 44, 49, 65

Triangle Integrated Fire Systems
Orchard House Orchard Street, Canterbury, CT2 8AJ
Tel: 01227-471473 **Fax:** 01227-471475
E-mail: info@triangle-integrated.co.uk
Website: http://www.triangle-integrated.co.uk
Directors: P. Boorman (Fin)
Immediate Holding Company: Triangle Integrated Services Ltd
Registration no: 03293140 **Date established:** 1996
No.of Employees: 1 - 10 **Product Groups:** 40, 52, 67

Viridian Envirosolutions Ltd
81 Thomas Way Lakesview International Business Park Hersden, Canterbury, CT3 4NH
Tel: 01227-713999 **Fax:** 01227-713607
E-mail: info@viridian.biz
Directors: C. Burton (MD), R. Walter (Dir)
Immediate Holding Company: VIRIDIAN ENVIROSOLUTIONS LTD
Registration no: 02354085 **Date established:** 1989
No.of Employees: 1 - 10 **Product Groups:** 31, 42

Date of Accounts	Dec 11	Dec 10	Dec 09
Working Capital	38	36	40
Current Assets	60	71	74

Chatham

A L Industrial Doors
6 Celestine Close, Chatham, ME5 9NG
Tel: 0783-675 5562 **Fax:** 01634-685029
Directors: A. Mitchell (Prop)
No.of Employees: 1 - 10 **Product Groups:** 26, 35

Airspace Avionics Ltd
7-8 New Road Avenue, Chatham, ME4 6BB
Tel: 01634-843878 **Fax:** 01634-401361
E-mail: peterfarrer@airspaceavionics.co.uk
Website: http://www.airspaceavionics.co.uk
Directors: P. Farrer (Dir)
Immediate Holding Company: AIRSPACE AVIONICS LIMITED
Registration no: 04206283 **Date established:** 2001
Turnover: Up to £250,000 **No.of Employees:** 11 - 20 **Product Groups:** 37, 39, 47

Date of Accounts	Apr 11	Apr 10	Apr 09
Working Capital	91	76	12
Fixed Assets	1	2	1
Current Assets	127	187	86

Astrosyn International Technolgy Ltd
The Old Courthouse New Road Avenue, Chatham, ME4 6BE
Tel: 01634-815175 **Fax:** 01634-826552
E-mail: astrosyn@btinternet.com
Website: http://www.astrosyn.com
Bank(s): Lloyds TSB Bank plc
Directors: D. Turner (Fin), S. Hunt (Dir)
Ultimate Holding Company: ASTROSYN LIMITED
Immediate Holding Company: ASTROSYN INTERNATIONAL TECHNOLOGY LIMITED
Registration no: 01188550 **VAT No.:** GB 204 5376 84
Date established: 1974 **Turnover:** Up to £250,000
No.of Employees: 11 - 20 **Product Groups:** 37, 38

Date of Accounts	Apr 11	Apr 10	Apr 09
Working Capital	123	552	459
Fixed Assets	196	202	183
Current Assets	623	1m	982

C Atkin
3 Princes Avenue, Chatham, ME5 8BA
Tel: 01634-687578 **Fax:** 01634-687578
Directors: C. Atkin (Prop)
Date established: 1995 **No.of Employees:** 1 - 10 **Product Groups:** 46, 48

Axia Consulting
17 New Road Avenue, Chatham, ME4 6BA
Tel: 01634-848894 **Fax:** 01634-868894
E-mail: info@axia-consulting.co.uk
Website: http://www.axia-consulting.co.uk
Directors: R. Starling (Dir)
Immediate Holding Company: AXIA CONSULTING LIMITED
Registration no: 02956595 **Date established:** 1994
Turnover: Up to £250,000 **No.of Employees:** 1 - 10 **Product Groups:** 44

Date of Accounts	Dec 11	Dec 10	Dec 09
Working Capital	18	21	16
Fixed Assets	1	N/A	1
Current Assets	20	24	19
Current Liabilities	1	3	2

C L Fabrications
Chatham Docks, Chatham, ME4 4SW
Tel: 01634-819787 **Fax:** 01634-891809
E-mail: ian@clfabs.co.uk
Website: http://www.clfabs.co.uk
Bank(s): National Westminster Bank Plc
Directors: I. Reynolds (Dir)
Immediate Holding Company: EUROPEAN ACTIVE PROJECTS LIMITED
Registration no: 03662185 **VAT No.:** GB 573 8164 17
Date established: 2005 **Turnover:** £500,000 - £1m
No.of Employees: 11 - 20 **Product Groups:** 48, 66

Date of Accounts	May 12	May 11	May 10
Working Capital	44	-100	-36
Fixed Assets	179	143	66
Current Assets	828	408	512

C P I Mackays
Badger Road, Chatham, ME5 8TD
Tel: 01634-673200 **Fax:** 01634-867742
E-mail: mackays@cpi-group.co.uk
Website: http://www.cpibooks.co.uk
Bank(s): National Westminster Bank Plc
Directors: J. Owen (Fin), M. Robson (Legal)
Ultimate Holding Company: CAMERON FRANCE HOLDING SAS (FRANCE)
Immediate Holding Company: CPI MACKAYS LTD
Registration no: 02196742 **VAT No.:** GB 304 2508 03
Date established: 1987 **Turnover:** £20m - £50m
No.of Employees: 101 - 250 **Product Groups:** 28

Date of Accounts	Mar 11	Mar 10	Mar 09
Sales Turnover	30m	29m	29m
Pre Tax Profit/Loss	1m	-912	-5m
Working Capital	-1m	3m	2m
Fixed Assets	15m	13m	12m
Current Assets	10m	13m	13m
Current Liabilities	1m	1m	1m

Callworth Ltd
35 Oakhurst Close, Chatham, ME5 9AN
Tel: 01634-402381 **Fax:** 01634-201770
E-mail: pj.crook@btinternet.com
Directors: P. Crook (Dir)
Immediate Holding Company: CALLWORTH LIMITED
Registration no: 01353110 **VAT No.:** GB 204 0403 35
Date established: 1978 **Turnover:** Up to £250,000
No.of Employees: 1 - 10 **Product Groups:** 80, 84

Date of Accounts	Dec 10	Dec 09	Dec 08
Working Capital	-34	-33	-32
Fixed Assets	46	46	47
Current Assets	N/A	N/A	1

Cardinal Health U.K. 232 Ltd
PO Box 6,, Chatham, ME4 4QY
Tel: 01634-893500 **Fax:** 01634-893600
E-mail: sales@micromedical.co.uk
Website: http://www.micromedical.co.uk
Bank(s): National Westminster Bank Plc
Registration no: 01761018 **VAT No.:** GB 372 5949 18
Date established: 1986 **Turnover:** £10m - £20m
No.of Employees: 101 - 250 **Product Groups:** 28, 31, 37, 38

Clinicare Supplies
Hopewell Drive, Chatham, ME5 7NP
Tel: 01634-812288 **Fax:** 01634-810760
E-mail: sales@clinicaresupplies.com
Website: http://www.clinicaresupplies.com
Directors: C. Campbell (Ptnr)
Immediate Holding Company: CLINICARE SUPPLIES LIMITED
Registration no: 07872692 **Date established:** 2011
No.of Employees: 21 - 50 **Product Groups:** 38, 67

Colorlites Ltd
Unit 23 Lordswood Industrial Estate Revenge Road, Chatham, ME5 8UD
Tel: 01634-862839 **Fax:** 01634-865285
E-mail: salesdesk@colorlites.com
Website: http://www.colouredbottles.co.uk
Directors: G. Sterling (MD)
Immediate Holding Company: COLORLITES LIMITED
Registration no: 01851465 **Date established:** 1984
Turnover: £250,000 - £500,000 **No.of Employees:** 11 - 20
Product Groups: 32, 33

Date of Accounts	Dec 11	Dec 10	Dec 09
Working Capital	177	130	78
Fixed Assets	130	142	134
Current Assets	334	271	254

Computer Terminal Services UK Ltd
16a Highview Drive, Chatham, ME5 9UN
Tel: 01634-681111 **Fax:** 01634-681158
E-mail: service@cts-business-solutions.com
Website: http://www.cts.uk.com
Directors: S. Spittle (MD), J. Spittle (Fin)
Managers: E. Edwards (I.T. Exec)
Immediate Holding Company: COMPUTER TERMINAL SERVICES (UK) LIMITED
Registration no: 04330918 **Date established:** 2001 **Turnover:** £1m - £2m
No.of Employees: 1 - 10 **Product Groups:** 44

Date of Accounts	Mar 11	Mar 10	Mar 09
Working Capital	41	43	12
Fixed Assets	19	42	49
Current Assets	85	174	160

Custom Wytelyne Powder Coating Ltd
88-90 Hopewell Drive, Chatham, ME5 7NL
Tel: 01634-819520 **Fax:** 01634-819510
E-mail: info@custom-powder.co.uk
Website: http://www.custom-powder.co.uk
Bank(s): HSBC, Bexleyheath
Directors: M. Gould (Dir), R. Smith (Dir), L. Callow (Co Sec)
Immediate Holding Company: CUSTOM WYTELYNE POWDER COATING LIMITED
Registration no: 02994947 **VAT No.:** GB 619 4901 27
Date established: 1994 **Turnover:** £250,000 - £500,000
No.of Employees: 11 - 20 **Product Groups:** 32, 48

Date of Accounts	Dec 11	Dec 10	Dec 09
Working Capital	87	67	81
Fixed Assets	56	88	92
Current Assets	263	195	226
Current Liabilities	N/A	N/A	29

Designed Storage Ltd
Oaks Business Village Revenge Road, Chatham, ME5 8LF
Tel: 01634-670470 **Fax:** 01634-868050
E-mail: chyril@designedstorage.com
Website: http://www.designedstorage.com
Directors: C. Young (MD), C. Adams (Co Sec)
Ultimate Holding Company: FAITHDEAN PLC
Immediate Holding Company: DESIGNED STORAGE LIMITED
Registration no: 01606188 **Date established:** 1981 **Turnover:** £2m - £5m
No.of Employees: 1 - 10 **Product Groups:** 35, 52, 67

Date of Accounts	Mar 12	Mar 11	Mar 10
Sales Turnover	N/A	2m	1m
Pre Tax Profit/Loss	N/A	70	-86
Working Capital	166	98	227
Fixed Assets	23	37	34
Current Assets	653	599	629
Current Liabilities	N/A	126	74

Designsmart UK Ltd
92 94 Hopewell Drive, Chatham, ME5 7PY
Tel: 0800-6127995 **Fax:** 01634-810610
E-mail: tony@smartdomaingroup.co.uk
Website: http://www.smartdomaingroup.co.uk
Directors: A. Spinks (Dir)
Registration no: 03945374 **Date established:** 2000
Turnover: £250,000 - £500,000 **No.of Employees:** 11 - 20
Product Groups: 44, 79

Eden Transformer Oil Ltd
8 Hopewell Business Centre Hopewell Drive, Chatham, ME5 7DX
Tel: 01634-305600 **Fax:** 01634-305601
E-mail: mail@edenoil.co.uk
Website: http://www.edenoil.co.uk
Directors: N. Denbow (Dir)
Immediate Holding Company: EDEN TRANSFORMER OIL LIMITED
Registration no: 05094065 **Date established:** 2004
No.of Employees: 1 - 10 **Product Groups:** 38, 42

Date of Accounts	Aug 11	Aug 10	Aug 09
Working Capital	-59	-114	-154
Fixed Assets	144	192	230
Current Assets	82	83	146

Emerson Process Management
Prince Regent House Quayside Chatham Maritime, Chatham, ME4 4QZ
Tel: 01634-895800 **Fax:** 01634-895844
E-mail: uksales@emersonprocess.com
Website: http://www.emerson.com
Directors: W. Vandormael (Fin), W. Nanncarrow (Dir)
Ultimate Holding Company: EMERSON ELECTRIC CO INC (USA)
Immediate Holding Company: EMERSON PROCESS MANAGEMENT LIMITED
Registration no: 00671801 **Date established:** 1960
Turnover: £125m - £250m **No.of Employees:** 21 - 50
Product Groups: 36, 38

Date of Accounts	Sep 11	Sep 10	Sep 09
Sales Turnover	143m	105m	125m
Pre Tax Profit/Loss	22m	16m	-515
Working Capital	67m	58m	70m
Fixed Assets	14m	14m	11m
Current Assets	123m	98m	109m
Current Liabilities	18m	21m	14m

Flowdrill UK Ltd
Unit 7 105 Hopewell Business Centre Hopewell Drive, Chatham, ME5 7DX
Tel: 01634-309422 **Fax:** 01634-303306
E-mail: flowdrill.uk@virgin.net
Website: http://www.flowdrill.com
Directors: J. Steffen (MD)
Immediate Holding Company: FLOWDRILL (UK) LIMITED
Registration no: 03163254 **VAT No.:** GB 702 7483 45
Date established: 1996 **Turnover:** Up to £250,000
No.of Employees: 1 - 10 **Product Groups:** 36, 40, 46, 48

Date of Accounts	Dec 11	Dec 10	Dec 09
Sales Turnover	135	177	113
Pre Tax Profit/Loss	13	17	7
Working Capital	-38	-52	-69
Current Assets	78	87	53
Current Liabilities	109	115	110

J A Glover Ltd
Unit 2 Lordswood Industrial Estate Revenge Road, Chatham, ME5 8UD
Tel: 01634-684419 **Fax:** 01634-200423
E-mail: richardlegge@jag-glover.demon.co.uk
Website: http://www.gloverventilation.net
Directors: M. Harrington (Fin), R. Legge (Dir)
Immediate Holding Company: J.A.GLOVER LIMITED
Registration no: 01333801 **Date established:** 1977 **Turnover:** £5m - £10m
No.of Employees: 51 - 100 **Product Groups:** 35, 36, 48

Date of Accounts	Dec 11	Dec 10	Dec 09
Sales Turnover	7m	6m	7m
Pre Tax Profit/Loss	-46	51	16
Working Capital	1m	1m	1m
Fixed Assets	162	166	206
Current Assets	3m	3m	2m
Current Liabilities	937	808	457

H D H Security Systems Ltd
Unit 2 Park House Hopewell Drive, Chatham, ME5 7PY
Tel: 01634-302616 **Fax:** 01634-852007
E-mail: accounts@hdhss.com
Website: http://www.hdhss.com
Directors: M. Hewitt (Dir), D. Bailey Hewitt (Fin)
Immediate Holding Company: H.D.H. SECURITY SYSTEMS LIMITED
Registration no: 03329149 **Date established:** 1997
Turnover: Up to £250,000 **No.of Employees:** 1 - 10 **Product Groups:** 22, 36, 40

Date of Accounts	Mar 11	Mar 10	Mar 09
Sales Turnover	265	299	355
Pre Tax Profit/Loss	63	101	70
Working Capital	15	47	31
Fixed Assets	7	8	8
Current Assets	124	133	154
Current Liabilities	24	60	47

Holiday Inn Ltd
Maidstone Road, Chatham, ME5 9SF
Tel: 08719-429069 **Fax:** 01634-673673
E-mail: rochester@6c.com
Website: http://www.ichotelsgroup.com/redirect?path=hd&hotelCode=rcske
Managers: M. Maxball (Chief Mgr)
Immediate Holding Company: HOLIDAY INN LIMITED
Registration no: 05479356 **Date established:** 2005 **Turnover:** £2m - £5m
No.of Employees: 101 - 250 **Product Groups:** 69

Hy-Ten Reinforcements Ltd
Portacabin Chatham Docks, Chatham, ME4 4SW
Tel: 01634-280504
E-mail: sales@hy-ten.co.uk
Website: http://www.hy-ten.co.uk

see next page

Hy-Ten Reinforcements Ltd - Cont'd

Managers: R. Allen (Mgr)
Immediate Holding Company: DOCKSIDE TRANSPORT AND REPAIR COMPANY LIMITED
Registration no: 00598988 **Date established:** 2010
No.of Employees: 11 - 20 **Product Groups:** 35

J H P Employability

Anchorage House High Street, Chatham, ME4 4LE
Tel: 01634-842299 **Fax:** 01634-841965
E-mail: chatham@jhptraining.com
Website: http://www.jhptraining.com
Managers: K. Bliss (Mgr)
Immediate Holding Company: THE SOUTH EAST INSTITUTE FOR THEOLOGICAL EDUCATION
Registration no: 03247918 **Date established:** 1983
Turnover: £250,000 - £500,000 **No.of Employees:** 1 - 10
Product Groups: 86

L N Radio Ltd

Unit B Jenkins Dale, Chatham, ME4 5RD
Tel: 01634-407200 **Fax:** 01634-407242
E-mail: sales@lnradio.co.uk
Website: http://www.lnradio.co.uk
Bank(s): Barclays, Tonbridge Wells
Directors: G. Lawrence (MD), S. Nixon (MD)
Immediate Holding Company: L & N RADIO LIMITED
Registration no: 01162048 **Date established:** 1974
Turnover: £500,000 - £1m **No.of Employees:** 11 - 20 **Product Groups:** 37

Date of Accounts	Jun 11	Jun 10	Jun 09
Working Capital	-16	-50	-44
Fixed Assets	19	23	13
Current Assets	447	305	227

Marshall & Wilson

37 Blenheim Avenue, Chatham, ME4 6UX
Tel: 01634-401492
No.of Employees: 1 - 10 **Product Groups:** 30, 48, 84

North Kent Joinery Ltd

Brunel Sawmill The Historic Dockyard, Chatham, ME4 4TQ
Tel: 01634-826903 **Fax:** 01634-826902
E-mail: kathy@nkj.co.uk
Website: http://www.nkj.co.uk
Directors: K. Collins (Co Sec)
Immediate Holding Company: NORTH KENT JOINERY LIMITED
Registration no: 01674814 **Date established:** 1982 **Turnover:** £1m - £2m
No.of Employees: 11 - 20 **Product Groups:** 25

Date of Accounts	Mar 11	Mar 10	Mar 09
Working Capital	103	91	123
Fixed Assets	4	11	17
Current Assets	272	174	289

Peach Contractors Ltd

6-8 Chestnut Avenue, Chatham, ME5 9AJ
Tel: 01634-660311 **Fax:** 01634-200843
E-mail: enquires@peach-contractors.co.uk
Website: http://www.peach-contractors.co.uk
Directors: A. Phipps (Co Sec)
Immediate Holding Company: PEACH (CONTRACTORS) LIMITED
Registration no: 00931623 **VAT No.:** GB 203 6421 09
Date established: 1968 **Turnover:** Up to £250,000
No.of Employees: 1 - 10 **Product Groups:** 84

Date of Accounts	Oct 11	Oct 10	Oct 09
Sales Turnover	53	81	39
Pre Tax Profit/Loss	16	17	12
Working Capital	-112	-129	-150
Fixed Assets	383	389	395
Current Assets	22	18	26
Current Liabilities	24	23	21

Process Plant Services Ltd

10a Revenge Road Lordswood, Chatham, ME5 8UD
Tel: 01634-686655 **Fax:** 01634-681371
E-mail: gary.bosson@process-plant.co.uk
Website: http://www.processplantservices.co.uk
Directors: B. Bosson (Fin), G. Bosson (MD)
Immediate Holding Company: PROCESS PLANT SERVICES LIMITED
Registration no: 04420071 **VAT No.:** GB 304 3944 75
Date established: 2002 **Turnover:** £250,000 - £500,000
No.of Employees: 1 - 10 **Product Groups:** 35, 36, 39, 46, 48, 49, 66, 67, 84

Date of Accounts	Apr 11	Apr 10	Apr 09
Working Capital	435	387	324
Fixed Assets	22	23	45
Current Assets	553	525	454

Switched On

179 Wayfield Road, Chatham, ME5 0HD
Tel: 01634-818192 **Fax:** 01634-818143
Directors: S. Keevil (Ptnr)
Date established: 2004 **No.of Employees:** 1 - 10 **Product Groups:** 36, 40

Thomas Fabrications

Unit 2 Beacon Road, Chatham, ME5 7BU
Tel: 01634-811553 **Fax:** 01634-401065
E-mail: dean@thomasfabrications.co.uk
Directors: D. Thomas (Prop)
No.of Employees: 1 - 10 **Product Groups:** 35, 52

Timeit Software Distribution Ltd

Orion House Unit 72 Riverside 3, Chatham, ME5 7PZ
Tel: 08450-942908 **Fax:** 0870-199 2627
E-mail: sales@timeitsoftware.co.uk
Website: http://www.timeitgroup.com
Directors: R. Clifford (MD)
Immediate Holding Company: TIMEIT SOFTWARE (DISTRIBUTION) LIMITED
Registration no: 06312817 **Date established:** 2007
Turnover: £250,000 - £500,000 **No.of Employees:** 1 - 10
Product Groups: 44, 49

Date of Accounts	Dec 10	Jul 09	Jul 08
Working Capital	-2	10	4
Fixed Assets	19	4	3
Current Assets	20	26	22

Tophouse Assessments

17 Albany Road, Chatham, ME4 5DL
Tel: 01634-566215
E-mail: martin.gill@tophouse.com
Website: http://www.pressuretests.co.uk
Turnover: Up to £250,000 **No.of Employees:** 11 - 20 **Product Groups:** 84, 85, 87

UK Mobility Services

11 Clover Street, Chatham, ME4 4DT
Tel: 01634-408420 **Fax:** 01634-408461
Website: http://www.ukmobility.com
Directors: W. Phillips (Dir)
No.of Employees: 1 - 10 **Product Groups:** 26, 38, 39

Watts Construction Ltd

Unit 1 & 2 Beacon Road 101-109 Beacon Road, Chatham, ME5 7BP
Tel: 01634-409149 **Fax:** 01634-403005
E-mail: wattsgroupltd@blueyonder.co.uk
Website: http://www.wattsgroupltd.com
Bank(s): Barclays
Directors: T. Varrall (MD)
Ultimate Holding Company: WATTS EQUIPMENT LIMITED
Immediate Holding Company: WATTS CONSTRUCTION LIMITED
Registration no: 02016960 **VAT No.:** GB 472 8606 25
Date established: 1986 **Turnover:** £500,000 - £1m
No.of Employees: 11 - 20 **Product Groups:** 40, 48

Date of Accounts	Apr 11	Apr 10	Apr 09
Working Capital	1m	880	848
Fixed Assets	122	124	143
Current Assets	2m	1m	1m

Wealden Rehab

113 Hopewell Drive, Chatham, ME5 7NP
Tel: 01634-813388 **Fax:** 01420-89227
E-mail: admin@wealdenrehab.com
Website: http://www.wealdenrehab.com
Directors: O. Campbell (Prop)
Immediate Holding Company: BOLDS BALANCE LIMITED
Registration no: 07567384 **Date established:** 2011
No.of Employees: 11 - 20 **Product Groups:** 26, 36, 39

Weldrite

101-109 Beacon Road, Chatham, ME5 7BP
Tel: 01634-409009
Directors: N. York (Prop)
No.of Employees: 21 - 50 **Product Groups:** 35

Westvic Enamellers

8 Ballards Industrial Estate Revenge Road, Chatham, ME5 8UD
Tel: 01634-660499 **Fax:** 01634-686692
E-mail: rachelweston@blueyonder.co.uk
Website: http://www.industrialpaintfinishers.com
Directors: G. Weston (Prop)
Date established: 1987 **No.of Employees:** 1 - 10 **Product Groups:** 46, 48

Chislehurst

Classic Video Services

Sunnymead 1 Bromley Lane, Chislehurst, BR7 6LH
Tel: 020-8464 5931 **Fax:** 01277-262695
E-mail: info@cvsinternational.co.uk
Website: http://cvsinternational.co.uk
Directors: J. Berry (Fin), C. Berry (MD)
Immediate Holding Company: CLASSIC VIDEO SERVICES INTERNATIONAL LIMITED
Registration no: 02683264 **Date established:** 1992
Turnover: £500,000 - £1m **No.of Employees:** 1 - 10 **Product Groups:** 37, 81, 83, 89

Date of Accounts	Mar 12	Mar 11	Mar 10
Working Capital	235	245	233
Fixed Assets	186	181	193
Current Assets	336	384	346

K S P Building Design Consultants Ltd

The Old Laundry Hawkwood Lane, Chislehurst, BR7 5PW
Tel: 020-8295 0033 **Fax:** 020-8295 0033
Directors: J. Gittins (Fin), R. Gittins (MD)
Immediate Holding Company: KSP BUILDING DESIGN CONSULTANTS LTD
Registration no: 04776070 **Date established:** 2003
No.of Employees: 1 - 10 **Product Groups:** 35

Cranbrook

A Bone

Parsons Farm Frittenden, Cranbrook, TN17 2DB
Tel: 01580-852588 **Fax:** 01580-852588
Directors: A. Bone (Prop)
Immediate Holding Company: RASPBERRY HOMES LIMITED
Registration no: 02789022 **Date established:** 2012
No.of Employees: 1 - 10 **Product Groups:** 35

Crofton House Associates

Crofton House The Moor, Hawkhurst, Cranbrook, TN18 4NN
Tel: 01580-752919 **Fax:** 01580-754173
E-mail: jim@crofton-house.co.uk
Website: http://www.crofton-house.co.uk
Managers: J. Wortley (Mgr)
Immediate Holding Company: CROFTON HOUSE ASSOCIATES LIMITED
Registration no: 02852036 **VAT No.:** GB 583 5608 15
Date established: 1993 **Turnover:** £500,000 - £1m
No.of Employees: 1 - 10 **Product Groups:** 40, 41, 45, 52

Edghurst Ltd

Brook House Cranbrook Road, Hawkhurst, Cranbrook, TN18 5EE
Tel: 01580-752330 **Fax:** 01580-752892
E-mail: dkelly@edghurst.co.uk
Directors: D. Kelly (Dir)
Ultimate Holding Company: TRICONTINENTAL LTD (JERSEY)
Immediate Holding Company: EDGHURST LIMITED
Registration no: 01636668 **Date established:** 1982 **Turnover:** £2m - £5m
No.of Employees: 1 - 10 **Product Groups:** 61

Date of Accounts	Mar 12	Mar 11	Mar 10
Working Capital	280	272	294
Fixed Assets	4	5	7
Current Assets	2m	1m	2m

Finders International Ltd

Orchard House Winchet Hill, Goudhurst, Cranbrook, TN17 1JY
Tel: 01580-211055 **Fax:** 01580-212062
E-mail: info@findershealth.com
Website: http://www.findershealth.com
Directors: J. Czik (Fin), K. Bunyan (Mkt Research)
Managers: G. Ashurst (Tech Serv Mgr), P. Morhen (Sales Prom Mgr)
Immediate Holding Company: FINDERS INTERNATIONAL LIMITED
Registration no: 02551332 **VAT No.:** GB 373 7266 30
Date established: 1990 **No.of Employees:** 11 - 20 **Product Groups:** 32, 49

Date of Accounts	Dec 11	Dec 10	Dec 09
Working Capital	669	680	612
Fixed Assets	281	265	307
Current Assets	1m	1m	1m

Fridays Ltd

Swattenden Lane, Cranbrook, TN17 3PN
Tel: 01580-710200 **Fax:** 01580-714760
E-mail: fridays@fridays.co.uk
Website: http://www.fridays.co.uk
Bank(s): National Westminster Bank Plc
Managers: K. Wilton
Immediate Holding Company: FRIDAYS LIMITED
Registration no: 01005611 **Date established:** 1971
Turnover: £20m - £50m **No.of Employees:** 251 - 500 **Product Groups:** 20

Date of Accounts	Dec 11	Dec 10	Dec 09
Sales Turnover	44m	44m	N/A
Pre Tax Profit/Loss	421	5m	N/A
Working Capital	9m	13m	12m
Fixed Assets	16m	13m	10m
Current Assets	12m	16m	15m
Current Liabilities	897	1m	2m

Genalog Ltd

Gills Green Oast Gills Green, Cranbrook, TN18 5ET
Tel: 01580-753754 **Fax:** 01580-752979
E-mail: sales@genalog.com
Website: http://www.genalog.com
Directors: G. Reed (MD)
Immediate Holding Company: GENALOG LIMITED
Registration no: 01350701 **Date established:** 1978
No.of Employees: 11 - 20 **Product Groups:** 37, 40, 44

Date of Accounts	Mar 11	Mar 10	Mar 09
Working Capital	624	772	973
Fixed Assets	312	311	331
Current Assets	1m	1m	1m
Current Liabilities	72	N/A	N/A

S W Kenyon

PO Box 71, Cranbrook, TN18 5ZR
Tel: 01580-850770 **Fax:** 01580-850225
E-mail: bob.houlden@btinternet.com
Website: http://www.swkenyon.com
Directors: R. Houlden (Prop)
Turnover: Up to £250,000 **No.of Employees:** 1 - 10 **Product Groups:** 32

Manufacturing Recruitment Ltd

Clayhill Marden Road, Cranbrook, TN17 2LP
Tel: 01580-715111 **Fax:** 01580-714718
E-mail: enquiries@manufacturingjobs.co.uk
Website: http://www.manufacturingjobs.co.uk
Directors: T. Cowell (MD), S. Cowell (Fin)
Immediate Holding Company: MANUFACTURING RECRUITMENT LTD
Registration no: 04023151 **Date established:** 2000
Turnover: £500,000 - £1m **No.of Employees:** 1 - 10 **Product Groups:** 80

Date of Accounts	Jun 12	Jun 11	Jun 10
Working Capital	603	442	184
Fixed Assets	25	22	20
Current Assets	729	726	266

Mobitech Fork Lift Trucks

Grandshore Wood Farm Grandshore Lane, Frittenden, Cranbrook, TN17 2BZ
Tel: 01580-852473 **Fax:** 01580-852580
E-mail: andrew@mobitechlifttrucks.co.uk
Directors: A. Barker (Prop)
Date established: 1984 **No.of Employees:** 1 - 10 **Product Groups:** 35, 39, 45

Peekay National Eyecare Group Ltd

Clermont House High Street, Cranbrook, TN17 3DN
Tel: 01580-713698 **Fax:** 01580-713178
E-mail: michael.wheeler@nationaleyecare.co.uk
Website: http://www.nationaleyecare.co.uk
Directors: M. Wheeler (Dir)
Ultimate Holding Company: PERCY KIRK GROUP LIMITED
Immediate Holding Company: PEEKAY PUBLISHING LIMITED
Registration no: 01906665 **VAT No.:** GB 583 7001 43
Date established: 1985 **No.of Employees:** 1 - 10 **Product Groups:** 61

Date of Accounts	Mar 11	Mar 10	Mar 06
Working Capital	1	-0	-1
Current Assets	19	19	9

S D S Group Ltd

Office Suite 3 Courtlands Farm Industrial Estate, Cranbrook, TN17 2QL
Tel: 01580-715038 **Fax:** 01580-712056
E-mail: sales@sdsgroupltd.co.uk
Website: http://www.sdsgroupltd.co.uk
Directors: C. Mather (Fin), S. Chambers (MD)
Ultimate Holding Company: PENTAGON PROTECTION PLC
Immediate Holding Company: SDS GROUP LIMITED
Registration no: 03348279 **VAT No.:** GB 200 5684 00
Date established: 1997 **Turnover:** £1m - £2m **No.of Employees:** 1 - 10
Product Groups: 37, 38, 40

Date of Accounts	Sep 11	Sep 10	Sep 09
Sales Turnover	1m	930	2m
Pre Tax Profit/Loss	-22	-113	15

Working Capital	73	83	194
Fixed Assets	7	9	11
Current Assets	373	496	647
Current Liabilities	61	41	158

N P Seymour
Avon Works Goudhurst Road, Cranbrook, TN17 2PT
Tel: 01580-712200 **Fax:** 01580-715191
E-mail: sales@npseymour.co.uk
Website: http://www.npseymour.co.uk
Directors: N. Seymour (Prop)
Immediate Holding Company: NP SEYMOUR LIMITED
Registration no: 06595567 **Date established:** 2008
No.of Employees: 1 - 10 **Product Groups:** 41

Date of Accounts	Jul 11	Jul 10	Jul 09
Working Capital	195	134	20
Current Assets	419	472	369

Winser Engineering Services
Flishinghurst Orchard Chalk Lane, Cranbrook, TN17 2QB
Tel: 01580-714460 **Fax:** 01580-715752
Website: http://www.winserengineering.co.uk
Directors: R. Winser (MD)
Date established: 1978 **No.of Employees:** 1 - 10 **Product Groups:** 35

Dartford

A C S Stainless Steel Fixings
Crown House Home Gardens, Dartford, DA1 1DZ
Tel: 01322-424510
E-mail: sales@acsstainless.co.uk
Website: http://www.acsstainless.co.uk
Directors: T. Higson (Comm)
Immediate Holding Company: KING AND CAMBRIDGE HOSPITALITY LTD
Registration no: 06849197 **Date established:** 2001
No.of Employees: 1 - 10 **Product Groups:** 35

Date of Accounts	Mar 04	Mar 03
Working Capital	1	-2
Fixed Assets	4	2
Current Assets	497	80

A D I Global
40 Acorn Industrial Park Crayford Road, Dartford, DA1 4AL
Tel: 01322-310736 **Fax:** 01322-310738
E-mail: jason.seal@adiglobal.com
Website: http://www.adiglobal.com
Managers: J. Seal (Mgr)
Immediate Holding Company: GARDINER SECURITY LIMITED
Registration no: 04124719 **Date established:** 2000
No.of Employees: 1 - 10 **Product Groups:** 37, 40

A Day 2 Remember
3 Bondfield Walk, Dartford, DA1 5JS
Tel: 01322-272747
E-mail: mail@aday-2-remember.co.uk
Website: http://www.aday-2-remember.co.uk
Directors: M. Tidy (Co Sec), M. Tidy (Prop)
Date established: 2008 **No.of Employees:** 1 - 10 **Product Groups:** 83

Abwood Machine Tools Ltd (Division of Atlanta Trust Ltd)
615 Princes Road, Dartford, DA2 6DY
Tel: 01322-225271 **Fax:** 01322-291862
E-mail: sales@abwoodcnc.co.uk
Website: http://www.abwoodcnc.co.uk
Bank(s): Barclays
Directors: C. Nicholas (Dir), K. Slater (Co Sec)
Ultimate Holding Company: ATLANTA TRUST LIMITED
Immediate Holding Company: ABWOOD MACHINE TOOLS LIMITED
Registration no: 01730319 **VAT No.:** GB 691 3161 38
Date established: 1983 **Turnover:** £500,000 - £1m
No.of Employees: 11 - 20 **Product Groups:** 46

Date of Accounts	Dec 11	Dec 10	Dec 09
Working Capital	400	400	400
Current Assets	400	400	400

Alpha Water Treatment
3 Millside Industrial Estate Lawson Road, Dartford, DA1 5BW
Tel: 01322-289398 **Fax:** 01322-223440
Directors: K. Cowdry (Dir)
Immediate Holding Company: ALPHA WATER TREATMENT LIMITED
Registration no: 02629532 **Date established:** 1991
No.of Employees: 1 - 10 **Product Groups:** 38, 42

Date of Accounts	Jun 11	Jun 10	Jun 09
Working Capital	N/A	-1	-3
Current Assets	12	9	3

Beck & Pollitzer
Sandpit Road, Dartford, DA1 5BD
Tel: 01322-528291 **Fax:** 01322-525461
E-mail: craford@beck-pollitzer.com
Website: http://www.beck-pollitzer.com
Bank(s): Bank of Scotland
Directors: D. Clarke (Plant), K. Anderson (Chief Op Offcr), S. Slater (Fin), T. Percival (MD)
Managers: R. Church (Chief Mgr)
Immediate Holding Company: BECK & POLLITZER LIMITED
Registration no: 06344191 **Date established:** 2007
Turnover: £50m - £75m **No.of Employees:** 21 - 50 **Product Groups:** 83

Blakley Electrics Ltd
1 Thomas Road Crayford, Dartford, DA1 4GA
Tel: 08450-740084 **Fax:** 01920-464682
E-mail: sales@blakley.co.uk
Website: http://www.blakley.co.uk
Bank(s): National Westminster Bank Plc
Directors: P. Blakley (MD), D. Slater (Fin), D. Mitchell (Fin), J. Lay (Tech Serv)
Managers: J. Arch (Purch Mgr), P. Dale, D. Mitchell (Tech Serv Mgr)
Immediate Holding Company: BLAKLEY ELECTRICS LIMITED
Registration no: 00592238 **VAT No.:** GB 407 7636 40
Date established: 1957 **Turnover:** £10m - £20m
No.of Employees: 21 - 50 **Product Groups:** 37

Date of Accounts	Dec 11	Dec 10	Dec 09
Sales Turnover	10m	14m	10m
Pre Tax Profit/Loss	303	403	297
Working Capital	3m	3m	3m
Fixed Assets	3m	3m	3m
Current Assets	6m	6m	7m
Current Liabilities	1m	2m	1m

Bradley Pulverizer Co.
15 Kennet Road, Dartford, DA1 4QN
Tel: 01322-559106 **Fax:** 01322-528690
E-mail: sales@bradleypulv.com
Website: http://www.bradleypulverizer.co.uk
Managers: K. Vereker, D. Thomas, R. Leeds (Purch Mgr)
Immediate Holding Company: BRADLEY PULVERIZER COMPANY
Registration no: FC000701 **VAT No.:** GB 235 5852 51
Date established: 2008 **Turnover:** £10m - £20m **No.of Employees:** 1 - 10
Product Groups: 42

British Loose Leaf Ltd
20 Kennet Road, Dartford, DA1 4QN
Tel: 01322-526262 **Fax:** 01322-558624
E-mail: sales@bll.co.uk
Website: http://www.bll.co.uk
Managers: J. Lee (Sales Prom Mgr), N. Dolling (Tech Serv Mgr), G. Sherrin (Fin Mgr)
Immediate Holding Company: BRITISH LOOSE LEAF LIMITED
Registration no: 00106750 **Date established:** 2009 **Turnover:** £5m - £10m
No.of Employees: 21 - 50 **Product Groups:** 28, 30, 49, 64

C G R Polythene Company Ltd
Unit 72 Powder Mill Lane Questor Trade Park, Questor, Dartford, DA1 1JA
Tel: 01322-292681 **Fax:** 0845-680 0084
E-mail: gary@cgrpolythene.co.uk
Website: http://www.cgrpolythene.co.uk
Directors: G. Brand (MD)
Immediate Holding Company: C.G.R. POLYTHENE COMPANY LIMITED
Registration no: 02485677 **VAT No.:** GB 566 3308 33
Date established: 1990 **Turnover:** £1m - £2m **No.of Employees:** 1 - 10
Product Groups: 27, 29, 30

Date of Accounts	Mar 11	Mar 10	Mar 09
Working Capital	114	115	68
Fixed Assets	50	39	36
Current Assets	516	443	357

C P P L M Ltd
Unit 38 Crayford Industrial Estate Swaisland Drive, Dartford, DA1 4HF
Tel: 01322-551940 **Fax:** 01322-550212
E-mail: sales@cpp-lm.com
Website: http://www.cpp-lm.com
Directors: A. Youseman (MD)
Immediate Holding Company: CPP - LM LIMITED
Registration no: 01463285 **Date established:** 1979
Turnover: £500,000 - £1m **No.of Employees:** 1 - 10 **Product Groups:** 48

Date of Accounts	Nov 11	Nov 10	Nov 09
Working Capital	-1	-55	-70
Fixed Assets	80	78	92
Current Assets	110	57	100

Car Air Conditioning Services
104 Bennett Way, Dartford, DA2 7JU
Tel: 01474-705370
E-mail: bobr@caraircon.co.uk
Website: http://www.caraircon.co.uk
Directors: R. Richardson (Prop)
No.of Employees: 1 - 10 **Product Groups:** 39, 40, 52, 66, 68, 85

J Clubb Ltd
Church Hill, Dartford, DA2 7DZ
Tel: 01322-225431 **Fax:** 01322-289932
E-mail: sales@jclubb.co.uk
Website: http://www.jclubb.co.uk
Bank(s): National Westminster Bank Plc
Directors: S. Clubb (MD)
Immediate Holding Company: J CLUBB HOLDINGS LIMITED
Registration no: 04835782 **VAT No.:** GB 202 9661 77
Date established: 2003 **Turnover:** £5m - £10m **No.of Employees:** 11 - 20
Product Groups: 14, 45, 52

Date of Accounts	Mar 11	Mar 10	Mar 09
Sales Turnover	8m	7m	N/A
Pre Tax Profit/Loss	-47	-126	135
Working Capital	1m	1m	N/A
Fixed Assets	5m	5m	480
Current Assets	4m	3m	N/A
Current Liabilities	732	571	N/A

Corus Engineering Steels
Station Road South Darenth, Dartford, DA4 9LD
Tel: 01322-227272 **Fax:** 01322-864893
Website: http://www.corus.com
Managers: M. Traylor (Sales Prom Mgr)
Ultimate Holding Company: TATA STEEL LIMITED (INDIA)
Immediate Holding Company: CORUS GROUP LIMITED
Registration no: 03811373 **Date established:** 1999 **Turnover:** £1m - £2m
No.of Employees: 21 - 50 **Product Groups:** 66

Crayford Tubes Ltd
Unit 33 Acorn Industrial Park Crayford Road, Dartford, DA1 4AL
Tel: 01322-526614 **Fax:** 01322-559462
E-mail: info@crayford-tubes.co.uk
Website: http://www.crayford-tubes.co.uk
Directors: K. Topliss (Co Sec), K. Topliss (Dir)
Immediate Holding Company: CRAYFORD TUBES LIMITED
Registration no: 02003489 **Date established:** 1986 **Turnover:** £1m - £2m
No.of Employees: 11 - 20 **Product Groups:** 27

Date of Accounts	Mar 12	Mar 11	Mar 10
Working Capital	221	151	121
Fixed Assets	36	44	29
Current Assets	422	398	282

Creative Audio Design
12 Harold Road Hawley, Dartford, DA2 7SA
Tel: 01322-224998
E-mail: j.burring@sky.com
Website: http://www.thecad.homecall.co.uk
Directors: J. Burring (Prop)
No.of Employees: 1 - 10 **Product Groups:** 26, 37, 89

D H L Global Forwarding UK Ltd
Persimmons House Anchor Boulevard, Crossways Business Park, Dartford, DA2 6QH
Tel: 01322-620900 **Fax:** 01322-620910
E-mail: glenda.spencer@dhl.com
Website: http://www.dhl.co.uk
Managers: G. Spencer (Sales Admin)
Ultimate Holding Company: DEUTSCHE POST AG (GERMANY)
Immediate Holding Company: DHL GLOBAL FORWARDING (UK) LIMITED
Registration no: 04056042 **Date established:** 2000
No.of Employees: 21 - 50 **Product Groups:** 74, 76

Date of Accounts	Dec 11	Dec 10	Dec 09
Sales Turnover	588m	563m	305m
Pre Tax Profit/Loss	32m	26m	24m
Working Capital	37m	21m	46m
Fixed Assets	28m	39m	36m
Current Assets	180m	168m	180m
Current Liabilities	73m	79m	67m

D P A Sound Hire
8 Hulberry Farm Lullingstone Lane, Eynsford, Dartford, DA4 0JB
Tel: 01322-863664 **Fax:** 01322-290588
E-mail: info@dpasound.co.uk
Website: http://www.dpasound.co.uk
Directors: L. Frisby (Prop)
Turnover: Up to £250,000 **No.of Employees:** 1 - 10 **Product Groups:** 37, 40

Darent Wax Co. (Proman Coatings)
Unit 1 Horton Kirby Trading Estate Station Road, South Darenth, Dartford, DA4 9BD
Tel: 01322-865892 **Fax:** 01322-864598
E-mail: acw@darentwax.com
Website: http://www.darentwax.com
Directors: A. Ward (Dir)
Immediate Holding Company: THE DARENT WAX COMPANY LIMITED
Registration no: 02635454 **Date established:** 1991
No.of Employees: 11 - 20 **Product Groups:** 31, 32

Date of Accounts	Dec 08	Mar 12	Mar 11
Working Capital	-67	213	4
Fixed Assets	458	608	564
Current Assets	805	2m	1m

Dartford Portable Buildings
Hawley Garden Centre Hawley Road, Dartford, DA2 7RB
Tel: 01322-229521 **Fax:** 01322-221948
E-mail: sales@dpbl.co.uk
Website: http://www.dpbl.co.uk
Bank(s): Lloyds TSB Bank plc
Managers: C. Beeby
Ultimate Holding Company: TERRIERS FARM SUPPLIES LIMITED
Immediate Holding Company: DARTFORD PORTABLE BUILDINGS LIMITED
Registration no: 03267557 **Date established:** 1996 **Turnover:** £1m - £2m
No.of Employees: 11 - 20 **Product Groups:** 25, 33, 35, 39, 83

Date of Accounts	Dec 11	Dec 10	Dec 09
Working Capital	-25	6	-3
Fixed Assets	164	156	149
Current Assets	282	219	165

Davies Turner & Co. Ltd
Eddison Park Crossways Business Park, Dartford, DA2 6QJ
Tel: 01322-277558 **Fax:** 01322-289063
E-mail: webmaster@daviesturner.co.uk
Website: http://www.daviesturner.com
Bank(s): National Westminster Bank Plc
Directors: M. Gransbury (Fin), M. Stephenson (MD)
Ultimate Holding Company: DAVIES TURNER HOLDINGS PLC
Immediate Holding Company: DAVIES TURNER & CO. LIMITED
Registration no: 04345197 **VAT No.:** GB 235 6746 45
Date established: 2001 **Turnover:** £50m - £75m
No.of Employees: 101 - 250 **Product Groups:** 72, 74, 76

Date of Accounts	Mar 11	Mar 10	Mar 09
Sales Turnover	100m	84m	93m
Pre Tax Profit/Loss	2m	1m	453
Working Capital	8m	7m	5m
Fixed Assets	1m	2m	2m
Current Assets	24m	22m	18m
Current Liabilities	4m	3m	3m

Decorative Iron Services
9 Parker Industrial Centre Watling Street, Dartford, DA2 6EP
Tel: 01322-276451 **Fax:** 01322-287689
E-mail: geofhand@btconnect.com
Directors: G. Hand (Prop)
Date established: 1981 **No.of Employees:** 1 - 10 **Product Groups:** 35

Detail Sheet Metal Ltd
Unit 9 Butterly Avenue, Questor, Dartford, DA1 1JQ
Tel: 01322-222121 **Fax:** 01322-291794
E-mail: sales@kentec.co.uk
Website: http://www.kentec.co.uk
Bank(s): Lloyds TSB Bank plc
Directors: R. King (MD)
Ultimate Holding Company: KENTEC ELECTRONICS LIMITED
Immediate Holding Company: DETAIL SHEET METAL (KENT) LIMITED
Registration no: 01110969 **VAT No.:** GB 204 2203 33
Date established: 1973 **Turnover:** £250,000 - £500,000
No.of Employees: 11 - 20 **Product Groups:** 48

Dole Fresh UK Ltd
Unit 12 Newtons Court Crossways, Crossways Business Park, Dartford, DA2 6QL
Tel: 01322-293355 **Fax:** 01322-299700
E-mail: admin@jpfruit.co.uk
Website: http://www.dolefreshuk.com
Bank(s): National Westminster Bank Plc
Directors: K. Scott (Fin)
Managers: S. Terry (Tech Serv Mgr), T. Reed (Personnel)
Ultimate Holding Company: DOLE FOOD COMPANY INC. (USA)
Immediate Holding Company: DOLE FRESH UK LIMITED
Registration no: 00969262 **VAT No.:** GB 205 4212 16
Date established: 1969 **Turnover:** £125m - £250m
No.of Employees: 101 - 250 **Product Groups:** 62

Date of Accounts	Dec 11	Dec 10	Dec 09
Sales Turnover	131m	128m	126m
Pre Tax Profit/Loss	4m	1m	729

see next page

Dole Fresh UK Ltd - Cont'd

Working Capital	13m	10m	8m
Fixed Assets	5m	7m	7m
Current Assets	37m	24m	26m
Current Liabilities	1m	1m	2m

Elan Lifts Ltd
Unit 8 Mulberry Court Bourne Industrial Park Bourne Road, Dartford, DA1 4BZ
Tel: 01322-559402 **Fax:** 01322-556108
E-mail: admin@elanlifts.co.uk
Website: http://www.elanlifts.co.uk
Directors: T. Fillery (Dir)
Immediate Holding Company: ELAN LIFTS LIMITED
Registration no: 04001679 **Date established:** 2000
No.of Employees: 11 - 20 **Product Groups:** 35, 39, 45

Date of Accounts	May 11	May 10	May 09
Working Capital	187	147	124
Fixed Assets	82	93	70
Current Assets	771	516	682

Electro Avionics
Unit 7 Millside Industrial Estate Lawson Road, Dartford, DA1 5BW
Tel: 01322-288698 **Fax:** 01322-277520
E-mail: c.t.purt@electroavionics.co.uk
Website: http://www.electroavionics.co.uk
Directors: C. Purt (Prop)
VAT No.: GB 707 3762 31 **Date established:** 1998
Turnover: £250,000 - £500,000 **No.of Employees:** 1 - 10
Product Groups: 37, 48

Electrobase RP Ltd
Unit 7 Avery Way, Questor, Dartford, DA1 1JZ
Tel: 01322-524498 **Fax:** 01322-290518
E-mail: sales@electrobaserp.co.uk
Website: http://www.electrobaserp.co.uk
Directors: D. Salmon (Co Sec), D. Chapman (MD)
Immediate Holding Company: ELECTROBASE RP LIMITED
Registration no: 04581317 **Date established:** 2002
No.of Employees: 21 - 50 **Product Groups:** 48

Date of Accounts	Sep 07	Sep 06	Sep 05
Working Capital	277	216	165
Fixed Assets	98	129	169
Current Assets	1031	723	772
Current Liabilities	754	507	607

Electrosonic Ltd
Hawley Mill Hawley Road, Dartford, DA2 7SY
Tel: 01322-222211 **Fax:** 01322-282282
E-mail: information@electrosonic.co.uk
Website: http://www.electrosonic.com
Bank(s): Clydesdale Bank PLC
Managers: G. Fabian
Ultimate Holding Company: ELECTROSONIC OY AB (FINLAND)
Immediate Holding Company: ELECTROSONIC LIMITED
Registration no: 00794221 **Date established:** 1964
Turnover: £20m - £50m **No.of Employees:** 101 - 250 **Product Groups:** 37

Date of Accounts	Dec 11	Dec 10	Dec 09
Sales Turnover	38m	22m	22m
Pre Tax Profit/Loss	11	255	630
Working Capital	2m	5m	6m
Fixed Assets	4m	1m	201
Current Assets	12m	9m	9m
Current Liabilities	6m	2m	2m

Eva - Trading Co.
94 London Road Crayford, Dartford, DA1 4DX
Tel: 01322-611 746 **Fax:** 01322-613 520
E-mail: info@evatrading.co.uk
Website: http://www.evatrading.co.uk
Directors: C. Smith (Ptnr)
Registration no: 07568656 **No.of Employees:** 1 - 10 **Product Groups:** 11, 12, 13, 17, 20, 22, 23, 24, 29, 31, 32, 33, 37, 61, 66, 80

Evridge Precison Engineering Ltd
Holmesdale Works Holmesdale Road, South Darenth, Dartford, DA4 9JP
Tel: 01322-868961 **Fax:** 01322-868962
E-mail: mailbox@evridgeengineering.com
Website: http://www.evridgeengineering.com
Bank(s): Barclays
Directors: J. Warner (MD)
Ultimate Holding Company: BUFFALO EVRIDGE LIMITED
Immediate Holding Company: EVRIDGE HOLDINGS LIMITED
Registration no: 02107401 **VAT No.:** GB 203 2180 25
Date established: 1987 **Turnover:** £1m - £2m **No.of Employees:** 21 - 50
Product Groups: 33, 39, 48

Date of Accounts	Mar 10	Mar 09	Mar 08
Working Capital	142	-14	-190
Fixed Assets	263	314	345
Current Assets	262	113	329

Findlay Media
Hawley Mill Hawley Road, Dartford, DA2 7TJ
Tel: 01322-221144 **Fax:** 01322-221188
E-mail: enquiries@findlay.co.uk
Website: http://www.findlay.co.uk
Bank(s): Barclays
Directors: P. Ring (Sales)
Managers: M. Keeley (Tech Serv Mgr), P. Knutton, S. Jeakins
Immediate Holding Company: FINDLAY MEDIA LIMITED
Registration no: 06779864 **Date established:** 2008
Turnover: £10m - £20m **No.of Employees:** 51 - 100 **Product Groups:** 28

Date of Accounts	Dec 10	Dec 09
Working Capital	176	125
Fixed Assets	25	49
Current Assets	1m	841

Fixmart Services
80 A The Brent, Dartford, DA1 1YW
Tel: 01322-274226 **Fax:** 01322-278178
Bank(s): Barclays
Managers: A. Reeves (Ops Mgr)
VAT No.: GB 207 3867 57 **Date established:** 1975 **Turnover:** £1m - £2m
No.of Employees: 11 - 20 **Product Groups:** 35, 37, 66

Fusion Media Europe
Crown House Home Gardens, Dartford, DA1 1DZ
Tel: 01322-424499 **Fax:** 01322-424515
E-mail: info@fusion-media.eu
Website: http://www.fusionmediaeurope.com
Directors: C. Bassett (MD)
Immediate Holding Company: KING AND CAMBRIDGE HOSPITALITY LTD
Date established: 2001 **No.of Employees:** 1 - 10 **Product Groups:** 25, 28, 29, 30, 37, 39, 44, 48, 49, 61, 75, 80, 81, 86, 87, 89

Date of Accounts	Mar 04	Mar 03
Working Capital	1	-2
Fixed Assets	4	2
Current Assets	497	80

Gasco International Ltd
Unit 5 Wilks Avenue Questor, Dartford, DA1 1JS
Tel: 01322-275559 **Fax:** 01322-274446
Website: http://www.gasco.org.uk
Managers: L. Springate (District Mgr)
Ultimate Holding Company: Gas And Components International Gcv (Belgium)
Registration no: SC120806 **Date established:** 1989
Turnover: £5m - £10m **No.of Employees:** 1 - 10 **Product Groups:** 40, 66

High Voltage Maintenance Services
Littlebrook Business Centre Littlebrook Manorway, Dartford, DA1 5PZ
Tel: 01322-273100 **Fax:** 01322-294413
E-mail: enquiries@hvms.co.uk
Website: http://www.hvms.co.uk
Directors: A. Pearce (MD), D. Swading (Sales)
Managers: T. O'Neil (I.T. Exec), D. Swadling (Sales & Mktg Mg)
Registration no: 05227977 **Turnover:** £2m - £5m
No.of Employees: 1 - 10 **Product Groups:** 37, 48, 51, 52, 84

Honeywell Control Systems Ltd
Honeywell House Anchor Boulevard Crossways, Crossways Business Park, Dartford, DA2 6QH
Tel: 01322-484800 **Fax:** 01322-484899
E-mail: bob.morris@honeywell.com
Website: http://honeywell.com
Directors: M. Nicholas (MD)
Managers: T. Leach (I.T. Exec), C. Wybrew (Personnel)
Ultimate Holding Company: HONEYWELL INTERNATIONAL INC (USA)
Immediate Holding Company: HONEYWELL CONTROL SYSTEMS LIMITED
Registration no: 00217803 **Date established:** 2026
No.of Employees: 21 - 50 **Product Groups:** 52

Date of Accounts	Dec 11	Dec 10	Dec 09
Sales Turnover	335m	348m	340m
Pre Tax Profit/Loss	16m	16m	2m
Working Capital	123m	111m	66m
Fixed Assets	13m	14m	16m
Current Assets	247m	227m	169m
Current Liabilities	47m	37m	33m

J & E Hall Ltd
Questor House 191 Hawley Road, Dartford, DA1 1PU
Tel: 01322-223456 **Fax:** 01322-394421
E-mail: helpline@jehall.co.uk
Website: http://www.jehall.co.uk
Bank(s): Barclays
Managers: C. Capozio
Ultimate Holding Company: DAIKIN INDUSTRIES LTD (JAPAN)
Immediate Holding Company: J & E HALL LIMITED
Registration no: 03120673 **Date established:** 1995 **Turnover:** £2m - £5m
No.of Employees: 101 - 250 **Product Groups:** 37, 39, 40, 41, 48, 52, 66

Date of Accounts	Dec 11	Dec 10	Dec 09
Sales Turnover	40m	36m	34m
Pre Tax Profit/Loss	672	-159	-251
Working Capital	4m	2m	2m
Fixed Assets	4m	4m	4m
Current Assets	17m	14m	13m
Current Liabilities	7m	6m	6m

Jetage Engineering Co 1991 Ltd
Pier House Thames Road, Crayford, Dartford, DA1 4RG
Tel: 01322-550666 **Fax:** 01322-558149
E-mail: jetageuk@btconnect.com
Directors: R. Noakes (MD)
Immediate Holding Company: JETAGE ENGINEERING CO (1991) LIMITED
Registration no: 02800404 **Date established:** 1993
Turnover: Up to £250,000 **No.of Employees:** 21 - 50 **Product Groups:** 48

Date of Accounts	Jun 10	Jun 09	Jun 08
Working Capital	-138	11	138
Fixed Assets	794	798	798
Current Assets	48	126	311
Current Liabilities	N/A	N/A	37

Jewson Ltd
Dewlands Estate London Road, Stone, Dartford, DA2 6AS
Tel: 01322-291414 **Fax:** 01322-291493
Website: http://www.jewson.co.uk
Managers: J. Wallis (Mgr)
Ultimate Holding Company: COMPAGNIE DE SAINT GOBAIN (FRANCE)
Immediate Holding Company: JEWSON LIMITED
Registration no: 00348407 **VAT No.:** GB 497 7184 83
Date established: 1939 **No.of Employees:** 1 - 10 **Product Groups:** 66

Date of Accounts	Dec 11	Dec 10	Dec 09
Sales Turnover	1606m	1547m	1485m
Pre Tax Profit/Loss	18m	100m	45m
Working Capital	-345m	-250m	-349m
Fixed Assets	496m	387m	461m
Current Assets	657m	1005m	1320m
Current Liabilities	66m	120m	64m

K L Contracts Ltd
The Old Laundry Mile End Green, Dartford, DA2 8EB
Tel: 01474-708000 **Fax:** 01474-708345
E-mail: keith@klcontracts.co.uk
Website: http://www.klcontracts.co.uk
Directors: K. Linton (MD)
Ultimate Holding Company: CITADEL SPARK EROSION LIMITED
Immediate Holding Company: K.L. CONTRACTS LIMITED
Registration no: 03198911 **Date established:** 1996
No.of Employees: 1 - 10 **Product Groups:** 25, 26, 33, 35, 49, 52, 67, 83, 84

Date of Accounts	May 11	May 10	May 09
Working Capital	93	89	-102
Fixed Assets	20	12	26
Current Assets	453	310	257

Keith's Lifts
32 Wyatt Road, Dartford, DA1 4SP
Tel: 01322-523931 **Fax:** 01322-551392
E-mail: keithslifts@yahoo.co.uk
Directors: K. Northwood (Prop)
Date established: 1994 **No.of Employees:** 1 - 10 **Product Groups:** 35, 39, 45

L M L Contracting Ltd
Unit D1-D2 Riverside Industrial Estate Riverside Way, Dartford, DA1 5BS
Tel: 01322-221813
E-mail: peter@craymetalfinishers.co.uk
Website: http://www.craymetalfinishers.co.uk
Directors: P. Podevin (Prop)
Immediate Holding Company: LML CONTRACTING LIMITED
Registration no: 04537201 **Date established:** 2002
Turnover: Up to £250,000 **No.of Employees:** 11 - 20 **Product Groups:** 35, 48

L P S Engineering
Unit 10 Millside Industrial Estate Lawson Road, Dartford, DA1 5BW
Tel: 01322-289430 **Fax:** 01322-289436
E-mail: info@lpsengineering.co.uk
Website: http://www.lpsengineering.co.uk
Directors: R. Liffen (Ptnr)
VAT No.: GB 527 3225 59 **Turnover:** Up to £250,000
No.of Employees: 1 - 10 **Product Groups:** 48

Landscape Supply Co.
115 Main Road Sutton at Hone, Dartford, DA4 9HQ
Tel: 01322-868646 **Fax:** 01322-420291
Website: http://www.lsc-uk.com
Directors: C. Ghinn (Ptnr)
Date established: 1998 **No.of Employees:** 11 - 20 **Product Groups:** 36

London Millwrights
The Forge Stonehill Green, Dartford, DA2 7HJ
Tel: 01322-667373 **Fax:** 01322-662544
Directors: R. Willie (Prop)
Immediate Holding Company: LONDON MILLWRIGHTS LIMITED
Registration no: 07535685 **Date established:** 2011
No.of Employees: 11 - 20 **Product Groups:** 39, 48

Long & Co Kent Ltd
Bybow Farm Orchard Way, Dartford, DA2 7ER
Tel: 01322-273028 **Fax:** 01322-228818
E-mail: ken@longandcokent.co.uk
Directors: K. Long (Dir), K. Long (MD)
Immediate Holding Company: LONG & CO (KENT) LIMITED
Registration no: 04708662 **VAT No.:** GB 203 9859 50
Date established: 2003 **Turnover:** £500,000 - £1m
No.of Employees: 1 - 10 **Product Groups:** 84

Date of Accounts	Mar 11	Mar 10	Mar 09
Working Capital	-9	-0	-13
Fixed Assets	8	11	16
Current Assets	83	101	78

Lyndees
105 Burnham Road, Dartford, DA1 5AZ
Tel: 01322-225147
E-mail: shop@lyndeesflorist.co.uk
Directors: L. Bremner (Ptnr)
No.of Employees: 1 - 10 **Product Groups:** 24, 62

Maybrey Reliance
16-18 Kennet Road, Dartford, DA1 4QN
Tel: 01322-550724 **Fax:** 01322-550724
E-mail: sales@maybrey.co.uk
Website: http://www.maybrey.co.uk
Directors: R. Wood (Fin), S. Virgo (Dir)
Managers: N. Watts (Mgr), S. Hanscombe (Sales Prom Mgr), T. Kidson (Prod Mgr)
Ultimate Holding Company: Compass Aerospace Corp. Longbeach, Ca. USA
Immediate Holding Company: Compass Aerospace Corporation UK Ltd
Registration no: 00720270 **Turnover:** £2m - £5m
No.of Employees: 1 - 10 **Product Groups:** 34

Metal Packs Ltd
The Old Parsonage Works High Street, Farningham, Dartford, DA4 0DG
Tel: 01322-862727 **Fax:** 01322-865580
E-mail: metalpacks@usa.net
Website: http://www.usa.net
Directors: P. Shand (MD)
Immediate Holding Company: METALPACKS LIMITED
Registration no: 00485631 **Date established:** 1950
No.of Employees: 1 - 10 **Product Groups:** 32, 34, 48

Date of Accounts	Mar 08	Mar 07	Mar 06
Working Capital	181	135	156
Fixed Assets	887	100	82
Current Assets	489	401	450

Metcraft Finished Products
Unit 22 Crayford Industrial Estate Swaisland Drive, Crayford, Dartford, DA1 4HS
Tel: 01322-550053 **Fax:** 01322-550053
E-mail: sthorne@live.co.uk
Directors: S. Thorne (Ptnr)
Date established: 1991 **No.of Employees:** 1 - 10 **Product Groups:** 46, 48

Mid Blue International Ltd
Laburnham Cottage Hawley Road, Dartford, DA1 1PX
Tel: 01322-407000 **Fax:** 07092-364351
E-mail: paul.williams@mid-blue.com
Website: http://www.mid-blue.com
Directors: P. Williams (Dir)
Immediate Holding Company: MID BLUE INTERNATIONAL LIMITED
Registration no: 02223957 **Date established:** 1988 **Turnover:** £2m - £5m
No.of Employees: 1 - 10 **Product Groups:** 26, 37, 44, 48, 52, 67, 83, 84, 86

Date of Accounts	Jun 11	Jun 10	Jun 09
Working Capital	71	57	72
Current Assets	310	76	146

Murex Biotech Ltd (a Subsidary of Abbott Laboratories)

Central Road, Dartford, DA1 5LR
Tel: 01322-277711 **Fax:** 01322-273288
Website: http://www.abbott.co.uk
Bank(s): Barclays, London EC2
Directors: S. Norrington (Co Sec), T. Reardon (Dir)
Ultimate Holding Company: ABBOTT LABORATORIES (USA)
Immediate Holding Company: MUREX BIOTECH LIMITED
Registration no: 02670649 **Date established:** 1991
Turnover: £10m - £20m **No.of Employees:** 251 - 500 **Product Groups:** 31

Date of Accounts	Dec 11	Dec 10	Nov 09
Sales Turnover	10m	17m	22m
Pre Tax Profit/Loss	2m	2m	4m
Working Capital	33m	31m	36m
Fixed Assets	33m	33m	39m
Current Assets	36m	37m	42m
Current Liabilities	2m	4m	3m

N C C T Ltd

Unit 7 Optima Park Thames Road, Crayford, Dartford, DA1 4QX
Tel: 01322-558806 **Fax:** 01322-558807
E-mail: info@ncct.co.uk
Website: http://www.ncct.co.uk
Directors: K. Timlin (MD)
Immediate Holding Company: NCCT LIMITED
Registration no: 05495459 **Date established:** 2005 **Turnover:** £2m - £5m
No.of Employees: 1 - 10 **Product Groups:** 07, 51, 52

Date of Accounts	Jun 11	Jun 10	Jun 09
Working Capital	660	267	577
Fixed Assets	186	174	570
Current Assets	849	443	922

New Horizon Systems Ltd

Unit 8 Thames Road Crayford, Dartford, DA1 4QX
Tel: 08456-250055
E-mail: info@newhorizon-systems.co.uk
Website: http://www.newhorizon-systems.co.uk
Directors: M. Nagpal (MD)
Immediate Holding Company: NEW HORIZON SYSTEMS LIMITED
Registration no: 04101208 **Date established:** 2000
Turnover: Up to £250,000 **No.of Employees:** 1 - 10 **Product Groups:** 27, 28, 37, 44, 48, 66, 67

Date of Accounts	Dec 11	Dec 10	Dec 09
Working Capital	10	39	33
Fixed Assets	20	10	N/A
Current Assets	112	96	62
Current Liabilities	N/A	18	N/A

E E Olley & Sons Ltd

Dartford Trade Park Questor, Dartford, DA1 1PE
Tel: 01322-227681 **Fax:** 01322-289724
E-mail: timolley@eeolley.co.uk
Website: http://www.eeolley.co.uk
Bank(s): Barclays
Directors: T. Olley (Dir)
Immediate Holding Company: E.E. OLLEY & SONS LIMITED
Registration no: 00513587 **Date established:** 1952 **Turnover:** £1m - £2m
No.of Employees: 11 - 20 **Product Groups:** 66

Date of Accounts	Nov 11	Nov 10	Nov 09
Working Capital	1m	1m	1m
Fixed Assets	213	202	212
Current Assets	2m	2m	2m

Owlett Jaton

Regus House Victory Way, Crossways Business Park, Dartford, DA2 6QD
Tel: 01322-277733 **Fax:** 01322-288043
E-mail: dartford.sales@owlett-jaton.com
Website: http://www.owlett-jaton.com
Bank(s): Barclays, Bexleyheath
Managers: J. Young (Sales Admin)
Ultimate Holding Company: BLACKFRIARS CORP (USA)
Immediate Holding Company: BROBUT LONGLEY ELECTRICAL SERVICES LIMITED
Registration no: 03112228 **VAT No.:** GB 299 5476 84
Date established: 2011 **Turnover:** £250,000 - £500,000
No.of Employees: 11 - 20 **Product Groups:** 26, 35

Date of Accounts	Aug 12	May 11	May 10
Working Capital	N/A	-0	-1
Fixed Assets	N/A	1	1
Current Assets	12	22	35

P P M Associates

Instone House Instone Road, Dartford, DA1 2AG
Tel: 01322-229912
E-mail: abbie@ppm-associates.com
Website: http://www.ppm-associates.com
Managers: A. Nie
Immediate Holding Company: P.P.M. AND ASSOCIATES LIMITED
Registration no: 03110510 **Date established:** 1995
No.of Employees: 1 - 10 **Product Groups:** 44

Date of Accounts	Oct 11	Oct 10	Oct 09
Working Capital	-358	46	N/A
Fixed Assets	3m	N/A	N/A
Current Assets	107	60	N/A

Premier Paper Group Ltd

Unit 1 Wilks Avenue Questor, Dartford, DA1 1JS
Tel: 01322-421940 **Fax:** 01322-227716
E-mail: graham.caistor@paper.co.uk
Website: http://www.paper.co.uk
Bank(s): Lloyds TSB Bank plc
Managers: G. Caistor (Sales Prom Mgr)
Ultimate Holding Company: G. C. PAPER LIMITED
Immediate Holding Company: PREMIER PAPER GROUP LIMITED
Registration no: 03672117 **Date established:** 1998
No.of Employees: 21 - 50 **Product Groups:** 27

Date of Accounts	Dec 11	Dec 10	Dec 09
Sales Turnover	155m	151m	141m
Pre Tax Profit/Loss	6m	6m	1m
Working Capital	18m	16m	7m
Fixed Assets	3m	3m	15m
Current Assets	62m	63m	53m
Current Liabilities	5m	4m	4m

Radflex Contract Services Ltd

Unit 35 Wilks Avenue Questor, Dartford, DA1 1JS
Tel: 01322-276363 **Fax:** 01322-270606
E-mail: grahamh@radflex.co.uk
Website: http://www.radflex.co.uk
Bank(s): National Westminster
Directors: G. Hedgecock (MD)
Immediate Holding Company: RADFLEX CONTRACT SERVICES LTD
Registration no: 01329156 **VAT No.:** GB 317 6254 60
Date established: 1977 **Turnover:** £1m - £2m **No.of Employees:** 21 - 50
Product Groups: 32, 66

Date of Accounts	Jan 12	Jan 11	Jan 10
Working Capital	1m	953	874
Fixed Assets	94	128	116
Current Assets	1m	1m	1m

Red Square Interactive Ltd

5 Sandpit Road, Dartford, DA1 5BU
Tel: 01322-628766 **Fax:** 01322-279216
E-mail: info@red-square.co.uk
Website: http://www.red-square.co.uk
Directors: B. Underhill (Dir)
Immediate Holding Company: RED SQUARE INTERACTIVE LIMITED
Registration no: 04109016 **Date established:** 2000
No.of Employees: 1 - 10 **Product Groups:** 81

Date of Accounts	Apr 11	Apr 10	Apr 09
Working Capital	-1	-8	29
Fixed Assets	3	9	14
Current Assets	43	39	79

Rolls Royce (Commercial Marine UK)

The Nucleus Brunel Way, Dartford, DA1 5GA
Tel: 01322-312028 **Fax:** 01322-312054
E-mail: alan.reid@rolls-royce.com
Website: http://www.rollsroyce.com
Managers: A. Reid (Sales Prom Mgr)
Ultimate Holding Company: ROLLS ROYCE
Registration no: 05694340 **VAT No.:** GB 239 6880 17
Date established: 2006 **Turnover:** £5m - £10m **No.of Employees:** 1 - 10
Product Groups: 37, 39, 40, 45

Safetell Ltd

Unit 46 Fawkes Avenue, Questor, Dartford, DA1 1JQ
Tel: 01322-223233 **Fax:** 01322-277751
E-mail: john.medlam@safetell.co.uk
Website: http://www.safetell.co.uk
Directors: B. Beecraft (Fin), A. Pieterse (MD)
Managers: N. Paget (Develop Mgr), S. Hewitt (Mats Contrlr), D. Rudkins (Sales Prom Mgr), A. Norris (Tech Serv Mgr), C. King (Personnel), G. Rouse (Comptroller)
Ultimate Holding Company: NEWMARK SECURITY PLC
Immediate Holding Company: SAFETELL INTERNATIONAL LIMITED
Registration no: 02421258 **Date established:** 1989 **Turnover:** £5m - £10m
No.of Employees: 51 - 100 **Product Groups:** 26, 35

Date of Accounts	Apr 11	Apr 10	Apr 09
Pre Tax Profit/Loss	N/A	N/A	-0
Working Capital	2m	2m	2m
Fixed Assets	N/A	N/A	107
Current Assets	2m	2m	2m

A Searle & Co. Ltd

Unit 24 Bourne Road Industrial Park Bourne Road, Dartford, DA1 4BZ
Tel: 01322-529119 **Fax:** 01322-528528
E-mail: info@asearle.co.uk
Website: http://www.asearle.co.uk
Directors: T. Oborne (Dir)
Immediate Holding Company: A. SEARLE & COMPANY LIMITED
Registration no: 06515709 **Date established:** 2008
No.of Employees: 1 - 10 **Product Groups:** 38, 42

Date of Accounts	Jun 11	Jun 10	Jun 09
Working Capital	376	105	26
Fixed Assets	40	37	43
Current Assets	1m	2m	1m

Seaweather Marine Services Ltd

625-649 Princes Road, Dartford, DA2 6EF
Tel: 01322-275513 **Fax:** 01322-292639
E-mail: safety@survitecgroup.com
Website: http://www.seaweather.co.uk
Directors: S. George (Co Sec), R. George (MD)
Managers: B. Clarke (Comm), B. Clarke (Sales Prom Mgr), A. Levack (Mktg Serv Mgr)
Ultimate Holding Company: SEAWEATHER HOLDINGS LIMITED
Immediate Holding Company: SEAWEATHER MARINE SERVICES LIMITED
Registration no: 01295131 **VAT No.:** GB 445 3297 40
Date established: 1977 **Turnover:** £1m - £2m **No.of Employees:** 11 - 20
Product Groups: 30, 32, 39, 40

Date of Accounts	Aug 10	Aug 09	Aug 08
Working Capital	189	401	442
Fixed Assets	260	225	185
Current Assets	1m	2m	2m

Shaw & Sons Ltd

Unit 21 Bourne Industrial Park Bourne Road, Dartford, DA1 4BZ
Tel: 01322-621100 **Fax:** 01322-550553
E-mail: sales@shaws.co.uk
Website: http://www.shaws.co.uk
Directors: R. Smith (Fin)
Managers: S. Bruty (Mgr)
Ultimate Holding Company: SHAW & SONS GROUP LIMITED
Immediate Holding Company: SHAW & SONS GROUP LIMITED
Registration no: 03416775 **VAT No.:** GB 701 5761 59
Date established: 1997 **Turnover:** £2m - £5m **No.of Employees:** 1 - 10
Product Groups: 28

Date of Accounts	Mar 11	Mar 10	Mar 09
Sales Turnover	N/A	N/A	2m
Pre Tax Profit/Loss	N/A	N/A	79
Working Capital	283	-1m	-210
Fixed Assets	3m	3m	44
Current Assets	283	284	655
Current Liabilities	N/A	N/A	620

Sherwen Engineering Co. Ltd

Mile End Green, Dartford, DA2 8EB
Tel: 01474-703220 **Fax:** 01474-705016
E-mail: sales@sherwen-engineering.co.uk
Website: http://www.gladetree.co.uk
Bank(s): Barclays
Directors: J. Sherwen (Dir)
Managers: I. Turner (Design Eng)
Ultimate Holding Company: GLADETREE LIMITED
Immediate Holding Company: SHERWEN ENGINEERING CO LIMITED
Registration no: 02064604 **VAT No.:** GB 203 6270 04
Date established: 1986 **Turnover:** £500,000 - £1m
No.of Employees: 11 - 20 **Product Groups:** 46

Date of Accounts	Jul 11	Jul 10	Jul 09
Working Capital	779	588	433
Fixed Assets	99	64	79
Current Assets	1m	997	725

Smithpack Ltd

Unit 8 Butterly Avenue, Questor, Dartford, DA1 1JG
Tel: 01322-311968 **Fax:** 01322-287183
E-mail: kent@smithpack.co.uk
Website: http://www.smithpack.co.uk
Directors: A. Brigstock (Sales), A. Brigstock (Dir), K. Allwood (MD), T. Coverdale (Fin)
Ultimate Holding Company: WSPH LIMITED
Immediate Holding Company: SMITHPACK LIMITED
Registration no: 01850712 **Date established:** 1984
Turnover: £10m - £20m **No.of Employees:** 11 - 20 **Product Groups:** 27, 49, 66

Date of Accounts	Apr 11	Apr 10	Apr 09
Sales Turnover	7m	7m	7m
Pre Tax Profit/Loss	105	73	-400
Working Capital	226	66	-187
Fixed Assets	431	528	752
Current Assets	2m	2m	2m
Current Liabilities	872	1m	1m

Solar Shield Ltd

10 Swan Business Park Sandpit Road, Dartford, DA1 5ED
Tel: 08451-306232 **Fax:** 08451-306232
E-mail: info@solarshield.co.uk
Website: http://www.solarshield.co.uk
Bank(s): HSBC
Directors: M. Townend (Dir)
Immediate Holding Company: SOLAR SHIELD LIMITED
Registration no: 01958075 **VAT No.:** 467 4500 38 **Date established:** 1985
Turnover: £1m - £2m **No.of Employees:** 11 - 20 **Product Groups:** 30

Date of Accounts	Mar 11	Mar 10	Mar 09
Working Capital	46	25	58
Fixed Assets	65	54	53
Current Assets	291	301	253

Spiral Packs London Ltd

Unit 22 Fawkes Avenue, Questor, Dartford, DA1 1JQ
Tel: 01322-425940 **Fax:** 01322-425942
E-mail: richardfrancis@spiralpacks.co.uk
Website: http://www.spiralpacks.co.uk
Bank(s): HSBC
Directors: S. Smith (Pers), R. Francis (MD)
Managers: P. Harris (Sales Prom Mgr)
Ultimate Holding Company: SPIRAL PACKS (HOLDINGS) LIMITED
Immediate Holding Company: SPIRAL PACKS (LONDON) LIMITED
Registration no: 01105821 **Date established:** 1973 **Turnover:** £5m - £10m
No.of Employees: 21 - 50 **Product Groups:** 27

Date of Accounts	Apr 11	Apr 10	Apr 09
Working Capital	624	612	529
Fixed Assets	124	131	161
Current Assets	1m	2m	1m

Splasher Pools

38 Acorn Industrial Park Crayford Road, Dartford, DA1 4AL
Tel: 01322-315732 **Fax:** 020-8303 1398
E-mail: sales@splasherpools.com
Website: http://garrarufacentre.co.uk
Directors: K. Hulbert (MD)
Registration no: 03651637 **Date established:** 1998
No.of Employees: 1 - 10 **Product Groups:** 30, 32, 33, 40

Stannah Lift Services Ltd

46-47 Acorn Industrial Park Crayford Road, Dartford, DA1 4AL
Tel: 01322-555777 **Fax:** 01322-555444
E-mail: julie_dutton@stannah.co.uk
Website: http://www.stannah.co.uk
Managers: J. Dutton (Mgr)
Ultimate Holding Company: STANNAH LIFTS HOLDINGS LIMITED
Immediate Holding Company: STANNAH LIFT SERVICES LIMITED
Registration no: 01189799 **Date established:** 1974
No.of Employees: 21 - 50 **Product Groups:** 35, 39, 45

Date of Accounts	Dec 11	Dec 10	Dec 09
Sales Turnover	84m	82m	87m
Pre Tax Profit/Loss	191	2m	2m
Working Capital	12m	14m	15m
Fixed Assets	4m	4m	3m
Current Assets	21m	24m	24m
Current Liabilities	6m	6m	7m

Stockgap Ltd

209 Watling Street, Dartford, DA2 6EG
Tel: 01322-291717 **Fax:** 01322-273939
E-mail: sales@stockgap.co.uk
Website: http://www.stockgap.co.uk
Bank(s): Barclays
Directors: A. Jones (MD)
Immediate Holding Company: STOCKGAP LIMITED
Registration no: 01540334 **VAT No.:** GB 358 2194 38
Date established: 1981 **Turnover:** £2m - £5m **No.of Employees:** 21 - 50
Product Groups: 66

Date of Accounts	Dec 11	Dec 10	Dec 09
Sales Turnover	N/A	N/A	5m
Pre Tax Profit/Loss	N/A	N/A	223
Working Capital	581	666	692
Fixed Assets	3m	3m	3m
Current Assets	1m	1m	1m
Current Liabilities	N/A	N/A	274

The Swift Lift Company UK Ltd

Unit 17 Mulberry Court Bourne Industrial Park Bourne Road, Dartford, DA1 4BF
Tel: 01322-551379 **Fax:** 01322-551381
E-mail: info@swiftlift-uk.com
Website: http://www.swiftlift-uk.com
Directors: S. McGregor (Co Sec), H. Eugene (Sales)
Immediate Holding Company: THE SWIFT LIFT COMPANY U.K. LIMITED
Registration no: 03116884 **Date established:** 1995
No.of Employees: 21 - 50 **Product Groups:** 35, 39, 45

Date of Accounts	Dec 11	Dec 10	Dec 09
Working Capital	539	481	434
Fixed Assets	57	44	44
Current Assets	1m	903	1m

T R S Ltd
Unit 2 Swan Business Park, Dartford, DA1 5ED
Tel: 08452-249000 **Fax:** 0845-224 9001
E-mail: service@trs.ltd.uk
Website: http://www.trs-online.co.uk
Directors: P. Dhaliwal (Fin), B. Bage (Dir), J. Kilgannon (Chief Op Offcr)
Managers: R. Chahal
Immediate Holding Company: TRS LIMITED
Registration no: 04931728 **VAT No.:** GB 335 8581 33
Date established: 2003 **Turnover:** £1m - £2m **No.of Employees:** 21 - 50
Product Groups: 52

Date of Accounts	Dec 11	Dec 10	Dec 09
Working Capital	78	-93	-67
Fixed Assets	285	452	421
Current Assets	671	588	612
Current Liabilities	N/A	N/A	4

Texcel Technology plc
Parkside Works Thames Road, Crayford, Dartford, DA1 4SB
Tel: 01322-621700 **Fax:** 01322-557733
E-mail: peter.shawyer@texceltechnology.com
Website: http://www.texceltechnology.com
Bank(s): Barclays
Directors: A. McLeod (I.T. Dir), A. McLeod (MD), P. Shawyer (Comm), S. Suckling (Fin)
Managers: B. Manager (Purch Mgr)
Ultimate Holding Company: TEXCEL (2011) LIMITED
Immediate Holding Company: TEXCEL TECHNOLOGY PLC
Registration no: 02607732 **VAT No.:** GB 547 8721 08
Date established: 1991 **Turnover:** £5m - £10m
No.of Employees: 51 - 100 **Product Groups:** 37, 38, 79, 80, 84

Date of Accounts	Jan 12	Jan 11	Jan 10
Sales Turnover	7m	7m	6m
Pre Tax Profit/Loss	36	132	123
Working Capital	1m	1m	1m
Fixed Assets	270	1m	1m
Current Assets	3m	3m	2m
Current Liabilities	315	349	250

Toolbank
Longreach Gallion Boulevard, Crossways Business Park, Dartford, DA2 6QE
Tel: 01322-321300 **Fax:** 01322-383641
E-mail: info@ecomerse.com
Website: http://www.toolbank.com
Directors: A. Strong (Grp Chief Exec), J. Twallin (Ch), N. Doyle (Dir)
Immediate Holding Company: TOOLBANK LIMITED
Registration no: 04679597 **VAT No.:** GB 202 9347 83
Date established: 2003 **Turnover:** £10m - £20m
No.of Employees: 101 - 250 **Product Groups:** 36, 37, 38

Westmeria Healthcare Ltd
Optima Park Thames Road, Crayford, Dartford, DA1 4QX
Tel: 01322-520560 **Fax:** 020-8658 9870
Website: http://www.westmeria.com
Directors: N. Rodker (MD)
Immediate Holding Company: WESTMERIA HEALTH CARE LIMITED
Registration no: 03144857 **Date established:** 1996 **Turnover:** £1m - £2m
No.of Employees: 21 - 50 **Product Groups:** 26, 38, 48, 83

Date of Accounts	Jan 12	Jan 11	Jan 10
Working Capital	2m	902	630
Fixed Assets	690	743	763
Current Assets	3m	2m	2m

Peter Westpfel
21 Walnut Tree Avenue Wilmington, Dartford, DA1 1LJ
Tel: 01322-401907 **Fax:** 01322-401907
E-mail: p.westpfel40@ntlworld.com
Website: http://www.thecorianman.co.uk
Directors: P. Westpfel (Prop)
Turnover: Up to £250,000 **No.of Employees:** 1 - 10 **Product Groups:** 24, 25, 27, 30, 33

Jacob White Packaging Ltd
Riverside Industrial Estate, Dartford, DA1 5BY
Tel: 01322-272531 **Fax:** 01322-270692
E-mail: jwhiteuk@aol.com
Website: http://www.jacobwhite.com
Bank(s): Barclays, Sevenoaks
Directors: P. Colwell (MD), C. Colwell (Co Sec), D. Smith (Fin)
Managers: J. Parris (Purch Mgr), M. West (Mktg Serv Mgr)
Immediate Holding Company: JACOB,WHITE(PACKAGING)LIMITED
Registration no: 01003647 **VAT No.:** GB 474 6189 13
Date established: 1971 **Turnover:** £2m - £5m **No.of Employees:** 21 - 50
Product Groups: 42

Date of Accounts	Dec 11	Dec 10	Dec 09
Working Capital	619	506	577
Fixed Assets	1m	1m	1m
Current Assets	2m	2m	1m

Wilhelmsen Ship Service
Unit 3a Newtons Court Crossways, Crossways Business Park, Dartford, DA2 6QL
Tel: 01322-282412 **Fax:** 01322-620660
E-mail: andy.millar@wilhelmsen.com
Website: http://www.wilhelmsen.com
Bank(s): Danske Bank, London
Managers: R. Freeman (Chief Mgr), A. Millar (Chief Mgr)
Ultimate Holding Company: WILH.WILHELMSEN LIMITED A (NORWAY)
Immediate Holding Company: WILHELMSEN SHIPS SERVICE LIMITED
Registration no: 00874720 **VAT No.:** GB 163 6571 53
Date established: 1966 **Turnover:** £10m - £20m
No.of Employees: 21 - 50 **Product Groups:** 20, 22, 23, 24, 29, 30, 31, 32, 35, 36, 37, 38, 39, 40, 42, 45, 46, 48, 66, 67, 68, 74, 76, 85

Date of Accounts	Dec 11	Dec 10	Dec 09
Sales Turnover	11m	9m	8m
Pre Tax Profit/Loss	718	12	778
Working Capital	816	158	214
Fixed Assets	153	103	35
Current Assets	2m	904	1m
Current Liabilities	724	464	343

A Winchester & Sons
9 Great Queen Street, Dartford, DA1 1TJ
Tel: 01322-221388 **Fax:** 01322-227659
E-mail: richardmay77@hotmail.co.uk
Managers: R. May (Mgr)
Turnover: £500,000 - £1m **No.of Employees:** 1 - 10 **Product Groups:** 66, 83

Deal

Advance Metal Components Ltd
Units 12-14 Minters Industrial Estate, Deal, CT14 9PZ
Tel: 01304-380574 **Fax:** 01304-380619
E-mail: sales@amc-cncmachining.com
Website: http://www.amc-cncmachining.com
Directors: S. Hambrook (MD), D. Hambrook (Fin)
Immediate Holding Company: ADVANCE METAL COMPONENTS LIMITED
Registration no: 04699783 **VAT No.:** GB **Date established:** 2003
Turnover: £250,000 - £500,000 **No.of Employees:** 1 - 10
Product Groups: 48

Date of Accounts	Apr 12	Apr 11	Apr 10
Working Capital	-107	-142	-139
Fixed Assets	172	152	181
Current Assets	88	90	49

Clark's Fabrications
A Deal Enterprise Centre Western Road, Deal, CT14 6PJ
Tel: 01304-360222
Directors: S. Clark (Prop)
Date established: 2002 **No.of Employees:** 1 - 10 **Product Groups:** 35

Creative Builders Deal Kent
66 Union Road, Deal, CT14 6AR
Tel: 01304-382349
E-mail: info@wezontheweb.co.uk
Website: http://www.creativebuilders.co.uk
Directors: W. Smith (Prop)
Date established: 1975 **No.of Employees:** 1 - 10 **Product Groups:** 25

F G S Engineering
Vine Lodge The Street, Northbourne, Deal, CT14 0LG
Tel: 01304-375956
Directors: S. Fletcher (Prop)
Date established: 2003 **No.of Employees:** 1 - 10 **Product Groups:** 35

Maurice Gill Blacksmith
42 Lydia Road Walmer, Deal, CT14 9JX
Tel: 01304-362771 **Fax:** 01304-362771
Directors: M. Gill (Prop)
Date established: 1988 **No.of Employees:** 1 - 10 **Product Groups:** 26, 35

Mongeham
174 Rectory Road, Deal, CT14 9NR
Tel: 01304-364855
E-mail: twrthomson@aol.com
Directors: W. Thomson (Prop)
No.of Employees: 1 - 10 **Product Groups:** 26, 35

Dover

A M S Engineering
Upton Wood Farm Upton Wood, Shepherdswell, Dover, CT15 7LE
Tel: 01304-830263 **Fax:** 01304-832066
Directors: G. Rolfe (Prop)
Date established: 1984 **No.of Employees:** 1 - 10 **Product Groups:** 41

Acorn Marketing Ltd
105 London Road River, Dover, CT16 3AA
Tel: 01304-827330 **Fax:** 01304-827080
E-mail: sales@acorn.uk.net
Website: http://www.acorn.uk.net
Directors: J. Baniack-Hollands (MD)
Managers: S. Dietpedalle (Mgr)
Registration no: 01648810 **VAT No.:** GB 377 9992 64
Turnover: £500,000 - £1m **No.of Employees:** 1 - 10 **Product Groups:** 27, 28, 49, 81

Date of Accounts	Mar 08	Mar 07	Mar 06
Sales Turnover	N/A	190	N/A
Pre Tax Profit/Loss	N/A	-3	N/A
Working Capital	-1	7	7
Fixed Assets	9	4	4
Current Assets	35	41	65
Current Liabilities	37	34	57
ROCE% (Return on Capital Employed)		-25.2	
ROT% (Return on Turnover)		-1.4	

Brightarc Welding Ltd
Newlands Farm Canterbury Road, Selsted, Dover, CT15 7HL
Tel: 01303-844319 **Fax:** 01303-844666
E-mail: glenn@brightarcwelding.wanadoo.co.uk
Website: http://www.brightarcwelding.co.uk
Directors: G. Jex (MD)
Immediate Holding Company: BRIGHTARC WELDING LIMITED
Registration no: 05726102 **VAT No.:** GB 472 7305 44
Date established: 2006 **Turnover:** Up to £250,000
No.of Employees: 1 - 10 **Product Groups:** 48

Date of Accounts	Apr 11	Apr 10	Apr 09
Working Capital	285	247	204
Fixed Assets	31	44	53
Current Assets	381	312	281

Charlton Bodies Ltd
Old Park Whitfield, Dover, CT16 2HQ
Tel: 01304-828680 **Fax:** 01304-824061
E-mail: admin@charltonbodies.co.uk
Website: http://www.charltonbodies.co.uk
Directors: S. Burton (MD)
Managers: K. Melrose (Works Gen Mgr), B. Olver
Ultimate Holding Company: THOMPSONS (UK) LIMITED
Immediate Holding Company: CHARLTON BODIES LIMITED
Registration no: 04056688 **Date established:** 2000
No.of Employees: 21 - 50 **Product Groups:** 45

Date of Accounts	Jan 11	Jan 10	Jan 09
Sales Turnover	3m	3m	N/A
Pre Tax Profit/Loss	-344	-271	N/A
Working Capital	-111	114	289
Fixed Assets	116	170	226
Current Assets	586	489	1m
Current Liabilities	195	94	N/A

Dicky Willis Fabrication & Welding
Coombe Road, Dover, CT17 0LQ
Tel: 01304-202227 **Fax:** 01304-202227
Managers: D. Willis (Mgr)
Immediate Holding Company: NORTHWALL DOVER LIMITED
Registration no: 02569731 **Date established:** 1990
No.of Employees: 1 - 10 **Product Groups:** 35

Date of Accounts	May 11	May 10	May 09
Working Capital	-205	42	-106
Fixed Assets	284	291	145
Current Assets	118	288	159

E D T Direct Ion Ltd
Unit 5 Waldershare Park, Waldershare, Dover, CT15 5DQ
Tel: 01304-829960 **Fax:** 01304-829970
E-mail: sales@edt.co.uk
Website: http://www.edt.co.uk
Directors: J. Chappell (MD)
Immediate Holding Company: EDT DIRECT ION LIMITED
Registration no: 04135318 **Date established:** 2001
No.of Employees: 1 - 10 **Product Groups:** 42

Date of Accounts	Dec 11	Dec 10	Dec 09
Working Capital	21	-22	-17
Fixed Assets	2	3	3
Current Assets	130	86	83

E E C Shipping & Forwarding
3 Market Square, Dover, CT16 1LZ
Tel: 01304-211011 **Fax:** 01304-214885
E-mail: info@eecshipping.com
Website: http://www.eecshipping.com
Managers: R. Baker (Chief Mgr)
Immediate Holding Company: EEC SHIPPING LIMITED
Registration no: 05833305 **Date established:** 2006
Turnover: £500,000 - £1m **No.of Employees:** 1 - 10 **Product Groups:** 76, 84

Date of Accounts	Dec 10	Dec 09	Jun 08
Sales Turnover	984	2m	1m
Pre Tax Profit/Loss	19	79	73
Working Capital	153	139	92
Fixed Assets	25	1	4
Current Assets	289	347	414
Current Liabilities	22	34	47

Freight Clearance Ltd
New Bridge House New Bridge, Dover, CT16 1JS
Tel: 01304-211020 **Fax:** 01304-209753
E-mail: info@freighttransport.co.uk
Website: http://www.freighttransport.co.uk
Directors: J. Kearns (MD), A. Miller (Fin)
Immediate Holding Company: FREIGHT CLEARANCE LIMITED
Registration no: 00989217 **VAT No.:** GB 238 5748 28
Date established: 1970 **Turnover:** £1m - £2m **No.of Employees:** 1 - 10
Product Groups: 76

Date of Accounts	Apr 11	Apr 10	Apr 09
Working Capital	361	319	280
Fixed Assets	19	23	30
Current Assets	1m	1m	1m

Friendly Soap
6 Church Hill Shepherdswell, Dover, CT15 7NR
Tel: 01304-830522
E-mail: info@friendlysoap.co.uk
Website: http://www.friendlysoap.co.uk
Directors: R. Wichall (Dir)
Date established: 2009 **Turnover:** Up to £250,000
No.of Employees: 1 - 10 **Product Groups:** 32, 63

GATIC
Poulton Close, Dover, CT17 0UF
Tel: 01304-203545 **Fax:** 01304-215001
E-mail: p.burnap@gatic.com
Website: http://www.gatic.com
Bank(s): Barclays
Directors: P. Burnap (Comm), N. Buckingham (MD), C. Little (Chief Op Offcr), D. Harvey (MD)
Managers: M. Stanway (Mktg Serv Mgr), J. Carter (I.T. Exec), I. Perkins (Works Gen Mgr)
Ultimate Holding Company: THE ALUMASC GROUP PLC
Immediate Holding Company: ELKINGTON GATIC LIMITED
Registration no: 02534229 **VAT No.:** GB 201 9417 96
Date established: 1990 **Turnover:** £5m - £10m **No.of Employees:** 21 - 50
Product Groups: 34, 35, 51

George Hammond plc
Aycliffe Business Centre Archcliffe Road, Dover, CT17 9EL
Tel: 01304-201201 **Fax:** 01304-240374
E-mail: info@georgehammond.plc.uk
Website: http://www.georgehammond.plc.uk
Bank(s): National Westminster Bank Plc
Directors: C. Madderson (MD), D. Ryeland (Ch), J. Ryeland (Dir), J. Ryeland (MD)
Managers: P. Dixon (I.T. Exec)
Immediate Holding Company: GEORGE HAMMOND PLC
Registration no: 00690947 **VAT No.:** GB 201 1156 39
Date established: 1961 **Turnover:** £50m - £75m
No.of Employees: 11 - 20 **Product Groups:** 74, 76, 82

Date of Accounts	Dec 10	Dec 09	Dec 08
Sales Turnover	67m	64m	67m
Pre Tax Profit/Loss	2m	982	2m
Working Capital	6m	5m	5m
Fixed Assets	10m	11m	10m
Current Assets	8m	7m	8m
Current Liabilities	585	464	684

Graham
Coombe Valley Road, Dover, CT17 0EN
Tel: 01304-216332 **Fax:** 01304-241121
E-mail: kevin.maynard@graham-group.co.uk
Website: http://www.graham-group.co.uk
Managers: K. Maynards (Mgr)
Registration no: 00307131 **VAT No.:** GB 497 7184 83
Turnover: £10m - £20m **No.of Employees:** 1 - 10 **Product Groups:** 66

The London Fancy Box Company Ltd
Poulton Close Coombe Valley, Dover, CT17 0XB
Tel: 01304-242001 **Fax:** 01304-240229
E-mail: sales@londonfancybox.co.uk
Website: http://www.londonfancybox.co.uk
Directors: C. Lawson (Grp Chief Exec), D. Dixon (Dir), M. Lawson (Fin), R. Terry (Dir)
Managers: S. McGarry (Personnel), Z. Haydon (Tech Serv Mgr)
Immediate Holding Company: THE LONDON FANCY BOX COMPANY LIMITED
Registration no: 00230692 **VAT No.:** GB 220 5331 19
Date established: 2028 **Turnover:** £10m - £20m
No.of Employees: 101 - 250 **Product Groups:** 27, 30, 31, 48, 49, 66

Date of Accounts	Dec 11	Dec 10	Dec 09
Sales Turnover	18m	17m	18m
Pre Tax Profit/Loss	927	-1m	306
Working Capital	2m	930	2m
Fixed Assets	2m	3m	3m
Current Assets	5m	5m	4m
Current Liabilities	2m	371	392

Megger Ltd
Archcliffe Road, Dover, CT17 9EN
Tel: 01304-502100 **Fax:** 01304-241491
E-mail: uksales@megger.com
Website: http://www.megger.com
Bank(s): National Westminster Bank Plc
Directors: L. Dyer (Fin), S. Drennan (Fin), J. Hewlett (Sales), A. Boughtwood (MD)
Managers: N. Hilditch (Mktg Serv Mgr), S. Martin, A. Munn (Personnel), A. Goggin (Tech Serv Mgr)
Ultimate Holding Company: TBG LIMITED
Immediate Holding Company: MEGGER LIMITED
Registration no: 02110613 **VAT No.:** GB 754 5261 26
Date established: 1987 **Turnover:** £20m - £50m
No.of Employees: 251 - 500 **Product Groups:** 38, 48, 67

Date of Accounts	Nov 11	Nov 10	Nov 09
Sales Turnover	29m	16m	N/A
Pre Tax Profit/Loss	734	635	3m
Working Capital	684	788	-6m
Fixed Assets	922	842	46m
Current Assets	8m	7m	73
Current Liabilities	1m	608	N/A

Olloquiegui UK Ltd
26-27 Market Square, Dover, CT16 1NG
Tel: 01304-206286 **Fax:** 01304-204914
E-mail: mpicamills@olloquiegui.es
Website: http://www.olloquiegui.es
Directors: J. Elorriaga Azpilicueta (Dir), F. Elorriaga (Co Sec), Picamills (Dir)
Managers: R. San Emeterio (Mgr)
Ultimate Holding Company: PRENIMEX LIMITED
Registration no: 01079872 **Date established:** 1994
Turnover: Up to £250,000 **No.of Employees:** 1 - 10 **Product Groups:** 72

Date of Accounts	Dec 05
Working Capital	73
Current Assets	176
Current Liabilities	104
Total Share Capital	1

P & O Ferries Administrative Offices
Channel House Channel View Road, Dover, CT17 9TJ
Tel: 01304-863000 **Fax:** 01482-708255
E-mail: sales@ponsf.com
Website: http://www.poferries.com
Directors: C. Cunningham (Dir), R. Lough (Dir), P. Van Den Brandhof (MD), J. Van Den Bor (Fin), G. Dunlop (Ch)
Managers: M. Brewin (Personnel), K. Hall (I.T. Exec), F. Wain (I.T. Exec), A. Hull (Mgr)
Ultimate Holding Company: DUBAI WORLD CORPORATION (DUBAI)
Immediate Holding Company: P&O FERRIES HOLDINGS LIMITED
Registration no: 06038077 **VAT No.:** GB 708 0286 46
Date established: 2006 **Turnover:** £75m - £125m
No.of Employees: 1 - 10 **Product Groups:** 74

Date of Accounts	Dec 11	Dec 10	Dec 09
Pre Tax Profit/Loss	812	-542	-2m
Working Capital	-237m	-239m	-240m
Fixed Assets	235m	237m	238m
Current Assets	5m	2m	20m
Current Liabilities	5	5	N/A

Priority Freight Ltd
6-7 Menzies Road White Cliffs Business Park, Whitfield, Dover, CT16 2HQ
Tel: 01304-828111 **Fax:** 01304-828112
E-mail: sales@priorityfreight.co.uk
Website: http://www.priorityfreight.com
Managers: P. Mercer (Fin Mgr), E. Benbridge (Transport), G. Williams (Transport)
Ultimate Holding Company: PRIORITY FREIGHT LIMITED
Immediate Holding Company: PRIORITY FREIGHT LIMITED
Registration no: 03436573 **Date established:** 1997
Turnover: £10m - £20m **No.of Employees:** 51 - 100 **Product Groups:** 76

Date of Accounts	Sep 11	Sep 10	Sep 09
Sales Turnover	14m	11m	7m
Pre Tax Profit/Loss	177	163	8
Working Capital	685	585	453
Fixed Assets	2m	2m	2m
Current Assets	4m	4m	3m
Current Liabilities	1m	538	790

Sea-Lift Diving Ltd
Weighside House Sandwich Road, Whitfield, Dover, CT16 3JX
Tel: 01304-829956 **Fax:** 01304-829958
E-mail: sea-lift@btconnect.com
Website: http://www.sea-liftdiving.co.uk
Directors: N. Morris (MD)
Immediate Holding Company: SEA-LIFT DIVING LIMITED
Registration no: 02576702 **Date established:** 1991
No.of Employees: 1 - 10 **Product Groups:** 35, 36, 39

Date of Accounts	Mar 12	Mar 11	Mar 10
Sales Turnover	N/A	231	212
Pre Tax Profit/Loss	N/A	16	-11
Working Capital	14	-5	-10
Fixed Assets	159	174	174
Current Assets	90	99	64
Current Liabilities	N/A	23	10

Sigma Security Devices Ltd
134-135 Snargate Street, Dover, CT17 9DA
Tel: 01304-205050 **Fax:** 01304-215563
E-mail: sigma@nightingale.co.uk
Website: http://www.sigmasecuritydevices.co.uk
Directors: D. Nightingale (MD), L. Nightingale (MD)
Ultimate Holding Company: NIGHTINGALE HOLDINGS (DOVER) LIMITED
Immediate Holding Company: SIGMA SECURITY DEVICES LIMITED
Registration no: 01449909 **Date established:** 1979
Turnover: £500,000 - £1m **No.of Employees:** 1 - 10 **Product Groups:** 38, 42

Date of Accounts	Dec 10	Dec 09	Dec 08
Sales Turnover	564	956	N/A
Pre Tax Profit/Loss	30	51	N/A
Working Capital	285	256	225
Fixed Assets	13	20	8
Current Assets	450	515	271
Current Liabilities	26	16	N/A

Smye Rumsby Ltd
123-125 Snargate Street, Dover, CT17 9AP
Tel: 01304-201187 **Fax:** 01304-240135
E-mail: info@smye-rumsby.com
Website: http://www.smye-rumsby.co.uk
Directors: C. Dymott (Co Sec), P. Smye-Rumsby (Dir)
Ultimate Holding Company: SMYE-RUMSBY LIMITED
Immediate Holding Company: SMYE-RUMSBY LIMITED
Registration no: 00624430 **VAT No.:** GB 378 0341 47
Date established: 1959 **Turnover:** £2m - £5m **No.of Employees:** 11 - 20
Product Groups: 37, 39, 40, 67, 83

Date of Accounts	Mar 12	Mar 11	Mar 10
Working Capital	54	33	16
Fixed Assets	168	223	253
Current Assets	547	619	649

Tempest Voice & Data Communications Ltd
Convergence House Lydden, Dover, CT15 7JN
Tel: 08700-056161 **Fax:** 08700-056166
E-mail: paul@tssip.co.uk
Website: http://www.tssip.co.uk
Directors: N. Perkins (Sales), P. Schelhaas (Fin)
Immediate Holding Company: TEMPEST VOICE & DATA COMMUNICATIONS LIMITED
Registration no: 04278435 **Date established:** 2001
No.of Employees: 1 - 10 **Product Groups:** 37, 38, 40, 67

Wheeler-Jefferiss
15 Holmstone Road, Dover, CT17 0UF
Tel: 01304-214196 **Fax:** 01304-216151
Directors: B. Wheeler (Ptnr)
Date established: 1989 **No.of Employees:** 1 - 10 **Product Groups:** 35

Edenbridge

Answerpak Ltd
Unit M Fircroft Way, Edenbridge, TN8 6EL
Tel: 01732-869930 **Fax:** 01732-869939
E-mail: sales@answerpak.co.uk
Website: http://www.answerpak.co.uk
Bank(s): National Westminster Bank Plc
Directors: L. Newman (MD)
Ultimate Holding Company: ALSAMEX PRODUCTS LIMITED
Immediate Holding Company: ANSWERPAK LIMITED
Registration no: 02773933 **VAT No.:** GB 625 7211 54
Date established: 1992 **Turnover:** £1m - £2m **No.of Employees:** 11 - 20
Product Groups: 25, 27, 30

Date of Accounts	Nov 11	Nov 10	Nov 09
Working Capital	-176	-128	-158
Fixed Assets	225	231	256
Current Assets	367	331	267

Bradford Electrical
Euro House Station Road, Edenbridge, TN8 6EY
Tel: 01732-867715
Website: http://www.bradfordelectrical.co.uk
Directors: P. Bradford (Prop)
Date established: 2005 **No.of Employees:** 1 - 10 **Product Groups:** 36, 40

Capital Springs & Pressings Ltd
Commerce Way, Edenbridge, TN8 6ED
Tel: 01732-867130 **Fax:** 01732-867140
E-mail: sales@capitalsprings.com
Website: http://www.capitalsprings.com
Bank(s): Barclays
Directors: A. Watts (MD)
Immediate Holding Company: CAPITAL SPRINGS AND PRESSINGS LIMITED
Registration no: 02022161 **Date established:** 1986
Turnover: £500,000 - £1m **No.of Employees:** 11 - 20
Product Groups: 34, 35

Date of Accounts	Mar 11	Mar 10	Mar 09
Working Capital	103	80	96
Fixed Assets	75	87	103
Current Assets	252	223	234

Colour Coatings South East Ltd
Unit 19 Warsop Trading Estate Hever Road, Edenbridge, TN8 5LD
Tel: 01732-866700 **Fax:** 01732-865983
E-mail: info@colour-coatings.co.uk
Website: http://www.colour-coatings.co.uk
Directors: C. Thurston Hobbs (Fin), G. Hobbs (MD)
Immediate Holding Company: COLOUR COATINGS (SOUTH EAST) LIMITED
Registration no: 04407660 **VAT No.:** GB 528 6660 20
Date established: 2002 **Turnover:** £250,000 - £500,000
No.of Employees: 1 - 10 **Product Groups:** 32

Date of Accounts	Mar 11	Mar 10	Mar 09
Working Capital	91	88	118
Fixed Assets	5	9	15
Current Assets	158	166	207

Eaton-Williams Group Ltd
Fircroft Way, Edenbridge, TN8 6EZ
Tel: 01732-866055 **Fax:** 01732-863461
E-mail: gerald.stapley@eaton-williams.com
Website: http://www.eaton-williams.com
Bank(s): Barclays, 93 Baker St, London, WIA 4SD
Directors: G. Stapley (MD)
Ultimate Holding Company: NORTEK INC (USA)
Immediate Holding Company: EATON-WILLIAMS (MILLBANK) LIMITED
Registration no: 00314514 **VAT No.:** GB 209 8701 54
Date established: 1936 **No.of Employees:** 101 - 250 **Product Groups:** 38, 40, 52, 66, 83, 84

Date of Accounts	Dec 09	Dec 08
Pre Tax Profit/Loss	-25	N/A
Working Capital	N/A	25
Current Assets	N/A	25

Eccles Technical Services Ltd
Eccles House Main Road, Edenbridge, TN8 6HZ
Tel: 01732-866776 **Fax:** 01732-863550
E-mail: ecclesuk@aol.com
Directors: V. Wells (Fin), B. Wells (MD)
Immediate Holding Company: ECCLES TECHNICAL SERVICES LIMITED
Registration no: 01250430 **VAT No.:** GB 204 9081 83
Date established: 1976 **Turnover:** £1m - £2m **No.of Employees:** 1 - 10
Product Groups: 28, 54, 61

Date of Accounts	Mar 11	Mar 10	Mar 09
Working Capital	99	43	43
Fixed Assets	N/A	1	2
Current Assets	531	348	444

Fi Glass Developments Ltd
Station Road, Edenbridge, TN8 6EB
Tel: 01732-863465 **Fax:** 01732-867287
E-mail: sales@fi-glass.co.uk
Website: http://www.fi-glass.co.uk
Bank(s): Lloyds TSB Bank plc
Directors: S. Humphries (MD)
Immediate Holding Company: FI-GLASS DEVELOPMENTS LIMITED
Registration no: 00699826 **VAT No.:** GB 210 5776 85
Date established: 1961 **Turnover:** £500,000 - £1m
No.of Employees: 11 - 20 **Product Groups:** 33

Date of Accounts	Sep 11	Sep 10	Sep 09
Working Capital	395	415	449
Fixed Assets	24	27	33
Current Assets	436	462	485

Greencare H20
Unit 1 Warsop Trading Estate Hever Road, Edenbridge, TN8 5LD
Tel: 01732-868296 **Fax:** 01732-867197
Directors: J. Isted (Fin), J. Highsted (Fin)
Immediate Holding Company: GREENCARE H20 LIMITED
Registration no: 07264290 **Date established:** 2010
No.of Employees: 1 - 10 **Product Groups:** 40, 66

Guest Medical Ltd
Enterprise Way, Edenbridge, TN8 6EW
Tel: 01732-867466 **Fax:** 01732-867476
E-mail: sales@guestmedical.co.uk
Website: http://www.guestmedical.com
Directors: R. Wakeford- Brown (Dir), S. Mew (Co Sec), S. Mew (Comm)
Ultimate Holding Company: ZURING AG (SWITZERLAND)
Immediate Holding Company: GUEST MEDICAL LIMITED
Registration no: 02137706 **VAT No.:** GB 602 3133 03
Date established: 1987 **Turnover:** £250,000 - £500,000
No.of Employees: 1 - 10 **Product Groups:** 31, 32, 67

Date of Accounts	Dec 09	Dec 08	Dec 07
Working Capital	391	346	295
Fixed Assets	12	12	21
Current Assets	816	780	627

Hallmark Servicing Ltd
South Barn Crockham Park, Edenbridge, TN8 6SR
Tel: 01732-782620 **Fax:** 01732-782621
E-mail: servicing@hallmarkkitchens.co.uk
Website: http://www.hallmarkgroup.net
Directors: K. Jennings (Dir), J. Darkes (Fin)
Registration no: 01732505 **No.of Employees:** 1 - 10 **Product Groups:** 20, 40, 41

Kemco Technology Limited
Acorn House Tonbridge Road, Bough Beech, Edenbridge, TN8 7AU
Tel: 01892-870077 **Fax:** 01892-870777
E-mail: info@kemcotech.com
Website: http://www.kemcotech.com
Directors: J. Gordon-Reid (MD)
Managers: R. Rayner (Sales Admin)
Registration no: 04353516 **Turnover:** £500,000 - £1m
No.of Employees: 11 - 20 **Product Groups:** 32

Date of Accounts	Mar 08	Mar 07	Mar 06
Sales Turnover	N/A	N/A	301
Pre Tax Profit/Loss	N/A	N/A	18
Working Capital	32	30	7
Fixed Assets	2	5	6
Current Assets	70	119	101
Current Liabilities	38	90	93
ROCE% (Return on Capital Employed)			135.8
ROT% (Return on Turnover)			6.1

Power Products International Ltd
Commerce Way, Edenbridge, TN8 6ED
Tel: 01732-866424 **Fax:** 01732-866399
E-mail: sales@ppi-uk.com
Website: http://www.ppi-uk.com
Bank(s): National Westminster Bank Plc
Directors: B. Chettle (Co Sec), A. Chettle (MD)
Managers: G. Robinson (Sales & Mktg Mg)
Immediate Holding Company: POWER PRODUCTS (INTERNATIONAL) LIMITED
Registration no: 01960827 **VAT No.:** GB 424 9986 07
Date established: 1985 **Turnover:** £2m - £5m **No.of Employees:** 11 - 20
Product Groups: 37, 67

Date of Accounts	Mar 12	Mar 11	Mar 10
Working Capital	589	558	547
Fixed Assets	255	273	286
Current Assets	931	923	859

T C Hillier Farmbike
Breezehurst Crouch House Road, Edenbridge, TN8 5LF
Tel: 01883-712355 **Fax:** 01883-714966
E-mail: nickistead@btinternet.com
Directors: N. Istead (Dir)
Date established: 1985 **No.of Employees:** 1 - 10 **Product Groups:** 41

Unicom Global
The Industrial Estate Enterprise Way, Edenbridge, TN8 6EW
Tel: 01732-865238 **Fax:** 01732-866820
E-mail: georgek@uni-com.uk.com
Website: http://www.uni-com.uk.com
Directors: G. Korbel (Prop)
Immediate Holding Company: UNI-COM (GLOBAL) LIMITED
Registration no: 01538329 **Date established:** 1981 **Turnover:** £2m - £5m
No.of Employees: 21 - 50 **Product Groups:** 80

Date of Accounts	Jun 11	Jun 10	Jun 09
Working Capital	925	929	915
Fixed Assets	523	560	598
Current Assets	2m	2m	2m

Unicorn Products Ltd
South Barn Crockham Park, Crockham Hill, Edenbridge, TN8 6UP
Tel: 0115-985 3500 **Fax:** 01732-782801
E-mail: elowy@unicorngroup.com
Website: http://www.unicorngroup.com
Bank(s): National Westminster
Directors: W. Stone (Co Sec), E. Lowy (MD), R. Lowy (Sales)
Immediate Holding Company: UNICORN PRODUCTS LIMITED
Registration no: 00370646 **VAT No.:** GB 217 8154 62
Date established: 1941 **Turnover:** £10m - £20m
No.of Employees: 51 - 100 **Product Groups:** 49

Date of Accounts	Dec 11	Dec 10	Dec 09
Sales Turnover	14m	13m	13m
Pre Tax Profit/Loss	-230	136	450
Working Capital	3m	4m	4m
Fixed Assets	2m	2m	2m
Current Assets	6m	6m	6m
Current Liabilities	802	753	790

Vapac Humidity Control Ltd
Fircroft Way, Edenbridge, TN8 6EZ
Tel: 01732-863447 **Fax:** 01732-865658
E-mail: gerry.stapley@eaton-williams.com
Website: http://www.eaton-williams.com
Directors: G. Stapley (MD)
Ultimate Holding Company: NORTEK INC (USA)
Immediate Holding Company: VAPAC HUMIDITY CONTROL LIMITED
Registration no: 01214521 **Date established:** 1975
No.of Employees: 51 - 100 **Product Groups:** 30, 40

Date of Accounts	Dec 09	Dec 08
Pre Tax Profit/Loss	-74	N/A
Working Capital	N/A	74
Current Assets	N/A	74

Whitehall Recruitment Ltd
37-41 High Street, Edenbridge, TN8 5AD
Tel: 01732-864777 **Fax:** 01732-865777
E-mail: enquiries@whitehall.uk.com
Website: http://www.whitehall.uk.com
Directors: E. Regan (MD)
Immediate Holding Company: WHITEHALL RECRUITMENT LIMITED
Registration no: 01677902 **VAT No.:** GB 367 5164 31
Date established: 1982 **No.of Employees:** 1 - 10 **Product Groups:** 80

Date of Accounts	Dec 10	Dec 09	Dec 08
Working Capital	43	3	51
Fixed Assets	2	3	4
Current Assets	131	66	125

Erith

A D M Pura Foods Ltd
Erith Oil Works Church Manorway, Erith, DA8 1DL
Tel: 01322-443000 **Fax:** 01322-443027
Website: http://www.adm.com
Directors: S. Manley (MD), S. Trowsdale (Sales), T. Saathoff (MD)
Ultimate Holding Company: ARCHER DANIELS MIDLAND COMPANY INC (USA)
Immediate Holding Company: ADM PURA LIMITED
Registration no: 00849405 **VAT No.:** GB 249 2679 23
Date established: 1965 **Turnover:** £250m - £500m
No.of Employees: 101 - 250 **Product Groups:** 20

Date of Accounts	Dec 11	Dec 10	Dec 09
Pre Tax Profit/Loss	75	14m	-234
Working Capital	40m	40m	30m
Fixed Assets	42m	41m	41m
Current Assets	45m	45m	46m
Current Liabilities	44	62	10m

ADM Trading (U.K.) Limited
Church Manorway, Erith, DA8 1DL
Tel: 01322-443000 **Fax:** 01482-386133
E-mail: ukinfo@adm.com
Website: http://www.admworld.com
Bank(s): Barclays, London
Directors: G. Legge (MD), A. Wilson (Fin), S. Sangerah (Eng Serv), V. Roberts (Fin)
Managers: K. Powell (Sales Prom Mgr), R. Thorsby (I.T. Exec)
Ultimate Holding Company: ARCHER DANIELS MIDLAND COMPANY INC (USA)
Immediate Holding Company: Adm Cocoa Processing Ltd
Registration no: 00818889 **VAT No.:** GB 245 1679 52
Date established: 1941 **Turnover:** £75m - £125m
No.of Employees: 51 - 100 **Product Groups:** 20

Alsford Timber Ltd
1 Ness Road, Erith, DA8 2LD
Tel: 01322-333004 **Fax:** 01322- 333058
E-mail: enquiries@alsfordtimber.com
Website: http://www.alsfordtimber.com
Bank(s): National Westminster Bank Plc
Directors: H. Mitchell (Dir), Q. Kemp (Purch)
Managers: E. Jones (Mgr), M. Tyler (Purch Mgr)
Ultimate Holding Company: GEO. KINGSBURY HOLDINGS LIMITED
Immediate Holding Company: ALSFORD TIMBER LIMITED
Registration no: 02827724 **Date established:** 1993
Turnover: £20m - £50m **No.of Employees:** 21 - 50 **Product Groups:** 66

Date of Accounts	Dec 10	Dec 09	Dec 08
Sales Turnover	26m	25m	32m
Pre Tax Profit/Loss	-1m	-1m	-37
Working Capital	4m	5m	6m
Fixed Assets	651	869	1m
Current Assets	8m	8m	9m
Current Liabilities	479	535	525

Archer Daniels Midland UK Ltd
Church Manorway, Erith, DA8 1DL
Tel: 01322-443030 **Fax:** 01322-437536
E-mail: info@admworld.com
Website: http://www.admworld.com
Directors: S. Filmer (Dir)
Ultimate Holding Company: ARCHER DANIELS MIDLAND COMPANY INC (USA)
Immediate Holding Company: ADM ELEVEN
Registration no: 03156449 **Date established:** 1996
Turnover: £20m - £50m **No.of Employees:** 1 - 10 **Product Groups:** 20, 31, 41, 62

Date of Accounts	Dec 10	Dec 09	Dec 05
Pre Tax Profit/Loss	N/A	N/A	43m

Base Enamellers Ltd
1 Power Works Slade Green Road, Erith, DA8 2HU
Tel: 01322-338052 **Fax:** 01322-334360
E-mail: info@base-enamellers.co.uk
Website: http://www.base-enamellers.co.uk
Bank(s): National Westminster Bank Plc
Directors: L. Topliffe (Fin), R. Topliffe (MD)
Immediate Holding Company: BASE ENAMELLERS LIMITED
Registration no: 01042168 **VAT No.:** GB 205 4352 00
Date established: 1972 **Turnover:** Up to £250,000
No.of Employees: 11 - 20 **Product Groups:** 48

Date of Accounts	Sep 11	Sep 10	Sep 09
Working Capital	68	109	193
Fixed Assets	211	91	104
Current Assets	524	458	639

Batt Cables plc
The Belfry Fraser Road, Erith, DA8 1QH
Tel: 01322-441166 **Fax:** 01322-440492
E-mail: steve.morrish@batt.co.uk
Website: http://www.batt.co.uk
Bank(s): Lloyds TSB Bank plc
Directors: S. Brown (Fin)
Managers: M. Wilson (Tech Serv Mgr), N. Francis (Purch Mgr), S. Hermitage (Sales Prom Mgr), S. Morrish (Ops Mgr), J. O'Grady (Personnel)
Immediate Holding Company: BATT CABLES PLC
Registration no: 01353688 **Date established:** 1978
Turnover: £75m - £125m **No.of Employees:** 101 - 250
Product Groups: 30, 35, 36, 37, 38, 44, 66, 67

Date of Accounts	Mar 12	Mar 11	Mar 10
Sales Turnover	106m	98m	84m
Pre Tax Profit/Loss	8m	9m	5m
Working Capital	41m	36m	31m
Fixed Assets	8m	9m	8m
Current Assets	69m	60m	54m
Current Liabilities	3m	3m	2m

Begg & Co Thermoplastics Ltd
71 Hailey Road, Erith, DA18 4AW
Tel: 020-8310 1236 **Fax:** 020-8310 4371
E-mail: info@beggandco.co.uk
Website: http://www.beggandco.co.uk
Directors: B. Begg (Dir), M. Begg (MD), M. Axell Nicholls (Co Sec), M. Axell-nicholls (Fin)
Managers: P. Neal (Buyer)
Immediate Holding Company: BEGG & CO. THERMOPLASTICS LIMITED
Registration no: 00574711 **VAT No.:** GB 205 4393 83
Date established: 1956 **Turnover:** £5m - £10m **No.of Employees:** 1 - 10
Product Groups: 31

Date of Accounts	Dec 11	Dec 10	Dec 09
Sales Turnover	6m	5m	5m
Pre Tax Profit/Loss	51	124	117
Working Capital	521	489	380
Fixed Assets	279	293	312
Current Assets	1m	2m	2m
Current Liabilities	245	174	119

Bexley Council For Racial Equality (Economic Development Unit)
1 Maran Way, Erith, DA18 4BP
Tel: 020-8310 0138 **Fax:** 020-8312 0238
E-mail: EDUBBC@bexley.gov.uk
Website: http://www.bexley.gov.uk/business
Managers: C. Tomlins, G. Williams, T. Tran (Mgr)
No.of Employees: 1 - 10 **Product Groups:** 80, 81, 86, 87

Bowes Scott & Western Ltd
Unit 6 Kencot Way, Erith, DA18 4AB
Tel: 020-8320 8722 **Fax:** 020-8317 0530
E-mail: bowesscottandwestern@gmail.com
Website: http://www.bowesscottandwestern.co.uk
Directors: L. Bonell (Dir)
Immediate Holding Company: BOWES SCOTT & WESTERN LTD
Registration no: 01901268 **Date established:** 1985
Turnover: Up to £250,000 **No.of Employees:** 1 - 10 **Product Groups:** 34, 35, 36, 45

Date of Accounts	Mar 11	Mar 10	Mar 09
Working Capital	-3	-15	2
Fixed Assets	2	2	3
Current Assets	16	15	20

Certex UK Ltd
Unit 2 Viking Way, Erith, DA8 1EW
Tel: 01322-446633 **Fax:** 01322-441044
E-mail: cdeaver@certex.co.uk
Website: http://www.certex.co.uk
Managers: C. Deaver
Ultimate Holding Company: AXEL JOHNSON INTERNATIONAL AB (SWEDEN)
Immediate Holding Company: CERTEX (UK) LIMITED
Registration no: 00928803 **Date established:** 1968
No.of Employees: 1 - 10 **Product Groups:** 23, 30, 35

Dartford Engraving & Screen Printing Ltd
4 Power Works Estate Slade Green Road, Erith, DA8 2HY
Tel: 01322-340194 **Fax:** 01322-347819
E-mail: mail@desp.co.uk
Website: http://www.desp.co.uk
Directors: M. Root (Dir), S. Root (Fin)
Immediate Holding Company: DARTFORD ENGRAVING & SCREENPRINTING LIMITED
Registration no: 01259868 **Date established:** 1976
Turnover: Up to £250,000 **No.of Employees:** 1 - 10 **Product Groups:** 28, 46, 48

Date of Accounts	Dec 11	Dec 10	Dec 09
Working Capital	-6	-5	-8
Fixed Assets	30	21	26
Current Assets	73	53	66

Euromaster Engineering Ltd
28 Hailey Road, Erith, DA18 4AP
Tel: 020-8312 2907
E-mail: info@euromaster.ltd.uk
Website: http://www.euromaster.ltd.uk
Directors: S. Chatterton (Co Sec), R. Berry (Dir), W. Todd (Dir)
Managers: K. Holmes (Admin Off)
Ultimate Holding Company: COMPAGNIE GENERALE DES ETABLISSEMENTS MICHELIN (FRANCE)
Immediate Holding Company: EUROMASTER LIMITED
Registration no: 02417972 **Date established:** 1989
No.of Employees: 21 - 50 **Product Groups:** 35

Date of Accounts	Oct 10	Oct 09	Oct 08
Working Capital	46	93	99
Fixed Assets	30	35	45
Current Assets	262	354	461

Europa Worldwide Logistics
Europa House 68 Hailey Road, Erith, DA18 4AU
Tel: 020-8311 5000 **Fax:** 020-8311 2660
E-mail: enquiries@europa-worldwide.co.uk
Website: http://www.europa-worldwide.co.uk
Bank(s): National Westminster Bank Plc
Directors: G. Turner (Dir), I. Hansford (Dir), R. Keep (Co Sec)
Ultimate Holding Company: EWG LIMITED
Immediate Holding Company: EUROPA FREIGHT CORPORATION LIMITED
Registration no: 01097287 **VAT No.:** GB 625 5124 59
Date established: 1973 **Turnover:** £250,000 - £500,000
No.of Employees: 251 - 500 **Product Groups:** 72, 74, 75, 76, 77, 79, 84

H S Door Systems Ltd
Unit 26 Kencot Close Business Park Waldriss Way, Erith, DA18 4AB
Tel: 0845-309355
E-mail: mark@hsdoors.com
Website: http://www.hsdoors.com
Managers: M. Sunders (Chief Mgr)
Immediate Holding Company: HS DOOR SYSTEMS LTD
Registration no: 06513363 **Date established:** 2008
No.of Employees: 1 - 10 **Product Groups:** 35, 36, 40, 48

Inter Steels Ltd
Landau Way Darent Industrial Park, Erith, DA8 2LF
Tel: 01322-337766 **Fax:** 01322-335662
E-mail: sales@intersteels.com
Website: http://www.intersteels.com
Bank(s): Barclays
Directors: A. Horgan (Sales), J. Horgan (Fin)
Immediate Holding Company: INTER-STEELS LIMITED
Registration no: 02179673 **VAT No.:** GB 566 2830 25
Date established: 1987 **Turnover:** £2m - £5m **No.of Employees:** 11 - 20
Product Groups: 34, 66

Date of Accounts	Jun 11	Jun 10	Jun 09
Working Capital	273	281	357
Fixed Assets	159	107	69
Current Assets	1m	852	875

Kort Propulsion Co. Ltd
The Boat House Erith High Street, Erith, DA8 1QY
Tel: 01322-346346 **Fax:** 01322-347346
E-mail: info@kortpropulsion.com
Website: http://www.kortpropulsion.com
Directors: D. Parsons (Ptnr)
Immediate Holding Company: KORT PROPULSION COMPANY LIMITED
Registration no: 00296528 **VAT No.:** GB 342 3166 81
Date established: 1935 **Turnover:** Up to £250,000
No.of Employees: 1 - 10 **Product Groups:** 39

Date of Accounts	Sep 11	Sep 10	Sep 09
Working Capital	-23	-38	-10
Fixed Assets	8	9	9
Current Assets	287	313	362

Landor Cartons Ltd
Church Manorway, Erith, DA8 1NP
Tel: 01322-435426 **Fax:** 01322-445830
E-mail: phil@landorcartons.co.uk
Website: http://www.landorcartons.co.uk
Bank(s): Barclays
Directors: P. Morley (MD)
Ultimate Holding Company: LANDOR CARTONS HOLDINGS LIMITED
Immediate Holding Company: LANDOR CARTONS LIMITED
Registration no: 03193683 **Date established:** 1996 **Turnover:** £5m - £10m
No.of Employees: 21 - 50 **Product Groups:** 27, 28

Date of Accounts	Mar 12	Mar 11	Mar 10
Working Capital	1m	2m	2m
Fixed Assets	937	712	753
Current Assets	2m	3m	2m

Lift Out Ltd
9 Landau Way Darent Industrial Park, Erith, DA8 2LF
Tel: 01322-331122 **Fax:** 01322-340536
E-mail: bill.lidsey@liftout.net
Website: http://www.liftout.net
Directors: W. Lidsey (MD), J. Lidsey (Fin)
Immediate Holding Company: LIFT OUT LIMITED
Registration no: 03593920 **Date established:** 1998
No.of Employees: 21 - 50 **Product Groups:** 35, 39, 45

Date of Accounts	Jul 11	Jul 10	Jul 09
Working Capital	365	550	513
Fixed Assets	142	157	158

Current Assets	558	741	833

The Logo Centre Embroidered & Printed Clothing

Unit 25 Kencot Close East Thamesmead Business Park, Erith, DA18 4AB
Tel: 020-8310 3030 **Fax:** 020-8310 8844
E-mail: sales@thelogocentre.co.uk
Website: http://www.thelogocentre.co.uk
Directors: S. Rouse (Dir)
Immediate Holding Company: THE LOGO CENTRE LTD
Registration no: 06449506 **Date established:** 2007
No.of Employees: 1 - 10 **Product Groups:** 23, 24, 30, 49, 63, 84

Date of Accounts	Jan 12	Jan 11	Jan 10
Working Capital	-16	-15	-14
Fixed Assets	23	27	32
Current Assets	42	53	42

M C B Imaging Services Ltd

14-16 Fraser Road, Erith, DA8 1QJ
Tel: 01322-440952 **Fax:** 01322-441654
E-mail: mcb@mcbimaging.co.uk
Website: http://www.mcbimaging.co.uk
Directors: M. Battell (Prop)
Immediate Holding Company: MCB IMAGING SERVICES LIMITED
Registration no: 04574981 **Date established:** 2002
No.of Employees: 1 - 10 **Product Groups:** 38, 44, 80, 81

Date of Accounts	Dec 11	Dec 10	Dec 07
Working Capital	2	3	-12
Fixed Assets	16	25	59
Current Assets	17	25	64

Mcnaughton James Paper Group Ltd

Jaymac House Church Manorway, Erith, DA8 1DF
Tel: 020-8320 3200 **Fax:** 020-8311 4162
E-mail: igeorge@mcnaughton-paper.com
Website: http://www.jmcpaper.com
Bank(s): Bank of Scotland
Directors: I. George (Ch), I. Pinks (Co Sec), I. George (MD), O. George (Grp Chief Exec), T. Porter (Mkt Research)
Managers: A. Bruguier (Mktg Serv Mgr), A. Pendreigh, A. Wade, J. Boyd (I.T. Exec), M. Smith (Mktg Serv Mgr), P. Gibson (Purch Mgr), V. Pond, J. Blackmore
Immediate Holding Company: JAMES MCNAUGHTON GROUP LIMITED
Registration no: 01131445 **Date established:** 1982
Turnover: £20m - £50m **No.of Employees:** 101 - 250
Product Groups: 23, 27, 28, 44

Mechanical & Ferrous Ltd

1 Church Road, Erith, DA8 1PG
Tel: 01322-447714 **Fax:** 01322-436228
E-mail: ian.hayes@mechanicalandferrous.co.uk
Website: http://www.mechanicalandferrous.co.uk
Managers: I. Hayes (Chief Mgr)
Immediate Holding Company: MECHANICAL & FERROUS LIMITED
Registration no: 02040027 **Date established:** 1986
Turnover: £500,000 - £1m **No.of Employees:** 11 - 20 **Product Groups:** 84

Date of Accounts	Jun 11	Jun 10	Jun 09
Working Capital	104	66	198
Fixed Assets	2	2	3
Current Assets	343	248	330

N K F Metal Services

Unit 5 East Thamesmead Business Park Kencot Close, Erith, DA18 4AB
Tel: 020-8310 2199 **Fax:** 020-8310 2204
E-mail: john@nkfmetals.com
Website: http://www.nkfmetals.com
Directors: J. O'shea (Prop)
Turnover: Up to £250,000 **No.of Employees:** 1 - 10 **Product Groups:** 48

Neville UK plc

Viking Way, Erith, DA8 1EW
Tel: 01322-443143 **Fax:** 01322-443153
E-mail: sales@nevilleuk.com
Website: http://www.nevilleuk.com
Directors: A. Neville (MD), P. Stratton (Fin)
Immediate Holding Company: NEVILLE UK PLC
Registration no: 04121817 **Date established:** 2000 **Turnover:** £5m - £10m
No.of Employees: 21 - 50 **Product Groups:** 30, 36, 40, 41, 63, 67

Date of Accounts	Dec 11	Dec 10	Dec 09
Sales Turnover	9m	9m	8m
Pre Tax Profit/Loss	703	380	318
Working Capital	3m	2m	2m
Fixed Assets	163	115	96
Current Assets	4m	4m	4m
Current Liabilities	1m	1m	1m

North Kent Recycling

Union Yard Manor Road, Erith, DA8 2AD
Tel: 01322-341088
E-mail: nkr-forktrucks@btconnect.com
Directors: M. Williams (Prop)
Immediate Holding Company: LOCK BROS (PLANT HIRE) LIMITED
Registration no: 01635123 **Date established:** 1993
Turnover: £500,000 - £1m **No.of Employees:** 1 - 10 **Product Groups:** 35, 39, 45

Date of Accounts	May 11	May 10	May 09
Working Capital	74	103	50
Fixed Assets	120	79	129
Current Assets	156	254	179

Pyramid Engineering Services Co. Ltd

25 Hailey Road, Erith, DA18 4AA
Tel: 020-8320 9590 **Fax:** 020-8311 2567
E-mail: chris.watkins@pyramideng.com
Website: http://www.pyramideng.com
Directors: C. Watkins (MD)
Managers: M. Heath (Sales Prom Mgr)
Immediate Holding Company: PYRAMID ENGINEERING SERVICES COMPANY LIMITED
Registration no: 02424442 **Date established:** 1989 **Turnover:** £2m - £5m
No.of Employees: 11 - 20 **Product Groups:** 37, 38, 42, 46, 47, 48

Date of Accounts	Sep 11	Sep 10	Sep 09
Working Capital	366	237	280
Fixed Assets	11	18	18
Current Assets	757	776	966

R K International Machine Tools Ltd

7 Europa Trading Estate Fraser Road, Erith, DA8 1PW
Tel: 01322-447611 **Fax:** 01322-447618
E-mail: sales@rk-int.com
Website: http://www.rk-int.com
Bank(s): National Westminter Bank plc
Directors: J. Schwarz (MD), R. Aldrich (Sales)
Immediate Holding Company: R.K.INTERNATIONAL MACHINE TOOLS LIMITED
Registration no: 00571795 **VAT No.:** GB 206 2366 90
Date established: 1956 **Turnover:** £5m - £10m **No.of Employees:** 21 - 50
Product Groups: 42, 46, 47, 48, 61, 67, 83

Date of Accounts	Sep 11	Sep 10	Sep 09
Working Capital	2m	1m	1m
Fixed Assets	167	143	155
Current Assets	3m	2m	2m

S L D Pumps & Power

2 Ness Road, Erith, DA8 2LD
Tel: 01322-350088 **Fax:** 01322-350066
E-mail: erith@sldpumpspower.co.uk
Website: http://www.sldpumpspower.co.uk
Bank(s): National Westminster, Uckfield
Managers: P. Starley (Depot Mgr)
Registration no: 01436404 **Date established:** 1979 **Turnover:** £2m - £5m
No.of Employees: 11 - 20 **Product Groups:** 37, 83

Sahara Presentation Systems plc

Williams House 61 Hailey Road, Erith, DA18 4AA
Tel: 020-8319 7700 **Fax:** 020-8319 7775
E-mail: info@saharaplc.com
Website: http://www.saharaplc.com
Bank(s): Barclays, Woolwich
Directors: K. Batley (MD)
Ultimate Holding Company: SAHARA HOLDINGS LIMITED
Immediate Holding Company: SAHARA PRESENTATION SYSTEMS PLC
Registration no: 01335211 **VAT No.:** GB 299 4892 75
Date established: 1977 **Turnover:** £10m - £20m
No.of Employees: 21 - 50 **Product Groups:** 28, 49

Date of Accounts	Dec 11	Dec 10	Dec 09
Sales Turnover	17m	16m	16m
Pre Tax Profit/Loss	742	797	1m
Working Capital	4m	4m	3m
Fixed Assets	429	418	457
Current Assets	6m	5m	5m
Current Liabilities	755	921	822

Star Anodising & Finishing Ltd

Unit 7 Power Works, Erith, DA8 2HY
Tel: 01322-335857 **Fax:** 01322-335868
E-mail: rodney.smith@staranodising.co.uk
Website: http://www.staranodising.co.uk
Directors: R. Smith (Prop)
Immediate Holding Company: STAR ANODISING & FINISHING LIMITED
Registration no: 02615858 **Date established:** 1991
No.of Employees: 1 - 10 **Product Groups:** 46, 48

Date of Accounts	Jun 12	Jun 11	Jun 10
Working Capital	107	87	43
Fixed Assets	11	13	17
Current Assets	171	189	110

Unitek Fabrications Ltd

Unit 5 Power Works Estate Slade Green Road, Erith, DA8 2HY
Tel: 01322-338100 **Fax:** 01322-333741
E-mail: kevin.baker@unitekfabs.co.uk
Website: http://www.unitekfabs.co.uk
Directors: K. Baker (MD)
Ultimate Holding Company: H.EVANS & SONS LIMITED
Immediate Holding Company: M & G TROLLIES LIMITED
Registration no: 05385835 **Date established:** 1973
No.of Employees: 1 - 10 **Product Groups:** 35, 45, 46, 48

Date of Accounts	Dec 10	Dec 09	Dec 08
Sales Turnover	N/A	428	336
Pre Tax Profit/Loss	N/A	-48	-65
Working Capital	91	232	260
Fixed Assets	368	413	436
Current Assets	197	435	407
Current Liabilities	N/A	100	89

Versapak International

Centurion Way, Erith, DA18 4AF
Tel: 020-8333 5353 **Fax:** 020-8312 2051
E-mail: sales@versapak.co.uk
Website: http://www.versapak.co.uk
Bank(s): HSBC
Directors: I. Denny-anderson (Prop), K. Gars (Fab), S. Waller (Sales)
Managers: N. Phillips (Purch Mgr), N. Cowell, N. Thomas (Tech Serv Mgr)
Immediate Holding Company: VERSAPAK HOLDINGS LTD
Registration no: 03566179 **Date established:** 2006 **Turnover:** £5m - £10m
No.of Employees: 21 - 50 **Product Groups:** 26, 27, 84

Date of Accounts	Aug 07	Aug 06
Working Capital	-22	40
Fixed Assets	N/A	453
Current Assets	63	1527
Current Liabilities	85	1486
Total Share Capital	9	9

Faversham

Ada & Ina Natural Fabrics and Curtains

Unit 2 B, Monks Granary Standard Quay, Faversham, CT5 1BX
Tel: 0843-2891180 **Fax:** 0151-526 0508
E-mail: info@linenfabrics.co.uk
Website: http://www.linenfabrics.co.uk
Product Groups: 24, 63

Allwick Patterns Ltd

The Shipyard Upper Brents, Faversham, ME13 7LB
Tel: 01795-532580 **Fax:** 01795-533707
E-mail: allwickpatterns@btconnect.com
Website: http://www.allwickpatternsltd.co.uk
Directors: J. Wicketts (MD)
Immediate Holding Company: ALLWICK PATTERNS LTD
Registration no: 04492023 **VAT No.:** GB 304 4892 63
Date established: 2002 **Turnover:** Up to £250,000
No.of Employees: 1 - 10 **Product Groups:** 46, 48

Date of Accounts	Jul 11	Jul 10	Jul 09
Sales Turnover	695	532	510
Working Capital	205	171	202
Fixed Assets	25	32	253
Current Assets	250	223	243

Andrews Decorating

104 Ospringe Road, Faversham, ME13 7LG
Tel: 07762-621300
E-mail: info@andrewsdecorating.co.uk
Website: http://www.andrewsdecorating.co.uk
Directors: L. Andrews (Prop)
Turnover: Up to £250,000 **No.of Employees:** 1 - 10 **Product Groups:** 52

B M M Weston Ltd

Weston Works Brent Hill, Faversham, ME13 7EB
Tel: 01795-533441 **Fax:** 01795-538891
E-mail: mail@bmmweston.com
Website: http://www.bmmweston.com
Bank(s): Lloyds TSB Bank plc
Directors: J. Dawson (MD)
Managers: D. Silvester (Fin Mgr), S. Bright (Chief Buyer)
Immediate Holding Company: BMM WESTON HOLDINGS LIMITED
Registration no: 03166621 **VAT No.:** GB 203 3000 48
Date established: 1996 **Turnover:** £5m - £10m
No.of Employees: 101 - 250 **Product Groups:** 38, 40, 41, 42, 43, 46, 48, 67, 84

Date of Accounts	Sep 08	Oct 09	Oct 10
Sales Turnover	N/A	7m	7m
Pre Tax Profit/Loss	-20	397	121
Working Capital	-1m	683	807
Fixed Assets	4m	630	620
Current Assets	11	3m	3m
Current Liabilities	N/A	1m	1m

Chaucer Group Ltd

67 Preston Street, Faversham, ME13 8PB
Tel: 01795-542500 **Fax:** 08450-724510
E-mail: rupert.laslett@chaucerconsulting.com
Website: http://www.chaucer.com
Directors: J. Freeman (Co Sec), C. Laslett (Tech Serv)
Managers: T. Pearson, D. Seakins (Develop Mgr), M. Grasar (Personnel)
Immediate Holding Company: CHAUCER GROUP LIMITED
Registration no: 02136429 **Date established:** 1987 **Turnover:** £5m - £10m
No.of Employees: 11 - 20 **Product Groups:** 80, 81, 84

Date of Accounts	Oct 11	Oct 10	Oct 09
Sales Turnover	9m	7m	8m
Pre Tax Profit/Loss	1m	932	-1m
Working Capital	1m	750	602
Fixed Assets	3m	3m	3m
Current Assets	4m	3m	2m
Current Liabilities	2m	1m	711

Cooks Auto Diesel Services Ltd

The Shipyard Upper Brents, Faversham, ME13 7DZ
Tel: 01795-538553 **Fax:** 01795-533988
Website: http://www.cooksautodiesel.co.uk
Directors: H. Cook (Dir)
Registration no: 04077071 **VAT No.:** GB 001 3616 37
No.of Employees: 1 - 10 **Product Groups:** 39, 40, 48, 68

Date of Accounts	Feb 08	Feb 07	Feb 06
Working Capital	29	-6	7
Fixed Assets	14	19	25
Current Assets	65	57	82
Current Liabilities	37	64	75
Total Share Capital	2	2	2

Cyberlux

4 Red Brick Cottages Rhode Common, Selling, Faversham, ME13 9PU
Tel: 01227-752406 **Fax:** 01227-752406
E-mail: spike@thelightingworkshop.co.uk
Directors: S. Gregor (Dir)
Immediate Holding Company: RANKIN MCGREGOR LIMITED
Registration no: 02902366 **Date established:** 1994
Turnover: Up to £250,000 **No.of Employees:** 1 - 10 **Product Groups:** 37, 67

Dooley

13-14 Upper Brents Indl-Est, Faversham, ME13 7DL
Tel: 01795-591100 **Fax:** 01795- 591100
E-mail: jjdooley@tiscali.co.uk
Directors: A. Alexander (Ptnr)
Date established: 1997 **No.of Employees:** 1 - 10 **Product Groups:** 46, 48

Gist Ltd

Oare Road, Faversham, ME13 7TW
Tel: 01795-594200
E-mail: dave.bowden@gistrail.com
Website: http://www.gistworld.com
Managers: D. Bowden (Chief Mgr), N. Atkin (Personnel), P. Kemp (Chief Acct), M. Gavin (Tech Serv Mgr)
Ultimate Holding Company: LINDE AG (GERMANY)
Immediate Holding Company: GIST LIMITED
Registration no: 00502669 **Date established:** 1951
No.of Employees: 251 - 500 **Product Groups:** 35, 45

Date of Accounts	Dec 11	Dec 10	Dec 09
Sales Turnover	407m	379m	340m
Pre Tax Profit/Loss	19m	24m	24m
Working Capital	76m	61m	34m
Fixed Assets	89m	90m	93m
Current Assets	153m	141m	104m
Current Liabilities	31m	33m	32m

J Coker Ltd (Rubber Moulding & Engineering)

Unit 11 The Shipyard Upper Brents, Faversham, ME13 7DZ
Tel: 01795-535008 **Fax:** 01795-532146
E-mail: info@j-coker.co.uk
Website: http://www.j-coker.co.uk
Directors: M. Baxter (Sales), A. Coker (MD)
Immediate Holding Company: J. COKER LIMITED
Registration no: 02638127 **Date established:** 1991
No.of Employees: 21 - 50 **Product Groups:** 29, 39

Date of Accounts	Sep 11	Sep 10	Sep 09
Working Capital	-204	-157	-120
Fixed Assets	244	198	152
Current Assets	282	248	131

Lambs Crener Whiting

Sumpter Way Lower Road, Faversham, ME13 7NT
Tel: 01795-532610 **Fax:** 01403-784663
E-mail: sales@lambsbricks.com
Website: http://www.lambsbricks.com
Managers: J. Mitchell (Works Gen Mgr)
Ultimate Holding Company: W.T. LAMB HOLDINGS LIMITED
Immediate Holding Company: CREMER,WHITING & CO.,LIMITED
Registration no: 00198546 **VAT No.:** GB 376 8218 18
Date established: 2024 **Turnover:** Up to £250,000
No.of Employees: 1 - 10 **Product Groups:** 33

Date of Accounts	Dec 10	Dec 09	Dec 08
Sales Turnover	87	243	323
Pre Tax Profit/Loss	-105	-49	-56
Working Capital	4m	4m	4m
Fixed Assets	217	248	272
Current Assets	4m	4m	4m
Current Liabilities	6	7	9

Lea Ray Retail Ltd

Hertford House 122 St Mary's Road, Faversham, ME13 8EG
Tel: 01795-535353 **Fax:** 01795-536991
E-mail: sales@learay.co.uk
Website: http://www.learay.co.uk
Directors: P. Allen (MD), S. Allen (Fin)
Immediate Holding Company: LEARAY RETAIL LIMITED
Registration no: 06285479 **VAT No.:** GB 301 7975 62
Date established: 2007 **Turnover:** £500,000 - £1m
No.of Employees: 1 - 10 **Product Groups:** 24

Date of Accounts	Jun 11	Jun 10	Jun 09
Working Capital	-17	3	-2
Fixed Assets	176	N/A	N/A
Current Assets	32	49	41

Meritronics Ltd

Otterden Place Otterden, Faversham, ME13 0BT
Tel: 01795-890341 **Fax:** 01795-890341
E-mail: contact@meritronics.co.uk
Website: http://www.meritronics.co.uk
Directors: D. Merifield (Dir), C. Merifield (Co Sec)
Immediate Holding Company: MERITRONICS LIMITED
Registration no: 01108599 **VAT No.:** 121 4532 16 **Date established:** 1973
Turnover: £250,000 - £500,000 **No.of Employees:** 1 - 10
Product Groups: 85

Date of Accounts	May 11	May 10	May 09
Working Capital	200	221	235
Fixed Assets	1	1	1
Current Assets	211	229	250

Shepherd Neame Ltd

17 Court Street, Faversham, ME13 7AX
Tel: 01795-532206 **Fax:** 01795-538907
E-mail: company@shepherd-neame.co.uk
Website: http://www.shepherd-neame.co.uk
Bank(s): National Westminster
Directors: F. Lester (Co Sec)
Ultimate Holding Company: SHEPHERD NEAME LIMITED
Immediate Holding Company: TODD VINTNERS LIMITED
Registration no: 02185226 **VAT No.:** GB 472 7817 17
Date established: 1987 **Turnover:** £75m - £125m
No.of Employees: 501 - 1000 **Product Groups:** 21

Date of Accounts	Jun 11	Jun 10	Jun 07
Working Capital	-53	-53	-53
Current Assets	N/A	N/A	-53

Stat Shop

87 South Road, Faversham, ME13 7LY
Tel: 01795-425424 **Fax:** 0870-7777827
E-mail: admin@statshop.co.uk
Website: http://www.statshop.co.uk
Directors: M. Hill (Prop), M. Hill (MD)
Immediate Holding Company: JAMES & BECKETT LLP
Registration no: 01163852 **Date established:** 2009
Turnover: £500,000 - £1m **No.of Employees:** 21 - 50
Product Groups: 49, 80

Date of Accounts	Sep 08	Sep 07	Sep 06
Working Capital	-23	-26	-32
Fixed Assets	36	42	48
Current Assets	73	66	85
Current Liabilities	96	92	117
Total Share Capital	39	39	39

Wilkinson Sails

Creek Side Workshop Swan Quay 1 Belvedere Road, Faversham, ME13 7LL
Tel: 01795-521503
E-mail: wilkinsonsails@yahoo.co.uk
Website: http://
Directors: C. Parker (Prop)
Date established: 1975 **Turnover:** **No.of Employees:** 1 - 10
Product Groups: 23, 24, 30, 39, 63

Folkestone

Church & Dwight UK Ltd

Wearbay Road, Folkestone, CT19 6PG
Tel: 01303-858700 **Fax:** 01303-858701
E-mail: info@carterproducts.co.uk
Website: http://www.churchdwight.com
Bank(s): Lloyds TSB Bank plc
Directors: G. Parsons (Sales), H. Cocker (MD), C. Cocker (MD)
Ultimate Holding Company: CHURCH AND DWIGHT CO INC (USA)
Immediate Holding Company: CHURCH & DWIGHT UK LIMITED
Registration no: 00375793 **Date established:** 1942
Turnover: £50m - £75m **No.of Employees:** 251 - 500
Product Groups: 31, 32

Date of Accounts	Dec 11	Nov 10	Nov 09
Sales Turnover	66m	58m	54m
Pre Tax Profit/Loss	2m	2m	2m
Working Capital	19m	20m	18m
Fixed Assets	7m	6m	8m
Current Assets	33m	28m	25m
Current Liabilities	2m	3m	2m

Cook Fabrications Ltd

Broomfield Works Fernfield Lane, Hawkinge, Folkestone, CT18 7AW
Tel: 01303-893011 **Fax:** 01303-893407
E-mail: info@cookfabrications.co.uk
Website: http://www.cookfabrications.co.uk
Bank(s): HSBC Bank plc
Directors: E. Cook (MD)
Managers: P. Perkins (Comptroller), R. Solley (Chief Mgr), S. Heath (Mktg Serv Mgr)
Immediate Holding Company: COOK FABRICATIONS LIMITED
Registration no: 01995879 **Date established:** 1986 **Turnover:** £2m - £5m
No.of Employees: 21 - 50 **Product Groups:** 48

Date of Accounts	Mar 12	Mar 11	Mar 10
Working Capital	2m	2m	2m
Fixed Assets	310	307	371
Current Assets	3m	3m	3m
Current Liabilities	1m	N/A	N/A

1st Call Plumbing & Heating Ltd

Unit 9 Folkestone Enterprise Centre Shearway Business Park, Folkestone, CT19 4RH
Tel: 01303-247593 **Fax:** 01303-298361
E-mail: trevor@1stcallgroup.co.uk
Website: http://www.1stcallgroup.co.uk
Directors: T. Baker (Dir)
Immediate Holding Company: 1ST CALL PLUMBING & HEATING LIMITED
Registration no: 04495312 **Date established:** 2002 **Turnover:** £2m - £5m
No.of Employees: 11 - 20 **Product Groups:** 40, 52, 66

Date of Accounts	Jul 07	Jul 06	Jul 05
Working Capital	-4	N/A	N/A
Fixed Assets	N/A	N/A	1
Current Assets	3	4	4
Current Liabilities	N/A	2	N/A

Folkestone & Dover

The Cherry Garden Cherry Garden Lane, Folkestone, CT19 4QB
Tel: 01303-298888 **Fax:** 01303- 276712
E-mail: sales@fdws.co.uk
Website: http://www.fdws.co.uk
Bank(s): National Westminster Bank Plc
Directors: D. Walton (MD)
Immediate Holding Company: FOLKESTONE AND DOVER WATER SERVICES LIMITED
Registration no: 03669198 **VAT No.:** GB 201 4758 93
Date established: 1998 **Turnover:** £10m - £20m
No.of Employees: 51 - 100 **Product Groups:** 18

Gordon Engineering

Fernlea Works Fernfield Lane, Hawkinge, Folkestone, CT18 7AW
Tel: 01303-892813 **Fax:** 01303-892742
E-mail: mcgregorgordon0@gmail.com
Website: http://www.gordonengineering.co.uk
Directors: M. Gordon (Ptnr)
No.of Employees: 1 - 10 **Product Groups:** 35

Graham

Kingsmead Park Farm Industrial Estate, Folkestone, CT19 5EU
Tel: 01303-850300 **Fax:** 01303-253330
Website: http://www.graham-group.co.uk
Managers: M. Reed (District Mgr)
Ultimate Holding Company: SAINT-GOBAIN PLC
Immediate Holding Company: GRAHAM GROUP LTD
Registration no: 00066738 **No.of Employees:** 1 - 10 **Product Groups:** 25, 66

J. S. Bradley Ltd

Park Farm Close Park Farm Industrial Estate, Folkestone, CT19 5ED
Tel: 01303-850011 **Fax:** 01303-244028
E-mail: info@bradleyfurniture.co.uk
Website: http://www.bradleyfurniture.co.uk
Directors: J. Wynn (MD), T. Hackett (Dir)
Managers: S. Price (Admin Off)
Immediate Holding Company: Bradley Furniture (Kent) Ltd
Registration no: 06188547 **Date established:** 2004 **Turnover:** £5m - £10m
No.of Employees: 1 - 10 **Product Groups:** 25

Date of Accounts	Jan 06
Sales Turnover	996
Pre Tax Profit/Loss	33
Working Capital	136
Fixed Assets	34
Current Assets	549
Current Liabilities	281

Kent Regional News & Media (a division of The Trinity Mirror Group)

Westcliff House West Cliff Gardens, Folkestone, CT20 1SZ
Tel: 01303-850999 **Fax:** 01303-226658
E-mail: newdesk.heraldexpress@kentregionalnewpaper.co.uk
Website: http://www.thisiskent.co.uk
Managers: S. Finlay
Ultimate Holding Company: TRINITY MIRROR PLC
Immediate Holding Company: THE ADSCENE GROUP LTD
Registration no: 01381259 **Turnover:** £1m - £2m
No.of Employees: 21 - 50 **Product Groups:** 28

M & S Linens

19-21 Rendezvous Street, Folkestone, CT20 1EY
Tel: 01303-223344
Directors: J. Underdown (Prop)
No.of Employees: 1 - 10 **Product Groups:** 23, 24

Martello Plastics Ltd (Glass Fibre Specialists)

Unit 11 Shorncliffe Industrial Estate Ross Way, Folkestone, CT20 3UJ
Tel: 01303-256848 **Fax:** 01303-246301
E-mail: mail@martelloplastics.co.uk
Website: http://www.martelloplastics.co.uk
Bank(s): National Westminster Bank Plc
Directors: L. Bray (MD)
Immediate Holding Company: MARTELLO PLASTICS LIMITED
Registration no: 00999397 **VAT No.:** GB 201 5695 86
Date established: 1971 **Turnover:** £500,000 - £1m
No.of Employees: 11 - 20 **Product Groups:** 30

Date of Accounts	Mar 12	Mar 11	Mar 10
Working Capital	113	98	81
Fixed Assets	196	206	218
Current Assets	170	179	150

N I C Instruments Ltd

Gladstone Road, Folkestone, CT19 5NF
Tel: 01303-851022 **Fax:** 01303-850155
E-mail: sales@nicltd.co.uk
Website: http://www.nicltd.co.uk
Bank(s): Barclays
Directors: S. Wisbey (MD)
Immediate Holding Company: NIC INSTRUMENTS LIMITED
Registration no: 00559230 **Date established:** 1955 **Turnover:** £2m - £5m
No.of Employees: 11 - 20 **Product Groups:** 40, 84

Date of Accounts	Dec 11	Dec 10	Dec 09
Sales Turnover	N/A	N/A	3m
Pre Tax Profit/Loss	N/A	N/A	850
Working Capital	528	398	358
Fixed Assets	622	643	550
Current Assets	820	788	1m
Current Liabilities	N/A	340	391

Ovenden Engineers

2 Radnor Street, Folkestone, CT19 6AQ
Tel: 01303-254387 **Fax:** 01303-254387
Directors: R. Parker (Prop)
Immediate Holding Company: OVENDENS ENGINEERS LTD
Registration no: 02984044 **VAT No.:** GB 397 8205 07
Date established: 1994 **Turnover:** £250,000 - £500,000
No.of Employees: 1 - 10 **Product Groups:** 48

Realia

Unit 3 Folkestone Enterprise Centre Shearway Business Park Shearway Road, Folkestone, CT19 4RH
Tel: 01303-298388 **Fax:** 01303-298389
E-mail: paul.williamson@realia-marketing.com
Website: http://www.team-realia.com
Directors: P. Williamson (Dir)
Immediate Holding Company: SHEPWAY ECONOMIC REGENERATION PARTNERSHIP (SERP) LTD
Registration no: 05375167 **Date established:** 2007
Turnover: Up to £250,000 **No.of Employees:** 1 - 10 **Product Groups:** 81

Date of Accounts	Mar 08	Mar 07	Mar 06
Working Capital	84	35	19
Fixed Assets	14	15	7
Current Assets	203	188	77
Current Liabilities	120	153	59

Reznor UK Ltd

Park Farm Road Park Farm Industrial Estate, Folkestone, CT19 5DR
Tel: 01303-259141 **Fax:** 01303-850002
E-mail: orders@reznor.co.uk
Website: http://www.reznor.co.uk
Bank(s): Lloyds TSB Bank plc
Managers: J. Kiernan (Sales Prom Mgr)
Ultimate Holding Company: AMBI-RAD GROUP LIMITED
Immediate Holding Company: REZNOR (UK) LIMITED
Registration no: 03275506 **Date established:** 1996 **Turnover:** £5m - £10m
No.of Employees: 21 - 50 **Product Groups:** 37, 40, 45, 48, 52, 54, 66, 84

Date of Accounts	Jul 10	Jul 09	Jul 08
Sales Turnover	7m	7m	8m
Pre Tax Profit/Loss	354	389	1m
Working Capital	2m	2m	2m
Fixed Assets	169	109	113
Current Assets	4m	4m	4m
Current Liabilities	646	815	855

Shepway District Council

Civic Centre Castle Hill Avenue, Folkestone, CT20 2QY
Tel: 01303-853000 **Fax:** 01303-245978
E-mail: jeremy.whittaker@shepway.gov.uk
Website: http://www.shepway.gov.uk
Directors: A. Stewart (Grp Chief Exec)
No.of Employees: 1 - 10 **Product Groups:** 80

Silver Spring Soft Drink Co. Ltd

Park Farm Road Park Farm Industrial Estate, Folkestone, CT19 5EA
Tel: 01303-856500 **Fax:** 01303-256524
E-mail: sales@silverspring.co.uk
Website: http://www.silverspring.co.uk
Bank(s): National Westminster Bank Plc
Directors: A. Hawker (Fin), G. West (Dir)
Managers: C. Rees (Buyer), M. Fletcher, H. Donovan
Immediate Holding Company: SSMW REALISATIONS (2009) LIMITED
Registration no: 00026463 **VAT No.:** GB 201 4692 00
Date established: 1988 **Turnover:** £20m - £50m
No.of Employees: 51 - 100 **Product Groups:** 21, 62

Date of Accounts	Jan 08	Jan 07
Sales Turnover	37070	40700
Pre Tax Profit/Loss	-2260	-3240
Working Capital	-2200	-2920
Fixed Assets	22700	25070
Current Assets	7520	9550
Current Liabilities	9720	12470
Total Share Capital	10	N/A
ROCE% (Return on Capital Employed)	-11.0	-14.6
ROT% (Return on Turnover)	-6.1	-8.0

Sytec Computers LTS

9 Castle Hill Court 21-23 Castle Hill Avenue, Folkestone, CT20 2QU
Tel: 01303-849329
E-mail: roger@sytecweb.co.uk
Website: http://www.sytecweb.co.uk
Directors: R. Weavers (Dir)
Immediate Holding Company: SYTEC COMPUTERS LIMITED
Registration no: 03271319 **Date established:** 1996
No.of Employees: 1 - 10 **Product Groups:** 44

Gillingham

Airnesco Group Ltd

Unit 2 Bredgar Road Industrial Estate Bredgar Road, Gillingham, ME8 6PL
Tel: 01634-267070 **Fax:** 01634-267079
E-mail: lorraine@airnesco.com
Website: http://www.airnesco.com
Managers: L. Waldron (Sales Admin)
Ultimate Holding Company: AIRNESCO GROUP LTD
Immediate Holding Company: AIRNESCO LIMITED
Registration no: 01459669 **VAT No.:** GB 304 3337 95
Date established: 1979 **Turnover:** £250,000 - £500,000
No.of Employees: 1 - 10 **Product Groups:** 37, 40, 45, 46

Date of Accounts	Dec 11	Dec 10	Dec 09
Working Capital	423	418	414
Current Assets	456	476	470

W & S Allely Ltd
Unit 6-7 Cloverlay Industrial Park, Rainham, Gillingham, ME8 8GL
Tel: 01634-379111 **Fax:** 01634-375666
E-mail: sales@allely.co.uk
Website: http://www.allely.co.uk
Managers: H. Bale (District Mgr)
Ultimate Holding Company: ALLELY EDEN HOLDINGS LIMITED
Immediate Holding Company: W. & S. ALLELY LIMITED
Registration no: 00292572 **VAT No.:** GB 547 6741 12
Date established: 1934 **Turnover:** £10m - £20m **No.of Employees:** 1 - 10
Product Groups: 34, 37, 49

Date of Accounts	Dec 11	Dec 10	Dec 09
Working Capital	465	401	371
Fixed Assets	22	25	43
Current Assets	3m	2m	2m
Current Liabilities	N/A	N/A	166

Arcola Products Ltd
311 Station Road Rainham, Gillingham, ME8 7PU
Tel: 01634-360562 **Fax:** 01634-232708
E-mail: info@arcolaproducts.co.uk
Website: http://www.arcolaproducts.co.uk
Directors: D. Bowra (MD)
Immediate Holding Company: ARCOLA PRODUCTS LIMITED
Registration no: 01006806 **VAT No.:** GB 204 6222 09
Date established: 1971 **Turnover:** £500,000 - £1m
No.of Employees: 1 - 10 **Product Groups:** 30, 48, 49

Date of Accounts	Sep 11	Sep 10	Sep 09
Sales Turnover	735	710	525
Pre Tax Profit/Loss	-6	6	-71
Working Capital	128	134	105
Fixed Assets	132	132	155
Current Assets	264	235	208
Current Liabilities	33	21	48

Bond Trading
2 Gillingham Green, Gillingham, ME7 1SS
Tel: 01634-580670 **Fax:** 01634-855455
E-mail: bondtradingltd@aol.com
Directors: N. Ahmad (MD), N. Ahmad (Fin)
Immediate Holding Company: BOND TRADING GB LIMITED
Registration no: 02665678 **VAT No.:** GB 619 2381 37
Date established: 1991 **Turnover:** Up to £250,000
No.of Employees: 1 - 10 **Product Groups:** 44, 61, 66, 67, 68, 80

Date of Accounts	Mar 10	Mar 09	Mar 08
Sales Turnover	22	29	16
Pre Tax Profit/Loss	N/A	-1	N/A
Working Capital	8	16	17
Fixed Assets	1	1	1
Current Assets	21	17	84
Current Liabilities	13	1	68

Bose Ltd
Unit 1 Ambley Green Gillingham Business Park, Gillingham, ME8 0NJ
Tel: 08707-414500 **Fax:** 08707-414545
E-mail: philip_carpenter@bose.com
Website: http://www.bose.com
Bank(s): HSBC Bank plc
Directors: P. Carpenter (MD)
Managers: D. McGrath (Nat Sales Mgr), M. Tasker (Tech Serv Mgr), S. Mighall (Comptroller), L. Rusbridge (Mktg Serv Mgr), J. Lemar (Personnel)
Ultimate Holding Company: BOSE CORPORATION (USA)
Immediate Holding Company: BOSE LIMITED
Registration no: 01187672 **VAT No.:** GB 204 5557 80
Date established: 1974 **Turnover:** £50m - £75m
No.of Employees: 51 - 100 **Product Groups:** 37

Date of Accounts	Mar 11	Mar 10	Mar 09
Sales Turnover	66m	66m	71m
Pre Tax Profit/Loss	2m	2m	3m
Working Capital	28m	27m	11m
Fixed Assets	530	525	15m
Current Assets	37m	40m	21m
Current Liabilities	7m	7m	6m

C Brewer & Sons
4-5 Matilda Close Gillingham Business Park, Gillingham, ME8 0RP
Tel: 01634-388351 **Fax:** 01634-231354
E-mail: gillingham@brewers.co.uk
Website: http://www.brewers.co.uk
Managers: A. Currington (Mgr)
Immediate Holding Company: C.BREWER & SONS LIMITED
Registration no: 00203852 **Date established:** 1925
No.of Employees: 1 - 10 **Product Groups:** 52

Fuji Copian
Unit 21a Bailey Drive Gillingham Business Park, Gillingham, ME8 0PZ
Tel: 01634-371137 **Fax:** 01634-366560
E-mail: sales@fujicopian.co.uk
Website: http://www.fujicopian.co.uk
Bank(s): National Westminster Bank Plc
Directors: P. Barker (Dir)
Ultimate Holding Company: FUJICOPIAN CO LIMITED (JAPAN)
Immediate Holding Company: FUJI COPIAN (UK) LIMITED
Registration no: 02380277 **Date established:** 1989 **Turnover:** £2m - £5m
No.of Employees: 11 - 20 **Product Groups:** 23, 28, 32, 44

Date of Accounts	Oct 11	Oct 10	Oct 09
Sales Turnover	3m	3m	3m
Pre Tax Profit/Loss	-486	-298	-547
Working Capital	966	1m	2m
Fixed Assets	233	266	307
Current Assets	2m	2m	2m
Current Liabilities	20	28	50

Hawkridge & Co.
39 Canterbury Street, Gillingham, ME7 5TR
Tel: 01634-854381 **Fax:** 01634-280200
E-mail: enquiries@hawklaw.co.uk
Website: http://www.hawklaw.co.uk
Directors: J. Hawkridge (Prop)
Immediate Holding Company: HAWKRIDGE & COMPANY LLP
Registration no: OC352849 **Date established:** 2010
No.of Employees: 1 - 10 **Product Groups:** 80

Date of Accounts	Mar 11
Working Capital	93
Fixed Assets	232
Current Assets	165

Hewi UK Ltd
Scimitar Close Gillingham Business Park, Gillingham, ME8 0RN
Tel: 01634-377688 **Fax:** 01634-370612
E-mail: info@hewi.co.uk
Website: http://www.hewi.co.uk
Bank(s): Bank of Scotland
Directors: V. Gant (Fin), L. Turner (MD)
Managers: J. Batters (Personnel), D. Graham (Sales Prom Mgr)
Immediate Holding Company: HEWI (UK) LIMITED
Registration no: 06266991 **VAT No.:** GB 921 4497 25
Date established: 2007 **Turnover:** £2m - £5m **No.of Employees:** 11 - 20
Product Groups: 25, 26, 30, 33, 35, 36, 61, 66

Date of Accounts	Dec 11	Dec 10	Dec 09
Working Capital	310	274	316
Fixed Assets	10	8	10
Current Assets	827	530	766

Kent Regional News & Media
Unit 4 Ambley Green Gillingham Business Park, Gillingham, ME8 0NJ
Tel: 01634-236320
Website: http://www.thisiskent.co.uk
Bank(s): National Westminster Bank Plc
Managers: J. Daker, A. Wiltshire, C. Rayner, E. Hayward (Sales & Mktg Mg), C. Lamming
Registration no: 02899725 **VAT No.:** GB 209 6240 74
Date established: 1994 **No.of Employees:** 51 - 100 **Product Groups:** 28

L Robinson Company Gillingham Ltd
Gads Hill, Gillingham, ME7 2RS
Tel: 01634-281200 **Fax:** 01634-280101
E-mail: sales@jubileeclips.co.uk
Website: http://www.jubileeclips.co.uk
Bank(s): HSBC, Chatham
Directors: J. Jennings (MD)
Immediate Holding Company: L. ROBINSON & CO (GILLINGHAM) LIMITED
Registration no: 00451655 **VAT No.:** GB 203 0200 55
Date established: 1948 **Turnover:** £2m - £5m
No.of Employees: 101 - 250 **Product Groups:** 35, 36, 37, 39

Date of Accounts	Dec 11	Dec 10	Dec 09
Sales Turnover	5m	4m	4m
Pre Tax Profit/Loss	194	106	-25
Working Capital	2m	2m	3m
Fixed Assets	3m	4m	2m
Current Assets	2m	2m	4m
Current Liabilities	341	273	184

London Bearings Kent Ltd
Unit 2 Sabre Court, Gillingham Business Park, Gillingham, ME8 0RW
Tel: 01634-235335 **Fax:** 01634-230268
E-mail: kevin.lane@lbk.co.uk
Website: http://www.lbk.co.uk
Directors: K. Lane (MD)
Immediate Holding Company: LONDON BEARINGS (KENT) LIMITED
Registration no: 02224336 **Date established:** 1988
Turnover: £500,000 - £1m **No.of Employees:** 1 - 10 **Product Groups:** 29, 30, 35, 45, 67

Date of Accounts	Mar 08	Mar 07	Mar 06
Sales Turnover	N/A	623	644
Pre Tax Profit/Loss	N/A	35	36
Working Capital	110	95	116
Fixed Assets	14	40	42
Current Assets	249	201	242
Current Liabilities	139	106	126
ROCE% (Return on Capital Employed)		26.2	22.9
ROT% (Return on Turnover)		5.7	5.6

Medway Optics
567 Mierscourt Road Rainham, Gillingham, ME8 8RB
Tel: 01634-373068 **Fax:** 01634-263253
E-mail: info@medwayoptics.com
Website: http://www.medwayoptics.com
Directors: A. Afran (Dir)
Registration no: 04541204 **Date established:** 2002
No.of Employees: 1 - 10 **Product Groups:** 38

Medway Portable Appliance Testing Ltd
70 Ellison Way Rainham, Gillingham, ME8 7PG
Tel: 01634-388966 **Fax:** 01634-388966
E-mail: info@medwaypattesting.co.uk
Website: http://www.medwaypattesting.co.uk
Directors: R. Brown (Prop)
Immediate Holding Company: MEDWAY PORTABLE APPLIANCE TESTING LIMITED
Registration no: 04800113 **Date established:** 2003
No.of Employees: 1 - 10 **Product Groups:** 38, 67, 85

Date of Accounts	Dec 10	Dec 09	Dec 07
Working Capital	1	2	2
Fixed Assets	3	4	2
Current Assets	4	6	7

Mems Power Generation
Beechings Way, Gillingham, ME8 6PS
Tel: 08452-230400 **Fax:** 01634-263666
E-mail: sales@memsgen.co.uk
Website: http://www.memsgen.co.uk
Directors: M. Diffey (Tech Serv), A. Rainer (Pers), P. Knight (Sales)
Managers: C. Jarvis (Fin Mgr), T. Dymott (I.T. Exec), R. Emerson (Buyer)
Immediate Holding Company: MEMS POWER GENERATION LIMITED
Registration no: 03690907 **Date established:** 1998 **Turnover:** £5m - £10m
No.of Employees: 51 - 100 **Product Groups:** 83

Metallic Wool Co. Ltd
Bredgar Road, Gillingham, ME8 6PL
Tel: 01634-239444 **Fax:** 01634-239888
E-mail: enquiries@metallic-wool.co.uk
Website: http://www.metallic-wool.co.uk
Directors: F. Shaw (Dir), P. Young (MD)
Managers: K. Holderness (Sales Prom Mgr), V. Batcheldor (Admin Off)
Immediate Holding Company: Metallic Wool Co. Limited(The)
Registration no: 02085672 **VAT No.:** GB 463 6217 47
Date established: 1987 **No.of Employees:** 11 - 20 **Product Groups:** 34, 35

Steelfields
Owens Way Gads Hill, Gillingham, ME7 2RT
Tel: 01634-280135 **Fax:** 01634-280689
E-mail: prentis.polhill@steelfield.co.uk
Website: http://www.steelfields.com
Bank(s): Barclays, Maidstone
Directors: P. Polhill (Sales)
Immediate Holding Company: STEELFIELDS (HOLDINGS) LIMITED
Registration no: 03483012 **VAT No.:** GB 203 9853 62
Date established: 1997 **Turnover:** £2m - £5m **No.of Employees:** 21 - 50
Product Groups: 35, 38, 45

Talon
Chieftain Close Gillingham Business Park, Gillingham, ME8 0PP
Tel: 08450-952828 **Fax:** 0845-095 2929
E-mail: sales@talon.co.uk
Website: http://www.talon.co.uk
Bank(s): National Westminster Bank Plc
Directors: D. Theobold (Comm)
Immediate Holding Company: TALON MANUFACTURING LTD
Registration no: 03796007 **VAT No.:** GB 304 3644 87
Date established: 1999 **Turnover:** £2m - £5m **No.of Employees:** 21 - 50
Product Groups: 25, 30, 35

Date of Accounts	Jul 08	Jul 07	Jul 06
Working Capital	1098	829	597
Fixed Assets	932	956	815
Current Assets	1700	1295	1019
Current Liabilities	602	466	422
Total Share Capital	50	50	50

21st Century Energy Publications Ltd
13 Lineacre Close, Gillingham, ME8 9NW
Tel: 01634-301418 **Fax:** 01634-301428
E-mail: energypublications@gmail.com
Website: http://www.21stcenturyenergy.co.uk
Directors: R. Hamacher (Fin), M. McIntyre (MD)
Immediate Holding Company: OIL & MARINE MEDIA LTD
Registration no: 05219899 **Date established:** 2012
Turnover: Up to £250,000 **No.of Employees:** 1 - 10 **Product Groups:** 28

Yiannis Avgerou
152 Edwin Road, Gillingham, ME8 0AQ
Tel: 01634-378523
No.of Employees: 1 - 10 **Product Groups:** 25, 36, 48

Gravesend

Abbey Fork Trucks Ltd
Unit B Denton Wharf Mark Lane, Gravesend, DA12 2QD
Tel: 01474-369379 **Fax:** 01474-369459
E-mail: terry@abbeyforktrucks.com
Website: http://www.abbeyforktrucks.com
Directors: T. Needham (Dir), L. Needham (Fin)
Immediate Holding Company: ABBEY FORK TRUCKS LIMITED
Registration no: 04179625 **Date established:** 2001
No.of Employees: 1 - 10 **Product Groups:** 35, 39, 45

Date of Accounts	Mar 11	Mar 10	Mar 09
Working Capital	-130	-94	-130
Fixed Assets	145	109	146
Current Assets	131	132	115

Access Communication Services Ltd
2 Westwood Farm Highcross Road, Southfleet, Gravesend, DA13 9PH
Tel: 01474-834834 **Fax:** 01474-834835
E-mail: info@accesscom.co.uk
Website: http://www.accesscom.co.uk
Directors: M. Clark (Fin)
Managers: B. Papworth (Projects), D. Bullock, I. Canning
Immediate Holding Company: O.C.S. Group Ltd
Registration no: 03154285 **Date established:** 2002
Turnover: £500m - £1,000m **No.of Employees:** 21 - 50
Product Groups: 35, 36, 39, 40

Date of Accounts	Mar 08	Mar 07	Mar 06
Sales Turnover	6069	5100	4028
Pre Tax Profit/Loss	-274	188	272
Working Capital	314	481	344
Fixed Assets	N/A	57	89
Current Assets	314	2159	1891
Current Liabilities	N/A	1679	1547
Total Share Capital	10	10	10
ROCE% (Return on Capital Employed)		35.0	62.9
ROT% (Return on Turnover)	-4.5	3.7	6.8

Ace Filtration Ltd
Air Flow Works Seymour Road, Northfleet, Gravesend, DA11 7BW
Tel: 01474-325666 **Fax:** 01474-333132
E-mail: sales@acefiltration.co.uk
Website: http://www.acefiltration.co.uk
Directors: A. Thain (Pers), M. Cowell (Fin), P. Gardner (Chief Op Offcr)
Immediate Holding Company: ACE FILTRATION LIMITED
Registration no: 01734727 **VAT No.:** GB 374 3371 47
Date established: 1983 **Turnover:** £1m - £2m **No.of Employees:** 11 - 20
Product Groups: 42

Date of Accounts	Jul 11	Jul 10	Jul 09
Working Capital	671	578	483
Fixed Assets	122	142	140
Current Assets	1m	1m	1m

Aintree Concrete Pumping
21 Aintree Close, Gravesend, DA12 5AS
Tel: 01474-333616 **Fax:** 01474-333616
E-mail: info@aintreeconcretepumping.co.uk
Website: http://www.aintreeconcretepumping.co.uk
Directors: K. Nelson (Dir)
No.of Employees: 1 - 10 **Product Groups:** 40, 52, 67

Appledore Packaging Ltd
Rose Dene Green Farm Lane, Shorne, Gravesend, DA12 3HL
Tel: 01474-770018 **Fax:** 01474-770019
E-mail: enquiries@appledore-packaging.co.uk
Website: http://www.appledore-packaging.co.uk
Managers: J. Dixon (Mgr)
Immediate Holding Company: APPLEDORE PACKAGING LIMITED
Registration no: 03074882 **Date established:** 1995
Turnover: £250,000 - £500,000 **No.of Employees:** 1 - 10
Product Groups: 27

Date of Accounts	Jun 11	Jun 10	Jun 09
Working Capital	-2	-1	-1
Fixed Assets	2	1	1
Current Assets	42	12	17

Bradley Shaw Ironwork
8 Park Avenue Northfleet, Gravesend, DA11 8DS
Tel: 01474-534952 **Fax:** 01474-537002
E-mail: sales@bradleyshawironwork.co.uk
Website: http://www.bradleyshawironwork.co.uk
Directors: P. Bradshaw (MD)
Immediate Holding Company: BARNEY, SANDS & HARTRIDGE LIMITED
Date established: 1946 **No.of Employees:** 1 - 10 **Product Groups:** 26, 35

Brise Fabrications
Unit Q3 Northfleet Industrial Estate Lower Road, Northfleet, Gravesend, DA11 9SN
Tel: 01322-277622 **Fax:** 01322-277623
E-mail: tim@brise.co.uk
Website: http://www.brise.co.uk
Directors: T. Brise (Prop)
Turnover: £250,000 - £500,000 **No.of Employees:** 1 - 10
Product Groups: 35, 37, 38, 39, 48, 67, 68

Britannia Refined Metals Ltd
Britannia Works Botany Road, Northfleet, Gravesend, DA11 9BG
Tel: 01474-538200 **Fax:** 01474-538203
Website: http://www.brm.co.uk
Bank(s): Lloyds TSB Bank plc
Directors: V. Surace (Fin)
Managers: T. Breeze (Personnel)
Ultimate Holding Company: XSTRATA PLC
Immediate Holding Company: BRITANNIA REFINED METALS LIMITED
Registration no: 00252455 **Date established:** 1930
Turnover: £250m - £500m **No.of Employees:** 101 - 250
Product Groups: 34

Date of Accounts	Dec 11	Dec 10	Dec 09
Sales Turnover	375m	381m	311m
Pre Tax Profit/Loss	10m	8m	11m
Working Capital	44m	37m	31m
Fixed Assets	20m	19m	19m
Current Assets	209m	203m	185m
Current Liabilities	4m	7m	3m

Captivair Pneumatics Ltd
Unit B2 West Mill Imperial Business Estate, Gravesend, DA11 0DL
Tel: 01474-334537 **Fax:** 01474-333657
E-mail: admin@captivair.co.uk
Website: http://www.captivair.co.uk
Directors: N. Jeffs (Prop)
Immediate Holding Company: CAPTIVAIR PNEUMATICS LIMITED
Registration no: 03527775 **Date established:** 1998 **Turnover:** £1m - £2m
No.of Employees: 1 - 10 **Product Groups:** 29, 30, 31, 35, 36, 37, 38, 39, 40, 41, 42, 43, 44, 45, 46, 48, 61, 67, 84

Date of Accounts	Mar 11	Mar 10	Mar 09
Working Capital	15	18	26
Fixed Assets	35	25	33
Current Assets	184	187	193

Causeway Steel Products Ltd
Five Ash Road, Gravesend, DA11 0RF
Tel: 01474-567871 **Fax:** 01474-328993
E-mail: causewaysteel@causeway-steel.co.uk
Website: http://www.causeway-steel.co.uk
Bank(s): Barclays
Directors: I. Allen (MD), I. Allen (Fin)
Ultimate Holding Company: CALEDONIA INVESTMENTS PLC
Immediate Holding Company: CAUSEWAY STEEL PRODUCTS LIMITED
Registration no: 04488987 **Date established:** 2002 **Turnover:** £2m - £5m
No.of Employees: 21 - 50 **Product Groups:** 33, 35

Date of Accounts	Jul 11	Jul 10	Jul 09
Working Capital	1m	1m	808
Fixed Assets	2m	2m	1m
Current Assets	2m	3m	3m

Comma Oil & Chemicals Ltd
Comma Works Dering Way, Gravesend, DA12 2QX
Tel: 01474-564311 **Fax:** 01474-333000
E-mail: enquiries@commaoil.com
Website: http://www.commaoil.com
Bank(s): National Westminster Bank Plc
Directors: D. Hopkinson (Dir), D. Seex (MD), K. McDonald (Fin), J. Corrish (MD), B. Morsso (Purch)
Managers: S. Medley (I.T. Exec), M. Bewsey (Publicity)
Ultimate Holding Company: EXXON MOBIL CORP (USA)
Immediate Holding Company: COMMA OIL & CHEMICALS LIMITED
Registration no: 02075698 **VAT No.:** GB 460 5422 69
Date established: 1986 **Turnover:** £50m - £75m
No.of Employees: 101 - 250 **Product Groups:** 31, 32, 66

Date of Accounts	Dec 11	Dec 10	Dec 09
Sales Turnover	78m	74m	69m
Pre Tax Profit/Loss	5m	6m	7m
Working Capital	27m	24m	22m
Fixed Assets	5m	8m	6m
Current Assets	36m	32m	28m
Current Liabilities	6m	4m	3m

Computertel Ltd
52 Bath Street, Gravesend, DA11 0DF
Tel: 01474-561111 **Fax:** 01474-561122
E-mail: info@computertel.co.uk
Website: http://www.computertel.co.uk
Bank(s): Lloyds
Directors: P. Haynes (MD)
Immediate Holding Company: COMPUTERTEL LIMITED
Registration no: 02311748 **VAT No.:** GB 527 3789 13
Date established: 1988 **Turnover:** £1m - £2m **No.of Employees:** 11 - 20
Product Groups: 37, 85

Date of Accounts	Mar 12	Mar 11	Mar 10
Working Capital	190	198	108
Fixed Assets	29	15	18
Current Assets	693	726	677
Current Liabilities	N/A	N/A	497

David Fry Piano Services
8 Longfield Road Meopham, Gravesend, DA13 0EN
Tel: 01474-814330
E-mail: workshop@davidfrypianos.co.uk
Website: http://www.davidfrypianos.co.uk
Directors: D. Fry (Prop)
No.of Employees: 1 - 10 **Product Groups:** 49

Double D Electronics Ltd
6 Robins Wharf Grove Road, Northfleet, Gravesend, DA11 9AX
Tel: 01474-333456 **Fax:** 01474-333414
E-mail: sales@ddelec.co.uk
Website: http://www.ddelec.co.uk
Directors: S. Davies (MD)
Immediate Holding Company: DOUBLE D ELECTRONICS LIMITED
Registration no: 01859875 **Date established:** 1984
Turnover: Up to £250,000 **No.of Employees:** 1 - 10 **Product Groups:** 37, 44

Date of Accounts	Oct 11	Oct 10	Oct 09
Working Capital	141	133	128
Fixed Assets	8	10	12
Current Assets	232	149	172

Ellis Rees & Co.
The Old Foundry Grove Road, Northfleet, Gravesend, DA11 9AX
Tel: 01474-567861 **Fax:** 01474-537056
Managers: R. Cousins (Mgr)
Ultimate Holding Company: MONITOR SERVICES LIMITED
Immediate Holding Company: MONITOR CLEANING SERVICES LIMITED
Registration no: 04699788 **Date established:** 1990 **Turnover:** £1m - £2m
No.of Employees: 1 - 10 **Product Groups:** 49

Date of Accounts	Dec 11	Dec 10	Dec 09
Sales Turnover	2m	2m	3m
Pre Tax Profit/Loss	1	46	77
Working Capital	102	101	56
Current Assets	297	506	502
Current Liabilities	110	141	166

Fire Protection Services
Unit B7 Imperial Business Estate West Mill, Gravesend, DA11 0DL
Tel: 01474-535555 **Fax:** 01474-535111
E-mail: info@fireprotectionservices.co.uk
Website: http://www.fireprotectionservices.co.uk
Directors: J. Stone (Prop)
Immediate Holding Company: FIRE PROTECTION SERVICES (UK) LIMITED
Registration no: 05382795 **Date established:** 2005
Turnover: £500,000 - £1m **No.of Employees:** 1 - 10 **Product Groups:** 38, 42

Date of Accounts	Mar 12	Mar 11	Mar 10
Sales Turnover	508	482	461
Pre Tax Profit/Loss	197	136	92
Working Capital	-30	-4	-11
Fixed Assets	61	61	69
Current Assets	84	130	107
Current Liabilities	80	65	55

HES UK Ltd
Unit P4 Northfleet Industrial Estate, Lower Road, Gravesend, DA11 9SN
Tel: 08000-754854 **Fax:** 08448-011066
E-mail: info@hesuk.com
Website: http://www.hesuk.co.uk
Product Groups: 30, 39, 40, 42, 52, 54, 84

Date of Accounts	Dec 07	Dec 06	Dec 05
Pre Tax Profit/Loss	200	450	300
Working Capital	-5	-5	-5
Fixed Assets	103	103	103
Current Liabilities	5	5	5
ROCE% (Return on Capital Employed)	204.0	458.9	305.9

Hollisters Electrical Contractors Ltd
54-56 Dover Road East, Gravesend, DA11 0RG
Tel: 01474-564088 **Fax:** 01474-560455
E-mail: martin@hollisterselectrical.co.uk
Website: http://www.hollisterselectrical.co.uk
Directors: M. Wheeler (MD)
Immediate Holding Company: HOLLISTERS (ELECTRICAL CONTRACTORS) LIMITED
Registration no: 00524780 **VAT No.:** GB 203 2493 04
Date established: 1953 **Turnover:** £250,000 - £500,000
No.of Employees: 1 - 10 **Product Groups:** 52

Date of Accounts	Mar 12	Mar 11	Mar 10
Sales Turnover	345	406	234
Working Capital	-18	-38	-21
Fixed Assets	5	5	5
Current Assets	32	37	34

Itab Shop Concept Ltd
Unit E2 Imperial Business Estate West Mill, Gravesend, DA11 0DL
Tel: 01474-537744 **Fax:** 01474-537860
E-mail: reception@itabuk.com
Website: http://www.itab.co.uk
Bank(s): National Westminster
Directors: A. Tweddle (Fin)
Ultimate Holding Company: ITAB SHOP CONCEPT AB (SWEDEN)
Immediate Holding Company: GWS GROUP LTD
Registration no: 03284213 **Date established:** 1996
Turnover: £20m - £50m **No.of Employees:** 101 - 250
Product Groups: 26, 52

Date of Accounts	Dec 11	Dec 10	Dec 09
Pre Tax Profit/Loss	9m	N/A	N/A
Fixed Assets	9m	N/A	N/A

Tasha Jacks
Oakland The Street, Shorne, Gravesend, DA12 3EA
Tel: 01474-823666 **Fax:** 01474-823777
E-mail: info@tashajacks.com
Website: http://www.tashajacks.com
Directors: N. Ratajczak (Prop)
Immediate Holding Company: TASHA JACKS LIMITED
Registration no: 04637998 **Date established:** 2003
Turnover: Up to £250,000 **No.of Employees:** 1 - 10 **Product Groups:** 30, 32, 36, 40, 49

Date of Accounts	Jan 12	Jan 11	Jan 10
Working Capital	6	24	25
Fixed Assets	3	2	1
Current Assets	40	41	64

Lafarge Cement UK
Northfleet Works The Shore, Northfleet, Gravesend, DA11 9AN
Tel: 01474-531200 **Fax:** 01474-531279
E-mail: info@lafargecement.co.uk
Website: http://www.lafargecement.co.uk
Managers: I. Bohill
Registration no: 00066558 **No.of Employees:** 21 - 50
Product Groups: 14, 29, 30, 33, 61

Mccomb Developments
Unit 3 Westwood Farm Highcross Road, Southfleet, Gravesend, DA13 9PH
Tel: 01474-833175 **Fax:** 01892-752161
E-mail: info@teleseal.co.uk
Website: http://www.teleseal.co.uk
Directors: B. Mccomb (Prop)
Immediate Holding Company: SPEECH & PRONUNCIATION LIMITED
Registration no: 06938001 **Date established:** 2010
No.of Employees: 1 - 10 **Product Groups:** 30, 36

Date of Accounts	Feb 08	Feb 10	Feb 09
Working Capital	43	-62	42
Fixed Assets	28	16	21
Current Assets	195	145	262

Mackey Bowley International Ltd
Norfolk Road Industrial Estate, Gravesend, DA12 2PT
Tel: 01474-363521 **Fax:** 01474-334818
E-mail: g.c.fenton@mackeybowley.co.uk
Website: http://www.mackeybowley.co.uk
Bank(s): National Westminster Bank Plc
Directors: G. Fenton (MD)
Ultimate Holding Company: MACKEY BOWLEY HOLDINGS LIMITED
Immediate Holding Company: MACKEY BOWLEY INTERNATIONAL LIMITED
Registration no: 01689390 **VAT No.:** GB 202 9658 66
Date established: 1982 **Turnover:** £2m - £5m **No.of Employees:** 11 - 20
Product Groups: 39, 41, 42, 45, 46, 47, 67

Date of Accounts	Dec 11	Dec 10	Dec 09
Working Capital	305	322	380
Fixed Assets	29	34	43
Current Assets	369	466	531

Mark 1 Locks
6 Ascot Road, Gravesend, DA12 5AL
Tel: 01474-747660
E-mail: 24hr@mark1locks.com
Website: http://www.mark1locks.com
Directors: M. Taylor (Prop)
Date established: 2004 **No.of Employees:** 1 - 10 **Product Groups:** 52

Meopham Welding Supplies Ltd
Railway Sidings Station Approach, Meopham, Gravesend, DA13 0LT
Tel: 01474-812050 **Fax:** 01474-813714
Directors: M. Mewett (Fin), A. Eastwood (MD)
Immediate Holding Company: MEOPHAM WELDING SUPPLIES LIMITED
Registration no: 01220955 **Date established:** 1975
No.of Employees: 1 - 10 **Product Groups:** 46

Date of Accounts	Jul 11	Jul 10	Jul 09
Working Capital	24	34	46
Fixed Assets	2	3	3
Current Assets	119	110	116

Metal Aspects Ltd
Unit 2 Wharf Road, Gravesend, DA12 2RU
Tel: 01474-536766 **Fax:** 01634-845775
E-mail: enquiries@metalaspects.com
Website: http://www.metalaspects.com
Directors: S. Whorlow (MD)
Immediate Holding Company: METAL ASPECTS LIMITED
Registration no: 04648525 **VAT No.:** GB 565 4890 03
Date established: 2003 **Turnover:** Up to £250,000
No.of Employees: 1 - 10 **Product Groups:** 26, 35

Date of Accounts	Dec 11	Dec 10	Dec 09
Working Capital	131	127	107
Fixed Assets	17	17	15
Current Assets	183	205	155

Muranda Electrical Services
Unit F13 Northfleet Industrial Estate Lower Road, Northfleet, Gravesend, DA11 9SW
Tel: 01322-386488 **Fax:** 01322-386985
E-mail: johnpalmer@muranda.net
Website: http://www.muranda.net
Directors: J. Palmer (MD), R. Palmer (Fin)
Immediate Holding Company: MURANDA ELECTRICAL SERVICES LTD
Registration no: 01688264 **VAT No.:** GB 373 7392 25
Date established: 1982 **Turnover:** £1m - £2m **No.of Employees:** 1 - 10
Product Groups: 52

Date of Accounts	Mar 12	Mar 11	Mar 10
Working Capital	194	198	156
Fixed Assets	43	34	44
Current Assets	615	1m	1m

Opal Fabrication
Mark Lane, Gravesend, DA12 2QB
Tel: 01474-568100
No.of Employees: 1 - 10 **Product Groups:** 35, 48, 52

Oriana & Company
Unit 3 Westwood Farm Highcross Road, Southfleet, Gravesend, DA13 9PH
Tel: 01474-833175 **Fax:** 01474-834457
E-mail: enquiries@orianaandcompany.co.uk
Website: http://www.orianaandcompany.co.uk
Directors: M. Lidden (Prop)
Immediate Holding Company: SPEECH & PRONUNCIATION LIMITED
Date established: 2010 **No.of Employees:** 1 - 10 **Product Groups:** 30, 48, 66

Date of Accounts	Feb 08	Feb 10	Feb 09
Working Capital	43	-62	42
Fixed Assets	28	16	21
Current Assets	195	145	262

Professional Design Consultancy Ltd
Pinnocks Avenue, Gravesend, DA11 7QD
Tel: 01474-745772 **Fax:** 01474-745772
E-mail: sales@plantroom.com
Website: http://www.plantroom.com
Directors: M. Martin (MD), J. Martin (Fin)
Immediate Holding Company: PROFESSIONAL DESIGN CONSULTANCY LIMITED
Registration no: 03393097 **Date established:** 1997
Turnover: Up to £250,000 **No.of Employees:** 1 - 10 **Product Groups:** 07, 26, 29, 30, 32, 35, 36, 37, 38, 39, 40, 42, 44, 47, 49, 52, 54, 66, 68, 81, 83, 84, 85, 86, 87

Date of Accounts	Jun 11	Jun 10	Jun 08
Working Capital	-6	-4	-2
Fixed Assets	6	4	6
Current Assets	8	15	12

R A Y Engineering Services
The White House Clifton Marine Parade, Gravesend, DA11 0DY
Tel: 01474-333360 **Fax:** 01474-320442
Directors: R. Wales (Prop)
Date established: 1986 **No.of Employees:** 1 - 10 **Product Groups:** 35

R J Rudd & Co.
Westwood Farm Highcross Road, Southfleet, Gravesend, DA13 9PH
Tel: 01474-833899 **Fax:** 01474-833799
Directors: S. Raines (Prop)
Registration no: 04532792 **Date established:** 2002
No.of Employees: 1 - 10 **Product Groups:** 35, 39, 45

Richco International Co. Ltd
Richco House Springhead Enterprise Park, Springhead Rd, Gravesend, DA11 8HE
Tel: 01474-327527 **Fax:** 01474-327455
E-mail: sales@richco.co.uk
Website: http://www.richco-int.com
Directors: T. Barfoot (MD), N. Lancaster (Sales)
Managers: T. Bourgeay, A. Woods (Accounts), P. Brookman (Purch Mgr)
Ultimate Holding Company: FILTRONA plc
Registration no: 02924696 **Date established:** 1975
Turnover: £20m - £50m **No.of Employees:** 101 - 250
Product Groups: 29, 30, 35, 37, 39, 67

Date of Accounts	Dec 11	Dec 10	Dec 09
Sales Turnover	10m	10m	8m
Pre Tax Profit/Loss	-3m	364	-846
Working Capital	-160	3m	3m
Fixed Assets	1m	2m	2m
Current Assets	8m	4m	4m
Current Liabilities	4m	519	425

Rodenstock UK Ltd
Springhead Enterprise Park Springhead Road, Northfleet, Gravesend, DA11 8HJ
Tel: 01474-325555 **Fax:** 01474-325537
E-mail: sales@rodenstock.co.uk
Website: http://www.rodenstock.co.uk
Directors: D. Rathbauer (MD)
Managers: M. Schneider, J. Burtscher (Personnel)
Ultimate Holding Company: EYEWEAR HOLDING GMBH (GERMANY)
Immediate Holding Company: RODENSTOCK (U.K.) LIMITED
Registration no: 00266467 **Date established:** 1932
Turnover: £10m - £20m **No.of Employees:** 101 - 250 **Product Groups:** 38

Date of Accounts	Dec 11	Dec 10	Dec 09
Sales Turnover	11m	11m	13m
Pre Tax Profit/Loss	66	280	-751
Working Capital	1m	1m	2m
Fixed Assets	908	1m	784
Current Assets	4m	4m	4m
Current Liabilities	706	638	1m

S I R S Navigation Ltd
Unit 1-2 Bowes Estate Wrotham Road, Meopham, Gravesend, DA13 0QB
Tel: 01474-816320 **Fax:** 01474-816321
E-mail: sales@sirs.co.uk
Website: http://www.sirs.co.uk
Directors: B. Eady (MD)
Ultimate Holding Company: SIRS PRODUCTS LIMITED
Immediate Holding Company: S.I.R.S. NAVIGATION LIMITED
Registration no: 01333068 **VAT No.:** GB 205 2325 30
Date established: 1977 **Turnover:** £500,000 - £1m
No.of Employees: 21 - 50 **Product Groups:** 38

Date of Accounts	Mar 11	Mar 10	Mar 09
Working Capital	745	850	819
Fixed Assets	635	119	101
Current Assets	935	1m	989

E A & H Sandford Lifting Ltd
Lock Entrance Works Albion Parade, Gravesend, DA12 2RR
Tel: 01474-365361 **Fax:** 01474-569036
E-mail: andy.woolford@sandfordlifting.co.uk
Website: http://www.sandfordlifting.co.uk
Directors: A. Woolford (MD)
Immediate Holding Company: E.A. & H. SANDFORD (LIFTING) LIMITED
Registration no: 01221099 **Date established:** 1975
Turnover: Up to £250,000 **No.of Employees:** 1 - 10 **Product Groups:** 23, 35, 45, 48, 83, 84

Date of Accounts	Sep 11	Sep 10	Sep 09
Working Capital	-28	-15	-33
Fixed Assets	29	35	44
Current Assets	160	194	183

Seacon Terminals
Tower Warf North Fleet, Northfleet, Gravesend, DA11 9BD
Tel: 01474-320000 **Fax:** 01474-329946
E-mail: cargo@seacon.co.uk
Website: http://www.seacongroup.co.uk
Bank(s): Barclays
Directors: K. Jeeves (Fin), T. Clark (Co Sec)
Ultimate Holding Company: SEACON GROUP LIMITED
Immediate Holding Company: SEACON TERMINALS LIMITED
Registration no: 01547396 **VAT No.:** GB 249 2852 35
Date established: 1981 **Turnover:** £10m - £20m
No.of Employees: 51 - 100 **Product Groups:** 74, 76, 77

Date of Accounts	Sep 11	Sep 10	Sep 09
Sales Turnover	14m	13m	13m
Pre Tax Profit/Loss	-506	-408	-400
Working Capital	3m	5m	3m
Fixed Assets	5m	6m	6m
Current Assets	6m	7m	6m
Current Liabilities	675	362	419

Sealtech Ltd
6 College Road Northfleet, Gravesend, DA11 9AU
Tel: 01474-320358 **Fax:** 01474-535809
Directors: J. Tiller (MD)
Immediate Holding Company: SEALTECH LIMITED
Registration no: 03453301 **Date established:** 1997
Turnover: Up to £250,000 **No.of Employees:** 1 - 10 **Product Groups:** 38, 42

Date of Accounts	Oct 11	Oct 10	Oct 09
Working Capital	61	50	38
Fixed Assets	23	12	15
Current Assets	110	82	62

South East Nut & Bolt
Lock Entrance Works Albion Parade, Gravesend, DA12 2RR
Tel: 01474-327017 **Fax:** 01474-333519
Managers: D. Creamer (Mgr)
Immediate Holding Company: SOUTH EAST ARC WELDING CO. LTD
Registration no: 01396394 **Date established:** 2001
No.of Employees: 1 - 10 **Product Groups:** 35

Sprint Engineering & Lubricant
Unit G3 Imperial Business Estate West Mill, Gravesend, DA11 0DL
Tel: 01474-534251 **Fax:** 01474-534566
E-mail: info@sprint-uk.com
Website: http://www.sprint-uk.com
Bank(s): HSBC Bank plc
Directors: A. Devine (MD)
Immediate Holding Company: SPRINT ENGINEERING AND LUBRICANTS LTD
Registration no: 02343919 **VAT No.:** GB 522 7093 60
Date established: 1989 **Turnover:** £2m - £5m **No.of Employees:** 11 - 20
Product Groups: 29, 30, 31, 32, 34, 35, 36, 38, 39, 40, 41, 43, 45, 46, 48

Date of Accounts	Apr 11	Apr 10	Apr 09
Working Capital	864	651	642
Fixed Assets	667	674	695
Current Assets	2m	2m	2m

Spro Turn
Highcross Road Southfleet, Gravesend, DA13 9PH
Tel: 01474-834077 **Fax:** 01474-834077
Directors: I. Sproul (Prop)
Date established: 2002 **No.of Employees:** 1 - 10 **Product Groups:** 41

Supernature
Kenway 17 Rhododendron Avenue, Meopham, Gravesend, DA13 0TU
Tel: 01732-820020 **Fax:** 01732-824747
E-mail: info@supernature.tv
Website: http://www.supernature.co.uk
Directors: M. Lord (Dir)
No.of Employees: 1 - 10 **Product Groups:** 26, 28, 37, 89

Thames Hose & Couplings Ltd
Units 1-2 Canal Industrial Park Canal Road, Gravesend, DA12 2PA
Tel: 01474-356485 **Fax:** 01474-320392
E-mail: thc.sales@btconnect.com
Directors: A. Cloke (Dir)
Immediate Holding Company: THAMES HOSE AND COUPLINGS LIMITED
Registration no: 02241372 **VAT No.:** GB 509 9583 05
Date established: 1988 **Turnover:** £500,000 - £1m
No.of Employees: 1 - 10 **Product Groups:** 29, 30, 36, 40

Date of Accounts	Apr 11	Apr 10	Apr 09
Working Capital	-36	-11	-51
Fixed Assets	260	268	276
Current Assets	213	207	218

Tube Gear Ltd
Unit B1 Springhead Enterprise Park Springhead Road, Northfleet, Gravesend, DA11 8HB
Tel: 01474-321954 **Fax:** 01474-321988
E-mail: sales@tube-gear.com
Website: http://www.tube-gear.com
Bank(s): Barclays
Directors: S. Schofield (Co Sec), A. Vandell (I.T. Dir)
Ultimate Holding Company: STANDELL COMPONENTS (HOLDINGS) LIMITED
Immediate Holding Company: TUBE GEAR LIMITED
Registration no: 01651618 **Date established:** 1982 **Turnover:** £2m - £5m
No.of Employees: 21 - 50 **Product Groups:** 30, 35, 36, 66

Date of Accounts	Feb 12	Feb 11	Feb 10
Working Capital	683	541	532
Fixed Assets	89	97	102
Current Assets	2m	2m	2m
Current Liabilities	N/A	583	455

Venesta
Imperial Business Estate West Mill, Gravesend, DA11 0DL
Tel: 01474-353333 **Fax:** 01474-533558
E-mail: jon.sherry@rsbpltd.co.uk
Website: http://www.venesta.co.uk
Bank(s): Barclays, Tunstall
Directors: J. Sherry (MD)
Managers: A. Harrington (Sales Prom Mgr)
Ultimate Holding Company: IDEAL STANDARD HOLDINGS (BC) UK LTD
Immediate Holding Company: IDEAL STANDARD UK LTD
Registration no: 02972916 **VAT No.:** GB 566 3121 49
Turnover: £10m - £20m **No.of Employees:** 21 - 50 **Product Groups:** 26, 30, 35, 36

Greenhithe

Access Control Services
20-26 High Street, Greenhithe, DA9 9NN
Tel: 01322-370777 **Fax:** 01322-370076
E-mail: info@xplan.com
Website: http://www.xplan.com
Bank(s): The Royal Bank of Scotland
Directors: M. Phillips (Prop)
Ultimate Holding Company: PLAN SYSTEMS LIMITED
Immediate Holding Company: ACCESS CONTROL SERVICES LIMITED
Registration no: 02793313 **VAT No.:** GB 335 8733 36
Date established: 1993 **No.of Employees:** 11 - 20 **Product Groups:** 35, 36, 37, 40, 44, 81

Date of Accounts	Feb 08	Feb 11	Feb 10
Working Capital	631	882	636
Fixed Assets	410	233	275
Current Assets	881	1m	1m

Antalis Mcnaughton
Unit C3 Crossways Boulevard, Greenhithe, DA9 9BT
Tel: 08706-073117 **Fax:** 01322-226297
Website: http://www.antalis.co.uk
Bank(s): National Westminster Bank Plc
Directors: H. Cubbon (MD), C. Candler (Fin), D. Jones (Mkt Research), G. Green (Gen Sec), G. Harrison (Fin)
Immediate Holding Company: ANTALIS HOLDINGS LTD
Registration no: 03990272 **VAT No.:** GB 580 5803 35
Turnover: £20m - £50m **No.of Employees:** 51 - 100 **Product Groups:** 66

Herne Bay

4 SQR Ltd
92 Margate Road, Herne Bay, CT6 7BJ
Tel: 01227-749593 **Fax:** 0870-242 3007
E-mail: info@4sqr.co.uk
Website: http://www.4sqr.co.uk
Directors: N. Panter (Prop)
Immediate Holding Company: 4 SQR LTD
Registration no: 04512383 **Date established:** 2002
Turnover: Up to £250,000 **No.of Employees:** 1 - 10 **Product Groups:** 44, 80

Date of Accounts	Aug 11	Aug 10	Aug 09
Sales Turnover	15	N/A	19
Pre Tax Profit/Loss	8	N/A	3
Working Capital	-0	-6	-5
Fixed Assets	1	1	1
Current Assets	8	2	1
Current Liabilities	3	N/A	3

C V K
9c Sweechbridge Road, Herne Bay, CT6 6TE
Tel: 01227-740763 **Fax:** 01227-373248
E-mail: cvk@btconnect.com
Directors: C. Leah (Dir)
Date established: 2004 **No.of Employees:** 1 - 10 **Product Groups:** 26, 35

Flexicon Europe Ltd
89 Lower Herne Road, Herne Bay, CT6 7PH
Tel: 01227-374710 **Fax:** 01227-365821
E-mail: sales@flexicon.co.uk
Website: http://www.flexicon.co.uk
Directors: K. Bourton (MD), G. Bourton (Co Sec)
Managers: A. Biggs (Purch Mgr), A. Walton (Sales Prom Mgr)
Immediate Holding Company: FLEXICON (EUROPE) LIMITED
Registration no: 02530915 **Date established:** 1990
No.of Employees: 21 - 50 **Product Groups:** 27, 30, 33, 35, 38, 39, 41, 42, 43, 44, 45, 46, 66, 67, 84

Date of Accounts	Sep 11	Sep 10	Sep 09
Working Capital	273	589	430
Fixed Assets	176	170	347
Current Assets	1m	1m	1m

G R Welding & Fabrication
238 Canterbury Road, Herne Bay, CT6 5UA
Tel: 01227-368951
Directors: G. Reynolds (Prop)
Date established: 1994 **No.of Employees:** 1 - 10 **Product Groups:** 26, 35

Gillespie & Adams
The South Room William Street, Herne Bay, CT6 5NR
Tel: 01227-371200 **Fax:** 01227-371220
E-mail: james@ga-net.co.uk
Website: http://www.ga-net.co.uk
Directors: J. Hurley (Fin)
Immediate Holding Company: GILLESPIE AND ADAMS LIMITED
Registration no: 04598020 **Date established:** 2002
No.of Employees: 1 - 10 **Product Groups:** 44

Date of Accounts	Mar 09	Mar 08	Mar 07
Working Capital	1	-1	-2
Fixed Assets	N/A	N/A	1
Current Assets	12	24	19

Icom UK Ltd
The Boulevard Altira Business Park, Herne Bay, CT6 6GZ
Tel: 01227-741741 **Fax:** 01227-741742
E-mail: info@icomuk.co.uk
Website: http://www.icomuk.co.uk
Bank(s): National Westminster Bank Plc
Managers: S. Taylor-nobbs (Sales Prom Mgr), D. Turner (Chief Mgr), I. Lockyear (Mktg Serv Mgr), I. Lockyer (Mktg Serv Mgr), J. Kelk (Tech Serv Mgr), L. Harris, R. Owen (Chief Acct)
Immediate Holding Company: ICOM (UK) LIMITED
Registration no: 01461875 **VAT No.:** GB 332 9756 37
Date established: 1979 **Turnover:** £5m - £10m **No.of Employees:** 21 - 50
Product Groups: 37, 40, 44, 67, 79, 84

Date of Accounts	Mar 12	Mar 11	Mar 10
Sales Turnover	6m	7m	7m
Pre Tax Profit/Loss	105	10	-14
Working Capital	6m	6m	6m
Fixed Assets	204	248	248
Current Assets	6m	6m	6m
Current Liabilities	479	237	213

R K D O Sound & Light
Unit 8g Hillborough Business Park Sweechbridge Road, Herne Bay, CT6 6TE
Tel: 01227-638085
E-mail: info@rkdo.co.uk
Website: http://www.rkdo.co.uk
Directors: S. Woodman (Prop)
Immediate Holding Company: RKDO LTD
Registration no: 07782838 **Date established:** 2011
Turnover: Up to £250,000 **No.of Employees:** 1 - 10 **Product Groups:** 83

Wahl UK Ltd
Herne Bay West Industrial Estate Sea Street, Herne Bay, CT6 8JZ
Tel: 01227-740066 **Fax:** 01227-367550
E-mail: customer.services@wahl.co.uk
Website: http://www.wahl.co.uk
Bank(s): Barclays Bank Plc, Canterbury
Directors: D. Goodman (MD)
Managers: M. Smith (Comptroller), S. Haggan, S. Bonnie
Ultimate Holding Company: WAHL CLIPPER CORPORATION (U.S.A)
Immediate Holding Company: WAHL (UK) LIMITED
Registration no: 02184515 **Date established:** 1987
Turnover: £10m - £20m **No.of Employees:** 51 - 100 **Product Groups:** 40, 49

Date of Accounts	Dec 11	Dec 10	Dec 09
Sales Turnover	19m	17m	16m
Pre Tax Profit/Loss	3m	3m	2m
Working Capital	10m	8m	6m
Fixed Assets	2m	2m	2m
Current Assets	14m	11m	9m
Current Liabilities	2m	2m	2m

www.babyassistant.co.uk
Goldfinch Farm Ford Road, Herne Bay, CT6 7AD
Tel: 01227-749838
E-mail: info@babyassistant.co.uk
Website: http://www.babyassistant.co.uk
Directors: V. Wain (Prop)
Turnover: Up to £250,000 **No.of Employees:** 1 - 10 **Product Groups:** 29, 30, 39

Hythe

Buckleys Uvral Ltd
Range Road Industrial Estate Range Road, Hythe, CT21 6HG
Tel: 01303-260127 **Fax:** 01303-262115
E-mail: sales@buckleys.co.uk
Website: http://www.buckleys.co.uk
Bank(s): HSBC, Hythe
Directors: J. Hoveman (MD), P. Hoveman (MD)
Managers: B. Green (I.T. Exec), D. Watkins (Purch Mgr), A. Marsh (Mktg Serv Mgr)
Immediate Holding Company: Buckleys (Uvral) Ltd
Registration no: 00374468 **VAT No.:** GB 215 9963 36
Date established: 1942 **Turnover:** £500,000 - £1m
No.of Employees: 11 - 20 **Product Groups:** 36

Date of Accounts	Mar 10	Mar 09	Mar 08
Working Capital	664	647	661
Fixed Assets	111	71	58
Current Assets	843	808	809

Gopak Ltd
Range Road Industrial Estate Range Road, Hythe, CT21 6HG
Tel: 01303-265751 **Fax:** 01303-268282
E-mail: andrewfieldwick@gopak.co.uk
Website: http://www.gopak.co.uk
Bank(s): Barclays
Directors: F. Fieldwick (Co Sec), D. Ponting (Sales & Mktg), A. Fieldwick (MD)
Immediate Holding Company: GOPAK LIMITED
Registration no: 00536385 **VAT No.:** GB 201 2924 15
Date established: 1954 **Turnover:** £5m - £10m **No.of Employees:** 21 - 50
Product Groups: 26, 49

Date of Accounts	Dec 11	Dec 10	Dec 09
Sales Turnover	7m	8m	8m
Pre Tax Profit/Loss	515	551	936
Working Capital	2m	2m	3m
Fixed Assets	2m	1m	1m
Current Assets	2m	3m	4m
Current Liabilities	352	470	525

Holiday Extras Ltd
Ashford Road Newingreen, Hythe, CT21 4JF
Tel: 01303-815300 **Fax:** 08708-444310
E-mail: cathy.beare@holidayextras.com
Website: http://www.holidayextras.co.uk
Directors: C. Beare (Fin)
Managers: N. Peiris, D. Stratton, A. Clarke-cowell, D. Turner (Tech Serv Mgr)
Ultimate Holding Company: HOLIDAY EXTRAS HOLDINGS LIMITED
Immediate Holding Company: HOLIDAY EXTRAS LIMITED
Registration no: 01693250 **Date established:** 1983
Turnover: £125m - £250m **No.of Employees:** 251 - 500
Product Groups: 72

Date of Accounts	Mar 11	Mar 10	Mar 09
Sales Turnover	143m	124m	124m
Pre Tax Profit/Loss	7m	3m	5m
Working Capital	17m	14m	9m
Fixed Assets	15m	11m	11m
Current Assets	46m	35m	24m
Current Liabilities	2m	1m	2m

Laser Transport International Ltd
Lympne Industrial Estate Lympne, Hythe, CT21 4LR
Tel: 01303-260471 **Fax:** 01303-264851
E-mail: office@laserint.co.uk
Website: http://www.laserint.co.uk
Bank(s): Midland, Folkestone
Directors: R. Arnold (Fin)
Managers: K. Wiltshire (Tech Serv Mgr)
Ultimate Holding Company: LASER TRANSPORT INTERNATIONAL LIMITED
Immediate Holding Company: LASER TRANSPORT INTERNATIONAL LIMITED
Registration no: 01726499 **VAT No.:** GB 202 3293 13
Date established: 1983 **Turnover:** £10m - £20m
No.of Employees: 101 - 250 **Product Groups:** 76

Date of Accounts	Dec 11	Dec 10	Dec 09
Sales Turnover	18m	17m	16m
Pre Tax Profit/Loss	546	238	8
Working Capital	563	204	200
Fixed Assets	1m	1m	1m
Current Assets	3m	2m	2m
Current Liabilities	648	615	540

Legend Signs Ltd
1 Benham Business Park Ashford Road, Newingreen, Hythe, CT21 4JD
Tel: 01303-261278 **Fax:** 01303-261280
E-mail: info@legendsigns.co.uk
Website: http://www.legendsigns.co.uk
Directors: K. Elcock (Dir)
Ultimate Holding Company: KULLASIGNS LTD
Immediate Holding Company: LEGEND SIGNS LIMITED
Registration no: 02312865 **Date established:** 1988
Turnover: Up to £250,000 **No.of Employees:** 1 - 10 **Product Groups:** 23, 28, 52, 81, 84

Date of Accounts	Mar 11	Mar 10	Mar 09
Working Capital	7	23	21
Fixed Assets	7	5	7
Current Assets	22	50	50

M V Services London Ltd
33 Harman Avenue Lympne, Hythe, CT21 4LB
Tel: 01303-237002 **Fax:** 01303-237003
Website: http://www.mvservices.biz
Directors: M. Varndell (Prop)
No.of Employees: 1 - 10 **Product Groups:** 40

Nationwide Access
Unit P3 Lympne Industrial Estate Lympne, Hythe, CT21 4LR
Tel: 01303-261901 **Fax:** 01303-262182
E-mail: mail@nationwideaccess.co.uk
Website: http://www.nationwideaccess.co.uk
Directors: D. Roebuck (Mkt Research), K. Appleton (Ch), P. Whittall (MD)
Managers: J. Miller (Mgr), L. Roberts (I.T. Exec)
Ultimate Holding Company: Lavendon Group P.L.C
Immediate Holding Company: NUSTEEL HOLDINGS LIMITED
Registration no: 04405299 **Date established:** 1984
Turnover: £10m - £20m **No.of Employees:** 1 - 10 **Product Groups:** 45, 83

Nusteel Structures Ltd
Lympne Industrial Estate Lympne, Hythe, CT21 4LR
Tel: 01303-268112 **Fax:** 01303-266098
E-mail: general@nusteelstructures.com
Website: http://www.nusteelstructures.com
Bank(s): Nat West
Directors: I. Benson (Ch)
Ultimate Holding Company: NUSTEEL HOLDINGS LIMITED
Immediate Holding Company: NUSTEEL STRUCTURES LIMITED
Registration no: 01851782 **VAT No.:** 571 8445 21 **Date established:** 1984
Turnover: £5m - £10m **No.of Employees:** 51 - 100 **Product Groups:** 35

Date of Accounts	Oct 11	Oct 10	Oct 09
Sales Turnover	9m	12m	11m
Pre Tax Profit/Loss	307	1m	575
Working Capital	3m	3m	2m
Fixed Assets	335	395	774
Current Assets	5m	6m	5m
Current Liabilities	1m	2m	2m

Sico-Europe Ltd
The Link Park Lympne Industrial Estate, Lympne, Hythe, CT21 4LR
Tel: 01303-234000 **Fax:** 01303-234001
E-mail: sales@sico-europe.com
Website: http://www.sico-europe.com
Directors: S. Mason (MD), M. Bundock (Fin)
Managers: D. Rafferty (Purch Mgr), S. Sarrasan (Mktg Serv Mgr), N. Bizley (Sales Prom Mgr)
Ultimate Holding Company: SICO INCORPORATED (USA)
Immediate Holding Company: MERRICKS SICO LIMITED
Registration no: 01015507 **VAT No.:** GB 218 1201 11
Date established: 1971 **Turnover:** £5m - £10m
No.of Employees: 51 - 100 **Product Groups:** 25, 26, 65, 66

Date of Accounts	Nov 99	Nov 98	Nov 11
Working Capital	1	1	1
Current Assets	1	1	1

Smiths Medical
Boundary Road, Hythe, CT21 6JL
Tel: 01303-260551 **Fax:** 01303-266761
E-mail: matt.sassone@smiths-medical.com
Website: http://www.smithsmedical.com
Bank(s): Lloyds TSB Bank plc
Directors: R. Bennett (Co Sec), M. Sassone (Dir), S. Eggleson (Fin), D. Patterson (Pers)
Ultimate Holding Company: SMITHS GROUP PLC
Immediate Holding Company: SMITHS MEDICAL INTERNATIONAL LIMITED
Registration no: 00362847 **VAT No.:** GB 571 9943 00
Date established: 1940 **Turnover:** £125m - £250m
No.of Employees: 101 - 250 **Product Groups:** 24, 29, 30, 36, 37, 38, 66

Date of Accounts	Jul 12	Jul 11	Jul 10
Sales Turnover	235m	233m	273m
Pre Tax Profit/Loss	20m	16m	44m
Working Capital	56m	52m	72m
Fixed Assets	29m	33m	41m
Current Assets	101m	95m	123m
Current Liabilities	6m	6m	7m

Wire & Plastic Products Ltd
Pennypot Industrial Estate Pennypot, Hythe, CT21 6PE
Tel: 01303-266061 **Fax:** 01303-261080
E-mail: sales@delfinware.co.uk
Website: http://www.delfinware.co.uk
Bank(s): HSBC Bank plc
Directors: M. Simmonds (Grp MD)
Ultimate Holding Company: WPP PLC (JERSEY)
Immediate Holding Company: WIRE & PLASTIC PRODUCTS LIMITED
Registration no: 00899099 **VAT No.:** GB 285 6152 39
Date established: 1967 **Turnover:** £500,000 - £1m
No.of Employees: 21 - 50 **Product Groups:** 30, 36

Date of Accounts	Dec 11	Dec 10	Dec 09
Sales Turnover	853	976	1m
Pre Tax Profit/Loss	-287	-197	-201
Working Capital	2m	2m	2m
Fixed Assets	434	461	489
Current Assets	2m	2m	2m
Current Liabilities	75	78	333

Keston

Double Parking Systems
132 Heathfield Road, Keston, BR2 6BA
Tel: 01689-856636 **Fax:** 01689-860429
E-mail: info@doubleparking.co.uk
Website: http://www.doubleparking.co.uk
Directors: D. Guyver (MD)
Immediate Holding Company: MAPLEDENE PROPERTY HOLDINGS LIMITED
Registration no: 03223652 **Date established:** 1977
Turnover: £250,000 - £500,000 **No.of Employees:** 1 - 10
Product Groups: 39, 48, 67, 80

Date of Accounts	Sep 11	Sep 10	Sep 09
Sales Turnover	N/A	56	53
Pre Tax Profit/Loss	N/A	-47	15
Working Capital	215	26	73
Fixed Assets	8	8	8
Current Assets	222	28	76
Current Liabilities	N/A	2	3

Solvent Solutions Ltd
Holmshaw Farm Layhams Road, Keston, BR2 6AR
Tel: 01332-691579 **Fax:** 01332-239627
E-mail: danny@solventsolutions.co.uk
Website: http://www.solventsolutions.co.uk
Directors: D. Lockhart (Sales), D. Lockhart (Prop)
Immediate Holding Company: SOLVENT SOLUTIONS LIMITED
Registration no: 02875336 **Date established:** 1993
Turnover: £250,000 - £500,000 **No.of Employees:** 1 - 10
Product Groups: 32, 52

Date of Accounts	Dec 10	Dec 09	Dec 08
Working Capital	7	7	7
Fixed Assets	3	4	4
Current Assets	48	63	83

Longfield

Admiral Signs London
71 Penenden New Ash Green, Longfield, DA3 8LS
Tel: 01474-874412 **Fax:** 01474-874412
E-mail: info@admiralsignslondon.co.uk
Website: http://www.admiralsignslondon.co.uk
Directors: J. Harris (Fin), M. Harris (Dir)
Immediate Holding Company: ADMIRAL SIGNS LONDON LTD.
Registration no: 06380201 **Date established:** 2007
No.of Employees: 1 - 10 **Product Groups:** 30, 49, 67

Date of Accounts	Sep 11	Sep 10	Sep 09
Working Capital	68	64	36
Fixed Assets	10	13	18
Current Assets	193	189	103

Mainserve Engineers Ltd
Chapelwood Enterprises Ash Road, Hartley, Longfield, DA3 8HA
Tel: 01474-708708 **Fax:** 01474-708700
E-mail: office@mainserve.co.uk
Directors: T. Geering (Fin), P. Smith (MD)
Immediate Holding Company: MAINSERVE ENGINEERS LIMITED
Registration no: 04887092 **Date established:** 2003
No.of Employees: 1 - 10 **Product Groups:** 35, 39, 45

Date of Accounts	Oct 11	Oct 10	Oct 09
Working Capital	59	31	44
Fixed Assets	27	23	6
Current Assets	115	78	129

MotorSport Vision
Brands Hatch Circuits Ltd Brands Hatch Road, Fawkham, Longfield, DA3 8NG
Tel: 01474-872331 **Fax:** 01474-874766
E-mail: marketing@motorsportvision.co.uk
Website: http://www.motorsportvision.co.uk
Directors: L. Bean (Co Sec), J. Palmer (Grp Chief Exec)
Managers: T. Harris, D. Nisbet, K. Dickens (Personnel), N. Sheldon (Fin Mgr), G. Carrier
Ultimate Holding Company: INTERPUBLIC GROUP OF COMPANIES INC (USA)
Immediate Holding Company: CAB (NO. 1) LIMITED
Registration no: 03031120 **Date established:** 1995
Turnover: £20m - £50m **No.of Employees:** 101 - 250 **Product Groups:** 89

Date of Accounts	Dec 09	Dec 08	Dec 07
Pre Tax Profit/Loss	-15	46	199
Working Capital	-6m	-6m	-6m
Current Assets	1m	1m	1m
Current Liabilities	17	18	34

N S P Coatings
Orchard Farm Fawkham Road, Longfield, DA3 7QP
Tel: 01474-707060 **Fax:** 01474-700260
E-mail: info@nspcoatings.co.uk
Website: http://www.nspcoatings.co.uk
Directors: N. Pearson (Dir), N. Pearson (MD), R. O'Reilly (Co Sec)
Immediate Holding Company: N S P COATINGS LIMITED
Registration no: 04781770 **Date established:** 2003
No.of Employees: 1 - 10 **Product Groups:** 23, 32, 33, 34, 35, 37, 44, 46, 48, 67, 86

Date of Accounts	May 09	May 08	May 07
Working Capital	-25	-27	-8
Fixed Assets	39	44	28
Current Assets	33	42	39

R A Engineering
Speedgate Farm Mussenden Lane, Fawkham, Longfield, DA3 8NJ
Tel: 01474-872856 **Fax:** 01474-872856
Directors: R. Aikenhead (Prop)
Date established: 1983 **No.of Employees:** 1 - 10 **Product Groups:** 36

Maidstone

A S B Aspire LLP
Horizon House 1 Eclipse Park Sittingbourne Road, Maidstone, ME14 3EN
Tel: 01622-356000 **Fax:** 01622-356099
E-mail: alison.parker@asb-aspire.com
Website: http://www.asb-law.com
Managers: A. Parker
Immediate Holding Company: ASB ASPIRE LIMITED LIABILITY PARTNERSHIP
Registration no: OC327667 **Date established:** 2007
Turnover: £5m - £10m **No.of Employees:** 1 - 10 **Product Groups:** 80

Date of Accounts	Apr 11	Apr 10	Apr 09
Working Capital	1m	1m	939
Fixed Assets	24	38	194
Current Assets	2m	2m	2m
Current Liabilities	94	108	171

A W Associates LLP
37 Postmill Drive, Maidstone, ME15 6FY
Tel: 01622-765847 **Fax:** 01622-208245
E-mail: enquiries@awassociates.co.uk
Website: http://www.awassociates.co.uk
Directors: A. Wessen (Prop)
Immediate Holding Company: A W ASSOCIATES LLP
Registration no: OC342874 **Date established:** 2009
Turnover: Up to £250,000 **No.of Employees:** 1 - 10 **Product Groups:** 84

Date of Accounts	Jan 12	Jan 11
Sales Turnover	58	60
Pre Tax Profit/Loss	27	-11

Working Capital	25	2
Fixed Assets	23	26
Current Assets	25	2

Acorn P V C Windows Doors & Conservatories

Unit 3 Heronden Road, Maidstone, ME15 9YR
Tel: 01622-752288 **Fax:** 01622-751880
Directors: S. Crayford (Prop)
Date established: 1997 **No.of Employees:** 1 - 10 **Product Groups:** 46

Alltype Hose & Couplings Ltd

Unit 14-15 Palace Industrial Estate Bircholt Road, Maidstone, ME15 9XU
Tel: 01622-757512 **Fax:** 01622-757663
E-mail: sales@alltypehose.co.uk
Website: http://www.alltypehose.co.uk
Directors: A. Daburn (MD)
Immediate Holding Company: ALLTYPE HOSE & COUPLINGS LTD
Registration no: 03132712 **Date established:** 1995
Turnover: £250,000 - £500,000 **No.of Employees:** 1 - 10
Product Groups: 22, 23, 29, 30, 31, 32, 33, 35, 36, 37, 38, 39, 40, 41, 42, 43, 45, 46, 63, 66

Date of Accounts	Apr 11	Apr 10	Feb 09
Working Capital	16	15	8
Fixed Assets	6	8	9
Current Assets	83	83	87

Alpha Electronics Southern Ltd

Unit 16 Wren Industrial Estate Coldred Road, Maidstone, ME15 9YT
Tel: 01622-690187 **Fax:** 01622-678827
E-mail: sales@alpha-electronics.com
Website: http://www.alpha-electronics.com
Directors: G. Biggs (Sales)
Immediate Holding Company: Alpha Electronics Group Ltd
Registration no: 01846199 **Date established:** 2002
Turnover: £500,000 - £1m **No.of Employees:** 1 - 10 **Product Groups:** 67, 85

Date of Accounts	Dec 08	Dec 07	Dec 06
Working Capital	52	41	33
Fixed Assets	213	186	175
Current Assets	476	537	466
Current Liabilities	423	496	433
Total Share Capital	33	33	33

Animalscan Ltd

21 Hockers Lane Detling, Maidstone, ME14 3JL
Tel: 01622-737408 **Fax:** 01622-737408
E-mail: m.jowen@onetel.net
Directors: M. Owen (Dir)
Immediate Holding Company: ANIMALSCAN LIMITED
Registration no: 03743397 **Date established:** 1999
Turnover: Up to £250,000 **No.of Employees:** 1 - 10 **Product Groups:** 31, 38

Date of Accounts	Mar 12	Mar 11	Mar 10
Sales Turnover	1	2	2
Pre Tax Profit/Loss	N/A	-3	-4
Working Capital	2	1	4
Current Assets	2	1	4
Current Liabilities	1	N/A	1

Answers & Solutions Kent

2 Freeman Way, Maidstone, ME15 8AN
Tel: 01622-201403 **Fax:** 01622-674529
E-mail: info@ask-kent.co.uk
Website: http://www.ask-kent.co.uk
Directors: T. Romain (Prop)
Immediate Holding Company: ASK KENT LIMITED
Registration no: OC321247 **Date established:** 2008
Turnover: Up to £250,000 **No.of Employees:** 1 - 10 **Product Groups:** 86

Date of Accounts	Mar 11	Mar 10
Working Capital	-1	1
Current Assets	14	6

Barminggraphics.Com

48 Heath Road, Maidstone, ME16 9JU
Tel: 01622-721933 **Fax:** 01622-721933
E-mail: info@barminggraphics.com
Website: http://www.barminggraphics.com
Directors: M. Codner (Prop)
No.of Employees: 1 - 10 **Product Groups:** 28, 44

Bedfont Scientific Ltd

Station Yard Station Road, Harrietsham, Maidstone, ME17 1JA
Tel: 01622-851122 **Fax:** 01634-673721
E-mail: ask@bedfont.com
Website: http://www.bedfont.com
Bank(s): National Westminster
Directors: B. Brummell (Fin)
Immediate Holding Company: BEDFONT SCIENTIFIC LIMITED
Registration no: 01289798 **VAT No.:** GB 224 6668 52
Date established: 1976 **Turnover:** £2m - £5m **No.of Employees:** 21 - 50
Product Groups: 38

Date of Accounts	Sep 11	Sep 10	Sep 09
Working Capital	1m	1m	944
Fixed Assets	179	139	111
Current Assets	2m	1m	1m

Biffa Waste Services Ltd Maidstone Customer Centre

The Caves Ashford Road, Hollingbourne, Maidstone, ME17 1XE
Tel: 01622-880432 **Fax:** 01622-735598
Website: http://www.biffa.co.uk
Managers: N. Fluet (Mgr)
Immediate Holding Company: BIFFA WASTE SERVICES LIMITED
Registration no: 00946107 **Date established:** 1969
No.of Employees: 1 - 10 **Product Groups:** 54, 72, 83

Date of Accounts	Mar 08	Mar 09	Apr 10
Sales Turnover	555m	574m	492m
Pre Tax Profit/Loss	23m	50m	30m
Working Capital	229m	271m	293m
Fixed Assets	371m	360m	378m
Current Assets	409m	534m	609m
Current Liabilities	50m	100m	115m

Boyer Bransden Electronics Ltd

Frinsbury House Cox Street, Detling, Maidstone, ME14 3HE
Tel: 01622-730939 **Fax:** 01622-730930
E-mail: sales@boyerbransden.com
Website: http://www.boyerbransden.com
Directors: E. Bransden (MD)
Immediate Holding Company: BOYER-BRANSDEN ELECTRONICS LIMITED
Registration no: 01087017 **VAT No.:** GB 206 2403 13
Date established: 1972 **Turnover:** £500,000 - £1m
No.of Employees: 1 - 10 **Product Groups:** 39

Date of Accounts	Mar 11	Mar 10	Mar 09
Working Capital	-61	-41	-53
Fixed Assets	191	197	209
Current Assets	112	115	104

Brachers Solicitors

57-59 London Road, Maidstone, ME16 8JH
Tel: 01622-690691 **Fax:** 020-7405 4352
E-mail: info@brachers.co.uk
Website: http://www.brachers.co.uk
Bank(s): National Westminster Bank Plc
Directors: J. Sheath (Snr Part)
Managers: I. Robertson (Tech Serv Mgr), P. Cunningham, J. Page (Personnel)
Immediate Holding Company: BRACHERS LLP
Registration no: OC336022 **Date established:** 2008
Turnover: £10m - £20m **No.of Employees:** 101 - 250
Product Groups: 80, 81, 82

Date of Accounts	Apr 11	Apr 10
Sales Turnover	10m	11m
Pre Tax Profit/Loss	2m	2m
Working Capital	2m	2m
Fixed Assets	3m	3m
Current Assets	4m	4m
Current Liabilities	1m	1m

Castacrete Concrete Products

Stone House Dean Street, East Farleigh, Maidstone, ME15 0PW
Tel: 01622-741333 **Fax:** 01622-741088
E-mail: simonking@castacrete.co.uk
Website: http://www.castacrete.co.uk
Managers: S. King (Fin Mgr)
Immediate Holding Company: CASTACRETE LIMITED
Registration no: 00875221 **Date established:** 1966 **Turnover:** £5m - £10m
No.of Employees: 1 - 10 **Product Groups:** 33

Date of Accounts	Dec 11	Dec 10	Dec 09
Sales Turnover	11m	10m	11m
Pre Tax Profit/Loss	841	757	741
Working Capital	2m	1m	1m
Fixed Assets	14m	14m	13m
Current Assets	3m	3m	3m
Current Liabilities	1m	433	1m

Chemicals & Feeds

Springfield House Sandling Road, Maidstone, ME14 2LP
Tel: 01622-764872 **Fax:** 01622-688481
E-mail: trading@chemifeed.com
Website: http://www.chemifeed.com
Directors: E. Butcher (MD), J. Belfrage (Dir)
Managers: M. Donnelly (Sales Admin)
Ultimate Holding Company: EDEN HOLDINGS LTD (GUERNSEY)
Immediate Holding Company: CHEMICALS AND FEEDS LIMITED
Registration no: 00520122 **VAT No.:** GB 205 6898 43
Date established: 1953 **Turnover:** £10m - £20m **No.of Employees:** 1 - 10
Product Groups: 17, 20, 31

Date of Accounts	May 12	May 11	May 10
Sales Turnover	13m	10m	12m
Pre Tax Profit/Loss	314	252	325
Working Capital	1m	912	757
Fixed Assets	42	49	31
Current Assets	6m	4m	3m
Current Liabilities	3m	2m	2m

Dempson Crooke

Hermitage Mills Hermitage Lane, Maidstone, ME16 9NP
Tel: 01622-727027 **Fax:** 01622-720768
E-mail: jonk@dempson.co.uk
Website: http://www.dempson.co.uk
Bank(s): Lloyds
Directors: D. Wright (Fab), J. Katzauer (MD)
Managers: N. Perkins (Comptroller)
Ultimate Holding Company: MEESDEN PROPERTIES LTD (ISLE OF MAN)
Immediate Holding Company: DEMPSON CROOKE LIMITED
Registration no: 00712226 **VAT No.:** 202 9113 11 **Date established:** 1962
Turnover: £10m - £20m **No.of Employees:** 101 - 250 **Product Groups:** 27

Date of Accounts	Jun 11	Jun 10	Jun 09
Sales Turnover	19m	18m	19m
Pre Tax Profit/Loss	136	57	-155
Working Capital	717	630	221
Fixed Assets	6m	6m	6m
Current Assets	9m	8m	7m
Current Liabilities	5m	1m	1m

Dutton Forshaw Ltd

Bircholt Road, Maidstone, ME15 9YN
Tel: 01622-699350 **Fax:** 01622-699204
E-mail: maidstone.skoda@duttonforshaw.com
Website: http://www.bristolaudi.co.uk
Bank(s): National Westminster Bank Plc
Directors: A. Leitch (MD), A. Leith (Dir), R. Dickenson (I.T. Dir), S. Bodium (Pers)
Ultimate Holding Company: Lookers plc
Immediate Holding Company: DUTTON-FORSHAW LIMITED
Registration no: 00199033 **Date established:** 1924
Turnover: £10m - £20m **No.of Employees:** 101 - 250
Product Groups: 38, 40, 54, 67, 68

Date of Accounts	Dec 07
Sales Turnover	395670
Pre Tax Profit/Loss	490
Working Capital	170
Fixed Assets	48070
Current Assets	111740
Current Liabilities	111570
Total Share Capital	14980
ROCE% (Return on Capital Employed)	1.0

Eriks UK (Maidstone Service Centre)

Unit 1 Heronden Road, Maidstone, ME15 9YR
Tel: 01622-757218 **Fax:** 01622-681900
E-mail: maidstone@eriks.co.uk
Website: http://www.eriks.com
Managers: N. Ashworth (Mgr)
Immediate Holding Company: HI-TEC SPRAY LIMITED
Date established: 1987 **Turnover:** £1m - £2m **No.of Employees:** 1 - 10
Product Groups: 66

Fike UK

4th Floor County House 35 Earl Street, Maidstone, ME14 1PF
Tel: 01622-677081 **Fax:** 01622-685737
E-mail: keithavila@fike.co.uk
Website: http://www.fike.co.uk
Managers: K. Avila (Chief Mgr)
Immediate Holding Company: FIKE EUROPE B.V.B.A.
Registration no: FC013112 **Date established:** 1984
Turnover: £250m - £500m **No.of Employees:** 1 - 10 **Product Groups:** 33, 35, 36, 37, 40, 45, 67, 84

Fileder Filter Systems Ltd

St Leonards Road Allington, Maidstone, ME16 0LS
Tel: 01622-691886 **Fax:** 01622-621932
E-mail: info@fileder.co.uk
Website: http://www.fileder.co.uk
Bank(s): Co-op
Directors: S. Warren (Fin)
Managers: C. Spashett, L. Perry (Mktg Serv Mgr)
Ultimate Holding Company: FILEDER HOLDINGS LIMITED
Immediate Holding Company: FILEDER FILTER SYSTEMS LIMITED
Registration no: 01595206 **VAT No.:** GB 304 4507 92
Date established: 1981 **Turnover:** £5m - £10m **No.of Employees:** 21 - 50
Product Groups: 33, 42

Date of Accounts	Dec 11	Dec 10	Dec 09
Sales Turnover	8m	7m	6m
Pre Tax Profit/Loss	430	625	477
Working Capital	1m	1m	1m
Fixed Assets	309	275	368
Current Assets	3m	3m	3m
Current Liabilities	242	422	252

FOCUS International

6 Tonbridge Road, Maidstone, ME16 8RP
Tel: 01622-351000 **Fax:** 01622-351001
E-mail: joanne.northen@focusfo.com
Website: http://www.focusfo.com
Directors: D. Tarr (Ch), C. Tarr (MD), A. Tarr (Sales), E. Dawson-Tarr (MD)
Managers: K. Thomas (Prod Mgr), J. Northen (Mktg Serv Mgr)
Immediate Holding Company: INTELLIGENT INTERIORS LIMITED
Registration no: 06420704 **VAT No.:** GB 226 3589 51
Date established: 2001 **Turnover:** £1m - £2m **No.of Employees:** 1 - 10
Product Groups: 37, 67

Date of Accounts	Nov 09	Nov 08
Working Capital	59	66
Fixed Assets	34	40
Current Assets	113	181

FOCUS Marketing

18 Wharf Road Bridge Industrial Estate, Tovil, Maidstone, ME15 6RD
Tel: 01622-755517
E-mail: sales@bandit.co.uk
Website: http://www.bandit.co.uk
Directors: M. Burt (MD), J. Ashton (Fin)
Immediate Holding Company: FOCUS MARKETING LIMITED
Registration no: 07914355 **Date established:** 2012
No.of Employees: 1 - 10 **Product Groups:** 29, 64, 66

Four Blank Walls Four Blank Walls

The Old Ice Cream Factory 112a Week Street, Maidstone, ME14 1RH
Tel: 01622-751596 **Fax:** 01634-319 000
E-mail: info@fourblankwalls.co.uk
Website: http://www.fourblankwalls.co.uk
Directors: J. Howard (Prop)
Turnover: £250,000 - £500,000 **No.of Employees:** 1 - 10
Product Groups: 31, 49, 66, 67

G M O Globalsign Ltd

Springfield House Sandling Road, Maidstone, ME14 2LP
Tel: 01622-766766 **Fax:** 01622-662255
E-mail: sales@globalsign.co.uk
Website: http://www.globalsign.co.uk
Directors: H. Kruims (Sales), P. Tourret (MD), S. Waite (Mkt Research)
Managers: C. Vidler (Fin Mgr), S. Rugg
Immediate Holding Company: GMO GLOBALSIGN LIMITED
Registration no: 04705639 **Date established:** 2003 **Turnover:** £2m - £5m
No.of Employees: 21 - 50 **Product Groups:** 44

Date of Accounts	Dec 11	Dec 10	Dec 09
Sales Turnover	5m	4m	3m
Pre Tax Profit/Loss	268	109	-114
Working Capital	390	119	19
Fixed Assets	956	959	951
Current Assets	3m	1m	726
Current Liabilities	1m	594	426

Glosrose Engineering Ltd

Old Mill Farm Old Mill Road, Hollingbourne, Maidstone, ME17 1XD
Tel: 01622-880669 **Fax:** 01622-880295
E-mail: info@glosrose.co.uk
Website: http://www.glosrose.co.uk
Directors: J. Butcher (MD)
Ultimate Holding Company: GLOSROSE HOLDINGS LIMITED
Immediate Holding Company: GLOSROSE ENGINEERING LIMITED
Registration no: 01252000 **Date established:** 1976 **Turnover:** £5m - £10m
No.of Employees: 21 - 50 **Product Groups:** 35, 39, 45

Date of Accounts	Dec 11	Dec 10	Dec 09
Sales Turnover	N/A	5m	7m
Pre Tax Profit/Loss	N/A	101	68
Working Capital	-413	-98	-565
Fixed Assets	3m	3m	3m
Current Assets	1m	1m	1m
Current Liabilities	N/A	284	163

P & D J Goacher

8 Tovil Green Business Park Burial Ground Lane, Tovil, Maidstone, ME15 6TA
Tel: 01622-682112
Website: http://www.goachers.com

see next page

***P & D J Goacher** - Cont'd*
Directors: P. Goacher (Prop)
Registration no: 06414717 **Date established:** 2007
Turnover: £250,000 - £500,000 **No.of Employees:** 1 - 10
Product Groups: 21

Gripworks
Units 11-13 Spectrum West 20-20 Maidstone Business Estate, Maidstone, ME16 0L
Tel: 01622-693200 **Fax:** 01622-693201
E-mail: sales@sinclair-rush.co.uk
Website: http://www.gripworks.co.uk
Managers: P. Boulton (Sales & Mktg Mg)
Registration no: 05102332 **No.of Employees:** 21 - 50
Product Groups: 29, 30, 39, 49

Haynes Of Maidstone
Ashford Road, Maidstone, ME14 5DQ
Tel: 01622-756781 **Fax:** 01622-678166
E-mail: t.pickard@haynesgrp.co.uk
Website: http://www.haynesofmaidstone.co.uk
Directors: T. Pickard (Fin)
Managers: A. Woods (Chief Mgr)
Ultimate Holding Company: HAYNES BROTHERS,LIMITED
Immediate Holding Company: HAYNES BROTHERS,LIMITED
Registration no: 00048511 **VAT No.:** GB 203 0849 01
Date established: 1996 **Turnover:** £50m - £75m
No.of Employees: 101 - 250 **Product Groups:** 39

Date of Accounts	Dec 11	Dec 10	Dec 09
Sales Turnover	69m	72m	69m
Pre Tax Profit/Loss	-397	-263	54
Working Capital	3m	-2m	4m
Fixed Assets	14m	14m	15m
Current Assets	18m	19m	17m
Current Liabilities	3m	3m	2m

Hi-Tec Spray Ltd
Unit 14 Heronden Road, Maidstone, ME15 9YR
Tel: 01622-356590 **Fax:** 01622-663555
E-mail: garry@hitecspray.co.uk
Website: http://www.hitecspray.co.uk
Directors: G. Dowling (MD)
Immediate Holding Company: HI-TEC SPRAY LIMITED
Registration no: 02088206 **VAT No.:** GB 460 5431 68
Date established: 1987 **Turnover:** £2m - £5m **No.of Employees:** 1 - 10
Product Groups: 40, 46

Date of Accounts	Mar 12	Mar 11	Mar 10
Sales Turnover	N/A	N/A	3m
Pre Tax Profit/Loss	N/A	N/A	-120
Working Capital	123	328	20
Fixed Assets	297	311	322
Current Assets	1m	2m	1m
Current Liabilities	N/A	N/A	356

Hunton Engineering Design Ltd
West Street Hunton, Maidstone, ME15 0RR
Tel: 01622-820643 **Fax:** 01622-820893
E-mail: info@huntonengineering.co.uk
Website: http://www.huntonengineering.co.uk
Directors: S. Trow (MD)
Immediate Holding Company: HUNTON ENGINEERING DESIGN LIMITED
Registration no: 03650936 **Date established:** 1998
No.of Employees: 11 - 20 **Product Groups:** 35, 36, 37, 39, 42, 45

Date of Accounts	Aug 11	Aug 10	Aug 09
Working Capital	155	188	134
Fixed Assets	117	102	30
Current Assets	570	722	606

Invicta Valves Ltd
Unit 10-11 Parkwood Industrial Estate Bircholt Road, Maidstone, ME15 9XT
Tel: 01622-754613 **Fax:** 01622-750436
E-mail: sales@invictavalves.co.uk
Website: http://www.invictavalves.co.uk
Bank(s): National Westminster Bank Plc
Directors: J. Sutcliffe (Sales), J. Anderton (Fin)
Immediate Holding Company: INVICTA VALVES LIMITED
Registration no: 01678942 **VAT No.:** GB 373 6668 15
Date established: 1982 **Turnover:** £2m - £5m **No.of Employees:** 11 - 20
Product Groups: 30, 36, 40

Date of Accounts	Oct 09	Oct 08	Sep 11
Working Capital	205	203	193
Fixed Assets	60	71	87
Current Assets	1m	2m	2m

Jewelultra Ltd
Diamondbrite House Ewell Lane, West Farleigh, Maidstone, ME15 0NG
Tel: 01622-815679 **Fax:** 01622-815321
E-mail: johnboseley@jewelultra.com
Website: http://www.jewelultra.com
Directors: J. Boseley (MD)
Ultimate Holding Company: JEWELULTRA HOLDINGS LIMITED
Immediate Holding Company: JEWELULTRA LIMITED
Registration no: 02732994 **VAT No.:** GB 583 9431 08
Date established: 1992 **Turnover:** £500,000 - £1m
No.of Employees: 1 - 10 **Product Groups:** 32, 68

Date of Accounts	Mar 11	Mar 10	Mar 09
Working Capital	842	1m	957
Fixed Assets	1m	703	658
Current Assets	2m	2m	2m

K E F
Eccleston Road Tovil, Maidstone, ME15 6QP
Tel: 01622-672261 **Fax:** 01622-750653
E-mail: info@kef.com
Website: http://www.kef.com
Bank(s): HSBC Bank plc
Directors: K. Liu (Fin), M. Hill (Fin), S. Halsall (Asst MD)
Managers: M. Bryant, D. Gathorne, P. Barnes (Personnel), M. Johnson, J. Sievenpiper, G. Shirley (I.T. Exec)
Ultimate Holding Company: GOLD PEAK INDUSTRIES {HOLDINGS} LIMITED {HONG KONG}
Immediate Holding Company: KEF AUDIO (UK) LIMITED
Registration no: 02711007 **Date established:** 1992
Turnover: £10m - £20m **No.of Employees:** 21 - 50 **Product Groups:** 37

K P Martin Fabrications
The Alders Seven Mile Lane, Mereworth, Maidstone, ME18 5JG
Tel: 01622-813901 **Fax:** 01622-813929
E-mail: info@kpmfab.co.uk
Website: http://www.kpmfab.co.uk
Managers: D. King (Mgr)
Date established: 1987 **No.of Employees:** 1 - 10 **Product Groups:** 35

Kemet International Ltd
Parkwood Trading Estate, Maidstone, ME15 9NJ
Tel: 01622-755287 **Fax:** 01622-670915
E-mail: sales@kemet.co.uk
Website: http://www.kemet.co.uk
Bank(s): Lloyds TSB Bank plc
Directors: G. Lloyd (Sales & Mktg), J. Park (MD)
Managers: A. Lemon (Accounts)
Registration no: 00344017 **VAT No.:** GB 202 9348 81
Date established: 1938 **Turnover:** £250,000 - £500,000
No.of Employees: 21 - 50 **Product Groups:** 33, 37, 46, 47, 49

Date of Accounts	Sep 07	Sep 06
Pre Tax Profit/Loss	450	270
Working Capital	1690	1580
Fixed Assets	2070	2080
Current Assets	2810	2560
Current Liabilities	1120	980
Total Share Capital	500	500
ROCE% (Return on Capital Employed)	12.0	7.4

The Kent Invicta Chamber Of Commerce
The Gatehouse The Old Palace Gardens Mill Street, Maidstone, ME15 6YE
Tel: 01622-695544 **Fax:** 01622-682513
E-mail: info@kentinvictachamber.co.uk
Website: http://www.kentinvictachamber.co.uk
Bank(s): National Westminster Bank Plc
Directors: J. James (Grp Chief Exec), P. Shillinglaw (Fin)
Registration no: 02851748 **VAT No.:** GB 304 3202 22
Date established: 1995 **Turnover:** £250,000 - £500,000
No.of Employees: 11 - 20 **Product Groups:** 87

Kersh Media Solutions Ltd
Business Solutions Barham Court, Teston, Maidstone, ME18 5BZ
Tel: 08453-707010
E-mail: admin@kershmedia.co.uk
Website: http://www.kershmedia.co.uk
Managers: G. Majin
Immediate Holding Company: KERSH MEDIA SOLUTIONS LIMITED
Registration no: 05594371 **Date established:** 2005
No.of Employees: 1 - 10 **Product Groups:** 37, 44, 89

Date of Accounts	Mar 11	Mar 10	Mar 09
Working Capital	11	4	43
Fixed Assets	3	8	14
Current Assets	33	24	73

Knight Optical UK Ltd
Unit 4 Roebuck Business Park Ashford Road, Harrietsham, Maidstone, ME17 1AB
Tel: 01622-859444 **Fax:** 01622-859555
E-mail: info@knightoptical.co.uk
Website: http://www.knightoptical.com
Directors: C. Overton (MD)
Immediate Holding Company: KNIGHT OPTICAL (UK) LIMITED
Registration no: 03755966 **Date established:** 1999
Turnover: £250,000 - £500,000 **No.of Employees:** 21 - 50
Product Groups: 33, 37, 38, 45, 65, 84, 85

Date of Accounts	Jul 11	Jul 10	Jul 09
Working Capital	289	194	-89
Fixed Assets	574	185	381
Current Assets	576	426	246

Kookaburra Reader Ltd
Unit 25 The Alders Seven Mile Lane, Mereworth, Maidstone, ME18 5JG
Tel: 01622-812230 **Fax:** 01622-814224
E-mail: sales@alfredreader.co.uk
Bank(s): National Westminster Bank Plc
Directors: B. Elliot (Fin)
Managers: A. Baker (Tech Serv Mgr), A. Baker (I.T. Exec), S. Waterson (Sales Prom Mgr), M. Wellbelove (Mgr), S. Waterson (Sales Prom Mgr)
Ultimate Holding Company: A G THOMPSON PTY LIMITED (AUSTRALIA)
Immediate Holding Company: KOOKABURRA READER LIMITED
Registration no: 02224095 **VAT No.:** GB 202 9823 77
Date established: 1988 **Turnover:** £2m - £5m **No.of Employees:** 21 - 50
Product Groups: 49

Date of Accounts	Jun 11	Jun 10	Jun 09
Sales Turnover	8m	8m	7m
Pre Tax Profit/Loss	962	788	221
Working Capital	2m	1m	571
Fixed Assets	2m	2m	2m
Current Assets	4m	3m	2m
Current Liabilities	524	647	352

Lenham Storage Ltd
Ham Lane Lenham, Maidstone, ME17 2LH
Tel: 01622-858441 **Fax:** 01622-850469
E-mail: info@lenham.com
Website: http://www.lenham.com
Bank(s): Barclays
Directors: A. Burgess (Fin), C. Tolhurst (I.T. Dir)
Immediate Holding Company: LENHAM STORAGE COMPANY LIMITED
Registration no: 00463800 **VAT No.:** GB 203 4630 10
Date established: 1949 **Turnover:** £20m - £50m
No.of Employees: 101 - 250 **Product Groups:** 48, 72, 76, 77

Date of Accounts	Aug 11	Aug 10	Aug 09
Sales Turnover	22m	19m	19m
Pre Tax Profit/Loss	553	519	240
Working Capital	-2m	-2m	-1m
Fixed Assets	17m	16m	16m
Current Assets	6m	5m	4m
Current Liabilities	4m	3m	2m

Lupofresh Ltd
Lupofresh Benover Road Yalding, Maidstone, ME18 6ET
Tel: 01622-815720 **Fax:** 01622-815730
E-mail: admin@lupofreshltd.com
Website: http://www.lupofreshltd.com
Bank(s): Barclays
Directors: D. Cowley (Fin), I. Ibbotson (MD), J. Smith (Dir)
Immediate Holding Company: LUPOFRESH LIMITED
Registration no: 00386719 **VAT No.:** GB 216 1872 73
Date established: 1944 **Turnover:** £10m - £20m
No.of Employees: 21 - 50 **Product Groups:** 02

Date of Accounts	Jun 11	Jun 10	Jun 09
Sales Turnover	10m	9m	11m
Pre Tax Profit/Loss	-2m	-412	96
Working Capital	-1m	1m	1m
Fixed Assets	3	3	2
Current Assets	7m	5m	6m
Current Liabilities	2m	2m	1m

M Steels Engineering
Laddingford Farm Dorman Lane, Laddingford, Maidstone, ME18 6BX
Tel: 01622-873100
Directors: M. O'donnell (MD)
Immediate Holding Company: CLOVAL LIMITED
Date established: 1983 **No.of Employees:** 1 - 10 **Product Groups:** 35

Date of Accounts	Mar 12	Mar 11	Mar 10
Sales Turnover	2	1	1
Pre Tax Profit/Loss	1	1	N/A
Working Capital	5	4	3
Current Assets	5	4	3

Maplin Electronics Ltd
79-85 Week Street, Maidstone, ME14 1QX
Tel: 08432-277324 **Fax:** 01622-690791
E-mail: customercare@maplin.co.uk
Website: http://www.maplin.co.uk
Managers: S. Gull (Mgr)
Ultimate Holding Company: MONTAGU PRIVATE EQUITY LLP
Immediate Holding Company: MAPLIN ELECTRONICS LIMITED
Registration no: 01264385 **Date established:** 1976
Turnover: £125m - £250m **No.of Employees:** 1 - 10 **Product Groups:** 37, 61

Date of Accounts	Dec 11	Dec 08	Dec 09
Sales Turnover	205m	204m	204m
Pre Tax Profit/Loss	25m	32m	35m
Working Capital	118m	49m	75m
Fixed Assets	27m	28m	28m
Current Assets	207m	108m	142m
Current Liabilities	78m	51m	59m

Mbe Fasteners
Unit D1 Bearsted Green Business Centre The Green, Bearsted, Maidstone, ME14 4DF
Tel: 01622-736868 **Fax:** 01622-730111
E-mail: info@mbefasteners.co.uk
Website: http://www.mbefasteners.co.uk
Directors: N. Parsons (Prop)
No.of Employees: 1 - 10 **Product Groups:** 35

Medway Insulations Ltd
7 Viewpoint Boxley Road, Penenden Heath, Maidstone, ME14 2DZ
Tel: 01622-764158 **Fax:** 01622-692205
E-mail: charles@medwayinsulations.co.uk
Website: http://www.medwayinsulations.com
Directors: C. Graves (MD)
Immediate Holding Company: MEDWAY INSULATIONS LIMITED
Registration no: 00549740 **Date established:** 1955
Turnover: £500,000 - £1m **No.of Employees:** 11 - 20
Product Groups: 33, 54, 80

Date of Accounts	May 11	May 10	May 09
Working Capital	679	521	525
Fixed Assets	70	117	135
Current Assets	1m	720	729

The Mid Kent Steel Centre
Station Road Harrietsham, Maidstone, ME17 1JA
Tel: 01622-859955 **Fax:** 01622-858333
Directors: M. Jones (Dir), C. Spence (Fin)
Immediate Holding Company: MID KENT STEEL FABRICATION LIMITED
Registration no: 06618300 **VAT No.:** GB 619 3495 17
Date established: 2008 **Turnover:** £2m - £5m **No.of Employees:** 1 - 10
Product Groups: 48

Date of Accounts	Jun 11	Jun 10	Jun 09
Working Capital	-68	-62	-8
Fixed Assets	12	16	21
Current Assets	62	117	41

Modus Vivendi
47 Beaconsfield Road, Maidstone, ME15 6RZ
Tel: 01622-201983 **Fax:** 01622-201983
E-mail: luke@mv-installations.com
Website: http://www.mv-installations.com
Directors: L. Emmott (MD), L. Emmott (Prop)
Turnover: Up to £250,000 **No.of Employees:** 1 - 10 **Product Groups:** 84

Newlands Engineering Ltd
Unit 13 Wren Industrial Estate Coldred Road, Maidstone, ME15 9XN
Tel: 01622-671229 **Fax:** 01622-671220
E-mail: sales@newlandsengineering.com
Website: http://www.newlands-engineering.co.uk
Directors: M. Larkin (Fin), R. Stevens (MD)
Immediate Holding Company: NEWLANDS ENGINEERING LIMITED
Registration no: 06225175 **Date established:** 2007
Turnover: £500,000 - £1m **No.of Employees:** 11 - 20
Product Groups: 46, 48, 67, 85

Date of Accounts	Sep 11	Apr 10
Working Capital	N/A	11
Fixed Assets	N/A	2
Current Assets	N/A	24

Obart Pumps Ltd
Obart House Twenty Twenty Industrial Estate, Maidstone, ME16 0FZ
Tel: 0800-092 4423 **Fax:** 01622-355019
E-mail: sales@obartpumps.co.uk
Website: http://www.obartpumps.co.uk
Bank(s): Barclays
Directors: M. Hill (MD)
Immediate Holding Company: OBART PUMPS LIMITED
Registration no: 02545121 **Date established:** 1990 **Turnover:** £1m - £2m
No.of Employees: 11 - 20 **Product Groups:** 39, 40, 46, 48

Date of Accounts	Mar 12	Mar 11	Mar 10
Working Capital	966	801	662
Fixed Assets	1m	2m	2m
Current Assets	2m	1m	1m
Current Liabilities	174	172	99

Paper Plant Services Engineering Ltd
Unit 16 Acorn Business Centre Milton Street, Maidstone, ME16 8LL
Tel: 01622-728066 **Fax:** 01622-728066
E-mail: trevor@ppsengineering.co.uk
Website: http://www.ppsengineering.co.uk
Directors: T. Savage (MD)
Immediate Holding Company: PAPER PLANT SERVICES (ENGINEERING) LTD

Registration no: 03770762 Date established: 1999
No.of Employees: 11 - 20 Product Groups: 35, 48, 52, 80

Date of Accounts	May 11	May 10	May 09
Sales Turnover	1m	1m	1m
Pre Tax Profit/Loss	5	-17	28
Working Capital	-66	-49	-39
Fixed Assets	34	34	41
Current Assets	381	356	332
Current Liabilities	267	242	178

Parker Hannifin plc
Hermitage Court Hermitage Lane, Maidstone, ME16 9NT
Tel: 01622-723300 **Fax:** 01622-728703
Website: http://www.parker.com
Managers: D. Wright (Mgr)
Ultimate Holding Company: Parker Hannifin (Holdings) Ltd
Immediate Holding Company: Parker Hannifin (GB) Ltd
Registration no: 04806503 **Date established:** 2007
No.of Employees: 11 - 20 **Product Groups:** 38, 42

Pegasus Training Services
6 Cobfields Chart Sutton, Maidstone, ME17 3SH
Tel: 01622-741300 **Fax:** 01622-741300
E-mail: peter@cobfields.freeuk.com
Website: http://www.pegasusforklifttraining.co.uk
Directors: P. Stott (Prop)
Date established: 1991 **No.of Employees:** 1 - 10 **Product Groups:** 35, 39, 45

Petron Welding & Fabrication
Haga Gravelly Bottom Road, Kingswood, Maidstone, ME17 3NS
Tel: 01622-842177 **Fax:** 01622-842177
E-mail: simon.read@dtn.ntl.com
Website: http://www.orantewaterwheel.co.uk
Directors: S. Read (Prop)
Date established: 1985 **No.of Employees:** 1 - 10 **Product Groups:** 35

Pharmarquip
Spectrum Business Estate Bircholt Road, Maidstone, ME15 9YP
Tel: 01622-686050
E-mail: leegifford74@hotmail.com
Website: http://www.pharmaquipe.co.uk
Directors: L. Gifford (Dir)
Registration no: 06714910 **Date established:** 2008 **Turnover:**
No.of Employees: 1 - 10 **Product Groups:** 31, 32

Phoenix Handling Ltd
6 The Alders Seven Mile Lane, Mereworth, Maidstone, ME18 5JG
Tel: 01622-817017 **Fax:** 01622-817018
E-mail: sales@phoenix-handling.co.uk
Directors: N. Quested (MD)
No.of Employees: 1 - 10 **Product Groups:** 27, 30

Preview Marketing LLP
21 Tovil Hill, Maidstone, ME15 6QS
Tel: 01622-766150
E-mail: luke@previewmarketing.co.uk
Website: http://www.previewmarketing.co.uk
Directors: L. Taylor (Dir)
Immediate Holding Company: PREVIEW MARKETING LLP
Registration no: OC327174 **Date established:** 2007
No.of Employees: 1 - 10 **Product Groups:** 27

Date of Accounts	Mar 11	Mar 10	Mar 09
Working Capital	-22	-24	-23
Fixed Assets	33	43	23
Current Assets	140	84	102
Current Liabilities	17	19	9

Primalec
Green Farm Cottage Maidstone Road, Nettlestead, Maidstone, ME18 5HD
Tel: 01622-816955 **Fax:** 01474-853968
E-mail: customers@primalec.co.uk
Website: http://www.primalec.com
Directors: R. Doran (MD), C. Siddall (Fin)
Immediate Holding Company: PRIMALEC LIMITED
Registration no: 02446347 **VAT No.:** GB 356 7949 95
Date established: 1989 **No.of Employees:** 1 - 10 **Product Groups:** 32, 37, 38, 39, 40, 44, 68, 83

Reliance Security Services Ltd
24 Hollingworth Court Turkey Mill, Maidstone, ME14 5PP
Tel: 01622-356530 **Fax:** 01622-691276
E-mail: info@reliancesecurity.co.uk
Website: http://www.reliancesecurity.co.uk
Directors: M. Carre (MD)
Ultimate Holding Company: RELIANCE CORPORATION LIMITED
Immediate Holding Company: RELIANCE PROPERTY HOLDINGS LIMITED
Registration no: 01033997 **Date established:** 1971
Turnover: Over £1,000m **No.of Employees:** 1 - 10 **Product Groups:** 81

Renson Fabrications Ltd
Fairfax Units 1-2-3 Bircholt Road Parkwood Industrial Estate, Maidstone, ME15 9SF
Tel: 01622-754123 **Fax:** 01622-689 478
E-mail: info@rensonuk.net
Website: http://www.uk.renson.be/solutions-for-ventilation-and-sun-protection-unite
Bank(s): National Westminster
Managers: F. Ruelens
Immediate Holding Company: RENSON FABRICATIONS LIMITED
Registration no: 02993317 **VAT No.:** GB 619 4748 09
Date established: 1994 **Turnover:** £500,000 - £1m
No.of Employees: 11 - 20 **Product Groups:** 23, 27, 33, 36, 48, 51, 52

Date of Accounts	Dec 11	Dec 10	Dec 09
Working Capital	476	449	3m
Fixed Assets	61	82	114
Current Assets	2m	3m	4m
Current Liabilities	820	N/A	N/A

Ringway Signs Ltd
Twenty Twenty Industrial Estate St Laurence Avenue, Allington, Maidstone, ME16 0LL
Tel: 01622-693476 **Fax:** 01622-685992
Website: http://www.ringway.co.uk
Managers: E. Girt (Admin Off)
Immediate Holding Company: Ringway Group Ltd
Registration no: 02283390 **No.of Employees:** 1 - 10 **Product Groups:** 30, 39, 40, 51, 84

S M B Sameday Couriers
683 Tonbridge Road, Maidstone, ME16 9DQ
Tel: 07930-281229
E-mail: burgum1@btinternet.com
Website: http://www.smbcouriers.vpweb.co.uk
Directors: N. Burgham (Prop), N. Burgum (Prop)
No.of Employees: 1 - 10 **Product Groups:** 79

Secom plc
5 The Progress Estate Bircholt Road, Maidstone, ME15 9YH
Tel: 01622-753735 **Fax:** 01622-753848
Website: http://www.secom.plc.uk
Managers: M. Wootton (Mgr)
Ultimate Holding Company: SECOM CO LTD (JAPAN)
Immediate Holding Company: SECOM PLC
Registration no: 02585807 **Date established:** 1991
No.of Employees: 1 - 10 **Product Groups:** 26, 35

Date of Accounts	Dec 11	Dec 10	Dec 09
Sales Turnover	40m	39m	35m
Pre Tax Profit/Loss	2m	2m	272
Working Capital	14m	13m	11m
Fixed Assets	14m	5m	6m
Current Assets	27m	24m	22m
Current Liabilities	11m	10m	10m

W H Skinner & Sons
Brishing Road Chart Sutton, Maidstone, ME17 3SP
Tel: 01622-744640 **Fax:** 01622-743307
E-mail: info@whskinner.co.uk
Website: http://www.whskinner.co.uk
Directors: P. Skinner (Prop), P. Skinner (Prop)
Immediate Holding Company: P M & J SKINNER BALLOONING LLP
Registration no: OC326967 **Date established:** 2007
No.of Employees: 1 - 10 **Product Groups:** 27, 28, 36, 38, 44, 49, 66, 85

Speedy Brush Co.
Mount Pleasant Farm Brishing Road, Chart Sutton, Maidstone, ME17 3SP
Tel: 01622-747299 **Fax:** 01622-743307
E-mail: info@speedybrush.com
Website: http://www.speedybrush.com
Directors: P. Skinner (Ptnr)
Immediate Holding Company: P M & J SKINNER BALLOONING LLP
Registration no: OC326967 **Date established:** 2007
No.of Employees: 1 - 10 **Product Groups:** 49

Date of Accounts	Dec 10	Dec 09	Dec 07
Working Capital	9	6	2
Fixed Assets	9	11	13
Current Assets	11	8	3

Summers PVC Ltd
Orchard Business Centre St Barnabas Close, Allington, Maidstone, ME16 0JZ
Tel: 01622-215456 **Fax:** 01622-754459
E-mail: bmmaidstone@summerspvc.co.uk
Website: http://www.summerspvc.co.uk
Directors: R. Monro (Co Sec)
Managers: J. Peacock (Mgr)
Ultimate Holding Company: SIG PLC
Immediate Holding Company: SUMMERS PVC LIMITED
Registration no: 02455530 **Date established:** 1989
No.of Employees: 1 - 10 **Product Groups:** 30, 31, 54

Swiss Valve Supply Ltd
2 Rose Court Maytum Farm, Linton, Maidstone, ME17 4BP
Tel: 01622-746945 **Fax:** 01622-749406
E-mail: sales@swissvalve.com
Website: http://www.swissvalve.com
Directors: J. Sutcliffe (Sales)
Immediate Holding Company: SWISS VALVE SUPPLY LIMITED
Registration no: 04205960 **Date established:** 2001
No.of Employees: 1 - 10 **Product Groups:** 36, 37, 38

Date of Accounts	May 11	May 10	May 09
Working Capital	-8	-11	12
Fixed Assets	23	7	9
Current Assets	97	98	110

Tarkett Ltd
Dickley Lane Lenham, Maidstone, ME17 2QX
Tel: 01622-854000 **Fax:** 01622-854500
E-mail: julie.watson@tarkett.com
Website: http://www.tarkett.co.uk
Bank(s): Lloyds TSB Bank plc, City Office
Directors: C. Holmes (Fin), J. Devine (Sales & Mktg)
Managers: S. Urwin (Mktg Serv Mgr), J. Watson, Y. Segal (Personnel), N. Coultrip (Purch Mgr)
Ultimate Holding Company: ETEX GROUP SA (BELGIUM)
Immediate Holding Company: MARLEY FLOORS LIMITED
Registration no: 00562641 **VAT No.:** GB 724 7570 24
Date established: 1956 **Turnover:** £20m - £50m
No.of Employees: 101 - 250 **Product Groups:** 30, 66

Date of Accounts	Dec 10	Dec 09	Dec 08
Pre Tax Profit/Loss	12	N/A	N/A
Working Capital	7m	7m	7m
Fixed Assets	N/A	150	150
Current Assets	7m	7m	7m

Techfil (Europe) Ltd
Hall Road Aylesford, Maidstone, ME20 7QZ
Tel: 01622-717780 **Fax:** 01622-710551
E-mail: info@techfil.co.uk
Website: http://www.techfil.co.uk
Directors: E. Blackmore (Dir)
Registration no: 06031269 **Date established:** 2007 **Turnover:** £1m - £2m
No.of Employees: 1 - 10 **Product Groups:** 14, 33, 66

The Ideal Cleaning Company
Woodcut Cottage Crismill Lane, Thurnham, Maidstone, ME14 3LY
Tel: 01622-735071 **Fax:** 01622-735097
E-mail: info@idealgroupuk.co.uk
Website: http://www.idealgroupuk.co.uk
Directors: K. Pedley (Fin), J. Ibrahim (MD)
Managers: J. Apps (Sales Admin), S. Stelmaczonek (Tech Serv Mgr), M. Weeks (Mktg Serv Mgr)
Immediate Holding Company: IDEAL RESPONSE GROUP LIMITED
Registration no: 04367515 **Date established:** 2002
No.of Employees: 21 - 50 **Product Groups:** 52, 83, 84

Date of Accounts	Jul 11	Jul 10	Jul 09
Working Capital	-37	-116	-35
Fixed Assets	260	277	264
Current Assets	322	185	147

UK Safety Compliance Ltd
3 Waters Edge, Maidstone, ME15 6SG
Tel: 01622-239127 **Fax:** 0870-7624008
E-mail: timcarr@uksafetycompliance.co.uk
Website: http://www.uksafetycompliance.co.uk
No.of Employees: 1 - 10 **Product Groups:** 84, 86

Wealden Hops Ltd
Congelow Benover Road, Yalding, Maidstone, ME18 6ET
Tel: 01622-817175 **Fax:** 01622-817014
E-mail: wealden.hops.ltd@unicombox.co.uk
Website: http://www.wealden-hops.co.uk
Managers: A. Unwin (Mgr)
Immediate Holding Company: BOTANICAL DEVELOPMENTS LIMITED
Registration no: 04953022 **Date established:** 2003
No.of Employees: 1 - 10 **Product Groups:** 20, 40, 41

Date of Accounts	Mar 11	Mar 10	Mar 09
Working Capital	-56	-35	-9
Current Assets	147	119	115

Margate

A1 Refrigeration Kent Ltd
48 Westbrook Avenue, Margate, CT9 5HB
Tel: 07860-268194
Directors: I. Smith (Prop)
Immediate Holding Company: A1 REFRIGERATION (KENT) LIMITED
Registration no: 07147334 **Date established:** 2010
No.of Employees: 1 - 10 **Product Groups:** 36, 40

Argoneon Ltd
Unit A6 Continental Approach Westwood Industrial Estate, Margate, CT9 4JG
Tel: 01843-226420 **Fax:** 01843-226420
E-mail: michael@argoneon.co.uk
Website: http://argoneon.co.uk
Directors: M. Bass (Fin), C. Mayhew (MD)
Immediate Holding Company: ARGONEON LIMITED
Registration no: 04501790 **Date established:** 2002
Turnover: Up to £250,000 **No.of Employees:** 1 - 10 **Product Groups:** 37

Date of Accounts	Aug 11	Aug 10	Aug 09
Sales Turnover	N/A	53	122
Pre Tax Profit/Loss	N/A	N/A	38
Working Capital	7	-5	12
Fixed Assets	4	5	6
Current Assets	73	29	61
Current Liabilities	N/A	2	11

Dugdale Plastics Ltd
2a Dane Hill, Margate, CT9 1QP
Tel: 01843-225789 **Fax:** 01843-227370
E-mail: sales@dugdaleplastics.co.uk
Website: http://www.dugdaleplastics.co.uk
Directors: M. Dally (MD)
Immediate Holding Company: DUGDALE PLASTICS LIMITED
Registration no: 01344978 **VAT No.:** GB 316 6780 45
Date established: 1977 **Turnover:** Up to £250,000
No.of Employees: 1 - 10 **Product Groups:** 30, 42, 48, 66

Date of Accounts	Apr 12	Apr 11	Apr 10
Working Capital	215	203	193
Fixed Assets	3	7	19
Current Assets	264	244	233

Emco Wheaton
Unit K Channel Road Westwood Industrial Estate, Margate, CT9 4JR
Tel: 01843-221521 **Fax:** 01843-295444
E-mail: gmurphy@emcowheaton.com
Website: http://www.emcowheaton.com
Bank(s): HSBC Bank plc
Directors: G. Murphy (MD), B. Armitage (Fin), M. Grummett (Co Sec)
Managers: P. Woloszynowicz (Tech Serv Mgr), M. Hubers (Purch Mgr)
Ultimate Holding Company: GARDNER DENVER INC (USA)
Immediate Holding Company: EMCO WHEATON U.K. LIMITED
Registration no: 00466276 **VAT No.:** GB 377 9545 89
Date established: 1949 **Turnover:** £5m - £10m **No.of Employees:** 21 - 50
Product Groups: 36

Date of Accounts	Dec 10	Dec 09	Dec 08
Sales Turnover	N/A	10m	N/A
Pre Tax Profit/Loss	626	11m	N/A
Working Capital	12m	12m	-1m
Fixed Assets	N/A	N/A	2m
Current Assets	12m	12m	3m
Current Liabilities	175	N/A	641

Hamilton Laboratory Glass Ltd
Unit A1 Continental Approach Westwood Industrial Estate, Margate, CT9 4JG
Tel: 01843-232633 **Fax:** 01843-232644
E-mail: sales@hamiltonlabglass.com
Website: http://www.hamiltonlabglass.com
Bank(s): HSBC, Canterbury
Directors: E. Bodley (MD), J. Bodley (Fin)
Immediate Holding Company: HAMILTON LABORATORY GLASS LIMITED
Registration no: 01112437 **VAT No.:** GB 202 0405 43
Date established: 1973 **Turnover:** £250,000 - £500,000
No.of Employees: 11 - 20 **Product Groups:** 33, 42, 63

Date of Accounts	Aug 11	Aug 10	Aug 09
Working Capital	55	8	13
Fixed Assets	18	31	34
Current Assets	137	89	94
Current Liabilities	N/A	12	8

Hilger Crystals Ltd
Unit R1 Westwood Industrial Estate Continental Approach, Margate, CT9 4JL
Tel: 01843-231166 **Fax:** 01843-290310
E-mail: sales@hilger-crystals.co.uk
Website: http://www.hilger-crystals.co.uk
Bank(s): Barclays, London

see next page

Hilger Crystals Ltd - *Cont'd*

Directors: A. Dudouit (Co Sec), J. Telfer (MD)
Managers: C. Smissen (Sales Prom Mgr)
Ultimate Holding Company: NEWPORT CORPORATION (USA)
Immediate Holding Company: HILGER CRYSTALS LIMITED
Registration no: 03412024 **Date established:** 1997 **Turnover:** £2m - £5m
No.of Employees: 21 - 50 **Product Groups:** 33, 37, 38, 66

Date of Accounts	Dec 09	Dec 08	Sep 11
Sales Turnover	1m	2m	2m
Pre Tax Profit/Loss	-202	213	-379
Working Capital	515	1m	378
Fixed Assets	794	602	715
Current Assets	927	1m	1m
Current Liabilities	61	61	51

Hornby Hobbies Ltd

H1-H2 Unit Enterprise Road Westwood Industrial Estate, Margate, CT9 4JX
Tel: 01843-233500 **Fax:** 01843-233513
E-mail: frank.martin@hornby.com
Website: http://www.hornby.com
Bank(s): Barclays
Directors: Martin (MD), F. Martin (Dir)
Managers: P. Bell (I.T. Exec), M. Moon (Sales Prom Mgr), J. Jefferys (Personnel), S. Cohler (Mktg Serv Mgr), J. Stansfield (Chief Acct), E. Edmunds (Mgr), C. Harwood (Sales Prom Mgr), A. Syme (Purch Mgr), S. Cowler (Mktg Serv Mgr)
Ultimate Holding Company: HORNBY PLC
Immediate Holding Company: HORNBY HOBBIES LIMITED
Registration no: 02065081 **VAT No.:** 445 1860 49 **Date established:** 1986
Turnover: £20m - £50m **No.of Employees:** 101 - 250 **Product Groups:** 49

Date of Accounts	Mar 11	Mar 10	Mar 09
Sales Turnover	51m	49m	47m
Pre Tax Profit/Loss	4m	3m	5m
Working Capital	17m	19m	13m
Fixed Assets	12m	13m	13m
Current Assets	33m	33m	28m
Current Liabilities	4m	4m	4m

Kent Scuba Ltd

274 Northdown Road, Margate, CT9 2PT
Tel: 01843-297430
E-mail: info@kentscuba.com
Website: http://www.kentscuba.com
Directors: S. Connell (MD)
Immediate Holding Company: KENT SCUBA LIMITED
Registration no: 04642390 **Date established:** 2003
Turnover: Up to £250,000 **No.of Employees:** 1 - 10 **Product Groups:** 40, 49, 89

Date of Accounts	Jan 11	Jan 10	Jan 09
Sales Turnover	N/A	66	66
Pre Tax Profit/Loss	N/A	4	7
Working Capital	-13	-10	-1
Fixed Assets	12	12	14
Current Assets	29	26	35
Current Liabilities	N/A	2	4

Pegasus Storage Solutions Ltd

11 High Street Garlinge, Margate, CT9 5LN
Tel: 01843-835999 **Fax:** 01843-835017
E-mail: enquiries@pegasus-storage.co.uk
Website: http://www.pegasusstorage.co.uk
Directors: S. Rutherford (Fin)
Immediate Holding Company: PEGASUS STORAGE SOLUTIONS LIMITED
Registration no: 03859534 **Date established:** 1999
No.of Employees: 1 - 10 **Product Groups:** 35, 42, 45

Date of Accounts	Mar 11	Mar 10	Mar 09
Working Capital	-58	29	115
Fixed Assets	11	15	19
Current Assets	204	187	396

Roe Ltd (Gang-Nail Systems Ltd)

Enterprise Road Westwood Industrial Estate, Margate, CT9 4JA
Tel: 01843-232888 **Fax:** 01843-232233
E-mail: info@roeltd.co.uk
Website: http://www.roeltd.co.uk
Directors: D. Roe (MD)
Managers: D. Macmillan (Sales Prom Mgr), R. Knowles (Factory Mgr), L. Caraccio
Immediate Holding Company: ROE LIMITED
Registration no: 03695845 **Date established:** 1999
Turnover: £10m - £20m **No.of Employees:** 101 - 250
Product Groups: 35, 66

Date of Accounts	Apr 11	Apr 10	Apr 09
Sales Turnover	10m	8m	9m
Pre Tax Profit/Loss	70	-196	-113
Working Capital	12	54	214
Fixed Assets	4m	4m	4m
Current Assets	2m	2m	2m
Current Liabilities	250	170	265

Thanet Press Ltd

Union Cresent, Margate, CT9 1NU
Tel: 01843-234800 **Fax:** 01843-228831
E-mail: enquiries@thanet-press.co.uk
Website: http://www.thanet-press.co.uk
Bank(s): Llyods TSB
Directors: D. Hurley (MD), K. Herbage (Fin), J. Davis (Fin), S. Dobbin (Co Sec), P. Yates (MD), K. Lindsay (Dir), C. Durrant (Sales), J. Bryant (Fin)
Managers: A. Clarke (Buyer), P. Gibson (I.T. Exec), G. Fordham (Sales Prom Mgr), D. Burton (Buyer)
Ultimate Holding Company: The Baird Group Limited
Immediate Holding Company: THANET PRESS LIMITED
Registration no: 03051768 **VAT No.:** GB 661 7964 01
Date established: 1995 **Turnover:** £5m - £10m
No.of Employees: 51 - 100 **Product Groups:** 28

Date of Accounts	Dec 08	Dec 07	Dec 06
Pre Tax Profit/Loss	-681	-319	-693
Working Capital	-697	-215	-234
Fixed Assets	853	1m	2m
Current Assets	1m	1m	1m
Current Liabilities	200	171	132

Xquisite Recruitment

Surrey Road Cliftonville, Margate, CT9 2JR
Tel: 01843-228440
E-mail: carole@xquisiterecruitment.co.uk
Website: http://www.xquisiterecruitment.co.uk
Directors: C. Clayton (Ptnr)
Date established: 2004 **No.of Employees:** 1 - 10 **Product Groups:** 80

New Romney

Access Fulfilment Ltd

The Distribution Centre Unit 1a & 1b, New Romney, TN28 8XU
Tel: 08700-601563 **Fax:** 0844-736 1531
E-mail: dave@accessfulfilment.com
Website: http://www.accessfulfilment.co.uk
Directors: D. Hughes (MD)
Immediate Holding Company: ACCESS FULFILMENT LIMITED
Registration no: 04273765 **Date established:** 2001 **Turnover:** £2m - £5m
No.of Employees: 11 - 20 **Product Groups:** 80

Date of Accounts	Aug 11	Aug 10	Aug 09
Working Capital	-8	-17	-8
Fixed Assets	5	6	9
Current Assets	91	213	255

Denton Containers 2000 Ltd

Mountfield Road Mountfield Industrial Estate, New Romney, TN28 8LH
Tel: 01797-361600 **Fax:** 01797-361700
E-mail: murray.cobb@dcl2000.com
Website: http://www.dcl2000.com
Bank(s): National Westminster Bank Plc
Directors: M. Cobb (MD)
Immediate Holding Company: DENTON CONTAINERS (2000) LIMITED
Registration no: 03959164 **Date established:** 2000 **Turnover:** £1m - £2m
No.of Employees: 21 - 50 **Product Groups:** 27, 30, 45

Date of Accounts	Jun 11	Jun 10	Jun 09
Working Capital	113	82	60
Fixed Assets	9	11	14
Current Assets	130	104	78

Echo Engineering Southern Ltd

Chapel Land Farm Ashford Road, New Romney, TN28 8TH
Tel: 01797-367670 **Fax:** 01797-367671
E-mail: roger.hooper@echo-eng.com
Website: http://www.echo-eng.com
Bank(s): Lloyds TSB Bank plc
Directors: D. Faulkner (Dir), M. Ouchford (Chief Op Offcr), R. Hooper (MD)
Managers: A. Kiernan (Tech Serv Mgr)
Immediate Holding Company: ECHO ENGINEERING (SOUTHERN) LIMITED
Registration no: 03389027 **VAT No.:** GB 571 7225 40
Date established: 1997 **Turnover:** £1m - £2m **No.of Employees:** 11 - 20
Product Groups: 48

Date of Accounts	May 11	May 10	May 09
Working Capital	69	80	-34
Fixed Assets	29	30	37
Current Assets	332	314	211

Hotel Complimentary Products

Mountfield House Mountfield Road, New Romney, TN28 8LH
Tel: 01797-362895 **Fax:** 01797-366722
E-mail: sales@hcp-ltd.com
Website: http://www.hcp-ltd.com
Directors: D. Deacon (Sales)
Immediate Holding Company: HOTEL COMPLIMENTARY PRODUCTS LIMITED
Registration no: 03513384 **Date established:** 1998 **Turnover:** £1m - £2m
No.of Employees: 1 - 10 **Product Groups:** 22, 24, 30, 32, 36, 49, 63

Date of Accounts	Jun 11	Jun 10	Jun 09
Sales Turnover	2m	1m	1m
Pre Tax Profit/Loss	309	225	106
Working Capital	551	446	369
Fixed Assets	237	213	228
Current Assets	1m	1m	1m
Current Liabilities	106	209	62

Orpington

Air Conditioning Contracts Ltd

79 Gillmans Road, Orpington, BR5 4LD
Tel: 020-8302 8637
E-mail: rayaircon@aol.com
Directors: R. Douglass (MD)
Immediate Holding Company: AIR CONDITIONING CONTRACTS LIMITED
Registration no: 03792695 **Date established:** 1999
No.of Employees: 1 - 10 **Product Groups:** 40, 66

Date of Accounts	Jun 10	Jun 09	Jun 08
Working Capital	205	59	41
Current Assets	205	297	268

Arco South East

Cray Avenue, Orpington, BR5 3QB
Tel: 01689-875411 **Fax:** 01689-876538
E-mail: watford.branch@arco.co.uk
Website: http://www.arco.co.uk
Managers: J. Bell (Mgr)
Immediate Holding Company: H AND D SUPPLIES LTD
Registration no: 07186870 **Date established:** 2007
Turnover: £125m - £250m **No.of Employees:** 21 - 50
Product Groups: 24, 29, 30, 40

Baselayer Ltd

11 Derry Downs, Orpington, BR5 4DT
Tel: 01689-603675
E-mail: baselayer@newerainternet.com
Website: http://www.baselayer.co.uk
Directors: P. Tagg (Fin)
Immediate Holding Company: BASELAYER LTD
Registration no: 05715227 **Date established:** 2006
No.of Employees: 1 - 10 **Product Groups:** 24

Date of Accounts	Mar 12	Mar 11	Mar 10
Working Capital	12	19	9
Fixed Assets	11	13	3
Current Assets	181	155	122

The Business Advantage Group plc

Pel House 33-35 Station Square, Petts Wood, Orpington, BR5 1LZ
Tel: 01689-873636 **Fax:** 01689-878070
E-mail: info@business-advantage.com
Website: http://www.business-advantage.com
Directors: D. Eaton (Dir), S. Turner (Fin), C. Turner (MD)
Immediate Holding Company: THE BUSINESS ADVANTAGE GROUP LIMITED
Registration no: 03548265 **Date established:** 1998
Turnover: £500,000 - £1m **No.of Employees:** 21 - 50 **Product Groups:** 81

Date of Accounts	Apr 11	Apr 10	Apr 09
Sales Turnover	558	774	1m
Pre Tax Profit/Loss	-119	-195	31
Working Capital	-162	-47	131
Fixed Assets	6	10	13
Current Assets	174	128	367
Current Liabilities	280	135	202

Channell Ltd

Fairway Petts Wood, Orpington, BR5 1EG
Tel: 01689-871522 **Fax:** 01689-833428
E-mail: info@channell.com
Website: http://www.channell.com
Directors: W. Channell Jr (Grp Chief Exec)
Ultimate Holding Company: CHANNELL COMMERCIAL CORPORATION (USA)
Immediate Holding Company: CHANNELL COMMERCIAL EUROPE LTD
Registration no: 02837910 **VAT No.:** GB 435 0768 49
Date established: 1993 **Turnover:** £2m - £5m **No.of Employees:** 1 - 10
Product Groups: 37

Date of Accounts	Dec 11	Dec 10	Dec 09
Working Capital	-775	-775	-775

Clarkson Wright & Jakes

Valiant House 12 Knoll Rise, Orpington, BR6 0PG
Tel: 01689-887887 **Fax:** 01689-887888
E-mail: peter.g@clarksons.co.uk
Website: http://www.cwj.co.uk
Directors: A. Wright (Snr Part), S. Helm (Pers)
Managers: D. Bassett (I.T. Exec), A. Grosvenor (Mktg Serv Mgr), N. Gunson (Tech Serv Mgr)
Immediate Holding Company: CLARKSON WRIGHT & JAKES LIMITED
Registration no: 07529406 **Date established:** 2011 **Turnover:** £5m - £10m
No.of Employees: 101 - 250 **Product Groups:** 80

Date of Accounts	Apr 10	Apr 09
Working Capital	2m	2m
Fixed Assets	218	317
Current Assets	2m	2m

Cockett Marine Oil Ltd

Carrick House 36 Station Square, Petts Wood, Orpington, BR5 1NA
Tel: 01689-883400 **Fax:** 01689-877666
E-mail: enquiries@cockett.co.uk
Website: http://www.cockett.co.uk
Directors: K. Beeson (MD)
Managers: A. Deer (Tech Serv Mgr), R. Nye (Fin Mgr), L. Jessops (Mktg Serv Mgr)
Ultimate Holding Company: GRINDROD LIMITED (SOUTH AFRICA)
Immediate Holding Company: COCKETT MARINE OIL LIMITED
Registration no: 01439075 **Date established:** 1979
Turnover: £500m - £1,000m **No.of Employees:** 21 - 50
Product Groups: 31

Date of Accounts	Nov 08	Nov 07	Nov 06
Sales Turnover	1365m	801m	572m
Pre Tax Profit/Loss	5m	2m	3m
Working Capital	15m	11m	9m
Fixed Assets	590	470	490
Current Assets	84m	105m	57m
Current Liabilities	69m	93m	48m
Total Share Capital	70	70	70

D P T S Group Holdings Ltd

Unit 2 02 Crayfields Industrial Park Main Road, Orpington, BR5 3HP
Tel: 01689-824777 **Fax:** 01689-834550
E-mail: richard.purves@dpts.co.uk
Website: http://www.dpts.co.uk
Bank(s): Barclays
Directors: J. Lee (Fin)
Managers: R. Purves (I.T. Exec), S. Murphy (Personnel)
Ultimate Holding Company: OVATION DATA SERVICES, INC.
Immediate Holding Company: DPTS GROUP HOLDINGS LIMITED
Registration no: 04317843 **VAT No.:** GB 367 3932 22
Date established: 2001 **Turnover:** £2m - £5m **No.of Employees:** 21 - 50
Product Groups: 44, 80

Date of Accounts	Dec 11	Dec 10	Dec 09
Working Capital	-41	-39	-52
Fixed Assets	311	311	311
Current Assets	1	1	172

David Newman Camshafts & Co.

Farnborough Way, Orpington, BR6 7DH
Tel: 01689-857109 **Fax:** 01689-855498
E-mail: info@newman-cams.com
Website: http://www.newman-cams.com
Directors: D. Newman (Snr Part)
VAT No.: GB 205 7497 56 **Turnover:** £1m - £2m **No.of Employees:** 11 - 20
Product Groups: 40

Econology Ltd

4 Norsted Lane Pratts Bottom, Orpington, BR6 7PG
Tel: 01689-860686
E-mail: cmaier@btconnect.com
Directors: C. Maier (Co Sec)
Immediate Holding Company: ECONOLOGY LIMITED
Registration no: 02214901 **Date established:** 1988
Turnover: Up to £250,000 **No.of Employees:** 1 - 10 **Product Groups:** 81, 84

Date of Accounts	Mar 11	Mar 10	Mar 09
Sales Turnover	N/A	N/A	3
Pre Tax Profit/Loss	N/A	-3	-5
Working Capital	-22	-20	-17
Fixed Assets	N/A	1	2
Current Liabilities	N/A	20	18

Foulds Clark London Ltd

PO Box 547, Orpington, BR6 7WP
Tel: 01689-860011 **Fax:** 01689-608738
E-mail: safety@fouldsclark.co.uk
Website: http://www.fouldsclark.co.uk
Directors: S. Clark (Dir)
Immediate Holding Company: FOULDS CLARK (LONDON) LIMITED
Registration no: 00926902 **Date established:** 1968
Turnover: Up to £250,000 **No.of Employees:** 1 - 10 **Product Groups:** 29, 30, 35, 36, 40

Date of Accounts	Mar 11	Mar 10	Mar 09
Working Capital	89	89	111
Fixed Assets	4	9	15
Current Assets	125	120	128

Hovercraft Rental
Po Box 755, Orpington, BR6 1DH
Tel: 0870-766 9125
E-mail: info@meridianmarine.co.uk
Website: http://www.hovercraftrental.co.uk
Directors: G. Roberts (Dir), D. Lensing (Dir)
Date established: 2006 **No.of Employees:** 1 - 10 **Product Groups:** 74

Meridian
PO Box 431, Orpington, BR5 4RG
Tel: 01689-824207 **Fax:** 01689-839905
E-mail: paulbowden@meridian-uk.com
Website: http://www.meridian-uk.com
Directors: P. Bowden (Prop)
VAT No.: GB 586 6423 04 **Date established:** 1991
No.of Employees: 1 - 10 **Product Groups:** 72, 76

Neilcott Construction Ltd
Excel House Cray Avenue, Orpington, BR5 3ST
Tel: 01689-832199 **Fax:** 01689-825745
E-mail: build@neilcott.co.uk
Website: http://www.neilcott.co.uk
Directors: M. Elster (Dir), L. Walls (Fin)
Managers: R. Cox, D. Holton (Mktg Serv Mgr), C. Bennett
Ultimate Holding Company: P. J. WALLS HOLDINGS LIMITED
Immediate Holding Company: NEILCOTT CONSTRUCTION LIMITED
Registration no: 01151561 **Date established:** 1973
Turnover: £50m - £75m **No.of Employees:** 21 - 50 **Product Groups:** 52, 84

Date of Accounts	Dec 11	Dec 10	Dec 09
Sales Turnover	57m	35m	36m
Pre Tax Profit/Loss	3m	1m	1m
Working Capital	3m	6m	5m
Fixed Assets	85	81	70
Current Assets	16m	17m	17m
Current Liabilities	2m	2m	3m

News Shopper
Mega House Crest View Drive, Petts Wood, Orpington, BR5 1BT
Tel: 01689-885619 **Fax:** 01689-877823
E-mail: dstuart@london.newsquest.co.uk
Website: http://www.newsshopper.co.uk
Managers: B. Turner (I.T. Exec), D. Stuart (Reg Sales Mgr), L. Anderson (Mktg Serv Mgr), S. Leigh (Sales Prom Mgr), K. Knight (Tech Serv Mgr), T. Mallett
Ultimate Holding Company: NEWS QUEST MEDIA GROUP
Registration no: 00839492 **VAT No.:** GB 574 0134 60
Turnover: £20m - £50m **No.of Employees:** 101 - 250 **Product Groups:** 28

P S Analytical Ltd
3 Crayfield Industrial Park Main Road, Orpington, BR5 3HP
Tel: 01689-891211 **Fax:** 01689-896009
E-mail: mas@psanalytical.com
Website: http://www.psanalytical.com
Bank(s): The Royal Bank of Scotland
Directors: M. Stockwell (Fin), P. Stockwell (I.T. Dir)
Managers: W. Corns, B. Edmonds, S. Azmi (Tech Serv Mgr)
Immediate Holding Company: P.S. ANALYTICAL LIMITED
Registration no: 01600004 **VAT No.:** GB 367 6490 13
Date established: 1981 **Turnover:** £2m - £5m **No.of Employees:** 21 - 50
Product Groups: 38, 44

Date of Accounts	Jun 11	Jun 10	Jun 09
Working Capital	2m	2m	2m
Fixed Assets	32	38	38
Current Assets	2m	2m	2m

Parker Bromley Ltd
5 Ravensquay Business Centre Cray Avenue, Orpington, BR5 4BQ
Tel: 01689-607607 **Fax:** 01689-604110
E-mail: enq@parkerbromley.co.uk
Website: http://www.parkerbromley.co.uk
Directors: P. Spicer (Co Sec), R. Parker (MD)
Managers: S. Holman (Develop Mgr), P. Hewagama (Fin Mgr)
Immediate Holding Company: PARKER BROMLEY LIMITED
Registration no: 01471810 **Date established:** 1980 **Turnover:** £5m - £10m
No.of Employees: 21 - 50 **Product Groups:** 52

Date of Accounts	Jun 11	Jun 10	Jun 09
Working Capital	668	743	705
Fixed Assets	195	107	164
Current Assets	3m	3m	2m

Prima Tapes & Labels Ltd
Prima House Faraday Way, Orpington, BR5 3QW
Tel: 01689-816111 **Fax:** 01689-816010
E-mail: sales@prima-tapes.com
Website: http://www.prima-tapes.com
Bank(s): HSBC
Directors: M. Lee (Ptnr)
Immediate Holding Company: PRIMA TAPES & LABELS LTD
Registration no: 01452786 **VAT No.:** GB 220 2444 21
Date established: 1979 **Turnover:** £2m - £5m **No.of Employees:** 21 - 50
Product Groups: 27

Date of Accounts	Dec 11	Dec 10	Dec 09
Working Capital	2m	2m	2m
Fixed Assets	586	625	661
Current Assets	3m	3m	3m

Pro Clothing
16b Grays Farm Production Village Grays Farm Road, Orpington, BR5 3BD
Tel: 01424-882467 **Fax:** 01689-819665
E-mail: sales@proclothing.co.uk
Website: http://www.proclothing.co.uk
Directors: J. Groombridge (Prop)
No.of Employees: 1 - 10 **Product Groups:** 23, 24, 63

Selectamark Security Systems plc
1 Locks Court 429 Crofton Road, Orpington, BR6 8NL
Tel: 01689-860757 **Fax:** 01689-860693
E-mail: sales@selectamark.co.uk
Website: http://www.selectadna.co.uk
Bank(s): National Westminster Bank Plc
Directors: T. Wood (Fin), J. Brown (Develop), J. Brown (Sales), A. Knights (MD)
Immediate Holding Company: SELECTAMARK SECURITY SYSTEMS PLC
Registration no: 01024280 **VAT No.:** GB 512 8043 77
Date established: 1971 **Turnover:** £1m - £2m **No.of Employees:** 11 - 20
Product Groups: 32, 37, 81

Date of Accounts	Oct 11	Oct 10	Oct 09
Sales Turnover	2m	2m	2m
Pre Tax Profit/Loss	47	104	81
Working Capital	611	579	513
Fixed Assets	459	413	426
Current Assets	904	935	800
Current Liabilities	150	143	115

Sem Ltd
Faraday House Faraday Way, Orpington, BR5 3QT
Tel: 01689-884700 **Fax:** 01689-884884
E-mail: info@sem.co.uk
Website: http://www.sem.co.uk
Bank(s): National Westminster Bank Plc
Directors: I. Wells (Fin), J. Bendall (Pers), M. Laming (MD)
Managers: S. Jackson (Sales & Mktg Mgr), D. Boydon
Ultimate Holding Company: DR JOHANNES HEIDENHAIN GMBH (GERMANY)
Immediate Holding Company: SEM LIMITED
Registration no: 00138006 **VAT No.:** GB 205 8785 46
Date established: 2014 **Turnover:** £10m - £20m
No.of Employees: 101 - 250 **Product Groups:** 37, 38

Date of Accounts	Dec 11	Dec 10	Dec 09
Sales Turnover	18m	11m	7m
Pre Tax Profit/Loss	1m	-1m	-895
Working Capital	4m	1m	1m
Fixed Assets	1m	683	733
Current Assets	7m	4m	2m
Current Liabilities	2m	654	409

Specac Ltd
River House 97 Cray Avenue, Orpington, BR5 4HE
Tel: 01689-873134 **Fax:** 01689-878527
E-mail: sales@specac.co.uk
Website: http://www.specac.co.uk
Bank(s): Barclays
Directors: D. Whiting (Co Sec), G. Poulter (Dir)
Managers: H. Hall (Mktg Serv Mgr), M. Goodall (Tech Serv Mgr), B. Self (Comptroller), E. Bramble (Purch Mgr)
Ultimate Holding Company: SMITHS GROUP PLC
Immediate Holding Company: SPECAC LIMITED
Registration no: 01008689 **VAT No.:** GB 226 6019 77
Date established: 1971 **Turnover:** £2m - £5m **No.of Employees:** 21 - 50
Product Groups: 38

Date of Accounts	Jul 11	Jul 10	Jul 09
Sales Turnover	4m	3m	3m
Pre Tax Profit/Loss	-170	-171	-451
Working Capital	2m	2m	4m
Fixed Assets	160	110	196
Current Assets	3m	2m	4m
Current Liabilities	103	74	56

Stanbridge
Cray Valley Road, Orpington, BR5 2UB
Tel: 01689-806500 **Fax:** 01689-806501
E-mail: admin@stanbridge.co.uk
Website: http://www.stanbridge.co.uk
Bank(s): National Westminster
Directors: J. Beaumont (MD)
Managers: M. Glover
Registration no: 00570388 **Date established:** 2005 **Turnover:** £2m - £5m
No.of Employees: 21 - 50 **Product Groups:** 37, 38, 67

Staples Dairy Products Ltd
The Mill House Main Road, Orpington, BR5 3HS
Tel: 01689-888700 **Fax:** 01689-888710
E-mail: geoff.pearce@stapledairy.co.uk
Website: http://www.stapledairy.co.uk
Bank(s): Barclays
Directors: D. Robbins (MD), G. Pearce (Asst MD), M. Venning (Mkt Research), P. Eburah (Fin)
Managers: C. Homewood (Tech Serv Mgr), P. Skelly
Ultimate Holding Company: STAPLE HOLDINGS (UK) LIMITED
Immediate Holding Company: STAPLE DAIRY PRODUCTS LIMITED
Registration no: 01881120 **Date established:** 1985
Turnover: £10m - £20m **No.of Employees:** 11 - 20 **Product Groups:** 20, 62

Date of Accounts	Mar 11	Mar 10	Mar 09
Sales Turnover	17m	15m	22m
Pre Tax Profit/Loss	111	215	155
Working Capital	1m	974	851
Current Assets	4m	3m	4m
Current Liabilities	358	367	248

Stora Enso UK Ltd
1 Kingfisher House Crayfields Business Park New Mill Road, Orpington, BR5 3QG
Tel: 01689-883200 **Fax:** 01992-788498
E-mail: james.barr@storaenso.com
Website: http://www.storaenso.com
Bank(s): Merita Bank
Directors: J. Barr (Fin)
Ultimate Holding Company: STORA ENSO OYJ {FINLAND}
Immediate Holding Company: STORA ENSO HOLDINGS UK LIMITED
Registration no: 00070861 **VAT No.:** GB 586 5306 13
Date established: 2001 **Turnover:** £2m - £5m **No.of Employees:** 11 - 20
Product Groups: 27, 66

Date of Accounts	Dec 11	Dec 10	Dec 09
Pre Tax Profit/Loss	-4m	705	-5m
Working Capital	21m	26m	25m
Fixed Assets	3m	3m	4m
Current Assets	28m	34m	34m
Current Liabilities	790	783	75

Harvey Waddington
Murray Road, Orpington, BR5 3RA
Tel: 01689-877020 **Fax:** 01689-877027
E-mail: smoon@teepol.co.uk
Website: http://www.teepol.co.uk
Immediate Holding Company: Supplytrade Ltd
Registration no: 03017608 **Product Groups:** 32, 63, 66

Queenborough

Concept Designs
Unit 1a Klondyke Industrial Estate Rushenden Road, Queenborough, ME11 5HH
Tel: 01795-660700
E-mail: edbedford@mail.com
Website: http://www.radiatorscoverintent.com
Directors: E. Bedford (Prop)
Ultimate Holding Company: SHEPPY LIMITED
Immediate Holding Company: M. & W. MUSIC LIMITED
Registration no: 00018098 **Date established:** 1971
No.of Employees: 1 - 10 **Product Groups:** 25, 26, 40, 63

Date of Accounts	May 11	May 10	May 09
Sales Turnover	533	537	N/A
Pre Tax Profit/Loss	-110	-499	N/A
Working Capital	345	471	-379
Fixed Assets	3m	4m	5m
Current Assets	3m	2m	1m
Current Liabilities	898	894	N/A

M I T Ltd
Queenborough Shipyard South Street, Queenborough, ME11 5EE
Tel: 01795-580808 **Fax:** 01795-580900
E-mail: reception@mitgroup.co.uk
Website: http://www.mitgroup.co.uk
Bank(s): Barclays Bank
Directors: M. Jackson (Mkt Research), P. Fenton (Fin)
Managers: A. Lough, S. Bartlett (Buyer)
Ultimate Holding Company: MARINE AND INDUSTRIAL TRANSMISSIONS LIMITED
Immediate Holding Company: M.I.T. (MACHINING) LIMITED
Registration no: 01177648 **VAT No.:** GB 204 5382 89
Date established: 1974 **Turnover:** £5m - £10m **No.of Employees:** 21 - 50
Product Groups: 35, 36, 39, 40, 45, 48, 84

Date of Accounts	Apr 08	Apr 07
Pre Tax Profit/Loss	631	175
Working Capital	1600	1217
Fixed Assets	245	162
Current Assets	4747	3117
Current Liabilities	3147	1900
Total Share Capital	8	8
ROCE% (Return on Capital Employed)	34.2	12.7

Pilkington Agr UK Ltd (Automotive)
Unit 4 Queenborough Business Park Main Road, Queenborough, ME11 5DY
Tel: 07802-204589 **Fax:** 01795-668059
E-mail: peter.swann@pilkington.com
Website: http://www.pilkington.com
Bank(s): Barclays, St. Helens
Directors: R. Hemingway (Fin)
Managers: P. Swann (Chief Mgr)
Ultimate Holding Company: NIPPON SHEET GLASS CO LTD (JAPAN)
Immediate Holding Company: PILKINGTON AGR (UK) LIMITED
Registration no: 02303036 **VAT No.:** GB 151 6225 91
Date established: 1988 **Turnover:** £2m - £5m **No.of Employees:** 11 - 20
Product Groups: 33, 39

Date of Accounts	Mar 11	Mar 10	Mar 07
Working Capital	13m	13m	13m
Current Assets	13m	13m	13m

Queenborough Forge Ltd
Unit 3 Klondyke Industrial Estate Rushenden Road, Queenborough, ME11 5HN
Tel: 01795-662266 **Fax:** 01795-669990
E-mail: info@eirikjohnsongateauto.co.uk
Bank(s): Natwest
Directors: E. Johnson (MD)
Immediate Holding Company: QUEENBOROUGH FORGE LIMITED
Registration no: 04657358 **VAT No.:** GB 619 0480 45
Date established: 2003 **Turnover:** £1m - £2m **No.of Employees:** 21 - 50
Product Groups: 35

Date of Accounts	Feb 11	Feb 10	Feb 09
Working Capital	-36	25	11
Fixed Assets	19	16	18
Current Assets	177	172	186

Sheppey Dental Laboratory
1a-2a Railway Terrace, Queenborough, ME11 5AY
Tel: 01795-662025 **Fax:** 01795-583593
Directors: A. Milton (Prop)
No.of Employees: 1 - 10 **Product Groups:** 38, 67

Sheppy Ltd
Klondyke Industrial Estate Rushenden Road, Queenborough, ME11 5HH
Tel: 01795-580181 **Fax:** 01795-580649
E-mail: sales@sheppy.ltd.uk
Website: http://www.sheppy.ltd.uk
Directors: M. Dowling (Dir), C. Poynter (Co Sec), P. Stevens (MD)
Ultimate Holding Company: SHEPPY LIMITED
Immediate Holding Company: SHEPPY LIMITED
Registration no: 01543842 **VAT No.:** GB 209 7633 50
Date established: 1981 **Turnover:** £250,000 - £500,000
No.of Employees: 1 - 10 **Product Groups:** 32, 80

Date of Accounts	May 11	May 10	May 09
Sales Turnover	355	226	N/A
Pre Tax Profit/Loss	-329	709	N/A
Working Capital	5	1m	348
Fixed Assets	1m	1m	1m
Current Assets	2m	2m	1m
Current Liabilities	730	47	N/A

Ramsgate

Apex Networks Ltd
Dundee House 23-26 Albion Place, Ramsgate, CT11 8HQ
Tel: 08715-223141 **Fax:** 0870-330 3151
E-mail: info@apex-networks.com
Website: http://www.apex-networks.com

see next page

***Apex Networks Ltd** - Cont'd*

Directors: C. White (Tech Serv)
Immediate Holding Company: APEX NETWORKS LIMITED
Registration no: 05573440 **Date established:** 2005
Turnover: £250,000 - £500,000 **No.of Employees:** 11 - 20
Product Groups: 44

Date of Accounts	Sep 11	Sep 10	Sep 09
Working Capital	53	69	2
Fixed Assets	61	13	12
Current Assets	337	270	139

Bosuns Locker

10 Military Road The Royal Harbour, Ramsgate, CT11 9LG
Tel: 01843-597158 **Fax:** 01843-597158
E-mail: accounts@whitstablemarine.co.uk
Website: http://www.whitstablemarine.co.uk
Directors: J. Fry (Ptnr)
Immediate Holding Company: THE DINGHY STORE
VAT No.: GB 624 6062 56 **Turnover:** Up to £250,000
No.of Employees: 1 - 10 **Product Groups:** 28, 74

The Bubble Factory & Convertors Ltd

Unit 5 Thorne Farm Thorne Hill, Ramsgate, CT12 5DS
Tel: 01227-722228 **Fax:** 01227-722399
E-mail: thebubble.factory@yahoo.co.uk
Website: http://www.thebubblefactoryuk.co.uk
Directors: B. Newark (Dir)
Immediate Holding Company: THE BUBBLE FACTORY AND CONVERTERS LIMITED
Registration no: 04902949 **Date established:** 2003
Turnover: £500,000 - £1m **No.of Employees:** 1 - 10 **Product Groups:** 20, 23, 30, 31, 48, 66, 76

Date of Accounts	Oct 10	Oct 09	Oct 08
Working Capital	6	-10	48
Fixed Assets	3	11	20
Current Assets	162	132	156

Chaos Lighting

36 Hollicondane Road, Ramsgate, CT11 7PH
Tel: 01843-596997 **Fax:** 01843-596997
E-mail: russell@chaoslighting.co.uk
Website: http://www.chaoslighting.co.uk
Registration no: 07564142 **Turnover:** Up to £250,000
No.of Employees: 1 - 10 **Product Groups:** 35, 37, 52, 67, 84

Cummins Power Generation Ltd

Manston Park Columbus Avenue, Manston, Ramsgate, CT12 5BF
Tel: 01843-255000 **Fax:** 01843-255902
Website: http://www.cumminstower.com
Bank(s): National Westminster Bank Plc
Directors: J. Berenzweig (Co Sec), P. Jenson-Muir (Comm)
Ultimate Holding Company: CUMMINS INC (USA)
Immediate Holding Company: CUMMINS POWER GENERATION LIMITED
Registration no: 00262310 **VAT No.:** GB 285 6634 21
Date established: 1932 **Turnover:** £250m - £500m
No.of Employees: 501 - 1000 **Product Groups:** 37, 83

Date of Accounts	Dec 10	Dec 09	Dec 08
Sales Turnover	343m	261m	342m
Pre Tax Profit/Loss	43m	12m	75m
Working Capital	26m	39m	27m
Fixed Assets	25m	23m	24m
Current Assets	121m	165m	166m
Current Liabilities	18m	7m	32m

Edge Enviro Services Ltd

Meeting Street, Ramsgate, CT11 9RT
Tel: 01843-852216 **Fax:** 01843-852827
E-mail: contract@edge-enviro.com
Website: http://www.edge-enviro.com
Directors: G. Evans (Fin), N. Collingwood (MD)
Immediate Holding Company: EDGE ENVIRO SERVICES LIMITED
Registration no: 03167825 **Date established:** 1996
Turnover: Up to £250,000 **No.of Employees:** 1 - 10 **Product Groups:** 29, 32

Date of Accounts	Mar 11	Mar 10	Mar 09
Sales Turnover	127	155	152
Pre Tax Profit/Loss	-12	10	38
Working Capital	-5	24	34
Fixed Assets	6	10	12
Current Assets	81	95	123
Current Liabilities	12	12	11

Flambeau Europlast Ltd

Manston Road, Ramsgate, CT12 6HW
Tel: 01843-854000 **Fax:** 01843-854010
E-mail: jwingfield@flambeau.com
Website: http://www.flambeau.co.uk
Bank(s): ABN Amro
Directors: I. Maine (Fin), J. Wingfield (MD)
Managers: M. Carney
Ultimate Holding Company: NORDIC GROUP OF COMPANIES LTD (USA)
Immediate Holding Company: FLAMBEAU EUROPLAST LTD
Registration no: 01216092 **VAT No.:** GB 202 6624 01
Date established: 1975 **Turnover:** £10m - £20m
No.of Employees: 101 - 250 **Product Groups:** 30

Date of Accounts	Jun 12	Jun 09	Jun 10
Sales Turnover	11m	5m	5m
Pre Tax Profit/Loss	141	-2m	-370
Working Capital	3m	1m	3m
Fixed Assets	4m	4m	4m
Current Assets	5m	2m	6m
Current Liabilities	543	125	775

Graham

59-63 Hopes Lane, Ramsgate, CT12 6UW
Tel: 01843-591561 **Fax:** 01843-851893
Website: http://www.graham-group.co.uk
Directors: G. Lightside (Prop)
Immediate Holding Company: JEWSONS
Registration no: 00066738 **Turnover:** £10m - £20m
No.of Employees: 1 - 10 **Product Groups:** 66

Anthony Jenkins Fuel Oil Ltd

Oil Storage Depot Canterbury Road West, Cliffsend, Ramsgate, CT12 5DU
Tel: 01843-596431 **Fax:** 01843-590946
Directors: J. Jenkins (Co Sec), T. Cardy-jenkins (MD), T. Jenkins (MD)
Immediate Holding Company: ANTHONY JENKINS FUEL OIL LIMITED
Registration no: 01010021 **Date established:** 1971 **Turnover:** £2m - £5m
No.of Employees: 1 - 10 **Product Groups:** 77

Date of Accounts	Mar 12	Mar 11	Mar 10
Sales Turnover	4m	3m	2m
Pre Tax Profit/Loss	56	9	-91
Working Capital	18	-15	-37
Fixed Assets	163	169	182
Current Assets	961	534	567
Current Liabilities	217	119	152

Maycoil Ltd

3 Wilton Road, Ramsgate, CT12 5HG
Tel: 01843-570044 **Fax:** 01843-570055
E-mail: info@maycoil.com
Website: http://www.maycoil.com
Directors: T. Wilkinson (MD), P. Ruranski (Fin)
Immediate Holding Company: MAYCOIL LIMITED
Registration no: 03660029 **Date established:** 1998
No.of Employees: 11 - 20 **Product Groups:** 35, 39, 45

Date of Accounts	Nov 11	Nov 10	Nov 09
Working Capital	-0	23	41
Fixed Assets	20	15	18
Current Assets	168	181	281

F K Moore Ltd

5 Wilton Road Haine Industrial Park, Ramsgate, CT12 5HD
Tel: 01843-593440 **Fax:** 01843-585883
E-mail: sales@fkmoore.com
Website: http://www.fkmoore.com
Directors: A. Stokes (Dir)
Immediate Holding Company: F K MOORE LTD
Registration no: 07078799 **VAT No.:** GB 202 5289 91
Date established: 2009 **Turnover:** £500,000 - £1m
No.of Employees: 1 - 10 **Product Groups:** 35

Date of Accounts	Dec 11	Dec 10
Sales Turnover	644	449
Pre Tax Profit/Loss	239	211
Working Capital	69	-62
Fixed Assets	223	229
Current Assets	259	240
Current Liabilities	80	61

Orbit Import Export Ltd

Ferry Terminal, Ramsgate, CT11 9FT
Tel: 01843-588899 **Fax:** 01843-850278
E-mail: orbit@btclick.com
Website: http://www.orbitimpex.co.uk
Directors: L. Wilkins (MD)
Registration no: 03676211 **VAT No.:** GB 397 8983 56
Turnover: £250,000 - £500,000 **No.of Employees:** 1 - 10
Product Groups: 76

Ramsgate Marina Harbour Authority (a division of Thanet District Council)

Harbour Offices Military Road, Ramsgate, CT11 9LQ
Tel: 01843-572100 **Fax:** 01843-590941
E-mail: portoframsgate@thanet.gov.uk
Website: http://www.portoframsgate.co.uk
Bank(s): National Westminster
Managers: R. Brown
Immediate Holding Company: THANET DISTRICT COUNCIL
Date established: 1907 **Turnover:** £1m - £2m **No.of Employees:** 21 - 50
Product Groups: 71, 74

Steelcraft Steel Fabricators

Unit 5 Monkton Road, Minster, Ramsgate, CT12 4JB
Tel: 01843-823888
E-mail: info@steelcraft.net
Website: http://www.steelcraft.net
Directors: D. Town (Prop)
No.of Employees: 1 - 10 **Product Groups:** 35

Surin Restaurant

30 Harbour Street, Ramsgate, CT11 8HA
Tel: 01843-592001 **Fax:** 01843-592001
E-mail: info@surinrestaurant.co.uk
Website: http://www.surinrestaurant.co.uk
Directors: D. Garbutts (Prop)
Registration no: 0000 **Date established:** 2002
Turnover: £250,000 - £500,000 **No.of Employees:** 1 - 10
Product Groups: 69

Thanet Plastics

1 Wilton Road Haine Industrial Park, Ramsgate, CT12 5HG
Tel: 01843-590950 **Fax:** 01843-590948
E-mail: sales@thanetplastics.co.uk
Website: http://www.thanetplastics.co.uk
Bank(s): National Westminster Bank Plc
Directors: D. Tritton (Prop)
Immediate Holding Company: THANET PLASTICS LIMITED
Registration no: 06529976 **VAT No.:** GB 202 1146 36
Date established: 2008 **No.of Employees:** 11 - 20 **Product Groups:** 28, 30, 48

Date of Accounts	Mar 11	Mar 10	Mar 09
Working Capital	180	133	74
Fixed Assets	9	8	8
Current Assets	233	228	183

Trimfix Mouldings Ltd

11 Leigh Road, Ramsgate, CT12 5EU
Tel: 01843-585698 **Fax:** 01843-594351
Website: http://www.transfix-mouldings.co.uk
Directors: L. Russell (Fin), G. Vickers (Dir)
Immediate Holding Company: TRIMFIX LIMITED
Registration no: 02078997 **Date established:** 1986
No.of Employees: 11 - 20 **Product Groups:** 30

Date of Accounts	Apr 11	Apr 09	Apr 08
Working Capital	564	442	443
Fixed Assets	21	34	22
Current Assets	733	520	554

Universal Machining

Unit 1 Whitehall Industrial Estate Whitehall Road, Ramsgate, CT12 6BU
Tel: 01843-599799 **Fax:** 01843-599799
E-mail: user@universal111.wanadoo.co.uk
Website: http://www.universal111.wanadoo.co.uk
Directors: M. Russell (Prop)
Date established: 1998 **No.of Employees:** 1 - 10 **Product Groups:** 35

W W Martin

Dane Park Road, Ramsgate, CT11 7LT
Tel: 01843-591584 **Fax:** 01843-596333
E-mail: enquiries@wwmartin.co.uk
Website: http://www.wwmartin.co.uk
Directors: N. Peck (Dir)
Managers: L. Fox (Mgr)
Immediate Holding Company: WW MARTIN LTD
Registration no: 00504927 **VAT No.:** GB 201 4407 25
Date established: 1952 **Turnover:** £20m - £50m **No.of Employees:** 1 - 10
Product Groups: 52

Date of Accounts	Feb 12	Feb 11	Feb 10
Sales Turnover	23m	19m	21m
Pre Tax Profit/Loss	86	-582	-714
Working Capital	96	-56	454
Fixed Assets	656	726	1000
Current Assets	3m	4m	5m
Current Liabilities	353	426	867

Rochester

Acorn Storage Equipment

Vulcan House Crown Wharf Whitewall Way, Medway City Estate, Rochester, ME2 4EN
Tel: 01634-296927 **Fax:** 01634-710089
E-mail: enquiries@acorn-storage.co.uk
Website: http://www.acorn-storage.co.uk
Directors: N. Wood (Dir)
Ultimate Holding Company: ACORN STORAGE SOLUTIONS LIMITED
Immediate Holding Company: ACORN STORAGE EQUIPMENT LIMITED
Registration no: 02081324 **Date established:** 1986 **Turnover:** £1m - £2m
No.of Employees: 11 - 20 **Product Groups:** 26, 35, 39, 67

Date of Accounts	Oct 11	Oct 10	Oct 09
Sales Turnover	N/A	2m	N/A
Pre Tax Profit/Loss	N/A	42	N/A
Working Capital	62	88	152
Fixed Assets	48	19	32
Current Assets	495	717	466
Current Liabilities	N/A	297	29

Advanced Petroleum Installations

12 Linton Dann Close Hoo, Rochester, ME3 9DQ
Tel: 01634-256622
Directors: M. Perez (Prop)
Date established: 1987 **No.of Employees:** 1 - 10 **Product Groups:** 40

Advanced Power Components plc

Medway City Estate, Rochester, ME2 4DP
Tel: 01634-290588 **Fax:** 01634-719672
E-mail: sales@apc-plc.co.uk
Website: http://www.apc-plc.co.uk
Bank(s): Barclays
Directors: D. Brown (Co Sec), P. Lancaster (Chief Op Offcr), R. Smith (Fin)
Managers: M. Robinson, P. Dale (Sales Prom Mgr), R. Devall (Tech Serv Mgr)
Immediate Holding Company: ADVANCED POWER COMPONENTS PUBLIC LIMITED COMPANY
Registration no: 01635609 **Date established:** 1982
Turnover: £10m - £20m **No.of Employees:** 51 - 100 **Product Groups:** 37, 44

Date of Accounts	Aug 11	Aug 10	Aug 09
Sales Turnover	14m	13m	14m
Pre Tax Profit/Loss	402	247	-491
Working Capital	277	413	-100
Fixed Assets	3m	3m	3m
Current Assets	3m	4m	4m
Current Liabilities	819	540	995

Air Cool Systems UK

13 Lakeside Neptune Close, Medway City Estate, Rochester, ME2 4LT
Tel: 01732-321661 **Fax:** 01732-321417
E-mail: sales@aircoolsystemsuk.co.uk
Website: http://www.aircoolsystemsuk.co.uk
Directors: M. Stewart (Prop)
Immediate Holding Company: AIRCOOL SYSTEMS UK LLP
Registration no: OC346335 **Date established:** 2009
No.of Employees: 1 - 10 **Product Groups:** 52, 84

Date of Accounts	Jun 11
Working Capital	55
Fixed Assets	36
Current Assets	101

Airconaire Ltd

Unit 6 Deacon Trading Centre Knight Road, Rochester, ME2 2AU
Tel: 01634-711264 **Fax:** 01634-717100
E-mail: info@airconaire.co.uk
Website: http://www.airconaire.co.uk
Directors: D. Allen (Fin), R. Allen (Dir), R. Allen (Dir), J. Allen (Ch)
Managers: J. Smith (Chief Mgr)
Ultimate Holding Company: CANEX REFRIGERATION LIMITED
Immediate Holding Company: AIRCONAIRE LIMITED
Registration no: 01350457 **Date established:** 1978 **Turnover:** £1m - £2m
No.of Employees: 21 - 50 **Product Groups:** 52

Date of Accounts	Aug 11	Aug 10	Aug 09
Working Capital	-33	-99	-49
Fixed Assets	163	186	231
Current Assets	1m	2m	841

All Pulley & Gear Developments

1 Kenden Business Park Maritime Close, Medway City Estate, Rochester, ME2 4JF
Tel: 01634-722420 **Fax:** 01634-722460
E-mail: sales@apgdev.com
Website: http://www.apgdev.com
Directors: L. Maynard (Fin)
Immediate Holding Company: ALL PULLEY & GEAR DEVELOPMENTS LIMITED
Registration no: 03752576 **VAT No.:** GB 515 5037 69
Date established: 1999 **Turnover:** £500,000 - £1m
No.of Employees: 1 - 10 **Product Groups:** 25, 29, 30, 35, 38, 39, 40, 45, 48

Date of Accounts	Mar 12	Mar 11	Mar 10
Working Capital	136	132	100
Fixed Assets	85	64	68
Current Assets	293	285	271

Allied Fabrications
Unit 85 Kingsnorth Industrial Estate, Hoo, Rochester, ME3 9ND
Tel: 01634-255266 **Fax:** 01634-255277
E-mail: mike.alliedfabs@btconnect.com
Website: http://www.alliedfabs.com
Directors: M. Butler (Prop)
No.of Employees: 21 - 50 **Product Groups:** 35, 40, 48, 52

Amberwood Publishing Ltd
Unit 4 Stirling House, Sunderland Quay Culpeper Close, Medway City Estate, Rochester, ME2 4HN
Tel: 01634-290115 **Fax:** 01634-290761
E-mail: info@amberwoodpublishing.com
Website: http://www.amberwoodpublishing.com
Directors: J. Crisp (MD)
Registration no: 02609769 **VAT No.:** GB 580 0802 62
Date established: 1991 **Turnover:** Up to £250,000
No.of Employees: 1 - 10 **Product Groups:** 28

Date of Accounts	May 08	May 07	May 06
Sales Turnover	25	34	67
Pre Tax Profit/Loss	-7	-3	N/A
Working Capital	23	30	35
Fixed Assets	1	1	2
Current Assets	28	36	53
Current Liabilities	2	2	6

Aset UK Ltd Conveyor & Mechanical Engineers
Unit 32b Sir Thomas Longley Road, Medway City Estate, Rochester, ME2 4DP
Tel: 01634-780056
E-mail: info@asetukltd.co.uk
Website: http://www.asetukltd.co.uk
Directors: S. Allen (Dir)
Immediate Holding Company: ASET (UK) LIMITED
Registration no: 06654487 **Date established:** 2008
No.of Employees: 21 - 50 **Product Groups:** 29, 30, 31, 33, 35, 38, 39, 40, 41, 42, 44, 45, 48, 49, 67, 83, 84

Date of Accounts	Jul 11	Jul 10	Jul 09
Sales Turnover	N/A	980	628
Pre Tax Profit/Loss	N/A	161	188
Working Capital	2	41	40
Fixed Assets	32	36	47
Current Assets	211	97	200
Current Liabilities	N/A	55	115

Atrium Gantrys Maintenance Ltd
Unit 18 Lakeside Park Neptune Close Medway City Estate, Rochester, ME2 4LT
Tel: 01634-295429 **Fax:** 01634-711452
E-mail: martin@atriumgantrys.co.uk
Website: http://www.atriumgantrys.co.uk
Directors: M. Batts (Dir)
Managers: J. Travis (Chief Mgr)
Immediate Holding Company: ATRIUM GANTRYS MAINTENANCE LIMITED
Registration no: 02640993 **Date established:** 1991
No.of Employees: 11 - 20 **Product Groups:** 33, 39, 45

Date of Accounts	Dec 11	Dec 10	Dec 09
Working Capital	63	-3	33
Fixed Assets	125	48	3
Current Assets	390	367	249

B A E Systems Ltd (Environmental & E M C Test Centre)
Airport Works, Rochester, ME1 2XX
Tel: 01634-844400 **Fax:** 01634-203647
E-mail: frank.ewen@baesystems.com
Website: http://www.baesystems.com
Directors: A. Start (MD), A. Holding (MD)
Immediate Holding Company: MEDWAY INNOVATION LTD
Registration no: 01470151 **VAT No.:** GB 641 4071 69
Date established: 1995 **No.of Employees:** 1 - 10 **Product Groups:** 32, 37, 39, 84

B L Castings
1 Valley View Road, Rochester, ME1 3PB
Tel: 01634-848187
Directors: M. Haines (Fin), M. Haines (MD)
Registration no: 04901574 **No.of Employees:** 1 - 10 **Product Groups:** 34, 35, 49

B S K Laminating Ltd
Commissioners Road, Rochester, ME2 4ED
Tel: 01634-292700 **Fax:** 01634-291029
E-mail: mike.speller@bsk-laminating.com
Website: http://www.bsk-laminating.com
Directors: K. Travis (Sales & Mktg)
Managers: B. Chavda (Comptroller), M. Speller (Works Gen Mgr)
Immediate Holding Company: BSK LAMINATING LIMITED
Registration no: 05797955 **Date established:** 2006
Turnover: £10m - £20m **No.of Employees:** 21 - 50 **Product Groups:** 27, 28, 30, 31, 32, 48, 66

Date of Accounts	Oct 09	Oct 08	Apr 08
Working Capital	1	1	1
Current Assets	1	1	1

Bryant Electrical Ltd
3 Shamel Business Centre Commissioners Road, Rochester, ME2 4HQ
Tel: 01634-297211 **Fax:** 01634-226863
E-mail: paul@bryantelectrical.co.uk
Website: http://www.bryantelectrical.com
Directors: R. Bryant (MD)
Immediate Holding Company: BRYANT ELECTRICAL LIMITED
Registration no: 02301003 **Date established:** 1988
Turnover: £250,000 - £500,000 **No.of Employees:** 1 - 10
Product Groups: 38, 39, 42, 44, 48

Date of Accounts	Mar 11	Mar 10	Mar 09
Sales Turnover	N/A	N/A	345
Pre Tax Profit/Loss	N/A	N/A	-11
Working Capital	96	138	151
Fixed Assets	17	20	24
Current Assets	209	262	284

Calibre Ltd
68 Sir Evelyn Road, Rochester, ME1 3LZ
Tel: 01256-475588 **Fax:** 01256-475599
E-mail: info@rubberbands.co.uk
Website: http://www.rubberbands.co.uk
Directors: D. Langridge (Prop), H. Burp (MD)
Managers: A. Marshall (Sales Off Mgr), D. Tricker (Chief Acct)
Immediate Holding Company: Altamar One Ltd
Registration no: 05279382 **VAT No.:** GB 189 9705 90
Date established: 1966 **Turnover:** £1m - £2m **No.of Employees:** 1 - 10
Product Groups: 29

Cats & Canines
PO Box 76, Rochester, ME2 4LT
Tel: 01634-710099 **Fax:** 01634-715274
E-mail: enquiries@catsandcanines.co.uk
Website: http://www.catsandcanines.co.uk
Managers: S. Betts (Mgr), S. Betts (Chief Mgr)
Turnover: Up to £250,000 **No.of Employees:** 1 - 10 **Product Groups:** 49, 62

Chatham Clearance & Transport Ltd
Laser Quay Culpeper Close, Medway City Estate, Rochester, ME2 4HU
Tel: 01634-711969 **Fax:** 01634-718702
E-mail: sales@chathamclearance.com
Website: http://www.cctgroupltd.com
Directors: M. Denny (MD)
Managers: G. Leverett (Fin Mgr)
Immediate Holding Company: CHATHAM CLEARANCE & TRANSPORT LIMITED
Registration no: 01883102 **Date established:** 1985 **Turnover:** £2m - £5m
No.of Employees: 1 - 10 **Product Groups:** 75, 76

Date of Accounts	Mar 11	Mar 10	Mar 09
Working Capital	835	760	836
Fixed Assets	16	18	20
Current Assets	1m	954	1m

Clark Electric Clutch & Controls Ltd
Unit 28 Victory Park Trident Close Medway City Estate, Rochester, ME2 4ER
Tel: 01634-297408 **Fax:** 020-8660 8845
E-mail: sales@clarkelectric.co.uk
Website: http://www.clarkelectric.co.uk
Directors: J. Reavell (Dir)
Ultimate Holding Company: WAYSTAR HOLDINGS LIMITED
Immediate Holding Company: CLARK ELECTRIC CLUTCH & CONTROLS LIMITED
Registration no: 00679900 **VAT No.:** GB 209 6207 72
Date established: 1961 **Turnover:** Up to £250,000
No.of Employees: 1 - 10 **Product Groups:** 35, 37, 43, 44, 45

Date of Accounts	Dec 11	Dec 10	Dec 09
Sales Turnover	143	193	196
Pre Tax Profit/Loss	6	28	3
Working Capital	43	36	10
Fixed Assets	2	3	N/A
Current Assets	83	93	93
Current Liabilities	29	9	63

Clean Room Construction Ltd
Unit K1-K2 Temple Court Knight Road, Rochester, ME2 2LT
Tel: 01634-295111 **Fax:** 01634-294100
E-mail: slawton@crc-ltd.co.uk
Website: http://www.crc-ltd.co.uk
Bank(s): Lloyds TSB Bank plc
Directors: S. Lawton (MD)
Managers: M. Webb (Ops Mgr), S. George
Immediate Holding Company: CLEAN ROOM CONSTRUCTION LIMITED
Registration no: 01176933 **VAT No.:** GB 206 9521 69
Date established: 1974 **Turnover:** £2m - £5m **No.of Employees:** 21 - 50
Product Groups: 29, 38, 40, 52, 84

Date of Accounts	Dec 11	Dec 10	Dec 09
Working Capital	718	631	584
Fixed Assets	100	123	144
Current Assets	1m	2m	2m

Coercive Systems Ltd
Unit C9 Laser Quay Culpeper Close, Medway City Estate, Rochester, ME2 4HU
Tel: 01634-713053 **Fax:** 01634-712541
E-mail: csl@coercive.com
Website: http://www.coercive.com
Bank(s): HSBC Bank plc
Directors: S. Jim (Dir)
Ultimate Holding Company: COERCIVE GROUP LIMITED
Immediate Holding Company: COERCIVE SYSTEMS LIMITED
Registration no: 02723273 **Date established:** 1992 **Turnover:** £2m - £5m
No.of Employees: 11 - 20 **Product Groups:** 37, 39

Date of Accounts	Mar 11	Mar 10	Mar 09
Working Capital	1m	1m	1m
Fixed Assets	37	42	41
Current Assets	2m	2m	2m

Communications Centre International Ltd
55-56 Riverside Estate Sir Thomas Longley Road, Medway City Estate, Rochester, ME2 4DP
Tel: 01634-291191 **Fax:** 01634-723895
E-mail: peter.krovina@commscentre.com
Website: http://www.commcentre.com
Directors: P. Krovina (MD)
Managers: S. Reardon (Chief Acct)
Immediate Holding Company: COMMUNICATIONS CENTRE INTERNATIONAL LIMITED
Registration no: 02355286 **VAT No.:** GB 460 6470 53
Date established: 1989 **Turnover:** £10m - £20m
No.of Employees: 21 - 50 **Product Groups:** 37

Date of Accounts	Dec 11	Dec 10	Dec 09
Working Capital	1m	1m	1m
Fixed Assets	330	314	316
Current Assets	3m	3m	2m

Component Force Ltd
Unit 19 Laker Road, Rochester, ME1 3QX
Tel: 01634-686504 **Fax:** 01622-245888
E-mail: sales@componentforce.co.uk
Website: http://www.componentforce.co.uk
Directors: L. Gardner (Fin), P. Gardner (MD)
Managers: N. Burrow (Cust Serv Mgr)
Immediate Holding Company: COMPONENT FORCE LIMITED
Registration no: 04082393 **Date established:** 2000
No.of Employees: 21 - 50 **Product Groups:** 30

Date of Accounts	Oct 11	Oct 10	Oct 09
Working Capital	384	212	267
Fixed Assets	123	70	46
Current Assets	768	524	509

Constructional Services
641 Maidstone Road, Rochester, ME1 3QJ
Tel: 01634-814257 **Fax:** 01634- 829833
E-mail: concrete.lab@mowlem.com
Website: http://www.mowlem.com
Managers: M. Collier (District Mgr)
Ultimate Holding Company: MOWLEM P.L.C.
Immediate Holding Company: MOWLEM CIVIL ENGINEERING
Registration no: 00190862 **No.of Employees:** 11 - 20 **Product Groups:** 85

Cradletech P J P Services
Unit 2.8 Medway Enterprise Centre Enterprise Close, Medway City Estate, Rochester, ME2 4SY
Tel: 01634-724393 **Fax:** 01634-724699
E-mail: info@cradletech.co.uk
Website: http://www.pjpservices.co.uk
Directors: C. Coole (MD), J. Coole (Fin)
Ultimate Holding Company: CRADLETECH LTD.
Immediate Holding Company: PJP SERVICES LIMITED
Registration no: 02911119 **Date established:** 1994
Turnover: £250,000 - £500,000 **No.of Employees:** 1 - 10
Product Groups: 35, 39, 45

Date of Accounts	Mar 11	Mar 10	Mar 09
Working Capital	38	147	71
Fixed Assets	1	1	4
Current Assets	260	362	284

D S L Fabrication Ltd
Unit 4 Vicarage Lane Hoo, Rochester, ME3 9LB
Tel: 01634-253296 **Fax:** 01634-251667
E-mail: services@dslmetalwork.co.uk
Website: http://www.dslmetalwork.co.uk
Bank(s): HSBC Bank plc
Directors: P. Edwards (Dir), D. Lucas (MD)
Managers: M. Hessenthaler (Fin Mgr)
Immediate Holding Company: D S L (FABRICATION) LIMITED
Registration no: 03766174 **VAT No.:** GB 304 3902 91
Date established: 1999 **Turnover:** £500,000 - £1m
No.of Employees: 21 - 50 **Product Groups:** 35, 36, 48

Date of Accounts	May 11	May 10	May 09
Working Capital	16	-59	43
Fixed Assets	47	64	88
Current Assets	394	462	426

Diamond Point International Ltd
Suite 13 Ashford House Beaufort Court Sir Thomas Longley Road, Medway City Estate, Rochester, ME2 4FA
Tel: 01634-300900 **Fax:** 01634-722398
E-mail: sales@dpie.com
Website: http://www.dpie.com
Bank(s): National Westminster Bank Plc
Directors: J. Vaines (MD)
Immediate Holding Company: DIAMOND POINT INTERNATIONAL (EUROPE) LIMITED
Registration no: 02168609 **VAT No.:** GB 384 3226 49
Date established: 1987 **Turnover:** £5m - £10m **No.of Employees:** 11 - 20
Product Groups: 44

Date of Accounts	Nov 11	Nov 10	Nov 09
Sales Turnover	5m	3m	2m
Pre Tax Profit/Loss	310	147	19
Working Capital	899	935	908
Fixed Assets	11	14	13
Current Assets	2m	1m	1m
Current Liabilities	671	149	24

Electraweld Ltd
Unit 1 Maritime Close Medway City Estate, Rochester, ME2 4AZ
Tel: 01634-291000 **Fax:** 01634-291004
E-mail: dale@theweld.fsnet.co.uk
Website: http://www.electraweld.co.uk
Directors: A. Westcott (MD)
Immediate Holding Company: ELECTRAWELD LIMITED
Registration no: 02654335 **VAT No.:** GB 573 7844 82
Date established: 1991 **Turnover:** £1m - £2m **No.of Employees:** 1 - 10
Product Groups: 24, 30, 32, 33, 34, 35, 37, 38, 40, 46, 85

Date of Accounts	Dec 11	Dec 10	Dec 09
Sales Turnover	N/A	1m	N/A
Pre Tax Profit/Loss	N/A	8	N/A
Working Capital	-18	56	56
Fixed Assets	35	29	36
Current Assets	249	306	254
Current Liabilities	N/A	32	N/A

Emkay Screw Supplies
74 Pepys Way Strood, Rochester, ME2 3LL
Tel: 01634-717256 **Fax:** 01634-717256
E-mail: emkaysupplies@talktalk.net
Website: http://www.emkaysupplies.co.uk
Directors: M. Kirsopp (Prop)
Date established: 1989 **Turnover:** Up to £250,000
No.of Employees: 1 - 10 **Product Groups:** 35

First Light London
9 Laker Road Rochester Airport Industrial Estate, Rochester, ME1 3QX
Tel: 01634-685500 **Fax:** 01634-685544
E-mail: info@firstlightlondon.co.uk
Website: http://www.mobideque.co.uk
Directors: D. Chapman (MD)
Immediate Holding Company: FIRST LIGHT (LONDON) LIMITED
Registration no: 03346497 **Date established:** 1997
No.of Employees: 1 - 10 **Product Groups:** 89

Date of Accounts	Apr 07	Apr 06
Working Capital	-47	-62
Fixed Assets	38	34
Current Assets	11	3
Current Liabilities	58	65

Fleet Design
Fleet House Upnor Road, Upnor, Rochester, ME2 4UP
Tel: 01634-294466
E-mail: chris@fleetdesign.com
Website: http://www.fleetdesign.com
Directors: C. Bentley (Head)
Immediate Holding Company: COLOUR MACHINE LTD.
Registration no: 03444951 **VAT No.:** GB 303 8498 53
Date established: 1997 **Turnover:** £250,000 - £500,000
No.of Employees: 1 - 10 **Product Groups:** 28, 81

Fleurwrap Ltd
Unit J2 Cuxton Industrial Estate Station Road, Cuxton, Rochester, ME2 1AJ
Tel: 01634-294091 **Fax:** 01634-295980
E-mail: sales@fleurwrap.co.uk
Website: http://www.fleurwrap.co.uk
Managers: M. Stevenson (Product)
Ultimate Holding Company: MEESDEN PROPERTIES LTD (ISLE OF MAN)
Immediate Holding Company: FLEURWRAP LIMITED
Registration no: 03679082 **Date established:** 1998
Turnover: £250,000 - £500,000 **No.of Employees:** 1 - 10
Product Groups: 38, 42

Date of Accounts	Mar 09	Mar 08	Jun 11
Sales Turnover	N/A	N/A	371
Pre Tax Profit/Loss	N/A	N/A	-12
Working Capital	-77	-40	-79
Fixed Assets	45	49	40
Current Assets	93	107	136
Current Liabilities	N/A	N/A	32

G S Polishing
Vicarage Lane Hoo, Rochester, ME3 9LB
Tel: 01634-251747
E-mail: gavin@gsowtr.orangehome.co.uk
Website: http://www.gspolishing.co.uk
Directors: G. Sowter (Prop)
Immediate Holding Company: CLEAN IMAGE SERVICING LIMITED
Registration no: 05577779 **Date established:** 2005 **Turnover:** £2m - £5m
No.of Employees: 1 - 10 **Product Groups:** 35

Date of Accounts	Sep 11	Sep 10	Sep 09
Sales Turnover	75	73	76
Pre Tax Profit/Loss	70	67	74
Working Capital	20	19	20
Fixed Assets	600	600	600
Current Assets	55	39	62
Current Liabilities	35	21	23

The Generator Company (Power Generation)
Unit 12 Stirling Park Laker Road, Rochester, ME1 3QR
Tel: 01634-668090 **Fax:** 01634-687039
E-mail: sales@tgc.uk.com
Website: http://www.tgc.uk.com
Directors: S. Allen (Pers), J. Stickings (MD)
Managers: T. Rodwell
Immediate Holding Company: TGC INTERNATIONAL LIMITED
Registration no: 04171318 **Date established:** 2001
No.of Employees: 21 - 50 **Product Groups:** 83

Date of Accounts	Mar 11	Mar 10	Mar 09
Working Capital	258	149	568
Fixed Assets	3m	2m	2m
Current Assets	3m	3m	2m

Global Translators UK Ltd
21 Jiniwin Road, Rochester, ME1 2DJ
Tel: 07854-169165 **Fax:** 01634-408040
E-mail: info@globaltranslators.co.uk
Website: http://www.globaltranslators.co.uk
Directors: M. Kaur (MD)
Immediate Holding Company: GLOBAL TRANSLATORS UK LTD
Registration no: 05918745 **Date established:** 2006
Turnover: Up to £250,000 **No.of Employees:** 1 - 10 **Product Groups:** 80

Date of Accounts	Aug 11	Aug 10	Aug 08
Working Capital	-2	N/A	-0
Fixed Assets	1	1	N/A
Current Assets	7	1	N/A

Gravesend Marine Ltd
Unit 14 Central Business Park Neptune Close, Medway City Estate, Rochester, ME2 4LW
Tel: 01634-296859 **Fax:** 01634-295822
E-mail: sales@gravesendmarine.com
Website: http://www.gravesendmarine.co.uk
Directors: J. Park (MD)
Immediate Holding Company: GRAVESEND MARINE LIMITED
Registration no: 01734560 **Date established:** 1983
No.of Employees: 1 - 10 **Product Groups:** 35, 36, 39

Date of Accounts	Jun 11	Jun 10	Jun 09
Working Capital	54	23	12
Fixed Assets	8	10	8
Current Assets	440	394	371

Hotchkiss Air Supply
2 Stirling Park Laker Road, Rochester, ME1 3QR
Tel: 01634-672730 **Fax:** 01634-686290
E-mail: hphilpott@hotchkissairsupply.co.uk
Website: http://www.hotchkissairsupply.co.uk
Managers: H. Philpott (Sales Prom Mgr)
Date established: 2002 **No.of Employees:** 1 - 10 **Product Groups:** 37, 40, 48

Hydraulic & Engineering Services Ltd
Unit 5-7 Victory Park Trident Close Medway City Estate, Rochester, ME2 4ER
Tel: 01634-295650 **Fax:** 01634-295670
E-mail: info@hydraulicandengineering.co.uk
Website: http://www.hydraulicandengineering.co.uk
Bank(s): HSBC Bank plc
Directors: S. Matthews (MD), A. Bute (Dir)
Managers: L. Morris
Immediate Holding Company: HYDRAULIC & ENGINEERING SERVICES LIMITED
Registration no: 02632578 **VAT No.:** GB 583 1866 13
Date established: 1991 **Turnover:** £1m - £2m **No.of Employees:** 21 - 50
Product Groups: 29, 36, 38, 40, 45, 48, 67, 85

Date of Accounts	Jun 11	Jun 10	Jun 09
Working Capital	140	142	88
Fixed Assets	64	51	79
Current Assets	520	370	338

Hydrotech Systems Ltd
Unit 11d Vicarage Lane Hoo, Rochester, ME3 9LB
Tel: 01634-252265 **Fax:** 01634-250755
E-mail: info@hydrotechsystemsltd.co.uk
Website: http://www.hydrotechsystems.eu
Directors: B. Chamberlain (MD)
Immediate Holding Company: HYDROTECH SYSTEMS LIMITED
Registration no: 01784422 **VAT No.:** GB 386 2251 43
Date established: 1984 **No.of Employees:** 1 - 10 **Product Groups:** 40, 46

Date of Accounts	Mar 10	Mar 09	Mar 08
Working Capital	-102	-111	-86
Fixed Assets	N/A	N/A	9
Current Assets	24	N/A	38

I C M Plastic Moulding Ltd
Enterprise Close Medway City Estate, Rochester, ME2 4LY
Tel: 01634-298500 **Fax:** 01634-714338
E-mail: info@icm-plasticmoulding.co.uk
Website: http://www.icm-plasticmoulding.co.uk
Bank(s): Lloyds TSB Bank plc
Directors: G. Goodhew (Sales & Mktg), R. Carter (Fin), G. Goodhew (Sales & Mktg)
Managers: M. Mitchelson (Comm)
Ultimate Holding Company: MERRIOTT PLASTICS LIMITED
Immediate Holding Company: ICM (PLASTIC MOULDING) LIMITED
Registration no: 04710572 **VAT No.:** GB 725 5021 61
Date established: 2003 **Turnover:** £5m - £10m
No.of Employees: 51 - 100 **Product Groups:** 30, 48

Date of Accounts	Mar 11	Mar 10	Mar 09
Working Capital	625	445	381
Fixed Assets	339	321	351
Current Assets	1m	1m	1m

Lift Support Services
Unit 11a Vicarage Lane Hoo, Rochester, ME3 9LB
Tel: 01634-255600 **Fax:** 01634-253112
Directors: M. Sheen (Prop)
Immediate Holding Company: CLEAN IMAGE SERVICING LIMITED
Registration no: 05577779 **Date established:** 2005 **Turnover:** £2m - £5m
No.of Employees: 1 - 10 **Product Groups:** 35, 39, 45

Date of Accounts	Sep 11	Sep 10	Sep 09
Sales Turnover	75	73	76
Pre Tax Profit/Loss	70	67	74
Working Capital	20	19	20
Fixed Assets	600	600	600
Current Assets	55	39	62
Current Liabilities	35	21	23

M I T Publishing Ltd
375 High Street, Rochester, ME1 1DA
Tel: 01634-830566 **Fax:** 01634-408488
E-mail: circulation@pesmag.co.uk
Website: http://www.aero-mag.com
Directors: D. Rose (Dir)
Immediate Holding Company: M.I.T. PUBLISHING LIMITED
Registration no: 03582315 **Date established:** 1998
No.of Employees: 11 - 20 **Product Groups:** 28, 87

Date of Accounts	Mar 12	Mar 11	Mar 10
Working Capital	325	193	184
Fixed Assets	80	58	77
Current Assets	669	410	356

Marina Mill
Cuxton Marina Station Road, Cuxton, Rochester, ME2 1AB
Tel: 01634-718871 **Fax:** 01634-714082
E-mail: info@marinamill.co.uk
Website: http://www.marinamill.co.uk
Directors: K. Rawkins (MD)
Managers: B. Crowhurst (Comptroller)
Immediate Holding Company: MARINAMILL LIMITED
Registration no: 02579849 **Date established:** 1991
No.of Employees: 11 - 20 **Product Groups:** 23, 84

Date of Accounts	Jul 11	Jul 10	Jul 09
Working Capital	193	195	186
Fixed Assets	7	13	18
Current Assets	329	300	270

Martinair Compressors
Unit 7 Enterprise Business Estate Whitewall Road, Medway City Estate, Rochester, ME2 4LQ
Tel: 01474-322737
E-mail: sales@martinairltd.com
Website: http://www.martinairltd.com
Directors: D. Rathburn (Fin), M. Rathburn (MD)
Immediate Holding Company: MARTINAIR COMPRESSORS LIMITED
Registration no: 04947434 **Date established:** 2003
No.of Employees: 1 - 10 **Product Groups:** 40, 67, 68

Date of Accounts	Nov 11	Nov 10	Nov 09
Working Capital	68	62	50
Fixed Assets	17	10	23
Current Assets	94	87	75

Masterhitch Europe Ltd
The Whitewall Centre Whitewall Road, Medway City Estate, Rochester, ME2 4DZ
Tel: 01634-290022 **Fax:** 01634-290024
E-mail: michael.wright@masterhitch.co.uk
Website: http://www.masterhitch.co.uk
Directors: M. Wright (Fin), N. Davis (MD)
Ultimate Holding Company: H.E. GROUP LTD
Immediate Holding Company: MASTERHITCH EUROPE LIMITED
Registration no: 02949004 **Date established:** 1994
No.of Employees: 11 - 20 **Product Groups:** 45

Date of Accounts	May 11	May 10	May 09
Working Capital	17	5	115
Fixed Assets	2	N/A	21
Current Assets	763	734	764

Medway Sling Company
Knight Road, Rochester, ME2 2AH
Tel: 01634-726400 **Fax:** 01634-726420
E-mail: sales@medwayslingcompany.co.uk
Website: http://www.medwayslingcompany.co.uk
Bank(s): National Westminster Bank Plc
Directors: E. Ashworth (MD)
Immediate Holding Company: MEDWAY SLING COMPANY MKT LIMITED
Registration no: 03217537 **VAT No.:** GB 662 1634 46
Date established: 1996 **Turnover:** £1m - £2m **No.of Employees:** 11 - 20
Product Groups: 23, 24, 35, 45, 66

Date of Accounts	Mar 12	Mar 11	Mar 10
Working Capital	71	67	109
Fixed Assets	66	89	39
Current Assets	242	258	239

Microformat UK Ltd
344 High Street, Rochester, ME1 1JE
Tel: 01634-813751 **Fax:** 01634-831557
E-mail: enquiries@microformat.co.uk
Website: http://www.microformat.co.uk
Directors: D. Chapman (MD), A. Murrin (MD)
Managers: M. Krolewiak (Personnel)
Ultimate Holding Company: MICROFORMAT GROUP BV (NETHERLANDS)
Immediate Holding Company: MICROFORMAT (UK) LIMITED
Registration no: 01021877 **Date established:** 1971
Turnover: £500,000 - £1m **No.of Employees:** 21 - 50
Product Groups: 38, 44

Date of Accounts	Dec 11	Dec 10	Dec 09
Sales Turnover	808	1m	2m
Pre Tax Profit/Loss	-450	-194	25
Working Capital	-134	291	445
Fixed Assets	549	142	179
Current Assets	296	424	623
Current Liabilities	99	50	78

N T A Monitor Ltd
14 Ashford House Beaufort Court Sir Thomas Longley Road, Medway City Estate, Rochester, ME2 4FA
Tel: 01634-721855 **Fax:** 01634-721844
E-mail: sales@nta-monitor.com
Website: http://www.nta-monitor.com
Directors: J. Hills (Fin), R. Hills (Tech Serv)
Immediate Holding Company: N T A MONITOR LIMITED
Registration no: 03297071 **Date established:** 1996
No.of Employees: 21 - 50 **Product Groups:** 44

Date of Accounts	Dec 11	Dec 10	Dec 09
Working Capital	498	337	296
Fixed Assets	296	299	267
Current Assets	750	598	555

P & W Nash Engineering Services Ltd
Vicarage Lane Hoo, Rochester, ME3 9LB
Tel: 01634-250986 **Fax:** 01634-251027
E-mail: sales@pwnash.co.uk
Website: http://www.pwnash.co.uk
Bank(s): National Westminster
Directors: S. Beaney (Prop), W. Nash (Co Sec)
Immediate Holding Company: P. & W. NASH (ENGINEERING SERVICES) LIMITED
Registration no: 02544800 **VAT No.:** GB 573 5327 30
Date established: 1990 **Turnover:** £1m - £2m **No.of Employees:** 11 - 20
Product Groups: 48

Date of Accounts	Sep 11	Sep 10	Sep 09
Sales Turnover	2m	2m	2m
Pre Tax Profit/Loss	118	149	165
Working Capital	612	516	538
Fixed Assets	89	113	127
Current Assets	942	789	769
Current Liabilities	172	131	85

Nestledown Beds
Knight Road, Rochester, ME2 2BP
Tel: 01634-723557 **Fax:** 01634-290257
E-mail: k.foulstone@simmonsbeds.co.uk
Website: http://www.nestledown.co.uk
Directors: K. Foulstone (Ch)
Ultimate Holding Company: CAUVAL INDUSTRIES SA (FRANCE)
Immediate Holding Company: NESTLEDOWN BEDS LIMITED
Registration no: 01478223 **Date established:** 1980
Turnover: £20m - £50m **No.of Employees:** 21 - 50 **Product Groups:** 26

Date of Accounts	Dec 11	Dec 10	Dec 09
Sales Turnover	9m	13m	14m
Pre Tax Profit/Loss	-2m	1	22
Working Capital	1m	-1m	-2m
Fixed Assets	636	505	599
Current Assets	12m	3m	4m
Current Liabilities	3m	657	652

New Phoenix Engineering Ltd
Unit 6a Nuralite Industrial Centre Canal Road, Higham, Rochester, ME3 7JA
Tel: 020-8663 6444
E-mail: steve@foxplating.co.uk
Website: http://www.newphoenixengineering.co.uk
Directors: S. Fox (MD), C. Briley (Fin)
Immediate Holding Company: NEW PHOENIX DEVELOPMENTS & ENGINEERING COMPANY LIMITED
Registration no: 00903222 **Date established:** 1967
No.of Employees: 1 - 10 **Product Groups:** 46, 48

Date of Accounts	Apr 11	Apr 10	Apr 09
Working Capital	29	3	10
Fixed Assets	9	8	17
Current Assets	44	22	29

P S I Euro Ltd
Unit 1.54 Medway Enterprise Centre Enterprise Close, Medway City Estate, Rochester, ME2 4SY
Tel: 01634-293054 **Fax:** 01634-713576
E-mail: psi@medwayenterprisecentre.co.uk
Website: http://www.medwayenterprisecentre.co.uk
Directors: J. Fewtrell (Dir)
Immediate Holding Company: QUATRO PRODUCTIONS LIMITED
Registration no: 02800958 **Date established:** 2008
No.of Employees: 1 - 10 **Product Groups:** 37

Date of Accounts	Dec 11	Dec 10	Dec 09
Sales Turnover	N/A	N/A	159
Pre Tax Profit/Loss	N/A	N/A	-19
Working Capital	4	6	-42
Fixed Assets	83	85	88
Current Assets	32	30	15
Current Liabilities	N/A	N/A	29

Palatine Precision Ltd
Airport Industrial Estate 45 Laker Road, Rochester, ME1 3QX
Tel: 01634-684571 **Fax:** 01634-200836
E-mail: sales@palatineprecision.co.uk
Website: http://www.palatineprecision.co.uk
Directors: C. Thomas (Fin), G. Thomas (MD)
Immediate Holding Company: PALATINE PRECISION LIMITED
Registration no: 00883226 **Date established:** 1966
Turnover: £500,000 - £1m **No.of Employees:** 11 - 20
Product Groups: 36, 40, 42

Date of Accounts	Oct 11	Oct 10	Oct 09
Working Capital	912	650	540
Fixed Assets	454	471	484
Current Assets	1m	963	738

Prior Packaging Ltd
Unit 87 Riverside Estate Sir Thomas Longley Road, Medway City Estate, Rochester, ME2 4BH
Tel: 01634-720222 **Fax:** 01634-720030
E-mail: sales@priorpackaging.com
Website: http://www.priorpackaging.com
Directors: R. Commissar (MD)
Ultimate Holding Company: PRIOR PACKAGING (HOLDINGS) LIMITED
Immediate Holding Company: PRIOR PACKAGING LIMITED
Registration no: 00966207 **Date established:** 1969 **Turnover:** £1m - £2m
No.of Employees: 1 - 10 **Product Groups:** 49, 84, 85

Date of Accounts	Sep 11	Sep 10	Sep 09
Working Capital	-9	43	70
Fixed Assets	14	16	18
Current Assets	266	351	339

Professional Technology UK Ltd
375 High Street, Rochester, ME1 1DA
Tel: 01634-815517 **Fax:** 01634-829032
E-mail: info@ptuk.co.uk
Website: http://www.ptuk.co.uk
Directors: C. Cunningham (Fin)
Immediate Holding Company: PROFESSIONAL TECHNOLOGY (UK) LTD
Registration no: 02026355 **VAT No.:** GB 445 8413 39
Date established: 1986 **No.of Employees:** 1 - 10 **Product Groups:** 28, 44

Date of Accounts	Jul 11	Jul 10	Jul 09
Working Capital	-12	-4	-3
Fixed Assets	14	20	11
Current Assets	37	33	23

R D Fabrications
Church Street Higham, Rochester, ME3 7LD
Tel: 01474-822166
Directors: R. Jones (Ptnr)
Date established: 2003 **No.of Employees:** 1 - 10 **Product Groups:** 35

G R Roberts & Son
Unit 7 Shamel Business Centre Commissioners Road, Rochester, ME2 4HQ
Tel: 01634-291340 **Fax:** 01634-291340
Directors: M. Roberts (Prop), M. Roberts (Prop)
Date established: 1990 **No.of Employees:** 1 - 10 **Product Groups:** 35

Rochester City Diesel
Miles Place, Rochester, ME1 2EW
Tel: 01634-813305 **Fax:** 01634-813305
Directors: P. Cross (Prop)
Date established: 1994 **No.of Employees:** 1 - 10 **Product Groups:** 40

Sandhurst Plant Ltd
Medway City Estate Enterprise Close, Rochester, ME2 4JW
Tel: 01634-739590 **Fax:** 0845-1206644
E-mail: info@sandhurst.co.uk
Website: http://www.sandhurst.co.uk
Directors: T. Dean (MD), P. Dean (Dir), J. Alison (Prop)
Managers: J. Young (Comptroller), D. Wong (I.T. Exec)
Immediate Holding Company: SANDHURST ON POWER LIMITED
Registration no: 02743466 **Date established:** 1992
No.of Employees: 11 - 20 **Product Groups:** 36, 37, 45

Date of Accounts	May 10	May 09
Working Capital	N/A	-154
Fixed Assets	3	303
Current Assets	42	43
Current Liabilities	42	N/A

V Scott
Unit 32 Nuralite Industrial Centre Canal Road, Higham, Rochester, ME3 7JA
Tel: 01474-824606 **Fax:** 01474-824606
Directors: V. Scott (Prop)
Immediate Holding Company: MEDWAY ULTRASONICS LIMITED
Registration no: 03080045 **Date established:** 1995
No.of Employees: 1 - 10 **Product Groups:** 35

Date of Accounts	Mar 11	Mar 10	Mar 09
Working Capital	18	14	12
Fixed Assets	38	42	51
Current Assets	23	17	14

Segezha Packaging
Priory Road, Rochester, ME2 2BD
Tel: 01634-716701 **Fax:** 01634-717468
E-mail: uk@segezha-packaging.com
Website: http://www.segezha-packaging.com
Managers: P. Crawley
Immediate Holding Company: SWAIN CONTRACTS LIMITED
Registration no: 05545888 **Date established:** 2009
Turnover: Up to £250,000 **No.of Employees:** 1 - 10 **Product Groups:** 27

Ships Electronic Services Ltd
Chichester House Waterside Court Neptune Way, Medway City Estate, Rochester, ME2 4NZ
Tel: 01634-295500 **Fax:** 01634-295537
E-mail: sales@ses-marine.com
Website: http://www.ses-marine.com
Bank(s): HSBC
Directors: P. Rees (Dir), S. Roper (MD), L. Murray (Co Sec)
Ultimate Holding Company: TICKETCOUCH LIMITED
Immediate Holding Company: SHIPS ELECTRONIC SERVICES LIMITED
Registration no: 01165320 **VAT No.:** GB 204 3833 92
Date established: 1974 **Turnover:** £5m - £10m **No.of Employees:** 21 - 50
Product Groups: 84

Date of Accounts	Dec 11	Dec 10	Dec 09
Sales Turnover	6m	5m	5m
Pre Tax Profit/Loss	294	353	305
Working Capital	972	776	511
Fixed Assets	70	83	88
Current Assets	2m	2m	1m
Current Liabilities	656	452	412

Smile Design Ltd
Unit 66 Riverside Estate Sir Thomas Longley Road Medway City Estate, Rochester, ME2 4BH
Tel: 01634-295557
Website: http://www.smiledesignltd.co.uk
Directors: P. Dumpleton (MD)
Immediate Holding Company: SMILE DESIGN LTD
Registration no: 04188134 **Date established:** 2001
No.of Employees: 11 - 20 **Product Groups:** 38, 88

Date of Accounts	Mar 11	Mar 10	Mar 09
Working Capital	31	30	35
Fixed Assets	28	35	42
Current Assets	87	88	104

Source It 4 Me Limited
156 Enterprise Centre Medway City Estate, Rochester, ME2 4SY
Tel: 01634-294432 **Fax:** 01634-294489
E-mail: steve.farrin@sourceit4me.co.uk
Product Groups: 25, 30, 33, 35, 36, 40, 66, 67, 81

Date of Accounts	Mar 08	Mar 07	Mar 06
Sales Turnover	324	218	N/A
Working Capital	-3	7	-7
Fixed Assets	13	7	1
Current Assets	84	47	16
Current Liabilities	N/A	N/A	5

Stangard Food Service Equipment Ltd
Suite A Vaillant House Trident Close, Medway City Estate, Rochester, ME2 4EZ
Tel: 01634-714141 **Fax:** 01634-714171
E-mail: enquiries@stangard.org
Website: http://www.stangard.org
Directors: R. Pucknell (MD)
Immediate Holding Company: STANGARD FOOD SERVICE EQUIPMENT LIMITED
Registration no: 03712830 **VAT No.:** GB 232 2014 27
Date established: 1999 **Turnover:** £5m - £10m **No.of Employees:** 1 - 10
Product Groups: 36, 40, 69

Date of Accounts	May 12	May 11	May 10
Working Capital	208	211	222
Fixed Assets	20	16	11
Current Assets	773	809	523

Sundridge Holdings
Vicarage Lane Hoo, Rochester, ME3 9LB
Tel: 01634-252104 **Fax:** 01634-250820
E-mail: sales@sundridge.co.uk
Website: http://www.sundridge.co.uk
Directors: J. Carroll (MD), J. Carrolle (MD), J. Carroll (Prop)
Managers: J. Stephens (Personnel)
Immediate Holding Company: SUNDRIDGE HOLDINGS LIMITED
Registration no: 01783754 **VAT No.:** GB 304 3713 94
Date established: 1984 **Turnover:** £500,000 - £1m
No.of Employees: 1 - 10 **Product Groups:** 24

Date of Accounts	May 11	May 10	May 09
Working Capital	378	190	188
Fixed Assets	23	25	24
Current Assets	873	717	952

T L C
3 Bergland Park Maritime Close, Medway City Estate, Rochester, ME2 4AD
Tel: 01634-711712 **Fax:** 01634-710666
E-mail: tlc@mw.vianw.co.uk
Website: http://www.tlc-direct.co.uk
Managers: T. Kurby (Mgr)
Date established: 1997 **No.of Employees:** 1 - 10 **Product Groups:** 36, 40

Teleporters Ltd
Higham Hall Farm (not Farmhouse) Taylors Lane, Rochester, ME3 7JU
Tel: 0845-4681325
E-mail: service@teleporters.co.uk
Website: http://www.teleporters.co.uk
Managers: D. Rochester ()
Registration no: 05454562 **Date established:** 2005
Turnover: Up to £250,000 **No.of Employees:** 1 - 10 **Product Groups:** 72

Date of Accounts	Mar 10	Mar 09	Mar 08
Working Capital	-33	-22	-23
Fixed Assets	3	4	5
Current Assets	2	1	1

Telspec plc
Lancaster Parker Road, Rochester, ME1 3QU
Tel: 01634-687133 **Fax:** 01634-684984
E-mail: fred.white@telspec.co.uk
Website: http://www.telspec.co.uk
Directors: F. White (Fin), J. May (Grp Sales), P. Thorpe (Grp Chief Exec)
Managers: J. Stephens (Mktg Serv Mgr), M. Sherwood (Comm), B. Deadman (Sales Admin)
Immediate Holding Company: TELSPEC EUROPE LIMITED
Registration no: 01227664 **Date established:** 1975
Turnover: Up to £250,000 **No.of Employees:** 11 - 20 **Product Groups:** 37, 38, 48, 79, 80, 84

Date of Accounts	Dec 07	Dec 06
Sales Turnover	3440	5870
Pre Tax Profit/Loss	-670	-1920
Working Capital	3840	2780
Fixed Assets	10	1770
Current Assets	4630	5060
Current Liabilities	790	2280
Total Share Capital	10130	10130
ROCE% (Return on Capital Employed)	-17.4	-42.2
ROT% (Return on Turnover)	-19.5	-32.7

Thermoseal Group Ltd
G 1 Unit Knights Park Industrial Estate Knight Road, Rochester, ME2 2LS
Tel: 01634-290240 **Fax:** 01634-724732
E-mail: sales@thermosealgroup.com
Website: http://www.thermosealgroup.com
Managers: M. Freeman (District Mgr)
Immediate Holding Company: THERMOSEAL GROUP LIMITED
Registration no: 01705619 **Date established:** 1983
No.of Employees: 11 - 20 **Product Groups:** 32, 33, 34

Date of Accounts	Dec 11	Dec 10	Dec 09
Sales Turnover	21m	19m	16m
Pre Tax Profit/Loss	2m	932	1m
Working Capital	7m	6m	5m
Fixed Assets	1m	1m	717
Current Assets	11m	10m	8m
Current Liabilities	1m	941	891

Tony Zemaitis Associates Ltd
278 City Way, Rochester, ME1 2BL
Tel: 01634-404903 **Fax:** 01634-404903
E-mail: info@zemaitis-uk.com
Website: http://www.zemaitis-uk.com
Directors: T. Zemaitis (Dir)
Immediate Holding Company: TONY ZEMAITIS ASSOCIATES LIMITED
Registration no: 04922784 **Date established:** 2003
No.of Employees: 1 - 10 **Product Groups:** 81

Date of Accounts	Oct 11	Oct 10	Oct 08
Working Capital	3	2	3
Fixed Assets	N/A	1	1
Current Assets	20	15	24

Totslots
14 The Braes Higham, Rochester, ME3 7NA
Tel: 0781-014 3381
E-mail: enquiries@totslots.co.uk
Website: http://www.totslots.co.uk
Directors: C. Bevan (Prop)
Date established: 2007 **Turnover:** Up to £250,000
No.of Employees: 1 - 10 **Product Groups:** 22, 40, 61

Ultrasonics Medway Ltd
Unit 15e Nuralite Industrial Centre, Higham, Rochester, ME3 7JA
Tel: 01474-824666 **Fax:** 01474-824770
E-mail: info@ultrasonic.co.uk
Website: http://www.ultrasonic.co.uk
Directors: C. Wallace (MD)
Immediate Holding Company: ULTRASONICS (MEDWAY) LIMITED
Registration no: 06119334 **Date established:** 2007
No.of Employees: 1 - 10 **Product Groups:** 38, 42, 48

Date of Accounts	Feb 08	Feb 10	Feb 09
Working Capital	22	43	45
Fixed Assets	61	77	84
Current Assets	38	49	55

Uniflo Systems Ltd
9 Neptune Industrial Estate Neptune Close, Medway City Estate, Rochester, ME2 4LT
Tel: 01634-716117 **Fax:** 01634-290235
E-mail: winifred.betts@uniflo.co.uk
Website: http://www.uniflow.co.uk
Directors: A. Betts (Prop), W. Betts (Fin)
Immediate Holding Company: AIRCOOL SYSTEMS UK LLP
Registration no: 02028423 **Date established:** 2009
Turnover: £500,000 - £1m **No.of Employees:** 21 - 50 **Product Groups:** 40

Date of Accounts	Mar 06	Mar 05	Mar 04
Working Capital	10	9	-9
Fixed Assets	4	2	30
Current Assets	242	202	195
Current Liabilities	232	192	204
Total Share Capital	10	10	10

Vaillant Ltd
Vaillant House Trident Close, Medway City Estate, Rochester, ME2 4EZ
Tel: 01634-292300 **Fax:** 0121-779 7141
E-mail: info@vaillant.co.uk
Website: http://www.vaillant.co.uk
Bank(s): HSBC
Directors: J. Collings (Mkt Research), J. Collins (Mkt Research), B. Thorpe (Sales), J. Bridge (Fin)
Ultimate Holding Company: VAILLANT GMBH (GERMANY)
Immediate Holding Company: VAILLANT LIMITED
Registration no: 01279010 **VAT No.:** GB 765 3678 87
Date established: 1976 **Turnover:** £250m - £500m
No.of Employees: 21 - 50 **Product Groups:** 40

Date of Accounts	Dec 11	Dec 10	Dec 09
Sales Turnover	279m	285m	259m
Pre Tax Profit/Loss	15m	16m	14m
Working Capital	14m	18m	14m
Fixed Assets	863	1m	746
Current Assets	69m	72m	70m
Current Liabilities	26m	30m	27m

Veetee Rice Ltd
Unit 21 Neptune Industrial Estate Neptune Close, Medway City Estate, Rochester, ME2 4LT
Tel: 01634-290092 **Fax:** 01634-297792
E-mail: mvarma@veetee.com
Website: http://www.veetee.com
Directors: M. Varma (MD)
Managers: V. Magoon, J. Newman (Mktg Serv Mgr), A. Ludick (Tech Serv Mgr), J. Kemp (Personnel), S. Surana (Comptroller)
Ultimate Holding Company: VEE TEE INVESTMENTS CORP (NASSAU)
Immediate Holding Company: VEETEE RICE LIMITED
Registration no: 02009019 **Date established:** 1986
Turnover: £50m - £75m **No.of Employees:** 51 - 100 **Product Groups:** 02, 20, 62, 63

Date of Accounts	Dec 11	Dec 10	Dec 09
Sales Turnover	71m	60m	62m
Pre Tax Profit/Loss	1m	4m	3m
Working Capital	8m	8m	5m
Fixed Assets	9m	7m	6m
Current Assets	44m	35m	30m
Current Liabilities	2m	2m	2m

Westwell Developments
Whitewall Road Medway City Estate, Rochester, ME2 4DZ
Tel: 01634-726148 **Fax:** 01634-727081
E-mail: sales@westwelldevelopments.com
Website: http://www.westwelldevelopments.com
Bank(s): Barclays
Directors: G. Smith (MD)
Ultimate Holding Company: H.E. GROUP LTD
Immediate Holding Company: H.E. CONSTRUCTION SERVICES LIMITED
Registration no: 01558352 **VAT No.:** GB 362 2336 73
Date established: 2006 **Turnover:** £1m - £2m **No.of Employees:** 11 - 20
Product Groups: 67, 68, 76, 83, 84

Whitton Marine Ltd
Vicarage Lane Hoo, Rochester, ME3 9LB
Tel: 01634-250593 **Fax:** 01634-250593
E-mail: info@whittonmarine.com
Website: http://www.whittonmarine.co.uk
Directors: M. Whitton (Dir)
Immediate Holding Company: WHITTON MARINE LIMITED
Registration no: 05321213 **Date established:** 2004 **Turnover:** £2m - £5m
No.of Employees: 1 - 10 **Product Groups:** 35, 36, 39

Date of Accounts	Dec 10	Dec 09	Dec 07
Sales Turnover	129	140	80
Pre Tax Profit/Loss	N/A	14	10
Working Capital	25	11	19
Fixed Assets	11	10	14
Current Assets	25	28	22
Current Liabilities	N/A	4	3

Xstream Ltd
Unit 1 Victory Park Trident Close, Medway City Estate, Rochester, ME2 4ER
Tel: 01634-305700 **Fax:** 0870-766 9287
E-mail: sales@xstreamgroup.co.uk
Website: http://www.xstreamgroup.co.uk
Directors: C. Hughes (MD), F. Hughes (Fin)
Immediate Holding Company: XSTREAM LIMITED
Registration no: 04130864 **Date established:** 2000
Turnover: Up to £250,000 **No.of Employees:** 1 - 10 **Product Groups:** 22, 23, 24, 61, 63, 65, 67, 83, 89

Date of Accounts	Dec 11	Dec 10	Dec 09
Working Capital	-6	-7	-8
Fixed Assets	6	7	9
Current Assets	45	44	39

Romney Marsh

Abraflex UK Ltd
Jessamine Farm Old Romney, Romney Marsh, TN29 9SG
Tel: 01797-366023 **Fax:** 01797-366962
E-mail: info@abraflexuk.co.uk
Website: http://www.abraflexuk.co.uk
Managers: D. Wilkins (Mgr)
Immediate Holding Company: ABRAFLEX UK LTD
Registration no: 05103363 **Date established:** 2004
No.of Employees: 1 - 10 **Product Groups:** 32, 33, 35, 46

Date of Accounts	May 12	May 11	May 10
Working Capital	-25	-15	-6
Fixed Assets	81	82	80
Current Assets	88	133	109

Dartpoint Ltd
Unit 1 Kitewell Lane, Lydd, Romney Marsh, TN29 9LP
Tel: 01797-320910 **Fax:** 01797-320571
E-mail: sales@dartpoint.co.uk
Website: http://www.dartpoint.co.uk
Directors: C. Watkinson (Fin), M. Watkinson (MD)
Immediate Holding Company: DARTPOINT LIMITED
Registration no: 01570282 **VAT No.:** GB 225 8579 35
Date established: 1981 **Turnover:** £500,000 - £1m
No.of Employees: 1 - 10 **Product Groups:** 37

Date of Accounts	Mar 12	Mar 11	Mar 10
Sales Turnover	752	556	567
Pre Tax Profit/Loss	5	1	3
Working Capital	21	20	23
Fixed Assets	42	39	40
Current Assets	221	154	134
Current Liabilities	145	101	83

Servo & Electronic Sales Ltd
Conector House Harden Road Lydd, Romney Marsh, TN29 9LX
Tel: 01797-322500 **Fax:** 01797-321569
E-mail: info@servoconnectors.co.uk
Website: http://www.servoconnectors.co.uk
Bank(s): National Westminster Bank Plc & Lloyds TSB Bank plc
Directors: P. Bendall (Fin)
Managers: W. Packer (Mktg Serv Mgr), M. Miles
Immediate Holding Company: SERVO & ELECTRONIC SALES LIMITED
Registration no: 00524572 **VAT No.:** GB 201 1296 23
Date established: 1953 **Turnover:** £2m - £5m **No.of Employees:** 11 - 20
Product Groups: 37, 38

Date of Accounts	Dec 11	Dec 10	Dec 09
Working Capital	1m	1m	1m
Fixed Assets	843	873	1m
Current Assets	2m	2m	2m

Westgate Group Ltd
Newchurch, Romney Marsh, TN29 0DZ
Tel: 01303-872277 **Fax:** 01303-874801
E-mail: sales@wefi.co.uk
Website: http://www.wefi.co.uk
Bank(s): The Royal Bank of Scotland
Directors: E. Vant (MD)
Immediate Holding Company: WESTGATE GROUP LIMITED
Registration no: 00699756 **VAT No.:** GB 201 1002 66
Date established: 1961 **Turnover:** £5m - £10m **No.of Employees:** 21 - 50
Product Groups: 30, 35, 38, 41, 49

Date of Accounts	Dec 11	Dec 10	Dec 09
Working Capital	867	827	794
Fixed Assets	1m	1m	1m
Current Assets	1m	968	963

Sandwich

A E I Compounds Ltd
Sandwich Industrial Estate, Sandwich, CT13 9LY
Tel: 01304-616171 **Fax:** 01304-616170
E-mail: sales@aeicompounds.co.uk
Website: http://www.aeicompounds.com
Bank(s): National Westminster Bank Plc
Directors: S. Garnett (Fin)
Ultimate Holding Company: TT ELECTRONICS PLC
Immediate Holding Company: AEI COMPOUNDS LIMITED
Registration no: 00163690 **Date established:** 2020
Turnover: £10m - £20m **No.of Employees:** 51 - 100 **Product Groups:** 30, 31, 32, 37, 67

Date of Accounts	Dec 11	Dec 10	Dec 09
Sales Turnover	20m	15m	15m
Pre Tax Profit/Loss	370	-169	317
Working Capital	5m	-2m	-1m
Fixed Assets	3m	3m	2m
Current Assets	11m	7m	6m
Current Liabilities	3m	569	476

Abird Ltd
Ramsgate Road, Sandwich, CT13 9ND
Tel: 01304-613221 **Fax:** 01304-614833
E-mail: info@abird.co.uk
Website: http://www.abird.co.uk
Bank(s): HSBC
Directors: C. Thurgate (Co Sec)
Ultimate Holding Company: ABIRD SUPERIOR LIMITED
Immediate Holding Company: ABIRD LIMITED
Registration no: 02559412 **VAT No.:** GB 571 8906 11
Date established: 1990 **Turnover:** £5m - £10m **No.of Employees:** 21 - 50
Product Groups: 40, 83

Date of Accounts	Dec 11	Dec 10	Dec 09
Sales Turnover	8m	N/A	N/A
Pre Tax Profit/Loss	550	N/A	N/A
Working Capital	-1m	-2m	-2m
Fixed Assets	10m	9m	8m
Current Assets	2m	2m	1m
Current Liabilities	540	N/A	N/A

Ted Kingsland
22 Moat Sole, Sandwich, CT13 9AU
Tel: 01304-612487
Directors: T. Kingsland (Prop)
Date established: 1995 **No.of Employees:** 1 - 10 **Product Groups:** 41

Pfizer Ltd
Ramsgate Road, Sandwich, CT13 9NJ
Tel: 01304-616161 **Fax:** 01304-656221
E-mail: matthew.sumner@pfizer.com
Website: http://www.pfizer.co.uk
Bank(s): Barclays
Directors: M. Sumner (Co Sec)
Ultimate Holding Company: PFIZER INC (USA)
Immediate Holding Company: PFIZER GROUP LIMITED
Registration no: 01143903 **Date established:** 1973
No.of Employees: 1501 & over **Product Groups:** 63

Date of Accounts	Nov 10	Nov 09	Nov 08
Pre Tax Profit/Loss	36	-119	4m
Working Capital	30m	-170m	10m
Fixed Assets	86m	287m	107m
Current Assets	425m	549m	730m
Current Liabilities	N/A	55	55

Reinforced Shuttlecocks Ltd
Sandown Road, Sandwich, CT13 9NU
Tel: 01304-612366 **Fax:** 01304-615484
E-mail: sales@maxsports.co.uk
Website: http://www.tennisdiscount.co.uk
Managers: C. Baker (Sales Admin)
Immediate Holding Company: REINFORCED SHUTTLECOCKS LIMITED
Registration no: 02611063 **VAT No.:** GB 571 9721 18
Date established: 1991 **Turnover:** £500,000 - £1m
No.of Employees: 1 - 10 **Product Groups:** 24, 49, 65

Date of Accounts	Jun 11	Jun 10	Jun 09
Working Capital	62	54	-170
Fixed Assets	95	101	107
Current Assets	113	143	171

Sandwich Mowers Ltd
Homestead Farm Woodnesborough Road, Sandwich, CT13 0AE
Tel: 01304-611000 **Fax:** 01304-611000
E-mail: sandwichmowersltd@btinternet.com
Website: http://www.sandwichmowers.co.uk
Directors: C. Bourner (Ptnr), P. Jones (Dir), T. Wilkinson (Ptnr)
Immediate Holding Company: SANDWICH MOWERS LIMITED
Registration no: 04485460 **VAT No.:** GB 621 9610 54
Date established: 2002 **Turnover:** Up to £250,000
No.of Employees: 1 - 10 **Product Groups:** 41, 45, 48

Date of Accounts	Jul 10	Jul 09	Jul 08
Working Capital	-7	-3	-8
Fixed Assets	7	11	13
Current Assets	35	50	36

Stevens & Carlotti Trading Ltd
Penbroke Works Ramsgate Road, Sandwich, CT13 9ST
Tel: 01304-612505 **Fax:** 01304-614636
E-mail: admin@stevens-and-carlotti.co.uk
Website: http://www.stevens-and-carlotti.co.uk
Directors: F. Carlotti (Fin), M. Carlotti (MD)
Immediate Holding Company: STEVENS & CARLOTTI LIMITED
Registration no: 00916841 **VAT No.:** GB 201 4058 24
Date established: 1967 **Turnover:** £5m - £10m **No.of Employees:** 21 - 50
Product Groups: 48

Date of Accounts	Sep 11	Sep 10	Sep 09
Sales Turnover	8m	N/A	N/A
Pre Tax Profit/Loss	1m	N/A	N/A
Working Capital	2m	2m	1m
Fixed Assets	1m	683	869
Current Assets	3m	3m	2m
Current Liabilities	1m	N/A	N/A

Transformer Equipment Ltd
Crystal Business Centre, Sandwich, CT13 9QX
Tel: 01304-612551 **Fax:** 01304-613630
E-mail: luke@transformer-equipment.co.uk
Website: http://www.transformer-equipment.co.uk
Directors: L. Horlick (Dir)
Immediate Holding Company: TRANSFORMER EQUIPMENT LIMITED
Registration no: 00507890 **VAT No.:** GB 201 5238 17
Date established: 1952 **Turnover:** £250,000 - £500,000
No.of Employees: 1 - 10 **Product Groups:** 37

Date of Accounts	Apr 12	Apr 11	Apr 10
Working Capital	10	11	8
Fixed Assets	6	8	9
Current Assets	56	71	68

Sevenoaks

1st Choice Garage Doors
The Barns Ford Lane, Wrotham Heath, Sevenoaks, TN15 7SE
Tel: 01732-843533 **Fax:** 01732-848634
E-mail: sales@1st-choice.co.uk
Website: http://www.1st-choice.co.uk
Directors: P. May (Dir), S. May (Co Sec)
Immediate Holding Company: 1ST CHOICE GARAGE DOORS LIMITED
Registration no: 02335784 **Date established:** 1989
Turnover: £500,000 - £1m **No.of Employees:** 1 - 10 **Product Groups:** 25, 30, 35, 36

Date of Accounts	Mar 12	Mar 11	Mar 10
Working Capital	114	131	176
Fixed Assets	43	41	43
Current Assets	277	279	276

Abacus Advice
3 Station Road Borough Green, Sevenoaks, TN15 8ER
Tel: 01732-881188 **Fax:** 020-8244 1747
E-mail: mhardy@aaltd.co.uk
Website: http://www.aaltd.co.uk
Directors: B. Barker (Fin), M. Hardy (Dir), M. Hardy (MD)
Immediate Holding Company: ABACUS ADVICE LTD
Registration no: 03694074 **Date established:** 1999
Turnover: £250,000 - £500,000 **No.of Employees:** 1 - 10
Product Groups: 82

Date of Accounts	Mar 11	Mar 10	Mar 09
Working Capital	6	6	3
Fixed Assets	5	7	8
Current Assets	66	78	72

Adsales Associates Ltd
Chart House 10 Western Road, Borough Green, Sevenoaks, TN15 8AG
Tel: 01883-734582 **Fax:** 01883-713640
E-mail: office@crier.co.uk
Website: http://www.crier.co.uk
Directors: A. Erasmus (MD)
Immediate Holding Company: ADSALES ASSOCIATES LTD
Registration no: 06054433 **Date established:** 2007 **Turnover:** £2m - £5m
No.of Employees: 1 - 10 **Product Groups:** 28, 44, 81

Date of Accounts	Jan 11	Jan 10	Jan 09
Working Capital	-16	-21	-11
Fixed Assets	18	23	N/A
Current Assets	62	97	13

Air Technics Ltd
Unit D3 Chaucer Business Park Watery Lane, Kemsing, Sevenoaks, TN15 6YU
Tel: 01732-760660 **Fax:** 01732-760 661
E-mail: sales@airtechnics.co.uk
Website: http://www.airtechnics.co.uk
Directors: C. Fletcher (MD)
Immediate Holding Company: AIRTECHNICS LTD
Registration no: 03860212 **Date established:** 1999
Turnover: £250,000 - £500,000 **No.of Employees:** 1 - 10
Product Groups: 29, 30, 35, 36, 37, 38, 39, 40, 42, 45, 46, 48, 61, 66, 67, 68, 84, 85, 86

Date of Accounts	Apr 11	Apr 10	Apr 09
Sales Turnover	261	198	236
Pre Tax Profit/Loss	1	N/A	-17
Working Capital	-25	-26	-27
Fixed Assets	8	11	13
Current Assets	77	62	51
Current Liabilities	44	30	13

Akita Systems Ltd
Unit 5 Chaucer Business Park Watery Lane Kemsing, Sevenoaks, TN15 6PL
Tel: 01732-762675 **Fax:** 01732-761741
E-mail: info@akitasystems.com
Website: http://www.AkitaSystems.com
Directors: C. Boudet (MD)
Managers: S. Champneys (Mktg Serv Mgr)
Immediate Holding Company: AKITA SYSTEMS LIMITED
Registration no: 03297540 **Date established:** 1996
Turnover: £500,000 - £1m **No.of Employees:** 1 - 10 **Product Groups:** 44

Date of Accounts	Dec 09	Dec 08	Dec 07
Sales Turnover	581	559	555
Pre Tax Profit/Loss	146	61	115
Working Capital	-39	-37	-27
Fixed Assets	136	139	157
Current Assets	240	177	201
Current Liabilities	236	185	205

Alpha Therm Ltd
Nepicar House London Road, Wrotham Heath, Sevenoaks, TN15 7RS
Tel: 01732-783000 **Fax:** 01732-783080
E-mail: info@alphatherm.co.uk
Website: http://www.alpha-innovation.co.uk
Directors: J. Studden (MD)
Managers: C. Lassnig (Systems Mgr), C. Earl (Mktg Serv Mgr), J. Templey (Fin Mgr), J. Easter
Ultimate Holding Company: IMMERFIN SPA (ITALY)
Immediate Holding Company: ALPHA THERM LIMITED
Registration no: 00882439 **VAT No.:** GB 205 4723 88
Date established: 1966 **Turnover:** £20m - £50m
No.of Employees: 11 - 20 **Product Groups:** 40, 66

Date of Accounts	Dec 11	Dec 10	Dec 09
Sales Turnover	28m	34m	27m
Pre Tax Profit/Loss	1m	2m	413
Working Capital	3m	4m	2m
Fixed Assets	129	226	333
Current Assets	11m	14m	9m
Current Liabilities	2m	2m	1m

Armourcoat Ltd
Morewood Close, Sevenoaks, TN13 2HU
Tel: 01732-460668 **Fax:** 01732-450930
E-mail: sales@armourcoat.co.uk
Website: http://www.armourcoat.co.uk
Directors: G. Whitehead (MD), D. Nevitt (Mkt Research)
Managers: C. Barnes, D. Parker (Fin Mgr)
Immediate Holding Company: ARMOURCOAT LIMITED
Registration no: 01997888 **Date established:** 1986 **Turnover:** £2m - £5m
No.of Employees: 21 - 50 **Product Groups:** 27, 30, 33, 52, 65, 66

Date of Accounts	Sep 11	Sep 10	Sep 09
Sales Turnover	5m	5m	5m
Pre Tax Profit/Loss	197	352	99
Working Capital	2m	2m	1m
Fixed Assets	301	329	350
Current Assets	3m	3m	2m
Current Liabilities	625	874	360

Ascom UK Ltd
Clockhouse Court Westerham Road, Sevenoaks, TN13 2QB
Tel: 01732-742014 **Fax:** 01732-455865
E-mail: sales@ascomtelenova.com
Website: http://www.ascomuk.com
Bank(s): National Westminster
Directors: S. Rea (Co Sec), F. Mumenthaler (Dir), J. Burns (MD)
Managers: T. Furgerson (Chief Acct), A. Smith (Personnel), R. Eldridge (I.T. Exec), P. Needham (Nat Sales Mgr)
Ultimate Holding Company: ASCOM HOLDING AG (SWITZERLAND)
Immediate Holding Company: ASCOM (UK) LTD
Registration no: 00599145 **Date established:** 1958 **Turnover:** £5m - £10m
No.of Employees: 11 - 20 **Product Groups:** 37, 79

Date of Accounts	Dec 10	Dec 09	Dec 08
Sales Turnover	10m	10m	13m
Pre Tax Profit/Loss	900	354	2m
Working Capital	3m	2m	2m
Fixed Assets	804	1m	2m
Current Assets	5m	5m	6m
Current Liabilities	1m	1m	3m

Assured Transcription & Typing Services
Teffont Long Mill Lane, Plaxtol, Sevenoaks, TN15 0QR
Tel: 01732-810502
E-mail: mae@assuredtranscription.co.uk
Website: http://www.assuredtranscription.co.uk
Directors: M. Evans (Prop)
Date established: 2008 **Turnover:** Up to £250,000
No.of Employees: 1 - 10 **Product Groups:** 80

B A S Components Ltd
Unit 9 Sevenoaks Business Centre Cramptons Road, Sevenoaks, TN14 5DQ
Tel: 01732-775820 **Fax:** 01732-775821
E-mail: lroberts@bas-components.co.uk
Website: http://www.bas-components.co.uk
Directors: L. Timbrell (MD)
Managers: L. Roberts (Sales Prom Mgr), S. Milner (Eng Serv Mgr), L. Roberts
Ultimate Holding Company: TT ELECTRONICS PLC
Immediate Holding Company: BAS COMPONENTS LIMITED
Registration no: 00375564 **Date established:** 1942 **Turnover:** £5m - £10m
No.of Employees: 1 - 10 **Product Groups:** 35

B P I Films Ltd
Moor Road, Sevenoaks, TN14 5EQ
Tel: 01732-450001 **Fax:** 01732-740043
E-mail: admin@bpipoly.com
Website: http://www.bpifilms.com
Directors: G. Buchalter (Dir)
Ultimate Holding Company: BRITISH POLYTHENE INDUSTRIES PLC
Immediate Holding Company: BRITISH POLYTHENE LTD
Registration no: 02318796 **VAT No.:** GB 268 9911 02
Date established: 1970 **Turnover:** £10m - £20m
No.of Employees: 51 - 100 **Product Groups:** 30, 80

Berger Tools Ltd
Units B1 B2 Chaucer Business Park Watery Lane, Kemsing, Sevenoaks, TN15 6QY
Tel: 01732-763377 **Fax:** 01732-763335
E-mail: sales@berger-tools.co.uk
Website: http://www.berger-tools.co.uk
Bank(s): Barclays
Directors: D. Goldsmith (MD)
Ultimate Holding Company: BERGER TOOL SERVICES LIMITED
Immediate Holding Company: BERGER TOOLS LIMITED
Registration no: 03058050 **Date established:** 1995 **Turnover:** £2m - £5m
No.of Employees: 11 - 20 **Product Groups:** 29, 30

Date of Accounts	Dec 11	Dec 10	Dec 09
Working Capital	171	163	178
Fixed Assets	23	27	6
Current Assets	801	716	603

Borough Green Plastic Surgery
4 Conyerd Road Borough Green, Sevenoaks, TN15 8RJ
Tel: 01732-886520
E-mail: craig@boroughgreenplasticsurgery.co.uk
Website: http://www.boroughgreenplasticsurgery.co.uk
Directors: C. Pattinson (Prop)
No.of Employees: 1 - 10 **Product Groups:** 27, 30, 33, 35, 52

John Chirnside & Son Ltd
73 Wrotham Road Borough Green, Sevenoaks, TN15 8DE
Tel: 01732-882367 **Fax:** 01732-885142
E-mail: enquiries@chirnsides.com
Website: http://www.chirnsides.co.uk
Directors: I. Chirnside (Dir)
Immediate Holding Company: JOHN CHIRNSIDE & SONS LIMITED
Registration no: 00583232 **VAT No.:** GB 202 9495 68
Date established: 1957 **Turnover:** £500,000 - £1m
No.of Employees: 1 - 10 **Product Groups:** 35, 49

Date of Accounts	Dec 11	Dec 10	Dec 09
Working Capital	151	118	86
Fixed Assets	161	163	174
Current Assets	288	273	231

Henry Cooch & Son Ltd
Unit 2 Platt Industrial Estate Maidstone Road, Platt, Sevenoaks, TN15 8JL
Tel: 01732-884484 **Fax:** 01732-882681
E-mail: t-links@dial.pipex.com
Website: http://www.henrycooch.co.uk
Directors: B. Chantler (Sales), S. Cooch (MD)
Immediate Holding Company: HENRY COOCH & SON LIMITED
Registration no: 03067308 **VAT No.:** GB 661 7262 33
Date established: 1995 **Turnover:** £250,000 - £500,000
No.of Employees: 1 - 10 **Product Groups:** 35, 37, 39, 45

Date of Accounts	Jun 11	Jun 10	Jun 09
Sales Turnover	457	502	690
Pre Tax Profit/Loss	24	8	52
Working Capital	46	56	82
Fixed Assets	1	2	2
Current Assets	113	112	173
Current Liabilities	9	21	12

R.J. Doran & Co. Ltd
Unit 1 West Kingsdown Industrial Estate London Road, West Kingsdown, Sevenoaks, TN15 6EL
Tel: 01474-854417 **Fax:** 01474-853968
E-mail: customers@primalec.co.uk
Website: http://www.primalec.com
Directors: J. Dufield (Mkt Research), R. Doran (Grp Chief Exec), R. Doran (MD)
Managers: D. Fitzgerald (Purch Mgr), D. Gerold (I.T. Exec), J. Duffield (Sales Prom Mgr), C. Siddle (Admin Off), J. Welch (Sales Prom Mgr)
Registration no: 01434222 **VAT No.:** GB 356 7949 95
Turnover: £500,000 - £1m **No.of Employees:** 1 - 10 **Product Groups:** 38

Elefant Gratings Ltd
Unit 9 Invicta Business Park London Road, Wrotham, Sevenoaks, TN15 7RJ
Tel: 08702-000992 **Fax:** 08702-000994
E-mail: sales@elefantgratings.com
Website: http://www.elefantgratings.com
Directors: P. Fahrsen Pedersen (Dir), P. Webster (Fin)
Immediate Holding Company: ELEFANT GRATINGS LIMITED
Registration no: 03626194 **VAT No.:** GB 726 5647 13
Date established: 1998 **Turnover:** £500,000 - £1m
No.of Employees: 1 - 10 **Product Groups:** 35

Date of Accounts	Dec 11	Dec 10	Dec 09
Working Capital	65	144	231
Fixed Assets	24	20	32
Current Assets	558	384	486

F Lane & Sons
138 Main Road Sundridge, Sevenoaks, TN14 6ET
Tel: 01959-563849 **Fax:** 01959-561201
Directors: R. Lane (Prop)
Date established: 1972 **No.of Employees:** 1 - 10 **Product Groups:** 35

Ayles Fernie International Ltd
Unit D5 Chaucer Business Park Watery Lane, Kemsing, Sevenoaks, TN15 6YU
Tel: 01732-762962 **Fax:** 01732-761961
E-mail: sales@aylesfernie.co.uk
Website: http://www.aylesfernie.co.uk
Directors: W. Fernie (Dir), E. Fernie (Fin)
Immediate Holding Company: AYLES FERNIE INTERNATIONAL LIMITED
Registration no: 02528916 **VAT No.:** GB 245 8841 34
Date established: 1990 **Turnover:** £500,000 - £1m
No.of Employees: 1 - 10 **Product Groups:** 39, 40

Date of Accounts	Dec 11	Dec 10	Dec 09
Working Capital	319	226	147
Fixed Assets	16	7	8
Current Assets	501	523	282

Fire Action Ltd
Unit 1b Beechcroft Farm Industrial Estate Chapel Wood Road, Ash, Sevenoaks, TN15 7HX
Tel: 01474-873556 **Fax:** 01474-873949
E-mail: enquiries@fireaction.co.uk
Website: http://www.fireaction.co.uk
Directors: M. Knaggs (MD), P. Garry (Fin)
Immediate Holding Company: FIRE ACTION LIMITED
Registration no: 04133367 **Date established:** 2000
No.of Employees: 1 - 10 **Product Groups:** 36, 37, 40

Date of Accounts	Mar 12	Mar 11	Mar 10
Working Capital	160	160	136
Fixed Assets	75	77	77
Current Assets	322	314	262

Flag Consultancy Ltd
8 Clearways Business Estate London Road, West Kingsdown, Sevenoaks, TN15 6ES
Tel: 01474-853822 **Fax:** 01474-853882
E-mail: info@flagconsultancy.co.uk
Website: http://www.flagconsultancy.co.uk
Directors: A. Farley (Fin), N. Farley (MD)
Immediate Holding Company: THE FLAG CONSULTANCY LIMITED
Registration no: 03653442 **Date established:** 1998
Turnover: Up to £250,000 **No.of Employees:** 1 - 10 **Product Groups:** 23, 24, 25, 26, 27, 28, 30, 33, 35, 37, 39, 40, 44, 45, 49, 66, 67, 68, 80, 81, 83

Date of Accounts	Mar 12	Mar 11	Mar 10
Sales Turnover	194	189	141
Pre Tax Profit/Loss	16	3	3
Working Capital	13	16	11
Fixed Assets	3	N/A	5
Current Assets	25	47	22
Current Liabilities	6	8	5

H J Fletcher & Newman Ltd
5 Bourne Enterprise Centre Wrotham Road, Borough Green, Sevenoaks, TN15 8DG
Tel: 01732-886555 **Fax:** 01732-884789
E-mail: john.sedgley@fletcher-newman.co.uk
Website: http://www.fletcher-newman.co.uk
Directors: J. Sedgley (Co Sec)
Immediate Holding Company: H.J. FLETCHER & NEWMAN LIMITED
Registration no: 00466234 **VAT No.:** GB 232 5384 76
Date established: 1949 **Turnover:** £1m - £2m **No.of Employees:** 1 - 10
Product Groups: 49

Date of Accounts	Mar 12	Mar 11	Mar 10
Working Capital	148	150	149
Fixed Assets	183	194	209
Current Assets	344	329	330

Geographers A Z Map Co. Ltd
197 Fairfield Road Borough Green, Sevenoaks, TN15 8PP
Tel: 01732-781000 **Fax:** 01732-780677
E-mail: tradesales@a-zmaps.co.uk
Website: http://www.a-zmaps.co.uk
Bank(s): The Royal Bank of Scotland
Directors: J. Syrett (Ch), J. Frankel (MD), M. Sanderson (Dir), D. Churchill (Co Sec), F. Barbor (Sales), J. Goy (Dir), N. Dennison (Dir), S. Berger (Fin), S. Barbor (Dir), S. Berger (MD), B. Woodhams (Pers), S. Berger (Co Sec)
Immediate Holding Company: GEOGRAPHERS MAP TRUSTEES LIMITED
Registration no: 00929975 **VAT No.:** GB 209 6060 76
Date established: 1968 **Turnover:** Up to £250,000
No.of Employees: 51 - 100 **Product Groups:** 28

Date of Accounts	Dec 07	Dec 06
Pre Tax Profit/Loss	1300	1197
Working Capital	23985	22791
Fixed Assets	3378	3618
Current Assets	25378	24117
Current Liabilities	1393	1326
ROCE% (Return on Capital Employed)	4.8	4.5

Graham Webb Iltd
Chapel House 31 London Road, Sevenoaks, TN13 1AR
Tel: 01732-741751 **Fax:** 01732-741918
E-mail: info@twinternational.com
Website: http://www.gwinternational.com
Directors: G. Hammill (Prop), G. Hamill (MD)
Immediate Holding Company: GRAHAM WEBB (SALONS) LIMITED
Registration no: 01217219 **Date established:** 1975
No.of Employees: 1 - 10 **Product Groups:** 32, 61

Grange Developments 2000 Ltd
Unit A4 Chaucer Business Park Watery Lane, Kemsing, Sevenoaks, TN15 6PW
Tel: 01732-760079
E-mail: info@grangedesign.com
Website: http://www.grangedesign.com
Directors: D. Hart (Dir)
Immediate Holding Company: GRANGE DEVELOPMENTS 2000 LIMITED
Registration no: 03731072 **Date established:** 1999
No.of Employees: 1 - 10 **Product Groups:** 36, 37, 38

Date of Accounts	Mar 11	Mar 10	Mar 09
Working Capital	238	242	258
Fixed Assets	42	24	27
Current Assets	415	307	332

Greenshields J C B Ltd
Unit 7 Invicta Business Park London Road, Wrotham, Sevenoaks, TN15 7RJ
Tel: 01732-783660 **Fax:** 01732-886051
Website: http://www.gjcb.co.uk
Directors: G. Greenshields (Prop)
Immediate Holding Company: GREENSHIELDS JCB LIMITED
Registration no: 03235098 **Date established:** 1996 **Turnover:** £2m - £5m
No.of Employees: 101 - 250 **Product Groups:** 39

Date of Accounts	Dec 11	Dec 10	Dec 09
Sales Turnover	84m	58m	44m
Pre Tax Profit/Loss	2m	1m	251
Working Capital	1m	-171	-1m
Fixed Assets	4m	5m	5m
Current Assets	14m	11m	10m
Current Liabilities	3m	2m	2m

Hoare Laboratory Engineering Ltd
Unit C5 Chaucer Business Park Watery Lane, Kemsing, Sevenoaks, TN15 6YT
Tel: 01732-763717 **Fax:** 01732-763827
E-mail: sales@hoare.co.uk
Website: http://www.hoare.co.uk
Directors: A. Hoare (Sales), M. Hoare (MD)
Immediate Holding Company: HOARE LABORATORY ENGINEERING LIMITED
Registration no: 01873446 **VAT No.:** GB 395 3915 13
Date established: 1984 **Turnover:** £1m - £2m **No.of Employees:** 1 - 10
Product Groups: 26, 30, 33, 35, 36, 37, 38, 42, 52

Date of Accounts	Dec 10	Dec 09	Dec 08
Working Capital	-146	-37	-16
Fixed Assets	211	215	221
Current Assets	79	160	332

John D Hotchkiss Ltd
Main Road West Kingsdown, Sevenoaks, TN15 6ER
Tel: 01474-853131 **Fax:** 01474-853288
E-mail: william@hotchkiss-engineers.co.uk
Website: http://www.hotchkiss-engineers.co.uk
Bank(s): Barclays
Directors: W. Hotchkiss (MD)
Immediate Holding Company: JOHN D. HOTCHKISS LIMITED
Registration no: 00401255 **Date established:** 1945 **Turnover:** £1m - £2m
No.of Employees: 11 - 20 **Product Groups:** 35, 44, 48, 84

Date of Accounts	Jun 11	Jun 10	Jun 09
Working Capital	-26	1m	1m
Fixed Assets	509	595	598
Current Assets	688	2m	2m

Hunter Neil Packaging Ltd
Unit 5 Hill Top Meadows Old London Road, Knockholt, Sevenoaks, TN14 7JW
Tel: 01959-532200 **Fax:** 01959-534400
E-mail: bill@hunterneil.com
Website: http://www.hunterneil.co.uk
Directors: V. O'Neill (MD)
Managers: B. Greenfield (Sales & Mktg Mg), W. Greenfield (Mgr), J. Hicks (Sec)
Registration no: 03641706 **VAT No.:** GB 437 4022 69
Turnover: £500,000 - £1m **No.of Employees:** 1 - 10 **Product Groups:** 48

Inspired By Light
Chapel Wood Road Ash, Sevenoaks, TN15 7HX
Tel: 08702-426232
E-mail: customerservice@inspiredbylight.co.uk
Website: http://www.inspiredbylight.co.uk
Managers: G. Catchpole (Mgr)
No.of Employees: 1 - 10 **Product Groups:** 37, 67

Invicta Containers Ltd
Stangate Quarry Quarry Hill Road, Borough Green, Sevenoaks, TN15 8RA
Tel: 01732-886973 **Fax:** 01732-885886
E-mail: invictacontainers@hotmail.com
Website: http://www.invictacontainers.co.uk
Directors: E. Moon (MD)
Immediate Holding Company: INVICTA CONTAINERS LTD.
Registration no: 03025521 **Date established:** 1995
No.of Employees: 11 - 20 **Product Groups:** 35, 42, 45

Date of Accounts	Mar 08	Mar 07	Mar 06
Working Capital	379	333	275
Fixed Assets	29	20	17
Current Assets	847	846	754
Current Liabilities	467	513	479
Total Share Capital	1	1	1

J Salmon Ltd
100-104 London Road, Sevenoaks, TN13 1BB
Tel: 01732-452381 **Fax:** 01732-450951
E-mail: enquiries@jsalmon.co.uk
Website: http://www.jsalmon.co.uk
Directors: H. Salmon (MD)
Immediate Holding Company: CAXTON & HOLMESDALE PRESS (SEVENOAKS) LIMITED(THE)
Registration no: 00461496 **VAT No.:** GB 209 6538 49
Date established: 1948 **Turnover:** Up to £250,000
No.of Employees: 51 - 100 **Product Groups:** 27, 28

Date of Accounts	Dec 11	Dec 10	Dec 09
Sales Turnover	N/A	N/A	116
Pre Tax Profit/Loss	N/A	N/A	12
Working Capital	18	37	36
Current Assets	57	40	42
Current Liabilities	N/A	N/A	6

Jardox Ltd
Jardox Products Ltd Vestry Road, Sevenoaks, TN14 5EL
Tel: 01732-456254 **Fax:** 01732-740805
E-mail: sales@jardox.com
Website: http://www.jardox.com
Bank(s): HSBC Bank plc

see next page

Jardox Ltd - Cont'd

Directors: A. Gardner (MD), K. Pattenden (Fin), K. Pattendon (Fin)
Managers: J. Allbury
Ultimate Holding Company: MOTE HALL LIMITED
Immediate Holding Company: JARDOX LIMITED
Registration no: 00181002 **VAT No.:** GB 209 6319 61
Date established: 2022 **Turnover:** £10m - £20m
No.of Employees: 21 - 50 **Product Groups:** 20

Date of Accounts	Mar 12	Mar 11	Mar 10
Sales Turnover	13m	12m	10m
Pre Tax Profit/Loss	397	308	206
Working Capital	2m	2m	1m
Fixed Assets	995	828	861
Current Assets	4m	3m	3m
Current Liabilities	919	661	268

Kent Leisure Buildings Halstead

London Road Halstead, Sevenoaks, TN14 7DY
Tel: 01959-534242 **Fax:** 01959-534242
E-mail: info@kentleisurebuildings.co.uk
Website: http://www.kentleisurebuildings.co.uk
Directors: B. Puri (Ptnr)
No.of Employees: 1 - 10 **Product Groups:** 25, 33, 35, 66

Kentinental Engineering Ltd

Platt Industrial Estate Maidstone Road, Borough Green, Sevenoaks, TN15 8JA
Tel: 01732-882345 **Fax:** 01732-885703
E-mail: sales@keg.co.uk
Website: http://www.kentinental.com
Directors: S. Ellis (Fin), T. Heaver (Sales), T. Smith (Sales), D. Betts (MD), E. Taylor (Co Sec)
Managers: J. King (Tech Serv Mgr), D. Nissan (Purch Mgr)
Ultimate Holding Company: K E GROUP LIMITED
Immediate Holding Company: KENTINENTAL ENGINEERING LIMITED
Registration no: 02188267 **VAT No.:** GB 472 9390 17
Date established: 1987 **Turnover:** £5m - £10m **No.of Employees:** 21 - 50
Product Groups: 26, 35, 36, 45, 48, 49, 67

Date of Accounts	Dec 11	Dec 10	Dec 09
Sales Turnover	7m	8m	6m
Pre Tax Profit/Loss	-197	124	-448
Working Capital	374	574	466
Fixed Assets	44	41	50
Current Assets	4m	4m	4m
Current Liabilities	1m	806	1m

Letchford Supplies Ltd

2 Bourne Enterprise Centre Wrotham Road, Borough Green, Sevenoaks, TN15 8DG
Tel: 01732-882633 **Fax:** 01732-884551
E-mail: lee@letchford-supplies.co.uk
Website: http://www.letchford-supplies.co.uk
Directors: L. Letchford (MD), S. Letchford (Fin)
Managers: G. Howard (Sales Prom)
Immediate Holding Company: LETCHFORD SUPPLIES LIMITED
Registration no: 03503823 **Date established:** 1998
Turnover: £250,000 - £500,000 **No.of Employees:** 1 - 10
Product Groups: 32

Date of Accounts	Sep 09	Sep 08	Sep 07
Working Capital	65	18	48
Fixed Assets	228	246	264
Current Assets	448	407	406
Current Liabilities	141	137	121

Macdonalds Catering Equipment Ltd

Frieslawn Farm Hodsoll Street, Sevenoaks, TN15 7LH
Tel: 01732-824444 **Fax:** 01732-824455
E-mail: info@macdonalds-online.com
Website: http://www.macdonalds-online.com
Directors: A. Macdonald (MD), J. Millard (Fin)
Immediate Holding Company: MACDONALDS (CATERING EQUIPMENT) LIMITED
Registration no: 01052813 **VAT No.:** GB 206 4527 82
Date established: 1972 **Turnover:** £2m - £5m **No.of Employees:** 1 - 10
Product Groups: 30, 36, 39, 40, 48, 67, 69, 83, 84

Date of Accounts	May 12	May 11	May 10
Working Capital	11	-32	21
Fixed Assets	28	31	33
Current Assets	48	21	68

Marshall F Pont & Associates

67 Mackerels Plain Ide Hill, Sevenoaks, TN14 6BW
Tel: 01732-750715 **Fax:** 01732-750692
E-mail: marshallpont@btconnect.com
Directors: M. Pont (Prop)
Date established: 1971 **No.of Employees:** 1 - 10 **Product Groups:** 35

Masters Exhibitions & Shows

Unit 3-4 North Downs Business Park Pilgrims Way, Dunton Green, Sevenoaks, TN13 2TL
Tel: 01732-740370 **Fax:** 01732-462854
E-mail: sales@mastersexhibitions.co.uk
Website: http://www.mastersexhibitions.co.uk
Bank(s): National Westminster
Directors: B. Cotton (Fin)
Managers: C. Bonwick (Purch Mgr), C. Kench (Sales Prom Mgr)
Immediate Holding Company: MASTERS OF BECKENHAM LTD
Registration no: 00512894 **VAT No.:** 205 6506 86 **Date established:** 1952
Turnover: £2m - £5m **No.of Employees:** 11 - 20 **Product Groups:** 26, 30, 35, 39, 49, 52, 81, 83, 84

Office Angels Commercial Cleaning House Angels

12 Armstrong Close Halstead, Sevenoaks, TN14 7BS
Tel: 0845-1084241
E-mail: officecleaning@houseangels.me.uk
Website: http://www.houseangels.me.uk
Turnover: £250,000 - £500,000 **No.of Employees:** 1 - 10
Product Groups: 32, 40, 52

Oscar Engineering Ltd

Michaels Lane Ash, Sevenoaks, TN15 7HT
Tel: 01474-873122 **Fax:** 01474-879554
E-mail: mail@oscar-acoustics.co.uk
Website: http://www.oscar-acoustics.co.uk
Managers: B. Hancock (Mgr)
Immediate Holding Company: OSCAR ENGINEERING LIMITED
Registration no: 01380508 **VAT No.:** GB 299 5957 68
Date established: 1978 **Turnover:** £500,000 - £1m
No.of Employees: 1 - 10 **Product Groups:** 33, 40, 52

Date of Accounts	Oct 11	Oct 10	Oct 09
Working Capital	235	188	162
Fixed Assets	89	57	60
Current Assets	428	264	342

Plain Sailing Communications Ltd

PO Box 335, Sevenoaks, TN13 3ZX
Tel: 01732-743746 **Fax:** 01732-743670
E-mail: info@psworld.co.uk
Website: http://www.psworld.co.uk
Directors: G. Cooper (Fin), M. Hart (Sales)
Immediate Holding Company: PLAIN SAILING COMMUNICATIONS LIMITED
Registration no: 04243309 **Date established:** 2001
Turnover: £250,000 - £500,000 **No.of Employees:** 1 - 10
Product Groups: 37, 79

Date of Accounts	Oct 11	Oct 10	Oct 09
Sales Turnover	N/A	N/A	255
Pre Tax Profit/Loss	N/A	N/A	7
Working Capital	27	16	36
Fixed Assets	2	2	11
Current Assets	91	82	92
Current Liabilities	N/A	N/A	20

Pre Mac International Ltd

Unit 5 Morewood Close, Sevenoaks, TN13 2HU
Tel: 01732-460333 **Fax:** 01732- 460222
E-mail: office@pre-mac.com
Website: http://www.pre-mac.com
Directors: C. Knox (Ch)
Ultimate Holding Company: GLOBAL ENVIRONMENTAL MANAGEMENT LTD.
Immediate Holding Company: PRE-MAC INTERNATIONAL LIMITED
Registration no: 01927161 **Date established:** 1985 **Turnover:** £5m - £10m
No.of Employees: 1 - 10 **Product Groups:** 30

Date of Accounts	Mar 09	Mar 08	Mar 07
Working Capital	267	244	4
Fixed Assets	32	25	35
Current Assets	332	567	185

Premier Alarms Ltd

Unit F4 Chaucer Business Park Kemsing, Sevenoaks, TN15 6PL
Tel: 01732-764444 **Fax:** 01732-740868
E-mail: sales1@premierprotects.co.uk
Website: http://www.premieralarms.co.uk
Directors: V. Humphreys (MD)
Managers: L. Humphreys
Ultimate Holding Company: PREMIER ALARMS LIMITED
Immediate Holding Company: LOCKSECURE LIMITED
Registration no: 01029674 **Date established:** 1971
No.of Employees: 21 - 50 **Product Groups:** 36, 67

Date of Accounts	May 05
Working Capital	-2
Fixed Assets	15
Current Assets	106

Procon Engineering Ltd

Vestry Estate Vestry Road, Sevenoaks, TN14 5EL
Tel: 01732-781300 **Fax:** 01732-781311
E-mail: sales@proconeng.com
Website: http://www.proconeng.com
Bank(s): Lloyds TSB Bank plc
Directors: C. O'Neil (Co Sec)
Managers: M. Stevens (Chief Mgr)
Ultimate Holding Company: NATIONAL OILWELL VARCO INC (USA)
Immediate Holding Company: PROCON ENGINEERING LIMITED
Registration no: 01201645 **VAT No.:** GB 206 9814 54
Date established: 1975 **Turnover:** £5m - £10m **No.of Employees:** 21 - 50
Product Groups: 38

Date of Accounts	Dec 08	Jun 12	Jun 11
Sales Turnover	7m	N/A	N/A
Pre Tax Profit/Loss	661	N/A	N/A
Working Capital	2m	N/A	N/A
Fixed Assets	276	N/A	N/A
Current Assets	5m	N/A	N/A
Current Liabilities	2m	N/A	N/A

Pumps UK Ltd

Unit A2 Chaucer Business Park Watery Lane, Kemsing, Sevenoaks, TN15 6PW
Tel: 01732-762541 **Fax:** 08707-505248
E-mail: info@pumpsukltd.com
Website: http://www.pumpsukltd.com
Directors: O. Gatto Bunton (Fin), P. Bunton (MD)
Immediate Holding Company: PUMPS (UK) LIMITED
Registration no: 04501085 **Date established:** 2002 **Turnover:** £2m - £5m
No.of Employees: 1 - 10 **Product Groups:** 02, 20, 22, 23, 26, 29, 30, 31, 33, 34, 35, 36, 37, 38, 39, 40, 41, 42, 43, 45, 46, 48, 49, 52, 54, 67, 68, 83, 84

Date of Accounts	Apr 11	Apr 10	Apr 09
Sales Turnover	2m	2m	2m
Pre Tax Profit/Loss	83	69	2
Working Capital	177	115	82
Fixed Assets	281	296	312
Current Assets	803	668	527
Current Liabilities	294	54	126

R T Quaife Engineering Ltd

Vestry Road Otsford, Sevenoaks, TN14 5EL
Tel: 01732-741144
E-mail: info@quaife.co.uk
Website: http://www.quaife.co.uk
Directors: S. Quaife (Dir)
Immediate Holding Company: R.T.QUAIFE ENGINEERING LIMITED
Registration no: 00853413 **VAT No.:** GB 209 8904 40
Date established: 1965 **Turnover:** £5m - £10m **No.of Employees:** 21 - 50
Product Groups: 39

Date of Accounts	Sep 11	Sep 10	Sep 09
Sales Turnover	8m	9m	8m
Pre Tax Profit/Loss	2m	3m	1m
Working Capital	1m	629	1m
Fixed Assets	4m	4m	3m
Current Assets	3m	4m	3m
Current Liabilities	701	2m	448

S & P Spanarc Ltd

Berwick House Dartford Road, Sevenoaks, TN13 3TQ
Tel: 01732-743456 **Fax:** 01732-742922
E-mail: chris.guinane@spanarc.co.uk
Website: http://www.spanarc.co.uk
Directors: H. Guinane (Fin), C. Guinane (MD)
Immediate Holding Company: S & P SPANARC LIMITED
Registration no: 00530575 **VAT No.:** GB 209 7964 27
Date established: 1954 **Turnover:** Up to £250,000
No.of Employees: 1 - 10 **Product Groups:** 36, 40

Date of Accounts	Mar 12	Mar 11	Mar 10
Sales Turnover	204	N/A	N/A
Pre Tax Profit/Loss	42	N/A	N/A
Working Capital	28	15	2
Fixed Assets	1	1	1
Current Assets	55	32	30
Current Liabilities	16	N/A	N/A

Sculpture Grain Ltd

Warren Court Farm Knockholt Road, Halstead, Sevenoaks, TN14 7ER
Tel: 01959-534060 **Fax:** 01959-522436
E-mail: mick.sculpturegrinds@virgin.net
Directors: C. Corp (Fin), M. Corp (Dir)
Immediate Holding Company: SCULPTURE GRAIN LIMITED
Registration no: 02415890 **VAT No.:** 550 3373 65 **Date established:** 1989
Turnover: Up to £250,000 **No.of Employees:** 1 - 10 **Product Groups:** 25

Date of Accounts	Dec 09	Dec 08	Dec 07
Working Capital	-2	-8	-7
Fixed Assets	9	10	13
Current Assets	26	12	22

Selwyn Electronics

Unit B8 Chaucer Business Park Watery Lane Kemsing, Sevenoaks, TN15 6QY
Tel: 01732-765100 **Fax:** 01732-765190
E-mail: connect@selwyn.co.uk
Website: http://www.selwyn.co.uk
Directors: P. Cooke (MD)
Registration no: 01777562 **VAT No.:** GB 395 2252 40
Date established: 1984 **Turnover:** £2m - £5m **No.of Employees:** 1 - 10
Product Groups: 37

Date of Accounts	Mar 08	Mar 07
Working Capital	497	541
Fixed Assets	33	46
Current Assets	874	760
Current Liabilities	378	219
Total Share Capital	20	20

Shortland Structures Ltd

4d Bradbourne Mews St Johns Hill, Sevenoaks, TN13 3NP
Tel: 01732-460912
E-mail: sales@shortlandstructures.com
Website: http://www.shortlandstructures.com
Directors: B. Shortland (Prop)
Immediate Holding Company: SHORTLAND STRUCTURES LIMITED
Registration no: 05495852 **Date established:** 2005
No.of Employees: 1 - 10 **Product Groups:** 35

Date of Accounts	Jul 11	Jul 10	Jul 09
Working Capital	-28	-10	-23
Fixed Assets	26	20	22
Current Assets	12	40	42

Shrink Sleeve Ltd

Camion House Mill Lane, Sevenoaks, TN14 5BX
Tel: 01732-462841 **Fax:** 01732-462851
E-mail: info@shrinksleeve.com
Website: http://www.shrinksleeve.co.uk
Directors: A. Sweeney (MD), J. Sweeney (Fin)
Immediate Holding Company: SHRINK SLEEVE LIMITED
Registration no: 02758419 **Date established:** 1992
No.of Employees: 1 - 10 **Product Groups:** 23, 28, 29, 30, 31, 37, 66

Date of Accounts	Nov 11	Nov 10	Nov 09
Working Capital	257	272	292
Fixed Assets	7	13	13
Current Assets	343	352	383

Skillclear Ltd

Top Floor 17 Granville Road, Sevenoaks, TN13 1EX
Tel: 0845-6801100 **Fax:** 0870-0512350
E-mail: info@skillclear.co.uk
Website: http://www.skillclear.co.uk
Directors: D. Marshall (MD), D. Schunker (Grp Chief Exec)
Managers: A. Carter (Personnel)
Immediate Holding Company: Wishbone Solutions Ltd
Registration no: 04430755 **Date established:** 2002
No.of Employees: 1 - 10 **Product Groups:** 80

Bill Skinner Studio Ltd

14 High Street Otford, Sevenoaks, TN14 5PQ
Tel: 01959-525505 **Fax:** 01959-525506
E-mail: sales@billskinnerstudio.co.uk
Website: http://www.billskinnerstudio.co.uk
Directors: G. Skinner (MD)
Immediate Holding Company: THE BILL SKINNER STUDIO LIMITED
Registration no: 03101806 **Date established:** 1995
Turnover: £500,000 - £1m **No.of Employees:** 1 - 10 **Product Groups:** 49

Date of Accounts	Oct 11	Oct 10	Oct 09
Working Capital	72	69	92
Fixed Assets	32	31	21
Current Assets	203	192	176

Specialist Lift Services Ltd

The Quadrant Victoria Road, Sevenoaks, TN13 1YD
Tel: 01732-455771 **Fax:** 01732-450530
E-mail: mail@specialistlifts.com
Website: http://www.specialistlifts.com
Managers: L. Shove (Sales Admin)
Immediate Holding Company: SPECIALIST LIFT SERVICES LIMITED
Registration no: 04071070 **Date established:** 2000 **Turnover:** £2m - £5m
No.of Employees: 1 - 10 **Product Groups:** 35, 39, 45

Date of Accounts	Apr 11	Apr 10	Apr 09
Sales Turnover	2m	2m	3m
Pre Tax Profit/Loss	190	174	158
Working Capital	-40	-93	-93
Fixed Assets	740	751	762
Current Assets	736	764	605
Current Liabilities	176	183	171

Spray Store
Clearways Industrial Estate London Road, West Kingsdown, Sevenoaks, TN15 6ES
Tel: 01474-853869
E-mail: spraystore@btconnect.com
Website: http://www.spraystore.co.uk
Directors: T. Allard (Prop)
No.of Employees: 1 - 10 **Product Groups:** 38, 42, 48

T M B International Ltd
Platt Industrial Estate Maidstone Road, Platt, Sevenoaks, TN15 8TB
Tel: 01732-887456 **Fax:** 01732-886345
E-mail: cos@tmbmailing.com
Website: http://www.tmbmailing.com
Managers: C. King (Mgr)
Registration no: 2292816 **Date established:** 1998 **Turnover:** £2m - £5m
No.of Employees: 21 - 50 **Product Groups:** 81

Tacwise Group plc
1 Connections Business Park Vestry Road, Sevenoaks, TN14 5DF
Tel: 01732-464800 **Fax:** 01732-464888
E-mail: sales@tacwise.com
Website: http://www.rapesco.com
Bank(s): HSBC
Directors: S. James (Jt MD), D. James (Ch & MD), N. Ward (Fin), A. Dawson (Fin), A. Frost (MD)
Managers: J. Godfrey (I.T. Exec)
Ultimate Holding Company: 05452341
Immediate Holding Company: TACWISE GROUP PLC
Registration no: 04747165 **Date established:** 2003 **Turnover:** £2m - £5m
No.of Employees: 51 - 100 **Product Groups:** 28, 30, 35, 49

Date of Accounts	May 08	May 07	May 06
Sales Turnover	5312	5349	4913
Pre Tax Profit/Loss	19	113	109
Working Capital	658	415	55
Fixed Assets	818	878	824
Current Assets	4339	4049	3083
Current Liabilities	3682	3634	3029
Total Share Capital	100	100	100
ROCE% (Return on Capital Employed)	1.3	8.7	12.4
ROT% (Return on Turnover)	0.4	2.1	2.2

Technical Treatments Ltd
Station Works Rye Lane, Dunton Green, Sevenoaks, TN14 5HD
Tel: 01732-462656 **Fax:** 01732-742602
E-mail: enquiries@technical-treatments.co.uk
Website: http://www.technical-treatments.co.uk
Bank(s): Barclays
Directors: A. Coldicott (Grp Chief Exec), S. Watson (Dir), P. Buckley (Ch), C. Watson (Dir)
Managers: W. Kent (Sales Prom Mgr), G. Wenban (Works Gen Mgr)
Registration no: 00421035 **Date established:** 1946 **Turnover:** £1m - £2m
No.of Employees: 11 - 20 **Product Groups:** 30, 66

Date of Accounts	Sep 11	Sep 10	Sep 09
Working Capital	662	653	788
Fixed Assets	276	285	148
Current Assets	740	730	902

Versatile Equipment Ltd
Units 1-3 Hornet Business Estate Quarry Hill Road, Borough Green, Sevenoaks, TN15 8RW
Tel: 08452-622280 **Fax:** 08452-622281
E-mail: enquiries@versatileequipment.co.uk
Website: http://www.versatileequipment.co.uk
Directors: P. Rolfe (MD)
Immediate Holding Company: VERSATILE EQUIPMENT LIMITED
Registration no: 04639625 **Date established:** 2003
No.of Employees: 11 - 20 **Product Groups:** 36, 39, 41, 45, 67, 82, 83

Date of Accounts	Mar 12	Mar 11	Mar 10
Working Capital	-83	-111	-90
Fixed Assets	861	564	502
Current Assets	941	602	453

W & Co Design Solutions Ltd
West Yoke Ash, Sevenoaks, TN15 7EP
Tel: 0845-6253545 **Fax:** 0870-1608071
E-mail: adam@w-co.co.uk
Website: http://www.w-co.co.uk
Directors: I. Vanovitch (Fin), A. Vanovitch (MD)
Immediate Holding Company: W & CO DESIGN SOLUTIONS LIMITED
Registration no: 04063394 **Date established:** 2000
No.of Employees: 1 - 10 **Product Groups:** 28, 37, 40, 49, 52, 67, 81, 84

W K D Storage Systems Ltd
3-4 Bourne Enterprise Centre Wrotham Road, Borough Green, Sevenoaks, TN15 8DF
Tel: 01732-882042 **Fax:** 01732-885763
E-mail: sales@wkdstorage.co.uk
Website: http://www.wkdstorage.co.uk
Directors: K. Mclean (Dir)
Immediate Holding Company: W.K.D. STORAGE SYSTEMS LIMITED
Registration no: 00906521 **VAT No.:** GB 210 1427 33
Date established: 1967 **Turnover:** £1m - £2m **No.of Employees:** 1 - 10
Product Groups: 25, 26, 27, 30, 35, 40, 45, 67

Date of Accounts	May 12	May 11	May 10
Working Capital	521	538	557
Fixed Assets	475	445	465
Current Assets	760	696	665

Waterbird Parakites
27 Blue Chalet Industrial Park West Kingsdown, Sevenoaks, TN15 6BQ
Tel: 01474-854352 **Fax:** 01474-854474
E-mail: info@waterbird.co.uk
Website: http://www.waterbird.co.uk
Directors: V. Gaskin (Prop)
Immediate Holding Company: WATERBIRD PARAKITE LTD
Registration no: 00002155 **VAT No.:** GB 662 0157 57
Turnover: £250,000 - £500,000 **No.of Employees:** 1 - 10
Product Groups: 24, 39

Wright Stone Granite Ltd
Crab Tree Court Farm Crab Tree Close Gravesend Road, Wrotham, Sevenoaks, TN15 7JL
Tel: 01732-824328 **Fax:** 05601-122076
E-mail: info@thewrightstone.com
Website: http://www.graniteshowroom.co.uk
Directors: J. Wright (MD)
Immediate Holding Company: WRIGHTSTONE GRANITE LIMITED
Registration no: 06843992 **Date established:** 2009
No.of Employees: 1 - 10 **Product Groups:** 33

Date of Accounts	Mar 11	Mar 10
Working Capital	52	5
Fixed Assets	43	20
Current Assets	147	107

Sheerness

A Y S Ltd
10 Marine Parade, Sheerness, ME12 2AL
Tel: 01795-669191 **Fax:** 01795-668040
E-mail: moss@aysltd.wanadoo.co.uk
Website: http://www.aysltd.co.uk
Directors: L. Moss (Fin), F. Moss (MD)
Immediate Holding Company: AYS LIMITED
Registration no: 04279039 **Date established:** 2001
No.of Employees: 1 - 10 **Product Groups:** 37, 52, 84, 85

Date of Accounts	Dec 11	Dec 10	Dec 09
Working Capital	21	28	43
Fixed Assets	23	27	35
Current Assets	84	76	108

Ateco Ltd
Bulldozer House New Road, Sheerness, ME12 1AU
Tel: 01795-660666 **Fax:** 01795-661559
E-mail: info@atecoaccess.com
Website: http://www.atecoaccess.com
Bank(s): Barclays
Managers: J. Spears (Mgr)
Immediate Holding Company: AZURE INTERNATIONAL LIMITED
Registration no: 02782479 **VAT No.:** GB 624 5094 48
Date established: 1993 **No.of Employees:** 11 - 20 **Product Groups:** 41, 45

Date of Accounts	Dec 11	Dec 10	Dec 09
Working Capital	-11	-64	-28
Fixed Assets	388	390	390
Current Assets	139	82	110

Burden Bros
Old Rides Farm Leysdown Road, Eastchurch, Sheerness, ME12 4BD
Tel: 01795-880224 **Fax:** 01795-880418
E-mail: guy@burdenbros.co.uk
Website: http://www.burdenbros.co.uk
Directors: J. Burden (Dir), G. Burden (MD)
Managers: C. Odgers (Mktg Serv Mgr), J. Rideout (Fin Mgr)
Immediate Holding Company: BURDEN BROS CONTRACTORS LTD
Registration no: 02912894 **Date established:** 1994
Turnover: Up to £250,000 **No.of Employees:** 21 - 50 **Product Groups:** 67, 84

Capespan Ltd
Lappel Bank Sheerness Docks, Sheerness, ME12 1RS
Tel: 01795-586100 **Fax:** 01795-580509
Website: http://www.capespan.com
Directors: G. Broomhall (Dir), R. Brighten (Dir), P. Misselbrook (Dir), N. Dockar (Dir), N. Oosthuizen (Dir), K. Ollier (Dir), G. Groenewald (Dir), E. Van Vlaanderen (Dir), A. Venter (Dir), A. Du Preez (Dir), A. De Haast (Fin), R. Lennon (Dir), J. Stanbury (Dir)
Ultimate Holding Company: CAPESPAN INTERNATIONAL HOLDINGS LIMITED
Immediate Holding Company: CAPESPAN LIMITED
Registration no: 03164511 **VAT No.:** GB 604 0062 03
Date established: 1996 **Turnover:** £75m - £125m
No.of Employees: 1 - 10 **Product Groups:** 21, 61

Checkmate Group
New Road, Sheerness, ME12 1PZ
Tel: 01795-580333 **Fax:** 01795-668280
E-mail: sales@checkmateuk.com
Website: http://www.checkmateuk.com
Bank(s): National Westminster Bank Plc
Directors: R. Price (Co Sec), O. Auston (MD), K. Sutcliffe (Fin)
Managers: D. Berier (Tech Serv Mgr), G. Nicolson (Buyer)
Ultimate Holding Company: CHECKMATE LIMITED
Immediate Holding Company: CHECKMATE UK LIMITED
Registration no: 01246358 **VAT No.:** GB 205 1835 92
Date established: 1976 **Turnover:** £2m - £5m **No.of Employees:** 51 - 100
Product Groups: 23

Date of Accounts	Dec 11	Dec 10	Dec 09
Working Capital	90	96	216
Current Assets	181	240	273
Current Liabilities	N/A	3	1

Kent Catering Service Ltd
Unit 7-8 Dorset Road Industrial Estate Dorset Road, Sheerness, ME12 1LT
Tel: 01795-668201 **Fax:** 01795-662667
E-mail: info@kentcateringservice.co.uk
Website: http://www.kentcateringservice.co.uk
Directors: M. Irwin (Fin), A. Irwin (MD)
Immediate Holding Company: KENT CATERING SERVICE LIMITED
Registration no: 03833609 **Date established:** 1999
Turnover: £250,000 - £500,000 **No.of Employees:** 1 - 10
Product Groups: 20, 40, 41

Date of Accounts	Aug 11	Aug 10	Aug 09
Sales Turnover	N/A	N/A	431
Pre Tax Profit/Loss	N/A	N/A	22
Working Capital	-10	-8	-2
Fixed Assets	28	24	17
Current Assets	99	78	83
Current Liabilities	N/A	N/A	37

Kent United Contractors Ltd
Unit 4 Regis Business Park New Road, Sheerness, ME12 1NB
Tel: 01795-583475 **Fax:** 01795-583476
E-mail: kuc@lineone.net
Website: http://www.kucltd.co.uk
Directors: J. Bellaque (Dir), I. Musk (Ch), L. Harris (Co Sec)
Immediate Holding Company: KENT UNITED CONTRACTORS LIMITED
Registration no: 02788556 **VAT No.:** GB 624 5372 46
Date established: 1993 **Turnover:** £250,000 - £500,000
No.of Employees: 1 - 10 **Product Groups:** 74, 76

Date of Accounts	Mar 09	Mar 08	Mar 07
Sales Turnover	N/A	2m	1m
Pre Tax Profit/Loss	N/A	7	31
Working Capital	131	177	169
Fixed Assets	88	91	94
Current Assets	232	505	446
Current Liabilities	N/A	328	277

Medway Marine Surveyors & Consultants Ltd
104 Anchor Lane Sheerness Docks, Sheerness, ME12 1HX
Tel: 01795-666633 **Fax:** 01795-666678
E-mail: medwaymsc@aol.com
Website: http://www.medwayports.com
Directors: M. Chilcott (Fin), C. Chilcott (MD)
Immediate Holding Company: MEDWAY MARINE SURVEYORS & CONSULTANTS LIMITED
Registration no: 04484195 **Date established:** 2002
No.of Employees: 1 - 10 **Product Groups:** 68, 71, 74, 76, 84

Date of Accounts	Mar 11	Mar 09	Mar 08
Working Capital	4	7	12
Fixed Assets	N/A	1	1
Current Assets	24	34	25

Monarch Chemicals Ltd
New Road, Sheerness, ME12 1LZ
Tel: 01795-583333 **Fax:** 01795-583300
E-mail: sales@monarchchemicals.co.uk
Website: http://www.monarchchemicals.co.uk
Date established: 1989 **Turnover:** £5m - £10m **No.of Employees:** 21 - 50
Product Groups: 31, 32, 66, 87

Date of Accounts	Mar 09	Mar 08	Mar 07
Sales Turnover	9m	7m	6m
Pre Tax Profit/Loss	854	656	564
Working Capital	-190	-274	-326
Fixed Assets	1m	1m	1m
Current Assets	2m	2m	1m
Current Liabilities	877	926	668

Monarch Chemicals Holdings Ltd
New Road, Sheerness, ME12 1LZ
Tel: 01795-583333 **Fax:** 01795-583300
E-mail: webenquiries@monarchchemicals.co.uk
Website: http://www.monarchchemicals.co.uk
Directors: V. Copeland (Co Sec)
Immediate Holding Company: Monarch Chemicals (Holdings) Ltd
Registration no: 02820075 **Date established:** 1993 **Turnover:** £5m - £10m
No.of Employees: 21 - 50 **Product Groups:** 32, 66

PDW Street Lighting
17 Court Tree Drive Eastchurch, Sheerness, ME12 4TR
Tel: 01795-881241
E-mail: info@pdwcontracting.com
Website: http://www.pdwcontracting.com
Product Groups: 37, 51, 52, 84

Scaffcad Structural Engineers
14 Bucklers Close Warden, Sheerness, ME12 4PT
Tel: 01795-511704 **Fax:** 01795-511729
Directors: P. Fitzgerald (Prop)
Date established: 1997 **No.of Employees:** 1 - 10 **Product Groups:** 35

Date of Accounts	Mar 11
Sales Turnover	58
Pre Tax Profit/Loss	37
Current Assets	11
Current Liabilities	10

Sidcup

Alsford Timber Ltd
Edgington Way, Sidcup, DA14 5AD
Tel: 020-8300 4375 **Fax:** 020-8308 0664
E-mail: sales@alsfordtimber.com
Website: http://www.alsfordtimber.com
Managers: I. Lumsden (District Mgr)
Ultimate Holding Company: GEO. KINGSBURY HOLDINGS LIMITED
Immediate Holding Company: ALSFORD TIMBER LIMITED
Registration no: 02827724 **Date established:** 1993
No.of Employees: 1 - 10 **Product Groups:** 25

Date of Accounts	Dec 11	Dec 10	Dec 09
Sales Turnover	28m	26m	25m
Pre Tax Profit/Loss	-577	-1m	-1m
Working Capital	4m	4m	5m
Fixed Assets	624	651	869
Current Assets	9m	8m	8m
Current Liabilities	532	479	535

Apex Lifts
Apex House Lefa Business Centre Edginton Way, Sidcup, DA14 5BH
Tel: 020-8300 2929 **Fax:** 020-8300 6868
E-mail: info@apex-lifts.co.uk
Website: http://www.apex-lifts.co.uk
Directors: K. Wakefield (Fin), L. Hughes (Mkt Research)
Managers: M. Holderness (Tech Serv Mgr)
Immediate Holding Company: APEX LIFT & ESCALATOR ENGINEERS LIMITED
Registration no: 01129631 **Date established:** 1973
Turnover: £10m - £20m **No.of Employees:** 21 - 50 **Product Groups:** 45, 67, 84

Date of Accounts	Aug 11	Aug 10	Aug 09
Sales Turnover	12m	13m	17m
Pre Tax Profit/Loss	284	-638	1m
Working Capital	3m	3m	3m
Fixed Assets	137	152	173
Current Assets	5m	5m	6m
Current Liabilities	1m	1m	1m

Astell Scientific Holdings Ltd
19 - 21 Powerscroft Road, Sidcup, DA14 5DT
Tel: 020-8300 4311 **Fax:** 020-8300 2247
E-mail: sales@astell.com
Website: http://www.astell.com
Bank(s): HSBC Bank plc
Directors: B. Sutcliffe (Fin), D. Pennock (MD), D. Thomas (Sales & Mktg), D. Pennock (Ch), G. Scarr (Tech Serv), J. Pennock (MD)
Ultimate Holding Company: Astell Scientific (Holdings) Ltd
Immediate Holding Company: Astell Scientific (Holdings) Ltd
Registration no: 01276179 **VAT No.:** GB 586 5033 22
Date established: 1976 **Turnover:** £2m - £5m **No.of Employees:** 21 - 50
Product Groups: 38, 40, 41, 42

Date of Accounts	Jun 10	Jun 09	Jun 08
Fixed Assets	575	575	N/A

Cralec Electrical Distributors Ltd

Foots Cray High Street, Sidcup, DA14 5HL
Tel: 020-8300 0186 **Fax:** 020-8302 5859
E-mail: quotes@cralec.com
Website: http://www.cralec.com
Directors: R. Law (Dir), L. Law (Fin)
Immediate Holding Company: CRALEC ELECTRICAL DISTRIBUTORS LIMITED
Registration no: 02760087 **Date established:** 1992
Turnover: £250,000 - £500,000 **No.of Employees:** 11 - 20
Product Groups: 35, 36, 37, 41, 66, 67

Date of Accounts	Dec 10	Dec 09	Dec 08
Sales Turnover	N/A	N/A	391
Pre Tax Profit/Loss	N/A	N/A	10
Working Capital	36	31	11
Fixed Assets	14	13	16
Current Assets	189	180	165
Current Liabilities	N/A	N/A	31

Donovan Brothers

Foots Cray High Street, Sidcup, DA14 5HP
Tel: 020-8302 6620 **Fax:** 020-8302 6621
E-mail: michael.donovan@donovanbros.com
Website: http://www.donovanbros.com
Bank(s): National Westminster Bank Plc
Directors: M. Donovan (MD)
Managers: M. Norris (Sales Prom Mgr)
Immediate Holding Company: DONOVAN BROS. LIMITED
Registration no: 00446154 **Date established:** 1947 **Turnover:** £5m - £10m
No.of Employees: 11 - 20 **Product Groups:** 27, 30

Date of Accounts	Sep 11	Sep 10	Sep 09
Sales Turnover	7m	8m	9m
Pre Tax Profit/Loss	-54	-30	36
Working Capital	388	389	415
Fixed Assets	2m	2m	2m
Current Assets	2m	2m	2m
Current Liabilities	228	377	408

Elevator Group Ltd

104 Station Road, Sidcup, DA15 7DE
Tel: 020-8302 7612 **Fax:** 020-8302 9864
E-mail: tina@theelevatorgroup.co.uk
Website: http://www.theelevatorgroup.co.uk
Directors: T. Wise (Fin), T. Nash (Dir)
Immediate Holding Company: THE ELEVATOR GROUP LTD
Registration no: 03989313 **Date established:** 2000
No.of Employees: 1 - 10 **Product Groups:** 35, 39, 45

Date of Accounts	Sep 11	Sep 10	Sep 09
Working Capital	-20	-18	-3
Fixed Assets	26	29	5
Current Assets	191	220	191

Envopak Group Ltd

Planmail House Edgington Way, Sidcup, DA14 5EF
Tel: 020-8308 8000 **Fax:** 020-8300 3832
E-mail: sales@itw-envopak.co.uk
Website: http://www.itw-envopak.com
Managers: J. Parker (Mktg Serv Mgr)
No.of Employees: 51 - 100 **Product Groups:** 27, 30, 35, 36, 37, 49

Harris Refrigeration

16 Days Lane, Sidcup, DA15 8JN
Tel: 020-8302 1582
Website: http://www.harrisrefrigeration.com
Directors: G. Harris (Prop)
Date established: 1984 **No.of Employees:** 1 - 10 **Product Groups:** 36, 40

Lowther Loudspeaker Systems Ltd

26 Footscary Lane, Sidcup, DA14 4NR
Tel: 020-8300 9166 **Fax:** 020-8308 0778
E-mail: diane@lowtherloudspeakers.com
Website: http://www.lowtherloudspeakers.com
Directors: D. Hanson (Co Sec)
Immediate Holding Company: HI-FERRIC TECHNOLOGY LIMITED
Registration no: 02671971 **VAT No.:** GB 527 4699 09
Date established: 1991 **Turnover:** Up to £250,000
No.of Employees: 1 - 10 **Product Groups:** 37, 40

Date of Accounts	Dec 10	Dec 02	Dec 01
Working Capital	-0	-9	-19
Fixed Assets	N/A	9	19
Current Liabilities	N/A	9	6

N E Plastics Ltd

1 Ruxley Corner Industrial Estate Edgington Way, Sidcup, DA14 5BL
Tel: 020-8308 9990 **Fax:** 020-8308 9995
E-mail: sales@neplastics.co.uk
Website: http://www.neplastics.co.uk
Directors: N. Warne (MD), E. Warne (Fin)
Immediate Holding Company: NE PLASTICS LIMITED
Registration no: 03348102 **VAT No.:** GB 586 8057 90
Date established: 1997 **Turnover:** £2m - £5m **No.of Employees:** 11 - 20
Product Groups: 66

Date of Accounts	May 11	May 10	May 09
Sales Turnover	N/A	3m	N/A
Pre Tax Profit/Loss	N/A	66	N/A
Working Capital	-48	-82	-40
Fixed Assets	214	139	170
Current Assets	1m	1m	1m
Current Liabilities	N/A	637	N/A

Nobel Electronics Ltd

Tudor Cottages Footscray High Street, Sidcup, DA14 5HN
Tel: 020-8309 0500 **Fax:** 020-8302 7901
E-mail: sales@nobelelectronics.co.uk
Website: http://www.nobelelectronics.co.uk
Managers: N. Noakes (Sec), S. Pinel (Sales Prom)
Registration no: 02371471 **VAT No.:** GB 205 8170 83
Date established: 1968 **Turnover:** £500,000 - £1m
No.of Employees: 1 - 10 **Product Groups:** 33, 37, 67

Date of Accounts	Apr 11	Apr 10	Apr 09
Working Capital	28	27	16
Fixed Assets	N/A	N/A	2
Current Assets	148	155	203

P S M Plant & Tool Hire Centres Ltd

253-255 Blackfen Road, Sidcup, DA15 8PR
Tel: 020-8850 5658 **Fax:** 020-8303 0436
E-mail: info@psmhire.co.uk
Website: http://www.psmhire.co.uk
Directors: M. Clegg (Fin)
Immediate Holding Company: PSM PLANT & TOOL HIRE CENTRES LIMITED
Registration no: 03503233 **Date established:** 1998
No.of Employees: 11 - 20 **Product Groups:** 36, 45, 83

Date of Accounts	Mar 11	Mar 10	Mar 09
Working Capital	632	443	308
Fixed Assets	2m	2m	2m
Current Assets	940	729	595

Pakt London Ltd

168 Blackfen Road Hawthorn Terrace, Sidcup, DA15 8PT
Tel: 020-8859 8877 **Fax:** 020-8859 8787
E-mail: sales@lspuk.com
Website: http://www.lspuk.com
Directors: K. Arnold (Dir)
Immediate Holding Company: L.S.P. LIMITED
Registration no: 02873983 **VAT No.:** GB 649 4012 37
Date established: 1993 **No.of Employees:** 1 - 10 **Product Groups:** 24, 29, 63

Date of Accounts	Dec 05	Dec 04	Dec 03
Working Capital	64	107	139
Fixed Assets	33	53	50
Current Assets	292	386	322

Progressive Media Group

Progressive House 2 Maidstone Road, Sidcup, DA14 5HZ
Tel: 020-8269 7700 **Fax:** 020-8269 7878
E-mail: wbp@progressivemediagroup.com
Website: http://www.progressivemediagroup.com
Directors: M. Danson (MD)
Managers: K. Prestidge (Fin Mgr), L. Hudson (Tech Serv Mgr), J. Chard, C. Denning (Personnel), K. Glaseby (Sales Prom Mgr)
Immediate Holding Company: PROGRESSIVE TITLES LIMITED
Registration no: 06381181 **VAT No.:** GB 586 6457 84
Date established: 2007 **Turnover:** £10m - £20m
No.of Employees: 51 - 100 **Product Groups:** 28

Rubax Lifts Ltd

Prospect House Foots Cray High Street, Sidcup, DA14 5HN
Tel: 020-8302 8800 **Fax:** 020-8302 6644
E-mail: sales@rubax.co.uk
Website: http://www.rubax.co.uk
Directors: P. Verey (MD), R. Adams (Dir)
Ultimate Holding Company: FROSTALL LIMITED
Immediate Holding Company: RUBAX LIFTS LIMITED
Registration no: 01509899 **Date established:** 1980
No.of Employees: 1 - 10 **Product Groups:** 35, 39, 45

Date of Accounts	Dec 07	Dec 06	Dec 05
Sales Turnover	5307	N/A	N/A
Pre Tax Profit/Loss	623	495	N/A
Working Capital	888	573	291
Fixed Assets	480	467	448
Current Assets	2514	1838	2314
Current Liabilities	1626	1264	2023
Total Share Capital	5	5	5
ROCE% (Return on Capital Employed)	45.5	47.6	
ROT% (Return on Turnover)	11.7		

Ruxley Manor Garden Centre

Maidstone Road, Sidcup, DA14 5BQ
Tel: 020-8300 0084 **Fax:** 020-8302 3879
E-mail: kevin@ruxley-manor.co.uk
Website: http://www.ruxley-manor.co.uk
Directors: A. Evans (MD), K. Baker (Fin)
Managers: S. Breakwell (Personnel), J. Evans (Mgr)
Ultimate Holding Company: H.EVANS & SONS LIMITED
Immediate Holding Company: RUXLEY MANOR GARDEN CENTRE LTD
Registration no: 01170687 **Date established:** 1974 **Turnover:** £5m - £10m
No.of Employees: 51 - 100 **Product Groups:** 25, 33, 35, 52, 66, 84

Date of Accounts	Dec 11	Dec 10	Dec 09
Sales Turnover	8m	8m	8m
Pre Tax Profit/Loss	404	445	925
Working Capital	3m	2m	3m
Fixed Assets	557	553	619
Current Assets	4m	4m	5m
Current Liabilities	474	194	653

S P Batteries

25-35 Birkbeck Road, Sidcup, DA14 4DD
Tel: 020-8309 1039 **Fax:** 020-8302 8941
Managers: S. Holder (Mgr)
Immediate Holding Company: REDLOH LIMITED
Registration no: 00560563 **Date established:** 2003
Turnover: £250,000 - £500,000 **No.of Employees:** 1 - 10
Product Groups: 37

Date of Accounts	Apr 11	Apr 10	Apr 09
Working Capital	-20	-19	2
Fixed Assets	140	144	147
Current Assets	6	11	12

Sabre Systems Heating Ltd

Ruxley Corner Indl-Est Edgington Way, Sidcup, DA14 5BL
Tel: 020-8308 0708 **Fax:** 020-8309 6727
E-mail: sales@sabre-spares.co.uk
Website: http://www.sabresystems.co.uk
Directors: A. Hammond (MD)
Immediate Holding Company: SABRE SYSTEMS (HEATING) LIMITED
Registration no: 01376093 **Date established:** 1978
Turnover: £500,000 - £1m **No.of Employees:** 1 - 10 **Product Groups:** 40, 66

Date of Accounts	Jun 11	Jun 10	Jun 09
Working Capital	-16	-139	-150
Fixed Assets	N/A	69	79
Current Assets	300	255	216

Security Cleared Jobs

Granville Court 75 Granville Road, Sidcup, DA14 4BT
Tel: 0845-270 3003 **Fax:** 0845-270 3004
E-mail: nfo@securityclearedjobs.com
Website: http://www.securityclearedjobs.com
Product Groups: 80

Stoneham plc

Powerscroft Road, Sidcup, DA14 5DZ
Tel: 020-8300 8181 **Fax:** 020-8300 8183
E-mail: info@stoneham.plc.uk
Website: http://www.stoneham-kitchens.co.uk
Bank(s): Midland
Directors: M. Stoneham (Fin), A. Stoneham (MD)
Managers: E. Chu (Purch Mgr)
Immediate Holding Company: STONEHAM PLC
Registration no: 00321764 **VAT No.:** GB 205 3020 30
Date established: 1936 **Turnover:** £5m - £10m
No.of Employees: 51 - 100 **Product Groups:** 26

Date of Accounts	Dec 11	Dec 10	Dec 09
Sales Turnover	6m	5m	5m
Pre Tax Profit/Loss	125	62	89
Working Capital	841	762	1m
Fixed Assets	1m	991	1m
Current Assets	2m	2m	2m
Current Liabilities	479	830	507

Team Weighing Co.

12 Rowley Avenue, Sidcup, DA15 9LA
Tel: 020-8302 9965 **Fax:** 01322-286515
E-mail: mike@teamweighing.fsnet.co.uk
Directors: M. Wickam (Prop)
Immediate Holding Company: 02665352
Registration no: 02665352 **Turnover:** Up to £250,000
No.of Employees: 1 - 10 **Product Groups:** 38, 45, 48, 67

Trans Oceanic Meat Co. Ltd

45 Sidcup Hill, Sidcup, DA14 6HJ
Tel: 020-8302 2544 **Fax:** 020-8309 0249
E-mail: peter.walk@transomeat.co.uk
Website: http://www.transomeat.co.uk
Managers: P. Walk (I.T. Exec)
Ultimate Holding Company: TRANS OCEANIC MEAT CO. LIMITED
Immediate Holding Company: TRANS OCEANIC MEAT COMPANY (MANCHESTER) LIMITED
Registration no: 01361697 **Date established:** 1978
Turnover: £75m - £125m **No.of Employees:** 11 - 20 **Product Groups:** 62

Date of Accounts	Oct 11	Oct 10	Oct 09
Working Capital	-225	-225	-224

Walsh & Jenkins plc

Power House Powerscroft Road, Sidcup, DA14 5EA
Tel: 020-8308 6300 **Fax:** 020-8308 6340
E-mail: sales@walsh-jenkins.co.uk
Website: http://www.walsh-jenkins.co.uk
Bank(s): National Westminster Bank PLC
Directors: R. Mills (MD)
Managers: S. Hunt (Mgr)
Registration no: 01195988 **Date established:** 1975
Turnover: £10m - £20m **No.of Employees:** 21 - 50 **Product Groups:** 27, 28, 30

Date of Accounts	Dec 07	Dec 06	Dec 05
Sales Turnover	8948	9524	8660
Pre Tax Profit/Loss	487	158	721
Working Capital	3713	3238	2913
Fixed Assets	85	213	329
Current Assets	6782	6033	4898
Current Liabilities	3069	2795	1984
Total Share Capital	50	50	50
ROCE% (Return on Capital Employed)	12.8	4.6	22.2
ROT% (Return on Turnover)	5.4	1.7	8.3

Sittingbourne

21st Century Logistics Ltd

Diana House Bonham Drive Eurolink Business Park, Sittingbourne, ME10 3RR
Tel: 01795-435000 **Fax:** 01795-418547
E-mail: sales@dodds.co.uk
Website: http://www.dodds.co.uk
Directors: D. Pink (MD), J. Dodd (Fin)
Ultimate Holding Company: DODDS GROUP LIMITED
Immediate Holding Company: 21ST CENTURY LOGISTICS LIMITED
Registration no: 02496182 **Date established:** 1990 **Turnover:** £5m - £10m
No.of Employees: 51 - 100 **Product Groups:** 77

Date of Accounts	Sep 10	Sep 09	Sep 08
Sales Turnover	8m	11m	13m
Pre Tax Profit/Loss	-397	-300	113
Working Capital	287	-263	-374
Fixed Assets	1m	2m	3m
Current Assets	2m	2m	3m
Current Liabilities	257	763	905

A P M Metals Ltd

Eurolink Way, Sittingbourne, ME10 3HH
Tel: 01795-426021 **Fax:** 01795-421858
E-mail: apmmetalsltd@btconnect.com
Website: http://www.apmmetalsltd.co.uk
Bank(s): HSBC Bank plc
Directors: P. Hyams (MD)
Immediate Holding Company: A.P.M. METALS LIMITED
Registration no: 00844605 **VAT No.:** GB 203 0909 09
Date established: 1965 **Turnover:** £1m - £2m **No.of Employees:** 11 - 20
Product Groups: 66

Date of Accounts	Apr 11	Apr 10	Apr 09
Working Capital	908	902	867
Fixed Assets	660	584	671
Current Assets	2m	2m	1m

Aeromet International plc

Eurolink Way, Sittingbourne, ME10 3RN
Tel: 01795-415000 **Fax:** 01795-415015
E-mail: andrew.king@aeromet.co.uk
Website: http://www.aeromet.co.uk
Bank(s): Barclays
Directors: A. King (Sales), D. Armour (Fin), N. Goddard (Develop), R. Chiese (Fin)
Managers: J. Smith, M. Rowlands (Tech Serv Mgr)
Ultimate Holding Company: AEROMET HOLDINGS INC (USA)
Immediate Holding Company: AEROMET INTERNATIONAL PLC
Registration no: 01626585 **VAT No.:** GB 373 5290 43
Date established: 1982 **Turnover:** £20m - £50m
No.of Employees: 101 - 250 **Product Groups:** 34, 39

Date of Accounts	Dec 11	Dec 10	Dec 09
Sales Turnover	29m	29m	33m
Pre Tax Profit/Loss	12m	2m	2m
Working Capital	14m	15m	14m
Fixed Assets	3m	6m	6m
Current Assets	18m	19m	19m
Current Liabilities	2m	1m	2m

Anglo Pacific Automation & Control Ltd
Unit 3 Saxonshaw Business Park Castle Road, Sittingbourne, ME10 3EU
Tel: 01795-477995 **Fax:** 01795-599700
E-mail: sales@apac-automation.com
Website: http://www.apac-automation.com
Directors: M. Myers (Co Sec), S. Mccabe (Dir)
Immediate Holding Company: ANGLO PACIFIC AUTOMATION AND CONTROL LIMITED
Registration no: 02880812 **Date established:** 1993
No.of Employees: 1 - 10 **Product Groups:** 35, 39, 45

Date of Accounts	Dec 11	Dec 10	Dec 09
Working Capital	39	45	38
Fixed Assets	3	3	4
Current Assets	242	283	250

Axminster Tool Centre
Sheppey Way Bobbing, Sittingbourne, ME9 8QP
Tel: 01795-437143 **Fax:** 01795-591642
E-mail: mike.jeffrey@axminster.co.uk
Website: http://www.axminster.co.uk
Managers: D. Johns (Mgr)
Registration no: 04758583 **Date established:** 2003
No.of Employees: 1 - 10 **Product Groups:** 37

Bale Pak Ltd
Unit 14 Church Road Business Centre Church Road, Sittingbourne, ME10 3RS
Tel: 01795-429484 **Fax:** 01795-429801
E-mail: info@balepak.co.uk
Website: http://www.balepak.co.uk
Directors: J. Smith (Dir)
Ultimate Holding Company: WOODWASTE SYSTEMS LIMITED
Immediate Holding Company: BALE-PAK LIMITED
Registration no: 04296214 **Date established:** 2001
No.of Employees: 1 - 10 **Product Groups:** 38, 42

Date of Accounts	Dec 10	Dec 09	Dec 08
Working Capital	84	90	72
Fixed Assets	19	30	32
Current Assets	477	192	142

Beam Industrial Fasteners Ltd
Eaves Court Bonham Drive Eurolink Commercial Park, Sittingbourne, ME10 3RY
Tel: 01795-435111 **Fax:** 01795-435222
E-mail: bob-nash@btconnect.com
Directors: P. Thurston (MD)
Managers: B. Nash (Chief Mgr)
Immediate Holding Company: BEAM INDUSTRIAL FASTENERS UK LIMITED
Registration no: 03039961 **VAT No.:** GB 702 5068 67
Date established: 1995 **Turnover:** £250,000 - £500,000
No.of Employees: 1 - 10 **Product Groups:** 30, 35, 66

Date of Accounts	Mar 12	Mar 11	Mar 10
Working Capital	3	-0	-0
Fixed Assets	1	2	2
Current Assets	123	103	89

Besco Industrial Supplies Ltd
Unit 3 The Glenmore Centre Castle Road, Eurolink, Sittingbourne, ME10 3GL
Tel: 0845-2960050 **Fax:** 0845-2960056
E-mail: sales@besco.co.uk
Website: http://www.besco.co.uk
Directors: M. Hodgson (MD)
Managers: K. Durling (Purch Mgr)
VAT No.: GB 733 7013 55 **No.of Employees:** 1 - 10 **Product Groups:** 32, 33, 36, 37, 38, 41

Capus UK Ltd
Unit B5 Staplehurst Lodge Industrial Estate Staplehurst Road, Sittingbourne, ME10 1XP
Tel: 01795-420333 **Fax:** 01795-424324
E-mail: d.gravener@capus.co.uk
Website: http://www.capus.co.uk
Directors: D. Gravener (MD)
Ultimate Holding Company: ROADLINK INTERNATIONAL LIMITED
Immediate Holding Company: CAPUS (U.K.) LIMITED
Registration no: 01661145 **Date established:** 1982
No.of Employees: 1 - 10 **Product Groups:** 35, 37, 39, 68

Date of Accounts	Mar 11	Mar 10	Mar 09
Working Capital	447	406	382
Fixed Assets	9	16	22
Current Assets	749	699	729

Carousel Logistics (Carousel)
Unit 14a Eurolink Industrial Centre Upper Field Road, Sittingbourne, ME10 3UP
Tel: 01795-413600 **Fax:** 01795-413610
E-mail: graham.martin@carousel.eu
Website: http://www.carousellogistics.co.uk
Directors: E. Weir (Fin), G. Martin (MD), M. Martin (Sales)
Managers: N. Alsop (Tech Serv Mgr), R. Syrett (Buyer)
Immediate Holding Company: CAROUSEL LOGISTICS LIMITED
Registration no: 01908712 **Date established:** 1985
Turnover: £10m - £20m **No.of Employees:** 51 - 100 **Product Groups:** 45, 75, 79

Cartridge World Ltd
5 Central Avenue, Sittingbourne, ME10 4BX
Tel: 01795-421212 **Fax:** 01795-421212
Website: http://www.sittingbourne.cartridgeworld.co.uk
Directors: C. Harms (Dir)
Immediate Holding Company: CARTRIDGE WORLD LIMITED
Registration no: 04124067 **Date established:** 2000 **Turnover:** £5m - £10m
No.of Employees: 21 - 50 **Product Groups:** 28, 30, 44

Date of Accounts	Dec 11	Dec 10	Dec 09
Sales Turnover	6m	7m	8m
Pre Tax Profit/Loss	373	164	210
Working Capital	1m	967	878
Fixed Assets	403	455	524
Current Assets	7m	7m	6m
Current Liabilities	4m	1m	2m

Clever Engineering (Kent) Limited Clever Air Conditioning Sales Limited
Winberg House Canterbury Road, Sittingbourne, ME10 4JA
Tel: 0845-0573097 **Fax:** 0845-280 1525
E-mail: sales@cleverengineering.co.uk
Website: http://www.factorycooling.com
Registration no: 06883394 **Product Groups:** 23, 40, 66

Computertel Ltd
Woodlands Dully Hill, Doddington, Sittingbourne, ME9 0BY
Tel: 01795-886333
E-mail: t.haynes@computertel.co.uk
Website: http://www.computertel.co.uk
Directors: P. Haynes (Dir)
Immediate Holding Company: COMPUTERTEL LIMITED
Registration no: 02311748 **Date established:** 1988
No.of Employees: 11 - 20 **Product Groups:** 37, 80

Date of Accounts	Mar 11	Mar 10	Mar 09
Working Capital	198	108	117
Fixed Assets	15	18	23
Current Assets	726	677	689
Current Liabilities	N/A	497	N/A

Crusader Packaging Services Ltd
Unit 5-6 Castleacres Industrial Park Castle Road, Sittingbourne, ME10 3RZ
Tel: 01795-429501 **Fax:** 01795-473736
E-mail: stuart@crusaderpackaging.co.uk
Website: http://www.crusaderpackaging.co.uk
Directors: S. Taylor (Dir)
Immediate Holding Company: CRUSADER PACKAGING SERVICES LIMITED
Registration no: 02110180 **Date established:** 1987
No.of Employees: 1 - 10 **Product Groups:** 27, 30

Date of Accounts	Mar 12	Mar 11	Mar 10
Working Capital	500	359	347
Fixed Assets	93	45	61
Current Assets	934	872	614

D S L Installations Ltd Disabled Supplies Ltd
Unit 3 D2 Trading Estate Castle Road, Sittingbourne, ME10 3RH
Tel: 01795-438545 **Fax:** 01795-438546
E-mail: enquiries@dsl-installations.co.uk
Website: http://www.dsl-installations.co.uk
Directors: A. Emery (Dir)
Immediate Holding Company: N.T.F.W. LIMITED
Date established: 2005 **Turnover:** £1m - £2m **No.of Employees:** 11 - 20
Product Groups: 30, 66, 67

Dodd's Group
Diana House Bonham Drive, Eurolink Commercial Pk, Sittingbourne, ME10 3RR
Tel: 01795-435000 **Fax:** 01795-479790
E-mail: sales@dodds.co.uk
Website: http://www.dodds.co.uk
Bank(s): National Westminster
Directors: D. Pink (MD)
Ultimate Holding Company: Dodds Group Ltd
Registration no: 02571068 **VAT No.:** GB 661 7343 33
Date established: 1905 **Turnover:** £20m - £50m
No.of Employees: 251 - 500 **Product Groups:** 45, 72, 74, 75, 76, 77, 84

Date of Accounts	Sep 09	Sep 08	Sep 07
Sales Turnover	11m	N/A	N/A
Pre Tax Profit/Loss	-300	825	144
Working Capital	-262	1	1
Fixed Assets	2m	843	843
Current Assets	2m	1	1
Current Liabilities	763	N/A	N/A

Dore Metal Services Ltd
Unit 2 Dolphin Park Cremers Road, Sittingbourne, ME10 3HB
Tel: 01795-473551 **Fax:** 01795-429473
E-mail: sales@doremetals.co.uk
Website: http://www.doremetals.co.uk
Bank(s): National Westminster Bank Plc
Directors: I. Hunter (MD), R. Hunter (Fin)
Ultimate Holding Company: HUNTER METAL HOLDINGS LIMITED
Immediate Holding Company: DORE METAL SERVICES SOUTHERN LIMITED
Registration no: 01789969 **VAT No.:** GB 414 1610 02
Date established: 1984 **Turnover:** £2m - £5m **No.of Employees:** 11 - 20
Product Groups: 66

Date of Accounts	Aug 11	Aug 10	Aug 09
Working Capital	241	320	283
Fixed Assets	2m	2m	2m
Current Assets	4m	3m	3m

Dyebrick
Ripley House Keycol Hill Newington, Sittingbourne, ME9 8NE
Tel: 01795-871972 **Fax:** 01795-871077
E-mail: mail@dyebrick.com
Website: http://www.dyebrick.com
Managers: D. Dempsey (Chief Mgr), D. Holland (Sales Admin)
Date established: 2003 **Turnover:** £500,000 - £1m
No.of Employees: 1 - 10 **Product Groups:** 52

E P S Logistics Technology Ltd
152 Staplehurst Road, Sittingbourne, ME10 1XS
Tel: 01795-424433 **Fax:** 01795-426970
E-mail: sales@epslt.co.uk
Website: http://www.epslt.co.uk
Bank(s): Barclays, Maidstone
Directors: R. Bonner (MD), T. Judge (Tech Serv)
Managers: M. Sage (Buyer), S. Chawner (Fin Mgr), S. Green
Ultimate Holding Company: WELLWINCH LIMITED
Immediate Holding Company: E.P.S. LOGISTICS TECHNOLOGY LIMITED
Registration no: 01328874 **VAT No.:** GB 530 8076 60
Date established: 1977 **Turnover:** £2m - £5m **No.of Employees:** 21 - 50
Product Groups: 24, 25, 28, 30, 35, 39

Date of Accounts	Mar 12	Mar 11	Mar 10
Sales Turnover	N/A	2m	3m
Pre Tax Profit/Loss	N/A	49	318
Working Capital	2m	2m	2m
Fixed Assets	3m	3m	3m
Current Assets	2m	2m	2m
Current Liabilities	N/A	111	141

Euro Bond Adhesives Ltd
Bonham Drive Eurolink Business Park, Sittingbourne, ME10 3RY
Tel: 01795-427888 **Fax:** 01795-479685
E-mail: sales@eurobond-adhesives.co.uk
Website: http://www.eurobond-adhesives.co.uk
Directors: S. Dearing (Prop), S. Speight (Fin)
Ultimate Holding Company: EUROBOND ADHESIVES HOLDINGS LIMITED
Immediate Holding Company: EUROBOND ADHESIVES LIMITED
Registration no: 01795491 **Date established:** 1984
No.of Employees: 1 - 10 **Product Groups:** 32

Date of Accounts	Mar 12	Mar 11	Mar 10
Working Capital	1m	1m	971
Fixed Assets	325	330	339
Current Assets	1m	1m	1m

Eurocoils Ltd
Unit D3 Eurolink Commercial Park Bonham Drive, Sittingbourne, ME10 3RX
Tel: 01795-475275 **Fax:** 01795-422210
E-mail: sales@eurocoils.co.uk
Website: http://www.eurocoils.co.uk
Directors: K. Murray (MD), T. Rayfield (Fin)
Ultimate Holding Company: RIBERIA LIMITED
Immediate Holding Company: EUROCOILS LIMITED
Registration no: 01149081 **Date established:** 1973 **Turnover:** £2m - £5m
No.of Employees: 1 - 10 **Product Groups:** 30, 36, 40, 48

Date of Accounts	Dec 11	Dec 10	Dec 09
Working Capital	119	170	65
Fixed Assets	1m	1m	1m
Current Assets	1m	1m	1m

Fedex
Gateway Centre Eurolink Industrial Centre Castle Road, Sittingbourne, ME10 3RN
Tel: 01795-479300 **Fax:** 01795-413609
E-mail: sales0008@anc.co.uk
Website: http://www.carousel-worldwide.com
Directors: M. Martin (Sales), G. Martin (MD)
Managers: E. Weir
Ultimate Holding Company: COLOMBIER GROUP NV (NETHERLANDS)
Immediate Holding Company: COLOMBIER (UK) LIMITED
Date established: 1968 **No.of Employees:** 21 - 50 **Product Groups:** 79, 87

Date of Accounts	Dec 11	Dec 10	Dec 09
Sales Turnover	11m	11m	13m
Pre Tax Profit/Loss	132	-747	2m
Working Capital	1m	883	706
Fixed Assets	5m	5m	5m
Current Assets	5m	4m	4m
Current Liabilities	356	925	1m

Freeway Signs Ltd
Mainstream House Bonham Drive Eurolink Business Park, Sittingbourne, ME10 3RY
Tel: 01795-426724 **Fax:** 01795-431180
E-mail: freewaysigns@lineone.net
Website: http://www.freewaysigns.co.uk
Directors: M. Perkins (Dir & Buyer), L. Perkins (MD), D. Mccarthy (MD), D. Mccarthy (Dir), E. Perkins (MD)
Managers: C. Jones (Mgr)
Immediate Holding Company: FREEWAY SIGNS LIMITED
Registration no: 03693823 **VAT No.:** GB 703 2417 77
Date established: 1999 **Turnover:** £500,000 - £1m
No.of Employees: 1 - 10 **Product Groups:** 28

Date of Accounts	Jan 10	Jan 09	Jan 08
Working Capital	-81	-0	19
Fixed Assets	5	13	18
Current Assets	60	91	62

Group Four Glass Fibre Co. Ltd
Unit 42 Church Road Business Centre Church Road, Sittingbourne, ME10 3RS
Tel: 01795-429424 **Fax:** 01795-476248
E-mail: sales@groupfourglassfibre.co.uk
Website: http://www.groupfourglassfibre.co.uk
Directors: T. Cox (MD), M. Cox (Fin)
Immediate Holding Company: GROUP FOUR GLASSFIBRE CO. LIMITED
Registration no: 01036836 **VAT No.:** GB 204 0562 15
Date established: 1972 **Turnover:** £500,000 - £1m
No.of Employees: 11 - 20 **Product Groups:** 30

Date of Accounts	Dec 11	Dec 10	Dec 09
Working Capital	449	386	368
Fixed Assets	81	92	71
Current Assets	613	597	595

Heras Ready Fence Service
Unit B1 Eurolink Industrial Estate, Sittingbourne, ME10 3RL
Tel: 01795-423261 **Fax:** 01795-426351
E-mail: tony.wells@readyfence.co.uk
Website: http://www.herasreadyfence.co.uk
Managers: T. Wells (Ops Mgr)
Ultimate Holding Company: CEMENT ROADSTONE HOLDINGS P.L.C.
Immediate Holding Company: CRH FENCING LTD
Registration no: 02840742 **Turnover:** £1m - £2m
No.of Employees: 1 - 10 **Product Groups:** 35, 40, 52, 66

J H Lifting
Unit Q London Road, Sittingbourne, ME10 1NQ
Tel: 01795-425760 **Fax:** 01795-429476
E-mail: info@jhlifting.co.uk
Website: http://www.jhlifting.co.uk
Directors: R. Oliveira (MD)
Immediate Holding Company: J.H. (LIFTING GEAR HIRE) LIMITED
Registration no: 01041586 **VAT No.:** GB 203 2419 16
Date established: 1972 **Turnover:** £500,000 - £1m
No.of Employees: 1 - 10 **Product Groups:** 23, 30, 35, 36, 37, 38, 39, 40, 41, 45, 48, 52, 66, 67, 68, 83, 85

Jaymech Food Machines
Unit 5 Church Road Business Centre Church Road, Sittingbourne, ME10 3RS
Tel: 01795-477747 **Fax:** 01795-471689
E-mail: info@jaymech.com
Website: http://www.jaymech.com
Directors: J. Hook (Prop)
Registration no: 02009161 **Turnover:** Up to £250,000
No.of Employees: 1 - 10 **Product Groups:** 20, 40, 41

Knauf Drywall
Kemsley Fields Business Park Ridham Dock, Iwade, Sittingbourne, ME9 8SR
Tel: 01795-424499 **Fax:** 01795-428651
E-mail: info@knauf.co.uk
Website: http://www.knauf.co.uk
Directors: S. Lindsay (Fin), I. Dean (Sales)
Managers: S. Drew (Purch Mgr), T. Kiley, D. Patrick (Mktg Serv Mgr), B. Findlay (Personnel), J. Wigley (Tech Serv Mgr)

see next page

***Knauf Drywall** - Cont'd*
Immediate Holding Company: KNAUF LIMITED
Registration no: 02292022 **Date established:** 1988
Turnover: £10m - £20m **No.of Employees:** 251 - 500
Product Groups: 33, 35

L M R Gear-Tech Ltd
Unit 9 Chapel Park Stadium Way, Sittingbourne, ME10 3RW
Tel: 01795-421040 **Fax:** 01795-439009
E-mail: enquiries@lmrgeartech.com
Website: http://www.lmrgeartech.com
Directors: D. Rungay (Prop)
Immediate Holding Company: L M R GEAR TECH LIMITED
Registration no: 02995696 **Date established:** 1994
No.of Employees: 1 - 10 **Product Groups:** 35, 45

Date of Accounts	Dec 11	Dec 10	Dec 09
Working Capital	-71	-83	-86
Fixed Assets	94	98	103
Current Assets	119	103	89

Lebus International Engineers Ltd
Kent Ambulance NHS Trust Crown Quay Lane, Sittingbourne, ME10 3HU
Tel: 01795-475324 **Fax:** 01795-428004
E-mail: enquiries@lebusintengineers.com
Website: http://www.lebusintengineers.com
Bank(s): Bank One NA
Directors: P. Dixon (Dir), P. Dixon (MD), S. Rossiter (Co Sec)
Managers: M. Case (Mgr)
Immediate Holding Company: LEBUS INTERNATIONAL ENGINEERS LIMITED
Registration no: 00716491 **VAT No.:** GB 203 3914 01
Date established: 1962 **Turnover:** £1m - £2m **No.of Employees:** 11 - 20
Product Groups: 35, 39, 40, 45, 46, 48, 84

Date of Accounts	Feb 08	Feb 11	Feb 10
Working Capital	-411	1m	911
Fixed Assets	63	119	131
Current Assets	2m	3m	2m

M K E Engineering Group
15b - 15c Dolphone Park Upper Field Road, Sittingbourne, ME10 3UP
Tel: 01795-471089 **Fax:** 01795-436611
E-mail: sales@mke.co.uk
Website: http://www.mke.co.uk
Directors: A. Savage (Dir)
No.of Employees: 51 - 100 **Product Groups:** 22, 29, 31, 33, 34, 35, 37, 38, 39, 40, 41, 42, 44, 45, 46, 47, 48, 49, 67, 68, 83, 84

McNealy Brown Ltd
Prentis Quay Mill Way, Sittingbourne, ME10 2QD
Tel: 01795-470592 **Fax:** 01795-471238
E-mail: info@mcnealybrown.co.uk
Website: http://www.mcnealybrown.com
Bank(s): National Westminster Bank Plc
Directors: R. Brown (Co Sec), V. Mcnealy (MD)
Managers: K. Drury (Personnel)
Ultimate Holding Company: MCNEALY BROWN GROUP LIMITED
Immediate Holding Company: MCNEALY BROWN LIMITED
Registration no: 01841649 **VAT No.:** GB 374 5245 42
Date established: 1984 **Turnover:** £5m - £10m
No.of Employees: 51 - 100 **Product Groups:** 25, 26, 33, 34, 35, 36, 39, 48, 49, 51, 52, 84

Date of Accounts	Jul 11	Jul 10	Jul 09
Sales Turnover	7m	N/A	N/A
Pre Tax Profit/Loss	36	N/A	N/A
Working Capital	1m	1m	1m
Fixed Assets	26	37	46
Current Assets	2m	3m	3m
Current Liabilities	538	N/A	N/A

Magna Exteriors & Interiors Ltd
Spade Lane Hartlip, Sittingbourne, ME9 7TT
Tel: 01634-385200 **Fax:** 01634-269840
Website: http://www.magna.com
Bank(s): Barclays, Sevenoaks
Managers: B. Edwards (Purch Mgr), R. Dowle (Mgr), R. Larcombe (Tech Serv Mgr), S. Margerum (Comptroller), K. Parker (Personnel)
Ultimate Holding Company: MAGNA INTERNATIONAL INC. (CANADA)
Immediate Holding Company: INTIER AUTOMOTIVE HOLDINGS LIMITED
Registration no: 01676532 **VAT No.:** GB 683 8198 82
Turnover: £75m - £125m **No.of Employees:** 251 - 500
Product Groups: 30, 39, 66

Medical & Cosmetic Mouldings Ltd
Gas Road, Sittingbourne, ME10 2QD
Tel: 01795-426452 **Fax:** 01795-422790
E-mail: informationmcm@aol.com
Website: http://www.medical-cosmetic.co.uk
Directors: D. Wise (Fin)
Immediate Holding Company: MEDICAL & COSMETIC MOULDINGS LIMITED
Registration no: 02538956 **VAT No.:** GB 571 7781 10
Date established: 1990 **Turnover:** £1m - £2m **No.of Employees:** 11 - 20
Product Groups: 30

Date of Accounts	Sep 11	Sep 10	Sep 09
Sales Turnover	1m	1m	893
Pre Tax Profit/Loss	238	184	158
Working Capital	171	115	90
Fixed Assets	306	305	318
Current Assets	365	282	244
Current Liabilities	114	92	79

Medway Galvanising & Powder Coating Ltd
9a-9c Eurolink Industrial Centre Castle Road, Sittingbourne, ME10 3RN
Tel: 01795-479489 **Fax:** 01795-477598
E-mail: info@medgalv.co.uk
Website: http://www.medgalv.co.uk
Directors: P. Roberts (Sales), N. Feliniak (Fin)
Managers: D. Wilsonham (Tech Serv Mgr), B. Cole (Personnel)
Immediate Holding Company: MEDWAY GALVANISING COMPANY LIMITED
Registration no: 01808205 **VAT No.:** GB 374 4247 43
Date established: 1984 **Turnover:** £5m - £10m
No.of Employees: 101 - 250 **Product Groups:** 26, 35, 48, 66

Date of Accounts	Mar 12	Mar 11	Mar 10
Sales Turnover	8m	8m	7m
Pre Tax Profit/Loss	214	164	8
Working Capital	634	756	936
Fixed Assets	3m	3m	3m
Current Assets	2m	2m	2m
Current Liabilities	796	556	494

Mid Kent Electrical Engineering Co. Ltd
Unit 15b & 15c Eurolink Industrial Estate Upper Field Road, Sittingbourne, ME10 3UP
Tel: 01795-471089 **Fax:** 01795-436611
E-mail: sales@mke.co.uk
Website: http://www.mke.co.uk
Directors: A. Savage (MD)
Immediate Holding Company: MID KENT ELECTRICAL ENGINEERING COMPANY LIMITED
Registration no: 01006814 **Date established:** 1971 **Turnover:** £5m - £10m
No.of Employees: 101 - 250 **Product Groups:** 67

Date of Accounts	Apr 11	Apr 10	Apr 09
Sales Turnover	8m	7m	8m
Pre Tax Profit/Loss	4	-590	33
Working Capital	-42	-51	338
Fixed Assets	229	290	378
Current Assets	3m	2m	2m
Current Liabilities	714	529	418

Milton Pipes Ltd
Cooks Lane, Sittingbourne, ME10 2QF
Tel: 01795-425191 **Fax:** 01795-420360
E-mail: sales@miltonprecast.com
Website: http://www.miltonprecast.com
Bank(s): Lloyds TSB
Managers: D. Mitchelle (Mgr)
Ultimate Holding Company: MPC PRECAST LIMITED
Immediate Holding Company: MILTON PIPES LIMITED
Registration no: 00755076 **VAT No.:** GB 201 6683 08
Date established: 1963 **Turnover:** £5m - £10m
No.of Employees: 51 - 100 **Product Groups:** 33

Date of Accounts	Mar 11	Mar 10	Mar 09
Sales Turnover	9m	7m	8m
Pre Tax Profit/Loss	-415	-2m	-1m
Working Capital	2m	1m	3m
Fixed Assets	6m	6m	7m
Current Assets	4m	3m	4m
Current Liabilities	2m	844	609

M-Real New Thames
Ridham Avenue Kemsley, Sittingbourne, ME10 2SG
Tel: 01795-564444 **Fax:** 01795-564555
E-mail: enquiries@m-real.com
Website: http://www.m-real.com
Bank(s): Lloyds TSB
Managers: J. Verajankorva (Chief Mgr), K. Wooton (Product), M. Elgar (Cust Serv Mgr)
Registration no: 00502493 **VAT No.:** GB 445 0263 72
Turnover: Over £1,000m **No.of Employees:** 251 - 500
Product Groups: 66

Plalite Ltd
Unit 9 Styles Close, Sittingbourne, ME10 3BF
Tel: 01795-476367 **Fax:** 01795-476369
E-mail: sales@plalite.com
Website: http://www.plalite.com
Bank(s): Barclays, Eltham
Directors: A. Bess (Dir), S. Hardman (Co Sec)
Immediate Holding Company: PLALITE LIMITED
Registration no: 00936082 **Date established:** 1968 **Turnover:** £2m - £5m
No.of Employees: 21 - 50 **Product Groups:** 30, 42, 48

Date of Accounts	Mar 11	Mar 10	Mar 09
Working Capital	173	-26	-69
Fixed Assets	2m	2m	2m
Current Assets	1m	871	676

Poolewood Machinery
Farriers Pett Lane, Stockbury, Sittingbourne, ME9 7RJ
Tel: 01622-884651 **Fax:** 01622-884520
E-mail: info@poolewood.co.uk
Website: http://www.poolewood.co.uk
Directors: T. Davis (MD)
Immediate Holding Company: HALLVALUE LIMITED
Registration no: 02165565 **VAT No.:** GB 472 7166 32
Date established: 1987 **Turnover:** Up to £250,000
No.of Employees: 1 - 10 **Product Groups:** 47, 48

Date of Accounts	Nov 11	Nov 10	Nov 09
Working Capital	75	52	47
Fixed Assets	69	71	73
Current Assets	158	102	106

Powakaddy International Ltd
Unit N1 Eurolink Industrial Centre Castle Road, Sittingbourne, ME10 3RN
Tel: 01795-473555 **Fax:** 01795-474586
E-mail: sales@powakaddy.co.uk
Website: http://www.powakaddy.co.uk
Bank(s): Bank of Scotland
Directors: S. Homer (Sales), R. Ledger (Fin)
Managers: L. Poppy (Personnel), A. Stelfox (Purch Mgr), E. Jeffery (Tech Serv Mgr), G. White
Ultimate Holding Company: POWAKADDY GROUP LIMITED
Immediate Holding Company: POWAKADDY INTERNATIONAL LIMITED
Registration no: 01978915 **Date established:** 1986
Turnover: £10m - £20m **No.of Employees:** 21 - 50 **Product Groups:** 49

Date of Accounts	Dec 10	Dec 09	Dec 08
Sales Turnover	18m	20m	16m
Pre Tax Profit/Loss	-2m	826	573
Working Capital	2m	3m	3m
Fixed Assets	920	924	997
Current Assets	5m	6m	6m
Current Liabilities	478	515	719

Product Support Ltd
152 Staplehurst Road, Sittingbourne, ME10 1XS
Tel: 01795-427242
E-mail: sales@walkerresidential.co.uk
Website: http://www.product-support.co.uk
Directors: C. Banfield (Co Sec), C. Phillips (Co Sec), G. Connell (Dir)
Ultimate Holding Company: WINCANTON PLC
Immediate Holding Company: PRODUCT SUPPORT LIMITED
Registration no: 02973863 **Date established:** 1994
Turnover: £10m - £20m **No.of Employees:** 1 - 10 **Product Groups:** 38, 42

Date of Accounts	Mar 11	Mar 10	Mar 09
Sales Turnover	N/A	N/A	24m
Pre Tax Profit/Loss	N/A	N/A	31m
Working Capital	34m	34m	34m
Current Assets	34m	34m	34m

Proquis Ltd
Building 1050 Cornforth Drive Kent Science Park, Sittingbourne, ME9 8PX
Tel: 01795-479001 **Fax:** 01795-479009
E-mail: info@proquis.com
Website: http://www.proquis.com/content/pages/why-proquis
Directors: B. Best (Dir)
Immediate Holding Company: PROQUIS LIMITED
Registration no: 02757521 **Date established:** 1992
Turnover: £250,000 - £500,000 **No.of Employees:** 1 - 10
Product Groups: 44, 80, 86

Date of Accounts	Sep 11	Sep 10	Sep 09
Sales Turnover	462	N/A	900
Pre Tax Profit/Loss	88	N/A	45
Working Capital	-10	-50	14
Fixed Assets	21	30	75
Current Assets	217	218	364
Current Liabilities	144	N/A	50

R & G Marine & Industrial Services
Units 1a-2a Brickmakers Industrial Estat Castle Road, Sittingbourne, ME10 3RL
Tel: 01795-470430 **Fax:** 01795-429722
E-mail: graham@randgmarine.co.uk
Website: http://www.randgmarine.co.uk
Directors: G. Newman (Ptnr)
Immediate Holding Company: R & G MARINE & INDUSTRIAL SERVICES LIMITED
Registration no: 04560586 **VAT No.:** GB 373 8446 23
Date established: 2002 **Turnover:** £250,000 - £500,000
No.of Employees: 1 - 10 **Product Groups:** 23, 35, 45, 48

Date of Accounts	Aug 11	Aug 10	Aug 09
Sales Turnover	399	358	532
Pre Tax Profit/Loss	-4	-20	-9
Working Capital	4	10	25
Fixed Assets	21	32	44
Current Assets	113	92	80
Current Liabilities	15	10	6

Scipac Ltd
Unit D7 Broad Oak Enterprise Village, Sittingbourne, ME9 8AQ
Tel: 01795-423077 **Fax:** 01795-426942
E-mail: mail@scipac.com
Website: http://www.scipac.com
Bank(s): HSBC
Directors: J. Lorimer (Fin)
Managers: C. Rapley (Purch Mgr)
Ultimate Holding Company: ALERE INC (USA)
Immediate Holding Company: SCIPAC LIMITED
Registration no: 01995896 **VAT No.:** GB 445 7097 28
Date established: 1986 **Turnover:** £5m - £10m
No.of Employees: 51 - 100 **Product Groups:** 31

Date of Accounts	Dec 11	Dec 10	Mar 10
Sales Turnover	6m	5m	N/A
Pre Tax Profit/Loss	1m	1m	N/A
Working Capital	4m	3m	2m
Fixed Assets	884	697	540
Current Assets	5m	4m	3m
Current Liabilities	175	430	N/A

Solaglas Ltd
Mill Way, Sittingbourne, ME10 2PD
Tel: 01795-421534 **Fax:** 01795-473651
E-mail: solaglas.gpd@saint-gobain-glass.com
Website: http://www.solaglas.sggs.com
Bank(s): Lloyds TSB Bank plc
Directors: A. Higgins (MD)
Managers: B. Baker (Mgr)
Ultimate Holding Company: Saint Gobain
Immediate Holding Company: Saint-Gobain Ltd
Registration no: 02442570 **VAT No.:** GB 544 9390 18
Date established: 1980 **Turnover:** £10m - £20m
No.of Employees: 51 - 100 **Product Groups:** 33, 54

Specialty Gases Ltd
Buiding 940 Kent Science Park, Sittingbourne, ME9 8PS
Tel: 01795-599099 **Fax:** 01795-411525
E-mail: sales@specialty-gases.com
Website: http://www.specialty-gases.com
Managers: K. Stoddart (Mgr)
Immediate Holding Company: SPECIALTY GASES LIMITED
Registration no: 01007149 **VAT No.:** GB 372 5949 18
Date established: 1971 **Turnover:** £500,000 - £1m
No.of Employees: 1 - 10 **Product Groups:** 31, 38, 66

Date of Accounts	Jun 11	Jun 10	Jun 09
Sales Turnover	N/A	N/A	601
Pre Tax Profit/Loss	N/A	N/A	31
Working Capital	51	14	-26
Fixed Assets	6	7	8
Current Assets	220	173	154
Current Liabilities	N/A	N/A	74

Structural & Welding Testing Ltd
19 Albany Road, Sittingbourne, ME10 1EB
Tel: 01795-420264 **Fax:** 0870-762 5588
E-mail: swtndt@msn.com
Directors: D. Hayre (Dir)
Managers: K. Hayre (Sales Admin), M. Hayre (Sec)
Immediate Holding Company: STRUCTURAL & WELD TESTING SERVICES LIMITED
Registration no: 05248231 **VAT No.:** GB 571 8390 20
Date established: 2004 **Turnover:** £250,000 - £500,000
No.of Employees: 11 - 20 **Product Groups:** 38, 54, 85, 86

Date of Accounts	Dec 10	Dec 09	Dec 08
Working Capital	219	374	171
Fixed Assets	68	85	95
Current Assets	426	596	387

Supreme Concrete Ltd
Crown Quay Lane, Sittingbourne, ME10 3SL
Tel: 01795-433580 **Fax:** 01795-433599
E-mail: enquiries@bourncrete.co.uk
Website: http://www.supremeconcrete.co.uk
Bank(s): Royal Bank of Scotland
Managers: S. France (Mgr)
Ultimate Holding Company: CRH PUBLIC LIMITED COMPANY
Immediate Holding Company: SUPREME CONCRETE LIMITED
Registration no: 01410463 **Date established:** 1979
Turnover: £20m - £50m **No.of Employees:** 21 - 50 **Product Groups:** 33

Date of Accounts	Dec 11	Dec 10	Dec 09
Sales Turnover	24m	23m	22m
Pre Tax Profit/Loss	3m	3m	2m

Working Capital	23m	21m	18m
Fixed Assets	4m	5m	5m
Current Assets	31m	27m	25m
Current Liabilities	5m	4m	5m

Swale Shutter & Door Services Ltd
Wises Oast Wises Lane, Borden, Sittingbourne, ME9 8LR
Tel: 01795-423716 **Fax:** 01795-426762
E-mail: enquiries@swaleshutters.co.uk
Website: http://www.swaleshutters.co.uk
Directors: C. Pengelly (Fin)
Immediate Holding Company: SWALE SHUTTER AND DOOR SERVICES LIMITED
Registration no: 03090172 **Date established:** 1995
No.of Employees: 1 - 10 **Product Groups:** 30, 35, 36, 48

Date of Accounts	Sep 11	Sep 10	Sep 09
Working Capital	9	-87	-56
Fixed Assets	7	9	12
Current Assets	159	94	141

Taylor Splice Co.
Unit A1-A2 Brickmakers Industrial Estate Castle Road, Sittingbourne, ME10 3RL
Tel: 01795-431235 **Fax:** 01795-431236
E-mail: deanna@randgmarine.co.uk
Website: http://www.randgmarine.co.uk
Directors: D. Newman (Dir)
Immediate Holding Company: RADIOACTIVE RISK MANAGEMENT LIMITED
Date established: 2007 **No.of Employees:** 1 - 10 **Product Groups:** 35

The Beat Project
10 Park Road, Sittingbourne, ME10 1DR
Tel: 01795-478401
E-mail: info@thebeatproject.org.uk
Website: http://www.thebeatproject.org.uk
Directors: S. Carley (Fab)
Immediate Holding Company: THE BEAT PROJECT LTD
Registration no: 04446363 **Date established:** 2002
Turnover: £250,000 - £500,000 **No.of Employees:** 11 - 20
Product Groups: 89

Date of Accounts	May 11	May 10	May 09
Sales Turnover	329	330	350
Pre Tax Profit/Loss	-19	22	38
Working Capital	134	154	130
Fixed Assets	4	3	5
Current Assets	151	171	149
Current Liabilities	7	6	6

Thermotron Industries
Newton House Unit 550 Winch Road Kent Science Park, Sittingbourne, ME9 8EF
Tel: 01795-436333 **Fax:** 01795-436777
E-mail: paul.bryant@thermotron.co.uk
Website: http://www.thermotron.co.uk
Bank(s): Lloyds, Sittingbourne
Managers: P. Bryant (Chief Mgr)
Immediate Holding Company: THERMOTRON (UK) LIMITED
Registration no: 02482295 **VAT No.:** GB 304 0559 93
Date established: 1990 **Turnover:** £2m - £5m **No.of Employees:** 11 - 20
Product Groups: 38

Vion Food N L Division Ltd
Syndale Court Stadium Way Eurolink Business Park, Sittingbourne, ME10 3SP
Tel: 01795-479131 **Fax:** 01795-424705
E-mail: tommy.bennett@vionfood.com
Website: http://www.vionfood.com
Managers: T. Bennett (Sales Admin)
Immediate Holding Company: VION FOOD (NL DIVISION) LIMITED
Registration no: 07330665 **VAT No.:** GB 472 6882 11
Date established: 2010 **Turnover:** Up to £250,000
No.of Employees: 11 - 20 **Product Groups:** 61

Date of Accounts	Dec 11
Sales Turnover	2m
Pre Tax Profit/Loss	109
Working Capital	66
Fixed Assets	14
Current Assets	121
Current Liabilities	51

Wire Belt Co. Ltd
Castle Road, Sittingbourne, ME10 3RF
Tel: 01795-421771 **Fax:** 01795-428905
E-mail: sales@wirebelt.co.uk
Website: http://www.wirebelt.co.uk
Bank(s): HSBC Bank plc
Directors: A. Munday (Fin)
Ultimate Holding Company: WIRE BELT COMPANY OF AMERICA INC (USA)
Immediate Holding Company: WIRE BELT COMPANY LIMITED
Registration no: 00716510 **VAT No.:** GB 202 9377 74
Date established: 1962 **Turnover:** £5m - £10m
No.of Employees: 51 - 100 **Product Groups:** 30, 35, 41, 43, 44, 45, 67, 84

Date of Accounts	Dec 11	Dec 10	Dec 09
Sales Turnover	7m	7m	6m
Pre Tax Profit/Loss	1m	955	287
Working Capital	7m	7m	7m
Fixed Assets	4m	4m	3m
Current Assets	8m	8m	7m
Current Liabilities	502	507	405

Snodland

Kingsdown
Mid Kent Business Park Brook Street, Snodland, ME6 5BB
Tel: 01634-249555 **Fax:** 01634-249550
E-mail: sales@kingsdownuk.com
Website: http://www.kingsdownuk.com
Bank(s): Lloyds TSB Bank plc
Directors: J. Wesson (MD), J. Darknell (Co Sec)
Immediate Holding Company: KINGSDALE LAND LIMITED
Registration no: 01771145 **VAT No.:** GB 573 5845 08
Date established: 1983 **Turnover:** £5m - £10m **No.of Employees:** 11 - 20
Product Groups: 35, 39, 40, 41, 45, 67, 68

Date of Accounts	Mar 11	Mar 10	Mar 09
Pre Tax Profit/Loss	14	6	-1
Working Capital	28	-21	-19
Fixed Assets	848	770	805
Current Assets	84	52	31
Current Liabilities	56	73	50

Smurfit Kappa Townsend Hook
Paper Mills Mill Street, Snodland, ME6 5AX
Tel: 01634-240205 **Fax:** 01634-243458
E-mail: info@smurfitkappa.co.uk
Website: http://www.smurfitkappa.co.uk
Directors: A. Richards (Fin), C. Allen (Grp Chief Exec), J. Hiscock (Co Sec)
Managers: N. Brookman (Buyer), R. McKenna (Personnel), R. Lustermans (Tech Serv Mgr)
Registration no: 01017013 **No.of Employees:** 101 - 250
Product Groups: 27

Swanley

A T B Computing Services Ltd
3 Manse Parade London Road, Swanley, BR8 8DA
Tel: 01322-614700 **Fax:** 01322-614777
E-mail: graham@atbltd.co.uk
Website: http://www.atbltd.co.uk
Directors: G. Hutson (MD), R. Hutson (Fin)
Immediate Holding Company: A.T.B. COMPUTING SERVICES LIMITED
Registration no: 03133350 **Date established:** 1995
Turnover: £250,000 - £500,000 **No.of Employees:** 1 - 10
Product Groups: 44

Date of Accounts	Dec 11	Dec 10	Dec 09
Working Capital	-17	-4	5
Fixed Assets	22	4	2
Current Assets	52	50	44

Aalco
Unit 7 The Interchange Wested Lane, Swanley, BR8 8TE
Tel: 01322-610900 **Fax:** 01322-610910
E-mail: swanley@aalco.co.uk
Website: http://www.aalco.co.uk
Bank(s): National Westminster Bank Plc
Managers: P. Temple, M. Dimmock (Sales Prom Mgr)
Ultimate Holding Company: UK STEESTOCK LTD
Immediate Holding Company: AMARI METALS LTD
Registration no: 03551533 **Date established:** 1994
Turnover: £125m - £250m **No.of Employees:** 21 - 50
Product Groups: 34, 35, 36, 66

Alpha R F Ltd
29 New Road Hextable, Swanley, BR8 7LS
Tel: 01322-666661 **Fax:** 01322-665828
E-mail: info@alpharf.co.uk
Website: http://www.alpharf.co.uk
Directors: A. Van Der Veen (Dir)
Immediate Holding Company: ALPHA R F LIMITED
Registration no: 03544127 **Date established:** 1998
No.of Employees: 1 - 10 **Product Groups:** 37, 49, 84

Date of Accounts	May 11	May 10	May 09
Working Capital	36	43	-5
Fixed Assets	5	6	7
Current Assets	118	69	77

Artscroll Security
26 Hotham Close, Swanley, BR8 7UX
Tel: 01322-664923 **Fax:** 01322-664923
Directors: W. Cope (Dir)
Date established: 1998 **No.of Employees:** 1 - 10 **Product Groups:** 26, 35

Automated Cable Solutions Ltd
44 A Tylers Green Road, Swanley, BR8 8LG
Tel: 0845-4288919 **Fax:** 01322-665718
E-mail: sales@automatedcablesolutions.co.uk
Website: http://www.automatedcablesolutions.co.uk
Managers: M. Warner (Sales Prom Mgr)
Registration no: 06755248 **Date established:** 2008
Turnover: Up to £250,000 **No.of Employees:** 1 - 10 **Product Groups:** 47

Eastwood Racing
London Road, Swanley, BR8 8BY
Tel: 01322-669469 **Fax:** 01322-614330
E-mail: wiseco.uk@btconnect.com
Website: http://www.wiseco.co.uk
Managers: A. Eastwood (Mgr)
Immediate Holding Company: WISECO PISTON (U.K.) LIMITED
Date established: 1987 **No.of Employees:** 1 - 10 **Product Groups:** 39, 40

Fugro Seismic Imaging Ltd
Horizon House Azalea Drive, Swanley, BR8 8JR
Tel: 01322-668011 **Fax:** 01322-613650
E-mail: andy.cowlard@fugro-fsi.com
Website: http://www.fugro.com
Directors: A. Cowlard (MD)
Managers: J. Sherriff, M. Carr (Develop Mgr), H. Davies (Mktg Serv Mgr), C. Schofield (Chief Acct)
Ultimate Holding Company: FUGRO NV (NETHERLANDS)
Immediate Holding Company: FUGRO SEISMIC IMAGING LIMITED
Registration no: 05314141 **VAT No.:** GB 654 0663 39
Date established: 2004 **Turnover:** £5m - £10m
No.of Employees: 51 - 100 **Product Groups:** 51

Date of Accounts	Dec 11	Dec 10	Dec 09
Sales Turnover	11m	8m	8m
Pre Tax Profit/Loss	4m	2m	2m
Working Capital	2m	389	72
Fixed Assets	2m	1m	811
Current Assets	4m	3m	2m
Current Liabilities	770	2m	2m

The General Lift Co. Ltd
Unit 4 Wested Farm Eynsford Road, Swanley, BR8 8EJ
Tel: 01322-614426 **Fax:** 01322-615123
E-mail: derrick@genlift.force9.co.uk
Website: http://www.general-lift.co.uk
Directors: D. Powis (MD)
Managers: J. Bennett (Fin Mgr), M. Becroft (Sales Prom Mgr)
Immediate Holding Company: GENERAL LIFT COMPANY LIMITED(THE)
Registration no: 02016081 **Date established:** 1986
Turnover: £250,000 - £500,000 **No.of Employees:** 11 - 20
Product Groups: 35, 39, 45

Date of Accounts	Apr 12	Apr 11	Apr 10
Working Capital	9	7	15
Fixed Assets	3	2	2
Current Assets	467	509	460

Gram UK
2 The Technology Centre London Road, Swanley, BR8 7AG
Tel: 01322-616900 **Fax:** 01322-616901
E-mail: glro@gramuk.co.uk
Website: http://www.gram-commercial.com
Directors: G. Roberts (MD)
Immediate Holding Company: GRAM (UK) LIMITED
Registration no: 00764216 **Date established:** 1963 **Turnover:** £2m - £5m
No.of Employees: 11 - 20 **Product Groups:** 38, 40, 41, 66, 67

Date of Accounts	Dec 11	Dec 10	Dec 09
Sales Turnover	3m	3m	3m
Pre Tax Profit/Loss	467	459	332
Working Capital	-223	-228	-130
Fixed Assets	384	394	319
Current Assets	232	287	211
Current Liabilities	198	271	185

Greenwich Instruments Limited
Meridian House Park Road, Swanley, BR8 8AH
Tel: 01322-668 724 **Fax:** 01322-660 352
E-mail: sales@greenwichinst.com
Website: http://www.greenwichinst.com
Bank(s): Lloyds TSB Bank plc
Directors: G. Dove (Dir), G. Dove (Ch & MD), J. Cutmore (Co Sec)
Managers: A. Jeffery (Sales Prom Mgr), A. Jeffrey (Sales Prom Mgr), B. Gold (Sales & Mktg Mg), L. Riches (Sales Admin)
Immediate Holding Company: Greenwich Instruments Ltd
Registration no: 01422005 **VAT No.:** GB 335 6564 43
Date established: 1979 **Turnover:** £2m - £5m **No.of Employees:** 11 - 20
Product Groups: 37, 44

Date of Accounts	Sep 09	Sep 08	Sep 07
Working Capital	226	78	174
Fixed Assets	32	41	51
Current Assets	245	147	215

I A Sound & Light
Unit C Old Forge Yard Swanley Village Road, Swanley, BR8 7NF
Tel: 01322-668681 **Fax:** 01322-668541
E-mail: info@iasoundandlight.co.uk
Website: http://www.iasoundandlight.co.uk
Directors: I. Adderley (Prop)
Turnover: Up to £250,000 **No.of Employees:** 1 - 10 **Product Groups:** 32, 35, 37, 38, 52, 67, 81, 83, 89

Image Grafix
8 Manse Parade London Road, Swanley, BR8 8DA
Tel: 01322-614669 **Fax:** 01322-614878
E-mail: imagegrafix@btconnect.com
Directors: J. Langdon (Prop)
Immediate Holding Company: IMAGE GRAFIX LIMITED
Registration no: 07107050 **Date established:** 2009
Turnover: Up to £250,000 **No.of Employees:** 1 - 10 **Product Groups:** 27, 28, 37, 39, 49

Date of Accounts	Dec 11	Dec 10
Working Capital	-1	-2
Fixed Assets	5	1
Current Assets	5	2

Kimber Allen UK Ltd
Broomfield Works London Road, Swanley, BR8 8DF
Tel: 01322-663234 **Fax:** 01322-668318
E-mail: ka@kimberallen.freeserve.co.uk
Website: http://www.kimberallen.8m.net
Bank(s): National Westminster Bank Plc
Directors: A. Ramsell (MD)
Managers: D. Andrews (Chief Mgr)
Immediate Holding Company: KIMBER-ALLEN LIMITED
Registration no: 00586450 **Date established:** 1957
Turnover: £500,000 - £1m **No.of Employees:** 21 - 50 **Product Groups:** 48

Date of Accounts	Jun 11	Jun 10	Jun 09
Working Capital	8	16	37
Fixed Assets	86	89	91
Current Assets	48	57	83

Newtech Tools
Unit B Park Road Industrial Estate Park Road, Swanley, BR8 8AH
Tel: 01322-665430 **Fax:** 01322-665430
E-mail: newtechtools@btconnect.com
Website: http://www.newtechtools.co.uk
Directors: R. Cordery (Prop)
Turnover: Up to £250,000 **No.of Employees:** 1 - 10 **Product Groups:** 35, 46, 47

Rydal Precision Tool Ltd
Unit 5 Technology Centre London Road, Swanley, BR8 7AG
Tel: 01322-614661 **Fax:** 01322-614760
E-mail: sales@rydal.co.uk
Website: http://www.mjallen.co.uk
Directors: B. Smith (MD)
Managers: C. Johnson, I. Hall (Buyer)
Immediate Holding Company: LIEMUR LIMITED
Registration no: 02196037 **VAT No.:** GB 201 1387 20
Date established: 2003 **Turnover:** £1m - £2m **No.of Employees:** 21 - 50
Product Groups: 46

Date of Accounts	Aug 10	Aug 09
Working Capital	-7	1
Fixed Assets	3	3
Current Assets	223	83

Rytech Metalcraft
Unit B Old Forge Yard Swanley Village Road, Swanley, BR8 7NF
Tel: 01322-664581 **Fax:** 01322-619107
Directors: R. Ryan (Prop)
Registration no: 06970176 **Date established:** 2009
No.of Employees: 1 - 10 **Product Groups:** 35

Swan Mill Paper Co. Ltd
Swan Mills Goldsel Road, Swanley, BR8 8EU
Tel: 01322-665566 **Fax:** 01322-666460
E-mail: sales@swantex.com
Website: http://www.swantex.com
Bank(s): National Westminster Bank Plc
Directors: A. Reeman (Co Sec), A. Barber (Sales), D. Byk (MD)
Ultimate Holding Company: SWAN MILL (HOLDINGS) LIMITED
Immediate Holding Company: SWAN MILL PAPER COMPANY LIMITED
Registration no: 01752881 **Date established:** 1983
Turnover: £20m - £50m **No.of Employees:** 101 - 250
Product Groups: 27, 30, 49

Date of Accounts	Mar 11	Mar 10	Mar 09
Sales Turnover	38m	33m	32m
Pre Tax Profit/Loss	1m	2m	309
Working Capital	12m	11m	11m
Fixed Assets	5m	5m	5m
Current Assets	18m	17m	17m
Current Liabilities	3m	3m	2m

Total Steel Solutions UK Ltd
168 Pinks Hill, Swanley, BR8 8NW
Tel: 01322-662353 **Fax:** 01322-614081
E-mail: kevin@totalsteel.co.uk
Directors: K. Green (MD)
Immediate Holding Company: TOTAL STEEL SOLUTIONS (UK) LIMITED
Registration no: 04571319 **Date established:** 2002
No.of Employees: 1 - 10 **Product Groups:** 35

Date of Accounts	Oct 11	Oct 10	Oct 09
Sales Turnover	N/A	N/A	70
Pre Tax Profit/Loss	N/A	N/A	4
Working Capital	-5	-3	-2
Fixed Assets	3	4	3
Current Assets	14	23	23
Current Liabilities	N/A	N/A	3

Transcover
Wested Lane, Swanley, BR8 8EE
Tel: 01322-666601 **Fax:** 01322-666615
E-mail: enquiries@transcover.com
Website: http://www.transcover.com
Directors: S. Hines (MD), S. Heins (MD), P. Hines (Purch)
Managers: C. Bartram (Sales Prom Mgr), L. Carey (Accounts), D. Bell (Sales Prom)
Immediate Holding Company: ECLATS DESIGN LIMITED
Registration no: 06679100 **Date established:** 2009
No.of Employees: 11 - 20 **Product Groups:** 38, 42, 52

William Whitmore & Sons
Tail Lifts 227 Swanley Lane, Swanley, BR8 7LD
Tel: 01322-662583 **Fax:** 01322- 665802
Directors: K. Whittemore (Ptnr)
Date established: 1974 **No.of Employees:** 1 - 10 **Product Groups:** 35, 39, 45

Swanscombe

Barton Willmore
The Observatory Southfleet Road, Swanscombe, DA10 0DF
Tel: 01322-374660 **Fax:** 01322-373660
E-mail: hew.edwards@bartonwillmore.co.uk
Website: http://www.bartonwillmore.co.uk
Directors: H. Edwards (Ptnr)
Ultimate Holding Company: BARTON WILLMORE HOLDINGS LTD
Immediate Holding Company: BARTON WILLMORE DESIGN LTD
Registration no: 02144444 **VAT No.:** GB 472 9467 08
Date established: 1999 **Turnover:** £5m - £10m **No.of Employees:** 11 - 20
Product Groups: 84

Date of Accounts	Jun 12	Jun 11	Jun 10
Sales Turnover	298	254	617
Pre Tax Profit/Loss	7	3	136
Working Capital	67	98	55
Fixed Assets	2	5	9
Current Assets	212	297	288
Current Liabilities	21	24	179

Wood Machines Ltd
1 Galley Hill Industrial Estate London Road, Swanscombe, DA10 0AA
Tel: 01322-385566 **Fax:** 01322-384449
E-mail: mail@uemcoltd.com
Website: http://www.uemcoltd.com
Directors: M. Moyes (MD), R. Cowling (MD)
Managers: M. Grimes (Chief Acct)
Immediate Holding Company: The Universal Electrical Manufacturing Company Ltd
Registration no: 00836254 **Date established:** 1965
Turnover: £500,000 - £1m **No.of Employees:** 1 - 10 **Product Groups:** 44

Date of Accounts	Jun 08	Jun 07	Jun 06
Working Capital	198	197	217
Fixed Assets	36	37	18
Current Assets	267	259	321
Current Liabilities	68	61	104
Total Share Capital	100	100	100

Tenterden

Applied Cutting Systems Ltd
Unit 4a Pickhill Business Centre Smallhythe Road, Tenterden, TN30 7LZ
Tel: 01580-761500 **Fax:** 01580-761700
E-mail: sales@appliedcutsys.com
Website: http://www.appliedcutsys.com
Directors: S. Langford-Smith (MD)
Immediate Holding Company: APPLIED CUTTING SYSTEMS LIMITED
Registration no: 04534529 **Date established:** 2002
No.of Employees: 1 - 10 **Product Groups:** 23, 25, 27, 28, 30, 33, 36, 37, 40, 42, 43, 44, 45, 46, 47, 48, 49, 51, 65, 66, 67, 68, 84

Date of Accounts	Mar 11	Mar 10	Mar 09
Working Capital	45	34	28
Fixed Assets	17	21	26
Current Assets	94	82	78

Cerium Group Ltd
Cerium House Cerium Technology Park Appledore Road, Tenterden, TN30 7DE
Tel: 01580-765211 **Fax:** 01580-765573
E-mail: clive@ceriumoptical.com
Website: http://www.ceriumoptical.com
Bank(s): Barclays, London
Directors: C. Sangster (MD), T. Snelling (Fin)
Managers: S. Pooley, E. Ashton (Sales Admin)
Immediate Holding Company: CERIUM GROUP LIMITED
Registration no: 01043567 **Date established:** 1972 **Turnover:** £2m - £5m
No.of Employees: 21 - 50 **Product Groups:** 33, 45

Date of Accounts	Sep 11	Sep 10	Sep 09
Working Capital	785	419	577
Fixed Assets	640	630	637
Current Assets	3m	3m	3m

H & H Engineering Ltd
51 Colonel Stephens Way, Tenterden, TN30 6EW
Tel: 0783-452 3344
E-mail: d.haisman@btopenworld.com
Directors: D. Haisman (Dir)
Immediate Holding Company: H & H ENGINEERING LIMITED
Registration no: 04965167 **Date established:** 2003
No.of Employees: 1 - 10 **Product Groups:** 35, 40, 48

Date of Accounts	Nov 10	Nov 09	Nov 08
Working Capital	-4	10	-4
Fixed Assets	4	6	8
Current Assets	4	18	1

L P G Auto Conversions
Island Works Island Cottage The Street, Stone, Tenterden, TN30 7JL
Tel: 01233-758014
E-mail: lpg@uk2.net
Website: http://www.lpgautoconversions.co.uk
Directors: S. Adams (Prop)
No.of Employees: 1 - 10 **Product Groups:** 35, 45, 68, 84

Maybourne & Russell Ltd
Unit 5 Leigh Green Industrial Estate, Tenterden, TN30 7DE
Tel: 01580-763264 **Fax:** 01580-765644
E-mail: enquiries@mandrgroup.com
Website: http://www.maybourneandrussell.com
Bank(s): National Westminster Bank Plc
Directors: N. Maybourne (Chief Op Offcr), B. Evans (Fin), M. Ingram (Prop)
Managers: S. Parr (Sales Admin)
Ultimate Holding Company: MAYBOURNE & RUSSELL GROUP LIMITED
Immediate Holding Company: MAYBOURNE & RUSSELL LIMITED
Registration no: 02626053 **VAT No.:** GB 583 8412 17
Date established: 1991 **Turnover:** £5m - £10m **No.of Employees:** 21 - 50
Product Groups: 52

Date of Accounts	Mar 12	Mar 11	Mar 10
Sales Turnover	N/A	7m	10m
Pre Tax Profit/Loss	N/A	-706	170
Working Capital	434	60	692
Fixed Assets	62	64	86
Current Assets	2m	3m	2m
Current Liabilities	N/A	351	274

Premier Marquees
Wittersham, Tenterden, TN30 7EH
Tel: 01797-270873
E-mail: info@premier-marquees.co.uk
Website: http://www.premier-marquees.co.uk
Directors: N. Harman (Prop)
No.of Employees: 1 - 10 **Product Groups:** 36, 49, 67, 69

Sartec
Century Farmhouse Reading Street, Tenterden, TN30 7HS
Tel: 01233-758157 **Fax:** 01233-758158
E-mail: sales@sartec.co.uk
Website: http://www.sartec.co.uk
Directors: R. Broadbank (Dir), A. Broadbank (Fin)
Immediate Holding Company: SARTEC LIMITED
Registration no: 01726196 **Date established:** 1983 **Turnover:** £1m - £2m
No.of Employees: 1 - 10 **Product Groups:** 38

Date of Accounts	Sep 11	Sep 10	Sep 09
Working Capital	87	147	112
Fixed Assets	21	23	18
Current Assets	237	407	171

Spazio Folding Door Co.
3 Barnfield St Michaels, Tenterden, TN30 6NH
Tel: 01580-763593 **Fax:** 01580-765883
E-mail: info@spazio.co.uk
Website: http://www.spazio.co.uk
Directors: S. Clarke (Co Sec), D. Tester (MD)
Date established: 1984 **Turnover:** £2m - £5m **No.of Employees:** 1 - 10
Product Groups: 29, 30, 33, 35, 36, 66

Tonbridge

A S D Metal Services
Pipers Business Centre 220 Vale Road, Tonbridge, TN9 1SP
Tel: 01732-362000 **Fax:** 01732-770730
E-mail: cambridge@asdmetalservices.co.uk
Website: http://www.asdmetalservices.co.uk
Managers: P. Eden (District Mgr)
Ultimate Holding Company: PIPER GROUP HOLDING LIMITED
Immediate Holding Company: CARWEB MANAGEMENT LIMITED
Registration no: 01019824 **Date established:** 1984
Turnover: £50m - £75m **No.of Employees:** 1 - 10 **Product Groups:** 66

Date of Accounts	Apr 11	Apr 10	Apr 09
Working Capital	7	7	65
Current Assets	7	7	269

A V Plastics Oldbury Plastics Ltd
Unit 1 Chiddingstone Causeway Chiddingstone Causeway, Tonbridge, TN11 8JU
Tel: 01892-870461 **Fax:** 01892-871262
E-mail: admin@avplastics.co.uk
Website: http://www.avplastics.co.uk
Directors: J. Torr (Dir)
Immediate Holding Company: RUBICON INTERIORS LIMITED
Registration no: 02746280 **Date established:** 2008
Turnover: £500,000 - £1m **No.of Employees:** 1 - 10 **Product Groups:** 29, 30, 48, 66, 84

Adsum Auxilium Limited
Bouncers Bank Half Moon Lane, Tudeley, Tonbridge, TN11 0PR
Tel: 01892-836969 **Fax:** 01892-836969
E-mail: info@adsumaux.co.uk
Website: http://www.adsumaux.co.uk
Directors: J. Leeper (MD)
Registration no: 03823517 **Date established:** 1999
Turnover: Up to £250,000 **No.of Employees:** 1 - 10 **Product Groups:** 80, 82

Airborne Balloon Flight Ltd
Hop Farm Country Park Maidstone Road Paddock Wood, Paddock Wood, Tonbridge, TN12 6PY
Tel: 01622-873200 **Fax:** 01622-871117
Website: http://www.airborneballoons.co.uk
Directors: S. Richards (Dir)
Immediate Holding Company: AIRBORNE BALLOON FLIGHTS LTD
Registration no: 03962276 **Date established:** 2000
No.of Employees: 1 - 10 **Product Groups:** 24, 37, 38

Anhydro UK Ltd
44-46 Morley Road, Tonbridge, TN9 1RA
Tel: 01732-362611 **Fax:** 01732-770776
E-mail: p.kennet@anhydro.com
Website: http://www.drytecdryers.com
Directors: P. Kennet (MD), L. Homewood (Co Sec), M. Kirby (MD)
Managers: T. Allen (Chief Mgr), S. Sheikh
Ultimate Holding Company: ANHYDRO HOLDING AS (DENMARK)
Immediate Holding Company: VETTERTEC LTD
Registration no: 01602355 **VAT No.:** GB 304 4658 71
Date established: 1981 **Turnover:** £2m - £5m **No.of Employees:** 1 - 10
Product Groups: 20, 32, 40, 41, 42, 45

Date of Accounts	Dec 11	Dec 10	Dec 09
Sales Turnover	5m	2m	2m
Pre Tax Profit/Loss	193	636	-207
Working Capital	395	186	-471
Fixed Assets	5	2	4
Current Assets	1m	863	2m
Current Liabilities	323	53	200

Aragon Locks
Roundel Way, Tonbridge, TN12 9TW
Tel: 0800-858642 **Fax:** 01622-831258
E-mail: aragonlocksmiths@aol.com
Website: http://www.locksmithkent.co.uk
Directors: J. Gillick (Prop), J. Gillitt (Prop)
Date established: 2001 **No.of Employees:** 1 - 10 **Product Groups:** 36

Arnolds Environmental Ltd
Unit 6e Longbrooks Knowle Road, Brenchley, Tonbridge, TN12 7DJ
Tel: 01892-725490
E-mail: sales@arnoldsenvironmental.co.uk
Website: http://www.arnoldsenvironmental.co.uk
Directors: R. Maggs (Dir)
Immediate Holding Company: ARNOLDS ENVIRONMENTAL LIMITED
Registration no: 04892379 **Date established:** 2003
No.of Employees: 1 - 10 **Product Groups:** 36, 48, 84

Date of Accounts	Feb 08	Feb 11	Feb 10
Working Capital	24	-71	-35
Fixed Assets	21	2	6
Current Assets	155	103	161

Baxall Construction Ltd
Eastlands Estate 2 Maidstone Road, Paddock Wood, Tonbridge, TN12 6BU
Tel: 01892-836755 **Fax:** 01892-834816
E-mail: sjsmith@baxallconstruction.co.uk
Website: http://www.baxallconstruction.co.uk
Bank(s): National Westminster Bank Plc
Directors: J. Exall (Purch), S. Smith (Comm), N. Exall (Ch), M. Clarke (MD), J. Exall (Fin)
Managers: A. Keen (Buyer), M. Clarke (Sales Prom Mgr)
Immediate Holding Company: BAXALL CONSTRUCTION LIMITED
Registration no: 01079105 **VAT No.:** GB 661 7608 23
Date established: 1972 **Turnover:** £5m - £10m **No.of Employees:** 21 - 50
Product Groups: 52

Date of Accounts	Mar 10	Mar 09	Mar 08
Sales Turnover	N/A	9m	10m
Pre Tax Profit/Loss	N/A	269	328
Working Capital	90	215	260
Fixed Assets	249	278	293
Current Assets	2m	2m	2m
Current Liabilities	N/A	126	134

BCS Luminaires Ltd
16 Sovereign Way, Tonbridge, TN9 1RS
Tel: 01732-357351 **Fax:** 01737-361088
E-mail: barwit@barwitcontrolsystems.co.uk
Website: http://www.bcs-luminaires.co.uk
Directors: D. Wittington (MD)
Managers: W. Holden (Sales Admin), C. Jeffery (Gen Contact)
Registration no: 03802274 **Product Groups:** 37, 52, 67, 84

Date of Accounts	Jun 08	Jun 07	Jun 06
Current Assets	1	1	1
Current Liabilities	1	1	1

Botanix Ltd
Hop Pocket Lane Paddock Wood, Tonbridge, TN12 6DQ
Tel: 01892-833415 **Fax:** 01892-836987
E-mail: sales@botanix.co.uk
Website: http://www.botanix.co.uk
Bank(s): National Westminster Bank Plc
Directors: A. Rice Tucker (Co Sec), C. Daws (Sales)
Managers: E. Downes, K. Yeo (Tech Serv Mgr), V. Lassetter (Personnel)
Ultimate Holding Company: JOH BARTH & SOHN GMBH & CO KG (GERMANY)
Immediate Holding Company: BOTANIX LIMITED
Registration no: 04079942 **Date established:** 2000
Turnover: £10m - £20m **No.of Employees:** 51 - 100 **Product Groups:** 02, 20, 31, 62, 66

Date of Accounts	Jul 11	Jul 10	Jul 09
Sales Turnover	15m	15m	16m
Pre Tax Profit/Loss	2m	2m	3m

Working Capital	7m	5m	5m
Fixed Assets	6m	7m	6m
Current Assets	9m	9m	8m
Current Liabilities	724	2m	2m

Building Product Design

North Frith Oasts Ashes Lane, Hadlow, Tonbridge, TN11 9QU
Tel: 01732-850770 **Fax:** 01732-355536
E-mail: lynnm@willantn.demon.co.uk
Website: http://www.buildingproductdesign.com
Bank(s): National Westminster
Directors: N. Rideout (Dir)
Immediate Holding Company: BOB WOOLMER SALES LIMITED
Registration no: 03944123 **VAT No.:** GB 437 8948 92
Date established: 1988 **Turnover:** £2m - £5m **No.of Employees:** 11 - 20
Product Groups: 40

Date of Accounts	Mar 12	Mar 11	Mar 10
Sales Turnover	N/A	2m	2m
Working Capital	637	539	503
Fixed Assets	13	16	20
Current Assets	844	801	503

Burnbright Fuels

Berisden Brenchley Road, Horsmonden, Tonbridge, TN12 8DN
Tel: 01892-836588 **Fax:** 01892-836589
E-mail: enquiries@burnbrightfuels.co.uk
Website: http://www.burnbrightfuels.co.uk
Directors: R. Berry (Prop)
Immediate Holding Company: BURNBRIGHT FUELS LIMITED
Registration no: 01427884 **Date established:** 1979
Turnover: £500,000 - £1m **No.of Employees:** 1 - 10 **Product Groups:** 25, 31, 42

Date of Accounts	Mar 96	Jun 99	Jun 98
Sales Turnover	252	N/A	N/A
Pre Tax Profit/Loss	-13	N/A	N/A
Working Capital	-150	-245	-181
Fixed Assets	71	48	67
Current Assets	25	21	25
Current Liabilities	175	267	206

C J Enterprises (t/a CJ Enterprises)

Infield House Old Hay, Brenchley, Tonbridge, TN12 7DG
Tel: 01892-838094 **Fax:** 01892-836182
E-mail: info@cjenterprises.co.uk
Website: http://www.cjenterprises.co.uk
Bank(s): Barclays
Directors: C. Jakes (Fin)
Immediate Holding Company: RDJ COLLOIDS LIMITED
Registration no: 01956377 **Date established:** 1985 **Turnover:** £1m - £2m
No.of Employees: 11 - 20 **Product Groups:** 40

Date of Accounts	Apr 12	Apr 11	Apr 10
Working Capital	-14	6	-46
Fixed Assets	166	162	179
Current Assets	235	201	185

C & K Extrusions Ltd

12 Drayton Road, Tonbridge, TN9 2BE
Tel: 01732-361434 **Fax:** 01732-771009
E-mail: admin@ckextrusions.co.uk
Website: http://www.ckextrusions.co.uk
Bank(s): HSBC Bank plc
Directors: N. Woodhams (MD)
Immediate Holding Company: C. & K. EXTRUSIONS LIMITED
Registration no: 01066745 **VAT No.:** GB 724 7674 12
Date established: 1972 **Turnover:** £500,000 - £1m
No.of Employees: 21 - 50 **Product Groups:** 30

Date of Accounts	Apr 11	Apr 10	Apr 09
Working Capital	2m	2m	2m
Fixed Assets	323	320	306
Current Assets	4m	3m	3m

C M S Kent Ltd

Ledgers Works Queens Street, Paddock Wood, Tonbridge, TN12 6NN
Tel: 01892-832418 **Fax:** 01892-836077
E-mail: sales@hasa.co.uk
Website: http://www.hasa.co.uk
Directors: K. Hollands (Fin), N. Ball (MD), D. Lane (Sales)
Immediate Holding Company: COMMERCIAL MOTOR SERVICES (KENT) LIMITED
Registration no: 00931021 **Date established:** 1968 **Turnover:** £2m - £5m
No.of Employees: 11 - 20 **Product Groups:** 68

Date of Accounts	Sep 11	Sep 10	Sep 09
Working Capital	1m	91	79
Fixed Assets	2m	2m	2m
Current Assets	1m	1m	1m

Campbell International

PO Box 57, Tonbridge, TN9 2NE
Tel: 01732-773364 **Fax:** 01732-362429
E-mail: info@campbelluk.co.uk
Website: http://www.campbelluk.co.uk
Directors: B. Dennison (MD), J. Dennison (Fin)
Immediate Holding Company: CAMPBELL INTERNATIONAL LIMITED
Registration no: 02757184 **Date established:** 1992
Turnover: Up to £250,000 **No.of Employees:** 1 - 10 **Product Groups:** 17, 22, 23, 24, 26, 27, 28, 30, 33, 38, 49, 64, 65, 66, 81

Date of Accounts	Oct 07	Oct 06	Oct 04
Sales Turnover	125	137	N/A
Pre Tax Profit/Loss	13	-0	N/A
Working Capital	62	64	-0
Fixed Assets	N/A	1	1
Current Assets	65	57	114

Camson Envelopes

Woodlands Mills Woodlands Road, Tonbridge, TN9 2NE
Tel: 01732-368949 **Fax:** 01732-362429
E-mail: info@camson.co.uk
Website: http://www.camson.co.uk
Directors: B. Dennison (MD)
Immediate Holding Company: CAMSON ENVELOPES LIMITED
Registration no: 02592870 **Date established:** 1991
Turnover: Up to £250,000 **No.of Employees:** 1 - 10 **Product Groups:** 27

Date of Accounts	Sep 97	Sep 11	Sep 04
Working Capital	-1	N/A	-1
Current Liabilities	N/A	N/A	1

Checkmate Corporate Gifts

The Granary Pullens Farm Lamberhurst Road, Horsmonden, Tonbridge, TN12 8ED
Tel: 01892-724474 **Fax:** 01892-724736
E-mail: checkmategifts@lineone.net
Website: http://www.checkmatecorporategifts.co.uk
Directors: F. Hope (MD), F. Hope (Prop)
Immediate Holding Company: THE SIMPLY WILD FOOD COMPANY LIMITED
Date established: 2002 **No.of Employees:** 1 - 10 **Product Groups:** 24, 25, 28, 30, 33, 35, 44, 49, 81

Chestnut Products Ltd

Unit 15 Gaza Trading Estate Scabharbour Road, Hildenborough, Tonbridge, TN11 8PL
Tel: 01732-463777 **Fax:** 01732-454636
E-mail: chestnutproducts@btconnect.com
Directors: M. Tyrrell (MD)
Immediate Holding Company: CHESTNUT PRODUCTS,LIMITED
Registration no: 00443848 **VAT No.:** GB 209 5544 59
Date established: 1947 **Turnover:** £2m - £5m **No.of Employees:** 1 - 10
Product Groups: 52

Date of Accounts	Mar 11	Mar 10	Mar 09
Working Capital	222	220	211
Fixed Assets	50	55	65
Current Assets	558	505	533

Christie & Grey Ltd

Morley Road, Tonbridge, TN9 1RA
Tel: 01732-371100 **Fax:** 01732-359666
E-mail: sales@christiegrey.com
Website: http://www.christiegrey.com
Bank(s): Lloyds TSB Bank plc
Directors: P. Turver (MD)
Immediate Holding Company: CHRISTIE & GREY LIMITED
Registration no: 00138071 **Date established:** 2014 **Turnover:** £1m - £2m
No.of Employees: 11 - 20 **Product Groups:** 29, 35

Date of Accounts	Oct 11	Oct 10	Oct 09
Working Capital	766	690	586
Fixed Assets	575	575	566
Current Assets	1m	966	843

Clayton First Aid Ltd

Chiddingstone Causeway, Tonbridge, TN11 8JP
Tel: 01892-871111 **Fax:** 01892-871122
E-mail: info@claytonfirstaid.com
Website: http://www.claytonfirstaid.com
Directors: P. Clayton (MD)
Immediate Holding Company: CLAYTON FIRST AID LIMITED
Registration no: 00591003 **VAT No.:** GB 209 6359 49
Date established: 1957 **Turnover:** £2m - £5m **No.of Employees:** 1 - 10
Product Groups: 24, 26, 38

Date of Accounts	Mar 11	Mar 10	Mar 09
Working Capital	257	312	369
Fixed Assets	806	811	815
Current Assets	389	463	595

Clovis Lande Associates Ltd

104 Branbridges Road East Peckham, Tonbridge, TN12 5HH
Tel: 01622-873900 **Fax:** 01622-873903
E-mail: info@clovis.co.uk
Website: http://www.clovis.co.uk
Bank(s): National Westminster Bank Plc
Directors: G. Revell (MD)
Immediate Holding Company: CLOVIS LANDE ASSOCIATES LIMITED
Registration no: 02210820 **Date established:** 1988 **Turnover:** £1m - £2m
No.of Employees: 21 - 50 **Product Groups:** 30, 35, 52, 84

Date of Accounts	Dec 11	Dec 09	Dec 08
Working Capital	391	326	401
Fixed Assets	127	103	88
Current Assets	858	1m	992
Current Liabilities	158	N/A	N/A

Cobwebb Communications Ltd

134 High Street, Tonbridge, TN9 1BB
Tel: 01732-447900 **Fax:** 01732-365604
E-mail: sales@cobwebb.com
Website: http://www.cobwebb.com
Directors: B. Webb (Dir)
Immediate Holding Company: COBWEBB COMMUNICATIONS LIMITED
Registration no: 02029183 **Date established:** 1986
Turnover: £500,000 - £1m **No.of Employees:** 1 - 10 **Product Groups:** 44

Date of Accounts	Jun 11	Jun 10	Jun 09
Working Capital	29	27	84
Fixed Assets	7	10	9
Current Assets	210	174	224

Codercom Radio Communications Ltd

P.O BOX 338 Staplehurst, Tonbridge, TN12 0WF
Tel: 0844-8099908 **Fax:** 01622-833399
E-mail: sales@codercom.com
Website: http://www.codercom.com
Registration no: 01752209 **No.of Employees:** 1 - 10 **Product Groups:** 37, 39, 67

Combined Book Services Ltd

Unit D Paddock Wood Distribution Centre, Paddock Wood, Tonbridge, TN12 6UU
Tel: 01892-837171 **Fax:** 01892-837272
E-mail: orders@combook.co.uk
Website: http://www.combook.co.uk
Directors: K. Neale (Dir)
Immediate Holding Company: COMBINED BOOK SERVICES LIMITED
Registration no: 02213087 **Date established:** 1988
No.of Employees: 11 - 20 **Product Groups:** 64

Date of Accounts	Mar 12	Mar 11	Mar 10
Working Capital	159	128	71
Fixed Assets	29	40	75
Current Assets	251	223	169

Compact & Bale Ltd

The Hop Kilns Unit 6 Boblands Farm Bizz Centre Cemetery Lane, Hadlow, Tonbridge, TN11 0LT
Tel: 01732-852244 **Fax:** 01732-851133
E-mail: info@compact-and-bale.com
Website: http://www.compact-and-bale.com
Directors: S. Burnett (MD)
Immediate Holding Company: COMPACT AND BALE LIMITED
Registration no: 04027675 **Date established:** 2000
No.of Employees: 1 - 10 **Product Groups:** 27, 30, 42, 44, 47, 54, 66

Date of Accounts	Jul 11	Jul 10	Jul 09
Working Capital	310	270	196
Fixed Assets	339	225	189
Current Assets	654	493	423

Control Design

Unit Z Paddock Wood Distribution Centre Paddock Wood, Tonbridge, TN12 6UU
Tel: 01892-836350 **Fax:** 01892-837292
E-mail: ian@controldesign.co.uk
Website: http://www.dialin.co.uk/control-design
Directors: A. Francis (MD), B. Clack (Sales), I. Mcarthur (Dir), M. Jones (Dir), T. Francis (Dir)
Immediate Holding Company: CONTROL DESIGN (A/C) LIMITED
Registration no: 01132663 **Date established:** 1973
Turnover: £500,000 - £1m **No.of Employees:** 11 - 20 **Product Groups:** 37

Date of Accounts	Feb 08	Feb 11	Feb 10
Sales Turnover	14m	N/A	N/A
Pre Tax Profit/Loss	555	N/A	N/A
Working Capital	1m	1m	980
Fixed Assets	28	51	52
Current Assets	2m	2m	3m
Current Liabilities	722	N/A	N/A

Copa Ltd

Unit 6 Crest Industrial Estate Pattenden Lane, Marden, Tonbridge, TN12 9QJ
Tel: 01622-833914 **Fax:** 01622-831466
E-mail: david.scale@copa.co.uk
Website: http://www.copa.co.uk
Bank(s): Lloyds TSB Bank plc
Directors: D. Scale (Dir), J. Thorne (Sales & Mktg)
Managers: J. Sommerville (Personnel)
Ultimate Holding Company: C D S Technologies
Registration no: 06548494 **VAT No.:** GB 754 5420 32
Date established: 1967 **Turnover:** £2m - £5m **No.of Employees:** 21 - 50
Product Groups: 32, 33, 35, 36, 38, 40, 41, 42, 44, 45, 47, 51, 52, 54, 66, 67, 84, 87

D K Holdings Ltd

Station Approach Staplehurst, Tonbridge, TN12 0QN
Tel: 01580-891662 **Fax:** 01580-893675
E-mail: info@dk-holdings.co.uk
Website: http://www.dk-holdings.co.uk
Bank(s): National Westminster Bank Plc
Directors: B. Salter (MD)
Immediate Holding Company: DIAFORCE LIMITED
Registration no: 02220852 **VAT No.:** GB 203 0596 04
Date established: 1988 **Turnover:** £5m - £10m
No.of Employees: 51 - 100 **Product Groups:** 33, 36, 47, 48, 49

Date of Accounts	Mar 11	Mar 10	Mar 07
Working Capital	6	6	6
Current Assets	6	6	6

Denton Pumps Ltd

191 Vale Road, Tonbridge, TN9 1ST
Tel: 01732-354847 **Fax:** 01732-770152
E-mail: martin@dentonpumps.co.uk
Website: http://www.dentonpumps.co.uk
Directors: P. Kearns (Fin), M. Kearns (MD)
Immediate Holding Company: DENTON PUMPS (KENT) LIMITED
Registration no: 01081280 **Date established:** 1972
No.of Employees: 1 - 10 **Product Groups:** 40

Date of Accounts	Dec 11	Dec 10	Dec 09
Working Capital	56	68	111
Fixed Assets	5	6	8
Current Assets	119	149	161

Easylog Ltd

40-42 Whetsted Road Five Oak Green, Tonbridge, TN12 6RS
Tel: 08452-257615 **Fax:** 01892-834202
E-mail: info@easylog.co.uk
Website: http://www.easylog.co.uk
Managers: G. Rolando (Mgr)
Immediate Holding Company: EASYLOG LIMITED
Registration no: 04988743 **Date established:** 2003
No.of Employees: 1 - 10 **Product Groups:** 44

Date of Accounts	Dec 11	Dec 10	Dec 09
Working Capital	-5	-5	-5
Current Assets	43	39	38

Elmor Supplies Ltd

104 Branbridges Road East Peckham, Tonbridge, TN12 5HH
Tel: 01622-871870 **Fax:** 01622-872024
Bank(s): National Westminster Bank Plc
Directors: B. Morel (MD), D. Morel (Fin)
Managers: A. Myers (Buyer)
Ultimate Holding Company: NEWVELL PRECISION ENGINEERING LIMITED
Immediate Holding Company: ELMOR SUPPLIES LIMITED
Registration no: 00749024 **VAT No.:** GB 209 6880 38
Date established: 1963 **Turnover:** Up to £250,000
No.of Employees: 21 - 50 **Product Groups:** 35

Date of Accounts	Sep 11	Sep 10	Sep 09
Working Capital	248	259	262
Fixed Assets	1	1	2
Current Assets	273	298	310

Enalon Ltd

PO Box 2, Tonbridge, TN9 1TB
Tel: 01732-358500 **Fax:** 01732-770463
E-mail: sr@enalon.co.uk
Website: http://www.enalon.co.uk
Bank(s): Barclays, Hanover Square, London
Directors: S. Ray (Tech Serv)
Ultimate Holding Company: NOLANE LIMITED
Immediate Holding Company: ENALON LIMITED
Registration no: 01389028 **VAT No.:** GB 367 5265 25
Date established: 1978 **Turnover:** £1m - £2m **No.of Employees:** 21 - 50
Product Groups: 30, 48, 66

Date of Accounts	Sep 10	Sep 09	Sep 08
Sales Turnover	1m	1m	2m
Pre Tax Profit/Loss	-74	3	20
Working Capital	40	130	138
Fixed Assets	82	37	27
Current Assets	337	307	371
Current Liabilities	138	77	90

Euler Hermes UK plc

Surety House Lyons Cresent, Tonbridge, TN9 1EN
Tel: 01732-770311 **Fax:** 01732-770361
E-mail: malcolm.jamieson@cgiplc.com
Website: http://www.ehgplc.com
Bank(s): National Westminster Bank Plc
Directors: M. Jamieson (Co Sec), A. Paton (Co Sec), A. Paton (Fin), H. Brown (MD)
Managers: M. Berry (Mgr), M. Jamieson (Mgr)
Ultimate Holding Company: ALLIANZ SE (GERMANY)
Immediate Holding Company: EULER HERMES GUARANTEE PLC
Registration no: 00956231 **Date established:** 1969 **Turnover:** £2m - £5m
No.of Employees: 11 - 20 **Product Groups:** 82

Date of Accounts	Dec 09	Dec 08	Dec 07
Pre Tax Profit/Loss	2m	5m	6m
Fixed Assets	38m	28m	32m
Current Assets	5m	13m	13m
Current Liabilities	7m	14m	16m

Eurohill Labels Ltd

195 Vale Road, Tonbridge, TN9 1SU
Tel: 01732-770700 **Fax:** 01732-770779
E-mail: sales@eurohill.com
Website: http://www.eurohill.com
Bank(s): National Westminster Bank Plc
Directors: A. Kirkpatrick (Fin), B. Tibbals (MD)
Ultimate Holding Company: EUROHILL HOLDINGS LIMITED
Immediate Holding Company: EUROHILL LABELS LIMITED
Registration no: 01372024 **Date established:** 1978 **Turnover:** £1m - £2m
No.of Employees: 21 - 50 **Product Groups:** 27, 42, 44, 84

Date of Accounts	Dec 11	Dec 10	Dec 09
Working Capital	69	61	42
Fixed Assets	11	14	15
Current Assets	291	246	229

Eurohill Traders Ltd (t/a Associated Packaging)

195 Vale Road, Tonbridge, TN9 1SU
Tel: 01732-770777 **Fax:** 01732-770757
E-mail: sales@apac.co.uk
Website: http://www.apac.co.uk
Bank(s): National Westminster Bank Plc
Directors: B. Tibblas (MD), A. Buckland (Chief Op Offcr), B. Tibbals (MD)
Registration no: 01114987 **Turnover:** £5m - £10m
No.of Employees: 21 - 50 **Product Groups:** 20, 27, 30, 48, 66

Date of Accounts	Dec 09	Dec 08	Dec 07
Working Capital	701	707	670
Fixed Assets	32	15	17
Current Assets	1m	2m	2m

Evolution Internet

Aspect House Pattenden Lane, Marden, Tonbridge, TN12 9QJ
Tel: 01622-831292 **Fax:** 01580-852181
E-mail: solutions@evolution-internet.com
Website: http://www.evolution-internet.com
Directors: G. Brown (Prop)
Immediate Holding Company: EVOLUTION INTERNET LIMITED
Registration no: 04385614 **Date established:** 2002
No.of Employees: 1 - 10 **Product Groups:** 44, 79, 80

Date of Accounts	Jul 11	Jul 10	Jul 09
Working Capital	55	33	56
Fixed Assets	28	17	22
Current Assets	103	95	101

Fenner Paper Co. Ltd

15 Orchard Business Centre Vale Road, Tonbridge, TN9 1QF
Tel: 01732-771100 **Fax:** 01732-771103
E-mail: lorna@fennerpaper.co.uk
Website: http://www.fennerpaper.co.uk
Directors: T. Fenner (MD), J. Hobson (Mkt Research)
Immediate Holding Company: FENNER PAPER COMPANY LIMITED
Registration no: 01934207 **VAT No.:** GB 426 7552 38
Date established: 1985 **Turnover:** £5m - £10m **No.of Employees:** 11 - 20
Product Groups: 25, 27, 28, 33, 42, 61, 63, 64, 66

Date of Accounts	Jul 11	Jul 10	Jul 09
Working Capital	1m	1m	1m
Fixed Assets	30	21	31
Current Assets	2m	1m	1m

Fidelity Investments International

Oakhill House 130 Tonbridge Road, Hildenborough, Tonbridge, TN11 9DZ
Tel: 01732-361144 **Fax:** 01732-838886
Website: http://www.fid-intl.com
Directors: G. Adams (Dir), S. Walden (Dir), N. Richards (Dir), S. Haslam (Dir), S. Fraser (Dir), R. Wane (Dir), G. Clapp (Dir), E. Boyle (Dir), E. Johnson (Dir), B. Bateman (Dir), A. Bolton (Dir), M. Cambridge (Dir)
Ultimate Holding Company: FIL LIMITED (BERMUDA)
Immediate Holding Company: FIDELITY INVESTMENTS LIMITED
Registration no: 04447198 **VAT No.:** GB 395 3090 35
Date established: 2002 **Turnover:** £5m - £10m
No.of Employees: 251 - 500 **Product Groups:** 82

G T S Europe

6a Arnolds Business Park Branbridges Road East Peckham, Tonbridge, TN12 5LG
Tel: 01622-873187 **Fax:** 01622-873287
E-mail: info@gtseurope.co.uk
Website: http://www.gtseurope.co.uk
Directors: D. Williams (MD)
No.of Employees: 1 - 10 **Product Groups:** 38, 42

Gabriel Chemie UK Ltd

Transfesa Road Paddock Wood, Tonbridge, TN12 6UT
Tel: 01892-836566 **Fax:** 01892-836979
E-mail: info@gabriel-chemie.com
Website: http://www.gabriel-chemie.com
Bank(s): National Westminster Bank Plc
Directors: P. Watkins (MD), M. Wilcox (Sales & Mktg)
Ultimate Holding Company: CLAROPE HOLDINGS NV (AUSTRIA)
Immediate Holding Company: GABRIEL-CHEMIE U.K. LIMITED
Registration no: 01017842 **VAT No.:** GB 204 3021 34
Date established: 1971 **Turnover:** £2m - £5m **No.of Employees:** 21 - 50
Product Groups: 32

Date of Accounts	Dec 11	Jun 10	Jun 09
Sales Turnover	8m	4m	5m
Pre Tax Profit/Loss	-300	-108	-312
Working Capital	700	930	970
Fixed Assets	1m	1m	1m
Current Assets	2m	2m	2m
Current Liabilities	272	186	215

Gard Plasticases Ltd

Unit 2 Arnolds Business Park Branbridges Road, East Peckham, Tonbridge, TN12 5LG
Tel: 01622-871887 **Fax:** 01622-871895
E-mail: info@gardplasticases.com
Website: http://www.gardplasticases.com
Bank(s): National Westminster Bank Plc
Directors: R. Chandler (Co Sec), G. Moon (Tech Serv), P. Fox (MD)
Ultimate Holding Company: GARD HOLDINGS LIMITED
Immediate Holding Company: GARD PLASTICASES LIMITED
Registration no: 01396896 **Date established:** 1978 **Turnover:** £1m - £2m
No.of Employees: 21 - 50 **Product Groups:** 22, 28, 30, 35

Date of Accounts	Mar 12	Mar 11	Mar 10
Working Capital	377	459	385
Fixed Assets	150	134	146
Current Assets	1m	995	858

Gardner Industrial Ltd

Vale Rise, Tonbridge, TN9 1TB
Tel: 01732-369792 **Fax:** 01732-362409
E-mail: sales@gardnerfloors.com
Website: http://www.gardnerfloors.com
Directors: G. Green (Dir)
Managers: B. Percy (Mgr), G. Green (Sales Prom Mgr), R. Brunning (I.T. Exec)
Immediate Holding Company: GARDNER INDUSTRIAL SUPPLIES LIMITED
Registration no: 02626929 **VAT No.:** GB 522 9320 65
Date established: 1991 **Turnover:** £250,000 - £500,000
No.of Employees: 1 - 10 **Product Groups:** 35

Date of Accounts	Mar 10	Mar 09	Mar 08
Sales Turnover	306	591	864
Pre Tax Profit/Loss	-99	-12	25
Working Capital	-136	-68	-80
Fixed Assets	63	98	128
Current Assets	130	118	101
Current Liabilities	131	63	38

Gas Compressors Ltd

Star Farm Golden Green, Tonbridge, TN11 0BE
Tel: 01732-852048 **Fax:** 01732-852376
E-mail: info@gascompressors.co.uk
Website: http://www.gascompressors.co.uk
Directors: C. Stevens (Co Sec), R. Easter (Dir)
Registration no: 04025913 **VAT No.:** GB 754 3435 29
Date established: 2000 **Turnover:** £1m - £2m **No.of Employees:** 1 - 10
Product Groups: 37, 40, 42, 54, 67, 84, 85

Date of Accounts	Mar 10	Mar 09	Mar 08
Sales Turnover	N/A	N/A	1m
Pre Tax Profit/Loss	N/A	N/A	405
Working Capital	1m	863	272
Fixed Assets	25	28	4
Current Assets	2m	2m	534
Current Liabilities	N/A	N/A	112

Genesa Ltd

56 Morley Road, Tonbridge, TN9 1RA
Tel: 01732-367030 **Fax:** 01732-378589
E-mail: gerard.garcia@sirti.co.uk
Website: http://www.genesa.co.uk
Directors: G. Garcia (MD), G. Garcia (MD)
Managers: S. Gibbons
Ultimate Holding Company: CYGNUS LIMITED
Immediate Holding Company: GENESA LIMITED
Registration no: 02254665 **Date established:** 1988 **Turnover:** £2m - £5m
No.of Employees: 1 - 10 **Product Groups:** 37, 40, 44, 52, 81

Date of Accounts	Dec 11	Dec 10	Dec 09
Sales Turnover	3m	2m	2m
Pre Tax Profit/Loss	221	10	57
Working Capital	525	315	287
Fixed Assets	214	159	178
Current Assets	961	654	625
Current Liabilities	240	268	172

Gibbs Dench

Longbrooks Farm Knowle Road, Brenchley, Tonbridge, TN12 7DJ
Tel: 01892-725523 **Fax:** 01892-724072
E-mail: stephengibbs@gibbsdench.co.uk
Website: http://www.gibbsdench.co.uk
Directors: S. Gibbs (Dir)
Immediate Holding Company: GIBBS DENCH ASSOCIATES LIMITED
Registration no: 02284538 **Date established:** 1988
Turnover: £250,000 - £500,000 **No.of Employees:** 1 - 10
Product Groups: 37, 79, 84

Date of Accounts	Jan 11	Jan 10	Jan 09
Sales Turnover	487	425	711
Pre Tax Profit/Loss	52	12	255
Working Capital	161	135	122
Fixed Assets	12	17	24
Current Assets	645	493	437
Current Liabilities	463	327	268

Grasslin UK Ltd

Tower House Vale Rise, Tonbridge, TN9 1TB
Tel: 01732-359888 **Fax:** 01732-354445
E-mail: rjo@tfc.uk.com
Website: http://www.grasslin-controls.co.uk
Directors: B. Gates (Sales), R. Ormand (MD), R. Ormond (MD), L. Ormond (Fin)
Ultimate Holding Company: TFC GROUP (UK) LIMITED
Immediate Holding Company: GRASSLIN (U.K.) LIMITED
Registration no: 01196987 **Date established:** 1975
No.of Employees: 21 - 50 **Product Groups:** 49

Date of Accounts	Mar 09	Mar 08	Mar 07
Working Capital	38	38	38
Current Assets	38	38	38

Groestar Ltd

1 Morley Business Centre, Tonbridge, TN9 1RA
Tel: 01732-771121 **Fax:** 01732-771124
E-mail: sales@groestar.co.uk
Website: http://www.groestar.co.uk
Bank(s): Lloyds TSB Bank plc
Directors: A. Grainger (Dir)
Immediate Holding Company: GROESTAR LIMITED
Registration no: 01202226 **VAT No.:** GB 293 8505 27
Date established: 1975 **Turnover:** £1m - £2m **No.of Employees:** 51 - 100
Product Groups: 52

Date of Accounts	Dec 11	Dec 10	Dec 09
Working Capital	730	267	218
Fixed Assets	438	404	302
Current Assets	3m	2m	746

Hoganas GB Ltd

Munday Works Morley Road, Tonbridge, TN9 1RP
Tel: 01732-362243 **Fax:** 01732-770262
E-mail: info@hoganas.com
Website: http://www.hoganas.com
Managers: L. Harrild (Mgr), A. Allen (Mgr), R. Carmichael (Comm)
Ultimate Holding Company: HOGANASGRUPPEN A.B. (SWEDEN).
Immediate Holding Company: HOGANAS (GREAT BRITAIN) LIMITED
Registration no: 00927351 **VAT No.:** GB 226 7318 62
Date established: 1968 **Turnover:** £10m - £20m
No.of Employees: 21 - 50 **Product Groups:** 34

Date of Accounts	Dec 11	Dec 10	Dec 09
Sales Turnover	18m	15m	9m
Pre Tax Profit/Loss	4m	3m	1m
Working Capital	12m	9m	7m
Fixed Assets	3m	3m	3m
Current Assets	15m	12m	8m
Current Liabilities	744	1m	505

Holmbury Ltd (Group Head Office)

Tower House Vale Rise, Tonbridge, TN9 1TB
Tel: 01732-378912 **Fax:** 01732-357666
E-mail: sales@holmbury.co.uk
Website: http://www.holmbury.co.uk
Directors: D. French (Ch), P. French (Dir)
Managers: A. Powell (Sales Prom Mgr)
Ultimate Holding Company: Holmbury Ltd
Registration no: 01849424 **Date established:** 1984 **Turnover:** £2m - £5m
No.of Employees: 11 - 20 **Product Groups:** 35, 36, 40

Date of Accounts	Feb 10	Feb 09	Feb 08
Pre Tax Profit/Loss	N/A	48	118
Working Capital	2m	2m	2m
Fixed Assets	107	120	97
Current Assets	2m	2m	3m
Current Liabilities	N/A	125	171

I M L Group

Blair House 184-186 High Street, Tonbridge, TN9 1BQ
Tel: 01732-359990 **Fax:** 01732-770049
E-mail: charlotte.sinclair@imlgroup.co.uk
Website: http://www.imlgrouponthenet.net
Directors: P. Jago (MD)
Managers: C. Sinclair (Sales Admin), M. Cura (I.T. Exec)
Immediate Holding Company: I M L GROUP PLC
Registration no: 02416272 **VAT No.:** GB 522 9376 38
Date established: 1989 **Turnover:** £2m - £5m **No.of Employees:** 21 - 50
Product Groups: 28

Date of Accounts	Mar 12	Mar 11	Mar 10
Sales Turnover	4m	3m	3m
Pre Tax Profit/Loss	86	66	29
Working Capital	-741	-729	-691
Fixed Assets	5m	5m	5m
Current Assets	2m	2m	2m
Current Liabilities	723	807	601

Icework Ltd

Lamberhurst Road Horsmonden, Tonbridge, TN12 8DP
Tel: 01892-722522 **Fax:** 01892-722578
E-mail: info@icework.co.uk
Website: http://www.icework.co.uk
Directors: V. Boon (Fin), R. Boom (MD)
Immediate Holding Company: ICE WORK LIMITED
Registration no: 02158638 **Date established:** 1987
No.of Employees: 1 - 10 **Product Groups:** 63, 81

Date of Accounts	Sep 11	Sep 10	Sep 09
Working Capital	-26	-36	-22
Fixed Assets	156	198	247
Current Assets	63	71	80

Industrial Waxes

Marle Place Marle Place Road, Brenchley, Tonbridge, TN12 7HS
Tel: 01892-724088 **Fax:** 01892-724099
E-mail: sales@marlinchemicals.ltd.uk
Website: http://www.marlinchemicals.co.uk
Directors: D. Reynolds (Dir)
Immediate Holding Company: MARLIN CHEMICALS LTD
Registration no: 01640117 **Date established:** 1993 **Turnover:** £2m - £5m
No.of Employees: 1 - 10 **Product Groups:** 20, 31, 32, 66

Date of Accounts	Jun 06
Working Capital	25
Current Assets	25
Total Share Capital	25

Kennedy's Publications Ltd

First Floor Offices Stafford House, 16 East Street, Tonbridge, TN9 1HG
Tel: 01732-371 510 **Fax:** 01732-352 438
E-mail: post@kennedys.co.uk
Website: http://www.kennedysconfection.com
Directors: J. Kennedy (MD), S. Kennedy (Co Sec)
Managers: N. Watson (Publishing), N. Dahanayake (Designer)
Registration no: 01160274 **Date established:** 1974
Turnover: £250,000 - £500,000 **No.of Employees:** 1 - 10
Product Groups: 28

Date of Accounts	Sep 08	Sep 07	Sep 06
Sales Turnover	N/A	N/A	481
Pre Tax Profit/Loss	N/A	N/A	165
Working Capital	135	44	6
Fixed Assets	9	13	11
Current Assets	264	151	112
Current Liabilities	129	107	106
ROCE% (Return on Capital Employed)			966.0
ROT% (Return on Turnover)			34.3

Ling Design Ltd

14-20 Eldon Way Paddock Wood, Tonbridge, TN12 6BE
Tel: 01892-838574 **Fax:** 01892-838676
E-mail: enquiries@lingdesign.co.uk
Website: http://www.lingdesign.co.uk
Bank(s): H S B C
Directors: C. Smith (Fin), M. Thomas (Chief Op Offcr), G. Parkinson (Fin), I. Banks (MD)

Managers: L. Craddock (Personnel), R. Dobson (Tech Serv Mgr)
Ultimate Holding Company: MATRIX PROPERTY LTD (GUERNSEY)
Immediate Holding Company: LING DESIGN LIMITED
Registration no: 03533652 **VAT No.:** GB 702 4688 42
Date established: 1998 **Turnover:** £5m - £10m
No.of Employees: 51 - 100 **Product Groups:** 27, 28, 64

Date of Accounts	Dec 11	Dec 10	Dec 09
Sales Turnover	10m	9m	10m
Pre Tax Profit/Loss	590	522	-455
Working Capital	3m	2m	2m
Fixed Assets	483	521	522
Current Assets	4m	4m	3m
Current Liabilities	841	724	691

M E C I Ltd
Orchard Business Centre Sanderson Way, Tonbridge, TN9 1QG
Tel: 01732-361335 **Fax:** 01732-770540
E-mail: info@mecint.co.uk
Website: http://www.mecint.co.uk
Managers: M. Jones (Mgr)
Immediate Holding Company: MECI LIMITED
Registration no: 01195675 **Date established:** 1975
Turnover: £500,000 - £1m **No.of Employees:** 1 - 10 **Product Groups:** 35, 37

Date of Accounts	May 12	May 11	May 10
Working Capital	184	174	162
Fixed Assets	17	26	35
Current Assets	238	278	277

M J Pallets
18-20 Pattenden Lane Marden, Tonbridge, TN12 9QJ
Tel: 01622-832015 **Fax:** 01622-833078
E-mail: enquiries@mjpallets.co.uk
Website: http://www.mjpallets.co.uk
Directors: M. Cloude (Prop)
Immediate Holding Company: M.J. PALLETS LLP
Registration no: OC342253 **Date established:** 2008
No.of Employees: 1 - 10 **Product Groups:** 45, 48, 76

Date of Accounts	Mar 11	Mar 10
Working Capital	114	84
Fixed Assets	110	97
Current Assets	214	164
Current Liabilities	90	N/A

Marlin Chemicals Ltd
Marle Place Marle Place Road, Brenchley, Tonbridge, TN12 7HS
Tel: 01892-724077 **Fax:** 01892-724099
E-mail: info@marlinchemicals.ltd.uk
Website: http://www.marlinchemicals.co.uk
Bank(s): HSBC
Directors: G. Williams (Dir), M. Williams (Co Sec), S. Ramsden (MD)
Immediate Holding Company: MARLIN CHEMICALS LIMITED
Registration no: 01640117 **VAT No.:** GB 367 6666 02
Date established: 1982 **Turnover:** £10m - £20m
No.of Employees: 11 - 20 **Product Groups:** 31, 32

Date of Accounts	Jun 11	Jun 10	Jun 09
Sales Turnover	19m	12m	12m
Pre Tax Profit/Loss	414	412	207
Working Capital	2m	2m	1m
Fixed Assets	699	377	412
Current Assets	7m	6m	4m
Current Liabilities	4m	3m	1m

Moltek Consultants Ltd
B F S House The Green, Horsmonden, Tonbridge, TN12 8JS
Tel: 01892-725000 **Fax:** 01892-724344
E-mail: recruit@moltek.net
Website: http://www.moltek.com
Directors: J. Picardat (Fin)
Immediate Holding Company: MOLTEK CONSULTANTS LIMITED
Registration no: 03033603 **Date established:** 1995
No.of Employees: 1 - 10 **Product Groups:** 84

Date of Accounts	Dec 11	Dec 10
Working Capital	726	660
Fixed Assets	25	87
Current Assets	1m	2m

New Force Ltd
6 Larkstore Park Lodge Road, Staplehurst, Tonbridge, TN12 0QY
Tel: 01580-895111 **Fax:** 01580-895222
E-mail: sales@new-force.co.uk
Website: http://www.newforce.com
Directors: J. Silvey (Fin), V. Silvey (MD)
Ultimate Holding Company: MILTONGLOW LIMITED
Immediate Holding Company: NEW FORCE LIMITED
Registration no: 01237762 **Date established:** 1975
Turnover: £250,000 - £500,000 **No.of Employees:** 1 - 10
Product Groups: 37, 47

Date of Accounts	Mar 12	Mar 11	Mar 10
Sales Turnover	N/A	N/A	256
Pre Tax Profit/Loss	N/A	N/A	19
Working Capital	76	83	84
Fixed Assets	3	4	6
Current Assets	115	148	144
Current Liabilities	N/A	N/A	22

One To One Business Services
61 Brookmead Hildenborough, Tonbridge, TN11 9EZ
Tel: 01732-833053 **Fax:** 07092-375881
E-mail: sjohnson@onetoone.co.uk
Website: http://www.onetoonebusiness.co.uk
Directors: S. Johnson (Prop)
Date established: 1992 **Turnover:** Up to £250,000
No.of Employees: 1 - 10 **Product Groups:** 80

P M C Marketing Ltd
Marle Place Marle Place Road, Brenchley, Tonbridge, TN12 7HS
Tel: 01892-725755 **Fax:** 01892-724099
E-mail: info@pmcmarketing.co.uk
Website: http://www.pmcmarketing.co.uk
Directors: M. Short (MD)
Ultimate Holding Company: Marlin Chemicals Ltd
Registration no: 03890652 **No.of Employees:** 1 - 10 **Product Groups:** 31

Paper Tigers
Woodlands Mills Woodlands Road, Tonbridge, TN9 2NE
Tel: 01732-771731 **Fax:** 01732-362429
E-mail: info@papertigers.co.uk
Website: http://www.papertigers.co.uk
Directors: B. Dennison (MD), B. Dennison (Prop)
Managers: L. Vulgar (Admin Off), G. Bunt (Accounts)
Immediate Holding Company: PAPER TIGERS LIMITED
Registration no: 03093215 **VAT No.:** GB 928 5956 69
Date established: 1995 **Turnover:** £500,000 - £1m
No.of Employees: 1 - 10 **Product Groups:** 23, 27, 28, 30, 38, 39, 40, 49

Powersense Technology (UPS & Generators)
Unit 3 Morley Business Centre Morley Road, Tonbridge, TN9 1RA
Tel: 01732-771818 **Fax:** 01732-771881
E-mail: alanbrailsford@talk21.com
Website: http://www.powersense.co.uk
Directors: A. Brailsford (Prop)
Registration no: 02089386 **VAT No.:** GB 442 5987 23
No.of Employees: 1 - 10 **Product Groups:** 37, 38, 44

Process Exchange
Unit 2 The Oast Pullens Farm Lamberhurst Road, Horsmonden, Tonbridge, TN12 8ED
Tel: 01892-724333 **Fax:** 01892-724888
E-mail: j-swain@processexchange.co.uk
Website: http://www.processexchange.co.uk
Directors: J. Swain (Prop)
Immediate Holding Company: THE SIMPLY WILD FOOD COMPANY LIMITED
Registration no: 03152019 **Date established:** 2002
Turnover: £250,000 - £500,000 **No.of Employees:** 1 - 10
Product Groups: 36, 37, 38

Date of Accounts	Mar 12
Working Capital	-212
Fixed Assets	288
Current Assets	382

Produce Packaging
Unit 10 Wheelbarrow Park Estate Pattenden Lane, Marden, Tonbridge, TN12 9QJ
Tel: 01622-833012 **Fax:** 01622-832500
Website: http://www.hlhltd.co.uk
Managers: J. Short (Mgr)
Turnover: £2m - £5m **No.of Employees:** 11 - 20 **Product Groups:** 38, 42

Pulp & Paper Machinery Ltd
Holman House Station Road, Staplehurst, Tonbridge, TN12 0QQ
Tel: 01580-893200 **Fax:** 01580-893229
E-mail: sales@pandpmachinery.com
Directors: S. Braganza (Dir)
Immediate Holding Company: PULP & PAPER MACHINERY LIMITED
Registration no: 00904021 **Date established:** 1967
No.of Employees: 1 - 10 **Product Groups:** 44

Date of Accounts	Dec 10	Dec 09	Dec 08
Working Capital	-19	-43	-98
Fixed Assets	N/A	N/A	5
Current Assets	7	22	5

Raster Vision Ltd
Unit 1 Crundalls Gedges Hill, Matfield, Tonbridge, TN12 7EA
Tel: 01892-722228 **Fax:** 01892-724228
E-mail: info@rastervision.co.uk
Website: http://www.rastervision.co.uk
Managers: R. Leman (Comptroller)
Immediate Holding Company: RASTER VISION LIMITED
Registration no: 02753356 **VAT No.:** 621 9314 58 **Date established:** 1992
Turnover: £250,000 - £500,000 **No.of Employees:** 11 - 20
Product Groups: 84, 85

Date of Accounts	Sep 11	Sep 10	Sep 09
Working Capital	265	220	742
Fixed Assets	9	17	26
Current Assets	2m	363	936

Rite Industrial Doors Ltd
Unit 9h Longbrooks Farm Knowle Road, Brenchley, Tonbridge, TN12 7DJ
Tel: 01892-725100 **Fax:** 01892-834887
E-mail: info@ritedoors.co.uk
Website: http://www.ritedoors.co.uk
Directors: R. Bright (Co Sec), R. Wright (Fin)
Immediate Holding Company: RITE INDUSTRIAL DOORS LTD
Registration no: 04136599 **Date established:** 2001
No.of Employees: 1 - 10 **Product Groups:** 26, 35

Date of Accounts	Apr 11	Apr 10	Apr 09
Working Capital	123	33	5
Fixed Assets	3	N/A	N/A
Current Assets	315	176	91

Derek Roberts Antiques
25 Shipbourne Road, Tonbridge, TN10 3DN
Tel: 01732-358986 **Fax:** 01732-771842
E-mail: drclocks@clara.net
Website: http://www.qualityantiqueclocks.com
Directors: P. Archard (Prop)
VAT No.: GB 210 3130 46 **No.of Employees:** 1 - 10 **Product Groups:** 65

Rodney Fletcher
Pullens Farm Lamberhurst Road, Horsmonden, Tonbridge, TN12 8ED
Tel: 01892-724314 **Fax:** 01892-724209
E-mail: wine@rfvintners.co.uk
Website: http://www.rfvintners.co.uk
Directors: R. Fletcher (MD)
Registration no: 07228117 **Turnover:** £500,000 - £1m
No.of Employees: 1 - 10 **Product Groups:** 62

Scarab Sweepers Ltd
Pattenden Lane Marden, Tonbridge, TN12 9QD
Tel: 01622-831006 **Fax:** 01622-831417
E-mail: dcassingham@scarab-sales.com
Website: http://www.scarab-sweepers.com
Bank(s): HSBC Bank plc
Directors: D. Cassingham (MD), S. Hoadley (Co Sec), D. Cassingham (Sales), J. Affleck (MD)
Managers: S. Myers (Personnel), N. Breen, D. Hoadley
Ultimate Holding Company: SCARAB HOLDINGS LIMITED
Immediate Holding Company: SCARAB HOLDINGS LIMITED
Registration no: 02086673 **VAT No.:** GB 374 5002 68
Date established: 1987 **Turnover:** £20m - £50m
No.of Employees: 101 - 250 **Product Groups:** 39, 40, 45

Date of Accounts	May 11	May 10	May 09
Sales Turnover	25m	23m	25m
Pre Tax Profit/Loss	2m	408	-443
Working Capital	7m	6m	5m
Fixed Assets	894	829	1m
Current Assets	12m	10m	9m
Current Liabilities	1m	679	485

Sciss Ltd
9 Larkstore Park Lodge Road, Staplehurst, Tonbridge, TN12 0QY
Tel: 01580-890582 **Fax:** 01580-890583
E-mail: sales@sciss.co.uk
Website: http://www.sciss.co.uk
Directors: K. Gray (Fin)
Immediate Holding Company: SCISS LIMITED
Registration no: 03870881 **VAT No.:** GB 725 0625 54
Date established: 1999 **No.of Employees:** 1 - 10 **Product Groups:** 33, 36, 48

Date of Accounts	Mar 12	Mar 11	Mar 10
Working Capital	-1	-45	-93
Fixed Assets	75	83	93
Current Assets	71	55	44

Seeder Sti
Becketts Grove Farm Sophurst Lane, Matfield, Tonbridge, TN12 7LH
Tel: 01892-724315 **Fax:** 01892-724319
E-mail: jpmiles@seedersti.co.uk
Website: http://www.seedersti.co.uk
Directors: J. Miles (MD)
Turnover: Up to £250,000 **No.of Employees:** 1 - 10 **Product Groups:** 41

Shirewater Joinery
Douglas Buildings Lodge Road, Staplehurst, Tonbridge, TN12 0QZ
Tel: 01580-893033 **Fax:** 01580-893033
E-mail: nickw@shearwaterkitchens.co.uk
Website: http://www.shearwaterkitchens.co.uk
Directors: N. Walsh (Prop), N. Walsh (MD)
No.of Employees: 1 - 10 **Product Groups:** 25, 26, 27, 30, 33, 35, 36, 52, 63, 66

Solid State Supplies plc
Unit 2 Eastlands Lane, Paddock Wood, Tonbridge, TN12 6BU
Tel: 01892-836836 **Fax:** 01892-837837
E-mail: sales@ssspl.com
Website: http://www.sssplc.com
Bank(s): HSBC, Croydon
Directors: J. Macmichael (MD), P. Haining (Fin), J. Macmicheal (MD)
Ultimate Holding Company: SOLID STATE PLC
Immediate Holding Company: SOLID STATE PLC
Registration no: 00771335 **VAT No.:** GB 619 4767 05
Date established: 1963 **Turnover:** £20m - £50m
No.of Employees: 21 - 50 **Product Groups:** 37, 44

Date of Accounts	Mar 12	Mar 11	Mar 10
Sales Turnover	26m	21m	14m
Pre Tax Profit/Loss	2m	1m	530
Working Capital	2m	1m	877
Fixed Assets	3m	3m	2m
Current Assets	10m	7m	5m
Current Liabilities	4m	3m	766

Sonance Ltd
12 Cornwallis Avenue, Tonbridge, TN10 4ES
Tel: 0870-005 5520 **Fax:** 0870-005 5521
E-mail: trade@sonance.biz
Website: http://www.sonance.biz
Directors: S. Baker (MD), M. Baker (Fin)
Immediate Holding Company: SONANCE LIMITED
Registration no: 04473642 **Date established:** 2002
No.of Employees: 1 - 10 **Product Groups:** 37, 44, 49

Date of Accounts	Dec 09	Dec 08	Dec 07
Working Capital	31	11	-1
Fixed Assets	N/A	1	1
Current Assets	84	48	82

Standex Electronics
40 Morley Road, Tonbridge, TN9 1RA
Tel: 01732-771023 **Fax:** 01732-770122
E-mail: sales@standex.co.uk
Website: http://www.standexelectronics.com
Bank(s): Lloyds
Managers: S. Brockett (Chief Mgr)
Immediate Holding Company: STANDEX HOLDINGS LTD
Registration no: 01034386 **VAT No.:** GB 210 0282 38
Date established: 1971 **Turnover:** £2m - £5m **No.of Employees:** 51 - 100
Product Groups: 37, 47

Style Tech
Unit 2 1 Vale Rise, Tonbridge, TN9 1TB
Tel: 01732-369368 **Fax:** 01732-352233
E-mail: info@styletechuk.com
Website: http://www.styletechuk.com
Directors: P. Woodcock (Snr Part)
Immediate Holding Company: TFC (INVESTMENT PROPERTIES) LLP
Date established: 2006 **Turnover:** **No.of Employees:** 11 - 20
Product Groups: 40

Date of Accounts	Mar 12	Mar 11	Mar 10
Working Capital	41	-67	-42
Fixed Assets	660	669	634
Current Assets	61	68	6

T F C Group
Tower House Vale Rise, Tonbridge, TN9 1TB
Tel: 01732-351680 **Fax:** 01732-354445
E-mail: info@tfc.uk.com
Website: http://www.tfc-group.co.uk
Bank(s): Barclays, Dartford
Directors: L. Ormond (Fin), B. Gates (Sales), R. Ormond (MD)
Ultimate Holding Company: TFC GROUP (UK) LIMITED
Immediate Holding Company: GRASSLIN (U.K.) LIMITED
Registration no: 01196987 **Date established:** 1975 **Turnover:** £5m - £10m
No.of Employees: 21 - 50 **Product Groups:** 38

Date of Accounts	Mar 11	Mar 10	Mar 09
Working Capital	38	38	38
Current Assets	38	38	38

Target Plastics Kent Ltd
Arnolds Business Park Branbridges Road, East Peckham, Tonbridge, TN12 5LG
Tel: 01622-873150 **Fax:** 020-8312 9191
E-mail: chris@targetplastics.co.uk
Website: http://www.targetplasticskent.co.uk
Bank(s): Barclays, Woolwich

see next page

Target Plastics Kent Ltd - Cont'd

Directors: C. Taylor (Fab)
Ultimate Holding Company: TARGET PLASTICS HOLDINGS LIMITED
Immediate Holding Company: TARGET PLASTICS (KENT) LIMITED
Registration no: 06857919 **VAT No.:** GB 467 5449 07
Date established: 2009 **Turnover:** £2m - £5m **No.of Employees:** 21 - 50
Product Groups: 30, 48

Date of Accounts	Jun 11	Jun 10	Jun 09
Working Capital	60	-11	-24
Fixed Assets	51	57	52
Current Assets	542	529	179

Tech Optics

6 Tannery Road, Tonbridge, TN9 1RF
Tel: 01732-770466 **Fax:** 01732-770476
E-mail: sales@techoptics.com
Website: http://www.techoptics.com
Bank(s): National Westminster Bank Plc
Directors: T. Parkinson (Fin), D. Paffey (Sales), S. Carter (MD)
Immediate Holding Company: TECH OPTICS FIRST COMPANY LIMITED
Registration no: 02257839 **VAT No.:** GB 510 0847 89
Date established: 1988 **Turnover:** £2m - £5m **No.of Employees:** 11 - 20
Product Groups: 37, 44, 45, 67

Date of Accounts	Dec 11	Dec 10	Dec 09
Working Capital	100	100	100
Current Assets	100	100	142

The Woodstove Trading Co LLP

Unit 5 Honeycrest Industrial Park Lodge Road, Staplehurst, Tonbridge, TN12 0RX
Tel: 01580-893510 **Fax:** 01580-893509
E-mail: sales@woodstovetrading.co.uk
Website: http://www.woodstovetrading.co.uk
Directors: L. Brice (Ptnr)
Immediate Holding Company: THE WOODSTOVE TRADING COMPANY LLP
Registration no: OC320817 **Date established:** 2006
No.of Employees: 1 - 10 **Product Groups:** 40

Date of Accounts	Jul 11	Jul 10	Jul 08
Working Capital	-146	-120	-110
Fixed Assets	49	52	47
Current Assets	96	98	61

Time Electronics

Unit 11 Sovereign Way Botany Industrial Estate, Tonbridge, TN9 1RH
Tel: 01732-355993 **Fax:** 01732-770312
E-mail: martin@timeelectronics.co.uk
Website: http://www.timelectronics.co.uk
Bank(s): National Westminster
Directors: S. Newby (Fin), M. Bailey (MD)
Managers: J. Carter (Sales Prom Mgr)
Registration no: 00904328 **VAT No.:** GB 356 6839 10
Date established: 1967 **Turnover:** £1m - £2m **No.of Employees:** 21 - 50
Product Groups: 38, 85

Tonbridge Diamond Cutting Ltd

15 Clare Avenue, Tonbridge, TN9 1XN
Tel: 01732-506064 **Fax:** 01732-770505
E-mail: diamondcut40@aol.com
Website: http://www.tonbridgediamondcutting.co.uk
Directors: H. Phillips (Fin), C. Phillips (MD)
Immediate Holding Company: TONBRIDGE DIAMOND CUTTING LIMITED
Registration no: 04445682 **Date established:** 2002
Turnover: Up to £250,000 **No.of Employees:** 1 - 10 **Product Groups:** 23, 28, 29, 30, 36, 38, 45, 46, 48, 49, 51, 67, 80, 83, 84, 85, 86, 87

Date of Accounts	Mar 11	Mar 10	Mar 09
Sales Turnover	143	355	268
Pre Tax Profit/Loss	-70	31	-21
Working Capital	2	67	42
Fixed Assets	14	19	25
Current Assets	33	87	86
Current Liabilities	13	5	16

United Business Media Ltd

Riverbank House Angel Lane, Tonbridge, TN9 1SE
Tel: 01732-362666 **Fax:** 01732-367301
Website: http://www.ubm.com
Directors: D. Clark (Comm)
Managers: L. Read (Personnel), S. Nelson
Ultimate Holding Company: UNITED NEWS & MEDIA CO. P.L.C.
Immediate Holding Company: MILLER FREEMAN UK LTD
Registration no: 00152298 **No.of Employees:** 1501 & over
Product Groups: 28

Harry Veall Ltd

Slaney Place Farmhouse Headcorn Road, Staplehurst, Tonbridge, TN12 0DT
Tel: 01580-895311 **Fax:** 01580-895311
E-mail: caroline.veall@btconnect.com
Directors: C. Veall (MD), O. Reynolds (Fin)
Immediate Holding Company: HARRY VEALL LIMITED
Registration no: 00623925 **Date established:** 1959
Turnover: Up to £250,000 **No.of Employees:** 1 - 10 **Product Groups:** 41

Date of Accounts	Mar 11	Mar 10	Mar 09
Sales Turnover	225	N/A	N/A
Pre Tax Profit/Loss	-46	N/A	N/A
Working Capital	-140	51	96
Fixed Assets	213	217	228
Current Assets	121	82	137

Wallace & Tiernan Ltd (Chemfeed Limited)

Priory Works Five Oak Green Road, Tonbridge, TN11 0QL
Tel: 01732-771777 **Fax:** 01732-771800
E-mail: sales@wallace-tiernan.com
Website: http://www.siemens.com
Bank(s): HSBC Bank plc
Directors: C. Dean (Dir), D. Parrish (Chief Op Offcr), R. Russ (Sales & Mktg)
Managers: D. Bourne (Develop Mgr), D. Rye (Purch Mgr), F. Roche (Export Sales Mg), P. Mcinulty (Comptroller), G. Brown
Ultimate Holding Company: SIEMENS AG (GERMANY)
Immediate Holding Company: USF HOLDING (UK) LIMITED
Registration no: 00212577 **VAT No.:** GB 754 0290 44
Date established: 1926 **Turnover:** £20m - £50m
No.of Employees: 101 - 250 **Product Groups:** 32, 38, 39, 40, 41, 42, 43, 45, 52, 54, 67

Date of Accounts	Sep 08	Sep 07
Sales Turnover	20650	18590
Pre Tax Profit/Loss	210	70
Working Capital	5440	-1410
Fixed Assets	6580	6710
Current Assets	11260	11330
Current Liabilities	5820	12740
Total Share Capital	2590	2590
ROCE% (Return on Capital Employed)	1.7	1.3
ROT% (Return on Turnover)	1.0	0.4

Ernest West & Beynon Ltd

Unit 25 Eldon Way Paddock Wood, Tonbridge, TN12 6BE
Tel: 01892-836455 **Fax:** 01892-834121
E-mail: sales@westbeynon.co.uk
Website: http://www.westbeynon.co.uk
Bank(s): National Westminster Bank Plc
Directors: I. Snowdon (Co Sec), C. Snowdon (MD)
Immediate Holding Company: ERNEST WEST & BEYNON,LIMITED
Registration no: 00101234 **VAT No.:** GB 205 9481 61
Date established: 2009 **Turnover:** £1m - £2m **No.of Employees:** 11 - 20
Product Groups: 38, 52, 66

Date of Accounts	Mar 11	Mar 10	Mar 09
Working Capital	247	229	204
Fixed Assets	74	122	125
Current Assets	821	888	1m

Whitebox3 Ltd

Unit 11 Durgates Lodge Clapper Lane, Staplehurst, Tonbridge, TN12 0JS
Tel: 01580-890747 **Fax:** 01580-890667
E-mail: sales@whitebox3.com
Website: http://www.whitebox3.com
Directors: J. Simpson (Dir)
Immediate Holding Company: WHITEBOX3 LIMITED
Registration no: 06265345 **Date established:** 2007
Turnover: £250,000 - £500,000 **No.of Employees:** 1 - 10
Product Groups: 49

Date of Accounts	Aug 11	Aug 10	Aug 09
Sales Turnover	N/A	N/A	312
Pre Tax Profit/Loss	N/A	N/A	16
Working Capital	-45	-28	-4
Fixed Assets	42	54	21
Current Assets	63	91	99
Current Liabilities	N/A	N/A	35

Paul Wilmhurst

117 Hadlow Road, Tonbridge, TN9 1QE
Tel: 01732-352949
E-mail: paulandrach@aol.com
Directors: P. Wilmhurst (Prop)
Immediate Holding Company: SEVENOAKS FENCING LTD
Date established: 2011 **No.of Employees:** 1 - 10 **Product Groups:** 25, 35, 52

George Wimpey South London Ltd

101-103 Tonbridge Road Hildenborough, Tonbridge, TN11 9HL
Tel: 01732-836000 **Fax:** 01732-836030
E-mail: phil.chapman@taylorwimpey.com
Website: http://www.wimpeyhomes.co.uk
Directors: E. Owens (MD), J. Stokes (Sales & Mktg), P. Carr (Fin), S. Livesey (Fin)
Managers: C. Scanes (Tech Serv Mgr), P. Hawkins (Chief Buyer), T. Fewsdale (Personnel)
Ultimate Holding Company: TAYLOR WIMPEY PLC
Immediate Holding Company: GEORGE WIMPEY SOUTH EAST LIMITED
Registration no: 01011967 **VAT No.:** GB 559 7983 61
Date established: 1971 **No.of Employees:** 51 - 100 **Product Groups:** 52, 80

Date of Accounts	Dec 11	Dec 10	Dec 09
Working Capital	17m	17m	17m
Current Assets	17m	17m	17m

Tunbridge Wells

C.O.H. Baines Ltd Rubber Extrusions

Unit 3 Buckingham House Longfield Road, Tunbridge Wells, TN2 3EY
Tel: 01892-543311 **Fax:** 01892-530682
E-mail: sales@coh-baines.co.uk
Website: http://www.coh-baines.co.uk
Bank(s): Barclays
Directors: R. Batt (MD)
Registration no: 00349854 **VAT No.:** GB 209 5098 56
Date established: 1939 **Turnover:** £2m - £5m **No.of Employees:** 21 - 50
Product Groups: 29, 42, 48

Date of Accounts	Dec 07	Dec 06	Dec 05
Working Capital	386	53	31
Fixed Assets	117	474	499
Current Assets	702	674	701
Current Liabilities	316	621	669
Total Share Capital	1	1	1

Bellingham & Stanley Ltd

Longfield Road, Tunbridge Wells, TN2 3EY
Tel: 01892-500400 **Fax:** 01892-543115
E-mail: sales@bellinghamandstanley.co.uk
Website: http://www.bellinghamandstanley.com
Bank(s): Barclays
Directors: M. Banks (Dir)
Managers: A. Darkins (Tech Serv Mgr), D. Bayliss (Buyer), K. Chapman, T. Ford (Sales Prom Mgr), A. Bertrand (Comptroller)
Ultimate Holding Company: ITT CORPORATION (USA)
Immediate Holding Company: BELLINGHAM & STANLEY LIMITED
Registration no: 00140250 **Date established:** 2015 **Turnover:** £2m - £5m
No.of Employees: 21 - 50 **Product Groups:** 28, 38, 42

Date of Accounts	Dec 11	Dec 10	Dec 09
Sales Turnover	4m	3m	3m
Pre Tax Profit/Loss	892	3m	379
Working Capital	5m	4m	1m
Fixed Assets	345	382	424
Current Assets	6m	5m	2m
Current Liabilities	163	261	171

Brimotor Ltd

10-12 Culverden Down, Tunbridge Wells, TN4 9SA
Tel: 01892-537588 **Fax:** 01892-527724
E-mail: info@brimotor.co.uk
Website: http://www.brimotor.co.uk
Directors: G. Mossery (MD)
Immediate Holding Company: BRIMOTOR LIMITED
Registration no: 01057050 **VAT No.:** GB 211 0857 07
Date established: 1972 **Turnover:** £250,000 - £500,000
No.of Employees: 11 - 20 **Product Groups:** 37, 40

Date of Accounts	Mar 11	Mar 10	Mar 09
Working Capital	14	15	29
Fixed Assets	49	53	58
Current Assets	20	21	41

Brown Knight & Truscott Ltd

North Farm Road, Tunbridge Wells, TN2 3BW
Tel: 01892-511678 **Fax:** 01892-511343
E-mail: maureen.burns@bkt.co.uk
Website: http://www.bkt.co.uk
Bank(s): HSBC Bank plc
Directors: M. Burns (MD)
Ultimate Holding Company: BROWN KNIGHT & TRUSCOTT HOLDINGS LIMITED
Immediate Holding Company: BROWN KNIGHT & TRUSCOTT LIMITED
Registration no: 02753137 **VAT No.:** GB 589 6165 79
Date established: 1992 **Turnover:** £5m - £10m
No.of Employees: 51 - 100 **Product Groups:** 44

Date of Accounts	Aug 11	Aug 10	Aug 09
Sales Turnover	8m	7m	7m
Pre Tax Profit/Loss	45	26	-102
Working Capital	16	-42	158
Fixed Assets	2m	2m	2m
Current Assets	2m	2m	2m
Current Liabilities	720	481	644

Brunning Newman Houghton Ltd

The Old Station Station Road, Groombridge, Tunbridge Wells, TN3 9RD
Tel: 01892-861002 **Fax:** 01892-863122
E-mail: info@bnhl.co.uk
Website: http://www.bnhl.co.uk
Directors: D. Brunning (MD)
Immediate Holding Company: BRUNNING NEWMAN HOUGHTON LIMITED
Registration no: 04853610 **Date established:** 2003
Turnover: £250,000 - £500,000 **No.of Employees:** 1 - 10
Product Groups: 82

Date of Accounts	Jun 11	Jun 10	Jun 09
Working Capital	40	56	35
Fixed Assets	9	9	8
Current Assets	93	110	78

Burgess C R Commissioning Ltd

19 Mount Ephraim, Tunbridge Wells, TN4 8AE
Tel: 01892-515169 **Fax:** 01892-547716
E-mail: burgesscomm@burgessgroup.co.uk
Website: http://www.burgessgroup.co.uk
Directors: R. Burgess (Dir), C. Burgess (MD)
Immediate Holding Company: C.R. BURGESS (COMMISSIONING) LIMITED
Registration no: 01326892 **VAT No.:** GB 312 8137 84
Date established: 1977 **No.of Employees:** 21 - 50 **Product Groups:** 80, 84

C Brewer & Sons

North Farm Road, Tunbridge Wells, TN2 3DY
Tel: 01892-530101 **Fax:** 01892-541423
E-mail: tunbridgewells@brewers.co.uk
Managers: M. Sallis (District Mgr)
Immediate Holding Company: C.BREWER & SONS LIMITED
Registration no: 00203852 **Date established:** 1925
No.of Employees: 11 - 20 **Product Groups:** 27, 30, 32, 36, 49, 66

C C Automation

11 Guildford Road, Tunbridge Wells, TN1 1SW
Tel: 01892-544789 **Fax:** 01892-544697
Website: http://www.ccautomation.com
Directors: D. Wilson (Prop)
Immediate Holding Company: CC AUTOMATION LIMITED
Registration no: 05740793 **Date established:** 2006
No.of Employees: 1 - 10 **Product Groups:** 38, 42

Date of Accounts	Mar 09	Mar 07
Working Capital	N/A	-3
Current Assets	5	10
Current Liabilities	N/A	12

Chilstone

Victoria Park Fordcombe Road, Fordcombe, Tunbridge Wells, TN3 0RD
Tel: 01892-740866 **Fax:** 01892-740249
E-mail: office@chilstone.com
Website: http://www.chilstone.com
Bank(s): Barclays
Directors: G. Gilbert (Fin)
Managers: S. Clark (Mgr), S. Clarke (Chief Mgr)
Immediate Holding Company: HESWAY LTD
Registration no: 00932477 **Turnover:** £500,000 - £1m
No.of Employees: 11 - 20 **Product Groups:** 33, 52

Choice Carpets Curtains & Blinds

Pantiles House 2 Nevill Street, Tunbridge Wells, TN2 5TT
Tel: 01892-536886 **Fax:** 01892-536657
E-mail: sales@choicecarpets.com
Website: http://www.choicecarpets.com
Managers: M. Orum (Mgr)
Registration no: 04427094 **Date established:** 2002 **Turnover:** £5m - £10m
No.of Employees: 1 - 10 **Product Groups:** 35, 36

Cicero Languages International

42 Upper Grosvenor Road, Tunbridge Wells, TN1 2ET
Tel: 01892-547077 **Fax:** 01892-522749
E-mail: info@cicero.co.uk
Website: http://www.cicero.co.uk
Managers: C. Reay (Mgr)
Immediate Holding Company: CICERO LANGUAGES INTERNATIONAL LIMITED
Registration no: 05859952 **VAT No.:** GB 339 8935 00
Date established: 2006 **Turnover:** £1m - £2m **No.of Employees:** 11 - 20
Product Groups: 80, 86

Date of Accounts	Sep 10	Sep 09	Sep 08
Working Capital	51	8	-7
Fixed Assets	21	21	23
Current Assets	156	110	77

Comtecs Ltd
Colebrook House 215a Upper Grosvenor Road, Tunbridge Wells, TN1 2EG
Tel: 01892-514636 **Fax:** 01892-543023
E-mail: info@comtecs.co.uk
Website: http://www.comtecs.co.uk
Directors: P. Charles (Fin), T. Blackden (Dir)
Immediate Holding Company: COMTECS LIMITED
Registration no: 04122678 **Date established:** 2000
No.of Employees: 1 - 10 **Product Groups:** 81

Date of Accounts	Dec 11	Dec 10	Dec 09
Working Capital	2	6	73
Fixed Assets	3	2	2
Current Assets	128	89	73

Creaseys Chartered Accountants
12-16 Lonsdale Gardens, Tunbridge Wells, TN1 1PA
Tel: 01892-546546 **Fax:** 01892-511232
E-mail: partners@creaseys.co.uk
Website: http://www.creaseys.co.uk
Bank(s): National Westminster Bank Plc
Directors: G. Turpin (Tech Serv), C. Manwaring (Pers), E. Roberts (Grp Chief Exec)
Managers: V. Wright (Personnel)
Immediate Holding Company: CREASEYS LLP
Registration no: OC319671 **VAT No.:** GB 203 0119 38
Date established: 2006 **Turnover:** £2m - £5m **No.of Employees:** 51 - 100
Product Groups: 80

Date of Accounts	Apr 11	Apr 10	Apr 09
Working Capital	688	915	920
Fixed Assets	65	63	68
Current Assets	1m	1m	2m

Denim Creative
55 Calverley Road, Tunbridge Wells, TN1 2TU
Tel: 01892-519777 **Fax:** 01892-519 778
E-mail: enquiries@denim-creative.co.uk
Website: http://www.denim-creative.co.uk
Directors: J. Oldfield (Ptnr)
Immediate Holding Company: CARBON CARE INVESTMENTS LIMITED
Registration no: 05764446 **Date established:** 2011
No.of Employees: 1 - 10 **Product Groups:** 81

Date of Accounts	Sep 10	Sep 09
Working Capital	N/A	1
Current Assets	40	38

Design Display Solutions
Budgeons Mead Willetts Lane, Blackham, Tunbridge Wells, TN3 9TU
Tel: 01892-740896 **Fax:** 01892-740930
E-mail: info@designdisplaysolutions.co.uk
Website: http://www.designdisplaysolutions.co.uk
Directors: M. Morley (MD)
Immediate Holding Company: DESIGN DISPLAY SOLUTIONS LIMITED
Registration no: 04328758 **Date established:** 2001
No.of Employees: 1 - 10 **Product Groups:** 26, 35, 49, 52, 81, 83, 84

Date of Accounts	Mar 12	Mar 11	Mar 10
Working Capital	14	10	6
Fixed Assets	N/A	1	1
Current Assets	49	70	45

Electrical Distributors Association
Union House Eridge Road, Tunbridge Wells, TN4 8HF
Tel: 01892-619990 **Fax:** 01892-619991
E-mail: nigel@eda.co.uk
Website: http://www.eda.org.uk
Directors: N. Ellis (Dir)
Immediate Holding Company: ELECTRICAL DISTRIBUTORS ASSOCIATION LIMITED
Registration no: 00466352 **Date established:** 1949
Turnover: £500,000 - £1m **No.of Employees:** 1 - 10 **Product Groups:** 87

Date of Accounts	Dec 11	Dec 10	Dec 09
Sales Turnover	713	389	420
Pre Tax Profit/Loss	103	47	51
Working Capital	525	446	403
Fixed Assets	8	7	15
Current Assets	678	582	494
Current Liabilities	138	135	91

Element 5 Systems (PA Loudspeakers)
202 Upper Grosvenor Road, Tunbridge Wells, TN1 2EH
Tel: 0800-5200972 **Fax:** 0870-4719925
E-mail: ross@element5systems.co.uk
Website: http://www.element5systems.co.uk
Turnover: Up to £250,000 **No.of Employees:** 1 - 10 **Product Groups:** 23, 25, 26, 33, 35, 37, 44, 67, 83

Environment Protection Ltd
114b London Road Southborough, Tunbridge Wells, TN4 0PN
Tel: 01892-513135
E-mail: sales@eplfilms.com
Website: http://www.eplfilms.com
Directors: F. Genery (Dir), N. Bradshaw (Fin)
Immediate Holding Company: ENVIRONMENT PROTECTION LIMITED
Registration no: 03164108 **Date established:** 1996
No.of Employees: 11 - 20 **Product Groups:** 37, 79

Date of Accounts	Oct 11	Oct 10	Oct 09
Working Capital	61	59	44
Fixed Assets	39	25	28
Current Assets	250	242	276

Epl Safety Solar Films For Windows
114b London Road Southborough, Tunbridge Wells, TN4 0PN
Tel: 01892-513135
Website: http://www.eplfilms.com
No.of Employees: 1 - 10 **Product Groups:** 27, 30, 33

Eurocareer Consultants
Century Place Lamberts Road, Tunbridge Wells, TN2 3EH
Tel: 01424-883022
E-mail: info@eurocareer.co.uk
Website: http://www.eurocareer.com
Directors: S. Edwards (MD)
Immediate Holding Company: APB MANAGEMENT LIMITED
Registration no: 02998436 **Date established:** 2005
Turnover: Up to £250,000 **No.of Employees:** 1 - 10 **Product Groups:** 80

Date of Accounts	Mar 11	Mar 10	Mar 09
Working Capital	377	156	95
Fixed Assets	6	146	146
Current Assets	382	162	100

Freight Transport Association
Hermes House St Johns Road, Tunbridge Wells, TN4 9UZ
Tel: 01892-526171 **Fax:** 01892-534989
E-mail: info@fta.co.uk
Website: http://www.fta.co.uk
Bank(s): National Westminster Bank Plc
Directors: T. De Pencier (Grp Chief Exec)
Managers: D. Wells
Immediate Holding Company: FREIGHT TRANSPORT ASSOCIATION LIMITED
Registration no: 00391957 **VAT No.:** GB 217 8535 50
Date established: 1944 **Turnover:** £20m - £50m
No.of Employees: 251 - 500 **Product Groups:** 87

Date of Accounts	Dec 11	Dec 10	Dec 09
Sales Turnover	24m	24m	25m
Pre Tax Profit/Loss	1m	946	2m
Working Capital	4m	4m	5m
Fixed Assets	3m	3m	3m
Current Assets	8m	8m	9m
Current Liabilities	3m	3m	3m

Grint Desgin
6 Benhall Mill Road, Tunbridge Wells, TN2 5JH
Tel: 07806-564026
E-mail: matt.grint@grintdesign.co.uk
Website: http://www.grintdesign.co.uk
Directors: M. Grint (Dir)
Registration no: 04187450 **Date established:** 2001
No.of Employees: 1 - 10 **Product Groups:** 44

C J Harris Electronic Components
Rosebank House Chafford Lane, Fordcombe, Tunbridge Wells, TN3 0SH
Tel: 01892-740000 **Fax:** 01892-740100
E-mail: chrisharris2@btconnect.com
Directors: C. Harris (Ptnr)
Turnover: £500,000 - £1m **No.of Employees:** 1 - 10 **Product Groups:** 37

Hendal Lighting Ltd
The Oast Hendal Farm, Groombridge, Tunbridge Wells, TN3 9NU
Tel: 01892-864499 **Fax:** 01892-863988
Directors: M. Ginman (Fin)
Immediate Holding Company: HENDAL LIGHTING LIMITED
Registration no: 02580652 **Date established:** 1991
No.of Employees: 1 - 10 **Product Groups:** 37, 67

Date of Accounts	Apr 11	Apr 10	Apr 09
Working Capital	29	37	23
Fixed Assets	3	4	5
Current Assets	65	73	62

Jiskoot Ltd
Jiskoot Technology Centre Longfield Road, Tunbridge Wells, TN2 3EY
Tel: 01892-518000 **Fax:** 01892-518100
E-mail: sales@jiskoot.com
Website: http://www.jiskoot.co.uk
Bank(s): Barclays
Directors: G. Mackie (Co Sec)
Managers: J. Blyth, M. Jiskoot (Chief Mgr), O. Prince-wright, S. Neal (Comptroller), S. Mills
Ultimate Holding Company: CAMERON INTERNATIONAL CORP (USA)
Immediate Holding Company: JISKOOT LIMITED
Registration no: 01834943 **Date established:** 1984 **Turnover:** £5m - £10m
No.of Employees: 51 - 100 **Product Groups:** 32, 38, 42, 84, 85

Date of Accounts	Dec 11	Dec 10	Dec 09
Sales Turnover	11m	8m	7m
Pre Tax Profit/Loss	1m	2m	1m
Working Capital	6m	5m	4m
Fixed Assets	996	394	92
Current Assets	10m	7m	6m
Current Liabilities	3m	855	1m

K2
Unit A4 Decimus Park Kingstanding Way, Tunbridge Wells, TN2 3GP
Tel: 01892-531530 **Fax:** 01892-519374
E-mail: us@k2-graphics.co.uk
Website: http://www.k2-graphics.co.uk
Directors: P. Kent (Fin), R. Harvey (MD)
Registration no: 04420002 **Date established:** 2002
Turnover: £20m - £50m **No.of Employees:** 1 - 10 **Product Groups:** 23, 26, 28, 30, 32, 35, 39, 44, 49, 52, 81, 83, 84

Kent Home Cinema Centre
69 London Road Southborough, Tunbridge Wells, TN4 0PA
Tel: 01892-535007 **Fax:** 01892-533334
E-mail: andrew@kenthomecinema.co.uk
Website: http://www.kenthomecinema.co.uk
Directors: A. Collie (Sales), F. Collie (Fin)
Immediate Holding Company: KENT HOME CINEMA CENTRE LTD
Registration no: 03407477 **Date established:** 1997
No.of Employees: 1 - 10 **Product Groups:** 26, 37

Date of Accounts	Jul 08	May 11	May 10
Working Capital	-2	41	47
Fixed Assets	332	319	316
Current Assets	291	237	219

Kent & Sussex Courier
Longfield Road, Tunbridge Wells, TN2 3HL
Tel: 01892-681000 **Fax:** 01892-543181
E-mail: editor@courier.co.uk
Website: http://www.thisiskent.co.uk
Directors: P. Collins (Co Sec), S. Lowe (Adv), D. Storer (Fin), R. Karn (MD), R. Karn (Dir)
Immediate Holding Company: INSITE LIMITED
Registration no: 00101944 **Date established:** 1994 **Turnover:** £5m - £10m
No.of Employees: 1 - 10 **Product Groups:** 28

Date of Accounts	Sep 10	Sep 09	Sep 08
Working Capital	67	57	29
Fixed Assets	9	12	16
Current Assets	163	161	159

Lamberhurst Engineering Ltd
Priory Farm Parsonage Lane, Lamberhurst, Tunbridge Wells, TN3 8DS
Tel: 01892-890364 **Fax:** 01892-890122
E-mail: accounts@lameng.com
Website: http://www.lameng.com
Managers: S. Fuller (Fin Mgr)
Immediate Holding Company: LAMBERHURST ENGINEERING LIMITED
Registration no: 03595260 **VAT No.:** GB 702 8949 20
Date established: 1998 **Turnover:** £1m - £2m **No.of Employees:** 1 - 10
Product Groups: 07, 24, 36, 39, 41, 45, 47, 48, 67, 83

Date of Accounts	Sep 11	Sep 10	Sep 09
Working Capital	862	746	660
Fixed Assets	27	18	21
Current Assets	1m	991	943

Lifestyle Ford
3 Mount Ephraim, Tunbridge Wells, TN4 8AG
Tel: 01892-515666 **Fax:** 01892-548441
E-mail: mail@lifestyleford.co.uk
Website: http://www.lifestyleeurope.co.uk
Bank(s): National Westminster Bank Plc
Managers: P. Rumsey (Chief Mgr)
Immediate Holding Company: LIFESTYLE FORD LIMITED
Registration no: 04071413 **VAT No.:** GB 697 4600 94
Date established: 2000 **Turnover:** £75m - £125m
No.of Employees: 21 - 50 **Product Groups:** 39, 68

M C L Group Ltd
77 Mount Ephraim, Tunbridge Wells, TN4 8BS
Tel: 01892-705600 **Fax:** 01892-536571
E-mail: dsisley@mclgroup.co.uk
Website: http://www.mclgroup.co.uk
Directors: R. Sisley (MD)
Managers: G. Hunter
Ultimate Holding Company: ITOCHU CORPORATION (JAPAN)
Immediate Holding Company: M C L GROUP LIMITED
Registration no: 00430530 **VAT No.:** GB 210 2014 53
Date established: 1947 **Turnover:** £75m - £125m
No.of Employees: 21 - 50 **Product Groups:** 77

Date of Accounts	Dec 09	Dec 08	Dec 07
Sales Turnover	74m	116m	155m
Pre Tax Profit/Loss	-5m	-10m	233
Working Capital	-8m	-18m	-3m
Fixed Assets	38m	47m	51m
Current Assets	19m	21m	32m
Current Liabilities	22m	8m	6m

M P Evans plc
3 Clanricarde Gardens, Tunbridge Wells, TN1 1HQ
Tel: 01892-516333 **Fax:** 01892-518639
E-mail: philipf@mpevans.co.uk
Website: http://www.mpevans.co.uk
Directors: T. Price (Fin), J. Elliott (Co Sec)
Ultimate Holding Company: M.P. EVANS GROUP PLC
Immediate Holding Company: BERTAM (U.K.) LIMITED
Registration no: 01574228 **Date established:** 1981
Turnover: £20m - £50m **No.of Employees:** 1 - 10 **Product Groups:** 84

Mainspring Marketing LLP
The Brewery Bells Yew Green Road, Bells Yew Green, Tunbridge Wells, TN3 9BD
Tel: 01892-752021 **Fax:** 01892-750458
E-mail: info@mainspring.uk.com
Website: http://www.mainspring.uk.com
Directors: M. Pursey (MD)
Immediate Holding Company: MAINSPRING MARKETING LIMITED
Registration no: 01182681 **VAT No.:** GB 445 7823 25
Date established: 1974 **No.of Employees:** 1 - 10 **Product Groups:** 44, 81

Date of Accounts	Dec 11	Dec 10	Dec 09
Working Capital	-28	-30	-19
Fixed Assets	82	77	49
Current Assets	N/A	N/A	4

Makrotest Ltd
29 Culverden Park, Tunbridge Wells, TN4 9QT
Tel: 01892-510711 **Fax:** 01892-511930
E-mail: makrotest@btopenworld.com
Website: http://www.makrotest.co.uk
Directors: N. Rubashow (MD), M. Wolff (Fin)
Registration no: 00882243 **Turnover:** £250,000 - £500,000
No.of Employees: 1 - 10 **Product Groups:** 81

Date of Accounts	Dec 07	Dec 06	Dec 05
Working Capital	33	21	1
Fixed Assets	3	3	4
Current Assets	42	31	21
Current Liabilities	9	10	20
Total Share Capital	187	187	187

Owl House Fruit Farm
Mount Pleasant Lamberhurst, Tunbridge Wells, TN3 8LY
Tel: 01892-890553 **Fax:** 01892-890370
E-mail: ccorfield@aol.com
Website: http://www.owletfruitjuice.co.uk
Directors: C. Corfield (Prop)
Turnover: £500,000 - £1m **No.of Employees:** 1 - 10 **Product Groups:** 62

Plastique
Unit 17-18 Decimus Park Kingstanding Way, Tunbridge Wells, TN2 3GP
Tel: 01892-543211 **Fax:** 01892-616713
E-mail: info@plastique.eu
Website: http://www.plastique.eu
Directors: P. Rigler (Sales)
Ultimate Holding Company: PLASTIQUE GROUP LIMITED
Immediate Holding Company: PLASTIQUE LIMITED
Registration no: 01407996 **Date established:** 1979 **Turnover:** £5m - £10m
No.of Employees: 21 - 50 **Product Groups:** 30

Date of Accounts	Dec 11	Dec 10	Dec 09
Sales Turnover	10m	9m	8m
Pre Tax Profit/Loss	-45	192	146
Working Capital	987	1m	1m
Fixed Assets	2m	2m	1m
Current Assets	3m	3m	3m
Current Liabilities	815	380	382

Reliance Mutual Insurance Society Ltd
Reliance House 6 Vale Avenue, Tunbridge Wells, TN1 1RG
Tel: 01892-510033 **Fax:** 01892-510676
E-mail: contact@reliancemutual.co.uk
Website: http://www.reliancemutual.co.uk
Bank(s): Barclays
Directors: C. Mills (Fin)
Managers: A. James, C. Lerpiniere, J. Tice, R. Eastwood (Personnel)
Immediate Holding Company: RELIANCE MUTUAL INSURANCE SOCIETY LIMITED
Registration no: 00491580 **VAT No.:** GB 339 8106 39
Date established: 1951 **Turnover:** £20m - £50m
No.of Employees: 51 - 100 **Product Groups:** 82

see next page

Reliance Mutual Insurance Society Ltd - *Cont'd*

Date of Accounts	Dec 11	Dec 10	Dec 09
Fixed Assets	1620m	1659m	1540m
Current Assets	20m	22m	21m
Current Liabilities	11m	4m	2m

S H Muffett Ltd

Ashdown House Lamberts Road, Tunbridge Wells, TN2 3EH
Tel: 01892-542111 **Fax:** 01892-545916
E-mail: sales@muffett.co.uk
Website: http://www.muffett.co.uk
Bank(s): National Westminster Bank Plc
Directors: A. Smith (MD)
Managers: C. Burlington (Chief Acct)
Ultimate Holding Company: SHM HOLDINGS LIMITED
Immediate Holding Company: S. H. MUFFETT LIMITED
Registration no: 00373545 **VAT No.:** GB 209 5528 57
Date established: 1942 **Turnover:** £1m - £2m **No.of Employees:** 21 - 50
Product Groups: 30, 35, 38, 39, 40, 43, 45, 46, 48, 49, 68

Date of Accounts	Mar 12	Mar 11	Mar 10
Working Capital	702	662	651
Fixed Assets	755	728	560
Current Assets	2m	1m	1m

Sitsmart Ltd

Unit 14 Decimus Park Kingstanding Way, Tunbridge Wells, TN2 3GP
Tel: 01892-510202 **Fax:** 01892-519834
E-mail: sales@sitsmart.co.uk
Website: http://www.sitsmart.co.uk
Directors: P. Flemming (MD)
Ultimate Holding Company: T.E.K. SEATING LIMITED
Immediate Holding Company: SITSMART LIMITED
Registration no: 02840837 **Date established:** 1993
No.of Employees: 1 - 10 **Product Groups:** 26, 39, 63, 65, 67, 84

Date of Accounts	Dec 11	Dec 10	Dec 09
Working Capital	9	9	9
Current Assets	9	9	9

Spa Aluminium Ltd

1 Chapmans Way, Tunbridge Wells, TN2 3EG
Tel: 01892-533911 **Fax:** 01892-542019
E-mail: sales@spaaluminium.co.uk
Website: http://www.spaaluminium.com
Bank(s): HSBC
Directors: J. Godbolt (Dir), S. Ives (Dir), R. Godbolt (Dir), G. Ives (MD)
Immediate Holding Company: SPA ALUMINIUM LIMITED
Registration no: 01014137 **VAT No.:** GB 426 7653 32
Date established: 1971 **Turnover:** £2m - £5m **No.of Employees:** 21 - 50
Product Groups: 34, 35, 48

Date of Accounts	Dec 11	Dec 10	Dec 09
Working Capital	504	475	462
Fixed Assets	138	86	110
Current Assets	1m	975	985

Sugar Marketing Ltd

Culverden Square, Tunbridge Wells, TN4 9NZ
Tel: 01892-539977
E-mail: info@sugarmarketing.co.uk
Website: http://www.sugarmarketing.co.uk
Directors: M. Long (MD)
Immediate Holding Company: SUGAR MARKETING LIMITED
Registration no: 06550726 **Date established:** 2008
Turnover: Up to £250,000 **No.of Employees:** 1 - 10 **Product Groups:** 44, 61

Date of Accounts	Mar 12	Mar 11	Mar 10
Working Capital	-1	-1	-3
Fixed Assets	2	3	4
Current Assets	53	36	27

T E K Seating Ltd

14 Decimus Park Kingstanding Way, Tunbridge Wells, TN2 3GP
Tel: 01892-515028 **Fax:** 01892-529751
E-mail: sales@tekseating.co.uk
Website: http://www.tekseating.co.uk
Directors: P. Fleming (MD), L. Fleming (Fin)
Managers: J. Hutchinson, R. Fleming (Sales Admin)
Immediate Holding Company: T.E.K. SEATING LIMITED
Registration no: 01014225 **Date established:** 1971 **Turnover:** £1m - £2m
No.of Employees: 11 - 20 **Product Groups:** 39, 63, 67, 68

Date of Accounts	Dec 11	Dec 10	Dec 09
Working Capital	211	128	121
Fixed Assets	67	74	96
Current Assets	900	839	723

Thermodiffusion Ltd

Hill Place London Road, Southborough, Tunbridge Wells, TN4 0PY
Tel: 01892-511533 **Fax:** 01892-515140
E-mail: enquiries@thermodiffusion.co.uk
Directors: R. Prince (MD)
Ultimate Holding Company: THERMODIFFUSION HOLDINGS LIMITED
Immediate Holding Company: THERMODIFFUSION LIMITED
Registration no: 01500117 **Date established:** 1980 **Turnover:** £1m - £2m
No.of Employees: 1 - 10 **Product Groups:** 52

Date of Accounts	Mar 12	Mar 11	Mar 10
Working Capital	223	224	213
Fixed Assets	13	6	21
Current Assets	352	382	395

V K H P Consulting Ltd

The Forge Little Mount Sion, Tunbridge Wells, TN1 1YS
Tel: 01892-521841 **Fax:** 01892-533149
E-mail: tw@vkhp.co.uk
Website: http://www.vkhp.co.uk
Directors: T. Robinson (Dir)
Immediate Holding Company: VKHP CONSULTING LIMITED
Registration no: 06445891 **VAT No.:** GB 367 4899 86
Date established: 2007 **Turnover:** £500,000 - £1m
No.of Employees: 11 - 20 **Product Groups:** 84

Date of Accounts	Mar 12	Mar 11	Mar 10
Working Capital	-55	45	26
Fixed Assets	948	984	1m
Current Assets	363	520	479

W A Turner

Broadwater Lane, Tunbridge Wells, TN2 5RD
Tel: 01892-509700 **Fax:** 01892-510028
E-mail: info@waturner.co.uk
Website: http://www.waturner.co.uk
Bank(s): H.S.B.C.
Directors: I. Bagnall (MD), B. Stebbon (Fin), A. Wotton (Sales & Mktg)
Managers: S. Mcivor (Personnel), S. McIvor (Personnel), J. Goddard, A. Travis (Supp Mgr), M. Baker (Tech Serv Mgr), A. Surve (Comptroller), M. Baker (I.T. Exec), K. Munyard (Buyer)
Immediate Holding Company: W.A. TURNER PROPERTY LTD
Registration no: 04813576 **VAT No.:** GB 445 8375 21
Date established: 1903 **Turnover:** £20m - £50m
No.of Employees: 251 - 500 **Product Groups:** 20

Date of Accounts	Mar 08	Sep 07	Sep 06
Sales Turnover	200	400	34218
Pre Tax Profit/Loss	88	-23	3342
Working Capital	-2747	-1695	-1531
Fixed Assets	3487	3521	3595
Current Assets	409	837	5
Current Liabilities	3156	2533	1536
Total Share Capital	250	250	250
ROCE% (Return on Capital Employed)	11.8	-1.3	161.9
ROT% (Return on Turnover)	43.8	-5.8	9.8

Weld Done

April Cottage The Lane, Fordcombe, Tunbridge Wells, TN3 0RP
Tel: 01892-740432
Directors: N. Davies (Prop)
Date established: 1997 **No.of Employees:** 1 - 10 **Product Groups:** 26, 35

Welling

A & L Movers

87 Burnell Avenue, Welling, DA16 3HP
Tel: 08454-741518
E-mail: sales@aandlmovers.co.uk
Website: http://www.aandlmovers.co.uk
Directors: L. MacKenzie (MD), A. Mackenzie (Prop)
Managers: A. MacKenzie (Mktg Serv Mgr)
No.of Employees: 1 - 10 **Product Groups:** 25, 35, 76

Artscroll Wrought Ironwork

Rear of 96 Upper Wickham Lane, Welling, DA16 3HQ
Tel: 020-8854 8944 **Fax:** 020-8854 1155
E-mail: sales@artscroll.ltd.uk
Website: http://www.artscroll.ltd.uk
Directors: W. Cope (Prop)
VAT No.: GB 378 4742 09 **Turnover:** £500,000 - £1m
No.of Employees: 1 - 10 **Product Groups:** 30, 35, 36, 37, 49, 66

Buckingham Gates & Railing Co. Ltd

98 Buckingham Avenue, Welling, DA16 2ND
Tel: 020-8298 1984 **Fax:** 020-8298 7763
E-mail: gary.patient@btinternet.com
Website: http://www.steelfabricationssoutheast.co.uk
Directors: G. Patient (Dir)
Immediate Holding Company: ZEUS FABRICATIONS LTD
Registration no: 04229389 **Date established:** 2012
No.of Employees: 1 - 10 **Product Groups:** 26, 35

Date of Accounts	Jun 06	Jun 05
Working Capital	10	-3
Fixed Assets	1	1
Current Assets	11	N/A
Current Liabilities	1	3

Cutler Freight Forwarding Ltd

Car Shipping House 2a South Gipsy Road, Welling, DA16 1JB
Tel: 020-8301 6626 **Fax:** 020-8301 2580
E-mail: nigel@milweb.net
Website: http://www.autoshipping.co.uk
Directors: N. Cutler (MD), S. Cutler (Fin)
Immediate Holding Company: CUTLER FREIGHT FORWARDING LIMITED
Registration no: 01632378 **VAT No.:** GB 358 4488 11
Date established: 1982 **Turnover:** £500,000 - £1m
No.of Employees: 1 - 10 **Product Groups:** 76

Date of Accounts	Mar 11	Mar 10	Mar 09
Working Capital	140	147	143
Fixed Assets	10	7	1
Current Assets	314	295	282

Intercoms R us Ltd

22 Swanley Road, Welling, DA16 1LH
Tel: 020-8301 1722
E-mail: info@intercomsrus.com
Website: http://www.intercomsrus.com
Directors: C. Wiltshire (Prop)
Immediate Holding Company: INTERCOMS.R.US LTD.
Registration no: 03331964 **Date established:** 1997
Turnover: Up to £250,000 **No.of Employees:** 1 - 10 **Product Groups:** 36

Date of Accounts	Mar 11	Mar 10	Mar 09
Sales Turnover	N/A	37	46
Pre Tax Profit/Loss	N/A	17	28
Working Capital	25	31	37
Fixed Assets	7	9	2
Current Assets	51	54	65
Current Liabilities	N/A	5	9

J F Guns

32 Park View Road, Welling, DA16 1RT
Tel: 020-8304 9922 **Fax:** 020-8303 5221
E-mail: phil@johnforsey.co.uk
Website: http://www.johnforsey.co.uk
Managers: P. Jackson (Mgr)
Date established: 1994 **No.of Employees:** 1 - 10 **Product Groups:** 36, 39, 40

Online Electrical Wholesalers

9 Welling High Street, Welling, DA16 1TR
Tel: 020-8303 8461 **Fax:** 020-8303 8681
E-mail: neil@onlineelctrical.co.uk
Website: http://www.onlineelctrical.co.uk
Directors: N. Waite (Dir), A. Greenwell (Prop), A. Varley (Dir)
Immediate Holding Company: ONLINE ELECTRICAL WHOLESALERS LIMITED
Registration no: 04200893 **Date established:** 2001 **Turnover:** £1m - £2m
No.of Employees: 1 - 10 **Product Groups:** 37

Date of Accounts	Apr 11	Apr 10	Apr 09
Sales Turnover	N/A	1m	1m
Pre Tax Profit/Loss	N/A	-36	50
Working Capital	-34	-0	55
Fixed Assets	14	19	24
Current Assets	216	178	469
Current Liabilities	N/A	30	53

Weighing Services

13 Dunstall Welling Estate Leigh Place, Welling, DA16 3JH
Tel: 020-8300 7009 **Fax:** 020-8300 7009
Website: http://www.weighingservices.co.uk
Managers: J. Riley (Mgr)
No.of Employees: 1 - 10 **Product Groups:** 38, 42

West Malling

ADT Fire & Security plc

11 Tower View Kings Hill, West Malling, ME19 4DQ
Tel: 0800-542 3108 **Fax:** 01732-587170
Website: http://www.adt.co.uk
Bank(s): HSBC Bank plc
Managers: G. Amato (Chief Mgr), R. Glendining (Sales Prom Mgr), L. Meadley (Cr Control), C. Hunter (Sales Prom Mgr)
Ultimate Holding Company: TYCO INTERNATIONAL LIMITED (SWITZERLAND)
Immediate Holding Company: ADT FIRE AND SECURITY PLC
Registration no: 01161045 **Date established:** 1974
No.of Employees: 21 - 50 **Product Groups:** 37, 40

Date of Accounts	Sep 11	Sep 08	Sep 09
Sales Turnover	363m	414m	384m
Pre Tax Profit/Loss	18m	4m	10m
Working Capital	450m	618m	561m
Fixed Assets	120m	193m	171m
Current Assets	710m	765m	722m
Current Liabilities	81m	57m	42m

H G Brunner Ltd

Unit 1 The Courtyard Business Centre Birling Road, Ryarsh, West Malling, ME19 5AA
Tel: 01732-873715 **Fax:** 01732-875610
E-mail: info@hgbrunner.com
Website: http://www.hgbrunner.com
Directors: M. Hart (MD)
Ultimate Holding Company: AUTOTEC MARKETING LIMITED
Immediate Holding Company: H.G. BRUNNER LIMITED
Registration no: 01306235 **Date established:** 1977
Turnover: £250,000 - £500,000 **No.of Employees:** 1 - 10
Product Groups: 30, 48, 66

Date of Accounts	Apr 11	Apr 10	Apr 09
Working Capital	156	164	168
Current Assets	254	228	232

Business Link

34 Tower View Kings Hill, West Malling, ME19 4UY
Tel: 01732-878000 **Fax:** 01732-841109
E-mail: bob.jones@businesssupportkent.co.uk
Website: http://www.businesslink.gov.uk
Directors: B. Jones (Dir), J. Faulkner (Dir), T. Buddin (Mkt Research)
Immediate Holding Company: BUSINESS SUPPORT KENT COMMUNITY INTEREST COMPANY
Registration no: 03000723 **Date established:** 1994 **Turnover:** £5m - £10m
No.of Employees: 51 - 100 **Product Groups:** 80, 81

Contacta Systems Ltd

11 Tower View Kings Hill, West Malling, ME19 4UY
Tel: 01732-223900 **Fax:** 01732-223909
E-mail: sales@contacta.co.uk
Website: http://www.contacta.co.uk
Directors: S. Thomas (MD)
Managers: P. Harrington (Prod Mgr), R. Delatouche (), C. Banfield (Mktg Serv Mgr)
Immediate Holding Company: CONTACTA SYSTEMS LIMITED
Registration no: 02994507 **Date established:** 1994
Turnover: £10m - £20m **No.of Employees:** 51 - 100 **Product Groups:** 37, 40

Date of Accounts	Dec 11	Dec 10	Dec 09
Working Capital	36	-101	N/A
Fixed Assets	117	133	N/A
Current Assets	2m	1m	N/A

Darcy Products Ltd

157 Mill Street East Malling, West Malling, ME19 6BP
Tel: 01732-843131 **Fax:** 01732-525500
E-mail: enqs@darcy.co.uk
Website: http://www.darcy.co.uk
Directors: P. Goff (Co Sec), R. Proctor (MD), J. Harp (Dir)
Managers: R. Jones (Develop Mgr)
Immediate Holding Company: DARCY PRODUCTS LIMITED
Registration no: 00472058 **VAT No.:** GB 203 3006 36
Date established: 1949 **Turnover:** £2m - £5m **No.of Employees:** 21 - 50
Product Groups: 30, 32, 38, 39, 40, 45, 54, 74, 77

Date of Accounts	Sep 10	Sep 09	Sep 08
Working Capital	413	520	609
Fixed Assets	2m	2m	2m
Current Assets	1m	1m	2m

Dynamic Video Ltd

70 Churchill Square Kings Hill, West Malling, ME19 4YU
Tel: 01227-752174
E-mail: mike@dv-production.co.uk
Website: http://www.dv-production.co.uk
Directors: M. Raycroft (MD)
Immediate Holding Company: DYNAMIC VIDEO LTD
Registration no: 03631710 **Date established:** 1998
No.of Employees: 1 - 10 **Product Groups:** 37, 44, 89

Date of Accounts	Sep 10	Sep 09	Sep 06
Sales Turnover	N/A	N/A	43
Pre Tax Profit/Loss	N/A	N/A	-2
Working Capital	-10	-23	-20
Fixed Assets	8	11	12
Current Assets	12	7	5
Current Liabilities	N/A	N/A	4

B E Ebdon

Leafdale London Road, Addington, West Malling, ME19 5PL
Tel: 01732-843351 **Fax:** 01732-843351

Directors: B. Ebdon (Prop)
Date established: 1967 **Turnover:** Up to £250,000
No.of Employees: 1 - 10 **Product Groups:** 30, 42

Elson Associates

5 Queen Street Kings Hill, West Malling, ME19 4DA
Tel: 01732-433433
E-mail: info@elsonassociates.com
Website: http://www.elsonassociates.com
Directors: M. Elson (Dir)
Immediate Holding Company: ELSON ASSOCIATES PLC
Registration no: 03595128 **Date established:** 1998 **Turnover:** £2m - £5m
No.of Employees: 11 - 20 **Product Groups:** 82

Date of Accounts	Oct 11	Oct 10	Oct 09
Sales Turnover	3m	2m	2m
Pre Tax Profit/Loss	901	1m	849
Working Capital	3m	3m	4m
Fixed Assets	20	21	25
Current Assets	4m	3m	4m
Current Liabilities	273	333	286

Flir Systems Ltd

2 Kings Hill Avenue Kings Hill, West Malling, ME19 4AQ
Tel: 01732-220011 **Fax:** 01732-220014
E-mail: info@flir.com
Website: http://www.flir.com
Bank(s): HSBC, Poultry & Princes St, London EC2P 2BX
Directors: C. Cooper (Fin), N. Bertram (Dir)
Managers: S. Giles (Buyer), A. Page (Personnel), T. Turner
Ultimate Holding Company: FLIR SYSTEMS INC (USA)
Immediate Holding Company: FLIR SYSTEMS LIMITED
Registration no: 01320288 **Date established:** 1977
Turnover: £20m - £50m **No.of Employees:** 21 - 50 **Product Groups:** 37, 38, 40, 85

Date of Accounts	Dec 11	Dec 10	Dec 09
Sales Turnover	37m	32m	38m
Pre Tax Profit/Loss	5m	3m	4m
Working Capital	11m	6m	3m
Fixed Assets	601	717	963
Current Assets	24m	15m	19m
Current Liabilities	5m	6m	6m

Grenco Refrigeration UK Ltd

Suite 1 40 Churchill Square Kings Hill, West Malling, ME19 4YU
Tel: 08706-001200 **Fax:** 0870-600 1277
E-mail: info@grenco.co.uk
Website: http://www.grenco.co.uk
Directors: V. Bostock (MD)
Managers: G. Young, M. Colley (Mgr)
Immediate Holding Company: CLAIMS MANAGEMENT AND ADJUSTING LIMITED
Registration no: 02955406 **Date established:** 1994
Turnover: £20m - £50m **No.of Employees:** 1 - 10 **Product Groups:** 40, 52

Locate In Kent

35 Kings Hill Avenue Kings Hill, West Malling, ME19 4DG
Tel: 01732-520700 **Fax:** 01732-520701
E-mail: enquiries@locateinkent.com
Website: http://www.locateinkent.com
Directors: P. Wookey (Grp Chief Exec)
Immediate Holding Company: LOCATE IN KENT LIMITED
Registration no: 03230721 **VAT No.:** GB 747 8879 54
Date established: 1996 **No.of Employees:** 1 - 10 **Product Groups:** 80, 81

Date of Accounts	Mar 11	Mar 10	Mar 09
Working Capital	477	322	358
Fixed Assets	1	1	4
Current Assets	593	676	598

Proquest Consulting Ltd

6 The Close Birling, West Malling, ME19 5WJ
Tel: 01732-842479
E-mail: info@proquest-consulting.co.uk
Website: http://www.proquest-consulting.co.uk
Directors: M. Collins (MD)
Immediate Holding Company: PROQUEST CONSULTING LIMITED
Registration no: 05035234 **Date established:** 2004
Turnover: Up to £250,000 **No.of Employees:** 1 - 10 **Product Groups:** 54, 61, 80, 81, 84, 86

Date of Accounts	Feb 12	Feb 11	Feb 10
Working Capital	87	45	45
Fixed Assets	N/A	1	1
Current Assets	122	68	73

Uniplex Machinery Sales Ltd

28-30 High Street, West Malling, ME19 6QR
Tel: 01732-841619 **Fax:** 01732-870190
E-mail: joanneivell@uniplexmachinery.co.uk
Website: http://www.uniplexmachinery.co.uk
Directors: K. Weddle (MD), J. Ivell (MD)
Managers: J. Ivell (Sales Off Mgr)
Immediate Holding Company: UNIPLEX MACHINERY SALES LIMITED
Registration no: 01228831 **Date established:** 1975
Turnover: £250,000 - £500,000 **No.of Employees:** 1 - 10
Product Groups: 42

Date of Accounts	Jun 11	Jun 10	Jun 09
Working Capital	218	242	241
Fixed Assets	10	16	22
Current Assets	691	467	419

Viridor Waste Management Ltd

42 Kings Hill Avenue Kings Hill, West Malling, ME19 4AJ
Tel: 01732-229200 **Fax:** 01732-229280
E-mail: enquiries@viridor.co.uk
Website: http://www.viridor.co.uk
Directors: B. Hurley (Dir)
Ultimate Holding Company: PENNON GROUP PLC
Immediate Holding Company: VIRIDOR WASTE MANAGEMENT LIMITED
Registration no: 00575069 **Date established:** 1956
Turnover: £125m - £250m **No.of Employees:** 51 - 100
Product Groups: 42, 51, 54

Date of Accounts	Mar 11	Mar 10	Mar 09
Sales Turnover	293m	230m	214m
Pre Tax Profit/Loss	45m	29m	33m
Working Capital	-49m	-33m	-78m
Fixed Assets	671m	615m	497m
Current Assets	251m	184m	150m
Current Liabilities	87m	49m	45m

Weidmuller Ltd

1 Abbey Wood Road Kings Hill, West Malling, ME19 4YT
Tel: 01732-877000 **Fax:** 01732- 521368
E-mail: ian.thorndycraft@weidmuller.co.uk
Website: http://www.weidmuller.co.uk
Bank(s): Barclays, Dudley, West Midlands
Directors: N. Clydesdale (MD), I. Thorndycraft (Fin)
Ultimate Holding Company: WEIDMULLER HOLDING AG & CO KGAA (GERMANY)
Immediate Holding Company: WEIDMULLER H LIMITED
Registration no: 02506190 **VAT No.:** GB 571 8014 48
Date established: 1990 **Turnover:** £75m - £125m
No.of Employees: 21 - 50 **Product Groups:** 27, 30, 36, 37, 38, 40, 42, 45, 46, 47, 66, 67, 81, 83

Ian Wright Organisation

Ashtree Farm Teston Road, Offham, West Malling, ME19 5RL
Tel: 01732-529511 **Fax:** 01732-529513
E-mail: info@thewrightevent.co.uk
Website: http://www.thewrightevent.co.uk
Directors: I. Wright (Prop)
Date established: 1999 **Turnover:** £500,000 - £1m
No.of Employees: 1 - 10 **Product Groups:** 89

West Wickham

ECU CLINIC

161 Langley Way, West Wickham, BR4 0DL
Tel: 020-8133 6164
E-mail: ecu-clinic@sky.com
Website: http://www.ecuclinic.com
Directors: A. Bigg (Prop), A. Bigg (Dir)
Date established: 2006 **No.of Employees:** 1 - 10 **Product Groups:** 39

Machinery Market Ltd

40 Croydon Road, West Wickham, BR4 9HZ
Tel: 020-8460 4224 **Fax:** 020-8290 1668
E-mail: info@machinery-market.co.uk
Website: http://www.machinery-market.co.uk
Directors: J. Bjorck (MD), P. Weaver (Fin)
Immediate Holding Company: MACHINERY MARKET LIMITED
Registration no: 00142483 **VAT No.:** GB 243 3212 05
Date established: 2015 **Turnover:** £1m - £2m **No.of Employees:** 1 - 10
Product Groups: 28

Date of Accounts	Dec 10	Dec 09	Dec 08
Working Capital	392	458	403
Fixed Assets	572	577	621
Current Assets	467	526	500

UK Solar Ltd

128 Queensway Coney Hall, West Wickham, BR4 9DY
Tel: 020-8325 3724 **Fax:** 020-8325 6265
E-mail: uksolar@uksolar.com
Website: http://www.uksolar.com
Directors: S. Sutton (Fin), P. Sutton (MD)
Immediate Holding Company: U.K. SOLAR LIMITED
Registration no: 03693057 **Date established:** 1999
No.of Employees: 1 - 10 **Product Groups:** 30, 33, 35, 49, 52, 66, 67, 81

Date of Accounts	Mar 11	Mar 10	Mar 09
Working Capital	24	36	44
Fixed Assets	13	18	25
Current Assets	72	95	77

Waterways

120 High Street, West Wickham, BR4 0LZ
Tel: 020-8777 6929
E-mail: sales@waterways.ltd.uk
Website: http://www.waterways.ltd.uk
Managers: J. Kelly (Mgr)
Date established: 1985 **No.of Employees:** 1 - 10 **Product Groups:** 38, 42

Westerham

Aqualisa Products Ltd Head Office

Westerham Trade Centre The Flyers Way, Westerham, TN16 1DE
Tel: 01959-560000 **Fax:** 01959-560030
E-mail: enquiries@aqualisa.co.uk
Website: http://www.aqualisa.co.uk
Directors: S. Dexter (Fin), S. Greenstreet (Sales & Mktg), C. Gee (Dir)
Managers: B. Simm (Purch Mgr), I. Sadlier (Tech Serv Mgr), K. Wells (Personnel)
Ultimate Holding Company: CBPE (GENERAL PARTNER) LIMITED
Immediate Holding Company: AQUALISA PRODUCTS LIMITED
Registration no: 01281596 **VAT No.:** GB 439 4758 08
Date established: 1976 **Turnover:** £20m - £50m
No.of Employees: 101 - 250 **Product Groups:** 36

Date of Accounts	Dec 10	Dec 09	Dec 08
Sales Turnover	35m	35m	36m
Pre Tax Profit/Loss	6m	6m	7m
Working Capital	49m	44m	39m
Fixed Assets	3m	4m	4m
Current Assets	53m	48m	43m
Current Liabilities	3m	3m	2m

Blagden Specialty Chemicals Ltd

Osprey House Black Eagle Square, Westerham, TN16 1PA
Tel: 01959-562000 **Fax:** 01959-565111
E-mail: sales@blagden.co.uk
Website: http://www.blagden.co.uk
Directors: G. Turton (MD), J. Wilkinson (Fin)
Immediate Holding Company: BLAGDEN SPECIALTY CHEMICALS LIMITED
Registration no: 03914333 **Date established:** 2000
Turnover: £20m - £50m **No.of Employees:** 21 - 50 **Product Groups:** 31

Date of Accounts	Jan 12	Jan 11	Jan 10
Sales Turnover	27m	23m	22m
Pre Tax Profit/Loss	1m	860	557
Working Capital	3m	2m	1m
Fixed Assets	2m	1m	1m
Current Assets	7m	6m	7m
Current Liabilities	2m	2m	2m

Brasted Forge

Park Garage High Street, Brasted, Westerham, TN16 1JN
Tel: 01959-565359 **Fax:** 01959-565359
E-mail: admin@brastedforge.com
Website: http://www.brastedforge.co.uk
Directors: D. Harman (Prop)
Immediate Holding Company: BRASTED FORGE LIMITED
Registration no: 00643212 **Date established:** 1959
No.of Employees: 1 - 10 **Product Groups:** 26, 35

Date of Accounts	Jul 11	Jul 10	Jul 09
Working Capital	45	40	47
Fixed Assets	6	13	16
Current Assets	63	43	52

Chartrite Ltd

Unit 2 Wireless Road Biggin Hill, Westerham, TN16 3PS
Tel: 01959-543680 **Fax:** 01959-543690
E-mail: john.davis@chartrite.com
Website: http://www.chartrite.com
Bank(s): Co-op, Cheshire
Directors: C. Laming (Dir), J. Davis (MD)
Immediate Holding Company: CHARTRITE LIMITED
Registration no: 02800732 **VAT No.:** GB 644 3591 30
Date established: 1993 **Turnover:** £2m - £5m **No.of Employees:** 21 - 50
Product Groups: 27, 28, 37, 38, 44, 64

Date of Accounts	Jul 11	Jul 10	Jul 09
Working Capital	348	272	190
Fixed Assets	231	356	413
Current Assets	990	938	886

D L H Timber Merchants

The Crown London Road, Westerham, TN16 1DL
Tel: 01959-561777 **Fax:** 01959-560399
Website: http://www.dlh-uk.com
Directors: S. Sullervan (MD), P. Riley (Co Sec), S. Sullivan (Dir), S. Sullivan (MD)
Immediate Holding Company: DLH UK LIMITED
Registration no: 01696690 **Date established:** 1983
Turnover: £10m - £20m **No.of Employees:** 11 - 20 **Product Groups:** 61

Date of Accounts	Dec 09	Dec 08	Dec 07
Sales Turnover	18m	22m	23m
Pre Tax Profit/Loss	-1m	-2m	630
Working Capital	438	6m	3m
Fixed Assets	28	99	81
Current Assets	6m	13m	10m
Current Liabilities	250	2m	442

R Durtnell & Sons Ltd

Rectory Lane Brasted, Westerham, TN16 1JR
Tel: 01959-564105 **Fax:** 01959-564756
E-mail: john.durtnell@durtnell.co.uk
Website: http://www.durtnell.co.uk
Bank(s): National Westminster, Sevenoaks
Directors: J. Durtnell (Ch), S. Routh (Fin)
Managers: K. Prescott (Chief Buyer), D. Warick
Ultimate Holding Company: R DURTNELL & SONS (HOLDINGS) LIMITED
Immediate Holding Company: R DURTNELL AND SONS LIMITED
Registration no: 01848570 **VAT No.:** 209 8037 61 **Date established:** 1984
Turnover: £50m - £75m **No.of Employees:** 101 - 250
Product Groups: 52, 84

Date of Accounts	Dec 11	Dec 10	Dec 09
Sales Turnover	36m	52m	50m
Pre Tax Profit/Loss	26	595	617
Working Capital	-995	-1m	-1m
Fixed Assets	3m	3m	3m
Current Assets	9m	11m	12m
Current Liabilities	829	2m	2m

European Music Co. Ltd

Unit 5/6, Concorde Business Centre Airport Industrial Estate, Main Road, Biggin Hill, Westerham, TN16 3YN
Tel: 01959-571600 **Fax:** 01959-572267
E-mail: marc@tanglewoodguitars.co.uk
Website: http://www.tanglewoodguitars.co.uk
Directors: D. Kommer (MD)
Managers: M. Kommer (Mgr)
Registration no: 02373931 **VAT No.:** GB 523 7853 34
Turnover: £1m - £2m **No.of Employees:** 1 - 10 **Product Groups:** 65

Fantasia Distribution Ltd

Unit B The Flyers Way, Westerham, TN16 1DE
Tel: 01959-564440 **Fax:** 01959-564829
E-mail: info@fantasiaceilingfans.com
Website: http://www.fantasiaceilingfans.com
Directors: T. Linger (MD), A. Linger (MD)
Managers: G. Smith (Chief Mgr), R. Moore (Mktg Serv Mgr)
Immediate Holding Company: FANTASIA DISTRIBUTION LIMITED
Registration no: 02726968 **Date established:** 1992 **Turnover:** £1m - £2m
No.of Employees: 11 - 20 **Product Groups:** 40

Date of Accounts	Dec 11	Dec 10	Dec 09
Working Capital	744	768	864
Fixed Assets	666	669	545
Current Assets	943	989	919

Interclad Ltd

173 Main Road Biggin Hill, Westerham, TN16 3JR
Tel: 01959-572447 **Fax:** 01959-576974
E-mail: sales@interclad.co.uk
Website: http://www.interclad.co.uk
Directors: R. Morgan Russell (MD)
Immediate Holding Company: INTERCLAD LIMITED
Registration no: 01948778 **Date established:** 1985 **Turnover:** £2m - £5m
No.of Employees: 11 - 20 **Product Groups:** 30

Joan Allen Electronics Ltd

190 Main Road Biggin Hill, Westerham, TN16 3BB
Tel: 01959-574234 **Fax:** 01959-576014
E-mail: sales@joanallen.co.uk
Website: http://www.joanallen.co.uk
Directors: L. Mahoney (MD)
Ultimate Holding Company: JOAN ALLEN (HOLDINGS) LIMITED
Immediate Holding Company: JOAN ALLEN (ELECTRONICS) LIMITED
Registration no: 01062542 **Date established:** 1972
No.of Employees: 1 - 10 **Product Groups:** 38, 61, 81

Date of Accounts	Dec 11	Dec 10	Jun 09
Working Capital	169	-17	17
Fixed Assets	19	19	5
Current Assets	296	406	1m

London Chemicals & Resources Ltd
Brewery House High Street, Westerham, TN16 1RG
Tel: 020-7183 0651 **Fax:** 020-7987 7980
E-mail: info@lcrl.net
Website: http://www.lcrl.net
Directors: R. Bartholomew (MD)
Immediate Holding Company: LONDON CHEMICALS & RESOURCES LIMITED
Registration no: 05594061 **VAT No.:** GB 718 6896 79
Date established: 2005 **Turnover:** £75m - £125m
No.of Employees: 1 - 10 **Product Groups:** 12, 31, 32, 34, 48, 66

Date of Accounts	Oct 11	Oct 10
Working Capital	2m	1m
Fixed Assets	5	8
Current Assets	4m	4m

Lukes Engineering Co. Ltd
79 Paynesfield Road Tatsfield, Westerham, TN16 2BQ
Tel: 01959-540944 **Fax:** 01959-540955
E-mail: lukesadmin@lukeseng.co.uk
Website: http://www.lukeseng.co.uk
Directors: B. Lukes (Prop)
Immediate Holding Company: LUKES ENGINEERING COMPANY LIMITED
Registration no: 00755398 **Date established:** 1963
Turnover: Up to £250,000 **No.of Employees:** 1 - 10 **Product Groups:** 37, 39, 40

Date of Accounts	Dec 10	Dec 09	Dec 08
Working Capital	42	40	64
Fixed Assets	1	2	3
Current Assets	67	82	103

Omega Valves
Concorde Business Centre Main Road Airport Industr, Biggin Hill, Westerham, TN16 3YN
Tel: 01959-571800 **Fax:** 01959-570695
Directors: C. Horton (Dir)
Date established: 1981 **No.of Employees:** 1 - 10 **Product Groups:** 36, 37, 38

P & R Roofing (Kent) Ltd
11A Melrose Road Biggin Hill, Westerham, TN16 3DA
Tel: 01959-540195 **Fax:** 01959-542609
E-mail: prroofskent@aol.com
Website: http://pandrroofingkent.co.uk
Managers: P. Rees (Chief Acct)
Registration no: 07292522 **Date established:** 1977
No.of Employees: 1 - 10 **Product Groups:** 25

Review Display Systems Ltd
Horton Place Hortons Way, Westerham, TN16 1BT
Tel: 01959-563345 **Fax:** 01959-564452
E-mail: info@review-displays.co.uk
Website: http://www.review-displays.co.uk
Bank(s): Barclays, Dartford
Directors: R. Smith (MD)
Managers: R. Gilbert (Chief Mgr)
Immediate Holding Company: REVIEW DISPLAY SYSTEMS LIMITED
Registration no: 01616402 **VAT No.:** GB 304 4800 94
Date established: 1982 **Turnover:** £5m - £10m **No.of Employees:** 21 - 50
Product Groups: 37, 38, 39, 40, 44, 49, 67

Date of Accounts	Mar 11	Mar 10	Mar 09
Pre Tax Profit/Loss	N/A	N/A	254
Working Capital	2m	2m	2m
Fixed Assets	11	35	68
Current Assets	2m	3m	3m
Current Liabilities	N/A	N/A	415

Surex International Ltd
Unit 5 Airport Trading Estate, Biggin Hill, Westerham, TN16 3BW
Tel: 01959-576000 **Fax:** 01959-571000
E-mail: info@surex.co.uk
Website: http://www.surex.co.uk
Directors: D. Acca (Dir), J. Acca (Dir)
Immediate Holding Company: SUREX INTERNATIONAL LIMITED
Registration no: 01274792 **Date established:** 1976 **Turnover:** £1m - £2m
No.of Employees: 1 - 10 **Product Groups:** 32, 42, 66

Date of Accounts	Dec 10	Dec 09	Dec 08
Working Capital	-60	155	54
Fixed Assets	28	34	40
Current Assets	318	437	560

Whitstable

Albion Office Interiors Ltd
Joseph Wilson Industrial Estate Millstrood Road, Whitstable, CT5 3PS
Tel: 01227-281281 **Fax:** 01227-282456
E-mail: mkg@albionoffice.co.uk
Website: http://www.albionoffice.co.uk
Directors: M. Golesworthy (MD), A. Wynn (Fin)
Immediate Holding Company: ALBION OFFICE INTERIORS LIMITED
Registration no: 03881847 **Date established:** 1999
No.of Employees: 1 - 10 **Product Groups:** 26, 37, 52, 67, 80, 83, 84

Date of Accounts	Mar 11	Mar 10	Mar 09
Working Capital	45	255	196
Fixed Assets	45	32	42
Current Assets	182	398	352

Amphenol Ltd
Thanet Way, Whitstable, CT5 3JF
Tel: 01227-773200 **Fax:** 01227-276571
E-mail: info@amphenol.com
Website: http://www.amphenol.co.uk
Bank(s): National Westminster Bank Plc
Directors: M. Garner (Fin)
Managers: A. Marsh (Purch Mgr), S. Osborne (Personnel)
Ultimate Holding Company: AMPHENOL CORPORATION INC (USA)
Immediate Holding Company: AMPHENOL LIMITED
Registration no: 00784278 **VAT No.:** GB 472 7739 11
Date established: 1963 **Turnover:** £20m - £50m
No.of Employees: 251 - 500 **Product Groups:** 37

Date of Accounts	Dec 11	Dec 10	Dec 09
Sales Turnover	33m	35m	35m
Pre Tax Profit/Loss	5m	5m	4m
Working Capital	23m	20m	16m
Fixed Assets	14m	14m	14m
Current Assets	42m	40m	38m
Current Liabilities	1m	2m	2m

Barton Marine Equipment Ltd
Tyler Way, Whitstable, CT5 2RS
Tel: 01227-792979 **Fax:** 01227-793555
E-mail: sales@bartonmarine.com
Website: http://www.bartonmarine.com
Bank(s): Barclays
Directors: D. Coleman (MD), P. Botterill (Dir)
Ultimate Holding Company: AKER SOLUTIONS ASA (NORWAY)
Immediate Holding Company: BARTON MARINE EQUIPMENT LIMITED
Registration no: 02020774 **VAT No.:** GB 444 9965 01
Date established: 1986 **Turnover:** £5m - £10m **No.of Employees:** 21 - 50
Product Groups: 45

Date of Accounts	Sep 11	Sep 10	Sep 09
Working Capital	105	54	52
Fixed Assets	863	916	967
Current Assets	452	492	426

Beam Engineering Ltd
Units 38-39 John Wilson Business Harvey Drive, Chestfield, Whitstable, CT5 3QY
Tel: 01227-282820 **Fax:** 01227-282830
E-mail: info@beammanufacturing.co.uk
Directors: G. Harvey (Dir)
Immediate Holding Company: BEAM ENGINEERING LIMITED
Registration no: 07755697 **VAT No.:** GB 725 2869 16
Date established: 2011 **Turnover:** £250,000 - £500,000
No.of Employees: 11 - 20 **Product Groups:** 48, 66, 84

Date of Accounts	Apr 08
Working Capital	-58
Fixed Assets	76
Current Assets	20
Current Liabilities	78

B & S Moulders Ltd
Unit 14 Joseph Wilson Industrial Estate Millstrood Road, Whitstable, CT5 3PS
Tel: 01227-262599 **Fax:** 01227-770767
E-mail: simon@bandsinjection.co.uk
Directors: B. Sumner (Prop)
Immediate Holding Company: B & S MOULDERS LTD
Registration no: 07242463 **VAT No.:** GB 202 8756 71
Date established: 2010 **Turnover:** £500,000 - £1m
No.of Employees: 1 - 10 **Product Groups:** 30

Date of Accounts	May 11
Working Capital	-57
Fixed Assets	84
Current Assets	115

George Wilson Holdings Ltd
PO Box 70, Whitstable, CT5 3RG
Tel: 01227-263077 **Fax:** 01227-262707
E-mail: george.wilson@gwholdings.co.uk
Directors: J. Wilson (Fin), G. Wilson (MD)
Ultimate Holding Company: GEORGE WILSON HOLDINGS LIMITED
Immediate Holding Company: GEORGE WILSON CONSTRUCTION LIMITED
Registration no: 01526704 **VAT No.:** GB 316 6695 36
Date established: 1980 **Turnover:** £2m - £5m **No.of Employees:** 1 - 10
Product Groups: 52

Date of Accounts	Oct 11	Oct 10	Oct 09
Sales Turnover	3m	6m	8m
Pre Tax Profit/Loss	-373	80	52
Working Capital	675	1m	967
Fixed Assets	16	9	12
Current Assets	2m	2m	6m
Current Liabilities	64	374	739

Greenlight Locksmith & Security
42 Preston Parade Seasalter, Whitstable, CT5 4AJ
Tel: 01227-274738
E-mail: greenlightlocks@btinternet.com
Website: http://www.greenlightlocks.co.uk
Directors: J. Selvey (MD), A. Selvey (Fin), J. Selvey (Prop)
Immediate Holding Company: GREENLIGHT LOCKSMITHS LIMITED
Registration no: 05943749 **Date established:** 2006
No.of Employees: 1 - 10 **Product Groups:** 30, 36, 37, 52

Date of Accounts	Apr 09	Apr 08	Apr 07
Working Capital	-1	-2	-8
Fixed Assets	12	16	17
Current Assets	36	28	27

Headway Doors & Windows Ltd
Crown House Pean Hill, Whitstable, CT5 3BJ
Tel: 01227-784971
E-mail: headwaywindows@tiscali.co.uk
Website: http://www.headwaywindows.co.uk
Directors: D. Marks (Dir), V. Marks (Dir)
Immediate Holding Company: HEADWAY DOORS AND WINDOWS LIMITED
Registration no: 04360629 **Date established:** 2002
No.of Employees: 11 - 20 **Product Groups:** 30, 35

Date of Accounts	Mar 11	Mar 10	Mar 09
Working Capital	-35	-32	-34
Fixed Assets	38	47	51
Current Assets	56	67	31

John Hellyar & Co. Ltd
Tyler Way, Whitstable, CT5 2RX
Tel: 01227-813200 **Fax:** 01227-792203
E-mail: sales@hellyar.co.uk
Website: http://www.hellyar.co.uk
Bank(s): Bank of Scotland, 38 Threadneedle St, London EC2
Directors: J. Hellyar (Prop), R. Cowling (MD), N. Guthrie (Fin)
Ultimate Holding Company: JOHN HELLYAR AND COMPANY LIMITED
Immediate Holding Company: JOHN HELLYAR AND COMPANY LIMITED
Registration no: 00694742 **VAT No.:** GB 201 2913 20
Date established: 1961 **Turnover:** £20m - £50m
No.of Employees: 21 - 50 **Product Groups:** 30, 31

Date of Accounts	Jun 12	Jun 11	Jun 10
Sales Turnover	22m	26m	19m
Pre Tax Profit/Loss	114	71	714
Working Capital	8m	8m	8m
Fixed Assets	1m	1m	1m
Current Assets	10m	12m	11m
Current Liabilities	268	658	876

J J Williams Ltd
1 Beresford Road, Whitstable, CT5 1JP
Tel: 01227-265522 **Fax:** 01227-770146
E-mail: joyce@jjwilliams.co.uk
Website: http://www.jjwilliams.co.uk
Bank(s): Barclays, West Wickham
Directors: J. Williams (Dir)
Immediate Holding Company: J. J. WILLIAMS (GASKETS) LTD
Registration no: 00488682 **VAT No.:** GB 235 9399 25
Date established: 1950 **No.of Employees:** 11 - 20 **Product Groups:** 22, 27, 29, 30

Date of Accounts	Dec 10	Dec 09	Dec 08
Working Capital	16	20	48
Fixed Assets	188	161	192
Current Assets	163	159	162

Jewson Ltd
Hamilton Road, Whitstable, CT5 1JX
Tel: 01227-263696 **Fax:** 01227-770652
Website: http://www.jewson.co.uk
Directors: P. Hindle (MD)
Managers: J. Taylor (District Mgr)
Ultimate Holding Company: COMPAGNIE DE SAINT GOBAIN (FRANCE)
Immediate Holding Company: JEWSON LIMITED
Registration no: 00348407 **VAT No.:** GB 394 1212 63
Date established: 1939 **Turnover:** £2m - £5m **No.of Employees:** 1 - 10
Product Groups: 66

Date of Accounts	Dec 11	Dec 10	Dec 09
Sales Turnover	1606m	1547m	1485m
Pre Tax Profit/Loss	18m	100m	45m
Working Capital	-345m	-250m	-349m
Fixed Assets	496m	387m	461m
Current Assets	657m	1005m	1320m
Current Liabilities	66m	120m	64m

M & B Engineering
Units 62 & 63 John Wilson Business Park, Chestfield, Whitstable, CT5 3QT
Tel: 01227-261917 **Fax:** 01227-770809
E-mail: robertacors@chessmail.co.uk
Managers: R. Acors (Mgr)
Immediate Holding Company: M&B ENGINEERING (WHITSTABLE) LLP
Registration no: OC301176 **VAT No.:** GB 316 6621 65
Date established: 2001 **Turnover:** £500,000 - £1m
No.of Employees: 1 - 10 **Product Groups:** 48

Medway Cutters
Unit 30 Joseph Wilson Industrial Estate Millstrood Road, Whitstable, CT5 3PS
Tel: 01227-273138 **Fax:** 01227-770344
E-mail: info@medwaycutters.co.uk
Website: http://www.medwaycutters.co.uk
Directors: M. Dawkins (Prop)
No.of Employees: 1 - 10 **Product Groups:** 44

Moore Services UK Ltd
4 Millstrood Road, Whitstable, CT5 1QQ
Tel: 01227-277477 **Fax:** 01227-770793
E-mail: mbishop@mooreservices.co.uk
Website: http://www.mooreservices.co.uk
Directors: B. Bishop (MD), M. Bishop (Dir), M. Bishop (MD)
Immediate Holding Company: MOORE SERVICES (UK) LIMITED
Registration no: 02569847 **VAT No.:** GB 571 8579 00
Date established: 1990 **No.of Employees:** 1 - 10 **Product Groups:** 67

Date of Accounts	Mar 11	Mar 10	Mar 09
Working Capital	-5	-10	-8
Fixed Assets	1	N/A	N/A
Current Assets	31	31	40

Morgans Pomade Company Ltd
Tyler Way, Whitstable, CT5 2RT
Tel: 01227-792761 **Fax:** 01227-794463
E-mail: admin@morganspomade.co.uk
Website: http://www.morganspomade.co.uk
Bank(s): Barclays, Canterbury
Managers: K. Mitchell (Fin Mgr), V. Rogers (Asst Gen Mgr), T. Matson (Chief Mgr), P. Noble, P. Standen (I.T. Exec)
Ultimate Holding Company: MARIE ANTOINETTE COMPANY (THE) LIMITED
Immediate Holding Company: MORGAN'S POMADE COMPANY LIMITED
Registration no: 00337419 **VAT No.:** GB 201 4930 10
Date established: 1938 **Turnover:** £1m - £2m **No.of Employees:** 21 - 50
Product Groups: 32

Date of Accounts	Dec 11	Dec 10	Dec 09
Sales Turnover	1m	1m	829
Pre Tax Profit/Loss	39	155	-143
Working Capital	238	191	99
Fixed Assets	133	141	95
Current Assets	871	860	564
Current Liabilities	18	35	22

P B I International Ltd
Unit 2 Tyler House Tyler Way, Whitstable, CT5 2RS
Tel: 01227-793334 **Fax:** 01227-794166
E-mail: yago@ball-bearings.biz
Website: http://www.ball-bearings.biz
Bank(s): National Westminster Bank Plc
Directors: Y. Zens (MD)
Immediate Holding Company: P.B.I. INTERNATIONAL LTD
Registration no: 03223753 **VAT No.:** GB 668 2608 22
Date established: 1996 **No.of Employees:** 11 - 20 **Product Groups:** 29, 30, 34, 35

Date of Accounts	Aug 11	Aug 10	Aug 09
Working Capital	229	219	213
Fixed Assets	5	5	3
Current Assets	995	822	776

P & B Metals
Tyler Way, Whitstable, CT5 2RR
Tel: 0114-262 6300 **Fax:** 01227-794612
E-mail: jonathan.howard@p-and-b.com
Website: http://www.p-and-b.com
Directors: J. Howard (Dir)
Immediate Holding Company: P & B METAL COMPONENTS LIMITED
Registration no: 00707502 **VAT No.:** GB 201 2698 95
Date established: 1961 **Turnover:** £10m - £20m
No.of Employees: 51 - 100 **Product Groups:** 30, 34, 37, 46, 48, 49

Date of Accounts	May 11	May 10	May 09
Sales Turnover	29m	19m	19m
Pre Tax Profit/Loss	2m	625	501

Working Capital	7m	5m	5m
Fixed Assets	7m	7m	7m
Current Assets	14m	10m	7m
Current Liabilities	1m	779	567

Rud Chains Ltd

Unit 10-14 John Wilson Business Park Harvey Drive, Chestfield, Whitstable, CT5 3QT
Tel: 01227-276611 **Fax:** 01227-276586
E-mail: sales@rud.co.uk
Website: http://www.rud.co.uk
Directors: C. Nelson (MD)
Ultimate Holding Company: RUD KETTENFABRIK GEBR RIEGER GMBH (GERMANY)
Immediate Holding Company: R U D CHAINS LIMITED
Registration no: 01104572 **Date established:** 1973 **Turnover:** £2m - £5m
No.of Employees: 1 - 10 **Product Groups:** 35, 45

Date of Accounts	Jun 12	Jun 11	Jun 10
Working Capital	67	-85	-118
Fixed Assets	254	263	274
Current Assets	2m	2m	2m

Ruskin Air Management Ltd (Part of Ruskin Air Management Ltd)

Joseph Wilson Industrial Estate South Street, Whitstable, CT5 3DU
Tel: 01227-276100 **Fax:** 01227-264262
E-mail: sales@actionair.co.uk
Website: http://www.actionair.co.uk
Directors: D. Watkins (Fin), A. Mackay (Fin), K. Munson (MD)
Managers: C. Shillpitoe (Sales & Mktg Mg), C. Shillpitoe (Sales & Mktg Mg), A. Barker (I.T. Exec), L. Roberts, L. Roberts, S. Bowen (Chief Buyer)
Ultimate Holding Company: PINAFORE COOPERATIEF U.A. (NETHERLANDS)
Immediate Holding Company: RUSKIN AIR MANAGEMENT LIMITED
Registration no: 00738495 **Date established:** 1962
No.of Employees: 101 - 250 **Product Groups:** 38, 39, 40, 66

Date of Accounts	Dec 11	Dec 10	Jan 10
Sales Turnover	20m	21m	22m
Pre Tax Profit/Loss	1m	2m	3m
Working Capital	18m	17m	16m
Fixed Assets	8m	8m	8m
Current Assets	21m	20m	19m
Current Liabilities	862	768	1m

Steel Construction

Molehill Road Chestfield, Whitstable, CT5 3PB
Tel: 01227-792556 **Fax:** 01227-794361
Directors: A. Cox (Ptnr)
VAT No.: GB 377 9714 92 **Date established:** 1981
Turnover: £250,000 - £500,000 **No.of Employees:** 1 - 10
Product Groups: 48

Taywest Control Systems Ltd

St Augustines Business Park Estuary Close, Whitstable, CT5 2QJ
Tel: 01227-794794 **Fax:** 01227-794949
E-mail: tom.westgarth@taywest.demon.co.uk
Website: http://www.taywest.co.uk
Directors: M. Taylor (MD)
Immediate Holding Company: TAYWEST CONTROL SYSTEMS LIMITED
Registration no: 02896528 **VAT No.:** GB 624 6951 25
Date established: 1994 **Turnover:** £500,000 - £1m
No.of Employees: 11 - 20 **Product Groups:** 38

Date of Accounts	Mar 11	Mar 10	Mar 09
Sales Turnover	N/A	N/A	911
Pre Tax Profit/Loss	N/A	N/A	98
Working Capital	130	84	77
Fixed Assets	183	183	184
Current Assets	791	476	522
Current Liabilities	N/A	N/A	326

Ventserv Ltd

Unit 126 John Wilson Business Park Harvey Drive, Chestfield, Whitstable, CT5 3QT
Tel: 01227-779273 **Fax:** 01227-281559
E-mail: accounts@ventserv.co.uk
Website: http://www.ventserv.co.uk
Directors: S. Maybourne (Dir)
Immediate Holding Company: VENTSERV LIMITED
Registration no: 02984635 **Date established:** 1994
No.of Employees: 1 - 10 **Product Groups:** 20, 40, 41

Date of Accounts	Sep 11	Sep 10	Sep 09
Working Capital	15	63	42
Fixed Assets	242	256	270
Current Assets	495	409	191

Washfreeze

21 Bayview Road, Whitstable, CT5 4NP
Tel: 08454-671215 **Fax:** 01227-263732
E-mail: repairs@washfreeze.co.uk
Website: http://www.washfreeze.co.uk
Directors: T. Emery (Prop)
Turnover: Up to £250,000 **No.of Employees:** 1 - 10 **Product Groups:** 40, 63

WBH Transport

1 Nightingale Avenue, Whitstable, CT4 5TR
Tel: 01227-266044
E-mail: info@wbht.co.uk
Website: http://www.wbht.co.uk
Managers: C. Feder (Chief Mgr)
Date established: 2001 **No.of Employees:** 1 - 10 **Product Groups:** 72

Whitstable Marine

Sea Wall, Whitstable, CT5 1BX
Tel: 01227-262525 **Fax:** 01227-772750
E-mail: jez@whitstablemarine.co.uk
Website: http://www.whitstablemarine.co.uk
Directors: J. Fry (Ptnr)
VAT No.: GB 430 8930 56 **Turnover:** Up to £250,000
No.of Employees: 1 - 10 **Product Groups:** 23, 39, 49

Woodfield Systems Ltd

Tyler Way, Whitstable, CT5 2RS
Tel: 01227-793351 **Fax:** 01227-793625
E-mail: richard.williams@akersolutions.com
Website: http://www.akersolutions.com
Bank(s): National Westminster Bank Plc
Directors: C. Collins (Co Sec), R. Williams (Dir)
Ultimate Holding Company: AKER SOLUTIONS ASA (NORWAY)
Immediate Holding Company: WOODFIELD SYSTEMS LIMITED
Registration no: 01645961 **VAT No.:** GB 377 9457 86
Date established: 1982 **Turnover:** £10m - £20m
No.of Employees: 21 - 50 **Product Groups:** 38, 39, 42, 48, 84

Date of Accounts	Dec 11	Dec 10	Dec 09
Sales Turnover	9m	11m	10m
Pre Tax Profit/Loss	2m	817	1m
Working Capital	4m	3m	2m
Fixed Assets	546	535	472
Current Assets	6m	7m	5m
Current Liabilities	1m	2m	1m

LANCASHIRE

Accrington

A S C Kitchens & Bathrooms Ltd
Whalley Road Clayton Le Moors, Accrington, BB5 5HE
Tel: 01254-234107 **Fax:** 01254-387259
E-mail: asckitchens@btconnect.com
Website: http://www.ascchorley.com
Directors: L. Mercer (Fin)
Managers: D. Carlisle (Chief Mgr)
Immediate Holding Company: ASC KITCHENS & BATHROOMS LIMITED
Registration no: 05516814 **Date established:** 2005
No.of Employees: 1 - 10 **Product Groups:** 26, 40, 66

Date of Accounts	Aug 11	Aug 10	Aug 09
Working Capital	40	50	76
Fixed Assets	34	40	46
Current Assets	103	100	132

Accrington Grinding Company Ltd
Victoria Mill Mount Street, Accrington, BB5 0PJ
Tel: 01254-383088 **Fax:** 01254-398180
E-mail: sales-accgrind@tiscali.co.uk
Website: http://www.accringtongrinding.co.uk
Directors: R. Kenyon (MD)
Immediate Holding Company: ACCRINGTON GRINDING COMPANY LIMITED
Registration no: 04016854 **Date established:** 2000
Turnover: Up to £250,000 **No.of Employees:** 1 - 10 **Product Groups:** 46

Date of Accounts	Apr 12	Apr 11	Apr 10
Sales Turnover	N/A	N/A	221
Working Capital	-16	-11	-9
Fixed Assets	29	24	24
Current Assets	94	72	77
Current Liabilities	92	50	24

Accurate Cutting Services
Metcalf Drive Clayton Business Park, Altham, Accrington, BB5 5AY
Tel: 01282-770913 **Fax:** 01282-770913
E-mail: sales@accurate-cutting.co.uk
Website: http://www.accurate-cutting.co.uk
Managers: I. Oliver (Mgr)
Ultimate Holding Company: MALEW INVESTMENTS LIMITED (ISLE OF MAN)
Immediate Holding Company: RLC (UK) LIMITED
Registration no: 01195730 **Date established:** 1975
Turnover: £20m - £50m **No.of Employees:** 11 - 20 **Product Groups:** 46, 48

Date of Accounts	May 12	May 11	May 10
Sales Turnover	86m	37m	25m
Pre Tax Profit/Loss	13m	4m	992
Working Capital	9m	12m	5m
Fixed Assets	18m	11m	5m
Current Assets	28m	27m	11m
Current Liabilities	5m	5m	864

Admagnetics
Unit D2 Bolton Avenue Huncoat Industrial Estate, Accrington, BB5 6NJ
Tel: 01254-381869 **Fax:** 01254-381674
E-mail: sales@admagnetics.co.uk
Website: http://www.admagnetics.co.uk
Bank(s): Lloyds TSB Bank plc
Directors: A. Sharples (Dir), S. Moorhouse (MD)
Registration no: 04940346 **VAT No.:** GB 597 8923 58
Date established: 2003 **Turnover:** £1m - £2m **No.of Employees:** 21 - 50
Product Groups: 37

All Electrical Supplies
65 Abbey Street, Accrington, BB5 1EH
Tel: 01254-875130 **Fax:** 01254-397840
E-mail: allelectrical.stores@talktalkbusiness.net
Directors: M. Langley (Prop)
Date established: 2004 **No.of Employees:** 1 - 10 **Product Groups:** 36, 40

Allspeeds Ltd
Royal Works Atlas Street Clayton Le Moors, Accrington, BB5 5LW
Tel: 01254-615100 **Fax:** 01254-615199
E-mail: info@allspeeds.co.uk
Website: http://www.allspeeds.co.uk
Bank(s): Bank of Scotland
Directors: J. Laycock (Fin)
Managers: D. Pilkington (Sales Prom Mgr), D. Fisher (Mktg Serv Mgr), D. Moore (Tech Serv Mgr)
Ultimate Holding Company: ALLSPEEDS HOLDINGS LIMITED
Immediate Holding Company: ALLSPEEDS LIMITED
Registration no: 04639403 **Date established:** 2003 **Turnover:** £2m - £5m
No.of Employees: 21 - 50 **Product Groups:** 35, 39, 40, 45, 46, 67

Date of Accounts	Mar 12	Mar 11	Mar 09
Working Capital	2m	1m	1m
Fixed Assets	412	227	236
Current Assets	3m	2m	2m
Current Liabilities	N/A	N/A	1

Architectual Fibre Glass Mouldings Ltd
Globe Works Richmond Street, Accrington, BB5 0RH
Tel: 01254-357000 **Fax:** 01254-357011
E-mail: info@fibreglassmouldings.co.uk
Website: http://www.fibreglassmouldings.co.uk
Directors: S. Hussain (MD)
Immediate Holding Company: ARCHITECTURAL FIBREGLASS MOULDINGS LIMITED
Registration no: 04979363 **Date established:** 2003
Turnover: £500,000 - £1m **No.of Employees:** 11 - 20 **Product Groups:** 30

Date of Accounts	Oct 11	Oct 10	Oct 09
Working Capital	884	606	561
Fixed Assets	59	73	79
Current Assets	1m	818	762

Ashley Engineering (Accrington) LLP
Stonebridge Mill Stonebridge Lane, Oswaldwistle, Accrington, BB5 3HX
Tel: 01254-356150 **Fax:** 01254-356151
E-mail: sales@ashleyengineering.com
Website: http://www.ashleyengineering.com
Product Groups: 30, 31, 34, 48, 66

Auto Motive Technology Ltd
PO Box 22, Accrington, BB5 0LA
Tel: 01254-357500 **Fax:** 01254-357600
E-mail: info@automotive-tech.co.uk
Website: http://www.automotive-tech.co.uk
Directors: C. Carter (Chief Op Offcr), G. Ellis (Fin)
Immediate Holding Company: G & A PLASTICS HOLDINGS LIMITED
Registration no: 01989498 **Date established:** 1971
Turnover: £10m - £20m **No.of Employees:** 51 - 100 **Product Groups:** 30

Baxenden Chemicals Ltd
Paragon Works Rising Bridge, Accrington, BB5 2SL
Tel: 01254-872278 **Fax:** 01254-871247
E-mail: mail@baxchem.co.uk
Website: http://www.baxenden.co.uk
Bank(s): National Westminster Bank Plc
Managers: M. Garrett (Sales Prom Mgr), J. Thompson, G. Warren (Tech Serv Mgr), K. Docherty (Personnel), S. Lewis (Mgr)
Ultimate Holding Company: CHEMTURA CORP (USA)
Immediate Holding Company: BAXENDEN CHEMICALS LIMITED
Registration no: 00147556 **VAT No.:** GB 149 7482 25
Date established: 2017 **Turnover:** £20m - £50m
No.of Employees: 101 - 250 **Product Groups:** 30, 31, 66

Date of Accounts	Dec 11	Dec 10	Dec 09
Sales Turnover	31m	34m	30m
Pre Tax Profit/Loss	2m	4m	695
Working Capital	12m	13m	9m
Fixed Assets	10m	11m	12m
Current Assets	15m	19m	14m
Current Liabilities	1m	2m	2m

William Blythe Ltd
Bridge Street Church, Accrington, BB5 4PD
Tel: 01254-320000 **Fax:** 01254-320001
E-mail: tim.hughes@williamblythe.com
Website: http://www.williamblythe.com
Bank(s): National Westminster Bank Plc
Directors: J. Davies (Sales), T. Hughes (MD), T. Pepper (Fin)
Managers: S. Kenyon, S. Kerfoot (Tech Serv Mgr)
Ultimate Holding Company: YULE CATTO & CO PUBLIC LIMITED COMPANY
Immediate Holding Company: WILLIAM BLYTHE LIMITED
Registration no: 02628212 **VAT No.:** GB 597 9390 62
Date established: 1991 **Turnover:** £20m - £50m
No.of Employees: 51 - 100 **Product Groups:** 31, 32

Date of Accounts	Dec 11	Dec 10	Dec 09
Sales Turnover	33m	31m	24m
Pre Tax Profit/Loss	5m	4m	754
Working Capital	9m	5m	2m
Fixed Assets	3m	2m	2m
Current Assets	15m	10m	9m
Current Liabilities	2m	1m	686

C & H Precision Measuring Systems Ltd
Unit 15 Gec Business Park Blackburn Road, Clayton le Moors, Accrington, BB5 5JW
Tel: 01254-301777 **Fax:** 01254-301777
E-mail: enquiries@ch-precision.co.uk
Website: http://www.ch-precision.co.uk.
Directors: J. Chatburn (MD)
Immediate Holding Company: C AND H PRECISION MEASURING SYSTEMS LIMITED
Registration no: 04492253 **Date established:** 2002
Turnover: Up to £250,000 **No.of Employees:** 1 - 10 **Product Groups:** 38, 48

Date of Accounts	Jul 11	Jul 10	Jul 09
Working Capital	15	N/A	2
Fixed Assets	2	1	2
Current Assets	65	38	32

Caligen Foam Ltd (A British Vita Company)
Broad Oak, Accrington, BB5 2BS
Tel: 01254-355000 **Fax:** 01254-355111
E-mail: sales@caligen.co.uk
Website: http://www.caligen.co.uk
Bank(s): Lloyds TSB Bank plc
Directors: G. Maundrell (Dir)
Ultimate Holding Company: VITA CAYMAN LIMITED (CAYMAN ISLANDS)
Immediate Holding Company: CALIGEN FOAM LIMITED
Registration no: 00800311 **VAT No.:** GB 606 3420 73
Date established: 1964 **Turnover:** £10m - £20m
No.of Employees: 51 - 100 **Product Groups:** 29, 30, 31, 36, 39, 42, 48, 49

Date of Accounts	Dec 11	Dec 10	Dec 09
Pre Tax Profit/Loss	-5	-4	-6
Working Capital	5m	5m	5m
Current Assets	5m	5m	5m

Cardboard Box
Clayton Business Park Petre Road Clayton Le Moors, Accrington, BB5 5JB
Tel: 01254-232223 **Fax:** 01254-232636
E-mail: enquiries@thecardboardbox.co.uk
Website: http://www.thecardboardbox.co.uk
Bank(s): National Westminster Bank Plc
Directors: K. Shackleton (MD)
Ultimate Holding Company: CBC HOLDINGS UK LIMITED
Immediate Holding Company: THE CARDBOARD BOX COMPANY LIMITED
Registration no: 04012577 **Date established:** 2000 **Turnover:** £2m - £5m
No.of Employees: 21 - 50 **Product Groups:** 27

Date of Accounts	Jun 12	Jun 11	Jun 10
Sales Turnover	12m	10m	8m
Pre Tax Profit/Loss	1m	1m	1m
Working Capital	-100	267	154
Fixed Assets	3m	3m	3m
Current Assets	4m	3m	2m
Current Liabilities	839	934	625

Chamber Of Commerce East Lancashire
Red Rose Court Clayton Le Moors, Accrington, BB5 5JR
Tel: 01254-356400 **Fax:** 01254-388900
E-mail: info@chamberelancs.co.uk
Website: http://www.chamberelancs.co.uk
Directors: M. Damms (Grp Chief Exec)
Immediate Holding Company: EAST LANCASHIRE CHAMBER OF COMMERCE AND INDUSTRY
Registration no: 00024084 **Date established:** 1987 **Turnover:** £1m - £2m
No.of Employees: 21 - 50 **Product Groups:** 86

Date of Accounts	Dec 11	Dec 10	Dec 09
Sales Turnover	1m	1m	1m
Pre Tax Profit/Loss	7	56	22
Working Capital	102	-107	-102
Fixed Assets	2m	2m	2m
Current Assets	289	374	341
Current Liabilities	60	333	309

Dapr Industrial Electronics
Junction 7 Business Park Blackburn Road, Clayton le Moors, Accrington, BB5 5JW
Tel: 01254-397939 **Fax:** 01254-397978
E-mail: agrice@daprind.co.uk
Website: http://www.daprind.co.uk
Directors: A. Grice (Co Sec)
Immediate Holding Company: J. O'BRIEN SEALANTS LIMITED
Registration no: 01808201 **Date established:** 2002
Turnover: £10m - £20m **No.of Employees:** 1 - 10 **Product Groups:** 84

Date of Accounts	Dec 10	Sep 09	Sep 08
Sales Turnover	22m	17m	N/A
Pre Tax Profit/Loss	2m	478	594

Working Capital	729	3m	3m
Fixed Assets	139	266	268
Current Assets	6m	9m	9m
Current Liabilities	3m	4m	5m

James Dewhurst Ltd

Altham Lane Altham, Accrington, BB5 5YA
Tel: 01282-775311 **Fax:** 01282-774717
E-mail: info@jamesdewhurst.com
Website: http://www.jamesdewhurst.com
Bank(s): Barclays, Bradford
Directors: S. Bentley (Fin)
Managers: B. Hogg, C. Parry-gannon (Buyer), M. Blackwell, L. Campbell (Tech Serv Mgr), N. Crofts (Sales & Mktg Mg)
Ultimate Holding Company: AAC CAPITAL PARTNERS HOLDING BV (NETHERLANDS)
Immediate Holding Company: JAMES DEWHURST LIMITED
Registration no: 00506170 **VAT No.:** GB 174 4012 86
Date established: 1952 **Turnover:** £20m - £50m
No.of Employees: 101 - 250 **Product Groups:** 23

Date of Accounts	Mar 12	Mar 11	Mar 10
Sales Turnover	49m	49m	44m
Pre Tax Profit/Loss	5m	4m	2m
Working Capital	19m	13m	8m
Fixed Assets	17m	19m	21m
Current Assets	24m	19m	16m
Current Liabilities	3m	2m	1m

Emerson & Renwick Ltd

Peel Bank Works Peel Bank, Church, Accrington, BB5 4EF
Tel: 01254-872727 **Fax:** 01254-871109
E-mail: office@eandr.com
Website: http://www.eandr.com
Bank(s): National Westminster Bank Plc
Directors: A. Pope (Co Sec), B. Clements (MD), C. Hargreaves (Ch), D. Hargreaves (Comm)
Managers: D. Wilkinson (Buyer), D. Wilson (Personnel)
Immediate Holding Company: EMERSON & RENWICK LIMITED
Registration no: 00205229 **VAT No.:** GB 174 4243 67
Date established: 2025 **Turnover:** £10m - £20m
No.of Employees: 101 - 250 **Product Groups:** 28, 44

Date of Accounts	Dec 11	Dec 10	Dec 09
Sales Turnover	14m	15m	9m
Pre Tax Profit/Loss	733	762	-9
Working Capital	991	1m	412
Fixed Assets	2m	2m	1m
Current Assets	8m	5m	5m
Current Liabilities	4m	2m	2m

Express Gifts

Church Bridge Works Mill Street, Church, Accrington, BB5 4EL
Tel: 01254-382121 **Fax:** 01254-352012
Website: http://www.24studio.co.uk
Bank(s): National Westminster Bank Plc
Directors: P. Maudsley (MD)
Ultimate Holding Company: FINDEL P.L.C.
Immediate Holding Company: EXPRESS GIFTS LIMITED
Registration no: 00718151 **VAT No.:** GB 125 6886 44
Date established: 1962 **Turnover:** £125m - £250m
No.of Employees: 251 - 500 **Product Groups:** 27

Date of Accounts	Mar 12	Apr 09	Apr 10
Sales Turnover	232m	229m	221m
Pre Tax Profit/Loss	7m	-17m	-9m
Working Capital	130m	-3m	25m
Fixed Assets	11m	18m	15m
Current Assets	246m	152m	142m
Current Liabilities	6m	4m	5m

F P W Axles Ltd

Unit D4 Enfield Road, Accrington, BB5 6NN
Tel: 01254-383413 **Fax:** 01254-390417
E-mail: len.wilson@fpw-axles.co.uk
Website: http://www.fpw-axles.co.uk
Bank(s): HSBC Bank plc
Directors: D. Mason (Mkt Research), L. Wilson (Fin), S. Taylor (Sales)
Ultimate Holding Company: FPW AXLES HOLDINGS LIMITED
Immediate Holding Company: FPW AXLES LIMITED
Registration no: 01657509 **VAT No.:** GB 375 1695 25
Date established: 1982 **No.of Employees:** 21 - 50 **Product Groups:** 39

Date of Accounts	Jan 12	Jan 11	Jan 10
Working Capital	146	139	139
Fixed Assets	372	432	471
Current Assets	819	829	817

Friction Components & Systems Ltd

Maudsley Mill Maudsley Street, Accrington, BB5 6AD
Tel: 01254-397561 **Fax:** 01254-389722
E-mail: friction@btconnect.com
Website: http://www.newtonfriction.co.uk
Directors: A. Keeney (Sales), D. Devlin (MD)
Immediate Holding Company: FRICTION COMPONENTS AND SYSTEMS LIMITED
Registration no: 01569429 **VAT No.:** GB 376 2529 31
Date established: 1981 **No.of Employees:** 1 - 10 **Product Groups:** 33

Date of Accounts	Jun 11	Jun 10	Jun 09
Working Capital	-36	-30	-47
Fixed Assets	101	105	109
Current Assets	133	156	105

G & A Plastics Holdings Ltd

Springhill Works Exchange Street Accrington, Accrington, BB5 0LE
Tel: 01254-871919 **Fax:** 01254-390967
E-mail: info@gandaplastics.co.uk
Website: http://www.gandaplastics.co.uk
Directors: S. Ashton (Fin), D. Challans (MD)
Immediate Holding Company: G & A PLASTICS HOLDINGS LIMITED
Registration no: 04419934 **VAT No.:** GB 175 1863 46
Date established: 2002 **Turnover:** £500,000 - £1m
No.of Employees: 1 - 10 **Product Groups:** 29, 30, 40, 48, 54

Date of Accounts	Apr 11	Apr 10	Apr 08
Working Capital	-1	-1	-1
Fixed Assets	269	269	269

Greenplant Stainless

Unit 3b Huncoat Business Park Huncoat Industrial Estate, Accrington, BB5 6NT
Tel: 01254-872287 **Fax:** 01254-385740
E-mail: sales@greenplant.co.uk
Website: http://www.greenplant.co.uk
Directors: L. Green (Dir), J. Green (Fin)
Immediate Holding Company: GREENPLANT STAINLESS LIMITED
Registration no: 02058391 **VAT No.:** GB 431 1891 69
Date established: 1986 **Turnover:** £250,000 - £500,000
No.of Employees: 1 - 10 **Product Groups:** 35

Date of Accounts	Sep 11	Sep 10	Sep 09
Working Capital	102	92	86
Fixed Assets	12	15	16
Current Assets	284	281	282

Walter Holland & Sons

Blackburn Road, Accrington, BB5 2SA
Tel: 01706-213591 **Fax:** 01706-228044
E-mail: enquiries@hollands-pies.co.uk
Website: http://www.northernfoods.com
Managers: S. Oldham (Personnel), D. Summons (Personnel), R. Chadwick, C. Barnes (Personnel), L. Holcroft (Mktg Serv Mgr), M. Gasgow
Immediate Holding Company: NORTHERN FOODS GROUP P.L.C.
Registration no: 00255912 **Date established:** 1851
Turnover: £20m - £50m **No.of Employees:** 251 - 500 **Product Groups:** 20

Homeheaven

Lodge Mill Victoria Street, Accrington, BB5 0PG
Tel: 01254-879998 **Fax:** 01254-394819
E-mail: enquiries@homeheaven.co.uk
Website: http://www.homeheaven.co.uk
Directors: J. Hawley (Prop)
Immediate Holding Company: HOMEHEAVEN LTD
Registration no: 03914537 **Date established:** 2000
Turnover: £250,000 - £500,000 **No.of Employees:** 51 - 100
Product Groups: 26, 63

Isothane Ltd

Newhouse Road Huncoat Industrial Estate, Accrington, BB5 6NT
Tel: 01254-872555 **Fax:** 01254-871522
E-mail: info@isothane.com
Website: http://www.isothane.com
Directors: C. Baxter (Fin), R. Spencer (Dir), R. Herridge (Tech Serv), P. Bullivant (MD)
Immediate Holding Company: ISOTHANE LIMITED
Registration no: 02975728 **VAT No.:** GB 548 2278 23
Date established: 1994 **Turnover:** £5m - £10m **No.of Employees:** 21 - 50
Product Groups: 30, 31, 32, 48, 66

Date of Accounts	Mar 12	Mar 11	Mar 10
Sales Turnover	9m	8m	N/A
Pre Tax Profit/Loss	123	254	N/A
Working Capital	766	663	484
Fixed Assets	882	948	1m
Current Assets	2m	3m	2m
Current Liabilities	477	599	N/A

Jet Rollers Ltd

Unit 7 Chester Street, Accrington, BB5 0SD
Tel: 01254-355230 **Fax:** 01254-231071
E-mail: sales@jet-rollers.co.uk
Website: http://www.jet-rollers.co.uk
Bank(s): National Westminster
Directors: W. Walker (MD)
Immediate Holding Company: JET ROLLERS (2005) LIMITED
Registration no: 05503153 **VAT No.:** GB 458 0920 37
Date established: 2005 **Turnover:** £1m - £2m **No.of Employees:** 11 - 20
Product Groups: 29, 44

Date of Accounts	Nov 11	Nov 10	Nov 09
Working Capital	-204	-211	-203
Fixed Assets	237	254	245
Current Assets	437	386	308

Langtec Ltd

Unit 1 Calder Court Altham, Accrington, BB5 5YB
Tel: 01282-772544 **Fax:** 01282-772740
E-mail: info@langtec.co.uk
Website: http://www.langtec.co.uk
Bank(s): National Westminster Bank Plc
Directors: A. Turner (MD)
Ultimate Holding Company: LANGTEC INTERNATIONAL LIMITED
Immediate Holding Company: LANGTEC LIMITED
Registration no: 00613374 **VAT No.:** GB 696 4786 60
Date established: 1958 **Turnover:** £2m - £5m **No.of Employees:** 21 - 50
Product Groups: 30, 31, 33, 37, 67, 84

Date of Accounts	Sep 11	Sep 10	Sep 09
Working Capital	478	465	340
Fixed Assets	388	347	373
Current Assets	1m	1m	822

Lantex Manufacturing Co. Ltd

Oxford Court Oxford Street, Accrington, BB5 1QX
Tel: 01254-398017 **Fax:** 01254-872363
E-mail: info@lantex.co.uk
Website: http://www.lantex.co.uk
Directors: J. Parker (MD)
Immediate Holding Company: LANTEX MANUFACTURING COMPANY LIMITED
Registration no: 00150264 **Date established:** 2018
No.of Employees: 11 - 20 **Product Groups:** 23, 24

Date of Accounts	Feb 12	Feb 11	Feb 10
Working Capital	140	145	140
Fixed Assets	229	238	202
Current Assets	483	449	379

Lift Aid Ltd

Fern Mill Duckworth Hall, Oswaldtwistle, Accrington, BB5 3RQ
Tel: 01254-729729 **Fax:** 01254-704135
Directors: K. Fenlan (Fin)
Immediate Holding Company: LIFT AID LIMITED
Registration no: 02172850 **Date established:** 1987
No.of Employees: 1 - 10 **Product Groups:** 35, 39, 45

Date of Accounts	Mar 11	Mar 10	Mar 09
Working Capital	-4	2	-4
Fixed Assets	2	3	4
Current Assets	4	10	4

M & F Components

PO Box 18, Accrington, BB5 5BE
Tel: 01254-301121 **Fax:** 01254-391416
E-mail: sales@mafcobell.co.uk
Website: http://www.mafcobell.co.uk
Directors: L. Monks (Sales)
Managers: A. Kay (Chief Mgr)
Ultimate Holding Company: MADWORTH LIMITED
Immediate Holding Company: M.& F.COMPONENTS LIMITED
Registration no: 00530699 **VAT No.:** GB 458 0649 25
Date established: 1954 **Turnover:** £5m - £10m **No.of Employees:** 1 - 10
Product Groups: 35, 39

Date of Accounts	Dec 11	Dec 10	Dec 09
Working Capital	-8	-66	-159
Fixed Assets	39	37	54
Current Assets	1m	1m	1m

Mckiernan Group Ltd

Crown St Works Crown Street, Accrington, BB5 0RW
Tel: 01254-398532 **Fax:** 01254-392157
E-mail: reception@themckiernangroup.co.uk
Website: http://www.themckiernangroup.co.uk
Bank(s): National Westminster, Great Harwood
Directors: A. Mckiernan (MD)
Immediate Holding Company: MCKIERNAN GROUP LIMITED
Registration no: 00482520 **VAT No.:** GB 174 6556 36
Date established: 1950 **Turnover:** £2m - £5m **No.of Employees:** 21 - 50
Product Groups: 52

Date of Accounts	Aug 11	Aug 10	Aug 09
Working Capital	60	27	204
Fixed Assets	68	92	255
Current Assets	410	316	594

Metalcraft Plastic Coatings

Grange Iron Works Back Wellington Street, Accrington, BB5 2NW
Tel: 01254-232063 **Fax:** 01254-871168
E-mail: sales@metalcraftpc.co.uk
Bank(s): HSBC
Managers: G. Hull (Mgr)
Immediate Holding Company: METALCRAFT PLASTIC COATINGS LIMITED
Registration no: 01320036 **VAT No.:** GB 291 1400 88
Date established: 1977 **Turnover:** £500,000 - £1m
No.of Employees: 11 - 20 **Product Groups:** 48

Date of Accounts	Aug 11	Aug 10	Aug 09
Working Capital	-38	-10	-54
Fixed Assets	92	102	100
Current Assets	202	226	202

Metcalfe Industrial Saws

436 Blackburn Road, Accrington, BB5 0DE
Tel: 01254-396633 **Fax:** 01254-388804
E-mail: metindsaws@hotmail.co.uk
Website: http://www.metcalfemodels.com
Directors: D. Metcalfe (Prop)
Date established: 2000 **No.of Employees:** 1 - 10 **Product Groups:** 36

Micro Peripherals Ltd

Shorten Brook Way Altham Business Park, Altham, Accrington, BB5 5YJ
Tel: 01282-776776 **Fax:** 01282-770001
E-mail: enquiries@micro-p.com
Website: http://www.micro-p.com
Bank(s): National Westminster
Directors: C. Warrington (I.T. Dir), J. Chibnall (I.T. Dir), M. Aldem (MD), M. Alden (MD), P. Meehan (Fin)
Ultimate Holding Company: DCC PUBLIC LIMITED COMPANY
Immediate Holding Company: Runsole Ltd
Registration no: 01511931 **VAT No.:** GB 314 7105 90
Date established: 1995 **Turnover:** £250m - £500m
No.of Employees: 251 - 500 **Product Groups:** 44, 67

Nayler Group Ltd

Aero Mill Kershaw Street, Church, Accrington, BB5 4JS
Tel: 01254-234247 **Fax:** 01254-383996
E-mail: alastair.nayler@marineworldmagazine.com
Website: http://www.printerslancashire.com
Bank(s): National Westminster Bank Plc
Directors: J. Nayler (Jt MD), A. Nayler (Jt MD), A. Nayler (MD)
Ultimate Holding Company: NAYLER GROUP LTD
Immediate Holding Company: ABSORBENT DRIPMATS LIMITED
Registration no: 00508469 **Date established:** 1952
Turnover: £500,000 - £1m **No.of Employees:** 11 - 20
Product Groups: 28, 64

Date of Accounts	Mar 11	Mar 10	Mar 09
Working Capital	N/A	-9	-9

Pennine Leisure Products

Unit 4 Chester Street, Accrington, BB5 0SD
Tel: 01254-385991
E-mail: sales@pennine-leisure.co.uk
Website: http://www.thepenninegroup.co.uk
Directors: C. Parkinson (Fin)
Managers: H. Walmsley
Immediate Holding Company: PENNINE LEISURE PRODUCTS LIMITED
Registration no: 01593421 **Date established:** 1981
No.of Employees: 51 - 100 **Product Groups:** 24, 39

Date of Accounts	Sep 11	Sep 10	Sep 09
Working Capital	398	693	601
Fixed Assets	1m	1m	1m
Current Assets	791	1m	999

Premier Environmental Ltd

14 Newhouse Road Huncoat Industrial Estate, Accrington, BB5 6NT
Tel: 01254-386776 **Fax:** 08714-340881
E-mail: sales@premier-env.co.uk
Website: http://www.premier-env.co.uk
Directors: A. Glover (MD)
Immediate Holding Company: PREMIER ENVIRONMENTAL LIMITED
Registration no: 04527450 **Date established:** 2002
No.of Employees: 1 - 10 **Product Groups:** 23, 40, 52

Date of Accounts	Sep 11	Sep 10	Sep 09
Working Capital	76	63	88
Fixed Assets	40	40	36
Current Assets	183	131	123

Production Glassfibre

Shorten Brook Way Altham Business Park, Altham, Accrington, BB5 5YJ
Tel: 01282-680444 **Fax:** 01282-680303
E-mail: sales@productionglassfibre.co.uk
Website: http://www.productionglassfibre.co.uk
Directors: S. Grossi (MD)
Managers: S. Grossey (Mgr)
Ultimate Holding Company: DCC PUBLIC LIMITED COMPANY
Registration no: 02379449 **Date established:** 1989
No.of Employees: 51 - 100 **Product Groups:** 30, 39, 48, 66, 68

Keith Prosser
Unit 22 Victoria Mill Victoria Street, Accrington, BB5 0PG
Tel: 01254-384898 **Fax:** 01254-384898
E-mail: kpcast@prosser.fslife.co.uk
Website: http://www.prosser.fslife.co.uk
Directors: K. Prosser (Prop)
VAT No.: GB 525 4481 48 **Turnover:** Up to £250,000
No.of Employees: 1 - 10 **Product Groups:** 34

Raven Manufacturing Ltd
Metcalf Drive Altham Industrial Estate, Accrington, BB5 5TU
Tel: 01282-770000 **Fax:** 01282-770022
E-mail: raven@raven.co.uk
Website: http://www.raven.co.uk
Directors: R. Davies (MD), S. Diggles (Fin), D. Grice (I.T. Dir), A. Whitehead (MD), A. Whitehead (Grp Chief Exec), R. Beagan (Sales)
Managers: R. Lambert (Sales Prom Mgr), R. Beagan (Sales & Mktg Mg)
Ultimate Holding Company: SATELLITE HOLDINGS LLC (USA)
Immediate Holding Company: RAVEN MANUFACTURING LIMITED
Registration no: 02113041 **VAT No.:** GB 375 2768 19
Date established: 1987 **Turnover:** £5m - £10m
No.of Employees: 101 - 250 **Product Groups:** 48

Date of Accounts	Dec 10	Dec 09	Dec 08
Sales Turnover	10m	9m	10m
Pre Tax Profit/Loss	61	-313	4m
Working Capital	602	240	1m
Fixed Assets	4m	4m	4m
Current Assets	3m	4m	7m
Current Liabilities	481	520	415

Robert Nicholas Steels
The Steel Works Charter Street, Accrington, BB5 0SA
Tel: 01254-872380 **Fax:** 01254-233455
E-mail: info@robnic-steel.co.uk
Website: http://www.robnic-steel.co.uk
Bank(s): The Royal Bank of Scotland
Directors: P. Rhind (Fin), W. Rhind (MD)
Immediate Holding Company: ROBERT NICHOLAS STEELS (BURNLEY) LIMITED
Registration no: 01188066 **Date established:** 1974 **Turnover:** £2m - £5m
No.of Employees: 11 - 20 **Product Groups:** 34

Date of Accounts	Jan 12	Jan 11	Jan 10
Working Capital	522	489	411
Fixed Assets	314	326	340
Current Assets	2m	2m	2m

Sally Hair & Beauty Supplies Ltd
Unit 1b Broadway, Accrington, BB5 1JZ
Tel: 01254-391002
E-mail: admin@sallybeauty.co.uk
Website: http://www.sallybeauty.com
Managers: F. Hussein (Mgr)
Ultimate Holding Company: SALLY BEAUTY HOLDING INC (USA)
Immediate Holding Company: SALLY SALON SERVICES LIMITED
Registration no: 01060763 **Date established:** 1972
No.of Employees: 1 - 10 **Product Groups:** 30, 36, 40

Date of Accounts	Sep 11	Sep 10	Sep 09
Sales Turnover	128m	107m	82m
Pre Tax Profit/Loss	3m	2m	1m
Working Capital	10m	7m	6m
Fixed Assets	11m	12m	9m
Current Assets	63m	50m	45m
Current Liabilities	10m	7m	4m

Senator International Ltd
Sykeside Drive Altham Business Park, Altham, Accrington, BB5 5YE
Tel: 01282-725000 **Fax:** 01282-775039
E-mail: jsimpson@senator.co.uk
Website: http://www.senatorinternational.co.uk
Directors: J. Simpson (Dir)
Immediate Holding Company: SENATOR INTERNATIONAL LIMITED
Registration no: 01323955 **Date established:** 1977
Turnover: £75m - £125m **No.of Employees:** 501 - 1000
Product Groups: 25, 26, 67

Date of Accounts	Dec 11	Dec 10	Dec 09
Sales Turnover	101m	92m	98m
Pre Tax Profit/Loss	3m	552	2m
Working Capital	12m	10m	9m
Fixed Assets	26m	24m	27m
Current Assets	33m	29m	27m
Current Liabilities	6m	5m	5m

Spa Web Ltd
Metcalf Drive Altham Industrial Estate, Accrington, BB5 5TU
Tel: 01282-688100 **Fax:** 01282-688105
E-mail: tom@spaweb.co.uk
Website: http://www.loadlok.com
Directors: J. Thompson (MD)
Immediate Holding Company: SPA WEB LIMITED
Registration no: 00778451 **Date established:** 1963 **Turnover:** £2m - £5m
No.of Employees: 11 - 20 **Product Groups:** 23

Date of Accounts	Dec 11	Dec 10	Dec 09
Working Capital	567	420	261
Fixed Assets	794	822	881
Current Assets	1m	1m	798
Current Liabilities	386	N/A	N/A

Tangye (All Speeds Group Ltd)
Royal Works Atlas Street, Clayton Le Moors, Accrington, BB5 5LW
Tel: 01254-615100 **Fax:** 01254-615199
E-mail: info@allspeeds.co.uk
Website: http://www.allspeeds.co.uk
Bank(s): The Royal Bank of Scotland
Directors: J. Laycock (Fin), M. Hollyhead (MD)
Managers: D. Moore (I.T. Exec), J. Pollock (Sales & Mktg Mg)
Immediate Holding Company: Allspeeds Ltd
Registration no: 04639403 **Turnover:** £2m - £5m
No.of Employees: 21 - 50 **Product Groups:** 38, 39, 40

3d Illustration
43 Queens Road, Accrington, BB5 6AR
Tel: 01254-381027
E-mail: studio@3dillustration.co.uk
Website: http://www.3dillustration.co.uk
Directors: B. Anderson (Prop)
Date established: 2002 **Turnover:** Up to £250,000
No.of Employees: 1 - 10 **Product Groups:** 81

R M Williams Accrington Ltd
21-25 Water Street, Accrington, BB5 6QZ
Tel: 01254-871911 **Fax:** 01254-395613
E-mail: sales@rmwaccltd.co.uk
Website: http://www.airtime.co.uk
Directors: G. Shears (MD), H. Cryer (Fin)
Immediate Holding Company: R.M. WILLIAMS (ACCRINGTON) LIMITED
Registration no: 00867720 **Date established:** 1965
Turnover: £500,000 - £1m **No.of Employees:** 1 - 10 **Product Groups:** 66

Date of Accounts	Mar 12	Mar 11	Mar 10
Working Capital	20	21	17
Fixed Assets	56	60	64
Current Assets	153	148	124

Graham Winterbottom Ltd
Unit 33 Victoria Business Centre Mount Street, Accrington, BB5 0PJ
Tel: 01254-390700 **Fax:** 01254-390800
E-mail: info@graham-winterbottom.co.uk
Website: http://www.graham-winterbottom.co.uk
Directors: P. Scates (MD), G. Scates (Co Sec)
Immediate Holding Company: GRAHAM WINTERBOTTOM LIMITED
Registration no: 01638003 **Date established:** 1982 **Turnover:** £1m - £2m
No.of Employees: 11 - 20 **Product Groups:** 24

Date of Accounts	Jan 12	Jan 11	Jan 10
Working Capital	856	877	843
Fixed Assets	23	29	36
Current Assets	1m	1m	1m

Ashton Under Lyne

A C P & D
86 Rose Hill Road, Ashton Under Lyne, OL6 8YF
Tel: 0161-343 1884 **Fax:** 0161-339 0650
E-mail: sales@acpd.co.uk
Website: http://www.acpd.co.uk
Directors: L. Pimlott (Fin), C. Pimlott (Dir)
Immediate Holding Company: A C P & D LIMITED
Registration no: 03245766 **Date established:** 1996
No.of Employees: 1 - 10 **Product Groups:** 35, 37, 38

Date of Accounts	Dec 11	Dec 10	Dec 09
Working Capital	15	19	-4
Fixed Assets	2	3	4
Current Assets	83	79	90

A U T Wheels & Castors Co. Ltd
The Wheelhouse Egmont Street, Mossley, Ashton Under Lyne, OL5 9NB
Tel: 01457-837772 **Fax:** 01457-832472
E-mail: ian_butterworth@aut.co.uk
Website: http://www.aut.co.uk
Bank(s): National Westminster Bank Plc
Directors: R. Glover (Dir)
Managers: I. Butterworth (Purch Mgr), I. Butterworth, D. Hatchard (Mktg Serv Mgr)
Immediate Holding Company: A.U.T. (WHEELS AND CASTORS) CO. LTD.
Registration no: 01472646 **VAT No.:** GB 317 8858 18
Date established: 1980 **Turnover:** £2m - £5m **No.of Employees:** 11 - 20
Product Groups: 29, 39

Date of Accounts	Dec 10	Dec 09	Dec 08
Working Capital	679	457	496
Fixed Assets	126	484	526
Current Assets	1m	1m	1m

Abbey Masterbatch Ltd
Whitelands Mill Whitelands Road, Ashton Under Lyne, OL6 6UG
Tel: 0161-308 2550 **Fax:** 0161-344 2345
E-mail: office@abbeymb.com
Website: http://www.abbeymasterbatch.com
Bank(s): National Westminster Bank Plc
Directors: M. Shirt (Dir), L. Mather (Co Sec), J. Shirt (MD)
Ultimate Holding Company: A.T.L. INDUSTRIES LIMITED
Immediate Holding Company: ABBEY THERMOSETS LIMITED
Registration no: 03563753 **VAT No.:** GB 678 5109 02
Date established: 1998 **Turnover:** £2m - £5m **No.of Employees:** 21 - 50
Product Groups: 31, 32, 33, 66

Airtec Air Systems Ltd
Valley House Lees Road, Mossley, Ashton Under Lyne, OL5 0PG
Tel: 01457-832724 **Fax:** 01457-832924
E-mail: info@airtecairsystems.ltd.uk
Website: http://www.airtecairsystems.ltd.uk
Directors: S. Cullen (MD), I. Cullen (Co Sec)
Immediate Holding Company: AIRTEC AIR SYSTEMS LIMITED
Registration no: 04298666 **Date established:** 2001
Turnover: £250,000 - £500,000 **No.of Employees:** 1 - 10
Product Groups: 40, 42

Date of Accounts	Sep 11	Sep 10	Sep 09
Working Capital	47	-5	-3
Fixed Assets	4	5	3
Current Assets	250	148	96

Amann Oxley Threads Ltd
Guide Mills South Street, Ashton Under Lyne, OL7 0PJ
Tel: 0161-339 6400 **Fax:** 0161-343 1705
E-mail: graham.hall@oxley-threads.com
Website: http://www.oxley-threads.com
Bank(s): National Westminster Bank Plc
Directors: G. Hall (I.T. Dir), M. McGowan (Fin)
Ultimate Holding Company: AMANN UND SOHNE GMBH (GERMANY)
Immediate Holding Company: AMANN THREADS UK LIMITED
Registration no: 00519347 **Date established:** 1953
Turnover: £10m - £20m **No.of Employees:** 101 - 250 **Product Groups:** 23

Date of Accounts	Dec 11	Dec 10	Dec 09
Sales Turnover	19m	18m	N/A
Pre Tax Profit/Loss	3m	2m	522
Working Capital	10m	8m	6m
Fixed Assets	965	812	423
Current Assets	12m	11m	9m
Current Liabilities	551	527	489

Arc Welding Products Ltd
Unit 7 Charlestown Industrial Estate Robinson Street, Ashton Under Lyne, OL6 8NS
Tel: 0161-330 1671 **Fax:** 0161-330 1714
Website: http://www.arcweldingproducts.co.uk
Directors: N. Fowler (Fin), P. Fowler (MD)
Immediate Holding Company: ARC WELDING PRODUCTS LIMITED
Registration no: 04386065 **Date established:** 2002
No.of Employees: 1 - 10 **Product Groups:** 46

Date of Accounts	Mar 12	Mar 11	Mar 10
Working Capital	53	20	47
Fixed Assets	43	52	48
Current Assets	288	243	194

Ashton Jig & Tool Company Ltd
Yorkshire Street, Ashton Under Lyne, OL6 8NR
Tel: 0161-330 4460 **Fax:** 0161-330 7040
E-mail: sales@ajt1.co.uk
Website: http://www.ajt1.co.uk
Directors: J. Clifton (MD)
Immediate Holding Company: ASHTON JIG AND TOOL COMPANY LIMITED
Registration no: 00604021 **Date established:** 1958
Turnover: £500,000 - £1m **No.of Employees:** 11 - 20
Product Groups: 46, 47, 67

Date of Accounts	May 11	May 10	May 09
Working Capital	92	77	80
Fixed Assets	809	590	585
Current Assets	300	286	276

Atlantic 2000
PO Box 11, Ashton Under Lyne, OL6 7TR
Tel: 0161-621 5960 **Fax:** 0161-621 5966
E-mail: info@atlanticboilers.com
Website: http://www.atlanticboilers.com
Managers: J. Baddeley
Turnover: £1m - £2m **No.of Employees:** 1 - 10 **Product Groups:** 40, 66

Audenshaw Steel Ltd
Unit 12 Wharf Parade Lower Wharf Street, Ashton Under Lyne, OL6 7PE
Tel: 0161-343 8550 **Fax:** 0161-343 8550
Directors: A. Nugent (Fin)
Immediate Holding Company: AUDENSHAW STEEL LIMITED
Registration no: 02144713 **VAT No.:** GB 458 3141 46
Date established: 1987 **Turnover:** Up to £250,000
No.of Employees: 1 - 10 **Product Groups:** 66

Date of Accounts	Jul 11	Jul 10	Jul 09
Working Capital	-36	-17	1
Fixed Assets	6	8	10
Current Assets	12	26	26

B & H Precision Tooling Ltd
Unit 14 Glover Estate, Mossley, Ashton Under Lyne, OL5 9PY
Tel: 01457-833434 **Fax:** 01457-835685
E-mail: sales@bh-precision.co.uk
Website: http://www.bh-precision.co.uk
Directors: A. Dutton (MD), I. Bethel (Fin)
Turnover: £2m - £5m **No.of Employees:** 21 - 50 **Product Groups:** 39, 48

Barcrest Group
Margaret Street, Ashton Under Lyne, OL7 0QQ
Tel: 0161-344 1000 **Fax:** 0161-308 2580
E-mail: info@barcrestgroup.com
Website: http://www.barcrestgroup.com
Directors: R. Lamb (Dep Pres), R. White (Fin), J. Duck (Prop), A. Wagstaff (Pers)
Managers: D. Wolstenholme (Ops Mgr), A. Wagstaff (Personnel), R. Littlewood (Mktg Serv Mgr)
Ultimate Holding Company: INTERNATIONAL GAME TECHNOLOGY INC (USA)
Immediate Holding Company: BARCREST GROUP TECHNOLOGY LIMITED
Registration no: 03132958 **Date established:** 1995
Turnover: £10m - £20m **No.of Employees:** 1 - 10 **Product Groups:** 49

Date of Accounts	Sep 09	Sep 08	Sep 07
Sales Turnover	33m	32m	40m
Pre Tax Profit/Loss	2m	-2m	3m
Working Capital	20m	23m	24m
Fixed Assets	26m	23m	23m
Current Assets	35m	35m	40m
Current Liabilities	4m	4m	5m

Besseges Valves Tubes & Fittings Ltd
Jackson House Turner Lane, Ashton Under Lyne, OL6 8LP
Tel: 0161-343 2225 **Fax:** 0161-339 0307
E-mail: sales@besseges-vtf.co.uk
Website: http://www.besseges-vtf.co.uk
Bank(s): Yorkshire Bank PLC
Directors: M. Savarizadeh (Dir)
Ultimate Holding Company: BESSEGES VALVES, TUBES & FITTINGS (HOLDINGS) LIMITED
Immediate Holding Company: BESSEGES (VALVES, TUBES AND FITTINGS) LIMITED
Registration no: 02265990 **Date established:** 1988 **Turnover:** £1m - £2m
No.of Employees: 11 - 20 **Product Groups:** 36

Date of Accounts	Sep 11	Sep 10	Sep 09
Working Capital	315	422	386
Fixed Assets	271	56	71
Current Assets	1m	1m	956

Chicago Coating Co.
Manchester Road Mossley, Ashton Under Lyne, OL5 9QA
Tel: 01457-832046 **Fax:** 01457-838697
Directors: R. Howarth (Dir)
Immediate Holding Company: CALCAM INVESTMENTS LIMITED
Registration no: 07090212 **Date established:** 2009
Turnover: Up to £250,000 **No.of Employees:** 1 - 10 **Product Groups:** 32, 48

Date of Accounts	Nov 07	Nov 06	Nov 05
Working Capital	N/A	1	24
Fixed Assets	28	33	39
Current Assets	44	35	66
Current Liabilities	44	34	43

Clonshall Ltd T/A Young & Co. (t/a Young & Co.)
Whiteacre House 97 Whiteacre Road, Ashton Under Lyne, OL6 9PJ
Tel: 0161-339 9637 **Fax:** 0161-343 1036
E-mail: roy.young@clonshall.co.uk
Website: http://www.roofingnorthwest.co.uk
Bank(s): National Westminster

Directors: R. Young (MD)
Immediate Holding Company: CLONSHALL LIMITED
Registration no: 01301838 **VAT No.:** GB 151 3923 82
Date established: 1977 **Turnover:** £1m - £2m **No.of Employees:** 11 - 20
Product Groups: 52

Date of Accounts	Mar 12	Mar 11	Mar 10
Working Capital	45	36	66
Fixed Assets	131	146	165
Current Assets	185	158	220

Dukinfield Induction Heating Services Ltd
Induction House Mossley Road, Ashton Under Lyne, OL6 9BX
Tel: 0161-343 5711 **Fax:** 0161-343 5808
E-mail: enquiries@dukinfield-induction.co.uk
Website: http://www.dukinfield-induction.co.uk
Directors: A. Walker (Fin)
Immediate Holding Company: DUKINFIELD INDUCTION HEATING SERVICES LIMITED
Registration no: 02231974 **Date established:** 1988
No.of Employees: 1 - 10 **Product Groups:** 40, 42, 46

Date of Accounts	Feb 11	Feb 10	Feb 09
Working Capital	83	92	154
Fixed Assets	55	68	64
Current Assets	166	158	194

Frank Fletcher Engineering Ltd
Unit 13 -15 Squire Mill Micklehurst Road, Mossley, Ashton Under Lyne, OL5 9JL
Tel: 01457-839111
E-mail: frank@squiremill.fsnet.co.uk
Website: http://www.squiremill.fsnet.co.uk
Directors: F. Fletcher (Prop)
Immediate Holding Company: FRANK FLETCHER ENGINEERING LIMITED
Registration no: 04943420 **Date established:** 2003
No.of Employees: 1 - 10 **Product Groups:** 35

Date of Accounts	Oct 11	Oct 10	Oct 09
Working Capital	-27	-24	-24
Fixed Assets	41	32	26
Current Assets	29	23	18

Gauge Developments
Langham Street, Ashton Under Lyne, OL7 9AX
Tel: 0161-343 3020 **Fax:** 0161-343 2969
E-mail: nick.smith06@btconnect.com
Website: http://www.gaugedevelopments.co.uk
Bank(s): Lloyds TSB Bank plc
Directors: N. Smith (MD)
Managers: K. Smith (Chief Acct)
Immediate Holding Company: GAUGE DEVELOPMENTS LIMITED
Registration no: 02069605 **Date established:** 1986
Turnover: £500,000 - £1m **No.of Employees:** 11 - 20
Product Groups: 38, 39, 67, 85

Date of Accounts	Apr 12	Apr 11	Apr 10
Sales Turnover	928	754	623
Pre Tax Profit/Loss	40	-66	8
Working Capital	256	205	301
Fixed Assets	143	191	106
Current Assets	395	404	386
Current Liabilities	60	121	40

Gericke Ltd
Victoria House Cavendish Street, Ashton Under Lyne, OL6 7DJ
Tel: 0161-344 1140 **Fax:** 0161-308 3403
E-mail: info@gericke.net
Website: http://www.gericke.net
Bank(s): National Westminster Bank Plc
Directors: N. Gooder (Co Sec), J. Obank (Fin), P. Brickenden (MD)
Managers: P. Brook (Sales Prom Mgr), J. Kinghorne (Works Gen Mgr)
Ultimate Holding Company: GERICKE HOLDING AG (SWITZERLAND)
Immediate Holding Company: GERICKE LIMITED
Registration no: 01015641 **VAT No.:** GB 146 7725 43
Date established: 1971 **Turnover:** £2m - £5m **No.of Employees:** 21 - 50
Product Groups: 38, 40, 41, 42, 45

Date of Accounts	Dec 11	Dec 10	Dec 09
Working Capital	359	123	471
Fixed Assets	67	108	156
Current Assets	2m	2m	2m

H M B Fabrication Services
Kayley Industrial Estate Richmond Street, Ashton Under Lyne, OL7 0AU
Tel: 0161-330 1546
E-mail: info@hmbfabrications.co.uk
Website: http://www.hmbfabrications.co.uk
Directors: A. Bartolo (Dir)
Immediate Holding Company: HMB FABRICATIONS SERVICES LIMITED
Registration no: 04341691 **Date established:** 2001
Turnover: £500,000 - £1m **No.of Employees:** 1 - 10 **Product Groups:** 35

Date of Accounts	Mar 11	Mar 10	Mar 09
Sales Turnover	587	342	450
Pre Tax Profit/Loss	133	10	61
Working Capital	42	-11	12
Fixed Assets	9	9	12
Current Assets	155	102	91
Current Liabilities	67	44	35

Hawke International
Oxford Street West, Ashton Under Lyne, OL7 0NA
Tel: 0161-830 6698 **Fax:** 0161-830 6648
E-mail: mconnolly@ehawke.com
Website: http://www.ehawke.com
Bank(s): National Westminster Bank Plc
Managers: M. Connolly
Ultimate Holding Company: HUBBELL HOLDINGS LIMITED
Immediate Holding Company: HAWKE CABLE GLANDS LIMITED
Registration no: 05879163 **VAT No.:** GB 792 4212 28
Date established: 2006 **Turnover:** £10m - £20m
No.of Employees: 101 - 250 **Product Groups:** 30, 35, 37, 40

High Society
23 Market Avenue, Ashton Under Lyne, OL6 6AL
Tel: 0161-339 0886
Directors: M. Azhar (MD)
Immediate Holding Company: HIGH SOCIETY LIMITED
Registration no: 01989733 **Date established:** 1986
Turnover: Up to £250,000 **No.of Employees:** 1 - 10 **Product Groups:** 63

Date of Accounts	May 11	May 10	May 09
Sales Turnover	5	9	9
Pre Tax Profit/Loss	-3	-4	-6
Working Capital	-137	-134	-130
Fixed Assets	1	2	2
Current Assets	26	27	26
Current Liabilities	36	36	35

Hill Biscuits Ltd
Smith Street, Ashton Under Lyne, OL7 0DB
Tel: 0161-330 3617 **Fax:** 0161-343 2108
E-mail: info@hillbiscuits.com
Website: http://www.hillbiscuits.com
Bank(s): Co-operative Bank
Directors: B. O'Donnell (Fin), S. Weatherby (MD)
Managers: D. Ravens Croft, P. Bennett (Buyer)
Immediate Holding Company: HILL BISCUITS LIMITED
Registration no: 00088544 **VAT No.:** GB 458 4249 21
Date established: 2006 **Turnover:** £10m - £20m
No.of Employees: 251 - 500 **Product Groups:** 20

Date of Accounts	Dec 11	Dec 10	Dec 09
Sales Turnover	13m	13m	13m
Pre Tax Profit/Loss	39	419	639
Working Capital	534	586	456
Fixed Assets	2m	2m	2m
Current Assets	3m	3m	3m
Current Liabilities	261	455	582

HSS Lift & Shift
Manchester Road, Ashton Under Lyne, OL7 0DA
Tel: 0161-339 0845 **Fax:** 0161-339 7356
Website: http://www.hss.com
Managers: P. Hargreaves (District Mgr)
Date established: 1996 **No.of Employees:** 1 - 10 **Product Groups:** 35, 39, 45

Impregnation Services Ltd
1 Cowhill Lane Industrial Estate Cowhill Lane, Ashton Under Lyne, OL6 6HH
Tel: 0161-344 1004 **Fax:** 0161-344 2428
E-mail: enquiries@impregnation.co.uk
Website: http://www.impregnation.co.uk
Directors: R. Benson (Fin), J. Benson (MD)
Immediate Holding Company: IMPREGNATION SERVICES LIMITED
Registration no: 00810867 **Date established:** 1964
Turnover: Up to £250,000 **No.of Employees:** 1 - 10 **Product Groups:** 47, 48

Date of Accounts	Aug 11	Aug 10	Aug 09
Working Capital	33	10	34
Fixed Assets	105	123	87
Current Assets	79	68	64

Itec Power Services Ltd
Itec House 2 Berkeley Street, Ashton Under Lyne, OL6 7DT
Tel: 0161-343 1595 **Fax:** 0161-343 2341
E-mail: sales@itecpower.co.uk
Website: http://www.itecpower.co.uk
Directors: J. Matthews (Chief Op Offcr)
Immediate Holding Company: ITEC POWER SERVICES LIMITED
Registration no: 02236627 **VAT No.:** GB 508 1158 66
Date established: 1988 **Turnover:** £1m - £2m **No.of Employees:** 1 - 10
Product Groups: 25, 29, 30, 35, 37, 45

Date of Accounts	Mar 11	Mar 10	Mar 09
Working Capital	38	2	39
Fixed Assets	73	68	45
Current Assets	389	367	349

K O Fabrication
Unit 9 Tramway Road, Ashton Under Lyne, OL6 9AN
Tel: 0161-339 0619 **Fax:** 0161-330 1435
Directors: K. Oldham (Prop)
Date established: 1993 **No.of Employees:** 1 - 10 **Product Groups:** 35

Lamplighter Plastic Mouldings Ltd
Unit L Mount Pleasant Street, Ashton Under Lyne, OL6 9HX
Tel: 0161-343 1113 **Fax:** 0161-339 5557
E-mail: mprady@lamplighterproducts.co.uk
Website: http://www.lamplighterproducts.co.uk
Directors: M. Prady (Prop), M. Prady (Dir)
Immediate Holding Company: LAMPLIGHTER PLASTIC MOULDINGS LIMITED
Registration no: 04263789 **VAT No.:** GB 847 1189 09
Date established: 2001 **Turnover:** £500,000 - £1m
No.of Employees: 1 - 10 **Product Groups:** 30, 37, 48, 49, 66

Date of Accounts	Sep 11	Sep 10	Sep 09
Working Capital	70	49	33
Fixed Assets	56	53	65
Current Assets	186	126	84

Lokfast Special Fasteners Ltd
Audley Street Works Audley Street, Mossley, Ashton Under Lyne, OL5 9HW
Tel: 01457-837514 **Fax:** 01457-832213
E-mail: john@lokfast.com
Website: http://www.lockfast.com
Directors: J. Warham (Dir)
Immediate Holding Company: LOKFAST LIMITED
Registration no: 01121119 **VAT No.:** GB 149 2394 47
Date established: 1973 **Turnover:** £500,000 - £1m
No.of Employees: 1 - 10 **Product Groups:** 35, 66

Date of Accounts	Sep 11	Sep 10	Sep 09
Working Capital	38	70	98
Fixed Assets	365	367	360
Current Assets	119	143	214

Manchester Electro Plating Ltd
Weir Mill Manchester Road, Mossley, Ashton Under Lyne, OL5 9QA
Tel: 01457-832776 **Fax:** 01457-833318
E-mail: mepworks@aol.com
Bank(s): HSBC Bank plc
Directors: J. Paul (MD)
Immediate Holding Company: MANCHESTER ELECTROPLATING LTD
Registration no: 03060447 **VAT No.:** GB 588 9976 33
Date established: 1995 **Turnover:** £500,000 - £1m
No.of Employees: 21 - 50 **Product Groups:** 48

Date of Accounts	Oct 11	Oct 10	Oct 09
Working Capital	88	63	57
Fixed Assets	233	230	235
Current Assets	200	225	198

William May Ltd
Cavendish Street, Ashton Under Lyne, OL6 7QW
Tel: 0161-330 3838 **Fax:** 0161-339 1097
E-mail: info@william-may.com
Website: http://www.william-may.com
Directors: J. May (I.T. Dir)
Immediate Holding Company: WILLIAM MAY (ASHTON) LIMITED
Registration no: 00665712 **VAT No.:** GB 146 2333 85
Date established: 1960 **Turnover:** £500,000 - £1m
No.of Employees: 1 - 10 **Product Groups:** 40, 52

Date of Accounts	Sep 11	Sep 10	Sep 09
Working Capital	138	154	179
Fixed Assets	241	246	252
Current Assets	178	199	213

Mossley Sheet Metal Co. Ltd
Squire Mill Micklehurst Road, Mossley, Ashton Under Lyne, OL5 9JL
Tel: 01457-832277 **Fax:** 01457-837030
E-mail: admin@mossleysheetmetal.co.uk
Website: http://www.mossleysheetmetal.co.uk
Directors: W. Jones (MD), F. Jones (Fin)
Immediate Holding Company: MOSSLEY SHEET METAL COMPANY LIMITED
Registration no: 00455695 **VAT No.:** GB 388 4023 34
Date established: 1948 **Turnover:** £500,000 - £1m
No.of Employees: 1 - 10 **Product Groups:** 35, 46, 48, 66, 67, 84

Date of Accounts	Jun 11	Jun 10	Jun 09
Working Capital	-72	-48	-23
Fixed Assets	341	355	335
Current Assets	162	187	125

Olympia Furniture Ltd
Whitelands Road, Ashton Under Lyne, OL6 6UX
Tel: 0161-331 4000 **Fax:** 0161-331 4029
E-mail: customer.service@olympia-furniture.co.uk
Website: http://www.olympia-furniture.co.uk
Bank(s): National Westminster Bank Plc
Directors: S. Carroll (Dir), T. Barrett (Dir)
Managers: T. Clarke (Personnel), T. Sedgwick (Sales Prom Mgr), G. Kalvert (Chief Buyer)
Ultimate Holding Company: SHOO 536 LIMITED
Immediate Holding Company: OLYMPIA FURNITURE LIMITED
Registration no: 02477674 **VAT No.:** GB 451 5970 39
Date established: 1990 **Turnover:** £20m - £50m
No.of Employees: 251 - 500 **Product Groups:** 26

Date of Accounts	Dec 10	Dec 09	Dec 08
Sales Turnover	22m	24m	22m
Pre Tax Profit/Loss	108	-138	-351
Working Capital	731	861	1m
Fixed Assets	4m	4m	4m
Current Assets	5m	6m	5m
Current Liabilities	1m	804	624

Ornamental Ironwork
6 Waggon Road Mossley, Ashton Under Lyne, OL5 9HL
Tel: 01457-832763 **Fax:** 01457-832763
E-mail: sales@forgework-bridlington.co.uk
Website: http://www.forgework-bridlington.co.uk
Directors: R. Lord (Prop)
Date established: 1969 **No.of Employees:** 1 - 10 **Product Groups:** 26, 35

P N P Motion Controls
Manchester Road Mossley, Ashton Under Lyne, OL5 9AY
Tel: 01457-831110
Website: http://www.p-n-p.co.uk
Directors: N. Hickling (Dir)
Registration no: 05092999 **Date established:** 2004
No.of Employees: 1 - 10 **Product Groups:** 37, 84, 86

Promota Logo
25 Stockport Road, Ashton Under Lyne, OL7 0LA
Tel: 0161-331 9777 **Fax:** 0161-331 9779
E-mail: info@promotalogo.co.uk
Website: http://www.promotalogo.co.uk
Directors: S. de Burgh (Mkt Research), M. Sharp (Ptnr)
Date established: 2005 **No.of Employees:** 1 - 10 **Product Groups:** 24, 49

Rael Brook Group Ltd
Rael Brook House Grosvenor Street, Ashton Under Lyne, OL7 0RE
Tel: 0161-344 5618 **Fax:** 0161-308 5060
E-mail: b.deas@raelbrookshirts.com
Website: http://www.raelbrookshirts.com
Directors: B. Deas (Dir)
Managers: J. Farnworth (Comptroller)
Ultimate Holding Company: RAEL BROOK (GROUP) LIMITED
Immediate Holding Company: RAEL BROOK (SHIRTS) LIMITED
Registration no: 02535898 **Date established:** 1990 **Turnover:** £5m - £10m
No.of Employees: 21 - 50 **Product Groups:** 24

Revelation & Liking Displays
Grosvenor Mill Business Centre Grosvenor Street, Ashton Under Lyne, OL7 0RG
Tel: 0161-330 0033 **Fax:** 0161- 3302843
Directors: R. Revell (Prop)
Immediate Holding Company: NHOM LTD
Date established: 1973 **No.of Employees:** 1 - 10 **Product Groups:** 37, 67

Date of Accounts	Mar 12	Mar 11	Mar 10
Working Capital	35	655	259
Fixed Assets	999	399	944
Current Assets	39	664	266

Ryecroft Engineering Co. Ltd
Ryecroft Street, Ashton Under Lyne, OL7 0BS
Tel: 0161-330 3623 **Fax:** 0161-343 2590
E-mail: enquiries@ryecroft.co.uk
Website: http://www.ryecroft.co.uk
Bank(s): National Westminster
Directors: A. Barber (MD)
Managers: G. Broadbent (Purch Mgr), A. Lyon (Sales Admin)
Immediate Holding Company: RYECROFT ENGINEERING COMPANY LIMITED
Registration no: 00371261 **VAT No.:** 146 0077 87 **Date established:** 1941
No.of Employees: 21 - 50 **Product Groups:** 48

Date of Accounts	Feb 11	Feb 10	Feb 09
Working Capital	-181	-126	-89
Fixed Assets	448	473	501
Current Assets	256	214	222

Scappa UK Ltd
Manchester Road, Ashton Under Lyne, OL7 0ED
Tel: 01582-478111 **Fax:** 01582-471085
E-mail: carole.price@scapatapes.com
Website: http://www.scappa.com

see next page

Scappa UK Ltd - Cont'd

Directors: J. McTaggert (Prop)
Ultimate Holding Company: SCAPA GROUP PUBLIC LIMITED COMPANY
Immediate Holding Company: PORRITTS & SPENCER LIMITED
Registration no: 03261510 **Date established:** 2014
Turnover: £125m - £250m **No.of Employees:** 1 - 10 **Product Groups:** 27, 30, 32

Date of Accounts	Mar 12	Mar 11	Mar 10
Pre Tax Profit/Loss	58	52	58
Working Capital	2m	2m	2m
Current Assets	2m	2m	2m
Current Liabilities	N/A	14	16

J Speake & Son

Woodend Mill Manchester Road, Mossley, Ashton Under Lyne, OL5 9AT
Tel: 01457-838262 **Fax:** 01457-838199
Directors: T. Speake (Ptnr)
Date established: 1989 **No.of Employees:** 1 - 10 **Product Groups:** 46, 48

Speedy Lifting Ltd

1 Albion Trading Estate Mossley Road, Ashton Under Lyne, OL6 6NQ
Tel: 0161-344 0182 **Fax:** 0161-330 3830
Website: http://www.speedyservices.com
Managers: B. Thomas (Mgr)
Ultimate Holding Company: SPEEDY HIRE PLC
Immediate Holding Company: SPEEDY LIFTING LIMITED
Registration no: 04529136 **Date established:** 2002
No.of Employees: 1 - 10 **Product Groups:** 35, 39, 45

Date of Accounts	Mar 12	Mar 11	Mar 10
Sales Turnover	N/A	N/A	21m
Pre Tax Profit/Loss	N/A	N/A	4m
Working Capital	20m	20m	20m
Current Assets	20m	20m	21m

P J Spencer Ltd

Langham House Langham Street, Ashton Under Lyne, OL7 9EA
Tel: 0161-343 1321 **Fax:** 0161-343 1856
E-mail: admin@pjspencerltd.co.uk
Directors: C. Spencer (MD)
Immediate Holding Company: P.J. SPENCER LIMITED
Registration no: 01432664 **Date established:** 1979 **Turnover:** £1m - £2m
No.of Employees: 1 - 10 **Product Groups:** 52

Date of Accounts	Sep 11	Sep 10	Sep 09
Working Capital	383	520	477
Fixed Assets	80	128	152
Current Assets	955	1m	2m

Steeladeal

70 Knowle Avenue, Ashton Under Lyne, OL7 9HW
Tel: 0161-331 9111 **Fax:** 0161-339 3453
E-mail: info@steeladeal.co.uk
Website: http://www.steeladeal.co.uk
Directors: K. Davenport (Ptnr)
Date established: 2003 **No.of Employees:** 1 - 10 **Product Groups:** 35

Tameside Libraries Information Service

Old Street, Ashton Under Lyne, OL6 7SG
Tel: 0161-342 2031 **Fax:** 0161-330 4762
E-mail: info@tameside.gov.uk
Website: http://www.tameside.gov.uk/libraries
Managers: K. Heathcote
Product Groups: 28, 44, 80, 81, 82, 89

Tameside Scale Services Ltd

Winton Street, Ashton Under Lyne, OL6 8NL
Tel: 0161-339 6501 **Fax:** 0161-339 6501
Directors: D. Jones (Dir)
Immediate Holding Company: TAMESIDE SCALE SERVICES LIMITED
Registration no: 07333128 **Date established:** 2010
No.of Employees: 1 - 10 **Product Groups:** 38, 42

Date of Accounts	Dec 11
Working Capital	-86
Fixed Assets	141
Current Assets	144

Taylors

150 Turner Lane, Ashton Under Lyne, OL6 8SZ
Tel: 0161-330 1495 **Fax:** 0161-339 9477
Directors: T. Talyor (Prop)
Managers: T. Taylour (Mgr)
No.of Employees: 1 - 10 **Product Groups:** 26, 32, 40, 62, 67

Tellure Rota

PO Box 29, Ashton Under Lyne, OL5 9NB
Tel: 01457-832556 **Fax:** 01457-832472
E-mail: sales@aut.co.uk
Website: http://www.aut.co.uk
Directors: R. Glover (MD)
Ultimate Holding Company: TELLURE ROTA (ITALY)
Immediate Holding Company: CASTORS DIRECT LIMITED
Registration no: 03416647 **Date established:** 1997
Turnover: £10m - £20m **No.of Employees:** 11 - 20 **Product Groups:** 29, 39, 66

Victoria Fan & Engineering Supplies Ltd

Audley Street Works Audley Street, Mossley, Ashton Under Lyne, OL5 9HW
Tel: 01457-835391 **Fax:** 01457-833378
E-mail: sales@victoriafans.co.uk
Website: http://www.victoriafans.co.uk
Directors: G. Garside (Dir)
Immediate Holding Company: VICTORIA FANS LIMITED
Registration no: 01808036 **VAT No.:** 408 7363 43 **Date established:** 1984
Turnover: £1m - £2m **No.of Employees:** 1 - 10 **Product Groups:** 40

Date of Accounts	Mar 12	Mar 11	Mar 10
Working Capital	82	74	75
Fixed Assets	17	20	24
Current Assets	401	343	364

Whitecroft Lighting Ltd

Burlington Street, Ashton Under Lyne, OL7 0AX
Tel: 08705-087087 **Fax:** 08705-084210
E-mail: info@whitecroftlight.com
Website: http://www.whitecroftlighting.com
Directors: M. Lester (Sales)
Managers: J. Farrow, P. Roden (Purch Mgr), T. Humphries (Tech Serv Mgr)
Ultimate Holding Company: FAGERHULT AB (SWEDEN)
Immediate Holding Company: WHITECROFT LIGHTING HOLDINGS LIMITED
Registration no: 03848868 **Date established:** 1999
Turnover: £20m - £50m **No.of Employees:** 101 - 250 **Product Groups:** 37

Date of Accounts	Dec 11	Dec 10	Dec 09
Pre Tax Profit/Loss	2m	4m	3m
Working Capital	2m	2m	2m
Fixed Assets	4m	4m	4m
Current Assets	2m	2m	2m

Wolf Filtration Ltd

81 Burlington Street, Ashton Under Lyne, OL6 7HJ
Tel: 0161-339 1604 **Fax:** 0161-343 1434
E-mail: sales@wolffiltration.co.uk
Website: http://www.wolffiltration.co.uk
Bank(s): The Royal Bank of Scotland
Directors: D. Oliver (MD)
Immediate Holding Company: WOLF FILTRATION LIMITED
Registration no: 02587335 **VAT No.:** GB 408 7890 20
Date established: 1991 **Turnover:** £1m - £2m **No.of Employees:** 21 - 50
Product Groups: 33, 34, 35, 37, 41, 42

Date of Accounts	Apr 12	Apr 11	Apr 10
Working Capital	185	194	161
Fixed Assets	96	103	111
Current Assets	292	286	257

Bacup

Alpha Rework & Warehousing

Atherton Holme Mill Railway Street, Bacup, OL13 0UF
Tel: 01706-871424 **Fax:** 01706-875007
E-mail: info@alpharework.co.uk
Website: http://www.alpharework.co.uk
Managers: J. Hodgson (Mgr), J. Hodgson (Mgr), K. Marsh (Sales Prom Mgr)
Ultimate Holding Company: TRAINTRACK LIMITED
Immediate Holding Company: ALPHA REWORK AND WAREHOUSING LIMITED
Registration no: 07443054 **Date established:** 2010
Turnover: £500,000 - £1m **No.of Employees:** 21 - 50 **Product Groups:** 77

Date of Accounts	Dec 11
Working Capital	10
Current Assets	114

John Ashworth & Partners Ltd

Park Road Business Centre, Bacup, OL13 0BW
Tel: 01706-879544 **Fax:** 01706-879481
E-mail: johnashworth.paint@virgin.net
Website: http://www.johnashworthltd.co.uk
Directors: J. Ashworth (MD)
Immediate Holding Company: JOHN ASHWORTH & PARTNERS LIMITED
Registration no: 04140217 **Date established:** 2001
Turnover: Up to £250,000 **No.of Employees:** 1 - 10 **Product Groups:** 85

Date of Accounts	Mar 11	Mar 10	Mar 09
Working Capital	332	288	256
Fixed Assets	22	25	28
Current Assets	347	300	283

Bacup Shoe Co. Ltd

Atherton Holme Mill Railway Street, Bacup, OL13 0UF
Tel: 01706-873304 **Fax:** 01706-873216
E-mail: stevensmith@bacupshoe.co.uk
Website: http://www.bacupshoe.co.uk
Bank(s): Barclays, Rawtenstall
Directors: C. Davy (Fin), S. Smith (Dir)
Managers: M. Ottley (Tech Serv Mgr)
Ultimate Holding Company: TRAINTRACK LIMITED
Immediate Holding Company: BACUP SHOE COMPANY LIMITED(THE)
Registration no: 00236042 **VAT No.:** GB 145 0551 91
Date established: 2029 **Turnover:** £10m - £20m
No.of Employees: 51 - 100 **Product Groups:** 22

Date of Accounts	Dec 11	Dec 10	Dec 09
Sales Turnover	8m	12m	11m
Pre Tax Profit/Loss	-100	130	-14
Working Capital	471	194	135
Fixed Assets	220	232	200
Current Assets	3m	4m	6m
Current Liabilities	304	396	628

Courtesy Shoes Ltd

Park Road Industrial Estate, Bacup, OL13 0BW
Tel: 01706-874752 **Fax:** 01706-874827
E-mail: brian@courtesy.co.uk
Website: http://www.wynsors.com
Directors: M. Richardson (MD), M. Kelly (Purch)
Managers: L. Houghton (Tech Serv Mgr)
Ultimate Holding Company: E.SUTTON & SON LIMITED
Immediate Holding Company: COURTESY SHOES LIMITED
Registration no: 00567238 **Date established:** 1956
Turnover: £20m - £50m **No.of Employees:** 101 - 250
Product Groups: 61, 63

Date of Accounts	Feb 08	Feb 11	Feb 10
Sales Turnover	28m	34m	35m
Pre Tax Profit/Loss	224	402	401
Working Capital	-191	2m	1m
Fixed Assets	7m	5m	5m
Current Assets	4m	6m	6m
Current Liabilities	2m	3m	3m

Glen Castings Ltd

Meadows Mill Burnley Road, Bacup, OL13 8BZ
Tel: 01706-873967 **Fax:** 01706-879234
E-mail: enquiries@glencastings.co.uk
Website: http://www.glencastings.co.uk
Directors: A. Butterworth (MD)
Ultimate Holding Company: GLEN CASTINGS HOLDINGS LIMITED
Immediate Holding Company: GLEN CASTINGS LIMITED
Registration no: 01083868 **VAT No.:** GB 146 5568 43
Date established: 1972 **Turnover:** £1m - £2m **No.of Employees:** 1 - 10
Product Groups: 34, 35, 45

Date of Accounts	Aug 11	Aug 10	Aug 09
Working Capital	39	60	75
Fixed Assets	57	63	67
Current Assets	232	312	326

Lancashire Sock Manufacturing Co.

Britannia Mill New Line, Bacup, OL13 9RZ
Tel: 01706-873188 **Fax:** 01706-879007
E-mail: sales@lancashiresock.com
Website: http://www.lancashiresock.com
Bank(s): Barclays
Directors: G. Ormerod (MD), G. Hardman (Fin)
Immediate Holding Company: LANCASHIRE SOCK MANUFACTURING COMPANY
Registration no: 00525682 **Date established:** 1953 **Turnover:** £2m - £5m
No.of Employees: 21 - 50 **Product Groups:** 22, 23, 24, 29

John Maden & Sons Ltd

Market Street, Bacup, OL13 0AU
Tel: 01706-873544 **Fax:** 01706-879130
E-mail: info@johnmaden.com
Directors: M. Stocks (MD)
Immediate Holding Company: JOHN MADEN & SON,LIMITED
Registration no: 00043234 **Date established:** 1995
Turnover: £500,000 - £1m **No.of Employees:** 1 - 10 **Product Groups:** 24

Date of Accounts	Oct 11	Oct 10	Oct 09
Working Capital	24	31	14
Fixed Assets	87	88	88
Current Assets	48	44	59

Spencer-Fire & Security Ltd

588a Newchurch Road, Bacup, OL13 0NH
Tel: 0845-4081694
E-mail: info@spencerfire.co.uk
Website: http://www.spencerfire.co.uk
No.of Employees: 1 - 10 **Product Groups:** 40, 54, 84

E Sutton & Son Ltd

Riverside, Bacup, OL13 0DT
Tel: 01706-874961 **Fax:** 01706-879268
E-mail: info@esutton.co.uk
Website: http://www.esutton.co.uk
Bank(s): National Westminster Bank Plc
Directors: B. Terry (Ch)
Managers: B. Miles, A. Ogorman (Personnel)
Immediate Holding Company: E.SUTTON & SON LIMITED
Registration no: 00395322 **VAT No.:** GB 145 0705 90
Date established: 1945 **Turnover:** £20m - £50m
No.of Employees: 51 - 100 **Product Groups:** 22

Date of Accounts	Feb 08	Feb 11	Feb 10
Sales Turnover	31m	38m	37m
Pre Tax Profit/Loss	647	306	430
Working Capital	6m	8m	8m
Fixed Assets	7m	5m	6m
Current Assets	10m	13m	13m
Current Liabilities	3m	4m	4m

Union Special (UK) Limited

Newline industrial Estate, Bacup, OL13 9RW
Tel: 0844-8542968 **Fax:** 0844-8542969
E-mail: sales@unionspecial.co.uk
Website: http://www.unionspecial.co.uk
Directors: P. Rodgers (Sales)
Registration no: 07439203 **Date established:** 1990 **Turnover:** £2m - £5m
No.of Employees: 21 - 50 **Product Groups:** 43

West Pennine Storage Equipment Ltd

West Pennine Business Park Burnley Road, Bacup, OL13 8PJ
Tel: 01706-875500 **Fax:** 01706-875600
E-mail: westpenninesd@aol.com
Website: http://www.westpenninesd.co.uk
Directors: A. Reed (MD)
Immediate Holding Company: WEST PENNINE STORAGE EQUIPMENT LIMITED
Registration no: 02248637 **VAT No.:** GB 498 0155 22
Date established: 1988 **Turnover:** £1m - £2m **No.of Employees:** 1 - 10
Product Groups: 26, 35, 45

Date of Accounts	Nov 11	Nov 10	Nov 09
Working Capital	20	-17	-41
Fixed Assets	18	41	50
Current Assets	198	280	102

Barnoldswick

Basically Doors

Unit 1 Rookery Road, Barnoldswick, BB18 6YH
Tel: 01282-816434 **Fax:** 01200-445576
E-mail: sales@basicallydoors.co.uk
Website: http://www.basicallydoors.co.uk
Directors: J. Ennis (Prop)
Immediate Holding Company: BASICALLY DOORS LTD
Registration no: 06961611 **Date established:** 2009
Turnover: Up to £250,000 **No.of Employees:** 1 - 10 **Product Groups:** 26

Carlson Ltd

The Butts Mill, Barnoldswick, BB18 5HP
Tel: 01282-811000 **Fax:** 01282-811001
E-mail: sales@carlson.co.uk
Website: http://www.carlson.co.uk
Bank(s): H S B C, Market St, Bradford
Directors: B. Gabbett (MD), R. Bikley (Fin)
Managers: S. Driver (Sales Prom Mgr)
Immediate Holding Company: CARLSON LTD
Registration no: 06410385 **VAT No.:** GB 508 2132 79
Date established: 2007 **Turnover:** £5m - £10m **No.of Employees:** 21 - 50
Product Groups: 27, 32, 33, 35, 40, 41, 42, 67

Date of Accounts	Dec 08
Working Capital	484
Fixed Assets	54
Current Assets	685

Ceratex Engineering Ltd

Church Lane Works Church Lane, Kelbrook, Barnoldswick, BB18 6UF
Tel: 01282-842900 **Fax:** 01282-844093
E-mail: mark.redwood@ceratex.co.uk
Website: http://www.ceratex.co.uk
Directors: M. Redwood (MD), R. Redwood (Fin)
Immediate Holding Company: CERATEX ENGINEERING LIMITED
Registration no: 03102060 **Date established:** 1995 **Turnover:** £1m - £2m
No.of Employees: 11 - 20 **Product Groups:** 33, 42, 46, 48

Date of Accounts	Jun 11	Jun 10	Jun 09
Working Capital	-223	353	208
Fixed Assets	540	564	536
Current Assets	565	556	438
Current Liabilities	N/A	91	144

Custom Colour Anodising

Unit 6 Ouzledale Business Park Long Ing Lane, Barnoldswick, BB18 6BJ
Tel: 01282-816633
E-mail: m.duerden@btinternet.com
Website: http://www.customcolouranodising.co.uk
Directors: M. Duerden (Prop)
Immediate Holding Company: CUSTOM COLOUR ANODISING LIMITED
Registration no: 04538453 **Date established:** 2002
No.of Employees: 1 - 10 **Product Groups:** 46, 48

Date of Accounts	Feb 11	Feb 10	Feb 09
Working Capital	-24	-22	-6
Fixed Assets	47	48	39
Current Assets	74	75	76

D & A Metalworks

Unit 4 Ouzledale Buiness Park, Barnoldswick, BB18 6BN
Tel: 01282-814330
Managers: D. Metcalfe (Mgr)
Date established: 2005 **No.of Employees:** 1 - 10 **Product Groups:** 35

Fernbank Shed Company Ltd

Fernbank Shed, Barnoldswick, BB18 5UY
Tel: 01282-813395 **Fax:** 01282-813172
Directors: I. Gill (Fin), I. Gill (Co Sec), J. Clark (Dir), J. Clark (MD)
Immediate Holding Company: FERNBANK SHED COMPANY,LIMITED
Registration no: 00131881 **VAT No.:** GB 179 7154 21
Date established: 1913 **Turnover:** Up to £250,000
No.of Employees: 1 - 10 **Product Groups:** 23

Date of Accounts	Mar 08
Working Capital	-4
Fixed Assets	155
Current Assets	31
Current Liabilities	36
Total Share Capital	24

M C Services

21a New Road Earby, Barnoldswick, BB18 6UY
Tel: 01282-844801 **Fax:** 01282-843159
E-mail: m.c_services@btconnect.com
Website: http://www.mcsweldfab.co.uk
Directors: M. Cowgill (Prop)
Date established: 2001 **No.of Employees:** 1 - 10 **Product Groups:** 35

R Soper Ltd

Crownest Mill Skipton Road, Barnoldswick, BB18 5RH
Tel: 01282-666000 **Fax:** 01282-666002
E-mail: sfinlay@alberthartley.co.uk
Website: http://www.sandown-bourne.co.uk
Bank(s): Barclays
Directors: C. Soper (MD)
Managers: A. Heaton
Ultimate Holding Company: R. SOPER LIMITED
Immediate Holding Company: ALBERT HARTLEY LIMITED
Registration no: 02944483 **Date established:** 1994
Turnover: £10m - £20m **No.of Employees:** 101 - 250
Product Groups: 23, 24

Wardle Storeys Earby Ltd

Grove Mill Grove Street Earby, Earby, Barnoldswick, BB18 6UT
Tel: 01282-842511 **Fax:** 01282-843170
E-mail: sales@wardlestoreys.com
Website: http://www.wardlestoreys.com
Directors: S. Quinn (Fin), A. Hall (MD)
Managers: I. Bolter (Purch Mgr), L. Willighan (Personnel)
Ultimate Holding Company: GWECO 478 LIMITED
Immediate Holding Company: WARDLE STOREYS (EARBY) LIMITED
Registration no: 04710820 **VAT No.:** GB 159 6596 08
Date established: 2003 **Turnover:** £20m - £50m
No.of Employees: 101 - 250 **Product Groups:** 30

Date of Accounts	Dec 11	Aug 10	Aug 09
Sales Turnover	38m	25m	18m
Pre Tax Profit/Loss	1m	2m	-3m
Working Capital	6m	5m	2m
Fixed Assets	2m	2m	3m
Current Assets	15m	14m	11m
Current Liabilities	4m	895	1m

Blackburn

A & B Catering

55-57 Devonport Road, Blackburn, BB2 1HW
Tel: 01254-671729 **Fax:** 01254-274871
E-mail: ibrar-hussain@ukonline.co.uk
Directors: I. Hussain (Prop)
No.of Employees: 1 - 10 **Product Groups:** 02, 20, 27, 30, 32, 35, 40, 61, 62

A Z Diesel Specialist

Throstle Street, Blackburn, BB2 1TQ
Tel: 01254-52544 **Fax:** 01254-52544
Directors: Z. Ulhaq (Prop)
Date established: 1995 **No.of Employees:** 11 - 20 **Product Groups:** 40

Able2

Moorgate Street, Blackburn, BB2 4PB
Tel: 01254-619000 **Fax:** 01254-619001
E-mail: enquiries@able2.eu
Website: http://www.able2.eu
Directors: D. Baxendale (Fin), M. Daij (MD)
Managers: V. Turner (Sales Admin), S. Hefford (Tech Serv Mgr)
Ultimate Holding Company: ADL HOLDINGS LIMITED
Immediate Holding Company: ABLE2 UK LIMITED
Registration no: 04882353 **Date established:** 2003 **Turnover:** £5m - £10m
No.of Employees: 21 - 50 **Product Groups:** 38

Date of Accounts	Aug 11	Aug 10	Aug 09
Sales Turnover	N/A	N/A	3m
Pre Tax Profit/Loss	N/A	N/A	-370
Working Capital	1m	1m	1m
Fixed Assets	2m	2m	2m
Current Assets	4m	4m	4m
Current Liabilities	N/A	N/A	780

Acme

H & H House Philips Road, Whitebirk Industrial Estate, Blackburn, BB1 5RL
Tel: 01254-277999 **Fax:** 01254-277988
E-mail: sales@acmerefrigeration.co.uk
Website: http://www.acmerefrigeration.co.uk
Bank(s): Barclays
Directors: S. Cooke (Fin)
Managers: P. Cheshire (Sales Admin), M. Wallis (Sales Prom Mgr), P. Wright (Personnel), S. Powderley (Purch Mgr), D. Finch, D. Finch (I.T. Exec), S. Eastham (Chief Acct), G. Morris (Sales & Mktg Mg)
Ultimate Holding Company: ROBERT STEPHEN HOLDINGS LTD
Immediate Holding Company: PENTLAND GROUP P.L.C.
Registration no: 00863661 **VAT No.:** GB 174 3835 47
Turnover: £5m - £10m **No.of Employees:** 51 - 100 **Product Groups:** 40, 63

Affordable Bar & Catering

Lomax Street Great Harwood, Blackburn, BB6 7DJ
Tel: 01254-888108 **Fax:** 01254-264679
E-mail: andy@abcdirect2u.co.uk
Website: http://www.abcdirect2u.co.uk
Managers: A. Sherrington (Mgr)
Immediate Holding Company: AFFORDABLE BAR & CATERING EQUIPMENT DIRECT LTD
Registration no: 04659985 **Date established:** 2003
No.of Employees: 1 - 10 **Product Groups:** 40, 67

Date of Accounts	Apr 11	Apr 10	Apr 09
Working Capital	81	45	-3
Fixed Assets	15	25	11
Current Assets	157	122	87
Current Liabilities	21	N/A	N/A

Akzo Nobel Decorative Coatings Ltd

Hollins Road, Blackburn, BB1 0BG
Tel: 01254-704951 **Fax:** 01254-774414
Website: http://www.akzonobel.com
Directors: J. Devitt (Dir), E. Mulholland (Dir), C. Bolland (Dir), R. Burton (Sales & Mktg), J. Branton (MD)
Managers: A. Biddle (Mgr), G. Branton
Ultimate Holding Company: FP003807
Immediate Holding Company: AKZO NOBEL DECORATIVE COATINGS LIMITED
Registration no: 00139914 **Date established:** 1915
Turnover: £125m - £250m **No.of Employees:** 1 - 10 **Product Groups:** 30, 32

Date of Accounts	Dec 07	Dec 06
Pre Tax Profit/Loss	51740	33280
Working Capital	-664140	-863470
Fixed Assets	779690	826980
Current Liabilities	664140	863470
Total Share Capital	533410	433410
ROCE% (Return on Capital Employed)	44.8	-91.2

Altitude Studio Ltd

Ravenswood Bank Hey Lane South, Blackburn, BB1 5QZ
Tel: 01254-56109
E-mail: info@altitudestudio.co.uk
Website: http://www.altitudestudio.co.uk
Directors: S. Snape (Prop)
Immediate Holding Company: ALTITUDE STUDIO LIMITED
Registration no: 06278126 **Date established:** 2007
Turnover: Up to £250,000 **No.of Employees:** 1 - 10 **Product Groups:** 52

Date of Accounts	Jul 10	Jul 09	Jul 08
Working Capital	1	4	-0
Fixed Assets	1	1	1
Current Assets	12	13	10

Artis Originals

Roe Lee Mills Whalley New Road, Blackburn, BB1 9SU
Tel: 01254-673733
E-mail: info@artisoriginals.co.uk
Website: http://www.artisoriginals.co.uk
Managers: M. Stevens (Mgr)
Date established: 2003 **Turnover:** Up to £250,000
No.of Employees: 1 - 10 **Product Groups:** 26

Auto Scales & Service Co. Ltd

Truweigh House Ordnance Street, Blackburn, BB1 3AE
Tel: 0800-169 1247 **Fax:** 01254-682374
E-mail: info@autoscales.co.uk
Website: http://www.autoscales.co.uk
Directors: A. Leman (MD)
Immediate Holding Company: AUTOSCALES LIMITED
Registration no: 06280114 **Date established:** 2007
No.of Employees: 1 - 10 **Product Groups:** 38, 45, 67

Autoscales & Service Co. Ltd

Truweigh House Ordnance Street, Blackburn, BB1 3AE
Tel: 01254-676938 **Fax:** 01254-682374
E-mail: info@autoscales.co.uk
Website: http://www.autoscales.co.uk
Directors: A. Leman (Dir), M. Leman (Dir), H. Leman (Dir)
Immediate Holding Company: AUTO SCALES & SERVICE CO.LIMITED
Registration no: 00627886 **Date established:** 1959 **Turnover:** £1m - £2m
No.of Employees: 1 - 10 **Product Groups:** 38, 48, 83

Date of Accounts	May 11	May 10	May 09
Working Capital	6	-19	15
Fixed Assets	76	73	69
Current Assets	180	193	205

B C P Fluted Packaging Ltd t/a B C P Fluted Packaging

Crompton House Nuttall Way Shadsworth, Shadsworth Business Park, Blackburn, BB1 2JT
Tel: 01254-677790 **Fax:** 01254-681736
E-mail: sales@bcpflute.com
Website: http://www.bcpflute.com
Bank(s): National Westminster Bank Plc
Directors: M. Jones (Sales), P. Redhead (Mkt Research), B. Jones (MD)
Managers: A. Leaming (Works Gen Mgr), A. Clifton (I.T. Exec)
Ultimate Holding Company: BCP HOLDINGS LIMITED
Immediate Holding Company: BCP FLUTED PACKAGING LIMITED
Registration no: 00248918 **VAT No.:** GB 174 3277 55
Date established: 1930 **Turnover:** £10m - £20m
No.of Employees: 51 - 100 **Product Groups:** 27, 48

Date of Accounts	Jun 11	Jun 10	Jun 09
Sales Turnover	12m	13m	10m
Pre Tax Profit/Loss	1m	2m	842
Working Capital	3m	2m	2m
Fixed Assets	3m	2m	1m
Current Assets	5m	4m	4m
Current Liabilities	908	510	606

B K S Plastics Ltd

Unit 2 Station Road Industrial Estate Great Harwood, Blackburn, BB6 7BB
Tel: 01254-889139 **Fax:** 01254-889187
E-mail: sales@bksplastics.co.uk
Website: http://bksplastics.co.uk
Directors: A. Dewhurst (MD)
Immediate Holding Company: BKS PLASTICS LIMITED
Registration no: 05886865 **Date established:** 2006
No.of Employees: 1 - 10 **Product Groups:** 30

Date of Accounts	Sep 11	Sep 10	Sep 09
Working Capital	58	87	66
Fixed Assets	85	58	61
Current Assets	158	153	136

B M S Vision Ltd

Capricorn Park Blakewater Road, Blackburn, BB1 5QR
Tel: 01254-662244 **Fax:** 01254-267100
E-mail: sales@barco.com
Website: http://www.visionbms.com
Bank(s): Lloyds TSB Bank plc
Directors: D. Robson (MD)
Managers: K. Ferguson (Sales Prom Mgr)
Ultimate Holding Company: BARCO NV (BELGIUM)
Immediate Holding Company: BMS VISION LIMITED
Registration no: 01501885 **VAT No.:** GB 614 6167 49
Date established: 1980 **Turnover:** £1m - £2m **No.of Employees:** 11 - 20
Product Groups: 44

Date of Accounts	Dec 10	Dec 09	Dec 08
Working Capital	869	746	707
Fixed Assets	628	660	694
Current Assets	1m	1m	1m

B S B Electronics Ltd

Queen Street Great Harwood, Blackburn, BB6 7AU
Tel: 01254-883348 **Fax:** 01254-889113
E-mail: ian.bend@progeny.co.uk
Website: http://www.progeny.co.uk
Bank(s): National Westminster Bank Plc
Directors: B. Burby (MD), S. Colquhoun (Sales & Mktg), I. Bend (Tech Serv), M. Ellison (Sales), B. Burby (Co Sec)
Managers: D. Holding (Tech Sales Eng), J. Dickenson (Purch Mgr)
Immediate Holding Company: B.S.B. ELECTRONICS LIMITED
Registration no: 02018255 **VAT No.:** GB 326 1055 90
Date established: 1986 **Turnover:** £250,000 - £500,000
No.of Employees: 11 - 20 **Product Groups:** 36, 40

Date of Accounts	May 11	May 10	May 09
Working Capital	99	78	103
Fixed Assets	73	101	111
Current Assets	442	377	333

Blackburn Chemicals Ltd

Cunliffe Road Whitebirk Industrial Estate, Blackburn, BB1 5SX
Tel: 01254-52222 **Fax:** 01254-664224
E-mail: sales@bbchem.co.uk
Website: http://www.bbchem.co.uk
Bank(s): National Westminster Bank Plc
Directors: A. Whalley (Fin), G. Lamb (Ch), S. Lamb (MD), A. Lamb (Mkt Research)
Registration no: 01112362 **VAT No.:** GB 175 5976 28
Date established: 1973 **Turnover:** £20m - £50m
No.of Employees: 21 - 50 **Product Groups:** 32, 66

Date of Accounts	May 10	May 09	May 08
Sales Turnover	23m	20m	N/A
Pre Tax Profit/Loss	4m	2m	3m
Working Capital	4m	5m	3m
Fixed Assets	72	39	44
Current Assets	8m	7m	6m
Current Liabilities	959	602	748

Blackburn Diesel Engineering

Carluke Street, Blackburn, BB1 3JR
Tel: 01254-56758
Managers: E. Booth (Mgr)
No.of Employees: 1 - 10 **Product Groups:** 35, 39

Blackburn With Darwen Borough Council

Town Hall King William Street, Blackburn, BB1 7DY
Tel: 01254-585585 **Fax:** 01254-697223
E-mail: info@blackburn.gov.uk
Website: http://www.blackburn.gov.uk
Directors: D. Fairclough (Pers), D. Park (Dir), G. Burgess (Grp Chief Exec)
Managers: T. Stannard
Turnover: £1m - £2m **No.of Employees:** 251 - 500 **Product Groups:** 80, 82

Date of Accounts	Mar 08	Mar 07	Mar 06
Sales Turnover	919	1601	1170
Pre Tax Profit/Loss	-292	341	160
Working Capital	10	301	189
Fixed Assets	305	323	47
Current Assets	285	546	387
Current Liabilities	275	245	198
ROCE% (Return on Capital Employed)	-92.8	54.6	67.8
ROT% (Return on Turnover)	-31.8	21.3	13.6

Blackburn Yarn Dyers Ltd

Blackburn Yarn Dyers Haslingden Road, Blackburn, BB2 3HN
Tel: 01254-53051 **Fax:** 01254- 672233
E-mail: info@bydltd.co.uk
Website: http://www.bydltd.co.uk
Bank(s): Barclays, Blackburn
Directors: D. Hodgson (Fin), G. Fern (MD), I. Peel (I.T. Dir)
Immediate Holding Company: BLACKBURN YARN DYERS,LIMITED
Registration no: 00139916 **Date established:** 2015
No.of Employees: 21 - 50 **Product Groups:** 23

Date of Accounts	Jan 12	Jan 11	Jan 10
Working Capital	2m	2m	2m
Fixed Assets	972	963	1m
Current Assets	2m	2m	2m

Bowker BMW & Mini

Trident Park Trident Way, Blackburn, BB1 3NU
Tel: 01254-274444 **Fax:** 01254-236373
E-mail: info@bowkerbmw.com
Website: http://www.bowkermotorgroup.com

see next page

***Bowker BMW & Mini** - Cont'd*

Managers: A. Uphill (Mktg Serv Mgr)
Ultimate Holding Company: W.H.BOWKER LIMITED
Immediate Holding Company: BOWKER BLACKBURN LIMITED
Registration no: 01364761 **Date established:** 1978
Turnover: £20m - £50m **No.of Employees:** 51 - 100 **Product Groups:** 68

Date of Accounts	Dec 11	Dec 10	Dec 09
Sales Turnover	36m	34m	35m
Pre Tax Profit/Loss	221	102	472
Working Capital	-102	6	167
Fixed Assets	4m	4m	4m
Current Assets	10m	9m	6m
Current Liabilities	3m	1m	2m

Boxes G H Ltd

Palatine Mill Meadow Street, Great Harwood, Blackburn, BB6 7EJ
Tel: 01254-888151 **Fax:** 01254-889569
E-mail: peterburgess@boxesgh.co.uk
Website: http://www.clondalkingroup.com
Directors: G. Ingram (Dir), P. Burgess (MD)
Managers: D. Settle
Ultimate Holding Company: CLONDALKIN GROUP HOLDINGS BV (NETHERLANDS)
Immediate Holding Company: BOXES (GH) LIMITED
Registration no: 02131455 **VAT No.:** GB 649 2574 05
Date established: 1987 **Turnover:** £10m - £20m
No.of Employees: 101 - 250 **Product Groups:** 20, 27

Date of Accounts	Dec 11	Dec 10	Dec 09
Sales Turnover	16m	14m	11m
Pre Tax Profit/Loss	845	269	56
Working Capital	2m	2m	2m
Fixed Assets	1m	1m	1m
Current Assets	6m	6m	5m
Current Liabilities	1m	685	570

C S Foods Ltd

Unit 9 Norden Court Alan Ramsbottom Way, Great Harwood, Blackburn, BB6 7UR
Tel: 01254-885188 **Fax:** 01254-829372
E-mail: kevincosgrove@tiscalli.co.uk
Website: http://www.tiscalli.co.uk
Directors: K. Cosgrove (Dir)
Immediate Holding Company: RISHTON WELDING & ENGINEERING COMPANY LIMITED
Registration no: 00404834 **Date established:** 1946
No.of Employees: 1 - 10 **Product Groups:** 20, 40, 41

Date of Accounts	Mar 11	Mar 10	Mar 09
Working Capital	472	348	489
Fixed Assets	91	99	110
Current Assets	924	783	944

The C W V Group

1 The Beehive Shadsworth Business Park, Blackburn, BB1 2QS
Tel: 01254-222800 **Fax:** 01254-222960
E-mail: enquiries@cwvgroup.com
Website: http://www.wallpapers-uk.com
Bank(s): HSBC Bank plc
Directors: M. Kellaway (MD)
Ultimate Holding Company: WORDON LTD (ISLE OF MAN)
Immediate Holding Company: CWV LIMITED
Registration no: 05297292 **Date established:** 2004 **Turnover:** £5m - £10m
No.of Employees: 21 - 50 **Product Groups:** 27, 30

Date of Accounts	Mar 09	Mar 10	Apr 11
Sales Turnover	11m	7m	6m
Pre Tax Profit/Loss	-2m	-1m	-1m
Working Capital	-4m	-5m	-4m
Fixed Assets	1m	1m	352
Current Assets	3m	3m	4m
Current Liabilities	407	1m	704

Car Communications

Saturn Centre Challenge Way, Blackburn, BB1 5QB
Tel: 08452-266454
E-mail: rafiq.ahmed@carcommunications.co.uk
Website: http://www.carcommunications.co.uk
Directors: R. Ahmed (MD)
Immediate Holding Company: CAR COMMUNICATIONS LIMITED
Registration no: 04021811 **Date established:** 2000
No.of Employees: 1 - 10 **Product Groups:** 26, 37, 38, 39

Date of Accounts	Jul 11	Jul 10	Jun 09
Working Capital	186	153	113
Fixed Assets	3	2	2
Current Assets	214	187	126

Catering Centre Ltd

Premier House Croft Head Road, Whitebirk Indl-Est, Blackburn, BB1 5UE
Tel: 01254-616600 **Fax:** 01254- 584715
E-mail: sales@thecateringcentre.co.uk
Website: http://www.thecateringcentre.co.uk
Directors: M. Mahony (Fin), S. Wulkan (MD)
Immediate Holding Company: THE CATERING CENTRE LIMITED
Registration no: 04603416 **Date established:** 2002 **Turnover:** £2m - £5m
No.of Employees: 21 - 50 **Product Groups:** 20, 40, 41

Date of Accounts	Aug 07	Dec 06
Working Capital	-264	-1279
Fixed Assets	307	734
Current Assets	1005	363
Current Liabilities	1269	1642
Total Share Capital	10	10

Cavalier Carpets Ltd

Thompson St Industrial Estate, Blackburn, BB2 1TX
Tel: 01254-268000 **Fax:** 01254-268001
E-mail: geraldl@cavalier-carpets.co.uk
Website: http://www.cavalier-carpets.co.uk
Bank(s): National Westminster
Directors: A. Pickstone (Chief Op Offcr), A. Todd (Fin), G. Lowe (Ch), H. Lowe (Sales & Mktg), J. Richardson (Sales)
Managers: B. Thomas (Personnel)
Ultimate Holding Company: MCCREERY LAWSON (JERSEY) LTD (JERSEY)
Immediate Holding Company: CAVALIER CARPETS LIMITED
Registration no: 01028083 **VAT No.:** GB 174 3319 65
Date established: 1971 **Turnover:** £20m - £50m
No.of Employees: 251 - 500 **Product Groups:** 23

Date of Accounts	Dec 11	Dec 10	Dec 09
Sales Turnover	31m	28m	34m
Pre Tax Profit/Loss	554	-170	61
Working Capital	2m	2m	3m
Fixed Assets	3m	3m	3m
Current Assets	8m	8m	8m
Current Liabilities	2m	1m	779

Cherry Tree Products Ltd

Barn Meadow House Barnmeadow Lane, Great Harwood, Blackburn, BB6 7AB
Tel: 01254-882544 **Fax:** 01254-882550
Directors: G. Neild (Fin), J. Neild (MD)
Immediate Holding Company: CHERRYTREE PRODUCTS LTD
Registration no: 08084390 **VAT No.:** GB 174 3483 52
Date established: 2012 **Turnover:** Up to £250,000
No.of Employees: 1 - 10 **Product Groups:** 49

Date of Accounts	Mar 10	Mar 09	Mar 07
Sales Turnover	N/A	2	10
Pre Tax Profit/Loss	-0	-0	-2
Working Capital	4	5	12
Current Assets	3	5	25
Current Liabilities	1	N/A	N/A

Chippendale & Co.

3 Daisyhill Mill Ashworth Street, Rishton, Blackburn, BB1 4JW
Tel: 01254-886658 **Fax:** 01254-886658
Directors: T. Bartley (Ptnr)
Registration no: 04402145 **Date established:** 1981
Turnover: Up to £250,000 **No.of Employees:** 1 - 10 **Product Groups:** 26, 30, 35, 37, 48, 66, 67

Cobble Blackburn Ltd

Gate Street Works Gate Street, Blackburn, BB1 3AH
Tel: 01254-55121 **Fax:** 01254- 671125
E-mail: info@cobble.co.uk
Website: http://www.cobble.co.uk
Bank(s): Barclays Bank PLC
Directors: C. Jones (Co Sec), G. Hemingway (Pres)
Managers: P. Whewell (Purch Mgr), J. Wallace (Personnel), C. Patton (Sales Prom Mgr), D. Marsden (Fin Mgr)
Ultimate Holding Company: SPENCER WRIGHT INDUSTRIES INC (USA)
Immediate Holding Company: COBBLE BLACKBURN LIMITED
Registration no: 01249134 **VAT No.:** GB 326 0584 68
Date established: 1976 **Turnover:** £5m - £10m
No.of Employees: 51 - 100 **Product Groups:** 43, 48

Date of Accounts	Dec 11	Dec 10	Dec 09
Sales Turnover	14m	9m	7m
Pre Tax Profit/Loss	-231	-958	-3m
Working Capital	2m	2m	3m
Fixed Assets	2m	2m	2m
Current Assets	6m	5m	6m
Current Liabilities	1m	1m	2m

Control Ability Business Equipment

Unit 2 Ashworth Buildings Heys Lane, Great Harwood, Blackburn, BB6 7BA
Tel: 01254-886685 **Fax:** 01254-886068
E-mail: j-almond@controlability.com
Website: http://www.controlability.com
Directors: J. Almond (MD), J. Almond (Dir)
Managers: G. Burrel (Mgr)
Registration no: 01135697 **VAT No.:** GB 149 5043 61
Turnover: £500,000 - £1m **No.of Employees:** 1 - 10 **Product Groups:** 38

Corus

Walker Industrial Estate Walker Road, Guide, Blackburn, BB1 2QE
Tel: 01254-55161 **Fax:** 01254-677505
E-mail: mike.forster@corusgroup.com
Website: http://www.corusgroup.com
Managers: D. Abbott (Mgr), D. Abbotts (Mgr), M. Forster (Mgr), M. Foster (Chief Mgr)
Ultimate Holding Company: British Steel P.L.C.
Immediate Holding Company: CORUS GROUP LIMITED
Registration no: 03811373 **Date established:** 1999
Turnover: £10m - £20m **No.of Employees:** 1 - 10 **Product Groups:** 48, 66, 77

Cosmotec

Highfield Road, Blackburn, BB2 3AS
Tel: 01254-56413 **Fax:** 01254- 682723
E-mail: sales@cosmo-tec.co.uk
Website: http://www.ctgplc.com
Managers: J. Winnre (Chief Mgr)
Immediate Holding Company: COSMOPOLITAN TEXTILE CO LTD
Registration no: 01177431 **VAT No.:** GB 159 1543 54
Date established: 1974 **Turnover:** £2m - £5m **No.of Employees:** 51 - 100
Product Groups: 23

Danley Engineering Services Ltd

Heys Lane Great Harwood, Blackburn, BB6 7UA
Tel: 01254-888401 **Fax:** 01254-884835
E-mail: info@danleyeng.co.uk
Website: http://www.danleyeng.co.uk
Directors: G. Wolstenholme (MD)
Ultimate Holding Company: DANLEY HOLDINGS LIMITED
Immediate Holding Company: DANLEY ENGINEERING SERVICES LIMITED
Registration no: 01509334 **Date established:** 1980
No.of Employees: 11 - 20 **Product Groups:** 43

Date of Accounts	Aug 11	Aug 10	Aug 09
Working Capital	251	194	230
Fixed Assets	143	155	171
Current Assets	327	304	324

The Depositry

Percliffe Way Off Philips Road, Blackburn, BB1 5PF
Tel: 01254-694207 **Fax:** 01254-262943
E-mail: info@the-depository.co.uk
Website: http://www.the-depository.co.uk
Directors: M. Patel (MD), A. Mangara (Purch), I. Patel (Fin)
Immediate Holding Company: M A CHIDLEY LIMITED
Registration no: 03746647 **VAT No.:** GB 174 8267 33
Date established: 2003 **No.of Employees:** 1 - 10 **Product Groups:** 72

Date of Accounts	Feb 12	Feb 11	Feb 10
Working Capital	9	10	10
Fixed Assets	2	2	3
Current Assets	27	22	21

Distributed Management Systems Ltd

Carmel Stockclough Lane, Feniscowles, Blackburn, BB2 5JR
Tel: 01254-208419 **Fax:** 01254-208418
E-mail: marg@casque.co.uk
Website: http://www.dms-soft.com
Directors: B. Philipsz (MD)
Immediate Holding Company: DISTRIBUTED MANAGEMENT SYSTEMS LIMITED
Registration no: SC064155 **VAT No.:** GB 327 4050 79
Date established: 1978 **Turnover:** £250,000 - £500,000
No.of Employees: 1 - 10 **Product Groups:** 44, 79

Date of Accounts	Dec 11	Dec 10	Dec 09
Working Capital	-106	-190	-121
Current Assets	141	82	123

J W Doody

Unit 19 Hamilton Street Industrial Estate, Blackburn, BB2 4AJ
Tel: 01254-679911
Directors: J. Doody (Prop)
No.of Employees: 1 - 10 **Product Groups:** 26, 35

East Lancashire Catering Equipment

20 St Peter Street, Blackburn, BB2 2HD
Tel: 01254-660400 **Fax:** 01254-660400
Directors: S. Rashid (Ptnr)
Immediate Holding Company: EAST LANCASHIRE CATERING EQUIPMENTS LIMITED
Registration no: 07823181 **Date established:** 2011
No.of Employees: 1 - 10 **Product Groups:** 20, 40, 41

East Lancashire Conveyor Co. Ltd (ELCO)

Oxford Works Montague Street, Blackburn, BB2 1EH
Tel: 01254-681872 **Fax:** 01254-682212
E-mail: elco@airtime.co.uk
Website: http://www.elcoconveyors.com
Directors: P. Jackson (MD)
Managers: P. Walsh (Sales Prom Mgr), W. Holmes
Immediate Holding Company: EAST LANCASHIRE CONVEYOR CO.LIMITED
Registration no: 00641288 **Date established:** 1959 **Turnover:** £1m - £2m
No.of Employees: 21 - 50 **Product Groups:** 41, 45, 84

Date of Accounts	Dec 11	Dec 10	Dec 09
Working Capital	80	28	58
Fixed Assets	466	4	492
Current Assets	496	177	404

Ensor Building Products Ltd

Blackamoor Road Guide, Blackburn, BB1 2LQ
Tel: 01254-52244 **Fax:** 01254- 682371
E-mail: p.brooke@ensorbuilding.com
Website: http://www.ensorbuilding.com
Bank(s): HSBC Bank plc
Directors: C. Beaver (Fin), P. Brooke (MD)
Ultimate Holding Company: ENSOR HOLDINGS P L C
Immediate Holding Company: ENSOR BUILDING PRODUCTS LIMITED
Registration no: 00241566 **VAT No.:** GB 603 7668 35
Date established: 2029 **Turnover:** £5m - £10m **No.of Employees:** 21 - 50
Product Groups: 66

Date of Accounts	Mar 12	Mar 11	Mar 10
Sales Turnover	7m	6m	6m
Pre Tax Profit/Loss	63	55	43
Working Capital	1m	894	1m
Fixed Assets	81	80	91
Current Assets	2m	2m	2m
Current Liabilities	252	231	200

Eriks UK

Unit 2 Blackburn Trading Estate, Blackburn, BB1 6JT
Tel: 01254-675538 **Fax:** 01254-676289
E-mail: jeff.deane@eriks.co.uk
Website: http://www.eriks.co.uk
Managers: J. Deane (District Mgr)
Registration no: 03142339 **Turnover:** £250m - £500m
No.of Employees: 1 - 10 **Product Groups:** 30

Europrint Promotions Ltd

Lancaster House 52 Preston New Road, Blackburn, BB2 6AH
Tel: 01254-588400 **Fax:** 01254-588401
E-mail: alan.rogers@gtech.com
Website: http://www.europrint-group.com
Directors: A. Rogers (Fin), A. Gray (MD)
Managers: J. Whalley (Sales Prom Mgr), I. Brame (Tech Serv Mgr)
Ultimate Holding Company: DE AGOSTINI SPA (ITALY)
Immediate Holding Company: EUROPRINT (PROMOTIONS) LIMITED
Registration no: 01780910 **Date established:** 1983 **Turnover:** £2m - £5m
No.of Employees: 21 - 50 **Product Groups:** 28

Date of Accounts	Dec 11	Dec 10	Dec 09
Sales Turnover	5m	4m	1m
Pre Tax Profit/Loss	276	605	127
Working Capital	490	436	148
Current Assets	1m	1m	535
Current Liabilities	213	242	121

Framar

44 King Street, Blackburn, BB2 2DH
Tel: 01254-264486 **Fax:** 01254-665013
E-mail: framarknives@googlemail.com
Website: http://www.framarcustomknives.co.uk
Directors: F. Kay (Prop)
Date established: 1993 **No.of Employees:** 1 - 10 **Product Groups:** 36, 39, 40

Fraser Adams Ltd

Resevoir Works Blackburn Road, Rishton, Blackburn, BB1 4ER
Tel: 01254-681177 **Fax:** 01254-689761
Website: http://www.fraser-adams.net
Directors: L. Eastwood (MD), D. Boardwell (Co Sec)
Immediate Holding Company: FRASER-ADAMS LIMITED
Registration no: 03165579 **Date established:** 1996
No.of Employees: 1 - 10 **Product Groups:** 27, 30, 67

Date of Accounts	Feb 08	Feb 11	Feb 10
Working Capital	336	411	387
Fixed Assets	328	346	321
Current Assets	731	843	719
Current Liabilities	396	N/A	N/A

Funzig Web Design

6 Brooklyn Road Clayton Le Dale, Blackburn, BB1 9PP
Tel: 07790-175266
E-mail: lee@akri.org
Website: http://www.funzig.com
Directors: L. Jorgensen (Prop)
Date established: 2005 **No.of Employees:** 1 - 10 **Product Groups:** 44

Gardner Engineering
Unit 12 Rosewood Park St James's Road, Blackburn, BB1 8ET
Tel: 01254-583338 **Fax:** 01254-670177
E-mail: info@gardnerengineering.co.uk
Website: http://www.gardner-engineering.net
Managers: K. Gardner (Mgr)
Immediate Holding Company: GARDNER ENGINEERING PRODUCTS LTD
Registration no: 07697008 **Date established:** 2011
Turnover: Up to £250,000 **No.of Employees:** 1 - 10 **Product Groups:** 26, 35, 37

Gas-Fire Com
15-17 High Street Rishton, Blackburn, BB1 4JZ
Tel: 0800-0281936 **Fax:** 01254-887569
E-mail: sales@gas-fire.com
Website: http://www.gas-fire.com
Directors: W. Cropper (Co Sec), Cropper (MD)
Managers: W. Cropper (Mgr), V. Walker (Sales Prom Mgr)
Immediate Holding Company: NORTH WESTERN GAS SAFETY SERVICES LIMITED
Registration no: 03138241 **Date established:** 1995
No.of Employees: 1 - 10 **Product Groups:** 35, 49, 52, 66

George Broughton & Co. Ltd
Whitebirk Road, Blackburn, BB1 3HZ
Tel: 01254-53644 **Fax:** 01254-690598
E-mail: sales@geo-broughton.co.uk
Website: http://www.geo-broughton.co.uk
Directors: K. Broughton (MD), I. Broughton (MD)
Managers: C. Turner (Accounts), A. Sumper (Sales Prom)
Registration no: 00372779 **Turnover:** £2m - £5m
No.of Employees: 1 - 10 **Product Groups:** 40, 66

Glass Scratch Repair
19 Harwood Lane Great Harwood, Blackburn, BB6 7SN
Tel: 01254-888557
E-mail: enquiries@glassscratchrepair.co.uk
Website: http://www.glassscratchrepair.co.uk
Directors: P. Cornwell (MD)
No.of Employees: 1 - 10 **Product Groups:** 33, 35, 39

Graham & Brown Ltd
PO Box 39, Blackburn, BB1 3DB
Tel: 01254-691321 **Fax:** 01254-582208
E-mail: andrew.graham@grahambrown.com
Website: http://www.grahambrown.com
Bank(s): National Westminster Bank Plc
Directors: G. Van Larrhoven (Fin), G. Shepherd (Fin)
Managers: A. Kemp (Mktg Serv Mgr), E. Green (Personnel), A. Graham, M. Williams (Tech Serv Mgr)
Ultimate Holding Company: GRAHAM & BROWN LIMITED
Immediate Holding Company: CATEGORY MERCHANDISING LIMITED
Registration no: 04687116 **VAT No.:** GB 174 7114 63
Date established: 2003 **Turnover:** £500,000 - £1m
No.of Employees: 251 - 500 **Product Groups:** 27, 30

Date of Accounts	Dec 11	Dec 10	Dec 09
Sales Turnover	677	668	613
Pre Tax Profit/Loss	3	26	19
Working Capital	183	178	N/A
Current Assets	237	235	N/A
Current Liabilities	42	42	N/A

Greenbank Technology Ltd
Unit 3 Greenbank Business Park, Blackburn, BB1 3AB
Tel: 01254-690555 **Fax:** 01254-690666
E-mail: info@greenbanktechnology.co.uk
Website: http://www.greenbanktechnology.co.uk
Bank(s): Co-operative Bank
Directors: B. Schofield (MD)
Managers: D. Carney (Chief Acct), A. Waugh (Purch Mgr)
Ultimate Holding Company: CPM HOLDINGS INC (USA)
Immediate Holding Company: GREENBANK TECHNOLOGY LIMITED
Registration no: 02566319 **VAT No.:** GB 597 8252 79
Date established: 1990 **Turnover:** £5m - £10m **No.of Employees:** 11 - 20
Product Groups: 40, 41, 42, 43, 44

Date of Accounts	Mar 08	Sep 11	Sep 10
Sales Turnover	N/A	5m	6m
Pre Tax Profit/Loss	2m	546	853
Working Capital	1m	3m	2939m
Fixed Assets	68	28	14m
Current Assets	5m	4m	5737m
Current Liabilities	2m	270	2797m

H & S Joinery Ltd
Thwaites Close Shadsworth Business Park, Blackburn, BB1 2QQ
Tel: 01254-696931 **Fax:** 01254-696932
E-mail: info@hsjoinery.co.uk
Website: http://www.hsjoinery.co.uk
Directors: S. Hudson (MD), S. McLaughlin (Co Sec)
Immediate Holding Company: H & S JOINERY LIMITED
Registration no: 04469787 **Date established:** 2002 **Turnover:** £1m - £2m
No.of Employees: 21 - 50 **Product Groups:** 66

Date of Accounts	Dec 11	Dec 10	Dec 09
Sales Turnover	2m	2m	3m
Pre Tax Profit/Loss	38	-69	-297
Working Capital	118	175	257
Fixed Assets	789	757	796
Current Assets	799	735	749
Current Liabilities	492	310	403

E Harding & Sons Ltd
Units 10 & 11 Walker Industrial Estate, Guide, Blackburn, BB1 2QE
Tel: 01254-581276 **Fax:** 01254-677012
E-mail: ben.lewis@timeplan.net
Website: http://www.eharding.co.uk
Bank(s): Royal Bank of Scotland, Bolton
Directors: I. Griffis (Ch), R. Whitehouse (MD)
Managers: D. McKinley, D. Mckinley
Ultimate Holding Company: A M CASTLE & CO (USA)
Immediate Holding Company: E.HARDING & SONS LIMITED
Registration no: 00144277 **VAT No.:** GB 146 1719 68
Date established: 2016 **Turnover:** £10m - £20m
No.of Employees: 51 - 100 **Product Groups:** 48

Date of Accounts	Dec 10	Dec 09	Dec 08
Sales Turnover	12m	8m	14m
Pre Tax Profit/Loss	579	-63	-311
Working Capital	846	657	645
Fixed Assets	777	435	658
Current Assets	6m	4m	4m
Current Liabilities	694	752	204

Harrison Verity Products Ltd
Veritas House Sett End Road, Shadsworth Business Park, Blackburn, BB1 2PT
Tel: 01254-662979 **Fax:** 01254-698580
E-mail: sales@hvp.co.uk
Website: http://www.polythene-packaging.com
Directors: J. Verity (MD)
Immediate Holding Company: HARRISON-VERITY PRODUCTS LIMITED
Registration no: 01171490 **Date established:** 1974
No.of Employees: 1 - 10 **Product Groups:** 30

Date of Accounts	Aug 11	Aug 10	Aug 09
Working Capital	304	465	557
Fixed Assets	522	606	593
Current Assets	415	579	657

The Hatchwell Co. Ltd
Unit G1 Riverside Industrial Estate Hermitage Street, Rishton, Blackburn, BB1 4NF
Tel: 01254-888479 **Fax:** 01254-883822
E-mail: info@hatchwell.co.uk
Website: http://www.hatchwell.co.uk
Directors: D. Taylor (MD), J. Taylor (Fin)
Immediate Holding Company: THE HATCHWELL COMPANY LIMITED
Registration no: 03531752 **VAT No.:** GB 174 4698 26
Date established: 1998 **Turnover:** £500,000 - £1m
No.of Employees: 1 - 10 **Product Groups:** 49, 62

Date of Accounts	Mar 12	Mar 11	Mar 10
Working Capital	125	114	110
Fixed Assets	88	98	81
Current Assets	283	264	265

Haworth Enterprises
Unit 1 Riverside Industrial Estate Hermitage Street, Rishton, Blackburn, BB1 4NF
Tel: 01254-888504 **Fax:** 01254-888628
E-mail: sales@haworth.co.uk
Website: http://www.haworth.co.uk
Directors: K. Haworth (MD)
Immediate Holding Company: L. T. CATERING SUPPLIES LIMITED
Registration no: 01853729 **Date established:** 1990 **Turnover:** £1m - £2m
No.of Employees: 1 - 10 **Product Groups:** 44, 66, 67

Date of Accounts	Dec 11	Dec 10	Dec 09
Working Capital	6	7	5
Fixed Assets	1	3	4
Current Assets	45	43	40

Heatmiser UK Ltd
Unit 8&9 Hurstwood Court, Mercer Way,, Shadsworth Business Park,, Blackburn, BB1 2QU
Tel: 01254-669090 **Fax:** 01254-704143
E-mail: info@heatmiser.co.uk
Website: http://www.heatmiser.co.uk
Bank(s): Lloyds TSB Bank plc
Directors: G. Kay (Dir), S. Greenwood (Co Sec)
Immediate Holding Company: Heatmiser Holdings Ltd
Registration no: 03747773 **VAT No.:** GB 174 6954 24
Date established: 1999 **No.of Employees:** 11 - 20 **Product Groups:** 38, 40, 52, 67

Date of Accounts	Feb 10	Feb 09	Feb 08
Working Capital	2m	1m	986
Fixed Assets	203	219	205
Current Assets	2m	2m	1m

Hollingsworth Service Co. Ltd
Unit 6 Norden Court Alan Ramsbottom Way, Great Harwood, Blackburn, BB6 7UR
Tel: 01254-881100 **Fax:** 01254-881101
E-mail: pat.turner@btconnect.com
Website: http://www.hollingsworth.co.uk
Directors: M. Lloyd (I.T. Dir), M. Lloyd (Dir), P. Turner (MD)
Managers: P. Turner (Mgr), P. Taylor (Sales Prom)
Ultimate Holding Company: HOLLINGSWORTH HOLDING COMPANY LIMITED
Immediate Holding Company: HOLLINGSWORTH COMPANY LIMITED
Registration no: 02798728 **Date established:** 1993
Turnover: £500,000 - £1m **No.of Employees:** 1 - 10 **Product Groups:** 30

Date of Accounts	Mar 11	Mar 10	Mar 09
Working Capital	-108	-47	-39
Fixed Assets	112	109	134
Current Assets	163	163	109

Jewson Ltd
Higher Barn Street, Blackburn, BB1 1JA
Tel: 01254-675331 **Fax:** 01254-670676
Website: http://www.jewson.co.uk
Bank(s): Barclays
Directors: T. Newman (Sales), C. Kenward (Fin), P. Hindle (MD)
Managers: S. Bracewell (District Mgr)
Ultimate Holding Company: COMPAGNIE DE SAINT GOBAIN (FRANCE)
Immediate Holding Company: JEWSON LIMITED
Registration no: 00348407 **Date established:** 1939
Turnover: £500m - £1,000m **No.of Employees:** 21 - 50
Product Groups: 66

Date of Accounts	Dec 11	Dec 10	Dec 09
Sales Turnover	1606m	1547m	1485m
Pre Tax Profit/Loss	18m	100m	45m
Working Capital	-345m	-250m	-349m
Fixed Assets	496m	387m	461m
Current Assets	657m	1005m	1320m
Current Liabilities	66m	120m	64m

K I Fasteners Blackburn Ltd
Unit 8 Pearson Street, Blackburn, BB2 2ES
Tel: 01254-678017 **Fax:** 01254-678018
Directors: B. Bright (MD)
Immediate Holding Company: K.I. FASTENERS (BLACKBURN) LIMITED
Registration no: 02055614 **VAT No.:** GB 444 8766 12
Date established: 1986 **Turnover:** Up to £250,000
No.of Employees: 1 - 10 **Product Groups:** 35, 66

Date of Accounts	Dec 11	Dec 10	Dec 09
Working Capital	57	53	57
Fixed Assets	N/A	1	2
Current Assets	61	58	63

L.C. Automation Ltd
Duttons Way Shadsworth Business Park, Blackburn, BB1 2QR
Tel: 01254-685900 **Fax:** 01254-685901
E-mail: sales@lca.co.uk
Website: http://www.lcautomation.com
Directors: K. Davies (MD), M. Chadwick (Sales)
Managers: M. Appleton (Tech Serv Mgr), N. Dean (Mktg Serv Mgr), P. Catherall (Sales Admin)
Registration no: 01166468 **VAT No.:** GB 155 9814 33
Date established: 1974 **Turnover:** £10m - £20m **No.of Employees:** 1 - 10
Product Groups: 38

Date of Accounts	Dec 09	Dec 08	Dec 07
Sales Turnover	7m	N/A	N/A
Pre Tax Profit/Loss	-129	-139	100
Working Capital	123	203	325
Fixed Assets	203	241	311
Current Assets	2m	2m	3m
Current Liabilities	897	1m	2m

Lancashire Saw Co. Ltd
Imperial Mill Gorse Street, Blackburn, BB1 3EU
Tel: 01254-51116 **Fax:** 01254- 672046
E-mail: info@lancashire-saw.co.uk
Website: http://www.lancashire-saw.co.uk
Bank(s): National Westminster Bank Plc
Directors: S. Bentley (Fin), P. Ashton (Sales)
Immediate Holding Company: LANCASHIRE SAW COMPANY LIMITED
Registration no: 00383301 **VAT No.:** GB 174 3286 54
Date established: 1943 **Turnover:** £2m - £5m **No.of Employees:** 21 - 50
Product Groups: 33, 34, 36, 37, 41, 46, 47, 48, 67, 84

Date of Accounts	Dec 11	Dec 10	Dec 09
Sales Turnover	2m	N/A	N/A
Working Capital	517	556	515
Fixed Assets	966	919	968
Current Assets	877	876	845

lancashire school of welding
Unit 45 Hollins Grove Mill, Darwen, Blackburn, BB3 1HG
Tel: 07543-958289
E-mail: welding_lst@live.co.uk
Website: http://www.lancashireschoolofwelding.co.uk
Managers: M. coogan (Chief Mgr)
Registration no: 9834722 **Date established:** 2009
Turnover: Up to £250,000 **No.of Employees:** 1 - 10 **Product Groups:** 86

Lancashire Textile Manufacturers Association
4 St Andrews Street, Blackburn, BB1 8AE
Tel: 01254-580248 **Fax:** 01254-580248
E-mail: all@ltma.co.uk
Website: http://www.ltma.co.uk
Directors: S. Walsh (MD)
Turnover: Up to £250,000 **No.of Employees:** 1 - 10 **Product Groups:** 23, 63

Lanfranchi Uk
34 Harrier Drive, Blackburn, BB1 8LW
Tel: 01254-694348 **Fax:** 01254-290054
E-mail: alex@lanfranchi.co.uk
Website: http://www.lanfranchi.co.uk
Directors: A. Jackson (Prop)
Date established: 2009 **Turnover:** £1m - £2m **No.of Employees:** 1 - 10
Product Groups: 67

B & M Longworth Edgeworth Ltd
Longworth House Sett End Road North, Shadsworth Business Park, Blackburn, BB1 2QG
Tel: 01254-680501 **Fax:** 01254-54041
E-mail: enquiries@bmlongworth.com
Website: http://www.bmlongworth.com
Bank(s): The Royal Bank of Scotland plc, Radcliffe
Directors: A. Reid (MD)
Managers: M. Longworth (Sales Prom Mgr)
Immediate Holding Company: B. & M. LONGWORTH (EDGWORTH) LIMITED
Registration no: 01259441 **Date established:** 1976 **Turnover:** £2m - £5m
No.of Employees: 11 - 20 **Product Groups:** 37, 40, 48

Date of Accounts	Mar 11	Mar 10	Mar 09
Working Capital	169	136	73
Fixed Assets	84	99	116
Current Assets	488	312	374

Lookers Blackburn
Quarry Street, Blackburn, BB1 5DE
Tel: 01254-511911 **Fax:** 01254-682546
E-mail: johndickson@lookersplc.co.uk
Website: http://www.lookers.co.uk
Bank(s): Barclays
Managers: I. May (Sales Prom Mgr), P. Del (Chief Mgr)
Immediate Holding Company: LOOKERS PUBLIC LIMITED COMPANY
Registration no: 00111876 **VAT No.:** GB 174 5928 30
Date established: 2010 **Turnover:** £10m - £20m
No.of Employees: 51 - 100 **Product Groups:** 68

M W Graphics
Vulcan Works Glebe Street, Great Harwood, Blackburn, BB6 7AA
Tel: 01254-876202 **Fax:** 08451-301518
E-mail: info@mwgraphics.co.uk
Website: http://www.mwgraphics.co.uk
Directors: G. Barker (MD), C. Barker (Fin)
Immediate Holding Company: MW GRAPHICS (NORTH WEST) LIMITED
Registration no: 06695702 **Date established:** 2008
Turnover: Up to £250,000 **No.of Employees:** 1 - 10 **Product Groups:** 28, 49

Date of Accounts	Feb 12	Feb 11	Feb 10
Working Capital	2	-2	-2
Fixed Assets	14	15	11
Current Assets	39	34	53
Current Liabilities	15	32	N/A

Mato Industries Ltd
Unit 1 Philips Road Whitebirk Industrial Estate, Blackburn, BB1 5PG
Tel: 01254-387638 **Fax:** 01254-238023
E-mail: info@mato.co.uk
Website: http://www.mato.co.uk
Bank(s): Bank of Ireland, Cardiff

see next page

***Mato Industries Ltd** - Cont'd*

Directors: D. Moore (Fin), R. Hill (MD)
Managers: G. Milner (Chief Mgr), A. Norton (Nat Sales Mgr), P. Savage
Ultimate Holding Company: MATO HOLDING GMBH (GERMANY)
Immediate Holding Company: MATO INDUSTRIES LIMITED
Registration no: 01950507 **VAT No.:** 419 9506 24 **Date established:** 1985
Turnover: £1m - £2m **No.of Employees:** 21 - 50 **Product Groups:** 45

Date of Accounts	Dec 11	Dec 10	Dec 09
Sales Turnover	N/A	6m	N/A
Pre Tax Profit/Loss	N/A	621	N/A
Working Capital	2m	2m	1m
Fixed Assets	601	674	643
Current Assets	3m	3m	3m
Current Liabilities	80	615	589

Mellor Electrics Ltd

Sett End Road Shadsworth Business Park, Blackburn, BB1 2NW
Tel: 01254-53854 **Fax:** 01254- 678625
E-mail: info@mellorelectrics.co.uk
Website: http://www.mellorelectrics.co.uk
Bank(s): HSBC Bank plc
Directors: S. Halliwell (MD)
Managers: A. Brearley (Sales Prom Mgr), H. Borrowdale (Buyer)
Immediate Holding Company: MELLOR ELECTRICS LIMITED
Registration no: 00822026 **VAT No.:** GB 174 9486 16
Date established: 1964 **Turnover:** £2m - £5m **No.of Employees:** 21 - 50
Product Groups: 30, 35, 37, 40

Date of Accounts	Sep 11	Sep 10	Sep 09
Working Capital	632	622	519
Fixed Assets	1m	759	761
Current Assets	2m	2m	1m

Metals UK Group Ltd

Unit 10-11 Walker Industrial Estate Walker Road Guide, Blackburn, BB1 2QE
Tel: 01254-586700 **Fax:** 01254-692063
E-mail: igriffiths@metalsuk.com
Website: http://www.metalsuk.com
Directors: J. Phillips (MD), R. Perna (Co Sec)
Ultimate Holding Company: A M CASTLE & CO (USA)
Immediate Holding Company: METALS UK GROUP LIMITED
Registration no: 04877041 **Date established:** 2003
Turnover: £10m - £20m **No.of Employees:** 101 - 250
Product Groups: 34, 66

Date of Accounts	Dec 10	Dec 09	Dec 08
Working Capital	-629	-629	-629
Fixed Assets	628	628	628
Current Assets	1	1	1

Metflex Precision Moulding Ltd

20 Alan Ramsbottom Way, Blackburn, BB6 7SE
Tel: 01254-884171 **Fax:** 01254-887753
E-mail: sales@metflex.co.uk
Website: http://www.metflex.co.uk
Bank(s): The Royal Bank of Scotland
Directors: D. McCarthy (Fin), J. Holland (MD)
Managers: D. Hudson, J. Whittaker (Mktg Serv Mgr)
Ultimate Holding Company: METFLEX HOLDING COMPANY LIMITED
Immediate Holding Company: METFLEX PRECISION MOULDINGS LIMITED
Registration no: 04744755 **VAT No.:** GB 785 3949 68
Date established: 2003 **Turnover:** £5m - £10m
No.of Employees: 51 - 100 **Product Groups:** 29, 30, 36

Date of Accounts	Dec 11	Dec 10	Dec 09
Sales Turnover	8m	8m	6m
Pre Tax Profit/Loss	874	216	347
Working Capital	3m	2m	4m
Fixed Assets	1m	1m	318
Current Assets	5m	4m	5m
Current Liabilities	1m	1m	1m

Micro Matic Ltd

Walker Industrial Estate Walker Road, Guide, Blackburn, BB1 2QE
Tel: 01254-669700 **Fax:** 01254-669701
E-mail: mmukd@micro-matic.co.uk
Website: http://www.micro-matic.co.uk
Bank(s): Royal Bank of Scotland
Managers: C. Bishop, S. Clare (Buyer), V. Edwards
Immediate Holding Company: MICRO MATIC LIMITED
Registration no: 04130684 **VAT No.:** GB 175 1279 55
Date established: 2000 **Turnover:** £5m - £10m
No.of Employees: 51 - 100 **Product Groups:** 30, 41, 42, 48

Date of Accounts	Apr 12	Apr 11	Apr 10
Sales Turnover	9m	8m	8m
Pre Tax Profit/Loss	311	-233	-11
Working Capital	2m	2m	2m
Fixed Assets	102	175	367
Current Assets	4m	4m	4m
Current Liabilities	469	438	569

Modern Bookbinders Ltd

Pringle Street, Blackburn, BB1 1SA
Tel: 01254-59371 **Fax:** 01254-59373
E-mail: binders@btclick.com
Website: http://www.modernbookbinders.co.uk
Directors: J. Eastwood (Works)
Immediate Holding Company: MODERN BOOKBINDERS LIMITED
Registration no: 00247220 **Date established:** 1930
Turnover: £500,000 - £1m **No.of Employees:** 21 - 50
Product Groups: 28, 30, 64

Date of Accounts	Mar 12	Mar 11	Mar 10
Working Capital	905	963	937
Fixed Assets	159	167	174
Current Assets	1m	1m	1m

Nationwide Platforms Ltd

Myerscough Road Mellor Brook, Blackburn, BB2 7LB
Tel: 0161-790 7442 **Fax:** 01254-813612
E-mail: blackburn.na@nationwideaccess.co.uk
Website: http://www.nationwideaccess.co.uk
Directors: R. Jones (Prop)
Ultimate Holding Company: LAVENDON GROUP PLC
Immediate Holding Company: NATIONWIDE PLATFORMS LIMITED
Registration no: 02268921 **Date established:** 1988
Turnover: £20m - £50m **No.of Employees:** 11 - 20 **Product Groups:** 45, 83

Date of Accounts	Dec 11	Dec 10	Dec 09
Sales Turnover	105m	93m	87m
Pre Tax Profit/Loss	13m	13m	-4m
Working Capital	-77m	-96m	-103m
Fixed Assets	120m	134m	157m
Current Assets	79m	65m	61m
Current Liabilities	17m	19m	16m

Newmans Footwear Ltd

Garden Street, Blackburn, BB2 1TZ
Tel: 01254-296540 **Fax:** 01254-296541
E-mail: info@nfw.co.uk
Website: http://www.nfw.co.uk
Bank(s): HSBC Bank plc
Directors: M. Newman (MD), N. Grainger (Chief Op Offcr), J. Procter (Co Sec)
Managers: M. Raine (Sales Prom Mgr)
Immediate Holding Company: Newman's Footwear Ltd
Registration no: 00315140 **VAT No.:** GB 174 6191 50
Date established: 1936 **Turnover:** £5m - £10m **No.of Employees:** 21 - 50
Product Groups: 22

Date of Accounts	Dec 09	Dec 08	Sep 07
Sales Turnover	8m	N/A	N/A
Pre Tax Profit/Loss	-9	-1m	154
Working Capital	1m	1m	2m
Fixed Assets	339	381	448
Current Assets	2m	3m	4m
Current Liabilities	418	446	538

Newsquest Blackburn

Newspaper House High Street, Blackburn, BB1 1HT
Tel: 01254-678678 **Fax:** 01254-682185
E-mail: timesads@london.newsquest.co.uk
Website: http://www.newsquest.co.uk
Directors: J. Lever (MD)
Managers: B. Leach (Sales & Mktg Mg), D. Kershaw (I.T. Exec), J. Baldwin (Mgr), N. Appleton (Fin Mgr)
Immediate Holding Company: Newsquest
Registration no: 01386277 **No.of Employees:** 101 - 250
Product Groups: 28

Northcote Manor

Northcote Road Langho, Blackburn, BB6 8BE
Tel: 01254-240555 **Fax:** 01254-246568
E-mail: reception@northcote.com
Website: http://www.northcotemanor.com
Bank(s): Barclays
Directors: C. Vancroft (MD)
Managers: K. Matthews (Mktg Serv Mgr), L. Charnley (Fin Mgr)
Ultimate Holding Company: SILVERCLIFF LIMITED (ISLE OF MAN)
Immediate Holding Company: SANDSHOW LIMITED
Registration no: 02002462 **Date established:** 1986
No.of Employees: 21 - 50 **Product Groups:** 69

Date of Accounts	Mar 11	Mar 10	Mar 09
Sales Turnover	4m	4m	N/A
Pre Tax Profit/Loss	-243	5	-307
Working Capital	-1m	-691	-751
Fixed Assets	3m	3m	3m
Current Assets	925	960	478
Current Liabilities	1m	736	475

Northern Industrial Electronics Ltd

Unit 115 Glenfields Park, Blackburn, BB1 5PF
Tel: 01254-673747 **Fax:** 01254-56177
E-mail: enquiries@n-i-e.co.uk
Website: http://www.n-i-e.co.uk
Bank(s): National Westminster, Blackburn
Directors: J. Lenehean (MD), J. Lennohen (MD), J. Lenehan (Prop), M. Cooper (Dir)
Managers: D. Lennohen (Sales & Mktg Mg), S. Park (I.T. Exec), J. Riches (Sales Admin)
Immediate Holding Company: NORTHERN INDUSTRIAL ELECTRONICS LIMITED
Registration no: 02772341 **VAT No.:** GB 375 1428 48
Date established: 1992 **Turnover:** £250,000 - £500,000
No.of Employees: 11 - 20 **Product Groups:** 48

Date of Accounts	Jul 11	Jul 10	Jul 09
Working Capital	425	288	213
Fixed Assets	47	48	50
Current Assets	612	484	338

P D Precision Grinding

Clarendon Road, Blackburn, BB1 9SS
Tel: 01254-663235 **Fax:** 01254-695222
E-mail: sales@prepol.com
Website: http://www.prepol.com
Directors: P. Duehurst (MD)
Immediate Holding Company: EAST LANCASHIRE REFRIGERATION LIMITED
Registration no: 01605243 **Date established:** 1981
No.of Employees: 1 - 10 **Product Groups:** 46

Date of Accounts	Feb 12	Feb 11	Feb 10
Working Capital	774	758	791
Fixed Assets	112	108	130
Current Assets	1m	1m	1m

P R I Ltd

Blackburn Technology Management Centre Challenge Way, Blackburn, BB1 5QB
Tel: 01254-697200
E-mail: john.cowburn@pri.co.uk
Website: http://www.pri.co.uk
Managers: J. Cowburn, J. Cowburn
Immediate Holding Company: EWOOD ENTERPRISES LIMITED
Registration no: 04224860 **Date established:** 2001
Turnover: £10m - £20m **No.of Employees:** 1 - 10 **Product Groups:** 38, 44, 49

Date of Accounts	Mar 06	Mar 05	Mar 04
Working Capital	76	75	72
Current Assets	77	107	152

Park Chemicals Ltd

15 Rowen Park, BLACKBURN, BB2 7BE
Tel: 01254-693962
E-mail: info@parkchemicals.co.uk
Website: http://www.parkchemicals.co.uk
Directors: P. Preston (Dir), C. Bennett (Dir)
Date established: 2005 **Turnover:** £250,000 - £500,000
No.of Employees: 1 - 10 **Product Groups:** 32, 42, 66, 84

Date of Accounts	Mar 08	Mar 07
Working Capital	7	11
Fixed Assets	5	5
Current Assets	44	51
Current Liabilities	37	41

Parkinson & Worden Ltd

12-14 Chapel Street, Blackburn, BB2 2EH
Tel: 01254-580166 **Fax:** 01254-664940
E-mail: chris@parkinson-worden.fsnet.co.uk
Website: http://www.parkinsonsigns.com
Bank(s): National Westminster
Directors: I. Parkinson (MD)
Ultimate Holding Company: PARKINSON HOLDINGS LIMITED
Immediate Holding Company: PARKINSON & WORDEN LIMITED
Registration no: 00412745 **VAT No.:** GB 174 7259 37
Date established: 1946 **No.of Employees:** 11 - 20 **Product Groups:** 49, 52

Date of Accounts	Sep 11	Sep 10	Sep 09
Working Capital	5	-1	-8
Current Assets	275	170	99

Partwell Cutting Technology Ltd

Bridge Works 120 Stanley Street, Blackburn, BB1 3BW
Tel: 01254-671875 **Fax:** 01254-674823
E-mail: info@partwell.com
Website: http://www.partwell.com
Bank(s): HSBC Bank plc
Directors: A. Bradburn (MD), K. Bradburn (Co Sec)
Ultimate Holding Company: PARTWELL HOLDINGS LIMITED
Immediate Holding Company: PARTWELL CUTTING TECHNOLOGY LIMITED
Registration no: 01405082 **Date established:** 1978 **Turnover:** £1m - £2m
No.of Employees: 11 - 20 **Product Groups:** 27, 41, 42, 48, 66

Date of Accounts	Jun 11	Jun 10	Jun 09
Working Capital	3	-51	-3
Fixed Assets	167	174	78
Current Assets	424	300	321
Current Liabilities	N/A	25	N/A

Pennine Trims

5 Rosewood Business Park St James's Road, Blackburn, BB1 8ET
Tel: 01254-582715 **Fax:** 01254-663309
Managers: M. Esser (Mgr)
VAT No.: GB 598 0734 95 **Turnover:** £250,000 - £500,000
No.of Employees: 1 - 10 **Product Groups:** 23, 30, 48

Penny Profit

77 Victoria Street, Blackburn, BB1 6DS
Tel: 01254-673533
Directors: A. Jawaid (Prop)
Date established: 1978 **No.of Employees:** 1 - 10 **Product Groups:** 20, 40, 41

Pentland Wholesale Ltd

Unit 13 Whitebirk Industrial Estate, Blackburn, BB2 3BA
Tel: 01254-614444 **Fax:** 01254-614477
E-mail: sales@pentlandwholesale.co.uk
Website: http://www.pentlandwholesale.co.uk
Directors: C. Allen (Fin), P. Campbell (Fin), M. Mason (Comm)
Managers: R. Taylor (Mktg Serv Mgr)
Ultimate Holding Company: PENTLAND GROUP PLC
Immediate Holding Company: PENTLAND WHOLESALE LIMITED
Registration no: 02761041 **Date established:** 1992
Turnover: £10m - £20m **No.of Employees:** 11 - 20 **Product Groups:** 26, 32, 36, 37, 40, 41, 63, 66, 67

Date of Accounts	Dec 11	Dec 10	Dec 09
Sales Turnover	10m	11m	10m
Pre Tax Profit/Loss	438	821	3m
Working Capital	6m	6m	6m
Fixed Assets	128	128	147
Current Assets	7m	7m	7m
Current Liabilities	452	369	363

Petre Process Plant Ltd

Carr Cottage Mill Whalley New Road, Blackburn, BB1 9SR
Tel: 01254-682030 **Fax:** 01254-55752
E-mail: sales@petreprocess.com
Website: http://www.petreprocess.com
Directors: C. Topham (Fin), K. Topham (Sales)
Immediate Holding Company: PETRE PROCESS PLANT LIMITED
Registration no: 01829233 **Date established:** 1984
Turnover: £250,000 - £500,000 **No.of Employees:** 1 - 10
Product Groups: 30, 35, 36, 37, 38, 39, 40, 41, 42, 45, 47, 48, 52, 66, 67, 68

Date of Accounts	Sep 11	Sep 10	Sep 09
Working Capital	1	-1	-12
Fixed Assets	9	13	18
Current Assets	99	77	100

Pets Choice Ltd

Gladstone Street, Blackburn, BB1 3ES
Tel: 01254-54545 **Fax:** 01254- 681446
E-mail: info@petschoice.co.uk
Website: http://www.petschoice.co.uk
Bank(s): Lloyds
Directors: T. Raeburn (Grp Chief Exec), S. Campbell (Co Sec), A. Raeburn (Sales)
Managers: S. Harrowell (Mktg Serv Mgr), D. Cook (Buyer), M. Hudson (Sales Admin)
Ultimate Holding Company: PET FOOD BRANDS LIMITED
Immediate Holding Company: PETS CHOICE LIMITED
Registration no: 02181268 **VAT No.:** GB 507 9093 34
Date established: 1987 **Turnover:** £20m - £50m
No.of Employees: 101 - 250 **Product Groups:** 20, 62

Date of Accounts	Jun 09	Jun 08	Jun 10
Sales Turnover	17m	N/A	18m
Pre Tax Profit/Loss	77	155	501
Working Capital	-915	-331	240
Fixed Assets	6m	6m	6m
Current Assets	5m	4m	6m
Current Liabilities	2m	2m	3m

Pheonix Dryers & Engineering Ltd

Carlinghurst Road, Blackburn, BB2 1PN
Tel: 01254-679944 **Fax:** 01254-681373
E-mail: info@phoenix-dryers.co.uk
Website: http://www.phoenix-dryers.co.uk
Bank(s): National Westminster
Directors: J. Beardsworth (MD)
Immediate Holding Company: PHOENIX DRYERS & ENGINEERING (BLACKBURN) LIMITED
Registration no: 01780599 **VAT No.:** GB 375 4029 47
Date established: 1983 **Turnover:** £2m - £5m **No.of Employees:** 11 - 20
Product Groups: 40, 42, 43

Date of Accounts	Dec 11	Dec 10	Dec 09
Working Capital	442	337	316
Fixed Assets	16	9	12
Current Assets	1m	708	733

Precision Polymer Engineering Ltd

Greenbank Road, Blackburn, BB1 3EA
Tel: 01254-295400 **Fax:** 01254-680182
E-mail: sales@prepol.com
Website: http://www.prepol.com
Bank(s): Lloyds TSB
Directors: P. Benedetto (Fin)
Managers: K. Healey (Purch Mgr), S. Corfield (Sales Prom Mgr), G. Rae (Personnel), G. Bradshaw (Tech Serv Mgr), B. Hogarth, D. Maskell (Mktg Serv Mgr)
Ultimate Holding Company: IDEX CORPORATION (USA)
Immediate Holding Company: PRECISION POLYMER ENGINEERING LIMITED
Registration no: 01476647 **VAT No.:** GB 792 4270 14
Date established: 1980 **Turnover:** £10m - £20m
No.of Employees: 101 - 250 **Product Groups:** 29

Date of Accounts	Dec 11	Dec 10	Jul 09
Sales Turnover	30m	16m	8m
Pre Tax Profit/Loss	8m	3m	2m
Working Capital	10m	4m	2m
Fixed Assets	5m	4m	4m
Current Assets	21m	14m	5m
Current Liabilities	4m	2m	1m

Presspart Manufacturing Ltd

Phillips Road, Blackburn, BB1 5RF
Tel: 01254-582233 **Fax:** 01254-584100
E-mail: blackburn@presspart.com
Website: http://www.presspart.com
Bank(s): The Royal Bank of Scotland
Directors: D. Schmitz (Fin), J. Hemy (Comm)
Ultimate Holding Company: HEITKAMP & THUMANN KG (GERMANY)
Immediate Holding Company: PRESSPART MANUFACTURING LIMITED
Registration no: 00995387 **Date established:** 1970
Turnover: £20m - £50m **No.of Employees:** 101 - 250
Product Groups: 35, 39, 48

Date of Accounts	Dec 11	Dec 10	Dec 09
Sales Turnover	28m	22m	19m
Pre Tax Profit/Loss	4m	3m	1m
Working Capital	383	3m	4m
Fixed Assets	7m	6m	7m
Current Assets	6m	6m	6m
Current Liabilities	2m	2m	1m

Promethean Ltd

Lower Phillips Road Whitebirk Industrial Estate, Blackburn, BB1 5TH
Tel: 01254-676921 **Fax:** 01254-581574
E-mail: neil.johnson@prometheanworld.com
Website: http://www.prometheanworld.com
Managers: N. Johnson (Comptroller), R. Degan, D. Murray
Ultimate Holding Company: PROMETHEAN WORLD PLC
Immediate Holding Company: PROMETHEAN LIMITED
Registration no: 01308938 **Date established:** 1977
No.of Employees: 251 - 500 **Product Groups:** 28, 37, 44

Date of Accounts	Dec 11	Dec 10	Dec 09
Sales Turnover	160m	175m	154m
Pre Tax Profit/Loss	8m	37m	24m
Working Capital	40m	48m	32m
Fixed Assets	50m	45m	35m
Current Assets	93m	85m	83m
Current Liabilities	10m	8m	8m

R P C Containers Ltd

Haslingden Road, Blackburn, BB1 2PX
Tel: 01254-682298 **Fax:** 01254-583752
E-mail: a.bloor@rpc-blackburn.co.uk
Website: http://www.rpc-containers.co.uk
Managers: A. Bloor (Mgr), C. Gardner, C. Lee (Personnel), S. Dyer (Sales & Mktg Mg), S. Dyer (Sales & Mktg Mgr), D. Wyke (Fin Mgr), D. Willis (Personnel), J. Bell (Purch Mgr)
Ultimate Holding Company: RPC GROUP PLC
Immediate Holding Company: RPC CONTAINERS LIMITED
Registration no: 02786492 **Date established:** 1993
No.of Employees: 251 - 500 **Product Groups:** 30, 66

Date of Accounts	Mar 11	Mar 10	Mar 09
Sales Turnover	189m	175m	183m
Pre Tax Profit/Loss	14m	15m	-1m
Working Capital	21m	17m	-37m
Fixed Assets	81m	77m	79m
Current Assets	76m	66m	68m
Current Liabilities	17m	13m	14m

Ralspeed Ltd

Hurstwood Court Mercer Way Shadsworth Business Park, Shadsworth Business Park, Blackburn, BB1 2QU
Tel: 01254-582345 **Fax:** 01254-668414
E-mail: sales@ralspeed.co.uk
Website: http://www.ralspeed.com
Bank(s): Yorkshire
Directors: P. Schaffel (Dir)
Immediate Holding Company: RALSPEED LIMITED
Registration no: 02291283 **VAT No.:** GB 498 0141 33
Date established: 1988 **Turnover:** £500,000 - £1m
No.of Employees: 11 - 20 **Product Groups:** 37

Date of Accounts	Mar 12	Mar 11	Mar 10
Working Capital	118	72	56
Fixed Assets	33	31	27
Current Assets	352	278	289
Current Liabilities	N/A	N/A	55

Readyspex Ltd

Glenfield Park Two Blakewater Road, Blackburn, BB1 5QH
Tel: 01254-680010 **Fax:** 01254-680241
Website: http://www.readyspex.co.uk
Directors: D. Singer (Sales), M. Lee (Fin)
Ultimate Holding Company: MOMENTAI PLC
Immediate Holding Company: READYSPEX LIMITED
Registration no: 02332312 **VAT No.:** GB 525 4665 38
Date established: 1989 **Turnover:** Up to £250,000
No.of Employees: 1 - 10 **Product Groups:** 38

Date of Accounts	Mar 12	Mar 11	Mar 10
Sales Turnover	143	167	484
Pre Tax Profit/Loss	7	3	-168

Working Capital	53	345	342
Fixed Assets	N/A	1	1
Current Assets	200	365	385
Current Liabilities	5	15	38

Regina International Ltd (Sales & Service Centre)

Unit 1 Greenbank Business Park Dyneley Road, Blackburn, BB1 3AB
Tel: 01254-661116 **Fax:** 01254-59456
E-mail: sales.uk@reginachain.net
Website: http://www.regina.it
Directors: D. Elliott (Sales)
Immediate Holding Company: REGINA INTERNATIONAL LIMITED
Registration no: 04706536 **Date established:** 2003 **Turnover:** £2m - £5m
No.of Employees: 1 - 10 **Product Groups:** 30, 35, 39, 45

Date of Accounts	Dec 11	Dec 10	Dec 09
Working Capital	-60	-62	-63
Fixed Assets	10	10	10
Current Assets	887	931	1m

Renown Gears Ltd

Dyneley Rd Greenbank Business Pk, Blackburn, BB1 3AB
Tel: 01254-679222 **Fax:** 01254-680534
E-mail: sales@renowngears.co.uk
Website: http://www.renowngears.co.uk
Bank(s): National Westminster Bank Plc
Directors: B. Simmons (Sales & Tech), J. Madden (MD)
Managers: M. Barton (Accounts), A. McMinn (Works Gen Mgr), T. Madden (Purch Mgr)
Registration no: 00902451 **VAT No.:** GB 174 7484 30
Turnover: £2m - £5m **No.of Employees:** 21 - 50 **Product Groups:** 35, 39, 40, 46

Date of Accounts	Mar 11	Mar 10	Mar 09
Working Capital	117	87	136
Fixed Assets	2m	2m	2m
Current Assets	1m	944	925

Rishton Welding & Engineering Co. Ltd

Heys Lane Great Harwood, Blackburn, BB6 7UA
Tel: 01254-886361 **Fax:** 01254-888530
E-mail: mrpilling@btconnect.com
Bank(s): Barclays
Directors: S. Pilling (MD)
Immediate Holding Company: RISHTON WELDING & ENGINEERING COMPANY LIMITED
Registration no: 00404834 **VAT No.:** GB 174 3414 71
Date established: 1946 **Turnover:** £1m - £2m **No.of Employees:** 11 - 20
Product Groups: 26, 35, 36, 40, 45, 48

Date of Accounts	Mar 12	Mar 11	Mar 10
Working Capital	543	472	348
Fixed Assets	86	91	99
Current Assets	1m	924	783

Rock Memorials

Monumental Yard 179 Blackburn Road, Great Harwood, Blackburn, BB6 7LU
Tel: 01254-884164
E-mail: info@rockmemorials.co.uk
Website: http://www.rockmemorials.co.uk
Directors: K. Howe (Prop)
Date established: 1971 **Turnover:** £250,000 - £500,000
No.of Employees: 1 - 10 **Product Groups:** 14, 33, 49, 52, 65, 66, 67

Rosenberger Micro Coax

9 Walker Industrial Estate Walker Road, Guide, Blackburn, BB1 2QE
Tel: 01254-660054 **Fax:** 01254-660053
E-mail: sales@rmcoax.com
Website: http://www.rmcoax.com
Managers: P. Lewis (Comptroller), J. Wailing (Purch Mgr), C. Bardsley (Personnel)
No.of Employees: 21 - 50 **Product Groups:** 37, 45

S A S Gas Services

21 Beech Street Great Harwood, Blackburn, BB6 7RB
Tel: 01254-882868 **Fax:** 01254-600561
Directors: S. Sykes (Prop)
No.of Employees: 1 - 10 **Product Groups:** 20, 40, 41

S G Aluminium Ltd

Unit B Sett End Road West Shadsworth Business Park, Blackburn, BB1 2QJ
Tel: 01254-691600 **Fax:** 01253-340526
E-mail: ken@sg-aluminium.co.uk
Website: http://www.sg-aluminium.co.uk
Bank(s): National Westminster
Directors: L. Ashurst (Co Sec), K. Smith (Dir), M. Hopkinson (Dir)
Managers: A. Leigh
Ultimate Holding Company: SG ALUMINIUM GROUP LIMITED
Immediate Holding Company: S.G. ALUMINIUM LIMITED
Registration no: 01234843 **Date established:** 1975 **Turnover:** £2m - £5m
No.of Employees: 51 - 100 **Product Groups:** 30, 35, 36

Date of Accounts	Mar 12	Mar 11	Mar 10
Sales Turnover	5m	8m	7m
Pre Tax Profit/Loss	179	238	444
Working Capital	1m	1m	1m
Fixed Assets	54	150	137
Current Assets	3m	3m	3m
Current Liabilities	318	252	317

S & J Welding

575 Preston Old Road Cherry Tree, Blackburn, BB2 5NU
Tel: 07973-417501 **Fax:** 01772-877444
E-mail: sandjwelding1981@aol.com
Website: http://www.sandjwelding.co.uk/
Directors: S. Turner (Prop)
No.of Employees: 1 - 10 **Product Groups:** 35, 48

Sharif Toolmakers

Barnmeadow Lane Great Harwood, Blackburn, BB6 7AB
Tel: 01254-884466 **Fax:** 01254-887290
Directors: O. Sharif (Prop)
Immediate Holding Company: CHERRY TREE PRODUCTS LIMITED
Registration no: 00429225 **Date established:** 1947
Turnover: Up to £250,000 **No.of Employees:** 1 - 10 **Product Groups:** 36

Silicone Engineering Ltd

Blakewater Road, Blackburn, BB1 3HU
Tel: 01254-261321 **Fax:** 01254-583519
E-mail: paul.kinsella@silicone.co.uk
Website: http://www.silicone.co.uk
Bank(s): National Westminster Bank Plc
Directors: P. Kinsella (MD), A. Peel (Sales), D. Beadman (Co Sec)
Managers: J. Mehta (Personnel), S. Aszal (Tech Serv Mgr), N. Moosa
Ultimate Holding Company: SILICONE HOLDINGS LIMITED
Immediate Holding Company: SILICONE ENGINEERING LIMITED
Registration no: 04340974 **VAT No.:** GB 792 5387 85
Date established: 2001 **Turnover:** £10m - £20m
No.of Employees: 101 - 250 **Product Groups:** 29, 30, 31, 32, 33, 36, 37, 48, 66

Date of Accounts	Dec 11	Dec 10	Dec 09
Sales Turnover	13m	11m	9m
Pre Tax Profit/Loss	867	1m	302
Working Capital	166	198	-9
Fixed Assets	1m	883	644
Current Assets	4m	3m	3m
Current Liabilities	2m	2m	2m

Specialist Skating Services

40 Wellington Road, Blackburn, BB2 2NQ
Tel: 01254-680937 **Fax:** 01254-916134
E-mail: ianrob99@googlemail.com
Website: http://www.specialistskatingservices.co.uk
Directors: I. Robertson (Prop)
No.of Employees: 1 - 10 **Product Groups:** 22, 49

Star Uretech Ltd

Enterprise House Hollin Bridge Street, Blackburn, BB2 4AY
Tel: 01254-663444 **Fax:** 01254-681886
E-mail: info@star-uretech.com
Website: http://www.star-uretech.com
Directors: T. Hughes (MD)
Immediate Holding Company: STAR URETECH LTD
Registration no: 04131266 **Date established:** 2000
Turnover: £250,000 - £500,000 **No.of Employees:** 11 - 20
Product Groups: 07, 30, 31, 32, 33, 52

Date of Accounts	Dec 11	Dec 10	Dec 09
Working Capital	233	216	136
Fixed Assets	149	171	180
Current Assets	662	702	554

Stevens Group Ltd

Greenback Technology Park, Blackburn, BB1 5QB
Tel: 01254-685200 **Fax:** 01254-685202
E-mail: info@stevensgroupltd.com
Website: http://www.stevensgroupltd.com
Bank(s): National Westminster Bank Plc
Managers: D. Fisher (Serv Mgr), M. Howe (Ops Mgr), T. Hawkins (Comm)
Ultimate Holding Company: DATALINKS SRL (ITALY)
Immediate Holding Company: STEVENS GROUP LIMITED
Registration no: 00745488 **Date established:** 1962 **Turnover:** £5m - £10m
No.of Employees: 21 - 50 **Product Groups:** 38, 48

Date of Accounts	Dec 11	Dec 10	Dec 09
Working Capital	248	208	140
Fixed Assets	1m	1m	1m
Current Assets	966	872	836

Styropack UK Ltd

Victoria Works Parker Street, Rishton, Blackburn, BB1 4NT
Tel: 01254-885946 **Fax:** 01254-889497
E-mail: blackburn@styropack.co.uk
Website: http://www.styropack.co.uk
Bank(s): National Westminster Bank Plc
Directors: K. Hutchins (Fin)
Ultimate Holding Company: SYNBRA GROUP BV (NETHERLANDS)
Immediate Holding Company: STYROPACK (UK) LIMITED
Registration no: SC041753 **VAT No.:** GB 265 4621 54
Date established: 1965 **Turnover:** £20m - £50m
No.of Employees: 21 - 50 **Product Groups:** 30, 31, 42

Date of Accounts	Dec 11	Dec 10	Dec 09
Sales Turnover	12m	13m	14m
Pre Tax Profit/Loss	-611	-44	-728
Working Capital	-2m	-2m	-2m
Fixed Assets	5m	5m	6m
Current Assets	4m	4m	4m
Current Liabilities	921	1m	1m

T T I Group

Lower Philips Road Whitebirk Industrial Estate, Blackburn, BB1 5RE
Tel: 01254-264901 **Fax:** 01254-662552
E-mail: joecadwallader@ttigroup.co.uk
Website: http://www.ttigroup.co.uk
Managers: J. Cadwallader (Works Gen Mgr)
Immediate Holding Company: AALBERTS INDUSTRIES U.K. LTD
Registration no: 00884462 **Turnover:** £10m - £20m
No.of Employees: 21 - 50 **Product Groups:** 40, 48, 84

Tensar International Ltd

Cunningham Court Shadsworth Business Park, Blackburn, BB1 2QX
Tel: 01254-262431 **Fax:** 01254-266868
E-mail: info@tensar.co.uk
Website: http://www.tensarinternational.com
Date established: 1957 **Turnover:** £20m - £50m
No.of Employees: 101 - 250 **Product Groups:** 23, 30, 33, 45, 51, 66, 84

Date of Accounts	Dec 11	Dec 10	Dec 09
Sales Turnover	39m	29m	27m
Pre Tax Profit/Loss	4m	936	3m
Working Capital	47m	44m	43m
Fixed Assets	3m	3m	3m
Current Assets	65m	74m	69m
Current Liabilities	6m	9m	8m

Thom Engineering Ltd

Mohawk Buildings Gorse Street, Blackburn, BB1 3EU
Tel: 01254-676222 **Fax:** 01254-672053
E-mail: bryn@thomengineering.co.uk
Website: http://www.thomengineering.co.uk
Bank(s): Midland Bank
Directors: B. Robert (MD), B. Roberts (MD)
Immediate Holding Company: THOM ENGINEERING LIMITED
Registration no: 01474781 **VAT No.:** 325 9643 39 **Date established:** 1980
Turnover: £1m - £2m **No.of Employees:** 11 - 20 **Product Groups:** 43

Date of Accounts	Mar 10	Mar 09	Mar 08
Working Capital	298	316	232
Fixed Assets	229	241	268
Current Assets	778	802	903

Daniel Thwaites plc
Star Brewery Penny Street, Blackburn, BB1 6HL
Tel: 01254-686868 **Fax:** 01254-681439
E-mail: info@danielthwaites.com
Website: http://www.thwaites.co.uk
Bank(s): Lloyds TSB Bank plc & HSBC Bank plc & The Royal Bank of Scotland
Directors: L. Jepson (Pers), B. Jenkins (Sales), S. Woodward (Co Sec)
Managers: C. Webb (Purch Mgr), R. Bailey, L. Williams, K. Wood, E. Kilbride
Immediate Holding Company: DANIEL THWAITES PUBLIC LIMITED COMPANY
Registration no: 00051702 **VAT No.:** GB 444 7390 36
Date established: 1997 **Turnover:** £125m - £250m
No.of Employees: 251 - 500 **Product Groups:** 21, 62

Date of Accounts	Mar 12	Mar 11	Mar 10
Sales Turnover	137m	127m	135m
Pre Tax Profit/Loss	7m	7m	1m
Working Capital	2m	7m	5m
Fixed Assets	285m	299m	310m
Current Assets	27m	31m	27m
Current Liabilities	14m	12m	11m

Two PlusTwo - Logical Business Solutions
86 Darwen Street, Blackburn, BB2 2AD
Tel: 07779-733364
E-mail: enquiries@twoplustwo.biz
Website: http://www.twoplustwo.biz
Managers: M. Gupta (Comm)
Turnover: Up to £250,000 **No.of Employees:** 1 - 10 **Product Groups:** 80

Tyson Lighting
Gibson House Walpole Street, Blackburn, BB1 1DB
Tel: 01254-266000 **Fax:** 01254-266001
E-mail: sales@tyson-lighting.co.uk
Website: http://www.tyson-lighting.co.uk
Bank(s): National Westminster Bank Plc
Directors: J. Gibson (Fin), P. Gibson (MD)
Managers: D. Day (Purch Mgr)
Immediate Holding Company: HAROLD TYSON & CO,LIMITED
Registration no: 00682184 **VAT No.:** GB 174 8044 53
Date established: 1961 **Turnover:** £1m - £2m **No.of Employees:** 21 - 50
Product Groups: 37

Date of Accounts	Dec 11	Dec 10	Dec 09
Working Capital	465	307	327
Fixed Assets	309	320	302
Current Assets	811	614	530

Usf Packaging
Number One The Beehive Lions Drive, Shadsworth Business Park, Blackburn, BB1 2QS
Tel: 01254-678988 **Fax:** 01254-699569
Website: http://www.unsa-uk.com
Managers: M. Atkinson (Mgr)
Immediate Holding Company: F.D. SIMS LIMITED
Registration no: 04139696 **Date established:** 2001
Turnover: £20m - £50m **No.of Employees:** 1 - 10 **Product Groups:** 38, 42

Verifyne Plastic Products Ltd
Unit 1 Lever Mill Slater Street, Blackburn, BB2 4PA
Tel: 01254-675639 **Fax:** 01254-673787
E-mail: enquiries@verifyne-plastics.co.uk
Website: http://www.verifyne-plastics.co.uk
Bank(s): National Westminster Bank Plc
Directors: S. McHugh (Dir), A. Holderness (MD)
Immediate Holding Company: VERIFYNE PLASTIC PRODUCTS LIMITED
Registration no: 01567034 **VAT No.:** GB 326 1279 68
Date established: 1981 **Turnover:** £500,000 - £1m
No.of Employees: 21 - 50 **Product Groups:** 30, 31, 39, 48, 66

Date of Accounts	Jul 11	Jul 10	Jul 09
Working Capital	217	333	320
Fixed Assets	210	220	157
Current Assets	467	578	624

Vogue Electrics
Back Hesketh Street Great Harwood, Blackburn, BB6 7DN
Tel: 01254-887321
Directors: P. Lewis (Prop)
Registration no: 02420841 **Date established:** 1989
No.of Employees: 1 - 10 **Product Groups:** 43

Warwick & Bailey Engineering
Witton Mill Stancliffe Street, Blackburn, BB2 2QU
Tel: 01254-662211 **Fax:** 01254-662277
E-mail: sales@warwick-bailey.com
Website: http://www.warwick-bailey.com
Bank(s): Midland
Managers: S. Draycott (Mgr), S. Draygott (Mgr), I. Davis (Chief Acct), S. Draycocktt (Chief Mgr)
Immediate Holding Company: PERMOID INDUSTRIES LTD
Turnover: £2m - £5m **No.of Employees:** 11 - 20 **Product Groups:** 35, 39, 48, 84

Weltonhurst Ltd
Centurion Way Roman Road, Blackburn, BB1 2LD
Tel: 01254-671177 **Fax:** 01254-671717
E-mail: cs@weltonhurst.co.uk
Website: http://www.weltonhurst.co.uk
Bank(s): Lloyds TSB
Managers: S. Wilding (Tech Serv Mgr), L. Bottomley (Comm), A. Fish (Comptroller), C. Slinger (Works Gen Mgr)
Immediate Holding Company: WELTONHURST LIMITED
Registration no: 00894340 **VAT No.:** 628 7677 87 **Date established:** 1966
Turnover: £5m - £10m **No.of Employees:** 101 - 250 **Product Groups:** 30

Date of Accounts	Dec 11	Dec 10	Dec 09
Sales Turnover	10m	9m	7m
Pre Tax Profit/Loss	182	-26	-137
Working Capital	-694	-1m	-1m
Fixed Assets	6m	6m	5m
Current Assets	3m	3m	2m
Current Liabilities	2m	2m	2m

Worswick Engineering
Philips Road, Blackburn, BB1 5SG
Tel: 01254-261351 **Fax:** 01254-682208
E-mail: sales@worswick.com
Website: http://www.worswick.com
Bank(s): Lloyds TSB Bank plc
Directors: A. Worswick (MD)
Immediate Holding Company: WORSWICK ENGINEERING LTD
Registration no: 04587329 **VAT No.:** GB 174 8007 59
Date established: 2002 **Turnover:** £2m - £5m **No.of Employees:** 11 - 20
Product Groups: 46

Date of Accounts	Dec 11	Dec 10	Dec 09
Working Capital	-0	-49	-14
Fixed Assets	614	618	18
Current Assets	988	139	465

Blackpool

adeptdoors Ltd
24-25 Squires Gate Industrial Estate Squires Gate Lane, Blackpool, FY4 3RN
Tel: 01253-403328 **Fax:** 01253-403329
E-mail: enquiries@adeptdoors.co.uk
Website: http://www.adeptdoors.co.uk
Directors: S. Abbott (Dir), J. Abbott (Asst MD)
Managers: C. Pickersgill (Sales Prom Mgr)
Immediate Holding Company: Adept Doors Ltd
Registration no: 05572617 **Date established:** 2005
No.of Employees: 1 - 10 **Product Groups:** 35

Ballroom Central & Dance Wear Central
PO Box 1246, Blackpool, FY1 9FJ
Tel: 08445-616664
E-mail: ballroomcentral@broadshire.com
Website: http://www.ballroomcentral.co.uk
Managers: E. O'Flannery (Mktg Serv Mgr), J. Hurley (Sales Prom Mgr)
Date established: 2008 **No.of Employees:** 1 - 10 **Product Groups:** 22

Blackpool Catering Equipment
195 Dickson Road, Blackpool, FY1 2HQ
Tel: 01253-622449 **Fax:** 01253-290740
E-mail: blackpoolcatering@hotmail.com
Website: http://www.catering-equipment-suppliers.co.uk
Directors: I. Brough (Prop)
Date established: 1990 **No.of Employees:** 1 - 10 **Product Groups:** 20, 40, 41

Blackpool Pleasure Beach Ltd
Ocean Boulevard, Blackpool, FY4 1EZ
Tel: 08712-221234 **Fax:** 01253-401098
E-mail: info@bpbltd.com
Website: http://www.blackpoolpleasurebeach.com
Bank(s): National Westminster Bank Plc
Managers: M. Wilkins (Sales Prom Mgr)
Ultimate Holding Company: BLACKPOOL PLEASURE BEACH (HOLDINGS) LIMITED
Immediate Holding Company: BLACKPOOL PLEASURE BEACH LIMITED
Registration no: 01876267 **Date established:** 1985
Turnover: £20m - £50m **No.of Employees:** 501 - 1000
Product Groups: 89

Date of Accounts	Mar 08	Apr 09	Apr 10
Sales Turnover	29m	24m	24m
Pre Tax Profit/Loss	3m	-4m	-521
Working Capital	-11m	-14m	-12m
Fixed Assets	25m	24m	23m
Current Assets	8m	7m	6m
Current Liabilities	2m	2m	2m

Booth Dispencers
Moor Park Avenue, Blackpool, FY2 0LZ
Tel: 01253-501800 **Fax:** 01253-501804
E-mail: sales@booth-dispensers.co.uk
Website: http://www.booth-dispensers.co.uk
Directors: S. Christopher (Fin)
Managers: M. Davis (Purch Mgr), M. Rogers (Tech Serv Mgr), J. Smart (Personnel)
Immediate Holding Company: BOOTH DISPENSERS LIMITED
Registration no: 03882967 **Date established:** 1999 **Turnover:** £5m - £10m
No.of Employees: 51 - 100 **Product Groups:** 49

Date of Accounts	Dec 11	Dec 10	Dec 09
Sales Turnover	7m	5m	4m
Pre Tax Profit/Loss	450	167	-287
Working Capital	709	562	494
Fixed Assets	873	974	1m
Current Assets	3m	2m	2m
Current Liabilities	866	507	236

Brighthouse Ltd
47-53 Abingdon Street, Blackpool, FY1 1DH
Tel: 01253-626919 **Fax:** 01253-299410
Website: http://www.brighthouse.info
Managers: S. Sykes (Mgr)
Ultimate Holding Company: VISION CAPITAL PARTNERS VI B LP
Immediate Holding Company: BRIGHTHOUSE LIMITED
Registration no: 06073794 **Date established:** 2007
No.of Employees: 11 - 20 **Product Groups:** 36, 40

Date of Accounts	Mar 12	Mar 11	Mar 10
Sales Turnover	266m	228m	197m
Pre Tax Profit/Loss	29m	25m	20m
Working Capital	57m	49m	68m
Fixed Assets	171m	161m	123m
Current Assets	97m	87m	98m
Current Liabilities	29m	26m	22m

Max Carlyle
61 Chorley Road, Blackpool, FY3 7XQ
Tel: 01253-398000 **Fax:** 01253-398000
Directors: D. Carlyle (Prop)
Immediate Holding Company: MAX CARLYLE LTD
Registration no: 05001101 **Date established:** 2003
No.of Employees: 1 - 10 **Product Groups:** 35

Date of Accounts	Dec 11	Dec 10	Dec 09
Working Capital	35	8	1
Fixed Assets	4	4	6
Current Assets	75	32	25

Caston PLC
Cornford Road, Blackpool, FY4 4QW
Tel: 01253-766411 **Fax:** 01253-691486
E-mail: paul@casdon.com
Website: http://www.casdon.co.uk
Directors: P. Cassidy (Ch), P. Cassidy (Dir)
Immediate Holding Company: CASDON PUBLIC LIMITED COMPANY
Registration no: 00565383 **Date established:** 1956 **Turnover:** £5m - £10m
No.of Employees: 1 - 10 **Product Groups:** 49

Date of Accounts	Apr 12	Apr 11	Apr 10
Sales Turnover	5m	5m	5m
Pre Tax Profit/Loss	215	-199	256
Working Capital	1m	873	1m
Fixed Assets	2m	2m	2m
Current Assets	2m	1m	2m
Current Liabilities	245	223	181

Challenger Security Products
4 Arkwright Court Blackpool & Fylde Industrial Estate, Blackpool, FY4 5DR
Tel: 01253-791888 **Fax:** 01253-791887
E-mail: stuart.burton@adivision.co.uk
Website: http://www.challenger.co.uk
Directors: I. Pain (Co Sec)
Managers: S. Burton (Ops Mgr)
Ultimate Holding Company: CANDOVER INVESTMENTS PLC
Immediate Holding Company: SECURE MAIL SERVICES LTD
Registration no: 02814516 **Turnover:** £1m - £2m
No.of Employees: 21 - 50 **Product Groups:** 35, 36

Chelsom Ltd
Heritage House Clifton Road, Blackpool, FY4 4QA
Tel: 01253-831400 **Fax:** 01253-698098
E-mail: sales@chelsom.co.uk
Website: http://www.chelsom.co.uk
Directors: G. Thompson (Fin)
Immediate Holding Company: CHELSOM LIMITED
Registration no: 00626933 **Date established:** 1959 **Turnover:** £5m - £10m
No.of Employees: 51 - 100 **Product Groups:** 33

Date of Accounts	Dec 11	Dec 10	Dec 09
Sales Turnover	N/A	N/A	7m
Pre Tax Profit/Loss	N/A	393	32
Working Capital	2m	2m	2m
Fixed Assets	47	44	49
Current Assets	3m	3m	3m
Current Liabilities	N/A	319	543

Cobblers Bench
128a Central Drive, Blackpool, FY1 5DY
Tel: 07890-307647
E-mail: cobblersbench@fsmail.net
Directors: P. Wilcoxson (Prop)
Turnover: Up to £250,000 **No.of Employees:** 1 - 10 **Product Groups:** 36, 52, 61

Coronation Rock Ltd
Unit 3 Wellington Point Amy Johnson Way, Blackpool, FY4 2RG
Tel: 01253-362810 **Fax:** 01253-407218
E-mail: sales@coronationrock.co.uk
Website: http://www.coronationrock.co.uk
Bank(s): HSBC Bank Plc
Directors: I. Atkinson (MD)
Ultimate Holding Company: GAINLOGIC LIMITED
Immediate Holding Company: CORONATION ROCK COMPANY,LIMITED
Registration no: 00220598 **VAT No.:** GB 534 3134 73
Date established: 2027 **Turnover:** £1m - £2m **No.of Employees:** 21 - 50
Product Groups: 20, 24, 25, 32, 33, 37, 46, 48, 62

Date of Accounts	Oct 10	Oct 09	Oct 08
Working Capital	99	102	138
Fixed Assets	513	512	525
Current Assets	543	505	486

Leonard Dews
18 Church Street, Blackpool, FY1 1EW
Tel: 01253-754940 **Fax:** 01253-294134
E-mail: enquiries@leonarddews.co.uk
Website: http://www.leonarddews.co.uk
Directors: M. Hyman (Prop)
No.of Employees: 1 - 10 **Product Groups:** 49, 65

Febland Group Ltd
Flag House Ashworth Road, Blackpool, FY4 4UN
Tel: 01253-600600 **Fax:** 01253-792211
E-mail: info@febland.co.uk
Website: http://www.febland.co.uk
Bank(s): National Westminster Bank Plc
Directors: T. Febland (MD)
Ultimate Holding Company: SIMMAN FEBLAND & CO.
Immediate Holding Company: FEBLAND GROUP LIMITED
Registration no: 00751678 **VAT No.:** GB 483 0227 60
Date established: 1963 **Turnover:** £2m - £5m **No.of Employees:** 21 - 50
Product Groups: 26, 33, 36, 63

Date of Accounts	Sep 11	Sep 10	Sep 09
Working Capital	1m	1m	1m
Fixed Assets	2m	2m	2m
Current Assets	2m	2m	2m

Fylde Hydraulics Ltd
6 Cornford Road, Blackpool, FY4 4QQ
Tel: 01253-694831 **Fax:** 01253-791191
Website: http://www.fyldehydraulics.co.uk
Directors: M. Picewicz (MD)
Immediate Holding Company: FYLDE HYDRAULICS LIMITED
Registration no: 01391643 **Date established:** 1978
No.of Employees: 1 - 10 **Product Groups:** 35, 45

Date of Accounts	Sep 11	Sep 10	Sep 09
Working Capital	92	90	94
Fixed Assets	4	1	N/A
Current Assets	124	113	114

Fylde Telecom Ltd
Unit 6 Whitehills Drive, Whitehills Business Park, Blackpool, FY4 5LW
Tel: 01253-600122 **Fax:** 01253-600121
E-mail: email@fyldetelecom.co.uk
Website: http://www.fyldetelecom.co.uk
Directors: L. McLinden (Fin), R. Dixson (Dir)
Immediate Holding Company: FYLDE LIMITED
Registration no: 04979731 **Date established:** 2003
No.of Employees: 1 - 10 **Product Groups:** 37, 67, 79, 80

Date of Accounts	Jun 11	Jun 10	Jun 09
Working Capital	421	271	64
Fixed Assets	498	475	490
Current Assets	504	339	96

Gilberts Blackpool Ltd
Gilair Works Clifton Road, Blackpool, FY4 4QT
Tel: 01253-766911 **Fax:** 01253-767941
E-mail: sales@gilbertsblackpool.com
Website: http://www.gilbertsblackpool.com
Bank(s): HSBC Bank plc
Directors: M. Wills (Sales), J. Haslam (Ch), G. Hodgson (Fin), J. Haslam (MD)
Managers: S. Riley (Buyer), S. Qualter (Snr Eng), A. Hornby (Tech Serv Mgr)
Immediate Holding Company: GILBERTS (BLACKPOOL) LIMITED
Registration no: 00673483 **Date established:** 1960
Turnover: £10m - £20m **No.of Employees:** 101 - 250
Product Groups: 35, 40, 46

Date of Accounts	Dec 11	Dec 10	Dec 09
Sales Turnover	16m	16m	18m
Pre Tax Profit/Loss	625	456	945
Working Capital	4m	4m	6m
Fixed Assets	1m	1m	1m
Current Assets	7m	9m	9m
Current Liabilities	2m	4m	2m

Glasdon Group Property Services (Holding Company)
Glasdon House Preston New Road, Blackpool, FY4 4WA
Tel: 01253-600430 **Fax:** 01253-761348
E-mail: property@glasdon.com
Website: http://www.aldonproperty.com
Bank(s): The Royal Bank of Scotland
Directors: A. Jackson (Co Sec)
Managers: S. Burns (Property Mgr)
Ultimate Holding Company: GLASDON GROUP LIMITED
Immediate Holding Company: GLASDON LIMITED
Registration no: 00797011 **VAT No.:** GB 155 8470 44
Date established: 1964 **Turnover:** £20m - £50m
No.of Employees: 11 - 20 **Product Groups:** 26, 33, 35

Date of Accounts	Oct 11	Oct 10	Oct 09
Working Capital	1m	1m	1m
Current Assets	1m	1m	1m

Glasdon International Ltd
Glasdon Inovation & Export Centre Preston New Road, Blackpool, FY4 4UY
Tel: 01253-600435 **Fax:** 01253-600436
E-mail: sales@glasdon.com
Website: http://www.glasdon.com
Bank(s): The Royal Bank of Scotland
Directors: A. Jackson (Fin)
Managers: W. Heart (Export Sales Mg)
Ultimate Holding Company: GLASDON GROUP LIMITED
Immediate Holding Company: GLASDON INTERNATIONAL LIMITED
Registration no: 02160568 **VAT No.:** GB 155 8470 44
Date established: 1987 **Turnover:** £10m - £20m
No.of Employees: 11 - 20 **Product Groups:** 26, 30, 39, 40, 45

Date of Accounts	Oct 11	Oct 10	Oct 09
Working Capital	2m	2m	2m
Fixed Assets	211	15	16
Current Assets	2m	2m	2m

Lebus International Engineers Ltd (Deck Machinery Division)
Pioneer House Shorebury Point, Blackpool, FY4 2RX
Tel: 01253-402402 **Fax:** 01253-894728
E-mail: enquiries@lebusinternational.com
Website: http://www.lebusintengineers.com
Directors: J. Wilson (Tech Serv)
Immediate Holding Company: LEBUS INTERNATIONAL ENGINEERS LIMITED
Registration no: 00716491 **Date established:** 1962
No.of Employees: 11 - 20 **Product Groups:** 45

Date of Accounts	Feb 08	Feb 11	Feb 10
Working Capital	-411	1m	911
Fixed Assets	63	119	131
Current Assets	2m	3m	2m

Maplin Electronics Ltd
Squires Gate Retail Park Amy Johnson Way, Blackpool, FY4 2RP
Tel: 01253-400839
Website: http://www.maplin.co.uk
Managers: C. Wright (Mgr)
Ultimate Holding Company: Maplin Electronics Group (Holdings) Ltd
Immediate Holding Company: MAPLIN ELECTRONICS LIMITED
Registration no: 01264385 **Date established:** 1976
Turnover: £125m - £250m **No.of Employees:** 11 - 20
Product Groups: 37, 61

Mobility Appliances Ltd
Foxs Garage Lichfield Road, Blackpool, FY1 2RR
Tel: 07889-197835 **Fax:** 01772-339174
Directors: J. Rayner (Dir)
Immediate Holding Company: MOBILITY APPLIANCES LIMITED
Registration no: 02603026 **Date established:** 1991
No.of Employees: 1 - 10 **Product Groups:** 35, 39, 45

Date of Accounts	Aug 11	Aug 10	Aug 07
Working Capital	3	3	N/A
Fixed Assets	1	1	1
Current Assets	11	15	9

North West Lifts Ltd
Progress Works Henry Street, Blackpool, FY1 5JG
Tel: 01253-344633 **Fax:** 01253-348382
E-mail: northwestlifts@aol.com
Website: http://www.northwestlifts.com
Managers: M. Roberts (Chief Mgr), M. Roberts (Mgr)
No.of Employees: 1 - 10 **Product Groups:** 35, 39, 45

Northern Neon Lights Blackpool Ltd
1 Chorley Road, Blackpool, FY3 7XQ
Tel: 01253-391462 **Fax:** 01253-302696
E-mail: j.cockerill@zeiss.co.uk
Bank(s): HSBC Bank plc
Directors: J. Cockerill (MD)
Immediate Holding Company: NORTHERN(NEON)LIGHTS,BLACKPOOL LIMITED
Registration no: 00617532 **VAT No.:** GB 153 5197 63
Date established: 1958 **Turnover:** £250,000 - £500,000
No.of Employees: 21 - 50 **Product Groups:** 37

Date of Accounts	Dec 11	Dec 10	Dec 09
Working Capital	362	196	131
Fixed Assets	808	850	933
Current Assets	957	722	439

F Parkinson Ltd
Mowbray Drive, Blackpool, FY3 7UN
Tel: 01253-394411 **Fax:** 01253-302088
E-mail: admin@fparkinson.co.uk
Website: http://www.fparkinson.co.uk
Directors: P. Glenn (Ch)
Ultimate Holding Company: WESTCLIFFE HOLDINGS LIMITED
Immediate Holding Company: F. PARKINSON LIMITED
Registration no: 00446626 **Date established:** 1947
Turnover: £20m - £50m **No.of Employees:** 101 - 250 **Product Groups:** 87

Date of Accounts	Sep 11	Sep 10	Sep 09
Sales Turnover	36m	26m	32m
Pre Tax Profit/Loss	307	147	261
Working Capital	695	665	564
Fixed Assets	390	392	395
Current Assets	11m	9m	11m
Current Liabilities	8m	7m	8m

Peake Fabrication Ltd
26 Cowley Road, Blackpool, FY4 4NE
Tel: 01253-762218 **Fax:** 01253-762218
Directors: S. Peake (Fin), J. Peake (MD)
Immediate Holding Company: PEAKE ENGINEERING LIMITED
Registration no: 04236096 **Date established:** 2001
No.of Employees: 1 - 10 **Product Groups:** 26, 35

Date of Accounts	Jul 08	Jul 07	Jul 06
Working Capital	-15	-14	-18
Fixed Assets	16	18	19
Current Assets	1	32	24

Pxwheels.Com
14 Piper Court Links Point Amy Johnson Way, Blackpool, FY4 2RT
Tel: 01253-400230 **Fax:** 01253-400130
E-mail: info@pxwheels.com
Website: http://www.pxwheels.com
Directors: G. Osgerby (Prop)
No.of Employees: 1 - 10 **Product Groups:** 35, 39, 48

R D S Garage Doors
14 Clifton Road, Blackpool, FY4 4QA
Tel: 01253-798665
E-mail: marcia.taylor@tiscali.co.uk
Website: http://www.rdsgaragedoors.co.uk
Directors: A. Taylor (Ptnr)
Ultimate Holding Company: M I INNOVATIONS LTD
Immediate Holding Company: RDS GARAGEDOORS LTD
Registration no: 07956197 **Date established:** 2012
No.of Employees: 1 - 10 **Product Groups:** 25, 30, 35, 36, 66

Rainbow Blinds Ltd
6 Keystone Court Hallam Way, Whitehills Business Park, Blackpool, FY4 5NZ
Tel: 01253-798512 **Fax:** 01253-798512
E-mail: david.gladwin@lycos.co.uk
Website: http://www.rainbowblindsuk.co.uk
Directors: S. Gladwin (MD)
Immediate Holding Company: RAINBOW BLINDS LIMITED
Registration no: 04741587 **Date established:** 2003
Turnover: £250,000 - £500,000 **No.of Employees:** 1 - 10
Product Groups: 30, 35

Date of Accounts	Apr 11	Apr 10	Apr 09
Working Capital	25	39	20
Fixed Assets	30	36	23
Current Assets	104	103	56

N A Robson Ltd
4a Robson Way Industrial Estate Robson Way, Blackpool, FY3 7PP
Tel: 01253-393406 **Fax:** 01253-300160
E-mail: i.robson@robson.uk.com
Website: http://www.robson.uk.com
Directors: I. Robson (MD)
Immediate Holding Company: N.A. ROBSON LIMITED
Registration no: 02366904 **Date established:** 1989
Turnover: £250,000 - £500,000 **No.of Employees:** 1 - 10
Product Groups: 46

Date of Accounts	Mar 11	Mar 10	Mar 09
Working Capital	74	65	39
Fixed Assets	55	79	102
Current Assets	370	396	327

U P L
90 Topping Street, Blackpool, FY1 3AD
Tel: 01253-290729 **Fax:** 01253-290729
Directors: S. Wilkins (Prop)
Date established: 2001 **No.of Employees:** 1 - 10 **Product Groups:** 36, 39, 40

Unicorn Chemicals Ltd
Unicorn House 141-151 Mowbray Drive, Blackpool, FY3 7UN
Tel: 01253-396101 **Fax:** 01253-302895
E-mail: tim@unicornchemicals.co.uk
Website: http://www.unicornchemicals.com
Directors: T. Kilpatrick (MD), L. Kilpatrick (Fin)
Ultimate Holding Company: A.V.E. LIMITED
Immediate Holding Company: UNICORN CHEMICALS LIMITED
Registration no: 01023873 **Date established:** 1971 **Turnover:** £1m - £2m
No.of Employees: 1 - 10 **Product Groups:** 31, 32, 66, 67

Date of Accounts	Sep 11	Sep 10	Sep 09
Working Capital	42	104	56
Fixed Assets	N/A	16	20
Current Assets	141	320	327
Current Liabilities	N/A	N/A	8

Urban Surveillance Ltd
4 Howe Avenue Marton, Blackpool, FY4 3HG
Tel: 01253-313257 **Fax:** 01253-313257
E-mail: urbansurveillance@blueyonder.co.uk
Directors: A. Hawksworth (Dir), A. Hawksworth (Fin)
Immediate Holding Company: URBAN SURVEILLANCE LTD
Registration no: 05701711 **Date established:** 2006 **Turnover:** £1m - £2m
No.of Employees: 1 - 10 **Product Groups:** 26, 37, 67

Date of Accounts	Mar 12	Mar 11	Mar 10
Working Capital	-6	-4	-6
Fixed Assets	7	5	6
Current Assets	12	11	24

Bolton

A P P H Bolton Filters Ltd (an ABBA Group Company)
Unit 1003 Great Bank Road Westhoughton, Bolton, BL5 3XU
Tel: 01942-850700 **Fax:** 01942-851901
E-mail: sales@apph.com
Website: http://www.apph.com
Bank(s): HSBC Bank plc
Directors: M. Cummings (Fin), M. Askew (MD)
Managers: Y. Riley
Ultimate Holding Company: BBA AVIATION PLC
Immediate Holding Company: APPH (BOLTON) LIMITED
Registration no: 01969231 **VAT No.:** GB 183 3721 61
Date established: 1985 **Turnover:** £10m - £20m
No.of Employees: 11 - 20 **Product Groups:** 39, 42

A T E Technology Ltd
48 Green Meadows Westhoughton, Bolton, BL5 2BN
Tel: 01942-815603 **Fax:** 01942-815321
Directors: E. Lee (Fin), M. Lee (MD)
Immediate Holding Company: A.T.E. TECHNOLOGY LIMITED
Registration no: 03094310 **Date established:** 1995
No.of Employees: 1 - 10 **Product Groups:** 44, 80, 81, 84, 86, 87

Date of Accounts	Aug 09	Aug 08	Aug 07
Sales Turnover	N/A	N/A	44
Pre Tax Profit/Loss	N/A	N/A	5
Working Capital	-1	-7	-27
Fixed Assets	19	25	32
Current Assets	28	30	6
Current Liabilities	N/A	N/A	5

A1 Mirrors Ltd
Swan Lane Mill Higher Swan Lane, Bolton, BL3 3AQ
Tel: 08448-843123 **Fax:** 0871-918 7826
E-mail: sales@a1mirrors.co.uk
Website: http://www.a1mirrors.co.uk
Directors: R. Adams (Dir)
Immediate Holding Company: A1 MIRRORS LIMITED
Registration no: 06900057 **Date established:** 2009
No.of Employees: 1 - 10 **Product Groups:** 33, 38, 63

Date of Accounts	May 11	May 10
Working Capital	3	N/A
Current Assets	3	N/A

Aalco Ltd
Express Trading Estate Stone Hill Road, Farnworth, Bolton, BL4 9NN
Tel: 01204-863456 **Fax:** 01204-863426
E-mail: manchester@aalco.co.uk
Website: http://www.aalco.co.uk
Bank(s): National Westminster Bank Plc
Managers: G. Brook (Mgr)
Ultimate Holding Company: UK STEELSTOCK LTD
Immediate Holding Company: AMARI METALS LTD
Registration no: 03551533 **Turnover:** £125m - £250m
No.of Employees: 21 - 50 **Product Groups:** 34, 35, 36, 66

Able Fire Security
Unit 8 Tonge Bridge Industrial Estate Tonge Bridge Way, Bolton, BL2 6BB
Tel: 01204-533643 **Fax:** 01204-531116
E-mail: info@ablefire.co.uk
Directors: G. Howarth (Prop)
Date established: 1982 **No.of Employees:** 1 - 10 **Product Groups:** 38, 42

ACDOCO Ltd
Mallison Street, Bolton, BL1 8PP
Tel: 01204-600500 **Fax:** 01204-600501
E-mail: specialist@acdo.co.uk
Website: http://www.acdo.co.uk
Bank(s): Lloyds TSB Bank plc
Directors: B. Pilling (MD)
Managers: V. Birtwistle (Purch Mgr), D. Pilling (I.T. Exec), E. Pilling (Personnel)
Immediate Holding Company: ACDOCO LIMITED
Registration no: 06174996 **VAT No.:** GB 144 9622 55
Date established: 2007 **Turnover:** £10m - £20m
No.of Employees: 21 - 50 **Product Groups:** 32, 63

Date of Accounts	Dec 11	Dec 10	Dec 09
Sales Turnover	N/A	N/A	10m
Pre Tax Profit/Loss	N/A	N/A	-34
Working Capital	592	436	376
Fixed Assets	121	144	156
Current Assets	4m	3m	3m
Current Liabilities	N/A	N/A	543

Add-A-Guard
Unit 6 Shepherd Cross St Industrial Estate, Bolton, BL1 3DE
Tel: 0161-480 8036 **Fax:** 0161- 4765463
Website: http://www.addaguard.com
Directors: G. Penson (MD)
Immediate Holding Company: ADD-A-GUARD LIMITED
Registration no: 03367366 **Date established:** 1997
No.of Employees: 1 - 10 **Product Groups:** 35, 49

Date of Accounts	Jul 10	Jul 09	Jul 08
Working Capital	-6	25	22
Fixed Assets	6	5	5
Current Assets	25	59	85

Advanced Ventilation Ltd
4 Tonge Bridge Indl-Est Tonge Bridge Way, Bolton, BL2 6BD
Tel: 01204-523384 **Fax:** 01204-389849
E-mail: jamie@advancedventilation.co.uk
Directors: J. Mccann (Prop)
Immediate Holding Company: ADVANCED VENTILATION LIMITED
Registration no: 04878489 **Date established:** 2003
No.of Employees: 21 - 50 **Product Groups:** 40, 66

Date of Accounts	Aug 09	Aug 08	Aug 07
Working Capital	-63	-37	-7
Fixed Assets	102	108	133
Current Assets	266	364	271

Aerotec Precision Finishing Ltd
8 Gladstone Road Farnworth, Bolton, BL4 7EH
Tel: 01204-571300 **Fax:** 01204-571300
Website: http://www.aerotecprecisionfinishing.co.uk
Directors: J. Wilton (MD)
Immediate Holding Company: AEROTEC PRECISION FINISHING LIMITED
Registration no: 02909223 **Date established:** 1994
No.of Employees: 1 - 10 **Product Groups:** 46, 48

Date of Accounts	Mar 12	Mar 11	Mar 10
Working Capital	124	103	101
Fixed Assets	13	14	15
Current Assets	154	129	118
Current Liabilities	30	25	17

Aesthetic World
Unit 4 Spa Road Industrial Estate, Bolton, BL1 4SS
Tel: 01204-365622 **Fax:** 01204-365622
E-mail: info@aestheticworld.co.uk
Website: http://www.aestheticworld.co.uk
Directors: D. Gee (Ptnr)
Immediate Holding Company: AESTHETIC WORLD HOLDINGS LIMITED
Registration no: 06695954 **Date established:** 2008
No.of Employees: 21 - 50 **Product Groups:** 38, 67

Date of Accounts	Aug 11	Aug 10	Aug 09
Working Capital	-513	-561	-605
Fixed Assets	2m	2m	2m
Current Assets	17	18	56

Airflow Measurements Ltd
72 Manchester Road Kearsley, Bolton, BL4 8NZ
Tel: 01204-571499 **Fax:** 01204-571734
E-mail: tony@airflowmeasurements.com
Website: http://www.airflowmeasurements.com
Directors: A. Leonard (MD)
Immediate Holding Company: AIRFLOW MEASUREMENTS LIMITED
Registration no: 01111677 **Date established:** 1973
Turnover: £250,000 - £500,000 **No.of Employees:** 1 - 10
Product Groups: 38, 48, 85

Date of Accounts	Apr 11	Apr 10	Apr 09
Working Capital	121	110	99
Fixed Assets	15	8	10
Current Assets	177	161	132

Ajax Equipment Ltd
Milton Works Mule Street, Bolton, BL2 2AR
Tel: 01204-386723 **Fax:** 01204-363706
E-mail: sales@ajax.co.uk
Website: http://www.ajax.co.uk
Directors: M. Waters (Dir), E. McGee (Dir)
Ultimate Holding Company: AJAX EQUIPMENT HOLDINGS LIMITED
Immediate Holding Company: AJAX EQUIPMENT LIMITED
Registration no: 00987764 **Date established:** 1970 **Turnover:** £1m - £2m
No.of Employees: 21 - 50 **Product Groups:** 45, 84

Date of Accounts	Mar 11	Mar 10	Mar 09
Working Capital	528	900	897
Fixed Assets	225	158	179
Current Assets	1m	1m	1m

Alliance Learning
The Hurst Building Horwich Business Park Chorley New Road, Horwich, Bolton, BL6 5UE
Tel: 01204-696744 **Fax:** 01204-669217
E-mail: info@alliancelearning.com
Website: http://www.alliancelearning.com
Bank(s): National Westminster Bank Plc
Directors: S. Whitehead (Dir)
Managers: P. Fulford (Fin Mgr), K. Wolfenden, V. Squires
Immediate Holding Company: ALLIANCE LEARNING
Registration no: 01619564 **VAT No.:** GB 673 4786 92
Date established: 1982 **Turnover:** £2m - £5m **No.of Employees:** 51 - 100
Product Groups: 86

Date of Accounts	Jul 11	Jul 10	Jul 09
Sales Turnover	3m	3m	4m
Pre Tax Profit/Loss	-106	3	323
Working Capital	840	1m	1m
Fixed Assets	2m	2m	2m
Current Assets	1m	2m	2m
Current Liabilities	271	184	179

Arboles UK Ltd (Laboratory Taps, Safety Showers & Eye Washes)
Unit 56 Evans Business Centre Manchester Road, Bolton, BL3 5EY
Tel: 01204-388814 **Fax:** 01204-388813
E-mail: sales@arboles.co.uk
Website: http://www.arboles.co.uk
Bank(s): Royal Bank of Scotland PLC
Directors: B. Haines (Dir), J. Buckley (Dir)
Immediate Holding Company: ARBOLES U.K. LTD.
Registration no: 03554674 **VAT No.:** GB 707 9502 27
Date established: 1998 **Turnover:** £250,000 - £500,000
No.of Employees: 21 - 50 **Product Groups:** 30, 31, 33, 36, 42

Date of Accounts	Mar 12	Mar 11	Mar 10
Working Capital	191	188	226
Fixed Assets	28	30	10
Current Assets	367	416	367

Ascot Doors Ltd
Unit 2 Britannia Way Industrial Park Union Road, Bolton, BL2 2HE
Tel: 01204-547799 **Fax:** 01204-545800
E-mail: sales@ascotdoors.co.uk
Website: http://www.ascotdoors.co.uk
Bank(s): Barclays
Directors: A. Ashworth (MD)
Immediate Holding Company: ASCOT DOORS LTD
Registration no: 01574755 **VAT No.:** GB 376 1110 73
Date established: 1981 **Turnover:** £5m - £10m
No.of Employees: 101 - 250 **Product Groups:** 25, 35, 36, 39, 49, 66

Date of Accounts	Jun 11	Jun 10	Jun 09
Sales Turnover	13m	13m	13m
Pre Tax Profit/Loss	336	151	200
Working Capital	1m	1m	1m
Fixed Assets	2m	1m	2m
Current Assets	4m	4m	4m
Current Liabilities	1m	1m	867

Atlas Guardrail Ltd
Unit 5b Lever Bridge Mills Radcliffe Road, Bolton, BL3 1RU
Tel: 01204-394204 **Fax:** 01204-394206
E-mail: atlasguardrail@hotmail.com
Website: http://www.atlasguardrail.co.uk
Directors: M. Jones (MD), D. Jones (Fin)
Immediate Holding Company: ATLAS GUARDRAIL LIMITED
Registration no: 03233280 **Date established:** 1996
No.of Employees: 1 - 10 **Product Groups:** 26, 35

Date of Accounts	Sep 11	Sep 10	Sep 09
Working Capital	20	24	25
Fixed Assets	5	4	4
Current Assets	63	61	59

B B F Bolton Ltd
Rasbottom Street Alma Works, Bolton, BL3 5BZ
Tel: 01204-535723 **Fax:** 01204-535723
Directors: P. Ince (MD)
Immediate Holding Company: BBF (BOLTON) LIMITED
Registration no: 04442989 **Date established:** 2002
Turnover: Up to £250,000 **No.of Employees:** 1 - 10 **Product Groups:** 20, 40, 41

Date of Accounts	Jul 11	Jul 10	Jul 09
Working Capital	-5	-0	-1
Fixed Assets	1	1	2
Current Assets	7	14	12
Current Liabilities	N/A	N/A	8

B I M UK Ltd
Prince Street, Bolton, BL1 2NP
Tel: 01204-366997 **Fax:** 01204-366998
E-mail: info@bimkemi.com
Website: http://www.bimkemi.com
Directors: J. Wood (MD), M. Wood (Co Sec)
Ultimate Holding Company: BIM KEMI AB (SWEDEN)
Immediate Holding Company: BIM UNITED KINGDOM LIMITED
Registration no: 00981321 **VAT No.:** GB 145 5247 69
Date established: 1970 **No.of Employees:** 21 - 50 **Product Groups:** 32

Date of Accounts	Dec 11	Dec 10	Dec 09
Pre Tax Profit/Loss	389	269	162
Working Capital	283	295	258
Fixed Assets	827	669	613
Current Assets	2m	2m	2m
Current Liabilities	324	935	327

Barton Lake Ltd
Nelson Mill Gaskell Street, Bolton, BL1 2QE
Tel: 01204-381200 **Fax:** 01204-364002
E-mail: info@bartonlake.co.uk
Website: http://www.bartonlake.co.uk
Directors: L. Nuttall (Fin)
Ultimate Holding Company: HARGREAVES HAMILTON HOLDINGS LTD
Immediate Holding Company: BARTON LAKE LIMITED
Registration no: 02607728 **Date established:** 1991 **Turnover:** £2m - £5m
No.of Employees: 1 - 10 **Product Groups:** 26, 32, 35, 38, 40, 66

Date of Accounts	Mar 11	Mar 10	Mar 09
Working Capital	-160	-188	-218
Fixed Assets	103	107	112
Current Assets	49	41	73

Benteler Distribution Ltd
New Progress Works Crompton Way, Bolton, BL1 8TY
Tel: 01204-301611 **Fax:** 01204-593074
E-mail: sales@benteler-distribution.co.uk
Website: http://www.benteler-distribution.co.uk
Bank(s): Barclays
Directors: S. Storer (Dir), W. Johnson (Fin), R. Heath (Sales), D. Skraskins (Comm)
Managers: A. Clayton (Personnel), D. Guest (Tech Serv Mgr)
Ultimate Holding Company: BENTELER INTERNATIONAL AG (AUSTRIA)
Immediate Holding Company: BENTELER HOLDINGS LIMITED
Registration no: 02848427 **Date established:** 1993
Turnover: £250,000 - £500,000 **No.of Employees:** 21 - 50
Product Groups: 36

Date of Accounts	Dec 11	Dec 10	Dec 09
Sales Turnover	461	450	20m
Pre Tax Profit/Loss	19	18	322
Working Capital	220	201	4m
Fixed Assets	3m	3m	2m
Current Assets	307	288	8m
Current Liabilities	88	86	384

Bettix Ltd
Lever Street, Bolton, BL3 6NZ
Tel: 01204-526241 **Fax:** 01204-521958
E-mail: sales@bettix.co.uk
Website: http://www.bettix.co.uk
Bank(s): Lloyds TSB Bank plc
Directors: D. Butler (MD), J. Middlehurst (Dir)
Managers: E. Peacock (Prod Mgr), I. Matthews (Tech Serv Mgr), N. Holland (Fin Mgr), S. Russell (Personnel)
Ultimate Holding Company: CLARY LIMITED (ISLE OF MAN)
Immediate Holding Company: BETTIX LIMITED
Registration no: 00345529 **Date established:** 1938 **Turnover:** £2m - £5m
No.of Employees: 51 - 100 **Product Groups:** 30

Date of Accounts	Dec 11	Dec 10	Dec 09
Sales Turnover	N/A	N/A	3m
Pre Tax Profit/Loss	N/A	N/A	56
Working Capital	494	672	727
Fixed Assets	245	290	146
Current Assets	1m	1m	1m
Current Liabilities	192	167	371

Biffa Waste Services Ltd
Lyon Road Industrial Estate Kearsley, Bolton, BL4 8NB
Tel: 01204-571671 **Fax:** 01204-575901
E-mail: derek.southwell@biffa.co.uk
Website: http://www.biffa.co.uk
Managers: D. Southwell (Mgr)
Immediate Holding Company: BIFFA WASTE SERVICES LIMITED
Registration no: 00946107 **Date established:** 1969
No.of Employees: 51 - 100 **Product Groups:** 54

Date of Accounts	Mar 08	Mar 09	Apr 10
Sales Turnover	555m	574m	492m
Pre Tax Profit/Loss	23m	50m	30m
Working Capital	229m	271m	293m
Fixed Assets	371m	360m	378m
Current Assets	409m	534m	609m
Current Liabilities	50m	100m	115m

Bilstein UK Ltd
5 Britannia Way, Bolton, BL2 2HH
Tel: 01204-399993 **Fax:** 01204-361620
E-mail: dnewnham99@yahoo.co.uk
Website: http://www.bilstein.net
Directors: D. Newnham (Dir), J. Bolderson (Fin)
Immediate Holding Company: BILSTEIN UK LTD
Registration no: 05384445 **Date established:** 2005
No.of Employees: 1 - 10 **Product Groups:** 46

Date of Accounts	Dec 11	Dec 10	Dec 09
Working Capital	189	143	100
Fixed Assets	23	26	20
Current Assets	269	261	208

Boldman Ltd
Unit 4 Britannia Way, Bolton, BL2 2HH
Tel: 01204-522123 **Fax:** 01204-522101
E-mail: info@boldman.co.uk
Website: http://www.boldman.co.uk
Directors: R. Benischke (Fin)
Immediate Holding Company: BOLDMAN LIMITED
Registration no: 07231075 **Date established:** 2010 **Turnover:** £2m - £5m
No.of Employees: 21 - 50 **Product Groups:** 34, 35

Date of Accounts	Mar 11
Working Capital	403
Fixed Assets	8
Current Assets	485

Bolton At Home
Adelaide House Adelaide Street, Bolton, BL3 3NY
Tel: 01204-335074 **Fax:** 01204-335639
E-mail: jim.higham@boltonathome.org.uk
Website: http://www.boltonathome.org.uk
Directors: J. Higham (Dir)
Managers: J. Davies (Fin Mgr), M. Lupton (Purch Mgr), K. Fenton
No.of Employees: 501 - 1000 **Product Groups:** 87

Bolton Central Library
Le Mans Crescent, Bolton, BL1 1SE
Tel: 01204-333173 **Fax:** 01204-332225
E-mail: central.library@bolton.gov.uk
Website: http://www.bolton.gov.uk/libraries
Managers: J. Spencer (District Mgr)
Immediate Holding Company: BOLTON FESTIVAL(THE)
Registration no: 01618850 **Date established:** 1997
No.of Employees: 11 - 20 **Product Groups:** 80, 89

Bolton Gate Co. Ltd
Waterloo Street, Bolton, BL1 2SP
Tel: 01204-871000 **Fax:** 01204-871049
E-mail: general@boltongate.co.uk
Website: http://www.boltongate.co.uk
Bank(s): HSBC Bank plc
Directors: A. Lloyd (MD), J. Cambray (Pers), A. Revell (Fin), D. Shepherd (Sales)
Managers: V. Patel, S. Sherrington (Buyer)
Ultimate Holding Company: BGC HOLDINGS LIMITED
Immediate Holding Company: BOLTON GATE COMPANY LIMITED
Registration no: 00348230 **Date established:** 1939 **Turnover:** £5m - £10m
No.of Employees: 101 - 250 **Product Groups:** 35, 36

Date of Accounts	Dec 11	Dec 10	Dec 09
Sales Turnover	7m	7m	7m
Pre Tax Profit/Loss	253	541	60
Working Capital	2m	2m	2m
Fixed Assets	128	90	127
Current Assets	4m	4m	5m
Current Liabilities	757	363	1m

Bolton Plastic Components Ltd
Lever Street, Bolton, BL3 6NZ
Tel: 01204-526241 **Fax:** 01204-521958
E-mail: dbutler@boltonplastics.co.uk
Website: http://www.boplas.co.uk
Bank(s): Lloyds TSB Bank plc
Directors: D. Butler (MD)
Ultimate Holding Company: CLARY LIMITED (ISLE OF MAN)
Immediate Holding Company: BOLTON PLASTIC COMPONENTS LIMITED
Registration no: 01770442 **VAT No.:** GB 389 8094 82
Date established: 1983 **Turnover:** £10m - £20m
No.of Employees: 101 - 250 **Product Groups:** 30

Date of Accounts	Dec 11	Dec 10	Dec 09
Sales Turnover	11m	8m	6m
Pre Tax Profit/Loss	564	363	-175
Working Capital	2m	1m	754
Fixed Assets	1m	1m	2m
Current Assets	5m	4m	2m
Current Liabilities	2m	2m	1m

Booth Industries
PO Box 50, Bolton, BL3 2RW
Tel: 01204-366333 **Fax:** 01204-380888
E-mail: marketing@booth-industries.co.uk
Website: http://www.booth-industries.co.uk
Bank(s): HSBC Bank plc
Directors: R. Edwards (MD)
Managers: E. Whittle (Buyer)
Ultimate Holding Company: REDHALL GROUP PLC
Immediate Holding Company: BOOTH INDUSTRIES LIMITED
Registration no: 01288302 **VAT No.:** GB 525 5940 37
Date established: 1976 **Turnover:** £10m - £20m
No.of Employees: 51 - 100 **Product Groups:** 33, 35, 36

Date of Accounts	Sep 11	Sep 10	Sep 09
Sales Turnover	15m	14m	14m
Pre Tax Profit/Loss	3m	3m	2m
Working Capital	7m	4m	2m
Fixed Assets	671	562	507
Current Assets	14m	9m	7m
Current Liabilities	4m	4m	3m

Bosch Rexroth Ltd
23 Queensbrook, Bolton, BL1 4AY
Tel: 01204-534083 **Fax:** 01204-534084
E-mail: info@boschrexroth.co.uk
Website: http://www.boschrexroth.co.uk
Managers: S. Smith (Sales Admin)
Ultimate Holding Company: ROBERT BOSCH GMBH (GERMANY)
Immediate Holding Company: BOSCH REXROTH LIMITED
Registration no: 00768471 **Date established:** 1963 **Turnover:** £5m - £10m
No.of Employees: 1 - 10 **Product Groups:** 34, 35

Date of Accounts	Dec 11	Dec 10	Dec 09
Sales Turnover	168m	117m	77m
Pre Tax Profit/Loss	13m	4m	-6m
Working Capital	21m	17m	13m
Fixed Assets	15m	13m	14m
Current Assets	53m	40m	28m
Current Liabilities	7m	6m	3m

Brabbin & Rudd Ltd

Walker Street, Bolton, BL1 4TB
Tel: 01204-521171 **Fax:** 01204-364972
E-mail: sales@brabbin-and-rudd.co.uk
Website: http://www.brabbin-and-rudd.co.uk
Directors: M. Brabbin (MD), P. Brabbin (Co Sec)
Immediate Holding Company: BRABBIN AND RUDD LIMITED
Registration no: 00684840 **VAT No.:** GB 145 0217 06
Date established: 1961 **Turnover:** £1m - £2m **No.of Employees:** 21 - 50
Product Groups: 66

Date of Accounts	Sep 11	Sep 10	Sep 09
Working Capital	596	637	734
Fixed Assets	245	235	248
Current Assets	1m	1m	1m

Bury Times Ltd Classified Advertising (a division of Newquest Ltd)

PO Box 22, Bolton, BL1 1DE
Tel: 01204-522333 **Fax:** 0161-797 3277
E-mail: sorrell@lancashire.newsquest.co.uk
Website: http://www.thisisbury.co.uk
Directors: E. Henshaw (MD)
Managers: P. Hilton (Chief Mgr)
Ultimate Holding Company: NEWSQUEST CAPITAL PLC
Immediate Holding Company: NEWSQUEST MEDIA GROUP LTD
Registration no: 00875708 **Turnover:** £2m - £5m
No.of Employees: 1 - 10 **Product Groups:** 28

Central Ceramics

44 Higher Bridge Street, Bolton, BL1 2HA
Tel: 01204-361887 **Fax:** 01204-362577
E-mail: sterobertson@fsmail.net
Directors: S. Robertson (MD)
Immediate Holding Company: CENTRAL CERAMICS LIMITED
Registration no: 04733098 **Date established:** 2003
No.of Employees: 1 - 10 **Product Groups:** 38, 67, 88

Date of Accounts	Mar 11	Mar 10	Mar 09
Working Capital	72	89	98
Fixed Assets	19	25	33
Current Assets	131	187	172

Chloride Motive Power C M P Batteries Ltd

Salford Road, Bolton, BL5 1BX
Tel: 01204-64111 **Fax:** 01204-62981
E-mail: elaine.mcleod@eu.exide.com
Website: http://www.exide.com
Bank(s): Bank of Scotland
Managers: L. Evans (Tech Serv Mgr), D. Morley (Mgr), M. Shaw, N. Dark (Mgr), E. McLeod (Mktg Serv Mgr)
Ultimate Holding Company: EXIDE TECHNOLOGIES INC (USA)
Immediate Holding Company: CMP BATTERIES LIMITED
Registration no: 02375355 **Date established:** 1989
Turnover: £75m - £125m **No.of Employees:** 51 - 100 **Product Groups:** 37

Date of Accounts	Mar 10	Mar 09	Mar 08
Sales Turnover	37m	73m	95m
Pre Tax Profit/Loss	-21m	539	2m
Working Capital	-8m	10m	19m
Fixed Assets	17m	25m	29m
Current Assets	13m	23m	43m
Current Liabilities	876	2m	2m

Chorley Electrical Traders

107 Halliwell Road, Bolton, BL1 3NE
Tel: 01204-535222 **Fax:** 01204-535118
E-mail: headoffice@chorleyelectrical.com
Website: http://www.chorleyelectrical.com
Directors: G. Gallagher (MD)
Immediate Holding Company: CHORLEY ELECTRICAL TRADERS LIMITED
Registration no: 01430809 **Date established:** 1979 **Turnover:** £1m - £2m
No.of Employees: 1 - 10 **Product Groups:** 77

Date of Accounts	Mar 12	Mar 11	Mar 10
Working Capital	344	323	305
Fixed Assets	63	54	58
Current Assets	880	797	759

Clean Air Ltd

Unit 16 Dunscar Industrial Estate Blackburn Road, Egerton, Bolton, BL7 9PQ
Tel: 01204-591115 **Fax:** 01204-591116
E-mail: john.bolton@cleanairltd.co.uk
Website: http://www.cleanairltd.co.uk
Directors: G. Findlay (Co Sec), J. Boulton (MD)
Ultimate Holding Company: HAVELOCK EUROPA PLC
Immediate Holding Company: CLEAN AIR LIMITED
Registration no: 02952082 **Date established:** 1994 **Turnover:** £2m - £5m
No.of Employees: 21 - 50 **Product Groups:** 40, 42, 54, 85

Date of Accounts	Dec 11	Dec 10	Dec 09
Sales Turnover	2m	3m	4m
Pre Tax Profit/Loss	-52	130	223
Working Capital	938	988	1m
Fixed Assets	30	19	35
Current Assets	1m	1m	2m
Current Liabilities	100	131	107

Coleman Milne Ltd

Wigan Road Westhoughton, Bolton, BL5 2EE
Tel: 01942-815600 **Fax:** 01942-815115
E-mail: paul.thompson@woodall-nicholson.co.uk
Website: http://www.woodall-nicholson.co.uk
Bank(s): HSBC Bank plc
Directors: P. Thompson (Fin), G. Hudson (Sales & Mktg), G. Hudson (Sales & Mktg)
Managers: C. Sorry (Commun Mgr), A. Hamilton (Purch Mgr)
Ultimate Holding Company: WOODALL NICHOLSON LIMITED
Immediate Holding Company: COLEMAN MILNE LIMITED
Registration no: 02700983 **Date established:** 1992 **Turnover:** £5m - £10m
No.of Employees: 101 - 250 **Product Groups:** 39

Combat Claims Ltd

21 Grange Road, Bolton, BL3 5QQ
Tel: 07721-678197
E-mail: andy@combatclaims.fsnet.co.uk
Directors: A. Farrell (MD)
Immediate Holding Company: COMBAT CLAIMS LTD.
Registration no: 04495998 **Date established:** 2002
Turnover: Up to £250,000 **No.of Employees:** 1 - 10 **Product Groups:** 84

Date of Accounts	Jul 04	Jul 03	Jan 08
Working Capital	N/A	N/A	-1
Fixed Assets	N/A	N/A	2
Current Assets	N/A	N/A	11
Current Liabilities	N/A	N/A	12

Compact Instruments

61-65 Lever Street, Bolton, BL3 2AB
Tel: 01204-532544 **Fax:** 01204-522285
E-mail: info@compactinstruments.co.uk
Website: http://www.compactinstruments.co.uk
Bank(s): Bank of Scotland
Directors: B. Jones (Dir)
Immediate Holding Company: COMPACT INSTRUMENTS LIMITED
Registration no: 04795150 **VAT No.:** GB 231 5681 76
Date established: 2003 **Turnover:** £1m - £2m **No.of Employees:** 21 - 50
Product Groups: 37, 38, 39, 67

Date of Accounts	Dec 11	Dec 10	Dec 09
Working Capital	349	223	180
Fixed Assets	13	13	4
Current Assets	452	377	259

Contamination Control Apparel Ltd

Northolt Drive, Bolton, BL3 6RE
Tel: 01204-528019 **Fax:** 01204-361549
E-mail: kareng@mikar.co.uk
Directors: K. Griffiths (Dir)
Immediate Holding Company: CONTAMINATION CONTROL APPAREL LIMITED
Registration no: 06707222 **VAT No.:** GB 597 8796 39
Date established: 2008 **Turnover:** £5m - £10m **No.of Employees:** 1 - 10
Product Groups: 24

Corus (Stockholders)

Union Road, Bolton, BL2 2HS
Tel: 01204-370999 **Fax:** 01204-396684
E-mail: chris.deacon@corusgroup.com
Website: http://www.corusgroup.com
Managers: C. Beardmore (Mgr), C. Beardmore (Comm)
Immediate Holding Company: CORUS GROUP LIMITED
Registration no: 03811373 **Date established:** 1999
Turnover: Up to £250,000 **No.of Employees:** 1 - 10 **Product Groups:** 34, 66

Cradlebay Ltd

490 St Helens Road, Bolton, BL3 3RS
Tel: 01204-650447
E-mail: mail@cradlebay.co.uk
Website: http://www.cradlebay.co.uk
Directors: K. Nogalski (Co Sec), D. Nogalski (Dir)
Managers: D. Nogalski (Chief Acct)
Immediate Holding Company: CRADLEBAY LIMITED
Registration no: 05251142 **Date established:** 2004
Turnover: Up to £250,000 **No.of Employees:** 1 - 10 **Product Groups:** 11, 29, 62

Date of Accounts	Oct 07	Oct 06	Oct 05
Working Capital	-8	-3	N/A
Current Liabilities	N/A	1	N/A

Creation Dental Labratory

300 Wigan Road, Bolton, BL3 5QT
Tel: 01204-656153 **Fax:** 01204-301162
E-mail: cdlharrison@hotmail.co.uk
Website: http://www.cdltd.net
Directors: M. Harrison (Prop)
Immediate Holding Company: CDL LTD
Registration no: 04922598 **Date established:** 2003
No.of Employees: 1 - 10 **Product Groups:** 37, 39, 88

Date of Accounts	Oct 11	Oct 10	Oct 09
Working Capital	1	1	3
Fixed Assets	4	5	5
Current Assets	21	28	23

D - Room Digital Marketing Solutions

14 Bark Street East, Bolton, BL1 2BQ
Tel: 01204-382599 **Fax:** 01204-382461
E-mail: paul@d-room.co.uk
Website: http://www.d-room.co.uk
Managers: P. Rignall
Immediate Holding Company: D-ROOM LIMITED
Registration no: 04691478 **Date established:** 2003
Turnover: Up to £250,000 **No.of Employees:** 1 - 10 **Product Groups:** 44, 81

Date of Accounts	Mar 11	Mar 10	Mar 09
Working Capital	-3	-9	14
Fixed Assets	20	28	37
Current Assets	89	158	154

D M Anderton Ltd

8 St Georges Street, Bolton, BL1 2EN
Tel: 01204-532618 **Fax:** 01204-532619
E-mail: d.singleton@the-dma.org.uk
Website: http://www.d-room.co.uk
Bank(s): The Royal Bank of Scotland
Directors: D. Singleton (Dir)
Immediate Holding Company: D.M. ANDERTON LIMITED
Registration no: 01642910 **VAT No.:** GB 380 4135 71
Date established: 1982 **Turnover:** £500,000 - £1m
No.of Employees: 11 - 20 **Product Groups:** 52

Date of Accounts	Aug 11	Aug 10	Aug 09
Working Capital	-1	-2	-3
Fixed Assets	3	3	3
Current Assets	96	85	107

Drew Brady & Co. Ltd

Dove Mill Dove Road, Bolton, BL3 4ET
Tel: 01204-854800 **Fax:** 01204-854854
E-mail: drewbrady@ruia.co.uk
Website: http://www.drewbrady.com
Bank(s): HSBC Bank plc & National Westminster Bank PLC
Directors: P. Campbell (Fin), S. Doughty (Purch)
Managers: C. Pringle (Personnel), R. Thompson (Tech Serv Mgr)
Ultimate Holding Company: RUIA GROUP LIMITED
Immediate Holding Company: DREW BRADY & CO. LIMITED
Registration no: 00429464 **Date established:** 1947
Turnover: £10m - £20m **No.of Employees:** 21 - 50 **Product Groups:** 24

Date of Accounts	Apr 12	Apr 11	Apr 10
Sales Turnover	21m	17m	12m
Pre Tax Profit/Loss	4m	2m	1m
Working Capital	4m	3m	3m
Fixed Assets	346	503	338
Current Assets	11m	10m	7m
Current Liabilities	2m	1m	642

Edbro plc

Nelson Street, Bolton, BL3 2JJ
Tel: 01204-528888 **Fax:** 01204-531957
E-mail: postmaster@edbro.co.uk
Website: http://www.edbro.co.uk
Bank(s): Barclays
Directors: D. Nesbitt (Dir), T. Bardet (Fin)
Managers: I. Clarke (Sales & Mktg Mg), C. Brookes (Tech Serv Mgr), Z. Dover (Purch Mgr)
Ultimate Holding Company: CARAVELLE SA (FRANCE)
Immediate Holding Company: EDBRO PLC.
Registration no: 00283933 **VAT No.:** GB 145 7833 46
Date established: 1934 **Turnover:** £20m - £50m
No.of Employees: 101 - 250 **Product Groups:** 40

Date of Accounts	Dec 11	Dec 10	Dec 09
Sales Turnover	26m	23m	24m
Pre Tax Profit/Loss	2m	1m	-2m
Working Capital	9m	11m	11m
Fixed Assets	4m	2m	2m
Current Assets	15m	16m	16m
Current Liabilities	2m	2m	2m

EK Williams Limited

1 Pavilion Square Cricketers Way, Westhoughton, Bolton, BL5 3AJ
Tel: 01942-811767 **Fax:** 01942-814636
E-mail: info@payepeople.co.uk
Website: http://www.ekwilliams.co.uk
Directors: B. Myers (Fin), C. Van De Velden (MD), C. Van-De-Veldem (MD), S. Lurie (Dir)
Managers: K. Howarth (I.T. Exec), H. Carr (Ops Mgr)
Ultimate Holding Company: BEECH BV (NETHERLANDS)
Registration no: 06057146 **Date established:** 1980 **Turnover:** £2m - £5m
No.of Employees: 51 - 100 **Product Groups:** 80

Date of Accounts	Dec 09	Dec 08	Dec 07
Working Capital	-968	-497	-142
Fixed Assets	1m	28	67
Current Assets	287	376	399

Electric Center

Lecturers Close, Bolton, BL3 6DG
Tel: 01204-541480 **Fax:** 01204-363695
E-mail: lee.huddart@wolseley.co.uk
Website: http://www.electric-center.co.uk
Managers: L. Huddart (District Mgr)
Ultimate Holding Company: WOLSELEY PLC (JERSEY)
Immediate Holding Company: A.C. ELECTRICAL WHOLESALE LIMITED
Registration no: 01204867 **Date established:** 1975
No.of Employees: 1 - 10 **Product Groups:** 63

Date of Accounts	Jul 11	Jul 10	Jul 09
Pre Tax Profit/Loss	315	292	891
Working Capital	20m	20m	20m
Current Assets	20m	20m	20m

Empire Tools & Abrasives

Unit G7 Bolton Enterprise Centre Washington Street, Bolton, BL3 5EY
Tel: 01204-388595 **Fax:** 01204-364550
Directors: P. Higgenson (Prop), P. Higinson (Prop)
Immediate Holding Company: CRUCIAL SYSTEMS LIMITED
Registration no: 03196629 **Date established:** 2002
No.of Employees: 1 - 10 **Product Groups:** 37

ERIKS Hose Technology

1 Queensbrook, Bolton, BL1 4AY
Tel: 01204-541500 **Fax:** 01204-541510
E-mail: sales@fhsb.co.uk
Website: http://www.eriks-hose-technology.com
Directors: R. Boulsbee (Site)
Managers: P. Harrison (District Mgr)
Ultimate Holding Company: FLEXIBLE HOSE SUPPLIES
Registration no: 01345495 **Date established:** 1977 **Turnover:** £2m - £5m
No.of Employees: 1 - 10 **Product Groups:** 29, 30

Eurobake Ltd

Bee Hive Industrial Estate Crescent Road Lostock, Bolton, BL6 4BU
Tel: 01204-468671 **Fax:** 01204-696665
E-mail: info@eurobake.co.uk
Website: http://www.eurobake.co.uk
Directors: D. Smart (Dir)
Immediate Holding Company: EUROBAKE LIMITED
Registration no: 01022225 **VAT No.:** GB 146 6657 39
Date established: 1971 **Turnover:** £5m - £10m **No.of Employees:** 1 - 10
Product Groups: 41

Date of Accounts	Jan 11	Jan 10	Jan 09
Working Capital	586	624	758
Fixed Assets	11	15	16
Current Assets	904	924	996

Exide Technologies Power Network

PO Box 1, Bolton, BL5 1DD
Tel: 01438-359090 **Fax:** 01438-727684
E-mail: sales@exidenetworkpower.co.uk
Website: http://www.exide.com
Bank(s): Royal Bank of Scotland
Managers: E. Mcleod (Mktg Serv Mgr), N. Dark (Sales Prom Mgr), S. Mitchell (District Mgr)
Immediate Holding Company: Exide Corporation
Registration no: 02316604 **VAT No.:** 572 3168 40
No.of Employees: 21 - 50 **Product Groups:** 37

F G Solutions (Fibreglass Gratings Solutions)

25 Marsh Road, Bolton, BL3 1RE
Tel: 01204-573230 **Fax:** 01204-573230
E-mail: ben@fibreglassgratingsolutions.co.uk
Website: http://www.fibreglassgratingsolutions.co.uk
Product Groups: 24, 29, 30, 35, 41, 45, 49, 51, 52, 66

Fibre Fillings
Albion Mill Cawdor Street, Farnworth, Bolton, BL4 7JE
Tel: 01204-578141 **Fax:** 01204-793087
E-mail: info@john-holden.com
Website: http://www.john-holden.com
Bank(s): The Royal Bank of Scotland
Directors: J. Isherwood (Co Sec), M. Sciama (Fin)
Managers: P. Woodcock (Ops Mgr), S. Boardman (Sales Prom Mgr)
Immediate Holding Company: POLYWARM PRODUCTS LTD
Registration no: 02872286 **VAT No.:** GB 262 1917 66
Date established: 1971 **Turnover:** £2m - £5m **No.of Employees:** 21 - 50
Product Groups: 23

Firwood Paints Ltd
Victoria Works Oakenbottom Road, Bolton, BL2 6DP
Tel: 01204-525231 **Fax:** 01204-362522
E-mail: asmith@firwoodpaints.com
Website: http://www.firwood.co.uk
Bank(s): National Westminster Bank Plc
Directors: M. Wallen (MD), A. Smith (Fin)
Immediate Holding Company: FIRWOOD PAINTS LIMITED
Registration no: 00207861 **Date established:** 2025 **Turnover:** £2m - £5m
No.of Employees: 21 - 50 **Product Groups:** 32

Date of Accounts	Sep 11	Sep 10	Sep 09
Sales Turnover	3m	3m	3m
Pre Tax Profit/Loss	-114	-173	-136
Working Capital	2m	2m	2m
Fixed Assets	895	923	923
Current Assets	2m	2m	2m
Current Liabilities	105	89	85

Clare Fishers Ltd
Hartford House Weston Street, Bolton, BL3 2AW
Tel: 01204-521631 **Fax:** 01204-527391
E-mail: info@clarefishers.co.uk
Directors: J. Smith (MD)
Ultimate Holding Company: EXCELSIOR COMMERCIAL AND INDUSTRIAL HOLDINGS LIMITED
Immediate Holding Company: CLARE FISHERS LIMITED
Registration no: 00115155 **Date established:** 2011
Turnover: Up to £250,000 **No.of Employees:** 1 - 10 **Product Groups:** 46, 67

Date of Accounts	Mar 11	Mar 10	Mar 09
Sales Turnover	N/A	N/A	26
Pre Tax Profit/Loss	N/A	N/A	-8
Working Capital	-113	-137	-134
Fixed Assets	4	5	5
Current Assets	280	298	291

L Fitton
12 Pendennis Avenue Lostock, Bolton, BL6 4RS
Tel: 01204-844429 **Fax:** 01204-844429
Directors: L. Fitton (Prop)
Immediate Holding Company: L. FITTON LIMITED
Registration no: 05883599 **Date established:** 2006
Turnover: Up to £250,000 **No.of Employees:** 1 - 10 **Product Groups:** 38, 42

Date of Accounts	Mar 11	Mar 10	Mar 09
Sales Turnover	35	42	38
Pre Tax Profit/Loss	2	-1	-2
Working Capital	-17	-19	-20
Fixed Assets	16	17	18
Current Assets	3	2	N/A
Current Liabilities	1	N/A	N/A

Fitzpatricks Conveyor Belting Ltd
Moss Hill Farm Bradshaw Road, Bradshaw, Bolton, BL2 4JP
Tel: 01204-852360 **Fax:** 01204-852340
E-mail: sales@nafitzpatrick.com
Website: http://www.nafitzpatrick.com
Product Groups: 23, 29, 30, 35, 41, 42, 45, 48, 66

FlowTech Design Ltd
355 Green Lane, Bolton, BL3 2LU
Tel: 01204-362622 **Fax:** 01204-362622
E-mail: enquiries@flowtechdesign.com
Website: http://www.flowtechdesign.com
Directors: C. Fenn (Co Sec)
Registration no: 02578182 **Turnover:** Up to £250,000
No.of Employees: 1 - 10 **Product Groups:** 30, 44, 48, 85

Date of Accounts	May 07	May 06	May 05
Sales Turnover	N/A	N/A	32
Pre Tax Profit/Loss	N/A	N/A	7
Working Capital	17	2	-12
Fixed Assets	66	68	70
Current Assets	31	20	14
Current Liabilities	N/A	N/A	6

Francis Searchlights Ltd
Union Road, Bolton, BL2 2HJ
Tel: 01204-558960 **Fax:** 01204-558979
E-mail: sales@francis.co.uk
Website: http://www.francis.co.uk
Bank(s): National Westminster Bank Plc
Directors: E. Drury (Co Sec), M. Dobson (MD)
Managers: P. Sadler (Chief Mgr), M. Thurston (Sales Prom Mgr)
Immediate Holding Company: FRANCIS SEARCHLIGHTS LIMITED
Registration no: 02503257 **VAT No.:** GB 572 2700 05
Date established: 1990 **Turnover:** £2m - £5m **No.of Employees:** 21 - 50
Product Groups: 33, 37, 38, 39, 40

Date of Accounts	Apr 11	Apr 10	Apr 09
Sales Turnover	4m	N/A	N/A
Pre Tax Profit/Loss	-674	N/A	N/A
Working Capital	422	-1m	204
Fixed Assets	423	3m	364
Current Assets	2m	1m	1m
Current Liabilities	189	N/A	N/A

G M D Catering & Business Machines
Unit 32 Darbishire Street, Bolton, BL1 2TN
Tel: 01204-382700
Website: http://www.gmdcatering.co.uk
Directors: G. Dilworth (Prop)
Immediate Holding Company: G.M.D. CATERING LIMITED
Registration no: 05220791 **Date established:** 2004
No.of Employees: 1 - 10 **Product Groups:** 20, 40, 41

Date of Accounts	Mar 11	Mar 10	Mar 09
Working Capital	16	4	N/A
Fixed Assets	11	15	17
Current Assets	24	10	17

G M P Baird Ltd
47 Tonge Bridge Way
off Hypatia Street
Bury Road, Bolton, BL2 6BD
Tel: 01204-399963 **Fax:** 01204-531195
E-mail: gmpbairdltd@aol.com
Website: http://www.gmpbairdltd.co.uk
Directors: G. Baird (MD)
Immediate Holding Company: G.M.P. BAIRD LIMITED
Registration no: 01300692 **Date established:** 1977
No.of Employees: 1 - 10 **Product Groups:** 37, 42, 54

Date of Accounts	Feb 08	Feb 11	Feb 10
Working Capital	163	5	30
Fixed Assets	204	155	193
Current Assets	385	199	173

GB Silicone Technology Ltd
Lynstock Way Lostock, Bolton, BL6 4QR
Tel: 01204-474333 **Fax:** 01204-474347
E-mail: sales@gbsilicone.com
Website: http://www.gbsilicone.com
Directors: D. Crompton (MD), S. Dunbar (Fin)
Managers: T. Howard (Tech Serv Mgr)
Ultimate Holding Company: RICHARD THRELFALL GROUP LIMITED
Immediate Holding Company: G.B. SILICONE TECHNOLOGY LIMITED
Registration no: 01000995 **Date established:** 1971 **Turnover:** £2m - £5m
No.of Employees: 21 - 50 **Product Groups:** 29, 31, 32, 33, 42, 48

Date of Accounts	Mar 12	Mar 11	Mar 10
Working Capital	221	236	196
Fixed Assets	148	150	130
Current Assets	715	772	594

Gem Engineering
Gemini House Bolton Road Industrial Estate Bolton Road, Westhoughton, Bolton, BL5 3JG
Tel: 01942-814464 **Fax:** 01942-842414
E-mail: gem.engineering@ic24.net
Directors: G. Shaw (Ptnr)
VAT No.: GB 497 9937 50 **Turnover:** Up to £250,000
No.of Employees: 1 - 10 **Product Groups:** 44

Georgia Pacific GB Ltd
Stadium House 2 Eastgate Approach, Horwich, Bolton, BL6 6SY
Tel: 01204-673300 **Fax:** 01204-673301
E-mail: lorraine.payne@gapac.com
Website: http://www.gp.com
Bank(s): Barclays, The Wellsprings
Directors: C. Jones (Dir), R. Bourdon (MD), L. Beavis (Fin), L. Payne (Co Sec)
Ultimate Holding Company: KOCH INDUSTRIES INC (USA)
Immediate Holding Company: GEORGIA-PACIFIC GB LIMITED
Registration no: 02186119 **Date established:** 1987
Turnover: £125m - £250m **No.of Employees:** 1001 - 1500
Product Groups: 27

Gordons Of Bolton
54-56 Higher Bridge Street, Bolton, BL1 2HQ
Tel: 01204-524474 **Fax:** 01204-524022
Website: http://www.gordonsford.co.uk
Managers: K. Allenby-Carr (Mgr)
Immediate Holding Company: GORDONS (BOLTON) LIMITED
Registration no: 00280366 **Date established:** 1933
Turnover: £50m - £75m **No.of Employees:** 1 - 10 **Product Groups:** 68

Date of Accounts	Dec 11	Dec 10	Dec 09
Sales Turnover	70m	62m	58m
Pre Tax Profit/Loss	-62	138	284
Working Capital	-4m	-4m	-3m
Fixed Assets	9m	9m	8m
Current Assets	20m	20m	18m
Current Liabilities	603	761	403

Grosvenor Windows Ltd
Lodge Bank Estate Crown Lane, Horwich, Bolton, BL6 5HY
Tel: 01204-664488 **Fax:** 01204-664499
E-mail: sales@grosvenorwindows.co.uk
Website: http://www.grosvenorwindows.co.uk
Directors: C. Mills (Fin)
Immediate Holding Company: MILLS PROPERTIES (NW) LIMITED
Registration no: 01888426 **Date established:** 1985 **Turnover:** £1m - £2m
No.of Employees: 1 - 10 **Product Groups:** 25, 30

Date of Accounts	Jul 11	Jul 10	Apr 09
Working Capital	64	722	451
Fixed Assets	795	854	1m
Current Assets	142	844	723

Halbro Sportswear Ltd
Chorley New Road Horwich, Bolton, BL6 7JG
Tel: 01204-696476 **Fax:** 01204-699479
E-mail: info@halbro.com
Website: http://www.halbro.com
Bank(s): The Royal Bank of Scotland
Directors: R. Moores (Dir), J. Moores (Dir)
Ultimate Holding Company: HALBRO HOLDINGS LIMITED
Immediate Holding Company: HALBRO SPORTSWEAR LIMITED
Registration no: 02309195 **VAT No.:** GB 146 2778 47
Date established: 1988 **Turnover:** £2m - £5m **No.of Employees:** 21 - 50
Product Groups: 24, 63

Date of Accounts	Dec 11	Dec 10	Dec 09
Working Capital	1m	1m	1m
Fixed Assets	427	533	547
Current Assets	2m	2m	1m

Hampson Composites Ltd
Vale Mill Vale Street, Bolton, BL2 6QF
Tel: 01204-381626 **Fax:** 01204-529457
E-mail: liz@hampson-composites.co.uk
Website: http://www.hampson-composites.co.uk
Directors: G. Entwistle (MD)
Immediate Holding Company: TO22.COM LIMITED
Registration no: 01056499 **VAT No.:** GB 146 8168 44
Date established: 1972 **Turnover:** £1m - £2m **No.of Employees:** 1 - 10
Product Groups: 30, 42

Date of Accounts	Jul 08	Jul 07	Jan 11
Working Capital	-99	-55	438
Fixed Assets	230	247	N/A
Current Assets	194	421	438

Harrison Lubrication Engineering Ltd
Lynstock Way Lostock, Bolton, BL6 4SA
Tel: 01204-691352 **Fax:** 01204-669200
E-mail: sales@hle.co.uk
Website: http://www.nippleshop.co.uk
Directors: P. Murray (Fin), P. Morris (MD)
Managers: A. Ronsfield (Purch Mgr)
Immediate Holding Company: HARRISON LUBRICATION ENGINEERING LIMITED
Registration no: 02821641 **Date established:** 1993
No.of Employees: 21 - 50 **Product Groups:** 27, 36, 42, 66, 67

Date of Accounts	May 11	May 10	May 09
Working Capital	110	165	286
Fixed Assets	352	386	391
Current Assets	390	499	662

Helman Workwear
Egerton Street Farnworth, Bolton, BL4 7ER
Tel: 01204-709400 **Fax:** 01204-862460
E-mail: sales@helmanworkwear.co.uk
Website: http://www.helmanworkwear.co.uk
Bank(s): National Westminster Bank Plc
Directors: P. Chadwick (MD)
Ultimate Holding Company: Helman Group Ltd
Immediate Holding Company: PERFECT FINISH LIMITED
Registration no: 01142253 **VAT No.:** GB 150 7660 74
Date established: 1997 **Turnover:** £2m - £5m **No.of Employees:** 21 - 50
Product Groups: 24, 63

Date of Accounts	Aug 11	Aug 10	Aug 09
Working Capital	-55	-43	-27
Fixed Assets	86	91	104
Current Assets	267	191	246

J & K Henderson Enterprises Ltd
Unit 45 Great Bank Road, Westhoughton, Bolton, BL5 3XU
Tel: 01942-845600 **Fax:** 01942-845601
E-mail: james@jkhenderson.co.uk
Website: http://www.jkhenderson.co.uk
Directors: J. Henderson (Prop)
Immediate Holding Company: J & K HENDERSON ENTERPRISES LIMITED
Registration no: 01403386 **Date established:** 1978
Turnover: £10m - £20m **No.of Employees:** 21 - 50 **Product Groups:** 65

Date of Accounts	May 11	May 10	May 09
Sales Turnover	14m	14m	13m
Pre Tax Profit/Loss	505	497	253
Working Capital	2m	2m	2m
Fixed Assets	88	98	136
Current Assets	4m	4m	4m
Current Liabilities	427	343	301

Hersil Fabrics
Union Mill Vernon Street, Bolton, BL1 2PT
Tel: 01204-399619 **Fax:** 01204-386513
E-mail: info@clearancefabrics.co.uk
Website: http://www.textileauctions.co.uk
Directors: S. Lee (Fin)
Managers: B. Bowker (Mgr)
Ultimate Holding Company: DEWHURST DENT P.L.C.
Immediate Holding Company: HERSIL FABRICS LIMITED
Registration no: 00871665 **Date established:** 1966 **Turnover:** £5m - £10m
No.of Employees: 1 - 10 **Product Groups:** 66

Hi Tec Controls Bolton Ltd
Unit 4 Riverside, Bolton, BL1 8TU
Tel: 01204-392172 **Fax:** 01204- 391660
E-mail: info@hiteccontrols.co.uk
Website: http://www.hiteccontrols.co.uk
Directors: J. Whicklen (MD), J. Wicklen (Dir)
Managers: A. Taylor (Sales Admin)
Immediate Holding Company: HI-TEC CONTROLS (BOLTON) LIMITED
Registration no: 04553503 **Date established:** 2002
Turnover: £250,000 - £500,000 **No.of Employees:** 11 - 20
Product Groups: 35, 36, 38, 39, 40, 49

Date of Accounts	Oct 11	Oct 10	Oct 09
Working Capital	-46	-72	-21
Fixed Assets	82	112	152
Current Assets	216	179	181

John Holden & Son Kearsley Ltd
Moss Rose Mill Springfield Road, Kearsley, Bolton, BL4 8JW
Tel: 01204-571686 **Fax:** 01204-861447
E-mail: info@john-holden.com
Website: http://www.john-holden.com
Bank(s): Barclays, Manchester
Directors: M. Sciama (Dir), M. Sciama (MD)
Immediate Holding Company: STORMPROOFINGS LIMITED
Registration no: 02295480 **Date established:** 1994 **Turnover:** £5m - £10m
No.of Employees: 101 - 250 **Product Groups:** 23, 24, 63, 84

Date of Accounts	Dec 11	Dec 10	Dec 09
Working Capital	61	242	558
Fixed Assets	2m	2m	2m
Current Assets	446	861	1m

Hoover Ltd
Industrial Estate Bury Road, Bolton, BL2 6PU
Tel: 01204-556100 **Fax:** 01204-365270
E-mail: carol.makinson@hoovercandy.com
Website: http://www.hoover.co.uk
Managers: S. Skinner (Comm)
Ultimate Holding Company: CANDY SPA (ITALY)
Immediate Holding Company: HOOVER LIMITED
Registration no: 02521528 **Date established:** 1990
No.of Employees: 101 - 250 **Product Groups:** 40, 63

Date of Accounts	Dec 11	Dec 10	Dec 09
Sales Turnover	187m	215m	216m
Pre Tax Profit/Loss	1m	13m	-642
Working Capital	54m	53m	41m
Fixed Assets	11m	11m	12m
Current Assets	108m	112m	98m
Current Liabilities	32m	38m	37m

Hyquip Ltd
New Brunswick Street Horwich, Bolton, BL6 7JB
Tel: 01204-699959 **Fax:** 01204-699542
E-mail: info@hyquip.co.uk
Website: http://www.hyquip.co.uk

Directors: P. Taylor (Dir), K. Yates (Chief Op Offcr)
Immediate Holding Company: HYQUIP LIMITED
Registration no: 04167649 **Date established:** 2001
No.of Employees: 21 - 50 **Product Groups:** 30, 31, 35, 36, 37, 38, 39, 40, 45, 46, 67

Date of Accounts	Mar 11	Mar 10	Mar 09
Working Capital	475	522	495
Fixed Assets	152	146	141
Current Assets	1m	1m	849

I T W Welding Products Group (a division of I T W Ltd)

Horwich Business Park Chorley New Road Unit 102 Rivington House, Horwich, Bolton, BL6 5UE
Tel: 01204-469058 **Fax:** 01204-473039
E-mail: sales@itw-welding.co.uk
Website: http://www.itw-welding.co.uk
Managers: T. Varley (Chief Mgr), J. Clark (Sales Prom Mgr), S. Plumtree (Cust Serv Mgr)
Immediate Holding Company: UK PRIVATE VEHICLE HIRE LIMITED
Date established: 2008 **Turnover:** £2m - £5m **No.of Employees:** 1 - 10
Product Groups: 67

Indespension Ltd (Head Office)

Paragon Business Park Chorley New Road, Horwich, Bolton, BL6 6HG
Tel: 01204-478500 **Fax:** 01204-478583
E-mail: info@indespension.co.uk
Website: http://www.indespension.co.uk
Bank(s): National Westminster Bank Plc
Directors: L. Mangnall (I.T. Dir), R. Graham (Pers), S. Sadler (Purch), D. Carroll (Fin), A. Graham (Ch)
Managers: S. Dunbar (Fin Mgr), M. Lowry (Tech Serv Mgr), N. Singleton (Mktg Serv Mgr)
Ultimate Holding Company: D.R.A. LTD
Immediate Holding Company: INDESPENSION LTD
Registration no: 02125263 **VAT No.:** GB 421 8277 59
Date established: 1987 **Turnover:** £10m - £20m
No.of Employees: 101 - 250 **Product Groups:** 39, 45, 68

Date of Accounts	Jun 11	Jun 10	Jun 09
Sales Turnover	17m	15m	19m
Pre Tax Profit/Loss	550	192	137
Working Capital	2m	1m	2m
Fixed Assets	4m	5m	6m
Current Assets	8m	8m	8m
Current Liabilities	3m	527	783

Indevent

Phoenix Works Lostock Lane, Lostock, Bolton, BL6 4BP
Tel: 08706-073460 **Fax:** 01204-592050
E-mail: b.murphy@physicalsecuritygroup.com
Website: http://www.indevent.com
Managers: B. Murphy (Sales Prom)
Immediate Holding Company: DUNSCAR SECURITY LTD
Registration no: 03037780 **Date established:** 1995
No.of Employees: 11 - 20 **Product Groups:** 26, 35

Date of Accounts	Mar 09	Mar 08	Mar 07
Working Capital	-380	-271	-137
Fixed Assets	30	36	59
Current Assets	409	339	371

Intech Ltd

Link House 273 Crown Lane, Horwich, Bolton, BL6 5HY
Tel: 01204-675675 **Fax:** 01204-695172
E-mail: ian.clough@intech.co.uk
Website: http://www.intech.co.uk
Directors: I. Clough (Dir)
Immediate Holding Company: INTECH LIMITED
Registration no: 01493542 **Date established:** 1980
Turnover: £500,000 - £1m **No.of Employees:** 1 - 10 **Product Groups:** 44

Date of Accounts	Jun 11	Jun 10	Jun 09
Working Capital	279	296	289
Fixed Assets	32	41	23
Current Assets	331	355	346

J J Haslam Ltd

Park Works Clegg Street, Bolton, BL2 6DU
Tel: 0161-320 9696 **Fax:** 0161-335 0918
E-mail: contact@jjhaslam.com
Website: http://www.jjhaslam.com
Directors: R. Barnshaw (MD), E. Hearn (Co Sec)
Managers: J. Donnally (Buyer), M. Green (Chief Mgr)
Immediate Holding Company: Section 5 Ltd
Registration no: 02614821 **Turnover:** £500,000 - £1m
No.of Employees: 11 - 20 **Product Groups:** 34, 35, 45, 46, 48

Date of Accounts	Dec 07	Dec 06	Dec 05
Working Capital	751	665	672
Fixed Assets	152	154	158
Current Assets	856	822	922
Current Liabilities	105	157	249

J S Liftrucks

193 Albert Road Farnworth, Bolton, BL4 9HZ
Tel: 01204-707790 **Fax:** 01204-707790
Directors: G. Smith (Ptnr), J. Smith (Ptnr)
Date established: 1977 **No.of Employees:** 1 - 10 **Product Groups:** 35, 39, 45

Jewson Ltd

Lever Street, Bolton, BL3 6NX
Tel: 01204-521261 **Fax:** 01204-532297
E-mail: paul.menzies@jewson.co.uk
Website: http://www.jewson.co.uk
Managers: P. Menzies
Ultimate Holding Company: COMPAGNIE DE SAINT GOBAIN (FRANCE)
Immediate Holding Company: JEWSON LIMITED
Registration no: 00348407 **VAT No.:** GB 497 7184 83
Date established: 1939 **Turnover:** £2m - £5m **No.of Employees:** 1 - 10
Product Groups: 66

Date of Accounts	Dec 11	Dec 10	Dec 09
Sales Turnover	1606m	1547m	1485m
Pre Tax Profit/Loss	18m	100m	45m
Working Capital	-345m	-250m	-349m
Fixed Assets	496m	387m	461m
Current Assets	657m	1005m	1320m
Current Liabilities	66m	120m	64m

W & S C Jobson

5 Dunscar Business Park Blackburn Road, Egerton, Bolton, BL7 9PQ
Tel: 01204-306212 **Fax:** 01204-306212
E-mail: info@jobsonsgarage.co.uk
Website: http://www.jobsonsgarage.co.uk
Directors: W. Jobson (Dir)
Date established: 1966 **No.of Employees:** 1 - 10 **Product Groups:** 39

Date of Accounts	Aug 08	Aug 07	Aug 06
Working Capital	14	21	-55
Fixed Assets	112	72	86
Current Assets	244	247	125
Current Liabilities	230	225	180

John Hunt Bolton Ltd

Alma Works Rasbottom Street, Bolton, BL3 5BZ
Tel: 01204-521831 **Fax:** 01204-527306
E-mail: spencer@johnhuntbolton.co.uk
Website: http://www.johnhuntbolton.co.uk
Bank(s): National Westminster Bank Plc
Directors: S. Cheetham (MD)
Managers: S. Cheetham (Sales Prom Mgr)
Immediate Holding Company: JOHN HUNT (BOLTON) LIMITED
Registration no: 00230080 **VAT No.:** GB 145 2046 94
Date established: 2028 **Turnover:** £1m - £2m **No.of Employees:** 11 - 20
Product Groups: 41

Date of Accounts	Aug 11	Aug 10	Aug 09
Working Capital	539	504	543
Fixed Assets	65	76	70
Current Assets	729	608	679

Krones UK Ltd

Westregen House Great Bank Road Wingates Industrial Estate, Westhoughton, Bolton, BL5 3XB
Tel: 01942-845000 **Fax:** 01942-845091
E-mail: info@krones.com
Website: http://www.krones.com
Directors: D. Hughes (Fin)
Managers: A. Wilson (Mgr), M. Riley (Purch Mgr), A. Albury (Mktg Serv Mgr)
Ultimate Holding Company: KRONES AG (GERMANY)
Immediate Holding Company: KRONES UK LIMITED
Registration no: 00521832 **VAT No.:** GB 519 5905 22
Date established: 1953 **Turnover:** £20m - £50m
No.of Employees: 51 - 100 **Product Groups:** 42, 67

Date of Accounts	Dec 11	Dec 10	Dec 09
Sales Turnover	38m	34m	26m
Pre Tax Profit/Loss	2m	2m	2m
Working Capital	5m	5m	5m
Fixed Assets	2m	2m	2m
Current Assets	12m	10m	9m
Current Liabilities	3m	3m	1m

Lancashire Fork Truck Services Ltd

Unit 1 Easter Park Wingates Westhoughton, Bolton, BL5 3XU
Tel: 0161-628 9977 **Fax:** 01254-672111
E-mail: info@lfts.co.uk
Website: http://www.lancashireforktruck.co.uk
Directors: D. Jones (MD)
Immediate Holding Company: LANCASHIRE (FORK TRUCK) SERVICES LIMITED
Registration no: 07001328 **Date established:** 2009
No.of Employees: 21 - 50 **Product Groups:** 35, 39, 45

Lancashire Gun Room Limited

394 Halliwell road, Bolton, BL1 8AP
Tel: 01204-848088 **Fax:** 01204-366236
E-mail: lancashireguns@aol.com
Website: http://www.shootingshack.com
Directors: C. Shack (Prop)
Registration no: 07054706 **Date established:** 2004
No.of Employees: 1 - 10 **Product Groups:** 36, 39, 40

Landers Recruitment

522 Blackburn Road, Bolton, BL1 8NW
Tel: 01204-309555 **Fax:** 01204-309595
E-mail: admin@landersrecruitment.co.uk
Website: http://www.landers-recruit.co.uk
Directors: L. Anderson (Dir)
Ultimate Holding Company: LANDERS SALES & MANAGEMENT RECRUITMENT LIMITED
Immediate Holding Company: LANDERS RECRUITMENT LIMITED
Registration no: 02733352 **Date established:** 1992
No.of Employees: 1 - 10 **Product Groups:** 80

Date of Accounts	Dec 11	Dec 10	Dec 09
Working Capital	90	-27	-54
Fixed Assets	N/A	63	65
Current Assets	201	154	78

Lantor UK

73 St Helens Road, Bolton, BL3 3PP
Tel: 01204-855000 **Fax:** 01204-61722
E-mail: sales@lantor.co.uk
Website: http://www.lantor.co.uk
Bank(s): National Westminster Bank Plc
Directors: A. Flint (Fin), G. Sethna (MD), J. Bickford (Comm)
Immediate Holding Company: LANTOR (UK) LIMITED
Registration no: 04180283 **VAT No.:** GB 588 8960 51
Date established: 2001 **Turnover:** £5m - £10m
No.of Employees: 51 - 100 **Product Groups:** 23, 24, 30, 33, 42

Date of Accounts	Nov 11	Dec 10	Dec 09
Sales Turnover	7m	7m	8m
Pre Tax Profit/Loss	-1m	-1m	-624
Working Capital	201	160	346
Fixed Assets	3m	2m	2m
Current Assets	2m	2m	2m
Current Liabilities	1m	830	969

Leadermac UK Ltd

Makinson Lodge Half Acre Lane, Blackrod, Bolton, BL6 5LR
Tel: 01942-859933 **Fax:** 01942-859944
E-mail: info@leadermac.uk.com
Website: http://www.leadermac.uk.com
Directors: K. Wright (Prop), J. Wright (Fin)
Immediate Holding Company: LEADERMAC UK LIMITED
Registration no: 04212410 **Date established:** 2001
No.of Employees: 1 - 10 **Product Groups:** 46

Date of Accounts	May 11	May 10	May 09
Working Capital	1m	991	1m
Fixed Assets	128	1	2
Current Assets	1m	1m	1m

Leighs Paints

Tower Works Kestor Street, Bolton, BL2 2AL
Tel: 01204-521771 **Fax:** 01332-371115
E-mail: enquiries@leighspaints.com
Website: http://www.leighspaints.com
Directors: A. Moon (Tech Serv), G. Bell (Prop), M. Snowball (Fin), M. Green (Pers), R. William (Sales)
Managers: S. Ball (Product), M. Hudson (Purch Mgr)
Ultimate Holding Company: THE SHERWIN-WILLIAMS CO
Immediate Holding Company: LEIGHS PAINTS
Registration no: 00893081 **VAT No.:** GB 146 0326 92
Date established: 1966 **Turnover:** £20m - £50m
No.of Employees: 101 - 250 **Product Groups:** 29, 30, 31, 32, 33, 40, 48

Date of Accounts	Dec 11	Dec 10	Dec 09
Sales Turnover	39m	32m	31m
Pre Tax Profit/Loss	-2m	-2m	-1m
Working Capital	3m	6m	8m
Fixed Assets	4m	10m	10m
Current Assets	17m	14m	11m
Current Liabilities	2m	3m	729

Leisuredrive Ltd

Unit 4 Fishbrook Industrial Estate, Kearsley, Bolton, BL4 8EL
Tel: 01204-574498 **Fax:** 01204-574488
E-mail: derek.andrews@leisuredrive.co.uk
Website: http://www.leisuredrive.co.uk
Directors: D. Andrews (Ch)
Immediate Holding Company: LEISUREDRIVE CAMPERVANS LTD
Registration no: 03324218 **Date established:** 1997 **Turnover:** £1m - £2m
No.of Employees: 11 - 20 **Product Groups:** 30

Date of Accounts	Jul 11	Jul 10	Jul 09
Working Capital	195	167	133
Fixed Assets	16	13	18
Current Assets	307	221	290
Current Liabilities	N/A	N/A	48

Lever Bridge Fabrications

Unit 5a Lever Bridge Mills Radcliffe Road, Bolton, BL3 1RU
Tel: 01204-392030 **Fax:** 01204-398479
Directors: R. Richardson (Prop)
Date established: 1997 **No.of Employees:** 1 - 10 **Product Groups:** 35

James Lever & Sons Ltd

Unit 26 Morris Green Business Park Fearnhead Street, Bolton, BL3 3PE
Tel: 01204-61121 **Fax:** 01204- 658154
E-mail: james@jameslever.co.uk
Website: http://www.jameslever.co.uk
Bank(s): National Westminster Bank Plc
Directors: J. Lever (MD)
Immediate Holding Company: JAMES LEVER & SONS LIMITED
Registration no: 00282949 **VAT No.:** GB 146 9641 39
Date established: 1933 **Turnover:** £2m - £5m **No.of Employees:** 11 - 20
Product Groups: 23

Date of Accounts	Sep 11	Sep 10	Sep 09
Working Capital	160	219	217
Fixed Assets	147	356	371
Current Assets	402	492	553

Lostock Electrical Projects Co. Ltd

Saviours Terrace Bankfield Street, Bolton, BL3 5NP
Tel: 01204-656811 **Fax:** 01204-61797
E-mail: admin@lostock-electrical.co.uk
Website: http://www.lostock-electrical.co.uk
Bank(s): Royal Bank of Scotland, Eccles
Directors: D. Simm (Dir), M. Nutter (Dir)
Managers: M. Williamson (Chief Acct)
Immediate Holding Company: LOSTOCK ELECTRICAL PROJECTS COMPANY LIMITED
Registration no: 02000662 **VAT No.:** GB 148 6337 45
Date established: 1986 **Turnover:** £2m - £5m **No.of Employees:** 21 - 50
Product Groups: 37

Date of Accounts	Jun 11	Jun 10	Jun 09
Sales Turnover	N/A	N/A	2m
Pre Tax Profit/Loss	N/A	N/A	244
Working Capital	615	630	507
Fixed Assets	48	72	90
Current Assets	1m	1m	951
Current Liabilities	N/A	N/A	160

Low Profile & Grinding

Unit 1 Britannia Way, Bolton, BL2 2HH
Tel: 01204-380560 **Fax:** 01204-548993
E-mail: jackie@lowprofiling.com
Directors: J. Low (Dir)
Immediate Holding Company: LOW PROFILING AND GRINDING LIMITED
Registration no: 02637534 **Date established:** 1991
No.of Employees: 1 - 10 **Product Groups:** 34, 66

Date of Accounts	Apr 11	Apr 10	Apr 09
Working Capital	-25	-42	-27
Fixed Assets	26	38	49
Current Assets	153	144	142

Luxia Catering Equipment

51 Higher Dunscar Egerton, Bolton, BL7 9TF
Tel: 01204-591111 **Fax:** 01204-595858
E-mail: sales@luxia-nce.co.uk
Website: http://www.luxia.co.uk
Directors: M. Lofthouse (Ptnr)
Immediate Holding Company: LUXIA (U.K.) LIMITED
Registration no: 01955664 **Date established:** 1985
No.of Employees: 1 - 10 **Product Groups:** 67

M B W UK Ltd

Unit 2-3 Cochrane Street, Bolton, BL3 6BN
Tel: 01204-387784 **Fax:** 01204-387797
E-mail: mbwuk@btinternet.com
Website: http://www.mbw.com
Managers: A. Gorozdy (Sales Admin)
Ultimate Holding Company: MBW INC (USA)
Immediate Holding Company: M. B. W. (U.K.) LIMITED
Registration no: 02107644 **Date established:** 1987
No.of Employees: 1 - 10 **Product Groups:** 42, 45

Date of Accounts	Dec 11	Dec 10	Dec 09
Working Capital	1m	945	963
Fixed Assets	58	57	33
Current Assets	1m	1m	1m

M H P Services
5 Valletts South Buildings Valletts Lane, Bolton, BL1 6DS
Tel: 01204-495313 **Fax:** 01204-495313
E-mail: enq@mhpservices.co.uk
Website: http://www.mhpservices.co.uk
Directors: P. Markland (Prop)
No.of Employees: 1 - 10 **Product Groups:** 52

M S C Copperflow Ltd
28 Hulme Street, Bolton, BL1 2SX
Tel: 01204-528206 **Fax:** 01204-366877
E-mail: sales@msc.uk.com
Website: http://www.msc.uk.com
Bank(s): Nat West
Directors: E. Nabb (Fin), D. Nabb (MD)
Managers: J. France (Sales Prom Mgr)
Ultimate Holding Company: COPPERFLOW LIMITED
Immediate Holding Company: MSC / COPPERFLOW LTD
Registration no: 02234352 **VAT No.:** GB 081 0520 01
Date established: 1988 **No.of Employees:** 21 - 50 **Product Groups:** 48

Date of Accounts	Jul 11	Jul 10	Jul 09
Working Capital	779	728	867
Fixed Assets	163	138	131
Current Assets	1m	936	1m
Current Liabilities	N/A	82	87

McGarrys Design Partnership
168 Victoria Raod Horwich, Bolton, BL6 5PQ
Tel: 01204-690160
E-mail: mcgarrysdesign@live.co.uk
Website: http://www.mcgarrysdesignpartnership.yolasite.com
Directors: A. McGarry (Prop)
Date established: 2008 **No.of Employees:** 1 - 10 **Product Groups:** 52, 81, 84

Machine Tool Supplies Ltd
302-304 Chorley Old Road, Bolton, BL1 4JU
Tel: 01204-840111 **Fax:** 01204-844407
E-mail: sales@mtsdriventools.co.uk
Website: http://www.MTSDRIVENTOOLS.CO.UK
Directors: D. Greenhalgh (MD)
Immediate Holding Company: MACHINE TOOL SUPPLIES LIMITED
Registration no: 02596083 **Date established:** 1991
No.of Employees: 1 - 10 **Product Groups:** 24, 36, 46, 47

Date of Accounts	Apr 12	Apr 11	Apr 10
Working Capital	139	81	40
Fixed Assets	2	N/A	N/A
Current Assets	425	252	139

Mayfran UK
Unit 38 Bradley Fold Trading Estate Radcliffe Moor Road, Bradley Fold, Bolton, BL2 6RT
Tel: 01204-366469 **Fax:** 01204-366840
E-mail: ksullivan@mayfran.eu
Website: http://www.mayfran.com
Managers: K. Sullivan (Mgr)
Ultimate Holding Company: MAYFRAN HOLDINGS INC (USA)
Immediate Holding Company: MAYFRAN U.K. LIMITED
Registration no: 01194008 **VAT No.:** GB 273 6820 43
Date established: 1974 **Turnover:** £500,000 - £1m
No.of Employees: 1 - 10 **Product Groups:** 42, 45

Date of Accounts	Dec 10	Dec 09	Dec 08
Sales Turnover	802	927	808
Pre Tax Profit/Loss	47	67	80
Working Capital	285	246	187
Fixed Assets	84	89	95
Current Assets	817	696	604
Current Liabilities	160	113	103

Merlin Coatings Ltd
Unit 7 Kirkhall Workshops, Bolton, BL1 4HH
Tel: 01204-940004
E-mail: paul@merlincoatings.com
Directors: P. Brough (Dir)
Immediate Holding Company: MERLIN COATINGS LIMITED
Registration no: 04809742 **Date established:** 2003
No.of Employees: 1 - 10 **Product Groups:** 34, 42, 52

Date of Accounts	Jun 11	Jun 10	Jun 09
Working Capital	N/A	-2	25
Fixed Assets	5	6	8
Current Assets	39	42	74

Michael Clothing Co
1 Amico Works 232-234 Waterloo Street, Bolton, BL1 8HU
Tel: 01204-524846 **Fax:** 01204-524846
Directors: S. Barker (Prop)
No.of Employees: 1 - 10 **Product Groups:** 22, 24

Midway Engineering North West Ltd
Unit 8 Shepherd Cross Street, Bolton, BL1 3DE
Tel: 01204-494121 **Fax:** 01204-493013
E-mail: midwayengineering@btconnect.com
Bank(s): Lloyds
Directors: J. Pasquill (Dir)
Managers: C. Holden (Chief Acct)
Immediate Holding Company: MIDWAY ENGINEERING (N.W.) LIMITED
Registration no: 02792912 **Date established:** 1993 **Turnover:** £1m - £2m
No.of Employees: 11 - 20 **Product Groups:** 33, 48

Date of Accounts	Mar 11	Mar 10	Mar 09
Working Capital	27	30	32
Fixed Assets	57	67	79
Current Assets	112	117	128

Monarch Catering Ltd
Vulcan Works Dixon Street, Horwich, Bolton, BL6 7PH
Tel: 0800-009 3290 **Fax:** 01204-669079
E-mail: info@monarch-direct.co.uk
Website: http://www.monarch-direct.co.uk
Managers: P. Shaw (Chief Mgr)
Immediate Holding Company: MONARCH CATERING EQUIPMENT LIMITED
Registration no: 01824304 **Date established:** 1984
No.of Employees: 1 - 10 **Product Groups:** 36, 40

Date of Accounts	Jun 11	Jun 10	Jun 09
Working Capital	454	449	470
Fixed Assets	55	52	53
Current Assets	678	670	717

Musco Lighting Europe
Unit 1005 Great Bank Road Wingates Industrial Estate, Westhoughton, Bolton, BL5 3XU
Tel: 01942-811777
E-mail: eurosales@musco.com
Website: http://www.musco.eu
Managers: J. Brown (Mgr)
Ultimate Holding Company: MUSCO SPORTS LIGHTING LLC (USA)
Immediate Holding Company: MUSCO LIGHTING EUROPE LTD.
Registration no: 02935540 **Date established:** 1994
No.of Employees: 11 - 20 **Product Groups:** 37, 67

Date of Accounts	Dec 11	Dec 10	Dec 09
Working Capital	874	415	425
Fixed Assets	113	156	190
Current Assets	2m	1m	2m

Newfoil Ltd
Bradford Street Farnworth, Bolton, BL4 9LS
Tel: 01204-861110 **Fax:** 01204-862201
E-mail: info@newfoil.co.uk
Website: http://www.newfoil.co.uk
Bank(s): Lloyds TSB Bank plc
Directors: P. Taylor (MD), T. Fletcher (Ch), J. Clarkson (Dir)
Managers: J. Clarkson (Develop Mgr), K. Scott (Accounts), G. Murphy (Purch Mgr)
Immediate Holding Company: NEWFOIL LIMITED
Registration no: 01427869 **Date established:** 1979 **Turnover:** £2m - £5m
No.of Employees: 21 - 50 **Product Groups:** 27, 28, 30, 44

Date of Accounts	Jun 08
Working Capital	387
Fixed Assets	1057
Current Assets	1010
Current Liabilities	623
Total Share Capital	24

Newtronic Controls International Ltd
Rockfield House 512 Darwen Road, Bromley Cross, Bolton, BL7 9DX
Tel: 01204-401105 **Fax:** 01204-401105
E-mail: newtroniccontrols@aol.com
Website: http://www.newtronic-controls.co.uk
Directors: G. Cotton (Dir)
Immediate Holding Company: NEWTRONIC CONTROLS INTERNATIONAL LIMITED
Registration no: 01287705 **Date established:** 1976
Turnover: £500,000 - £1m **No.of Employees:** 1 - 10 **Product Groups:** 38

Date of Accounts	Dec 11	Dec 10	Dec 09
Working Capital	13	6	5
Fixed Assets	N/A	N/A	1
Current Assets	38	32	35

Niagra Lasalle Ltd
Stone Hill Road Farnworth, Bolton, BL4 7NN
Tel: 01204-576321 **Fax:** 01204-574511
E-mail: sales@man.macreadys.niag.com
Website: http://www.niag.com
Directors: G. Rawlson (MD), J. Lycett (Fin)
Managers: A. Hart (Mgr), S. Chester (Mgr)
Ultimate Holding Company: Niagara Corporation
Immediate Holding Company: Niagara Lasalle (UK) Ltd
Registration no: 03725308 **Date established:** 1978
No.of Employees: 21 - 50 **Product Groups:** 34

North West Metalcraft
Unit 25 Bradley Fold Trading Estate Radcliffe Moor Road, Bradley Fold, Bolton, BL2 6RT
Tel: 07973-500669
E-mail: i.hayes@northwestmetalcraft.com
Website: http://www.northwestmetalcraft.com
Directors: I. Hayes (MD)
Immediate Holding Company: NORTH WEST METALCRAFT LIMITED
Registration no: 03494171 **Date established:** 1998
No.of Employees: 1 - 10 **Product Groups:** 26, 35

Date of Accounts	Mar 10	Mar 09	Mar 08
Working Capital	-5	-10	-8
Fixed Assets	5	6	8
Current Assets	23	16	19

Norville Optical
Turner Bridge Folds Road, Bolton, BL1 2TU
Tel: 01204-381224 **Fax:** 01204-388906
E-mail: info@norville.co.uk
Website: http://www.norville.co.uk
Managers: M. Walters (District Mgr)
No.of Employees: 21 - 50 **Product Groups:** 37, 38, 65

One Stop Hire Ltd
135 Bridgeman Street, Bolton, BL3 6BS
Tel: 01204-366555 **Fax:** 01204-368020
E-mail: info@onestophire.com
Website: http://www.onestophire.com
Directors: S. Hitchen (MD)
Immediate Holding Company: ONE STOP HIRE LIMITED
Registration no: 04857939 **Date established:** 2003
No.of Employees: 1 - 10 **Product Groups:** 39, 44, 54, 61, 67, 72, 74, 76, 83, 89

Date of Accounts	May 09	Mar 12	Mar 11
Working Capital	N/A	17	125
Fixed Assets	N/A	2m	2m
Current Assets	N/A	1m	984

Orseal Ltd (Orseal Valve Specialists)
Lynstock Way Lostock, Bolton, BL6 4QR
Tel: 01204-474300 **Fax:** 01204-474347
E-mail: sales@orseal.com
Website: http://www.orseal.com
Bank(s): National Westminster Bank Plc
Directors: D. Crompton (MD)
Ultimate Holding Company: RICHARD THRELFALL GROUP LIMITED
Immediate Holding Company: ORSEAL LIMITED
Registration no: 00707869 **VAT No.:** GB 145 2667 62
Date established: 1961 **Turnover:** £2m - £5m **No.of Employees:** 11 - 20
Product Groups: 35, 36, 39, 40

Date of Accounts	Mar 12	Mar 11	Mar 10
Working Capital	541	542	628
Fixed Assets	50	62	48
Current Assets	3m	957	995

Outright Fire Protection
25 Lower Drake Fold Westhoughton, Bolton, BL5 2RE
Tel: 01942-817148 **Fax:** 01942-817148
Directors: J. Harris (Prop)
Date established: 1979 **No.of Employees:** 1 - 10 **Product Groups:** 38, 42

P J H Group Ltd
Alder House Slackey Brow, Kearsley, Bolton, BL4 8SL
Tel: 01204-707070 **Fax:** 01204-573140
E-mail: info@pjhgroup.com
Website: http://www.pjhgroup.co.uk
Directors: R. George (Tech Serv), S. Johnstone (Sales), R. Higgins (Purch), A. Yates (Grp Chief Exec), M. Cameron (Pers), M. Errington (Fin)
Ultimate Holding Company: GLOBE UNION INDUSTIRAL CORP (TAIWAN)
Immediate Holding Company: P.J.H. GROUP LIMITED
Registration no: 01056008 **VAT No.:** 588 7086 67 **Date established:** 1972
Turnover: £125m - £250m **No.of Employees:** 51 - 100
Product Groups: 26

Date of Accounts	Dec 11	Dec 10	Dec 09
Sales Turnover	140m	164m	163m
Pre Tax Profit/Loss	3m	6m	7m
Working Capital	52m	48m	44m
Fixed Assets	2m	2m	1m
Current Assets	89m	96m	92m
Current Liabilities	8m	10m	9m

P T F E Developments Ltd
Seymour Drive Bradshaw, Bolton, BL2 3HB
Tel: 01204-309784
E-mail: david@ptfe.org
Website: http://www.ptfe-developments.co.uk
Directors: D. Howarth (Dir)
Immediate Holding Company: P.T.F.E. DEVELOPMENTS LTD.
Registration no: 02533134 **Date established:** 1990
No.of Employees: 1 - 10 **Product Groups:** 30, 33, 36

Date of Accounts	Nov 11	Nov 10	Nov 09
Working Capital	23	19	-15
Fixed Assets	44	49	54
Current Assets	88	114	90

P T Fabrications
159 Springfield Road Kearsley, Bolton, BL4 8JZ
Tel: 07779-286517
E-mail: sales@p-t-fabrications.co.uk
Website: http://www.p-t-fabrications.co.uk
Directors: P. Tebay (Prop)
Registration no: 06366858 **Date established:** 2003
No.of Employees: 1 - 10 **Product Groups:** 26, 35

Panalux Ltd
Sunset Business Park Manchester Road, Kearsley, Bolton, BL4 8RL
Tel: 01204-794000 **Fax:** 0117-923 5745
E-mail: info@panalux.biz
Website: http://www.panalux.biz
Directors: J. Lawton (MD)
Ultimate Holding Company: PANAVISION INC (USA)
Immediate Holding Company: PANALUX LIMITED
Registration no: 04197837 **Date established:** 2001 **Turnover:** £2m - £5m
No.of Employees: 11 - 20 **Product Groups:** 37

Date of Accounts	Dec 11	Dec 10	Dec 09
Sales Turnover	32m	34m	29m
Pre Tax Profit/Loss	3m	4m	2m
Working Capital	7m	3m	2m
Fixed Assets	13m	13m	12m
Current Assets	17m	15m	13m
Current Liabilities	8m	3m	2m

Pathway Scooters Ltd
Chorley New Road Horwich, Bolton, BL6 7JG
Tel: 01204-697899
Website: http://www.pathwayscooters.co.uk
Directors: C. Matthews (Prop)
Registration no: 04722460 **Date established:** 2003
No.of Employees: 1 - 10 **Product Groups:** 37, 38, 39

Paylor Controls Ltd
Unit 7 Waters Meeting Britannia Way, Bolton, BL2 2HH
Tel: 01204-370067 **Fax:** 0161-764 2745
E-mail: sales@paylor.co.uk
Website: http://www.paylor.co.uk
Directors: M. Clayton (MD), B. Clayton (Fin)
Immediate Holding Company: PAYLOR CONTROLS LIMITED
Registration no: 01242923 **VAT No.:** GB 150 5990 63
Date established: 1976 **No.of Employees:** 1 - 10 **Product Groups:** 37, 45

Date of Accounts	Jan 12	Jan 11	Jan 10
Working Capital	175	116	91
Fixed Assets	2	9	16
Current Assets	293	211	159

Pennine Products
Fold Mill Bradley Lane, Bolton, BL2 6RR
Tel: 01204-361547 **Fax:** 01204-380 872
E-mail: info@pennineindustries.com
Website: http://www.pennineindustries.com
Bank(s): National Westminster
Managers: A. Coates (Tech Serv Mgr), M. Seddon (Mgr), M. Bee (Personnel), P. Ashcroft (Buyer)
Immediate Holding Company: PENNINE INDUSTRIES LIMITED
Registration no: 01279313 **VAT No.:** GB 151 1262 13
Date established: 1976 **Turnover:** £2m - £5m
No.of Employees: 101 - 250 **Product Groups:** 29, 30

Date of Accounts	Mar 08	Sep 06
Pre Tax Profit/Loss	N/A	-194
Working Capital	114	306
Fixed Assets	340	105
Current Assets	2156	1874
Current Liabilities	2042	1568
Total Share Capital	34	34
ROCE% (Return on Capital Employed)		-47.2

Peron Plastics
Unit 10 Dunscar Industrial Estate Blackburn Road, Egerton, Bolton, BL7 9PQ
Tel: 01204-597546 **Fax:** 01204-596928
E-mail: sales@peronplastics.co.uk
Website: http://www.peronplastics.co.uk
Directors: R. Wadeson (Prop)
VAT No.: GB 325 8862 32 **Turnover:** Up to £250,000
No.of Employees: 1 - 10 **Product Groups:** 30, 49

Philadelphia Scientific
188 Oxford Grove, Bolton, BL1 3BH
Tel: 01204-467777
Website: http://www.philadelphiascientific.com
Immediate Holding Company: PHILADELPHIA SCIENTIFIC (U.K.) LIMITED
Registration no: 03380727 **Date established:** 1997
No.of Employees: 21 - 50 **Product Groups:** 37, 49

Date of Accounts	Dec 11	Dec 10	Dec 09
Working Capital	521	85	10
Fixed Assets	289	240	243
Current Assets	1m	390	266

Planters Clayton Ltd
Unit 6, Rivington House Horwich Business Park, Chorley New Road, Horwich, Bolton, BL6 5UE
Tel: 01204-690003 **Fax:** 01204-690170
E-mail: carl.g@plantersclayton.com
Website: http://www.plantersclayton.com
Managers: C. Greenhalgh (Mgr), A. Harrison
Registration no: 02981416 **VAT No.:** GB 633 9933 11
Turnover: £1m - £2m **No.of Employees:** 1 - 10 **Product Groups:** 41, 42, 43, 46, 67

Date of Accounts	Mar 12	Mar 11	Mar 10
Working Capital	650	193	197
Fixed Assets	53	60	14
Current Assets	1m	2m	798

Portman Doors Ltd
Unit 3 Bradshaw Works Printers Lane, Bolton, BL2 3DW
Tel: 01204-596026 **Fax:** 01204-669094
E-mail: info@portmandoors.co.uk
Website: http://www.portmandoors.co.uk
Bank(s): Barclays
Directors: R. Allport (MD)
Immediate Holding Company: PORTMAN DOORS LIMITED
Registration no: 02594915 **VAT No.:** GB 598 8920 64
Date established: 1991 **Turnover:** £1m - £2m **No.of Employees:** 11 - 20
Product Groups: 35, 36

Date of Accounts	Mar 11	Mar 10	Mar 09
Working Capital	98	163	216
Fixed Assets	106	129	143
Current Assets	211	281	392

Proton Glass & Dishwashers
3 Moorlands View, Bolton, BL3 3TN
Tel: 01204-650046 **Fax:** 01204-650046
E-mail: sterodgers@yahoo.co.uk
Website: http://www.protonwashrite.co.uk
Managers: S. Rodgers (Mgr)
No.of Employees: 1 - 10 **Product Groups:** 20, 40, 41

Purepages Group Ltd
7a Church Bank, Bolton, BL1 1HX
Tel: 01204-375500
E-mail: sales@purepagesgroup.com
Website: http://www.purepages.com
Directors: M. Phillips (MD)
Immediate Holding Company: PUREPAGES GROUP LIMITED
Registration no: 04414898 **Date established:** 2002
No.of Employees: 1 - 10 **Product Groups:** 44

Date of Accounts	Sep 11	Sep 10	Sep 09
Working Capital	-3	-37	-43
Fixed Assets	572	551	530
Current Assets	2	1	4

Q-Lab Corporation
Express Trading Estate Stone Hill Road, Farnworth, Bolton, BL4 9TP
Tel: 01204-861616 **Fax:** 01204-861617
E-mail: info.eu@q-lab.com
Website: http://www.q-lab.com
Directors: D. Grossman (Prop)
Immediate Holding Company: Q-LAB CORPORATION
Registration no: FC010692 **VAT No.:** GB 306 4172 85
Date established: 1980 **No.of Employees:** 1 - 10 **Product Groups:** 38, 67

R D K Mobility
190 Tonge Moor Road, Bolton, BL2 2HN
Tel: 0800-107 5118 **Fax:** 01204-387638
E-mail: bolton@rdkmobility.co.uk
Website: http://www.rdkmobility.co.uk
Managers: C. Pratt (Mgr)
Ultimate Holding Company: GWYNDAL PROPERTIES LIMITED
Immediate Holding Company: RADCLIFFE (HOMEMAKERS) LIMITED
Registration no: 01189254 **Date established:** 1974
Turnover: Up to £250,000 **No.of Employees:** 1 - 10 **Product Groups:** 39, 45, 67, 85

Date of Accounts	Jan 11	Jan 10	Jan 09
Working Capital	128	150	199
Fixed Assets	13	17	22
Current Assets	280	273	322

Remondis UK Ltd
Scot Lane Industrial Estate Scot Lane, Blackrod, Bolton, BL6 5SL
Tel: 01942-831362 **Fax:** 01942-833051
E-mail: sales@remondisuk.co.uk
Website: http://www.remondis.co.uk
Bank(s): Barclays
Directors: W. Stell (Fin), D. Winstanley (MD), W. Sandiland (Fin)
Managers: R. Marsland (Sales Prom Mgr), K. Hargreaves, A. Andrews, R. Marsland (Sales Prom Mgr), G. Schwanz (Mktg Serv Mgr)
Ultimate Holding Company: REDMONDIS ASSETS & SERVICES GMBH & CO KG (GERMANY)
Immediate Holding Company: REMONDIS U.K. LIMITED
Registration no: 00728631 **VAT No.:** GB 147 9719 22
Date established: 1962 **Turnover:** £5m - £10m
No.of Employees: 51 - 100 **Product Groups:** 33, 46, 80

Date of Accounts	Dec 11	Dec 10	Dec 09
Sales Turnover	7m	4m	4m
Pre Tax Profit/Loss	392	113	-53
Working Capital	1m	940	513
Fixed Assets	1m	1m	897
Current Assets	3m	3m	3m
Current Liabilities	222	619	312

Roe
Salop Street, Bolton, BL2 1DZ
Tel: 01204-523188 **Fax:** 01204-523178
E-mail: p_roe@btconnect.com
Directors: I. Lynsey (MD), P. Roe (Prop)
Immediate Holding Company: URBAN OUTREACH (BOLTON)
Registration no: 01639168 **Date established:** 1995
No.of Employees: 1 - 10 **Product Groups:** 27, 29, 42

Date of Accounts	Dec 10	Dec 09	Dec 08
Working Capital	9	28	5
Fixed Assets	2	2	3
Current Assets	16	36	7

S P H Europe plc
Rothwell Mill Rothwell Street, Bolton, BL3 6HY
Tel: 01204-398400 **Fax:** 01204-398211
E-mail: info@sph.co.uk
Website: http://www.sph.co.uk
Directors: J. Bentley (Dir)
Managers: M. Williams (Personnel), M. Williams (Personnel), J. Hughes, S. Anderson (Fin Mgr), S. Anderson (Fin Mgr)
Ultimate Holding Company: SPH (2003) LIMITED
Immediate Holding Company: SPH EUROPE PLC
Registration no: 01568664 **Date established:** 1981 **Turnover:** £1m - £2m
No.of Employees: 21 - 50 **Product Groups:** 84

Date of Accounts	Apr 12	Apr 11	Apr 10
Sales Turnover	1m	1m	743
Pre Tax Profit/Loss	141	221	-42
Working Capital	2m	2m	422
Fixed Assets	2m	3m	3m
Current Assets	2m	2m	2m
Current Liabilities	183	195	66

Samoa Ltd
Asturias House Barrs Fold Road Wingates Industrial Estate, Westhoughton, Bolton, BL5 3XP
Tel: 01942-850600 **Fax:** 01204-812160
E-mail: sales@samoa.ltd.uk
Website: http://www.samoa.ltd.uk
Bank(s): Lloyds TSB Bank plc
Directors: W. Fletcher (Dir), J. Fletcher (MD)
Managers: N. O'Dell (Sales Prom Mgr)
Immediate Holding Company: Samoa S.A.
Registration no: 02306519 **VAT No.:** GB 483 2808 30
Turnover: £2m - £5m **No.of Employees:** 11 - 20 **Product Groups:** 36, 39, 40

Date of Accounts	Dec 07	Dec 06	Dec 05
Working Capital	829	800	599
Fixed Assets	1683	1056	1082
Current Assets	1658	1433	1147
Current Liabilities	829	633	548
Total Share Capital	10	10	160

Sanber Ltd
3 Newnham Street, Bolton, BL1 8QA
Tel: 01204-596015 **Fax:** 01204-598751
E-mail: bernard.coates@sanberlabservices.co.uk
Website: http://www.sanberlabservices.co.uk
Directors: B. Coates (MD), A. Coates (Fin)
Immediate Holding Company: SANBER LIMITED
Registration no: 04220267 **Date established:** 2001
No.of Employees: 1 - 10 **Product Groups:** 30, 31, 38, 40, 41, 42, 46, 54, 67, 85

Date of Accounts	May 12	May 11	May 10
Working Capital	204	151	141
Fixed Assets	33	51	77
Current Assets	475	417	520

Saraco Industries
PO Box 190, Bolton, BL1 8AH
Tel: 01204-381990 **Fax:** 01204-525190
E-mail: info@saraco-industries.com
Directors: S. Bapu (Fin)
Immediate Holding Company: SARACO INDUSTRIES LIMITED
Registration no: 05446285 **Date established:** 2005
No.of Employees: 1 - 10 **Product Groups:** 24, 66

Date of Accounts	Dec 11	Dec 10	Dec 09
Working Capital	665	398	442
Fixed Assets	93	75	86
Current Assets	1m	972	942

Schneider Electric Ltd
4 Queensbrook, Bolton, BL1 4AY
Tel: 01204-385552 **Fax:** 01204-385535
E-mail: pm-divisiongb@schneider.co.uk
Website: http://www.schneider-electric.com
Managers: P. Woods (Ops Mgr), P. Woods (Ops Mgr)
Ultimate Holding Company: SCHNEIDER ELECTRIC SA (FRANCE)
Immediate Holding Company: SCHNEIDER ELECTRIC LIMITED
Registration no: 01407228 **Date established:** 1978
No.of Employees: 1 - 10 **Product Groups:** 37, 67

Date of Accounts	Dec 11	Dec 10	Dec 09
Sales Turnover	444m	407m	357m
Pre Tax Profit/Loss	28m	37m	38m
Working Capital	188m	164m	124m
Fixed Assets	35m	32m	20m
Current Assets	314m	263m	219m
Current Liabilities	48m	39m	34m

Scorewell UK Ltd
Lorne Street Ivy Mill, Farnworth, Bolton, BL4 7LW
Tel: 01204-572000 **Fax:** 01204-793445
E-mail: sales@hometextile.co.uk
Website: http://www.hometextile.co.uk
Directors: A. Makim (Sales & Mktg), S. Makim (Sales & Mktg)
Managers: S. Makim (Sales Prom Mgr), A. Makin (Sec)
Immediate Holding Company: SCOREWELL (UK) LIMITED
Registration no: 06632911 **VAT No.:** GB 748 8650 80
Date established: 2008 **Turnover:** £1m - £2m **No.of Employees:** 1 - 10
Product Groups: 23, 24, 26, 62

Scorpion Compressed Air Co. Ltd
Unit 1 24 Smethurst Lane, Bolton, BL3 3QE
Tel: 01204-431846
E-mail: info@supportscorpioncompressors.co.uk
Website: http://www.scorpioncompressors.co.uk
Directors: J. Mcfarland (Dir)
Immediate Holding Company: SCORPION COMPRESSED AIR LIMITED
Registration no: 05327342 **Date established:** 2005
Turnover: Up to £250,000 **No.of Employees:** 1 - 10 **Product Groups:** 40, 68

Date of Accounts	Jan 12	Jan 11	Jan 10
Working Capital	-12	-0	-2
Fixed Assets	4	12	15
Current Assets	67	99	94

Seddons Plant & Engineers Ltd (Head Office)
PO Box 41, Bolton, BL4 0LR
Tel: 01204-854600 **Fax:** 01204-570401
E-mail: sales@seddondirect.co.uk
Website: http://www.seddondirect.co.uk
Bank(s): Barclays, Manchester
Directors: J. Smith (Sales & Mktg), P. Winnington (Sales & Mktg)
Managers: J. Wetherby, S. Lythcoe, T. Shehan (Tech Serv Mgr)
Ultimate Holding Company: SEDDON GROUP LIMITED
Immediate Holding Company: SEDDONS (PLANT AND ENGINEERS) LIMITED
Registration no: 00499299 **VAT No.:** GB 147 6277 43
Date established: 1951 **Turnover:** £10m - £20m
No.of Employees: 21 - 50 **Product Groups:** 67

Date of Accounts	Dec 11	Dec 10	Dec 09
Sales Turnover	14m	12m	10m
Pre Tax Profit/Loss	182	152	-124
Working Capital	4m	4m	4m
Fixed Assets	561	522	481
Current Assets	6m	6m	6m
Current Liabilities	340	304	245

Service Offset Supplies NW Ltd
6 Burnden Industrial Estate Manchester Road, Bolton, BL3 2NG
Tel: 01204-396595 **Fax:** 01204-387800
Website: http://www.sosnorthwest.com
Bank(s): National westminster
Directors: D. Mccormick (Fin), D. Owens (Dir), E. Mordin (MD)
Managers: P. McLein (Admin Off)
Ultimate Holding Company: Sos North Ltd
Immediate Holding Company: SERVICE OFFSET SUPPLIES (NW) LIMITED
Registration no: 01408215 **Date established:** 1979
No.of Employees: 21 - 50 **Product Groups:** 67

Date of Accounts	Dec 09	Dec 08	Dec 07
Working Capital	403	647	791
Fixed Assets	94	145	130
Current Assets	2m	2m	1m

Shopmobility
81 Knowsley Street, Bolton, BL1 2BJ
Tel: 01204-382408 **Fax:** 01204-382408
E-mail: johnseddon@ukgateway.net
Directors: J. Seddon (Ch)
Registration no: 02194128 **Date established:** 1987
Turnover: Up to £250,000 **No.of Employees:** 21 - 50 **Product Groups:** 38, 67

Shutter Maintenance Northern
Millfield House Boundary Industrial Estate Millfield Road, Bolton, BL2 6QY
Tel: 01204-534543 **Fax:** 01204-534448
No.of Employees: 11 - 20 **Product Groups:** 35, 36

Sigma Electrical
Woodbine Road, Bolton, BL3 3JH
Tel: 01204-64322 **Fax:** 01204-64612
E-mail: harold@sigma-electrical.co.uk
Website: http://www.sigma-electrical.co.uk
Directors: H. Hayes (Ptnr)
No.of Employees: 1 - 10 **Product Groups:** 35, 37, 40, 67

Silcoms
Victoria Mill Piggott Street, Farnworth, Bolton, BL4 9QN
Tel: 01204-466070 **Fax:** 01204-861723
E-mail: keith.harrison@silcoms.co.uk
Website: http://www.silcoms.co.uk
Bank(s): The Royal Bank of Scotland
Directors: C. Winby (Comm), K. Harrison (MD), J. Cottam (Fin)
Managers: S. Jones (Tech Serv Mgr), K. Burke (Purch Mgr), K. Davies (Sales Admin)
Ultimate Holding Company: BOLTON ENGINEERING (HOLDINGS) LIMITED
Immediate Holding Company: SILCOMS LIMITED
Registration no: 00350911 **VAT No.:** GB 560 6122 68
Date established: 1939 **Turnover:** £10m - £20m
No.of Employees: 101 - 250 **Product Groups:** 41, 48

Date of Accounts	Mar 12	Mar 11	Mar 10
Sales Turnover	17m	14m	11m
Pre Tax Profit/Loss	552	293	-154
Working Capital	3m	3m	2m
Fixed Assets	2m	2m	2m
Current Assets	8m	6m	5m
Current Liabilities	2m	1m	1m

Andrew & Mark Smith Metals Ltd
Darbishire Street, Bolton, BL1 2TN
Tel: 01204-533662 **Fax:** 01204-392480
E-mail: info@smithmetals.co.uk
Website: http://www.smithmetals.co.uk
Directors: B. Carey (Dir), S. Holburn (Co Sec)
Immediate Holding Company: ONE51 ES METALS (NORTH) LIMITED
Registration no: 01447460 **VAT No.:** GB 633 7741 30
Date established: 1979 **Turnover:** £20m - £50m
No.of Employees: 11 - 20 **Product Groups:** 66

Date of Accounts	Dec 11	Dec 10	Dec 09
Sales Turnover	54m	37m	5m
Pre Tax Profit/Loss	839	-2m	-933
Working Capital	4m	4m	-820
Fixed Assets	18m	19m	1m
Current Assets	10m	8m	1m
Current Liabilities	1m	1m	646

Smith Gates
12 Whiteland Avenue, Bolton, BL3 5QB
Tel: 01204-63774
Directors: A. Smith (Prop)
Date established: 1990 **No.of Employees:** 1 - 10 **Product Groups:** 26, 35

Spectrum Products Ltd
Plantation Farm Plantation Road Turton, Bolton, BL7 0BY
Tel: 01204-853520 **Fax:** 01204-853029
E-mail: mark@spectrumproductsltd.co.uk
Website: http://www.spectrumproductsltd.co.uk

see next page

Spectrum Products Ltd - Cont'd

Directors: M. Worsley (Dir)
Immediate Holding Company: SPECTRUM PRODUCTS LIMITED
Registration no: 05172847 **Date established:** 2004
Turnover: £250,000 - £500,000 **No.of Employees:** 1 - 10
Product Groups: 35, 36, 48, 66

Date of Accounts	Jul 11	Jul 10	Jul 09
Working Capital	12	-1	-0
Fixed Assets	3	4	3
Current Assets	170	144	144

spraytrain.com

53 Smith Lane Egerton, Bolton, BL7 9EZ
Tel: 0781-514 6622
E-mail: mick@spraytrain.com
Website: http://www.spraytrain.com
Directors: M. Warren (Prop)
Immediate Holding Company: WARREN EDUCATIONAL CONSULTANCY LIMITED
Registration no: 07127782 **Date established:** 2010
No.of Employees: 1 - 10 **Product Groups:** 46

Date of Accounts	Jan 11
Working Capital	11
Current Assets	16

S R C L

The Incinerator Minerva Road, Farnworth, Bolton, BL4 0JR
Tel: 03332-404024 **Fax:** 01204-524220
E-mail: info@srcl.com
Website: http://www.srcl.com
Managers: A. Clewer (Mgr)
No.of Employees: 11 - 20 **Product Groups:** 30, 40, 42, 54

Stephensons Enterprise Fork Trucks

Unit 1 Easter Park Wingates Industrial Estate, Westhoughton, Bolton, BL5 3XU
Tel: 01942-276711 **Fax:** 01942-276728
E-mail: enquiries@sefit.co.uk
Website: http://www.stephensons-forktrucks.co.uk
Managers: A. Jones (Sales Off Mgr), A. Jones
Immediate Holding Company: LANSINGE LINDE STERLING
Registration no: 04006912 **Turnover:** £1m - £2m
No.of Employees: 11 - 20 **Product Groups:** 45, 48, 67, 83

Syntech Europe Ltd

351 Wigan Road, Bolton, BL3 5QU
Tel: 01204-659899 **Fax:** 01204-659941
E-mail: afane.syntech@googlemail.com
Website: http://www.syntech-europe.co.uk
Directors: C. Shin (Dir)
Immediate Holding Company: SYNTECH EUROPE LTD
Registration no: 04400891 **VAT No.:** GB 744 4069 30
Date established: 2002 **Turnover:** £250,000 - £500,000
No.of Employees: 1 - 10 **Product Groups:** 27, 48

Date of Accounts	Mar 12	Mar 11	Mar 10
Working Capital	92	81	84
Fixed Assets	1	2	2
Current Assets	125	121	162

T C H Vending Ltd

Unit 2 Bridgebank Industrial Estate Taylor Street, Horwich, Bolton, BL6 7PD
Tel: 01204-450160 **Fax:** 01204-450160
Directors: P. Baugh (Fin), S. Baugh (Dir)
Immediate Holding Company: TCH VENDING LIMITED
Registration no: 04586117 **Date established:** 2002
No.of Employees: 1 - 10 **Product Groups:** 38, 42

Date of Accounts	Mar 11	Nov 09	Nov 08
Working Capital	11	-13	-14
Fixed Assets	8	37	42
Current Assets	151	186	155

Taurus Promotions Ltd

Derby Mill 13 Thomas Street, Bolton, BL3 6JU
Tel: 01204-396555
Directors: S. Birchall (Dir), S. Birchall (Co Sec)
Immediate Holding Company: OCEAN IMAGES (BOLTON) LIMITED
Registration no: 02064722 **Date established:** 1986
No.of Employees: 11 - 20 **Product Groups:** 24, 84

Date of Accounts	Oct 11	Oct 10	Oct 09
Working Capital	2	-15	-8
Fixed Assets	N/A	16	21
Current Assets	2	20	36

Tek Dry Systems Ltd

Unit 9a Horwich Business Park Chorley New Road, Horwich, Bolton, BL6 5UE
Tel: 01204-667011 **Fax:** 01204-667013
E-mail: info@tek-dry.co.uk
Website: http://www.tek-dry.co.uk
Directors: T. Fryars (MD), I. Fryars (Co Sec)
Immediate Holding Company: TEK-DRY SYSTEMS LIMITED
Registration no: 02566391 **Date established:** 1990
No.of Employees: 1 - 10 **Product Groups:** 40, 42, 46

Date of Accounts	Dec 11	Dec 10	Dec 09
Working Capital	781	794	517
Fixed Assets	20	12	5
Current Assets	870	2m	809

The Awning Co UK Ltd

Vale Mill, Bolton, BL2 6QF
Tel: 01204-544900 **Fax:** 01204-363041
E-mail: info@theawningcompany.co.uk
Website: http://www.theawningcompany.co.uk
Managers: S. Watson
Immediate Holding Company: THE AWNING COMPANY (UK) LIMITED
Registration no: 02652500 **Date established:** 1991
No.of Employees: 11 - 20 **Product Groups:** 24, 35

Date of Accounts	Oct 10	Oct 09	Oct 08
Working Capital	106	120	160
Fixed Assets	172	144	118
Current Assets	409	421	520

Richard Threlfall Group Ltd

Lynstock Way Lostock, Bolton, BL6 4QR
Tel: 01204-474300 **Fax:** 01204-474347
E-mail: dennis@orseal.com
Website: http://www.roseal.com
Directors: D. Crompton (Dir), D. Crompton (MD)
Managers: S. Dunbar (Chief Acct)
Immediate Holding Company: RICHARD THRELFALL GROUP LIMITED
Registration no: 05352510 **Date established:** 2005
No.of Employees: 21 - 50 **Product Groups:** 36, 37, 38

Date of Accounts	Mar 11	Mar 10	Mar 09
Working Capital	1m	2m	2m
Fixed Assets	2m	2m	2m
Current Assets	2m	3m	3m

TI Protective Coating Systems

Unit 6, Lodge Bank Estate Crown Lane, Horwich, Bolton, BL6 5HY
Tel: 01204-468080
E-mail: sales@ticoatings.co.uk
Website: http://www.ticoatings.co.uk
Managers: N. Slanzky (Mktg Serv Mgr)
Registration no: 07029029 **Date established:** 1994
No.of Employees: 21 - 50 **Product Groups:** 32

Till & Whitehead

2 Lonsdale Road, Bolton, BL1 4PW
Tel: 01204-493000 **Fax:** 01204-493888
E-mail: jalfrey@tillwite.com
Website: http://www.tillwite.com
Managers: J. Alfrey (Mgr)
Immediate Holding Company: TILL AND WHITEHEAD LIMITED
Registration no: 00046963 **Date established:** 2018
No.of Employees: 1 - 10 **Product Groups:** 35, 49

Date of Accounts	Mar 07	Mar 06
Pre Tax Profit/Loss	108	150
Working Capital	-150	150
Fixed Assets	3698	3006
Current Assets	3510	2290
Current Liabilities	3661	2140
Total Share Capital	100	100
ROCE% (Return on Capital Employed)	3.0	4.8

Toyk Design

10 Bleak Street, Bolton, BL2 2JP
Tel: 01204-388261
E-mail: gary@toykdesign.co.uk
Website: http://www.toykdesign.co.uk
Directors: G. Bosstock (Prop)
Registration no: 05514143 **Date established:** 2005
Turnover: Up to £250,000 **No.of Employees:** 1 - 10 **Product Groups:** 84

Travel Counsellors PLC

Travel House 43 Churchgate, Bolton, BL1 1TH
Tel: 01204-536000 **Fax:** 01204-536050
E-mail: steve.byrne@travelcounsellors.com
Website: http://www.travelcounsellors.co.uk
Directors: S. Burns (MD), S. Byrne (MD)
Ultimate Holding Company: TRAVEL COUNSELLORS GROUP LIMITED
Immediate Holding Company: TRAVEL COUNSELLORS LIMITED
Registration no: 02133414 **Date established:** 1987
Turnover: £50m - £75m **No.of Employees:** 101 - 250 **Product Groups:** 69

Date of Accounts	Oct 11	Oct 10	Oct 09
Sales Turnover	70m	65m	54m
Pre Tax Profit/Loss	4m	4m	2m
Working Capital	7m	5m	3m
Fixed Assets	7m	7m	7m
Current Assets	47m	48m	51m
Current Liabilities	16m	16m	14m

Unique Dutch Light Company Ltd

Bent Spur Road Kearsley, Bolton, BL4 8PD
Tel: 01204-571800 **Fax:** 01204-862412
E-mail: enquiries@elite-greenhouses.co.uk
Website: http://www.elite-greenhouses.co.uk
Bank(s): National Westminster
Directors: J. Hannant (MD), R. Hannant (Fin)
Immediate Holding Company: UNIQUE DUTCH LIGHT COMPANY LTD
Registration no: 01293367 **VAT No.:** GB 305 9901 96
Date established: 1977 **No.of Employees:** 21 - 50 **Product Groups:** 30

Date of Accounts	Mar 07	Mar 06
Working Capital	140	138
Fixed Assets	46	48
Current Assets	220	217
Current Liabilities	80	79
Total Share Capital	50	50

V I L Resins Ltd

Union Road Tonge Moor, Bolton, BL2 2DT
Tel: 01204-388800 **Fax:** 01204-362775
E-mail: enquiries@vilresins.co.uk
Website: http://www.vilresins.com
Bank(s): National Westminster Bank Plc
Directors: R. Wallen (MD), S. Richardson (Co Sec)
Ultimate Holding Company: VIL HOLDINGS LIMITED
Immediate Holding Company: VIL HOLDINGS LIMITED
Registration no: 02909297 **VAT No.:** GB 145 8365 48
Date established: 1994 **Turnover:** £5m - £10m **No.of Employees:** 11 - 20
Product Groups: 31, 32

Date of Accounts	Sep 11	Sep 10	Sep 09
Sales Turnover	10m	9m	9m
Pre Tax Profit/Loss	158	2m	1m
Working Capital	13m	13m	12m
Fixed Assets	2m	3m	3m
Current Assets	15m	15m	13m
Current Liabilities	329	505	479

Vanden Powder Coatings Ltd

79 Manchester Road Westhoughton, Bolton, BL5 3QD
Tel: 01942-818953 **Fax:** 01942-840678
Directors: M. Taylor (Dir)
Immediate Holding Company: VANDEN POWDER COATINGS LIMITED
Registration no: 02682604 **VAT No.:** GB 354 6986 09
Date established: 1992 **Turnover:** £250,000 - £500,000
No.of Employees: 1 - 10 **Product Groups:** 36, 48

Date of Accounts	Jul 11	Jul 10	Jul 09
Working Capital	7	-9	7
Fixed Assets	4	2	4
Current Assets	44	48	57

Vapor Tek Ltd

Fairclough Street, Bolton, BL3 2AF
Tel: 01204-521795 **Fax:** 01204-364576
E-mail: info@vapor-tek.co.uk
Website: http://www.vapor-tek.co.uk
Directors: A. Parkinson (MD)
Immediate Holding Company: VAPOR-TEK LIMITED
Registration no: 00921537 **VAT No.:** GB 146 9535 38
Date established: 1967 **Turnover:** £250,000 - £500,000
No.of Employees: 1 - 10 **Product Groups:** 31, 32, 66, 68

Date of Accounts	Aug 11	Aug 10	Aug 09
Working Capital	601	568	503
Fixed Assets	24	22	26
Current Assets	685	624	566

Vernacare Ltd (a division of Verna Ltd)

Folds Road, Bolton, BL1 2TX
Tel: 01204-529494 **Fax:** 01204-521862
E-mail: info@vernagroup.com
Website: http://www.vernagroup.com
Bank(s): Lloyds
Directors: L. Webster (MD)
Ultimate Holding Company: VERNA GROUP INTERNATIONAL LIMITED
Immediate Holding Company: VERNACARE LIMITED
Registration no: 00796740 **Date established:** 1964
Turnover: £20m - £50m **No.of Employees:** 101 - 250
Product Groups: 24, 38

Date of Accounts	Mar 11	Mar 10	Mar 09
Sales Turnover	26m	27m	26m
Pre Tax Profit/Loss	3m	5m	4m
Working Capital	23m	21m	17m
Fixed Assets	6m	6m	6m
Current Assets	60m	57m	53m
Current Liabilities	4m	4m	3m

Vernagroup

Folds Road, Bolton, BL1 2TX
Tel: 01204-529494 **Fax:** 01204-521862
E-mail: sales@vernacare.com
Website: http://www.vernagroup.com
Bank(s): Lloyds TSB Bank plc
Directors: C. Attrill (Dir), K. Haslam (Grp Chief Exec)
Managers: C. Ratchford (Sales Prom Mgr), S. Brownlee (I.T. Exec), P. Cottcroft (Mktg Serv Mgr)
Ultimate Holding Company: Verna Group International Ltd
Immediate Holding Company: VGH Acquisitions Ltd
Registration no: 02259514 **Date established:** 1990 **Turnover:** £5m - £10m
No.of Employees: 1501 & over **Product Groups:** 36, 38

Vizcom Design

Bolton Enterprise Centre Washington Street, Bolton, BL3 5EY
Tel: 01204-383599
E-mail: info@vizcomdesign.co.uk
Website: http://www.vizcomdesign.co.uk
Directors: D. Robinson (Dir)
Immediate Holding Company: STREETWISE SOCCER COMMUNITY INTEREST COMPANY
Registration no: 03196629 **Date established:** 2009
Turnover: Up to £250,000 **No.of Employees:** 1 - 10 **Product Groups:** 81

Date of Accounts	Mar 11	Mar 10	Mar 09
Working Capital	300	314	309
Fixed Assets	2	2	1
Current Assets	338	356	358

Walkden Group Ltd

Unit 10 Watermead Works Slater Lane, Bolton, BL1 2TE
Tel: 01204-371116 **Fax:** 01204-306069
E-mail: info@walkdengroup.co.uk
Website: http://www.walkdengroup.co.uk
Directors: B. Walkden (Dir)
Immediate Holding Company: WALKDEN GROUP LIMITED
Registration no: 04784905 **Date established:** 2003
Turnover: Up to £250,000 **No.of Employees:** 1 - 10 **Product Groups:** 39

Date of Accounts	Mar 11	Mar 10	Mar 09
Sales Turnover	N/A	N/A	106
Pre Tax Profit/Loss	N/A	N/A	18
Working Capital	17	15	16
Fixed Assets	23	15	14
Current Assets	25	30	28
Current Liabilities	N/A	N/A	2

Warbutons Ltd

Rear of Bank House Hereford Street, Bolton, BL1 8HJ
Tel: 01204-531004 **Fax:** 01204-528883
Website: http://www.warburtons.co.uk
Directors: B. Warburton (MD), J. Healey (Co Sec), J. Warburton (Dir), W. Warburton (Dir)
Managers: W. Pickering (Chief Mgr), D. Gee (I.T. Exec)
Ultimate Holding Company: WARBURTONS HOLDINGS LIMITED
Immediate Holding Company: WARBURTONS LIMITED
Registration no: 06500892 **Date established:** 2021
Turnover: £250m - £500m **No.of Employees:** 1 - 10 **Product Groups:** 20

Date of Accounts	Sep 10	Sep 09	Sep 08
Sales Turnover	492m	510m	498m
Pre Tax Profit/Loss	29m	63m	32m
Working Capital	130m	34m	112m
Fixed Assets	211m	270m	214m
Current Assets	208m	130m	209m
Current Liabilities	60m	85m	72m

Watson Steel Structures Ltd

Lostock Lane Lostock, Bolton, BL6 4BL
Tel: 01204-699999 **Fax:** 01204-694543
E-mail: carl.cardwell@watsonsteel.co.uk
Website: http://www.watsonsteel.co.uk
Bank(s): Royal Bank of Scotland, 38 Mosey St, Manchester, M60 2BE
Directors: J. Baridale (Purch), S. Day (MD), C. Cardwell (Fin), C. Cardwell (Fin), P. Miller (Sales)
Managers: M. Moore (Commun Mgr)
Ultimate Holding Company: SEVERFIELD-ROWEN PLC
Immediate Holding Company: WATSON STEEL STRUCTURES LIMITED
Registration no: 04313355 **VAT No.:** GB 163 2707 74
Date established: 2001 **Turnover:** £75m - £125m
No.of Employees: 251 - 500 **Product Groups:** 48

Date of Accounts	Dec 11	Dec 10	Dec 09
Sales Turnover	121m	120m	103m
Pre Tax Profit/Loss	3m	8m	17m
Working Capital	15m	15m	15m
Fixed Assets	2m	3m	3m
Current Assets	76m	78m	75m
Current Liabilities	5m	17m	34m

Webster Drives (A Gardner Denver Product)

Folds Road, Bolton, BL1 2SE
Tel: 01204-382121 **Fax:** 01204-386100
E-mail: sales@websterdrives.co.uk
Website: http://www.websterdrives.co.uk
Bank(s): The Royal Bank of Scotland
Directors: D. Jackson (MD), M. Grummett (Fin)
Managers: A. Flanagan (Sales & Mktg Mg), S. Bottomley
Ultimate Holding Company: GARDNER DENVER INC (USA)
Immediate Holding Company: WEBSTER DRIVES LIMITED
Registration no: 00553051 **Date established:** 1955 **Turnover:** £5m - £10m
No.of Employees: 51 - 100 **Product Groups:** 39

Date of Accounts	Dec 10	Dec 09	Dec 08
Sales Turnover	N/A	7m	7m
Pre Tax Profit/Loss	635	9m	2m
Working Capital	13m	12m	2m
Fixed Assets	N/A	N/A	2m
Current Assets	13m	12m	4m
Current Liabilities	178	N/A	823

Winget Ltd

Plodder Lane Farnworth, Bolton, BL4 0LR
Tel: 01204-854650 **Fax:** 01204-854663
E-mail: sales@winget.co.uk
Website: http://www.winget.co.uk
Bank(s): National Westminster
Directors: S. Hodge (Dir)
Ultimate Holding Company: SEDDON GROUP LIMITED
Immediate Holding Company: WINGET LIMITED
Registration no: 01977110 **Date established:** 1986 **Turnover:** £2m - £5m
No.of Employees: 11 - 20 **Product Groups:** 42

Date of Accounts	Dec 11	Dec 10	Dec 09
Sales Turnover	3m	2m	2m
Pre Tax Profit/Loss	117	91	-410
Working Capital	1m	1m	1m
Fixed Assets	19	14	26
Current Assets	2m	2m	1m
Current Liabilities	57	52	39

Woodley Equipment Co. Ltd

Unit 7 Locomotive House Chorley New Road, Horwich, Bolton, BL6 5UE
Tel: 08456-777001 **Fax:** 08456-777002
E-mail: sales@woodleyequipment.com
Website: http://www.woodleyequipment.com
Managers: C. Woof (Projects), C. Wooff (Projects)
Registration no: 4669537 **Date established:** 1989
No.of Employees: 21 - 50 **Product Groups:** 83

Date of Accounts	May 08	May 07	May 06
Working Capital	567	482	306
Fixed Assets	231	179	124
Current Assets	1535	1475	1091
Current Liabilities	968	993	786

World of Brass

9 Hebble Close, Bolton, BL2 3FS
Tel: 0845-260 9009 **Fax:** 0845-260 9008
E-mail: info@worldofbrass.co.uk
Website: http://www.worldofbrass.co.uk
Product Groups: 25, 30, 33

Wrought Iron Specialist

159 Chorley New Road Horwich, Bolton, BL6 5QE
Tel: 01204-699310
Website: http://www.wroughtironservices.co.uk
Directors: R. Mahon (Prop)
No.of Employees: 1 - 10 **Product Groups:** 34, 39, 49

Yateson Stainless

Osman House Prince Street, Bolton, BL1 2NP
Tel: 01204-370099 **Fax:** 01204-392634
E-mail: info@yateson-stainless.com
Website: http://www.yateson-stainless.com
Bank(s): National Westminster Bank Plc
Directors: S. Avent (Prop)
Registration no: 03958033 **VAT No.:** GB 732 8722 27
Date established: 2000 **Turnover:** £1m - £2m **No.of Employees:** 11 - 20
Product Groups: 34, 35, 36, 38, 40, 41, 42, 45, 46, 48, 66, 67, 84

Burnley

A 1 Plastic Extrusions Ltd

Brindley Close Network 65 Business Park, Hapton, Burnley, BB11 5TD
Tel: 01282-446010 **Fax:** 01282-446055
E-mail: sales@a1plastic.co.uk
Website: http://www.a1plastic.co.uk
Directors: S. Woodcock (Dir)
Immediate Holding Company: A1 PLASTIC EXTRUSIONS LIMITED
Registration no: 04859429 **Date established:** 2003
Turnover: £500,000 - £1m **No.of Employees:** 1 - 10 **Product Groups:** 30, 31, 35, 42, 66

Date of Accounts	Dec 11	Dec 10	Dec 09
Working Capital	15	8	6
Fixed Assets	57	65	56
Current Assets	201	260	191

A M S Neve Ltd

Billington Road, Burnley, BB11 5UB
Tel: 01282-457011 **Fax:** 01282-417282
E-mail: info@ams-neve.com
Website: http://www.ams-neve.com
Bank(s): National Westminster Bank Plc
Directors: M. Crabtree (MD)
Managers: M. Tyrer (Purch Mgr), S. Hindle (Tech Serv Mgr), L. Jackson
Immediate Holding Company: AMS NEVE LIMITED
Registration no: 05478352 **VAT No.:** GB 597 8799 33
Date established: 2005 **Turnover:** £2m - £5m **No.of Employees:** 51 - 100
Product Groups: 37

Date of Accounts	Dec 11	Dec 10	Dec 09
Working Capital	1m	498	170
Fixed Assets	859	1m	1m
Current Assets	2m	2m	2m

Acewell Electronics Ltd

Farrington Close, Burnley, BB11 5SH
Tel: 01282-412340 **Fax:** 01282-412358
E-mail: andrew.hodson@acewellelectronics.co.uk
Website: http://www.acewellelectronics.co.uk
Directors: A. Hodson (MD)
Immediate Holding Company: ACEWELL ELECTRONICS LIMITED
Registration no: 01758253 **Date established:** 1983
Turnover: Up to £250,000 **No.of Employees:** 1 - 10 **Product Groups:** 40

Date of Accounts	Sep 11	Sep 10	Sep 09
Working Capital	112	300	344
Fixed Assets	154	3	3
Current Assets	176	371	380
Current Liabilities	N/A	18	N/A

Althams Travel Services

Riverside Offices Netherwood Road, Burnley, BB10 2AN
Tel: 01282-434431 **Fax:** 01282-831535
E-mail: scunthorpe@althams.co.uk
Website: http://www.althams.co.uk
Bank(s): Barclays
Directors: D. Ball (Co Sec), E. Starkie (MD)
Immediate Holding Company: ALTHAMS TRAVEL SERVICES LIMITED
Registration no: 00042478 **VAT No.:** GB 174 3878 29
Date established: 1994 **Turnover:** £5m - £10m **No.of Employees:** 21 - 50
Product Groups: 39, 69

Date of Accounts	Sep 11	Sep 10	Sep 09
Sales Turnover	6m	6m	6m
Pre Tax Profit/Loss	56	215	180
Working Capital	48	384	197
Fixed Assets	6m	6m	6m
Current Assets	4m	5m	5m
Current Liabilities	699	797	841

Anglo Carleton

30 Tabor Street, Burnley, BB12 0HL
Tel: 01282-453342 **Fax:** 01282- 453342
Directors: I. Spencer (Prop)
Date established: 1990 **No.of Employees:** 1 - 10 **Product Groups:** 35, 39, 45

Apico International

Unit 2 Bridgewater Close Network 65 Business Park, Hapton, Burnley, BB11 5TE
Tel: 01282-473190 **Fax:** 08707-779202
E-mail: sales@apico.co.uk
Website: http://www.apico.co.uk
Bank(s): HSBC
Directors: Y. Vesterinen (MD)
Managers: S. Cannon (Mktg Serv Mgr)
Registration no: 04304681 **VAT No.:** GB 413 1986 60
No.of Employees: 21 - 50 **Product Groups:** 24, 30

Date of Accounts	Sep 09	Sep 08	Sep 07
Working Capital	1m	885	702
Fixed Assets	51	89	89
Current Assets	2m	2m	2m

Ascotex Ltd

Calder Works Simonstone, Burnley, BB12 7NL
Tel: 01282-773609 **Fax:** 01282-773600
E-mail: sales@ascotex.com
Website: http://www.ascotex.com
Bank(s): National Westminster
Directors: A. Ashworth (Dir)
Immediate Holding Company: ASCOTEX LIMITED
Registration no: 00874811 **VAT No.:** GB 174 3239 63
Date established: 1966 **Turnover:** £2m - £5m **No.of Employees:** 11 - 20
Product Groups: 46, 67, 84

Date of Accounts	Mar 12	Mar 11	Mar 10
Working Capital	4m	4m	3m
Fixed Assets	63	56	63
Current Assets	4m	4m	4m

Bauschlinnemann UK

Widow Hill Road Heasandford Industrial Estate, Burnley, BB10 2TB
Tel: 01282-686850 **Fax:** 01282-412361
E-mail: info@uk.bauschlinnemann.com
Website: http://www.uk.bauschlinnemann.com
Bank(s): National Westminster, Edinburgh
Directors: T. Barber (Dir), D. Fleming (MD)
Managers: P. Reynolds (Factory Mgr), C. Fort
Ultimate Holding Company: SURTEGO AG (GERMANY)
Immediate Holding Company: BAUSCHLINNEMANN UK LIMITED
Registration no: 00694799 **Date established:** 1961 **Turnover:** £5m - £10m
No.of Employees: 21 - 50 **Product Groups:** 30, 34

Date of Accounts	Dec 11	Dec 10	Dec 09
Sales Turnover	9m	10m	9m
Pre Tax Profit/Loss	594	277	111
Working Capital	2m	2m	2m
Fixed Assets	2m	2m	3m
Current Assets	4m	4m	4m
Current Liabilities	931	1m	827

Bemis Ltd

Farrington Road, Burnley, BB11 5SW
Tel: 01282-438717 **Fax:** 01282-412717
E-mail: uksales@bemiseurope.com
Website: http://www.bemiseurope.com
Directors: Bemis (Prop)
Ultimate Holding Company: BEMIS MANUFACTURING COMPANY INC (USA)
Immediate Holding Company: BEMIS LIMITED
Registration no: 00918517 **Date established:** 1967
Turnover: £10m - £20m **No.of Employees:** 21 - 50 **Product Groups:** 30, 35

Date of Accounts	Dec 11	Dec 10	Dec 09
Sales Turnover	13m	14m	14m
Pre Tax Profit/Loss	11	-675	-474
Working Capital	4m	4m	5m
Fixed Assets	2m	1m	1m
Current Assets	7m	7m	8m
Current Liabilities	1m	2m	1m

Blazes Fireplace Centres Ltd

23 Standish Street, Burnley, BB11 1AP
Tel: 01282-831176 **Fax:** 01282-424411
E-mail: info@blazes.co.uk
Website: http://www.blazes.co.uk
Directors: M. Eyre (MD)
Immediate Holding Company: HEATING SOLUTIONS YORKSHIRE LIMITED
Registration no: 07258897 **Date established:** 2010
No.of Employees: 1 - 10 **Product Groups:** 33, 35

Date of Accounts	May 08	May 07	May 06
Working Capital	-104	-99	-86
Fixed Assets	3	3	4
Current Assets	16	7	14
Current Liabilities	120	106	101
Total Share Capital	100	100	100

Boydell & Jacks Ltd

Marlborough Street, Burnley, BB11 2HW
Tel: 01282-456411 **Fax:** 01282-437496
E-mail: sales@featherwing.com
Website: http://www.featherwing.com
Directors: C. Starkey (Fin), P. Halstead (Works)
Managers: D. Rushton (Sales Prom Mgr)
Immediate Holding Company: BOYDELL & JACKS LIMITED
Registration no: 01438861 **Date established:** 1979 **Turnover:** £2m - £5m
No.of Employees: 21 - 50 **Product Groups:** 39

Date of Accounts	Dec 11	Dec 10	Dec 09
Working Capital	706	627	705
Fixed Assets	452	455	503
Current Assets	1m	1m	1m

British Velvets Ltd

Wyre Street Padiham, Burnley, BB12 8DQ
Tel: 01282-778134 **Fax:** 01282-772168
E-mail: sales@britishvelvets.co.uk
Website: http://www.britishvelvets.co.uk
Bank(s): Barclays
Directors: K. Prytharch (Dir), K. Prypherch (MD), K. Wells (Dir)
Managers: J. Smith (Prod Mgr), K. Prythargh (Mgr)
Ultimate Holding Company: MOTTRAM NV (HOLLAND)
Immediate Holding Company: BRITISH VELVETS LIMITED
Registration no: 00547526 **VAT No.:** GB 174 8718 26
Date established: 1955 **Turnover:** £5m - £10m
No.of Employees: 51 - 100 **Product Groups:** 23

Date of Accounts	Jan 10	Jan 09	Jan 08
Working Capital	940	1m	931
Fixed Assets	295	375	486
Current Assets	2m	2m	2m

Burnley Metal Treatments

Unit 16 Balderstone Close, Burnley, BB10 2TA
Tel: 01282-830221 **Fax:** 01282-830224
E-mail: glenn.dickinson@btconnect.com
Directors: G. Dickinson (Ptnr)
Date established: 1991 **No.of Employees:** 1 - 10 **Product Groups:** 46, 48

C Pack Packaging Machinery Ltd

Unit 2 Progress House Athletic Street, Burnley, BB10 4LP
Tel: 01282-422485 **Fax:** 01282-422512
Directors: C. Rilley (MD)
Immediate Holding Company: C PACK PACKAGING MACHINERY LIMITED
Registration no: 04491052 **Date established:** 2002
No.of Employees: 1 - 10 **Product Groups:** 38, 42

Date of Accounts	Dec 11	Dec 10	Dec 09
Working Capital	32	52	35
Fixed Assets	33	23	26
Current Assets	92	85	38

Carr Reinforcements

Gordon Street Mill Gordon Street, Worsthorne, Burnley, BB10 3NA
Tel: 01282-420924 **Fax:** 0161-443 3388
E-mail: erictaylor@btconnect.com
Website: http://www.carr-reinforcements.com
Directors: E. Taylor (Dir)
Immediate Holding Company: CARR REINFORCEMENTS LIMITED
Registration no: 02507015 **VAT No.:** GB 570 6388 23
Date established: 1990 **Turnover:** £1m - £2m **No.of Employees:** 1 - 10
Product Groups: 23

Date of Accounts	Sep 11	Sep 10	Sep 09
Working Capital	112	39	-12
Fixed Assets	53	50	60
Current Assets	639	536	499

Clifford Packaging Ltd

Bentley Wood Way Network 65 Business Park, Hapton, Burnley, BB11 5ST
Tel: 01282-458550 **Fax:** 01282-410650
E-mail: mike@cliffordpackaging.com
Website: http://www.cliffordpackaging.com
Managers: M. Gordon (Chief Mgr)
Immediate Holding Company: CLIFFORD PACKAGING LIMITED
Registration no: 07485911 **Date established:** 2011 **Turnover:** £5m - £10m
No.of Employees: 1 - 10 **Product Groups:** 27

Date of Accounts	Jan 12
Working Capital	217
Fixed Assets	25
Current Assets	985

Commtech Trading Co Lancs Ltd

Bentley Wood Way Network 65 Business Park, Hapton, Burnley, BB11 5ST
Tel: 01254-232638 **Fax:** 01254-301197
E-mail: sales@commtechcommunications.co.uk
Website: http://www.commtechcommunications.co.uk
Bank(s): HSBC Bank plc
Managers: L. Newman Ridehough (Mgr)
Ultimate Holding Company: CONCORD HOLDINGS LIMITED
Immediate Holding Company: COMMTECH TRADING CO. (LANCS) LIMITED
Registration no: 05647953 **VAT No.:** GB 375 3044 56
Date established: 2005 **Turnover:** £2m - £5m **No.of Employees:** 51 - 100
Product Groups: 37

Date of Accounts	Mar 11	Mar 10	Mar 09
Sales Turnover	N/A	7m	7m
Pre Tax Profit/Loss	N/A	113	2
Working Capital	N/A	404	363
Fixed Assets	N/A	120	48
Current Assets	N/A	3m	2m
Current Liabilities	N/A	168	279

J Conlan

Wyre Street Padiham, Burnley, BB12 8DF
Tel: 01282-771458 **Fax:** 01282-771458

see next page

J Conlan - Cont'd

Directors: J. Conlan (Prop)
Ultimate Holding Company: SC REALISATIONS 2012 LIMITED
Immediate Holding Company: MERSEY OIL COMPANY LTD
Registration no: 02978942 **Date established:** 2002
Turnover: £10m - £20m **No.of Employees:** 1 - 10 **Product Groups:** 26, 35

Date of Accounts	Dec 10	Dec 09	Dec 08
Sales Turnover	N/A	N/A	20m
Pre Tax Profit/Loss	N/A	N/A	40
Working Capital	13	13	13
Current Assets	13	13	22
Current Liabilities	N/A	N/A	9

Crystal Plastics Ltd

Grove Mill Grove Lane, Padiham, Burnley, BB12 8DN
Tel: 01282-777717 **Fax:** 01282-777765
E-mail: crystalplastics@btconnect.com
Website: http://www.crystalplastics.co.uk
Directors: J. Maddock (MD)
Immediate Holding Company: CRYSTAL PLASTICS LIMITED
Registration no: 05580650 **Date established:** 2005
Turnover: Up to £250,000 **No.of Employees:** 1 - 10 **Product Groups:** 30

Date of Accounts	Sep 11	Sep 10	Sep 09
Sales Turnover	N/A	150	98
Pre Tax Profit/Loss	N/A	17	-3
Working Capital	-23	-29	-39
Fixed Assets	26	34	36
Current Assets	78	36	22
Current Liabilities	N/A	32	21

Customfit Signs

Mayfield House St Matthew Street, Burnley, BB11 4JJ
Tel: 07708-701361 **Fax:** 01282-439937
E-mail: pac@customfitservices.co.uk
Website: http://www.customfitservices.co.uk
Directors: P. Cicero (Prop)
Immediate Holding Company: LANCASHIRE SLATE & TILE LTD
Registration no: 03864287 **Date established:** 2009 **Turnover:** £1m - £2m
No.of Employees: 1 - 10 **Product Groups:** 30, 37, 40, 49, 67

Date of Accounts	Jul 12	Jul 11	Jul 10
Working Capital	-24	2	-14
Fixed Assets	21	33	39
Current Assets	15	29	39

E R C Scrap Metals

2-7 Rexington Buildings Phoenix Way, Burnley, BB11 5SX
Tel: 01282-455698 **Fax:** 01282-459241
E-mail: info@ercscrap.co.uk
Website: http://www.ercscrap.co.uk
Directors: B. Critchley (Ptnr)
No.of Employees: 1 - 10 **Product Groups:** 54, 66

East Lancashire Platers Ltd

Oxford Mill Oxford Road, Burnley, BB11 3BA
Tel: 01282-425621 **Fax:** 01282-433618
E-mail: john@eastlancashireplaters.co.uk
Website: http://www.eastlancashireplaters.co.uk
Directors: J. Duxbury (MD), D. Duxbury (Fin)
Ultimate Holding Company: MINELASER LIMITED
Immediate Holding Company: EAST LANCASHIRE PLATERS LIMITED
Registration no: 01278186 **VAT No.:** GB 375 4540 39
Date established: 1976 **Turnover:** Up to £250,000
No.of Employees: 11 - 20 **Product Groups:** 48

Date of Accounts	Oct 11	Oct 10	Oct 09
Working Capital	16	2	39
Fixed Assets	36	44	55
Current Assets	262	212	222

E-Reg Coatings Ltd

4 Trans Britannia Industrial Estate Farrington Road, Burnley, BB11 5SW
Tel: 01282-838378 **Fax:** 01282-838015
E-mail: eregcoatings@aol.com
Website: http://www.eregcoatings.com
Directors: B. Slater (MD)
Managers: M. Larkin (Ops Mgr)
Immediate Holding Company: E- REG COATINGS LIMITED
Registration no: 02750600 **Date established:** 1992
No.of Employees: 21 - 50 **Product Groups:** 30, 48, 52, 66

Date of Accounts	Sep 11	Sep 10	Sep 09
Working Capital	588	612	419
Fixed Assets	190	227	264
Current Assets	669	886	579

Everest Cooling Services

11 Brunshaw Avenue, Burnley, BB10 4LT
Tel: 01282-685223 **Fax:** 01282-685223
E-mail: info@everestcooling.com
Website: http://www.everestcooling.com
Directors: M. Gentile (Prop)
No.of Employees: 1 - 10 **Product Groups:** 38, 40, 48, 52, 66

Fagan & Whalley Ltd

Unit 9a-9b Mead Way, Padiham, Burnley, BB12 7NG
Tel: 01282-771983 **Fax:** 01282-771428
E-mail: graham.fagan@faganwhalley.co.uk
Website: http://www.faganwhalley.co.uk
Directors: G. Fagan (MD), S. Fagan (Fin)
Immediate Holding Company: FAGAN & WHALLEY LIMITED
Registration no: 00366737 **Date established:** 1941
Turnover: £10m - £20m **No.of Employees:** 101 - 250 **Product Groups:** 77

Date of Accounts	Apr 11	Apr 10	Apr 09
Sales Turnover	15m	13m	12m
Pre Tax Profit/Loss	1m	297	359
Working Capital	1m	1m	1m
Fixed Assets	8m	7m	7m
Current Assets	4m	4m	3m
Current Liabilities	984	943	769

Filtaco UK Ltd

7 Brookford Close, Burnley, BB12 0XH
Tel: 01282-830501 **Fax:** 01282-546363
Directors: A. Challen (Dir)
No.of Employees: 1 - 10 **Product Groups:** 38, 42

Flexible Reinforcements Ltd

Bancroft Road, Burnley, BB10 2TP
Tel: 01282-478222 **Fax:** 01282-478210
E-mail: sales@flexr.co.uk
Website: http://www.flexr.co.uk
Bank(s): Barclays, Manchester
Directors: I. Pendleborough (Grp Chief Exec), I. Pendlebury (Fin), L. Eventhall (MD)
Managers: D. Eventhall (Prod Mgr), T. Carswell, J. Montwill (Sales Prom Mgr), J. Montwill (Sales Prom Mgr), P. Keighley (Buyer)
Immediate Holding Company: Tellar Holdings Ltd
Registration no: 00876491 **VAT No.:** GB 375 3105 62
Turnover: Up to £250,000 **No.of Employees:** 21 - 50 **Product Groups:** 23, 29, 30

Hambledon Studios

Unit 1a Parkhill Business Centre Padiham Road, Burnley, BB12 6TG
Tel: 01282-686000 **Fax:** 01282-686001
E-mail: hambledon@aol.com
Directors: D. Dean (MD)
Registration no: 00602400 **Turnover:** £20m - £50m
No.of Employees: 51 - 100 **Product Groups:** 27, 28

Heatsense Cables Ltd

Bentley Wood Way Network 65 Business Park, Hapton, Burnley, BB11 5ST
Tel: 01706-355330 **Fax:** 01706-657691
E-mail: gina@heatsensecables.co.uk
Website: http://www.heatsensecables.co.uk
Directors: P. Mcgreevy (Dir)
Managers: J. Devine (Sales & Mktg Mg)
Ultimate Holding Company: 00074416
Immediate Holding Company: HEATSENSE CABLES LTD.
Registration no: 01839647 **Date established:** 1984
Turnover: £500,000 - £1m **No.of Employees:** 1 - 10 **Product Groups:** 37

Date of Accounts	Mar 08	Mar 07	Mar 06
Sales Turnover	1225	1036	991
Pre Tax Profit/Loss	93	105	133
Working Capital	395	331	206
Fixed Assets	41	23	42
Current Assets	758	609	427
Current Liabilities	363	278	221
ROCE% (Return on Capital Employed)	21.2	29.6	53.6
ROT% (Return on Turnover)	7.6	10.1	13.5

Hi Chrome Europe Ltd

Heathenford Industrial Estate Widowhill Road, Burnley, BB10 2TT
Tel: 01282-418300 **Fax:** 01282-418310
E-mail: sales@hycrome.com
Website: http://www.hichrome.com
Bank(s): Clydesdale Bank PLC
Directors: A. Bailey (MD), S. Pollard (Dir)
Managers: S. Kelly (Works Gen Mgr)
Ultimate Holding Company: Score Group plc
Immediate Holding Company: Score (Europe) Ltd
Registration no: SC122201 **VAT No.:** GB 498 5817 74
Turnover: £2m - £5m **No.of Employees:** 51 - 100 **Product Groups:** 32, 35, 46, 48, 51, 68

I A C Plastics Ltd (Industrial Anti-Corrosives Ltd)

Oak Mill Manchester Road, Dunnockshaw, Burnley, BB11 5PW
Tel: 01706-212225 **Fax:** 01706-229926
E-mail: sales@iacplastics.com
Website: http://www.iacplastics.com
Bank(s): Yorkshire Bank PLC
Directors: C. Holland (Dir), T. McPherson (Co Sec)
Managers: A. Grady
Ultimate Holding Company: INDUSTRIAL ANTI-CORROSIVES LTD
Registration no: 01290597 **VAT No.:** GB 151 1533 08
Date established: 1980 **Turnover:** £1m - £2m **No.of Employees:** 21 - 50
Product Groups: 23, 30, 31, 35, 42, 48, 66, 84

J G Coates Ltd (t/a Cotel Mouldings)

Trafalgar Street, Burnley, BB11 1TH
Tel: 01282-424376 **Fax:** 01282-456166
E-mail: sales@cotel.co.uk
Website: http://www.cotel.co.uk
Directors: J. Coates (MD)
Immediate Holding Company: J.G. COATES (BURNLEY) LIMITED
Registration no: 00822572 **VAT No.:** GB 174 3057 69
Date established: 1964 **Turnover:** £500,000 - £1m
No.of Employees: 1 - 10 **Product Groups:** 30, 66

Date of Accounts	Sep 11	Sep 10	Sep 09
Working Capital	240	188	161
Fixed Assets	44	51	63
Current Assets	426	323	263

Jewson Ltd

Eastham Place, Burnley, BB11 3DA
Tel: 01282-450721 **Fax:** 01282-450332
Website: http://www.jewson.co.uk
Managers: B. Seddon (Mgr)
Ultimate Holding Company: COMPAGNIE DE SAINT GOBAIN (FRANCE)
Immediate Holding Company: JEWSON LIMITED
Registration no: 00348407 **Date established:** 1939
Turnover: £500m - £1,000m **No.of Employees:** 1 - 10
Product Groups: 66

Date of Accounts	Dec 11	Dec 10	Dec 09
Sales Turnover	1606m	1547m	1485m
Pre Tax Profit/Loss	18m	100m	45m
Working Capital	-345m	-250m	-349m
Fixed Assets	496m	387m	461m
Current Assets	657m	1005m	1320m
Current Liabilities	66m	120m	64m

Kavia Mouldings Ltd

Unit 8-9 Balderstone Close, Burnley, BB10 2TA
Tel: 01282-423935 **Fax:** 01282-426105
E-mail: kavia.mouldingsltd@virgin.net
Directors: P. Worthington (MD)
Immediate Holding Company: KAVIA MOULDINGS LIMITED
Registration no: 01799293 **VAT No.:** GB 375 4270 42
Date established: 1984 **Turnover:** £1m - £2m **No.of Employees:** 11 - 20
Product Groups: 28, 30, 66

Date of Accounts	Jun 11	Jun 10	Jun 09
Working Capital	54	30	56
Fixed Assets	166	157	195
Current Assets	238	201	195
Current Liabilities	N/A	N/A	51

Lancashire Board & Paper Ltd

Balderstone Lane Heasandford Industrial Estate, Burnley, BB10 2AL
Tel: 01282-835033 **Fax:** 01282-835044
E-mail: info@lancsboard.co.uk
Website: http://www.lancsboard.co.uk
Directors: H. Thane (Fin), B. Thane (MD)
Managers: M. Bush (Personnel)
Ultimate Holding Company: BELLANN BOARD & PACKAGING CO.LIMITED
Immediate Holding Company: LANCASHIRE BOARD & PAPER CO. LIMITED
Registration no: 01454613 **VAT No.:** GB 305 9476 46
Date established: 1979 **Turnover:** £2m - £5m **No.of Employees:** 21 - 50
Product Groups: 27

Date of Accounts	Oct 11	Oct 10	Oct 09
Working Capital	735	682	610
Fixed Assets	313	360	416
Current Assets	2m	2m	2m

Laserworld Engineering Co. Ltd

Brownside Mill Brun Terrace, Burnley, BB10 3JR
Tel: 01282-425999 **Fax:** 01282-426739
E-mail: info@laserworldengineering.co.uk
Website: http://www.laserworldengineering.com
Directors: A. Masterson (Co Sec), H. Masterson (MD)
Immediate Holding Company: LASERWORLD ENGINEERING CO. LIMITED
Registration no: 02778423 **VAT No.:** GB 598 2687 68
Date established: 1993 **Turnover:** £250,000 - £500,000
No.of Employees: 1 - 10 **Product Groups:** 48

Date of Accounts	Aug 12	Aug 11	Aug 10
Working Capital	108	155	102
Fixed Assets	330	30	32
Current Assets	237	241	176

Lectros International Ltd

Unit 3 Boran Court Network 65 Business Park, Hapton, Burnley, BB11 5TH
Tel: 0845-4006666 **Fax:** 0845-4003333
E-mail: sales@lectros.com
Website: http://www.lectros.com
Directors: C. Taylor (Sales), A. Street (MD), T. Street (MD)
Managers: D. Burtewell (Purch Mgr)
Registration no: 03289540 **Turnover:** £250,000 - £500,000
No.of Employees: 21 - 50 **Product Groups:** 27, 52

Date of Accounts	Apr 08	Apr 07	Apr 06
Working Capital	387	392	327
Fixed Assets	292	94	114
Current Assets	1732	1536	1325
Current Liabilities	1346	1144	997
Total Share Capital	1	1	1

Learoyd Packaging Ltd

Heasandford Mill Netherwood Road, Burnley, BB10 2EJ
Tel: 01282-438016 **Fax:** 01282-430289
E-mail: learoyd@learoyd.co.uk
Website: http://www.learoyd.co.uk
Bank(s): Barclays, Macclesfield
Directors: A. Turner (Dir)
Ultimate Holding Company: API GROUP PLC
Immediate Holding Company: LEAROYD GROUP LIMITED
Registration no: 03037060 **VAT No.:** GB 174 3993 29
Date established: 1995 **Turnover:** £5m - £10m
No.of Employees: 101 - 250 **Product Groups:** 30

Date of Accounts	Mar 11	Mar 10	Sep 05
Working Capital	-163	-163	-163

Lupton & Place Ltd

Norcastal Works Athletic Street, Burnley, BB10 4LR
Tel: 01282-422361 **Fax:** 01282-428107
E-mail: sales@lupton-place.co.uk
Website: http://www.lupton-place.co.uk
Bank(s): HSBC
Directors: S. Gill (MD)
Immediate Holding Company: LUPTON & PLACE LIMITED
Registration no: 01605457 **VAT No.:** GB 546 3819 22
Date established: 1981 **Turnover:** £5m - £10m
No.of Employees: 101 - 250 **Product Groups:** 34

Date of Accounts	Mar 11	Mar 10	Mar 09
Sales Turnover	9m	7m	8m
Pre Tax Profit/Loss	526	165	3
Working Capital	-230	-362	-474
Fixed Assets	3m	3m	3m
Current Assets	2m	2m	2m
Current Liabilities	430	399	329

M & L Tooling

Unit B1 Farrington Close, Burnley, BB11 5SH
Tel: 01282-831058 **Fax:** 01282-415058
Website: http://www.mltooling.co.uk
Directors: H. Miles (Co Sec)
Immediate Holding Company: M & L TOOLING LTD
Registration no: 04721577 **Date established:** 2003
No.of Employees: 1 - 10 **Product Groups:** 46

Date of Accounts	Jul 12	Jul 11	Jul 10
Working Capital	22	14	-1
Fixed Assets	3	6	10
Current Assets	84	55	105

Marbill Developments Isabdeni Ltd

Unit O B 1 Time Technology Park Blackburn Road, Simonstone, Burnley, BB12 7NQ
Tel: 01282-778031 **Fax:** 01282-779507
E-mail: info@marbill.co.uk
Website: http://www.marbill.co.uk
Bank(s): National Westminster Bank Plc
Directors: M. Hargreaves (MD)
Managers: L. Lonsdale, P. Marvin (Prod Mgr)
Ultimate Holding Company: MARBILL HOLDINGS (SABDEN) LIMITED
Immediate Holding Company: MARBILL DEVELOPMENTS (SABDEN) LIMITED
Registration no: 01162732 **VAT No.:** GB 175 4379 36
Date established: 1974 **Turnover:** £1m - £2m **No.of Employees:** 21 - 50
Product Groups: 29, 30, 31, 48

Date of Accounts	May 12	May 11	May 10
Working Capital	494	484	421
Fixed Assets	252	262	272
Current Assets	788	820	795

Morplate Ltd

Hammerton Street, Burnley, BB11 1LE
Tel: 01282-428571 **Fax:** 01282-413600
Directors: G. Morris (Ch), M. Hodgson (MD), G. Morris (Dir)
Immediate Holding Company: MORPLATE LIMITED
Registration no: 00486204 **VAT No.:** 174 6255 50 **Date established:** 1950
Turnover: Up to £250,000 **No.of Employees:** 11 - 20 **Product Groups:** 32, 48

Date of Accounts	Oct 09	Oct 08	Oct 07
Working Capital	62	66	71
Fixed Assets	N/A	1	5
Current Assets	76	81	92

Packaging Machinery Ltd

8 Sweet Clough Drive, Burnley, BB12 6LY
Tel: 01282-414954 **Fax:** 01282-452580
E-mail: andrew.bannister@alliedpharma.com
Website: http://www.alliedpharma.com
Directors: A. Bannister (Dir)
Immediate Holding Company: PACKAGING MACHINERY LIMITED
Registration no: 06971892 **Date established:** 2009
No.of Employees: 1 - 10 **Product Groups:** 38, 42

Date of Accounts	Jul 11	Jul 10
Working Capital	N/A	11
Fixed Assets	N/A	1
Current Assets	1	22

Padiham Glass Ltd

Unit 10a Shuttleworth Mead Business Park Mead Way, Padiham, Burnley, BB12 7NG
Tel: 01282-774124 **Fax:** 01282-774951
E-mail: jkemp@padihamglass.co.uk
Website: http://www.padihamglass.co.uk
Bank(s): National Westminster
Directors: W. Clarkson (Sales), T. Clarkson (Co Sec), A. Clarkson (MD), J. Kemp (Chief Op Offcr)
Immediate Holding Company: PADIHAM GLASS LIMITED
Registration no: 01520736 **VAT No.:** GB 326 0529 76
Date established: 1980 **No.of Employees:** 21 - 50 **Product Groups:** 33

Date of Accounts	Sep 11	Sep 10	Sep 09
Working Capital	-5	37	138
Fixed Assets	2m	2m	2m
Current Assets	1m	1m	886

Panaz Ltd

Spring Mill 422 Wheatley Lane Road, Fence, Burnley, BB12 9HP
Tel: 01282-696969 **Fax:** 01282-611519
E-mail: admin@panaz.co.uk
Website: http://www.panaz.co.uk
Bank(s): HSBC
Directors: A. Attard (Sales), M. Berry (Fin), T. Attard (Grp Chief Exec)
Managers: C. Satterthwaite, K. Fairhurst, N. Memon (Tech Serv Mgr), S. Cleary (Purch Mgr)
Ultimate Holding Company: PANAZ HOLDINGS LIMITED
Immediate Holding Company: PANAZ LIMITED
Registration no: 01944865 **Date established:** 1985
Turnover: £10m - £20m **No.of Employees:** 51 - 100 **Product Groups:** 23

Date of Accounts	Mar 11	Mar 10	Mar 09
Sales Turnover	10m	11m	12m
Pre Tax Profit/Loss	290	564	529
Working Capital	4m	3m	4m
Fixed Assets	370	349	801
Current Assets	6m	6m	6m
Current Liabilities	547	488	434

Pentagon Bakery Systems Ltd

1 Susan Mill Junction Street, Burnley, BB12 0LZ
Tel: 01282-448992 **Fax:** 01282-448993
E-mail: ron.greenwood@btinternet.com
Directors: R. Greenwood (MD), M. Greenwood (Fin)
Immediate Holding Company: PENTAGON BAKERY SYSTEMS LTD.
Registration no: 03887807 **Date established:** 1999
No.of Employees: 1 - 10 **Product Groups:** 20, 40, 41

Date of Accounts	Dec 10	Dec 09	Dec 08
Working Capital	-2	-12	-23
Fixed Assets	2	2	2
Current Assets	23	21	27

Phoenix Engineering

Unit 1a Summit Works Manchester Road, Burnley, BB11 5HG
Tel: 01282-831539 **Fax:** 01282-413193
E-mail: rpilling123@aol.com
Website: http://www.phoenixengin.com
Directors: R. Pilling (Dir)
No.of Employees: 1 - 10 **Product Groups:** 23, 29, 30, 36, 43, 44, 45, 48

Pipeline Induction Heat Ltd

Farrington Road, Burnley, BB11 5SW
Tel: 01282-415323 **Fax:** 01282-415326
E-mail: sales@pih.co.uk
Website: http://www.pih.co.uk
Directors: G. Laake (Fin), P. Robinson (Co Sec), P. Bond (MD)
Managers: D. Bell (Sales & Mktg Mg), R. Fullard, L. Niccalles (Personnel)
Ultimate Holding Company: CRC HOLDINGS CORP (USA)
Immediate Holding Company: PIPELINE INDUCTION HEAT LIMITED
Registration no: 01478556 **VAT No.:** GB 344 7874 22
Date established: 1980 **Turnover:** £20m - £50m
No.of Employees: 51 - 100 **Product Groups:** 29, 30, 31, 39, 46, 48, 54

Date of Accounts	Dec 11	Dec 10	Mar 10
Sales Turnover	26m	23m	24m
Pre Tax Profit/Loss	2m	4m	3m
Working Capital	8m	10m	6m
Fixed Assets	4m	3m	3m
Current Assets	18m	20m	18m
Current Liabilities	8m	8m	8m

Precision Weighing Systems Ltd

International House Springhill Road, Burnley, BB11 2LQ
Tel: 01282-878250 **Fax:** 01282-699237
E-mail: ben.blackburn@precisionweighinguk.co.uk
Website: http://www.pwsscales.co.uk
Directors: J. Blackburn (MD)
Immediate Holding Company: PRECISION WEIGHING SYSTEMS LTD
Registration no: 04929521 **Date established:** 2003
Turnover: Up to £250,000 **No.of Employees:** 1 - 10 **Product Groups:** 38, 42

Date of Accounts	Dec 08	Dec 07	Jun 11
Sales Turnover	148	150	N/A
Pre Tax Profit/Loss	3	5	N/A
Working Capital	-9	-16	-5
Fixed Assets	14	19	8
Current Assets	27	16	56

printing.com @ Burnley Creative

4 Hargreaves Street, Burnley, BB11 1EA
Tel: 01282-437574
E-mail: design@burnley-printing.com
Website: http://www.burnley-printing.com
Directors: M. Girven (Dir)
Date established: 2006 **No.of Employees:** 1 - 10 **Product Groups:** 28

James Proctor Ltd

P O Box 19, Burnley, BB11 1NN
Tel: 01282-453816 **Fax:** 01282-416178
E-mail: info@jamesproctor.com
Website: http://www.jamesproctor.com
Directors: D. Proctor (MD), M. Proctor (Fin)
Immediate Holding Company: JAMES PROCTOR,LIMITED
Registration no: 00074028 **VAT No.:** GB 174 3045 76
Date established: 2002 **Turnover:** £500,000 - £1m
No.of Employees: 1 - 10 **Product Groups:** 40, 42, 45, 46, 84

Date of Accounts	Mar 10	Mar 09	Mar 08
Working Capital	25	23	17
Current Assets	366	219	256

Proplas International Ltd

Lancashire Digital Technology Centre Bancroft Road, Burnley, BB10 2TP
Tel: 01282-872450 **Fax:** 01282-872501
E-mail: info@proplasint.com
Website: http://www.proplasint.com
Directors: B. Green (Dir), S. Anderson (Dir)
Registration no: 04955460 **Turnover:** Up to £250,000
No.of Employees: 1 - 10 **Product Groups:** 37, 38, 42, 54

Date of Accounts	Nov 08	Nov 07	Nov 06
Working Capital	6	-26	-30
Fixed Assets	1	1	1
Current Assets	22	5	4
Current Liabilities	16	31	34

Quest Ltd

Victoria House Accrington Road, Burnley, BB11 5EF
Tel: 01282-838000 **Fax:** 01282-452121
E-mail: sales@questelectrical.co.uk
Website: http://www.questelectrical.co.uk
Bank(s): HSBC
Directors: I. Briggs (Fin), A. Davies (Chief Op Offcr)
Managers: J. Marriot (Personnel), C. Holly (Purch Mgr)
Immediate Holding Company: HOLLYCO LIMITED
Registration no: 02616061 **VAT No.:** GB 597 9836 48
Date established: 1992 **Turnover:** £2m - £5m **No.of Employees:** 21 - 50
Product Groups: 67

Date of Accounts	Aug 11	Aug 10	Aug 09
Working Capital	65	53	57
Fixed Assets	344	356	369
Current Assets	1m	863	809

Remec Engineering Services

Summit Works Manchester Road, Burnley, BB11 5HG
Tel: 01282-414263 **Fax:** 01282-412576
E-mail: remeceng@aol.com
Directors: P. Furness (MD)
Immediate Holding Company: REMEC ENGINEERING SERVICES (BURNLEY) LIMITED
Registration no: 02908470 **Date established:** 1994
No.of Employees: 11 - 20 **Product Groups:** 35, 39, 45

Remploy Packaging

Accrington Road, Burnley, BB11 5DR
Tel: 01282-411220 **Fax:** 01282-412213
E-mail: steve.wellens@remploy.co.uk
Website: http://www.remploy.co.uk
Managers: D. Kay (Mgr), L. Roberts
Immediate Holding Company: REMPLOY LIMITED
Registration no: NF003194 **Date established:** 1995
No.of Employees: 21 - 50 **Product Groups:** 27

B Rourke & Co. Ltd

Accrington Road, Burnley, BB11 5QD
Tel: 01282-422841 **Fax:** 01282-458901
E-mail: margaret.rourke@rourkes.co.uk
Website: http://www.rourkes.co.uk
Directors: M. Rourke (Sales), E. Rourke (Dir & Co Sec), B. Rourke (MD), M. Rourke (Dir), E. Rourke (Co Sec)
Managers: J. Gibbons (Export Sales Mg), S. Hunt (I.T. Exec), J. Nicholson (Sales Prom Mgr)
Immediate Holding Company: B. ROURKE & CO. LIMITED
Registration no: 01151730 **VAT No.:** GB 175 4072 62
Date established: 1973 **Turnover:** £2m - £5m **No.of Employees:** 51 - 100
Product Groups: 35, 49

Date of Accounts	Apr 11	Apr 10	Apr 09
Sales Turnover	3m	4m	4m
Pre Tax Profit/Loss	-145	-535	-565
Working Capital	-741	-1m	-499
Fixed Assets	2m	2m	3m
Current Assets	1m	921	1m
Current Liabilities	81	189	169

Sceptor Engineering Services

Unit 7 Balderstone Close, Burnley, BB10 2TA
Tel: 01282-422999 **Fax:** 01282-832964
Directors: P. Connearn (Prop)
Date established: 1988 **No.of Employees:** 1 - 10 **Product Groups:** 35

Sofos Design

29 Loughrigg Close, Burnley, BB12 8AS
Tel: 07732-075102
E-mail: office@sofos-design.co.uk
Website: http://www.sofos-design.co.uk
Directors: J. Molnar (Fin)
Registration no: 6221946 **Date established:** 2007
No.of Employees: 1 - 10 **Product Groups:** 44

Specialist Anodising Ltd

New Hall Works Elm Street, Burnley, BB10 1NY
Tel: 01282-412500 **Fax:** 01282-422804
E-mail: info@sacoltd.com
Website: http://www.sacoltd.com
Bank(s): National Westminster
Directors: M. Duffel (MD), M. Duffell (Co Sec), H. Lomax (Fin)
Managers: M. Hollis (Mktg Serv Mgr), V. Moody
Ultimate Holding Company: LENDLOCK GROUP LIMITED
Immediate Holding Company: SPECIALIST ANODISING COMPANY LIMITED
Registration no: 01849981 **VAT No.:** GB 375 4745 21
Date established: 1984 **Turnover:** £10m - £20m
No.of Employees: 101 - 250 **Product Groups:** 35, 48

Date of Accounts	Jul 11	Jul 10	Jul 09
Sales Turnover	12m	12m	9m
Pre Tax Profit/Loss	2m	55	11
Working Capital	5m	3m	3m
Fixed Assets	3m	3m	3m
Current Assets	7m	6m	6m
Current Liabilities	926	447	2m

John Spencer Textiles Ltd

Ashfield Mill Active Way, Burnley, BB11 1BS
Tel: 01282-423111 **Fax:** 01282-416283
E-mail: sales@johnspencer.com
Website: http://www.johnspencer.com
Bank(s): National Westminster Bank Plc
Directors: C. Pollard (Co Sec)
Immediate Holding Company: JOHN SPENCER (TEXTILES) LIMITED
Registration no: 01031371 **VAT No.:** GB 174 3930 53
Date established: 1971 **Turnover:** £2m - £5m **No.of Employees:** 21 - 50
Product Groups: 23, 24, 63

Date of Accounts	Apr 11	Apr 10	Apr 09
Working Capital	1m	1m	1m
Fixed Assets	1m	1m	1m
Current Assets	2m	2m	2m

Stanworth Engineers Ltd

Brown Street, Burnley, BB11 1PN
Tel: 01282-421427 **Fax:** 01282-458318
E-mail: john@stanworth.co.uk
Website: http://www.stanworth.co.uk
Bank(s): National Westminster Bank Plc
Directors: J. Stanworth (MD)
Immediate Holding Company: STANWORTH ENGINEERS LIMITED
Registration no: 00991178 **Date established:** 1970 **Turnover:** £1m - £2m
No.of Employees: 21 - 50 **Product Groups:** 85

Date of Accounts	Oct 11	Oct 10	Oct 09
Working Capital	385	663	670
Fixed Assets	51	86	174
Current Assets	674	1m	1m

Stockbridge Mill Co. Ltd

Green Lane Padiham, Burnley, BB12 7AE
Tel: 01282-772231 **Fax:** 01282-771084
E-mail: ann.hume@stockbridgemill.com
Website: http://www.stockbridgemill.com
Directors: A. Hume (MD), V. Morley (Co Sec)
Immediate Holding Company: STOCKBRIDGE MILL COMPANY LIMITED
Registration no: 00935499 **VAT No.:** GB 175 4092 56
Date established: 1968 **Turnover:** £500,000 - £1m
No.of Employees: 1 - 10 **Product Groups:** 24, 27, 63

Date of Accounts	Dec 10	Dec 09	Dec 08
Working Capital	-16	134	39
Fixed Assets	258	263	170
Current Assets	492	617	680
Current Liabilities	N/A	78	N/A

Streamline Engineering

2 Brownside Mill Worsthorne, Burnley, BB10 3JR
Tel: 01282-832032 **Fax:** 01282-832032
Directors: J. Duerden (Prop)
Date established: 2003 **No.of Employees:** 1 - 10 **Product Groups:** 46

Tankmaster UK Ltd

North Street Hapton, Burnley, BB12 7LD
Tel: 01282-681930
E-mail: info@alphatanks.co.uk
Website: http://www.alphatanks.co.uk
Directors: A. French (Dir)
Immediate Holding Company: TANKMASTER (UK) LTD
Registration no: 07077518 **Date established:** 2009
No.of Employees: 1 - 10 **Product Groups:** 35, 42, 45

Date of Accounts	Oct 10	Mar 12
Working Capital	8	-0
Fixed Assets	2	N/A
Current Assets	85	25

Trantec Solids Handling Ltd

45 Bank Street Padiham, Burnley, BB12 8HQ
Tel: 01282-777566 **Fax:** 01282-772422
E-mail: sales@trantec.info
Website: http://www.trantec.info
Directors: M. Harrison (Fin), G. Harrison (MD)
Immediate Holding Company: TRANTEC (SOLIDS HANDLING) LIMITED
Registration no: 03233202 **Date established:** 1996
Turnover: Up to £250,000 **No.of Employees:** 1 - 10 **Product Groups:** 41

Date of Accounts	Jan 11	Jan 10	Jan 09
Working Capital	51	44	39
Fixed Assets	6	8	11
Current Assets	70	68	66

Trapp Forge

Trapp Lane Simonstone, Burnley, BB12 7QW
Tel: 01282-771025 **Fax:** 01282-779500
E-mail: info@trappforge.co.uk
Website: http://www.trappforge.co.uk
Directors: F. Carter (MD), A. Tomlinson (Co Sec)
Immediate Holding Company: TRAPP FORGE LIMITED
Registration no: 04637897 **Date established:** 2003
Turnover: Up to £250,000 **No.of Employees:** 1 - 10 **Product Groups:** 26, 35

Date of Accounts	Jan 12	Jan 11	Jan 10
Working Capital	-44	-43	-40
Fixed Assets	101	105	111
Current Assets	22	20	10

Upgrade Windows

Elm Street, Burnley, BB10 1NY
Tel: 01282-441227 **Fax:** 01282-437966
E-mail: info@upgradewindows.co.uk
Website: http://www.upgradewindows.co.uk
Directors: S. Rassool (MD)
Immediate Holding Company: UPGRADE WINDOWS (BURNLEY) LTD
Registration no: 04474383 **Date established:** 2002
No.of Employees: 1 - 10 **Product Groups:** 46

Date of Accounts	Jun 12	Jun 11	Jun 10
Working Capital	-12	-11	-16
Fixed Assets	25	16	19
Current Assets	21	25	22

Veka plc
Farrington Road Rossendale Road Industrial Estate, Burnley, BB11 5DA
Tel: 01282-716611 **Fax:** 01282-718490
E-mail: djones@veka.com
Website: http://www.vekauk.com
Bank(s): Barclays
Directors: C. Torley (Sales & Mktg), D. Jones (MD), G. Fitton (Fin)
Managers: R. Walsh, G. Hammond (Personnel), N. Woods
Ultimate Holding Company: VEKA AG (GERMANY)
Immediate Holding Company: VEKA PLC
Registration no: 01626563 **VAT No.:** GB 497 9515 76
Date established: 1982 **Turnover:** £20m - £50m
No.of Employees: 101 - 250 **Product Groups:** 30

Date of Accounts	Dec 11	Dec 10	Dec 09
Sales Turnover	29m	28m	26m
Pre Tax Profit/Loss	-3m	-2m	-1m
Working Capital	7m	538	3m
Fixed Assets	26m	10m	11m
Current Assets	17m	12m	11m
Current Liabilities	532	848	578

Whitehead & Wood Ltd (Head Office)
Brindley Close Network 65 Business Park, Hapton, Burnley, BB11 5TD
Tel: 01282-446000 **Fax:** 01282-446044
E-mail: simon@wwcom.co.uk
Website: http://www.wwcom.co.uk
Bank(s): Barclays
Directors: S. Woodcock (MD)
Ultimate Holding Company: DOTCOM PARTNERSHIP LIMITED
Immediate Holding Company: WHITEHEAD & WOOD LIMITED
Registration no: 02229365 **VAT No.:** GB 174 6816 36
Date established: 1988 **Turnover:** £2m - £5m **No.of Employees:** 11 - 20
Product Groups: 27, 28

Date of Accounts	Dec 11	Dec 10	Dec 09
Working Capital	40	-63	-119
Fixed Assets	204	207	217
Current Assets	392	277	194

Worms Eye Site Investigation Ltd
52 Bank Parade, Burnley, BB11 1TS
Tel: 01282-414649 **Fax:** 01282-721916
E-mail: info@wormseye.co.uk
Website: http://www.wormseye.co.uk
Directors: G. Cannon (Dir)
Immediate Holding Company: WORMS EYE GEOTECHNICAL LTD
Registration no: 02902025 **Date established:** 1994
No.of Employees: 1 - 10 **Product Groups:** 85

Bury

Abbey Attachments Ltd
Nuttall Square Manchester Road, Bury, BL9 9SX
Tel: 0161-766 8885 **Fax:** 0161-767 9017
E-mail: info@abbey-attachments.co.uk
Website: http://www.abbey-attachments.co.uk
Bank(s): HSBC
Directors: P. Saunders (MD)
Managers: A. Shaw (Chief Acct)
Immediate Holding Company: ABBEY ATTACHMENTS LIMITED
Registration no: 01788300 **Date established:** 1984 **Turnover:** £1m - £2m
No.of Employees: 21 - 50 **Product Groups:** 45

Date of Accounts	Mar 11	Mar 10	Mar 09
Working Capital	451	146	191
Fixed Assets	2m	2m	2m
Current Assets	1m	600	519

Ainsworth Maguire
Unit 28 Peel Industrial Estate Chamberhall Street, Bury, BL9 0LU
Tel: 0161-447 8550
E-mail: kevinainsworth@ainsmag.co.uk
Website: http://www.ainsmag.co.uk
Directors: K. Ainsworth (Ptnr)
Registration no: 02021691 **Date established:** 1986
Turnover: Up to £250,000 **No.of Employees:** 1 - 10 **Product Groups:** 81

Alphatek Hyperformance Coatings Ltd
Unit 5a Cuba Industrial Estate Bolton Road North, Ramsbottom, Bury, BL0 0NE
Tel: 01706-821021 **Fax:** 01706-821023
E-mail: postbox@alphatek.co.uk
Website: http://www.alphatek.co.uk
Directors: S. Greenwood (Fin)
Immediate Holding Company: ALPHATEK HYPERFORMANCE COATINGS LTD.
Registration no: 02847431 **VAT No.:** GB 633 7816 25
Date established: 1993 **Turnover:** £500,000 - £1m
No.of Employees: 11 - 20 **Product Groups:** 32, 34, 46, 48, 67

Date of Accounts	Aug 11	Aug 10	Aug 09
Working Capital	232	229	268
Fixed Assets	218	266	278
Current Assets	372	387	567

Andrew Webron Ltd
Walshaw Road, Bury, BL8 1NG
Tel: 0161-761 1411 **Fax:** 0161-763 1156
E-mail: info@andrewwebron.com
Website: http://www.andrewwebronltd.com
Bank(s): Barclays
Directors: I. Dixon (MD)
Managers: R. Butterworth (Chief Acct)
Ultimate Holding Company: ANDREW INDUSTRIES LIMITED
Immediate Holding Company: ANDREW TEXTILE INDUSTRIES LIMITED
Registration no: 02458598 **Date established:** 1990
Turnover: £10m - £20m **No.of Employees:** 51 - 100 **Product Groups:** 23, 42

Date of Accounts	Mar 11	Mar 10	Mar 09
Working Capital	256	256	256
Fixed Assets	343	343	343
Current Assets	256	256	256

Antler Ltd
Pilot Works Alfred Street, Bury, BL9 9EF
Tel: 0161-764 0721 **Fax:** 0161-764 0723
E-mail: custserv@antler.co.uk
Website: http://www.antler.co.uk
Bank(s): The Royal Bank of Scotland
Directors: P. Bridge (MD), K. Twine (Grp Chief Exec), R. Woodcock (Jt MD), P. Eglin (Sales), N. Stevens (Sales), G. Capell (MD), A. Woodcock (MD)
Managers: R. Kellett (Tech Serv Mgr), R. Keller (Publicity), C. Gainley (Mktg Serv Mgr), P. Rigge (I.T. Exec), K. Walker (Chief Mgr), M. Wrigley (Transport), B. Wreford (Import Mgr), P. Rigg (I.T. Exec)
Ultimate Holding Company: LLOYDS TSB BANK PLC
Immediate Holding Company: ANTLER LIMITED
Registration no: 07111190 **VAT No.:** GB 144 9201 79
Date established: 2009 **Turnover:** £20m - £50m
No.of Employees: 251 - 500 **Product Groups:** 22

Date of Accounts	Dec 10
Sales Turnover	27m
Pre Tax Profit/Loss	-462
Working Capital	8m
Fixed Assets	9m
Current Assets	14m
Current Liabilities	2m

B D M Surface Coatings
Unit 2 Hudcar Mill, Bury, BL9 6HD
Tel: 0161-764 1200 **Fax:** 0161-764 1235
E-mail: bdmmetal@absonline.net
Directors: B. Morgan (Dir), J. Williamson (Fin)
Immediate Holding Company: BDM SURFACE COATINGS LTD
Registration no: 06291770 **VAT No.:** GB 151 2704 02
Date established: 2007 **Turnover:** £500,000 - £1m
No.of Employees: 1 - 10 **Product Groups:** 48

Date of Accounts	Aug 09	Aug 08
Working Capital	-44	-22
Fixed Assets	20	25
Current Assets	136	135

Baerlocher UK
Moss Hall Road, Bury, BL9 7JJ
Tel: 0161-764 3155 **Fax:** 0161-764 0250
E-mail: admin@baerlocher.co.uk
Website: http://www.baerlocheruk.com
Bank(s): Barclays
Managers: D. Hadfield (Fin Mgr), A. Schulle
Ultimate Holding Company: MRF MICHAEL ROSENTHAL GMBH (GERMANY)
Immediate Holding Company: BAERLOCHER UK LIMITED
Registration no: 01109873 **VAT No.:** GB 211 2400 42
Date established: 1973 **Turnover:** £10m - £20m
No.of Employees: 21 - 50 **Product Groups:** 66

Date of Accounts	Dec 11	Dec 10	Dec 09
Sales Turnover	13m	12m	12m
Pre Tax Profit/Loss	18	99	108
Working Capital	1m	2m	1m
Fixed Assets	2m	2m	2m
Current Assets	4m	4m	3m
Current Liabilities	631	562	240

Bartec UK Ltd
Arundel House Hollins Brook Park, Bury, BL9 8RN
Tel: 08444-992710 **Fax:** 0844-499 2715
E-mail: info@bartec.co.uk
Website: http://www.bartec.co.uk
Bank(s): Barclays, 1 Yorkshire St, Rochdale
Directors: K. Morris (MD)
Ultimate Holding Company: CAPVIS GENERAL PARTNERS 111 LIMITED (JERSEY)
Immediate Holding Company: BARTEC (U.K.) LIMITED
Registration no: 01700764 **Date established:** 1983 **Turnover:** £5m - £10m
No.of Employees: 11 - 20 **Product Groups:** 37, 40, 44, 47

Date of Accounts	Apr 12	Apr 11	Apr 10
Sales Turnover	6m	6m	4m
Pre Tax Profit/Loss	718	187	-124
Working Capital	-1m	-2m	-2m
Fixed Assets	58	81	109
Current Assets	2m	2m	1m
Current Liabilities	313	315	208

Beechfield Brands Ltd
Unit 3 Warth Park Radcliffe Road, Bury, BL9 9NB
Tel: 0161-762 9444 **Fax:** 0161-762 9555
E-mail: sales@beechfield.com
Website: http://www.beechfield.com
Directors: R. McHugh (Fin), P. Mchugh (Dir)
Ultimate Holding Company: BEECHFIELD BRANDS HOLDINGS LIMITED
Immediate Holding Company: BEECHFIELD BRANDS LIMITED
Registration no: 02953704 **Date established:** 1994 **Turnover:** £5m - £10m
No.of Employees: 11 - 20 **Product Groups:** 22, 24

Date of Accounts	Dec 10	Dec 09	Dec 08
Sales Turnover	9m	N/A	N/A
Pre Tax Profit/Loss	1m	N/A	N/A
Working Capital	3m	5m	4m
Fixed Assets	102	95	101
Current Assets	4m	6m	5m
Current Liabilities	1m	N/A	N/A

Benito UK
Unit 9 Bridge Mills Rochdale Road, Ramsbottom, Bury, BL0 0RE
Tel: 01706-821010 **Fax:** 01706-826324
E-mail: bschofield@benitouk.com
Website: http://www.benitouk.com
Managers: B. Schofield (Mgr), B. Schofield (Sales Prom Mgr)
Immediate Holding Company: JOHN SCHOFIELD (TEXTILE MACHINERY) LIMITED
Date established: 1977 **Turnover:** £1m - £2m **No.of Employees:** 1 - 10
Product Groups: 26

Date of Accounts	Apr 10	Apr 09	Apr 08
Working Capital	54	75	76
Fixed Assets	13	17	21
Current Assets	115	138	202

Brown & Co EE Ltd
7 The Pavilions Bridge Hall Drive, Bury, BL9 7NX
Tel: 0161-761 0118 **Fax:** 0161-797 5297
E-mail: brown@brownelectrical.co.uk
Website: http://www.brownelectrical.co.uk
Bank(s): National Westminster Bank Plc
Directors: C. Rhodes (MD)
Managers: C. Hutton (Sales & Mktg Mg)
Immediate Holding Company: BROWN & CO (ELECTRICAL ENGINEERS) LIMITED
Registration no: 00228005 **Date established:** 2028 **Turnover:** £1m - £2m
No.of Employees: 21 - 50 **Product Groups:** 52

Date of Accounts	May 11	May 10	May 09
Working Capital	37	4	243
Fixed Assets	294	316	102
Current Assets	853	1m	1m

Bury Dental 2000
12 Manchester Old Road, Bury, BL9 0TB
Tel: 0161-764 0329 **Fax:** 0161-761 1352
Directors: A. Irvin (Prop)
No.of Employees: 1 - 10 **Product Groups:** 38, 67

Card & Party Store Ltd
574 Manchester Road Blackford Bridge, Bury, BL9 9SW
Tel: 0161-796 7353 **Fax:** 0161-766 7678
E-mail: info@card-party.co.uk
Website: http://www.card-party.co.uk
Directors: J. O'boyle (Dir), N. Brooks (Sales)
Managers: W. McAteer
Immediate Holding Company: CARD & PARTY STORE (CASH & CARRY) LIMITED
Registration no: 03338435 **VAT No.:** GB 147 5373 54
Date established: 1997 **Turnover:** £5m - £10m **No.of Employees:** 21 - 50
Product Groups: 27, 28, 64, 65, 66

Date of Accounts	Jun 11	Jun 10	Jun 09
Working Capital	634	671	726
Fixed Assets	402	427	329
Current Assets	1m	1m	1m

Chadwicks of Bury Ltd
Villiers Street, Bury, BL9 6BS
Tel: 0161-763 2100 **Fax:** 0161-763 2125
E-mail: sales@chadwicks-lids.com
Website: http://www.chadwicks-lids.com
Bank(s): Barclays, Cheltenham
Directors: J. Chadwick (MD), M. Hardman (Sales & Mktg), J. Marriott (Fab)
Managers: P. Whelan (Mgr), P. Starling, D. Benjamin (Mgr), R. Cutworth (Mgr)
Ultimate Holding Company: Clondalkin Ltd
Immediate Holding Company: Clondalkin Ltd
Registration no: 00418902 **VAT No.:** GB 145 8198 41
Date established: 1954 **No.of Employees:** 101 - 250 **Product Groups:** 28, 30, 35

Date of Accounts	Dec 11	Dec 10	Dec 09
Sales Turnover	14m	13m	15m
Pre Tax Profit/Loss	640	906	1m
Working Capital	8m	8m	8m
Fixed Assets	5m	4m	4m
Current Assets	11m	12m	11m
Current Liabilities	756	866	988

CLICKintoPR.com
Unit 28 Peel Indl-Est Chamberhall Street, Bury, BL9 0LU
Tel: 0161-408 0152
E-mail: moreinfo@clickintopr.com
Website: http://www.clickintopr.com
Directors: A. Maguire (Ptnr), K. Ainsworth (Ptnr)
Immediate Holding Company: SALON FUSION LIMITED
Date established: 2002 **Turnover:** Up to £250,000
No.of Employees: 1 - 10 **Product Groups:** 81

College Sewing Machine Parts Ltd
Waterfold Park Ratcliffe Way, Bury, BL9 7BR
Tel: 0161-763 6969
E-mail: rickysnr@college-sewing.co.uk
Website: http://www.college-sewing.co.uk
Directors: R. Atherton (Dir)
Immediate Holding Company: COLLEGE SEWING MACHINE PARTS LIMITED
Registration no: 02124853 **Date established:** 1987
No.of Employees: 11 - 20 **Product Groups:** 35, 36, 61

Date of Accounts	Jun 11	Jun 10	Jun 09
Working Capital	182	151	126
Fixed Assets	44	63	85
Current Assets	557	539	547

Corcoran Fabrications
6 Dunsters Avenue, Bury, BL8 1EF
Tel: 07957-285208
E-mail: tommy.corcoran@hotmail.co.uk
Directors: T. Corcoran (Prop)
No.of Employees: 1 - 10 **Product Groups:** 35

Cormar Carpets (Cormar Carpets)
Brookhouse Mill Holcombe Road, Greenmount, Bury, BL8 4HR
Tel: 01204-881234 **Fax:** 01706-827633
E-mail: info@cormarcarpets.co.uk
Website: http://www.cormarcarpets.co.uk
Directors: D. Cormake (Mkt Research), N. Cormack (Grp Chief Exec)
Immediate Holding Company: GREENWOOD & COOPE LIMITED
Registration no: 00200956 **VAT No.:** GB 146 0981 60
Date established: 2024 **Turnover:** £75m - £125m
No.of Employees: 101 - 250 **Product Groups:** 23

Date of Accounts	Sep 11	Sep 10	Sep 09
Sales Turnover	80m	70m	63m
Pre Tax Profit/Loss	2m	687	3m
Working Capital	12m	11m	13m
Fixed Assets	9m	9m	10m
Current Assets	21m	21m	19m
Current Liabilities	4m	4m	4m

D R M Industrial Fabrics Ltd
Bond Street, Bury, BL9 7BE
Tel: 0161-763 1776 **Fax:** 0161-763 1778
E-mail: info@drm.co.uk
Website: http://www.drm.co.uk
Bank(s): Barclays Bank PLC
Directors: P. Mcguinness (MD), R. Hoyle (Sales), J. McGuinness (Fin)
Managers: P. Heap (Tech Serv Mgr)
Ultimate Holding Company: D R M LIMITED
Immediate Holding Company: D.R.M.INDUSTRIAL FABRICS LIMITED
Registration no: 00983478 **VAT No.:** GB 145 3105 02
Date established: 1970 **Turnover:** £1m - £2m **No.of Employees:** 21 - 50
Product Groups: 23, 24, 40, 41, 42, 45

Date of Accounts	Dec 11	Dec 10	Dec 09
Working Capital	330	267	307
Fixed Assets	174	190	68
Current Assets	872	776	777

Data Clinic Ltd
The Pavilions, Bridge Hall Lane, Bury, BL9 7NX
Tel: 0871-977 2525 **Fax:** 0871-2316810
E-mail: customer.services@dataclinic.co.uk
Website: http://www.dataclinic.co.uk

Directors: C. Seeley (Jt MD), R. Burrows (Co Sec)
Managers: J. Done (Cust Serv Mgr)
Immediate Holding Company: Data Clinic Ltd
Registration no: 04417174 **Date established:** 2002
Turnover: £250,000 - £500,000 **No.of Employees:** 1 - 10
Product Groups: 44

Date of Accounts	Apr 09	Apr 08	Apr 07
Working Capital	-19	-0	5
Fixed Assets	52	23	36
Current Assets	144	126	115

Delta Batteries Bury

3 Bolholt Industrial Park Walshaw Road, Bury, BL8 1PL
Tel: 0161-762 9777 **Fax:** 0161-762 9793
E-mail: sales@deltabatteries.co.uk
Website: http://www.deltabatteries.co.uk
Directors: J. Whyle (MD), A. Lord (Fin)
Immediate Holding Company: DELTA BATTERIES (OF BURY) LIMITED
Registration no: 03487410 **VAT No.:** GB 588 6844 65
Date established: 1997 **Turnover:** Up to £250,000
No.of Employees: 1 - 10 **Product Groups:** 37

Date of Accounts	Mar 12	Mar 11	Mar 10
Working Capital	30	31	26
Fixed Assets	3	3	4
Current Assets	53	52	50

Expersys Ltd

305a Bolton Road, Bury, BL8 2NZ
Tel: 0845-0940014 **Fax:** 0161-762 1040
E-mail: gkellett@expersys.co.uk
Website: http://www.expersys.co.uk/
Registration no: 05498703 **Product Groups:** 44

Date of Accounts	Jul 07	Jul 06
Working Capital	-1	-1
Fixed Assets	7	3
Current Assets	18	8
Current Liabilities	18	9

Extinguishers Direct Ltd

Uk Dry Risers Ltd Albion Courtyard, Albion Street, Bury, BL8 2AD
Tel: 0161-764 0002 **Fax:** 0161-763 7419
E-mail: sales@extinguishers-direct.com
Website: http://www.extinguishers-direct.com
Directors: M. Charlton (Dir)
Registration no: 05702520 **Product Groups:** 36, 38, 40, 67

Fabricad Designs Ltd

258 Bolton Road West Ramsbottom, Bury, BL0 9PX
Tel: 01706-827771 **Fax:** 01706-828529
E-mail: info@fabricaddesign.com
Website: http://www.fabricaddesign.com
Directors: J. Forshaw (Dir), R. Forshaw (Fin)
Immediate Holding Company: FABRICAD DESIGN LIMITED
Registration no: 02746256 **Date established:** 1992
Turnover: £250,000 - £500,000 **No.of Employees:** 1 - 10
Product Groups: 23

Date of Accounts	Dec 11	Dec 10	Dec 09
Working Capital	86	108	118
Fixed Assets	82	85	92
Current Assets	196	195	280

Finishing Aids & Tools Ltd

Unit 25 Woolfold Industrial Estate Mitchell Street, Bury, BL8 1SF
Tel: 0161-705 1300 **Fax:** 0161-763 1959
E-mail: johnp@finaid.com
Website: http://www.finaids.com
Directors: C. Howcroft (MD)
Immediate Holding Company: FINISHING AIDS AND TOOLS LIMITED
Registration no: 00660087 **VAT No.:** GB 216 1047 07
Date established: 1960 **Turnover:** £1m - £2m **No.of Employees:** 1 - 10
Product Groups: 33

Date of Accounts	Dec 11	Dec 10	Dec 09
Working Capital	73	100	121
Fixed Assets	347	412	377
Current Assets	862	719	594

Finishing Techniques Ltd

Halter Inn Works Holcombe Brook, Ramsbottom, Bury, BL0 9SA
Tel: 01706-825819 **Fax:** 01706-825748
E-mail: jonathan@fintek.co.uk
Website: http://www.fintek.co.uk
Directors: J. Dean (MD), R. Ainsworth (Co Sec)
Immediate Holding Company: FINISHING TECHNIQUES LIMITED
Registration no: 01574671 **VAT No.:** GB 383 1435 56
Date established: 1981 **Turnover:** £500,000 - £1m
No.of Employees: 1 - 10 **Product Groups:** 46, 48

Date of Accounts	Jun 11	Jun 10	Jun 09
Working Capital	158	143	160
Fixed Assets	123	79	43
Current Assets	292	204	273

Floor-Tech O'Neill Ltd

8 Woodroyd Drive, Bury, BL9 7NH
Tel: 0161-272 0455 **Fax:** 0161-763 9349
E-mail: floortec_contact@hotmail.com
Website: http://floortechonline.com
Directors: R. O'neill (Prop)
Immediate Holding Company: FLOOR-TEC (O'NEILL) LIMITED
Registration no: 06570282 **Date established:** 2008
No.of Employees: 1 - 10 **Product Groups:** 29, 30, 52

Fork Lift Training Ltd

52 Radcliffe Road, Bury, BL9 9JY
Tel: 0161-797 3959 **Fax:** 0161-797 3272
E-mail: sales@f-l-t.co.uk
Website: http://www.f-l-t.co.uk
Directors: C. Jones (Prop)
Registration no: 05060246 **Date established:** 2003
No.of Employees: 1 - 10 **Product Groups:** 35, 39, 45

Formulated Polymer Products Ltd

8 Garden Street Ramsbottom, Bury, BL0 9BQ
Tel: 01706-828208 **Fax:** 01706-828820
E-mail: neil@polymers.co.uk
Website: http://www.polymers.co.uk
Directors: N. Howarth (MD)
Immediate Holding Company: FORMULATED POLYMER PRODUCTS LIMITED
Registration no: 02308906 **Date established:** 1988 **Turnover:** £2m - £5m
No.of Employees: 1 - 10 **Product Groups:** 02, 22, 23, 27, 29, 31, 32, 66

Date of Accounts	Jun 12	Jun 11	Jun 10
Working Capital	458	450	229
Fixed Assets	120	91	57
Current Assets	2m	2m	2m

Thomas French Ltd

James Street, Bury, BL9 7EG
Tel: 0161-764 5356 **Fax:** 0161-764 6416
E-mail: peter.owen@thomasfrench.com
Website: http://www.thomasfrench.com
Directors: J. Sedgewick (Sales)
Managers: P. Owen (Chief Mgr)
Immediate Holding Company: SOFTWARE SOLUTIONS NORTH WEST LIMITED
Registration no: 04361287 **Date established:** 1998
Turnover: Up to £250,000 **No.of Employees:** 51 - 100
Product Groups: 24, 63

Date of Accounts	Aug 08	Aug 07	Aug 06
Working Capital	-63	-29	-10
Fixed Assets	132	118	133
Current Assets	1158	1555	964
Current Liabilities	1221	1585	974

Joshua Greaves & Sons Ltd

Atlas Engineering Works Garden Street Ramsbottom, Bury, BL0 9BG
Tel: 01706-824191 **Fax:** 01706-823000
E-mail: ross.g@greaves.co.uk
Website: http://www.greaves.co.uk
Bank(s): The Royal Bank of Scotland
Directors: R. Greaves (Dir)
Immediate Holding Company: JOSHUA GREAVES & SONS LIMITED
Registration no: 00481060 **Date established:** 1950 **Turnover:** £2m - £5m
No.of Employees: 11 - 20 **Product Groups:** 41, 43, 45

Date of Accounts	Mar 11	Mar 10	Mar 09
Working Capital	2m	2m	2m
Fixed Assets	372	703	438
Current Assets	2m	2m	2m

Handling & Laying Systems Nw Ltd

26 Whitelegge Street, Bury, BL8 1SW
Tel: 0161-272 0111
E-mail: marcus@handlingandlayingsystemsltd.co.uk
Website: http://www.handlingandlayingsystemsltd.co.uk
Directors: P. Marriott (MD), S. Marriot (Fin)
Immediate Holding Company: HANDLING & LAYING SYSTEMS (N.W.) LIMITED
Registration no: 04871320 **Date established:** 2003
No.of Employees: 1 - 10 **Product Groups:** 35, 39, 45

Date of Accounts	Aug 09	Aug 08	Aug 07
Working Capital	18	43	31
Fixed Assets	7	16	18
Current Assets	33	80	75

Interquartz UK Ltd

Pennine House Salford Street, Bury, BL9 6YA
Tel: 0161-763 3122 **Fax:** 0161-763 4029
E-mail: roy.stephenson@interquartz.co.uk
Website: http://www.interquartz.co.uk
Directors: C. Williams (Dir)
Ultimate Holding Company: PENNINE TELECOM (HOLDINGS) LIMITED
Immediate Holding Company: INTERQUARTZ (U K) LIMITED
Registration no: 01538605 **Date established:** 1981
No.of Employees: 1 - 10 **Product Groups:** 28

Date of Accounts	Dec 11	Dec 10	Dec 09
Working Capital	487	600	707
Current Assets	648	633	1m

J L Lord & Son Ltd

Wellington Cement Works Ainsworth Road, Bury, BL8 2RS
Tel: 0161-764 4617 **Fax:** 0161-763 1873
E-mail: enquiries@john-lord.co.uk
Website: http://www.john-lord.co.uk
Bank(s): Barclays
Directors: E. Lord (MD), K. Porter (Fin)
Immediate Holding Company: JOHN LORD HOLDINGS LIMITED
Registration no: 03254155 **VAT No.:** GB 560 6644 38
Date established: 1996 **Turnover:** £10m - £20m
No.of Employees: 11 - 20 **Product Groups:** 30, 33, 48, 52

Date of Accounts	Aug 11	Aug 10	Aug 09
Sales Turnover	N/A	12m	12m
Pre Tax Profit/Loss	144	359	139
Working Capital	1m	3m	3m
Fixed Assets	2m	2m	3m
Current Assets	1m	5m	5m
Current Liabilities	48	780	997

Jason Plastics

Prettywood, Bury, BL9 7HZ
Tel: 0161-763 8000 **Fax:** 0161-763 8052
E-mail: sales@jasonplastics.com
Website: http://www.jasonplastics.com
Bank(s): The Royal Bank of Scotland
Directors: B. Walshaw (MD), D. Walshaw (MD)
Immediate Holding Company: JASON PLASTICS LIMITED
Registration no: 01062457 **VAT No.:** GB 145 6158 63
Date established: 1972 **Turnover:** £10m - £20m
No.of Employees: 51 - 100 **Product Groups:** 30

Date of Accounts	Mar 11	Mar 10	Mar 09
Sales Turnover	11m	9m	N/A
Pre Tax Profit/Loss	543	491	142
Working Capital	750	472	206
Fixed Assets	3m	3m	4m
Current Assets	4m	3m	2m
Current Liabilities	935	486	368

JDJ Communications Ltd (This entry will not appear in the book)

24 Northfield Road Limefield, Bury, BL9 6QD
Tel: 0161-761 3814 **Fax:** 0161-761 3814
E-mail: john@jdjcommunications.co.uk
Website: http://www.jdjcommunications.co.uk
Directors: J. Jones (MD)
Registration no: 04773638 **Date established:** 2003
Turnover: Up to £250,000 **No.of Employees:** 1 - 10 **Product Groups:** 81

Date of Accounts	Aug 10	Aug 09	Aug 08
Working Capital	2	3	1
Fixed Assets	1	3	1
Current Assets	17	21	44

Jetchem Systems Ltd

Cuba Industrial Estate Bolton Road North Ramsbottom, Bury, BL0 0NE
Tel: 01706-828888 **Fax:** 01706-828000
E-mail: kevin@jetchem.com
Website: http://www.jetchem.com
Managers: K. Troughton (Mgr)
Immediate Holding Company: JETCHEM SYSTEMS LIMITED
Registration no: 02636413 **Date established:** 1991 **Turnover:** £2m - £5m
No.of Employees: 1 - 10 **Product Groups:** 32, 36, 38, 39, 40, 47, 48, 83, 84

Date of Accounts	Aug 11	Aug 10	Aug 09
Working Capital	-25	40	131
Fixed Assets	913	775	824
Current Assets	2m	2m	2m

Jewson Ltd

Higher Mills Bridge Street, Bury, BL9 6HH
Tel: 0161-764 6011 **Fax:** 0161-764 8977
E-mail: andy.sunter@jewson.co.uk
Website: http://www.hirepoint.co.uk
Bank(s): Barclays
Directors: D. McArthy (Dir)
Ultimate Holding Company: COMPAGNIE DE SAINT GOBAIN (FRANCE)
Immediate Holding Company: JEWSON LIMITED
Registration no: 00348407 **VAT No.:** GB 497 7184 83
Date established: 1939 **No.of Employees:** 11 - 20 **Product Groups:** 66

Date of Accounts	Dec 11	Dec 10	Dec 09
Sales Turnover	1606m	1547m	1485m
Pre Tax Profit/Loss	18m	100m	45m
Working Capital	-345m	-250m	-349m
Fixed Assets	496m	387m	461m
Current Assets	657m	1005m	1320m
Current Liabilities	66m	120m	64m

Kadant UK Ltd

PO Box 6, Bury, BL8 1DF
Tel: 0161-764 9111 **Fax:** 0161-797 1496
E-mail: ron.chambers@kadant.com
Website: http://www.kadant.com
Bank(s): Barclays
Directors: R. Chambers (MD), J. Davidson (Fin)
Managers: B. Williams (Sales Prom Mgr), K. Bulmer (Purch Mgr)
Ultimate Holding Company: KADANT INC (USA)
Immediate Holding Company: KADANT U.K. LIMITED
Registration no: 01741735 **Date established:** 1983
Turnover: £10m - £20m **No.of Employees:** 51 - 100 **Product Groups:** 44

Date of Accounts	Dec 11	Dec 10	Dec 09
Sales Turnover	11m	10m	9m
Pre Tax Profit/Loss	1m	976	635
Working Capital	3m	3m	2m
Fixed Assets	5m	5m	5m
Current Assets	6m	5m	4m
Current Liabilities	1m	664	690

Kays Ramsbottom Ltd

Britannia Works Kenyon Street, Ramsbottom, Bury, BL0 0AE
Tel: 01706-822216 **Fax:** 01706-828615
E-mail: sales@kays-soap.com
Website: http://www.kays-soap.com
Bank(s): Barclays
Directors: R. Kenyon (MD), A. Kenyon (Fab), S. Yates (Mkt Research)
Managers: G. Dennis (Personnel), S. Holt (Chief Acct)
Immediate Holding Company: KAY S(RAMSBOTTOM)LIMITED
Registration no: 00501154 **Date established:** 1951 **Turnover:** £2m - £5m
No.of Employees: 21 - 50 **Product Groups:** 32, 63

Date of Accounts	Oct 11	Oct 10	Oct 09
Working Capital	765	760	622
Fixed Assets	761	823	833
Current Assets	2m	2m	2m

L & D Mortimer Ltd

Birch Street, Bury, BL9 5AL
Tel: 0161-764 1362 **Fax:** 0161-761 6836
Directors: D. Mortimer (MD)
Immediate Holding Company: L. & D. MORTIMER LIMITED
Registration no: 02435324 **VAT No.:** GB 146 9475 30
Date established: 1989 **Turnover:** £250,000 - £500,000
No.of Employees: 1 - 10 **Product Groups:** 52, 83

Date of Accounts	Mar 11	Mar 10	Mar 09
Working Capital	112	125	48
Fixed Assets	104	66	77
Current Assets	273	237	107

Lab M Ltd

Topley House 52 Wash Lane, Bury, BL9 6AS
Tel: 0161-797 5729 **Fax:** 0161-762 9322
E-mail: info@labm.com
Website: http://www.labm.com
Bank(s): HSBC Bank plc
Directors: C. Goodwill (Ch), C. Goodwille (Ch), C. Goodwille (Prop), R. McDougal (MD)
Managers: M. Iddon (Sales & Mktg Mg), M. Sullivan (I.T. Exec), K. Bootell (Ops Mgr)
Ultimate Holding Company: LAB M HOLDINGS LIMITED
Immediate Holding Company: LAB M LIMITED
Registration no: 02903063 **Date established:** 1994 **Turnover:** £2m - £5m
No.of Employees: 21 - 50 **Product Groups:** 38

Date of Accounts	Apr 11	Apr 10	Apr 09
Sales Turnover	3m	3m	3m
Pre Tax Profit/Loss	249	208	3m
Working Capital	782	552	329
Fixed Assets	154	133	148
Current Assets	1m	1m	1m
Current Liabilities	314	301	360

Leighmans.com Ltd

Warth Business Centre Warth Road, Bury, BL9 9NB
Tel: 0161-763 2690 **Fax:** 0161-763 2783
E-mail: sales@leighmans.com
Website: http://www.leighmans.com
Managers: A. Showman (Chief Acct)
Registration no: 04894490 **Date established:** 2003
No.of Employees: 11 - 20 **Product Groups:** 65

The LK Group

Bury Business Centre Kay Street, Bury, BL9 6BU
Tel: 0161-763 7200 **Fax:** 0161-763 7318
E-mail: C.Leyden@thelkgroup.com
Website: http://www.thelkgroup.com

see next page

The LK Group - Cont'd
Managers: C. O'Reilly (Mgr)
Date established: 2002 **No.of Employees:** 21 - 50 **Product Groups:** 40, 54, 85, 86

Martin & Taylor Engineers Ltd

Limefield Works Limefield Brow, Bury, BL9 6QR
Tel: 0161-764 5698 **Fax:** 0161-763 1372
E-mail: enquiries@roller-manufacturers.co.uk
Website: http://www.roller-manufacturers.co.uk
Directors: D. Stumbilich (Dir), M. Stumbilich (MD), A. Stumbilich (Co Sec)
Managers: D. Stumbilich, K. Williams (Sales Admin)
Immediate Holding Company: MARTIN & TAYLOR ENGINEERS LIMITED
Registration no: 00727986 **VAT No.:** GB 146 4422 76
Date established: 1962 **Turnover:** £250,000 - £500,000
No.of Employees: 1 - 10 **Product Groups:** 27, 29, 30, 34, 35, 40, 41, 42, 43, 44, 45, 48

Date of Accounts	Apr 12	Apr 11	Apr 10
Working Capital	517	484	460
Fixed Assets	24	26	27
Current Assets	603	583	528

Matsdirect UK Ltd

Unit 2 Bolholt Industrial Park Walshaw Road, Bury, BL8 1PL
Tel: 0161-797 6785 **Fax:** 0161-797 6349
E-mail: info@matsdirect.co.uk
Website: http://www.matsdirect.co.uk
Directors: J. Bleakley (Dir)
Immediate Holding Company: MATSDIRECT UK LIMITED
Registration no: 05745665 **Date established:** 2006 **Turnover:** £1m - £2m
No.of Employees: 1 - 10 **Product Groups:** 23, 29

Date of Accounts	Mar 12	Mar 11	Mar 10
Working Capital	13	7	-4
Fixed Assets	4	5	6
Current Assets	135	102	61

Melba Swintex Ltd

Derby Works Manchester Road, Bury, BL9 9NX
Tel: 0161-761 4933 **Fax:** 0161-797 1146
E-mail: sales@melbaswintex.co.uk
Website: http://www.melbaswintex.co.uk
Directors: D. Clegg (Purch), J. Dawson (Dir), P. Harrison (Fin), L. Hay (Sales)
Managers: S. Gilligan (Personnel)
Ultimate Holding Company: MELBA PRODUCTS LIMITED
Immediate Holding Company: SWINTEX LIMITED
Registration no: 00670973 **Date established:** 1960 **Turnover:** £5m - £10m
No.of Employees: 101 - 250 **Product Groups:** 30, 39, 40

Date of Accounts	Mar 10	Mar 09
Pre Tax Profit/Loss	128	-163
Working Capital	N/A	-39
Fixed Assets	N/A	1m
Current Assets	N/A	91
Current Liabilities	N/A	1

Microwavesdirect.Com

72 Bolton Road Hawkshaw, Bury, BL8 4JA
Tel: 01204-887396 **Fax:** 01204-887396
E-mail: info@microwavesdirect.com
Website: http://www.microwavesdirect.com
Directors: D. Horrocks (Prop)
No.of Employees: 1 - 10 **Product Groups:** 40, 42, 67

Mident Ltd

Remmets House Lord Street, Bury, BL9 0RE
Tel: 0161-761 1111 **Fax:** 0161-763 1005
E-mail: midentuk@aol.com
Bank(s): Whiteaway Laidlaw
Directors: P. Thompson (Prop)
Immediate Holding Company: MIDENT LIMITED
Registration no: 07001287 **Date established:** 2009 **Turnover:** £1m - £2m
No.of Employees: 11 - 20 **Product Groups:** 30

Date of Accounts	Sep 11	Sep 10
Working Capital	17	-10
Fixed Assets	45	50
Current Assets	219	211

Millers Vanguard

Bridge Hall Works Bridge Hall Lane, Bury, BL9 7NY
Tel: 0161-764 7888 **Fax:** 0161-761 5002
Website: http://www.millersvanguard.co.uk
Managers: A. Watson (Mktg Serv Mgr), R. Jones (Mgr), P. Jones (Fin Mgr), M. Naylor
Registration no: 04215829 **Date established:** 2001
No.of Employees: 11 - 20 **Product Groups:** 20, 40, 41

Mistermarble

Unit 1 J2 Business Park Bridge Hall Lane, Heap Bridge, Bury, BL9 7NY
Tel: 0161-764 5601 **Fax:** 0161-272 0110
E-mail: mistermarble@tiscali.co.uk
Website: http://www.mistermarble.co.uk/
Managers: M. Jonson (I.T. Exec)
Date established: 2000 **No.of Employees:** 1 - 10 **Product Groups:** 14, 33

Moorepay Ltd

Warwick House Hollins Brook Way, Bury, BL9 8RR
Tel: 0151-928 0767 **Fax:** 0151-920 1755
Website: http://www.moorepay.co.uk
Bank(s): Barclays
Directors: C. Stone (Grp Chief Exec), J. Richardson (Co Sec)
Ultimate Holding Company: NIS HOLDINGS SARL (LUXEMBOURG)
Immediate Holding Company: MOOREPAY LIMITED
Registration no: 00891686 **VAT No.:** GB 133 4197 82
Date established: 1966 **Turnover:** £10m - £20m
No.of Employees: 251 - 500 **Product Groups:** 44, 80

Date of Accounts	Apr 11	Apr 10	Apr 09
Sales Turnover	16m	17m	19m
Pre Tax Profit/Loss	2m	2m	-107
Working Capital	927	-704	-1m
Fixed Assets	18m	19m	18m
Current Assets	6m	19m	16m
Current Liabilities	3m	2m	2m

Moseley Rubber Company Pty Ltd

Europa House Barcroft Street, Bury, BL9 5BT
Tel: 0161-447 8867 **Fax:** 0161-447 8868
E-mail: info@moseleysrubber.com
Website: http://www.moseleyrubber.com

Managers: P. Fisher (Mgr)
Ultimate Holding Company: HWL HOLDINGS LIMITED
Immediate Holding Company: MCM SALES & DESIGN LTD
Registration no: 03024372 **Date established:** 2006 **Turnover:** £1m - £2m
No.of Employees: 1 - 10 **Product Groups:** 29, 30, 48

Date of Accounts	Jan 12	Jan 11	Jan 10
Working Capital	9	N/A	2
Current Assets	39	49	28

P & S Textiles Ltd

Hornby Street, Bury, BL9 5BL
Tel: 0161-764 8617 **Fax:** 0161-763 7260
E-mail: info@pstextiles.co.uk
Website: http://www.pstextiles.co.uk
Bank(s): HSBC Bank plc
Managers: J. Hirst (Comptroller)
Ultimate Holding Company: ARVILLE HOLDINGS LIMITED
Immediate Holding Company: P & S TEXTILES LIMITED
Registration no: 00347271 **VAT No.:** GB 323 8961 42
Date established: 1938 **No.of Employees:** 11 - 20 **Product Groups:** 23, 48

Date of Accounts	May 08	May 09	May 10
Working Capital	-47	-102	-163
Fixed Assets	477	424	380
Current Assets	678	486	506

Pacific Valve Ltd

Unit 2b Lowercroft Business Park Lowercroft Road, Bury, BL8 3PA
Tel: 0161-763 6557
E-mail: info@pacificvalves.co.uk
Website: http://www.pacificvalves.co.uk
Managers: M. Richardson (Mgr)
Immediate Holding Company: PACIFIC VALVE COMPANY LTD.
Registration no: 02869295 **Date established:** 1993 **Turnover:** £1m - £2m
No.of Employees: 1 - 10 **Product Groups:** 36, 37, 38

Date of Accounts	Dec 11	Dec 10	Dec 09
Working Capital	66	11	49
Current Assets	405	236	304

Paper Industry Technical Association

5 Frecheville Court, Bury, BL9 0UF
Tel: 0161-764 5858 **Fax:** 0161-764 5353
E-mail: info@pita.co.uk
Website: http://www.pita.co.uk
Directors: B. Read (Dir)
Immediate Holding Company: PAPER INDUSTRY TECHNICAL ASSOCIATION
Registration no: 04300838 **Date established:** 2001
Turnover: Up to £250,000 **No.of Employees:** 1 - 10 **Product Groups:** 28

Date of Accounts	Dec 10	Dec 09	Dec 08
Sales Turnover	132	158	243
Pre Tax Profit/Loss	-47	-19	-59
Working Capital	294	334	344
Fixed Assets	219	225	235
Current Assets	362	384	387
Current Liabilities	40	36	36

Parkland Machines Ltd

6 Portland Street, Bury, BL9 6EY
Tel: 0161-762 9737 **Fax:** 0161-762 9738
E-mail: sales@parkland-international.com
Website: http://www.parkland-international.com
Directors: P. Kelly (MD)
Immediate Holding Company: PARKLAND MACHINES LIMITED
Registration no: 02035387 **Date established:** 1986
No.of Employees: 11 - 20 **Product Groups:** 44

Date of Accounts	Aug 11	Aug 10	Aug 09
Working Capital	-168	-135	-159
Fixed Assets	36	44	62
Current Assets	175	634	288

PC World

Waterfold Park, Bury, BL9 7BJ
Tel: 08445-610000 **Fax:** 0161-763 6056
E-mail: info@pcwbd.com
Website: http://www.pcworld.co.uk
Bank(s): The Royal Bank of Scotland, Middleton
Directors: D. Lloyd (MD), N. Roberts (Fin), R. Mark (Pers)
Managers: B. Payne (Publicity), B. Payne, H. Afzal (Sales Prom), M. Ainsworth (Purch Mgr), R. Lisles (Mgr), J. Kane (Sales Prom Mgr)
Ultimate Holding Company: DSG International plc
Immediate Holding Company: DSG RETAIL LIMITED
Registration no: 00504877 **Date established:** 1952
Turnover: £20m - £50m **No.of Employees:** 101 - 250
Product Groups: 26, 27, 44

Pennine Telecom Ltd

Pennine House Salford Street, Bury, BL9 6YA
Tel: 0161-763 3333 **Fax:** 0161-763 3332
E-mail: sales@penninetelecom.com
Website: http://www.penninetelecom.com
Directors: A. Roberts (MD), G. King (Sales), G. King (Sales), N. Beaumont (Fin)
Managers: G. Hutchinson, X. Sennelle (Tech Serv Mgr), A. Barnes (Personnel), B. McGee (Mktg Serv Mgr)
Ultimate Holding Company: PENNINE TELECOM (HOLDINGS) LIMITED
Immediate Holding Company: PENNINE TELECOM LIMITED
Registration no: 01763970 **VAT No.:** GB 388 4552 07
Date established: 1983 **Turnover:** £5m - £10m
No.of Employees: 51 - 100 **Product Groups:** 37

Date of Accounts	Dec 11	Dec 10	Dec 09
Sales Turnover	6m	7m	6m
Pre Tax Profit/Loss	145	258	242
Working Capital	2m	2m	2m
Fixed Assets	764	703	712
Current Assets	4m	4m	4m
Current Liabilities	1m	1m	1m

Penning Springs

Bolton Road North Ramsbottom, Bury, BL0 0LY
Tel: 01706-824614 **Fax:** 01706-821636
E-mail: mike.pendrigh@btconnect.com
Directors: M. Pendry (Prop)
Date established: 1978 **No.of Employees:** 1 - 10 **Product Groups:** 35

Polytec

Ormrod Street, Bury, BL9 7HF
Tel: 0161-705 1901 **Fax:** 0161-705 1935
E-mail: enquiries@polytec.co.uk
Website: http://www.polytec.co.uk

Directors: M. Worseley (Ptnr)
VAT No.: GB 560 7512 50 **Date established:** 1969
Turnover: Up to £250,000 **No.of Employees:** 1 - 10 **Product Groups:** 30

Printpack Enterprises Ltd T/A Printpack

Bridge Hall Mills Bridge Hall Lane, Bury, BL9 7PA
Tel: 0161-764 5441 **Fax:** 0161-705 1624
E-mail: jaustin@printpack.com
Website: http://www.printpack.eu.com
Directors: J. Austin (MD), D. Read (Dir)
Ultimate Holding Company: PRINTPACK HOLDINGS INC (USA)
Immediate Holding Company: PRINTPACK LIMITED
Registration no: 05022184 **Date established:** 2004
Turnover: £20m - £50m **No.of Employees:** 251 - 500
Product Groups: 27, 30

Date of Accounts	Jun 08	Jun 09	Jun 10
Sales Turnover	38m	33m	39m
Pre Tax Profit/Loss	-580	-3m	-669
Working Capital	5m	3m	2m
Fixed Assets	5m	5m	5m
Current Assets	17m	13m	17m
Current Liabilities	5m	4m	5m

Psychologica Career Guidance Services

26 Albert Street Ramsbottom, Bury, BL0 9EL
Tel: 01706-823997
E-mail: phil@psychologica.co.uk
Website: http://www.psychologica.co.uk
Directors: J. Bardzil (Fin), P. Bardzil (MD)
Immediate Holding Company: PSYCHOLOGICA LIMITED
Registration no: 01759537 **VAT No.:** GB 560 3502 73
Date established: 1983 **Turnover:** Up to £250,000
No.of Employees: 1 - 10 **Product Groups:** 33, 48

Date of Accounts	Mar 12	Mar 11	Mar 10
Working Capital	6	3	1
Fixed Assets	11	2	2
Current Assets	11	7	5

Rayhome Ltd

Rayhome House Walshaw Road, Bury, BL8 1PY
Tel: 0161-761 1132 **Fax:** 0161-764 6015
E-mail: sales@rayshim.co.uk
Website: http://www.rayshim.co.uk
Directors: E. Byrom (Fin), Y. White (MD)
Immediate Holding Company: RAYHOME LIMITED
Registration no: 01832805 **Date established:** 1984 **Turnover:** £1m - £2m
No.of Employees: 1 - 10 **Product Groups:** 34, 35, 38

Date of Accounts	Dec 11	Dec 10	Dec 09
Working Capital	21	-12	-2
Fixed Assets	512	511	502
Current Assets	263	211	202

Rileys Crane Services

Unit 18 Croft Industrial Estate Hollins Vale, Bury, BL9 8QG
Tel: 0161-796 5515 **Fax:** 0161-796 5516
Directors: D. Brockbank (Dir)
Immediate Holding Company: RILEY'S CRANE SERVICES LIMITED
Registration no: 04743282 **Date established:** 2003
No.of Employees: 1 - 10 **Product Groups:** 35, 39, 45

Date of Accounts	May 12	May 11	May 10
Working Capital	70	66	45
Fixed Assets	33	31	42
Current Assets	98	95	64

Rota Engineering Ltd

Wellington Street, Bury, BL8 2BD
Tel: 0161-764 0424 **Fax:** 0161-762 9729
E-mail: info@rota-eng.com
Website: http://www.rota-eng.com
Directors: R. Gething (Dir)
Ultimate Holding Company: WHARTON HOLDINGS LIMITED
Immediate Holding Company: ROTA ENGINEERING LIMITED
Registration no: 00415416 **Date established:** 1946 **Turnover:** £1m - £2m
No.of Employees: 21 - 50 **Product Groups:** 37, 38, 39

Date of Accounts	Aug 11	Aug 10	Aug 09
Working Capital	803	349	757
Fixed Assets	672	457	405
Current Assets	2m	2m	1m

Roxtec Ltd

C1 Waterfold Park, Bury, BL9 7BQ
Tel: 0161-761 5280 **Fax:** 0161-763 6065
E-mail: info@uk.roxtec.com
Website: http://www.roxtec.com
Managers: S. Turner (Mgr)
Immediate Holding Company: ROXTEC LTD.
Registration no: 05267114 **Date established:** 2004
Turnover: £250,000 - £500,000 **No.of Employees:** 11 - 20
Product Groups: 29, 30, 35, 37, 39, 40, 44, 54, 66

Date of Accounts	Jun 11	Jun 10	Jun 09
Working Capital	211	67	118
Fixed Assets	219	276	260
Current Assets	1m	981	1m

Ryalux Carpets Ltd

Mossfield Mill Chesham Fold Road, Bury, BL9 6JZ
Tel: 0161-762 3030 **Fax:** 01706-716035
E-mail: sales@ryalux.com
Website: http://www.ryalux.com
Directors: J. Gaverham (MD), K. Henry (Dir), P. Jackson (Sales)
Managers: P. Bevis (Mktg Serv Mgr), S. Agnew (I.T. Exec), A. Martin (Personnel)
Ultimate Holding Company: Airea plc
Immediate Holding Company: Airea Floor Coverings Ltd
Registration no: 00988948 **VAT No.:** GB 785 3970 77
Turnover: Up to £250,000 **No.of Employees:** 101 - 250
Product Groups: 23

Safety Products Online.co.uk Crossfield Excalibur Ltd

Unit 21 Woolfold Ind Est, Mitchell St, Bury, BL8 1SF
Tel: 0161-763 4377 **Fax:** 0161-763 4926
E-mail: sales@excalibur-rm.co.uk
Website: http://www.safetyproductsonline.co.uk
Turnover: £500,000 - £1m **No.of Employees:** 11 - 20
Product Groups: 22, 24, 63

Scale Services T W T Ltd
18 Dearden Fold Edenfield, Ramsbottom, Bury, BL0 0LH
Tel: 01706-822486 **Fax:** 01706-822486
E-mail: admin@scaleservices.co.uk
Website: http://www.scaleservicestwt.co.uk
Directors: C. Mitchell (Dir)
Immediate Holding Company: SCALE SERVICES TWT LIMITED
Registration no: 04628364 **Date established:** 2003
Turnover: Up to £250,000 **No.of Employees:** 1 - 10 **Product Groups:** 38, 42

Date of Accounts	Mar 11	Mar 10	Mar 08
Working Capital	4	7	4
Current Assets	64	68	58

Scottex Precision Textiles Ltd
Unit 1 Bolholt Industrial Estate Walshaw Road, Bury, BL8 1PY
Tel: 0161-763 6550 **Fax:** 0161-764 1365
E-mail: sales@scottex-filters.com
Website: http://www.scottex-filters.com
Directors: S. Parkinson (Prop)
Immediate Holding Company: SCOTTEX PRECISION TEXTILES LIMITED
Registration no: 01375545 **Date established:** 1978
No.of Employees: 11 - 20 **Product Groups:** 38, 42

Date of Accounts	Dec 11	Dec 10	Dec 09
Working Capital	-116	-85	-73
Fixed Assets	13	13	13
Current Assets	172	166	142

Sefar Ltd
Bury Business Centre Kay Street, Bury, BL9 6BU
Tel: 0161-765 3530 **Fax:** 0161-763 1382
E-mail: sales@sefar.co.uk
Website: http://www.sefar.com
Directors: R. Nuttall (MD)
Immediate Holding Company: SEFAR LTD
Registration no: 01885061 **VAT No.:** GB 408 2406 76
Date established: 1985 **No.of Employees:** 1 - 10 **Product Groups:** 23, 42, 63

Date of Accounts	Dec 11	Dec 10	Dec 09
Working Capital	504	350	328
Fixed Assets	49	97	127
Current Assets	868	696	552

Senior Hargreaves Ltd
Lord Street, Bury, BL9 0RG
Tel: 0161-764 5082 **Fax:** 0161-762 2333
E-mail: sales@senior-hargreaves.co.uk
Website: http://www.hargreaves-ductwork.co.uk
Bank(s): Midland, London
Directors: K. White (MD), D. Lutkevitch (Fin), P. Johnson (Mkt Research)
Managers: A. Kinsey (Personnel), L. Antrobus (Purch Mgr), R. Whittle (Tech Serv Mgr)
Ultimate Holding Company: SENIOR PLC
Immediate Holding Company: SENIOR HARGREAVES LIMITED
Registration no: 00288899 **Date established:** 1934
Turnover: £10m - £20m **No.of Employees:** 101 - 250
Product Groups: 35, 36, 40

Date of Accounts	Dec 11	Dec 10	Dec 09
Sales Turnover	18m	15m	15m
Pre Tax Profit/Loss	731	1m	533
Working Capital	1m	547	-1m
Fixed Assets	2m	2m	2m
Current Assets	6m	6m	4m
Current Liabilities	2m	942	1m

Solar Tech
Alexander House 197 Market Street, Tottington, Bury, BL8 3HF
Tel: 01204-881402 **Fax:** 0161-792 9775
E-mail: solartech@onetel.net
Website: http://www.solartechuk.co.uk
Directors: D. Lindenberg (Prop)
Immediate Holding Company: SOLARTECH (UK) LIMITED
Registration no: 03637792 **VAT No.:** GB 645 4141 50
Date established: 1998 **Turnover:** Up to £250,000
No.of Employees: 1 - 10 **Product Groups:** 37, 39, 40, 49

Date of Accounts	Sep 11	Sep 10	Sep 09
Working Capital	-42	-36	-52
Current Assets	5	5	5

Tetrosyl (International Division)
Bevis Green Works Walmersley, Bury, BL9 6RE
Tel: 0161-764 5981 **Fax:** 0161-797 5899
E-mail: info@tetrosyl.com
Website: http://www.tetrosyl.com
Bank(s): Barclays Bank
Directors: M. Oconnor (Fin), S. Brennan (Fin)
Managers: E. Jenkins (Personnel), G. Lawson (Tech Serv Mgr), I. Tench (Mktg Serv Mgr), J. McArthy (Purch Mgr)
Ultimate Holding Company: TETROSYL GROUP LIMITED
Immediate Holding Company: TETROSYL LEASING LIMITED
Registration no: 01148534 **VAT No.:** GB 149 7227 41
Date established: 1973 **Turnover:** Up to £250,000
No.of Employees: 251 - 500 **Product Groups:** 32

Date of Accounts	Dec 10	Dec 09	Dec 08
Sales Turnover	N/A	5	7
Pre Tax Profit/Loss	N/A	23	7
Working Capital	62	62	42
Current Assets	62	62	42

Stuart Tod & Sons Ltd
94 Victoria Street, Bury, BL8 1LE
Tel: 0161-761 2451 **Fax:** 0161-761 2451
Directors: M. Tod (MD)
Immediate Holding Company: STUART TOD & SONS LIMITED
Registration no: 01112282 **Date established:** 1973
No.of Employees: 1 - 10 **Product Groups:** 40, 42, 46

Date of Accounts	Mar 11	Mar 10	Mar 09
Working Capital	14	16	10
Fixed Assets	35	39	34
Current Assets	56	59	47

Ukfineart.Com
Europa House Barcroft Street, Bury, BL9 5BT
Tel: 0161-447 8957 **Fax:** 0161-447 8961
E-mail: sales@ukfineart.com
Website: http://www.ukfineart.com
Directors: S. Tibbs (MD), S. Tibbs (Dir)
Ultimate Holding Company: HWL HOLDINGS LIMITED
Immediate Holding Company: HAIRCLOTH WEAVING & FINISHING COMPANY LIMITED
Registration no: 05626388 **Date established:** 1951
No.of Employees: 1 - 10 **Product Groups:** 64

Valves & Engineered Products Ltd
Kay Buildings Kay Street, Bury, BL9 6BQ
Tel: 0161-761 5100 **Fax:** 0161-761 5110
E-mail: info@vepltd.co.uk
Website: http://www.vepltd.co.uk
Bank(s): National Westminster
Directors: A. Derby (Dir)
Ultimate Holding Company: SCHOFIELD & DERBY LIMITED
Immediate Holding Company: VALVES AND ENGINEERED PRODUCTS LIMITED
Registration no: 03004425 **VAT No.:** GB 652 5733 31
Date established: 1994 **Turnover:** £1m - £2m **No.of Employees:** 11 - 20
Product Groups: 36

Date of Accounts	Mar 11	Mar 10	Mar 09
Working Capital	277	197	120
Fixed Assets	17	28	28
Current Assets	429	331	348

Wallwork Heat Treatment Ltd
Lord Street, Bury, BL9 0RE
Tel: 0161-797 9111 **Fax:** 0161-763 1861
E-mail: sales@wallworkht.com
Website: http://www.wallworkht.com
Bank(s): National Westminster Bank Plc
Directors: R. Burslem (Fin), P. Carpenter (Dir), S. Collins (Sales), I. Griffiths (Works), R. Carpenter (Mkt Research)
Managers: Y. McKenna (Purch Mgr), D. Robins
Immediate Holding Company: WALLWORK HEAT TREATMENT LIMITED
Registration no: 00640305 **VAT No.:** GB 519 0363 03
Date established: 1959 **Turnover:** £5m - £10m
No.of Employees: 51 - 100 **Product Groups:** 34, 40, 48

Date of Accounts	Mar 11	Mar 10	Mar 09
Sales Turnover	7m	5m	6m
Pre Tax Profit/Loss	399	-489	2
Working Capital	524	329	-2m
Fixed Assets	1m	958	4m
Current Assets	3m	3m	3m
Current Liabilities	413	307	271

Carnforth

Dennis Barnfield Ltd
Lodge Quarry, Carnforth, LA5 9DW
Tel: 01524-733422 **Fax:** 01524-736450
E-mail: info@dennisbarnfield.co.uk
Website: http://www.dennisbarnfield.co.uk
Directors: T. Barnfield (Dir)
Immediate Holding Company: DENNIS BARNFIELD LIMITED
Registration no: 00920487 **Date established:** 1967 **Turnover:** £2m - £5m
No.of Employees: 11 - 20 **Product Groups:** 42, 45, 46, 48, 67

Date of Accounts	Apr 12	Apr 11	Apr 10
Working Capital	1m	1m	1m
Fixed Assets	437	450	462
Current Assets	2m	2m	2m

Black Sheep Iron Works Ltd
Unit 15 Holme Mills Industrial Estate, Holme, Carnforth, LA6 1RD
Tel: 01524-781093 **Fax:** 01524-782375
Directors: A. Townley (MD), K. Townley (Fin)
Immediate Holding Company: BLACK SHEEP IRONWORKS LIMITED
Registration no: 04508565 **Date established:** 2002
Turnover: Up to £250,000 **No.of Employees:** 1 - 10 **Product Groups:** 26, 35

Date of Accounts	Aug 11	Aug 10	Aug 09
Working Capital	-14	-7	-10
Fixed Assets	37	45	37
Current Assets	42	51	46
Current Liabilities	29	28	34

Hillside Garage
Laundry Lane Ingleton, Carnforth, LA6 3DA
Tel: 01524-241595 **Fax:** 01524-241595
E-mail: graham@hillsidegarage.f9.co.uk
Website: http://www.hillsidegarage.f9.co.uk
Directors: G. Bullock (Prop)
No.of Employees: 1 - 10 **Product Groups:** 25, 35, 39

E & R M Middleton
Yarlsber House Ingleton, Carnforth, LA6 3JB
Tel: 01524-241317 **Fax:** 01524-241317
Directors: K. Middleton (Ptnr)
Date established: 1973 **No.of Employees:** 1 - 10 **Product Groups:** 41

Mountainstone Forge
2 The Old Co-Op Yard Kellet Road, Carnforth, LA5 9LR
Tel: 01524-736565 **Fax:** 01524-401292
Website: http://www.mountainstoneforge.co.uk
Directors: A. Constantine (Prop)
Date established: 2002 **No.of Employees:** 1 - 10 **Product Groups:** 26, 35

North Fork Ltd
1 Leapers View Over Kellet, Carnforth, LA6 1HL
Tel: 01524-720011 **Fax:** 01706-655750
E-mail: info@north-fork.co.uk
Website: http://www.north-fork.co.uk
Directors: D. Griffiths (Ptnr)
Immediate Holding Company: NORTH - FORK LIMITED
Registration no: 05846864 **Date established:** 2006
No.of Employees: 1 - 10 **Product Groups:** 35, 39, 45

Date of Accounts	Jun 11	Jun 10	Jun 09
Working Capital	51	28	18
Fixed Assets	17	20	22
Current Assets	100	87	81

P Mcgaffigan & Sons Ltd
101 Main Road Bolton Le Sands, Carnforth, LA5 8EQ
Tel: 01524-822325 **Fax:** 01524-822382
E-mail: sales@mcgaffigans.com
Website: http://www.mcgaffigans.co.uk
Directors: S. Modley (Dir)
Immediate Holding Company: P. MCGAFFIGAN & SONS LIMITED
Registration no: 02055088 **Date established:** 1986
No.of Employees: 1 - 10 **Product Groups:** 26, 35

Date of Accounts	Sep 11	Sep 10	Sep 09
Working Capital	-78	-43	5
Fixed Assets	319	324	316
Current Assets	214	218	223

Savant Ltd
Dalton Hall Business Centre Dalton Lane, Burton, Carnforth, LA6 1BL
Tel: 01524-784400 **Fax:** 0870-460 1023
E-mail: info@savant.co.uk
Website: http://www.savant.co.uk
Directors: I. Henderson (Fin), I. Gray (MD)
Managers: J. Pearson (Admin Off), G. Jones (Develop Mgr)
Ultimate Holding Company: SAVANT GROUP LIMITED
Immediate Holding Company: SAVANT LIMITED
Registration no: 02077844 **VAT No.:** GB 708 3225 51
Date established: 1986 **No.of Employees:** 21 - 50 **Product Groups:** 44

Date of Accounts	Sep 11	Sep 10	Sep 09
Working Capital	1m	2m	2m
Fixed Assets	617	185	269
Current Assets	3m	3m	3m

Sicoma OMG
Beach Helm Beach Helm, Arnside, Carnforth, LA5 0AX
Tel: 01524-762762
E-mail: info@sicomaomg.co.uk
Website: http://www.sicomaomg.co.uk
Directors: S. Willis (Dir), B. Hebblethwaite (Dir)
Registration no: 4588860 **Date established:** 1990 **Turnover:** £1m - £2m
No.of Employees: 1 - 10 **Product Groups:** 45

P Singleton
Midland Unit 4 Scotland Road, Carnforth, LA5 9RE
Tel: 01524-733303 **Fax:** 01524- 733303
Directors: P. Singleton (Prop)
Ultimate Holding Company: ASHLEA LIMITED
Immediate Holding Company: ASHLEA LANDSCAPING HOLDINGS LIMITED
Registration no: 01646393 **Date established:** 2010
No.of Employees: 1 - 10 **Product Groups:** 41, 46

W C F Fuels North West
Station Goods Yard Warton Road, Carnforth, LA5 9EU
Tel: 01524-733669 **Fax:** 01524-720077
E-mail: sales@wcfnw.co.uk
Website: http://www.wcfnw.co.uk
Managers: D. Spencer (Mgr)
No.of Employees: 11 - 20 **Product Groups:** 31, 72

Walling UK Ltd
Kirk House Over Kellet, Carnforth, LA6 1DX
Tel: 01524-732370 **Fax:** 01524-720113
E-mail: sales@wallinguk.com
Website: http://www.wallinguk.com
Directors: J. Walling (Fin), D. Walling (MD)
Immediate Holding Company: WALLING UK LIMITED
Registration no: 04482141 **Date established:** 2002
Turnover: £500,000 - £1m **No.of Employees:** 1 - 10 **Product Groups:** 48

Date of Accounts	Jun 12	Jun 11	Jun 10
Working Capital	210	150	112
Fixed Assets	163	151	130
Current Assets	1m	884	815

Chorley

4a Solutions Ltd
41 Earls Way Euxton, Chorley, PR7 6QA
Tel: 01257-268351 **Fax:** 01257-268351
E-mail: andrew.holt@4asolutions.co.uk
Website: http://www.4asolutions.co.uk
Directors: A. Holt (Fin), A. Holt (MD)
Immediate Holding Company: 4A SOLUTIONS LTD
Registration no: 05264277 **Date established:** 2004
No.of Employees: 1 - 10 **Product Groups:** 44

Date of Accounts	Oct 08	Oct 07	Oct 06
Working Capital	15	13	17
Fixed Assets	5	5	3
Current Assets	28	26	31

AKM Fabrications Ltd
Unit 6 Yarrow Business Centre, Yarrow Road, Chorley, PR6 0LP
Tel: 01257-260441 **Fax:** 01257-233866
E-mail: info@akmfabrications.co.uk
Website: http://www.akmfabrications.co.uk
No.of Employees: 1 - 10 **Product Groups:** 30, 33, 35, 45, 47, 52

Date of Accounts	Jul 08
Working Capital	20
Fixed Assets	156
Current Assets	233
Current Liabilities	212

Alan Gordon Engineering Ltd
George Street, Chorley, PR7 2BE
Tel: 01257-274723 **Fax:** 01257-241342
E-mail: sales@alangordoneng.co.uk
Website: http://www.alangordoneng.co.uk
Bank(s): National Westminster Bank Plc
Directors: L. Lavin (Dir), J. Waterworth (Sales)
Immediate Holding Company: ALAN GORDON ENGINEERING CO. LIMITED
Registration no: 02112664 **VAT No.:** GB 323 1330 15
Date established: 1987 **Turnover:** £1m - £2m **No.of Employees:** 21 - 50
Product Groups: 48

Date of Accounts	Apr 11	Apr 10	Apr 09
Working Capital	1m	1m	1m
Fixed Assets	215	169	206
Current Assets	2m	2m	2m

B R T Bearings Ltd
Unit 9 Ackhurst Road, Chorley, PR7 1NH
Tel: 01257-264266 **Fax:** 01257-274698
E-mail: chorley@brt-group.com
Website: http://www.brtbearings.com

see next page

B R T Bearings Ltd - Cont'd

Directors: T. Wilson (Dir)
Ultimate Holding Company: N.I.S. HOLDINGS LIMITED
Immediate Holding Company: HOLD ENGINEERING LIMITED
Registration no: 00912230 **Date established:** 1994
Turnover: £10m - £20m **No.of Employees:** 1 - 10 **Product Groups:** 35, 39, 66, 68

Date of Accounts	Mar 11	Mar 10	Mar 08
Working Capital	438	440	440
Fixed Assets	243	243	243
Current Assets	440	440	572

Bailcast Ltd

Unit 8 Chorley North Industrial Pk, Chorley, PR6 7BX
Tel: 01257-266060 **Fax:** 01257-261034
E-mail: enquiry@bailcast.com
Website: http://www.bailcast.com
Bank(s): The Royal Bank of Scotland
Directors: D. Hartley (Dir), L. Alty (Dir), P. Hayward (Dir)
Registration no: 01526605 **VAT No.:** GB 349 8709 02
Date established: 1981 **Turnover:** £1m - £2m **No.of Employees:** 21 - 50
Product Groups: 29, 39, 68

Date of Accounts	Dec 11	Dec 10	Dec 09
Sales Turnover	N/A	N/A	2m
Pre Tax Profit/Loss	N/A	N/A	388
Working Capital	2m	1m	1m
Fixed Assets	307	325	314
Current Assets	2m	2m	2m
Current Liabilities	N/A	N/A	233

Bill Beaumont Textiles Ltd

Unit 4 Chorley North Business Park Drumhead Road, Chorley, PR6 7BX
Tel: 01257-263065 **Fax:** 01257-241348
E-mail: sales@billbeaumont.co.uk
Website: http://www.billbeaumont.co.uk
Bank(s): Barclays, Chorley
Directors: D. Beaumont (Chief Op Offcr), H. Berry (Co Sec)
Immediate Holding Company: BILL BEAUMONT TEXTILES LTD
Registration no: 00430970 **VAT No.:** GB 153 4570 72
Date established: 1947 **Turnover:** £5m - £10m **No.of Employees:** 11 - 20
Product Groups: 23

Date of Accounts	Mar 11	Mar 10	Mar 09
Working Capital	1m	1m	445
Fixed Assets	718	769	767
Current Assets	2m	2m	2m

Biffa Waste Services Ltd

Bolton Road Withnell, Chorley, PR6 8BP
Tel: 01254-831389 **Fax:** 01254-831791
E-mail: peter.lunt@biffa.co.uk
Website: http://www.biffa.co.uk
Managers: P. Lunt (Mgr), G. Dunn (Mgr)
Immediate Holding Company: BIFFA WASTE SERVICES LIMITED
Registration no: 00946107 **Date established:** 1969
No.of Employees: 1 - 10 **Product Groups:** 54

Date of Accounts	Mar 08	Mar 09	Apr 10
Sales Turnover	555m	574m	492m
Pre Tax Profit/Loss	23m	50m	30m
Working Capital	229m	271m	293m
Fixed Assets	371m	360m	378m
Current Assets	409m	534m	609m
Current Liabilities	50m	100m	115m

Brothers Of Charity

Dawson Lane Whittle-le-woods, Chorley, PR6 7DX
Tel: 01257-266311 **Fax:** 01257-265671
E-mail: info@brothersofcharity.org.uk
Website: http://www.brothersofcharity.org.uk
Directors: R. Swarbrick (Fin)
Managers: N. Howell, A. Atherton
No.of Employees: 251 - 500 **Product Groups:** 86

Brysdales Ltd

Brysdale House Drumhead Road Chorley North Business Park, Chorley, PR6 7DE
Tel: 01257-240000 **Fax:** 01257-240024
E-mail: sales@brysdales.co.uk
Website: http://www.brysdales.co.uk
Bank(s): Lloyds TSB Bank plc
Directors: E. Porter (Co Sec)
Ultimate Holding Company: BRYSDALES H LIMITED
Immediate Holding Company: BRYSDALES LIMITED
Registration no: 01016437 **VAT No.:** GB 379 7641 91
Date established: 1971 **Turnover:** £2m - £5m **No.of Employees:** 11 - 20
Product Groups: 26

Date of Accounts	Dec 11	Dec 10	Dec 09
Sales Turnover	N/A	2m	N/A
Pre Tax Profit/Loss	N/A	-34	N/A
Working Capital	326	262	247
Fixed Assets	158	97	172
Current Assets	878	663	646
Current Liabilities	N/A	111	N/A

Cal Software

Rivington House Drumhead Road, Chorley, PR6 7BX
Tel: 01257-234826 **Fax:** 01257-230927
E-mail: info@calsoftware.com
Website: http://www.calsoftware.co.uk
Directors: R. Clay (Co Sec), F. Noble (Dir)
Ultimate Holding Company: CONSTELLATION SOFTWARE INC (CANADA)
Immediate Holding Company: CULTURA TECHNOLOGIES LTD
Registration no: 01250877 **VAT No.:** GB 175 6617 36
Date established: 1976 **Turnover:** £1m - £2m **No.of Employees:** 1 - 10
Product Groups: 44

Date of Accounts	Dec 11	Dec 10	Dec 09
Working Capital	1m	273	229
Fixed Assets	88	26	42
Current Assets	6m	2m	1m

Carrington Career & Work Wear

Market Street Adlington, Chorley, PR7 4HE
Tel: 01257-476850 **Fax:** 01257-476868
E-mail: sales@carrington-cww.co.uk
Website: http://www.carrington-cww.co.uk
Bank(s): The Royal Bank of Scotland
Directors: J. Vareldzis (MD)
Ultimate Holding Company: ROCHDALE TEXTILE SUPPLIES (JERSEY)
Immediate Holding Company: HOWE & COATES LIMITED
Registration no: 02880498 **VAT No.:** GB 696 2921 90
Date established: 1993 **No.of Employees:** 21 - 50 **Product Groups:** 23, 24

Catering Plus

Unit 10 Chorley Central Business Park Stump Lane, Chorley, PR6 0BL
Tel: 01257-230004 **Fax:** 0845-056 0161
E-mail: sales@cateringplus.co.uk
Website: http://www.cateringplus.co.uk
Directors: D. Knights (Dir)
Immediate Holding Company: CATERING PLUS U.K. LIMITED
Registration no: 04919788 **Date established:** 2003
No.of Employees: 1 - 10 **Product Groups:** 20, 40, 41

Date of Accounts	Dec 11	Dec 10	Dec 09
Working Capital	-45	-46	47
Fixed Assets	26	18	7
Current Assets	41	78	282

Cavendish Upholstery Ltd

Mayfield Mill Briercliffe Road, Chorley, PR6 0DA
Tel: 01257-277664 **Fax:** 01257-261665
E-mail: sales@cavendish-upholstery.co.uk
Website: http://www.cavendish-upholstery.co.uk
Bank(s): Lloyds TSB Bank plc
Directors: M. McCann (Sales & Mktg), R. Hodgkinson (Fin)
Ultimate Holding Company: AIRSPRUNG GROUP PLC
Immediate Holding Company: CAVENDISH UPHOLSTERY LIMITED
Registration no: 01912412 **VAT No.:** GB 137 6009 75
Date established: 1985 **Turnover:** £2m - £5m **No.of Employees:** 21 - 50
Product Groups: 26

Date of Accounts	Mar 10
Working Capital	30
Current Assets	2m

Celebration Lighting

North Street, Chorley, PR7 1QD
Tel: 01257-260606
E-mail: chorley@celebrationelectrical.com
Managers: B. Houghton (Mgr)
Immediate Holding Company: ADLINGTON WELDING SUPPLIES LIMITED
Date established: 1973 **No.of Employees:** 1 - 10 **Product Groups:** 37, 67

Date of Accounts	Aug 11	Aug 10	Aug 09
Pre Tax Profit/Loss	261	151	181
Working Capital	-1m	-1m	-1m
Fixed Assets	5m	5m	5m
Current Assets	3m	3m	2m
Current Liabilities	964	1m	985

G W Chadwick Ltd

Unit 40 Chorley North Industrial Park, Chorley, PR6 7BX
Tel: 01257-234242 **Fax:** 01257-234213
E-mail: philip@gwchadwick.co.uk
Website: http://www.gwchadwick.co.uk
Bank(s): Barclays
Directors: P. Seagrave (Sales)
Immediate Holding Company: G W CHADWICK LIMITED
Registration no: 00100113 **VAT No.:** GB 147 5727 43
Date established: 2008 **Turnover:** £1m - £2m **No.of Employees:** 11 - 20
Product Groups: 20, 23, 25, 27

Date of Accounts	Mar 11	Mar 10	Mar 09
Working Capital	166	170	127
Fixed Assets	8	12	16
Current Assets	620	508	561

J Charnley & Sons Ltd

Marsh Lane Brindle, Chorley, PR6 8NY
Tel: 01254-852122 **Fax:** 01254-852794
E-mail: will@charnleys.com
Website: http://www.charnleys.com
Directors: W. Charnley (MD)
Immediate Holding Company: J. CHARNLEY & SONS
Registration no: 03727216 **Date established:** 1999
No.of Employees: 1 - 10 **Product Groups:** 41

Date of Accounts	Aug 07
Working Capital	1m
Fixed Assets	109
Current Assets	1m

Droyt Products Ltd

Progress Mill Progress Street, Chorley, PR6 0RZ
Tel: 01257-417251 **Fax:** 01257-261066
E-mail: chris@droyt.com
Website: http://www.droyt.com
Bank(s): The Royal Bank of Scotland
Directors: A. McCracken (Sales), C. Effendowicz (MD)
Immediate Holding Company: DROYT PRODUCTS LIMITED
Registration no: 00322883 **VAT No.:** GB 154 0069 91
Date established: 1937 **Turnover:** £500,000 - £1m
No.of Employees: 11 - 20 **Product Groups:** 32

Date of Accounts	Mar 11	Mar 10	Mar 09
Working Capital	34	6	-75
Fixed Assets	133	138	144
Current Assets	214	221	183

F & P Wholesale

Chorley North Industrial Park, Chorley, PR6 7BT
Tel: 01257-238100 **Fax:** 01257-232885
E-mail: chorley@fpwholesale.co.uk
Website: http://www.fpwholesale.co.uk
Managers: G. Barnish (Mgr)
Registration no: 00704322 **Date established:** 1992
No.of Employees: 21 - 50 **Product Groups:** 36, 40

Fairport Holdings Ltd

Market Place Adlington, Chorley, PR7 4EZ
Tel: 01257-476060 **Fax:** 01257-484071
E-mail: ian.wakefield@fairportholdings.co.uk
Website: http://www.fairportholdings.co.uk
Directors: I. Wakefield (Fin)
Immediate Holding Company: FAIRPORT HOLDINGS LIMITED
Registration no: 02510535 **Date established:** 1990 **Turnover:** £5m - £10m
No.of Employees: 1 - 10 **Product Groups:** 82

Date of Accounts	Mar 11	Mar 10	Mar 09
Sales Turnover	8m	7m	8m
Pre Tax Profit/Loss	272	132	-35
Working Capital	2m	2m	2m
Fixed Assets	5m	3m	4m
Current Assets	4m	4m	4m
Current Liabilities	598	619	467

G D W Engineering & Plant Services Ltd

Low Mill Town Lane, Whittle-le-Woods, Chorley, PR6 7DJ
Tel: 01257-262491 **Fax:** 01257-241174
E-mail: sales@gdwengineering.co.uk
Website: http://www.gdwengineering.co.uk
Bank(s): Barclays
Directors: G. Watkinson (MD), S. Watkinson (Fin)
Managers: A. Green (Buyer), B. McGhee (Eng), N. Watkinson (Tech Serv Mgr), M. Clayton (Sales Admin)
Ultimate Holding Company: GDW HOLDINGS LIMITED
Immediate Holding Company: GDW ENGINEERING AND PLANT SERVICES LIMITED
Registration no: 02973304 **VAT No.:** GB 534 2174 66
Date established: 1994 **Turnover:** £1m - £2m **No.of Employees:** 21 - 50
Product Groups: 48

Date of Accounts	Nov 11	Nov 10	Nov 09
Working Capital	351	712	412
Fixed Assets	N/A	N/A	194
Current Assets	1m	1m	974

Heracles E E S Ltd

20 Thirlmere Close Adlington, Chorley, PR6 9QD
Tel: 01257-483733 **Fax:** 01257-483732
E-mail: sales@heracles.org.uk
Website: http://www.heracles.org.uk
Directors: V. Mccully (MD)
Immediate Holding Company: HERACLES ELECTRONIC EQUIPMENT SUPPLIES LIMITED
Registration no: 02450095 **Date established:** 1989 **Turnover:** £2m - £5m
No.of Employees: 1 - 10 **Product Groups:** 38

Date of Accounts	Dec 11	Dec 10	Dec 09
Working Capital	-13	-15	-12
Fixed Assets	2	2	3
Current Assets	11	8	9

K W Designed Solutions Ltd

Unit 18 Adlington South Business Park Huyton Road, Adlington, Chorley, PR7 4JR
Tel: 01257-474507 **Fax:** 01257-482318
E-mail: sales@kwdesign.co.uk
Website: http://www.kwdesign.co.uk
Directors: M. Kay (MD)
Immediate Holding Company: KW DESIGNED SOLUTIONS LTD
Registration no: 05252152 **Date established:** 2004
Turnover: £250,000 - £500,000 **No.of Employees:** 1 - 10
Product Groups: 30, 35, 37, 38, 40, 41, 42, 67, 85

Date of Accounts	Mar 12	Mar 11	Mar 10
Working Capital	67	49	73
Fixed Assets	21	28	37
Current Assets	182	233	198

Kerax Ltd

Cowling Road, Chorley, PR6 9DR
Tel: 01257-237500 **Fax:** 01257-237334
E-mail: sales@kerax.co.uk
Website: http://www.kerax.co.uk
Directors: G. Strettle (Fin), I. Appleton (MD)
Managers: A. Crawford (Comptroller), A. Fisk (Sales Prom Mgr), K. Whittle (Sales Prom Mgr)
Ultimate Holding Company: KERAX (CHORLEY) LIMITED
Immediate Holding Company: KERAX LIMITED
Registration no: 04968239 **Date established:** 2003
Turnover: £10m - £20m **No.of Employees:** 21 - 50 **Product Groups:** 31, 32, 66

Date of Accounts	Dec 11	Dec 10	Dec 09
Sales Turnover	17m	13m	10m
Pre Tax Profit/Loss	551	291	435
Working Capital	2m	1m	2m
Fixed Assets	699	724	3m
Current Assets	5m	5m	4m
Current Liabilities	3m	828	1m

Logma Systems Design Ltd

Logic Centre Cunliffe Street, Chorley, PR7 2BA
Tel: 01257-233123 **Fax:** 01257-237215
E-mail: sales@logma.co.uk
Website: http://www.logma.co.uk
Managers: W. Hindle (Ops Mgr)
Immediate Holding Company: LOGMA SYSTEMS DESIGN LIMITED
Registration no: 02321865 **Date established:** 1988
No.of Employees: 1 - 10 **Product Groups:** 37, 44, 49, 67, 79, 80, 84, 86

Date of Accounts	Mar 11	Mar 10	Mar 09
Working Capital	-20	9	58
Fixed Assets	127	144	16
Current Assets	85	122	167

Managing For Quality Ltd

249 Spendmore Lane Coppull, Chorley, PR7 5DF
Tel: 01257-471345 **Fax:** 01257-471343
E-mail: david.edwards@mfq.co.uk
Website: http://www.mfq.co.uk
Directors: D. Edwards (Dir)
Immediate Holding Company: MANAGING FOR QUALITY LIMITED
Registration no: 02287860 **VAT No.:** GB 482 9160 27
Date established: 1988 **Turnover:** £500,000 - £1m
No.of Employees: 1 - 10 **Product Groups:** 85, 86

Date of Accounts	Jun 11	Jun 10	Jun 09
Working Capital	53	54	66
Fixed Assets	2	1	31
Current Assets	93	106	119
Current Liabilities	31	N/A	N/A

M K Profile Systems

9 Cowling Business Park Canal Side, Chorley, PR6 0QL
Tel: 0115-922 1296 **Fax:** 01257-271409
E-mail: info@mkprofiles.co.uk
Website: http://www.mkprofiles.co.uk
Managers: D. Whiteside (Sales Prom Mgr), J. Loud (Ops Mgr), J. Loud (Sales Prom Mgr), S. Fagan (Admin Off)
Registration no: 04063338 **Turnover:** £2m - £5m
No.of Employees: 1 - 10 **Product Groups:** 34, 35, 36, 37, 40, 45

Date of Accounts	Dec 07	Dec 06	Dec 05
Working Capital	-262	-91	51
Fixed Assets	3	3	3

Current Assets	194	250	250
Current Liabilities	456	341	199
Total Share Capital	10	10	10

Morgan Bros Ltd
Unit 7 Primrose Bank Mill Friday Street, Chorley, PR6 0AA
Tel: 01257-264041 **Fax:** 01257-241092
E-mail: sales@morgan-bros.co.uk
Website: http://www.morgan-bros.co.uk
Bank(s): Barclays
Directors: P. Morgan (Dir)
Immediate Holding Company: MORGAN BROS (METALWORK SOLUTIONS) LTD
Registration no: 07037174 **VAT No.:** GB 154 4927 51
Date established: 2009 **Turnover:** £500,000 - £1m
No.of Employees: 21 - 50 **Product Groups:** 48

Date of Accounts	Jan 12	Jan 11
Working Capital	-29	-110
Fixed Assets	327	259
Current Assets	394	281

N I S Ltd (Alumas)
Common Bank Industrial Estate Ackhurst Road, Chorley, PR7 1NH
Tel: 01257-265656 **Fax:** 01257-275501
E-mail: sales@nisltd.com
Website: http://www.nisltd.com
Directors: C. Nicholson (Co Sec)
Managers: I. Hardman
Ultimate Holding Company: N.I.S. HOLDINGS LIMITED
Immediate Holding Company: N.I.S. LIMITED
Registration no: 03345114 **Date established:** 1997
Turnover: £10m - £20m **No.of Employees:** 101 - 250 **Product Groups:** 84

Date of Accounts	Mar 11	Mar 10	Mar 09
Sales Turnover	11m	11m	7m
Pre Tax Profit/Loss	-55	-494	-976
Working Capital	3m	3m	899
Fixed Assets	291	579	383
Current Assets	8m	5m	4m
Current Liabilities	3m	969	741

N S G Environmental Ltd
Matrix Park Western Avenue, Buckshaw Village, Chorley, PR7 7NB
Tel: 01772-458818 **Fax:** 01772-458819
E-mail: mailbox@environmental.co.uk
Website: http://www.nsgltd.co.uk
Directors: J. Morris (MD)
Ultimate Holding Company: N.I.S. HOLDINGS LIMITED
Immediate Holding Company: NSG ENVIRONMENTAL LIMITED
Registration no: 02769182 **Date established:** 1992 **Turnover:** £2m - £5m
No.of Employees: 1 - 10 **Product Groups:** 33, 54

Date of Accounts	Mar 11	Mar 10	Mar 09
Sales Turnover	12m	12m	8m
Pre Tax Profit/Loss	1m	984	805
Working Capital	2m	2m	3m
Fixed Assets	1m	666	145
Current Assets	4m	5m	5m
Current Liabilities	1m	1m	932

Naylor & Walkden Ltd
Hatton Street Adlington, Chorley, PR7 4HT
Tel: 01257-480222 **Fax:** 01257-482696
E-mail: info@naylorwalkden.co.uk
Website: http://www.naylorwalkden.co.uk
Bank(s): Barclays,Wigan
Directors: C. Stephenson (Fin), C. Stevenson (Fin), S. Lee (MD)
Managers: S. Fairclough (Buyer)
Ultimate Holding Company: NAYLOR AND WALKDEN (HOLDINGS) LIMITED
Immediate Holding Company: NAYLOR & WALKDEN,LIMITED
Registration no: 00433999 **VAT No.:** GB 154 3137 85
Date established: 1947 **Turnover:** £10m - £20m
No.of Employees: 51 - 100 **Product Groups:** 52

Date of Accounts	Mar 11	Mar 10	Mar 09
Sales Turnover	13m	14m	N/A
Pre Tax Profit/Loss	183	1m	595
Working Capital	7m	7m	6m
Fixed Assets	218	330	282
Current Assets	11m	11m	11m
Current Liabilities	2m	1m	2m

Mick Ogden
Holden Street Adlington, Chorley, PR7 4JJ
Tel: 01257-474393 **Fax:** 01257-474898
Directors: M. Ogden (Prop)
Date established: 1995 **No.of Employees:** 1 - 10 **Product Groups:** 40, 68

Owon Technology Ltd
69 Studfold, Chorley, PR7 1UA
Tel: 0845-050 8168 **Fax:** 0845-050 8169
E-mail: info@owon.co.uk
Website: http://www.owon.co.uk
Directors: M. Zou (Fin), B. Zou (Dir)
Immediate Holding Company: OWON TECHNOLOGY LIMITED
Registration no: 05993216 **Date established:** 2006
Turnover: Up to £250,000 **No.of Employees:** 1 - 10 **Product Groups:** 38

Date of Accounts	Oct 11	Oct 10	Oct 09
Working Capital	6	29	32
Fixed Assets	N/A	2	3
Current Assets	77	106	118

P B Mechanical Services
The Boatyard Rawlinson Lane, Heath Charnock, Chorley, PR7 4DE
Tel: 01257-474422 **Fax:** 01257-475422
E-mail: info@pbmechanical.co.uk
Website: http://www.pbmechanical.co.uk
Directors: L. Burkhardt (Ptnr)
Immediate Holding Company: MARINE PROPULSION SERVICES LIMITED
Registration no: 01973318 **Date established:** 1985
No.of Employees: 1 - 10 **Product Groups:** 35, 36, 39

Date of Accounts	Oct 11	Oct 10	Oct 07
Working Capital	22	24	30
Fixed Assets	51	50	50
Current Assets	24	26	42

paramelt
Cowling Road, Chorley, PR6 9DR
Tel: 01257-274232 **Fax:** 01257-275333
E-mail: info@paramelt.com
Website: http://www.paramelt.com
Directors: M. Dahlström (Comm)
Managers: A. Marcus (Sales Prom Mgr)
Product Groups: 32

Petrie Technologies Ltd
Common Bank Industrial Estate Ackhurst Road, Chorley, PR7 1NH
Tel: 01257-241206 **Fax:** 01257-267562
E-mail: sales@petrieltd.com
Website: http://www.nisltd.com
Directors: C. Nicholson (Fin), C. Nicholson (Co Sec), K. Branton (MD), N. Meffan (Ch)
Managers: M. Sims (Elec Mgr), D. Spillsbury (Sales Prom Mgr), A. Woodward (I.T. Exec), A. Jennings (Purch Mgr), R. Bailey (Chief Mgr)
Immediate Holding Company: PETRIE TECHNOLOGIES LIMITED
Registration no: 02982082 **Date established:** 1994
Turnover: Up to £250,000 **No.of Employees:** 1 - 10 **Product Groups:** 40, 41, 42

Date of Accounts	Mar 10	Mar 09	Mar 08
Sales Turnover	101	468	269
Pre Tax Profit/Loss	-465	-78	-164
Working Capital	-598	-366	-96
Fixed Assets	38	235	43
Current Assets	210	102	160
Current Liabilities	6	14	5

Porter-Lancastrian Ltd
Lower Healey Business Park Froom Street, Chorley, PR6 9AR
Tel: 08708-710113 **Fax:** 08708-710114
E-mail: andrew.brown@porta.co.uk
Website: http://www.porta.co.uk
Bank(s): National Westminster Bank Plc
Directors: A. Brown (MD)
Managers: L. Blackledge (Personnel), V. Marsden
Immediate Holding Company: PORTER-LANCASTRIAN LIMITED
Registration no: 02179724 **VAT No.:** GB 497 9290 74
Date established: 1987 **Turnover:** £2m - £5m **No.of Employees:** 21 - 50
Product Groups: 26, 27, 30, 37, 40, 49, 66

Date of Accounts	Feb 12	Feb 11	Feb 10
Working Capital	124	-58	-164
Fixed Assets	804	844	890
Current Assets	921	1m	1m

Rema Tip Top Industry UK Ltd
Mill Lane Coppull, Chorley, PR7 5AW
Tel: 01257-793487 **Fax:** 01257-793930
E-mail: steve.norris@tip-top.co.uk
Website: http://tiptop.co.uk
Bank(s): Nat West
Managers: S. Norris (Mgr)
Immediate Holding Company: REMA TIP TOP INDUSTRY UK LIMITED
Registration no: 01176719 **VAT No.:** GB 210 4736 05
Date established: 1974 **Turnover:** £500,000 - £1m
No.of Employees: 21 - 50 **Product Groups:** 29, 30

Date of Accounts	Dec 11	Dec 10	Dec 09
Sales Turnover	10m	10m	11m
Pre Tax Profit/Loss	293	-151	-154
Working Capital	-587	-948	-1000
Fixed Assets	1m	1m	2m
Current Assets	4m	4m	4m
Current Liabilities	750	661	426

Rustic Touch Ltd
453 Preston Road Clayton-Le-Woods, Chorley, PR6 7JD
Tel: 01772-698175 **Fax:** 01257-220498
E-mail: sales@rustictouch.co.uk
Website: http://www.rustictouch.co.uk
Directors: R. Oliver (MD)
Immediate Holding Company: RUSTIC TOUCH LIMITED
Registration no: 05709533 **Date established:** 2006
Turnover: Up to £250,000 **No.of Employees:** 1 - 10 **Product Groups:** 39

Date of Accounts	Apr 11	Apr 10	Apr 09
Working Capital	-4	13	N/A
Fixed Assets	7	7	9
Current Assets	46	63	38

Ruttle Plant Ltd
Lancaster House Ackhurst Road, Chorley, PR7 1NH
Tel: 01257-266511 **Fax:** 01257-260625
E-mail: sales@ruttle.co.uk
Website: http://www.ruttle.co.uk
Directors: G. Ruttle (Dir), M. Ruttle (Dir)
Managers: N. Deal
Ultimate Holding Company: RUTTLE PLANT HOLDINGS LIMITED
Immediate Holding Company: RUTTLE PLANT HOLDINGS LIMITED
Registration no: 01333237 **Date established:** 1977 **Turnover:** £5m - £10m
No.of Employees: 51 - 100 **Product Groups:** 41, 45, 67, 83

Date of Accounts	Sep 11	Sep 10	Sep 09
Sales Turnover	6m	7m	17m
Pre Tax Profit/Loss	-602	-488	1m
Working Capital	5m	4m	-2m
Fixed Assets	21m	22m	23m
Current Assets	23m	21m	26m
Current Liabilities	7m	4m	6m

Rxpharma
17 Bury Lane Withnell, Chorley, PR6 8RX
Tel: 01254-832321 **Fax:** 01254-832322
E-mail: info@rxpharma.co.uk
Website: http://www.rxpharma.com
Directors: P. Williams (Prop)
Date established: 2006 **No.of Employees:** 1 - 10 **Product Groups:** 31

S & S Northern Ltd
Dickinsons Industrial Estate Moss Lane, Coppull, Chorley, PR7 5AL
Tel: 01257-470 983 **Fax:** 01257-471 937
E-mail: steve@snsnorthern.com
Website: http://www.snsnorthern.com
Directors: S. McMahon (MD)
Immediate Holding Company: S & S NORTHERN LIMITED
Registration no: 03000888 **Date established:** 1994
No.of Employees: 1 - 10 **Product Groups:** 38

Date of Accounts	Mar 11	Mar 10	Mar 09
Working Capital	-27	-47	-78
Fixed Assets	55	56	44
Current Assets	196	179	116

Sal Abrasives Technologies
44-45 Drumhead Road Chorley North Industrial Park, Chorley, PR6 7BX
Tel: 01257-271914 **Fax:** 01257-260702
E-mail: abrasives@salgroup.co.uk
Website: http://www.salgroup.co.uk
Bank(s): Lloyds TSB, Wigan
Directors: J. Handley (MD)
Ultimate Holding Company: SAL GROUP 2008 LIMITED
Immediate Holding Company: SAL ABRASIVE TECHNOLOGIES GROUP LIMITED
Registration no: 00939860 **Date established:** 1968 **Turnover:** £2m - £5m
No.of Employees: 11 - 20 **Product Groups:** 33, 36, 40, 47

Date of Accounts	Sep 11	Sep 10	Sep 09
Working Capital	416	430	515
Fixed Assets	94	90	82
Current Assets	2m	1m	1m
Current Liabilities	528	423	353

Scorpion Automotive Ltd
Drumhead Road Chorley North Business Park, Chorley, PR6 7DE
Tel: 01257-249928 **Fax:** 01257-249938
E-mail: info@scorpionauto.com
Website: http://www.scorpionauto.com
Managers: G. Cirby (Sales Prom Mgr), R. Andrews (Sales & Mktg Mg), K. Hicklen (Purch Mgr), S. Kavanagh
Immediate Holding Company: SCORPION AUTOMOTIVE LIMITED
Registration no: 06969452 **Date established:** 2009
No.of Employees: 21 - 50 **Product Groups:** 37, 40, 67, 68

Date of Accounts	Aug 11	Aug 10
Working Capital	339	81
Fixed Assets	517	459
Current Assets	2m	2m

Shackerley Holdings Group Ltd
139 Wigan Road Euxton, Chorley, PR7 6JH
Tel: 01257-273114 **Fax:** 01257-262386
E-mail: info@shackerley.com
Website: http://www.shackerley.com
Directors: S. Newell (Comm)
Ultimate Holding Company: SHACKERLEY (HOLDINGS) GROUP LIMITED
Immediate Holding Company: SHACKERLEY (HOLDINGS) GROUP LIMITED
Registration no: 01704765 **VAT No.:** 379 7940 81 **Date established:** 1983
Turnover: £2m - £5m **No.of Employees:** 101 - 250 **Product Groups:** 33

Date of Accounts	Dec 11	Dec 10	Dec 09
Working Capital	1m	1m	763
Fixed Assets	444	253	308
Current Assets	2m	2m	1m

P Singleton
Holmes Farm Sandy Lane, Brindle, Chorley, PR6 8LZ
Tel: 01772-324268 **Fax:** 01772-620770
Directors: P. Singleton (Prop)
Date established: 1966 **No.of Employees:** 1 - 10 **Product Groups:** 41, 46

Solarfilm Sales Ltd
Common Bank Industrial Estate Ackhurst Road, Chorley, PR7 1NH
Tel: 01257-267418 **Fax:** 01257-276203
E-mail: info@solarfilm.co.uk
Website: http://www.solarfilm.co.uk
Directors: S. Lord (Fin)
Managers: V. Hardman (Sales Admin)
Immediate Holding Company: ANDREW HARDMAN SOLARFILM LIMITED
Registration no: 01717493 **VAT No.:** GB 379 8196 81
Date established: 1983 **Turnover:** £1m - £2m **No.of Employees:** 1 - 10
Product Groups: 30

Date of Accounts	Mar 11	Mar 10	Mar 09
Working Capital	130	123	68
Current Assets	170	344	690

Tapeswitch Ltd
38 Drumhead Road Chorley North Industrial Park, Chorley, PR6 7BX
Tel: 01257-249777 **Fax:** 01257-246600
E-mail: info@tapeswitch.co.uk
Website: http://www.tapeswitch.co.uk
Bank(s): National Westminster Bank Plc
Directors: J. Park (Co Sec), J. Wignall (MD)
Managers: G. Davies (Sales Prom Mgr), J. Cowley (Tech Serv Mgr)
Ultimate Holding Company: ROWAN TECHNOLOGIES INC (USA)
Immediate Holding Company: TAPESWITCH LTD.
Registration no: 02481808 **VAT No.:** GB 534 3745 44
Date established: 1990 **Turnover:** £1m - £2m **No.of Employees:** 21 - 50
Product Groups: 40

Date of Accounts	Dec 11	Dec 10	Dec 09
Working Capital	800	919	979
Fixed Assets	687	719	741
Current Assets	993	1m	1m

Taylor & Taylor
Unit 1 1 Mill Lane Whittle-le-Woods, Chorley, PR6 7LX
Tel: 01257-260360 **Fax:** 01257-260360
E-mail: enquiries@gtaylorandtaylor.co.uk
Website: http://www.gtaylorandtaylor.co.uk
Directors: G. Taylor (Prop)
Date established: 1979 **No.of Employees:** 1 - 10 **Product Groups:** 26, 35

Taylor Transformers Ltd
Unit 2-6 Common Bank Industrial Estate Ackhurst Road, Chorley, PR7 1NH
Tel: 01257-270230 **Fax:** 01257-241049
E-mail: sales@taylor-transformers.co.uk
Website: http://www.taylor-transformers.co.uk
Directors: A. Taylor (MD), D. Taylor (Dir), R. Taylor (Dir)
Immediate Holding Company: TAYLOR TRANSFORMERS LIMITED
Registration no: 02053809 **Date established:** 1986 **Turnover:** £1m - £2m
No.of Employees: 21 - 50 **Product Groups:** 27, 30, 35, 37, 49, 67

Date of Accounts	Mar 12	Mar 11	Mar 10
Working Capital	10	-1	1
Fixed Assets	90	99	107
Current Assets	400	408	354
Current Liabilities	73	67	N/A

Unit Two Systems
25-27 Foster Street, Chorley, PR6 0AY
Tel: 01257-268628 **Fax:** 01257-268628
E-mail: glynnhughes2004@yahoo.co.uk
Directors: B. Hughes (Ptnr)
Date established: 1980 **No.of Employees:** 1 - 10 **Product Groups:** 52

Verde Sports Cricket Ltd
Gabbotts Farm Bury Lane, Withnell, Chorley, PR6 8SW
Tel: 01254-831666 **Fax:** 01254-831066
E-mail: sales@verdesports.com
Website: http://www.verdesports.com

see next page

***Verde Sports Cricket Ltd** - Cont'd*

Directors: P. Dury (MD)
Immediate Holding Company: VERDE SPORTS (CRICKET) LIMITED
Registration no: 03013348 **VAT No.:** GB 483 0908 36
Date established: 1995 **No.of Employees:** 1 - 10 **Product Groups:** 23, 49

Date of Accounts	Mar 12	Mar 11	Mar 10
Working Capital	80	80	77
Fixed Assets	N/A	1	1
Current Assets	141	231	188

W L Cunliffe Southport Ltd
Unit K1-K4 Buckshaw Link Ordnance Road, Buckshaw Village, Chorley, PR7 7EL
Tel: 01772-622444 **Fax:** 01695-711811
E-mail: north@productionglassfibre.co.uk
Website: http://www.productionglassfibre.co.uk
Bank(s): Royal Bank of Scotland, Ormskirk
Directors: I. Khan (Fin), S. Grossi (MD)
Managers: A. Hill (Sales & Mktg Mg), C. Mellor (Buyer)
Ultimate Holding Company: CARLINGNOSE LIMITED
Immediate Holding Company: W.L.CUNLIFFE(SOUTHPORT)LIMITED
Registration no: 00740787 **VAT No.:** GB 152 1539 87
Date established: 1962 **Turnover:** £2m - £5m **No.of Employees:** 51 - 100
Product Groups: 30, 33, 39, 40, 48

Date of Accounts	May 11	May 10	May 09
Working Capital	-582	416	469
Fixed Assets	599	76	115
Current Assets	965	822	989

W S Electrical Contractors
Unit 6 East Chorley Business Centre East Way, Chorley, PR6 0BJ
Tel: 01257-272688 **Fax:** 01257-272698
Directors: S. Wright (Ptnr), S. Wright (Snr Part)
Date established: 2004 **No.of Employees:** 11 - 20 **Product Groups:** 36, 40

Woodfit Ltd
Kem Mill Kem Mill Lane, Whittle-le-Woods, Chorley, PR6 7EA
Tel: 01257-266421 **Fax:** 01257-264271
E-mail: sales@woodfit.com
Website: http://www.woodfit.com
Bank(s): HSBC Bank plc
Directors: B. Robinson (MD), W. Robinson (MD)
Managers: P. Robinson (Sales Admin), P. Marland (Purch Mgr)
Ultimate Holding Company: DOVEMENS LIMITED
Immediate Holding Company: WOODFIT LIMITED
Registration no: 01174678 **VAT No.:** GB 156 1633 71
Date established: 1974 **Turnover:** £2m - £5m **No.of Employees:** 21 - 50
Product Groups: 25, 26, 30, 35, 36

Date of Accounts	Jun 11	Jun 10	Jun 09
Working Capital	842	936	877
Fixed Assets	1m	1m	1m
Current Assets	2m	2m	2m

Xyone LTD
P.O Box 495, Chorley, PR6 6DL
Tel: 0845-6154400 **Fax:** 01257-417280
E-mail: info@xyone.co.uk
Website: http://www.xyone.com
Directors: S. Robinson (MD)
Managers: A. Lancaster (Mktg Serv Mgr), B. Lomax (I.T. Exec)
Registration no: 04086209 **No.of Employees:** 1 - 10 **Product Groups:** 80, 81

Clitheroe

Alexanders
9 Woodlands Drive Whalley, Clitheroe, BB7 9TG
Tel: 01254-825880
E-mail: jonathen@alexanders-uk.com
Website: http://www.alexanders-uk.com
Directors: A. McCrerie (Prop)
Date established: 1993 **No.of Employees:** 1 - 10 **Product Groups:** 35

Autool Grinders Ltd
Padiham Road Sabden, Clitheroe, BB7 9EW
Tel: 01282-775000 **Fax:** 01282-773486
E-mail: p.varley@autool.co.uk
Website: http://www.autool.co.uk
Directors: P. Varley (MD), E. Smith (Fin)
Immediate Holding Company: AUTOOL GRINDERS LIMITED
Registration no: 04105508 **Date established:** 2000
Turnover: £250,000 - £500,000 **No.of Employees:** 1 - 10
Product Groups: 46, 47

Date of Accounts	Mar 11	Mar 10	Mar 09
Working Capital	38	30	34
Fixed Assets	7	8	9
Current Assets	140	119	126

Clitheroe Light Engineering
Unit C Up Brooks, Clitheroe, BB7 1PL
Tel: 01200-422707 **Fax:** 01200-425517
E-mail: info@clitheroelightengineering.co.uk
Website: http://www.clitheroelightengineering.co.uk
Bank(s): National Westminster Bank Plc
Managers: H. Meloy (Chief Mgr)
VAT No.: GB 175 4730 50 **Date established:** 1973 **Turnover:** £1m - £2m
No.of Employees: 21 - 50 **Product Groups:** 48

Date of Accounts	Dec 07	Dec 06	Dec 05
Working Capital	-320	-280	-236
Fixed Assets	1563	1450	1165
Current Assets	410	308	328
Current Liabilities	730	588	563

Clitheroe Lighting Centre
14 Moor Lane, Clitheroe, BB7 1BE
Tel: 01200-423757 **Fax:** 01200-423757
E-mail: leeisherwood@live.co.uk
Website: http://www.clitheroelightingcentre.co.uk
Directors: L. Isherwood (Prop)
Date established: 1983 **No.of Employees:** 1 - 10 **Product Groups:** 37, 38

Date of Accounts	May 06	May 05
Working Capital	-2	2
Fixed Assets	18	20
Current Assets	55	57
Current Liabilities	57	55

Dugdale Nutrition Ltd
Bellman Mill Salthill, Clitheroe, BB7 1QW
Tel: 01200-420200 **Fax:** 01200-428975
E-mail: info@dugdalenutrition.com
Website: http://www.dugdalenutrition.com
Bank(s): Barclays, Clitheroe
Directors: M. Dugdale (MD), M. Townend (Fin)
Managers: R. Dugdale, H. Dugdale, M. Collinge (Tech Serv Mgr)
Ultimate Holding Company: B. DUGDALE & SON LIMITED
Immediate Holding Company: DUGDALE NUTRITION LIMITED
Registration no: 00294023 **Date established:** 1934
Turnover: £20m - £50m **No.of Employees:** 21 - 50 **Product Groups:** 62

Date of Accounts	Apr 12	Apr 11	Apr 10
Sales Turnover	27m	24m	19m
Pre Tax Profit/Loss	600	1m	530
Working Capital	165	191	518
Fixed Assets	2m	2m	2m
Current Assets	5m	5m	4m
Current Liabilities	475	772	346

First Exhibitions Direct Ltd
Unit 14 The Sidings Whalley, Clitheroe, BB7 9SE
Tel: 07721-619123 **Fax:** 01254-824854
E-mail: sales@designer-gifts.co.uk
Immediate Holding Company: FIRST EXHIBITIONS DIRECT LIMITED
Registration no: 04680010 **Date established:** 2003
No.of Employees: 1 - 10 **Product Groups:** 81

Date of Accounts	Apr 11	Apr 10	Apr 09
Working Capital	-8	-6	-6
Fixed Assets	6	7	7
Current Assets	1	7	10

L Gooding
High Beech House Crow Trees Brow, Chatburn, Clitheroe, BB7 4AA
Tel: 01200-440322 **Fax:** 01200-440323
Directors: L. Gooding (Prop)
Immediate Holding Company: PRIMET PARKLANDS LIMITED
Registration no: 03297662 **Date established:** 1997
No.of Employees: 1 - 10 **Product Groups:** 35

Date of Accounts	Sep 11	Sep 10	Sep 09
Working Capital	23	8	4
Fixed Assets	4	4	5
Current Assets	40	25	20

Harrison Welding & Engineering Supplies
Kendal Street, Clitheroe, BB7 1PA
Tel: 01200-424360 **Fax:** 01200-427529
E-mail: peter@hcwes.co.uk
Website: http://www.hcwes.co.uk
Directors: P. Croft (Prop)
Date established: 1974 **No.of Employees:** 1 - 10 **Product Groups:** 46

L I P Harrison
North Street, Clitheroe, BB7 1PG
Tel: 01200-426185 **Fax:** 01200-426185
E-mail: laurieharrison@talktalk.net
Directors: L. Harrison (Prop)
Immediate Holding Company: 4KIDS LIMITED
Date established: 2007 **No.of Employees:** 1 - 10 **Product Groups:** 37, 67

Date of Accounts	Mar 11	Mar 10
Working Capital	-23	-24
Fixed Assets	22	23
Current Assets	6	3

Lodematic Group
1-3 Works Primrose Road, Clitheroe, BB7 1BS
Tel: 01200-422233 **Fax:** 01200-429292
E-mail: clive@lodematic.co.uk
Website: http://www.lodematic.co.uk
Directors: C. Thompson (MD)
Registration no: 00716807 **No.of Employees:** 21 - 50
Product Groups: 40, 84

Mantle Packaging Machinery Ltd
Units 1-2 The Sidings Whalley, Clitheroe, BB7 9SE
Tel: 01254-824992 **Fax:** 01254-824994
E-mail: info@mantlepackaging.co.uk
Website: http://www.mantlepackaging.co.uk
Directors: C. Mantle (Dir)
Immediate Holding Company: MANTLE PACKAGING MACHINERY LIMITED
Registration no: 03371709 **Date established:** 1997
No.of Employees: 1 - 10 **Product Groups:** 42

Date of Accounts	Apr 12	Apr 11	Apr 10
Working Capital	114	110	72
Fixed Assets	21	25	28
Current Assets	239	257	189

N & J Aluminium Linings Ltd
Unit 9-11 Deanfield Court Link 59 Business Park, Clitheroe, BB7 1QS
Tel: 01200-429955 **Fax:** 01200-427680
E-mail: info@njaluminiumlinings.co.uk
Website: http://www.nj4x4.co.uk
Directors: J. Buchanan (Dir)
Immediate Holding Company: N & J ALUMINIUM LININGS LTD
Registration no: 04451912 **Date established:** 2002
No.of Employees: 1 - 10 **Product Groups:** 35, 39, 48

Date of Accounts	May 11	May 10	May 09
Working Capital	-65	-58	-52
Fixed Assets	300	328	344
Current Assets	125	80	54

R V Fire Systems
Unit 17 Deanfield Court Link 59 Business Park, Clitheroe, BB7 1QS
Tel: 01200-428400 **Fax:** 01200-428004
E-mail: info@rvfiresystems.co.uk
Website: http://www.rvfiresystems.co.uk
Directors: F. Potter (Ptnr)
Immediate Holding Company: R V FIRE SYSTEMS LIMITED
Registration no: 06390266 **Date established:** 2007
Turnover: £250,000 - £500,000 **No.of Employees:** 1 - 10
Product Groups: 40, 67

Ribble Valley Homes Ltd
21 Manor Road, Clitheroe, BB7 2LH
Tel: 01200-427966
E-mail: a.hodgson1@gmail.com
Website: http://hogroastlancashire.co.uk
Managers: L. Baldwin (Mgr)
Date established: 2004 **Turnover:** Up to £250,000
No.of Employees: 1 - 10 **Product Groups:** 69

Spiroflow Ltd
Lincoln Way, Clitheroe, BB7 1QG
Tel: 01200-422525 **Fax:** 01200-429165
E-mail: sales@spiroflow.com
Website: http://www.spiroflow.com
Bank(s): Lloyds TSB Bank plc
Directors: A. Wilson (Fin)
Managers: F. Iqbal (Tech Serv Mgr), K. Vincent (Sales Prom Mgr)
Ultimate Holding Company: SPIROFLOW LIMITED
Immediate Holding Company: SPIROFLOW UK LIMITED
Registration no: 03976317 **VAT No.:** GB 732 9112 49
Date established: 2000 **Turnover:** £1m - £2m **No.of Employees:** 21 - 50
Product Groups: 41, 42, 45

Suppression Devices
Unit 8 York Street Business Centre, Clitheroe, BB7 2DL
Tel: 01200-444497 **Fax:** 01200-444330
E-mail: sales@suppression-devices.com
Website: http://www.suppression-devices.com
Directors: C. Barker (Prop)
Immediate Holding Company: SUPPRESSION DEVICES LIMITED
Registration no: 05355828 **Date established:** 2005
Turnover: Up to £250,000 **No.of Employees:** 1 - 10 **Product Groups:** 37, 38

Telsa Sheet Metal Ltd
Fishes & Peggy Hill Farm Henthorn Road, Clitheroe, BB7 3BY
Tel: 07803-587714
E-mail: tommoathome47@btinternet.com
Directors: S. Tomlinson (MD)
No.of Employees: 1 - 10 **Product Groups:** 37, 40, 48

Trutex plc
Jubilee Mill Taylor Street, Clitheroe, BB7 1NL
Tel: 01200-421200 **Fax:** 01200-421209
E-mail: sales@trutex.com
Website: http://www.trutex.com
Directors: M. Betts (Fin)
Managers: R. Mullings (Buyer), C. Riggs (Mktg Serv Mgr), J. Broadley (Personnel)
Ultimate Holding Company: TRUTEX INVESTMENTS LIMITED
Immediate Holding Company: TRUTEX LIMITED
Registration no: 07132787 **VAT No.:** GB 690 0377 36
Date established: 2010 **Turnover:** £10m - £20m
No.of Employees: 101 - 250 **Product Groups:** 24

Date of Accounts	Dec 11	Dec 10
Sales Turnover	20m	16m
Pre Tax Profit/Loss	-222	-991
Working Capital	729	1m
Fixed Assets	3m	2m
Current Assets	5m	3m
Current Liabilities	2m	2m

Ultraframe
Enterprise Works Salthill Road, Clitheroe, BB7 1PE
Tel: 01200-443311 **Fax:** 01200-442991
E-mail: info@ultraframe.co.uk
Website: http://www.ultraframe-conservatories.co.uk
Directors: D. Saunders (Fin), I. Thomson (MD), J. Martoccia (Sales)
Managers: G. Ferguson (Chief Mgr), S. Holt (Personnel)
Ultimate Holding Company: LATIUM PLASTICS ENTERPRISES LIMITED
Immediate Holding Company: ULTRAFRAME LIMITED
Registration no: 03330992 **VAT No.:** GB 628 9454 00
Date established: 1997 **Turnover:** £75m - £125m
No.of Employees: 101 - 250 **Product Groups:** 35

Date of Accounts	Oct 10	Oct 09	Oct 08
Pre Tax Profit/Loss	N/A	N/A	-21m
Working Capital	4	4	4
Fixed Assets	14m	14m	14m
Current Assets	4	4	4

Whalley Catering Equipment
Unit 1 Meadow Court Whalley Industrial Park Clitheroe Road, Barrow, Clitheroe, BB7 9AE
Tel: 01254-822165 **Fax:** 01254-823113
Directors: I. Collier (Prop)
Date established: 1980 **No.of Employees:** 1 - 10 **Product Groups:** 20, 40, 41

Colne

Brian Sutcliffe Packaging Ltd
Clarence Street, Colne, BB8 0PP
Tel: 01282-863088 **Fax:** 01282-870390
E-mail: sales@bs-packaging.co.uk
Website: http://www.bs-packaging.co.uk
Directors: A. Sutcliffe (Fin), B. Sutcliffe (MD)
Immediate Holding Company: BRIAN SUTCLIFFE PACKAGING LIMITED
Registration no: 03934867 **Date established:** 2000
No.of Employees: 1 - 10 **Product Groups:** 27, 30, 45

Date of Accounts	Mar 11	Mar 10	Mar 09
Working Capital	36	40	46
Fixed Assets	17	25	9
Current Assets	210	202	179

Builder Center Ltd
Regent Street, Colne, BB8 8LJ
Tel: 01282-869899 **Fax:** 01282-831723
E-mail: admin@buildercenter.co.uk
Website: http://www.buildcenter.co.uk
Directors: S. Davies (MD)
Managers: A. Scarborough (District Mgr), J. Walters (District Mgr), M. Slater (District Mgr)
Ultimate Holding Company: Wolseley plc
Immediate Holding Company: BUILD CENTER LIMITED
Registration no: 00462397 **Date established:** 1948
Turnover: Over £1,000m **No.of Employees:** 11 - 20 **Product Groups:** 66

Calderbank Coach Painters
Calderbank Mill Greenfield Road, Colne, BB8 9PD
Tel: 01282-864050 **Fax:** 01282-864050
E-mail: calderbankcp@btconnect.com

Directors: G. Wearden (MD), E. Wearden (Fin)
Immediate Holding Company: CALDERBANK COACH PAINTERS LIMITED
Registration no: 04945214 **Date established:** 2003
No.of Employees: 1 - 10 **Product Groups:** 46, 48

Date of Accounts	Dec 11	Dec 10	Dec 09
Working Capital	-9	-14	-14
Fixed Assets	10	16	22
Current Assets	6	6	11

Colne Anodising Co. Ltd
Calder Mill Green Road, Colne, BB8 8AL
Tel: 01282-867300 **Fax:** 01282-867407
E-mail: sales@colneanodising.co.uk
Website: http://www.colneanodising.co.uk
Directors: P. Starkie (Prop), P. Starky (MD), B. Pickles (MD), G. Pickles (Fin), P. Starkie (MD)
Immediate Holding Company: COLNE ANODISING COMPANY LIMITED
Registration no: 04358957 **Date established:** 2002 **Turnover:** £1m - £2m
No.of Employees: 11 - 20 **Product Groups:** 48

Date of Accounts	Jan 07	Jan 06
Working Capital	-200	-296
Fixed Assets	376	415
Current Assets	392	349
Current Liabilities	592	645
Total Share Capital	124	124

Dent Instrumentation Ltd
Enterprise Way Whitewalls Industrial Estate, Colne, BB8 8LY
Tel: 01282-862703 **Fax:** 01282-862037
E-mail: andrew.dent@dentsensors.com
Website: http://www.dentsensors.com
Directors: A. Dent (MD), D. Thwaites (I.T. Dir), I. Farquhar (Fin)
Immediate Holding Company: DENT INSTRUMENTATION LIMITED
Registration no: 01539660 **Date established:** 1981
No.of Employees: 21 - 50 **Product Groups:** 38

Date of Accounts	Feb 12	Feb 11	Feb 10
Working Capital	698	672	505
Fixed Assets	826	647	599
Current Assets	998	1m	793

E A Foulds Ltd
Clifton Street, Colne, BB8 9AE
Tel: 01282-861500 **Fax:** 01282-869655
E-mail: info@fouldslifts.co.uk
Website: http://www.fouldslifts.co.uk
Directors: E. Foulds (Co Sec)
Managers: H. Foulds (Chief Mgr)
Immediate Holding Company: E.A. FOULDS LIMITED
Registration no: 00274169 **VAT No.:** GB 174 3069 62
Date established: 1933 **Turnover:** £2m - £5m **No.of Employees:** 1 - 10
Product Groups: 45

Date of Accounts	Dec 11	Dec 10	Dec 09
Sales Turnover	3m	N/A	N/A
Pre Tax Profit/Loss	172	N/A	N/A
Working Capital	238	45	5
Fixed Assets	342	364	431
Current Assets	627	507	494
Current Liabilities	138	N/A	N/A

Kelbrook Shooting Lodge
Foulridge, Colne, BB8 7QH
Tel: 01282-861632 **Fax:** 01282-861632
E-mail: aaronmeggison@hotmail.com
Website: http://www.kelbrook.com
Directors: A. Meggison (Ptnr)
Date established: 1982 **No.of Employees:** 1 - 10 **Product Groups:** 36, 39, 40

Kevin Guy Plant Hire Ltd
Shaygate Farm Skipton Old Road, Colne, BB8 7EW
Tel: 01282-861166 **Fax:** 01282-866879
E-mail: kevinguyplanthire@googlemail.com
Website: http://www.tower-crane-hire.com
Directors: K. Guy (MD)
Immediate Holding Company: KEVIN GUY PLANT HIRE LIMITED
Registration no: 04509531 **Date established:** 2002
No.of Employees: 1 - 10 **Product Groups:** 45, 83, 86

Date of Accounts	Sep 11	Sep 10	Sep 09
Working Capital	-15	54	33
Fixed Assets	531	373	417
Current Assets	183	198	136

M.C. TEC Limited
PO Box 1067, Colne, BB9 4DD
Tel: 01282-798086 **Fax:** 01282-798224
E-mail: info@mctec.nl
Website: http://www.mctec.nl
Managers: M. Warner (Sales Prom Mgr)
Registration no: 05095274 **Date established:** 2007
No.of Employees: 1 - 10 **Product Groups:** 67

Mitchell Interflex Ltd
County Brook Mill County Brook Lane, Foulridge, Colne, BB8 7LT
Tel: 01282-813221 **Fax:** 01282-813633
E-mail: adrian@mitchell-interflex.co.uk
Website: http://www.mitchell-interflex.co.uk
Bank(s): National Westminster
Directors: A. Mitchell (Fin), L. Mitchell (Dir)
Ultimate Holding Company: COUNTY BROOK LIMITED
Immediate Holding Company: MITCHELL INTERFLEX LIMITED
Registration no: 02724470 **VAT No.:** GB 325 4341 80
Date established: 1992 **Turnover:** £2m - £5m **No.of Employees:** 21 - 50
Product Groups: 23

Date of Accounts	Aug 11	Aug 10	Aug 09
Working Capital	836	789	698
Fixed Assets	218	177	931
Current Assets	2m	2m	1m

Northstar Design & Printing.Com
Suite 1 The Exchange, 15 Spring Lane, Colne, BB8 9BD
Tel: 01282-865333 **Fax:** 01282-860201
E-mail: ideas@northstardesign.co.uk
Website: http://www.northstardesign.co.uk
Directors: J. Lambley (Ptnr), M. Lamle (Dir)
Turnover: £250,000 - £500,000 **No.of Employees:** 1 - 10
Product Groups: 81

Pendle Nu Tech
Old School House School Lane, Laneshawbridge, Colne, BB8 7EQ
Tel: 01282-861111 **Fax:** 01282-871113
Directors: D. Hadfield (MD)
Immediate Holding Company: PENDLE NU TECH LIMITED
Registration no: 03995386 **Date established:** 2000
No.of Employees: 1 - 10 **Product Groups:** 38, 42

Date of Accounts	Mar 12	Mar 11	Mar 10
Working Capital	72	71	68
Fixed Assets	13	15	18
Current Assets	110	105	108

Pendle Polymer Engineering Ltd
Vulcan Works Warehouse Lane, Foulridge, Colne, BB8 7PP
Tel: 01282-868916 **Fax:** 01282-870529
E-mail: tony.bielby@pendlepolymer.co.uk
Website: http://www.pendlepolymer.co.uk
Bank(s): HSBC
Directors: N. Burton (Fin), A. Bielby (MD)
Managers: S. Bielby
Ultimate Holding Company: PENDLE FLUID SEALING LIMITED
Immediate Holding Company: PENDLE POLYMER ENGINEERING LIMITED
Registration no: 02265026 **VAT No.:** GB 498 0069 15
Date established: 1988 **Turnover:** £2m - £5m **No.of Employees:** 51 - 100
Product Groups: 29, 30

Date of Accounts	May 11	May 10	May 09
Working Capital	922	765	669
Fixed Assets	426	497	583
Current Assets	2m	1m	1m

Pennine Blade Polishers
3 Enterprise Way Whitewalls Industrial Estate, Colne, BB8 8LY
Tel: 01282-865005 **Fax:** 01282-865335
E-mail: wayne@pennineblade polishers.co.uk
Website: http://www.pennineblade polishers.co.uk
Directors: W. Miles (Dir)
Date established: 1999 **No.of Employees:** 11 - 20 **Product Groups:** 46, 48

Riley Lifting Equipment Ltd
Hope Building Dockray Street, Colne, BB8 9HT
Tel: 01282-867177 **Fax:** 01282-863698
E-mail: info@superclamp.co.uk
Website: http://www.superclamp.co.uk
Bank(s): HSBC
Directors: S. Riley (MD)
Immediate Holding Company: RILEY (LIFTING EQUIPMENT) LIMITED
Registration no: 01526219 **VAT No.:** GB 326 1380 79
Date established: 1980 **Turnover:** £500,000 - £1m
No.of Employees: 11 - 20 **Product Groups:** 35, 36, 45

Date of Accounts	May 11	May 10	May 09
Working Capital	908	958	785
Fixed Assets	275	282	267
Current Assets	1m	1m	875

Studio Bretherton Artworks & Photography
4 Sydney Terrace Trawden, Colne, BB8 8RH
Tel: 01282-861741
E-mail: maxbretherton@onetel.net.uk
Directors: M. Bretherton (Prop)
Date established: 2006 **Turnover:** Up to £250,000
No.of Employees: 1 - 10 **Product Groups:** 37, 44, 79, 81, 89

Trevon Industrial Finishers Ltd
Unit 4 Regent Street Whitewalls Industrial Estate, Colne, BB8 8LJ
Tel: 01282-861786 **Fax:** 01282-863829
E-mail: trevor.crabtree@virgin.net
Website: http://www.trevonpowdercoaters.co.uk
Directors: J. Crabtree (Co Sec), T. Crabtree (MD)
Ultimate Holding Company: TREVON INDUSTRIAL FINISHERS (HOLDINGS) LIMITED
Immediate Holding Company: TREVON INDUSTRIAL FINISHERS LIMITED
Registration no: 01209523 **Date established:** 1975
No.of Employees: 21 - 50 **Product Groups:** 46, 48

Date of Accounts	May 11	May 10	May 09
Working Capital	179	140	209
Fixed Assets	80	55	194
Current Assets	295	275	291

Venchem Ltd
Green Road, Colne, BB8 8AJ
Tel: 01282-861198 **Fax:** 01282-860020
E-mail: sales@venchem.co.uk
Website: http://www.venchem.co.uk
Directors: G. Ashworth (Co Sec), J. Ashworth (MD)
Immediate Holding Company: VENCHEM LIMITED
Registration no: 02063397 **VAT No.:** GB 634 1290 61
Date established: 1986 **Turnover:** £250,000 - £500,000
No.of Employees: 1 - 10 **Product Groups:** 31, 32

Date of Accounts	Dec 11	Dec 10	Dec 09
Working Capital	111	69	31
Fixed Assets	29	27	19
Current Assets	223	139	97

Wolseley Timber Center
Timber Centre Regent Street, Colne, BB8 8LJ
Tel: 01204-385232 **Fax:** 01204-392306
E-mail: t2e.colne@wolseley.co.uk
Website: http://www.capperplastics.com
Bank(s): Llyods
Managers: R. Nash (District Mgr)
Registration no: 00636445 **VAT No.:** GB 351 0233 93
Turnover: £250m - £500m **No.of Employees:** 11 - 20
Product Groups: 08, 25, 66

Darwen

Art Metals Darwen
Unit 9 Gillibrand Mill Hollins Grove Street, Darwen, BB3 1HG
Tel: 01254-706706 **Fax:** 01254-706706
E-mail: info@artmetalsdarwen.co.uk
Directors: S. Shore (Prop)
Date established: 1972 **No.of Employees:** 1 - 10 **Product Groups:** 26, 35

Astley Bank Welding
Unit 1a Cotton Hall Street, Darwen, BB3 0DW
Tel: 01254-775066 **Fax:** 01254-775066
E-mail: astleybank@fsmail.net
Directors: J. Kelly (Prop)
Immediate Holding Company: BROOKS & COMPANY (BODYBUILDERS) LIMITED
Registration no: 04809699 **Date established:** 2003
Turnover: £250,000 - £500,000 **No.of Employees:** 1 - 10
Product Groups: 26, 35

Date of Accounts	Mar 12	Mar 11	Mar 10
Working Capital	13	23	32
Fixed Assets	14	11	13
Current Assets	53	65	80

Canopies Scotland
1 Chanters Way, Darwen, BB3 0GY
Tel: 01254-761294 **Fax:** 01254-775747
E-mail: info@canopies-uk.com
Website: http://www.canopiesuk.co.uk
Directors: R. Eastwood (Ch), E. Morris (MD)
Immediate Holding Company: CANOPIES UK LIMITED
Registration no: 02472327 **VAT No.:** GB 572 2392 40
Date established: 1990 **Turnover:** £1m - £2m **No.of Employees:** 1 - 10
Product Groups: 30

Date of Accounts	Dec 11	Dec 10	Dec 09
Working Capital	467	1m	2m
Fixed Assets	228	2m	2m
Current Assets	1m	2m	3m

Chapman Envelopes Ltd
Waterside Business Park Johnson Road, Eccleshill, Darwen, BB3 3RT
Tel: 01254-682387 **Fax:** 01254-775920
E-mail: sales@heritage-envelopes.co.uk
Website: http://www.chapman-envelopes.co.uk
Directors: T. Whittaker (MD), S. Bromley (Co Sec), R. Kavangh (MD), R. Kavanagh (MD), P. Blasenheur (Ch), J. Pettier (Grp Chief Exec), F. Glaizal (Dir)
Managers: P. Bryan (Sales Prom Mgr), M. Gwilt (Purch Mgr), C. Burche (I.T. Exec), C. Clapier (Mktg Serv Mgr)
Ultimate Holding Company: GPV SA (FRANCE)
Immediate Holding Company: CHAPMAN ENVELOPES LIMITED
Registration no: 03800352 **VAT No.:** GB 217 8528 47
Date established: 1999 **Turnover:** £10m - £20m
No.of Employees: 51 - 100 **Product Groups:** 27

Date of Accounts	Dec 10	Dec 09	Dec 08
Sales Turnover	12m	14m	13m
Pre Tax Profit/Loss	-787	303	-469
Working Capital	-979	-303	-1m
Fixed Assets	388	532	1m
Current Assets	5m	8m	7m
Current Liabilities	2m	3m	3m

Ekm Systems Ltd
Unit 6 Arkwright Court Commercial Road, Darwen, BB3 0FG
Tel: 0844-8588580
E-mail: sales@ekmsystems.co.uk
Website: http://www.ekmsystems.co.uk
Directors: A. Chesworth (MD)
Registration no: 04774091 **Date established:** 1997
Turnover: £250,000 - £500,000 **No.of Employees:** 1 - 10
Product Groups: 44

Date of Accounts	May 07	May 06
Sales Turnover	N/A	467
Pre Tax Profit/Loss	N/A	143
Working Capital	216	119
Fixed Assets	37	3
Current Assets	384	173
Current Liabilities	168	54
ROCE% (Return on Capital Employed)		117.3
ROT% (Return on Turnover)		30.7

Frank Barnes Darwen Ltd
Albert & Hope Mills Cross Street, Darwen, BB3 2PN
Tel: 01254-702748 **Fax:** 01254-773968
E-mail: info@frank-barnes.co.uk
Website: http://www.frank-barnes.co.uk
Directors: S. Barnes (MD)
Immediate Holding Company: FRANK BARNES (DARWEN) LIMITED
Registration no: 00505225 **Date established:** 1952 **Turnover:** £5m - £10m
No.of Employees: 51 - 100 **Product Groups:** 14, 35, 40, 42, 45, 46, 52, 54, 66, 67, 72, 83

Date of Accounts	Mar 11	Mar 10	Mar 09
Sales Turnover	10m	7m	N/A
Pre Tax Profit/Loss	458	54	34
Working Capital	1m	561	215
Fixed Assets	3m	3m	4m
Current Assets	3m	3m	2m
Current Liabilities	664	773	627

Guide Security Services Ltd
Arkwright Courtblackburn Interchange Commercial Road, Darwen, BB1 2QE
Tel: 0845-0580011 **Fax:** 0845-0580018
E-mail: info@guidesecurity.co.uk
Website: http://www.guidesecurity.co.uk
Directors: A. Tomlinson (Co Sec), E. Cusack (MD)
Managers: R. Pogson (Sales Prom Mgr)
Registration no: 03246838 **Date established:** 2007
Turnover: Up to £250,000 **No.of Employees:** 21 - 50 **Product Groups:** 36, 40, 84

Date of Accounts	Mar 08	Mar 07	Mar 06
Working Capital	2	-150	-185
Fixed Assets	1342	644	514
Current Assets	1371	834	880
Current Liabilities	1368	984	1065
Total Share Capital	880	880	5

Heritage Steel Fabricators Ltd
Unit 12 Albert Mill Albert Place, Lower Darwen, Darwen, BB3 0QE
Tel: 01254-664759 **Fax:** 01254-664759
E-mail: d.hayden@lindanengineering.com
Directors: D. Hayden (Dir)
Immediate Holding Company: HERITAGE STEEL FABRICATORS LIMITED
Registration no: 06369765 **Date established:** 2007
No.of Employees: 1 - 10 **Product Groups:** 35

Date of Accounts	May 11	May 10	May 09
Working Capital	N/A	-0	-0
Current Assets	100	140	141

John Lawson Distributers
Scotshaw Brook House Branch Road, Lower Darwen, Darwen, BB3 0PR
Tel: 01254-677121 **Fax:** 01254-665922
E-mail: sales@johnlawsondist.co.uk
Website: http://www.johnlawsondist.co.uk
Managers: S. Riches (Mgr)
Immediate Holding Company: JOHN LAWSON DISTRIBUTORS LIMITED
Registration no: 01508597 **VAT No.:** 326 0298 69 **Date established:** 1980
Turnover: £500,000 - £1m **No.of Employees:** 11 - 20 **Product Groups:** 30

Date of Accounts	Oct 11	Oct 10	Oct 09
Working Capital	419	455	473
Fixed Assets	30	40	16
Current Assets	632	723	554

J & A Kay Ltd
Cotton Hall Mill Cotton Hall Street, Darwen, BB3 0DP
Tel: 01254-873535 **Fax:** 01254-873463
E-mail: info@jakay.co.uk
Website: http://www.jakay.co.uk
Directors: D. Kay (Dir), J. Kay (Fin)
Managers: A. Collinge (Purch Mgr)
Immediate Holding Company: J. & A. KAY LIMITED
Registration no: 00579425 **Date established:** 1957
No.of Employees: 21 - 50 **Product Groups:** 30, 49, 66

Date of Accounts	Apr 11	Apr 10	Apr 09
Working Capital	-10	-28	-287
Fixed Assets	1m	1m	1m
Current Assets	1m	955	1m

Leofixings.Com
Unit 6, Scotshaw Brook Industrial Estate Branch Road, Lower Darwen, Darwen, BB3 0PR
Tel: 01254-916203 **Fax:** 01254-916161
E-mail: info@leofixings.com
Website: http://www.leofixings.com
Directors: R. Dickinson (Dir)
No.of Employees: 1 - 10 **Product Groups:** 35, 66

Metal Fabrications Darwen Ltd
Taylor Street, Darwen, BB3 1DQ
Tel: 01254-701829 **Fax:** 01254-701829
Directors: J. Taylor (MD), J. Taylor (Fin)
Immediate Holding Company: METAL FABRICATIONS (DARWEN) LIMITED
Registration no: 00512575 **VAT No.:** GB 174 6605 49
Date established: 1952 **Turnover:** Up to £250,000
No.of Employees: 1 - 10 **Product Groups:** 48

Moorfield Of Lancashire Ltd
Perseverance House Olive Lane, Darwen, BB3 3DQ
Tel: 01254-704131 **Fax:** 01254-704141
E-mail: donelana@aol.com
Directors: A. Donelan (Grp Chief Exec), A. Donelan (Dir)
Immediate Holding Company: MOORFIELD OF LANCASHIRE LIMITED
Registration no: 02104252 **Date established:** 1987
Turnover: Up to £250,000 **No.of Employees:** 1 - 10 **Product Groups:** 24

Date of Accounts	Oct 07	Oct 06
Working Capital	-37	-41
Fixed Assets	88	100
Current Assets	11	14
Current Liabilities	48	54

S D S Albion Engineering Ltd
Goose House Lane, Darwen, BB3 0EH
Tel: 01254-703432 **Fax:** 01254-703456
E-mail: sds.albion@virgin.net
Website: http://www.sds-ltd.com
Directors: D. Aston (MD)
Immediate Holding Company: S.D.S. ALBION ENGINEERING LIMITED
Registration no: 01352150 **Date established:** 1978
Turnover: £250,000 - £500,000 **No.of Employees:** 1 - 10
Product Groups: 48

Date of Accounts	Feb 12	Feb 11	Feb 10
Working Capital	28	11	5
Fixed Assets	56	32	36
Current Assets	96	48	20

Sabar UK Ltd
17 Duckworth Street, Darwen, BB3 1AR
Tel: 01254-702456 **Fax:** 01254-702456
E-mail: sabaruk@ntlworld.com
Website: http://www.sabarpumps.com
Directors: K. Moosa (Fin)
Immediate Holding Company: SABAR (UK) LIMITED
Registration no: 04569320 **Date established:** 2002
No.of Employees: 1 - 10 **Product Groups:** 37, 40, 67

Date of Accounts	Mar 09	Mar 08	Mar 07
Working Capital	-10	2	-12
Fixed Assets	104	109	115
Current Assets	40	65	55

Shaws Of Darwen Ltd (a division of Shires Ltd)
Higher Waterside Waterside, Darwen, BB3 3NX
Tel: 01254-775111 **Fax:** 01254-873462
E-mail: sales@shawsofdarwen.com
Website: http://www.shawsofdarwen.com
Bank(s): National Westminster Bank Plc
Directors: D. Dare (MD)
Immediate Holding Company: SHAWS OF DARWEN LIMITED
Registration no: 06870273 **VAT No.:** GB 557 1140 56
Date established: 2009 **No.of Employees:** 51 - 100 **Product Groups:** 33

Date of Accounts	Dec 11	Dec 10	Dec 09
Working Capital	670	455	222
Fixed Assets	268	297	184
Current Assets	1m	1m	2m
Current Liabilities	319	496	1m

Software4biz Ltd
Tower View Cranberry Bottoms, Darwen, BB3 2HY
Tel: 01254-761336
E-mail: sales@software4biz.co.uk
Website: http://www.software4biz.co.uk
Directors: L. Anderson (MD), P. Hodgson (Fin)
Immediate Holding Company: SOFTWARE4BIZ LTD
Registration no: 01883660 **Date established:** 1985
No.of Employees: 1 - 10 **Product Groups:** 44

Date of Accounts	Mar 11	Mar 10	Mar 09
Working Capital	-24	-24	-26
Fixed Assets	90	91	91
Current Assets	17	15	17

Stainless Metric Stock Ltd
Bolton Road, Darwen, BB3 2TT
Tel: 01254-775133 **Fax:** 01254-873460
E-mail: phil.cowley@stainlessmetricstock.co.uk
Website: http://www.stainlessmetricstock.com
Bank(s): Nat West
Directors: S. Pilkington (Co Sec), P. Cowley (MD)
Ultimate Holding Company: SAPATOIL HOLDINGS LIMITED
Immediate Holding Company: STAINLESS METRIC STOCK LIMITED
Registration no: 01507556 **Date established:** 1980 **Turnover:** £5m - £10m
No.of Employees: 11 - 20 **Product Groups:** 36, 66

Date of Accounts	Jun 12	Jun 11	Jun 10
Working Capital	124	-23	56
Fixed Assets	30	50	67
Current Assets	2m	2m	2m

A J Watson Electrical Services Ltd
Browning Street Hoddlesden, Darwen, BB3 3NE
Tel: 01254-760048 **Fax:** 01254-760034
E-mail: info@ajelectricals.co.uk
Website: http://www.ajelectricals.co.uk
Directors: T. Watson (Dir)
Immediate Holding Company: A.J. WATSON (ELECTRICAL SERVICES) LIMITED
Registration no: 01278168 **VAT No.:** GB 175 7665 20
Date established: 1976 **Turnover:** £250,000 - £500,000
No.of Employees: 1 - 10 **Product Groups:** 37, 81

Date of Accounts	Jan 12	Jan 11	Jan 10
Working Capital	-35	-43	-44
Fixed Assets	56	57	58
Current Assets	34	31	34

Wheelbase Engineering Ltd
Lower Eccleshill Road, Darwen, BB3 0RP
Tel: 01254-819399 **Fax:** 01254-776920
E-mail: sales@wheelbase.net
Website: http://www.wheelbase.net
Directors: C. Pickles (Dir), S. Pickles (MD)
Managers: G. Barker (Personnel)
Ultimate Holding Company: WHEELBASE HOLDINGS LIMITED
Immediate Holding Company: WHEELBASE ENGINEERING LIMITED
Registration no: 01816735 **Date established:** 1984
No.of Employees: 21 - 50 **Product Groups:** 39

Date of Accounts	Sep 11	Sep 10	Sep 09
Working Capital	917	924	1m
Fixed Assets	53	80	114
Current Assets	2m	2m	2m

Fleetwood

Archbell Greenwood Structures
1 St Peters Place, Fleetwood, FY7 6EB
Tel: 01253-779062
E-mail: hq@archbellgreenwood.com
Directors: D. Norman (Dir)
No.of Employees: 1 - 10 **Product Groups:** 35

Boris Net Co. Ltd
Copse Road, Fleetwood, FY7 6RP
Tel: 01253-779291 **Fax:** 01253-778203
E-mail: john@borisnet.co.uk
Website: http://www.borisnet.co.uk
Bank(s): Barclays
Directors: J. Howard (MD)
Immediate Holding Company: BORIS NET COMPANY LIMITED
Registration no: 00607513 **VAT No.:** GB 154 0949 61
Date established: 1958 **Turnover:** £1m - £2m **No.of Employees:** 21 - 50
Product Groups: 23, 35

Date of Accounts	Jun 11	Jun 10	Jun 09
Working Capital	154	163	202
Fixed Assets	80	88	84
Current Assets	836	604	823

E T F Fylde Ltd
Unit 1 Navigation Way, Fleetwood, FY7 6RS
Tel: 01253-777145 **Fax:** 01253-777146
E-mail: sales@e-t-f.co.uk
Website: http://www.e-t-f.co.uk
Directors: J. Beckett (Ptnr)
Immediate Holding Company: E T F (FYLDE) LIMITED
Registration no: 04698477 **Date established:** 2003
No.of Employees: 1 - 10 **Product Groups:** 46

Date of Accounts	Mar 11	Mar 10	Mar 09
Working Capital	-30	-43	-38
Fixed Assets	30	44	100
Current Assets	196	186	160

Roger Eaves Building Ltd
London Street, Fleetwood, FY7 6JQ
Tel: 01253-874216 **Fax:** 01253-773635
E-mail: rogereaves@btconnect.com
Website: http://www.rogereaves.com
Bank(s): Royal Bank of Scotland
Directors: R. Eaves (Dir), J. Eaves (Fin)
Ultimate Holding Company: ROGER EAVES & SON.LIMITED
Immediate Holding Company: ROGER EAVES & SON.LIMITED
Registration no: 00403877 **VAT No.:** GB 153 7321 78
Date established: 1946 **Turnover:** £2m - £5m **No.of Employees:** 11 - 20
Product Groups: 52

Date of Accounts	Sep 11	Sep 10	Sep 09
Working Capital	131	121	100
Fixed Assets	215	223	230
Current Assets	179	127	106

Fleetwood Trawlers Supply Company
1 Denham Way, Fleetwood, FY7 6PR
Tel: 01253-873476 **Fax:** 01253-773230
E-mail: info@ftsgroup.co.uk
Website: http://www.ftsgroup.co.uk
Directors: A. Dennison (Co Sec), T. Amor (MD)
Immediate Holding Company: FLEETWOOD TRAWLERS SUPPLY COMPANY,LIMITED(THE)
Registration no: 00122033 **VAT No.:** GB 151 1677 63
Date established: 1912 **Turnover:** £2m - £5m **No.of Employees:** 51 - 100
Product Groups: 74

Date of Accounts	May 08	May 07	May 06
Sales Turnover	4138	N/A	N/A
Pre Tax Profit/Loss	72	-495	-408
Working Capital	273	104	376
Fixed Assets	2121	2123	2195
Current Assets	1316	1062	1231
Current Liabilities	1044	958	855
Total Share Capital	8	8	8
ROCE% (Return on Capital Employed)	3.0	-22.2	-15.9
ROT% (Return on Turnover)	1.7		

Great British Lighting
Denham Way, Fleetwood, FY7 6PR
Tel: 01253-873503 **Fax:** 01253-778895
E-mail: sales@greatbritishlighting.co.uk
Website: http://www.greatbritishlighting.co.uk
Managers: T. Burman (Chief Mgr)
Immediate Holding Company: FLEETWOOD SHEET METAL LIMITED
Registration no: 00122033 **Date established:** 2011 **Turnover:** £2m - £5m
No.of Employees: 1 - 10 **Product Groups:** 37

Halsall Toys Europe Ltd
Eastham House Copse Road, Fleetwood, FY7 7NY
Tel: 01253-778888 **Fax:** 01253-878711
E-mail: general@htigroup.co.uk
Website: http://www.htigroup.co.uk
Directors: M. Walls (Dir)
Ultimate Holding Company: J R HUTT HOLDINGS LIMITED
Immediate Holding Company: HALSALL TOYS EUROPE LTD
Registration no: 00514002 **Date established:** 1952
Turnover: £20m - £50m **No.of Employees:** 51 - 100 **Product Groups:** 49, 61

Date of Accounts	Mar 11	Mar 10	Mar 09
Sales Turnover	21m	31m	30m
Pre Tax Profit/Loss	5m	15m	516
Working Capital	23m	18m	3m
Fixed Assets	3m	4m	4m
Current Assets	29m	27m	12m
Current Liabilities	3m	3m	4m

Hesketh Press Ltd
Warren Street, Fleetwood, FY7 6JU
Tel: 01253-875484 **Fax:** 01253-776206
E-mail: sales@heskethpress.com
Website: http://www.heskethpress.com
Directors: R. Poulter (MD), C. Polter (MD), M. Poulter (MD)
Immediate Holding Company: HESKETH PRESS LIMITED
Registration no: 01983175 **Date established:** 1986
Turnover: £500,000 - £1m **No.of Employees:** 1 - 10 **Product Groups:** 28

Date of Accounts	Mar 10	Mar 09	Mar 08
Working Capital	151	153	143
Fixed Assets	213	240	267
Current Assets	260	274	273

Lofthouse Of Fleetwood Ltd
Maritime Street, Fleetwood, FY7 7LP
Tel: 01253-872435 **Fax:** 01253-778725
E-mail: dlofthouse@fishermansfriend.com
Website: http://www.fishermansfriend.co.uk
Bank(s): National Westminster
Directors: D. Lofthouse (MD), J. Lofthouse (MD)
Immediate Holding Company: LOFTHOUSE OF FLEETWOOD LIMITED
Registration no: 00781277 **VAT No.:** GB 157 0499 45
Date established: 1963 **Turnover:** £20m - £50m
No.of Employees: 251 - 500 **Product Groups:** 63

Date of Accounts	Dec 11	Dec 10	Dec 09
Sales Turnover	39m	36m	34m
Pre Tax Profit/Loss	5m	6m	6m
Working Capital	40m	40m	41m
Fixed Assets	34m	29m	29m
Current Assets	51m	53m	48m
Current Liabilities	908	1m	1m

Packaged Ice Co. Ltd
Dock Avenue, Fleetwood, FY7 6NN
Tel: 01253-873249 **Fax:** 01253-777752
E-mail: frank@party-ice.co.uk
Website: http://www.fyldecoldstores.co.uk
Directors: C. Sutcliffe (Sales)
Managers: F. Turley (Chief Mgr)
Ultimate Holding Company: J. MARR LTD
Immediate Holding Company: FYLDE ICE & COLD STORAGE COMPANY,LIMITED
Registration no: 02104659 **VAT No.:** GB 077 3407 26
No.of Employees: 21 - 50 **Product Groups:** 21

Date of Accounts	Dec 07	Dec 06	Dec 05
Working Capital	1122	1050	939
Fixed Assets	9	16	12
Current Assets	2080	2126	1667
Current Liabilities	957	1077	728

Port Catering Equipment Services Ltd
172 Dock Street, Fleetwood, FY7 6JB
Tel: 01253-776173 **Fax:** 01253-770969
E-mail: info@portcatering.co.uk
Website: http://www.portcatering.co.uk
Directors: D. Williamson (Dir), H. Williamson (Fin)
Immediate Holding Company: PORT CATERING EQUIPMENT SERVICES LIMITED
Registration no: 04205673 **Date established:** 2001
No.of Employees: 1 - 10 **Product Groups:** 20, 40, 41

Date of Accounts	Oct 11	Oct 10	Apr 09
Working Capital	-9	-8	-11
Fixed Assets	11	13	23
Current Assets	274	187	146

Pro-Fix
64 Princes Way, Fleetwood, FY7 8DB
Tel: 01253-681202 **Fax:** 01253-300365
E-mail: p1dux@aol.com
Website: http://www.profixwindows.co.uk
Directors: P. Duxbury (Prop)
No.of Employees: 1 - 10 **Product Groups:** 30

Redmans Engine Centre
Rydal House Copse Road, Fleetwood, FY7 6RP
Tel: 01253-872296 **Fax:** 01253-878282
E-mail: redmansengines@hotmail.co.uk
Website: http://www.redmansenginecentre.co.uk
Managers: D. Howarth (Mgr)
Immediate Holding Company: REDMAN'S ENGINE CENTRE LIMITED
Registration no: 01608769 **Date established:** 1982
No.of Employees: 1 - 10 **Product Groups:** 35, 36, 39

Date of Accounts	Feb 12	Feb 11	Feb 10
Working Capital	N/A	8	12
Fixed Assets	11	12	12
Current Assets	74	74	76

Shakespeare Monofilament UK Ltd
Enterprise Way Off Venture Road, Fleetwood, FY7 8RY
Tel: 01253-858787 **Fax:** 01253-859595
E-mail: gary.walsh@jardenuk.co.uk
Website: http://www.monofilament.co.uk
Bank(s): Barclays
Directors: R. Evans (MD), G. Walsh (Fin)
Ultimate Holding Company: JARDEN CORPORATION LTD (NEW ZEALAND)
Immediate Holding Company: SHAKESPEARE INTERNATIONAL LIMITED
Registration no: 02461465 **Date established:** 1990 **Turnover:** £5m - £10m
No.of Employees: 21 - 50 **Product Groups:** 23

Date of Accounts	Dec 11	Dec 10	Dec 09
Fixed Assets	2m	2m	2m

Wellam Forge Ltd
Merlin House Copse Road, Fleetwood, FY7 6RP
Tel: 01253-874615 **Fax:** 01253-773292
E-mail: sales@wellamforge.com
Website: http://www.wellamforge.com
Directors: M. Wilding (MD)
Immediate Holding Company: WELLAM FORGE LIMITED
Registration no: 00858125 **VAT No.:** GB 154 7389 38
Date established: 1965 **Turnover:** £500,000 - £1m
No.of Employees: 1 - 10 **Product Groups:** 39, 48

Date of Accounts	Dec 11	Dec 10	Dec 09
Working Capital	21	-2	-6
Fixed Assets	6	8	10
Current Assets	118	79	58

Wyre Wrought Iron
Unit A Siding Road, Fleetwood, FY7 6NS
Tel: 01253-777889 **Fax:** 01253-777889
E-mail: wyrewroughtiron@hotmail.com
Website: http://www.wyrewroughtiron.co.uk
Directors: L. Horabin (Prop)
Immediate Holding Company: SHELL RECYCLING UK LLP
Registration no: OC332824 **Date established:** 2007
No.of Employees: 1 - 10 **Product Groups:** 26, 35

Heywood

A C S Lining Ltd
2-4 Middleton Road, Heywood, OL10 2HT
Tel: 01706-628524 **Fax:** 01706-628318
Website: http://www.acslining.co.uk
Directors: S. Mcconnell (MD)
Immediate Holding Company: ACS LINING LIMITED
Registration no: 02956502 **Date established:** 1994
No.of Employees: 1 - 10 **Product Groups:** 40, 66

Date of Accounts	Sep 11	Sep 10	Sep 09
Working Capital	634	525	513
Fixed Assets	16	10	17
Current Assets	1m	712	710

Advance Computer Repairs Ltd
208 Phoenix Park Industrial Estate Phoenix Close, Heywood, OL10 2JG
Tel: 01706-627233 **Fax:** 01706-627250
E-mail: service@acrlimited.com
Website: http://www.acrlimited.com
Directors: R. Allen (MD)
Immediate Holding Company: ADVANCE COMPUTER REPAIRS LIMITED
Registration no: 02519356 **Date established:** 1990
Turnover: £500,000 - £1m **No.of Employees:** 1 - 10 **Product Groups:** 44

Date of Accounts	Aug 11	Aug 10	Aug 09
Working Capital	60	63	78
Fixed Assets	14	17	21
Current Assets	101	96	124

All Tools Direct
Poor Peg Mill Buckley Street, Heywood, OL10 4HZ
Tel: 01706-692410
E-mail: sales@alltoolsdirect.co.uk
Website: http://www.alltoolsdirect.co.uk
Managers: J. Blakeley (Mgr)
Immediate Holding Company: FRANK BLAKELEY & SON LIMITED
Date established: 1979 **No.of Employees:** 21 - 50 **Product Groups:** 37, 40, 41

Date of Accounts	Dec 11	Dec 10	Dec 09
Working Capital	394	428	321
Fixed Assets	238	132	113
Current Assets	2m	1m	1m

Anochrome Finishing
Unit 202 Phoenix Park Industrial Estate Phoenix Close, Heywood, OL10 2JG
Tel: 01706-629983 **Fax:** 01706-629986
E-mail: info@anochromefinishing.co.uk
Website: http://www.anochromefinishing.co.uk
Directors: K. Pearn (Ptnr)
Date established: 1999 **No.of Employees:** 1 - 10 **Product Groups:** 46, 48

Biwater Services Ltd
Gregge Street, Heywood, OL10 2DX
Tel: 01706-367555 **Fax:** 01706-365598
E-mail: vicky.gillibrand@biwater.com
Website: http://www.biwater.co.uk
Bank(s): Barclays
Directors: J. Abraham (Dir), M. Studholme (Ch), M. Studholme (MD), B. Armstrong (MD), B. Armstrong (Ch), C. Hull (Fin), A. Williams (Sales & Mktg), T. Standring (Sales & Mktg)
Managers: M. Finch (Mktg Serv Mgr), J. Boffey (Buyer), P. Dawson (I.T. Exec), D. Wood (Sales Prom Mgr), T. Butler (I.T. Exec), V. Gillibrand (Mktg Serv Mgr), M. Manning (Personnel), V. Jones (Mktg Serv Mgr), F. Jackson (Chief Buyer)
Immediate Holding Company: MWH TREATMENT LIMITED
Registration no: 01535477 **VAT No.:** GB 606 4050 75
Date established: 1980 **Turnover:** £75m - £125m
No.of Employees: 251 - 500 **Product Groups:** 39, 42, 51

Date of Accounts	Mar 10	Mar 09	Mar 08
Sales Turnover	81m	131m	116m
Pre Tax Profit/Loss	3m	4m	4m
Working Capital	14m	14m	11m
Fixed Assets	5m	6m	7m
Current Assets	43m	63m	61m
Current Liabilities	18m	35m	28m

Frank Blakeley & Son Ltd
Buckley Street, Heywood, OL10 4HZ
Tel: 01706-692420 **Fax:** 01706-626022
E-mail: sales@frank-blakeley.com
Website: http://www.frank-blakeley.com
Directors: A. Blakeley (Ptnr)
Immediate Holding Company: FRANK BLAKELEY & SON LIMITED
Registration no: 01428943 **Date established:** 1979 **Turnover:** £2m - £5m
No.of Employees: 21 - 50 **Product Groups:** 66

Date of Accounts	Dec 11	Dec 10	Dec 09
Working Capital	394	428	321
Fixed Assets	238	132	113
Current Assets	2m	1m	1m

E A P International Ltd
Junction 19 Industrial Park Green Lane, Heywood, OL10 1NB
Tel: 01706-624422 **Fax:** 0161-835 2619
E-mail: sales@eapseals.com
Website: http://www.eapseals.com
Directors: S. Glover (MD), G. Hill (Fin)
Immediate Holding Company: E-A-P INTERNATIONAL LIMITED
Registration no: 01592211 **VAT No.:** GB 248 4731 43
Date established: 1981 **Turnover:** £1m - £2m **No.of Employees:** 1 - 10
Product Groups: 29, 30

Date of Accounts	Mar 12	Mar 11	Mar 10
Working Capital	549	483	464
Fixed Assets	691	724	719
Current Assets	805	725	690

Falcon Fire Ltd
PO Box 114, Heywood, OL10 9AD
Tel: 0800-612 3595 **Fax:** 0844-567 8685
E-mail: info@falconfire.co.uk
Website: http://www.falcon-fire.co.uk
Directors: S. Williams (MD)
Immediate Holding Company: FALCON FIRE LIMITED
Registration no: 07129808 **Date established:** 2010 **Turnover:**
No.of Employees: 1 - 10 **Product Groups:** 33, 38, 40, 52

Date of Accounts	Jan 11
Working Capital	22
Fixed Assets	5
Current Assets	61

Fitters Friend Ltd
Unit B8f Broadlands Heywood Distribution Park, Heywood, OL10 2TS
Tel: 0161-761 5055 **Fax:** 0161-761 2050
E-mail: sales@thefittersmate.com
Website: http://www.thefittersmate.com
Directors: R. Tate (Sales), F. Tate (Fin)
Immediate Holding Company: THE FITTER'S FRIEND LIMITED
Registration no: 03492568 **Date established:** 1998
No.of Employees: 1 - 10 **Product Groups:** 08, 30

Date of Accounts	Mar 11	Mar 10	Mar 09
Working Capital	-39	-117	-144
Fixed Assets	91	121	151
Current Assets	885	705	495

General Vacuum Equipment Ltd
Pennine Business Park Pilsworth Rd, Heywood, OL10 2TL
Tel: 01706-622442 **Fax:** 01706-622772
E-mail: sales.general@bobst.com
Website: http://www.bobst.com
Directors: B. Duckham (Sales & Mktg), S. Carey (MD)
Ultimate Holding Company: Bobst Group, Switzerland
Registration no: 02055148 **Date established:** 1986
Turnover: £10m - £20m **No.of Employees:** 51 - 100 **Product Groups:** 40, 42, 44, 47, 48, 67, 84

Date of Accounts	Dec 11	Dec 10	Dec 09
Sales Turnover	31m	20m	18m
Pre Tax Profit/Loss	4m	2m	-45
Working Capital	6m	2m	-2m
Fixed Assets	2m	2m	2m
Current Assets	12m	11m	8m
Current Liabilities	2m	2m	874

H Breakell Company Ltd
Heywood Distribution Park Pilsworth Road, Heywood, OL10 2TT
Tel: 01706-369272 **Fax:** 01706-629448
E-mail: sales@breakell-lifts.co.uk
Website: http://www.breakell-lifts.co.uk
Bank(s): HSBC Bank plc
Directors: J. Beevers (MD)
Immediate Holding Company: H. BREAKELL & CO. (BLACKBURN) LIMITED
Registration no: 00353915 **VAT No.:** GB 174 6761 35
Date established: 1939 **Turnover:** £1m - £2m **No.of Employees:** 11 - 20
Product Groups: 45, 84

Date of Accounts	May 11	May 10	May 09
Working Capital	107	102	8
Fixed Assets	25	53	59
Current Assets	200	274	388
Current Liabilities	N/A	N/A	361

Harris Hart & Co. Ltd
Gregge Street Works Gregge Street, Heywood, OL10 2EJ
Tel: 01706-625355 **Fax:** 01706-360570
E-mail: info@epsom-salts.com
Website: http://www.epsom-salts.com
Directors: A. Tyson (Dir)
Immediate Holding Company: HARRIS,HART & COMPANY LIMITED
Registration no: 00150296 **Date established:** 2018
Turnover: £250,000 - £500,000 **No.of Employees:** 1 - 10
Product Groups: 31

Date of Accounts	Dec 11	Dec 10	Dec 09
Working Capital	107	82	65
Fixed Assets	274	302	308
Current Assets	133	111	99

Paul Hartman Ltd
P2 Pilsworth Road Heywood Distribution Park, Heywood, OL10 2TT
Tel: 01706-363200 **Fax:** 01706-363201
E-mail: bengt.gustafson@uk.hartmann.info
Website: http://www.hartmann.co.uk
Bank(s): Barclays
Directors: B. Gustafson (MD), C. Turner (Tech Serv), T. Coupe (Dir)
Managers: P. Fewtrell (Purch Mgr), M. Ripley (Personnel)
Ultimate Holding Company: PAUL HARTMANN AG (GERMANY)
Immediate Holding Company: PAUL HARTMANN LIMITED
Registration no: 01523121 **VAT No.:** GB 362 3417 68
Date established: 1980 **Turnover:** £20m - £50m
No.of Employees: 51 - 100 **Product Groups:** 23, 24, 29, 33, 38, 68

Date of Accounts	Dec 11	Dec 10	Dec 09
Sales Turnover	25m	25m	23m
Pre Tax Profit/Loss	-1m	-783	-877
Working Capital	752	282	92
Fixed Assets	457	550	522
Current Assets	6m	6m	5m
Current Liabilities	1m	1m	1m

Hawker Siddeley Switchgear
Unit 2 Warfield Distribution Centre Manchester Road, Heywood, OL10 2TU
Tel: 01706-632051 **Fax:** 01706-674001
E-mail: sales@hss-ltd.com
Website: http://www.hss-ltd.com
Bank(s): Barclays, Bradford
Directors: S. Lane (Eng Serv)
Registration no: 00370559 **VAT No.:** GB 184 4733 43
Date established: 1991 **Turnover:** £10m - £20m
No.of Employees: 21 - 50 **Product Groups:** 35, 37

Date of Accounts	Mar 08	Mar 07
Pre Tax Profit/Loss	-136430	-55980
Working Capital	-1427m	-966690
Fixed Assets	1127m	1161m
Current Assets	413820	482550
Current Liabilities	1841m	1449m
ROCE% (Return on Capital Employed)	45.5	-28.9

Ibex Marina Ropes
Cartridge Ropery Brunswick Street, Heywood, OL10 1HA
Tel: 01706-360363 **Fax:** 01706-622986
E-mail: sales@ibexmarina.com
Website: http://www.ibexmarina.com
Bank(s): Barclays
Directors: M. Earp (Fin)
Managers: J. Wild (Comm)
Ultimate Holding Company: ENGLISH BRAIDS LIMITED
Immediate Holding Company: IBEX MARINA ROPES LIMITED
Registration no: 02194192 **VAT No.:** GB 377 1091 45
Date established: 1987 **Turnover:** £2m - £5m **No.of Employees:** 21 - 50
Product Groups: 23

Date of Accounts	Dec 11	Dec 10	Dec 09
Sales Turnover	3m	3m	2m
Pre Tax Profit/Loss	705	473	137
Working Capital	2m	1m	919
Fixed Assets	45	92	152
Current Assets	3m	2m	1m
Current Liabilities	599	412	253

Intercover (E Hampson) Ltd
Unit B12a, Broadlands Heywood Distribution Park, Pilsworth Road, Heywood, OL10 2TS
Tel: 01706-623344 **Fax:** 01706-623345
E-mail: sales@intercover.co.uk
Website: http://www.intercover.co.uk
Directors: E. Hampson (MD)
Managers: R. Hampson (Admin Off)
Registration no: 03946853 **VAT No.:** GB 425 5710 62
Date established: 1993 **Turnover:** £1m - £2m **No.of Employees:** 1 - 10
Product Groups: 67

J D P
Green Lane, Heywood, OL10 2EU
Tel: 01204-396052 **Fax:** 01706-366402
E-mail: heywood@jdpipes.co.uk
Website: http://www.jdpipes.co.uk
Managers: M. Perry (Reg Mgr), S. Collins (Depot Mgr), S. Collins
Immediate Holding Company: DYKA UK LTD
Registration no: 01863996 **VAT No.:** GB 425 7776 22
Turnover: £20m - £50m **No.of Employees:** 11 - 20 **Product Groups:** 30, 66

Jost Great Britain Ltd
B7 Broadlands Heywood Distribution Park, Heywood, OL10 2TS
Tel: 0161-763 0200 **Fax:** 0161-763 0234
E-mail: sales@jostgb.co.uk
Website: http://www.jostgb.co.uk
Bank(s): Barclays, Manchester
Directors: D. Deri (Tech Serv)
Ultimate Holding Company: CINVEN LIMITED
Immediate Holding Company: JOST (GREAT BRITAIN) LIMITED
Registration no: 00953466 **Date established:** 1969 **Turnover:** £5m - £10m
No.of Employees: 11 - 20 **Product Groups:** 39, 45

Date of Accounts	Dec 11	Dec 10	Dec 09
Sales Turnover	6m	6m	5m
Pre Tax Profit/Loss	571	567	140
Working Capital	2m	2m	2m
Fixed Assets	33	53	86
Current Assets	3m	2m	2m
Current Liabilities	327	317	180

Mike Goldrick Window Blinds Ltd
Dawson Street, Heywood, OL10 4ND
Tel: 01706-628451 **Fax:** 01706-625525
E-mail: contact@mikegoldrick.co.uk
Website: http://www.mikegoldrick.co.uk
Directors: M. Goldrick (Fin), D. Goldrick (Dir)
Immediate Holding Company: MIKE GOLDRICK WINDOW BLINDS LIMITED
Registration no: 04415521 **Date established:** 2002
No.of Employees: 21 - 50 **Product Groups:** 24, 25, 35

Date of Accounts	Apr 11	Apr 10	Apr 09
Working Capital	323	294	250
Fixed Assets	473	496	505

see next page

Mike Goldrick Window Blinds Ltd - *Cont'd*

Current Assets	567	562	440

Partners In Packaging Machine Systems Ltd

Unit 7 Southgate Industrial Park Green Lane, Heywood, OL10 1ND
Tel: 01706-369000 **Fax:** 01706-369555
E-mail: sales@partnersinpackaging.com
Website: http://www.partnersinpackaging.com
Directors: D. Macintyre (MD)
Immediate Holding Company: PARTNERS IN PACKAGING LIMITED
Registration no: 04058163 **Date established:** 2000 **Turnover:** £1m - £2m
No.of Employees: 1 - 10 **Product Groups:** 38, 42

Date of Accounts	Aug 09	Aug 08	Aug 07
Sales Turnover	N/A	N/A	1m
Pre Tax Profit/Loss	N/A	N/A	-23
Working Capital	-65	-74	-117
Fixed Assets	17	22	23
Current Assets	292	275	234
Current Liabilities	N/A	N/A	71

Pillar Wedge Ltd

Green Lane, Heywood, OL10 2DY
Tel: 01706-366191 **Fax:** 01706-625939
E-mail: pillar-wedge@wedge-galv.co.uk
Website: http://www.wedge-galv.co.uk
Bank(s): National Westminster, Bradford
Managers: M. Davies (Mgr)
Ultimate Holding Company: B.E. WEDGE HOLDINGS LIMITED
Immediate Holding Company: PILLAR-WEDGE LIMITED
Registration no: 00539872 **VAT No.:** 100 6706 19 **Date established:** 1954
Turnover: £2m - £5m **No.of Employees:** 51 - 100 **Product Groups:** 48

Date of Accounts	Mar 11	Mar 10	Mar 09
Pre Tax Profit/Loss	12	12	12
Working Capital	105	105	105
Current Assets	107	107	107
Current Liabilities	3	3	2

Precision Components & Equipment Ltd

Railway Street Works, Heywood, OL10 1LX
Tel: 01706-621421 **Fax:** 01706-621319
E-mail: mike-pce@johnbradleygroup.co.uk
Website: http://www.johnbradleygroup.co.uk
Directors: N. Bradley (MD), S. Booth (Sales)
Managers: S. Robb (Buyer)
Immediate Holding Company: PRECISION COMPONENTS & EQUIPMENT (HEYWOOD) LIMITED
Registration no: 00584296 **Date established:** 1957 **Turnover:** £2m - £5m
No.of Employees: 21 - 50 **Product Groups:** 22, 28, 30, 48

Date of Accounts	Jun 11	Jun 10	Jun 09
Working Capital	-90	-189	28
Fixed Assets	1m	1m	1m
Current Assets	1m	1m	913

Ravenfield Designs Ltd

Russell Street, Heywood, OL10 1NX
Tel: 01706-369307 **Fax:** 01706-360472
E-mail: post@ravenfield.com
Website: http://www.ravenfield.com
Directors: E. Taylor (Fin)
Immediate Holding Company: RAVENFIELD DESIGNS LIMITED
Registration no: 01568226 **VAT No.:** GB 307 7323 75
Date established: 1981 **Turnover:** Up to £250,000
No.of Employees: 1 - 10 **Product Groups:** 38

Date of Accounts	Feb 08	Feb 11	Feb 10
Working Capital	122	70	127
Fixed Assets	74	83	87
Current Assets	177	165	220

Reach BCS Web Design Manchester

1st Floor, Longford House, Heywood, OL10 1DP
Tel: 01706-369894 **Fax:** 01706-365056
E-mail: derek@reachbcs.com
Website: http://www.reachbcs.com
Directors: D. Meyerson (Mkt Research)
Date established: 2005 **No.of Employees:** 11 - 20 **Product Groups:** 44

Roch Valley Examination Dancewear

Unit 3 Pennine Business Park Pilsworth Road, Heywood, OL10 2TL
Tel: 01706-362501 **Fax:** 01706-362525
E-mail: sales@roch-valley.co.uk
Website: http://www.roch-valley.co.uk
Directors: D. Golding (Mkt Research)
Immediate Holding Company: ROCH VALLEY LIMITED
Registration no: 02049641 **Date established:** 1986 **Turnover:** £5m - £10m
No.of Employees: 21 - 50 **Product Groups:** 65

Date of Accounts	Jul 11	Jul 10	Jul 09
Sales Turnover	6m	6m	6m
Pre Tax Profit/Loss	554	214	221
Working Capital	16	245	-432
Fixed Assets	2m	2m	2m
Current Assets	2m	2m	2m
Current Liabilities	1m	354	779

Sherwood Agencies Ltd

Sherwood House Mutual Mills Aspinall Street, Heywood, OL10 4HW
Tel: 01706-898100 **Fax:** 01706-898101
E-mail: sales@sherwoodagencies.com
Website: http://www.sherwoodagencies.com
Directors: D. Mehta (Dir), J. Patel (Fin), M. Mehta (MD)
Managers: L. Watson (Personnel)
Immediate Holding Company: SHERWOOD AGENCIES LIMITED
Registration no: 01168790 **Date established:** 1974
Turnover: £10m - £20m **No.of Employees:** 21 - 50 **Product Groups:** 36, 49, 65

Date of Accounts	May 11	May 10	May 09
Sales Turnover	11m	12m	15m
Pre Tax Profit/Loss	-786	-361	-2m
Working Capital	3m	3m	3m
Fixed Assets	1m	1m	1m
Current Assets	11m	11m	12m
Current Liabilities	227	1m	1m

T S C Ltd

Microbiology House Fir Street, Heywood, OL10 1NW
Tel: 01706-620600 **Fax:** 01706-620445
E-mail: sales@tscswabs.co.uk
Website: http://www.tscswabs.co.uk

Directors: E. Cooper (Fin), J. Rainbow (Pers)
Managers: D. Lewis (Sales Prom Mgr), G. Campbell (Buyer)
Ultimate Holding Company: S & J (CHATTERIS) HOLDINGS LIMITED
Immediate Holding Company: T.S.C. LIMITED
Registration no: 02947038 **Date established:** 1994 **Turnover:** £1m - £2m
No.of Employees: 21 - 50 **Product Groups:** 67

Date of Accounts	Dec 98	Dec 96	Jul 98
Sales Turnover	2m	N/A	3m
Pre Tax Profit/Loss	52	N/A	-139
Working Capital	-166	77	-187
Fixed Assets	161	22	123
Current Assets	1m	649	809
Current Liabilities	376	N/A	264

Thyssen Krupp Materails (UK) Ltd

Phoenix Close Industrial Estate Phoenix Close, Heywood, OL10 2JG
Tel: 01706-361000 **Fax:** 01706-693933
Website: http://www.thyssen.co.uk
Bank(s): Barclays
Directors: P. Rawlinson (Dir), W. Street (Fin)
Managers: D. Adams (Comm), I. Lochhead (Comm), C. Meiklen (Sales Prom Mgr)
Ultimate Holding Company: Thyssen Krupp
Immediate Holding Company: Thyssen Garfield Ltd
Registration no: 00645702 **Date established:** 1991 **Turnover:** £2m - £5m
No.of Employees: 21 - 50 **Product Groups:** 34, 35, 36, 48, 66

Wayland Sheet Metal & Fabrications Ltd

Premier Iron Works Rochdale Road, Heywood, OL10 1LD
Tel: 01706-360345 **Fax:** 01706-621661
E-mail: sales@waylandsheetmetal.co.uk
Website: http://www.waylandsheetmetal.co.uk
Directors: L. Booth (Dir)
Immediate Holding Company: WAYLAND SHEET METAL & FABRICATIONS LIMITED
Registration no: 04735662 **Date established:** 2003
Turnover: £500,000 - £1m **No.of Employees:** 11 - 20
Product Groups: 35, 48, 84

Date of Accounts	May 11	May 10	May 09
Working Capital	27	6	79
Fixed Assets	251	272	224
Current Assets	314	255	286

Woodford Sheet Metal Ltd

14 Wham Street, Heywood, OL10 4QU
Tel: 01706-364295 **Fax:** 01706-621996
E-mail: woodford-sm@lineone-net.co.uk
Website: http://www.woodfordsm.co.uk
Directors: A. Whitehead (MD)
Immediate Holding Company: WOODFORD SHEET METAL LIMITED
Registration no: 01840487 **VAT No.:** GB 408 8109 52
Date established: 1984 **Turnover:** £250,000 - £500,000
No.of Employees: 1 - 10 **Product Groups:** 48, 52

Date of Accounts	Sep 11	Sep 10	Sep 09
Working Capital	12	12	31
Fixed Assets	10	11	12
Current Assets	166	164	156

Lancaster

Albion Ironworks

9a King Street, Lancaster, LA1 1JN
Tel: 01524-382249
Directors: M. Woods (Prop)
Date established: 1999 **No.of Employees:** 1 - 10 **Product Groups:** 26, 35

Amusement Ride Services

189 High Road Halton, Lancaster, LA2 6QB
Tel: 01524-811323
E-mail: info@amusementrideservices.com
Website: http://www.amusementrideservices.com
Directors: T. Harling (Dir)
Date established: 0012 **Turnover:** Up to £250,000
No.of Employees: 1 - 10 **Product Groups:** 49, 52, 84, 89

S J Bargh Ltd

Hornby Road Caton, Lancaster, LA2 9JA
Tel: 01524-770439 **Fax:** 01524-770487
E-mail: traffic@sjbargh.co.uk
Website: http://www.sjbargh.co.uk
Directors: J. Renaghan (Fin), S. Corthwaite (MD)
Managers: G. Openshaw (Personnel)
Immediate Holding Company: S.J.BARGH LIMITED
Registration no: 00532272 **Date established:** 1954
Turnover: £20m - £50m **No.of Employees:** 101 - 250 **Product Groups:** 77

Date of Accounts	Apr 11	Apr 10	Apr 09
Sales Turnover	28m	24m	17m
Pre Tax Profit/Loss	2m	2m	2m
Working Capital	7m	5m	5m
Fixed Assets	8m	8m	6m
Current Assets	11m	8m	8m
Current Liabilities	1m	1m	1m

C P L Petroleum

Marsh Point New Quay Road, Lancaster, LA1 5QW
Tel: 01524-847455 **Fax:** 01524-847466
E-mail: lancaster@cplpetroleum.co.uk
Website: http://www.cplpetroleum.co.uk
Bank(s): National Westminster Bank Plc
Managers: T. Manifold (Mgr)
Ultimate Holding Company: CPL INDUSTRIES HOLDINGS LIMITED
Immediate Holding Company: CPL PETROLEUM LIMITED
Registration no: 03003860 **VAT No.:** GB 721 5764 39
Date established: 1994 **No.of Employees:** 11 - 20 **Product Groups:** 66

Date of Accounts	Mar 12	Mar 11	Mar 10
Pre Tax Profit/Loss	N/A	878	904
Working Capital	31	30m	30m
Fixed Assets	26	26m	26m
Current Assets	57	56m	56m
Current Liabilities	26	246	253

Choose-Hosting

32 Aldrens Lane, Lancaster, LA1 2DU
Tel: 0844-8700328 **Fax:** 0844-8700329
E-mail: kompass.co.uk@upforit.org
Website: http://www.choose-a-domain.com

Managers: D. Wright (I.T. Exec)
Registration no: 04936485 **Date established:** 2004
Turnover: £250,000 - £500,000 **No.of Employees:** 11 - 20
Product Groups: 79

Condex Ltd

White Cross Industrial Estate South Road, Lancaster, LA1 4XQ
Tel: 01524-61601 **Fax:** 01524- 381515
E-mail: info@condex.co.uk
Website: http://www.pelletmills.com
Directors: D. Connor (MD)
Immediate Holding Company: CONDEX (UK) LIMITED
Registration no: 03464935 **Date established:** 1997
No.of Employees: 1 - 10 **Product Groups:** 41

Date of Accounts	Jan 11	Jan 10	Jan 09
Working Capital	1	-9	27
Fixed Assets	33	42	8
Current Assets	207	135	227

Department Of Continuing Education

Lonsdale College Bailrigg, Lancaster, LA1 4YN
Tel: 01524-592624 **Fax:** 01524- 592448
E-mail: managementlearning@lancaster.ac.uk
Website: http://www.lancs.ac.uk/depts/conted
Directors: D. Collinson (Grp Chief Exec)
Managers: S. Balshaw (Sales Admin), K. Pursey (), M. Reynolds, M. Easterby-Smith (Ind Relations), V. Hodgson
Turnover: £1m - £2m **No.of Employees:** 21 - 50 **Product Groups:** 86

Fat Media

Fat Media Storey Creative Industry Centre Meeting House Lane, Lancaster, LA1 1TH
Tel: 01524-590430
E-mail: info@fatmedia.co.uk
Website: http://www.fatmedia.co.uk
Directors: J. Cocker (Dir), J. French (Dir), D. Whiteford (Dir)
Immediate Holding Company: FAT MEDIA LIMITED
Registration no: 05645611 **Date established:** 2005
No.of Employees: 21 - 50 **Product Groups:** 44

Date of Accounts	Dec 11	Dec 10	Dec 09
Working Capital	247	151	106
Fixed Assets	13	7	8
Current Assets	510	380	294

Fibaform Products Ltd

22a Caton Road Lansil Industrial Estate, Lancaster, LA1 3PQ
Tel: 01524-60182 **Fax:** 01524- 389829
E-mail: info@fibaform.co.uk
Website: http://www.fibaform.co.uk
Bank(s): National Westminster Bank Plc
Directors: D. Bentley (Fin), G. Wheeldon (MD)
Ultimate Holding Company: FIBAFORM SHELTERS LIMITED
Immediate Holding Company: FIBAFORM PRODUCTS LIMITED
Registration no: 03384811 **VAT No.:** GB 693 3382 10
Date established: 1997 **Turnover:** £500,000 - £1m
No.of Employees: 21 - 50 **Product Groups:** 30, 35, 37

Date of Accounts	Mar 11	Mar 10	Mar 09
Working Capital	214	138	220
Fixed Assets	45	26	34
Current Assets	415	397	432

Filltech Systems Ltd

8 Endsleigh Grove, Lancaster, LA1 2TX
Tel: 01524-221665 **Fax:** 01524-380933
E-mail: sales@filltechsystems.co.uk
Website: http://www.filltechsystems.co.uk
Directors: G. Jackson (MD)
Registration no: 04969520 **Date established:** 2003
Turnover: Up to £250,000 **No.of Employees:** 1 - 10 **Product Groups:** 67, 84

Date of Accounts	Mar 08	Mar 07	Mar 06
Working Capital	-7	-9	22
Fixed Assets	16	21	27
Current Assets	26	18	44
Current Liabilities	33	26	22

Flexible Medical Packaging Ltd CliniMed (Holdings) Ltd

Unit 8 White Cross Industrial Estate South Road, Lancaster, LA1 4XS
Tel: 01524-68737 **Fax:** 01524-67110
E-mail: cgoodall@flexible-medical.com
Website: http://www.flexible-medical.com
Directors: S. Bryden (Fin), S. Shaw (Fin), C. Goodall (MD)
Managers: C. Sigee, C. Bell (Personnel), L. Banks, S. Wood (Cust Serv Mgr)
Ultimate Holding Company: CLINIMED (HOLDINGS) LIMITED
Immediate Holding Company: FLEXIBLE MEDICAL PACKAGING LIMITED
Registration no: 01022136 **VAT No.:** GB 534 5276 43
Date established: 1971 **Turnover:** £5m - £10m
No.of Employees: 51 - 100 **Product Groups:** 23, 24, 27, 28, 30, 31, 48, 84

Date of Accounts	Dec 11	Dec 10	Dec 09
Sales Turnover	8m	8m	7m
Pre Tax Profit/Loss	1m	1m	2m
Working Capital	1m	2m	1m
Fixed Assets	971	909	978
Current Assets	3m	3m	3m
Current Liabilities	328	283	261

Forsberg Services Ltd

1b Waterview White Cross Industrial Estate South Road, Lancaster, LA1 4XS
Tel: 01524-848374 **Fax:** 01524-382939
Website: http://www.forsbergservices.co.uk
Directors: F. Forsberg (MD)
Registration no: SC104949 **No.of Employees:** 1 - 10 **Product Groups:** 37, 38, 44

Gardner Jones

Claremont Cottage Bowerham Road, Lancaster, LA1 4AA
Tel: 01524-67212 **Fax:** 01524-67212
E-mail: enquiries@gardnerjones.com
Website: http://www.gardnerjones.com
Directors: R. Jones (Ptnr)
Date established: 1987 **Turnover:** Up to £250,000
No.of Employees: 1 - 10 **Product Groups:** 80

Glasson Electronics Ltd

Harbour House Glasson Dock, Lancaster, LA2 0BU
Tel: 01524-752208
E-mail: info@glassonelectronics.co.uk
Website: http://www.glassonelectronics.co.uk

Directors: M. Hornshaw (Fin), S. Bibby (MD)
Immediate Holding Company: GLASSON ELECTRONICS LIMITED
Registration no: 03269349 **Date established:** 1996
No.of Employees: 1 - 10 **Product Groups:** 37, 84

Date of Accounts	Dec 11	Dec 10	Dec 09
Working Capital	-70	-87	-69
Fixed Assets	42	50	58
Current Assets	20	26	35

W H Inman Ltd

38-42 North Road, Lancaster, LA1 1NY
Tel: 01524-32082 **Fax:** 01524- 846513
Website: http://www.inmanslighting.co.uk
Directors: M. Drake (MD)
Immediate Holding Company: W.H. INMAN LIMITED
Registration no: 00517742 **Date established:** 1953
Turnover: £500,000 - £1m **No.of Employees:** 1 - 10 **Product Groups:** 67

Date of Accounts	Jun 11	Jun 10	Jun 09
Working Capital	-32	-1	30
Fixed Assets	8	9	11
Current Assets	97	114	139

Iron Awe

Unit 24 Lansil Walk Lansil Industrial Estate, Lancaster, LA1 3PQ
Tel: 01524-845511 **Fax:** 01524-845511
E-mail: petersmalley@ironawe.com
Website: http://www.ironawe.com
Directors: P. Smalley (Prop)
Immediate Holding Company: RUSHCLIFFE DAY NURSERIES LIMITED
Date established: 2008 **Turnover:** £250,000 - £500,000
No.of Employees: 1 - 10 **Product Groups:** 26, 35, 46, 49

Kara-Jalmarit International Ltd

Europa House Lune Industrial Estate, Lancaster, LA1 5QP
Tel: 01524-840804 **Fax:** 01524-36450
E-mail: esapirttijarvi@aol.com
Website: http://www.karajalmarit.com
Directors: E. Pirttijarvi (MD)
Immediate Holding Company: KARA JALMARIT INTERNATIONAL LIMITED
Registration no: 03769747 **Date established:** 1999
Turnover: £250,000 - £500,000 **No.of Employees:** 1 - 10
Product Groups: 37, 38, 39, 49

Date of Accounts	May 11	May 10	May 09
Working Capital	42	55	95
Fixed Assets	1	1	1
Current Assets	56	63	146

Kidde Products

Station Road Bentham, Lancaster, LA2 7NA
Tel: 01524-264000 **Fax:** 01524-264180
E-mail: general.enquiries@kiddeuk.co.uk
Website: http://www.kiddeproducts.co.uk
Directors: P. Williams (MD), C. Boon (Sales)
Managers: B. Keeble, C. Thorp (Tech Serv Mgr), I. Ross (Purch Mgr), N. Hanson (Personnel)
No.of Employees: 101 - 250 **Product Groups:** 38, 42

Lancaster University Business Enterprises Ltd

University House Bailrigg, Lancaster, LA1 4YW
Tel: 01524-65201 **Fax:** 01524-65201
E-mail: g.fielding@lancaster.ac.uk
Website: http://www.lancaster.ac.uk
Directors: A. Neal (Fin), G. Fielding (Co Sec), J. Dwyer (I.T. Dir), V. Walsh (Dir), T. McMillan (Dir)
Managers: H. Holt (Purch Mgr), P. Wellens
Ultimate Holding Company: LANCASTER UNIVERSITY
Immediate Holding Company: LANCASTER UNIVERSITY BUSINESS ENTERPRISES LTD
Registration no: 00968581 **Date established:** 1969
Turnover: Up to £250,000 **No.of Employees:** 1501 & over
Product Groups: 86

Date of Accounts	Jul 11	Jul 10	Jul 09
Sales Turnover	41	44	72
Pre Tax Profit/Loss	-10	-23	-7
Working Capital	-214	-204	-191
Fixed Assets	46	46	56
Current Assets	24	20	65
Current Liabilities	2	5	9

Lancaster University Management School

Bailrigg, Lancaster, LA1 4YX
Tel: 01524-510752 **Fax:** 01524-594060
E-mail: r.newton@lancaster.ac.uk
Website: http://www.lums.lancs.ac.uk/bino/default.htm
Managers: B. Bloomfield
No.of Employees: 11 - 20 **Product Groups:** 86

A Macari & Sons

55 St Leonards Gate, Lancaster, LA1 1QS
Tel: 01524-66724
Directors: A. Macari (Prop)
No.of Employees: 1 - 10 **Product Groups:** 20, 40, 41

Martec Environmental Consultants Ltd

Waterbrow Wood Gressingham, Lancaster, LA2 8LX
Tel: 01524-222000 **Fax:** 07970-137469
E-mail: info@martecenviro.co.uk
Website: http://www.martecenviro.co.uk
Bank(s): Royal Bank of Scotland
Directors: D. Kenyon (Fin), M. Kenyon (MD)
Immediate Holding Company: MARTEC ENVIRONMENTAL CONSULTANTS LIMITED
Registration no: 04774068 **VAT No.:** GB 166 2605 64
Date established: 2003 **Turnover:** Up to £250,000
No.of Employees: 11 - 20 **Product Groups:** 54

Date of Accounts	Apr 11	Apr 09	Apr 08
Working Capital	-4	22	24
Fixed Assets	19	17	27
Current Assets	38	64	69

G Robertson Lancaster Ltd

10 Sun Street, Lancaster, LA1 1EW
Tel: 01524-63855 **Fax:** 01524- 843234
E-mail: kevin.mcloughlin@robertsons.ac
Website: http://www.robertsons.ac
Bank(s): The Royal Bank of Scotland
Directors: M. Davies (MD)
Immediate Holding Company: G.ROBERTSON(LANCASTER)LIMITED
Registration no: 00574209 **VAT No.:** GB 154 5017 85
Date established: 1956 **Turnover:** £500,000 - £1m
No.of Employees: 11 - 20 **Product Groups:** 52, 84

Date of Accounts	May 11	May 10	May 09
Working Capital	58	35	71
Fixed Assets	85	91	97
Current Assets	232	244	271

S W S

Hornby Road Claughton, Lancaster, LA2 9LA
Tel: 01524-772400 **Fax:** 01524-772411
E-mail: info@swsuk.co.uk
Website: http://www.swsuk.co.uk
Directors: C. Reoch (MD)
Managers: D. Edmondson (Personnel), K. Corrigan (Personnel), P. Cooper (Mktg Serv Mgr), M. Fletcher (Purch Mgr), D. Edmondson (Fin Mgr), V. Hawley (Mktg Serv Mgr), A. Wilson (Tech Serv Mgr), K. Lindeque (Sales Prom Mgr)
Immediate Holding Company: SECURITY WINDOW SHUTTERS LIMITED
Registration no: 02125993 **Date established:** 1987
Turnover: £10m - £20m **No.of Employees:** 101 - 250
Product Groups: 26, 35

Date of Accounts	Dec 11	Dec 10	Dec 09
Sales Turnover	12m	12m	12m
Pre Tax Profit/Loss	749	873	1m
Working Capital	4m	4m	3m
Fixed Assets	359	424	481
Current Assets	7m	6m	6m
Current Liabilities	1m	1m	944

J Storey & Co. Ltd (part of Petrofern Inc.)

Heron Chemical Works Moor Lane, Lancaster, LA1 1QQ
Tel: 01524-63252 **Fax:** 01524- 381805
E-mail: sales@samuelbanner.co.uk
Website: http://www.josephstorey.com
Directors: A. Howarth (Fin), S. Lovatt (Comm)
Ultimate Holding Company: PETROFERM INC.
Registration no: 00099615 **Date established:** 1908 **Turnover:** £2m - £5m
No.of Employees: 11 - 20 **Product Groups:** 31, 32

Robert Taylor & Sons

Green Smithy Bentham, Lancaster, LA2 7DH
Tel: 01524-261353 **Fax:** 01524-262051
E-mail: info@roberttaylorandsons.co.uk
Website: http://www.roberttaylorandsons.co.uk
Directors: P. Tallentine (Dir), B. Taylor (Dir), P. Taylor (Dir)
Immediate Holding Company: J.G. PAXTON AND SONS LIMITED
Registration no: 01696152 **Date established:** 1983
No.of Employees: 11 - 20 **Product Groups:** 41

Date of Accounts	Dec 11	Dec 10	Dec 09
Sales Turnover	18m	16m	15m
Pre Tax Profit/Loss	314	289	121
Working Capital	1m	1m	894
Fixed Assets	3m	3m	3m
Current Assets	5m	4m	4m
Current Liabilities	413	679	519

The Bronze Company

Unit 2 Standfast Complex Caton Road, Lancaster, LA1 3PE
Tel: 01524-381611 **Fax:** 01524-381611
E-mail: sales@lancasterbronze.co.uk
Website: http://www.lancasterbronze.com
Directors: S. Cockburn (Dir)
No.of Employees: 1 - 10 **Product Groups:** 46, 48

W F Wades plc

Unit 63 White Cross Industrial Estate, Lancaster, LA1 4XQ
Tel: 01524-32323 **Fax:** 01524-37846
E-mail: ray.rimmer@hagemeyer.co.uk
Directors: A. Rose (MD), B. Smithers (MD)
Managers: R. Rimmer (District Mgr)
Ultimate Holding Company: TELECONOMY RESEARCH LIMITED
Immediate Holding Company: LUNE ENGINEERING LIMITED
Registration no: 03650472 **Date established:** 2006
Turnover: Up to £250,000 **No.of Employees:** 1 - 10 **Product Groups:** 67

M Wilson

Grove Hill Smithy Station Road, Bentham, Lancaster, LA2 7LH
Tel: 01524-262828 **Fax:** 01524-262828
Directors: M. Wilson (Prop)
Immediate Holding Company: GROVE HILL GARAGE LIMITED
Registration no: 06187501 **Date established:** 2007
No.of Employees: 1 - 10 **Product Groups:** 41

Date of Accounts	Mar 11	Mar 10	Mar 09
Working Capital	-16	17	40
Fixed Assets	98	73	51
Current Assets	229	228	233

Brian Yates

Lansil Way Lansil Industrial Estate, Lancaster, LA1 3QY
Tel: 01524-35035 **Fax:** 01524-32232
E-mail: sales@brian-yates.co.uk
Website: http://www.brian-yates.co.uk
Bank(s): National Westminster Bank Plc
Directors: S. Coombes (Fin)
Managers: C. Murphy, L. Taylor (Sales Prom Mgr)
Ultimate Holding Company: CALCHAS SOPARFI SA (LUXEMBOURG)
Immediate Holding Company: NORTHERN TISSUE GROUP LIMITED
Registration no: 05082006 **VAT No.:** GB 334 9206 60
Date established: 2004 **Turnover:** £10m - £20m
No.of Employees: 21 - 50 **Product Groups:** 52

Date of Accounts	Dec 11	Dec 10	Dec 09
Sales Turnover	15m	24m	17m
Pre Tax Profit/Loss	-1m	-491	-525
Working Capital	1m	2m	2m
Fixed Assets	2m	2m	2m
Current Assets	6m	7m	6m
Current Liabilities	2m	2m	494

Leigh

AB World Foods Ltd

Kiribati Way, Leigh, WN7 5RS
Tel: 01942-267000 **Fax:** 01942-267070
E-mail: info@abworldfoods.com
Website: http://www.abworldfoods.com
Managers: S. Ward (Fin Mgr), M. Travis (Tech Serv Mgr), G. Blocks (Chief Mgr), C. Kendell (Purch Mgr), C. Sherriden (Personnel)
Ultimate Holding Company: WITTINGTON INVESTMENTS LIMITED
Immediate Holding Company: AB WORLD FOODS LIMITED
Registration no: 01400901 **VAT No.:** GB 235 5035 83
Date established: 1978 **Turnover:** £20m - £50m
No.of Employees: 251 - 500 **Product Groups:** 62

Date of Accounts	Sep 10	Sep 11	Sep 08
Sales Turnover	136m	145m	84m
Pre Tax Profit/Loss	13m	15m	306
Working Capital	4m	13m	-7m
Fixed Assets	13m	14m	10m
Current Assets	35m	44m	44m
Current Liabilities	19m	22m	16m

Cosaf Environments Ltd

The Lodge 421 Manchester Road, Leigh, WN7 2NP
Tel: 01942-680080 **Fax:** 01942-680081
E-mail: info@cosaf.co.uk
Website: http://www.cosaf.co.uk
Directors: M. Sullivan (MD)
Immediate Holding Company: COSAF ENVIRONMENTS LIMITED
Registration no: 02614582 **Date established:** 1991 **Turnover:** £1m - £2m
No.of Employees: 11 - 20 **Product Groups:** 30, 38

Date of Accounts	Mar 11	Mar 10	Mar 09
Working Capital	92	108	42
Fixed Assets	22	36	52
Current Assets	636	861	649

Danfield Ltd

Unit 1 Penfield Road, Leigh, WN7 3PF
Tel: 01942-675316 **Fax:** 01942-670063
E-mail: sales@danfield.co.uk
Website: http://www.danfield.co.uk
Bank(s): Barclays, Manchester
Directors: A. Forshaw (Dir)
Managers: C. Stott (Purch Mgr)
Immediate Holding Company: DANFIELD LIMITED
Registration no: 00851458 **Date established:** 1965 **Turnover:** £2m - £5m
No.of Employees: 21 - 50 **Product Groups:** 23

Date of Accounts	Apr 11	Apr 10	Apr 09
Working Capital	1m	2m	2m
Fixed Assets	952	274	293
Current Assets	2m	3m	3m
Current Liabilities	N/A	N/A	47

Deva Tap Co

Brooklands Mill English Street, Leigh, WN7 3EH
Tel: 01942-680177 **Fax:** 01942-680190
E-mail: nigel.darbyshire@devatap.com
Website: http://www.deva.org.uk
Directors: N. Darbyshire (Fin), R. Pryde (Dir)
Managers: P. Makin (Buyer), S. Pilkington (I.T. Exec), C. Stokes (Mktg Serv Mgr), P. Patterson (Sales Prom Mgr)
Immediate Holding Company: DEVA TAP COMPANY LIMITED
Registration no: 02610491 **Date established:** 1991
Turnover: £10m - £20m **No.of Employees:** 101 - 250
Product Groups: 36, 63, 66

Date of Accounts	Mar 08	Dec 06	Dec 05
Sales Turnover	N/A	N/A	6547
Pre Tax Profit/Loss	2061	2057	1157
Working Capital	5421	2559	1776
Fixed Assets	98	141	274
Current Assets	13501	11559	7605
Current Liabilities	8080	9000	5829
Total Share Capital	98	78	78
ROCE% (Return on Capital Employed)	37.3	76.2	56.4
ROT% (Return on Turnover)			17.7

Expert Rule Software Ltd

Newlands Road, Leigh, WN7 4HN
Tel: 0870-6060870 **Fax:** 0870-6040156
E-mail: info@expertrule.com
Website: http://www.expertrule.com
Directors: E. White (Dir), A. Attar (MD)
Registration no: 01885600 **VAT No.:** GB 403 6063 90
No.of Employees: 1 - 10 **Product Groups:** 44

Grundfos Pumps Ltd

Orford Court Green Fold Way, Leigh, WN7 3XJ
Tel: 08707-503888 **Fax:** 01942-605970
Website: http://www.grundfos.com
Directors: P. Reynolds (Dir)
Managers: B. Williams (Sales Prom Mgr)
Ultimate Holding Company: GROUPE NORBERT DENTRESSANGLE SA (FRANCE)
Immediate Holding Company: GRUNDFOS PUMPS LIMITED
Registration no: 00805960 **Date established:** 1964
Turnover: £500,000 - £1m **No.of Employees:** 1 - 10 **Product Groups:** 40

J P Whitter Ltd

Smallbrook Service Station Smallbrook Lane, Leigh, WN7 5PZ
Tel: 01942-871900 **Fax:** 01942-896843
E-mail: sally@waterwell-engineers.co.uk
Website: http://www.waterwell-engineers.co.uk
Managers: S. Whitter (Mgr)
Immediate Holding Company: OCP MOTORS LIMITED
Date established: 2010 **No.of Employees:** 21 - 50 **Product Groups:** 40

J & S Lewis Ltd

Hope Carr Lane, Leigh, WN7 3XA
Tel: 01942-682828 **Fax:** 01942-680101
E-mail: enquiries@jslewis.co.uk
Website: http://www.jslewis.co.uk
Directors: J. Ganley (Fin), J. Lewis (Dir)
Immediate Holding Company: J. & S. LEWIS LIMITED
Registration no: 01362875 **Date established:** 1978 **Turnover:** £1m - £2m
No.of Employees: 11 - 20 **Product Groups:** 07

see next page

J & S Lewis Ltd - Cont'd

Date of Accounts	Jan 12	Jan 11	Jan 10
Working Capital	101	185	96
Fixed Assets	1m	424	497
Current Assets	2m	2m	2m

Jacobi Carbons

Croft Court Unit E12 Moss Industrial Estate, Moss Industrial Estate, Leigh, WN7 3PT
Tel: 01942-670600 **Fax:** 01942-670605
E-mail: info@jacobi.net
Website: http://www.jacobi.net
Managers: J. Davies (Sales Admin), M. Currier (Sales Prom Mgr), S. Mahony (Mgr)
Immediate Holding Company: JACOBI CARBONS LIMITED
Registration no: 03185100 **Date established:** 1996 **Turnover:** £2m - £5m
No.of Employees: 11 - 20 **Product Groups:** 31, 32, 33, 42

Date of Accounts	Dec 10	Dec 09	Dec 08
Working Capital	810	289	29
Fixed Assets	115	73	85
Current Assets	2m	2m	1m

Laltex & Co. Ltd

Leigh Commerce Park Green Fold Way, Leigh, WN7 3XH
Tel: 01942-687000 **Fax:** 01942-687070
E-mail: mail@laltex.com
Website: http://www.laltex.com
Bank(s): HSBC Bank plc
Directors: R. Mulchand (MD), D. Chorley (Co Sec)
Managers: J. Brennan (Mktg Serv Mgr), P. Bentley (Tech Serv Mgr)
Immediate Holding Company: LALTEX & CO.LIMITED
Registration no: 00741075 **Date established:** 1962
Turnover: £20m - £50m **No.of Employees:** 51 - 100 **Product Groups:** 63

Date of Accounts	Feb 12	Feb 11	Feb 10
Sales Turnover	22m	22m	20m
Pre Tax Profit/Loss	1m	1m	253
Working Capital	16m	15m	14m
Fixed Assets	2m	2m	2m
Current Assets	22m	23m	21m
Current Liabilities	6m	7m	6m

Legacy Telecom

6 Acorn Business Centre Acorn Court Butts Street, Leigh, WN7 3DD
Tel: 01942-686260 **Fax:** 01942-679847
E-mail: sales@legacytelecom.co.uk
Website: http://www.legacytelecom.co.uk
Directors: L. Wynn (Fin)
Immediate Holding Company: LEGACY TELECOM LIMITED
Registration no: 04674154 **Date established:** 2003
No.of Employees: 1 - 10 **Product Groups:** 37, 38, 40, 44, 48, 83

Date of Accounts	Jun 11	Jun 10	Jun 09
Working Capital	4	1	34
Fixed Assets	11	13	14
Current Assets	115	115	122

Leigh Spinners Ltd

Park Lane, Leigh, WN7 2LB
Tel: 01942-673232 **Fax:** 01942-261694
E-mail: sales@leighspinners.com
Website: http://www.leighspinners.com
Bank(s): National Westminster Bank Plc
Directors: P. Horrocks (MD), S. Houston (Co Sec), P. Smith (Sales), J. Morrison (Sales)
Managers: T. Walsh (Chief Mgr)
Immediate Holding Company: LEIGH SPINNERS LIMITED
Registration no: 00529628 **VAT No.:** GB 151 8887 35
Date established: 1954 **Turnover:** £2m - £5m **No.of Employees:** 21 - 50
Product Groups: 23

Date of Accounts	Feb 09	Feb 10	Feb 11
Sales Turnover	5m	4m	N/A
Pre Tax Profit/Loss	-836	-328	N/A
Working Capital	2m	2m	2m
Fixed Assets	351	282	181
Current Assets	3m	2m	2m
Current Liabilities	229	187	N/A

P E Systems Ltd

Victoria Street, Leigh, WN7 5SE
Tel: 01942-260330 **Fax:** 01942-261835
E-mail: sales@pe-systems.co.uk
Website: http://www.pe-systems.co.uk
Bank(s): The Royal Bank of Scotland
Directors: J. Smith (Fin), M. Smith (MD)
Managers: J. Nuttall (Purch Mgr), S. Kendall (I.T. Exec), A. Gee (Comptroller), P. Aldred (Sales Prom Mgr), S. Aldred (Sales Prom Mgr)
Immediate Holding Company: P.E. SYSTEMS LIMITED
Registration no: 02117413 **VAT No.:** GB 457 9678 76
Date established: 1987 **Turnover:** £2m - £5m **No.of Employees:** 21 - 50
Product Groups: 37, 48, 67

Date of Accounts	Jun 11	Jun 10	Jun 09
Working Capital	469	385	336
Fixed Assets	865	883	917
Current Assets	2m	1m	1m
Current Liabilities	770	531	427

Pentre Group Ltd

Unit 2 Moss Industrial Estate Off St Helens Road, Leigh, WN7 3PF
Tel: 01942-607080 **Fax:** 01942-261878
E-mail: sales@pentrereels.co.uk
Bank(s): National Westminster
Directors: J. Meal (Fin)
Managers: R. Johnstone (Sales Prom Mgr), C. Balmer (Factory Mgr), D. Jackson (Purch Mgr)
Ultimate Holding Company: PENTRE HOLDINGS LIMITED
Immediate Holding Company: PENTRE HOLDINGS LIMITED
Registration no: 04918239 **Date established:** 2003
Turnover: £20m - £50m **No.of Employees:** 101 - 250
Product Groups: 25, 27, 30, 43, 46

Date of Accounts	Mar 11	Mar 10	Mar 09
Sales Turnover	21m	20m	25m
Pre Tax Profit/Loss	2m	2m	3m
Working Capital	5m	3m	5m
Fixed Assets	5m	4m	5m
Current Assets	9m	7m	9m
Current Liabilities	815	839	2m

Plus Opto Ltd

Unit B13 Moss Industrial Estate, Leigh, WN7 3PT
Tel: 01942-671122 **Fax:** 01942-671133
E-mail: sales@plusopto.co.uk
Website: http://www.plusopto.co.uk
Managers: G. Gore
Immediate Holding Company: PLUS OPTO (HOLDINGS) LIMITED
Registration no: 03864381 **Date established:** 1999 **Turnover:** £2m - £5m
No.of Employees: 11 - 20 **Product Groups:** 37, 38, 84

Date of Accounts	Oct 10	Oct 09	Oct 08
Working Capital	-190	-190	-190
Fixed Assets	220	220	220

Quadwall Ltd

Unit B5 Walter Leigh Way, Moss Industrial Estate, Leigh, WN7 3PT
Tel: 01942-674012 **Fax:** 01942-260167
E-mail: sales@quadwall.co.uk
Website: http://www.quadwall.co.uk
Directors: C. Anderson (Fin), S. Anderson (MD)
Immediate Holding Company: QUADWALL LTD
Registration no: 03156958 **Date established:** 1996
No.of Employees: 11 - 20 **Product Groups:** 27, 30, 66, 85

Date of Accounts	Aug 11	Aug 10	Aug 09
Working Capital	4	39	32
Fixed Assets	11	13	15
Current Assets	102	106	99
Current Liabilities	N/A	25	14

Rapid Colour Services Ltd

D 2 Moss Industrial Estate Moss Industrial Estate, Leigh, WN7 3PT
Tel: 01942-675932 **Fax:** 01942-602229
E-mail: sales@rapidcolour.co.uk
Website: http://www.rapidcolour.co.uk
Directors: K. Fenn (MD)
Immediate Holding Company: RAPID COLOUR SERVICES LIMITED
Registration no: 02455419 **VAT No.:** GB 519 9858 82
Date established: 1989 **No.of Employees:** 1 - 10 **Product Groups:** 32

Date of Accounts	Jun 11	Jun 10	Jun 09
Working Capital	618	576	538
Fixed Assets	347	379	421
Current Assets	1m	943	837

Sedco Ltd

Unit 1 Commonwealth Close, Leigh, WN7 3BD
Tel: 01942-673184 **Fax:** 0161-876 5267
Website: http://www.sedco.co.uk
Directors: C. Stead (Sales)
Immediate Holding Company: SEDCO LIMITED
Registration no: 01539798 **Date established:** 1981
No.of Employees: 1 - 10 **Product Groups:** 38, 42

Date of Accounts	Mar 11	Mar 10	Mar 09
Working Capital	462	448	451
Fixed Assets	362	372	126
Current Assets	753	750	694

Shutter Master

PO Box 104, Leigh, WN7 3WQ
Tel: 01942-676722
E-mail: info@shuttermaster.co.uk
Website: http://www.shuttermaster.co.uk
Managers: C. wilson (Chief Mgr)
Date established: 2004 **No.of Employees:** 1 - 10 **Product Groups:** 25

Sporting Lodge Greyhound Hotel

Warrington Road, Leigh, WN7 3XQ
Tel: 01942-671256 **Fax:** 01942-261949
E-mail: info@sportinglodgeinns.co.uk
Website: http://www.sportinglodgeinns.co.uk
Bank(s): National Westminster Bank Plc
Directors: A. Thurstan (Fin), P. Kelly (Fin), T. Bird (MD)
Managers: C. Skilton (Sales Prom Mgr)
Ultimate Holding Company: ASHDOWN INVESTORS LTD (GUERNSEY)
Immediate Holding Company: YARD GLASS PUB COMPANY LIMITED
Registration no: 03589841 **Date established:** 2002 **Turnover:** £2m - £5m
No.of Employees: 101 - 250 **Product Groups:** 69

Date of Accounts	Apr 09
Working Capital	1m
Current Assets	1m

Travtec Ltd

Unit 11 Commonwealth Close, Leigh, WN7 3BD
Tel: 01942-261100 **Fax:** 01942-261101
E-mail: info@travtec.co.uk
Website: http://www.travtec.co.uk
Directors: H. Thomason (Dir)
Ultimate Holding Company: TRAVTEC HOLDINGS LIMITED
Immediate Holding Company: TRAVTEC LIMITED
Registration no: 03009875 **Date established:** 1995
No.of Employees: 11 - 20 **Product Groups:** 38, 42

Date of Accounts	Jan 12	Jan 11	Jan 10
Working Capital	28	83	-0
Fixed Assets	25	26	12
Current Assets	181	259	116

Weldfast Services Ltd

Unit 1-2 Waterside Trading Estate Mill Lane, Leigh, WN7 2BG
Tel: 01942-261631 **Fax:** 01942-261631
E-mail: info@weldfastservices.co.uk
Website: http://www.weldfastservices.co.uk
Directors: S. Hugo (Fin), W. Brabbs (MD)
Immediate Holding Company: WELDFAST SERVICES LIMITED
Registration no: 03855847 **Date established:** 1999
No.of Employees: 11 - 20 **Product Groups:** 26, 35

Date of Accounts	Jan 12	Jan 11	Jan 10
Working Capital	89	113	143
Fixed Assets	22	28	25
Current Assets	178	196	252

Westland Fork Trucks

46 Smallbrook Lane, Leigh, WN7 5QA
Tel: 01942-886353 **Fax:** 01942-630022
Directors: B. Naylor (Prop)
Immediate Holding Company: SERVICEPLAN CONTRACTS LIMITED
Registration no: 02987971 **Date established:** 1994
Turnover: £250,000 - £500,000 **No.of Employees:** 1 - 10
Product Groups: 35, 39, 45

Leyland

Ainscough Vanguard Ltd

Farington Business Park Golden Hill Lane, Leyland, PR25 1XX
Tel: 01772-622116 **Fax:** 01772-622210
E-mail: general@ainscough.co.uk
Website: http://www.ainscoughengineering.co.uk
Directors: B. Ainscough (Ch), B. Ainsco (Prop), D. Cheers (Fin), M. Ainscough (MD)
Immediate Holding Company: AINSCOUGH VANGUARD LIMITED
Registration no: 04266687 **VAT No.:** GB 582 0259 45
Date established: 2001 **Turnover:** £10m - £20m **No.of Employees:** 1 - 10
Product Groups: 83

Anderton & Kitchen Plant Hire Ltd

Braconash Road, Leyland, PR25 3ZE
Tel: 01772-433583 **Fax:** 01772-622402
E-mail: anderton-kitchen@btclick.com
Website: http://www.anderton-kitchen.com
Directors: B. Anderton (Dir), C. Woodford (Fin), I. Mcfaite (Co Sec), M. Widders (Dir)
Ultimate Holding Company: BRACONASH PLANT LIMITED
Immediate Holding Company: ANDERTON & KITCHEN (PLANT HIRE) LIMITED
Registration no: 02208073 **VAT No.:** GB 483 1864 25
Date established: 1987 **Turnover:** £2m - £5m **No.of Employees:** 51 - 100
Product Groups: 83

Date of Accounts	Mar 12	Mar 11	Mar 10
Working Capital	273	273	273
Current Assets	967	273	678

Croston Conservatories

Unit 85 Bison Place Moss Side Industrial Estate, Leyland, PR26 7QR
Tel: 01772-435353 **Fax:** 01772-452525
E-mail: paul@phowarth.co.uk
Website: http://www.crostonconservatories.co.uk
Directors: J. Latimer (Dir), M. Davies (Fin), P. Howarth (MD), S. Williams (Fin)
Immediate Holding Company: CROSTON CONSERVATORIES LIMITED
Registration no: 02611980 **Date established:** 1991
No.of Employees: 1 - 10 **Product Groups:** 08, 30

Date of Accounts	Mar 07	Mar 06	Sep 09
Working Capital	N/A	N/A	-381
Fixed Assets	N/A	N/A	398
Current Assets	N/A	N/A	395

Custom Tape Ltd

Unit 27 Centurion Industrial Estate Centurion Way, Farington, Leyland, PR25 4GU
Tel: 01772-434444 **Fax:** 01772-436363
E-mail: sales@customtape.co.uk
Website: http://www.customtape.co.uk
Directors: A. Abram (Prop)
Immediate Holding Company: CUSTOM TAPE LIMITED
Registration no: 05457578 **VAT No.:** GB 878 5775 46
Date established: 2005 **No.of Employees:** 1 - 10 **Product Groups:** 27

Date of Accounts	Jul 11	Jul 10	Jul 09
Working Capital	108	145	134
Fixed Assets	263	17	5
Current Assets	469	421	295

Eurocraft Ltd

Unit 1 Titan Way, Leyland, PR26 7EW
Tel: 01772-622856 **Fax:** 01772-622857
E-mail: sales@eurocraft.com
Website: http://www.eurocraft.com
Bank(s): HSBC
Directors: G. Downie (Co Sec), C. Burrows (MD), C. Moores (Dir), D. Race (Fin)
Immediate Holding Company: EUROCRAFT LIMITED
Registration no: 07020943 **VAT No.:** GB 534 2161 75
Date established: 2009 **Turnover:** £1m - £2m **No.of Employees:** 11 - 20
Product Groups: 29, 30

Date of Accounts	Sep 10
Working Capital	8
Fixed Assets	19
Current Assets	189
Current Liabilities	42

Framework Events Ltd

Earnshaw Business Centre Hugh Lane, Leyland, PR26 6PD
Tel: 01772-624321
E-mail: tracey@frameworkevents.com
Website: http://www.frameworkevents.com
Directors: T. Larkin (Dir)
Immediate Holding Company: FRAMEWORK EVENTS LTD
Registration no: 06055973 **Date established:** 2007
Turnover: Up to £250,000 **No.of Employees:** 1 - 10 **Product Groups:** 81

Date of Accounts	Feb 11	Feb 10	Feb 09
Working Capital	-35	-41	-48
Fixed Assets	46	50	56
Current Assets	33	14	27

Heskin Fabrications Ltd

6 Centurion Court Farington, Leyland, PR25 3UQ
Tel: 01772-457733 **Fax:** 01772-457740
E-mail: heskinfabs@btconnect.com
Website: http://www.heskinfabs.co.uk
Bank(s): Barclays
Directors: M. Baldwin (Co Sec), P. Baldwin (Dir)
Managers: M. Baldwin (Personnel)
Immediate Holding Company: HESKIN FABRICATIONS LTD
Registration no: 03160006 **VAT No.:** GB 628 8697 76
Date established: 1996 **Turnover:** £1m - £2m **No.of Employees:** 21 - 50
Product Groups: 48

Date of Accounts	Mar 12	Mar 11	Mar 10
Working Capital	284	231	194
Fixed Assets	227	269	282
Current Assets	564	552	453

N F M Iddon Ltd

Quin Street, Leyland, PR25 2TB
Tel: 01772-421258 **Fax:** 01772-431114
E-mail: sales@nfmiddon.co.uk
Website: http://www.nfm.net
Bank(s): HSBC - Hough Lane, Leyland

Directors: D. Iddon (Dir), S. Swallen (MD)
Immediate Holding Company: NFM IDDON LIMITED
Registration no: 03703984 **VAT No.:** GB 732 9658 05
Date established: 1999 **No.of Employees:** 11 - 20 **Product Groups:** 42, 46

Date of Accounts	Apr 11	Apr 10	Apr 09
Working Capital	-213	-50	9
Fixed Assets	288	210	216
Current Assets	574	540	1m

Lancs & Cumbria Lifts Ltd
30 Yarrow Close Croston, Leyland, PR26 9SJ
Tel: 01772-601912 **Fax:** 01772-600762
E-mail: brian@lancsandcumbrialifts.co.uk
Directors: B. Fishwick (Prop), B. Fishwick (MD)
Immediate Holding Company: LANCS & CUMBRIA LIFTS LIMITED
Registration no: 06133844 **Date established:** 2007
No.of Employees: 1 - 10 **Product Groups:** 35, 39, 45

Date of Accounts	Mar 11	Mar 10	Mar 09
Working Capital	-5	-13	-6
Fixed Assets	9	13	17
Current Assets	59	39	162

Laptop Express Ltd
17 Midge Hall Lane Midge Hall, Leyland, PR26 6TN
Tel: 01772-454300 **Fax:** 01772-455366
E-mail: sales@laptopexpress.co.uk
Website: http://www.laptopexpress.co.uk
Directors: T. Brocklebank (MD)
Immediate Holding Company: LAPTOP EXPRESS LIMITED
Registration no: 05078890 **Date established:** 2004
Turnover: £500,000 - £1m **No.of Employees:** 1 - 10 **Product Groups:** 67

Leyland Exports
Centurion Court Farington, Leyland, PR25 3UQ
Tel: 01772-621321 **Fax:** 01772-621333
E-mail: info@leyland.co.uk
Website: http://www.leylandexports.com
Directors: P. Kirkman (MD), I. Lowe (Comm)
Ultimate Holding Company: LEYLAND HOLDING COMPANY LIMITED
Immediate Holding Company: LEYLAND EXPORTS LIMITED
Registration no: 02840119 **Date established:** 1993
Turnover: £10m - £20m **No.of Employees:** 51 - 100 **Product Groups:** 40, 68

Date of Accounts	Sep 11	Sep 10	Sep 09
Sales Turnover	11m	11m	11m
Pre Tax Profit/Loss	414	1m	1m
Working Capital	259	286	31
Fixed Assets	127	98	935
Current Assets	4m	3m	4m
Current Liabilities	2m	553	1m

Leyland Rubber Components Ltd
1a-1b Centurion House Leyland Business Park Centurion Way, Farington, Leyland, PR25 3GR
Tel: 01772-433751 **Fax:** 01772-623742
E-mail: info@lrcltd.co.uk
Website: http://www.lrcltd.co.uk
Directors: J. Burdett (MD)
Managers: C. Robinson (Sales Prom Mgr)
Immediate Holding Company: LEYLAND RUBBER COMPONENTS LIMITED
Registration no: 06051766 **Date established:** 2007 **Turnover:** £1m - £2m
No.of Employees: 21 - 50 **Product Groups:** 29, 34

Date of Accounts	Jan 11	Jan 10	Jan 09
Sales Turnover	2m	2m	N/A
Working Capital	-34	-8	33
Fixed Assets	574	607	607
Current Assets	560	535	533

Leyland Trucks Ltd
Croston Road Leyland, Farington Moss, Leyland, PR26 6LZ
Tel: 01772-621400 **Fax:** 01772-625910
E-mail: sales@packar.com
Website: http://www.leylandtrucksltd.co.uk
Bank(s): Barclays
Managers: P. Jones (Mgr)
Ultimate Holding Company: PACCAR PARTS U.K. LIMITED
Immediate Holding Company: LEYLAND TRUCKS LIMITED
Registration no: 02814092 **VAT No.:** GB 604 7086 51
Date established: 1993 **Turnover:** £125m - £250m
No.of Employees: 51 - 100 **Product Groups:** 39, 68

Date of Accounts	Dec 11	Dec 10	Dec 09
Sales Turnover	546m	338m	308m
Pre Tax Profit/Loss	19m	13m	7m
Working Capital	102m	91m	89m
Fixed Assets	29m	31m	35m
Current Assets	205m	179m	172m
Current Liabilities	2m	4m	4m

Leyprint
Leyland Lane, Leyland, PR25 1UT
Tel: 01772-425000 **Fax:** 01772-457353
E-mail: info@leyprint.co.uk
Website: http://www.leyprint.co.uk
Bank(s): National Westminster Bank Plc
Directors: E. Mould (MD)
Immediate Holding Company: SCENESTOCK LIMITED
Registration no: 04416609 **VAT No.:** GB 153 9927 32
Date established: 2002 **Turnover:** £5m - £10m
No.of Employees: 51 - 100 **Product Groups:** 27, 28

Date of Accounts	Jan 12	Jan 11	Jan 10
Working Capital	142	65	-2
Fixed Assets	2m	527	558
Current Assets	3m	2m	1m

Lifting Gear UK Ltd
Unit D3 Leyland Business Park Centurion Way, Farington, Leyland, PR25 3GR
Tel: 01772-699880 **Fax:** 01772-623852
E-mail: info@lg-uk.com
Website: http://www.lg-uk.com
Directors: M. Turner (Dir)
Immediate Holding Company: LIFTING GEAR UK LIMITED
Registration no: 06416624 **Date established:** 2007
No.of Employees: 11 - 20 **Product Groups:** 23, 29, 30, 35, 36, 37, 38, 39, 40, 41, 45, 66, 67, 83, 84, 85

Date of Accounts	Oct 11	Oct 10	Oct 09
Working Capital	117	124	228
Fixed Assets	750	598	496
Current Assets	731	466	408

Main Road Sheet Metal Ltd
Unit 2 Lancashire Enterprise Business Park, Leyland, PR26 6TZ
Tel: 01772-424172 **Fax:** 01772-456245
E-mail: graham@mainroadsheetmetal.com
Website: http://www.mainroadsheetmetal.com
Bank(s): National Westminster
Directors: E. John (Dir), G. John (Dir), J. John (Co Sec)
Ultimate Holding Company: MAIN ROAD (C.N.C.) LIMITED
Immediate Holding Company: MAIN ROAD (SHEET METAL) LIMITED
Registration no: 01574514 **VAT No.:** GB 349 9914 93
Date established: 1981 **No.of Employees:** 21 - 50 **Product Groups:** 34, 35, 36, 40, 46, 48, 49, 66, 67, 84

Date of Accounts	Oct 11	Oct 10	Oct 09
Working Capital	-186	-365	-645
Fixed Assets	678	784	917
Current Assets	1m	947	678
Current Liabilities	N/A	420	132

MSDS Services Ltd
38 Sandringham Avenue Farington, Leyland, PR25 4YH
Tel: 01772-978021
E-mail: sales@msds365.com
Website: http://www.msds365.com
Directors: D. Walker (Fin), D. Allen (Dir)
Immediate Holding Company: SEVRON LTD
Registration no: 06053767 **Date established:** 2007
No.of Employees: 1 - 10 **Product Groups:** 84

Date of Accounts	Jan 11	Jan 10	Jan 09
Working Capital	80	-38	3
Fixed Assets	29	17	N/A
Current Assets	148	39	30

N T S
121 Clydesdale Place Moss Side Industrial Estate, Leyland, PR26 7QS
Tel: 01772-331900 **Fax:** 01772-331901
E-mail: sales@ntslimited.co.uk
Website: http://www.ntslimited.co.uk
Immediate Holding Company: NORTH WEST TRANSPORT SUPPLIES LIMITED
Registration no: 04575299 **Date established:** 2002
No.of Employees: 21 - 50 **Product Groups:** 37, 39, 48

S & S Refrigeration
55 Stanifield Lane Farington, Leyland, PR25 4QA
Tel: 01772-434443
Directors: C. Sicuse (Prop)
No.of Employees: 1 - 10 **Product Groups:** 36, 40

Sorbothane
Unit 3 Lostock House Lancashire Enterprise Business Park, Leyland, PR26 6TZ
Tel: 08709-901357 **Fax:** 08709-901358
Website: http://www.sorbothane.co.uk
Directors: R. Aldred (MD)
No.of Employees: 21 - 50 **Product Groups:** 22, 24, 38

Still Materials Handling Ltd
Aston Way Moss Side, Leyland, PR26 7UX
Tel: 01772-644300 **Fax:** 01772-454668
E-mail: info@still.co.uk
Website: http://www.still.co.uk
Directors: A. Chadwick (Dir), N. Smith (Dir), C. Booth (MD)
Managers: A. Snook
Ultimate Holding Company: H. M. WHITTLE (HOLDINGS) LIMITED
Immediate Holding Company: TYCERRIG LIMITED
Registration no: 01463301 **Date established:** 1999
Turnover: £20m - £50m **No.of Employees:** 21 - 50 **Product Groups:** 35, 39, 45

Date of Accounts	Apr 11	Apr 10	Apr 09
Working Capital	2m	2m	2m
Fixed Assets	400	560	494
Current Assets	4m	4m	3m

Style Machine Tools Ltd
30a Centurion Industrial Estate Centurion Way, Farington, Leyland, PR25 4GU
Tel: 01772-624114 **Fax:** 01722-624114
E-mail: enquiries@stylemachinetools.co.uk
Website: http://www.stylemachinetools.co.uk
Directors: D. Metherell (MD), N. Fearnley (Fin)
Immediate Holding Company: STYLE MACHINE TOOLS LIMITED
Registration no: 03473249 **Date established:** 1997
No.of Employees: 1 - 10 **Product Groups:** 46

Date of Accounts	Feb 12	Feb 11	Feb 10
Working Capital	136	93	90
Fixed Assets	50	55	61
Current Assets	214	157	155

Swift
5 Drinkhouse Road Croston, Leyland, PR26 9JE
Tel: 01772-600923 **Fax:** 01772-601923
E-mail: steven@swift-design.net1.co.uk
Website: http://www.swift-design.net1.co.uk
Directors: S. Swift (Prop)
Date established: 1981 **No.of Employees:** 1 - 10 **Product Groups:** 35

Taylor Dental Technology Centre
Independence House Golden Hill Lane, Leyland, PR25 3NP
Tel: 01772-623623 **Fax:** 01772-493493
E-mail: info@taylordental.co.uk
Directors: S. Taylor (Prop)
Registration no: 06649752 **Date established:** 2008
No.of Employees: 11 - 20 **Product Groups:** 38, 67

Teslatest Systems
3 Bamfords Fold Bretherton, Leyland, PR26 9AL
Tel: 01772-600771 **Fax:** 01772-600771
E-mail: sales@teslatest.co.uk
Website: http://www.teslatest.co.uk
Directors: A. Burnett (Prop)
VAT No.: GB 823 5244 45 **Turnover:** Up to £250,000
No.of Employees: 1 - 10 **Product Groups:** 38, 40, 42

V-SOL Ltd
Centurion House Leyland Business Park Centurion Way, Farington, Leyland, PR25 3GR
Tel: 01772-699980 **Fax:** 01772-623634
E-mail: info@v-sol.co.uk
Website: http://www.v-sol.co.uk
Directors: D. Isom (MD)
Immediate Holding Company: V-SOL LIMITED
Registration no: 03390461 **Date established:** 1997 **Turnover:** £1m - £2m
No.of Employees: 1 - 10 **Product Groups:** 37, 39

Date of Accounts	Oct 08	Apr 12	Apr 11
Working Capital	445	316	363
Fixed Assets	31	7	5
Current Assets	563	388	489

Western Truck Ltd
123 Clydesdale Place Moss Side Industrial Estate, Leyland, PR26 7QS
Tel: 01772-454124 **Fax:** 01772-456075
E-mail: tb@westerntruck.co.uk
Directors: T. Bobola (MD)
Immediate Holding Company: WESTERN TRUCK LIMITED
Registration no: 01581676 **VAT No.:** GB 350 0715 94
Date established: 1981 **Turnover:** £500,000 - £1m
No.of Employees: 1 - 10 **Product Groups:** 39, 45, 61, 68

Date of Accounts	Mar 11	Mar 10	Mar 09
Sales Turnover	917	845	1m
Pre Tax Profit/Loss	16	6	172
Working Capital	329	317	325
Fixed Assets	N/A	N/A	2
Current Assets	415	447	588
Current Liabilities	20	21	77

Littleborough

Air Fabrications Ltd
Ebor Street, Littleborough, OL15 9AS
Tel: 01706-377866 **Fax:** 01706-377332
E-mail: sales@airfabs.co.uk
Website: http://www.airfabs.co.uk
Directors: S. Shepherd (Co Sec), M. Shepherd (MD)
Immediate Holding Company: AIR FABRICATIONS LIMITED
Registration no: 02400433 **VAT No.:** GB 508 5924 31
Date established: 1989 **Turnover:** Up to £250,000
No.of Employees: 1 - 10 **Product Groups:** 48

Date of Accounts	Nov 11	Nov 10	Nov 09
Working Capital	5	-1	-13
Fixed Assets	100	99	102
Current Assets	71	65	53

Broadfield Plastics Ltd
Foxcroft Street, Littleborough, OL15 8LB
Tel: 01706-378636 **Fax:** 01706-377131
E-mail: sales@broadfieldplastics.co.uk
Website: http://www.broadfieldplastic.co.uk
Directors: A. Docker (MD), J. Docker (Fin)
Immediate Holding Company: BROADFIELD PLASTICS LIMITED
Registration no: 00816119 **VAT No.:** GB 145 5959 34
Date established: 1964 **Turnover:** £250,000 - £500,000
No.of Employees: 1 - 10 **Product Groups:** 30, 48

Date of Accounts	Aug 11	Aug 10	Aug 09
Working Capital	56	13	-127
Fixed Assets	381	365	366
Current Assets	98	72	69

Alan Bush
Todmorden Road, Littleborough, OL15 9EG
Tel: 01706-377300 **Fax:** 01706-377488
E-mail: alan@alanbush.co.uk
Website: http://www.alanbush.co.uk
Directors: A. Bush (Prop)
Date established: 2003 **No.of Employees:** 11 - 20 **Product Groups:** 36, 40

C R P
Todmorden Road, Littleborough, OL15 9EG
Tel: 01706-756400 **Fax:** 01706-379567
E-mail: enquiry@crp.co.uk
Website: http://www.crp.co.uk
Managers: R. Barlow (Fin Mgr)
Immediate Holding Company: CORROSION RESISTANT PRODUCTS LIMITED
Registration no: 03564229 **Date established:** 1998 **Turnover:** £5m - £10m
No.of Employees: 21 - 50 **Product Groups:** 29, 36

Date of Accounts	Dec 11	Dec 10	Dec 09
Sales Turnover	8m	7m	6m
Pre Tax Profit/Loss	2m	748	46
Working Capital	-440	690	346
Fixed Assets	4m	2m	2m
Current Assets	3m	2m	2m
Current Liabilities	672	613	806

Circus Jim
61 Drake Road, Littleborough, OL15 9PS
Tel: 01706-377393
E-mail: jim@circusjim.co.uk
Website: http://www.circusjim.co.uk
Directors: J. Riley (Prop)
Date established: 2006 **Turnover:** Up to £250,000
No.of Employees: 1 - 10 **Product Groups:** 89

Durosil Products Ltd
5 Gatehouse Blackstone Edge Old Road, Littleborough, OL15 0JJ
Tel: 01706-838868 **Fax:** 01706-838868
E-mail: rogerbowmer@durosil.co.uk
Website: http://www.durosil.co.uk
Directors: R. Bowmer (MD), J. Bowmer (Fin)
Immediate Holding Company: DUROSIL PRODUCTS LIMITED
Registration no: 05186383 **Date established:** 2004
No.of Employees: 1 - 10 **Product Groups:** 46, 48

Date of Accounts	Aug 11	Aug 10	Aug 09
Working Capital	-9	-8	-8
Fixed Assets	5	6	8
Current Assets	24	21	17

Falconex Ltd
Greenvale Business Park Todmorden Road, Littleborough, OL15 9FG
Tel: 01706-378173 **Fax:** 01706-378073
E-mail: sales@falconex.co.uk
Website: http://www.falconex.co.uk

see next page

Falconex Ltd - *Cont'd*

Directors: P. Roux (Prop)
Immediate Holding Company: FALCONEX LTD
Registration no: 03517038 **Date established:** 1998
No.of Employees: 11 - 20 **Product Groups:** 35, 39, 45

Date of Accounts	Feb 08	Feb 11	Feb 10
Working Capital	81	89	77
Fixed Assets	6	20	23
Current Assets	269	348	354

Fothergill Crenette Ltd

Greenvale Mill Summit, Littleborough, OL15 9QP
Tel: 01706-371137 **Fax:** 01706-371821
Website: http://www.porcher-ind.com
Bank(s): Barclays Ltd
Directors: R. Porcher (MD)
Managers: N. Garner (Prod Mgr), E. Butterworth (Admin Off)
Immediate Holding Company: FOTHERGILL-CRENETTE LIMITED.
Registration no: 02763262 **VAT No.:** GB 606 5645 39
Date established: 1992 **Turnover:** £2m - £5m **No.of Employees:** 11 - 20
Product Groups: 23

Date of Accounts	Dec 10	Dec 09	Dec 08
Working Capital	617	442	615
Fixed Assets	967	1m	1m
Current Assets	1m	1m	1m

Fothergill Engineered Fabrics Ltd

Summit, Littleborough, OL15 0LR
Tel: 01706-372414 **Fax:** 01706-376422
E-mail: sales@fothergill.co.uk
Website: http://www.fothergill.co.uk
Directors: J. Boam (Fin)
Managers: N. Cawley (Tech Serv Mgr), C. Lamb (Personnel), V. Moran (Purch Mgr), N. Midani (Chief Mgr), P. Brennan (Chief Acct)
Ultimate Holding Company: BRENNAN ENTERPRISE LIMITED
Immediate Holding Company: FOTHERGILL ENGINEERED FABRICS LIMITED
Registration no: 02986454 **Date established:** 1994
Turnover: £10m - £20m **No.of Employees:** 101 - 250
Product Groups: 23, 33, 63

Date of Accounts	Jan 12	Jan 11	Jan 10
Sales Turnover	11m	10m	10m
Pre Tax Profit/Loss	1m	473	216
Working Capital	4m	3m	3m
Fixed Assets	514	673	886
Current Assets	6m	6m	5m
Current Liabilities	1m	1m	2m

Mag-Tech

53 Wordsworth Crescent, Littleborough, OL15 0RB
Tel: 07952-587246 **Fax:** 01706-371266
E-mail: sales@mag-tech.co.uk
Website: http://www.mag-tech.co.uk
Directors: M. Horrocks (Prop)
Registration no: 6325438 **Date established:** 2003
Turnover: Up to £250,000 **No.of Employees:** 1 - 10 **Product Groups:** 67

Pressed Flights Ltd

Unit 6 Python Industrial Estate Todmorden Road, Littleborough, OL15 9EG
Tel: 01706-372551 **Fax:** 01706-377598
E-mail: kevin.pearson@pressedflights.co.uk
Website: http://www.pressedflights.co.uk
Directors: K. Pearson (MD)
Ultimate Holding Company: PRESSED FLIGHTS (HOLDINGS) LIMITED
Immediate Holding Company: PRESSED FLIGHTS LIMITED
Registration no: 02225111 **Date established:** 1988 **Turnover:** £1m - £2m
No.of Employees: 11 - 20 **Product Groups:** 41, 45, 67

Date of Accounts	Mar 12	Mar 11	Mar 10
Working Capital	168	130	105
Fixed Assets	152	100	57
Current Assets	456	373	309

J Priestley & Son

Williams Street, Littleborough, OL15 8JP
Tel: 01706-370642 **Fax:** 01706-378119
E-mail: sales@woodmachine.co.uk
Website: http://www.woodmachine.co.uk
Directors: N. Priestley (Prop)
Immediate Holding Company: MIKROSPIN LIMITED
Registration no: 01980816 **Date established:** 1986
No.of Employees: 1 - 10 **Product Groups:** 46

Date of Accounts	Dec 11	Dec 10	Dec 09
Working Capital	34	16	-1
Fixed Assets	36	37	43
Current Assets	346	332	256

PTI Plastics Ltd

22 Milbury Drive Hollingworth Lake, Littleborough, OL15 0BZ
Tel: 01706-375919 **Fax:** 01706-375919
E-mail: enquiries@ptiplastics.co.uk
Website: http://www.ptiplastics.co.uk
Product Groups: 23, 27, 30, 31, 32, 36, 37, 38, 42, 48, 61, 66, 84

Surface Protection Coatings Ltd

66 Church Street, Littleborough, OL15 8AU
Tel: 01706-838500 **Fax:** 01706-838055
E-mail: sales@surfaceprotection.co.uk
Website: http://www.surfaceprotection.co.uk
Directors: J. Kennedy (Prop)
Immediate Holding Company: SURFACE PROTECTION COATINGS LIMITED
Registration no: 04542956 **Date established:** 2002
Turnover: £250,000 - £500,000 **No.of Employees:** 1 - 10
Product Groups: 30, 31, 32

Date of Accounts	Dec 11	May 11	May 10
Working Capital	190	308	391
Fixed Assets	68	57	4
Current Assets	935	699	711

Vacuubrand G M B H & Co.

Sales Office PO Box 111, Littleborough, OL15 0FG
Tel: 01706-370707 **Fax:** 01706-370886
E-mail: info@vacuubrand.com
Website: http://www.vacuubrand.com
Managers: G. Cape (Mgr)
Date established: 1999 **No.of Employees:** 1 - 10 **Product Groups:** 40

Lytham St Annes

B J Ltd

Adele House 32-34 Park Road, Lytham St Annes, FY8 1RE
Tel: 01253-721262 **Fax:** 01253-711765
E-mail: david.corlton@beaverbrooks.co.uk
Website: http://www.beaverbrooks.co.uk
Managers: D. Carlton (Mktg Serv Mgr), J. Smith, P. Walker, P. Jepson (Personnel), C. Spencer (Fin Mgr)
Immediate Holding Company: B. J. LIMITED
Registration no: 05185982 **Date established:** 2004
Turnover: £75m - £125m **No.of Employees:** 51 - 100
Product Groups: 35, 46, 49

Date of Accounts	Jul 11	Jul 10	Jul 09
Working Capital	N/A	8	1
Current Assets	13	22	14

Compass Point

PO Box 274, Lytham St Annes, FY8 9FX
Tel: 01253-795597 **Fax:** 01253-739460
E-mail: rick@compasspoint-online.co.uk
Website: http://www.compasspoint-online.co.uk
Directors: R. Houghton (MD)
Registration no: 04256084 **Date established:** 2001
Turnover: £10m - £20m **No.of Employees:** 1 - 10 **Product Groups:** 49, 61, 65

Douglas Storrie Labels Ltd

Tudor Works Tudor Rd, Lytham St Annes, FY8 2LA
Tel: 01253-643000 **Fax:** 01253-643001
E-mail: sales@storrielabels.com
Website: http://www.storrielabels.com
Bank(s): National Westminster Bank Plc
Directors: N. Storrie (MD), P. Storrie (Co Sec)
Managers: N. Livermore (Sales Prom Mgr)
Registration no: 00491524 **VAT No.:** GB 154 7237 61
Turnover: £1m - £2m **No.of Employees:** 11 - 20 **Product Groups:** 23, 27, 28, 30, 42, 49

Date of Accounts	Mar 11	Mar 10	Mar 09
Working Capital	481	450	475
Fixed Assets	538	453	448
Current Assets	778	738	720

Dudley Industries Ltd

Preston Road, Lytham St Annes, FY8 5AT
Tel: 01253-738311 **Fax:** 01253-794393
E-mail: sales@rentokil-initial.com
Website: http://www.dudleyindustries.com
Bank(s): HSBC, London
Directors: G. Higham (Dir), M. Carnell (Fin)
Managers: G. Scott (Sales Prom Mgr), K. Syner (Tech Serv Mgr), P. Shorthouse (Personnel), S. Meakin (Purch Mgr)
Ultimate Holding Company: RENTOKIL INITIAL PLC
Immediate Holding Company: DUDLEY INDUSTRIES LIMITED
Registration no: 00375137 **VAT No.:** GB 190 6214 74
Date established: 1942 **Turnover:** £20m - £50m
No.of Employees: 101 - 250 **Product Groups:** 36, 40

Date of Accounts	Dec 11	Dec 10	Dec 09
Sales Turnover	22m	21m	26m
Pre Tax Profit/Loss	79	-940	601
Working Capital	14m	14m	14m
Fixed Assets	3m	3m	4m
Current Assets	17m	16m	19m
Current Liabilities	301	260	1m

Energy 2000 Marketing Ltd

9 Bannister Street, Lytham St Annes, FY8 5HP
Tel: 01253-739333 **Fax:** 01253-794947
E-mail: alexander.whiteside@energy2000.co.uk
Website: http://www.energy2000.co.uk
Directors: P. Whiteside (Dir), J. Dickins (Co Sec), A. Williams (Co Sec), L. Johnstone (Co Sec), A. Whiteside (Dir), J. Morton (Co Sec), N. Williams (Dir)
Ultimate Holding Company: ENSERVE GROUP LIMITED
Immediate Holding Company: ENERGY 2000 MARKETING LIMITED
Registration no: 03061610 **Date established:** 1995 **Turnover:** £1m - £2m
No.of Employees: 11 - 20 **Product Groups:** 54

Date of Accounts	Oct 06	Apr 10	Apr 09
Sales Turnover	N/A	2m	1m
Pre Tax Profit/Loss	N/A	807	276
Working Capital	87	1m	321
Fixed Assets	326	N/A	18
Current Assets	241	1m	1m
Current Liabilities	N/A	N/A	574

Fylde Executive Cars

2 Deal Place, Lytham St Annes, FY8 3EN
Tel: 01772-632020 **Fax:** 01772-632020
E-mail: info@fyldeexecutivecars.co.uk
Website: http://www.fyldeexecutivecars.co.uk
Directors: J. Coombes (Dir), J. Coombes (Dir), M. Coombes (Fin), S. Coombes (Fin)
Immediate Holding Company: FYLDE EXECUTIVE CARS LIMITED
Registration no: 04290016 **Date established:** 2001
Turnover: £500,000 - £1m **No.of Employees:** 21 - 50 **Product Groups:** 72

Date of Accounts	Sep 11	Sep 10	Sep 09
Working Capital	28	10	15
Fixed Assets	48	25	32
Current Assets	109	74	84

Grand Hotel (Shoe Repairs & Key Cutting)

South Promenade, Lytham St Annes, FY8 1NB
Tel: 01253-643424 **Fax:** 01253-714459
E-mail: derrick@the-grand.co.uk
Website: http://www.the-grand.co.uk
Directors: R. Webb (Prop)
Immediate Holding Company: GRAND HOTEL (ST. ANNES) LIMITED
Registration no: 02829190 **Date established:** 1993
Turnover: Up to £250,000 **No.of Employees:** 21 - 50 **Product Groups:** 22, 36, 52, 61

Date of Accounts	Sep 11	Sep 10	Sep 09
Working Capital	-396	-296	-189
Fixed Assets	7m	7m	7m
Current Assets	431	465	663

Helical Technology

Dock Road, Lytham St Annes, FY8 5AQ
Tel: 01253-733122 **Fax:** 01253-794880
E-mail: sales@helical-technology.co.uk
Website: http://www.helical-technology.co.uk
Bank(s): Yorkshire Bank PLC
Directors: A. Morris (MD), A. Morris (Tech Serv), P. Spall (Fin)
Managers: J. Cookson (Sales & Mktg Mg), J. Ryle (Personnel)
Ultimate Holding Company: HELICAL INDUSTRIES LTD.
Immediate Holding Company: HELICAL TECHNOLOGY LTD.
Registration no: 01413643 **VAT No.:** GB 350 1031 22
Date established: 1979 **Turnover:** £20m - £50m
No.of Employees: 101 - 250 **Product Groups:** 33, 35, 36, 38, 40, 66

Date of Accounts	Dec 11	Dec 10	Dec 09
Sales Turnover	28m	22m	13m
Pre Tax Profit/Loss	3m	1m	294
Working Capital	6m	3m	3m
Fixed Assets	3m	3m	2m
Current Assets	11m	8m	6m
Current Liabilities	958	1m	591

Peter A Hodson

The Cove 20 Shalbourn Road, Lytham St Annes, FY8 1DN
Tel: 01253-780808 **Fax:** 01253-780808
E-mail: peter@peterahodson.co.uk
Website: http://www.peterahodson.co.uk
Directors: P. Hodson (Prop)
Date established: 1988 **No.of Employees:** 1 - 10 **Product Groups:** 35

Inenco Ltd

Petros House Street Andrews Road North Lytham Street Annes, Lytham St Annes, FY8 2NF
Tel: 01253-785000 **Fax:** 01253-785001
E-mail: marketing@inenco.com
Website: http://www.inenco.com
Bank(s): Barclays
Directors: M. Abbott (MD), J. Morton (Co Sec)
Ultimate Holding Company: CILANTRO MIDCO LIMITED
Immediate Holding Company: INENCO GROUP LIMITED
Registration no: 02435678 **VAT No.:** GB 529 5409 27
Date established: 1989 **Turnover:** £10m - £20m
No.of Employees: 101 - 250 **Product Groups:** 54, 80

Date of Accounts	Apr 11	Apr 10	Apr 09
Sales Turnover	19m	14m	13m
Pre Tax Profit/Loss	5m	4m	3m
Working Capital	-7m	5m	7m
Fixed Assets	26m	27m	22m
Current Assets	14m	11m	10m
Current Liabilities	9m	5m	3m

New Pet Express

12-13 Lidun Park Industrial Estate Boundary Road, Lytham St Annes, FY8 5HU
Tel: 01253-795353 **Fax:** 01253-795353
Directors: P. Sumner (MD), P. Sumner (Prop)
Registration no: 02596831 **Date established:** 1996
No.of Employees: 1 - 10 **Product Groups:** 20, 61

Performance Springs Ltd

Queensway Industrial Estate Scafell Road, Lytham St Annes, FY8 3HE
Tel: 01253-716900 **Fax:** 01253-716911
E-mail: sales@performance-springs.com
Website: http://www.performance-springs.com
Bank(s): National Westminster Bank Plc
Directors: S. Williams (MD)
Managers: D. Prestwich (Chief Acct)
Ultimate Holding Company: SHANNON COILED SPRINGS LIMITED
Immediate Holding Company: PERFORMANCE SPRINGS LIMITED
Registration no: 03250268 **VAT No.:** GB 678 5851 72
Date established: 1996 **Turnover:** £1m - £2m **No.of Employees:** 21 - 50
Product Groups: 35, 39, 66

Date of Accounts	Dec 11	Dec 10	Dec 09
Working Capital	302	144	172
Fixed Assets	626	664	746
Current Assets	898	662	479

Q E P Ltd

Everest Road Queensway Industrial Estate, Lytham St Annes, FY8 3AZ
Tel: 01253-789180 **Fax:** 01253-789182
E-mail: pboyce@vitrex.co.uk
Website: http://www.qep.com
Bank(s): HSBC
Directors: S. Kenny (Fin)
Managers: P. Boyce
Ultimate Holding Company: QEP INC (USA)
Immediate Holding Company: Q.E.P. CO. U.K. LIMITED
Registration no: 04988177 **VAT No.:** GB 153 5819 55
Date established: 2003 **Turnover:** £5m - £10m **No.of Employees:** 11 - 20
Product Groups: 36

Date of Accounts	Feb 08	Feb 11	Feb 10
Sales Turnover	6m	8m	8m
Pre Tax Profit/Loss	-529	452	698
Working Capital	726	2m	1m
Fixed Assets	20	24	13
Current Assets	3m	4m	3m
Current Liabilities	308	1m	1m

Read Management Services Ltd

International House 35 St Davids Road South, Lytham St Annes, FY8 1TJ
Tel: 01253-780000 **Fax:** 01253-781111
E-mail: rms@rms-group.com
Website: http://www.rms-group.com
Directors: T. Read (Prop)
Immediate Holding Company: READ MANAGEMENT SERVICES LIMITED
Registration no: 01272687 **VAT No.:** GB 156 5774 33
Date established: 1976 **Turnover:** £1m - £2m **No.of Employees:** 1 - 10
Product Groups: 81

Date of Accounts	Jul 12	Jul 11	Jul 10
Working Capital	-49	-43	-48
Fixed Assets	8	10	13
Current Assets	113	58	148
Current Liabilities	N/A	6	N/A

Statestrong Ltd

Boundary Road, Lytham St Annes, FY8 5LT
Tel: 01253-741806 **Fax:** 01253-794542
E-mail: sales@statestrong.com
Website: http://www.statestrong.com
Bank(s): Abbey national

Directors: K. Baptist (Co Sec), S. Baptist (MD)
Managers: S. Baptist (Sales Prom Mgr), N. Defty (Purch Mgr)
Ultimate Holding Company: HANKEY'S LIMITED
Immediate Holding Company: STATESTRONG LIMITED
Registration no: 01771174 **Date established:** 1983 **Turnover:** £5m - £10m
No.of Employees: 51 - 100 **Product Groups:** 32

Date of Accounts	Jun 08	Jun 09	Jun 10
Sales Turnover	N/A	10m	9m
Pre Tax Profit/Loss	15	254	-1m
Working Capital	5m	5m	4m
Fixed Assets	6m	6m	6m
Current Assets	7m	6m	5m
Current Liabilities	352	320	309

Virtual Living Ltd
The Grove Serpentine Walk, Lytham St Annes, FY8 5PB
Tel: 07968-353989
E-mail: info@virtual-living.co.uk
Website: http://www.virtual-living.co.uk
Directors: M. Sugden (MD)
Immediate Holding Company: VIRTUAL LIVING LTD
Registration no: 05516421 **Date established:** 2005
No.of Employees: 1 - 10 **Product Groups:** 44

Date of Accounts	Mar 11	Mar 10
Working Capital	-0	-3
Fixed Assets	1	3
Current Assets	25	8

Manchester

A I International Laminates Ltd
Unit 15 Shield Drive Wardley Industrial Estate Worsley, Manchester, M28 2QB
Tel: 0161-727 0250 **Fax:** 0161-727 0259
E-mail: sales@aiplastics.com
Website: http://www.aiplastics.com
Managers: P. Atherton (Chief Mgr)
Ultimate Holding Company: BLACKFRIARS CORP (USA)
Immediate Holding Company: A.I. INTERNATIONAL LAMINATES LIMITED
Registration no: 01511231 **Date established:** 1980 **Turnover:** £2m - £5m
No.of Employees: 1 - 10 **Product Groups:** 48

Date of Accounts	Dec 10	Dec 08	Apr 08
Sales Turnover	N/A	N/A	2m
Pre Tax Profit/Loss	N/A	N/A	86
Working Capital	44	614	614
Current Assets	44	614	614

A & K Engineering Services Ltd
Unit 4 Greenside Trading Estate Greenside Lane, Droylsden, Manchester, M43 7AJ
Tel: 0161-301 1550
E-mail: akeng@hotmail.co.uk
Website: http://www.akengineeringservices.co.uk
Directors: A. Corbishley (MD)
Immediate Holding Company: A & K ENGINEERING SERVICES LTD
Registration no: 04521123 **Date established:** 2002
No.of Employees: 1 - 10 **Product Groups:** 40, 48, 52

Date of Accounts	Aug 11	Aug 10	Aug 09
Working Capital	10	1	2
Fixed Assets	2	3	3
Current Assets	29	23	19

A M R Textiles Ltd
Unit F1-F2 Europa Trading Estate Stoneclough Road, Radcliffe, Manchester, M26 1GG
Tel: 01204-799910 **Fax:** 01204-799919
E-mail: bill.radburn@john-holden.com
Website: http://www.amrtextiles.co.uk
Directors: M. Sciama (Fin)
Immediate Holding Company: AMR TEXTILES LIMITED
Registration no: 04140877 **Date established:** 2001
Turnover: £10m - £20m **No.of Employees:** 21 - 50 **Product Groups:** 23, 30, 31

Date of Accounts	Mar 12	Mar 11	Mar 10
Sales Turnover	12m	11m	9m
Pre Tax Profit/Loss	670	372	847
Working Capital	353	-127	-556
Fixed Assets	3m	4m	4m
Current Assets	3m	3m	3m
Current Liabilities	247	526	234

A & Co Shutters Ltd
Monton Street, Manchester, M14 4LS
Tel: 0161-226 9955 **Fax:** 0161-226 9911
Website: http://www.aandcoltd.co.uk
Directors: Z. Aslam (Fin)
Immediate Holding Company: A & CO. SHUTTERS LIMITED
Registration no: 02897979 **Date established:** 1994
No.of Employees: 1 - 10 **Product Groups:** 26, 35

Date of Accounts	Feb 08	Feb 07	Feb 06
Working Capital	15	6	-1
Fixed Assets	16	20	18
Current Assets	131	109	97
Current Liabilities	116	102	98

Abal Engineering UK
Unit 6 Parkway 4 Trading Estate, Trafford Park, Manchester, M17 1SW
Tel: 0161-874 3100 **Fax:** 0161-874 3101
E-mail: sales@abal.co.uk
Website: http://www.abal.co.uk
Directors: M. Luby (Dir), D. Luby (Fin)
Immediate Holding Company: ABAL ENGINEERING (UK) LIMITED
Registration no: 06220823 **VAT No.:** GB 259 4742 25
Date established: 2007 **Turnover:** £5m - £10m **No.of Employees:** 1 - 10
Product Groups: 34, 39

Date of Accounts	Mar 09	Mar 08
Working Capital	-12	60
Fixed Assets	107	133
Current Assets	1m	987

Able Fabrication Services Ltd
Unit C2 Victoria Mill Buckley Street, Droylsden, Manchester, M43 6DU
Tel: 0161-301 4552 **Fax:** 0161-301 4071
E-mail: ableservicesdes@aol.com
Directors: D. Mickleburgh (Dir)
No.of Employees: 1 - 10 **Product Groups:** 26, 35

Able Hydraulics Ltd
Unit 1a Broadoak Business Park Ashburton Road West, Trafford Park, Manchester, M17 1RW
Tel: 0161-872 3022 **Fax:** 0161-872 9756
E-mail: sales@ablehydraulics.co.uk
Website: http://www.ablehydraulics.co.uk
Bank(s): National Westminster Bank Plc
Directors: R. Gawthorpe (MD)
Ultimate Holding Company: ABLE HYDRAULICS HOLDINGS LIMITED
Immediate Holding Company: ABLE HYDRAULICS LIMITED
Registration no: 01593258 **VAT No.:** GB 350 0265 02
Date established: 1981 **Turnover:** £1m - £2m **No.of Employees:** 11 - 20
Product Groups: 30, 35, 36, 40

Date of Accounts	Feb 12	Feb 11	Feb 10
Working Capital	556	569	568
Fixed Assets	150	108	107
Current Assets	851	827	771

A.B.O.M.S.
Progress Centre Charlton Place, Ardwick, Manchester, M12 6HS
Tel: 0161-273 4441 **Fax:** 0161-273 8390
E-mail: aboms@hotmail.com
Website: http://www.aboms.co.uk
Directors: T. Christian (Prop)
Immediate Holding Company: TOWER CONSULTING SERVICES LIMITED
Registration no: 06079354 **Date established:** 2005
No.of Employees: 1 - 10 **Product Groups:** 44

Date of Accounts	Nov 11	Nov 10	Nov 08
Working Capital	-1	-15	-13
Fixed Assets	N/A	1	1
Current Assets	14	5	5

Accent Hansen (Sales Office)
Unit 2 Chadderton Industrial Estate Greenside Way, Middleton, Manchester, M24 1SW
Tel: 0161-284 4100 **Fax:** 0161-655 3119
E-mail: sales@accenthansen.com
Website: http://www.hansengroup.biz
Directors: P. Steele (Fin), T. Anderson (MD)
Managers: P. Warde (Sales Prom Mgr), A. Buckley (Mktg Serv Mgr)
Ultimate Holding Company: HANSENGROUP A/S (DENMARK)
Immediate Holding Company: ACCENTHANSEN LIMITED
Registration no: 05472410 **VAT No.:** GB 605 4994 25
Date established: 2005 **Turnover:** £2m - £5m **No.of Employees:** 21 - 50
Product Groups: 35

Date of Accounts	Jun 11	Jun 10	Jun 09
Sales Turnover	3m	3m	3m
Pre Tax Profit/Loss	64	-401	-254
Working Capital	N/A	215	448
Fixed Assets	191	223	77
Current Assets	1m	1m	1m
Current Liabilities	128	258	186

Access Cleaning Specialist Ltd
Access House Hanson Street, Middleton, Manchester, M24 2HW
Tel: 0161-655 3390 **Fax:** 0161-655 3418
E-mail: info@accesscleaning.co.uk
Website: http://www.accesscleaningspecialist.com
Directors: M. Carr (Prop)
Immediate Holding Company: ACCESS CLEANING SPECIALISTS LIMITED
Registration no: 03743050 **Date established:** 1999
No.of Employees: 1 - 10 **Product Groups:** 52

Date of Accounts	Mar 11	Mar 10	Mar 09
Working Capital	-56	-42	-67
Fixed Assets	60	63	107
Current Assets	97	90	73

Acco East Light Ltd
Ashton Road Denton, Manchester, M34 3LR
Tel: 0161-336 9431 **Fax:** 0161-320 8012
E-mail: mark.winstanley@acco-eastlight.co.uk
Website: http://www.accoeastlight.com
Bank(s): HSBC Bank plc
Directors: M. Winstanley (Mkt Research), P. Maher (Dir), S. Butler (Sales)
Ultimate Holding Company: ACCO BRANDS CORP (USA)
Immediate Holding Company: ACCO EASTLIGHT LIMITED
Registration no: 00475543 **VAT No.:** GB 221 0851 20
Date established: 1949 **Turnover:** £20m - £50m
No.of Employees: 101 - 250 **Product Groups:** 26, 27, 28, 30, 49, 64, 67

Date of Accounts	Dec 11	Dec 10	Dec 09
Working Capital	N/A	N/A	1m
Current Assets	N/A	N/A	1m

Adam Kluj Transport
51c Albert Road Whitefield, Manchester, M45 8NN
Tel: 07966-873354 **Fax:** 0161-796 8995
E-mail: adamkluj@btinternet.com
Website: http://www.adamklujtransport.co.uk
Directors: A. Kluj (Prop)
No.of Employees: 1 - 10 **Product Groups:** 45, 72, 74, 76, 84

Advance Filtration Systems Ltd
3 Ordinal Street Trafford Park, Manchester, M17 1GB
Tel: 08458-722222 **Fax:** 0844-225 0401
E-mail: info@afs-limited.com
Website: http://www.afs-limited.com
Directors: A. Ryan (Dir)
Immediate Holding Company: ADVANCE FILTRATION SYSTEMS LIMITED
Registration no: 03124146 **Date established:** 1995
No.of Employees: 11 - 20 **Product Groups:** 38, 42

Date of Accounts	Dec 11	Dec 10	Dec 09
Working Capital	100	87	109
Fixed Assets	42	33	5
Current Assets	458	220	276

Advanced Cladding & Insulation Group Ltd
3 Stokes Street, Manchester, M11 4QU
Tel: 0161-231 0001 **Fax:** 0161-231 1055
E-mail: sales@advancedcladding.com
Website: http://www.advancedcladding.com
Directors: D. Hall (Sales)
Immediate Holding Company: ADVANCED CLADDING & INSULATION GROUP LIMITED
Registration no: 01555763 **Date established:** 1981 **Turnover:** £2m - £5m
No.of Employees: 1 - 10 **Product Groups:** 25, 30, 35, 66

Date of Accounts	Mar 12	Mar 11	Mar 10
Working Capital	253	423	161
Fixed Assets	99	90	86
Current Assets	2m	2m	1m
Current Liabilities	75	N/A	37

Advanced Protective Packaging Ltd
Unit 58 Pioneer Mill Milltown Street, Radcliffe, Manchester, M26 1WN
Tel: 0161-724 8080 **Fax:** 0161-725 9074
E-mail: salesnorth@advanced-pp.co.uk
Website: http://www.advanced-pp.co.uk
Directors: B. Garsden (Fin)
Managers: M. Lancaster (Sales Off Mgr)
Registration no: 02052369 **VAT No.:** GB 444 8953 13
Date established: 1960 **Turnover:** £2m - £5m **No.of Employees:** 11 - 20
Product Groups: 30

Akcros Chemicals Ltd
Lankro Way Eccles, Manchester, M30 0LX
Tel: 0161-785 1111 **Fax:** 0161-788 7886
E-mail: webadmin@akcros.com
Website: http://www.akcros.com
Bank(s): Barclays
Directors: R. Catchpole (MD)
Ultimate Holding Company: AKCROS HOLDINGS LIMITED
Immediate Holding Company: AKCROS CHEMICALS LIMITED
Registration no: 00995767 **VAT No.:** GB 603 6145 72
Date established: 1970 **Turnover:** £20m - £50m
No.of Employees: 51 - 100 **Product Groups:** 12, 23, 24, 25, 27, 29, 30, 31, 32, 33, 34, 35, 36, 38, 42, 48, 49

Date of Accounts	Dec 11	Dec 10	Dec 09
Sales Turnover	46m	46m	39m
Pre Tax Profit/Loss	113	2m	1m
Working Capital	8m	8m	7m
Fixed Assets	4m	3m	3m
Current Assets	19m	18m	16m
Current Liabilities	1m	2m	2m

Alanco Alamatic Ltd
Wilton Street Denton, Manchester, M34 3WH
Tel: 0161-336 4702 **Fax:** 0161-335 0100
E-mail: info@alanco-alamatic.co.uk
Website: http://www.alanco-alamatic.com
Directors: N. Breeze (Dir)
Immediate Holding Company: ALANCO-ALAMATIC LIMITED
Registration no: 01089743 **VAT No.:** GB 158 2140 77
Date established: 1973 **Turnover:** £2m - £5m **No.of Employees:** 1 - 10
Product Groups: 35, 39, 45

Date of Accounts	Mar 11	Mar 10	Mar 09
Working Capital	211	203	200
Fixed Assets	57	59	61
Current Assets	221	213	211

J Allcock & Sons Ltd
Oak Chemical Works Textile Street, Manchester, M12 5DL
Tel: 0161-223 7181 **Fax:** 0161-223 0173
E-mail: ja@allcocks.co.uk
Website: http://www.allcocks.co.uk
Directors: L. Hunter (Co Sec), A. Rushden (MD)
Immediate Holding Company: J.ALLCOCK & SONS LIMITED
Registration no: 00228726 **VAT No.:** GB 145 5252 76
Date established: 2028 **Turnover:** £250,000 - £500,000
No.of Employees: 1 - 10 **Product Groups:** 17, 29, 31, 32, 33, 66

Date of Accounts	Dec 11	Dec 10	Dec 09
Working Capital	-48	-20	-580
Fixed Assets	951	962	978
Current Assets	344	298	283

Alloy Bodies Ltd
Jubilee Works Clifton Street, Miles Platting, Manchester, M40 8HN
Tel: 0161-205 7612 **Fax:** 0161-202 1917
E-mail: accounts@alloybodies.co.uk
Website: http://www.alloybodies.co.uk
Bank(s): Lloyds TSB Bank plc
Directors: S. Riddiford (Dir), J. Henderson (Co Sec), M. Bragg (Fin)
Immediate Holding Company: ALLOY BODIES LIMITED
Registration no: 05567800 **VAT No.:** GB 145 7924 43
Date established: 2005 **Turnover:** £5m - £10m
No.of Employees: 51 - 100 **Product Groups:** 30, 39, 45, 68

Date of Accounts	Oct 10	Nov 09	Nov 08
Sales Turnover	5m	7m	N/A
Pre Tax Profit/Loss	-124	-1	872
Working Capital	570	699	716
Fixed Assets	2m	2m	2m
Current Assets	2m	3m	4m
Current Liabilities	793	1m	1m

Alpha Electronics Northern Ltd
35 Gibfield Park Avenue Atherton, Manchester, M46 0SY
Tel: 01942-886993 **Fax:** 01942-886450
E-mail: north@alpha-electronics.com
Website: http://www.alpha-electronics.com
Directors: S. Hartley (Dir)
Ultimate Holding Company: ALPHA ELECTRONICS GROUP LIMITED
Immediate Holding Company: ALPHA ELECTRONICS (NORTHERN) LIMITED
Registration no: 03139920 **Date established:** 1995
Turnover: £500,000 - £1m **No.of Employees:** 1 - 10 **Product Groups:** 37, 38, 39, 49, 67, 83, 85, 87

Date of Accounts	Dec 11	Dec 10	Dec 09
Sales Turnover	N/A	N/A	1m
Pre Tax Profit/Loss	N/A	N/A	51
Working Capital	11	34	81
Fixed Assets	156	156	129
Current Assets	309	274	267
Current Liabilities	N/A	N/A	36

Amalgamated Ltd
Systems House Dawson Street Swinton, Manchester, M27 4FJ
Tel: 0161-728 2228 **Fax:** 0161-794 5102
Website: http://www.amalgamatedltd.co.uk
Directors: G. Teader (Dir), A. Teader (Fin)
Immediate Holding Company: AMALGAMATED LTD
Registration no: 00978651 **Date established:** 1970
Turnover: £500,000 - £1m **No.of Employees:** 11 - 20
Product Groups: 37, 38, 40, 46, 47

Date of Accounts	Mar 11	Mar 10	Mar 09
Working Capital	731	709	638
Fixed Assets	21	29	93
Current Assets	1m	1m	1m

American & Efird GB Ltd
Chapelfield Radcliffe, Manchester, M26 1JF
Tel: 0161-766 1544 **Fax:** 0161-766 9965
E-mail: paul.dhenin@amefird.co.uk
Website: http://www.amefird.co.uk
Directors: F. Jackson (Pres), I. Peterson (Dir), P. D'henin (MD), R. Rowe (Sales)
Managers: S. Probert (Chief Mgr)
Ultimate Holding Company: FP014338
Immediate Holding Company: AMERICAN & EFIRD (G.B.) LIMITED
Registration no: 01423914 **VAT No.:** GB 328 1707 61
Date established: 1979 **Turnover:** £2m - £5m **No.of Employees:** 1 - 10
Product Groups: 23

Date of Accounts	Sep 07
Sales Turnover	7578
Pre Tax Profit/Loss	-142
Working Capital	2151
Fixed Assets	341
Current Assets	3854
Current Liabilities	1703
Total Share Capital	2420
ROCE% (Return on Capital Employed)	-5.7

Americhem Europe Ltd
Cawdor Street Eccles, Manchester, M30 0QF
Tel: 0161-789 7832 **Fax:** 0161-787 7832
E-mail: cmacdougall@americhem.com
Website: http://www.americhem.com
Directors: C. Macdougall (MD), I. McCoy (Fin), J. Berner (Fin)
Managers: C. Crosby (Purch Mgr), J. O'Carroll (Personnel)
Ultimate Holding Company: AMERICHEM INC (USA)
Immediate Holding Company: AMERICHEM EUROPE LIMITED
Registration no: 01009410 **VAT No.:** GB 638 8141 19
Date established: 1971 **Turnover:** £10m - £20m
No.of Employees: 21 - 50 **Product Groups:** 30, 32

Date of Accounts	Sep 11	Sep 10	Sep 09
Sales Turnover	15m	12m	8m
Pre Tax Profit/Loss	2m	1m	-124
Working Capital	3m	5m	4m
Fixed Assets	3m	2m	2m
Current Assets	6m	8m	6m
Current Liabilities	282	301	348

Anderson Greenwood Instrumentation (a division of Tyco Engineered Products (UK) Ltd)
Sharp Street Worsley, Manchester, M28 3NA
Tel: 0161-790 7741 **Fax:** 0161-703 1859
E-mail: info@stafetysytemsuk.com
Website: http://www.andersongreenwood.com
Bank(s): National Westminster Bank Plc
Managers: P. Stevenson (Sales Prom Mgr)
Ultimate Holding Company: Tyco International Ltd
Immediate Holding Company: Tyco Engineered Products (UK) Ltd
Registration no: 03814871 **VAT No.:** GB 716 0578 38
Turnover: £10m - £20m **No.of Employees:** 101 - 250
Product Groups: 30, 36, 39, 40

Andrew Engineering Leigh Ltd
14 Lodge Road Atherton, Manchester, M46 9BL
Tel: 01942-888848 **Fax:** 01942-888878
E-mail: enquiries@andrew-engineering.co.uk
Website: http://www.andrew-engineering.co.uk
Directors: M. Lee (Fin), J. Lee (MD)
Immediate Holding Company: ANDREW ENGINEERING (LEIGH) LIMITED
Registration no: 01668542 **Date established:** 1982
No.of Employees: 1 - 10 **Product Groups:** 46

Date of Accounts	Dec 10	Dec 09	Dec 07
Working Capital	-18	-4	29
Fixed Assets	52	59	75
Current Assets	91	88	101

Andrew's Air Conditioning Ltd
Claverton Road Roundthorn Industrial Estate, Manchester, M23 9FT
Tel: 08457-697987 **Fax:** 0161-945 7412
E-mail: andy.whiteley@andrews-sykes.com
Website: http://www.airconditioningservices.com
Directors: A. Whiteley (MD)
Immediate Holding Company: KLICK TECHNOLOGY LIMITED
Registration no: 06282339 **VAT No.:** GB 100 4295 24
Date established: 1981 **Turnover:** £75m - £125m
No.of Employees: 21 - 50 **Product Groups:** 38, 40, 66

Date of Accounts	Sep 11	Sep 10	Sep 09
Working Capital	420	328	267
Fixed Assets	51	41	47
Current Assets	2m	2m	2m

Anvil Masters Wrought Iron
1 Wild Street Denton, Manchester, M34 3AD
Tel: 0161-336 3285 **Fax:** 0161-336 3285
E-mail: info@anvilmasters.co.uk
Website: http://www.anvilmasters.co.uk
Directors: A. Lowe (Prop)
Date established: 1995 **No.of Employees:** 1 - 10 **Product Groups:** 26, 35

Aon Ltd
Arkwright House Parsonage Gardens, Manchester, M3 2LF
Tel: 0161-910 5100 **Fax:** 0161-833 9071
Website: http://www.aon.com
Directors: P. Mellor (Dir), P. Tompsett (MD)
Immediate Holding Company: AON LIMITED
Registration no: 00210725 **Date established:** 1925
No.of Employees: 101 - 250 **Product Groups:** 82

APMG Ltd
Mount Skip Lane Little Hulton, Manchester, M38 9AL
Tel: 0161-799 2200 **Fax:** 0161-799 2220
E-mail: enquiries@apmg.co.uk
Website: http://www.apmg.co.uk
Bank(s): Lloyds TSB Bank plc
Directors: W. Perrott (MD), G. Perrott (Fin), W. Perrott (Dir)
Managers: R. Shanks (Chief Acct), C. Brown (Sales Prom Mgr)
Immediate Holding Company: A P M G LIMITED
Registration no: 00358231 **Date established:** 1939 **Turnover:** £2m - £5m
No.of Employees: 21 - 50 **Product Groups:** 30, 31, 40, 42, 48, 66

Date of Accounts	Oct 11	Oct 10	Oct 09
Working Capital	582	400	288
Fixed Assets	175	165	225
Current Assets	847	1m	1m

Apple Display & Shopfitting Ltd
King Street Denton Denton, Manchester, M34 6PF
Tel: 0161-335 0660 **Fax:** 0161-335 9114
E-mail: sales@appledisplay.co.uk
Website: http://www.appledisplay.co.uk
Directors: J. Smyth (Dir), L. Heap (Dir)
Immediate Holding Company: APPLE DISPLAY & SHOPFITTING LIMITED
Registration no: 02414652 **Date established:** 1989 **Turnover:** £1m - £2m
No.of Employees: 1 - 10 **Product Groups:** 52

Date of Accounts	Mar 11	Mar 10	Mar 09
Working Capital	-54	-35	-16
Fixed Assets	111	115	142
Current Assets	353	395	430

Applewood Data Services
20 Wheel Forge Way Trafford Park, Manchester, M17 1EH
Tel: 08458-381038
E-mail: enquiries@applewooddata.co.uk
Website: http://www.applewooddata.co.uk
Directors: P. Moran (Prop)
Date established: 2004 **No.of Employees:** 1 - 10 **Product Groups:** 37

Date of Accounts	Mar 08	Mar 07	Mar 06
Working Capital	3	-16	-14
Fixed Assets	53	58	38
Current Assets	96	90	20
Current Liabilities	94	106	34

Applied Fusion
Fielding Street Eccles, Manchester, M30 0GJ
Tel: 0161-789 1469 **Fax:** 0161-787 8226
E-mail: gedheavey@supanet.com
Website: http://www.heaveyeng.co.uk
Bank(s): National Westminster Bank Plc
Directors: I. Hogg (Ptnr), T. Heavey (MD), D. Heavey (Fin)
Managers: F. Appleby (Works Gen Mgr)
Immediate Holding Company: HEAVEY PROPERTIES LIMITED
Registration no: 00442785 **VAT No.:** GB 145 6810 63
Date established: 1947 **No.of Employees:** 11 - 20 **Product Groups:** 48

Approved Fabricators
16 Debdale Lane Astley, Tyldesley, Manchester, M29 7FL
Tel: 08448-845213
E-mail: info@approvedfabricators.co.uk
Website: http://www.approvedfabricators.co.uk
Directors: J. Loxham (Prop)
Managers: J. Loxham (Chief Mgr)
Date established: 2007 **Turnover:** Up to £250,000
No.of Employees: 1 - 10 **Product Groups:** 35

Aquaculture Equipment Ltd
36 Foxdenton Lane Middleton, Manchester, M24 1QG
Tel: 0161-683 5869 **Fax:** 0161-683 5869
E-mail: sales@aquacultureequipment.co.uk
Website: http://www.aquacultureequipment.co.uk
Directors: M. Stockton (Dir)
Registration no: 04470461 **Date established:** 2002
Turnover: Up to £250,000 **No.of Employees:** 1 - 10 **Product Groups:** 41, 84

Aramex
Unit 10 Ringway Trading Estate, Manchester, M22 5LH
Tel: 0161-908 3900 **Fax:** 0161-908 3929
E-mail: jim.armour@aramex.com
Website: http://www.aramex.com
Directors: E. Elayan (Co Sec), J. Armour (MD)
Managers: T. Alkharouf (Fin Mgr), E. Cobden (Personnel)
Ultimate Holding Company: ARAMEX PJSC (UNITED ARAB EMIRATES)
Immediate Holding Company: VANGUARD FREIGHT SYSTEMS LIMITED
Registration no: 02431789 **Date established:** 1989
No.of Employees: 51 - 100 **Product Groups:** 76

Arcelormittal Ltd
Avis House Highfield Road, Little Hulton, Manchester, M38 9ST
Tel: 0161-703 9073 **Fax:** 0161-703 9037
Website: http://www.arcelormittal.com
Bank(s): Yorkshire Bank PLC
Directors: A. Bowen (MD)
Managers: A. Pety (Sales Prom Mgr), P. Taylor (Tech Serv Mgr), S. Allen, S. Taylor (Fin Mgr), K. Bevan (Personnel)
Ultimate Holding Company: ARCELORMITTAL SA (LUXEMBOURG)
Immediate Holding Company: ARCELORMITTAL DISTRIBUTION SOLUTIONS UK LIMITED
Registration no: 01669950 **VAT No.:** GB 383 2095 49
Date established: 1982 **Turnover:** £75m - £125m
No.of Employees: 51 - 100 **Product Groups:** 66

Date of Accounts	Dec 11	Dec 10	Dec 09
Sales Turnover	211m	117m	35m
Pre Tax Profit/Loss	3m	4m	-10
Working Capital	17m	-183	4m
Fixed Assets	13m	10m	2m
Current Assets	73m	39m	12m
Current Liabilities	4m	4m	732

Arco Ltd
Tenax Circle Trafford Park, Manchester, M17 1EZ
Tel: 0161-869 5807 **Fax:** 0161-869 5858
E-mail: martin.emery@arco.co.uk
Website: http://www.arco.co.uk
Managers: I. Martin (District Mgr), M. Emery (Mgr)
Immediate Holding Company: ARCO LIMITED
Registration no: 00133804 **Date established:** 2014 **Turnover:** £2m - £5m
No.of Employees: 21 - 50 **Product Groups:** 24, 29, 30, 40

Date of Accounts	Jun 11	Jun 10	Jun 09
Sales Turnover	229m	216m	214m
Pre Tax Profit/Loss	8m	6m	260
Working Capital	32m	27m	29m
Fixed Assets	19m	21m	23m
Current Assets	82m	67m	62m
Current Liabilities	12m	13m	8m

Arivatex Ltd
17 Chatley Street, Manchester, M3 1HX
Tel: 0161-834 9191 **Fax:** 0161-834 9161
E-mail: info@arivatex.co.uk
Website: http://www.arivatex.co.uk
Directors: R. Smith (MD)
Immediate Holding Company: ARIVATEX LIMITED
Registration no: 04994464 **VAT No.:** GB 473 4228 45
Date established: 2003 **Turnover:** £500,000 - £1m
No.of Employees: 1 - 10 **Product Groups:** 24

Date of Accounts	Mar 11	Mar 10	Mar 09
Working Capital	-20	-15	-13
Fixed Assets	13	14	16
Current Assets	372	99	145

Armquest Industrial Services Ltd
Invar Road Swinton, Manchester, M27 9HD
Tel: 0161-727 8578 **Fax:** 0161-728 3190
E-mail: stevegroves@armquest.co.uk
Website: http://www.armquest.co.uk
Directors: S. Groves (MD)
Immediate Holding Company: ARMQUEST INDUSTRIAL SERVICES LIMITED
Registration no: 02399808 **Date established:** 1989
No.of Employees: 21 - 50 **Product Groups:** 25, 27, 33, 37, 42, 45, 48, 51, 52, 72, 76, 80, 83, 87

Date of Accounts	Mar 11	Mar 10	Mar 09
Working Capital	162	132	84
Fixed Assets	251	228	258
Current Assets	384	353	314

Armstrong Controls Ltd
Wenlock Way, Manchester, M12 5JL
Tel: 08444-145145 **Fax:** 0121-550 1679
E-mail: marketing@holdenbrooke.com
Website: http://www.armstrongcontrols.co.uk
Bank(s): Barclays
Directors: R. Stroude (MD), P. Gwilliams (Fin), C. Buchanan (Mkt Research), A. Kilmister (Fin)
Managers: P. Chilteton (Sales & Mktg Mg), N. Livesy (Personnel), S. Howlett (Tech Serv Mgr), I. Frank, R. Gill (I.T. Exec)
Ultimate Holding Company: ARMSTRONG INTEGRATED LIMITED
Immediate Holding Company: ARMSTRONG HOLDEN BROOKE PULLEN LIMITED
Registration no: 07261626 **VAT No.:** GB 677 3986 65
Date established: 2010 **Turnover:** £10m - £20m
No.of Employees: 51 - 100 **Product Groups:** 39, 40

Arriva North West
6 St Andrews Square, Manchester, M1 2NS
Tel: 0161-272 6565 **Fax:** 0161-272 7333
Website: http://www.arriva.co.uk
Directors: H. Hughes (Dir)
Ultimate Holding Company: ARRIVA PLC
Immediate Holding Company: ARRIVA (2007) LTD
Registration no: 02405347 **Turnover:** £5m - £10m
No.of Employees: 51 - 100 **Product Groups:** 72

Artisan Sintered Products Ltd
Unit 15 Shepley Industrial Estate South Audenshaw, Manchester, M34 5DW
Tel: 0161-336 5911 **Fax:** 0161-335 0280
E-mail: sales@artisnacarbide.co.uk
Website: http://www.artisancarbide.co.uk
Managers: P. Flynn (Mgr)
Ultimate Holding Company: HARDMETAL PRODUCTS LIMITED
Immediate Holding Company: ARTISAN SINTERED PRODUCTS LIMITED
Registration no: 00916766 **Date established:** 1967 **Turnover:** £1m - £2m
No.of Employees: 1 - 10 **Product Groups:** 34, 36, 45, 46

Date of Accounts	Mar 11	Mar 10	Mar 09
Working Capital	201	242	389
Fixed Assets	34	48	61
Current Assets	691	615	659

Arup
St James Buildings 79 Oxford Street, Manchester, M1 6EL
Tel: 0161-228 2331 **Fax:** 0161-236 1057
E-mail: manchester@arup.com
Website: http://www.arup.com
Directors: K. Rudd (Dir), R. Milburn (Dir)
Immediate Holding Company: BRANKGATE PROPERTIES LIMITED
Registration no: SC062237 **Date established:** 1965
No.of Employees: 101 - 250 **Product Groups:** 44

Aspin Engineering Ltd
Unit 5 Egremont Close Moss Lane Industrial Estate, Whitefield, Manchester, M45 8FH
Tel: 0161-766 9622 **Fax:** 0161-766 1423
E-mail: enquiries@aspin-engineering.com
Website: http://www.aspin-engineering.com
Directors: A. Aspin (MD)
Ultimate Holding Company: ASPIN DEVELOPMENTS LIMITED
Immediate Holding Company: ASPIN DEVELOPMENTS LIMITED
Registration no: 01808439 **Date established:** 1984
Turnover: £500,000 - £1m **No.of Employees:** 11 - 20
Product Groups: 30, 36, 48

Associated Home Fabrics Ltd
Hyline House Tilson Road, Roundthorn Industrial Estate, Manchester, M23 9JD
Tel: 0161-998 1526 **Fax:** 0161-946 0407
E-mail: sales@a-h-f.co.uk
Website: http://www.a-h-f.co.uk
Bank(s): National Westminster Bank Plc
Directors: S. Hughes (MD)
Immediate Holding Company: ASSOCIATED HOME FABRICS LIMITED
Registration no: 00551895 **VAT No.:** GB 145 0988 52
Date established: 1955 **Turnover:** £5m - £10m **No.of Employees:** 11 - 20
Product Groups: 23, 24

Date of Accounts	Jun 12	Jun 11	Jun 10
Working Capital	517	579	663
Fixed Assets	231	235	244
Current Assets	613	594	698

Association of Hot Foil Printers
15 Hunt Street Atherton, Manchester, M46 9JF
Tel: 01942-873574 **Fax:** 01942-873574
E-mail: association@hotfoilprinting.org
Website: http://www.hotfoilprinting.org
Directors: L. Knight (Dir), P. Foreshaw (Ch)
Turnover: Up to £250,000 **No.of Employees:** 1 - 10 **Product Groups:** 28

Astra Signs Ltd
204 Dantzic Street, Manchester, M4 4DD
Tel: 0161-832 2429 **Fax:** 0161-839 9004
E-mail: info@astrasigns.com
Website: http://www.astrasigns.com
Directors: D. Derbyshire (MD)
Immediate Holding Company: ASTRA SIGNS LIMITED
Registration no: 03115547 **Date established:** 1995 **Turnover:** £1m - £2m
No.of Employees: 51 - 100 **Product Groups:** 27, 28, 30, 37, 39, 40, 49, 67, 81

Date of Accounts	Dec 11	Dec 10	Dec 09
Working Capital	-166	-289	-170
Fixed Assets	1m	1m	1m
Current Assets	733	629	644

ATM Import Export Ltd
Unit 4 29 Cheetwood Road, Manchester, M8 8 AQ
Tel: 0161-834 9155 **Fax:** 0161-831 9178
E-mail: info@mashgroup.co.uk
Website: http://www.mashgroup.co.uk
Directors: S. Irving (Dir)
Immediate Holding Company: ATM IMPORT EXPORT LIMITED
Registration no: 07756165 **Date established:** 2011
No.of Employees: 1 - 10 **Product Groups:** 28, 67

Austin Trumanns Steel Ltd (Austin Division)
Moss Lane Walkden, Manchester, M28 3NH
Tel: 0161-799 8882 **Fax:** 0161-790 1848
E-mail: sales@austin-trumanns.co.uk
Website: http://www.austin-trumanns.co.uk
Bank(s): National Westminster Bank Plc
Directors: B. Gregory (MD), G. Hill (Grp Chief Exec)
Managers: T. Simpson (Sales & Mktg Mg)
Ultimate Holding Company: Murray International Holdings Ltd
Immediate Holding Company: Murray General Steels Group Ltd
Registration no: 01220846 **Turnover:** £50m - £75m
No.of Employees: 51 - 100 **Product Groups:** 66

Date of Accounts	Jan 08	Jan 07
Sales Turnover	83230	67130
Pre Tax Profit/Loss	6540	3210
Working Capital	21020	16410
Fixed Assets	740	840
Current Assets	40010	37460
Current Liabilities	18990	21050
Total Share Capital	2000	2000
ROCE% (Return on Capital Employed)	30.1	18.6
ROT% (Return on Turnover)	7.9	4.8

Auto Marine Cables Ltd
Unit 32 Oakhill Trading Estate Devonshire Road, Worsley, Manchester, M28 3PT
Tel: 01204-575234 **Fax:** 01204-861740
E-mail: sales@automarinecables.co.uk
Website: http://www.automarinecables.co.uk
Bank(s): The Royal Bank of Scotland
Directors: G. Holt (Fin), P. Hammond (MD), J. Fincham (Fin), D. Hammond (Sales)
Managers: J. Rhoads (Purch Mgr)
Immediate Holding Company: AUTO MARINE CABLES LIMITED
Registration no: 00804767 **VAT No.:** GB 354 7037 53
Date established: 1964 **Turnover:** £10m - £20m
No.of Employees: 51 - 100 **Product Groups:** 30, 36, 37, 39, 68

Date of Accounts	Sep 11	Sep 10	Sep 09
Sales Turnover	11m	9m	7m
Pre Tax Profit/Loss	1m	557	339
Working Capital	1m	1m	1m
Fixed Assets	376	398	340
Current Assets	4m	4m	3m
Current Liabilities	620	459	301

AVS MOT
1 Hall Street Off Hobson Street, Failsworth, Manchester, M35 0JH
Tel: 0161-681 6511 **Fax:** 0161-684 8975
E-mail: pete@avs.com
Website: http://www.avsautos.com
Managers: C. Laycock (Mgr)
No.of Employees: 1 - 10 **Product Groups:** 68, 72, 85

Axiom Displays Ltd
Mersey Road North Failsworth, Manchester, M35 9LT
Tel: 0161-681 1371 **Fax:** 0161-683 4641
E-mail: info@axiom-displays.co.uk
Website: http://www.axiom-displays.co.uk
Bank(s): National Westminster Bank Plc
Directors: I. Price (Fin), R. Jarvis (Sales)
Managers: D. Walton (Buyer)
Ultimate Holding Company: AXIOM MARKETING SERVICES LIMITED
Immediate Holding Company: AXIOM DISPLAYS LIMITED
Registration no: 02191874 **VAT No.:** GB 508 2310 81
Date established: 1987 **No.of Employees:** 51 - 100 **Product Groups:** 49, 81

Date of Accounts	Nov 11	Nov 10	Nov 09
Working Capital	175	152	134
Current Assets	2m	2m	2m

B K W Instruments Ltd
Weymouth Road Eccles, Manchester, M30 8SH
Tel: 0161-707 4838 **Fax:** 0161-787 7580
E-mail: sales@bkwinstruments.co.uk
Website: http://www.bkwinstruments.co.uk
Bank(s): Lloyds TSB Bank plc
Directors: M. Honeyford (Chief Op Offcr)
Immediate Holding Company: BKW INSTRUMENTS LIMITED
Registration no: 01207254 **Date established:** 1975 **Turnover:** £1m - £2m
No.of Employees: 21 - 50 **Product Groups:** 38, 40

Date of Accounts	Dec 11	Dec 10	Dec 09
Working Capital	-94	-145	-215
Fixed Assets	723	715	714
Current Assets	1m	1m	991

B M Commercials
724 Hyde Road, Manchester, M18 7EF
Tel: 0161-230 6002 **Fax:** 0161-230 6060
E-mail: bmcommercials@aol.com
Website: http://www.bmcommercials.co.uk
Directors: K. Murray (Dir)
Date established: 1969 **No.of Employees:** 1 - 10 **Product Groups:** 40, 45

B & M Electronics
23 New Mount Street, Manchester, M4 4DE
Tel: 0161-953 4070
Directors: B. Morris (Prop)
Immediate Holding Company: HOLT BERRY LIMITED
Registration no: 06807399 **Date established:** 2009 **Turnover:** £1m - £2m
No.of Employees: 1 - 10 **Product Groups:** 36, 40

Date of Accounts	Aug 11
Working Capital	-24
Fixed Assets	25
Current Assets	13

B & M Industrial Floor Cleaning Machinery
6 Town Lane Denton, Manchester, M34 6LE
Tel: 0161-320 4291 **Fax:** 0161-320 4291
Directors: M. Sidebotham (Prop)
Date established: 1998 **Turnover:** Up to £250,000
No.of Employees: 1 - 10 **Product Groups:** 40, 52, 83

B P M Engineering Services Ltd
Unit 18 Failsworth Industrial Estate Morton Street, Failsworth, Manchester, M35 0BN
Tel: 0161-682 3377 **Fax:** 0161-682 7711
E-mail: brian.bpm@btconnect.com
Website: http://www.bpmengineering.co.uk
Directors: B. Mawson (Prop)
Immediate Holding Company: B P M ENGINEERING SERVICES LIMITED
Registration no: 03184799 **VAT No.:** GB 628 7629 01
Date established: 1996 **Turnover:** Up to £250,000
No.of Employees: 1 - 10 **Product Groups:** 27, 42, 44

Date of Accounts	Apr 11	Apr 10	Apr 09
Working Capital	-3	20	9
Fixed Assets	1	2	2
Current Assets	14	61	31

B S H Industries Ltd
Rutland Street Swinton, Manchester, M27 6AU
Tel: 0161-793 5148 **Fax:** 0161-794 4793
E-mail: bsh@boltblue.com
Directors: S. Waller (Fin), D. Waller (MD)
Immediate Holding Company: BSH INDUSTRIES LIMITED
Registration no: 01262603 **VAT No.:** GB 150 9658 51
Date established: 1976 **Turnover:** £500,000 - £1m
No.of Employees: 1 - 10 **Product Groups:** 37, 39

Date of Accounts	Dec 11	Dec 10	Dec 09
Working Capital	-120	-135	-164
Fixed Assets	1m	1m	1m
Current Assets	28	29	19

B3 Cable Solutions
Delaunays Road, Manchester, M9 8FP
Tel: 0161-740 9151 **Fax:** 0161-795 8393
E-mail: info@b3cables.com
Website: http://www.b3cables.com
Bank(s): HSBC Bank plc
Directors: C. Allen (Co Sec), C. Sykes (Grp Chief Exec), D. Powell (Fin)
Managers: A. Dar (Tech Serv Mgr), I. Clements (Buyer), P. Farrell (Sales Prom Mgr), H. Mansbridge (Personnel)
Ultimate Holding Company: BELDEN INC (USA)
Immediate Holding Company: BELDEN UK LIMITED
Registration no: 02882171 **VAT No.:** GB 641 5389 33
Date established: 1993 **Turnover:** £5m - £10m
No.of Employees: 101 - 250 **Product Groups:** 35, 37, 44, 67

Date of Accounts	Dec 11	Dec 10	Dec 09
Sales Turnover	6m	5m	4m
Pre Tax Profit/Loss	69	899	438
Working Capital	-132	4m	11m
Fixed Assets	4m	3m	2m
Current Assets	6m	6m	18m
Current Liabilities	302	387	706

Banico Ltd
Tilson Road Roundthorn Industrial Estate, Manchester, M23 9GF
Tel: 08451-700740 **Fax:** 0845-170 0750
E-mail: info@banico.co.uk
Website: http://www.banico.co.uk
Directors: A. Bani (MD)
Immediate Holding Company: BANICO LIMITED
Registration no: 02440630 **Date established:** 1989
Turnover: £500,000 - £1m **No.of Employees:** 1 - 10 **Product Groups:** 36, 37, 38, 39, 40, 66, 67

Date of Accounts	Mar 11	Mar 10	Mar 09
Working Capital	1m	936	645
Fixed Assets	16	18	22
Current Assets	1m	1m	819

Barratt Homes Manchester
4 Brindley Road, Manchester, M16 9HQ
Tel: 0161-872 0161 **Fax:** 0161-848 7332
E-mail: neil.goodwin@barratthomes.co.uk
Website: http://www.barratthomes.co.uk
Directors: J. Newton (Sales), N. Goodwin (MD), M. Cleary (Fin)
Managers: J. Griffin, J. Adams
Immediate Holding Company: E-BONDED LIMITED
Registration no: 00658155 **Date established:** 2001
Turnover: £50m - £75m **No.of Employees:** 51 - 100 **Product Groups:** 80

Date of Accounts	Dec 11	Dec 10	Dec 09
Working Capital	-1m	-671	-1m
Fixed Assets	3m	3m	3m
Current Liabilities	1m	N/A	N/A

Basic Elements
PO Box 439, Manchester, M14 0BH
Tel: 0845-0263639 **Fax:** 0845-0263640
E-mail: basicelements@piranha-internet.co.uk
Website: http://www.basicelements.co.uk
Registration no: 05214352 **No.of Employees:** 1 - 10 **Product Groups:** 24, 63

Basic Welding Services
48 Cambrian Street, Manchester, M40 7EG
Tel: 0161-273 8150 **Fax:** 0161-273 3042
E-mail: roger@basicwelding.co.uk
Website: http://www.basicwelding.co.uk
Directors: R. Jones (MD)
Immediate Holding Company: BASIC WELDING SERVICES LIMITED
Registration no: 03334319 **Date established:** 1997
No.of Employees: 11 - 20 **Product Groups:** 46

Date of Accounts	Jul 11	Jul 10	Jul 09
Working Capital	54	51	37
Fixed Assets	3	3	4
Current Assets	205	264	154

Baskerville Reactors Autoclaves Ltd
Unit 30 Long Wood Road, Trafford Park, Manchester, M17 1PZ
Tel: 0161-848 5960 **Fax:** 0161-888 2345
E-mail: admin@baskervilleautoclaves.co.uk
Website: http://www.baskervilleautoclaves.co.uk
Directors: C. Fleming (Dir)
Immediate Holding Company: BASKERVILLE REACTORS & AUTOCLAVES LIMITED
Registration no: 05701913 **VAT No.:** GB 603 7682 41
Date established: 2006 **Turnover:** £500,000 - £1m
No.of Employees: 1 - 10 **Product Groups:** 30, 35, 37, 38, 40, 41, 42, 48, 84

Date of Accounts	Jun 11	Jun 10	Jun 09
Working Capital	-55	-77	-110
Fixed Assets	164	196	175
Current Assets	431	380	367

Bath Surgeon
102 Ewood House St Marys Road, Eccles, Manchester, M30 0BA
Tel: 0161-788 0182 **Fax:** 0161-707 6634
E-mail: enquiries@bathsurgeon.co.uk
Website: http://www.bathsurgeon.co.uk
Directors: G. Johnson (Prop)
No.of Employees: 1 - 10 **Product Groups:** 46, 48

Batt Cables plc
Unit 64-66 Oakhill Trading Estate Devonshire Road, Worsley, Manchester, M28 3PT
Tel: 01204-793111 **Fax:** 01204-576245
E-mail: rob.waddington@batt.co.uk
Website: http://www.batt.co.uk
Directors: R. Waddington (Dir)
Immediate Holding Company: BATT CABLES PLC
Registration no: 01353688 **Date established:** 1978
No.of Employees: 21 - 50 **Product Groups:** 30, 35, 36, 37, 38, 44, 66, 67

Date of Accounts	Mar 12	Mar 11	Mar 10
Sales Turnover	106m	98m	84m
Pre Tax Profit/Loss	8m	9m	5m
Working Capital	41m	36m	31m
Fixed Assets	8m	9m	8m
Current Assets	69m	60m	54m
Current Liabilities	3m	3m	2m

Battery Force Ltd
4 Beacon Road Trafford Park, Manchester, M17 1AF
Tel: 01892-888135 **Fax:** 01892-730659
E-mail: webmaster@battery-force.co.uk
Website: http://www.battery-force.co.uk
Managers: O. Davis (Mgr), S. Dowd
Ultimate Holding Company: SUPREME IMPORTS LTD
Immediate Holding Company: BATTERY FORCE LTD.
Registration no: 04642418 **Date established:** 2003
Turnover: £250,000 - £500,000 **No.of Employees:** 1 - 10
Product Groups: 37, 38

Date of Accounts	Dec 08	Mar 12	Mar 11
Working Capital	51	76	76
Fixed Assets	4	N/A	N/A
Current Assets	113	76	76
Current Liabilities	33	N/A	N/A

B C Design Engineers Ltd
26 Carrington Road Urmston, Manchester, M41 6HX
Tel: 0161-746 9111 **Fax:** 0161-746 9222
E-mail: admin@bcdesignengineers.co.uk
Website: http://www.bcdesignengineers.co.uk
Directors: H. Clarkin (Fin), A. Smith (MD)
Immediate Holding Company: B. C. DESIGN ENGINEERS LIMITED
Registration no: 01012994 **Date established:** 1971
Turnover: £500,000 - £1m **No.of Employees:** 11 - 20
Product Groups: 44, 84

Date of Accounts	Aug 11	Aug 10	Aug 09
Working Capital	52	146	196
Fixed Assets	4	13	20
Current Assets	86	196	267

Beachcroft Wansbroughs
St Anns House St Anns Street, Manchester, M2 7LP
Tel: 0161-934 3000 **Fax:** 0161- 9343288
Website: http://www.bwlaw.co.uk
Bank(s): Lloyds TSB Bank plc
Directors: C. Charles (Fin), I. Moore (MD)
Managers: N. Attree
Registration no: 06113320 **Date established:** 2007 **Turnover:** £5m - £10m
No.of Employees: 101 - 250 **Product Groups:** 80

Beamech Group Ltd
5 Orion Trading Estate Tenax Road, Trafford Park, Manchester, M17 1JT
Tel: 0161-848 0316 **Fax:** 0161-873 7718
E-mail: email@beamech.com
Website: http://www.beamech.com
Bank(s): National Westminster Bank Plc
Directors: J. Blackwell (MD), S. Blackwell (Sales), G. Buckley (Eng Serv), J. Blackwell (Dir), S. Blackwell (Tech Sales)
Managers: A. Stanley (Purch Mgr)
Immediate Holding Company: BEAMECH GROUP LIMITED
Registration no: 01405763 **VAT No.:** GB 298 8309 94
Date established: 1978 **Turnover:** £2m - £5m **No.of Employees:** 21 - 50
Product Groups: 30

Date of Accounts	Apr 11	Apr 10	Apr 09
Working Capital	-540	-186	-302
Fixed Assets	2m	787	797
Current Assets	2m	2m	1m

Belden UK Ltd
Manchester International Office Centre Styal Road, Manchester, M22 5WB
Tel: 0161-498 3754 **Fax:** 0121-329 5001
Website: http://www.hirschmann.co.uk
Directors: V. Schicker (Fin)
Managers: C. Clews, S. Doyle (Personnel)
Ultimate Holding Company: BELDEN INC (USA)
Immediate Holding Company: BELDEN UK LIMITED
Registration no: 02882171 **Date established:** 1993 **Turnover:** £2m - £5m
No.of Employees: 21 - 50 **Product Groups:** 37, 38, 44, 67

see next page

Belden UK Ltd - Cont'd

Date of Accounts	Dec 11	Dec 10	Dec 09
Sales Turnover	6m	5m	4m
Pre Tax Profit/Loss	69	899	438
Working Capital	-132	4m	11m
Fixed Assets	4m	3m	2m
Current Assets	6m	6m	18m
Current Liabilities	302	387	706

Beldorm Ltd

Kearsley Mill Crompton Road, Radcliffe, Manchester, M26 1RH
Tel: 01204-702300 **Fax:** 01204-854854
E-mail: sunil@ruia.co.uk
Website: http://www.ruia.co.uk
Bank(s): HSBC Bank plc & National Westminster Bank PLC
Directors: J. Ruia (Dir), S. Ruia (MD)
Managers: K. Pringle (Personnel), K. Parker (Mktg Serv Mgr), C. Jackson (Sales Prom Mgr), R. Thompson (I.T. Exec)
Ultimate Holding Company: RUIA GROUP LIMITED
Immediate Holding Company: DREW BRADY & CO. LIMITED
Registration no: 00883804 **Date established:** 1947
Turnover: £10m - £20m **No.of Employees:** 21 - 50 **Product Groups:** 23, 24

Date of Accounts	Apr 11	Apr 10	Apr 09
Sales Turnover	48m	42m	41m
Pre Tax Profit/Loss	7m	5m	313
Working Capital	14m	15m	12m
Fixed Assets	6m	7m	7m
Current Assets	29m	26m	24m
Current Liabilities	8m	9m	9m

Bendex Plastics

Europa Trading Estate Stoneclough Road, Radcliffe, Manchester, M26 1GG
Tel: 01204-861337 **Fax:** 01204-791872
E-mail: sales@bendex-plastics.co.uk
Website: http://www.bendex-plastics.co.uk
Managers: J. Hamer
Immediate Holding Company: TOTAL FLEET UK LTD
Registration no: 01062820 **VAT No.:** GB 668 4611 07
Date established: 2009 **No.of Employees:** 11 - 20 **Product Groups:** 30

Date of Accounts	May 11	May 09	May 08
Working Capital	-350	10	-8
Fixed Assets	391	63	67
Current Assets	46	94	95

Benson Components Ltd

Saxon Works South Street, Openshaw, Manchester, M11 2FY
Tel: 0161-952 8888 **Fax:** 0161-231 6866
E-mail: sales@bensonexhausts.com
Website: http://www.bensonexhausts.com
Bank(s): National Westminster Bank Plc
Directors: B. Hewitson (Dir)
Ultimate Holding Company: FINAL FLOURISH LIMITED
Immediate Holding Company: BENSON COMPONENTS LIMITED
Registration no: 00503682 **VAT No.:** GB 145 3008 00
Date established: 1952 **Turnover:** £5m - £10m
No.of Employees: 51 - 100 **Product Groups:** 35, 40, 48, 68

Date of Accounts	Dec 11	Dec 10	Dec 09
Sales Turnover	7m	6m	5m
Pre Tax Profit/Loss	343	387	173
Working Capital	172	2m	2m
Fixed Assets	1m	743	734
Current Assets	3m	3m	3m
Current Liabilities	508	455	173

Biffa Waste Services Ltd

Lumns Lane Swinton, Manchester, M27 8LN
Tel: 0161-793 1400 **Fax:** 0161-793 9259
E-mail: marketing@biffa.co.uk
Website: http://www.biffa.co.uk
Managers: J. Ratcliffe (Mgr)
Immediate Holding Company: BIFFA WASTE SERVICES LIMITED
Registration no: 00946107 **Date established:** 1969
No.of Employees: 1 - 10 **Product Groups:** 32, 54

Date of Accounts	Mar 08	Mar 09	Apr 10
Sales Turnover	555m	574m	492m
Pre Tax Profit/Loss	23m	50m	30m
Working Capital	229m	271m	293m
Fixed Assets	371m	360m	378m
Current Assets	409m	534m	609m
Current Liabilities	50m	100m	115m

Bifold Group

Greengate Industrial Estate Middleton, Manchester, M24 1SW
Tel: 0161-345 4777 **Fax:** 0161-345 4780
E-mail: gjacobson@bifold.co.uk
Website: http://www.bifold.co.uk
Bank(s): Barclays
Directors: G. Bancroft (Mkt Research), B. Pazzard (Sales)
Managers: A. Revans (Fin Mgr), S. Humphreys (Personnel), G. Jacobson
Ultimate Holding Company: BIFOLD FLUIDPOWER LIMITED
Immediate Holding Company: FLUIDPOWER (STAINLESS STEEL) LIMITED
Registration no: 01928457 **VAT No.:** GB 374 1828 38
Date established: 1985 **Turnover:** £10m - £20m
No.of Employees: 101 - 250 **Product Groups:** 40

Biodata Ltd

10 Stocks Street, Manchester, M8 8QG
Tel: 0161-834 6688 **Fax:** 0161-833 2190
E-mail: g.collins@microlink.co.uk
Website: http://www.microlink.co.uk
Directors: G. Collins (MD)
Immediate Holding Company: BIODATA LIMITED
Registration no: 01107155 **VAT No.:** GB 149 1487 45
Date established: 1973 **Turnover:** £500,000 - £1m
No.of Employees: 1 - 10 **Product Groups:** 44, 84

Date of Accounts	Jun 12	Jun 11	Jun 10
Working Capital	78	74	62
Fixed Assets	139	153	170
Current Assets	192	140	267

Blackburn & Murgatroyd Ltd

7 Poplar Road Stretford, Manchester, M32 9AN
Tel: 0161-865 2292 **Fax:** 0161-865 4992
E-mail: info@blackmurg.com
Website: http://www.blackmurg.com
Directors: M. Guest (Prop)
Immediate Holding Company: BLACKBURN & MURGATROYD LIMITED
Registration no: 00582248 **VAT No.:** GB 145 0680 80
Date established: 1957 **Turnover:** £250,000 - £500,000
No.of Employees: 1 - 10 **Product Groups:** 52

Date of Accounts	Apr 12	Apr 11	Apr 10
Working Capital	62	43	37
Fixed Assets	41	44	41
Current Assets	185	145	139

Boardman Bros Ltd

50 Red Bank, Manchester, M4 4HF
Tel: 0161-832 2381 **Fax:** 0161-833 2456
E-mail: phil@boardmanbros.co.uk
Website: http://www.boardmanbros.co.uk
Directors: N. Bell (Fin)
Ultimate Holding Company: PESHAWEAR (U.K.) LIMITED
Immediate Holding Company: BOARDMAN BROS LIMITED
Registration no: 00204341 **Date established:** 2025
Turnover: £10m - £20m **No.of Employees:** 51 - 100 **Product Groups:** 24, 63

Date of Accounts	Jan 11	Jan 10	Jan 09
Sales Turnover	13m	12m	11m
Pre Tax Profit/Loss	313	562	467
Working Capital	2m	2m	2m
Fixed Assets	199	170	116
Current Assets	5m	4m	4m
Current Liabilities	2m	1m	1m

Bolton Engineering & Manufacturing Co. Ltd

Unit R Highfield Road Little Hulton, Manchester, M38 9ST
Tel: 0161-790 1365 **Fax:** 0161-703 8632
Website: http://www.percydoughty.co.uk
Directors: R. Hollman (MD)
Ultimate Holding Company: BOLTON ENGINEERING (HOLDINGS) LIMITED
Immediate Holding Company: BOLTON ENGINEERING COMPANY
Registration no: 02701605 **VAT No.:** GB 354 7836 23
Date established: 1992 **Turnover:** £1m - £2m **No.of Employees:** 11 - 20
Product Groups: 36

Date of Accounts	Mar 12	Mar 11	Mar 10
Working Capital	N/A	N/A	-281
Fixed Assets	931	931	931

Bond IT Ltd

Unit 11b Enterprise House Manchester Science Park, LLoyd Street North, Manchester, M5 6 SE
Tel: 0161-737 6270 **Fax:** 0161-226 9995
E-mail: info@bonditltd.com
Website: http://bonditltd.com
Directors: G. Rawlinson (Dir)
Registration no: 05560257 **Date established:** 2005
No.of Employees: 1 - 10 **Product Groups:** 32

Botraco Ltd (a division of Wrengate House)

Wrengate House 221 Palatine Road, Manchester, M20 2EE
Tel: 0161-438 1015 **Fax:** 0161-438 1020
E-mail: botraco@wrengate.co.uk
Website: http://www.wrengate.co.uk
Bank(s): ABN AMRO Bank NV
Directors: A. Ruia (Dir), A. Desai (Co Sec), A. Ruia (Ch), G. Prichard (Sales), M. Ruia (Dir), T. Purcel (MD)
Managers: N. Gates (Sales Admin), D. Grimshaw (Personnel), M. Keyes (Accounts)
Ultimate Holding Company: Wrengate Ltd
Immediate Holding Company: Wrengate Ltd
Registration no: 00578230 **VAT No.:** GB 145 2770 69
Date established: 1957 **Turnover:** £250,000 - £500,000
No.of Employees: 11 - 20 **Product Groups:** 23

Date of Accounts	Apr 09	Apr 08	Apr 07
Sales Turnover	441	629	857
Pre Tax Profit/Loss	-268	-186	-146
Working Capital	6m	6m	6m
Fixed Assets	2	4	4
Current Assets	6m	7m	7m
Current Liabilities	85	195	260

Bowers Ltd

Unit 5 Longley Lane Sharston Industrial Area, Manchester, M22 4WT
Tel: 0161-945 3126 **Fax:** 0161-946 0384
E-mail: mark@bowerssemiconductors.com
Website: http://www.bowerssemiconductors.com
Directors: M. Bowers (MD)
Registration no: 01469270 **Date established:** 1984
Turnover: £500,000 - £1m **No.of Employees:** 1 - 10 **Product Groups:** 37, 38, 40, 45, 67

Brammer Ltd

Unit 26 Westbrook Road Trafford Park, Manchester, M17 1AY
Tel: 0161-848 8484 **Fax:** 0161-872 8718
E-mail: cm@brammer.plc.uk
Website: http://www.brammer.co.uk/
Managers: T. Hanna (Mgr)
Ultimate Holding Company: CITY TRANSPORT HOLDINGS LIMITED
Immediate Holding Company: CITY AIR EXPRESS (NORTHERN) LTD.
Registration no: 00162925 **Date established:** 1990
Turnover: £250m - £500m **No.of Employees:** 1 - 10 **Product Groups:** 22, 23, 29, 30, 35, 36, 39, 40, 45, 48, 84

Breeze Ltd

Breeze House Albert Close Trading Estate, Whitefield, Manchester, M45 8EH
Tel: 0161-796 3600 **Fax:** 0161-796 3700
E-mail: info@breez.co.uk
Website: http://www.breeze.co.uk
Directors: N. Stern (MD)
Immediate Holding Company: BREEZE LIMITED
Registration no: 01789286 **VAT No.:** GB 408 1035 90
Date established: 1984 **Turnover:** £500,000 - £1m
No.of Employees: 1 - 10 **Product Groups:** 81

Date of Accounts	Mar 12	Mar 11	Mar 10
Working Capital	-16	-107	-69
Fixed Assets	156	173	220
Current Assets	253	153	212

Bridgestone Charter Surveyors Ltd

Clayton House 59-61 Piccadilly, Manchester, M1 2AQ
Tel: 0161-906 3500 **Fax:** 0161-906 3501
Website: http://www.bridgestonesurveyors.com
Directors: L. MacFadyan (MD), M. Gilbert (Fin)
Immediate Holding Company: BRIDGESTONE SURVEYORS LIMITED
Registration no: 05370895 **Date established:** 2005
No.of Employees: 21 - 50 **Product Groups:** 80

Bridgewater Laminate Products Ltd

Bridgewater House Barlow Street, Worsley, Manchester, M28 3BQ
Tel: 0161-703 3980 **Fax:** 0161-703 3981
E-mail: sales@bridgewatergroup.co.uk
Website: http://www.bridgewatergroup.co.uk
Directors: M. Mcnulty (MD)
Immediate Holding Company: BRIDGEWATER LAMINATE PRODUCTS LIMITED
Registration no: 03537823 **Date established:** 1998
No.of Employees: 1 - 10 **Product Groups:** 25, 27, 30, 38, 52, 66

Date of Accounts	Mar 12	Mar 11	Mar 10
Working Capital	139	120	-2
Fixed Assets	44	54	57
Current Assets	343	333	233

Brimar Ltd

Chadderton Industrial Estate Greenside Way, Middleton, Manchester, M24 1SN
Tel: 0161-681 7072 **Fax:** 0161-682 3818
E-mail: gary.payne@brimar.ltd.uk
Website: http://www.brimar-ltd.com
Bank(s): The Royal Bank of Scotland
Directors: D. Eldridge (Sales), G. Payne (Fin)
Managers: D. Braywood (Tech Serv Mgr), J. Macleod (Personnel)
Ultimate Holding Company: P H GILES & CO LIMITED
Immediate Holding Company: BRIMAR LIMITED
Registration no: 03230282 **VAT No.:** GB 628 8951 88
Date established: 1996 **Turnover:** £10m - £20m
No.of Employees: 51 - 100 **Product Groups:** 37, 38, 39, 44, 52

Date of Accounts	Dec 11	Dec 10	Dec 09
Sales Turnover	12m	11m	13m
Pre Tax Profit/Loss	-1m	-139	432
Working Capital	2m	3m	3m
Fixed Assets	2m	2m	2m
Current Assets	6m	5m	6m
Current Liabilities	N/A	2m	2m

British Vita plc

Central Industrial Estate Oldham Road, Middleton, Manchester, M24 1QZ
Tel: 0161-643 1133 **Fax:** 0161-653 5411
E-mail: info@britishvita.com
Website: http://www.britishvita.com
Directors: S. Cox (Dir), M. Cosgrove (Procurement)
Managers: J. Frankish (Personnel), P. Morton (Tech Serv Mgr)
Ultimate Holding Company: VITA CAYMAN LIMITED (CAYMAN ISLANDS)
Immediate Holding Company: BRITISH VITA UNLIMITED
Registration no: 00871669 **Date established:** 1966
Turnover: £500m - £1,000m **No.of Employees:** 1 - 10
Product Groups: 26, 29, 30

Date of Accounts	Dec 11	Dec 10	Dec 09
Pre Tax Profit/Loss	N/A	15m	-2m
Working Capital	154m	150m	123m
Fixed Assets	335m	278m	251m
Current Assets	161m	156m	128m
Current Liabilities	3m	3m	3m

Brooks Ltd

Causeway Park Manchester Road, Audenshaw, Manchester, M34 5UU
Tel: 0161-666 5000 **Fax:** 0161-666 5050
E-mail: benw@brooks.ltd.uk
Website: http://www.brooks.ltd.uk
Bank(s): HSBC Bank plc
Directors: P. Bainbridge (Dir), B. Whitham (MD)
Immediate Holding Company: BROOKS LIMITED
Registration no: 01097593 **VAT No.:** GB 158 1504 70
Date established: 1973 **Turnover:** £5m - £10m
No.of Employees: 51 - 100 **Product Groups:** 25, 30, 33, 35, 36, 38, 39, 40, 43, 45, 46, 48, 66, 68

Date of Accounts	Oct 11	Oct 10	Oct 09
Working Capital	812	548	393
Fixed Assets	1m	967	908
Current Assets	2m	2m	1m

Broome & Wellington

86 Princess Street, Manchester, M1 6NG
Tel: 0161-236 2317 **Fax:** 0161-228 1326
E-mail: info@broomwell.com
Website: http://www.broomwell.com
Bank(s): HSBC, King St, Manchester
Directors: J. Rowe (Dir), M. Rowe (Fin)
Immediate Holding Company: BROOME & WELLINGTON (AVIATION) LIMITED
Registration no: 02028702 **Date established:** 1986
Turnover: £125m - £250m **No.of Employees:** 21 - 50 **Product Groups:** 23

Date of Accounts	Mar 11	Mar 10	Mar 09
Working Capital	86	87	87
Current Assets	87	87	88

Broomstair Metal Co.

328 Hyde Road Denton, Manchester, M34 3EH
Tel: 0161-336 3240 **Fax:** 0161-336 8888
Managers: J. Schofield (Mgr)
Immediate Holding Company: JOHKAR LIMITED
Registration no: 07022825 **Date established:** 1993
Turnover: Up to £250,000 **No.of Employees:** 1 - 10 **Product Groups:** 48

Date of Accounts	Mar 11	Mar 10
Working Capital	122	17
Current Assets	315	69

Brother International Europe Ltd

1 Tame Street Audenshaw, Manchester, M34 5JE
Tel: 0161-330 6531 **Fax:** 0161-931 2209
E-mail: yuji.ishiguro@brother-uk.com
Website: http://www.brother.com
Directors: Y. Ishiguro (MD), G. Lockton (Fin)
Managers: A. Peart, J. Dixon (Personnel), D. Bailey
Ultimate Holding Company: BROTHER INDUSTRIES LTD (JAPAN)
Immediate Holding Company: BROTHER INTERNATIONAL EUROPE LIMITED
Registration no: 00664172 **VAT No.:** GB 145 9375 40
Date established: 1960 **Turnover:** £500m - £1,000m
No.of Employees: 101 - 250 **Product Groups:** 43, 64, 67

Date of Accounts	Mar 11	Mar 10	Mar 09
Sales Turnover	666m	612m	672m
Pre Tax Profit/Loss	10m	4m	10m

Working Capital	39m	32m	26m
Fixed Assets	6m	7m	9m
Current Assets	135m	121m	133m
Current Liabilities	4m	5m	8m

Bruntwood Wrought Iron

2 Bankley Street, Manchester, M19 3PP
Tel: 0161-257 2660 **Fax:** 0161-257 2660
Directors: G. Ashworth (Prop)
Date established: 1997 **No.of Employees:** 1 - 10 **Product Groups:** 26, 35

BS&B Safety Systems (UK) Ltd

Adamson House Tower Business Pk, Wilmslow Rd, Didsbury, Manchester, M20 2YY
Tel: 0161-955 4202 **Fax:** 0161-955 4282
E-mail: sales@bsb-systems.co.uk
Website: http://www.bsb.ie
Registration no: 02254064 **Date established:** 1987
No.of Employees: 1 - 10 **Product Groups:** 33, 36, 40

Date of Accounts	Jun 08	Jun 07	Jun 06
Working Capital	296	-504	-205
Current Assets	349	453	635
Current Liabilities	53	957	840

B S B

Unit 10 Vaughan Street Industrial Estate, Manchester, M12 5BT
Tel: 0161-230 7030 **Fax:** 0161-220 8038
E-mail: sales@bsbrollers.co.uk
Website: http://www.bsbrollers.co.uk
Directors: I. McNeil (Prop)
Immediate Holding Company: BSB ROLLERS LTD
Registration no: 07274593 **Date established:** 2010
Turnover: Up to £250,000 **No.of Employees:** 1 - 10 **Product Groups:** 29, 44, 48, 66

Date of Accounts	Jun 11
Sales Turnover	212
Working Capital	48
Fixed Assets	10
Current Assets	74

Buck & Hickman Ltd

Unit 5 Waterside Trafford Park, Manchester, M17 1WD
Tel: 0161-877 7888 **Fax:** 0161-877 7111
E-mail: manchester@buckandhickman.com
Website: http://www.buckandhickman.com
Managers: M. Emmerson (District Mgr)
Ultimate Holding Company: TRAVIS PERKINS PLC
Immediate Holding Company: BOSTON (2011) LIMITED
Registration no: 06028304 **Date established:** 2006
No.of Employees: 11 - 20 **Product Groups:** 24, 29, 30, 33, 36, 37, 41, 46

Date of Accounts	Dec 10	Mar 10	Mar 09
Working Capital	6m	6m	6m
Current Assets	27m	27m	27m

Budenberg Gauge Co. Ltd

4 Gilchrist Road Irlam, Manchester, M44 5AY
Tel: 08443-728900 **Fax:** 08443-728925
E-mail: sales@budenberg.co.uk
Website: http://www.budenberg.co.uk
Bank(s): Lloyds TSB Bank plc
Directors: I. Paterson (Fin), T. Batt (MD), L. Tomlinson (Fin)
Managers: P. Cropps (Personnel), P. Holland (Sales & Mktg Mg)
Ultimate Holding Company: BUDENBERG 4B GROUP LIMITED
Immediate Holding Company: BUDENBERG GAUGE COMPANY LIMITED
Registration no: 00072396 **Date established:** 2002 **Turnover:** £2m - £5m
No.of Employees: 21 - 50 **Product Groups:** 36, 38, 40, 85

Date of Accounts	Dec 11	Dec 10	Dec 09
Sales Turnover	3m	3m	3m
Pre Tax Profit/Loss	38	11	53
Working Capital	638	584	579
Fixed Assets	62	79	73
Current Assets	1m	2m	1m
Current Liabilities	116	216	229

D H Budenburg

PO Box 224, Manchester, M44 5AY
Tel: 08707-877370 **Fax:** 08707-877369
E-mail: info@dh-budenberg.co.uk
Website: http://www.dh-budenberg.co.uk
Bank(s): Lloyds TSB Bank plc
Directors: J. Hackney (MD)
Immediate Holding Company: ELECTROCAL LTD
Registration no: 03239293 **VAT No.:** GB 682 0514 47
Date established: 2002 **Turnover:** £2m - £5m **No.of Employees:** 21 - 50
Product Groups: 38, 85

Builder Center Ltd

1 Knowsley Street, Manchester, M8 8QN
Tel: 0161-834 9437 **Fax:** 0161-839 7470
E-mail: wolseley@center.co.uk
Website: http://www.buildcenter.co.uk
Directors: M. White (Fin), N. Sibley (MD)
Managers: P. Kenneddy (District Mgr), T. Hollerlan (District Mgr)
Ultimate Holding Company: Wolseley plc
Immediate Holding Company: BUILD CENTER LIMITED
Registration no: 00462397 **Date established:** 1948 **Turnover:** £5m - £10m
No.of Employees: 11 - 20 **Product Groups:** 66

Building Chemical Research Ltd

Mount Sion Road Radcliffe, Manchester, M26 3SJ
Tel: 0161-723 2237 **Fax:** 0161-724 7699
E-mail: brooksc@buildchem.co.uk
Website: http://www.buildchem.co.uk
Directors: C. Reich (Co Sec), C. Brooks (MD)
Immediate Holding Company: BUILDING CHEMICAL RESEARCH (1984) LIMITED
Registration no: 01849473 **VAT No.:** GB 408 1719 60
Date established: 1984 **Turnover:** £1m - £2m **No.of Employees:** 11 - 20
Product Groups: 66

Date of Accounts	Dec 11	Dec 10	Dec 09
Working Capital	-118	-120	-130
Fixed Assets	420	419	426
Current Assets	319	423	375
Current Liabilities	287	313	N/A

Building Design Partnership

PO Box 85, Manchester, M60 3JA
Tel: 0161-828 2200 **Fax:** 0161-832 4280
E-mail: manchester@bdp.com
Website: http://www.bdp.com
Directors: H. Wells (Fin), J. Parker (Fin)
Managers: L. Ferguson (Mktg Serv Mgr), C. Boe (Personnel), S. Peary (Tech Serv Mgr), G. Elliott, K. Sutton (Sales Admin), J. Hobson (Mktg Serv Mgr), M. Jones (Personnel)
Ultimate Holding Company: BDP HOLDINGS LIMITED
Immediate Holding Company: BUILDING DESIGN PARTNERSHIP LIMITED
Registration no: 02207415 **Date established:** 1987
Turnover: £75m - £125m **No.of Employees:** 101 - 250
Product Groups: 54, 80, 84, 85

Date of Accounts	Jun 12	Jun 11	Jun 10
Sales Turnover	68m	80m	96m
Pre Tax Profit/Loss	2m	3m	7m
Working Capital	15m	13m	9m
Fixed Assets	5m	7m	10m
Current Assets	38m	45m	58m
Current Liabilities	21m	31m	47m

Bunzl Vending Services Ltd

Unit 3 Kiwi Park, Trafford Park, Manchester, M17 1HW
Tel: 0161-848 6700 **Fax:** 0161-877 8054
E-mail: steve@bunzlvending.com
Website: http://www.bunzlvending.com
Managers: S. Hartland (Mgr)
Immediate Holding Company: BUNZL VENDING SERVICES LIMITED
Registration no: 02605313 **Date established:** 1991
No.of Employees: 21 - 50 **Product Groups:** 49, 61

Date of Accounts	Dec 10	Dec 09	Dec 08
Sales Turnover	68m	80m	110m
Pre Tax Profit/Loss	-6m	-6m	-2m
Working Capital	-36m	-33m	-32m
Fixed Assets	28m	29m	32m
Current Assets	43m	45m	49m
Current Liabilities	3m	4m	4m

By Design plc

Unit 6 Mountheath Industrial Park Prestwich, Manchester, M25 9WB
Tel: 0161-281 4400 **Fax:** 0161-281 4481
E-mail: worldwide@by-design.co.uk
Website: http://www.by-design.co.uk
Directors: S. Passi (MD), A. Bhandari (Dir), D. Passi (Ch), M. Patel (Fin), R. Coutts (Mkt Research), R. Passi (Ch)
Managers: B. Grayshon (Sales Prom Mgr), K. Rimmer (Shipping Mgr), W. Yunus (I.T. Exec)
Ultimate Holding Company: BY DESIGN HOLDINGS UK LIMITED
Immediate Holding Company: By Design Holdings UK Ltd
Registration no: 01492174 **Date established:** 1980 **Turnover:** £1m - £2m
No.of Employees: 21 - 50 **Product Groups:** 63

C B R E

12 5th Floor Booth Street, Manchester, M2 4AW
Tel: 0161-455 7666 **Fax:** 0161-455 0161
E-mail: info@cbre.com
Website: http://www.cbre.co.uk
Directors: J. Ogden (MD)
Managers: A. Errington
Immediate Holding Company: J BOOTH (METAL FABRICATIONS) LIMITED
Registration no: 01415100 **Date established:** 1960
Turnover: £10m - £20m **No.of Employees:** 51 - 100 **Product Groups:** 80, 82

C P D Distribution

8 Commerce Way Trafford Park, Manchester, M17 1HW
Tel: 0161-874 5311 **Fax:** 0161-874 5312
E-mail: manchester@cpdplc.co.uk
Website: http://www.cpdplc.co.uk
Bank(s): HSBC Bank plc
Managers: C. Mitchell (Mgr)
Immediate Holding Company: S I G LTD
Registration no: 01493505 **VAT No.:** GB 487 0173 33
Turnover: Over £1,000m **No.of Employees:** 11 - 20 **Product Groups:** 33, 35

C P M Engineering Ltd

Clarke Industrial Estate St Modwen Road, Stretford, Manchester, M32 0ZF
Tel: 0161-865 6161 **Fax:** 0161-864 2344
E-mail: info@cpm-uk.com
Website: http://www.cpm-uk.com
Directors: C. Mccallister (Dir)
Immediate Holding Company: CPM ENGINEERING LIMITED
Registration no: 03687274 **VAT No.:** GB 603 6791 41
Date established: 1998 **Turnover:** £500,000 - £1m
No.of Employees: 21 - 50 **Product Groups:** 48

C S G Lanstar

Liverpool Road Cadishead, Manchester, M44 5DT
Tel: 0161-775 2644 **Fax:** 0161-908 1727
E-mail: neil.richards@csg.co.uk
Website: http://www.csg.co.uk
Bank(s): HSBC
Directors: N. Richards (MD), P. Quigley (Co Sec)
Ultimate Holding Company: CLEANSING SERVICE GROUP LTD
Immediate Holding Company: LANSTAR HOLDINGS LTD
Registration no: 02318907 **VAT No.:** GB 519 5743 72
Date established: 1984 **Turnover:** £20m - £50m
No.of Employees: 51 - 100 **Product Groups:** 54

Cannon Confidential

Units 8-9 Fairhills Industrial Estate Woodrow Way, Irlam, Manchester, M44 6BP
Tel: 0161-777 4950 **Fax:** 0161-776 2345
E-mail: harry.harrison@ocs.co.uk
Website: http://www.cannonhygiene.com
Directors: H. Harrison (Dir)
Immediate Holding Company: NULIFE GLASS EQUIPMENT SALES LIMITED
Registration no: N0544959 **Date established:** 2009 **Turnover:** £2m - £5m
No.of Employees: 1 - 10 **Product Groups:** 27, 44, 80

Date of Accounts	Sep 10
Working Capital	-30
Fixed Assets	962
Current Assets	8

Cargill Flavor Systems UK Ltd

Old Trafford Essence Distillery 416 Chester Road, Manchester, M16 9HJ
Tel: 0161-872 0225 **Fax:** 0161-848 7331
E-mail: sales_enquiries@cargi.com
Website: http://www.cargillflavorsystems.com
Bank(s): Barclays
Directors: P. Bruggink (MD)
Ultimate Holding Company: CARGILL INCORPORATED (USA)
Immediate Holding Company: KERRY FLAVOURS UK LIMITED
Registration no: 00358462 **VAT No.:** GB 166 6904 34
Date established: 1939 **Turnover:** £10m - £20m
No.of Employees: 101 - 250 **Product Groups:** 20, 31, 32

Date of Accounts	May 11	May 10	May 09
Sales Turnover	20m	18m	20
Pre Tax Profit/Loss	663	3m	-5
Working Capital	-5m	-7m	-7
Fixed Assets	5m	6m	7
Current Assets	7m	6m	7
Current Liabilities	962	1m	1

CeeT UK

31 Mount Street Swinton, Manchester, M27 5NG
Tel: 07793-537512 **Fax:** 0161-794 1175
E-mail: info@ceetuk.co.uk
Website: http://www.barrierfilm.co.uk
Directors: M. Kwidzinski (Prop)
No.of Employees: 1 - 10 **Product Groups:** 23, 30

Cemb Hofmann UK Ltd

1 Long Wood Road Trafford Park, Manchester, M17 1PZ
Tel: 0161-872 3122 **Fax:** 0161-872 9247
E-mail: sales@cembhofmann.co.uk
Website: http://www.cembhofmann.co.uk
Directors: M. Davies (Dir), R. Jeffery (Co Sec)
Immediate Holding Company: CEMB-HOFMANN (UK) LIMITED
Registration no: 03602667 **VAT No.:** GB 725 7619 14
Date established: 1998 **Turnover:** £20m - £50m **No.of Employees:** 1 - 10
Product Groups: 29, 37, 38, 39, 46, 48

Date of Accounts	Dec 11	Dec 10	Dec 09
Working Capital	-131	-199	-62
Fixed Assets	149	135	84
Current Assets	660	418	543
Current Liabilities	N/A	476	N/A

Centaur Fuel Management

251 Manchester Road Walkden, Worsley, Manchester, M28 3HE
Tel: 08448-586323 **Fax:** 08448-248031
E-mail: da@centauronline.co.uk
Website: http://www.centauronline.co.uk
Directors: D. Allender (MD)
Ultimate Holding Company: CLEARINTO LIMITED
Immediate Holding Company: CENTAUR FUEL MANAGEMENT LIMITED
Registration no: 02389675 **VAT No.:** GB 712 5248 58
Date established: 1989 **Turnover:** £500,000 - £1m
No.of Employees: 1 - 10 **Product Groups:** 38

Date of Accounts	Jul 11	Jul 10	Jul 09
Working Capital	106	96	81
Fixed Assets	71	59	60
Current Assets	426	428	262

Chadtex Limited

1 Edward Street Cambridge Industrial Area, Manchester, M7 1FN
Tel: 0161-830 1919 **Fax:** 0161-830 1909
E-mail: info@chadtex.co.uk
Website: http://www.chadtex.co.uk
Directors: J. Jackson (Fin), D. Chadwick (Ch & MD), D. Chadwicks (Prop)
Immediate Holding Company: C. T. Holdings Ltd
Registration no: 05669131 **Date established:** 1973
No.of Employees: 21 - 50 **Product Groups:** 24, 63

Chaintec Ltd

Unit 43 & 38 Westbrook Trading Estate, Trafford Park, Manchester, M17 1AY
Tel: 0161-877 7373 **Fax:** 0161-876 0365
E-mail: info@chaintec.co.uk
Website: http://www.chaintec.co.uk
Bank(s): Lloyds TSB
Directors: D. Hassan (MD)
Managers: D. Hassan (Sales Prom Mgr), S. Hill (Export Sales Mg)
Registration no: 02646338 **VAT No.:** GB 584 9134 08
Date established: 1991 **Turnover:** £1m - £2m **No.of Employees:** 11 - 20
Product Groups: 35, 36, 39, 45, 66, 67

Chamber Link Limited

Merchants Exchange 17-19 Whitworth Street West, Manchester, M1 5WG
Tel: 0845-6083388 **Fax:** 0161-241 5381
E-mail: busadvice@business-support-solutions.co.uk
Website: http://www.chamber-link.co.uk
Directors: M. Ashdon (Grp Chief Exec)
Managers: G. Richardson (Sales Prom), R. Haig (Mgr)
Registration no: 03922575 **Date established:** 2002
Turnover: £20m - £50m **No.of Employees:** 11 - 20 **Product Groups:** 80

Chemtura

PO Box 44, Manchester, M17 1WT
Tel: 0161-872 2323 **Fax:** 01407-830001
Website: http://www.greatlakesfine.com
Managers: M. Kidman (Sales Prom Mgr)
Ultimate Holding Company: CHEMTURA CORP (USA)
Immediate Holding Company: CHEMTURA SALES UK LIMITED
Registration no: 03447394 **Date established:** 1997
Turnover: £20m - £50m **No.of Employees:** 101 - 250
Product Groups: 31, 32, 66

Date of Accounts	Dec 10	Dec 09	Dec 08
Sales Turnover	44m	41m	14m
Pre Tax Profit/Loss	1m	997	-203
Working Capital	4m	4m	3m
Current Assets	11m	9m	7m
Current Liabilities	1m	831	401

Chess Logistics Technology Ltd

Commerce Way Trafford Park, Manchester, M17 1HW
Tel: 0161-888 2580 **Fax:** 0161-888 2590
E-mail: info@chess.uk.com
Website: http://www.chess.uk.com
Bank(s): National Westminster Bank Plc
Directors: A. Mills (Sales & Mktg), N. Abbott (Tech Serv), J. Burton (Dir)
Immediate Holding Company: CHESS LOGISTICS TECHNOLOGY LIMITED
Registration no: 01448826 **VAT No.:** GB 305 8817 51
Date established: 1979 **Turnover:** £1m - £2m **No.of Employees:** 21 - 50
Product Groups: 44

Date of Accounts	Dec 11	Dec 10	Dec 09
Working Capital	274	170	153
Fixed Assets	677	694	719
Current Assets	1m	1m	858

Chi Yip Group Ltd
Treasure House Greengate Industrial Estate, Middleton, Manchester, M24 1SW
Tel: 0161-655 3600 **Fax:** 0161-655 3188
E-mail: info@chiyip.co.uk
Website: http://www.chiyip.co.uk
Directors: J. Lui (MD), N. Ghaznabi (Fin)
Managers: K. Wong (Buyer), W. Tang (Tech Serv Mgr)
Ultimate Holding Company: CHI YIP HOLDINGS LIMITED
Immediate Holding Company: CHI YIP GROUP LIMITED
Registration no: 02487941 **Date established:** 1990
Turnover: £20m - £50m **No.of Employees:** 51 - 100 **Product Groups:** 20, 61, 62

Date of Accounts	May 11	May 10	May 09
Sales Turnover	39m	35m	33m
Pre Tax Profit/Loss	347	264	409
Working Capital	4m	4m	3m
Fixed Assets	75	93	114
Current Assets	11m	9m	8m
Current Liabilities	575	221	657

Christie Hospital N H S Foundation Trust
550 Wilmslow Road, Manchester, M20 4BX
Tel: 0161-446 3000 **Fax:** 0161-446 3352
E-mail: caroline.shaw@christie.nhs.uk
Website: http://www.christie.nhs.uk
Directors: C. Shaw (Grp Chief Exec)
VAT No.: GB 654 9161 18 **Date established:** 1991
No.of Employees: 1501 & over **Product Groups:**

Churchill Machine Tools Ltd
Empress Street Old Trafford, Manchester, M16 9EN
Tel: 0161-848 9539 **Fax:** 0161-872 9234
E-mail: info@churchill-grinders.co.uk
Website: http://www.churchill-grinders.co.uk
Directors: W. Coplin (MD)
Managers: P. Cooke, T. Harrision, K. McLaren (Sales Admin)
Registration no: 04186074 **Turnover:** £500,000 - £1m
No.of Employees: 21 - 50 **Product Groups:** 32, 46, 48

Cleanaway Ltd
Fifth Avenue Trafford Park, Manchester, M17 1TR
Tel: 0161-877 3463 **Fax:** 0161-877 2354
E-mail: info@cleanaway.com
Website: http://www.cleanaway.com
Managers: S. Huzzey, J. Howarth (Mgr)
Registration no: OC342199 **VAT No.:** GB 352 1129 90
Date established: 2008 **No.of Employees:** 11 - 20 **Product Groups:** 54

Clearcoat Northwest Ltd
Unit 8 Castle Industrial Estate Louvain Street, Failsworth, Manchester, M35 0XB
Tel: 0161-684 7700 **Fax:** 0161-684 7700
Website: http://www.clearcoatnw.com
Directors: A. Beach (Ptnr)
Immediate Holding Company: CLEARCOAT (NORTH WEST) LIMITED
Registration no: 05870662 **Date established:** 2006
No.of Employees: 1 - 10 **Product Groups:** 46, 48

Date of Accounts	Mar 11	Mar 10	Mar 08
Working Capital	-18	-17	31
Fixed Assets	18	22	30
Current Assets	57	66	76

Clynder Cables Ltd
3 Lord North Street, Manchester, M40 8AD
Tel: 0161-629 9333 **Fax:** 0161-629 9444
E-mail: sales@clyndercables.co.uk
Website: http://www.clyndercables.co.uk
Directors: A. Crossley (Fin)
Ultimate Holding Company: HOSTOMBE GROUP LIMITED
Immediate Holding Company: CLYNDER CABLES LIMITED
Registration no: 01724832 **Date established:** 1983 **Turnover:** £2m - £5m
No.of Employees: 1 - 10 **Product Groups:** 30, 35, 37, 44, 48, 67

Date of Accounts	Mar 11	Mar 10	Mar 09
Working Capital	388	330	583
Fixed Assets	620	627	45
Current Assets	2m	2m	1m

The Co Op
PO Box 53, Manchester, M60 4ES
Tel: 0161-834 1212
Website: http://www.co-operative.coop
Directors: Z. Morgan (Mkt Research), M. Beaumont (Grp Chief Exec)
Ultimate Holding Company: CO-OPERATIVE GROUP LIMITED
Immediate Holding Company: CO-OPERATIVE GROUP PENSION FUND TRUSTEES LIMITED
Registration no: 03430283 **Date established:** 1997
Turnover: Up to £250,000 **No.of Employees:** 1501 & over
Product Groups: 26, 62, 63

Co-Operative Banking Group (Head Office)
1 Balloon Street, Manchester, M60 4EP
Tel: 0161-832 3456 **Fax:** 0161-829 4475
Website: http://www.cfs.co.uk
Directors: R. Burlton (Dir), M. Lees (Co Sec), H. Sweeney (Pers), C. Shannon (Mkt Research), K. Lewis (Dir)
Managers: G. Pennell (), H. Sweeney, J. Sheerin (), G. Bennett (I.T. Exec), G. Pennell
Ultimate Holding Company: CO-OPERATIVE GROUP LIMITED
Immediate Holding Company: CO-OPERATIVE BANK FINANCIAL ADVISERS LIMITED
Registration no: 00718903 **VAT No.:** GB 403 3096 90
Date established: 1962 **No.of Employees:** 1 - 10 **Product Groups:** 82

Date of Accounts	Dec 11	Dec 10	Dec 09
Sales Turnover	N/A	N/A	2m
Pre Tax Profit/Loss	344	-17m	-11m
Working Capital	1m	3m	9m
Fixed Assets	N/A	200	N/A
Current Assets	10m	15m	11m
Current Liabilities	8m	12m	2m

W L Coller Ltd
Unit 1-4 Holloway Drive Worsley, Manchester, M28 2LA
Tel: 0161-799 5353 **Fax:** 0161-703 7180
E-mail: caroline.merry@wlcoller.co.uk
Website: http://www.wlcoller.co.uk
Bank(s): Natwest, City Branch
Directors: D. Merry (Dir), P. Merry (Dir), S. Merry (Dir)
Immediate Holding Company: W.L. COLLER LIMITED
Registration no: 00357066 **VAT No.:** GB 145 5519 62
Date established: 1939 **Turnover:** £2m - £5m **No.of Employees:** 11 - 20
Product Groups: 66

Date of Accounts	Jun 11	Jun 10	Jun 09
Working Capital	3m	3m	3m
Fixed Assets	2m	324	342
Current Assets	4m	4m	3m

Collinson Grant
Ryecroft Aviary Road, Worsley, Manchester, M28 2WF
Tel: 0161-703 5600 **Fax:** 0161-790 9177
E-mail: acollinson@collinsongrant.com
Website: http://www.collinsongrant.com
Bank(s): Co-operative
Directors: A. Collinson (Prop), D. Brown (Co Sec), R. Hendry (Pers)
Managers: T. Bennett, M. Davis (Sales Admin)
Ultimate Holding Company: COLLINSON GRANT GROUP LIMITED
Immediate Holding Company: COLLINSON GRANT LIMITED
Registration no: 03097916 **VAT No.:** GB 673 3393 19
Date established: 1995 **Turnover:** £5m - £10m **No.of Employees:** 21 - 50
Product Groups: 80

Date of Accounts	Dec 11	Dec 10	Dec 09
Sales Turnover	7m	7m	10m
Pre Tax Profit/Loss	821	-975	-3m
Working Capital	-417	-1m	-294
Fixed Assets	3	11	28
Current Assets	776	3m	5m
Current Liabilities	709	4m	5m

Colour Anodising Ltd
Holland Street Radcliffe, Manchester, M26 2RH
Tel: 0161-723 2637 **Fax:** 0161-725 9252
E-mail: info@anodising.com
Website: http://www.anodising.com
Bank(s): HSBC Bank plc
Directors: J. Buckley (Fin), D. Buckley (MD)
Ultimate Holding Company: ANODISING & PLATINGS LTD
Immediate Holding Company: COLOUR ANODISING LTD
Registration no: 00336599 **Date established:** 1938 **Turnover:** £1m - £2m
No.of Employees: 51 - 100 **Product Groups:** 48

Date of Accounts	Apr 11	Apr 10	Apr 09
Working Capital	360	394	395
Fixed Assets	696	706	725
Current Assets	728	758	751

Colourtone Ltd
250 Mauldeth Road West Withington, Manchester, M20 1BE
Tel: 0161-448 0273 **Fax:** 0161-448 7331
Website: http://www.colourtone.com
Directors: P. Pickstone (MD)
Immediate Holding Company: COLOURTONE LIMITED
Registration no: 01685283 **Date established:** 1982
No.of Employees: 11 - 20 **Product Groups:** 38, 42

Date of Accounts	Apr 11	Apr 10	Apr 09
Working Capital	52	31	5
Fixed Assets	30	37	44
Current Assets	232	232	228

M Comar & Sons Ltd
37 Broughton Street, Manchester, M8 8LZ
Tel: 0161-834 8049 **Fax:** 0161-833 1798
E-mail: sales@comars.co.uk
Website: http://www.comars.co.uk
Directors: S. Comar (MD), P. Comar (Dir)
Immediate Holding Company: M. COMAR & SONS LIMITED
Registration no: 01158312 **VAT No.:** GB 149 6357 33
Date established: 1974 **Turnover:** £500,000 - £1m
No.of Employees: 1 - 10 **Product Groups:** 24, 63

Date of Accounts	Jan 12	Jan 11	Jan 10
Working Capital	70	55	40
Fixed Assets	5	6	7
Current Assets	85	80	67

Comfy Quilts Ltd
Old Hall Street Middleton, Manchester, M24 1AG
Tel: 08707-662324 **Fax:** 0161-655 3362
E-mail: info@comfyquilts.com
Website: http://www.comfyquilts.com
Directors: G. Moryoussef (Co Sec)
Managers: T. Cornthwaite (Fin Mgr), M. Williams (Ops Mgr), D. Coulman (Buyer)
Ultimate Holding Company: COMFY QUILTS LIMITED
Immediate Holding Company: BEDCREST LIMITED
Registration no: 04137953 **VAT No.:** GB 562 5922 29
Date established: 2001 **Turnover:** £10m - £20m
No.of Employees: 101 - 250 **Product Groups:** 24

Date of Accounts	Jun 10	Jun 09	Jun 08
Working Capital	125	125	125
Current Assets	125	125	125

Connect Engineering Ltd
Thomas Brown House Edwin Road, Manchester, M11 3ER
Tel: 0161-273 6333 **Fax:** 0161-273 8351
E-mail: connectengineering@yahoo.co.uk
Directors: H. Gowrie (Fin), P. Gowrie (MD)
Ultimate Holding Company: THOMAS BROWN HOLDINGS LIMITED
Immediate Holding Company: CONNECT ENGINEERING LIMITED
Registration no: 03122582 **VAT No.:** GB 628 6825 06
Date established: 1995 **Turnover:** £500,000 - £1m
No.of Employees: 1 - 10 **Product Groups:** 48

Date of Accounts	Feb 12	Feb 11	Feb 10
Working Capital	-34	-32	-31
Fixed Assets	18	20	25
Current Assets	54	60	42

Controlled Event Solutions Ltd
Unit 13a-13b United Trading Estate, Manchester, M16 0RJ
Tel: 0161-868 8181 **Fax:** 0161-868 8171
E-mail: admin@controlledsolutions.net
Website: http://www.controlledsolutionsgroup.com
Directors: H. Kirkland (Dir)
Immediate Holding Company: CONTROLLED EVENT SOLUTIONS LIMITED
Registration no: 04480079 **Date established:** 2002 **Turnover:** £5m - £10m
No.of Employees: 11 - 20 **Product Groups:** 86

Date of Accounts	Jul 11	Jul 10	Jul 09
Sales Turnover	N/A	7m	8m
Pre Tax Profit/Loss	N/A	410	982
Working Capital	170	330	552
Fixed Assets	835	681	870
Current Assets	1000	1m	1m
Current Liabilities	N/A	554	631

Cope Engineering Ltd
Sion Street Radcliffe, Manchester, M26 3SF
Tel: 0161-723 6500 **Fax:** 0161-723 6501
E-mail: sales@cope-engineering.co.uk
Website: http://www.cope-engineering.co.uk
Bank(s): HSBC Bank plc
Directors: A. Cope (MD), J. Cope (Purch)
Managers: M. Regan
Immediate Holding Company: COPE ENGINEERING (RADCLIFFE) LIMITED
Registration no: 00519961 **Date established:** 1953 **Turnover:** £5m - £10m
No.of Employees: 21 - 50 **Product Groups:** 29, 35, 42, 44, 45

Date of Accounts	May 11	May 10	May 09
Working Capital	276	-164	-361
Fixed Assets	700	1m	2m
Current Assets	1m	1m	2m

Costain Energy & Process
Costain House Styal Road, Manchester, M22 5WN
Tel: 0161-910 3444 **Fax:** 0161-910 3399
E-mail: info@costain.com
Website: http://www.costain.com
Directors: C. Sweeney (MD), C. Franks (Fin)
Managers: C. Winstanley (Fin Mgr), S. Hall, C. Ross (Personnel)
Ultimate Holding Company: COSTAIN GROUP PLC
Immediate Holding Company: COSTAIN OIL, GAS & PROCESS LIMITED
Registration no: 00786418 **VAT No.:** GB 235 9835 31
Date established: 1964 **Turnover:** £125m - £250m
No.of Employees: 251 - 500 **Product Groups:** 36, 37, 40, 42, 48, 54, 84

Date of Accounts	Dec 11	Dec 10	Dec 09
Sales Turnover	146m	145m	86m
Pre Tax Profit/Loss	12m	15m	7m
Working Capital	22m	16m	5m
Fixed Assets	10m	854	822
Current Assets	62m	58m	44m
Current Liabilities	17m	18m	18m

Crew Industrial Flooring
Walkden, Manchester, M28 3BT
Tel: 07914-743755 **Fax:** 0871-2636818
E-mail: info@crewflooring.co.uk
Website: http://www.crewflooring.co.uk
Product Groups: 25, 32, 33, 52, 66

Crosbie Casco Coating
Wood Lane Partington, Manchester, M31 4BT
Tel: 0161-775 3025 **Fax:** 0161-777 9076
E-mail: sales@crosbie-casco.co.uk
Website: http://www.crosbie-casco.co.uk
Bank(s): The Royal Bank of Scotland
Managers: D. Davenport (Buyer), M. Varty (Chief Mgr)
Immediate Holding Company: CROSBIE CASCO COATINGS LTD
Registration no: 06034927 **Date established:** 2006 **Turnover:** £2m - £5m
No.of Employees: 21 - 50 **Product Groups:** 32

Date of Accounts	Dec 10	Dec 09	Dec 08
Sales Turnover	2m	N/A	N/A
Pre Tax Profit/Loss	74	N/A	N/A
Working Capital	98	N/A	N/A
Fixed Assets	60	N/A	N/A
Current Assets	1m	N/A	N/A
Current Liabilities	505	N/A	N/A

Crosland Laser Guarding Ltd
4 Lyons Road Trafford Park, Manchester, M17 1RN
Tel: 0161-877 8668 **Fax:** 0161-876 5234
E-mail: sales@croslandvk.com
Website: http://www.croslandvk.com
Directors: S. Waterhouse (Pers), J. Briggs (MD), J. Whiteside (Fin)
Ultimate Holding Company: AVOCET CROSLAND LIMITED
Immediate Holding Company: CROSLAND VK LIMITED
Registration no: 02490083 **Date established:** 1990 **Turnover:** £2m - £5m
No.of Employees: 21 - 50 **Product Groups:** 23, 27, 38, 42, 43, 44, 46, 67, 76

Date of Accounts	May 09	May 08	May 07
Working Capital	1m	1m	1m
Fixed Assets	47	67	90
Current Assets	2m	2m	2m

Crowcroft Wrought Ironwork
3 Crowcroft Road, Manchester, M12 4QZ
Tel: 0161-256 1951 **Fax:** 0161-257 2452
Directors: G. Ormord (Prop)
Date established: 1979 **No.of Employees:** 1 - 10 **Product Groups:** 26, 35

Cunningham & Jepson Packaging Ltd
3 Westbrook Trading Estate Westbrook Road, Trafford Park, Manchester, M17 1AY
Tel: 0161-872 6390 **Fax:** 0161-872 8141
Directors: A. Jepson (MD)
Immediate Holding Company: CUNNINGHAM & JEPSON PACKAGING LIMITED
Registration no: 01625181 **Date established:** 1982
No.of Employees: 1 - 10 **Product Groups:** 38, 42

Date of Accounts	Mar 11	Mar 10	Mar 09
Working Capital	15	27	11
Fixed Assets	12	6	7
Current Assets	82	118	75

Customised Packaging Ltd
Windmill Lane Denton, Manchester, M34 3SP
Tel: 0161-320 8318 **Fax:** 0161-320 8201
E-mail: grahamlord@customisedpackaging.co.uk
Website: http://www.customisedpackaging.co.uk
Directors: G. Lord (Dir)
Managers: D. Watson (Chief Acct)
Immediate Holding Company: CUSTOMISED PACKAGING LIMITED
Registration no: 05248623 **Date established:** 2004
No.of Employees: 21 - 50 **Product Groups:** 30, 66

Date of Accounts	Dec 11	Dec 10	Dec 09
Working Capital	92	74	-130
Fixed Assets	352	372	448
Current Assets	860	561	609
Current Liabilities	N/A	N/A	419

D B M
Barnett House 53 Fountain Street, Manchester, M2 2AN
Tel: 08454-562279 **Fax:** 0161-237 1129
Website: http://www.dbm.co.uk
Directors: W. Nash (MD)
Immediate Holding Company: HARVEY WEBB ASSOCIATES LTD
Registration no: 00001776 **Date established:** 2011 **Turnover:** £2m - £5m
No.of Employees: 1 - 10 **Product Groups:** 80, 81, 86

Date of Accounts	Nov 11	Nov 10
Working Capital	1	1
Current Assets	1	1

D T Z
1 Marsden Street, Manchester, M2 1HW
Tel: 0161-236 9595 **Fax:** 0161-228 7097
E-mail: mike.mitchell@dtz.com
Website: http://www.dtz.com
Directors: M. Mitchell (MD)
Managers: J. Hindle (Personnel), J. Brummell (Sales Admin), K. Hough
Immediate Holding Company: DTZ MCCOMBE PIERCE LLP
Registration no: NC000516 **Date established:** 2009 **Turnover:** £2m - £5m
No.of Employees: 101 - 250 **Product Groups:** 54, 80, 84

Date of Accounts	Apr 12	Apr 11	Apr 10
Working Capital	544	613	968
Fixed Assets	68	105	156
Current Assets	1m	1m	3m

Dale & Company Ancoats Ltd
2 Kelbrook Road, Manchester, M11 2QA
Tel: 0161-223 1990 **Fax:** 0161-223 6767
E-mail: info@dale-lifting.co.uk
Website: http://www.dale-lifting.co.uk
Managers: J. Wright (Mgr)
Immediate Holding Company: DALE & COMPANY (ANCOATS) LIMITED
Registration no: 00610341 **Date established:** 1958
No.of Employees: 11 - 20 **Product Groups:** 35, 39, 45

Date of Accounts	Dec 11	Dec 10	Dec 09
Working Capital	249	167	178
Fixed Assets	731	735	737
Current Assets	743	730	628

Dale Lifting and Handling
2 Kelbrook Road Off Stainburn Road, Parkhouse Industrial Estate, Manchester, M11 2QA
Tel: 0161-223 1990 **Fax:** 0161-223 6767
E-mail: info@dale-lifting.co.uk
Website: http://www.dale-lifting.co.uk
Bank(s): The Royal Bank of Scotland
Directors: J. Whitehead (Prop), J. Whitehead (Dir), M. Bradley (MD)
Managers: B. Billington (Chief Acct), J. Wright (Purch Mgr), P. Wilmot (Mktg Serv Mgr), S. Blackshaw (Sales Prom Mgr)
Registration no: 00610341 **VAT No.:** GB 145 5891 42
Turnover: £1m - £2m **No.of Employees:** 21 - 50 **Product Groups:** 45

Dale Lifting and Handling Equipment Specialists
2 Kelbrook Road, Manchester, M11 2QA
Tel: 0845-270 2919 **Fax:** 0161-223 6767
E-mail: sales@dale-lifting.co.uk
Website: http://www.dale-lifting.co.uk
Managers: P. Wilmot (Mgr), W. Billington (Accounts)
Immediate Holding Company: Dale & Co. Ancoats Ltd
Registration no: 00610341 **Turnover:** £1m - £2m
No.of Employees: 21 - 50 **Product Groups:** 23, 30, 35, 36, 37, 38, 45, 67

Date of Accounts	Dec 07	Dec 06	Dec 05
Current Assets	1	6	5
Current Liabilities	1	6	5

Danzer Ltd
Windmill Lane Denton, Manchester, M34 2JF
Tel: 08000-350 443 **Fax:** 0161-337 4537
E-mail: info@danzer.ltd.uk
Website: http://www.danzer.ltd.uk
Product Groups: 25, 26, 33, 35, 51, 52, 66, 80, 83

Date of Accounts	Sep 08	Sep 07	Sep 06
Working Capital	288	234	166
Fixed Assets	703	641	616
Current Assets	1893	1916	1877
Current Liabilities	1605	1682	1712
Total Share Capital	160	160	160

Darnell Consultants Ltd
14a Kenworthy Lane, Manchester, M22 4EJ
Tel: 0161-945 6996 **Fax:** 0161-945 6997
E-mail: cabling@darnellconsultants.com
Website: http://www.darnellconsultants.co.uk
Directors: B. Cronshaw (MD), L. Cronshaw (Fin)
Immediate Holding Company: DARNELL CONSULTANTS LIMITED
Registration no: 01466013 **VAT No.:** GB 560 9570 26
Date established: 1979 **Turnover:** Up to £250,000
No.of Employees: 1 - 10 **Product Groups:** 30, 35, 37, 40, 44, 51, 67

Date of Accounts	Sep 11	Sep 10	Sep 09
Working Capital	11	-0	18
Fixed Assets	58	63	70
Current Assets	33	47	54

Datlabs Data Recovery Services
One Central Park Northampton Road, Manchester, M40 5WW
Tel: 08701-402999
E-mail: info@datlabs.co.uk
Website: http://www.datlabs.co.uk
Managers: A. McQuoid (Ops Mgr)
Immediate Holding Company: PROCESS INTEGRATION LIMITED
Registration no: 07042359 **Date established:** 2004
Turnover: £500,000 - £1m **No.of Employees:** 1 - 10 **Product Groups:** 26

Date of Accounts	Sep 11	Sep 10	Sep 09
Working Capital	196	189	260
Fixed Assets	25	44	62
Current Assets	435	303	302

Davies Arnold Cooper
60 Fountain Street, Manchester, M2 2FE
Tel: 0161-839 8396 **Fax:** 0161-839 8309
E-mail: sgorman@dac.co.uk
Website: http://www.dac.co.uk
Directors: A. Megaw (Ptnr)
Immediate Holding Company: L SPORTS INVESTMENTS LIMITED
Registration no: OC343237 **Date established:** 2007
No.of Employees: 11 - 20 **Product Groups:** 80

Date of Accounts	Dec 11	Dec 10	Dec 09
Pre Tax Profit/Loss	N/A	N/A	2
Working Capital	-7	-6	-5
Fixed Assets	1	1	1
Current Assets	7	7	7
Current Liabilities	N/A	N/A	13

Davies Turner & Co. Ltd
Unit 8 Manchester International Freight Terminal Westinghouse Road, Trafford Park, Manchester, M17 1DY
Tel: 0161-872 7651 **Fax:** 0161-848 0539
E-mail: wendybarlow@daviesturner.co.uk
Website: http://www.daviesturner.com
Bank(s): National Westminster Bank Plc
Managers: W. Barlow (Admin Off)
Ultimate Holding Company: DAVIES TURNER HOLDINGS PLC
Immediate Holding Company: DAVIES TURNER & CO. LIMITED
Registration no: 04345197 **Date established:** 2001
Turnover: £75m - £125m **No.of Employees:** 51 - 100
Product Groups: 72, 74, 76, 77, 84

Date of Accounts	Mar 12	Mar 11	Mar 10
Sales Turnover	97m	100m	84m
Pre Tax Profit/Loss	2m	2m	1m
Working Capital	3m	8m	7m
Fixed Assets	2m	1m	2m
Current Assets	20m	24m	22m
Current Liabilities	3m	4m	3m

Davies Turner Air Cargo Ltd
Unit 10 301 World Freight Terminal, Manchester Airport, Manchester, M90 5BF
Tel: 0161-498 0777 **Fax:** 0161-498 9777
E-mail: sales@daviesturner.co.uk
Website: http://www.daviesturneraircargo.com
Managers: S. Mcgovers (District Mgr)
Ultimate Holding Company: DAVIES TURNER HOLDINGS PLC
Immediate Holding Company: DAVIES TURNER AIR CARGO LIMITED
Registration no: 02513979 **VAT No.:** GB 235 6746 45
Date established: 1990 **No.of Employees:** 11 - 20 **Product Groups:** 76

Date of Accounts	Mar 12	Mar 11	Mar 10
Sales Turnover	50m	48m	41m
Pre Tax Profit/Loss	2m	1m	952
Working Capital	6m	5m	5m
Fixed Assets	365	433	436
Current Assets	16m	15m	13m
Current Liabilities	4m	4m	3m

Davies Wallis Foyster ltd
1 Scott Place 2 Hardman Street, Manchester, M3 3AA
Tel: 0161-603 5000 **Fax:** 0161-835 2407
E-mail: enquiries@dwf.co.uk
Website: http://www.dwf.co.uk
Bank(s): Royal of Scotland
Directors: J. Davies (Grp Chief Exec)
Registration no: 03163046 **VAT No.:** GB 166 7216 50
Turnover: £10m - £20m **No.of Employees:** 101 - 250 **Product Groups:** 80

Date of Accounts	May 07	May 06	May 05
Working Capital	N/A	N/A	111
Current Assets	N/A	N/A	146
Current Liabilities	N/A	N/A	34

Dawson Home Group Limited
PO Box 60 Deansgate, Manchester, M3 2QG
Tel: 0844-800 3744 **Fax:** 0161-251 4417
E-mail: info@dorma.co.uk
Website: http://www.dorma.co.uk
Bank(s): Barclays, 68 Lombard St, London EC3
Directors: M. Hartley (Dir), M. Mann (MD), R. Binch (Pers), W. Smyth (Dir)
Managers: F. McDougal (Mgr), S. Alexander (I.T. Exec), S. Wiliamson (Mktg Serv Mgr), S. Williamson (Mgr)
Ultimate Holding Company: Dawson International plc
Immediate Holding Company: Vantona Ltd
Registration no: 00011136 **Date established:** 1877
Turnover: Up to £250,000 **No.of Employees:** 101 - 250
Product Groups: 23, 24, 26, 27, 30

Date of Accounts	Dec 07
Sales Turnover	44870
Pre Tax Profit/Loss	-3050
Working Capital	6560
Fixed Assets	1200
Current Assets	23040
Current Liabilities	16480
Total Share Capital	33770
ROCE% (Return on Capital Employed)	-39.3

Dean Group International
Brinell Drive Northbank Industrial Park, Irlam, Manchester, M44 5BL
Tel: 0161-775 1633 **Fax:** 0161-777 9221
E-mail: info@deangroup-int.co.uk
Website: http://www.deangroup-int.co.uk
Directors: C. Hutchinson (Dir), C. Dean (MD)
Managers: C. Giblin (Purch Mgr)
Registration no: 01062820 **VAT No.:** GB 146 3074 78
No.of Employees: 101 - 250 **Product Groups:** 34, 38, 46, 48, 66, 84

Date of Accounts	Jun 08	Jun 07	Jun 06
Working Capital	984	805	603
Fixed Assets	754	757	812
Current Assets	1610	1162	913
Current Liabilities	626	357	310
Total Share Capital	7	7	7

Debdale Colour & Chemical Ltd
Waterhouse Road Gorton, Manchester, M18 7JF
Tel: 0161-231 1504 **Fax:** 0161-223 2763
E-mail: info@debdale.com
Website: http://www.debdale.com
Directors: D. Lewis (Sales & Mktg), J. Lewis (MD), M. Lewis (MD)
Managers: S. Howard (Chief Acct), F. Howard (Sales Admin)
Ultimate Holding Company: Deldale Ltd
Immediate Holding Company: Debdale Ltd
Registration no: 02819508 **VAT No.:** GB 606 6146 52
Date established: 1973 **Turnover:** £2m - £5m **No.of Employees:** 1 - 10
Product Groups: 32, 34, 49

Date of Accounts	Apr 07	Apr 06	Apr 05
Working Capital	23	21	18
Current Assets	383	341	317

Degussa Construction Chemicals UK Ltd
Albany House Swinton Hall Road, Swinton, Manchester, M27 4DT
Tel: 0161-794 7411 **Fax:** 0161-727 8547
E-mail: mbcfeb@basf.com
Website: http://www.basf-cc.co.uk
Bank(s): Lloyds TSB
Directors: G. McMannus (MD), M. Horsefield (Mkt Research)
Ultimate Holding Company: S.K.W. - VIAG TROTSBERG
Immediate Holding Company: P.C.I. GERMANY
Registration no: 00514077 **No.of Employees:** 101 - 250
Product Groups: 48

Delta Containers Manchester Ltd
Preston Street, Manchester, M18 8DB
Tel: 0161-231 2875 **Fax:** 0161-230 7352
E-mail: enquiries@deltacontainers.com
Website: http://www.deltacontainers.com
Directors: W. White (MD)
Immediate Holding Company: D.C. REALISATIONS 2011 LIMITED
Registration no: 01758860 **Date established:** 1983 **Turnover:** £1m - £2m
No.of Employees: 1 - 10 **Product Groups:** 27, 30, 35, 45, 66, 77

Date of Accounts	Apr 10	Apr 09	Apr 08
Working Capital	-183	-214	-205
Fixed Assets	266	332	367
Current Assets	550	605	609

Denial Design
112 Venwood Road Prestwich, Manchester, M25 9UH
Tel: 07908-964992
E-mail: mike@denialdesign.co.uk
Website: http://www.denialdesign.co.uk
Directors: M. Beckett (Dir), M. Beckett (Prop)
Date established: 2000 **Turnover:** Up to £250,000
No.of Employees: 1 - 10 **Product Groups:** 44

Design Services N W Ltd
42 Long Street Middleton, Manchester, M24 6UQ
Tel: 0161-643 0088 **Fax:** 0161-643 6254
E-mail: info@designservicesltd.co.uk
Website: http://www.designservicesltd.co.uk
Directors: D. Collinson (MD)
Immediate Holding Company: DESIGN SERVICES (NW) LIMITED
Registration no: 01267600 **Date established:** 1976 **Turnover:** £5m - £10m
No.of Employees: 1 - 10 **Product Groups:** 80

Date of Accounts	Mar 12	Mar 11	Mar 10
Working Capital	387	369	369
Fixed Assets	58	60	60
Current Assets	1m	739	650

Deva Composites Ltd (a division of Cope Engineering (Radcliffe) Ltd)
Sion Street Works Radcliffe, Manchester, M26 3SF
Tel: 0161-723 5105 **Fax:** 0161-723 6501
E-mail: info@devacomposites.com
Website: http://www.devacomposites.com
Directors: B. Burrows (Dir)
Registration no: 06481331 **VAT No.:** GB 836 7622 04
Date established: 1994 **No.of Employees:** 1 - 10 **Product Groups:** 30, 33, 36, 37, 39, 84

Date of Accounts	Mar 07	Mar 06
Working Capital	372	-714
Fixed Assets	784	717
Current Assets	917	184
Current Liabilities	544	898

Development Processes Group plc
93 Walkden Road Worsley, Manchester, M28 7BQ
Tel: 0161-975 7777 **Fax:** 0161-975 7575
E-mail: info@dpgplc.co.uk
Website: http://www.dpgplc.co.uk
Directors: R. Wagner (MD)
Managers: T. Taylor (Mktg Serv Mgr)
Immediate Holding Company: DEVELOPMENT PROCESSES GROUP PLC
Registration no: 02708805 **Date established:** 1992 **Turnover:** £1m - £2m
No.of Employees: 1 - 10 **Product Groups:** 28, 64

Date of Accounts	Mar 12	Mar 11	Mar 10
Sales Turnover	2m	2m	1m
Pre Tax Profit/Loss	141	155	18
Working Capital	-353	-354	-288
Fixed Assets	432	431	406
Current Assets	841	507	479
Current Liabilities	885	404	464

Dezign Steelwork Solutions
Palmerston Road Denton, Manchester, M34 2NY
Tel: 0161-336 1933
E-mail: info@dezignsolutions.co.uk
Website: http://www.dezignsolutions.com
Directors: M. Mcaleese (Dir)
No.of Employees: 1 - 10 **Product Groups:** 26, 35, 63

Direct Access Platforms
Unit 3 Gorton Crescent Windmill Lane Industrial Estate, Denton, Manchester, M34 3RB
Tel: 0161-336 4336 **Fax:** 0161-336 4343
Website: http://www.directaccessplatforms.com
Directors: D. Cholmondeley (MD)
Immediate Holding Company: TOM CHANDLEY LIMITED
Registration no: 05482578 **Date established:** 1944
No.of Employees: 11 - 20 **Product Groups:** 37, 40, 45, 84

Direct Route
36 Fairway Prestwich, Manchester, M25 0JH
Tel: 0161-773 5178 **Fax:** 0161-773 5178
E-mail: d.glickman@directroute.uk.com
Website: http://www.directroute.uk.com
Directors: D. Glickman (Prop), D. Glickman (Develop)
No.of Employees: 1 - 10 **Product Groups:** 82

Dolphin Bathrooms
2 Brindley Road, Manchester, M16 9HQ
Tel: 0800-626717
E-mail: customersupport@dolphinbathrooms.co.uk
Website: http://www.dolphinbathrooms.co.uk/contact-us/

see next page

Dolphin Bathrooms - Cont'd

Directors: B. Ponting (Sales)
Managers: T. Burdon (Mgr)
Ultimate Holding Company: SUN CAPITAL PARTNERS IV LP (UNITED STATES)
Immediate Holding Company: HOMEFORM GROUP LIMITED
Registration no: 06132417 **Date established:** 2007
Turnover: £20m - £50m **No.of Employees:** 1 - 10 **Product Groups:** 36

Date of Accounts	Mar 08	Mar 09	Mar 10
Sales Turnover	164m	148m	151m
Pre Tax Profit/Loss	-27m	-12m	-6m
Working Capital	-31m	-26m	-31m
Fixed Assets	8m	9m	8m
Current Assets	34m	28m	29m
Current Liabilities	21m	18m	16m

Drugasar Service Ltd

2 Deans Trading Estate Deans Road, Swinton, Manchester, M27 0JH
Tel: 0161-793 8700 **Fax:** 0161-727 8057
E-mail: info@drugasar.co.uk
Website: http://www.druservice.co.uk
Directors: N. Deiraniya (Fin)
Ultimate Holding Company: BRUGAKKER NV (NETHERLANDS)
Immediate Holding Company: DRUGASAR LIMITED
Registration no: 01072512 **VAT No.:** GB 677 5353 94
Date established: 1972 **Turnover:** £2m - £5m **No.of Employees:** 11 - 20
Product Groups: 37, 52, 66

Date of Accounts	Dec 11	Dec 10	Dec 09
Sales Turnover	3m	3m	3m
Pre Tax Profit/Loss	-3	5	-2
Working Capital	141	148	142
Fixed Assets	4	N/A	1
Current Assets	1m	1m	1m
Current Liabilities	197	169	121

Duffy Civils & Utillities Ltd

93 Hazelhurst Road Worsley, Manchester, M28 2SW
Tel: 0161-728 3656 **Fax:** 0161-728 3656
E-mail: info@duffycul.co.uk
Website: http://www.duffycul.co.uk
Directors: B. Duffy (Dir)
Turnover: £250,000 - £500,000 **No.of Employees:** 1 - 10
Product Groups: 30, 36, 54

Date of Accounts	Mar 08	Mar 07
Working Capital	-25	45
Fixed Assets	51	19
Current Assets	53	84
Current Liabilities	78	39

Dunbar & Boardman Partnership

Imex House 40 Princess Street, Manchester, M1 6DE
Tel: 0161-236 3968 **Fax:** 0161-236 3969
E-mail: k.young@dunbarboardman.com
Website: http://www.dunbarboardman.com
Managers: K. Young (Mgr)
Immediate Holding Company: HENG FENG MECHANICAL AND ELECTRICAL CO. LTD.
Registration no: 06754700 **Date established:** 2006
No.of Employees: 1 - 10 **Product Groups:** 35, 39, 45

Date of Accounts	Apr 11	Apr 10	Apr 09
Working Capital	95	85	48
Fixed Assets	7	9	13
Current Assets	131	105	108

E B V Elektronik

Suite 3e Manchester International Office Centre Styal Road, Manchester, M22 5WB
Tel: 0161-499 3434 **Fax:** 0161-499 3474
Website: http://www.ebv.com
Managers: I. Bhaiyat (Mgr)
Immediate Holding Company: GENERIS TECHNOLOGY HOLDINGS LIMITED
Registration no: 01187438 **Date established:** 2004
No.of Employees: 11 - 20 **Product Groups:** 36, 37

E M S Cargo Ltd

Unit 5 Ringway Trading Estate, Manchester, M22 5LH
Tel: 0161-499 1344 **Fax:** 0161-499 0847
E-mail: paule@ems-cargo.co.uk
Website: http://www.ems-cargo.com
Directors: P. Evans (MD)
Immediate Holding Company: EMS CARGO LIMITED
Registration no: 01309488 **VAT No.:** GB 151 5639 69
Date established: 1977 **Turnover:** £2m - £5m **No.of Employees:** 11 - 20
Product Groups: 76

Date of Accounts	Dec 11	Dec 10	Dec 09
Working Capital	181	188	113
Fixed Assets	20	11	15
Current Assets	873	1m	841

East Lancs Chemical Co. Ltd

Edge Lane Droylsden, Manchester, M43 6AU
Tel: 0161-371 5585 **Fax:** 0161-301 1990
E-mail: info@eastlancschemical.com
Website: http://www.eastlancschemical.com
Bank(s): National Westminster Bank Plc
Managers: F. Guffogg (Mgr)
Immediate Holding Company: EAST LANCASHIRE CHEMICAL (HOLDINGS) LTD
Registration no: 00228405 **VAT No.:** GB 145 1987 49
Turnover: £1m - £2m **No.of Employees:** 21 - 50 **Product Groups:** 32, 63

Date of Accounts	Sep 08	Sep 07	Sep 06
Working Capital	364	353	335
Fixed Assets	633	677	690
Current Assets	700	672	681
Current Liabilities	336	319	347
Total Share Capital	79	79	79

Eastland Compounding

Bank Street Clayton, Manchester, M11 4AS
Tel: 0161-223 3241 **Fax:** 0161-223 3240
E-mail: info@eastlandcompounding.com
Website: http://www.eastlandcompounding.com
Bank(s): National Westminster
Managers: R. Turner
Immediate Holding Company: EASTLAND COMPOUNDING LIMITED
Registration no: 04387263 **VAT No.:** GB 606 3418 60
Date established: 2002 **Turnover:** £10m - £20m
No.of Employees: 51 - 100 **Product Groups:** 29

Edm Ltd

1 Thorp Road, Manchester, M40 5BJ
Tel: 0161-203 3150 **Fax:** 0161-202 2500
E-mail: info@edm.ltd.uk
Website: http://www.edm.ltd.uk
Bank(s): The Royal Bank of Scotland
Directors: D. Garner (Tech Serv), G. Moss (Fin)
Managers: M. Bonney (Develop Mgr), N. Bonney (Sales Prom Mgr)
Ultimate Holding Company: EDM HOLDINGS LIMITED
Immediate Holding Company: EDM LIMITED
Registration no: 01001465 **Date established:** 1971
Turnover: £10m - £20m **No.of Employees:** 101 - 250
Product Groups: 28, 49

Date of Accounts	Dec 11	Dec 10	Dec 09
Sales Turnover	12m	12m	8m
Pre Tax Profit/Loss	1m	1m	149
Working Capital	5m	3m	2m
Fixed Assets	1m	1m	1m
Current Assets	7m	7m	4m
Current Liabilities	1m	2m	858

Elcometer Instruments Ltd

Elcometer Edge Lane, Droylsden, Manchester, M43 6BU
Tel: 0161-371 6000 **Fax:** 0161-371 6010
E-mail: catherine.lund-barker@elcometer.com
Website: http://www.elcometer.com
Bank(s): Lloyds TSB Bank plc
Directors: P. Dodgeson (Pers), I. Sellers (MD), I. Sellars (Ch)
Managers: M. Sellers (Sales Prom Mgr), N. Sellers (Mgr), C. Lund-Barker (Mktg Serv Mgr), L. Kenyan (I.T. Exec), P. Dodgeson
Ultimate Holding Company: SELLARS ELECTRONICS LTD
Immediate Holding Company: ELCOMETER LIMITED
Registration no: 01729726 **Date established:** 1983
Turnover: £10m - £20m **No.of Employees:** 101 - 250
Product Groups: 37, 38, 44, 67, 85

Date of Accounts	Mar 11	Mar 10	Mar 09
Sales Turnover	22m	19m	N/A
Pre Tax Profit/Loss	2m	2m	2m
Working Capital	7m	6m	3m
Fixed Assets	8m	6m	7m
Current Assets	12m	10m	6m
Current Liabilities	2m	1m	1m

Electrium Sales Ltd

Sharston Road Wythenshawe, Manchester, M22 4RA
Tel: 0161-998 5454 **Fax:** 0161-945 1587
Website: http://www.electrium.co.uk
Directors: G. Gent (Dir), E. Lovebridge (Fin)
Managers: K. McLoud (Personnel), J. Benson (Purch Mgr)
Ultimate Holding Company: SIEMENS AG (GERMANY)
Immediate Holding Company: ELECTRIUM SALES LIMITED
Registration no: 02226729 **Date established:** 1988
Turnover: £75m - £125m **No.of Employees:** 101 - 250
Product Groups: 30, 37

Date of Accounts	Sep 11	Sep 10	Sep 09
Sales Turnover	100m	111m	114m
Pre Tax Profit/Loss	-4m	-15m	11m
Working Capital	13m	17m	31m
Fixed Assets	10m	6m	11m
Current Assets	75m	69m	81m
Current Liabilities	7m	20m	5m

Elliott Group Ltd

Chaddock Lane Worsley, Manchester, M28 1DP
Tel: 0161-790 3721 **Fax:** 0161-703 8294
E-mail: info@elliotthire.co.uk
Website: http://www.elliotthire.co.uk
Managers: I. Candeland (Mgr)
Ultimate Holding Company: TDR CAPITAL LLP
Immediate Holding Company: ELLIOTT GROUP LIMITED
Registration no: 00147207 **Date established:** 2017
No.of Employees: 21 - 50 **Product Groups:** 39

Date of Accounts	Dec 10	Dec 09	Dec 08
Sales Turnover	135m	137m	165m
Pre Tax Profit/Loss	-2m	3m	3m
Working Capital	16m	49m	7m
Fixed Assets	264m	230m	260m
Current Assets	79m	122m	80m
Current Liabilities	31m	32m	14m

Emerge Recycling

E1-E4 New Smithfield Market, Manchester, M11 2WJ
Tel: 0161-223 8200 **Fax:** 0161-231 2141
E-mail: office@emergemanchester.co.uk
Website: http://www.emergemanchester.co.uk
Directors: L. Danger (Grp Chief Exec)
Managers: K. Clayton (Fin Mgr), G. Jones (Chief Mgr), A. Quinn (Develop Mgr)
Immediate Holding Company: EMERGE 3RS
Registration no: 03556346 **Date established:** 1998
Turnover: £500,000 - £1m **No.of Employees:** 21 - 50
Product Groups: 42, 54

Date of Accounts	Mar 11	Mar 10	Mar 09
Sales Turnover	701	761	N/A
Pre Tax Profit/Loss	-61	-28	N/A
Working Capital	-33	-15	11
Fixed Assets	59	78	104
Current Assets	98	110	124
Current Liabilities	66	49	N/A

Endress Hauser Ltd

Floats Road Roundthorn Industrial Estate, Manchester, M23 9NF
Tel: 0161-286 5000 **Fax:** 0161-998 1841
E-mail: sales@uk.endress.com
Website: http://www.uk.endress.com
Bank(s): Lloyds TSB Bank plc
Directors: D. Newell (MD), R. Stone (Fin)
Managers: C. Smith (Personnel), R. O'Sullivan (Tech Serv Mgr)
Ultimate Holding Company: ENDRESS + HAUSER HOLDING AG (SWITZERLAND)
Immediate Holding Company: ENDRESS + HAUSER LIMITED
Registration no: 00942157 **VAT No.:** GB 146 1934 64
Date established: 1968 **Turnover:** £20m - £50m
No.of Employees: 101 - 250 **Product Groups:** 38

Date of Accounts	Dec 11	Dec 10	Dec 09
Sales Turnover	34m	33m	31m
Pre Tax Profit/Loss	2m	2m	2m
Working Capital	7m	6m	6m
Fixed Assets	7m	8m	8m
Current Assets	10m	9m	9m
Current Liabilities	945	1m	1m

Energy & Environment Ltd

91 Claude Road, Manchester, M21 8DE
Tel: 0161-881 1383
E-mail: sales@energyenv.co.uk
Website: http://www.energyenv.co.uk
Directors: T. Kennedy (MD)
Immediate Holding Company: ENERGY AND ENVIRONMENT LTD
Registration no: 04091971 **Date established:** 2000
Turnover: £250,000 - £500,000 **No.of Employees:** 1 - 10
Product Groups: 37

Date of Accounts	Apr 12	Apr 11	Apr 09
Working Capital	7	10	-0
Fixed Assets	1	1	1
Current Assets	96	63	40

Enterprise Q Ltd

1 Tallow Way Irlam, Manchester, M44 6RJ
Tel: 0161-777 4888 **Fax:** 0161-777 4899
E-mail: info@enterprise-q.co.uk
Website: http://www.enterprise-q.co.uk
Directors: J. Miller (Fin), D. Cathie (MD)
Immediate Holding Company: ENTERPRISE Q LTD.
Registration no: 03166763 **Date established:** 1996
No.of Employees: 11 - 20 **Product Groups:** 17, 33, 37, 38

Date of Accounts	Mar 11	Mar 10	Mar 09
Working Capital	632	640	757
Fixed Assets	597	608	800
Current Assets	939	825	949

Equal Response T/d Extragas

1 Trafford Road Eccles, Manchester, M30 0JX
Tel: 0161-789 0000 **Fax:** 0161-788 8111
E-mail: ralph@extragas.co.uk
Website: http://WWW.EXTRAGAS.CO.UK
Registration no: 04464490 **Date established:** 1992 **Turnover:** £2m - £5m
No.of Employees: 21 - 50 **Product Groups:** 18, 31

Eriks UK

Unit 4 Littlers Point, Trafford Park, Manchester, M17 1LT
Tel: 0161-872 2946 **Fax:** 0161-872 9905
E-mail: manchester@eriks.co.uk
Website: http://www.eriks.co.uk
Directors: R. Mcmullen (Prop)
Registration no: 03142338 **No.of Employees:** 1 - 10 **Product Groups:** 30

Ernest & Young LLP

100 Barbirolli Square, Manchester, M2 3EY
Tel: 0161-333 3000 **Fax:** 0161-333 3001
E-mail: info@uk.ey.com
Website: http://www.ey.com
Directors: S. Allport (Ptnr)
Managers: M. Hilton (I.T. Exec), K. Tetlow (Mktg Serv Mgr), L. Zukswoki (Personnel)
Ultimate Holding Company: FLP2 LIMITED
Immediate Holding Company: DO IT ALL (HOLDINGS) LIMITED
Registration no: 05458987 **Date established:** 1990 **Turnover:** £1m - £2m
No.of Employees: 251 - 500 **Product Groups:** 80

Date of Accounts	Jul 08	Jul 07	Jul 06
Working Capital	-2	-2	2
Fixed Assets	491	489	490
Current Assets	1	N/A	4

Etde Contracting

One Didsbury Point 2 The Avenue, Manchester, M20 2EY
Tel: 0161-279 1000 **Fax:** 0161-249 1001
E-mail: ttglossop@compuserve.co.uk
Website: http://www.etde.co.uk
Bank(s): Clydesdale Bank PLC
Directors: Z. Ahmed (Dir)
Managers: M. Short (Mktg Serv Mgr), S. Heyes (Sales Prom Mgr)
Ultimate Holding Company: SCOTTISH AND SOUTHERN ENERGY P.L.C.
Immediate Holding Company: SCOTTISH & SOUTHERN ENERGY P.L.C.
Registration no: SC087174 **VAT No.:** GB 261 5400 89
Turnover: £20m - £50m **No.of Employees:** 21 - 50 **Product Groups:** 38, 40, 52, 84

Euro Car Parks Ltd

31 Byrom Street, Manchester, M3 4PF
Tel: 0161-832 9777 **Fax:** 0161-831 7088
E-mail: humanresources@eurocarparks.com
Website: http://www.eurocarparks.com
Bank(s): National Westminster Bank Plc
Directors: G. Lomas (Co Sec), B. Tucker (MD)
Ultimate Holding Company: ECP (HOLDINGS) PLC
Immediate Holding Company: EURO CAR PARKS LIMITED
Registration no: 01270612 **VAT No.:** GB 451 5697 31
Date established: 1976 **Turnover:** £2m - £5m
No.of Employees: 501 - 1000 **Product Groups:** 80

Date of Accounts	Dec 11	Dec 10	Dec 09
Sales Turnover	24m	25m	27m
Pre Tax Profit/Loss	1m	1m	979
Working Capital	2m	2m	2m
Fixed Assets	613	669	892
Current Assets	9m	10m	9m
Current Liabilities	6m	6m	5m

Euro Fluid Hydraulics Ltd

7 Harp Trading Estate Guinness Road, Trafford Park, Manchester, M17 1SR
Tel: 0161-876 5257 **Fax:** 0161-876 5259
Directors: W. Wood (Dir)
Immediate Holding Company: EURO (FLUID) HYDRAULICS LIMITED
Registration no: 02935105 **Date established:** 1994
No.of Employees: 1 - 10 **Product Groups:** 36, 38, 40

Date of Accounts	Dec 11	Dec 10	Dec 09
Working Capital	148	122	115
Fixed Assets	41	29	26
Current Assets	656	544	526

Europasonic UK Ltd

11 Sherbourne Street, Manchester, M3 1JS
Tel: 0161-831 7879 **Fax:** 0161-835 2125
E-mail: jill.prendergast@panasonic.co.uk
Website: http://www.europasonic.com
Bank(s): The Royal Bank of Scotland
Directors: J. Prendergast (Co Sec), Z. Khan (Tech Serv)
Immediate Holding Company: EUROPASONIC (U.K.) LIMITED
Registration no: 01394171 **VAT No.:** GB 305 6274 73
Date established: 1978 **Turnover:** £20m - £50m
No.of Employees: 51 - 100 **Product Groups:** 37

Date of Accounts	Mar 11	Mar 10	Mar 09
Sales Turnover	27m	27m	N/A
Pre Tax Profit/Loss	634	-62	124
Working Capital	1m	672	20
Fixed Assets	3m	4m	4m
Current Assets	10m	11m	5m
Current Liabilities	2m	2m	1m

European Metals Recycling Ltd

Irlam Street, Manchester, M40 2BP
Tel: 0161-205 1735 **Fax:** 0161-203 4532
Website: http://www.emrltd.com
Managers: J. Bissett (Mgr)
Immediate Holding Company: EUROPEAN METAL RECYCLING LIMITED
Registration no: 02954623 **Date established:** 1994
Turnover: £10m - £20m **No.of Employees:** 1 - 10 **Product Groups:** 42, 66

Date of Accounts	Dec 11	Dec 10	Dec 09
Sales Turnover	3032m	2431m	1843m
Pre Tax Profit/Loss	116m	155m	91m
Working Capital	414m	371m	167m
Fixed Assets	518m	483m	480m
Current Assets	1027m	717m	557m
Current Liabilities	124m	118m	185m

Evans Textiles Sales Ltd

Helmet Street, Manchester, M1 2NT
Tel: 0161-274 4147 **Fax:** 0161-274 4322
E-mail: peter@kgchristys.co.uk
Website: http://www.kgchristys.co.uk
Bank(s): National Westminster Bank Plc
Directors: P. Callan (MD), P. Christys (MD)
Immediate Holding Company: K.G. CHRISTYS & CO. LIMITED
Registration no: 01410626 **VAT No.:** GB 145 6491 53
Date established: 1979 **Turnover:** £5m - £10m **No.of Employees:** 21 - 50
Product Groups: 23, 24, 32, 63, 66

Date of Accounts	Jan 11	Jan 10	Jan 09
Working Capital	-341	-357	-383
Fixed Assets	N/A	7	16
Current Assets	7	9	22

Everlast Flat Roofing Systems

198 Liverpool Road Irlam, Manchester, M44 6FE
Tel: 0161-771 2305 **Fax:** 0845-680 1251
E-mail: info@everlastgrp.co.uk
Website: http://www.everlastgrp.co.uk
Product Groups: 30, 32, 66

Eversheds LLP

Eversheds House 70 Great Bridgewater Street, Manchester, M1 5ES
Tel: 0161-831 8000 **Fax:** 0161-831 8888
E-mail: bryanhughes@eversheds.com
Website: http://www.eversheds.com
Bank(s): Barclays
Directors: A. Macgregor (Pers), G. Osborne (Mkt Research), K. Fleming (Fin)
Managers: W. Stevens (Sales Admin), L. Hart (Sales Admin)
Immediate Holding Company: EVERSHEDS LLP
Registration no: OC304065 **VAT No.:** GB 169 2808 32
Date established: 2003 **Turnover:** £250m - £500m
No.of Employees: 251 - 500 **Product Groups:** 80

Date of Accounts	Apr 11	Apr 10	Apr 09
Sales Turnover	355m	355m	366m
Pre Tax Profit/Loss	110m	105m	95m
Working Capital	113m	128m	119m
Fixed Assets	50m	54m	61m
Current Assets	201m	191m	180m
Current Liabilities	52m	52m	47m

Executive Status Ltd

Darnell House 14a Kenworthy Lane, Manchester, M22 4EJ
Tel: 0161-613 9300 **Fax:** 0161-613 9310
E-mail: reservations@executivestatus.co.uk
Website: http://www.executivestatus.co.uk
Directors: L. Cronshaw (MD)
Immediate Holding Company: EXECUTIVE STATUS LIMITED
Registration no: 03538819 **VAT No.:** GB 712 6111 80
Date established: 1998 **Turnover:** £2m - £5m **No.of Employees:** 1 - 10
Product Groups: 69, 81

Date of Accounts	Mar 12	Mar 11	Mar 10
Working Capital	26	25	12
Fixed Assets	4	5	7
Current Assets	117	120	208

F G F Insulation Ltd

8 Fourways Trading Estate Longbridge Road, Trafford Park, Manchester, M17 1SW
Tel: 0161-873 7445 **Fax:** 0161-872 9120
E-mail: scott.heesom@fgflimited.co.uk
Website: http://www.fgflimited.co.uk
Bank(s): Barclays, Yardley
Managers: S. Heesom (Mgr)
Immediate Holding Company: F.G.F. LTD
Registration no: 00530903 **VAT No.:** GB 559 0806 21
Turnover: £20m - £50m **No.of Employees:** 11 - 20 **Product Groups:** 23, 25, 32, 33, 36, 66

F1 Mobile Valeting

92-96 Deansgate, Manchester, M3 2QG
Tel: 07766-526153
E-mail: info@f1mobilevaleting.co.uk
Website: http://www.f1mobilevaleting.co.uk
Directors: S. Swindells (Prop)
Date established: 2002 **Turnover:** Up to £250,000
No.of Employees: 1 - 10 **Product Groups:** 32, 39, 68

Failsworth Hats Ltd

Crown Street Failsworth, Manchester, M35 9BD
Tel: 0161-681 3131 **Fax:** 0161-683 4754
E-mail: sales@failsworth-hats.co.uk
Website: http://www.failsworth-hats.co.uk
Bank(s): National Westminster Bank Plc
Directors: C. Eccles (Fin), D. Puleikis (Sales & Mktg), P. Lynch (MD)
Managers: M. Clegg (Sales Admin)
Immediate Holding Company: FAILSWORTH HATS LIMITED
Registration no: 00079310 **Date established:** 2003 **Turnover:** £2m - £5m
No.of Employees: 21 - 50 **Product Groups:** 24

Date of Accounts	Dec 10	Dec 09	Dec 08
Working Capital	2m	2m	2m
Fixed Assets	339	359	347
Current Assets	3m	3m	3m

Faith Products Ltd

Faith House James Street, Radcliffe, Manchester, M26 1LN
Tel: 0161-724 4016 **Fax:** 0161-724 8210
E-mail: info@faithinnature.co.uk
Website: http://www.faithinnature.co.uk
Bank(s): The Royal Bank of Scotland
Managers: S. Anderton (Sales Admin)
Immediate Holding Company: FAITH PRODUCTS LIMITED
Registration no: SC068493 **VAT No.:** GB 327 4674 41
Date established: 1979 **Turnover:** £500,000 - £1m
No.of Employees: 21 - 50 **Product Groups:** 31, 32, 49, 63, 85

Date of Accounts	Jun 11	Jun 10	Jun 09
Working Capital	1m	893	789
Fixed Assets	166	175	194
Current Assets	1m	1m	1m

Thomas Fattorini(Namebadges)

Westbourne Road Urmston, Manchester, M41 0TR
Tel: 0161-748 0441 **Fax:** 0161-755 3258
E-mail: sales@fattorini.co.uk
Website: http://www.fattorini.co.uk/Namebadges.aspx
Directors: G. Fattorini (MD), T. Fattorini (Sales)
Immediate Holding Company: THOMAS FATTORINI LIMITED
Registration no: 00153351 **VAT No.:** GB 343 4128 78
Date established: 1963 **Turnover:** £2m - £5m **No.of Employees:** 11 - 20
Product Groups: 23, 27, 28, 30, 40, 49

Date of Accounts	Dec 11	Dec 10	Dec 09
Sales Turnover	10m	N/A	N/A
Pre Tax Profit/Loss	1m	N/A	N/A
Working Capital	3m	3m	2m
Fixed Assets	734	429	386
Current Assets	5m	5m	3m
Current Liabilities	795	N/A	N/A

Feather Brooksbank

Cardinal House St Marys Parsonage, Manchester, M3 2LY
Tel: 0161-834 9793 **Fax:** 0161-835 1363
E-mail: sbell@featherbrookbank.co.uk
Website: http://www.featherbrooksbank.co.uk
Directors: R. Sweedey (Dir), S. Bell (Dir), C. Broadbent (Dir), C. Downing (Dir), J. Brickhill (Dir), M. Cox (Dir), M. Conry (Dir), R. Kelly (Dir)
Immediate Holding Company: JOHNNY GREEN PRODUCTIONS LIMITED
Registration no: 04594996 **Date established:** 2010
Turnover: £10m - £20m **No.of Employees:** 21 - 50 **Product Groups:** 81

Fife Tidland Ltd

Millennium House Progress Way, Denton, Manchester, M34 2GP
Tel: 0161-320 2000 **Fax:** 0161-320 4513
E-mail: sales_uk@maxcess.eu
Website: http://www.tidland.co.uk
Directors: B. Ryan (Dir), G. Mathes (Grp Chief Exec)
Managers: D. Bold (Sales Prom Mgr), L. Smith (Sales Admin)
Ultimate Holding Company: MAXCESS INTERNATIONAL CORP (USA)
Immediate Holding Company: Maxcess International Corporation (USA)
Registration no: 01315614 **Date established:** 1977 **Turnover:** £1m - £2m
No.of Employees: 11 - 20 **Product Groups:** 44, 46

Date of Accounts	Jun 08	Jun 07	Jun 06
Sales Turnover	N/A	1636	1681
Pre Tax Profit/Loss	N/A	348	331
Working Capital	552	391	417
Fixed Assets	19	58	63
Current Assets	857	784	712
Current Liabilities	305	393	296
ROCE% (Return on Capital Employed)		77.6	69.0
ROT% (Return on Turnover)		21.3	19.7

Film Solutions Ltd

Highfield Road Industrial Estate Highfield Road, Little Hulton, Manchester, M38 9ST
Tel: 0161-799 1111 **Fax:** 0161-799 1100
E-mail: sales@filmsolutions.co.uk
Website: http://www.filmsolutions.co.uk
Bank(s): National Westminster Bank Plc
Directors: R. Bottomley (MD)
Managers: S. Walsh (Sales & Mktg Mg)
Registration no: 05908123 **VAT No.:** GB 468 0544 32
Turnover: £2m - £5m **No.of Employees:** 11 - 20 **Product Groups:** 23, 27, 30, 33, 34

Finglands Coachway

261 Wilmslow Road, Manchester, M14 5LJ
Tel: 0161-225 3333 **Fax:** 0161-257 3154
E-mail: shurden@finglands.co.uk
Website: http://www.finglands.co.uk
Directors: D. Shurden (MD), P. Leeman (Co Sec)
Ultimate Holding Company: EYMS GROUP LIMITED
Immediate Holding Company: FINGLANDS COACHWAYS LIMITED
Registration no: 00243051 **Date established:** 2029 **Turnover:** £2m - £5m
No.of Employees: 101 - 250 **Product Groups:** 68, 72

Date of Accounts	Dec 11	Dec 10	Dec 09
Sales Turnover	5m	5m	5m
Pre Tax Profit/Loss	-266	-454	-361
Working Capital	-1m	-1m	-846
Fixed Assets	3m	3m	4m
Current Assets	263	399	307
Current Liabilities	320	225	329

Fisher Audio Visual

Carrington Business Park Manchester Road, Carrington, Manchester, M31 4ZU
Tel: 0151-482 8700 **Fax:** 0151-482 8739
E-mail: info@fisherav.co.uk
Website: http://www.fisheraudiovisual.co.uk
Bank(s): HSBC Bank plc
Directors: B. Fisher (Prop)
Immediate Holding Company: DATASYS INTEGRATION LIMITED
Registration no: 06865024 **VAT No.:** GB 673 3165 32
Date established: 2009 **Turnover:** £1m - £2m **No.of Employees:** 11 - 20
Product Groups: 37, 81, 83

Date of Accounts	May 11	May 10	May 09
Working Capital	682	600	158
Fixed Assets	565	833	1m
Current Assets	1m	938	531

Flintnine Fasteners Ltd

Highfield Road Little Hulton, Manchester, M38 9ST
Tel: 0161-790 7817 **Fax:** 0161-703 8314
E-mail: sales@flintnine.co.uk
Website: http://www.flintnine.co.uk
Directors: P. Howarth (Fin)
Immediate Holding Company: FLINTNINE FASTENERS LIMITED
Registration no: 03386891 **VAT No.:** GB 693 2928 94
Date established: 1997 **Turnover:** £500,000 - £1m
No.of Employees: 1 - 10 **Product Groups:** 30, 35, 66

Date of Accounts	Dec 11	Dec 10	Dec 09
Working Capital	-97	-106	-112
Fixed Assets	102	106	113
Current Assets	258	243	214

Fluorocarbon Co. Ltd

Excalibur Way Irlam, Manchester, M44 5DL
Tel: 0161-777 6300 **Fax:** 0161-776 2503
E-mail: seals@fluorocarbon.co.uk
Website: http://www.fluorocarbon.co.uk
Bank(s): Lloyds TSB Bank plc
Directors: J. Cumins (Fin), S. Lewis (Dir), T. Wells (Dir)
Managers: R. Owuen (Chief Mgr), C. Woodham (Buyer)
Immediate Holding Company: CHARLES MITCHELL WINES LIMITED
Registration no: 01588333 **Date established:** 1981
Turnover: £20m - £50m **No.of Employees:** 101 - 250
Product Groups: 30, 36, 66

Date of Accounts	Jan 12	Jan 11	Jan 10
Working Capital	-59	-45	-63
Fixed Assets	189	198	205
Current Assets	137	149	116
Current Liabilities	176	N/A	N/A

Forsyth Bros Ltd

126 Deansgate, Manchester, M3 2GR
Tel: 0161-834 3281 **Fax:** 0161-834 0630
E-mail: info@forsyths.co.uk
Website: http://www.forsyths.co.uk
Directors: D. Loat (MD)
Managers: S. Loat (Chief Mgr)
Immediate Holding Company: FORSYTH BROTHERS LIMITED
Registration no: 00068072 **VAT No.:** GB 145 4970 51
Date established: 2000 **Turnover:** £1m - £2m **No.of Employees:** 21 - 50
Product Groups: 28, 65, 83

Date of Accounts	Jun 11	Jun 10	Jun 09
Working Capital	2m	1m	1m
Fixed Assets	55	48	58
Current Assets	2m	2m	2m

Fragrance Oils International Ltd

Eton Hill Road Radcliffe, Manchester, M26 2FR
Tel: 0161-724 9311 **Fax:** 0161-725 5225
E-mail: uk.sales@fragrance-oils.com
Website: http://www.fragrance-oils.com
Bank(s): Co-operative Bank P.L.C.
Directors: M. Hogan (Purch)
Managers: J. Slavin
Ultimate Holding Company: FRAGRANCE OILS PLC
Immediate Holding Company: FRAGRANCE OILS (INTERNATIONAL) LIMITED
Registration no: 01180568 **VAT No.:** GB 431 2605 91
Date established: 1974 **Turnover:** £20m - £50m
No.of Employees: 101 - 250 **Product Groups:** 20, 31, 32, 66

Date of Accounts	Feb 12	Feb 11	Feb 10
Sales Turnover	34m	33m	29m
Pre Tax Profit/Loss	922	937	2m
Working Capital	8m	7m	7m
Current Assets	15m	11m	18m
Current Liabilities	1m	1m	1m

Franke UK Ltd

Manchester Int Office Centre Styal Road, Manchester, M22 5WB
Tel: 0161-436 6280 **Fax:** 0161-436 2180
E-mail: info.uk@franke.com
Website: http://www.franke.co.uk
Directors: C. Brindle (Fin)
Managers: L. Jones, L. Jones (Mgr), J. Swain, A. Dwan
Ultimate Holding Company: FRANKE HOLDING AG (SWITZERLAND)
Immediate Holding Company: FRANKE U.K. LIMITED
Registration no: SC126669 **Date established:** 1990
Turnover: £20m - £50m **No.of Employees:** 11 - 20 **Product Groups:** 33, 36, 66

Date of Accounts	Dec 11	Dec 10	Dec 09
Sales Turnover	34m	31m	32m
Pre Tax Profit/Loss	5m	5m	5m
Working Capital	4m	4m	5m
Fixed Assets	263	453	644
Current Assets	10m	8m	9m
Current Liabilities	3m	2m	2m

Frazer

Higher Ainsworth Road Radcliffe, Manchester, M26 4AF
Tel: 0161-723 6342 **Fax:** 0161-723 6266
Website: http://www.frazer.eu.com
Managers: M. Nixen (Mgr)
Ultimate Holding Company: SAINT GOBAIN PIPE SYSTEMS
Registration no: 02065074 **Turnover:** £75m - £125m
No.of Employees: 1 - 10 **Product Groups:** 66

Freddies Forge Ltd

Unit 3 Bank Street, Whitefield, Manchester, M45 7JF
Tel: 0161-766 1502
E-mail: sales@gateexpectations.co.uk
Website: http://www.gateexpectations.co.uk
Directors: F. Goddard (Prop), R. Dixon (Prop)
Immediate Holding Company: FREDDIES FORGE LTD
Registration no: 04486076 **Date established:** 2002
No.of Employees: 1 - 10 **Product Groups:** 26, 35

Future Forwarding Co. Ltd

Building 308 World Freight Terminal, Manchester Airport, Manchester, M90 5PZ
Tel: 0161-436 8181 **Fax:** 0161-499 0654
E-mail: andreadelves@futureforwarding.com
Website: http://www.futureforwarding.com
Directors: D. Holland (Co Sec), P. Holland (Dir)
Immediate Holding Company: FUTURE FORWARDING COMPANY LTD
Registration no: 01376547 **VAT No.:** GB 399 4269 86
No.of Employees: 1 - 10 **Product Groups:** 76

Date of Accounts	Sep 10	Sep 09	Sep 08
Working Capital	35	35	35
Current Assets	35	50	599

G A Engineering

Unit C Barton Hall Industrial Estate Hardy Street, Eccles, Manchester, M30 7NB
Tel: 0161-788 8666 **Fax:** 0161-788 8857
E-mail: peterwooff@gaeng.co.uk
Website: http://www.gaeng.co.uk
Directors: P. Wooff (Dir)
Ultimate Holding Company: TEXAS HOLDINGS LIMITED
Immediate Holding Company: TEXAS HOLDINGS LIMITED
Registration no: 03546550 **Date established:** 1973 **Turnover:** £5m - £10m
No.of Employees: 11 - 20 **Product Groups:** 35

Date of Accounts	Nov 11	Nov 10	Nov 09
Sales Turnover	4m	4m	4m
Pre Tax Profit/Loss	208	-1m	503
Working Capital	-5m	-5m	-20m
Fixed Assets	29m	29m	42m
Current Assets	2m	2m	779
Current Liabilities	786	919	548

G B M Group

2 Heyrod Street Ancoats, Manchester, M1 2WW
Tel: 0161-273 5562 **Fax:** 0161-273 3597
E-mail: info@gbm.co.uk
Website: http://www.gbm.co.uk
Directors: J. Payne (Fin), M. Ealand (MD)
Ultimate Holding Company: GBM GROUP HOLDINGS LIMITED
Immediate Holding Company: G B M GROUP LIMITED
Registration no: 02231732 **Date established:** 1988 **Turnover:** £2m - £5m
No.of Employees: 21 - 50 **Product Groups:** 28, 81

Date of Accounts	Mar 11	Mar 10	Mar 09
Sales Turnover	N/A	3m	3m
Pre Tax Profit/Loss	N/A	-71	-115
Working Capital	-154	-366	-457
Fixed Assets	1m	1m	1m
Current Assets	729	544	561
Current Liabilities	N/A	185	183

G C Supplies UK Ltd

13-15a Reliance Trading Estate Reliance Street, Manchester, M40 3ET
Tel: 0161-681 8114 **Fax:** 0161-947 0148
E-mail: gcsuppliesukats@googlemail.com
Website: http://www.stainlessvalves.co.uk
Bank(s): Barclays
Directors: A. Steeles (Dir), S. Glover (Co Sec)
Immediate Holding Company: G.C.SUPPLIES UK LIMITED
Registration no: 01871479 **Date established:** 1984 **Turnover:** £1m - £2m
No.of Employees: 11 - 20 **Product Groups:** 48

Date of Accounts	Dec 11	Dec 10	Dec 09
Working Capital	3m	3m	2m
Fixed Assets	287	302	317
Current Assets	3m	3m	2m

G J Plastics Ltd

Unit 2 Eton Hill Works Eton Hill Road, Radcliffe, Manchester, M26 2US
Tel: 0161-723 1374 **Fax:** 0161-723 5064
E-mail: info@gjplastics.co.uk
Website: http://www.gjplastics.co.uk
Directors: G. Croston (Dir)
Immediate Holding Company: G.J. PLASTICS LIMITED
Registration no: 04484916 **Date established:** 2002
Turnover: Up to £250,000 **No.of Employees:** 11 - 20 **Product Groups:** 30, 49

Date of Accounts	Aug 11	Aug 10	Aug 09
Working Capital	-6	11	6
Fixed Assets	88	89	59
Current Assets	110	124	85

G S G

Unit 5 Cathrine Street West Denton, Manchester, M34 3SY
Tel: 0161-320 6605 **Fax:** 0161-320 6605
E-mail: gsgmetalfabrications@btconnect.com
Directors: G. Gibson (Prop)
No.of Employees: 1 - 10 **Product Groups:** 20, 40, 41

G V A Grimley Ltd

81 Fountain Street, Manchester, M2 2EE
Tel: 08709-008990 **Fax:** 0161-956 4009
Website: http://www.gvagrimley.co.uk
Directors: D. Smith (Fin), J. Coates (Pers), G. Fairhurst (Dir), K. Marriott (MD)
Managers: S. Doughty (Tech Serv Mgr), P. Cherry (Sales Admin)
Ultimate Holding Company: GVA GRIMLEY HOLDINGS LIMITED
Immediate Holding Company: GVA GRIMLEY LIMITED
Registration no: 06382509 **VAT No.:** GB 109 632 476
Date established: 2007 **No.of Employees:** 51 - 100 **Product Groups:** 54, 80, 84

Date of Accounts	Apr 11	Apr 10	Apr 09
Sales Turnover	115m	112m	118m
Pre Tax Profit/Loss	574	4m	3m
Working Capital	9m	11m	7m
Fixed Assets	113m	114m	117m
Current Assets	42m	42m	35m
Current Liabilities	22m	22m	16m

G V E Ltd

Ashburton House Ashburton Road East, Trafford Park, Manchester, M17 1BN
Tel: 0161-872 0777 **Fax:** 0161-872 9324
E-mail: info@gvepumps.co.uk
Website: http://www.gvepumps.co.uk
Directors: H. Towers (Dir), S. Oliver (Dir)
Immediate Holding Company: G.V.E. LIMITED
Registration no: 02080836 **VAT No.:** GB 453 2010 96
Date established: 1986 **Turnover:** £250,000 - £500,000
No.of Employees: 1 - 10 **Product Groups:** 40, 42

Date of Accounts	Dec 11	Dec 10	Dec 09
Working Capital	-131	-146	-159
Fixed Assets	609	699	710
Current Assets	72	81	150

Gap PR & Marketing

Paradise Wharf Ducie Street, Manchester, M1 2JN
Tel: 0161-273 8931 **Fax:** 0845-241 5411
E-mail: info@gapgb.com
Website: http://www.gapgb.com
Directors: G. Parker (MD)
Immediate Holding Company: GAP PR AND MARKETING LIMITED
Registration no: 05580069 **Date established:** 2005
Turnover: £250,000 - £500,000 **No.of Employees:** 1 - 10
Product Groups: 81

Date of Accounts	Mar 11	Mar 10	Mar 09
Working Capital	-19	-16	-16
Fixed Assets	1	2	2
Current Assets	15	N/A	N/A

Gardner Denver Ltd

Unit 7 Whitefield, Manchester, M45 8FJ
Tel: 0161-767 1555 **Fax:** 0161-767 1545
E-mail: charles.howden@gardnerdenver.com
Website: http://www.gardendenver.com
Ultimate Holding Company: GARDNER DENVER INC (USA)
Immediate Holding Company: GARDNER DENVER LTD
Registration no: 03047245 **Date established:** 1995 **Turnover:** £1m - £2m
No.of Employees: 1 - 10 **Product Groups:** 39, 40, 41, 42, 43, 46, 66, 67

Date of Accounts	Dec 11	Dec 10	Dec 09
Sales Turnover	136m	136m	67m
Pre Tax Profit/Loss	8m	2m	-668
Working Capital	-11m	-23m	26m
Fixed Assets	86m	92m	101m
Current Assets	45m	44m	63m
Current Liabilities	11m	6m	10m

Gaselle Central Heating

1 Mather Avenue Prestwich, Manchester, M25 0ND
Tel: 07931-401825
Directors: Y. Nahari (Prop)
No.of Employees: 1 - 10 **Product Groups:** 40, 48, 52

Glasses Complete Ltd

14 Hulton District Centre Worsley, Manchester, M28 0AU
Tel: 0161-790 0800 **Fax:** 0161-790 0100
E-mail: districtopticians@hotmail.co.uk
Website: http://www.glassescomplete.co.uk
Directors: I. Mohamad (Dir)
Immediate Holding Company: GLASSES COMPLETE LIMITED
Registration no: 05787935 **Date established:** 2006
Turnover: Up to £250,000 **No.of Employees:** 1 - 10 **Product Groups:** 38

Date of Accounts	Apr 12	Apr 11	Apr 10
Working Capital	1	2	10
Fixed Assets	N/A	3	5
Current Assets	1	6	14

Joseph Gleave & Son Ltd

995 Chester Road Stretford, Manchester, M32 0NB
Tel: 0161-865 6025 **Fax:** 0161-865 0879
E-mail: david.shaw@gleave.co.uk
Website: http://www.gleave.co.uk
Bank(s): National Westminster Bank Plc
Directors: J. Shaw (MD)
Managers: A. Jameson (Purch Mgr), S. Causer
Immediate Holding Company: JOSEPH GLEAVE & SON LIMITED
Registration no: 00582735 **VAT No.:** GB 150 5672 77
Date established: 1957 **Turnover:** £20m - £50m
No.of Employees: 51 - 100 **Product Groups:** 66

Date of Accounts	Dec 11	Dec 10	Dec 09
Sales Turnover	22m	28m	27m
Pre Tax Profit/Loss	3m	1m	1m
Working Capital	7m	5m	4m
Fixed Assets	4m	4m	4m
Current Assets	10m	8m	8m
Current Liabilities	1m	889	2m

Global Investment Group plc

413 Bury Old Road Prestwich, Manchester, M25 1PS
Tel: 0161-798 6602 **Fax:** 0161-773 6358
E-mail: info@global-inv-group.co.uk
Website: http://www.global-inv-group.co.uk
Directors: D. Booth (MD), S. Booth (MD), R. Ristic (Sales), R. Ristic (Fin)
Immediate Holding Company: GLOBAL INVESTMENT GROUP PLC
Registration no: 03539290 **Date established:** 1998 **Turnover:** £5m - £10m
No.of Employees: 101 - 250 **Product Groups:** 61

Date of Accounts	Mar 10	Mar 09	Mar 08
Sales Turnover	6m	6m	6m
Pre Tax Profit/Loss	-278	-590	-620
Working Capital	-2m	-2m	-2m
Fixed Assets	11m	11m	13m
Current Assets	849	906	782
Current Liabilities	984	1m	822

R Gorton & Associates Electronics Ltd

308-310 Slade Lane, Manchester, M19 2BY
Tel: 0161-224 5650 **Fax:** 0161-257 2761
E-mail: accounts@gortonelectronics.com
Website: http://www.gortonelectronics.com
Bank(s): National Westminster
Directors: P. Gorton (MD), E. Gorton (Fin)
Immediate Holding Company: R. GORTON AND ASSOCIATES (ELECTRONICS) LIMITED
Registration no: 01292983 **Date established:** 1976
Turnover: £500,000 - £1m **No.of Employees:** 11 - 20
Product Groups: 37, 84

Date of Accounts	Mar 11	Mar 10	Mar 09
Working Capital	-19	-22	35
Fixed Assets	58	59	60
Current Assets	92	83	141

Green Brothers Signs Ltd

Shentonfield Road Sharston Industrial Area, Manchester, M22 4TJ
Tel: 0161-741 7270 **Fax:** 0161-741 7272
E-mail: sales@greensigns.co.uk
Website: http://www.greensigns.co.uk
Bank(s): The Royal Bank of Scotland
Directors: P. Keep (MD), J. Keep (Co Sec)
Immediate Holding Company: GREEN BROTHERS SIGNS LTD
Registration no: 07433026 **Date established:** 2010 **Turnover:** £1m - £2m
No.of Employees: 21 - 50 **Product Groups:** 30, 35, 37, 39, 40, 45, 48, 49

Date of Accounts	Jan 12
Working Capital	11
Fixed Assets	60
Current Assets	351

Greenoaks Ltd

Greenoaks House Siemens Road, Irlam, Manchester, M44 5AH
Tel: 0161-775 7178 **Fax:** 0161-776 1951
E-mail: info@greenoaks.ltd.uk
Website: http://www.greenoaks.ltd.uk
Directors: G. Rogerson (Dir)
Immediate Holding Company: GREENOAKS LIMITED
Registration no: 02008299 **VAT No.:** GB 437 6351 40
Date established: 1986 **Turnover:** £1m - £2m **No.of Employees:** 11 - 20
Product Groups: 26, 67

Date of Accounts	May 11	May 10	May 09
Working Capital	-109	-97	-111
Fixed Assets	293	280	294
Current Assets	567	510	590

Ernest Griffith & Sons Ltd

Praed Road Trafford Park, Manchester, M17 1PQ
Tel: 0161-877 1655 **Fax:** 0161-877 6577
E-mail: pdbrearley@aol.com
Website: http://www.griffithdustsheets.co.uk
Directors: P. Brearley (Dir)
Registration no: 03680507 **Turnover:** £250,000 - £500,000
No.of Employees: 1 - 10 **Product Groups:** 24, 30, 66

Date of Accounts	Sep 11	Sep 10	Sep 09
Working Capital	99	105	107
Fixed Assets	31	30	67
Current Assets	402	289	527

Middleton Guardian

1 Scott Place, Manchester, M3 3RN
Tel: 0161-643 3615 **Fax:** 0161-653 9968
Website: http://www.middletonguardian.co.uk
Directors: B. Hibbert (I.T. Dir), C. Marland (MD), E. Forgan (Non Exec), P. Myners (Ch), P. Broadman (Co Sec), R. Gavron (Ch), N. Castro (Fin), J. Clay (Non Exec), J. Bullmore (Non Exec), I. Ashcroft (MD), A. Karney (Non Exec), C. McColl (MD), R. Phillis (Grp Chief Exec)
Managers: E. Derbyshire (Mktg Serv Mgr), G. Sammon (Mgr), J. Harris
Immediate Holding Company: THE SCOTT TRUST LIMITED
Registration no: 00094531 **VAT No.:** GB 145 7744 45
Date established: 2007 **Turnover:** £250m - £500m
No.of Employees: 1 - 10 **Product Groups:** 28

H & C Storage Ltd

3 Martingale Way Droylsden, Manchester, M43 7ES
Tel: 0161-371 1458 **Fax:** 0161-371 8072
E-mail: sales@hcstorage.co.uk
Website: http://www.hcstorage.co.uk
Directors: H. Robinson (Fin)
Immediate Holding Company: H & C STORAGE LIMITED
Registration no: 05898539 **Date established:** 2006
No.of Employees: 1 - 10 **Product Groups:** 26

Date of Accounts	Aug 11	Aug 10	Aug 08
Working Capital	20	14	6
Current Assets	40	35	20

H M G Paints Ltd

Riverside Works Collyhurst Road, Manchester, M40 7RU
Tel: 0161-205 7631 **Fax:** 0161-205 8823
E-mail: sales@hmgpaint.com
Website: http://www.hmgpaint.com
Bank(s): National Westminster Bank Plc
Directors: J. Falder (Prop), D. Cleary (Sales), A. Burton (Fin), A. Burton (Fin)
Managers: A. Patterson (Mktg Serv Mgr), I. Burwin (Personnel), B. Wood, H. Clark (Buyer)
Ultimate Holding Company: H. MARCEL GUEST, LIMITED
Immediate Holding Company: H. MARCEL GUEST, LIMITED
Registration no: 00251148 **Date established:** 1930
Turnover: £10m - £20m **No.of Employees:** 101 - 250 **Product Groups:** 32

Date of Accounts	Sep 11	Sep 10	Sep 09
Sales Turnover	14m	13m	11m
Pre Tax Profit/Loss	512	21	-301
Working Capital	2m	1m	2m
Fixed Assets	2m	2m	2m
Current Assets	6m	6m	6m
Current Liabilities	2m	1m	1m

Halliday Meecham

Rodwell Tower 111 Piccadilly, Manchester, M1 2HY
Tel: 0161-661 5566 **Fax:** 0161-661 5567
E-mail: apd@hallidaymeecham.com
Website: http://www.hallidaymeecham.com
Directors: A. Parry Davies (Dir)
Ultimate Holding Company: HALLIDAY MEECHAM HOLDINGS LIMITED
Immediate Holding Company: HALLIDAY MEECHAM HOLDINGS LIMITED
Registration no: 05073812 **Date established:** 2004
No.of Employees: 21 - 50 **Product Groups:** 84

Date of Accounts	Mar 12	Mar 11	Mar 10
Fixed Assets	172	172	172

James Halstead Group plc

Beechfield Hollinhurst Road, Radcliffe, Manchester, M26 1JN
Tel: 0161-767 2500 **Fax:** 0161-766 7499
E-mail: enquiries@jameshalstead.co.uk
Website: http://www.jameshalstead.com
Directors: G. Oliver (Fin)
Managers: T. Froggatt
Immediate Holding Company: JAMES HALSTEAD PLC
Registration no: 00140269 **Date established:** 2015
Turnover: £125m - £250m **No.of Employees:** 11 - 20 **Product Groups:** 82

Date of Accounts	Jun 11	Jun 10	Jun 09
Sales Turnover	214m	186m	169m
Pre Tax Profit/Loss	38m	36m	33m
Working Capital	57m	48m	44m
Fixed Assets	43m	37m	36m
Current Assets	115m	99m	81m
Current Liabilities	27m	25m	21m

Hanah UK Ltd

Northbank Industrial Estate Huntsman Drive Irlam, Manchester, M44 5EG
Tel: 0161-775 7098 **Fax:** 0161-775 7101
E-mail: info@hanahuk.co.uk
Website: http://www.hanahuk.co.uk
Directors: K. Kavat (Dir), K. Khabat (MD), K. Khvat (MD), S. Khvat (Fin)
Managers: A. Kavat (Buyer)
Immediate Holding Company: HANAH PROPERTIES LIMITED
Registration no: 07193932 **Date established:** 2010
No.of Employees: 1 - 10 **Product Groups:** 49

Date of Accounts	Mar 11
Working Capital	25
Current Assets	25

Hanix Europe Ltd

Unit B Alliance Industrial Estate Windmill Lane, Denton, Manchester, M34 3SP
Tel: 0161-335 2330 **Fax:** 0161-335 0336
E-mail: sales@hanixeurope.com
Website: http://www.hanixeurope.com

Directors: H. Ogasahara (Co Sec), K. Walker (Dir), P. Hyslop (Sales)
Managers: Asal (Mgr)
Ultimate Holding Company: HAJUNI BANK LTD (JAPAN)
Immediate Holding Company: HANIX EUROPE LTD.
Registration no: 02197128 **Date established:** 1987
Turnover: £10m - £20m **No.of Employees:** 11 - 20 **Product Groups:** 41, 45, 67, 83

Date of Accounts	Mar 11	Mar 10	Mar 09
Sales Turnover	9m	10m	9m
Pre Tax Profit/Loss	-3m	-2m	-4m
Working Capital	-5m	-1m	280
Fixed Assets	279	76	222
Current Assets	5m	6m	11m
Current Liabilities	53	98	990

Hansen Group

Greengate Industrial Estate Greenside Way, Middleton, Manchester, M24 1SW
Tel: 0161-653 3030 **Fax:** 0161-653 3031
E-mail: s.barnes@hansengroup.biz
Website: http://www.hansengroup.biz
Directors: K. Pedersen (Fin)
Managers: S. Townsend (Tech Serv Mgr), G. Lynch (Buyer)
Ultimate Holding Company: HANSENGROUP A/S (DENMARK)
Immediate Holding Company: HANSENGROUP LIMITED
Registration no: 02802131 **Date established:** 1993
Turnover: £10m - £20m **No.of Employees:** 21 - 50 **Product Groups:** 26, 35

Date of Accounts	Jun 11	Jun 10	Jun 09
Sales Turnover	13m	16m	21m
Pre Tax Profit/Loss	-2m	-2m	-1m
Working Capital	867	3m	4m
Fixed Assets	961	1m	1m
Current Assets	7m	12m	10m
Current Liabilities	1m	1m	1m

Hardwood Dimensions Holdings Ltd

Trafford Park Road Trafford Park, Manchester, M17 1WH
Tel: 0161-872 5111 **Fax:** 0161-873 7004
E-mail: sales@hardwooddimensions.ltd.uk
Website: http://www.hardwooddimensions.ltd.uk
Bank(s): National Westminster Bank Plc
Directors: A. Waterhouse (MD), J. Marsden (Dir), J. Waterhouse (Dir), S. Marsden (MD)
Ultimate Holding Company: WATERHOUSE (F. & M.) LIMITED
Immediate Holding Company: HARDWOOD DIMENSIONS (HOLDINGS) LIMITED
Registration no: 00673095 **Date established:** 1960 **Turnover:** £5m - £10m
No.of Employees: 11 - 20 **Product Groups:** 61

Date of Accounts	Mar 12	Mar 11	Mar 10
Sales Turnover	9m	9m	8m
Pre Tax Profit/Loss	73	196	-69
Working Capital	847	784	584
Fixed Assets	1m	1m	1m
Current Assets	4m	4m	3m
Current Liabilities	1m	971	258

J A Harrison & Co Manchester Ltd

Britain Works Sherborne Street, Manchester, M8 8HP
Tel: 0161-832 2282 **Fax:** 0161-832 3263
E-mail: enquiries@jaharrison.co.uk
Website: http://www.jaharrison.co.uk
Bank(s): The Royal Bank of Scotland
Directors: K. Shepherd (MD)
Immediate Holding Company: J.A. HARRISON & COMPANY (MANCHESTER) LIMITED
Registration no: 01236981 **VAT No.:** GB 150 5076 93
Date established: 1975 **Turnover:** £1m - £2m **No.of Employees:** 11 - 20
Product Groups: 23, 25, 29, 33, 35, 36, 45

Date of Accounts	Sep 11	Sep 10	Sep 09
Working Capital	1m	1m	978
Fixed Assets	1m	971	981
Current Assets	2m	2m	2m

Harry Seymour & Associates Ltd

26 Minster Drive Urmston, Manchester, M41 5HA
Tel: 07801-233925 **Fax:** 01625-828131
Website: http://www.hsal.fsbusiness.co.uk
Directors: J. Seymour (Fin)
Immediate Holding Company: HARRY SEYMOUR & ASSOCIATES LIMITED
Registration no: 02587477 **Date established:** 1991
No.of Employees: 1 - 10 **Product Groups:** 35

Date of Accounts	Sep 11	Sep 10	Sep 09
Working Capital	6	3	5
Fixed Assets	8	11	14
Current Assets	21	11	15

Harvey Engineering

Unit B 12 Dewey Street Openshaw, Manchester, M11 2NT
Tel: 0161-223 6220 **Fax:** 0161-223 8013
E-mail: barry.harvey@btconnect.com
Website: http://www.harveyengineering.co.uk
Directors: B. Harvey (Prop)
No.of Employees: 1 - 10 **Product Groups:** 40, 46, 48

Hay Group

Sovereign House 12-18 Queen Street, Manchester, M2 5HS
Tel: 0161-831 2460 **Fax:** 0161-835 2616
Website: http://www.haygroup.co.uk
Managers: L. Boots (Sales Admin), J. Blanire (Sales Admin)
Registration no: 02673374 **No.of Employees:** 11 - 20 **Product Groups:** 80

Haynes International Ltd

Parkhouse Street, Manchester, M11 2JX
Tel: 0161-230 7777 **Fax:** 0161-223 2412
E-mail: pcrawshaw@haynesintl.com
Website: http://www.haynesintl.com
Bank(s): RBS
Directors: A. Chapman (I.T. Dir), P. Crawshaw (MD)
Managers: T. Barfoot (Develop Mgr), J. Sairbrother (Comptroller), J. Rotherford (Personnel)
Ultimate Holding Company: HAYNES INTERNATIONAL INC (USA)
Immediate Holding Company: HAYNES INTERNATIONAL LTD
Registration no: 01209891 **VAT No.:** GB 359 8881 80
Date established: 1975 **Turnover:** £20m - £50m
No.of Employees: 21 - 50 **Product Groups:** 34, 35, 36, 48

Date of Accounts	Sep 11	Sep 10	Sep 09
Sales Turnover	39m	27m	33m
Pre Tax Profit/Loss	5m	2m	2m
Working Capital	20m	17m	15m
Fixed Assets	700	361	496
Current Assets	28m	21m	19m
Current Liabilities	1m	922	889

Hays Education (K.I.T.E.)

Ninth Floor Portland Tower Portland Street, Manchester, M1 3LF
Tel: 0161-228 7300 **Fax:** 0161-832 6240
E-mail: sales@hays-education.com
Website: http://www.hays.com/education
Directors: M. Best (Dir)
Immediate Holding Company: NEW MEDIA INTELLIGENCE LIMITED
Registration no: 02732451 **Date established:** 1999 **Turnover:** £2m - £5m
No.of Employees: 21 - 50 **Product Groups:** 44, 80, 86

Date of Accounts	Sep 10	Sep 09	Sep 08
Working Capital	-56	-18	6
Fixed Assets	3	4	2
Current Assets	13	10	33

Headen & Quarmby Ltd

Sadler Street Middleton, Manchester, M24 5UJ
Tel: 0161-643 2576 **Fax:** 0161-653 0554
E-mail: ho@headen-quarmby.co.uk
Website: http://www.headen-quarmby.co.uk
Bank(s): Barclays, Middleton Branch
Directors: H. Moore (Fin), D. Moore (Dir)
Managers: P. Robert (Mktg Serv Mgr)
Immediate Holding Company: HEADEN & QUARMBY LIMITED
Registration no: 03375522 **VAT No.:** GB 145 2775 59
Date established: 1997 **Turnover:** £1m - £2m **No.of Employees:** 11 - 20
Product Groups: 24

Date of Accounts	Sep 11	Sep 10	Sep 09
Working Capital	92	-4	2
Fixed Assets	388	394	402
Current Assets	1m	940	1m

Healthy Spirit

37 Barlow Moor Road, Manchester, M20 6TW
Tel: 0161-434 6784 **Fax:** 0161-434 6784
E-mail: healthyspirit37@ntlworld.com
Website: http://www.healthy-spirit.com
Directors: S. Casey (Prop)
No.of Employees: 1 - 10 **Product Groups:** 31, 32

Heimbach UK

Bradnor Road Sharston Industrial Area, Manchester, M22 4TS
Tel: 0161-998 6911 **Fax:** 0161-998 8095
E-mail: info@heimbach.com
Website: http://www.heimbach-group.com
Bank(s): National Westminster Bank Plc
Directors: R. Martin (Dir), G. Hanson (Co Sec)
Managers: L. Johnson (Personnel), P. Burgess (Fin Mgr), D. Hannon (Tech Serv Mgr), R. Whitehead (Purch Mgr)
Ultimate Holding Company: HEIMBACH GMBH (GERMANY)
Immediate Holding Company: HEIMBACH UK LIMITED
Registration no: 00055771 **VAT No.:** GB 145 8913 43
Date established: 1998 **Turnover:** £10m - £20m
No.of Employees: 101 - 250 **Product Groups:** 44

Date of Accounts	Dec 11	Dec 10	Dec 09
Sales Turnover	12m	9m	9m
Pre Tax Profit/Loss	2m	1m	2m
Working Capital	905	332	-1m
Fixed Assets	10m	9m	10m
Current Assets	3m	4m	3m
Current Liabilities	672	420	711

Hellermann Tyton

1 Robeson Way, Manchester, M22 4TY
Tel: 0161-945 4181 **Fax:** 0161-947 2233
E-mail: sales@hellermanntyton.co.uk
Website: http://www.hellermanntyton.co.uk
Bank(s): HSBC Bank plc
Directors: S. Pemberton (Fin)
Managers: R. Kynnersley (Sales & Mktg Mg), S. Slater, T. Lambert (Tech Serv Mgr), M. Cunliff (Sales Off Mgr), G. Carr (Personnel)
Ultimate Holding Company: SPIRENT PLC
Immediate Holding Company: SPIRENT P.L.C.
Registration no: 05652018 **Turnover:** £2m - £5m
No.of Employees: 101 - 250 **Product Groups:** 29, 30, 35, 36, 37, 46, 47

Henderson Engineering Ltd

307 Manchester Road West Little Hulton, Manchester, M38 9XH
Tel: 0161-799 0900 **Fax:** 0161-799 7524
E-mail: sales@henderson-engineering.co.uk
Website: http://www.henderson-engineering.co.uk
Directors: G. Jones (MD)
Ultimate Holding Company: ENHANCED BUSINESS LIMITED
Immediate Holding Company: HENDERSON ENGINEERING LIMITED
Registration no: 03511584 **Date established:** 1998
No.of Employees: 11 - 20 **Product Groups:** 42, 43, 44, 47, 67

Date of Accounts	Jun 11	Jun 10	Jun 09
Working Capital	-332	-381	-238
Fixed Assets	496	505	566
Current Assets	894	466	375

Henri Lloyd Ltd

Smithfold Lane Worsley, Manchester, M28 0GP
Tel: 0161-799 1212 **Fax:** 0161-975 2500
E-mail: mstrzelecki@henrilloyd.co.uk
Website: http://www.henrilloyd.com
Directors: M. Strzelecki (Grp Chief Exec), H. Ford (Fin)
Managers: S. Hurst (Personnel), D. Williams (Mktg Serv Mgr), A. Leebetter
Immediate Holding Company: HENRI-LLOYD INTERNATIONAL LIMITED
Registration no: 01994135 **Date established:** 1986
Turnover: £20m - £50m **No.of Employees:** 101 - 250
Product Groups: 24, 81

Date of Accounts	Dec 11	Dec 10	Dec 09
Sales Turnover	26m	27m	27m
Pre Tax Profit/Loss	658	653	-2m
Working Capital	6m	6m	6m
Fixed Assets	3m	4m	4m
Current Assets	12m	12m	12m
Current Liabilities	1m	1m	3m

Hewden

Trafford House Chester Road, Stretford, Manchester, M32 0RL
Tel: 08456-070111 **Fax:** 0161-848 2298
E-mail: info@hewden.co.uk
Website: http://www.hewden.co.uk
Directors: M. Pen (Sales), M. Davies (Dir), J. Schofield (Mkt Research), B. Sherlock (MD), S. Shardlow (Fin), C. Vikes (Purch)
Managers: T. Reynolds (Sales Admin), P. Burns (I.T. Exec), R. O'Connor
Ultimate Holding Company: SUN CAPITAL PARTNERS V LP (CAYMAN ISLANDS)
Immediate Holding Company: HEWDEN TOWER CRANES LIMITED
Registration no: 00967197 **VAT No.:** GB 145 6518 59
Date established: 1969 **Turnover:** £2m - £5m **No.of Employees:** 1 - 10
Product Groups: 25, 30, 83

Date of Accounts	Dec 10	Dec 09	Dec 08
Pre Tax Profit/Loss	N/A	N/A	20
Working Capital	947	947	947
Current Assets	947	19m	19m
Current Liabilities	N/A	5	N/A

Hill Farm Forge

20 Hanson Close Middleton, Manchester, M24 2HD
Tel: 0161-653 0811 **Fax:** 0161-653 0848
Managers: C. Walsh (Mgr)
Date established: 1991 **No.of Employees:** 1 - 10 **Product Groups:** 26, 35

Hilson Ltd

Shentonfield Road Sharston Industrial Area, Manchester, M22 4SD
Tel: 0161-491 7800 **Fax:** 0161-428 1179
E-mail: vasant@hilson.co.uk
Website: http://www.hilson.co.uk
Bank(s): Barclays
Directors: J. Cartwright (Fin), V. Mistry (MD)
Managers: S. Mistry (Sec), M. Taylor (Sales & Mktg Mg)
Immediate Holding Company: HILSON LIMITED
Registration no: 04224733 **Date established:** 2001 **Turnover:** £1m - £2m
No.of Employees: 21 - 50 **Product Groups:** 35

Date of Accounts	Sep 09	Sep 08	Sep 07
Working Capital	28	114	73
Fixed Assets	330	282	229
Current Assets	1m	2m	1m

Hilti GB Ltd (Head Office)

1 Trafford Wharf Road Trafford Park, Manchester, M17 1BY
Tel: 0800-886100 **Fax:** 0161-872 1240
E-mail: gbsales@hilti.com
Website: http://www.hilti.com
Bank(s): National Westminster Bank Plc
Directors: R. Van Der Feltz Van Der Sloot (Dir)
Ultimate Holding Company: HILTI AG (LIECHTENSTEIN)
Immediate Holding Company: HILTI (GT.BRITAIN) LIMITED
Registration no: 00479786 **VAT No.:** GB 146 0352 91
Date established: 1950 **Turnover:** £50m - £75m
No.of Employees: 101 - 250 **Product Groups:** 30, 35, 37, 46, 66

Date of Accounts	Dec 11	Dec 10	Dec 09
Sales Turnover	87m	65m	66m
Pre Tax Profit/Loss	838	766	-379
Working Capital	12m	12m	15m
Fixed Assets	6m	5m	5m
Current Assets	45m	33m	25m
Current Liabilities	10m	6m	4m

The Hira Company Ltd

Hira House 1 Elizabeth Street, Manchester, M8 8PR
Tel: 0161-834 2868 **Fax:** 0161-832 4566
E-mail: reception@hira.co.uk
Website: http://www.hira.co.uk
Bank(s): HSBC Bank plc
Directors: M. Shah (Fin), M. Hira (Dir)
Managers: C. Smith (Chief Mgr)
Ultimate Holding Company: HIRA COMPANY LIMITED(THE)
Immediate Holding Company: TEXET SALES LIMITED
Registration no: 01656138 **VAT No.:** GB 560 4160 70
Date established: 1982 **Turnover:** £10m - £20m
No.of Employees: 11 - 20 **Product Groups:** 27, 37

Date of Accounts	Apr 10	Apr 09	Apr 08
Working Capital	117	117	117
Current Assets	117	117	117

Hirex Ltd

1 Lomax Street Radcliffe, Manchester, M26 1PX
Tel: 0161-723 6100 **Fax:** 0161-723 4744
E-mail: sales@hirex.co.uk
Website: http://www.hirex.co.uk
Directors: J. McWilliams (Sales), M. Mc Williams (Co Sec)
Immediate Holding Company: HIREX LIMITED
Registration no: 01878510 **Date established:** 1985
No.of Employees: 11 - 20 **Product Groups:** 26, 35, 44, 49, 52, 69, 80, 81, 83, 84

Date of Accounts	Jul 11	Jul 10	Jul 09
Working Capital	-192	-164	-151
Fixed Assets	956	223	246
Current Assets	141	165	149

Hockley International Ltd

Hockley House
Ashbrook Office Park
3 Longstone Road, Manchester, M22 5LB
Tel: 0161-2097400 **Fax:** 0161-2097401
E-mail: mail@hockley.co.uk
Website: http://www.hockley.co.uk
Bank(s): The Royal Bank of Scotland plc
Directors: F. Howard (MD)
Managers: M. Murphy (Sales Prom Mgr)
Registration no: 02566845 **VAT No.:** GB 593 6473 00
Date established: 1991 **Turnover:** £10m - £20m
No.of Employees: 11 - 20 **Product Groups:** 30, 32, 41, 61, 66

Date of Accounts	Jun 11	Jun 10	Jun 09
Sales Turnover	16m	13m	18m
Pre Tax Profit/Loss	233	624	672
Working Capital	1m	1m	807
Fixed Assets	260	142	97
Current Assets	5m	4m	4m
Current Liabilities	170	254	337

Joseph Holt Ltd

Derby Brewery Empire Street, Cheetham, Manchester, M3 1JD
Tel: 0161-834 3285 **Fax:** 0161-834 6458
E-mail: therichmond@joseph-holt.com
Website: http://www.joseph-holt.com
Bank(s): Royal Bank of Scotland
Directors: P. Rowan (Co Sec), T. Dempsey (Chief Op Offcr)
Immediate Holding Company: Joseph Holt Group Ltd
Registration no: 00182757 **VAT No.:** GB 146 0643 80
Date established: 1922 **Turnover:** £20m - £50m
No.of Employees: 51 - 100 **Product Groups:** 21

Holt Lloyd International Ltd (Holt Lloyd International Ltd)

Unit 100 Barton Dock Road Stretford, Manchester, M32 0YQ
Tel: 0161-866 4800 **Fax:** 0161-866 4854
E-mail: info@holtsauto.com
Website: http://www.holtsauto.com
Directors: M. Baff (Sales), A. Holland (Fin), D. Hales (Mkt Research)
Managers: P. Lof, S. Blackburn (Personnel), M. Johns
Ultimate Holding Company: HONEYWELL INTERNATIONAL INC (USA)
Immediate Holding Company: HOLT LLOYD INTERNATIONAL LIMITED
Registration no: 01235124 **Date established:** 1975
Turnover: £20m - £50m **No.of Employees:** 21 - 50 **Product Groups:** 32, 49, 68

Date of Accounts	Dec 10	Dec 09	Dec 08
Sales Turnover	32m	19m	21m
Pre Tax Profit/Loss	-622	-3m	-4m
Working Capital	-17m	-15m	-11m
Fixed Assets	13m	13m	13m
Current Assets	14m	6m	7m
Current Liabilities	2m	2m	1m

Homes4u

Armstrong House Oxford Road, Manchester, M1 7ED
Tel: 0161-236 0202 **Fax:** 0161-236 8202
E-mail: sales@homes4u.co.uk
Website: http://www.homes4u.co.uk
Managers: A. Durrell (Chief Mgr)
Ultimate Holding Company: NATIONAL COMPUTING CENTRE LIMITED(THE)
Immediate Holding Company: CONFERENCEPAGE.COM LIMITED
Registration no: 04148609 **Date established:** 2000
No.of Employees: 1 - 10 **Product Groups:** 80

Dave Hopton

32 Braemar Avenue Urmston, Manchester, M41 6HP
Tel: 0161-748 7256 **Fax:** 0161-748 7256
E-mail: dave_hopton@hotmail.com
Website: http://www.davehopton.com
Directors: D. Hopton (Prop)
Date established: 1970 **Turnover:** Up to £250,000
No.of Employees: 1 - 10 **Product Groups:** 30, 52

John Howard & Sons Ltd

Unit 6 Linnyshaw Indl-Est Sharp Street, Worsley, Manchester, M28 3LY
Tel: 0161-790 2149 **Fax:** 0161-703 8253
E-mail: contact@johnhowardwalkden.com
Website: http://www.johnhowardwalkden.com
Directors: G. Howard (MD), S. Howard (MD)
Immediate Holding Company: JOHN HOWARD & SONS (WALKDEN) LIMITED
Registration no: 00496709 **VAT No.:** GB 145 8011 83
Date established: 1951 **Turnover:** £500,000 - £1m
No.of Employees: 1 - 10 **Product Groups:** 26, 35, 36, 48

Date of Accounts	Jul 11	Jul 10	Jul 09
Working Capital	109	112	118
Fixed Assets	21	22	23
Current Assets	255	271	228

Howgate Sable LLP

Arkwright House Parsonage Gardens, Manchester, M3 2LF
Tel: 0161-839 2000 **Fax:** 0161-839 0064
E-mail: manchester@howgate-sable.com
Website: http://www.howgate-sable.com
Directors: A. Sharman (Fin)
Immediate Holding Company: HOWGATE SABLE (UK) LTD
Registration no: 03586599 **Date established:** 1998 **Turnover:** £2m - £5m
No.of Employees: 11 - 20 **Product Groups:** 80

Hub Le Bas (a division of Caparo Precision Tubes Ltd)

Bower Street Newton Heath, Manchester, M40 2AF
Tel: 0161-203 4410 **Fax:** 0161-203 4426
E-mail: sally.atkins@hublebas.co.uk
Website: http://www.hublebas.co.uk
Managers: S. Atkins (Mgr), J. Curran (Sales Prom Mgr), J. Renshaw (Purch Mgr)
Ultimate Holding Company: TYCO INTERNATIONAL LTD
Immediate Holding Company: TYCO EUROPEAN TUBING LTD
Registration no: 02168228 **No.of Employees:** 21 - 50 **Product Groups:** 36

Hubron Speciality Ltd

Albion Street Failsworth, Manchester, M35 0FP
Tel: 0161-681 2691 **Fax:** 0161-683 4045
E-mail: info@hubron.com
Website: http://www.hubron.com
Bank(s): National Westminster Bank Plc
Managers: L. Hurst (Purch Mgr), D. Dunworhty (I.T. Exec), D. Hanvey (Personnel)
Ultimate Holding Company: OBG PHARMACEUTICALS LIMITED
Immediate Holding Company: HUBRON SPECIALITY LIMITED
Registration no: 05138283 **Date established:** 2004
Turnover: £20m - £50m **No.of Employees:** 11 - 20 **Product Groups:** 32

Date of Accounts	Dec 11	Dec 10	Dec 09
Sales Turnover	9m	8m	6m
Pre Tax Profit/Loss	463	361	149
Working Capital	567	635	362
Fixed Assets	146	190	208
Current Assets	3m	2m	2m
Current Liabilities	2m	1m	1m

J Hughes Welding & Engineering Ltd

59a Clifton Road Eccles, Manchester, M30 9QS
Tel: 0161-788 9443 **Fax:** 0161-788 9443
Directors: S. Cottrill (Fin), G. Cottrill (MD)
Immediate Holding Company: J HUGHES WELDING & ENGINEERING LIMITED
Registration no: 04618575 **Date established:** 2002
No.of Employees: 1 - 10 **Product Groups:** 26, 35

Date of Accounts	Dec 11	Dec 09	Dec 08
Working Capital	23	34	51
Fixed Assets	2	5	5
Current Assets	42	66	95
Current Liabilities	N/A	19	N/A

Hyde Precision Components Ltd

Oldham Street Denton, Manchester, M34 3SA
Tel: 0161-337 9242 **Fax:** 0161-335 0787
E-mail: sales@hyde-precision.co.uk
Website: http://www.hydeprecision.com
Directors: A. Sharples (MD), M. Ford (Dir), P. Beard (MD)
Ultimate Holding Company: Hyde Industrial Holdings Ltd
Immediate Holding Company: HYDE PRECISION COMPONENTS LIMITED
Registration no: 03145450 **Date established:** 1996 **Turnover:** £2m - £5m
No.of Employees: 21 - 50 **Product Groups:** 30, 33, 34, 39, 46, 48

Date of Accounts	Sep 11	Sep 10	Sep 09
Working Capital	3m	3m	3m
Fixed Assets	55	29	147
Current Assets	5m	5m	5m

Hydes' Brewery Trustee Ltd

46 Moss Lane West, Manchester, M15 5PH
Tel: 0161-226 1317 **Fax:** 0161-227 9593
E-mail: info@hydesbrewery.com
Website: http://www.hydesbrewery.com
Bank(s): Barclays, Manchester
Directors: C. Hyde (Fin), P. Johnson (Ch)
Immediate Holding Company: HYDES' BREWERY (TRUSTEE) LIMITED
Registration no: 05003811 **VAT No.:** GB 145 8239 53
Date established: 2003 **Turnover:** £20m - £50m
No.of Employees: 51 - 100 **Product Groups:** 21

I M I Scott Ltd

Dallimore Road Roundthorn Industrial Estate, Manchester, M23 9WJ
Tel: 0161-998 5533 **Fax:** 0161-946 0538
E-mail: sales@imiscott.co.uk
Website: http://www.imiscott.co.uk
Bank(s): Lloyds TSB Bank plc
Directors: D. Austin (MD)
Managers: M. Barr, S. Holt, C. Oldham (Tech Serv Mgr)
Ultimate Holding Company: IMI PLC
Immediate Holding Company: IMI SCOTT LIMITED
Registration no: 00190744 **Date established:** 2023 **Turnover:** £5m - £10m
No.of Employees: 21 - 50 **Product Groups:** 34, 35

Date of Accounts	Dec 11	Dec 10	Dec 09
Sales Turnover	7m	7m	4m
Pre Tax Profit/Loss	242	228	144
Working Capital	1m	963	799
Current Assets	1m	1m	839
Current Liabilities	64	64	40

I T A C Ltd

Bankfield Mills Bankfield Street, Radcliffe, Manchester, M26 1AS
Tel: 01204-573736 **Fax:** 01204-862332
E-mail: sales@itac.uk.com
Website: http://www.itacadhesives.com
Bank(s): HSBC
Directors: P. Armitt (MD)
Managers: W. Finch
Immediate Holding Company: ITAC LIMITED
Registration no: 00499145 **VAT No.:** GB 145 4337 73
Date established: 1951 **No.of Employees:** 21 - 50 **Product Groups:** 32, 66

Date of Accounts	Sep 08	Oct 09	Oct 10
Working Capital	510	416	556
Fixed Assets	699	646	613
Current Assets	987	848	1m

I T V Granada

Quay Street, Manchester, M60 9EA
Tel: 0161-952 1000 **Fax:** 0161-827 2029
E-mail: mike.blair@itv.com
Website: http://www.itv.com
Directors: M. Blair (Reg MD)
Immediate Holding Company: RED PRODUCTION COMPANY LIMITED
Registration no: 00840590 **Date established:** 1997
No.of Employees: 1 - 10 **Product Groups:** 89

Icopal Ltd (t/a Vulcanite Ltd)

Barton Dock Road Stretford, Manchester, M32 0YL
Tel: 08432-247400 **Fax:** 0161-864 1178
E-mail: ukmla@icopal.com
Website: http://www.monarflexgeomembranes.co.uk
Managers: D. Kane (Purch Mgr), M. Lawrence, P. Stel (Comptroller), P. Walsh (Tech Serv Mgr)
Ultimate Holding Company: INVESTCORP BANK EC (BAHRAIN)
Immediate Holding Company: ICOPAL LIMITED
Registration no: 02472635 **VAT No.:** GB 207 8505 66
Date established: 1990 **Turnover:** £20m - £50m
No.of Employees: 101 - 250 **Product Groups:** 31, 32

Date of Accounts	Dec 11	Dec 10	Dec 09
Sales Turnover	35m	35m	36m
Pre Tax Profit/Loss	-4m	-4m	-5m
Working Capital	5m	4m	4m
Fixed Assets	14m	12m	12m
Current Assets	15m	14m	11m
Current Liabilities	2m	2m	3m

Inal Metals North Ltd

Smithfold Lane Worsley, Manchester, M28 0GP
Tel: 0161-790 0118 **Fax:** 0161-790 5887
E-mail: lynn@inal.com
Website: http://www.inal.com
Directors: L. Nicklin (Dir), E. Collier (Fin)
Ultimate Holding Company: INAL METALS LIMITED
Immediate Holding Company: INAL METALS NORTH LIMITED
Registration no: 02043010 **Date established:** 1986
No.of Employees: 11 - 20 **Product Groups:** 66

Date of Accounts	Nov 11	Nov 10	Nov 09
Working Capital	-407	-466	-656
Fixed Assets	1m	1m	1m
Current Assets	752	489	557

Industrial Door Repair

Unit 13 Denton Enterprise Centre Pitt Street, Denton, Manchester, M34 6PT
Tel: 0161-336 2228 **Fax:** 0161-336 8742
Directors: B. Cox (Ptnr)
Immediate Holding Company: INDUSTRIAL DOOR REPAIRS LIMITED
Registration no: 06530195 **Date established:** 2008 **Turnover:** £5m - £10m
No.of Employees: 1 - 10 **Product Groups:** 35, 48, 52

Date of Accounts	Mar 11	Mar 10	Mar 09
Working Capital	-18	-24	-30
Fixed Assets	21	28	32
Current Assets	5	10	13

Industrial Labelling Systems

Unit D 4 Brookside Industrial Estate Greengate, Middleton, Manchester, M24 1GS
Tel: 0161-655 4846 **Fax:** 08701-608413
E-mail: sales@ilsystems.co.uk
Website: http://www.ilsystems.co.uk
Directors: N. Greene (Co Sec)
Immediate Holding Company: INDUSTRIAL LABELLING SYSTEMS LTD
Registration no: 04379042 **Date established:** 2002 **Turnover:** £1m - £2m
No.of Employees: 1 - 10 **Product Groups:** 42

Date of Accounts	Dec 11	Dec 10	Dec 09
Working Capital	7	-5	-11
Fixed Assets	9	11	14
Current Assets	234	268	301

Industrial Latex Compounds Ltd

Chadderton Industrial Estate Greenside Way, Middleton, Manchester, M24 1SW
Tel: 0161-688 7221 **Fax:** 0161-684 9147
E-mail: enquiries@indlatex.co.uk
Website: http://www.industrialatex.com
Bank(s): National Westminster
Directors: G. Treaner (Sales & Mktg), J. Davison (MD)
Immediate Holding Company: Jacques Products Ltd
Registration no: 02821941 **VAT No.:** 606 5843 35 **Date established:** 1993
Turnover: £10m - £20m **No.of Employees:** 11 - 20 **Product Groups:** 29, 32

Date of Accounts	Dec 07
Sales Turnover	13390
Pre Tax Profit/Loss	310
Working Capital	-200
Fixed Assets	1450
Current Assets	4000
Current Liabilities	4200
Total Share Capital	100
ROCE% (Return on Capital Employed)	24.8

Industrial Maintenance Products Ltd

Hulme Road Radcliffe, Manchester, M26 1EY
Tel: 01204-793422 **Fax:** 01204-793336
E-mail: sales@impuk.net
Website: http://www.impuk.net
Bank(s): Barclays
Directors: A. Foot (Dir), B. Stout (MD), J. Walker (Dir), H. Stout (Co Sec)
Immediate Holding Company: INDUSTRIAL MAINTENANCE PRODUCTS LIMITED
Registration no: 01332080 **VAT No.:** GB 305 1248 02
Date established: 1977 **Turnover:** £2m - £5m **No.of Employees:** 21 - 50
Product Groups: 31, 35, 66

Date of Accounts	Sep 07	Sep 06	Sep 05
Working Capital	361	286	64
Fixed Assets	705	347	337
Current Assets	2207	1862	1338
Current Liabilities	1846	1577	1273
Total Share Capital	13	13	13

Industrial Trucks

10 Dewey Street, Manchester, M11 2NT
Tel: 08453-651535 **Fax:** 0161-230 7042
E-mail: info@its-forklifts.co.uk
Website: http://www.its-forklifts.co.uk
Directors: S. Conaghan (Dir)
Immediate Holding Company: INDUSTRIAL TRUCK SERVICES LIMITED
Registration no: 04070726 **Date established:** 2000
No.of Employees: 1 - 10 **Product Groups:** 35, 39, 45

Date of Accounts	Mar 11	Mar 10	Mar 09
Working Capital	256	219	180
Fixed Assets	244	263	281
Current Assets	467	422	309

Industria Engineering Products Ltd

Unit A3 Lyntown Trading Estate Eccles, Manchester, M30 9QG
Tel: 0161-788 9922 **Fax:** 0161-787 7634
E-mail: export@industria.co.uk
Website: http://www.industria.co.uk
Directors: C. Williams (Fin), V. Leach (MD), A. Wilkinson (Fab)
Managers: S. Pilkington (District Mgr), S. Pilkington (Depot Mgr)
Ultimate Holding Company: RITRAMA SPA (ITALY)
Immediate Holding Company: INDUSTRIA ENGINEERING PRODUCTS LIMITED
Registration no: 00513697 **Date established:** 1952
Turnover: £20m - £50m **No.of Employees:** 1 - 10 **Product Groups:** 35

Date of Accounts	Mar 05	Mar 04	Mar 03
Pre Tax Profit/Loss	-258	-69	-316
Working Capital	295	544	593
Fixed Assets	138	147	167
Current Assets	4m	4m	4m
Current Liabilities	192	149	150

Inflite Engineering Services Ltd

Unit B Broadlink Middleton, Manchester, M24 1UB
Tel: 0161-643 6668 **Fax:** 0161-655 3375
E-mail: enquiries@ultratools.co.uk
Website: http://www.ultratools.co.uk
Bank(s): Midland
Directors: K. Gibson (Sales)
Ultimate Holding Company: SWAN INVESTMENTS GROUP LIMITED
Immediate Holding Company: INFLITE ENGINEERING SERVICES LIMITED
Registration no: 02171334 **VAT No.:** GB 150 4644 87
Date established: 1987 **Turnover:** £2m - £5m **No.of Employees:** 21 - 50
Product Groups: 48

Date of Accounts	Mar 11	Mar 10	Mar 09
Sales Turnover	37m	51m	56m
Pre Tax Profit/Loss	-758	1m	4m
Working Capital	10m	10m	12m
Fixed Assets	9m	9m	7m
Current Assets	18m	19m	22m
Current Liabilities	4m	5m	4m

Intadex Ltd

Alex J Cheetham Morton Street, Failsworth, Manchester, M35 0BP
Tel: 0161-681 1115 **Fax:** 0161-681 0339
E-mail: mark@alexjcheetham.co.uk
Website: http://www.intadex.co.uk
Bank(s): HSBC Bank plc
Directors: A. Cheetham (MD)
Registration no: 00403641 **VAT No.:** GB 704 1672 60
Turnover: £1m - £2m **No.of Employees:** 21 - 50 **Product Groups:** 27, 28, 30

Integer Computers

167-169 Heywood Road Prestwich, Manchester, M25 1LB
Tel: 0161-798 7307 **Fax:** 0161-773 3151
E-mail: office@integeruk.com
Website: http://www.integeruk.com

Directors: G. Whittle (Ptnr)
Turnover: £500,000 - £1m **No.of Employees:** 1 - 10 **Product Groups:** 44

Intego Packaging

Unit 1 Oakhill Trading Estate Devonshire Road, Worsley, Manchester, M28 3PT
Tel: 08707-543322 **Fax:** 08707-543366
E-mail: sales@integopackaging.co.uk
Website: http://www.integopackaging.co.uk
Directors: P. Barlow (Dir), P. Barlow (Prop)
Managers: S. Whitton (Sales Prom Mgr)
Turnover: £1m - £2m **No.of Employees:** 1 - 10 **Product Groups:** 66

Integral UK Ltd

Unit C5 Broadoak Business Park Ashburton Road West, Trafford Park, Manchester, M17 1RW
Tel: 0161-872 7925 **Fax:** 0161-872 9508
Website: http://www.integral.co.uk
Bank(s): National Westminster Bank Plc
Directors: A. Nichol (Reg)
Ultimate Holding Company: INTEGRAL UK HOLDINGS LIMITED
Immediate Holding Company: INTEGRAL UK LIMITED
Registration no: 05307588 **VAT No.:** GB 239 3550 53
Date established: 2004 **Turnover:** £10m - £20m
No.of Employees: 21 - 50 **Product Groups:** 52

Date of Accounts	Dec 11	Dec 10	Dec 09
Sales Turnover	196m	175m	182m
Pre Tax Profit/Loss	9m	16m	9m
Working Capital	19m	14m	17m
Fixed Assets	773	701	N/A
Current Assets	73m	62m	51m
Current Liabilities	30m	26m	20m

Interactive Special Projects Ltd

Unit 10 The Schoolhouse Second Avenue Trafford Park, Trafford Park, Manchester, M17 1DZ
Tel: 0161-873 8482
E-mail: general@interactivespecialprojects.co.uk
Website: http://www.interactivespecialprojects.co.uk
Directors: B. Maddick (MD)
Immediate Holding Company: INTERACTIVE VENTILATION LIMITED
Registration no: 03352160 **Date established:** 1997
No.of Employees: 11 - 20 **Product Groups:** 40, 66

Date of Accounts	Jun 11	Jun 10	Jun 09
Working Capital	-50	-29	-7
Fixed Assets	10	12	16
Current Assets	94	68	48

Investment Tooling International Ltd

4a Moston Road Middleton, Manchester, M24 1SL
Tel: 0161-653 8066 **Fax:** 0161-655 3095
E-mail: ray@iti-manchester.co.uk
Website: http://www.iti-manchester.co.uk
Bank(s): HSBC Bank plc
Directors: A. Bunyan (Co Sec), R. Golson (MD)
Ultimate Holding Company: INTEGRATED MANUFACTURING GROUP LIMITED
Immediate Holding Company: INVESTMENT TOOLING INTERNATIONAL LIMITED
Registration no: 06772202 **VAT No.:** GB 340 1992 70
Date established: 2008 **Turnover:** £1m - £2m **No.of Employees:** 21 - 50
Product Groups: 48

Date of Accounts	Jun 11	Jun 10	Jun 09
Working Capital	915	771	N/A
Fixed Assets	31	1	N/A
Current Assets	2m	1m	N/A

Isola Manufacturing Co Wythenshawe Ltd

Harper Road Northenden, Sharston Industrial Area, Manchester, M22 4SH
Tel: 0161-998 2294 **Fax:** 0161-946 0390
E-mail: isola.sales@nu-pax.com
Website: http://www.nu-pax.com
Directors: D. Tonge (MD), P. Tonge (Co Sec)
Immediate Holding Company: ISOLA MANUFACTURING CO.(WYTHENSHAWE)LIMITED
Registration no: 00331245 **VAT No.:** GB 145 1765 67
Date established: 1937 **Turnover:** £1m - £2m **No.of Employees:** 1 - 10
Product Groups: 23, 24, 27, 31

Date of Accounts	Dec 11	Dec 10	Dec 09
Working Capital	25	155	235
Fixed Assets	713	728	699
Current Assets	48	184	247

Iss Group Services

Pellowe House Francis Road, Manchester, M20 4XP
Tel: 0161-445 5442 **Fax:** 0161-445 4914
E-mail: info@iss-group.co.uk
Website: http://www.iss-group.co.uk
Bank(s): National Westminster
Managers: J. Turner
Ultimate Holding Company: INDUSTRIAL & SCIENTIFIC HOLDINGS LIMITED
Immediate Holding Company: ISS GROUP SERVICES LIMITED
Registration no: 01372232 **VAT No.:** GB 603 3366 57
Date established: 1978 **Turnover:** £1m - £2m **No.of Employees:** 11 - 20
Product Groups: 37, 38, 83, 85

Date of Accounts	Apr 11	Apr 10	Apr 09
Working Capital	-184	-219	-297
Fixed Assets	234	247	291
Current Assets	578	639	803

J B Fabrications Ltd

Newhaven Business Park Barton Lane, Eccles, Manchester, M30 0HH
Tel: 0161-707 9400 **Fax:** 0161-707 9401
E-mail: enquiries@jbfabrications.co.uk
Website: http://jbfabrications.co.uk
Directors: S. Boon (Fin)
Immediate Holding Company: JB FABRICATIONS LIMITED
Registration no: 02642126 **Date established:** 1991
No.of Employees: 1 - 10 **Product Groups:** 35, 39, 45

Date of Accounts	Nov 11	Nov 10	Nov 09
Working Capital	102	85	80
Fixed Assets	44	50	57
Current Assets	193	202	196

J C S Pallets Repairs Services Sales

Lord North Street, Manchester, M40 8AD
Tel: 0161-203 5450 **Fax:** 0161-205 5302
E-mail: jcspallets@btinternet.com
Website: http://www.palletsuppliers.co.uk
Directors: S. Cornforth (Prop)
Turnover: Up to £250,000 **No.of Employees:** 1 - 10 **Product Groups:** 45, 48, 67, 76

J D Williams Mail Order Group

Griffin House 40 Lever Street, Manchester, M60 6ES
Tel: 0161-238 2000 **Fax:** 0161-238 2030
E-mail: info@jdwilliams.co.uk
Website: http://www.nbrown.co.uk
Bank(s): HSBC Bank plc
Directors: D. Moore (Fin), D. Alliance (Ch)
Managers: S. Stansfield, W. Ryan, S. Smith (Personnel), J. Hinchcliffe, P. Short
Ultimate Holding Company: N BROWN GROUP PLC
Immediate Holding Company: N BROWN GROUP PLC
Registration no: 00814103 **Date established:** 1964
Turnover: £500m - £1,000m **No.of Employees:** 1501 & over
Product Groups: 61

Date of Accounts	Feb 09	Feb 10	Feb 11
Sales Turnover	663m	690m	719m
Pre Tax Profit/Loss	92m	86m	95m
Working Capital	470m	456m	433m
Fixed Assets	113m	109m	128m
Current Assets	590m	586m	618m
Current Liabilities	66m	81m	86m

J & H Lift Co.

Heaton Mills Heaton Street, Denton, Manchester, M34 3RG
Tel: 0161-336 1042 **Fax:** 0161-320 7909
E-mail: sales@psliftservices.co.uk
Website: http://www.psliftservices.co.uk
Directors: D. Johnston (Prop)
Immediate Holding Company: J & H LIFT CO. LIMITED
Registration no: 05634701 **Date established:** 2005
No.of Employees: 1 - 10 **Product Groups:** 35, 39, 45

Date of Accounts	Nov 11	Nov 10	Nov 09
Working Capital	14	9	18
Fixed Assets	3	2	3
Current Assets	41	28	33

J & J Tooling Services Ltd

Bridge House Railway Street, Radcliffe, Manchester, M26 3AA
Tel: 0161-724 7799 **Fax:** 0161-724 0722
E-mail: sales@jjtooling.co.uk
Website: http://www.jjtooling.co.uk
Directors: E. Hartley (Fin), D. Brennan (MD)
Ultimate Holding Company: J. & J. TOOLING HOLDINGS CO. LTD.
Immediate Holding Company: J. & J. TOOLING SERVICES (BURY) LIMITED
Registration no: 01193528 **VAT No.:** GB 149 9859 91
Date established: 1974 **Turnover:** £1m - £2m **No.of Employees:** 1 - 10
Product Groups: 36, 37, 40, 46

Date of Accounts	Dec 11	Dec 10	Dec 09
Working Capital	518	461	475
Fixed Assets	53	29	36
Current Assets	943	759	748

J 1 Technologies Ltd

Unit 6 Off Marshall Stevens Way, Trafford Park, Manchester, M17 1PP
Tel: 0161-875 2110 **Fax:** 0161-776 4111
E-mail: sales@j1technologies.com
Website: http://www.j1technologies.com
Bank(s): Barclays
Directors: K. Burgess (MD), P. Minister (Mkt Research)
Immediate Holding Company: J1 TECHNOLOGIES LIMITED
Registration no: 03796737 **VAT No.:** GB 726 9900 07
Date established: 1999 **Turnover:** £1m - £2m **No.of Employees:** 11 - 20
Product Groups: 31, 32, 41, 66

Date of Accounts	Jun 11	Jun 10	Jun 09
Working Capital	225	183	177
Fixed Assets	300	339	37
Current Assets	2m	2m	1m

J W Lees & Co Brewers Ltd

Greengate Brewery Middleton Junction, Middleton, Manchester, M24 2AX
Tel: 0161-643 2487 **Fax:** 0161-655 3731
E-mail: mail@jwlees.co.uk
Website: http://www.jwlees.co.uk
Bank(s): The Royal Bank of Scotland
Directors: W. Lees Jones (MD)
Ultimate Holding Company: J.W.LEES & CO.(BREWERS)LIMITED
Immediate Holding Company: J.W.LEES & CO.(BREWERS)LIMITED
Registration no: 00557225 **VAT No.:** GB 145 2393 73
Date established: 1955 **Turnover:** £50m - £75m
No.of Employees: 501 - 1000 **Product Groups:** 21

Date of Accounts	Mar 11	Mar 10	Mar 09
Sales Turnover	53m	51m	50m
Pre Tax Profit/Loss	4m	3m	3m
Working Capital	3m	3m	2m
Fixed Assets	71m	69m	58m
Current Assets	18m	16m	13m
Current Liabilities	11m	9m	8m

Jacques Products

Greengate Industrial Estate Greenside Way, Middleton, Manchester, M24 1SW
Tel: 0161-688 7744 **Fax:** 0161-688 6060
E-mail: sbell@indlatex.co.uk
Bank(s): Barclays
Directors: S. Bell (MD)
Immediate Holding Company: JACQUES PRODUCTS LIMITED
Registration no: 03256362 **VAT No.:** GB 673 5705 16
Date established: 1996 **Turnover:** £10m - £20m
No.of Employees: 11 - 20 **Product Groups:** 48

Date of Accounts	Dec 11	Dec 10	Dec 09
Sales Turnover	17m	15m	13m
Pre Tax Profit/Loss	-110	18	393
Working Capital	119	186	109
Fixed Assets	964	1m	1m
Current Assets	4m	4m	3m
Current Liabilities	424	2m	2m

Jamak Fabrication Europe Ltd

Unit 53 Oakhill Trading Estate Devonshire Road, Worsley, Manchester, M28 3PT
Tel: 01204-794554 **Fax:** 01204-574521
E-mail: sales@jamak.co.uk
Website: http://www.jamak.com
Managers: J. Blundell (Sales Prom Mgr)
Ultimate Holding Company: J M K INTERNATIONAL INC (USA)
Immediate Holding Company: JAMAK FABRICATION EUROPE LIMITED
Registration no: 01336691 **Date established:** 1977 **Turnover:** £5m - £10m
No.of Employees: 1 - 10 **Product Groups:** 29, 39

Date of Accounts	Dec 11	Dec 10	Dec 09
Working Capital	303	115	316
Fixed Assets	361	376	420
Current Assets	970	831	785

Jewellery World Ltd

5 Chatley Street, Manchester, M3 1HU
Tel: 0161-834 5007 **Fax:** 0161-835 3238
E-mail: jewelleryworld@btinternet.com
Website: http://www.jewellery-world.co.uk
Directors: I. Geller (MD)
Immediate Holding Company: JEWELLERY WORLD LIMITED
Registration no: 02703752 **Date established:** 1992
Turnover: Up to £250,000 **No.of Employees:** 11 - 20 **Product Groups:** 49, 65

Date of Accounts	Feb 08	Feb 11	Feb 10
Working Capital	1m	633	995
Fixed Assets	749	599	646
Current Assets	1m	1m	1m

Jewson Ltd

Beckford Street, Manchester, M40 5AJ
Tel: 0161-205 8812 **Fax:** 0161-203 4934
Website: http://www.jewson.co.uk
Directors: P. Hindle (Ch)
Ultimate Holding Company: COMPAGNIE DE SAINT GOBAIN (FRANCE)
Immediate Holding Company: JEWSON LIMITED
Registration no: 00348407 **VAT No.:** GB 497 7184 83
Date established: 1939 **Turnover:** £500m - £1,000m
No.of Employees: 11 - 20 **Product Groups:** 66

Date of Accounts	Dec 11	Dec 10	Dec 09
Sales Turnover	1606m	1547m	1485m
Pre Tax Profit/Loss	18m	100m	45m
Working Capital	-345m	-250m	-349m
Fixed Assets	496m	387m	461m
Current Assets	657m	1005m	1320m
Current Liabilities	66m	120m	64m

JLG Industries, Inc.

Units 4 & 5 Bentley Avenue, Middleton, Manchester, M24 2GP
Tel: 0870-2007700 **Fax:** 0870-2007711
E-mail: jlguk@jlg.com
Website: http://www.jlg.com
Directors: W. Lawson (Ch), G. Campbell (MD)
Managers: D. Sumerling (Mktg Serv Mgr), L. Van Ooijien (I.T. Exec), J. Powell, C. Pearson
Ultimate Holding Company: J.L.G. Industries Inc (USA)
Immediate Holding Company: J.L.G. Industries (Europe)
Registration no: SF000430 **VAT No.:** 245 0750 77
Turnover: £75m - £125m **No.of Employees:** 21 - 50 **Product Groups:** 35, 39, 45, 48

John Staniar & Co. Ltd

34 Stanley Road Whitefield, Manchester, M45 8QX
Tel: 0161-767 1500 **Fax:** 0161-767 1502
E-mail: info@johnstaniar.co.uk
Website: http://www.johnstaniar.co.uk
Directors: M. Bolton (MD)
Immediate Holding Company: JOHN STANIAR & CO. LTD.
Registration no: 02422356 **VAT No.:** GB 146 9155 48
Date established: 1989 **Turnover:** £2m - £5m **No.of Employees:** 11 - 20
Product Groups: 23, 35, 40, 41, 42, 66

Date of Accounts	Jun 11	Jun 10	Jun 09
Working Capital	721	10	N/A
Fixed Assets	376	N/A	N/A
Current Assets	1m	10	N/A

Neville Johnson Ltd

Unit 4 Broadoak Business Park Ashburton Road West, Trafford Park, Manchester, M17 1RW
Tel: 0161-873 8333 **Fax:** 0161-873 8335
E-mail: sales@nevillejohnson.co.uk
Website: http://www.nevillejohnson.co.uk
Bank(s): National Westminster Bank Plc
Directors: W. Bennett (Fin), N. Pailing (Sales), K. Bennett (Fin)
Managers: A. Hawkes (Purch Mgr), L. Lalor (Mktg Serv Mgr)
Ultimate Holding Company: NEVILLE JOHNSON HOLDINGS LIMITED
Immediate Holding Company: NEVILLE JOHNSON LIMITED
Registration no: 01701103 **VAT No.:** GB 403 6602 86
Date established: 1983 **Turnover:** £10m - £20m
No.of Employees: 251 - 500 **Product Groups:** 26

Date of Accounts	Apr 11	Apr 10	Apr 09
Sales Turnover	18m	16m	17m
Pre Tax Profit/Loss	2m	2m	2m
Working Capital	6m	5m	3m
Fixed Assets	1m	888	1m
Current Assets	11m	9m	7m
Current Liabilities	3m	3m	3m

Jones Lang Lasalle

50 Brown Street, Manchester, M2 2JT
Tel: 0161-828 6440 **Fax:** 0161-828 6490
E-mail: jonathan.mills@eu.jll.com
Website: http://www.joneslanglasalle.com
Directors: M. Jagger (Dir), S. Williams (MD)
Managers: A. Guy (Sales Admin), J. Mills (), J. Mills
Immediate Holding Company: JONES LANG LASALLE LTD
Registration no: 02176622 **Date established:** 1910 **Turnover:** £1m - £2m
No.of Employees: 21 - 50 **Product Groups:** 80, 82

S E Jones & Son

95 Swinton Hall Road Swinton, Manchester, M27 4AU
Tel: 0161-794 3172 **Fax:** 0161-794 3562
Directors: S. Jones (Ptnr)
Immediate Holding Company: WHATS YOUR NUMBER LTD
VAT No.: GB 148 3253 66 **Date established:** 2011
Turnover: Up to £250,000 **No.of Employees:** 1 - 10 **Product Groups:** 64

Juice Coperation Ltd

16 Bury New Road, Manchester, M8 8FR
Tel: 0161-832 4951 **Fax:** 0161-835 1446
E-mail: mail@juicecorp.co.uk
Website: http://www.juicecorporation.co.uk

see next page

Juice Coperation Ltd - Cont'd
Directors: K. Ahmed (MD)
Managers: J. Rose (Purch Mgr), P. Ragigan (Fin Mgr), B. Ahmed (Sales & Mktg Mg)
Immediate Holding Company: THE LEGENDARY JOE BLOGGS PLC
Registration no: 03413909 **VAT No.:** GB 305 1843 85
Date established: 1997 **Turnover:** £10m - £20m
No.of Employees: 21 - 50 **Product Groups:** 63

K B Import & Export Ltd
43-45 North Street, Manchester, M8 8RE
Tel: 0161-834 8485 **Fax:** 0161-832 8057
E-mail: sales@kbie.co.uk
Website: http://www.plustron.com
Directors: R. Khemlani (Dir), S. Khemlani (Co Sec)
Ultimate Holding Company: KB GROUP HOLDINGS LTD.
Immediate Holding Company: K B (IMPORT & EXPORT) LIMITED
Registration no: 01490164 **VAT No.:** GB 306 6409 70
Date established: 1980 **Turnover:** £10m - £20m **No.of Employees:** 1 - 10
Product Groups: 24, 26, 27, 29, 32, 34, 35, 36, 61, 63, 65

Date of Accounts	Mar 08	Mar 07	Mar 06
Sales Turnover	N/A	16m	16m
Pre Tax Profit/Loss	-199	323	212
Working Capital	-1m	-8	3
Fixed Assets	2m	1m	2m
Current Assets	9m	8m	8m
Current Liabilities	1m	2m	1m

K M O Medical & Dental Laboratory
Unit 35 Phoenix Industrial Estate Failsworth, Manchester, M35 9DS
Tel: 0161-688 9000 **Fax:** 0161-688 9000
E-mail: sales@kmodental-lab.co.uk
Website: http://www.kmodental-lab.co.uk
Directors: G. Whitehead (Prop)
No.of Employees: 1 - 10 **Product Groups:** 38, 63, 88

Karpelle Ltd
Varley Business Centre Varley Street, Manchester, M40 8EE
Tel: 0161-203 2400 **Fax:** 0161-205 1583
E-mail: hklepper@karpelleltd.co.uk
Website: http://www.karpelle.co.uk
Directors: D. Hughes (Fin), H. Klepper (MD)
Immediate Holding Company: KARPELLE LIMITED
Registration no: 01983060 **VAT No.:** GB 431 2225 04
Date established: 1986 **Turnover:** Up to £250,000
No.of Employees: 21 - 50 **Product Groups:** 24, 63

Date of Accounts	Jan 09	Feb 12	Feb 11
Pre Tax Profit/Loss	-84	N/A	N/A
Working Capital	293	683	581
Fixed Assets	75	37	28
Current Assets	2m	3m	3m
Current Liabilities	859	N/A	N/A

Kaumagraph Transfers UK Ltd
Unit 7 Leestone Road Sharston Industrial Area, Manchester, M22 4RN
Tel: 0161-428 0626 **Fax:** 0161-428 0033
E-mail: info@kaumagraphtransfers.co.uk
Website: http://www.kaumagraphtransfers.co.uk
Directors: T. Millington (Fin)
Managers: J. Ryan (Mgr)
Immediate Holding Company: KAUMAGRAPH TRANSFERS UK LIMITED
Registration no: 03857105 **Date established:** 1999
Turnover: Up to £250,000 **No.of Employees:** 1 - 10 **Product Groups:** 23, 27

Date of Accounts	Dec 11	Dec 10	Dec 09
Working Capital	52	34	45
Fixed Assets	26	39	52
Current Assets	123	127	103

W.J. Kenyon Group
3000 Manchester Business Park Aviator Way, Manchester Airport, Manchester, M22 5TG
Tel: 0870-7607751 **Fax:** 0161-266 1001
E-mail: sales@autopsyequipment.co.uk
Website: http://www.autopsyequipment.co.uk
Directors: J. Hanson (Sales), P. Rossi (Ch)
Managers: A. Mclaren (Purch Mgr), J. Davenport (Export Sales Mg)
Turnover: £1m - £2m **No.of Employees:** 21 - 50 **Product Groups:** 38, 67

Kerry Logistics Ltd (Kerry Logistics Network)
Broadoak Trading Estate Ashburton Road West Trafford Park, Manchester, M17 1RW
Tel: 0161-873 8777 **Fax:** 0161-872 9016
E-mail: gary.wilcock@kerrylogistics.com
Website: http://www.kerrylogistics.com
Directors: G. Wilcock (MD)
Ultimate Holding Company: KERRY GROUP LTD (COOK ISLANDS)
Immediate Holding Company: KERRY LOGISTICS (UK) LIMITED
Registration no: 01571804 **Date established:** 1981
Turnover: £50m - £75m **No.of Employees:** 51 - 100 **Product Groups:** 77

Date of Accounts	Dec 11	Dec 10	Dec 09
Sales Turnover	71m	88m	56m
Pre Tax Profit/Loss	3m	4m	3m
Working Capital	7m	7m	4m
Fixed Assets	11m	8m	8m
Current Assets	24m	24m	20m
Current Liabilities	8m	6m	5m

Kin Ltd
140 Higher Road Urmston, Manchester, M41 9AZ
Tel: 0161-747 7077 **Fax:** 0161-747 1147
E-mail: sales@kinltd.com
Website: http://www.kinltd.co.uk
Directors: S. Scott (Dir)
Immediate Holding Company: KIN LIMITED
Registration no: 03016726 **Date established:** 1995
No.of Employees: 1 - 10 **Product Groups:** 35, 39, 45

Date of Accounts	Feb 08	Feb 11	Feb 10
Working Capital	231	272	290
Fixed Assets	127	183	138
Current Assets	466	574	460

Kinetic plc
3rd Floor Duckworth House The Lancastrian Office Centre Talbot Road, Stretford, Manchester, M32 0FP
Tel: 0161-874 1645 **Fax:** 0161-228 1949
E-mail: info@kinetic-plc.co.uk
Website: http://www.kinetic-plc.co.uk
Managers: S. Taggart (Mgr)
Ultimate Holding Company: KINETIC RECRUITMENT SERVICES LIMITED
Immediate Holding Company: THE KINETIC EMPLOYEE BENEFIT TRUST LIMITED
Registration no: 03248307 **Date established:** 1996
Turnover: £20m - £50m **No.of Employees:** 1 - 10 **Product Groups:** 80

Date of Accounts	Mar 12
Working Capital	63
Fixed Assets	15
Current Assets	409

Kipfold Ltd
Cheetwood House Cheetwood Road, Manchester, M8 8AQ
Tel: 0161-792 4040 **Fax:** 0161-792 2280
E-mail: sales@kipfoldgroup.com
Website: http://www.kipfoldgroup.com
Directors: B. Mehta (Fin), S. Sebastian (Fin)
Managers: M. Mehta (Personnel)
Ultimate Holding Company: KIPFOLD (HOLDINGS) LTD.
Immediate Holding Company: KIPFOLD LIMITED
Registration no: 01085712 **VAT No.:** GB 147 3666 47
Date established: 1972 **Turnover:** £5m - £10m **No.of Employees:** 11 - 20
Product Groups: 23, 61

Date of Accounts	Mar 11	Mar 10	Mar 09
Sales Turnover	6m	6m	13m
Pre Tax Profit/Loss	-433	-429	-56
Working Capital	2m	3m	3m
Fixed Assets	69	80	93
Current Assets	3m	4m	5m
Current Liabilities	519	1m	2m

Knowsley S K Ltd
Centrepoint Marshall Stevens Way, Trafford Park, Manchester, M17 1AE
Tel: 0161-872 7511 **Fax:** 0161-848 8508
E-mail: sales@knowsleysk.co.uk
Website: http://www.knowsleysk.co.uk
Bank(s): National Westminster Bank Plc
Managers: T. Green (Cust Serv Mgr), T. Morrisey (Mktg Serv Mgr), S. Jackson (Tech Serv Mgr), M. Paul (Purch Mgr), S. Lake
Ultimate Holding Company: IMTECH NV (NETHERLANDS)
Immediate Holding Company: KNOWSLEY S.K. LIMITED
Registration no: 01789152 **VAT No.:** GB 383 4751 31
Date established: 1984 **Turnover:** £5m - £10m **No.of Employees:** 21 - 50
Product Groups: 39, 40

Date of Accounts	Dec 11	Dec 10	Dec 09
Sales Turnover	8m	9m	8m
Pre Tax Profit/Loss	899	866	659
Working Capital	5m	4m	2m
Fixed Assets	181	213	190
Current Assets	8m	8m	4m
Current Liabilities	2m	2m	871

Kobo UK Ltd
Ketten House Leestone Road Sharston Industrial Area, Manchester, M22 4RB
Tel: 0161-491 9840 **Fax:** 0161-428 1999
E-mail: info@kobo.co.uk
Website: http://www.kobo.co.uk
Bank(s): HSBC, Manchester
Directors: C. McDonald (Dir), S. Mort (MD)
Immediate Holding Company: KOBO (UK) LIMITED
Registration no: 00942977 **VAT No.:** GB 157 4491 44
Date established: 1968 **Turnover:** £2m - £5m **No.of Employees:** 21 - 50
Product Groups: 29, 30, 35, 39, 40, 41, 42, 43, 44, 45, 46

Date of Accounts	Dec 11	Dec 10	Dec 09
Working Capital	2m	2m	2m
Fixed Assets	42	40	37
Current Assets	3m	2m	3m
Current Liabilities	N/A	N/A	100

KPMG UK Ltd
St James's Square, Manchester, M2 6DS
Tel: 0161-838 4000 **Fax:** 0161-838 4040
E-mail: malcolm.edge@kpmg.co.uk
Website: http://www.kpmg.co.uk
Directors: J. Hurst (Snr Part)
Ultimate Holding Company: KPMG EUROPE LLP
Immediate Holding Company: KPMG UK LIMITED
Registration no: 03580549 **Date established:** 1998 **Turnover:** £2m - £5m
No.of Employees: 251 - 500 **Product Groups:** 80

Date of Accounts	Sep 11	Sep 10	Sep 09
Sales Turnover	698m	632m	624m
Pre Tax Profit/Loss	655	593	584
Working Capital	1m	847	419
Current Assets	23m	21m	25m
Current Liabilities	22m	20m	20m

Kratos Analytical Ltd
Trafford Wharf Road Trafford Park, Manchester, M17 1GP
Tel: 0161-888 4400 **Fax:** 0161-888 4401
E-mail: info@kratos.co.uk
Website: http://www.kratos.co.uk
Directors: J. Birtwistle (Co Sec), B. Adamson (Fin), J. Jones (Fin)
Managers: D. Dingley (Sales Prom Mgr), K. McCafferey (Purch Mgr), P. Dowlington (Tech Serv Mgr)
Ultimate Holding Company: SHIMADZU CORP (JAPAN)
Immediate Holding Company: KRATOS ANALYTICAL LIMITED
Registration no: 00563161 **VAT No.:** GB 403 4909 70
Date established: 1956 **Turnover:** £20m - £50m
No.of Employees: 101 - 250 **Product Groups:** 38, 40, 48, 61

Date of Accounts	Dec 11	Dec 10	Dec 09
Sales Turnover	42m	29m	21m
Pre Tax Profit/Loss	3m	1m	1m
Working Capital	9m	6m	8m
Fixed Assets	6m	5m	5m
Current Assets	20m	13m	11m
Current Liabilities	4m	5m	2m

Kuehne & Nagel UK Ltd (Branch)
Building 317 World Freight Terminal, Manchester Airport, Manchester, M90 5NA
Tel: 0161-436 9400 **Fax:** 0161-436 9429
E-mail: neil.robinson@kuehne-nagel.com
Website: http://www.kuehne-nagel.com
Bank(s): Lloyds TSB Bank plc
Managers: N. Robinson (District Mgr)
Ultimate Holding Company: KUEHNE & NAGEL INTERNATIONAL AG (SWITZERLAND)
Immediate Holding Company: KUEHNE + NAGEL (UK) LIMITED
Registration no: 01463105 **VAT No.:** GB 584 6403 22
Date established: 1979 **Turnover:** £10m - £20m
No.of Employees: 51 - 100 **Product Groups:** 75, 76

Date of Accounts	Dec 11	Dec 10	Dec 09
Sales Turnover	958m	948m	833m
Pre Tax Profit/Loss	22m	27m	15m
Working Capital	20m	18m	16m
Fixed Assets	17m	12m	18m
Current Assets	175m	177m	148m
Current Liabilities	68m	73m	74m

Lakeland Laboratories Ltd (Head Office)
Peel Lane Astley, Tyldesley, Manchester, M29 7FE
Tel: 01942-873555 **Fax:** 01942-884409
E-mail: mailbox@lakeland-labs.co.uk
Website: http://www.lakeland-labs.co.uk
Bank(s): Barclays, Leeds
Directors: P. Clark (MD), C. Mallard (Co Sec), P. McCormack (Sales)
Ultimate Holding Company: LAKELAND CHEMICALS LIMITED
Immediate Holding Company: LAKELAND LABORATORIES LIMITED
Registration no: 02875769 **VAT No.:** GB 151 7256 75
Date established: 1993 **Turnover:** £2m - £5m **No.of Employees:** 21 - 50
Product Groups: 31, 32, 66

Date of Accounts	Dec 11	Dec 10	Dec 09
Working Capital	999	1m	1m
Fixed Assets	182	213	251
Current Assets	2m	2m	2m

Lambert Smith Hampton
3 Hardman Street, Manchester, M3 3HF
Tel: 0161-228 6411 **Fax:** 0161-228 7354
E-mail: rtunnicliffe@lsh.co.uk
Website: http://www.lsh.co.uk
Bank(s): Bank of Scotland
Directors: R. Tunnicliffe (Dir)
Immediate Holding Company: LAMBERT SMITH HAMPTON
Registration no: NF002871 **VAT No.:** GB 524 3182 69
Date established: 1990 **Turnover:** £10m - £20m
No.of Employees: 51 - 100 **Product Groups:** 52, 80, 82, 84

Laptop Screen Online
Flat 1 Cutberth Court 7 Malvern Grove, Manchester, M20 1HT
Tel: 0161-4347449 **Fax:** 0161-8840048
E-mail: sales@laptopscreenonline.co.uk
Website: http://www.laptopscreenonline.com
Managers: D. Tjituaiza (Sales Admin)
Date established: 2008 **Turnover:** **No.of Employees:** 1 - 10
Product Groups: 37

Lee Floorstok Ltd
Unit B1 The Dresser Centre Whitworth Street, Openshaw, Manchester, M11 2NE
Tel: 0161-231 8080 **Fax:** 0161-231 8787
E-mail: leefloor@aol.com
Website: http://www.leefloorstok.co.uk
Bank(s): Barclays
Directors: T. Baxendell (MD)
Managers: A. Mawdesley (Chief Mgr), L. Whitworth
Immediate Holding Company: LEE FLOORSTOK LIMITED
Registration no: 01012402 **VAT No.:** GB 146 6893 27
Date established: 1971 **Turnover:** £1m - £2m **No.of Employees:** 21 - 50
Product Groups: 23, 30, 35, 36, 49, 63

Date of Accounts	Mar 12	Mar 11	Mar 10
Sales Turnover	9m	N/A	N/A
Pre Tax Profit/Loss	315	N/A	N/A
Working Capital	2m	2m	2m
Fixed Assets	1m	1m	191
Current Assets	3m	3m	2m
Current Liabilities	173	N/A	N/A

Lee-Healey
Unit 1 Bentley Avenue, Middleton, Manchester, M24 2GP
Tel: 0161-655 0303 **Fax:** 0161-655 0304
E-mail: info@lee-healey.com
Website: http://www.lee-healey.com
Directors: C. Hargreaves (Co Sec)
Turnover: £1m - £2m **No.of Employees:** 21 - 50 **Product Groups:** 29, 30, 66

Lees Newsome Ltd
Rule Business Park Grimshaw Lane, Middleton, Manchester, M24 2AE
Tel: 08450-708005 **Fax:** 0845-070 8006
E-mail: philip@leesnewsome.co.uk
Website: http://www.leesnewsome.co.uk
Bank(s): National Westminster Bank Plc
Directors: K. Warburton (Fin)
Managers: N. Sultana, P. Lees (Mgr)
Immediate Holding Company: LEES-NEWSOME LIMITED
Registration no: 00074666 **VAT No.:** GB 145 1235 96
Date established: 2002 **Turnover:** £2m - £5m **No.of Employees:** 21 - 50
Product Groups: 23, 24

Date of Accounts	Oct 09	Oct 08	Oct 10
Working Capital	514	571	569
Fixed Assets	110	133	96
Current Assets	914	1m	1m

Leo Display & Exhibitions Ltd
Unit 38 Stretford Motorway Estate Barton Dock Road, Stretford, Manchester, M32 0ZH
Tel: 0161-866 8060 **Fax:** 0161-866 8061
E-mail: info@leo-exhibitions.com
Website: http://www.leo-exhibitions.com
Directors: M. Broadhurst (MD)
Immediate Holding Company: LEO DISPLAY & EXHIBITIONS LIMITED
Registration no: 03150511 **Date established:** 1996
No.of Employees: 1 - 10 **Product Groups:** 26, 30, 35

Date of Accounts	Mar 11	Mar 10	Mar 09
Working Capital	-37	-44	-55
Fixed Assets	12	14	18
Current Assets	94	104	81

Leybold Optics UK Ltd (Branch Office)
St Modwen Road Trafford Park, Stretford, Manchester, M32 0ZE
Tel: 0161-866 2800 **Fax:** 0161-866 2801
E-mail: info@leyboldoptics.com
Website: http://www.leyboldoptics.com
Bank(s): Barclays

Directors: D. Clegg (MD)
Immediate Holding Company: LEYBOLD OPTICS UK LIMITED
Registration no: 04023277 **Date established:** 2000 **Turnover:** £2m - £5m
No.of Employees: 11 - 20 **Product Groups:** 38, 40, 46

Date of Accounts	Dec 11	Dec 10	Dec 09
Working Capital	219	336	448
Fixed Assets	2	1	27
Current Assets	984	1m	1m

Lindab
Unit 11b Central Park Estate Mosley Road, Trafford Park, Manchester, M17 1PG
Tel: 0161-876 0688 **Fax:** 0161-876 0858
E-mail: michelle.jones@lindab.co.uk
Website: http://www.lindab.co.uk
Bank(s): National Westminster Bank Plc
Managers: M. Jones (Mgr)
Ultimate Holding Company: LINDAB AB (SWEDEN)
Immediate Holding Company: LINDAB LIMITED
Registration no: 01641399 **VAT No.:** GB 589 7030 00
Date established: 1982 **Turnover:** £10m - £20m
No.of Employees: 11 - 20 **Product Groups:** 23, 32, 35, 36

Date of Accounts	Dec 11	Dec 10	Dec 09
Sales Turnover	51m	47m	49m
Pre Tax Profit/Loss	1m	-204	354
Working Capital	16m	-3m	-4m
Fixed Assets	16m	20m	22m
Current Assets	22m	20m	23m
Current Liabilities	1m	980	775

Ray Ling
Weymouth Road Eccles, Manchester, M30 8BT
Tel: 0161-787 8785
Website: http://www.raylings.co.uk
Directors: R. Parks (Prop)
Immediate Holding Company: A P R WINDOWS AND CONSERVATORIES LIMITED
Registration no: 05428140 **Date established:** 2005
No.of Employees: 1 - 10 **Product Groups:** 26, 35

Date of Accounts	Apr 11	Apr 10	Apr 09
Working Capital	-138	-118	-81
Fixed Assets	112	140	168
Current Assets	47	56	61
Current Liabilities	N/A	N/A	67

Little Giants Ltd
Unit 2 30 Broughton Street, Manchester, M8 8NN
Tel: 0161-832 1526 **Fax:** 0161-839 1754
E-mail: littlegiantsltd@hotmail.com
Bank(s): National Westminster
Directors: A. Ghafoor (MD), M. Ghafoor (Fin)
Immediate Holding Company: LITTLE GIANTS LIMITED
Registration no: 01834717 **VAT No.:** GB 323 7645 01
Date established: 1984 **Turnover:** £500,000 - £1m
No.of Employees: 251 - 500 **Product Groups:** 24

Date of Accounts	Apr 11	Apr 10	Apr 09
Working Capital	284	265	243
Fixed Assets	3	4	4
Current Assets	543	511	441
Current Liabilities	N/A	21	N/A

Lock Alarm & Safe Company
1 Edwin Road, Manchester, M11 3NQ
Tel: 0161-273 7749 **Fax:** 0161-276 0035
E-mail: mike@commsec.co.uk
Website: http://www.communitysecurity.co.uk
Directors: A. Nuttall (MD)
Ultimate Holding Company: COMMUNITY SECURITY (NORTH WEST) LIMITED
Immediate Holding Company: LOCK ALARM SAFE COMPANY LTD
Registration no: 03081617 **Date established:** 1995
No.of Employees: 11 - 20 **Product Groups:** 36, 40, 52, 67

M Lodge & Son
Failsworth Mill Ashton Road West, Failsworth, Manchester, M35 0FR
Tel: 0161-934 4050 **Fax:** 0161-683 4280
E-mail: indo@fabric.co.uk
Directors: A. Kapadia (Prop)
Ultimate Holding Company: ANDREW MERCER LIMITED
Immediate Holding Company: M.LODGE & SON LIMITED
Registration no: 00175661 **Date established:** 2021
Turnover: £10m - £20m **No.of Employees:** 1 - 10 **Product Groups:** 23, 63

Logstrup UK Ltd
Unit A3 Wardley Industrial Estate Priestley Road Worsley, Manchester, M28 2LY
Tel: 0161-728 1261 **Fax:** 0161-794 9485
E-mail: sales@logstrup.co.uk
Website: http://www.logstrup.com
Bank(s): Royal Bank of Scotland
Directors: J. Logstrup (MD), C. Myall (Co Sec)
Ultimate Holding Company: LOGSTRUP STEEL A/S (DENMARK)
Immediate Holding Company: LOGSTRUP (UK) LIMITED
Registration no: 01208295 **VAT No.:** GB 150 1937 87
Date established: 1975 **Turnover:** £1m - £2m **No.of Employees:** 11 - 20
Product Groups: 35, 37

Date of Accounts	Aug 11	Aug 10	Aug 09
Working Capital	36	100	-170
Fixed Assets	19	22	6
Current Assets	665	568	759

London Scottish Bank plc
24 Mount Street, Manchester, M2 3LS
Tel: 0161-834 2861 **Fax:** 0161-834 2536
Website: http://www.london-scottish.com
Directors: J. Freel (Sales), J. Rodwell (I.T. Dir), P. Cawdrey (Ch), M. Tattersall (MD), R. Reece (Grp Chief Exec), M. Coates (Mkt Research)
Managers: K. Harford (Mktg Serv Mgr)
Registration no: 00973008 **Date established:** 1903
No.of Employees: 1 - 10 **Product Groups:** 82

Date of Accounts	Oct 07
Pre Tax Profit/Loss	-15730
Fixed Assets	19910
Current Assets	360880
Current Liabilities	318680
Total Share Capital	14240
ROCE% (Return on Capital Employed)	-25.3

Longworth Ltd
Leltex House Longley Lane, Manchester, M22 4SY
Tel: 0161-945 1333 **Fax:** 0161-946 0026
E-mail: info@longworth.co.uk
Website: http://www.longworth.co.uk
Bank(s): Royal Bank of Scotland
Directors: V. O'Brien (Fin), K. Rae (Sales), V. O Brien (Fin)
Ultimate Holding Company: LONGWORTH (UK) LIMITED
Immediate Holding Company: LONGWORTH LTD
Registration no: 00336890 **VAT No.:** 146 1775 58 **Date established:** 1938
Turnover: £5m - £10m **No.of Employees:** 11 - 20 **Product Groups:** 24, 29, 40

Date of Accounts	Apr 11	Apr 10	Apr 09
Working Capital	-479	-441	-613
Fixed Assets	2m	2m	2m
Current Assets	357	283	399

Lookers plc
776 Chester Road Stretford, Manchester, M32 0QH
Tel: 0161-291 0043 **Fax:** 0161-864 2363
E-mail: robingregson@lookers.co.uk
Website: http://www.lookers.co.uk
Bank(s): Barclays Bank PLC, National Westminster, Northern Bank, National Austriali Bank, Lloyds, HSBC, Bank
Directors: P. Jones (Grp Chief Exec)
Immediate Holding Company: LOOKERS PUBLIC LIMITED COMPANY
Registration no: 00111876 **Date established:** 2010
Turnover: Over £1,000m **No.of Employees:** 51 - 100 **Product Groups:** 30, 39, 40, 68

Date of Accounts	Dec 11	Dec 10	Dec 09
Sales Turnover	1899m	1884m	1749m
Pre Tax Profit/Loss	31m	31m	12m
Working Capital	47m	42m	34m
Fixed Assets	253m	255m	260m
Current Assets	480m	429m	375m
Current Liabilities	294m	246m	205m

Lucchini UK Ltd (Wheel Systems Division)
Gate 2 Wheel Forge Way Trafford Park, Manchester, M17 1EH
Tel: 0161-886 0300 **Fax:** 0161-872 2895
E-mail: salesuk@lucchini.co.uk
Website: http://www.lucchini.it
Bank(s): National Westminster
Directors: C. Fawdry (MD), V. Montgomery (Co Sec)
Managers: C. Toms, M. Wood (Sales Prom Mgr), E. Martin (Personnel), H. Montgomery (Fin Mgr), R. Brooke
Ultimate Holding Company: OAO SEVERSTAL (RUSSIA)
Immediate Holding Company: LUCCHINI UK LIMITED
Registration no: 03120940 **Date established:** 1995
Turnover: £20m - £50m **No.of Employees:** 101 - 250 **Product Groups:** 39

Date of Accounts	Dec 11	Dec 10	Dec 09
Sales Turnover	22m	24m	26m
Pre Tax Profit/Loss	3m	3m	2m
Working Capital	8m	7m	7m
Fixed Assets	8m	8m	8m
Current Assets	11m	10m	12m
Current Liabilities	817	785	1m

Lucid Innovation
Unit 32 Greenheys Business Centre Pencroft Way, Manchester, M15 6JJ
Tel: 0161-860 0058
E-mail: ideas@lucidinnovation.com
Website: http://www.lucidinnovation.com
Directors: A. Williamson (MD)
Immediate Holding Company: LUCID GROUP LIMITED
Registration no: 04533078 **VAT No.:** GB 797 9053 64
Date established: 2002 **Turnover:** £250,000 - £500,000
No.of Employees: 1 - 10 **Product Groups:** 80, 84, 85

Date of Accounts	Mar 11	Mar 10	Mar 09
Working Capital	126	110	84
Fixed Assets	28	7	7
Current Assets	206	186	146

Lunex Ltd
151-153 Cheetham Hill Road, Manchester, M8 8LY
Tel: 0161-833 3435 **Fax:** 0161-833 3332
E-mail: sales@lunex.co.uk
Website: http://www.microcityuk.com
Directors: R. Malik (MD)
Immediate Holding Company: LUNEX LIMITED
Registration no: 05837936 **Date established:** 2006
Turnover: £500,000 - £1m **No.of Employees:** 1 - 10 **Product Groups:** 30, 66

Date of Accounts	Jun 11	Jun 10	Jun 09
Working Capital	-25	-75	-27
Fixed Assets	22	32	27
Current Assets	503	134	114

Luton Engineering Services Ltd
6 Swan Street, Manchester, M4 5JN
Tel: 0161-834 6577
Website: http://www.luton-eng.com
Directors: M. Ashar (Dir)
No.of Employees: 11 - 20 **Product Groups:** 37, 52

Luxonic Lighting
Unit 25 Wilsons Park Monsall Road, Manchester, M40 8WN
Tel: 0161-277 9861
E-mail: rayc@luxonic.co.uk
Website: http://www.luxonic.co.uk
Directors: R. Conboy (Reg Sales)
Immediate Holding Company: LUXONIC LIGHTING PLC
Registration no: 02024289 **Date established:** 1986 **Turnover:** £5m - £10m
No.of Employees: 1 - 10 **Product Groups:** 37, 67

Date of Accounts	Aug 11	Aug 10	Aug 09
Sales Turnover	10m	10m	8m
Pre Tax Profit/Loss	165	498	160
Working Capital	37	122	-9
Fixed Assets	3m	2m	2m
Current Assets	3m	3m	3m
Current Liabilities	2m	1m	1m

Luxus Loft Conversions
Luxus House 275 Deansgate, Manchester, M3 4EL
Tel: 0844-800 4165
E-mail: info@luxuslofts.co.uk
Website: http://www.luxuslofts.co.uk
Directors: J. Sales (Dir), L. Preston (Prop)
Registration no: 06265945 **Date established:** 2007
No.of Employees: 1 - 10 **Product Groups:** 52

M E L Chemicals
PO Box 6, Manchester, M27 8LS
Tel: 0161-911 1100 **Fax:** 0161-911 1090
E-mail: joy.walters@melchemicals.com
Website: http://www.zrchem.com
Bank(s): Midland
Directors: A. McClusky (Fin)
Managers: D. McWhinnie (Tech Serv Mgr), J. Walters (Admin Off)
Immediate Holding Company: BRITISH ALUMINIUM LTD
Registration no: 03141950 **Turnover:** £20m - £50m
No.of Employees: 51 - 100 **Product Groups:** 12, 31, 34, 35

M E N Media
1 Scott Place, Manchester, M3 3RN
Tel: 0161-832 7200 **Fax:** 0161-475 4893
E-mail: stockportadvertising@gmwn.co.uk
Website: http://www.mortons.co.uk
Directors: M. Dodson (Grp Chief Exec), D. Sharrocks (MD)
Managers: A. Wood (Publicity), S. Earnshaw (I.T. Exec)
Ultimate Holding Company: STAGECOACH GROUP PLC
Immediate Holding Company: GREATER MANCHESTER BUSES SOUTH LIMITED
Registration no: 00308157 **Date established:** 1935
Turnover: £250,000 - £500,000 **No.of Employees:** 1 - 10
Product Groups: 28

M G F Trench Construction Systems Ltd
Chaddock Lane Astley, Tyldesley, Manchester, M29 7JT
Tel: 01942-896282 **Fax:** 01942-894152
E-mail: enquiries@mgf.ltd.uk
Website: http://www.mgf.ltd.uk
Directors: E. Kelly (Sales), G. Nowicki (Fin)
Managers: N. Pickup (Tech Serv Mgr), M. Lord (Purch Mgr)
Ultimate Holding Company: MGF LIMITED
Immediate Holding Company: M.G.F. (TRENCH CONSTRUCTION SYSTEMS) LIMITED
Registration no: 01546198 **Date established:** 1981
Turnover: £20m - £50m **No.of Employees:** 51 - 100 **Product Groups:** 33, 34, 35, 83

Date of Accounts	Jun 11	Jun 10	Jun 09
Sales Turnover	23m	22m	24m
Pre Tax Profit/Loss	5m	6m	7m
Working Capital	4m	2m	3m
Fixed Assets	13m	11m	12m
Current Assets	9m	6m	7m
Current Liabilities	3m	3m	3m

M Gordon & Sons
Lawrence House Derby Street, Manchester, M8 8AT
Tel: 0161-834 4528 **Fax:** 0161-834 0111
E-mail: sales@gordons-manchester.co.uk
Website: http://www.gordons-manchester.co.uk
Directors: I. Sarwar (MD), M. Dean (Sales), P. Gordon (MD)
Managers: A. Staton (Chief Mgr), J. Green (I.T. Exec)
Immediate Holding Company: M. GORDON & SONS LIMITED
Registration no: 01243836 **VAT No.:** GB 305 0560 05
Date established: 1976 **Turnover:** £250,000 - £500,000
No.of Employees: 1 - 10 **Product Groups:** 65

M & I Materials Ltd
Stretford, Manchester, M32 0ZD
Tel: 0161-864 5422 **Fax:** 0161-875 2695
E-mail: kimwhittle@mimaterials.com
Website: http://www.mimaterials.com
Bank(s): HSBC Bank plc
Directors: E. Salt Melis (Co Sec), C. Salt (MD)
Managers: M. Greyson-Wood (Mktg Serv Mgr), S. Jeffery (Prod Mgr), K. Whittle (Comm)
Immediate Holding Company: M & I MATERIALS LIMITED
Registration no: 02772838 **VAT No.:** GB 560 7207 55
Date established: 1992 **Turnover:** £10m - £20m
No.of Employees: 101 - 250 **Product Groups:** 31, 34, 36, 37

Date of Accounts	Mar 11	Mar 10	Mar 09
Sales Turnover	26m	19m	20m
Pre Tax Profit/Loss	4m	2m	1m
Working Capital	4m	4m	4m
Fixed Assets	5m	4m	4m
Current Assets	10m	9m	8m
Current Liabilities	3m	3m	2m

M K D Holdings Ltd
Cornbrook 2 Brindley Road, Manchester, M16 9HQ
Tel: 0161-872 2422 **Fax:** 0161-848 7733
E-mail: custserv@mkdh.co.uk
Website: http://www.homeform.co.uk
Directors: A. Stanway (Prop), J. White (Mkt Research), A. Lewis (Dir), N. Slowey (MD), P. Lynskey (Dir), P. Hill (Dir), A. Stanway (Grp Chief Exec)
Managers: S. Hughes (Sales Prom Mgr), S. Evans (I.T. Exec)
Immediate Holding Company: SAGE & CO LIMITED
Registration no: 02340362 **Date established:** 2011
Turnover: £50m - £75m **No.of Employees:** 251 - 500 **Product Groups:** 26

Date of Accounts	Dec 05
Sales Turnover	78050
Pre Tax Profit/Loss	-6810
Working Capital	-11640
Fixed Assets	12350
Current Assets	7870
Current Liabilities	19510
Total Share Capital	700
ROCE% (Return on Capital Employed)	-959.2

M & N Textiles Ltd
Wrengate House 221 Palatine Road, Manchester, M20 2EE
Tel: 0161-438 1050 **Fax:** 0161-438 1021
E-mail: ngates@wrengate.co.uk
Website: http://www.wrengate.co.uk
Managers: N. Gates (Ops Mgr)
Immediate Holding Company: M.& N.TEXTILES LIMITED
Registration no: 00633335 **VAT No.:** GB 145 2774 61
Date established: 1959 **Turnover:** £5m - £10m **No.of Employees:** 1 - 10
Product Groups: 23, 63

Date of Accounts	Apr 11	Apr 10	Apr 09
Pre Tax Profit/Loss	N/A	N/A	83
Working Capital	7m	7m	7m
Fixed Assets	2m	2m	2m
Current Assets	8m	7m	7m
Current Liabilities	N/A	N/A	154

M S S Products Ltd

Bankfield Road Tyldesley, Manchester, M29 8QH
Tel: 0161-703 2200 **Fax:** 0161-702 6454
E-mail: enquiries@mssproducts.com
Website: http://www.mssproducts.com
Directors: A. Barker (Dir)
Managers: J. Dunn (Fin Mgr), S. Sankey (Personnel), K. Vennard (Tech Serv Mgr), R. Calvin (Mktg Serv Mgr)
Ultimate Holding Company: PGL (FORTY-FOUR) LIMITED
Immediate Holding Company: MAXIM INDUSTRIES LIMITED
Registration no: 02607738 **Date established:** 1991 **Turnover:** £5m - £10m
No.of Employees: 51 - 100 **Product Groups:** 12, 32, 34, 35, 36, 37, 48, 66, 84

Date of Accounts	Dec 11	Oct 10	Oct 09
Sales Turnover	10m	9m	7m
Pre Tax Profit/Loss	992	801	783
Working Capital	4m	3m	2m
Fixed Assets	182	92	108
Current Assets	6m	5m	4m
Current Liabilities	1m	1m	397

M S S Watch Company

Labtec Street Pendlebury, Swinton, Manchester, M27 8SE
Tel: 0161-794 7310 **Fax:** 0161-794 7311
E-mail: soamesclocks@tesco.net
Website: http://www.msswatch.co.uk
Directors: G. Frost (MD)
Ultimate Holding Company: SNB 06 LIMITED
Immediate Holding Company: SNB 06 LIMITED
Registration no: 03280435 **Date established:** 2006 **Turnover:** £2m - £5m
No.of Employees: 21 - 50 **Product Groups:** 65

Date of Accounts	Dec 11	Dec 10	Dec 09
Working Capital	-192	-192	-177
Fixed Assets	292	292	292
Current Assets	10	10	10

M W Wire Products Ltd

Unit 1 Smithfield Enterprise Estate Whitworth Street East, Manchester, M11 2NQ
Tel: 0161-223 8861 **Fax:** 0161-223 8861
E-mail: walkerswireproducts@yahoo.co.uk
Website: http://www.mwwireproducts.co.uk
Directors: M. Walker (Prop)
Managers: M. walker (Chief Acct)
Registration no: 233456 **Date established:** 1980 **No.of Employees:** 1 - 10
Product Groups: 48

Mac Fabrications

Old Coop Yard Warwick Street, Prestwich, Manchester, M25 3HB
Tel: 0161-773 0200 **Fax:** 0161-773 0200
Directors: M. Moore (MD)
Date established: 2001 **No.of Employees:** 1 - 10 **Product Groups:** 35

Maceplast UK Ltd

347 Moorside Road Swinton, Manchester, M27 9HH
Tel: 0161-793 7628 **Fax:** 0161-793 7629
E-mail: sales@maceplastuk.com
Website: http://www.maceplastuk.com
Directors: G. Mazza (Pres), G. Lynch (MD), G. Mazza (Prop)
Managers: F. Saladini (), J. Ward (Sales Prom Mgr), M. Nocera (Tech Serv Mgr)
Immediate Holding Company: MACEPLAST U.K. LIMITED
Registration no: 03650193 **VAT No.:** GB 725 6219 35
Date established: 1998 **Turnover:** £2m - £5m **No.of Employees:** 8
Product Groups: 27, 30, 31, 32, 40, 42, 48

Date of Accounts	Dec 11	Dec 10	Dec 09
Working Capital	-281	-400	-273
Fixed Assets	854	874	841
Current Assets	2m	1m	868

McKenzie Martin Ltd

Eton Hill Works Eton Hill Road, Radcliffe, Manchester, M26 2US
Tel: 0161-723 2234 **Fax:** 0161-725 9531
E-mail: general@mckenziemartin.co.uk
Website: http://www.mckenziemartin.co.uk
Directors: M. Pearse (Fab), G. Waite (Dir)
Immediate Holding Company: MCKENZIE-MARTIN LIMITED
Registration no: 00886296 **VAT No.:** GB 148 1238 72
Date established: 1966 **Turnover:** £1m - £2m **No.of Employees:** 21 - 50
Product Groups: 30, 33, 35, 40, 66

Date of Accounts	Jul 11	Jul 10	Jul 09
Working Capital	73	70	118
Current Assets	365	376	460

Magnesium Elektron

PO Box 23, Manchester, M27 8DD
Tel: 0161-911 1000 **Fax:** 0161-911 1010
E-mail: info@magnesium-elektron.com
Website: http://www.magnesium-elektron.com
Bank(s): The Royal Bank of Scotland
Directors: L. Seddon (Co Sec), C. Dagger (MD), N. Kershaw (Fin)
Managers: R. Baird (Purch Mgr), A. Duffield
Ultimate Holding Company: LUXFER HOLDINGS PLC
Immediate Holding Company: MAGNESIUM ELEKTRON LIMITED
Registration no: 03141950 **Date established:** 1995
Turnover: £75m - £125m **No.of Employees:** 101 - 250
Product Groups: 32, 34, 35

Date of Accounts	Dec 11	Dec 10	Dec 09
Sales Turnover	89m	65m	55m
Pre Tax Profit/Loss	13m	8m	5m
Working Capital	28m	18m	11m
Fixed Assets	45m	44m	45m
Current Assets	46m	28m	21m
Current Liabilities	8m	6m	6m

Malbern U P V C Windows & Doors Ltd

Malbern Industrial Estate Holland Street, Denton, Manchester, M34 3WE
Tel: 0161-320 5801 **Fax:** 0161-337 9507
E-mail: wayneclarke@malbernwindows.co.uk
Website: http://www.malbernwindows.co.uk
Directors: W. Clarke (Sales), A. Mitchell (Fin), P. Thackeray (Fin)
Managers: C. Kelly, E. Robinson (Purch Mgr)
Immediate Holding Company: MALBERN UPVC WINDOWS & DOORS LTD
Registration no: 02024805 **Date established:** 1986 **Turnover:** £5m - £10m
No.of Employees: 21 - 50 **Product Groups:** 30, 33, 36

Date of Accounts	Mar 07	Mar 06	Mar 05
Pre Tax Profit/Loss	62	53	157
Working Capital	-1m	-1m	-946
Fixed Assets	2m	692	2m
Current Assets	2m	2m	2m
Current Liabilities	687	483	883

Manchester Airguns

470 Oldham Road Failsworth, Manchester, M35 0FH
Tel: 0161-681 7947 **Fax:** 0161-684 8092
Directors: A. Hamer (Ptnr)
Date established: 1978 **No.of Employees:** 1 - 10 **Product Groups:** 36, 39, 40

The Manchester Conference Centre

Trading Services Umist, Manchester, M60 1QD
Tel: 0161-955 8000 **Fax:** 0161-275 2223
Website: http://www.meeting.co.uk
Bank(s): National Westminster, Manchester
Managers: A. Stephens (Mgr), H. Whitman (Sales Prom), D. Taylor
Immediate Holding Company: WESTON CONFERENCE CENTRE LTD
VAT No.: GB 519 8089 11 **Turnover:** £5m - £10m
No.of Employees: 101 - 250 **Product Groups:** 69, 81

Manchester Coppersmiths

Garland Works Bennett Street, Manchester, M12 5BW
Tel: 0161-223 0303 **Fax:** 0161-231 6558
E-mail: d-quin@manchestercoppersmiths.co.uk
Website: http://www.manchestercoppersmiths.co.uk
Directors: D. Quin (Ptnr)
Managers: P. Sidebottom (Sales Prom Mgr)
Date established: 1989 **No.of Employees:** 21 - 50 **Product Groups:** 35, 42, 45

Manchester Light & Stage Co LGTD

77 North Western Street, Manchester, M12 6DY
Tel: 0161-273 2662 **Fax:** 0161-273 2664
E-mail: info@manchesterlightandstage.com
Website: http://www.manchesterlightandstage.com
Directors: B. Mitchell (Prop)
No.of Employees: 21 - 50 **Product Groups:** 37, 67

Manchester Microwave

Unit 1 Albany Trading Estate, Manchester, M21 0AZ
Tel: 0161-881 3258 **Fax:** 0161-881 3356
Website: http://www.manchestermicrowave.co.uk
Directors: L. Bonner (Ptnr)
Date established: 1984 **No.of Employees:** 1 - 10 **Product Groups:** 36, 40

Manchester Paper Company Ltd

Victoria Works Williams Road, Gorton, Manchester, M18 7AY
Tel: 0161-223 9363 **Fax:** 0161-223 9291
E-mail: sales@manchesterpaper.co.uk
Website: http://www.manchesterpaper.co.uk
Directors: M. Sarwar (Fin)
Immediate Holding Company: MANCHESTER PAPER (CONVERTERS) CO. LIMITED
Registration no: 02917644 **Date established:** 1994
Turnover: £500,000 - £1m **No.of Employees:** 1 - 10 **Product Groups:** 66

Date of Accounts	Jun 11	Jun 10	Jun 09
Sales Turnover	N/A	575	N/A
Working Capital	217	235	231
Fixed Assets	53	53	56
Current Assets	424	455	642

Manchester Refractory

Highfield Road Little Hulton, Manchester, M38 9SS
Tel: 0161-703 9757 **Fax:** 0161-703 9737
E-mail: georgedodd@btconnect.com
Website: http://www.manchesterrefractory.co.uk
Directors: G. Dodd (Prop)
Immediate Holding Company: HODGKINSON BENNIS LIMITED
Registration no: 00357540 **Date established:** 1939
Turnover: £500,000 - £1m **No.of Employees:** 1 - 10 **Product Groups:** 33, 52

Date of Accounts	Sep 11	Sep 10	Sep 09
Working Capital	29	-28	-84
Fixed Assets	794	801	807
Current Assets	535	570	534

Manchester Wholesale Tools

5 Sagar Street, Manchester, M8 8EU
Tel: 0161-834 1123 **Fax:** 0161-834 1123
Managers: D. Hall (Mgr)
Immediate Holding Company: ABBRIA LIMITED
Registration no: 06953769 **Date established:** 2009
No.of Employees: 1 - 10 **Product Groups:** 46

Manplas Ltd

28 Coldfield Drive Roundthorn Industrial Estate, Manchester, M23 9GG
Tel: 0161-946 7800 **Fax:** 0161-946 7809
E-mail: sales@manplas.co.uk
Bank(s): The Royal Bank of Scotland
Directors: J. Green (MD), J. Green (MD)
Managers: P. Skerrett (Tech Serv Mgr), T. Martin
Ultimate Holding Company: MANPLAS HOLDINGS LIMITED
Immediate Holding Company: MANPLAS LIMITED
Registration no: 01109553 **VAT No.:** GB 158 5451 45
Date established: 1973 **Turnover:** £2m - £5m **No.of Employees:** 21 - 50
Product Groups: 30, 42, 48, 66

Date of Accounts	Sep 09	Sep 08	Jun 11
Working Capital	2m	2m	2m
Fixed Assets	423	483	279
Current Assets	3m	4m	4m

Mansam Products

49-51 Broughton Lane, Manchester, M8 9UE
Tel: 0161-834 1356 **Fax:** 0161-835 1024
E-mail: sales@mansam.com
Website: http://www.mansam.com
Directors: L. Stern (Dir)
Immediate Holding Company: MANSAM PRODUCTS LIMITED
Registration no: 06784892 **Date established:** 2009
No.of Employees: 1 - 10 **Product Groups:** 22, 23, 24, 27, 29, 30, 35, 43, 49, 61, 63, 65, 66

Date of Accounts	Jan 11	Jan 10
Working Capital	103	18
Fixed Assets	8	10
Current Assets	1m	1m

Maplin Electronics Ltd

Unit 17 The Fort Retail Park Cheetham Hill, Manchester, M8 8EP
Tel: 08432-277380 **Fax:** 0161-832 2380
E-mail: customercare@maplin.co.uk
Website: http://www.maplin.co.uk
Managers: Y. Mohammed (Mgr)
Ultimate Holding Company: MONTAGU PRIVATE EQUITY LLP
Immediate Holding Company: MAPLIN ELECTRONICS LIMITED
Registration no: 01264385 **Date established:** 1976
Turnover: £125m - £250m **No.of Employees:** 11 - 20
Product Groups: 37, 61

Date of Accounts	Dec 11	Dec 08	Dec 09
Sales Turnover	205m	204m	204m
Pre Tax Profit/Loss	25m	32m	35m
Working Capital	118m	49m	75m
Fixed Assets	27m	28m	28m
Current Assets	207m	108m	142m
Current Liabilities	78m	51m	59m

Marshall Tufflex Ltd

Tufflex House Europa Trading Estate Stoneclough Road, Radcliffe, Manchester, M26 1GG
Tel: 08702-403200
Website: http://www.marshall-tufflex.com
Managers: P. Booker (Mgr)
Immediate Holding Company: MARSHALL-TUFFLEX LIMITED
Registration no: 01007764 **Date established:** 1971
No.of Employees: 11 - 20 **Product Groups:** 30, 37, 66

Date of Accounts	May 11	May 10	May 09
Working Capital	25	36	86
Current Assets	184	58	230

Matrix Control Solutions Ltd

Unit1d Littlemoss Road Droylsden, Manchester, M43 7EF
Tel: 0161-371 0111 **Fax:** 0161-371 0880
E-mail: phil.middlebrook@matrixcontrolsolutions.com
Website: http://www.matrixcontrolsolutions.com
Directors: P. Middlebrook (MD), P. Middlebrook (Dir)
Ultimate Holding Company: 07023717
Immediate Holding Company: MATRIX CONTROL SOLUTIONS LIMITED
Registration no: 04681451 **Date established:** 2003
Turnover: £10m - £20m **No.of Employees:** 51 - 100 **Product Groups:** 37, 38, 52

Date of Accounts	Dec 07	Dec 06	Dec 05
Pre Tax Profit/Loss	3872	N/A	N/A
Working Capital	3273	3530	1006
Fixed Assets	90	118	51
Current Assets	7405	7313	2709
Current Liabilities	4132	3783	1703
Total Share Capital	3	3	3
ROCE% (Return on Capital Employed)	115.1		

Maxi Haulage Ltd

Oldham Road, Manchester, M40 5AF
Tel: 0161-205 9000 **Fax:** 0161-205 9191
Website: http://www.maxihaulage.co.uk
Directors: A. Miles (MD)
Managers: D. Ellis (Mgr)
Ultimate Holding Company: MAXI CALEDONIAN LIMITED
Immediate Holding Company: MAXI HAULAGE LIMITED
Registration no: SC054932 **Date established:** 1974
Turnover: £5m - £10m **No.of Employees:** 1 - 10 **Product Groups:** 72

Date of Accounts	Sep 10	Sep 09	Sep 08
Sales Turnover	35m	34m	31m
Pre Tax Profit/Loss	2m	2m	1m
Working Capital	6m	5m	2m
Fixed Assets	5m	4m	5m
Current Assets	8m	8m	7m
Current Liabilities	1m	1m	955

E Mesrie & Sons Ltd

3 Brazil Street, Manchester, M1 3PJ
Tel: 0161-236 6274 **Fax:** 0161-236 8086
E-mail: m.mesrie@mdmresourcing.com
Website: http://www.mdmresourcing.com
Directors: M. Mesrie (Dir)
Immediate Holding Company: E MESRIE & SONS LIMITED
Registration no: 00494030 **VAT No.:** GB 693 6479 77
Date established: 1951 **Turnover:** Up to £250,000
No.of Employees: 1 - 10 **Product Groups:** 23, 63

Date of Accounts	Mar 11	Mar 10	Mar 09
Working Capital	1m	1m	1m
Fixed Assets	648	630	637
Current Assets	2m	1m	2m
Current Liabilities	N/A	31	N/A

Methodist Insurance plc

Brazennose House West Brazennose Street, Manchester, M2 5AS
Tel: 0161-833 9696 **Fax:** 0161-833 1287
E-mail: enquiries@micmail.com
Website: http://www.methodistinsurance.co.uk
Bank(s): HSBC
Directors: R. Hall (Co Sec)
Immediate Holding Company: METHODIST INSURANCE PUBLIC LIMITED COMPANY
Registration no: 00006369 **Date established:** 1972 **Turnover:** £5m - £10m
No.of Employees: 21 - 50 **Product Groups:** 82

Date of Accounts	Dec 11	Dec 10	Dec 09
Pre Tax Profit/Loss	572	2m	2m
Working Capital	N/A	N/A	25m
Fixed Assets	18m	19m	16m
Current Assets	21m	22m	27m
Current Liabilities	24m	25m	2m

Midnite Express

6 Sidcup Road Roundthorn Industrial Estate, Manchester, M23 9PH
Tel: 0161-998 7700 **Fax:** 0161-998 7799
E-mail: sales@mnx.uk.com
Website: http://www.mnx.com
Directors: J. Best (Dir)
Turnover: Up to £250,000 **No.of Employees:** 1 - 10 **Product Groups:** 79

Midwest Plastic Products Ltd

2 Astley Park Estate Chaddock Lane Tyldesley, Manchester, M29 7JY
Tel: 01942-894657 **Fax:** 01942-897483
E-mail: sales@metalandplastics.co.uk
Website: http://www.metalsandplastics.co.uk
Bank(s): Barclays

Directors: H. Ward (MD)
Ultimate Holding Company: GABBOTTS FARM LIMITED
Immediate Holding Company: MIDWEST PLASTIC PRODUCTS LIMITED
Registration no: 07382096 **VAT No.:** 383 3893 16 **Date established:** 2010
Turnover: £500,000 - £1m **No.of Employees:** 21 - 50 **Product Groups:** 30

Date of Accounts	Dec 11
Working Capital	-85
Fixed Assets	69
Current Assets	233

Molygran & Co. Ltd
115-119 Bury Road Radcliffe, Manchester, M26 2UT
Tel: 0161-724 4771 **Fax:** 0161-724 8855
E-mail: sales@molygran.com
Website: http://www.molygran.com
Directors: I. Hitchon (MD)
Immediate Holding Company: MOLYGRAN & CO. LIMITED
Registration no: 01636930 **VAT No.:** GB 354 6930 36
Date established: 1982 **Turnover:** £500,000 - £1m
No.of Employees: 1 - 10 **Product Groups:** 30

Date of Accounts	May 11	May 10	May 09
Working Capital	83	36	4
Fixed Assets	337	350	365
Current Assets	161	130	94

Mono Pumps Ltd
Martin Street Audenshaw, Manchester, M34 5JA
Tel: 0161-339 9000 **Fax:** 0161-344 0727
E-mail: pnaylon@mono-pumps.com
Website: http://www.mono-pumps.com
Bank(s): Lloyds TSB Bank plc
Directors: S. Valentine (Fin), K. Holland (Fin), P. Naylon (MD)
Managers: P. Smith (Personnel), M. Beaver, E. Jacobs (Mktg Serv Mgr)
Ultimate Holding Company: NATIONAL OILWELL VARCO INC (USA)
Immediate Holding Company: MONO PUMPS LIMITED
Registration no: 00300721 **VAT No.:** GB 508 1666 47
Date established: 1935 **Turnover:** £50m - £75m
No.of Employees: 251 - 500 **Product Groups:** 39, 40, 41, 42, 45, 46, 54

Date of Accounts	Dec 11	Dec 10	Dec 09
Sales Turnover	64m	44m	41m
Pre Tax Profit/Loss	14m	7m	3m
Working Capital	35m	26m	21m
Fixed Assets	4m	4m	4m
Current Assets	47m	36m	38m
Current Liabilities	4m	4m	3m

Mruk Research Ltd
40 Princess Street, Manchester, M1 6DE
Tel: 08451-304576 **Fax:** 0161-234 0129
E-mail: rachel@mruk.co.uk
Website: http://www.cellomruk.co.uk
Directors: R. Cope (Research), R. Cope (Dir)
Immediate Holding Company: XL PRO AUDIO LTD
Registration no: 02693794 **Date established:** 2007
No.of Employees: 1 - 10 **Product Groups:** 81

Multiple Winding Co Ltd
Taylor Lane Denton, Manchester, M34 3NR
Tel: 0161-336 6125 **Fax:** 0161-335 9134
E-mail: chris@multiplewinding.co.uk
Website: http://www.multiplewinding.co.uk
Directors: C. Shaw (MD)
Managers: S. Yarwood (Admin Off)
Ultimate Holding Company: Shavian Investments Co. Ltd
Immediate Holding Company: Shavian Investments Company Limited(The)
Registration no: 00642251 **VAT No.:** 508 3941 41 **Date established:** 1959
Turnover: £2m - £5m **No.of Employees:** 21 - 50 **Product Groups:** 23

Date of Accounts	Mar 08	Mar 07	Mar 06
Working Capital	311	435	204
Fixed Assets	4568	3120	2831
Current Assets	2234	2186	1537
Current Liabilities	1923	1752	1333
Total Share Capital	900	900	900

N C C Group
Manchester Technology Centre Oxford Road, Manchester, M1 7EF
Tel: 0161-209 5200 **Fax:** 0161-209 5400
E-mail: info@nccglobal.com
Website: http://www.nccgroup.com
Bank(s): National Westminster
Managers: J. Lee
Ultimate Holding Company: NCC GROUP PLC
Immediate Holding Company: NCC GROUP SECURITY SERVICES LIMITED
Registration no: 04474600 **Date established:** 2002
Turnover: £10m - £20m **No.of Employees:** 51 - 100 **Product Groups:** 80

Date of Accounts	May 12	May 11	May 10
Sales Turnover	26m	17m	11m
Pre Tax Profit/Loss	4m	2m	2m
Working Capital	308	272	1m
Fixed Assets	776	653	472
Current Assets	8m	7m	4m
Current Liabilities	3m	3m	1m

N S C Programming Ltd
4th Floor Piccadilly House 49 Piccadilly, Manchester, M1 2AP
Tel: 0161-236 0535 **Fax:** 0161-236 2088
E-mail: info@nscgroup.co.uk
Website: http://www.nscgroup.co.uk
Directors: H. Sherrington (MD)
Immediate Holding Company: LEGACY RENOVATION LTD
Registration no: 01456224 **VAT No.:** GB 560 6938 21
Date established: 1979 **Turnover:** £500,000 - £1m
No.of Employees: 11 - 20 **Product Groups:** 44

Date of Accounts	Mar 11	Mar 10	Mar 09
Working Capital	-123	-122	-57
Fixed Assets	882	809	729
Current Assets	95	122	118

Nail It
Hope Street Swinton, Manchester, M27 4ES
Tel: 0161-794 9030 **Fax:** 0161-794 9755
Directors: P. Kershaw (Ptnr)
No.of Employees: 1 - 10 **Product Groups:** 35

North East Manchester Advertiser
1 Scott Place, Manchester, M3 3RN
Tel: 0161-832 7200 **Fax:** 0161-223 5447
Website: http://www.manchestereveningnews.co.uk
Directors: D. Benjamin (MD)
Managers: K. McMahon (Bldg Mgr), A. Lord (Mgr)
Ultimate Holding Company: THE HOTGROUP LIMITED
Immediate Holding Company: GUARDIAN MEDIA GROUP PLC
Registration no: 02631443 **Date established:** 1991
Turnover: £50m - £75m **No.of Employees:** 1 - 10 **Product Groups:** 28

North West Prototypes Ltd
The Little Mill Palatine Street, Denton, Manchester, M34 3LY
Tel: 0161-320 5529 **Fax:** 0161-335 0928
E-mail: sales@nwproto.co.uk
Website: http://www.nwproto.co.uk
Directors: M. Lee (Fin), W. Lee (MD)
Immediate Holding Company: NORTH WEST PROTOTYPES LIMITED
Registration no: 04477937 **Date established:** 2002
Turnover: £250,000 - £500,000 **No.of Employees:** 1 - 10
Product Groups: 42, 49

Date of Accounts	Jun 11	Jun 10	Jun 09
Working Capital	139	171	156
Fixed Assets	12	19	7
Current Assets	203	229	284

Northern Drives & Controls Ltd
Unit 26 Stretford Motorway Estate Stretford, Manchester, M32 0ZH
Tel: 0161-865 6026 **Fax:** 0161-865 3260
E-mail: j.griffin@ndc.uk.com
Website: http://www.ndc-uk.com
Directors: D. Griffin (Fin), J. Griffin (Dir)
Ultimate Holding Company: COMPLETE PLANT MAINTENANCE ENGINEERING LIMITED
Immediate Holding Company: NORTHERN DRIVES & CONTROLS LIMITED
Registration no: 03098497 **Date established:** 1995
No.of Employees: 11 - 20 **Product Groups:** 18, 37

Date of Accounts	Dec 11	Dec 10	Dec 09
Working Capital	69	-38	17
Fixed Assets	75	73	43
Current Assets	483	421	412

Northern Fan Supplies Ltd
Unit E1 Longford Trading Estate Thomas Street, Stretford, Manchester, M32 0JT
Tel: 0161-864 1777 **Fax:** 0161-864 2777
E-mail: jonathan.parry@nfan.co.uk
Website: http://www.nfan.co.uk
Directors: J. Parry (MD), D. Parry (Fin)
Ultimate Holding Company: NORTHERN FAN SUPPLIES HOLDINGS LIMITED
Immediate Holding Company: NORTHERN FAN SUPPLIES LIMITED
Registration no: 01904592 **VAT No.:** GB 408 2472 63
Date established: 1985 **Turnover:** £1m - £2m **No.of Employees:** 1 - 10
Product Groups: 30, 34, 35, 36, 37, 39, 40, 42, 46, 48, 66, 68

Date of Accounts	Jul 11	Jul 10	Jul 09
Working Capital	732	648	552
Fixed Assets	34	28	29
Current Assets	2m	1m	1m
Current Liabilities	N/A	770	N/A

Nothern Gas Installation UK Ltd
7 Alder Road Failsworth, Manchester, M35 0GH
Tel: 0161-682 8323 **Fax:** 0161-682 0043
E-mail: info@northerngasinstallations.com
Website: http://www.northerngasinstallations.com
Directors: D. Braithwaite (Dir)
Immediate Holding Company: NORTHERN GAS INSTALLATIONS (UK) LIMITED
Registration no: 06351348 **Date established:** 2007
No.of Employees: 1 - 10 **Product Groups:** 31, 38, 40, 52, 67

Date of Accounts	Sep 11	Sep 10	Sep 09
Working Capital	26	17	11
Fixed Assets	7	17	25
Current Assets	71	70	36

Nova Alarms
18 Spingclough Drive Worsley, Manchester, M28 3HS
Tel: 0161-702 8643 **Fax:** 0114-276 6644
E-mail: info@nova-alarms.co.uk
Website: http://www.nova-alarms.co.uk
Directors: D. Lee (Dir), J. Hickling (Dir), K. Lee (MD)
Immediate Holding Company: G.F.Wells Ltd
Registration no: SC338000 **Date established:** 1944
Turnover: Up to £250,000 **No.of Employees:** 1 - 10 **Product Groups:** 66

Date of Accounts	Dec 10	Dec 09	Dec 08
Working Capital	217	241	261
Fixed Assets	55	55	55
Current Assets	245	269	293

Nova Non Ferrous Ltd
Unit 13 Worsley Business Park, Worsley, Manchester, M28 1NL
Tel: 0161-799 4108 **Fax:** 0161-703 7294
E-mail: sales@novametals.co.uk
Website: http://www.novametals.co.uk
Directors: S. Carter (Dir)
Immediate Holding Company: NOVA METALS LTD.
Registration no: 01870601 **VAT No.:** GB 408 2055 79
Date established: 1984 **Turnover:** £500,000 - £1m
No.of Employees: 1 - 10 **Product Groups:** 48

Date of Accounts	Feb 12	Feb 11	Feb 10
Working Capital	74	76	51
Fixed Assets	13	15	21
Current Assets	201	173	162

Novinit Ltd
56 Lever Street, Manchester, M1 1FJ
Tel: 0161-236 1223 **Fax:** 0161-211 0090
E-mail: samsainz@ntlworld.com
Directors: A. Hussain (Dir)
Immediate Holding Company: NON STOP FASHIONS LIMITED
Registration no: 05806530 **Date established:** 2006
Turnover: £250,000 - £500,000 **No.of Employees:** 1 - 10
Product Groups: 63

Date of Accounts	Sep 08	Sep 07
Sales Turnover	N/A	457
Pre Tax Profit/Loss	N/A	-15
Working Capital	-21	-15
Current Assets	329	162
Current Liabilities	N/A	103

Noyna School Aprons
222 Stretford Road Urmston, Manchester, M41 9NT
Tel: 0161-748 2724 **Fax:** 0161-747 8775
E-mail: info@noyna.com
Website: http://www.noyna.com
Directors: R. Birtwistle (Prop)
Turnover: £250,000 - £500,000 **No.of Employees:** 1 - 10
Product Groups: 24

Nuoe Ltd (Trafford Branch)
100 Chorlton Road, Manchester, M15 4AN
Tel: 0161-227 7733 **Fax:** 0161-227 7733
E-mail: sales@nuoe.co.uk
Website: http://www.nuoe.co.uk
Directors: J. O'leary (Ptnr)
Immediate Holding Company: N.U.O.E. LIMITED
Registration no: 06959980 **Date established:** 2009
No.of Employees: 1 - 10 **Product Groups:** 26

Date of Accounts	Aug 11	Aug 10
Working Capital	-6	-8
Fixed Assets	17	18
Current Assets	36	41

Oldham Caravans
Oldham Road Failsworth, Manchester, M35 0HP
Tel: 0161-683 5555 **Fax:** 0161-683 5005
Managers: S. Bennett (Mgr)
No.of Employees: 1 - 10 **Product Groups:** 37, 67

Omega Engineering Ltd
Omega Drive Irlam, Manchester, M44 5BD
Tel: 0161-777 6611 **Fax:** 0161-777 6622
E-mail: zuk-kellysearch@omega.co.uk
Website: http://www.omega.co.uk
Directors: M. Hollander (Dir), B. Hollander (Prop), R. Kremheller (Co Sec)
Ultimate Holding Company: OMEGA ENGINEERING INC (USA)
Immediate Holding Company: OMEGA ENGINEERING LIMITED
Registration no: 02564017 **VAT No.:** GB 620 0439 89
Date established: 1990 **Turnover:** £10m - £20m
No.of Employees: 51 - 100 **Product Groups:** 29, 30, 32, 34, 35, 36, 37, 38, 39, 40, 41, 42, 45, 48, 49, 66, 67, 84, 85

Date of Accounts	Dec 11	Dec 10	Dec 09
Sales Turnover	2	2	2
Pre Tax Profit/Loss	2	2	2
Working Capital	-26	305	304
Fixed Assets	321	318	318
Current Assets	N/A	334	333
Current Liabilities	1	N/A	N/A

Open Control Solutions
Suite 2 Morston Close Worsley, Manchester, M28 1PB
Tel: 08708-810595 **Fax:** 08708-810594
E-mail: info@opencontrolsolutions.co.uk
Website: http://www.opencontrolsolutions.co.uk
Managers: P. Hamlon (Mgr)
Immediate Holding Company: OPEN CONTROL SOLUTIONS LIMITED
Registration no: 05190062 **Date established:** 2004
No.of Employees: 11 - 20 **Product Groups:** 40, 66

Date of Accounts	Aug 11	Aug 10	Aug 09
Working Capital	200	146	131
Fixed Assets	8	6	5
Current Assets	785	599	562

Opinion Research Corporation International
City Point 701 Chester Road, Stretford, Manchester, M32 0RW
Tel: 0161-877 6781 **Fax:** 0161-872 3997
E-mail: info@orcinternational.co.uk
Website: http://www.orcinternational.co.uk
Bank(s): HSBC Bank plc
Directors: R. Cornelius (MD)
Immediate Holding Company: OPINION RESEARCH CORPORATION, (USA)
Registration no: 01088226 **Date established:** 1997
No.of Employees: 11 - 20 **Product Groups:** 81

Orca Divers Ltd
557 Barlow Moor Road, Manchester, M21 8AN
Tel: 0161-718 3118
E-mail: enquiries@orcadivers.com
Website: http://www.orcadivers.com
Directors: C. Robertson-Brown (MD)
Immediate Holding Company: ORCA DIVERS LIMITED
Registration no: 05203885 **Date established:** 2004
No.of Employees: 1 - 10 **Product Groups:** 24, 40, 49

Ottoman Textiles Ltd
4 Alexandra Trading Estate Alexandra Road, Denton, Manchester, M34 3DX
Tel: 0161-320 7644 **Fax:** 0161-320 3747
E-mail: info@ottomantextiles.com
Website: http://www.ottomantextiles.com
Directors: M. Kaygusaz (MD), L. Kaygusuz (Fin)
Immediate Holding Company: OTTOMAN TEXTILES LIMITED
Registration no: 02066022 **Date established:** 1986
No.of Employees: 11 - 20 **Product Groups:** 24, 29

Date of Accounts	Oct 10	Oct 09	Oct 08
Working Capital	1m	1m	1m
Fixed Assets	154	189	213
Current Assets	1m	2m	2m

Overseas Courier
Unit 2 Cornishway Industrial Estate, Manchester, M22 0WT
Tel: 0161-498 9000 **Fax:** 0161-436 4205
E-mail: manchester@ocsworldwide.co.uk
Website: http://www.ocscourier.com
Managers: L. Birch (Mgr)
Ultimate Holding Company: OVERSEAS COURIER SERVICE (LONDON) LTD
No.of Employees: 1 - 10 **Product Groups:** 76, 79

Oxylitre Medical Services Ltd
Morton House, Manchester, M16 0WJ
Tel: 0161-872 6322 **Fax:** 0161-848 7914
E-mail: sales@oxylitre.co.uk
Website: http://www.oxylitre.co.uk
Bank(s): Barclays

see next page

Oxylitre Medical Services Ltd - Cont'd

Directors: S. Bell (Fin)
Managers: D. Mitchell
Immediate Holding Company: OXYLITRE (MEDICAL SERVICES) LIMITED
Registration no: 02111115 **VAT No.:** GB 146 6892 29
Date established: 1987 **Turnover:** £1m - £2m **No.of Employees:** 21 - 50
Product Groups: 38

Date of Accounts	Mar 11	Mar 10	Mar 09
Working Capital	760	673	709
Fixed Assets	26	18	30
Current Assets	930	1m	1m
Current Liabilities	3	120	216

P B S I Group Ltd

Belle Vue Works Boundary Street, Manchester, M12 5NG
Tel: 0161-230 6363 **Fax:** 0161-230 6464
E-mail: mail@pbsigroup.com
Website: http://www.pbsigroup.com
Bank(s): National Westminster Bank Plc
Directors: D. Hampson (Fin), K. Hamilton (Grp MD)
Managers: J. Hall (Prod Mgr), P. York (Develop Mgr), J. Beaumont
Immediate Holding Company: PBSI GROUP LIMITED
Registration no: 02030212 **VAT No.:** GB 519 5499 07
Date established: 1986 **Turnover:** £5m - £10m
No.of Employees: 51 - 100 **Product Groups:** 37, 38, 39

Date of Accounts	Jun 11	Jun 10	Jun 09
Sales Turnover	6m	7m	8m
Pre Tax Profit/Loss	-148	201	409
Working Capital	2m	3m	2m
Fixed Assets	2m	2m	2m
Current Assets	3m	4m	3m
Current Liabilities	434	456	466

P F & F Ltd

Environmental House Bag Lane, Atherton, Manchester, M46 0LY
Tel: 01942-896966 **Fax:** 01942-896990
E-mail: sales@pfandf.co.uk
Website: http://www.pfandf.co.uk
Bank(s): National Westminster Bank Plc
Directors: D. Bamber (Dir), G. Bamber (Co Sec)
Ultimate Holding Company: P F & F HOLDINGS LTD.
Immediate Holding Company: P F &F LTD
Registration no: 02621098 **Date established:** 1991 **Turnover:** £2m - £5m
No.of Employees: 21 - 50 **Product Groups:** 42, 61, 85

Date of Accounts	Jun 11	Jun 10	Jun 09
Working Capital	106	194	184
Fixed Assets	25	29	33
Current Assets	468	542	453

P G A Rewinds

58 Temperance Street, Manchester, M12 6DP
Tel: 0161-273 4484 **Fax:** 0161-273 4484
Directors: V. Moss (Prop)
Turnover: Up to £250,000 **No.of Employees:** 1 - 10 **Product Groups:** 48

P H S Services & Supplies

Hurds Garage Broomgrove Lane, Denton, Manchester, M34 3DU
Tel: 0161-320 4467
E-mail: peter@magicmerchants.co.uk
Website: http://www.phsservices.co.uk
Directors: P. Hall (Prop)
Registration no: 03462419 **Date established:** 1997
No.of Employees: 1 - 10 **Product Groups:** 38, 42

Date of Accounts	Aug 11	Aug 10	Aug 09
Working Capital	9	15	19
Fixed Assets	1	3	4
Current Assets	9	48	51

P J P Plant Hire

Mill Bank Radcliffe, Manchester, M26 1AJ
Tel: 0161-959 0000 **Fax:** 0161-959 9011
E-mail: hire@pjpuk.com
Website: http://www.pjpuk.com
Directors: C. Power (MD)
Managers: D. Foster (Fin Mgr)
Immediate Holding Company: PJP PLANT HIRE LIMITED
Registration no: 04103779 **Date established:** 2000
No.of Employees: 21 - 50 **Product Groups:** 45

P P M Recruitment Ltd

37 Cross Street Sale, Manchester, M33 7FT
Tel: 0845-0132303 **Fax:** 0161-905 0334
E-mail: info@ppmrecruit.com
Website: http://www.ppmrecruit.com
Directors: M. Foggarty (MD), B. Horrocks (Dir)
Managers: P. Todhunter (Chief Acct)
Registration no: 04421827 **Turnover:** £1m - £2m
No.of Employees: 1 - 10 **Product Groups:** 80

Packaging Products Ltd

Collyhurst Road, Manchester, M40 7RT
Tel: 0161-205 4181 **Fax:** 0161-203 4678
E-mail: sales@packagingproducts.co.uk
Website: http://www.packagingproducts.co.uk
Directors: D. Cornford (Dir), G. McNeeley (Sales), P. Cornford (Comm)
Managers: J. Witherland (Tech Serv Mgr), M. Ollerenshaw (Purch Mgr)
Ultimate Holding Company: PACKAGING PRODUCTS (COATINGS) LTD
Immediate Holding Company: PACKAGING PRODUCTS LIMITED
Registration no: 00900216 **Date established:** 1967
Turnover: £500,000 - £1m **No.of Employees:** 51 - 100
Product Groups: 27

Date of Accounts	Dec 11	Dec 10	Dec 09
Working Capital	40	40	648
Fixed Assets	N/A	N/A	136
Current Assets	40	42	1m

Pak Nylon Hosiery Co.

31 Broughton Street, Manchester, M8 8LZ
Tel: 0161-832 7371 **Fax:** 0161-839 5134
E-mail: c_m_afzal_khan@hotmail.co.uk
Website: http://www.paknylon.co.uk
Directors: A. Khan (Ptnr)
Date established: 1955 **No.of Employees:** 1 - 10 **Product Groups:** 24, 63

Panavision Video Filming Equipment

Unit 3 Littlers Point Second Avenue, Trafford Park, Manchester, M17 1LT
Tel: 0161-872 4766 **Fax:** 0161-872 6637
E-mail: dean.oram@panavision.co.uk
Website: http://www.panavision.co.uk
Managers: D. Oram (Mktg Serv Mgr)
No.of Employees: 1 - 10 **Product Groups:** 37, 38

Pannone LLP

123 Deansgate, Manchester, M3 2BU
Tel: 0161-909 2000 **Fax:** 0161-909 4444
E-mail: law@pannone.co.uk
Website: http://www.pannone.com
Directors: J. Muir (Fin), T. Dixon-phillips (Mkt Research), E. Holt (Snr Part)
Managers: R. Dobson
Immediate Holding Company: PANNONE LLP
Registration no: OC317202 **VAT No.:** GB 145 4350 81
Date established: 2006 **Turnover:** £50m - £75m
No.of Employees: 501 - 1000 **Product Groups:** 80

Paramount Electroplating Ltd

Morton House Skerton Road, Manchester, M16 0WJ
Tel: 0161-872 6581 **Fax:** 0161-848 7914
E-mail: tony.bell@oxyliter.co.uk
Directors: C. Bell (MD)
Immediate Holding Company: PARAMOUNT ELECTROPLATING LIMITED
Registration no: 03238888 **Date established:** 1996
No.of Employees: 1 - 10 **Product Groups:** 46, 48

Date of Accounts	Mar 11	Mar 10	Mar 09
Working Capital	45	43	34
Fixed Assets	1	1	2
Current Assets	270	223	119
Current Liabilities	169	116	28

Parat UK Ltd

Unit C1 Europa Trading Estate Europaway Stoneclough Road, Radcliffe, Manchester, M26 1GG
Tel: 01204-868630 **Fax:** 01204-868631
E-mail: ra@paratuk.co.uk
Website: http://www.paratuk.co.uk
Bank(s): HSBC Bank plc
Directors: R. Atkins (Dir), S. Qureshi (Sales)
Managers: M. Mikleticova (Mktg Serv Mgr), J. Kenyon (Buyer)
Immediate Holding Company: PARAT UK LIMITED
Registration no: 02344308 **VAT No.:** GB 562 4606 44
Date established: 1989 **Turnover:** £1m - £2m **No.of Employees:** 11 - 20
Product Groups: 22, 35, 38, 44

Date of Accounts	Dec 10	Dec 09	Dec 08
Working Capital	88	49	65
Fixed Assets	76	83	92
Current Assets	331	243	561

Park Cross (Engineering) Ltd

Unit 7Bealey Industrial Estate Off Dumers Lane, Radcliffe, Manchester, M26 9QE
Tel: 0161-724 2940 **Fax:** 0161-724 2941
E-mail: mail@park-cross.co.uk
Website: http://www.park-cross.co.uk
Bank(s): Barclays
Directors: A. Cope (MD), P. Currie (Dir)
Managers: R. Clegg (Buyer), T. Handley (Sales Prom Mgr), S. Tongue (Accounts)
Immediate Holding Company: C P C Group
Registration no: 00493581 **Date established:** 1968 **Turnover:** £2m - £5m
No.of Employees: 21 - 50 **Product Groups:** 30, 44, 48

Parker Body Builders Ltd

Chapel Street Levenshulme, Manchester, M19 3QA
Tel: 0161-224 0205 **Fax:** 0161-225 8035
E-mail: info@parkerbodybuilders.co.uk
Website: http://www.parkerbodybuilders.co.uk
Directors: B. Parker (Fin)
Immediate Holding Company: PARKER BODYBUILDERS LIMITED
Registration no: 01284375 **VAT No.:** GB 151 0700 20
Date established: 1976 **Turnover:** Up to £250,000
No.of Employees: 1 - 10 **Product Groups:** 39

Date of Accounts	Jan 11	Jan 10	Jan 09
Working Capital	35	30	31
Fixed Assets	27	28	29
Current Assets	123	122	134

R & J Partington

Failsworth Mill Ashton Road West, Failsworth, Manchester, M35 0FR
Tel: 0161-934 4040 **Fax:** 0161-683 4280
E-mail: partington@fabric.co.uk
Website: http://www.fabric.co.uk
Directors: M. Kapadia (Prop)
Ultimate Holding Company: ANDREW MERCER LIMITED
Immediate Holding Company: R.& J.PARTINGTON(1920)LIMITED
Registration no: 00170892 **VAT No.:** GB 145 0397 75
Date established: 2020 **Turnover:** £5m - £10m **No.of Employees:** 1 - 10
Product Groups: 23, 61

Passion Knitwear Ltd

Unit 2 Dark Lane, Manchester, M12 6FA
Tel: 0161-274 3786 **Fax:** 0161-273 7499
E-mail: tiberius66@yahoo.com
Directors: M. Rashid (Co Sec), B. Majid (Sales)
Immediate Holding Company: PASSION KNITWEAR LIMITED
Registration no: 02284901 **Date established:** 1988 **Turnover:** £1m - £2m
No.of Employees: 21 - 50 **Product Groups:** 24

Date of Accounts	Oct 11	Oct 10	Oct 09
Working Capital	1m	1m	1m
Fixed Assets	176	193	174
Current Assets	2m	2m	2m

Peek Traffic Ltd

6 Commerce Way Trafford Park, Manchester, M17 1HW
Tel: 0161-868 2040 **Fax:** 0161-868 2041
E-mail: mike.elwell@peek-traffic.co.uk
Website: http://www.peek-traffic.co.uk
Managers: M. Elwell (Mgr)
Ultimate Holding Company: IMTECH NV (NETHERLANDS)
Immediate Holding Company: PEEK TRAFFIC LIMITED
Registration no: 01490333 **Date established:** 1980
Turnover: Up to £250,000 **No.of Employees:** 21 - 50 **Product Groups:** 37, 38, 39, 44, 51

Date of Accounts	Dec 11	Dec 10	Dec 09
Sales Turnover	63m	63m	58m
Pre Tax Profit/Loss	6m	6m	2m
Working Capital	17m	14m	7m
Fixed Assets	2m	2m	6m
Current Assets	29m	27m	16m
Current Liabilities	9m	9m	4m

Peel Mount Contract Furnishing

27 Ellesmere Street, Manchester, M15 4LZ
Tel: 0161-817 2500 **Fax:** 0161-832 0216
E-mail: mbartlett@peelmount.co.uk
Website: http://www.peelmount.co.uk
Bank(s): Barclays
Directors: M. Bartlett (Prop), D. Worthington (Ch)
Managers: A. Hasington (Mktg Serv Mgr)
Immediate Holding Company: PEEL MOUNT CONTRACT FURNISHINGS LIMITED
Registration no: 01421081 **Date established:** 1979
Turnover: £500,000 - £1m **No.of Employees:** 21 - 50
Product Groups: 23, 24, 26, 35, 39

Date of Accounts	May 11	May 10	May 09
Working Capital	68	112	197
Fixed Assets	33	42	44
Current Assets	599	499	595

Perdaw Engineering Co. Ltd

4 Liverpool Road Cadishead, Manchester, M44 5AF
Tel: 0161-775 4133 **Fax:** 0161-777 9634
E-mail: b.perrin@perdaw.co.uk
Website: http://www.perdaw.co.uk
Bank(s): Barclays
Directors: B. Perrin (MD)
Immediate Holding Company: PERDAW ENGINEERING COMPANY LIMITED
Registration no: 01244162 **VAT No.:** GB 153 2927 67
Date established: 1976 **Turnover:** Up to £250,000
No.of Employees: 11 - 20 **Product Groups:** 35

Date of Accounts	Jul 11	Jul 10	Jul 09
Working Capital	140	156	257
Fixed Assets	82	87	94
Current Assets	248	230	329

Perkins Engines Co.

Perkins Powerpart Distribution Centre Frank Perkins Way, Irlam, Manchester, M44 5PP
Tel: 0161-776 5000 **Fax:** 0161-776 5100
E-mail: frost.neil@perkins.com
Website: http://www.perkins.com
Managers: N. Frost (Chief Mgr), R. Newton (Purch Mgr), L. Hood, A. Rainford (Tech Serv Mgr), A. Rainford (Tech Serv Mgr), I. Pugh (Fin Mgr)
Registration no: 02089227 **VAT No.:** GB 239 0382 63
Date established: 1998 **Turnover:** £75m - £125m
No.of Employees: 101 - 250 **Product Groups:** 68

Permanoid Ltd

107 Hulme Hall Lane, Manchester, M40 8HH
Tel: 0161-205 6161 **Fax:** 0161-205 9325
E-mail: sales@permanoid.co.uk
Website: http://www.permanoid.co.uk
Directors: J. Monello Jr (Fin), D. Cresswell (Co Sec)
Managers: G. Taylor (Purch Mgr), S. Hibbs (Sales & Mktg Mg)
Ultimate Holding Company: DAVRO INVESTMENTS LIMITED
Immediate Holding Company: PERMANOID LIMITED
Registration no: 00352908 **Date established:** 1939
Turnover: £10m - £20m **No.of Employees:** 51 - 100 **Product Groups:** 37

Date of Accounts	Sep 11	Sep 08	Oct 09
Sales Turnover	12m	N/A	8m
Pre Tax Profit/Loss	371	-45	-236
Working Capital	-520	-880	-984
Fixed Assets	536	609	453
Current Assets	3m	3m	2m
Current Liabilities	449	362	490

Perscent

Churchill Point Lake Edge Green, Trafford Park, Manchester, M17 1BL
Tel: 08702-084444 **Fax:** 08702-085555
E-mail: accounts@per-scent.co.uk
Website: http://www.per-scent.co.uk
Directors: S. Vadera (Grp Chief Exec)
Ultimate Holding Company: FRAGRANCE ACQUISITIONS LIMITED
Immediate Holding Company: PER-SCENT LIMITED
Registration no: 05245148 **Date established:** 2004
Turnover: £50m - £75m **No.of Employees:** 101 - 250 **Product Groups:** 63

Date of Accounts	Apr 12	Apr 11	Apr 10
Sales Turnover	57m	56m	56m
Pre Tax Profit/Loss	6m	6m	6m
Working Capital	28m	23m	19m
Fixed Assets	1m	1m	1m
Current Assets	41m	38m	31m
Current Liabilities	4m	4m	4m

Phoenix Abrasive Wheel Co. Ltd

Shepley Industrial Estate South Audenshaw, Manchester, M34 5DW
Tel: 0161-320 9580 **Fax:** 0161-335 9074
E-mail: grant.roberts@phoenixabrasives.co.uk
Website: http://www.phoenixabrasives.co.uk
Bank(s): National Westminster Bank Plc
Directors: G. Roberts (MD), K. Lawless (Fab), L. Gibson (Fin)
Immediate Holding Company: PHOENIX ABRASIVE WHEEL CO.LIMITED(THE)
Registration no: 00929557 **VAT No.:** GB 457 4114 50
Date established: 1968 **Turnover:** £1m - £2m **No.of Employees:** 21 - 50
Product Groups: 33

Date of Accounts	Mar 11	Mar 10	Mar 09
Working Capital	769	654	639
Fixed Assets	388	423	424
Current Assets	1m	1m	962

Phoenix Electroplating Ltd

Milltown Street Radcliffe, Manchester, M26 1WN
Tel: 0161-725 9479 **Fax:** 0161-725 9714
E-mail: enquiries@electroplating.co.uk
Website: http://www.electroplating.co.uk
Directors: M. Oates (Dir)
Immediate Holding Company: PHOENIX ELECTROPLATING LIMITED
Registration no: 02302218 **Date established:** 1988
No.of Employees: 1 - 10 **Product Groups:** 46, 48

Date of Accounts	Jan 12	Jan 11	Jan 10
Working Capital	-10	7	45
Fixed Assets	79	78	83
Current Assets	120	115	131

Phoenix Utility Services Ltd

44 Windsor Road Denton, Manchester, M34 2HD
Tel: 0161-320 7202 **Fax:** 0161-320 7202
E-mail: shaun.ellam@pusl.co.uk
Website: http://www.pusl.co.uk
Registration no: 04860109 **Product Groups:** 36, 39, 41, 45, 54, 67, 68, 83

Date of Accounts	Sep 08	Sep 07	Sep 06
Sales Turnover	103	46	33
Pre Tax Profit/Loss	44	-7	-19
Working Capital	-21	8	12
Fixed Assets	77	91	106
Current Assets	6	22	20
Current Liabilities	22	9	2

William Pinder & Sons Ltd

4 Harling Road Sharston Industrial Estate, Sharston Industrial Area, Manchester, M22 4UZ
Tel: 0161-998 1729 **Fax:** 0161-946 0734
E-mail: info@pinderblades.com
Website: http://www.pinderblades.com
Directors: R. Peacock (MD), C. Barratt (Co Sec)
Immediate Holding Company: WILLIAM PINDER & SONS LIMITED
Registration no: 00502332 **VAT No.:** GB 157 5480 44
Date established: 1951 **Turnover:** £250,000 - £500,000
No.of Employees: 1 - 10 **Product Groups:** 28, 30, 36, 41, 42, 43, 44, 45, 46, 47

Date of Accounts	Mar 11	Mar 10	Mar 09
Working Capital	55	43	48
Fixed Assets	10	14	12
Current Assets	168	155	147

Pinewood Associates

Barton Hall Works Hardy Street Eccles, Manchester, M30 7NB
Tel: 0161-707 7076 **Fax:** 0161-707 6766
E-mail: sales@pinewoodassociates.com
Website: http://www.pinewoodassociates.com
Directors: M. Rappaport (Dir), J. Blaskey (Sales)
Ultimate Holding Company: PANEL HOLDINGS LIMITED
Immediate Holding Company: PINEWOOD ASSOCIATES LIMITED
Registration no: 01998934 **Date established:** 1986
Turnover: £250,000 - £500,000 **No.of Employees:** 11 - 20
Product Groups: 26, 30

Date of Accounts	Jun 11	Jun 10	Jun 09
Working Capital	267	105	88
Fixed Assets	67	83	112
Current Assets	750	720	649

Pipe Center (a division of Wolseley UK)

2 Raven Street, Manchester, M12 6PP
Tel: 0161-276 0210 **Fax:** 01925-851444
E-mail: anthony.peers@wolseley.co.uk
Website: http://www.pipecenter.co.uk
Managers: A. Pierce (District Mgr)
Immediate Holding Company: PROFIT FOCUS (UK) LIMITED
Registration no: 03244411 **Date established:** 1996
No.of Employees: 1 - 10 **Product Groups:** 30, 31, 36, 39, 40, 42, 48, 66

Date of Accounts	Jun 11	Jun 10	Jun 09
Sales Turnover	87m	96m	96m
Pre Tax Profit/Loss	-2m	5m	5m
Working Capital	-2m	1m	4m
Fixed Assets	36m	34m	26m
Current Assets	34m	33m	45m
Current Liabilities	9m	7m	9m

Pipe & Climate Center

Unit 1 Severnside Trading Estate Textilose Road, Trafford Park, Manchester, M17 1WA
Tel: 0161-872 8431 **Fax:** 0161-872 0265
Website: http://www.climatecenter.co.uk
Managers: A. Rigby (District Mgr)
No.of Employees: 11 - 20 **Product Groups:** 40, 66

Date of Accounts	Jun 11	Jun 10	Jun 09
Sales Turnover	87m	96m	96m
Pre Tax Profit/Loss	-2m	5m	5m
Working Capital	-2m	1m	4m
Fixed Assets	36m	34m	26m
Current Assets	34m	33m	45m
Current Liabilities	9m	7m	9m

Plasman Laminate Products Ltd

Plasman Industrial Centre Marquis Street, Manchester, M19 3JH
Tel: 0161-224 0333 **Fax:** 0161-224 9961
E-mail: sales@plasman.co.uk
Website: http://www.plasman.co.uk
Directors: R. Moss (MD), S. Moss (MD), R. Sherratt (Sales), R. Sherratt (Asst MD), K. Ashdown (Fin), K. Ashdown (Co Sec)
Immediate Holding Company: PLASMAN (LAMINATE PRODUCTS) LIMITED
Registration no: 02256242 **Date established:** 1988 **Turnover:** £5m - £10m
No.of Employees: 21 - 50 **Product Groups:** 25, 26

Date of Accounts	Mar 12	Mar 11	Mar 10
Sales Turnover	7m	7m	7m
Pre Tax Profit/Loss	24	28	18
Working Capital	-652	-976	-1m
Fixed Assets	1m	1m	1m
Current Assets	2m	2m	2m
Current Liabilities	296	269	384

Plastic Art Co.

92 Temperance Street, Manchester, M12 6HU
Tel: 0161-273 3766 **Fax:** 0161-236 3201
E-mail: plasticartco@gmail.com
Website: http://www.plasticartmcr.co.uk
Directors: J. Kithchingman (Prop)
Immediate Holding Company: THE PLASTIC ART COMPANY (LEEDS) LTD
Registration no: 06234313 **VAT No.:** GB 403 4034 10
Date established: 2001 **Turnover:** £250,000 - £500,000
No.of Employees: 1 - 10 **Product Groups:** 37

Platt Haworth & Co. Ltd

Fourways House 18 Tariff Street, Manchester, M1 2FN
Tel: 0161-236 0764 **Fax:** 0161-236 7543
E-mail: sales@platthaworth.com
Website: http://www.platthaworth.com
Directors: R. Haworth (MD)
Immediate Holding Company: PLATT, HAWORTH & CO. LIMITED
Registration no: 00624568 **VAT No.:** GB 146 7784 27
Date established: 1959 **Turnover:** £2m - £5m **No.of Employees:** 1 - 10
Product Groups: 23

Date of Accounts	Oct 11	Oct 10	Oct 09
Working Capital	183	278	416
Fixed Assets	21	28	3
Current Assets	255	380	435

Portman Travel Ltd

Adlington Court Greencourts Business Park Styal Road, Manchester, M22 5LG
Tel: 0161-437 0300 **Fax:** 0161-437 0400
E-mail: sales@portmantravel.com
Website: http://www.portmantravel.com
Managers: M. Sore (Mgr), M. Soar (Chief Mgr)
Ultimate Holding Company: Portman Group Holdings Ltd
Immediate Holding Company: Fleet Street Travel Ltd
Registration no: 00620104 **VAT No.:** GB 680 4034 53
Turnover: £125m - £250m **No.of Employees:** 21 - 50 **Product Groups:** 69

Powell Marketing Ltd

P M House Cromer Industrial Estate Hilton Fold Lane, Middleton, Manchester, M24 2LE
Tel: 0161-653 7770 **Fax:** 0161-655 3795
E-mail: enq@powellmarketing.com
Website: http://www.powellmarketing.com
Directors: A. Powell (MD)
Immediate Holding Company: POWELL MARKETING LIMITED
Registration no: 02108961 **VAT No.:** GB 147 6771 50
Date established: 1987 **Turnover:** £2m - £5m **No.of Employees:** 1 - 10
Product Groups: 81

Date of Accounts	Dec 10	Dec 09	Mar 09
Working Capital	23	170	73
Fixed Assets	22	30	37
Current Assets	467	674	405

Power Fire Protection

17 Mountside Cresent Prestwich, Manchester, M25 3JF
Tel: 0161-798 7451 **Fax:** 0161-798 7451
Directors: M. Power (Prop)
Date established: 1987 **No.of Employees:** 1 - 10 **Product Groups:** 38, 42

Power Gems Ltd

Unit 1 Fairhills Road Irlam, Manchester, M44 6BA
Tel: 0161-776 7030 **Fax:** 0161-776 7039
E-mail: patrick.mcguane@powergems.com
Website: http://www.powergems.com
Directors: P. Mcguaine (Sales)
Immediate Holding Company: POWER GEMS LIMITED
Registration no: 05807625 **Date established:** 2006 **Turnover:** £2m - £5m
No.of Employees: 11 - 20 **Product Groups:** 23, 33, 37, 83

Date of Accounts	Apr 10	Apr 09	Feb 12
Working Capital	9	-154	452
Fixed Assets	168	190	222
Current Assets	536	513	662

Precise Pro Audio Hire

Unit 5 Concept Green Business Park 16 George Street, Eccles, Manchester, M30 0RG
Tel: 0161-789 2246 **Fax:** 0161-425 7651
E-mail: info@preciseaudiohire.com
Website: http://www.preciseaudiohire.com
Directors: A. Boothe (Dir)
Date established: 2003 **Turnover:** Up to £250,000
No.of Employees: 1 - 10 **Product Groups:** 37

Premier Rainwear

46 Stanley Street, Manchester, M8 8SH
Tel: 0161-834 9481
Immediate Holding Company: MOHANS (WAREHOUSES) LIMITED
Registration no: 01105475 **Date established:** 1973
No.of Employees: 1 - 10 **Product Groups:** 24, 63

Date of Accounts	Mar 10	Mar 09	Mar 08
Working Capital	396	558	691
Fixed Assets	416	421	425
Current Assets	762	914	1m

Presbar Diecastings Ltd

Store Street, Manchester, M1 2WD
Tel: 0161-273 4381 **Fax:** 0161-273 3235
E-mail: sales@presbar-diecastings.co.uk
Website: http://www.presbar-diecastings.co.uk
Bank(s): Barclays
Directors: D. Kitching (MD)
Ultimate Holding Company: PRESBAR GROUP LIMITED
Immediate Holding Company: PRESBAR DIECASTINGS LIMITED
Registration no: 03798597 **Date established:** 1999
Turnover: £10m - £20m **No.of Employees:** 101 - 250
Product Groups: 34, 46, 48, 66

Date of Accounts	Oct 11	Oct 10	Oct 09
Sales Turnover	10m	8m	7m
Pre Tax Profit/Loss	702	399	315
Working Capital	4m	4m	4m
Fixed Assets	705	799	932
Current Assets	5m	6m	4m
Current Liabilities	513	785	486

Pro Trainers UK Ltd

7 Willow Road Prestwich, Manchester, M25 3DZ
Tel: 07968-287552 **Fax:** 0161-773 3677
E-mail: forklifttrainer@aol.com
Website: http://www.pro-trainersuk.co.uk
Directors: M. Jones (Dir)
Immediate Holding Company: PRO-TRAINERS UK LIMITED
Registration no: 06929025 **Date established:** 2009
Turnover: Up to £250,000 **No.of Employees:** 1 - 10 **Product Groups:** 86

Date of Accounts	Jun 11	Jun 10
Sales Turnover	40	29
Pre Tax Profit/Loss	N/A	-0
Working Capital	N/A	-0
Current Assets	2	2
Current Liabilities	2	2

Professional Chauffeur Services

Atlas House Atlas Business Park Simonsway, Manchester, M22 5PP
Tel: 08703-807060 **Fax:** 08703-807060
E-mail: info@pcsshuttles.co.uk
Website: http://www.pcslimited.org
Directors: J. Murphy (Prop)
No.of Employees: 1 - 10 **Product Groups:** 72

Proseat

Site A Stakehill Industrial Estate Touchet Hall Road Middleton, Manchester, M24 2SJ
Tel: 0161-654 2500 **Fax:** 0161-655 4433
Website: http://www.proseat.de
Directors: R. Magee (Grp Chief Exec), M. Manseau (Fin)
Ultimate Holding Company: WOODBRIDGE FOAM CORPORATION (CANADA)
Immediate Holding Company: WOODBRIDGE FOAM (UK) LIMITED
Registration no: 03173516 **VAT No.:** GB 003 1735 16
Date established: 1996 **Turnover:** £20m - £50m
No.of Employees: 101 - 250 **Product Groups:** 30, 39

Date of Accounts	Oct 11	Oct 10	Oct 09
Sales Turnover	21m	21m	15m
Pre Tax Profit/Loss	617	2m	3m
Working Capital	-14m	-14m	-8m
Fixed Assets	859	736	736
Current Assets	9m	10m	11m
Current Liabilities	467	257	167

Public Address Systems Ltd

Unit 5 Leestone Road Sharston Sharston Industrial Area, Manchester, M22 4RN
Tel: 0161-611 7171 **Fax:** 0161-611 7170
E-mail: sales@pad.co.uk
Website: http://www.pad.co.uk
Directors: M. Thilo (MD), C. Kenyon (Jt MD)
Managers: D. Harding (Tech Serv Mgr), J. Perez (Prod Mgr), J. Kenyon (Prod Mgr)
Registration no: 03911804 **Date established:** 2005 **Turnover:** £1m - £2m
No.of Employees: 1 - 10 **Product Groups:** 37

Date of Accounts	Oct 05
Working Capital	-118
Fixed Assets	10
Current Assets	191
Current Liabilities	309

Pump Supply & Repair Group Ltd

Unit 3 The Furrows Trafford Park, Stretford, Manchester, M32 0SZ
Tel: 0161-864 4678 **Fax:** 0161-794 8052
E-mail: sales@pumpgroup.co.uk
Website: http://www.pumpgroup.co.uk
Directors: I. Pendleton (MD)
Ultimate Holding Company: PUMP SUPPLY & REPAIR GROUP HOLDINGS LTD
Immediate Holding Company: PUMP SUPPLY & REPAIR GROUP LIMITED
Registration no: 04464897 **Date established:** 2002
No.of Employees: 21 - 50 **Product Groups:** 29, 30, 33, 35, 36, 37, 38, 39, 40, 41, 42, 43, 45, 46, 48, 49, 52, 54, 67, 68, 83, 84

Date of Accounts	Jan 11	Jan 10	Jan 09
Working Capital	224	154	56
Current Assets	1m	942	850

Quiligotti Terrazzo Ltd

PO Box 4, Manchester, M27 8LP
Tel: 0161-727 1189 **Fax:** 0161- 7931173
E-mail: sales@pilkingtons.com
Website: http://www.quiligotti.co.uk
Directors: D. Gratrix (Sales)
Immediate Holding Company: QUILIGOTTI TERRAZZO LIMITED
Registration no: 00450328 **Date established:** 1948
Turnover: £20m - £50m **No.of Employees:** 21 - 50 **Product Groups:** 33

R D M Industrial Services Ltd

Stakehill Lane Middleton, Manchester, M24 2RW
Tel: 0161-643 9333 **Fax:** 0161-655 3467
E-mail: sales@rdmengineering.co.uk
Website: http://www.rdmengineering.co.uk
Directors: S. Horwich (Sales), R. Horwich (MD)
Managers: G. Smith (Sales Prom Mgr), A. Bagshaw (Accounts), C. Sheldon (Sales Admin)
Ultimate Holding Company: Horwich RDM Group
Immediate Holding Company: R.D.M. Industrial Services Ltd
Registration no: 01149853 **Date established:** 1973 **Turnover:** £2m - £5m
No.of Employees: 51 - 100 **Product Groups:** 35, 36, 37, 40, 41, 42, 46

Date of Accounts	Dec 07	Dec 06	Dec 05
Working Capital	525	202	155
Fixed Assets	279	300	260
Current Assets	2307	2093	1483
Current Liabilities	1782	1891	1328
Total Share Capital	35	35	35

R M S International Ltd

66 Pendlebury Road Swinton, Manchester, M27 4GY
Tel: 0161-727 8182 **Fax:** 0161-727 8191
E-mail: enquiries@rmsint.com
Website: http://www.rmsint.com
Bank(s): Hong Kong & Shanghai
Directors: J. Hammond (Fin), M. Taylor (Sales)
Managers: E. Turner (Personnel), M. Jones (Tech Serv Mgr)
Ultimate Holding Company: RMS INTERNATIONAL PLC
Immediate Holding Company: RMS INTERNATIONAL UK LTD
Registration no: 01161241 **VAT No.:** 588 8638 58 **Date established:** 1974
Turnover: £10m - £20m **No.of Employees:** 21 - 50 **Product Groups:** 27

Date of Accounts	Dec 11	Dec 10	Dec 09
Sales Turnover	13m	11m	14m
Pre Tax Profit/Loss	459	-193	55
Working Capital	190	-49	16
Fixed Assets	3m	3m	4m
Current Assets	7m	5m	5m
Current Liabilities	4m	3m	3m

R & S Electroplating Ltd

The Smithy Crown Street, Failsworth, Manchester, M35 9BD
Tel: 0161-683 4908 **Fax:** 0161-683 4908
E-mail: info@rschrome.co.uk
Website: http://www.rschrome.co.uk
Directors: M. Bray Cotton (Dir)
Immediate Holding Company: R. & S. ELECTRO PLATING LIMITED
Registration no: 01310043 **Date established:** 1977
No.of Employees: 1 - 10 **Product Groups:** 46, 48

Date of Accounts	Aug 11	Aug 10	Aug 09
Working Capital	-8	-19	-14
Fixed Assets	63	67	48
Current Assets	7	9	8

Radcliffe Engineering Services

101 Church Street West Radcliffe, Manchester, M26 2SX
Tel: 0161-723 4331 **Fax:** 0161-723 0300
E-mail: john.green@radcliffeengineering.co.uk
Directors: A. Green (Fin)
Immediate Holding Company: RADCLIFFE ENGINEERING SERVICES LIMITED

see next page

Radcliffe Engineering Services - Cont'd

Registration no: 04605559 **Date established:** 2002
No.of Employees: 1 - 10 **Product Groups:** 45, 84

Date of Accounts	Feb 08	Feb 11	Feb 10
Working Capital	-164	-109	-167
Fixed Assets	169	114	132
Current Assets	32	86	81

Rainbow Cosmetics Manchester Ltd

61 Stanley Road Edward House Whitefield, Manchester, M45 8GZ
Tel: 0161-767 7878 **Fax:** 0161-767 7679
E-mail: john.sharman@rainbowcosmetics.co.uk
Website: http://www.rainbowcosmetics.co.uk
Directors: J. Sharman (Ch)
Managers: R. Collins (Develop Mgr)
Ultimate Holding Company: RAINBOW COSMETICS (HOLDINGS) LIMITED
Immediate Holding Company: RAINBOW COSMETICS (MANCHESTER) LIMITED
Registration no: 04352003 **Date established:** 2002
Turnover: £20m - £50m **No.of Employees:** 21 - 50 **Product Groups:** 32

Date of Accounts	Dec 11	Dec 10	Dec 09
Sales Turnover	27m	34m	28m
Pre Tax Profit/Loss	294	479	294
Working Capital	649	702	378
Current Assets	13m	14m	11m
Current Liabilities	1m	754	1m

Really Useful Research & Development

Balmoral House 9 Balmoral Grange, Prestwich, Manchester, M25 0GZ
Tel: 0161-720 9924 **Fax:** 0161-740 0561
E-mail: john@reallyusefulresearch.co.uk
Website: http://www.reallyusefulconsultency.co.uk
Directors: J. Ardern (Snr Part)
Registration no: 04459545 **Turnover:** £250,000 - £500,000
No.of Employees: 1 - 10 **Product Groups:** 80, 81

Record Electrical Associates

Unit C1 Longford Trading Estate, Thomas Street, Stretford, Manchester, M32 0JT
Tel: 0845-257 1053 **Fax:** 0845-257 1054
E-mail: sales@reauk.com
Website: http://www.reauk.com
Directors: C. Mcgrau (Dir), J. Evans (Dir), A. Johnson (Dir)
Registration no: 04885349 **Product Groups:** 27, 35, 36, 37, 38, 39, 40, 42, 45, 48, 49, 67, 84

Date of Accounts	Jan 10	Jan 09	Jan 08
Sales Turnover	1m	1m	1m
Pre Tax Profit/Loss	239	167	121
Working Capital	87	86	65
Fixed Assets	4	8	18
Current Assets	219	246	191
Current Liabilities	90	107	80

Rectella

Unit 2 Blackmore Road, Stretford, Manchester, M32 0QY
Tel: 0161-866 2610 **Fax:** 0161-866 2620
E-mail: sales@rectella.co.uk
Website: http://www.rectella.co.uk
Bank(s): Barclays, Manchester
Directors: K. Spencer (Fin), F. Greicach (Dir)
Managers: D. Muir (Tech Serv Mgr), T. Graham (Personnel), A. Greicbach (Sales Prom Mgr)
Immediate Holding Company: RICHMOND GROUP LTD
Registration no: 00430344 **VAT No.:** GB 154 1452 87
Turnover: Over £1,000m **No.of Employees:** 21 - 50 **Product Groups:** 23, 24, 26, 63

Date of Accounts	Apr 08	Apr 07	Apr 06
Working Capital	10	10	10
Current Assets	10	10	10
Total Share Capital	10	10	10

Reed Accountancy Personnel Ltd

37 King Street, Manchester, M2 7AT
Tel: 0161-834 6207 **Fax:** 0161-237 1733
E-mail: rapmanchester@reed.co.uk
Website: http://www.reed.co.uk
Managers: K. Southward (Comm)
Ultimate Holding Company: REED EXECUTIVE P.L.C.
Immediate Holding Company: REED PERSONNEL SERVICES LTD
Registration no: 00973629 **Turnover:** £125m - £250m
No.of Employees: 21 - 50 **Product Groups:** 80

Reed Health Group P.L.C.

4th Floor 55 Spring Gardens, Manchester, M2 2BY
Tel: 0161-228 2421 **Fax:** 0161-238 8579
Website: http://www.reedglobal.com
Directors: J. Reed (Grp Chief Exec), M. Sallon (Sales), T. Millar (MD), K. Nicholson (Mkt Research), P. Drake (I.T. Dir)
Registration no: 03974512 **Turnover:** £500m - £1,000m
No.of Employees: 11 - 20 **Product Groups:** 80

Reed Nursing Personnel

33 Cross St, Manchester, M2 1NL
Tel: 0161-831 9110 **Fax:** 0161-835 2878
E-mail: katherine.brindley@reedhealth.co.uk
Website: http://www.reedhealth.co.uk
No.of Employees: 1 - 10 **Product Groups:** 80

Regalead Ltd

Columbus House Altrincham Road, Manchester, M22 9AF
Tel: 0161-946 1164 **Fax:** 0161-946 1033
E-mail: guy.hubble@regalead.co.uk
Website: http://www.regalead.co.uk
Bank(s): National Westminster Bank Plc
Directors: G. Hubble (MD)
Managers: P. Duffle (Buyer), S. Sheldon (Fin Mgr)
Immediate Holding Company: REGALEAD LIMITED
Registration no: 04211244 **Date established:** 2001 **Turnover:** £5m - £10m
No.of Employees: 21 - 50 **Product Groups:** 34

Date of Accounts	Sep 11	Sep 10	Sep 09
Sales Turnover	8m	N/A	N/A
Pre Tax Profit/Loss	313	N/A	N/A
Working Capital	1m	1m	868
Fixed Assets	969	1m	847
Current Assets	4m	3m	2m
Current Liabilities	1m	N/A	N/A

Regatta Ltd

Risol House Mercury Park Mercury Way, Urmston, Manchester, M41 7RR
Tel: 0161-749 1200 **Fax:** 0161-749 1210
E-mail: mweisz@regatta.com
Website: http://www.regatta.com
Bank(s): Midland
Directors: C. Bulmer (Tech Serv), H. Kahan (Sales), K. Black (MD), M. Ifould (Fin)
Managers: A. Edgerton (Buyer)
Ultimate Holding Company: RISOL IMPORTS LIMITED
Immediate Holding Company: REGATTA LTD
Registration no: 01063450 **VAT No.:** GB 150 9673 55
Date established: 1972 **Turnover:** £75m - £125m
No.of Employees: 251 - 500 **Product Groups:** 24

Date of Accounts	Jan 12	Jan 11	Jan 10
Sales Turnover	113m	102m	80m
Pre Tax Profit/Loss	5m	11m	7m
Working Capital	23m	22m	21m
Fixed Assets	11m	9m	9m
Current Assets	67m	53m	40m
Current Liabilities	12m	11m	8m

Reliance Security Services Ltd

Adamson House Pomona Strand, Old Trafford, Manchester, M16 0TT
Tel: 0161-874 7606 **Fax:** 0161-877 7344
E-mail: info@reliancesecurity.co.uk
Website: http://www.reliancesecurity.co.uk
Directors: C. Glover (Dir), K. Allison (Ch), R. Ban (Fin), S. Glover (Fin)
Managers: A. Anchors (Chief Mgr)
Ultimate Holding Company: Barclays plc
Immediate Holding Company: RELIANCE SECURITY SERVICES LIMITED
Registration no: 01146486 **Date established:** 1973
Turnover: Over £1,000m **No.of Employees:** 11 - 20 **Product Groups:** 81

Renew-All Bath Re-Enamelling

89 Moorside Road Urmston, Manchester, M41 5UH
Tel: 0161-747 2412 **Fax:** 0161-747 2412
E-mail: davidrostron@hotmail.com
Directors: D. Rostron (Prop)
Date established: 1994 **No.of Employees:** 1 - 10 **Product Groups:** 46, 48

Reynards UK Ltd

Greengate Middleton, Manchester, M24 1RU
Tel: 0161-653 7700 **Fax:** 0161-655 3891
E-mail: swood@reynards.com
Website: http://www.reynards.com
Bank(s): Barclays
Directors: A. Reynard (Co Sec), J. Reynard (Ch), R. Perkins (Comm), J. Ward (Fin)
Managers: D. Lee (Purch Mgr), I. Doggart (Depot Mgr), J. Bellshaw (Tech Serv Mgr)
Ultimate Holding Company: REYNARDS LIMITED
Immediate Holding Company: REYNARDS (U.K) LIMITED
Registration no: 00828877 **VAT No.:** GB 145 5289 53
Date established: 1964 **Turnover:** £10m - £20m
No.of Employees: 51 - 100 **Product Groups:** 25, 27, 30, 35, 41

Date of Accounts	Mar 12	Mar 11	Mar 10
Sales Turnover	15m	15m	15m
Pre Tax Profit/Loss	-84	-193	-211
Working Capital	-404	-321	-312
Fixed Assets	2m	2m	3m
Current Assets	3m	4m	4m
Current Liabilities	380	399	366

Richard Haworth & Co. Ltd

Kearsley Mill Stoneclough, Radcliffe, Manchester, M26 1RH
Tel: 01204-702300 **Fax:** 01204-705772
E-mail: info@richardhaworth.co.uk
Website: http://www.richardhaworth.co.uk
Bank(s): National Westminster Bank Plc & HSBC Bank plc
Directors: R. Ruia (Prop), R. Ruia (MD), S. Ruia (Jt MD)
Managers: C. Moore (Sales Prom Mgr), R. Thompson (I.T. Exec), K. Pringle (Personnel), Elliott (Mktg Serv Mgr)
Immediate Holding Company: RICHARD HAWORTH LIMITED
Registration no: 00883804 **Date established:** 1966
Turnover: £10m - £20m **No.of Employees:** 101 - 250
Product Groups: 23, 24

Date of Accounts	Apr 10	Apr 09	Apr 08
Sales Turnover	15m	17m	22m
Pre Tax Profit/Loss	1m	-989	-324
Working Capital	9m	8m	9m
Fixed Assets	143	235	306
Current Assets	11m	15m	16m
Current Liabilities	726	2m	2m

Richardson & Co. Ltd

Smithfold Lane Worsley, Manchester, M28 0GP
Tel: 0161-702 7002 **Fax:** 0161-790 8263
Bank(s): National Westminster Bank Plc
Directors: F. Richardson (Dir)
Managers: H. Richardson (Sales & Mktg Mg)
Immediate Holding Company: RICHARDSON & COMPANY STEELY PRODUCTS
Registration no: 01837283 **VAT No.:** GB 589 8559 47
Date established: 1984 **Turnover:** Up to £250,000
No.of Employees: 11 - 20 **Product Groups:** 43, 45

Date of Accounts	Sep 93	Sep 92	Sep 91
Fixed Assets	292	111	112
Current Assets	209	293	196

Ritrama UK Ltd

Lynwell Road Lyntown Trading Estate, Eccles, Manchester, M30 9QG
Tel: 0161-786 1700 **Fax:** 0161-786 1701
E-mail: mark.evans@ritrama.co.uk
Website: http://www.ritrama.co.uk
Bank(s): Barclays, Bury
Directors: M. Attwood (I.T. Dir), A. McManus (Fin), L. Ward (Sales), M. Evans (MD), P. Burton (Fin)
Ultimate Holding Company: RITRAMA SPA (ITALY)
Immediate Holding Company: RITRAMA (U.K.) LIMITED
Registration no: 01547937 **VAT No.:** GB 359 2905 25
Date established: 1981 **Turnover:** £20m - £50m
No.of Employees: 51 - 100 **Product Groups:** 27, 30, 44, 48, 49

Date of Accounts	Dec 11	Dec 10	Dec 09
Sales Turnover	30m	29m	25m
Pre Tax Profit/Loss	2m	784	423
Working Capital	5m	5m	2m
Fixed Assets	941	652	4m
Current Assets	12m	14m	10m
Current Liabilities	2m	1m	1m

Rodo Ltd

Lumb Lane Droylsden, Manchester, M43 7BU
Tel: 0161-371 6400 **Fax:** 0161-371 6401
E-mail: sales@rodo.co.uk
Website: http://www.rodo.co.uk
Bank(s): Midland
Directors: C. Thomason (Sales), P. Brierley (MD)
Managers: G. Bent, P. Ellor (Purch Mgr), C. Thorpe (Tech Serv Mgr)
Immediate Holding Company: RODO LIMITED
Registration no: 01832828 **VAT No.:** GB 146 3867 43
Date established: 1984 **Turnover:** £10m - £20m
No.of Employees: 51 - 100 **Product Groups:** 24, 49

Date of Accounts	Mar 11	Mar 10	Mar 09
Sales Turnover	18m	18m	N/A
Pre Tax Profit/Loss	948	1m	1m
Working Capital	8m	8m	7m
Fixed Assets	3m	3m	3m
Current Assets	10m	10m	10m
Current Liabilities	1m	1m	997

Rollcut Services

Tilson Road Roundthorn Industrial Estate, Manchester, M23 9GF
Tel: 0161-945 6002 **Fax:** 0161-903 9869
E-mail: peter@rollcutservices.co.uk
Directors: P. Roberts (Snr Part)
Immediate Holding Company: JON RICHARD HOLDINGS LIMITED
Date established: 2010 **No.of Employees:** 1 - 10 **Product Groups:** 23, 31, 63

J Rosenthal & Son Ltd

158 Bury Road Radcliffe, Manchester, M26 2JR
Tel: 0161-723 0404 **Fax:** 0161-724 5358
E-mail: info@jrosenthal.co.uk
Website: http://www.jrosenthal.co.uk
Bank(s): National Westminster Bank Plc
Directors: G. Crolla (Co Sec), N. Anderson (Sales), H. Rosenthal (MD)
Ultimate Holding Company: J ROSENTHAL HOLDINGS LIMITED
Immediate Holding Company: J. ROSENTHAL AND SON LIMITED
Registration no: 02415151 **Date established:** 1989
Turnover: £20m - £50m **No.of Employees:** 21 - 50 **Product Groups:** 24, 63

Date of Accounts	Sep 11	Sep 10	Sep 09
Sales Turnover	28m	31m	31m
Pre Tax Profit/Loss	1m	234	515
Working Capital	770	-674	-399
Fixed Assets	1m	2m	2m
Current Assets	13m	12m	14m
Current Liabilities	1m	2m	2m

Rotalac Plastics Ltd

Southmoor Road Roundhorn Industrial Estate, Roundthorn Industrial Estate, Manchester, M23 9DS
Tel: 0161-946 9460 **Fax:** 0161-946 9461
E-mail: enq@rotalac.com
Website: http://www.rotalac.com
Bank(s): Barclays
Directors: L. Jimmins (MD)
Immediate Holding Company: ROTALAC PLASTICS LIMITED
Registration no: 04081363 **Date established:** 2000 **Turnover:** £2m - £5m
No.of Employees: 21 - 50 **Product Groups:** 23, 25, 30, 31, 35, 36, 39, 66

Date of Accounts	Dec 11	Dec 10	Dec 09
Sales Turnover	3m	3m	4m
Pre Tax Profit/Loss	241	132	316
Working Capital	342	349	456
Fixed Assets	746	743	705
Current Assets	1m	1m	1m
Current Liabilities	164	110	91

Rowan Technologies Ltd

216 Church Road Urmston, Manchester, M41 9DX
Tel: 0161-748 3644 **Fax:** 0161-748 3644
E-mail: mail@rowantechnologies.co.uk
Website: http://www.rowantechnologies.co.uk
Directors: K. Farrell (Fin)
Immediate Holding Company: ROWAN TECHNOLOGIES LIMITED
Registration no: 02653333 **Date established:** 1991
No.of Employees: 1 - 10 **Product Groups:** 46, 48

Date of Accounts	Oct 11	Oct 10	Oct 09
Working Capital	109	92	89
Fixed Assets	5	6	11
Current Assets	179	125	117
Current Liabilities	71	33	N/A

A Rowe Ltd

Unit 21 Newhaven Business Park Barton Lane, Eccles, Manchester, M30 0HH
Tel: 0161-787 8150 **Fax:** 0161-787 8140
E-mail: info@arowe.co.uk
Website: http://www.arowe.co.uk
Directors: P. Gray (MD)
Immediate Holding Company: A. ROWE LIMITED
Registration no: 04055611 **VAT No.:** GB 144 9447 47
Date established: 2000 **Turnover:** £2m - £5m **No.of Employees:** 1 - 10
Product Groups: 23, 31

Date of Accounts	Sep 11	Sep 10	Sep 09
Working Capital	138	119	108
Current Assets	345	338	284
Current Liabilities	N/A	N/A	67

Rowham Steel Products

Lyons Road Trafford Park, Manchester, M17 1RN
Tel: 0161-786 3700 **Fax:** 0161-786 3707
E-mail: sales@rowhamsteel.co.uk
Website: http://www.rowhamsteel.co.uk
Bank(s): Lloyds TSB Bank plc
Directors: H. Spooner (Fin), T. Mizon (Dir)
Managers: L. Bland
Immediate Holding Company: ROWHAM STEEL PRODUCTS LIMITED
Registration no: 01426207 **VAT No.:** GB 305 7998 26
Date established: 1979 **Turnover:** £2m - £5m **No.of Employees:** 11 - 20
Product Groups: 66, 87

Date of Accounts	Jul 12	Jul 11	Jul 10
Working Capital	341	313	446
Fixed Assets	153	87	90
Current Assets	2m	1m	1m

Royal Treecare

40 Palm Street Droylsden, Manchester, M43 6WJ
Tel: 07917-713749
E-mail: phillip@royaltreecare.co.uk
Website: http://www.royaltreecare.co.uk

Product Groups: 07, 29, 30, 35, 62

R T K Grab Hire Limited

Kane House Sharp Street, Worsley, Manchester, M28 3LY
Tel: 0844-800 1047 **Fax:** 0161-799 9799
E-mail: enquiries@rtkgrabhire.com
Website: http://www.rtk-grabhire.co.uk
Directors: J. Bottomley (Prop)
Immediate Holding Company: RTK Grab Hire Ltd
Registration no: 05519526 **Date established:** 1990
Turnover: £500,000 - £1m **No.of Employees:** 1 - 10 **Product Groups:** 54

Date of Accounts	Oct 09	Oct 08	Oct 07
Working Capital	4	2	-36
Fixed Assets	148	212	350
Current Assets	121	128	96

Rufflette Ltd

Sharston Road Sharston Industrial Area, Manchester, M22 4TH
Tel: 0161-998 1811 **Fax:** 0161-945 1123
E-mail: phil.dawson@rufflette.com
Website: http://www.rufflette.com
Bank(s): National Westminster Bank Plc
Directors: P. Dawson (Sales), S. Manrai (Fin)
Managers: P. Earnshaw (Tech Serv Mgr)
Ultimate Holding Company: BANDEX TEXTIL & HANDELS GMBH (AUSTRIA)
Immediate Holding Company: RUFFLETTE LIMITED
Registration no: 03868897 **Date established:** 1999 **Turnover:** £2m - £5m
No.of Employees: 51 - 100 **Product Groups:** 23, 24, 30, 35, 36, 61, 63, 83

Date of Accounts	Dec 11	Dec 10	Dec 09
Sales Turnover	3m	3m	3m
Pre Tax Profit/Loss	-155	1m	-469
Working Capital	361	316	26
Fixed Assets	398	672	383
Current Assets	1m	1m	1m
Current Liabilities	226	182	225

S & B UK Ltd

Labtec Street Swinton, Manchester, M27 8SE
Tel: 0161-793 9333 **Fax:** 0161-728 9149
E-mail: jim_burgess@splusb.co.uk
Website: http://www.splusb.co.uk
Bank(s): HSBC Bank plc
Directors: J. Burgess (Dir)
Ultimate Holding Company: SNB 06 LIMITED
Immediate Holding Company: S + B UK LIMITED
Registration no: 03280435 **VAT No.:** GB 628 8639 93
Date established: 1996 **Turnover:** £5m - £10m **No.of Employees:** 21 - 50
Product Groups: 26, 37, 42, 52, 67

Date of Accounts	Dec 11	Dec 10	Dec 09
Working Capital	1m	2m	1m
Fixed Assets	612	86	91
Current Assets	2m	3m	2m

S G Cuttings

Unit H1 Europa Trading Estate Stoneclough Road, Radcliffe, Manchester, M26 1GG
Tel: 01204-574030 **Fax:** 01204-574031
E-mail: simon.leigh@john-holden.com
Website: http://www.john-holden.com
Directors: S. Leigh (MD)
No.of Employees: 11 - 20 **Product Groups:** 23, 24, 43, 48

S G Equipment

Delta Point Groby Road, Audenshaw, Manchester, M34 5UP
Tel: 0161-371 6130 **Fax:** 0161-371 7587
E-mail: brian@sgequipment.co.uk
Website: http://www.sgequipment.co.uk
Directors: A. Dobson (Dir), P. Cannings (Co Sec)
Managers: T. Jennings
Ultimate Holding Company: HYDE INDUSTRIAL HOLDINGS LIMITED
Immediate Holding Company: S G EQUIPMENT LIMITED
Registration no: 04301129 **Date established:** 2001 **Turnover:** £5m - £10m
No.of Employees: 21 - 50 **Product Groups:** 36, 37, 38, 39, 68

Date of Accounts	Sep 11	Sep 10	Sep 09
Sales Turnover	N/A	6m	6m
Pre Tax Profit/Loss	N/A	655	115
Working Capital	5m	5m	4m
Fixed Assets	176	255	215
Current Assets	5m	6m	5m
Current Liabilities	N/A	736	613

S H Metal Finishing

Unit 2 Albert Street Works Albert Street, Droylsden, Manchester, M43 7BA
Tel: 0161-371 1876 **Fax:** 0161-285 0765
Website: http://www.shmetalfinishing.co.uk
Directors: S. Holmes (Prop)
Immediate Holding Company: TAMESIDE AUTOMATICS LIMITED
Date established: 1997 **No.of Employees:** 1 - 10 **Product Groups:** 46, 48

Date of Accounts	Apr 11	Apr 09	Apr 08
Working Capital	11	18	22
Fixed Assets	11	17	21
Current Assets	55	56	52

S J L Print Media

St James House Fifth Street, Trafford Park, Manchester, M17 1JX
Tel: 0161-872 2801 **Fax:** 0161-872 2794
E-mail: sales@printmedia.com
Website: http://www.printmedialtd.com
Directors: R. Denton (Ptnr)
Immediate Holding Company: ST. JAMES LABEL COMPANY LIMITED
Registration no: 03118539 **Date established:** 1995
No.of Employees: 1 - 10 **Product Groups:** 38, 42

Date of Accounts	Oct 11	Oct 10	Oct 09
Working Capital	551	464	398
Fixed Assets	296	270	313
Current Assets	966	828	732

S J Translift Ltd

Unit 9 Manor Farm Industrial Estate, Stretford, Manchester, M32 9AN
Tel: 0161-866 8565 **Fax:** 0161-866 8565
E-mail: info@sjtranslift.co.uk
Website: http://www.sjtranslift.co.uk
Directors: S. Jackson (Dir)
Immediate Holding Company: SJ TRANSLIFT LIMITED
Registration no: 05408198 **Date established:** 2005
No.of Employees: 1 - 10 **Product Groups:** 35, 36, 38, 39, 40, 41, 43, 44, 45, 46, 47, 48, 49, 61, 66, 68, 69

Date of Accounts	Mar 11	Mar 10	Mar 09
Sales Turnover	N/A	109	96
Working Capital	25	15	29
Fixed Assets	42	42	43
Current Assets	69	67	29

S K Wiring Products Ltd

Unit 5 Denton Business Park Windmill Lane, Denton, Manchester, M34 3SP
Tel: 0161-320 9237 **Fax:** 0161-320 3663
E-mail: skwiringproducts@btconnect.com
Website: http://www.skwiringproducts.com
Directors: G. Hamilton (MD), S. Hamilton (Co Sec)
Ultimate Holding Company: SOVEREIGN STRANDS LIMITED
Immediate Holding Company: S.K. WIRING PRODUCTS LIMITED
Registration no: 02105823 **Date established:** 1987
Turnover: £500,000 - £1m **No.of Employees:** 1 - 10 **Product Groups:** 38

Date of Accounts	Mar 12	Mar 11	Mar 09
Working Capital	337	245	188
Fixed Assets	126	73	86
Current Assets	575	485	381

S & N Stainless Pipeline Products Ltd

Unit B4 Fallons Road, Wardley Road Industrial Estate, Swinton, Manchester, M28 2NY
Tel: 0161-728 1148 **Fax:** 0161-728 1149
E-mail: sales@snstainless.com
Website: http://www.snstainless.com
Registration no: 04391871 **VAT No.:** GB 794 6594 63
Turnover: £1m - £2m **No.of Employees:** 1 - 10 **Product Groups:** 34, 35, 36, 48, 66

Date of Accounts	Mar 08	Mar 07	Mar 06
Working Capital	252	249	192
Fixed Assets	42	22	19
Current Assets	688	755	588
Current Liabilities	436	505	397

S R H Lifting Equipment

Brook Business Complex Bennett Street, Manchester, M12 5AU
Tel: 0161-272 6944 **Fax:** 0161-272 6647
E-mail: srhlifting@btconnect.com
Website: http://www.srhliftingequipment.com
Directors: E. Maly (Prop), E. Maly (MD)
Immediate Holding Company: PHILIP SHOVLIN PLANT HIRE LIMITED
Registration no: 01299993 **VAT No.:** GB 786 6038 88
Date established: 1977 **Turnover:** £5m - £10m **No.of Employees:** 1 - 10
Product Groups: 23, 26, 29, 30, 34, 35, 36, 37, 38, 39, 40, 41, 42, 43, 45, 46, 48, 66, 67, 68, 83

S W S Metal Treatments Ltd

Second Avenue Trafford Park, Manchester, M17 1EE
Tel: 0161-872 3569 **Fax:** 0161-848 7356
E-mail: enquiries@swsmetaltreatments.co.uk
Website: http://www.swsmetaltreatments.co.uk
Bank(s): Barclays
Directors: A. Bennett (MD)
Managers: S. Bennett
Immediate Holding Company: CROMIE LTD
Registration no: 01056142 **VAT No.:** GB 157 7994 03
Turnover: £1m - £2m **No.of Employees:** 11 - 20 **Product Groups:** 48

Date of Accounts	Mar 08	Mar 07	Mar 06
Working Capital	73	30	80
Fixed Assets	577	582	43
Current Assets	268	239	203
Current Liabilities	195	210	124
Total Share Capital	1	1	1

Safety Systems UK Ltd

Sharp Street Worsley, Manchester, M28 3NA
Tel: 0161-790 7741 **Fax:** 0161-799 4335
E-mail: support@safetysystemsuk.com
Website: http://www.safetysystemsuk.com
Directors: L. Cook (Sales & Mktg)
Managers: A. Lamin (Tech Serv Mgr), J. Wainwright (Chief Mgr), M. Boardman (Chief Acct), K. Taylor (Personnel)
Ultimate Holding Company: TYCO INTERNATIONAL LIMITED (SWITZERLAND)
Immediate Holding Company: SAFETY SYSTEMS UK LIMITED
Registration no: 00030037 **VAT No.:** GB 405 2661 78
Date established: 1989 **Turnover:** £20m - £50m
No.of Employees: 101 - 250 **Product Groups:** 30, 40

Date of Accounts	Sep 11	Sep 08	Sep 09
Sales Turnover	30m	25m	26m
Pre Tax Profit/Loss	1m	2m	3m
Working Capital	25m	18m	40m
Fixed Assets	3m	3m	3m
Current Assets	32m	24m	48m
Current Liabilities	2m	2m	3m

Salford Van Hire

43 Sherborne Street Strangeways, Manchester, M3 1EJ
Tel: 0161-833 0771 **Fax:** 0161-833 0420
E-mail: sales@salfordvanhire.com
Website: http://www.salfordvanhire.com
Bank(s): HSBC
Directors: G. Bacci Evers (Co Sec), R. Bacci (MD)
Managers: N. Evers
Ultimate Holding Company: SALFORD VAN HIRE LIMITED
Immediate Holding Company: SALFORD VAN HIRE (CONTRACTS) LIMITED
Registration no: 01874061 **VAT No.:** GB 147 2757 49
Date established: 1984 **Turnover:** £50m - £75m
No.of Employees: 51 - 100 **Product Groups:** 72

Date of Accounts	Dec 11	Dec 10	Dec 09
Working Capital	200	200	200
Current Assets	200	200	200

Samsung Telecom UK Ltd

Unit B2 Brookside Business Park Greengate, Middleton, Manchester, M24 1GS
Tel: 0161-655 1100 **Fax:** 0161-655 1166
E-mail: info@samsungelectronics.co.uk
Directors: H. Roh (Fin)
Ultimate Holding Company: SAMSUNG ELECTRONICS CO LTD (S KOREA)
Immediate Holding Company: SAMSUNG TELECOMS (U.K.) LIMITED
Registration no: 03562489 **Date established:** 1998
Turnover: £50m - £75m **No.of Employees:** 1 - 10 **Product Groups:** 37

Sauter Automation

Trafford House Chester Road, Stretford, Manchester, M32 0RS
Tel: 0161-874 1300 **Fax:** 0161-848 0855
E-mail: info@uk.sauter-bc.com
Website: http://www.sautercontrols.com
Bank(s): Barclays
Managers: I. Sherburn (Mgr)
Ultimate Holding Company: OMX AB (SWEDEN)
Immediate Holding Company: FI SOFTWARE LIMITED
Registration no: 02777448 **Date established:** 1998
Turnover: £20m - £50m **No.of Employees:** 11 - 20 **Product Groups:** 49

Date of Accounts	Sep 11	Sep 10	Sep 09
Sales Turnover	7m	6m	3m
Pre Tax Profit/Loss	744	1m	-2m
Working Capital	3m	3m	2m
Fixed Assets	604	682	659
Current Assets	37m	30m	41m
Current Liabilities	33m	26m	39m

Scott-Grant Ltd

Portland Tower Portland Street, Manchester, M1 3LD
Tel: 0161-234 2121 **Fax:** 0161-234 2125
E-mail: info@scott-grant.co.uk
Website: http://www.scott-grant.co.uk
Directors: J. Hare (Co Sec), R. Taylor (MD)
Immediate Holding Company: SCOTT-GRANT LIMITED
Registration no: 05214287 **Date established:** 2004
No.of Employees: 1 - 10 **Product Groups:** 80, 86, 89

Date of Accounts	Dec 11	Dec 10	Dec 09
Working Capital	5	-29	-49
Fixed Assets	68	41	53
Current Assets	529	470	408
Current Liabilities	260	6	192

Service Point

Vicus Building 73-83 Liverpool Road, Manchester, M3 4AQ
Tel: 0161-817 4860 **Fax:** 0161-817 4870
E-mail: manchester@servicepointuk.com
Website: http://www.servicepointuk.com
Managers: A. Overland (District Mgr), J. Frangleton (District Mgr)
Immediate Holding Company: U D O Holdings Ltd
Registration no: 01093958 **Turnover:** £20m - £50m
No.of Employees: 21 - 50 **Product Groups:** 64

S F D Welding & Fabrication

Unit 9a Vaughan Street Industrial Estate, Manchester, M12 5BP
Tel: 0161-220 7678 **Fax:** 0161-220 7678
Directors: S. Davies (Prop)
Date established: 1999 **No.of Employees:** 1 - 10 **Product Groups:** 26, 35

Sheathed Heating Elements Holdings Ltd

Wardley Industrial Estate North Worsley, Manchester, M28 2DP
Tel: 0161-794 6122 **Fax:** 0161-794 8601
E-mail: sales@sheauk.free.com
Website: http://www.shelluk.com
Bank(s): Midland, Manchester
Directors: H. Hansson (Dir)
Immediate Holding Company: SHEATHED HEATING ELEMENTS (HOLDINGS) LIMITED
Registration no: 01309597 **VAT No.:** GB 408 1536 68
Date established: 1977 **Turnover:** £5m - £10m
No.of Employees: 101 - 250 **Product Groups:** 37, 40

Date of Accounts	Dec 07	Dec 06	Dec 05
Pre Tax Profit/Loss	-666	N/A	-1494
Working Capital	190	183	183
Current Assets	190	183	1677
Current Liabilities	N/A	N/A	1494
Total Share Capital	68	68	68
ROCE% (Return on Capital Employed)			-815.5

Sheridan Lifts Ltd

Windmill Lane Denton, Manchester, M34 3QS
Tel: 0161-336 0800 **Fax:** 0161-336 0800
E-mail: info@sheridanlifts.com
Website: http://www.sheridanlifts.com
Directors: A. Sheridan (Prop), T. Sheridan (Dir)
Managers: P. Knight (Chief Mgr)
Immediate Holding Company: SHERIDAN LIFTS LIMITED
Registration no: 05286889 **Date established:** 2004
No.of Employees: 11 - 20 **Product Groups:** 48

Date of Accounts	Nov 07
Working Capital	-50
Fixed Assets	60
Current Assets	191
Current Liabilities	241

Shonn Bros Manchester Ltd

Emperor House 151 Great Ducie Street, Manchester, M3 1FB
Tel: 0161-834 1394 **Fax:** 0161-832 1875
E-mail: shonnbros@yahoo.co.uk
Website: http://www.shonnbrotherswholesalers.co.uk
Directors: M. Shonn (Dir), I. George (Fin)
Managers: J. French (Personnel), J. Shonn, J. Boss (Tech Serv Mgr)
Ultimate Holding Company: RED BOLT CONSTRUCTION LIMITED
Immediate Holding Company: SHONN BROTHERS (MANCHESTER) LIMITED
Registration no: 00593397 **VAT No.:** GB 146 9229 45
Date established: 1957 **Turnover:** £250,000 - £500,000
No.of Employees: 11 - 20 **Product Groups:** 65

Date of Accounts	Dec 11	Dec 10	Dec 09
Working Capital	504	605	1m
Fixed Assets	548	572	764
Current Assets	1m	1m	2m

Shop Direct Ltd

Universal House Devonshire St, Manchester, M60 6EL
Tel: 0844-292 1000 **Fax:** 0161-277 4881
E-mail: supplier.enquiries@shopdirect.com
Website: http://www.shopdirect.com
Directors: K. Jones (Fin), W. Blackwood (MD)
Ultimate Holding Company: Experian Investment Holdings Ltd
Immediate Holding Company: Experian 2006 plc
Registration no: 04730752 **Turnover:** £20m - £50m
No.of Employees: 1 - 10 **Product Groups:** 61

Siemens Industry Automation & Drive Technology
Sir William Siemens House Princess Road, Manchester, M20 2UR
Tel: 0161-446 5000 **Fax:** 0161-446 5742
E-mail: david.wheeler@siemens.com
Website: http://www.siemens.co.uk
Directors: R. Phillips (Fin)
Managers: R. Wheeler (Mgr), T. Harris (Sales Prom Mgr), M. Lunn, A. Fletcher (Personnel), D. Wheeler (Mgr)
Immediate Holding Company: SIEMENS HOLDINGS PLC
Registration no: 00727817 **No.of Employees:** 501 - 1000
Product Groups: 37

Sietech Hearing Ltd
Ultravox House Styal Road, Manchester, M22 5WY
Tel: 0161-209 7002
E-mail: info@amplivox.com
Website: http://www.amplivox.com
Ultimate Holding Company: AMPLIFON SPA
Immediate Holding Company: AMPLIFON LIMITED
Registration no: 06132082 **Date established:** 1977
No.of Employees: 1 - 10 **Product Groups:** 28, 37, 86

Signs Express Stockport
Unit 9 Alpha Court Windmill Lane Industrial Estate, Denton, Manchester, M34 3RB
Tel: 0161-337 9988 **Fax:** 0161-337 0088
E-mail: stockport@signsexpress.co.uk
Website: http://www.signsexpress.co.uk
Managers: S. Ahmed (District Mgr)
Immediate Holding Company: TOM CHANDLEY LIMITED
Registration no: 00387243 **Date established:** 1944
No.of Employees: 1 - 10 **Product Groups:** 28, 40

Date of Accounts	May 11	May 10	May 09
Sales Turnover	9m	N/A	5m
Pre Tax Profit/Loss	1m	N/A	184
Working Capital	1m	1m	982
Fixed Assets	740	789	887
Current Assets	3m	3m	2m
Current Liabilities	778	N/A	390

Simpson Ready Foods Ltd
Stretford Road Urmston, Manchester, M41 9WH
Tel: 0161-865 2241 **Fax:** 0161-865 2893
E-mail: william.simpson@simpsonsfoods.co.uk
Website: http://www.simpsonsfoods.co.uk
Bank(s): National Westminster
Directors: W. Simpson (MD), B. Cooke (Comm)
Managers: C. Simpson (Tech Serv Mgr), A. Pembroke (Purch Mgr)
Immediate Holding Company: SIMPSON READY FOODS LIMITED
Registration no: 00114121 **VAT No.:** GB 146 5019 76
Date established: 2011 **Turnover:** £10m - £20m
No.of Employees: 51 - 100 **Product Groups:** 20

Date of Accounts	Dec 11	Dec 10	Dec 09
Sales Turnover	16m	13m	10m
Pre Tax Profit/Loss	-173	172	146
Working Capital	608	487	172
Fixed Assets	2m	2m	2m
Current Assets	5m	3m	3m
Current Liabilities	262	318	262

Samuel Simpson & Co. Ltd
30 Broughton Street, Manchester, M8 8NN
Tel: 0161-834 4920 **Fax:** 0161-834 3056
E-mail: sales@samuelsimpson.com
Website: http://www.samuelsimpson.com
Directors: D. Yorke (Co Sec)
Managers: S. Backler (Accounts)
Immediate Holding Company: Samuel Simpson & Co Ltd
Registration no: 04069206 **VAT No.:** GB 468 1095 30
Date established: 1993 **Turnover:** £2m - £5m **No.of Employees:** 1 - 10
Product Groups: 23

Date of Accounts	Apr 04
Sales Turnover	20
Pre Tax Profit/Loss	-4
Working Capital	131
Current Assets	137
Current Liabilities	6
Total Share Capital	25
ROCE% (Return on Capital Employed)	-3.1

Skytronic Ltd
Containerbase Barton Dock Road, Manchester, M41 7BQ
Tel: 0161-749 8180 **Fax:** 0161-749 8181
E-mail: sales@skytronic.co.uk
Website: http://skytroni.en.china.cn
Directors: S. Orr (Co Sec), P. Williams (MD), B. Goulding (Sales)
Immediate Holding Company: Avsl Group Ltd
Registration no: 06886306 **VAT No.:** GB 229 1036 84
Date established: 2005 **Turnover:** £500,000 - £1m
No.of Employees: 1 - 10 **Product Groups:** 37

Date of Accounts	Dec 07	Dec 06	Dec 05
Pre Tax Profit/Loss	1204	871	647
Working Capital	1888	1502	1022
Fixed Assets	211	684	643
Current Assets	5950	5775	3810
Current Liabilities	4062	4273	2788
Total Share Capital	55	70	70
ROCE% (Return on Capital Employed)	57.4	39.8	38.9

Smart Form
Unit 11 Vaughan Street, Manchester, M12 5DU
Tel: 08451-309100 **Fax:** 07003-909100
Website: http://www.smartformuk.com
Registration no: 06214531 **Date established:** 2007
No.of Employees: 51 - 100 **Product Groups:** 35, 48

Smartruck UK
105 Thirlmere Road Partington, Manchester, M31 4PS
Tel: 0161-775 6549 **Fax:** 0161-775 7515
E-mail: smartruck@aol.com
Website: http://www.smartruck-uk.com
Directors: R. Finney (Prop)
Immediate Holding Company: SMARTRUCK UK LTD
Registration no: 05490013 **Date established:** 2005
No.of Employees: 1 - 10 **Product Groups:** 35, 39, 45

Date of Accounts	Jun 11	Jun 10	Jun 07
Working Capital	1	3	7
Fixed Assets	1	1	5
Current Assets	5	9	12

Smith's Blinds
Unit B7 Newhaven Business Park Barton Lane, Eccles, Manchester, M30 0HH
Tel: 0161-787 7102 **Fax:** 0161-787 7102
E-mail: info@smithsblinds.co.uk
Website: http://www.smithsblinds.co.uk
Directors: T. Mulgrew (Prop)
Immediate Holding Company: SMITHS BLINDS LTD
Registration no: 06154305 **Date established:** 2007
No.of Employees: 1 - 10 **Product Groups:** 24, 25, 63

Date of Accounts	Mar 11	Mar 10	Mar 09
Working Capital	-45	-55	-65
Fixed Assets	27	8	10
Current Assets	65	33	26

Solar Guard Tinting
134 Higher Road Urmston, Manchester, M41 9AZ
Tel: 0800-0965500 **Fax:** 07970-381 668
E-mail: info@solarguardtinting.co.uk
Website: http://www.solarguardtinting.co.uk
Managers: D. Wood (Chief Mgr), S. Cunnigham (Mgr), R. Wood (Accounts)
Date established: 2005 **Turnover:** Up to £250,000
No.of Employees: 1 - 10 **Product Groups:** 30

Speciality Linens
Unit 2 Albert Close Trading Estate, Whitefield, Manchester, M45 8EH
Tel: 0161-796 7111 **Fax:** 0161-796 3337
E-mail: sales@specialitylinens.co.uk
Website: http://www.specialitylinens.co.uk
Directors: R. Crammer (Prop)
Date established: 1980 **No.of Employees:** 21 - 50 **Product Groups:** 24, 83

Speedy Lifting Ltd
Guinness Road Trading Estate Guinness Road Trafford Park, Manchester, M17 1SB
Tel: 0161-877 3330 **Fax:** 0161-848 9312
Website: http://www.speedyhire.com
Managers: L. Montuague (Mgr)
Ultimate Holding Company: SPEEDY HIRE PLC
Immediate Holding Company: SPEEDY LIFTING LIMITED
Registration no: 04529136 **Date established:** 2002
Turnover: £20m - £50m **No.of Employees:** 1 - 10 **Product Groups:** 35, 37, 38, 39, 45, 48, 83

Date of Accounts	Mar 12	Mar 11	Mar 10
Sales Turnover	N/A	N/A	21m
Pre Tax Profit/Loss	N/A	N/A	4m
Working Capital	20m	20m	20m
Current Assets	20m	20m	21m

Spoken Image Ltd
Studio 6 Riverside Mews 4 Commercial Street, Manchester, M15 4RQ
Tel: 0161-236 7522 **Fax:** 0161-236 3386
E-mail: geoff@spoken-image.com
Website: http://www.spoken-image.com
Directors: G. Ollman (MD)
Immediate Holding Company: SPOKEN IMAGE LIMITED
Registration no: 01668713 **VAT No.:** GB 150 5092 95
Date established: 1982 **Turnover:** £500,000 - £1m
No.of Employees: 1 - 10 **Product Groups:** 44, 80, 81

Date of Accounts	Apr 11	Apr 10	Apr 09
Working Capital	2	1	41
Fixed Assets	5	6	10
Current Assets	67	74	105

Spraysafe Automatic Sprinklers
6 Westpoint Enterprise Park Clarence Avenue, Trafford Park, Manchester, M17 1QS
Tel: 0161-875 0500 **Fax:** 0161-875 0509
E-mail: kate.scourfield@centralsprinkler.com
Website: http://www.centralsprinkler.com
Managers: C. Prideaux (Sales Prom Mgr), I. Brough (Sales Prom Mgr), K. Scourfield (Sales Prom Mgr)
Ultimate Holding Company: Tyco International (USA)
Immediate Holding Company: DALLIMORE PROPERTIES LLP
Registration no: 01050090 **VAT No.:** GB 129 4336 65
Date established: 2008 **Turnover:** £2m - £5m **No.of Employees:** 1 - 10
Product Groups: 23, 29, 30, 36, 40, 67

St James Label Company Ltd
St James House Fifth Street, Trafford Park, Manchester, M17 1JX
Tel: 0161-877 7931 **Fax:** 0161-876 4473
E-mail: sales@sjl.co.uk
Website: http://www.sjl.co.uk
Directors: D. Bickley (MD)
Managers: C. Hulme (Comptroller)
Immediate Holding Company: ST. JAMES LABEL COMPANY LIMITED
Registration no: 03118539 **Date established:** 1995 **Turnover:** £1m - £2m
No.of Employees: 21 - 50 **Product Groups:** 27, 28, 30

Date of Accounts	Oct 11	Oct 10	Oct 09
Working Capital	551	464	398
Fixed Assets	296	270	313
Current Assets	966	828	732

Start Training Ltd
Wesley Street Swinton, Manchester, M27 6AD
Tel: 0161-728 2438 **Fax:** 0161-794 8261
E-mail: start.training@virgin.net
Website: http://www.starttraining.co.uk
Bank(s): Nat West
Directors: M. Jenkinson (MD), J. Robinson (Ch)
Managers: L. Fisher (Sales & Mktg Mg), D. Doherty (Personnel)
Immediate Holding Company: START TRAINING LTD
Registration no: 05905954 **VAT No.:** GB 588 8009 89
Date established: 2006 **Turnover:** Up to £250,000
No.of Employees: 11 - 20 **Product Groups:** 86

Date of Accounts	Jul 11	Jul 10	Jul 08
Working Capital	196	163	43
Fixed Assets	10	14	18
Current Assets	260	317	292

Steroplast Ltd
Alpha Point Bradnor Road, Sharston Industrial Area, Manchester, M22 4TE
Tel: 0161-902 3030 **Fax:** 0161-902 3040
E-mail: sales@steroplast.co.uk
Website: http://www.steroplast.co.uk
Bank(s): National Westminster, Manchester
Directors: H. Richbell (Fin)
Managers: H. Jones (Admin Off)
Immediate Holding Company: STEROPLAST HEALTHCARE LIMITED
Registration no: 00504340 **VAT No.:** GB 145 0772 75
Date established: 1952 **Turnover:** £2m - £5m **No.of Employees:** 21 - 50
Product Groups: 24

Date of Accounts	Mar 11	Mar 10	Mar 09
Working Capital	1m	1m	918
Fixed Assets	898	928	938
Current Assets	2m	2m	1m

Stormproofings Ltd
8 Vale Park Industrial Estate Hazel Bottom Road, Manchester, M8 0GF
Tel: 0161-205 5354 **Fax:** 0161-205 8057
E-mail: info@john-holden.com
Website: http://www.stormproofing.co.uk
Bank(s): Barclays
Managers: M. Matthew (Chief Mgr), N. Matthew (Chief Mgr), C. Bowie
Immediate Holding Company: STORMPROOFINGS LIMITED
Registration no: 02997151 **Date established:** 1994 **Turnover:** £2m - £5m
No.of Employees: 11 - 20 **Product Groups:** 23, 24, 27, 32, 66

Date of Accounts	Mar 12	Mar 11	Mar 10
Sales Turnover	N/A	7m	N/A
Pre Tax Profit/Loss	N/A	285	N/A
Working Capital	2m	1m	1m
Fixed Assets	4	16	33
Current Assets	3m	3m	2m
Current Liabilities	N/A	221	629

Stuart Photronics Ltd
4 Haslam Street Middleton, Manchester, M24 1GT
Tel: 0161-643 7673 **Fax:** 0161-643 0391
E-mail: stuartphot@aol.com
Website: http://www.amglo.com
Directors: S. Riding (MD)
Managers: M. Kennedy (Sales Admin)
Ultimate Holding Company: Amgo-kenlite Labs Inc
Immediate Holding Company: STUART (PHOTRONICS) LIMITED
Registration no: 01057439 **VAT No.:** GB 147 4764 42
Date established: 1972 **Turnover:** £250,000 - £500,000
No.of Employees: 1 - 10 **Product Groups:** 37

Sun Chemical Ltd (Sun Chemical Group Ltd)
Taylor Road Urmston, Manchester, M41 7SW
Tel: 0161-748 7340 **Fax:** 0161-748 7685
E-mail: david.garrighan@sunchemical.com
Website: http://www.sunchemical.com
Bank(s): Barclays
Managers: D. Garrighan (Site Co-ord)
Ultimate Holding Company: DAINIPPON INK & CHEMICALS INC (JAPAN)
Immediate Holding Company: SUN CHEMICAL LIMITED
Registration no: 02647054 **Date established:** 1991
Turnover: £20m - £50m **No.of Employees:** 51 - 100 **Product Groups:** 32

Date of Accounts	Dec 11	Dec 10	Dec 09
Sales Turnover	277m	282m	271m
Pre Tax Profit/Loss	2m	6m	-23m
Working Capital	17m	20m	27m
Fixed Assets	59m	62m	65m
Current Assets	100m	98m	104m
Current Liabilities	11m	13m	12m

Swinton Electro Plating Lancs Ltd
Royal Oak Works Oak Street, Swinton, Manchester, M27 4FL
Tel: 0161-794 8426 **Fax:** 0161-794 0155
E-mail: sales@swintonplating.com
Website: http://www.swintonplating.com
Directors: G. Evans (MD)
Ultimate Holding Company: DORSET INDUSTRIES LIMITED
Immediate Holding Company: SWINTON ELECTRO-PLATING (LANCS) LIMITED
Registration no: 00723561 **Date established:** 1962
No.of Employees: 21 - 50 **Product Groups:** 46, 48

Date of Accounts	Dec 11	Dec 10	Dec 09
Working Capital	311	150	363
Fixed Assets	84	110	88
Current Assets	1m	848	917

Swinton Holdings Ltd
Swinton House 6 Great Marlborough Street, Manchester, M1 5SW
Tel: 0161-236 1222 **Fax:** 0161-237 9214
Website: http://www.swinton.co.uk
Directors: S. Hargreaves (Co Sec)
Ultimate Holding Company: RSA INSURANCE GROUP PLC
Immediate Holding Company: SWINTON (HOLDINGS) LIMITED
Registration no: 01741892 **Date established:** 1983
Turnover: £250m - £500m **No.of Employees:** 1501 & over
Product Groups: 82

Date of Accounts	Dec 11	Dec 10	Dec 09
Sales Turnover	329m	278m	272m
Pre Tax Profit/Loss	51m	34m	36m
Working Capital	32m	-22m	-49m
Fixed Assets	120m	149m	164m
Current Assets	391m	305m	225m
Current Liabilities	358m	115m	212m

T B S Fabrications
Martens Road Irlam, Manchester, M44 5AX
Tel: 0161-775 1871 **Fax:** 0161-775 8929
E-mail: info@tbs-fabrications.com
Website: http://www.abp-tbswashrooms.co.uk
Managers: R. Nelson
Ultimate Holding Company: ABP-TBS PARTNERSHIP LIMITED
Immediate Holding Company: T.B.S. FABRICATIONS LIMITED
Registration no: 01230092 **Date established:** 1975 **Turnover:** £5m - £10m
No.of Employees: 51 - 100 **Product Groups:** 26, 30, 35, 36, 49, 66

Date of Accounts	Mar 11	Mar 10	Mar 09
Sales Turnover	7m	7m	N/A
Pre Tax Profit/Loss	153	75	202
Working Capital	2m	2m	2m
Fixed Assets	253	212	276
Current Assets	4m	4m	4m
Current Liabilities	549	464	555

T E R Calibration Ltd
2 Peel Lane Tyldesley, Manchester, M29 7QX
Tel: 01942-882275 **Fax:** 01942-897958
E-mail: al@ter.co.uk
Website: http://www.ter.co.uk
Bank(s): Nat West

Directors: S. Hibbert (Dir)
Immediate Holding Company: T E R CALIBRATION LTD.
Registration no: 07597709 **VAT No.:** 152 1866 72 **Date established:** 2011
Turnover: £1m - £2m **No.of Employees:** 11 - 20 **Product Groups:** 48, 85

Date of Accounts	Apr 10	Apr 09	Apr 08
Working Capital	-36	28	-30
Fixed Assets	171	180	157
Current Assets	227	256	296

T G Nuttall Packaging Ltd

Unit N1-N2 Central Park Estate Mosley Road, Trafford Park, Manchester, M17 1PG
Tel: 0161-872 7745 **Fax:** 0161-872 0354
E-mail: chris@nuttall-packaging.co.uk
Website: http://www.nuttall-packaging.co.uk
Bank(s): The Royal Bank of Scotland
Directors: C. Bywater (Dir), C. Bywater (MD), M. Whittaker (Dir)
Managers: R. Bradford (Sales Admin)
Ultimate Holding Company: NUTTALL PACKAGING LIMITED
Immediate Holding Company: T.G. NUTTALL PACKAGING LIMITED
Registration no: 01088106 **VAT No.:** GB 146 7231 68
Date established: 1972 **Turnover:** £2m - £5m **No.of Employees:** 21 - 50
Product Groups: 25, 26, 27, 28, 30, 33, 36, 44, 45, 48, 49, 66, 84, 85, 87

Date of Accounts	Dec 11	Dec 10	Dec 09
Working Capital	478	400	365
Fixed Assets	253	184	159
Current Assets	838	806	655
Current Liabilities	3	3	3

T & J Conservatories

35-37 Church Street Atherton, Manchester, M46 9DE
Tel: 01942-876047 **Fax:** 01942-876051
E-mail: sales@tandjconservatories.co.uk
Website: http://www.tandjconservatories.co.uk
Directors: T. Davies (Dir)
Immediate Holding Company: T + J CONSERVATORY AND WINDOW CENTRE LTD.
Registration no: 04593244 **Date established:** 2002
No.of Employees: 1 - 10 **Product Groups:** 30

Date of Accounts	Dec 11	Dec 10	Mar 10
Working Capital	N/A	N/A	1
Fixed Assets	9	9	11
Current Assets	44	11	70

T Stensby & Co. Ltd

1 Shudehill, Manchester, M4 2AF
Tel: 0161-834 6589 **Fax:** 0161-834 6589
E-mail: info@stensby.co.uk
Website: http://www.stensby.co.uk
Directors: A. Bayley (MD)
Immediate Holding Company: T. STENSBY & CO. LIMITED
Registration no: 00555147 **Date established:** 1955
No.of Employees: 1 - 10 **Product Groups:** 36, 39, 40

Date of Accounts	Mar 07	Mar 06	Mar 05
Working Capital	-65	-58	-53
Fixed Assets	180	181	181
Current Assets	27	29	28
Current Liabilities	92	88	81
Total Share Capital	8	8	8

Tecflo Ltd

Unit C Highfield Industrial Estate Highfield Road, Little Hulton, Manchester, M38 9ST
Tel: 0161-703 7185 **Fax:** 0161-703 7186
E-mail: info@tec-flo.co.uk
Website: http://www.tec-flo.co.uk
Directors: M. Whittaker (Dir)
Immediate Holding Company: TECFLO LIMITED
Registration no: 01977972 **Date established:** 1986
No.of Employees: 1 - 10 **Product Groups:** 38, 42

Date of Accounts	Feb 12	Feb 11	Feb 10
Working Capital	426	424	358
Fixed Assets	53	67	67
Current Assets	625	612	509

Techmarkets Manchester Ltd

Fourth Avenue Trafford Park, Manchester, M17 1DB
Tel: 0161-876 4125 **Fax:** 0161-876 4146
E-mail: techmarkets@btconnect.com
Website: http://www.techmarkets.co.uk
Bank(s): National Westminster Bank Plc
Directors: B. Hammond (Dir), D. Chell (Co Sec)
Immediate Holding Company: TECHMARKETS (MANCHESTER) LIMITED
Registration no: 02324603 **VAT No.:** GB 511 6812 72
Date established: 1988 **Turnover:** £1m - £2m **No.of Employees:** 11 - 20
Product Groups: 30, 35, 66

Date of Accounts	Mar 11	Mar 10	Mar 09
Working Capital	-88	-223	-234
Fixed Assets	1m	1m	1m
Current Assets	406	387	305

Tekhniseal Ltd

Unit 1 Allbion Business Centre Priestley Road, Worsley, Manchester, M28 2LY
Tel: 0161-794 6063 **Fax:** 0161-794 4773
E-mail: sales@tekhniseal.com
Website: http://www.tekhniseal.com
Directors: H. Haslam (Fin)
Immediate Holding Company: TEKHNISEAL LIMITED
Registration no: 02024647 **VAT No.:** GB 437 6785 07
Date established: 1986 **Turnover:** £250,000 - £500,000
No.of Employees: 1 - 10 **Product Groups:** 29, 30, 31, 33, 34, 35, 36, 38, 39, 40

Date of Accounts	Dec 11	Dec 10	Dec 09
Working Capital	-14	-13	-1
Fixed Assets	16	18	21
Current Assets	99	112	97

Tenmat Ltd (Head Office)

Ashburton Road West Trafford Park, Manchester, M17 1RU
Tel: 0161-872 2181 **Fax:** 0161-872 7596
E-mail: info@tenmat.com
Website: http://www.tenmat.com
Bank(s): Barclays
Directors: A. Moore (MD)
Ultimate Holding Company: MODULAR STOCK LIMITED
Immediate Holding Company: TENMAT LIMITED
Registration no: 03342498 **VAT No.:** GB 951 7690 01
Date established: 1997 **Turnover:** £20m - £50m
No.of Employees: 101 - 250 **Product Groups:** 30, 32, 33, 35, 39, 40, 42, 48, 66, 67

Date of Accounts	Jul 10	Jul 11	Aug 08
Sales Turnover	19m	24m	19m
Pre Tax Profit/Loss	2m	8m	5m
Working Capital	1m	5m	5m
Fixed Assets	6m	6m	7m
Current Assets	6m	9m	9m
Current Liabilities	1m	2m	2m

D Tetlow

9 Savio Way Middleton, Manchester, M24 1FZ
Tel: 0161-626 2782 **Fax:** 0161-626 2782
E-mail: tetlow4@aol.com
Directors: D. Tetlow (Prop)
Date established: 2000 **No.of Employees:** 1 - 10 **Product Groups:** 35

The Textile Institute

1st Floor St James Building 79 Oxford Street, Manchester, M1 6FQ
Tel: 0161-237 1188 **Fax:** 0161-236 1991
E-mail: tiihq@textileinst.org.uk
Website: http://www.textileinstitute.org
Directors: R. Unsworth (MD)
Immediate Holding Company: CASCADE FINANCIAL LIMITED
Registration no: 00839425 **VAT No.:** GB 146 6379 41
Date established: 2011 **Turnover:** £500,000 - £1m
No.of Employees: 1 - 10 **Product Groups:** 80, 87

Thomas Kneale & Company Ltd

Arbry House 6 Piccadilly Trading Estate, Manchester, M1 2NP
Tel: 0161-274 4464
E-mail: info@thomaskneale.co.uk
Website: http://www.thomaskneale.co.uk
Managers: C. Sherriff
Date established: 1947 **No.of Employees:** 11 - 20 **Product Groups:** 24, 26, 63

Thorn Lighting (Northern Region) Ltd

The Towers Wilmslow Road, Manchester, M20 2SE
Tel: 0161-448 0505
Directors: S. Island (Dir)
No.of Employees: 1 - 10 **Product Groups:** 37, 67

3i Group plc

3 Hardman Street, Manchester, M3 3HF
Tel: 0161-839 3131 **Fax:** 0161-833 9182
E-mail: manchester@3i.com
Website: http://www.3i.com
Directors: K. Parker (Ptnr), K. Parry (MD)
Managers: J. Morris (Mktg Serv Mgr)
Immediate Holding Company: 3I GROUP PLC
Registration no: 01142830 **Date established:** 1973
No.of Employees: 1 - 10 **Product Groups:** 82

Thyssenkrupp Aerospace

Bankfield Road Tyldesley, Manchester, M29 8QH
Tel: 0161-911 2800 **Fax:** 0161-911 2899
Website: http://www.alcoa.com
Managers: G. Lowe (Mgr)
Immediate Holding Company: ONE PRODUCTS LTD
Date established: 2000 **No.of Employees:** 21 - 50 **Product Groups:** 34, 36

Date of Accounts	Aug 11	Aug 10	Aug 09
Working Capital	190	136	97
Fixed Assets	4	13	24
Current Assets	1m	1m	890
Current Liabilities	236	139	62

Tie Rack Ltd

Terminal 1, Manchester, M90 3XG
Tel: 0161-498 9620
Managers: S. Atkinsons (Mgr)
Immediate Holding Company: TIE RACK LIMITED
Registration no: 01524977 **Date established:** 1980 **Turnover:** £1m - £2m
No.of Employees: 1 - 10 **Product Groups:** 24, 49

Tile Mart

165a Great Ducie Street, Manchester, M3 1FF
Tel: 0161-839 1777 **Fax:** 0161-839 1777
Managers: L. Ishmale, L. Ishmale
No.of Employees: 1 - 10 **Product Groups:** 33, 40

Timpson Ltd

Timpson House Claverton Road, Roundthorn Industrial Estate, Manchester, M23 9TT
Tel: 0161-946 6200 **Fax:** 0161-946 0135
E-mail: callcentre@timpsonlocksmiths.co.uk
Website: http://www.bbg.co.uk
Directors: J. Timpson (MD)
Managers: J. Martin (Mgr)
Ultimate Holding Company: Offerhappy Ltd
Immediate Holding Company: TIMPSON LIMITED
Registration no: 00675216 **Date established:** 1960 **Turnover:** £2m - £5m
No.of Employees: 1 - 10 **Product Groups:** 36, 52, 66, 86

Date of Accounts	Sep 09	Sep 08	Sep 07
Sales Turnover	87m	84m	81m
Pre Tax Profit/Loss	5m	-189	8m
Working Capital	19m	14m	16m
Fixed Assets	31m	31m	31m
Current Assets	52m	36m	36m
Current Liabilities	8m	8m	8m

Touchstar Technologies Ltd

7 Commerce Way Trafford Park, Manchester, M17 1HW
Tel: 0161-874 5050 **Fax:** 0161-874 5088
E-mail: mark.hardy@touchstar.co.uk
Website: http://www.touchstar.co.uk
Directors: J. Austin (Sales)
Managers: N. Rouke (Comptroller), M. Turner (Mktg Serv Mgr), W. Shipman (Buyer)
Ultimate Holding Company: BELGRAVIUM TECHNOLOGIES PLC
Immediate Holding Company: TOUCHSTAR TECHNOLOGIES LIMITED
Registration no: 04731086 **Date established:** 2003 **Turnover:** £5m - £10m
No.of Employees: 21 - 50 **Product Groups:** 39, 44

Date of Accounts	Dec 11	Dec 10	Dec 09
Sales Turnover	8m	6m	5m
Pre Tax Profit/Loss	1m	438	419
Working Capital	4m	3m	5m
Fixed Assets	309	258	299
Current Assets	7m	6m	8m
Current Liabilities	1m	2m	866

Townson Mercer Ltd

Unit C1 Longford Industrial Trading Estate, Thomas Street, Stretford, Manchester, M32 0JT
Tel: 0845-2571053 **Fax:** 0845-2571054
E-mail: info@townson-mercer.co.uk
Website: http://www.townson-mercer.co.uk
Registration no: 04885349 **No.of Employees:** 11 - 20
Product Groups: 28, 30, 37, 38, 42, 46, 65, 67, 84

Trafford Lifting Services Ltd

Unit 2-Naval Street, Manchester, M4 6AX
Tel: 0161-205 9317 **Fax:** 0161-205 8569
E-mail: j.stapleton@trafford-lifting.co.uk
Website: http://www.trafford-lifting.co.uk
Directors: A. Spiteri (Works), J. Stapleton (MD)
Immediate Holding Company: TRAFFORD LIFTING SERVICES LIMITED
Registration no: 01186290 **Date established:** 1974
Turnover: Up to £250,000 **No.of Employees:** 1 - 10 **Product Groups:** 35, 39, 45

Date of Accounts	Dec 10	Dec 09	Dec 08
Sales Turnover	206	234	334
Pre Tax Profit/Loss	-14	1	4
Working Capital	27	131	124
Fixed Assets	26	50	58
Current Assets	140	165	163

Trafford Rubber Products

Greengate Works Broadoak Industrial Estate, Trafford Park, Manchester, M17 1RW
Tel: 0161-873 7172 **Fax:** 0161-848 9762
E-mail: website@traffordrubberproducts.co.uk
Website: http://www.traffordrubber.com
Directors: L. Birkett (Fin), L. Cotton (Chief Op Offcr)
Managers: C. Matthews (Sales Prom Mgr), S. Lowes
Immediate Holding Company: TRAFFORD RUBBER PRODUCTS LIMITED
Registration no: 01980202 **VAT No.:** GB 437 6928 11
Date established: 1986 **Turnover:** £2m - £5m **No.of Employees:** 21 - 50
Product Groups: 27, 29, 37

Date of Accounts	Dec 11	Dec 10	Dec 09
Working Capital	648	611	525
Fixed Assets	1m	1m	1m
Current Assets	2m	1m	1m

Transcript Services

7 Oakcliffe Road Baguley, Manchester, M23 1DA
Tel: 0161-945 6188
E-mail: carol@transcript-services.co.uk
Website: http://www.transcript-services.co.uk
Directors: C. Dicello (Prop)
Date established: 2000 **Turnover:** Up to £250,000
No.of Employees: 1 - 10 **Product Groups:** 80

Transformation

413 Bury Old Road Prestwich, Manchester, M25 1PS
Tel: 0161-773 4477 **Fax:** 0161-773 6358
E-mail: info@tranformation.co.uk
Website: http://www.transformationshops.co.co.uk
Directors: S. Booth (MD)
Ultimate Holding Company: GLOBAL INVESTMENT GROUP PLC
Immediate Holding Company: CDC (RETAIL) LIMITED
Registration no: 03323202 **Date established:** 1997
Turnover: £500,000 - £1m **No.of Employees:** 11 - 20 **Product Groups:** 61

Date of Accounts	Mar 10	Mar 09	Mar 08
Sales Turnover	609	701	708
Pre Tax Profit/Loss	21	28	8
Working Capital	200	177	145
Fixed Assets	10	12	16
Current Assets	1m	1m	1m
Current Liabilities	17	12	24

The Translation People Limited

Adamson House Towers Business Park Wilmslow Road, Manchester, M20 2YY
Tel: 0845-6430489 **Fax:** 0870-759 8449
E-mail: manchester@thetranslationpeople.com
Website: http://www.thetranslationpeople.com
Directors: S. Wilde (MD)
Managers: L. Athey (Ops Mgr)
Registration no: 06646116 **Date established:** 2009 **Turnover:** £2m - £5m
No.of Employees: 1 - 10 **Product Groups:** 80

Travis Perkins plc

281 Liverpool Road Eccles, Manchester, M30 0QN
Tel: 0161-789 2631 **Fax:** 0161-787 7579
E-mail: jim.nuttall@travisperkins.co.uk
Website: http://www.travisperkins.co.uk
Managers: J. Nuttell (District Mgr)
Immediate Holding Company: TRAVIS PERKINS PLC
Registration no: 00824821 **Date established:** 1964
Turnover: Up to £250,000 **No.of Employees:** 1 - 10 **Product Groups:** 66

Date of Accounts	Dec 11	Dec 10	Dec 09
Sales Turnover	4779m	3153m	2931m
Pre Tax Profit/Loss	270m	197m	213m
Working Capital	133m	159m	248m
Fixed Assets	2771m	2749m	2108m
Current Assets	1421m	1329m	1035m
Current Liabilities	473m	412m	109m

Trendsetter Home Furnishings Ltd

Cobra Court 10 Blackmore Road, Trafford Park, Manchester, M32 0QY
Tel: 0161-864 5610 **Fax:** 0161-865 0133
E-mail: sales@trendsetter.co.uk
Website: http://www.the-fine-bedding-company.co.uk
Directors: M. Crichton (Fin), P. Wagstaff (Chief Op Offcr), R. Black (Ch), C. Black (Sales & Mktg)
Managers: B. Suttcliffe (Chief Acct)
Registration no: 01298570 **VAT No.:** GB 562 4806 36
Date established: 1977 **Turnover:** £10m - £20m
No.of Employees: 101 - 250 **Product Groups:** 24

Trimline Valves

6 Dales Park Drive Swinton, Manchester, M27 0FP
Tel: 0161-727 8128 **Fax:** 0161-727 9060
E-mail: harrycope@trimlinevalveslimited.co.uk
Website: http://www.trimlinevalveslimited.co.uk
Directors: H. Cope (Prop)
Registration no: 02144331 **VAT No.:** GB 451 5753 47
Turnover: Up to £250,000 **No.of Employees:** 1 - 10 **Product Groups:** 38, 40

see next page

Trimline Valves - Cont'd

Date of Accounts	Jul 08	Jul 07	Jul 06
Working Capital	20	19	27
Fixed Assets	1	1	N/A
Current Assets	37	36	46
Current Liabilities	17	16	19
Total Share Capital	10	10	10

Trumeter Co Ltd

Milltown Street Radcliffe, Manchester, M26 1NX
Tel: 0161-724 6311 **Fax:** 0161-724 9455
E-mail: sales@trumeter.com
Website: http://www.trumeter.com
Bank(s): HSBC Midland
Directors: R. Weidenbaum (Dir), J. Allen (MD), P. Weidenbaum (Ch)
Managers: D. Lewis (Accounts), M. O'Keeffe (Sales Prom Mgr), G. Norris (Purch Mgr)
Registration no: 00493430 **VAT No.:** GB 145 6679 35
Date established: 1937 **Turnover:** £10m - £20m
No.of Employees: 51 - 100 **Product Groups:** 30, 35, 37, 38, 39, 45, 46, 47, 49, 67, 84, 85

Date of Accounts	Apr 08	Apr 07	Apr 06
Pre Tax Profit/Loss	39	-85	106
Working Capital	-359	-331	91
Fixed Assets	1473	1686	2039
Current Assets	2804	2321	2971
Current Liabilities	3163	2652	2880
Total Share Capital	11	11	11
ROCE% (Return on Capital Employed)	3.5	-6.3	5.0

Tupman & Hainey Ltd

Louisa Street Worsley, Manchester, M28 3GA
Tel: 0161-790 2664 **Fax:** 0161-703 8435
E-mail: geoff@tupmanhainey.co.uk
Website: http://www.tupmanhainey.co.uk
Directors: G. Horrocks (MD)
Ultimate Holding Company: T & H PROPERTIES LIMITED
Immediate Holding Company: TUPMAN & HAINEY LIMITED
Registration no: 00566844 **VAT No.:** GB 146 5381 59
Date established: 1956 **Turnover:** £500,000 - £1m
No.of Employees: 1 - 10 **Product Groups:** 48

Date of Accounts	Dec 09	Dec 08	May 11
Working Capital	97	107	54
Fixed Assets	58	57	46
Current Assets	243	275	225

Turboflame Ltd

Unit 68 792 Wilmslow Road, Manchester, M20 6UG
Tel: 0161-428 1077 **Fax:** 0161-428 7692
E-mail: enquieries@turboflame.co.uk
Website: http://www.turboflame.co.uk
Directors: S. Shakarchy (MD)
Registration no: 05198202 **Date established:** 2000
No.of Employees: 1 - 10 **Product Groups:** 49

Tyco

Tyco Park Grimshaw Lane, Manchester, M40 2WL
Tel: 0161-455 4400 **Fax:** 0161-455 4541
E-mail: jandreu@tycoint.com
Website: http://www.tycofis.com
Bank(s): Barclays Bank PLC
Directors: J. Andreu (MD), M. Brough (Pers), J. Bramall (Fin)
Managers: G. Hunter (Mktg Serv Mgr), I. Monks
Ultimate Holding Company: TYCO INTERNATIONAL LIMITED (SWITZERLAND)
Immediate Holding Company: TYCO FIRE & INTEGRATED SOLUTIONS (UK) LIMITED
Registration no: 01952517 **VAT No.:** GB 416 3058 73
Date established: 1985 **Turnover:** £5m - £10m
No.of Employees: 501 - 1000 **Product Groups:** 30, 37, 39, 40, 44, 67, 80

Tyco Fire Protection Products

6 Westpoint Enterprise Park Clarence Avenue, Trafford Park, Manchester, M17 1QS
Tel: 0161-875 0400 **Fax:** 0161-875 0509
E-mail: jtingle@tyco-bspd.com
Website: http://www.centralsprinkler.com
Directors: C. Owen (Co Sec), S. Broadley (Dir)
Managers: B. Sheeran (Sales Admin), G. Wells (Mgr), K. Scourfield (Mgr)
Immediate Holding Company: RUSSELLS PROPERTY LLP
Registration no: 02559027 **VAT No.:** GB 555 1027 64
Date established: 2006 **Turnover:** £10m - £20m **No.of Employees:** 1 - 10
Product Groups: 32, 40

Date of Accounts	Sep 07	Sep 06	Sep 05
Sales Turnover	11128	9920	25591
Pre Tax Profit/Loss	2292	1827	1154
Working Capital	7899	5064	3275
Fixed Assets	43	64	93
Current Assets	12070	10216	14568
Current Liabilities	4171	5152	11293
Total Share Capital	501	501	501
ROCE% (Return on Capital Employed)	28.9	35.6	34.3
ROT% (Return on Turnover)	20.6	18.4	4.5

Tye Mann Limited

Customer Services Po Box 411, Manchester, M16 0YB
Tel: 0845-6521505 **Fax:** 0845-6521505
E-mail: enquiries@homme-rock.com
Website: http://www.homme-rock.com
Managers: J. Tye (Accounts)
Registration no: 05933222 **Date established:** 2006
Turnover: Up to £250,000 **No.of Employees:** 1 - 10 **Product Groups:** 24

Date of Accounts	Sep 09	Sep 08	Sep 07
Working Capital	4	4	4
Current Assets	8	8	4

Universal Container Services Ltd

Unit 12 Barton Industrial Estate Eccles, Manchester, M30 7RT
Tel: 08450-500330 **Fax:** 0161-775 9079
E-mail: george.woolley@universal-containers.com
Website: http://www.universal-containers.com
Directors: D. Holmes (Co Sec), G. Woolley (Dir)
Managers: G. Tarburton
Immediate Holding Company: UNIVERSAL CONTAINER SERVICES LIMITED
Registration no: 02565098 **Date established:** 1990
Turnover: Up to £250,000 **No.of Employees:** 21 - 50 **Product Groups:** 24, 26, 33, 54, 76

Date of Accounts	Dec 11	Dec 10	Dec 09
Working Capital	2m	2m	2m
Fixed Assets	247	189	117
Current Assets	3m	2m	2m

University Of Manchester Incubator Company Ltd

48 Grafton Street, Manchester, M13 9XX
Tel: 0161-606 7200 **Fax:** 0161-606 7300
E-mail: yvonne.loughlin@umic.co.uk
Website: http://www.umic.co.uk
Managers: Y. Loughlin
Ultimate Holding Company: UNIVERSITY OF MANCHESTER
Immediate Holding Company: MANCHESTER INNOVATION LIMITED
Registration no: 01594344 **Date established:** 1981
Turnover: £500,000 - £1m **No.of Employees:** 11 - 20 **Product Groups:** 86

Date of Accounts	Jul 11	Jul 10	Jul 09
Sales Turnover	516	516	707
Pre Tax Profit/Loss	-10	-13	108
Working Capital	-2m	-2m	-2m
Fixed Assets	23m	24m	24m
Current Assets	347	349	353
Current Liabilities	361	363	362

Vacuum Engineering Services Ltd

St Modwen Road Stretford, Manchester, M32 0ZE
Tel: 0161-866 8860 **Fax:** 0161-866 8861
E-mail: info@vac-eng.com
Website: http://www.vac-eng.com
Directors: E. Garner (Sales), G. Benson (MD), S. Derbyshire (Purch)
Immediate Holding Company: VACUUM ENGINEERING SERVICES LIMITED
Registration no: 02897361 **Date established:** 1994 **Turnover:** £2m - £5m
No.of Employees: 21 - 50 **Product Groups:** 38, 40, 48

Date of Accounts	Mar 11	Mar 10	Mar 09
Working Capital	633	716	571
Fixed Assets	155	161	191
Current Assets	947	1m	1m
Current Liabilities	85	182	450

Vacuum Scientific Services Ltd

44 Ellesmere Street, Manchester, M15 4JY
Tel: 0161-833 9108 **Fax:** 0161-835 1443
E-mail: mail@vacuum-scientific.com
Website: http://www.vacuum-scientific.com
Directors: H. Bance (MD), P. Bance (Fin)
Immediate Holding Company: VACUUM SCIENTIFIC SERVICES LIMITED
Registration no: 01528740 **Date established:** 1980
Turnover: Up to £250,000 **No.of Employees:** 1 - 10 **Product Groups:** 38, 40, 48

Date of Accounts	Dec 10	Dec 08	Dec 07
Working Capital	11	7	11
Fixed Assets	7	7	7
Current Assets	21	63	49

Valves Instruments Plus Ltd

Chaddock Lane Astley, Tyldesley, Manchester, M29 7JT
Tel: 01942-885700 **Fax:** 0161-832 8099
E-mail: sales@vip-ltd.co.uk
Website: http://www.vip-ltd.co.uk
Bank(s): Royal Bank of Scotland
Directors: K. Wood (Fin), S. Wood (MD)
Immediate Holding Company: VALVES INSTRUMENTS PLUS LIMITED
Registration no: 01909945 **Date established:** 1985 **Turnover:** £1m - £2m
No.of Employees: 11 - 20 **Product Groups:** 36, 38

Date of Accounts	Mar 12	Mar 11	Mar 10
Working Capital	85	103	125
Fixed Assets	83	92	107
Current Assets	1m	1m	976

Veolia Environmental Services Ltd

Second Avenue Trafford Park, Manchester, M17 1DZ
Tel: 0161-877 5017 **Fax:** 0161-877 5019
Website: http://www.veoilaenvironmentalservices.co.uk
Managers: P. Makinson (Mgr)
Immediate Holding Company: VEOLIA ENVIRONMENTAL SERVICES (UK) PLC
Registration no: 02215767 **Date established:** 1988
No.of Employees: 51 - 100 **Product Groups:** 34, 39, 42, 54

Victoria Veneered Doors Ltd

20-21 Long Wood Road Trafford Park, Manchester, M17 1PZ
Tel: 0161-877 8612 **Fax:** 0161-848 7970
Directors: P. Babington (Dir)
Immediate Holding Company: VICTORIA VENEERED DOORS LIMITED
Registration no: 02825567 **Date established:** 1993
No.of Employees: 1 - 10 **Product Groups:** 26, 35

Date of Accounts	Jun 11	Jun 10	Jun 09
Working Capital	34	76	64
Current Assets	120	173	126

Videonations Ltd

Unit 20, Edward Court Altrincham Business Park, Altrincham, Manchester, WA14 5GL
Tel: 0845-084 3010 **Fax:** 0845-084 3020
E-mail: info@videonations.com
Website: http://www.videonations.com
Directors: I. Carter (MD)
Registration no: 03821559 **Turnover:** £1m - £2m
No.of Employees: 1 - 10 **Product Groups:** 37, 38, 40, 44, 67, 80

Date of Accounts	Sep 08	Sep 07	Sep 06
Sales Turnover	N/A	2723	1609
Pre Tax Profit/Loss	N/A	579	116
Working Capital	482	668	379
Fixed Assets	818	803	72
Current Assets	1381	1200	691
Current Liabilities	899	532	312
ROCE% (Return on Capital Employed)		39.4	25.7
ROT% (Return on Turnover)		21.3	7.2

Vita Liquid Polymers

Harling Road Sharston Industrial Area, Manchester, M22 4SZ
Tel: 0161-998 3226 **Fax:** 0161-946 0118
E-mail: info@vita-liquid.co.uk
Website: http://www.vita-liquid.co.uk
Bank(s): Lloyds TSB Bank plc
Directors: I. Bragg (Fin), G. Maundrell (Dir)
Managers: A. Murray (Purch Mgr), D. Bishop (Tech Serv Mgr)
Ultimate Holding Company: VITA CAYMAN LIMITED (CAYMAN ISLANDS)
Immediate Holding Company: VITA LIQUID POLYMERS LIMITED
Registration no: 00268760 **Date established:** 1932
Turnover: £10m - £20m **No.of Employees:** 51 - 100 **Product Groups:** 02, 22, 23, 24, 26, 27, 29, 30, 31, 32, 33, 36, 38, 39, 40, 41, 42, 47, 48, 66, 68, 72

Date of Accounts	Dec 11	Dec 10	Dec 09
Sales Turnover	19m	14m	15m
Pre Tax Profit/Loss	-229	-645	543
Working Capital	8m	6m	5m
Fixed Assets	746	738	297
Current Assets	12m	11m	8m
Current Liabilities	287	210	430

Vitco Ltd

Vitco House 58 Derby Street, Manchester, M8 8HF
Tel: 0161-834 3579 **Fax:** 0161-834 0471
E-mail: admin@vitco.co.uk
Website: http://www.vitco.co.uk
Directors: P. Vithlani (MD), D. Vithlani (MD)
Immediate Holding Company: VITCO LIMITED
Registration no: 01485864 **Date established:** 1980
No.of Employees: 21 - 50 **Product Groups:** 24, 40, 63

Date of Accounts	Dec 10	Dec 09	Dec 08
Working Capital	-425	-225	-132
Fixed Assets	2m	2m	2m
Current Assets	624	816	874

Vitec (British Vita)

Oldham Road Middleton, Manchester, M24 2DB
Tel: 0161-643 1133 **Fax:** 0161-654 8942
E-mail: info@vcfuk.com
Website: http://www.vitecuk.com
Bank(s): National Westminster Bank Plc
Managers: D. Darkins (Ops Mgr)
Ultimate Holding Company: BRITISH VITA UNLIMITED
Registration no: 01557037 **VAT No.:** GB 606 3421 71
Date established: 1981 **Turnover:** £5m - £10m **No.of Employees:** 21 - 50
Product Groups: 22, 27, 29, 30, 32, 33, 36, 42, 49, 68

W A Cooke & Sons

Ellesmere Works Southern Street, Worsley, Manchester, M28 3QN
Tel: 01204-574721 **Fax:** 01204-861778
E-mail: admin@wacooke.co.uk
Website: http://www.wacooke.co.uk
Directors: S. Cooke (MD)
Ultimate Holding Company: W.A. COOKE AND SONS ENGINEERS (ESTABLISHED 1926) LIMITED
Immediate Holding Company: W.A. COOKE & SONS (SITE SERVICES) LIMITED
Registration no: 01573639 **VAT No.:** GB 323 9062 71
Date established: 1981 **Turnover:** £1m - £2m **No.of Employees:** 21 - 50
Product Groups: 35, 48, 52

Date of Accounts	Dec 11	Dec 10	Dec 09
Working Capital	116	109	64
Fixed Assets	29	37	39
Current Assets	704	478	342

W Y G Engineering Ltd

Quay West Trafford Wharf Road, Trafford Park, Manchester, M17 1HH
Tel: 0161-872 3223 **Fax:** 0161-872 3193
E-mail: info@wyg.com
Website: http://www.wyg.com
Bank(s): Lloyds TSB Bank plc
Directors: A. Fuller (MD)
Ultimate Holding Company: WYG PLC
Immediate Holding Company: WYG ENGINEERING LIMITED
Registration no: 01959704 **Date established:** 1985
Turnover: £20m - £50m **No.of Employees:** 51 - 100 **Product Groups:** 42, 54, 80, 81, 84, 85

Date of Accounts	Mar 12	Mar 11	Jun 10
Sales Turnover	17m	24m	53m
Pre Tax Profit/Loss	-243	-21m	4m
Working Capital	15m	225	5m
Fixed Assets	N/A	N/A	22m
Current Assets	20m	6m	16m
Current Liabilities	4m	6m	9m

Walkers Instore

Crabtree Lane Clayton, Manchester, M11 1BR
Tel: 0161-223 7814 **Fax:** 0161-231 7212
E-mail: gary.herrington@walkers-of-manchester.co.uk
Website: http://www.walkersinstore.co.uk
Bank(s): The Royal Bank of Scotland
Directors: G. Herrington (MD), S. Currigan (Co Sec)
Ultimate Holding Company: BEALAW (MAN) 31 LIMITED
Immediate Holding Company: WALKERS MCR LIMITED
Registration no: 00303014 **VAT No.:** GB 673 6050 34
Date established: 1935 **No.of Employees:** 21 - 50 **Product Groups:** 27, 28, 37, 40, 49

Date of Accounts	Apr 07	Apr 06	Apr 05
Pre Tax Profit/Loss	430	447	503
Working Capital	3m	2m	2m
Fixed Assets	2m	2m	1m
Current Assets	6m	4m	3m
Current Liabilities	2m	518	417

Washington Mills Electro Minerals Ltd

Mosley Road Trafford Park, Manchester, M17 1NR
Tel: 0161-848 0271 **Fax:** 0161-872 2974
E-mail: sales@washingtonmills.co.uk
Website: http://www.washingtonmills.co.uk
Bank(s): National Westminster Bank Plc
Directors: R. Painter (MD)
Managers: K. Hine (Comptroller), P. Johnson (Personnel)
Ultimate Holding Company: WASHINGTON MILLS COMPANY (USA)
Immediate Holding Company: WASHINGTON MILLS ELECTRO MINERALS LIMITED
Registration no: 01436144 **VAT No.:** GB 383 3896 10
Date established: 1979 **Turnover:** £10m - £20m
No.of Employees: 51 - 100 **Product Groups:** 33, 39, 48

Date of Accounts	Dec 11	Dec 10	Dec 09
Sales Turnover	14m	16m	12m
Pre Tax Profit/Loss	-268	-2	-1m
Working Capital	8m	8m	8m
Fixed Assets	1m	1m	1m
Current Assets	10m	13m	12m
Current Liabilities	58	73	88

Watkins Hire Ltd
48 Grange Park Road, Manchester, M9 7AH
Tel: 0161-795 8666 **Fax:** 0161-795 8008
E-mail: mark.whittle@watkinshire.co.uk
Website: http://www.watkinshire.co.uk
Directors: M. Whittle (Prop)
Immediate Holding Company: WATKINS HIRE LIMITED
Registration no: 03599314 **Date established:** 1998
Turnover: £10m - £20m **No.of Employees:** 1 - 10 **Product Groups:** 39, 40

Weir Materials & Foundries
Park Works Grimshaw Lane, Newton Heath, Manchester, M40 2BA
Tel: 0161-203 4262 **Fax:** 0161-954 4739
E-mail: wmlinfo@wml.weir.co.uk
Website: http://www.weirclearliquid.com
Bank(s): Royal Bank of Scotland
Directors: G. Byrne (Sales & Tech), A. Hollis (MD)
Ultimate Holding Company: The Weir Group P.L.C.
Registration no: SC107219 **Date established:** 1988
Turnover: £10m - £20m **No.of Employees:** 101 - 250
Product Groups: 36, 45, 67

Robert Werner Ltd
Rex Mill Don Street, Middleton, Manchester, M24 2GG
Tel: 0161-653 0000 **Fax:** 0161- 6531000
Directors: A. Nassimi (MD), C. Hannah (MD)
Registration no: 01539870 **VAT No.:** GB 306 4916 63
Date established: 1981 **Turnover:** Up to £250,000
No.of Employees: 1 - 10 **Product Groups:** 61

Date of Accounts	Dec 05
Working Capital	-861
Fixed Assets	23
Current Assets	57
Current Liabilities	918
Total Share Capital	449

West & Senior Ltd
Milltown Street Radcliffe, Manchester, M26 1WE
Tel: 0161-724 7131 **Fax:** 0161-724 9519
E-mail: info@westsenior.co.uk
Website: http://www.westsenior.co.uk
Bank(s): Barclays
Directors: D. Brown (Fin), S. Senior (MD)
Immediate Holding Company: WEST & SENIOR LIMITED
Registration no: 00508673 **VAT No.:** GB 147 8950 25
Date established: 1952 **Turnover:** £10m - £20m
No.of Employees: 51 - 100 **Product Groups:** 32

Date of Accounts	May 12	May 11	May 10
Sales Turnover	12m	10m	8m
Pre Tax Profit/Loss	682	310	332
Working Capital	1m	1m	884
Fixed Assets	2m	2m	2m
Current Assets	3m	3m	3m
Current Liabilities	821	233	285

West Village Ltd
48 Broughton Street, Manchester, M8 8NN
Tel: 0161-834 6509 **Fax:** 0161-834 9452
E-mail: xited@hotmail.co.uk
Website: http://www.x-ited.co.uk
Directors: K. Banga (Dir), S. Modlin (Co Sec)
Immediate Holding Company: X-ITED (M/CR) LIMITED
Registration no: 5899703 **Date established:** 2008
No.of Employees: 1 - 10 **Product Groups:**

Westwood Security Shutters Ltd
24 Ardwick Green South, Manchester, M13 9XE
Tel: 0161-272 9333
E-mail: info@rollershutter.co.uk
Website: http://www.rollershutter.co.uk
Directors: M. Dinnie (MD)
Immediate Holding Company: WESTWOOD SECURITY SHUTTERS LIMITED
Registration no: 04128851 **Date established:** 2000
No.of Employees: 1 - 10 **Product Groups:** 26, 35

Date of Accounts	Dec 11	Dec 10	Dec 09
Working Capital	15	-12	-15
Fixed Assets	26	25	30
Current Assets	114	102	90

J & W Whewell Ltd (Head Office)
Radcliffe, Manchester, M26 9GJ
Tel: 0161-796 6333 **Fax:** 0161-766 3017
E-mail: sales@jwwhewell.co.uk
Website: http://www.jwwhewell.co.uk
Bank(s): The Royal Bank of Scotland
Directors: J. Walker (MD)
Ultimate Holding Company: WALKER BROTHERS BURY LIMITED
Immediate Holding Company: J AND W WHEWELL LIMITED
Registration no: 00221593 **VAT No.:** GB 707 7980 01
Date established: 2027 **Turnover:** £2m - £5m **No.of Employees:** 11 - 20
Product Groups: 31, 32, 42, 43, 63, 66

Date of Accounts	Dec 11	Dec 10	Dec 09
Working Capital	1m	807	626
Fixed Assets	441	524	482
Current Assets	2m	2m	1m

White Recyling Ltd
New Hall Farm Liverpool Road, Eccles, Manchester, M30 7LJ
Tel: 0161-789 3268 **Fax:** 0161-707 5909
E-mail: info@thewhitegroup.co.uk
Website: http://www.thewhitegroup.co.uk
Bank(s): National Westminster Bank Plc
Directors: D. White (MD), C. Naylon (Comm)
Managers: D. Wilde, K. Deighan (Tech Serv Mgr), L. Galloway (Sales Prom Mgr), S. Fowler
Ultimate Holding Company: WHITE GROUP HOLDINGS LIMITED
Immediate Holding Company: WHITE RECYCLING LIMITED
Registration no: 00596397 **VAT No.:** GB 147 2441 76
Date established: 1958 **Turnover:** £10m - £20m
No.of Employees: 51 - 100 **Product Groups:** 66

Date of Accounts	Sep 11	Sep 10	Sep 09
Sales Turnover	11m	11m	11m
Pre Tax Profit/Loss	47	-172	61
Working Capital	-3m	-2m	-1m
Fixed Assets	6m	5m	4m
Current Assets	3m	3m	3m
Current Liabilities	2m	1m	2m

Wilkinson Star
Shield Drive Wardley Industrial Estate, Worsley, Manchester, M28 2WD
Tel: 0161-728 7900 **Fax:** 0161-727 8297
E-mail: steve.murray@wilkinsonstar.com
Website: http://www.wilkinsonstar.com
Directors: E. Wilkinson (Co Sec), S. Murray (Dir), P. Snape (Fin)
Managers: C. Ashcroft, A. Smith (Transport), S. Ross (Sales Prom Mgr), J. Kelly (Mktg Serv Mgr)
Ultimate Holding Company: THE WILKINSON CORPORATION LIMITED
Immediate Holding Company: WILKINSON STAR LIMITED
Registration no: 01768127 **Date established:** 1983 **Turnover:** £5m - £10m
No.of Employees: 51 - 100 **Product Groups:** 67

Date of Accounts	Nov 11	Nov 10	Nov 09
Sales Turnover	8m	8m	7m
Pre Tax Profit/Loss	100	109	-295
Working Capital	3m	3m	2m
Fixed Assets	311	365	419
Current Assets	8m	7m	7m
Current Liabilities	3m	3m	3m

Wisla Narrow Fabrics
Unit 1 Littlemoss Road Droylsden, Manchester, M43 7EF
Tel: 0161-301 4747 **Fax:** 0161-301 5757
E-mail: info@wisla-webbings.co.uk
Website: http://www.wisla-webbings.co.uk
Directors: E. Kozaczek (MD)
Immediate Holding Company: WISLA NARROW FABRICS LIMITED
Registration no: 05184655 **Date established:** 2004 **Turnover:** £5m - £10m
No.of Employees: 11 - 20 **Product Groups:** 23, 29, 33, 43

Date of Accounts	Dec 11	Dec 10	Dec 09
Working Capital	100	211	182
Fixed Assets	154	190	229
Current Assets	310	380	409

Wolseley UK Limited
Unit 14 Harp Road Harp Trading Estate, Trafford Park, Manchester, M17 1SR
Tel: 0161-848 0546 **Fax:** 0161-872 0265
E-mail: phil.davies@wolseley.co.uk
Website: http://www.wolseley.co.uk
Directors: G. Richardson (MD)
Managers: A. Brown (Admin Off), P. Davies (District Mgr)
Registration no: 00636445 **Turnover:** £2m - £5m
No.of Employees: 1 - 10 **Product Groups:** 40, 47, 66, 67

Richard Wood Babywear
Sherbourne Street, Manchester, M8 8HF
Tel: 0161-832 2734 **Fax:** 0161-835 1547
E-mail: rwbabywear@btconnect.com
Website: http://www.richwoodbabywear.co.uk
Directors: M. Lawton (Prop)
Immediate Holding Company: VITCO IMPORTS LIMITED
Date established: 2002 **No.of Employees:** 1 - 10 **Product Groups:** 24

World Transport Agency Ltd
Manchester International Office Centre Styal Road, Manchester, M22 5WB
Tel: 0161-493 1160 **Fax:** 0161-499 1145
E-mail: info@wta.co.uk
Website: http://www.wta.co.uk
Directors: A. Hilton (Dir)
Ultimate Holding Company: SOMMER HOLDINGS LTD
Immediate Holding Company: WORLD TRANSPORT AGENCY LIMITED
Registration no: 00129014 **VAT No.:** GB 235 9766 24
Date established: 2013 **Turnover:** Up to £250,000
No.of Employees: 1 - 10 **Product Groups:** 72, 76

Date of Accounts	Jun 11	Jun 10	Jun 09
Sales Turnover	58m	48m	48m
Pre Tax Profit/Loss	2m	1m	2m
Working Capital	3m	3m	3m
Fixed Assets	146	227	311
Current Assets	10m	10m	9m
Current Liabilities	872	477	754

Wormald Fire Systems
Wormald Park Grimshaw Lane, Manchester, M40 2WL
Tel: 0161-455 4550
Website: http://www.tycoint.com
Directors: M. Clegg (Dir)
Ultimate Holding Company: Tyco International Limited
Registration no: 01699654 **Date established:** 1983
No.of Employees: 501 - 1000 **Product Groups:** 37, 40, 84

Wrengate
Wrengate House 221 Palatine Road, Manchester, M20 2EE
Tel: 0161-438 6900 **Fax:** 0161-438 1020
E-mail: botraco@wrengate.co.uk
Website: http://www.wrengate.co.uk
Bank(s): ABN
Directors: N. Musry (Ch), R. Ruia (Jt MD), M. Ruia (Dir)
Immediate Holding Company: Wrengate Ltd
Registration no: 01172978 **VAT No.:** GB 145 2770 69
Date established: 1974 **Turnover:** £20m - £50m
No.of Employees: 1001 - 1500 **Product Groups:** 61

Date of Accounts	Apr 09	Apr 08	Apr 07
Sales Turnover	29m	26m	29m
Pre Tax Profit/Loss	408	-226	1m
Working Capital	24m	25m	29m
Fixed Assets	25m	23m	22m
Current Assets	32m	35m	39m
Current Liabilities	3m	4m	4m

Wyko Industrial Services Ltd (Manchester Service Centre)
Unit 4 Littlers Point Second Avenue, Trafford Park, Manchester, M17 1LT
Tel: 0161-872 2946 **Fax:** 0161-872 9905
E-mail: manchester@eriks.co.uk
Website: http://www.wyko.co.uk
Directors: R. Mccoellen (Prop)
Managers: R. McMullen (District Mgr)
Immediate Holding Company: WYKO INDUSTRIAL SERVICES LIMITED
Registration no: 00917112 **Date established:** 1967
Turnover: £250m - £500m **No.of Employees:** 1 - 10 **Product Groups:** 66

Morecambe

Alfa Aesar (a Johnson Matthey Co.)
Shore Road Heysham, Morecambe, LA3 2XY
Tel: 01524-850506 **Fax:** 01524-850608
E-mail: uksales@alfa.com
Website: http://www.alfa.com
Directors: S. Farrant (Co Sec)
Ultimate Holding Company: JOHNSON MATTHEY PLC
Immediate Holding Company: AVOCADO RESEARCH CHEMICALS LIMITED
Registration no: 02682211 **Date established:** 1992
Turnover: £20m - £50m **No.of Employees:** 101 - 250
Product Groups: 31, 32

Date of Accounts	Mar 12	Mar 11	Mar 10
Sales Turnover	19m	20m	18m
Pre Tax Profit/Loss	4m	4m	4m
Working Capital	-4m	552	18m
Fixed Assets	7m	7m	8m
Current Assets	27m	20m	24m
Current Liabilities	2m	2m	1m

Barclay & Mathieson Ltd
Unit 2a Southgate White Lund Industrial Estate, Morecambe, LA3 3PB
Tel: 01524-67241 **Fax:** 01524-382641
E-mail: morecambe@bmsteel.co.uk
Website: http://www.bmsteel.co.uk
Managers: S. Brainsby (Mgr)
Ultimate Holding Company: STEMCOR HOLDINGS LIMITED
Immediate Holding Company: BARCLAY & MATHIESON LIMITED
Registration no: SC030987 **VAT No.:** GB 723 9322 39
Date established: 1955 **Turnover:** £250,000 - £500,000
No.of Employees: 1 - 10 **Product Groups:** 66

Date of Accounts	Dec 11	Dec 10	Dec 09
Sales Turnover	55m	48m	35m
Pre Tax Profit/Loss	2m	2m	-865
Working Capital	11m	13m	13m
Fixed Assets	19m	16m	18m
Current Assets	24m	25m	20m
Current Liabilities	4m	5m	713

Robert Briggs & Son Lancaster Ltd
369a Lancaster Road, Morecambe, LA4 6LZ
Tel: 01524-412875 **Fax:** 01524-423739
E-mail: sales@robertbriggsandson.co.uk
Website: http://www.robertbriggsandson.co.uk
Directors: S. Briggs (MD)
Immediate Holding Company: ROBERT BRIGGS AND SON (LANCASTER) LIMITED
Registration no: 00952531 **VAT No.:** GB 155 7597 25
Date established: 1969 **Turnover:** £500,000 - £1m
No.of Employees: 1 - 10 **Product Groups:** 52

Date of Accounts	May 11	May 10	May 09
Working Capital	1m	1m	822
Fixed Assets	192	188	429
Current Assets	1m	1m	932

Exco Industries
Southgate White Lund Industrial Estate, Morecambe, LA3 3PB
Tel: 01524-388822 **Fax:** 01524-388877
Directors: D. Sallis (Sales)
Immediate Holding Company: EXCO INDUSTRIES LIMITED
Registration no: 03884213 **Date established:** 1999
No.of Employees: 1 - 10 **Product Groups:** 40, 66, 83

Date of Accounts	Apr 11	Apr 10	Apr 09
Working Capital	338	298	244
Fixed Assets	2	3	3
Current Assets	498	485	448

Fuel Proof Ltd
Middleton Business Park Middleton Road, Middleton, Morecambe, LA3 3FH
Tel: 01524-850685 **Fax:** 01524-859681
E-mail: info@fuelproof.co.uk
Website: http://www.fuelproof.co.uk
Directors: A. Hargreaves (Dir)
Managers: B. Pilkington (Tech Serv Mgr)
Immediate Holding Company: FUEL PROOF LIMITED
Registration no: 03991145 **Date established:** 2000
Turnover: Up to £250,000 **No.of Employees:** 21 - 50 **Product Groups:** 29, 38, 39, 42, 67

Date of Accounts	Dec 11	Dec 10	Dec 09
Working Capital	581	527	487
Fixed Assets	26	18	26
Current Assets	1m	1m	869

Gates Architectual Metal Work
Alice Street Works Alice Street, Morecambe, LA4 5NH
Tel: 01524-413513
E-mail: keithdugdale@yahoo.co.uk
Directors: K. Dugdale (Prop)
Date established: 2002 **No.of Employees:** 1 - 10 **Product Groups:** 35, 48

Graham The Plumber Merchants (t/a Graham Builders Merchants)
Southgate White Lund Industrial Estate, Morecambe, LA3 3PB
Tel: 01524-68881 **Fax:** 01524- 841984
E-mail: neville.buckley@graham-group.co.uk
Website: http://www.graham-group.co.uk
Managers: N. Buckley (Mgr)
Immediate Holding Company: ROOF SUPPORT SYSTEMS LIMITED
Registration no: 00066738 **VAT No.:** GB 394 1212 63
Date established: 2011 **No.of Employees:** 1 - 10 **Product Groups:** 40, 63, 66

Lines & Jones Ltd
1 Freightway Southgate, White Lund Industrial Estate, Morecambe, LA3 3PB
Tel: 01524-841260 **Fax:** 01524-841795
E-mail: sales@landj.co.uk
Website: http://www.landj.co.uk
Bank(s): HSBC
Directors: I. Kennon (Dir), P. Shelling (Co Sec)
Immediate Holding Company: LINES AND JONES,LIMITED
Registration no: 00433081 **VAT No.:** GB 154 3638 63
Date established: 1947 **Turnover:** £500,000 - £1m
No.of Employees: 11 - 20 **Product Groups:** 26, 67

see next page

Lines & Jones Ltd - Cont'd

Date of Accounts	Jun 12	Jun 11	Jun 10
Working Capital	380	347	327
Fixed Assets	379	396	422
Current Assets	614	638	612

Major Equipment Ltd

Unit 5 Major Industrial Estate Middleton Road, Middleton, Morecambe, LA3 3JJ
Tel: 01524-850501 **Fax:** 01524-850502
E-mail: ukinfo@major-equipment.com
Website: http://www.major-equipment.com
Directors: J. Murphy (Dir)
Immediate Holding Company: MAJOR EQUIPMENT LIMITED
Registration no: 02566836 **Date established:** 1990
Turnover: Up to £250,000 **No.of Employees:** 1 - 10 **Product Groups:** 41, 67

Date of Accounts	Dec 11	Dec 10	Dec 09
Working Capital	-48	-40	-48
Fixed Assets	76	67	65
Current Assets	898	1m	1m

Meters UK Ltd

Whitegate White Lund Industrial Estate, Morecambe, LA3 3BT
Tel: 01524-555929 **Fax:** 01524-847009
E-mail: sales@meters.co.uk
Website: http://www.meters.co.uk
Directors: M. Pye (MD)
Immediate Holding Company: METERS UK LTD
Registration no: 04454106 **Date established:** 2002
Turnover: £50m - £75m **No.of Employees:** 1 - 10 **Product Groups:** 35, 38

Date of Accounts	Dec 11	Dec 10	Dec 09
Working Capital	435	352	276
Fixed Assets	1	2	2
Current Assets	529	392	339

Bill Moore

15 Woodlands Drive Heysham, Morecambe, LA3 1LZ
Tel: 01524-854692 **Fax:** 01524-851566
E-mail: sales@bmlt.co.uk
Website: http://www.bmlt.ndo.co.uk
Directors: B. Moore (Prop), F. Moore (MD), K. Platts (Co Sec)
Immediate Holding Company: BILL MOORE (LIFTING TACKLE) LIMITED
Registration no: 01482196 **Date established:** 1980
Turnover: £250,000 - £500,000 **No.of Employees:** 1 - 10
Product Groups: 45, 48, 84

Date of Accounts	Jun 11	Jun 10	Jun 09
Working Capital	124	115	106
Fixed Assets	61	63	63
Current Assets	241	217	205

Optimum Coatings Ltd

Unit 5 Newgate, White Lund Industrial Estate, Morecambe, LA3 3PT
Tel: 01524-541540
E-mail: info@optimumcoatings.co.uk
Website: http://www.optimumcoatings.co.uk
Directors: M. Harwood (Fin), P. Bailey (MD)
Immediate Holding Company: OPTIMUM COATINGS LIMITED
Registration no: 04204670 **Date established:** 2001
No.of Employees: 21 - 50 **Product Groups:** 37, 38, 65

Date of Accounts	Mar 12	Sep 11	Sep 10
Working Capital	-115	-133	-40
Fixed Assets	498	530	643
Current Assets	260	233	313

Rhino Scaffolding Northern Ltd

Unit 5 Vickers Industrial Estate Mellishaw Lane, Morecambe, LA3 3EN
Tel: 01524-39978 **Fax:** 01524-39979
E-mail: info@rhinoscaffolding.co.uk
Website: http://www.rhinoscaffolding.co.uk
Directors: S. Mcguire (MD)
Immediate Holding Company: RHINO SCAFFOLDING NORTHERN LTD
Registration no: 04333514 **Date established:** 2001
Turnover: £500,000 - £1m **No.of Employees:** 11 - 20 **Product Groups:** 35

Date of Accounts	Jan 11	Jan 10	Feb 08
Sales Turnover	N/A	N/A	808
Pre Tax Profit/Loss	N/A	N/A	230
Working Capital	-103	-52	228
Fixed Assets	2m	2m	719
Current Assets	197	129	482
Current Liabilities	N/A	N/A	55

Tradebe Solvent Recycling

Middleton Road Middleton, Morecambe, LA3 3JW
Tel: 01524-853053 **Fax:** 01524-851284
E-mail: sales@tradebe.com
Website: http://www.tradebe.com
Bank(s): Skandinavisika Enskilda Banken, London
Directors: P. Mason (Fin), R. Butcher (Sales & Mktg)
Managers: S. Mcgowan (Mgr), A. Sutcliffe (Personnel)
Ultimate Holding Company: HEIDELBERG CEMENT AG (GERMANY)
Immediate Holding Company: TRADEBE SOLVENT RECYCLING LIMITED
Registration no: 03890526 **VAT No.:** GB 217 9157 51
Date established: 1999 **Turnover:** £20m - £50m
No.of Employees: 51 - 100 **Product Groups:** 31, 32, 54

Date of Accounts	Dec 10	Dec 09	Dec 08
Sales Turnover	35m	32m	40m
Pre Tax Profit/Loss	2m	-1m	4m
Working Capital	7m	6m	6m
Fixed Assets	11m	10m	12m
Current Assets	17m	16m	16m
Current Liabilities	2m	4m	4m

Van Bodies Lancs Ltd

East Gate White Lund Trading Estate, White Lund Industrial Estate, Morecambe, LA3 3DY
Tel: 01524-34422 **Fax:** 01524- 381432
E-mail: vanbodies@btconnect.com
Website: http://www.vanbodies.co.uk
Bank(s): Royal Bank of Scotland
Directors: R. Stevenson (MD)
Immediate Holding Company: VAN BODIES (LANCS) LIMITED
Registration no: 01221795 **Date established:** 1975
No.of Employees: 11 - 20 **Product Groups:** 39

Date of Accounts	Aug 08	Aug 07	Feb 11
Working Capital	-86	-18	151
Fixed Assets	99	105	34
Current Assets	204	74	613

Nelson

A C D C Led Ltd

Innovation Works Gisburn Road, Barrowford, Nelson, BB9 8NB
Tel: 08458-626400 **Fax:** 01282-608401
E-mail: sales@acdclighting.co.uk
Website: http://www.acdclighting.co.uk
Directors: G. Franklin (Sales)
Managers: G. Frankland
Immediate Holding Company: AC/DC LIGHTING SYSTEMS LIMITED
Registration no: 05005498 **Date established:** 2004 **Turnover:** £2m - £5m
No.of Employees: 51 - 100 **Product Groups:** 37, 67

Date of Accounts	Dec 11	Dec 10	Dec 09
Working Capital	184	-124	-82
Fixed Assets	507	2m	2m
Current Assets	1m	1m	1m

Adpak Machinery Systems Ltd

3 Pendleside Lomeshaye Industrial Estate, Nelson, BB9 6RY
Tel: 01282-601444 **Fax:** 01282-612201
E-mail: info@adpak.co.uk
Website: http://www.adpak.co.uk
Directors: J. Farrow (Dir), R. Hartley (Fin)
Managers: A. Jenkins (Personnel), K. Furmston (Mktg Serv Mgr)
Immediate Holding Company: ADPAK MACHINERY SYSTEMS LIMITED
Registration no: 02179444 **VAT No.:** GB 497 9285 67
Date established: 1987 **Turnover:** £2m - £5m **No.of Employees:** 21 - 50
Product Groups: 30, 42, 44, 67

Date of Accounts	Mar 12	Mar 11	Mar 10
Working Capital	233	29	15
Fixed Assets	1m	1m	1m
Current Assets	2m	1m	2m

Bearing Factors

Progress Road Whitewalls Industrial Estate, Nelson, BB9 8TE
Tel: 01282-693540 **Fax:** 01282-691881
E-mail: sales@bearingfactors.co.uk
Website: http://www.onlinebearings.co.uk
Directors: S. Egar (Ptnr)
Turnover: £250,000 - £500,000 **No.of Employees:** 1 - 10
Product Groups: 31, 34, 35, 39, 66

Blackburn Distributions

19 Barnfield Business Centre Brunswick Street, Nelson, BB9 0HT
Tel: 08451-161285 **Fax:** 01282-699237
E-mail: sales@blackburndistributions.com
Website: http://www.blackburndistrubutions.com
Directors: B. Blackburn (MD)
Immediate Holding Company: BLACKBURN AND DISTRICT ENTERPRISE TRUST LIMITED (THE)
Date established: 1984 **Turnover:** £250,000 - £500,000
No.of Employees: 1 - 10 **Product Groups:** 31, 38

Blakey J H & Sons Ltd

Burnley Road Brierfield, Nelson, BB9 5AD
Tel: 01282-613593 **Fax:** 01282-617550
E-mail: sales@jhblakey.co.uk
Website: http://www.jhblakey.co.uk
Directors: N. Blakey (Dir)
Immediate Holding Company: J H BLAKEY & SONS (SECURITY) LIMITED
Registration no: 00753087 **Date established:** 1963
No.of Employees: 11 - 20 **Product Groups:** 35, 36

Date of Accounts	Apr 12	Apr 11	Apr 10
Working Capital	118	82	74
Fixed Assets	180	224	234
Current Assets	316	340	336

Buoyant Upholstery Ltd

Hallam Road, Nelson, BB9 8AJ
Tel: 01282-691631 **Fax:** 01282-697298
E-mail: maramayo@buoyant-upholstery.co.uk
Website: http://www.buoyant-upholstery.co.uk
Directors: M. Aramayo (MD), S. Bracewell (Fin), C. Wade (Ch), B. Carrahar (MD)
Managers: M. Aramayo (Sales Prom Mgr), P. Mellor (Mgr)
Ultimate Holding Company: BUOYANT HOLDINGS LIMITED
Immediate Holding Company: BUOYANT UPHOLSTERY LIMITED
Registration no: 03690496 **Date established:** 1998
Turnover: Up to £250,000 **No.of Employees:** 251 - 500
Product Groups: 26

Date of Accounts	Sep 08	Sep 09	Oct 10
Sales Turnover	20m	21m	29m
Pre Tax Profit/Loss	-2m	-405	2m
Working Capital	637	386	3m
Fixed Assets	535	381	276
Current Assets	6m	6m	9m
Current Liabilities	4m	4m	4m

Carpets Direct

Unit 3 Hendon Business Centre Waterford Street, Nelson, BB9 8AQ
Tel: 01282-690400 **Fax:** 01282-690400
E-mail: admin@carpetsdirect.co.uk
Website: http://www.carpetsdirect.co.uk
Directors: M. Kimber (Prop)
Immediate Holding Company: Carpets Direct UK Ltd
Registration no: 03317121 **No.of Employees:** 1 - 10 **Product Groups:** 35, 36

Carradice Of Nelson Ltd

St Marys Street, Nelson, BB9 7BA
Tel: 01282-615886 **Fax:** 01282-602329
E-mail: info@carradice.co.uk
Website: http://www.carradice.co.uk
Directors: D. Chadwick (MD)
Immediate Holding Company: CARRADICE OF NELSON LIMITED
Registration no: 01269407 **VAT No.:** GB 175 7297 23
Date established: 1976 **No.of Employees:** 1 - 10 **Product Groups:** 37

Date of Accounts	Aug 11	Aug 10	Aug 09
Working Capital	175	136	68
Fixed Assets	25	24	26
Current Assets	287	250	165
Current Liabilities	58	N/A	N/A

Colin Blakey's Fireplace Galleries Ltd

115 Manchester Road, Nelson, BB9 7HB
Tel: 01282-614941 **Fax:** 01282-698511
E-mail: enquiries@fireplaceseastlancashire.com
Website: http://www.colinblakeyfireplaces.com
Directors: C. Blakey (Fin), P. Blakey (MD), G. Cooper (Sales)
Managers: M. Spencer (Sales Admin)
Immediate Holding Company: Colin Blakey Galleries Ltd
Registration no: 07404440 **Date established:** 2010
Turnover: Up to £250,000 **No.of Employees:** 1 - 10 **Product Groups:** 25, 33

Contenur

Unit 189 191 Imex Spaces Business Centre Lomeshaye Business, Nelson, BB9 7DR
Tel: 01282-604400 **Fax:** 01282-604404
E-mail: enquiries@contenur.com
Website: http://www.contenur.com
Directors: R. Lockley (MD)
Immediate Holding Company: CONTENUR (UK) LIMITED
Registration no: 03892289 **Date established:** 1999
No.of Employees: 1 - 10 **Product Groups:** 35, 42, 45

Date of Accounts	Dec 11	Dec 10	Dec 09
Working Capital	800	797	771
Fixed Assets	12	12	11
Current Assets	2m	2m	1m

S Dawes Weaving Ltd

Manor Mill Hallam Road, Nelson, BB9 8DN
Tel: 01282-612325 **Fax:** 01282-690466
E-mail: l.smith@sdawesweaving.co.uk
Website: http://www.sdawesweaving.co.uk
Bank(s): Barclays, Uxbridge
Managers: L. Smith (Chief Acct)
Immediate Holding Company: S. DAWES WEAVING LIMITED
Registration no: 05482607 **VAT No.:** GB 741 1469 47
Date established: 2005 **Turnover:** £1m - £2m **No.of Employees:** 11 - 20
Product Groups: 23

Date of Accounts	Jun 11	Jun 10	Jun 09
Working Capital	21	50	-165
Fixed Assets	88	102	124
Current Assets	515	546	360

Delta Electrical Repairs Ltd

2 Lindred Road Brierfield, Nelson, BB9 5SR
Tel: 01282-617771 **Fax:** 01282-616622
E-mail: mario@delta-electrical.co.uk
Website: http://www.delta-electrical.co.uk
Directors: M. Burian (Fin)
Immediate Holding Company: DELTA ELECTRICAL REPAIRS LIMITED
Registration no: 01770708 **Date established:** 1983 **Turnover:** £1m - £2m
No.of Employees: 11 - 20 **Product Groups:** 48

Date of Accounts	Dec 11	Dec 10	Dec 09
Working Capital	747	760	736
Fixed Assets	120	58	131
Current Assets	914	905	899

Door Care Systems

4 Saffron Close Barrowford, Nelson, BB9 6DL
Tel: 01282-617220 **Fax:** 01282-447598
E-mail: doorcare.systems@ntlworld.com
Directors: G. Smith (Prop)
Turnover: Up to £250,000 **No.of Employees:** 1 - 10 **Product Groups:** 25, 30, 35

E Reg Sheet Metal Fabricators Ltd

7 Kirby Road Lomeshaye Industrial Estate, Nelson, BB9 6RS
Tel: 01282-697748 **Fax:** 01282-697749
E-mail: eregbarry@aol.com
Website: http://www.eregsheermetal.co.uk
Directors: B. Slater (Dir)
Immediate Holding Company: E-REG SHEET METAL FABRICATORS LIMITED
Registration no: 02166334 **Date established:** 1987 **Turnover:** £1m - £2m
No.of Employees: 1 - 10 **Product Groups:** 40, 48

Date of Accounts	Jul 11	Jul 10	Jul 09
Working Capital	141	121	224
Fixed Assets	28	31	27
Current Assets	216	199	279

Excelsior Retail Systems Ltd

25 Hill Street Brierfield, Nelson, BB9 5AT
Tel: 01282-696144 **Fax:** 01282- 696122
Directors: K. Rogers (MD)
No.of Employees: 1 - 10 **Product Groups:** 38, 42

Farmhouse Biscuits Ltd (a division of Kippax Biscuits)

Brook Street, Nelson, BB9 9PX
Tel: 01282-613520 **Fax:** 01282-694796
E-mail: sales@farmhouse-biscuits.co.uk
Website: http://www.farmhouse-biscuits.co.uk
Bank(s): Barclays, Clitheroe
Directors: G. Mcivor (Dir)
Managers: L. Mayor, P. O'Sullivan (Personnel)
Immediate Holding Company: FARMHOUSE BISCUITS LIMITED
Registration no: 01145352 **VAT No.:** GB 175 3722 54
Date established: 1973 **Turnover:** £10m - £20m
No.of Employees: 101 - 250 **Product Groups:** 20

Date of Accounts	Dec 11	Dec 10	Dec 09
Sales Turnover	11m	10m	9m
Pre Tax Profit/Loss	307	545	157
Working Capital	2m	2m	2m
Fixed Assets	4m	4m	4m
Current Assets	3m	3m	3m
Current Liabilities	460	498	409

Ferguson Engineering Northern Ltd

2 Coulton Road Brierfield, Nelson, BB9 5ST
Tel: 01282-447500 **Fax:** 01282-447600
E-mail: rferguson@f-e-n.com
Website: http://www.f-e-n.com
Directors: T. Fullard (Dir), R. Ferguson (Dir)
Managers: D. Smith, R. Barlow (Personnel), S. James (Purch Mgr), E. Dyson (Chief Acct)
Ultimate Holding Company: FERGUSON ENGINEERING (HOLDINGS) LIMITED
Immediate Holding Company: FERGUSON ENGINEERING (NORTHERN) LIMITED

Registration no: 02161479 **Date established:** 1987 **Turnover:** £2m - £5m
No.of Employees: 51 - 100 **Product Groups:** 40, 45

Date of Accounts	Sep 11	Sep 10	Sep 09
Sales Turnover	N/A	N/A	4m
Pre Tax Profit/Loss	N/A	N/A	-86
Working Capital	-73	-213	-130
Fixed Assets	389	418	268
Current Assets	2m	2m	932
Current Liabilities	N/A	N/A	155

Fibet Rubber Bonding UK Ltd

Unit 9 Dale Mill Hallam Road, Nelson, BB9 8AN
Tel: 01282-878200 **Fax:** 01282-878201
E-mail: sales@fibet.co.uk
Website: http://www.fibet.co.uk
Managers: M. Connor (Chief Mgr)
Immediate Holding Company: FIBET RUBBER BONDING (U.K.) LIMITED
Registration no: 02762838 **VAT No.:** GB 607 0467 56
Date established: 1992 **Turnover:** £1m - £2m **No.of Employees:** 1 - 10
Product Groups: 29, 30, 33, 35, 38, 39, 40, 42, 45, 46, 54, 66, 68, 85

Date of Accounts	Dec 11	Dec 10	Dec 09
Working Capital	215	184	155
Fixed Assets	19	6	1
Current Assets	599	479	309

Graham Engineering Ltd

Edward Street Whitewalls Industrial Estate, Nelson, BB9 8SY
Tel: 01282-695121 **Fax:** 01282-698498
E-mail: info@graham-eng.co.uk
Website: http://www.graham-eng.co.uk
Bank(s): National Westminster Bank Plc
Directors: S. Fraser (Dir), F. Kelly (Fin)
Managers: B. Watson (Purch Mgr), P. Ashworth (Tech Serv Mgr), M. Hubbert
Immediate Holding Company: GRAHAM ENGINEERING LIMITED
Registration no: 01329239 **VAT No.:** GB 291 1734 59
Date established: 1977 **Turnover:** £10m - £20m
No.of Employees: 101 - 250 **Product Groups:** 35, 37, 46, 48

Date of Accounts	Aug 11	Aug 10	Aug 08
Sales Turnover	12m	10m	N/A
Pre Tax Profit/Loss	715	559	-239
Working Capital	659	514	178
Fixed Assets	6m	6m	6m
Current Assets	3m	3m	4m
Current Liabilities	843	768	764

Green Light Vehicles Ltd

Unit 3 Brook Street, Nelson, BB9 9PU
Tel: 08454-508440 **Fax:** 0845-450 8443
E-mail: sales@greenlightvehicles.co.uk
Website: http://www.greenlightvehicles.co.uk
Directors: L. Sutton (Prop)
No.of Employees: 1 - 10 **Product Groups:** 68, 72, 82

Date of Accounts	Jul 07	Jul 06	Jul 05
Working Capital	-92	-53	-22
Fixed Assets	18	22	30
Current Assets	10	8	7
Current Liabilities	102	61	29

J Rostron Engineering Ltd

Lindred Road Brierfield, Nelson, BB9 5SR
Tel: 01282-611110 **Fax:** 01282-619961
E-mail: sales@rostron.co.uk
Website: http://www.rostron.co.uk
Bank(s): The Royal Bank of Scotland
Directors: B. Rostron (Dir), G. Rostron (Dir), J. Rostron (Ch & MD), K. Grimshaw (Tech Sales)
Immediate Holding Company: J. Rostron Engineering Ltd
Registration no: 02002153 **Date established:** 1986 **Turnover:** £1m - £2m
No.of Employees: 21 - 50 **Product Groups:** 42, 43, 44, 52

Date of Accounts	May 08	May 07	May 06
Working Capital	56	82	-17
Fixed Assets	376	403	533
Current Assets	207	469	388
Current Liabilities	150	387	405

Jewson Ltd

Coal Wharf Scotland Road, Nelson, BB9 7XR
Tel: 01282-692815 **Fax:** 01282-693212
E-mail: dennis.ross@jewson.co.uk
Website: http://www.jewson.co.uk
Directors: P. Hindle (MD)
Managers: S. Walling (District Mgr)
Ultimate Holding Company: COMPAGNIE DE SAINT GOBAIN (FRANCE)
Immediate Holding Company: JEWSON LIMITED
Registration no: 00348407 **VAT No.:** GB 497 7184 83
Date established: 1939 **Turnover:** £2m - £5m **No.of Employees:** 1 - 10
Product Groups: 66

Date of Accounts	Dec 11	Dec 10	Dec 09
Sales Turnover	1606m	1547m	1485m
Pre Tax Profit/Loss	18m	100m	45m
Working Capital	-345m	-250m	-349m
Fixed Assets	496m	387m	461m
Current Assets	657m	1005m	1320m
Current Liabilities	66m	120m	64m

Loubec Sheet Metal Ltd

Throstle Nest Mill Leeds Road, Nelson, BB9 9XG
Tel: 01282-604737 **Fax:** 01282-611897
Directors: C. Bradbury (MD), W. Bradbury (Fin)
Registration no: 03258182 **VAT No.:** GB 685 9823 68
Date established: 2004 **Turnover:** £250,000 - £500,000
No.of Employees: 1 - 10 **Product Groups:** 48

Lynteck Ltd

Protec House Churchill Way, Nelson, BB9 6RT
Tel: 01282-717490 **Fax:** 01282-698020
E-mail: sales@lynteck.co.uk
Website: http://www.lynteck.co.uk
Directors: B. Russell (Dir), T. Fairnie (Fin)
Ultimate Holding Company: PROTEC FIRE AND SECURITY GROUP LIMITED
Immediate Holding Company: LYNTECK LIMITED
Registration no: 02206469 **Date established:** 1987 **Turnover:** £1m - £2m
No.of Employees: 1 - 10 **Product Groups:** 36, 37, 44

Date of Accounts	Aug 11	Aug 10	Aug 09
Sales Turnover	1m	1m	1m
Pre Tax Profit/Loss	112	128	139
Working Capital	893	820	724
Current Assets	2m	2m	1m
Current Liabilities	73	64	74

Nelson Double Glazing

Unit 2 Pendle Industrial Estate Southfield Street, Nelson, BB9 0LD
Tel: 01282-692639 **Fax:** 01282-611255
Website: http://www.nelsondoubleglazing.co.uk
Directors: D. Hodgson (Dir)
Immediate Holding Company: NELSON DOUBLE GLAZING LIMITED
Registration no: 04478179 **Date established:** 2002
Turnover: Up to £250,000 **No.of Employees:** 1 - 10 **Product Groups:** 26, 35

Date of Accounts	Jul 12	Jul 11	Jul 10
Sales Turnover	N/A	N/A	244
Pre Tax Profit/Loss	N/A	N/A	29
Working Capital	64	13	3
Fixed Assets	8	11	15
Current Assets	64	55	41

Nelson Packaging Ltd

Townsley Street, Nelson, BB9 0RY
Tel: 01282-690215 **Fax:** 01282-699976
E-mail: richardjones@nelson-packaging.co.uk
Website: http://www.nelson-packaging.co.uk
Directors: R. Jones (MD)
Immediate Holding Company: RETAIL PACKAGING SOLUTIONS LIMITED
Registration no: 05932560 **Date established:** 2006 **Turnover:** £5m - £10m
No.of Employees: 51 - 100 **Product Groups:** 30

Date of Accounts	Nov 11	Nov 10	Nov 09
Working Capital	215	109	88
Fixed Assets	15	20	N/A
Current Assets	2m	2m	1m

Norfolk Street Garage

52 Norfolk Street, Nelson, BB9 7FG
Tel: 01282-611790 **Fax:** 01282-611790
Directors: N. Mahmood (Prop)
No.of Employees: 1 - 10 **Product Groups:** 25, 35, 39

North Valley Forge Ltd

Unit 1 Valley Forge Business Park Reedyford Road, Nelson, BB9 8TU
Tel: 01282-677300 **Fax:** 01282-691583
E-mail: sales@nvf.co.uk
Website: http://www.nvf.co.uk
Directors: P. Ratcliffe (MD)
Immediate Holding Company: NORTH VALLEY FORGE LTD
Registration no: 07577833 **Date established:** 2011
No.of Employees: 11 - 20 **Product Groups:** 26, 35

Date of Accounts	Mar 12
Working Capital	479
Fixed Assets	522
Current Assets	739

North West Sheeting Supplies

Unit 23 Bizspace Lomeshaye Business Village Turner Road, Nelson, BB9 7DR
Tel: 01282-619430 **Fax:** 01282-619431
E-mail: sales@steelroofing.co.uk
Website: http://www.steelroofing.co.uk
Directors: R. Ellis (Ptnr)
Date established: 1991 **Turnover:** £250,000 - £500,000
No.of Employees: 1 - 10 **Product Groups:** 27, 35, 52, 66

Pendle Frozen Foods Ltd

40 Churchill Way, Nelson, BB9 6RT
Tel: 01282-691177 **Fax:** 01282-690011
E-mail: aplatt@pendlefrozenfoods.co.uk
Website: http://www.pendlefrozenfoods.co.uk
Directors: A. Platt (Dir)
Managers: J. Platt (Tech Serv Mgr), A. Bray (Sales Prom Mgr)
Immediate Holding Company: PENDLE FROZEN FOODS LIMITED
Registration no: 01096475 **Date established:** 1973 **Turnover:** £1m - £2m
No.of Employees: 21 - 50 **Product Groups:** 20, 62

Date of Accounts	Mar 11	Mar 10	Mar 09
Working Capital	-139	-132	-119
Fixed Assets	1m	1m	2m
Current Assets	483	507	501

Professional Retail Systems Ltd T/A Prs-Epos

Systems House 5 Vantage Court Riverside Business Park, Barrowford, Nelson, BB9 6BP
Tel: 01282-425566 **Fax:** 01282-423831
E-mail: info@prs-epos.co.uk
Website: http://www.prs-epos.co.uk
Directors: G. Tierney (MD), S. Tierney (Fin)
Immediate Holding Company: PROFESSIONAL RETAIL SYSTEMS LIMITED
Registration no: 04292179 **Date established:** 2001
Turnover: £500,000 - £1m **No.of Employees:** 1 - 10 **Product Groups:** 44

Date of Accounts	Mar 11	Mar 10	Mar 09
Working Capital	74	92	93
Fixed Assets	14	17	31
Current Assets	120	143	184

Protec Fire Detection

Lomeshaye Industrial Estate, Nelson, BB9 6RT
Tel: 01282-717171 **Fax:** 01282-717273
E-mail: sales@protec.co.uk
Website: http://www.protec.co.uk
Bank(s): Barclays
Directors: C. Hore (Sales)
Ultimate Holding Company: PROTEC FIRE AND SECURITY GROUP LIMITED
Immediate Holding Company: PROTEC FIRE DETECTION (EXPORT) LIMITED
Registration no: 02985633 **VAT No.:** GB 175 4469 35
Date established: 1994 **Turnover:** £2m - £5m
No.of Employees: 251 - 500 **Product Groups:** 37, 38, 40

Date of Accounts	Aug 11	Aug 10	Aug 09
Sales Turnover	3m	2m	2m
Pre Tax Profit/Loss	819	735	583
Working Capital	2m	1m	836
Current Assets	2m	2m	1m
Current Liabilities	139	107	129

R E M UK Ltd

Glenfield Road, Nelson, BB9 8AW
Tel: 01282-619977 **Fax:** 01282-619617
E-mail: cmb@rem.co.uk
Website: http://www.rem.co.uk
Bank(s): Coutts & Co.
Directors: C. Blakey (Fin), M. Roach (Sales)
Managers: J. Braithwaite, R. Ingram (Purch Mgr), J. Lowe (Personnel)
Ultimate Holding Company: BRAITHWAITE HOLDINGS LIMITED
Immediate Holding Company: R.E.M. (UK) LIMITED
Registration no: 03094826 **VAT No.:** GB 437 2639 38
Date established: 1995 **Turnover:** £5m - £10m
No.of Employees: 51 - 100 **Product Groups:** 32

Date of Accounts	Sep 11	Sep 10	Sep 09
Sales Turnover	9m	10m	10m
Pre Tax Profit/Loss	175	217	379
Working Capital	1m	1m	1m
Fixed Assets	421	485	405
Current Assets	3m	3m	4m
Current Liabilities	864	1m	1m

Rapid Air Filtration

328 Railway Street, Nelson, BB9 0JD
Tel: 01282-618700
E-mail: rapid-air@tiscali.co.uk
Directors: A. Greenwood (Prop)
No.of Employees: 1 - 10 **Product Groups:** 38, 42

Riggs Autopack Ltd

Southfield Street, Nelson, BB9 0LD
Tel: 01282-440040 **Fax:** 01282-440041
E-mail: info@autopack.co.uk
Website: http://www.autopack.co.uk
Bank(s): Nat West
Directors: I. Wilson (MD)
Managers: N. Matthews (Chief Mgr), R. Lumb (Sales Prom Mgr), S. Farnhill (Sales Admin)
Registration no: 05715991 **VAT No.:** GB 174 7819 25
Date established: 1950 **Turnover:** £1m - £2m **No.of Employees:** 11 - 20
Product Groups: 42

Date of Accounts	Mar 08	Mar 07	Mar 06
Working Capital	709	633	377
Fixed Assets	833	926	1180
Current Assets	938	830	877
Current Liabilities	229	197	500
Total Share Capital	1	1	1

Robinson & Lawlor Ltd

Hope House Lomeshaye Road, Nelson, BB9 7AP
Tel: 01282-612189 **Fax:** 01282-617192
E-mail: admin@robinsonandlawlor.co.uk
Managers: A. Blake (Chief Acct), J. Ashworth (Buyer)
Immediate Holding Company: ROBINSON & LAWLOR LIMITED
Registration no: 02300663 **Date established:** 1988 **Turnover:** £2m - £5m
No.of Employees: 21 - 50 **Product Groups:** 52

Date of Accounts	Mar 11	Sep 11	Sep 10
Working Capital	159	363	96
Fixed Assets	271	266	272
Current Assets	1m	957	937

Standel Dawman Ltd

Pasture Lane Works Pasture Lane, Barrowford, Nelson, BB9 6ES
Tel: 01282-613175 **Fax:** 01282-615429
E-mail: sales@standeldawman.uk.com
Website: http://www.standeldawman.net
Bank(s): National Westminster Bank Plc
Directors: P. Kyle (MD)
Managers: A. Bradley, M. Morley
Immediate Holding Company: STANDEL DAWMAN LIMITED
Registration no: 05005337 **VAT No.:** GB 831 6456 30
Date established: 2004 **Turnover:** £1m - £2m **No.of Employees:** 21 - 50
Product Groups: 29, 30, 35, 37, 39, 44, 49, 65, 66

Date of Accounts	Apr 12	Apr 11	Apr 10
Working Capital	445	473	-402
Fixed Assets	902	959	1m
Current Assets	806	733	630

Straight Line Engineering

Unit 30 Churchill Way, Nelson, BB9 6RT
Tel: 01282-693424 **Fax:** 01282-698138
E-mail: sales@straight-line.co.uk
Website: http://www.straight-line.co.uk
Directors: F. Greenwood (MD)
Immediate Holding Company: STRAIGHT LINE ENGINEERING LIMITED
Registration no: 01550924 **Date established:** 1981
No.of Employees: 21 - 50 **Product Groups:** 46

Date of Accounts	May 11	May 10	May 09
Working Capital	2m	1m	1m
Fixed Assets	1m	1m	1m
Current Assets	3m	2m	2m

Sugden Ltd

Pasture Lane Barrowford, Nelson, BB9 6ES
Tel: 01282-611199 **Fax:** 01282-613373
E-mail: sales@sugden.ltd.uk
Website: http://www.sugden.ltd.uk
Bank(s): Barclays
Directors: G. Sutcliffe (MD), J. Buck (Co Sec)
Immediate Holding Company: SUGDEN LIMITED
Registration no: 01313718 **VAT No.:** GB 326 0606 84
Date established: 1977 **Turnover:** £2m - £5m **No.of Employees:** 11 - 20
Product Groups: 41

Date of Accounts	Aug 09	Apr 12	Apr 11
Working Capital	354	538	452
Fixed Assets	458	497	566
Current Assets	941	773	702

Voltek Automation

Unit 39C, Churchill Way, Lomeshaye Industrial Estate, Nelson, BB9 6RT
Tel: 01282-695500 **Fax:** 01282-695511
E-mail: sales@voltek.co.uk
Website: http://www.voltek.co.uk
Bank(s): Barclays
Directors: D. Watkins (Sales), J. Iqbal (Fin)
Immediate Holding Company: Voltek Automation Ltd
Registration no: 01935848 **VAT No.:** GB 435 6548 33
Date established: 2005 **Turnover:** £1m - £2m **No.of Employees:** 21 - 50
Product Groups: 37, 38, 40

see next page

***Voltek Automation** - Cont'd*

Date of Accounts	Jun 09	Jun 08	Jun 07
Working Capital	1m	1m	983
Fixed Assets	1	17	35
Current Assets	2m	1m	1m

W J C Ltd

John Street Works John Street, Brierfield, Nelson, BB9 5NX
Tel: 01282-613985 **Fax:** 01282-698677
E-mail: sales@wjc.co.uk
Website: http://www.wjc.co.uk
Directors: A. Arnold (Ch)
Immediate Holding Company: W.J.C. DIP MOULDINGS LIMITED
Registration no: 01530678 **Date established:** 1980
No.of Employees: 11 - 20 **Product Groups:** 30, 42, 46, 48

Date of Accounts	Feb 11	Feb 10	Feb 08
Working Capital	38	38	38
Current Assets	38	38	38

William Reed Weaving (Branch of Allied Textile Companies P.L.C.)

Spring Bank Mill Every Street, Nelson, BB9 7DA
Tel: 01282-603666 **Fax:** 01282-695207
E-mail: john@wreed.co.uk
Website: http://www.alliedtextiles.com
Bank(s): HSBC Bank plc
Directors: J. Reed (MD)
Managers: D. Evans (Personnel), A. Gill (Ops Mgr), B. Roberts (Chief Acct)
Immediate Holding Company: ALLIED TEXTILES COMPANIES P.L.C.
Registration no: 00176518 **VAT No.:** GB 185 0589 38
Date established: 1888 **Turnover:** £10m - £20m
No.of Employees: 51 - 100 **Product Groups:** 23, 63

Oldham

2 M Automation

Meridian Centre King Street, Oldham, OL8 1EZ
Tel: 0161-785 0267 **Fax:** 0161-785 9287
E-mail: info@2m-automation.co.uk
Website: http://www.2m-automation.co.uk
Directors: M. Mirshafiei (MD)
Immediate Holding Company: 2M AUTOMATION LTD
Registration no: 04750866 **Date established:** 2003
Turnover: £250,000 - £500,000 **No.of Employees:** 1 - 10
Product Groups: 44

Date of Accounts	May 11	May 10	May 09
Working Capital	31	6	-4
Current Assets	79	82	26

A A K Bakery Services

Falcon Street, Oldham, OL8 1JU
Tel: 0161-652 6311 **Fax:** 0161-627 2346
E-mail: steve.hamilton@aak.com
Website: http://www.aak.com
Directors: A. Fowler (Sales)
Managers: S. Hamilton
Ultimate Holding Company: CRODA INTERNATIONAL PLC
No.of Employees: 51 - 100 **Product Groups:** 20, 32, 41

Advanced Biomedical Ltd

Saddleworth Business Centre Huddersfield Road Delph, Delph, Oldham, OL3 5DF
Tel: 01457-875798 **Fax:** 01457-871088
E-mail: info@advanced-biomedical.co.uk
Website: http://www.advanced-biomedical.co.uk
Directors: H. Aojula (MD)
Immediate Holding Company: ADVANCED BIOMEDICAL LIMITED
Registration no: 04690930 **Date established:** 2003
No.of Employees: 1 - 10 **Product Groups:** 31

Date of Accounts	Mar 11	Mar 10	Mar 09
Working Capital	13	27	47
Fixed Assets	17	15	19
Current Assets	31	47	71

Advanced Detection Systems

The Workshop 3 Atherton Street, Springhead, Oldham, OL4 5TF
Tel: 0161-628 4781 **Fax:** 0161-620 5601
Website: http://www.advanceddetection.co.uk
Directors: J. Coleman (MD)
Immediate Holding Company: Advanced Detection Systems Ltd
Registration no: 04789786 **Date established:** 2003
No.of Employees: 1 - 10 **Product Groups:** 37, 40, 52

Advanced Metallurgical Services Ltd

Mosshey Street Shaw, Oldham, OL2 8QL
Tel: 01706-882891 **Fax:** 01706-882893
E-mail: ken@amsshaw.co.uk
Website: http://www.pdnorthern.co.uk
Managers: K. Glaister (Lab Mgr)
Immediate Holding Company: ADVANCED METALLURGICAL SERVICES LIMITED
Registration no: 02558234 **Date established:** 1990
Turnover: £250,000 - £500,000 **No.of Employees:** 1 - 10
Product Groups: 38, 42, 67, 84, 85

Date of Accounts	Oct 11	Oct 10	Oct 09
Working Capital	235	159	181
Fixed Assets	8	7	8
Current Assets	282	228	220

AGD Shutters Ltd

Vanguard Works Mold Street, Oldham, OL1 2DN
Tel: 01204-656755 **Fax:** 01204-656009
E-mail: sales@agdshutters.co.uk
Website: http://www.agdshutters.co.uk
Directors: A. Bollard (Prop)
Managers: M. Burke (Ops Mgr)
Ultimate Holding Company: DOVER VANGUARD ROLLER SHUTTERS LIMITED
Immediate Holding Company: AGD ROLLER SHUTTERS LIMITED
Registration no: 05038905 **Date established:** 2008
Turnover: £250,000 - £500,000 **No.of Employees:** 11 - 20
Product Groups: 26, 35

Date of Accounts	Mar 08	Mar 07	Mar 06
Sales Turnover	407	N/A	N/A
Pre Tax Profit/Loss	43	N/A	N/A
Working Capital	N/A	-6	-12
Fixed Assets	N/A	11	5
Current Assets	188	101	66
Current Liabilities	188	107	77

Almic Engineering Co. Ltd

Mossdown Road Royton, Oldham, OL2 6HS
Tel: 01706-846343 **Fax:** 01706-849613
E-mail: paula.marland@btconnect.com
Website: http://www.almic-engineering.co.uk
Bank(s): Barclays, Oldham
Managers: P. Marland (Mgr)
Immediate Holding Company: ALMIC ENGINEERING CO.LIMITED
Registration no: 00709281 **VAT No.:** GB 692 3446 16
Date established: 1961 **Turnover:** £500,000 - £1m
No.of Employees: 11 - 20 **Product Groups:** 48

Date of Accounts	Nov 11	Nov 10	Nov 09
Working Capital	470	413	313
Fixed Assets	395	367	332
Current Assets	625	560	475

Andrews Sykes Hire Ltd

Railway Road, Oldham, OL9 6HA
Tel: 0161-652 5380 **Fax:** 0161-620 1910
E-mail: depot.old@andrews-sykes.com
Website: http://www.andrew-sykes.com
Managers: D. Alcock (Mgr)
Immediate Holding Company: ANDREWS SYKES HIRE LIMITED
Registration no: 02985657 **VAT No.:** GB 100 4295 24
Date established: 1994 **Turnover:** £10m - £20m **No.of Employees:** 1 - 10
Product Groups: 40

Date of Accounts	Dec 11	Dec 10	Dec 09
Sales Turnover	35m	36m	34m
Pre Tax Profit/Loss	10m	10m	8m
Working Capital	8m	6m	2m
Fixed Assets	7m	7m	9m
Current Assets	33m	35m	35m
Current Liabilities	7m	7m	5m

Ansa Elevators Ltd

Unit 21 Broadgate Oldham Broadway Business Park, Chadderton, Oldham, OL9 9XA
Tel: 0161-688 6500 **Fax:** 0161-681 8083
E-mail: info@ansaelevators.co.uk
Website: http://www.ansaelevators.co.uk
Directors: M. Dunning (Fin)
Managers: J. Taylor (Sales Prom Mgr)
Ultimate Holding Company: ANSA GROUP HOLDINGS LIMITED
Immediate Holding Company: ANSA ELEVATORS LIMITED
Registration no: 03785224 **Date established:** 1999 **Turnover:** £5m - £10m
No.of Employees: 51 - 100 **Product Groups:** 35, 39, 45

Date of Accounts	Oct 11	Oct 10	Oct 09
Sales Turnover	8m	5m	7m
Pre Tax Profit/Loss	799	155	206
Working Capital	249	556	512
Fixed Assets	412	201	220
Current Assets	2m	1m	1m
Current Liabilities	1m	415	413

Alan Appleton Oldham Ltd

Kilburn Street, Oldham, OL1 4JF
Tel: 0161-652 0327 **Fax:** 0161-633 0019
E-mail: info@alanappleton.com
Website: http://www.alanappleton.com
Bank(s): National Westminster Bank Plc
Directors: A. Appleton (MD), I. Appleton (MD), J. Appleton (Dir)
Immediate Holding Company: ALAN APPLETON (OLDHAM) LIMITED
Registration no: 01365171 **Date established:** 1978
No.of Employees: 21 - 50 **Product Groups:** 23, 24

Date of Accounts	Aug 11	Aug 10	Aug 09
Working Capital	576	416	390
Fixed Assets	816	849	959
Current Assets	1m	986	687
Current Liabilities	N/A	N/A	6

Armour Sheet Metal

Red Rose Works Shaw Road, Royton, Oldham, OL2 6EF
Tel: 0161-624 9496 **Fax:** 0161-624 9496
Directors: M. Hughes (Ptnr)
Immediate Holding Company: EQUINE MANIA LIMITED
Registration no: 05919179 **Date established:** 2006
No.of Employees: 1 - 10 **Product Groups:** 26, 35

Austin Wolstencroft & Co. Ltd

56 Broadbent Road, Oldham, OL1 4HY
Tel: 0161-624 5236 **Fax:** 0161-620 8413
E-mail: avrilbrooks20944@aol.com
Directors: A. Brooks (Fin), D. Wolstencroft (MD)
Immediate Holding Company: AUSTIN, WOLSTENCROFT & CO. LIMITED
Registration no: 00539260 **VAT No.:** GB 146 2426 78
Date established: 1954 **Turnover:** Up to £250,000
No.of Employees: 1 - 10 **Product Groups:** 35, 36

Date of Accounts	Oct 11	Oct 10	Oct 09
Working Capital	359	299	258
Fixed Assets	22	25	28
Current Assets	462	431	384

Autokontrol Ltd

Quantum House Salmon Fields Royton, Oldham, OL2 6JG
Tel: 0161-626 4271 **Fax:** 0870-241 7161
E-mail: sales@autokontrol.com
Website: http://www.autokontrol.com
Managers: M. Gray (Mgr)
Immediate Holding Company: AUTOKONTROL LIMITED
Registration no: 04077820 **Date established:** 2000 **Turnover:** £1m - £2m
No.of Employees: 11 - 20 **Product Groups:** 36, 39

Date of Accounts	Oct 11	Oct 10	Oct 09
Working Capital	311	317	225
Fixed Assets	182	189	220
Current Assets	622	430	391

Autolok Security

52 Park Lane Royton, Oldham, OL2 6PU
Tel: 0161-624 8171 **Fax:** 0161-627 3742
E-mail: david.brearley@autolok.co.uk
Website: http://www.autolock.co.uk
Directors: D. Brearley (MD)
Ultimate Holding Company: A.K.HUGHES LIMITED
Immediate Holding Company: AUTOLOK SECURITY PRODUCTS LIMITED
Registration no: 03504836 **Date established:** 1998
No.of Employees: 1 - 10 **Product Groups:** 36

Date of Accounts	Mar 11	Mar 10	Mar 09
Working Capital	664	668	848
Fixed Assets	N/A	N/A	10
Current Assets	665	801	936

B & B Enamellers Ltd

91 Middleton Road Royton, Oldham, OL2 5JJ
Tel: 0161-624 5530 **Fax:** 0161-624 5973
Directors: B. Heacock (Prop)
Immediate Holding Company: B & B ENAMELLERS LTD
Registration no: 05225675 **Date established:** 2004
No.of Employees: 1 - 10 **Product Groups:** 46, 48

Date of Accounts	Sep 11	Sep 10	Sep 09
Working Capital	-25	-70	-101
Fixed Assets	132	154	155
Current Assets	245	174	82

Builder Center Ltd

Coldhurst Street, Oldham, OL1 2PX
Tel: 0161-621 4000 **Fax:** 0161-621 4040
Website: http://www.buildcenter.co.uk
Managers: R. Elliott (Mgr), R. Elliott (Chief Mgr)
Ultimate Holding Company: Wolseley plc
Immediate Holding Company: BUILD CENTER LIMITED
Registration no: 00462397 **Date established:** 1948
No.of Employees: 21 - 50 **Product Groups:** 66

C J Windows

22 Mossley Road Grasscroft, Oldham, OL4 4HE
Tel: 01457-872752
Managers: C. Allen (Mgr)
No.of Employees: 1 - 10 **Product Groups:** 35, 36

Carpenters Ltd

Bee Mill Shaw Road, Royton, Oldham, OL2 6EH
Tel: 0161-627 0044 **Fax:** 0161-627 0951
E-mail: ian.owen@carpenter.com
Website: http://www.carpenter.com
Bank(s): Royal Bank of Scotland, Manchester
Directors: B. Messer (Fin), I. Owen (Sales)
Managers: J. Bolton (Personnel), P. Meat (Tech Serv Mgr), S. Redford (Buyer)
Immediate Holding Company: CARPENTERS LIMITED
Registration no: 06532413 **Date established:** 2008
No.of Employees: 51 - 100 **Product Groups:** 26

Cash Fabrication

Belmont Works Franklin Street, Oldham, OL1 2DP
Tel: 0161-652 8666 **Fax:** 0161-652 8777
E-mail: john@mezzaninefloor.co.uk
Website: http://www.mezzaninefloor.co.uk
Directors: J. Aspinall (Dir)
Ultimate Holding Company: CORAL DESIGN & BUILD LTD
Immediate Holding Company: CASH FABRICATIONS AND ERECTION SERVICES LIMITED
Registration no: 02848691 **Date established:** 1993
No.of Employees: 11 - 20 **Product Groups:** 35

Date of Accounts	Sep 07	Sep 06	Mar 10
Working Capital	47	4	13
Fixed Assets	81	117	76
Current Assets	323	275	179

Central Diesel

Unit 15 Hawksley Industrial Estate Hawksley Street, Oldham, OL8 4PQ
Tel: 0161-620 7070 **Fax:** 0161-620 6007
E-mail: steve.kay@central-diesel.co.uk
Website: http://www.central-diesel.co.uk
Bank(s): Barclays
Managers: S. Kay (Mgr)
Ultimate Holding Company: TURNER MITCHELL GROUP GLASGOW
Immediate Holding Company: MITCHELL DIESEL GROUP
Registration no: 01179564 **VAT No.:** GB 118 2891 60
Turnover: £250m - £500m **No.of Employees:** 11 - 20
Product Groups: 38, 40

Comid Engineering Ltd

Greenacres Road, Oldham, OL4 2AB
Tel: 0161-624 9592 **Fax:** 0161-627 1620
E-mail: sales@comid.co.uk
Website: http://www.comid.co.uk
Bank(s): Yorkshire Bank PLC
Directors: P. Rowbotham (MD), J. Rowbotham (Fin)
Immediate Holding Company: COMID ENGINEERING LIMITED
Registration no: 01664479 **Date established:** 1982
Turnover: £500,000 - £1m **No.of Employees:** 11 - 20 **Product Groups:** 48

Date of Accounts	Sep 11	Sep 10	Sep 09
Working Capital	1m	1m	1m
Fixed Assets	600	624	621
Current Assets	1m	1m	1m

Constellation Luggage Ltd

Constellation Works Fernhurst Street, Chadderton, Oldham, OL1 2RN
Tel: 0161-620 4231 **Fax:** 0161-627 0914
E-mail: constellation@japinda.co.uk
Website: http://www.japinda.co.uk
Directors: R. Levene (MD), H. Silver (Dir), L. Levene (Co Sec)
Managers: N. Burnes (Sales Admin)
Immediate Holding Company: SKIPWORTH LIMITED
Registration no: 00714891 **VAT No.:** GB 145 1365 83
Date established: 1997 **No.of Employees:** 1 - 10 **Product Groups:** 22

Date of Accounts	Dec 09	Dec 08	Dec 06
Working Capital	1	1	1
Current Assets	1	1	1

Cotec Converting Machinery Ltd

Unit 20 St Johns Industrial Estate, Lees, Oldham, OL4 3DZ
Tel: 0161-626 5350 **Fax:** 0161-626 5450
E-mail: jackcotten@btconnect.com
Directors: J. Cotton (Prop), E. Cotton (Co Sec)
Immediate Holding Company: COTEC CONVERTING MACHINERY LIMITED
Registration no: 02327427 **Date established:** 1988
Turnover: Up to £250,000 **No.of Employees:** 1 - 10 **Product Groups:** 44, 84

Date of Accounts	Jan 11	Jan 10	Jan 09
Working Capital	5	7	19
Fixed Assets	1	N/A	1

Current Assets	27	24	40

Crackdown Drug Testing

Unit 11 Boarshurst Business Park Boarshurst Lane, Greenfield, Oldham, OL3 7ER
Tel: 01457-877988 **Fax:** 01457-877080
E-mail: sales@crackdown-drugtesting.com
Website: http://www.crackdown-drugtesting.com
Directors: K. Rigg (Dir)
Immediate Holding Company: CRACKDOWN DRUG TESTING LIMITED
Registration no: 03177783 **Date established:** 1996
Turnover: Up to £250,000 **No.of Employees:** 1 - 10 **Product Groups:** 81

Date of Accounts	Apr 11	Apr 10	Apr 09
Working Capital	-3	-4	-6
Fixed Assets	4	5	6
Current Assets	30	24	26
Current Liabilities	33	29	N/A

J Crowther Royton Ltd (t/a Crowther Marine)

Eden Works Belgrave Mill Honeywell Lane, Oldham, OL8 2JP
Tel: 0161-652 4234 **Fax:** 0161-627 4265
E-mail: crowther.marine@tiscali.co.uk
Website: http://www.crowthermarine.co.uk
Directors: K. Hickson (Dir)
Immediate Holding Company: J CROWTHER (ROYTON) LIMITED
Registration no: 00757484 **VAT No.:** 145 2715 77 **Date established:** 1963
Turnover: Up to £250,000 **No.of Employees:** 1 - 10 **Product Groups:** 35, 39

Date of Accounts	Nov 11	Nov 10	Nov 09
Working Capital	298	304	328
Fixed Assets	4	5	7
Current Assets	306	321	343

D & P Tuck

56 Schofield Street, Oldham, OL8 1QJ
Tel: 0161-678 7864 **Fax:** 0161-678 7864
Directors: D. Tuck (Prop)
Date established: 1989 **No.of Employees:** 1 - 10 **Product Groups:** 20, 40, 41

Dawnvale Catering Equipment

Units 1-2 Albert Street, Oldham, OL8 3QP
Tel: 0161-684 7879 **Fax:** 0161-684 8789
E-mail: sales@dawnvale.com
Website: http://www.dawnvale.com
Managers: M. Jagger (Sales Prom Mgr)
Immediate Holding Company: ATLAS TUBE BENDING LIMITED
Registration no: 03162842 **Date established:** 1996
No.of Employees: 1 - 10 **Product Groups:** 84

Date of Accounts	Jun 11	Jun 10	Jun 09
Working Capital	197	220	251
Fixed Assets	249	224	234
Current Assets	462	419	515

Dawson Precision Components Ltd

Greenfield Lane Shaw, Oldham, OL2 8QP
Tel: 01706-842311 **Fax:** 01706-849584
E-mail: sales@dpc.co.uk
Website: http://www.dpc.co.uk
Bank(s): Nat West Plc
Directors: J. Hughes (Fin)
Managers: H. Dawson (Fin Mgr), L. Dawson (Mats Contrlr)
Immediate Holding Company: DAWSON PRECISION COMPONENTS LIMITED
Registration no: 00857801 **VAT No.:** GB 146 8796 15
Date established: 1965 **Turnover:** £1m - £2m **No.of Employees:** 21 - 50
Product Groups: 30, 35, 46, 48

Date of Accounts	Sep 11	Sep 10	Sep 09
Working Capital	343	278	471
Fixed Assets	522	472	574
Current Assets	728	636	812
Current Liabilities	263	N/A	N/A

Diodes Zetex Semiconductors Ltd

Zetex Technology Park Chadderton, Oldham, OL9 9LL
Tel: 0161-622 4400 **Fax:** 0161-622 4446
E-mail: colin_greene@eu.diodes.com
Website: http://www.zetex.com
Directors: C. Greene (Dir)
Managers: P. Baxendale (Tech Serv Mgr), K. Bouch (Purch Mgr), R. Vig (Mktg Serv Mgr), D. Benstead (Personnel), S. Brady (Fin Mgr)
Ultimate Holding Company: DIODES INC (USA)
Immediate Holding Company: DIODES ZETEX SEMICONDUCTORS LIMITED
Registration no: 02387949 **Date established:** 1989
Turnover: £75m - £125m **No.of Employees:** 251 - 500
Product Groups: 37

Date of Accounts	Dec 11	Dec 10	Dec 09
Sales Turnover	93m	92m	63m
Pre Tax Profit/Loss	12m	29m	6m
Working Capital	-66	-9m	15m
Fixed Assets	18m	18m	23m
Current Assets	42m	43m	40m
Current Liabilities	40m	10m	4m

James Dunkerley Steels Ltd

Holyrood Sidings Shaw Road, Oldham, OL1 4AN
Tel: 0161-624 3168 **Fax:** 0161-627 4653
E-mail: sales@dunkerley.co.uk
Website: http://www.dunkerley.co.uk
Bank(s): Lloyds
Directors: C. Walton (Sales), J. Dunkerley (MD)
Managers: D. Simpson (Sales Prom Mgr), J. Boon (Tech Serv Mgr)
Immediate Holding Company: JAMES DUNKERLEY STEELS LIMITED
Registration no: 00506171 **VAT No.:** GB 146 3720 73
Date established: 1952 **Turnover:** £2m - £5m **No.of Employees:** 21 - 50
Product Groups: 35, 66

Date of Accounts	Jun 11	Jun 10	Jun 09
Working Capital	621	636	573
Fixed Assets	958	883	958
Current Assets	2m	2m	2m

Dynamic Controls Ltd

Union Street Royton, Oldham, OL2 5JD
Tel: 0161-633 3933 **Fax:** 0161-633 4113
E-mail: sales@dynamiccontrols.co.uk
Website: http://www.dynamiccontrols.co.uk
Bank(s): HSBC Bank plc
Directors: R. Ariss (Fin), A. Hill (Dir)
Managers: A. Kirk (Sales & Mktg Mg)
Immediate Holding Company: DYNAMIC CONTROLS LIMITED
Registration no: 01689259 **VAT No.:** GB 145 6459 49
Date established: 1982 **Turnover:** £1m - £2m **No.of Employees:** 21 - 50
Product Groups: 29, 30, 36

Date of Accounts	Nov 11	Nov 10	Nov 09
Working Capital	2m	1m	1m
Fixed Assets	632	534	557
Current Assets	2m	2m	2m

Eco-Gifts

Promotional Choice Limited, Falcon Business Centre Victoria Street, Chadderton, OLDHAM, OL9 0HB
Tel: 0161-345 9103 **Fax:** 0161-345 9108
E-mail: sales@eco-gifts.co.uk
Website: http://www.eco-gifts.co.uk
Directors: L. Hunt (Sales), K. Needham (Dir), D. Foster (MD)
Date established: 1997 **No.of Employees:** 1 - 10 **Product Groups:** 49

Electrotec International Ltd

Manchester Road, Oldham, OL9 7AA
Tel: 0161-688 1542
E-mail: lheywood@electrotec-ltd.co.uk
Website: http://www.electrical-deals.co.uk
Managers: L. Heywood (Mgr)
Ultimate Holding Company: SERVICECARE SUPPORT SERVICES LIMITED
Immediate Holding Company: ELECTROTEC INTERNATIONAL LIMITED
Registration no: 02150434 **Date established:** 1987
No.of Employees: 1 - 10 **Product Groups:** 48

Date of Accounts	Sep 11	Sep 10	Sep 09
Working Capital	324	169	173
Fixed Assets	7	6	9
Current Assets	920	916	1m

EPower Trucks

Unit F Prince of Wales Business Park, Vulcan Street, Oldham, OL1 4ER
Tel: 0161-626 9628 **Fax:** 0161-626 9728
E-mail: info@epowertrucks.co.uk
Website: http://www.epowertrucks.co.uk
Managers: D. Redfern (Mgr)
Date established: 2000 **No.of Employees:** 1 - 10 **Product Groups:** 39

F E P Shelman

Unit K Oldham Central Trading Park Coulton Close, Oldham, OL1 4EB
Tel: 0161-628 0628 **Fax:** 0161-628 0555
E-mail: fep@holscot.com
Website: http://www.holscot.com
Managers: C. King (Chief Mgr)
Immediate Holding Company: HOLSCOT INDUSTRIAL LININGS LTD
Registration no: 01721982 **VAT No.:** GB 116 6730 76
Date established: 1988 **Turnover:** £500,000 - £1m
No.of Employees: 1 - 10 **Product Groups:** 30, 31, 36, 38, 40, 48

F & F Drum Reconditioners

Cobden Street Chadderton, Oldham, OL9 9LE
Tel: 0161-626 5555 **Fax:** 0161-622 1654
Directors: G. Foster (Ptnr)
Date established: 1992 **No.of Employees:** 1 - 10 **Product Groups:** 35, 36, 45

F M C G Ltd (Personal Care Division)

Prospect House Featherstall Road South, Oldham, OL9 6HT
Tel: 0161-627 3061 **Fax:** 0161-627 3134
E-mail: info@fmcgltd.com
Website: http://www.fmcgltd.com
Directors: G. Rudd (Dir), P. Bennett (Dir)
Managers: P. McDonnell (Export Sales Mg), A. Tabner, P. Lever
Immediate Holding Company: FMCG Ltd
Registration no: 05374362 **VAT No.:** GB 508 3395 42
Date established: 1989 **Turnover:** £2m - £5m **No.of Employees:** 1 - 10
Product Groups: 30, 31, 32, 61, 63

Ferguson Polycom Ltd

Windsor Mill Hollinwood, Oldham, OL8 3RA
Tel: 0161-681 2206 **Fax:** 0161-947 1326
E-mail: info@fergusonpolycom.co.uk
Website: http://www.fergusonpolycom.co.uk
Bank(s): Barclays
Directors: P. Brennan (Prop), A. Cramb (Dir), J. Boam (Dir)
Ultimate Holding Company: BRENNAN ENTERPRISE LIMITED
Immediate Holding Company: FERGUSON POLYCOM LIMITED
Registration no: 03977194 **VAT No.:** GB 145 0708 84
Date established: 2000 **Turnover:** £5m - £10m
No.of Employees: 51 - 100 **Product Groups:** 23, 26, 29

Date of Accounts	Jan 12	Jan 11	Jan 10
Sales Turnover	8m	7m	6m
Pre Tax Profit/Loss	590	336	128
Working Capital	3m	2m	2m
Fixed Assets	294	287	332
Current Assets	4m	4m	4m
Current Liabilities	975	1m	897

Ferranti Technologies Ltd

Cairo House Greenacres Road, Oldham, OL4 3JA
Tel: 0161-624 0281 **Fax:** 0161-624 5244
E-mail: sales@ferranti-technologies.co.uk
Website: http://www.ferranti-technologies.co.uk
Directors: F. Brinksman (Fin), S. Warren (MD)
Managers: G. Booth (Mktg Serv Mgr), B. Saint (Purch Mgr), J. Lewis (Personnel)
Ultimate Holding Company: ELBIT SYSTEMS (ISRAEL)
Immediate Holding Company: FERRANTI TECHNOLOGIES LIMITED
Registration no: 02968071 **VAT No.:** GB 652 5626 32
Date established: 1994 **Turnover:** £20m - £50m
No.of Employees: 101 - 250 **Product Groups:** 85

Date of Accounts	Dec 11	Dec 10	Dec 09
Sales Turnover	26m	26m	28m
Pre Tax Profit/Loss	970	969	2m
Working Capital	13m	12m	11m
Fixed Assets	4m	3m	3m
Current Assets	20m	21m	17m
Current Liabilities	2m	2m	2m

Florsheim Consultants Ltd

Unit 14 Pennant Industrial Estate Pennant Street, Oldham, OL1 3NP
Tel: 0161-633 8246 **Fax:** 0161-628 2392
E-mail: mnield@florsheim.co.uk
Website: http://www.florcons.co.uk
Directors: M. Nield (Co Sec)
Immediate Holding Company: FLORSHEIM CONSULTANTS LIMITED
Registration no: 02734674 **VAT No.:** GB 606 5566 35
Date established: 1992 **Turnover:** £500,000 - £1m
No.of Employees: 1 - 10 **Product Groups:** 35, 48

Date of Accounts	Mar 12	Mar 11	Mar 10
Working Capital	56	-5	7
Fixed Assets	63	66	68
Current Assets	111	102	117

K & A Furness Ltd

Trent Industrial Estate Duchess Street, Shaw, Oldham, OL2 7UT
Tel: 01706-843411 **Fax:** 01706-882289
E-mail: admin@kafurness.co.uk
Website: http://www.jet-vac.co.uk
Directors: L. Furness (MD), P. Brown (Co Sec)
Ultimate Holding Company: KAF CONSULTANTS LIMITED (ISLE OF MAN)
Immediate Holding Company: K.AND A.FURNESS LIMITED
Registration no: 00661182 **VAT No.:** GB 145 2003 15
Date established: 1960 **Turnover:** £2m - £5m **No.of Employees:** 1 - 10
Product Groups: 40, 48

Date of Accounts	May 11	May 10	May 09
Working Capital	130	138	103
Fixed Assets	16	10	12
Current Assets	220	240	177

G & J Powder Coating

Linney Lane Shaw, Oldham, OL2 8HD
Tel: 01706-843350 **Fax:** 01706-843350
Managers: J. Matherson (Mgr)
Ultimate Holding Company: PAUL ROBINSON HOLDINGS LIMITED
Immediate Holding Company: W.SHUTTLEWORTH & CO.(METAL WORKERS)LIMITED
Registration no: 03456006 **Date established:** 1953
No.of Employees: 1 - 10 **Product Groups:** 46, 48

Date of Accounts	May 11	May 10	May 09
Working Capital	402	367	270
Fixed Assets	100	104	100
Current Assets	886	867	869

G R Labels Ltd

Signum House Terrace Street, Oldham, OL4 1HG
Tel: 0161-624 4835 **Fax:** 0161-628 2778
E-mail: admin@grlabels4signs.co.uk
Website: http://www.grlabels4signs.co.uk
Bank(s): Royal Bank of Scotland, Oldham
Directors: G. Ralphs (Comm)
Immediate Holding Company: G.R. LABELS LIMITED
Registration no: 02594665 **VAT No.:** GB 562 6061 50
Date established: 1991 **Turnover:** £250,000 - £500,000
No.of Employees: 11 - 20 **Product Groups:** 30, 40, 49

Date of Accounts	Mar 12	Mar 11	Mar 10
Working Capital	199	257	310
Fixed Assets	462	476	502
Current Assets	252	297	349

R Gledhill Ltd

Pingle Mill Pingle Lane, Delph, Oldham, OL3 5EX
Tel: 01457-874651 **Fax:** 01457-872428
E-mail: general@rgledhill.co.uk
Website: http://www.rgledhill.co.uk
Bank(s): National Westminster Bank Plc
Directors: J. Gledhill (Fin), P. Gledhill (Dir)
Immediate Holding Company: R.GLEDHILL LIMITED
Registration no: 00313566 **VAT No.:** GB 145 5365 63
Date established: 1936 **Turnover:** £5m - £10m
No.of Employees: 51 - 100 **Product Groups:** 23

Date of Accounts	Oct 11	Oct 10	Oct 09
Sales Turnover	6m	N/A	N/A
Pre Tax Profit/Loss	133	N/A	N/A
Working Capital	1m	1m	1m
Fixed Assets	675	664	669
Current Assets	3m	3m	3m
Current Liabilities	510	N/A	N/A

Graphisign Ltd

B Castle Park Industrial Estate Bower Street, Oldham, OL1 3LN
Tel: 0161-628 9997 **Fax:** 0161-628 9992
E-mail: alant@graphisign.co.uk
Website: http://www.graphisign.co.uk
Directors: A. Tupman (Dir), C. Tupman (Dir), T. Stead (Mkt Research), A. Tupman (MD)
Managers: S. Hand (Sales Prom Mgr), M. Mason (I.T. Exec)
Immediate Holding Company: GRAPHISIGN UK LIMITED
Registration no: 02675187 **Date established:** 1992
No.of Employees: 11 - 20 **Product Groups:** 28, 29, 30

Date of Accounts	Dec 08
Working Capital	-112
Fixed Assets	120
Current Assets	460

Hartley Botanic Ltd

Wellington Road Greenfield, Oldham, OL3 7AG
Tel: 01457-873244 **Fax:** 01457-821968
E-mail: info@hartleybotanic.co.uk
Website: http://www.hartley-botanic.co.uk
Bank(s): Lloyds TSB Bank plc
Directors: J. Mobashaer (MD)
Managers: C. Jackson, R. Plumber (Purch Mgr), C. Stevens (Chief Acct)
Immediate Holding Company: HARTLEY BOTANIC LIMITED
Registration no: 03054175 **Date established:** 1995 **Turnover:** £5m - £10m
No.of Employees: 21 - 50 **Product Groups:** 35

Date of Accounts	Dec 11	Dec 10	Dec 09
Working Capital	1m	1m	323
Fixed Assets	654	684	992
Current Assets	3m	3m	2m

Harveys Nursery

Glodwick Road, Oldham, OL4 1YU
Tel: 0161-624 9535 **Fax:** 0161-627 2028
E-mail: sales@harveys.co.uk
Website: http://www.harveys.co.uk
Managers: K. Greensides (Mgr)
Ultimate Holding Company: HARVEYS OF OLDHAM (HOLDINGS) LIMITED
Immediate Holding Company: HARVEYS OF OLDHAM (HOLDINGS) LIMITED

see next page

Harveys Nursery - Cont'd

Registration no: 00525619 **VAT No.:** GB 508 4779 19
Date established: 2002 **Turnover:** £5m - £10m **No.of Employees:** 1 - 10
Product Groups: 24

Date of Accounts	Nov 11	Nov 10	Nov 09
Working Capital	2m	3m	2m
Fixed Assets	932	991	739
Current Assets	3m	3m	3m

Hirst Kidd & Rennie Ltd

172 Union Street, Oldham, OL1 1EQ
Tel: 0161-633 2121 **Fax:** 0161-627 0905
E-mail: francesh@oldham-chronicle.co.uk
Website: http://www.oldham-chronicle.co.uk
Bank(s): HSBC Bank plc
Directors: B. Stone (Co Sec), H. Hirst (Ch), P. Hirst (MD)
Immediate Holding Company: HIRST, KIDD & RENNIE LIMITED
Registration no: 00170327 **Date established:** 2020 **Turnover:** £2m - £5m
No.of Employees: 51 - 100 **Product Groups:** 27, 28

Date of Accounts	Mar 11	Mar 10	Mar 09
Sales Turnover	3m	4m	N/A
Pre Tax Profit/Loss	-749	-718	-1m
Working Capital	573	937	1m
Fixed Assets	3m	3m	3m
Current Assets	1m	1m	2m
Current Liabilities	405	250	273

Dave Hobin Ltd

273 Shaw Road Royton, Oldham, OL2 6DY
Tel: 0161-633 3728 **Fax:** 0161-633 3728
Directors: V. Teece (Fin), D. Hobin (MD)
Immediate Holding Company: DAVE HOBIN LIMITED
Registration no: 04431450 **Date established:** 2002
No.of Employees: 1 - 10 **Product Groups:** 20, 40, 41

Date of Accounts	May 11	May 10	May 09
Working Capital	-30	-21	-13
Fixed Assets	23	22	13
Current Assets	15	45	66

Howard & Street Engineering

Unit 2 Red Rose Business Park Shaw Road, Royton, Oldham, OL2 6EF
Tel: 0161-652 1124 **Fax:** 0161-628 8048
E-mail: enquiries@howardandstreet.co.uk
Directors: G. Street (Prop)
Immediate Holding Company: EQUINE MANIA LIMITED
Registration no: 01371699 **Date established:** 2006
No.of Employees: 1 - 10 **Product Groups:** 20, 40, 41

Howarth Timber & Building Supplies

Medlock Sawmills Shaw Road, Oldham, OL1 3LJ
Tel: 08448-013310 **Fax:** 0161-620 9527
E-mail: sales.oldham@howarth-timber.co.uk
Website: http://www.howarth-timber.co.uk
Managers: J. Cosslett (Mgr)
Immediate Holding Company: HOWARTH TIMBER & BUILDING SUPPLIES LIMITED
Registration no: 00201929 **Date established:** 1924
No.of Employees: 1 - 10 **Product Groups:** 25, 35, 66

Hyma UK Ltd

Unit 2-3 Hargreaves Street, Oldham, OL9 9ND
Tel: 0161-620 4137 **Fax:** 0161-627 0713
Managers: G. Walker (Mgr)
Ultimate Holding Company: DAN/CUT HOLDINGS APS (DENMARK)
Immediate Holding Company: HYMA (UK) LIMITED
Registration no: 02506900 **Date established:** 1990 **Turnover:** £2m - £5m
No.of Employees: 1 - 10 **Product Groups:** 42, 43

Date of Accounts	Dec 11	Dec 10	Dec 09
Working Capital	106	255	340
Fixed Assets	182	189	196
Current Assets	229	362	481

I P S Converters Ltd

Featherstall Road South, Oldham, OL9 6HS
Tel: 0161-626 1844 **Fax:** 0161-627 5202
E-mail: info@ipsconverters.co.uk
Website: http://www.ipsconverters.co.uk
Directors: H. Cooke (Prop)
Immediate Holding Company: I P S CONVERTERS LIMITED
Registration no: 00751905 **Date established:** 1963 **Turnover:** £1m - £2m
No.of Employees: 11 - 20 **Product Groups:** 23, 24, 27, 32, 35, 36, 61, 63

Date of Accounts	Jan 12	Jan 11	Jan 10
Working Capital	530	542	607
Fixed Assets	141	171	205
Current Assets	757	834	999

J B H Property Consulting Ltd

Broseley House 81 Union Street, Oldham, OL1 1PF
Tel: 0161-336 5068 **Fax:** 0161-320 0512
E-mail: info@jbh-property.co.uk
Website: http://www.jbh-property.co.uk
Directors: A. Barton (MD)
Immediate Holding Company: JBH PROPERTY CONSULTING LIMITED
Registration no: 06606124 **Date established:** 2008
Turnover: Up to £250,000 **No.of Employees:** 1 - 10 **Product Groups:** 80

Date of Accounts	Mar 11	Mar 10	Mar 09
Working Capital	6	1	N/A
Fixed Assets	5	4	N/A
Current Assets	61	45	N/A

J M Lawton & Co

Tylon House Middleton Road West, Chadderton, Oldham, OL9 0PA
Tel: 0161-626 6764 **Fax:** 0161-627 4431
Directors: T. Lawton (Dir)
Date established: 1989 **No.of Employees:** 1 - 10 **Product Groups:** 37, 40, 48

Jacobsons

Werneth Ring Mills Henley Street, Oldham, OL1 2AE
Tel: 0161-624 3894 **Fax:** 0161-620 0261
Website: http://www.jacobsongroup.co.uk
Directors: P. Blay (Co Sec)
Managers: M. Shannon (Warehouse Mgr)
Ultimate Holding Company: AMANN OXLEY HOLDINGS LTD
Immediate Holding Company: AMANN OXLEY THREADS LTD
Registration no: 00008985 **No.of Employees:** 51 - 100
Product Groups: 22

The Jordon Group

Refrigeration House Quebec Street, Oldham, OL9 6QL
Tel: 0161-622 9700 **Fax:** 0161-622 9709
E-mail: sales@jordon.co.uk
Website: http://www.jordon.co.uk
Directors: P. Jordon (MD)
Immediate Holding Company: E.JORDON(REFRIGERATION)LIMITED
Registration no: 00876775 **Date established:** 1966
Turnover: £10m - £20m **No.of Employees:** 51 - 100 **Product Groups:** 52

Date of Accounts	Dec 11	Dec 10	Dec 09
Sales Turnover	11m	8m	7m
Pre Tax Profit/Loss	222	181	-63
Working Capital	1m	1m	939
Fixed Assets	1m	1m	969
Current Assets	4m	3m	3m
Current Liabilities	896	630	594

K B Electronics

20 Ryefields Drive Uppermill, Oldham, OL3 6BX
Tel: 01457-870506 **Fax:** 01457-870520
E-mail: p.blakeley@zen.co.uk
Website: http://www.kbelectronics.com
Managers: P. Blakeley (Sales Prom Mgr)
Immediate Holding Company: HEGEMON COMPONENTS LIMITED
Date established: 2008 **No.of Employees:** 1 - 10 **Product Groups:** 37, 67

Date of Accounts	Dec 11	Dec 10	Dec 09
Sales Turnover	71	60	87
Pre Tax Profit/Loss	35	16	47
Working Capital	-7	14	56
Fixed Assets	15	17	13
Current Assets	41	58	67
Current Liabilities	8	4	10

K W Fire Protection

Unit 38-39 The Acorn Centre Barry Street, Oldham, OL1 3NE
Tel: 0161-628 9379 **Fax:** 0161-620 5354
E-mail: karl.worswick@kwfire.co.uk
Website: http://www.kwfire.co.uk
Directors: K. Worswick (Prop)
Immediate Holding Company: K.W. FIRE PROTECTION LIMITED
Registration no: 04987313 **Date established:** 2003
Turnover: £250,000 - £500,000 **No.of Employees:** 1 - 10
Product Groups: 40, 44, 67, 84, 86

Date of Accounts	Dec 11	Dec 10	Dec 09
Working Capital	53	39	48
Fixed Assets	31	26	17
Current Assets	113	92	105
Current Liabilities	N/A	53	52

Kee Valves

Greenacres Road, Oldham, OL4 2AB
Tel: 01782-523388 **Fax:** 01782-523399
E-mail: sales@keevalves.co.uk
Website: http://www.keevalves.co.uk
Bank(s): National Westminster Bank Plc
Directors: P. Rowbotham (MD), A. Keeley (MD)
Immediate Holding Company: KEE-VALVES LIMITED
Registration no: 03285781 **VAT No.:** GB 670 7894 92
Date established: 1996 **Turnover:** Up to £250,000
No.of Employees: 11 - 20 **Product Groups:** 36, 38, 39, 40

Date of Accounts	Nov 07	Nov 06	Nov 05
Working Capital	-2	-8	-25
Fixed Assets	7	9	11
Current Assets	31	51	7
Current Liabilities	33	59	32

L T E Scientific Ltd

Greenbridge Lane Greenfield, Oldham, OL3 7EN
Tel: 01457-876221 **Fax:** 01457-870131
E-mail: info@lte-scientific.co.uk
Website: http://www.lte-scientific.co.uk
Bank(s): Royal Bank of Scotland
Directors: J. Lees (MD), K. Cooper (Fin)
Managers: S. Henthorn (Purch Mgr)
Immediate Holding Company: LTE SCIENTIFIC LIMITED
Registration no: 02648370 **VAT No.:** GB 562 7943 11
Date established: 1991 **Turnover:** £2m - £5m **No.of Employees:** 51 - 100
Product Groups: 38, 40, 42

Date of Accounts	Dec 11	Dec 10	Dec 09
Sales Turnover	4m	4m	4m
Pre Tax Profit/Loss	-8	349	288
Working Capital	763	844	707
Fixed Assets	2m	2m	1m
Current Assets	2m	2m	2m
Current Liabilities	760	867	838

Laboratory Servicing

21 Dacres Drive Greenfield, Oldham, OL3 7HP
Tel: 01457-875794 **Fax:** 01457-875569
E-mail: sgh@laboratoryservicing.co.uk
Website: http://www.laboratoryservicing.co.uk
Directors: S. Holland (Prop)
Date established: 1983 **No.of Employees:** 1 - 10 **Product Groups:** 38, 42

Lees Lifting Ltd

24 Owls Gate Lees, Oldham, OL4 3FL
Tel: 0161-785 9903 **Fax:** 0161-785 0567
Directors: L. Albison (Dir), J. Albison (MD)
Managers: L. Albison (Mgr)
Immediate Holding Company: LEES LIFTING LIMITED
Registration no: 04453798 **Date established:** 2002
No.of Employees: 1 - 10 **Product Groups:** 35, 39, 45

Date of Accounts	Jun 08	Jun 07	Jun 06
Working Capital	-26	-7	-2
Fixed Assets	6	8	3
Current Assets	11	30	29
Current Liabilities	38	37	31
Total Share Capital	1	1	1

Liftech UK Ltd

19 Lydgate Drive, Oldham, OL4 5HH
Tel: 0161-628 8777 **Fax:** 0161-624 7083
E-mail: liftech@btconnect.com
Directors: O. Kovacevic (MD)
Immediate Holding Company: LIFTECH (U.K.) LIMITED
Registration no: 04376698 **Date established:** 2002
Turnover: Up to £250,000 **No.of Employees:** 1 - 10 **Product Groups:** 35, 39, 45

Date of Accounts	Feb 11	Feb 10	Feb 09
Sales Turnover	39	26	34
Pre Tax Profit/Loss	2	N/A	8
Working Capital	5	7	4
Fixed Assets	N/A	N/A	3
Current Assets	74	64	67
Current Liabilities	25	13	13

Linco P C Ltd

Calico House Edge Lane Street, Royton, Oldham, OL2 6DS
Tel: 0161-624 7098 **Fax:** 0161-678 6162
E-mail: info@lincopc.com
Website: http://www.lincopc.com
Directors: A. Foy-Thackwell (Dir)
Immediate Holding Company: LINCO PC LIMITED
Registration no: 04991751 **VAT No.:** GB 150 2716 01
Date established: 2003 **Turnover:** £1m - £2m **No.of Employees:** 1 - 10
Product Groups: 26, 35

Date of Accounts	Mar 11	Mar 10	Mar 09
Working Capital	-26	11	9
Fixed Assets	38	46	56
Current Assets	152	178	211

Lloyd & Jones Engineers Ltd

Wrigley Street, Oldham, OL4 1HW
Tel: 0161-287 8118 **Fax:** 0161-287 5226
E-mail: oldham_branch@lloyd-jones.com
Website: http://www.lloyd-jones.com
Bank(s): Barclays
Directors: K. Warren (Co Sec)
Managers: B. Lees (Depot Mgr)
Ultimate Holding Company: LLOYD & JONES ENGINEERS (HOLDINGS) LIMITED
Immediate Holding Company: LLOYD & JONES ENGINEERS LIMITED
Registration no: 01751835 **Date established:** 1983
No.of Employees: 11 - 20 **Product Groups:** 37, 67

Date of Accounts	Oct 11	Oct 10	Oct 09
Sales Turnover	13m	10m	10m
Pre Tax Profit/Loss	570	135	47
Working Capital	2m	1m	1m
Fixed Assets	516	813	616
Current Assets	4m	5m	4m
Current Liabilities	1m	1m	1m

Lock Inspection Systems Ltd

Lock House Neville Street, Chadderton, Oldham, OL9 6LF
Tel: 0161-624 0333 **Fax:** 0161-624 5181
E-mail: sales@lockinspection.com
Website: http://www.lockinspection.com
Managers: D. Garnett
Ultimate Holding Company: LOCK INSPECTION HOLDINGS LIMITED
Immediate Holding Company: LOCK INSPECTION GROUP LIMITED
Registration no: 03671954 **VAT No.:** GB 306 9593 36
Date established: 1998 **Turnover:** £500,000 - £1m
No.of Employees: 51 - 100 **Product Groups:** 38, 41

Date of Accounts	Dec 11	Dec 10	Dec 09
Sales Turnover	N/A	500	538
Pre Tax Profit/Loss	94	7	-9
Working Capital	-2m	-2m	-922
Fixed Assets	6m	6m	6m
Current Assets	1m	1m	2m
Current Liabilities	55	66	30

Luwa UK Ltd

Wrigley Street, Oldham, OL4 1HN
Tel: 0161-624 8185 **Fax:** 0161-626 4609
E-mail: sales@luwa.co.uk
Website: http://www.luwa.com
Directors: B. Vonarburg (Fin)
Managers: M. Davies (Chief Mgr)
Immediate Holding Company: LUWA (U.K.) LIMITED
Registration no: 00642994 **VAT No.:** GB 218 2316 86
Date established: 1959 **Turnover:** £2m - £5m **No.of Employees:** 1 - 10
Product Groups: 40, 41, 42, 43, 44, 46, 47, 52

Date of Accounts	Apr 12	Apr 11	Apr 10
Working Capital	257	233	243
Fixed Assets	28	35	13
Current Assets	310	341	350
Current Liabilities	N/A	15	N/A

M C M Conveyor Systems

Crompton Street Chadderton, Oldham, OL9 9AA
Tel: 0161-284 2222 **Fax:** 0161-627 0075
E-mail: info@amber-industries.ltd.uk
Website: http://www.amber-industries.ltd.uk
Bank(s): HSBC
Directors: K. Moden (MD)
Managers: R. Hughs (Personnel), M. Adams (Sales Prom Mgr)
Registration no: 01529235 **VAT No.:** 741 2682 42 **Date established:** 1983
Turnover: £5m - £10m **No.of Employees:** 21 - 50 **Product Groups:** 45

Mallinson's Of Oldham Ltd

Trent Industrial Estate Duchess Street, Shaw, Oldham, OL2 7UT
Tel: 01706-299000 **Fax:** 01706-299700
E-mail: mallinsons@o2.co.uk
Website: http://www.mallinsonsofoldham.co.uk
Directors: T. Cowell (Co Sec)
Ultimate Holding Company: KAF CONSULTANTS LIMITED (ISLE OF MAN)
Immediate Holding Company: MALLINSON'S OF OLDHAM LIMITED
Registration no: 01699029 **Date established:** 1983
No.of Employees: 11 - 20 **Product Groups:** 20, 40, 41

Date of Accounts	Feb 11	Feb 10	Feb 09
Working Capital	-3	-4	-1
Fixed Assets	44	29	31
Current Assets	170	115	202

Manchester Gate Company Ltd

4 Watts Street Chadderton, Oldham, OL9 9LQ
Tel: 0161-628 7550 **Fax:** 0161-628 7550
E-mail: info@manchestergatecompany.co.uk
Website: http://www.manchestergatecompany.co.uk
Managers: W. Beswick (Mgr)
Immediate Holding Company: MANCHESTER GATE CO LTD
Registration no: 07041186 **Date established:** 2009
No.of Employees: 1 - 10 **Product Groups:** 26, 35

Date of Accounts	Oct 10
Working Capital	-7
Fixed Assets	7
Current Assets	4

Manhatten Heights
425 Milnrow Road Shaw, Oldham, OL2 8BU
Tel: 01706-849752 **Fax:** 01706-299209
E-mail: sales@manheights.co.uk
Website: http://www.manheights.co.uk
Directors: W. Cunningham (Prop)
No.of Employees: 1 - 10 **Product Groups:** 40, 48, 52, 66

Marshall Pumps Systems Ltd
Rhodes Bank, Oldham, OL1 1UA
Tel: 0161-609 8888 **Fax:** 0161-627 0913
E-mail: info@marshallpumps.co.uk
Website: http://www.marshallpumps.co.uk
Bank(s): Barclays, High Street, Oldham
Directors: N. Hursthouse (Dir), N. Hursthouse (Dir)
Immediate Holding Company: MARSHALL PUMP SYSTEMS LIMITED
Registration no: 00859839 **VAT No.:** GB 144 9128 63
Date established: 1965 **Turnover:** £2m - £5m **No.of Employees:** 21 - 50
Product Groups: 36, 38, 39, 40

Date of Accounts	Sep 11	Sep 10	Sep 09
Working Capital	325	143	63
Fixed Assets	695	710	712
Current Assets	785	667	632

Masterpeace (a division of Pennine Systems Ltd)
Crossley Works Walsh Street, Chadderton, Oldham, OL9 9LR
Tel: 0161-678 2998 **Fax:** 0161-678 2997
E-mail: ian.torr@penninesystems.co.uk
Website: http://www.penninesystems.co.uk
Bank(s): National Westminster
Directors: I. Torr (Dir), I. Torr (MD), S. Torr (Dir)
Managers: J. Larton (Sales Prom Mgr), L. Holt (Sales Admin), L. Torr (Sales Admin)
Immediate Holding Company: B.T. TECHNICAL SYSTEMS LIMITED
Registration no: 01076827 **VAT No.:** GB 652 6584 17
Date established: 1972 **Turnover:** £1m - £2m **No.of Employees:** 21 - 50
Product Groups: 26, 84

Medical Air Technology Ltd
Gateway Crescent Broadway Business Park, Chadderton, Oldham, OL9 9XB
Tel: 08448-712100 **Fax:** 0161-624 7547
E-mail: sales@medicalairtechnology.com
Website: http://www.medicalairtechnology.com
Bank(s): HSBC
Directors: S. Taylor (Sales & Mktg), N. Hay (Contracts)
Managers: D. Booth (Comptroller)
Immediate Holding Company: MEDICAL AIR LIMITED
Registration no: 07391186 **VAT No.:** GB 468 1476 18
Date established: 2010 **Turnover:** £2m - £5m **No.of Employees:** 21 - 50
Product Groups: 40

Midas Plating & Engineering Co. Ltd
Woodend Mills Hartshead Street, Lees, Oldham, OL4 5EE
Tel: 0161-620 0939 **Fax:** 0161-678 8614
Directors: J. Day (Co Sec), P. Butler (MD)
Immediate Holding Company: MIDAS PLATING & ENGINEERING CO LIMITED
Registration no: 01452372 **VAT No.:** GB 306 0000 37
Date established: 1979 **Turnover:** £250,000 - £500,000
No.of Employees: 1 - 10 **Product Groups:** 48

Date of Accounts	Mar 11	Mar 10	Mar 09
Working Capital	34	33	39
Fixed Assets	38	39	41
Current Assets	84	66	69

Millstek
44 Denbydale Way Royton, Oldham, OL2 5TJ
Tel: 0161-620 8563 **Fax:** 0161-333 3250
E-mail: info@millstek.com
Website: http://www.millstek.com
Directors: H. Mills (Prop)
VAT No.: GB 792 8638 71 **Date established:** 2001
Turnover: Up to £250,000 **No.of Employees:** 1 - 10 **Product Groups:** 23, 43

Monarch Shelving Ltd
Unit 7 Moss Lane Industrial Estate Royton, Oldham, OL2 6HR
Tel: 01706-880355 **Fax:** 01706-880520
E-mail: sales@monarchdirect.co.uk
Website: http://www.monarchdirect.co.uk
Directors: N. Hare (MD)
Immediate Holding Company: MONARCH SHELVING LIMITED
Registration no: 05429662 **Date established:** 2005
Turnover: £500,000 - £1m **No.of Employees:** 1 - 10 **Product Groups:** 26, 30, 36, 39, 45

Date of Accounts	Apr 11	Apr 10	Apr 09
Sales Turnover	529	416	632
Pre Tax Profit/Loss	2	-4	28
Working Capital	283	281	293
Fixed Assets	19	23	11
Current Assets	351	324	339
Current Liabilities	12	8	15

Money Controls Ltd
Coin House New Coin Street, Royton, Oldham, OL2 6JZ
Tel: 0161-678 0111 **Fax:** 0161-626 7674
E-mail: slindon@moneycontrols.com
Website: http://www.moneycontrols.com
Bank(s): Bank of Scotland
Directors: A. Morrison (Sales), K. Collett (Dir), R. Wilkinson (Fin)
Managers: A. Vidguard (Personnel), B. Barker (Tech Serv Mgr), D. Harrison, D. John (Mktg Serv Mgr)
Ultimate Holding Company: CRANE CO. (USA)
Immediate Holding Company: MONEY CONTROLS HOLDINGS LIMITED
Registration no: 02549191 **VAT No.:** GB 341 7015 88
Date established: 1990 **Turnover:** £20m - £50m
No.of Employees: 1001 - 1500 **Product Groups:** 44, 49

Date of Accounts	Dec 11	Sep 10	Sep 09
Pre Tax Profit/Loss	15	30	61
Working Capital	15m	14m	14m
Fixed Assets	14m	15m	15m
Current Assets	15m	15m	15m
Current Liabilities	N/A	10	260

J Moran Precision Grinding
Bleasby Street, Oldham, OL4 2AJ
Tel: 0161-620 1284 **Fax:** 0161-627 4985
E-mail: michael-moran@btconnect.com
Website: http://www.jamesmoranprecisiongrinders.co.uk
Directors: M. Moran (Prop)
Immediate Holding Company: G J K TRANSPORT LIMITED
Registration no: 02416945 **Date established:** 1989
Turnover: Up to £250,000 **No.of Employees:** 1 - 10 **Product Groups:** 48

Date of Accounts	Sep 90
Working Capital	-22
Fixed Assets	13
Current Assets	7

Neo Electronics Ltd
Shaw Road, Oldham, OL1 4AW
Tel: 0161-633 2148 **Fax:** 0161-627 5324
E-mail: info@neo.co.uk
Website: http://www.neo.co.uk
Directors: P. Hurst (Fin), C. Schofield (MD)
Ultimate Holding Company: NEO SYSTEMS LIMITED
Immediate Holding Company: NEO ELECTRONICS LIMITED
Registration no: 01882260 **Date established:** 1985
Turnover: £500,000 - £1m **No.of Employees:** 11 - 20
Product Groups: 37, 44, 48, 49, 84, 85

Date of Accounts	May 11	May 10	May 09
Working Capital	370	609	695
Fixed Assets	364	29	49
Current Assets	676	839	953

Newfoil Machines
Moorhey Street, Oldham, OL4 1JE
Tel: 0161-627 0550 **Fax:** 0161-627 0551
E-mail: sales@newfoilmachines.co.uk
Website: http://www.newfoilmachines.co.uk
Bank(s): National Westminster Bank Plc
Directors: D. Evans (Dir)
Immediate Holding Company: NEWFOIL MACHINES LIMITED
Registration no: 01611761 **VAT No.:** GB 376 1397 27
Date established: 1982 **Turnover:** £500,000 - £1m
No.of Employees: 11 - 20 **Product Groups:** 44

Date of Accounts	Aug 11	Aug 10	Aug 09
Working Capital	2m	2m	1m
Fixed Assets	600	608	629
Current Assets	2m	2m	2m

Nicholson Group (Holdings) Ltd
Hollinwood Business Centre Albert Street Hollinwood, Oldham, OL8 3QL
Tel: 0161-684 2319 **Fax:** 0161-684 2318
E-mail: enquiries@nicholson-group.co.uk
Website: http://www.nicholson-group.co.uk
Directors: P. Hobwood (MD)
Managers: A. Reid (Contracts Mgr), C. Eaton (Sales Prom), B. Collinge (Fin Mgr)
Registration no: 02056060 **Date established:** 1972
Turnover: £500,000 - £1m **No.of Employees:** 1 - 10 **Product Groups:** 43

John E Noone & Associates
11 Queen Street, Oldham, OL1 1RD
Tel: 0161-627 3746 **Fax:** 0161-627 1056
E-mail: john.noone@jenassoc.co.uk
Directors: J. Noone (Prop)
Immediate Holding Company: JOHN E NOONE AND ASSOCIATES LTD
Registration no: 06836054 **Date established:** 2009
Turnover: Up to £250,000 **No.of Employees:** 1 - 10 **Product Groups:** 35

Date of Accounts	Mar 11	Mar 10
Sales Turnover	128	89
Pre Tax Profit/Loss	29	N/A
Working Capital	-14	-23
Fixed Assets	20	23
Current Assets	37	22
Current Liabilities	21	13

Normesh Ltd
18-20 Miles Street, Oldham, OL1 3NU
Tel: 0161-628 9849 **Fax:** 0161-627 5732
E-mail: sales@normesh.co.uk
Website: http://www.normesh.co.uk
Directors: N. Clokey (MD)
Immediate Holding Company: NORMESH LIMITED
Registration no: 04446478 **VAT No.:** GB 425 7596 30
Date established: 2002 **No.of Employees:** 1 - 10 **Product Groups:** 23, 30, 35, 36, 42, 66

Date of Accounts	Jul 11	Jul 10	Jul 09
Working Capital	44	36	48
Fixed Assets	46	50	55
Current Assets	100	97	97

Northern Counties Housing Association
Bower House Unit 1 Stable Street, Chadderton, Oldham, OL9 7LH
Tel: 0161-219 7000 **Fax:** 0161-244 6801
E-mail: customer.service@guinness.org.uk
Website: http://www.ncha.co.uk
Directors: J. Thomson (Ch)
Managers: J. Cockerham (Mgr), S. Would Not Provide
Immediate Holding Company: PEAKNINE RESIDENTS ASSOCIATION LTD
Registration no: FP051630 **Date established:** 1993
No.of Employees: 101 - 250 **Product Groups:** 87

Northern Wall & Floor Ltd
Bismark House Bower Street, Oldham, OL1 3XB
Tel: 0161-626 3366 **Fax:** 0161-627 3306
E-mail: sales@thetileshop.co.uk
Website: http://www.thetileshop.co.uk
Bank(s): Yorkshire Bank PLC
Directors: C. Ellis (Co Sec)
Managers: M. Tindale (Mgr)
Immediate Holding Company: NORTHERN WALL & FLOOR LIMITED
Registration no: 01808993 **VAT No.:** GB 519 1571 45
Date established: 1984 **Turnover:** £1m - £2m **No.of Employees:** 11 - 20
Product Groups: 30, 33

Date of Accounts	Dec 10	Dec 09	Dec 08
Working Capital	847	816	924
Fixed Assets	235	250	255
Current Assets	1m	1m	1m

Nortonics Foxtam Ltd
Foxtam House Watts Street, Chadderton, Oldham, OL9 9LQ
Tel: 0161-626 5316 **Fax:** 0161-627 0929
E-mail: julie@nortonicsfoxtam.co.uk
Website: http://www.nortonicsfoxtam.co.uk
Bank(s): National Westminster Bank Plc
Directors: J. Tribe (Sales), J. Carter (Fin)
Managers: I. Birch (Tech Serv Mgr), S. Cooper (Prod Mgr)
Immediate Holding Company: NORTONICS FOXTAM LIMITED
Registration no: 01736622 **VAT No.:** GB 151 2631 03
Date established: 1983 **Turnover:** £250,000 - £500,000
No.of Employees: 21 - 50 **Product Groups:** 38, 49

Date of Accounts	May 11	May 10	May 09
Working Capital	668	643	584
Fixed Assets	52	61	88
Current Assets	948	1m	973

Oldham Electroplating Co. Ltd
Argyle Street, Oldham, OL1 3PQ
Tel: 0161-624 5473 **Fax:** 0161-624 5473
Directors: P. Mollard (MD)
Immediate Holding Company: OLDHAM ELECTROPLATING COMPANY LIMITED
Registration no: 01348203 **Date established:** 1978
No.of Employees: 1 - 10 **Product Groups:** 46, 48

Date of Accounts	Mar 12	Mar 11	Mar 10
Working Capital	103	88	83
Fixed Assets	40	41	43
Current Assets	116	98	91

Oldham Hire Centre Oldham Plant Hire & Sales Ltd
50 Oldham Road Royton, Oldham, OL2 5PF
Tel: 0161-627 0427 **Fax:** 0161-633 6590
E-mail: sales@oldhamhirecentre.co.uk
Website: http://www.oldhamplanthire.co.uk
Directors: N. Mooney (MD)
Immediate Holding Company: OLDHAM PLANT HIRE & SALES LIMITED
Registration no: 02151116 **Date established:** 1987
No.of Employees: 1 - 10 **Product Groups:** 40, 83

Date of Accounts	Jul 11	Jul 10	Jul 08
Working Capital	28	17	25
Fixed Assets	30	38	47
Current Assets	80	66	81

Oldham Industrial
Hadfield Works Hadfield Street, Oldham, OL8 3BU
Tel: 0161-620 5499 **Fax:** 0161-678 6782
E-mail: oldhamradiators@btconnect.com
Website: http://www.oldhamindustrialheatexchangers.com
Directors: R. Salisbury (MD)
Immediate Holding Company: OLDHAM RADIATORS LIMITED
Registration no: 01630638 **Date established:** 1982
No.of Employees: 1 - 10 **Product Groups:** 37, 40, 48

Date of Accounts	May 11	May 10	May 09
Working Capital	96	72	50
Fixed Assets	73	66	60
Current Assets	219	208	154

Oldham Trade Plastics
Unit 5 Victoria Trading Estate Drury Lane, Chadderton, Oldham, OL9 7PJ
Tel: 0161-683 3250 **Fax:** 0161-683 3259
E-mail: sales@oldhamtradeplastics.co.uk
Website: http://www.oldhamtradeplastics.co.uk
Directors: K. Tupaea (MD)
Date established: 2006 **No.of Employees:** 1 - 10 **Product Groups:** 30

P & D Northern Steels Ltd
Mosshey Street Shaw, Oldham, OL2 8QL
Tel: 01706-848811 **Fax:** 01706-841153
E-mail: sales@pdnorthern.co.uk
Website: http://www.pdnorthern.co.uk
Bank(s): National Westminster Bank Plc
Directors: P. Martin (MD)
Immediate Holding Company: P.& D.NORTHERN STEELS LIMITED
Registration no: 00584986 **Date established:** 1957 **Turnover:** £5m - £10m
No.of Employees: 11 - 20 **Product Groups:** 34, 66

Date of Accounts	Oct 11	Oct 10	Oct 09
Working Capital	1m	1m	1m
Fixed Assets	481	412	470
Current Assets	3m	2m	2m
Current Liabilities	32	N/A	N/A

P D Q Lifting Ltd
Unit 73 The Acorn Centre Barry Street, Oldham, OL1 3NE
Tel: 0161-678 1212 **Fax:** 0161-678 1313
E-mail: nick@pdqlifting.co.uk
Website: http://www.pdqlifting.co.uk
Directors: N. Johnson (Dir)
Immediate Holding Company: PDQ LIFTING LIMITED
Registration no: 03841262 **Date established:** 1999
No.of Employees: 1 - 10 **Product Groups:** 35, 39, 45

Date of Accounts	Feb 08	Feb 11	Feb 10
Working Capital	-18	-4	13
Fixed Assets	110	39	54
Current Assets	382	275	344

P & R Fire & Security
Sherwood House 119 Lees Road, Oldham, OL4 1JW
Tel: 0161-620 8111 **Fax:** 0161-620 8111
E-mail: sales@pandrsecurities.co.uk
Website: http://www.pandrfireandsecurity.co.uk
Directors: K. Pearson (MD)
Immediate Holding Company: P & R SECURITY SYSTEMS LIMITED
Registration no: 03783088 **Date established:** 1999 **Turnover:** £1m - £2m
No.of Employees: 1 - 10 **Product Groups:** 37, 40, 48, 52, 67

Date of Accounts	Dec 10	Dec 09	Dec 08
Working Capital	-882	-879	-576
Fixed Assets	112	119	134
Current Assets	717	620	947

Pan Amusements
Austerlands Mill Huddersfield Road, Austerlands, Oldham, OL4 3QB
Tel: 0161-652 8092 **Fax:** 0161-627 5357
E-mail: info@panamusements.com
Website: http://www.panamusements.com
Bank(s): National Westminster Oldham

see next page

Pan Amusements - Cont'd
Directors: P. Whittaker (Prop)
Immediate Holding Company: PORVALE LIMITED
Registration no: 01790854 **VAT No.:** GB 408 7343 49
Date established: 1984 **No.of Employees:** 11 - 20 **Product Groups:** 49

Date of Accounts	Sep 11	Sep 10	Sep 09
Working Capital	2	16	-18
Fixed Assets	39	25	28
Current Assets	301	350	264

Park Cakes Bakeries Ltd
Ashton Road, Oldham, OL8 2ND
Tel: 0161-633 1181 **Fax:** 0161-626 6199
E-mail: steve.ford@parkcakes.com
Website: http://www.northernfoods.com
Bank(s): Barclays
Directors: R. Paul (Fin), A. Allen (MD), B. Mitchell (Sales & Mktg)
Managers: K. Buckley (Chief Acct), M. Wilford (Mktg Serv Mgr), R. Reynolds, S. Carter, A. McGuirk (Personnel), C. Whitehead, J. Whitticker (Personnel)
Ultimate Holding Company: ELIOT LUXEMBOURG HOLDCO SARL (LUXEMBOURG)
Immediate Holding Company: PARK CAKES LIMITED
Registration no: 05998327 **VAT No.:** GB 168 7433 30
Date established: 2006 **Turnover:** £75m - £125m
No.of Employees: 1001 - 1500 **Product Groups:** 20

Date of Accounts	Mar 08	Mar 09	Mar 10
Sales Turnover	119m	99m	100m
Pre Tax Profit/Loss	-6m	-3m	-10m
Working Capital	-12m	-19m	-27m
Fixed Assets	7m	10m	10m
Current Assets	30m	29m	23m
Current Liabilities	3m	4m	4m

Patterson & Rothwell Ltd
Mount Pleasant Street, Oldham, OL4 1HH
Tel: 0161-621 5000 **Fax:** 0161-621 5001
E-mail: sales@patterson-rothwell.co.uk
Website: http://www.patterson-rothwell.co.uk
Bank(s): HSBC
Directors: R. Anderson (Fin), A. Rothwell (MD)
Managers: D. Bowden (Sales & Mktg Mgr), B. Kennally (Tech Serv Mgr), A. Flynn (Personnel)
Ultimate Holding Company: MAKEMORE LIMITED
Immediate Holding Company: PATTERSON AND ROTHWELL LIMITED
Registration no: 01848302 **Date established:** 1984
Turnover: £10m - £20m **No.of Employees:** 51 - 100 **Product Groups:** 30, 42, 48

Date of Accounts	Dec 11	Dec 10	Dec 09
Sales Turnover	13m	12m	10m
Pre Tax Profit/Loss	760	126	75
Working Capital	2m	2m	1m
Fixed Assets	3m	2m	3m
Current Assets	6m	6m	6m
Current Liabilities	2m	3m	2m

Peter Cox Ltd
Unit 2 Broadgate Chadderton, Oldham, OL9 9XA
Tel: 0845-370899 **Fax:** 0191-487 4804
E-mail: headoffice@petercox.com
Website: http://www.petercox.com
Directors: L. Wales (Cust Serv)
Managers: S. Hall (Mgr)
Immediate Holding Company: PETER COX LIMITED
Registration no: 02438126 **Date established:** 1989
Turnover: £10m - £20m **No.of Employees:** 1 - 10 **Product Groups:** 07, 32, 52, 66

Philmar Fabrications
Lion Mill Fitton Street, Royton, Oldham, OL2 5JX
Tel: 0161-633 1409 **Fax:** 0161-620 4612
E-mail: mark@philmar.co.uk
Website: http://www.philmar.co.uk
Directors: M. Mills (Dir)
Immediate Holding Company: PHILMAR FABRICATIONS LIMITED
Registration no: 04438779 **Date established:** 2002
No.of Employees: 11 - 20 **Product Groups:** 20, 40, 41

Date of Accounts	Jul 11	Jul 10	Jul 09
Working Capital	574	458	389
Fixed Assets	113	89	122
Current Assets	893	702	738

Platt & Hill Ltd
Belgrave Mill Fitton Hill Road, Oldham, OL8 2LZ
Tel: 0161-621 4400 **Fax:** 0161-621 4408
E-mail: sales@phfillings.co.uk
Website: http://www.phfillings.com
Bank(s): Barclays
Directors: A. Hill (Sales), J. Platt (Fab), M. Iwanowytsch (Fin)
Managers: D. Hill (), N. Bonner (), N. Hill (), A. Hill (), M. Iwanowytsch (Accounts), C. Yelland-Hey (Purch Mgr)
Registration no: 00060275 **VAT No.:** GB 306 3667 63
Date established: 1889 **Turnover:** £10m - £20m
No.of Employees: 101 - 250 **Product Groups:** 23, 24, 26, 29, 30, 63

Date of Accounts	Dec 11	Dec 10	Dec 09
Sales Turnover	9m	9m	9m
Pre Tax Profit/Loss	236	-21	-225
Working Capital	198	114	151
Fixed Assets	724	749	796
Current Assets	3m	2m	2m
Current Liabilities	661	460	476

Polymeric Labels Ltd
12 Greenacres Road, Oldham, OL4 1HA
Tel: 0161-678 9005 **Fax:** 0161-627 1378
E-mail: sales@polymeric.co.uk
Website: http://www.polymeric.co.uk
Bank(s): Lloyds
Directors: J. Buckley (Co Sec), I. Buckley (MD)
Managers: P. Clarke (Prod Mgr)
Immediate Holding Company: POLYMERIC LABELS LIMITED
Registration no: 02015901 **VAT No.:** GB 440 2102 19
Date established: 1986 **Turnover:** £2m - £5m **No.of Employees:** 21 - 50
Product Groups: 29, 30

Date of Accounts	Dec 09	Dec 08	Dec 07
Working Capital	-36	-66	-72
Fixed Assets	1m	1m	1m
Current Assets	10	N/A	N/A

Promotional Choice Ltd
Chambers Business Centre Chapel Road, Oldham, OL8 4QQ
Tel: 0161-345 9103 **Fax:** 0161-345 9108
E-mail: sales@promochoice.co.uk
Website: http://www.promochoice.co.uk
Directors: D. Foster (MD)
Immediate Holding Company: PROMOTIONAL CHOICE LIMITED
Registration no: 03354720 **Date established:** 1997
Turnover: £500,000 - £1m **No.of Employees:** 1 - 10 **Product Groups:** 24, 49, 65

Date of Accounts	Apr 11	Apr 10	Apr 09
Working Capital	215	233	289
Fixed Assets	3	2	3
Current Assets	359	305	417

Pulse Home Products Ltd
Vine Mill Middleton Road, Royton, Oldham, OL2 5LN
Tel: 0161-652 1211 **Fax:** 0161-626 0391
E-mail: info@pulse-uk.co.uk
Website: http://www.pulse-uk.co.uk
Bank(s): National Westminster
Directors: D. Allen (MD), M. Davison (Sales), M. Weems (Fin)
Managers: M. Bird (Tech Serv Mgr)
Ultimate Holding Company: RUTLAND PARTNERS LLP
Immediate Holding Company: PULSE HOME PRODUCTS LIMITED
Registration no: 00713656 **Date established:** 1962
Turnover: £50m - £75m **No.of Employees:** 101 - 250 **Product Groups:** 40

Date of Accounts	Mar 11	Mar 10	Mar 09
Sales Turnover	63m	67m	72m
Pre Tax Profit/Loss	3m	3m	1m
Working Capital	14m	11m	7m
Fixed Assets	6m	7m	7m
Current Assets	23m	22m	27m
Current Liabilities	4m	2m	5m

Q Plant Hire Ltd
Queghan House Stampstone Street, Oldham, OL1 3PW
Tel: 0161-620 2115 **Fax:** 0161-652 8342
E-mail: matt@qplanthire.co.uk
Website: http://www.qplanthire.co.uk
Directors: A. Quinn (MD)
Ultimate Holding Company: Q CRANE HIRE LIMITED
Immediate Holding Company: Q PLANT HIRE LIMITED
Registration no: 01068623 **Date established:** 1972
Turnover: £500,000 - £1m **No.of Employees:** 1 - 10 **Product Groups:** 51, 83

Date of Accounts	Aug 09	Aug 08	Aug 07
Working Capital	-843	-732	-546
Fixed Assets	4m	4m	3m
Current Assets	1m	1m	1m

Quantum Profile Systems
Salmon Fields Royton, Oldham, OL2 6JG
Tel: 0161-627 4222 **Fax:** 0161-627 4333
E-mail: sales@quantum-ps.co.uk
Website: http://www.dacatie.co.uk
Managers: S. Keane (Sales Prom Mgr)
Immediate Holding Company: QUANTUM PROFILE SYSTEMS LIMITED
Registration no: 04057656 **VAT No.:** GB 110 6214 33
Date established: 2000 **Turnover:** £5m - £10m
No.of Employees: 51 - 100 **Product Groups:** 30, 35, 66

Date of Accounts	Dec 11	Dec 10	Dec 09
Sales Turnover	N/A	6m	6m
Pre Tax Profit/Loss	N/A	57	154
Working Capital	-288	-191	-142
Fixed Assets	908	747	870
Current Assets	2m	2m	1m
Current Liabilities	N/A	692	581

R M D Creative Displays
Thornham Works Oozewood Road, Royton, Oldham, OL2 5SQ
Tel: 0781-321 5527 **Fax:** 0161-627 3787
Website: http://www.rmd-display.co.uk
Directors: S. Willis (MD)
Immediate Holding Company: THORNHAM PAINTS (YORKSHIRE) LIMITED
Registration no: 02784863 **Date established:** 1993
No.of Employees: 1 - 10 **Product Groups:** 26, 35

Date of Accounts	Mar 12	Mar 11	Mar 10
Working Capital	124	113	91
Fixed Assets	11	13	24
Current Assets	207	187	155

Reece Safety Products Ltd
Unit 3 Gatehead Business Park Delph New Road, Delph, Oldham, OL3 5DE
Tel: 01457-871148 **Fax:** 01457-831144
E-mail: sales@reecesafety.co.uk
Website: http://www.reecesafety.co.uk
Directors: J. Reece (MD)
Immediate Holding Company: REECE SAFETY PRODUCTS LTD
Registration no: 04372283 **VAT No.:** GB 787 0410 21
Date established: 2002 **Turnover:** £2m - £5m **No.of Employees:** 1 - 10
Product Groups: 30, 35, 36, 40

Date of Accounts	Apr 12	Apr 11	Apr 10
Sales Turnover	4m	3m	3m
Pre Tax Profit/Loss	679	546	232
Working Capital	901	531	131
Fixed Assets	342	329	326
Current Assets	2m	919	469
Current Liabilities	241	211	104

Reel Appeal
Unit 3 Milking Green Hartshead Street, Lees, Oldham, OL4 5EE
Tel: 0161-620 6764 **Fax:** 0161-620 6764
E-mail: sales@reelappeal.co.uk
Website: http://www.reelappeal.co.uk
Directors: M. Lewis (Co Sec), B. Lewis (Dir)
Immediate Holding Company: REEL APPEAL LIMITED
Registration no: 05139751 **VAT No.:** GB 841 2851 37
Date established: 2004 **No.of Employees:** 1 - 10 **Product Groups:** 27, 28, 30, 66

Date of Accounts	Jun 12	Jun 11	Jun 10
Working Capital	133	105	53
Fixed Assets	51	54	22
Current Assets	209	249	139

Remote Estimating Ltd
2 Cherry Grove Royton, Oldham, OL2 5YL
Tel: 0780-9158186
E-mail: info@remoteestimating.co.uk
Website: http://remoteestimating.co.uk
Managers: I. Whetham (Eng)
Registration no: 6719769 **Date established:** 2008
Turnover: Up to £250,000 **No.of Employees:** 1 - 10 **Product Groups:** 44, 84

Remploy Building Products
Ashton Road Bardsley, Oldham, OL8 3JG
Tel: 0161-627 3355 **Fax:** 0161-620 6610
E-mail: stevebottomley@remploy.co.uk
Website: http://www.remploy.co.uk
Managers: S. Bottomley (Prod Mgr), D. Paget (Sales Prom Mgr), A. Hughes (Purch Mgr)
No.of Employees: 101 - 250 **Product Groups:** 36, 40

Ribble Packaging Ltd
Greengate Street, Oldham, OL4 1DF
Tel: 0161-284 9000 **Fax:** 0161-627 5049
E-mail: stephen@ribble-pack.co.uk
Website: http://www.ribble-pack.co.uk
Bank(s): The Royal Bank of Scotland
Directors: M. Kernaghan (Fin), S. Rector (MD)
Managers: R. Hunter (Sales Prom Mgr), S. Barber (Personnel), B. Parkin (Tech Serv Mgr)
Ultimate Holding Company: RIBBLE INVESTMENTS LIMITED
Immediate Holding Company: RIBBLE PACKAGING LIMITED
Registration no: 00521820 **Date established:** 1953
Turnover: £20m - £50m **No.of Employees:** 101 - 250 **Product Groups:** 27

Date of Accounts	Dec 11	Dec 10	Dec 09
Sales Turnover	22m	19m	15m
Pre Tax Profit/Loss	504	-19	672
Working Capital	2m	2m	2m
Fixed Assets	5m	5m	6m
Current Assets	11m	11m	8m
Current Liabilities	4m	5m	3m

Charles Robinson Cutting Tools Ltd
Unit C1 Castle Park Industrial Estate, Oldham, OL1 3LN
Tel: 0161-628 5550 **Fax:** 0161-628 5599
E-mail: sales@c-robinson.co.uk
Website: http://www.cut-tools.co.uk
Directors: D. Robinson (MD)
Immediate Holding Company: CHARLES ROBINSON (CUTTING TOOLS) LIMITED
Registration no: 01536566 **Date established:** 1980
Turnover: £500,000 - £1m **No.of Employees:** 11 - 20
Product Groups: 24, 27, 28, 36, 37, 42, 43, 44

Date of Accounts	Dec 11	Dec 10	Dec 09
Working Capital	57	27	53
Fixed Assets	25	29	34
Current Assets	204	125	142

S A Meats
2 Summers Street Chadderton, Oldham, OL9 9EQ
Tel: 07798-793993 **Fax:** 0161-860 0727
E-mail: fasi@email.com
Website: http://www.fasi.4mg.com
Directors: M. Fasi (Snr Part), M. Fasi (Ptnr), M. Rafi (Dir)
No.of Employees: 1 - 10 **Product Groups:** 20, 62

S G & M Worthington & Co.
7 Lansdowne Road Chadderton, Oldham, OL9 9EG
Tel: 0161-620 9653 **Fax:** 0161-678 6979
E-mail: sales@sgmw.co.uk
Website: http://www.sgmw.co.uk
Directors: T. Macdonald (Dir)
Immediate Holding Company: KAB SYSTEMS UK LTD
Registration no: 05520869 **Date established:** 2005
No.of Employees: 1 - 10 **Product Groups:** 37, 67

Date of Accounts	Jul 11	Jul 10	Jul 09
Working Capital	27	34	-16
Fixed Assets	17	17	17
Current Assets	126	128	75

S K Electronics Ltd
Regent Street, Oldham, OL1 3TZ
Tel: 0161-620 5414 **Fax:** 0161-627 3237
E-mail: sales@skelectronics.co.uk
Website: http://www.skelectronics.co.uk
Directors: A. Ashton (MD), A. Jones (MD)
Managers: S. Walker (Mgr)
Immediate Holding Company: S K ELECTRONICS LIMITED
Registration no: 04153109 **VAT No.:** GB 306 3596 60
Date established: 2001 **Turnover:** £1m - £2m **No.of Employees:** 11 - 20
Product Groups: 30, 37

Date of Accounts	Mar 11	Mar 10	Mar 09
Working Capital	151	125	125
Fixed Assets	133	111	112
Current Assets	886	458	496

Safeguard Refrigeration Services
Units 1-2 Albert Street, Oldham, OL8 3QP
Tel: 0161-626 2202
E-mail: service@safeguard.uk.com
Website: http://www.safeguard.uk.com
Directors: S. Ingham (Prop)
Immediate Holding Company: JESCO (MANCHESTER) LIMITED
Date established: 2007 **No.of Employees:** 11 - 20 **Product Groups:** 36, 40

Saras Process Ltd
Trent Industrial Estate Duchess Street, Shaw, Oldham, OL2 7UT
Tel: 01706-845960 **Fax:** 01706-882403
E-mail: sales@sarasprocess.co.uk
Website: http://www.sarasprocess.co.uk
Directors: J. Gates (MD)
Ultimate Holding Company: KAF CONSULTANTS LIMITED (ISLE OF MAN)
Immediate Holding Company: SARAS PROCESS LIMITED
Registration no: 04643614 **VAT No.:** GB 150 1114 34
Date established: 2003 **No.of Employees:** 1 - 10 **Product Groups:** 48

Date of Accounts	Dec 11	Dec 10	Dec 09
Working Capital	27	23	20
Fixed Assets	25	29	32
Current Assets	70	57	52

Scientific Glass Blowing Co. Ltd
163-165 Higginshaw Lane Royton, Oldham, OL2 6HQ
Tel: 0161-621 4700 **Fax:** 0161-627 0493
E-mail: sales@sciglass.co.uk
Website: http://www.sciglass.co.uk
Directors: N. Stuart (Fin), L. Stuart (MD)
Immediate Holding Company: SCIENTIFIC GLASS BLOWING CO. LIMITED
Registration no: 01296425 **VAT No.:** GB 151 1314 20
Date established: 1977 **Turnover:** £1m - £2m **No.of Employees:** 1 - 10
Product Groups: 33, 36, 38, 40, 42, 47, 63, 66, 67

Date of Accounts	Jan 12	Jan 11	Jan 10
Sales Turnover	355	1m	1m
Pre Tax Profit/Loss	12	22	12
Working Capital	63	52	32
Fixed Assets	41	42	46
Current Assets	200	221	142
Current Liabilities	92	95	51

Robert Scott & Sons
Oakview Mills Manchester Road, Greenfield, Oldham, OL3 7HG
Tel: 01457-873931 **Fax:** 01457-819490
E-mail: sales@robert-scott.co.uk
Website: http://www.robert-scott.co.uk
Bank(s): Nat West
Directors: A. Scott (Sales & Mktg), A. Scott (Fin), F. Murphy (Purch), P. Scott (Dir)
Managers: B. Beckett
Ultimate Holding Company: ROBERT SCOTT & SONS LIMITED
Immediate Holding Company: HAROLD WATSON LIMITED
Registration no: 03218088 **VAT No.:** GB 148 5566 35
Date established: 1996 **Turnover:** £20m - £50m
No.of Employees: 101 - 250 **Product Groups:** 24, 32, 33, 49

Date of Accounts	Sep 11	Sep 10	Sep 09
Working Capital	921	921	921
Current Assets	921	921	921

Servemet N W Ltd
Unit D Westwood Industrial Estate Arkwright Street, Oldham, OL9 9LZ
Tel: 0161-626 4145 **Fax:** 0161-626 4146
E-mail: peter@servemet.co.uk
Website: http://www.servicemetals.co.uk
Bank(s): National Westminster Bank Plc
Directors: H. Webb (Sales), P. Brady (Dir)
Immediate Holding Company: SERVEMET (N.W.) LIMITED
Registration no: 01576526 **VAT No.:** GB 361 5126 75
Date established: 1981 **Turnover:** £5m - £10m **No.of Employees:** 21 - 50
Product Groups: 66

Date of Accounts	Dec 11	Dec 10	Dec 09
Working Capital	863	798	756
Fixed Assets	90	129	125
Current Assets	3m	2m	2m

Shaw Sheet Metal Co. Ltd
Thomas Street Shaw, Oldham, OL2 8PG
Tel: 01706-847172 **Fax:** 01706-848411
E-mail: shawsheetmetal@btconnect.com
Directors: R. Hartley (MD)
Ultimate Holding Company: SHAW SHEET METAL (HOLDINGS) LIMITED
Immediate Holding Company: SHAW SHEET METAL COMPANY LIMITED
Registration no: 04907446 **VAT No.:** GB 146 8707 40
Date established: 2003 **Turnover:** £250,000 - £500,000
No.of Employees: 1 - 10 **Product Groups:** 48

Date of Accounts	Oct 11	Oct 10	Oct 09
Working Capital	76	6	38
Current Assets	397	255	296

Smart Metals Ltd
Unit 3 Victoria Trading Estate Drury Lane, Chadderton, Oldham, OL9 7PJ
Tel: 0161-684 9545 **Fax:** 0161-684 9969
E-mail: smartmetals@yahoo.co.uk
Website: http://www.smart-metals.co.uk
Directors: A. Griffiths (Ptnr)
No.of Employees: 1 - 10 **Product Groups:** 26, 35

Sourcing Vantage Ltd
4 Lower Knoll Road Diggle, Oldham, OL3 5PD
Tel: 0845-6026322
E-mail: david@sourcingvantage.com
Website: http://www.sourcingvantage.com
Directors: D. MacKellar (Dir), D. Turner (Dir)
Registration no: 06806798 **Date established:** 2009
Turnover: £500,000 - £1m **No.of Employees:** 1 - 10 **Product Groups:** 44, 61, 80

Special Equipment Ltd
Unit 1 United Mill Suffolk Street, Oldham, OL9 7DJ
Tel: 0161-624 6636 **Fax:** 0161-628 6340
Directors: A. Stafford (MD)
Immediate Holding Company: SPECIAL EQUIPMENT LIMITED
Registration no: 02992635 **VAT No.:** GB 146 7383 45
Date established: 1994 **Turnover:** £250,000 - £500,000
No.of Employees: 1 - 10 **Product Groups:** 84

Date of Accounts	Dec 11	Dec 10	Dec 09
Working Capital	77	78	87
Fixed Assets	1	1	2
Current Assets	88	90	95

Standring Brothers Ltd
Wellington Road Greenfield, Oldham, OL3 7AG
Tel: 01457-877227 **Fax:** 01457-877204
E-mail: sales@standringbrothers.co.uk
Website: http://www.standringbrothers.co.uk
Bank(s): Natwest
Directors: J. Standring (Dir)
Immediate Holding Company: STANDRING BROTHERS LIMITED
Registration no: 02694601 **VAT No.:** GB 606 3734 50
Date established: 1992 **Turnover:** £500,000 - £1m
No.of Employees: 11 - 20 **Product Groups:** 30

Date of Accounts	May 11	May 10	May 09
Working Capital	34	-34	-25
Fixed Assets	158	151	170
Current Assets	312	263	208

Star In A Car Ltd
1 Kent Close Diggle, Oldham, OL3 5PN
Tel: 08456-123863 **Fax:** 0560-341 3285
E-mail: enquiries@starinacar.co.uk
Website: http://www.starinacar.co.uk
Directors: J. Gittins (MD), S. Gittins (Fin)
Immediate Holding Company: STAR IN A CAR LTD
Registration no: 05333802 **Date established:** 2005
Turnover: Up to £250,000 **No.of Employees:** 1 - 10 **Product Groups:** 72

Date of Accounts	Jan 11	Jan 10	Jan 09
Sales Turnover	103	77	117
Pre Tax Profit/Loss	30	10	14
Working Capital	-5	-9	-8
Fixed Assets	12	14	14
Current Assets	27	19	21
Current Liabilities	10	6	6

Sterling Sensors Ltd
Hawksley Industrial Estate Manchester Road, Oldham, OL8 4PQ
Tel: 0161-620 0410 **Fax:** 0161-627 0507
E-mail: sales@sterlingsensors.co.uk
Website: http://www.sterlingsensors.co.uk
Bank(s): Barclays
Directors: J. Murray (MD)
Ultimate Holding Company: PRECISION 21 LIMITED
Immediate Holding Company: STERLING SENSORS LIMITED
Registration no: 02497036 **VAT No.:** GB 562 7047 39
Date established: 1990 **Turnover:** £500,000 - £1m
No.of Employees: 11 - 20 **Product Groups:** 38

Date of Accounts	Nov 11	Nov 10	Nov 09
Working Capital	376	310	248
Fixed Assets	41	38	47
Current Assets	621	592	463

Stigwood & Sons
Grafton Street, Oldham, OL1 4SD
Tel: 0161-633 3398 **Fax:** 0161-633 3398
Directors: D. Stigwood (Prop)
Date established: 1962 **No.of Employees:** 1 - 10 **Product Groups:** 20, 40, 41

Stream Measurement Ltd
Unit 5 St Johns Industrial Estate Lees, Oldham, OL4 3DZ
Tel: 0161-622 0777 **Fax:** 0161-622 0777
E-mail: sales@stream-measurement.com
Website: http://www.stream-measurement.com
Managers: K. Cooper (Mgr)
Immediate Holding Company: STREAM MEASUREMENT LIMITED
Registration no: 03808602 **Date established:** 1999 **Turnover:** £1m - £2m
No.of Employees: 11 - 20 **Product Groups:** 38, 48, 83, 85

Date of Accounts	Apr 12	Apr 11	Apr 10
Working Capital	448	446	342
Fixed Assets	69	60	51
Current Assets	1m	985	933

George Sumner Ltd
4 Rhodes Bank, Oldham, OL1 1UA
Tel: 0161-609 8888 **Fax:** 0161-627 0913
E-mail: info@marshallpumps.co.uk
Website: http://www.marshallpumps.co.uk
Directors: N. Hursthouse (MD)
Ultimate Holding Company: MARSHALL PUMP SYSTEMS LIMITED
Immediate Holding Company: GEORGE SUMNER LIMITED
Registration no: 00134279 **VAT No.:** GB 144 9079 50
Date established: 2014 **Turnover:** £500,000 - £1m
No.of Employees: 1 - 10 **Product Groups:** 48

Date of Accounts	Sep 11	Sep 10	Sep 09
Working Capital	96	56	37
Fixed Assets	12	12	16
Current Assets	138	136	108

Swirl Products Ltd
Prospect House Featherstall Road South, Oldham, OL9 6HT
Tel: 0161-627 3061
E-mail: sales@fmcgltd.com
Website: http://www.fmcgltd.com
Directors: H. Rees (Dir), D. Rees (Co Sec)
Immediate Holding Company: SWIRL PRODUCTS LIMITED
Registration no: 03150346 **Date established:** 1996 **Turnover:** £2m - £5m
No.of Employees: 11 - 20 **Product Groups:** 32

Date of Accounts	Dec 11	Dec 10	Dec 09
Sales Turnover	N/A	N/A	5m
Pre Tax Profit/Loss	N/A	N/A	270
Working Capital	2m	1m	1m
Fixed Assets	19	26	25
Current Assets	2m	2m	2m
Current Liabilities	N/A	N/A	251

Synergy Healthcare plc
Lion Mill Fitton Street Royton, Oldham, OL2 5JX
Tel: 0161-624 5641 **Fax:** 0161-627 0902
Website: http://www.synergyhealthplc.com
Managers: A. Hamer (Quality Control), J. McClean (Grp Mktg Mgr), J. Wilson (Mktg Serv Mgr)
Ultimate Holding Company: Shiloh P.L.C.
Immediate Holding Company: U.K. ELECTRONICS LIMITED
Registration no: 01753503 **VAT No.:** GB 146 9637 30
Date established: 1983 **No.of Employees:** 1 - 10 **Product Groups:** 22, 24, 27

Talentum Development Ltd
Beal Lane Shaw, Oldham, OL2 8PF
Tel: 01706-844714 **Fax:** 01706-882612
E-mail: info@talentum.co.uk
Website: http://www.talentum.co.uk
Bank(s): Barclays
Directors: J. Broadbent (MD)
Immediate Holding Company: TALENTUM DEVELOPMENTS LIMITED
Registration no: 00940267 **VAT No.:** GB 146 1723 77
Date established: 1968 **Turnover:** £500,000 - £1m
No.of Employees: 11 - 20 **Product Groups:** 38

Date of Accounts	Mar 12	Mar 11	Mar 10
Working Capital	547	407	339
Fixed Assets	669	667	588
Current Assets	903	819	663

Tanner Business Centre
Waterside Mill Chew Valley Road, Greenfield, Oldham, OL3 7NH
Tel: 01457-872273 **Fax:** 01457-870133
E-mail: info@tannerbrothers.co.uk
Website: http://www.tender-care.com
Directors: J. Tanner (MD)
Immediate Holding Company: TANNER BROS. (GREENFIELD) LIMITED
Registration no: 00517732 **VAT No.:** GB 145 1908 71
Date established: 1953 **No.of Employees:** 1 - 10 **Product Groups:** 84

Date of Accounts	Mar 11	Mar 10	Mar 09
Working Capital	264	319	351
Fixed Assets	2m	2m	2m
Current Assets	518	550	503

C H Thompson Ltd
Westpoint Industrial Estate Hargreaves Street, Oldham, OL9 9ND
Tel: 0161-620 0211 **Fax:** 0161-627 4480
E-mail: info@boiler-repairs.co.uk
Website: http://www.boiler-repairs.co.uk
Directors: S. Mak (Fin), R. Kolbuck (MD)
Immediate Holding Company: C H THOMPSON LIMITED
Registration no: 03484686 **VAT No.:** GB 146 7118 64
Date established: 1997 **Turnover:** £1m - £2m **No.of Employees:** 1 - 10
Product Groups: 48

Date of Accounts	Dec 11	Dec 10	Dec 09
Working Capital	207	264	321
Fixed Assets	5	5	6
Current Assets	331	455	497

Transdrive Engineering Ltd
Milton Street Royton, Oldham, OL2 6QU
Tel: 0161-628 8497 **Fax:** 0161-628 4366
E-mail: sales@transdrive.co.uk
Website: http://www.transdrive.co.uk
Bank(s): Yorkshire
Directors: P. Wren (Dir)
Immediate Holding Company: TECHNODRIVES LIMITED
Registration no: 03372342 **VAT No.:** GB 380 4596 35
Date established: 1997 **Turnover:** £2m - £5m **No.of Employees:** 11 - 20
Product Groups: 35, 37

Trouvay & Cauvin Ltd
Broadgate Oldham Broadway Business Park, Chadderton, Oldham, OL9 9XA
Tel: 0161-684 7488 **Fax:** 0161-684 7487
E-mail: sales@trouvay-cauvin.co.uk
Website: http://www.trouvay-cauvin.com
Bank(s): HSBC
Directors: S. Pickup (Fin)
Managers: G. Lumley (Comm)
Ultimate Holding Company: TROUVAY & CAUVIN (HOLDINGS) LIMITED
Immediate Holding Company: TROUVAY & CAUVIN LIMITED
Registration no: 00966219 **VAT No.:** 222 9973 44 **Date established:** 1969
Turnover: £10m - £20m **No.of Employees:** 11 - 20 **Product Groups:** 36, 38, 40

Date of Accounts	Oct 11	Oct 10	Oct 09
Working Capital	796	1m	1m
Fixed Assets	25	3	6
Current Assets	2m	2m	2m

Tunnel Engineering Services UK Ltd
Heywood Street, Oldham, OL4 2HA
Tel: 0161-626 6005 **Fax:** 0161-627 0993
E-mail: geoffrey.clarke@tesuk.co.uk
Website: http://www.tesuk.co.uk
Directors: G. Clarke (Dir)
Managers: A. Worsley (Admin Off), A. Worsley
Immediate Holding Company: TUNNEL ENGINEERING SERVICES (U.K.) LTD.
Registration no: 02696865 **Date established:** 1992
No.of Employees: 11 - 20 **Product Groups:** 42, 45

Date of Accounts	May 11	May 10	May 09
Working Capital	369	243	161
Fixed Assets	66	62	67
Current Assets	565	482	746
Current Liabilities	97	N/A	N/A

Turner Bianca
Bell Mill Claremont Street, Oldham, OL8 3EJ
Tel: 0161-627 0045 **Fax:** 0161-627 0660
E-mail: admin@turner-bianca.co.uk
Website: http://www.turner-bianca.co.uk
Directors: K. Walmsley (Fin), R. Bullbrook (Ch)
Managers: T. Young, P. Fitzpatrick, S. Leeson (Tech Serv Mgr), L. Rich (Personnel)
Ultimate Holding Company: TURNER BIANCA PLC
Immediate Holding Company: BIANCA TEXTILES LIMITED
Registration no: 01343042 **VAT No.:** GB 150 1977 75
Date established: 1977 **Turnover:** £50m - £75m
No.of Employees: 101 - 250 **Product Groups:** 61

Date of Accounts	Mar 11	Mar 10	Mar 07
Working Capital	100	100	100
Current Assets	100	100	100

UK Electronics Ltd
Schofield House Lion Mill Yard Fitton Street, Royton, Oldham, OL2 5JX
Tel: 0161-626 4117 **Fax:** 0161-627 4870
E-mail: neil.carr@ukelectronics.co.uk
Website: http://www.ukelectronics.co.uk
Bank(s): Barclays
Directors: N. Carr (Fin)
Managers: A. Evans (Tech Serv Mgr), G. Jones (Prod Mgr), S. McKown (Tech Sales Mgr), H. Kwuka (Purch Mgr)
Immediate Holding Company: U.K. ELECTRONICS LIMITED
Registration no: 01753503 **VAT No.:** GB 388 4535 07
Date established: 1983 **Turnover:** £1m - £2m **No.of Employees:** 21 - 50
Product Groups: 84

Date of Accounts	Jul 11	Jul 10	Jul 09
Working Capital	342	215	217
Fixed Assets	1m	1m	978
Current Assets	1m	1m	766

Unity Plating Co. Ltd
Mount Pleasant Street, Oldham, OL4 1HH
Tel: 0161-287 8714 **Fax:** 0161-287 8715
E-mail: peterwilson@hotmail.co.uk
Directors: E. Wilson (Fin), P. Wilson (MD)
Immediate Holding Company: UNITY PLATING CO. LIMITED
Registration no: 00614019 **VAT No.:** GB 147 1374 70
Date established: 1958 **Turnover:** £250,000 - £500,000
No.of Employees: 1 - 10 **Product Groups:** 48

Date of Accounts	Nov 11	Nov 10	Nov 09
Working Capital	27	25	42
Fixed Assets	22	25	30
Current Assets	48	48	58
Current Liabilities	N/A	19	N/A

W Shuttleworth & Co. Ltd

Linney Lane Shaw, Oldham, OL2 8HD
Tel: 01706-845966 **Fax:** 01706-844966
E-mail: sales@wshuttleworth.co.uk
Website: http://www.wshuttleworth.co.uk
Bank(s): National Westminster
Directors: J. Atkinson (Co Sec), P. Robinson (MD)
Managers: S. Robinson (Mktg Serv Mgr)
Immediate Holding Company: W.SHUTTLEWORTH & CO.(METAL WORKERS)LIMITED
Registration no: 00519143 **VAT No.:** GB 145 2708 74
Date established: 1953 **No.of Employees:** 11 - 20 **Product Groups:** 48

Date of Accounts	May 11	May 10	May 09
Working Capital	402	367	270
Fixed Assets	100	104	100
Current Assets	886	867	869

Waldor Door Manufacturers

Unit 35 Acorn Enterprise Centre Barry Street, Oldham, OL1 3NE
Tel: 0161-626 0352 **Fax:** 0161-626 0352
Directors: D. Wallwork (Prop)
Date established: 1984 **No.of Employees:** 1 - 10 **Product Groups:** 26, 35

Whittaker Brothers

Rutland Way Linney Lane, Shaw, Oldham, OL2 8HE
Tel: 01706-847531 **Fax:** 01706-848871
E-mail: sales@whittakers.co.uk
Website: http://www.whittakers.co.uk
Managers: J. Whittaker (Mgr)
Immediate Holding Company: WHITTAKER BROTHERS (LEISURE) LIMITED
Registration no: 01192560 **Date established:** 1974 **Turnover:** £1m - £2m
No.of Employees: 1 - 10 **Product Groups:** 49, 65, 83, 89

Date of Accounts	Dec 11	Dec 10	Dec 09
Working Capital	516	545	496
Fixed Assets	455	63	74
Current Assets	542	611	542

Widdop Bingham & Co. Ltd

Broadgate Broadway Business Park, Chadderton, Oldham, OL9 9XE
Tel: 0161-688 1200 **Fax:** 0161-682 6808
E-mail: sales@widdop.co.uk
Website: http://www.widdop.co.uk
Bank(s): Lloyds TSB Bank plc
Directors: M. Illingworth (Dir)
Ultimate Holding Company: WOODCLAY LIMITED
Immediate Holding Company: WIDDOP BINGHAM & CO. LIMITED
Registration no: 00171327 **VAT No.:** GB 145 0672 79
Date established: 2020 **Turnover:** £20m - £50m
No.of Employees: 51 - 100 **Product Groups:** 49, 65

Date of Accounts	Sep 11	Sep 10	Sep 09
Sales Turnover	23m	24m	23m
Pre Tax Profit/Loss	3m	673	838
Working Capital	9m	7m	8m
Fixed Assets	470	274	185
Current Assets	13m	13m	13m
Current Liabilities	1m	690	3m

Williamsons

16 Brook Street, Oldham, OL1 3HG
Tel: 0161-624 2080 **Fax:** 0161-627 1716
E-mail: sales@williamsons-conveyors.co.uk
Website: http://www.williamsons-conveyors.co.uk
Directors: M. Steer (MD)
Immediate Holding Company: WILLIAMSON'S CONVEYORS AND HANDLING EQUIPMENT LIMITED
Registration no: 01910223 **VAT No.:** GB 425 7356 44
Date established: 1985 **Turnover:** £1m - £2m **No.of Employees:** 11 - 20
Product Groups: 45

Date of Accounts	Jun 11	Jun 10	Jun 09
Working Capital	91	138	148
Fixed Assets	136	147	158
Current Assets	226	362	364

Wilmslow Express

Mitchell Henry House Hollinwood Avenue, Chadderton, Oldham, OL9 8EF
Tel: 0161-211 2944 **Fax:** 01625-549660
E-mail: macclesfield@menmedia.co.uk
Website: http://www.wilmslowexpress.co.uk
Managers: J. Gordon
Ultimate Holding Company: GUARDIAN MEDIA GROUP
Immediate Holding Company: LANCS & CHESIRE COUNTY NEWSPAPERS LTD
Registration no: 00103931 **VAT No.:** GB 145 7744 45
Date established: 1900 **No.of Employees:** 1 - 10 **Product Groups:** 28

Ormskirk

Aerocool Ltd

Unit 301 Merlin Park Burscough Industrial Estate, Ormskirk, L40 8JY
Tel: 01704-897520 **Fax:** 01704-897521
E-mail: enquiries@aerocool.co.uk
Website: http://www.aerocool.co.uk
Directors: A. Hafez (Dir), I. Jones (Co Sec)
Immediate Holding Company: HAFEZ & JONES LIMITED
Registration no: 02799357 **Date established:** 1993
No.of Employees: 21 - 50 **Product Groups:** 40, 66

Apex Interior Systems Ltd

Unit 10 Plantation Road, Burscough Industrial Estate, Ormskirk, L40 8JT
Tel: 01704-896600 **Fax:** 01704-896611
E-mail: sales@apexinteriorsystems.co.uk
Website: http://www.apexinteriorsystems.co.uk
Directors: A. Ashworth (MD)
Managers: C. Hartley-montron (Sales Prom Mgr)
Ultimate Holding Company: ASHWORTH HOLDINGS LTD
Immediate Holding Company: APEX INTERIOR SYSTEMS LIMITED
Registration no: 03023695 **Date established:** 1995
No.of Employees: 51 - 100 **Product Groups:** 26, 30, 33

Date of Accounts	Apr 12	Apr 11	Apr 10
Working Capital	1m	1m	887
Fixed Assets	552	676	806
Current Assets	2m	2m	2m

Derek Ashcroft Ltd

Guys Indl-Est Tollgate Road, Burscough, Ormskirk, L40 8TG
Tel: 01704-892279 **Fax:** 01704- 895276
Directors: R. Wood (MD), A. Parks (Fin), C. Wood (MD)
Ultimate Holding Company: RICHARD WOOD LIMITED
Immediate Holding Company: DEREK ASHCROFT LIMITED
Registration no: 03299576 **Date established:** 1997
Turnover: £250,000 - £500,000 **No.of Employees:** 1 - 10
Product Groups: 25, 45

Date of Accounts	Jan 11	Jan 10	Jan 09
Sales Turnover	882	N/A	N/A
Pre Tax Profit/Loss	20	N/A	N/A
Working Capital	654	636	622
Fixed Assets	20	23	25
Current Assets	770	703	706
Current Liabilities	21	N/A	6

Atkinson & Kirby Ltd

Unit 1 Atkinson Road, Ormskirk, L39 2AJ
Tel: 01695-573234 **Fax:** 01695-573859
E-mail: sales@akirby.co.uk
Website: http://www.akirby.co.uk
Directors: D. Ellams (Mkt Research), R. Lincoln (Fin), R. Scott (MD)
Managers: P. Singh (Tech Serv Mgr), A. Birkett (Buyer)
Ultimate Holding Company: RIPAT LIMITED
Immediate Holding Company: ATKINSON & KIRBY LIMITED
Registration no: 00215881 **Date established:** 2026
Turnover: £10m - £20m **No.of Employees:** 51 - 100 **Product Groups:** 25

Date of Accounts	Sep 08	Oct 09	Oct 10
Sales Turnover	10m	9m	9m
Pre Tax Profit/Loss	1m	606	-997
Working Capital	2m	3m	3m
Fixed Assets	4m	4m	2m
Current Assets	5m	6m	5m
Current Liabilities	428	686	886

Bins-n-Benches

Smithy Lane Holmeswood, Ormskirk, L40 1UH
Tel: 01704-821136 **Fax:** 01704-821136
E-mail: sales@bins-n-benches.co.uk
Website: http://www.bins-n-benches.co.uk
Directors: A. Forrest (Prop)
Immediate Holding Company: BINS-N-BENCHES LIMITED
Registration no: 05421623 **Date established:** 2005
No.of Employees: 1 - 10 **Product Groups:** 30, 35, 36

Date of Accounts	Apr 12	Apr 11	Apr 10
Working Capital	229	175	157
Fixed Assets	164	150	165
Current Assets	277	229	210

Burscough Rewinds

Unit 1-10 Red Cat Lane, Burscough, Ormskirk, L40 0RA
Tel: 01704-894501 **Fax:** 01704-897787
E-mail: sales@burscough-rewinds.co.uk
Website: http://www.burscough-rewinds.co.uk
Directors: S. Fox (Prop)
Registration no: 04151273 **Turnover:** £250,000 - £500,000
No.of Employees: 1 - 10 **Product Groups:** 37, 48

C M Hesford & Co. Ltd

Moorgate, Ormskirk, L39 4RU
Tel: 01695-572564 **Fax:** 01695-571002
E-mail: info@22club.co.uk
Website: http://www.hesfordsdiy.co.uk
Bank(s): Barclays
Directors: M. Hesford (Dir)
Immediate Holding Company: C.M. HESFORD & COMPANY LIMITED
Registration no: 00252866 **VAT No.:** GB 164 4951 47
Date established: 1930 **Turnover:** £500,000 - £1m
No.of Employees: 11 - 20 **Product Groups:** 35, 66

Date of Accounts	Mar 12	Mar 11	Mar 10
Working Capital	-31	-26	-19
Fixed Assets	267	284	292
Current Assets	186	158	166

Clarke & Pulman

Langley Place Burscough Industrial Estate, Ormskirk, L40 8JS
Tel: 01704-897507 **Fax:** 01704-897163
E-mail: info@clarkeandpulman.com
Website: http://www.clarkeandpulman.com
Directors: G. Clarke (MD), S. Clarke (Fin)
Immediate Holding Company: CLARKE AND PULMAN LIMITED
Registration no: 04637003 **Date established:** 2003
No.of Employees: 11 - 20 **Product Groups:** 41

Date of Accounts	Dec 11	Dec 10	Dec 09
Sales Turnover	9m	N/A	N/A
Pre Tax Profit/Loss	143	N/A	N/A
Working Capital	704	888	610
Fixed Assets	2m	975	877
Current Assets	3m	3m	3m
Current Liabilities	261	N/A	N/A

Clayton Commercials Ltd

Langley Road Burscough Industrial Estate, Ormskirk, L40 8JR
Tel: 01704-894244 **Fax:** 01704-894226
E-mail: sales@claytoncommercials.com
Website: http://www.claytoncommercials.com
Bank(s): The Royal Bank of Scotland
Directors: T. Kelts (Fin), S. Barrett (Pers)
Managers: C. Horrocks (Buyer), P. Norris (Chief Mgr)
Ultimate Holding Company: CLAYTON COMMERCIALS HOLDINGS LIMITED
Immediate Holding Company: CLAYTON COMMERCIALS LIMITED
Registration no: 01047357 **Date established:** 1972 **Turnover:** £2m - £5m
No.of Employees: 51 - 100 **Product Groups:** 39

Date of Accounts	Dec 11	Dec 10	Dec 09
Sales Turnover	5m	3m	4m
Pre Tax Profit/Loss	151	-429	-1m
Working Capital	873	465	853
Fixed Assets	153	195	247
Current Assets	2m	1m	2m
Current Liabilities	139	275	433

Geoff Dale Woodwork Machinery

95a Causeway Lane Rufford, Ormskirk, L40 1SL
Tel: 01704-821821 **Fax:** 01704-821999
E-mail: geoff.dale@woodmachines.fsnet.co.uk
Website: http://www.woodmachines.fsnet.co.uk
Directors: G. Dale (Ptnr)
Date established: 1993 **No.of Employees:** 1 - 10 **Product Groups:** 46

Direct Instrument Hire Ltd

16 Swordfish Close Swordfish Business Park, Burscough, Ormskirk, L40 8JW
Tel: 01704-896966 **Fax:** 01704-896956
E-mail: sales@instrument-hire.co.uk
Website: http://www.instrument-hire.co.uk
Directors: D. Wilson (Dir), K. Carine (Fin)
Ultimate Holding Company: TEST & MEASUREMENT HIRE LIMITED
Immediate Holding Company: DIRECT INSTRUMENT HIRE LIMITED
Registration no: 03176208 **Date established:** 1996
Turnover: £500,000 - £1m **No.of Employees:** 1 - 10 **Product Groups:** 37, 38, 39, 44, 85

Date of Accounts	Mar 11	Mar 10	Mar 09
Working Capital	2	45	3
Fixed Assets	N/A	85	40
Current Assets	2	208	195
Current Liabilities	N/A	N/A	20

Fox Fabrication

Towngate Works Dark Lane, Mawdesley, Ormskirk, L40 2QU
Tel: 01704-822050 **Fax:** 01257-471492
E-mail: chris@foxfab.co.uk
Website: http://www.foxfab.co.uk
Directors: C. Fox (Prop)
Immediate Holding Company: FOX FABRICATION & CONSTRUCTION LIMITED
Registration no: 05570705 **Date established:** 2005
No.of Employees: 21 - 50 **Product Groups:** 35

Date of Accounts	Dec 11	Dec 10	Dec 09
Working Capital	76	51	1
Fixed Assets	232	250	233
Current Assets	224	159	136

F W S Supplies Ltd

Unit 2 Ringtail Place Burscough Industrial Estate, Ormskirk, L40 8LA
Tel: 01704-897755 **Fax:** 01704-897555
Directors: K. Tabran (Prop), P. Tabarn (Co Sec)
Immediate Holding Company: F.W.S. SUPPLIES LTD
Registration no: 03103171 **Date established:** 1995
No.of Employees: 1 - 10 **Product Groups:** 46

Date of Accounts	Sep 11	Sep 10	Sep 09
Working Capital	121	118	127
Fixed Assets	18	21	21
Current Assets	209	189	186

Hylands Packaging Ltd

Plantation Road Burscough Industrial Estate, Ormskirk, L40 8JT
Tel: 01704-897222 **Fax:** 01704-897333
E-mail: sales@hylands-packaging.com
Website: http://www.hylands-packaging.com
Directors: S. Hyland (MD)
Immediate Holding Company: HYLANDS PACKAGING LIMITED
Registration no: 02807374 **VAT No.:** GB 618 6548 13
Date established: 1993 **No.of Employees:** 1 - 10 **Product Groups:** 66

Date of Accounts	Jun 12	Jun 11	Jun 10
Working Capital	68	67	53
Fixed Assets	15	15	19
Current Assets	273	328	272

M C B Fabrications Ltd

Wood Lane Mawdesley, Ormskirk, L40 2RL
Tel: 01704-823055 **Fax:** 01704-823055
Directors: M. Culshaw (Dir)
Immediate Holding Company: MCB FABRICATIONS LIMITED
Registration no: 04181306 **Date established:** 2001
No.of Employees: 1 - 10 **Product Groups:** 35

Date of Accounts	Aug 11	Aug 09	Aug 08
Working Capital	9	22	66
Fixed Assets	31	26	25
Current Assets	72	50	140

Nittel UK Ltd

Unit 10 Swordfish Close, Burscough, Ormskirk, L40 8JW
Tel: 01704-897077 **Fax:** 01704-897999
E-mail: rob.thompson@nittel.com
Website: http://www.nittel.co.uk
Managers: J. Gwynne (Mgr), R. Thompson (Sales Prom Mgr)
Immediate Holding Company: NITTEL UK LIMITED
Registration no: 03373773 **Date established:** 1997 **Turnover:** £1m - £2m
No.of Employees: 1 - 10 **Product Groups:** 27, 30, 34, 35, 36, 40, 45, 48, 66

Date of Accounts	Dec 11	Dec 10	Dec 09
Sales Turnover	1m	1m	983
Pre Tax Profit/Loss	53	32	N/A
Working Capital	287	284	263
Fixed Assets	18	28	75
Current Assets	476	492	402
Current Liabilities	57	52	36

Ormskirk Microwaves & Kitchen Appliances

Ormskirk Market Hall Moorgate, Ormskirk, L39 4RT
Tel: 01695-570277
Directors: H. Morrison (Prop)
Date established: 1995 **No.of Employees:** 1 - 10 **Product Groups:** 36, 40

Pilkington Group Limited

European Technical Centre Hall Lane, Lathom, Ormskirk, L40 5UF
Tel: 01744-692837 **Fax:** 01744-692550
E-mail: info@pilkington.com
Website: http://www.pilkington.com
Bank(s): National Westminster Bank Plc
Managers: C. Nolan (Chief Mgr), D. Harding (Transport), J. Davis (Sales & Mktg Mg)
Immediate Holding Company: Pilkington United Kingdom Ltd
Registration no: 00041495 **Turnover:** £5m - £10m
No.of Employees: 51 - 100 **Product Groups:** 33, 66

Process Valve Supplies Ltd

PO Box 295, Ormskirk, L40 7WW
Tel: 01704-894403 **Fax:** 01704-897046
E-mail: sales@processvalve.co.uk
Website: http://www.processvalve.co.uk
Directors: P. Millward (Dir)
Immediate Holding Company: PROCESS VALVE SUPPLIES LIMITED
Registration no: 02701447 **Date established:** 1992
Turnover: £500,000 - £1m **No.of Employees:** 1 - 10 **Product Groups:** 40, 66

Date of Accounts	Apr 11	Apr 10	Apr 09
Working Capital	8	19	30
Fixed Assets	6	1	1
Current Assets	93	131	92

R J Engineering
Derby Works Liverpool Road South, Burscough, Ormskirk, L40 7SU
Tel: 01704-897771 **Fax:** 01704-897772
E-mail: r.j.engineering@amserve.net
Directors: R. Edge (Prop), R. Edge (MD)
Immediate Holding Company: G & M ANDREWS LIMITED
Registration no: 04704955 **VAT No.:** GB 166 0012 04
Date established: 2003 **Turnover:** Up to £250,000
No.of Employees: 1 - 10 **Product Groups:** 66

Date of Accounts	Jun 11	Jun 08	Jul 10
Working Capital	-1	8	-1
Fixed Assets	1	2	1
Current Assets	12	26	16

Sarah Louise Ltd
10-14 Green Lane, Ormskirk, L39 1SL
Tel: 01695-576069 **Fax:** 01695-574805
E-mail: dgiven@sarah-louise.co.uk
Website: http://www.sarah-louise.co.uk
Directors: L. Given (MD)
Immediate Holding Company: SARAH LOUISE LIMITED
Registration no: 01163548 **VAT No.:** GB 165 8943 20
Date established: 1974 **No.of Employees:** 11 - 20 **Product Groups:** 23, 24

Date of Accounts	Jun 11	Jun 10	Jun 09
Working Capital	1m	1m	1m
Fixed Assets	185	195	206
Current Assets	1m	1m	1m

Smithy Mushrooms Ltd
229 Smithy Lane Scarisbrick, Ormskirk, L40 8HL
Tel: 01704-840982 **Fax:** 01704-841138
E-mail: enquiries@smithymushrooms.co.uk
Website: http://www.smithymushrooms.co.uk
Directors: J. Dorrian (Dir)
Ultimate Holding Company: PREMIERBLEND LIMITED
Immediate Holding Company: SMITHY MUSHROOMS LIMITED
Registration no: 02480783 **Date established:** 1990 **Turnover:** £2m - £5m
No.of Employees: 21 - 50 **Product Groups:** 02, 41

Date of Accounts	Dec 11	Dec 10	Dec 09
Sales Turnover	N/A	3m	3m
Pre Tax Profit/Loss	N/A	138	111
Working Capital	217	199	133
Fixed Assets	291	281	270
Current Assets	781	634	533
Current Liabilities	N/A	64	52

T R M Packaging Ltd
Red Cat Lane Burscough, Ormskirk, L40 0SY
Tel: 01704-892811 **Fax:** 01704-895546
E-mail: sales@trmpack.co.uk
Website: http://www.trmpack.co.uk
Bank(s): National Westminster Bank Plc
Directors: D. Plant (Fin), M. Giles (Sales), M. Jarvis (Sales)
Managers: N. Swift (Purch Mgr), R. Wright (Tech Serv Mgr)
Immediate Holding Company: TRM PACKAGING LIMITED
Registration no: 04256359 **VAT No.:** GB 164 2396 59
Date established: 2001 **Turnover:** £20m - £50m
No.of Employees: 101 - 250 **Product Groups:** 27

Date of Accounts	Aug 11	Aug 10	Aug 09
Sales Turnover	34m	28m	25m
Pre Tax Profit/Loss	1m	-233	474
Working Capital	-2m	-2m	-2m
Fixed Assets	8m	7m	4m
Current Assets	11m	10m	8m
Current Liabilities	7m	6m	5m

Test & Measurement Hire Ltd
Unit 16 Swordfish Close, Burscough, Ormskirk, L40 8JW
Tel: 08707-870105 **Fax:** 08707-870106
E-mail: ken.carine@instruments4hire.co.uk
Website: http://www.instruments4hire.co.uk
Directors: K. Carine (Dir)
Immediate Holding Company: TEST & MEASUREMENT HIRE LIMITED
Registration no: 05508572 **Date established:** 2005 **Turnover:** £1m - £2m
No.of Employees: 1 - 10 **Product Groups:** 27, 37, 38, 40, 48, 67, 83, 85

Date of Accounts	Apr 12	Apr 11	Apr 10
Working Capital	232	56	-128
Fixed Assets	811	886	886
Current Assets	749	680	415

U B H International Ltd
Orrell Lane Burscough, Ormskirk, L40 0SL
Tel: 01704-898500 **Fax:** 01704-898518
E-mail: tanks@ubh.co.uk
Website: http://www.ubh.co.uk
Bank(s): HSBC
Directors: J. Lyons (MD), K. Bragg (Fin), P. Harding (Sales & Mktg)
Managers: A. Craven (Purch Mgr)
Ultimate Holding Company: UBH INTERNATIONAL LIMITED
Immediate Holding Company: UBH INTERNATIONAL LIMITED
Registration no: 03742928 **VAT No.:** 738 5862 87 **Date established:** 1999
Turnover: £5m - £10m **No.of Employees:** 101 - 250 **Product Groups:** 39, 45

Date of Accounts	Sep 11	Sep 10	Sep 09
Sales Turnover	10m	6m	10m
Pre Tax Profit/Loss	2m	-349	1m
Working Capital	5m	4m	4m
Fixed Assets	127	201	314
Current Assets	7m	6m	6m
Current Liabilities	1m	944	364

Richard Wood Packaging Ltd
Guys Industrial Estate Tollgate Road Burscough, Ormskirk, L40 8TG
Tel: 01704-893073 **Fax:** 01704-895276
E-mail: woodpackaging@aol.co.uk
Directors: C. Wood (MD), A. Parks (Fin)
Immediate Holding Company: DODDS LANE INVESTMENTS LIMITED
Registration no: 03285847 **Date established:** 1996 **Turnover:** £1m - £2m
No.of Employees: 1 - 10 **Product Groups:** 25, 27, 45

Date of Accounts	Jan 12	Jan 11	Jan 10
Sales Turnover	N/A	1m	N/A
Pre Tax Profit/Loss	N/A	80	N/A
Working Capital	671	577	568
Fixed Assets	26	5	6
Current Assets	1m	882	1m
Current Liabilities	N/A	128	N/A

Poulton Le Fylde

Deltec Industries Ltd
Unit 8 Wyrefields Poulton Industrial Estate, Poulton Le Fylde, FY6 8JX
Tel: 01253-885747 **Fax:** 01253-899713
E-mail: sales@deltec.net
Website: http://www.deltec.net
Directors: J. Mcgregor (Dir)
Immediate Holding Company: DELTEC INDUSTRIES LIMITED
Registration no: 03890699 **Date established:** 1999
No.of Employees: 11 - 20 **Product Groups:** 36, 37, 44, 49, 61, 67

Date of Accounts	Dec 11	Dec 10	Dec 09
Working Capital	195	131	105
Fixed Assets	211	118	138
Current Assets	739	616	378

Glasdon Manufacturing Ltd
Poulton Business Park Clark Street, Poulton Industrial Estate, Poulton Le Fylde, FY6 8JW
Tel: 01253-891131 **Fax:** 01253-891923
E-mail: sales@glasdon-manufacturing.co.uk
Website: http://www.glasdon.com
Bank(s): The Royal Bank of Scotland
Directors: A. Jackson (Co Sec), N. Barnett (Dir)
Managers: P. Thwaites (Sales Prom Mgr)
Ultimate Holding Company: GLASDON GROUP LIMITED
Immediate Holding Company: GLASDON MANUFACTURING LIMITED
Registration no: 02161573 **VAT No.:** GB 155 8470 44
Date established: 1987 **Turnover:** £5m - £10m
No.of Employees: 51 - 100 **Product Groups:** 30, 33, 35

Date of Accounts	Oct 11	Oct 10	Oct 09
Sales Turnover	9m	8m	6m
Pre Tax Profit/Loss	407	179	-398
Working Capital	2m	1m	1m
Fixed Assets	411	308	283
Current Assets	4m	4m	3m
Current Liabilities	318	247	181

Hambleton Signs
Shard Lane Hambleton, Poulton Le Fylde, FY6 9BX
Tel: 01253-702721 **Fax:** 01253-702721
E-mail: info@hambletonsigns.co.uk
Website: http://www.hambletonsigns.co.uk
Directors: P. Butt (Ptnr)
No.of Employees: 1 - 10 **Product Groups:** 20, 31, 61

Micro Safe
3 Sandicroft Place Preesall, Poulton Le Fylde, FY6 0PB
Tel: 01253-810001
Directors: P. Prop (Prop)
No.of Employees: 1 - 10 **Product Groups:** 36, 40

Plasmaparts.Com
Spiro House Cocker Avenue, Poulton Industrial Estate, Poulton Le Fylde, FY6 8JU
Tel: 01253-884970 **Fax:** 01253-890083
E-mail: andy@plasmaparts.com
Website: http://www.plasma-parts.com
Directors: A. Zakrzewski (Prop)
Immediate Holding Company: BRIAN ORMROD ENGINEERING LIMITED
Registration no: 01346725 **Date established:** 1978
Turnover: £250,000 - £500,000 **No.of Employees:** 1 - 10
Product Groups: 46

Date of Accounts	Mar 11	Mar 10	Mar 09
Working Capital	41	20	-42
Fixed Assets	65	82	105
Current Assets	435	416	354

Poulton Trade Windows Ltd
Cocker Avenue Poulton Industrial Estate, Poulton Le Fylde, FY6 8JU
Tel: 01253-890800 **Fax:** 01253-890999
Directors: G. Rowe (Prop)
Immediate Holding Company: POULTON WINDOWS DIRECT LIMITED
Registration no: 04759236 **Date established:** 2003
No.of Employees: 1 - 10 **Product Groups:** 33, 35, 66

Date of Accounts	Apr 08	Apr 07	Apr 06
Working Capital	-57	-37	-21
Fixed Assets	69	81	97
Current Assets	77	68	75

Silverfield Ltd
Aldon Road Poulton Industrial Estate, Poulton Le Fylde, FY6 8JL
Tel: 01253-891733 **Fax:** 01253-894404
E-mail: mail@silverfield.co.uk
Website: http://www.silverfield.co.uk
Directors: G. Barclay (MD), G. Berkley (MD)
Managers: B. Blake (Tech Serv Mgr)
Ultimate Holding Company: SILVERFIELD HOLDINGS LIMITED
Immediate Holding Company: SILVERFIELD LIMITED
Registration no: 02922036 **Date established:** 1994
No.of Employees: 51 - 100 **Product Groups:** 46, 48

Date of Accounts	Sep 11	Sep 10	Sep 09
Working Capital	221	206	122
Fixed Assets	399	375	409
Current Assets	776	776	673

Preston

A A Packaging Ltd
Light Industrial Estate Liverpool Road, Walmer Bridge, Preston, PR4 5HY
Tel: 01772-617481 **Fax:** 01772-614856
E-mail: sales@aapackaging.co.uk
Website: http://www.aapackaging.co.uk
Directors: D. Parkinson (MD)
Immediate Holding Company: A.A. PACKAGING LIMITED
Registration no: 01718996 **VAT No.:** GB 379 7769 65
Date established: 1983 **Turnover:** £1m - £2m **No.of Employees:** 1 - 10
Product Groups: 30, 32

Date of Accounts	Jun 12	Jun 11	Jun 10
Working Capital	344	322	280
Fixed Assets	197	210	225
Current Assets	623	602	557

A B Fire Protection Ltd
87-91 Waterloo Road Ashton-On-Ribble, Preston, PR2 1BH
Tel: 01772-726126 **Fax:** 01772-726111
E-mail: sales@abfireprotection.com
Directors: A. Heaps (Dir)
Immediate Holding Company: A.B FIRE PROTECTION LIMITED
Registration no: 04811703 **Date established:** 2003
No.of Employees: 1 - 10 **Product Groups:** 38, 42

Date of Accounts	Jul 11	Jul 10	Jul 09
Working Capital	131	126	79
Fixed Assets	333	156	163
Current Assets	250	204	136

A R T GB Ltd
231 Eldon Street Ashton-On-Ribble, Preston, PR2 2BB
Tel: 01772-204504 **Fax:** 01772-202283
E-mail: sales@alisterreidties.com
Website: http://www.alisterreidties.com
Directors: W. Stokes (MD)
Immediate Holding Company: A.R.T.(G.B.) LIMITED
Registration no: 02483784 **VAT No.:** GB 534 2508 63
Date established: 1990 **No.of Employees:** 1 - 10 **Product Groups:** 24

Date of Accounts	May 12	May 11	May 10
Working Capital	312	265	216
Fixed Assets	16	21	27
Current Assets	402	352	326

Accolade Signs
Unit 42-43 Old Mill Industrial Estate, Bamber Bridge, Preston, PR5 6SY
Tel: 01772-628666
Directors: S. Preston (Fin), M. Stephenson (Dir)
Immediate Holding Company: ACCOLADE SIGNS LIMITED
Registration no: 05951875 **Date established:** 2006
No.of Employees: 1 - 10 **Product Groups:** 40, 49, 80

Advanced Steel Services Ltd
South Ribble Industrial Estate Grove Road, Walton-Le-Dale, Preston, PR5 4AJ
Tel: 01772-259822 **Fax:** 01772-259561
E-mail: sales@advanced-steel.co.uk
Website: http://www.advanced-steel.co.uk
Bank(s): HSBC Bank plc
Directors: C. Grundy (MD)
Ultimate Holding Company: BARRETT STEEL LIMITED
Immediate Holding Company: ADVANCED STEEL SERVICES LIMITED
Registration no: 02762749 **VAT No.:** GB 607 1489 41
Date established: 1992 **Turnover:** £10m - £20m
No.of Employees: 11 - 20 **Product Groups:** 66

Date of Accounts	Sep 08
Working Capital	1
Current Assets	1

Air Power Centre Limited
Unit B4 Anchorage Business Park Chain Caul Way, Ashton-on-Ribble, Preston, PR2 2YL
Tel: 01772-728513 **Fax:** 01772-736506
E-mail: apcpreston@airpowercentre.com
Website: http://www.airpowercentre.com
Bank(s): The Royal Bank of Scotland
Directors: S. Kernohan (Fin), T. Dawson Jnr (Jt MD), T. Dawson (Jt MD), S. Kernohan (Fin), T. Dawson (Jt MD), T. Dawson (Junior) (MD)
Managers: G. Pollitt (Purch Mgr), M. Elston (Comm), R. Hempton
Ultimate Holding Company: Air Power Centre
Immediate Holding Company: Heaps, Collis & Harrison Ltd
Registration no: 00395178 **VAT No.:** GB 153 8456 50
Date established: 1972 **Turnover:** £5m - £10m **No.of Employees:** 21 - 50
Product Groups: 40, 46

Allthread Tools & Fasteners Ltd
Owen Street, Preston, PR1 5DN
Tel: 01772-651511 **Fax:** 01772-651305
E-mail: peter@atfltd.com
Website: http://www.atfltd.com
Directors: P. Rogers (Dir)
Immediate Holding Company: ALLTHREAD TOOLS & FASTENERS LIMITED
Registration no: 04330958 **Date established:** 2001
Turnover: Up to £250,000 **No.of Employees:** 1 - 10 **Product Groups:** 35, 66

Date of Accounts	Dec 11	Dec 10	Dec 09
Working Capital	43	54	54
Fixed Assets	454	457	443
Current Assets	364	371	389

AMC Diesel Engineering Ltd
Beverley House Hall Lane, Longton, Preston, PR4 5ZD
Tel: 01772-613003 **Fax:** 01772-616364
E-mail: sales@amcdiesel.co.uk
Website: http://www.amcdiesel.co.uk
Directors: P. McConnell (Fin), S. Mcconnell (Fin)
Immediate Holding Company: A. M. C. DIESEL ENGINEERING LIMITED
Registration no: 02151529 **Date established:** 1987
Turnover: £250,000 - £500,000 **No.of Employees:** 1 - 10
Product Groups: 68

Date of Accounts	Jul 11	Jul 10	Jul 09
Working Capital	214	470	429
Fixed Assets	86	84	95
Current Assets	357	524	484

Amey Datel
Albert Edward House 3 The Pavilions, Ashton-On-Ribble, Preston, PR2 2YB
Tel: 01772-901700 **Fax:** 01772-901701
E-mail: val.williamson@amey.co.uk
Website: http://www.amey.co.uk
Managers: V. Williamson (Contracts Mgr)
Immediate Holding Company: ACCIDENT MATE LIMITED
Date established: 2012 **No.of Employees:** 51 - 100 **Product Groups:** 40, 44, 80, 84

see next page

Amey Datel - Cont'd

Date of Accounts	Dec 07	Dec 06	Dec 05
Sales Turnover	6175	5318	6060
Pre Tax Profit/Loss	-899	372	277
Working Capital	-2211	-1592	-1967
Fixed Assets	N/A	N/A	3
Current Assets	4038	2715	6635
Current Liabilities	6249	4307	8602
Total Share Capital	8584	8584	8584
ROCE% (Return on Capital Employed)	40.7	-23.4	-14.1
ROT% (Return on Turnover)	-14.6	7.0	4.6

Andrews Sykes Hire Ltd
Unit 5 Roman Way Longridge Road, Preston, PR2 5BB
Tel: 01772-651668 **Fax:** 01772-651645
E-mail: info@andrews-sykes.com
Website: http://www.andrews-sykes.com
Directors: K. Fogwill (Sales & Mktg), N. Burson (Pers), R. Stevens (Grp Chief Exec)
Managers: E. Danby (Sales Admin), N. Drelincourt, N. Zanotti (Purch Mgr), P. Stubbs (I.T. Exec), J. Maxwell (Depot Mgr)
Immediate Holding Company: Andrews Sykes Group plc
Registration no: 02985657 **VAT No.:** GB 100 4295 24
No.of Employees: 1 - 10 **Product Groups:** 40

Askews & Holts Library Services Ltd
218-222 North Road, Preston, PR1 1SY
Tel: 01772-555947 **Fax:** 01772-492768
E-mail: enquiries@askewsandholts.com
Website: http://www.askewsandholts.com
Bank(s): Barclays
Directors: K. Pattinson (Dir), A. Holland (Sales & Mktg)
Managers: T. Robinson (Fin Mgr), G. Jones (Tech Serv Mgr), A. Lakeland
Ultimate Holding Company: THE LITTLE GROUP LIMITED
Immediate Holding Company: ASKEWS AND HOLTS LIBRARY SERVICES LTD.
Registration no: 02745298 **VAT No.:** GB 153 4009 95
Date established: 1992 **Turnover:** £10m - £20m
No.of Employees: 101 - 250 **Product Groups:** 64

Date of Accounts	Feb 08	Feb 11	Feb 10
Sales Turnover	N/A	20m	22m
Pre Tax Profit/Loss	1m	355	479
Working Capital	3m	3m	3m
Fixed Assets	2m	254	309
Current Assets	5m	5m	5m
Current Liabilities	378	265	277

Assystem UK Group
Club Street Bamber Bridge, Preston, PR5 6FN
Tel: 01772-645000 **Fax:** 01772-645001
E-mail: lstewart@assystemuk.com
Website: http://www.assystem.com
Bank(s): Lloyds TSB Bank plc
Directors: D. Caunce (Fin)
Managers: I. Gibb (Tech Serv Mgr), L. Stewart
Ultimate Holding Company: ASSYSTEM SA (FRANCE)
Immediate Holding Company: ASSYSTEM GROUP UK LIMITED
Registration no: 03218561 **Date established:** 1996
Turnover: £50m - £75m **No.of Employees:** 251 - 500
Product Groups: 35, 36, 37, 38, 39, 44, 46, 47, 48, 52, 54, 67, 68, 76, 80, 81, 83, 84, 85

Date of Accounts	Dec 11	Dec 10	Dec 09
Sales Turnover	82m	62m	48m
Pre Tax Profit/Loss	7m	5m	2m
Working Capital	19m	14m	9m
Fixed Assets	2m	2m	2m
Current Assets	29m	24m	18m
Current Liabilities	7m	6m	5m

Atlantic Industrial
Unit 6 Bannister Hall Works Higher Walton, Preston, PR5 4DZ
Tel: 01772-311311 **Fax:** 01772-311211
E-mail: sales@atlantic-ind.com
Website: http://www.atlantic-ind.com
Managers: C. Johnson (Mgr)
VAT No.: GB 604 6705 54 **Turnover:** £1m - £2m **No.of Employees:** 1 - 10
Product Groups: 35

Attwater Group Ltd
Hopwood Street, Preston, PR1 1UN
Tel: 01772-258245 **Fax:** 01772-203361
E-mail: info@attwater.com
Website: http://www.attwater.com
Bank(s): National Westminster Bank Plc
Directors: R. Kennedy (Sales & Mktg), R. Attwater (Dir)
Managers: M. Bate (Chief Acct), S. Eland (Tech Serv Mgr)
Immediate Holding Company: ATTWATER & SONS LIMITED
Registration no: 00354338 **VAT No.:** GB 153 4585 59
Date established: 1939 **No.of Employees:** 21 - 50 **Product Groups:** 17, 30, 31, 33, 37, 39, 47, 66

Date of Accounts	Dec 11	Dec 10	Dec 09
Working Capital	183	163	112
Fixed Assets	1m	1m	1m
Current Assets	2m	1m	1m

Austin Walmsley
Unit 12 Leachfield Industrial Estate Green Lane, Garstang, Preston, PR3 1PR
Tel: 01995-602173 **Fax:** 01995-602080
E-mail: annwalmsley_07@hotmail.com
Website: http://www.austinwalmsley.co.uk
Directors: A. Walmsley (Snr Part)
Immediate Holding Company: AUSTIN WALMSLEY LTD
Registration no: 04556651 **Date established:** 2002
No.of Employees: 1 - 10 **Product Groups:** 35, 42, 45

Date of Accounts	Dec 11	Dec 10	Dec 09
Working Capital	114	100	115
Fixed Assets	17	18	12
Current Assets	141	120	139

Banister Bros & Co. Ltd
Bee Mill Preston Road, Ribchester, Preston, PR3 3XJ
Tel: 01254-878355 **Fax:** 01254-878119
E-mail: sales@beemill.co.uk
Website: http://www.beemill.co.uk
Directors: M. Banister (MD), J. Banister (Fin)
Immediate Holding Company: BANISTER BROS. & CO. LIMITED
Registration no: 00448757 **VAT No.:** GB 153 4016 01
Date established: 1948 **Turnover:** £2m - £5m **No.of Employees:** 1 - 10
Product Groups: 23

Date of Accounts	Jan 12	Jan 11	Jan 10
Working Capital	-77	-111	-113
Fixed Assets	1m	1m	1m
Current Assets	72	58	45

Barber Pumps Ltd
Jacksons Yard Douglas Road North, Fulwood, Preston, PR2 3QH
Tel: 01772-715502 **Fax:** 01772- 712716
E-mail: s.barber@barberpumps.co.uk
Website: http://www.barberpumps.co.uk
Directors: S. Barber (MD)
Immediate Holding Company: BARBER PUMPS (SUPPLIES AND REPAIRS) LIMITED
Registration no: 01673009 **Date established:** 1982
Turnover: £500,000 - £1m **No.of Employees:** 1 - 10 **Product Groups:** 40, 48, 67

Date of Accounts	Oct 11	Oct 10	Oct 09
Working Capital	712	706	722
Fixed Assets	241	230	133
Current Assets	929	1m	921

Biffa Waste Services Ltd
Green Place Walton Summit Centre, Bamber Bridge, Preston, PR5 8AY
Tel: 01772-334847 **Fax:** 01772-334841
E-mail: marketing@biffa.co.uk
Website: http://www.biffa.co.uk
Managers: P. Turner (Mgr), D. Brown (Transport)
Immediate Holding Company: BIFFA WASTE SERVICES LIMITED
Registration no: 00946107 **Date established:** 1969 **Turnover:** £5m - £10m
No.of Employees: 11 - 20 **Product Groups:** 54

Date of Accounts	Mar 08	Mar 09	Apr 10
Sales Turnover	555m	574m	492m
Pre Tax Profit/Loss	23m	50m	30m
Working Capital	229m	271m	293m
Fixed Assets	371m	360m	378m
Current Assets	409m	534m	609m
Current Liabilities	50m	100m	115m

Bildabin Agricultural Machinery
Harrison House Benson Lane, Catforth, Preston, PR4 0HY
Tel: 01772-690575 **Fax:** 01772-691681
E-mail: roger@bildabin.co.uk
Website: http://www.bildabin.co.uk
Directors: R. Wicks (Prop)
Immediate Holding Company: BILDABIN LIMITED
Registration no: 04703670 **Date established:** 2003
Turnover: £250,000 - £500,000 **No.of Employees:** 1 - 10
Product Groups: 38

Date of Accounts	Dec 11	Mar 11	Mar 10
Working Capital	295	222	74
Fixed Assets	92	63	62
Current Assets	541	513	359

Bonar Floors Ltd
Unit 92 Seedlee Road Walton Summit Centre, Bamber Bridge, Preston, PR5 8AE
Tel: 020-7033 0335 **Fax:** 0870-855 0535
Website: http://www.bonarfloors.co.uk
Managers: L. Binns (Personnel)
Immediate Holding Company: GASKELL P.L.C.
Registration no: 02087618 **VAT No.:** 305 8856 41 **Turnover:** £20m - £50m
No.of Employees: 1 - 10 **Product Groups:** 23

Bond & Bywater
91-92 St Pauls Road, Preston, PR1 1UH
Tel: 01772-258980 **Fax:** 01772-258980
Website: http://www.bondandbywater.co.uk
Directors: P. Brooks (Prop)
Date established: 1993 **No.of Employees:** 1 - 10 **Product Groups:** 36, 39, 40

Bosal UK Ltd
Unit 330 Four Oaks Road, Bamber Bridge, Preston, PR5 8AP
Tel: 01772-771000 **Fax:** 01772-312750
E-mail: buk.marketing@eur.bosal.com
Website: http://www.bosal.com
Bank(s): National Westminster, Manchester
Directors: A. Shaffer (Sales), R. Sweetnam (MD), R. Sweetnam (Dir), K. Bos (Ch)
Managers: I. Muncaster (I.T. Exec)
Ultimate Holding Company: JENDA HOLDINGS AG (LIECHTENSTEIN)
Immediate Holding Company: BOSAL (U.K.) LIMITED
Registration no: 01303096 **VAT No.:** GB 604 7131 72
Date established: 1977 **Turnover:** £20m - £50m
No.of Employees: 101 - 250 **Product Groups:** 26, 36, 39, 40

Date of Accounts	Dec 10	Dec 09	Dec 08
Sales Turnover	32m	30m	39m
Pre Tax Profit/Loss	-3m	-3m	-3m
Working Capital	4m	2m	5m
Fixed Assets	2m	2m	2m
Current Assets	13m	15m	19m
Current Liabilities	2m	1m	4m

Bowker Preston Ltd
Channel Way Ashton-on-Ribble, Preston, PR2 2YA
Tel: 01772-769976 **Fax:** 01772-766600
E-mail: darren@bowkermail.com
Website: http://www.bowkerprestonbmw.co.uk
Directors: A. Bowker (Sales), D. Thomason (Fin)
Managers: T. Fox
Ultimate Holding Company: W.H.BOWKER LIMITED
Immediate Holding Company: BOWKER PRESTON LIMITED
Registration no: 00805059 **Date established:** 1964
Turnover: £20m - £50m **No.of Employees:** 51 - 100 **Product Groups:** 68

Date of Accounts	Dec 11	Dec 10	Dec 09
Sales Turnover	38m	34m	36m
Pre Tax Profit/Loss	423	322	467
Working Capital	2m	2m	2m
Fixed Assets	3m	3m	3m
Current Assets	11m	10m	8m
Current Liabilities	3m	2m	2m

W H Bowker Ltd
Holme Road Bamber Bridge, Preston, PR5 6BP
Tel: 01772-628800 **Fax:** 01772-628801
E-mail: enquiries@bowkergroup.co.uk
Website: http://www.bowkertransport.co.uk
Bank(s): Lloyds TSB, Blackburn
Directors: D. Thomason (Fin)
Managers: C. Kay (Tech Serv Mgr), P. Lewis (Sales Prom Mgr)
Immediate Holding Company: W.H.BOWKER LIMITED
Registration no: 00364757 **VAT No.:** GB 175 6964 15
Date established: 1941 **Turnover:** £75m - £125m
No.of Employees: 251 - 500 **Product Groups:** 72, 77

Date of Accounts	Dec 11	Dec 10	Dec 09
Sales Turnover	87m	81m	85m
Pre Tax Profit/Loss	1m	725	912
Working Capital	840	443	147
Fixed Assets	10m	10m	10m
Current Assets	24m	22m	17m
Current Liabilities	8m	5m	5m

Boxes & Packaging
Gorse Lane Tarleton, Preston, PR4 6LH
Tel: 01772-815689 **Fax:** 01772-812234
E-mail: steve.hughes@boxesandpackaging.co.uk
Website: http://www.boxesandpackaging.co.uk
Managers: M. Raw (Chief Mgr), P. Hampson (Sales Prom), S. Hughes (Mgr)
Registration no: 05562632 **Turnover:** £1m - £2m
No.of Employees: 11 - 20 **Product Groups:** 27

C C A Group Ltd
Eastway Fulwood, Preston, PR2 9WS
Tel: 01772-662800 **Fax:** 01772-662987
E-mail: sales@ccagroup.co.uk
Website: http://www.ccagroup.com
Bank(s): Bank of Scotland
Directors: M. Seekins (MD), M. Swkins (MD), S. Greenwood (Co Sec)
Managers: C. Sharman (I.T. Exec), G. Whitfield (I.T. Exec), S. Vicars
Ultimate Holding Company: CCA Group Ltd
Registration no: 02667669 **VAT No.:** GB 379 7453 92
Date established: 1906 **Turnover:** £20m - £50m
No.of Employees: 251 - 500 **Product Groups:** 64

Date of Accounts	Dec 05	Jun 05	Jun 04
Working Capital	1744	1744	1744
Current Assets	1744	1744	1744
Total Share Capital	36	36	36

C H F Supplies (Tank Suppliers & Manufacturers)
Crane Hall Wyreside, Out Rawcliffe, Preston, PR3 6TP
Tel: 01995-670888 **Fax:** 01995-670305
E-mail: iain@chfsupplies.co.uk
Website: http://www.chfsupplies.co.uk
Directors: I. Mackie (Ptnr)
Registration no: 04015425 **Turnover:** £1m - £2m
No.of Employees: 1 - 10 **Product Groups:** 30, 35

C M D Ltd (CMD Ltd)
Claughton Industrial Estate Brockholes Way, Claughton-On-Brock, Preston, PR3 0PZ
Tel: 01995-640844 **Fax:** 01995-640798
E-mail: enquiries@cmd-ltd.com
Website: http://www.powerplan.co.uk
Bank(s): The Royal Bank of Scotland Plc
Directors: R. Cooper (Fin)
Ultimate Holding Company: HAMSARD 3120 LIMITED
Immediate Holding Company: CMD LIMITED
Registration no: 02290387 **Date established:** 1988
Turnover: £10m - £20m **No.of Employees:** 101 - 250 **Product Groups:** 37

Date of Accounts	Dec 11	Dec 10	Dec 09
Sales Turnover	16m	16m	14m
Pre Tax Profit/Loss	1m	1m	1m
Working Capital	16m	14m	12m
Fixed Assets	3m	4m	4m
Current Assets	19m	17m	15m
Current Liabilities	2m	2m	2m

C S Storage Ltd
1a Round House Court Bamberbridge, Preston, PR5 6DA
Tel: 01772-641964
E-mail: jim.jardine@csstorage.co.uk
Website: http://www.csstorage.co.uk
Directors: J. Jardine (MD), C. Blunt (Fin)
Immediate Holding Company: C S STORAGE LIMITED
Registration no: 05281274 **Date established:** 2004
No.of Employees: 1 - 10 **Product Groups:** 35, 42, 45

Date of Accounts	Mar 12	Mar 11	Mar 10
Working Capital	263	278	218
Fixed Assets	9	3	2
Current Assets	427	391	315

Care Shop Mobility
1 Lytham Road Fulwood, Preston, PR2 8JE
Tel: 01772-788128 **Fax:** 01772-788914
Website: http://www.careshop.co.uk
Managers: I. Topping (Mgr)
No.of Employees: 1 - 10 **Product Groups:** 24, 30, 61

Cartridge World Ltd
49 Water Lane Ashton-On-Ribble, Preston, PR2 2NL
Tel: 01772-659007 **Fax:** 01772-729289
Website: http://www.preston.cartridgeworld.co.uk
Managers: C. Dixon (Develop Mgr)
Immediate Holding Company: CARTRIDGE WORLD LIMITED
Registration no: 04124067 **Date established:** 2000 **Turnover:** £5m - £10m
No.of Employees: 1 - 10 **Product Groups:** 28, 30, 44

Date of Accounts	Dec 11	Dec 10	Dec 09
Sales Turnover	6m	7m	8m
Pre Tax Profit/Loss	373	164	210
Working Capital	1m	967	878
Fixed Assets	403	455	524
Current Assets	7m	7m	6m
Current Liabilities	4m	1m	2m

Central Power Services Ltd
Garstang Road Claughton-on-Brock, Preston, PR3 0PH
Tel: 01995-642600 **Fax:** 01995-642601
E-mail: sales@central-power.co.uk
Website: http://www.central-power.co.uk
Directors: J. Brakewell (Dir)
Managers: J. Brakewell (Comptroller)
Immediate Holding Company: CENTRAL POWER SERVICES LIMITED
Registration no: 01980449 **Date established:** 1986 **Turnover:** £2m - £5m
No.of Employees: 21 - 50 **Product Groups:** 37, 40, 67

Date of Accounts	Mar 11	Mar 10	Mar 09
Working Capital	465	97	43
Fixed Assets	938	1m	1m

Current Assets	2m	1m	1m

Chemical Innovations Ltd

211 Walton Summit Road Walton Summit Centre, Bamber Bridge, Preston, PR5 8AQ
Tel: 01772-322888 **Fax:** 01772-315853
E-mail: sales@polycil.co.uk
Website: http://www.polycil.co.uk
Bank(s): Barclays, Manchester
Directors: A. Benarous (MD)
Managers: M. Hunter (Mktg Serv Mgr), P. Horton (Tech Serv Mgr), S. Martin (Comptroller), C. Coyne
Ultimate Holding Company: VITA CAYMAN LIMITED (CAYMAN ISLANDS)
Immediate Holding Company: CHEMICAL INNOVATIONS LIMITED
Registration no: 00637686 **Date established:** 1959
Turnover: £10m - £20m **No.of Employees:** 21 - 50 **Product Groups:** 29, 31, 32, 48

Date of Accounts	Dec 11	Dec 10	Dec 09
Sales Turnover	11m	10m	7m
Pre Tax Profit/Loss	2m	2m	1m
Working Capital	14m	15m	13m
Fixed Assets	7m	3m	4m
Current Assets	18m	19m	16m
Current Liabilities	2m	1m	546

Clear Debt Solutions

Anchorage Business Park Chain Caul Way, Ashton-On-Ribble, Preston, PR2 2YL
Tel: 01772-333340 **Fax:** 01772-731974
E-mail: pcrilly@cleardebtsolutions.co.uk
Website: http://www.cleardebtsolutions.com
Directors: R. Morgan (Prop)
Immediate Holding Company: CLEAR DEBT SOLUTIONS LIMITED
Registration no: 05940444 **Date established:** 2006 **Turnover:** £1m - £2m
No.of Employees: 21 - 50 **Product Groups:** 82

Date of Accounts	Mar 11	Mar 10	Sep 08
Working Capital	-118	-73	-40
Fixed Assets	130	75	33
Current Assets	241	183	82

Coars Ltd

Cobre Business Park Green Lane West, Garstang, Preston, PR3 1NU
Tel: 01995-603555 **Fax:** 01995-603666
E-mail: sales@coars.co.uk
Website: http://www.coars.co.uk
Directors: A. Coar (Dir), S. Reid (Dir)
Immediate Holding Company: COARS LIMITED
Registration no: 03431705 **Date established:** 1997
No.of Employees: 11 - 20 **Product Groups:** 41

Date of Accounts	Jan 12	Jan 11	Jan 10
Working Capital	670	554	416
Fixed Assets	120	124	94
Current Assets	1m	1m	959

Complete Property Management Solutions Ltd

41 Dilworth Lane Longridge, Preston, PR3 3ST
Tel: 08432-084492 **Fax:** 08719-002883
E-mail: info@completepropertymanagement.co.uk
Website: http://www.completepropertymanagement.co.uk
Directors: D. Norris (MD)
Immediate Holding Company: COMPLETE PROPERTY MANAGEMENT SOLUTIONS LIMITED
Registration no: 05236404 **Date established:** 2004
Turnover: Up to £250,000 **No.of Employees:** 1 - 10 **Product Groups:** 80

Date of Accounts	Oct 11	Oct 10	Oct 09
Working Capital	17	3	-1
Fixed Assets	10	N/A	1
Current Assets	83	55	26

Control Center NRS

428 Oakshott Place Bamber Bridge, Preston, PR5 8AT
Tel: 01772-628608 **Fax:** 01772-628599
Website: http://www.climatecentre.co.uk
Managers: J. Rushton (Mgr)
No.of Employees: 1 - 10 **Product Groups:** 40, 66

Cool & Heat Ltd

A22 Red Scar Industrial Estate Longridge Road, Ribbleton, Preston, PR2 5NB
Tel: 01772-703999 **Fax:** 01772-703999
E-mail: marcus@coolandheatltd.co.uk
Website: http://www.coolandheatltd.co.uk
Directors: M. Walsh (Ptnr), K. Aldren (Fin)
Immediate Holding Company: COOL & HEAT LTD
Registration no: 04665531 **Date established:** 2003
No.of Employees: 1 - 10 **Product Groups:** 52

Date of Accounts	Mar 12	Mar 11	Mar 10
Working Capital	117	111	108
Fixed Assets	32	39	37
Current Assets	282	216	212

Coote Lane Garage

Coote Lane Whitestake, Preston, PR4 4LJ
Tel: 01772-335385 **Fax:** 01772-335385
Directors: J. Longson (Prop)
Date established: 1967 **Turnover:** Up to £250,000
No.of Employees: 1 - 10 **Product Groups:** 39, 44, 72

Cortman Textiles Ltd

450 Carr Place Walton Summit Centre, Bamber Bridge, Preston, PR5 8AU
Tel: 01772-627262 **Fax:** 01772-627570
E-mail: ann@cortman.co.uk
Website: http://www.cortman.co.uk
Bank(s): National Westminster Bank Plc
Directors: C. Harrison (Co Sec)
Managers: N. Davey (Sales Prom Mgr)
Immediate Holding Company: CORTMAN TEXTILES LIMITED
Registration no: 01389217 **Date established:** 1978 **Turnover:** £2m - £5m
No.of Employees: 11 - 20 **Product Groups:** 23, 29, 63

Date of Accounts	Oct 11	Oct 10	Oct 09
Working Capital	795	660	540
Fixed Assets	44	44	53
Current Assets	2m	2m	1m

Coupe Foundry Ltd

The Foundry Kittlingbourne Brow, Higher Walton, Preston, PR5 4DQ
Tel: 01772-338151 **Fax:** 01772-627609
E-mail: reception@coupefoundry.co.uk
Website: http://www.coupefoundry.co.uk
Bank(s): Barclays, Preston
Directors: N. Winn (Fin), P. Wieckowicz (MD)
Managers: S. Carol (Sales Admin), B. Davis (Sales Prom Mgr)
Immediate Holding Company: COUPE FOUNDRY LIMITED
Registration no: 05047429 **VAT No.:** GB 534 5704 48
Date established: 2004 **Turnover:** £5m - £10m
No.of Employees: 51 - 100 **Product Groups:** 34, 48

Date of Accounts	Mar 10	Mar 09	Mar 08
Sales Turnover	6m	N/A	N/A
Pre Tax Profit/Loss	380	868	356
Working Capital	-22	367	-117
Fixed Assets	91	128	209
Current Assets	2m	2m	1m
Current Liabilities	901	1m	453

D R Fabrications

188 Chapel Lane New Longton, Preston, PR4 4AE
Tel: 01772-613540
Directors: D. Richardson (Prop)
Date established: 1994 **No.of Employees:** 1 - 10 **Product Groups:** 35

Dale Pianos

Cann Bridge Street Higher Walton, Preston, PR5 4DJ
Tel: 01772-321992 **Fax:** 01772-321993
Directors: M. Fenton (MD)
Registration no: 01346731 **VAT No.:** 322 8244 76 **Date established:** 1978
Turnover: £250,000 - £500,000 **No.of Employees:** 1 - 10
Product Groups: 49

Dixon Group Europe Ltd

Dixon House 350 Walton Summit Centre, Bamber Bridge, Preston, PR5 8AS
Tel: 01772-323529 **Fax:** 01772-314664
E-mail: enquiries@dixoneurope.co.uk
Website: http://www.dixoneurope.co.uk
Bank(s): National Westminster Bank Plc
Directors: T. Spencer (MD)
Managers: S. Beniston (Export Sales Mg)
Ultimate Holding Company: Dixon Valve & Coupling Company (USA)
Registration no: 00328298 **VAT No.:** GB 199 3577 96
Date established: 1950 **Turnover:** £5m - £10m
No.of Employees: 51 - 100 **Product Groups:** 29, 35, 36, 39, 40, 45

Date of Accounts	Dec 11	Dec 10	Dec 09
Sales Turnover	11m	9m	7m
Pre Tax Profit/Loss	435	-491	-1m
Working Capital	2m	2m	2m
Fixed Assets	11m	11m	11m
Current Assets	7m	6m	5m
Current Liabilities	471	348	266

E D V Reinforcements Ltd

Unit C17 & C20 Red Scar Industrial Estate Longridge Road, Ribbleton, Preston, PR2 5NQ
Tel: 01772-790060
E-mail: info@edv.co.uk
Website: http://www.edv.co.uk
Directors: D. Balchin (MD)
Immediate Holding Company: E.D.V. REINFORCEMENTS LIMITED
Registration no: 01888161 **Date established:** 1985
No.of Employees: 11 - 20 **Product Groups:** 33, 35, 52

Date of Accounts	Feb 11	Feb 10	Feb 09
Working Capital	713	609	484
Fixed Assets	83	96	102
Current Assets	1m	1m	725

E E Thompson & Son Ltd

402-404 Blackpool Road Ashton-on-Ribble, Preston, PR2 2DX
Tel: 01772-726962 **Fax:** 01772-721164
Website: http://www.ethompson.co.uk
Directors: S. Thompson (Dir), J. Greenwood (Fin), A. Thompson (MD)
Managers: T. Smith (Contracts Eng)
Immediate Holding Company: E.E.THOMPSON & SON LIMITED
Registration no: 01051028 **Date established:** 1972
Turnover: £500,000 - £1m **No.of Employees:** 1 - 10 **Product Groups:** 52

Date of Accounts	Apr 11	Apr 10	Apr 09
Working Capital	588	532	531
Fixed Assets	71	54	84
Current Assets	977	822	756

Eorigen Com Ltd

Belgrave Court Caxton Road, Fulwood, Preston, PR2 9PL
Tel: 01772-651555 **Fax:** 01772-651777
E-mail: info@eorigen.com
Website: http://www.eorigen.com
Directors: M. Mulvihill (MD)
Immediate Holding Company: EORIGEN.COM LIMITED
Registration no: 05088347 **VAT No.:** GB 741 2580 50
Date established: 2004 **Turnover:** £250,000 - £500,000
No.of Employees: 1 - 10 **Product Groups:** 89

Date of Accounts	Sep 11	Sep 10	Sep 09
Working Capital	-93	-177	-169
Fixed Assets	279	240	232
Current Assets	181	222	189
Current Liabilities	43	N/A	N/A

equip2work.com

Unit 1, Astra Business Centre Roman Way, Preston, PR2 5AP
Tel: 01772-759061 **Fax:** 01772-653991
E-mail: sales@equip2work.com
Website: http://www.equip2work.com
Managers: P. Wilmot (Mgr), W. Billington (Accounts)
No.of Employees: 21 - 50 **Product Groups:** 24, 30, 35, 40, 43, 45, 66, 83

Eurolite

Unit 21 Progress Business Park Orders Lane, Kirkham, Preston, PR4 2TZ
Tel: 01772-672020 **Fax:** 01772-672030
E-mail: sales@eurolite.co.uk
Website: http://www.eurolite.co.uk
Managers: I. Schofield (Chief Mgr)
Date established: 2004 **No.of Employees:** 11 - 20 **Product Groups:** 36, 40

European Freeze Dry

Roman Way Industrial Estate Longridge Road, Ribbleton, Preston, PR2 5BD
Tel: 01772-654441 **Fax:** 01772-655004
E-mail: sales@europeanfreezedry.com
Website: http://www.europeanfreezedry.com
Managers: M. Harvey (Chief Mgr), D. Morris (Sales Prom Mgr), S. Bell (Fin Mgr)
Immediate Holding Company: EUROPEAN FREEZE DRY LIMITED
Registration no: 02979293 **Date established:** 1994 **Turnover:** £2m - £5m
No.of Employees: 21 - 50 **Product Groups:** 20

Date of Accounts	Dec 11	Dec 10	Dec 09
Working Capital	2m	2m	2m
Fixed Assets	833	735	678
Current Assets	2m	2m	2m

Evans Vanodine International plc

Brierley Road Walton Summit Centre, Bamber Bridge, Preston, PR5 8AH
Tel: 01772-322200 **Fax:** 01772-626000
E-mail: devans@evansvanodine.co.uk
Website: http://www.evansvanodine.co.uk
Bank(s): The Royal Bank of Scotland
Directors: P. Evans (Mkt Research), A. Evans (Tech Serv), C. Evans (Purch), D. Evans (MD)
Managers: J. Fishwick (Fin Mgr)
Immediate Holding Company: EVANS VANODINE INTERNATIONAL PLC
Registration no: 00518504 **VAT No.:** GB 305 5067 83
Date established: 1953 **Turnover:** £20m - £50m
No.of Employees: 101 - 250 **Product Groups:** 31, 32

Date of Accounts	Mar 12	Mar 11	Mar 10
Sales Turnover	23m	22m	21m
Pre Tax Profit/Loss	828	1m	1m
Working Capital	8m	7m	6m
Fixed Assets	2m	2m	2m
Current Assets	11m	11m	9m
Current Liabilities	851	633	808

Express Instrument Hire Ltd

Express House Church Road, Tarleton, Preston, PR4 6UP
Tel: 01772-815600 **Fax:** 01772-815937
E-mail: sales@expresshire.net
Website: http://www.expresshire.net
Directors: A. Griffiths (Fin), L. Myers (MD)
Ultimate Holding Company: EXPRESS INSTRUMENT HIRE (HOLDINGS) LIMITED
Immediate Holding Company: EXPRESS INSTRUMENT HIRE LIMITED
Registration no: 02593280 **Date established:** 1991
Turnover: £500,000 - £1m **No.of Employees:** 1 - 10 **Product Groups:** 37, 38, 39, 40, 85

Date of Accounts	Mar 11	Mar 10	Mar 09
Working Capital	386	287	314
Fixed Assets	213	218	135
Current Assets	625	581	620

Eyecatchers

The Hayloft, Mill Farm Fleetwood Road, Preston, PR4 3HD
Tel: 01772-681000
E-mail: mlt@eyecatchers.co.uk
Website: http://www.eyecatchers.co.uk
Directors: M. Louise Taylor (Dir)
No.of Employees: 11 - 20 **Product Groups:** 28, 30, 40

First Trace Heating Direct Ltd

Chain Caul Road Ashton-On-Ribble, Preston, PR2 2PD
Tel: 01772-761333 **Fax:** 01772-761222
E-mail: sales@first-traceheating.co.uk
Website: http://www.first-traceheating.co.uk
Directors: R. Dunne (MD)
Immediate Holding Company: FIRST TRACE HEATING DIRECT LIMITED
Registration no: 03492441 **Date established:** 1998
Turnover: £250,000 - £500,000 **No.of Employees:** 1 - 10
Product Groups: 40

Date of Accounts	Jun 11	Jun 10	Jun 09
Working Capital	336	126	108
Fixed Assets	6	6	7
Current Assets	2m	703	557

FlyTek Fly Fishing

Taenross Orchard Close, Wrea Green, Preston, PR4 2NH
Tel: 01772-684003 **Fax:** 01772-684003
E-mail: info@flytek.co.uk
Website: http://www.flytek.co.uk
Product Groups: 35, 36

Friedenthals Ltd

Marine Propeller Works Croft Street, Preston, PR1 8XD
Tel: 01772-254255 **Fax:** 01772-204829
Directors: C. Foster (Fin), G. Friedenthal (MD)
Immediate Holding Company: FRIEDENTHALS,LIMITED
Registration no: 00145448 **Date established:** 2016
Turnover: Up to £250,000 **No.of Employees:** 1 - 10 **Product Groups:** 29, 34, 39

Date of Accounts	Dec 11	Dec 10	Dec 09
Working Capital	-172	-165	-157
Fixed Assets	136	136	136
Current Assets	9	14	21

G P Fleet Solutions

23 Valley View Walton Le Dale, Walton-le-dale, Preston, PR5 4LU
Tel: 0845-467 6095 **Fax:** 01772-483420
E-mail: info@gpfleetsolutions.co.uk
Website: http://www.gpfleetsolutions.co.uk
Directors: I. Pearson (Fin)
Immediate Holding Company: GP FLEET SOLUTIONS LIMITED
Registration no: 06347213 **Date established:** 2007
No.of Employees: 1 - 10 **Product Groups:** 44

Garage Doors Lancashire

Aspden Street Bamber Bridge, Preston, PR5 6TL
Tel: 01772-334828 **Fax:** 01772-627877
E-mail: post@garagedoorslancs.co.uk
Website: http://www.garagedoorslancs.co.uk
Directors: J. Chester (Dir)
Immediate Holding Company: GARAGE DOORS (NORTHERN) LIMITED
Registration no: 01359652 **Date established:** 1978
No.of Employees: 11 - 20 **Product Groups:** 25, 30, 35

Date of Accounts	Jul 11	Jul 10	Jul 09
Working Capital	1m	962	2m
Fixed Assets	881	922	99
Current Assets	1m	1m	2m

Gardiner Security Ltd
2 Preston Enterprise Centre Salter Street, Preston, PR1 1NT
Tel: 01772-561444 **Fax:** 01772-252529
Website: http://www.gardinersecurity.co.uk
Managers: P. O'Donnell (Mgr)
Immediate Holding Company: ADI-Gardiner Emea Ltd
Registration no: 04124719 **Date established:** 2000
No.of Employees: 1 - 10 **Product Groups:** 37, 40

G Gordon
Shay Lane Industrial Estate Shay Lane, Longridge, Preston, PR3 3BT
Tel: 01772-782070 **Fax:** 01772-786237
Directors: G. Gordon (Prop)
Immediate Holding Company: EASTHAMS BUILDING CONTRACTORS LIMITED
Registration no: 00983646 **Date established:** 1970
No.of Employees: 1 - 10 **Product Groups:** 40

Date of Accounts	Jul 11	Jul 10	Jul 09
Working Capital	625	755	700
Fixed Assets	1m	864	783
Current Assets	1m	1m	1m
Current Liabilities	N/A	N/A	40

Granuldisk
PO Box 437 Tarleton, Preston, PR4 6YU
Tel: 07765-244447
E-mail: david.barton@granuldisk.com
Website: http://www.granuldisk.com
Directors: D. Barton (Dir)
No.of Employees: 51 - 100 **Product Groups:** 40, 45, 46

H R T Hand Pallet Trucks Ltd
172 Station Road Hesketh Bank, Preston, PR4 6ST
Tel: 01772-814967 **Fax:** 01772-814967
E-mail: hrt.ltd@talktalk.net
Directors: A. Cottam (MD)
Immediate Holding Company: HAND ROLLER TRUCKS LIMITED
Registration no: 04924293 **Date established:** 2003
No.of Employees: 1 - 10 **Product Groups:** 35, 39, 45

Date of Accounts	Mar 12	Mar 11	Mar 10
Working Capital	-8	-12	-7
Fixed Assets	7	8	8
Current Assets	8	8	8

H T B Packaging Ltd
Unit 8 Electron Works Brook Street, Preston, PR1 7NH
Tel: 01772-561137 **Fax:** 01772-200001
Directors: J. Turner (MD)
Immediate Holding Company: HTB PACKAGING LTD.
Registration no: 03524079 **Date established:** 1998
No.of Employees: 1 - 10 **Product Groups:** 38, 42

Date of Accounts	Mar 11	Mar 10	Mar 09
Working Capital	-27	-19	-27
Fixed Assets	3	3	7
Current Assets	4	4	7

Hallis Hudson Group Ltd
Unit B1 Red Scar Business Park, Ribbleton, Preston, PR2 5NJ
Tel: 01772-909500 **Fax:** 01772-909599
E-mail: info@hallishudson.com
Website: http://www.hallishudson.co.uk
Bank(s): Royal Bank of Scotland P.L.C., Preston
Directors: J. Soper (MD), J. Soaper (Dir)
Managers: A. Soper (Personnel), R. Soper (Mktg Serv Mgr), I. Gregory (Purch Mgr), L. Soper (Sales Prom Mgr), G. Hill (Tech Serv Mgr), R. Stanford (Fin Mgr)
Ultimate Holding Company: HARPER INDUSTRIES PLC
Immediate Holding Company: HALLIS-HUDSON GROUP LIMITED
Registration no: 01290285 **VAT No.:** GB 322 9409 65
Date established: 1976 **Turnover:** £10m - £20m
No.of Employees: 51 - 100 **Product Groups:** 23, 24, 30, 36

Date of Accounts	Jun 11	Jun 10	Jun 09
Sales Turnover	15m	14m	13m
Pre Tax Profit/Loss	503	385	278
Working Capital	1m	802	832
Fixed Assets	399	271	171
Current Assets	5m	4m	4m
Current Liabilities	2m	1m	1m

Henry Halstead Fasteners Ltd
492 Holly Place Walton Summit Centre, Bamber Bridge, Preston, PR5 8AX
Tel: 01772-339521 **Fax:** 01772-332233
E-mail: sales@henry-halstead.co.uk
Website: http://www.kanbanexperts.co.uk
Bank(s): Bank of Scotland, Glasgow
Directors: M. Mchugh (MD)
Managers: A. Morris (Purch Mgr), S. Savage (Fin Mgr)
Ultimate Holding Company: SHANCASTLE INVESTMENTS LIMITED
Immediate Holding Company: HENRY HALSTEAD LIMITED
Registration no: 00725298 **VAT No.:** GB 174 9714 29
Date established: 1962 **Turnover:** £10m - £20m
No.of Employees: 21 - 50 **Product Groups:** 35, 66

Date of Accounts	Mar 12	Mar 11	Mar 10
Sales Turnover	14m	13m	10m
Pre Tax Profit/Loss	2m	1m	1m
Working Capital	3m	2m	3m
Fixed Assets	235	115	95
Current Assets	7m	6m	5m
Current Liabilities	588	739	476

Holland House Electrical
161-163 Eldon Street Ashton-On-Ribble, Preston, PR2 2AD
Tel: 01772-257975 **Fax:** 01772-201897
E-mail: preston@hh-electrical.co.uk
Website: http://www.hollandhouseelectrical.co.uk
Directors: I. Smith (Fin)
Managers: A. Barron (Mgr)
Immediate Holding Company: HOLLAND HOUSE ELECTRICAL CO. LTD
Registration no: 00265679 **VAT No.:** GB 232 1940 92
No.of Employees: 1 - 10 **Product Groups:** 29, 37

Housesafe Fire Alarm Systems
470 Ranglet Road Walton Summit Centre, Bamber Bridge, Preston, PR5 8AR
Tel: 01772-336335 **Fax:** 01772-336445
E-mail: sales@housesafe.com
Website: http://www.housesafe.com
Directors: J. Cowland (Fin)
Immediate Holding Company: HOUSESAFE LIMITED
Registration no: 04368683 **Date established:** 2002
No.of Employees: 1 - 10 **Product Groups:** 37, 38, 40

Date of Accounts	Feb 11	Feb 10	Feb 09
Working Capital	-25	-24	-34
Fixed Assets	15	14	5
Current Assets	48	26	17
Current Liabilities	N/A	1	1

Howick Forge Limited
Crossley House Industrial Estate Leyland Road, Penwortham, Preston, PR1 9QP
Tel: 01772-748948 **Fax:** 01772-751821
E-mail: info@howickforge.co.uk
Website: http://www.howickforge.co.uk
Directors: M. Smith (Prop)
Registration no: 07359842 **Date established:** 1988
No.of Employees: 11 - 20 **Product Groups:** 26, 35

HSS Lift & Shift
170 Ribbleton Lane, Preston, PR2 2DQ
Tel: 01772-798877 **Fax:** 01772-798855
Website: http://www.hss.com
Managers: K. Jow (Mgr)
Date established: 1996 **No.of Employees:** 1 - 10 **Product Groups:** 35, 39, 45

W H Hull Ltd
Canal Works Plox Brow, Tarleton, Preston, PR4 6HE
Tel: 01772-812126 **Fax:** 01772-812037
E-mail: sales@whhull.com
Website: http://www.whhull.com
Directors: G. Perplus (MD)
Ultimate Holding Company: FORCESTATE LIMITED
Immediate Holding Company: W. H. HULL LIMITED
Registration no: 00754820 **VAT No.:** GB 163 6981 34
Date established: 1963 **Turnover:** £1m - £2m **No.of Employees:** 1 - 10
Product Groups: 39, 45

Date of Accounts	Mar 12	Mar 11	Feb 10
Working Capital	-644	-647	-664
Fixed Assets	2m	2m	2m
Current Assets	868	585	781

Hygienic Stainless Steel Ltd
8 Charnley Fold Industrial Estate School Lane, Bamber Bridge, Preston, PR5 6PS
Tel: 01772-315277 **Fax:** 01772-626011
E-mail: sales@hss-ltd.co.uk
Website: http://www.hss-ltd.co.uk
Directors: M. Linford (Fin)
Immediate Holding Company: HYGIENIC STAINLESS STEEL LIMITED
Registration no: 02027413 **Date established:** 1986 **Turnover:** £1m - £2m
No.of Employees: 1 - 10 **Product Groups:** 36

Date of Accounts	Dec 11	Dec 10	Dec 09
Working Capital	303	295	293
Fixed Assets	2	3	5
Current Assets	691	613	637

Incorez Ltd
Sika House Miller Street, Preston, PR1 1EA
Tel: 01772-201964 **Fax:** 01772-255194
E-mail: info@incorez.co.uk
Website: http://www.incorez.com
Bank(s): Barclays, Fishergate, Preston
Managers: C. Lynch (Sales & Mktg Mg), L. Daniels (Chief Mgr), M. Ideson (Tech Serv Mgr), L. Waite (Purch Mgr), S. Lowe (Personnel)
Ultimate Holding Company: SIKA AG (SWITZERLAND)
Immediate Holding Company: INCOREZ LIMITED
Registration no: 02033501 **VAT No.:** GB 448 1939 18
Date established: 1986 **Turnover:** £10m - £20m
No.of Employees: 21 - 50 **Product Groups:** 30

Date of Accounts	Dec 11	Dec 10	Dec 09
Sales Turnover	12m	11m	11m
Pre Tax Profit/Loss	339	1m	1m
Working Capital	-565	-543	5m
Fixed Assets	2m	2m	1m
Current Assets	3m	4m	7m
Current Liabilities	374	416	881

James Hall & Co. Ltd
Bowland View, Preston, PR2 5QT
Tel: 01772-706666 **Fax:** 01772-706667
E-mail: customer.service@jameshall.co.uk
Website: http://www.jameshall.co.uk
Bank(s): National Westminster Bank Plc
Directors: C. Collins (Fin), S. Niven (Fin)
Managers: P. Huartson (Buyer)
Ultimate Holding Company: JAMES HALL AND COMPANY (HOLDINGS) LIMITED
Immediate Holding Company: JAMES HALL AND COMPANY (PROPERTIES) LIMITED
Registration no: 00204303 **VAT No.:** GB 350 0469 83
Date established: 2025 **Turnover:** £2m - £5m
No.of Employees: 251 - 500 **Product Groups:** 85

Date of Accounts	Mar 11	Mar 10	Mar 09
Sales Turnover	N/A	N/A	4m
Pre Tax Profit/Loss	N/A	N/A	1m
Working Capital	-441	-238	-294
Fixed Assets	37m	34m	34m
Current Assets	N/A	N/A	110
Current Liabilities	N/A	N/A	403

Jewson Ltd
Raglan Street Ashton-on-Ribble, Preston, PR2 2AX
Tel: 01772-254091 **Fax:** 01772-250686
Website: http://www.jewson.co.uk
Bank(s): Barclays
Directors: J. Burrows (MD)
Ultimate Holding Company: COMPAGNIE DE SAINT GOBAIN (FRANCE)
Immediate Holding Company: JEWSON LIMITED
Registration no: 00348407 **VAT No.:** GB 497 7184 83
Date established: 1939 **No.of Employees:** 21 - 50 **Product Groups:** 66

Date of Accounts	Dec 11	Dec 10	Dec 09
Sales Turnover	1606m	1547m	1485m
Pre Tax Profit/Loss	18m	100m	45m
Working Capital	-345m	-250m	-349m
Fixed Assets	496m	387m	461m
Current Assets	657m	1005m	1320m
Current Liabilities	66m	120m	64m

Jones Stroud Insulations Ltd
Queen Street Longridge, Preston, PR3 3BS
Tel: 01772-783011 **Fax:** 01772-784200
E-mail: n.currie@jsi.krempel.com
Website: http://www.krempel-group.com
Bank(s): National Westminster
Directors: N. Currie (Fin)
Managers: I. Grimshaw (Tech Serv Mgr), L. Fitzsimmons, M. Hems (Sales Prom Mgr), D. Hamridings (Personnel)
Ultimate Holding Company: KREMPEL BETEILIGUNGSGESELLSHEFT (GERMANY)
Immediate Holding Company: JONES STROUD INSULATIONS LIMITED
Registration no: 03989743 **VAT No.:** GB 153 4405 87
Date established: 2000 **Turnover:** £20m - £50m
No.of Employees: 101 - 250 **Product Groups:** 30, 33, 36, 37

Date of Accounts	Dec 11	Dec 10	Dec 09
Sales Turnover	25m	20m	15m
Pre Tax Profit/Loss	3m	2m	774
Working Capital	4m	4m	3m
Fixed Assets	9m	6m	7m
Current Assets	10m	10m	8m
Current Liabilities	794	2m	620

Jonesco (Preston) Ltd
Pittman Way Fulwood, Preston, PR2 9ZD
Tel: 01772-706809 **Fax:** 01772-702209
E-mail: dstark@jonesco-plastics.com
Website: http://www.jonesco-plastics.com
Bank(s): The Royal Bank of Scotland
Directors: C. Shiers (Co Sec), R. Jones (Ch), H. Jones (Jt MD), A. Jones (Jt MD), P. Williams (Sales)
Managers: M. Consterdine (Export Sales Mg), R. Calverley (Chief Design)
Registration no: 00901751 **VAT No.:** GB 154 3042 96
Date established: 1966 **No.of Employees:** 101 - 250 **Product Groups:** 30, 32, 36, 39, 40, 45, 48, 66, 68

Date of Accounts	Mar 12	Mar 11	Mar 10
Sales Turnover	15m	13m	11m
Pre Tax Profit/Loss	585	151	224
Working Capital	3m	2m	2m
Fixed Assets	3m	3m	3m
Current Assets	6m	5m	4m
Current Liabilities	818	873	643

Knight Air Products Ltd
Richard Street Kirkham, Preston, PR4 2HU
Tel: 01772-687707 **Fax:** 01772-686633
E-mail: info@knight-air.co.uk
Website: http://www.knight-air.co.uk
Directors: S. Macnamara (Dir)
Immediate Holding Company: KNIGHT AIR PRODUCTS LIMITED
Registration no: 03969512 **Date established:** 2000
Turnover: £250,000 - £500,000 **No.of Employees:** 1 - 10
Product Groups: 27, 29, 30

Date of Accounts	Apr 11	Apr 10	Apr 09
Working Capital	72	62	47
Fixed Assets	6	8	11
Current Assets	186	183	148

L S Systems Ltd
188 Blackgate Lane Tarleton, Preston, PR4 6UU
Tel: 01772-812484 **Fax:** 01772-815417
E-mail: sales@lssystems.co.uk
Website: http://www.lssystems.co.uk
Directors: K. Ball (Dir)
Managers: D. Scott (Fin Mgr), S. Myerscough (Tech Serv Mgr)
Immediate Holding Company: L.S. SYSTEMS LIMITED
Registration no: 02329261 **Date established:** 1988
No.of Employees: 21 - 50 **Product Groups:** 07, 35, 38, 41

Date of Accounts	Dec 10	Dec 09	Dec 08
Working Capital	857	846	762
Fixed Assets	212	207	229
Current Assets	2m	2m	2m

Lancashire Police Federation
15-17 Hutton Hall Avenue Hutton, Preston, PR4 5TJ
Tel: 0845-125 3545
Website: http://www.lancashire.police.uk
Immediate Holding Company: POWER ENGINEERING CONSULTANTS PUBLIC LIMITED COMPANY
Date established: 1990 **No.of Employees:** 1 - 10 **Product Groups:** 37, 67, 87

Linear Motion Systems Ltd
Unit 5 90 Berry Lane, Longridge, Preston, PR3 3WH
Tel: 01772-780200 **Fax:** 01772-733777
E-mail: sales@linearmotionsystems.co.uk
Website: http://www.linearmotionsystems.co.uk
Managers: J. Moffatt (Mgr)
Immediate Holding Company: LINEAR MOTION SYSTEMS LIMITED
Registration no: 02327201 **Date established:** 1988
No.of Employees: 1 - 10 **Product Groups:** 35

Date of Accounts	Mar 12	Mar 11	Mar 10
Working Capital	374	330	253
Fixed Assets	12	13	20
Current Assets	459	463	318

Mcarthur Group Ltd
Raglan Street Ashton-On-Ribble, Preston, PR2 2AX
Tel: 01772-556042 **Fax:** 0113-242 1150
E-mail: alan.curme@mcarthur-group.com
Website: http://www.mcarthur-group.com
Bank(s): HSBC Bank plc
Managers: A. Curme (District Mgr), K. Sheehan (District Mgr)
Immediate Holding Company: MCARTHUR GROUP LIMITED
Registration no: 00394222 **Date established:** 1945 **Turnover:** £5m - £10m
No.of Employees: 21 - 50 **Product Groups:** 22

Date of Accounts	Dec 11	Dec 10	Dec 09
Sales Turnover	82m	79m	79m
Pre Tax Profit/Loss	-1m	-529	-2m
Working Capital	-1m	144	10
Fixed Assets	13m	14m	15m
Current Assets	25m	26m	22m
Current Liabilities	1m	2m	11m

Manmart Ltd
Rough Hey Road Grimsargh, Preston, PR2 5AR
Tel: 01772-705060 **Fax:** 01772-792474
E-mail: sales@pakawaste.co.uk
Website: http://www.manmart.co.uk

Directors: A. Smith (Fin), B. Martland (MD), D. Hamer (Grp MD)
Managers: A. Astley (Mktg Serv Mgr), A. Ekins (Buyer), P. Harding
Ultimate Holding Company: MOORCO FIVE LIMITED
Immediate Holding Company: MANMART LIMITED
Registration no: 01616292 **Date established:** 1982
No.of Employees: 51 - 100 **Product Groups:** 23, 30, 34, 35, 38, 39, 40, 41, 42, 43, 44, 45, 46, 47, 48, 49, 61, 67, 83, 84

Date of Accounts	Jan 12	Jan 11	Jan 10
Working Capital	N/A	N/A	102
Fixed Assets	N/A	N/A	2
Current Assets	N/A	19	130
Current Liabilities	N/A	19	N/A

Maplin Electronics Ltd
Corporation Street, Preston, PR1 2UQ
Tel: 01772-258484 **Fax:** 01772-258686
Website: http://www.maplin.co.uk
Ultimate Holding Company: Maplin Electronics Group (Holdings) Ltd
Immediate Holding Company: Maplin Electronics (Holdings) Ltd
Registration no: 01264385 **Date established:** 1976
Turnover: £125m - £250m **No.of Employees:** 1 - 10 **Product Groups:** 37, 61

Tom Martin & Co. Ltd
123 Seedlee Road Walton Summit Centre, Bamber Bridge, Preston, PR5 8AE
Tel: 01772-626828 **Fax:** 01772-627491
E-mail: info@tom-martin.co.uk
Website: http://www.tom-martin.co.uk
Directors: C. Mcneil (Works), G. Brettle (MD), S. Hallinan (Fin)
Ultimate Holding Company: TOM MARTIN METAL HOLDINGS LIMITED
Immediate Holding Company: TOM MARTIN & COMPANY LIMITED
Registration no: 00990667 **Date established:** 1970
Turnover: £50m - £75m **No.of Employees:** 51 - 100 **Product Groups:** 66

Date of Accounts	Dec 11	Dec 10	Dec 09
Sales Turnover	54m	47m	31m
Pre Tax Profit/Loss	4m	3m	781
Working Capital	7m	5m	3m
Fixed Assets	2m	2m	2m
Current Assets	17m	16m	10m
Current Liabilities	3m	5m	3m

Merlin Diesel Systems Ltd
189-191 Bradkirk Place Walton Summit Centre, Bamber Bridge, Preston, PR5 8AJ
Tel: 01772-627676 **Fax:** 01772-626220
E-mail: sales@merlinint.co.uk
Website: http://www.merlindiesel.com
Bank(s): National Westminster Bank Plc
Directors: L. Bramley (MD)
Immediate Holding Company: MERLIN DIESEL SYSTEMS LTD
Registration no: 02539463 **VAT No.:** GB 534 4133 70
Date established: 1990 **Turnover:** £10m - £20m
No.of Employees: 51 - 100 **Product Groups:** 39, 40, 68

Date of Accounts	Jul 11	Jul 10	Jul 09
Sales Turnover	11m	10m	9m
Pre Tax Profit/Loss	507	658	549
Working Capital	3m	2m	2m
Fixed Assets	693	571	260
Current Assets	5m	4m	4m
Current Liabilities	278	420	218

Metcalf Agricultural Engineers
Height Lane Chipping, Preston, PR3 2NU
Tel: 01995-61166 **Fax:** 01995-61166
Directors: R. Metcalf (Prop)
Date established: 1983 **No.of Employees:** 1 - 10 **Product Groups:** 41

Mezz Barriers & Gates
Unit 1 Astra Business Centre, Roman Way, Preston, PR2 5AP
Tel: 01772-759061 **Fax:** 01772-653991
E-mail: info@mezzbarriers.co.uk
Website: http://www.mezzbarriers.co.uk
Managers: P. Wilmot (Mgr), W. Billington (Accounts)
Registration no: 00610341 **Turnover:** Up to £250,000
Product Groups: 35, 36, 51, 66

National Clamps
PO Box 208, Preston, PR1 2AE
Tel: 01772-882992 **Fax:** 01772-882882
E-mail: sales@national-clamps.com
Website: http://www.national-clamps.com
Directors: T. Whitehouse (Ch)
Date established: 1989 **Turnover:** £250,000 - £500,000
No.of Employees: 1 - 10 **Product Groups:** 36

Nederman Ltd
91 Seedlee Road Walton Summit Centre, Bamber Bridge, Preston, PR5 8AE
Tel: 08452-743434 **Fax:** 01772-315273
E-mail: info@nederman.co.uk
Website: http://www.nederman.com
Bank(s): National Westminster Bank Plc
Directors: L. Neary (Fin)
Ultimate Holding Company: NEDERMAN HOLDINGS AB (SWEDEN)
Immediate Holding Company: NEDERMAN LIMITED
Registration no: 01393492 **Date established:** 1978 **Turnover:** £5m - £10m
No.of Employees: 21 - 50 **Product Groups:** 30, 34, 35, 36, 42, 45, 46

Date of Accounts	Dec 11	Dec 10	Dec 09
Sales Turnover	13m	10m	N/A
Pre Tax Profit/Loss	446	545	-477
Working Capital	57	2m	2m
Fixed Assets	3m	739	816
Current Assets	6m	4m	3m
Current Liabilities	2m	652	599

New City Fire
83 Marsh Way Penwortham, Preston, PR1 9PJ
Tel: 01772-751448
E-mail: dave@newcityfire.co.uk
Website: http://www.newcityfire.co.uk
Directors: D. O'hara (Dir)
Immediate Holding Company: NEW CITY FIRE LIMITED
Registration no: 06292623 **Date established:** 2007
No.of Employees: 1 - 10 **Product Groups:** 52, 67, 84

Date of Accounts	Jun 11	Jun 09	Jun 08
Working Capital	-5	-5	-1
Fixed Assets	2	3	1
Current Assets	2	1	N/A

Noblett Steel
Toad Hall Farm Moss Lane, Inskip, Preston, PR4 0UA
Tel: 01995-679500
Managers: T. Noblett (Mgr)
No.of Employees: 1 - 10 **Product Groups:** 35

North & Western Lancashire Chamber Of Commerce
9-10 Eastway Business Village Olivers Place, Fulwood, Preston, PR2 9WT
Tel: 01772-653000 **Fax:** 01772-655544
E-mail: sales@lancschamber.co.uk
Website: http://www.lancschamber.co.uk
Directors: B. Murphy (Grp Chief Exec)
Immediate Holding Company: NORTH & WESTERN LANCASHIRE CHAMBER OF COMMERCE
Registration no: 00145454 **Date established:** 2016
Turnover: £500,000 - £1m **No.of Employees:** 11 - 20 **Product Groups:** 87

Date of Accounts	Dec 11	Dec 10	Dec 09
Working Capital	170	166	127
Fixed Assets	792	800	812
Current Assets	425	512	497

Norwesco Coffee
12 Powis Road Ashton-on-Ribble, Preston, PR2 1AD
Tel: 01772-729413
E-mail: matt@fischealthcare.co.uk
Directors: S. White (Ptnr)
Turnover: Up to £250,000 **No.of Employees:** 1 - 10 **Product Groups:** 40, 62, 67

P J F Ltd
Samlesbury Mill Samlesbury Bottoms, Preston, PR5 0RN
Tel: 01254-853824 **Fax:** 01254-851824
E-mail: info@pjfltd.com
Website: http://www.pjfltd.com
Directors: S. Jewes (Fin), P. Jewes (MD)
Immediate Holding Company: P J F LIMITED
Registration no: 04678578 **Date established:** 2003
No.of Employees: 1 - 10 **Product Groups:** 26, 35

Date of Accounts	Apr 11	Apr 10	Apr 09
Working Capital	-16	-27	-25
Fixed Assets	15	24	21
Current Assets	52	52	48

Pakawaste
Rough Hey Road Grimsargh, Preston, PR2 5AR
Tel: 01772-654348 **Fax:** 01772-792474
E-mail: sales@pakawaste.co.uk
Website: http://www.pakawaste.co.uk
Bank(s): The Royal Bank of Scotland
Directors: D. Hamer (MD), A. Smith (Fin)
Managers: C. Calderbank (Sales Off Mgr), A. Ekins (Purch Mgr)
Ultimate Holding Company: MOORCO FIVE LIMITED
Immediate Holding Company: PAKAWASTE ENGINEERING SERVICES LIMITED
Registration no: 02568736 **VAT No.:** GB 156 5511 65
Date established: 1990 **Turnover:** £5m - £10m **No.of Employees:** 21 - 50
Product Groups: 41, 42, 43, 44, 45, 54, 67, 83

Date of Accounts	Jan 12	Jan 11	Jan 10
Working Capital	216	178	52
Fixed Assets	89	76	71
Current Assets	530	385	318

Palmer Publicity Services Ltd
Unit A5 Chain Caul Way Ashton-on-Ribble, Preston, PR2 2YL
Tel: 01772-733213 **Fax:** 01772-733613
E-mail: info@palmerpublicity.co.uk
Website: http://www.palmerpublicity.co.uk
Directors: N. Palmer (MD)
Immediate Holding Company: PALMER PUBLICITY SERVICES LIMITED
Registration no: 04493066 **Date established:** 2002
Turnover: £500,000 - £1m **No.of Employees:** 11 - 20 **Product Groups:** 49

Date of Accounts	Sep 11	Sep 10	Sep 09
Working Capital	-125	-142	-322
Fixed Assets	338	355	355
Current Assets	196	187	266

Parker Merchanting Ltd
J Guild Trading Estate Ribbleton Lane, Preston, PR1 5DP
Tel: 01772-796939 **Fax:** 01772-793138
E-mail: info.parker@hagemeyer.co.uk
Website: http://www.parker-merchanting.com
Managers: A. Hinks (Warehouse Mgr)
Ultimate Holding Company: RAY INVESTMENT SARL (LUXEMBOURG)
Immediate Holding Company: PARKER MERCHANTING LIMITED
Registration no: 00224779 **VAT No.:** GB 614 2136 80
Date established: 2027 **No.of Employees:** 11 - 20 **Product Groups:** 22, 24, 29, 30, 33, 37, 39, 40, 45, 63, 66, 68

Date of Accounts	Dec 10	Dec 09	Dec 08
Working Capital	51	51	51
Current Assets	51	51	51

Tom Parker Ltd
PO Box 36, Preston, PR1 1HY
Tel: 01772-251405 **Fax:** 01772-827088
E-mail: richard.parker@tom-parker.co.uk
Website: http://www.tom-parker.co.uk
Bank(s): Yorkshire Bank PLC
Directors: T. Parker (Fin), R. Parker (Sales), T. Parker (MD)
Managers: P. Brown (I.T. Exec), L. Lawrence (Mktg Serv Mgr), I. Howarth (Sales Prom Mgr)
Immediate Holding Company: TOM PARKER LIMITED
Registration no: 01068402 **VAT No.:** GB 154 6770 48
Date established: 1972 **Turnover:** £5m - £10m
No.of Employees: 51 - 100 **Product Groups:** 29, 30

Date of Accounts	Apr 11	Apr 10	Apr 09
Sales Turnover	9m	8m	7m
Pre Tax Profit/Loss	279	275	275
Working Capital	3m	3m	2m
Fixed Assets	970	1m	967
Current Assets	5m	4m	4m
Current Liabilities	1m	448	1m

H H Pedder & Son
Lympstone Snape Wood Lane, Cabus, Preston, PR3 0JP
Tel: 01995-603224 **Fax:** 01995-606001
Website: http://www.tankfabrication.co.uk
Directors: I. Pedder (Prop)
Date established: 1946 **No.of Employees:** 1 - 10 **Product Groups:** 35, 42, 45

Photo First Aid
4 Park Avenue New Longton, Preston, PR4 4AY
Tel: 01772-744566
E-mail: info@photofirstaid.co.uk
Website: http://www.photofirstaid.co.uk
Directors: O. Harper (Prop)
Date established: 2000 **No.of Employees:** 1 - 10 **Product Groups:** 81, 89

Pilkingtons Ltd (t/a Weitzer Parket UK)
Belgrave Court Caxton Road Fulwood, Preston, PR2 9PL
Tel: 01772-790990 **Fax:** 01772-701044
E-mail: info@pilkingtonsltd.com
Website: http://www.pilkingtons.co.uk
Bank(s): Barclays
Directors: R. Pilkington (MD)
Immediate Holding Company: PILKINGTONS LIMITED
Registration no: 00098076 **VAT No.:** GB 145 8244 60
Date established: 2008 **Turnover:** £1m - £2m **No.of Employees:** 11 - 20
Product Groups: 22, 30, 43

Date of Accounts	Dec 11	Dec 10	Dec 09
Working Capital	839	-6	-78
Fixed Assets	2m	2m	4m
Current Assets	1m	236	191

Plumbs
Brookhouse Mill Old Lancaster Lane, Preston, PR1 7PZ
Tel: 01772-838301 **Fax:** 01772-838396
E-mail: geoffrey.plumb@plumbs.ltd.uk
Website: http://www.plumbs.co.uk
Directors: G. Plumb (Ch), S. Page (MD)
Ultimate Holding Company: PLUMBS LIMITED
Immediate Holding Company: HERITAGE COVERS LIMITED
Registration no: 02109342 **Date established:** 1987
Turnover: £20m - £50m **No.of Employees:** 251 - 500 **Product Groups:** 23

Date of Accounts	Dec 11	Dec 10	Dec 09
Sales Turnover	26m	26m	26m
Pre Tax Profit/Loss	407	-150	774
Working Capital	1m	1m	1m
Fixed Assets	696	795	862
Current Assets	5m	4m	5m
Current Liabilities	2m	2m	3m

Polytank Ltd
Naze Lane East Freckleton, Preston, PR4 1UN
Tel: 01772-632850 **Fax:** 01772-679615
E-mail: sales@polytank.co.uk
Website: http://www.polytank.co.uk
Bank(s): National Westminster Bank Plc
Directors: S. Mckew (Fin), S. McHugh (Comm)
Immediate Holding Company: POLYTANK GROUP LIMITED
Registration no: 01016434 **VAT No.:** GB 154 3210 04
Date established: 1971 **Turnover:** £250,000 - £500,000
No.of Employees: 21 - 50 **Product Groups:** 30

Date of Accounts	Sep 11	Sep 10	Sep 09
Working Capital	-846	-608	-581
Fixed Assets	4m	4m	4m
Current Assets	2m	2m	1m

Powerspray
Wynbald House Smallwood Hey, Pilling, Preston, PR3 6HJ
Tel: 01253-790600 **Fax:** 01253-790021
Directors: P. Smith (Prop)
Date established: 2001 **No.of Employees:** 1 - 10 **Product Groups:** 38, 42

Premitec Ltd
PO Box 1220, Preston, PR2 0HX
Tel: 0845-0066210 **Fax:** 0845-0066213
E-mail: info@premitec.co.uk
Website: http://www.premitec.co.uk
Directors: I. Pickles (MD)
Registration no: 04573574 **Turnover:** £250,000 - £500,000
No.of Employees: 1 - 10 **Product Groups:** 45, 46

Date of Accounts	Mar 08	Mar 07	Mar 06
Working Capital	80	55	-17
Fixed Assets	23	25	27
Current Assets	129	116	22
Current Liabilities	50	61	39

Preston Board & Packaging Ltd
Arkwright Mill Greenbank Street, Preston, PR1 7JS
Tel: 01772-254187 **Fax:** 01772-253264
E-mail: sales@prestonboard.co.uk
Website: http://www.prestonboard.co.uk
Directors: C. Ingham (MD)
Managers: C. Ingham (Sales Prom Mgr)
Ultimate Holding Company: MARBLEGRANGE LIMITED
Immediate Holding Company: PRESTON BOARD AND PACKAGING LIMITED
Registration no: 01567779 **Date established:** 1981
Turnover: £20m - £50m **No.of Employees:** 21 - 50 **Product Groups:** 27

Date of Accounts	Dec 11	Dec 10	Dec 09
Sales Turnover	22m	20m	17m
Pre Tax Profit/Loss	206	583	207
Working Capital	264	293	651
Fixed Assets	6m	6m	5m
Current Assets	6m	6m	5m
Current Liabilities	968	2m	503

Preston Harley-Davidson
West Strand Park Strand Road, Preston, PR1 8UY
Tel: 01772-551800 **Fax:** 01772-551801
E-mail: sales@preston-harleydavidson.com
Website: http://www.preston-harleydavidson.com
Managers: A. Uphill (Grp Mktg Mgr)
Ultimate Holding Company: PROTOPLAN LIMITED
Registration no: 04587859 **Date established:** 2002
No.of Employees: 11 - 20 **Product Groups:** 68

Preston Plywood Supplies (Nationwide)
River Street Off Bow Lane, Preston, PR1 8NS
Tel: 01772-561656 **Fax:** 01772-561256
E-mail: liam@prestonplywood.co.uk
Website: http://www.cubiclesanddoors.co.uk

see next page

***Preston Plywood Supplies (Nationwide)** - Cont'd*
Managers: L. Byrne (Mgr)
No.of Employees: 1 - 10 **Product Groups:** 08, 25, 26, 30, 35, 37, 47, 66, 76

Preston Welding Supplies

136 Roebuck Street Ashton-on-Ribble, Preston, PR2 2JN
Tel: 01772-722611 **Fax:** 01772-722590
E-mail: prestonweldingsupplies@googlemail.com
Directors: F. Embrey (Prop)
Date established: 1990 **No.of Employees:** 1 - 10 **Product Groups:** 46

Prestoplan Ltd

366 Four Oaks Road Walton Summit Centre, Bamber Bridge, Preston, PR5 8AP
Tel: 01772-627373 **Fax:** 01772-627575
E-mail: john.bedford@prestoplan.co.uk
Website: http://www.prestoplan.co.uk
Directors: P. Hoyle (Fin), J. Bedford (MD), A. Black (Fin)
Managers: N. Webb (Purch Mgr), S. Cowell, I. Loughnane
Ultimate Holding Company: TAYLOR WIMPEY PLC
Immediate Holding Company: PRESTOPLAN LIMITED
Registration no: 03521811 **Date established:** 1998
No.of Employees: 101 - 250 **Product Groups:** 35

Date of Accounts	Dec 11	Dec 10	Dec 09
Sales Turnover	20m	24m	22m
Pre Tax Profit/Loss	-2m	17	949
Working Capital	2m	4m	4m
Fixed Assets	398	563	794
Current Assets	7m	7m	7m
Current Liabilities	1m	1m	2m

Protec Workwear & Safety Ltd

29-31 School Lane Bamber Bridge, Preston, PR5 6QE
Tel: 01772-316060 **Fax:** 01772-316622
E-mail: bill@protecpreston.com
Website: http://www.protecworkwear.com
Directors: W. Rawlinson (MD), N. Rawlinson (Fin)
Immediate Holding Company: PROTEC WORKWEAR AND SAFETY LIMITED
Registration no: 04196231 **Date established:** 2001
No.of Employees: 21 - 50 **Product Groups:** 22, 23, 24, 29, 30, 35, 38, 40, 43, 49, 63, 67, 83

Date of Accounts	Jun 08	Jun 07	Jun 06
Working Capital	71	40	10
Fixed Assets	50	45	39
Current Assets	326	340	290
Current Liabilities	255	300	280

Proview Presentation Solutions

North View Skitham Lane, Pilling, Preston, PR3 6BD
Tel: 01995-601571 **Fax:** 01995-602612
E-mail: info@proviewps.fsnet.co.uk
Website: http://www.proviewps.fsnet.co.uk
Directors: A. McCormick (Prop)
Date established: 2002 **No.of Employees:** 1 - 10 **Product Groups:** 37, 67, 83

Pyro Glass Ltd

Unit 5 Astra Business Centre Longridge Road, Ribbleton, Preston, PR2 5AP
Tel: 01772-651265 **Fax:** 01772-654912
E-mail: sales@pyroglass.com
Website: http://www.pyroglass.com
Bank(s): Royal Bank of Scotland
Directors: P. Atkinson (Dir)
Immediate Holding Company: PYROGLASS LIMITED
Registration no: 02176681 **VAT No.:** GB 477 3510 33
Date established: 1987 **Turnover:** £500,000 - £1m
No.of Employees: 11 - 20 **Product Groups:** 23, 33

Date of Accounts	Dec 11	Dec 10	Dec 09
Working Capital	370	251	274
Fixed Assets	41	33	45
Current Assets	558	432	454
Current Liabilities	N/A	96	N/A

R S Micro

129 Brookfield Place Walton Summit Centre, Bamber Bridge, Preston, PR5 8BF
Tel: 01772-628000 **Fax:** 01772-628888
E-mail: gregw@rstechnology.co.uk
Website: http://www.rstechnology.co.uk
Managers: G. Winlett (Mgr)
Date established: 1990 **No.of Employees:** 1 - 10 **Product Groups:** 45, 46

R W H Iron Design Ltd

Bleasdale Road Whitechapel, Preston, PR3 2ER
Tel: 01995-640444 **Fax:** 01995-643253
E-mail: rwhirondesign@btinternet.com
Website: http://www.rwhirondesign.co.uk
Directors: R. Hayton (Dir), S. Hayton (Fin)
Immediate Holding Company: RWH IRON DESIGN LIMITED
Registration no: 04457712 **Date established:** 2002
No.of Employees: 1 - 10 **Product Groups:** 46, 48

Date of Accounts	Jun 11	Jun 10	Jun 09
Working Capital	-18	-6	15
Fixed Assets	46	56	54
Current Assets	33	61	75

Reed Specalist Recruitment

First Floor 81 Fishergate, Preston, PR1 2UH
Tel: 01772-200843 **Fax:** 01772-251912
E-mail: preston@reed.co.uk
Website: http://www.reed.co.uk
Managers: D. Finch (Mgr)
Registration no: 00669854 **Date established:** 1994
Turnover: £75m - £125m **No.of Employees:** 1 - 10 **Product Groups:** 80

Regal Amusement Machine Sales Limited

139 Brookfield Place Walton Summit Centre, Bamber Bridge, Preston, PR5 8BF
Tel: 01772-694242 **Fax:** 01257-234343
E-mail: info@regalamusements.co.uk
Website: http://www.regalamusements.co.uk
Directors: K. Turner (MD), T. Yate (Dir)
Immediate Holding Company: BRYSDALES H LIMITED
Registration no: 03329800 **Date established:** 1999
No.of Employees: 51 - 100 **Product Groups:** 37, 49, 65

Richards Hose Ltd

Unit 7 Roman Way Centre Longridge Road, Preston, PR2 5BB
Tel: 01772-651550 **Fax:** 01772-651325
E-mail: info@richardsfire.co.uk
Website: http://www.richardsfire.co.uk
Directors: T. Hatton (MD)
Registration no: 02534702 **VAT No.:** GB 534 4788 21
Date established: 1991 **No.of Employees:** 1 - 10 **Product Groups:** 23, 29, 30, 36, 39, 40, 51, 67, 74

Date of Accounts	Dec 11	Dec 10	Dec 09
Working Capital	510	480	454
Fixed Assets	2	3	4
Current Assets	713	647	644

Road Safety Services

Brackenwood Centre Bradshaw Lane, Greenhalgh, Preston, PR4 3HQ
Tel: 01253-596388 **Fax:** 01253-596388
E-mail: shaun@road-safety.net
Website: http://www.road-safety.net
Directors: S. Foy (MD), D. Foy (Dir), C. Foy (Dir)
Immediate Holding Company: ROAD SAFETY SERVICES LIMITED
Registration no: 03719045 **Date established:** 1999
No.of Employees: 11 - 20 **Product Groups:** 39, 40, 51

Date of Accounts	Apr 11	Apr 10	Apr 09
Working Capital	410	394	257
Fixed Assets	1m	1m	1m
Current Assets	878	876	739

John Robson Metals Ltd

Stump Cross Works Eaves Green Lane, Goosnargh, Preston, PR3 2FE
Tel: 01772-865272 **Fax:** 01772-861819
E-mail: jrr@johnrobsonltd.co.uk
Website: http://www.johnrobsonmetals.co.uk
Directors: J. Robson (MD), L. Slater (Fin)
Managers: A. Walton (Buyer)
Immediate Holding Company: JOHN ROBSON LIMITED
Registration no: 04936214 **Date established:** 2003 **Turnover:** £1m - £2m
No.of Employees: 21 - 50 **Product Groups:** 66, 84

Sabre Triad Ltd

42 Roman Way Industrial Estate Ribbleton, Preston, PR2 5BD
Tel: 01772-655325 **Fax:** 01772-655326
E-mail: j.morgan@eggconnect.net
Website: http://www.sabretriad.co.uk
Bank(s): HSBC Bank plc
Directors: A. Treverton (Fin), C. Chamberlain (MD), C. Chamberlain (MD)
Ultimate Holding Company: SABRE TRIAD HOLDINGS LIMITED
Immediate Holding Company: SABRE TRIAD LIMITED
Registration no: 02171454 **VAT No.:** GB 477 3588 93
Date established: 1987 **Turnover:** £5m - £10m **No.of Employees:** 21 - 50
Product Groups: 27, 30

Date of Accounts	Dec 11	Dec 10	Dec 09
Sales Turnover	7m	7m	7m
Pre Tax Profit/Loss	390	483	346
Working Capital	1m	1m	841
Fixed Assets	886	937	1m
Current Assets	3m	3m	3m
Current Liabilities	669	793	826

The Sachet Co

Red Scar Industrial Estate Longridge Road, Ribbleton, Preston, PR2 5NE
Tel: 01772-797121
Website: http://www.thesachetcompany.co.uk
Directors: D. Hartley (Prop)
No.of Employees: 1 - 10 **Product Groups:** 31, 32

Safe Shop

29 New Hall Lane, Preston, PR1 5NX
Tel: 01772-793792 **Fax:** 01772-651886
E-mail: anthony@thesafeshop.co.uk
Website: http://www.thesafeshop.co.uk
Directors: A. Neary (Ptnr)
Immediate Holding Company: THE SAFE SHOP LIMITED
Registration no: 06771208 **Date established:** 2008
No.of Employees: 1 - 10 **Product Groups:** 22, 26, 87

Sharples Stress Engineers Ltd

Unit 29 Old Mill Industrial Estate Bamber Bridge, Preston, PR5 6SY
Tel: 01772-323359 **Fax:** 01772-316017
E-mail: sharplesstress@aol.com
Website: http://www.sharplesstress.com
Directors: E. Sharples (MD)
Immediate Holding Company: SHARPLES STRESS ENGINEERS LIMITED
Registration no: 01682034 **VAT No.:** GB 379 7103 22
Date established: 1982 **Turnover:** £250,000 - £500,000
No.of Employees: 1 - 10 **Product Groups:** 38, 85

Date of Accounts	Jan 11	Jan 10	Jan 09
Working Capital	363	317	337
Fixed Assets	22	N/A	N/A
Current Assets	411	331	365

Sika Liquid Plastics

Iotech House Miller Street Fishwick Park, Preston, PR1 1EA
Tel: 01772-259781 **Fax:** 01772-255670
E-mail: info@liquidplastics.co.uk
Website: http://www.liquidplastics.co.uk
Bank(s): Barclays, 38 Fishergate
Directors: J. Gregson (Co Sec)
Managers: S. Sullivan (Chief Mgr)
Ultimate Holding Company: SIKA LIMITED
Immediate Holding Company: LIQUID PLASTICS LIMITED
Registration no: 00696057 **VAT No.:** GB 154 0837 72
Date established: 1961 **Turnover:** £20m - £50m
No.of Employees: 101 - 250 **Product Groups:** 30, 32, 33

Date of Accounts	Dec 11	Dec 10	Dec 09
Sales Turnover	26m	25m	28m
Pre Tax Profit/Loss	2m	4m	1m
Working Capital	3m	4m	9m
Fixed Assets	1m	1m	1m
Current Assets	7m	8m	14m
Current Liabilities	2m	2m	2m

Simmal Head Quarters

Unit 479-480 Ranglet Road, Bamber Bridge, Preston, PR5 8AR
Tel: 01772-324277 **Fax:** 01772-627486
E-mail: simmal@btconect.com
Website: http://www.simmal.co.uk
Bank(s): National Westminster Bank Plc
Directors: J. Simmons (MD), S. Simmons (Fin)
Managers: C. Lever (Buyer)
Immediate Holding Company: SIMMAL LIMITED
Registration no: 01741450 **VAT No.:** GB 379 8567 72
Date established: 1983 **Turnover:** £5m - £10m **No.of Employees:** 21 - 50
Product Groups: 66

Date of Accounts	Sep 11	Sep 10	Sep 09
Sales Turnover	10m	8m	8m
Pre Tax Profit/Loss	245	118	-187
Working Capital	2m	2m	2m
Fixed Assets	942	863	832
Current Assets	5m	5m	4m
Current Liabilities	463	322	243

Somic Textiles

New Hall Lane - Alliance Works, Preston, PR1 5NY
Tel: 01772-790000 **Fax:** 01772-795677
E-mail: sales@somic.co.uk
Website: http://www.somic.co.uk
Bank(s): HSBC
Directors: H. Borking (Fin), D. Holt (Co Sec), R. Blackburn (MD), P. Blackburn (Sales)
Managers: T. Gillespie (Purch Mgr)
Immediate Holding Company: SOMIC TEXTILES LIMITED
Registration no: 06866449 **VAT No.:** GB 401 2362 15
Date established: 2009 **Turnover:** £2m - £5m **No.of Employees:** 21 - 50
Product Groups: 23, 27, 30, 63, 66

Date of Accounts	Mar 12	Mar 11	Mar 10
Working Capital	439	476	277
Fixed Assets	189	111	54
Current Assets	575	784	564

Speedy Services

Unit 3 15-19 Sedgwick Street, Preston, PR1 1TP
Tel: 01772-204666 **Fax:** 01772-204888
Website: http://www.speedyservices.co.uk
Managers: I. Baxter (Depot Mgr)
Immediate Holding Company: LIFTING GEAR HIRE LIMITED
Registration no: 05566506 **Date established:** 2005
No.of Employees: 1 - 10 **Product Groups:** 35, 39, 45

Sub Surface Ltd

3 Peel Street Ashton-On-Ribble, Preston, PR2 2QS
Tel: 01772-561135 **Fax:** 01772-204907
E-mail: preston@subsurface.co.uk
Website: http://www.subsurface.co.uk
Directors: C. Marsden (MD)
Immediate Holding Company: SUB SURFACE NORTH EAST LIMITED
Registration no: 02472687 **VAT No.:** GB 732 4887 15
Date established: 1990 **Turnover:** £500,000 - £1m
No.of Employees: 11 - 20 **Product Groups:** 84

Date of Accounts	May 11	May 10	May 09
Working Capital	-3	1	26
Fixed Assets	2	2	3
Current Assets	229	234	256
Current Liabilities	185	185	180

Submarine Manufacturing & Products Ltd

Blackpool Road Newton, Preston, PR4 3RE
Tel: 01772-687775 **Fax:** 01772-687774
E-mail: dormsby@smp-ltd.co.uk
Website: http://www.smp-ltd.co.uk
Directors: D. Ormsby (Fin)
Managers: T. Duncan (Personnel), S. Simpson (Tech Serv Mgr), K. Adams (Purch Mgr), R. Connolly (Sales & Mktg Mg)
Ultimate Holding Company: MSS HOLDINGS (UK) LIMITED
Immediate Holding Company: SUBMARINE MANUFACTURING AND PRODUCTS LIMITED
Registration no: 02608984 **Date established:** 1991 **Turnover:** £1m - £2m
No.of Employees: 21 - 50 **Product Groups:** 35, 37, 39, 40, 49, 67, 68

Date of Accounts	Dec 11	Dec 10	Dec 09
Working Capital	2m	2m	1m
Fixed Assets	146	161	168
Current Assets	4m	4m	3m

Super Lizzy (PAKAWASTE)

Unit 6 Rough Hey Road Grimsargh, Preston, PR2 5AR
Tel: 01772-796688 **Fax:** 01772-792474
E-mail: sales@pakawaste.co.uk
Website: http://www.pakawaste.co.uk
Product Groups: 40, 67, 69, 83, 84, 89

T F L International Ltd

Chain Caul Way Ashton-On-Ribble, Preston, PR2 2TL
Tel: 01772-733211 **Fax:** 01772-722771
E-mail: roger@tflinternational.co.uk
Website: http://www.tflinternational.co.uk
Directors: R. Moyle (Dir), J. Chalker (Design), K. Ziemer (MD), B. Cox (Ch)
Immediate Holding Company: TFL INTERNATIONAL LIMITED
Registration no: 00848757 **Date established:** 1965 **Turnover:** £5m - £10m
No.of Employees: 1 - 10 **Product Groups:** 52

Taylor & Russell Ltd

Stonebridge Mill Preston Road, Longridge, Preston, PR3 3AN
Tel: 01772-782295 **Fax:** 01772-785341
Website: http://www.taylorandrussell.co.uk
Bank(s): HSBC Bank plc
Directors: D. Taylor (Dir), P. Taylor (Fin)
Managers: I. Taylor (Sales Admin), C. Porter (Accounts)
Immediate Holding Company: TAYLOR & RUSSELL LIMITED
Registration no: 00495202 **VAT No.:** GB 154 6598 34
Date established: 1951 **Turnover:** £500,000 - £1m
No.of Employees: 11 - 20 **Product Groups:** 26, 30, 34, 35, 36, 39, 45, 48, 49

Date of Accounts	May 11	May 10	May 09
Working Capital	191	220	336
Fixed Assets	61	63	69
Current Assets	396	447	565

Tetrad plc

Hartford Mill Swan Street, Preston, PR1 5PQ
Tel: 01772-792936 **Fax:** 01772-798319
E-mail: sales@tetrad.co.uk
Website: http://www.tetrad.co.uk
Bank(s): Yorkshire Bank PLC
Directors: C. Lodge (Fin), J. Cooper (Sales), M. Griffin (MD), S. Nield (Tech Serv)
Managers: H. Marriott (Mktg Serv Mgr), A. Robinson (Purch Mgr), P. Sherliker (Personnel)

Immediate Holding Company: TETRAD LIMITED
Registration no: 00936239 **VAT No.:** GB 604 4513 73
Date established: 1968 **Turnover:** £10m - £20m
No.of Employees: 251 - 500 **Product Groups:** 26

Date of Accounts	Apr 09	Apr 08	Apr 10
Sales Turnover	18m	34m	14m
Pre Tax Profit/Loss	-4m	-570	108
Working Capital	-890	492	-385
Fixed Assets	6m	8m	7m
Current Assets	4m	10m	4m
Current Liabilities	1m	2m	1m

Thompsons Paper

5 Kenyon Farm Units Gough Lane, Bamber Bridge, Preston, PR5 6AQ
Tel: 01772-627469 **Fax:** 01772-620764
E-mail: richard@thompsonspap.co.uk
Website: http://www.arranmarketing.co.uk
Directors: F. Thompson (Prop)
Date established: 1993 **No.of Employees:** 1 - 10 **Product Groups:** 38, 42

ThyssenKrupp Aerospace UK Ltd

76-80 Banksfield Place Walton Summit Centre, Bamber Bridge, Preston, PR5 8AD
Tel: 01772-648017
E-mail: info@thyssenkrupp.com
Website: http://www.thyssenkrupp.com
Ultimate Holding Company: THYSSEN KRUPP AG (GERMANY)
Immediate Holding Company: THYSSENKRUPP AEROSPACE UK LTD
Registration no: 01914559 **Date established:** 1985
No.of Employees: 1 - 10 **Product Groups:** 34, 36

Date of Accounts	Sep 11	Sep 10	Sep 09
Sales Turnover	101m	95m	101m
Pre Tax Profit/Loss	5m	3m	7m
Working Capital	27m	26m	27m
Fixed Assets	3m	4m	4m
Current Assets	64m	59m	68m
Current Liabilities	7m	8m	10m

Total Bitumen (a division of Total UK)

Chain Caul Way Preston Riversway, Ashton-on-Ribble, Preston, PR2 2TZ
Tel: 01772-729302 **Fax:** 01772-724713
E-mail: info@total.co.uk
Website: http://www.total.co.uk
Bank(s): Barclays, Epsom
Directors: L. Young (Co Sec)
Managers: M. Linley (Chief Mgr)
Ultimate Holding Company: TOTAL SAFETY INC (USA)
Immediate Holding Company: TOTAL BITUMEN UK LIMITED
Registration no: 00105979 **VAT No.:** GB 483 2918 23
Date established: 2009 **Turnover:** £2m - £5m **No.of Employees:** 51 - 100
Product Groups: 17, 31

Date of Accounts	Dec 11	Dec 10	Dec 09
Sales Turnover	2m	2m	2m
Working Capital	18m	18m	18m
Current Assets	18m	18m	18m

Unique Enamelling Services Ltd

Unit J Bee Mill Preston Road, Ribchester, Preston, PR3 3XL
Tel: 01254-878265 **Fax:** 01524-792299
E-mail: info@ues-ltd.co.uk
Website: http://www.ues-ltd.co.uk
Directors: D. Shaw (MD)
Immediate Holding Company: UNIQUE ENAMELLING SERVICES LIMITED
Registration no: 04535192 **Date established:** 2002
Turnover: Up to £250,000 **No.of Employees:** 1 - 10 **Product Groups:** 46, 48

Date of Accounts	Sep 11	Sep 10	Sep 09
Sales Turnover	99	98	110
Pre Tax Profit/Loss	37	33	43
Working Capital	7	10	15
Fixed Assets	10	11	2
Current Assets	27	24	38
Current Liabilities	12	9	21

Veolia Enviromental Services PLC

Unit D4-D5 Red Scar Industrial Estate Longridge Road, Ribbleton, Preston, PR2 5NQ
Tel: 01772-798748 **Fax:** 01772-798762
E-mail: helen.orson@vieola.co.uk
Website: http://www.cleanaway.com
Managers: G. Dunford (Mgr)
Ultimate Holding Company: VEOLIA ENVIRONNEMENT SA (FRANCE)
Immediate Holding Company: VEOLIA ENVIRONMENTAL SERVICES (UK) PLC
Registration no: 02215767 **VAT No.:** 352 1129 90 **Date established:** 1988
No.of Employees: 21 - 50 **Product Groups:** 42, 54

Date of Accounts	Dec 11	Dec 10	Dec 09
Sales Turnover	1223m	1210m	1173m
Pre Tax Profit/Loss	124m	104m	85m
Working Capital	557m	514m	481m
Fixed Assets	1583m	1063m	1043m
Current Assets	1181m	1085m	1065m
Current Liabilities	164m	132m	151m

W Bateman & Co.

Garstang Road Barton, Preston, PR3 5AA
Tel: 01772-862948 **Fax:** 01772-861639
E-mail: sales@bateman-sellarc.co.uk
Website: http://www.bateman-sellarc.co.uk
Managers: S. Cox (Mgr)
Immediate Holding Company: W.BATEMAN & CO.
Registration no: 00481111 **VAT No.:** GB 153 4648 61
Date established: 1950 **Turnover:** £500,000 - £1m
No.of Employees: 1 - 10 **Product Groups:** 39, 40, 41, 52, 68

Date of Accounts	May 10	May 09	May 08
Working Capital	149	147	183
Fixed Assets	23	36	45
Current Assets	193	187	245

Walki Ltd

Ray Lane Barnacre, Preston, PR3 1GG
Tel: 01995-604227 **Fax:** 01995-605222
E-mail: graham.hogben@walki.com
Website: http://www.walki.com
Bank(s): HSBC Bank plc
Directors: J. Grundy (Co Sec), P. Capstick (Co Sec), D. Ingham (Sales), G. Hogben (MD)
Managers: C. O'Neill (Purch Mgr)
Ultimate Holding Company: WALKI GROUP OY (FINLAND)
Immediate Holding Company: WALKI LIMITED
Registration no: SC014320 **VAT No.:** GB 154 0283 89
Date established: 2026 **Turnover:** £20m - £50m
No.of Employees: 21 - 50 **Product Groups:** 27

Date of Accounts	Dec 11	Dec 10	Dec 09
Sales Turnover	24m	25m	22m
Pre Tax Profit/Loss	2m	2m	730
Working Capital	5m	5m	4m
Fixed Assets	1m	2m	2m
Current Assets	8m	8m	6m
Current Liabilities	902	1m	1m

Westmead International Ltd

Highfield Blackpool Road, Clifton, Preston, PR4 0XL
Tel: 01772-671000 **Fax:** 01772-671660
E-mail: alan.emery@btclick.com
Directors: A. Emery (MD), R. Emery (Fin)
Immediate Holding Company: WESTMEAD INTERNATIONAL LIMITED
Registration no: 01885618 **VAT No.:** 407 1748 59 **Date established:** 1985
Turnover: £250,000 - £500,000 **No.of Employees:** 1 - 10
Product Groups: 61, 77

Date of Accounts	Dec 11	Dec 10	Dec 09
Working Capital	51	51	49
Current Assets	93	77	71

Alfred Whiteside

1 Warbrick Cottage Taylors Lane, Pilling, Preston, PR3 6AB
Tel: 01253-790700
Directors: A. Whiteside (Prop)
Date established: 1989 **No.of Employees:** 1 - 10 **Product Groups:** 35

S J Wilkinson

Blundellbrook Farm Cumeragh Lane, Whittingham, Preston, PR3 2JB
Tel: 01772-784330 **Fax:** 01772-785970
Directors: C. Wilkinson (Ptnr)
Date established: 2000 **No.of Employees:** 1 - 10 **Product Groups:** 41

Williamsons Of Nateby

Longmoor Lane Nateby, Preston, PR3 0JB
Tel: 01995-604434 **Fax:** 01995-604434
Directors: A. Williamson (Prop)
Ultimate Holding Company: COLLINSON HOLDINGS LIMITED
Immediate Holding Company: J. & M. COLLINSON LIMITED
Registration no: 02967743 **Date established:** 1981
No.of Employees: 1 - 10 **Product Groups:** 26, 35

Date of Accounts	Dec 11	Dec 10	Dec 09
Sales Turnover	10m	11m	11m
Pre Tax Profit/Loss	616	1m	159
Working Capital	6m	5m	4m
Fixed Assets	459	476	620
Current Assets	7m	7m	6m
Current Liabilities	938	816	1m

Y P H Welding Supplies Ltd

Unit 1 Stubbins Lane Claughton-on-Brock, Preston, PR3 0QH
Tel: 01995-604057 **Fax:** 01995-604018
E-mail: sales@yphltd.co.uk
Website: http://www.yphltd.co.uk
Directors: A. Thornton (MD)
Immediate Holding Company: YPH LIMITED
Registration no: 03703132 **Date established:** 1999
No.of Employees: 1 - 10 **Product Groups:** 46

Date of Accounts	Jan 12	Jan 11	Jan 10
Working Capital	34	17	-3
Fixed Assets	26	38	46
Current Assets	209	190	150

Rochdale

A & M Associates 1994 Ltd

Unit 2 Stuart Street, Rochdale, OL16 5NB
Tel: 01706-710747 **Fax:** 01706-710746
E-mail: amasso@zen.co.uk
Directors: A. Grime (Dir)
Immediate Holding Company: A & M ASSOCIATES (1994) LIMITED
Registration no: 08116384 **Date established:** 2012
Turnover: Up to £250,000 **No.of Employees:** 1 - 10 **Product Groups:** 63

A1 Extinguisher Services Ltd

149 Queens Drive, Rochdale, OL11 2NW
Tel: 01706-343963 **Fax:** 01706-341562
E-mail: a1extinguishers@live.co.uk
Website: http://www.alextinguisherservices.co.uk
Directors: J. Fieldhouse (Fin), P. Fieldhouse (MD)
Immediate Holding Company: P & J FIRE PROTECTION (ROCHDALE) LIMITED
Registration no: 04840415 **Date established:** 2003
Turnover: Up to £250,000 **No.of Employees:** 1 - 10 **Product Groups:** 38, 42

Date of Accounts	Jul 12	Jul 11	Jul 10
Working Capital	-16	-28	-32
Fixed Assets	4	5	6
Current Assets	4	7	8

Ace Polishing Services Ltd

Unit 1-3 The Landings 143 Oldham Road, Rochdale, OL16 5QY
Tel: 01706-630878 **Fax:** 01706-630878
E-mail: info@acepolishingservices.co.uk
Website: http://www.acepolishingservices.co.uk
Directors: P. Kirk (Ptnr)
Immediate Holding Company: ACE POLISHING SERVICES LIMITED
Registration no: 06235025 **Date established:** 2007
No.of Employees: 1 - 10 **Product Groups:** 46

Date of Accounts	May 11	May 10	May 09
Working Capital	8	12	74
Fixed Assets	27	11	4
Current Assets	58	47	78

Adi Gardiner Emea Ltd

Transpennine Trading Estate, Rochdale, OL11 2PX
Tel: 01706-343343 **Fax:** 01706-646600
E-mail: ehorton@gardinersecurity.co.uk
Website: http://www.gardinersecurity.co.uk
Bank(s): The Royal Bank of Scotland, Liverpool
Directors: J. Gazielly (Dir)
Managers: A. Connell (Chief Acct)
Ultimate Holding Company: HONEYWELL INTERNATIONAL INC (USA)
Immediate Holding Company: ADI-GARDINER EMEA LIMITED
Registration no: 02005506 **VAT No.:** GB 508 1246 69
Date established: 1986 **Turnover:** £2m - £5m **No.of Employees:** 21 - 50
Product Groups: 36, 40

Date of Accounts	Dec 11	Dec 10	Dec 09
Sales Turnover	2m	132	147
Pre Tax Profit/Loss	771	20m	160
Working Capital	60	-53	23m
Fixed Assets	8m	8m	8m
Current Assets	685	809	24m
Current Liabilities	333	544	800

Advanced Engineering Middleton Ltd

Unit 5d Transpennine Trading Estate Gorrels Way, Rochdale, OL11 2PX
Tel: 01706-759003 **Fax:** 01706-759004
E-mail: info@aemixers.com
Website: http://www.aemixers.com
Bank(s): The Royal Bank of Scotland
Directors: A. Hudson (MD)
Ultimate Holding Company: QUALTECH ENGINEERING SERVICES LIMITED
Immediate Holding Company: ADVANCED ENGINEERING (MIDDLETON) LIMITED
Registration no: 00940726 **Date established:** 1968 **Turnover:** £1m - £2m
No.of Employees: 11 - 20 **Product Groups:** 41, 42, 43

Date of Accounts	Oct 09	Oct 08	Mar 11
Working Capital	233	123	278
Fixed Assets	14	60	33
Current Assets	333	173	329

W & S Allely Ltd

Unit 9 Albion Road Industrial Estate, Rochdale, OL11 4JB
Tel: 01706-353770 **Fax:** 01706-654198
E-mail: rochdale@allely.co.uk
Website: http://www.allely.co.uk
Managers: M. Butterworth (Mgr)
Ultimate Holding Company: ALLELY EDEN HOLDINGS LIMITED
Immediate Holding Company: W. & S. ALLELY LIMITED
Registration no: 00292572 **VAT No.:** GB 547 6741 12
Date established: 1934 **Turnover:** £10m - £20m **No.of Employees:** 1 - 10
Product Groups: 34, 49, 66

Date of Accounts	Dec 11	Dec 10	Dec 09
Working Capital	465	401	371
Fixed Assets	22	25	43
Current Assets	3m	2m	2m
Current Liabilities	N/A	N/A	166

Anglo Recycling Technology Ltd

Bridge End Mills Tong Lane, Whitworth, Rochdale, OL12 8BG
Tel: 01706-853513 **Fax:** 01706-853625
E-mail: simon.macaulay@anglofelt.com
Website: http://www.anglorecycling.com
Bank(s): National Westminster Bank Plc
Directors: S. Macaulay (Dir)
Managers: R. Macaulay (Chief Acct)
Ultimate Holding Company: ANGLO FAMILY LIMITED
Immediate Holding Company: ANGLO RECYCLING TECHNOLOGY LIMITED
Registration no: 02143970 **VAT No.:** GB 458 3043 46
Date established: 1987 **Turnover:** £2m - £5m **No.of Employees:** 21 - 50
Product Groups: 23

Date of Accounts	Oct 11	Oct 10	Oct 09
Working Capital	513	530	549
Fixed Assets	221	166	203
Current Assets	819	910	854

Applications Tape Company Ltd

Calf Hey South, Rochdale, OL11 2JS
Tel: 01706-633043 **Fax:** 01706-710086
E-mail: sales@apptape.co.uk
Website: http://www.apptape.co.uk
Directors: L. Brand (MD), P. Holt (Dir)
Immediate Holding Company: APPLICATION TAPE COMPANY LIMITED
Registration no: 04771213 **Date established:** 2003
No.of Employees: 11 - 20 **Product Groups:** 49

Date of Accounts	May 11	May 10	May 09
Working Capital	-1	-10	-303
Fixed Assets	217	225	386
Current Assets	664	699	462

Aquacheck Ltd

Royle Barn Road, Rochdale, OL11 3DT
Tel: 01706-712593 **Fax:** 01706-641653
E-mail: info@aqua-check.co.uk
Website: http://www.aqua-check.co.uk
Directors: P. Carrington (Dir)
Ultimate Holding Company: BRIDGEPOINT CAPITAL LIMITED (BELGIUM)
Immediate Holding Company: AQUACHECK LIMITED
Registration no: 04651692 **Date established:** 2003
No.of Employees: 11 - 20 **Product Groups:** 36, 37, 38

Date of Accounts	Mar 11	Mar 10	Mar 09
Working Capital	N/A	N/A	150
Current Assets	N/A	N/A	150

Atlantic Project Co

828 Manchester Road, Rochdale, OL11 3AW
Tel: 01706-345661 **Fax:** 01706-648243
E-mail: aslack@apcpower.com
Website: http://www.atlanticprojects.com
Directors: M. Wall (Dir), P. Healy (MD)
Managers: A. Matcham (Admin Off)
Immediate Holding Company: MIDDLETON SCAFFOLDING COMPANY LIMITED
Registration no: 04231473 **Date established:** 2001
No.of Employees: 1 - 10 **Product Groups:** 48

B T G Plastics Ltd

Corporation Road, Rochdale, OL11 4HJ
Tel: 01706-640400 **Fax:** 01706-653434
E-mail: btg.plastics@tiscali.co.uk
Website: http://www.hoops4fitness.co.uk
Directors: B. Gooding (MD)
Immediate Holding Company: B.T.G. PLASTICS LIMITED
Registration no: 04833974 **VAT No.:** GB 408 7632 42
Date established: 2003 **Turnover:** £250,000 - £500,000
No.of Employees: 1 - 10 **Product Groups:** 30

see next page

B T G Plastics Ltd - Cont'd

Date of Accounts	Oct 11	Oct 10	Oct 09
Sales Turnover	319	378	367
Working Capital	28	46	26
Fixed Assets	173	148	140
Current Assets	103	127	137

Barton Kendal

122 Yorkshire Street, Rochdale, OL16 1LA
Tel: 01706-653214 **Fax:** 01706-341476
E-mail: sales@barton-kendal.co.uk
Website: http://www.barton-kendal.co.uk
Managers: S. Barton (Comm)
Immediate Holding Company: BARTON KENDAL RESIDENTIAL LIMITED
Registration no: 06447887 **Date established:** 2007
Turnover: £250,000 - £500,000 **No.of Employees:** 1 - 10
Product Groups: 80

Date of Accounts	Jan 12	Jan 11	Jan 10
Sales Turnover	N/A	N/A	274
Pre Tax Profit/Loss	N/A	N/A	86
Working Capital	23	-10	-36
Fixed Assets	234	286	353
Current Assets	80	44	143
Current Liabilities	N/A	18	65

BCH Ltd

Spring Place Millfold, Whitworth, Rochdale, OL12 8DN
Tel: 01706-852122 **Fax:** 01706-853010
E-mail: info@bchltd.com
Website: http://www.bchltd.com
Bank(s): Bank of Scotland
Directors: P. Jaimeson (Dir), K. Branton (Dir)
Registration no: 01943231 **Turnover:** £5m - £10m **Product Groups:** 35, 37, 41, 48, 67, 84, 85

Date of Accounts	Mar 10	Mar 09	Mar 08
Working Capital	20	20	20
Current Assets	854	747	950

Beeweb Ltd

Ambrose Street, Rochdale, OL11 1QX
Tel: 01706-648717 **Fax:** 01706-653012
E-mail: beeweb@btconnect.com
Website: http://www.beewebltd.com
Directors: H. Beedham (Fin), M. Beedham (MD)
Immediate Holding Company: BEEWEB LIMITED
Registration no: 04037261 **VAT No.:** GB 306 6582 56
Date established: 2000 **Turnover:** £250,000 - £500,000
No.of Employees: 1 - 10 **Product Groups:** 23, 30, 35

Date of Accounts	Jul 11	Jul 10	Jul 09
Working Capital	45	48	29
Fixed Assets	20	26	33
Current Assets	178	171	137

Brennard Textiles

Unit 2h Moss Industrial Estate Woodbine Street East, Rochdale, OL16 5LB
Tel: 01706-868444 **Fax:** 01706-269003
E-mail: info@brennardtextiles.co.uk
Website: http://www.brennardtextiles.co.uk
Directors: A. Shone (Prop)
No.of Employees: 1 - 10 **Product Groups:** 23, 24, 63, 65

The British Millerain Company Ltd

Broad Shaw Farm Broad Shaw Lane, Milnrow, Rochdale, OL16 4NR
Tel: 01706-649242 **Fax:** 01706-527611
E-mail: sales@britishmillerain.com
Website: http://www.britishmillerain.com
Directors: K. Laird (Sales), M. Miller (MD), D. Littler (Mkt Research)
Managers: T. Hall
Immediate Holding Company: THE BRITISH MILLERAIN COMPANY LIMITED
Registration no: 00185953 **VAT No.:** GB 508 4601 60
Date established: 2022 **Turnover:** £10m - £20m **No.of Employees:** 1 - 10
Product Groups: 23, 24, 29, 32, 43, 63, 66, 85

Date of Accounts	Nov 11	Nov 10	Nov 09
Sales Turnover	23m	18m	16m
Pre Tax Profit/Loss	541	703	243
Working Capital	7m	7m	6m
Fixed Assets	4m	5m	4m
Current Assets	11m	11m	9m
Current Liabilities	2m	2m	1m

C Norris Spring Specialists Ltd

Ladyhouse Spring Works Newhey Road Milnrow, Rochdale, OL16 4JD
Tel: 01706-642555 **Fax:** 01706-648347
E-mail: andrewward@btconnect.com
Website: http://www.norris-springs.co.uk
Bank(s): Barclays
Directors: A. Ward (Jt MD), A. Ward (MD), J. Armstead (Dir)
Immediate Holding Company: C. NORRIS (SPRING SPECIALISTS) LIMITED
Registration no: 00722551 **VAT No.:** GB 147 0633 77
Date established: 1962 **Turnover:** £1m - £2m **No.of Employees:** 11 - 20
Product Groups: 35, 36, 66

Date of Accounts	Apr 11	Apr 10	Apr 09
Working Capital	376	254	523
Fixed Assets	357	332	353
Current Assets	798	838	726

C R Solutions

1 Holmes Street, Rochdale, OL12 6AQ
Tel: 01706-357444 **Fax:** 01706-357444
E-mail: admin@crsolutions.com
Website: http://www.crsolutions.com
Directors: R. Nothard (Dir)
No.of Employees: 1 - 10 **Product Groups:** 37, 45, 67

Carter International

Unit B6-B7 Fieldhouse Industrial Estate Fieldhouse Road, Rochdale, OL12 0AA
Tel: 01706-638301 **Fax:** 01706-526569
E-mail: info@carter-mixers.co.uk
Website: http://www.carter-mixers.co.uk
Bank(s): HSBC
Directors: D. Hargreaves (Fin), P. Fletcher (MD)
Managers: N. Slater
Immediate Holding Company: CARTER INTERNATIONAL LIMITED
Registration no: 04980621 **Date established:** 2003
Turnover: £250,000 - £500,000 **No.of Employees:** 21 - 50
Product Groups: 36

Date of Accounts	Jun 11	Jun 10	Jun 09
Working Capital	621	128	101
Fixed Assets	444	238	286
Current Assets	2m	2m	1m
Current Liabilities	1m	N/A	223

Carter Origin Ltd

Holmes Street, Rochdale, OL12 6AQ
Tel: 01706-647049 **Fax:** 01706-524909
E-mail: sales@carterorigin.co.uk
Website: http://www.carterorigin.co.uk
Directors: R. Carter (MD), C. Carter (Co Sec)
Immediate Holding Company: CARTER ORIGIN LIMITED
Registration no: 00375173 **Date established:** 1942
Turnover: Up to £250,000 **No.of Employees:** 11 - 20 **Product Groups:** 30, 35, 48

Date of Accounts	Sep 11	Sep 10	Sep 09
Working Capital	185	161	230
Fixed Assets	24	29	39
Current Assets	297	230	363
Current Liabilities	N/A	N/A	71

Casey Group Ltd

Rydings Road, Rochdale, OL12 9PS
Tel: 01706-341121 **Fax:** 01706-861156
E-mail: info@casey.co.uk
Website: http://www.casey.co.uk
Directors: J. Warren (Fin), A. Chell (Grp)
Managers: C. Williams (Mktg Serv Mgr), A. Roland (Tech Serv Mgr), P. Butler (Buyer)
Immediate Holding Company: MASTER SPORT SURFACES LIMITED
Registration no: 01737168 **Date established:** 1983
Turnover: £20m - £50m **No.of Employees:** 21 - 50 **Product Groups:** 52, 84

Date of Accounts	Jul 11	Jul 10	Jul 09
Working Capital	-6	-8	72
Current Assets	N/A	N/A	82
Current Liabilities	6	N/A	N/A

Carcraft

Nixon Street, Rochdale, OL11 3JW
Tel: 0800-923 9418 **Fax:** 01706-752530
E-mail: sales@carcraft.co.uk
Website: http://www.carcraft.co.uk
Directors: J. Phipps (Mkt Research), D. McKee (Purch), M. Walsh (Sales), N. McKee (Grp Chief Exec), S. Nobes (Co Sec)
Managers: M. Brook (Tech Serv Mgr), R. White (Personnel)
Ultimate Holding Company: PENNINE METALS A LIMITED
Immediate Holding Company: CC AUTOMOTIVE GROUP LIMITED
Registration no: 00819414 **Date established:** 1964
Turnover: £75m - £125m **No.of Employees:** 251 - 500
Product Groups: 68

Date of Accounts	Sep 11	Sep 10	Sep 09
Sales Turnover	124m	127m	132m
Pre Tax Profit/Loss	-5m	4m	-2m
Working Capital	7m	12m	8m
Fixed Assets	2m	3m	4m
Current Assets	36m	35m	34m
Current Liabilities	10m	10m	10m

Chelburn Precision Ltd

Trans Pennine Trading Estate Gorrells Way, Rochdale, OL11 2PX
Tel: 01706-350479 **Fax:** 01706-861733
E-mail: n.travis@chelburn.co.uk
Website: http://www.chelburn.co.uk
Bank(s): Yorkshire Bank PLC
Directors: N. Travis (MD)
Managers: A. Bower (Chief Acct)
Ultimate Holding Company: CHELBURN HOLDINGS LIMITED
Immediate Holding Company: CHELBURN PRECISION LIMITED
Registration no: 01666113 **VAT No.:** GB 388 3782 92
Date established: 1982 **Turnover:** £2m - £5m **No.of Employees:** 21 - 50
Product Groups: 48

Date of Accounts	Jun 11	Jun 10	Jun 09
Working Capital	612	-301	-566
Fixed Assets	1m	2m	3m
Current Assets	2m	1m	830
Current Liabilities	N/A	605	485

Coates Engineering International Ltd

Millfold Whitworth, Rochdale, OL12 8DN
Tel: 01706-852122 **Fax:** 01706-853629
E-mail: info@bchltd.com
Website: http://www.bchltd.com
Bank(s): Barclays
Directors: T. Eve (Dir), A. Hunter (Fin)
Managers: C. Kershaw (Tech Serv Mgr), D. Stansfield (Mats Contrlr), D. Tod (Sales Prom Mgr), S. Barker, S. Graves (Personnel)
Ultimate Holding Company: COATES ENGINEERING GROUP LIMITED
Immediate Holding Company: COATES ENGINEERING (INTERNATIONAL) LIMITED
Registration no: 02163525 **VAT No.:** GB 306 0550 02
Date established: 1987 **Turnover:** £5m - £10m
No.of Employees: 51 - 100 **Product Groups:** 35, 37, 41, 48, 84, 85

Date of Accounts	Mar 12	Mar 11	Mar 10
Sales Turnover	9m	9m	8m
Pre Tax Profit/Loss	348	428	217
Working Capital	3m	2m	2m
Fixed Assets	1m	1m	1m
Current Assets	5m	5m	5m
Current Liabilities	1m	924	1m

Colourcode Group

10 Regent Street, Rochdale, OL12 0HQ
Tel: 01706-671168 **Fax:** 01706-671169
E-mail: john@colourcode.net
Website: http://www.colourcode.net
Directors: J. Wood (MD), G. Wood (Fin)
Immediate Holding Company: PIER PLASTICS LIMITED
Registration no: 04036419 **Date established:** 2000
No.of Employees: 11 - 20 **Product Groups:** 46, 48

Date of Accounts	Jul 09	Jul 08	Jul 07
Working Capital	66	67	151
Fixed Assets	53	45	41
Current Assets	173	222	277

Composite Textiles Ltd

Moss Mill Industrial Estate, Rochdale, OL16 5LB
Tel: 01706-750045 **Fax:** 01706-356694
E-mail: info@compotexuk.com
Website: http://www.compotexuk.com
Directors: W. Hobhouse (Co Sec), A. Burford (Dir)
Immediate Holding Company: COMPOSITE TEXTILES LIMITED
Registration no: 02919450 **Date established:** 1994 **Turnover:**
No.of Employees: 1 - 10 **Product Groups:** 29, 39

Date of Accounts	Mar 11	Mar 10	Mar 09
Working Capital	-14	-20	-12
Fixed Assets	4	4	5
Current Assets	45	21	24

Constell Engineering Ltd

Eagle Buildings Crawford Street, Rochdale, OL16 5NU
Tel: 01706-646936 **Fax:** 01706-647817
E-mail: office@constell.co.uk
Website: http://www.constell.co.uk
Directors: K. Cheetham (Dir)
Immediate Holding Company: CONSTELL ENGINEERS LIMITED
Registration no: 03526455 **VAT No.:** GB 712 2982 45
Date established: 1998 **Turnover:** £500,000 - £1m
No.of Employees: 1 - 10 **Product Groups:** 46

Date of Accounts	Dec 11	Dec 10	Dec 09
Working Capital	92	41	13
Fixed Assets	439	426	350
Current Assets	391	285	213
Current Liabilities	N/A	55	22

Custom Composites Ltd

Ensor Mill Queensway, Rochdale, OL11 2NU
Tel: 01706-526255 **Fax:** 01706-350187
E-mail: mail@customcom.co.uk
Website: http://www.customcom.co.uk
Bank(s): National Westminster Bank Plc
Directors: M. Bate (Co Sec)
Managers: J. Saunders (Ops Mgr)
Ultimate Holding Company: ATTWATER & SONS LIMITED
Immediate Holding Company: CUSTOM COMPOSITES LIMITED
Registration no: 01677195 **VAT No.:** GB 376 2280 43
Date established: 1982 **Turnover:** £500,000 - £1m
No.of Employees: 21 - 50 **Product Groups:** 30, 33, 37, 39

Date of Accounts	Dec 11	Dec 10	Dec 09
Working Capital	102	140	116
Fixed Assets	99	106	131
Current Assets	300	257	233

D.T.P. Supplies

242 Whitworth Rd, Rochdale, OL12 0SA
Tel: 01706-522113 **Fax:** 01706-647624
E-mail: sales@dtpsupplies.com
Website: http://www.dtpsupplies.com
Directors: V. Meech (Ptnr), D. Preston (Ptnr), H. Preston (Ptnr), J. Preston (Ptnr), R. Preston (Ptnr), G. Meech (Ptnr)
VAT No.: GB 151 1615 06 **Turnover:** £2m - £5m **No.of Employees:** 11 - 20
Product Groups: 22, 23, 27, 30, 35, 43, 44, 46, 63, 66

Dale Fire Proctection

10 Foot Mill Crescent, Rochdale, OL12 6PF
Tel: 01706-351608 **Fax:** 01706-351608
E-mail: info@dalefireprotection.co.uk
Website: http://www.dalefireprotection.co.uk
Directors: D. Reilly (Prop)
Immediate Holding Company: DALE FIRE PROTECTION LIMITED
Registration no: 05731740 **Date established:** 2006
No.of Employees: 1 - 10 **Product Groups:** 38, 42

Date of Accounts	Mar 11	Mar 09	Mar 07
Working Capital	-22	-35	-63
Fixed Assets	15	30	54
Current Assets	61	25	22

Dexine Rubber Co. Ltd

Jape Two Business Centre Dell Road, Rochdale, OL12 6BZ
Tel: 01706-640011 **Fax:** 01706-527714
E-mail: info@dexine.com
Website: http://www.dexine.com
Bank(s): Barclays, Rochdale
Directors: G. Guite (Fin), T. O'reilly (Grp Chief Exec)
Immediate Holding Company: DEXINE RUBBER COMPANY LIMITED
Registration no: 00059730 **VAT No.:** GB 145 2085 84
Date established: 1998 **Turnover:** £2m - £5m **No.of Employees:** 21 - 50
Product Groups: 29

Date of Accounts	Mar 11	Mar 10	Mar 09
Working Capital	435	711	877
Fixed Assets	362	389	657
Current Assets	817	1m	1m

Direct Coated Products Ltd

Unit 1a Eagle Technology Park Queensway, Rochdale, OL11 1TQ
Tel: 01706-651112 **Fax:** 01706-651113
E-mail: sales@directcoatedproducts.co.uk
Website: http://www.directcoatedproducts.co.uk
Directors: D. Platt (MD)
Immediate Holding Company: DIRECT COATED PRODUCTS LIMITED
Registration no: 02862334 **Date established:** 1993
Turnover: £500,000 - £1m **No.of Employees:** 1 - 10 **Product Groups:** 48

Date of Accounts	Sep 11	Sep 10	Sep 09
Working Capital	527	351	430
Fixed Assets	303	285	299
Current Assets	1m	1m	625

Dunphy Combustion Ltd

Queensway, Rochdale, OL11 2SL
Tel: 01706-649217 **Fax:** 01706-655512
E-mail: info@dunphy.co.uk
Website: http://www.dunphy.co.uk
Bank(s): Barclays, 1 Yorkshire St, Rochdale
Directors: S. Kuligowski (Dir)
Managers: K. Richardson, M. Brierely (Tech Serv Mgr), A. Martins (Mktg Serv Mgr), D. Morris (Purch Mgr)
Ultimate Holding Company: DUNPHY TECHNOLOGY LIMITED
Immediate Holding Company: DUNPHY COMBUSTION LIMITED
Registration no: 01016230 **VAT No.:** GB 145 5557 54
Date established: 1971 **Turnover:** £2m - £5m **No.of Employees:** 51 - 100
Product Groups: 40

Date of Accounts	Sep 11	Sep 10	Sep 09
Working Capital	992	1m	1m
Fixed Assets	199	90	119
Current Assets	2m	2m	2m

Dunphy Ecclesiastical Heating
Mitre House Willbutts Lane, Rochdale, OL11 5BE
Tel: 01706-522702 **Fax:** 01706-354815
E-mail: info@dunphychurchheating.co.uk
Website: http://www.dunphychurchheating.co.uk
Directors: C. Dunphy (Prop)
Registration no: 03380840 **Date established:** 1997
No.of Employees: 1 - 10 **Product Groups:** 40, 52

Eaga Insulations
Unit 12 Scotts Industrial Park Fishwick Street, Rochdale, OL16 5NA
Tel: 01706-759543 **Fax:** 01706-759765
E-mail: rochdale@eaga.com
Website: http://www.milfoldgroup.com
Managers: C. Renouf (Mgr), D. Cope (Sales Prom)
Date established: 1982 **Turnover:** £20m - £50m
No.of Employees: 11 - 20 **Product Groups:** 30, 33, 52, 66

Edward Keirby & Co. Ltd
Vine Works Chichester Street, Rochdale, OL16 2BG
Tel: 01706-645330 **Fax:** 01706-352882
E-mail: info@edwardkeirby.co.uk
Website: http://www.edwardkeirby.co.uk
Directors: T. Jenkins (MD), I. Jenkins (Co Sec)
Immediate Holding Company: EDWARD KEIRBY & CO LIMITED
Registration no: 00128371 **Date established:** 2013 **Turnover:** £1m - £2m
No.of Employees: 1 - 10 **Product Groups:** 66

Date of Accounts	Dec 10	Dec 09	Dec 08
Working Capital	71	110	196
Fixed Assets	64	72	78
Current Assets	258	227	410

Elliott Absorbent Products Ltd
Unit 4 Blueberry Business Park Kingsway, Rochdale, OL16 5DB
Tel: 01706-643122 **Fax:** 01706-354575
E-mail: sally@elliottabsorbents.co.uk
Website: http://www.elliottabsorbents.co.uk
Directors: S. Creevy (Fin)
Immediate Holding Company: ELLIOTT ABSORBENT PRODUCTS LIMITED
Registration no: 03786926 **Date established:** 1999
No.of Employees: 11 - 20 **Product Groups:** 38, 42

Date of Accounts	Dec 11	Dec 10	Dec 09
Working Capital	1m	1m	1m
Fixed Assets	1m	1m	1m
Current Assets	2m	2m	2m

Employment Links
99-101 Drake Street, Rochdale, OL16 1PZ
Tel: 01706-646471 **Fax:** 01706-753653
E-mail: j21@lancsinternet.com
Website: http://www.j21.org.uk
Managers: H. Darwent (Mgr)
Date established: 2006 **No.of Employees:** 21 - 50 **Product Groups:** 80

European Metals Recycling Ltd
Uncouth Road, Rochdale, OL16 3DD
Tel: 01706-341623 **Fax:** 01706-659434
Website: http://www.emrltd.com
Directors: C. Sheppard (MD), N. Warren (Co Sec)
Immediate Holding Company: EUROPEAN METAL RECYCLING LIMITED
Registration no: 02954623 **Date established:** 1994
Turnover: Over £1,000m **No.of Employees:** 1 - 10 **Product Groups:** 42, 66

Date of Accounts	Dec 11	Dec 10	Dec 09
Sales Turnover	3032m	2431m	1843m
Pre Tax Profit/Loss	116m	155m	91m
Working Capital	414m	371m	167m
Fixed Assets	518m	483m	480m
Current Assets	1027m	717m	557m
Current Liabilities	124m	118m	185m

Expert Electrical Supplies
Buckley Road Industrial Estate, Rochdale, OL12 9EF
Tel: 01706-860011
E-mail: stuart@expert-electrical.co.uk
Website: http://www.expertelec.co.uk
Directors: S. Hindle (MD)
No.of Employees: 1 - 10 **Product Groups:** 37

Farrel Ltd
PO Box 27, Rochdale, OL11 2PF
Tel: 01706-647434 **Fax:** 01706-638982
E-mail: ashaio@farrel.com
Website: http://www.farrel.com
Directors: A. Newell (Fin), P. Gaskell (Dir)
Managers: S. Brawn (Tech Serv Mgr)
Ultimate Holding Company: HARBURG-FREUDENBERGER MASGINEENBAU GMBH(GERMANY)
Immediate Holding Company: FARREL LIMITED
Registration no: 01922655 **VAT No.:** GB 425 7768 21
Date established: 1985 **Turnover:** £20m - £50m
No.of Employees: 101 - 250 **Product Groups:** 40, 42, 48, 67

Date of Accounts	Dec 11	Dec 10	Dec 09
Sales Turnover	30m	28m	21m
Pre Tax Profit/Loss	3m	2m	2m
Working Capital	7m	8m	6m
Fixed Assets	5m	4m	3m
Current Assets	18m	19m	14m
Current Liabilities	4m	5m	5m

Freudenberg Household Products
2 Chichester Street, Rochdale, OL16 2AX
Tel: 01706-759597 **Fax:** 01706-350143
E-mail: peter.gough@fhp-ww.com
Website: http://www.vileda.com
Managers: S. Butterworth (Sales Prom Mgr), C. Coyle, G. Greenwood (Tech Serv Mgr), H. Sternberg (Mgr), H. Spink (Personnel), K. Barker (Mktg Serv Mgr)
Ultimate Holding Company: FREUDENBERG AND CO KG (GERMANY)
Immediate Holding Company: FREUDENBERG VILEDA LIMITED
Registration no: 00940747 **Date established:** 1968
Turnover: £10m - £20m **No.of Employees:** 21 - 50 **Product Groups:** 23, 24, 29, 30, 33, 35, 36, 40, 45, 63

Date of Accounts	Dec 11	Dec 10	Dec 09
Pre Tax Profit/Loss	6	32	-32
Working Capital	-196	-228	-247
Fixed Assets	397	424	412
Current Assets	62	34	161

Frost Auto Restorations
Eagle Iron Works Crawford Street, Rochdale, OL16 5NU
Tel: 01706-658619 **Fax:** 01706-860338
E-mail: info@frost.co.uk
Website: http://www.frost.co.uk
Directors: M. Wood (MD)
Immediate Holding Company: FROST AUTO RESTORATION TECHNIQUES LTD
Registration no: 01936145 **Date established:** 1985 **Turnover:** £1m - £2m
No.of Employees: 1 - 10 **Product Groups:** 39

Date of Accounts	Jul 11	Jul 10	Jul 09
Sales Turnover	1m	1m	N/A
Pre Tax Profit/Loss	11	34	N/A
Working Capital	271	279	248
Fixed Assets	28	12	16
Current Assets	423	452	423
Current Liabilities	42	42	N/A

G A Electrical Distributors (a division of Edmundson Electrical)
Unit 9 Magnum Centre Fishwick Street, Rochdale, OL16 5NP
Tel: 01706-654321 **Fax:** 01706-642109
E-mail: lee.muskett@eel.co.uk
Website: http://www.edmundson-electrical.co.uk/
Managers: L. Muskett (Mgr)
Turnover: £2m - £5m **No.of Employees:** 1 - 10 **Product Groups:** 77

GB Ductwork Ltd
Station Road Facit, Rochdale, OL12 8LJ
Tel: 01706-854900 **Fax:** 01706-854990
Directors: J. Gibson (Dir)
Immediate Holding Company: G. B. DUCTWORK LIMITED
Registration no: 04148947 **VAT No.:** GB 147 5510 68
Date established: 2001 **Turnover:** £500,000 - £1m
No.of Employees: 1 - 10 **Product Groups:** 36

Date of Accounts	Jan 12	Jan 11	Jan 10
Working Capital	117	193	303
Fixed Assets	30	40	47
Current Assets	174	237	341

George Culley
8 WADDINGTON FOLD, Rochdale, OL16 4QB
Tel: 0161-622 0020 **Fax:** 0161-622 0010
E-mail: gculley251@aol.com
Website: http://www.rubber-extrusions-seals.co.uk
Directors: G. Culley (MD)
Registration no: 04451728 **VAT No.:** GB 798 0432 95
Turnover: £500,000 - £1m **No.of Employees:** 1 - 10 **Product Groups:** 29, 30, 49

Granada Material Handling Ltd
Sherwood Industrial Park Queensway, Rochdale, OL11 2NU
Tel: 01706-653620 **Fax:** 01706-523943
E-mail: info@gmh.co.uk
Website: http://www.gmh.co.uk
Directors: M. Sidwell (Sales), A. Cantrell (Sales), M. Cantrell (Fin)
Managers: P. Pinder (Works Gen Mgr)
Immediate Holding Company: GRANADA MATERIAL HANDLING LIMITED
Registration no: 01536663 **Date established:** 1980 **Turnover:** £5m - £10m
No.of Employees: 51 - 100 **Product Groups:** 30, 35, 37, 38, 39, 43, 45, 48, 51, 52, 61, 67, 84, 85, 86

Date of Accounts	Sep 11	Sep 10	Sep 09
Sales Turnover	8m	7m	6m
Pre Tax Profit/Loss	360	280	171
Working Capital	2m	1m	1m
Fixed Assets	299	313	348
Current Assets	4m	3m	2m
Current Liabilities	789	780	324

P W Greenhalgh & Co. Ltd
Ogden Mill Milnrow, Rochdale, OL16 3TH
Tel: 01706-847911 **Fax:** 01706-881217
E-mail: information@pwgreenhalgh.com
Website: http://www.pwgreenhalgh.com
Bank(s): Co-Operative
Directors: B. Greenhalgh (MD), S. Greenhalgh (Sales), A. Green Halgh (Co Sec)
Managers: T. Malkin (Chief Acct)
Ultimate Holding Company: P. W. GREENHALGH HOLDINGS LIMITED
Immediate Holding Company: P.W.GREENHALGH & CO.LIMITED
Registration no: 00199153 **VAT No.:** GB 145 1169 83
Date established: 2024 **Turnover:** £5m - £10m
No.of Employees: 51 - 100 **Product Groups:** 23

Date of Accounts	Dec 11	Dec 10	Dec 09
Sales Turnover	7m	7m	5m
Pre Tax Profit/Loss	-22	-250	-27
Working Capital	2m	2m	3m
Fixed Assets	603	1m	990
Current Assets	3m	3m	4m
Current Liabilities	481	494	501

Greenwood Lonsdale Ltd
Scotts Industrial Park Fishwick Street, Rochdale, OL16 5NA
Tel: 01706-759763 **Fax:** 01706-759764
E-mail: enquiries@greenwoodeng.co.uk
Website: http://www.greenwoodengineering.co.uk
Directors: J. Moore (Dir), K. Bevan (Fin)
Ultimate Holding Company: BUFFALO HOLDINGS LIMITED
Immediate Holding Company: GREENWOOD LONSDALE LIMITED
Registration no: 07571956 **Date established:** 2011
Turnover: £500,000 - £1m **No.of Employees:** 21 - 50
Product Groups: 29, 43, 67

Date of Accounts	May 10	Jun 09	Jun 08
Working Capital	273	293	265
Fixed Assets	98	111	115
Current Assets	493	424	500
Current Liabilities	N/A	N/A	212

Greenwood Magnetics Ltd
Unit 4c Buckley Road Industrial Estate, Rochdale, OL12 9EF
Tel: 01706-645824 **Fax:** 01706-642458
E-mail: sales@greenwoodmagnetics.com
Website: http://www.greenwoodmagnetics.com
Directors: G. Greenwood (Fin)
Immediate Holding Company: GREENWOOD MAGNETICS LIMITED
Registration no: 00449828 **Date established:** 1948
No.of Employees: 1 - 10 **Product Groups:** 37, 42, 45

Date of Accounts	Feb 12	Feb 11	Feb 10
Working Capital	180	103	91
Fixed Assets	251	254	253
Current Assets	296	228	180

Hanolex Ltd
246 Whitworth Road, Rochdale, OL12 0JL
Tel: 01706-656789 **Fax:** 01706-659911
E-mail: info@atwellengineering.co.uk
Website: http://www.eyelets.co.uk
Directors: M. Guttridge (Dir)
Immediate Holding Company: HANOLEX LIMITED
Registration no: 03180078 **VAT No.:** GB 431 2875 62
Date established: 1996 **Turnover:** £1m - £2m **No.of Employees:** 1 - 10
Product Groups: 22, 23, 27, 30, 34, 35, 36, 38, 39, 42, 43, 46, 49, 63, 66

Date of Accounts	Apr 11	Apr 10	Apr 09
Working Capital	91	118	133
Fixed Assets	42	33	46
Current Assets	286	293	284

Heap Dawson Ltd
2 Oldham Road, Rochdale, OL11 1BU
Tel: 01706-656222 **Fax:** 01706-641852
E-mail: enquiries@heapdawson.co.uk
Website: http://www.heapdawson.co.uk
Bank(s): Barclays Bank, Heywood
Directors: M. Heap (MD)
Immediate Holding Company: HEAP DAWSON LIMITED
Registration no: 01052214 **Date established:** 1972
No.of Employees: 11 - 20 **Product Groups:** 40

Date of Accounts	Apr 12	Apr 11	Apr 10
Working Capital	253	251	222
Fixed Assets	100	94	117
Current Assets	536	484	439

Hi-5 Electronics
Sherwood Industrial Park Queensway, Rochdale, OL11 2NU
Tel: 01706-647006 **Fax:** 01706-646853
E-mail: sales@hi5electronics.co.uk
Website: http://www.hi5electronics.co.uk
Managers: R. Houghton (Mgr)
Date established: 1999 **No.of Employees:** 21 - 50 **Product Groups:** 37, 44, 84

Date of Accounts	Jul 08	Jul 07	Jul 06
Working Capital	143	78	16
Fixed Assets	24	32	38
Current Assets	399	313	336
Current Liabilities	256	235	320

Holroyd Machine Tools & Rotors
Harbour Lane North Milnrow, Rochdale, OL16 3LQ
Tel: 01706-526590 **Fax:** 01706-353350
E-mail: info@holroyd.com
Website: http://www.holroyd.com
Directors: I. Emery (Fin), N. Jones (Develop), P. Hannah (Sales & Mktg)
Managers: S. Henshaw (Comptroller), S. Johnson (Tech Serv Mgr), S. Potts (Buyer), S. Johnson (I.T. Exec), D. Wittle (Personnel), D. Whittle (Personnel)
Ultimate Holding Company: DELMOR LIMITED
Immediate Holding Company: HOLROYD PRECISION LTD
Registration no: 05844176 **Date established:** 2006 **Turnover:** £5m - £10m
No.of Employees: 101 - 250 **Product Groups:** 46

Date of Accounts	Dec 11	Dec 10	Mar 09
Sales Turnover	10m	5m	11m
Pre Tax Profit/Loss	615	721	2m
Working Capital	5m	3m	971
Fixed Assets	108	115	102
Current Assets	18m	11m	6m
Current Liabilities	5m	4m	1m

Honnor Marine Ltd
Marine House Miall Street, Rochdale, OL11 1HY
Tel: 01706-715986 **Fax:** 01706-342576
E-mail: info@honnormarine.co.uk
Website: http://www.honnormarine.co.uk
Directors: B. Brown (MD)
Immediate Holding Company: HONNOR MARINE LIMITED
Registration no: 03450021 **Date established:** 1997
No.of Employees: 11 - 20 **Product Groups:** 30, 39, 84

Date of Accounts	Dec 11	Dec 10	Dec 09
Working Capital	49	63	24
Fixed Assets	22	30	37
Current Assets	190	169	183

Innovative Solutions
Mayfield Centre Off Belfield Road, Rochdale, OL16 2UZ
Tel: 01706-746713 **Fax:** 01706-746713
E-mail: info@innovative-solutions.org.uk
Website: http://www.innovativesolutions.co.uk
Bank(s): National Westminster Bank Plc
Directors: A. Rigby (MD)
Managers: D. McGee (Fin Mgr), P. Devenny (Purch Mgr)
Ultimate Holding Company: RICHARD WHITTAKER LIMITED
Immediate Holding Company: INNOVATIVE SOLUTIONS (UK) LIMITED
Registration no: 03654087 **VAT No.:** GB 146 8505 52
Date established: 1998 **Turnover:** £2m - £5m **No.of Employees:** 21 - 50
Product Groups: 20, 32

Date of Accounts	May 11	May 10	May 09
Working Capital	3	3	3
Fixed Assets	1	N/A	N/A
Current Assets	31	29	32

K S K Fabrications
Unit 8 Gorrell Street, Rochdale, OL11 1AP
Tel: 01706-718080 **Fax:** 01706-718081
Website: http://www.saltsep.co.uk
Directors: S. Grindrod (Co Sec), K. Dingley (Prop), K. Shackleton (Dir)
Immediate Holding Company: K S K FABRICATIONS LTD
Registration no: 06892008 **Date established:** 2009
No.of Employees: 1 - 10 **Product Groups:** 35

Date of Accounts	Apr 11	Apr 10
Working Capital	22	N/A
Fixed Assets	10	16
Current Assets	179	164

Kerf Developments Ltd
Unit 4d Buckley Road Industrial Estate, Rochdale, OL12 9EF
Tel: 01706-757670 **Fax:** 01706-372923
E-mail: info@kerfdevelopments.com
Website: http://www.kerfdevelopments.com

see next page

Kerf Developments Ltd - Cont'd

Managers: S. Townend (Chief Mgr)
Immediate Holding Company: KERF DEVELOPMENTS LIMITED
Registration no: 04492096 **Date established:** 2002
No.of Employees: 1 - 10 **Product Groups:** 42, 45, 46, 48

Date of Accounts	Jul 12	Jul 11	Jul 10
Working Capital	672	504	427
Fixed Assets	91	62	82
Current Assets	1m	773	654

Keytech Managed Services Ltd

Millgate House Market Street, Shawforth, Rochdale, OL12 8NX
Tel: 01706-897100 **Fax:** 01706-897101
E-mail: marketing@keytech.co.uk
Website: http://www.keytech.co.uk
Bank(s): National Westminster, Bolton
Directors: B. Paterson (Fin), S. Critchley (MD)
Immediate Holding Company: KEYTECH MANAGED SERVICES LTD
Registration no: 03540919 **VAT No.:** GB 444 8816 23
Date established: 1998 **Turnover:** £2m - £5m **No.of Employees:** 21 - 50
Product Groups: 44

Date of Accounts	Mar 11	Mar 10	Mar 09
Working Capital	52	48	99
Fixed Assets	238	228	263
Current Assets	500	359	527

L E W Diecastings Ltd

Trows Lane, Rochdale, OL11 2UF
Tel: 01706-632218 **Fax:** 01706-643714
E-mail: alan@lew.co.uk
Website: http://www.lew.co.uk
Directors: A. Scarfe (MD)
Immediate Holding Company: L.E.W. DIECASTINGS LIMITED
Registration no: 05240207 **Date established:** 2004
Turnover: £500,000 - £1m **No.of Employees:** 21 - 50 **Product Groups:** 34

Date of Accounts	Sep 11	Sep 10	Sep 09
Working Capital	155	215	-37
Fixed Assets	34	40	47
Current Assets	642	609	566

Laboratory Sales UK Ltd

Unit 20-21 Trans Pennine Trading Estate Gorrells Way, Rochdale, OL11 2PX
Tel: 01706-356444 **Fax:** 01706-860885
E-mail: sales@ls-uk.com
Website: http://www.ls-uk.com
Bank(s): National Westminster Bank Plc
Directors: J. Hill (Fin), D. Burrows (Sales)
Managers: M. Kerai, J. Camps, K. Hickey-fareed (Fin Mgr)
Ultimate Holding Company: E-VIALS EUROPE LIMITED
Immediate Holding Company: LABORATORY SALES (U.K.) LIMITED
Registration no: 01515665 **VAT No.:** GB 306 3440 91
Date established: 1980 **Turnover:** £5m - £10m
No.of Employees: 51 - 100 **Product Groups:** 30

Date of Accounts	Dec 11	Oct 10	Oct 09
Sales Turnover	9m	7m	7m
Pre Tax Profit/Loss	831	833	1m
Working Capital	4m	3m	3m
Fixed Assets	711	795	873
Current Assets	5m	4m	4m
Current Liabilities	373	402	487

Lancashire Security

6 Roefield Terrace, Rochdale, OL12 7BJ
Tel: 01706-342569
Directors: M. Holden (Ptnr)
No.of Employees: 1 - 10 **Product Groups:** 37, 38, 67

Lew Castings Group

Trows Lane Castleton, Rochdale, OL11 2UF
Tel: 01706-632218 **Fax:** 01706-643714
E-mail: alan@lew.co.uk
Website: http://www.lew.co.uk
Product Groups: 34, 66

Lion Springs Ltd

Summer Street, Rochdale, OL16 1SY
Tel: 01706-861352 **Fax:** 01706-657863
E-mail: sales@lionsprings.co.uk
Website: http://lionsprings.co.uk
Bank(s): Yorkshire Bank
Directors: P. Harrison (Dir), M. Harrison (Co Sec)
Immediate Holding Company: LION SPRINGS LIMITED
Registration no: 01842409 **VAT No.:** GB 408 8085 40
Date established: 1984 **Turnover:** £250,000 - £500,000
No.of Employees: 11 - 20 **Product Groups:** 35, 48

Date of Accounts	Sep 11	Sep 10	Sep 09
Working Capital	138	125	121
Fixed Assets	82	85	89
Current Assets	299	271	235

M H 4 Drains

38 Moss Avenue, Rochdale, OL16 4AA
Tel: 01706-868876
E-mail: mh4drains@btconnect.com
Website: http://www.mh4drains.co.uk
Directors: M. Holland (Dir)
Turnover: Up to £250,000 **No.of Employees:** 1 - 10 **Product Groups:** 29, 30, 33

M S Microwaves

367a Oldham Road, Rochdale, OL16 5LN
Tel: 01706-861121
Directors: S. Karim (Prop)
Immediate Holding Company: M S MICROWAVE SERVICES LIMITED
Registration no: 04723881 **Date established:** 2003
No.of Employees: 1 - 10 **Product Groups:** 36, 40

M Whitaker Spray Polishing

5 Daniel Street Whitworth, Rochdale, OL12 8BX
Tel: 01706-854500 **Fax:** 01706-854500
Directors: M. Whitaker (Prop)
Immediate Holding Company: M WHITAKER SPRAY POLISHING LTD
Registration no: 08000584 **Date established:** 2012
No.of Employees: 1 - 10 **Product Groups:** 46, 48

Makin Metal Powders UK Ltd

Buckley Road, Rochdale, OL12 9DT
Tel: 01706-717317 **Fax:** 01706-717303
E-mail: derek.oldham@makin-metals.com
Website: http://www.makin-metals.com
Bank(s): Barclays, Silver St, Bury
Directors: B. Hope (Fin)
Managers: H. Dawson (Personnel), D. Oldham (Buyer), J. Hood (Mktg Serv Mgr), S. Taylor (Tech Serv Mgr)
Ultimate Holding Company: UNITED STATES BRONZE POWDERS INC
Immediate Holding Company: MAKIN METAL POWDERS LIMITED
Registration no: 03227469 **VAT No.:** GB 148 0033 95
Date established: 1996 **Turnover:** £20m - £50m
No.of Employees: 21 - 50 **Product Groups:** 34

Date of Accounts	Aug 11	Aug 10
Sales Turnover	33m	21m
Pre Tax Profit/Loss	2m	1m
Working Capital	2m	-606
Fixed Assets	3m	3m
Current Assets	7m	6m
Current Liabilities	1m	2m

Marathon Belting Ltd

Healey Mill Whitworth Road, Rochdale, OL12 0TF
Tel: 01706-657052 **Fax:** 01706-525143
E-mail: sales@marathonbelting.co.uk
Website: http://www.marathonbelting.co.uk
Bank(s): National Westminster Bank Plc
Directors: G. Hanson (Fin), K. Beese (Sales)
Managers: M. Brecht (Buyer), M. Mitchell (Comm), P. Racliffe (Tech Serv Mgr), D. Payne (Sales Prom Mgr)
Ultimate Holding Company: HEIMBACH GMBH (GERMANY)
Immediate Holding Company: MARATHON BELTING LIMITED
Registration no: 01265916 **VAT No.:** GB 300 1905 22
Date established: 1976 **Turnover:** £5m - £10m **No.of Employees:** 21 - 50
Product Groups: 23, 35, 45, 66

Date of Accounts	Dec 11	Dec 10	Dec 09
Sales Turnover	5m	5m	5m
Pre Tax Profit/Loss	561	671	498
Working Capital	2m	2m	1m
Fixed Assets	414	405	472
Current Assets	2m	2m	2m
Current Liabilities	264	282	313

Matterson Cranes

45 Regent Street, Rochdale, OL12 0HQ
Tel: 01706-649321 **Fax:** 01706-657452
Website: http://www.pctgroup.co.uk
Managers: J. Colshaw (Mgr)
Immediate Holding Company: BITTLESTON LIMITED
Registration no: 04544583 **Date established:** 2002
No.of Employees: 1 - 10 **Product Groups:** 35, 39, 45

Mellor Coachcraft

Miall Street, Rochdale, OL11 1HY
Tel: 01706-860610 **Fax:** 01706-860402
E-mail: mellersales@woodall-nicholson.co.uk
Website: http://www.mellor-coachcraft.co.uk
Bank(s): Midland
Directors: N. Crowther (MD)
Managers: S. Jones (Purch Mgr), A. Prince (Sales & Mktg Mg)
Immediate Holding Company: CREATIVE NETWORKS LIMITED
Registration no: 05565620 **Date established:** 2005
No.of Employees: 51 - 100 **Product Groups:** 39, 45

Date of Accounts	Mar 11	Mar 10	Mar 09
Working Capital	1	-3	9
Fixed Assets	3	3	1
Current Assets	34	22	23

Metallia Waste Management Ltd

Unit 1h Moss Indl-Est Woodbine Street East, Rochdale, OL16 5LB
Tel: 01706-750172 **Fax:** 01706-750146
E-mail: info@metallia.co.uk
Website: http://www.metallia-waste.co.uk
Directors: Z. Anjum (Fin), A. Anjum (Fin)
Managers: N. Anjum (Mgr), N. Anjum (Purch Mgr)
Immediate Holding Company: METALLIA WASTE MANAGEMENT LIMITED
Registration no: 06785290 **Date established:** 2009
Turnover: £500,000 - £1m **No.of Employees:** 1 - 10 **Product Groups:** 61

Metrolift UK Ltd

Old Smithy Walker Street, Rochdale, OL16 2AB
Tel: 01706-644309 **Fax:** 01706-868223
E-mail: info@metroliftuk.co.uk
Managers: J. Wood (Sales Admin)
Immediate Holding Company: METROLIFT (UK) LTD.
Registration no: 00878251 **Date established:** 1966
Turnover: Up to £250,000 **No.of Employees:** 1 - 10 **Product Groups:** 35, 39, 45

Date of Accounts	Dec 11	Dec 10	Dec 09
Sales Turnover	88	115	82
Pre Tax Profit/Loss	29	47	26
Working Capital	6	13	-2
Fixed Assets	17	4	5
Current Assets	22	40	15
Current Liabilities	12	23	14

Micris

Green Grove Mill Dyehouse Lane, Rochdale, OL16 2QN
Tel: 01706-753500 **Fax:** 01706-753501
E-mail: sales@micris.co.uk
Website: http://www.micris.co.uk
Directors: M. Boyle (Tech Serv)
Managers: A. Clarke, S. Salmon (Chief Acct)
Immediate Holding Company: MICRIS LIMITED
Registration no: 03814387 **Date established:** 1999 **Turnover:** £1m - £2m
No.of Employees: 11 - 20 **Product Groups:** 39, 40, 45, 67

Date of Accounts	Dec 10	Dec 09	Dec 08
Working Capital	60	50	32
Fixed Assets	37	27	24
Current Assets	244	249	230

N H Fabrications

Unit 4 Firgrove Business Park Bellfield Mill Lane, Firgrove, Rochdale, OL16 2UJ
Tel: 01706-351228
E-mail: neil@nhfabrications.co.uk
Website: http://www.nhfabrications.co.uk
Directors: N. Hull (Prop), P. Burrell (Prop)
No.of Employees: 1 - 10 **Product Groups:** 35

Nationwide Fire Prevention Ltd

Dodgson Street, Rochdale, OL16 5SJ
Tel: 01706-358392 **Fax:** 01706- 353092
Directors: K. Bunter (Fin), D. Bunter (MD)
Immediate Holding Company: ATLANTIS CORPORATION LIMITED
Registration no: 04558021 **Date established:** 2009
Turnover: Up to £250,000 **No.of Employees:** 1 - 10 **Product Groups:** 38, 42

Date of Accounts	Jun 11	Jun 10
Sales Turnover	1m	107
Pre Tax Profit/Loss	22	8
Working Capital	72	6
Current Assets	332	125
Current Liabilities	210	87

Nema Ltd

Townhead Works Lomax Street, Rochdale, OL12 0HD
Tel: 01706-640442 **Fax:** 01706-640444
E-mail: jane@nema.ltd.uk
Website: http://www.nemaltd.co.uk
Directors: J. Richardson (Dir)
Managers: P. Greenwood
Immediate Holding Company: NEMA LIMITED
Registration no: 00576760 **VAT No.:** GB 652 6185 31
Date established: 1957 **Turnover:** £500,000 - £1m
No.of Employees: 21 - 50 **Product Groups:** 35

Date of Accounts	Jan 12	Jan 11	Jan 10
Working Capital	386	82	437
Fixed Assets	390	429	397
Current Assets	907	772	940

North West Refrigeration

7 Stonehill Drive, Rochdale, OL12 7JN
Tel: 01706-860279
Managers: A. Arain (Mgr)
No.of Employees: 1 - 10 **Product Groups:** 36, 40

Northern Joinery

Daniel Street Whitworth, Rochdale, OL12 8DA
Tel: 01706-852345 **Fax:** 01706-853114
E-mail: office@northernjoinery.co.uk
Website: http://www.northernjoinery.co.uk
Bank(s): Lloyds TSB Bank plc
Directors: P. Davenport (Co Sec), A. Broadbent (Dir)
Ultimate Holding Company: NORTHERN JOINERY (HOLDINGS) LIMITED
Immediate Holding Company: NORTHERN JOINERY LIMITED
Registration no: 02862733 **VAT No.:** GB 146 3861 55
Date established: 1993 **Turnover:** £2m - £5m **No.of Employees:** 21 - 50
Product Groups: 25, 48

Date of Accounts	Oct 11	Oct 10	Oct 09
Sales Turnover	N/A	2m	N/A
Pre Tax Profit/Loss	N/A	-20	N/A
Working Capital	549	479	428
Fixed Assets	977	1m	1m
Current Assets	1m	2m	1m
Current Liabilities	N/A	618	N/A

Northern Technical Services UK Ltd

2 Dell Side Way, Rochdale, OL12 6XX
Tel: 01706-665886 **Fax:** 08714-331643
E-mail: montypython44@hotmail.com
Website: http://www.ntsukltd.co.uk
Directors: D. Williams (Fin), S. Williams (MD)
Immediate Holding Company: NORTHERN TECHNICAL SERVICES (UK) LIMITED
Registration no: 03646637 **Date established:** 1998
No.of Employees: 1 - 10 **Product Groups:** 38, 42

Date of Accounts	Oct 11	Oct 10	Oct 09
Working Capital	30	18	15
Fixed Assets	3	4	1
Current Assets	60	48	37

Ormerod Ltd

Ormerod House Caldershaw Business Park, Rochdale, OL12 7LQ
Tel: 01706-646808 **Fax:** 01706-640694
E-mail: sales@ormerods.com
Website: http://www.ormerods.com
Bank(s): HSBC Bank plc
Directors: R. Ward (Dir)
Managers: P. Dawson (Est)
Ultimate Holding Company: ORMERODS HOLDINGS LIMITED
Immediate Holding Company: ORMERODS LIMITED
Registration no: 00153954 **VAT No.:** GB 146 6090 65
Date established: 2019 **Turnover:** £2m - £5m **No.of Employees:** 21 - 50
Product Groups: 28

Date of Accounts	Mar 11	Mar 10	Mar 09
Working Capital	2m	2m	2m
Fixed Assets	3m	3m	3m
Current Assets	3m	3m	3m

Penco Catering Systems

6 Rilldene Walk Norden, Rochdale, OL11 5WF
Tel: 01706-711744 **Fax:** 01706-711744
E-mail: sales@penco.co.uk
Website: http://www.CATERING-EQUIPMENT-SUPPLIES.COM
Directors: M. Pendlebury (Dir), I. Pendlebury (Fin)
Immediate Holding Company: PENCO CATERING SYSTEMS LIMITED
Registration no: 02104204 **Date established:** 1987 **Turnover:** £1m - £2m
No.of Employees: 1 - 10 **Product Groups:** 20, 40, 41

Date of Accounts	Mar 11	Mar 10	Mar 09
Working Capital	423	416	455
Fixed Assets	N/A	1	1
Current Assets	561	430	575

Penthouse Carpets Ltd

Buckley Carpet Mill Buckley Road, Rochdale, OL12 9DU
Tel: 01706-341231 **Fax:** 01706-860577
E-mail: alex.dyson@penthousecarpets.co.uk
Website: http://www.penthousecarpets.co.uk
Directors: P. Speakman (Sales), S. Yu (Fin), A. Dyson (MD)
Managers: J. Buck (Personnel), N. Rozie (Purch Mgr)
Ultimate Holding Company: PENTHOUSE CARPETS HOLDINGS LIMITED
Immediate Holding Company: PENTHOUSE CARPETS LIMITED
Registration no: 01059087 **VAT No.:** 652 6063 45 **Date established:** 1972
Turnover: £10m - £20m **No.of Employees:** 51 - 100 **Product Groups:** 63

Date of Accounts	Jun 11	Jun 10	Jun 09
Sales Turnover	13m	13m	15m
Pre Tax Profit/Loss	261	265	415
Working Capital	3m	3m	3m
Fixed Assets	3m	3m	3m
Current Assets	5m	5m	5m
Current Liabilities	643	620	696

Peter Stott & Company

3 Moor View Close, Rochdale, OL12 7SY
Tel: 01706-648526 **Fax:** 01706-648526
E-mail: peter.stott@peter-stott.co.uk
Website: http://www.peter-stott.co.uk
Directors: P. Stott (Prop)
Immediate Holding Company: PETER STOTT LIMITED
Registration no: 04710961 **Date established:** 2003
No.of Employees: 1 - 10 **Product Groups:** 20, 40, 41

Date of Accounts	Mar 11	Mar 10	Mar 09
Working Capital	2	-1	-4
Fixed Assets	2	3	4
Current Assets	50	64	50

Polux Ltd

Elliott Street, Rochdale, OL12 0LH
Tel: 01706-358466 **Fax:** 01706-642841
E-mail: info@polux.co.uk
Website: http://www.polux.co.uk
Bank(s): Barclays, Yorkshire Street
Directors: F. Paolucci (MD), A. Paolucci (Dir)
Managers: E. O'Keeffe, T. Mungroo ()
Registration no: 00867381 **VAT No.:** GB 146 2649 58
Date established: 1968 **Turnover:** £1m - £2m **No.of Employees:** 11 - 20
Product Groups: 23, 35, 37, 38

Date of Accounts	Dec 11	Dec 10	Dec 09
Working Capital	329	302	267
Fixed Assets	141	147	151
Current Assets	577	505	460

Pressed Parts Co. Ltd

Unit C3 Fieldhouse Industrial Estate Fieldhouse Road, Rochdale, OL12 0AA
Tel: 01706-359414 **Fax:** 01706-654817
E-mail: pressedparts@zen.co.uk
Website: http://www.pressedparts.co.uk
Directors: R. Barlow (MD)
Immediate Holding Company: PRESSED PARTS COMPANY LIMITED
Registration no: 01581988 **VAT No.:** 306 3996 44 **Date established:** 1981
Turnover: £1m - £2m **No.of Employees:** 1 - 10 **Product Groups:** 37, 66

Date of Accounts	Mar 12	Mar 11	Mar 10
Working Capital	428	426	403
Fixed Assets	56	56	63
Current Assets	567	653	580
Current Liabilities	N/A	202	N/A

R G S Engineering

Unit 1 Buckley Road Industrial Estate, Rochdale, OL12 9EF
Tel: 0161-763 4000 **Fax:** 0161-763 4000
E-mail: info@rgses.co.uk
Website: http://www.rgses.co.uk
Directors: J. Haynes (Dir)
Immediate Holding Company: RGS ENGINEERING SOLUTIONS LIMITED
Registration no: 06947448 **Date established:** 2009
No.of Employees: 1 - 10 **Product Groups:** 29, 30, 31, 38, 42, 43, 48

Date of Accounts	Dec 11	Dec 10	Jun 10
Working Capital	-35	-42	-86
Fixed Assets	97	110	107
Current Assets	154	174	83

Renold Gears

Station Road Milnrow, Rochdale, OL16 3LS
Tel: 01706-751000 **Fax:** 01706-751001
E-mail: sales@gears.renold.com
Website: http://www.renold.com
Bank(s): Lloyds TSB Bank plc
Directors: H. Byrne (Pers), R. Godson (Sales), A. Brown (Tech Serv), R. Core (Fin)
Managers: N. Cook (Buyer), T. Simon (Mktg Serv Mgr), R. Core, C. Newton (I.T. Exec)
Immediate Holding Company: RENOLD P.L.C.
Registration no: 00182382 **Date established:** 1896
Turnover: £10m - £20m **No.of Employees:** 101 - 250
Product Groups: 35, 38, 39, 40, 43

Rentruck Car & Truck Hire Ltd (J.R. Ashworth & Sons Ltd)

Blueberry Business Park Wallhead Road, Rochdale, OL16 5AF
Tel: 01706-640055 **Fax:** 01706-640067
E-mail: info@rentruck.co.uk
Website: http://www.rentruck.co.uk
Directors: R. Cotton (Dir)
Ultimate Holding Company: J.R. ASHWORTH & SONS LIMITED
Immediate Holding Company: RENTRUCK (ROCHDALE) LIMITED
Registration no: 00740150 **Date established:** 1962
No.of Employees: 1 - 10 **Product Groups:** 72

Rochdale Power Tool Services

Unit 1 Primrose Street Off Spotland Road, Rochdale, OL12 6AW
Tel: 01706-642466 **Fax:** 01706-860022
E-mail: m_lonsdale@sky.com
Directors: J. Lonsdale (Prop)
Date established: 1991 **No.of Employees:** 1 - 10 **Product Groups:** 37

Rochdale Re-Tool Ltd

Unit 5e Princess Street, Rochdale, OL12 0HA
Tel: 01706-711430 **Fax:** 01706-860807
Directors: J. Haigherty (MD)
Immediate Holding Company: ROCHDALE RE-TOOL LIMITED
Registration no: 05116531 **Date established:** 2004
No.of Employees: 1 - 10 **Product Groups:** 37

Date of Accounts	Jun 11	Jun 10	Jun 09
Working Capital	36	57	28
Fixed Assets	25	20	23
Current Assets	120	123	119

Rochdale Springs Company Ltd

Unit 14 Hollows Works Shawclough Road, Rochdale, OL12 6LN
Tel: 01706-648550 **Fax:** 01706-648850
E-mail: sales@rochdalesprings.co.uk
Website: http://www.rochdalesprings.co.uk
Directors: A. Horner (Fin)
Managers: J. Kirkbride (Mgr)
Ultimate Holding Company: IMPRESSIVESTYLE LIMITED
Immediate Holding Company: ROCHDALE SPRING COMPANY HOLDINGS LIMITED
Registration no: 03792748 **Date established:** 1999
No.of Employees: 1 - 10 **Product Groups:** 34, 35, 36, 38, 39, 40, 43, 48, 66, 68, 85

Date of Accounts	Aug 12	Aug 11	Aug 10
Working Capital	366	330	267
Fixed Assets	48	48	42
Current Assets	407	406	296

Salt Separation Services Ltd

Grosvenor House Gorrell Street, Rochdale, OL11 1AP
Tel: 01706-655522 **Fax:** 01706-654475
E-mail: sales@saltsep.co.uk
Website: http://www.saltsep.co.uk
Directors: S. Grindrod (Dir)
Immediate Holding Company: SALT SEPARATION SERVICES LIMITED
Registration no: 02457981 **Date established:** 1990 **Turnover:** £1m - £2m
No.of Employees: 21 - 50 **Product Groups:** 42

Date of Accounts	Apr 11	Apr 10	Apr 09
Working Capital	917	748	419
Fixed Assets	93	76	85
Current Assets	3m	2m	1m

Arnold Sharrocks Ltd

229 Spotland Road, Rochdale, OL12 7AQ
Tel: 01706-655411 **Fax:** 01706-642452
E-mail: arnold-sharrocks@2binternet.co.uk
Website: http://www.sharrocks.co.uk
Directors: G. Greenhalgh (Dir), D. Greenhalgh (Ch)
Managers: D. Madely (Sales Admin)
Immediate Holding Company: ARNOLD SHARROCKS LIMITED
Registration no: 02489606 **VAT No.:** GB 306 3657 66
Date established: 1990 **Turnover:** Up to £250,000
No.of Employees: 1 - 10 **Product Groups:** 52

Date of Accounts	Apr 11	Apr 10	Apr 09
Sales Turnover	N/A	N/A	138
Pre Tax Profit/Loss	N/A	N/A	48
Working Capital	1m	988	880
Fixed Assets	894	1m	1m
Current Assets	1m	1m	895
Current Liabilities	N/A	N/A	15

Showtech Sound & Light

Unit 1k Moss Industrial Estate Woodbine Street East, Rochdale, OL16 5LB
Tel: 01706-347159 **Fax:** 01706-347912
E-mail: info@showtechuk.com
Website: http://www.showtechuk.com
Directors: S. Sutcliffe (MD)
Date established: 2007 **Turnover:** £250,000 - £500,000
No.of Employees: 1 - 10 **Product Groups:** 37, 67, 83

Sidewinder Crains

Shawclough Road, Rochdale, OL12 7HR
Tel: 01706-343873 **Fax:** 01706-343873
Directors: P. Howarth (Prop)
Immediate Holding Company: OPEN SYSTEMS PEOPLE LIMITED
Registration no: 02251578 **Date established:** 1988
No.of Employees: 1 - 10 **Product Groups:** 35, 39, 45

Date of Accounts	Mar 11	Mar 10	Mar 09
Working Capital	-3	-3	-9
Fixed Assets	3	4	6
Current Assets	34	20	8

Simtek UK

1-2 Daniel Street Whitworth, Rochdale, OL12 8BX
Tel: 01706-854857 **Fax:** 01706-521926
E-mail: sales@simtekuk.co.uk
Website: http://www.simtekuk.co.uk
Directors: G. Simkins (Dir)
Immediate Holding Company: SIMTEK (UK) LTD.
Registration no: 05668459 **Date established:** 2006
No.of Employees: 1 - 10 **Product Groups:** 35

Date of Accounts	Jan 12	Jan 11	Jan 10
Working Capital	-10	-8	-2
Fixed Assets	11	8	8
Current Assets	87	61	15
Current Liabilities	N/A	N/A	7

Sun Chemicals Ltd

Ellen Road Site Elizabethan Way, Newhey, Rochdale, OL16 4LE
Tel: 01706-889600 **Fax:** 01706-889700
E-mail: michael.whitaker@sunchemical.com
Website: http://www.sunchemical.com
Managers: M. Bridesdale (Buyer), A. Chung (Chief Acct), L. Guilfoyle (Personnel), M. Whitaker (Site Co-ord)
Immediate Holding Company: SUN CHEMICAL LIMITED
Registration no: 02647054 **Date established:** 1991
No.of Employees: 101 - 250 **Product Groups:** 32

T B A Electro Conductive Products

Unit 3 Trans Pennine Trading Estate Gorrells Way, Rochdale, OL11 2PX
Tel: 01706-647718 **Fax:** 01706-646170
E-mail: davidhurst@tbaecp.co.uk
Website: http://www.tbaecp.co.uk
Managers: D. Hurst (Comm)
Immediate Holding Company: TBA ELECTRO CONDUCTIVE PRODUCTS LIMITED
Registration no: 05882227 **Date established:** 2006
Turnover: £10m - £20m **No.of Employees:** 1 - 10 **Product Groups:** 26, 29, 30, 32, 35, 37, 38, 48

Date of Accounts	Dec 11	Dec 10	Dec 09
Working Capital	-20	-32	-11
Fixed Assets	30	36	3
Current Assets	295	281	229

T B A Textiles

Unit 3 Trans Pennine Trading Estate Gorrells Way, Rochdale, OL11 2PX
Tel: 01706-647422 **Fax:** 01706-354295
E-mail: info@tbatextiles.co.uk
Website: http://www.tbatextiles.co.uk
Bank(s): Bank of Scotland
Directors: B. Smith (MD), C. Smith (Fin)
Managers: D. Mawson (Tech Serv Mgr), P. Ingham (Works Gen Mgr), B. Lowe (Purch Mgr)
Ultimate Holding Company: FEROTEC LIMITED
Immediate Holding Company: TBA TEXTILES LIMITED
Registration no: 03425139 **Date established:** 1997 **Turnover:** £5m - £10m
No.of Employees: 51 - 100 **Product Groups:** 23, 24, 40, 63, 66

Date of Accounts	Dec 11	Dec 10	Dec 09
Sales Turnover	9m	8m	7m
Pre Tax Profit/Loss	247	215	-150
Working Capital	919	870	691
Fixed Assets	296	136	158
Current Assets	4m	4m	3m
Current Liabilities	912	1m	890

Telford Rubber (Granulated Rubber)

PO Box 21, Rochdale, OL12 7EU
Tel: 01706-527793 **Fax:** 01706-527808
E-mail: enquiries@telfordrubber.co.uk
Website: http://www.telfordrubber.co.uk
Managers: T. Alban (Mgr)
Ultimate Holding Company: FLEXITALLIC GROUP
Immediate Holding Company: FLEXITALLIC LTD
Registration no: 03308289 **Date established:** 1938
Turnover: £500,000 - £1m **No.of Employees:** 1 - 10 **Product Groups:** 29, 32, 66

Temperature Electronics Ltd

388-400 Manchester Road, Rochdale, OL11 4NW
Tel: 01706-633438 **Fax:** 01706-524609
E-mail: tempelec@btinternet.com
Website: http://www.tel-uk.com
Bank(s): Royal Bank of Scotland
Directors: J. Eady (MD), R. Eady (Fin)
Managers: A. Boyd (Prod Mgr), S. Carburtt (Chief Mgr), S. Justyn (Buyer), Chadwick (Sales Admin)
Immediate Holding Company: TEMPERATURE ELECTRONICS LIMITED
Registration no: 00968772 **VAT No.:** GB 146 2611 83
Date established: 1969 **Turnover:** £1m - £2m **No.of Employees:** 11 - 20
Product Groups: 37, 38, 40, 54

Date of Accounts	Apr 10	Apr 09	Apr 08
Working Capital	876	635	367
Fixed Assets	99	97	84
Current Assets	1m	1m	1m

Tenon plc

Cedar House Sandbrook Way, Rochdale, OL11 1LQ
Tel: 01706-355505 **Fax:** 01706-659486
E-mail: rochdale@rsmtenon.com
Website: http://www.tenongroup.com
Directors: P. Donnelley (Dir)
Immediate Holding Company: BENTLEY JENNISON LIMITED
Registration no: 02894171 **Date established:** 1994 **Turnover:** £2m - £5m
No.of Employees: 51 - 100 **Product Groups:** 44, 80, 81, 82, 86

Testometric Co. Ltd

1 Lincoln Business Park Lincoln Close, Rochdale, OL11 1NR
Tel: 01706-654039 **Fax:** 01706-646089
E-mail: info@testometric.co.uk
Website: http://www.testometric.co.uk
Bank(s): National Westminster Bank Plc
Directors: K. Harwood (MD)
Managers: A. Harwood (Sales Admin), J. Thompson (Tech Serv Mgr)
Immediate Holding Company: TESTOMETRIC COMPANY LIMITED(THE)
Registration no: 01112862 **Date established:** 1973 **Turnover:** £2m - £5m
No.of Employees: 21 - 50 **Product Groups:** 38, 44, 64, 84

Date of Accounts	Jul 11	Jul 10	Jul 09
Working Capital	69	90	93
Fixed Assets	73	75	72
Current Assets	1m	883	638

Texchem

Holmes Mill Holmes Street, Rochdale, OL12 6AQ
Tel: 01706-711990 **Fax:** 01706-710985
E-mail: info@texchem.co.uk
Website: http://www.texchem.co.uk
Directors: M. Bower (MD)
Immediate Holding Company: TEXCHEM UK HOLDINGS LIMITED
Registration no: 05546529 **Date established:** 2005 **Turnover:** £2m - £5m
No.of Employees: 1 - 10 **Product Groups:** 66, 67

Date of Accounts	May 12	May 11	May 10
Fixed Assets	10	10	10

Thermal Memory

6 Dodd Croft, Rochdale, OL16 4QX
Tel: 01706-522611
E-mail: jaroslaw@shrinkfit.co.uk
Website: http://www.shrinkfit.co.uk
Directors: J. Pidburskyj (Dir), A. Pidburskyj (Fin)
Immediate Holding Company: THERMAL MEMORY LIMITED
Registration no: 06153820 **Date established:** 2007
Turnover: Up to £250,000 **No.of Employees:** 1 - 10 **Product Groups:** 61

Date of Accounts	Apr 11	Apr 10	Apr 09
Working Capital	21	19	24
Fixed Assets	1	1	1
Current Assets	36	44	48

Thiel Technics Limited

Tonacliffe Road Whitworth, Rochdale, OL12 8SS
Tel: 01706-868822 **Fax:** 01706-343402
E-mail: sales@thiel-technics.co.uk
Website: http://www.thiel-technics.co.uk
Directors: P. Hewitt (MD)
Immediate Holding Company: Thiel Technics Ltd
Registration no: 03504082 **VAT No.:** GB 606 7192 40
Date established: 1998 **Turnover:** £250,000 - £500,000
No.of Employees: 1 - 10 **Product Groups:** 26, 36, 45

Date of Accounts	Mar 10	Mar 09	Mar 08
Working Capital	135	154	149
Fixed Assets	N/A	1	1
Current Assets	175	202	179

Thorite Group Ltd

Unit 11 The Landings Oldham Road, Rochdale, OL16 5QY
Tel: 01706-860919 **Fax:** 01706-861731
E-mail: rochdale@thorite.co.uk
Website: http://www.thorite.co.uk
Managers: B. Day (District Mgr)
Ultimate Holding Company: THOMAS WRIGHT/THORITE GROUP LTD
No.of Employees: 1 - 10 **Product Groups:** 35, 36, 38, 40

Triad Fabrications
Globe Works Queensway, Rochdale, OL11 2QY
Tel: 01706-655099 **Fax:** 01706-658712
E-mail: enquiries@triadfabs.com
Website: http://www.triadfabs.co.uk
Bank(s): Barclays
Directors: J. Leech (Dir)
Immediate Holding Company: TRIAD FABRICATIONS LIMITED
Registration no: 05112537 **VAT No.:** GB 305 4557 71
Date established: 2004 **Turnover:** £250,000 - £500,000
No.of Employees: 11 - 20 **Product Groups:** 35, 36, 46, 48

Date of Accounts	Jun 11	Jun 10	Jun 09
Sales Turnover	N/A	474	857
Pre Tax Profit/Loss	N/A	2	51
Working Capital	-17	-24	6
Fixed Assets	60	67	70
Current Assets	106	73	130
Current Liabilities	N/A	15	79

Twin Automating Ltd
River House North Street, Whitworth, Rochdale, OL12 8RE
Tel: 01706-852108 **Fax:** 01706-852591
E-mail: adrianpennin@btconnect.com
Website: http://www.twin-automating.co.uk
Directors: A. Pennington (MD)
Immediate Holding Company: TWIN AUTOMATING LIMITED
Registration no: 03864856 **Date established:** 1999
Turnover: Up to £250,000 **No.of Employees:** 21 - 50 **Product Groups:** 46

Date of Accounts	Oct 11	Oct 10	Oct 09
Sales Turnover	247	283	227
Pre Tax Profit/Loss	-25	18	3
Working Capital	-37	-12	-31
Fixed Assets	1	1	1
Current Assets	85	84	46
Current Liabilities	60	37	33

United Springs Ltd
Mandale Park Norman Road, Rochdale, OL11 4HP
Tel: 01706-644551 **Fax:** 01706-630516
E-mail: sales@united-springs.co.uk
Website: http://www.united-springs.co.uk
Bank(s): Barclays
Directors: A. Marastoni (Fin), D. Shaw (Co Sec)
Managers: A. May, S. Ratcliffe (Personnel), J. Law (Fin Mgr)
Ultimate Holding Company: CIR SPA (ITALY)
Immediate Holding Company: UNITED SPRINGS LIMITED
Registration no: 04080381 **VAT No.:** GB 764 5171 20
Date established: 2000 **Turnover:** £2m - £5m **No.of Employees:** 51 - 100
Product Groups: 34, 35, 38, 39, 48, 66

Date of Accounts	Dec 11	Dec 10	Dec 09
Sales Turnover	4m	4m	4m
Pre Tax Profit/Loss	151	75	-326
Working Capital	2m	2m	2m
Fixed Assets	5m	5m	5m
Current Assets	3m	3m	2m
Current Liabilities	214	218	180

Vindon Scientific Ltd
Unit E2a1 John Boyd Dunlop Drive, Rochdale, OL16 4NG
Tel: 01706-716710 **Fax:** 01706-716740
E-mail: info@vindon.co.uk
Website: http://www.vindon.co.uk
Bank(s): National Westminster Bank Plc
Directors: J. Scopes (Fin), P. Jackson (MD)
Managers: M. Whatmough (Tech Serv Mgr), A. Cuff (Buyer)
Ultimate Holding Company: VINDON HEALTHCARE PLC
Immediate Holding Company: VINDON SCIENTIFIC LIMITED
Registration no: 00878160 **Date established:** 1966 **Turnover:** £5m - £10m
No.of Employees: 21 - 50 **Product Groups:** 38, 88

Date of Accounts	Dec 11	Dec 10	Dec 09
Sales Turnover	6m	5m	5m
Pre Tax Profit/Loss	1m	927	772
Working Capital	2m	1m	288
Fixed Assets	5m	5m	5m
Current Assets	4m	3m	3m
Current Liabilities	777	508	611

Wireless CCTV
Mitchell Hey Place College Road, Rochdale, OL12 6AE
Tel: 01706-631166 **Fax:** 01706-631122
E-mail: sales@wcctv.com
Website: http://www.wcctv.com
Directors: T. Williams (Dir), H. Williams (Co Sec)
Ultimate Holding Company: WIRELESS HOLDINGS LIMITED
Immediate Holding Company: WIRELESS CCTV LIMITED
Registration no: 04192399 **Date established:** 2001 **Turnover:** £2m - £5m
No.of Employees: 21 - 50 **Product Groups:** 37, 40, 67

Date of Accounts	Jul 11	Jul 10	Jul 09
Working Capital	195	540	467
Fixed Assets	572	520	572
Current Assets	1m	2m	2m

Mark Wynn Fabrications
Unit 14 Two Bridges Industrial Park Newhey, Rochdale, OL16 3SR
Tel: 01706-843757 **Fax:** 01706-843757
E-mail: mark.wynne@talk21.com
Directors: M. Wynne (Prop)
Immediate Holding Company: F. & A. DUNBAR LIMITED
Registration no: 00432839 **Date established:** 1947
No.of Employees: 1 - 10 **Product Groups:** 26, 35

Date of Accounts	Mar 11	Mar 10	Mar 09
Working Capital	110	155	240
Fixed Assets	107	111	113
Current Assets	172	216	274

Martin Yaffe International
Arrow Mill Queensway, Rochdale, OL11 2QN
Tel: 01706-717800 **Fax:** 01706-717801
E-mail: info@martinyaffe.com
Website: http://www.martinyaffe.com
Bank(s): Midland
Directors: A. Balkin (Dir), R. Yaffe (MD), R. Yaffie (Prop), J. Whitehead (Co Sec)
Immediate Holding Company: MARTIN YAFFE SHANGHAI LIMITED
Registration no: 05414736 **VAT No.:** GB 451 554 62
Date established: 2005 **Turnover:** £20m - £50m
No.of Employees: 101 - 250 **Product Groups:** 49

Rossendale

Acre Packaging Supplies Ltd
102 Laneside Road Haslingden, Rossendale, BB4 6PG
Tel: 01706-213197 **Fax:** 01706-213197
Website: http://www.acrepackaging.co.uk
Directors: J. Spencer (I.T. Dir)
Managers: D. Mann
Immediate Holding Company: ACRE PACKAGING SUPPLIES LIMITED
Registration no: 01749004 **Date established:** 1983
No.of Employees: 1 - 10 **Product Groups:** 38, 42

Date of Accounts	Jan 12	Jan 11	Jan 10
Working Capital	19	14	17
Fixed Assets	16	21	14
Current Assets	131	121	105

Andrew Webron Ltd
Hareholme Mill Bacup Road Rawtenstall, Rossendale, BB4 7JL
Tel: 01706-214001 **Fax:** 01706-830003
E-mail: sales@andrewwebron.com
Website: http://www.andrewwebron.com
Bank(s): Barclays
Directors: I. Cropper (Fin)
Managers: M. Briggs (Personnel)
Ultimate Holding Company: ANDREW INDUSTRIES LIMITED
Immediate Holding Company: ANDREW WEBRON LIMITED
Registration no: 03685494 **VAT No.:** GB 725 7924 09
Date established: 1998 **No.of Employees:** 21 - 50 **Product Groups:** 23, 42

Date of Accounts	Mar 11	Mar 10	Mar 09
Sales Turnover	15m	14m	N/A
Pre Tax Profit/Loss	983	83	69
Working Capital	2m	3m	4m
Fixed Assets	2m	2m	2m
Current Assets	6m	5m	6m
Current Liabilities	494	283	288

Apple Transcription Ltd
Suite 204 Kingfisher Centre Burnley Road, Rawtenstall, Rossendale, BB4 8ES
Tel: 08456-045642 **Fax:** 01706-870838
E-mail: info@appletranscription.co.uk
Website: http://www.appletranscription.co.uk
Directors: D. Mitchell (Dir)
Immediate Holding Company: APPLE TRANSCRIPTION LIMITED
Registration no: 05761195 **Date established:** 2006
No.of Employees: 11 - 20 **Product Groups:** 80

Date of Accounts	Mar 11	Mar 10	Mar 09
Working Capital	29	13	-3
Fixed Assets	7	10	4
Current Assets	79	40	15

Autocross Plastics
Unit 3-4 New Hall Hey Business Park New Hall Hey Road, Rossendale, BB4 6HL
Tel: 01706-216794 **Fax:** 01706-230758
E-mail: bill.cross@euroshel.com
Website: http://www.euroshel.co.uk
Directors: B. Cross (Prop)
VAT No.: GB 146 1229 85 **Turnover:** Up to £250,000
No.of Employees: 1 - 10 **Product Groups:** 33, 39

Brooklands Metalcraft
Hargreaves Mill Chapel Street, Haslingden, Rossendale, BB4 5QR
Tel: 01706-225740 **Fax:** 01706-225740
Website: http://www.brooklandsmetalcraft.co.cc
Directors: S. White (MD), S. White (Fin)
Immediate Holding Company: BROOKLANDS METALCRAFT LIMITED
Registration no: 04105159 **Date established:** 2000
No.of Employees: 1 - 10 **Product Groups:** 20, 40, 41

Date of Accounts	Nov 11	Nov 10	Nov 09
Working Capital	26	25	41
Fixed Assets	10	14	17
Current Assets	29	29	68

Cheshire Style Ltd
Unit 3 Myrtle Grove Mill Lench Road, Rossendale, BB4 7JJ
Tel: 01706-229909 **Fax:** 01706-221144
Directors: K. Mcgall (MD)
Immediate Holding Company: CHESHIRE STYLE LIMITED
Registration no: 01908026 **Date established:** 1985
No.of Employees: 1 - 10 **Product Groups:** 63

Date of Accounts	May 12	May 11	May 10
Working Capital	31	57	53
Fixed Assets	1	1	1
Current Assets	275	376	389

Domus Furnishings
17-19 Bacup Road, Rossendale, BB4 7NG
Tel: 01706-212298 **Fax:** 01706-220674
E-mail: sales@domusfurnishings.com
Website: http://www.domusfurnishings.com
Directors: C. Nuttall (Prop)
Date established: 1980 **No.of Employees:** 1 - 10 **Product Groups:** 26

Ducting Supplies Lancs
Unit 5 Waterside Road, Haslingden, Rossendale, BB4 5EN
Tel: 01706-227747 **Fax:** 01706-222838
Directors: S. Yates (Prop)
Ultimate Holding Company: AB FUTURITAS KARISKRONA (SWEDEN)
Immediate Holding Company: LODGE SHEET METAL FABRICATIONS LIMITED
Registration no: 02202034 **Date established:** 1987
No.of Employees: 1 - 10 **Product Groups:** 37, 40, 48

Eborall Fork Trucks
Gordon Works Piercy Road, Waterfoot, Rossendale, BB4 9JW
Tel: 01706-213995 **Fax:** 01706-230477
E-mail: sales@eborall.co.uk
Website: http://www.eborall.co.uk
Managers: H. Eborall (Mgr)
Date established: 1988 **No.of Employees:** 1 - 10 **Product Groups:** 35, 39, 45

Envair Ltd
York Avenue Haslingden, Rossendale, BB4 4HX
Tel: 01706-228416 **Fax:** 01706-242205
E-mail: info@envair.co.uk
Website: http://www.envair.co.uk
Bank(s): Lloyds TSB Bank plc
Directors: G. Bagshaw (MD)
Managers: S. Baraird (Fin Mgr), M. Bamber (Mktg Serv Mgr)
Ultimate Holding Company: BASSAIRE HOLDINGS LIMITED
Immediate Holding Company: ENVAIR LIMITED
Registration no: 05892537 **VAT No.:** GB 145 7477 42
Date established: 2006 **Turnover:** £5m - £10m **No.of Employees:** 21 - 50
Product Groups: 38, 40, 52, 84

Date of Accounts	May 12	May 11	May 10
Working Capital	798	645	488
Fixed Assets	74	121	106
Current Assets	2m	1m	2m

John Fenwick Rossendale Ltd
Vine Grove Works Commerce Street, Haslingden, Rossendale, BB4 5JT
Tel: 01706-210300 **Fax:** 01706-210325
E-mail: dwrudd@lineone.net
Directors: J. Shorrock (Fin)
Immediate Holding Company: JOHN FENWICK (ROSSENDALE) LTD.
Registration no: 02480803 **Date established:** 1990
No.of Employees: 1 - 10 **Product Groups:** 29

Date of Accounts	Mar 12	Mar 11	Mar 10
Working Capital	312	309	316
Fixed Assets	41	44	20
Current Assets	377	387	379
Current Liabilities	20	N/A	N/A

Flexipol Packaging Ltd
14 Bentwood Road Haslingden, Rossendale, BB4 5HH
Tel: 01706-222792 **Fax:** 01706-224683
E-mail: info@flexipol.co.uk
Website: http://www.flexipol.co.uk
Bank(s): Co-op, Manchester
Directors: D. Griffiths (Fin), P. Connelly (Sales & Mktg)
Managers: D. Crozier (Tech Serv Mgr), I. Sim, J. Hindle
Immediate Holding Company: FLEXIPOL PACKAGING LIMITED
Registration no: 02963868 **VAT No.:** GB 634 0007 87
Date established: 1994 **Turnover:** £10m - £20m
No.of Employees: 51 - 100 **Product Groups:** 30

Date of Accounts	Oct 08	Oct 09	Oct 10
Sales Turnover	11m	10m	13m
Pre Tax Profit/Loss	615	349	817
Working Capital	2m	2m	2m
Fixed Assets	2m	3m	3m
Current Assets	4m	4m	6m
Current Liabilities	933	626	1m

Gemini Dispersions Ltd
Holt Mill Road, Rossendale, BB4 7JB
Tel: 01706-214751 **Fax:** 01706-218152
E-mail: p.gabriel@geminidispersions.com
Website: http://www.geminidispersions.com
Bank(s): National Westminster Bank Plc
Directors: P. Gabriel (Dir), S. Cummins (Fin), S. Grennan (Fin)
Immediate Holding Company: GEMINI DISPERSIONS LIMITED
Registration no: 05452955 **VAT No.:** GB 634 1451 63
Date established: 2005 **Turnover:** £5m - £10m **No.of Employees:** 21 - 50
Product Groups: 32

Date of Accounts	Mar 11	Mar 10	Mar 09
Working Capital	794	557	506
Fixed Assets	317	295	130
Current Assets	3m	2m	2m

Harrison Saw & Tool Ltd
Underbank Way Haslingden, Rossendale, BB4 5HR
Tel: 01706-225221 **Fax:** 01706-831409
E-mail: sales@harrisonsaw.co.uk
Website: http://www.harrisonsaw.co.uk
Bank(s): HSBC Bank plc
Directors: A. Cookson (MD), J. Cookston (Sales)
Managers: L. Booth (Chief Acct)
Immediate Holding Company: HARRISON SAW AND TOOL LIMITED
Registration no: 01914115 **Date established:** 1985 **Turnover:** £5m - £10m
No.of Employees: 21 - 50 **Product Groups:** 36, 37, 48

Date of Accounts	Mar 11	Mar 10	Mar 09
Working Capital	314	35	121
Fixed Assets	321	332	392
Current Assets	3m	3m	3m

J B Broadley
Reeds Holme Works Burnley Road, Rawtenstall, Rossendale, BB4 8LN
Tel: 01706-213661 **Fax:** 01706-227786
E-mail: sales@jbbroadley.co.uk
Website: http://www.jbbroadley.co.uk
Bank(s): HSBC Bank plc
Directors: D. Boyden (MD), K. Mitchelle (Pers), S. Robertshaw (Sales), G. Rowanwild (I.T. Dir), J. Smith (MD)
Managers: G. Rowan-wilde (Buyer), M. Hayman (Chief Acct)
Immediate Holding Company: Allied Textile Companies P.L.C.
Registration no: 00081338 **Turnover:** £10m - £20m
No.of Employees: 101 - 250 **Product Groups:** 23, 48, 63

D Jacobson & Sons Ltd
Bacup Road, Rossendale, BB4 7PA
Tel: 01706-219444 **Fax:** 01706-214324
E-mail: admin@jacobsongroup.co.uk
Website: http://www.jacobsongroup.co.uk
Directors: D. Green (Fin), R. Sisson (Purch), T. Couchman (Sales)
Managers: D. Hill, A. Patel, G. Pedder (Personnel)
Ultimate Holding Company: JACOBSON GROUP LIMITED
Immediate Holding Company: D. JACOBSON & SONS LIMITED
Registration no: 01647853 **Date established:** 1982
Turnover: £20m - £50m **No.of Employees:** 101 - 250 **Product Groups:** 63

Date of Accounts	Sep 11	Sep 10	Sep 09
Sales Turnover	53m	47m	45m
Pre Tax Profit/Loss	4m	2m	924
Working Capital	18m	21m	20m
Fixed Assets	6m	6m	6m
Current Assets	39m	34m	29m
Current Liabilities	9m	4m	4m

K Steels Ltd
Jubilee Works Holme Lane, Rossendale, BB4 6JB
Tel: 01706-217722 **Fax:** 01254-704173
E-mail: sales@ksteels.co.uk
Website: http://www.ksteels.co.uk

Bank(s): HSBC Bank plc
Directors: A. Nuttall (Co Sec)
Managers: R. Harris
Ultimate Holding Company: K STEELS HOLDINGS LIMITED
Immediate Holding Company: K STEELS LIMITED
Registration no: 02284684 **VAT No.:** GB 525 4259 49
Date established: 1988 **Turnover:** £5m - £10m **No.of Employees:** 21 - 50
Product Groups: 34

Date of Accounts	Sep 11	Sep 10	Sep 09
Sales Turnover	9m	8m	8m
Pre Tax Profit/Loss	119	3	-573
Working Capital	2m	2m	2m
Fixed Assets	170	225	278
Current Assets	5m	4m	3m
Current Liabilities	459	585	563

K Supplies
Hill End Lane, Rossendale, BB4 7PP
Tel: 01706-217441 **Fax:** 01706-831772
E-mail: sales@ksupplies.co.uk
Website: http://www.ksupplies.co.uk
Bank(s): HSBC
Managers: C. Hardman (Buyer), K. Doublard (Mgr), R. Roundell (Tech Serv Mgr)
Immediate Holding Company: K SUPPLIES LIMITED
Registration no: 02284686 **VAT No.:** GB 525 4260 64
Date established: 1988 **No.of Employees:** 11 - 20 **Product Groups:** 66

Date of Accounts	Dec 10	Dec 09	Jan 09
Working Capital	N/A	N/A	655
Fixed Assets	N/A	N/A	113
Current Assets	N/A	N/A	1m

Kenross Containers Ltd
Kippax Mill Goodshawfold Road, Rossendale, BB4 8QW
Tel: 01706-228381 **Fax:** 01706-831523
E-mail: darren@kenross.co.uk
Website: http://www.kenross.co.uk
Bank(s): Yorkshire Bank PLC
Directors: D. Turner (MD), L. Turner (Co Sec)
Managers: C. Donnolly, P. Markey (Sales Prom Mgr), J. Flynn (Chief Acct)
Immediate Holding Company: KENROSS CONTAINERS LIMITED
Registration no: 02539994 **VAT No.:** GB 597 9362 67
Date established: 1990 **Turnover:** £2m - £5m **No.of Employees:** 21 - 50
Product Groups: 27, 28, 30, 45

Date of Accounts	Sep 11	Sep 10	Sep 09
Working Capital	-9	-23	185
Fixed Assets	2m	2m	2m
Current Assets	1m	1m	922

Konvekta Ltd
Knowsley Road Industrial Estate Haslingden, Rossendale, BB4 4RR
Tel: 01706-227018 **Fax:** 01706-831124
E-mail: sales@konvekta.co.uk
Website: http://www.konvekta.co.uk
Directors: C. Coxen (Dir), C. Branagan (Dir), C. Branagan (Fin)
Managers: M. Duplain (Buyer), A. Unwin (Sales Prom Mgr)
Immediate Holding Company: KONVEKTA LIMITED
Registration no: 01572877 **Date established:** 1981
Turnover: £500,000 - £1m **No.of Employees:** 21 - 50
Product Groups: 38, 40

Date of Accounts	Apr 11	Apr 10	Apr 09
Working Capital	238	236	240
Fixed Assets	143	184	223
Current Assets	264	302	373

L H Safety Ltd
Greenbridge Works Fallbarn Road, Rossendale, BB4 7NX
Tel: 01706-235100 **Fax:** 01706-235150
E-mail: enquiries@lhsafety.co.uk
Website: http://www.lhsafety.co.uk
Bank(s): Lloyds TSB Bank plc
Directors: S. Hill (Dir)
Managers: J. Tuplin (Personnel), C. Boyce (Sales Prom Mgr), A. Walmsley
Ultimate Holding Company: DELTA PLUS GROUP SA (FRANCE)
Immediate Holding Company: L H SAFETY LIMITED
Registration no: 04180687 **VAT No.:** GB 703 4318 27
Date established: 2001 **Turnover:** £5m - £10m **No.of Employees:** 21 - 50
Product Groups: 22, 24, 61, 63

Date of Accounts	Dec 11	Dec 10	Dec 09
Sales Turnover	6m	7m	7m
Pre Tax Profit/Loss	136	385	447
Working Capital	3m	2m	2m
Fixed Assets	100	22	3
Current Assets	4m	5m	4m
Current Liabilities	246	274	210

Macmillan Quality Bedding
16 Downham Avenue, Rossendale, BB4 8JY
Tel: 01706-215185
E-mail: yvonne@macmillanqualitybedding.co.uk
Website: http://www.macmillanqualitybedding.co.uk
Directors: Y. Fanshaw (Ptnr)
No.of Employees: 1 - 10 **Product Groups:** 23, 24, 63

Madison Filter
Knowsley Road Industrial Estate Haslingden, Rossendale, BB4 4EJ
Tel: 01706-213421 **Fax:** 01706-221916
E-mail: info@madisonfilter.com
Website: http://www.madisonfilter.com
Bank(s): HSBC Bank plc
Directors: M. Jordan (Dir)
Managers: K. Cocker
Ultimate Holding Company: GAMMA HOLDING NV (NETHERLANDS)
Immediate Holding Company: CLEAR EDGE - UK LTD
Registration no: 00939480 **Date established:** 1968 **Turnover:** £5m - £10m
No.of Employees: 11 - 20 **Product Groups:** 23, 40, 42, 45

Date of Accounts	Dec 10	Dec 09	Dec 08
Sales Turnover	5m	5m	9m
Pre Tax Profit/Loss	-493	-1m	-633
Working Capital	840	1m	-915
Fixed Assets	60	75	287
Current Assets	3m	2m	4m
Current Liabilities	259	259	181

Mainland Catering Equipment Ltd
Unit 1a Fountain Mill Rakefoot, Haslingden, Rossendale, BB4 5RE
Tel: 01706-244810 **Fax:** 01706-244811
E-mail: sales@mainlandcatering.co.uk
Website: http://www.mainlandcatering.co.uk
Directors: A. Haworth (MD)
Immediate Holding Company: MAINLAND CATERING EQUIPMENT LIMITED
Registration no: 03398535 **Date established:** 1997
No.of Employees: 1 - 10 **Product Groups:** 20, 40, 41

Date of Accounts	Aug 11	Aug 10	Aug 09
Working Capital	-193	-187	-29
Fixed Assets	222	203	37
Current Assets	738	685	691

Mobile UK Ltd
PO Box 286, Rossendale, BB4 0EQ
Tel: 01706-868160 **Fax:** 01706-868969
E-mail: sales@mukl.com
Website: http://www.mukl.com
Managers: M. Connell (Mgr)
Immediate Holding Company: MOBILE UK LIMITED
Registration no: 03255475 **Date established:** 1996
No.of Employees: 1 - 10 **Product Groups:** 20, 40, 41

Date of Accounts	Dec 11	Dec 10	Dec 09
Working Capital	337	258	212
Fixed Assets	18	12	10
Current Assets	585	347	300

P R S S Solutions UK Ltd
Unit 8 Scout Bottom Industrial Estate Burnley Road East, Rossendale, BB4 9JR
Tel: 01706-220786 **Fax:** 01706-220786
E-mail: info@prss-solutions.co.uk
Website: http://www.prss-solutions.co.uk
Directors: D. Shauhan (MD)
Immediate Holding Company: PRSS SOLUTIONS (UK) LIMITED
Registration no: 05155441 **Date established:** 2004
Turnover: Up to £250,000 **No.of Employees:** 1 - 10 **Product Groups:** 31, 32, 63, 66

Date of Accounts	Jun 11	Jun 10	Jun 09
Working Capital	-25	-25	-22
Fixed Assets	34	38	38
Current Assets	30	24	19

R C S
The Hanger Bury Road, Rawtenstall, Rossendale, BB4 6DJ
Tel: 01706-230727 **Fax:** 01706-230728
E-mail: sales@rcsdoors.co.uk
Website: http://www.rcsdoors.co.uk
Directors: S. Kenney (Prop)
Immediate Holding Company: ROLLERSHUTTERS COMPONENTS & SPRINGS LIMITED
Registration no: 06548614 **Date established:** 2008
No.of Employees: 1 - 10 **Product Groups:** 26, 35

Date of Accounts	Mar 11	Mar 10	Mar 09
Working Capital	56	109	N/A
Fixed Assets	60	63	N/A
Current Assets	326	296	N/A

R T E Electronics
568 Burnley Road, Rossendale, BB4 8AJ
Tel: 01706-227234 **Fax:** 01706-227531
Directors: B. Parsonage (Prop)
Immediate Holding Company: R.T.E. POWER LIMITED
Registration no: 03214547 **VAT No.:** GB 158 8818 60
Date established: 1996 **Turnover:** £250,000 - £500,000
No.of Employees: 1 - 10 **Product Groups:** 37, 40, 44

Recontainers Ltd
4 Taylors Court Todd Hall Road, Haslingden, Rossendale, BB4 5LA
Tel: 01706-211112 **Fax:** 01706-211102
Website: http://www.recontainers.com
Directors: P. Pritchard (Co Sec)
Immediate Holding Company: RECONTAINERS LIMITED
Registration no: 02640530 **Date established:** 1991
No.of Employees: 11 - 20 **Product Groups:** 35, 36, 45

Date of Accounts	Aug 11	Aug 10	Aug 09
Working Capital	-70	-88	-72
Fixed Assets	140	121	199
Current Assets	108	51	46

S D F Electronics Ltd
Unit 2 Unicon Park Todd Hall Road, Haslingden, Rossendale, BB4 5LA
Tel: 01706-224026 **Fax:** 01706-224024
E-mail: sales@sdfelectronics.co.uk
Website: http://www.sdf.elect.zen.co.uk
Directors: S. Fitton (MD)
Immediate Holding Company: S D F ELECTRONICS LTD
Registration no: 03288672 **Date established:** 1996
Turnover: £500,000 - £1m **No.of Employees:** 1 - 10 **Product Groups:** 37, 38, 40

Date of Accounts	Jun 11	Jun 10	Jun 09
Working Capital	26	42	46
Fixed Assets	11	14	16
Current Assets	85	92	90

Setco Automotive UK Ltd
York Avenue Haslingden, Rossendale, BB4 4HU
Tel: 01706-237200 **Fax:** 01706-229585
E-mail: salesuk@setcoauto.com
Website: http://www.setcoauto.com/uk
Bank(s): HSBC Bank plc
Directors: B. Parry (Fin), M. Coote (Sales & Mktg)
Managers: D. Harrison, M. Toote (Mktg Serv Mgr)
Immediate Holding Company: SETCO AUTOMOTIVE (UK) LIMITED
Registration no: 05628324 **VAT No.:** GB 149 6776 13
Date established: 2005 **Turnover:** £2m - £5m **No.of Employees:** 21 - 50
Product Groups: 39, 68

Date of Accounts	Mar 11	Mar 10	Mar 09
Sales Turnover	4m	3m	3m
Pre Tax Profit/Loss	72	-123	254
Working Capital	133	142	497
Fixed Assets	2m	2m	2m
Current Assets	3m	3m	3m
Current Liabilities	88	120	173

Sparta Ltd
Victoria Works Hill End Lane, Rossendale, BB4 7AG
Tel: 01706-235200 **Fax:** 01706-222309
E-mail: enquiries@sparta.co.uk
Website: http://www.sparta.co.uk
Bank(s): National Westminster Bank Plc
Directors: E. Drury (Fin)
Managers: S. Lord, G. Barnes (Works Gen Mgr)
Immediate Holding Company: SPARTA LIMITED
Registration no: 02607524 **VAT No.:** GB 597 8766 48
Date established: 1991 **Turnover:** £2m - £5m **No.of Employees:** 51 - 100
Product Groups: 34, 48

Date of Accounts	Apr 11	Apr 10	Apr 09
Working Capital	111	198	322
Fixed Assets	1m	1m	1m
Current Assets	2m	1m	1m

Techmould Ltd
9 Knowsley Road Industrial Estate Knowsley Road, Haslingden, Rossendale, BB4 4RX
Tel: 01706-227717 **Fax:** 01706-830204
E-mail: sales@techmould.co.uk
Website: http://www.techmould.co.uk
Directors: M. Wainwright (Dir)
Ultimate Holding Company: UNICON HOLDINGS LIMITED
Immediate Holding Company: TECHMOULD LIMITED
Registration no: 01499651 **VAT No.:** GB 421 8532 69
Date established: 1980 **Turnover:** £500,000 - £1m
No.of Employees: 1 - 10 **Product Groups:** 29

Date of Accounts	Jun 11	Jun 10	Jun 09
Working Capital	242	228	205
Fixed Assets	66	42	44
Current Assets	370	336	310

Tele Control Ltd
Unit 21 Three Point Business Park Charles Lane, Haslingden, Rossendale, BB4 5EH
Tel: 01706-226333 **Fax:** 01706-226444
E-mail: sales@tele-control.co.uk
Website: http://www.tele-power-net.com
Directors: M. Slorick (Fin), E. Threlfall (Dir), H. Haase (MD)
Managers: J. Von Speyr (Chief Mgr), N. Isherwood, Y. Threlfall (Sales Admin)
Ultimate Holding Company: MODUL UMBH (AUSTRIA)
Immediate Holding Company: TELE-CONTROL LIMITED
Registration no: 01604675 **Date established:** 1981 **Turnover:** £1m - £2m
No.of Employees: 1 - 10 **Product Groups:** 37, 38, 49

Date of Accounts	Dec 08	Dec 07	Dec 06
Working Capital	-333	-294	-306
Fixed Assets	37	44	27
Current Assets	189	187	120
Current Liabilities	522	481	426
Total Share Capital	112	112	112

Texecom
Bradwood Court St Crispin Way, Haslingden, Rossendale, BB4 4PW
Tel: 01706-234800
E-mail: sales@texe.com
Website: http://www.texe.com
Directors: D. Cummins (Fin), J. Ludwig (MD), P. Harris (Sales & Mktg)
Managers: S. Ash, S. Jansen (Purch Mgr), S. Bolger (Personnel)
Ultimate Holding Company: HALMA PUBLIC LIMITED COMPANY
Immediate Holding Company: TEXECOM LIMITED
Registration no: 02084170 **Date established:** 1986
Turnover: £20m - £50m **No.of Employees:** 51 - 100 **Product Groups:** 37, 40

Date of Accounts	Mar 12	Mar 09	Apr 10
Sales Turnover	26m	17m	18m
Pre Tax Profit/Loss	2m	1m	2m
Working Capital	5m	2m	5m
Fixed Assets	2m	3m	2m
Current Assets	10m	6m	10m
Current Liabilities	856	690	796

Thorpe Tractors
6 Higher Boarsgreave Cowpe Road, Rossendale, BB4 7AB
Tel: 01706-227679
Managers: S. Thorpe (Mgr)
No.of Employees: 1 - 10 **Product Groups:** 41

W H Good Automation Ltd
Carrs Indl-Est Commerce Street, Haslingden, Rossendale, BB4 5JT
Tel: 08703-600110 **Fax:** 08703-600446
E-mail: group@whgood.co.uk
Website: http://www.whgood.co.uk
Directors: P. Sumner (MD), P. Sumner (Co Sec)
Managers: B. Pursglove (Chief Mgr)
Ultimate Holding Company: W.H.GOOD GROUP LIMITED
Immediate Holding Company: W H GOOD AUTOMATION LTD
Registration no: 02289519 **VAT No.:** GB 145 5981 41
Date established: 1988 **Turnover:** £2m - £5m **No.of Employees:** 51 - 100
Product Groups: 52

Date of Accounts	Apr 11	Apr 10	Apr 09
Working Capital	498	588	517
Fixed Assets	80	95	98
Current Assets	1m	1m	1m

Salford

A P I Holographics Ltd
Astor Road, Salford, M50 1BB
Tel: 0161-789 8131 **Fax:** 0161-707 5315
E-mail: enquiries@apigroup.com
Website: http://www.apigroup.com
Bank(s): Barclays
Directors: S. Clarke (MD), R. Bell (Fin)
Managers: P. Cairns (Mktg Serv Mgr), R. Stageman (Tech Serv Mgr), J. Cunningham (Purch Mgr), D. Stephens (Personnel)
Ultimate Holding Company: API GROUP PLC
Immediate Holding Company: API HOLOGRAPHICS LIMITED
Registration no: 03503309 **VAT No.:** GB 345 1022 00
Date established: 1998 **Turnover:** £20m - £50m
No.of Employees: 51 - 100 **Product Groups:** 34, 81

Date of Accounts	Mar 12	Mar 11	Mar 10
Sales Turnover	13m	11m	9m
Pre Tax Profit/Loss	734	75	-826
Working Capital	3m	2m	1m
Fixed Assets	4m	4m	4m
Current Assets	4m	4m	2m
Current Liabilities	513	436	435

Aldridge & Son Wholesale Ltd
50 Queen Street, Salford, M3 7DQ
Tel: 08444-125101 **Fax:** 0161-828 0838
E-mail: sales@e-aldridge.co.uk
Website: http://www.ealdridge.co.uk
Managers: G. Hall (District Mgr)
Immediate Holding Company: E. ALDRIDGE & SON (LOCKSMITHS) LTD
Registration no: 00257714 **Turnover:** £5m - £10m
No.of Employees: 1 - 10 **Product Groups:** 36, 66

Allday P A
Michigan Avenue Isher House, Salford, M50 2GY
Tel: 08450-561234 **Fax:** 0161-877 4207
E-mail: info@customerservice.alldaypa.com
Website: http://www.alldaypa.com
Managers: K. Thompson
Turnover: £500,000 - £1m **No.of Employees:** 11 - 20 **Product Groups:** 80

Alma Laboratories
Unit 3 Buffalo Court, Salford, M50 2QL
Tel: 0161-848 7289 **Fax:** 0161-872 7637
Managers: D. Latham (Mgr)
No.of Employees: 1 - 10 **Product Groups:** 38, 67

Archer Catering Systems
2 Mode Wheel Road, Salford, M5 5DQ
Tel: 0161-737 8307 **Fax:** 0161-736 8307
E-mail: archercatering@hotmail.co.uk
Directors: N. Archer (Ptnr)
Immediate Holding Company: ARCHER CATERING SYSTEMS LIMITED
Registration no: 05924276 **Date established:** 2006
No.of Employees: 1 - 10 **Product Groups:** 20, 40, 41

Date of Accounts	Sep 11	Sep 10	Sep 09
Working Capital	-17	-6	-24
Fixed Assets	31	20	27
Current Assets	106	147	129

Ariel Maritime UK Ltd
Unit 26 Waters Edge Business Park, Salford, M5 3EZ
Tel: 0161-848 9009 **Fax:** 0161-848 9511
E-mail: manchester@arielmaritime.co.uk
Website: http://www.arielmaritime.com
Directors: A. Sethi (MD)
Ultimate Holding Company: Saville International Investments
Immediate Holding Company: ARIEL MARITIME (U.K.) LIMITED
Registration no: 01533534 **VAT No.:** GB 306 4213 00
Date established: 1980 **Turnover:** £2m - £5m **No.of Employees:** 1 - 10
Product Groups: 39, 45, 76

Date of Accounts	Dec 11	Dec 10	Dec 09
Working Capital	104	80	54
Fixed Assets	128	132	143
Current Assets	517	411	593

Artegy Ltd
Suite G1, Building 8 Exchange Quay, Salford Quays, Salford, M5 3EJ
Tel: 0845-266 6010 **Fax:** 0845-2666043
E-mail: info@artegy.co.uk
Website: http://www.artegy.co.uk
Directors: M. Lewis (Dir), N. James (Co Sec)
Managers: J. Bell, M. Taylor (Sales Prom Mgr)
Ultimate Holding Company: BNP PARIBAS S.A. (FRANCE)
Registration no: 04960923 **Date established:** 2003
Turnover: £10m - £20m **No.of Employees:** 21 - 50 **Product Groups:** 72

Date of Accounts	Dec 09	Dec 08	Dec 07
Sales Turnover	13m	14m	16m
Pre Tax Profit/Loss	2m	2m	103
Working Capital	-5m	-4m	-5m
Fixed Assets	21m	22m	21m
Current Assets	2m	1m	2m
Current Liabilities	3m	3m	2m

Bardon Aggregates Ltd
Mode Wheel Road South, Salford, M50 1DG
Tel: 0161-872 6071 **Fax:** 0161-872 0220
Website: http://www.bardonaggregates.co.uk
Managers: R. Stott (Mgr), S. Paryington (Mgr)
Immediate Holding Company: BARDON AGGREGATES LIMITED
Registration no: 00836912 **VAT No.:** GB 532 3679 43
Date established: 1965 **No.of Employees:** 1 - 10 **Product Groups:** 31

Bowdon Office Equipment Ltd
63 Waybridge Industrial Estate Daniel Adamson Road, Salford, M50 1DS
Tel: 0161-848 9990 **Fax:** 0161-848 9979
E-mail: enquiries@bowdonoffice.co.uk
Website: http://www.bowdenoffice.co.uk
Directors: D. Monks (MD), A. Howarth (Co Sec)
Managers: A. St Clair (Sales Admin), N. Low (Purch Mgr)
Immediate Holding Company: BOWDON OFFICE EQUIPMENT LIMITED
Registration no: 02783264 **Date established:** 1993
Turnover: £500,000 - £1m **No.of Employees:** 21 - 50 **Product Groups:** 48

Britch & Associates Ltd
31 The Crescent, Salford, M5 4PF
Tel: 0161-736 1447 **Fax:** 0161-745 7564
E-mail: jasmine.allsop@britch.co.uk
Website: http://www.britch.co.uk
Directors: P. Allsop (MD)
Immediate Holding Company: BRITCH & ASSOCIATES LIMITED
Registration no: 01551632 **VAT No.:** GB 145 5186 63
Date established: 1981 **Turnover:** Up to £250,000
No.of Employees: 1 - 10 **Product Groups:** 84

Date of Accounts	Mar 11	Mar 10	Mar 09
Working Capital	3	10	17
Fixed Assets	1	1	2
Current Assets	131	137	116

Brock Signs & Graphics Ltd
32 Kansas Avenue, Salford, M50 2GL
Tel: 0161-877 8484 **Fax:** 0161-877 8444
E-mail: p-harris@brocksigns.co.uk
Website: http://www.brocksigns.co.uk
Directors: P. Harris (MD)
Immediate Holding Company: BROCK SIGNS AND GRAPHICS LIMITED
Registration no: 05087446 **VAT No.:** GB 145 0211 18
Date established: 2004 **Turnover:** £250,000 - £500,000
No.of Employees: 1 - 10 **Product Groups:** 39

Date of Accounts	Mar 12	Mar 11	Mar 10
Working Capital	-3	3	-31
Fixed Assets	N/A	N/A	2
Current Assets	5	7	9

Cancarp Automation Ltd
28 Willan Industrial Estate Vere Street, Salford, M50 2GR
Tel: 0161-736 9026 **Fax:** 0161-745 8657
E-mail: bisc@cancart.com
Website: http://www.cancarp.com
Directors: K. Greenhalgh (Dir), L. Roscoe (Co Sec), L. Roscoe (Fin)
Managers: L. Roscoe (Purch Mgr)
Immediate Holding Company: CANCARP LIMITED
Registration no: 01678621 **VAT No.:** GB 376 2341 49
Date established: 1982 **Turnover:** Up to £250,000
No.of Employees: 1 - 10 **Product Groups:** 34, 37, 38, 39

Date of Accounts	Mar 11	Mar 10	Mar 09
Working Capital	56	58	113
Fixed Assets	7	12	17
Current Assets	132	91	148

Carry Lift Material Handling Ltd
Unit 10 Waters Edge Business Park Modwen Road, Salford, M5 3EZ
Tel: 0161-877 4000 **Fax:** 0161-877 4007
E-mail: info@carryliftgroup.com
Website: http://www.carryliftgroup.com
Managers: G. Green (Sales Admin)
No.of Employees: 11 - 20 **Product Groups:** 35, 39, 45

Chemipat Ltd (t/a Adhesive & Coating Supplies)
Casablanca Mill Sherborne Street West, Salford, M3 7LF
Tel: 0161-835 1420 **Fax:** 0161-839 3543
E-mail: sales@chemipat.co.uk
Website: http://www.chemipat.co.uk
Directors: J. Woodruff (Dir), T. Woodruff (Fin)
Immediate Holding Company: CHEMIPAT LIMITED
Registration no: 01287421 **Date established:** 1976 **Turnover:** £2m - £5m
No.of Employees: 11 - 20 **Product Groups:** 32

Date of Accounts	Feb 08	Feb 11	Feb 10
Working Capital	123	142	122
Fixed Assets	85	93	110
Current Assets	886	781	624

The Corps
Osprey House 217-227 Broadway, Salford, M50 2UE
Tel: 0161-869 9800 **Fax:** 0161-869 9805
E-mail: manchesteroffice@the-corp.co.uk
Website: http://www.corpssecurity.co.uk
Managers: J. Eaton (Contracts Mgr)
Date established: 1995 **No.of Employees:** 1 - 10 **Product Groups:** 81

Creative Logistics
Duncan Street, Salford, M5 3SQ
Tel: 0161-873 7101 **Fax:** 0161-872 1447
E-mail: enquiries@creative-logistics.co.uk
Website: http://www.creative-logistics.co.uk
Directors: M. Clynes (Dir)
Immediate Holding Company: CREATIVE LOGISTICS (WAREHOUSING) LTD
Registration no: 02666898 **Turnover:** £1m - £2m
No.of Employees: 1 - 10 **Product Groups:** 72

Date of Accounts	Dec 07	Dec 06	Dec 05
Working Capital	94	-1	-4
Fixed Assets	10	11	9
Current Assets	150	87	283
Current Liabilities	56	88	287
Total Share Capital	1	1	1

Cromwell Industrial Supplies
651 Eccles New Road, Salford, M50 1BA
Tel: 0161-786 2500 **Fax:** 0161-787 7113
E-mail: manchester@cromwell.co.uk
Website: http://www.cromwell.co.uk
Directors: S. Carmichael (Fin)
Managers: C. Musgrave (District Mgr)
Ultimate Holding Company: CROMWELL GROUP (HOLDINGS) LIMITED
Immediate Holding Company: CROMWELL LOGISTICS LIMITED
Registration no: 01220889 **Date established:** 1975 **Turnover:** £2m - £5m
No.of Employees: 21 - 50 **Product Groups:** 36, 37, 41, 42, 46, 47

Date of Accounts	Aug 11	Aug 10	Aug 09
Sales Turnover	12m	11m	11m
Pre Tax Profit/Loss	1m	1m	1m
Working Capital	5m	4m	3m
Fixed Assets	432	627	885
Current Assets	6m	5m	4m
Current Liabilities	507	321	304

Cubic Modular Systems (UK) Ltd
Unit 8 Boston Court Kansas Avenue, Salford, M50 2GN
Tel: 0161-876 4742 **Fax:** 0161-876 4746
E-mail: info@cubic-uk.co.uk
Website: http://www.cubic.dk
Bank(s): Jyske
Managers: D. Flynn (Sales Prom Mgr)
Ultimate Holding Company: Cubic Modulsystem A/S (Denmark)
Immediate Holding Company: Cubic Modular Systems U.K. Ltd
Registration no: 03770846 **VAT No.:** GB **Date established:** 1999
Turnover: £20m - £50m **No.of Employees:** 11 - 20 **Product Groups:** 37

Cussons Technology Ltd
102 Great Clowes Street, Salford, M7 1RH
Tel: 0161-833 0036 **Fax:** 0161-834 4688
E-mail: sales@cussons.co.uk
Website: http://www.cussons.co.uk
Managers: S. Curtis (Mgr), D. Todd (Buyer)
Ultimate Holding Company: CUSSONS TECHNOLOGY HOLDINGS LIMITED
Immediate Holding Company: CUSSONS TECHNOLOGY LIMITED
Registration no: 04271888 **VAT No.:** GB 519 0125 73
Date established: 2001 **Turnover:** £2m - £5m **No.of Employees:** 21 - 50
Product Groups: 28, 38, 39

Date of Accounts	Mar 11	Mar 10	Mar 09
Working Capital	857	1m	886
Fixed Assets	673	736	517
Current Assets	3m	2m	2m

11 Out Of 10 Ltd
The Innovation Forum Frederick Road, Salford, M6 6AR
Tel: 0161-798 7977
E-mail: info@11outof10.com
Website: http://www.11outof10.com
Directors: V. Holt (Dir)
Immediate Holding Company: 11OUTOF10 LIMITED
Registration no: 05003669 **VAT No.:** GB 835 8161 15
Date established: 2003 **No.of Employees:** 11 - 20 **Product Groups:** 44

Date of Accounts	Mar 12	Mar 11	Mar 10
Working Capital	86	26	58
Fixed Assets	6	8	7
Current Assets	204	127	101
Current Liabilities	N/A	N/A	35

Ener-G Combined Power
Ener G House Daniel Adamson Road, Salford, M50 1DT
Tel: 0161-745 7450 **Fax:** 0161-745 7457
E-mail: info@energ.co.uk
Website: http://www.energ.co.uk
Directors: A. Barlow (MD), T. Wadhams (Tech Serv), D. Evans (Pers)
Managers: T. Baker (Mktg Serv Mgr), T. Roe (Purch Mgr), M. Wallace (Fin Mgr)
Ultimate Holding Company: ENER-G PLC
Immediate Holding Company: ENER-G COMBINED POWER LIMITED
Registration no: 01874716 **Date established:** 1984
Turnover: £20m - £50m **No.of Employees:** 51 - 100 **Product Groups:** 37, 38, 40, 42, 67, 84, 85

Date of Accounts	Mar 12	Mar 11	Mar 10
Sales Turnover	37m	37m	30m
Pre Tax Profit/Loss	2m	3m	2m
Working Capital	16m	21m	15m
Fixed Assets	14m	15m	14m
Current Assets	28m	33m	26m
Current Liabilities	7m	6m	4m

European Metals Recycling Ltd
West Egerton Street, Salford, M5 4DY
Tel: 0161-745 7555 **Fax:** 0161-745 9961
E-mail: brian.moreton@emrltd.com
Website: http://www.emrltd.com
Bank(s): HSBC
Managers: B. Moreton (Mgr)
Immediate Holding Company: EUROPEAN METAL RECYCLING LIMITED
Registration no: 02954623 **Date established:** 1994
No.of Employees: 51 - 100 **Product Groups:** 34, 42, 54, 66

Date of Accounts	Dec 11	Dec 10	Dec 09
Sales Turnover	3032m	2431m	1843m
Pre Tax Profit/Loss	116m	155m	91m
Working Capital	414m	371m	167m
Fixed Assets	518m	483m	480m
Current Assets	1027m	717m	557m
Current Liabilities	124m	118m	185m

F A B Recording Studios
15 Knoll Street, Salford, M7 2EQ
Tel: 0161-792 0203 **Fax:** 0161-792 0203
E-mail: chris@fabstudios.co.uk
Website: http://www.fabstudios.co.uk
Directors: C. Galbraith (Prop)
No.of Employees: 1 - 10 **Product Groups:** 26, 37, 44, 67

Flowserve Corporation
Dakota Avenue, Salford, M50 2PU
Tel: 0161-869 1200 **Fax:** 0161-869 1235
Website: http://www.flowserve.com
Directors: M. Headford (Mkt Research)
Managers: G. Crossland (Admin Off), S. Bhatt (Applic Eng), S. Petter (Chief Mgr), M. Round (Chief Acct)
Immediate Holding Company: Flowserve International Ltd
Registration no: 06748072 **Date established:** 2008
Turnover: Over £1,000m **No.of Employees:** 21 - 50 **Product Groups:** 33, 36, 39

Forest Sofa
Newbury House Greenwood Street, Salford, M6 6PD
Tel: 0161-737 6918 **Fax:** 0161-745 7830
E-mail: david.foster@forestsofa.co.uk
Website: http://www.forestsofa.co.uk
Directors: C. Smith (Fin), D. Foster (MD), R. Mohieddin (Mkt Research)
Immediate Holding Company: FOREST CONTRACT LIMITED
Registration no: 06219743 **VAT No.:** GB 146 1279 70
Date established: 2007 **No.of Employees:** 21 - 50 **Product Groups:** 26

Date of Accounts	Dec 11	Dec 10	Dec 09
Current Assets	45	35	56

Frank Pine
1 Crown Street, Salford, M3 7DH
Tel: 0161-834 0456 **Fax:** 0161-832 0385
E-mail: reception@frankpine.co.uk
Website: http://www.frankpine.co.uk
Bank(s): Barclays
Directors: J. Pine (Prop)
Immediate Holding Company: FRANK PINE LIMITED
Registration no: 00421390 **Date established:** 1946 **Turnover:** £2m - £5m
No.of Employees: 11 - 20 **Product Groups:** 23

Date of Accounts	Oct 11	Oct 10	Oct 09
Working Capital	1m	1m	1m
Fixed Assets	1m	1m	1m
Current Assets	2m	2m	2m

G E Robinson & Co.
Thurlow Mills Montford Street, Salford, M50 2XD
Tel: 0161-872 0435 **Fax:** 0161-872 9045
E-mail: sales@ge-robinson.co.uk
Website: http://www.ge-robinson.co.uk
Bank(s): National Westminster Bank Plc
Directors: A. Gerrard (MD), G. Foster (Sales)
Managers: D. Rossall (Buyer)
Ultimate Holding Company: HALDANE SHIELLS AND COMPANY LIMITED
Immediate Holding Company: G E ROBINSON (TIMBER) LIMITED
Registration no: 00298984 **VAT No.:** GB 146 8067 50
Date established: 1935 **Turnover:** £10m - £20m
No.of Employees: 51 - 100 **Product Groups:** 61, 66

Date of Accounts	Dec 11	Dec 10	Dec 09
Working Capital	1m	1m	1m
Current Assets	1m	1m	1m

Gerber Technology Ltd
302 Metroplex Business Park Broadway, Salford, M50 2UE
Tel: 0161-772 2000 **Fax:** 0161-772 2020
Website: http://www.gerbertechnology.com

Directors: Y. Heinen (Mkt Research), A. Geldart (Fin)
Managers: C. Moore (Sales Admin), D. Vickers (Sales Prom Mgr)
Ultimate Holding Company: GERBER SCIENTIFIC INC (USA)
Immediate Holding Company: GERBER TECHNOLOGY LIMITED
Registration no: 00976330 **Date established:** 1970 **Turnover:** £5m - £10m
No.of Employees: 21 - 50 **Product Groups:** 43, 44

Date of Accounts	Apr 11	Apr 10	Apr 09
Sales Turnover	6m	5m	6m
Pre Tax Profit/Loss	131	376	335
Working Capital	1m	2m	7m
Fixed Assets	18	6	30
Current Assets	5m	4m	8m
Current Liabilities	560	1m	922

H & S

Mode Wheel Road South, Salford, M50 1DG
Tel: 0161-872 6235 **Fax:** 0161-872 6293
Managers: C. Henderson (Mgr)
Immediate Holding Company: PALMER DEMOLITION LTD
Date established: 1983 **No.of Employees:** 1 - 10 **Product Groups:** 36, 40

Date of Accounts	Dec 11	Dec 10	Dec 09
Working Capital	508	457	353
Fixed Assets	352	386	476
Current Assets	663	629	624

Hach Lange Ltd

5 Pacific Way, Salford, M50 1DL
Tel: 0161-872 1487 **Fax:** 0161-848 7324
E-mail: info@hach-lange.co.uk
Website: http://www.hach-lange.co.uk
Bank(s): Barclays
Directors: D. Stell (Dir), D. Tunley (Fin), M. Dillon (Sales)
Managers: S. Blyads (Mktg Serv Mgr)
Ultimate Holding Company: DANAHER CORPORATION (DELAWARE U.S.A)
Immediate Holding Company: HACH LANGE LTD
Registration no: 01029281 **VAT No.:** GB 174 5572 43
Date established: 1971 **Turnover:** £10m - £20m
No.of Employees: 21 - 50 **Product Groups:** 38

Date of Accounts	Dec 11	Dec 10	Dec 09
Sales Turnover	20m	18m	15m
Pre Tax Profit/Loss	1m	958	631
Working Capital	3m	10m	9m
Fixed Assets	1m	2m	2m
Current Assets	7m	14m	11m
Current Liabilities	1m	1m	919

Hafele UK Ltd

Unit 11-12 Salford University Business Park Leslie Hough Way, Salford, M6 6AJ
Tel: 0161-745 8242 **Fax:** 0161-736 3288
E-mail: martin.poulton@hafele.co.uk
Website: http://www.hafele.co.uk
Managers: M. Poulton (Mgr)
Ultimate Holding Company: HAFELE HOLDING GMBH (GERMANY)
Immediate Holding Company: HAFELE U.K. LIMITED
Registration no: 01486136 **Date established:** 1980
No.of Employees: 1 - 10 **Product Groups:** 35, 36

Date of Accounts	Dec 11	Dec 10	Dec 09
Sales Turnover	77m	79m	73m
Pre Tax Profit/Loss	8m	10m	9m
Working Capital	24m	23m	20m
Fixed Assets	20m	20m	21m
Current Assets	33m	34m	29m
Current Liabilities	5m	4m	3m

Harland Machine Systems Ltd

2 Michigan Avenue, Salford, M50 2GY
Tel: 0161-848 4800 **Fax:** 0161-848 4830
E-mail: enquiries@harland-hms.com
Website: http://www.harland-hms.com
Bank(s): Bank of Scotland, 19-21 Spring Gardens,Manchester, M2 1FB
Directors: D. Latham (Sales), F. Dean (Co Sec)
Managers: R. Argent (Tech Serv Mgr), S. Whittingham (Chief Buyer), C. Hamilton (Personnel)
Ultimate Holding Company: HARLAND SYSTEMS GROUP LIMITED
Immediate Holding Company: HARLAND MACHINE SYSTEMS LIMITED
Registration no: 04124774 **VAT No.:** GB 748 3319 14
Date established: 2000 **Turnover:** £5m - £10m
No.of Employees: 51 - 100 **Product Groups:** 37, 42, 43, 44, 48, 76

Date of Accounts	Dec 11	Dec 10	Dec 09
Sales Turnover	12m	9m	8m
Pre Tax Profit/Loss	852	815	462
Working Capital	3m	2m	966
Fixed Assets	471	540	666
Current Assets	8m	6m	3m
Current Liabilities	504	493	434

Heath Lambert Group

Cloister House New Bailey Street, Salford, M3 5AG
Tel: 0161-935 2935 **Fax:** 0161-839 2839
Website: http://www.heathlambert.com
Directors: N. Kerr (Dir), D. Rudman (Grp Chief Exec)
Managers: R. Darby (Sales Admin)
Immediate Holding Company: LIBERTY HOUSE MANAGEMENT COMPANY LIMITED
Registration no: 01199129 **Date established:** 2011
No.of Employees: 21 - 50 **Product Groups:** 80, 82

Hercules Holding Ii Ltd

Langley Road Pendelbury, Salford, M6 6JU
Tel: 0161-745 8905 **Fax:** 0161-745 7009
E-mail: name@herc.com
Website: http://www.herc.com
Bank(s): Citibank International plc
Directors: M. Maxwell (Fin)
Ultimate Holding Company: ASHLAND INC (USA)
Immediate Holding Company: HERCULES HOLDING II LIMITED
Registration no: 04352568 **Date established:** 2002
Turnover: £20m - £50m **No.of Employees:** 21 - 50 **Product Groups:** 32

Date of Accounts	Sep 11	Sep 10	Sep 09
Pre Tax Profit/Loss	-6	N/A	-17m
Working Capital	-10m	-10m	-10m
Fixed Assets	2m	2m	2m
Current Assets	N/A	6	6
Current Liabilities	N/A	10m	N/A

Highlead Ltd

5 Cheltenham Street, Salford, M6 6WY
Tel: 0870-139 8869 **Fax:** 0870-139 8869
E-mail: info@highlead.co.uk
Website: http://www.highlead.co.uk
Directors: A. Trainor (Fin), J. Trainor (MD)
Immediate Holding Company: HIGHLEAD LIMITED
Registration no: 04987004 **Date established:** 2003
No.of Employees: 1 - 10 **Product Groups:** 43, 44, 48, 61, 67

Date of Accounts	Mar 07	Mar 06	Mar 05
Working Capital	N/A	1	1
Current Assets	N/A	1	1

Hilti GT Britain Ltd

4 Hagley Road, Salford, M5 3EY
Tel: 0800-886100 **Fax:** 0800-886200
Website: http://www.hilti.co.uk
Ultimate Holding Company: HILTI AG (LIECHTENSTEIN)
Immediate Holding Company: HILTI (GT.BRITAIN) LIMITED
Registration no: 00479786 **Date established:** 1950
Turnover: £75m - £125m **No.of Employees:** 1 - 10 **Product Groups:** 35, 37, 48

Date of Accounts	Dec 11	Dec 10	Dec 09
Sales Turnover	87m	65m	66m
Pre Tax Profit/Loss	838	766	-379
Working Capital	12m	12m	15m
Fixed Assets	6m	5m	5m
Current Assets	45m	33m	25m
Current Liabilities	10m	6m	4m

Hoselines & Industrial Supplies North West Ltd

Unit 8 & 9 Knoll Street Industrial Park, Salford, M7 2BL
Tel: 0161-792 0481 **Fax:** 0161-792 5328
E-mail: sales@hoselines.com
Website: http://www.hoselines.com
Directors: D. Fairclough (Sales), M. Wild (MD)
Immediate Holding Company: HOSELINES AND INDUSTRIAL SUPPLIES (NORTH WEST) LIMITED
Registration no: 04768254 **Date established:** 2003
No.of Employees: 1 - 10 **Product Groups:** 23, 29, 30, 36, 66

Date of Accounts	Dec 09	Dec 08	Dec 07
Working Capital	-7	41	24
Fixed Assets	62	26	31
Current Assets	192	167	172

Hydraulic Transmission Services Ltd

9 Cannon Street, Salford, M3 6JH
Tel: 0161-834 7666 **Fax:** 0113-279 5505
E-mail: joanm@hts-ltd.co.uk
Website: http://www.hts-ltd.co.uk
Managers: J. Morgridge, J. Mugbridge (Sales Prom Mgr)
Immediate Holding Company: HYDRAULIC & TRANSMISSION SERVICES LIMITED
Registration no: 01051404 **Date established:** 1972
No.of Employees: 21 - 50 **Product Groups:** 22, 23, 24, 27, 29, 30, 31, 32, 33, 34, 35, 36, 37, 38, 39, 40, 41, 42, 43, 44, 45, 46, 47, 48, 49, 51, 52, 54, 61, 62, 63, 66, 67, 68, 83, 84, 85, 86

Date of Accounts	Jul 11	Jul 10	Jul 09
Working Capital	875	617	934
Fixed Assets	488	513	524
Current Assets	1m	1m	1m

Janus Steel Door Systems Ltd

Unit 3-4 Westlink Business Park James Corbett Road, Salford, M50 1DE
Tel: 0161-745 5000 **Fax:** 0161-745 5001
E-mail: sales@janusdoors.co.uk
Website: http://www.janusdoors.co.uk
Directors: P. Gibson (MD), J. Gibson (Fin)
Immediate Holding Company: JANUS STEEL DOOR SYSTEMS LIMITED
Registration no: 04816477 **Date established:** 2003
Turnover: Up to £250,000 **No.of Employees:** 1 - 10 **Product Groups:** 33, 35, 36, 39, 66

Date of Accounts	Jul 11	Jul 10	Jul 09
Working Capital	-26	7	-1
Fixed Assets	79	41	50
Current Assets	290	281	251

K3 Business Technology Group plc

50 Kansas Avenue, Salford, M50 2GL
Tel: 0161-876 4498 **Fax:** 01362-691710
E-mail: info@k3btg.com
Website: http://www.k3btg.com
Directors: P. Murray (Fin), G. Ormerod (Dir)
Immediate Holding Company: K3 BUSINESS TECHNOLOGY GROUP PLC
Registration no: 02641001 **Date established:** 1991
Turnover: £50m - £75m **No.of Employees:** 51 - 100 **Product Groups:** 28, 37, 44, 67, 79

Date of Accounts	Dec 08	Dec 07	Jun 11
Sales Turnover	38m	34m	53m
Pre Tax Profit/Loss	4m	4m	5m
Working Capital	-6m	-5m	-6m
Fixed Assets	47m	46m	59m
Current Assets	14m	14m	23m
Current Liabilities	13m	13m	20m

Kone Bolton Brady

11 Lord Byron Square, Salford, M50 2XH
Tel: 0161-745 9627 **Fax:** 0161- 7370940
Website: http://www.kone.com
Managers: I. Charman (Mgr)
No.of Employees: 1 - 10 **Product Groups:** 45, 48, 67

Krupa Engineering Ltd

18 Upper Camp Street, Salford, M7 2ZN
Tel: 0161-792 8588 **Fax:** 0161-792 8588
E-mail: krupaeng@gmail.com
Directors: P. Pacholek (MD), I. Pacholek (Fin)
Immediate Holding Company: KRUPA ENGINEERING LIMITED
Registration no: 04688826 **Date established:** 2003
No.of Employees: 1 - 10 **Product Groups:** 46

Date of Accounts	Mar 11	Mar 10	Mar 09
Working Capital	59	55	57
Fixed Assets	4	5	5
Current Assets	82	65	64

Labmedics UK Llp

Telegraphic House Waterfront Quay, Salford, M50 3XW
Tel: 0161-869 0420 **Fax:** 0161-869 0421
E-mail: sales@labmedics.co.uk
Website: http://www.labmedics.co.uk
Directors: T. O'Reilly (Ptnr), T. Pike (Dir), T. O'reilly (Dir), R. Haslehurst (Dir)
Managers: N. Humphries (Admin Off)
Immediate Holding Company: LABMEDICS (UK) LLP
Registration no: OC342725 **VAT No.:** GB 473 5316 43
Date established: 2009 **Turnover:** £2m - £5m **No.of Employees:** 1 - 10
Product Groups: 38, 44

Date of Accounts	Oct 08	Dec 07	Dec 06
Sales Turnover	N/A	3m	4m
Pre Tax Profit/Loss	N/A	530	308
Working Capital	694	559	724
Fixed Assets	56	62	128
Current Assets	1m	2m	2m
Current Liabilities	433	1m	1m
Total Share Capital	324	324	324

Langfields Ltd

158 Liverpool Street, Salford, M5 4LJ
Tel: 0161-736 4506 **Fax:** 0161-745 7108
E-mail: sales@langfields.com
Website: http://www.langfields.com
Bank(s): National Westminster Bank Plc
Directors: I. Dean (MD), K. Dean (Fin)
Immediate Holding Company: LANGFIELDS LIMITED
Registration no: 01901403 **VAT No.:** GB 403 6007 03
Date established: 1985 **Turnover:** £2m - £5m **No.of Employees:** 21 - 50
Product Groups: 31, 34, 35, 36, 37, 40, 42, 48, 54

Date of Accounts	Mar 11	Mar 10	Mar 09
Working Capital	738	554	1m
Fixed Assets	313	266	268
Current Assets	2m	2m	2m

Linden Textiles Ltd

Linden Court House 52 Liverpool Street, Salford, M5 4LT
Tel: 0161-745 9268 **Fax:** 0161-737 6061
E-mail: accounts@thomasfrederick.co.uk
Managers: J. Shasha
Immediate Holding Company: LINDEN TEXTILES LIMITED
Registration no: 03890544 **VAT No.:** 145 4158 73 **Date established:** 1999
Turnover: £5m - £10m **No.of Employees:** 1 - 10 **Product Groups:** 24, 63

Date of Accounts	May 09	May 08	Nov 11
Working Capital	70	55	-3m
Fixed Assets	2	10	N/A
Current Assets	3m	3m	813

Maplin Electronics Ltd

Unit E1 Regent Retail Park Regent Road, Salford, M5 3TP
Tel: 08432-277356 **Fax:** 0161-839 3803
E-mail: customercare@maplin.co.uk
Website: http://www.maplin.co.uk
Managers: C. Twamley (Mgr)
Ultimate Holding Company: MONTAGU PRIVATE EQUITY LLP
Immediate Holding Company: MAPLIN ELECTRONICS LIMITED
Registration no: 01264385 **Date established:** 1976
Turnover: £125m - £250m **No.of Employees:** 11 - 20
Product Groups: 37, 61

Date of Accounts	Dec 11	Dec 08	Dec 09
Sales Turnover	205m	204m	204m
Pre Tax Profit/Loss	25m	32m	35m
Working Capital	118m	49m	75m
Fixed Assets	27m	28m	28m
Current Assets	207m	108m	142m
Current Liabilities	78m	51m	59m

Markem-Imaje Ltd

Astor Road, Salford, M50 1DA
Tel: 0161-333 8400 **Fax:** 0161-707 5566
E-mail: kappleton@markem.com
Website: http://www.markem-imaje.com
Bank(s): Royal Bank of Scotland
Directors: K. Appleton (Co Sec)
Ultimate Holding Company: DOVER CORPORATION (U.S.A.)
Immediate Holding Company: MARKEM-IMAJE LIMITED
Registration no: 01940732 **Date established:** 1985
Turnover: £20m - £50m **No.of Employees:** 51 - 100 **Product Groups:** 27, 28, 42, 44

Date of Accounts	Dec 10	Dec 09	Dec 08
Sales Turnover	58m	58m	40m
Pre Tax Profit/Loss	14m	13m	16m
Working Capital	44m	50m	46m
Fixed Assets	15m	15m	5m
Current Assets	55m	60m	52m
Current Liabilities	9m	8m	4m

Mawdsley Brooks Ltd

Unit 3 South Langworthy Road, Salford, M50 2PW
Tel: 0161-742 3300 **Fax:** 0161-742 3301
E-mail: info@mawdsleys.co.uk
Website: http://www.mawdsleys.co.uk
Directors: S. Westall (Dir)
Ultimate Holding Company: MAWDSLEYS GROUP INVESTMENTS LIMITED
Immediate Holding Company: MAWDSLEY-BROOKS & COMPANY LIMITED
Registration no: 00044701 **Date established:** 1995
Turnover: £125m - £250m **No.of Employees:** 101 - 250
Product Groups: 31, 63

Date of Accounts	Mar 11	Mar 10	Mar 09
Sales Turnover	187m	322m	302m
Pre Tax Profit/Loss	4m	5m	4m
Working Capital	8m	11m	5m
Fixed Assets	9m	18m	16m
Current Assets	44m	70m	61m
Current Liabilities	3m	8m	7m

Brian Milligan Associates (Consultants in Occupational & Environmental Hygiene)

57 Wensley Road, Salford, M7 3GJ
Tel: 0161-792 2269 **Fax:** 0161-792 2269
E-mail: brian@brian-milligan.co.uk
Website: http://www.brian-milligan.co.uk
Directors: B. Milligan (Prop)
Turnover: Up to £250,000 **No.of Employees:** 1 - 10 **Product Groups:** 38, 54, 84, 85

N G K Berylco UK Ltd
Houston Park, Salford, M50 2RP
Tel: 0161-745 7162 **Fax:** 0161-745 7520
E-mail: enquiries@ngkberylco.co.uk
Website: http://www.ngkberylco.co.uk
Directors: S. Emsley (Prop), L. Mcnichol (MD)
Managers: L. Reising (Chief Acct)
Ultimate Holding Company: N G K INSULATORS LTD (JAPAN)
Immediate Holding Company: NGK BERYLCO UK, LTD.
Registration no: 02085285 **VAT No.:** GB 457 4017 48
Date established: 1986 **Turnover:** £2m - £5m **No.of Employees:** 1 - 10
Product Groups: 34, 35, 36, 37, 66

N T Stainless
Unit 6 Boston Court, Salford, M50 2GN
Tel: 0161-848 8990 **Fax:** 0161-848 6080
E-mail: sales@ntstainless.co.uk
Website: http://www.ntstainless.co.uk
Directors: C. Taylor (MD), M. Taylor (Dir)
Managers: N. Taylor (Mgr), T. Bond (Mgr)
Ultimate Holding Company: Canberra Wells Ltd
Immediate Holding Company: Canberra Wells Ltd
Registration no: 07407784 **VAT No.:** GB 306 9390 50
Date established: 1981 **No.of Employees:** 1 - 10 **Product Groups:** 26, 30, 34, 35, 36, 38, 39, 49, 61, 63, 66

Nortest Ltd
1 West Ashton Street, Salford, M50 2XS
Tel: 0161-745 9525 **Fax:** 0161-745 9527
E-mail: info@nortest.ltd.uk
Website: http://www.nortest.ltd.uk
Bank(s): National Westminster
Managers: S. Thompson (Admin Off)
Immediate Holding Company: NORTEST LIMITED
Registration no: 01502537 **VAT No.:** GB 325 0482 82
Date established: 1980 **Turnover:** £500,000 - £1m
No.of Employees: 11 - 20 **Product Groups:** 34, 37, 38, 39, 48, 52, 54, 83, 85, 86

Date of Accounts	Jun 11	Jun 10	Jun 09
Working Capital	-38	-48	-51
Fixed Assets	286	250	269
Current Assets	284	229	205

Parker Merchanting Ltd Depot
74 Liverpool Street, Salford, M5 4QP
Tel: 08451-202454 **Fax:** 0161-745 7152
E-mail: info.parker@hagemeyer.co.uk
Website: http://www.parker-direct.com
Directors: R. Farrington (Fin), R. Williams (MD)
Managers: M. Parsons (Ops Mgr), N. Brook, D. Tymon (Depot Mgr), D. Timans (Mgr)
Ultimate Holding Company: Hagemeyer N.V.
Immediate Holding Company: PARKER MERCHANTING LIMITED
Registration no: 00224779 **VAT No.:** GB 614 2136 80
Date established: 1927 **Turnover:** £75m - £125m
No.of Employees: 1 - 10 **Product Groups:** 22, 23, 24, 29, 30, 33, 37, 39, 40, 45, 63, 66, 68

Pellstrand Ltd
397 Bury New Road, Salford, M7 2BT
Tel: 0161-708 9459 **Fax:** 0161-792 2186
Directors: A. Vogiel (MD)
Immediate Holding Company: PELLSTRAND LIMITED
Registration no: 00870002 **VAT No.:** GB 147 1963 51
Date established: 1966 **No.of Employees:** 1 - 10 **Product Groups:** 23

Date of Accounts	Dec 11	Dec 10	Dec 09
Working Capital	-60	-40	-18
Fixed Assets	225	225	225
Current Assets	110	133	96

Pin Mill Textiles Ltd
Dreamscene House Park House Bridge Estate, Salford, M6 6JQ
Tel: 0161-737 3300 **Fax:** 0161-737 3100
E-mail: info@pinmill.com
Website: http://www.pinmill.com
Directors: M. Cowen (Prop)
Immediate Holding Company: PIN MILL TEXTILES LIMITED
Registration no: 00511181 **Date established:** 1952 **Turnover:** £5m - £10m
No.of Employees: 1 - 10 **Product Groups:** 63

Date of Accounts	Sep 11	Sep 10	Sep 09
Working Capital	617	583	500
Fixed Assets	588	603	606
Current Assets	3m	3m	4m

Premier Installation MCR Ltd
Unit Q1 Buffalo Court, Salford, M50 2QL
Tel: 0161-877 9575 **Fax:** 0161-877 6133
E-mail: mail@premier-installation.co.uk
Website: http://www.premier-installation.co.uk
Directors: N. Hampton (Dir)
Immediate Holding Company: PREMIER INSTALLATION M/CR LIMITED
Registration no: 03183374 **Date established:** 1996
No.of Employees: 1 - 10 **Product Groups:** 52

Date of Accounts	Nov 11	Nov 10	Nov 09
Working Capital	234	190	96
Fixed Assets	201	204	217
Current Assets	343	336	179

Prestige Fabrications UK Ltd
Cobden Street, Salford, M6 6 NA
Tel: 0161-736 7358 **Fax:** 0161-736 7358
Managers: D. Worthington (Mgr)
Immediate Holding Company: PRESTIGE FABRICATIONS (UK) LIMITED
Registration no: 05555701 **Date established:** 2005
No.of Employees: 1 - 10 **Product Groups:** 26, 35

Date of Accounts	Sep 11	Sep 10	Sep 09
Working Capital	-5	-8	-9
Fixed Assets	7	8	10
Current Assets	16	14	14

R P S Laboratories Ltd
Unit 12 Waters Edge Business Park Modwen Road, Salford, M5 3EZ
Tel: 0161-872 2443 **Fax:** 0161-877 3959
E-mail: rpsma@rpsgroup.com
Website: http://www.rpsgroup.com
Directors: G. Young (Fin), S. Cambell (Chief Op Offcr)
Ultimate Holding Company: R P S GROUP PLC
Immediate Holding Company: RPS LABORATORIES LIMITED
Registration no: 02368537 **Date established:** 1989
Turnover: £10m - £20m **No.of Employees:** 21 - 50 **Product Groups:** 40, 54, 85

Rapid Technologys
77 Pendleton Way, Salford, M6 5FW
Tel: 0161-736 6120
E-mail: sales@rapide-repro.co.uk
Website: http://www.rapide-repro.co.uk
Managers: M. Masoori (Mgr)
No.of Employees: 1 - 10 **Product Groups:** 37, 44, 77

Rehau Ltd
The Lowry, Pier 8 Salford Quays, Salford, M50 3AZ
Tel: 0121-344 2300 **Fax:** 0121-344 2301
E-mail: sheila.monaghan@rehau.com
Website: http://www.rehau.com
Managers: C. Haworth (Chief Mgr), C. Howarth (Chief Mgr), C. Pearson (Mgr)
Ultimate Holding Company: STAPLES INC (USA)
Immediate Holding Company: CORPORATE EXPRESS (HOLDINGS) LIMITED
Registration no: 00722004 **Date established:** 1948
Turnover: £75m - £125m **No.of Employees:** 21 - 50 **Product Groups:** 30, 31, 33

Resistance Technology Ltd
8 Worrall Street, Salford, M5 4TH
Tel: 0161-877 7345 **Fax:** 0161-877 8711
E-mail: info@resistance-technology.co.uk
Website: http://www.resistance-technology.co.uk
Bank(s): Barclays
Directors: P. Hartley (Dir)
Immediate Holding Company: RESISTANCE TECHNOLOGY LIMITED
Registration no: 02589015 **VAT No.:** GB 561 0936 49
Date established: 1991 **Turnover:** £500,000 - £1m
No.of Employees: 11 - 20 **Product Groups:** 29, 37, 40, 41

Date of Accounts	Mar 11	Mar 10	Mar 09
Working Capital	600	524	481
Fixed Assets	45	42	45
Current Assets	691	600	596

S M F Ltd
Willow Bank Works Whit Lane, Salford, M6 6JJ
Tel: 0161-736 4211 **Fax:** 0161-745 9367
E-mail: smfltd@hotmail.com
Website: http://www.smfltd.co.uk
Directors: A. Brooks (Dir)
Immediate Holding Company: S M F LIMITED
Registration no: 03853650 **Date established:** 1999
No.of Employees: 11 - 20 **Product Groups:** 46, 48

Date of Accounts	Oct 11	Oct 10	Oct 09
Working Capital	-63	-40	-23
Fixed Assets	71	18	23
Current Assets	283	287	275

Scan Coin
Dutch House 110 Broadway, Salford, M50 2UW
Tel: 0161-873 0500 **Fax:** 0161-873 0501
E-mail: dthornber@scancoin.co.uk
Website: http://www.scancoin.co.uk
Bank(s): HSBC Bank plc
Directors: J. Carr (MD), S. Fitton (Sales)
Managers: J. Yates (Fin Mgr), G. Pilch (Personnel)
Ultimate Holding Company: SCAN COIN AB (SWEDEN)
Immediate Holding Company: SCAN COIN LTD.
Registration no: 00518608 **Date established:** 1953 **Turnover:** £5m - £10m
No.of Employees: 51 - 100 **Product Groups:** 44, 49

Date of Accounts	Dec 11	Dec 10	Dec 09
Sales Turnover	8m	9m	7m
Pre Tax Profit/Loss	458	574	312
Working Capital	1m	2m	1m
Fixed Assets	447	478	433
Current Assets	4m	4m	3m
Current Liabilities	2m	2m	1m

Schawk Ltd
Kansas Avenue Boston Court, Salford, M50 2GN
Tel: 0161-872 9449 **Fax:** 0161-848 8441
E-mail: robert.moore@schawk.com
Website: http://www.schawk.com
Bank(s): Royal Bank of Scotland
Directors: I. Banks (Sales), J. Earl (Develop), R. Moore (MD), A. Seddon (Fin)
Immediate Holding Company: WEIR TECHNOLOGY
Registration no: 01008765 **VAT No.:** GB 698 8304 72
Date established: 1903 **Turnover:** £5m - £10m
No.of Employees: 101 - 250 **Product Groups:** 28

Scott Packaging Ltd
Hulme Street, Salford, M5 4PX
Tel: 0161-736 1337 **Fax:** 0161-745 7724
E-mail: sales@hsltd.co.uk
Website: http://www.hsltd.co.uk
Bank(s): Barclays, Manchester
Directors: T. Trotter (Fin), G. Gillies (Sales), N. Scott (Fin)
Managers: D. Holmes (Tech Serv Mgr)
Ultimate Holding Company: SCOTT GROUP INVESTMENTS LIMITED
Immediate Holding Company: HENRY SUTCLIFFE LIMITED
Registration no: 00339323 **VAT No.:** GB 145 7705 55
Date established: 1938 **Turnover:** £1m - £2m **No.of Employees:** 11 - 20
Product Groups: 25

Date of Accounts	Dec 11	Dec 10	Dec 09
Working Capital	51	564	463
Fixed Assets	N/A	28	34
Current Assets	51	991	909

Simon & Simon Security Ltd
Unit 12 95-103 Broughton Lane, Salford, M7 1UH
Tel: 0161-833 3232 **Fax:** 0161-833 3434
E-mail: joelmonath@aol.com
Directors: J. Monath (MD), M. Monath (Fin)
Immediate Holding Company: SIMON & SIMON SECURITY LIMITED
Registration no: 03838284 **VAT No.:** GB 741 3096 50
Date established: 1999 **Turnover:** £500,000 - £1m
No.of Employees: 1 - 10 **Product Groups:** 66

Date of Accounts	Dec 07	Dec 06	Dec 05
Working Capital	6	1	3
Fixed Assets	8	9	11
Current Assets	91	96	54
Current Liabilities	85	94	51

Smatex Ltd
Merlyn House Bridge Mills, Holland Street, Salford, M6 6EL
Tel: 0161-742280 **Fax:** 0161-737 5615
E-mail: info@smatex.co.uk
Website: http://www.smatex.com
Directors: D. Moss (Dir), A. Moss (Co Sec)
Managers: D. Moss (Sales Prom Mgr), A. Moss (Accounts)
Registration no: 01211656 **VAT No.:** GB 150 2636 96
Date established: 1983 **Turnover:** Up to £250,000
No.of Employees: 1 - 10 **Product Groups:** 37, 38

Date of Accounts	Jun 08	Jun 07	Jun 06
Sales Turnover	N/A	N/A	232
Pre Tax Profit/Loss	N/A	N/A	24
Working Capital	29	67	28
Fixed Assets	2	3	7
Current Assets	52	84	62
Current Liabilities	23	17	35
ROCE% (Return on Capital Employed)			68.2
ROT% (Return on Turnover)			10.2

Southern & Darwent
Frederick Road, Salford, M6 6BR
Tel: 0161-745 9287 **Fax:** 0161-745 9854
E-mail: salford@travisperkins.co.uk
Website: http://www.southern-darwent.co.uk
Managers: R. Kuzemko (Mgr), R. Wagner (Mgr)
Immediate Holding Company: Traus Perkins P.L.C.
Registration no: 00733503 **Turnover:** £2m - £5m
No.of Employees: 21 - 50 **Product Groups:** 25, 48

J D Stoward Salford Ltd
Dymun Works Missouri Avenue, Salford, M50 2NP
Tel: 0161-736 1238 **Fax:** 0161-736 8700
Directors: W. Mundy (MD)
Immediate Holding Company: J. D. STOWARD (SALFORD) LIMITED
Registration no: 01186491 **VAT No.:** GB 148 3711 62
Date established: 1974 **Turnover:** Up to £250,000
No.of Employees: 1 - 10 **Product Groups:** 34

Date of Accounts	Dec 11	Dec 10	Dec 09
Working Capital	-89	-86	-86
Fixed Assets	95	99	102
Current Assets	69	53	58
Current Liabilities	N/A	86	86

Swift
Matthew Elliott House 64 Broadway, Salford, M50 2TS
Tel: 0161-872 6262 **Fax:** 0161-877 2424
E-mail: info@swiftsecurity.com
Website: http://www.swiftsecurity.com
Directors: S. Bottomley (Fin), N. Jackson (Co Sec)
Managers: S. Barett (Personnel), C. Prunty (Tech Serv Mgr), M. Solman
Ultimate Holding Company: ELVERE LTD
Immediate Holding Company: SWIFT FIRE AND SECURITY GROUP PLC
Registration no: 01609444 **Date established:** 1982
Turnover: £10m - £20m **No.of Employees:** 101 - 250
Product Groups: 37, 40, 52, 67

Date of Accounts	May 11	May 10	May 09
Sales Turnover	15m	16m	15m
Pre Tax Profit/Loss	582	462	446
Working Capital	-78	-142	-556
Fixed Assets	7m	7m	7m
Current Assets	4m	5m	5m
Current Liabilities	3m	3m	3m

Tarmac Central
Fax Langley Road, Salford, M6 6JQ
Tel: 0161-737 5221 **Fax:** 0161-745 8035
E-mail: info@tarmac-central.co.uk
Website: http://www.tarmac.co.uk
Bank(s): Barclays
Managers: M. Elford (Chief Mgr)
Ultimate Holding Company: ANGLO AMERICAN PLC
Immediate Holding Company: TARMAC LIMITED
Registration no: 00453791 **VAT No.:** GB 532 3679 43
Date established: 1948 **Turnover:** £20m - £50m
No.of Employees: 21 - 50 **Product Groups:** 37

Date of Accounts	Dec 10	Dec 09	Dec 08
Sales Turnover	1069m	1247m	1566m
Pre Tax Profit/Loss	75m	-47m	-29m
Working Capital	-24m	25m	2m
Fixed Assets	1244m	1391m	1434m
Current Assets	321m	431m	447m
Current Liabilities	93m	168m	213m

Thomas Frederick & Co. Ltd
Linden Court House 52 Liverpool Street, Salford, M5 4LT
Tel: 0161-745 7761 **Fax:** 0161-737 6061
E-mail: jonathanshasha@tiscali.co.uk
Directors: J. Shasha (MD)
Managers: M. Yodaiken (Fin Mgr), J. Warhurst, S. Quinlivan (Sales Prom Mgr), M. Yodaiken (Fin Mgr)
Immediate Holding Company: THOMAS FREDERICK & COMPANY LIMITED
Registration no: 00361476 **VAT No.:** GB 145 7757 36
Date established: 1940 **Turnover:** £5m - £10m **No.of Employees:** 1 - 10
Product Groups: 63

Date of Accounts	Feb 12	Feb 11	Feb 10
Sales Turnover	N/A	6m	9m
Pre Tax Profit/Loss	N/A	-982	21
Working Capital	5m	5m	3m
Fixed Assets	58	80	96
Current Assets	6m	9m	9m
Current Liabilities	N/A	500	480

Toltec Systems
Exchange Quay, Salford, M5 3EQ
Tel: 0161-876 4447 **Fax:** 0161-876 4448
E-mail: admin@coltecsystems.co.uk
Website: http://www.toltec.it
Directors: S. Cornforth (Co Sec), T. Hughes (I.T. Dir)
Immediate Holding Company: TOLTEC SYSTEMS LIMITED
Registration no: 04085224 **VAT No.:** GB 764 8193 92
Date established: 2000 **Turnover:** £1m - £2m **No.of Employees:** 1 - 10
Product Groups: 37, 38, 39, 44, 52, 79, 84

Date of Accounts	Oct 11	Oct 10	Oct 09
Working Capital	21	28	203
Fixed Assets	76	51	68
Current Assets	142	182	203

The Training Centre
48 Kansas Avenue Salford Quays, Salford, M50 2GL
Tel: 0161-876 6027 **Fax:** 0161-876 6028
Website: http://www.thetrainingcentre.co.uk
Managers: D. Kellett (Trng Mgr)
Date established: 2001 **No.of Employees:** 1 - 10 **Product Groups:** 35, 39, 45

Travis Perkins plc
Lissadel Street Frederick Road, Salford, M6 6BR
Tel: 0161-736 8751 **Fax:** 0161-737 9744
E-mail: mark.cohen@travisperkin.co.uk
Website: http://www.travisperkins.co.uk
Bank(s): The Royal Bank of Scotland
Managers: C. Billington (Mgr)
Immediate Holding Company: TRAVIS PERKINS PLC
Registration no: 00824821 **Date established:** 1964 **Turnover:** £5m - £10m
No.of Employees: 21 - 50 **Product Groups:** 66

Date of Accounts	Dec 11	Dec 10	Dec 09
Sales Turnover	4779m	3153m	2931m
Pre Tax Profit/Loss	270m	197m	213m
Working Capital	133m	159m	248m
Fixed Assets	2771m	2749m	2108m
Current Assets	1421m	1329m	1035m
Current Liabilities	473m	412m	109m

Turner & Coates Ltd (Quality & Engineering Consultants)
34 Haddon Street Salford, Salford, M6 6BN
Tel: 0845-890 9870 **Fax:** 0845-890 9871
E-mail: info@turnerandcoates.com
Website: http://www.turnerandcoates.com
Directors: N. Coulborn (MD), N. Coulborn (Fin)
Immediate Holding Company: TURNER & COATES LIMITED
Registration no: 05395659 **Date established:** 2005
Turnover: £500,000 - £1m **No.of Employees:** 1 - 10 **Product Groups:** 85

Date of Accounts	Mar 11	Mar 10	Mar 09
Working Capital	4	5	10
Fixed Assets	3	1	1
Current Assets	78	25	55

Valbruna UK Ltd
Unit 1 Bute Street, Salford, M50 1DU
Tel: 0161-745 9190 **Fax:** 0161-745 9183
E-mail: david.lukeman@valbruna-uk.com
Website: http://www.valbruna-uk.com
Managers: D. Lukeman (District Mgr)
Ultimate Holding Company: AMENDUNI ACCIAIO SPA (ITALY)
Immediate Holding Company: VALBRUNA UK LIMITED
Registration no: 02015096 **Date established:** 1986
Turnover: £10m - £20m **No.of Employees:** 1 - 10 **Product Groups:** 34, 35

Date of Accounts	Dec 11	Dec 10	Dec 09
Sales Turnover	31m	24m	20m
Pre Tax Profit/Loss	1m	632	35
Working Capital	10m	7m	4m
Fixed Assets	4m	4m	4m
Current Assets	24m	20m	18m
Current Liabilities	1m	904	311

Versasteel
41 Cobden Street, Salford, M6 6WF
Tel: 0161-736 2297 **Fax:** 0161-745 7897
E-mail: adam@jwentwistle.com
Website: http://www.jwentwistle.com
Directors: A. Smallwood (Sales)
Ultimate Holding Company: HEYS-SHAW LIMITED
Immediate Holding Company: J.W. ENTWISTLE CO. LIMITED
Registration no: 00645276 **VAT No.:** GB 145 1760 77
Date established: 1959 **Turnover:** £500,000 - £1m
No.of Employees: 1 - 10 **Product Groups:** 48

Date of Accounts	Dec 09	Dec 08	Oct 11
Working Capital	505	481	5
Fixed Assets	376	405	N/A
Current Assets	911	869	613

Western Automation R&D
Unit 1 Boston Court, Salford, M50 2GN
Tel: 0161-877 0910 **Fax:** 0161-876 5243
E-mail: info@westernautomation.com
Website: http://www.westernautomation.com
Managers: J. Stephenson (District Mgr), P. Hitchin (Sales Prom Mgr)
Immediate Holding Company: U.K. Electric Ltd
Registration no: 00775728 **VAT No.:** GB 338 2468 41
Turnover: £250m - £500m **No.of Employees:** 1 - 10 **Product Groups:** 30, 37

Williams Fasteners
1 Missouri Avenue, Salford, M50 2NP
Tel: 0161-737 1628 **Fax:** 0161-848 7296
E-mail: phil.simpson@williamsfasteners.com
Website: http://www.williamsfasteners.com
Managers: P. Simpson (Mgr)
Immediate Holding Company: ALSECURE GROUP LIMITED
Registration no: 05880257 **Date established:** 1972
Turnover: £500,000 - £1m **No.of Employees:** 1 - 10 **Product Groups:** 30, 35, 49

Skelmersdale

The AA Group Ltd
Priorswood Place East Pimbo, Skelmersdale, WN8 9QB
Tel: 01695-50123 **Fax:** 01695-50133
E-mail: aa@taag.co.uk
Website: http://www.taag.co.uk
Directors: A. Prince (MD), A. Smith (Dir)
Managers: A. Lamb (Chief Acct), A. Harrison (Personnel)
Immediate Holding Company: The A.A. Group (Holdings) Ltd
Registration no: 04127100 **VAT No.:** GB 294 9633 07
Date established: 2000 **Turnover:** £10m - £20m **Product Groups:** 51, 52

Date of Accounts	Dec 07	Dec 06	Dec 05
Sales Turnover	14517	N/A	N/A
Pre Tax Profit/Loss	708	395	558
Working Capital	614	-9	66
Fixed Assets	485	493	429
Current Assets	3255	2676	2642
Current Liabilities	2641	2685	2576
Total Share Capital	1	1	1
ROCE% (Return on Capital Employed)	64.4	81.6	112.7
ROT% (Return on Turnover)	4.9		

Arena Access Ltd
15 Greenhey Place, Skelmersdale, WN8 9SA
Tel: 01695-559785 **Fax:** 01695-559826
E-mail: enquiries@arenaaccess.co.uk
Website: http://www.arenaaccess.co.uk
Registration no: 06537651 **Product Groups:** 14, 25, 27, 30, 33, 35, 37, 39, 40, 45, 49, 68, 83

Asco Numatics
2 Pit Hey Place, Skelmersdale, WN8 9PG
Tel: 01695-713600 **Fax:** 01695-729477
E-mail: steve.meadows@emerson.com
Website: http://www.asconumatics.co.uk
Managers: B. Kelly, K. Wright (Purch Mgr), S. Patterson (Comptroller), S. Meadows (Sales Prom Mgr), C. Blackledge (Personnel)
Ultimate Holding Company: EMERSON ELECTRIC CO INC (USA)
Immediate Holding Company: ASCO JOUCOMATIC LIMITED
Registration no: 02861557 **VAT No.:** GB 151 6534 78
Date established: 1993 **Turnover:** £10m - £20m
No.of Employees: 101 - 250 **Product Groups:** 36, 40, 66

Automation Supplies Ltd
Unit 1 Allied Business Centre Potter Place, Skelmersdale, WN8 9PW
Tel: 01772-681106 **Fax:** 08708-386591
E-mail: info@automation-supplies.com
Website: http://www.asconveyorsystems.co.uk
Directors: T. Murphy (MD)
Immediate Holding Company: AUTOMATION SUPPLIES LIMITED
Registration no: 04573357 **Date established:** 2002
Turnover: £250,000 - £500,000 **No.of Employees:** 1 - 10
Product Groups: 66

Date of Accounts	Mar 12	Mar 11	Mar 10
Working Capital	185	86	56
Fixed Assets	5	5	1
Current Assets	415	280	245

Beaconsfield Footwear Ltd
2 Peel Road, Skelmersdale, WN8 9PT
Tel: 01695-712720 **Fax:** 01695-712715
E-mail: admin@hotter.co.uk
Website: http://www.hottershoes.com
Directors: N. Davis (Co Sec), P. Davis (Co Sec), S. Houlgrave (Dir)
Managers: D. Ainsworth (Tech Serv Mgr), P. Spillane (Mktg Serv Mgr), K. Terry (Personnel), M. Pearce (Purch Mgr)
Ultimate Holding Company: HOTTER GROUP HOLDINGS LIMITED
Immediate Holding Company: BEACONSFIELD FOOTWEAR LIMITED
Registration no: 00641365 **Date established:** 1959
Turnover: £50m - £75m **No.of Employees:** 251 - 500 **Product Groups:** 22

Date of Accounts	Jan 10	Jan 09	Jan 08
Sales Turnover	44m	38m	37m
Pre Tax Profit/Loss	8m	5m	5m
Working Capital	16m	15m	11m
Fixed Assets	4m	3m	3m
Current Assets	20m	20m	16m
Current Liabilities	2m	3m	3m

Bodycote Heating Treatment Ltd
18 Westgate, Skelmersdale, WN8 8AZ
Tel: 01695-721361 **Fax:** 01695-50105
E-mail: derek.alty@bodycote.com
Website: http://www.bodycote.com
Bank(s): HSBC, Manchester
Managers: D. Alty, D. Cross (Admin Off), D. Webster (Personnel)
Immediate Holding Company: BODYCOTE INTERNATIONAL P.L.C.
Registration no: 01025652 **Turnover:** £5m - £10m
No.of Employees: 51 - 100 **Product Groups:** 48

Bodycote Metallurgical Coatings
13 Glebe Road, Skelmersdale, WN8 9JP
Tel: 01695-724474 **Fax:** 01695-558498
E-mail: info@bodycote.com
Website: http://www.bodycote.com
Managers: K. Roper (Mgr)
Ultimate Holding Company: BODYCOTE INTERNATIONAL P.L.C.
Immediate Holding Company: BODYCOTE PLC
Registration no: 00519057 **VAT No.:** GB 222 4882 72
No.of Employees: 21 - 50 **Product Groups:** 48

Buswell Machine Electronics
Peel House Peel Road, Skelmersdale, WN8 9PT
Tel: 01695-726518 **Fax:** 01695-726518
E-mail: rbuswell@buswell.co.uk
Website: http://www.buswell.co.uk
Directors: R. Buswell (Dir), R. Buswell (MD), C. Buswell (Co Sec), C. Buswell (Fin)
Ultimate Holding Company: SURETANK GROUP LIMITED
Immediate Holding Company: BUSWELL MACHINE ELECTRONICS LIMITED
Registration no: 04733562 **VAT No.:** GB 344 1969 41
Date established: 2003 **Turnover:** Up to £250,000
No.of Employees: 1 - 10 **Product Groups:** 37, 84

Date of Accounts	Apr 08	Apr 07
Working Capital	6	6
Fixed Assets	16	16
Current Assets	23	26
Current Liabilities	17	20

C M E Services
44 Bearncroft, Skelmersdale, WN8 9HG
Tel: 07904-162496 **Fax:** 07904-162496
E-mail: neilcmeservices@aol.com
Directors: N. Cartmill (Prop)
Turnover: Up to £250,000 **No.of Employees:** 1 - 10 **Product Groups:** 35, 48

Carrylift Materials Handling Ltd
Peel Road, Skelmersdale, WN8 9PT
Tel: 01695-455000 **Fax:** 01695-455099
E-mail: info@carryliftgroup.com
Website: http://www.carryliftgroup.com
Directors: D. Martin (Fin)
Managers: R. Thorp (Tech Serv Mgr), S. Routledge (Sales Prom Mgr), J. Houghton (Mktg Serv Mgr), A. Walker (Personnel)
Ultimate Holding Company: CORPACQ PLC
Immediate Holding Company: CARRYLIFT MATERIALS HANDLING LIMITED
Registration no: 02221891 **Date established:** 1988
Turnover: £10m - £20m **No.of Employees:** 101 - 250 **Product Groups:** 68

Date of Accounts	Dec 11	Dec 10	Mar 10
Sales Turnover	17m	14m	18m
Pre Tax Profit/Loss	4m	3m	103
Working Capital	9m	7m	5m
Fixed Assets	3m	3m	3m
Current Assets	15m	14m	15m
Current Liabilities	2m	3m	5m

Cordstrap Ltd
Paddock Road, Skelmersdale, WN8 9PL
Tel: 01695-554700 **Fax:** 01695-556644
E-mail: sales.uk@cordstrap.net
Website: http://www.cordstrap.net
Managers: D. Pilkington (Purch Mgr), D. Boult (Nat Sales Mgr), A. Green (Comm)
Ultimate Holding Company: CORDSTRAP BV (NETHERLANDS)
Immediate Holding Company: CORDSTRAP LIMITED
Registration no: 02211068 **Date established:** 1988 **Turnover:** £5m - £10m
No.of Employees: 11 - 20 **Product Groups:** 23, 29, 32, 45

Date of Accounts	Mar 12	Mar 11	Mar 10
Sales Turnover	6m	5m	5m
Pre Tax Profit/Loss	460	456	368
Working Capital	452	1m	790
Fixed Assets	382	414	427
Current Assets	2m	2m	2m
Current Liabilities	346	327	276

Dynamic Battery Services Ltd
Unit 1 Gillibrands Road, Skelmersdale, WN8 9TA
Tel: 01695-557575 **Fax:** 01695-557676
E-mail: paul.buttrick@dynamicbatteries.co.uk
Website: http://www.dynamicbatteries.com
Directors: P. Buttrick (Co Sec)
Ultimate Holding Company: ALTRON LTD (REPUBLIC OF SOUTH AFRICA)
Immediate Holding Company: DYNAMIC BATTERY SERVICES LIMITED
Registration no: 02902484 **Date established:** 1994 **Turnover:** £5m - £10m
No.of Employees: 11 - 20 **Product Groups:** 37, 68

Date of Accounts	Feb 08	Feb 11	Feb 10
Working Capital	2m	3m	2m
Fixed Assets	24	20	24
Current Assets	3m	3m	3m

Europanel UK Ltd
1 Gerrard Place, Skelmersdale, WN8 9SU
Tel: 01695-731033 **Fax:** 01695-727489
E-mail: info@europanelonline.co.uk
Website: http://www.europanelonline.co.uk
Directors: P. Rooney (MD)
Ultimate Holding Company: DOORPOINT LIMITED
Immediate Holding Company: EUROPANEL (HOLDINGS) LIMITED
Registration no: 04016487 **VAT No.:** GB 643 6547 24
Date established: 2000 **Turnover:** £5m - £10m **No.of Employees:** 1 - 10
Product Groups: 25, 27, 30, 31

Date of Accounts	May 12	May 11	May 10
Working Capital	-160	-160	-160
Fixed Assets	177	177	177
Current Liabilities	N/A	160	160

Fasttrack Fasteners
4 Pilling Place, Skelmersdale, WN8 9PF
Tel: 01695-556611 **Fax:** 01695-556633
E-mail: fastracksales@btconnect.com
Directors: R. Gater (Dir), B. Rigby (Sales)
Immediate Holding Company: FASTRACK FASTENERS LIMITED
Registration no: 04389379 **Date established:** 2002
No.of Employees: 1 - 10 **Product Groups:** 29, 35, 36, 66

Date of Accounts	Aug 11	Aug 10	Aug 09
Working Capital	273	253	264
Fixed Assets	N/A	3	10
Current Assets	440	381	380

Glaston Compressor Services Ltd
Greenhey Place, Skelmersdale, WN8 9SA
Tel: 01695-51010 **Fax:** 01695-50055
E-mail: michael@glaston.com
Website: http://www.glastoncompressors.co.uk
Directors: M. Douglas (MD)
Managers: J. Noon (Chief Mgr)
Ultimate Holding Company: MICALTON LIMITED
Immediate Holding Company: GLASTON COMPRESSOR SERVICES LIMITED
Registration no: 01431973 **Date established:** 1979 **Turnover:** £2m - £5m
No.of Employees: 11 - 20 **Product Groups:** 36, 40, 68

Date of Accounts	Jun 11	Jun 10	Jun 09
Working Capital	1m	28	840
Fixed Assets	297	289	310
Current Assets	3m	2m	3m

Gouldhall Computer Services Ltd
6 Pikelaw Place, Skelmersdale, WN8 9PP
Tel: 01695-716550 **Fax:** 01695-723711
E-mail: info@gouldhall.com
Website: http://www.gouldhall.com
Directors: B. Gray (Ptnr)
Immediate Holding Company: GOULD HALL COMPUTER SERVICES LIMITED
Registration no: 07574113 **VAT No.:** GB 401 2099 04
Date established: 2011 **Turnover:** £1m - £2m **No.of Employees:** 21 - 50
Product Groups: 44, 79

J K Guest
Stanley Way Stanley Industrial Estate, Skelmersdale, WN8 8EA
Tel: 01257-425742 **Fax:** 01257-426042
E-mail: jkguestpro@gmail.com
Website: http://www.jkguest.co.uk

see next page

J K Guest - Cont'd

Directors: J. Guest (MD)
Immediate Holding Company: LOCKHURST HOLDINGS LIMITED
Registration no: 02179787 **Date established:** 1987
No.of Employees: 21 - 50 **Product Groups:** 33, 45, 51

Date of Accounts	May 11	May 10	May 03
Working Capital	26	26	26
Current Assets	26	26	26

Kirkham Engineering Co. Ltd

Prestwood Place, Skelmersdale, WN8 9QE
Tel: 01695-727401 **Fax:** 01695-50407
E-mail: email@kirkhamengineering.co.uk
Website: http://www.kirkhamengineering.co.uk
Bank(s): Barclays
Directors: B. Lynam (Fin)
Immediate Holding Company: KIRKHAM ENGINEERING (HOLDINGS) LIMITED
Registration no: 00554106 **VAT No.:** GB 164 0618 77
Date established: 1955 **Turnover:** £1m - £2m **No.of Employees:** 21 - 50
Product Groups: 35, 48

Date of Accounts	Feb 12	Feb 11	Feb 10
Working Capital	342	412	387
Fixed Assets	275	275	275
Current Assets	349	419	420

M & D Cleaning Supplies Ltd

Grove Road Upholland, Skelmersdale, WN8 0LH
Tel: 01695-632765 **Fax:** 01695-632760
E-mail: sales@mandd.co.uk
Website: http://www.mandd.co.uk
Directors: M. Trevarton (Dir)
Immediate Holding Company: M & D CLEANING SUPPLIES LIMITED
Registration no: 02095989 **Date established:** 1987 **Turnover:** £1m - £2m
No.of Employees: 11 - 20 **Product Groups:** 24, 27, 30, 40, 63, 66

Date of Accounts	Apr 12	Apr 11	Apr 10
Working Capital	297	291	233
Fixed Assets	997	1m	996
Current Assets	1m	1m	1m

Matalan Ltd

Gillibrands Road, Skelmersdale, WN8 9TB
Tel: 01695-552400 **Fax:** 01695-552401
Website: http://www.matalan.co.uk
Bank(s): Barclays
Directors: J. Mills (Dir), P. Gilbert (Fin)
Ultimate Holding Company: MISSOURI TOP CO LTD (GUERNSEY)
Immediate Holding Company: MATALAN LIMITED
Registration no: 01579910 **VAT No.:** GB 534 5886 16
Date established: 1981 **Turnover:** £2m - £5m
No.of Employees: 501 - 1000 **Product Groups:** 61

Date of Accounts	Feb 09	Feb 10	Feb 11
Pre Tax Profit/Loss	-100	19m	60m
Working Capital	65m	85m	85m
Fixed Assets	14m	14m	14m
Current Assets	67m	86m	146m
Current Liabilities	300	300	300

Mechan Controls plc

14 Seddon Place Stanley Industrial Estate, Skelmersdale, WN8 8EB
Tel: 01695-722264 **Fax:** 01695-729664
E-mail: sales@mechancontrols.co.uk
Website: http://www.mechancontrols.co.uk
Bank(s): National Westminster Bank Plc
Directors: P. Knowles (Sales & Mktg), R. Parkinson (Co Sec), W. Boardman (MD)
Immediate Holding Company: MECHAN CONTROLS PLC
Registration no: 03802853 **Date established:** 1999 **Turnover:** £2m - £5m
No.of Employees: 11 - 20 **Product Groups:** 37, 40

Date of Accounts	Dec 11	Dec 10	Dec 09
Sales Turnover	3m	3m	3m
Pre Tax Profit/Loss	400	506	421
Working Capital	867	709	460
Fixed Assets	2m	1m	1m
Current Assets	2m	1m	963
Current Liabilities	350	318	238

Metal Deck Ltd

1a Prestwood Place, Skelmersdale, WN8 9QE
Tel: 01695-555070 **Fax:** 01695-555180
E-mail: sales@metaldeck.ltd.uk
Website: http://www.metaldeck.ltd.uk
Directors: G. Hewitt (MD), A. Price (MD)
Managers: J. Dougal (Chief Mgr), A. Harris (Mgr)
Ultimate Holding Company: METALDECK HOLDINGS LIMITED
Immediate Holding Company: METALDECK LIMITED
Registration no: 01752918 **Date established:** 1983 **Turnover:** £5m - £10m
No.of Employees: 21 - 50 **Product Groups:** 25, 29, 30, 35, 45, 48, 52, 66

Date of Accounts	Dec 10	Dec 09	Dec 08
Sales Turnover	8m	8m	11m
Pre Tax Profit/Loss	-209	109	634
Working Capital	-199	-39	635
Fixed Assets	855	951	1m
Current Assets	1m	2m	3m
Current Liabilities	282	436	550

J K Middleton Surgical Engineering & Research Centre

9a School Lane Upholland, Skelmersdale, WN8 0LW
Tel: 01695-632519 **Fax:** 01695-625743
Managers: J. Middleton (Mgr)
Date established: 1972 **No.of Employees:** 1 - 10 **Product Groups:** 36, 42, 67

Molecular Control Systems Ltd

Unit 1 Greetby Place, Skelmersdale, WN8 9UL
Tel: 01695-566700 **Fax:** 01695-50329
E-mail: mary.webb@porpoise.co.uk
Website: http://www.porpoise.co.uk/service.html
Directors: M. Webb (Fin)
Immediate Holding Company: MOLECULAR CONTROL SYSTEMS LIMITED
Registration no: 05059068 **VAT No.:** GB 374 1341 66
Date established: 2004 **Turnover:** Up to £250,000
No.of Employees: 1 - 10 **Product Groups:** 37, 38, 44, 45

Date of Accounts	Dec 11	Dec 10	Dec 09
Working Capital	48	63	25
Fixed Assets	3	4	6
Current Assets	77	83	85

Noble Engineering Services Ltd

Greenhey Place, Skelmersdale, WN8 9SA
Tel: 01695-724764 **Fax:** 01695-557573
E-mail: enquiries@nobleeng.co.uk
Website: http://www.nobleeng.co.uk
Bank(s): National Westminster
Directors: S. Barker (MD), V. Lewis (Fin)
Ultimate Holding Company: MICALTON LIMITED
Immediate Holding Company: NOBLE ENGINEERING SERVICES LIMITED
Registration no: 06554867 **Date established:** 2008
No.of Employees: 21 - 50 **Product Groups:** 38, 84

Date of Accounts	Jan 12	Apr 10	Apr 09
Working Capital	-12	N/A	N/A
Fixed Assets	89	N/A	N/A
Current Assets	445	N/A	N/A

Northern Packaging Ltd

Selby Place Stanley Industrial Estate, Skelmersdale, WN8 8EF
Tel: 01695-731445 **Fax:** 01695-51865
E-mail: info@northern-packaging.co.uk
Website: http://www.northern-packaging.co.uk
Bank(s): Royal Bank of Scotland
Directors: J. McEvoy (Fin), P. Bunting (MD), J. Mcevoy (Fin)
Managers: B. Dack (Comm), M. Gogerty (Ops Mgr)
Immediate Holding Company: NORTHERN PACKAGING LIMITED
Registration no: 01471317 **VAT No.:** GB 344 0562 76
Date established: 1980 **Turnover:** £10m - £20m
No.of Employees: 51 - 100 **Product Groups:** 27

Date of Accounts	Dec 11	Dec 10	Dec 09
Sales Turnover	12m	10m	8m
Pre Tax Profit/Loss	1m	68	100
Working Capital	2m	2m	2m
Fixed Assets	2m	3m	3m
Current Assets	4m	3m	3m
Current Liabilities	705	908	653

Nutriculture

3-5 Paddock Road, Skelmersdale, WN8 9PL
Tel: 01695-554080 **Fax:** 01695-554081
E-mail: sales@nutriculture.com
Website: http://www.nutriculture.com
Bank(s): Barclays
Directors: C. Molyneaux (MD), J. Neely (Co Sec), M. Molyneux (Fin)
Managers: G. Jones (Sales Prom Mgr)
Registration no: 01281894 **VAT No.:** GB 166 6480 38
Date established: 1975 **Turnover:** £1m - £2m **No.of Employees:** 21 - 50
Product Groups: 30, 40, 41, 42, 66

Date of Accounts	Nov 07	Nov 06	Nov 05
Working Capital	474	531	762
Fixed Assets	1427	1157	944
Current Assets	1001	984	1109
Current Liabilities	527	453	347
Total Share Capital	50	50	50

Ormrod Diesel

Unit 4 Peel Industrial Estate Peel Road, Skelmersdale, WN8 9PT
Tel: 01695-731847 **Fax:** 01695-51925
E-mail: julie@ormrod-diesels.co.uk
Website: http://www.ormroddiesels.com
Directors: D. Ormrod (MD)
Managers: J. Swift (Fin Mgr)
Immediate Holding Company: ORMROD ENGINEERING SERVICES LIMITED
Registration no: 05003478 **Date established:** 2003
Turnover: £500,000 - £1m **No.of Employees:** 11 - 20 **Product Groups:** 84

Date of Accounts	May 09
Working Capital	-3
Current Liabilities	3

P E S Ltd (Perimeter Equipment Services)

15 Greenhey Place, Skelmersdale, WN8 9SA
Tel: 01695-559785 **Fax:** 01695-559826
E-mail: post@perimeterequipmentservices.co.uk
Website: http://www.perimeterequipmentservices.co.uk
Registration no: 04362110 **Date established:** 2002 **Product Groups:** 25, 30, 33, 35, 36, 37, 39, 45, 49, 66, 68, 83

Phoenix Lighting

18 Grimrod Place, Skelmersdale, WN8 9UU
Tel: 01695-733068
Website: http://www.phoenix-lighting.co.uk
Directors: N. Davies (Fin), N. Davies (MD)
Immediate Holding Company: HAMSARD 2663 LIMITED
Registration no: 04732250 **Date established:** 2003
No.of Employees: 1 - 10 **Product Groups:** 37, 67

Date of Accounts	Sep 10	Sep 09	Sep 08
Working Capital	-178	-176	-151
Fixed Assets	32	39	45
Current Assets	39	84	163
Current Liabilities	N/A	N/A	184

Plastic Sheets

West Lancashire Investment Centre Maple View, Skelmersdale, WN8 9TG
Tel: 0800-3284299
E-mail: contact@plastic-sheets.co.uk
Website: http://www.plastic-sheets.co.uk
Managers: D. Kay (Mgr), J. Jakes
Immediate Holding Company: PLASTIC MAN MORECAMBE LTD
Registration no: 04211121 **Date established:** 2001
No.of Employees: 1 - 10 **Product Groups:** 80

Power Efficient Systems Ltd

15 Greenhey Place, Skelmersdale, WN8 9SA
Tel: 01695-559785 **Fax:** 01695-559826
E-mail: post@pesgroupltd.co.uk
Website: http://www.powerefficientsystems.co.uk
Directors: G. Vizard (MD)
Immediate Holding Company: POWER EFFICIENT SYSTEMS LIMITED
Registration no: 04362110 **Date established:** 2002
No.of Employees: 1 - 10 **Product Groups:** 37, 39, 40, 54, 67

Date of Accounts	Jan 12	Jan 11	Jan 10
Working Capital	81	98	71
Fixed Assets	20	20	22
Current Assets	169	214	128

Riverdale Colour

Unit 6 Greetby Place, Skelmersdale, WN8 9UL
Tel: 01695-550115
Website: http://www.riverdalecolor.com
Directors: I. Bentley (Fin)
Immediate Holding Company: RIVERDALE COLOUR LIMITED
Registration no: 05297474 **Date established:** 2004
Turnover: Up to £250,000 **No.of Employees:** 1 - 10 **Product Groups:** 32, 38

Date of Accounts	Nov 10	Nov 09	Nov 08
Working Capital	2	-16	-7
Fixed Assets	20	24	27
Current Assets	105	59	95

S B Training UK Ltd

7 Glebe Road, Skelmersdale, WN8 9JP
Tel: 01695-735335 **Fax:** 01695-735287
E-mail: info@sbtrainingltd.co.uk
Website: http://www.sbtrainingltd.co.uk
Directors: J. Beaumont (MD)
Immediate Holding Company: SB TRAINING UK LIMITED
Registration no: 05792049 **Date established:** 2006
Turnover: Up to £250,000 **No.of Employees:** 11 - 20 **Product Groups:** 35, 39, 45

Date of Accounts	Apr 11	Apr 10	Apr 09
Working Capital	44	57	34
Fixed Assets	88	81	68
Current Assets	372	241	208

S V R Plastics Ltd

Units 5-6 Greenhey Place, Skelmersdale, WN8 9SA
Tel: 01695-50717 **Fax:** 01695-50052
E-mail: sales@svrplastics.co.uk
Website: http://www.svrplastics.co.uk
Bank(s): National Westminster
Directors: J. Rose (Sales), S. Rose (MD)
Immediate Holding Company: SVR PLASTICS LIMITED
Registration no: 04102611 **Date established:** 2000
Turnover: £500,000 - £1m **No.of Employees:** 11 - 20
Product Groups: 29, 30, 33, 34, 36, 38, 39, 40, 42

Date of Accounts	Dec 11	Dec 10	Dec 09
Working Capital	22	-28	-42
Fixed Assets	85	45	60
Current Assets	208	149	142

Scott International Ltd

Pimbo Road, Skelmersdale, WN8 9RA
Tel: 01695-727171 **Fax:** 01695-711775
E-mail: plarge@tycoint.com
Website: http://www.scottint.com
Bank(s): Barclays
Directors: A. Martin (Dir), S. Burns (Fin)
Ultimate Holding Company: TYCO INTERNATIONAL LIMITED (SWITZERLAND)
Immediate Holding Company: SCOTT HEALTH & SAFETY LIMITED
Registration no: 00413886 **VAT No.:** GB 864 4260 18
Date established: 1946 **Turnover:** £500m - £1,000m
No.of Employees: 251 - 500 **Product Groups:** 24, 30, 31, 33, 37, 38, 39, 40, 41, 42, 45, 49, 52, 54, 63, 66, 67, 84

Date of Accounts	Sep 11	Sep 10	Sep 09
Sales Turnover	57m	45m	35m
Pre Tax Profit/Loss	5m	3m	1m
Working Capital	12m	32m	30m
Fixed Assets	6m	6m	6m
Current Assets	24m	43m	38m
Current Liabilities	3m	3m	2m

Set Europe Ltd

15-17 Seddon Place Stanley Industrial Estate, Skelmersdale, WN8 8EB
Tel: 01695-455400 **Fax:** 0870-750 3440
E-mail: wayne.ash@sanko.co.uk
Website: http://www.sankogosei.com
Directors: J. Harris (Fin), L. Tabner (MD)
Managers: P. Gault (Tech Serv Mgr)
Immediate Holding Company: SET EUROPE LIMITED
Registration no: 04684150 **VAT No.:** GB 812 5183 52
Date established: 2003 **Turnover:** £5m - £10m **No.of Employees:** 11 - 20
Product Groups: 29, 30, 32, 33, 36, 38, 39, 40, 42, 46, 48, 68, 84

Date of Accounts	May 11	May 10	May 09
Sales Turnover	5m	2m	4m
Pre Tax Profit/Loss	317	22	49
Working Capital	961	745	804
Fixed Assets	109	95	14
Current Assets	4m	2m	2m
Current Liabilities	2m	541	1m

Shad Fork Trucks Ltd

2 Garnett Place, Skelmersdale, WN8 9UB
Tel: 01695-724651 **Fax:** 01695-50592
E-mail: sales@shadgroup.co.uk
Website: http://www.shadgroup.co.uk
Directors: P. Byrne (MD)
Immediate Holding Company: SHAD FORK TRUCKS (LIVERPOOL) LIMITED
Registration no: 01276700 **Date established:** 1976
No.of Employees: 1 - 10 **Product Groups:** 35, 39, 45

Date of Accounts	Oct 11	Oct 10	Oct 09
Working Capital	-157	-549	-382
Fixed Assets	903	1m	1m
Current Assets	460	817	954

Leroy Somer

2 Potter Place Pimbo, Skelmersdale, WN8 9PW
Tel: 01695-554100 **Fax:** 01695-554117
E-mail: skelmersdale@leroysomer.co.uk
Website: http://www.leroysomer.com
Directors: K. Court (MD)
Managers: Z. Wilson (Personnel), K. Hauthon (Mgr)
Ultimate Holding Company: EMERSON ELECTRIC CO INC (USA)
Immediate Holding Company: LEROY SOMER LIMITED
Registration no: 00649756 **VAT No.:** GB 222 7516 82
Date established: 1960 **Turnover:** £20m - £50m
No.of Employees: 21 - 50 **Product Groups:** 48

Date of Accounts	Aug 11	Aug 10	Aug 09
Sales Turnover	30m	26m	24m
Pre Tax Profit/Loss	984	265	961
Working Capital	5m	4m	4m
Fixed Assets	41	32	6
Current Assets	11m	9m	8m
Current Liabilities	1m	695	578

Standish Metal Treatments

Potter Place, Skelmersdale, WN8 9PW
Tel: 01695-455977 **Fax:** 01695-728835
E-mail: stuart.croft@standishmetal.co.uk
Website: http://www.standishmetal.co.uk
Bank(s): Natwest
Directors: S. Croft (Dir), S. Croft (Dir)
Managers: S. Waywell (Mktg Serv Mgr), H. Croft (Buyer)
Immediate Holding Company: STANDISH METAL TREATMENT LIMITED
Registration no: 02607774 **VAT No.:** GB 535 0893 38
Date established: 1991 **Turnover:** £1m - £2m **No.of Employees:** 21 - 50
Product Groups: 48

Date of Accounts	May 11	May 10	May 09
Working Capital	-416	-477	-461
Fixed Assets	631	675	689
Current Assets	2m	2m	1m

Tammer UK Ltd

34 Greenhey Place East Gillibrands, Skelmersdale, WN8 9SA
Tel: 01695-727994 **Fax:** 01695-724456
E-mail: sales@tammer.co.uk
Website: http://www.tammeruk.co.uk
Directors: S. Taylor (Fin), J. Taylor (MD)
Immediate Holding Company: TAMMER UK LIMITED
Registration no: 04498909 **Date established:** 2002
Turnover: £500,000 - £1m **No.of Employees:** 1 - 10 **Product Groups:** 68

Date of Accounts	Aug 11	Aug 10	Aug 09
Working Capital	23	28	32
Fixed Assets	5	8	13
Current Assets	164	119	131

Trak-Rap

Unit 6 Greetby Place, Skelmersdale, WN8 9UL
Tel: 01695-555576
E-mail: sales@trakrap.com
Website: http://www.trakrap.com
Managers: A. Bumferque (Mgr)
Ultimate Holding Company: MICALTON LIMITED
Immediate Holding Company: GLASTON COMPRESSOR SERVICES LIMITED
Registration no: 02848795 **Date established:** 1979
No.of Employees: 1 - 10 **Product Groups:** 38, 42

Trelleborg Offshore Ltd

Stanley Way Stanley Industrial Estate, Skelmersdale, WN8 8EA
Tel: 01695-712000 **Fax:** 01695-712 111
E-mail: offshore@trelleborg.com
Website: http://www.trelleborg.com
Directors: M. Buxton (Fin)
Managers: D. Harmer (Tech Serv Mgr), D. McDonnell (Personnel), S. Dorrington (Mgr), C. Kelsall (Purch Mgr)
Ultimate Holding Company: LOCKHURST HOLDINGS LIMITED
Immediate Holding Company: LOCKHURST HOLDINGS LIMITED
Registration no: 00978141 **Date established:** 1987 **Turnover:** £5m - £10m
No.of Employees: 251 - 500 **Product Groups:** 32

Date of Accounts	May 11	May 10	May 03
Working Capital	26	26	26
Current Assets	26	26	26

Turtle Wax Ltd

East Gillibrands, Skelmersdale, WN8 9TX
Tel: 01695-722161 **Fax:** 01695-716621
E-mail: mwilliams@turtlewax.ltd.uk
Website: http://www.turtlewax.ltd.uk
Bank(s): Barclays, St. Helens
Directors: M. Williams (Dir), P. Smith (Sales & Mktg)
Managers: J. White (Tech Serv Mgr), R. Aston (Personnel), M. Williams
Immediate Holding Company: TURTLE WAX LIMITED
Registration no: 00836643 **VAT No.:** GB 151 6156 84
Date established: 1965 **Turnover:** £10m - £20m
No.of Employees: 51 - 100 **Product Groups:** 32, 68

Date of Accounts	Dec 11	Dec 10	Dec 09
Sales Turnover	11m	11m	10m
Pre Tax Profit/Loss	553	472	103
Working Capital	4m	4m	3m
Fixed Assets	555	591	712
Current Assets	6m	6m	5m
Current Liabilities	2m	2m	2m

Tyco Valves & Controls Distribution UK Ltd

White Moss Business Park Moss Lane View, Skelmersdale, WN8 9TN
Tel: 01695-554800 **Fax:** 01695-554835
E-mail: eudirectors@tyco.com
Website: http://www.tyco.com
Bank(s): National Westminster Bank Plc
Directors: I. Gascull (Sales & Mktg), J. Millar (MD), S. Redford (MD)
Managers: J. Chandler (I.T. Exec)
Ultimate Holding Company: Tyco International Ltd
Immediate Holding Company: Keystone Valve (U.K.) Ltd
Registration no: SC202028 **VAT No.:** GB 707 9842 03
Date established: 2000 **Turnover:** £20m - £50m
No.of Employees: 101 - 250 **Product Groups:** 36

Unique Integrated Systems

3a-3b Selby Place Stanley Industrial Estate, Skelmersdale, WN8 8EF
Tel: 01695-50332 **Fax:** 01695-50644
E-mail: sales@uis-security.co.uk
Website: http://www.uis-security.co.uk
Directors: J. Hewson (Co Sec), P. Brown (Dir), M. Ashall (Dir)
Immediate Holding Company: UNIQUE INTEGRATED SYSTEMS LIMITED
Registration no: 02621698 **Date established:** 1991
Turnover: £250,000 - £500,000 **No.of Employees:** 21 - 50
Product Groups: 36, 40, 52

Date of Accounts	Jun 12	Jun 11	Jun 10
Working Capital	174	164	264
Fixed Assets	287	295	216
Current Assets	639	684	793

Vivalis Ltd

22 Grimrod Place, Skelmersdale, WN8 9UU
Tel: 01695-727317 **Fax:** 01932-733401
E-mail: contactus@vivalis.co.uk
Website: http://www.vivalis.co.uk
Directors: M. Hooper (Sales), A. Kokshoorn (Mkt Research), G. Lynch Staunton (Dir), L. Ring (Co Sec)
Managers: D. Hill (Tech Serv Mgr), N. Parkinson (Personnel)
Ultimate Holding Company: IWP INTERNATIONAL PUBLIC LIMITED COMPANY
Immediate Holding Company: CONSTANCE CARROLL HOLDINGS LIMITED
Registration no: 01637008 **Date established:** 1982
Turnover: £10m - £20m **No.of Employees:** 101 - 250 **Product Groups:** 63

Date of Accounts	Mar 11	Mar 10	Mar 09
Pre Tax Profit/Loss	N/A	406	N/A
Working Capital	13	13m	12
Fixed Assets	N/A	150	N/A
Current Assets	13	13m	12

West Lancashire Forklift Co.

Pendle Place, Skelmersdale, WN8 9PN
Tel: 01695-728826 **Fax:** 01695-728826
E-mail: sales@westlancsforklift.com
Website: http://www.westlancsforklift.com
Directors: R. Dee (Dir)
Immediate Holding Company: WEST LANCASHIRE FORKLIFT COMPANY LIMITED
Registration no: 06125555 **Date established:** 2007
No.of Employees: 1 - 10 **Product Groups:** 35, 39, 45

Date of Accounts	Feb 12	Feb 11	Feb 10
Working Capital	-169	-171	-173
Fixed Assets	170	172	178
Current Assets	77	87	95

Thornton Cleveleys

AGC Chemicals Ltd

Hill House International, Thornton Cleveleys, FY5 4QD
Tel: 01253-861800 **Fax:** 01253-861950
E-mail: susie.claridge@fluon.co.uk
Website: http://www.fluon.co.uk
Bank(s): National Westminster Bank Plc
Managers: S. Claridge
Ultimate Holding Company: ASAHI GLASS CO LTD (JAPAN)
Immediate Holding Company: AGC CHEMICALS EUROPE, LTD.
Registration no: 03825057 **VAT No.:** GB 732 8037 42
Date established: 1999 **Turnover:** £75m - £125m
No.of Employees: 101 - 250 **Product Groups:** 30, 31, 32, 42

Date of Accounts	Dec 11	Dec 10	Dec 09
Sales Turnover	92m	82m	64m
Pre Tax Profit/Loss	7m	582	-15m
Working Capital	1m	113	-23m
Fixed Assets	24m	25m	26m
Current Assets	41m	34m	24m
Current Liabilities	5m	3m	3m

Amcron Pipework

Preston House Long Meadow Lane, Red Marsh Industrial Estate, Thornton Cleveleys, FY5 4JT
Tel: 01253-829878 **Fax:** 01253-856175
Website: http://www.amcron.com
Directors: M. Alves (Prop)
Immediate Holding Company: J.PRESTON & SONS,LIMITED
Registration no: 05387021 **Date established:** 2012
Turnover: Up to £250,000 **No.of Employees:** 1 - 10 **Product Groups:** 35

Date of Accounts	Mar 12	Mar 11	Mar 10
Working Capital	1m	963	759
Fixed Assets	204	80	68
Current Assets	2m	1m	1m

Belmont Blinds

41 Kirkstone Drive, Thornton Cleveleys, FY5 1QQ
Tel: 01253-820084 **Fax:** 01253-820084
E-mail: pculley3@aol.com
Website: http://www.belmontblinds.co.uk
Directors: M. Culley (Prop)
Immediate Holding Company: BELMONT BLINDS & CURTAINS CONTRACTS LIMITED
Date established: 2011 **Turnover:** £250,000 - £500,000
No.of Employees: 1 - 10 **Product Groups:** 24, 63, 66

Fast Fix

62-64 Victoria Road East, Thornton Cleveleys, FY5 5HQ
Tel: 01253-850400 **Fax:** 01253-850200
E-mail: fastfixworkshop@btconnect.com
Directors: K. Webster (MD)
Managers: P. Killenn (Chief Mgr)
Turnover: £500,000 - £1m **No.of Employees:** 1 - 10 **Product Groups:** 30, 40, 49

Date of Accounts	Jul 12	Jul 11	Jul 10
Working Capital	157	166	119
Fixed Assets	26	16	20
Current Assets	225	245	216

T & J Hooley

34 Rossall Road, Thornton Cleveleys, FY5 1EE
Tel: 01253-866606 **Fax:** 01253-866606
E-mail: jannetahooley@yahoo.co.uk
Website: http://www.tjhooley.co.uk
Directors: J. Hooley (Ptnr)
No.of Employees: 1 - 10 **Product Groups:** 24, 81

Kilgour Metal Treatments

Holly Close Holly Road, Thornton Cleveleys, FY5 4LR
Tel: 01253-864609 **Fax:** 01253-852237
Website: http://www.kilgour.co.uk
Directors: F. Kilgour (Fin)
Managers: C. Sweeney (Purch Mgr)
Immediate Holding Company: KILGOUR METAL TREATMENTS LIMITED
Registration no: 03712091 **Date established:** 1999
No.of Employees: 11 - 20 **Product Groups:** 46, 48

Date of Accounts	Mar 08	Jun 11	Jun 10
Working Capital	154	238	112
Fixed Assets	48	36	40
Current Assets	973	1m	1m

J B Masters Ltd

Dorset Avenue, Thornton Cleveleys, FY5 2DB
Tel: 01253-856096 **Fax:** 01253-856096
E-mail: jb@mastersltd.freeserve.co.uk
Directors: J. Masters (MD)
Immediate Holding Company: J.B. MASTERS LIMITED
Registration no: 01233193 **Date established:** 1975
Turnover: Up to £250,000 **No.of Employees:** 1 - 10 **Product Groups:** 38

Date of Accounts	Mar 11	Mar 10	Mar 09
Working Capital	4	16	32
Fixed Assets	56	58	61
Current Assets	25	44	86

Onsite Kitchen Rentals Ltd

Hill House International Business Park North Road, Thornton Cleveleys, FY5 4QD
Tel: 01253-863305 **Fax:** 01253-857139
E-mail: info@onsitekitchens.com
Website: http://www.onsitekitchens.com
Directors: D. Burns (MD)
Registration no: 03592065 **Date established:** 2007
Turnover: £20m - £50m **No.of Employees:** 1 - 10 **Product Groups:** 20, 40, 41

Date of Accounts	Oct 07	Oct 06	Oct 05
Sales Turnover	742	N/A	476
Pre Tax Profit/Loss	183	N/A	145
Working Capital	12	-49	8
Fixed Assets	267	233	144
Current Assets	221	172	157
Current Liabilities	209	221	149
ROCE% (Return on Capital Employed)	65.5		94.9
ROT% (Return on Turnover)	24.6		30.4

Taurus Farbrication Ltd

Red Marsh Drive Red Marsh Industrial Estate, Thornton Cleveleys, FY5 4HR
Tel: 01253-868152
Directors: J. Ronson (Co Sec)
Immediate Holding Company: TAURUS FABRICATION LIMITED
Registration no: 02068402 **Date established:** 1986
No.of Employees: 1 - 10 **Product Groups:** 35

Date of Accounts	Feb 12	Feb 11	Feb 10
Working Capital	20	16	31
Fixed Assets	13	16	18
Current Assets	47	41	55
Current Liabilities	N/A	N/A	2

Todmorden

Brisbane Moss Corduroy Manufacturers

Bridgeroyd Works Halifax Road, Todmorden, OL14 6DF
Tel: 01706-815121 **Fax:** 01706-818598
E-mail: info@brisbanemoss.co.uk
Website: http://www.brisbanemoss.co.uk
Bank(s): Barclays, Stockport
Managers: D. Ellison (Sales Admin)
Immediate Holding Company: M. CHAPMAN & SONS (TEXTILES) LTD
Registration no: 02214074 **VAT No.:** GB 157 1727 56
Turnover: £5m - £10m **No.of Employees:** 11 - 20 **Product Groups:** 23

Creative Graphics Ltd

Ridge House Ridge Road, Todmorden, OL14 7AW
Tel: 01706-818163 **Fax:** 01706-818159
E-mail: info@creativegraphicsuk.com
Website: http://www.creativegraphicsuk.com
Directors: G. Fisher (MD)
Immediate Holding Company: CREATIVE GRAPHICS LTD
Registration no: 05085426 **Date established:** 2004
Turnover: £500,000 - £1m **No.of Employees:** 1 - 10 **Product Groups:** 81

Date of Accounts	Aug 10	Aug 09	Aug 08
Working Capital	5	-9	15
Fixed Assets	11	37	19
Current Assets	132	81	117

Disegno

7 Haven Street, Todmorden, OL14 6AD
Tel: 01706-817724
E-mail: info@disegno.uk.com
Website: http://www.disegno.uk.com
Directors: M. Bowers (Dir)
Date established: 2005 **No.of Employees:** 1 - 10 **Product Groups:** 44

Foodmac International

Stoodley Bridge Mill Stoodley Lane, Todmorden, OL14 6HA
Tel: 01706-815040 **Fax:** 01706-815506
E-mail: sales@foodmac.co.uk
Website: http://www.foodmac.co.uk
Directors: A. Haigh (MD), L. Haigh (Fin)
Immediate Holding Company: FOODMAC INTERNATIONAL LIMITED
Registration no: 04627871 **Date established:** 2003
No.of Employees: 1 - 10 **Product Groups:** 20, 40, 41

Date of Accounts	Nov 11	Nov 10	Nov 09
Working Capital	87	91	88
Fixed Assets	97	112	113
Current Assets	144	190	185

Frostholme Furniture Ltd

Frostholme Mill Burnley Road, Todmorden, OL14 7ED
Tel: 01706-815133 **Fax:** 01706-818701
E-mail: linda.hooper@sutcliffegroup.co.uk
Website: http://www.sutcliffegroup.co.uk
Bank(s): Barclays
Directors: J. Michell (Co Sec), R. Smith (Sales)
Managers: W. Dunmore (Mktg Serv Mgr), L. Hooper, J. Redmond (Personnel), C. Henry (Purch Mgr), P. Clark (Fin Mgr)
Ultimate Holding Company: JHS REALISATIONS LIMITED
Immediate Holding Company: JHS REALISATIONS LIMITED
Registration no: 00249314 **VAT No.:** GB 427 4351 57
Date established: 1930 **Turnover:** £2m - £5m **No.of Employees:** 21 - 50
Product Groups: 26

Date of Accounts	Mar 10	Mar 09	Mar 08
Sales Turnover	5m	N/A	N/A
Pre Tax Profit/Loss	-38	-348	44
Working Capital	-537	-571	-269
Fixed Assets	2m	2m	2m
Current Assets	2m	2m	2m
Current Liabilities	937	1m	1m

Harmsworth Townley & Co. Ltd

The Melting Pot White Hart Fold, Todmorden, OL14 7BD
Tel: 01706-814931 **Fax:** 01706-812382
E-mail: glen@harmsworth-townley.co.uk
Website: http://www.highpowersemiconductors.com

see next page

Harmsworth Townley & Co. Ltd - *Cont'd*
Directors: G. Mattock (Dir)
Ultimate Holding Company: THE GREEN TOY COMPANY LIMITED
Immediate Holding Company: HARMSWORTH TOWNLEY AND COMPANY LIMITED
Registration no: 00598048 **Date established:** 1958
Turnover: £500,000 - £1m **No.of Employees:** 1 - 10 **Product Groups:** 37

Date of Accounts	Jan 11	Jan 10	Jan 09
Working Capital	177	200	234
Fixed Assets	248	261	265
Current Assets	254	270	338

Kavia Moulded Products Ltd
Unit 1c & 2a Walsden Industrial Estate Rochdale Road, Todmorden, OL14 6UD
Tel: 01706-816696 **Fax:** 01706-813822
E-mail: sylvia.spence@kavia.info
Website: http://www.kavia.info
Bank(s): Barclays
Directors: H. Spence (Dir)
Ultimate Holding Company: KAVIA HOLDINGS LIMITED
Immediate Holding Company: KAVIA MOULDED PRODUCTS LIMITED
Registration no: 01445437 **VAT No.:** GB 325 9202 69
Date established: 1979 **Turnover:** £500,000 - £1m
No.of Employees: 11 - 20 **Product Groups:** 29, 30, 48

Date of Accounts	Dec 11	Dec 10	Dec 09
Working Capital	323	307	301
Fixed Assets	263	276	285
Current Assets	601	581	545

Mardan Products Ltd
Sandholme Mill Commercial Street, Todmorden, OL14 5RG
Tel: 01706-816692 **Fax:** 01706-818101
E-mail: sales@mardan.co.uk
Website: http://www.mardan.co.uk
Directors: G. Hughes (MD)
Managers: A. Martin (Comm)
Immediate Holding Company: MARDAN PRODUCTS LIMITED
Registration no: 02351808 **VAT No.:** GB 516 2079 62
Date established: 1989 **Turnover:** £500,000 - £1m
No.of Employees: 11 - 20 **Product Groups:** 49

Date of Accounts	Mar 12	Mar 11	Mar 10
Working Capital	71	119	111
Fixed Assets	65	51	60
Current Assets	273	272	190

Menzolit
Perseverance Works Halifax Road, Todmorden, OL14 6EG
Tel: 01706-814714 **Fax:** 01706-814717
E-mail: richard.fiddling@menzolit.com
Website: http://www.menzolit-uk.co.uk
Bank(s): Lloyds TSB Bank plc
Directors: R. Fiddling (Fin), S. Stokes (Co Sec)
Managers: B. Ram (Sales Prom Mgr)
Ultimate Holding Company: PLASTAL GROUP AB (SWEDEN)
Immediate Holding Company: MENZOLIT LTD.
Registration no: 02184127 **Date established:** 1987 **Turnover:** £2m - £5m
No.of Employees: 21 - 50 **Product Groups:** 30, 31

Date of Accounts	Dec 07	Dec 06	Dec 05
Sales Turnover	6911	5287	5497
Pre Tax Profit/Loss	364	106	205
Working Capital	1663	1341	1175
Fixed Assets	686	751	815
Current Assets	3039	2348	1914
Current Liabilities	1375	1007	739
Total Share Capital	2550	2550	2550
ROCE% (Return on Capital Employed)	15.5	5.1	10.3
ROT% (Return on Turnover)	5.3	2.0	3.7

Newtech Hardware Ltd
Vale Mill Stansfield Road, Todmorden, OL14 5DL
Tel: 01706-813071 **Fax:** 01706-814196
E-mail: sales@newtechshelving.co.uk
Website: http://www.newtechshelving.co.uk
Directors: C. Gillies (MD)
Ultimate Holding Company: RMU HOLDINGS LIMITED
Immediate Holding Company: NEWTECH HARDWARE LIMITED
Registration no: 02916332 **Date established:** 1994
No.of Employees: 21 - 50 **Product Groups:** 35, 42, 45

Date of Accounts	Jan 12	Jan 11	Jan 10
Working Capital	499	478	473
Fixed Assets	19	24	9
Current Assets	693	659	649

Parkside Metal Finishers
Parkside Mill Parkside Road, Todmorden, OL14 8PF
Tel: 01706-815778 **Fax:** 01706-817917
E-mail: daniellejones1998@yahoo.co.uk
Directors: D. Johns (Fin), B. Johns (MD)
Immediate Holding Company: PARKSIDE METAL FINISHERS LTD
Registration no: 04713252 **Date established:** 2003
No.of Employees: 1 - 10 **Product Groups:** 46, 48

Date of Accounts	Feb 08	Feb 11	Feb 10
Working Capital	-45	-25	-37
Fixed Assets	55	29	38
Current Assets	29	28	29

Rochdale Metal Units Ltd
Stansfield Road, Todmorden, OL14 5DL
Tel: 01706-813071 **Fax:** 01706-814196
E-mail: sales@trendsure.co.uk
Website: http://www.trendsure.co.uk
Managers: B. Brookes (Develop Mgr)
Ultimate Holding Company: RMU HOLDINGS LIMITED
Immediate Holding Company: ROCHDALE METAL UNITS LIMITED
Registration no: 02850873 **VAT No.:** GB 183 9257 30
Date established: 1993 **Turnover:** £1m - £2m **No.of Employees:** 21 - 50
Product Groups: 26, 48

Date of Accounts	Jan 12	Jan 11	Jan 10
Working Capital	257	207	147
Fixed Assets	568	654	578
Current Assets	798	768	556

Superspray Lube
Unit 2 Salford Indl-Est Salford, Todmorden, OL14 7LF
Tel: 01706-839911 **Fax:** 01706- 839922
E-mail: mrscreenwash@aol.com

Directors: P. Thornton (Ptnr), P. Thornton (Ch), S. Thornton (Ptnr)
Ultimate Holding Company: P & S THORNTON (PARTNERSHIP)
Date established: 1984 **Turnover:** £1m - £2m **No.of Employees:** 1 - 10
Product Groups: 66

White & Newton Furniture Ltd
Frostholme Mill Burnley Road, Todmorden, OL14 7ED
Tel: 01706-812596 **Fax:** 01706-818701
E-mail: info@sutcliffefurniture.co.uk
Website: http://www.sutcliffegroup.co.uk
Directors: R. Smith (MD), P. Flecther (Sales)
Managers: S. Wilke (Mktg Serv Mgr), L. Hooper (Sec)
Ultimate Holding Company: JHS REALISATIONS LIMITED
Immediate Holding Company: WHITE & NEWTON (FURNITURE) LIMITED
Registration no: 00877672 **Date established:** 1966 **Turnover:** £5m - £10m
No.of Employees: 101 - 250 **Product Groups:** 52

Date of Accounts	Mar 10	Mar 09	Mar 08
Fixed Assets	1	1	1

Wigan

A & A Fire Protection
154 City Road, Wigan, WN5 0BG
Tel: 01942-323473 **Fax:** 01942-202600
Directors: A. Cassidy (Ptnr)
Date established: 1995 **No.of Employees:** 1 - 10 **Product Groups:** 38, 42

A B C Aerials Ltd
Lamberhead Industrial Estate Leopold Street, Pemberton, Wigan, WN5 8DH
Tel: 01942-224839 **Fax:** 01942-226682
E-mail: andrew@abcaerials.ltd.uk
Website: http://www.abcaerials.ltd.uk
Directors: A. Harrison (MD)
Immediate Holding Company: WILLJO LTD
Registration no: 01136976 **Date established:** 1973
Turnover: £250,000 - £500,000 **No.of Employees:** 21 - 50
Product Groups: 37

Date of Accounts	Sep 11	Sep 10	Sep 09
Working Capital	33	105	208
Fixed Assets	786	831	796
Current Assets	281	419	523

A S G Stage Products Ltd
Redgate Road Ashton-In-Makerfield, Wigan, WN4 8DT
Tel: 01942-718347 **Fax:** 01942-718219
E-mail: post@asgstage.co.uk
Website: http://www.asgstage.co.uk
Directors: S. Mcferran (MD)
Immediate Holding Company: ASG STAGE PRODUCTS LIMITED
Registration no: 01260457 **Date established:** 1976 **Turnover:** £1m - £2m
No.of Employees: 11 - 20 **Product Groups:** 37

Date of Accounts	May 11	May 10	May 09
Working Capital	848	868	673
Fixed Assets	39	50	34
Current Assets	1m	2m	1m

Abex Power Components Ltd
The Warehouse Smethurst Lane, Wigan, WN5 8BL
Tel: 01942-222928 **Fax:** 01942-221200
E-mail: sales@abexpower.co.uk
Website: http://www.abexpower.co.uk
Bank(s): The Royal Bank of Scotland
Managers: J. Spargo (Mgr)
Immediate Holding Company: ABEX POWER COMPONENTS LTD.
Registration no: 01905949 **Date established:** 1985 **Turnover:** £2m - £5m
No.of Employees: 11 - 20 **Product Groups:** 22, 23, 25, 29, 33, 35, 37, 39, 45

Date of Accounts	Apr 12	Apr 11	Apr 10
Working Capital	226	217	198
Fixed Assets	241	244	240
Current Assets	961	967	1m

Able Plastering
24 Elkwood Close, Wigan, WN1 2PD
Tel: 0783-825 1505
E-mail: enquiries@getplastered.biz
Website: http://www.getplastered.biz
Directors: D. O'Tool (Prop)
No.of Employees: 1 - 10 **Product Groups:** 33, 45, 52

Airmat Machinery Ltd
43 Bridgeman Terrace, Wigan, WN1 1TT
Tel: 01942-493563 **Fax:** 01942-496276
E-mail: info@airmat-machinery.co.uk
Website: http://www.airmat-machinery.co.uk
Directors: R. Waller (Dir)
Immediate Holding Company: AIRMAT MACHINERY LIMITED
Registration no: 01413191 **VAT No.:** GB 295 0948 21
Date established: 1979 **Turnover:** Up to £250,000
No.of Employees: 1 - 10 **Product Groups:** 44

Date of Accounts	Mar 11	Mar 10	Mar 09
Working Capital	10	10	13
Fixed Assets	1	1	1
Current Assets	13	18	19

Allenbuild Northwest Ltd (North West)
Jubilee House Waterside Drive, Wigan, WN3 5AZ
Tel: 01942-246265 **Fax:** 01942-821573
E-mail: steve.kelly@allenbuild.co.uk
Website: http://www.allenbuild.co.uk
Bank(s): Barclays
Directors: A. Moss (Contracts), B. Rive (Develop), J. Sawyer (MD), S. Kelly (Dir), J. Redfarn (Fin)
Managers: A. Wright, C. Andrew (Comm)
Ultimate Holding Company: RENEW HOLDINGS PLC.
Immediate Holding Company: ALLENBUILD (NORTH WEST) LIMITED
Registration no: 06887595 **VAT No.:** GB 208 0334 04
Date established: 2009 **Turnover:** £125m - £250m
No.of Employees: 21 - 50 **Product Groups:** 52, 80

Anglo Scot Abrasives
5 Bolton Road Ashton-in-Makerfield, Wigan, WN4 8AA
Tel: 01942-270729 **Fax:** 01942-273395
Directors: J. Whalley (Prop)
Date established: 1991 **No.of Employees:** 1 - 10 **Product Groups:** 38, 42

B B K Labelling & Coding Solutions Ltd
Unit 30 Cinnamon Brow Business Park Makerfield Way, Ince, Wigan, WN2 2PR
Tel: 01942-367262 **Fax:** 01942-226301
E-mail: info@bbk-labelling.co.uk
Website: http://www.bbk-labelling.co.uk
Directors: S. Jarmesty (MD)
Immediate Holding Company: BBK LABELLING AND CODING SOLUTIONS LIMITED
Registration no: 05185996 **Date established:** 2004
Turnover: £250,000 - £500,000 **No.of Employees:** 1 - 10
Product Groups: 42

Date of Accounts	Dec 10	Dec 09	Dec 08
Working Capital	382	135	-81
Fixed Assets	16	21	22
Current Assets	425	453	300

Balmoral Ornamental Wrought Iron
Unit 2 Major Street, Wigan, WN5 8AD
Tel: 01942-221828
Directors: G. Derbyshire (Prop)
Date established: 2001 **No.of Employees:** 1 - 10 **Product Groups:** 26, 35

Bitrez Ltd
Bradley Hall Trading Estate Bradley Lane, Standish, Wigan, WN6 0XQ
Tel: 01257-425512 **Fax:** 01257-422863
E-mail: bitrez@aol.com
Website: http://bitrez.com
Directors: C. Holgate (Pers), B. Allen (Fin), P. Jones (MD)
Managers: C. Charnock
Ultimate Holding Company: BITREZ GROUP LIMITED
Immediate Holding Company: BITREZ LIMITED
Registration no: 04138468 **VAT No.:** GB 373 9719 09
Date established: 2001 **Turnover:** £20m - £50m
No.of Employees: 51 - 100 **Product Groups:** 32

Date of Accounts	Dec 11	Dec 10	Dec 09
Sales Turnover	21m	20m	17m
Pre Tax Profit/Loss	499	472	432
Working Capital	2m	2m	1m
Fixed Assets	19	24	29
Current Assets	7m	7m	6m
Current Liabilities	297	234	262

Bollard Tech
10 Miles Lane Shevington, Wigan, WN6 8EB
Tel: 01257-255446 **Fax:** 01925-234373
Website: http://www.bollardtech.com
Managers: N. Rotledge (Mgr)
No.of Employees: 1 - 10 **Product Groups:** 35, 39

Brian Hughes Plant
43 moores lane standish, wigan, WN6 0JD
Tel: 01257-426761 **Fax:** 01257-400610
E-mail: bhplant@blueyonder.co.uk
Website: http://
Directors: B. Hughes (Fin), A. Hughes (Dir)
Immediate Holding Company: BRIAN HUGHES PLANT LTD
Registration no: 06209750 **Date established:** 2007
Turnover: £500,000 - £1m **No.of Employees:** 1 - 10 **Product Groups:** 45, 67

C P A Ironworks
Bradley Hall Bradley Hall Trading Estate Bradley Lane, Standish, Wigan, WN6 0XQ
Tel: 0800-093 3548 **Fax:** 05602-048647
E-mail: info@cpagates.co.uk
Website: http://www.cpagates.co.uk
Managers: J. Prescott (Mgr)
Ultimate Holding Company: BRADLEY HALL HOLDINGS LIMITED
Immediate Holding Company: NATIONWIDE CRANE HIRE LIMITED
Date established: 1984 **Turnover:** Up to £250,000
No.of Employees: 1 - 10 **Product Groups:** 35

C-Tec Security Ltd
Challenge Way Martland Mill Industrial Estate, Wigan, WN5 0LD
Tel: 01942-322744 **Fax:** 01942-829867
E-mail: info@c-tec.co.uk
Website: http://www.c-tec.co.uk
Bank(s): The Royal Bank of Scotland
Directors: A. Foster (MD)
Managers: G. Owen, G. Haselden (Comptroller), J. Darlington (Purch Mgr)
Registration no: 01559261 **VAT No.:** GB 344 0372 81
Turnover: £5m - £10m **No.of Employees:** 51 - 100 **Product Groups:** 37, 38, 40, 67, 81

Captrad Ltd
Unit 19 Hewitt Business Park Winstanley Road, Billinge, Wigan, WN5 7XB
Tel: 01695-680010 **Fax:** 01695-680009
E-mail: phil.capstick@captrad-ltd.co.uk
Website: http://www.captrad-ltd.co.uk
Directors: P. Capstick (MD), R. Capstick (Fin)
Immediate Holding Company: CAPTRAD LIMITED
Registration no: 03775179 **Date established:** 1999
No.of Employees: 1 - 10 **Product Groups:** 22, 30

Date of Accounts	Feb 08	Feb 11	Feb 10
Working Capital	36	75	72
Fixed Assets	8	3	4
Current Assets	260	280	250

Cheeky Chums
49 Broadway Hindley, Wigan, WN2 4JP
Tel: 01942-254259
E-mail: cheekychms@yahoo.co.uk
Website: http://cheekychumsonline.co.uk
Directors: S. Sudlow (Prop)
No.of Employees: 1 - 10 **Product Groups:** 22, 24, 61

Chemviron Carbon Ltd
Edgar House Locket Road, Ashton-In-Makerfield, Wigan, WN4 8DE
Tel: 01942-275400 **Fax:** 01942-275600
E-mail: info@chemvironcarbon.com
Website: http://www.chemvironcarbon.com
Directors: N. Taylor (Sales)
Managers: G. Baron (Personnel), D. Reay (Mktg Serv Mgr), M. Graham (Fin Mgr), A. Addison
Ultimate Holding Company: CALGON CARBON CORPORATION (USA)
Immediate Holding Company: CHEMVIRON CARBON LIMITED
Registration no: 02208285 **Date established:** 1987
Turnover: £10m - £20m **No.of Employees:** 21 - 50 **Product Groups:** 31, 33, 40, 42, 49

Date of Accounts	Dec 11	Dec 10	Dec 09
Sales Turnover	33m	28m	24m
Pre Tax Profit/Loss	4m	2m	988
Working Capital	8m	9m	7m
Fixed Assets	7m	5m	6m
Current Assets	15m	12m	10m
Current Liabilities	2m	2m	1m

Clariant UK Ltd

Unit C7-C8 Haslemere Industrial Estate Wigan Road, Ashton-in-Makerfield, Wigan, WN4 0BZ
Tel: 01942-296200 **Fax:** 01942-494555
E-mail: kelly.morrisey@clariant.com
Website: http://www.clariant.com
Bank(s): National Westminster Bank Plc
Managers: K. Morrisey, A. Peck (Fin Mgr), G. Alecock (Mgr), M. Hurst (Chief Mgr), P. Brookston (Lab Mgr), S. Mansheder (I.T. Exec), T. Lyford (Ops Mgr), S. Bennett, K. Sinclair (Sales & Mktg Mg)
Immediate Holding Company: CLARIANT UK LTD
Registration no: 04213887 **Date established:** 2001
No.of Employees: 51 - 100 **Product Groups:** 32

Climavent Systems Ltd

Units 1-3 Cairngorm Business Park Liverpool Road, Ashton-In-Makerfield, Wigan, WN4 0YU
Tel: 01942-726164 **Fax:** 01942-722300
E-mail: info@climavent.co.uk
Website: http://www.climavent.co.uk
Directors: I. Ratcliffe (MD)
Immediate Holding Company: CLIMAVENT SYSTEMS LIMITED
Registration no: 03423175 **Date established:** 1997
Turnover: £500,000 - £1m **No.of Employees:** 1 - 10 **Product Groups:** 40, 46

Date of Accounts	Jan 12	Jan 11	Jan 10
Working Capital	306	219	210
Fixed Assets	78	60	49
Current Assets	616	833	631

Codamatic Ltd

Unit 4 Wigan Road Ashton-In-Makerfield, Wigan, WN4 0BW
Tel: 01942-724805 **Fax:** 01942-724829
Directors: P. Snape (Dir), A. Snape (Co Sec)
Immediate Holding Company: CODAMATIC LIMITED
Registration no: 03026319 **Date established:** 1995
No.of Employees: 1 - 10 **Product Groups:** 37

Date of Accounts	Sep 11	Sep 10	Sep 09
Working Capital	12	21	20
Fixed Assets	16	14	15
Current Assets	95	85	60

Collins Containers Ltd

Unit 19 Bradley Hall Trading Estate Bradley Lane, Standish, Wigan, WN6 0XQ
Tel: 01257-473463 **Fax:** 01257-450400
E-mail: enquiries@collinscontainers.co.uk
Website: http://www.collinscontainers.co.uk
Directors: K. Collins (Dir)
Immediate Holding Company: COLLINS CONTAINERS LIMITED
Registration no: 07192500 **Date established:** 2010
No.of Employees: 1 - 10 **Product Groups:** 35, 36, 45

Date of Accounts	Mar 12	Mar 11
Working Capital	-244	-381
Fixed Assets	404	436
Current Assets	261	172

Compressed Air Parts

Swan Lane Hindley Green, Wigan, WN2 4EZ
Tel: 01772-455266 **Fax:** 01772-622310
E-mail: sales@compressedairparts.co.uk
Website: http://www.compressedairparts.co.uk
Bank(s): Lloyds TSB Bank plc
Managers: C. Noakes (Chief Mgr)
Ultimate Holding Company: INGERSOLL-RAND CO LTD (BERMUDA)
Immediate Holding Company: COMPRESSED AIR PARTS LIMITED
Registration no: 01821415 **Date established:** 1984 **Turnover:** £1m - £2m
No.of Employees: 21 - 50 **Product Groups:** 40, 48

Date of Accounts	Dec 06	Dec 05	Dec 04
Sales Turnover	2m	2m	2m
Pre Tax Profit/Loss	-1	-15	-405
Working Capital	N/A	-152	-155
Fixed Assets	N/A	30	44
Current Assets	N/A	679	807
Current Liabilities	N/A	36	129

Contitech PTS (Power Transmission Systems) Ltd

Unit 1 Hindley Green Business Park, Leigh Road, Hindley Green, Wigan, WN2 4TN
Tel: 01942-524028 **Fax:** 01942-524000
E-mail: lisa.donohue@ptg.contitech.co.uk
Website: http://www.contitech.co.uk/industrial_powertransmission.html
Immediate Holding Company: Continental Group
Turnover: £10m - £20m **No.of Employees:** 101 - 250
Product Groups: 29, 30, 35, 38, 39, 45, 66, 68

Conway Trailer Division

Skull House Lane Appley Bridge, Wigan, WN6 9DW
Tel: 01257-254535 **Fax:** 01257-254547
E-mail: sales@conwaytrailers.com
Website: http://www.conwaytrailers.com
Managers: S. Pennington (Mgr)
Immediate Holding Company: APEX BUILDING CONTRACTORS LIMITED
Registration no: 04628033 **Date established:** 1997 **Turnover:** £5m - £10m
No.of Employees: 1 - 10 **Product Groups:** 39

Corlett Electrical Engineering Co 1981 Ltd

208 Gidlow Lane, Wigan, WN6 7BN
Tel: 01942-241333 **Fax:** 01942-820958
E-mail: gary@corlett-elec.com
Website: http://www.corlett-elec.com
Bank(s): Barclays, Wigan
Directors: G. Freeman (Fin)
Immediate Holding Company: CORLETT ELECTRICAL ENGINEERING COMPANY (1981) LIMITED
Registration no: 01561012 **VAT No.:** GB 344 0129 90
Date established: 1981 **Turnover:** £500,000 - £1m
No.of Employees: 21 - 50 **Product Groups:** 52

Date of Accounts	Mar 11	Mar 10	Mar 09
Working Capital	242	206	168
Fixed Assets	89	93	85

Current Assets	683	537	482

Creative Photo Shop & Portrait Studio

Unit 16 Greensway Shopping Arcade 34 Gerard Street, Ashton-In-Makerfield, Wigan, WN4 9AE
Tel: 01942-725847
E-mail: geoff.beattie@creativephotoshop.co.uk
Website: http://www.creativephotoshop.co.uk
Directors: G. Beattie (Prop)
Managers: G. Beattie (Chief Mgr)
Immediate Holding Company: GREENSWAY (HOLDINGS) LIMITED
Registration no: 01590249 **Date established:** 1981
No.of Employees: 1 - 10 **Product Groups:** 27, 37, 81

D & D Fabrications

Off Moat House Street Ince, Wigan, WN2 2EH
Tel: 01942-821642
Directors: G. Scrivens (Prop)
Date established: 1994 **No.of Employees:** 1 - 10 **Product Groups:** 26, 35

D P I Services

33 Moores Lane Standish, Wigan, WN6 0JD
Tel: 01257-424340 **Fax:** 01257-424340
E-mail: ian@dpiservices.co.uk
Directors: P. Speakman (Ptnr)
Date established: 1988 **Turnover:** Up to £250,000
No.of Employees: 1 - 10 **Product Groups:** 48

E S K Industrial Roofing Ltd

5 Linton Avenue, Wigan, WN6 7PR
Tel: 01942-820377 **Fax:** 01942-244076
E-mail: esk@blueyonder.co.uk
Website: http://www.eskroofing.co.uk
Directors: E. Campbell (MD), K. Campbell (Fin)
Immediate Holding Company: E.S.K. INDUSTRIAL ROOFING LIMITED
Registration no: 03120432 **Date established:** 1995
Turnover: Up to £250,000 **No.of Employees:** 1 - 10 **Product Groups:** 52, 66

Date of Accounts	Jul 11	Jul 10	Jul 09
Working Capital	178	161	69
Fixed Assets	11	12	12
Current Assets	256	161	157

Elf Productivity

The Stables Skull House Lane, Appley Bridge, Wigan, WN6 9DJ
Tel: 01257-256000 **Fax:** 01257-256010
E-mail: sales@elf.uk.com
Website: http://www.elf.uk.com
Directors: P. Obrien (Co Sec), P. O'brien (Dir)
Immediate Holding Company: ELF PRODUCTIVITY LIMITED
Registration no: 01677934 **Date established:** 1982 **Turnover:** £1m - £2m
No.of Employees: 11 - 20 **Product Groups:** 44, 86

Date of Accounts	Dec 11	Dec 10	Dec 09
Working Capital	44	167	104
Fixed Assets	1m	1m	113
Current Assets	724	708	460

Entwistle & Joynt

62 Darlington Street East, Wigan, WN1 3AT
Tel: 01942-527477 **Fax:** 01942-243330
E-mail: info@entys.co.uk
Website: http://www.entys.co.uk
Bank(s): National Westminster Bank Plc
Directors: I. Entwhistle (Dir), P. Entwistle (Ptnr), S. Marrow (Dir)
Immediate Holding Company: ENTWISTLE & JOYNT LIMITED
Registration no: 01001233 **VAT No.:** GB 152 1101 31
Date established: 1971 **Turnover:** £5m - £10m **No.of Employees:** 21 - 50
Product Groups: 37

Date of Accounts	Jan 12	Jan 11	Jan 10
Sales Turnover	N/A	8m	6m
Pre Tax Profit/Loss	221	65	-310
Working Capital	3m	2m	2m
Fixed Assets	794	1m	1m
Current Assets	4m	3m	3m
Current Liabilities	95	132	117

Euromark Marking & Coding Ltd

5 Croftwood Square Martland Mill Industrial Estate, Wigan, WN5 0LG
Tel: 01942-228882 **Fax:** 01942-228802
E-mail: info@euromark.biz
Website: http://www.euromark.biz
Directors: S. Luck (MD)
Immediate Holding Company: EUROMARK CODING AND MARKING LIMITED
Registration no: 03258285 **Date established:** 1996 **Turnover:** £1m - £2m
No.of Employees: 11 - 20 **Product Groups:** 27, 28, 38, 44, 67

Date of Accounts	Oct 09	Oct 08	Oct 07
Working Capital	58	46	40
Fixed Assets	26	38	56
Current Assets	424	422	525

European Tubes Ltd

Unit 9 Pagefield Industrial Estate Miry Lane, Wigan, WN6 7LA
Tel: 01942-615130 **Fax:** 0870-202 0244
E-mail: sales@europeantubes.co.uk
Website: http://www.europeantubes.co.uk
Managers: K. Gratton (Mgr), V. Flannery (Fin Mgr)
Immediate Holding Company: EUROPEAN TUBES LIMITED
Registration no: 02276395 **Date established:** 1988 **Turnover:** £5m - £10m
No.of Employees: 21 - 50 **Product Groups:** 66

Date of Accounts	Dec 11	Dec 10	Dec 09
Sales Turnover	9m	7m	6m
Pre Tax Profit/Loss	404	191	210
Working Capital	2m	2m	1m
Fixed Assets	236	138	100
Current Assets	5m	3m	3m
Current Liabilities	2m	1m	1m

Exel Industrial UK Ltd

Unit 4 Lockflight Buildings Wheatlea Industrial Estate, Wigan, WN3 6XR
Tel: 01942-829111 **Fax:** 01942-820491
E-mail: enquiries@exel-uk.com
Website: http://www.exel-uk.com
No.of Employees: 21 - 50 **Product Groups:** 25, 32, 33, 37, 40, 42, 46, 47, 48, 83

Date of Accounts	Aug 08
Working Capital	810
Fixed Assets	66

Current Assets	1459		
Current Liabilities	649		
Total Share Capital	171		

Falcoe Software

Enterprise House Pemberton Business Centre Richmond Hill, Wigan, WN5 8AA
Tel: 01942-217801 **Fax:** 01942-216592
E-mail: admin@falcoe.com
Website: http://www.falcoe.com
Managers: P. Darwen (Mgr)
Immediate Holding Company: CREATE CREATIVE CONSULTANTS LIMITED
Registration no: 06978478 **Date established:** 2009
Turnover: £250,000 - £500,000 **No.of Employees:** 1 - 10
Product Groups: 44

Date of Accounts	Mar 11	Mar 10	Mar 09
Working Capital	4	4	1
Fixed Assets	20	20	20
Current Assets	9	6	3

Flavour Master Ltd

Unit 17d Makerfield Way Ince, Wigan, WN2 2PR
Tel: 01942-498500
E-mail: sales@flavourmaster.co.uk
Website: http://www.flavourmaster.co.uk
Directors: A. Hulme (Dir)
Immediate Holding Company: FLAVOUR MASTER LIMITED
Registration no: 06048144 **Date established:** 2007
Turnover: Up to £250,000 **No.of Employees:** 1 - 10 **Product Groups:** 21, 32

Date of Accounts	Mar 12	Mar 11	Mar 10
Working Capital	22	8	3
Fixed Assets	85	85	84
Current Assets	201	190	112

Guardian Technical Maintenance Ltd

Unit 26 Hewitt Business Park Winstanley Road, Billinge, Wigan, WN5 7XB
Tel: 01942-208101 **Fax:** 01942-704777
E-mail: info@guardian-technical.co.uk
Website: http://www.guardian-technical.co.uk
Directors: A. Lines (MD), J. Lines (Fin)
Immediate Holding Company: GUARDIAN TECHNICAL MAINTENANCE LIMITED
Registration no: 03410595 **Date established:** 1997
No.of Employees: 11 - 20 **Product Groups:** 32, 37, 40

Date of Accounts	Jul 11	Jul 10	Jul 09
Working Capital	59	70	21
Fixed Assets	45	59	48
Current Assets	151	181	189

H H Valves Ltd

Unit 4 Leopold Street, Wigan, WN5 8EG
Tel: 01942-218111 **Fax:** 01942-224800
Website: http://www.hhvalve.com
Directors: C. Hosie (MD)
Immediate Holding Company: HH VALVES LIMITED
Registration no: 04007454 **Date established:** 2000
No.of Employees: 11 - 20 **Product Groups:** 36, 37, 38

Date of Accounts	Nov 11	Nov 10	Nov 09
Working Capital	246	311	392
Fixed Assets	202	223	242
Current Assets	790	743	1m

Hose Tech Ltd

3 Wheatlea Industrial Estate Wheatlea Road, Wigan, WN3 6XP
Tel: 01942-233036 **Fax:** 01942-322915
E-mail: admin@hose-tech.co.uk
Website: http://hose-tech.co.uk
Bank(s): National Westminster Bank Plc
Directors: I. Charnock (MD), E. Hilton (Fin)
Immediate Holding Company: HOSE-TECH LIMITED
Registration no: 01560056 **VAT No.:** GB 349 9727 92
Date established: 1981 **No.of Employees:** 11 - 20 **Product Groups:** 29, 30

Date of Accounts	Jul 11	Jul 10	Jul 09
Working Capital	58	49	17
Fixed Assets	38	37	32
Current Assets	198	160	111

Interlink Import Export Ltd

The Rodings Lancaster Lane, Parbold, Wigan, WN8 7HQ
Tel: 01257-463211 **Fax:** 01257-464220
E-mail: peter@interlink.uk.com
Directors: J. Large (MD), J. Westhead (Fin)
Immediate Holding Company: INTERLINK IMPORT - EXPORT LIMITED
Registration no: 01209496 **VAT No.:** GB 153 2333 96
Date established: 1975 **Turnover:** Up to £250,000
No.of Employees: 1 - 10 **Product Groups:** 30, 32, 34, 35, 37, 42

Date of Accounts	Mar 09	Mar 08	Mar 11
Working Capital	125	113	293
Fixed Assets	17	22	28
Current Assets	164	157	324

Interserve Construction

Woodhouse Drive, Wigan, WN6 7NT
Tel: 01942-236434 **Fax:** 01942-824159
E-mail: john.godfrey@interserve.com
Website: http://www.interserve.com
Bank(s): HSBC Bank plc
Directors: J. Godfrey (Div)
Managers: J. Greenhall, N. Jones, S. Herring
Immediate Holding Company: DOUGLAS PRINTERS LIMITED
Registration no: 02254163 **Date established:** 1988
Turnover: £500m - £1,000m **No.of Employees:** 51 - 100
Product Groups: 51, 52

Date of Accounts	May 11	May 10	May 09
Working Capital	36	32	64
Fixed Assets	67	85	40
Current Assets	101	93	98

J T & E Castings Ltd

Leyland Mill Lane, Wigan, WN1 2SA
Tel: 01942-241966 **Fax:** 01942-492136
E-mail: enquiries@jte-castings.co.uk
Website: http://www.jte-castings.co.uk
Bank(s): Royal Bank of Scotland

see next page

J T & E Castings Ltd - Cont'd

Directors: M. Bradley (Dir)
Immediate Holding Company: J.T. & E. CASTINGS LIMITED
Registration no: 00631385 **VAT No.:** GB 151 7253 81
Date established: 1959 **Turnover:** £250,000 - £500,000
No.of Employees: 11 - 20 **Product Groups:** 34, 48

Date of Accounts	Jun 12	Jun 11	Jun 10
Working Capital	453	426	438
Fixed Assets	60	64	65
Current Assets	502	509	513

Jewson Ltd

Rosebridge Way Ince, Wigan, WN1 3DG
Tel: 01942-246341 **Fax:** 01942-821787
E-mail: kieran.burke@jewson.co.uk
Website: http://www.jewson.co.uk
Managers: K. Burke (District Mgr)
Ultimate Holding Company: COMPAGNIE DE SAINT GOBAIN (FRANCE)
Immediate Holding Company: JEWSON LIMITED
Registration no: 00348407 **Date established:** 1939
Turnover: Over £1,000m **No.of Employees:** 1 - 10 **Product Groups:** 66

Date of Accounts	Dec 11	Dec 10	Dec 09
Sales Turnover	1606m	1547m	1485m
Pre Tax Profit/Loss	18m	100m	45m
Working Capital	-345m	-250m	-349m
Fixed Assets	496m	387m	461m
Current Assets	657m	1005m	1320m
Current Liabilities	66m	120m	64m

Jewson Ltd (Central Division)

Victoria Street, Wigan, WN5 9BX
Tel: 01942-214741 **Fax:** 01942-216746
E-mail: mark.nuttall@jewson.co.uk
Website: http://www.hirepoint.co.uk
Managers: M. Nuttall (Mgr)
Ultimate Holding Company: COMPAGNIE DE SAINT GOBAIN (FRANCE)
Immediate Holding Company: JEWSON LIMITED
Registration no: 00348407 **VAT No.:** GB 394 1212 63
Date established: 1939 **No.of Employees:** 1 - 10 **Product Groups:** 66

Date of Accounts	Dec 11	Dec 10	Dec 09
Sales Turnover	1606m	1547m	1485m
Pre Tax Profit/Loss	18m	100m	45m
Working Capital	-345m	-250m	-349m
Fixed Assets	496m	387m	461m
Current Assets	657m	1005m	1320m
Current Liabilities	66m	120m	64m

Joy Mining Machinery Ltd

PO Box 12, Wigan, WN1 3DD
Tel: 08702-526000 **Fax:** 08702-526888
E-mail: rbailey@joy.co.uk
Website: http://www.joy.com
Bank(s): National Westminster Bank Plc
Directors: C. Hibbert (Eng Serv)
Managers: H. Gibson (Personnel)
Ultimate Holding Company: JOY GLOBAL INC (USA)
Immediate Holding Company: JOY MINING MACHINERY LIMITED
Registration no: 02546087 **VAT No.:** GB 535 5644 34
Date established: 1990 **Turnover:** £1m - £2m
No.of Employees: 101 - 250 **Product Groups:** 36, 38, 45

Date of Accounts	Oct 08	Oct 09	Oct 10
Sales Turnover	319m	332m	290m
Pre Tax Profit/Loss	56m	43m	88m
Working Capital	27m	57m	76m
Fixed Assets	203m	202m	201m
Current Assets	169m	159m	201m
Current Liabilities	33m	33m	38m

K B Rebar Ltd

Unit 5 Dobson Park Industrial Estate Dobson Park Way, Ince, Wigan, WN2 2DY
Tel: 0161-790 8635 **Fax:** 0161-799 7083
E-mail: sales@kbrebar.co.uk
Website: http://www.kbrebar.co.uk
Bank(s): Lloyds TSB Bank plc
Directors: M. Collins (Dir)
Immediate Holding Company: K B REBAR LIMITED
Registration no: 06467776 **VAT No.:** GB 305 2764 76
Date established: 2008 **Turnover:** £10m - £20m
No.of Employees: 11 - 20 **Product Groups:** 34, 35

Date of Accounts	Sep 11	Sep 10	Sep 09
Working Capital	12	-2	-61
Fixed Assets	16	29	87
Current Assets	208	205	208

L B Materials Handling Equipment

Challenge Way Martland Mill Industrial Estate, Wigan, WN5 0LD
Tel: 01942-223456 **Fax:** 01942-223453
E-mail: sales@1blifttrucks.co.uk
Website: http://www.lblifttrucks.co.uk
Managers: M. Evans (Comptroller), M. Farrimond (Comptroller)
Ultimate Holding Company: JJB SPORTS PLC
Immediate Holding Company: THE GOLF CHANNEL (UK) LIMITED
Registration no: 04175859 **Date established:** 2004
Turnover: Up to £250,000 **No.of Employees:** 21 - 50 **Product Groups:** 35, 39, 45

Date of Accounts	Jan 11	Jan 10	Jan 12
Working Capital	20m	20m	20m
Current Assets	25m	25m	25m

Laycocks Timber Merchants Ltd

Warrington Road Ince, Wigan, WN3 4QJ
Tel: 01942-242344 **Fax:** 01942-820705
E-mail: info@laycockstimber.co.uk
Website: http://www.laycockstimber.co.uk
Directors: S. High (MD), S. High (Fin), J. Atherton (MD)
Managers: A. O'Connor (Sales Prom Mgr)
Immediate Holding Company: LAYCOCKS TIMBER MERCHANTS LIMITED
Registration no: 03104408 **VAT No.:** GB 647 9558 77
Date established: 1995 **Turnover:** £500,000 - £1m
No.of Employees: 1 - 10 **Product Groups:** 25, 66

Date of Accounts	Nov 11	Nov 10	Nov 09
Working Capital	164	176	196
Fixed Assets	66	55	53
Current Assets	251	246	267

Le Aco Ltd

Lamberhead Industrial Estate Leopold Street, Pemberton, Wigan, WN5 8DH
Tel: 01942-221188 **Fax:** 01942-226682
E-mail: sales@leaco.ltd.uk
Website: http://www.leaco.ltd.uk
Bank(s): Royal Bank of Scotland, St. Helens
Directors: A. Harrison (MD)
Ultimate Holding Company: WILLJO LTD
Immediate Holding Company: LEACO LIMITED
Registration no: 00580389 **VAT No.:** GB 153 1773 73
Date established: 1957 **Turnover:** £500,000 - £1m
No.of Employees: 21 - 50 **Product Groups:** 30, 48

Date of Accounts	Sep 11	Sep 10	Sep 09
Working Capital	-365	-387	-448
Fixed Assets	830	834	866
Current Assets	293	227	198

Limelite Design Ltd

4 Dalby Road Hindley Green, Wigan, WN2 4RJ
Tel: 01942-522964
E-mail: sales@limelitedesign.com
Website: http://www.limelitedesign.com
Immediate Holding Company: LIMELITE DESIGN LIMITED
Registration no: 02666836 **Date established:** 1991
No.of Employees: 1 - 10 **Product Groups:** 37

Date of Accounts	Dec 11	Dec 10	Dec 09
Working Capital	35	25	17
Fixed Assets	6	5	7
Current Assets	284	238	250

Limelite Design

Unit 3 Swan Lane Hindley Green, Wigan, WN2 4HD
Tel: 01942-523330 **Fax:** 01942-522515
E-mail: sales@limelitedesign.com
Website: http://www.limelitedesign.com
Directors: G. Elliott (MD)
Immediate Holding Company: LIMELITE DESIGN LIMITED
Registration no: 02666836 **Date established:** 1991
No.of Employees: 1 - 10 **Product Groups:** 67

Date of Accounts	Dec 11	Dec 10	Dec 09
Working Capital	35	25	17
Fixed Assets	6	5	7
Current Assets	284	238	250

Lloyds British Testing Ltd

Wheatlea Road, Wigan, WN3 6XR
Tel: 01942-405600 **Fax:** 01942-239709
E-mail: wigan@lloydsbritish.com
Website: http://www.lloydsbritish.com
Directors: L. Speight (Dir)
Ultimate Holding Company: LLOYDS BRITISH GROUP LIMITED
Immediate Holding Company: LLOYDS BRITISH TESTING LIMITED
Registration no: 04444099 **Date established:** 2002
Turnover: £20m - £50m **No.of Employees:** 1 - 10 **Product Groups:** 39, 45, 48

Date of Accounts	Dec 11	Dec 10	Dec 09
Sales Turnover	16m	15m	15m
Pre Tax Profit/Loss	86	75	142
Working Capital	3m	3m	3m
Fixed Assets	2m	2m	2m
Current Assets	9m	8m	9m
Current Liabilities	1m	3m	4m

M P K

Unit 1j Bradley Hall Trading Estate Bradley Lane, Standish, Wigan, WN6 0XQ
Tel: 01257-425566 **Fax:** 01257- 425566
Directors: G. West (Ptnr)
Ultimate Holding Company: BRADLEY HALL HOLDINGS LIMITED
Immediate Holding Company: NATIONWIDE CRANE HIRE LIMITED
Date established: 1984 **No.of Employees:** 1 - 10 **Product Groups:** 35

T & J J Mcavoy

33 School Lane Standish, Wigan, WN6 0TG
Tel: 01257-426129 **Fax:** 01257-472248
E-mail: admin@guns.gb.com
Website: http://www.guns.gb.com
Directors: T. Mcavoy (Ptnr)
Immediate Holding Company: T & JJ MCAVOY LTD
Registration no: 07129184 **Date established:** 2010
No.of Employees: 1 - 10 **Product Groups:** 36, 39, 40

Martland Ltd

Unit 1h Cricket Street Business Centre Cricket Street, Wigan, WN6 7TP
Tel: 01942-497064 **Fax:** 01942-497075
E-mail: martland-ltd@tiscali.co.uk
Website: http://www.martlandltd.co.uk
Directors: J. Binns (Ptnr)
Managers: M. Draper
Immediate Holding Company: MARTLAND LIMITED
Registration no: 04612348 **Date established:** 2002
Turnover: £500,000 - £1m **No.of Employees:** 11 - 20
Product Groups: 29, 63, 66

Date of Accounts	Dec 11	Dec 10	Dec 09
Working Capital	-93	13	-55
Fixed Assets	120	131	88
Current Assets	476	342	247
Current Liabilities	225	14	126

Medisponge

35 Water Drive Standish, Wigan, WN6 0EH
Tel: 01257-473175 **Fax:** 01257-473175
Directors: M. Jameson (Prop)
VAT No.: GB 505 6664 44 **Turnover:** Up to £250,000
No.of Employees: 1 - 10 **Product Groups:** 49

Metering Solutions

Unit 13/14 Kingfisher Court, Bryn, Wigan, WN4 9DW
Tel: 01942-273333 **Fax:** 01942-271316
E-mail: warren@meteringsolutions.co.uk
Website: http://www.meteringsolutions.co.uk
Registration no: 02300848 **Product Groups:** 38, 44

Microface Ltd

Woodcock Hall Cobbs Brow Lane, Newburgh, Wigan, WN8 7NB
Tel: 01257-463225 **Fax:** 01257-463416
E-mail: sales@microface.com
Website: http://www.microface.com
Directors: A. Slevin (MD)
Immediate Holding Company: MICROFACE LIMITED
Registration no: 01576383 **VAT No.:** 344 1548 65 **Date established:** 1981
Turnover: £250,000 - £500,000 **No.of Employees:** 1 - 10
Product Groups: 38, 44

Date of Accounts	Dec 11	Dec 10	Dec 09
Working Capital	-60	-35	-7
Fixed Assets	222	224	226
Current Assets	151	136	174

Micron Electrical Contracting Ltd

Unit 2f Cricket Street Business Centre Cricket Street, Wigan, WN6 7TP
Tel: 01942-242887 **Fax:** 01942-820978
E-mail: john@micronvideo.co.uk
Bank(s): Natwest
Directors: J. Oakes (Dir)
Immediate Holding Company: MICRON ELECTRICAL (CONTRACTING) LIMITED
Registration no: 02363751 **VAT No.:** GB 534 6749 21
Date established: 1989 **Turnover:** £500,000 - £1m
No.of Employees: 11 - 20 **Product Groups:** 52

Date of Accounts	Mar 12	Sep 10	Sep 09
Working Capital	133	3	54
Fixed Assets	27	19	14
Current Assets	224	78	129

Milliken Industrials Ltd

Beech Hill Plant Gidlow Lane, Wigan, WN6 8RN
Tel: 01942-826073 **Fax:** 01942-826570
Website: http://www.milliken.com
Bank(s): Barclays, Silver St, Bury, National Westminster, Bury
Directors: J. Graham (Pers), J. Wakefield (Sales), J. Salley (Dir), M. Haworth (Fin), N. West (Tech Serv), A. Kitchingman (Mkt Research)
Managers: L. Furclough
Ultimate Holding Company: MILLIKEN AND CO. (U.S.A.)
Immediate Holding Company: MILLIKEN INDUSTRIALS LIMITED
Registration no: 00172105 **VAT No.:** GB 145 9283 45
Date established: 2020 **Turnover:** £75m - £125m
No.of Employees: 101 - 250 **Product Groups:** 23

Date of Accounts	Nov 08	Nov 09	Nov 10
Sales Turnover	95m	87m	103m
Pre Tax Profit/Loss	9m	5m	7m
Working Capital	33m	38m	45m
Fixed Assets	22m	19m	18m
Current Assets	60m	61m	70m
Current Liabilities	5m	4m	7m

Multilink Resources Ltd

22 Upper Dicconson Street, Wigan, WN1 2AD
Tel: 01942-244404 **Fax:** 01942-244404
E-mail: enquire@multilink.co.uk
Website: http://www.multilink.co.uk
Directors: S. Hanlon (Dir), P. Hanlon (Dir), T. Hanlon (MD)
Managers: J. Hanlon
Registration no: 03159999 **VAT No.:** GB 674 5075 17
Turnover: Up to £250,000 **No.of Employees:** 1 - 10 **Product Groups:** 36, 37, 40, 52, 54, 66

Nyquest Video Production Companies

Unit 21 Observer Building Rowbottom Square, Wigan, WN1 1LN
Tel: 01942-235349
E-mail: nyquest@btconnect.com
Website: http://www.nyquestlimited.com
Directors: D. Meehan (Prop)
Turnover: £250,000 - £500,000 **No.of Employees:** 1 - 10
Product Groups: 28

Orica UK Ltd

4 Stonecrop North Quarry Business Park, Appley Bridge, Wigan, WN6 9DL
Tel: 01257-256100 **Fax:** 01257-256166
E-mail: enquiries@orica.com
Website: http://www.orica.com
Directors: I. Ferguson (MD)
Managers: C. Ducker (Fin Mgr)
Ultimate Holding Company: ORICA LIMITED (AUSTRALIA)
Immediate Holding Company: ORICA UK LIMITED
Registration no: 03499102 **Date established:** 1998
Turnover: £10m - £20m **No.of Employees:** 21 - 50 **Product Groups:** 32

Date of Accounts	Sep 11	Sep 10	Sep 09
Sales Turnover	16m	15m	16m
Pre Tax Profit/Loss	2m	1m	3m
Working Capital	26m	26m	26m
Fixed Assets	10m	10m	10m
Current Assets	36m	36m	37m
Current Liabilities	350	1m	2m

Orrell Marketing Co

The Lakes Hall Orrell Road, Orrell, Wigan, WN5 8QZ
Tel: 01695-627719 **Fax:** 01695-627729
E-mail: jdlomc@aol.com
Directors: D. Leather (Prop)
Immediate Holding Company: WIGAN CARAVANS LIMITED
Registration no: 05344654 **Date established:** 1986
No.of Employees: 1 - 10 **Product Groups:** 38, 42

Date of Accounts	Dec 10	Dec 09	Dec 08
Working Capital	-15	3	-1
Current Assets	64	72	89

P & H Minepro Services

PO Box 12, Wigan, WN1 3DD
Tel: 01942-614400 **Fax:** 01942-614419
E-mail: ph-min@phmining.com
Website: http://www.minepro.com
Bank(s): The Royal Bank of Scotland
Managers: I. Grant (Chief Mgr)
Ultimate Holding Company: P & H NINEPRO SERVICES
Immediate Holding Company: P & H MINING EQUIPMENT
Registration no: 02484112 **VAT No.:** GB 621 1131 09
Turnover: £10m - £20m **No.of Employees:** 11 - 20 **Product Groups:** 67

Pier Steel Fabrications

Faraday Close Miry Lane Industrial Estate, Wigan, WN6 7TJ
Tel: 01942-239526
Website: http://www.piersteelfabrications.co.uk
Directors: D. Curtin (Ptnr)
No.of Employees: 1 - 10 **Product Groups:** 35, 48, 52

Pierhead Gates Ltd
Park Street, Wigan, WN3 5HE
Tel: 01942-495027 **Fax:** 01942-495027
Website: http://www.pierheadgatesandwelding.co.uk
Directors: R. Partington (Prop), R. Partington (MD)
Immediate Holding Company: PIERHEADGATES LIMITED
Registration no: 05907420 **Date established:** 2006
No.of Employees: 1 - 10 **Product Groups:** 26, 35

Date of Accounts	Aug 08	Aug 07
Working Capital	N/A	2
Current Assets	N/A	2

Plan Profiling Ltd
Bickerstaffs Yard Wilcock Street, Wigan, WN3 4AP
Tel: 01942-491782 **Fax:** 01942-825715
E-mail: enquiries@planprofiling.co.uk
Website: http://www.planprofiling.co.uk
Directors: L. Ashcroft (Fin), C. Sumner (MD)
Immediate Holding Company: PLAN PROFILING LIMITED
Registration no: 01417462 **Date established:** 1979
No.of Employees: 1 - 10 **Product Groups:** 46, 48

Date of Accounts	Apr 11	Apr 10	Apr 09
Working Capital	196	206	206
Fixed Assets	53	42	46
Current Assets	237	236	243

Polyfab & Formings Ltd
Unit 3 Hindley Green Business Park Leigh Road, Hindley Green, Wigan, WN2 4TN
Tel: 01942-523617 **Fax:** 01942-523533
E-mail: carol@polyfab.co.uk
Website: http://www.polyfab.co.uk
Directors: C. Goulding (Dir)
Immediate Holding Company: POLYFAB & FORMINGS LIMITED
Registration no: 02235374 **VAT No.:** GB 483 4642 28
Date established: 1988 **Turnover:** £500,000 - £1m
No.of Employees: 21 - 50 **Product Groups:** 30

Date of Accounts	Apr 11	Apr 10	Apr 09
Working Capital	73	4	2
Fixed Assets	47	55	48
Current Assets	349	201	149

Potters
1 Botanic Court Martland Park, Wigan, WN5 0JZ
Tel: 01942-219960 **Fax:** 01942-219966
E-mail: info@pottersherbals.co.uk
Website: http://www.potterspoultry.co.uk
Bank(s): National Westminster Bank Plc
Directors: P. Weigerstorfer (Dir), J. Flatley (Co Sec)
Ultimate Holding Company: GALENICA AG (SWITZERLAND)
Immediate Holding Company: POTTERS LIMITED
Registration no: 00510338 **VAT No.:** GB 151 8929 45
Date established: 1952 **Turnover:** £5m - £10m
No.of Employees: 51 - 100 **Product Groups:** 20

Date of Accounts	Dec 11	Dec 10	Dec 09
Sales Turnover	6m	8m	9m
Pre Tax Profit/Loss	448	2m	-4m
Working Capital	N/A	3m	-9m
Fixed Assets	N/A	9m	18m
Current Assets	N/A	4m	6m
Current Liabilities	N/A	694	691

P P G Industries UK Ltd
PO Box 132, Wigan, WN2 4XG
Tel: 01942-257161 **Fax:** 01942-522385
E-mail: b.pollock@ppg.com
Website: http://www.ppg.com
Bank(s): HSBC Bank plc
Directors: B. Pollock (MD)
Ultimate Holding Company: P P G INDUSTRIES INC (USA)
Immediate Holding Company: PPG INDUSTRIES (UK) LIMITED
Registration no: 02110620 **VAT No.:** GB 559 0132 48
Date established: 1987 **No.of Employees:** 251 - 500 **Product Groups:** 23, 33, 66

Date of Accounts	Dec 11	Dec 10	Dec 09
Sales Turnover	150m	137m	131m
Pre Tax Profit/Loss	5m	17m	-6m
Working Capital	22m	21m	22m
Fixed Assets	73m	78m	86m
Current Assets	143m	94m	95m
Current Liabilities	7m	7m	6m

Pqe Ltd
Units 4-5 Appleton Srtreet, Wigan, WN3 4BZ
Tel: 01942-513900 **Fax:** 01942-513001
E-mail: harold@pqeltd.com
Website: http://www.pqeltd.com
Directors: H. Whistle (MD)
Immediate Holding Company: PQE LIMITED
Registration no: 03490185 **Date established:** 1998
No.of Employees: 1 - 10 **Product Groups:** 37, 38, 67

Date of Accounts	Mar 11	Mar 10	Mar 09
Working Capital	84	110	82
Fixed Assets	30	9	12
Current Assets	218	247	239

Premier Lift Trucks Ltd
Unit 17 Cinnamon Brow Business Park Makerfield Way, Ince, Wigan, WN2 2PR
Tel: 01942-825757 **Fax:** 0161-745 7779
E-mail: info@fork-lift.co.uk
Website: http://www.fork-lift.co.uk
Directors: R. Geddes (Dir)
Immediate Holding Company: PREMIER LIFT TRUCKS LIMITED
Registration no: 03045143 **Date established:** 1995 **Turnover:** £2m - £5m
No.of Employees: 1 - 10 **Product Groups:** 39, 45, 48, 67, 68, 71, 83, 86

Date of Accounts	Apr 11	Apr 10	Apr 09
Working Capital	451	465	430
Fixed Assets	45	37	110
Current Assets	654	573	544

Pro Care Shower & Bathroom Ltd
Unit 5&6 Enfield Industrial Estate Enfield Street, Wigan, WN5 8DB
Tel: 01942-206004
E-mail: brianl@procare-ltd.co.uk
Website: http://www.procare-ltd.co.uk
Managers: A. Balmer (Tech Serv Mgr), B. Lee (Mgr)
Immediate Holding Company: PRO CARE SHOWER AND BATHROOM CENTRE LIMITED
Registration no: 04300621 **Date established:** 2001
No.of Employees: 11 - 20 **Product Groups:** 30, 36, 63

Date of Accounts	Mar 11	Mar 10	Mar 09
Working Capital	612	649	526
Fixed Assets	308	210	217
Current Assets	1m	1m	1m

Pyramid Tool & Die Co.
Unit A Leopold Street Pemberton, Wigan, WN5 8DH
Tel: 01942-227938 **Fax:** 01942-211179
E-mail: paul@pyramid-tool.co.uk
Website: http://www.pyramid-tool.co.uk
Bank(s): The Royal Bank of Scotland
Directors: E. O'brien (Prop), P. O'Brien (Co Sec)
Ultimate Holding Company: WILLJO LTD
Immediate Holding Company: LEACO LIMITED
Registration no: 00580389 **VAT No.:** GB 374 2937 28
Date established: 1957 **Turnover:** £1m - £2m **No.of Employees:** 11 - 20
Product Groups: 29, 30, 42, 44, 46, 48

Date of Accounts	Sep 10	Sep 09	Sep 08
Working Capital	105	208	350
Fixed Assets	831	796	772
Current Assets	419	523	675

Rapid Pump Hydraulics
5 Stoneygate Appleby Bridge, Wigan, WN6 9ED
Tel: 07827-434777 **Fax:** 01257-254947
E-mail: info@rapidpump.co.uk
Website: http://www.rapidpump.co.uk
No.of Employees: 1 - 10 **Product Groups:** 40, 48, 84

Ravenhead Catering Equipment
Newton Road Billinge, Wigan, WN5 7TA
Tel: 01744-893880
Directors: V. Newton (Prop)
Immediate Holding Company: AJM WINDOWS LIMITED
Registration no: 03077265 **Date established:** 1995
No.of Employees: 21 - 50 **Product Groups:** 20, 40, 41

Rollins Bulldog Tools
Clarington Forge Darlington Street East, Wigan, WN1 3BT
Tel: 01942-244281 **Fax:** 01942-824316
E-mail: sales@rollins.co.uk
Website: http://www.bulldog.com
Managers: G. Robinson (Factory Mgr)
Date established: 1904 **No.of Employees:** 51 - 100 **Product Groups:** 36

Ross Electric Vehicles Ltd
Unit 1h Bradley Hall Trading Estate Bradley Lane, Standish, Wigan, WN6 0XQ
Tel: 01257-472066 **Fax:** 01257-472070
E-mail: info@rosselectricvehicles.co.uk
Website: http://www.rosselectricvehicles.co.uk
Directors: V. Johnson (MD)
Immediate Holding Company: ROSS ELECTRIC VEHICLES LIMITED
Registration no: 02336408 **Date established:** 1989
No.of Employees: 1 - 10 **Product Groups:** 35, 39, 45

Date of Accounts	Dec 11	Dec 10	Dec 09
Working Capital	113	90	111
Fixed Assets	N/A	N/A	1
Current Assets	184	132	152

S R B Joinery Ltd
232 Mossy Lea Road Wrightington, Wigan, WN6 9RL
Tel: 01257-424362 **Fax:** 0845-867 4760
E-mail: sales@srbltd.co.uk
Website: http://www.srbltd.co.uk
Directors: M. Boocock (Fin), S. Boocock (MD)
Immediate Holding Company: SRB JOINERY LTD
Registration no: 04763632 **Date established:** 2003
Turnover: Up to £250,000 **No.of Employees:** 1 - 10 **Product Groups:** 47, 48

Date of Accounts	Dec 11	Dec 10	Dec 09
Working Capital	21	3	6
Fixed Assets	11	9	12
Current Assets	48	33	40

Sandbrook Engineering Ltd
17 Sandbrook Road Orrell Orrell, Wigan, WN5 8UD
Tel: 01695-632409
Registration no: 05703269 **Date established:** 2006
No.of Employees: 1 - 10 **Product Groups:** 35, 45, 48, 52

Satronic Online
Unit 4 Swan Lane Hindley Green, Wigan, WN2 4HD
Tel: 01942-203981 **Fax:** 01942-769621
Directors: M. Whittle (Ptnr)
Immediate Holding Company: K.K.D. TRAILERS LTD.
Date established: 2006 **No.of Employees:** 1 - 10 **Product Groups:** 40

Date of Accounts	Jun 11	Jun 10	Jun 09
Working Capital	-38	-23	-27
Fixed Assets	39	33	33
Current Assets	60	15	9

Speedy Power Ltd
Lamberhead Industrial Estate Leopold Street, Wigan, WN5 8EG
Tel: 01942-217888 **Fax:** 01942-217888
E-mail: andrew@abexpower.co.uk
Website: http://www.speedypower.co.uk
Managers: J. Ping (Sales & Mktg Mg), A. Teanby (Mgr)
Immediate Holding Company: SPEEDY POWER LIMITED
Registration no: 03923249 **Date established:** 2000
No.of Employees: 1 - 10 **Product Groups:** 40, 83

Teckna Group
Saddle Hill Farm 277 Preston Road, Standish, Wigan, WN6 0NZ
Tel: 01257-421700 **Fax:** 01257-472647
E-mail: enquiries@tecknagroup.co.uk
Website: http://www.tecknagroup.co.uk
Managers: M. Shrigley
Immediate Holding Company: TECKNA GROUP LIMITED
Registration no: 01480853 **Date established:** 1980 **Turnover:** £1m - £2m
No.of Employees: 11 - 20 **Product Groups:** 37, 45, 51, 84

Date of Accounts	May 11	May 10	May 09
Working Capital	7	56	92
Fixed Assets	268	339	303
Current Assets	210	348	218

Tracks & Poles & Things Windmill Furnishings
The Old Windmill 1 Mill Lane, Parbold, Wigan, WN8 7NW
Tel: 01257-462787 **Fax:** 01257-463438
E-mail: sales@tracksandpoles.com
Website: http://www.tracksandpoles.com
Directors: J. Bennett (MD)
Immediate Holding Company: MILL HOUSE GALLERY LTD
Registration no: 06865556 **Date established:** 2009
Turnover: Up to £250,000 **No.of Employees:** 1 - 10 **Product Groups:** 24, 35, 36

Date of Accounts	Apr 11	Apr 10
Working Capital	-36	-49
Fixed Assets	47	49
Current Assets	24	20

Tremco Illbruck Ltd (Factory)
Coupland Road Hindley Green, Wigan, WN2 4HT
Tel: 01942-251400 **Fax:** 01942-251410
E-mail: info@tremco-illbruck.com
Website: http://www.tremco-illbruck.com
Bank(s): HSBC
Directors: R. Hill (Sales), A. Metcalfe (Dir), D. Johnson (Fin)
Managers: R. Toase (Mktg Serv Mgr), D. Mullerworth (Personnel), M. Deaville, M. Dillon
Ultimate Holding Company: RPM INTERNATIONAL INC (USA)
Immediate Holding Company: TREMCO ILLBRUCK LIMITED
Registration no: 02802593 **Date established:** 1993
Turnover: £20m - £50m **No.of Employees:** 51 - 100 **Product Groups:** 30, 31, 32, 33

Date of Accounts	May 11	May 10	May 09
Sales Turnover	24m	23m	20m
Pre Tax Profit/Loss	-40	21	579
Working Capital	240	42	-35
Fixed Assets	664	981	1m
Current Assets	10m	6m	5m
Current Liabilities	2m	2m	2m

UK Car Source
Martland Mill Garage Martland Mill Lane, Wigan, WN5 0LZ
Tel: 01942-248 000 **Fax:** 01942-248 099
E-mail: info@ukcarsource.co.uk
Website: http://www.ukcarsource.co.uk
Managers: D. Bickerton (Sales Prom Mgr)
Registration no: 05591552 **Turnover:** £1m - £2m
No.of Employees: 1 - 10 **Product Groups:** 61

Gary Wainwrights Gardens By Design Ltd
217 Upholland Road Billinge, Wigan, WN5 7DL
Tel: 01695-623444 **Fax:** 01695-623444
E-mail: wainwrightsgardensltd@tiscali.co.uk
Directors: G. Wainwright (MD)
Registration no: 03311721 **Turnover:** Up to £250,000
No.of Employees: 1 - 10 **Product Groups:** 07

Waller Eurosel
43 Bridgeman Terrace, Wigan, WN1 1TT
Tel: 01942-234897 **Fax:** 01942-496276
E-mail: info@waller-eurosel.co.uk
Website: http://www.waller-eurosel.co.uk
Directors: R. Waller (Prop)
Managers: D. Waller (Chief Acct)
Immediate Holding Company: AIRMAT MACHINERY LIMITED
Registration no: 01419260 **Date established:** 1979
Turnover: Up to £250,000 **No.of Employees:** 1 - 10 **Product Groups:** 42

Date of Accounts	Mar 11	Mar 10	Mar 09
Working Capital	10	10	13
Fixed Assets	1	1	1
Current Assets	13	18	19

Warisa Distribution Services International Road Haulage
Leopold Street Pemberton, Wigan, WN5 8DH
Tel: 01942-226545 **Fax:** 01942-225454
E-mail: granville@warisa.co.uk
Website: http://www.warisa.co.uk
Bank(s): Yorkshire Bank
Directors: G. Myers (MD)
Immediate Holding Company: WARISA DISTRIBUTION SERVICES LIMITED
Registration no: 02767118 **VAT No.:** GB 295 0220 71
Date established: 1992 **Turnover:** £1m - £2m **No.of Employees:** 11 - 20
Product Groups: 76

Date of Accounts	Apr 11	Apr 10	Apr 09
Working Capital	-94	-45	161
Fixed Assets	83	110	168
Current Assets	276	258	378

Whittle Valve Repairs Ltd
Unit 3 Tower Enterprise Park Great George Street, Wigan, WN3 4DP
Tel: 01942-493495 **Fax:** 01942-825392
E-mail: info@whittle-valves.co.uk
Website: http://www.whittle-valves.co.uk
Directors: P. Whittle (MD)
Immediate Holding Company: WHITTLE VALVE REPAIRS LIMITED
Registration no: 03272673 **Date established:** 1996
No.of Employees: 11 - 20 **Product Groups:** 36, 37, 38

Date of Accounts	Dec 11	Dec 10	Dec 09
Working Capital	922	711	486
Fixed Assets	12	16	21
Current Assets	1m	940	670

Wigan Timber Ltd
Unit 21 Swan Meadow Industrial Estate Swan Meadow Road, Wigan, WN3 5BE
Tel: 01942-235353 **Fax:** 01942-235363
E-mail: info@wigantimber.co.uk
Website: http://www.wigantimber.co.uk
Directors: J. Bentham (Fin)
Immediate Holding Company: WIGAN TIMBER LIMITED
Registration no: 03229726 **Date established:** 1996
No.of Employees: 11 - 20 **Product Groups:** 25, 32, 35, 41, 47, 52, 61, 66, 67, 74, 76, 80, 84, 85, 87

Date of Accounts	Dec 11	Dec 10	Dec 09
Working Capital	250	229	247
Fixed Assets	39	54	57
Current Assets	465	399	432

LEICESTERSHIRE

Incorporating **Rutland**

Ashby De La Zouch

A T P Instrumentation (Test & Measurement)

Ivanhoe Industrial Estate Tournament Way, Ashby De La Zouch, LE65 2UU
Tel: 01530-566800 **Fax:** 01530-560373
E-mail: sales@atp-instruments.co.uk
Website: http://www.atp-instrumentation.co.uk
Directors: G. Clarkson (Dir)
Immediate Holding Company: A.T.P. INSTRUMENTATION LTD.
Registration no: 02570899 **Date established:** 1990 **Turnover:** £1m - £2m
No.of Employees: 11 - 20 **Product Groups:** 31, 38, 39, 49, 85

Date of Accounts	Jan 12	Jan 11	Jan 10
Working Capital	218	204	161
Fixed Assets	336	335	347
Current Assets	454	432	429

Arla Foods Ltd

Smisby Road, Ashby De La Zouch, LE65 2UG
Tel: 01530-412858 **Fax:** 01530-411237
Website: http://www.arlafoods.co.uk
Managers: P. Carter (Chief Mgr)
Ultimate Holding Company: ARLA FOODS AMBA (DENMARK)
Immediate Holding Company: ARLA FOODS LIMITED
Registration no: 02143253 **Date established:** 1987
Turnover: £500m - £1,000m **No.of Employees:** 251 - 500
Product Groups: 20, 41, 42

Date of Accounts	Dec 11	Dec 10	Dec 09
Sales Turnover	1587m	1482m	1435m
Pre Tax Profit/Loss	31m	31m	29m
Working Capital	31m	67m	79m
Fixed Assets	310m	297m	276m
Current Assets	229m	289m	317m
Current Liabilities	11m	5m	158m

Biosil Ltd

Tournament Way, Ashby De La Zouch, LE65 2UU
Tel: 01530-560204 **Fax:** 01530-412715
E-mail: julia.f@biosil.co.uk
Website: http://www.biosil.co.uk
Managers: J. Hill (Fin Mgr), J. Foley (Mgr)
Ultimate Holding Company: GLOBAL CONSOLIDATED AESTHETICS LIMITED
Immediate Holding Company: BIOSIL LIMITED
Registration no: FC015985 **VAT No.:** GB 000 9538 07
Date established: 1991 **Turnover:** £500,000 - £1m
No.of Employees: 21 - 50 **Product Groups:** 38

Date of Accounts	Dec 10	Jun 09	Jun 08
Sales Turnover	8m	5m	4m
Pre Tax Profit/Loss	766	451	1m
Working Capital	986	311	-156
Fixed Assets	527	465	487
Current Assets	3m	1m	807
Current Liabilities	2m	709	806

British Sanitized Ltd

19 Babelake Street Packington, Ashby De La Zouch, LE65 1WD
Tel: 01530-415533 **Fax:** 01530-411180
E-mail: ian.dring@actifresh.freeserve.co.uk
Website: http://www.sanitized.com
Directors: I. Dring (MD)
Immediate Holding Company: BRITISH SANITIZED LIMITED
Registration no: 00587378 **Date established:** 1957
Turnover: £500,000 - £1m **No.of Employees:** 1 - 10 **Product Groups:** 32

Date of Accounts	Dec 11	Dec 10	Dec 09
Sales Turnover	848	687	621
Pre Tax Profit/Loss	29	51	31
Working Capital	16	55	25
Fixed Assets	6	7	9
Current Assets	215	248	157
Current Liabilities	11	15	10

Electrolube (a division of H.K. Wentworth Ltd)

Ashby Park Coalfield Way, Ashby De La Zouch, LE65 1JF
Tel: 0844-3759700 **Fax:** 0844-3759799
E-mail: info@hkw.co.uk
Website: http://www.electrolube.com
Bank(s): National Westminster Bank Plc
Directors: L. Finlay (Sales)
Ultimate Holding Company: H.K. Wentworth Ltd
Immediate Holding Company: H K Wentworth Ltd
Registration no: 00575334 **Turnover:** £5m - £10m
No.of Employees: 51 - 100 **Product Groups:** 31, 32, 47, 66

Hallmark Tractors Ltd

Smisby Road, Ashby De La Zouch, LE65 2UE
Tel: 01530-412811 **Fax:** 01530-412512
E-mail: sales@tractors.co.uk
Website: http://www.tractors.co.uk
Directors: J. Hall (Fin)
Immediate Holding Company: HALLMARK TRACTORS LIMITED
Registration no: 00756888 **Date established:** 1963
No.of Employees: 21 - 50 **Product Groups:** 84

Date of Accounts	Dec 10	Dec 09	Dec 08
Working Capital	907	931	828
Fixed Assets	407	412	197
Current Assets	3m	3m	3m
Current Liabilities	7	N/A	N/A

Hill-Rom Ltd

Clinitron House Excelsior Road, Ashby De La Zouch, LE65 1JG
Tel: 01530-411000 **Fax:** 01530-411555
E-mail: rachel.apsey@hill-rom.com
Website: http://www.hill-rom.com
Bank(s): Lloyds TSB Bank plc
Directors: D. Gittings (Fin), R. Apsey (Sales)
Ultimate Holding Company: HILL ROM HOLDINGS INC (USA)
Immediate Holding Company: HILL-ROM (UK) LIMITED
Registration no: 01702696 **VAT No.:** GB 341 2753 77
Date established: 1983 **Turnover:** £10m - £20m
No.of Employees: 101 - 250 **Product Groups:** 26

Date of Accounts	Sep 11	Sep 10	Sep 09
Sales Turnover	N/A	N/A	11m
Pre Tax Profit/Loss	160	153	1m
Working Capital	6m	6m	6m
Current Assets	6m	6m	6m

Nottingham Rehab Ltd

Clinitron House Excelsior Road, Ashby De La Zouch, LE65 1JG
Tel: 08451-218111
E-mail: customerservice@nrs-uk.co.uk
Website: http://www.nrs-uk.co.uk
Bank(s): Lloyds TSB Bank plc
Directors: G. Martell (Jt MD), P. Isherwood (MD), I. Lamb (Jt MD), J. Bonn (MD), G. Korosi (Jt MD)
Managers: T. McPhillips (Buyer), J. Hurley (Sales Prom Mgr)
Ultimate Holding Company: FINDEL P.L.C.
Immediate Holding Company: NOTTINGHAM REHAB LIMITED
Registration no: 01948041 **VAT No.:** GB 227 1642 77
Date established: 1985 **No.of Employees:** 21 - 50 **Product Groups:** 38, 40, 42, 85

Date of Accounts	Mar 08	Apr 09	Apr 10
Sales Turnover	52m	61m	60m
Pre Tax Profit/Loss	-927	5m	3m
Working Capital	-7m	-4m	18m
Fixed Assets	7m	7m	7m
Current Assets	26m	32m	27m
Current Liabilities	2m	3m	3m

Plastribution

Findel House 5 Ashby Park, Ashby De La Zouch, LE65 1XY
Tel: 01530-560560 **Fax:** 01530-560303
E-mail: sales@plastribution.co.uk
Website: http://www.plastribution.co.uk
Bank(s): Barclays, Burton on Trent
Directors: M. Boswell (MD)
Ultimate Holding Company: ITOCHU CORPORATION (JAPAN)
Immediate Holding Company: PLASTRIBUTION LIMITED
Registration no: 01461218 **VAT No.:** GB 345 8381 34
Date established: 1979 **Turnover:** £75m - £125m
No.of Employees: 21 - 50 **Product Groups:** 31

Date of Accounts	Dec 10	Dec 09	Dec 08
Sales Turnover	52m	41m	45m
Pre Tax Profit/Loss	2m	970	897
Working Capital	5m	4m	4m
Fixed Assets	285	240	282
Current Assets	18m	14m	13m
Current Liabilities	2m	664	653

R T Environmental Services

5 Rouen Way, Ashby De La Zouch, LE65 2QX
Tel: 01530-563888
E-mail: richard@rtinstall.co.uk
Website: http://www.rtinstall.co.uk
Managers: R. Bithell (Mgr)
Immediate Holding Company: R.T. ENVIRONMENTAL SERVICES LIMITED
Registration no: 02854132 **Date established:** 1993
Turnover: Up to £250,000 **No.of Employees:** 1 - 10 **Product Groups:** 26, 49, 79, 84

The Royal Hotel

Station Road, Ashby De La Zouch, LE65 2GP
Tel: 01530-412833 **Fax:** 01530-564548
E-mail: reservations@royalhotelashby.com
Website: http://www.royalhotelashby.com
Bank(s): HSBC Bank plc
Managers: D. Flanagan (Chief Mgr)
Ultimate Holding Company: ALLIED SANIS
VAT No.: GB 232 1538 95 **No.of Employees:** 21 - 50 **Product Groups:** 69

Standard Soap Co

Derby Road, Ashby De La Zouch, LE65 2HG
Tel: 01530-410000 **Fax:** 01530-410001
E-mail: helen.suwannawongse@standardsoap.co.uk
Website: http://www.standardsoap.co.uk
Directors: E. Yeoh (Dir), D. Gutteridge (MD), H. Suwannawongse (Pers)
Managers: P. Higgins (Personnel), H. Suwannawongse, S. Perry (I.T. Exec)
Ultimate Holding Company: KUALA LUMPUR KEPONG BERHAD (MALAYSIA)
Immediate Holding Company: STANDARD SOAP COMPANY LIMITED
Registration no: 03081008 **VAT No.:** GB 646 6473 09
Date established: 1995 **Turnover:** £10m - £20m
No.of Employees: 101 - 250 **Product Groups:** 32, 44

Date of Accounts	Sep 10	Sep 09	Sep 08
Sales Turnover	10m	10m	11m
Pre Tax Profit/Loss	-5m	-3m	-1m
Working Capital	-2m	-148	-119
Fixed Assets	1m	3m	3m
Current Assets	4m	4m	4m
Current Liabilities	2m	298	329

Ways & Means

Clinitron House Excelsior Road, Ashby De La Zouch, LE65 1JG
Tel: 08456-060911 **Fax:** 01530-419150
E-mail: customerservice@nrs-uk.co.uk
Website: http://www.nrs-uk.co.uk
Managers: H. Moreley (Mgr)
Ultimate Holding Company: HILL ROM HOLDINGS INC (USA)
Immediate Holding Company: HILL-ROM LIMITED
Date established: 1988 **No.of Employees:** 11 - 20 **Product Groups:** 38, 67

Date of Accounts	Sep 11	Sep 10	Sep 09
Sales Turnover	26m	25m	12m
Pre Tax Profit/Loss	852	-356	-257
Working Capital	8m	7m	7m
Fixed Assets	14m	15m	15m
Current Assets	13m	14m	12m
Current Liabilities	2m	2m	2m

Coalville

Advance Workwear & Disposables Ltd

Unit 12a South Leicester Industrial Estate Ellistown, Coalville, LE67 1EU
Tel: 01530-263321 **Fax:** 01530-262623
E-mail: advanceworkwear@hotmail.com
Website: http://www.advanceworkwear.com
Directors: V. Roberts (Fin), D. Thompson (MD)
Immediate Holding Company: ADVANCE WORKWEAR & DISPOSABLES LIMITED
Registration no: 01545626 **Date established:** 1981
Turnover: £500,000 - £1m **No.of Employees:** 1 - 10 **Product Groups:** 24

Date of Accounts	Aug 11	Aug 10	Aug 09
Working Capital	-6	-11	-38
Fixed Assets	217	228	242
Current Assets	298	302	269

Aggregate Industries Ltd

Bardon Road Bardon Hill, Coalville, LE67 1TL
Tel: 01530-510066 **Fax:** 01530-510259
E-mail: ukenquiries@ukaggregate.com
Website: http://www.aggregate.com
Directors: B. Bolsover (MD), C. Jenkins (Jt MD), J. Bowater (Fin), M. Allen (Mkt Research), P. Barltrop (Grp Chief Exec), P. Tom (Ch), P. Ton (Ch), S. Tagg (Pers), W. Bolsover (Grp Chief Exec)
Managers: A. Robinson (Mgr), G. Smith (Mgr), G. Smith, J. Coussins (Purch Mgr), M. Gibbins (I.T. Exec), K. White (Admin Off)

Immediate Holding Company: AGGREGATE INDUSTRIES LIMITED
Registration no: 05655952 **Date established:** 2005
Turnover: £500m - £1,000m **No.of Employees:** 101 - 250
Product Groups: 14

Alvey & Towers

Unit A12 The Springboard Centre Mantle Lane, Coalville, LE67 3DW
Tel: 01530-450011 **Fax:** 01530-450011
E-mail: office@alveyandtowers.com
Website: http://www.alveyandtowers.com
Directors: P. Alvey (Ptnr), E. Rowen (Ptnr)
Turnover: £250,000 - £500,000 **No.of Employees:** 1 - 10
Product Groups: 81

Antalis Mcnaughton

Gateway House Interlink Way West Bardon Hill, Coalville, LE67 1LE
Tel: 01530-505150 **Fax:** 08706-073160
E-mail: contact@antalis-mcnaughton.co.uk
Website: http://www.antalis-mcnaughton.co.uk
Bank(s): Barclays
Managers: B. Munro, C. Green (Product)
Immediate Holding Company: ANTALIS PENSION SCHEME TRUSTEE LIMITED
Registration no: 06609581 **Date established:** 2008
Turnover: £250m - £500m **No.of Employees:** 101 - 250
Product Groups: 27, 30, 31, 32, 34, 35, 36, 66, 68

Associated Recycling Solutions Ltd

Unit 1 Station Road Bagworth, Coalville, LE67 1BH
Tel: 01530-231861 **Fax:** 01530-230984
E-mail: mike@rslplant.com
Website: http://www.rslplant.com
Directors: M. Johnson (Dir)
Immediate Holding Company: ASSOCIATED RECYCLING SOLUTIONS LIMITED
Registration no: 04791323 **Date established:** 2003
No.of Employees: 1 - 10 **Product Groups:** 40, 45, 51, 66, 67, 83

Date of Accounts	Dec 10	Dec 08	Dec 09
Working Capital	84	34	-18
Fixed Assets	323	183	283
Current Assets	916	524	555

Benson Box Ltd

Interlink Park Bardon Hill, Coalville, LE67 1PE
Tel: 01530-518200 **Fax:** 01530-518222
E-mail: n.benson@bensonbox.co.uk
Website: http://www.bensonbox.co.uk
Bank(s): Royal Bank of Scotland
Directors: C. Kunz (Fin), N. Benson (Comm)
Managers: D. Cook (Chief Buyer), P. Towersey (Tech Serv Mgr), L. Webster (Personnel)
Ultimate Holding Company: SHOO 553 LIMITED
Immediate Holding Company: BENSON BOX COMPANY LIMITED(THE)
Registration no: 00550953 **VAT No.:** GB 705 3298 42
Date established: 1955 **Turnover:** £20m - £50m
No.of Employees: 101 - 250 **Product Groups:** 27, 42

Date of Accounts	May 11	May 10	May 09
Sales Turnover	49m	39m	33m
Pre Tax Profit/Loss	5m	4m	2m
Working Capital	8m	7m	7m
Fixed Assets	6m	7m	5m
Current Assets	27m	23m	21m
Current Liabilities	4m	2m	2m

Bywater Services Ltd

Unit 7 Telford Way Stephenson Industrial Estate, Coalville, LE67 3HE
Tel: 01530-833469 **Fax:** 01530-810795
E-mail: admin@bywaterservices.co.uk
Website: http://www.bywaterservices.co.uk
Directors: N. Bywater (MD)
Immediate Holding Company: BYWATER SERVICES LIMITED
Registration no: 03749948 **Date established:** 1999
No.of Employees: 11 - 20 **Product Groups:** 32, 36, 39, 40, 42, 66, 67

Date of Accounts	Apr 11	Apr 10	Apr 09
Working Capital	59	156	33
Fixed Assets	244	228	219
Current Assets	330	374	206

Camarc Ltd

Unit 6 Old Station Close, Coalville, LE67 3FH
Tel: 01530-831444 **Fax:** 024-7646 2442
E-mail: industrial301@aol.com
Website: http://www.camarc.co.uk
Directors: S. Parks (Prop)
Immediate Holding Company: CAMARC LIMITED
Registration no: 02045552 **Date established:** 1986
Turnover: Up to £250,000 **No.of Employees:** 1 - 10 **Product Groups:** 37, 48, 67, 83

Date of Accounts	Oct 11	Oct 10	Oct 09
Working Capital	61	104	80
Fixed Assets	26	15	18
Current Assets	327	320	452

Charnwood Instrumentation Services

81 Park Road, Coalville, LE67 3AF
Tel: 01530-510615 **Fax:** 01530-510950
E-mail: karen@instrumentationservices.net
Website: http://www.instrumentationservices.net
Directors: K. Watson (Co Sec)
Immediate Holding Company: CHARNWOOD INSTRUMENTATION SERVICES LIMITED
Registration no: 02048275 **Date established:** 1986
Turnover: £500,000 - £1m **No.of Employees:** 1 - 10 **Product Groups:** 38, 85

Date of Accounts	Apr 12	Apr 11	Apr 10
Working Capital	303	253	146
Fixed Assets	41	38	32
Current Assets	378	344	220

David Wilson Homes East Midlands

Forest Business Park Cartwright Way, Bardon Hill, Coalville, LE67 1GL
Tel: 01530-276700 **Fax:** 01530-276780
E-mail: john.reddington@dwh.co.uk
Website: http://www.davidwilsonhomes.co.uk
Directors: J. Reddington (MD), S. Burgess (Fin)
Ultimate Holding Company: BARRATT DEVELOPMENTS P L C
Immediate Holding Company: DAVID WILSON HOMES (EAST MIDLANDS) LIMITED
Registration no: 01139570 **VAT No.:** GB 113 7575 75
Date established: 1973 **Turnover:** £125m - £250m
No.of Employees: 51 - 100 **Product Groups:** 52

Electract Ltd

Walker Road Bardon Hill, Coalville, LE67 1TU
Tel: 01530-510011 **Fax:** 01530-811224
E-mail: pete.connor@electract.co.uk
Website: http://www.electract.co.uk
Bank(s): HSBC Bank plc
Directors: P. Connor (MD), R. Malpas (Fin)
Managers: C. Walker (Personnel)
Ultimate Holding Company: ELECTRACT HOLDINGS LIMITED
Immediate Holding Company: ELECTRACT LIMITED
Registration no: 00479653 **Date established:** 1950
Turnover: £10m - £20m **No.of Employees:** 101 - 250 **Product Groups:** 52

Date of Accounts	Mar 12	Mar 11	Mar 10
Sales Turnover	14m	14m	13m
Pre Tax Profit/Loss	365	216	458
Working Capital	2m	2m	2m
Fixed Assets	120	66	88
Current Assets	4m	4m	4m
Current Liabilities	648	546	699

Fleet Auction Group

Stephenson Court Brindley Road Stephenson Industrial Estate, Coalville, LE67 3HG
Tel: 01530-833535 **Fax:** 01530-813425
E-mail: info@fleetauctiongroup.com
Website: http://www.fleetauctiongroup.com
Directors: K. Clarke (Chief Op Offcr)
Managers: D. Betts (Tech Serv Mgr), D. Bush (Chief Acct), A. Walker
Immediate Holding Company: THE FLEET AUCTION GROUP LIMITED
Registration no: 04053278 **Date established:** 2000 **Turnover:** £5m - £10m
No.of Employees: 21 - 50 **Product Groups:** 68

Date of Accounts	Dec 11	Dec 10	Dec 09
Sales Turnover	6m	6m	3m
Pre Tax Profit/Loss	690	671	148
Working Capital	-2m	-2m	-2m
Fixed Assets	7m	6m	6m
Current Assets	579	629	627
Current Liabilities	1m	2m	N/A

Flex-It

Unit 3 Wylam Court Telford Way, Coalville, LE67 3HP
Tel: 01530-812195 **Fax:** 01530-817191
E-mail: sales@flex-it.co.uk
Website: http://www.flex-it.co.uk
Directors: A. Dickinson (Ptnr)
Turnover: £250,000 - £500,000 **No.of Employees:** 1 - 10
Product Groups: 30, 33, 35, 36, 37, 45, 46, 47, 68

Flint Distribution Ltd

Walker Road Bardon Hill, Coalville, LE67 1TU
Tel: 01530-510333 **Fax:** 01530-510275
E-mail: enq@flint.co.uk
Website: http://www.flint.co.uk
Bank(s): Lloyds TSB Bank plc
Directors: C. Barton (MD)
Managers: N. Brown (Tech Serv Mgr), R. Wavy (Personnel), R. Wavy (Personnel), P. Wyles (Sales Prom Mgr), M. Dealtry (I.T. Exec), V. Synnott (Sales & Mktg Mg)
Ultimate Holding Company: AVNET INC (USA)
Immediate Holding Company: FLINT DISTRIBUTION LIMITED
Registration no: 01927634 **VAT No.:** GB 436 3433 59
Date established: 1985 **Turnover:** £500,000 - £1m
No.of Employees: 21 - 50 **Product Groups:** 33, 35, 37, 38, 39, 44, 67

Date of Accounts	Jun 08	Jun 09	Jul 10
Sales Turnover	13m	11m	11m
Pre Tax Profit/Loss	-383	-13	542
Working Capital	2m	2m	3m
Fixed Assets	61	109	101
Current Assets	6m	5m	6m
Current Liabilities	359	330	507

Greasley Electronics Ltd

The Springboard Centre Mantle Lane, Coalville, LE67 3DW
Tel: 01530-835823 **Fax:** 01530-810231
E-mail: info@greasley.co.uk
Website: http://www.greasley.co.uk
Directors: K. Courtney (Co Sec)
Immediate Holding Company: GREASLEY ELECTRONICS LIMITED
Registration no: 01968483 **VAT No.:** GB 339 5018 51
Date established: 1985 **Turnover:** £250,000 - £500,000
No.of Employees: 1 - 10 **Product Groups:** 37, 48

Date of Accounts	Mar 12	Mar 11	Mar 10
Working Capital	80	65	52
Fixed Assets	8	10	12
Current Assets	132	106	85

Greygate Chemical Products

Brunel Way Stephenson Industrial Estate, Coalville, LE67 3HF
Tel: 01530-839222 **Fax:** 01530-837084
E-mail: sales@greygate.com
Website: http://www.greygate.com
Bank(s): Lloyds TSB Bank plc
Directors: A. Brown (Co Sec), R. Stenhouse (Dir), R. Stenhouse (MD)
Immediate Holding Company: GREYGATE CHEMICAL PRODUCTS LIMITED
Registration no: 00951847 **Date established:** 1969
Turnover: £500,000 - £1m **No.of Employees:** 21 - 50 **Product Groups:** 32

Date of Accounts	Aug 11	Aug 10	Aug 09
Working Capital	87	84	80
Fixed Assets	9	12	16
Current Assets	242	240	227

Home IQ

279 Thornborough rd, Coalville, LE67 3TN
Tel: 01530-460091 **Fax:** 01530-460091
E-mail: home-iq@home-iq.co.uk
Website: http://www.home-iq.co.uk
Directors: C. Nycz (Ptnr)
Registration no: 06103779 **Date established:** 2006
Turnover: Up to £250,000 **No.of Employees:** 1 - 10 **Product Groups:** 37, 40, 49

Hörmann (UK) Ltd

Gee Road, Coalville, LE67 4JW
Tel: 01530-513000 **Fax:** 01530-513051
E-mail: marketing.lei@hormann.co.uk
Website: http://www.hormann.co.uk
Bank(s): Barclays Bank plc
Directors: R. Warom (MD), T. Langley (Dir)
Managers: D. Newcombe (), A. Jenkins, P. Kanabar (Mgr), J. Smith (Mgr)
Immediate Holding Company: Hormann KG (Germany)
Registration no: 01440638 **VAT No.:** GB 330 3172 08
No.of Employees: 101 - 250 **Product Groups:** 25, 29, 30, 35, 36, 37, 40

Date of Accounts	Dec 11	Dec 10	Dec 09
Sales Turnover	41m	40m	34m
Pre Tax Profit/Loss	-348	500	-142
Working Capital	4m	5m	4m
Fixed Assets	4m	4m	4m
Current Assets	16m	16m	14m
Current Liabilities	2m	2m	2m

J H L Sales UK Ltd

Unit A Brunel Way, Coalville, LE67 3HF
Tel: 01530-815687 **Fax:** 01530-815686
E-mail: info@jhluk.co.uk
Website: http://www.jhluk.co.uk
Managers: A. Delaney (Mgr)
Immediate Holding Company: JHL SALES (UK) LIMITED
Registration no: 05359099 **Date established:** 2005
No.of Employees: 1 - 10 **Product Groups:** 18, 42

Date of Accounts	Mar 11	Mar 10	Mar 09
Working Capital	-32	-33	36
Fixed Assets	6	10	30
Current Assets	360	247	202

Lastolite Ltd

18 Atlas Road, Coalville, LE67 3FQ
Tel: 01530-813381 **Fax:** 01530-830408
E-mail: sales@lastolite.com
Website: http://www.lastolite.com
Bank(s): National Westminster Bank Plc
Directors: C. Henry (Co Sec), M. Davis (MD), S. Henry (Sales)
Ultimate Holding Company: THE VITEC GROUP PLC.
Immediate Holding Company: MANFROTTO LIGHTING LIMITED
Registration no: 01959633 **VAT No.:** GB 424 4818 53
Date established: 1985 **Turnover:** £5m - £10m
No.of Employees: 51 - 100 **Product Groups:** 37, 38, 65

Date of Accounts	Dec 11	Dec 10	Dec 09
Sales Turnover	9m	8m	N/A
Pre Tax Profit/Loss	1m	2m	N/A
Working Capital	3m	2m	2m
Fixed Assets	382	428	387
Current Assets	4m	3m	3m
Current Liabilities	528	226	N/A

Matsuura Machinery Ltd

Gee Road, Coalville, LE67 4NH
Tel: 01530-511400 **Fax:** 01530-511440
E-mail: marketing@matsuura.co.uk
Website: http://www.matsuura.co.uk
Managers: I. Mitchie (Mktg Serv Mgr)
Ultimate Holding Company: MATSUURA MACHINERY CORP (JAPAN)
Immediate Holding Company: MATSUURA MACHINERY LIMITED
Registration no: 02592156 **Date established:** 1991
Turnover: £20m - £50m **No.of Employees:** 51 - 100 **Product Groups:** 46

Date of Accounts	Dec 11	Dec 10	Dec 09
Sales Turnover	33m	17m	10m
Pre Tax Profit/Loss	2m	459	147
Working Capital	4m	2m	2m
Fixed Assets	661	734	555
Current Assets	16m	14m	9m
Current Liabilities	3m	6m	2m

Midland Lift Services Ltd

343 Station Road Bagworth, Coalville, LE67 1BL
Tel: 01530-230555 **Fax:** 01530-231555
E-mail: sales@midlandliftservices.co.uk
Website: http://www.midlandliftservices.co.uk
Directors: L. Martin (Dir)
Immediate Holding Company: MIDLAND LIFT SERVICES LIMITED
Registration no: 04411093 **Date established:** 2002
Turnover: Up to £250,000 **No.of Employees:** 1 - 10 **Product Groups:** 35, 39, 45

Date of Accounts	Mar 11	Mar 10	Mar 09
Working Capital	8	25	14
Fixed Assets	32	36	24
Current Assets	229	150	121

Midland Metal Sawing Services

Old Station Close, Coalville, LE67 3FH
Tel: 01530-839939
Directors: S. James (Prop)
Immediate Holding Company: SPRINGFIELDS (UK) LIMITED
Registration no: 03156028 **Date established:** 2003
No.of Employees: 1 - 10 **Product Groups:** 35

Date of Accounts	Jun 11	Jun 10	Jun 09
Working Capital	776	543	572
Fixed Assets	1m	1m	1m
Current Assets	788	555	586

P O S Direct Ltd

Samson Road, Coalville, LE67 3FP
Tel: 01530-518980 **Fax:** 01530-518999
Website: http://www.posdirect.co.uk
Directors: R. Crosse (MD), P. Halam (Dir)
Immediate Holding Company: P.O.S. DIRECT LIMITED
Registration no: 02579623 **Date established:** 1991
No.of Employees: 11 - 20 **Product Groups:** 49

Date of Accounts	May 11	May 10	May 09
Sales Turnover	6m	6m	7m
Pre Tax Profit/Loss	400	93	366
Working Capital	-193	-240	-85
Fixed Assets	3m	3m	3m
Current Assets	2m	1m	2m
Current Liabilities	520	444	471

Precision Balance Services

3 Atlas Court, Coalville, LE67 3FL
Tel: 01530-834650 **Fax:** 01530-834650
E-mail: sales@precisionbalance.co.uk
Website: http://www.precisionbalance.co.uk
Directors: L. Exell (Dir)
Immediate Holding Company: PRECISION BALANCE SERVICES LIMITED
Registration no: 04562574 **Date established:** 2002
No.of Employees: 1 - 10 **Product Groups:** 38, 42

see next page

***Precision Balance Services** - Cont'd*

Date of Accounts	Mar 11	Mar 10	Mar 09
Working Capital	-10	-29	-39
Fixed Assets	21	32	41
Current Assets	106	68	62

Process Technology Europe Ltd
18 North Street Whitwick, Coalville, LE67 5HA
Tel: 01530-810333 **Fax:** 08717- 504327
E-mail: tony.bolton@process-technology.co.uk
Website: http://www.process-technology.co.uk
Directors: T. Bolton (Prop)
Immediate Holding Company: PROCESS TECHNOLOGY (EUROPE) LIMITED
Registration no: 04749500 **Date established:** 2003
Turnover: £250,000 - £500,000 **No.of Employees:** 1 - 10
Product Groups: 46

Date of Accounts	Apr 11	Apr 10	Apr 09
Working Capital	-123	-100	-72
Fixed Assets	132	106	88
Current Assets	N/A	1	16

Radiant Control Ltd
Unit 6 Cartwright Court Cartwright Way, Bardon Hill, Coalville, LE67 1UE
Tel: 01530-519666 **Fax:** 01530-519667
E-mail: sales@radiantcontrol.co.uk
Website: http://www.radiantcontrol.co.uk
Directors: A. Sipika (Dir)
Immediate Holding Company: RADIANT CONTROL LTD
Registration no: 05157988 **Date established:** 2004
No.of Employees: 1 - 10 **Product Groups:** 36, 37, 38, 39, 40, 66, 84, 86

Date of Accounts	Jul 11	Jul 10	Jul 09
Working Capital	77	70	59
Fixed Assets	1	2	4
Current Assets	179	175	186

Revolution
43 North Avenue, Coalville, LE67 3QX
Tel: 01530-510080 **Fax:** 01530-833700
E-mail: sales@revolutionshirts.co.uk
Website: http://www.revolutionshirts.co.uk
Directors: J. Edgecombe (Dir)
Registration no: 04218893 **Turnover:** £250,000 - £500,000
No.of Employees: 11 - 20 **Product Groups:** 23

Russell's Garden Buildings (Shedland)
Gelsmoor Road Coleorton, Coalville, LE67 8JF
Tel: 01530-222295
E-mail: russellboam@yahoo.com
Website: http://www.shedland.co.uk
Directors: R. Boam (Prop)
Immediate Holding Company: FINNINGLEY ESTATES LIMITED
Registration no: 00352306 **Date established:** 1939
No.of Employees: 1 - 10 **Product Groups:** 25, 35, 41

Date of Accounts	Mar 11	Mar 10	Mar 06
Working Capital	53	57	66
Fixed Assets	923	555	479
Current Assets	82	93	104

H Seal & Co. Ltd
Church Lane Whitwick, Coalville, LE67 5DH
Tel: 01530-832351 **Fax:** 01530-813382
E-mail: sales@hseal.co.uk
Website: http://www.hseal.co.uk
Bank(s): National Westminster Bank Plc
Directors: P. Seal (MD)
Immediate Holding Company: H.SEAL & CO.,LIMITED
Registration no: 00166525 **VAT No.:** GB 114 9146 82
Date established: 2020 **Turnover:** £1m - £2m **No.of Employees:** 11 - 20
Product Groups: 23

Date of Accounts	Sep 11	Sep 10	Sep 09
Working Capital	746	460	427
Fixed Assets	190	225	268
Current Assets	880	520	502

Shermond Surgical Supplies
New Frontier House Interlink Park, Bardon Hill, Coalville, LE67 1PB
Tel: 01530-278111 **Fax:** 01530-278117
E-mail: sales@shermond.com
Website: http://www.shermond.com
Managers: D. Black (Sales Admin)
Turnover: £10m - £20m **No.of Employees:** 11 - 20 **Product Groups:** 24, 29, 30

Sunshine Display Group Ltd
Unit 6 Coalville Business Park Jackson Street, Coalville, LE67 3NR
Tel: 01530-811671 **Fax:** 01530-815743
E-mail: info@sunshine-uk.com
Website: http://www.sunshine-uk.com
Turnover: £500,000 - £1m **No.of Employees:** 1 - 10 **Product Groups:** 26, 28, 30, 49, 75

Date of Accounts	Jul 08
Working Capital	12
Fixed Assets	1
Current Assets	47
Current Liabilities	35

Terex (BL Pegson)
Mammoth Street, Coalville, LE67 3GN
Tel: 01530-518600 **Fax:** 01530-518618
Website: http://www.bl-pegson.com
Directors: K. Tuder (MD)
Managers: G. Horn (Fin Mgr), L. Axten (Tech Serv Mgr), P. Fisher (Mktg Serv Mgr), Z. Staniforth (Personnel)
Immediate Holding Company: POWERSCREEN INTERNATIONAL LTD
Registration no: 03087561 **VAT No.:** GB 616 8291 26
Date established: 1931 **Turnover:** £125m - £250m
No.of Employees: 51 - 100 **Product Groups:** 45

Date of Accounts	Dec 07	Dec 06	Dec 05
Sales Turnover	149710	124690	105450
Pre Tax Profit/Loss	25400	16540	16450
Working Capital	77470	58740	47700
Fixed Assets	4540	3400	3310
Current Assets	137570	113200	96330
Current Liabilities	60100	54460	48630
Total Share Capital	2530	2530	2530
ROCE% (Return on Capital Employed)	31.0	26.6	32.2
ROT% (Return on Turnover)	17.0	13.3	15.6

Tornos Technologies UK Ltd
Tornos House Garden Road, Coalville, LE67 4JQ
Tel: 01530-513100 **Fax:** 01530-814212
E-mail: sales@tornos.co.uk
Website: http://www.tornos.com
Managers: J. Mcbride
Ultimate Holding Company: TORNOS HOLDINGS SA (SWITZERLAND)
Immediate Holding Company: TORNOS TECHNOLOGIES UK LIMITED
Registration no: 01420750 **VAT No.:** GB 228 9172 42
Date established: 1979 **Turnover:** £500,000 - £1m
No.of Employees: 1 - 10 **Product Groups:** 46

Date of Accounts	Dec 11	Dec 10	Dec 09
Sales Turnover	N/A	549	524
Pre Tax Profit/Loss	N/A	36	27
Working Capital	-44	-49	-58
Fixed Assets	514	537	565
Current Assets	58	44	33
Current Liabilities	N/A	33	29

TriMark Europe Ltd
Cedar Court Bardon Hill, Coalville, LE67 1TU
Tel: 01530-512460 **Fax:** 01530-512461
E-mail: sales@trimarkeu.com
Website: http://www.trimarkeu.com
Directors: K. Dolbear (MD)
Ultimate Holding Company: TRI/MARK CORPORATION (USA)
Immediate Holding Company: TRIMARK EUROPE LIMITED
Registration no: 03403771 **Date established:** 1997 **Turnover:** £5m - £10m
No.of Employees: 11 - 20 **Product Groups:** 24, 25, 29, 30, 33, 34, 35

Date of Accounts	Dec 11	Dec 10	Dec 09
Sales Turnover	8m	6m	4m
Pre Tax Profit/Loss	1	573	-673
Working Capital	2m	942	604
Fixed Assets	1m	2m	2m
Current Assets	3m	3m	2m
Current Liabilities	240	297	220

The Valve Alliance Ltd
Unit 6 Interlink Way South, Bardon Hill, Coalville, LE67 1PH
Tel: 01530-834270 **Fax:** 01530-838986
E-mail: sales@acvalvealliance.com
Website: http://www.acvalvealliance.com
Directors: J. Calvert (Fin), S. Craddock (Sales), A. Calvert (MD)
Managers: M. Conway (Sales Eng)
Immediate Holding Company: THE VALVE ALLIANCE LIMITED
Registration no: 03596499 **Date established:** 1998
No.of Employees: 21 - 50 **Product Groups:** 36, 37, 38

Date of Accounts	Mar 12	Mar 11	Mar 10
Working Capital	2m	2m	1m
Fixed Assets	79	49	67
Current Assets	2m	3m	2m

Vitax Ltd
Owen Street, Coalville, LE67 3DE
Tel: 01530-510060 **Fax:** 01530-510299
E-mail: julian.plews@vitax.co.uk
Website: http://www.vitax.co.uk
Bank(s): National Westminster
Directors: C. Platt (I.T. Dir), J. Plews (Co Sec)
Managers: P. Gooding (Chief Acct)
Ultimate Holding Company: SYNCHEMICALS LIMITED
Immediate Holding Company: VITAX LIMITED
Registration no: 02010696 **VAT No.:** GB 238 0325 81
Date established: 1986 **Turnover:** £5m - £10m **No.of Employees:** 21 - 50
Product Groups: 32

Date of Accounts	Aug 11	Aug 10	Aug 09
Sales Turnover	9m	9m	8m
Pre Tax Profit/Loss	214	616	261
Working Capital	4m	4m	4m
Fixed Assets	212	355	308
Current Assets	5m	6m	5m
Current Liabilities	1m	1m	1m

Vivid Laminating Technologies
St Georges House Whitwick Road, Coalville, LE67 3FA
Tel: 01530-510946 **Fax:** 01530-510979
E-mail: sales@vivid-online.com
Website: http://www.vivid-online.com
Directors: M. Evans (MD)
Immediate Holding Company: VIVID LAMINATING TECHNOLOGIES LIMITED
Registration no: 02063018 **Date established:** 1986
Turnover: Up to £250,000 **No.of Employees:** 21 - 50 **Product Groups:** 30, 44

Date of Accounts	Apr 11	Apr 10	Apr 09
Working Capital	1m	1m	771
Fixed Assets	173	171	144
Current Assets	2m	2m	2m

Winbro Group Technologies
Whitwick Business Park Stenson Road, Coalville, LE67 4JP
Tel: 01530-516000 **Fax:** 01530-516001
E-mail: reception@winbrogroup.com
Website: http://www.winbrogroup.com
Directors: T. Box (Fin), T. Barnett (Fin)
Managers: A. Lawson (Sales Prom Mgr), P. Antill (I.T. Exec)
Ultimate Holding Company: WINBRO GROUP LTD (USA)
Immediate Holding Company: WINBRO GROUP UK LIMITED
Registration no: 03742577 **VAT No.:** GB 558 7846 77
Date established: 1999 **Turnover:** £5m - £10m
No.of Employees: 101 - 250 **Product Groups:** 46

Date of Accounts	Dec 11	Dec 10	Oct 09
Sales Turnover	19m	10m	12m
Pre Tax Profit/Loss	3m	183	3m
Working Capital	5m	3m	6m
Fixed Assets	3m	2m	1m
Current Assets	8m	7m	7m
Current Liabilities	1m	1m	1m

Hinckley

A D I Midlands Ltd
Cold Comfort Farm Rogues Lane, Hinckley, LE10 3DX
Tel: 01455-213812 **Fax:** 01455-213813
E-mail: accounts@a-d-i.co.uk
Website: http://www.a-d-i.co.uk
Managers: C. Mcmanus (Ops Mgr)
Immediate Holding Company: ADI MIDLANDS LIMITED
Registration no: 07143347 **Date established:** 2010
No.of Employees: 11 - 20 **Product Groups:** 25, 30, 35, 41, 49, 52, 66

Date of Accounts	Feb 12	Feb 11
Working Capital	18	20
Fixed Assets	50	34
Current Assets	157	176

A M System UK Ltd
8 Watling Drive, Hinckley, LE10 3EY
Tel: 01455-250550 **Fax:** 01455-250072
E-mail: sales@amsystem.co.uk
Website: http://www.amsystem.co.uk
Bank(s): Jyske, London
Directors: M. Maxted (MD)
Managers: C. Henriksen (Chief Mgr), S. Maxted (Personnel)
Ultimate Holding Company: XAM 1042 LIMITED
Immediate Holding Company: AM SYSTEM (UK) LIMITED
Registration no: 00604883 **Date established:** 1958 **Turnover:** £1m - £2m
No.of Employees: 11 - 20 **Product Groups:** 26

Date of Accounts	Dec 11	Dec 10	Dec 09
Working Capital	872	1m	961
Fixed Assets	111	105	115
Current Assets	2m	2m	2m

Access Plus
Wheatfield Way, Hinckley, LE10 1YG
Tel: 0113-252 9922 **Fax:** 0113-252 2864
E-mail: healthcheck@accessplus.co.uk
Website: http://www.accessplus.co.uk
Directors: J. Cromak (Grp Chief Exec)
Immediate Holding Company: HERITAGE WOODCRAFT LIMITED
Registration no: 00469211 **Date established:** 1989
No.of Employees: 21 - 50 **Product Groups:** 27, 28, 44, 64, 80, 81

Advanced Carbide Tooling Ltd
Unit 8 Sketchley Meadows Business Park, Hinckley, LE10 3EZ
Tel: 01455-234000 **Fax:** 01455-234022
E-mail: sales@advancedcarbidetooling.co.uk
Website: http://www.advancedcarbidetooling.co.uk
Directors: D. Houghton (Dir)
Immediate Holding Company: ADVANCED CARBIDE TOOLING LIMITED
Registration no: 01788846 **Date established:** 1984 **Turnover:** £1m - £2m
No.of Employees: 1 - 10 **Product Groups:** 33, 34, 36, 46

Date of Accounts	Sep 11	Sep 10	Sep 09
Working Capital	222	169	160
Fixed Assets	294	297	313
Current Assets	376	316	372

Automatic Engineers Hinckley Ltd
Burbage Road Burbage, Hinckley, LE10 2TP
Tel: 01455-238033 **Fax:** 01455-615101
E-mail: sales@automaticengineers.com
Website: http://www.automaticengineers.com
Directors: R. Clayfield (MD)
Immediate Holding Company: AUTOMATIC ENGINEERS (HINCKLEY) LIMITED
Registration no: 02695945 **Date established:** 1992
No.of Employees: 11 - 20 **Product Groups:** 46, 48

Date of Accounts	Mar 11	Mar 10	Mar 09
Working Capital	158	101	56
Fixed Assets	402	408	406
Current Assets	360	315	218

Burgess Architectural Products Ltd
PO Box 11, Hinckley, LE10 2LL
Tel: 01455-618787 **Fax:** 01455-251061
E-mail: info@burgessceilings.co.uk
Website: http://www.burgessceilings.co.uk
Bank(s): National Westminster Bank Plc
Directors: D. Palmer (Fin), J. Higgins (Dir)
Managers: G. White (Personnel)
Ultimate Holding Company: BAP HOLDINGS LIMITED
Immediate Holding Company: BURGESS ARCHITECTURAL PRODUCTS LIMITED
Registration no: 01129056 **VAT No.:** GB 424 3898 34
Date established: 1973 **Turnover:** £5m - £10m
No.of Employees: 51 - 100 **Product Groups:** 35, 36, 40, 42

Date of Accounts	Dec 11	Dec 10	Dec 09
Sales Turnover	7m	7m	8m
Pre Tax Profit/Loss	243	255	242
Working Capital	2m	1m	1m
Fixed Assets	969	973	445
Current Assets	4m	4m	4m
Current Liabilities	784	767	937

Cabbola Food Service Equipment
47 New Street, Hinckley, LE10 1QY
Tel: 01455-612020 **Fax:** 01455-636364
E-mail: sales@cabbola.com
Website: http://www.cateringequipment.com
Directors: P. Woodford (MD), R. Duncan (MD), S. Dixon (Sales), C. McDermott (Co Sec)
Immediate Holding Company: LAMP ENTERPRISES LIMITED
Registration no: 02200740 **Date established:** 2007 **Turnover:** £2m - £5m
No.of Employees: 1 - 10 **Product Groups:** 40, 67

Date of Accounts	Sep 10	Sep 09	Sep 08
Working Capital	20	15	N/A
Fixed Assets	3	1	1
Current Assets	29	23	6

Canner & Sons
32 Brindley Road Dodwells Bridge Industrial Estate, Hinckley, LE10 3BY
Tel: 01455-890282 **Fax:** 01455-891283
Managers: J. Canner (Mgr)
Date established: 1983 **No.of Employees:** 11 - 20 **Product Groups:** 35

Crane Electronics Ltd

Open House 3 Watling Drive, Hinckley, LE10 3EY
Tel: 01455-251488 **Fax:** 01455-614717
E-mail: info@crane-electronics.com
Website: http://www.crane-electronics.com
Bank(s): HSBC Bank plc
Directors: A. Duffin (MD)
Managers: C. Branson (Tech Serv Mgr), I. Brown (Sales & Mktg Mg), J. Morgan (Buyer)
Ultimate Holding Company: COBCO 812 LIMITED
Immediate Holding Company: CRANE ELECTRONICS LIMITED
Registration no: 01029811 **Date established:** 1971 **Turnover:** £2m - £5m
No.of Employees: 21 - 50 **Product Groups:** 35, 36, 37, 38, 40, 44, 85

Date of Accounts	Nov 08	Nov 09	Nov 10
Sales Turnover	5m	3m	4m
Pre Tax Profit/Loss	214	212	356
Working Capital	2m	2m	2m
Fixed Assets	1m	1m	1m
Current Assets	3m	3m	3m
Current Liabilities	924	597	764

Direct Signs UK Ltd

Unit 6 Venture Court, Hinckley, LE10 3BT
Tel: 01455-230122 **Fax:** 01455-634333
E-mail: sales@directsigns.co.uk
Website: http://www.directsigns.co.uk
Directors: E. Glen (Dir)
Immediate Holding Company: DIRECT SIGNS (UK) LIMITED
Registration no: 03637488 **Date established:** 1998
Turnover: £250,000 - £500,000 **No.of Employees:** 1 - 10
Product Groups: 27, 28, 30, 39, 40, 49, 52, 81, 84

Date of Accounts	Dec 11	Dec 10	Dec 09
Sales Turnover	N/A	N/A	418
Pre Tax Profit/Loss	N/A	N/A	53
Working Capital	-11	15	-35
Fixed Assets	62	62	77
Current Assets	175	209	139

East Midland Coatings Ltd

Barleyfield, Hinckley, LE10 1YE
Tel: 01455-619176 **Fax:** 01455-619051
E-mail: sales@eastmidlandcoatings.co.uk
Website: http://www.eastmidlandcoatings.co.uk
Directors: S. Moore (Fin)
Immediate Holding Company: EAST MIDLAND COATINGS LIMITED
Registration no: 01825193 **Date established:** 1984 **Turnover:** £1m - £2m
No.of Employees: 11 - 20 **Product Groups:** 30, 32

Date of Accounts	Jul 12	Jul 11	Jul 10
Working Capital	1m	1m	1m
Fixed Assets	87	71	75
Current Assets	1m	1m	1m

Fridge Freezer Direct Company Ltd

41-43 Brookside Burbage, Hinckley, LE10 2TG
Tel: 08456-800695 **Fax:** 01454-250434
E-mail: enquiries@fridgefreezerdirect.co.uk
Website: http://www.fridgefreezerdirect.co.uk
Directors: C. Greenhough (MD)
Immediate Holding Company: FRIDGE FREEZER DIRECT LTD
Registration no: 07357723 **Date established:** 2010
Turnover: £500,000 - £1m **No.of Employees:** 1 - 10 **Product Groups:** 40

Date of Accounts	Aug 11
Working Capital	57
Fixed Assets	7
Current Assets	121

H J Sock Group Ltd

57 Coventry Road, Hinckley, LE10 0JX
Tel: 01455-638800 **Fax:** 01455-610535
E-mail: enquiries@hjhall.com
Website: http://www.hjhall.com
Bank(s): The Royal Bank of Scotland
Directors: A. Jenkins (Sales & Mktg)
Managers: G. Bennett (Chief Acct), R. Gray (Tech Serv Mgr)
Ultimate Holding Company: H J HALL LTD
Immediate Holding Company: H J SOCK GROUP LIMITED
Registration no: 02412782 **VAT No.:** GB 350 3491 75
Date established: 1989 **Turnover:** £2m - £5m **No.of Employees:** 21 - 50
Product Groups: 24

Date of Accounts	Jun 11	Jun 10	Jun 09
Sales Turnover	4m	6m	6m
Pre Tax Profit/Loss	273	-480	677
Working Capital	4m	4m	4m
Fixed Assets	330	381	422
Current Assets	4m	4m	5m
Current Liabilities	293	593	426

H J Hall

Coventry Road, Hinckley, LE10 0JX
Tel: 01455-638800 **Fax:** 01455-610535
E-mail: enquiries@hjhall.com
Website: http://www.hjhall.com
Bank(s): Bank of Scotland
Directors: A. Jenkins (Sales & Mktg), G. Marsh (MD), N. Hall (Ch)
Immediate Holding Company: H J Hall Ltd
Registration no: 05906935 **VAT No.:** GB 350 3491 75
Date established: 2006 **Turnover:** £5m - £10m
No.of Employees: 101 - 250 **Product Groups:** 24

A.O. Henton Engineering Co. Ltd

Cotes Road Burbage, Hinckley, LE10 2HJ
Tel: 01455-238331 **Fax:** 01455-254323
E-mail: david.english@aohenton.co.uk
Bank(s): Barclays, Birmiingham
Directors: R. Hipkins (Co Sec), J. Atkinson (Dir)
Managers: R. Tolley (Buyer), D. Halliday (Chief Mgr), D. English (Sales Prom Mgr)
Ultimate Holding Company: J.S. Chinn Holdings Ltd
Immediate Holding Company: J.S. Chinn Holdings Ltd
Registration no: 00539384 **Turnover:** £5m - £10m
No.of Employees: 51 - 100 **Product Groups:** 39, 48

Date of Accounts	Dec 06	Dec 05
Sales Turnover	6395	5433
Pre Tax Profit/Loss	189	75
Working Capital	1453	1132
Fixed Assets	1527	1577
Current Assets	3985	3806
Current Liabilities	2532	2674
Total Share Capital	4	4
ROCE% (Return on Capital Employed)	6.3	2.8
ROT% (Return on Turnover)	2.9	1.4

Hollis Packaging

Unit 11 Sketchley Meadows, Hinckley, LE10 3EN
Tel: 01455-234235 **Fax:** 01455-251607
E-mail: sales@hollispackaging.co.uk
Website: http://www.hollispackaging.co.uk
Directors: V. Moore (Ptnr)
Registration no: 06024479 **Date established:** 2006
Turnover: Up to £250,000 **No.of Employees:** 11 - 20 **Product Groups:** 30, 48

Lemar Wrought Ironwork

Newton Road, Hinckley, LE10 3DS
Tel: 01455-637077 **Fax:** 01455-251972
E-mail: info@lemar.co.uk
Website: http://www.lemar.co.uk
Directors: G. Mayberry (Ptnr)
Immediate Holding Company: HINCKLEY GLASS AND GLAZING COMPANY LIMITED
Registration no: 02032102 **VAT No.:** GB 328 0149 74
Date established: 1983 **Turnover:** £250,000 - £500,000
No.of Employees: 1 - 10 **Product Groups:** 35, 40, 48

Date of Accounts	Mar 12	Mar 11	Mar 10
Working Capital	-8	-14	-13
Fixed Assets	18	21	17
Current Assets	34	21	22

Live Wire Marketing Ltd

The Lawns Business Centre The Lawns, Hinckley, LE10 1DY
Tel: 01455-234468 **Fax:** 01455-444493
E-mail: ideas@livewiredirect.co.uk
Website: http://www.livewiredirect.co.uk
Directors: P. Hoggard (Dir), M. Levell (Fin)
Immediate Holding Company: LIVE WIRE MARKETING LIMITED
Registration no: 03772944 **Date established:** 1999
Turnover: Up to £250,000 **No.of Employees:** 1 - 10 **Product Groups:** 81

M F X Design

19 Glebe Road Hinckley, Hinckley, LE10 1HF
Tel: 01827-255306
E-mail: mfxkitchendesign@yahoo.co.uk
Website: http://www.mfxdesign.co.uk
Directors: A. Cattell (Prop)
Date established: 2006 **Turnover:** Up to £250,000
No.of Employees: 1 - 10 **Product Groups:** 84

Manchester Hosiery A Division Of Aikon Europe Group Ltd

Queens Road, Hinckley, LE10 1EE
Tel: 01455-632161 **Fax:** 01455-635390
E-mail: info@palmunderwear.co.uk
Website: http://www.palmunderwear.co.uk
Bank(s): Royal Bank of Scotland
Directors: Finn (Dir)
Ultimate Holding Company: THE MANCHESTER HOSIERY GROUP LIMITED
Immediate Holding Company: WHITE SWAN KNITWEAR LIMITED
Registration no: 01062541 **Date established:** 1972 **Turnover:** £2m - £5m
No.of Employees: 21 - 50 **Product Groups:** 24

Date of Accounts	Dec 11	Dec 10	Dec 09
Working Capital	-6	-6	-6

Milturn Precision Engineers

Unit 1 Stirling Park 0 Jacknell Road, Hinckley, LE10 3BS
Tel: 01455-611444 **Fax:** 01455-615777
E-mail: admin@milturn.net
Website: http://www.milturn.net
Directors: B. Kemp (Dir)
Immediate Holding Company: MILTURN (PRECISION ENGINEERS) LIMITED
Registration no: 04236207 **Date established:** 2001
Turnover: £500,000 - £1m **No.of Employees:** 11 - 20
Product Groups: 28, 35, 39, 44, 48, 66, 68, 87

Date of Accounts	Jul 11	Jul 10	Jul 09
Working Capital	-145	-154	-81
Fixed Assets	287	205	194
Current Assets	356	219	154

The Mobility Equipment Company Ltd

136 Ashby Road, Hinckley, LE10 1SN
Tel: 01455-632222 **Fax:** 08700-118234
E-mail: sales@tmecuk.co.uk
Directors: T. Fergus (Dir)
Immediate Holding Company: THE MOBILITY EQUIPMENT COMPANY LIMITED
Registration no: 04234000 **Date established:** 2001
No.of Employees: 11 - 20 **Product Groups:** 35, 39, 45

Date of Accounts	Jun 11	Jun 10	Jun 09
Working Capital	-77	17	199
Fixed Assets	248	210	123
Current Assets	406	490	582

Multi Industrial Doors Ltd

M I D Business Centre Sapcote Road, Burbage, Hinckley, LE10 2AU
Tel: 01455-891929 **Fax:** 01455-891974
E-mail: sales@multiindustrialdoors.co.uk
Website: http://www.multiindustrialdoors.co.uk
Directors: C. Husthwaite (Fin), M. Husthwaite (MD)
Immediate Holding Company: MULTI INDUSTRIAL DOORS LIMITED
Registration no: 03027847 **Date established:** 1995
No.of Employees: 11 - 20 **Product Groups:** 26, 35

Date of Accounts	Sep 11	Sep 10	Sep 09
Working Capital	397	333	327
Fixed Assets	30	38	38
Current Assets	561	567	512

Nylon Hosiery

44 Upper Bond Street, Hinckley, LE10 1RJ
Tel: 01455-631413 **Fax:** 01455-636345
E-mail: rob@nylonhosiery.co.uk
Website: http://www.webleicester.co.uk
Directors: R. Murray (Prop)
Immediate Holding Company: SAMABI LTD
Registration no: 00536463 **VAT No.:** GB 232 7854 55
Turnover: £1m - £2m **No.of Employees:** 1 - 10 **Product Groups:** 24, 63

Date of Accounts	Mar 07	Mar 06
Working Capital	554	3653
Fixed Assets	38	333
Current Assets	1277	3893
Current Liabilities	723	240
Total Share Capital	75	75

O L D Engineering Co. Ltd

Plot 1 Sketchley Lane Industrial Estate, Hinckley, LE10 3EN
Tel: 01455-612521 **Fax:** 01455-635790
E-mail: enquiries@oldengineering.co.uk
Website: http://www.oldengineering.co.uk
Bank(s): HSBC Bank plc
Directors: M. Topp (MD)
Ultimate Holding Company: O.L.D. HOLDINGS LIMITED
Immediate Holding Company: O.L.D. ENGINEERING COMPANY LIMITED
Registration no: 01009395 **VAT No.:** GB 114 2418 13
Date established: 1971 **Turnover:** £10m - £20m
No.of Employees: 51 - 100 **Product Groups:** 48

Date of Accounts	Apr 12	Apr 11	Apr 10
Sales Turnover	11m	N/A	N/A
Pre Tax Profit/Loss	574	N/A	N/A
Working Capital	2m	1m	1m
Fixed Assets	1m	470	227
Current Assets	4m	4m	2m
Current Liabilities	405	N/A	N/A

P E S UK Ltd

Unit 1 Watling Close, Hinckley, LE10 3EZ
Tel: 01455-251251 **Fax:** 01455-251252
E-mail: sales@pesukltd.com
Website: http://www.pesukltd.com
Bank(s): National Westminster Bank Plc
Directors: R. Elsey (MD)
Immediate Holding Company: PES (UK) LIMITED
Registration no: 01492922 **VAT No.:** GB 343 4516 69
Date established: 1980 **No.of Employees:** 11 - 20 **Product Groups:** 26, 29, 30, 32, 33, 34, 35, 36, 38, 39, 40, 44, 45, 46, 66, 85

Date of Accounts	May 11	May 10	May 09
Working Capital	439	446	462
Fixed Assets	286	231	246
Current Assets	1m	965	868

Paynes Of Hinckley

Watling Street, Hinckley, LE10 3ED
Tel: 01455-237777 **Fax:** 01455-237774
E-mail: stuartspalding@paynes-garages.co.uk
Website: http://www.paynes-garages.co.uk
Bank(s): National Westminster Bank Plc
Directors: S. Spalding (MD)
Ultimate Holding Company: PAYNES GARAGE(HOLDINGS) LIMITED
Immediate Holding Company: PAYNES VEHICLE CONTRACTS LIMITED
Registration no: 00811277 **Date established:** 1964
Turnover: £20m - £50m **No.of Employees:** 51 - 100 **Product Groups:** 68, 72

Date of Accounts	Dec 11	Dec 10	Dec 09
Working Capital	1	1	1
Current Assets	1	1	1

Plastic Paint Shop Ltd (Finishing Division)

Unit 4-6 Southways Industrial Estate Coventry Road, Hinckley, LE10 0NJ
Tel: 01455-234202 **Fax:** 01455-251335
E-mail: richard@plasticspaintshop.co.uk
Website: http://www.plasticpaintshop.co.uk
Directors: R. Butler (Dir)
Immediate Holding Company: PLASTIC PAINT SHOP LIMITED
Registration no: 06440918 **VAT No.:** GB 220 4153 22
Date established: 2007 **No.of Employees:** 1 - 10 **Product Groups:** 28, 48

Date of Accounts	Jan 12	Jan 11	Jan 10
Working Capital	24	7	3
Fixed Assets	12	15	3
Current Assets	101	84	63

Recognition Express

Wheatfield Way, Hinckley, LE10 1YG
Tel: 01455-445555 **Fax:** 01455-445566
E-mail: manchester@re-trade.co.uk
Website: http://www.re-trade.co.uk
Bank(s): Natwest
Directors: P. Mitchell (Dir), L. Bagley (Fin)
Ultimate Holding Company: THE BARDON GROUP LIMITED
Immediate Holding Company: RECOGNITION EXPRESS LIMITED
Registration no: 01457120 **Date established:** 1979 **Turnover:** £1m - £2m
No.of Employees: 11 - 20 **Product Groups:** 23

Date of Accounts	Mar 11	Mar 10	Mar 09
Working Capital	592	707	752
Fixed Assets	14	8	16
Current Assets	811	951	929

Rushlift Ltd

Hinckley Fields Industrial Estate Barleyfield, Hinckley, LE10 1YE
Tel: 01455-623420
E-mail: sales@rushliftuk.co.uk
Website: http://www.rushlift.co.uk
Directors: L. Cosgrove (Fin)
Managers: K. Frost (Mgr)
Ultimate Holding Company: THE SPECIALIST HIRE GROUP LIMITED
Immediate Holding Company: RUSHLIFT LIMITED
Registration no: 05493140 **Date established:** 2005
No.of Employees: 1 - 10 **Product Groups:** 35, 39, 45

Date of Accounts	Aug 11	Aug 10	Aug 09
Sales Turnover	18m	15m	16m
Pre Tax Profit/Loss	1m	757	1m
Working Capital	-3m	928	316
Fixed Assets	28m	11m	12m
Current Assets	6m	6m	6m
Current Liabilities	2m	2m	2m

Shapecraft Sheet Metal Co. Ltd

Wheatfield Way, Hinckley, LE10 1YG
Tel: 01455-618593 **Fax:** 01455-618593
E-mail: denise.johnson@hotmail.co.uk
Website: http://www.shapecraftsheetmetal.co.uk
Directors: D. Johnson (MD)
Immediate Holding Company: SHAPECRAFT SHEETMETAL COMPANY LIMITED

see next page

Shapecraft Sheet Metal Co. Ltd - Cont'd
Registration no: 01932968 **VAT No.:** GB 424 3811 72
Date established: 1985 **Turnover:** £250,000 - £500,000
No.of Employees: 1 - 10 **Product Groups:** 35, 48, 84

Date of Accounts	Jul 11	Jul 10	Jul 09
Working Capital	31	41	61
Fixed Assets	165	148	148
Current Assets	112	109	116

Software Stationery Specialists Ltd
Wheatfield Way, Hinckley, LE10 1YG
Tel: 01455-615564 **Fax:** 01455-616246
E-mail: sales@bsdstat.co.uk
Website: http://www.bsdstat.co.uk
Directors: F. McGoldrick (MD), J. Cromack (Dir)
Managers: D. Caldwell (Fin Mgr)
Ultimate Holding Company: Office2office plc
Immediate Holding Company: Software Stationery Holdings Ltd
Registration no: 02736545 **Date established:** 1949
Turnover: £20m - £50m **No.of Employees:** 1 - 10 **Product Groups:** 28, 81

Date of Accounts	Dec 06	Dec 05
Working Capital	749	749
Current Assets	3355	3355
Current Liabilities	2605	2605
Total Share Capital	749	749

Soho Paper Products
Unit 2 Teal Business Park Dodwells Road, Hinckley, LE10 3BZ
Tel: 01455-636242
E-mail: burdett45@aol.com
Website: http://www.sohopaper.co.uk
Directors: J. Burdett (Prop)
Immediate Holding Company: GET BIZZING LIMITED
Date established: 2011 **Turnover:** Up to £250,000
No.of Employees: 1 - 10 **Product Groups:** 27

Survey Express Services
7 Sunnyside Park, Hinckley, LE10 1PJ
Tel: 01455-890892 **Fax:** 01455-890893
Managers: J. Walker (Mgr)
No.of Employees: 1 - 10 **Product Groups:** 38

Swift J & R Ltd
Parsons Lane, Hinckley, LE10 1XT
Tel: 01455-238398 **Fax:** 01455-238866
E-mail: ask@swiftsuniforms.co.uk
Website: http://www.swiftsuniforms.co.uk
Directors: C. Swift (Dir), K. Swift (MD)
Immediate Holding Company: A V B MILLS LIMITED
Registration no: 00758633 **VAT No.:** GB 114 1526 15
Date established: 1993 **Turnover:** £250,000 - £500,000
No.of Employees: 1 - 10 **Product Groups:** 24

Date of Accounts	Aug 10	Aug 09	Aug 08
Sales Turnover	160	221	113
Pre Tax Profit/Loss	15	52	15
Working Capital	33	44	37
Fixed Assets	1	1	2
Current Assets	130	102	76
Current Liabilities	73	51	32

Veolia Environmental Services
Watling Street, Hinckley, LE10 3ED
Tel: 01455-251101 **Fax:** 01455-891045
Website: http://www.onyxgroup.co.uk
Managers: D. Moore (Ops Mgr)
Immediate Holding Company: FREEWAY PETROLEUM LIMITED
Registration no: 01980687 **VAT No.:** GB 530 0088 93
Date established: 1997 **No.of Employees:** 21 - 50 **Product Groups:** 34, 39, 54

Date of Accounts	Jun 08	Jun 07	Jun 06
Working Capital	114	78	47
Fixed Assets	1	1	1
Current Assets	187	149	116

Vision Packaging Ltd
Workshops Sketchley Meadows, Hinckley, LE10 3ES
Tel: 01455-637734 **Fax:** 01455-637724
E-mail: info@visionpackagingltd.co.uk
Website: http://www.visionpackagingltd.co.uk
Directors: D. Long (Dir)
Immediate Holding Company: VISION PACKAGING LIMITED
Registration no: 05989716 **Date established:** 2006
No.of Employees: 1 - 10 **Product Groups:** 28, 30, 31, 48

Date of Accounts	Dec 11	Dec 10	Dec 09
Working Capital	65	38	29
Fixed Assets	3	12	20
Current Assets	180	145	131

Warwick Wireless Ltd
Unit 16 Sapcote Road Industrial Estate Burbage, Hinckley, LE10 2AU
Tel: 01455-233616 **Fax:** 01455-233179
E-mail: sales@radiotelemetry.co.uk
Website: http://www.radiotelemetry.co.uk
Directors: A. Wiggin (Dir)
Immediate Holding Company: WARWICK WIRELESS LTD
Registration no: 02103088 **VAT No.:** GB 307 5531 72
Date established: 1987 **Turnover:** £500,000 - £1m
No.of Employees: 1 - 10 **Product Groups:** 37, 38, 44, 67

Date of Accounts	Mar 12	Mar 11	Mar 10
Working Capital	169	169	186
Fixed Assets	1	1	2
Current Assets	218	217	249

Weigh Till
Unit 45 Sparkenhoe House Southfield Road, Hinckley, LE10 1UB
Tel: 01455-617227 **Fax:** 01455-617227
E-mail: sales@weigh-till.co.uk
Website: http://www.weigh-till.co.uk
Directors: D. Darlison (Ptnr)
Registration no: 01802545 **Date established:** 1984
Turnover: £250,000 - £500,000 **No.of Employees:** 1 - 10
Product Groups: 38, 42

Wolvey Refrigeration
Glendower Lodge Coventry Road, Wolvey, Hinckley, LE10 3LD
Tel: 01455-220577 **Fax:** 01455-220577
E-mail: phillips@phillipsalan262.orangehome.co.uk
Directors: A. Phillips (Prop)
Date established: 1979 **No.of Employees:** 1 - 10 **Product Groups:** 36, 40

Ibstock

ATI Garryson Limited
Spring Road, Ibstock, LE67 6LR
Tel: 01530-261145 **Fax:** 01530-262801
E-mail: sales@garryson.co.uk
Website: http://www.atigarryson.co.uk
Bank(s): Royal Bank of Scotland, London
Directors: M. Everett (Fin), S. Drain (Mkt Research), J. Pickering (Dir), S. McGarry (Sales), A. Newitt (Fab), M. Herbert (MD)
Managers: H. Burdett (Purch Mgr), S. Taylor (Mktg Serv Mgr), C. Marsden (Sales Admin), G. Gray (Cust Serv Mgr), A. Pollard (Sales Prom Mgr), D. Marron (I.T. Exec)
Immediate Holding Company: B. Elliott Group Ltd
Registration no: 01323084 **Date established:** 1977
Turnover: £10m - £20m **No.of Employees:** 101 - 250
Product Groups: 33, 36, 37, 46, 48

Ibstock Brick Ltd
Leicester Road, Ibstock, LE67 6HS
Tel: 01530-261999 **Fax:** 01530-257457
E-mail: marketing@ibstock.co.uk
Website: http://www.ibstock.com
Directors: J. Richards (Sales), K. Sims (Dir), S. Hardy (Co Sec), W. Shepard (MD), W. Sheppard (MD)
Managers: A. Halstead-Smith (Mktg Serv Mgr), C. Phillips (I.T. Exec)
Ultimate Holding Company: CRH PUBLIC LIMITED COMPANY
Immediate Holding Company: IBSTOCK BUILDING PRODUCTS LIMITED
Registration no: 00784339 **Date established:** 1963 **Turnover:** £2m - £5m
No.of Employees: 101 - 250 **Product Groups:** 33

Jellybean Creative Ltd
58 Copson Street, Ibstock, LE67 6LB
Tel: 01530-263025
E-mail: jellybeancreative@tiscali.co.uk
Website: http://www.jellybeancreative.com
Directors: J. Mudge (MD)
Immediate Holding Company: JELLYBEAN CREATIVE LIMITED
Registration no: 05352206 **Date established:** 2005
Turnover: £250,000 - £500,000 **No.of Employees:** 1 - 10
Product Groups: 26, 44, 49, 52, 81, 84

Date of Accounts	Feb 08	Feb 11	Feb 10
Working Capital	3	-14	-12
Fixed Assets	7	18	13
Current Assets	37	33	10

Leicester

A C Hydraulics Ltd
12 Mandervell Road Oadby, Leicester, LE2 5LQ
Tel: 0116-271 0561 **Fax:** 0116-272 0561
E-mail: sales@achydraulics.co.uk
Website: http://www.achydraulics.co.uk
Bank(s): Barclays
Directors: S. I'anson (Sales)
Ultimate Holding Company: ABWICH LIMITED
Immediate Holding Company: A.C. HYDRAULICS LIMITED
Registration no: 01329434 **VAT No.:** GB 290 2469 63
Date established: 1977 **Turnover:** £2m - £5m **No.of Employees:** 11 - 20
Product Groups: 29, 30, 35, 36, 38, 39, 40, 45, 46, 47, 48, 76, 83, 84

Date of Accounts	Sep 11	Sep 10	Sep 09
Working Capital	682	598	614
Fixed Assets	49	15	19
Current Assets	1m	1m	1m

ADT Fire & Security plc
Bridge Park Plaza Bridge Park Road, Thurmaston, Leicester, LE4 8BL
Tel: 0800-542 3108 **Fax:** 0116-264 1777
Website: http://www.adt.co.uk
Managers: Hodgeson (Chief Mgr), R. Taunton (Sales Prom Mgr)
Ultimate Holding Company: TYCO INTERNATIONAL LIMITED (SWITZERLAND)
Immediate Holding Company: ADT FIRE AND SECURITY PLC
Registration no: 01161045 **Date established:** 1974
No.of Employees: 101 - 250 **Product Groups:** 37, 38, 39, 40, 47, 52, 81

Date of Accounts	Sep 11	Sep 08	Sep 09
Sales Turnover	363m	414m	384m
Pre Tax Profit/Loss	18m	4m	10m
Working Capital	450m	618m	561m
Fixed Assets	120m	193m	171m
Current Assets	710m	765m	722m
Current Liabilities	81m	57m	42m

A & L Springs
Unit 2 29 Wigston Street Countesthorpe, Leicester, LE8 5RP
Tel: 0116-278 8100 **Fax:** 0116-278 8200
E-mail: mitchalsprings@talktalkbusiness.net
Website: http://www.aandlsprings.co.uk
Directors: M. Dare (Ptnr)
No.of Employees: 1 - 10 **Product Groups:** 29, 33, 34, 35, 36, 38, 39, 40, 43, 46, 48, 49, 66, 68, 85

A & M Grinding
6 Windsor Avenue Groby, Leicester, LE6 0YF
Tel: 0116-287 0389 **Fax:** 0116-287 0389
Directors: M. Kyriacou (Prop)
Date established: 2002 **No.of Employees:** 1 - 10 **Product Groups:** 36

A1 Metal Fabrications
22 Boston Road, Leicester, LE4 1AU
Tel: 0116-235 0444 **Fax:** 0116-235 0444
Managers: D. Channel (Mgr)
Immediate Holding Company: A1 METAL FABRICATIONS LIMITED
Registration no: 04716879 **Date established:** 2003
Turnover: £250,000 - £500,000 **No.of Employees:** 1 - 10
Product Groups: 48, 52

Date of Accounts	Mar 11	Mar 10	Mar 09
Working Capital	-19	-16	-4
Fixed Assets	19	20	21
Current Assets	29	29	39

A P Y
104 Uppingham Road, Leicester, LE5 0QF
Tel: 0116-276 9200 **Fax:** 0116-276 9200
E-mail: office@apy2000.com
Website: http://www.apy2000.co.uk
Directors: F. Jassat (Prop)
Immediate Holding Company: APY LIMITED
Registration no: 03610928 **VAT No.:** GB 715 2594 36
Date established: 1998 **Turnover:** £500,000 - £1m
No.of Employees: 1 - 10 **Product Groups:** 23

Date of Accounts	Dec 10	Dec 08	Dec 07
Working Capital	33	47	31
Fixed Assets	5	2	2
Current Assets	117	148	127

A S M UK Ltd
Imperial House St Nicholas Circle, Leicester, LE1 4LF
Tel: 0116-242 4032 **Fax:** 0116-242 4049
Website: http://www.asm-sensor.co.uk
Directors: K. Steinich (MD)
Immediate Holding Company: ASM UK Ltd
Registration no: 06201404 **Date established:** 2007
No.of Employees: 1 - 10 **Product Groups:** 37, 38

A T A Group
Unit 2 Meridian West, Meridian Business Park, Leicester, LE19 1WX
Tel: 0844-9670702 **Fax:** 0844-8261140
E-mail: sales@atagroupuk.com
Website: http://www.atagroupuk.com
Directors: B. Lemond (Fin)
Managers: R. Cunningham
Turnover: £2m - £5m **No.of Employees:** 11 - 20 **Product Groups:** 46

Abaloid Plastics Ltd
165 Scudamore Road, Leicester, LE3 1UQ
Tel: 0116-232 0212 **Fax:** 0116-232 0569
E-mail: enquiries@abaloidplastics.co.uk
Website: http://www.abaloidplastics.co.uk
Directors: A. Cowley (MD)
Managers: P. Hammond (Prod Mgr)
Immediate Holding Company: ABALOID PLASTICS LIMITED
Registration no: 01207928 **VAT No.:** GB 115 7806 70
Date established: 1975 **Turnover:** £2m - £5m **No.of Employees:** 1 - 10
Product Groups: 30, 48

Abel Alarm Company Ltd
Detection House 4 Vaughan Way, Leicester, LE1 4ST
Tel: 0116-265 4200 **Fax:** 0116-251 5341
E-mail: info@abelalarm.co.uk
Website: http://www.abelalarm.co.uk
Bank(s): National Westminster Bank Plc
Directors: A. Warner (Fin), P. Tansey (Dir)
Managers: A. Smith (Purch Mgr)
Ultimate Holding Company: ABEL GROUP LIMITED
Immediate Holding Company: ABEL ALARM COMPANY LIMITED
Registration no: 00857251 **VAT No.:** GB 399 8033 95
Date established: 1965 **Turnover:** £10m - £20m
No.of Employees: 51 - 100 **Product Groups:** 36, 37, 40

Date of Accounts	Dec 11	Dec 10	Dec 09
Sales Turnover	12m	11m	11m
Pre Tax Profit/Loss	364	379	-397
Working Capital	-1m	-2m	-2m
Fixed Assets	4m	4m	4m
Current Assets	3m	3m	3m
Current Liabilities	3m	4m	4m

AC2000 Limited
North Bridge Place Frog Island, Leicester, LE3 5BG
Tel: 0116-262 0411 **Fax:** 0116-251 8967
E-mail: aircon@ac2000.co.uk
Website: http://www.ac2000.co.uk
Bank(s): HSBC Bank plc
Directors: T. Norman (MD), R. Francis (Fin), T. Norman (Dir), Thurnham (Ch), S. Thurnham (Ch), H. Sutton (Fin)
Managers: C. Galand (Chief Mgr), K. Dunne, R. Paice (Sales & Mktg Mg)
Immediate Holding Company: Electrum Holdings Ltd
Registration no: 00541159 **VAT No.:** GB 705 3188 49
Date established: 1954 **Turnover:** £5m - £10m
No.of Employees: 51 - 100 **Product Groups:** 52

Access & Security 24Hr Locksmiths
Key House Coombe Rise Oadby, Leicester, LE2 5TT
Tel: 0116-271 9003 **Fax:** 0116-271 9229
E-mail: info@leicesterlocksmith.com
Website: http://www.leicesterlocksmith.com
Directors: I. Muddimer (Prop)
No.of Employees: 1 - 10 **Product Groups:** 36, 52

Ace Electro-Plating Company Ltd
110 Wordsworth Road, Leicester, LE2 6EE
Tel: 0116-270 8651 **Fax:** 0116-270 2593
Directors: S. Sandhu (Co Sec), J. Sandhu (Dir)
Immediate Holding Company: ACE ELECTRO-PLATING COMPANY LIMITED
Registration no: 02016174 **VAT No.:** GB 536 2176 50
Date established: 1986 **Turnover:** £250,000 - £500,000
No.of Employees: 1 - 10 **Product Groups:** 48

Date of Accounts	Jul 08	Jul 07	Jul 06
Working Capital	310	256	332
Fixed Assets	55	67	81
Current Assets	416	362	393
Current Liabilities	107	106	62

Ace Leicester Ltd
Gemini House Winston Avenue Croft, Leicester, LE9 3GQ
Tel: 01455-289001 **Fax:** 01455-284481
E-mail: dave.crumbie@aceleicester.co.uk
Website: http://www.aceleicester.co.uk
Directors: D. Crumbie (MD)
Immediate Holding Company: SAMBELL ENGINEERING LIMITED
Registration no: 01327546 **Date established:** 1976
No.of Employees: 1 - 10 **Product Groups:** 35

Date of Accounts	Sep 11	Sep 10	Sep 09
Working Capital	901	732	527
Fixed Assets	197	245	319
Current Assets	1m	1m	820

Ackwa Ltd
Unit 2a Trevanth Road, Leicester, LE4 9LS
Tel: 0116-246 0880 **Fax:** 0800-634 8121
E-mail: jackie@ackwa.co.uk
Website: http://www.ackwa.co.uk
Directors: J. Miles (MD)
Immediate Holding Company: ACKWA LTD
Registration no: 05766807 **Date established:** 2006
No.of Employees: 1 - 10 **Product Groups:** 20, 32, 36, 40, 41, 42, 48, 49, 61, 62, 63, 66, 67

Date of Accounts	Sep 11	Sep 10	Sep 09
Working Capital	1	N/A	-0
Fixed Assets	1	N/A	N/A
Current Assets	30	24	19

Adams Glass
St George Street, Leicester, LE1 1QG
Tel: 0116-251 1715
Directors: L. Taylor (Ptnr)
No.of Employees: 11 - 20 **Product Groups:** 25, 35, 66

Adept Vacuum Formers & Patterns Ltd
141 Waterside Road Hamilton, Leicester, LE5 1TL
Tel: 0116-246 0552 **Fax:** 0116-246 0987
E-mail: enquiries@adeptvp.co.uk
Website: http://www.adeptvp.co.uk
Directors: J. Brindley (MD), E. Brindley (Fin)
Ultimate Holding Company: NO. 608 LEICESTER LIMITED
Immediate Holding Company: ADEPT (VACUUM FORMERS & PATTERNS) LIMITED
Registration no: 03253196 **Date established:** 1996
Turnover: £500,000 - £1m **No.of Employees:** 1 - 10 **Product Groups:** 30, 31, 48, 49

Date of Accounts	Jun 11	Jun 10	Jun 09
Working Capital	51	N/A	-16
Fixed Assets	27	31	36
Current Assets	147	119	118

Advance Tapes Group Ltd
PO Box 122, Leicester, LE4 5RA
Tel: 0116-251 0191 **Fax:** 0116-265 3070
E-mail: info@advancetapes.com
Website: http://www.advancetapes.com
Bank(s): Lloyds TSB
Managers: K. Robinson (Fin Mgr), M. Ayres, V. Woolley (Personnel), S. Boyle (Sales Prom Mgr), M. Brown (Purch Mgr), J. Page (Tech Serv Mgr), A. Ratcliffe (Mktg Serv Mgr)
Ultimate Holding Company: Advance Tape Group
Immediate Holding Company: ADVANCE TAPES GROUP LIMITED
Registration no: 00808986 **VAT No.:** GB 115 6143 00
Date established: 1964 **Turnover:** £20m - £50m
No.of Employees: 101 - 250 **Product Groups:** 23, 27, 34, 42

Date of Accounts	Dec 11	Dec 10	Dec 09
Sales Turnover	22m	21m	20m
Pre Tax Profit/Loss	1m	708	198
Working Capital	4m	3m	4m
Fixed Assets	2m	2m	1m
Current Assets	7m	6m	6m
Current Liabilities	801	741	430

Advanced Machinery Services
Green Lane Road, Leicester, LE5 4PF
Tel: 08448-449949 **Fax:** 0844-844 4744
E-mail: sales@advancedmachinery.co.uk
Website: http://www.advancedmachinery.co.uk
Directors: S. Foster (Prop)
Immediate Holding Company: ADVANCED MACHINERY SERVICES LIMITED
Registration no: 06405798 **Date established:** 2007
Turnover: £500,000 - £1m **No.of Employees:** 21 - 50
Product Groups: 33, 40, 47, 48, 67, 84

Date of Accounts	Dec 11	Dec 10	Dec 09
Working Capital	143	165	77
Fixed Assets	143	46	33
Current Assets	454	399	247

Air Conditioning Wright Favell Ltd
Winston Avenue Croft, Leicester, LE9 3GQ
Tel: 01455-283011 **Fax:** 01455-285198
E-mail: stuart@aircon-wf.co.uk
Website: http://www.aircon-wf.co.uk
Bank(s): Bank of Scotland
Directors: S. Orgill (MD), E. Orgill (Fin)
Immediate Holding Company: WRIGHT FAVELL LIMITED
Registration no: 02247892 **VAT No.:** GB 113 9728 66
Date established: 1988 **Turnover:** £1m - £2m **No.of Employees:** 11 - 20
Product Groups: 52

Date of Accounts	Oct 11	Oct 10	Oct 09
Working Capital	260	372	384
Fixed Assets	53	44	38
Current Assets	614	825	930

Air Movement Systems Ltd
34 The Meer Fleckney, Leicester, LE8 8UN
Tel: 0845-680 0852 **Fax:** 08456-800851
E-mail: stephen@airmovementsystems.co.uk
Website: http://www.airmovementsystems.co.uk
Directors: S. Day (Ptnr)
Immediate Holding Company: AIR MOVEMENT SYSTEMS LTD
Registration no: 05913019 **Date established:** 2006
No.of Employees: 1 - 10 **Product Groups:** 40, 41, 44, 45, 52, 54, 66, 83

Date of Accounts	Jan 11	Jan 10	Jan 09
Working Capital	63	85	14
Fixed Assets	24	1	1
Current Assets	119	173	43

Alchemy Carta
Hazel Drive, Leicester, LE3 2JE
Tel: 0116-282 4824 **Fax:** 0116-282 5202
E-mail: sales@alchemygroup.com
Website: http://www.alchemygroup.co.uk
Directors: T. Phillipson (Dir), S. Phillipson (Sales)
Managers: M. Dunkley, L. Emery (Fin Mgr)
Immediate Holding Company: THE ALCHEMY CARTA LIMITED
Registration no: 01492076 **Date established:** 1980
No.of Employees: 51 - 100 **Product Groups:** 49

Date of Accounts	May 11	May 10	May 09
Working Capital	784	836	824
Fixed Assets	166	6	8
Current Assets	1m	1m	1m

Aldeby Painting Services Co. Ltd
Britannia Way Thurmaston, Leicester, LE4 8JY
Tel: 0116-269 5699 **Fax:** 0116-260 2887
E-mail: kevinbarry23@yahoo.co.uk
Website: http://www.aldebypainting.co.uk
Directors: K. Barry (MD)
Ultimate Holding Company: ALDEBY SHOT BLASTING LIMITED
Immediate Holding Company: ALDEBY PAINTING SERVICES CO. LIMITED
Registration no: 01217213 **VAT No.:** GB 372 2660 57
Date established: 1975 **Turnover:** £250,000 - £500,000
No.of Employees: 1 - 10 **Product Groups:** 48, 52

Date of Accounts	Feb 12	Feb 11	Feb 10
Working Capital	295	296	304
Fixed Assets	21	28	31
Current Assets	344	341	341

Alentec Orion Ltd
Bruce Way Whetstone, Leicester, LE8 6HP
Tel: 0116-284 6040 **Fax:** 0116-284 6070
E-mail: tony.hale@alentec-orion.co.uk
Website: http://www.alentec-orion.co.uk
Directors: T. Hale (Sales)
Ultimate Holding Company: LINTER HOLDINGS LIMITED
Immediate Holding Company: ALENTEC ORION LIMITED
Registration no: 00231713 **Date established:** 2028 **Turnover:** £1m - £2m
No.of Employees: 1 - 10 **Product Groups:** 36, 39, 40

Date of Accounts	Dec 11	Dec 10	Dec 09
Sales Turnover	1m	1m	984
Pre Tax Profit/Loss	49	35	-1
Working Capital	913	876	848
Fixed Assets	2	3	7
Current Assets	1m	1m	1m
Current Liabilities	114	87	48

Alliance & Leicester plc (Customer Service Centre)
Carlton Park Narborough, Leicester, LE19 0AL
Tel: 0116-201 1000 **Fax:** 0116-200 4040
E-mail: admin@alliance-leicestergroup.co.uk
Website: http://www.alliance-leicestergroup.co.uk
Directors: J. Barker (Dir), F. Rodford (Dir), C. Rhodes (MD)
Managers: J. Aspinwall (I.T. Exec)
Ultimate Holding Company: FP047516
Immediate Holding Company: ALLIANCE & LEICESTER PUBLIC LIMITED COMPANY
Registration no: 03263713 **Date established:** 1996
Turnover: Over £1,000m **No.of Employees:** 1501 & over
Product Groups: 80, 81, 82

Alliance & Leicester plc
Heritage House 61 Southgates, Leicester, LE1 5RR
Tel: 08705-785131 **Fax:** 0116-253 2333
Website: http://www.alliance-leicester.co.uk
Directors: D. Patton (MD)
Immediate Holding Company: ALLIANCE & LEICESTER PUBLIC LIMITED COMPANY
Registration no: 03263713 **Date established:** 1996
Turnover: £75m - £125m **No.of Employees:** 1 - 10 **Product Groups:** 82

Alpha Seating Ltd
Unit 10 The Konfidence Works Arthur Street, Barwell, Leicester, LE9 8GZ
Tel: 01455-851425 **Fax:** 01455-851934
E-mail: peter_reynalt_morgan@hotmail.com
Website: http://www.alphaseating.com
Directors: P. Morgan (MD), P. Gazey (Fin)
Immediate Holding Company: ALPHA SEATING LIMITED
Registration no: 04490420 **Date established:** 2002
No.of Employees: 1 - 10 **Product Groups:** 26, 38, 39

Date of Accounts	Jul 11	Jul 10	Jul 09
Working Capital	-12	-11	-13
Fixed Assets	15	13	15
Current Assets	167	165	149

Amber Valley Development Ltd
12 Churchill Way Fleckney, Leicester, LE8 8UD
Tel: 0116-240 2968 **Fax:** 0116-240 2941
E-mail: sales@amber-valley.co.uk
Website: http://www.amber-valley.co.uk
Directors: D. Morewood (MD)
Managers: E. Vandelli (Personnel), N. Davies (Purch Mgr)
Immediate Holding Company: AMBER VALLEY LIMITED
Registration no: 03010792 **Date established:** 1995
No.of Employees: 21 - 50 **Product Groups:** 39, 40, 67, 68

Date of Accounts	Jan 12	Jan 11	Jan 10
Working Capital	169	182	166
Fixed Assets	149	162	60
Current Assets	560	537	553

Ambit Precision Grinding
38a Kenilworth Drive Oadby, Leicester, LE2 5LG
Tel: 0116-271 1011 **Fax:** 0161-627 1101
E-mail: sheldrakeadam@yahoo.com
Directors: A. Sheldrake (Prop)
Date established: 1998 **Turnover:** Up to £250,000
No.of Employees: 1 - 10 **Product Groups:** 32, 48

Andrews Hydraulics Ltd
Unit 27-28 Craftmans Way East Goscote, Leicester, LE7 3SL
Tel: 0116-260 1001 **Fax:** 0116-264 0186
E-mail: design@andrewshydraulics.co.uk
Website: http://www.andrewshydraulics.co.uk
Bank(s): Lloyds TSB
Directors: K. Andrews (MD)
Immediate Holding Company: ANDREWS HYDRAULICS LIMITED
Registration no: 01771624 **VAT No.:** GB 395 6034 03
Date established: 1983 **Turnover:** £1m - £2m **No.of Employees:** 11 - 20
Product Groups: 38

Date of Accounts	Jan 11	Jan 10	Jan 09
Working Capital	195	201	190
Fixed Assets	58	37	44
Current Assets	1m	1m	1m

Angraves Cane Furniture Ltd
Brook Street Thurmaston, Leicester, LE4 8DB
Tel: 0116-269 2255 **Fax:** 0116-269 4701
E-mail: jen@angrave.com
Website: http://www.angraves.com
Directors: D. Angrave (Dir), J. Mobbs (Dir), N. Angrave (Jt MD)
Immediate Holding Company: ANGRAVES CANE FURNITURE LIMITED
Registration no: 02900149 **VAT No.:** GB 114 0431 31
Date established: 1994 **Turnover:** £1m - £2m **No.of Employees:** 21 - 50
Product Groups: 25, 26

Date of Accounts	Jul 07	Jul 06
Working Capital	20	25
Fixed Assets	181	177
Current Assets	635	594
Current Liabilities	615	569
Total Share Capital	10	10

Annalex Bute Ltd
Unit B6 Blaby Industrial Park Winchester Avenue, Blaby, Leicester, LE8 4GZ
Tel: 0116-277 9537 **Fax:** 0116-277 8623
E-mail: sales@annalexbute.co.uk
Website: http://www.annalexbute.co.uk
Directors: A. Hunter (Fin)
Ultimate Holding Company: ANNALEX UK LIMITED
Immediate Holding Company: ANNALEX UK LIMITED
Registration no: 02606368 **Date established:** 1991
Turnover: £500,000 - £1m **No.of Employees:** 1 - 10 **Product Groups:** 35

Date of Accounts	Jun 11	Jun 10	Jun 09
Working Capital	34	36	32
Fixed Assets	9	11	10
Current Assets	81	85	91

Aramark Ltd
Grange Business Park Enderby Road, Whetstone, Leicester, LE8 6EP
Tel: 0116-278 0108 **Fax:** 0116-278 0037
Website: http://www.aramark.co.uk
Directors: D. Bradbury (Dir)
Ultimate Holding Company: ARAMARK HOLDINGS CORPORATION (USA)
Immediate Holding Company: ARAMARK LIMITED
Registration no: 00983951 **Date established:** 1970
Turnover: £20m - £50m **No.of Employees:** 21 - 50 **Product Groups:** 49, 52, 69

Date of Accounts	Sep 11	Oct 08	Oct 09
Sales Turnover	341m	425m	410m
Pre Tax Profit/Loss	17m	9m	9m
Working Capital	56m	37m	41m
Fixed Assets	46m	60m	55m
Current Assets	107m	110m	126m
Current Liabilities	22m	18m	25m

Arc Euro Trade Ltd
10 Archdale Street Syston, Leicester, LE7 1NA
Tel: 0116-269 5693 **Fax:** 0116-260 5805
E-mail: information@arceurotrade.co.uk
Website: http://www.arceurotrade.co.uk
Directors: S. Swali (Fin), K. Swali (Dir)
Immediate Holding Company: ARC EURO TRADE LTD
Registration no: 05060731 **VAT No.:** GB 442 0102 17
Date established: 2004 **No.of Employees:** 1 - 10 **Product Groups:** 35, 39

Date of Accounts	Mar 11	Mar 10	Mar 09
Working Capital	311	242	149
Fixed Assets	31	34	43
Current Assets	436	388	369

Arriva Midlands North Ltd
852 Melton Road Thurmaston, Leicester, LE4 8BT
Tel: 01543-466123 **Fax:** 0116-260 5605
Website: http://www.arrivabus.co.uk
Directors: J. Barlow (Fin)
Managers: K. Myatt (Commun Mgr), P. Dowley, C. Grierson (Purch Mgr), L. Starling (Personnel)
Ultimate Holding Company: DEUTSCHE BAHN AG (GERMANY)
Immediate Holding Company: ARRIVA MIDLANDS NORTH LIMITED
Registration no: 01556305 **VAT No.:** GB 541 8320 62
Date established: 1981 **Turnover:** £20m - £50m
No.of Employees: 101 - 250 **Product Groups:** 72

Date of Accounts	Dec 11	Dec 10	Dec 09
Sales Turnover	37m	32m	32m
Pre Tax Profit/Loss	4m	2m	2m
Working Capital	11m	8m	6m
Fixed Assets	2m	3m	3m
Current Assets	40m	21m	31m
Current Liabilities	4m	4m	4m

Articlinic
91 Jacklin Drive Rushey Mead, Leicester, LE4 7SU
Tel: 0116-266 3906 **Fax:** 0116-266 3906
E-mail: admin@articlinic.com
Website: http://www.articlinic.com
Directors: N. Trivedi (Prop)
Date established: 2004 **No.of Employees:** 1 - 10 **Product Groups:** 88

Artizan Steelworkers
Artizan Steelworkers Ltd Brook Street, Thurmaston, Leicester, LE4 8DA
Tel: 0116-260 6655 **Fax:** 0116-260 2130
Website: http://www.artizansteelworkersltd.co.uk
Directors: T. Atton (MD)
Date established: 1999 **No.of Employees:** 1 - 10 **Product Groups:** 35

Asfordby Doors Ltd
Unit 112 The Burrows East Goscote, Leicester, LE7 3XD
Tel: 0116-269 7174 **Fax:** 0116-260 3475
Directors: S. Murphy (Fin)
Immediate Holding Company: ASFORDBY DOORS LIMITED
Registration no: 04416928 **Date established:** 2002
No.of Employees: 1 - 10 **Product Groups:** 35

Date of Accounts	Jan 11	Jan 10	Jan 09
Working Capital	189	99	140
Fixed Assets	58	70	89
Current Assets	402	339	340

Ashfield UK Ltd
Mangochi House 107-115 Gwendolen Road, Leicester, LE5 5FL
Tel: 08454-301234 **Fax:** 0116-273 3396
E-mail: info@ashfielduk.com
Website: http://www.ashfielduk.com
Directors: A. Mohamed (MD), A. Mohammed (MD), I. Mahomed (Fin), I. Mohammed (Fin), S. Widdowson (Sales)

see next page

Ashfield UK Ltd - *Cont'd*
Immediate Holding Company: ASHFIELD (UK) LIMITED
Registration no: 02034549 **Date established:** 1986
No.of Employees: 21 - 50 **Product Groups:** 24

Date of Accounts	Sep 11	Sep 10	Sep 09
Working Capital	-130	-201	-172
Fixed Assets	556	596	636
Current Assets	312	292	382

Ashwell Electrical Contractors
13 Springwell Lane Whetstone, Leicester, LE8 6LT
Tel: 0116-275 3860
Website: http://www.ashwellelectrical.co.uk
Directors: P. Davies (Dir), P. Davies (Prop)
Immediate Holding Company: ASHWELL ELECTRICAL CONTRACTORS LIMITED
Registration no: 05837433 **Date established:** 2006
Turnover: Up to £250,000 **No.of Employees:** 1 - 10 **Product Groups:** 36, 37, 40, 52

Date of Accounts	Jun 11	Jun 10	Jun 09
Working Capital	6	-20	-26
Fixed Assets	8	11	16
Current Assets	38	18	12
Current Liabilities	N/A	N/A	16

Ask Miller
19 Dukes Close Thurmaston, Leicester, LE4 8EY
Tel: 0116-264 0440 **Fax:** 0116-264 0135
E-mail: sales@askmillers.co.uk
Directors: M. Miller (Prop)
Registration no: 05019838 **Date established:** 2004
Turnover: Up to £250,000 **No.of Employees:** 1 - 10 **Product Groups:** 37

Assured Fire Protection
22 Spring Gardens Littlethorpe, Leicester, LE19 2JH
Tel: 0116-275 0966 **Fax:** 0116-275 0966
E-mail: info@assuredfireprotection.co.uk
Website: http://www.assuredfireprotection.co.uk
Directors: C. Thirlby (Prop)
Date established: 1997 **No.of Employees:** 1 - 10 **Product Groups:** 38, 42

Atkinson Design Associates Ltd
1 Abbey Gate, Leicester, LE4 0AA
Tel: 0116-262 9494 **Fax:** 0116-251 0836
E-mail: cs@atkdesign.co.uk
Website: http://www.atkdesign.co.uk
Directors: P. Sutton (Fin), P. Atkinson (MD), J. Hinton (Sales & Mktg)
Ultimate Holding Company: ATKINSON DESIGN HOLDINGS LIMITED
Immediate Holding Company: ATKINSON DESIGN ASSOCIATES LIMITED
Registration no: 01607185 **Date established:** 1982
Turnover: £500,000 - £1m **No.of Employees:** 1 - 10 **Product Groups:** 85

Date of Accounts	Mar 11	Mar 10	Mar 09
Working Capital	18	161	311
Fixed Assets	173	16	26
Current Assets	100	233	372

Atlas Transfer Printers Ltd
9 Wanstead Road, Leicester, LE3 1TR
Tel: 0116-231 4500 **Fax:** 0116-231 4600
E-mail: atpl@btconnect.com
Managers: G. Johnson (Mgr)
Immediate Holding Company: ATLAS TRANSFER PRINTERS LIMITED
Registration no: 02838309 **Date established:** 1993
Turnover: Up to £250,000 **No.of Employees:** 1 - 10 **Product Groups:** 27

Date of Accounts	Dec 08	Dec 07	Mar 11
Sales Turnover	168	180	N/A
Pre Tax Profit/Loss	-3	2	N/A
Working Capital	41	42	43
Fixed Assets	4	5	1
Current Assets	90	108	111
Current Liabilities	25	31	N/A

B S Attwall & Co. Ltd
14-20 Cannock Street, Leicester, LE4 9HR
Tel: 0116-276 3800 **Fax:** 0116-246 0139
E-mail: noni@bsattwall.com
Website: http://www.bsattwall.com
Directors: K. Attwal (Co Sec), B. Attwal (Dir)
Immediate Holding Company: B.S. ATTWALL & CO. LIMITED
Registration no: 00795149 **VAT No.:** GB 339 4195 34
Date established: 1964 **Turnover:** £2m - £5m **No.of Employees:** 51 - 100
Product Groups: 24

Date of Accounts	Jul 11	Jul 10	Jul 09
Sales Turnover	5m	4m	3m
Pre Tax Profit/Loss	-272	22	N/A
Working Capital	-647	-110	-493
Fixed Assets	1m	1m	2m
Current Assets	3m	4m	2m
Current Liabilities	631	592	627

Autal 2000 Ltd
3 Kings Court Kingsfield Road, Barwell, Leicester, LE9 8NZ
Tel: 01455-850333 **Fax:** 01455-850335
E-mail: sales@autal.co.uk
Website: http://www.autal.co.uk
Managers: J. Winsper (Chief Mgr)
Immediate Holding Company: AUTAL 2000 LIMITED
Registration no: 03866974 **Date established:** 1999
No.of Employees: 1 - 10 **Product Groups:** 46

Date of Accounts	Dec 11	Dec 10	Dec 09
Working Capital	370	334	294
Fixed Assets	35	39	49
Current Assets	539	452	416

Automatic Precision Turning (Leicester) Limited
Rookery Lane Groby, Leicester, LE6 0GL
Tel: 0116-287 0051 **Fax:** 0116-287 0053
E-mail: sales@aptleicester.co.uk
Website: http://www.aptleicester.co.uk
Directors: A. Clayton (Admin), B. Debbenham (Fab), D. Bailey (Dir), S. Bailey (Fin)
Managers: N. Baller (Prod Mgr), R. Simmons (Eng Serv Mgr)
Registration no: 00976903 **VAT No.:** GB 114 1274 16
Turnover: £1m - £2m **No.of Employees:** 1 - 10 **Product Groups:** 30, 35, 48

Date of Accounts	Mar 08	Mar 07	Mar 06
Working Capital	12	15	27
Fixed Assets	43	44	46
Current Assets	17	21	32
Current Liabilities	5	5	5
Total Share Capital	3	3	3

B H Tungsten Grinders
89 Sycamore Way Littlethorpe, Leicester, LE19 2HW
Tel: 0116-286 4342
E-mail: sales@tungstengrinders.co.uk
Website: http://www.tungstengrinders.co.uk
Directors: D. White (Prop)
Date established: 2000 **No.of Employees:** 1 - 10 **Product Groups:** 46

B L Scaffolding Ltd
Spa Building Queen Street, Leicester, LE1 1QW
Tel: 0116-253 0197 **Fax:** 0116-253 2752
E-mail: blscaffolding@btconnect.com
Website: http://www.blscaffolding.co.uk
Bank(s): Barclays
Directors: A. Broadbent (MD), A. Broadben (Dir), A. Broadbenp (Dir)
Immediate Holding Company: B.L. SCAFFOLDING LIMITED
Registration no: 01967300 **VAT No.:** GB 670 3416 51
Date established: 1985 **Turnover:** £500,000 - £1m
No.of Employees: 21 - 50 **Product Groups:** 52, 83

Date of Accounts	Dec 11	Dec 10	Dec 09
Working Capital	-68	-91	-164
Fixed Assets	257	281	366
Current Assets	207	210	225
Current Liabilities	N/A	123	122

B P X Electro Mechanical Company Ltd
124 Ross Walk, Leicester, LE4 5HA
Tel: 0116-299 9100 **Fax:** 0116-299 9201
E-mail: rogercollins@bpx.co.uk
Website: http://www.bpx.co.uk
Directors: A. Collins (MD), N. Collins (Tech Serv), R. Collins (Dir)
Ultimate Holding Company: BPX GROUP LIMITED
Immediate Holding Company: BPX ELECTRO-MECHANICAL COMPANY LIMITED
Registration no: 00863458 **VAT No.:** GB 113 7064 03
Date established: 1965 **Turnover:** £20m - £50m
No.of Employees: 21 - 50 **Product Groups:** 37

Date of Accounts	Oct 11	Oct 10	Oct 09
Sales Turnover	22m	18m	15m
Pre Tax Profit/Loss	60	179	73
Working Capital	4m	4m	4m
Fixed Assets	570	551	628
Current Assets	9m	7m	6m
Current Liabilities	678	350	393

B S S Pipe Fitting Stockholders Head Office
Fleet House Lee Circle, Leicester, LE1 3QQ
Tel: 0116-262 3232 **Fax:** 0116-253 1343
E-mail: andy.vaughan@bssgroup.com
Website: http://www.bssgroup.com
Directors: P. Wood (Dir), F. Elkins (MD)
Managers: A. Vaughan (Mgr)
Ultimate Holding Company: TRAVIS PERKINS PLC
Immediate Holding Company: BSS (UK) LIMITED
Registration no: 00579814 **VAT No.:** GB 316 0004 22
Date established: 1957 **Turnover:** £75m - £125m
No.of Employees: 1 - 10 **Product Groups:** 30, 32, 36, 38, 40, 66

Date of Accounts	Dec 10	Mar 10	Mar 09
Working Capital	4m	N/A	N/A
Current Assets	4m	N/A	N/A

Beaumanor Press Ltd
23 Bath Lane, Leicester, LE3 5BF
Tel: 0116-233 1337 **Fax:** 0116-233 5337
E-mail: info@beaumanor.co.uk
Website: http://www.beaumanor.co.uk
Directors: P. Millrain (MD), A. Aspinall (Fin)
Immediate Holding Company: BEAUMANOR PRESS LIMITED
Registration no: 01102836 **Date established:** 1973
Turnover: £250,000 - £500,000 **No.of Employees:** 1 - 10
Product Groups: 27, 28, 64, 80

Date of Accounts	Mar 11	Mar 10	Mar 09
Working Capital	51	58	82
Fixed Assets	56	67	79
Current Assets	80	89	105

Beckdale Shipping Ltd
Unit G3 Charter Street, Leicester, LE1 3UD
Tel: 0116-253 0022 **Fax:** 0116-253 0777
E-mail: sales@beckdale.co.uk
Website: http://www.beckdale.co.uk
Directors: M. Frankton (Dir)
Immediate Holding Company: BECKDALE PACKAGING & DESIGN LIMITED
Registration no: 06875218 **Date established:** 2009
No.of Employees: 1 - 10 **Product Groups:** 27, 30, 66

Belgrave Timber & Steele Ltd
Plot 3-4 Abbey Court Industrial Estate Wallingford Road, Leicester, LE4 5RD
Tel: 0116-266 2774 **Fax:** 0116-266 2774
E-mail: edward@campbell313.orangehome.co.uk
Directors: E. Campbell (Prop)
Date established: 1987 **No.of Employees:** 1 - 10 **Product Groups:** 25, 30, 66

Benlowe Windows
Park Road Ratby, Leicester, LE6 0JL
Tel: 0116-239 5353 **Fax:** 0116-238 7295
E-mail: sales@benlowe.co.uk
Website: http://www.benlowe.co.uk
Directors: M. Harris (MD), N. James (Fin)
Managers: S. Tyers (Personnel), J. Page (I.T. Exec), N. James (Chief Acct), S. Billings (Buyer), S. Billings (Buyer), S. Pollard (Personnel)
Ultimate Holding Company: BENLOWE GROUP HOLDINGS LIMITED
Immediate Holding Company: BENLOWE GROUP LIMITED
Registration no: 03779009 **Date established:** 1999 **Turnover:** £5m - £10m
No.of Employees: 51 - 100 **Product Groups:** 25

Date of Accounts	Sep 11	Sep 10	Sep 09
Fixed Assets	15	15	15
Current Assets	3	3	3
Current Liabilities	3	3	3

Benninghoven UK Ltd
Incendium House Centurion Way Meridian Business Park, Leicester, LE19 1WH
Tel: 0116-263 0345 **Fax:** 0116-282 8741
E-mail: enquiries@benninghoven.co.uk
Website: http://www.benninghoven.com
Directors: P. Bolley (MD)
Managers: B. Long (Fin Mgr), J. Cooper, D. Gregson
Immediate Holding Company: BENNINGHOVEN U.K. LIMITED
Registration no: 02188376 **Date established:** 1987
Turnover: £10m - £20m **No.of Employees:** 21 - 50 **Product Groups:** 40, 45

Date of Accounts	Dec 11	Dec 10	Dec 09
Sales Turnover	10m	13m	11m
Pre Tax Profit/Loss	366	619	-769
Working Capital	550	568	58
Fixed Assets	718	756	756
Current Assets	4m	4m	5m
Current Liabilities	1m	891	552

E. Berry & Sons
Unit 19 308A Melton Road, Leicester, LE4 7SL
Tel: 0845-1306862 **Fax:** 0845-3892144
E-mail: info@premierpioneer.co.uk
Website: http://www.premierpioneer.co.uk
Directors: J. Berry (MD)
Registration no: 00089024 **Turnover:** Up to £250,000
No.of Employees: 1 - 10 **Product Groups:** 38, 49

Bibielle
11 Oaks Industrial Estate Coventry Road, Narborough, Leicester, LE19 2GF
Tel: 0116-275 3131 **Fax:** 0116-275 3130
Website: http://www.bibielle.com
Directors: M. Wright (MD)
No.of Employees: 1 - 10 **Product Groups:** 32, 33

Biffa Waste Services Ltd
90 High Street Syston, Leicester, LE7 1GQ
Tel: 0116-269 6492 **Fax:** 0116-269 6496
E-mail: leicester@biffa.co.uk
Website: http://www.biffa.co.uk
Managers: N. Coutts (Mgr)
Immediate Holding Company: BIFFA WASTE SERVICES LIMITED
Registration no: 00946107 **Date established:** 1969
No.of Employees: 21 - 50 **Product Groups:** 32, 54

Date of Accounts	Mar 08	Mar 09	Apr 10
Sales Turnover	555m	574m	492m
Pre Tax Profit/Loss	23m	50m	30m
Working Capital	229m	271m	293m
Fixed Assets	371m	360m	378m
Current Assets	409m	534m	609m
Current Liabilities	50m	100m	115m

Blanson Ltd
Coventry Road Narborough, Leicester, LE19 2GG
Tel: 0116-286 7007 **Fax:** 0116-286 5791
E-mail: blanson@blanson.com
Website: http://www.blanson.com
Bank(s): Barclays
Directors: C. Johnstone (MD)
Ultimate Holding Company: ADATIF INTERNATIONAL LIMITED (CANADA)
Immediate Holding Company: BLANSON LIMITED
Registration no: 05323799 **Date established:** 2005 **Turnover:** £2m - £5m
No.of Employees: 11 - 20 **Product Groups:** 28, 30

Date of Accounts	Dec 11	Dec 10	Dec 09
Working Capital	688	641	738
Fixed Assets	404	213	255
Current Assets	1m	927	1m

Bostik Ltd
Ulverscroft Road, Leicester, LE4 6BW
Tel: 01785-272727 **Fax:** 0116-268 9299
E-mail: sales@bostik.co.uk
Website: http://www.bostik.co.uk
Bank(s): Barclays, Town Hall Square
Directors: H. Murray (MD), K. Charlesworth (Fin), T. Davidson (MD)
Ultimate Holding Company: TOTAL SAFETY INC (USA)
Registration no: 00068328 **Date established:** 2000
Turnover: £125m - £250m **No.of Employees:** 251 - 500
Product Groups: 29, 31, 32

Date of Accounts	Dec 09	Dec 08	Dec 07
Sales Turnover	124m	131m	138m
Pre Tax Profit/Loss	2m	2m	9m
Working Capital	-592	3m	10m
Fixed Assets	59m	62m	67m
Current Assets	39m	42m	52m
Current Liabilities	9m	8m	7m

Bosworth Marketing Ltd
162 Shilton Road Barwell, Leicester, LE9 8BN
Tel: 01455-841288 **Fax:** 01455-840744
E-mail: info@bosworthmarketing.co.uk
Website: http://www.bosworthmarketing.co.uk
Directors: A. Barber (MD), R. Barber (Fin)
Immediate Holding Company: BOSWORTH MARKETING LIMITED
Registration no: 04851793 **Date established:** 2003
Turnover: Up to £250,000 **No.of Employees:** 1 - 10 **Product Groups:** 81

Date of Accounts	Aug 11	Aug 10	Aug 08
Working Capital	-3	N/A	-10
Fixed Assets	3	3	4
Current Assets	7	13	8

Bosworth Wright Anstey Ltd
Express Works Hollow Road, Anstey, Leicester, LE7 7FP
Tel: 0116-236 2231 **Fax:** 0116-235 2230
E-mail: bosworthwright@hotmail.com
Website: http://www.bosworthwright.com
Directors: D. Thompson (MD)
Immediate Holding Company: BOSWORTH WRIGHT (ANSTEY) LIMITED
Registration no: 03638841 **VAT No.:** GB 715 3041 72
Date established: 1998 **Turnover:** Up to £250,000
No.of Employees: 1 - 10 **Product Groups:** 27

Date of Accounts	Dec 11	Dec 10	Dec 09
Working Capital	247	206	186
Fixed Assets	36	37	28
Current Assets	293	234	226

Boxes & Packaging Ltd
11 Uxbridge Road, Leicester, LE4 7ST
Tel: 0116-266 2666 **Fax:** 0116-266 2555
E-mail: sales@boxesandpackaging.co.uk
Website: http://www.boxesandpackaging.co.uk
Bank(s): Barclays
Directors: G. Troup (MD)
Ultimate Holding Company: BOXES AND PACKAGING (UK) LIMITED
Immediate Holding Company: BOXES AND PACKAGING LIMITED
Registration no: 05291434 **VAT No.:** 637 1876 13 **Date established:** 2004
Turnover: £2m - £5m **No.of Employees:** 21 - 50 **Product Groups:** 27

British Precast Concrete Federation Ltd
60 Charles Street, Leicester, LE1 1FB
Tel: 0116-253 6161 **Fax:** 0116-251 4568
E-mail: info@britishprecast.org
Website: http://www.britishprecast.org
Directors: A. Carey (Sales), D. Szimanski (Dir), D. Zanker (Gen Sec), M. Clarke (MD)
Immediate Holding Company: British Precast Concrete Federation Limited(The)
Registration no: 01209092 **VAT No.:** GB 687 7988 34
Date established: 1975 **Turnover:** Up to £250,000
No.of Employees: 1 - 10 **Product Groups:** 87

Broctone Design Ltd
8 Broctone Close Broughton Astley, Leicester, LE9 6XX
Tel: 01455-289389 **Fax:** 01455-289389
Website: http://www.leisuregasservices.co.uk
Directors: J. Williamson (MD), S. Williamson (Fin)
Immediate Holding Company: INSIDE EDGE LIMITED
Registration no: 04788443 **Date established:** 1996
Turnover: Up to £250,000 **No.of Employees:** 1 - 10 **Product Groups:** 35, 39, 45

Bromford Industries
129 Scudamore Road, Leicester, LE3 1UQ
Tel: 0116-232 2233 **Fax:** 0116-232 2311
E-mail: ben.hambleton@bromfordindustries.co.uk
Website: http://www.bromfordindustries.co.uk
Managers: B. Hambleton (Ops Mgr)
Ultimate Holding Company: Hampson Industries plc
Immediate Holding Company: Hampson Aerospace Machining Ltd
Registration no: 00474681 **No.of Employees:** 51 - 100
Product Groups: 30, 33, 34, 39, 48

Burton Mccall Ltd
163 Parker Drive, Leicester, LE4 0JP
Tel: 0116-234 4600 **Fax:** 0116-235 8031
E-mail: sales@burton-mccall.co.uk
Website: http://www.burton-mccall.co.uk
Directors: C. Cooper (Co Sec), S. Davey (MD)
Managers: M. Urch (Tech Serv Mgr), M. Dickinson (Mktg Serv Mgr), P. Penton (Personnel)
Ultimate Holding Company: BOLLIN GROUP LIMITED
Immediate Holding Company: BURTON MCCALL LIMITED
Registration no: 02168907 **VAT No.:** GB 544 5824 31
Date established: 1987 **Turnover:** £20m - £50m
No.of Employees: 51 - 100 **Product Groups:** 36, 37, 49

Date of Accounts	Jun 11	Jun 10	Jun 09
Sales Turnover	24m	22m	20m
Pre Tax Profit/Loss	515	1m	471
Working Capital	3m	3m	2m
Fixed Assets	338	279	405
Current Assets	11m	8m	7m
Current Liabilities	984	532	464

C B M Designs Ltd
6a Fir Tree Lane Groby, Leicester, LE6 0FH
Tel: 0116-287 4201 **Fax:** 0116-287 5999
E-mail: dave@cbmdesigns.co.uk
Website: http://www.cbmdesigns.co.uk
Directors: D. Copson (Dir)
Immediate Holding Company: C.B.M. DESIGNS LIMITED
Registration no: 01926955 **VAT No.:** GB 355 2980 35
Date established: 1985 **No.of Employees:** 1 - 10 **Product Groups:** 44, 84

Date of Accounts	Apr 12	Apr 11	Apr 10
Working Capital	114	69	131
Fixed Assets	3	3	4
Current Assets	199	147	221

C G P Engineering Ltd
Cross Street Oadby, Leicester, LE2 4DD
Tel: 0116-271 7715 **Fax:** 0116-272 0701
E-mail: phil@cgp-engineering.com
Website: http://www.cgp-engineering.com
Directors: P. Harrison (MD)
Immediate Holding Company: C.G.P. ENGINEERING LTD
Registration no: 02033559 **Date established:** 1986
Turnover: £500,000 - £1m **No.of Employees:** 1 - 10 **Product Groups:** 48

Date of Accounts	Oct 11	Oct 10	Oct 09
Working Capital	63	33	76
Fixed Assets	182	125	165
Current Assets	196	141	138

C I Logistics (a division of Portec Rail Products (UK) Ltd)
43 Wenlock Way Troon Industrial Area, Leicester, LE4 9HU
Tel: 0116-276 1691 **Fax:** 0116-276 9836
E-mail: sales@conveyors.co.uk
Website: http://www.conveyors.co.uk
Directors: M. Cartwright (Fin), G. Bale (MD)
Managers: A. Ralph (Sales Prom Mgr), A. Pryte (Sales Prom Mgr), R. Greatorex (Purch Mgr), A. Ralf (Sales & Mktg Mg), C. Pearson (Personnel)
Registration no: 00393942 **Turnover:** £2m - £5m
No.of Employees: 21 - 50 **Product Groups:** 35, 38, 39, 40, 41, 42, 45

C P I UK Ltd
107 Boston Road Gorse Hill, Leicester, LE4 1AW
Tel: 0116-234 0600 **Fax:** 0116-235 2592
E-mail: mike.fentem@cpiglobal.co.uk
Website: http://www.cpiglobal.co.uk
Directors: K. Ryan (Ch), M. Fentem (Fin), J. Wojciechowski (MD), M. Fentem (Co Sec)
Managers: S. Wagstaff (Mktg Serv Mgr)
Immediate Holding Company: CPI UK LIMITED
Registration no: 02229986 **Date established:** 1988
Turnover: £10m - £20m **No.of Employees:** 51 - 100 **Product Groups:** 26, 28, 30, 42, 48, 49, 66, 81

Date of Accounts	Dec 08	Dec 07	Nov 06
Sales Turnover	N/A	3m	3m
Pre Tax Profit/Loss	N/A	-325	170
Working Capital	209	33	2m
Fixed Assets	46	103	211
Current Assets	924	637	3m
Current Liabilities	N/A	84	202

C & R Printing Services
Bruce House, Warren Park Way Enderby, Leicester, LE19 4SA
Tel: 0116-284 7464 **Fax:** 0116-284 7440
E-mail: info@candr.co.uk
Website: http://www.candr.co.uk
Managers: C. Johnstone (Mgr)
Registration no: 03955084 **Date established:** 2000 **Turnover:** £2m - £5m
No.of Employees: 1 - 10 **Product Groups:** 28, 32

C S Milne Engineering Ltd
Peckleton Lane Business Park Peckleton Common, Peckleton, Leicester, LE9 7RN
Tel: 01455-822569 **Fax:** 01455-824012
E-mail: rob@cs-milne.co.uk
Website: http://www.cs-milne.co.uk
Directors: R. Carnall (Tech Serv)
Immediate Holding Company: C.S. MILNE ENGINEERING LIMITED
Registration no: 04045865 **Date established:** 2000
No.of Employees: 1 - 10 **Product Groups:** 46

Date of Accounts	Aug 11	Aug 10	Aug 09
Working Capital	-11	52	53
Fixed Assets	23	29	38
Current Assets	147	243	161

Camloc Motion Control Ltd
15 New Star Road, Leicester, LE4 9JD
Tel: 0116-274 3600 **Fax:** 0116-274 3620
E-mail: tracy.ayres@camloc.com
Website: http://www.camloc.com
Directors: T. Calvert (Dir), A. Calvert (MD), D. Marshall (Co Sec), T. Calvert (MD)
Managers: T. Orgill (Mats Contrlr)
Immediate Holding Company: CAMLOC MOTION CONTROL LIMITED
Registration no: 03773109 **VAT No.:** GB 738 8577 71
Date established: 1999 **Turnover:** £2m - £5m **No.of Employees:** 21 - 50
Product Groups: 35, 36, 38, 39, 40

Date of Accounts	Sep 11	Sep 10	Sep 09
Sales Turnover	N/A	3m	3m
Pre Tax Profit/Loss	N/A	179	63
Working Capital	2m	650	2m
Fixed Assets	N/A	136	177
Current Assets	4m	3m	2m
Current Liabilities	N/A	2m	111

Carlton Laser Services Ltd
470 Thurmaston Boulevard Troon Industrial Estate, Leicester, LE4 9LN
Tel: 0116-222 3190 **Fax:** 0116-233 9992
E-mail: sales@carltonlaser.co.uk
Website: http://www.carltonlaser.co.uk
Bank(s): National Westminster Bank Plc
Directors: M. Jassi (Fab)
Managers: A. Brainbridge (Buyer)
Registration no: 01514280 **Date established:** 1980 **Turnover:** £2m - £5m
No.of Employees: 21 - 50 **Product Groups:** 30, 35, 39, 40, 44, 45, 46, 48, 49, 65, 68

Date of Accounts	Sep 11	Sep 10	Sep 08
Working Capital	1m	678	237
Fixed Assets	585	1m	1m
Current Assets	2m	2m	1m

Cartem Ltd
Viaduct Works Cannon Street, Leicester, LE4 6GH
Tel: 0870-0665122 **Fax:** 0870-0665133
E-mail: info@cartem.co.uk
Website: http://www.cartem.co.uk
Bank(s): Barclays
Directors: C. Tharapton (Sales), K. Mckay (Dir), L. Dolby (Co Sec)
Registration no: 05835704 **VAT No.:** GB 202 9657 68
No.of Employees: 11 - 20 **Product Groups:** 40, 42, 45

Date of Accounts	Dec 07	Dec 06
Working Capital	-20	-128
Fixed Assets	182	201
Current Assets	309	169
Current Liabilities	329	297
Total Share Capital	10	10

Castle Building Services
12 Gullet Lane Kirby Muxloe, Leicester, LE9 2BL
Tel: 0116-239 2939 **Fax:** 0116-239 2525
E-mail: info@castlebuildingservices.co.uk
Website: http://www.castlebuildingservices.co.uk
Directors: K. Dalzell (Ptnr)
Date established: 1997 **No.of Employees:** 1 - 10 **Product Groups:** 52

Cessar Catering Equiptment Ltd
50 The Fleet Stoney Stanton, Leicester, LE9 4DY
Tel: 01455-272807 **Fax:** 01455-272807
E-mail: clivetaylor@ndo.co.uk
Directors: M. Taylor (Fin), C. Taylor (MD)
Immediate Holding Company: CESSAR LIMITED
Registration no: 04718847 **Date established:** 2003
No.of Employees: 1 - 10 **Product Groups:** 20, 40, 41

Date of Accounts	Apr 11	Apr 10	Apr 09
Working Capital	-3	-4	-5
Fixed Assets	5	6	8
Current Assets	12	13	16

Chapman Fraser & Co. Ltd
10 Pinfold Road Thurmaston, Leicester, LE4 8BF
Tel: 0116-269 3856 **Fax:** 0116-264 0349
E-mail: william@chapmanfraser.com
Bank(s): National Westminster Bank Plc
Directors: W. Fraser (MD), H. Herniman (Fin)
Immediate Holding Company: CHAPMAN FRASER & COMPANY LIMITED
Registration no: 00541726 **VAT No.:** GB 113 7100 25
Date established: 1954 **Turnover:** £2m - £5m **No.of Employees:** 11 - 20
Product Groups: 23

Date of Accounts	Dec 11	Dec 10	Dec 09
Working Capital	663	616	563
Fixed Assets	74	96	103
Current Assets	899	868	788

Clinical Print Finishers
Glenbarr Avenue, Leicester, LE4 0AE
Tel: 0116-262 0050 **Fax:** 0116-251 9843
E-mail: estimating@clinical-print.co.uk
Website: http://www.clinical-print.co.uk
Directors: A. Pickles (Chief Op Offcr), A. Brown (Co Sec), J. Court (MD), J. Cunningham Court (MD)
Managers: N. Dobney
Immediate Holding Company: CLINICAL PRINT FINISHERS (U.K.) LIMITED
Registration no: 02823604 **Date established:** 1993
Turnover: £500,000 - £1m **No.of Employees:** 21 - 50 **Product Groups:** 44

Date of Accounts	Feb 08	Feb 11	Feb 10
Working Capital	-111	-166	-77
Fixed Assets	2m	2m	2m
Current Assets	412	529	644

Coba Plastics Ltd
Marlborough Drive Fleckney, Leicester, LE8 8UR
Tel: 0116-240 1000 **Fax:** 0116-240 3871
E-mail: sales@cobaplastics.com
Website: http://www.cobaplastics.com
Bank(s): Barclays, Coventry
Directors: M. Cooke (MD), B. Dowsett (Co Sec)
Managers: R. Lambert (Sales & Mktg Mg), S. Elliott (Tech Serv Mgr), Y. Copson (Personnel), S. Hutchinson (Purch Mgr)
Ultimate Holding Company: COBA INTERNATIONAL LIMITED
Immediate Holding Company: COBA PLASTICS LIMITED
Registration no: 00885482 **VAT No.:** GB 119 6396 44
Date established: 1966 **Turnover:** £10m - £20m
No.of Employees: 101 - 250 **Product Groups:** 23, 25, 27, 29, 30, 33, 37, 39, 66

Date of Accounts	Jun 11	Jun 10	Jun 09
Sales Turnover	17m	15m	13m
Pre Tax Profit/Loss	1m	1m	50
Working Capital	4m	3m	2m
Fixed Assets	1m	1m	968
Current Assets	7m	5m	4m
Current Liabilities	354	711	255

Ray Cole Doors
1 George Street Barwell, Leicester, LE9 8GN
Tel: 01455-842880 **Fax:** 01455-842881
Website: http://www.raycoledoors.co.uk
Directors: J. Cole (Fin), R. Cole (Dir)
Immediate Holding Company: RAY COLE DOORS LIMITED
Registration no: 03414378 **Date established:** 1997
No.of Employees: 1 - 10 **Product Groups:** 26, 35

Date of Accounts	Jul 11	Jul 10	Jul 09
Working Capital	15	-1	-14
Fixed Assets	1	7	15
Current Assets	46	26	18

Comer Industries UK Ltd
Unit 2 Merrylees Industrial Estate Heath Road Desford, Leicester, LE9 9FE
Tel: 01530-231504 **Fax:** 01530-231503
E-mail: sales@comer.co.uk
Website: http://www.comerindustries.com
Directors: V. Venni (MD)
Immediate Holding Company: COMER INDUSTRIES (UK) LTD
Registration no: 02297178 **Date established:** 1988 **Turnover:** £2m - £5m
No.of Employees: 1 - 10 **Product Groups:** 35, 39, 40, 41

Date of Accounts	Dec 11	Dec 10	Dec 09
Working Capital	2m	2m	1m
Fixed Assets	22	23	31
Current Assets	4m	3m	3m
Current Liabilities	N/A	N/A	2m

Completely Independent Distribution
11 Waterside Road Hamilton, Leicester, LE5 1TL
Tel: 0116-276 6577 **Fax:** 0116-274 7199
Website: http://www.cidmerch.com
Directors: N. Wastell (MD)
Immediate Holding Company: COMPLETELY INDEPENDENT DISTRIBUTION LIMITED
Registration no: 04528350 **Date established:** 2002
No.of Employees: 21 - 50 **Product Groups:** 24, 61

Computalabel International Ltd
PO Box 8867, Leicester, LE21 3DA
Tel: 0116-270 0881 **Fax:** 0116-270 4427
E-mail: info@computalabel.com
Website: http://www.computalabel.com
Directors: S. Urquhart (MD)
Immediate Holding Company: COMPUTALABEL INTERNATIONAL LIMITED
Registration no: 03198516 **VAT No.:** 670 4375 34 **Date established:** 1996
Turnover: Up to £250,000 **No.of Employees:** 1 - 10 **Product Groups:** 42, 44

Date of Accounts	Oct 11	Oct 10	Oct 09
Working Capital	-18	-23	-28
Current Assets	6	4	3

Construction Chemicals
75 Town Green Street Rothley, Leicester, LE7 7NW
Tel: 0116-230 1955
E-mail: sales@constructionchemicals.co.uk
Website: http://www.constructionchemicals.co.uk
Directors: J. Beadman (MD)
Immediate Holding Company: CONSTRUCTION CHEMICALS (UK) LIMITED
Registration no: 03361820 **Date established:** 1997 **Turnover:** £5m - £10m
No.of Employees: 1 - 10 **Product Groups:** 32

Date of Accounts	Apr 11	Apr 10	Apr 09
Working Capital	25	13	19
Fixed Assets	12	11	17
Current Assets	280	300	301

Conveyors International (CI Logistics) (a division of Portec Rail Products (UK) Ltd)
43 Wenlock Way Troon Industrial Area, Leicester, LE4 9HU
Tel: 0116-276 1691 **Fax:** 0116-276 9836
E-mail: sales@conveyors.co.uk
Website: http://www.conveyors.co.uk
Bank(s): National Westminster Bank Plc
Managers: A. Pryce (Sales Prom Mgr), G. Hings (Prod Mgr), R. Greatorex (Purch Mgr)

see next page

Conveyors International (CI Logistics) (a division of Portec Rail Products (UK) Ltd) - Cont'd
Ultimate Holding Company: Portec Rail Products Inc. (USA)
Immediate Holding Company: Torvale Fisher
Registration no: 03939427 **VAT No.:** GB 159 3019 61
Turnover: £2m - £5m **No.of Employees:** 51 - 100 **Product Groups:** 38, 39, 41, 43, 44, 45, 84

Date of Accounts	Dec 04
Working Capital	1063
Current Assets	1063
Total Share Capital	90

Cookson Ltd
16 Morris Road, Leicester, LE2 6BR
Tel: 0116-270 6288 **Fax:** 0116-270 6882
Directors: N. Clarke (Dir)
Immediate Holding Company: COOKSON LIMITED
Registration no: 00788793 **VAT No.:** GB 290 1255 77
Date established: 1964 **Turnover:** £250,000 - £500,000
No.of Employees: 1 - 10 **Product Groups:** 23

Date of Accounts	Mar 11	Mar 10	Mar 09
Working Capital	14	12	-1
Fixed Assets	63	65	66
Current Assets	36	37	33

J M Cooper Knitwear
Unit B The Konfidence Works Arthur Street, Barwell, Leicester, LE9 8GZ
Tel: 01455-841660 **Fax:** 01455-841660
E-mail: cooperlm@btconnect.com
Website: http://www.cooperknitwear.co.uk
Directors: J. Cooper (Prop)
No.of Employees: 1 - 10 **Product Groups:** 24, 61, 63

Copely Developments Ltd
54 Wenlock Way, Leicester, LE4 9HU
Tel: 0116-276 5881 **Fax:** 0116-246 0117
E-mail: sales@copely.com
Website: http://www.copely.com
Bank(s): Lloyds TSB Bank plc
Directors: M. Ball (Fin)
Ultimate Holding Company: COBA INTERNATIONAL LIMITED
Immediate Holding Company: COPELY DEVELOPMENTS LIMITED
Registration no: 07035172 **VAT No.:** GB 115 0616 13
Date established: 2009 **Turnover:** Up to £250,000
No.of Employees: 101 - 250 **Product Groups:** 30

Date of Accounts	Jun 11	Jun 10
Sales Turnover	5m	3m
Pre Tax Profit/Loss	-587	-202
Working Capital	314	614
Fixed Assets	359	267
Current Assets	2m	2m
Current Liabilities	142	136

County Diesel Ltd
Unit 10 The Half Croft High Street, Syston, Leicester, LE7 1LD
Tel: 0116-260 0096 **Fax:** 0116-264 0293
Website: http://www.dieselinjection.glo.cc
Directors: P. Thompson (Dir)
Immediate Holding Company: COUNTY DIESEL LIMITED
Registration no: 07343188 **Date established:** 2010
No.of Employees: 1 - 10 **Product Groups:** 40

Date of Accounts	Aug 11
Working Capital	-46
Fixed Assets	50
Current Assets	48

Martin Cowman Ltd
Gaddesby Lane Rearsby, Leicester, LE7 4YH
Tel: 01664-424840 **Fax:** 01664-424064
E-mail: info@cowman.co.uk
Website: http://www.cowman.co.uk
Managers: L. Barke (Sales Admin)
Ultimate Holding Company: UROC LIMITED
Immediate Holding Company: MARTIN COWMAN LIMITED
Registration no: 00418670 **Date established:** 1946
No.of Employees: 1 - 10 **Product Groups:** 31, 33

Date of Accounts	Feb 12	Feb 11	Feb 10
Working Capital	404	366	363
Fixed Assets	17	65	134
Current Assets	803	889	771

Creative Triangle
31 Rutland Street, Leicester, LE1 1RE
Tel: 0116-253 3426
E-mail: enquiries@creativetriangle.co.uk
Website: http://www.creativetriangle.co.uk
Directors: J. Mcbean (Dir)
Immediate Holding Company: CREATIVE TRIANGLE LIMITED
Registration no: 05961904 **Date established:** 2006
Turnover: Up to £250,000 **No.of Employees:** 1 - 10 **Product Groups:** 84

Date of Accounts	Oct 11	Oct 10	Oct 09
Working Capital	114	46	15
Fixed Assets	9	9	7
Current Assets	261	168	132

Criptic Arvis Ltd
16 Bridge Park Road Thurmaston, Leicester, LE4 8BL
Tel: 0116-260 9700 **Fax:** 0116-264 0147
E-mail: sales@arvis.co.uk
Website: http://www.arvis.co.uk
Managers: D. Chhatralia
Immediate Holding Company: CRIPTIC-ARVIS LIMITED
Registration no: 01538148 **VAT No.:** GB 355 2093 62
Date established: 1981 **No.of Employees:** 11 - 20 **Product Groups:** 33, 35, 46

Date of Accounts	May 11	May 10	May 09
Working Capital	115	88	111
Fixed Assets	124	138	162
Current Assets	263	223	241

Crown Crest Holdings
101 Cobden Street, Leicester, LE1 2LB
Tel: 0116-253 2866 **Fax:** 0116-233 9933
E-mail: azib.tayub@leicester.gov.uk
Directors: A. Tayub (MD)
Immediate Holding Company: CROWN CREST (HOLDINGS) PLC
Registration no: 02971805 **Date established:** 1994 **Turnover:** £2m - £5m
No.of Employees: 1 - 10 **Product Groups:** 62

Date of Accounts	Mar 12	Mar 11	Mar 10
Sales Turnover	2m	2m	2m
Pre Tax Profit/Loss	410	649	258
Working Capital	2m	-599	-747
Fixed Assets	8m	14m	14m
Current Assets	3m	2	33
Current Liabilities	163	185	82

D B I Plastics Ltd
Unit 5a Swannington Road Cottage Lane Industrial Estate, Broughton Astley, Leicester, LE9 6TU
Tel: 01455-283380 **Fax:** 01455-283384
E-mail: info@dbiplastics.co.uk
Website: http://www.dbiplastics.co.uk
Directors: H. Hellstrom Henningsen (Fin), H. Henningsen (MD)
Ultimate Holding Company: D B I HOLDINGS A/S (DENMARK)
Immediate Holding Company: DBI PLASTICS LIMITED
Registration no: 03368590 **Date established:** 1997 **Turnover:** £1m - £2m
No.of Employees: 1 - 10 **Product Groups:** 27, 30, 39, 66

Date of Accounts	Dec 11	Dec 10	Dec 09
Working Capital	694	605	559
Fixed Assets	369	375	381
Current Assets	1m	1m	1m

D G Springs Ltd
64 Cannock Street, Leicester, LE4 9HR
Tel: 0116-276 3616 **Fax:** 0116-276 3626
E-mail: sales@dgsprings.com
Website: http://www.dgsprings.com
Directors: D. Clarke (MD)
Managers: R. Frearson (Chief Mgr), A. Thompson
Immediate Holding Company: D G SPRINGS LIMITED
Registration no: 01688883 **Date established:** 1982
Turnover: £500,000 - £1m **No.of Employees:** 11 - 20 **Product Groups:** 35

Date of Accounts	Dec 11	Dec 10	Dec 09
Working Capital	379	313	304
Fixed Assets	124	145	166
Current Assets	566	448	431

D & H Engineering Ltd
36-38 Great Central Street, Leicester, LE1 4JT
Tel: 0116-251 6200 **Fax:** 0116-251 6120
E-mail: sales@dhengineering.co.uk
Website: http://www.dhengineering.com
Directors: V. Mistry (Fin)
Immediate Holding Company: D & H ENGINEERING LIMITED
Registration no: 02721894 **Date established:** 1992
No.of Employees: 1 - 10 **Product Groups:** 30, 35, 41, 45, 48, 68, 84, 85

Date of Accounts	Sep 11	Sep 10	Sep 09
Working Capital	89	114	164
Fixed Assets	2m	2m	2m
Current Assets	910	993	716

D Potter
23 Rosebery Road Anstey, Leicester, LE7 7EL
Tel: 0116-262 2998 **Fax:** 0116- 2629689
Directors: A. Potter (Prop)
Date established: 1979 **No.of Employees:** 1 - 10 **Product Groups:** 20, 40, 41

D R M T Leicester Ltd
F5 Waterside Road Hamilton, Leicester, LE5 1TL
Tel: 0116-246 0066 **Fax:** 0116-246 4006
E-mail: sales@drmtsolutions.com
Website: http://www.drmtsolutions.com
Directors: P. Brennan (Fin)
Immediate Holding Company: DRMT (LEICESTER) LIMITED
Registration no: 04829444 **VAT No.:** GB 371 7022 70
Date established: 2003 **Turnover:** £1m - £2m **No.of Employees:** 1 - 10
Product Groups: 46, 67

Date of Accounts	Jul 11	Jul 10	Jul 09
Working Capital	222	249	244
Fixed Assets	4	5	5
Current Assets	368	373	363

D S Commodities Ltd
Rannoch House 4 Main Street, Queniborough, Leicester, LE7 3DA
Tel: 0116-264 0461 **Fax:** 0116-264 0584
E-mail: derek@dscommodities.co.uk
Directors: D. Smith (Dir)
Immediate Holding Company: D S COMMODITIES LIMITED
Registration no: 02155638 **VAT No.:** GB 404 0172 12
Date established: 1987 **No.of Employees:** 1 - 10 **Product Groups:** 61, 82

Date of Accounts	Sep 11	Sep 10	Sep 09
Working Capital	-71	-81	-164
Fixed Assets	394	397	406
Current Assets	574	730	324

Danro Ltd
Unit 68 Jaydon Industrial Estate Station Road, Earl Shilton, Leicester, LE9 7GA
Tel: 01455-847061 **Fax:** 01455-841272
E-mail: info@danroltd.co.uk
Website: http://www.danroltd.co.uk
Directors: M. Tansey (Fin)
Immediate Holding Company: DANRO LIMITED
Registration no: 01530820 **VAT No.:** GB 350 3932 71
Date established: 1980 **Turnover:** £1m - £2m **No.of Employees:** 1 - 10
Product Groups: 27, 28, 42, 44

Date of Accounts	Oct 11	Oct 10	Oct 09
Working Capital	498	466	428
Fixed Assets	81	89	83
Current Assets	635	606	562

Dansart Ltd
19 Lees Side Merrylees Industrial Estate, Desford, Leicester, LE9 9FE
Tel: 01530-230058 **Fax:** 01530-230064
E-mail: enquiries@dansart.co.uk
Website: http://www.dansart.co.uk
Directors: P. Davies (MD)
Immediate Holding Company: DANSART LIMITED
Registration no: 02602047 **Date established:** 1991
Turnover: £500,000 - £1m **No.of Employees:** 1 - 10 **Product Groups:** 26, 30, 49, 66

Date of Accounts	Jan 11	Jan 10	Jan 09
Working Capital	539	511	443
Fixed Assets	14	18	22
Current Assets	671	677	577

Data Academy Ltd
187 Scudamore Road, Leicester, LE3 1UQ
Tel: 0116-287 7692 **Fax:** 0116-287 4906
E-mail: training@dataacademy.co.uk
Website: http://www.dataacademy.co.uk
Directors: R. Field-Naldrett (MD)
Immediate Holding Company: DATA ACADEMY LIMITED
Registration no: 05620934 **Date established:** 2005
No.of Employees: 1 - 10 **Product Groups:** 51

Date of Accounts	Dec 11	Dec 10	Dec 09
Working Capital	-18	-59	-31
Current Assets	36	10	19

Dekton Components Leicester Ltd
All Saints Road, Leicester, LE3 5AB
Tel: 0116-251 8387 **Fax:** 0116-253 2824
E-mail: a-bullock@dekton.co.uk
Website: http://www.dekton.co.uk
Directors: T. Bullock (Dir)
Immediate Holding Company: DEKTON COMPONENTS (LEICESTER) LIMITED
Registration no: 01237783 **Date established:** 1975 **Turnover:** £1m - £2m
No.of Employees: 1 - 10 **Product Groups:** 47

Date of Accounts	Jan 11	Jan 10	Jan 09
Working Capital	-36	-57	-81
Current Assets	26	11	6
Current Liabilities	N/A	52	N/A

Dellian Engineering Co.
140 Marjorie Street, Leicester, LE4 5GX
Tel: 0116-266 1821 **Fax:** 0116-266 1821
Directors: I. Randell (Prop)
Date established: 1964 **No.of Employees:** 1 - 10 **Product Groups:** 35

Direct Baggage
52 Park Rise, Leicester, LE3 6SH
Tel: 0116-291 1270 **Fax:** 0116-231 3820
E-mail: info@directbaggage.com
Website: http://www.directbaggage.com
Directors: J. Henry (Prop)
No.of Employees: 1 - 10 **Product Groups:** 22, 28, 45, 84

Direct Engineering Co. Ltd
Parva House Regent Road, Countesthorpe, Leicester, LE8 5RF
Tel: 0116-277 7922 **Fax:** 0116-247 7731
E-mail: admin@cncdirect.co.uk
Website: http://www.cncdirect.co.uk
Bank(s): National Westminster Bank Plc
Directors: A. Suffolk (MD)
Managers: J. Hitchman (Sales Admin)
Immediate Holding Company: LEICESTER G.B. TOOLS LIMITED
Registration no: 04594605 **VAT No.:** GB 424 4652 61
Date established: 1983 **Turnover:** £1m - £2m **No.of Employees:** 21 - 50
Product Groups: 48

Date of Accounts	Oct 11	Oct 10	Oct 09
Working Capital	28	26	30
Fixed Assets	68	74	80
Current Assets	50	42	47

Discretely Different
21 Ferndale Drive Ratby, Leicester, LE6 0LH
Tel: 0116-238 6338
E-mail: info@discretelydifferent.com
Website: http://www.underwearfordisabled.co.uk
Directors: J. Reeve (Prop)
Date established: 2008 **No.of Employees:** 1 - 10 **Product Groups:** 24

Display Coatings
13 Marlow Road, Leicester, LE3 2BQ
Tel: 0116-263 1411 **Fax:** 0116-263 1411
Managers: P. Williamson (Mgr)
Immediate Holding Company: ARTSPACE LLP
Date established: 2002 **No.of Employees:** 1 - 10 **Product Groups:** 46, 48

Date of Accounts	Mar 04	Mar 03
Working Capital	N/A	3
Fixed Assets	1	1
Current Assets	N/A	4

Donaldson Filteration GB Ltd
Humberstone Lane Thurmaston, Leicester, LE4 8HP
Tel: 0116-269 6161 **Fax:** 0116-269 3028
E-mail: info@donaldson.com
Website: http://www.donaldson.com
Bank(s): National Westminster Bank Plc
Managers: D. Croff (Tech Serv Mgr), S. Day, N. Hirani (Personnel), S. Brown (Buyer)
Immediate Holding Company: DONALDSON FILTRATION (GB) LIMITED
Registration no: 03914641 **VAT No.:** GB 295 9798 66
Date established: 2000 **Turnover:** £10m - £20m
No.of Employees: 101 - 250 **Product Groups:** 40, 54, 66

Date of Accounts	May 08	May 07	May 06
Sales Turnover	28155	26129	20462
Pre Tax Profit/Loss	1935	1322	484
Working Capital	4820	3311	2693
Fixed Assets	2633	3973	3489
Current Assets	12876	12235	8075
Current Liabilities	8055	8924	5382
ROCE% (Return on Capital Employed)	26.0	18.1	7.8
ROT% (Return on Turnover)	6.9	5.1	2.4

Drive Vauxhall plc
5 Freemens Common Aylestone Road, Leicester, LE2 7SL
Tel: 0116-255 7567 **Fax:** 0116-247 1006
E-mail: vikkiknight@drivevauxhall.co.uk
Website: http://www.drivevauxhall.co.uk
Bank(s): Barclays
Directors: C. Elvidge (Fin)
Managers: G. Palmer (Personnel), A. Carnell, S. Reeves (Mgr), V. Meadows
Immediate Holding Company: DRIVE INVESTMENTS LIMITED
Registration no: 04340383 **VAT No.:** GB 176 0950 50
Date established: 2011 **Turnover:** £125m - £250m
No.of Employees: 501 - 1000 **Product Groups:** 68

Date of Accounts	Dec 11	Dec 10	Dec 09
Sales Turnover	202m	183m	191m
Pre Tax Profit/Loss	2m	3m	4m
Working Capital	196	-2m	505
Fixed Assets	29m	29m	26m
Current Assets	30m	33m	28m
Current Liabilities	3m	3m	5m

Ductform Engineering Ltd

141 Barkby Road, Leicester, LE4 9LW
Tel: 0116-276 6636 **Fax:** 0116-246 0426
Website: http://www.mellorbromley.co.uk
Bank(s): Midland
Directors: D. Bloxam (Sales & Mktg), D. Chapman (MD), P. Kinal (Fin), C. Lapidge (Ch)
Ultimate Holding Company: MELLOR BROMLEY LIMITED
Immediate Holding Company: VENDUCT AIR CONDITIONING SUPPLIES LIMITED
Registration no: 01158280 **Date established:** 1986 **Turnover:** £2m - £5m
No.of Employees: 21 - 50 **Product Groups:** 26, 35, 36

Date of Accounts	Mar 07	Mar 06	Mar 05
Pre Tax Profit/Loss	N/A	-2	N/A
Working Capital	27	27	28
Current Assets	43	43	1073
Current Liabilities	16	16	1045
Total Share Capital	5	5	5
ROCE% (Return on Capital Employed)		-5.6	

Duplus Architectural Systems Ltd

370 Melton Road, Leicester, LE4 7SL
Tel: 0116-261 0710 **Fax:** 0116-261 0539
E-mail: sales@duplus.co.uk
Website: http://www.duplus.co.uk
Directors: P. Gregory (MD)
Ultimate Holding Company: WILLIAM FREER LIMITED
Immediate Holding Company: DUPLUS ARCHITECTURAL SYSTEMS LIMITED
Registration no: 00587805 **VAT No.:** GB 790 0380 18
Date established: 1957 **Turnover:** £5m - £10m
No.of Employees: 51 - 100 **Product Groups:** 33, 35

Date of Accounts	Dec 11	Dec 10	Dec 09
Sales Turnover	7m	5m	7m
Pre Tax Profit/Loss	135	-251	255
Working Capital	1m	2m	2m
Fixed Assets	518	530	568
Current Assets	3m	3m	2m
Current Liabilities	173	81	305

Dustraction Ltd

1 Pomeroy Drive Oadby, Leicester, LE2 5NE
Tel: 0116-271 3212 **Fax:** 0116-271 3215
E-mail: info@dustraction.co.uk
Website: http://www.dustraction.co.uk
Bank(s): HSBC Bank plc
Directors: S. Henson (Ptnr), S. Matuska (Sales)
Managers: K. Swift
Immediate Holding Company: DUSTRACTION LIMITED
Registration no: 03905418 **Date established:** 2000 **Turnover:** £1m - £2m
No.of Employees: 21 - 50 **Product Groups:** 40, 46, 48, 54

Date of Accounts	May 12	May 11	May 10
Working Capital	296	341	378
Fixed Assets	377	376	404
Current Assets	576	638	681

E V L Design & Distribution

48 Boston Road, Leicester, LE4 1AA
Tel: 0116-236 7711 **Fax:** 0116-236 8868
E-mail: sales@evl-design.com
Website: http://www.evl-design.com
Directors: G. Sanghera (Fin), M. Sanghera (Sales)
Managers: M. Pitt (Sales Prom Mgr), V. Nathwani (Fin Mgr), R. Raja (Purch Mgr), R. Devereox (Personnel), H. Paulinski (Mktg Serv Mgr)
Immediate Holding Company: BPC (HOLDINGS) LIMITED
Date established: 2011 **No.of Employees:** 21 - 50 **Product Groups:** 37, 67

Eagle Plastics Ltd

3 Highmeres Road, Leicester, LE4 9LZ
Tel: 0116-276 6363 **Fax:** 0116-276 6366
E-mail: sales@eagleplastics.co.uk
Website: http://www.eagleplastics.co.uk
Managers: A. Skinner (Sales Admin)
Immediate Holding Company: EAGLE PLASTICS LIMITED
Registration no: 02915093 **Date established:** 1994
No.of Employees: 1 - 10 **Product Groups:** 26, 30, 31, 44, 49

Date of Accounts	Dec 11	Dec 10	Dec 09
Working Capital	475	481	487
Fixed Assets	128	120	119
Current Assets	887	815	790

Econosto UK Ltd

Unit D1 Whiteacres, Whetstone, Leicester, LE8 6ZG
Tel: 0116-272 7300 **Fax:** 0116-272 7345
E-mail: sales@econosto.uk.com
Website: http://www.econosto.uk.com
Directors: M. Hemsley (Co Sec), J. Van Os (Dir)
Managers: S. Underhill (Sales & Mktg Mg), J. Clark (Tech Serv Mgr), G. Pollard (Comptroller), R. Talmer
Ultimate Holding Company: SHV HOLDINGS NV (NETHERLANDS)
Immediate Holding Company: ECONOSTO UK LIMITED
Registration no: 01826762 **Date established:** 1984
Turnover: £10m - £20m **No.of Employees:** 21 - 50 **Product Groups:** 36, 40, 41

Date of Accounts	Dec 11	Dec 10	Dec 09
Sales Turnover	11m	11m	14m
Pre Tax Profit/Loss	301	143	1m
Working Capital	2m	2m	2m
Fixed Assets	234	191	141
Current Assets	7m	5m	7m
Current Liabilities	667	407	698

Electro Mech Design & Assembly Ltd

13 Dartford Road, Leicester, LE2 7PQ
Tel: 0116-283 8883 **Fax:** 0116-283 8884
E-mail: sales@electromechltd.co.uk
Directors: A. Bates (Fin), P. Bates (MD)
Managers: M. Bretherton (Sales Prom Mgr)
Immediate Holding Company: ELECTROMECH DESIGN AND ASSEMBLY LIMITED
Registration no: 01475096 **Date established:** 1980 **Turnover:** £1m - £2m
No.of Employees: 21 - 50 **Product Groups:** 37

Date of Accounts	Mar 11	Mar 10	Mar 09
Working Capital	687	543	487
Fixed Assets	196	201	204
Current Assets	966	816	655

Electro Motion UK (Export) Ltd

161 Barkby Road, Leicester, LE4 9LX
Tel: 0116-276 6341 **Fax:** 0116-274 3048
E-mail: darwin@electromotion.co.uk
Website: http://www.electromotion.co.uk
Bank(s): Lloyds, Roundway
Directors: D. Gadsden (MD), E. Murray (Dir), E. Seemann (Dir), D. Gadsden (Fin)
Managers: A. Karia (Sales Prom Mgr)
Immediate Holding Company: ELECTRO-MOTION UK (EXPORT) LIMITED
Registration no: 00448241 **VAT No.:** 115 0411 31 **Date established:** 1948
Turnover: £5m - £10m **No.of Employees:** 51 - 100 **Product Groups:** 36, 39, 42, 46, 47, 48, 67, 83

Date of Accounts	Mar 11	Mar 10	Mar 09
Sales Turnover	6m	6m	N/A
Pre Tax Profit/Loss	123	-96	-138
Working Capital	972	1m	1m
Fixed Assets	2m	2m	2m
Current Assets	3m	3m	3m
Current Liabilities	130	114	105

Electroforms & Components Ltd

61 Narborough Road Cosby, Leicester, LE9 1TB
Tel: 0116-286 4832 **Fax:** 0116-286 4298
E-mail: elforms@aol.com
Bank(s): National Westminster Bank Plc
Directors: C. Margetts (MD)
Immediate Holding Company: ELECTROFORMS & COMPONENTS LIMITED
Registration no: 00930205 **Date established:** 1968 **Turnover:** £1m - £2m
No.of Employees: 11 - 20 **Product Groups:** 34, 37, 48, 67

Date of Accounts	Sep 11	Sep 10	Sep 09
Working Capital	1m	795	795
Fixed Assets	988	1m	1m
Current Assets	1m	2m	2m

Elliot Group Ltd

St Georges House Gaddesby Lane Rearsby, Leicester, LE7 4YH
Tel: 01664-424888 **Fax:** 01664-424955
E-mail: events@as.elliotuk.com
Website: http://www.elliotuk.com
Managers: L. Buswell
Registration no: 01805542 **Date established:** 1947 **Turnover:** £5m - £10m
No.of Employees: 11 - 20 **Product Groups:** 83

Date of Accounts	Dec 07
Sales Turnover	754
Pre Tax Profit/Loss	-268
Working Capital	-334
Fixed Assets	3551
Current Assets	936
Current Liabilities	1270
Total Share Capital	50
ROCE% (Return on Capital Employed)	-8.3

Emusol Products Ltd

7b Trevanth Road, Leicester, LE4 9LS
Tel: 0116-274 1114 **Fax:** 0116-274 1114
E-mail: sales@emusolproducts.com
Website: http://www.emusolproducts.com
Directors: D. Tebbatt (Fab)
Managers: M. Sampey (Mktg Serv Mgr), P. Hacker (Export Sales Mg), A. Teagle (Accounts)
Registration no: 00722693 **Turnover:** £500,000 - £1m
No.of Employees: 1 - 10 **Product Groups:** 29, 30, 31, 32, 33, 49, 52, 85

Enterprise Graphics Ltd

1 Earls Close Earls Close Industrial Estate, Thurmaston, Leicester, LE4 8FZ
Tel: 0116-260 0879 **Fax:** 0116-269 7729
E-mail: fiona@enterprisegraphics.wannado.co.uk
Website: http://www.enterprisegraphics.co.uk
Directors: F. Ryan (Prop)
Immediate Holding Company: ENTERPRISE GRAPHICS LIMITED
Registration no: 01256315 **Date established:** 1976
Turnover: Up to £250,000 **No.of Employees:** 1 - 10 **Product Groups:** 44

Date of Accounts	May 11	May 10	May 09
Working Capital	1	30	-39
Fixed Assets	75	79	81
Current Assets	145	155	118

Entrex Door Services

119-125 Bridge Road, Leicester, LE5 3QP
Tel: 0116-274 0466 **Fax:** 0116-246 0462
E-mail: info@leicesterglass.co.uk
Website: http://www.leicesterglass.co.uk
Directors: B. Hill (MD)
Date established: 1992 **No.of Employees:** 11 - 20 **Product Groups:** 26, 35

Eriks UK (Leicester Service Centre)

12 Cannock Street, Leicester, LE4 9HR
Tel: 0116-276 6211 **Fax:** 0116-246 0184
E-mail: leicester@eriks.co.uk
Website: http://www.eriks.co.uk
Managers: A. Ayres (Sales Admin)
Turnover: £250m - £500m **No.of Employees:** 1 - 10 **Product Groups:** 66

Euro Energy Resources Ltd

Unit 10 Barrington Business Park Leycroft Road, Leicester, LE4 1ET
Tel: 0116-234 0567 **Fax:** 0116-235 4183
E-mail: info@euroenergy.co.uk
Website: http://www.euroenergy.co.uk
Directors: L. Raynor (Tech Serv)
Managers: J. Masters (Sales & Mktg Mg)
Immediate Holding Company: EURO ENERGY RESOURCES LIMITED
Registration no: 01576945 **VAT No.:** GB 355 3065 62
Date established: 1981 **Turnover:** £1m - £2m **No.of Employees:** 11 - 20
Product Groups: 37

Date of Accounts	Jan 12	Jan 11	Jan 10
Working Capital	468	415	666
Fixed Assets	45	53	60
Current Assets	723	673	901

European Thermodynamics

8 Priory Business Park Wistow, Kibworth, Leicester, LE8 0RX
Tel: 0116-279 6899 **Fax:** 0116-279 3490
E-mail: info@etdyn.com
Website: http://www.etdyn.com
Directors: N. Porter (Dir), P. Stirley (Co Sec)
Immediate Holding Company: EUROPEAN THERMODYNAMICS LIMITED
Registration no: 04345086 **Date established:** 2001
No.of Employees: 1 - 10 **Product Groups:** 27, 33, 37, 38, 39, 40, 44, 66, 67, 84, 85

Date of Accounts	Dec 11	Dec 10	Dec 09
Working Capital	2m	2m	1m
Fixed Assets	78	64	78
Current Assets	2m	2m	2m

Eurotool Express Ltd

22 Broome Avenue East Goscote, Leicester, LE7 3SA
Tel: 0116-260 3400 **Fax:** 0116-260 3400
Directors: J. Jennaway (Prop)
Date established: 1995 **No.of Employees:** 1 - 10 **Product Groups:** 37

Everards Brewery Ltd

Castle Acres Everard Way, Enderby, Leicester, LE19 1BY
Tel: 0116-201 4100 **Fax:** 0116-281 4199
E-mail: info@everards.co.uk
Website: http://www.everards.co.uk
Bank(s): National Westminster Bank Plc
Directors: N. Allen (Fin), N. Arthur (Sales), M. Allen (Fin)
Managers: J. Shepherd (Personnel), S. Tice, E. Hardy, G. Armston
Immediate Holding Company: EVERARDS BREWERY LIMITED
Registration no: 00319261 **Date established:** 1936
Turnover: £20m - £50m **No.of Employees:** 101 - 250
Product Groups: 21, 62

Date of Accounts	Sep 08	Sep 09	Sep 10
Sales Turnover	31m	30m	29m
Pre Tax Profit/Loss	3m	2m	4m
Working Capital	-22m	-8m	-8m
Fixed Assets	86m	86m	86m
Current Assets	8m	7m	7m
Current Liabilities	4m	5m	5m

Exclusive Leisure Ltd

28 Cannock Street, Leicester, LE4 9HR
Tel: 0116-233 2255 **Fax:** 0116-246 1561
E-mail: info@exclusiveleisure.co.uk
Website: http://www.exclusiveleisure.co.uk
Directors: D. Bell (Fin)
Immediate Holding Company: EXCLUSIVE LEISURE LIMITED
Registration no: 04048455 **Date established:** 2000
Turnover: £500,000 - £1m **No.of Employees:** 1 - 10 **Product Groups:** 30

Date of Accounts	Aug 11	Aug 10	Aug 09
Working Capital	495	484	469
Fixed Assets	70	106	72
Current Assets	662	772	710

Express Furniture (t/a EOS Ltd)

260-266 Humberstone Road, Leicester, LE5 0EG
Tel: 0116-262 7153 **Fax:** 01474-853163
E-mail: faranjust4u@gmail.com
Website: http://www.expressfurniture.co.uk
Directors: S. Peacock (Dir), S. Beacock (Dir)
Managers: F. Kardame
Immediate Holding Company: EXPRESS FURNITURE (LEICESTER) LIMITED
Registration no: 07122190 **Date established:** 2010
No.of Employees: 1 - 10 **Product Groups:** 26, 83

F1 Manufacturing Ltd

350 Melton Road, Leicester, LE4 7SL
Tel: 0116-268 8484 **Fax:** 0116-268 8489
E-mail: sales@f1manufacturing.com
Website: http://www.f1manufacturing.com
Bank(s): The Royal Bank of Scotland
Directors: J. McNulty (Co Sec), T. Mcnulty (Dir)
Managers: L. Talbot, S. Souter (Buyer)
Ultimate Holding Company: STARKSTROM GROUP LIMITED
Immediate Holding Company: F1 MANUFACTURING LTD
Registration no: 04663333 **VAT No.:** GB 485 6687 81
Date established: 2003 **Turnover:** £2m - £5m **No.of Employees:** 21 - 50
Product Groups: 49

Date of Accounts	Dec 09	Dec 08	Dec 07
Working Capital	202	187	126
Fixed Assets	135	140	128
Current Assets	738	981	868

Fastener Technology Ltd

2 Rochester Close Kibworth Harcourt, Leicester, LE8 0JS
Tel: 0116-279 2820 **Fax:** 0116-279 6409
E-mail: rikharwood123@btinternet.com
Website: http://www.fastenertech.co.uk
Directors: V. Harwood (Fin), R. Harwood (MD)
Immediate Holding Company: FASTENER TECHNOLOGY LIMITED
Registration no: 04191340 **Date established:** 2001
No.of Employees: 1 - 10 **Product Groups:** 25, 30, 35

Date of Accounts	Mar 12	Mar 11	Mar 09
Working Capital	3	-2	-3
Fixed Assets	2	2	2
Current Assets	48	28	32

Flow Mech Products Ltd

Charter Street, Leicester, LE1 3UD
Tel: 0116-242 5425 **Fax:** 0116-242 5555
E-mail: info@flowmech.co.uk
Website: http://www.flowmech.co.uk
Managers: J. Woodward (Admin Off)
Immediate Holding Company: FLOW MECH PRODUCTS LIMITED
Registration no: 02726033 **Date established:** 1992 **Turnover:** £1m - £2m
No.of Employees: 11 - 20 **Product Groups:** 22, 29, 30, 38, 40, 42, 48, 67

Date of Accounts	Jun 11	Jun 10	Jun 09
Working Capital	323	266	300
Fixed Assets	247	262	270
Current Assets	688	608	566

Formseal South Ltd

23 Snowdrop Close Narborough, Leicester, LE19 3YB
Tel: 0116-275 0052 **Fax:** 0116-286 5808
E-mail: colin.towers@sky.com
Website: http://www.formseal.co.uk
Directors: P. Towers (Fin), C. Towers (Dir)
Immediate Holding Company: FORMSEAL (SOUTH) LIMITED
Registration no: 02116045 **VAT No.:** GB 459 9749 67
Date established: 1987 **Turnover:** Up to £250,000
No.of Employees: 1 - 10 **Product Groups:** 30, 36, 49

see next page

Formseal South Ltd - Cont'd

Date of Accounts	Aug 10	Aug 08	Aug 07
Working Capital	5	5	5
Fixed Assets	N/A	N/A	1
Current Assets	17	18	16

Formwell Plastics Ltd
Unit L4 0 Humberstone Lane, Leicester, LE4 9HA
Tel: 0116-276 0958 **Fax:** 0116-222 3892
E-mail: sales@formwell.co.uk
Website: http://www.formwell.co.uk
Directors: J. Timson (Dir)
Immediate Holding Company: FORMWELL PLASTICS LIMITED
Registration no: 02588988 **VAT No.:** GB 565 8506 10
Date established: 1991 **Turnover:** £2m - £5m **No.of Employees:** 1 - 10
Product Groups: 30, 42

Date of Accounts	Apr 11	Apr 10	Apr 09
Working Capital	136	117	150
Fixed Assets	20	25	28
Current Assets	210	194	208

Forst UK Ltd
14 Dartford Road, Leicester, LE2 7PR
Tel: 0116-245 2000 **Fax:** 0116-245 2037
E-mail: sales@alpineabrasives.com
Website: http://www.forst.co.uk
Directors: S. Evans (MD)
Immediate Holding Company: ALPINE ABRASIVES LIMITED
Registration no: 01561649 **Date established:** 1981 **Turnover:** £2m - £5m
No.of Employees: 21 - 50 **Product Groups:** 46, 48

Date of Accounts	Jul 08	Jul 07	Jul 06
Working Capital	-301	-518	-425
Fixed Assets	1m	1m	1m
Current Assets	3m	3m	2m

Forward Micro Systems Ltd
40-42 Northgate Street, Leicester, LE3 5BY
Tel: 0116-262 7974 **Fax:** 0116-251 5524
E-mail: info@formicro.co.uk
Website: http://www.formicro.co.uk
Directors: N. Patel (Comm)
Ultimate Holding Company: APPLECROSS HOLDINGS LIMITED
Immediate Holding Company: FORWARD ELECTRONICS LIMITED
Registration no: 01498627 **Date established:** 1980
Turnover: £250,000 - £500,000 **No.of Employees:** 11 - 20
Product Groups: 38

G D M S UK Ltd
14 The Meadway Syston, Leicester, LE7 2BD
Tel: 0116-264 0381 **Fax:** 0116-264 0381
E-mail: sales@gdms.org.uk
Website: http://www.gdms.org.uk
Directors: W. Duncan (Dir)
Immediate Holding Company: G.D.M.S. UK Ltd
Registration no: 04588625 **Date established:** 2002
Turnover: £250,000 - £500,000 **No.of Employees:** 1 - 10
Product Groups: 32

Date of Accounts	Dec 07	Dec 06	Dec 05
Working Capital	9	10	7
Fixed Assets	1	2	2
Current Assets	19	19	20
Current Liabilities	10	9	13

G E Sensing
Fir Tree Lane Groby, Leicester, LE6 0FH
Tel: 0116-231 7100 **Fax:** 0116-231 7101
E-mail: tim.povall@ge.com
Website: http://www.geinfrastructure.com
Bank(s): Barclays, Town Hall Square
Directors: T. Povall (Prop)
Managers: S. Philips
Ultimate Holding Company: GENERAL ELECTRIC COMPANY (USA)
Immediate Holding Company: DRUCK LIMITED
Registration no: 01590333 **Date established:** 1981
Turnover: £50m - £75m **No.of Employees:** 501 - 1000
Product Groups: 37, 38, 39

Date of Accounts	Dec 11	Dec 10	Dec 09
Sales Turnover	87m	76m	68m
Pre Tax Profit/Loss	16m	16m	11m
Working Capital	74m	59m	45m
Fixed Assets	15m	14m	14m
Current Assets	88m	74m	55m
Current Liabilities	10m	8m	5m

G & J Woodworking
52 Cannock Street Troon Industrial Estate, Leicester, LE4 9HR
Tel: 0116-276 6761 **Fax:** 0116-276 6762
E-mail: gjwoodworking@btconnect.com
Website: http://www.gjwoodworking.co.uk
Directors: K. Jones (Ptnr)
No.of Employees: 1 - 10 **Product Groups:** 25, 30, 48, 49

Gafbros Ltd
Littleholme Street, Leicester, LE3 5NG
Tel: 0116-253 0380 **Fax:** 0116-251 0377
E-mail: sales@gafbros.com
Website: http://www.gafbros.com
Directors: I. Gassar (MD)
Immediate Holding Company: GAFBROS LIMITED
Registration no: 01256243 **Date established:** 1976 **Turnover:** £2m - £5m
No.of Employees: 1 - 10 **Product Groups:** 27, 30

Date of Accounts	Apr 11	Apr 10	Apr 09
Working Capital	699	665	661
Fixed Assets	58	86	72
Current Assets	2m	2m	2m

Glen Quarrying Plant Ltd
39a Saddington Road Fleckney, Leicester, LE8 8AX
Tel: 0116-240 2996
E-mail: glenquarrying@dsl.pipex.com
Website: http://www.glenquarryingplant.com
Date established: 1992 **Product Groups:** 14, 45, 67

Glendower Cutting Tools Ltd
Unit 3 Pinfold Road Thurmaston, Leicester, LE4 8AS
Tel: 0116-269 5999 **Fax:** 0116-269 3442
E-mail: sales@glendower.co.uk
Website: http://www.glendower.co.uk
Bank(s): Barclays
Directors: C. Sanders (Co Sec), A. Pallett (Dir)
Managers: D. Chattaway (Admin Off)
Immediate Holding Company: GLENDOWER CUTTING TOOLS LIMITED
Registration no: 01047217 **VAT No.:** GB 114 0601 32
Date established: 1972 **Turnover:** £2m - £5m **No.of Employees:** 21 - 50
Product Groups: 34, 36, 46, 47

Date of Accounts	Dec 11	Dec 10	Dec 09
Working Capital	352	306	211
Fixed Assets	418	252	269
Current Assets	890	682	549

Greenshires Group Ltd
160-164 Barkby Road, Leicester, LE4 9LF
Tel: 0116-202 2600 **Fax:** 0116-202 2601
E-mail: paul.heath@greenshires.com
Website: http://www.greenshires.com
Bank(s): National Westminster Bank Plc
Directors: P. Heath (MD)
Managers: T. Bottomley (Mktg Serv Mgr), T. Coulson (Accounts), M. Cross (Sales & Mktg Mg)
Ultimate Holding Company: GREENSHIRES HOLDINGS LIMITED
Immediate Holding Company: GREENSHIRES GROUP LIMITED
Registration no: 00759321 **VAT No.:** GB 313 0580 04
Date established: 1963 **Turnover:** £10m - £20m
No.of Employees: 101 - 250 **Product Groups:** 28

Date of Accounts	Dec 10	Dec 09	Mar 09
Sales Turnover	14m	9m	13m
Pre Tax Profit/Loss	200	91	-441
Working Capital	316	-60	-274
Fixed Assets	3m	3m	4m
Current Assets	3m	3m	3m
Current Liabilities	761	637	495

Greyblue Ltd
PO Box 8790, Leicester, LE3 7BG
Tel: 08459-005790
E-mail: information@greyblue.co.uk
Website: http://www.greyblue.co.uk
Directors: P. Gardner (Dir)
Immediate Holding Company: GREYBLUE LTD
Registration no: 04890772 **Date established:** 2003
No.of Employees: 1 - 10 **Product Groups:** 84

Date of Accounts	Jan 12	Jan 11	Jan 10
Working Capital	-22	-32	-36
Fixed Assets	1	1	2
Current Assets	1	N/A	N/A

Guardian Finance Ltd
207 Barkby Road, Leicester, LE4 9HZ
Tel: 0116-276 6631 **Fax:** 0116-246 0447
E-mail: sales@guardian-finance.co.uk
Website: http://www.guardian-finance.co.uk
Directors: M. Bent (MD)
Ultimate Holding Company: GUARDIAN HOLDINGS (LEICESTER) LIMITED
Immediate Holding Company: GUARDIAN FINANCE LIMITED
Registration no: 00373207 **VAT No.:** GB 113 8897 48
Date established: 1942 **Turnover:** £500,000 - £1m
No.of Employees: 1 - 10 **Product Groups:** 82

Date of Accounts	Mar 12	Mar 11	Mar 10
Working Capital	1m	1m	1m
Fixed Assets	30	40	53
Current Assets	2m	2m	2m

Guildea Welding Engineering Supplies
642 Aylestone Road, Leicester, LE2 8JD
Tel: 0116-283 2221 **Fax:** 0116-283 2221
E-mail: sales@guildea-welding-supplies.co.uk
Website: http://www.guildea-welding-supplies.co.uk
Directors: M. Guildea (Ptnr)
Date established: 1989 **No.of Employees:** 1 - 10 **Product Groups:** 46

W N Gutteridge Ltd
11 Wellington Street, Leicester, LE1 6HH
Tel: 0116-254 3825 **Fax:** 0116-247 0276
E-mail: chris@gutteridge.co.uk
Website: http://www.gutteridge.co.uk
Directors: C. Gutteridge (Ptnr)
Immediate Holding Company: W.N. GUTTERIDGE LIMITED
Registration no: 00338775 **VAT No.:** GB 113 9655 67
Date established: 1938 **Turnover:** £2m - £5m **No.of Employees:** 1 - 10
Product Groups: 23, 30, 35

Date of Accounts	Mar 11	Mar 10	Mar 09
Working Capital	201	174	233
Fixed Assets	22	23	31
Current Assets	321	234	300

Hands Cleaners Ltd
93 Humberstone Gate, Leicester, LE1 1WB
Tel: 0116-222 9333 **Fax:** 0116-224 6608
E-mail: mailsupportservices@handsgroup.co.uk
Website: http://www.handsgroup.co.uk
Directors: W. Argraves (MD)
Immediate Holding Company: HANDS (CLEANERS) LIMITED
Registration no: 00993117 **Date established:** 1970
Turnover: £500,000 - £1m **No.of Employees:** 11 - 20 **Product Groups:** 52

Date of Accounts	Oct 11	Oct 10	Oct 09
Working Capital	206	158	170
Fixed Assets	168	165	103
Current Assets	502	451	473

Harleys Corrugated Cases Ltd
Lonsdale Road Thurmaston, Leicester, LE4 8JF
Tel: 0116-269 3303 **Fax:** 0116-269 2828
E-mail: sales@harleys-boxes.com
Website: http://www.harleys-boxes.com
Bank(s): Lloyds TSB Bank plc
Directors: P. Harley (Sales), T. Harley (MD)
Immediate Holding Company: HARLEYS CORRUGATED CASES LIMITED
Registration no: 00880424 **Date established:** 1966 **Turnover:** £2m - £5m
No.of Employees: 21 - 50 **Product Groups:** 27, 85

Date of Accounts	May 12	May 11	May 10
Working Capital	1m	1m	1m
Fixed Assets	516	536	541
Current Assets	2m	2m	2m

Harrison Castings Ltd
Gough Road, Leicester, LE5 4AP
Tel: 0116-276 9351 **Fax:** 0116-246 0199
E-mail: martin.beach@harrisoncastings.com
Website: http://www.harrisoncastings.com
Bank(s): Barclays
Directors: M. Beach (Fin), M. Cole (MD), M. Cole (MD)
Immediate Holding Company: HARRISON CASTINGS LIMITED
Registration no: 00370237 **Date established:** 1941
Turnover: £10m - £20m **No.of Employees:** 51 - 100 **Product Groups:** 34

Date of Accounts	Jun 11	Jun 10	Jun 09
Sales Turnover	12m	7m	8m
Pre Tax Profit/Loss	530	87	72
Working Capital	2m	2m	1m
Fixed Assets	3m	3m	3m
Current Assets	5m	3m	2m
Current Liabilities	899	441	361

Hewitt Ladders Ltd
37 Melrose Street, Leicester, LE4 6FD
Tel: 0116-266 3304 **Fax:** 0116-261 3033
E-mail: hewittladdersltd@btconnect.com
Website: http://www.hewittladders.co.uk
Registration no: 01424921 **Turnover:** Up to £250,000
No.of Employees: 1 - 10 **Product Groups:** 23, 25, 30, 35, 36, 39, 40, 45, 66, 83

Date of Accounts	Feb 08
Working Capital	-38
Fixed Assets	26
Current Assets	35
Current Liabilities	73

Hex Holdings Ltd
10 Charter Street, Leicester, LE1 3UD
Tel: 0116-253 8251 **Fax:** 0116-253 8201
E-mail: sales@hex.co.uk
Website: http://www.hex.co.uk
Managers: K. Brown (Mgr)
Immediate Holding Company: HEX HOLDINGS LIMITED
Registration no: 01285161 **VAT No.:** GB 507 7067 39
Date established: 1976 **Turnover:** £500,000 - £1m
No.of Employees: 1 - 10 **Product Groups:** 39

Date of Accounts	Apr 10	Apr 09	Apr 08
Sales Turnover	20m	21m	N/A
Pre Tax Profit/Loss	32	105	23
Working Capital	1m	767	771
Fixed Assets	3m	3m	3m
Current Assets	11m	11m	9m
Current Liabilities	3m	3m	4m

Hi Tech Coatings UK Ltd
19 Progress Way, Leicester, LE4 9LQ
Tel: 0116-246 1522 **Fax:** 0116-246 1533
Directors: A. Premji (MD)
Immediate Holding Company: HI-TECH COATINGS (U.K.) LIMITED
Registration no: 02602897 **Date established:** 1991
No.of Employees: 1 - 10 **Product Groups:** 46, 48

Date of Accounts	Mar 11	Mar 10	Mar 09
Working Capital	41	47	87
Fixed Assets	8	9	11
Current Assets	41	64	216

R & J Hill Engineering Ltd
153 Parker Drive, Leicester, LE4 0JP
Tel: 0116-236 6888 **Fax:** 0116-236 8777
E-mail: sales@hillsport.com
Website: http://www.hillsport.com
Bank(s): National Westminster
Directors: J. Hancock (Dir), D. Gilbert (Co Sec)
Immediate Holding Company: R. & J. HILL ENGINEERING LIMITED
Registration no: 01100148 **VAT No.:** GB 115 1972 83
Date established: 1973 **Turnover:** £500,000 - £1m
No.of Employees: 11 - 20 **Product Groups:** 34

Date of Accounts	Mar 11	Mar 10	Mar 09
Working Capital	368	373	362
Fixed Assets	264	281	301
Current Assets	508	526	542

Hilti GT Britain Ltd (Midlands)
22 Charter Street, Leicester, LE1 3UD
Tel: 0800-886100 **Fax:** 0800-886200
Website: http://www.hilti.co.uk
Directors: J. Rood (MD), R. Hudspeth (Sales), R. Dannheim (Fin)
Ultimate Holding Company: HILTI AG (LIECHTENSTEIN)
Immediate Holding Company: HILTI (GT.BRITAIN) LIMITED
Registration no: 00479786 **Date established:** 1950
No.of Employees: 1 - 10 **Product Groups:** 30, 35, 36, 37, 40

Date of Accounts	Dec 10	Dec 09	Dec 08
Sales Turnover	65m	66m	79m
Pre Tax Profit/Loss	766	-379	-48
Working Capital	12m	15m	12m
Fixed Assets	5m	5m	6m
Current Assets	33m	25m	23m
Current Liabilities	6m	4m	5m

Hiva Products (High Voltage Applications Ltd)
Disraeli Street, Leicester, LE2 8LX
Tel: 0116-283 6977 **Fax:** 0116-283 5265
E-mail: info@hiva.co.uk
Website: http://www.hiva.co.uk
Managers: A. Woodcock (Mgr)
Immediate Holding Company: GRANBY EXTRUDERS LIMITED
Registration no: 01409157 **VAT No.:** GB 114 3904 96
Date established: 1979 **Turnover:** £2m - £5m **No.of Employees:** 11 - 20
Product Groups: 23, 27, 28, 30, 48, 63

Date of Accounts	Mar 11	Mar 10	Mar 09
Working Capital	6	1	12
Current Assets	206	131	46

Honeywell
140 Waterside Road Hamilton, Leicester, LE5 1TN
Tel: 0116-246 2000 **Fax:** 0116-246 2300
E-mail: mark.ayton@gent.co.uk
Website: http://www.honeywell.com
Bank(s): HSBC Bank plc
Directors: D. Whittaker (Fin), M. Ayton (MD)
Managers: N. Morgan (Mktg Serv Mgr), C. Scott (Tech Serv Mgr), D. Sanders

Immediate Holding Company: CARADON P.L.C.
Registration no: 00264047 **VAT No.:** GB 661 5534 36
Date established: 1932 **Turnover:** £20m - £50m
No.of Employees: 101 - 250 **Product Groups:** 37, 40

Stewart Houston

Brookbridge Court Melton Road, Syston, Leicester, LE7 2JT
Tel: 0116-269 8001 **Fax:** 0116-269 8001
E-mail: shouston_design@btconnect.com
Directors: S. Houston (Prop)
Registration no: 05906414 **Date established:** 2006
Turnover: Up to £250,000 **No.of Employees:** 1 - 10 **Product Groups:** 35

Hub Le Bas (a division of Caparo Precision Tubes Ltd)

11 New Star Road, Leicester, LE4 9JD
Tel: 0116-276 9171 **Fax:** 0116-274 3473
E-mail: andy.bott@hublebas.co.uk
Website: http://www.hublebas.co.uk
Managers: A. Bott (Reg Mgr)
Ultimate Holding Company: TYCO INTERNATIONAL LTD
Immediate Holding Company: TYCO EUROPEAN TUBING LTD
Registration no: 02168228 **Turnover:** £5m - £10m
No.of Employees: 11 - 20 **Product Groups:** 36

U & P Hughes Precision Engineers

Unit 7 Belgrave Business Centre 308a Melton Road, Leicester, LE4 7SL
Tel: 0116-233 1661 **Fax:** 0116-233 1662
Directors: P. Hughes (Ptnr)
Date established: 1980 **Turnover:** Up to £250,000
No.of Employees: 1 - 10 **Product Groups:** 48

Industrial & Marine Silencers Ltd

Syston Road Cossington, Leicester, LE7 4UZ
Tel: 0116-260 4985 **Fax:** 0116-260 5151
E-mail: sales@silencers.co.uk
Website: http://www.silencers.co.uk
Directors: G. Rennocks (MD)
Managers: M. Vidler, V. Williams (Purch Mgr), P. Wroe (Sales Prom Mgr), D. Rennocks (Prod Mgr), T. Jones (Tech Serv Mgr)
Immediate Holding Company: Bradgate Containers Ltd
Registration no: 02605553 **Turnover:** £2m - £5m
No.of Employees: 21 - 50 **Product Groups:** 39, 40

Date of Accounts	Aug 11	Aug 10	Aug 09
Working Capital	2m	2m	2m
Fixed Assets	374	334	377
Current Assets	4m	3m	3m

Infinity Group

Tara House Hilltop Road, Hamilton, Leicester, LE5 1TT
Tel: 0116-222 5300 **Fax:** 0844-779 8778
E-mail: info@infinitygrp.co.uk
Website: http://www.infinitygrp.co.uk
Managers: A. Gosai (Ops Mgr), D. Hodgson (Tech Serv Mgr), E. Hodgson (Personnel)
Date established: 1998 **Turnover:** £2m - £5m **No.of Employees:** 11 - 20
Product Groups: 37

Harvey Ingram LLP

20-40 New Walk, Leicester, LE1 6TX
Tel: 0116-254 5454 **Fax:** 0116-255 4559
E-mail: stephen.woolfe@harveyingram.com
Website: http://www.harveyingram.com
Bank(s): National Westminster
Directors: W. Irving (Fin), S. Woolfe (Snr Part), M. Jones (Ptnr), R. Bowder (Snr Part)
Managers: T. Spicer (Tech Serv Mgr), A. Thorne, R. Seal (Buyer), D. Flora (Mktg Serv Mgr), C. Burgeson (Sales & Mktg Mg), S. Mennell (Personnel), I. Smit (Tech Serv Mgr)
Immediate Holding Company: NEW WALK REALISATIONS LLP
Registration no: OC308609 **Date established:** 2004
Turnover: £10m - £20m **No.of Employees:** 101 - 250 **Product Groups:** 80

Date of Accounts	Mar 11	Mar 10	Mar 09
Sales Turnover	14m	14m	14m
Pre Tax Profit/Loss	3m	3m	3m
Working Capital	7m	6m	5m
Fixed Assets	630	557	781
Current Assets	10m	7m	7m
Current Liabilities	2m	1m	946

International Lift Equipment Ltd

Unit 3a Wanlip Road, Syston, Leicester, LE7 1PD
Tel: 0116-269 0900 **Fax:** 0116-269 0939
E-mail: p.lycett@ilem.co.uk
Website: http://www.ileweb.com
Bank(s): Lloyds TSB Bank plc
Directors: P. Lycett (Fin)
Managers: G. Stevenson (Sales Prom Mgr), J. Tinsley (Tech Serv Mgr), L. Hooper (Purch Mgr)
Ultimate Holding Company: ILE HOLDINGS LIMITED
Immediate Holding Company: INTERNATIONAL LIFT EQUIPMENT LTD
Registration no: 01236448 **VAT No.:** GB 355 3843 40
Date established: 1975 **No.of Employees:** 51 - 100 **Product Groups:** 45

Date of Accounts	Sep 11	Sep 10	Sep 09
Sales Turnover	13m	14m	15m
Pre Tax Profit/Loss	70	106	10
Working Capital	2m	2m	2m
Fixed Assets	1m	1m	1m
Current Assets	6m	5m	6m
Current Liabilities	528	538	435

Intertek Testing Services Leicester Ltd

Centre Court Meridian North, Meridian Business Park, Leicester, LE19 1WD
Tel: 0116-263 0330 **Fax:** 0116-263 0311
E-mail: gary.mawston@intertek.com
Website: http://www.intertek.com
Bank(s): National Westminster Bank Plc
Directors: G. Mawston (MD), M. Mellor (Fin)
Managers: M. Hill (Personnel)
Ultimate Holding Company: INTERTEK GROUP PLC
Immediate Holding Company: INTERTEK LABTEST UK LIMITED
Registration no: 03287320 **VAT No.:** GB 672 7639 96
Date established: 1996 **Turnover:** £5m - £10m
No.of Employees: 51 - 100 **Product Groups:** 38, 80, 85

Date of Accounts	Dec 09	Dec 08	Dec 07
Sales Turnover	8m	8m	7m
Pre Tax Profit/Loss	514	328	201
Working Capital	1m	784	1m
Fixed Assets	5m	5m	5m
Current Assets	3m	2m	2m
Current Liabilities	819	889	756

J P L Steel Stock Ltd

Pinfold Road Thurmaston, Leicester, LE4 8AS
Tel: 0116-260 6464 **Fax:** 0116-260 6808
E-mail: john@jplsteelstock.co.uk
Website: http://www.jplsteelstock.co.uk
Directors: P. Gent (Fin), J. Boulby (Dir)
Ultimate Holding Company: IDEALREVIEW LIMITED
Immediate Holding Company: J P L STEEL STOCK LIMITED
Registration no: 03355390 **VAT No.:** GB 687 4188 81
Date established: 1997 **Turnover:** £1m - £2m **No.of Employees:** 1 - 10
Product Groups: 66

Date of Accounts	Dec 11	Dec 10	Dec 09
Working Capital	590	551	515
Fixed Assets	11	N/A	3
Current Assets	1m	1m	952

J Thomas & Co.

6 Wilemans Close Earl Shilton, Leicester, LE9 7GW
Tel: 01455-842599 **Fax:** 01455-842599
Directors: M. Thomas (Prop)
Date established: 1991 **No.of Employees:** 1 - 10 **Product Groups:** 43

Jack Electrical Ltd

27 High Street Barwell, Leicester, LE9 8DQ
Tel: 07985-884499
E-mail: chippendalegroup@googlemail.com
Website: http://www.jackltd.com
Directors: P. Chippendale (Prop)
Immediate Holding Company: JACK ELECTRICAL LIMITED
Registration no: 06872430 **Date established:** 2009
Turnover: Up to £250,000 **No.of Employees:** 1 - 10 **Product Groups:** 52

Date of Accounts	Apr 11	Apr 10
Working Capital	-33	-28
Fixed Assets	17	21
Current Assets	3	1

Jelson Holdings Ltd

370 Loughborough Road, Leicester, LE4 5PR
Tel: 0116-266 1541 **Fax:** 0116-266 4589
E-mail: info@jelson.co.uk
Website: http://www.jelson.co.uk
Directors: R. Jelley (MD), G. Jelley (Sales), B. Doherty (Fin)
Managers: V. Hunt, P. Radnell (Chief Buyer), J. Bradbury (Tech Serv Mgr)
Immediate Holding Company: JELSON HOLDINGS LIMITED
Registration no: 00419442 **Date established:** 1946
Turnover: £50m - £75m **No.of Employees:** 501 - 1000
Product Groups: 52

Date of Accounts	Apr 12	Apr 11	Apr 10
Sales Turnover	65m	61m	61m
Pre Tax Profit/Loss	4m	2m	5m
Working Capital	47m	68m	72m
Fixed Assets	76m	71m	65m
Current Assets	105m	109m	103m
Current Liabilities	22m	22m	22m

Jessops plc

Jessop House 98 Scudamore Road, Leicester, LE3 1TZ
Tel: 0116-232 6000 **Fax:** 0116-232 0060
E-mail: ghenson@jessops.com
Website: http://www.jessops.co.uk
Directors: C. Langley (Grp Chief Exec)
Managers: G. Henson (Mgr), K. Lamerick (Mktg Serv Mgr)
Ultimate Holding Company: CAMERA EQUITY LIMITED
Immediate Holding Company: JESSOPS PLC
Registration no: 04487170 **VAT No.:** GB 350 3281 86
Date established: 2002 **Turnover:** £125m - £250m
No.of Employees: 1501 & over **Product Groups:** 22, 37, 38

Jewson Ltd

Welford Road, Leicester, LE2 6BA
Tel: 0116-254 1434 **Fax:** 0116-255 1696
Website: http://www.jewson.co.uk
Managers: W. Bates (Mgr)
Ultimate Holding Company: COMPAGNIE DE SAINT GOBAIN (FRANCE)
Immediate Holding Company: JEWSON LIMITED
Registration no: 00348407 **Date established:** 1939
Turnover: £500m - £1,000m **No.of Employees:** 11 - 20
Product Groups: 66

Date of Accounts	Dec 11	Dec 10	Dec 09
Sales Turnover	1606m	1547m	1485m
Pre Tax Profit/Loss	18m	100m	45m
Working Capital	-345m	-250m	-349m
Fixed Assets	496m	387m	461m
Current Assets	657m	1005m	1320m
Current Liabilities	66m	120m	64m

Jones & Shipman Grinding Ltd (a division of Renold Engineering Products Co.)

Murrayfield Road, Leicester, LE3 1UW
Tel: 0116-201 3000 **Fax:** 0116-201 3002
E-mail: michael.duignan@jonesshipman.com
Website: http://www.jonesshipman.com
Bank(s): Barclays
Directors: G. Newton (Co Sec), H. Rhodes (Fin), M. Duignan (MD)
Managers: J. Taylor (Personnel), T. Kaubi (Buyer), M. Simpkin (Tech Serv Mgr)
Immediate Holding Company: JONES & SHIPMAN GRINDING LIMITED
Registration no: 07203012 **Date established:** 2010 **Turnover:** £5m - £10m
No.of Employees: 51 - 100 **Product Groups:** 46

Date of Accounts	Dec 11	Dec 10
Sales Turnover	10m	5m
Pre Tax Profit/Loss	753	-192
Working Capital	3m	2m
Fixed Assets	201	151
Current Assets	7m	5m
Current Liabilities	2m	1m

K & A Fashions

22-24 Russell Square, Leicester, LE1 2DS
Tel: 0116-262 6229 **Fax:** 0116-251 2982
E-mail: info@ka-fashion.com
Website: http://www.ka-fashions.com
Managers: A. Pancholi (Mgr)
Immediate Holding Company: K & A FASHIONS (MANUFACTURING) LIMITED
Registration no: 05001515 **VAT No.:** GB 115 5566 74
Date established: 2003 **Turnover:** £2m - £5m **No.of Employees:** 1 - 10
Product Groups: 24, 63

Date of Accounts	Mar 12	Mar 11	Mar 10
Working Capital	-168	-191	-184
Fixed Assets	110	126	142
Current Assets	342	281	307

K J N Ltd

Unit 5 Peckleton Lane Business Park Peckleton Common Peckleton, Leicester, LE9 7RN
Tel: 01455-823304 **Fax:** 01455-828186
E-mail: sales@kjnltd.co.uk
Website: http://www.aluminium-profile.co.uk
Directors: J. Nelsey (MD)
Immediate Holding Company: K.J.N. AUTOMATION LIMITED
Registration no: 03741649 **Date established:** 1999
No.of Employees: 1 - 10 **Product Groups:** 34, 48, 66

Date of Accounts	Mar 11	Mar 10	Mar 09
Working Capital	178	114	211
Fixed Assets	66	35	44
Current Assets	424	385	420

K M D Company Ltd

140 Queens Road, Leicester, LE2 3FX
Tel: 0116-270 9221 **Fax:** 0116-270 2334
E-mail: info@kmd-company.co.uk
Website: http://www.kmdcompany.co.uk
Bank(s): Bank of Scotland
Directors: P. Carden (Comm), S. Jarrom (MD)
Ultimate Holding Company: KMD INVESTORS LIMITED
Immediate Holding Company: KMD COMPANY LIMITED
Registration no: 01219774 **VAT No.:** GB 565 9305 15
Date established: 1975 **Turnover:** £2m - £5m **No.of Employees:** 21 - 50
Product Groups: 27, 28, 44, 48, 49

Date of Accounts	Dec 11	Dec 10	Dec 09
Working Capital	543	526	452
Fixed Assets	100	144	200
Current Assets	779	854	1m

Kaby Engineers Ltd

14-16 Upper Charnwood Street, Leicester, LE2 0AU
Tel: 0116-253 6353 **Fax:** 0116-251 5237
E-mail: kaby@kaby.co.uk
Website: http://www.kaby.co.uk
Bank(s): Yorkshire Bank PLC
Directors: B. Sanghera (MD)
Managers: S. Bruce (Sales Prom Mgr), S. Hartshorn (Prod Mgr), H. Patel (Personnel), D. Edwards (Works Gen Mgr), G. Frith (I.T. Exec)
Immediate Holding Company: KABY ENGINEERS LIMITED
Registration no: 01211144 **VAT No.:** GB 115 7445 76
Date established: 1975 **Turnover:** £10m - £20m
No.of Employees: 101 - 250 **Product Groups:** 35, 48, 85

Date of Accounts	Mar 10	Mar 09	Mar 08
Sales Turnover	10m	N/A	N/A
Pre Tax Profit/Loss	-1m	-380	595
Working Capital	3m	5m	6m
Fixed Assets	5m	4m	4m
Current Assets	8m	9m	10m
Current Liabilities	2m	2m	2m

Keenpac Independent Ltd

29 Centurion Way Meridian Business Park, Leicester, LE19 1WH
Tel: 08448-261737 **Fax:** 020-8308 6340
E-mail: info@keenpac.co.uk
Website: http://www.keenpac.co.uk
Bank(s): Lloyds TSB Bank plc
Managers: E. Brown (Mgr)
Immediate Holding Company: KEENPAC LIMITED
Registration no: 01418926 **VAT No.:** GB 339 4231 56
Date established: 1979 **Turnover:** £20m - £50m
No.of Employees: 51 - 100 **Product Groups:** 27, 30

Date of Accounts	Dec 07	Dec 06	Dec 05
Sales Turnover	46151	41778	39444
Pre Tax Profit/Loss	1676	925	2860
Working Capital	9237	8105	5583
Fixed Assets	934	1191	1346
Current Assets	32336	29162	19785
Current Liabilities	23099	21057	14202
Total Share Capital	24	24	24
ROCE% (Return on Capital Employed)	16.5	10.0	41.3
ROT% (Return on Turnover)	3.6	2.2	7.3

Keswick Trays

Forest View Farm Peckleton Lane, Desford, Leicester, LE9 9JU
Tel: 01455-828990 **Fax:** 01455-828999
E-mail: d.crocker@keswicktrays.f9.co.uk
Website: http://www.keswicktrays.f9.co.uk
Directors: D. Crocker (Prop)
Immediate Holding Company: HIGHFIELDS SEEDS LIMITED
Registration no: 04236948 **VAT No.:** GB 670 0415 68
Date established: 2001 **Turnover:** £250,000 - £500,000
No.of Employees: 1 - 10 **Product Groups:** 33

Date of Accounts	May 11	May 10	May 09
Working Capital	206	157	161
Fixed Assets	61	75	60
Current Assets	466	443	427

Kings Welding Supplies Ltd

10 Chiswick Road Freemens Common, Leicester, LE2 7SX
Tel: 0116-247 0599 **Fax:** 0116-247 0202
Website: http://www.kingsweldingsupplies.co.uk
Directors: D. King (Dir), J. Percival (Co Sec)
Immediate Holding Company: KINGS WELDING SUPPLIES LIMITED
Registration no: 04590138 **Date established:** 2002
No.of Employees: 1 - 10 **Product Groups:** 46

Date of Accounts	Mar 12	Mar 11	Mar 10
Working Capital	28	-7	-10
Fixed Assets	8	15	10
Current Assets	76	76	68

Kingsway Domestic Appliances

124 Humberstone Road, Leicester, LE5 0AT
Tel: 0116-253 9060 **Fax:** 0116-221 8336
Directors: Z. Ahmani (Prop)
Date established: 2004 **No.of Employees:** 1 - 10 **Product Groups:** 36, 40

Kirkbride Metal Fabrications Ltd
47 Wenlock Way, Leicester, LE4 9HU
Tel: 0116-276 0131 **Fax:** 0116-246 1001
E-mail: kirkmfabs@aol.com
Bank(s): HSBC Bank plc
Directors: K. Kirkbride (Dir), P. Kirkbride (Fin)
Immediate Holding Company: KIRKBRIDE METAL FABRICATIONS LIMITED
Registration no: 03082088 **VAT No.:** GB 114 9275 71
Date established: 1995 **Turnover:** £500,000 - £1m
No.of Employees: 11 - 20 **Product Groups:** 48

Date of Accounts	Jul 11	Jul 10	Jul 09
Working Capital	558	362	310
Fixed Assets	247	283	311
Current Assets	1m	763	659

Knighton Tool Supplies
17 Lothair Road, Leicester, LE2 7QE
Tel: 0116-283 4021 **Fax:** 0116-244 0289
E-mail: sales@knighton-tools.co.uk
Website: http://www.knighton-tools.co.uk
Directors: R. Heap (MD)
Immediate Holding Company: KNIGHTON TOOL SUPPLIES LIMITED
Registration no: 05538099 **Date established:** 2005
No.of Employees: 1 - 10 **Product Groups:** 22, 23, 24, 27, 29, 30, 31, 32, 33, 34, 35, 36, 37, 38, 39, 40, 41, 42, 43, 44, 45, 46, 47, 48, 49, 51, 63, 64, 65, 66, 67, 68, 83, 86

KPMG UK Ltd
1 Waterloo Way, Leicester, LE1 6LP
Tel: 0116-256 6000 **Fax:** 0116-256 6050
E-mail: ian.borley@kpmg.co.uk
Website: http://www.kpmg.co.uk
Bank(s): Lloyds TSB Bank plc
Directors: I. Borley (Snr Part)
Managers: D. Stephens (Mktg Serv Mgr)
Ultimate Holding Company: KPMG EUROPE LLP
Immediate Holding Company: KPMG UK LIMITED
Registration no: 03580549 **Date established:** 1998
Turnover: £20m - £50m **No.of Employees:** 101 - 250 **Product Groups:** 80

Date of Accounts	Apr 11	Apr 10	Apr 09
Sales Turnover	106	102	105
Pre Tax Profit/Loss	77	77	75
Working Capital	-41	-46	-52
Fixed Assets	1m	1m	1m
Current Assets	22	22	16
Current Liabilities	24	27	25

L J F UK Ltd
Centurion Way Meridian Business Park, Leicester, LE19 1WH
Tel: 0116-289 1888 **Fax:** 0116-289 2283
E-mail: info@ljfm.com
Website: http://www.ljfm.com
Directors: J. King (MD), N. Peplow (Fin)
Managers: P. Brown (Mats Contrlr)
Ultimate Holding Company: TOTAL SAFETY INC (USA)
Immediate Holding Company: LJF (UK) LIMITED
Registration no: 02796513 **Date established:** 1993 **Turnover:** £5m - £10m
No.of Employees: 1 - 10 **Product Groups:** 32, 35, 37, 45, 68

Date of Accounts	Dec 11	Dec 10	Dec 09
Sales Turnover	5m	5m	6m
Pre Tax Profit/Loss	85	-15	141
Working Capital	395	528	533
Fixed Assets	5	9	20
Current Assets	1m	2m	2m
Current Liabilities	281	253	224

L & M Spray
18-20 Gladstone Street, Leicester, LE1 2BN
Tel: 0116-253 7577 **Fax:** 0116-253 2922
E-mail: team@lmspray.co.uk
Website: http://www.lmspray.co.uk
Directors: M. Cutkelvin (Ptnr)
Immediate Holding Company: L & M SPRAY FINISHERS LIMITED
Registration no: 05603411 **Date established:** 2005
No.of Employees: 11 - 20 **Product Groups:** 46, 48

Date of Accounts	Mar 12	Mar 11	Mar 10
Working Capital	147	78	9
Fixed Assets	63	69	83
Current Assets	344	203	105

L M W Electronics Ltd
L M W House Merrylees Industrial Estate Lee Side, Desford, Leicester, LE9 9FS
Tel: 01530-231141 **Fax:** 01530-231143
E-mail: enquiries@lmw.co.uk
Website: http://www.lmw.co.uk
Bank(s): Barclays
Directors: A. Baum (Dir), C. Smith (MD), H. Smith (Co Sec)
Managers: P. Daines (Tech Serv Mgr)
Immediate Holding Company: LMW ELECTRONICS LIMITED
Registration no: 01971947 **VAT No.:** GB 428 4867 16
Date established: 1985 **Turnover:** £2m - £5m **No.of Employees:** 11 - 20
Product Groups: 33, 37

Date of Accounts	Jan 12	Sep 11	Sep 10
Working Capital	166	141	250
Fixed Assets	2	6	161
Current Assets	587	550	815

Labelsco
29 Moat Way Barwell, Leicester, LE9 8EY
Tel: 01455-852400 **Fax:** 01455-841444
E-mail: sales@labelsco.co.uk
Website: http://www.labelsco.co.uk
Directors: D. Seymour (Dir), D. Gillies (Grp Sales)
Managers: D. Bailey (Purch Mgr), N. Robinson (Tech Serv Mgr), P. Dowling (Personnel), D. Walsh
Ultimate Holding Company: PRINTCAST LIMITED
Immediate Holding Company: LABELSCO LIMITED
Registration no: 01251298 **Date established:** 1976
Turnover: £10m - £20m **No.of Employees:** 101 - 250
Product Groups: 27, 28

Date of Accounts	Dec 11	Dec 10	Dec 09
Sales Turnover	12m	11m	13m
Pre Tax Profit/Loss	-1m	-1m	-933
Working Capital	-5m	-5m	-4m
Fixed Assets	5m	5m	6m
Current Assets	3m	3m	4m
Current Liabilities	716	430	428

Ledwell Plastics Ltd
33 Cannock Street, Leicester, LE4 9HR
Tel: 0116-276 6221 **Fax:** 0116-246 0134
E-mail: sales@ledwellplastics.com
Website: http://www.ledwellplastics.com
Directors: C. Simms (Fin)
Immediate Holding Company: LEDWELL PLASTICS LIMITED
Registration no: 00931055 **VAT No.:** GB 115 4235 05
Date established: 1968 **Turnover:** £2m - £5m **No.of Employees:** 11 - 20
Product Groups: 29

Date of Accounts	Dec 11	Dec 10	Dec 09
Working Capital	319	296	333
Fixed Assets	497	478	509
Current Assets	673	610	585

Leengate Industrial & Welding Supplies Ltd
4 Cannock Street, Leicester, LE4 9HR
Tel: 0116-276 4981 **Fax:** 0116-246 0492
Website: http://www.nexusweld.com
Directors: C. Bowler (Sales)
Ultimate Holding Company: LINDE AG (GERMANY)
Immediate Holding Company: LEENGATE INDUSTRIAL & WELDING SUPPLIES LTD
Registration no: 02350403 **VAT No.:** GB 715 3003 80
Date established: 1989 **Turnover:** £1m - £2m **No.of Employees:** 1 - 10
Product Groups: 35, 40

Date of Accounts	Dec 11	Dec 10	Dec 09
Sales Turnover	2m	2m	2m
Pre Tax Profit/Loss	51	20	12
Working Capital	162	127	89
Fixed Assets	58	57	77
Current Assets	794	769	572
Current Liabilities	49	45	28

Leicester Mail Ltd
St Georges Street, Leicester, LE1 9FQ
Tel: 0116-251 2512 **Fax:** 0116-262 4687
E-mail: enquiries@leicestermercury.co.uk
Website: http://www.thisisleicestershire.co.uk
Bank(s): National Westminster Bank Plc
Directors: D. Simms (MD)
Ultimate Holding Company: DAILY MAIL GEN TRUST P.L.C.
Immediate Holding Company: NORTHCLIFFE NEWSPAPERS
Registration no: 00226937 **Turnover:** £20m - £50m
No.of Employees: 251 - 500 **Product Groups:** 28

Leicester Optical
Unit 3 Victoria Mills Fowke Street, Rothley, Leicester, LE7 7PJ
Tel: 0116-237 5646 **Fax:** 0116-237 6449
E-mail: orders@leicesteroptical.co.uk
Website: http://www.leicesteroptical.co.uk
Directors: T. Keily (Ptnr)
No.of Employees: 11 - 20 **Product Groups:** 38

The Leicester Plating Co. Ltd
Wesley Street, Leicester, LE4 5QG
Tel: 0116-266 1344 **Fax:** 0116-266 2716
E-mail: office@leicesterplating.co.uk
Website: http://www.leicesterplating.co.uk
Bank(s): Lloyds TSB Bank plc
Directors: I. Ovington (MD), A. Marshall (Fin)
Ultimate Holding Company: AMJA LIMITED
Immediate Holding Company: LEICESTER PLATING COMPANY LIMITED(THE)
Registration no: 00432557 **VAT No.:** GB 114 9334 81
Date established: 1947 **Turnover:** £500,000 - £1m
No.of Employees: 11 - 20 **Product Groups:** 48

Date of Accounts	Sep 11	Sep 10	Sep 09
Working Capital	99	128	118
Fixed Assets	123	9	13
Current Assets	319	246	274

Leicester Switch & Control Ltd
126 Ross Walk, Leicester, LE4 5HH
Tel: 0116-299 9277 **Fax:** 0116-299 9278
E-mail: sales@lsandc.co.uk
Website: http://www.lsandc.co.uk
Directors: G. Collins (Dir)
Ultimate Holding Company: BPX GROUP LIMITED
Immediate Holding Company: LEICESTER SWITCH & CONTROL CO. LIMITED
Registration no: 01253904 **VAT No.:** 113 7064 03 **Date established:** 1976
Turnover: £1m - £2m **No.of Employees:** 1 - 10 **Product Groups:** 35, 37, 38

Date of Accounts	Oct 11	Oct 10	Oct 09
Working Capital	1m	1m	1m
Current Assets	2m	2m	2m

Leversedge Telecom Services Ltd
23 Slater Street, Leicester, LE3 5AS
Tel: 0116-262 5116 **Fax:** 0116-251 4314
E-mail: sales@leversedge.co.uk
Website: http://www.leversedge.co.uk
Bank(s): National Westminster
Directors: R. Scott-Gordon (MD)
Immediate Holding Company: LEVERSEDGE TELECOM SERVICES LIMITED
Registration no: 01207776 **Date established:** 1975 **Turnover:** £2m - £5m
No.of Employees: 11 - 20 **Product Groups:** 37

Date of Accounts	Apr 12	Apr 11	Apr 10
Working Capital	57	-25	23
Fixed Assets	165	231	181
Current Assets	513	455	414

Lewis & Hill
Lazarus Court Woodgate, Rothley, Leicester, LE7 7NR
Tel: 0116-230485
E-mail: enquiries@lewisandhill.co.uk
Website: http://www.lewisandhill.co.uk
Directors: G. Hill (Ptnr), G. Hills (Ptnr)
Immediate Holding Company: LEWIS&HILL LIMITED
Registration no: 07668425 **Date established:** 2011
Turnover: £250,000 - £500,000 **No.of Employees:** 1 - 10
Product Groups: 26

Lift Components Ltd
123 Abbey Lane, Leicester, LE4 5QX
Tel: 08447-782348 **Fax:** 0844-778 2349
E-mail: sales@liftcomponents.co.uk
Website: http://www.liftcomponents.co.uk
Managers: S. Cufflin (Mgr)
Ultimate Holding Company: UNITED TECHNOLOGIES CORP INC (USA)
Immediate Holding Company: LIFT COMPONENTS LIMITED
Registration no: 00154755 **Date established:** 2019 **Turnover:** £1m - £2m
No.of Employees: 1 - 10 **Product Groups:** 29, 35, 37, 38, 40, 45

Lines Keogh Pos Ltd
St Marks Works Foundry Lane, Leicester, LE1 3WU
Tel: 0116-262 3098 **Fax:** 05603-423756
E-mail: info@lineskeogh.co.uk
Website: http://www.lineskeogh.co.uk
Directors: R. Concannon (Dir)
Immediate Holding Company: LINES KEOGH (POS) LIMITED
Registration no: 06764707 **Date established:** 2008
Turnover: Up to £250,000 **No.of Employees:** 1 - 10 **Product Groups:** 22, 26, 30, 38, 42, 48, 49, 64, 67, 81, 84

Date of Accounts	May 11	May 10	May 09
Working Capital	8	8	N/A
Fixed Assets	16	9	N/A
Current Assets	60	69	N/A

Linic Products Ltd
Victoria Works Saddington Road, Fleckney, Leicester, LE8 8AW
Tel: 0116-240 3400 **Fax:** 0116-240 3300
E-mail: sales@linic.co.uk
Website: http://www.linic.co.uk
Bank(s): Midland
Directors: N. Burdett (MD), N. Burdett (MD)
Ultimate Holding Company: LINIC HOLDINGS LIMITED
Immediate Holding Company: LINIC PRODUCTS LIMITED
Registration no: 02118074 **VAT No.:** GB 330 3665 82
Date established: 1987 **Turnover:** £1m - £2m **No.of Employees:** 21 - 50
Product Groups: 30, 66

Date of Accounts	Oct 11	Oct 10	Oct 09
Working Capital	25	23	42
Fixed Assets	1	1	1
Current Assets	520	513	540

Linpic Storage & Shelving Systems
67 Auburn Road Blaby, Leicester, LE8 4DA
Tel: 0116-277 0077 **Fax:** 0116-277 0088
E-mail: graham@linpic.com
Website: http://www.linpic.com
Directors: G. Beitch (Snr Part)
Date established: 2003 **No.of Employees:** 11 - 20 **Product Groups:** 35, 42, 45

Livingston & Doughty Ltd
17 Mandervell Road Oadby, Leicester, LE2 5LR
Tel: 0116-271 4221 **Fax:** 0116-271 6977
E-mail: paul@flexofil.co.uk
Website: http://www.flexofil.co.uk
Directors: P. Murray (MD)
Immediate Holding Company: LIVINGSTON & DOUGHTY LIMITED
Registration no: 00080205 **VAT No.:** GB 114 5583 80
Date established: 2004 **Turnover:** £500,000 - £1m
No.of Employees: 1 - 10 **Product Groups:** 47

Date of Accounts	Dec 11	Dec 10	Dec 09
Working Capital	309	351	326
Fixed Assets	581	591	600
Current Assets	448	434	420

Lotan Ltd
108 Cannock Street, Leicester, LE4 9HR
Tel: 0116-276 4559 **Fax:** 0116-276 4904
E-mail: george.wan@btinternet.com
Directors: G. Wan (MD)
Immediate Holding Company: LOTAN LIMITED
Registration no: 01948114 **Date established:** 1985
No.of Employees: 1 - 10 **Product Groups:** 38, 42

Date of Accounts	Mar 11	Mar 10	Mar 09
Working Capital	842	786	489
Fixed Assets	2m	2m	2m
Current Assets	2m	1m	919

M C R Systems Ltd
14 High View Close, Leicester, LE4 9LJ
Tel: 0116-299 7000 **Fax:** 0116-299 7001
E-mail: sales@mcr-systems.co.uk
Website: http://www.mcr-systems.co.uk
Directors: B. Archer (Dir)
Ultimate Holding Company: DUTYLOG LIMITED
Immediate Holding Company: MCR SYSTEMS LIMITED
Registration no: 01349701 **Date established:** 1978
No.of Employees: 11 - 20 **Product Groups:** 44, 48, 67

Date of Accounts	Oct 11	Oct 10	Oct 09
Working Capital	2m	1m	1m
Fixed Assets	428	421	398
Current Assets	3m	2m	2m

M E D Engineering Services
6 Tithe Street, Leicester, LE5 4BN
Tel: 0116-246 1641
Directors: L. Whitton (Dir)
Immediate Holding Company: MED GROUP INCORPORATED LIMITED
Registration no: 05375654 **Date established:** 2005
No.of Employees: 1 - 10 **Product Groups:** 35, 39, 40

Date of Accounts	Feb 08	Feb 07
Working Capital	-5	-5

M E S International Ltd
11 Copdale Road, Leicester, LE5 4FG
Tel: 0116-249 0333 **Fax:** 0116-249 0142
E-mail: sales@mesinternational.uk.com
Website: http://www.mesinternational.uk.com
Directors: P. Anderson (Dir), J. Anderson (Sales), S. Davison (Fin), J. Grimmett (Tech Serv)
Managers: S. Thompson (Purch Mgr), T. Anderson (Sales Prom Mgr)
Immediate Holding Company: MES INTERNATIONAL LIMITED
Registration no: 01556587 **VAT No.:** GB 355 3697 25
Date established: 1981 **Turnover:** £2m - £5m **No.of Employees:** 1 - 10
Product Groups: 61

Date of Accounts	Mar 11	Mar 10	Mar 09
Working Capital	580	539	505
Fixed Assets	538	530	534

Current Assets	2m	2m	1m

M F Hire Ltd
2 Highmeres Road, Leicester, LE4 7LZ
Tel: 0116-276 3807 **Fax:** 0116-246 0198
E-mail: ele@mfhgroup.co.uk
Website: http://www.mfhgroup.co.uk
Directors: I. Davis (Dir)
Managers: A. Taylor, B. Carey (Mktg Serv Mgr), D. Reilly (Eng Serv Mgr), M. Bugg (I.T. Exec), R. Linford (Comm), A. Loy (Personnel)
Immediate Holding Company: M.F.H. Engineering (Holdings) Ltd
Registration no: 01362202 **Turnover:** £1m - £2m
No.of Employees: 11 - 20 **Product Groups:** 45, 83

M I K Engineering
5 Cannock Street, Leicester, LE4 9HR
Tel: 0116-233 3740 **Fax:** 0116-233 3740
Directors: M. King (Prop)
Date established: 1987 **No.of Employees:** 1 - 10 **Product Groups:** 46

Marshall Deacon Knitwear Ltd
122 Fairfax Road, Leicester, LE4 9EL
Tel: 0116-246 1260 **Fax:** 0116-274 3528
E-mail: info@marshalldeacon.com
Website: http://marshalldeacon.com
Directors: K. Khosla (MD), R. Khosla (Fin)
Immediate Holding Company: H.K. CATERING SUPPLIERS LIMITED
Registration no: 00702531 **VAT No.:** GB 113 7244 01
Date established: 1990 **Turnover:** Up to £250,000
No.of Employees: 1 - 10 **Product Groups:** 24, 63

Date of Accounts	Jun 11	Jun 10	Jun 09
Sales Turnover	N/A	146	160
Working Capital	25	26	19
Fixed Assets	5	3	5
Current Assets	38	44	38

Percy Martin Ltd
Church Hill Road Thurmaston, Leicester, LE4 8DJ
Tel: 0116-260 5582 **Fax:** 0116-264 0227
E-mail: info@percymartin.co.uk
Website: http://www.percymartin.co.uk
Directors: I. Martin (Mkt Research)
Immediate Holding Company: PERCY MARTIN LIMITED
Registration no: 00507125 **VAT No.:** GB 113 7759 65
Date established: 1952 **Turnover:** £1m - £2m **No.of Employees:** 1 - 10
Product Groups: 67

Date of Accounts	Jul 11	Jul 10	Jul 09
Working Capital	993	722	513
Fixed Assets	76	86	55
Current Assets	2m	2m	821

Media Plastics
Unit 6 Mill Hill Industrial Estate Quarry Lane, Enderby, Leicester, LE19 4AU
Tel: 0116-286 1224 **Fax:** 0116-286 7603
E-mail: info@mediaplastics.co.uk
Website: http://www.mediaplastics.co.uk
Directors: I. Millen (Ptnr)
Immediate Holding Company: MEDIA PLASTICS LIMITED
Registration no: 06845877 **Date established:** 2009
Turnover: Up to £250,000 **No.of Employees:** 1 - 10 **Product Groups:** 22, 27, 28, 30, 49, 63, 64, 67

Date of Accounts	Jul 07	Jul 06
Working Capital	3	7
Fixed Assets	17	34
Current Assets	40	69
Current Liabilities	37	62
Total Share Capital	10	10

Mellor Bromley
141 Barkby Road, Leicester, LE4 9LW
Tel: 0116-276 6636 **Fax:** 0116-246 0426
E-mail: mail@mellorbromley.co.uk
Website: http://www.mellorbromley.co.uk
Bank(s): HSBC
Directors: D. Bloxam (Dir), P. Kinal (Fin)
Managers: D. Lurdeloudihi (Contracts Mgr)
Immediate Holding Company: MELLOR BROMLEY LIMITED
Registration no: 02048177 **VAT No.:** GB 535 9504 30
Date established: 1986 **Turnover:** £10m - £20m
No.of Employees: 51 - 100 **Product Groups:** 38

Date of Accounts	Mar 11	Mar 10	Mar 09
Sales Turnover	11m	11m	11m
Pre Tax Profit/Loss	-116	-199	83
Working Capital	794	876	1m
Fixed Assets	2m	2m	2m
Current Assets	3m	3m	4m
Current Liabilities	406	223	197

Merrow Sales UK Ltd
17 Glebe Road Groby, Leicester, LE6 0GT
Tel: 0116-232 1779 **Fax:** 0116-287 8099
Website: http://www.merrow-uk.com
Directors: M. Knight (Fin)
Immediate Holding Company: MERROW SALES UK LTD
Registration no: 03488986 **Date established:** 1998
No.of Employees: 1 - 10 **Product Groups:** 43

Date of Accounts	Jan 12	Jan 11	Jan 10
Working Capital	7	6	5
Current Assets	45	42	40

Metalite Ltd
121 Barkby Road, Leicester, LE4 9LU
Tel: 0116-276 7874 **Fax:** 0116-233 0337
Directors: K. Gawera (Dir)
Immediate Holding Company: METALITE LIMITED
Registration no: 02517892 **VAT No.:** GB 536 2818 36
Date established: 1990 **Turnover:** Up to £250,000
No.of Employees: 1 - 10 **Product Groups:** 35, 46

Date of Accounts	Aug 11	Aug 10	Aug 09
Working Capital	279	240	266
Fixed Assets	44	52	7
Current Assets	341	322	293

Mettler Toledo Ltd
64 Boston Road, Leicester, LE4 1AW
Tel: 0116-235 7070 **Fax:** 0116-235 2837
E-mail: nigel.mason@mt.com
Website: http://www.mt.com
Directors: N. Mason (Fin)
Ultimate Holding Company: METTLER TOLEDO INTERNATIONAL INC (USA)
Immediate Holding Company: METTLER-TOLEDO LIMITED
Registration no: 00959974 **Date established:** 1969
Turnover: £20m - £50m **No.of Employees:** 101 - 250
Product Groups: 38, 41

Date of Accounts	Dec 10	Dec 09	Dec 08
Sales Turnover	27m	24m	27m
Pre Tax Profit/Loss	1m	287	196
Working Capital	1m	559	600
Fixed Assets	2m	1m	1m
Current Assets	10m	9m	8m
Current Liabilities	3m	3m	3m

Micron Engineering Ltd
Unit 5 Earls Way Earls Way Industrial Estate, Thurmaston, Leicester, LE4 8DL
Tel: 0116-264 0040 **Fax:** 0116-260 4441
E-mail: e.muddimer@btconnect.com
Directors: E. Muddimer (MD)
Immediate Holding Company: MICRON ENGINEERING LIMITED
Registration no: 02707241 **VAT No.:** GB 566 0478 23
Date established: 1992 **Turnover:** £250,000 - £500,000
No.of Employees: 1 - 10 **Product Groups:** 48, 85

Date of Accounts	Apr 11	Apr 10	Apr 09
Working Capital	129	127	109
Fixed Assets	22	8	1
Current Assets	230	217	202

Midland Diving Equipment Ltd
57 Sparkenhoe Street, Leicester, LE2 0TD
Tel: 0116-212 4262 **Fax:** 0116-212 4263
E-mail: sales@midlanddiving.com
Website: http://www.midlanddiving.com
Bank(s): HSBC
Directors: R. Poll (MD)
Managers: A. Sturling (Tech Serv Mgr), M. Humphries (Sales Prom Mgr), T. Jarram (Purch Mgr)
Immediate Holding Company: MIDLAND DIVING EQUIPMENT LIMITED
Registration no: 00706216 **VAT No.:** GB 115 2272 09
Date established: 1961 **No.of Employees:** 21 - 50 **Product Groups:** 24, 40, 49

Date of Accounts	Dec 11	Dec 10	Dec 09
Working Capital	1m	1m	1m
Fixed Assets	144	152	264
Current Assets	2m	2m	1m

Midland Enamellers
Unit 1 Pinfold Road Thurmaston, Leicester, LE4 8AS
Tel: 0116-269 7861 **Fax:** 0116-264 0739
Directors: S. Cox (MD)
Immediate Holding Company: MIDLAND ENAMELLERS LIMITED
Registration no: 02651268 **Date established:** 1991
Turnover: £250,000 - £500,000 **No.of Employees:** 1 - 10
Product Groups: 46, 48

Date of Accounts	May 11	May 10	May 08
Working Capital	35	28	38
Fixed Assets	7	10	17
Current Assets	105	86	107

Midland Handling Equipment Ltd
Stretton Road Great Glen, Leicester, LE8 9GN
Tel: 0116-259 3175 **Fax:** 0116-259 2820
E-mail: enquiry@mhel.co.uk
Website: http://www.mhel.co.uk
Bank(s): Barclays
Directors: M. Deacon (MD), M. Deacon (Sales), R. Deacon (Fin), E. Deacon (Fin), K. Deacon (MD)
Immediate Holding Company: MIDLAND HANDLING EQUIPMENT LIMITED
Registration no: 01096847 **Date established:** 1973 **Turnover:** £1m - £2m
No.of Employees: 11 - 20 **Product Groups:** 45, 84

Date of Accounts	Feb 11	Feb 10	Feb 09
Working Capital	549	498	481
Fixed Assets	23	19	17
Current Assets	690	672	610

Midland Idustrial Supplies Ltd
Unit 1d Mill Lane Industrial Estate Glenfield, Leicester, LE3 8DX
Tel: 0116-287 5202 **Fax:** 0116-231 4319
E-mail: pa.jackson@miscompany.co.uk
Website: http://www.miscompany.co.uk
Directors: P. Jackson (Dir)
Registration no: 05539047 **Turnover:** £500,000 - £1m
No.of Employees: 1 - 10 **Product Groups:** 27, 48

Date of Accounts	Apr 08	Apr 07
Working Capital	69	11
Fixed Assets	50	55
Current Assets	367	266
Current Liabilities	299	254

Midland Signs Leicester Ltd (t/a G & G Signs)
15 Foxholes Road Golfcourse Lane, Leicester, LE3 1TH
Tel: 0116-254 4445 **Fax:** 0116-254 2020
E-mail: info@ggstreetnameplates.com
Website: http://www.ggstreetnameplates.com
Bank(s): T.S.B.Lloyds
Directors: G. Greet (MD)
Registration no: 01778323 **VAT No.:** GB 399 6697 55
Turnover: Up to £250,000 **No.of Employees:** 21 - 50 **Product Groups:** 30, 39

Date of Accounts	Mar 10	Mar 09	Mar 08
Working Capital	892	959	1m
Fixed Assets	56	74	83
Current Assets	1m	1m	1m

Midland Transmissions Ltd
887 Melton Road Thurmaston, Leicester, LE4 8EF
Tel: 0116-260 6200 **Fax:** 0116-260 2548
E-mail: fosse.bearings@btinternet.com
Directors: J. Stock (MD)
Immediate Holding Company: MIDLAND TRANSMISSIONS LIMITED
Registration no: 01428337 **VAT No.:** GB 115 7472 73
Date established: 1979 **Turnover:** £500,000 - £1m
No.of Employees: 1 - 10 **Product Groups:** 48

Date of Accounts	Oct 11	Oct 10	Oct 03
Working Capital	-3	-3	-3
Current Liabilities	3	3	3

Midlands Advice & Training Services Ltd
36 Bloomfield Road, Leicester, LE2 6LA
Tel: 07703-885305
E-mail: karl@craig-west.co.uk
Website: http://www.midsats.co.uk
Directors: K. Craig West (Dir)
Immediate Holding Company: MIDLANDS ADVICE & TRAINING SERVICES LTD
Registration no: 06877564 **Date established:** 2009
Turnover: Up to £250,000 **No.of Employees:** 1 - 10 **Product Groups:** 86

Midlands Co Op Food
170 Evington Road, Leicester, LE2 1HL
Tel: 0116-273 6251 **Fax:** 0116-273 4162
E-mail: jbishop@tomorrows-world.co.uk
Website: http://www.co-operative.coop
Managers: J. Bishop (Stores Mgr), F. Makwana (Mgr)
Date established: 1994 **No.of Employees:** 1 - 10 **Product Groups:** 69

Miles Platts Ltd
Unit Z Blaby Industrial Park Winchester Avenue Blaby, Leicester, LE8 4GZ
Tel: 0116-262 2593 **Fax:** 0116-253 7889
E-mail: dplatts@milesplatts.co.uk
Website: http://www.milesplatts.co.uk
Directors: D. Platt (MD)
Managers: B. Hatley (Sales Prom Mgr), M. Marriott (Fin Mgr)
Immediate Holding Company: MILES PLATTS LIMITED
Registration no: 01092078 **Date established:** 1973 **Turnover:** £5m - £10m
No.of Employees: 51 - 100 **Product Groups:** 29

Date of Accounts	Mar 11	Mar 10	Mar 09
Working Capital	714	393	405
Fixed Assets	252	289	393
Current Assets	1m	842	780
Current Liabilities	1	51	N/A

Mitchell Grieve
129 Parker Drive, Leicester, LE4 0HZ
Tel: 0116-235 0512 **Fax:** 0116-234 0273
E-mail: sales@mitchell-grieve.co.uk
Website: http://www.mitchell-grieve.co.uk
Bank(s): National Westminster Bank Plc
Managers: A. Upton (Chief Acct), B. Brumby (Tech Serv Mgr), C. Cashmore (Sales & Mktg Mg)
Ultimate Holding Company: WILLIAM MITCHELL SINKERS LTD
Immediate Holding Company: RICAL LTD
Registration no: 01632078 **VAT No.:** 683 9765 68 **Date established:** 1982
Turnover: £5m - £10m **No.of Employees:** 21 - 50 **Product Groups:** 43

Geoff Moore Engraving
Unit W5 The Beaumont Enterprise Centre Boston Road, Leicester, LE4 1HB
Tel: 0116-236 6266 **Fax:** 0116-235 1844
Website: http://www.gmengraver.co.uk
Directors: G. Moore (Prop)
Immediate Holding Company: REACHING PEOPLE
Registration no: 03576786 **Date established:** 2011
Turnover: £500,000 - £1m **No.of Employees:** 1 - 10 **Product Groups:** 46, 48

Date of Accounts	Mar 12
Sales Turnover	360
Pre Tax Profit/Loss	72
Working Capital	77
Fixed Assets	19
Current Assets	87
Current Liabilities	6

Motor Cycle Accessories Ltd
160-162 Belgrave Gate, Leicester, LE1 3XL
Tel: 0116-262 4983 **Fax:** 0116-253 1712
E-mail: info@mcaleicester.co.uk
Website: http://www.mcaleicester.co.uk
Directors: P. Britain (Prop), L. Brittan (Co Sec)
Managers: D. Hall (Mgr)
Immediate Holding Company: MOTOR CYCLE ACCESSORIES LIMITED
Registration no: 02004687 **Date established:** 1986
No.of Employees: 1 - 10 **Product Groups:** 24, 39

Date of Accounts	Feb 08	Feb 11	Feb 10
Working Capital	-46	13	-13
Fixed Assets	54	50	49
Current Assets	292	263	310

Moulding Bros & Merry Leicester Ltd
11 Hilltop Road Hamilton, Leicester, LE5 1TT
Tel: 0116-276 5112 **Fax:** 0116-276 6596
Directors: D. White (Fin)
Immediate Holding Company: MOULDING BROS & MERRY (LEICESTER) LIMITED
Registration no: 02110731 **Date established:** 1987
No.of Employees: 11 - 20 **Product Groups:** 46

Date of Accounts	Feb 08	Feb 12	Feb 11
Working Capital	-4	5	-3
Fixed Assets	3	1	1
Current Assets	23	14	12

Moveman S K G
Prospect Works 123 Abbey Lane, Leicester, LE4 5QX
Tel: 0116-225 2100 **Fax:** 0116-266 5353
E-mail: sales@movemanskg.co.uk
Website: http://www.movemanskg.co.uk
Managers: W. Blyghton (Chief Mgr)
Ultimate Holding Company: UNITED TECHNOLOGIES CORP INC (USA)
Immediate Holding Company: MOVEMANSKG LIMITED
Registration no: 01761761 **Date established:** 1983
No.of Employees: 11 - 20 **Product Groups:** 35, 39, 45

Date of Accounts	Nov 07	Nov 06	Nov 05
Working Capital	-18	-18	-18
Current Liabilities	N/A	18	N/A

Movement 2 Ltd
Unit 8 The Warren East Goscote, Leicester, LE7 3XA
Tel: 08449-802281 **Fax:** 0870-705 9953
E-mail: mail@movement2.co.uk
Website: http://www.movement2.co.uk
Directors: C. Williams (MD), L. Daines (Sales & Mktg)
Managers: L. Daines (Mktg Serv Mgr)
Immediate Holding Company: MOVEMENT 2 LIMITED
Registration no: 05243793 **Date established:** 2004
No.of Employees: 11 - 20 **Product Groups:** 26, 45, 66, 67

see next page

Movement 2 Ltd - *Cont'd*

Date of Accounts	Oct 09	Oct 08	Oct 07
Working Capital	69	-7	-25
Fixed Assets	57	30	45
Current Assets	380	237	176

N & B Fabrications
Lutterworth Road Blaby, Leicester, LE8 4DP
Tel: 0116-277 4543 **Fax:** 0116- 2774543
Directors: N. Brewis (Prop)
Date established: 1997 **No.of Employees:** 1 - 10 **Product Groups:** 35

N P Services Sheet Metal Fabrication Ltd
Brook House Cross Street, Syston, Leicester, LE7 2JG
Tel: 0116-269 6977
E-mail: sales@food-fabrications.co.uk
Website: http://www.food-fabrications.co.uk
Directors: N. Pickering (MD)
Immediate Holding Company: N P SERVICES (LEICESTER) LIMITED
Registration no: 04993420 **Date established:** 2003
No.of Employees: 11 - 20 **Product Groups:** 35

Date of Accounts	Dec 11	Dec 10	Dec 09
Working Capital	-72	-74	-101
Fixed Assets	103	133	160
Current Assets	172	217	325

Nags Welding Shop
27b Main Street Humberstone, Leicester, LE5 1AE
Tel: 0116-276 2380 **Fax:** 0116-276 2380
Directors: N. Mistry (Prop)
Date established: 1989 **No.of Employees:** 1 - 10 **Product Groups:** 26, 35

The Neoknitting & Trim Ltd
Peter Pal House Albion Street, Oadby, Leicester, LE2 5DE
Tel: 0116-271 4923 **Fax:** 0116-271 4422
E-mail: paresh@neotrims.com
Website: http://www.neotrims.com
Managers: P. Raja (Mgr)
Immediate Holding Company: THE NEO KNITTING & TRIMS CO. LIMITED
Registration no: 04121337 **VAT No.:** GB 531 9547 36
Date established: 2000 **Turnover:** £250,000 - £500,000
No.of Employees: 1 - 10 **Product Groups:** 23, 24, 49, 63

Date of Accounts	Mar 11	Mar 10	Mar 09
Working Capital	4	-12	-18
Fixed Assets	14	16	20
Current Assets	53	37	34

Next plc
Desford Road Enderby, Leicester, LE19 4AT
Tel: 08448-448888 **Fax:** 0116-284 8998
Website: http://www.next.co.uk
Directors: S. Wolfston (Grp Chief Exec), S. Myatt (Dir), J. Barton (Ch & MD), D. Keens (Fin), A. McKinley (Fin), A. Varley (Dir)
Ultimate Holding Company: NEXT PLC
Immediate Holding Company: NEXT PLC
Registration no: 04412362 **VAT No.:** GB 179 7658 90
Date established: 2002 **Turnover:** Over £1,000m **No.of Employees:** 1 - 10
Product Groups: 61

Date of Accounts	Jan 10	Jan 11	Jan 12
Sales Turnover	3407m	3454m	3444m
Pre Tax Profit/Loss	505m	551m	580m
Working Capital	283m	234m	398m
Fixed Assets	653m	725m	714m
Current Assets	1041m	1067m	1140m
Current Liabilities	578m	512m	549m

Noiseair Acoustic Consultants
5 Fritchley Close Huncote, Leicester, LE9 3AR
Tel: 0116-272 5908
E-mail: sales@noiseairconsultants.co.uk
Website: http://www.noiseairconsultants.co.uk
Directors: N. Malone (Prop)
Date established: 2005 **No.of Employees:** 1 - 10 **Product Groups:** 40

Northvale Korting Ltd
2 Uxbridge Road, Leicester, LE4 7ST
Tel: 0116-266 5911 **Fax:** 0116-261 0050
E-mail: sales@northvalekorting.co.uk
Website: http://www.northvalekorting.co.uk
Bank(s): Lloyds TSB
Directors: S. Wright (MD)
Immediate Holding Company: NORTHVALE KORTING LIMITED
Registration no: 02091066 **VAT No.:** GB 459 9212 13
Date established: 1987 **Turnover:** £2m - £5m **No.of Employees:** 21 - 50
Product Groups: 36, 40

Date of Accounts	Dec 11	Dec 10	Dec 09
Working Capital	38	-72	-114
Fixed Assets	16	20	30
Current Assets	652	588	686

Nylacast
200 Hastings Road, Leicester, LE5 0HL
Tel: 0116-276 4048 **Fax:** 0116-274 1954
E-mail: malvin.fookes@nylacast.com
Website: http://www.nylacast.com
Bank(s): The RBS
Directors: M. Fookes (Dir)
Ultimate Holding Company: NYLACAST HOLDINGS LIMITED
Immediate Holding Company: NYLACAST LIMITED
Registration no: 05949301 **VAT No.:** GB 565 7769 80
Date established: 2006 **Turnover:** £20m - £50m
No.of Employees: 51 - 100 **Product Groups:** 30, 35, 39, 48, 66

Date of Accounts	Dec 11	Dec 10	Dec 09
Sales Turnover	24m	21m	18m
Pre Tax Profit/Loss	191	-563	-12m
Working Capital	-6m	2m	2m
Fixed Assets	8m	10m	11m
Current Assets	9m	8m	7m
Current Liabilities	2m	3m	2m

O B Carpenters & Joiners
2 St Davids Close Leicester Forest East, Leicester, LE3 3LU
Tel: 07808-910717
E-mail: santokh.obhi@hotmail.co.uk
Directors: S. Obhi (Dir)
No.of Employees: 1 - 10 **Product Groups:** 26, 37, 52, 63

Oak Refrigeration Service
51 Iliffe Avenue Oadby, Leicester, LE2 5LH
Tel: 0116-272 1299 **Fax:** 0116-272 1351
E-mail: info@oak-refrigeration.co.uk
Website: http://www.oak-refrigeration.co.uk
Directors: L. Collins (Dir), L. Cordale (Prop)
Registration no: 04556976 **Date established:** 2002
Turnover: £500,000 - £1m **No.of Employees:** 1 - 10 **Product Groups:** 40, 52

Oakland Excelsior
6 Mandervell Road Oadby, Leicester, LE2 5LL
Tel: 0116-272 0800 **Fax:** 0115-989 9016
E-mail: sales@oakland-elevators.co.uk
Website: http://www.oakland-elevators.co.uk
Bank(s): HSBC
Directors: K. Chilton (MD), A. Walker (Fin), D. Holmes (Chief Op Offcr), J. Wallwork (MD), T. Wallwork (Dir)
Managers: M. Marmoy (Purch Mgr), N. Byrne (Estimating), S. Freer (I.T. Exec), M. Byrne (Mktg Serv Mgr), A. Karim (Mgr)
Immediate Holding Company: Otis Ltd
Registration no: 00612633 **VAT No.:** GB 113 7867 62
Turnover: £10m - £20m **No.of Employees:** 51 - 100 **Product Groups:** 45

Date of Accounts	Nov 07	Nov 06	Nov 05
Sales Turnover	14310	14552	16915
Pre Tax Profit/Loss	1564	1888	1979
Working Capital	3143	2044	1273
Fixed Assets	280	328	322
Current Assets	9052	7036	5891
Current Liabilities	5909	4992	4618
Total Share Capital	2	2	2
ROCE% (Return on Capital Employed)	45.7	79.6	124.1
ROT% (Return on Turnover)	10.9	13.0	11.7

Oem - Automatic Ltd
Whiteacres Cambridge Road, Whetstone, Leicester, LE8 6ZG
Tel: 0116-284 9900 **Fax:** 0116-284 1721
E-mail: information@uk.oem.se
Website: http://www.oem.co.uk
Bank(s): Svenska Handelsbanken
Directors: R. Armstrong (Dir), S. Mills (Co Sec)
Managers: D. Jesscoatt (Mgr), A. Massey (Mktg Serv Mgr)
Ultimate Holding Company: OEM INTERNATIONAL AB (SWEDEN)
Immediate Holding Company: OEM - AUTOMATIC LIMITED
Registration no: 02240242 **VAT No.:** GB 487 5621 07
Date established: 1988 **Turnover:** £5m - £10m **No.of Employees:** 21 - 50
Product Groups: 37

Date of Accounts	Dec 11	Dec 10	Dec 09
Sales Turnover	8m	7m	5m
Pre Tax Profit/Loss	801	808	242
Working Capital	802	1m	1m
Fixed Assets	604	48	45
Current Assets	3m	2m	2m
Current Liabilities	743	500	278

Ohaus UK Ltd
64 Boston Road, Leicester, LE4 1AW
Tel: 0116-235 7070 **Fax:** 0116-235 9256
Website: http://www.ohaus.com
Directors: G. Eley (MD), M. Pearl (MD), N. Mason (Fin)
Ultimate Holding Company: METTLER TOLEDO INTERNATIONAL INC (USA)
Immediate Holding Company: OHAUS (UK) LIMITED
Registration no: 03270452 **Date established:** 1996 **Turnover:** £1m - £2m
No.of Employees: 1 - 10 **Product Groups:** 38, 42

Date of Accounts	Dec 10	Dec 09	Dec 08
Pre Tax Profit/Loss	34	33	39
Working Capital	765	741	717
Current Assets	816	773	744
Current Liabilities	51	32	27

Ones & Zeros
30 Dulverton Road, Leicester, LE3 0SA
Tel: 08707-705592 **Fax:** 08707-705593
E-mail: j-rogers@oneszeros.biz
Website: http://www.oneszeros.biz
Directors: J. Rogers (Prop)
Date established: 2003 **No.of Employees:** 1 - 10 **Product Groups:** 37, 44, 79

Opsec Security Ltd
2 Penman Way Enderby, Leicester, LE19 1ST
Tel: 0116-282 2000 **Fax:** 0116-282 2100
E-mail: sales@opsecsecurity.co.uk
Website: http://www.appliedopsec.com
Directors: P. Warwick (Fab)
Ultimate Holding Company: OPSEC SECURITY GROUP PLC
Immediate Holding Company: OPSEC SECURITY LIMITED
Registration no: 01997954 **VAT No.:** GB 448 9476 89
Date established: 1986 **Turnover:** £20m - £50m **No.of Employees:** 1 - 10
Product Groups: 28, 34, 81

Date of Accounts	Mar 12	Mar 11	Mar 10
Sales Turnover	13m	16m	9m
Pre Tax Profit/Loss	42	1m	118
Working Capital	-967	-3m	-5m
Fixed Assets	7m	9m	9m
Current Assets	4m	6m	3m
Current Liabilities	2m	3m	2m

P A C S
113 Barkby Road, Leicester, LE4 9LG
Tel: 0116-276 8555 **Fax:** 0116-246 1090
E-mail: david@p-a-c-s.co.uk
Website: http://www.p-a-c-s.co.uk
Directors: D. Wigley (Ch), M. Robotham (MD)
Immediate Holding Company: B.W.S. EXPORT PACKAGING SERVICES LIMITED
Registration no: 00929932 **Date established:** 1968
Turnover: £500,000 - £1m **No.of Employees:** 1 - 10 **Product Groups:** 29, 30, 84

P D S Consultants
82 London Road, Leicester, LE2 0QR
Tel: 0116-254 4645 **Fax:** 0116-247 0092
E-mail: philip.drew@pds-consultants.co.uk
Website: http://www.pds-consultants.co.uk
Directors: P. Drew (Prop), P. Drew (MD)
Managers: P. Drew (Consultant)
Immediate Holding Company: VISUAL READ MEDICAL SOFTWARE LIMITED
Registration no: 04557405 **VAT No.:** GB 372 1180 76
Date established: 2002 **Turnover:** Up to £250,000
No.of Employees: 1 - 10 **Product Groups:** 44

P 15 Plastics Ltd
161 Waterside Road Hamilton, Leicester, LE5 1TL
Tel: 0116-276 1495 **Fax:** 0116-246 0489
E-mail: info@p15uk.com
Website: http://www.p15uk.com
Directors: P. Gamble (MD)
Ultimate Holding Company: STENE HOLDINGS LIMITED
Immediate Holding Company: P.15 PLASTICS LTD.
Registration no: 01469316 **Date established:** 1979
Turnover: £500,000 - £1m **No.of Employees:** 1 - 10 **Product Groups:** 30, 49

Date of Accounts	Mar 11	Mar 10	Mar 09
Working Capital	536	416	347
Fixed Assets	57	69	87
Current Assets	706	565	455

P M A Group
181 Waterside Road Hamilton, Leicester, LE5 1TL
Tel: 0116-246 1808 **Fax:** 0116-276 1600
E-mail: mike.westwood@pmagroup.co.uk
Website: http://www.pmagroup.co.uk
Bank(s): HSBC
Directors: M. Westwood (Dir)
Ultimate Holding Company: TOOLING AND DEVELOPMENTS LIMITED
Immediate Holding Company: FRASER PRODUCTS LIMITED
Registration no: 02906945 **Date established:** 1994 **Turnover:** £5m - £10m
No.of Employees: 51 - 100 **Product Groups:** 68

P O S Direct Ltd (Logistics)
99 Boston Road, Leicester, LE4 1AW
Tel: 0116-234 4400 **Fax:** 0116-235 8947
E-mail: rogercrosse@posdirect.co.uk
Website: http://www.posdirect.co.uk
Directors: G. Newman (Dir), R. Crosse (Dir)
Managers: S. Wilkins (Tech Serv Mgr), C. Clarke (Fin Mgr), J. Perkins (Personnel)
Immediate Holding Company: P.O.S. DIRECT LIMITED
Registration no: 02579623 **Date established:** 1991 **Turnover:** £5m - £10m
No.of Employees: 21 - 50 **Product Groups:** 30, 38, 72, 76, 77, 81, 84

Date of Accounts	May 11	May 10	May 09
Sales Turnover	6m	6m	7m
Pre Tax Profit/Loss	400	93	366
Working Capital	-193	-240	-85
Fixed Assets	3m	3m	3m
Current Assets	2m	1m	2m
Current Liabilities	520	444	471

Paramount Knitwear Leicester Ltd
Unit 22a Centurion Way Meridian Business Park, Leicester, LE19 1WH
Tel: 0116-263 0044 **Fax:** 0116-263 0101
E-mail: sales@paramountknitwear.com
Website: http://www.paramountknitwear.com
Bank(s): Barclays
Directors: A. Omar (MD)
Ultimate Holding Company: PARAMOUNT HOLDINGS (UK) LIMITED
Immediate Holding Company: PARAMOUNT KNITWEAR (LEICESTER) LIMITED
Registration no: 01174794 **VAT No.:** GB 115 7092 83
Date established: 1974 **No.of Employees:** 11 - 20 **Product Groups:** 63

Date of Accounts	Mar 11	Mar 10	Mar 09
Working Capital	7m	7m	7m
Fixed Assets	145	130	117
Current Assets	8m	9m	8m

Parker Fine Foods Services
Winkadale House Knights Road, Leicester, LE4 1JX
Tel: 0116-235 5666 **Fax:** 0116-235 5777
E-mail: quality@parkerfinefoods.com
Website: http://www.parkerfinefoods.com
Directors: A. Parker (MD)
Registration no: 00566000 **No.of Employees:** 21 - 50 **Product Groups:** 62

Parker Plant Ltd
Viaduct Works Canon Street, Leicester, LE4 6GH
Tel: 0116-266 5999 **Fax:** 0116-268 1254
E-mail: info@parkerplant.com
Website: http://www.parkerplant.com
Bank(s): HSBC Bank plc
Directors: G. Wheeler (Fin)
Managers: B. Dalby (Mktg Serv Mgr), D. Reynolds (Tech Serv Mgr), J. White (Sales Prom Mgr), M. Forte (Purch Mgr), S. Wilkinson (Personnel)
Ultimate Holding Company: PHOENIX PARKER HOLDINGS LIMITED
Immediate Holding Company: PARKER PLANT LIMITED
Registration no: 04908756 **VAT No.:** GB 705 3139 62
Date established: 2003 **Turnover:** £10m - £20m
No.of Employees: 101 - 250 **Product Groups:** 45

Date of Accounts	Dec 11	Dec 10	Dec 09
Sales Turnover	16m	16m	17m
Pre Tax Profit/Loss	726	2m	3m
Working Capital	4m	3m	2m
Fixed Assets	2m	1m	2m
Current Assets	10m	9m	8m
Current Liabilities	2m	2m	2m

Parkers Of Leicester Ltd
254 Braunstone Lane, Leicester, LE3 3AS
Tel: 0116-289 9555 **Fax:** 0116-282 5060
E-mail: paul.marriage@parkers-leic.co.uk
Directors: P. Marriage (Co Sec)
Immediate Holding Company: PARKERS OF LEICESTER LIMITED
Registration no: 02138495 **Date established:** 1987 **Turnover:** £5m - £10m
No.of Employees: 1 - 10 **Product Groups:** 02

Date of Accounts	Sep 11	Sep 10	Sep 09
Sales Turnover	8m	6m	7m
Pre Tax Profit/Loss	2m	776	4m
Working Capital	10m	11m	11m
Fixed Assets	21m	18m	17m
Current Assets	15m	15m	14m
Current Liabilities	925	398	627

Parmeko plc
Percy Road, Leicester, LE2 8FT
Tel: 0116-244 0044 **Fax:** 0116-244 0000
E-mail: info@parmeko.co.uk
Website: http://www.parmeko.co.uk
Bank(s): National Westminster Bank Plc

Directors: B. Cox (Fin)
Ultimate Holding Company: PARMEKO HOLDINGS LIMITED
Immediate Holding Company: PARMEKO LIMITED
Registration no: 02486122 **Date established:** 1990 **Turnover:** £1m - £2m
No.of Employees: 51 - 100 **Product Groups:** 37

Date of Accounts	Nov 08	Dec 09	Dec 10
Sales Turnover	3m	2m	N/A
Pre Tax Profit/Loss	989	-350	N/A
Working Capital	-40	-292	-123
Fixed Assets	921	531	428
Current Assets	2m	973	1m
Current Liabilities	229	187	N/A

Peek Traffic Ltd
Meridian Business Park Centurion Way, Leicester, LE19 1WH
Tel: 0116-282 8500 **Fax:** 0116-282 8528
E-mail: steve.wright@peek.co.uk
Website: http://www.peekglobal.com
Directors: S. Wright (Dir)
Ultimate Holding Company: IMTECH NV (NETHERLANDS)
Immediate Holding Company: PEEK TRAFFIC LIMITED
Registration no: 01490333 **Date established:** 1980
No.of Employees: 21 - 50 **Product Groups:** 37, 38, 39, 44, 51

Date of Accounts	Dec 11	Dec 10	Dec 09
Sales Turnover	63m	63m	58m
Pre Tax Profit/Loss	6m	6m	2m
Working Capital	17m	14m	7m
Fixed Assets	2m	2m	6m
Current Assets	29m	27m	16m
Current Liabilities	9m	9m	4m

Pegasus Mechanical Lifting
30 Great Central Street, Leicester, LE1 4JT
Tel: 0116-253 7411 **Fax:** 0116-253 9751
E-mail: sales@pegasuslifting.co.uk
Website: http://www.pegasuslifting.co.uk
Directors: S. Platts (MD)
Turnover: £1m - £2m **No.of Employees:** 1 - 10 **Product Groups:** 35, 39, 45

Pen Logistics Ltd
Unit C Britannia Way, Leicester, LE4 8JY
Tel: 0116-260 8989 **Fax:** 0116-260 6224
E-mail: pen-logistics@btconnect.com
Website: http://www.penlogisticsltd.com
Product Groups: 39, 45, 71, 75, 76, 77, 80, 84

Peterkin UK Ltd
85 Commercial Square, Leicester, LE2 7SR
Tel: 0116-254 3645 **Fax:** 0116-247 0618
E-mail: sales@peterkin.co.uk
Website: http://www.peterkin.co.uk
Directors: N. Seary (MD)
Ultimate Holding Company: W J BROWN LIMITED
Immediate Holding Company: PETERKIN (U.K.) LIMITED
Registration no: 00566155 **Date established:** 1956 **Turnover:** £2m - £5m
No.of Employees: 11 - 20 **Product Groups:** 61

Date of Accounts	Dec 11	Dec 10	Dec 09
Working Capital	2m	1m	1m
Fixed Assets	97	84	75
Current Assets	2m	2m	2m

Pinnacle International Freight Ltd
C Mortimer Road Narborough, Leicester, LE19 2GA
Tel: 08456-216111 **Fax:** 0116-286 7928
E-mail: enquiry@pif.co.uk
Website: http://www.pif.co.uk
Directors: P. Huston (Chief Op Offcr), P. Huston (MD), N. Burrell (Dir), C. Bannister (Fin), C. Bannister (Dir), N. Burrell (MD)
Ultimate Holding Company: PINNACLE INTERNATIONAL FREIGHT HOLDINGS LIMITED
Immediate Holding Company: PINNACLE INTERNATIONAL FREIGHT LIMITED
Registration no: 01059368 **Date established:** 1972
Turnover: £10m - £20m **No.of Employees:** 51 - 100 **Product Groups:** 61, 72, 74, 75, 76, 77

Date of Accounts	Dec 10	Dec 09	Dec 08
Sales Turnover	17m	11m	N/A
Pre Tax Profit/Loss	882	232	582
Working Capital	3m	3m	3m
Fixed Assets	809	93	119
Current Assets	7m	5m	6m
Current Liabilities	2m	612	754

Robert Pochin Ltd
18 Samuel Street, Leicester, LE1 1RU
Tel: 0116-262 3419 **Fax:** 0116-253 8829
E-mail: simon.froggatt@robertpochin.co.uk
Website: http://www.pochin.com
Bank(s): National Westminster
Directors: S. Froggatt (Dir)
Immediate Holding Company: ROBERT POCHIN LIMITED
Registration no: 00179511 **VAT No.:** GB 113 7690 75
Date established: 2022 **Turnover:** £10m - £20m
No.of Employees: 11 - 20 **Product Groups:** 36, 66

Date of Accounts	Dec 11	Dec 10	Dec 09
Sales Turnover	12m	12m	12m
Pre Tax Profit/Loss	270	119	45
Working Capital	-150	-111	135
Fixed Assets	5m	4m	4m
Current Assets	3m	3m	3m
Current Liabilities	303	402	201

Pollard Boxes
Feldspar Close Enderby, Leicester, LE19 4SD
Tel: 0116-275 2666 **Fax:** 0116-275 2888
E-mail: info@pollardboxes.co.uk
Website: http://www.pollardboxes.co.uk
Directors: P. Conner (Comm)
Managers: M. Stanfield (Comptroller), J. Smith (Personnel), S. Keen (Buyer)
Ultimate Holding Company: LEICESTER FANCY BOX COMPANY LIMITED
Immediate Holding Company: POLLARD BOXES LIMITED
Registration no: 00158917 **VAT No.:** 620 2818 71 **Date established:** 2019
Turnover: £10m - £20m **No.of Employees:** 251 - 500 **Product Groups:** 27

Date of Accounts	Dec 11	Dec 10	Dec 09
Sales Turnover	14m	13m	10m
Pre Tax Profit/Loss	227	167	270
Working Capital	3m	3m	3m
Fixed Assets	3m	4m	4m
Current Assets	7m	7m	6m
Current Liabilities	1m	2m	1m

Gregory Pollard Ltd
Regent Road Countesthorpe, Leicester, LE8 5RF
Tel: 0116-277 3857 **Fax:** 0116-278 4395
E-mail: david@magicfit.co.uk
Website: http://www.magicfit.co.uk
Bank(s): HSBC Bank plc
Directors: D. Winterton (MD)
Immediate Holding Company: DAVID WINTERTON LEISURE WEAR LIMITED
Registration no: 01762028 **VAT No.:** GB 114 2721 12
Date established: 1983 **Turnover:** £1m - £2m **No.of Employees:** 11 - 20
Product Groups: 24

Date of Accounts	Dec 11	Dec 10	Dec 09
Working Capital	N/A	N/A	-279
Fixed Assets	335	335	335
Current Assets	N/A	N/A	1

Polybags Direct
30 wakerley road Evington, leicester, LE5 6AQ
Tel: 07989-605047
E-mail: info@polybagsdirect.com
Website: http://www.polybagsonline.co.uk
Managers: M. Billing (Chief Acct)
Date established: 1981 **Turnover:** Up to £250,000
No.of Employees: 11 - 20 **Product Groups:** 30

Potterton Pacs Trading as Potterton Cases
103 Coleman Road, Leicester, LE5 4LE
Tel: 0116-276 7562 **Fax:** 0116-246 0445
E-mail: sales@pottertonscases.co.uk
Website: http://www.pottertonscases.co.uk
Bank(s): Barclays, Town Hall Square
Directors: T. Pickering (MD)
Immediate Holding Company: POTTERTONPACS LIMITED
Registration no: 07938336 **Date established:** 2012
No.of Employees: 21 - 50 **Product Groups:** 22, 27, 30, 49, 63

Date of Accounts	Jan 11	Jan 10	Jan 09
Working Capital	84	86	-83
Fixed Assets	416	423	429
Current Assets	380	352	311

Potton-Delph
Lazarus Court 16 Woodgate, Rothley, Leicester, LE7 7NR
Tel: 0116-230 3327 **Fax:** 0116-230 3327
E-mail: phil@potton-delph.co.uk
Website: http://www.potton-delph.co.uk
Directors: P. Buxton (MD)
Date established: 2005 **No.of Employees:** 1 - 10 **Product Groups:** 38, 42

Powerdrive PSR
Forward Park Sheene Road, Leicester, LE4 1BF
Tel: 0116-235 5887
E-mail: info@powerdrive.co.uk
Website: http://www.powerdrive.co.uk
Managers: S. Wilson (Mgr)
Registration no: 03835632 **Date established:** 1999
No.of Employees: 1 - 10 **Product Groups:** 35

Prince Petroleum Ltd
139 Abbey Lane, Leicester, LE4 5QZ
Tel: 0116-266 1828 **Fax:** 0116-261 0727
E-mail: enquiries@prince-petroleum.co.uk
Website: http://www.prince-petroleum.co.uk
Bank(s): National Westminster Bank Plc
Directors: D. Prince (Dir)
Immediate Holding Company: PRINCE PETROLEUM LIMITED
Registration no: 00749966 **VAT No.:** GB 113 7259 85
Date established: 1963 **Turnover:** £10m - £20m
No.of Employees: 11 - 20 **Product Groups:** 30, 31, 40, 42, 48, 72, 82

Date of Accounts	Aug 08	Jun 11	Jun 10
Working Capital	-329	-322	-377
Fixed Assets	651	734	650
Current Assets	1m	3m	2m

Pro Impressions
Imperial House St Nicholas Circle, Leicester, LE1 4LF
Tel: 0116-276 5150 **Fax:** 0116-276 5121
E-mail: info@proimpressions.com
Website: http://www.proimpressions.com
Directors: R. Mistry (Dir)
Immediate Holding Company: PRO IMPRESSIONS (UK) LIMITED
Registration no: 04429197 **Date established:** 2002
No.of Employees: 11 - 20 **Product Groups:** 32, 49, 63, 66

Procorr Packaging Ltd
Unit One Park Farm Business Centre, Skeffington, Leicester, LE7 9YE
Tel: 0116-259 9302
Directors: J. Webb (MD)
Registration no: 05299174 **No.of Employees:** 1 - 10 **Product Groups:** 38, 42

The Professional Lamp Company
Unit 11a St Marks Works Foundry Lane, Leicester, LE1 3WU
Tel: 0116-262 7345 **Fax:** 0116-262 7346
E-mail: sales@prolamp.co.uk
Website: http://www.prolamp.co.uk
Directors: N. D'amore (Prop)
Turnover: Up to £250,000 **No.of Employees:** 1 - 10 **Product Groups:** 30, 33, 36, 37, 38, 39, 41, 45, 49, 67, 84

Prospray Spraying
Tooley Park Lodge 12 Peckleton Common Road, Peckleton, Leicester, LE9 7RF
Tel: 01455-828599 **Fax:** 01455-828515
E-mail: clint@spiraltd.com
Website: http://www.spiraltd.com
Directors: S. Houchin (Dir)
Date established: 2002 **No.of Employees:** 1 - 10 **Product Groups:** 46, 48

Provenair Sales Ltd
20 Dukes Close Thurmaston, Leicester, LE4 8EY
Tel: 0116-269 7373 **Fax:** 0116-269 7371
E-mail: carol.allen@provenairsalesltd.co.uk
Website: http://www.provenairsalesltd.co.uk
Directors: C. Allen (Co Sec)
Immediate Holding Company: PROVENAIR SALES LIMITED
Registration no: 02552054 **VAT No.:** GB 536 2914 40
Date established: 1990 **Turnover:** £500,000 - £1m
No.of Employees: 11 - 20 **Product Groups:** 40, 66

Date of Accounts	May 11	May 10	May 09
Working Capital	218	225	228
Fixed Assets	92	66	83
Current Assets	305	327	364

Pulse Lighting Ltd
39a Highmeres Road, Leicester, LE4 9LZ
Tel: 0116-260 1010 **Fax:** 0116-264 0444
E-mail: info@pulselighting.co.uk
Website: http://www.pulselighting.co.uk
Directors: D. Soulsby (MD)
Immediate Holding Company: PULSE LIGHTING LIMITED
Registration no: 05300806 **Date established:** 2004
Turnover: £500,000 - £1m **No.of Employees:** 11 - 20 **Product Groups:** 37

Date of Accounts	Feb 08	Feb 11	Feb 10
Working Capital	56	291	198
Fixed Assets	4	16	9
Current Assets	246	522	433

Q C Mould Tools
King Street Buildings King Street, Enderby, Leicester, LE19 4NT
Tel: 0116-286 2816 **Fax:** 0116-286 2816
Directors: J. Coulson (Prop)
Date established: 2002 **No.of Employees:** 1 - 10 **Product Groups:** 36

Quality Electroplaters Ltd
118 Marjorie Street, Leicester, LE4 5GX
Tel: 0116-268 1421 **Fax:** 0116-268 1421
E-mail: qep.arvind@yahoo.co.uk
Directors: A. Solanki (Dir)
Date established: 1980 **No.of Employees:** 1 - 10 **Product Groups:** 46, 48

Quality Graphics Midlands Ltd
1 Fletcher Road Stoney Stanton, Leicester, LE9 4DE
Tel: 01455-272413 **Fax:** 01455-274510
E-mail: info@quality-graphics.co.uk
Website: http://www.quality-graphics.co.uk
Directors: M. Ashby (Dir)
Immediate Holding Company: QUALITY GRAPHICS (MIDLANDS) LIMITED
Registration no: 05914070 **Date established:** 2006
Turnover: Up to £250,000 **No.of Employees:** 1 - 10 **Product Groups:** 37, 80, 83

Date of Accounts	Aug 11	Aug 10	Aug 09
Working Capital	-27	-41	-48
Fixed Assets	30	37	43
Current Assets	14	8	4

Qualvis Packaging Ltd
854 Melton Road Thurmaston, Leicester, LE4 8BT
Tel: 0116-260 2220 **Fax:** 0116-260 1066
E-mail: jason@qualvis.co.uk
Website: http://www.qualvis.co.uk
Bank(s): Royal Bank of Scotland
Directors: J. Short (MD), P. Bartlett (Fin)
Managers: A. Bruce (Personnel), S. George (Mktg Serv Mgr)
Immediate Holding Company: QUALVIS PACKAGING LIMITED
Registration no: 01615940 **VAT No.:** GB 371 7525 44
Date established: 1982 **Turnover:** £5m - £10m
No.of Employees: 101 - 250 **Product Groups:** 27, 66, 67

Date of Accounts	Jan 12	Jan 11	Jan 10
Sales Turnover	11m	9m	7m
Pre Tax Profit/Loss	146	141	-143
Working Capital	695	384	-869
Fixed Assets	634	798	943
Current Assets	3m	4m	3m
Current Liabilities	1m	1m	215

Quarry Plant Installations
56 Boston Road, Leicester, LE4 1AA
Tel: 0116-235 0323 **Fax:** 0116-235 1323
Directors: R. Palfrey (MD)
Immediate Holding Company: QUARRY PLANT INSTALLATIONS LIMITED
Registration no: 03711434 **Date established:** 1999
No.of Employees: 11 - 20 **Product Groups:** 35

R G Attachments
86 Belper Street, Leicester, LE4 6EA
Tel: 0116-261 1038 **Fax:** 0116-261 2403
E-mail: info@rga.co.uk
Website: http://www.rga.co.uk
Directors: R. Gent (Dir)
Immediate Holding Company: RG ATTACHMENTS LIMITED
Registration no: 05457648 **Date established:** 2005
No.of Employees: 1 - 10 **Product Groups:** 43

Date of Accounts	Jul 11	Jul 10	Jul 09
Working Capital	39	38	16
Fixed Assets	83	57	71
Current Assets	210	107	108

R & J Machinery
Mallory Park Circuit Church Road, Kirkby Mallory, Leicester, LE9 7QE
Tel: 01455-840224 **Fax:** 01455-840225
E-mail: justin.inman@rjmachinery.co.uk
Website: http://www.rjmachinery.co.uk
Directors: J. Inman (Prop)
Turnover: £2m - £5m **No.of Employees:** 1 - 10 **Product Groups:** 46

Ram Catering Equipment Services
79 Glenfield Road, Leicester, LE3 6AW
Tel: 0116-299 0299
Directors: J. Hindocha (Ptnr)
Date established: 1991 **No.of Employees:** 1 - 10 **Product Groups:** 20, 40, 41

Ram Universal Ltd
19 Swannington Road Broughton Astley, Leicester, LE9 6TU
Tel: 01455-285428 **Fax:** 01455-285404
E-mail: sales@ramuniversal.co.uk
Website: http://www.ramuniversal.co.uk

see next page

Ram Universal Ltd - Cont'd
Directors: R. James (MD)
Immediate Holding Company: RAM UNIVERSAL LIMITED
Registration no: 01642089 **Date established:** 1982 **Turnover:** £1m - £2m
No.of Employees: 11 - 20 **Product Groups:** 30, 36

Date of Accounts	Dec 11	Dec 10	Dec 09
Working Capital	264	220	268
Fixed Assets	17	19	35
Current Assets	928	647	566

Ramon Hygiene Products
380 Thurmaston Boulevard, Leicester, LE4 9LE
Tel: 0116-276 1881 **Fax:** 0116-246 0224
E-mail: admin@ramonhygiene.co.uk
Website: http://www.ramonhygiene.com
Bank(s): Bank of Scotland
Directors: G. Peters (Fin), R. Smith (Fin), R. Flowers (MD), S. Baldock (Sales)
Managers: S. Amilton (Mktg Serv Mgr), D. Collins, J. Butler
Immediate Holding Company: RAMON HYGIENE PRODUCTS LIMITED
Registration no: 04219151 **VAT No.:** GB 661 5543 35
Date established: 2001 **Turnover:** £10m - £20m
No.of Employees: 101 - 250 **Product Groups:** 24, 30, 49

Date of Accounts	Apr 08	Apr 09	Apr 10
Sales Turnover	12m	N/A	N/A
Pre Tax Profit/Loss	1m	N/A	N/A
Fixed Assets	6m	6m	6m

Raven Forge
Unit 12 Trading Estate Maidstone Road, Leicester, LE2 0UB
Tel: 0116-262 9499
Directors: R. Atkins (MD)
Date established: 1999 **No.of Employees:** 1 - 10 **Product Groups:** 26, 35

Raw
Marlone House Churchill Way, Fleckney, Leicester, LE8 8UD
Tel: 0116-240 2282 **Fax:** 0116-240 4277
E-mail: enquiries@rawshoe.co.uk
Website: http://www.rawshoe.co.uk
Directors: G. Brown (MD)
Immediate Holding Company: RAW SHOES LIMITED
Registration no: 03159148 **Date established:** 1996
Turnover: £250,000 - £500,000 **No.of Employees:** 1 - 10
Product Groups: 22

Reed Employment Ltd
54 Market Place, Leicester, LE1 5GF
Tel: 0116-253 1471 **Fax:** 0116-262 2542
Website: http://www.reeds.co.uk
Directors: T. Brian (MD)
Managers: J. Walls (District Mgr), A. Murrey (District Mgr), P. Smith (Mgr), P. Bellingham (Mgr)
Ultimate Holding Company: REED GLOBAL LTD (MALTA)
Immediate Holding Company: REED EMPLOYMENT LIMITED
Registration no: 00669854 **Date established:** 1960
Turnover: Over £1,000m **No.of Employees:** 1 - 10 **Product Groups:** 80

Regent Engineers Ltd
Regent Street Narborough, Leicester, LE19 2DT
Tel: 0116-286 2209 **Fax:** 0116-275 0293
E-mail: j.horsfall@regentengineers.co.uk
Website: http://www.regentengineers.co.uk
Bank(s): Barclays
Directors: S. Iles (Fin), H. Dalby (MD)
Managers: R. Tipping (Develop Mgr), S. Keel (Buyer)
Ultimate Holding Company: DALBY HOLDINGS LIMITED
Immediate Holding Company: REGENT ENGINEERS LIMITED
Registration no: 00914011 **Date established:** 1967 **Turnover:** £2m - £5m
No.of Employees: 21 - 50 **Product Groups:** 48

Date of Accounts	Mar 11	Mar 10	Mar 09
Working Capital	453	470	409
Fixed Assets	591	657	704
Current Assets	1m	941	691

Ride2success Driving School Leicester Driving Lessons
103 Sunbury Green, Leicester, LE5 2QL
Tel: 07708-809708
E-mail: info@ride2success.co.uk
Website: http://www.ride2success.co.uk
Directors: F. Ahmed (Prop)
Immediate Holding Company: MADRASATUL BARKAAT LIMITED
Date established: 2010 **No.of Employees:** 1 - 10 **Product Groups:** 28

Date of Accounts	Sep 11
Working Capital	-0

Roberts Of Churchgate
47 Church Gate, Leicester, LE1 3AL
Tel: 0116-262 9061 **Fax:** 0116-262 9062
E-mail: robertsofchurchgates@fsmail.net
Directors: A. Mcclelland (Dir)
Registration no: 02799254 **Turnover:** Up to £250,000
No.of Employees: 1 - 10 **Product Groups:** 65

Rock Kitchen Harris Ltd
31 Lower Brown Street, Leicester, LE1 5TH
Tel: 0116-233 7500 **Fax:** 0116-233 7533
E-mail: dmoore@rkh.co.uk
Website: http://www.rkh.co.uk
Bank(s): Barclays
Directors: D. Moore (Fin), P. Sculthorpe (Dir), J. Mollard (Dir)
Immediate Holding Company: ROCK KITCHEN HARRIS LIMITED
Registration no: 01589727 **VAT No.:** GB 565 7496 89
Date established: 1981 **Turnover:** £1m - £2m **No.of Employees:** 21 - 50
Product Groups: 81

Date of Accounts	Dec 11	Dec 10	Dec 09
Working Capital	240	307	283
Fixed Assets	150	20	27
Current Assets	854	747	782

Rollings Buildbase (Head Office and Depot)
15-21 Cannock Street, Leicester, LE4 9HR
Tel: 0116-276 0275 **Fax:** 0116-246 0554
Website: http://www.buildbase.co.uk
Managers: S. Hill (Mgr)
Immediate Holding Company: CIRCLE TOWERS LIMITED
Registration no: 00620514 **VAT No.:** GB 114 5677 71
Date established: 2006 **Turnover:** £2m - £5m **No.of Employees:** 1 - 10
Product Groups: 66

Date of Accounts	Jul 10	Jul 09	Jul 08
Working Capital	244	-21	-17
Current Assets	250	250	249
Current Liabilities	N/A	267	N/A

David Ross Fabrications Ltd
Unit 1e Peckleton Lane Business Park Peckleton Common, Peckleton, Leicester, LE9 7RN
Tel: 01455-823721 **Fax:** 01455-828339
E-mail: info@davidrossfabrications.co.uk
Website: http://www.davidrossfabrications.co.uk
Bank(s): TSB, Leicester
Directors: J. Ross (Fin), D. Ross (MD)
Immediate Holding Company: DAVID ROSS FABRICATIONS LIMITED
Registration no: 03925912 **VAT No.:** GB 536 2986 15
Date established: 2000 **Turnover:** £250,000 - £500,000
No.of Employees: 11 - 20 **Product Groups:** 48

Date of Accounts	Oct 11	Oct 10	Oct 09
Working Capital	205	209	208
Fixed Assets	24	24	31
Current Assets	682	492	404

Ross Handling Ltd
71 Cannock Street, Leicester, LE4 9HR
Tel: 0116-276 4987 **Fax:** 0116-274 1751
E-mail: sales@rosshandling.co.uk
Website: http://www.rosshandling.co.uk
Directors: C. Fitzpatrick (MD)
Immediate Holding Company: ROSS HANDLING LIMITED
Registration no: 01343301 **Date established:** 1977
No.of Employees: 1 - 10 **Product Groups:** 23, 26, 29, 30, 35, 36, 39, 41, 42, 45, 46, 49, 66

Date of Accounts	Mar 11	Mar 10	Mar 09
Working Capital	226	226	293
Fixed Assets	29	12	14
Current Assets	412	393	405

S B A Ltd
Leicester Leicestershire, Leicester, LE2 7SQ
Tel: 0116-257 6595 **Fax:** 0116-247 0072
E-mail: sales@sba.co.uk
Website: http://www.sba.co.uk
Bank(s): HSBC Bank plc
Directors: K. Webber (Mkt Research), J. Belgrave (Purch), K. Webber (Dir)
Managers: T. Hawkes (Comptroller), S. Jackson (Tech Serv Mgr)
Immediate Holding Company: S B A LTD.
Registration no: 00381000 **Date established:** 1943 **Turnover:** £5m - £10m
No.of Employees: 21 - 50 **Product Groups:** 29, 30, 33, 36, 40, 49

Date of Accounts	Nov 11	Nov 10	Nov 09
Sales Turnover	8m	7m	6m
Pre Tax Profit/Loss	86	42	-54
Working Capital	-518	-583	-647
Fixed Assets	215	185	221
Current Assets	2m	2m	1m
Current Liabilities	1m	134	179

S J Event Consultancy Ltd
6 Cross Hedge Rothley, Leicester, LE7 7RR
Tel: 0116-230 2040 **Fax:** 0116-230 2341
E-mail: steve@sjeventconsultancy.com
Website: http://www.sjeventconsultancy.com
Directors: S. Spillane (MD)
Immediate Holding Company: S.J. EVENT CONSULTANCY LIMITED
Registration no: 05270640 **Date established:** 2004 **Turnover:** £1m - £2m
No.of Employees: 1 - 10 **Product Groups:** 69, 89

Date of Accounts	Dec 11	Dec 10	Dec 09
Sales Turnover	1m	937	845
Working Capital	34	12	8
Fixed Assets	N/A	1	1
Current Assets	499	405	185

S M C Sites Services
Syston Mill 16 Mill Lane, Syston, Leicester, LE7 1NS
Tel: 0116-260 5567 **Fax:** 0116-239 0160
E-mail: smcsiteservices@aol.com
Website: http://www.smc-site-services.co.uk
Directors: I. Roos (Ptnr)
No.of Employees: 1 - 10 **Product Groups:** 35

S & P Coil Products Ltd
Evington Valley Road, Leicester, LE5 5LU
Tel: 0116-249 0044 **Fax:** 0116-249 0033
E-mail: peter.teasdale@spcoils.co.uk
Website: http://www.spcoils.co.uk
Bank(s): National Westminster Bank Plc
Directors: P. Teasdale (Fin), W. Taylor (Sales), M. Madden (Pers)
Managers: K. Pytherch, E. Hustings (Tech Serv Mgr), T. Johnston
Immediate Holding Company: S & P COIL PRODUCTS LIMITED
Registration no: 05015411 **VAT No.:** GB 328 1976 34
Date established: 2004 **Turnover:** £10m - £20m
No.of Employees: 51 - 100 **Product Groups:** 36, 40

Date of Accounts	Mar 08	Mar 09	Apr 10
Sales Turnover	6m	6m	9m
Pre Tax Profit/Loss	545	614	707
Working Capital	-407	-469	463
Fixed Assets	4m	4m	3m
Current Assets	2m	3m	3m
Current Liabilities	815	1m	1m

S P L Blacking Ltd
420 Thurmaston Boulevard, Leicester, LE4 9LE
Tel: 0116-223 6100 **Fax:** 0116-246 0803
E-mail: office@splblacking.co.uk
Website: http://www.splblacking.co.uk
Directors: A. Foss (Fin), S. Lane (MD)
Immediate Holding Company: SPL BLACKING LTD
Registration no: 04815174 **Date established:** 2003
No.of Employees: 1 - 10 **Product Groups:** 46, 48

Date of Accounts	Aug 11	Aug 10	Aug 09
Working Capital	35	15	6
Fixed Assets	77	71	78
Current Assets	74	75	48

S P S Technologies Ltd
Troon Industrial Area 191 Barkby Road, Leicester, LE4 9HX
Tel: 0116-276 8261 **Fax:** 0116-274 0243
Website: http://www.sps.com
Bank(s): National Westminster
Directors: D. Bullivant (Sales), D. Parkes (Fin), K. Smith (Pers), P. Watson (Mkt Research), M. Wallis (Co Sec)
Managers: M. Willey (Tech Serv Mgr), D. Pearsall (Purch Mgr)
Ultimate Holding Company: PRECISION CASTPARTS CORP (USA)
Immediate Holding Company: SPS TECHNOLOGIES LIMITED
Registration no: 00303951 **VAT No.:** GB 765 3347 13
Date established: 1935 **Turnover:** £50m - £75m
No.of Employees: 251 - 500 **Product Groups:** 35, 67

Date of Accounts	Mar 11	Mar 10	Mar 09
Sales Turnover	57m	65m	74m
Pre Tax Profit/Loss	10m	25m	28m
Working Capital	14m	13m	16m
Fixed Assets	30m	31m	36m
Current Assets	25m	26m	27m
Current Liabilities	3m	3m	3m

S S R Fashions
8-14 Raymond Road, Leicester, LE3 2AS
Tel: 0116-282 4854 **Fax:** 0116-282 4854
E-mail: info@ssr-fashions.co.uk
Website: http://www.ssr-fashions.co.uk
Managers: R. Singh (Mgr)
Date established: 1983 **Turnover:** £250,000 - £500,000
No.of Employees: 1 - 10 **Product Groups:** 63

Safe Computing Ltd
20 Freeschool Lane, Leicester, LE1 4FY
Tel: 08445-832134 **Fax:** 0116-251 5535
E-mail: sandy.scott@safecomputing.co.uk
Website: http://www.safecomputing.co.uk
Bank(s): Barclays Bank Plc, Leicester
Directors: M. James (Co Sec), S. Scott (MD), A. Scott (MD)
Managers: J. Horlock (Chief Mgr), A. Simpson (Sales & Mktg Mg)
Ultimate Holding Company: SAFE COMPUTING HOLDINGS LIMITED
Immediate Holding Company: SAFE COMPUTING LIMITED
Registration no: 01202124 **VAT No.:** GB 485 7231 22
Date established: 1975 **Turnover:** £5m - £10m
No.of Employees: 101 - 250 **Product Groups:** 44

Date of Accounts	Dec 10	Dec 09	Dec 08
Sales Turnover	8m	7m	7m
Pre Tax Profit/Loss	973	1m	2m
Working Capital	6m	5m	5m
Fixed Assets	783	659	1m
Current Assets	10m	8m	8m
Current Liabilities	4m	3m	3m

Safety Source
24 Pasture Lane, Leicester, LE1 4EY
Tel: 0116-253 3598 **Fax:** 0116-262 7090
E-mail: sales@safety-source.co.uk
Website: http://www.safety-source.co.uk
Managers: P. Eames (Nat Sales Mgr)
Date established: 1973 **No.of Employees:** 21 - 50 **Product Groups:** 40

Sammic
Unit 2 Trevanth Road, Leicester, LE4 9LS
Tel: 0116-246 1900 **Fax:** 0116-246 0619
E-mail: uksales@sammic.com
Website: http://www.sammic.co.uk
Directors: J. Pena Neira (Co Sec), I. Houldsworth (MD)
Ultimate Holding Company: IGARPE TRADING SL (SPAIN)
Immediate Holding Company: SAMMIC LIMITED
Registration no: 02765706 **Date established:** 1992
No.of Employees: 1 - 10 **Product Groups:** 20, 40, 41

Date of Accounts	Dec 11	Dec 10	Dec 09
Working Capital	210	236	272
Fixed Assets	4	5	10
Current Assets	448	422	717

Sandwell Polybags Ltd
Unit 17 Elizabeth Street, Leicester, LE5 4FL
Tel: 0121-553 0244 **Fax:** 0121-553 0247
E-mail: ksingh@hotmail.co.uk
Directors: K. Singh (Co Sec)
Immediate Holding Company: SANDWELL POLYBAGS LIMITED
Registration no: 02135927 **Date established:** 1987
Turnover: £500,000 - £1m **No.of Employees:** 1 - 10 **Product Groups:** 30

Date of Accounts	Aug 11	Aug 10	Aug 09
Working Capital	38	102	166
Fixed Assets	9	11	13
Current Assets	260	212	178

Scaleways Leicester Ltd
35 Carlisle Street, Leicester, LE3 6AH
Tel: 0116-255 5092 **Fax:** 0116-255 5143
E-mail: sales@scaleways.co.uk
Website: http://www.scaleways.co.uk
Directors: J. Miller (Fin)
Immediate Holding Company: SCALEWAYS (LEICESTER) LIMITED
Registration no: 01816784 **VAT No.:** GB 114 9158 75
Date established: 1984 **Turnover:** Up to £250,000
No.of Employees: 1 - 10 **Product Groups:** 37, 38, 45, 48, 83

Date of Accounts	Jun 11	Jun 10	Jun 09
Working Capital	83	76	79
Fixed Assets	16	19	16
Current Assets	145	141	135

ScanSense
Bekkeveien 163 Queniborough, Leicester, LE7 3FP
Tel: 0116-260 9757
Website: http://WWW.SCANSENSE.NO
Date established: 1986 **Turnover:** £5m - £10m **No.of Employees:** 21 - 50
Product Groups: 38

SDI designs
James House Thurmaston Boulevard, Leicester, LE4 9LD
Tel: 0844-499 0121 **Fax:** 0844-499 0181
E-mail: info@sdidisplays.co.uk
Website: http://www.sdidisplays.co.uk
Bank(s): TSB, Litchfield

Directors: S. Hill (MD), G. Pullen (Comm), A. Elshout (MD), P. Elshout (Ch)
Managers: A. Litchfield (Accounts)
Immediate Holding Company: Sdi Displays Ltd
Registration no: 01195722 **Date established:** 1975
Turnover: £10m - £20m **No.of Employees:** 51 - 100 **Product Groups:** 30, 49, 81

Date of Accounts	Dec 09	Aug 08	Aug 07
Working Capital	402	462	-210
Fixed Assets	N/A	N/A	564
Current Assets	402	462	2m

Seac Ltd
46 Chesterfield Road, Leicester, LE5 5LP
Tel: 0116-273 9501 **Fax:** 0116-273 8373
E-mail: david.buckley@seac.uk.com
Website: http://www.seac.uk.com
Bank(s): National Westminster Bank Plc
Directors: D. Buckley (MD), R. Beer (Fin)
Managers: C. Kaye (Sales & Mktg Mg)
Ultimate Holding Company: SEAC HOLDINGS LIMITED
Immediate Holding Company: SEAC LIMITED
Registration no: 00145362 **Date established:** 2016 **Turnover:** £5m - £10m
No.of Employees: 21 - 50 **Product Groups:** 30, 35, 36

Date of Accounts	Apr 09	Apr 10	Apr 11
Working Capital	2m	2m	2m
Fixed Assets	783	746	707
Current Assets	3m	3m	3m

Seagas Industries Ltd
152 Abbey Lane, Leicester, LE4 0DA
Tel: 0116-266 9988 **Fax:** 0116-268 2557
E-mail: sales@seagas.net
Website: http://www.seagas.net
Directors: D. Heffernan (Dir)
Immediate Holding Company: SEAGAS INDUSTRIES LIMITED
Registration no: 01133222 **VAT No.:** GB 114 8082 87
Date established: 1973 **Turnover:** £2m - £5m **No.of Employees:** 1 - 10
Product Groups: 37

Date of Accounts	Dec 11	Dec 10	Dec 09
Working Capital	2m	2m	2m
Fixed Assets	9	10	13
Current Assets	2m	2m	2m

Securi Grille
Hollin Top Main Street, Illston, Leicester, LE7 9EG
Tel: 0116-259 9191 **Fax:** 0116-259 9191
E-mail: info@securi-grille.co.uk
Website: http://www.securi-grille.co.uk
Directors: J. Wetherill (Prop)
Immediate Holding Company: FOX & GOOSE (2010) LTD
Date established: 2010 **No.of Employees:** 1 - 10 **Product Groups:** 26, 35

Sequence Controls Ltd
Omni House Sheene Road, Leicester, LE4 1BF
Tel: 0116-299 8000 **Fax:** 0116-299 8001
E-mail: info@circuitcontroltechnology.com
Website: http://www.circuitcontroltechnology.com
Directors: K. Fisher (Dir)
Registration no: 02444011 **No.of Employees:** 11 - 20
Product Groups: 40, 67

Serjeants
25 The Crescent, Leicester, LE1 6RX
Tel: 0116-233 2626 **Fax:** 0116-233 0551
E-mail: mail@serjeants.co.uk
Website: http://www.serjeants.co.uk
Directors: I. Mckelvey (Snr Part)
Immediate Holding Company: SERJEANTS LLP
Registration no: OC371845 **VAT No.:** GB 339 4083 45
Date established: 2012 **Turnover:** £1m - £2m **No.of Employees:** 11 - 20
Product Groups: 80

Shenu Fashions
3 Western Road, Leicester, LE3 0GD
Tel: 0116-254 3440 **Fax:** 0116-247 0979
E-mail: info@shenugroup.co.uk
Website: http://www.shenugroup.co.uk
Directors: S. Sattar (MD)
Immediate Holding Company: SHENU ENTERPRISES LIMITED
Registration no: 02008070 **Date established:** 1986 **Turnover:** £2m - £5m
No.of Employees: 11 - 20 **Product Groups:** 24

Date of Accounts	Dec 11	Dec 10	Dec 09
Working Capital	1m	1m	1m
Fixed Assets	6	8	11
Current Assets	2m	2m	2m

shop4retail.com
The Manor, Main Street Tur Langton, Market Harborough, Leicester, LE8 0PJ
Tel: 0845-450 7966
E-mail: contact@shop4retail.com
Website: http://www.shop4retail.com
Date established: 2006 **No.of Employees:** 1 - 10 **Product Groups:** 30

Paul Sibary Hibberd
9 Six Acres Broughton Astley, Leicester, LE9 6PX
Tel: 01455-282177 **Fax:** 01455-285514
E-mail: paul.hibberd@btconnect.com
Directors: P. Hibberd (Prop)
Date established: 1983 **No.of Employees:** 1 - 10 **Product Groups:** 41

Silkjet Plastics Ltd
12-18 Lewisher Road, Leicester, LE4 9LR
Tel: 0116-276 2350 **Fax:** 0116-276 1152
E-mail: sales@silkjet.co.uk
Website: http://www.silkjet.co.uk
Bank(s): Co-Operative, Birmingham
Directors: M. Hayes (MD), R. Smith (Tech Serv), D. Seaby (Fin), D. Grove (Dir), G. Wells (MD), T. Middleton (Fin)
Managers: I. Humphries (Sales & Mktg Mg)
Immediate Holding Company: SILKJET PLASTICS LTD
Registration no: 04627716 **VAT No.:** GB 666 3201 43
Date established: 2003 **Turnover:** £1m - £2m **No.of Employees:** 51 - 100
Product Groups: 39, 40

Date of Accounts	Dec 08	Dec 07	Aug 10
Working Capital	-305	-135	-51
Fixed Assets	451	414	332
Current Assets	702	710	729

Smith Bros Stores Ltd
Batten Street Aylestone Road, Leicester, LE2 7PB
Tel: 0116-283 3511 **Fax:** 0116-244 0430
E-mail: sales@sbs.co.uk
Website: http://www.sbs.co.uk
Bank(s): National Westminster
Directors: J. Robertshaw (MD), D. Bryson (Fin)
Ultimate Holding Company: SMITH BROTHERS (LEICESTER) LIMITED
Immediate Holding Company: SMITH BROTHERS STORES LIMITED
Registration no: 00962846 **VAT No.:** GB 114 4051 21
Date established: 1969 **Turnover:** £20m - £50m
No.of Employees: 21 - 50 **Product Groups:** 36

Date of Accounts	Sep 11	Sep 10	Sep 09
Sales Turnover	37m	27m	19m
Pre Tax Profit/Loss	2m	1m	923
Working Capital	280	116	79
Fixed Assets	500	515	389
Current Assets	16m	14m	9m
Current Liabilities	3m	2m	920

E H Smith Builders Merchants Ltd
57 Mill Hill Enderby, Leicester, LE19 4AJ
Tel: 0116-275 0999 **Fax:** 0116-275 0135
E-mail: dave.keeling@ehsmith.co.uk
Website: http://www.ehsmith.co.uk
Bank(s): Barclays, Acocks Green, Birmingham
Managers: D. Keeling (District Mgr)
Ultimate Holding Company: E H SMITH HOLDINGS LTD
Immediate Holding Company: E H SMITH (BUILDERS MERCHANTS) LIMITED
Registration no: 00800907 **Date established:** 1964
Turnover: £10m - £20m **No.of Employees:** 21 - 50 **Product Groups:** 14, 51, 66

Date of Accounts	Jun 11	Jun 10	Jun 09
Sales Turnover	95m	80m	82m
Pre Tax Profit/Loss	218	-795	-2m
Working Capital	10m	9m	10m
Fixed Assets	9m	10m	10m
Current Assets	26m	21m	20m
Current Liabilities	1m	977	1m

Spectro Analytical UK Ltd
2 New Star Road, Leicester, LE4 9JD
Tel: 0116-246 2950 **Fax:** 0116-274 0160
E-mail: spectro-uk.sales@ametek.com
Website: http://www.spectro.com
Managers: S. Allott
Immediate Holding Company: SPECTRO ANALYTICAL UK LIMITED
Registration no: 01766726 **VAT No.:** GB 384 4071 47
Date established: 1983 **Turnover:** £1m - £2m **No.of Employees:** 1 - 10
Product Groups: 38

Date of Accounts	Dec 11	Dec 10	Dec 09
Sales Turnover	1m	1m	1m
Pre Tax Profit/Loss	220	124	-41
Working Capital	362	178	1
Fixed Assets	120	128	238
Current Assets	635	449	377
Current Liabilities	200	170	144

Springfield Pressings Ltd
378 Thurmaston Boulevard, Leicester, LE4 9LE
Tel: 0116-276 9953 **Fax:** 0116-276 2704
E-mail: sales@springfieldpressings.co.uk
Website: http://www.springfieldpressings.co.uk
Directors: T. Holt (MD)
Immediate Holding Company: SPRINGFIELD PRESSINGS LIMITED
Registration no: 01181130 **Date established:** 1974
Turnover: Up to £250,000 **No.of Employees:** 11 - 20 **Product Groups:** 34, 35, 36, 39, 48

Date of Accounts	Sep 11	Sep 10	Sep 09
Working Capital	105	27	-23
Fixed Assets	360	111	128
Current Assets	405	427	263

Sprint Lifting Equipment Ltd
16 Pinfold Road Thurmaston, Leicester, LE4 8AS
Tel: 0116-260 4100 **Fax:** 0116-260 4111
E-mail: sales@sprint-lifting.co.uk
Website: http://www.sprint-lifting.co.uk
Directors: D. Carey (Dir)
Immediate Holding Company: SPRINT LIFTING EQUIPMENT LIMITED
Registration no: 02774822 **Date established:** 1992
No.of Employees: 11 - 20 **Product Groups:** 35, 39, 45

Date of Accounts	Dec 11	Dec 10	Dec 09
Working Capital	484	375	303
Fixed Assets	349	374	354
Current Assets	786	778	553

Stephens Midlands Ltd
17 Herrick Close Enderby, Leicester, LE19 4RU
Tel: 0116-284 8621 **Fax:** 0116-286 4957
Website: http://www.stephenslube.co.uk
Managers: P. Cherry (Chief Mgr)
Immediate Holding Company: STEPHENS (MIDLANDS) LIMITED
Registration no: 02687911 **Date established:** 1992
No.of Employees: 1 - 10 **Product Groups:** 38, 42

K Stevens Leicester Ltd
Portishead Road, Leicester, LE5 0JL
Tel: 0116-276 6416 **Fax:** 0116-246 0570
E-mail: info@biasbinding.com
Website: http://www.biasbinding.com
Bank(s): Barclays Bank PLC
Directors: K. Stevens (Fin), R. Stevens (Dir)
Immediate Holding Company: K STEVENS (LEICESTER) LIMITED
Registration no: 03125088 **VAT No.:** GB 785 0739 94
Date established: 1995 **Turnover:** £1m - £2m **No.of Employees:** 11 - 20
Product Groups: 23

Date of Accounts	Dec 11	Dec 10	Dec 09
Working Capital	155	142	123
Fixed Assets	56	58	58
Current Assets	362	334	238

Stoney Cove Diver Training Centre Ltd
Sapcote Road Stoney Stanton, Leicester, LE9 4DW
Tel: 01455-273089 **Fax:** 01455-274000
Website: http://www.stoneycove.com

Directors: A. King (MD)
Managers: P. Bryan (Tech Serv Mgr), B. Foreman
Immediate Holding Company: G.T. TRAILERS LIMITED
Registration no: 05984826 **VAT No.:** GB 566 0753 27
Date established: 2006 **Turnover:** £1m - £2m **No.of Employees:** 21 - 50
Product Groups: 24, 40, 49, 51

Date of Accounts	Mar 11	Mar 10
Working Capital	-8	-15
Fixed Assets	N/A	5
Current Assets	N/A	4

Strategic Marketing Solutions
97 Newport Street, Leicester, LE3 9FU
Tel: 0116-242 5781
E-mail: paul@smsols.co.uk
Website: http://www.smsols.co.uk
Directors: P. McDermott (Prop)
Managers: P. McDermott (Accounts)
Date established: 2006 **No.of Employees:** 1 - 10 **Product Groups:** 22, 24, 30, 44, 49

Structural Precast Association
60 Charles Street, Leicester, LE1 1FB
Tel: 0116-253 6161 **Fax:** 0116-251 4568
E-mail: spa@britishprecast.org
Website: http://www.structural-precast-association.org.uk
Directors: C. Budge (Tech Serv), D. Zanker (Fin), M. Clarke (Grp Chief Exec)
Managers: A. Ladva (Public Relation)
Turnover: Up to £250,000 **No.of Employees:** 1 - 10 **Product Groups:** 87

Sub Zero Technology Ltd
Unit 35 Churchill Way Fleckney, Leicester, LE8 8UD
Tel: 0116-240 2634 **Fax:** 0116-240 4099
E-mail: sales@subzero.co.uk
Website: http://www.subzero.co.uk
Directors: D. Laxton (Dir)
Registration no: 01297686 **Date established:** 1977 **Turnover:** £1m - £2m
No.of Employees: 1 - 10 **Product Groups:** 24

Date of Accounts	Mar 10	Mar 09	Mar 08
Working Capital	219	-17	-38
Fixed Assets	56	34	40
Current Assets	219	153	222

Summit Engineering Co.
Wharf Way Glen Parva, Leicester, LE2 9TF
Tel: 0116-277 1083 **Fax:** 0116-277 3518
E-mail: summit@webleicester.co.uk
Website: http://www.summitgroup.co.uk
Bank(s): Natwest
Directors: G. Frankham (Ch), M. Frankham (Dir)
Managers: G. Bond (I.T. Exec), R. McVey (Comm)
Immediate Holding Company: Frankham Bros Ltd
Registration no: 03053803 **VAT No.:** GB 566 0323 52
Date established: 1962 **Turnover:** £2m - £5m
No.of Employees: 101 - 250 **Product Groups:** 48

Super Turn UK Ltd
6 Clipper Road Troon Industrial Area, Leicester, LE4 9JE
Tel: 0116-246 0118 **Fax:** 0870-851 8826
E-mail: s.hanif@superturn.co.uk
Website: http://www.superturn.co.uk
Directors: S. Hanif (Prop), S. Henif (Dir)
Managers: K. Parlmer (Sales Prom Mgr)
Immediate Holding Company: SUPER TURN UK LIMITED
Registration no: 04492225 **Date established:** 2002
No.of Employees: 1 - 10 **Product Groups:** 35, 48

Date of Accounts	Sep 10	Sep 09	Sep 08
Working Capital	11	18	20
Fixed Assets	151	120	126
Current Assets	221	138	168

Supply Point Systems Ltd
Units 3 & 4 Churchill Way Fleckney, Leicester, LE8 8UD
Tel: 0844-5761247 **Fax:** 0844-5761248
E-mail: info@supplypointsystems.com
Website: http://www.supplypointsystems.com
Directors: S. Guppy (Co Sec)
Registration no: 03495308 **Date established:** 1998
No.of Employees: 1 - 10 **Product Groups:** 38, 42

Date of Accounts	Aug 07	Aug 06
Working Capital	1747	1411
Fixed Assets	645	617
Current Assets	2683	2420
Current Liabilities	936	1009
Total Share Capital	100	100

Systemair Fans & Spares Ltd
Unit 10 The Beaver Centre Putney Road West, Leicester, LE2 7TD
Tel: 0116-254 9898 **Fax:** 0116-247 0590
E-mail: leicester@fansandspares.co.uk
Website: http://www.fansandspares.co.uk
Managers: M. Knox (District Mgr)
Ultimate Holding Company: SYSTEMAIR AB (SWEDEN)
Immediate Holding Company: SYSTEMAIR FANS & SPARES LTD
Registration no: 04997065 **VAT No.:** GB 300 0687 11
Date established: 2003 **Turnover:** £1m - £2m **No.of Employees:** 1 - 10
Product Groups: 39, 40, 48, 52

Date of Accounts	Apr 12	Apr 11	Apr 10
Sales Turnover	16m	14m	9m
Pre Tax Profit/Loss	763	-2m	-41
Working Capital	2m	1m	845
Fixed Assets	893	970	921
Current Assets	6m	6m	3m
Current Liabilities	619	665	273

Syston Rolling Shutters Ltd
33 Albert Street Syston, Leicester, LE7 2JB
Tel: 0116-260 8841 **Fax:** 0116-264 0846
E-mail: sales@syston.com
Website: http://www.syston.com
Directors: J. Gunn (Dir)
Managers: A. Cook (Mgr)
Immediate Holding Company: SYSTON ROLLING SHUTTERS LIMITED
Registration no: 02240153 **Date established:** 1988
No.of Employees: 11 - 20 **Product Groups:** 26, 35

Date of Accounts	Dec 11	Dec 10	Dec 09
Working Capital	632	583	652
Fixed Assets	727	763	751
Current Assets	1m	1m	1m

Sytner Group Ltd
2 Penman Way Enderby, Leicester, LE19 1ST
Tel: 0116-282 1000 **Fax:** 0116-282 1010
E-mail: info@sytner.co.uk
Website: http://www.sytner.co.uk
Directors: G. Nieuwenhuys (MD)
Ultimate Holding Company: PENSKE AUTOMOTIVE GROUP INC (USA)
Immediate Holding Company: SYTNER GROUP LIMITED
Registration no: 02883766 **Date established:** 1993
Turnover: Over £1,000m **No.of Employees:** 51 - 100 **Product Groups:** 68

Date of Accounts	Dec 11	Dec 10	Dec 09
Sales Turnover	2659m	2399m	2175m
Pre Tax Profit/Loss	49m	52m	45m
Working Capital	-76m	-98m	-67m
Fixed Assets	292m	281m	287m
Current Assets	476m	388m	379m
Current Liabilities	287m	206m	191m

T M Machinery Sales Ltd
49 Iliffe Avenue Oadby, Leicester, LE2 5LH
Tel: 0116-271 7155 **Fax:** 0116-271 5862
E-mail: matt@tmservices.co.uk
Website: http://www.tmpartnership.co.uk
Bank(s): Barclays
Directors: M. Pearce (Dir), A. Morris (MD), C. Dexter (Dir)
Registration no: 01867584 **VAT No.:** GB 399 8492 63
Date established: 1996 **Turnover:** £1m - £2m **No.of Employees:** 11 - 20
Product Groups: 36, 37, 40, 42, 47, 48, 67

Date of Accounts	Jan 10	Jan 09	Jan 08
Working Capital	623	658	578
Fixed Assets	4	5	7
Current Assets	655	841	774

Taskmaster Ltd
Morris Road, Leicester, LE2 6BR
Tel: 0116-270 4286 **Fax:** 0116-270 6992
E-mail: info@taskmasteronline.co.uk
Website: http://www.taskmasteronline.co.uk
Directors: T. Chell (MD)
Immediate Holding Company: TASKMASTER LIMITED
Registration no: 00454017 **VAT No.:** GB 114 2923 00
Date established: 1948 **Turnover:** £1m - £2m **No.of Employees:** 1 - 10
Product Groups: 28, 64

Date of Accounts	Dec 08	Dec 07	Jun 11
Working Capital	683	649	531
Fixed Assets	53	89	8
Current Assets	906	875	801

Taylor Hobson Ltd (Head Office)
2 New Star Road, Leicester, LE4 9JD
Tel: 0116-276 3771 **Fax:** 0116-274 1350
E-mail: kathy.sena@ametek.com
Website: http://www.taylor-hobson.com
Bank(s): National Westminster Bank Plc
Directors: K. Sena (Co Sec), D. Chilton (Fin), C. Howarth (MD), N. Curtis (Sales)
Managers: I. Lee-bennett (Mktg Serv Mgr), G. Raby (Personnel), S. Males (Purch Mgr), S. Packwood (Tech Serv Mgr)
Ultimate Holding Company: AMETEK INC (USA)
Immediate Holding Company: TAYLOR HOBSON HOLDINGS LIMITED
Registration no: 03230257 **Date established:** 1996
Turnover: £20m - £50m **No.of Employees:** 101 - 250
Product Groups: 38, 85

Date of Accounts	Dec 11	Dec 10	Dec 09
Pre Tax Profit/Loss	252	253	1m
Working Capital	22m	22m	22m
Fixed Assets	5m	5m	5m
Current Assets	22m	22m	22m
Current Liabilities	85	70	3

The Alexandra Stone Co.
Kirby Muxloe, Leicester, LE9 2BR
Tel: 0116-239 2513 **Fax:** 0116-239 3993
E-mail: collins@castacrete.co.uk
Website: http://www.castacrete.co.uk
Managers: H. Collins (Mgr)
Ultimate Holding Company: CASTACRETE LIMITED
Immediate Holding Company: THE ALEXANDRA STONE COMPANY LIMITED
Registration no: 00126382 **Date established:** 2013 **Turnover:** £2m - £5m
No.of Employees: 21 - 50 **Product Groups:** 33

Date of Accounts	Dec 10	Dec 09	Dec 08
Sales Turnover	N/A	N/A	4m
Pre Tax Profit/Loss	N/A	N/A	166
Working Capital	26	26	39
Fixed Assets	N/A	N/A	2m
Current Assets	26	26	39

Thermal Exchange Ltd
Chiswick Road Freemens Common, Leicester, LE2 7SX
Tel: 0116-254 6652 **Fax:** 0116-255 9176
E-mail: sales@thermalexchange.co.uk
Website: http://www.thermalexchange.co.uk
Directors: C. Walker (Sales)
Immediate Holding Company: THERMAL EXCHANGE LIMITED
Registration no: 02619819 **VAT No.:** GB 399 7918 60
Date established: 1991 **No.of Employees:** 11 - 20 **Product Groups:** 38, 40, 41, 42, 44, 46, 52

Date of Accounts	Jun 12	Jun 11	Jun 10
Working Capital	100	-0	-21
Fixed Assets	61	36	21
Current Assets	395	296	279

Thermograve Ltd
171 Scudamore Road, Leicester, LE3 1UQ
Tel: 0116-291 9000 **Fax:** 0116-291 9001
E-mail: enquiries@thermograve.co.uk
Website: http://www.thermograve.co.uk
Directors: H. Moscetano (Co Sec), A. Gilmartin (MD)
Ultimate Holding Company: GILMARTIN HOLDINGS LIMITED
Immediate Holding Company: THERMOGRAVE LIMITED
Registration no: 01280983 **VAT No.:** GB 115 8793 48
Date established: 1976 **Turnover:** £1m - £2m **No.of Employees:** 21 - 50
Product Groups: 49

Date of Accounts	Mar 12	Mar 11	Mar 10
Sales Turnover	N/A	2m	N/A
Pre Tax Profit/Loss	N/A	220	N/A
Working Capital	547	392	339
Fixed Assets	160	123	114
Current Assets	1m	616	600
Current Liabilities	N/A	210	N/A

Albert Thurston Ltd
3 Frog Island, Leicester, LE3 5AG
Tel: 0116-262 7515 **Fax:** 0116-251 3607
E-mail: sales@albertthurston.com
Website: http://www.albertthurston.com
Bank(s): HSBC Bank plc
Directors: B. Panahy (Dir)
Immediate Holding Company: ALBERT THURSTON LIMITED
Registration no: 00271221 **Date established:** 1932
Turnover: £500,000 - £1m **No.of Employees:** 11 - 20
Product Groups: 24, 38

Date of Accounts	Feb 12	Feb 11	Feb 10
Working Capital	376	360	332
Current Assets	463	444	430

Tiernan Automation Ltd
308a Melton Road, Leicester, LE4 7SL
Tel: 0116-266 4000 **Fax:** 0116-261 0090
E-mail: david@t-automation.fsnet.co.uk
Website: http://www.tiernanautomation.co.uk
Bank(s): Lloyds
Directors: J. Tiernan (Co Sec), D. Tiernan (Dir)
Managers: M. Reid
Immediate Holding Company: TIERNAN AUTOMATION LIMITED
Registration no: 01896993 **VAT No.:** GB 424 3287 63
Date established: 1985 **Turnover:** £250,000 - £500,000
No.of Employees: 21 - 50 **Product Groups:** 48

Date of Accounts	Jun 11	Jun 10	Jun 09
Working Capital	63	-9	72
Fixed Assets	736	532	309
Current Assets	890	563	296

Timber Team Machinery Ltd
The Knoll Leicester Road, Earl Shilton, Leicester, LE9 7TJ
Tel: 01455-846888 **Fax:** 01455-848808
E-mail: sales@timber-team.com
Website: http://www.timber-team.com
Directors: D. Watts (MD)
Immediate Holding Company: TIMBER TEAM (MACHINERY) LIMITED
Registration no: 03239496 **Date established:** 1996
No.of Employees: 1 - 10 **Product Groups:** 46

Date of Accounts	Aug 11	Aug 10	Aug 09
Working Capital	55	17	13
Fixed Assets	1	2	2
Current Assets	55	54	44

Timberwise UK Ltd
1 Norman Road Thurmaston, Leicester, LE4 8EL
Tel: 0800-991100 **Fax:** 0116-269 3678
E-mail: leics@timberwise.co.uk
Website: http://www.timberwise.co.uk
Managers: A. Manson (District Mgr)
Immediate Holding Company: TIMBERWISE (UK) LIMITED
Registration no: 03230356 **Date established:** 1996
No.of Employees: 1 - 10 **Product Groups:** 07, 32, 52

Topps Tiles UK Ltd
Barnsdale Way Enderby, Leicester, LE19 1SU
Tel: 0116-289 4577 **Fax:** 0116-282 8100
E-mail: enquiries@toppstiles.co.uk
Website: http://www.toppstiles.co.uk
Managers: M. Ban-Sittert
Ultimate Holding Company: TOPPS TILES PLC
Immediate Holding Company: TOPPS TILES (UK) LIMITED
Registration no: 04781209 **Date established:** 2003
Turnover: £10m - £20m **No.of Employees:** 1 - 10 **Product Groups:** 33

Date of Accounts	Sep 08	Sep 09	Oct 10
Sales Turnover	175m	159m	165m
Pre Tax Profit/Loss	16m	11m	8m
Working Capital	39m	63m	66m
Fixed Assets	151m	140m	131m
Current Assets	182m	115m	104m
Current Liabilities	7m	10m	11m

Torclad Ltd
Rose Park Lutterworth Road, Blaby, Leicester, LE8 4DP
Tel: 0116-277 9577 **Fax:** 0116- 2779804
E-mail: adam@torclad.com
Website: http://www.torclad.com
Bank(s): Alied Irish Bank P.L.C.
Directors: A. Johnson (MD), K. Smith (MD), J. Smith (Co Sec)
Managers: D. Wardrop (Sales Prom), I. Smith (Sales & Mktg Mg)
Immediate Holding Company: TORCLAD LIMITED
Registration no: 01443274 **Date established:** 1979 **Turnover:** £5m - £10m
No.of Employees: 51 - 100 **Product Groups:** 30

Date of Accounts	Oct 10	Oct 09	Oct 08
Sales Turnover	9m	9m	9m
Pre Tax Profit/Loss	196	450	769
Working Capital	1m	945	971
Fixed Assets	541	533	553
Current Assets	4m	4m	4m
Current Liabilities	213	301	434

Total Butler Ltd
Winston Avenue Croft, Leicester, LE9 3GQ
Tel: 01455-282180 **Fax:** 01455-285530
E-mail: croft.depot@totalbutler.co.uk
Website: http://www.totalbutler.co.uk
Bank(s): Barclays
Managers: K. Manship (District Mgr)
Immediate Holding Company: TOTAL BUTLER LIMITED
Registration no: 01162536 **VAT No.:** GB 232 6481 73
Date established: 1974 **Turnover:** £20m - £50m
No.of Employees: 11 - 20 **Product Groups:** 31

Toyota Material Handling UK Ltd
Meridian West Meridian Business Park, Leicester, LE19 1WX
Tel: 0116-289 4411 **Fax:** 0116-282 7002
E-mail: we.deliver@uk.toyota-industries.eu
Website: http://www.toyota-forklifts.co.uk
Managers: D. New
Ultimate Holding Company: TOYOTA INDUSTRIES CORP (JAPAN)
Immediate Holding Company: TOYOTA MATERIAL HANDLING UK LIMITED
Registration no: 00699993 **Date established:** 1961
No.of Employees: 1 - 10 **Product Groups:** 45, 67

Date of Accounts	Mar 11	Mar 10	Mar 09
Sales Turnover	147m	131m	157m
Pre Tax Profit/Loss	13m	11m	6m
Working Capital	18m	7m	-359
Fixed Assets	43m	44m	47m
Current Assets	66m	50m	54m
Current Liabilities	21m	19m	26m

Trace Machining Ltd
Unit 4-5 Thurmaston Village Court 651 Melton Road, Thurmaston, Leicester, LE4 8EB
Tel: 0116-269 7992 **Fax:** 0116-269 7993
Directors: D. Sharpe (Dir)
Immediate Holding Company: TRACE MACHINING LIMITED
Registration no: 07122998 **Date established:** 2010
No.of Employees: 1 - 10 **Product Groups:** 35

Date of Accounts	Mar 12	Mar 11
Working Capital	-218	-241
Fixed Assets	463	496
Current Assets	58	57

Transfra Graphics Ltd
Unit 13-14 Abbey Court Wallingford Road, Leicester, LE4 5RD
Tel: 0116-234 0440 **Fax:** 0116-235 1881
E-mail: sales@transfragraphics.com
Website: http://www.transfragraphics.com
Directors: G. Baker (Dir)
Immediate Holding Company: BKH ENTERPRISES LIMITED
Registration no: 02022492 **VAT No.:** GB 424 6411 73
Date established: 1986 **Turnover:** £500,000 - £1m
No.of Employees: 1 - 10 **Product Groups:** 23

Date of Accounts	Jul 11	Sep 10	Sep 09
Working Capital	142	25	45
Fixed Assets	N/A	52	43
Current Assets	218	88	92

Transmon Engineering Ltd
2a The Half Croft Syston, Leicester, LE7 1LD
Tel: 0116-260 4200 **Fax:** 0116-264 1964
E-mail: info@transmon.co.uk
Website: http://www.transmon.co.uk
Directors: S. Coley (MD), E. Middleton (Fin)
Immediate Holding Company: TRANSMON ENGINEERING LIMITED
Registration no: 04216742 **Date established:** 2001
No.of Employees: 1 - 10 **Product Groups:** 35, 39, 45

Date of Accounts	Dec 11	Dec 10	Dec 09
Working Capital	632	539	467
Fixed Assets	20	29	39
Current Assets	742	621	568

Trelleborg Industrial A V S Ltd
1 Hoods Close, Leicester, LE4 2BN
Tel: 0116-267 0300 **Fax:** 0116-267 0301
E-mail: ron.smith@trelleborg.com
Website: http://www.trelleborg.com
Bank(s): SEB
Directors: I. Dew (Fin), C. Billinge (Sales & Mktg), A. Pahtinen (Dir)
Managers: D. Burlingham (Purch Mgr), D. Howart (Tech Serv Mgr), C. Bbradshaw (Personnel)
Registration no: 00995293 **Turnover:** £20m - £50m
No.of Employees: 101 - 250 **Product Groups:** 25, 29, 35, 36, 37, 38, 39, 40, 41, 46, 49, 84

Trifibre Ltd (t/a Smith Sample Cases Ltd)
17 Boston Road, Leicester, LE4 1AW
Tel: 0116-232 3166 **Fax:** 01473-811873
E-mail: info@trifibre.co.uk
Website: http://www.trifibre.co.uk
Bank(s): HSBC Bank plc
Managers: S. Roberts (Sales Prom Mgr)
Ultimate Holding Company: TRIFIBRE GROUP LIMITED
Immediate Holding Company: TRIFIBRE LIMITED
Registration no: 01890698 **Date established:** 1985
No.of Employees: 21 - 50 **Product Groups:** 22, 25, 30, 35, 38, 49, 66, 76

Date of Accounts	Mar 12	Mar 11	Mar 10
Working Capital	74	-45	-56
Fixed Assets	547	490	462
Current Assets	2m	1m	1m

Turbine Controls Ltd
52 Kenilworth Drive Oadby, Leicester, LE2 5LG
Tel: 0116-271 7248 **Fax:** 0116-271 7248
E-mail: chrisr@tcluk.net
Website: http://www.turbinecontrolsltd.com
Directors: C. Rees (Sales)
Managers: R. Dhiman
Immediate Holding Company: TURBINE CONTROLS LIMITED
Registration no: 01947922 **Date established:** 1985 **Turnover:** £1m - £2m
No.of Employees: 21 - 50 **Product Groups:** 37, 38, 40, 44, 48

Date of Accounts	Aug 11	Aug 10	Aug 09
Working Capital	127	110	-80
Fixed Assets	65	58	84
Current Assets	894	800	820

UK Distributors Footwear Ltd
Churchill Way Fleckney, Leicester, LE8 8UD
Tel: 0116-403232 **Fax:** 0116-240 2762
E-mail: derek@ukdistributors.co.uk
Website: http://www.ukdistributors.co.uk
Directors: D. Marlow (Fin), J. Marlow (MD), P. Hill (Export)
Managers: B. Holders (Accounts)
Immediate Holding Company: UK DISTRIBUTORS (FOOTWEAR) LIMITED
Registration no: 04120969 **VAT No.:** GB 114 1165 21
Date established: 2000 **Turnover:** £10m - £20m
No.of Employees: 51 - 100 **Product Groups:** 63

Date of Accounts	Apr 09	Apr 08	Apr 07
Sales Turnover	14m	N/A	N/A
Pre Tax Profit/Loss	1m	1m	1m
Working Capital	11m	11m	10m
Fixed Assets	2m	2m	2m
Current Assets	14m	13m	12m
Current Liabilities	2m	697	709

UK Internet Marketing
39 Wigston Road Oadby, Leicester, LE2 5QF
Tel: 0116-221 5615
E-mail: bobash@ntlworld.com
Website: http://www.ukinternet-marketing.co.uk

Directors: R. Ashford (Prop)
No.of Employees: 1 - 10 **Product Groups:** 37, 38, 40, 80

Ultra Sealed Windows Ltd
Combine House 7 Woodboy Street, Leicester, LE1 3NJ
Tel: 0116-262 8208 **Fax:** 0116-233 3900
Directors: J. Chudasama (Dir)
Immediate Holding Company: ULTRA SHIELD WINDOWS LIMITED
Registration no: 04028606 **Date established:** 2000
No.of Employees: 1 - 10 **Product Groups:** 30, 48

Date of Accounts	Jul 11	Jul 10	Jul 09
Working Capital	-7	-10	-14
Fixed Assets	8	11	14
Current Assets	81	75	87

Unique Window Systems Ltd
87 Parker Drive, Leicester, LE4 0JP
Tel: 0116-236 4656 **Fax:** 0116-236 4237
E-mail: sales@uniquewindowsystems.com
Website: http://www.uniquewindowsystems.com
Directors: A. Patel (MD), S. Patel (Fin)
Managers: R. Patel (Personnel)
Immediate Holding Company: UNIQUE WINDOW SYSTEMS LTD
Registration no: 05060094 **Date established:** 2004 **Turnover:** £5m - £10m
No.of Employees: 51 - 100 **Product Groups:** 35, 36

Date of Accounts	Sep 09	Sep 08	Apr 11
Sales Turnover	5m	N/A	6m
Pre Tax Profit/Loss	-498	138	10
Working Capital	-57	120	354
Fixed Assets	635	710	225
Current Assets	2m	2m	2m
Current Liabilities	439	287	405

Universal Flexible Packaging Ltd
61 Lunsford Road, Leicester, LE5 0HJ
Tel: 0116-276 9992 **Fax:** 0116-276 9631
E-mail: admin@uniflex.co.uk
Website: http://www.uniflex.co.uk
Directors: A. Durrani (Dir)
Managers: A. Rossell (Personnel), J. Palmer (Comptroller)
Ultimate Holding Company: UNIVERSAL DEVELOPMENTS (LEICESTER) LIMITED
Immediate Holding Company: UNIVERSAL FLEXIBLE PACKAGING LIMITED
Registration no: 03092987 **Date established:** 1995
Turnover: £10m - £20m **No.of Employees:** 51 - 100 **Product Groups:** 28, 30

Date of Accounts	Dec 11	Dec 10	Dec 09
Sales Turnover	11m	8m	7m
Pre Tax Profit/Loss	225	337	288
Working Capital	15	195	342
Fixed Assets	2m	2m	1m
Current Assets	4m	4m	4m
Current Liabilities	1m	1m	2m

Universal Instrument Services Ltd
Unit 69 Cambridge Road, Whetstone, Leicester, LE8 6PA
Tel: 0116-275 0123 **Fax:** 0116-275 0262
E-mail: sales@uiscal.co.uk
Website: http://www.uiscal.co.uk
Directors: D. Homewood (MD), M. Chester (Ch), H. Horn (Sales), S. Homewood (Dir), S. Sykes (Dir)
Ultimate Holding Company: TRISTRAM HOLDINGS LIMITED
Immediate Holding Company: UNIVERSAL INSTRUMENT SERVICES LIMITED
Registration no: 01554448 **VAT No.:** GB 355 2894 28
Date established: 1981 **No.of Employees:** 1 - 10 **Product Groups:** 38, 67, 85

Date of Accounts	Sep 11	Sep 10	Sep 09
Working Capital	565	374	258
Fixed Assets	144	151	243
Current Assets	898	733	450

Unsworth Sugden Advertising Ltd
De Montfort House 19b De Montfort Street, Leicester, LE1 7GE
Tel: 0116-247 1777 **Fax:** 0116-254 1222
E-mail: info@unsworthsugden.co.uk
Website: http://www.unsworthsugden.co.uk
Directors: D. Watts (Dir)
Managers: S. Sugden
Immediate Holding Company: UNSWORTH SUGDEN ADVERTISING LIMITED
Registration no: 02601076 **Date established:** 1991
No.of Employees: 11 - 20 **Product Groups:** 44, 81

Date of Accounts	Mar 12	Mar 11	Mar 10
Working Capital	-83	-81	-3
Fixed Assets	447	454	470
Current Assets	510	349	418

Velan Valves Ltd
Unit 1 Lakeside Business Park Thurmaston, Leicester, LE4 8AS
Tel: 0116-269 5172 **Fax:** 0116-269 3695
E-mail: sales@velan.co.uk
Website: http://www.velan.com
Managers: L. Vincent, B. Sunnar (Purch Mgr)
Ultimate Holding Company: VELAN INC (CANADA)
Immediate Holding Company: VELAN VALVES LIMITED
Registration no: 00537156 **Date established:** 1954 **Turnover:** £5m - £10m
No.of Employees: 21 - 50 **Product Groups:** 36, 37, 38

Date of Accounts	Feb 12	Feb 11	Feb 10
Sales Turnover	5m	8m	18m
Pre Tax Profit/Loss	4m	-1m	1m
Working Capital	8m	7m	8m
Fixed Assets	5m	5m	5m
Current Assets	9m	8m	11m
Current Liabilities	310	410	1m

Verivide Ltd
Quartz Close Enderby, Leicester, LE19 4SG
Tel: 0116-284 7790 **Fax:** 0116-284 7799
E-mail: p.dakin@verivide.com
Website: http://www.verivide.com
Bank(s): National Westminster Bank Plc
Directors: P. Dakin (Dir)
Immediate Holding Company: VERIVIDE LIMITED
Registration no: 00827815 **VAT No.:** GB 114 1191 20
Date established: 1964 **Turnover:** £1m - £2m **No.of Employees:** 11 - 20
Product Groups: 38

Date of Accounts	Nov 11	Nov 10	Nov 09
Working Capital	162	118	-2
Fixed Assets	245	256	273
Current Assets	787	820	635

Vibration Isolation Products Ltd
51 Nursery Road, Leicester, LE5 2HQ
Tel: 0116-241 8604 **Fax:** 0116-243 3396
E-mail: sales@vibrationisolationproducts.co.uk
Website: http://www.vibrationisolationproducts.co.uk
Directors: R. Goodman (Fin), P. Goodman (MD)
Immediate Holding Company: VIBRATION ISOLATION PRODUCTS LTD
Registration no: 04591159 **Date established:** 2002
Turnover: £500,000 - £1m **No.of Employees:** 1 - 10 **Product Groups:** 23, 29

Date of Accounts	Mar 12	Mar 11	Mar 09
Working Capital	33	24	19
Fixed Assets	1	1	2
Current Assets	72	63	41

Vinola Knitwear
191 Ross Walk, Leicester, LE4 5HH
Tel: 0116-268 1461 **Fax:** 0116-266 5280
Website: http://www.vinola.co.uk
Directors: C. Chawla (Dir), J. Chawla (MD), S. Chawla (Dir)
Immediate Holding Company: VINOLA (KNITWEAR) MANUFACTURING CO. LIMITED
Registration no: 02035613 **Date established:** 1986 **Turnover:** £2m - £5m
No.of Employees: 21 - 50 **Product Groups:** 63

Date of Accounts	Aug 11	Aug 10	Aug 09
Sales Turnover	N/A	2m	2m
Pre Tax Profit/Loss	N/A	-109	-140
Working Capital	137	142	239
Fixed Assets	315	308	320
Current Assets	3m	2m	1m
Current Liabilities	N/A	995	662

Vulcan Fire Safety Ltd
3 Court Road Glen Parva, Leicester, LE2 9JB
Tel: 0116-222 0870 **Fax:** 0116-222 0870
E-mail: info@vulcanfiresafety.com
Website: http://www.vulcanfiresafety.com
Directors: C. McMahon (MD), M. Weston (Fin)
Immediate Holding Company: VULCAN FIRE SAFETY LTD
Registration no: 05037108 **Date established:** 2004
No.of Employees: 1 - 10 **Product Groups:** 38, 42

Date of Accounts	Feb 08	Feb 11	Feb 09
Working Capital	31	-0	2
Fixed Assets	3	N/A	2
Current Assets	64	26	25

W R Refrigeration
1 Heanor Street, Leicester, LE1 4DB
Tel: 0116-251 2700 **Fax:** 0116-251 2800
Managers: S. Gibbons (Mgr)
Ultimate Holding Company: Huurre Group Oy (Finland)
Immediate Holding Company: WR Group Holdings Ltd
Registration no: 00594746 **Date established:** 1957
Turnover: £50m - £75m **No.of Employees:** 1 - 10 **Product Groups:** 40, 66

Watling J C B Ltd
Dog & Gun Lane Whetstone, Leicester, LE8 6LJ
Tel: 0116-286 3621 **Fax:** 0116-286 3171
E-mail: sales.info@watling.co.uk
Website: http://www.watling.co.uk
Bank(s): Royal Bank of Scotland
Directors: J. King (Fin), R. Telfer (MD)
Managers: G. Cox, M. Goodwin
Ultimate Holding Company: HAJCO 199 LIMITED
Immediate Holding Company: WATLING JCB LIMITED
Registration no: 01245540 **Date established:** 1976
Turnover: £75m - £125m **No.of Employees:** 101 - 250
Product Groups: 41, 45, 48

Date of Accounts	Dec 11	Dec 10	Dec 09
Sales Turnover	85m	59m	42m
Pre Tax Profit/Loss	2m	1m	531
Working Capital	4m	3m	3m
Fixed Assets	2m	2m	1m
Current Assets	16m	12m	9m
Current Liabilities	3m	3m	2m

Weighing Technology Services Ltd
Unit 16b Iliffe House 12 Iliffe Avenue, Oadby, Leicester, LE2 5LS
Tel: 0116-271 3228 **Fax:** 0116-271 3229
E-mail: richard.fahey@wts-ltd.co.uk
Website: http://www.wts-ltd.co.uk
Directors: C. Adams (Fin), C. Casey (Dir)
Immediate Holding Company: WEIGHING TECHNOLOGY SERVICES LIMITED
Registration no: 02812436 **Date established:** 1993
Turnover: £250,000 - £500,000 **No.of Employees:** 1 - 10
Product Groups: 38, 42

Date of Accounts	Mar 11	Mar 10	Mar 07
Working Capital	37	33	8
Fixed Assets	11	15	5
Current Assets	95	88	52

Welland By Drive
22 Cannock Street, Leicester, LE4 9HR
Tel: 0116-276 1440 **Fax:** 0116-276 4449
E-mail: t.beaumont@wellandmedical-leicester.co.uk
Website: http://www.wellandmedical-leicester.co.uk
Directors: T. Beaumont (MD)
Managers: M. Wayne (Comptroller)
No.of Employees: 21 - 50 **Product Groups:** 38, 67

Welland Machinery Sales Ltd
Court Cottage Court Road, Thurnby, Leicester, LE7 9PA
Tel: 0116-243 3113 **Fax:** 0116-241 2023
E-mail: wellmac@webleicester.co.uk
Website: http://www.wellandmachinery.co.uk
Directors: P. Gregory (MD), S. Gregory (Fin)
Immediate Holding Company: WELLAND MACHINERY SALES LIMITED
Registration no: 04517194 **Date established:** 2002
No.of Employees: 1 - 10 **Product Groups:** 46

Date of Accounts	Mar 11	Mar 10	Mar 08
Working Capital	76	50	27
Fixed Assets	1	N/A	N/A
Current Assets	106	76	73

John Wigfull & Co. Ltd
First Hangings Blaby Road, Enderby, Leicester, LE19 4AQ
Tel: 0116-286 2287 **Fax:** 0116-275 1232
E-mail: wigfull@btinternet.com
Website: http://www.johnwigfull.co.uk
Directors: T. Wigfull (Dir)
Immediate Holding Company: JOHN WIGFULL & CO.LIMITED
Registration no: 00729474 **VAT No.:** GB 114 2583 95
Date established: 1962 **Turnover:** £250,000 - £500,000
No.of Employees: 1 - 10 **Product Groups:** 42, 52, 85

Date of Accounts	Mar 12	Mar 11	Mar 10
Working Capital	9	2	-3
Fixed Assets	43	52	34
Current Assets	164	173	211

Willprints Ltd
7 Pomeroy Drive Oadby, Leicester, LE2 5NE
Tel: 0116-271 0574 **Fax:** 0116-271 0550
E-mail: sales@willprints.co.uk
Website: http://www.willprints.co.uk
Directors: J. Wills (Dir)
Immediate Holding Company: WILLPRINTS LIMITED
Registration no: 04890210 **VAT No.:** GB 339 5375 27
Date established: 2003 **No.of Employees:** 1 - 10 **Product Groups:** 28, 40

Date of Accounts	Oct 11	Oct 10	Oct 09
Working Capital	55	44	25
Fixed Assets	56	70	85
Current Assets	129	115	88

Windowfix
73 Grange Drive Glen Parva, Leicester, LE2 9PH
Tel: 0116-223 0483 **Fax:** 0116-223 0403
E-mail: info@windowfixers.co.uk
Website: http://www.windowfixers.co.uk
Managers: J. Clarke (Admin Off)
No.of Employees: 1 - 10 **Product Groups:** 30, 35, 52, 66

Winterton Leisurewear Ltd
Regent Road Countesthorpe, Leicester, LE8 5RF
Tel: 0116-277 9789 **Fax:** 0116-278 4395
E-mail: david@magicfit.co.uk
Website: http://www.magicfit.co.uk
Directors: D. Winterton (MD), D. Winterton (Prop), E. Winterton (Dir)
Managers: C. Dunn (Ops Mgr), T. Hurd (Accounts), S. Walton (Admin Off)
Immediate Holding Company: LEICESTER G.B. TOOLS LIMITED
Registration no: 04594605 **VAT No.:** GB 371 7995 07
Date established: 1983 **Turnover:** £250,000 - £500,000
No.of Employees: 1 - 10 **Product Groups:** 24

Wykes International Ltd
434-442 Thurmaston Boulevard, Leicester, LE4 9LD
Tel: 0116-276 8282 **Fax:** 0116-274 2506
E-mail: sales@wykes.co.uk
Website: http://www.wykes.co.uk
Bank(s): National Westminster
Managers: M. Mellor (Mgr)
Immediate Holding Company: WYKES INTERNATIONAL LIMITED
Registration no: 04108663 **VAT No.:** GB 113 9216 93
Date established: 2000 **No.of Employees:** 21 - 50 **Product Groups:** 23

Date of Accounts	Dec 11	Dec 10	Dec 09
Working Capital	358	-108	-205
Fixed Assets	196	244	295
Current Assets	760	1m	900

Zipex UK Ltd
15 Abbey Gate, Leicester, LE4 0AA
Tel: 0116-262 4988 **Fax:** 0116-251 3745
E-mail: sales@zipex.co.uk
Website: http://www.zipex.co.uk
Directors: D. Zeitouni (Dir)
Immediate Holding Company: ZIPEX (U.K.) LIMITED
Registration no: 02029998 **Date established:** 1986
No.of Employees: 11 - 20 **Product Groups:** 30

Date of Accounts	Jun 11	Jun 10	Jun 08
Working Capital	64	33	83
Fixed Assets	339	350	373
Current Assets	321	269	248

Loughborough

3 M Healthcare Ltd
3 M House 1 Morley Street, Loughborough, LE11 1EP
Tel: 01509-611611 **Fax:** 01509-613253
E-mail: jsmith123@mmm.com
Website: http://www.3m.com
Bank(s): Lloyds TSB Bank plc
Managers: M. Boxley, M. Dawson (Chief Mgr), S. Doughty (Sales & Mktg Mg), T. Fletcher (Personnel), R. Smith (Commun Mgr), M. Ellison
Ultimate Holding Company: 3M COMPANY (USA)
Immediate Holding Company: 3M HEALTH CARE LIMITED
Registration no: 00968166 **Date established:** 1969
Turnover: £125m - £250m **No.of Employees:** 501 - 1000
Product Groups: 24, 30, 31, 37, 38

Date of Accounts	Dec 11	Dec 10	Dec 09
Sales Turnover	179m	242m	260m
Pre Tax Profit/Loss	42m	59m	65m
Working Capital	182m	184m	148m
Fixed Assets	104m	41m	46m
Current Assets	264m	231m	208m
Current Liabilities	11m	11m	13m

Able Engineering
Station Works Rempstone Road, Normanton On Soar, Loughborough, LE12 5EW
Tel: 01509-646491 **Fax:** 01509-646491
Website: http://www.able-engineering-midlands.co.uk
Directors: N. Parker (Dir)
No.of Employees: 1 - 10 **Product Groups:** 34, 35, 46

Air Plasma Ltd
3 Limehurst Avenue, Loughborough, LE11 1PE
Tel: 01509-237369 **Fax:** 01509-234942
E-mail: service@air-plasma.com
Website: http://www.air-plasma.com

see next page

Air Plasma Ltd - Cont'd
Directors: S. Goodwin (Fin), D. Goodwin (MD)
Ultimate Holding Company: GOODWIN AIR PLASMA LIMITED
Immediate Holding Company: SUBSEA PLASMA LIMITED
Registration no: 01371585 **VAT No.:** GB 308 1468 67
Date established: 1987 **No.of Employees:** 1 - 10 **Product Groups:** 46, 48

Air Technology Ltd
Unit 1 Oaks Industrial Estate Festival Drive, Loughborough, LE11 5XN
Tel: 01509-264900 **Fax:** 01509-264800
E-mail: eric.harding@airtechnology.co.uk
Website: http://www.airtechnology.co.uk
Directors: E. Harding (MD)
Immediate Holding Company: AIR TECHNOLOGY LIMITED
Registration no: 02157358 **VAT No.:** GB 479 3269 00
Date established: 1987 **Turnover:** £250,000 - £500,000
No.of Employees: 1 - 10 **Product Groups:** 40, 52

Date of Accounts	Dec 11	Dec 10	Dec 09
Working Capital	195	121	108
Fixed Assets	13	9	12
Current Assets	305	293	176

Allan & Bertram Ltd
Vantage Point Unit 16 Loughborough Motorway Trading Estate Gelders Hall Road, Shepshed, Loughborough, LE12 9NH
Tel: 01509-509509 **Fax:** 01509-509510
E-mail: enquiries@allanandbertram.com
Website: http://www.allanandbertram.com
Bank(s): HSBC Bank plc
Directors: V. Evershed (Mkt Research)
Immediate Holding Company: ALLAN & BERTRAM LIMITED
Registration no: 00777054 **VAT No.:** GB 220 4942 92
Date established: 1963 **Turnover:** £2m - £5m **No.of Employees:** 11 - 20
Product Groups: 28

Date of Accounts	Jul 11	Jul 10	Jul 09
Working Capital	773	762	705
Fixed Assets	805	847	894
Current Assets	2m	2m	2m

Altimed Ltd
74 Sullington Road Shepshed, Loughborough, LE12 9JJ
Tel: 01509-501720 **Fax:** 01509-501721
E-mail: champamistry@altimed.co.uk
Website: http://www.altimed.co.uk
Bank(s): Royal Bank of Scotland, London
Managers: C. Mistry (Mgr), K. Purdey (Ops Mgr)
Ultimate Holding Company: VIVA SANTE (FRANCE)
Immediate Holding Company: ALTIMED LIMITED
Registration no: 00259746 **VAT No.:** GB 113 8671 74
Date established: 1931 **Turnover:** £1m - £2m **No.of Employees:** 21 - 50
Product Groups: 23, 24

Date of Accounts	Dec 10	Dec 09	Dec 08
Sales Turnover	2m	1m	N/A
Pre Tax Profit/Loss	521	69	N/A
Working Capital	1m	402	305
Fixed Assets	168	233	267
Current Assets	1m	713	623
Current Liabilities	98	260	264

Archtechnik Architectural Engineers, Architectural Metalwork
Hathern Industrial Estate Rempstone Road, Normanton On Soar, Loughborough, LE12 5EW
Tel: 0870-4604831 **Fax:** 0870-4604832
E-mail: info@archtechnik.co.uk
Website: http://www.archtechnik.co.uk
No.of Employees: 1 - 10 **Product Groups:** 33, 35, 37

Date of Accounts	Jan 10	Jan 09	Jan 08
Working Capital	-9	-30	-38
Fixed Assets	26	44	57
Current Assets	147	105	91

Arnolds
63 Beardsley Road Quorn, Loughborough, LE12 8UX
Tel: 01509-416198 **Fax:** 01509-416198
E-mail: arnoldsplastering@btinternet.com
Directors: S. Arnold (Prop)
Immediate Holding Company: ALLIED SURVEYORS PLC
Registration no: 02622864 **No.of Employees:** 1 - 10 **Product Groups:** 30, 52

Artform International Ltd
Bishop Meadow Road, Loughborough, LE11 5TH
Tel: 01509-232426 **Fax:** 01509-236186
E-mail: sales@artform.co.uk
Website: http://www.artform.co.uk
Bank(s): The Royal Bank of Scotland plc
Directors: P. Mcwilliam (MD), M. Hawkins (Co Sec)
Managers: L. Cartwright (Personnel)
Ultimate Holding Company: IMI PLC
Immediate Holding Company: ARTFORM INTERNATIONAL LIMITED
Registration no: 01144080 **Date established:** 1973
Turnover: £20m - £50m **No.of Employees:** 251 - 500
Product Groups: 26, 30, 49

Date of Accounts	Dec 11	Dec 10	Dec 09
Sales Turnover	31m	29m	34m
Pre Tax Profit/Loss	2m	1m	3m
Working Capital	3m	12m	16m
Fixed Assets	2m	2m	2m
Current Assets	12m	17m	20m
Current Liabilities	3m	2m	3m

Atol Racking & Building Ltd
Unit A3 Wymeswold Industrial Park Wymeswold Road, Burton-on-the-wolds, Loughborough, LE12 5TY
Tel: 01509-881345 **Fax:** 01509-881064
E-mail: keith.walker@atol.co.uk
Website: http://www.atol.co.uk
Directors: A. Furby (Fin), K. Walker (MD)
Managers: B. Maxwell (Mgr)
Immediate Holding Company: ATOL RACKING AND BUILDINGS LIMITED
Registration no: 02515798 **Date established:** 1990 **Turnover:** £5m - £10m
No.of Employees: 11 - 20 **Product Groups:** 26

Date of Accounts	Jun 11	Jun 10	Jun 09
Working Capital	3m	3m	3m
Fixed Assets	259	116	75
Current Assets	3m	4m	3m

John Boyes Consulting
May House Tanners Lane, Hathern, Loughborough, LE12 5JG
Tel: 01509-646530 **Fax:** 01509-646530
Website: http://www.sterlingmanagement.co.uk
Directors: J. Boyes (Head)
Ultimate Holding Company: STERLING CONSULTING GROUP LTD
Date established: 2005 **Turnover:** £250,000 - £500,000
No.of Employees: 1 - 10 **Product Groups:** 80

Bradgate Containers Ltd
Leicester Road Shepshed, Loughborough, LE12 9EG
Tel: 01509-508678 **Fax:** 01509-503224
E-mail: sales@bradgate.co.uk
Website: http://www.bradgate.co.uk
Bank(s): National Westminster
Directors: J. Bexon (Sales), P. Stapleton (MD), D. Gallacher (Dir)
Managers: I. Harris (Tech Serv Mgr), M. Smith (Purch Mgr), B. Davies (Personnel)
Ultimate Holding Company: BRADGATE CONTAINERS (HOLDINGS) LIMITED
Immediate Holding Company: BRADGATE CONTAINERS LIMITED
Registration no: 01624460 **VAT No.:** GB 371 8179 32
Date established: 1982 **Turnover:** £10m - £20m
No.of Employees: 101 - 250 **Product Groups:** 40, 48

Date of Accounts	Aug 11	Aug 10	Aug 09
Sales Turnover	20m	16m	20m
Pre Tax Profit/Loss	3m	2m	3m
Working Capital	737	120	3m
Fixed Assets	3m	3m	3m
Current Assets	9m	7m	7m
Current Liabilities	2m	1m	2m

Bristish Gypsum
Gypsum Head Office East Leake, Loughborough, LE12 6HX
Tel: 0115-945 1000 **Fax:** 0115-945 1901
E-mail: bgtechnical.enquiries@bpb.com
Website: http://www.british-gypsum.com
Directors: G. Thompson (Fin), M. Chaldicott (MD), M. Chaldecott (MD)
Managers: P. Deacon, S. O'Connell (Personnel), D. Travill (Sales Prom Mgr)
Immediate Holding Company: BPB UK LTD
Registration no: 00701564 **Turnover:** £20m - £50m
No.of Employees: 251 - 500 **Product Groups:** 33

Date of Accounts	Dec 07	Dec 06	Dec 05
Working Capital	4140	4140	4140
Current Assets	4140	4140	4140
Total Share Capital	1000	1000	1000

Brush Electrical Machines Ltd
Falcoln Works Nottingham Road, Loughborough, LE11 1EX
Tel: 01509-611511 **Fax:** 01509-610440
E-mail: sales@brushtransformers.com
Website: http://www.brushtransformers.com
Bank(s): Barclays
Directors: J. Monckton (Purch), M. Vaughan (MD), P. Guice (Fin), K. Sallis (Ptnr)
Managers: R. Poole, T. Hill (Tech Serv Mgr)
Ultimate Holding Company: MELROSE PLC
Immediate Holding Company: BRUSH ELECTRICAL MACHINES LIMITED
Registration no: 00111849 **VAT No.:** GB 184 4733 43
Date established: 2010 **Turnover:** £125m - £250m
No.of Employees: 501 - 1000 **Product Groups:** 37

Date of Accounts	Dec 11	Dec 10	Dec 09
Sales Turnover	166m	197m	187m
Pre Tax Profit/Loss	41m	24m	17m
Working Capital	344m	332m	327m
Fixed Assets	10m	10m	9m
Current Assets	414m	409m	391m
Current Liabilities	14m	13m	12m

Bunzl Vending Services Ltd
34 Jubilee Drive, Loughborough, LE11 5TU
Tel: 01509-230481 **Fax:** 01509-233572
Website: http://www.bunzlvend.com
Bank(s): Barclays
Directors: P. Hussey (Dir)
Managers: T. Jinnivar (District Mgr)
Ultimate Holding Company: BUNZL PUBLIC LIMITED COMPANY
Immediate Holding Company: MIDLAND VENDING SERVICES LIMITED
Registration no: 01144648 **VAT No.:** GB 115 4260 06
Date established: 1973 **Turnover:** £5m - £10m
No.of Employees: 101 - 250 **Product Groups:** 61

Date of Accounts	Dec 07
Working Capital	3
Current Assets	3

C N Promotions
16 Coniston Crescent, Loughborough, LE11 3RH
Tel: 01509-235550 **Fax:** 01509-554126
E-mail: sales@cn-promotions.co.uk
Website: http://www.cn-promotions.co.uk
Directors: C. Willis (Ptnr)
No.of Employees: 1 - 10 **Product Groups:** 22, 23, 24, 25, 27, 28, 29, 30, 44, 49, 65, 75, 77, 80, 81, 89

C P S Interiors Ltd
Chairman House 16 Cradock Street, Loughborough, LE11 1AJ
Tel: 01509-230429 **Fax:** 01509-610617
E-mail: enquiries@cpsinteriors.com
Website: http://www.cpsinteriors.com
Bank(s): Barclays, Loughborough
Directors: A. Howell (Dir)
Immediate Holding Company: CPS INTERIORS LIMITED
Registration no: 04378210 **VAT No.:** GB 115 3227 09
Date established: 2002 **Turnover:** £1m - £2m **No.of Employees:** 11 - 20
Product Groups: 30, 35, 52

Date of Accounts	Apr 12	Apr 11	Apr 10
Working Capital	20	-59	-25
Fixed Assets	528	540	565
Current Assets	356	250	211

C T S U Ltd
Lighting House Station Road, East Leake, Loughborough, LE12 6LQ
Tel: 01509-820888 **Fax:** 01509-820886
Directors: T. Sadler (Prop)
Immediate Holding Company: CTSU Ltd
Registration no: 05830302 **Date established:** 2006
No.of Employees: 11 - 20 **Product Groups:** 37, 67

Cavill Fabrications Ltd
Station Avenue, Loughborough, LE11 5DZ
Tel: 01509-260220 **Fax:** 01509-260552
E-mail: jackie@cavillfabs.co.uk
Website: http://www.cavillfabs.co.uk
Directors: N. Cavill (Mkt Research), R. Cavill (MD), J. Belcher (Fin)
Immediate Holding Company: CAVILL FABRICATIONS LIMITED
Registration no: 02694615 **Date established:** 1992 **Turnover:** £1m - £2m
No.of Employees: 21 - 50 **Product Groups:** 35, 48

Date of Accounts	Sep 09	Sep 08	Sep 07
Working Capital	130	392	397
Fixed Assets	193	253	235
Current Assets	1m	2m	1m

Centrator UK Ltd
Albion Rd Sileby, Loughborough, LE12 7RA
Tel: 01509-814626 **Fax:** 01509-814626
E-mail: centrator@supanet.com
Website: http://www.centrator.com
Directors: D. Jarvis (MD)
Registration no: 02883439 **Turnover:** Up to £250,000
No.of Employees: 1 - 10 **Product Groups:** 36, 46

Date of Accounts	Dec 11	Dec 10	Dec 09
Working Capital	160	127	202
Fixed Assets	3	3	4
Current Assets	211	159	236

Centre For Hazard & Risk Management (CEMMNT)
Loughborough University, Loughborough, LE11 3TU
Tel: 01509-222175 **Fax:** 01509-223991
E-mail: enquiry@cemmnt.co.uk
Website: http://cemmnt.co.uk
Directors: E. Vogt (Grp Chief Exec), C. Hancocks (Dir)
Date established: 2005 **No.of Employees:** 11 - 20 **Product Groups:** 38, 85

Charles Bentley & Son Ltd
1 Monarch Way, Loughborough, LE11 5XG
Tel: 01509-232757 **Fax:** 01509-233861
E-mail: sales@bentleybrushware.co.uk
Website: http://www.bentleybrushware.co.uk
Bank(s): National Westminster Bank Plc
Directors: T. Robinson (Pers), C. Bentley (Ptnr)
Managers: T. Robinson (Tech Serv Mgr), S. Graham (Mktg Serv Mgr), P. Godwin (I.T. Exec), F. Graham (Sales Prom Mgr), B. Woodley (Comptroller), B. Woodley (Comptroller), F. Graham (Sales Prom Mgr)
Immediate Holding Company: CHARLES BENTLEY & SON LIMITED
Registration no: 01409627 **VAT No.:** GB 115 6747 65
Date established: 1979 **Turnover:** £20m - £50m
No.of Employees: 101 - 250 **Product Groups:** 49, 63

Date of Accounts	Mar 11	Mar 10	Mar 09
Sales Turnover	20m	19m	N/A
Pre Tax Profit/Loss	690	1m	397
Working Capital	2m	2m	1m
Fixed Assets	3m	4m	4m
Current Assets	8m	8m	8m
Current Liabilities	2m	2m	1m

Charnwood Fasteners Ltd
15 Prince William Road, Loughborough, LE11 5GU
Tel: 01509-237280 **Fax:** 01509-262428
E-mail: charnwoodfasteners@btconnect.com
Website: http://www.charnwoodfasteners.co.uk
Directors: J. Nicholson (Fin)
Managers: P. Measures (Mgr)
Immediate Holding Company: CHARNWOOD FASTENERS LIMITED
Registration no: 01581632 **VAT No.:** GB 355 3157 57
Date established: 1981 **No.of Employees:** 1 - 10 **Product Groups:** 35, 66

Date of Accounts	Aug 09	Aug 08	Sep 11
Working Capital	24	37	12
Fixed Assets	4	5	7
Current Assets	77	90	69

Charnwood Forest Brick Ltd
Old Station Close Shepshed, Loughborough, LE12 9NJ
Tel: 01509-503203 **Fax:** 01509-507566
E-mail: sales@charnwoodforest.com
Website: http://www.mbhplc.co.uk
Bank(s): Lloyds TSB Bank plc
Managers: K. Johnson (Fin Mgr)
Ultimate Holding Company: MICHELMERSH BRICK HOLDINGS PLC
Immediate Holding Company: CHARNWOOD FOREST BRICK LIMITED
Registration no: 03690069 **VAT No.:** GB 115 1279 00
Date established: 1998 **Turnover:** £2m - £5m **No.of Employees:** 51 - 100
Product Groups: 33

Date of Accounts	Dec 11	Dec 10	Dec 09
Sales Turnover	N/A	3m	2m
Pre Tax Profit/Loss	2	281	-42
Working Capital	334	332	-1m
Fixed Assets	3m	3m	5m
Current Assets	334	3m	2m
Current Liabilities	N/A	N/A	427

Cooper Bussmann Cooper (UK) Ltd
Melton Road Burton-on-the-Wolds, Loughborough, LE12 5TH
Tel: 01509-882600 **Fax:** 01509-882786
E-mail: eurosales@bussmann.co.uk
Website: http://www.bussmann.co.uk
Bank(s): National Westminster Bank Plc
Directors: D. Baker (Fin), S. Pinkney (Mkt Research), D. Reece (Sales), B. Milford (MD)
Managers: J. Clark (Personnel), C. Scarborough
Ultimate Holding Company: COOPER INDUSTRIES (AMERICA)
Immediate Holding Company: COOPER (UK) LTD
Registration no: FC014457 **VAT No.:** GB 501 6757 61
Turnover: £20m - £50m **No.of Employees:** 251 - 500
Product Groups: 30, 37, 39, 67, 68

Creoseal Ltd
7-11 Brook Street Sileby, Loughborough, LE12 7RF
Tel: 01509-812473 **Fax:** 01509-816970
E-mail: sales@creoseal.co.uk
Website: http://www.creoseal.co.uk
Directors: J. Middleton (Fin), P. Middleton (MD)
Immediate Holding Company: CREOSEAL LIMITED
Registration no: 04348566 **Date established:** 2002
Turnover: Up to £250,000 **No.of Employees:** 1 - 10 **Product Groups:** 32

Date of Accounts	Jan 11	Jan 10	Jan 09
Working Capital	17	21	19
Current Assets	60	69	74

Cromaston Ltd

17 Swan Street Sileby, Loughborough, LE12 7NN
Tel: 01509-812840 **Fax:** 01509-813494
E-mail: info@cromaston.co.uk
Website: http://www.cromaston.co.uk
Directors: M. Smart (MD), R. Mason (Fin)
Immediate Holding Company: CROMASTON LIMITED
Registration no: 06756487 **Date established:** 2008
Turnover: £250,000 - £500,000 **No.of Employees:** 11 - 20
Product Groups: 38, 46, 48

Date of Accounts	Jan 12	Jan 11	Jan 10
Working Capital	1	-10	-38
Fixed Assets	2	12	39
Current Assets	190	132	96

Cross & Sansam Ltd

63 Ashby Road Shepshed, Loughborough, LE12 9BS
Tel: 01509-651414 **Fax:** 01509-651115
E-mail: david.sansam@crossandsansam.co.uk
Website: http://www.crossandsansam.co.uk
Bank(s): National Westminster Bank Plc
Directors: D. Sansam (MD)
Immediate Holding Company: CROSS & SANSAM LIMITED
Registration no: 00482486 **VAT No.:** GB 113 8890 62
Date established: 1950 **Turnover:** £500,000 - £1m
No.of Employees: 21 - 50 **Product Groups:** 33, 46, 48

Date of Accounts	Jun 11	Jun 10	Jun 09
Working Capital	215	232	221
Fixed Assets	295	194	225
Current Assets	583	542	637

Dartnall Design Associates

34 De Verdun Avenue Belton, Loughborough, LE12 9TY
Tel: 01530-223049 **Fax:** 01530-223049
E-mail: info@dartnalldesign.co.uk
Website: http://www.dartnalldesign.co.uk
Directors: A. Dartnall (Prop)
Date established: 1983 **Turnover:** Up to £250,000
No.of Employees: 1 - 10 **Product Groups:** 84, 85

Datalink Electronics Ltd

8 Jubilee Drive, Loughborough, LE11 5XS
Tel: 01509-231023 **Fax:** 01509-234849
E-mail: info@datalink-electronics.co.uk
Website: http://www.datalink-electronics.co.uk
Bank(s): HSBC Bank plc
Directors: I. Wilson (Sales), F. Wood (MD), J. Ottey (Fin), E. Luckwell (Tech Serv)
Managers: P. Kinbar, M. Nasi (Personnel)
Immediate Holding Company: DATALINK ELECTRONICS LIMITED
Registration no: 01664664 **Date established:** 1982 **Turnover:** £2m - £5m
No.of Employees: 21 - 50 **Product Groups:** 35, 37, 44

Date of Accounts	Mar 12	Mar 11	Mar 10
Sales Turnover	N/A	N/A	3m
Pre Tax Profit/Loss	N/A	N/A	37
Working Capital	145	210	139
Fixed Assets	125	46	17
Current Assets	2m	2m	1m
Current Liabilities	N/A	730	N/A

Jonathan Dean Textiles Ltd

The Old Coach House Wharncliffe Road, Loughborough, LE11 1SN
Tel: 01509-235251 **Fax:** 01509-611121
E-mail: jonathan.dean@btinternet.com
Directors: J. Dean (MD), M. Dean (Dir), M. Dean (Fin)
Managers: A. Osbourne (Mgr)
Immediate Holding Company: JONATHAN DEAN TEXTILES LIMITED
Registration no: 01501223 **Date established:** 1980
Turnover: £500,000 - £1m **No.of Employees:** 1 - 10 **Product Groups:** 23

Date of Accounts	Jun 10	Dec 08	Dec 07
Working Capital	4	88	99
Current Assets	16	103	135

E M C F Die Cutting

8 Oaks Industrial Estate Festival Drive, Loughborough, LE11 5XN
Tel: 01509-262342 **Fax:** 01509-210331
Directors: J. Adcock (Ptnr)
VAT No.: GB 380 1865 49 **Turnover:** £500,000 - £1m
No.of Employees: 1 - 10 **Product Groups:** 23, 24, 27, 33, 48, 85

E T S Distribution & Storage Services

175 Meadow Lane, Loughborough, LE11 1NF
Tel: 01509-615050 **Fax:** 01509-269792
E-mail: transport@etsltd.co.uk
Website: http://www.etsltd.co.uk
Bank(s): Barclays Bank plc
Managers: R. Ward (Mgr)
Immediate Holding Company: ETS ELLIOTT TRANSPORT SERVICES LIMITED
Registration no: 01340529 **VAT No.:** GB 316 0390 88
Date established: 1977 **Turnover:** £5m - £10m
No.of Employees: 51 - 100 **Product Groups:** 72, 76, 77, 84

Date of Accounts	Nov 11	Nov 10	Nov 09
Working Capital	41	8	-136
Fixed Assets	1m	1m	2m
Current Assets	928	1m	779

Eazzee Workwear

Unit 4 Station Road East Leake, Loughborough, LE12 6LQ
Tel: 08456-010253 **Fax:** 01509-852371
E-mail: sales@eazzee.co.uk
Website: http://www.eazzee.co.uk
Directors: S. Haslan (Ptnr)
Immediate Holding Company: EAZZEE.CO.UK LLP
Registration no: OC364837 **Date established:** 2011 **Turnover:** £2m - £5m
No.of Employees: 1 - 10 **Product Groups:** 24, 63

Event Engineering Ltd

Unit 8-9 Windmill Road Industrial Estate Windmill Road, Loughborough, LE11 1RA
Tel: 08450-525282 **Fax:** 0845-052 5285
E-mail: enquiry@eventengineering.co.uk
Website: http://www.eventengineering.co.uk
Directors: M. Thornton (Dir)
Immediate Holding Company: EVENT ENGINEERING LIMITED
Registration no: 04214514 **Date established:** 2001
No.of Employees: 1 - 10 **Product Groups:** 81, 83

Date of Accounts	May 11	May 10	May 09
Working Capital	15	28	18
Fixed Assets	72	68	51
Current Assets	72	94	49

Farm Tours

Devonshire House Devonshire Lane, Loughborough, LE11 3DF
Tel: 01509-618810 **Fax:** 01509-610585
E-mail: sales@farm-tours.co.uk
Website: http://www.farm-tours.co.uk
Managers: M. Peasnall (Mgr)
Immediate Holding Company: UNI-TRAVEL LTD
Registration no: 02238595 **Turnover:** £2m - £5m
No.of Employees: 1 - 10 **Product Groups:** 69

Fisher Scientific UK Ltd

Bishop Meadow Road, Loughborough, LE11 5RG
Tel: 01509-231166 **Fax:** 01509-231893
E-mail: info@fisher.co.uk
Website: http://www.fisher.co.uk
Bank(s): National Westminster Bank Plc
Directors: J. Coley (Dir), N. Ward (Co Sec)
Ultimate Holding Company: THERMO FISHER SCIENTIFIC INC (USA)
Immediate Holding Company: FISHER SCIENTIFIC UK HOLDING COMPANY LIMITED
Registration no: 03947481 **Date established:** 2000
Turnover: £75m - £125m **No.of Employees:** 251 - 500
Product Groups: 33, 38, 40, 42, 47, 63, 67

Date of Accounts	Dec 10	Dec 09	Dec 08
Sales Turnover	126m	118m	111m
Pre Tax Profit/Loss	2m	7m	9m
Working Capital	19m	27m	25m
Fixed Assets	29m	19m	17m
Current Assets	37m	43m	39m
Current Liabilities	4m	6m	3m

Fistreem International Ltd

Monarch Way Belton Park, Loughborough, LE11 5XG
Tel: 01509-224613 **Fax:** 01509-260210
E-mail: sales@fistreem.co.uk
Website: http://www.fistreeminternational.com
Bank(s): HSBC Bank plc
Managers: R. Farmery (Mgr)
Registration no: 05136733 **VAT No.:** GB 845 2060 44
Date established: 2004 **Turnover:** £500,000 - £1m **Product Groups:** 31, 32, 33, 38, 42

Date of Accounts	Aug 11	Aug 10	Aug 09
Working Capital	344	205	382
Fixed Assets	2	3	3
Current Assets	511	439	537

Force Engineering International Ltd

Old Station Close Shepshed, Loughborough, LE12 9NJ
Tel: 01509-506025 **Fax:** 01509-505433
E-mail: stanley.proverbs@kirton.co.uk
Website: http://www.force.co.uk
Directors: A. Foster (MD), N. Foster (Co Sec), S. Proverbs (Dir), S. Foster (Comm)
Immediate Holding Company: FORCE ENGINEERING (INTERNATIONAL) LIMITED
Registration no: 04620874 **Date established:** 2002 **Turnover:** £1m - £2m
No.of Employees: 1 - 10 **Product Groups:** 37, 40

Date of Accounts	Oct 08	Oct 07	Oct 06
Working Capital	78	74	164
Fixed Assets	68	65	83
Current Assets	390	203	261
Current Liabilities	312	129	97

GL Noble Denton

Holywell Park Ashby Road, Loughborough, LE11 3GR
Tel: 01509-282000 **Fax:** 01509-283131
E-mail: glnobledenton@gl-group.com
Website: http://www.gl-nobledenton.com
Bank(s): Barclays
Ultimate Holding Company: Germanischer LLoyd
Registration no: 03294136 **VAT No.:** GB 757 2365 11
Turnover: £50m - £75m **No.of Employees:** 3'000 **Product Groups:** 13, 44, 54, 84, 85

Date of Accounts	Dec 07
Sales Turnover	30660
Pre Tax Profit/Loss	-3320
Working Capital	17270
Fixed Assets	2440
Current Assets	35420
Current Liabilities	18150
Total Share Capital	30880
ROCE% (Return on Capital Employed)	-16.8

Groeneveld UK Ltd

Unit 29a Loughborough Motorway Trading Estate Gelders Hall Road, Shepshed, Loughborough, LE12 9NH
Tel: 01509-600033 **Fax:** 01509-602000
E-mail: hendrikus@groeneveld.uk.com
Website: http://www.groeneveld-group.com/en
Bank(s): National Westminster Bank Plc
Directors: G. Hewitt (MD), G. Hewitt (Co Sec), D. Mercurio (MD), H. Groeneveld (Dir)
Managers: D. Booth (Product)
Ultimate Holding Company: FP034421
Immediate Holding Company: GROENEVELD UK LIMITED
Registration no: 02498107 **VAT No.:** GB 558 4241 29
Date established: 1990 **Turnover:** £50m - £75m
No.of Employees: 21 - 50 **Product Groups:** 36, 39, 40, 68

Date of Accounts	Dec 11	Dec 10	Dec 09
Working Capital	429	337	498
Fixed Assets	322	332	355
Current Assets	734	586	660

H S M Engineering Technology Ltd

3 Beaumont Court Belton Park Industrial Estate, Loughborough, LE11 5DA
Tel: 01509-211233 **Fax:** 01509-269061
E-mail: iain@hsm-engineering.demon.co.uk
Website: http://www.hsm-engineering.demon.co.uk
Directors: I. Middlebrook (Co Sec)
Immediate Holding Company: H.S.M. ENGINEERING TECHNOLOGY LIMITED
Registration no: 02230970 **Date established:** 1988
No.of Employees: 21 - 50 **Product Groups:** 39, 40, 51, 68, 85

Date of Accounts	Jun 11	Jun 10	Jun 09
Working Capital	81	90	88
Fixed Assets	2	3	1
Current Assets	88	103	111

Hancocks Cash & Carry Ltd

25 Jubilee Drive, Loughborough, LE11 5TX
Tel: 01509-216644 **Fax:** 01509-237104
E-mail: info@hancocks.co.uk
Website: http://www.hancocks.co.uk
Directors: R. Garner (Fin)
Managers: J. Johnson, S. Colley (Tech Serv Mgr), J. Oliver (Personnel)
Ultimate Holding Company: HANCOCKS GROUP HOLDINGS LIMITED
Immediate Holding Company: HANCOCKS HOLDINGS LIMITED
Registration no: 02884267 **Date established:** 1994 **Turnover:** £2m - £5m
No.of Employees: 21 - 50 **Product Groups:** 61

Date of Accounts	Dec 11	Dec 10	Dec 09
Sales Turnover	3m	3m	4m
Pre Tax Profit/Loss	3m	2m	3m
Working Capital	2m	1m	-64
Fixed Assets	7m	8m	7m
Current Assets	13m	15m	19m
Current Liabilities	1m	582	1m

Harlequin

Ladybird House Beeches Road, Loughborough, LE11 2HA
Tel: 08445-430100 **Fax:** 0844-543 0101
E-mail: harsales@harlequin.uk.com
Website: http://www.harlequin.uk.com
Managers: J. Hicks (Sales Prom Mgr)
Ultimate Holding Company: WALKER GREENBANK PLC.
Immediate Holding Company: ABARIS HOLDINGS LTD
Registration no: 01089191 **Turnover:** £10m - £20m
No.of Employees: 1 - 10 **Product Groups:** 23, 30, 66

Harlow Brothers Ltd

Hathern Road Long Whatton, Loughborough, LE12 5DE
Tel: 01509-842561 **Fax:** 01509-843577
E-mail: sales@harlowbros.co.uk
Website: http://www.harlowbros.co.uk
Bank(s): Barclays
Directors: P. Harlow (Dir)
Immediate Holding Company: HARLOW BROS. LIMITED
Registration no: 00907445 **VAT No.:** GB 114 2004 40
Date established: 1967 **Turnover:** £20m - £50m
No.of Employees: 251 - 500 **Product Groups:** 08, 25, 31, 35, 66

Date of Accounts	Jun 11	Jun 10	Jun 09
Sales Turnover	33m	27m	22m
Pre Tax Profit/Loss	2m	1m	170
Working Capital	12m	14m	15m
Fixed Assets	15m	10m	9m
Current Assets	18m	18m	18m
Current Liabilities	3m	2m	1m

Hatco Corporation

9 Pavilion Way, Loughborough, LE11 5GW
Tel: 01509-260140 **Fax:** 01509-260151
E-mail: info@hatcocorp.com
Website: http://www.hatcocorp.com
Directors: M. Poultney (MD)
Immediate Holding Company: TOOLGEAR LIMITED
Date established: 2004 **No.of Employees:** 11 - 20 **Product Groups:** 37, 40, 41

I R L Group Ltd

Unit C1 Swingbridge Road, Loughborough, LE11 5JD
Tel: 01509-217101 **Fax:** 01509-611004
E-mail: info@irlgroup.co.uk
Website: http://www.irlgroup.co.uk
Bank(s): Barclays
Directors: S. Jones (MD)
Immediate Holding Company: IRL GROUP LIMITED
Registration no: 02615625 **VAT No.:** GB 428 4056 53
Date established: 1991 **Turnover:** £1m - £2m **No.of Employees:** 21 - 50
Product Groups: 52

Date of Accounts	Apr 12	Apr 11	Apr 10
Working Capital	244	152	164
Fixed Assets	776	738	675
Current Assets	1m	995	972

Imperial Catering Equipment Ltd

Elite House Castle Business Park, Loughborough, LE11 5GW
Tel: 01509-260150 **Fax:** 01664-424955
E-mail: sales@imperialrange.co.uk
Website: http://www.imperialrange.co.uk
Directors: M. Poultney (Dir), R. Gamble (Fin)
Immediate Holding Company: IMPERIAL CATERING EQUIPMENT LIMITED
Registration no: 02449623 **Date established:** 1989
Turnover: £10m - £20m **No.of Employees:** 11 - 20 **Product Groups:** 40, 41, 42, 67

Date of Accounts	Apr 12	Apr 11	Apr 10
Working Capital	44	-3	-31
Fixed Assets	193	167	168
Current Assets	2m	2m	2m

Intelligent Energy Solutions

7 Aerodrome Close, Loughborough, LE11 5RJ
Tel: 01509-768565 **Fax:** 01509-808159
E-mail: sales@iesolutions.co.uk
Website: http://www.iesolutions.co.uk
Directors: M. Searancke (Fin), P. Searancke (Dir)
Managers: P. Searancke (Mgr)
Immediate Holding Company: 1NTELLIGENT ENERGY SOLUTIONS LTD
Registration no: 05927695 **Date established:** 2006
Turnover: Up to £250,000 **No.of Employees:** 1 - 10 **Product Groups:** 37

Jewson Ltd

25-29 Bakewell Road, Loughborough, LE11 5QY
Tel: 01509-212121 **Fax:** 01509-610218
E-mail: simon.hall@jewson.co.uk
Website: http://www.jewson.co.uk
Managers: S. Hall (Mgr)
Ultimate Holding Company: COMPAGNIE DE SAINT GOBAIN (FRANCE)
Immediate Holding Company: JEWSON LIMITED
Registration no: 00348407 **Date established:** 1939
Turnover: Over £1,000m **No.of Employees:** 1 - 10 **Product Groups:** 66

Date of Accounts	Dec 11	Dec 10	Dec 09
Sales Turnover	1606m	1547m	1485m
Pre Tax Profit/Loss	18m	100m	45m

see next page

Jewson Ltd - Cont'd

Working Capital	-345m	-250m	-349m
Fixed Assets	496m	387m	461m
Current Assets	657m	1005m	1320m
Current Liabilities	66m	120m	64m

John Taylor & Co Ltd
The Bell Foundry Freehold Street, Loughborough, LE11 1AR
Tel: 01509-212241 **Fax:** 01509-263305
E-mail: office@taylorbells.co.uk
Website: http://www.taylorbells.co.uk
Bank(s): Barclays
Directors: R. Lester (Fin)
Managers: C. Banton (Develop Mgr), A. Higson, G. Flatters, M. Spencer (Chief Mgr)
Immediate Holding Company: Bellfounders Ltd
Registration no: 05756978 **VAT No.:** GB 316 0541 93
No.of Employees: 21 - 50 **Product Groups:** 34

K S B Ltd
2 Cotton Way, Loughborough, LE11 5TF
Tel: 01509-231872 **Fax:** 01509-215228
E-mail: sales@ksb.com
Website: http://www.ksb.com
Bank(s): Barclays
Directors: J. Walsh (Fin), A. Ratcliffe (Dir), J. Walsh (Co Sec)
Managers: S. Wallis (Sales Prom Mgr), R. Stockley (Tech Serv Mgr), P. Smith (Personnel)
Ultimate Holding Company: KSB AKTIENGESELLSCHAFT (GERMANY)
Immediate Holding Company: KSB LIMITED
Registration no: 00188357 **VAT No.:** GB 374 3530 53
Date established: 2023 **Turnover:** £10m - £20m
No.of Employees: 101 - 250 **Product Groups:** 36, 39, 40, 42, 45, 46

Date of Accounts	Dec 11	Dec 10	Dec 09
Sales Turnover	19m	17m	18m
Pre Tax Profit/Loss	420	439	511
Working Capital	1m	746	756
Fixed Assets	2m	2m	2m
Current Assets	7m	6m	6m
Current Liabilities	2m	2m	2m

Kesbond
100 Kingfisher Road Mountsorrel, Loughborough, LE12 7FS
Tel: 0116-237 5767 **Fax:** 0116-237 5797
E-mail: barry@kesbond.com
Website: http://www.kesbond.com
Directors: B. Disler (Prop)
No.of Employees: 1 - 10 **Product Groups:** 22, 30, 35, 63

Loughborough University Enterprises Ltd
Rutland Hall, Loughborough, LE11 3TP
Tel: 01509-222597 **Fax:** 01509-211516
E-mail: consultancy@lboro.ac.uk
Website: http://www.lboro.ac.uk/enterprise
Directors: K. Walsh (Dir)
Ultimate Holding Company: LOUGHBOROUGH UNIVERSITY DEVELOPMENT TRUST
Immediate Holding Company: LOUGHBOROUGH UNIVERSITY ENTERPRISES LIMITED
Registration no: 03139948 **Date established:** 1995 **Turnover:** £1m - £2m
No.of Employees: 1 - 10 **Product Groups:** 54, 80, 84

Date of Accounts	Jul 12	Jul 11	Jul 10
Working Capital	18	18	16
Fixed Assets	1	1	1
Current Assets	772	625	584

LPL Systems
Unit C4 Swingbridge Road, Loughborough, LE11 5JB
Tel: 01509-262042 **Fax:** 01509-262517
E-mail: clive.bass@lplsystems.co.uk
Website: http://www.lplsystems.co.uk
Bank(s): The Bank of Scotland plc
Managers: A. Sanders (Sales Prom Mgr)
Registration no: 01674887 **VAT No.:** GB 380 1543 71
No.of Employees: 21 - 50 **Product Groups:** 37, 38, 39, 45, 84

Date of Accounts	Dec 11	Dec 10	Dec 09
Working Capital	2m	2m	2m
Fixed Assets	145	24	49
Current Assets	2m	2m	2m

Master Control UK Ltd
Unit 4m Loughborough Motorway Trading Estate Gelders Hall Road, Shepshed, Loughborough, LE12 9NH
Tel: 01509-650750 **Fax:** 01509-600075
E-mail: info@mastercontrol.co.uk
Website: http://www.mastercontrol.co.uk
Directors: J. Farley (MD)
Immediate Holding Company: MASTER CONTROL (U.K.) LIMITED
Registration no: 01944964 **Date established:** 1985
Turnover: £500,000 - £1m **No.of Employees:** 1 - 10 **Product Groups:** 45

Date of Accounts	Oct 11	Oct 10	Oct 09
Working Capital	89	57	40
Fixed Assets	53	51	12
Current Assets	163	142	79

Karl Mayer Textile Machinery Ltd
35 Kings Road Shepshed, Loughborough, LE12 9HT
Tel: 01509-502056 **Fax:** 01509-508065
E-mail: info@karlmayer.co.uk
Website: http://www.karlmayer.co.uk
Bank(s): National Westminster Bank Plc
Directors: K. Priestley (Fin)
Managers: P. Frise (Mgr)
Immediate Holding Company: KARL MAYER TEXTILE MACHINERY LIMITED
Registration no: 00950132 **VAT No.:** GB 114 0175 23
Date established: 1969 **Turnover:** £10m - £20m
No.of Employees: 21 - 50 **Product Groups:** 67

Date of Accounts	Dec 11	Dec 10	Dec 09
Sales Turnover	11m	12m	12m
Pre Tax Profit/Loss	-439	-26	-666
Working Capital	5m	6m	5m
Fixed Assets	3m	3m	3m
Current Assets	6m	7m	6m
Current Liabilities	684	574	389

Mentioncourt Ltd
Wymeswold Road Burton-on-the-Wolds, Loughborough, LE12 5TR
Tel: 01509-881223 **Fax:** 0115-984 6947
Directors: T. Bourne (MD), M. Hull (MD)
Registration no: 01693225 **No.of Employees:** 1 - 10 **Product Groups:** 30

Merlin Tools Ltd
Unit 21 North Road, Loughborough, LE11 1LE
Tel: 01509-610300 **Fax:** 01509-610400
E-mail: sales@merlintools.ltd.uk
Website: http://www.merlintools.ltd.uk
Directors: S. Ward (MD)
Immediate Holding Company: MERLIN TOOLS LIMITED
Registration no: 03493385 **Date established:** 1998
No.of Employees: 1 - 10 **Product Groups:** 46

Date of Accounts	Mar 11	Mar 10	Mar 09
Working Capital	174	142	138
Fixed Assets	58	38	42
Current Assets	517	383	439

Midlands Testing Services
3 Hollis Meadow East Leake, Loughborough, LE12 6RU
Tel: 01509-854444 **Fax:** 01509-854444
E-mail: kevinspencer@thepowerservice.com
Website: http://www.thepowerservice.com
Directors: K. Spencer (Prop)
No.of Employees: 1 - 10 **Product Groups:** 38, 80, 84, 88

Migatronic Welding Equipment Ltd
21 Jubilee Drive Belton Park, Loughborough, LE11 5XS
Tel: 01509-267499 **Fax:** 01509-231959
E-mail: sales@migatronic.co.uk
Website: http://www.migatronic.co.uk
Directors: P. Roed (MD)
Managers: G. Clark (Sales Admin)
Ultimate Holding Company: SVEJSEMASKINEFABRIKKEN MIGRATRONIC A/S (DENMARK)
Immediate Holding Company: MIGATRONIC WELDING EQUIPMENT LIMITED
Registration no: 01352109 **VAT No.:** GB 324 2629 74
Date established: 1978 **Turnover:** £500,000 - £1m
No.of Employees: 1 - 10 **Product Groups:** 46

Date of Accounts	Dec 11	Dec 10	Dec 09
Sales Turnover	1m	800	703
Pre Tax Profit/Loss	-117	194	-215
Working Capital	68	180	-195
Fixed Assets	16	22	203
Current Assets	442	437	327
Current Liabilities	72	49	27

Morelli Group
1 Viking Court Shepshed Road, Hathern, Loughborough, LE12 5LZ
Tel: 01509-842627 **Fax:** 01509-843782
E-mail: enquiries@morelli.co.uk
Website: http://www.morelli.co.uk
Managers: P. Taylor
Immediate Holding Company: FINELIST GROUP P.L.C.
Registration no: 02533343 **Turnover:** Up to £250,000
No.of Employees: 1 - 10 **Product Groups:** 32

Morning Side
5 Pavilion Way, Loughborough, LE11 5GW
Tel: 01509-217705 **Fax:** 01509-217706
E-mail: info@morningsidepharm.com
Website: http://www.morningsidepharm.com
Managers: E. Dodd (Mgr)
Registration no: 02672877 **VAT No.:** GB 565 9777 71
Date established: 2005 **Turnover:** £2m - £5m **No.of Employees:** 11 - 20
Product Groups: 24, 63

Motiv Business Gifts
Prospect House 4 Old Station Close Shepshed, Loughborough, LE12 9NJ
Tel: 01509-509220 **Fax:** 01509-267276
E-mail: sales@motivbg.com
Website: http://www.motivbg.com
Directors: R. Wilson (Ptnr)
Turnover: £500,000 - £1m **No.of Employees:** 1 - 10 **Product Groups:** 28, 49

Newtons 4th Ltd
30 Loughborough Road Mountsorrel, Loughborough, LE12 7AT
Tel: 0116-230 1066 **Fax:** 0116-230 1061
E-mail: sales@newtons4th.com
Website: http://www.newtons4th.com
Directors: S. Chappell (MD)
Immediate Holding Company: NEWTONS4TH LTD
Registration no: 03463832 **Date established:** 1997
Turnover: £250,000 - £500,000 **No.of Employees:** 11 - 20
Product Groups: 37, 38, 67

Date of Accounts	Nov 11	Nov 10	Nov 09
Working Capital	960	761	484
Fixed Assets	77	13	13
Current Assets	1m	1m	702

O D U UK Ltd
Loughborough Technology Centre Epinal Way, Loughborough, LE11 3GE
Tel: 01509-266433 **Fax:** 01509-266777
E-mail: sales@odu-uk.co.uk
Website: http://www.odu.de
Directors: K. Woelfl (Pres), S. O'donnell (MD)
Immediate Holding Company: ODU-UK LIMITED
Registration no: 03546482 **Date established:** 1998 **Turnover:** £1m - £2m
No.of Employees: 1 - 10 **Product Groups:** 35, 37

Date of Accounts	Dec 11	Dec 10	Dec 09
Working Capital	574	584	435
Fixed Assets	95	81	83
Current Assets	1m	1m	795

P R S Services
79 Barrow Road Quorn, Loughborough, LE12 8DH
Tel: 01509-414107 **Fax:** 01509-414107
E-mail: enquiries@prs-services.co.uk
Website: http://www.prs-services.co.uk
Directors: J. Clare (Prop)
No.of Employees: 1 - 10 **Product Groups:** 38, 44

Permarock Products Ltd
Jubilee Drive, Loughborough, LE11 5TW
Tel: 01509-262924 **Fax:** 01509-230063
E-mail: info@permarock.com
Website: http://www.permarock.com
Bank(s): National Westminster Bank Plc
Directors: S. Waldrum (MD), R. Tocher (Develop)
Managers: V. Smith, D. Elton (Mktg Serv Mgr), M. Barlow (Cust Serv Mgr)
Ultimate Holding Company: CARILLION PLC
Immediate Holding Company: PERMAROCK PRODUCTS LIMITED
Registration no: 01867923 **VAT No.:** GB 616 6734 28
Date established: 1984 **Turnover:** £5m - £10m **No.of Employees:** 21 - 50
Product Groups: 30, 33, 37

Date of Accounts	Oct 08	May 10	May 09
Sales Turnover	7m	7m	3m
Pre Tax Profit/Loss	758	536	81
Working Capital	1m	1m	1m
Fixed Assets	700	653	676
Current Assets	2m	3m	2m
Current Liabilities	306	219	206

Piab Ltd
Vacuum Innovation House Station Road, East Leake, Loughborough, LE12 6LQ
Tel: 01509-857010 **Fax:** 01509-814647
E-mail: info@piab.co.uk
Website: http://www.piab.co.uk
Directors: H. Fryer (Fin), M. Leitch (MD)
Ultimate Holding Company: ALTOR FUND II (SWEDEN)
Immediate Holding Company: PIAB LIMITED
Registration no: 03706878 **Date established:** 1999
No.of Employees: 1 - 10 **Product Groups:** 35, 39, 45

Date of Accounts	Dec 11	Dec 10	Dec 09
Working Capital	281	406	460
Fixed Assets	14	15	8
Current Assets	354	637	644

Prosser Flooring Ltd (Pharma/Biotech)
Greenoak Wysall Lane, Rempstone, Loughborough, LE12 6RW
Tel: 01509-881175 **Fax:** 01509-881175
E-mail: mail@prosserflooring.com
Website: http://www.prosserflooring.com
Directors: T. Prosser (Ptnr)
Immediate Holding Company: PROSSER FLOORING LIMITED
Registration no: 08151361 **Date established:** 2012
Turnover: £500,000 - £1m **No.of Employees:** 1 - 10 **Product Groups:** 52

Q E D
4 Soar Road Quorn, Loughborough, LE12 8BW
Tel: 01509-412317 **Fax:** 01509-416555
E-mail: sales@qedmotorsport.co.uk
Website: http://www.qedmotorsport.co.uk
Directors: S. Lea (Dir)
Registration no: 04097967 **Date established:** 2000
Turnover: Up to £250,000 **No.of Employees:** 1 - 10 **Product Groups:** 39

Rhondama Ltd
Unit 6 Windmill Road, Loughborough, LE11 1RA
Tel: 01509-218149 **Fax:** 01509-210162
E-mail: enquiries@rhondamaltd.com
Website: http://www.rhondamaltd.com
Managers: K. Smalley
Immediate Holding Company: RHONDAMA LIMITED
Registration no: 01171504 **VAT No.:** GB 115 6249 81
Date established: 1974 **Turnover:** £1m - £2m **No.of Employees:** 11 - 20
Product Groups: 29, 30, 32, 33, 34, 35, 36, 38, 39, 40, 42

Date of Accounts	Nov 11	Nov 10	Nov 09
Working Capital	171	160	122
Fixed Assets	95	71	85
Current Assets	346	343	348

S C S Machine Tool Services
18 Deeming Drive Quorn, Loughborough, LE12 8NF
Tel: 01509-412108 **Fax:** 01509-412108
Directors: W. Salmon (Prop)
Date established: 1987 **No.of Employees:** 1 - 10 **Product Groups:** 46

S I P Industrial Products Ltd
Gelders Hall Road Shepshed, Loughborough, LE12 9NH
Tel: 01509-500500 **Fax:** 01509-503154
E-mail: info@sip-group.com
Website: http://www.sip-group.com
Bank(s): HSBC
Directors: E. Ippaso (MD), A. Ippaso (MD), R. Povoas (Pers), G. Gittus (Fin), P. Ippaso (Dir)
Ultimate Holding Company: S.I.P. (INVESTMENTS) LIMITED
Immediate Holding Company: S.I.P.(INDUSTRIAL PRODUCTS)LIMITED
Registration no: 00942287 **VAT No.:** GB 395 3792 90
Date established: 1968 **Turnover:** £5m - £10m **No.of Employees:** 21 - 50
Product Groups: 40

Date of Accounts	Dec 11	Dec 10	Dec 09
Sales Turnover	9m	8m	7m
Pre Tax Profit/Loss	540	389	219
Working Capital	-446	-3m	-2m
Fixed Assets	3m	3m	3m
Current Assets	5m	4m	4m
Current Liabilities	3m	2m	970

Sanyo Gallenkamp plc
Monarch Way Belton Park, Loughborough, LE11 5XG
Tel: 01509-265265 **Fax:** 01509-269770
E-mail: sales@sanyogallenkamp.com
Website: http://www.sanyogallenkamp.com
Directors: M. Haslan (I.T. Dir), R. Kokubo (MD), Z. Millington (Dir)
Managers: K. Bowling (Sales & Mktg Mg)
Immediate Holding Company: FISTREEM INTERNATIONAL LIMITED
Registration no: 05136733 **VAT No.:** GB 524 2217 81
Date established: 2004 **Turnover:** £20m - £50m
No.of Employees: 11 - 20 **Product Groups:** 38, 40, 42

Date of Accounts	Aug 11	Aug 10	Aug 09
Working Capital	344	205	382
Fixed Assets	2	3	3
Current Assets	511	439	537

Satalight Videography
35-37 High Street Barrow Upon Soar, Loughborough, LE12 8PY
Tel: 0845-1307317 **Fax:** 01509-853111
E-mail: sales@satalight.co.uk
Website: http://www.weddingsonvideo.co.uk
Directors: T. Wilcox (MD)
Date established: 1993 **Turnover:** Up to £250,000
No.of Employees: 1 - 10 **Product Groups:** 85

Securitas Ltd
87 Derby Road, Loughborough, LE11 5AE
Tel: 01509-265556 **Fax:** 01509-265558
E-mail: info@reliancesecurity.co.uk
Website: http://www.securitas.co.uk
Managers: M. Millership (Fin Mgr), N. Coates (Chief Mgr), R. McKeon (Develop Mgr), R. Clegg (Personnel)
Immediate Holding Company: RELIANCE SECURITY SERVICES LIMITED
Registration no: 01146486 **Date established:** 1973
Turnover: Over £1,000m **No.of Employees:** 1 - 10 **Product Groups:** 81

Date of Accounts	Dec 10	Dec 09	Dec 08
Sales Turnover	N/A	2m	849
Pre Tax Profit/Loss	20	-991	-1m
Working Capital	-3m	-3m	-2m
Fixed Assets	N/A	683	494
Current Assets	N/A	539	890
Current Liabilities	N/A	110	131

Siba UK Ltd
19 Duke Street, Loughborough, LE11 1ED
Tel: 01509-269719 **Fax:** 01509-236024
E-mail: sales@siba.de
Website: http://www.sibauk.co.uk
Directors: R. Van Woerden (MD)
Ultimate Holding Company: SIBA GMBH & CO KG (GERMANY)
Immediate Holding Company: SIBA
Registration no: 03163350 **Date established:** 1996
Turnover: £250,000 - £500,000 **No.of Employees:** 1 - 10
Product Groups: 30, 37, 39, 67, 68

Date of Accounts	Sep 11	Sep 10	Sep 09
Working Capital	272	256	62
Fixed Assets	5	5	6
Current Assets	309	289	124

Stage Systems Ltd
Stage House Prince William Road, Loughborough, LE11 5GU
Tel: 01509-611021 **Fax:** 01509-233146
E-mail: info@stagesystems.co.uk
Website: http://www.stagesystems.co.uk
Managers: D. Mawdsley (Sales Prom Mgr), E. Goode (Personnel), R. Thorpe (Chief Acct)
Ultimate Holding Company: HAVELOCK EUROPA PLC
Immediate Holding Company: STAGE SYSTEMS LIMITED
Registration no: 00882644 **Date established:** 1966 **Turnover:** £2m - £5m
No.of Employees: 21 - 50 **Product Groups:** 26

Date of Accounts	Dec 11	Dec 10	Dec 09
Sales Turnover	3m	3m	4m
Pre Tax Profit/Loss	316	389	600
Working Capital	2m	2m	3m
Fixed Assets	80	92	114
Current Assets	3m	2m	3m
Current Liabilities	176	103	136

Starchild Shoes
Unit 18 The Oak Business Centre 79-93 Ratcliffe Road, Sileby, Loughborough, LE12 7PU
Tel: 01509-817601 **Fax:** 01509-817601
E-mail: info@starchildshoes.co.uk
Website: http://www.starchildshoes.co.uk
Directors: S. Bryant (Dir)
Immediate Holding Company: STARCHILD SHOES LIMITED
Registration no: 05273702 **Date established:** 2004
Turnover: £500,000 - £1m **No.of Employees:** 11 - 20 **Product Groups:** 63

Date of Accounts	Oct 11	Oct 10	Oct 08
Working Capital	85	72	29
Fixed Assets	36	49	62
Current Assets	199	210	150

J Alex Swift Ltd
Cross Street Hathern, Loughborough, LE12 5LB
Tel: 01509-842284 **Fax:** 01509-646106
E-mail: jgander@uk.estee.com
Website: http://www.jalexswift.co.uk
Bank(s): Yorkshire Bank PLC
Directors: I. Swift (Dir), N. Swift (Dir)
Immediate Holding Company: J.ALEX SWIFT LIMITED
Registration no: 00582072 **Date established:** 1957
Turnover: £500,000 - £1m **No.of Employees:** 21 - 50 **Product Groups:** 24

Date of Accounts	Mar 11	Mar 10	Mar 09
Working Capital	402	432	436
Fixed Assets	118	110	104
Current Assets	533	541	536

Synergy Logistics Ltd
Synergy House Lisle Street, Loughborough, LE11 1AW
Tel: 01509-232706 **Fax:** 01509-610186
E-mail: info@synergy-logistics.co.uk
Website: http://www.synergy-logistics.co.uk
Bank(s): Barclays
Directors: G. Clark (Comm), M. Darley Usmar (MD)
Managers: P. Price
Ultimate Holding Company: SYNERGY LIMITED
Immediate Holding Company: SYNERGY LOGISTICS LIMITED
Registration no: 01077180 **VAT No.:** GB 558 7088 93
Date established: 1972 **Turnover:** £1m - £2m **No.of Employees:** 21 - 50
Product Groups: 44

Date of Accounts	Mar 12	Mar 11	Mar 10
Sales Turnover	2m	2m	1m
Pre Tax Profit/Loss	358	102	23
Working Capital	454	380	672
Fixed Assets	65	63	81
Current Assets	1m	910	795
Current Liabilities	684	458	75

Szabo Software & Engineering UK Ltd
43 Angrave Road East Leake, Loughborough, LE12 6JA
Tel: 01509-854467 **Fax:** 01509-856787
E-mail: info@szabo-engineering.co.uk
Website: http://www.szabo-software.co.uk
Immediate Holding Company: Szabo Software & Engineering. Uk. Ltd
Registration no: 04075769 **No.of Employees:** 1 - 10 **Product Groups:** 37, 38, 40, 44, 49, 67, 84

Date of Accounts	Dec 07	Dec 06	Dec 05
Working Capital	10	38	17
Fixed Assets	9	6	6
Current Assets	35	53	64
Current Liabilities	25	15	48

T P Power Services Ltd
Rempstone Road Wymeswold, Loughborough, LE12 6UE
Tel: 01509-889410 **Fax:** 01509-889445
E-mail: enquiries@tppowerservices.com
Website: http://www.tppowerservices.com
Directors: S. Pidcock (MD)
Immediate Holding Company: TP POWER SERVICES LTD
Registration no: 04757171 **Date established:** 2003 **Turnover:** £2m - £5m
No.of Employees: 11 - 20 **Product Groups:** 37

Date of Accounts	Oct 11	Oct 10	Oct 09
Working Capital	229	101	152
Fixed Assets	49	50	55
Current Assets	465	218	945

Thomas Automation
Weldon Road, Loughborough, LE11 5RN
Tel: 01509-219912 **Fax:** 01509-266836
E-mail: service@thomasa.co.uk
Website: http://www.thomasa.co.uk
Bank(s): HSBC
Directors: A. McCourt (MD)
Immediate Holding Company: WHITTAKER OFFICE SUPPLIES LIMITED
Registration no: 02318185 **VAT No.:** GB 616 7301 54
Date established: 1987 **Turnover:** £2m - £5m **No.of Employees:** 11 - 20
Product Groups: 49

Date of Accounts	Dec 11	Dec 10	Dec 09
Working Capital	289	208	113
Fixed Assets	334	377	416
Current Assets	1m	1m	727

Vertical Height Safety Ltd
145 Byron Street, Loughborough, LE11 5JN
Tel: 01509-218747 **Fax:** 01509-218749
E-mail: mark@verticalheightsafety.com
Website: http://www.verticalheightsafety.com
Directors: J. Felstead (Dir)
Immediate Holding Company: VERTICAL HEIGHT SAFETY LIMITED
Registration no: 06636614 **Date established:** 2008
No.of Employees: 1 - 10 **Product Groups:** 35, 39, 40, 52, 54, 80, 84, 86

Date of Accounts	Jul 09
Working Capital	-3
Fixed Assets	4
Current Assets	12

Weatherford Group Reeves Oilfield Services Ltd
East Leake, Loughborough, LE12 6JX
Tel: 0115-945 7800 **Fax:** 0115-940 7921
E-mail: martin.endstone@eu.weatherford.com
Website: http://www.weatheford.com
Managers: C. Howle, M. Draicchio (Personnel), I. Jones (Comptroller), A. Wain (Tech Serv Mgr), M. Endstone (Chief Mgr)
Ultimate Holding Company: WEATHERFORD INTERNATIONAL LIMITED (BERMUDA)
Immediate Holding Company: REEVES OILFIELD SERVICES LTD
Registration no: 00134347 **Date established:** 1995
No.of Employees: 101 - 250 **Product Groups:** 11, 61

Date of Accounts	Dec 11	Dec 10	Dec 09
Sales Turnover	3m	3m	2m
Pre Tax Profit/Loss	331	379	-8
Working Capital	-1m	-1m	-2m
Fixed Assets	1m	2m	1m
Current Assets	2m	2m	1m
Current Liabilities	201	229	84

Weiss Gallenkamp Ltd
Unit 37-38 Loughborough Technology Centre Epinal Way, Loughborough, LE11 3GE
Tel: 01509-631590 **Fax:** 01509-211133
E-mail: enquiries@weiss-gallenkamp.com
Website: http://www.weiss-gallenkamp.com
Directors: M. Reilly (MD)
Managers: G. Taylor (Sales Prom Mgr), J. Walton (Mktg Serv Mgr), S. Jones (Serv Mgr), A. Fox (Fin Mgr)
Immediate Holding Company: WEISS GALLENKAMP LTD
Registration no: 03659232 **Date established:** 1998 **Turnover:** £5m - £10m
No.of Employees: 21 - 50 **Product Groups:** 38

Date of Accounts	Dec 11	Dec 10	Dec 09
Sales Turnover	7m	6m	7m
Pre Tax Profit/Loss	229	27	365
Working Capital	2m	2m	1m
Fixed Assets	243	155	225
Current Assets	3m	3m	3m
Current Liabilities	1m	1m	1m

M Wright & Sons Ltd
Quorn Mills Leicester Road, Quorn, Loughborough, LE12 8FZ
Tel: 01509-412365 **Fax:** 01509-415618
E-mail: info@mwright.co.uk
Website: http://www.mwright.co.uk
Bank(s): Yorkshire
Directors: M. Carver (Fin), J. James (Dir), M. Wright (Ch)
Managers: J. Green (Prod Mgr)
Immediate Holding Company: M. WRIGHT & SONS LIMITED
Registration no: 04105474 **VAT No.:** GB 114 3491 95
Date established: 2000 **Turnover:** £5m - £10m
No.of Employees: 51 - 100 **Product Groups:** 23

Date of Accounts	Nov 09	Nov 08	Nov 11
Sales Turnover	4m	N/A	5m
Pre Tax Profit/Loss	133	129	238
Working Capital	2m	2m	2m
Fixed Assets	1m	1m	1m
Current Assets	3m	2m	3m
Current Liabilities	406	333	460

Lutterworth

Bromley Enterprises UK Ltd
Unit 7 Bruntingthorpe Industrial Estate Upper Bruntingthorpe, Lutterworth, LE17 5QZ
Tel: 0116-247 8912 **Fax:** 0116-247 8969
E-mail: bromleyenterprises@googlemail.com
Directors: A. Felton (Fin), J. Briggs (Dir)
Managers: K. Deacon (Systems Mgr)
Ultimate Holding Company: HARBORO RUBBER COMPANY LIMITED(THE)
Immediate Holding Company: BROMLEY ENTERPRISES (U.K.) LIMITED
Registration no: 01838565 **Date established:** 1984
Turnover: Up to £250,000 **No.of Employees:** 1 - 10 **Product Groups:** 32

Date of Accounts	Oct 11	Oct 10	Oct 09
Working Capital	112	142	133
Fixed Assets	65	21	22
Current Assets	156	196	168

Clarke Translift Ltd
Bilton Way, Lutterworth, LE17 4HJ
Tel: 01455-552801 **Fax:** 01455-554112
E-mail: sales@clarke-transport.co.uk
Website: http://www.clarke-transport.co.uk
Directors: H. Smith (Dir)
Immediate Holding Company: CLARKE TRANSLIFT LIMITED
Registration no: 00693306 **VAT No.:** GB 113 8074 92
Date established: 1961 **Turnover:** £250,000 - £500,000
No.of Employees: 11 - 20 **Product Groups:** 72

Date of Accounts	Apr 12	Apr 11	Apr 10
Working Capital	347	319	324
Fixed Assets	577	598	631
Current Assets	458	448	457

Cre8 Associates Ltd
Bruntingthorpe Proving Ground Bath Lane, Lutterworth, LE17 5QS
Tel: 01162-479787 **Fax:** 08700-517401
E-mail: sales@cre8associates.com
Website: http://cre8-associates.com
Managers: D. Hobbs (Comm)
Date established: 2003 **Turnover:** Up to £250,000
No.of Employees: 1 - 10 **Product Groups:** 37, 84, 85

Date of Accounts	Mar 09	Mar 08	Mar 07
Sales Turnover	N/A	238	109
Pre Tax Profit/Loss	N/A	30	25
Working Capital	-10	6	30
Fixed Assets	20	19	4
Current Assets	13	42	74
Current Liabilities	N/A	21	38

Creative Laser Services
The Bakehouse 17b High Street, Lutterworth, LE17 4AT
Tel: 01455-559229 **Fax:** 01455-554712
E-mail: barry@clsmail.co.uk
Website: http://www.creativelaserservices.co.uk
Directors: B. Briggs (Dir)
Immediate Holding Company: CREATIVE LASER SERVICES LIMITED
Registration no: 05145038 **Date established:** 2004
No.of Employees: 1 - 10 **Product Groups:** 47, 48

Date of Accounts	Jun 11	Jun 10	Jun 09
Working Capital	-3	-4	-7
Fixed Assets	4	5	7
Current Assets	40	34	26

Dudley Associates
Unit 3 Elizabethan Way, Lutterworth, LE17 4ND
Tel: 01455-558825 **Fax:** 01455-558780
E-mail: sales@dudleyassociates.com
Website: http://www.dudleyassociates.com
Directors: J. Churchard (MD)
Managers: A. Topiwala, B. Holland
Immediate Holding Company: DUDLEY ASSOCIATES LIMITED
Registration no: 02508699 **Date established:** 1990 **Turnover:** £1m - £2m
No.of Employees: 21 - 50 **Product Groups:** 30, 46

Date of Accounts	Sep 08	Jun 11	Jun 10
Sales Turnover	N/A	2m	2m
Pre Tax Profit/Loss	N/A	-151	488
Working Capital	-16	300	364
Fixed Assets	350	411	396
Current Assets	754	551	627
Current Liabilities	N/A	115	90

Electroustic Ltd
1 Eaglesfield Industrial Estate Main Street, Leire, Lutterworth, LE17 5HF
Tel: 01455-202364 **Fax:** 01455-209043
E-mail: sales@electroustic.co.uk
Website: http://www.electroustic.co.uk
Directors: D. Collins (MD), K. Greening (Dir), K. Greening (MD)
Immediate Holding Company: ELECTROUSTIC HOLDINGS LIMITED
Registration no: 04534147 **Date established:** 2002
Turnover: £500,000 - £1m **No.of Employees:** 1 - 10 **Product Groups:** 37, 38

Date of Accounts	Jun 08	Jun 07	Jun 06
Sales Turnover	N/A	12	16
Pre Tax Profit/Loss	N/A	8	9
Working Capital	48	73	82
Fixed Assets	1	N/A	N/A
Current Assets	58	85	88
Current Liabilities	10	12	5
Total Share Capital	41	41	41
ROCE% (Return on Capital Employed)		11.6	10.5
ROT% (Return on Turnover)		71.7	54.0

Euro Catering Equipment
3 Turnpike Close, Lutterworth, LE17 4YB
Tel: 01455-559969 **Fax:** 01455-559979
E-mail: sales@euro-catering.co.uk
Website: http://www.chefsrange.co.uk
Directors: M. Charlton (Fin)
Immediate Holding Company: EURO CATERING EQUIPMENT LTD
Registration no: 02755032 **Date established:** 1992 **Turnover:** £1m - £2m
No.of Employees: 1 - 10 **Product Groups:** 28, 30, 36, 37, 40, 41, 42, 63, 66, 67

Date of Accounts	Mar 12	Mar 11	Mar 10
Working Capital	22	10	-40
Fixed Assets	34	25	19
Current Assets	485	359	312

Export Ltd
37 Station Road, Lutterworth, LE17 4AP
Tel: 01455-555340 **Fax:** 01455-555381
Website: http://www.husky-products.com
Directors: S. Bentley (Sales), A. David (Fin)
Ultimate Holding Company: JUPITER INDUSTRIES LIMITED
Immediate Holding Company: HUSKY GROUP LIMITED
Registration no: 00669115 **Date established:** 1960 **Turnover:** £5m - £10m
No.of Employees: 51 - 100 **Product Groups:** 40, 67

Date of Accounts	Dec 06	Dec 05	Dec 04
Sales Turnover	16m	13m	16m
Pre Tax Profit/Loss	390	-47	153

see next page

Export Ltd - Cont'd

Working Capital	766	508	506
Fixed Assets	311	437	564
Current Assets	5m	6m	5m
Current Liabilities	2m	2m	2m

F A Simms & Partners Ltd

Insol House 39 Station Road, Lutterworth, LE17 4AP
Tel: 01455-555444 **Fax:** 01455-552572
E-mail: info@fasimms.com
Website: http://www.fasimms.com
Directors: R. Simms (Dir)
Immediate Holding Company: F A SIMMS & PARTNERS LIMITED
Registration no: 06003034 **VAT No.:** GB 602 0836 79
Date established: 2006 **Turnover:** £500,000 - £1m
No.of Employees: 21 - 50 **Product Groups:** 80, 81, 82

Date of Accounts	Apr 11	Apr 10	Apr 09
Working Capital	189	462	575
Fixed Assets	162	182	193
Current Assets	531	714	778

Federated Ltd

Station Road North Kilworth, Lutterworth, LE17 6HY
Tel: 01858-881133 **Fax:** 01858-881144
E-mail: timkirby@federated.ltd.uk
Directors: T. Kirby (MD), J. Kirby (Fin)
Immediate Holding Company: FEDERATED LTD
Registration no: 03232800 **Date established:** 1996
No.of Employees: 1 - 10 **Product Groups:** 46, 48

Date of Accounts	May 11	May 10	May 09
Working Capital	125	97	59
Fixed Assets	30	39	57
Current Assets	315	216	140

Freudenberg Simrit LP

Simrit Service Centre Lutterworth Unit 7 Wycliffe Industrial Park, Lutterworth, LE17 4HG
Tel: 01455-204444 **Fax:** 01455-204455
E-mail: info@simrit.com
Website: http://www.simrit.com
Bank(s): Barclays, Elland
Directors: A. Mulac (MD)
Managers: T. Coles (Buyer), K. Swatton (Mktg Serv Mgr), N. Masters (Comptroller)
Ultimate Holding Company: FREUDENBERG & CO. (GERMANY)
Immediate Holding Company: FREUDENBERG TECHNICAL PRODUCTS L.P, NOK UK
Registration no: LP007952 **Turnover:** £10m - £20m
No.of Employees: 21 - 50 **Product Groups:** 29, 30, 31, 33, 36, 39, 40, 63, 66

Giromax Technology Ltd

Eagle House Bilton Way, Lutterworth, LE17 4JA
Tel: 01455-558969 **Fax:** 01455-558787
E-mail: enquiries@giromax.co.uk
Website: http://www.giromax.co.uk
Directors: R. Ennett (MD)
Immediate Holding Company: GIROMAX TECHNOLOGY LTD
Registration no: 03207074 **Date established:** 1996
No.of Employees: 1 - 10 **Product Groups:** 46, 48

Date of Accounts	Jul 11	Jul 10	Jul 09
Working Capital	227	214	137
Fixed Assets	3	2	3
Current Assets	2m	1m	776

Goratu UK Ltd (Goratu Maquinas Herramienta S.A.)

Unit 3 Cosford Business Park, Lutterworth, LE17 4QU
Tel: 01455-207801 **Fax:** 0845-612 1494
E-mail: sales@goratu.co.uk
Website: http://www.goratu.co.uk
Directors: M. Randall (MD)
Immediate Holding Company: GORATU UK LIMITED
Registration no: 04186371 **Date established:** 2001 **Turnover:** £1m - £2m
No.of Employees: 1 - 10 **Product Groups:** 46

Date of Accounts	Dec 11	Dec 10	Dec 09
Working Capital	31	23	64
Fixed Assets	16	36	22
Current Assets	520	379	153

Lifeplan Products Ltd

Unit 1 Elizabethan Way, Lutterworth, LE17 4ND
Tel: 01455-556281 **Fax:** 01455-556261
E-mail: enquiries@lifeplan.co.uk
Website: http://www.lifeplan.co.uk
Bank(s): Natwest
Directors: J. Christie (MD), M. Sadofsky (Fin), J. Robinson (Fin)
Managers: K. Maccanney, M. Hyde (Personnel), H. Christie (Buyer)
Ultimate Holding Company: MSW GROUP LTD.
Immediate Holding Company: LIFEPLAN PRODUCTS LIMITED
Registration no: 01843973 **VAT No.:** GB 424 3193 72
Date established: 1984 **Turnover:** £2m - £5m **No.of Employees:** 21 - 50
Product Groups: 20, 31

Date of Accounts	May 11	May 10	May 09
Sales Turnover	N/A	4m	4m
Pre Tax Profit/Loss	N/A	-294	47
Working Capital	165	258	287
Fixed Assets	2m	2m	2m
Current Assets	2m	2m	2m
Current Liabilities	N/A	521	838

Lister Industrial Power Tools Ltd

Bell Lane Husbands Bosworth, Lutterworth, LE17 6LA
Tel: 01858-880333 **Fax:** 01858-880333
Directors: H. Essajee (MD), M. Essajee (Fin)
Immediate Holding Company: LISTER INDUSTRIAL POWER TOOLS LIMITED
Registration no: 05258987 **Date established:** 2004
No.of Employees: 1 - 10 **Product Groups:** 37

Date of Accounts	Mar 11	Mar 10	Mar 09
Working Capital	-52	-50	-5
Fixed Assets	N/A	3	6
Current Assets	21	32	72

Nationwide Platforms

15 Midland Court Central Park, Lutterworth, LE17 4PN
Tel: 01455-558874 **Fax:** 01327-832809
E-mail: northampton.na@nationwideaccess.co.uk
Website: http://www.nationwideaccess.co.uk
Directors: H. Walters (Mkt Research)
Managers: A. Wright
Ultimate Holding Company: Lavendon Group PLC
Immediate Holding Company: THE PLATFORM COMPANY (HOLDINGS) LIMITED
Registration no: 04340206 **Date established:** 2001
Turnover: £20m - £50m **No.of Employees:** 1 - 10 **Product Groups:** 45, 83

Notts Sport Ltd

Innovation House Magna Park, Lutterworth, LE17 4XH
Tel: 01455-883730 **Fax:** 01455-883755
E-mail: info@nottssport.com
Website: http://www.nottssport.com
Directors: S. Patrick (Prop)
Ultimate Holding Company: NOTTS SPORT LIMITED
Immediate Holding Company: NOTTS SPORT (INTERNATIONAL) LIMITED
Registration no: 04586506 **Date established:** 2002 **Turnover:** £2m - £5m
No.of Employees: 21 - 50 **Product Groups:** 49

Date of Accounts	Oct 11	Oct 10	Apr 09
Working Capital	40	40	36
Current Assets	792	755	764

Pal International Ltd

Bilton Way, Lutterworth, LE17 4JA
Tel: 01455-555700 **Fax:** 01455-555777
E-mail: info@palinternational.com
Website: http://www.palinternational.com
Bank(s): National Westminster
Directors: R. Brucciani (MD)
Managers: S. Donaghy (Sales Prom Mgr), V. Human (Mktg Serv Mgr), P. Bryan, J. Wright (Chief Mgr), A. Wilson (Prod Mgr), A. Phippen (Export Sales Mg)
Immediate Holding Company: PAL INTERNATIONAL LIMITED
Registration no: 03272370 **Date established:** 1996
Turnover: £10m - £20m **No.of Employees:** 51 - 100 **Product Groups:** 22, 23, 24, 27, 29, 30

Date of Accounts	Dec 11	Dec 10	Dec 09
Sales Turnover	10m	11m	13m
Pre Tax Profit/Loss	28	174	695
Working Capital	3m	3m	3m
Fixed Assets	5m	5m	5m
Current Assets	5m	5m	5m
Current Liabilities	445	481	755

Select Engineering Midlands Ltd

Unit 2a Vedonis Works Gilmorton Road, Lutterworth, LE17 4PL
Tel: 01455-553778 **Fax:** 01455-553778
Directors: R. Stringer (Fin), R. Stringer (Prop), M. Stringer (MD)
Immediate Holding Company: SELECT ENGINEERING (MIDLANDS) LIMITED
Registration no: 04842184 **Date established:** 2003
No.of Employees: 1 - 10 **Product Groups:** 35

Date of Accounts	Jul 08	Jul 07	Jul 06
Working Capital	-8	-6	-8
Fixed Assets	13	14	17
Current Assets	35	26	23

Semelab Ltd

Coventry Road, Lutterworth, LE17 4JB
Tel: 01455-552505 **Fax:** 01455-558843
E-mail: sales@magnatec.co.uk
Website: http://www.magnatec.co.uk
Bank(s): Barclays
Directors: R. Bacon (MD), M. Mccabe (MD)
Managers: H. Joshi (Comptroller), A. Grigg (Personnel), W. Jackson (Tech Serv Mgr), S. Denton-beaumont (Serv Mgr), R. Rhodes, K. Stodart (Purch Mgr)
Ultimate Holding Company: TT ELECTRONICS PLC
Immediate Holding Company: SEMELAB LIMITED
Registration no: 06649272 **Date established:** 2008
Turnover: Up to £250,000 **No.of Employees:** 101 - 250
Product Groups: 37

Date of Accounts	Dec 11	Dec 10	Dec 09
Sales Turnover	15	13m	12m
Pre Tax Profit/Loss	1	513	897
Working Capital	3	3m	3m
Fixed Assets	6	6m	7m
Current Assets	8	5m	5m
Current Liabilities	1	737	633

Tech-Ni-Fold

2 St Johns Business Park, Lutterworth, LE17 4HB
Tel: 01455-554491 **Fax:** 01455-554526
E-mail: info@technifold.com
Website: http://www.technifold.com
Directors: G. Harris (Dir)
Registration no: 03939210 **Date established:** 2002
No.of Employees: 1 - 10 **Product Groups:** 44

Vintage Tractor Spares

Manor Farm Park Lane, Walton, Lutterworth, LE17 5RQ
Tel: 01455-556784
E-mail: mail@vintagetractorspares.co.uk
Website: http://www.vintagetractorspares.co.uk
Directors: D. Sumner (Ptnr)
Date established: 1999 **No.of Employees:** 1 - 10 **Product Groups:** 41

Wearparts UK Ltd

Oaks Industrial Estate Gilmorton Road, Lutterworth, LE17 4HA
Tel: 01455-553551 **Fax:** 01455-550907
E-mail: sales@wearparts.com
Website: http://www.wearparts.com
Directors: A. Pezzotti (MD), N. Morrell (Fin), S. Morel (Sales)
Immediate Holding Company: WEARPARTS UK LTD
Registration no: 05764530 **VAT No.:** GB 294 3093 43
Date established: 2006 **Turnover:** £5m - £10m
No.of Employees: 51 - 100 **Product Groups:** 45

Date of Accounts	Jun 08	Jun 07
Sales Turnover	5327	5243
Pre Tax Profit/Loss	82	-80
Working Capital	564	481
Fixed Assets	288	139
Current Assets	2174	2187
Current Liabilities	1610	1706
Total Share Capital	200	200
ROCE% (Return on Capital Employed)	9.6	-12.9
ROT% (Return on Turnover)	1.5	-1.5

Westfield Farm Equipment

Westfield Lodge Rugby Road, Swinford, Lutterworth, LE17 6BP
Tel: 01788-860336 **Fax:** 01788-860336
Website: http://www.wfes.co.uk
Directors: P. Robottom (Prop)
Date established: 1978 **No.of Employees:** 1 - 10 **Product Groups:** 41

Whitmores Timber Co. Ltd

Main Road Claybrooke Magna, Lutterworth, LE17 5AQ
Tel: 01455-209121 **Fax:** 01455-209041
E-mail: sales@whitmores.co.uk
Website: http://www.whitmores.co.uk
Bank(s): Bank of Scotland, Edinburgh
Directors: A. Rankine (Chief Op Offcr), N. Bazeley (Fin), R. Loveridge (Dir)
Managers: J. Reynolds (Tech Serv Mgr)
Immediate Holding Company: WHITMORE'S TIMBER CO. LIMITED
Registration no: 02359578 **Date established:** 1989
Turnover: £10m - £20m **No.of Employees:** 21 - 50 **Product Groups:** 25

Date of Accounts	Jul 11	Jul 10	Jul 09
Sales Turnover	11m	7m	6m
Pre Tax Profit/Loss	49	-57	12
Working Capital	2m	891	912
Fixed Assets	700	759	791
Current Assets	5m	5m	2m
Current Liabilities	979	2m	615

Market Harborough

2U Ltd

Sunderland Court 36 Main Street, Lubenham, Market Harborough, LE16 9TF
Tel: 0844-8044455
E-mail: olivere021@02.co.uk
Website: http://www.getyourmobilehere.2u.co.uk
Managers: O. Richmond (Mgr)
No.of Employees: 1 - 10 **Product Groups:** 67

Access & Lifting Services Ltd

Anchor House Riverside Industrial Estate, Market Harborough, LE16 7PT
Tel: 01858-465599 **Fax:** 01858-465379
E-mail: stevejwattsltd@gmail.com
Directors: S. Watts (Dir)
Immediate Holding Company: S J WATTS LIMITED
Registration no: 05100020 **Date established:** 2004
No.of Employees: 1 - 10 **Product Groups:** 35, 39, 45

Date of Accounts	Mar 11	Mar 10	Mar 09
Working Capital	-25	-33	-22
Fixed Assets	239	248	235
Current Assets	127	115	121

Aplab Power Systems

5 Heygate Street, Market Harborough, LE16 7JR
Tel: 01858-431288 **Fax:** 01858-439959
E-mail: bryan@aplabpowersystems.co.uk
Website: http://www.aplabpowersystems.co.uk
Directors: B. Powell (MD), B. Powell (MD)
Registration no: 03129898 **Turnover:** £250,000 - £500,000
No.of Employees: 1 - 10 **Product Groups:** 37, 38

Arkel Computer Services Ltd

38 Granville Street, Market Harborough, LE16 9EX
Tel: 01858-432495 **Fax:** 01858-467613
E-mail: info@arkel.co.uk
Website: http://www.arkel.co.uk
Directors: P. Arnold (MD)
Immediate Holding Company: ARKEL COMPUTER SERVICES LIMITED
Registration no: 01666681 **VAT No.:** GB 360 1791 66
Date established: 1982 **Turnover:** £1m - £2m **No.of Employees:** 1 - 10
Product Groups: 44

Date of Accounts	Jun 11	Jun 10	Jun 09
Working Capital	222	235	232
Fixed Assets	50	34	36
Current Assets	288	298	332

Banks Amenity Products Ltd

4 The Point, Market Harborough, LE16 7QU
Tel: 01858-464346 **Fax:** 01858-434734
E-mail: sales@banksamenity.co.uk
Website: http://www.banksamenity.co.uk
Directors: T. Banks (Ch)
Ultimate Holding Company: BANKS HOLDINGS LIMITED
Immediate Holding Company: BANKS AMENITY PRODUCTS LIMITED
Registration no: 00690835 **Date established:** 1961 **Turnover:** £2m - £5m
No.of Employees: 1 - 10 **Product Groups:** 14, 25, 32, 52

Date of Accounts	Dec 11	Dec 10	Dec 09
Working Capital	701	449	392
Fixed Assets	277	247	237
Current Assets	4m	4m	3m

The C S L Print Centre

84 St Marys Road, Market Harborough, LE16 7DX
Tel: 01858-433499 **Fax:** 01858-465208
E-mail: sstirland@thecslgroup.com
Website: http://www.thecslgroup.com
Managers: S. Stirland (Mgr)
Immediate Holding Company: COPYING SERVICES (LEICS) LTD
Registration no: 00953247 **No.of Employees:** 1 - 10 **Product Groups:** 44, 46, 48, 67, 79, 80, 83

Cadar Ltd

Unit 3 The Point, Market Harborough, LE16 7QU
Tel: 01858-410101 **Fax:** 01858-433934
E-mail: sales@cadar.ltd.uk
Website: http://www.cadar.ltd.uk
Directors: D. Thomas (Sales), T. McCleave (Fin), C. Ryder (MD)
Immediate Holding Company: CADAR LIMITED
Registration no: 01954475 **Date established:** 1985 **Turnover:** £1m - £2m
No.of Employees: 1 - 10 **Product Groups:** 20, 30, 32, 33, 36, 40, 42

Date of Accounts	Oct 11	Oct 10	Oct 09
Working Capital	126	143	401
Fixed Assets	33	34	38
Current Assets	977	915	1m

Darian Trading Ltd
Darian House Roman Way, Market Harborough, LE16 7PQ
Tel: 01858-433096 **Fax:** 01858-465409
E-mail: sales@dariangllobalsourcing.co.uk
Website: http://www.darianglobalsourcing.co.uk
Directors: E. Samandi (MD)
Ultimate Holding Company: STUDIO ENTERPRISE LIMITED
Immediate Holding Company: DARIAN TRADING LIMITED
Registration no: 02021071 **VAT No.:** GB 445 6069 38
Date established: 1986 **Turnover:** £2m - £5m **No.of Employees:** 1 - 10
Product Groups: 34, 48, 66, 80

Date of Accounts	Oct 11	Oct 10	Oct 09
Working Capital	30	12	-9
Fixed Assets	2	3	156
Current Assets	201	83	229

Elite Thermal Systems Ltd
6 Stuart Road, Market Harborough, LE16 9PQ
Tel: 01858-469834 **Fax:** 01858-410085
E-mail: sales@elitefurnaces.com
Website: http://www.elitefurnaces.com
Directors: J. Roberts (Fin), A. Roberts (MD)
Immediate Holding Company: ELITE THERMAL SYSTEMS LIMITED
Registration no: 03679821 **Date established:** 1998
No.of Employees: 1 - 10 **Product Groups:** 40, 42, 46

Date of Accounts	Apr 11	Apr 10	Apr 09
Working Capital	125	61	34
Fixed Assets	255	263	256
Current Assets	270	238	249

Elliot Design
3 Nobold Court Gold Street, Clipston, Market Harborough, LE16 9RR
Tel: 01858-525664
Directors: B. Towneno (Prop)
No.of Employees: 1 - 10 **Product Groups:** 36, 40

Em Secure (Commercial Vehicle Security Locks Installation)
3 Rolleston Close, Market Harborough, LE16 8BZ
Tel: 07891-340168 **Fax:** 01858-432756
E-mail: info@emsecure.co.uk
Website: http://www.emsecure.co.uk
Directors: R. Breslin (Prop)
Immediate Holding Company: EMSECURE GARRISON LIMITED
Registration no: 06967481 **Date established:** 2009
No.of Employees: 1 - 10 **Product Groups:** 36

Date of Accounts	Jul 11	Jul 10
Working Capital	-3	N/A
Fixed Assets	4	N/A
Current Assets	78	N/A

Euromec Ltd
Unit A1 Welland Indl-Est Valley Way, Market Harborough, LE16 7PS
Tel: 01858-434011 **Fax:** 01858-464910
E-mail: sales@euromec.co.uk
Website: http://www.euromec.co.uk
Directors: P. Crew (MD), P. Crewe (MD)
Managers: H. Crewe (Mktg Serv Mgr)
Immediate Holding Company: EUROMEC CONTRACTS LIMITED
Registration no: 03328632 **Date established:** 1997 **Turnover:** £1m - £2m
No.of Employees: 11 - 20 **Product Groups:** 37, 40, 45

Date of Accounts	Dec 08	Dec 07	Dec 06
Working Capital	34	-14	3
Fixed Assets	130	6	N/A
Current Assets	487	31	73
Current Liabilities	452	45	69
Total Share Capital	50	N/A	N/A

The Harborough Rubber Co. Ltd
Riverside, Market Harborough, LE16 7PZ
Tel: 01858-410610 **Fax:** 01858-410006
E-mail: help@harboro.co.uk
Website: http://www.harboro.co.uk
Bank(s): HSBC Bank plc
Directors: N. Tulloch (Dir)
Immediate Holding Company: HARBORO ENTERPRISES LIMITED
Registration no: 00257353 **Date established:** 2010 **Turnover:** £5m - £10m
No.of Employees: 51 - 100 **Product Groups:** 22, 29, 63

Date of Accounts	Oct 08	Oct 09	Oct 10
Sales Turnover	7m	4m	6m
Pre Tax Profit/Loss	469	-307	233
Working Capital	3m	3m	2m
Fixed Assets	3m	3m	3m
Current Assets	4m	3m	3m
Current Liabilities	954	299	620

Henley Structural Steel Systems Ltd
Riverside House Riverside, Market Harborough, LE16 7PT
Tel: 01858-433770
Website: http://www.henleybs.com
Immediate Holding Company: Greys Secretarial Services Ltd
Registration no: 05496411 **Date established:** 2005
No.of Employees: 21 - 50 **Product Groups:** 34, 44, 48, 52

Hunting Lodge Hotel
High Street Cottingham, Market Harborough, LE16 8XN
Tel: 01536-771370 **Fax:** 01536-771942
E-mail: info@huntinglodgehotel.com
Website: http://www.huntinglodgehotel.com
Directors: J. Weedall (Sales)
Managers: Z. Collins
Immediate Holding Company: THE HUNTING LODGE COTTINGHAM LIMITED
Registration no: 03212655 **Date established:** 1996
No.of Employees: 21 - 50 **Product Groups:** 69

Date of Accounts	Oct 11	Oct 10	Oct 09
Working Capital	-186	-186	-141
Fixed Assets	2m	2m	2m
Current Assets	94	113	127

Jendico Ltd
Unit G3 Welland Industrial Estate Valley Way, Market Harborough, LE16 7PS
Tel: 01858-464888 **Fax:** 01858-464030
E-mail: sales@jendico.co.uk
Website: http://www.jendico.co.uk
Directors: M. Peacock (MD), D. Allinson (Sales)
Managers: J. Hubble (Sales Admin)
Immediate Holding Company: JENDICO LIMITED
Registration no: 03823656 **Date established:** 1999 **Turnover:** £2m - £5m
No.of Employees: 1 - 10 **Product Groups:** 30, 36, 40

Date of Accounts	Dec 07	Dec 06	Dec 05
Working Capital	-174	-171	19
Fixed Assets	99	126	146
Current Assets	410	380	508
Current Liabilities	584	552	488
Total Share Capital	221	221	221

King Trailers Ltd
Riverside, Market Harborough, LE16 7PX
Tel: 01858-467361 **Fax:** 01858-467161
E-mail: sales@kingtrailers.co.uk
Website: http://www.kingtrailers.co.uk
Bank(s): HSBC Bank plc
Directors: M. Carrington (MD), R. Brown (Fin), R. Spreckley (Fab)
Managers: S. Wright
Immediate Holding Company: KING TRAILERS LIMITED
Registration no: 03503886 **VAT No.:** GB 727 9350 10
Date established: 1998 **Turnover:** £5m - £10m
No.of Employees: 51 - 100 **Product Groups:** 39, 45

Date of Accounts	Mar 11	Mar 10	Mar 09
Sales Turnover	6m	6m	N/A
Pre Tax Profit/Loss	245	250	180
Working Capital	694	581	292
Fixed Assets	105	98	133
Current Assets	2m	2m	2m
Current Liabilities	283	784	627

King Vehicle Engineering Ltd
Riverside, Market Harborough, LE16 7PX
Tel: 01858-467361 **Fax:** 01858-467161
E-mail: sales@kingtrailers.co.uk
Website: http://www.kingtrailers.co.uk
Managers: R. Bryant (Chief Mgr)
Registration no: 05543840 **VAT No.:** GB 775 6696 63
Date established: 2000 **No.of Employees:** 11 - 20 **Product Groups:** 36, 39, 45, 83

Date of Accounts	Mar 10	Mar 09	Mar 08
Working Capital	-84	-84	-84
Fixed Assets	191	191	191
Current Assets	17	N/A	N/A

Market Harborough Building Society
15-17 The Square, Market Harborough, LE16 7PD
Tel: 01858-412250 **Fax:** 01858-410169
E-mail: mrobinson@mhbs.co.uk
Website: http://www.mhbs.co.uk
Directors: M. Robinson (Grp Chief Exec)
Immediate Holding Company: MARKET HARBOROUGH BUILDING SOCIETY CHARITABLE FOUN
Registration no: 03885898 **Date established:** 1999
Turnover: Up to £250,000 **No.of Employees:** 21 - 50 **Product Groups:** 82

Needalocksmith.com
Rolleston Close, Market Harborough, LE16 8BZ
Tel: 07891-340168
E-mail: info@needalocksmith.com
Website: http://www.needalocksmith.com
Directors: R. Breslin (Mkt Research)
No.of Employees: 11 - 20 **Product Groups:** 52, 66

Nomad Ltd (Head Office)
Rockingham Industrial Estate Rockingham Road, Market Harborough, LE16 7QE
Tel: 01858-464878 **Fax:** 01253-291834
E-mail: sales@nomadplc.co.uk
Website: http://www.nomadplc.co.uk
Directors: S. Rumsey (MD)
Managers: Y. Tinkler (Chief Acct)
Ultimate Holding Company: NO CHANGE LIMITED
Immediate Holding Company: NOMAD LIMITED
Registration no: 00705998 **Date established:** 1961 **Turnover:** £1m - £2m
No.of Employees: 21 - 50 **Product Groups:** 22, 25, 27, 30, 35, 38, 44, 49, 63

Date of Accounts	Mar 11	Mar 10	Mar 09
Working Capital	184	178	170
Fixed Assets	289	303	338
Current Assets	535	446	536

D G Norman
Cottons Farm Buildings The Cottons, Rockingham, Market Harborough, LE16 8TF
Tel: 01536-770966 **Fax:** 01536-771696
E-mail: dgnorman@hotmail.com
Directors: D. Norman (Prop)
Date established: 2002 **No.of Employees:** 1 - 10 **Product Groups:** 41

Orthos Engineering Ltd
2 The Point, Market Harborough, LE16 7QU
Tel: 01858-464246 **Fax:** 01858-434480
E-mail: sales@orthos.uk.com
Website: http://www.orthos.uk.com
Directors: K. Scott (Dir), E. Davis (I.T. Dir)
Immediate Holding Company: ORTHOS (ENGINEERING) LIMITED
Registration no: 00560412 **VAT No.:** GB 120 6488 86
Date established: 1956 **Turnover:** £1m - £2m **No.of Employees:** 1 - 10
Product Groups: 36, 40, 41, 42, 43, 44, 45, 46, 67

Date of Accounts	Feb 12	Feb 11	Feb 10
Working Capital	132	192	258
Fixed Assets	57	55	59
Current Assets	363	421	546

Orthos Projects Ltd
Fernie Road, Market Harborough, LE16 7PH
Tel: 01858-462806 **Fax:** 01858-464403
E-mail: nick.hall@orthosprojects.com
Website: http://www.orthosprojects.com
Directors: N. Hall (Dir)
Immediate Holding Company: ORTHOS (PROJECTS) LIMITED
Registration no: 01316160 **Date established:** 1977 **Turnover:** £1m - £2m
No.of Employees: 11 - 20 **Product Groups:** 32, 38, 40, 41, 42, 44, 45, 66, 84

Date of Accounts	May 12	May 11	May 10
Working Capital	1m	1m	1m
Fixed Assets	32	55	88
Current Assets	1m	2m	1m

Pact Services
4 Court Yard Workshops Bath Street, Market Harborough, LE16 9EW
Tel: 01858-432841 **Fax:** 01858-432841
E-mail: ianathompson@btconnect.com
Website: http://www.pactservices.co.uk
Directors: I. Thompson (Prop)
Immediate Holding Company: P.A.C.T. SERVICES LIMITED
Registration no: 03876764 **Date established:** 1999
No.of Employees: 1 - 10 **Product Groups:** 38, 48

Date of Accounts	Mar 12	Mar 11	Mar 10
Working Capital	-28	-37	-19
Fixed Assets	25	36	24
Current Assets	112	65	65

Page & Moy General Enquiries
Compass House Rockingham Road, Market Harborough, LE16 7QD
Tel: 01858-410456 **Fax:** 01858-461956
E-mail: info@travelsphere.co.uk
Website: http://www.pageandmoy.co.uk
Directors: H. Thomas (Fin)
Managers: P. Shepherd, W. Burton
Ultimate Holding Company: KALEIDOSCOPE TOPCO LIMITED
Immediate Holding Company: PAGE & MOY TRAVEL GROUP AIR HOLIDAYS LIMITED
Registration no: 01329030 **VAT No.:** GB 313 0600 24
Date established: 1977 **Turnover:** £75m - £125m
No.of Employees: 251 - 500 **Product Groups:** 69

Date of Accounts	Nov 11	Nov 10	Nov 09
Sales Turnover	95m	77m	79m
Pre Tax Profit/Loss	-6m	3m	-2m
Working Capital	31	11m	12m
Fixed Assets	4m	5m	5m
Current Assets	20m	31m	30m
Current Liabilities	15m	16m	15m

Q P I Ltd
Melton Road East Langton, Market Harborough, LE16 7TG
Tel: 01858-540121 **Fax:** 01858-540133
E-mail: sales@qpiltd.co.uk
Website: http://www.qpiltd.co.uk
Managers: S. Green (Mgr)
Immediate Holding Company: QPI LTD
Registration no: 06442416 **Date established:** 2007 **Turnover:** £2m - £5m
No.of Employees: 11 - 20 **Product Groups:** 30, 45, 46, 48, 67

Date of Accounts	Nov 10	Nov 09
Working Capital	-0	-0

Rhewum GB Ltd
3 The Point, Market Harborough, LE16 7QU
Tel: 01858-468088 **Fax:** 01858-433934
E-mail: info@rhewum.de
Website: http://www.rhewum.com
Directors: C. Ryder (MD), T. McCleave (Co Sec)
Ultimate Holding Company: CADAR LIMITED
Immediate Holding Company: RHEWUM (GB) LIMITED
Registration no: 02848465 **Date established:** 1993
No.of Employees: 1 - 10 **Product Groups:** 35, 39, 45

Date of Accounts	Dec 11	Dec 10	Dec 09
Working Capital	73	43	24
Current Assets	84	75	45

T G W Ltd
1 The Point, Market Harborough, LE16 7QU
Tel: 01858-468855 **Fax:** 01858-419613
E-mail: ukenquiries@tgw-group.com
Website: http://www.tgw-group.com
Directors: P. Steeds (Sales), A. Smith (MD), I. Powell (Chief Op Offcr), G. Kirchmayr (Dir)
Immediate Holding Company: TGW Logistics Group GmbH, AT-Wels
Registration no: 02860436 **VAT No.:** GB 038 2891 06
Date established: 1969 **Turnover:** £125m - £250m
No.of Employees: 51 - 100 **Product Groups:** 41, 44, 45

Date of Accounts	Jun 11	Jun 10	Jun 09
Sales Turnover	30m	N/A	N/A
Pre Tax Profit/Loss	2m	N/A	N/A
Working Capital	3m	736	136
Fixed Assets	142	111	103
Current Assets	8m	6m	3m
Current Liabilities	1m	N/A	N/A

Texane Ltd
Unit D4 Welland Industrial Estate Valley Way, Market Harborough, LE16 7PS
Tel: 01858-462040 **Fax:** 01858-410029
E-mail: info@texane.com
Website: http://www.texane.com
Directors: A. Dutt (Fin), A. Dutt (MD)
Ultimate Holding Company: NEWSVILLE LIMITED
Immediate Holding Company: TEXANE LIMITED
Registration no: 00880347 **VAT No.:** 114 5422 07 **Date established:** 1966
Turnover: £1m - £2m **No.of Employees:** 1 - 10 **Product Groups:** 48

Date of Accounts	Sep 11	Sep 10	Sep 09
Working Capital	117	112	64
Fixed Assets	45	50	59
Current Assets	460	497	534

Towrite Electric Vehicles Harborough Ltd
Albert Road, Market Harborough, LE16 7LU
Tel: 01858-467805 **Fax:** 01858-434209
E-mail: sales@towrite.co.uk
Website: http://www.towrite.co.uk
Bank(s): National Westminster
Managers: A. Raimi (Mgr)
Immediate Holding Company: TOWRITE ELECTRIC VEHICLES (HARBOROUGH) LIMITED
Registration no: 02370915 **VAT No.:** GB 514 0106 10
Date established: 1989 **Turnover:** £250,000 - £500,000
No.of Employees: 11 - 20 **Product Groups:** 39

Date of Accounts	Aug 11	Aug 10	Aug 09
Working Capital	460	467	540
Fixed Assets	36	32	26
Current Assets	590	571	607

Tyco Valves & Controls Ltd
Crosby Road, Market Harborough, LE16 9EE
Tel: 01858-467281 **Fax:** 01858-434728
E-mail: sales_uk@tyco-valves.com
Website: http://www.tyco.com

see next page

Tyco Valves & Controls Ltd - Cont'd

Directors: N. Petty (MD)
Managers: R. Forbes (Purch Mgr), G. Knight (Fin Mgr), D. Strang (Tech Serv Mgr), R. Gibson (Personnel)
Immediate Holding Company: ALLEN GLENOLD LIMITED
Registration no: 01702360 **Date established:** 1983
Turnover: £10m - £20m **No.of Employees:** 51 - 100 **Product Groups:** 30, 36, 39, 40

Date of Accounts	Mar 11	Mar 10	Mar 09
Working Capital	333	384	395
Fixed Assets	33	42	46
Current Assets	852	680	671

Wash Tech Services Ltd

Unit 3 1 Fernie Road, Market Harborough, LE16 7PH
Tel: 01858-464748 **Fax:** 01858-467506
E-mail: washtech@btconnect.com
Website: http://www.washtechservices.co.uk
Directors: A. Evans (MD)
Immediate Holding Company: WASHTECH SERVICES LIMITED
Registration no: 03707377 **Date established:** 1999
No.of Employees: 1 - 10 **Product Groups:** 20, 40, 41

Date of Accounts	Feb 08	Feb 11	Feb 10
Working Capital	N/A	-57	75
Fixed Assets	N/A	59	69
Current Assets	N/A	62	75

Wright Plastics Ltd

Fernie Road, Market Harborough, LE16 7PH
Tel: 01858-465661 **Fax:** 01858-431831
E-mail: sales@wplastic.co.uk
Website: http://www.wplastic.co.uk
Bank(s): Lloyds
Directors: S. Walsh (MD), M. Best (Chief Op Offcr)
Managers: S. Timpton (Fin Mgr), N. Skidmore (Sales Prom Mgr)
Immediate Holding Company: WRIGHT PLASTICS LIMITED
Registration no: 01095422 **VAT No.:** GB 119 9410 61
Date established: 1973 **Turnover:** Up to £250,000
No.of Employees: 21 - 50 **Product Groups:** 30, 42, 48

Date of Accounts	Mar 11	Mar 10	Mar 09
Working Capital	235	62	524
Fixed Assets	244	262	273
Current Assets	2m	2m	1m

Markfield

Briton Supplies

Unit 19 Hill Lane Industrial Estate, Markfield, LE67 9PN
Tel: 01530-249100 **Fax:** 01530-249400
E-mail: britsupplies@tiscali.co.uk
Directors: T. Baird (Prop)
Date established: 1979 **No.of Employees:** 1 - 10 **Product Groups:** 38, 42

Coolmation Services Ltd

Unit 5b Hill Lane Close, Markfield, LE67 9PY
Tel: 01530-244334 **Fax:** 01530-242807
E-mail: enquiries@service4chillers.co.uk
Website: http://www.service4chillers.co.uk
Directors: G. Franklin (Co Sec)
Managers: A. Wait (Sales Admin)
Ultimate Holding Company: COOLMATION LIMITED
Immediate Holding Company: COOLMATION SERVICE LTD
Registration no: 03443661 **Date established:** 1997 **Turnover:** £5m - £10m
No.of Employees: 21 - 50 **Product Groups:** 40, 41, 42, 52

Date of Accounts	Jan 12	Jan 11	Jan 10
Working Capital	1m	1m	1m
Fixed Assets	246	284	107
Current Assets	2m	2m	2m

C J Upton & Sons Ltd

Shaw Lane, Markfield, LE67 9PU
Tel: 01530-242116 **Fax:** 01530-245626
E-mail: james.upton@uptonsteel.com
Website: http://www.uptonsteel.com
Directors: J. Upton (Dir)
Ultimate Holding Company: C.J. UPTON HOLDINGS LTD.
Immediate Holding Company: C.J. UPTON & SONS LIMITED
Registration no: NI009719 **VAT No.:** GB 295 4769 01
Date established: 1973 **Turnover:** £20m - £50m
No.of Employees: 51 - 100 **Product Groups:** 34, 48, 66

Date of Accounts	Dec 11	Dec 10	Dec 09
Sales Turnover	55m	43m	34m
Pre Tax Profit/Loss	158	952	470
Working Capital	3m	4m	3m
Fixed Assets	3m	2m	2m
Current Assets	20m	14m	11m
Current Liabilities	6m	1m	634

Vickers Sporting Services

Unit 9a Hill Lane Close, Markfield, LE67 9PY
Tel: 01530-249996 **Fax:** 01530- 249996
E-mail: shimlin@hotmail.co.uk
Website: http://www.shimlin.freeserve.co.uk
Directors: S. Vickers (Prop)
Turnover: £250,000 - £500,000 **No.of Employees:** 1 - 10
Product Groups: 36, 39, 40

Melton Mowbray

A G S Noise Control Ltd

16 Digby Drive, Melton Mowbray, LE13 0RQ
Tel: 01664-568728 **Fax:** 01664-481190
E-mail: sales@agsnoisecontrol.co.uk
Website: http://www.agsnoisecontrol.co.uk
Directors: A. Grummitt (MD)
Immediate Holding Company: A G S NOISE CONTROL LIMITED
Registration no: 04594070 **Date established:** 2002
Turnover: £250,000 - £500,000 **No.of Employees:** 1 - 10
Product Groups: 54

Date of Accounts	Dec 11	Dec 10	Dec 09
Working Capital	87	140	87
Fixed Assets	170	167	177
Current Assets	287	585	444

Alstom Midlands Test Centre

St. Bartholomews Way Welby, Melton Mowbray, LE14 3JP
Tel: 01664-814111 **Fax:** 01664-814104
Website: http://www.transport.alstom.com
No.of Employees: 11 - 20 **Product Groups:** 18, 37, 39, 72

Anglo Adhesives & Services Ltd

Anglo House Dalby Road, Melton Mowbray, LE13 0BL
Tel: 01664-480866 **Fax:** 0116-448 0963
E-mail: sales@anglo-adhesives.co.uk
Website: http://www.anglo-adhesives.co.uk
Directors: P. Kinder (MD)
Immediate Holding Company: ANGLO ADHESIVES & SERVICES LIMITED
Registration no: 03842448 **Date established:** 1999 **Turnover:** £2m - £5m
No.of Employees: 1 - 10 **Product Groups:** 29, 31, 32, 66

Date of Accounts	Apr 11	Apr 10	Apr 09
Working Capital	-100	-83	-56
Fixed Assets	793	790	792
Current Assets	185	187	176

Approved Fire Protection Ltd

Lime Street Burton Lazars, Melton Mowbray, LE14 2UP
Tel: 01664-560256 **Fax:** 01664-560256
Website: http://www.afpltd.org.uk
Directors: S. Tagg (Fin)
Immediate Holding Company: APPROVED FIRE PROTECTION LIMITED
Registration no: 02989095 **Date established:** 1994
No.of Employees: 1 - 10 **Product Groups:** 38, 42

Date of Accounts	Dec 11	Dec 10	Dec 09
Sales Turnover	23	N/A	N/A
Pre Tax Profit/Loss	4	N/A	N/A
Working Capital	2	-1	7
Fixed Assets	2	1	2
Current Assets	6	21	14
Current Liabilities	4	N/A	N/A

Bramlage - Wiko UK

The Crown Business Park Station Road, Old Dalby, Melton Mowbray, LE14 3NQ
Tel: 08707-516670 **Fax:** 08707-516679
E-mail: sales@rpc-bramlagewiko.co.uk
Website: http://www.rpc-group.com
Managers: I. Smith (Sales Prom Mgr)
Date established: 2003 **No.of Employees:** 1 - 10 **Product Groups:** 30

Brobot Petroleum Ltd

Thorpe Road, Melton Mowbray, LE13 1SQ
Tel: 01664-480000 **Fax:** 01664-410504
E-mail: sales@brobot.co.uk
Website: http://www.brobot.co.uk
Bank(s): National Westminster Bank Plc
Directors: B. Smith (Fin), E. Bright (MD)
Managers: H. Chapman (Personnel), K. Newton (Purch Mgr)
Ultimate Holding Company: BROBOT GROUP LIMITED
Immediate Holding Company: BROBOT PETROLEUM LIMITED
Registration no: 01349544 **Date established:** 1978
Turnover: £125m - £250m **No.of Employees:** 21 - 50 **Product Groups:** 61

Date of Accounts	Mar 12	Mar 11	Mar 10
Sales Turnover	127m	148m	127m
Pre Tax Profit/Loss	239	1m	973
Working Capital	-8m	-6m	-6m
Fixed Assets	21m	20m	20m
Current Assets	5m	9m	11m
Current Liabilities	805	1m	1m

Cavat Tools Ltd

7 New Road Burton Lazars, Melton Mowbray, LE14 2UU
Tel: 01664-561761 **Fax:** 01664-410280
E-mail: cavattools@cavattools.co.uk
Website: http://www.cavattools.co.uk
Directors: R. Kemm (MD)
Immediate Holding Company: CAVAT TOOLS LIMITED
Registration no: 01614086 **Date established:** 1982
Turnover: Up to £250,000 **No.of Employees:** 1 - 10 **Product Groups:** 45, 46

Date of Accounts	Jan 12	Jan 11	Jan 10
Working Capital	-14	-17	-16
Current Assets	31	23	38

Dual Pumps Ltd

47 Norman Way, Melton Mowbray, LE13 1JE
Tel: 01664-567226 **Fax:** 01664-410127
E-mail: info@dualpumps.co.uk
Website: http://www.dualpumps.co.uk
Bank(s): National Westminster Bank Plc
Managers: A. Cudit (Purch Mgr), C. Wake (Chief Mgr)
Immediate Holding Company: DUAL PUMPS LIMITED
Registration no: 01216746 **Date established:** 1975 **Turnover:** £5m - £10m
No.of Employees: 21 - 50 **Product Groups:** 39, 40

Date of Accounts	May 11	May 10	May 09
Sales Turnover	N/A	N/A	6m
Pre Tax Profit/Loss	N/A	N/A	151
Working Capital	3m	3m	3m
Fixed Assets	941	900	1m
Current Assets	4m	4m	3m
Current Liabilities	N/A	N/A	416

Elster-Instromet

4 Pate Road, Melton Mowbray, LE13 0RG
Tel: 01664-567797 **Fax:** 01664-410254
E-mail: sales@elster.com
Website: http://www.elster-instromet.com
Bank(s): Nat West
Managers: P. Morris (Mgr), A. Pead (Sales Prom Mgr), M. Herus (Purch Mgr)
Ultimate Holding Company: INSTUMET INTERNATIONAL
Immediate Holding Company: NV ROBSA INTERNATIONAL SA (BELGIUM)
Registration no: 01300800 **VAT No.:** 118 2239 86 **Date established:** 1977
Turnover: £500,000 - £1m **No.of Employees:** 21 - 50 **Product Groups:** 84

Flextraction Ltd

10 Digby Drive, Melton Mowbray, LE13 0RQ
Tel: 01664-410641 **Fax:** 01664-480244
E-mail: wpg@flextraction.co.uk
Website: http://www.flextraction.co.uk
Directors: W. Gilder (Prop)
Immediate Holding Company: FLEXTRACTION LIMITED
Registration no: 03486736 **Date established:** 1997
Turnover: £250,000 - £500,000 **No.of Employees:** 11 - 20
Product Groups: 40, 54

Date of Accounts	Nov 11	Nov 10	Nov 09
Working Capital	-10	-19	44
Fixed Assets	14	24	33
Current Assets	389	399	432
Current Liabilities	193	187	197

Hortus Ligneous

The Willows Ironstone Lane, Holwell, Melton Mowbray, LE14 4SU
Tel: 01664-444724 **Fax:** 01664-444334
E-mail: samclemons@hortuslig.co.uk
Website: http://www.hortuslig.co.uk
Directors: S. Clemons (Prop)
Immediate Holding Company: HORTUS LIGNEOUS LIMITED
Registration no: 04721089 **Date established:** 2003
No.of Employees: 1 - 10 **Product Groups:** 26, 35

Date of Accounts	Mar 08
Working Capital	-25
Fixed Assets	28
Current Assets	66
Current Liabilities	91

Long Clawson Dairy Ltd

Hickling Lane Long Clawson, Melton Mowbray, LE14 4PJ
Tel: 01664-822332 **Fax:** 01664-823236
E-mail: enquiries@clawson.co.uk
Website: http://www.clawson.co.uk
Bank(s): Midland
Managers: S. Thompson
Registration no: 0005419r **VAT No.:** GB 416 1169 95
Date established: 1911 **Turnover:** £10m - £20m
No.of Employees: 101 - 250 **Product Groups:** 20

M A S Welding Supplies

Manor Farm Cottage 10 Manor Lane, Somerby, Melton Mowbray, LE14 2QD
Tel: 01664-454403 **Fax:** 01664-454803
Directors: C. Crankshaw (Prop)
Date established: 1984 **No.of Employees:** 1 - 10 **Product Groups:** 46

Metal World Engineering

Unit 3 Stapleford Estate, Saxby, Melton Mowbray, LE14 2SB
Tel: 01572-787333 **Fax:** 01572-787555
E-mail: sales@metalworldeng.com
Website: http://www.metalworldeng.com
Directors: R. Parnell (Prop)
Turnover: Up to £250,000 **No.of Employees:** 1 - 10 **Product Groups:** 36, 48

Premier Fork Lift Trucks

Unit 6a Rural Industrial Estate Station Road, John O' Gaunt, Melton Mowbray, LE14 2RE
Tel: 0116-230 1000 **Fax:** 01509-551911
Directors: S. Cotterell (Prop)
Registration no: 04107307 **Date established:** 2000
No.of Employees: 1 - 10 **Product Groups:** 35, 39, 45

R P C Containers Ltd

The Crown Business Park Station Road, Old Dalby, Melton Mowbray, LE14 3NQ
Tel: 01664-821210 **Fax:** 01664-821214
E-mail: t.roper@rpc-olddalby.co.uk
Website: http://www.rpc-containers.co.uk
Managers: T. Roper (Mgr)
Ultimate Holding Company: RPC GROUP PLC
Immediate Holding Company: RPC CONTAINERS LIMITED
Registration no: 02786492 **Date established:** 1993
No.of Employees: 21 - 50 **Product Groups:** 30

Date of Accounts	Mar 11	Mar 10	Mar 09
Sales Turnover	189m	175m	183m
Pre Tax Profit/Loss	14m	15m	-1m
Working Capital	21m	17m	-37m
Fixed Assets	81m	77m	79m
Current Assets	76m	66m	68m
Current Liabilities	17m	13m	14m

Rural Energy

21 Burrough Court Burrough On The Hill, Melton Mowbray, LE14 2QS
Tel: 01664-454989 **Fax:** 01664-454230
E-mail: info@ruralenergy.co.uk
Website: http://www.ruralenergy.co.uk
Directors: R. Harvey (Fin)
Managers: A. Medjber
Immediate Holding Company: MYRIAD CEG LIMITED
Registration no: 04391926 **Date established:** 2002 **Turnover:** £2m - £5m
No.of Employees: 21 - 50 **Product Groups:** 40, 67, 86

Date of Accounts	Aug 09	Aug 08	Mar 11
Sales Turnover	N/A	N/A	4m
Pre Tax Profit/Loss	N/A	N/A	83
Working Capital	1m	452	1m
Fixed Assets	71	43	582
Current Assets	2m	1m	2m
Current Liabilities	N/A	N/A	849

Sweat Guard Ltd

Sycamore House Debdale Hill, Old Dalby, Melton Mowbray, LE14 3LF
Tel: 0844-2510335
E-mail: info@sweatguard.co.uk
Website: http://www.sweatguard.co.uk
Managers: D. Tebb (Chief Acct)
Registration no: 05998898 **Date established:** 1996
No.of Employees: 1 - 10 **Product Groups:** 24, 32, 38

Synergy Food Ingredients Ltd

46 Abingdon Road, Melton Mowbray, LE13 0SB
Tel: 01664-567169
E-mail: info@sfi-ltd.com
Website: http://www.sfi-ltd.com
Directors: D. Primrose (MD)
Immediate Holding Company: SYNERGY FOOD INGREDIENTS LTD
Registration no: 05703685 **Date established:** 2006
Turnover: Up to £250,000 **No.of Employees:** 1 - 10 **Product Groups:** 20

Date of Accounts	Jun 11	Jun 10	Jun 09
Working Capital	28	12	5
Fixed Assets	N/A	N/A	1
Current Assets	37	18	6

Tuxford & Tebbutt
46-56 Thorpe End, Melton Mowbray, LE13 1RB
Tel: 01664-502900 **Fax:** 01664-502901
E-mail: stuart.scott@milklink.com
Website: http://www.milklink.com
Bank(s): Barclays
Directors: D. Thomson (Fin)
Managers: S. Scott (Site Co-ord)
Immediate Holding Company: THE GLANBIA GROUP
Registration no: 02670609 **Turnover:** £5m - £10m
No.of Employees: 51 - 100 **Product Groups:** 20

Walker
6a Digby Drive, Melton Mowbray, LE13 0RQ
Tel: 01664-410354 **Fax:** 01664-410354
E-mail: david@djwalker.go-plus.net
Directors: D. Walker (Prop)
Turnover: Up to £250,000 **No.of Employees:** 1 - 10 **Product Groups:** 30, 49

Waltham Electronics
34 Cranmere Road, Melton Mowbray, LE13 1TB
Tel: 01664-850061 **Fax:** 01664-850062
Website: http://www.scalemanager.co.uk
Directors: J. Aley (Fin)
Immediate Holding Company: WALTHAM PREMIER LTD
Registration no: 05514940 **Date established:** 2005
No.of Employees: 1 - 10 **Product Groups:** 37, 40, 42

Date of Accounts	Jul 09	Jul 08	Jul 07
Working Capital	-25	-22	-15
Fixed Assets	33	24	17
Current Assets	61	81	54

Oakham

C B S Products Ltd
Pillings Road, Oakham, LE15 6QF
Tel: 01572-723665 **Fax:** 01572-756009
E-mail: sales@cbsproducts.com
Website: http://www.cbsproducts.com
Bank(s): Barclays, Nottingham
Directors: R. Cobley (Co Sec), T. Lewis (Chief Op Offcr)
Managers: R. Bull (Buyer)
Ultimate Holding Company: GENERAL MACHINE PRODUCTS CO INC (USA)
Immediate Holding Company: CBS PRODUCTS LIMITED
Registration no: 02160870 **VAT No.:** GB 486 5008 29
Date established: 1987 **Turnover:** £2m - £5m **No.of Employees:** 21 - 50
Product Groups: 35, 37, 45

Date of Accounts	Dec 11	Dec 10	Dec 09
Sales Turnover	3m	3m	3m
Pre Tax Profit/Loss	46	51	139
Working Capital	103	165	226
Fixed Assets	43	47	54
Current Assets	1m	1m	1m
Current Liabilities	50	43	94

C J F Ceramics
Thistleton Road Indl-Est Market Overton, Oakham, LE15 7PP
Tel: 01572-768476
Directors: J. Francis (Prop)
Ultimate Holding Company: KNILL HOLDING GMBH (AUSTRIA)
Immediate Holding Company: C.C.L. SYSTEMS LIMITED
Date established: 1935 **No.of Employees:** 1 - 10 **Product Groups:** 37, 67

Robin Church Engineering
11 Main Street Whitwell, Oakham, LE15 8BW
Tel: 01780-460709
Directors: R. Church (Prop)
No.of Employees: 1 - 10 **Product Groups:** 35, 36

GB Welding Services Rutland Ltd
Unit 4-6 Pillings Road Industrial Estate, Oakham, LE15 6QF
Tel: 01572-722764 **Fax:** 01572-724347
E-mail: admin@gbwelding.co.uk
Website: http://www.gbwelding.co.uk
Bank(s): Barclays, Oakham
Managers: A. Salt (Mgr)
Immediate Holding Company: G.B. WELDING SERVICES (RUTLAND) LIMITED
Registration no: 02657647 **VAT No.:** GB 425 6804 48
Date established: 1991 **Turnover:** £500,000 - £1m
No.of Employees: 11 - 20 **Product Groups:** 48

Date of Accounts	Oct 11	Oct 10	Oct 09
Working Capital	8	13	3
Fixed Assets	17	13	150
Current Assets	132	153	97

Marathon Electric
6 Thistleton Road Market Overton, Oakham, LE15 7PP
Tel: 01572-768206 **Fax:** 01572-768217
E-mail: barry.mills@marathonelectric.com
Website: http://www.marathonelectric.com
Directors: B. Mills (Sales)
Immediate Holding Company: M Y A CONSULTING LIMITED
Registration no: FC015074 **Date established:** 2002
Turnover: £250m - £500m **No.of Employees:** 1 - 10 **Product Groups:** 37, 67

Mecc Alte UK Ltd
Lands End Way, Oakham, LE15 6RF
Tel: 01572-771160 **Fax:** 01572-771161
E-mail: info@meccalte.it
Website: http://www.meccalte.it
Bank(s): National Westminster Bank Plc
Directors: A. Bell (MD)
Managers: F. Taylor (Personnel), S. Dalby, J. Stokes (Sales & Mktg Mg)
Immediate Holding Company: MECC ALTE (UK) LIMITED
Registration no: 03320100 **VAT No.:** GB 690 7302 32
Date established: 1997 **Turnover:** £20m - £50m
No.of Employees: 101 - 250 **Product Groups:** 37

Date of Accounts	Dec 11	Dec 10	Dec 09
Sales Turnover	29m	19m	20m
Pre Tax Profit/Loss	813	1m	2m
Working Capital	2m	2m	2m
Fixed Assets	6m	5m	5m
Current Assets	15m	12m	9m
Current Liabilities	2m	659	384

Orchard Technologies Ltd
Unit F5 Market Overton Industrial Estate Thistleton Road, Market Overton, Oakham, LE15 7PP
Tel: 01572-768489 **Fax:** 01572-768181
Website: http://www.orchard56.freeserve.co.uk
Directors: R. Vincent (MD), R. Vincent (Fin)
Managers: J. Vincent (Purch Mgr)
Ultimate Holding Company: KNILL HOLDING GMBH (AUSTRIA)
Immediate Holding Company: ORCHARD TECHNOLOGIES LIMITED
Registration no: 02262293 **Date established:** 1988
Turnover: £250,000 - £500,000 **No.of Employees:** 1 - 10
Product Groups: 30, 36, 37, 40

Date of Accounts	May 11	May 10	May 09
Working Capital	-8	1	12
Fixed Assets	2	2	2
Current Assets	19	18	27
Current Liabilities	11	7	N/A

P D Fabrications
59 Pillings Road, Oakham, LE15 6QF
Tel: 01572-756511 **Fax:** 01572-756511
Directors: P. Danes (Prop)
Date established: 1982 **No.of Employees:** 1 - 10 **Product Groups:** 35

Rutland Electric Fencing Co. Ltd
8 Lands End Way, Oakham, LE15 6RF
Tel: 01572-722558 **Fax:** 01572-757614
E-mail: enquiries@rutland-electric-fencing.co.uk
Website: http://www.rutland-electric-fencing.co.uk
Bank(s): Barclays
Managers: C. Barrow (Admin Off)
Ultimate Holding Company: WOODSTREAM GROUP INC (UNITED STATES OF AMERICA)
Immediate Holding Company: WOODSTREAM EUROPE LIMITED
Registration no: 01942940 **VAT No.:** GB 313 1238 10
Date established: 1985 **Turnover:** £5m - £10m **No.of Employees:** 21 - 50
Product Groups: 35, 40, 41

Date of Accounts	Jun 09	Jun 08	Nov 11
Sales Turnover	5m	5m	N/A
Pre Tax Profit/Loss	-56	111	N/A
Working Capital	3m	2m	4m
Fixed Assets	121	945	468
Current Assets	6m	5m	7m
Current Liabilities	303	353	N/A

Rutland Plastics Ltd
Cold Overton Road, Oakham, LE15 6NU
Tel: 01572-723476 **Fax:** 01572-757700
E-mail: enquiry@rutlandplastics.co.uk
Website: http://www.rutlandplastics.co.uk
Bank(s): HSBC, Gallowtree Gate
Directors: S. Ayre (MD)
Managers: S. Lovett (Mktg Serv Mgr), S. Johnston (Sales Prom Mgr), A. Forbes (Prod Mgr), C. Martin, M. Dolby (Accounts)
Registration no: 00560131 **Turnover:** £5m - £10m
No.of Employees: 101 - 250 **Product Groups:** 30

Date of Accounts	Dec 11	Dec 10	Dec 09
Sales Turnover	9m	9m	7m
Pre Tax Profit/Loss	322	462	124
Working Capital	4m	4m	4m
Fixed Assets	6m	6m	5m
Current Assets	5m	5m	5m
Current Liabilities	446	264	319

Rutlands Sheds & Leisure Buildings
1 Langham Place Ashwell Road, Oakham, LE15 7QN
Tel: 01572-755938
E-mail: rutlandsheds@sky.com
Website: http://www.comptonbuildings.co.uk
Directors: G. Boyd (Prop)
No.of Employees: 1 - 10 **Product Groups:** 25, 33, 35, 66

SensorsONE Ltd
PO Box 8286, Oakham, LE15 0AW
Tel: 01780-721569
E-mail: enquiries@sensorsone.co.uk
Website: http://www.sensorsone.co.uk
Directors: W. Bishop (MD)
Registration no: 5805666 **Date established:** 2006
No.of Employees: 1 - 10 **Product Groups:** 37, 38

Technelec
Edison House Station Approach Industrial Estate Station Approach, Oakham, LE15 6QW
Tel: 01572-771199 **Fax:** 01572-771196
E-mail: sales@technelec.co.uk
Website: http://www.technelec.co.uk
Directors: H. Pollock (Fin)
Immediate Holding Company: TECHNELEC LIMITED
Registration no: 02753595 **Date established:** 1992
No.of Employees: 1 - 10 **Product Groups:** 37, 44, 84

Date of Accounts	Oct 11	Oct 10	Oct 09
Working Capital	64	15	15
Fixed Assets	16	18	23
Current Assets	117	52	36

Vaughan Technology Ltd
26 Catmose Park Road, Oakham, LE15 6HN
Tel: 01572-757352 **Fax:** 01572-757446
Website: http://www.vauntec.co.uk
Directors: R. Vaughan (MD), L. Vaughan (Fin)
Registration no: 03707932 **Date established:** 1999
No.of Employees: 1 - 10 **Product Groups:** 46

Arnold Wills & Co. Ltd
10 Station Road Uppingham, Oakham, LE15 9TZ
Tel: 01572-822261 **Fax:** 01572-821059
E-mail: david.couldwell@arnoldwills.net
Website: http://www.arnoldwills.co.uk
Directors: R. Wills (MD), M. Payne (Sales & Mktg)
Managers: P. Southam (Chief Acct), D. Couldwell (Tech Serv Mgr), M. Beaver (Factory Mgr)
Immediate Holding Company: ARNOLD WILLS AND COMPANY LIMITED
Registration no: 00417612 **Date established:** 1946
Turnover: £10m - £20m **No.of Employees:** 51 - 100 **Product Groups:** 22, 24, 49, 66

Date of Accounts	May 11	May 10	May 09
Sales Turnover	18m	24m	20m
Pre Tax Profit/Loss	917	3m	1m
Working Capital	9m	12m	10m
Fixed Assets	4m	3m	3m
Current Assets	11m	13m	12m
Current Liabilities	897	1m	1m

Wigston

ADS Laser Cutting
Radnor Road, Wigston, LE18 4XY
Tel: 0116-244 4999 **Fax:** 0116-244 4998
E-mail: sales@adslaser.co.uk
Website: http://www.adslasercutting.co.uk
Directors: D. Keates (Ptnr), S. Keates (MD), A. Keates (Co Sec)
Immediate Holding Company: TOWER TOOL COMPANY LIMITED
Date established: 1980 **No.of Employees:** 21 - 50 **Product Groups:** 46, 48

Date of Accounts	Aug 11	Aug 10	Aug 09
Working Capital	35	5	-24
Fixed Assets	331	349	368
Current Assets	203	132	169

The Anodising Co. Ltd
North Street, Wigston, LE18 1PS
Tel: 0116-288 1333 **Fax:** 0116-251 1351
E-mail: info@theanodisingco.co.uk
Website: http://www.theanodisingco.co.uk
Directors: M. Rogers (Fin), N. Rogers (MD)
Immediate Holding Company: THE ANODISING COMPANY LIMITED
Registration no: 04173780 **Date established:** 2001
No.of Employees: 1 - 10 **Product Groups:** 46, 48

Date of Accounts	Mar 12	Mar 11	Mar 10
Working Capital	37	17	12
Fixed Assets	4	N/A	N/A
Current Assets	79	55	45

David Beaumont & Associates
78 Thirlmere Road, Wigston, LE18 3RR
Tel: 0116-281 2865 **Fax:** 0116-242 1095
E-mail: davidjbeaumont@ricsonline.org
Website: http://www.dbandaltd.co.uk
Directors: D. Beaumont (Dir)
Immediate Holding Company: ARTS TRAINING CENTRAL
Registration no: 03195195 **Date established:** 1996
No.of Employees: 1 - 10 **Product Groups:** 38, 80, 84

Consort Displays (Leicester) Ltd
Magna Road, Wigston, LE18 4ZH
Tel: 0116-278 5075 **Fax:** 0116-278 7888
E-mail: andy@consortdisplays.com
Website: http://www.consortdisplays.com
Directors: H. Goodwin (Dir), A. Smith (MD)
Registration no: 05421215 **Date established:** 2005 **Turnover:** £1m - £2m
No.of Employees: 21 - 50 **Product Groups:** 22, 25, 28, 30, 31, 37, 38, 39, 42, 44, 48, 49, 67, 81, 84

Date of Accounts	Apr 11	Apr 10	Apr 09
Working Capital	324	224	186
Fixed Assets	67	73	82
Current Assets	739	638	366
Current Liabilities	N/A	N/A	5

The Cooke Patterns & Castings
West Avenue, Wigston, LE18 2FB
Tel: 0116-288 1234 **Fax:** 0116-288 1238
E-mail: cookejohn@hotmail.com
Directors: J. Cooke (Dir)
Immediate Holding Company: F W STEVENS (ELECTRICAL) LIMITED
Date established: 2003 **Turnover:** £500,000 - £1m
No.of Employees: 21 - 50 **Product Groups:** 46

Cromwell Group Holdings
65 Chartwell Drive, Wigston, LE18 2FS
Tel: 0116-288 8000 **Fax:** 0116-288 5050
E-mail: hq@cromwell-tools.co.uk
Website: http://www.apexindustrial.co.uk
Bank(s): Lloyds
Directors: D. Sealey (Dir), M. Cook (Dir), M. Gregory (MD), M. Gregory (Grp Chief Exec), M. Kerins (MD)
Ultimate Holding Company: 01756362
Immediate Holding Company: CROMWELL GROUP (INTERNATIONAL) LIMITED
Registration no: 04835122 **Date established:** 2003
Turnover: £50m - £75m **No.of Employees:** 251 - 500 **Product Groups:** 47

Delifrance UK Ltd
17 Chartwell Drive, Wigston, LE18 2FL
Tel: 0116-257 1871 **Fax:** 0116-257 1608
E-mail: info@delifrance.co.uk
Website: http://www.delifrance.com
Directors: A. Moutter (Comm), I. Dobbie (MD), R. Turner (Fin), L. Daunizeau (Fin)
Managers: K. Dusdaux (Tech Serv Mgr), J. Simpson (Purch Mgr), S. Wilson (Personnel)
Ultimate Holding Company: NUTRIXO SA (FRANCE)
Immediate Holding Company: DELIFRANCE (UK) LIMITED
Registration no: 02186392 **Date established:** 1987
Turnover: £125m - £250m **No.of Employees:** 51 - 100
Product Groups: 42, 67

Date of Accounts	Dec 11	Dec 10	Dec 09
Sales Turnover	129m	129m	106m
Pre Tax Profit/Loss	-541	-702	3m
Working Capital	7m	1m	5m
Fixed Assets	9m	8m	5m
Current Assets	27m	25m	29m
Current Liabilities	2m	3m	3m

DMC Creative World

13 Leicester Road, Wigston, LE18 1NR
Tel: 0116-288 3133 **Fax:** 0116-281 3592
E-mail: kim@kimscrafts.co.uk
Website: http://www.dmc.com
Bank(s): Lloyds TSB Bank plc
Directors: D. Hughes (MD), J. Hames (Fin), J. Thompson (Co Sec), O. Bishop (Sales), D. Dempsey (MD)
Managers: A. Tallis (I.T. Exec), J. Cooke (Comptroller), J. Drew, E. Weirs, M. Knight (Chief Mgr)
Ultimate Holding Company: D M C (France)
Immediate Holding Company: Double Arch Ltd
Registration no: 01838869 **Date established:** 2007
Turnover: Up to £250,000 **No.of Employees:** 21 - 50 **Product Groups:** 23

Date of Accounts	Dec 06	Dec 05
Sales Turnover	2459	4803
Pre Tax Profit/Loss	224	-779
Working Capital	6	-38
Fixed Assets	383	377
Current Assets	1608	1633
Current Liabilities	1602	1671
Total Share Capital	77	77
ROCE% (Return on Capital Employed)	57.6	-229.8
ROT% (Return on Turnover)	9.1	-16.2

Full Metal Fabrications Ltd

Unit 46 Radnor Road, Wigston, LE18 4XY
Tel: 0116-278 9564 **Fax:** 0116-278 9601
Product Groups: 35, 36, 40, 48, 66, 84

Date of Accounts	Aug 10	Aug 09	Aug 08
Sales Turnover	N/A	262	368
Working Capital	5	29	2
Fixed Assets	33	22	31
Current Assets	5	93	72

Groz-Beckert UK

Groz-Beckert House 139-139a Gloucester Crescent, Wigston, LE18 4YL
Tel: 0116-264 3500 **Fax:** 0116-264 3505
E-mail: contact@groz-beckert.com
Website: http://www.groz-beckert.com
Directors: J. Elson (MD)
Immediate Holding Company: GROZ-BECKERT U.K. LIMITED
Registration no: 00493485 **Date established:** 1951 **Turnover:** £1m - £2m
No.of Employees: 1 - 10 **Product Groups:** 35, 43

Date of Accounts	Dec 11	Dec 10	Dec 09
Sales Turnover	2m	3m	222
Pre Tax Profit/Loss	1m	760	787
Working Capital	1m	1m	1m
Fixed Assets	423	4m	413
Current Assets	1m	1m	2m
Current Liabilities	58	165	122

James Latham plc

13 Chartwell Drive, Wigston, LE18 2FN
Tel: 0116-288 9161 **Fax:** 0116-281 3806
E-mail: andrew.craig@lathams.co.uk
Website: http://www.lathamtimber.co.uk
Bank(s): National Westminster Bank Plc
Directors: A. Craig (Dir)
Immediate Holding Company: JAMES LATHAM PUBLIC LIMITED COMPANY
Registration no: 00065619 **VAT No.:** GB 169 6943 06
Date established: 2000 **Turnover:** £10m - £20m
No.of Employees: 21 - 50 **Product Groups:** 61

Date of Accounts	Mar 12	Mar 11	Mar 10
Sales Turnover	144m	130m	115m
Pre Tax Profit/Loss	7m	8m	6m
Working Capital	40m	39m	36m
Fixed Assets	23m	19m	19m
Current Assets	62m	60m	53m
Current Liabilities	5m	7m	5m

Jubb Ltd

3 Chartwell Drive Chartwell House, Wigston, LE18 2FL
Tel: 0116-212 1212 **Fax:** 0116-212 1313
E-mail: sales@jubbuk.com
Website: http://www.jubbuk.com
Bank(s): HSBC Bank plc
Managers: P. Wake
Immediate Holding Company: JUBB (UK) LIMITED
Registration no: 05662791 **VAT No.:** GB 669 8681 57
Date established: 2005 **Turnover:** £2m - £5m **No.of Employees:** 21 - 50
Product Groups: 66

Date of Accounts	Dec 11	Dec 10	Dec 09
Working Capital	174	-55	-248
Fixed Assets	292	474	608
Current Assets	916	1m	1m
Current Liabilities	N/A	N/A	1m

Know It All Ltd

13 Long Meadow, Wigston, LE18 3TY
Tel: 07769-697858 **Fax:** 0116-281 2002
E-mail: lisa@knowitall.co.uk
Website: http://www.knowitall.co.uk
Directors: L. Bhardwaj (Fin)
Immediate Holding Company: KNOW IT ALL LIMITED
Registration no: 05261139 **Date established:** 2004
No.of Employees: 1 - 10 **Product Groups:** 80, 86

Date of Accounts	Mar 08	Mar 07	Mar 06
Working Capital	41	-1	1
Fixed Assets	15	3	4
Current Assets	229	29	17

Kwik-Fit GB Ltd

Bullhead Street, Wigston, LE18 1PE
Tel: 0116-281 2801
Website: http://www.kwik-fit.com
Managers: P. Johal (District Mgr)
Ultimate Holding Company: FINANCIERE DAUNOU 2 SA (LUXEMBOURG)
Immediate Holding Company: KWIK-FIT (GB) LIMITED
Registration no: 01009184 **Date established:** 1971
No.of Employees: 1 - 10 **Product Groups:** 29, 39, 85

Date of Accounts	Dec 10	Dec 09	Dec 08
Sales Turnover	527m	495m	449m
Pre Tax Profit/Loss	269m	56m	97m
Working Capital	197m	201m	154m
Fixed Assets	106m	115m	110m
Current Assets	375m	368m	329m
Current Liabilities	36m	36m	38m

Measom Freer Company

37-41 Chartwell Drive, Wigston, LE18 2FL
Tel: 0116-288 1588 **Fax:** 0116-281 3000
E-mail: sales@measomfreer.co.uk
Website: http://www.measomfreer.co.uk
Directors: M. Freer (Dir)
Immediate Holding Company: MEASOM FREER & COMPANY LIMITED
Registration no: 00654605 **VAT No.:** GB 290 1842 62
Date established: 1960 **Turnover:** £5m - £10m **No.of Employees:** 1 - 10
Product Groups: 30, 66

Date of Accounts	Mar 12	Mar 11	Mar 10
Working Capital	364	325	2m
Fixed Assets	695	581	622
Current Assets	881	836	2m

Newall Measurement Systems Ltd

Technology Gateway Cornwall Road, Wigston, LE18 4XH
Tel: 0116-264 2730 **Fax:** 0116-264 2731
E-mail: sales@newall.co.uk
Website: http://www.newall.co.uk
Bank(s): Bank of Scotland
Directors: S. De Peretti (MD), G. Prime (Fin), D. Hall (Fin)
Managers: C. Hurst (Personnel), M. Garbett (Tech Serv Mgr), M. Bennett (Purch Mgr)
Ultimate Holding Company: SCHNEIDER ELECTRIC SA (FRANCE)
Immediate Holding Company: NEWALL MEASUREMENT SYSTEMS LIMITED
Registration no: 05199004 **VAT No.:** GB 848 4219 05
Date established: 2004 **Turnover:** £5m - £10m **No.of Employees:** 21 - 50
Product Groups: 37, 38, 46

Date of Accounts	Dec 11	Dec 10	Dec 09
Sales Turnover	9m	7m	5m
Pre Tax Profit/Loss	2m	1m	169
Working Capital	3m	2m	841
Fixed Assets	2m	3m	3m
Current Assets	4m	3m	2m
Current Liabilities	952	707	492

P W Circuits Ltd

Shelmer Works Canal Street, Wigston, LE18 4PN
Tel: 0116-278 5241 **Fax:** 0116-277 1072
E-mail: pcbs@pwcircuits.co.uk
Website: http://www.pwcircuits.co.uk
Directors: C. Oconnor (MD), C. O'connor (MD)
Managers: A. O'Connor (Tech Serv Mgr), S. Quinn (Personnel)
Immediate Holding Company: P.W. CIRCUITS LIMITED
Registration no: 01462752 **Date established:** 1979
No.of Employees: 21 - 50 **Product Groups:** 37, 48

Date of Accounts	Oct 11	Oct 10	Oct 09
Working Capital	80	62	102
Fixed Assets	61	65	78
Current Assets	442	425	464
Current Liabilities	N/A	N/A	26

Pandet Ltd

1 Premier Drum Works Canal Street, Wigston, LE18 4PL
Tel: 0116-277 2372 **Fax:** 0116-277 2672
E-mail: sales@kuroma.com
Website: http://www.kuroma.com
Directors: J. Davies (MD)
Immediate Holding Company: PANDET LIMITED
Registration no: 01513652 **VAT No.:** GB 350 3246 88
Date established: 1980 **Turnover:** £250,000 - £500,000
No.of Employees: 1 - 10 **Product Groups:** 84

Date of Accounts	Oct 11	Oct 10	Oct 09
Working Capital	136	109	108
Fixed Assets	8	10	17
Current Assets	190	175	132

Time Products UK Ltd

Alexander House Chartwell Drive, Wigston, LE18 2EZ
Tel: 0116-288 2500 **Fax:** 0870-850 8201
E-mail: info@timeproducts.co.uk
Website: http://www.timeproducts.co.uk
Bank(s): National Westminster Bank Plc
Directors: P. Sibson (Fin), N. Adatia (Admin), D. Merriman (MD)
Managers: J. Adcock (Personnel), T. James, A. Boothroyd (Tech Serv Mgr)
Ultimate Holding Company: ALMAR PLC
Immediate Holding Company: TIME PRODUCTS (UK) LIMITED
Registration no: 00746690 **Date established:** 1963
No.of Employees: 51 - 100 **Product Groups:** 35, 47, 65

Date of Accounts	Jan 12	Jan 11	Jan 10
Sales Turnover	31m	27m	26m
Pre Tax Profit/Loss	6m	4m	5m
Working Capital	7m	7m	7m
Fixed Assets	1m	1m	1m
Current Assets	23m	21m	22m
Current Liabilities	6m	5m	6m

Triumph Needle Co. Ltd

14 Albion Street, Wigston, LE18 4SA
Tel: 0116-222 9222 **Fax:** 0116-222 9200
E-mail: triumphneedle@btclick.com
Directors: A. Gibson (MD), J. Neale (Jt MD), A. Gibson (Jt MD), J. Neale (MD)
Immediate Holding Company: TRIUMPH NEEDLE CO LIMITED
Registration no: 01349975 **VAT No.:** 371 7326 50 **Date established:** 1978
Turnover: £500,000 - £1m **No.of Employees:** 1 - 10 **Product Groups:** 35, 43, 46, 61

Date of Accounts	Mar 11	Mar 10	Mar 09
Working Capital	161	148	144
Fixed Assets	27	22	42
Current Assets	414	363	392

Upstage Theatre Supplies Ltd

Drapers Yard 33 Saffron Road, South Wigston, Wigston, LE18 4UL
Tel: 0116-278 3084 **Fax:** 0116-278 6869
E-mail: darren@upstagesupplies.co.uk
Website: http://www.upstage.biz
Directors: D. Parlby (Dir), D. Brooks (Dir)
Registration no: 03667968 **VAT No.:** GB 738 9434 88
Date established: 1999 **No.of Employees:** 3 **Product Groups:** 24, 26, 32, 37, 38, 52, 65, 81, 83, 89

Date of Accounts	Apr 12	Apr 11	Apr 10
Working Capital	7	7	4
Fixed Assets	20	23	28
Current Assets	71	97	90
Current Liabilities	57	N/A	N/A

Victoria Hydraulic Services Ltd

Unit 13a Branston House West Avenue, Wigston, LE18 2FB
Tel: 0116-288 6678 **Fax:** 0116-281 6679
E-mail: info@victoriahydraulics.co.uk
Website: http://www.victoriahydraulics.co.uk
Directors: E. Osbourne (Dir)
Immediate Holding Company: VICTORIA HYDRAULIC SERVICES LTD
Registration no: 05981346 **Date established:** 2006
Turnover: Up to £250,000 **No.of Employees:** 1 - 10 **Product Groups:** 40

Date of Accounts	Dec 11	Dec 10	Dec 09
Working Capital	25	6	7
Fixed Assets	26	28	23
Current Assets	63	29	35
Current Liabilities	23	N/A	N/A

LINCOLNSHIRE

Alford

Act Fire & Safety
C/O Safelincs Ltd, Alford, LN13 9PS
Tel: 0800-6124829 **Fax:** 08453-305407
E-mail: service@actfire.co.uk
Website: http://www.actfire.co.uk
Directors: N. Link (MD)
Registration no: 04715788 **Date established:** 2007
No.of Employees: 1 - 10 **Product Groups:** 38, 42

Date of Accounts	Mar 06
Working Capital	-116
Fixed Assets	30
Current Assets	119
Current Liabilities	234
Total Share Capital	20

Finnveden Powertrain Components Ltd
West Street, Alford, LN13 9DQ
Tel: 01507-463427 **Fax:** 01507-466942
E-mail: stuart.shaw@finnvedenpowertrain.com
Website: http://www.finnvedenpowertrain.com
Bank(s): Lloyds TSB Bank plc
Directors: H. Linner (MD), J. Linnell (MD), M. Gnutti (Dir)
Managers: J. Fulwood (Quality Control), P. Calvert (Eng Serv Mgr), S. Shaw (Comm), S. Shaw
Ultimate Holding Company: FINNVEDEN AB (SWEDEN)
Immediate Holding Company: FINNVEDEN POWERTRAIN LIMITED
Registration no: 03047921 **VAT No.:** GB 598 7878 36
Date established: 1995 **Turnover:** £10m - £20m
No.of Employees: 21 - 50 **Product Groups:** 61

Date of Accounts	Dec 09	Dec 08	Dec 07
Sales Turnover	10m	21m	19m
Pre Tax Profit/Loss	-4m	2m	596
Working Capital	-463	3m	1m
Fixed Assets	2m	3m	3m
Current Assets	5m	7m	6m
Current Liabilities	2m	658	493

Foureyez
Unit 3 Norman Terrace Beechings Way, Alford, LN13 9JE
Tel: 0845-2997202 **Fax:** 01472-882933
E-mail: enquiries@foureyez.com
Website: http://www.foureyez.com
Registration no: 06651122 **Product Groups:** 32, 33, 38, 47

Keyline Builders Merchants
Unit 7 Beechings Way Industrial Estate, Alford, LN13 9JE
Tel: 01507-462741 **Fax:** 01507-462746
E-mail: alford0281@keyline.co.uk
Website: http://www.keyline.co.uk
Managers: W. Bishell (Asst Gen Mgr), K. Hewson (District Mgr)
Immediate Holding Company: DIRECT BUILDING SUPPLIES TRURO LIMITED
Registration no: 02711617 **VAT No.:** GB 408 5567 37
Date established: 1992 **No.of Employees:** 1 - 10 **Product Groups:** 66

Nationwide Fire Extinguishers (Safelincs Ltd)
Unit 1 Farlesthorpe Road, Alford, LN13 9PS
Tel: 0800-6122947
E-mail: info@nationwidefireextinguishers.co.uk
Website: http://www.nationwidefireextinguishers.co.uk
Directors: R. McCarthy (Dir)
Registration no: 06417603 **Date established:** 2004
Turnover: Up to £250,000 **No.of Employees:** 21 - 50 **Product Groups:** 39, 40, 67, 68

P Coppin & Son
The Spinneys Hanby Lane, Willoughby, Alford, LN13 9NN
Tel: 01507-462357 **Fax:** 01507-462357
Directors: J. Coppin (Prop)
Immediate Holding Company: PETER COPPIN & SON LIMITED
Registration no: 05503166 **Date established:** 2005
No.of Employees: 1 - 10 **Product Groups:** 36, 39, 40

Date of Accounts	Aug 11	Aug 10	Aug 09
Working Capital	24	37	44
Fixed Assets	11	11	9
Current Assets	135	122	123

R M Construction Co
5 The Maltings, Alford, LN13 9TS
Tel: 01507-477240 **Fax:** 01507-462031
Website: http://www.rmconstruction.co.uk
Directors: S. Crow (Dir)
Registration no: 02727538 **Date established:** 1992
No.of Employees: 1 - 10 **Product Groups:** 35

Boston

Apollo Plant Holdings Ltd
Redstone Industrial Estate, Boston, PE21 8AL
Tel: 01205-351722 **Fax:** 01205-360432
E-mail: enquiries@apollo-plant.co.uk
Website: http://www.impact-handling.com
Bank(s): Barclays
Directors: I. Merry (Sales), M. Neale (Chief Op Offcr), H. Hemens (Ch), R. Haunch (MD), T. Kendrew (Fin)
Managers: R. Wilson
Immediate Holding Company: Impact Fork Trucks Ltd
Registration no: 02903349 **VAT No.:** GB 455 4660 35
Date established: 1979 **Turnover:** £2m - £5m **No.of Employees:** 21 - 50
Product Groups: 26, 40, 44, 45, 48, 67, 80, 83, 86

W S Barrett & Son Ltd
Riverside Industrial Estate Marsh Lane, Boston, PE21 7PJ
Tel: 01205-362585 **Fax:** 01205-310831
E-mail: info@wsbarrett.co.uk
Website: http://www.barrettofboston.co.uk
Bank(s): National Westminster
Directors: C. Bramwell Royale (Dir), C. Bramwell-royale (MD)
Managers: A. Ellis (Tech Serv Mgr), M. Clare (Personnel)
Immediate Holding Company: W.S.BARRETT & SON LIMITED
Registration no: 00472359 **VAT No.:** GB 128 9739 24
Date established: 1949 **Turnover:** £1m - £2m **No.of Employees:** 21 - 50
Product Groups: 38, 39, 41, 45

Date of Accounts	Mar 12	Mar 11	Mar 10
Working Capital	-12	22	61
Fixed Assets	471	473	481
Current Assets	582	484	507

Cable Ties - Online
105 Wyberton West Road, Boston, PE21 7JU
Tel: 08450-949680
E-mail: sales@cableties-online.co.uk
Website: http://www.cableties-online.co.uk
Directors: D. Baker (Prop)
Date established: 2005 **No.of Employees:** 1 - 10 **Product Groups:** 30, 35, 39

Craven & Nicholas Structural Ltd
St Johns Road, Boston, PE21 6BG
Tel: 01205-364004 **Fax:** 01205-310798
E-mail: info@carven-nicholas.co.uk
Website: http://www.craven-nicholas.co.uk
Directors: C. Budge (MD), G. Mc Intosh (MD), L. Smith (Co Sec)
Managers: L. Smith (Admin Off)
Immediate Holding Company: CRAVEN AND NICHOLAS (STRUCTURAL) LIMITED
Registration no: 04777635 **VAT No.:** GB 127 7337 60
Date established: 2003 **No.of Employees:** 1 - 10 **Product Groups:** 32, 48

Dynamic Cassette International Ltd
Marsh Lane, Boston, PE21 7TX
Tel: 01205-355555 **Fax:** 01205-354823
E-mail: sales@dci.co.uk
Website: http://www.dci.co.uk
Directors: J. Studholme (Dir), A. Butler (Fin)
Managers: P. Sawka (Tech Serv Mgr), P. Sneath (Sales & Mktg Mg), M. Ferreira (Buyer)
Immediate Holding Company: DYNAMIC CASSETTE INTERNATIONAL LIMITED
Registration no: 01757389 **VAT No.:** GB 364 6930 29
Date established: 1983 **Turnover:** £20m - £50m
No.of Employees: 101 - 250 **Product Groups:** 30

Date of Accounts	Dec 11	Dec 10	Dec 09
Sales Turnover	34m	38m	34m
Pre Tax Profit/Loss	4m	2m	8m
Working Capital	12m	9m	10m
Fixed Assets	1m	1m	1m
Current Assets	16m	15m	14m
Current Liabilities	842	1m	3m

Finn Forest Ltd
The Old Golf Course Site Fishtoft Road, Boston, PE21 0BJ
Tel: 01205-362461 **Fax:** 01205-310026
E-mail: stuart.parker@finnforest.com
Website: http://www.finnforest.co.uk
Directors: R. Allan (MD), W. Dudding (Mkt Research), T. Tong (Mkt Research), N. Davenport (MD), C. Smith (I.T. Dir)
Managers: S. Clarke (Ops Mgr), S. Parker (Ops Mgr)
Immediate Holding Company: FINNFOREST UK LIMITED
Registration no: 03071064 **Date established:** 1995 **Turnover:** £2m - £5m
No.of Employees: 251 - 500 **Product Groups:** 08, 25

Fitmykitchen
Moulton Chantry House Southfields, Old Leake, Boston, PE22 9LP
Tel: 01205-871987
E-mail: sales@fitmykitchen.co.uk
Website: http://www.fitmykitchen.co.uk
Directors: N. Howarth (Prop)
No.of Employees: 1 - 10 **Product Groups:** 36, 40, 66

Fogarty Filled Products Ltd
Havenside Fishtoft Road, Boston, PE21 0AH
Tel: 01205-361122 **Fax:** 01205-353202
E-mail: stuart.macdonald@fogarty.co.uk
Website: http://www.fogarty.co.uk
Bank(s): Barclays
Directors: A. Mathews (Sales), G. Tawton (Fin), S. Macdonald (MD)
Managers: B. Richards (Tech Serv Mgr), S. Grundy
Ultimate Holding Company: FOGARTY HOLDINGS LIMITED
Immediate Holding Company: FOGARTY (FILLED PRODUCTS) LIMITED
Registration no: 04346056 **VAT No.:** GB 555 7119 29
Date established: 2001 **Turnover:** £20m - £50m
No.of Employees: 251 - 500 **Product Groups:** 63

Date of Accounts	Sep 11	Sep 10	Sep 09
Sales Turnover	34m	32m	26m
Pre Tax Profit/Loss	-1m	-990	-648
Working Capital	-2m	-577	564
Fixed Assets	3m	2m	1m
Current Assets	14m	12m	11m
Current Liabilities	12m	7m	5m

Grimme UK Ltd
Station Road Swineshead, Boston, PE20 3PS
Tel: 01205-821182 **Fax:** 01205-821196
E-mail: b.white@grimme.co.uk
Website: http://www.grimmeuk.com
Directors: B. Baker (Sales), M. Baumber (Fin)
Managers: N. White (Admin Off), R. Powell (Mktg Serv Mgr), R. Everett
Ultimate Holding Company: GRIMME HOLDING GMBH (GERMANY)
Immediate Holding Company: GRIMME (U.K.) LIMITED
Registration no: 02846291 **Date established:** 1993
Turnover: £20m - £50m **No.of Employees:** 21 - 50 **Product Groups:** 41

Date of Accounts	Dec 11	Dec 10	Dec 09
Sales Turnover	33m	22m	26m
Pre Tax Profit/Loss	3m	1m	-35
Working Capital	8m	6m	5m
Fixed Assets	1m	1m	1m
Current Assets	15m	12m	10m
Current Liabilities	1m	1m	570

Guildway Ltd
194 London Road, Boston, PE21 7HJ
Tel: 01205-350555 **Fax:** 01205-359261
E-mail: mail@guildway.ltd.uk
Website: http://www.walkertimbergroup.com
Bank(s): National Westminster Bank Plc
Directors: J. Campbell (Fin), N. Simpson (Dir)
Managers: M. Vaughan (Purch Mgr)
Ultimate Holding Company: JAMES WALKER (LEITH) LIMITED
Immediate Holding Company: GUILDWAY LIMITED
Registration no: SC179909 **Date established:** 1997
Turnover: £10m - £20m **No.of Employees:** 51 - 100 **Product Groups:** 25, 52

Date of Accounts	Mar 11	Mar 10	Mar 09
Sales Turnover	14m	11m	N/A
Pre Tax Profit/Loss	-111	-125	103
Working Capital	990	958	968
Fixed Assets	292	413	505
Current Assets	4m	4m	3m
Current Liabilities	545	409	363

Howard Tenens
Riverside Industrial Estate Marsh Lane, Boston, PE21 7SZ
Tel: 01205-311808 **Fax:** 01205-354086
E-mail: bill.smith@grimme.co.uk
Website: http://www.tenens.com

see next page

Howard Tenens - Cont'd
Bank(s): Barclays
Managers: B. Smith
Ultimate Holding Company: HOWARD TENENS LIMITED
Immediate Holding Company: HOWARD TENENS (BOSTON) LIMITED
Registration no: 02159726 **VAT No.:** GB 391 9766 95
Date established: 1987 **Turnover:** £5m - £10m **No.of Employees:** 21 - 50
Product Groups: 72, 77, 84

Date of Accounts	Sep 11	Sep 10	Sep 09
Sales Turnover	9m	8m	7m
Pre Tax Profit/Loss	465	362	398
Working Capital	1m	867	652
Fixed Assets	742	994	967
Current Assets	3m	2m	2m
Current Liabilities	1m	726	927

JAMES ISAAC STOVE & CHIMNEY LINING SERVICES
65 SPILSBY RD, Boston, PE21 9NX
Tel: 01205-352148
E-mail: enquiries@jamesisaacstovesandchimneys.co.uk
Website: http://www.jamesisaacstoves.vpweb.co.uk
Product Groups: 35, 40, 63, 66

Jewson Ltd
Nelson Way, Boston, PE21 8UA
Tel: 01205-362451 **Fax:** 01205-365898
Website: http://www.jewson.co.uk
Managers: S. Cannzinaro (Mgr)
Ultimate Holding Company: COMPAGNIE DE SAINT GOBAIN (FRANCE)
Immediate Holding Company: JEWSON LIMITED
Registration no: 00348407 **VAT No.:** GB 394 1212 63
Date established: 1939 **Turnover:** Over £1,000m
No.of Employees: 11 - 20 **Product Groups:** 66

Date of Accounts	Dec 11	Dec 10	Dec 09
Sales Turnover	1606m	1547m	1485m
Pre Tax Profit/Loss	18m	100m	45m
Working Capital	-345m	-250m	-349m
Fixed Assets	496m	387m	461m
Current Assets	657m	1005m	1320m
Current Liabilities	66m	120m	64m

Derek Lee Gunsmiths Ltd
Toft Hill Tumby, Boston, PE22 7TB
Tel: 01526-354505 **Fax:** 01526-354902
E-mail: derek@dl-gunsmiths.com
Directors: M. Lee (Fin), D. Lee (MD)
Immediate Holding Company: DEREK LEE GUNSMITHS LIMITED
Registration no: 04217715 **Date established:** 2001
No.of Employees: 1 - 10 **Product Groups:** 36, 39, 40

Date of Accounts	Jul 11	Jul 10	Jul 09
Working Capital	134	104	106
Fixed Assets	63	69	59
Current Assets	412	400	422

Mastenbroek Ltd
Swineshead Road Wyberton Fen, Boston, PE21 7JG
Tel: 01205-311313 **Fax:** 01205-310016
E-mail: info@mastenbroek.com
Website: http://www.mastenbroek.com
Bank(s): National Westminster Bank Plc
Directors: H. Gauntlet (Fin)
Managers: M. Taylor (Tech Serv Mgr), H. Townsend (Sales Admin), C. Pett (Chief Mgr), G. Bastow (Purch Mgr)
Ultimate Holding Company: MASTENBROEK HOLDING COMPANY LIMITED
Immediate Holding Company: MASTENBROEK HOLDING COMPANY LIMITED
Registration no: 03288619 **VAT No.:** GB 737 6893 77
Date established: 1996 **Turnover:** £5m - £10m **No.of Employees:** 21 - 50
Product Groups: 36, 39, 41, 45

Date of Accounts	Dec 11	Dec 10	Dec 09
Working Capital	-541	-547	-552
Fixed Assets	3m	3m	3m

Mayday Engineering Concepts
Brinsworth Farm Kirton Holme, Boston, PE20 1SY
Tel: 01205-290792 **Fax:** 01205-290793
Website: http://www.maydaymixers.com
Directors: A. Cheeseman (MD)
Immediate Holding Company: Mayday Engineering Concepts Ltd
Registration no: 03421586 **Date established:** 1997
Turnover: Up to £250,000 **No.of Employees:** 1 - 10 **Product Groups:** 20, 40, 41

Date of Accounts	Aug 08	Aug 07	Aug 06
Sales Turnover	11	19	11
Pre Tax Profit/Loss	-3	-4	-3
Working Capital	-6	-3	-13
Fixed Assets	5	6	14
Current Assets	N/A	4	2
Current Liabilities	6	7	14

Mirade Studios
The Shrublands Bell Lane, Fosdyke, Boston, PE20 2BS
Tel: 01205-260437 **Fax:** 01205-260529
E-mail: mike@miradestudios.co.uk
Website: http://www.miradestudios.co.uk
Directors: M. Deal (Prop)
Turnover: Up to £250,000 **No.of Employees:** 1 - 10 **Product Groups:** 89

Mowbray & Son Ltd
North End Business Park Station Road, Swineshead, Boston, PE20 3PW
Tel: 01205-820284 **Fax:** 01205-820976
E-mail: julie.mowbrayltd@tiscali.co.uk
Website: http://www.mowbraybuildingcontractors.co.uk
Bank(s): HSBC
Directors: J. Piggins (Fin)
Ultimate Holding Company: LYNSDALE HOLDINGS LIMITED
Immediate Holding Company: MOWBRAY & SON LIMITED
Registration no: 01500254 **VAT No.:** GB 351 8374 48
Date established: 1980 **Turnover:** £2m - £5m **No.of Employees:** 11 - 20
Product Groups: 52

Date of Accounts	Mar 12	Mar 11	Mar 10
Sales Turnover	3m	N/A	2m
Pre Tax Profit/Loss	248	N/A	131
Working Capital	691	1m	932
Fixed Assets	174	192	205
Current Assets	2m	2m	2m
Current Liabilities	231	N/A	142

N N Z Ltd
Lowgate Lane Bicker, Boston, PE20 3DG
Tel: 01332-696966 **Fax:** 01775-821908
Website: http://www.nnz.com
Directors: B. Keasey (MD)
Managers: P. Bright (Mgr)
Immediate Holding Company: NNZ LTD
Registration no: 01864778 **Date established:** 1984
No.of Employees: 1 - 10 **Product Groups:** 38, 42

Neal Pestforce Ltd
Unit 1 North End Business Park Station Road, Swineshead, Boston, PE20 3PW
Tel: 01205-822970 **Fax:** 01205-460886
E-mail: anninkirton@aol.com
Directors: J. Neal (Dir)
Immediate Holding Company: NEAL PESTFORCE LIMITED
Registration no: 03269016 **VAT No.:** GB 677 0098 12
Date established: 1996 **Turnover:** Up to £250,000
No.of Employees: 1 - 10 **Product Groups:** 52

Date of Accounts	Nov 11	Nov 10	Nov 09
Working Capital	-60	-56	-56
Fixed Assets	23	13	13
Current Assets	32	33	32

Oldrids Co. Ltd
11 Strait Bargate, Boston, PE21 6UF
Tel: 01205-361251 **Fax:** 01205-356402
E-mail: lesley.mcgarry@oldrids.co.uk
Website: http://www.oldrids.co.uk
Directors: M. Issac (Dir), J. Young (Pers), M. Isaac (MD), D. Simpson (Dir)
Managers: S. Bause (Publicity), L. Bracey, L. Mcgarry (Mgr), R. Turner (I.T. Exec), D. Turner (I.T. Exec), A. Mcclingtok (Mgr), S. Fowler (Comptroller)
Immediate Holding Company: OLDRID & CO.,LIMITED
Registration no: 00284283 **VAT No.:** GB 351 8731 50
Date established: 1934 **Turnover:** £20m - £50m
No.of Employees: 101 - 250 **Product Groups:** 77

Date of Accounts	Jan 09	Jan 10	Jan 11
Sales Turnover	46m	43m	42m
Pre Tax Profit/Loss	4m	3m	4m
Working Capital	7m	8m	10m
Fixed Assets	26m	26m	25m
Current Assets	13m	14m	16m
Current Liabilities	4m	3m	2m

Paladin Radiators
West Skirbeck House London Road, Boston, PE21 7HF
Tel: 01205-350070 **Fax:** 01205-356733
E-mail: sales@paladinradiators.com
Website: http://www.paladinradiators.com
Directors: H. Proctor (MD)
No.of Employees: 1 - 10 **Product Groups:** 38, 40

Richard Pearson Ltd
Priory Road Freiston, Boston, PE22 0JZ
Tel: 01205-760383 **Fax:** 01205-760822
E-mail: info@richardpearson.com
Website: http://www.richardpearson.com
Directors: R. Bainbridge (Dir)
Immediate Holding Company: RICHARD PEARSON LIMITED
Registration no: 00611568 **VAT No.:** GB 127 9578 28
Date established: 1958 **Turnover:** £1m - £2m **No.of Employees:** 1 - 10
Product Groups: 67

Date of Accounts	Dec 11	Dec 10	Dec 09
Working Capital	-40	-400	-242
Fixed Assets	2m	2m	2m
Current Assets	221	208	286

Philip Cowan Interiors
Sutterton Enterprise Park Sutterton, Boston, PE20 2JA
Tel: 01205-461111 **Fax:** 01205-461119
E-mail: enquiries@cowans.co.uk
Website: http://www.cowans.co.uk
Managers: P. Cowan (Mgr)
Ultimate Holding Company: M G S MANAGEMENT SERVICES LIMITED
Immediate Holding Company: R & D PROPERTY INVESTMENTS LIMITED
Registration no: 03656819 **Date established:** 1990
No.of Employees: 1 - 10 **Product Groups:** 63

Porcher Abrasive Coatings Ltd
Nursery Road Industrial Estate, Boston, PE21 7TN
Tel: 01205-356666 **Fax:** 01205-351646
E-mail: info@porcher.co.uk
Website: http://www.porcher.co.uk
Directors: E. Porcher (Dir)
Immediate Holding Company: PORCHER ABRASIVE COATINGS LIMITED
Registration no: 03298201 **VAT No.:** GB 694 2796 79
Date established: 1996 **No.of Employees:** 11 - 20 **Product Groups:** 25, 29, 30, 32, 33, 35, 36, 40, 41, 67

Date of Accounts	Apr 11	Apr 10	Apr 09
Working Capital	412	229	253
Fixed Assets	515	513	524
Current Assets	600	584	384

Robert H Crawford & Son
Frithville, Boston, PE22 7DU
Tel: 01205-750367 **Fax:** 01205-750369
E-mail: sales@rhcrawford.com
Website: http://www.rhcrawford.com
Directors: R. Crawford (MD)
Immediate Holding Company: ROBERT H. CRAWFORD & SON
Registration no: 00572971 **Date established:** 1956
No.of Employees: 21 - 50 **Product Groups:** 41

Date of Accounts	Dec 99	Dec 00
Working Capital	683	662
Fixed Assets	76	63
Current Assets	1m	1m

S C L
Norwood Yard Church Green Road, Fishtoft, Boston, PE21 0RN
Tel: 01205-351531 **Fax:** 01205-351531
E-mail: laurance.lee@btconnect.com
Directors: L. Lee (Prop)
Date established: 2003 **No.of Employees:** 1 - 10 **Product Groups:** 35

S Dodson
80 Cherry Walk, Boston, PE21 8AZ
Tel: 01205-360341 **Fax:** 01205-360341
Directors: S. Dodson (Prop)
Date established: 1983 **No.of Employees:** 1 - 10 **Product Groups:** 35, 39, 45

United Fork Trucks
Unity House Nursery Road Industrial Estate, Boston, PE21 7TN
Tel: 01205-355050 **Fax:** 01205-353033
Website: http://www.unitedforktrucks.co.uk
Managers: G. Taylor (Serv Mgr)
Immediate Holding Company: UNITED FORKTRUCKS (1992) LTD
Registration no: 02693495 **No.of Employees:** 11 - 20
Product Groups: 35, 39, 45

Bourne

Bourne Skip Hire & Recycling Ltd
Cherry Holt Road, Bourne, PE10 9LA
Tel: 01778-394044 **Fax:** .
E-mail: info@bourneskiphire.biz
Website: http://www.bourneskiphire.biz
Directors: C. Seggie (MD)
Immediate Holding Company: BOURNE SKIP HIRE AND RECYCLING LIMITED
Registration no: 04545691 **Date established:** 2002
No.of Employees: 1 - 10 **Product Groups:** 39, 45, 83

Date of Accounts	Sep 11	Sep 10	Sep 09
Working Capital	-438	-325	-358
Fixed Assets	655	534	576
Current Assets	210	233	259

Bourne Textile Services Ltd
Cherry Holt Road, Bourne, PE10 9LA
Tel: 01778-423483 **Fax:** 01778-420910
E-mail: david.johnson@bournegroup.co.uk
Website: http://www.bournegroup.co.uk
Bank(s): Barclays P.L.C., Spalding
Directors: D. Johnson (MD), H. Stroud (Fin)
Ultimate Holding Company: BOURNE SERVICES GROUP LIMITED
Immediate Holding Company: BOURNE TEXTILE SERVICES LIMITED
Registration no: 03017579 **Date established:** 1995
Turnover: £10m - £20m **No.of Employees:** 251 - 500
Product Groups: 23, 83

Date of Accounts	Feb 08	Feb 11	Feb 10
Sales Turnover	N/A	13m	12m
Pre Tax Profit/Loss	847	2m	1m
Working Capital	599	1m	776
Fixed Assets	3m	4m	4m
Current Assets	3m	3m	4m
Current Liabilities	951	1m	1m

Eduard Hueck
1 Manor Crown Business Centre Meadow Drove, Bourne, PE10 0BP
Tel: 01780-762914 **Fax:** 01780-765631
Managers: D. Barritt (Mgr)
Immediate Holding Company: ROSEDALE LETTING AGENTS LIMITED
Date established: 2011 **No.of Employees:** 1 - 10 **Product Groups:** 35, 40

Date of Accounts	Apr 11	Apr 10	Apr 09
Working Capital	-13	-5	2
Fixed Assets	24	13	6
Current Assets	27	14	10

Exmol Manufacturing
Meadow Drove Farm, Bourne, PE10 0AL
Tel: 01778-426670 **Fax:** 01778-426670
E-mail: gmoss@exmol.com
Website: http://www.exmol.com
Directors: G. Moss (Prop)
Date established: 1999 **No.of Employees:** 1 - 10 **Product Groups:** 35

Field Box More Labels
Roman Bank, Bourne, PE10 9LQ
Tel: 01778-426444 **Fax:** 01778-421862
E-mail: spencer.johnston@chesapeakecorp.com
Website: http://www.fieldboxmore.com
Bank(s): Barclays
Directors: R. Smith (MD), S. Johnston (Chief Op Offcr), P. Rous (MD), M. Brown (Fin)
Managers: K. Taytor (Buyer), I. Coles (Sales Prom Mgr), D. Tilley (Purch Mgr), D. Bills (Tech Serv Mgr), A. Tate (Accounts)
Immediate Holding Company: THE FIELD GROUP P.L.C.
Registration no: 01821587 **VAT No.:** GB 395 9072 07
Turnover: £1m - £2m **No.of Employees:** 51 - 100 **Product Groups:** 30

Fusion Software UK Ltd
Phoenix House 32 Main Road, Dowsby, Bourne, PE10 0TL
Tel: 0845-094 4470 **Fax:** 01327-300336
E-mail: enquiry@fusionsoftwareuk.co.uk
Website: http://www.fusionsoftwareuk.co.uk
Directors: H. Muscroft (Fin), L. Ottaway (MD)
Registration no: 04627293 **Turnover:** Up to £250,000
No.of Employees: 1 - 10 **Product Groups:** 38, 44

Date of Accounts	Jan 08	Jan 07	Jan 06
Working Capital	42	29	13
Fixed Assets	N/A	1	1
Current Assets	72	50	29
Current Liabilities	30	21	16

Jewson Ltd
1 South Road, Bourne, PE10 9JB
Tel: 01778-421167 **Fax:** 01778-422634
E-mail: nick.franklin@jewsons.co.uk
Website: http://www.jewson.co.uk
Managers: M. Durham (Mgr)
Ultimate Holding Company: COMPAGNIE DE SAINT GOBAIN (FRANCE)
Immediate Holding Company: JEWSON LIMITED
Registration no: 00348407 **Date established:** 1939 **Turnover:** £2m - £5m
No.of Employees: 1 - 10 **Product Groups:** 66

Date of Accounts	Dec 11	Dec 10	Dec 09
Sales Turnover	1606m	1547m	1485m
Pre Tax Profit/Loss	18m	100m	45m
Working Capital	-345m	-250m	-349m
Fixed Assets	496m	387m	461m
Current Assets	657m	1005m	1320m
Current Liabilities	66m	120m	64m

Links Labels & Tapes (SLPP Ltd)
Pinfold Road, Bourne, PE10 9HT
Tel: 01778-426282 **Fax:** 01778-391638
E-mail: enquiries@linkslabels-tapes.co.uk
Website: http://www.linkslabels-tapes.co.uk
Bank(s): Lloyds TSB Bank plc
Directors: R. Rudd (MD), D. Shale (Dir), D. Dutton (Dir)
Ultimate Holding Company: SLPP LIMITED
Immediate Holding Company: NRB ROADPHONE GROUP LIMITED
Registration no: 03591734 **VAT No.:** GB 310 8040 14
Date established: 2002 **No.of Employees:** 21 - 50 **Product Groups:** 28

Date of Accounts	Apr 11	Apr 10	Apr 09
Working Capital	-8	-9	-9
Fixed Assets	7	10	8
Current Assets	16	11	13

Martin Lishman
Roman Bank, Bourne, PE10 9LQ
Tel: 01778-426600 **Fax:** 01778-426555
E-mail: sales@martinlishman.com
Website: http://www.martinlishman.com
Directors: C. Lishman (Fin), G. Lishman (MD)
Immediate Holding Company: MARTIN LISHMAN LIMITED
Registration no: 03793534 **Date established:** 1999
Turnover: £500,000 - £1m **No.of Employees:** 11 - 20 **Product Groups:** 41

Date of Accounts	Dec 11	Dec 10	Dec 09
Working Capital	441	456	443
Fixed Assets	80	71	72
Current Assets	586	720	708

Opico Ltd
Cherry Holt Road, Bourne, PE10 9LA
Tel: 01778-421111 **Fax:** 01778-425080
E-mail: james.woolway@opico.co.uk
Website: http://www.opico.co.uk
Directors: J. Woolway (MD)
Immediate Holding Company: OPICO LIMITED
Registration no: 06175803 **VAT No.:** GB 119 1309 90
Date established: 2007 **Turnover:** £2m - £5m **No.of Employees:** 21 - 50
Product Groups: 41, 67

Date of Accounts	Dec 11	Dec 10	Dec 09
Working Capital	999	740	625
Fixed Assets	985	929	975
Current Assets	2m	2m	2m

Progreen Weed Control Solutions Ltd
Kellington House South Fen Business Park South Fen Road, Bourne, PE10 0DN
Tel: 01778-394052 **Fax:** 01778-394499
E-mail: info@progreen.co.uk
Website: http://www.progreen.co.uk
Managers: L. Boothman (Comm)
Immediate Holding Company: PROGREEN WEED CONTROL SOLUTIONS LIMITED
Registration no: 07375409 **Date established:** 2010
No.of Employees: 1 - 10 **Product Groups:** 32

Date of Accounts	Jan 12
Working Capital	126
Fixed Assets	1
Current Assets	181

B W Riddle
South Fen Road, Bourne, PE10 0DN
Tel: 01775-670257 **Fax:** 01775-670301
E-mail: admin@bwriddle.co.uk
Website: http://www.bwriddle.co.uk
Bank(s): Barclays
Directors: C. Riddle (Prop)
Immediate Holding Company: PETERBOROUGH METAL RECYCLING LIMITED
Registration no: 03365414 **VAT No.:** GB 312 6186 81
Date established: 1997 **Turnover:** Up to £250,000
No.of Employees: 21 - 50 **Product Groups:** 34, 54

Date of Accounts	Apr 12	Apr 11	Apr 10
Sales Turnover	7m	N/A	N/A
Pre Tax Profit/Loss	543	N/A	N/A
Working Capital	1m	2m	2m
Fixed Assets	3m	1m	1m
Current Assets	2m	3m	2m
Current Liabilities	386	N/A	N/A

Trackline International
Pinfold Road, Bourne, PE10 9HT
Tel: 01778-426057 **Fax:** 01778-393682
E-mail: sales@tracklineinternational.com
Website: http://www.tracklineinternational.com
Directors: B. O'Connell (MD)
Managers: D. Williams (Mgr), G. Griffiths (Mgr)
Immediate Holding Company: L S BAKER LIMITED
Registration no: 04347622 **VAT No.:** GB 425 6296 41
Date established: 1998 **No.of Employees:** 11 - 20 **Product Groups:** 30, 35, 36, 39, 45, 48

Date of Accounts	Apr 11	Apr 10	Apr 09
Working Capital	-8	-9	-9
Fixed Assets	7	10	8
Current Assets	16	11	13

Gainsborough

Neville Barnes Ltd
Padmoor Lane Upton, Gainsborough, DN21 5NH
Tel: 01427-838245 **Fax:** 01427-838417
Website: http://www.nevillebarnes.co.uk
Directors: J. Martinson (MD)
Immediate Holding Company: NEVILLE BARNES LIMITED
Registration no: 01541640 **Date established:** 1981
No.of Employees: 1 - 10 **Product Groups:** 41

Date of Accounts	Dec 11	Dec 10	Dec 09
Working Capital	146	143	141
Fixed Assets	63	68	75
Current Assets	236	228	241

G W Belton Ltd
Heaton Street, Gainsborough, DN21 2ED
Tel: 01427-612291 **Fax:** 01427- 810520
E-mail: ian.burgess@gwbelton.co.uk
Website: http://www.gwbelton.com
Bank(s): HSBC
Directors: I. Burgess (Co Sec)
Immediate Holding Company: G.W.BELTON LIMITED
Registration no: 00510366 **VAT No.:** GB 127 7723 55
Date established: 1952 **Turnover:** £2m - £5m **No.of Employees:** 21 - 50
Product Groups: 28, 80

Date of Accounts	Dec 09	Dec 08	Dec 07
Working Capital	-235	-287	-111
Fixed Assets	942	1m	1m
Current Assets	206	263	220

T Bland Welding Ltd
Sandars Road Heapham Road Industrial Estate, Gainsborough, DN21 1RZ
Tel: 01427-610116 **Fax:** 01427-810287
E-mail: t.bland@virgin.net
Website: http://www.tbland.co.uk
Directors: T. Bland (MD)
Immediate Holding Company: T. BLAND WELDING LIMITED
Registration no: 04969478 **VAT No.:** GB 555 3102 66
Date established: 2003 **Turnover:** Up to £250,000
No.of Employees: 1 - 10 **Product Groups:** 48

Date of Accounts	Dec 11	Dec 10	Dec 09
Working Capital	-12	-19	-26
Fixed Assets	20	27	33
Current Assets	94	100	54

Chafer Machinery Ltd
Upton, Gainsborough, DN21 5PB
Tel: 01427-838341 **Fax:** 01427-838507
E-mail: rob.starkey@cropsprayers.com
Website: http://www.cropsprayers.com
Directors: C. Allen (MD)
Managers: S. Robertson (Mgr), J. Allen (Mgr), R. Searkey (Mgr)
Immediate Holding Company: CHAFER MACHINERY LIMITED
Registration no: 04055546 **Date established:** 2000
No.of Employees: 21 - 50 **Product Groups:** 41

Date of Accounts	Sep 11	Sep 10	Sep 09
Working Capital	1m	1m	957
Fixed Assets	102	99	100
Current Assets	2m	2m	2m

Diamond Power Specialty
Unit 5b Sandars Road, Heapham Road Industrial Estate, Gainsborough, DN21 1RZ
Tel: 01427-810497 **Fax:** 01427-810498
E-mail: cbrown@diamondpower.co.uk
Website: http://www.diamondpower.co.uk
Managers: C. Brown (Mgr)
Ultimate Holding Company: MCDERMOTT INTERNATIONAL INC (PANAMA)
Immediate Holding Company: DIAMOND POWER SPECIALTY LIMITED
Registration no: 00127571 **Date established:** 2013
Turnover: £20m - £50m **No.of Employees:** 11 - 20 **Product Groups:** 37, 40, 48

Date of Accounts	Dec 11	Dec 10	Dec 09
Sales Turnover	29m	26m	29m
Pre Tax Profit/Loss	2m	2m	2m
Working Capital	18m	16m	14m
Fixed Assets	7m	8m	8m
Current Assets	23m	21m	20m
Current Liabilities	4m	3m	4m

Eminox Ltd
North Warren Road, Gainsborough, DN21 2TU
Tel: 01427-810088 **Fax:** 01427-810061
E-mail: enquiries@eminox.com
Website: http://www.eminox.com
Directors: D. Hodgson (Co Sec), A. Whitehouse (Fin), D. Milles (Ch)
Managers: A. Mills (Tech Serv Mgr), K. Henderson (Mktg Serv Mgr), M. Martley (Purch Mgr), D. Hulley (Sales Prom Mgr), J. Varley-hill (Personnel)
Ultimate Holding Company: HEXADEX LIMITED
Immediate Holding Company: EMINOX LIMITED
Registration no: 01349209 **Date established:** 1978
Turnover: £20m - £50m **No.of Employees:** 101 - 250
Product Groups: 31, 39, 68

Date of Accounts	Dec 11	Dec 10	Dec 09
Sales Turnover	43m	34m	34m
Pre Tax Profit/Loss	5m	4m	5m
Working Capital	12m	11m	15m
Fixed Assets	2m	3m	2m
Current Assets	19m	16m	19m
Current Liabilities	3m	825	1m

Flexadux Plastics Ltd
Corringham Road Industrial Estate Grange Road, Gainsborough, DN21 1QB
Tel: 01427-617547 **Fax:** 01427-811170
E-mail: sales@flexadux.co.uk
Website: http://www.flexadux.co.uk
Bank(s): National Westminster
Directors: J. Simon (Co Sec), F. Schauenburg (Dir)
Ultimate Holding Company: SCHAUENBURG SERVICE GMBH (GERMANY)
Immediate Holding Company: FLEXADUX PLASTICS LIMITED
Registration no: 04126555 **Date established:** 2000 **Turnover:** £2m - £5m
No.of Employees: 11 - 20 **Product Groups:** 23, 30, 40

Date of Accounts	Dec 11	Dec 10	Dec 09
Working Capital	727	565	443
Fixed Assets	35	29	34
Current Assets	1m	790	945

Gleadell Agriculture Ltd
Lindsey House Hemswell Cliff, Gainsborough, DN21 5TH
Tel: 01427-421200 **Fax:** 01427-421230
E-mail: michael.thompson@gleadellagriculture.co.uk
Website: http://www.gleadellagriculture.co.uk
Directors: S. Shand (Sales), M. Thompson (Fin)
Managers: J. Martin (Tech Serv Mgr)
Immediate Holding Company: GLEADELL AGRICULTURE LIMITED
Registration no: 00534118 **VAT No.:** 555 6831 16 **Date established:** 1954
Turnover: £250m - £500m **No.of Employees:** 51 - 100
Product Groups: 61

Date of Accounts	Jun 11	Jun 10	Jun 09
Sales Turnover	433m	291m	359m
Pre Tax Profit/Loss	6m	4m	9m
Working Capital	7m	5m	9m
Fixed Assets	6m	6m	2m
Current Assets	60m	37m	41m
Current Liabilities	4m	3m	4m

Hall Farm Nursery
Hall Farm Harpswell, Gainsborough, DN21 5UU
Tel: 01427-668412 **Fax:** 01427-667478
E-mail: marktatam@hall-farm.co.uk
Website: http://www.hall-farm.co.uk
Directors: M. Tatam (Prop)
Turnover: Up to £250,000 **No.of Employees:** 1 - 10 **Product Groups:** 35, 41, 46, 48, 49

Horstine Farmery
1 Cow Lane Upton, Gainsborough, DN21 5PB
Tel: 01427-838383 **Fax:** 01427-838507
E-mail: c.allen@horstinefarmery.com
Website: http://www.horstinefarmery.com
Directors: C. Allen (Prop)
Managers: R. Starkey (Comm), S. Robertson (Ops Mgr)
Registration no: 03125238 **VAT No.:** GB 647 4567 04
Turnover: £1m - £2m **No.of Employees:** 21 - 50 **Product Groups:** 67

Interfuse Ltd
Unit 19 Corringham Road Industrial Estate Corringham Road, Gainsborough, DN21 1QB
Tel: 01427-810290 **Fax:** 01427-810405
E-mail: rogerjones@interfuseblocks.com
Website: http://www.interfuseblocks.com
Managers: R. Jones (Sales Prom Mgr)
Ultimate Holding Company: JELSON HOLDINGS LIMITED
Immediate Holding Company: INTERFUSE LIMITED
Registration no: 00850109 **VAT No.:** GB 115 0808 04
Date established: 1965 **Turnover:** £2m - £5m **No.of Employees:** 1 - 10
Product Groups: 33

Date of Accounts	Apr 12	Apr 11	Apr 10
Sales Turnover	10m	9m	9m
Pre Tax Profit/Loss	462	246	32
Working Capital	9m	9m	9m
Fixed Assets	1m	1m	1m
Current Assets	11m	10m	10m
Current Liabilities	243	262	106

Kern-Liebers Ltd
Unit 7 Corringham Road Industrial Estate Corringham Road, Gainsborough, DN21 1QB
Tel: 01427-612085 **Fax:** 01427-610301
E-mail: adrian.nicoll@kern-liebers.co.uk
Website: http://www.kern-liebers.co.uk
Bank(s): HSBC Bank plc
Directors: A. Nicoll (MD), K. Scheuble (Co Sec)
Managers: C. Cowell (Ops Mgr), J. Hinder (Sales & Mktg Mg)
Ultimate Holding Company: HUGO-KERN UND LIEBERS AND CO GMBH (GERMA
Immediate Holding Company: KERN-LIEBERS LIMITED
Registration no: 01326455 **VAT No.:** GB 316 8408 55
Date established: 1977 **Turnover:** £2m - £5m **No.of Employees:** 21 - 50
Product Groups: 35, 42, 48

Date of Accounts	Jun 11	Jun 10	Jun 09
Working Capital	582	210	106
Fixed Assets	284	778	1m
Current Assets	1m	1m	1m

Kirkstons Packaging Insulatione Midlands Ltd
Unit 16 Corringham Road Industrial Estate, Gainsborough, DN21 1QB
Tel: 01427-612007 **Fax:** 01427-810952
E-mail: kirkston@packaging.fsworld.co.uk
Bank(s): Yorkshire Bank PLC
Directors: C. Webster (Works), E. Doughty (MD), E. Doughty (Prop)
Managers: D. Heywood (Sales Prom Mgr)
Registration no: 01405182 **VAT No.:** GB 313 5756 65
Turnover: £1m - £2m **No.of Employees:** 11 - 20 **Product Groups:** 30, 31

Peacock & Binnington
High Street Corringham, Gainsborough, DN21 5QP
Tel: 01427-838696 **Fax:** 01427-838411
E-mail: jonathan.jones@peacock.co.uk
Website: http://www.peacock.co.uk
Managers: J. Jones (Mgr)
Ultimate Holding Company: PEACOCK & BINNINGTON HOLDINGS LIMITED
Immediate Holding Company: PEACOCK & BINNINGTON
Registration no: 00328944 **Date established:** 1937
No.of Employees: 1 - 10 **Product Groups:** 41

Date of Accounts	Dec 11	Dec 10	Dec 09
Sales Turnover	36m	35m	34m
Pre Tax Profit/Loss	361	202	267
Working Capital	2m	2m	1m
Fixed Assets	2m	1m	1m
Current Assets	8m	8m	7m
Current Liabilities	653	231	599

Ping Europe Ltd
Corringham Road, Gainsborough, DN21 1XZ
Tel: 01427-615405 **Fax:** 01427-617259
E-mail: johnc@pingeurope.co.uk
Website: http://www.pingeurope.co.uk
Bank(s): SEB
Directors: A. Burton (Fin), J. Clark (MD)
Managers: N. Dear (Personnel), M. Waring (Purch Mgr), T. Jenkins (Mktg Serv Mgr), N. Cottingham (Tech Serv Mgr)
Immediate Holding Company: PING EUROPE LIMITED
Registration no: 01129505 **VAT No.:** GB 613 6261 63
Date established: 1973 **Turnover:** £50m - £75m
No.of Employees: 101 - 250 **Product Groups:** 49

Date of Accounts	Dec 11	Dec 10	Dec 09
Sales Turnover	54m	52m	48m
Pre Tax Profit/Loss	2m	2m	1m
Working Capital	13m	14m	13m
Fixed Assets	6m	5m	5m
Current Assets	19m	21m	21m
Current Liabilities	4m	4m	5m

Playhouse Gainsborough Ltd
Corringham Road Industrial Estate Corringham Road, Gainsborough, DN21 1QB
Tel: 01427-810148 **Fax:** 01427-810443
E-mail: info@playhousegainsborough.co.uk
Website: http://www.playhousegainsborough.co.uk
Bank(s): National Westminster Bank Plc
Directors: R. Fall (Dir)
Immediate Holding Company: PLAYHOUSE GAINSBOROUGH LIMITED
Registration no: 07399485 **VAT No.:** GB 288 3501 37
Date established: 2010 **Turnover:** £2m - £5m **No.of Employees:** 11 - 20
Product Groups: 42

Date of Accounts	Mar 12
Working Capital	-90
Fixed Assets	79
Current Assets	10

Silvaperl
Ropery Road Albion Works, Gainsborough, DN21 2QB
Tel: 01427-610160 **Fax:** 01427-811838
E-mail: guy.sinclair@william-sinclair.co.uk
Website: http://www.silvaperl.co.uk
Bank(s): Lloyds TSB Bank plc
Directors: R. Sinclair (Dir)
Managers: R. Sinclair (Comm)
Ultimate Holding Company: William Sinclair Holdings PLC
Immediate Holding Company: William Sinclair Horticulture Ltd
Registration no: 04436927 **Date established:** 2002
Turnover: £20m - £50m **No.of Employees:** 21 - 50 **Product Groups:** 14, 17, 20, 32, 33

Date of Accounts	Dec 11	Dec 10	Dec 09
Sales Turnover	13m	15m	15m
Pre Tax Profit/Loss	477	938	789
Working Capital	2m	1m	1m
Fixed Assets	2m	3m	3m
Current Assets	4m	5m	5m
Current Liabilities	704	998	831

Smiffy's (R.H. Smith & Sons (Wigmakers)
Heapham Road South Caldicott Drive, Heapham Road Industrial Estate, Gainsborough, DN21 1FJ
Tel: 01427-616831 **Fax:** 01427-617190
E-mail: sales@smiffys.com
Website: http://www.smiffys.com
Bank(s): HSBC
Directors: G. Peckett (Co Sec), E. Peckett (Dir)
Managers: P. Barker (Buyer), M. George (Mktg Serv Mgr), J. Noble (Personnel), H. Corfield (Sales Prom Mgr), D. Braisby (Buyer), D. Wain (Sales Prom Mgr), D. Wadhams (Tech Serv Mgr), A. Sharp (Fin Mgr), J. Green
Immediate Holding Company: RACETORATIONS LIMITED
Registration no: 02600284 **VAT No.:** GB 129 5795 28
Date established: 1998 **Turnover:** £250,000 - £500,000
No.of Employees: 251 - 500 **Product Groups:** 24, 27, 30, 32, 49, 61, 63, 65, 89

Date of Accounts	Mar 11	Mar 10	Mar 09
Working Capital	-75	36	-35
Fixed Assets	5	6	5
Current Assets	39	36	50

Spiroflex Ltd
Unit 7 Lusher Way Corringham Road Industrial Estate, Gainsborough, DN21 1QB
Tel: 0870-3333503 **Fax:** 0870-3333513
E-mail: info@spiroflex.com
Website: http://www.spiroflex.com
Bank(s): Skandinaviska Enskilda Banken (London) Swift/ BIC: ESSEGB2L IBAN: GB46 ESSE 4048 6522 7750 07
Directors: E. Reading (MD)
Managers: A. Stead (Chief Mgr), R. Clough (Sales Eng), R. Green (Accounts)
Immediate Holding Company: Autoliv
Registration no: 06931475 **VAT No.:** GB 785 2245 12
No.of Employees: 51 - 100 **Product Groups:** 35

Stairlift Spares Ltd
Cliff Road Snitterby, Gainsborough, DN21 4UA
Tel: 01673-818003
E-mail: sales@stairlift-spares.co.uk
Website: http://www.stairlift-spares.co.uk
Directors: M. Hulbert (Prop)
Immediate Holding Company: STAIRLIFT SPARES LIMITED
Registration no: 04680064 **Date established:** 2003
No.of Employees: 1 - 10 **Product Groups:** 35, 39, 45

Date of Accounts	Mar 11	Mar 10	Mar 09
Sales Turnover	N/A	N/A	146
Pre Tax Profit/Loss	N/A	N/A	26
Working Capital	14	2	-0
Fixed Assets	1	1	1
Current Assets	101	72	52
Current Liabilities	31	18	22

T M S Gainsborough Ltd
Track Marshalls Building Corringham Road, Gainsborough, DN21 1QH
Tel: 01427-612301 **Fax:** 01427-612672
E-mail: mail@tmsgainsborough.co.uk
Directors: M. Lighton (Dir)
Immediate Holding Company: T.M.S. GAINSBOROUGH LIMITED
Registration no: 02543978 **VAT No.:** GB 555 5983 95
Date established: 1990 **No.of Employees:** 1 - 10 **Product Groups:** 42, 45, 46, 67

Date of Accounts	May 10	May 09	May 08
Working Capital	127	216	221
Fixed Assets	42	40	44
Current Assets	640	661	550

T W Logistics Ltd
The Old Ship Yard, Gainsborough, DN21 1NQ
Tel: 01427-614551 **Fax:** 01427-613770
E-mail: pgsargent@twlogistics.co.uk
Website: http://www.twlogistics.co.uk
Bank(s): Midland
Directors: J. Daubney (Fin), P. Sargent (Co Sec)
Managers: S. Wain (Tech Serv Mgr), J. Ledsham (Mgr)
Immediate Holding Company: T W LOGISTICS LIMITED
Registration no: 03150116 **Date established:** 1996 **Turnover:** £5m - £10m
No.of Employees: 51 - 100 **Product Groups:** 72

Date of Accounts	Dec 11	Dec 10	Dec 09
Sales Turnover	6m	5m	4m
Pre Tax Profit/Loss	173	161	76
Working Capital	-105	22	105
Fixed Assets	4m	4m	4m
Current Assets	2m	2m	1m
Current Liabilities	293	381	205

Technosys Ltd
C Off Sandars Road Heapham Road Industrial Estate, Gainsborough, DN21 1RZ
Tel: 01427-811567 **Fax:** 01427-811555
Website: http://www.nosys.freeserve.co.uk
Directors: G. King (Dir), J. Wrath (Dir)
Immediate Holding Company: AMP TECHNOSYS LIMITED
Registration no: 07440120 **Date established:** 2010
No.of Employees: 1 - 10 **Product Groups:** 38, 42

Date of Accounts	Mar 06	Dec 04
Pre Tax Profit/Loss	590	N/A
Working Capital	N/A	-590
Current Liabilities	N/A	590
Total Share Capital	16	16

UK Fire Security Ltd
18 Littleborough Lane Marton, Gainsborough, DN21 5AB
Tel: 01427-717000 **Fax:** 01427-717000
Directors: G. Airey (Dir)
Immediate Holding Company: U.K. FIRE SECURITIES LIMITED
Registration no: 03275712 **Date established:** 1996
No.of Employees: 1 - 10 **Product Groups:** 38, 42

Date of Accounts	Dec 11	Dec 10	Dec 09
Working Capital	4	-2	-7
Fixed Assets	3	4	5
Current Assets	13	12	16
Current Liabilities	8	12	N/A

Grantham

Anbar Trading Company
44 Belton Lane Great Gonerby, Grantham, NG31 8NA
Tel: 01476-571966 **Fax:** 01476-592093
E-mail: anbar@globalnet.co.uk
Directors: T. Barnett (Prop)
No.of Employees: 1 - 10 **Product Groups:** 45, 48, 67

Armstrong & Holmes Ltd
South Heath Lane Fulbeck, Grantham, NG32 3HX
Tel: 01400-261061 **Fax:** 01400-262289
E-mail: sales@farmtrailers.co.uk
Website: http://www.farmtrailers.co.uk
Directors: A. Armstrong (MD)
Immediate Holding Company: ARMSTRONG & HOLMES LIMITED
Registration no: 01340588 **Date established:** 1977
No.of Employees: 1 - 10 **Product Groups:** 39

Date of Accounts	Feb 12	Feb 11	Feb 10
Working Capital	95	93	84
Fixed Assets	88	94	100
Current Assets	150	216	174
Current Liabilities	22	N/A	N/A

Arraquip Ltd
Withambrook Industrial Estate, Grantham, NG31 9ST
Tel: 01476-573637 **Fax:** 01476-590192
E-mail: gdewey@nascr.net
Website: http://www.nacr.net
Directors: G. Dewey (MD)
Immediate Holding Company: ARRAQUIP LIMITED
Registration no: 01391300 **VAT No.:** GB 309 4051 79
Date established: 1978 **Turnover:** £1m - £2m **No.of Employees:** 1 - 10
Product Groups: 66

Date of Accounts	Apr 12	Apr 11	Apr 10
Working Capital	603	626	584
Fixed Assets	636	624	623
Current Assets	1m	1m	1m

Associated Timber Services Ltd
Honey Pot Lane Colsterworth, Grantham, NG33 5LT
Tel: 01476-860117 **Fax:** 01476-861348
E-mail: sales@associatedtimber.co.uk
Website: http://www.associatedtimber.co.uk
Directors: G. Rattcliff (Fin)
Immediate Holding Company: ASSOCIATED TIMBER SERVICES LIMITED
Registration no: 02099199 **Date established:** 1987 **Turnover:** £2m - £5m
No.of Employees: 11 - 20 **Product Groups:** 08

Date of Accounts	Jun 11	Jun 10	Jun 09
Sales Turnover	N/A	N/A	5m
Pre Tax Profit/Loss	N/A	N/A	228
Working Capital	2m	889	846
Fixed Assets	1m	2m	2m
Current Assets	4m	3m	3m
Current Liabilities	933	848	1m

Autocraft Drivetrain Solutions Ltd (t/a Autocraft Industries UK)
Syston Lane Belton, Grantham, NG32 2LY
Tel: 01476-581300 **Fax:** 01476-70589
E-mail: sharris@autocraftds.com
Website: http://www.autocraftds.co.uk
Directors: M. Hague-morgan (Dir), A. Dorr (Fin), S. Harris (MD)
Managers: P. Charlesworth (Tech Serv Mgr), A. Howitt (Personnel)
Ultimate Holding Company: HARMOR LIMITED
Immediate Holding Company: AUTOCRAFT DRIVETRAIN SOLUTIONS LIMITED
Registration no: 02847178 **Date established:** 1993
Turnover: £10m - £20m **No.of Employees:** 101 - 250
Product Groups: 40, 48

Date of Accounts	Dec 11	Dec 10	Dec 09
Sales Turnover	12m	6m	N/A
Pre Tax Profit/Loss	506	3m	3
Working Capital	-4m	-4m	-3m
Fixed Assets	9m	8m	7m
Current Assets	6m	6m	89
Current Liabilities	940	1m	13

Bell & Webster Concrete Ltd
Alma Park Road, Grantham, NG31 9SE
Tel: 01476-562277 **Fax:** 01476-562944
E-mail: shaun.brown@eleco.com
Website: http://www.bellandwebster.co.uk
Bank(s): Lloyds TSB Bank plc
Directors: J. Stothard (MD)
Managers: C. Lound, D. Dannhauser (Chief Acct)
Ultimate Holding Company: ELECO PUBLIC LIMITED COMPANY
Immediate Holding Company: BELL & WEBSTER CONCRETE LIMITED
Registration no: 02255867 **Date established:** 1988
Turnover: £20m - £50m **No.of Employees:** 21 - 50 **Product Groups:** 33

Date of Accounts	Dec 11	Jun 10	Jun 09
Sales Turnover	22m	21m	23m
Pre Tax Profit/Loss	-7m	-5m	-150
Working Capital	6	-5m	-420
Fixed Assets	3m	4m	4m
Current Assets	3m	5m	8m
Current Liabilities	1m	3m	3m

Beta Training Ltd
Thompsons Lane Hough-on-the-Hill, Grantham, NG32 2BB
Tel: 01400-250423 **Fax:** 01400-251849
E-mail: david@betatraining.com
Website: http://www.betatraining.com
Directors: D. Silver (MD)
Immediate Holding Company: BETA TRAINING LIMITED
Registration no: 01366747 **Date established:** 1978
Turnover: Up to £250,000 **No.of Employees:** 1 - 10 **Product Groups:** 86

Date of Accounts	May 11	May 10	May 09
Sales Turnover	16	18	42
Pre Tax Profit/Loss	2	5	-0
Working Capital	6	4	-1
Fixed Assets	2	1	2
Current Assets	8	8	13
Current Liabilities	1	2	5

Bridal Fashions Ltd
Springfield Business Park Springfield Road, Grantham, NG31 7BG
Tel: 01476-593311 **Fax:** 01476-574396
Website: http://www.berketexbride.com
Managers: R. Oke (Mktg Serv Mgr)
Immediate Holding Company: BRIDAL FASHIONS LIMITED
Registration no: 03287579 **Date established:** 1996 **Turnover:** £5m - £10m
No.of Employees: 101 - 250 **Product Groups:** 24

Date of Accounts	Dec 11	Dec 10	Dec 09
Sales Turnover	8m	7m	8m
Pre Tax Profit/Loss	110	-130	117
Working Capital	2m	671	639
Fixed Assets	214	337	314
Current Assets	6m	3m	3m
Current Liabilities	2m	781	1m

Caddy Castings Ltd
Springfield Road, Grantham, NG31 7BQ
Tel: 01476-566667 **Fax:** 01476-570220
E-mail: enquiries@caddycastings.co.uk
Bank(s): HSBC Bank plc
Directors: K. Hutchinson (Dir), L. Cockerton (MD)
Immediate Holding Company: CADDY CASTINGS LIMITED
Registration no: 00046914 **VAT No.:** GB 116 2898 58
Date established: 1996 **Turnover:** £1m - £2m **No.of Employees:** 11 - 20
Product Groups: 34

Date of Accounts	Jun 11	Jun 10	Jun 09
Working Capital	62	-2	53
Fixed Assets	16	12	23
Current Assets	375	278	169

Castle Dataware Ltd
7 Partnership House Withambrook Park Industrial Estate, Grantham, NG31 9ST
Tel: 01476-592123 **Fax:** 01476-592992
E-mail: sales@culmak.co.uk
Website: http://www.culmak.co.uk
Directors: R. Handley (MD), E. Handley (Fin)
Immediate Holding Company: CASTLE DATAWARE LIMITED
Registration no: 03742149 **VAT No.:** GB 729 6546 93
Date established: 1999 **Turnover:** £250,000 - £500,000
No.of Employees: 1 - 10 **Product Groups:** 45, 48

Date of Accounts	Mar 11	Mar 10	Mar 09
Working Capital	14	14	15
Fixed Assets	1	1	1
Current Assets	15	15	16

Cathodic Protection Co. Ltd
Venture Way, Grantham, NG31 7XS
Tel: 01476-590666 **Fax:** 01476-570605
E-mail: rob.holden@cathodic.co.uk
Website: http://www.cathodic.co.uk
Directors: P. Righton (Fin), R. Holden (Dir), A. Arnold (Dir)
Ultimate Holding Company: HOSTOMBE GROUP LIMITED
Immediate Holding Company: CATHODIC PROTECTION CO. LIMITED
Registration no: 00478098 **Date established:** 1950
Turnover: £10m - £20m **No.of Employees:** 51 - 100 **Product Groups:** 84, 85

Date of Accounts	Mar 11	Mar 10	Mar 09
Sales Turnover	10m	7m	N/A
Pre Tax Profit/Loss	1m	986	N/A
Working Capital	2m	2m	1m
Fixed Assets	705	358	113
Current Assets	4m	4m	3m
Current Liabilities	606	661	N/A

Cutter Grinding Services
Unit 1-2 Withambrook Park Industrial Estate, Grantham, NG31 9ST
Tel: 01476-576486 **Fax:** 01476-579490
Directors: P. Hourd (Snr Part)
Date established: 1993 **No.of Employees:** 11 - 20 **Product Groups:** 46

David Wilson Trailers Ltd
Jubilee Park Honey Pot Lane, Colsterworth, Grantham, NG33 5LZ
Tel: 01476-860833 **Fax:** 01476-862813
E-mail: info@dwt-exhibitions.co.uk
Website: http://www.dwt-exhibitions.co.uk
Directors: D. Wilson (MD)
Immediate Holding Company: DAVID WILSON'S TRAILERS LIMITED
Registration no: 03033642 **Date established:** 1995 **Turnover:** £2m - £5m
No.of Employees: 1 - 10 **Product Groups:** 39, 45, 72, 81

Date of Accounts	Mar 12	Mar 11	Mar 10
Working Capital	-163	-162	-424
Fixed Assets	1m	1m	2m
Current Assets	154	93	156

Electro-Tech C P Ltd
Unit 3b Dysart Road Industrial Estate Dysart Road, Grantham, NG31 7EJ
Tel: 01476-564650 **Fax:** 01476-563630
E-mail: info@electrotechcp.com
Website: http://www.electrotechcp.com
Directors: P. Gibbs (MD)
Immediate Holding Company: ELECTRO-TECH CP LIMITED
Registration no: 04995041 **Date established:** 2003
No.of Employees: 11 - 20 **Product Groups:** 46, 48

Date of Accounts	Sep 11	Sep 10	Sep 09
Working Capital	372	844	899
Fixed Assets	48	64	70
Current Assets	996	1m	1m

Falcon Sales & Marketing
8 Waterloo Close Caythorpe, Grantham, NG32 3DL
Tel: 01400-272848 **Fax:** 01400-273447
E-mail: falconsm@btconnect.com
Directors: P. Taylor (Prop)
Date established: 1988 **No.of Employees:** 1 - 10 **Product Groups:** 38, 42

Farm Electronics Ltd
Woodland Drive Alma Park Road, Grantham, NG31 9SR
Tel: 01476-591592 **Fax:** 01476-591188
E-mail: paul@farmelec.co.uk
Website: http://www.farmelectronics.co.uk
Bank(s): Barclays
Directors: P. Jackson (Dir)
Immediate Holding Company: FARM ELECTRONICS LIMITED
Registration no: 01390214 **Date established:** 1978
No.of Employees: 11 - 20 **Product Groups:** 38, 40

Date of Accounts	Dec 11	Dec 10	Dec 09
Working Capital	338	241	276
Fixed Assets	53	37	35
Current Assets	750	466	588

Gilder Grids
Unit 11 Withambrook Park Industrial Estate, Grantham, NG31 9ST
Tel: 01476-560052 **Fax:** 01476-568165
E-mail: enquiries@gildergrids.co.uk
Website: http://www.gildergrids.co.uk
Directors: G. Gilder (Prop)
Turnover: Up to £250,000 **No.of Employees:** 1 - 10 **Product Groups:** 30, 32, 35, 38

Grantham Engineering Ltd
Harlaxton Road, Grantham, NG31 7SF
Tel: 01476-566301 **Fax:** 01476-590145
E-mail: sales@invictavibrators.co.uk
Website: http://www.invictavibrators.co.uk
Bank(s): Lloyds TSB Bank plc
Directors: P. Turley (I.T. Dir), A. Bailey (MD)
Managers: M. Caldwell (Mktg Serv Mgr), A. Sleaford (Tech Serv Mgr), S. Round
Ultimate Holding Company: JACK HARRIS (GRANTHAM) LIMITED
Immediate Holding Company: GRANTHAM ENGINEERING LTD.
Registration no: 00415925 **VAT No.:** GB 610 4250 96
Date established: 1946 **Turnover:** £5m - £10m
No.of Employees: 51 - 100 **Product Groups:** 30, 41, 42, 45

Date of Accounts	Sep 11	Sep 10	Sep 09
Sales Turnover	10m	8m	8m
Pre Tax Profit/Loss	888	301	207
Working Capital	2m	2m	3m
Fixed Assets	2m	2m	1m
Current Assets	4m	4m	4m
Current Liabilities	635	408	416

Grantham Manufacturing Ltd
Alma Park Industrial Estate, Grantham, NG31 9SW
Tel: 01476-566414 **Fax:** 01476-590225
E-mail: sales@gmluk.com
Website: http://www.gmluk.com
Bank(s): Barclays
Directors: M. Howitt (Dir)
Immediate Holding Company: GRANTHAM MANUFACTURING LIMITED
Registration no: 01929256 **Date established:** 1985 **Turnover:** £2m - £5m
No.of Employees: 21 - 50 **Product Groups:** 25, 27, 28, 29, 32

Date of Accounts	Apr 12	Apr 11	Apr 10
Working Capital	-12	-93	-91
Fixed Assets	303	312	322
Current Assets	409	422	363

Henry Bell & Co Grantham Ltd
Dysart Road, Grantham, NG31 7DB
Tel: 01476-565761 **Fax:** 01476-566950
E-mail: tom@henry-bell.co.uk
Website: http://www.henrybell-services.com
Directors: R. Fox (Ch), R. Lee (Ch), T. Lee (Ch), T. Lee (MD), C. Foster (Dir)
Immediate Holding Company: HENRY BELL & CO. (MORLEY) LIMITED
Registration no: 00479661 **Date established:** 1950
Turnover: Up to £250,000 **No.of Employees:** 21 - 50 **Product Groups:** 14, 20, 41, 62

Date of Accounts	Jun 08	Jun 07	Jun 06
Sales Turnover	N/A	N/A	11942
Pre Tax Profit/Loss	242	278	539
Working Capital	1393	1331	1096
Fixed Assets	1023	1104	1169
Current Assets	3273	2684	3150
Current Liabilities	1880	1353	2054
Total Share Capital	3	3	3
ROCE% (Return on Capital Employed)	10.0	11.4	23.8
ROT% (Return on Turnover)			4.5

Ichchus Canine Centre
5 The Crescent Wilsford, Grantham, NG32 3NT
Tel: 01400-230965
E-mail: lorraine@iccdogtraining.co.uk
Website: http://www.iccdogtraining.co.uk
Directors: C. Oxtoby (Prop), L. Rohland (Prop)
Date established: 2004 **No.of Employees:** 1 - 10 **Product Groups:** 01

Interlink Express Parcels Ltd
Unit 2 Earlesfield Lane, Grantham, NG31 7NT
Tel: 01476-570263 **Fax:** 01476-750268
E-mail: depot634@interlinkexpress.com
Website: http://www.rsexpress.co.uk
Managers: A. Thompson
Ultimate Holding Company: LA POSTE (FRANCE)
Immediate Holding Company: INTERLINK EXPRESS PARCELS LIMITED
Registration no: 01421773 **Date established:** 1979
No.of Employees: 1 - 10 **Product Groups:** 24, 72, 79

Date of Accounts	Dec 08	Jan 10	Jan 11
Sales Turnover	129m	128m	135m
Pre Tax Profit/Loss	15m	15m	15m
Working Capital	17m	20m	21m
Current Assets	27m	29m	31m
Current Liabilities	9m	8m	9m

Invictas Group
Invicta Works Houghton Road, Grantham, NG31 6JE
Tel: 01476-515500 **Fax:** 01476-515540
E-mail: info@invictasgroup.co.uk
Website: http://www.sitedumpers.com
Directors: D. Snowdin (Grp MD)
Immediate Holding Company: INVICTAS GROUP LTD
Registration no: 07132432 **VAT No.:** GB 183 7822 35
Date established: 2010 **Turnover:** £2m - £5m **No.of Employees:** 51 - 100
Product Groups: 36

J T T Equipment Services Ltd
Unit 6 Belton Lane, Grantham, NG31 9HN
Tel: 01476-576704 **Fax:** 01476-576217
E-mail: jenni.towning@btconnect.com
Website: http://www.jttltd.co.uk
Directors: R. Benson (Sales), T. Towning (Dir)
Immediate Holding Company: J.T.T. EQUIPMENT SERVICES LIMITED
Registration no: 01670572 **Date established:** 1982 **Turnover:** £1m - £2m
No.of Employees: 1 - 10 **Product Groups:** 40, 66

Date of Accounts	Mar 11	Mar 10	Mar 09
Working Capital	113	130	161
Fixed Assets	79	88	97
Current Assets	310	264	281

Jewson Ltd
Wharf Road, Grantham, NG31 6BJ
Tel: 01476-591007 **Fax:** 01476-592965
E-mail: james.truman@jewson.co.uk
Website: http://www.jewson.co.uk
Bank(s): Barclays
Managers: J. Truman (District Mgr)
Ultimate Holding Company: COMPAGNIE DE SAINT GOBAIN (FRANCE)
Immediate Holding Company: JEWSON LIMITED
Registration no: 00348407 **VAT No.:** GB 497 7184 83
Date established: 1939 **Turnover:** £2m - £5m **No.of Employees:** 11 - 20
Product Groups: 66

Date of Accounts	Dec 11	Dec 10	Dec 09
Sales Turnover	1606m	1547m	1485m
Pre Tax Profit/Loss	18m	100m	45m
Working Capital	-345m	-250m	-349m
Fixed Assets	496m	387m	461m
Current Assets	657m	1005m	1320m
Current Liabilities	66m	120m	64m

Julian Graves Ltd
Unit 24 Isaac Newton Centre, Grantham, NG31 6EE
Tel: 01476-594529 **Fax:** 01476-594529
E-mail: customercare@juliangraves.co.uk
Website: http://www.juliangraves.co.uk
Managers: A. Codling
Ultimate Holding Company: THE CARLYLE GROUP LLC (USA)
Immediate Holding Company: JULIAN GRAVES LIMITED
Registration no: 02109178 **Date established:** 1987
No.of Employees: 1 - 10 **Product Groups:** 31, 32

Date of Accounts	Mar 08	Mar 07	Sep 10
Sales Turnover	70m	62m	64m
Pre Tax Profit/Loss	-2m	700	3m
Working Capital	-10m	-1m	-6m
Fixed Assets	14m	13m	3m
Current Assets	15m	19m	12m
Current Liabilities	3m	2m	3m

M L P S
3 Wharf Road, Grantham, NG31 6BA
Tel: 01476-578654 **Fax:** 01476-590400
E-mail: enquiries@mlps.co.uk
Website: http://www.printingsystemsuk.com
Directors: C. Moreton (Prop)
Turnover: Up to £250,000 **No.of Employees:** 1 - 10 **Product Groups:** 27, 28, 30, 35, 37, 38, 42, 44, 49, 64, 65, 67

Marston Agricultural Services Ltd
Toll Bar Road Marston, Grantham, NG32 2HG
Tel: 01400-250226 **Fax:** 01400-250540
E-mail: sales@marstontrailers.co.uk
Website: http://www.marstontrailers.co.uk
Bank(s): HSBC
Directors: D. Green (MD)
Managers: A. Jones (Fin Mgr), C. Owen (Sales & Mktg Mg), N. Gibson (Purch Mgr), H. Cadwallader (Personnel)
Immediate Holding Company: MARSTON AGRICULTURAL SERVICES LIMITED
Registration no: 01169693 **Date established:** 1974 **Turnover:** £5m - £10m
No.of Employees: 51 - 100 **Product Groups:** 41, 67

Date of Accounts	Sep 10	Sep 09	Sep 08
Sales Turnover	6m	7m	7m
Pre Tax Profit/Loss	-424	220	115
Working Capital	304	712	524
Fixed Assets	2m	2m	2m
Current Assets	2m	2m	2m
Current Liabilities	471	349	380

Metron Eledyne
Unit 18 Autumn Park Dysart Road, Grantham, NG31 7DD
Tel: 01476-516120 **Fax:** 01476-516121
E-mail: info@metroneledyne.co.uk
Website: http://www.metroneledyne.co.uk
Bank(s): National Westminster
Directors: D. Carter (MD)
Managers: D. Chilvers (Sales & Mktg Mg), L. Hewerdine (Purch Mgr), M. Heard (Comptroller), P. Martino (Tech Serv Mgr)

Ultimate Holding Company: TECKNIT (USA)
Immediate Holding Company: TECHNICAL WIRE PRODUCTS INC (USA)
Registration no: 03444205 **VAT No.:** 417 5094 53 **Date established:** 2008
Turnover: £1m - £2m **No.of Employees:** 21 - 50 **Product Groups:** 37

Moy Park Ltd
Gonerby Hill Foot, Grantham, NG31 8HZ
Tel: 01476-571015 **Fax:** 01476-579713
E-mail: adrian.downs@moypark.com
Website: http://www.moypark.com
Managers: N. Laing (Chief Mgr)
Ultimate Holding Company: OSI GROUP LLC (USA)
Immediate Holding Company: MOY PARK LIMITED
Registration no: FC006640 **Date established:** 1970
Turnover: £125m - £250m **No.of Employees:** 501 - 1000
Product Groups: 01

Date of Accounts	Dec 07	Dec 06	Dec 05
Sales Turnover	652m	623m	467m
Pre Tax Profit/Loss	-15m	-6m	8m
Working Capital	-29m	-19m	173
Fixed Assets	163m	163m	147m
Current Assets	128m	98m	105m
Current Liabilities	12m	20m	25m

Mumford & Mumford
7a Market Place, Grantham, NG31 6LJ
Tel: 01476-590603 **Fax:** 01476-590609
Directors: L. Manford (Prop)
Registration no: 03691732 **Date established:** 1999
No.of Employees: 1 - 10 **Product Groups:** 35

Opsis Practice Management Solutions
Summit House Alma Park Road, Grantham, NG31 9SP
Tel: 0844-815 5751 **Fax:** 01476-567716
E-mail: sales@opsisltd.co.uk
Website: http://www.opsisltd.co.uk
Directors: A. Cutforth (Tech Serv), B. O'Neil (MD), M. Leuw (Dir)
Managers: E. Jenkins (Sales & Mktg Mg)
Immediate Holding Company: Opsis Ltd
Registration no: 02498463 **VAT No.:** GB 550 8875 16
Turnover: £500,000 - £1m **No.of Employees:** 1 - 10 **Product Groups:** 44

P E Charity
33-34 Westgate, Grantham, NG31 6LY
Tel: 01476-563074
Directors: P. Charity (Prop)
Date established: 1954 **No.of Employees:** 1 - 10 **Product Groups:** 36, 39, 40

Parts Export Ltd
Unit 8a Isaac Newton Way, Grantham, NG31 9RT
Tel: 01476-560161 **Fax:** 01476-577623
E-mail: sales@partsexport.co.uk
Website: http://www.partsexport.co.uk
Directors: A. Beecroft (MD)
Immediate Holding Company: PARTS EXPORT LIMITED
Registration no: 01784699 **VAT No.:** 385 3732 28 **Date established:** 1984
Turnover: £1m - £2m **No.of Employees:** 1 - 10 **Product Groups:** 61

Date of Accounts	Feb 12	Feb 11	Feb 10
Working Capital	9	-16	45
Fixed Assets	13	16	19
Current Assets	257	200	253

Postpack Ltd
Units 1, 2 & 4, Hollis Road, Grantham, NG31 7QH
Tel: 0845-071 0754 **Fax:** 0845-0710759
E-mail: sales@postpack.co.uk
Website: http://www.postpack.co.uk
Directors: M. Reid (MD)
Immediate Holding Company: Postpack Ltd
Registration no: 04446988 **Date established:** 2002 **Turnover:** £1m - £2m
No.of Employees: 11 - 20 **Product Groups:** 27, 30

Date of Accounts	May 08	May 07	May 06
Working Capital	N/A	-7	20
Fixed Assets	6	10	1
Current Assets	203	81	38
Current Liabilities	203	88	18

R C Setchfield Ltd
Unit 10 Withambrook Park Industrial Estate, Grantham, NG31 9ST
Tel: 01476-560784 **Fax:** 01476-570151
E-mail: sales@setchfield.co.uk
Website: http://www.setchfield.co.uk
Directors: H. Setchfield (Fin)
Immediate Holding Company: R. C. SETCHFIELD LIMITED
Registration no: 04580768 **Date established:** 2002 **Turnover:** £2m - £5m
No.of Employees: 11 - 20 **Product Groups:** 41

Date of Accounts	Dec 11	Dec 10	Dec 09
Working Capital	324	210	197
Fixed Assets	104	119	116
Current Assets	1m	1m	817

RFDS Consultants
253 Dysart Road, Grantham, NG31 7LP
Tel: 01476-409929 **Fax:** 01476-409929
E-mail: office@quenvhas.co.uk
Website: http://www.rfdsconsultants.com
Directors: R. Fountain (MD)
Date established: 1987 **No.of Employees:** 1 - 10 **Product Groups:** 84

S S T Process Engineering Ltd
Unit 22 Autumn Park Dysart Road, Grantham, NG31 7DD
Tel: 01476-590112 **Fax:** 01476-590113
E-mail: sales@sstpe.co.uk
Website: http://www.sstprocessengineering.co.uk
Directors: C. Talton (Fin)
Immediate Holding Company: S.S.T. PROCESS ENGINEERING LIMITED
Registration no: 02982634 **Date established:** 1994
Turnover: £500,000 - £1m **No.of Employees:** 1 - 10 **Product Groups:** 35, 37, 40, 48

Date of Accounts	Oct 11	Oct 10	Oct 09
Working Capital	98	136	2
Fixed Assets	37	23	10
Current Assets	196	273	147

Stanborough Press Ltd
Londonthorpe Road, Grantham, NG31 9SN
Tel: 01476-591700 **Fax:** 01476-577144
E-mail: ppodder@stanpress.co.uk
Website: http://www.stanboroughpress.co.uk
Bank(s): National Westminster
Managers: P. Podder (Mgr)
Immediate Holding Company: STANBOROUGH PRESS LIMITED
Registration no: 00041819 **VAT No.:** GB 385 2622 40
Date established: 1994 **Turnover:** £2m - £5m **No.of Employees:** 11 - 20
Product Groups: 28

Date of Accounts	Dec 10	Dec 09	Dec 08
Sales Turnover	2m	3m	3m
Pre Tax Profit/Loss	40	195	429
Working Capital	3m	3m	2m
Fixed Assets	170	172	185
Current Assets	3m	4m	3m
Current Liabilities	461	593	616

Staples Disposables Ltd
Hurlingham Business Park Fulbeck Heath, Grantham, NG32 3HL
Tel: 01400-262800 **Fax:** 01529-411607
E-mail: orders@staplesdisposables.com
Website: http://www.staplesdisposables.com
Bank(s): National Westminster Bank Plc
Directors: A. Staples (MD), R. Leatherland (Fin), L. Edney (Sales)
Managers: C. McDonald (Personnel), A. Boseley
Ultimate Holding Company: STAPLES HOLDINGS LIMITED
Immediate Holding Company: STAPLES DISPOSABLES LIMITED
Registration no: 01576051 **VAT No.:** GB 648 0243 44
Date established: 1981 **Turnover:** £20m - £50m
No.of Employees: 101 - 250 **Product Groups:** 24, 27

Date of Accounts	Mar 08	Mar 09	Mar 10
Sales Turnover	20m	31m	32m
Pre Tax Profit/Loss	3m	2m	1m
Working Capital	7m	6m	6m
Fixed Assets	1m	2m	3m
Current Assets	16m	15m	16m
Current Liabilities	2m	3m	2m

Today Interiors Ltd
Unit 5 Orchard Park Isaac Newton Way, Grantham, NG31 9RT
Tel: 01476-574401 **Fax:** 01476-590208
E-mail: info@today-interiors.co.uk
Website: http://www.today-interiors.co.uk
Bank(s): HSBC
Directors: A. Bolt (Sales), S. Davis (MD), W. Cook (Co Sec), H. Anderson (Sales)
Immediate Holding Company: TODAY INTERIORS LIMITED
Registration no: 01090241 **VAT No.:** GB 310 9766 60
Date established: 1973 **Turnover:** £2m - £5m **No.of Employees:** 21 - 50
Product Groups: 23

Date of Accounts	Dec 11	Dec 10	Dec 09
Working Capital	501	640	868
Fixed Assets	1m	1m	1m
Current Assets	1m	2m	2m

Vacu Lug Traction Tyres Ltd
Gonerby Road Gonerby Hill Foot, Grantham, NG31 8HE
Tel: 01476-593095 **Fax:** 01476-513809
E-mail: info@vaculug.com
Website: http://www.vaculug.com
Bank(s): HSBC
Directors: T. Hercock (MD)
Immediate Holding Company: VACU-LUG TRACTION TYRES LIMITED
Registration no: 00488961 **VAT No.:** GB 116 9981 36
Date established: 1950 **Turnover:** £20m - £50m
No.of Employees: 101 - 250 **Product Groups:** 29

Date of Accounts	Dec 11	Dec 10	Dec 09
Sales Turnover	23m	21m	19m
Pre Tax Profit/Loss	239	-55	-89
Working Capital	3m	3m	3m
Fixed Assets	2m	2m	2m
Current Assets	10m	9m	9m
Current Liabilities	4m	4m	4m

Vaderstad Ltd
Unit 1 Ellesmere Business Park Swingbridge Road, Grantham, NG31 7XT
Tel: 01476-581900 **Fax:** 01476-568994
E-mail: elaine.prince@vaderstad.com
Website: http://www.vaderstad.com
Directors: M. Alsop (MD)
Managers: E. Prince (Fin Mgr), A. Gamble (Mktg Serv Mgr)
Ultimate Holding Company: VADERSTAD - VERKEN AB (SWEDEN)
Immediate Holding Company: VADERSTAD LIMITED
Registration no: 02768478 **Date established:** 1992
Turnover: £20m - £50m **No.of Employees:** 11 - 20 **Product Groups:** 41

Date of Accounts	Dec 11	Dec 10	Dec 09
Sales Turnover	24m	22m	21m
Pre Tax Profit/Loss	1m	1m	1m
Working Capital	5m	5m	4m
Fixed Assets	721	190	219
Current Assets	13m	12m	12m
Current Liabilities	1m	1m	906

The Vintners Selection Ltd
The Barn Church Street, Corby Glen, Grantham, NG33 4NJ
Tel: 01476-550476 **Fax:** 01476-550777
E-mail: sales@vintners.co.uk
Website: http://www.vintners.co.uk
Directors: J. Marshall Roberts (MD)
Immediate Holding Company: THE VINTNERS SELECTION LIMITED
Registration no: 02785930 **Date established:** 1993
Turnover: Up to £250,000 **No.of Employees:** 1 - 10 **Product Groups:** 21, 62

Date of Accounts	Aug 11	Aug 10	Aug 09
Sales Turnover	174	173	201
Pre Tax Profit/Loss	-1	2	11
Working Capital	8	6	5
Fixed Assets	25	32	25
Current Assets	72	73	96
Current Liabilities	32	17	33

Westminster Machine Tools Ltd
The Mine Site Unit 8 Mill Lane, South Witham, Grantham, NG33 5QN
Tel: 01572-767922 **Fax:** 01572-768321
E-mail: sales@wmtg.co.uk
Website: http://www.wmtg.co.uk
Directors: D. Iveson (MD), G. Chelley (MD)
Registration no: 00845694 **No.of Employees:** 11 - 20 **Product Groups:** 46

Date of Accounts	Dec 08	Dec 07	Dec 06
Working Capital	727	976	-850
Fixed Assets	77	44	1212
Current Assets	764	1038	511
Current Liabilities	37	62	1361
Total Share Capital	100	100	100

Woodland Trust
Kempton Way, Grantham, NG31 6LL
Tel: 01476-581111 **Fax:** 01476-590808
E-mail: julian.purvis@woodland-trust.org.uk
Website: http://www.dailymail.co.uk
Directors: J. Purvis (Co Sec)
Ultimate Holding Company: WOODLAND TRUST(THE)
Immediate Holding Company: WOODLAND TRUST(THE)
Registration no: 01982873 **Date established:** 1986
Turnover: £20m - £50m **No.of Employees:** 1 - 10 **Product Groups:** 35, 46, 48, 49

Date of Accounts	Dec 11	Dec 10	Dec 09
Sales Turnover	27m	20m	26m
Pre Tax Profit/Loss	616	6m	8m
Working Capital	10m	10m	11m
Fixed Assets	98m	97m	90m
Current Assets	12m	13m	13m
Current Liabilities	526	646	440

Horncastle

A Foster & Son Ltd
8 High Street, Horncastle, LN9 5BL
Tel: 01507-522334 **Fax:** 01507-524024
E-mail: postbox@afosterandson.co.uk
Website: http://www.afosterandson.co.uk
Directors: P. Foster (MD)
Immediate Holding Company: A. FOSTER AND SONS (HORNCASTLE) LIMITED
Registration no: 01370042 **VAT No.:** GB 310 7472 87
Date established: 1978 **Turnover:** £1m - £2m **No.of Employees:** 1 - 10
Product Groups: 81

Date of Accounts	Dec 11	Dec 10	Dec 06
Working Capital	-89	-93	-125
Fixed Assets	45	55	190
Current Assets	11	13	46

B A Bush & Sons Ltd
Station Yard, Horncastle, LN9 5AQ
Tel: 0800-801054 **Fax:** 01507- 525439
E-mail: accounts@bushtyres.co.uk
Website: http://www.bushtyres.co.uk
Directors: N. Bush (MD)
Immediate Holding Company: B.A.BUSH & SON LIMITED
Registration no: 00976405 **VAT No.:** GB 127 7208 71
Date established: 1970 **Turnover:** £10m - £20m **No.of Employees:** 1 - 10
Product Groups: 29, 39, 68

Date of Accounts	Dec 11	Dec 10	Dec 09
Sales Turnover	21m	19m	16m
Pre Tax Profit/Loss	90	391	154
Working Capital	1m	1m	1m
Fixed Assets	3m	3m	3m
Current Assets	8m	7m	5m
Current Liabilities	478	600	356

Nelson Butler & Son Ltd
Elmhirst Road, Horncastle, LN9 5AU
Tel: 01507-523451 **Fax:** 01507-522182
Website: http://www.nelsonbutlertimber.com
Directors: C. Butler (Dir), C. Butler (Co Sec)
Immediate Holding Company: NELSON BUTLER & SON LIMITED
Registration no: 00471035 **VAT No.:** GB 128 1898 44
Date established: 1949 **Turnover:** £1m - £2m **No.of Employees:** 1 - 10
Product Groups: 66

Date of Accounts	Dec 11	Dec 10	Dec 09
Working Capital	480	468	429
Fixed Assets	175	170	183
Current Assets	642	624	574

Forum Packaging Ltd (a division of D.S. Smith P.L.C.)
Mareham Road, Horncastle, LN9 6NG
Tel: 01507-523434 **Fax:** 01507-523431
E-mail: enquire@forumpkg.com
Website: http://www.forumpackaging.com
Bank(s): Lloyds TSB
Directors: M. Spivey (MD)
Managers: P. Newsham (Tech Serv Mgr), R. Massey (Fin Mgr), J. Topley (Personnel), G. Newson (Tech Serv Mgr)
Ultimate Holding Company: LINPAC GROUP LTD
Immediate Holding Company: FORUM PACKAGING LIMITED
Registration no: 07536149 **VAT No.:** 129 1823 69 **Date established:** 2011
Turnover: £5m - £10m **No.of Employees:** 51 - 100 **Product Groups:** 27

Date of Accounts	Apr 12	Apr 11
Sales Turnover	11m	N/A
Pre Tax Profit/Loss	917	N/A
Working Capital	454	N/A
Fixed Assets	1m	N/A
Current Assets	3m	N/A
Current Liabilities	924	N/A

Gymphlex
Boston Road, Horncastle, LN9 6HU
Tel: 01507-523243 **Fax:** 01507-524421
E-mail: sales@gymphlex.co.uk
Website: http://www.gymphlex.co.uk
Bank(s): HSBC Bank plc
Directors: J. Greenlees (MD)
Ultimate Holding Company: RYLAND DICKSON LIMITED
Immediate Holding Company: GYMPHLEX LIMITED
Registration no: 00299638 **Date established:** 1935 **Turnover:** £5m - £10m
No.of Employees: 21 - 50 **Product Groups:** 24, 63

Date of Accounts	Nov 11	Nov 10	Nov 09
Working Capital	591	440	603
Fixed Assets	73	77	177
Current Assets	948	1m	2m

Lincolnshire Leisure Buildings
36 Elmhirst Road, Horncastle, LN9 5LU
Tel: 01507-522205
E-mail: sales@compton-buildings.co.uk
Website: http://www.comptonbuildings.co.uk
Directors: V. Atkinson (Prop)
No.of Employees: 1 - 10 **Product Groups:** 25, 33, 35, 66

Mortons Media Group Ltd (Part of Mortons Media Group Ltd)
Media Centre, Horncastle, LN9 6JR
Tel: 01507-524004 **Fax:** 01507-529499
E-mail: lmaltby@mortons.co.uk
Website: http://www.mortons.co.uk
Bank(s): Lloyds
Directors: K. Pinder (Fin)
Managers: D. England (Sales Prom Mgr), D. Shaw (Tech Serv Mgr), M. Gill (Personnel), L. Maltby, C. Park (Mktg Serv Mgr)
Ultimate Holding Company: MORTONS OF HORNCASTLE LIMITED
Immediate Holding Company: MORTONS MEDIA GROUP LTD
Registration no: 03676192 **VAT No.:** GB 128 2930 69
Date established: 1998 **Turnover:** £10m - £20m
No.of Employees: 101 - 250 **Product Groups:** 28

Date of Accounts	Jan 10	Jan 11	Jan 12
Sales Turnover	11m	11m	13m
Pre Tax Profit/Loss	1m	1m	1m
Working Capital	4m	2m	4m
Fixed Assets	6m	8m	8m
Current Assets	7m	5m	7m
Current Liabilities	2m	3m	3m

Phillard Pump Co. Ltd
A Church Road Boston Road Industrial Estate, Horncastle, LN9 6AS
Tel: 01507-523281 **Fax:** 01507-527437
E-mail: paul@phillips-animal-health-ltd.co.uk
Website: http://www.phillips-animal-health-ltd.co.uk
Bank(s): HSBC
Directors: P. Phillips (Dir)
Immediate Holding Company: PHILLIPS ANIMAL HEALTH LTD
Registration no: 01245416 **VAT No.:** GB 129 8384 34
Date established: 1973 **Turnover:** £1m - £2m **No.of Employees:** 11 - 20
Product Groups: 39, 40

Noel J H Robinson & Co. Ltd
The Garage Mareham on the Hill, Horncastle, LN9 6PQ
Tel: 01507-523334 **Fax:** 01507-526919
E-mail: paul@noeljhrobinson.com
Website: http://www.noeljhrobinson.com
Directors: P. Robinson (MD)
Immediate Holding Company: NOEL J. H. ROBINSON & CO. LIMITED
Registration no: 02618628 **Date established:** 1991
No.of Employees: 11 - 20 **Product Groups:** 07, 40

Date of Accounts	Mar 11	Mar 10	Mar 09
Working Capital	-82	62	52
Fixed Assets	109	120	131
Current Assets	18	162	151

Lincoln

A L S Group
The Workshop Freisthorpe Road, Buslingthorpe, Lincoln, LN3 5AQ
Tel: 01522-821525 **Fax:** 01522-821524
E-mail: alsents@hotmail.com
Website: http://www.als-group.co.uk
Directors: A. Allison (Prop)
Immediate Holding Company: UNION DECORATORS LIMITED
Date established: 2007 **No.of Employees:** 1 - 10 **Product Groups:** 40, 49, 69

Allied Bakeries Ltd
Deacon Road, Lincoln, LN2 4JE
Tel: 01522-528334 **Fax:** 01522-537391
E-mail: ab_houghton@alliedbakeries.co.uk
Website: http://www.alliedbakeries.co.uk
Directors: G. Weston (Prop)
Managers: G. Weston (Mgr), T. Norton (Depot Mgr)
Ultimate Holding Company: WITTINGTON INVESTMENTS LIMITED
Immediate Holding Company: ALLIED BAKERIES LIMITED
Registration no: 00214377 **Date established:** 1926 **Turnover:** £5m - £10m
No.of Employees: 21 - 50 **Product Groups:** 20, 41

Date of Accounts	Sep 10	Sep 11	Sep 08
Working Capital	10	10	10
Current Assets	10	10	10

Asc Metals Lincoln Ltd
Westminster Trading Estate Station Road, North Hykeham, Lincoln, LN6 3QY
Tel: 01522-501777 **Fax:** 01522-501700
E-mail: sales@ascmetals.com
Website: http://www.ascmetals.com
Bank(s): National Westminster Bank Plc
Directors: A. Hoole (MD), R. Hall (MD)
Immediate Holding Company: ASC METALS LINCOLN LIMITED
Registration no: 03443750 **Date established:** 1997
Turnover: £10m - £20m **No.of Employees:** 11 - 20 **Product Groups:** 66

Date of Accounts	Dec 11	Dec 10	Dec 09
Working Capital	1m	1m	997
Fixed Assets	744	660	737
Current Assets	3m	3m	2m

Assisted Health & Mobility
Moorland Way, Lincoln, LN6 7TN
Tel: 01522-500288 **Fax:** 01636-674305
E-mail: info@assistedhealthandmobility.co.uk
Website: http://www.ahminstallations.co.uk
Directors: S. Symcox (Prop)
Date established: 2001 **No.of Employees:** 1 - 10 **Product Groups:** 38, 67

Bardney Racing
20 Station Road Bardney, Lincoln, LN3 5UA
Tel: 01526-398118 **Fax:** 01526-398118
E-mail: sales@bardneyracing.co.uk
Website: http://www.fairingsdirect.co.uk

Directors: R. Lintin (Prop)
Date established: 2000 **Turnover:** Up to £250,000
No.of Employees: 1 - 10 **Product Groups:** 30, 39, 40, 68

Biffa Waste Services Ltd

4 Dale Street, Lincoln, LN5 8LL
Tel: 0800-601601 **Fax:** 01522- 576565
E-mail: customer.services@biffa.co.uk
Website: http://www.biffa.co.uk
Managers: S. Evans (Mgr)
Immediate Holding Company: BIFFA WASTE SERVICES LIMITED
Registration no: 00946107 **Date established:** 1969
No.of Employees: 1 - 10 **Product Groups:** 54, 72, 83

Date of Accounts	Mar 08	Mar 09	Apr 10
Sales Turnover	555m	574m	492m
Pre Tax Profit/Loss	23m	50m	30m
Working Capital	229m	271m	293m
Fixed Assets	371m	360m	378m
Current Assets	409m	534m	609m
Current Liabilities	50m	100m	115m

Bluebird Fixings Ltd

Westminster Trading Estate Station Road, North Hykeham, Lincoln, LN6 3QY
Tel: 01522-697776 **Fax:** 01522-697771
E-mail: info@bluebird-fixings.ltd.uk
Website: http://www.bluebird-fixings.ltd.uk
Bank(s): National Westminster Bank Plc
Directors: P. Hodder (MD)
Immediate Holding Company: BLUEBIRD FIXINGS LIMITED
Registration no: 02286714 **VAT No.:** GB 497 8737 63
Date established: 1988 **No.of Employees:** 11 - 20 **Product Groups:** 35, 52, 66

Date of Accounts	Jan 12	Jan 11	Jan 10
Working Capital	58	-9	-91
Fixed Assets	191	199	207
Current Assets	187	165	160

Bowser Bros

Stainton Manor Stainton By Langworth, Lincoln, LN3 5BL
Tel: 01673-862423 **Fax:** 01673-862423
E-mail: peterbowser@hotmail.com
Website: http://www.bowserbros.com
Directors: P. Bowser (Prop)
Immediate Holding Company: MUMMY & LITTLE ME LIMITED
Registration no: 06787352 **Date established:** 2006
No.of Employees: 1 - 10 **Product Groups:** 25, 40, 67

Brayford Plastics

Horncastle Lane Dunholme, Lincoln, LN2 3QF
Tel: 01522-530557 **Fax:** 01522-730372
E-mail: info@brayfordplastics.com
Website: http://www.brayfordplastics.com
Bank(s): Barclays
Directors: G. Edmonds (Co Sec), N. Grawal (Dir)
Managers: H. Cripps (Admin Off)
Ultimate Holding Company: SUPREME PLASTICS HOLDINGS LTD
Immediate Holding Company: SUPREME PLASTICS LTD
Registration no: 00762772 **VAT No.:** GB 127 7555 50
Date established: 1969 **Turnover:** £2m - £5m **No.of Employees:** 21 - 50
Product Groups: 30

Brown Butlin Group Ltd

Sales Office 77 Sleaford Road, Dorrington, Lincoln, LN4 3PU
Tel: 01526-832771 **Fax:** 01526-834531
E-mail: john.harris@brownbutlin.co.uk
Bank(s): HSBC Bank plc
Directors: J. Harris (Dir)
Ultimate Holding Company: HUTCHINSON GROUP LIMITED
Immediate Holding Company: BROWN BUTLIN GROUP PENSION TRUST LIMITED
Registration no: 02055105 **Date established:** 1986
No.of Employees: 21 - 50 **Product Groups:** 32, 61

Burton Mobility

Unit 19 Roman Way Gateway Park, South Hykeham, Lincoln, LN6 9UH
Tel: 01522-509781 **Fax:** 01522-509877
Website: http://www.burton-mobility.co.uk
Managers: R. Gibbon (Mgr)
No.of Employees: 1 - 10 **Product Groups:** 26, 30, 39, 67

Chameleon Coatings Ltd

Western Lane High Street, Skellingthorpe, Lincoln, LN6 5TS
Tel: 01522-698111 **Fax:** 01522-698222
E-mail: w.jenner@chameleoncoatings.co.uk
Website: http://www.chameleoncoatings.co.uk
Directors: S. Jenner (Fin), W. Jenner (MD)
Immediate Holding Company: CHAMELEON COATINGS LIMITED
Registration no: 03873871 **Date established:** 1999
Turnover: £500,000 - £1m **No.of Employees:** 1 - 10 **Product Groups:** 46, 48

Date of Accounts	Mar 11	Mar 10	Mar 09
Working Capital	22	47	71
Fixed Assets	73	56	43
Current Assets	113	114	126

Cleanaway Ltd

Albion Works Long Leys Road, Lincoln, LN1 1DS
Tel: 0845-6060460 **Fax:** 01522-511088
Website: http://www.cleanaway.com
Managers: R. Mead
Immediate Holding Company: CLEANAWAY LIMITED
Registration no: NF002533 **Date established:** 1981 **Turnover:** £2m - £5m
No.of Employees: 1 - 10 **Product Groups:** 33, 42, 54, 83

Cold Hanworth Forge

The Forge Cold Hanworth, Lincoln, LN2 3RE
Tel: 01673-866700
Website: http://www.teachblacksmithing.com
Directors: R. Oakes (Prop)
Date established: 2002 **No.of Employees:** 1 - 10 **Product Groups:** 26, 35

County Industrial Doors Ltd

16 High Street Scampton, Lincoln, LN1 2SD
Tel: 01522-731342 **Fax:** 01522-730127
Website: http://www.cidoors.co.uk
Directors: C. Nicholson (MD), J. Nicholson (Fin)
Immediate Holding Company: COUNTY INDUSTRIAL DOORS LIMITED
Registration no: 03795322 **Date established:** 1999
No.of Employees: 1 - 10 **Product Groups:** 26, 35

Date of Accounts	Mar 12	Mar 11	Mar 10
Working Capital	-9	19	13
Fixed Assets	15	19	20
Current Assets	116	134	117

Peter Cox Ltd

103 Sadler Road, Lincoln, LN6 3RS
Tel: 01522-500214 **Fax:** 01522-688838
E-mail: graham.warnes@petercox.com
Website: http://www.petercox.com
Managers: G. Warnes (District Mgr)
Ultimate Holding Company: GERALDTON SERVICES INC (USA)
Immediate Holding Company: PETER COX LIMITED
Registration no: 02438126 **Date established:** 1989
No.of Employees: 21 - 50 **Product Groups:** 07, 32, 52, 66

Date of Accounts	Dec 11	Dec 10	Dec 09
Sales Turnover	15m	15m	14m
Pre Tax Profit/Loss	645	282	-350
Working Capital	3m	3m	2m
Fixed Assets	459	542	643
Current Assets	6m	5m	4m
Current Liabilities	2m	2m	961

Cromwell Tools Ltd

Station Road North Hykeham, Lincoln, LN6 9AL
Tel: 01522-500888 **Fax:** 01522-500857
E-mail: lincoln@cromwell.co.uk
Website: http://www.cromwell.co.uk
Bank(s): Royal Bank of Scotland, Lincoln
Managers: A. Nicholson (District Mgr)
Ultimate Holding Company: CROMWELL GROUP (HOLDINGS) LIMITED
Immediate Holding Company: CROMWELL TOOLS LIMITED
Registration no: 00986161 **VAT No.:** GB 763 7660 01
Date established: 1970 **Turnover:** £1m - £2m **No.of Employees:** 11 - 20
Product Groups: 35, 36, 37, 46, 66, 67

Date of Accounts	Aug 11	Aug 10	Aug 09
Sales Turnover	201m	175m	160m
Pre Tax Profit/Loss	10m	5m	461
Working Capital	43m	36m	32m
Fixed Assets	4m	4m	5m
Current Assets	100m	84m	80m
Current Liabilities	4m	3m	3m

Danwood Group

Danwood House Harrison Place Whisby Road, Lincoln, LN6 3DG
Tel: 01522-882288 **Fax:** 01522-884488
E-mail: mail@danwood.co.uk
Website: http://www.danwood.co.uk
Directors: E. Daniels (Pers), G. Reeve (Mkt Research)
Managers: R. Coles (Sales Prom Mgr), P. Hopton, S. Wilson, A. Owen (Tech Serv Mgr), G. Smalls
Ultimate Holding Company: DANWOOD GROUP HOLDINGS LIMITED
Immediate Holding Company: DANWOOD GROUP HOLDINGS LIMITED
Registration no: 06548014 **VAT No.:** GB 310 6982 69
Date established: 2008 **Turnover:** £125m - £250m
No.of Employees: 251 - 500 **Product Groups:** 48, 64, 67

Date of Accounts	Sep 10	Sep 09	Sep 08
Sales Turnover	220m	194m	86
Pre Tax Profit/Loss	4m	2m	-1
Working Capital	39m	24m	17
Fixed Assets	106m	92m	90
Current Assets	98m	62m	58
Current Liabilities	29m	16m	17

Data Cabling Ltd

Unit 2 Whisby Way, Lincoln, LN6 3LQ
Tel: 01522-500699 **Fax:** 01522-500882
E-mail: sales@data-cabling.co.uk
Website: http://www.data-cabling.co.uk
Managers: D. White (Chief Mgr)
Ultimate Holding Company: TRISOFT LIMITED
Immediate Holding Company: DATA CABLING LIMITED
Registration no: 02266088 **Date established:** 1988 **Turnover:** £1m - £2m
No.of Employees: 11 - 20 **Product Groups:** 35, 37, 44

Date of Accounts	Dec 11	Dec 10	Dec 09
Sales Turnover	N/A	N/A	1m
Pre Tax Profit/Loss	N/A	N/A	118
Working Capital	197	201	213
Fixed Assets	11	20	32
Current Assets	471	367	384
Current Liabilities	N/A	N/A	114

James Dawson & Son Ltd

Tritton Road, Lincoln, LN6 7AF
Tel: 01522-781800 **Fax:** 01522-510029
E-mail: sales@james-dawson.com
Website: http://www.james-dawson.com
Bank(s): Barclays
Directors: T. Faulkner (Co Sec), P. Edwards (Sales & Mktg), S. Hateley (Fin)
Managers: S. Veal, C. Evans (Purch Mgr), P. Elsender (Personnel), M. Williams (Tech Serv Mgr)
Ultimate Holding Company: FENNER PLC
Immediate Holding Company: JAMES DAWSON & SON,LIMITED
Registration no: 00047152 **Date established:** 1996
Turnover: £20m - £50m **No.of Employees:** 251 - 500
Product Groups: 23, 29, 30, 35, 38, 45, 48, 49, 63, 66

Date of Accounts	Aug 11	Aug 10	Aug 09
Sales Turnover	29m	23m	20m
Pre Tax Profit/Loss	1m	-826	-5m
Working Capital	4m	3m	4m
Fixed Assets	5m	6m	7m
Current Assets	9m	9m	7m
Current Liabilities	3m	1m	1m

Denby Transport Ltd

73 Sadler Road, Lincoln, LN6 3JR
Tel: 01522-503900 **Fax:** 01522-686372
E-mail: sales@denbytransport.co.uk
Website: http://www.denbytransport.co.uk
Bank(s): HSBC Bank plc
Directors: S. Judge (Sales), C. Dickinson (Dir), P. Denby (MD)
Managers: N. Metcalfe
Immediate Holding Company: DENBY TRANSPORT LIMITED
Registration no: 00687151 **VAT No.:** GB 127 7470 58
Date established: 1961 **Turnover:** £5m - £10m
No.of Employees: 51 - 100 **Product Groups:** 72, 77, 84

Date of Accounts	Apr 12	Apr 11	Apr 10
Sales Turnover	8m	7m	6m
Pre Tax Profit/Loss	527	391	243

Working Capital	-70	-27	-208
Fixed Assets	3m	2m	2m
Current Assets	2m	1m	1m
Current Liabilities	997	880	691

Denholm Valve Care Ltd

North End Welbourn, Lincoln, LN5 0ND
Tel: 01400-272273 **Fax:** 01400-273510
E-mail: info@valvecare.com
Website: http://www.valvecare.com
Directors: R. Wood (MD)
Ultimate Holding Company: J. & J. DENHOLM LIMITED
Immediate Holding Company: DENHOLM VALVECARE LIMITED
Registration no: 02468254 **Date established:** 1990 **Turnover:** £2m - £5m
No.of Employees: 21 - 50 **Product Groups:** 36, 37, 38

Date of Accounts	Dec 11	Dec 10	Dec 09
Sales Turnover	6m	4m	5m
Pre Tax Profit/Loss	-683	-911	-281
Working Capital	1m	2m	1m
Fixed Assets	942	852	235
Current Assets	4m	3m	2m
Current Liabilities	448	194	180

Destec Engineering Ltd

Five Mile Lane Washingborough, Lincoln, LN4 1AF
Tel: 01522-791721 **Fax:** 01522-790033
E-mail: barry.porter@destec.co.uk
Website: http://www.destec.co.uk
Bank(s): Barclays, Crawley
Directors: B. Porter (Dir)
Managers: K. Andrews (Tech Serv Mgr), W. Kennedy (Fin Mgr), S. Cowan (Purch Mgr), A. Chadwick (Sales & Mktg Mg)
Immediate Holding Company: DESTEC ENGINEERING LIMITED
Registration no: 00946573 **Date established:** 1969 **Turnover:** £5m - £10m
No.of Employees: 51 - 100 **Product Groups:** 35, 36, 48, 54, 67, 84

Date of Accounts	Feb 12	Feb 11	Feb 10
Sales Turnover	8m	6m	9m
Pre Tax Profit/Loss	1m	700	2m
Working Capital	6m	5m	5m
Fixed Assets	2m	2m	2m
Current Assets	7m	6m	6m
Current Liabilities	695	400	826

Direct Pocket Bikes

Cliffside Wellingore, Lincoln, LN5 0DR
Tel: 01522-813680
Directors: M. Clarke (Prop)
No.of Employees: 1 - 10 **Product Groups:** 39

Ducted Air Systems Ltd

101 Sadler Road, Lincoln, LN6 3RS
Tel: 01522-682239 **Fax:** 01522-883002
E-mail: nev@ductedair.com
Website: http://www.ductedair.com
Directors: N. Williams (Dir), S. Zealand (Co Sec)
Immediate Holding Company: DUCTED AIR SYSTEMS LIMITED
Registration no: 03529413 **VAT No.:** GB 613 9138 47
Date established: 1998 **Turnover:** £500,000 - £1m
No.of Employees: 1 - 10 **Product Groups:** 35, 36

Date of Accounts	Aug 11	Aug 10	Aug 09
Working Capital	-92	-61	-86
Fixed Assets	2	4	52
Current Assets	226	196	239

ECi Software Solutions Limited

Building C
West Central
Runcorn Road, Lincoln, LN6 3QP
Tel: 0333-123 0333 **Fax:** 0333-123 0313
E-mail: eu-info@ecisolutions.com
Website: http://www.ipuk.com
Directors: K. Hunter (MD), P. White (Sales), S. Howes (Develop)
Immediate Holding Company: CORDIC LTD
Registration no: 0416072 **VAT No.:** GB 915 8252 18
Date established: 2002 **Turnover:** £2m - £5m **No.of Employees:** 51 - 100
Product Groups: 44

Date of Accounts	Nov 11	Nov 10	Nov 09
Working Capital	1m	1m	662
Fixed Assets	1m	2m	2m
Current Assets	2m	2m	1m

Eaga Insulation

4 Monks Way, Lincoln, LN2 5LN
Tel: 01522-563550 **Fax:** 01522-563551
E-mail: enquiries@eaga.co.uk
Website: http://www.eaga.co.uk
Directors: P. Horan (Prop)
Registration no: 01931510 **Date established:** 1982
Turnover: £20m - £50m **No.of Employees:** 1 - 10 **Product Groups:** 33, 45, 52, 66, 84

Elesa (UK) Ltd

26 Moorlands Estate Metheringham, Lincoln, LN4 3HX
Tel: 01526-322670 **Fax:** 01526-322669
E-mail: sales@elesa.co.uk
Website: http://www.elesanow.co.uk
Bank(s): The Royal Bank of Scotland
Directors: A. Mosca (Dir), C. Bertani (Dir), A. Bertani (Dir), N. Pritchett (MD)
Managers: R. Griffths, A. Cooke (Purch Mgr), E. Mourao (Accounts)
Ultimate Holding Company: Elesa S.p.A.
Immediate Holding Company: Elesa (UK) Holdings Ltd
Registration no: 00577223 **Turnover:** £1m - £2m
No.of Employees: 11 - 20 **Product Groups:** 30, 33, 35, 36, 38, 39, 46, 66

Date of Accounts	Dec 07	Dec 06	Dec 05
Working Capital	790	504	333
Fixed Assets	258	258	258
Current Assets	809	741	726
Current Liabilities	19	237	393
Total Share Capital	60	60	60

Elpeeko

Wrightsway Outer Circle Road, Lincoln, LN2 4JY
Tel: 01522-512111 **Fax:** 01522-541796
E-mail: steve@elpeeko.com
Website: http://www.elpeeko.com
Bank(s): HSBC Bank plc

see next page

***Elpeeko** - Cont'd*

Directors: S. Turner (MD)
Immediate Holding Company: ELPEEKO LIMITED
Registration no: 00280712 **Date established:** 1933
Turnover: £500,000 - £1m **No.of Employees:** 11 - 20 **Product Groups:** 28

Date of Accounts	Oct 11	Oct 10	Oct 09
Working Capital	-41	-51	-19
Fixed Assets	160	179	201
Current Assets	91	128	117

Eriks Industrial Distribution (Lincoln Service Centre)

Unit 3 Crofton Close, Lincoln, LN3 4PG
Tel: 01522-534631 **Fax:** 01522-534635
E-mail: lincoln@eriks.co.uk
Website: http://www.eriks.co.uk
Managers: A. Archers (District Mgr)
Immediate Holding Company: WYKO GROUP LTD
Registration no: 00917112 **No.of Employees:** 1 - 10 **Product Groups:** 66

Fire Engineering Services

Ophira Chapel Lane, Harmston, Lincoln, LN5 9TB
Tel: 01522-720454 **Fax:** 01522- 721822
Directors: J. Stead (Prop)
Managers: J. Stead (Mgr)
No.of Employees: 1 - 10 **Product Groups:** 38, 42

Fixfirm Ltd

Pyke Road, Lincoln, LN6 3QS
Tel: 01522-500002 **Fax:** 0870-777 3828
E-mail: sales@fixfirmlincoln.com
Website: http://www.fixfirmlincoln.com
Bank(s): HSBC Bank plc
Directors: W. Haughton (MD)
Managers: C. Haughton (Sales Prom Mgr), B. Haughton (Fin Mgr)
Immediate Holding Company: FIXFIRM LIMITED
Registration no: 07998761 **VAT No.:** GB 125 7010 07
Date established: 2012 **Turnover:** £1m - £2m **No.of Employees:** 11 - 20
Product Groups: 35

Game Engineering Ltd

Witham St Hughs Business Park Witham St Hughs, Lincoln, LN6 9TW
Tel: 01522-868021 **Fax:** 01522-868027
E-mail: sales@game-security-engineering.com
Website: http://www.game-engineering.com
Directors: V. Wing (Fin), P. Ablewhite (MD)
Ultimate Holding Company: GAME HOLDINGS LIMITED
Immediate Holding Company: GAME ENGINEERING LIMITED
Registration no: 01872121 **Date established:** 1984
Turnover: £10m - £20m **No.of Employees:** 51 - 100 **Product Groups:** 35, 36

Date of Accounts	Mar 11	Mar 10	Mar 09
Sales Turnover	11m	9m	N/A
Pre Tax Profit/Loss	237	329	206
Working Capital	163	180	-30
Fixed Assets	216	214	280
Current Assets	4m	3m	2m
Current Liabilities	778	827	1m

GB Logan Fabrications Ltd

Deacon Road, Lincoln, LN2 4JB
Tel: 01522-523622 **Fax:** 01522-527408
E-mail: logan@enterprise.net
Website: http://www.enterprise.net
Directors: G. Logan (MD), M. Logan (Co Sec), S. Logan (Dir)
Managers: P. Baggley, V. Munroe (Accounts), N. Mundin (Chief Mgr)
Immediate Holding Company: G.B. LOGAN FABRICATIONS LIMITED
Registration no: 02765848 **VAT No.:** GB 364 9305 37
Date established: 1992 **Turnover:** £2m - £5m **No.of Employees:** 21 - 50
Product Groups: 36, 48

Date of Accounts	Dec 09	Dec 08	Dec 07
Working Capital	-76	40	96
Fixed Assets	382	426	474
Current Assets	30	159	271

Steve Gilman

28 High Street Bassingham, Lincoln, LN5 9EY
Tel: 01522-788000
Directors: S. Gilman (Dir), H. Gilman (Fin)
Immediate Holding Company: STEVE GILMAN DESIGN LIMITED
Registration no: 05337463 **Date established:** 2005
No.of Employees: 1 - 10 **Product Groups:** 35

Date of Accounts	Jan 12	Jan 11	Jan 10
Working Capital	-3	15	21
Fixed Assets	19	20	23
Current Assets	24	42	42
Current Liabilities	N/A	26	16

Grundy Agricultural

Five Mile Lane Washingborough, Lincoln, LN4 1AF
Tel: 01522-790720 **Fax:** 01522-793550
Website: http://www.grundyagricultural.co.uk
Directors: M. Grundy (Ptnr)
Date established: 1984 **No.of Employees:** 1 - 10 **Product Groups:** 41

J.A. Harvey (Bassingham) Ltd

Navenby Lane Bassingham, Lincoln, LN5 9JF
Tel: 01522-304134 **Fax:** 01522-788195
E-mail: ja.harvey@btconnect.com
Website: http://www.jaharveybassinghamlincoln.co.uk
Directors: D. Harvey (Jt MD), P. Harvey (Jt MD)
Registration no: 01144914 **No.of Employees:** 21 - 50
Product Groups: 34, 35, 36, 38, 48, 49

Holmes Lincoln

1-2 Sadler Road, Lincoln, LN6 3RS
Tel: 01522-500510 **Fax:** 01522-500551
E-mail: rayholmeslincoln@hotmail.co.uk
Directors: N. Bratton (Dir), A. Warren (Co Sec)
Registration no: 02452591 **VAT No.:** GB 555 6989 78
Turnover: £500,000 - £1m **No.of Employees:** 1 - 10 **Product Groups:** 66

Househam Sprayers Ltd

The New Forge Leadenham, Lincoln, LN5 0PE
Tel: 01400-276000 **Fax:** 01400-273388
E-mail: info@househamsprayers.com
Website: http://www.househamsprayers.com
Directors: R. Willey (MD)
Managers: S. Fox (Buyer), Y. Johnson (Personnel)
Immediate Holding Company: HOUSEHAM SPRAYERS LIMITED
Registration no: 02651880 **Date established:** 1991
Turnover: £10m - £20m **No.of Employees:** 51 - 100 **Product Groups:** 40, 41, 46, 48, 67

Date of Accounts	Dec 11	Dec 10	Dec 09
Sales Turnover	16m	13m	12m
Pre Tax Profit/Loss	940	631	405
Working Capital	2m	2m	953
Fixed Assets	906	693	881
Current Assets	5m	4m	3m
Current Liabilities	934	1m	782

Humidity Control Systems Ltd

Units 7 & 8 22 The Green, Nettleham, Lincoln, LN2 2NR
Tel: 01522-753722 **Fax:** 01522-753822
E-mail: sales@humiditycontrol.co.uk
Website: http://www.humiditycontrol.co.uk
Directors: G. Jones (MD), R. Jones (Fin)
Immediate Holding Company: HUMIDITY CONTROL SYSTEMS LIMITED
Registration no: 03177097 **Date established:** 1996
Turnover: £500,000 - £1m **No.of Employees:** 1 - 10 **Product Groups:** 40, 42

Date of Accounts	Jul 11	Jul 10	Jul 09
Working Capital	343	273	280
Fixed Assets	28	38	30
Current Assets	445	358	327

Industrial & Marine Power Services Ltd

Whisby Way North Hykeham, Lincoln, LN6 3LQ
Tel: 01522-881000 **Fax:** 01522-883555
E-mail: chris@ind-marpower.co.uk
Website: http://www.ind-marpower.co.uk
Bank(s): Yorkshire Bank
Directors: C. Woolley (MD), P. Wheeler (Sales)
Managers: A. Gore (Export Sales Mg), D. Penney (Mgr), D. Atkin (Mgr)
Registration no: 02675226 **VAT No.:** GB 555 7833 07
Date established: 1990 **Turnover:** £2m - £5m **No.of Employees:** 21 - 50
Product Groups: 37, 40, 46, 67, 68

Date of Accounts	Apr 08	Apr 07	Apr 06
Sales Turnover	N/A	3294	3903
Pre Tax Profit/Loss	N/A	187	562
Working Capital	625	612	626
Fixed Assets	462	508	510
Current Assets	2658	1696	1688
Current Liabilities	2033	1084	1061
ROCE% (Return on Capital Employed)		16.7	49.4
ROT% (Return on Turnover)		5.7	14.4

J G R Building Services Ltd

J G R House Exchange Road, Lincoln, LN6 3JZ
Tel: 01522-698883 **Fax:** 01522-688789
E-mail: sales@jgr1.com
Website: http://www.jgr1.com
Directors: J. Wood (Prop)
Immediate Holding Company: JGR BUILDING SERVICES LIMITED
Registration no: 04268701 **Date established:** 2001 **Turnover:** £1m - £2m
No.of Employees: 21 - 50 **Product Groups:** 40, 52

Date of Accounts	Dec 11	Dec 10	Dec 09
Working Capital	85	-259	-498
Fixed Assets	1m	1m	1m
Current Assets	1m	755	652

Jewson Ltd

Chieftain Way Tritton Road Trading Estate, Lincoln, LN6 7RY
Tel: 01522-543705 **Fax:** 01522-513061
Website: http://www.jewson.co.uk
Managers: R. Jarvis (District Mgr)
Ultimate Holding Company: COMPAGNIE DE SAINT GOBAIN (FRANCE)
Immediate Holding Company: JEWSON LIMITED
Registration no: 00348407 **Date established:** 1939
Turnover: £500m - £1,000m **No.of Employees:** 21 - 50
Product Groups: 66

Date of Accounts	Dec 11	Dec 10	Dec 09
Sales Turnover	1606m	1547m	1485m
Pre Tax Profit/Loss	18m	100m	45m
Working Capital	-345m	-250m	-349m
Fixed Assets	496m	387m	461m
Current Assets	657m	1005m	1320m
Current Liabilities	66m	120m	64m

Kone Cranes Machine Tool Services

1 Farrier Road, Lincoln, LN6 3RU
Tel: 01522-687878 **Fax:** 01522-687879
E-mail: service@kandbmts.com
Website: http://www.konecranes.co.uk
Directors: R. Beale (Co Sec)
Managers: V. Jeal (Serv Mgr)
Ultimate Holding Company: KONECRANES PLC (FINLAND)
Immediate Holding Company: K & B MACHINE TOOL SERVICES LIMITED
Registration no: 02843089 **VAT No.:** GB 613 8020 75
Date established: 1993 **Turnover:** Up to £250,000
No.of Employees: 1 - 10 **Product Groups:** 48

Date of Accounts	Dec 09	Dec 08	Dec 07
Pre Tax Profit/Loss	-18	N/A	N/A
Working Capital	N/A	18	107
Fixed Assets	N/A	N/A	4
Current Assets	N/A	18	423

Krystals Premier

Krystals Pyke Road, Lincoln, LN6 3QS
Tel: 01522-882266 **Fax:** 01522-882268
E-mail: mike@krystals.co.uk
Website: http://www.krystals.co.uk
Managers: J. Lucchese, M. Burrows (Sales Prom Mgr), M. Hanby
Immediate Holding Company: PREMIER PACKAGING SUPPLIES LIMITED
Registration no: 03151623 **Date established:** 1996 **Turnover:** £2m - £5m
No.of Employees: 21 - 50 **Product Groups:** 27, 30, 33, 66

Leengate Welding Ltd

6 Pioneer Way, Lincoln, LN6 3DH
Tel: 01522-690692 **Fax:** 01522-690706
E-mail: nick.scrafton@boc.com
Website: http://www.leengate.com
Directors: N. Scrafton (Dir), P. Dixon (Fin)
Ultimate Holding Company: LINDE AG (GERMANY)
Immediate Holding Company: LEENGATE INDUSTRIAL & WELDING SUPPLIES (LINCOLN) LTD
Registration no: 02160043 **Date established:** 1987
Turnover: £500,000 - £1m **No.of Employees:** 1 - 10 **Product Groups:** 40, 46, 67

Date of Accounts	Dec 11	Dec 10	Dec 09
Sales Turnover	774	654	677
Pre Tax Profit/Loss	-3	-3	5
Working Capital	-20	-24	-26
Fixed Assets	224	230	234
Current Assets	201	208	161
Current Liabilities	19	16	13

Limagrain UK Ltd

Camp Road Witham St Hughs, Lincoln, LN6 9TW
Tel: 01522-861300 **Fax:** 01522-869703
E-mail: limagrain@advanta-seeds.co.uk
Website: http://www.limagrain.co.uk
Directors: P. Thompson (Fin), T. Jolliffe (MD)
Ultimate Holding Company: COOPERATIVE LIMAGRAIN (FRANCE)
Immediate Holding Company: LIMAGRAIN UK LIMITED
Registration no: 01305690 **VAT No.:** GB 103 5004 38
Date established: 1977 **Turnover:** £20m - £50m **No.of Employees:** 1 - 10
Product Groups: 02, 20

Date of Accounts	Jun 11	Jun 10	Jun 09
Sales Turnover	43m	41m	45m
Pre Tax Profit/Loss	2m	1m	4m
Working Capital	15m	13m	11m
Fixed Assets	5m	5m	6m
Current Assets	21m	21m	19m
Current Liabilities	2m	816	2m

Lincat Ltd

Whisby Road, Lincoln, LN6 3QZ
Tel: 01522-875555 **Fax:** 01522-875530
E-mail: sales@lincat.co.uk
Website: http://www.lincat.co.uk
Bank(s): Royal Bank of Scotland
Directors: S. Mitchell (MD), T. Storey (Fin), T. Aston (Sales)
Managers: N. McDonald, S. Flaherty (Purch Mgr), V. Body (Tech Serv Mgr)
Ultimate Holding Company: MIDDLEBY CORPORATION (THE) (USA)
Immediate Holding Company: LINCAT GROUP EBT LIMITED
Registration no: 06337729 **VAT No.:** GB 526 1746 47
Date established: 2007 **Turnover:** £10m - £20m
No.of Employees: 101 - 250 **Product Groups:** 40

Date of Accounts	Dec 11	Dec 10	Jan 09
Pre Tax Profit/Loss	-18	-0	N/A
Working Capital	-20	-17	-17
Fixed Assets	N/A	16	16

Lincoln Diesels Ltd

Great Northern Terrace, Lincoln, LN5 8HJ
Tel: 01522-511512 **Fax:** 01522-512935
E-mail: iansmith@lincolndiesels.com
Website: http://www.lincolndiesels.com
Bank(s): Royal Bank of Scotland
Directors: I. Smith (MD)
Ultimate Holding Company: SIMPLEX-TURBULO COMPANY LIMITED
Immediate Holding Company: LINCOLN DIESELS LIMITED
Registration no: 03313019 **VAT No.:** GB 351 9359 39
Date established: 1997 **Turnover:** £2m - £5m **No.of Employees:** 11 - 20
Product Groups: 40

Date of Accounts	Sep 11	Sep 10	Sep 09
Sales Turnover	N/A	N/A	3m
Pre Tax Profit/Loss	N/A	N/A	195
Working Capital	567	450	412
Fixed Assets	13	15	16
Current Assets	2m	1m	965
Current Liabilities	N/A	N/A	253

Lincolnshire Chamber Of Commerce & Industry

Commerce House Outer Circle Road, Lincoln, LN2 4HY
Tel: 01522-523333 **Fax:** 01522-546667
E-mail: enquiries@lincs-chamber.co.uk
Website: http://www.lincs-chamber.co.uk
Bank(s): National Westminster Bank Plc
Managers: B. Holden (Fin Mgr)
Immediate Holding Company: LINCOLNSHIRE CHAMBER OF COMMERCE & INDUSTRY
Registration no: 00028997 **Date established:** 1989
Turnover: Up to £250,000 **No.of Employees:** 11 - 20 **Product Groups:** 80, 87

Date of Accounts	Mar 11	Mar 10	Mar 09
Working Capital	405	417	343
Fixed Assets	864	843	842
Current Assets	571	580	581

Mccomb Coachwork

22 Market Place Tattershall, Lincoln, LN4 4LJ
Tel: 01526-342292 **Fax:** 01526-344411
E-mail: simon.naggs@mccombcoachwork.co.uk
Website: http://www.mccombcoachwork.co.uk
Bank(s): Midland
Directors: S. Hampstom (Ch)
Managers: S. Knaggs (Chief Mgr), S. Naggs (Mgr)
VAT No.: GB 129 6208 64 **Turnover:** £500,000 - £1m
No.of Employees: 21 - 50 **Product Groups:** 39

Micrometric Ltd

Doddington Road, Lincoln, LN6 3RX
Tel: 01522-509999 **Fax:** 01522-501901
E-mail: rosiedesmit@micrometric.co.uk
Website: http://www.micrometric.uk.com
Directors: N. Main (MD), R. De Smit (Fin)
Managers: C. Walters (Ops Mgr)
Immediate Holding Company: MICROMETRIC LIMITED
Registration no: 03667443 **VAT No.:** GB 364 4749 26
Date established: 1998 **Turnover:** £2m - £5m **No.of Employees:** 21 - 50
Product Groups: 37, 46, 48, 84

Date of Accounts	Dec 09	Dec 08	Jun 11
Working Capital	-100	63	2
Fixed Assets	142	300	118
Current Assets	375	604	619

Morton Engineering

Westminster Industrial Estate Station Road, North Hykeham, Lincoln, LN6 3QY
Tel: 01522-685719 **Fax:** 01522-685719
Website: http://www.mortonengineering.co.uk

Directors: R. Westlake (Dir)
Immediate Holding Company: DOLPHIN MOBILITY EAST MIDLANDS LIMITED
Registration no: 01427004 **Date established:** 2001
No.of Employees: 1 - 10 **Product Groups:** 35, 39, 45

Date of Accounts	Mar 12	Mar 11	Mar 10
Working Capital	-23	-25	-27
Fixed Assets	24	25	27
Current Assets	7	5	4

Mr Tyre Ltd

Proctors Road, Lincoln, LN2 4HQ
Tel: 01522-530477 **Fax:** 01522-543373
E-mail: gareth@mrtyre.com
Website: http://www.mrtyre.com
Managers: G. Lomax (District Mgr)
Ultimate Holding Company: M.T. DEVELOPMENTS LIMITED
Immediate Holding Company: MR. TYRE LIMITED
Registration no: 02602575 **Date established:** 1991
No.of Employees: 1 - 10 **Product Groups:** 29, 68

Date of Accounts	Dec 11	Dec 10	Dec 09
Sales Turnover	42m	40m	41m
Pre Tax Profit/Loss	437	598	409
Working Capital	2m	2m	2m
Fixed Assets	2m	2m	2m
Current Assets	16m	15m	13m
Current Liabilities	3m	2m	2m

Newland Chiropractic Clinic

82 Newland, Lincoln, LN1 1YA
Tel: 01522-538450 **Fax:** 01522-538450
Website: http://www.newlandchiropractic.co.uk
Directors: D. Barnes-Heath (Prop)
Immediate Holding Company: NEWLAND CHIROPRACTIC CLINIC LIMITED
Registration no: 05086513 **Date established:** 2004
Turnover: £250,000 - £500,000 **No.of Employees:** 1 - 10
Product Groups: 88

Date of Accounts	Mar 11	Mar 10	Mar 09
Working Capital	3	10	-2
Fixed Assets	106	103	122
Current Assets	21	26	15

Nmb-Minebea UK Ltd

2 Sadler Road, Lincoln, LN6 3RA
Tel: 01522-500933 **Fax:** 01522-500975
E-mail: mark.stansfield@nmb-minebea.com
Website: http://www.minebea.co.uk
Bank(s): Lloyds TSB Bank plc
Directors: M. Stansfield (MD)
Managers: M. Batty (Tech Serv Mgr), S. Ray (Purch Mgr), A. Robinson (Fin Mgr)
Ultimate Holding Company: MINEBEA CO LIMITED
Immediate Holding Company: NMB-MINEBEA UK LTD
Registration no: 02194706 **Date established:** 1987
Turnover: £20m - £50m **No.of Employees:** 251 - 500 **Product Groups:** 35

Date of Accounts	Mar 12	Mar 11	Mar 10
Sales Turnover	25m	20m	21m
Pre Tax Profit/Loss	1m	648	1m
Working Capital	16m	15m	15m
Fixed Assets	10m	10m	10m
Current Assets	24m	22m	20m
Current Liabilities	2m	1m	2m

Nutrel Products Ltd

Park Farm Park Farm Road, Kettlethorpe, Lincoln, LN1 2LD
Tel: 01522-704747 **Fax:** 01522-704748
E-mail: sales@nutrelgroup.co.uk
Website: http://www.nutrelgroup.co.uk
Directors: D. Wilkinson (MD), J. Plews (Co Sec)
Ultimate Holding Company: SYNCHEMICALS LIMITED
Immediate Holding Company: NUTREL PRODUCTS LIMITED
Registration no: 02120895 **Date established:** 1987 **Turnover:** £5m - £10m
No.of Employees: 21 - 50 **Product Groups:** 32

Date of Accounts	Aug 11	Aug 10	Aug 09
Sales Turnover	6m	5m	5m
Pre Tax Profit/Loss	211	308	405
Working Capital	1m	1m	709
Fixed Assets	69	111	489
Current Assets	2m	2m	2m
Current Liabilities	365	570	716

P C C Associates

Brunel House Deepdale Enterprise Park, Nettleham, Lincoln, LN2 2LL
Tel: 01522-596910 **Fax:** 01522-596911
E-mail: info@pcoleconsult.co.uk
Website: http://www.pcoleconsult.co.uk
Managers: R. Cole (Eng), R. Cole (Mktg Serv Mgr)
Immediate Holding Company: PETER COLE CONSULTANTS LIMITED
Registration no: 02506401 **Date established:** 1990
Turnover: £500,000 - £1m **No.of Employees:** 1 - 10 **Product Groups:** 84

Date of Accounts	Jun 08	Jun 07	Jun 06
Working Capital	83	47	76
Fixed Assets	68	61	65
Current Assets	373	313	268

Pearson Hydraulics Ltd

11 Cardinal Close, Lincoln, LN2 4SY
Tel: 01522-846846 **Fax:** 01522-510508
E-mail: sales@pearson-hyds.co.uk
Website: http://www.pearson-hyds.co.uk
Bank(s): Lloyds TSB Bank plc
Managers: J. Walters (Depot Mgr)
Immediate Holding Company: PEARSON HYDRAULICS LIMITED
Registration no: 00809034 **VAT No.:** GB 128 2603 84
Date established: 1964 **Turnover:** £2m - £5m **No.of Employees:** 21 - 50
Product Groups: 29, 30, 36, 38, 40

Date of Accounts	Mar 12	Mar 11	Mar 10
Working Capital	2m	2m	2m
Fixed Assets	653	638	634
Current Assets	3m	3m	3m

Polytop Europe Ltd

PO Box 613, Lincoln, LN6 0GS
Tel: 01522-689598
E-mail: rpeters@polytop.com
Website: http://www.polytop.com
Directors: R. Peters (MD)
Immediate Holding Company: POLYTOP EUROPE LIMITED
Registration no: 03895244 **Date established:** 1999
Turnover: Up to £250,000 **No.of Employees:** 1 - 10 **Product Groups:** 35, 45

Date of Accounts	Dec 11	Dec 10	Dec 09
Sales Turnover	178	N/A	N/A
Pre Tax Profit/Loss	-59	N/A	N/A
Working Capital	82	98	123
Fixed Assets	N/A	1	N/A
Current Assets	97	107	135
Current Liabilities	8	N/A	N/A

Praxair

Whisby Road North Hykeham, Lincoln, LN6 3DL
Tel: 01522-878200 **Fax:** 01522-878250
E-mail: enquiries@sermatech.com
Website: http://www.praxair.com
Managers: S. Ashley (Purch Mgr), C. Lobban (Purch Mgr)
Immediate Holding Company: SERMATECH INTERNATIONAL UK LIMITED
Registration no: 05349513 **Date established:** 2005
Turnover: £10m - £20m **No.of Employees:** 101 - 250
Product Groups: 32, 48

Date of Accounts	Dec 11	Dec 10	Dec 09
Sales Turnover	N/A	N/A	13m
Pre Tax Profit/Loss	11	6	-692
Working Capital	4m	4m	1m
Fixed Assets	N/A	N/A	6m
Current Assets	4m	4m	5m
Current Liabilities	3	N/A	1m

R & L Executive Network

Howard House The Point Office Park Weaver Road, Lincoln, LN6 3QN
Tel: 08718-718714 **Fax:** 01522-690322
E-mail: cbaker@fmcgexecutive.com
Website: http://www.fmcgexecutive.co.uk
Directors: N. Dudley (Co Sec), R. Moore (MD), R. Moore (Ptnr)
Ultimate Holding Company: NETWORK GROUP HOLDINGS PLC
Immediate Holding Company: R & L EXECUTIVE NETWORK LIMITED
Registration no: 04394176 **Date established:** 2002
Turnover: £250,000 - £500,000 **No.of Employees:** 1 - 10
Product Groups: 80

Date of Accounts	Nov 10	Nov 09	Nov 08
Sales Turnover	372	379	551
Pre Tax Profit/Loss	5	4	82
Working Capital	-29	44	38
Fixed Assets	10	12	16
Current Assets	124	97	101
Current Liabilities	68	51	37

Rossendale Group Ltd

Roman Way South Hykeham, Lincoln, LN6 9UH
Tel: 01522-693423 **Fax:** 01522-693988
E-mail: info@rossendalegroup.co.uk
Website: http://www.rossendalegroup.co.uk
Directors: C. Meakin (Dir)
Immediate Holding Company: ROSSENDALE GROUP LIMITED
Registration no: 00463320 **Date established:** 1949
No.of Employees: 21 - 50 **Product Groups:** 35, 39, 45

Date of Accounts	Mar 12	Mar 11	Mar 10
Working Capital	686	384	490
Fixed Assets	455	513	635
Current Assets	1m	1m	1m

J W Ruddock & Sons Ltd

56 Great Northern Terrace, Lincoln, LN5 8HL
Tel: 01522-529591 **Fax:** 01522-535108
E-mail: sales@ruddocks.co.uk
Website: http://www.ruddocks.co.uk
Bank(s): Barclays
Directors: P. Banton (MD), T. Humphrys (Sales)
Managers: J. Burton, C. Smallbones (Sales Admin)
Ultimate Holding Company: RUDDOCKS 1884 LIMITED
Immediate Holding Company: J. W. RUDDOCK & SONS LIMITED
Registration no: 02686386 **VAT No.:** GB 613 5307 70
Date established: 1992 **Turnover:** £2m - £5m **No.of Employees:** 21 - 50
Product Groups: 28

Date of Accounts	Sep 11	Sep 10	Sep 09
Working Capital	514	408	195
Fixed Assets	387	515	497
Current Assets	1m	769	571

S P E International Ltd

Honeyholes Lane Dunholme, Lincoln, LN2 3SU
Tel: 01673-860709 **Fax:** 01673-861119
E-mail: sales@spe-int.com
Website: http://www.spe-int.com
Bank(s): Royal Bank of Scotland
Directors: P. Mansfield (Sales), K. Mansfield (Fin)
Managers: R. Clarke, P. Nicholson (Personnel)
Ultimate Holding Company: SPE WORLDWIDE LIMITED
Immediate Holding Company: SPE INTERNATIONAL LIMITED
Registration no: 01717706 **VAT No.:** 37 4115 75 **Date established:** 1983
Turnover: £2m - £5m **No.of Employees:** 51 - 100 **Product Groups:** 46

Date of Accounts	Jun 11	Jun 10	Jun 09
Working Capital	113	68	74
Fixed Assets	1	2	2
Current Assets	2m	2m	2m

Sax Lift

12 Cockerels Roost Newton-On-Trent, Lincoln, LN1 2FY
Tel: 01777-228661 **Fax:** 01777-228865
E-mail: saxlift@saxlift.co.uk
Website: http://www.SAXLIFT.CO.UK
Directors: E. Madsen (Prop)
Ultimate Holding Company: SAX LIFT APS, DENMARK
Date established: 2008 **No.of Employees:** 1 - 10 **Product Groups:** 45

Shipaid Diesel Services Ltd

Unit 1-2 Westminster Industrial Estate Station Road, North Hykeham, Lincoln, LN6 3QY
Tel: 01522-696642 **Fax:** 01522-695153
E-mail: service@shipaid.co.uk
Website: http://www.shipaid.co.uk
Directors: T. Rampton (Dir)
Immediate Holding Company: SHIPAID DIESEL SERVICES LIMITED
Registration no: 01273981 **Date established:** 1976
Turnover: £500,000 - £1m **No.of Employees:** 1 - 10 **Product Groups:** 35, 36, 39

Date of Accounts	Sep 11	Sep 10	Sep 09
Working Capital	125	110	134
Fixed Assets	21	26	33
Current Assets	390	407	377

Sje Engineering Ltd

Unit 25 Lyndon Business Park Farrier Road, Lincoln, LN6 3RU
Tel: 01522-889911 **Fax:** 01522-889922
E-mail: info@sje-engineering.co.uk
Website: http://www.sje-engineering.co.uk
Directors: B. Sowden (MD), W. Sowden (Fin)
Managers: J. Sowden (Chief Mgr)
Immediate Holding Company: S.J.E. ENGINEERING LIMITED
Registration no: 02533505 **VAT No.:** GB 555 6481 17
Date established: 1990 **Turnover:** £500,000 - £1m
No.of Employees: 1 - 10 **Product Groups:** 37, 39, 40, 48

Date of Accounts	Dec 11	Dec 10	Dec 09
Sales Turnover	N/A	N/A	714
Pre Tax Profit/Loss	N/A	N/A	70
Working Capital	240	223	170
Fixed Assets	11	11	12
Current Assets	559	418	278
Current Liabilities	N/A	N/A	33

Spaldings Ltd

25-35 Sadler Road, Lincoln, LN6 3XJ
Tel: 01522-500600 **Fax:** 01522-509300
E-mail: sales@spaldings.co.uk
Website: http://www.spaldings.co.uk
Bank(s): Lloyds P.L.C.
Directors: J. Sorby (Fin)
Ultimate Holding Company: SPALDINGS HOLDINGS LIMITED
Immediate Holding Company: SPALDINGS LIMITED
Registration no: 01558147 **VAT No.:** GB 389 0124 42
Date established: 1981 **Turnover:** £20m - £50m
No.of Employees: 51 - 100 **Product Groups:** 07, 41

Date of Accounts	Dec 11	Dec 10	Dec 09
Sales Turnover	24m	22m	22m
Pre Tax Profit/Loss	3m	3m	3m
Working Capital	9m	8m	7m
Fixed Assets	760	978	795
Current Assets	12m	11m	10m
Current Liabilities	448	809	1m

Specialised Injection Services

5 Exchange Road, Lincoln, LN6 3JZ
Tel: 01522-691182 **Fax:** 01522-689611
Directors: C. Spencer (Prop)
Date established: 1987 **No.of Employees:** 1 - 10 **Product Groups:** 40

Sugarworks

82 Sewell Road, Lincoln, LN2 5LY
Tel: 01522-538999 **Fax:** 08719-002781
E-mail: christian@sugarworks.co.uk
Website: http://www.sugarworks.co.uk
Directors: C. Hanvey (Prop)
Date established: 1992 **Turnover:** £500,000 - £1m
No.of Employees: 1 - 10 **Product Groups:** 49, 81

Swallow Cleaning Contractors

Spa Road, Lincoln, LN2 5TB
Tel: 01522-540056 **Fax:** 01522-546846
E-mail: enquiries@swallowcleaning.com
Directors: C. Sleath (MD)
Managers: S. Last (Chief Mgr)
Immediate Holding Company: SWALLOW CLEANING CONTRACTORS LIMITED
Registration no: 04956152 **VAT No.:** GB 310 6230 19
Date established: 2003 **Turnover:** £1m - £2m **No.of Employees:** 1 - 10
Product Groups: 52

Date of Accounts	Feb 08	Feb 11	Feb 10
Working Capital	-17	-4	62
Fixed Assets	128	124	121
Current Assets	170	202	257

T R Weston & Son Ltd

Westminster Industrial Estate Station Road, North Hykeham, Lincoln, LN6 3QY
Tel: 01522-688436 **Fax:** 01522-501169
E-mail: claire.weston@btconnect.com
Directors: C. Weston (Co Sec)
Immediate Holding Company: T.R.WESTON & SON LIMITED
Registration no: 03728108 **Date established:** 1999
No.of Employees: 1 - 10 **Product Groups:** 35

Date of Accounts	Mar 12	Mar 11	Mar 10
Working Capital	391	335	273
Fixed Assets	481	488	523
Current Assets	506	378	308
Current Liabilities	98	35	29

Travis Perkins plc

Long Leys Road, Lincoln, LN1 1DU
Tel: 01522-527113 **Fax:** 01522-567905
E-mail: steve.redmile@travisperkins.co.uk
Website: http://www.travisperkins.co.uk
Bank(s): HSBC
Managers: S. Redmile (District Mgr)
Immediate Holding Company: TRAVIS PERKINS PLC
Registration no: 00824821 **VAT No.:** GB 408 5567 37
Date established: 1964 **Turnover:** £5m - £10m **No.of Employees:** 11 - 20
Product Groups: 66

Date of Accounts	Dec 11	Dec 10	Dec 09
Sales Turnover	4779m	3153m	2931m
Pre Tax Profit/Loss	270m	197m	213m
Working Capital	133m	159m	248m
Fixed Assets	2771m	2749m	2108m
Current Assets	1421m	1329m	1035m
Current Liabilities	473m	412m	109m

V X I Power Ltd

Westminster Industrial Estate Station Road, North Hykeham, Lincoln, LN6 3QY
Tel: 01522-500511 **Fax:** 01522-500515
E-mail: sales@vxipower.com
Website: http://www.vxipower.com
Bank(s): National Westminster Bank Plc

see next page

V X I Power Ltd - Cont'd

Directors: G. Ashley (Tech Serv), T. McCann (Chief Op Offcr)
Managers: R. Twell (Tech Serv Mgr)
Immediate Holding Company: VXI POWER LIMITED
Registration no: 04615501 **Date established:** 2002 **Turnover:** £2m - £5m
No.of Employees: 21 - 50 **Product Groups:** 37, 38

Date of Accounts	Mar 12	Mar 11	Mar 10
Working Capital	163	140	104
Fixed Assets	93	55	52
Current Assets	768	696	600

Welvent Ltd

Whisby Way, Lincoln, LN6 3LQ
Tel: 01522-693008 **Fax:** 01522-500429
E-mail: enquiries@welvent.com
Website: http://www.welvent.com
Directors: J. Sharp (MD), J. Sharp (MD), J. Gardiner (MD)
Managers: G. Wilson (Sales Admin)
Immediate Holding Company: WELVENT LIMITED
Registration no: 02350569 **Date established:** 1989 **Turnover:** £2m - £5m
No.of Employees: 21 - 50 **Product Groups:** 41

Date of Accounts	Dec 11	Dec 10	Dec 09
Working Capital	946	782	663
Fixed Assets	138	78	104
Current Assets	2m	2m	1m

William Sinclair Horticulture Ltd

Firth Road, Lincoln, LN6 7AH
Tel: 01522-537561 **Fax:** 01522-560648
E-mail: info@william-sinclair.co.uk
Website: http://www.william-sinclair.co.uk
Directors: P. Davenport (MD), P. Williams (Dir), B. Burns (Grp Chief Exec)
Managers: B. Denton (I.T. Exec), S. Harper (Sales Prom Mgr), V. Carrington (Mktg Serv Mgr)
Ultimate Holding Company: WILLIAM SINCLAIR HOLDINGS PUBLIC LIMITED COMPANY
Immediate Holding Company: BARK PRODUCTS LIMITED
Registration no: 00993617 **Date established:** 1970
Turnover: £20m - £50m **No.of Employees:** 1 - 10 **Product Groups:** 49

Windscreen Repair Service

27 Hazel Grove Welton, Lincoln, LN2 3LG
Tel: 01673-861314 **Fax:** 01673-862022
E-mail: info@gtglass.co.uk
Website: http://diamondfast.co.uk
Directors: R. Tucker (Ptnr), G. Tucker (Prop)
Date established: 1991 **Turnover:** Up to £250,000
No.of Employees: 1 - 10 **Product Groups:** 33, 45, 48

Wyman Gordon

Tower Works Spa Road, Lincoln, LN2 5TB
Tel: 01522-565000 **Fax:** 01522-521701
E-mail: chris.thomas@wyman-uk.com
Website: http://www.wyman-gordon.com
Bank(s): Clydesdale Bank PLC
Directors: N. Tutton (Mkt Research), S. Sinclair (Fin)
Managers: N. Abby (Tech Serv Mgr), A. Wright (Personnel), C. Hobday, C. Thomas
Immediate Holding Company: WYMAN-GORDON LIMITED
Registration no: 02889486 **VAT No.:** GB 634 8609 19
Date established: 1994 **Turnover:** £75m - £125m
No.of Employees: 51 - 100 **Product Groups:** 34, 35, 36, 48

Date of Accounts	Mar 08	Mar 07	Mar 06
Sales Turnover	104430	97050	76950
Pre Tax Profit/Loss	21150	8060	-1690
Working Capital	-4470	-19880	-34470
Fixed Assets	27480	24020	25220
Current Assets	40420	47140	39800
Current Liabilities	44890	67020	74270
Total Share Capital	12900	12900	12900
ROCE% (Return on Capital Employed)	91.9	194.7	18.3
ROT% (Return on Turnover)	20.3	8.3	-2.2

Louth

Britton Merlin Ltd

101 Brackenborough Road, Louth, LN11 0AX
Tel: 01507-617800 **Fax:** 01507-601681
E-mail: mark.finneran@britton-group.com
Website: http://www.britton-group.com
Directors: M. Finneran (Chief Op Offcr)
Managers: R. Richardson (Tech Serv Mgr), E. Moorhouse (Personnel)
Ultimate Holding Company: BRAVO BIDCO LIMITED
Immediate Holding Company: BRITTON MERLIN LIMITED
Registration no: 00815053 **VAT No.:** GB 651 5630 47
Date established: 1964 **Turnover:** £20m - £50m
No.of Employees: 251 - 500 **Product Groups:** 24, 30

Date of Accounts	Apr 11	Apr 10	Apr 09
Sales Turnover	55m	48m	48m
Pre Tax Profit/Loss	2m	2m	1m
Working Capital	4m	5m	6m
Fixed Assets	11m	11m	11m
Current Assets	22m	19m	20m
Current Liabilities	2m	2m	3m

Cawmc Engineering Ltd

Manor Farm Scupholme, Louth, LN11 7EJ
Tel: 01507-328333 **Fax:** 01507-328444
E-mail: sales@cawmc.com
Website: http://www.cawmc.com
Directors: J. Cawkwell (Prop)
Immediate Holding Company: CAWMC ENGINEERING LIMITED
Registration no: 04692075 **Date established:** 2003
No.of Employees: 1 - 10 **Product Groups:** 35

Date of Accounts	Mar 11	Mar 10	Mar 09
Working Capital	17	-14	-8
Fixed Assets	79	80	98
Current Assets	152	91	135

Compass Estate Agents

7 Cornmarket, Louth, LN11 9PY
Tel: 01507-604712 **Fax:** 01507-604252
E-mail: sales@compass-homes.co.uk
Website: http://www.compass-homes.co.uk
Directors: M. Jones (Prop)
Immediate Holding Company: COMPASS DAMP PROOFING UK LIMITED
Registration no: 07394139 **Date established:** 2010
Turnover: Up to £250,000 **No.of Employees:** 1 - 10 **Product Groups:** 61, 80

Date of Accounts	Mar 11
Working Capital	-17
Fixed Assets	9
Current Assets	4

Douglas Electronic Industries Ltd

55 Eastfield Road, Louth, LN11 7AL
Tel: 01507-603643 **Fax:** 01507-600502
E-mail: sales@douglas-transformers.co.uk
Website: http://www.douglas-transformers.co.uk
Bank(s): Yorkshire Bank PLC
Directors: M. Chapman (MD), E. Bullock (Fin)
Immediate Holding Company: DOUGLAS ELECTRONIC INDUSTRIES LIMITED
Registration no: 00407703 **VAT No.:** GB 128 0408 92
Date established: 1946 **Turnover:** £250,000 - £500,000
No.of Employees: 11 - 20 **Product Groups:** 37, 39, 44, 48

Date of Accounts	Jul 11	Jul 10	Jul 09
Sales Turnover	447	391	411
Pre Tax Profit/Loss	89	44	64
Working Capital	-23	-87	-111
Fixed Assets	701	701	706
Current Assets	260	229	233
Current Liabilities	119	154	134

Eastern Box

2 Belvoir Court, Louth, LN11 0UD
Tel: 01507-600533 **Fax:** 01507-610510
E-mail: andy.goulsbra@easternbox.co.uk
Website: http://www.easternbox.co.uk
Bank(s): Lloyds TSB Bank plc
Directors: A. Goulsbra (MD)
Managers: A. Ball (Comptroller)
Registration no: 00002562 **VAT No.:** GB 555 6968 86
Turnover: £250,000 - £500,000 **No.of Employees:** 21 - 50
Product Groups: 27

Date of Accounts	Aug 07	Aug 06
Working Capital	-18	-26
Fixed Assets	300	300
Current Assets	3	3
Current Liabilities	21	30
Total Share Capital	10	10

Electrical Services

38 Northgate, Louth, LN11 0LY
Tel: 01507-606837 **Fax:** 01507-600409
E-mail: sales@grs-electrical.co.uk
Website: http://www.grs-electrical.co.uk
Directors: I. Gilliatt (Fin), R. Pestell (Dir)
Ultimate Holding Company: NORTHGATE MEWS LIMITED
Immediate Holding Company: G R S ELECTRICAL SERVICES LIMITED
Registration no: 03670457 **Date established:** 1998 **Turnover:** £2m - £5m
No.of Employees: 1 - 10 **Product Groups:** 52, 84

Date of Accounts	May 12	May 11	May 10
Working Capital	292	241	182
Fixed Assets	160	111	65
Current Assets	1m	1m	970

G Howard & Sons

83 Upgate, Louth, LN11 9HF
Tel: 01507-603267 **Fax:** 01507-603267
Managers: B. Bradley (Mgr)
Date established: 1944 **No.of Employees:** 1 - 10 **Product Groups:** 41

Green Ant Plastic Recycling

Office 1 Fairfield Enterprise Centre Lincoln Way, Fairfield Industrial Estate, Louth, LN11 0LS
Tel: 01507-418111 **Fax:** 01507-418222
E-mail: admin@greenantplasticrecycling.co.uk
Website: http://www.greenantplasticrecycling.co.uk
Directors: A. Matthews (MD)
Immediate Holding Company: TIPPABUSH LIMITED
Registration no: 04962098 **Date established:** 2003
Turnover: £250,000 - £500,000 **No.of Employees:** 1 - 10
Product Groups: 30, 42

Date of Accounts	May 11	May 10	May 09
Working Capital	15	10	2
Fixed Assets	4	6	N/A
Current Assets	117	56	29

Hi-Lite Signs Ltd

28 Bolingbroke Road, Louth, LN11 0WA
Tel: 01507-600500 **Fax:** 01507-600309
E-mail: sales@hi-litesigns.com
Website: http://www.hi-litesigns.com
Directors: D. Bradshaw (MD), A. Bradshaw (Fin)
Immediate Holding Company: HI-LITE SIGNS LIMITED
Registration no: 00886857 **Date established:** 1966 **Turnover:** £1m - £2m
No.of Employees: 11 - 20 **Product Groups:** 27, 30, 39, 40

Date of Accounts	Jul 11	Jul 10	Jul 09
Working Capital	30	-18	-21
Fixed Assets	2m	1m	995
Current Assets	259	241	239

Javelin Irrigation Systems Ltd

The Pump House Belvoir Way, Louth, LN11 0YA
Tel: 01507-607175 **Fax:** 01507-607521
E-mail: mail@javelinirrigation.co.uk
Website: http://www.javelinirrigation.co.uk
Directors: D. Bird (Dir)
Immediate Holding Company: JAVELIN IRRIGATION SYSTEMS LIMITED
Registration no: 05710116 **Date established:** 2006
Turnover: £250,000 - £500,000 **No.of Employees:** 1 - 10
Product Groups: 41

Date of Accounts	Dec 11	Dec 10	Dec 09
Working Capital	333	266	241
Fixed Assets	67	4	9
Current Assets	503	425	447

Jewson Ltd

Belvoir Way Fairfield Industrial Estate Fairfield Industrial Estate, Louth, LN11 0LQ
Tel: 01507-604041 **Fax:** 01507-600879
E-mail: andy.craven@jewson.co.uk
Website: http://www.jewson.co.uk
Managers: A. Craven (District Mgr)
Ultimate Holding Company: COMPAGNIE DE SAINT GOBAIN (FRANCE)
Immediate Holding Company: JEWSON LIMITED
Registration no: 00348407 **Date established:** 1939
Turnover: £500,000 - £1m **No.of Employees:** 11 - 20 **Product Groups:** 66

Date of Accounts	Dec 11	Dec 10	Dec 09
Sales Turnover	1606m	1547m	1485m
Pre Tax Profit/Loss	18m	100m	45m
Working Capital	-345m	-250m	-349m
Fixed Assets	496m	387m	461m
Current Assets	657m	1005m	1320m
Current Liabilities	66m	120m	64m

Leakes Masonry Ltd

15 James Street, Louth, LN11 0JW
Tel: 01507-604828 **Fax:** 01507-600826
E-mail: diruschristopher@aol.com
Website: http://www.leakes-masonry.com
Directors: R. Christopher (Ptnr)
Immediate Holding Company: LEAKES MASONRY LIMITED
Registration no: 01099282 **VAT No.:** GB 129 2761 60
Date established: 1973 **Turnover:** £250,000 - £500,000
No.of Employees: 1 - 10 **Product Groups:** 52

Date of Accounts	Apr 11	Apr 10	Apr 09
Working Capital	-1	6	41
Fixed Assets	93	112	130
Current Assets	138	142	206

Louth Transformer Co. Ltd

Belvoir Way Fairfield Industrial Estate, Louth, LN11 0LQ
Tel: 01507-606436 **Fax:** 01507-600168
E-mail: info@louthtransformers.co.uk
Website: http://www.louthtransformers.co.uk
Directors: K. Mead (Dir)
Immediate Holding Company: LOUTH TRANSFORMER COMPANY LIMITED
Registration no: 02180587 **VAT No.:** GB 288 6743 95
Date established: 1987 **Turnover:** £500,000 - £1m
No.of Employees: 11 - 20 **Product Groups:** 37

Date of Accounts	Oct 11	Oct 10	Oct 09
Working Capital	537	547	521
Fixed Assets	81	84	86
Current Assets	618	592	561

Louth Wrought Iron Centre

81a Upgate, Louth, LN11 9HF
Tel: 01507-605145
Directors: P. Johnson (Prop)
Date established: 1976 **No.of Employees:** 1 - 10 **Product Groups:** 26, 35

Luxus Ltd

Belvoir Way Fairfield Industrial Estate, Louth, LN11 0LQ
Tel: 01507-604941 **Fax:** 01507-609154
E-mail: info@luxus.co.uk
Website: http://www.luxus.co.uk
Directors: N. Page (Fin)
Managers: G. Jackson (Tech Serv Mgr), J. Ballantyne (Sales Prom Mgr), M. Odlin (Purch Mgr), C. Sykes
Immediate Holding Company: LUXUS LIMITED
Registration no: 00834329 **VAT No.:** GB 120 1276 29
Date established: 1965 **Turnover:** £20m - £50m
No.of Employees: 101 - 250 **Product Groups:** 30, 31

Date of Accounts	Sep 11	Sep 10	Sep 09
Sales Turnover	21m	15m	11m
Pre Tax Profit/Loss	918	711	-890
Working Capital	962	779	-18
Fixed Assets	5m	4m	5m
Current Assets	7m	5m	4m
Current Liabilities	1m	1m	1m

Macdonald's Engineers Ltd

11-13 Linden Walk, Louth, LN11 9HT
Tel: 01507-603566 **Fax:** 01507-603565
Directors: S. Macdonald (Co Sec)
Managers: D. Macdonald
Immediate Holding Company: MACDONALD'S ENGINEERS LIMITED
Registration no: 04508951 **Date established:** 2002
No.of Employees: 1 - 10 **Product Groups:** 41

Date of Accounts	Feb 12	Feb 11	Feb 10
Working Capital	-40	-48	-64
Fixed Assets	52	57	62
Current Assets	36	48	33

Machinery Products UK Ltd

Four Trees South Elkington, Louth, LN11 0RU
Tel: 01507-610108 **Fax:** 01507-610044
E-mail: jonny.walker@btconnect.com
Website: http://www.machineryproducts.co.uk
Directors: J. Walker (MD)
Immediate Holding Company: MACHINERY PRODUCTS UK LIMITED
Registration no: 02911783 **VAT No.:** 650 8058 40 **Date established:** 1994
Turnover: £500,000 - £1m **No.of Employees:** 1 - 10 **Product Groups:** 42, 67

Date of Accounts	Jun 11	Jun 10	Jun 08
Working Capital	-90	-77	-49
Fixed Assets	1	1	3
Current Assets	17	15	17

Martin Manufacturing UK plc

Belvoir Way Fairfield Industrial Estate, Louth, LN11 0LQ
Tel: 01507-604399 **Fax:** 01507-601956
E-mail: info@martin.dk
Website: http://www.martin.dk
Bank(s): Unibank
Managers: J. Andrews (Ops Mgr), J. Boyall (Purch Mgr), C. Price (Fin Mgr)
Ultimate Holding Company: AKTIESELSKABET SCHOUW & CO (DENMARK)
Immediate Holding Company: MARTIN MANUFACTURING (UK) PLC
Registration no: 01913440 **VAT No.:** 366 9836 91 **Date established:** 1985
Turnover: £2m - £5m **No.of Employees:** 21 - 50 **Product Groups:** 32, 37

Date of Accounts	Dec 11	Dec 10	Dec 09
Sales Turnover	4m	4m	3m
Pre Tax Profit/Loss	50	-242	-582
Working Capital	-530	-681	-393
Fixed Assets	235	338	333
Current Assets	2m	2m	2m
Current Liabilities	18	14	31

MPW Group

Manby Business Park, Louth, LN11 8UT
Tel: 01507-328031 **Fax:** 01507-328039
E-mail: sales@manby.com
Website: http://www.mpw-group.net
Bank(s): Barclays Bank Plc
Directors: A. Sarkissian (Develop), B. Broughton (Mkt Research), M. Chapman (Fin)
Managers: R. Copp, S. Mettam, D. Short (Mats Contrlr), T. Paul (Accounts), J. Kennedy
Registration no: 04687500 **VAT No.:** GB 455 4107 59
Date established: 1984 **Turnover:** £2m - £5m **No.of Employees:** 51 - 100
Product Groups: 30, 33, 37

Mr Tyre Ltd

Belvorr Way Fairfield Industrial Estate, Louth, LN11 0YF
Tel: 01507-602484 **Fax:** 01507-606404
Website: http://www.mrtyre.com
Managers: S. Cresswell (Mgr)
Ultimate Holding Company: M.T. DEVELOPMENTS LIMITED
Immediate Holding Company: MR. TYRE LIMITED
Registration no: 02602575 **Date established:** 1991
No.of Employees: 1 - 10 **Product Groups:** 29, 68

Date of Accounts	Dec 11	Dec 10	Dec 09
Sales Turnover	42m	40m	41m
Pre Tax Profit/Loss	437	598	409
Working Capital	2m	2m	2m
Fixed Assets	2m	2m	2m
Current Assets	16m	15m	13m
Current Liabilities	3m	2m	2m

North Lincs Engineering Ltd

College View Works Manby Middlegate, Grimoldby, Louth, LN11 8HE
Tel: 01507-328787 **Fax:** 01507-329306
E-mail: petlam@nle.demon.co.uk
Website: http://www.northlincseng.co.uk
Bank(s): Barclays
Directors: A. Garlant (MD), P. Lamin (Dir)
Managers: M. Jefford (Tech Serv Mgr), K. Goodyear
Immediate Holding Company: NORTH LINCS. ENGINEERING LIMITED
Registration no: 00756037 **VAT No.:** GB 128 2807 68
Date established: 1963 **Turnover:** £500,000 - £1m
No.of Employees: 11 - 20 **Product Groups:** 37, 39, 40, 48

Date of Accounts	Mar 12	Mar 11	Mar 10
Working Capital	196	134	200
Fixed Assets	245	240	225
Current Assets	546	655	557

Peacock & Binnington Ltd

Grimsby Road, Louth, LN11 0SY
Tel: 01507-353500 **Fax:** 01507-600719
E-mail: kevin.gladding@peacock.co.uk
Website: http://www.peacock.co.uk
Managers: A. Whiteley (Sales Prom Mgr)
Ultimate Holding Company: PEACOCK & BINNINGTON HOLDINGS LIMITED
Immediate Holding Company: PEACOCK & BINNINGTON
Registration no: 00328944 **Date established:** 1937
No.of Employees: 11 - 20 **Product Groups:** 41

Date of Accounts	Dec 10	Dec 09	Dec 08
Sales Turnover	35m	34m	28m
Pre Tax Profit/Loss	202	267	-55
Working Capital	2m	1m	1m
Fixed Assets	1m	1m	1m
Current Assets	8m	7m	6m
Current Liabilities	231	599	277

Power Systems Warehouse Ltd

Powerguard House Grimsby Road, Louth, LN11 0SX
Tel: 01507-600688 **Fax:** 01507-600621
E-mail: sales@powerguard.co.uk
Website: http://www.powerguard.co.uk
Directors: G. Chapman (MD)
Managers: R. Lindsey (Mktg Serv Mgr)
Registration no: 03714546 **Date established:** 1985
Turnover: Up to £250,000 **No.of Employees:** 1 - 10 **Product Groups:** 37

Date of Accounts	May 08	May 07	May 06
Sales Turnover	N/A	1101	946
Pre Tax Profit/Loss	N/A	76	49
Working Capital	60	73	24
Fixed Assets	43	6	5
Current Assets	324	519	267
Current Liabilities	264	446	244
ROCE% (Return on Capital Employed)		95.5	171.1
ROT% (Return on Turnover)		6.9	5.2

Ralegh

Airs House Manby Park, Manby, Louth, LN11 8UT
Tel: 01507-600400 **Fax:** 01507-327039
E-mail: peter.white@ralegh.co.uk
Website: http://www.ralegh.co.uk
Managers: L. Santhorpe (Comm), M. Topley (Tech Serv Mgr), P. Willows (Prod Mgr), P. White (Mgr)
Ultimate Holding Company: LINPAC SENIOR HOLDINGS LTD
Immediate Holding Company: LINPAC FINANCE LTD
Registration no: 01124217 **Date established:** 1995
No.of Employees: 51 - 100 **Product Groups:** 46

M W Shepherd

Furze Lane Legbourne, Louth, LN11 8LR
Tel: 01507-609060 **Fax:** 01507-607833
E-mail: marcus@mwshepherd.co.uk
Website: http://www.mwshepherd.co.uk
Managers: M. Shepherd (Mgr)
Date established: 1975 **No.of Employees:** 1 - 10 **Product Groups:** 41

Sportique Ski Boats

Fire Beacon Bridge Fire Beacon Lane, Covenham St Bartholomew, Louth, LN11 0PA
Tel: 01472-388296 **Fax:** 01472-388944
E-mail: info@sportiqueboats.co.uk
Website: http://www.sportiqueboats.co.uk
Directors: Y. Keeton (Dir)
Immediate Holding Company: SPORTIQUE BOATS LIMITED
Registration no: 04489027 **VAT No.:** GB 310 7781 74
Date established: 2002 **Turnover:** Up to £250,000
No.of Employees: 1 - 10 **Product Groups:** 39

Date of Accounts	Sep 11	Sep 10	Sep 09
Working Capital	14	13	-10
Fixed Assets	37	43	48
Current Assets	41	48	76

Steve Graves Steelworks & Cladding Ltd

Corner Cottage Chapel Lane, Great Carlton, Louth, LN11 8JR
Tel: 01507-450321 **Fax:** 01507-450321
E-mail: sgraves1@btconnect.com
Directors: S. Graves (MD)
Immediate Holding Company: STEVE GRAVES STEELWORK & CLADDING LTD
Registration no: 04682477 **Date established:** 2003
No.of Employees: 1 - 10 **Product Groups:** 35

Date of Accounts	Mar 11	Mar 10	Mar 09
Working Capital	18	18	34
Fixed Assets	60	73	67
Current Assets	92	71	75

Watson Fuels

Nottingham Road, Louth, LN11 0WB
Tel: 01507-606498 **Fax:** 01507-606090
Website: http://www.watsonfuels.co.uk
Managers: A. Scaman (Mgr)
Immediate Holding Company: WATSON PETROLEUM LIMITED
Registration no: 00594001 **Date established:** 1957 **Turnover:** £1m - £2m
No.of Employees: 1 - 10 **Product Groups:** 31, 66

Mablethorpe

Keetch Factors 1984 Ltd

Alexandra Road, Mablethorpe, LN12 1BJ
Tel: 01507-477177 **Fax:** 01507-473878
E-mail: keetchfactors@aol.com
Website: http://www.keetchfactors.com
Directors: J. Carter (MD)
Immediate Holding Company: KEETCH FACTORS (1984) LIMITED
Registration no: 01773182 **Date established:** 1983 **Turnover:** £1m - £2m
No.of Employees: 1 - 10 **Product Groups:** 33, 35, 40, 67

Date of Accounts	Mar 11	Mar 10	Mar 09
Working Capital	40	60	75
Fixed Assets	47	50	54
Current Assets	260	249	226

Market Rasen

P Burley & Son

Magna Mile Ludford, Market Rasen, LN8 6AH
Tel: 01507-313620 **Fax:** 01507-313620
Directors: B. Burley (Dir)
Immediate Holding Company: PL BURLEY & SON LIMITED
Registration no: 04687805 **Date established:** 2003
No.of Employees: 1 - 10 **Product Groups:** 41

Date of Accounts	May 11	May 09	May 08
Working Capital	11	65	67
Fixed Assets	166	71	84
Current Assets	122	116	127

C & G Construction Solutions (C & G Quarried Products)

Mansgate Hill Nettleton, Market Rasen, LN7 6NT
Tel: 01472-851281 **Fax:** 01472-851117
Website: http://www.candgconcrete.co.uk
Bank(s): National Westminster Bank Plc
Directors: F. Gilman (MD), N. Poole (Co Sec)
Managers: M. Cummins (I.T. Exec), R. Mason (Sales Prom Mgr), R. Brocklesby (Prod Mgr)
Immediate Holding Company: C & G Concrete Ltd
VAT No.: GB 127 7839 36 **No.of Employees:** 11 - 20 **Product Groups:** 45

Cherry Valley Farms Ltd

Rothwell, Market Rasen, LN7 6BJ
Tel: 01472-371271 **Fax:** 01472-362422
E-mail: kate.butler@cherryvalley.co.uk
Website: http://www.cherryvalley.co.uk
Bank(s): Lloyds TSB Bank plc
Directors: E. Jagger (Sales & Mktg), R. Bird (MD), K. Butler (Fin)
Managers: T. Boundry (I.T. Exec), C. Kropacz (Purch Mgr)
Ultimate Holding Company: NICKERSON GROUP ROTHWELL LIMITED(THE)
Immediate Holding Company: CHERRY VALLEY FARMS LIMITED
Registration no: 00642385 **Date established:** 1959
Turnover: £20m - £50m **No.of Employees:** 21 - 50 **Product Groups:** 62

Date of Accounts	Mar 10	Apr 08	Dec 10
Sales Turnover	56m	52m	44m
Pre Tax Profit/Loss	8m	790	5m
Working Capital	10m	-3m	12m
Fixed Assets	18m	17m	20m
Current Assets	28m	21m	29m
Current Liabilities	8m	3m	3m

Fox Plant Owmby Ltd

Caenby Corner, Market Rasen, LN8 2AR
Tel: 01673-878444 **Fax:** 01673-878644
E-mail: office@foxowmby.com
Website: http://www.foxowmby.co.uk
Bank(s): The Royal Bank of Scotland
Directors: W. Bean (Co Sec), S. Fox (MD)
Managers: M. Dady (Mktg Serv Mgr), T. Allen (Contracts Mgr), R. Durrant (Tech Serv Mgr)
Immediate Holding Company: FOX PLANT (OWMBY) LIMITED
Registration no: 06166342 **Date established:** 2007
Turnover: £10m - £20m **No.of Employees:** 101 - 250 **Product Groups:** 51

Date of Accounts	Mar 12	Mar 11	Mar 10
Working Capital	-10	-10	-16

Holton Tractor

Poplar Farm Skinners Lane, Middle Rasen, Market Rasen, LN8 3JD
Tel: 01673-843743 **Fax:** 01673-844241
E-mail: sales@holtontractors.com
Website: http://www.holtontractors.co.uk
Directors: M. Hansard (Dir)
Registration no: 04579793 **Date established:** 2002
Turnover: £250,000 - £500,000 **No.of Employees:** 1 - 10
Product Groups: 41, 67

Nickerson Bros Ltd

Binbrook Hill Binbrook, Market Rasen, LN8 6BL
Tel: 01472-398498 **Fax:** 01472-398111
E-mail: nickersonbrothersltd@hotmail.co.uk
Directors: P. Barr (Dir)
Immediate Holding Company: NICKERSON BROTHERS LTD.
Registration no: 01935311 **VAT No.:** GB 365 1004 85
Date established: 1985 **Turnover:** Up to £250,000
No.of Employees: 1 - 10 **Product Groups:** 41

Date of Accounts	Dec 11	Dec 10	Dec 09
Working Capital	44	49	33
Fixed Assets	1	N/A	N/A
Current Assets	62	106	105

Parallel Flooring Accessories Ltd

Frontier House Pasture Lane, Market Rasen, LN8 3DT
Tel: 01673-844424 **Fax:** 01673-843135
E-mail: sales@flooring-trims.com
Website: http://www.flooring-trims.com
Directors: J. Bell (Fin), A. Bell (MD)
Immediate Holding Company: PARALLEL FLOORING ACCESSORIES LIMITED
Registration no: 03192959 **Date established:** 1996
Turnover: £500,000 - £1m **No.of Employees:** 1 - 10 **Product Groups:** 33

Date of Accounts	Apr 12	Apr 11	Apr 10
Working Capital	215	224	226
Fixed Assets	161	156	198
Current Assets	426	398	415

R P C Containers Ltd

Gallamore Lane, Market Rasen, LN8 3HZ
Tel: 01673-840200 **Fax:** 01673-840240
E-mail: sales@rpc-marketrasen.co.uk
Website: http://www.rpc-containers.co.uk
Managers: A. Bearn (I.T. Exec), A. Swan, B. Margetts (Mgr), P. Lindsay (Sales & Mktg Mg), S. Baird (Personnel), T. Cochrane (Fin Mgr), T. Cochrane (Fin Mgr)
Ultimate Holding Company: RPC GROUP PLC
Immediate Holding Company: RPC CONTAINERS LIMITED
Registration no: 02786492 **Date established:** 1993
No.of Employees: 101 - 250 **Product Groups:** 30, 66

Date of Accounts	Mar 11	Mar 10	Mar 09
Sales Turnover	189m	175m	183m
Pre Tax Profit/Loss	14m	15m	-1m
Working Capital	21m	17m	-37m
Fixed Assets	81m	77m	79m
Current Assets	76m	66m	68m
Current Liabilities	17m	13m	14m

Trackside Guns & Archery Ltd

Station Road North Kelsey Moor, Market Rasen, LN7 6HD
Tel: 01652-678895 **Fax:** 01652-678020
E-mail: tracksideairguns@supanet.com
Website: http://www.tracksidegunsandarchery.com
Directors: G. Goulsbra (MD)
Immediate Holding Company: TRACKSIDE GUNS AND ARCHERY LTD
Registration no: 03898651 **Date established:** 1999
No.of Employees: 1 - 10 **Product Groups:** 36, 39, 40

Date of Accounts	Dec 10	Dec 08	Dec 07
Working Capital	-3	-5	-1
Fixed Assets	4	5	6
Current Assets	25	26	35

Wold Engineering Ltd

Swinhope, Market Rasen, LN8 6HT
Tel: 01472-398236 **Fax:** 01472-398827
E-mail: info@wold-engineering.co.uk
Website: http://www.wold-engineering.co.uk
Directors: L. Dame (Co Sec)
Registration no: 02549741 **Date established:** 1990
No.of Employees: 1 - 10 **Product Groups:** 41

Date of Accounts	Feb 10	Feb 09	Feb 08
Working Capital	-23	-23	-18
Fixed Assets	49	50	31
Current Assets	130	132	110

Skegness

George Bateman & Son Ltd

Salem Bridge Brewery Mill Lane, Wainfleet, Skegness, PE24 4JE
Tel: 01754-880317 **Fax:** 01754-880939
E-mail: info@bateman.co.uk
Website: http://www.bateman.co.uk
Directors: J. Bateman (Mkt Research), A. Reed (Sales), S. Bateman (MD)
Managers: J. Woodward (Comptroller), S. Raymond, N. Hutchinson (Tech Serv Mgr)
Immediate Holding Company: GEORGE BATEMAN & SON LIMITED
Registration no: 00232213 **VAT No.:** GB 657 7526 93
Date established: 2028 **Turnover:** £10m - £20m
No.of Employees: 51 - 100 **Product Groups:** 62

Date of Accounts	Jan 12	Jan 11	Jan 10
Sales Turnover	15m	13m	N/A
Pre Tax Profit/Loss	74	122	-12
Working Capital	203	-2m	-730
Fixed Assets	13m	13m	13m
Current Assets	3m	3m	3m
Current Liabilities	1m	992	908

C F N Packaging Group Ltd

Heath Road, Skegness, PE25 3ST
Tel: 01754-897700 **Fax:** 01754-897715
E-mail: sales@cfnpackaging.co.uk
Website: http://www.cfnpackaging.co.uk
Bank(s): Lloyds TSB Bank plc
Directors: B. Yardy (MD)
Immediate Holding Company: CFN PACKAGING GROUP LIMITED
Registration no: 02264841 **VAT No.:** GB 497 8297 65
Date established: 1988 **Turnover:** £5m - £10m **No.of Employees:** 21 - 50
Product Groups: 30, 48

see next page

C F N Packaging Group Ltd - Cont'd

Date of Accounts	Mar 12	Mar 11	Mar 10
Sales Turnover	5m	8m	7m
Pre Tax Profit/Loss	-693	285	275
Working Capital	-938	-451	-393
Fixed Assets	3m	3m	3m
Current Assets	2m	3m	2m
Current Liabilities	1m	275	271

Chocolate Graphics Ltd
Hawthorn Road, Skegness, PE25 3TD
Tel: 01754-896668 **Fax:** 01754-896668
E-mail: info@sweetthoughts.co.uk
Website: http://www.chocolategraphics.co.uk
Directors: E. Haynes (MD)
Date established: 2005 **No.of Employees:** 11 - 20 **Product Groups:** 20, 27

Classy Products Ltd
Hassall Road, Skegness, PE25 3TB
Tel: 01754-764200 **Fax:** 01754-768394
E-mail: enquiries@classyproducts.co.uk
Website: http://www.classyproducts.co.uk
Directors: A. Ladlow (Fin), J. Ladlow (MD)
Immediate Holding Company: CLASSY PRODUCTS LIMITED
Registration no: 01118954 **VAT No.:** GB 129 3924 53
Date established: 1973 **Turnover:** £250,000 - £500,000
No.of Employees: 1 - 10 **Product Groups:** 30

Date of Accounts	Aug 12	Aug 11	Aug 10
Working Capital	32	34	40
Fixed Assets	212	212	212
Current Assets	38	37	45
Current Liabilities	N/A	N/A	5

Drapers Ltd
23 Lumley Road, Skegness, PE25 3LN
Tel: 01754-763206 **Fax:** 01754-765917
Directors: C. Draper (Dir)
Immediate Holding Company: J.E.DRAPER LIMITED
Registration no: 00557899 **Date established:** 1955
Turnover: £500,000 - £1m **No.of Employees:** 1 - 10 **Product Groups:** 61

Date of Accounts	Jan 11	Jan 10	Jan 09
Working Capital	92	93	113
Fixed Assets	40	46	52
Current Assets	399	371	360
Current Liabilities	N/A	53	N/A

Fenland Laundries Ltd
Roman Bank, Skegness, PE25 1SQ
Tel: 01754-767171 **Fax:** 01754-610344
E-mail: keith.brown@fenlandlaundries.co.uk
Website: http://www.bournegroup.co.uk
Bank(s): Barclays
Directors: R. Parker (Fin), J. Berry (Fin), P. Brenon (Sales & Mktg), K. Brown (Dir), P. Brenon (Sales & Mktg)
Managers: G. Stock (Personnel), J. Stock (Personnel), L. Penrose (Purch Mgr), J. Liley (Tech Serv Mgr), J. Liley (I.T. Exec)
Immediate Holding Company: FENLAND LAUNDRIES LIMITED
Registration no: 00176558 **VAT No.:** GB 128 1599 54
Date established: 2021 **Turnover:** £10m - £20m
No.of Employees: 251 - 500 **Product Groups:** 83

Date of Accounts	Dec 11	Dec 10	Dec 09
Sales Turnover	16m	16m	16m
Pre Tax Profit/Loss	827	1m	887
Working Capital	5m	5m	2m
Fixed Assets	6m	6m	7m
Current Assets	8m	8m	6m
Current Liabilities	2m	2m	2m

Foundations & Buildings
Manor Farm Skegness Road, Hogsthorpe, Skegness, PE24 5NR
Tel: 01754-871919 **Fax:** 01754-871911
E-mail: fablimited@hotmail.co.uk
Directors: P. Stevenson Joyce (Dir)
Immediate Holding Company: FOUNDATIONS AND BUILDINGS LIMITED
Registration no: 05342541 **Date established:** 2005
No.of Employees: 1 - 10 **Product Groups:** 35

Date of Accounts	Aug 11	Aug 10	Aug 09
Working Capital	108	64	17
Fixed Assets	12	14	17
Current Assets	218	281	200

Jewson Ltd
Albert Road, Skegness, PE25 3RB
Tel: 01754-763238 **Fax:** 01754-610581
E-mail: richardw@jewson.co.uk
Website: http://www.jewson.co.uk
Bank(s): Barclays
Managers: M. Turton (Sales Prom Mgr)
Ultimate Holding Company: COMPAGNIE DE SAINT GOBAIN (FRANCE)
Immediate Holding Company: JEWSON LIMITED
Registration no: 00348407 **VAT No.:** GB 497 7184 83
Date established: 1939 **No.of Employees:** 11 - 20 **Product Groups:** 33, 66

Date of Accounts	Dec 11	Dec 10	Dec 09
Sales Turnover	1606m	1547m	1485m
Pre Tax Profit/Loss	18m	100m	45m
Working Capital	-345m	-250m	-349m
Fixed Assets	496m	387m	461m
Current Assets	657m	1005m	1320m
Current Liabilities	66m	120m	64m

Micronclean Laundry
Roman Bank, Skegness, PE25 1SQ
Tel: 01754-767377 **Fax:** 01754-610344
E-mail: simon.fry@micronclean.co.uk
Website: http://www.micronclean.co.uk
Directors: S. Fry (MD)
Managers: L. Cartwright (Buyer), J. Stock (Personnel), J. Liley (Tech Serv Mgr)
Immediate Holding Company: MICRONCLEAN LIMITED
Registration no: 01525661 **Date established:** 1980
No.of Employees: 101 - 250 **Product Groups:** 66, 67, 83

Date of Accounts	Dec 11	Dec 10	Dec 09
Working Capital	-1	-5	-18
Current Assets	25	8	10

R & B Catering Equipment Company
1b Barkers Yard Heather Road, Skegness, PE25 3SR
Tel: 01754-766451 **Fax:** 01754-766451
E-mail: rbcater@btconnect.com
Website: http://www.cateringequipmentskegness.co.uk
Directors: B. Mason (Prop)
Date established: 1987 **No.of Employees:** 1 - 10 **Product Groups:** 20, 40, 41

Skegness Springs Ltd
Hassall Road, Skegness, PE25 3TB
Tel: 08454-305000 **Fax:** 01754-610584
E-mail: sales@skegsprings.co.uk
Website: http://www.skegsprings.co.uk
Bank(s): Barclays
Directors: I. Johnson (Ptnr)
Immediate Holding Company: SKEGNESS SPRINGS LIMITED
Registration no: 01170209 **Date established:** 1974
Turnover: £500,000 - £1m **No.of Employees:** 11 - 20 **Product Groups:** 35

Date of Accounts	Apr 11	Apr 10	Apr 09
Working Capital	431	304	298
Fixed Assets	147	145	168
Current Assets	533	391	375

Skegness Steel Services
Clifton Mews Drummond Road, Skegness, PE25 3EA
Tel: 01754-760338 **Fax:** 01754-761888
Directors: A. Davidson (Prop)
Date established: 1986 **No.of Employees:** 1 - 10 **Product Groups:** 35

Storit Ltd
Church Lane Croft, Skegness, PE24 4RW
Tel: 01754-882222 **Fax:** 01754-880904
E-mail: enquiries@storavan.co.uk
Website: http://www.storavan.co.uk
Directors: N. Sanderson (MD)
Registration no: 03483669 **Turnover:** £500,000 - £1m
No.of Employees: 11 - 20 **Product Groups:** 77

Truckmasters Handling Ltd
Boston Road Wainfleet St Mary, Skegness, PE24 4HA
Tel: 01754-880481 **Fax:** 01754-880601
E-mail: mail@truckmasters.co.uk
Website: http://www.truckmasters.co.uk
Bank(s): The Royal Bank of Scotland
Directors: J. Aiken (Fin)
Ultimate Holding Company: WILLOUGHBY (30) LIMITED
Immediate Holding Company: TRUCKMASTERS HANDLING LIMITED
Registration no: 02555001 **VAT No.:** GB 598 6488 54
Date established: 1990 **Turnover:** £2m - £5m **No.of Employees:** 51 - 100
Product Groups: 45

Date of Accounts	Dec 11	Dec 10	Dec 09
Working Capital	882	742	640
Fixed Assets	168	216	283
Current Assets	2m	2m	2m

Wrappin' & Bags
8 Heather Road, Skegness, PE25 3SR
Tel: 01754-764663 **Fax:** 01754-767283
Website: http://www.packaginglincs.co.uk
Managers: A. Thoman (Mgr)
Date established: 1996 **No.of Employees:** 1 - 10 **Product Groups:** 38, 42

Sleaford

Carlight Caravans Ltd
28 Carre Street, Sleaford, NG34 7TR
Tel: 01529-415056 **Fax:** 01529-415057
E-mail: mail@carlight.co.uk
Website: http://www.carlight.co.uk
Directors: J. White (Ptnr), R. Hodgson (MD)
Immediate Holding Company: J Hodgson & Sons Ltd
Registration no: 02151039 **VAT No.:** GB 610 6370 76
Date established: 1987 **No.of Employees:** 1 - 10 **Product Groups:** 39

Drayton Welding & Tool Connections Ltd
The Coachworks Woodbridge Road, Sleaford, NG34 7EW
Tel: 01529-414774 **Fax:** 01529-414452
E-mail: sales@draytonwelding.co.uk
Website: http://www.draytonwelding.co.uk
Directors: W. Drayton (MD)
Immediate Holding Company: DRAYTON WELDING & TOOL CONNECTIONS LIMITED
Registration no: 02295125 **Date established:** 1988
No.of Employees: 1 - 10 **Product Groups:** 46

Date of Accounts	Mar 12	Mar 11	Mar 10
Working Capital	-121	-140	-121
Fixed Assets	264	271	263
Current Assets	340	231	203

Eastern Harvesters Ltd
London Road, Sleaford, NG34 8NX
Tel: 01529-303093 **Fax:** 01529-413363
E-mail: g.cummings@rwmarsh.co.uk
Website: http://www.easternharvesters.co.uk
Directors: G. Cummings (Sales)
Managers: G. Cummings (Chief Mgr)
Ultimate Holding Company: CLAAS KGAA (GERMANY)
Immediate Holding Company: EASTERN HARVESTERS LTD
Registration no: 02917927 **Date established:** 1994
No.of Employees: 11 - 20 **Product Groups:** 41

Date of Accounts	Sep 11	Sep 10	Sep 09
Sales Turnover	53m	47m	47m
Pre Tax Profit/Loss	723	1m	2m
Working Capital	3m	3m	3m
Fixed Assets	462	416	410
Current Assets	8m	6m	7m
Current Liabilities	2m	1m	2m

Jewson Ltd
East Road, Sleaford, NG34 7EQ
Tel: 01529-304235 **Fax:** 01529-307666
E-mail: john.padley@jewson.co.uk
Website: http://www.jewson.co.uk
Managers: J. Padley (Mgr)
Ultimate Holding Company: COMPAGNIE DE SAINT GOBAIN (FRANCE)
Immediate Holding Company: JEWSON LIMITED
Registration no: 00348407 **VAT No.:** GB 497 7184 83
Date established: 1939 **Turnover:** £2m - £5m **No.of Employees:** 1 - 10
Product Groups: 66

Date of Accounts	Dec 11	Dec 10	Dec 09
Sales Turnover	1606m	1547m	1485m
Pre Tax Profit/Loss	18m	100m	45m
Working Capital	-345m	-250m	-349m
Fixed Assets	496m	387m	461m
Current Assets	657m	1005m	1320m
Current Liabilities	66m	120m	64m

M & G Fabrications Ltd
South View South Fen Road Helpringham Fen, Sleaford, NG34 0BP
Tel: 01529-421652
E-mail: mandgfabrications@hotmail.com
Website: http://www.mandgfabrications.co.uk
Directors: M. Stanley (MD)
Immediate Holding Company: M & G FABRICATIONS LIMITED
Registration no: 04777356 **Date established:** 2003
No.of Employees: 1 - 10 **Product Groups:** 35, 48, 52

Date of Accounts	May 11	May 10	May 09
Working Capital	541	420	414
Fixed Assets	106	117	137
Current Assets	790	815	626

Moy Park
Main Street Anwick, Sleaford, NG34 9SL
Tel: 01526-832661 **Fax:** 01526-833180
E-mail: philip.biddle@moypark.com
Website: http://www.moypark.com
Managers: P. Biddle (Chief Mgr)
Immediate Holding Company: G W PADLEY HOLDINGS LIMITED
Registration no: 00633999 **Date established:** 1959 **Turnover:** £5m - £10m
No.of Employees: 1001 - 1500 **Product Groups:** 20

Date of Accounts	Jul 11	Jul 10	Jul 09
Sales Turnover	9m	8m	8m
Pre Tax Profit/Loss	731	959	2m
Working Capital	19m	21m	28m
Fixed Assets	9m	7m	4m
Current Assets	24m	26m	33m
Current Liabilities	5m	5m	5m

N B Fabrications
6 Little Hale Road Great Hale, Sleaford, NG34 9LH
Tel: 01529-460064 **Fax:** 01529-460064
E-mail: nbfabs@tiscali.co.uk
Directors: N. Brandreth (Prop)
Date established: 1990 **No.of Employees:** 1 - 10 **Product Groups:** 26, 35

Simba International Ltd
Unit 11 Woodbridge Road, Sleaford, NG34 7EW
Tel: 01529-304654 **Fax:** 01529-413468
E-mail: info@simba.co.uk
Website: http://www.simba.co.uk
Bank(s): Bank of Scotland
Directors: C. Adams (MD), D. Holmes (Sales)
Managers: S. Haresign (Purch Mgr), A. Naismith (Sales Admin), R. Matthews (Comptroller)
Ultimate Holding Company: SECKLOE 168 LIMITED
Immediate Holding Company: SIMBA INTERNATIONAL LIMITED
Registration no: 03378135 **VAT No.:** GB 610 4165 87
Date established: 1997 **Turnover:** £10m - £20m
No.of Employees: 101 - 250 **Product Groups:** 41

Date of Accounts	Dec 11	Dec 10	Dec 09
Sales Turnover	16m	20m	22m
Pre Tax Profit/Loss	-248	606	1m
Working Capital	3m	3m	2m
Fixed Assets	4m	3m	2m
Current Assets	8m	5m	6m
Current Liabilities	1m	875	2m

Sleaford Quality Foods Ltd
Woodbridge Road East Road Industrial Estate, Sleaford, NG34 7JX
Tel: 01529-305000 **Fax:** 01529-413720
E-mail: sales@sleafordqf.com
Website: http://www.sleafordqf.com
Managers: A. Bailey, P. Lawlor, L. Pearson (Mktg Serv Mgr), Y. Ashman (Personnel)
Ultimate Holding Company: JAIN IRRIGATION SYSTEMS LTD (INDIA)
Immediate Holding Company: SLEAFORD QUALITY FOODS LIMITED
Registration no: 00943156 **VAT No.:** GB 698 1198 31
Date established: 1968 **Turnover:** £20m - £50m
No.of Employees: 51 - 100 **Product Groups:** 20, 42

Date of Accounts	Dec 10	Dec 09	Dec 08
Sales Turnover	28m	26m	22m
Pre Tax Profit/Loss	1m	277	643
Working Capital	2m	2m	1m
Fixed Assets	3m	3m	3m
Current Assets	10m	9m	9m
Current Liabilities	461	210	252

Turnbull & Co. Ltd
95 Southgate, Sleaford, NG34 7RQ
Tel: 01529-303025 **Fax:** 01529-413364
E-mail: gary.hopkins@turnbullsonline.co.uk
Bank(s): Lloyds
Directors: G. Hopkins (Dir)
Ultimate Holding Company: HOPKINS GROUP LIMITED
Immediate Holding Company: TURNBULL AND COMPANY LIMITED
Registration no: 00536685 **VAT No.:** GB 450 0260 04
Date established: 1954 **Turnover:** £10m - £20m
No.of Employees: 101 - 250 **Product Groups:** 66

Date of Accounts	Dec 11	Dec 10	Dec 09
Sales Turnover	18m	16m	15m
Pre Tax Profit/Loss	346	132	131
Working Capital	2m	1m	2m
Fixed Assets	2m	2m	2m
Current Assets	6m	5m	5m
Current Liabilities	865	703	586

Spalding

Andrew & Co Spalding Ltd
Welland Sawmills Little London, Spalding, PE11 2UJ
Tel: 01775-723016 **Fax:** 01775-722499
E-mail: sales@andrewsdiy.co.uk
Website: http://www.andrewsdiy.co.uk
Bank(s): HSBC Bank plc

Directors: D. Richardson (Dir), G. Richardson (MD)
Immediate Holding Company: ANDREW & CO (SPALDING) LIMITED
Registration no: 00592501 **Date established:** 1957
Turnover: £500,000 - £1m **No.of Employees:** 11 - 20 **Product Groups:** 66

Date of Accounts	Dec 11	Dec 10	Dec 09
Working Capital	-11	29	81
Fixed Assets	135	137	146
Current Assets	288	258	278

Art Gen Halta
Belchmire Lane Gosberton, Spalding, PE11 4HG
Tel: 01775-840020 **Fax:** 01775-843063
E-mail: info@sandhurst-mfg.com
Website: http://www.sandhurst-rent.co.uk
Directors: M. Hodges (Prop), T. Cooper (MD), T. Dean (Ch)
Managers: N. Hodges (Mgr), R. Brand (Tech Serv Mgr)
No.of Employees: 11 - 20 **Product Groups:** 45

B T Blinds
26 Winsover Road, Spalding, PE11 1EJ
Tel: 01775-760620 **Fax:** 01775-760620
E-mail: info@btblinds.co.uk
Website: http://www.bt-blinds.co.uk
Directors: B. Topham (Ptnr)
Turnover: Up to £250,000 **No.of Employees:** 1 - 10 **Product Groups:** 66

George Barnsdale & Sons Ltd
24 High Street Donington, Spalding, PE11 4TA
Tel: 01775-823000 **Fax:** 01775-823010
E-mail: sgammons@georgebarnsdale.co.uk
Website: http://www.georgebarnsdale.co.uk
Directors: S. Gammons (Co Sec)
Managers: T. Morgan (Chief Acct), O. Bunton (Tech Serv Mgr), S. Dixon (Mktg Serv Mgr)
Immediate Holding Company: GEORGE BARNSDALE & SONS LIMITED
Registration no: 02487250 **Date established:** 1990 **Turnover:** £1m - £2m
No.of Employees: 21 - 50 **Product Groups:** 25

Date of Accounts	Mar 11	Mar 10	Mar 09
Working Capital	61	74	114
Fixed Assets	545	397	432
Current Assets	524	762	487

Boud Minerals Ltd
West Bank Sutton Bridge, Spalding, PE12 9QH
Tel: 01406-351988 **Fax:** 01406-350897
E-mail: sales@boud.com
Website: http://www.boud.com
Directors: F. Boud (Dir)
Managers: M. Phillips (Chief Acct)
Immediate Holding Company: BOUD MINERALS LIMITED
Registration no: 01936377 **Date established:** 1985 **Turnover:** £2m - £5m
No.of Employees: 11 - 20 **Product Groups:** 14, 17, 31, 32, 33, 66

Date of Accounts	Dec 11	Dec 10	Dec 09
Working Capital	93	255	320
Fixed Assets	2m	2m	2m
Current Assets	1m	1m	1m

Bridge Greenhouses Ltd
Bridge Grenhouses Park Lane, Donington, Spalding, PE11 4UE
Tel: 01775-821191 **Fax:** 01775-820306
Website: http://www.bridgegreenhouses.co.uk
Directors: E. Bridge (Fin)
Managers: N. Watson (Mgr)
Immediate Holding Company: BRIDGE GREENHOUSES LIMITED
Registration no: 01681524 **Date established:** 1982
No.of Employees: 1 - 10 **Product Groups:** 26, 35

Date of Accounts	Dec 11	Dec 10	Dec 09
Working Capital	511	552	445
Fixed Assets	61	49	77
Current Assets	1m	1m	984

Bunn Engineering Services
9 Benner Road Pinchbeck, Spalding, PE11 3TZ
Tel: 01775-766917 **Fax:** 01775-712575
E-mail: adrian.bunn@bunnengineeringservices.co.uk
Website: http://www.bunnengineeringservices.co.uk
Directors: A. Bunn (Ptnr)
VAT No.: GB 363 5139 54 **Turnover:** £250,000 - £500,000
No.of Employees: 1 - 10 **Product Groups:** 30, 40, 48

Butters Group Ltd
1 Kellet Gate Fulney, Low Fulney, Spalding, PE12 6EH
Tel: 01775-714737 **Fax:** 01775-761848
Website: http://www.butters.co.uk
Directors: S. Phillips (Fin), M. Bodenham (Dir)
Immediate Holding Company: BUTTERS GROUP LIMITED
Registration no: 06055242 **VAT No.:** D.G.M. **Date established:** 2007
Turnover: £20m - £50m **No.of Employees:** 101 - 250 **Product Groups:** 62

Date of Accounts	Sep 09	Sep 08	Jun 11
Sales Turnover	37m	36m	40m
Pre Tax Profit/Loss	-820	-2m	-371
Working Capital	167	-159	2m
Fixed Assets	8m	9m	8m
Current Assets	7m	6m	13m
Current Liabilities	1m	1m	2m

C S B Engineering Services Ltd
56 Roman Bank Saracens Head, Holbeach, Spalding, PE12 8BB
Tel: 01406-425201
E-mail: csbeng@valves66.fsnet.co.uk
Directors: C. McCormack (Ptnr), D. McCormack (Prop)
Immediate Holding Company: CSB ENGINEERING SERVICES LIMITED
Registration no: 04580397 **Date established:** 2002
No.of Employees: 1 - 10 **Product Groups:** 66

Date of Accounts	Nov 11	Nov 10	Nov 09
Working Capital	-20	-8	-9
Fixed Assets	8	11	11
Current Assets	1	14	6

David Chapman
Lynn House Mill Lane, Sutton St James, Spalding, PE12 0EJ
Tel: 01945-440273 **Fax:** 01945-440273
Directors: D. Chapman (MD), D. Chapman (Prop)
Date established: 1967 **No.of Employees:** 1 - 10 **Product Groups:** 84

Chislett Hire
Enterprise Way Pinchbeck, Spalding, PE11 3YR
Tel: 01775-725778 **Fax:** 01775-767523
E-mail: sales@chislett.co.uk
Website: http://www.chislett.co.uk
Directors: J. Woodfield (Dir)
Immediate Holding Company: CHISLETTS (SPALDING) LIMITED
Registration no: 02948937 **Date established:** 1994
Turnover: £75m - £125m **No.of Employees:** 1 - 10 **Product Groups:** 83

Date of Accounts	Jun 11	Jun 10	Jun 09
Working Capital	61	12	134
Fixed Assets	522	476	446
Current Assets	351	301	298

A Culpin & Son Ltd
Northgate Garage Northgate, Pinchbeck, Spalding, PE11 3SE
Tel: 01775-725038 **Fax:** 01775-761383
E-mail: sculpin@culpins.co.uk
Directors: S. Culpin (MD)
Immediate Holding Company: A. CULPIN & SON LIMITED
Registration no: 03270563 **Date established:** 1996
Turnover: £250,000 - £500,000 **No.of Employees:** 11 - 20
Product Groups: 39

Date of Accounts	Dec 11	Dec 10	Dec 09
Working Capital	2m	2m	2m
Fixed Assets	477	443	410
Current Assets	2m	2m	2m

Deister Electronic
Stapleton Way Pinchbeck, Spalding, PE11 3YQ
Tel: 01775-717100 **Fax:** 01775-717101
E-mail: info@deister.co.uk
Website: http://www.deister.com
Directors: L. Scheler (Co Sec)
Managers: D. Harrold (Chief Mgr)
Ultimate Holding Company: DEISTER ELECTRONIC GMBH (GERMANY)
Immediate Holding Company: DEISTER ELECTRONIC (UK) LIMITED
Registration no: 02120680 **Date established:** 1987 **Turnover:** £5m - £10m
No.of Employees: 11 - 20 **Product Groups:** 40

Date of Accounts	Dec 11	Dec 10	Dec 09
Working Capital	2m	2m	2m
Fixed Assets	158	175	179
Current Assets	3m	3m	3m

E P H Edmundson Ltd
Venture Court Elsoms Way, Pinchbeck, Spalding, PE11 3JG
Tel: 01775-723546 **Fax:** 01775-769640
E-mail: sales@eph-supplies.co.uk
Website: http://www.edmundson-electrical.co.uk/
Managers: G. Robinson (Mgr)
Date established: 1982 **No.of Employees:** 11 - 20 **Product Groups:** 39, 40, 66, 67

E & S Forklift Sales
Malting Lane Donington, Spalding, PE11 4XA
Tel: 01775-822000 **Fax:** 01775-822009
E-mail: e.elam@e-s-forklifts.co.uk
Website: http://www.eands-forklifts.co.uk
Managers: E. Elam (Mgr)
Turnover: Up to £250,000 **No.of Employees:** 1 - 10 **Product Groups:** 45, 48, 67, 83

Eastern Forge Agriculture Ltd
Eastern Forge Stockwell Gate, Whaplode, Spalding, PE12 6UE
Tel: 01406-422731 **Fax:** 01406-424245
E-mail: eforge@nippymail.co.uk
Directors: W. Barker (MD), J. Barker (Dir)
Immediate Holding Company: EASTERN FORGE AGRICULTURE LIMITED
Registration no: 02451068 **Date established:** 1989
Turnover: Up to £250,000 **No.of Employees:** 1 - 10 **Product Groups:** 61

Date of Accounts	Dec 11	Dec 10	Dec 09
Working Capital	335	252	196
Fixed Assets	1	1	1
Current Assets	428	421	271

Elsam Cross & Co.
5-6 London Road, Spalding, PE11 2TA
Tel: 01775-723758 **Fax:** 01775-768575
E-mail: sales@newtonpress.co.uk
Website: http://www.elsamcross.co.uk
Directors: N. Ward (Prop)
Date established: 1957 **Turnover:** Up to £250,000
No.of Employees: 1 - 10 **Product Groups:** 28, 49, 64, 66, 67, 81

Feldbinder UK Ltd
Tydd Bank Sutton Bridge, Spalding, PE12 9XE
Tel: 01406-353500 **Fax:** 01606-832525
E-mail: i.swann@feldbinder.com
Website: http://www.feldbinder.co.uk
Bank(s): National Westminster Bank Plc
Managers: I. Swann (Mgr)
Ultimate Holding Company: FELDBINDER SPEZIALFAHRZEUGWERKE GMBH (GERMANY)
Immediate Holding Company: FELDBINDER (UK) LIMITED
Registration no: 00346642 **Date established:** 1938
Turnover: £10m - £20m **No.of Employees:** 11 - 20 **Product Groups:** 39

Date of Accounts	Dec 11	Dec 10	Dec 09
Sales Turnover	15m	11m	6m
Pre Tax Profit/Loss	16	66	-241
Working Capital	706	639	531
Fixed Assets	354	386	445
Current Assets	3m	4m	2m
Current Liabilities	2m	1m	66

Fruitex Ltd
Station Street Donington, Spalding, PE11 4UQ
Tel: 01775-820538 **Fax:** 01775-821343
E-mail: agrimer@fruitex.co.uk
Website: http://www.fruitex-spalding.co.uk
Directors: A. Grimer (Dir), J. Miller (Co Sec), W. Day (Dir)
Managers: G. Wand (Transport)
Ultimate Holding Company: TURNERS (SOHAM) LIMITED
Immediate Holding Company: FRUITEX (SPALDING) LIMITED
Registration no: 01094418 **Date established:** 1973
Turnover: Up to £250,000 **No.of Employees:** 51 - 100
Product Groups: 72

Date of Accounts	Dec 11	Jan 09	Jan 10
Sales Turnover	61	60	61
Pre Tax Profit/Loss	37	35	37

Working Capital	-20	-17	-18
Fixed Assets	314	384	361
Current Assets	1	1	N/A
Current Liabilities	21	18	18

Gardman Ltd
High Street Moulton, Spalding, PE12 6QD
Tel: 01406-372222 **Fax:** 01406-372233
E-mail: sales@gardman.co.uk
Website: http://www.gardman.co.uk
Directors: P. Tushingham (Develop), R. Browne (Fin), J. Lawler (Mkt Research)
Managers: I. Mountain (I.T. Exec), C. Rendi (Purch Mgr)
Ultimate Holding Company: GHL 1 LIMITED
Immediate Holding Company: GARDMAN LIMITED
Registration no: 02606680 **Date established:** 1991
Turnover: £75m - £125m **No.of Employees:** 251 - 500
Product Groups: 26, 33

Date of Accounts	Jan 11	Jan 10	Jan 09
Sales Turnover	76m	72m	68m
Pre Tax Profit/Loss	7m	9m	9m
Working Capital	10m	10m	9m
Fixed Assets	1m	1m	1m
Current Assets	47m	42m	41m
Current Liabilities	9m	23m	10m

GB Security Group
Security House, High Street Donington, Spalding, PE11 4TA
Tel: 01775-821100 **Fax:** 01775-821395
E-mail: enquiries@gbsg.co.uk
Website: http://www.gbsecurity.co.uk
Directors: O. Bunton (I.T. Dir), S. Wright (Dir), S. Gammons (Co Sec)
Managers: N. Jackson (Sales & Mktg Mg), S. Field (Sec)
Immediate Holding Company: GB Alarms Ltd
Registration no: 07262902 **Date established:** 1990 **Turnover:** £1m - £2m
No.of Employees: 1 - 10 **Product Groups:** 40, 52

Date of Accounts	Dec 08	Dec 07	Dec 06
Working Capital	164	151	172
Fixed Assets	119	137	107
Current Assets	571	470	548
Current Liabilities	407	319	376
Total Share Capital	7	7	7

D A Green & Sons Ltd
High Road Whaplode, Spalding, PE12 6TL
Tel: 01406-370585 **Fax:** 01406- 370766
E-mail: pc@dagreen.co.uk
Website: http://www.dagreen.co.uk
Bank(s): Lloyds TSB Bank plc
Directors: P. Coote (Fin)
Managers: C. Clow (Purch Mgr), I. Burchnall, J. Bell (Tech Serv Mgr)
Immediate Holding Company: D.A.GREEN & SONS LIMITED
Registration no: 00537720 **Date established:** 1954
Turnover: £10m - £20m **No.of Employees:** 101 - 250
Product Groups: 35, 52

Date of Accounts	Apr 09	Apr 08	Apr 07
Sales Turnover	15m	16m	18m
Pre Tax Profit/Loss	-704	296	369
Working Capital	2m	3m	3m
Fixed Assets	2m	2m	2m
Current Assets	5m	6m	7m
Current Liabilities	198	485	567

Greenaway Amenity Ltd
7 Browntoft Lane Donington, Spalding, PE11 4TQ
Tel: 01775-821031 **Fax:** 01775-821034
E-mail: greenawayamenity@aol.com
Website: http://www.greenawaycda.com
Directors: D. Woodcock (Dir)
Immediate Holding Company: GREENAWAY AMENITY LIMITED
Registration no: 04058574 **Date established:** 2000
No.of Employees: 1 - 10 **Product Groups:** 41

Date of Accounts	Dec 11	Dec 10	Dec 09
Working Capital	-95	-97	-131
Fixed Assets	26	10	39
Current Assets	22	43	25

Guttridge Ltd
Wardentree Park Pinchbeck, Spalding, PE11 3UU
Tel: 01775-765300 **Fax:** 01775-765301
E-mail: sales@guttridge.co.uk
Website: http://www.guttridge.co.uk
Directors: S. Spratt (Fin), P. Guttridge (Ch)
Managers: K. Weetman (Personnel), T. Berryman (Tech Serv Mgr), B. O'Leary (Purch Mgr), P. Gott (Sales & Mktg Mg)
Ultimate Holding Company: GUTTRIDGE LIMITED
Immediate Holding Company: GUTTRIDGE LIMITED
Registration no: 00731549 **Date established:** 1962
Turnover: £10m - £20m **No.of Employees:** 51 - 100 **Product Groups:** 35, 44, 46, 47, 48, 51, 52, 66, 84

Date of Accounts	Dec 11	Dec 10	Dec 09
Sales Turnover	11m	10m	8m
Pre Tax Profit/Loss	620	232	198
Working Capital	1m	731	607
Fixed Assets	2m	2m	3m
Current Assets	3m	3m	2m
Current Liabilities	771	574	354

Hallgate Timber
Red Mays Farm Lime Walk, Long Sutton, Spalding, PE12 9HG
Tel: 01406-363978 **Fax:** 01406-365689
E-mail: mark@hallgate-timber.co.uk
Website: http://www.hallgate-timber.co.uk
Directors: M. Harris (Prop), E. Harris (Prop)
Managers: M. Harris (Mgr)
Immediate Holding Company: HALLGATE TIMBER LIMITED
Registration no: 06597108 **Date established:** 2008
Turnover: £250,000 - £500,000 **No.of Employees:** 1 - 10
Product Groups: 25

Date of Accounts	Jun 11	Jun 10	Jun 09
Working Capital	-75	-147	-139
Fixed Assets	71	81	79
Current Assets	66	57	41

Hargrave Agriculture Ltd
Unit 29 Fleet Road Industrial Estate Holbeach, Spalding, PE12 8LY
Tel: 01406-422003 **Fax:** 01406-490995
E-mail: sales@hargraveagri.co.uk
Website: http://www.hargraveagri.co.uk

see next page

***Hargrave Agriculture Ltd** - Cont'd*

Directors: D. Hargrave (MD), A. Hargrave (Co Sec), A. Barnsdale (Sales)
Immediate Holding Company: HARGRAVE AGRICULTURE LIMITED
Registration no: 03340649 **Date established:** 1997
Turnover: £500,000 - £1m **No.of Employees:** 1 - 10 **Product Groups:** 67

Date of Accounts	Mar 12	Mar 11	Mar 10
Working Capital	245	205	173
Fixed Assets	33	24	4
Current Assets	383	394	320
Current Liabilities	38	29	25

Hart-Marler Leisure

The Flaxmill Flaxmill Lane, Pinchbeck, Spalding, PE11 3YP
Tel: 01775-725670 **Fax:** 01775-714670
E-mail: office@hmleisure.co.uk
Managers: B. Hart (Mgr)
No.of Employees: 1 - 10 **Product Groups:** 49

I T W Pro Media

Unit 6 Apex Court, Pinchbeck, Spalding, PE11 3UL
Tel: 01775-713460 **Fax:** 01775-712908
Website: http://www.itwpromedia.com
Managers: G. Price (Mgr), D. Wade (Sales Admin)
Date established: 1995 **No.of Employees:** 1 - 10 **Product Groups:** 38, 42

Infotel

Infotel House Boston Road, Gosberton, Spalding, PE11 4NR
Tel: 01775-843413 **Fax:** 08707-522236
E-mail: hotels@infotel.co.uk
Website: http://www.infotel.co.uk
Directors: K. Graham (MD)
Managers: K. Graham (Mgr)
Immediate Holding Company: INFOTEL SOLUTIONS LIMITED
Registration no: 04185660 **Date established:** 2001
No.of Employees: 51 - 100 **Product Groups:** 69

Date of Accounts	Mar 11	Mar 10	Mar 09
Sales Turnover	2m	2m	3m
Pre Tax Profit/Loss	5	6	18
Working Capital	-126	-139	-172
Fixed Assets	806	852	893
Current Assets	290	235	195
Current Liabilities	82	116	101

Jewson Ltd

Boston Road South Holbeach, Spalding, PE12 7LR
Tel: 01406-422037 **Fax:** 01406-426099
Website: http://www.jewson.co.uk
Managers: S. Parker (District Mgr)
Ultimate Holding Company: COMPAGNIE DE SAINT GOBAIN (FRANCE)
Immediate Holding Company: JEWSON LIMITED
Registration no: 00348407 **VAT No.:** GB 497 7184 83
Date established: 1939 **No.of Employees:** 1 - 10 **Product Groups:** 66

Date of Accounts	Dec 11	Dec 10	Dec 09
Sales Turnover	1606m	1547m	1485m
Pre Tax Profit/Loss	18m	100m	45m
Working Capital	-345m	-250m	-349m
Fixed Assets	496m	387m	461m
Current Assets	657m	1005m	1320m
Current Liabilities	66m	120m	64m

Jewson Ltd

Wardentree Lane Pinchbeck, Spalding, PE11 3UY
Tel: 01775-724741 **Fax:** 01775-711210
E-mail: tim.atkins@jewson.co.uk
Website: http://www.jewson.co.uk
Managers: T. Atkins (District Mgr)
Ultimate Holding Company: COMPAGNIE DE SAINT GOBAIN (FRANCE)
Immediate Holding Company: JEWSON LIMITED
Registration no: 00348407 **Date established:** 1939
Turnover: £500m - £1,000m **No.of Employees:** 1 - 10
Product Groups: 66

Date of Accounts	Dec 11	Dec 10	Dec 09
Sales Turnover	1606m	1547m	1485m
Pre Tax Profit/Loss	18m	100m	45m
Working Capital	-345m	-250m	-349m
Fixed Assets	496m	387m	461m
Current Assets	657m	1005m	1320m
Current Liabilities	66m	120m	64m

L C Packaging Ltd

Bridge Road Long Sutton, Spalding, PE12 9EF
Tel: 01406-362511 **Fax:** 01406-362811
E-mail: info@lcpackaging.com
Website: http://www.lcpackaging.com
Directors: P. Giles (Co Sec), M. Shroder (MD)
Ultimate Holding Company: LAMMERS & VAN CLEEFF BV (NETHERLANDS)
Immediate Holding Company: LC PACKAGING UK LTD
Registration no: 01558016 **Date established:** 1981
No.of Employees: 11 - 20 **Product Groups:** 38, 42

Date of Accounts	Dec 11	Dec 10	Dec 09
Pre Tax Profit/Loss	501	N/A	N/A
Working Capital	1m	987	846
Fixed Assets	66	57	60
Current Assets	4m	4m	4m
Current Liabilities	1m	N/A	N/A

Lincs Pumps & Pipeline

Water Gate Quadring, Spalding, PE11 4PY
Tel: 01775-821163 **Fax:** 01775-821613
E-mail: helclyde@yahoo.com
Directors: D. Webster (Ptnr)
Immediate Holding Company: LINCS PUMPS & PIPELINES LIMITED
Registration no: 04961529 **Date established:** 2003
No.of Employees: 1 - 10 **Product Groups:** 51

Date of Accounts	Jan 12	Jan 11	Jan 10
Working Capital	221	216	190
Fixed Assets	88	92	94
Current Assets	301	279	273

Lucksbridge Horticulture Ltd

Broadgate Drove Moulton Chapel, Spalding, PE12 0XU
Tel: 01406-389055 **Fax:** 01406-380767
E-mail: enquiries@lucksbridge.com
Website: http://www.lucksbridge.com
Directors: T. Ball (Prop)
Immediate Holding Company: LUCKSBRIDGE HORTICULTURE LIMITED
Registration no: 06762548 **Date established:** 2008
Turnover: £250,000 - £500,000 **No.of Employees:** 1 - 10
Product Groups: 02

Date of Accounts	Dec 11	Dec 10	Dec 09
Working Capital	-162	-25	123
Fixed Assets	64	66	71
Current Assets	246	354	320

M B E Fabrications Ltd

Town Drove Quadring, Spalding, PE11 4PU
Tel: 01775-821222 **Fax:** 01775-820914
E-mail: enquiries@mbefabs.com
Website: http://www.mbefabs.com
Directors: M. Burrell (MD), M. Burrell (MD), K. Burrell (Fin)
Managers: G. Thompson (Tech Serv Mgr), L. Burrell (Mktg Serv Mgr)
Immediate Holding Company: MBE (FABRICATIONS) LIMITED
Registration no: 02688124 **VAT No.:** GB 599 5192 74
Date established: 1992 **Turnover:** £250,000 - £500,000
No.of Employees: 21 - 50 **Product Groups:** 48

Date of Accounts	Nov 11	Sep 10	Sep 09
Working Capital	-228	-222	-198
Fixed Assets	312	389	447
Current Assets	2m	928	954

Magnum Fabrications Ltd

Magnum House 18 High Street Donington, Spalding, PE11 4TA
Tel: 01775-822505
E-mail: magnumfabs@fsmail.net
Website: http://www.magnumltd.co.uk
Directors: M. Chambers (Dir)
Immediate Holding Company: MAGNUM FABRICATIONS LIMITED
Registration no: 04798715 **Date established:** 2003
Turnover: £250,000 - £500,000 **No.of Employees:** 1 - 10
Product Groups: 35

Date of Accounts	Mar 12	Mar 11	Mar 10
Working Capital	-80	1	211
Fixed Assets	433	349	41
Current Assets	137	146	274

Motivated Engineering Techniques Ltd

Roseville Tongue End, Spalding, PE11 3JJ
Tel: 01775-670361 **Fax:** 01775- 670371
Directors: A. Welch (Dir), P. Firkin (Fin)
Immediate Holding Company: MOTIVATED ENGINEERING TECHNIQUES LIMITED
Registration no: 02615902 **Date established:** 1991
No.of Employees: 1 - 10 **Product Groups:** 35, 40, 48

Date of Accounts	May 08	May 07	May 06
Working Capital	-16	-19	-10
Fixed Assets	2	3	4
Current Assets	58	63	79
Current Liabilities	74	82	89
Total Share Capital	1	1	1

Moulton Bulb Co. Ltd

Long Lane Moulton, Spalding, PE12 6PP
Tel: 01406-370380 **Fax:** 01406-371678
E-mail: robert.oldershaw@oldershawgroup.co.uk
Website: http://www.oldershawgroup.co.uk
Directors: R. Oldershaw Junior (Dir), J. Grimwood (Grp Chief Exec), R. Greetham (Sales)
Managers: C. Crowfoot
Immediate Holding Company: MOULTON BULB COMPANY LIMITED
Registration no: 00793018 **Date established:** 1964
Turnover: £50m - £75m **No.of Employees:** 101 - 250 **Product Groups:** 20

Date of Accounts	Sep 11	Sep 10	Sep 09
Sales Turnover	55m	49m	48m
Pre Tax Profit/Loss	2m	2m	989
Working Capital	2m	1m	1m
Fixed Assets	8m	7m	7m
Current Assets	9m	9m	8m
Current Liabilities	2m	3m	1m

Nationwide Produce plc

Northons Lane Holbeach, Spalding, PE12 7QS
Tel: 01406-490490 **Fax:** 01406-490888
E-mail: enquiries@nationwideproduce.com
Website: http://www.nationwideproduce.com
Directors: T. O'malley (MD)
Managers: C. Haunch (Tech Serv Mgr)
Ultimate Holding Company: NATIONWIDE PRODUCE HOLDINGS PLC
Immediate Holding Company: NATIONWIDE PRODUCE PLC
Registration no: 01972264 **Date established:** 1985
No.of Employees: 21 - 50 **Product Groups:** 02

Date of Accounts	May 10	May 09	May 11
Sales Turnover	64m	60m	74m
Pre Tax Profit/Loss	601	1m	803
Working Capital	748	-141	632
Fixed Assets	2m	3m	3m
Current Assets	13m	10m	13m
Current Liabilities	531	803	876

Neil Brown Engineering

Walding Tree Industrial Estate Benner Road Pinchbeck, Spalding, PE11 3TZ
Tel: 01775-723052 **Fax:** 01775-710570
E-mail: admin@nbe.co.uk
Website: http://www.nbe.co.uk
Directors: N. Brown (Dir), F. Brown (Dir)
Ultimate Holding Company: NEIL BROWN ENGINEERING DEVELOPMENTS LIMITED
Immediate Holding Company: NEIL BROWN ENGINEERING DEVELOPMENTS LIMITED
Registration no: 06515551 **Date established:** 2008
Turnover: Up to £250,000 **No.of Employees:** 21 - 50 **Product Groups:** 40

Date of Accounts	Dec 11	Dec 10	Dec 09
Working Capital	-1m	-2m	-2m
Fixed Assets	3m	3m	3m

Newbrook Engineering Co. Ltd

Church Street Donington, Spalding, PE11 4UA
Tel: 01775-820583 **Fax:** 01775-820487
E-mail: newbrook-eng@tiscali.co.uk
Directors: R. Newhouse (Dir)
Immediate Holding Company: NEWBROOK ENGINEERING COMPANY LIMITED (THE)
Registration no: 00978838 **Date established:** 1970
No.of Employees: 1 - 10 **Product Groups:** 35, 45

Date of Accounts	Mar 12	Mar 11	Mar 10
Working Capital	131	214	187
Fixed Assets	132	142	206
Current Assets	310	413	215

Paragon Labels Ltd

Enterprise Way Pinchbeck, Spalding, PE11 3YR
Tel: 01775-712233 **Fax:** 01775-710800
E-mail: sales@paragonprintandpackaging.com
Website: http://www.paragon-labels.co.uk
Directors: K. Bostock (Fin), A. Lennon (MD)
Managers: J. Gibson (Tech Serv Mgr), S. Smith (Personnel)
Ultimate Holding Company: PARAGON PRINT AND PACKAGING (HOLDINGS) LIMITED
Immediate Holding Company: PARAGON LABELS LIMITED
Registration no: 02925612 **VAT No.:** GB 598 5668 57
Date established: 1994 **Turnover:** £75m - £125m
No.of Employees: 51 - 100 **Product Groups:** 27, 28, 30, 49

Date of Accounts	Dec 11	Dec 10	Dec 09
Sales Turnover	134m	117m	110m
Pre Tax Profit/Loss	6m	6m	5m
Working Capital	24m	16m	32m
Fixed Assets	23m	21m	20m
Current Assets	49m	38m	52m
Current Liabilities	11m	8m	12m

W & W H Pettit

Cowbit Road, Spalding, PE12 6AB
Tel: 01775-722674 **Fax:** 01775-713064
E-mail: pettitrjpettit@aol.com
Directors: R. Pettit (Prop), R. Pettit (Prop)
No.of Employees: 1 - 10 **Product Groups:** 41

Promech Engineering Ltd

Cleylands Burr Lane, Spalding, PE12 6AZ
Tel: 01775-711611 **Fax:** 01775-712634
E-mail: info@promechengineering.co.uk
Website: http://www.promechengineering.co.uk
Directors: J. Hunns (Prop)
Immediate Holding Company: PROMECH ENGINEERING LTD
Registration no: 04203436 **Date established:** 2001
No.of Employees: 1 - 10 **Product Groups:** 35

Date of Accounts	Jun 11	Jun 10	Jun 09
Working Capital	181	132	21
Fixed Assets	114	85	48
Current Assets	250	241	84

Pulling

Sweetlands Way Gosberton, Spalding, PE11 4HH
Tel: 01775-841070 **Fax:** 01775-840167
E-mail: info@andypullingengineering.co.uk
Website: http://www.andypullingengineering.co.uk
Directors: A. Pulling (Prop)
No.of Employees: 1 - 10 **Product Groups:** 31, 40

R P S Construction Ltd

Kingston Lodge Jekylls Gate Holbeach Fen, Holbeach, Spalding, PE12 8QS
Tel: 01406-424406 **Fax:** 01406-426260
E-mail: rps@rpsconstruction.co.uk
Website: http://www.rpsconstruction.co.uk
Directors: R. Pratt (Fin), R. Sanderson (MD)
Immediate Holding Company: RPS CONSTRUCTION LIMITED
Registration no: 04691419 **Date established:** 2003 **Turnover:** £2m - £5m
No.of Employees: 1 - 10 **Product Groups:** 52

Date of Accounts	Mar 12	Mar 11	Mar 10
Working Capital	447	434	406
Fixed Assets	4m	4m	4m
Current Assets	939	1m	791

S V R Ltd

Holland Place Wardentree Park, Pinchbeck, Spalding, PE11 3ZN
Tel: 01775-760999 **Fax:** 01775-724547
E-mail: spares@svrspalding.co.uk
Website: http://www.svrspalding.co.uk
Directors: P. Semmence (Dir)
Immediate Holding Company: SVR LIMITED
Registration no: 04567039 **Date established:** 2002
No.of Employees: 1 - 10 **Product Groups:** 36, 37, 38

Date of Accounts	Mar 12	Mar 11	Mar 10
Working Capital	67	84	89
Fixed Assets	467	446	365
Current Assets	268	302	259

Shoebridge Engineering

Kellett Gate Low Fulney, Spalding, PE12 6EH
Tel: 01775-725351 **Fax:** 01775-710298
E-mail: office@crane-spalding.freeserve.co.uk
Website: http://www.shoebridges.com
Directors: R. Knight (MD), L. Going (Fin)
Ultimate Holding Company: BUTTERS GROUP LIMITED
Immediate Holding Company: SHOEBRIDGE ENGINEERING LIMITED
Registration no: 04584341 **Date established:** 2002
No.of Employees: 11 - 20 **Product Groups:** 36, 37, 38

Date of Accounts	Mar 12	Mar 11	Mar 10
Working Capital	71	5	-55
Fixed Assets	196	205	181
Current Assets	451	358	281

T N Sneath & Sons

Sneath Cross Lanes, Pinchbeck, Spalding, PE11 3SN
Tel: 01775-640373 **Fax:** 01775-640125
E-mail: richard@tn-sneath.co.uk
Website: http://www.tn-sneath.co.uk
Directors: R. Sneath (Ptnr)
Turnover: £500,000 - £1m **No.of Employees:** 1 - 10 **Product Groups:** 07, 39, 48, 84

South Lincs Construction Ltd

Bars Bridge Bourne Road, West Pinchbeck, Spalding, PE11 3NQ
Tel: 01775-640555 **Fax:** 01775-640679
E-mail: lyn@sldesignandbuild.co.uk
Website: http://www.sldesignandbuild.co.uk
Directors: J. Fitzjohn (Fin)
Managers: L. Atkin (Sales Admin)
Immediate Holding Company: South Lincs Construction Ltd.
Registration no: 01725879 **Date established:** 1983
Turnover: £500,000 - £1m **No.of Employees:** 1 - 10 **Product Groups:** 35, 52, 66

Date of Accounts	May 11	May 10	May 09
Working Capital	-13	-77	-46
Fixed Assets	26	33	35
Current Assets	429	220	256

South Lincs Patterns

Ivanhoe Spalding Common, Spalding, PE11 3AS
Tel: 01775-722988 **Fax:** 01775-760386
E-mail: sales@southlincsfoundry.co.uk
Website: http://www.southlincsfoundry.co.uk
Bank(s): National Westminster Bank Plc
Managers: D. Harriman (Mgr)
Turnover: £1m - £2m **No.of Employees:** 21 - 50 **Product Groups:** 34, 48

Spalding Pallets Ltd

Barr Farm Main Road, Deeping St Nicholas, Spalding, PE11 3BW
Tel: 01775-630011 **Fax:** 01775-630073
E-mail: info@spaldingrecycling.co.uk
Website: http://www.spaldingrecycling.co.uk
Directors: P. Turner (Fin), R. Turner (MD)
Immediate Holding Company: SPALDING PALLETS LIMITED
Registration no: 03295849 **Date established:** 1996 **Turnover:** £1m - £2m
No.of Employees: 1 - 10 **Product Groups:** 25, 42, 45, 47

Date of Accounts	May 12	May 11	May 10
Working Capital	33	17	-6
Fixed Assets	103	141	157
Current Assets	95	105	134

Specialist On Site Services Ltd

3 Park Lane Surfleet, Spalding, PE11 4BP
Tel: 01775-680608 **Fax:** 01775-680825
E-mail: enquiries@specialistonsite.myzen.co.uk
Website: http://www.specialistonsiteservices.sagenet.co.uk
Directors: J. De Heveningham (Fin), P. Semmence (MD)
Ultimate Holding Company: SVR LIMITED
Immediate Holding Company: SPECIALIST ON SITE SERVICES LIMITED
Registration no: 07216368 **Date established:** 2010
No.of Employees: 1 - 10 **Product Groups:** 36, 37, 38

Date of Accounts	Mar 12	Mar 11
Working Capital	25	-12
Fixed Assets	32	66
Current Assets	154	113

Superseal Anglia Ltd

40 Mansell Close, Spalding, PE11 1NE
Tel: 01775-722116 **Fax:** 07883-399444
E-mail: info@supersealanglia.co.uk
Website: http://www.supersealanglia.co.uk
Directors: V. Tweed (Fin)
Registration no: 05591981 **Date established:** 2005
Turnover: Up to £250,000 **No.of Employees:** 1 - 10 **Product Groups:** 29

Systemford Overseas Recruitment Ltd

Sandy Gate Sandygate, Sutton St James, Spalding, PE12 0HG
Tel: 01945-440652 **Fax:** 01945-440689
E-mail: recruitment@systemford.co.uk
Website: http://www.systemford.co.uk
Directors: A. Lemon (Fin)
Immediate Holding Company: SYSTEMFORD LIMITED
Registration no: 01732899 **Date established:** 1983
Turnover: Up to £250,000 **No.of Employees:** 1 - 10 **Product Groups:** 80

Date of Accounts	Mar 11	Mar 10	Mar 03
Working Capital	-40	-37	-16
Fixed Assets	4	4	10
Current Assets	22	19	23

T G Contractors Holbeach Ltd

Bramley House Hurn Road Holbeach Hurn, Holbeach, Spalding, PE12 8JD
Tel: 01406-422500 **Fax:** 01406-422784
Directors: J. Green (Fin)
Immediate Holding Company: T.G. CONTRACTORS (HOLBEACH) LIMITED
Registration no: 02047053 **Date established:** 1986
No.of Employees: 1 - 10 **Product Groups:** 51

Date of Accounts	Mar 11	Mar 10	Mar 09
Working Capital	1m	1m	1m
Fixed Assets	43	52	45
Current Assets	1m	1m	1m

Terry Johnson Ltd

31 Cranmore Lane Holbeach, Spalding, PE12 7HT
Tel: 01406-422286 **Fax:** 01406-426372
E-mail: accounts@terryjohnsonltd.co.uk
Website: http://www.terryjohnsonltd.co.uk
Directors: M. Johnson (Fin), P. Johnson (MD)
Immediate Holding Company: TERRY JOHNSON LIMITED
Registration no: 02062273 **Date established:** 1986
Turnover: £500,000 - £1m **No.of Employees:** 11 - 20
Product Groups: 39, 41

Date of Accounts	Jan 12	Jan 10	Jan 09
Working Capital	100	128	126
Fixed Assets	39	31	38
Current Assets	449	440	405
Current Liabilities	N/A	N/A	16

Tomtech UK Ltd

Red May Farm 317 Broadgate, Sutton St Edmund, Spalding, PE12 0LR
Tel: 01945-700553 **Fax:** 01945-700866
E-mail: a.thompson@tomtech.co.uk
Website: http://www.tomtech.co.uk
Directors: A. Thompson (Prop)
Immediate Holding Company: TOMTECH (UK) LIMITED
Registration no: 07847786 **VAT No.:** 448 5400 45 **Date established:** 2011
Turnover: Up to £250,000 **No.of Employees:** 1 - 10 **Product Groups:** 44

Totalprint Ltd

Station Road Gedney Hill, Spalding, PE12 0NP
Tel: 01406-330122 **Fax:** 01406-330123
E-mail: grant@totalprintltd.com
Website: http://www.totalprintltd.com
Bank(s): HSBC
Directors: G. Wilson (MD)
Immediate Holding Company: TOTALPRINT LIMITED
Registration no: 01548206 **Date established:** 1981
Turnover: Up to £250,000 **No.of Employees:** 11 - 20 **Product Groups:** 28

Date of Accounts	Mar 12	Mar 11	Mar 10
Working Capital	-33	-24	-14
Fixed Assets	209	216	200
Current Assets	77	111	70

Vantage Windows

Bankhouse Farm The Delph, Spalding, PE11 3JH
Tel: 01775-670111 **Fax:** 01775-670160
E-mail: christine@vantagewindows.com
Website: http://www.vantagewindows.com
Directors: R. Grocock (Dir)
Immediate Holding Company: VANTAGE BUSINESSES LIMITED
Registration no: 05657427 **Date established:** 2005
No.of Employees: 1 - 10 **Product Groups:** 30, 35, 66

Date of Accounts	Dec 11	Dec 10	Dec 09
Working Capital	-0	-0	-0
Current Assets	22	12	32

Veeract Portapack Ltd

Allenbys Chase Sutton Bridge, Spalding, PE12 9SY
Tel: 01406-350720 **Fax:** 01406-350903
E-mail: kspiller@portapack.co.uk
Website: http://www.portapack.co.uk
Directors: K. Spiller (MD)
Immediate Holding Company: VEERACT (PORTAPACK) LIMITED
Registration no: 01887021 **VAT No.:** GB 426 1295 62
Date established: 1985 **Turnover:** £250,000 - £500,000
No.of Employees: 1 - 10 **Product Groups:** 30, 32, 36, 39, 40, 41, 42, 44, 45, 67, 83

Date of Accounts	Mar 12	Mar 11	Mar 10
Working Capital	-9	-9	-1
Fixed Assets	29	30	31
Current Assets	51	40	49

Vegetable Harvesting Systems MBE Fabrications, premier pit

Town Drove Quadring, Spalding, PE11 4PU
Tel: 01775-821222
E-mail: kate@mbefabs.com
Website: http://www.vhsharvesting.co.uk
Directors: M. Burrell (MD)
No.of Employees: 21 - 50 **Product Groups:** 41

W R Refrigeration Ltd

2 Woolram Wygate, Spalding, PE11 1NX
Tel: 01775-768978 **Fax:** 01775-768713
E-mail: chriscocks@wrspalding.com
Website: http://www.wrref.com
Managers: J. King (Mgr)
Ultimate Holding Company: HUURRE GROUP OY (FINLAND)
Immediate Holding Company: WR REFRIGERATION LIMITED
Registration no: 00594746 **Date established:** 1957
Turnover: £250,000 - £500,000 **No.of Employees:** 1 - 10
Product Groups: 38, 40, 52, 66

Date of Accounts	Dec 11	Dec 10	Dec 09
Sales Turnover	45m	44m	57m
Pre Tax Profit/Loss	412	-2m	1m
Working Capital	29m	21m	23m
Fixed Assets	3m	4m	3m
Current Assets	52m	45m	36m
Current Liabilities	4m	2m	2m

W S K Spalding Ltd

Enterprise Way Pinchbeck, Spalding, PE11 3YR
Tel: 01775-769921 **Fax:** 01775-769075
Directors: M. Sternham (Dir)
Immediate Holding Company: W.S.K. (SPALDING) LIMITED
Registration no: 01661845 **VAT No.:** GB 395 7235 13
Date established: 1982 **Turnover:** £75m - £125m
No.of Employees: 1 - 10 **Product Groups:** 18

Date of Accounts	Dec 11	Dec 10	Dec 09
Working Capital	519	487	450
Fixed Assets	19	10	13
Current Assets	920	980	951

Welland Engineering Ltd

31a Cranmore Lane Holbeach, Spalding, PE12 7HT
Tel: 01406-490660 **Fax:** 01406-490444
E-mail: sales@wellandpower.net
Website: http://www.wellandpower.net
Bank(s): Barclays, Hall Place.
Directors: E. Farrow (MD)
Immediate Holding Company: WELLAND ENGINEERING COMPANY LIMITED
Registration no: 00479009 **Date established:** 1950 **Turnover:** £5m - £10m
No.of Employees: 11 - 20 **Product Groups:** 37, 83

Date of Accounts	Mar 12	Mar 11	Mar 10
Working Capital	604	735	909
Fixed Assets	2m	1m	803
Current Assets	883	920	1m

A S Whitaker & Sons

Stephenson Avenue Pinchbeck, Spalding, PE11 3SW
Tel: 01775-722789 **Fax:** 01775-710519
E-mail: info@whitakers-bodyshop.co.uk
Website: http://www.whitakers-bodyshop.co.uk
Directors: D. Whitaker (Prop), D. Whittaker (Prop)
Immediate Holding Company: CPT DISTRIBUTION LIMITED
Registration no: 03141619 **Date established:** 1995
No.of Employees: 21 - 50 **Product Groups:** 39

Date of Accounts	Dec 11	Dec 10	Dec 09
Working Capital	9	17	11
Fixed Assets	840	593	545
Current Assets	277	221	188

R W White

Cradge Bank, Spalding, PE11 3AQ
Tel: 01775-769063 **Fax:** 01775-761142
Directors: R. White (Prop)
Immediate Holding Company: ASSOCIATED BRITISH BULBS
Registration no: 03153950 **Date established:** 1963
No.of Employees: 1 - 10 **Product Groups:** 35

Date of Accounts	Jan 12	Jan 11	Jan 10
Working Capital	56	69	95
Fixed Assets	6	7	10
Current Assets	97	130	172

Spilsby

Bullet Engineering Ltd

Vale Road Industrial Estate, Spilsby, PE23 5HE
Tel: 01790-753320 **Fax:** 01790-754530
E-mail: bullet.sales@tiscali.co.uk
Website: http://www.bulletengineering.co.uk
Directors: S. Harvey (Fin)
Immediate Holding Company: BULLET ENGINEERING LIMITED
Registration no: 03143329 **VAT No.:** GB 555 3652 31
Date established: 1996 **Turnover:** £500,000 - £1m
No.of Employees: 1 - 10 **Product Groups:** 48

Date of Accounts	Jun 11	Jun 10	Jun 09
Working Capital	-41	-9	103
Fixed Assets	316	356	131
Current Assets	161	142	270
Current Liabilities	92	N/A	N/A

G P C Industries Ltd

21 Halton Road, Spilsby, PE23 5JZ
Tel: 01790-753835 **Fax:** 01790-752109
E-mail: sales@gpcind.co.uk
Website: http://www.gpcind.co.uk
Bank(s): Barclays
Directors: G. Clarke (Prop)
Managers: P. Young (Chief Mgr)
Immediate Holding Company: G P C INDUSTRIES LIMITED
Registration no: 01844293 **VAT No.:** GB 364 8460 30
Date established: 1984 **Turnover:** £1m - £2m **No.of Employees:** 21 - 50
Product Groups: 35, 40, 45

Date of Accounts	Dec 11	Dec 10	Dec 09
Working Capital	613	565	548
Fixed Assets	31	41	37
Current Assets	1m	1m	1m

J & A International Ltd

Vale Road, Spilsby, PE23 5HE
Tel: 01790-752757 **Fax:** 01790-754132
E-mail: ja-int@ja-int.co.uk
Website: http://www.ja-int.co.uk
Directors: M. Kemp (MD), V. Nixon (Comm), C. Fry (Dir), A. Apletree (Mkt Research), S. Holderness (Sales)
Managers: P. Law (Comptroller)
Immediate Holding Company: J & A (INTERNATIONAL) LIMITED
Registration no: 01567572 **Date established:** 1981 **Turnover:** £5m - £10m
No.of Employees: 101 - 250 **Product Groups:** 23

Date of Accounts	Dec 11	Dec 10	Dec 09
Sales Turnover	7m	6m	5m
Pre Tax Profit/Loss	620	443	363
Working Capital	3m	3m	3m
Fixed Assets	2m	2m	1m
Current Assets	4m	4m	4m
Current Liabilities	745	599	454

Tong Peal Engineering Ltd

Ashby Road, Spilsby, PE23 5DW
Tel: 01790-752771 **Fax:** 01790-753611
E-mail: sales@tongpeal.com
Website: http://www.tongpeal.com
Directors: C. Tong (MD), D. McArthur (Co Sec)
Managers: C. Metcalfe (Mktg Serv Mgr), E. Tong (Tech Serv Mgr), I. Hodgson (Purch Mgr)
Immediate Holding Company: TONG ENGINEERING LTD
Registration no: 01957036 **Date established:** 1985 **Turnover:** £5m - £10m
No.of Employees: 101 - 250 **Product Groups:** 41

Date of Accounts	Jan 12	Jan 11	Jan 10
Sales Turnover	11m	10m	10m
Pre Tax Profit/Loss	80	-89	159
Working Capital	1m	1m	2m
Fixed Assets	2m	2m	2m
Current Assets	4m	3m	3m
Current Liabilities	793	952	801

Stamford

Alltech UK Ltd

Ryhall Road, Stamford, PE9 1TZ
Tel: 01780-764512 **Fax:** 01780-764506
Website: http://www.alltech.com
Directors: N. Hohman (Fin)
Managers: I. Brown (Mktg Serv Mgr), C. Brown (Tech Serv Mgr)
Ultimate Holding Company: ALLTECH INC (USA)
Immediate Holding Company: ALLTECH (U.K.) LIMITED
Registration no: 01634012 **Date established:** 1982 **Turnover:** £5m - £10m
No.of Employees: 51 - 100 **Product Groups:** 20

Date of Accounts	Dec 10	Dec 09	Dec 08
Sales Turnover	6m	7m	6m
Pre Tax Profit/Loss	314	318	-2m
Working Capital	-3m	-3m	-3m
Fixed Assets	2m	2m	2m
Current Assets	3m	3m	3m
Current Liabilities	314	317	250

Ambiance Home Improvements

4 Broad Street, Stamford, PE9 1PB
Tel: 01780-483969
E-mail: enquiries@ambiancehi.co.uk
Website: http://www.ambiancehi.co.uk
Directors: P. Cushing (Prop)
Immediate Holding Company: AXIOM BUSINESS SYSTEMS LTD.
Date established: 1998 **No.of Employees:** 1 - 10 **Product Groups:** 25, 36

Date of Accounts	Nov 10
Working Capital	-7
Fixed Assets	1
Current Assets	7

Awin Barratt Siegel Wine Agencies

28 Recreation Ground Road, Stamford, PE9 1EW
Tel: 01780-755810 **Fax:** 01780-482721
E-mail: admin@abswineagencies.co.uk
Website: http://www.abswineagencies.co.uk

see next page

Awin Barratt Siegel Wine Agencies - Cont'd

Directors: J. Barratt (Ptnr), M. Awin (Ptnr)
Managers: D. Wright (Chief Mgr), D. Wright (Mgr)
Immediate Holding Company: AWIN BARRATT SIEGEL WINE AGENCIES LLP
Registration no: OC307303 **VAT No.:** GB 239 2422 67
Date established: 2004 **Turnover:** £1m - £2m **No.of Employees:** 1 - 10
Product Groups: 62

C J Carpets & Lighting

53 Scotgate, Stamford, PE9 2YQ
Tel: 01780-754825 **Fax:** 01780-754825
E-mail: cahillcpts@aol.com
Website: http://www.cjcarpetsandlighting.com
Directors: S. Cahill (Ptnr)
Date established: 2003 **Turnover:** Up to £250,000
No.of Employees: 1 - 10 **Product Groups:** 23, 37

Cummins Generator Technologies

PO Box 17, Stamford, PE9 2NB
Tel: 01780-484000 **Fax:** 01780-484100
E-mail: info@cummins.com
Website: http://www.cummins.com
Directors: T. Ede (Co Sec), R. Eyres (Co Sec), S. Patch (Fin)
Managers: L. Middleton (Personnel), J. Stephenson, S. Bendall (Purch Mgr), C. Wong (Tech Serv Mgr)
Ultimate Holding Company: CUMMINS INC (USA)
Immediate Holding Company: NEWAGE LIMITED
Registration no: 02125770 **VAT No.:** GB 776 5392 82
Date established: 1987 **Turnover:** £125m - £250m
No.of Employees: 501 - 1000 **Product Groups:** 37, 39

Geoff Steels Fabrications

Unit 1a Station Road, Barnack, Stamford, PE9 3DW
Tel: 01780-740861 **Fax:** 01780-749344
Directors: G. Steels (Prop)
Date established: 1993 **No.of Employees:** 1 - 10 **Product Groups:** 35

Hanson Cement & Packed Products

Ketton Works Ketton, Stamford, PE9 3SX
Tel: 08456-001616 **Fax:** 01780-727070
E-mail: kent.stuehmer@hanson.biz
Website: http://www.castlecement.com
Managers: M. Cox (Plant), A. Mytton (Personnel)
Immediate Holding Company: HEIDELBERGCEMENT UK LTD
Registration no: 02182762 **No.of Employees:** 251 - 500
Product Groups: 33

Klingair Ltd

Unit 3 Station Road Business Park Station Road, Barnack, Stamford, PE9 3DW
Tel: 01780-740644 **Fax:** 01780-740881
E-mail: klingair@btconnect.com
Website: http://www.klingair.co.uk
Managers: C. Darby (Mgr)
Immediate Holding Company: KLINGAIR LIMITED
Registration no: 01344759 **Date established:** 1977
Turnover: Up to £250,000 **No.of Employees:** 1 - 10 **Product Groups:** 39

Date of Accounts	Jun 11	Jun 10	Jun 09
Working Capital	-4	-0	-3
Fixed Assets	1	2	3
Current Assets	37	47	39

Kyal Machine Tools Ltd

Foundry Road, Stamford, PE9 2PP
Tel: 01780-765965 **Fax:** 01780-765877
E-mail: office@kyalmachinetools.co.uk
Website: http://www.kyalmachinetools.co.uk
Directors: S. Pollard (MD)
Immediate Holding Company: KYAL MACHINE TOOLS LIMITED
Registration no: 01937586 **VAT No.:** GB 452 5431 66
Date established: 1985 **Turnover:** £1m - £2m **No.of Employees:** 1 - 10
Product Groups: 46, 67

Date of Accounts	Jul 11	Jul 10	Jul 09
Working Capital	320	370	303
Fixed Assets	4	7	1
Current Assets	888	663	553

Lawson Consulting

Church Gables Wilsthorpe, Stamford, PE9 4PE
Tel: 01778-429553 **Fax:** 07092-252676
E-mail: info@lawsonconsulting.co.uk
Website: http://www.lawsonconsulting.co.uk
Directors: T. Lawson (Dir), V. Hirst (Fin)
Immediate Holding Company: LAWSON CONSULTING LIMITED
Registration no: 06059792 **Date established:** 2007
Turnover: Up to £250,000 **No.of Employees:** 1 - 10 **Product Groups:** 80

Date of Accounts	Jan 11	Jan 10	Jan 09
Working Capital	61	47	72
Fixed Assets	1	2	3
Current Assets	88	56	101

Luckins

Cherryholt Road, Stamford, PE9 2EP
Tel: 01780-750500 **Fax:** 01780-750567
E-mail: donna.ward@luckins.co.uk
Website: http://www.luckins.co.uk
Bank(s): Natwest
Directors: C. Pyle (Ch), D. Ward (MD)
Managers: K. Gutteridge (Systems Mgr), A. Cummings (Comm), D. Moore (Accounts)
Ultimate Holding Company: DE FACTO 1731 LIMITED
Immediate Holding Company: BOWMAN (HERITAGE) LTD
Registration no: 00857447 **VAT No.:** GB 120 4684 96
Date established: 2011 **Turnover:** £2m - £5m **No.of Employees:** 21 - 50
Product Groups: 28, 44, 64, 80, 81

Date of Accounts	Dec 10	Dec 09	Dec 08
Sales Turnover	11m	11m	10m
Pre Tax Profit/Loss	3m	2m	2m
Working Capital	318	-5m	-4m
Fixed Assets	19m	20m	21m
Current Assets	5m	3m	3m
Current Liabilities	5m	8m	6m

Pro Machine Tools Ltd

17 Station Road Barnack, Stamford, PE9 3DW
Tel: 01780-740956 **Fax:** 01780-740957
E-mail: promachuk@aol.com
Website: http://www.inputmachinetools.co.uk
Directors: B. Tate (MD), P. Tierney Tate (Fin)
Immediate Holding Company: PRO MACHINE TOOLS LIMITED
Registration no: 03278527 **Date established:** 1996
Turnover: £500,000 - £1m **No.of Employees:** 1 - 10 **Product Groups:** 67

Date of Accounts	Oct 11	Oct 10	Oct 09
Working Capital	183	186	189
Fixed Assets	13	17	22
Current Assets	242	255	287

Proline Botanicals Ltd

Meadow Park Industrial Estate Bourne Road, Essendine, Stamford, PE9 4LT
Tel: 01780-753366 **Fax:** 01780-759060
E-mail: tony.carter@prolinebotanials.com
Website: http://www.prolinebotanicals.com
Directors: B. Carter (Fin), T. Carter (Comm), A. Carter (MD)
Immediate Holding Company: PROLINE BOTANICALS LIMITED
Registration no: 04226789 **Date established:** 2001
No.of Employees: 21 - 50 **Product Groups:** 32, 63

Date of Accounts	May 09	Nov 08	Nov 07
Working Capital	-177	29	84
Fixed Assets	537	151	156
Current Assets	682	558	767
Current Liabilities	N/A	148	196

Ritelite Systems Ltd

Meadow Park Industrial Estate Bourne Road, Essendine, Stamford, PE9 4LT
Tel: 01780-765600 **Fax:** 01780-765700
E-mail: sales@ritelite.co.uk
Website: http://www.ritelite.co.uk
Bank(s): Barclays, Stamford
Directors: M. Batty (MD), S. Batty (Fin)
Managers: A. Sumner
Immediate Holding Company: RITELITE (SYSTEMS) LIMITED
Registration no: 02225641 **VAT No.:** GB 510 9157 69
Date established: 1988 **Turnover:** £5m - £10m **No.of Employees:** 21 - 50
Product Groups: 37, 39

Date of Accounts	Apr 11	Apr 10	Apr 09
Sales Turnover	6m	6m	7m
Pre Tax Profit/Loss	723	729	716
Working Capital	8m	7m	7m
Fixed Assets	383	385	399
Current Assets	12m	11m	11m
Current Liabilities	1m	1m	2m

Starfish

738, Stamford, PE9 1PB
Tel: 08450-645555 **Fax:** 01780-480666
E-mail: info@starfish-uk.com
Website: http://www.starfish-uk.com
Directors: P. Cowley (Dir)
Immediate Holding Company: AXIOM BUSINESS SYSTEMS LTD.
Registration no: 03601370 **Date established:** 1998
No.of Employees: 1 - 10 **Product Groups:** 84

Date of Accounts	Nov 10
Working Capital	-7
Fixed Assets	1
Current Assets	7

Tarmac Precast Concrete Ltd

Tallington Factory Barholm Road, Tallington, Stamford, PE9 4RL
Tel: 01778-381000 **Fax:** 01778-348041
E-mail: nd@tarmacprecast.co.uk
Website: http://www.tarmac.co.uk
Bank(s): HSBC Bank plc
Directors: G. Loader (Fin), N. Claxton (Dir)
Managers: M. Parnham (Sales & Mktg Mg)
Immediate Holding Company: TARMAC PRECAST CONCRETE LIMITED
Registration no: 03224010 **VAT No.:** GB 532 3679 43
Date established: 1996 **No.of Employees:** 21 - 50 **Product Groups:** 33

Tinwell Forge

27 Main Street Tinwell, Stamford, PE9 3UD
Tel: 01780-756341 **Fax:** 01780-756341
E-mail: tinwellforge@aol.com
Directors: D. O'Regan (Prop)
Date established: 1962 **No.of Employees:** 1 - 10 **Product Groups:** 26, 35

Woodhall Spa

Charles H Hill Ltd

Moor Lane Horsington, Woodhall Spa, LN10 5HH
Tel: 01526-388281 **Fax:** 01526-388311
E-mail: info@charleshhill.co.uk
Website: http://www.charleshhill.co.uk
Directors: G. Hill (MD)
Immediate Holding Company: CHARLES H HILL LIMITED
Registration no: 04614596 **Date established:** 2002
No.of Employees: 1 - 10 **Product Groups:** 37

Date of Accounts	Dec 11	Dec 10	Dec 09
Working Capital	771	704	600
Fixed Assets	136	133	141
Current Assets	1m	1m	1m

M G R Guns

1 Witham Road, Woodhall Spa, LN10 6RW
Tel: 01526-351750 **Fax:** 01526-351749
E-mail: john@wortley9490.fsnet.co.uk
Directors: A. Wortley (Prop)
Date established: 2004 **No.of Employees:** 1 - 10 **Product Groups:** 36, 39, 40

Poultry First Ltd

The Manor House Greenways Manor Estate, Woodhall Spa, LN10 6PY
Tel: 01526-352471 **Fax:** 01526-352022
Website: http://www.poultryfirst.co.uk
Directors: J. Sabberton (Fin), R. Haynes (Prop), R. Haynes (MD), S. Donson (MD)
Managers: J. Wright (Admin Off)
Immediate Holding Company: POULTRY FIRST LIMITED
Registration no: 00155566 **Date established:** 1919
No.of Employees: 1 - 10 **Product Groups:** 62

Date of Accounts	Dec 07	Dec 06
Working Capital	190	190
Current Assets	190	190

E Skinns Ltd

Witham Road, Woodhall Spa, LN10 6QX
Tel: 01526-352120 **Fax:** 01526-352684
Directors: D. Shelton (MD)
Immediate Holding Company: E. SKINNS LIMITED
Registration no: 02006120 **Date established:** 1986
No.of Employees: 1 - 10 **Product Groups:** 41

Date of Accounts	Dec 11	Dec 10	Dec 09
Working Capital	123	114	115
Fixed Assets	97	102	106
Current Assets	164	136	138

GREATER LONDON

London

1st Communications Ltd
15 Bowling Green Lane, London, EC1R 0BD
Tel: 020-7553 4488
E-mail: info@1st-comms.com
Website: http://www.1st-comms.com
Managers: B. Byrne, G. Howard
Immediate Holding Company: 1ST COMMUNICATIONS INSTALLATION AND MAINTENANCE LIMITED
Registration no: 03119270 **Date established:** 1995
No.of Employees: 1 - 10 **Product Groups:** 37, 44, 48, 67

Date of Accounts	Dec 11	Dec 10	Dec 09
Working Capital	15	35	32
Fixed Assets	4	5	9
Current Assets	188	204	170

1st Translation Co. Ltd
Gresham House 24 Holborn Viaduct, London, EC1A 2BN
Tel: 020-7329 0032 **Fax:** 020-7329 0035
E-mail: welcome@1st-translation-co.com
Website: http://www.1st-translation-co.com
Directors: F. Glader (MD)
Immediate Holding Company: TRANSLATION ORGANISATION LIMITED
Registration no: 08140820 **VAT No.:** GB 524 0940 68
Date established: 2012 **Turnover:** Up to £250,000
No.of Employees: 1 - 10 **Product Groups:** 80

Date of Accounts	Mar 11	Mar 10	Mar 09
Working Capital	17	20	23
Fixed Assets	13	18	23
Current Assets	43	74	62

24 Hour Electrician
The Call Centre, London, W1W 7AB
Tel: 0701-743 4930
Website: http://www.london.electrician247.co.uk
Managers: P. Harrison (Mgr)
No.of Employees: 1 - 10 **Product Groups:** 38, 52, 84

3 I Group plc
16 Palace Street, London, SW1E 5JD
Tel: 020-7928 3131 **Fax:** 01223-420459
E-mail: info@3i.com
Website: http://www.3i.com
Directors: L. Garrett (Dir)
Immediate Holding Company: 3I GROUP PLC
Registration no: 01142830 **Date established:** 1973
Turnover: £250m - £500m **No.of Employees:** 101 - 250
Product Groups: 82

Date of Accounts	Mar 12	Mar 11	Mar 10
Sales Turnover	202m	261m	343m
Pre Tax Profit/Loss	20m	35m	72m
Working Capital	-74m	-24m	-7m
Fixed Assets	73m	64m	22m
Current Assets	151m	235m	294m
Current Liabilities	112m	148m	132m

4 Business Ltd
72 New Bond Street, London, W1S 1RR
Tel: 020-7514 9900 **Fax:** 020-7514 9910
E-mail: mc@4bs.com
Website: http://www.base4business.com
Directors: M. Clifford (Dir), M. Clifford (MD), R. John (Dir)
Ultimate Holding Company: 4 BUSINESS GROUP HOLDINGS LTD (SEYCHELLES)
Immediate Holding Company: 4 BUSINESS LIMITED
Registration no: 03782650 **Date established:** 1999
Turnover: £500,000 - £1m **No.of Employees:** 21 - 50
Product Groups: 44, 61

Date of Accounts	Dec 10	Dec 09	Dec 08
Sales Turnover	N/A	923	1m
Pre Tax Profit/Loss	N/A	18	-24
Working Capital	105	89	63
Fixed Assets	N/A	26	34
Current Assets	105	196	232
Current Liabilities	N/A	71	51

4Logistics Ltd
2nd Floor 145-157 St Johns Street, London, EC1V 4PY
Tel: 0845-8621162 **Fax:** 0845-8672685
E-mail: solutions@4logistics.com
Website: http://www.4logistics.com
Directors: R. Davies (Dir)
Registration no: 05898878 **Date established:** 2006
Turnover: £500,000 - £1m **No.of Employees:** 1 - 10 **Product Groups:** 84

Date of Accounts	Dec 07
Working Capital	14
Fixed Assets	2
Current Assets	93
Current Liabilities	79

A B A Consultants
7 Salmon Street, London, NW9 8PP
Tel: 020-8205 0989 **Fax:** 020-8205 2921
Directors: H. Abbei (Prop)
Immediate Holding Company: RELEVET LIMITED
Registration no: 01639042 **Date established:** 1982
No.of Employees: 1 - 10 **Product Groups:** 35, 39, 45

Date of Accounts	Jul 11	Jul 10	Jul 09
Working Capital	108	102	75
Fixed Assets	1	2	2
Current Assets	118	146	121

A B C Selfstore
Unit 3 Wandsworth Trading Estate 118-120 Garratt Lane, London, SW18 4DJ
Tel: 0800-015 0787
E-mail: wandsworth@abcselfstore.co.uk
Website: http://www.abcselfstore.co.uk
Directors: D. Milton (MD)
Date established: 2001 **Turnover:** **No.of Employees:** 1 - 10
Product Groups: 77

A B Fine Art Foundry Ltd
1 Fawe Street, London, E14 6PD
Tel: 020-7515 8052 **Fax:** 020-7987 7339
Website: http://www.abfineart.com
Directors: H. Abercrombie (Dir)
Immediate Holding Company: A B FINE ART FOUNDRY LIMITED
Registration no: 02762230 **Date established:** 1992
No.of Employees: 1 - 10 **Product Groups:** 35, 48, 89

Date of Accounts	Oct 11	Oct 10	Oct 09
Working Capital	836	799	804
Fixed Assets	165	151	162
Current Assets	1m	926	1m

A B Integration Ltd
South Bank Technopark 90 London Road, London, SE1 6LN
Tel: 020-7252 1490
E-mail: mail@abintegration.co.uk
Website: http://www.abintegration.co.uk
Directors: A. Thomson (Eng Serv)
Immediate Holding Company: A B INTEGRATION LIMITED
Registration no: 06628829 **Date established:** 2008
Turnover: Up to £250,000 **No.of Employees:** 1 - 10 **Product Groups:** 45, 84

Date of Accounts	Mar 11	Mar 10	Mar 09
Working Capital	8	30	13
Fixed Assets	2	1	N/A
Current Assets	36	52	21

A C Buckoke & Sons Ltd
11-25 Chatfield Road, London, SW11 3SE
Tel: 020-7223 3746 **Fax:** 020-7223 3746
E-mail: acbuckoke@yahoo.co.uk
Directors: P. Buckoke (MD), L. Buckoke (Fin)
Immediate Holding Company: A.C.BUCKOKE & SONS LIMITED
Registration no: 01047978 **Date established:** 1972
Turnover: Up to £250,000 **No.of Employees:** 1 - 10 **Product Groups:** 25, 26, 48, 49

Date of Accounts	Mar 12	Mar 11	Mar 10
Working Capital	76	75	66
Fixed Assets	8	10	3
Current Assets	99	82	72

A Elder Reed & Co. Ltd (t/a Reed Harris)
Riverside House Unit 5 Carnwath Road Industrial Estate 27 Carnwath Road, London, SW6 3HR
Tel: 020-7736 7511 **Fax:** 020-7736 2988
E-mail: martyn@reed-harris.co.uk
Website: http://www.reedharris.co.uk
Bank(s): National Westminster Bank Plc
Directors: J. Reed (MD), M. Legg (MD), N. Brimacombe (MD)
Immediate Holding Company: A. ELDER REED & CO. LIMITED
Registration no: 00226982 **Date established:** 1927
No.of Employees: 11 - 20 **Product Groups:** 33

Date of Accounts	Dec 07	Dec 06	Dec 05
Sales Turnover	N/A	N/A	2739
Pre Tax Profit/Loss	N/A	N/A	-49
Working Capital	183	172	124
Fixed Assets	85	76	103
Current Assets	628	586	465
Current Liabilities	445	414	341
Total Share Capital	228	216	216
ROCE% (Return on Capital Employed)			-21.8
ROT% (Return on Turnover)			-1.8

A F C O Products
122-124 High Road, London, NW10 2PN
Tel: 020-8930 1100 **Fax:** 020-8459 0320
Directors: R. Gupta (Dir)
Ultimate Holding Company: RNG INVESTMENTS LTD
Immediate Holding Company: NEW CITIZEN PUBLICATIONS LIMITED
Registration no: 01668033 **VAT No.:** GB 226 6506 66
Date established: 1982 **Turnover:** £500,000 - £1m
No.of Employees: 1 - 10 **Product Groups:** 32, 63

Date of Accounts	Jun 11	Jun 10	Jun 09
Working Capital	5	-1	5
Fixed Assets	2	3	N/A
Current Assets	36	36	40

A & G Metal Works
11a Powell Road, London, E5 8DJ
Tel: 020-8985 9625
Directors: S. Andreas (Prop)
Date established: 1973 **No.of Employees:** 1 - 10 **Product Groups:** 35

A Holt & Sons Ltd
115 Whitecross Street, London, EC1Y 8JQ
Tel: 020-7256 2222 **Fax:** 020-7638 3578
E-mail: office@aholt.co.uk
Website: http://www.aholt.co.uk
Directors: S. Holt (Prop)
Immediate Holding Company: A. HOLT & SONS LIMITED
Registration no: 00175385 **Date established:** 2021
Turnover: £500,000 - £1m **No.of Employees:** 1 - 10 **Product Groups:** 23, 24, 66

Date of Accounts	Dec 11	Dec 10	Dec 09
Working Capital	418	295	273
Fixed Assets	391	397	416
Current Assets	713	803	504

A & J Infrastructure Services Ltd
Unit 3 Greenshield Industrial Estate Bradfield Road, London, E16 2AU
Tel: 020-7366 6519 **Fax:** 020-7476 3638
E-mail: info@aje-ltd.com
Website: http://www.aje-ltd.com
Directors: J. Short (MD), T. Baldry (Dir)
Managers: K. Bellotti
Immediate Holding Company: FASTRACK XPRESS LTD
Date established: 2008 **No.of Employees:** 21 - 50 **Product Groups:** 36, 38, 40, 84

A & K Tractor Sales
5 Vines Avenue, London, N3 2QD
Tel: 020-8349 1757 **Fax:** 020-8343 1218
E-mail: aktractors@msn.com
Directors: A. Gee (Prop)
No.of Employees: 1 - 10 **Product Groups:** 48

A N S Export Ltd
15 Brockley Rise, London, SE23 1JG
Tel: 020-8291 4900 **Fax:** 020-8291 1950
E-mail: sales@ansexport.com
Website: http://www.tradezone.ltd.uk
Directors: M. Dave (Fin)
Immediate Holding Company: A.N.S. EXPORT LIMITED
Registration no: 02367253 **Date established:** 1989
Turnover: £500,000 - £1m **No.of Employees:** 1 - 10 **Product Groups:** 65, 87

Date of Accounts	Mar 11	Mar 09	Mar 08
Sales Turnover	N/A	N/A	80
Pre Tax Profit/Loss	N/A	N/A	-2
Working Capital	-3	-17	-9
Current Assets	2	11	14

A Nelson & Co. (Head Office)
Nelsons House 83 Wimbledon Park Side, London, SW19 5LP
Tel: 020-8780 4200 **Fax:** 020-8780 5871
E-mail: enquiries@nelsons.net
Website: http://www.nelsonsnaturalworld.com
Bank(s): Lloyds TSB Bank plc

see next page

A Nelson & Co. (Head Office) - Cont'd

Directors: M. Dunne (Fin), R. Wilson (Ch), C. Sundberg-cox (Mkt Research)
Ultimate Holding Company: NELSON & RUSSELL HOLDINGS LIMITED
Immediate Holding Company: A NELSON & CO LIMITED
Registration no: 00249879 **VAT No.:** GB 318 5994 19
Date established: 1930 **Turnover:** £20m - £50m
No.of Employees: 101 - 250 **Product Groups:** 31, 63

Date of Accounts	Dec 11	Dec 10	Dec 09
Sales Turnover	46m	40m	37m
Pre Tax Profit/Loss	12m	12m	10m
Working Capital	9m	11m	4m
Fixed Assets	6m	6m	6m
Current Assets	14m	16m	9m
Current Liabilities	4m	3m	3m

A P G Atlantic Paper Ltd

7 Earls Court Square, London, SW5 9BY
Tel: 020-7373 3132 **Fax:** 020-7373 3880
E-mail: sales@wastepaper.com
Website: http://www.waste-paper.co.uk
Directors: B. Beckett Terrell (Fin), P. Serfaty (MD)
Ultimate Holding Company: WASTE PAPER HOLDINGS LTD
Immediate Holding Company: APG ATLANTIC PAPER LTD
Registration no: 03531171 **VAT No.:** GB 239 2017 76
Date established: 1998 **Turnover:** Up to £250,000
No.of Employees: 1 - 10 **Product Groups:** 14, 61, 66, 80

Date of Accounts	Apr 11	Apr 10	Apr 09
Sales Turnover	6	1m	3m
Pre Tax Profit/Loss	-6	-22	138
Working Capital	170	174	1m
Fixed Assets	N/A	2	2
Current Assets	177	906	2m
Current Liabilities	7	718	310

A P T Controls Ltd

Unit 1 Bow Enterprise Park, London, E3 3QY
Tel: 020-7538 1871 **Fax:** 020-7538 2693
E-mail: dholden@westminster.gov.uk
Website: http://www.aptcontrols.co.uk
Directors: A. Samson (MD)
Managers: D. Demarquet, D. Holden (Site Co-ord), S. Story (I.T. Exec)
Immediate Holding Company: APT CONTROLS LIMITED
Registration no: 02754698 **Date established:** 1992
Turnover: Up to £250,000 **No.of Employees:** 1 - 10 **Product Groups:** 39

Date of Accounts	Dec 11	Dec 10	Dec 09
Sales Turnover	25m	26m	27m
Pre Tax Profit/Loss	2m	3m	3m
Working Capital	6m	6m	5m
Fixed Assets	9m	9m	9m
Current Assets	14m	15m	15m
Current Liabilities	4m	4m	5m

A P T N

The Interchange Oval Road, London, NW1 7DZ
Tel: 020-7482 7400 **Fax:** 020-7413 8302
E-mail: ncampbell@ap.org
Website: http://www.ap.org
Directors: D. Wilkinson (Fin), D. Veerasingham (Sales)
Managers: S. Dixon (Personnel), J. Howe, N. Campbell
Ultimate Holding Company: ASSOCIATED PRESS (THE) (USA)
Immediate Holding Company: ASSOCIATED PRESS TELEVISION NEWS LIMITED
Registration no: 03589918 **Date established:** 1998
Turnover: £500m - £1,000m **No.of Employees:** 251 - 500
Product Groups: 67, 79, 81, 89

Date of Accounts	Dec 06
Sales Turnover	108990
Pre Tax Profit/Loss	27320
Working Capital	52650
Fixed Assets	14020
Current Assets	91490
Current Liabilities	38840
ROCE% (Return on Capital Employed)	41.0

A P T Transtelex Ltd

Unit F The Mews 6 Putney Common, London, SW15 1HL
Tel: 020-8246 4050 **Fax:** 020-8246 4059
E-mail: marketing@aptlimited.co.uk
Website: http://www.aptlimited.gov.uk
Directors: C. Jamieson (MD)
Ultimate Holding Company: APT TRANSLATIONS LTD
Immediate Holding Company: APT TRANSTELEX LTD
Registration no: 01174742 **Date established:** 1974
No.of Employees: 21 - 50 **Product Groups:** 28, 80

Date of Accounts	Dec 11	Dec 10	Dec 09
Working Capital	358	300	189
Fixed Assets	339	340	349
Current Assets	979	853	529

A R M Direct

1 Bentinck Mews, London, W1U 2AF
Tel: 020-7317 3230 **Fax:** 020-7224 3041
E-mail: digby@arm-direct.co.uk
Website: http://www.arm-direct.co.uk
Bank(s): National Westminster Bank Plc
Directors: D. Orsmond (Prop), A. Luggeri (Co Sec)
Immediate Holding Company: A R M DIRECT LIMITED
Registration no: 01843038 **Date established:** 1984 **Turnover:** £5m - £10m
No.of Employees: 11 - 20 **Product Groups:** 80, 81

Date of Accounts	Mar 12	Mar 11	Mar 10
Working Capital	837	655	549
Fixed Assets	1	2	7
Current Assets	3m	2m	2m

A S D Metal Services plc

Thames Wharf Dock Road, London, E16 1AF
Tel: 020-7474 7854 **Fax:** 020-7476 0239
E-mail: enquiries@asdmetalservices.co.uk
Website: http://www.asdmetalservices.co.uk
Bank(s): National Westminster Bank Plc
Managers: J. Viggiano (Chief Mgr), J. Philpot
Ultimate Holding Company: ASD GROUP LTD
Immediate Holding Company: ASD METAL SERVICES LIMITED
Registration no: 02680562 **Date established:** 1992 **Turnover:** £2m - £5m
No.of Employees: 21 - 50 **Product Groups:** 48, 66, 77

A T On Line Computing Ltd

65 Clerkenwell Road, London, EC1R 5BL
Tel: 020-7454 1254 **Fax:** 020-7454 1253
E-mail: paulb@onlinecomputing.co.uk
Website: http://www.onlinecomputing.co.uk
Directors: O. Byrne (Fin), P. Bryne (Dir)
Immediate Holding Company: AT ON LINE COMPUTING LIMITED
Registration no: 02855399 **Date established:** 1993 **Turnover:** £1m - £2m
No.of Employees: 21 - 50 **Product Groups:** 44

Date of Accounts	Oct 11	Oct 10	Oct 09
Sales Turnover	N/A	2m	2m
Pre Tax Profit/Loss	N/A	-29	126
Working Capital	305	286	324
Fixed Assets	110	51	42
Current Assets	648	791	1m
Current Liabilities	N/A	402	470

Aashish Motors

374 High Road, London, N17 9HY
Tel: 020-8808 2407 **Fax:** 020-8885 3127
Directors: P. Chikhlia (Prop)
VAT No.: GB 375 6869 90 **Turnover:** £250,000 - £500,000
No.of Employees: 1 - 10 **Product Groups:** 27, 28, 29, 35, 36, 39, 40, 42, 45, 49, 61, 68

Abacus Air Conditioning Ltd

27 Cambridge Park Wanstead, London, E11 2PU
Tel: 0800-848 8035 **Fax:** 0207-197 8171
E-mail: nick@abacusairconditioning.co.uk
Website: http://www.abacusairconditioning.co.uk
Managers: K. Knight (Mktg Serv Mgr)
Registration no: 06507686 **Date established:** 1986
No.of Employees: 101 - 250 **Product Groups:** 40

Abacus Printing Company Ltd

Gloucester House 34-38 Gloucester Way, London, EC1R 0BN
Tel: 020-7278 4637 **Fax:** 020-7278 8535
E-mail: sales@abacusprinting.com
Website: http://www.abacusprinting.com
Bank(s): National Westminster Bank Plc
Directors: S. Raja (MD), S. Raja (Co Sec), J. Raja (Fin)
Immediate Holding Company: ABACUS PRINTING COMPANY LIMITED
Registration no: 00958331 **VAT No.:** GB 447 2660 40
Date established: 1969 **Turnover:** £1m - £2m **No.of Employees:** 21 - 50
Product Groups: 28

Date of Accounts	Mar 11	Mar 10	Mar 09
Working Capital	839	998	1m
Fixed Assets	412	435	463
Current Assets	1m	1m	1m

Abbey Current Accounts (Head Office)

2-3 Triton Square, London, NW1 3AN
Tel: 0800-5875045 **Fax:** 020-7612 4010
Website: http://www.abbey.com
Directors: A. Horto-Osorio (Ch)
Immediate Holding Company: Santander UK plc
Registration no: 02294747 **VAT No.:** GB 466 2647 24
Date established: 1996 **Turnover:** Over £1,000m **No.of Employees:** 1 - 10
Product Groups: 82

Abbott Mead Vickers Group Ltd

151 Marylebone Road, London, NW1 5QE
Tel: 020-7616 3500 **Fax:** 020-7616 3600
E-mail: pearmani@amvbbdo.com
Website: http://www.amvbbdo.com
Bank(s): Lloyds TSB Bank plc
Directors: P. Smith (Tech Serv), V. Allard (Gen Sec), K. Wilkins (Pers), C. Fleming (Fin)
Managers: I. Pearman, M. Mitchell
Ultimate Holding Company: OMNICOM GROUP INC (USA)
Immediate Holding Company: ABBOTT MEAD VICKERS GROUP LIMITED
Registration no: 01336553 **Date established:** 1977
Turnover: £20m - £50m **No.of Employees:** 251 - 500 **Product Groups:** 81

Date of Accounts	Dec 11	Dec 10	Dec 09
Pre Tax Profit/Loss	-2m	3m	89m
Working Capital	4m	6m	3m
Fixed Assets	164m	164m	164m
Current Assets	67m	63m	75m
Current Liabilities	1m	1m	956

Abee Signs Ltd

Unit 15c Winchester Buildings Rivermead Road Stonehill Business Park, London, N18 3QW
Tel: 020-8345 5122 **Fax:** 020-8181 6113
E-mail: sales@abeesigns.co.uk
Website: http://www.abeesigns.co.uk
Directors: A. Bhatt (MD)
Immediate Holding Company: ABEE SIGNS (LONDON) LTD
Registration no: 02247135 **Turnover:** Up to £250,000
No.of Employees: 1 - 10 **Product Groups:** 27, 28, 49

Date of Accounts	Apr 08	Apr 07	Apr 06
Working Capital	67	92	89
Fixed Assets	35	11	13
Current Assets	131	156	129
Current Liabilities	64	64	41
Total Share Capital	1	1	1

Aberdeen Asset Management

Bowbells 1 Bread Street, London, EC4M 9HH
Tel: 020-7463 6000 **Fax:** 020-7463 6001
E-mail: officeservices@aberdeen-asset.com
Website: http://www.aberdeen-asset.co.uk
Directors: L. Quinn (Dir)
Managers: P. Sharp (), P. Sharp
Ultimate Holding Company: ABERDEEN ASSET MANAGEMENT PLC
Immediate Holding Company: ABERDEEN ASSET MANAGEMENT LIFE AND PENSIONS LIMITED
Registration no: 03526143 **Date established:** 1998 **Turnover:** £2m - £5m
No.of Employees: 501 - 1000 **Product Groups:** 82

Date of Accounts	Dec 04	Sep 09	Sep 08
Pre Tax Profit/Loss	11m	2m	4m
Fixed Assets	4018m	10m	15m
Current Assets	21m	1400m	1138m
Current Liabilities	40m	671	325

Abis Systems Limited

Albert Buildings 49 Queen Victoria Street, London, EC4N 4SA
Tel: 020-7489 8123 **Fax:** 020-7489 8117
E-mail: admin@abis-systems.com
Website: http://www.abis-systems.com
Directors: D. King (MD)
Registration no: 01548330 **Date established:** 2008
No.of Employees: 1 - 10 **Product Groups:** 33, 35, 36, 37, 38, 39, 40, 41, 42, 46, 47, 49, 52, 64, 67, 83, 84

Able Internet Payroll Ltd

Unit 101, China House 395 Edgware Road, London, NW2 6LN
Tel: 020-8438 9791 **Fax:** 0871-9896099
E-mail: sally.wells@ableinternetpayroll.com
Website: http://www.ableinternetpayroll.com
Managers: S. Wells (Mktg Serv Mgr)
Registration no: 04773140 **Date established:** 1999
No.of Employees: 21 - 50 **Product Groups:** 44

Date of Accounts	May 08	May 07	May 06
Working Capital	-29	-33	-11
Current Assets	24	14	21
Current Liabilities	53	46	32
Total Share Capital	1	1	1

Abrahamson & Associates

10 North End Road, London, NW11 7PH
Tel: 020-8458 1100 **Fax:** 020-8458 1588
E-mail: postoffice@abrahamsons.co.uk
Website: http://www.abrahamsons.co.uk
Directors: B. Abrahamson (Head)
Immediate Holding Company: UNIONGATE INVESTMENTS (UK) LIMITED
Registration no: 05520523 **Date established:** 2005
Turnover: Up to £250,000 **No.of Employees:** 1 - 10 **Product Groups:** 80

Date of Accounts	Jul 10	Jul 09	Jul 08
Sales Turnover	65	99	47
Pre Tax Profit/Loss	3	30	6
Working Capital	24	15	8
Fixed Assets	16	21	16
Current Assets	31	26	13

Abrasive Technology Ltd

Roxby Place Fulham, London, SW6 1RT
Tel: 020-7471 0200 **Fax:** 020-7471 0202
E-mail: customerservices@abrasive-tech.com
Website: http://www.abrasive-tech.com
Bank(s): Bank of Wales, Cardiff
Directors: P. Gurney (Fin), K. Hall (Site), S. Swords (MD)
Managers: P. Brearey (I.T. Exec)
Immediate Holding Company: Abrasive Technology Inc (USA)
Registration no: 02874855 **VAT No.:** GB 628 4782 08
Turnover: £2m - £5m **No.of Employees:** 51 - 100 **Product Groups:** 36, 45, 47

ABS Energy Research

8 Quarry Road, London, SW18 2QJ
Tel: 020-8871 2752 **Fax:** 020-8328 7117
E-mail: melanykrangle@absenergyresearch.com
Website: http://www.absenergyresearch.com
VAT No.: GB 572 5135 45 **No.of Employees:** 1 - 10 **Product Groups:** 38, 51, 54, 80, 81, 85

Abucon Marketing Consultants Ltd

33 Jamestown Way, London, E14 2DE
Tel: 020-7834 1066
E-mail: info@abucon.co.uk
Website: http://www.abucon.co.uk
Bank(s): Lloyds TSB Bank plc
Directors: L. Jones (MD)
Immediate Holding Company: ABUCON LIMITED
Registration no: 03655616 **Date established:** 1998
Turnover: £250,000 - £500,000 **No.of Employees:** 11 - 20
Product Groups: 80, 81, 82, 86

Date of Accounts	Apr 08	Apr 07	Apr 06
Working Capital	-16	5	20
Fixed Assets	17	12	16
Current Assets	50	57	73
Current Liabilities	66	52	52

Abwood Contract Support Ltd

1 Onega Gate, London, SE16 7PF
Tel: 020-7740 2323 **Fax:** 020-7740 2340
E-mail: marcus@abwood.co.uk
Website: http://www.abwood.co.uk
Directors: M. Earle (MD)
Ultimate Holding Company: ABWOOD GROUP LIMITED
Immediate Holding Company: ABWOOD MARINE LIMITED
Registration no: 03239889 **Date established:** 1996
No.of Employees: 1 - 10 **Product Groups:** 35, 36, 39

Date of Accounts	Mar 09	Mar 08	Mar 07
Working Capital	222	36	-15
Fixed Assets	55	29	33
Current Assets	562	270	142

Academy

410 Coldharbour Lane Brixton, London, SW9 8LF
Tel: 020-7274 2602 **Fax:** 020-7733 8924
E-mail: academyphotos@hotmail.com
Website: http://www.academyimaging.com
Directors: C. Pereira (Dir), R. Pereira (Fin)
Immediate Holding Company: ACADEMY PHOTOS LIMITED
Registration no: 04536315 **Date established:** 2002
Turnover: Up to £250,000 **No.of Employees:** 1 - 10 **Product Groups:** 28, 65, 86

Date of Accounts	Dec 11	Dec 10	Dec 09
Working Capital	-15	-17	-11
Fixed Assets	8	9	12
Current Assets	5	4	3

Academy Class Ltd

99 Waterloo Road, London, SE1 8UL
Tel: 0800-043 8889 **Fax:** 0870-330 5722
E-mail: info@academyclass.com
Website: http://www.academyclass.com
Directors: M. Young (MD)
Immediate Holding Company: ACADEMY CLASS LIMITED
Registration no: 05878400 **Date established:** 2006
No.of Employees: 11 - 20 **Product Groups:** 44, 86

Date of Accounts	Jul 11	Jul 10	Jul 09
Working Capital	21	-32	-35
Fixed Assets	46	41	45
Current Assets	415	302	261

Access Logistics UK Ltd

Unit 28 Leyton Business Centre, London, E10 7BT
Tel: 020-8539 0707 **Fax:** 020-8539 0706
E-mail: info@accesslogistics.co.uk
Website: http://www.accesslogistics.co.uk

Directors: R. Badul (MD)
Immediate Holding Company: ACCESS LOGISTICS (UK) LIMITED
Registration no: 04308141 **Date established:** 2001 **Turnover:** £1m - £2m
No.of Employees: 1 - 10 **Product Groups:** 76

Date of Accounts	Oct 11	Oct 10	Oct 09
Working Capital	-16	-23	-21
Fixed Assets	3	4	5
Current Assets	2	3	14

Access Plant Hire & Sales Ltd

9 Orient Industrial Park Simonds Road Leyton, London, E10 7DE
Tel: 020-8518 7400 **Fax:** 020-8503 0500
E-mail: hire@accessplant.fsnet.co.uk
Website: http://www.accessplant.co.uk
Directors: C. Wright (Fin)
Managers: T. Fox (Mgr)
Ultimate Holding Company: KENRICH GROUP HOLDINGS P.L.C.
Immediate Holding Company: ACCESS PLANT (HIRE & SALES) LIMITED
Registration no: 01613269 **Date established:** 1982
Turnover: £250,000 - £500,000 **No.of Employees:** 1 - 10
Product Groups: 37, 40, 83

Date of Accounts	Jan 11	Jan 10	Jan 09
Sales Turnover	259	240	274
Pre Tax Profit/Loss	-103	-121	-161
Working Capital	60	156	283
Fixed Assets	140	148	159
Current Assets	111	197	329
Current Liabilities	30	33	33

Accor Services

50 Vauxhall Bridge Road, London, SW1V 2RS
Tel: 020-7834 6666 **Fax:** 020-7931 0700
E-mail: webmaster@accor-services.com
Website: http://www.accor-services.com
Bank(s): National Westminster Bank Plc
Directors: L. Fourier (MD), D. Hardman (Sales), L. Delmas (MD)
Managers: K. Brooks (Sales Prom Mgr)
Ultimate Holding Company: ACCOR SA (FRANCE)
Immediate Holding Company: CHILDCARE VOUCHERS LIMITED
Registration no: 00540144 **VAT No.:** GB 238 4227 61
Date established: 1989 **Turnover:** £1m - £2m **No.of Employees:** 51 - 100
Product Groups: 80

Date of Accounts	Dec 10	Dec 09	Dec 08
Sales Turnover	17m	16m	15m
Pre Tax Profit/Loss	11m	11m	10m
Working Capital	15m	15m	12m
Fixed Assets	N/A	N/A	2
Current Assets	84m	74m	60m
Current Liabilities	65m	54m	45m

Accuracast Ltd

64 Elmshurst Crescent, London, N2 0LP
Tel: 0800-019 6813
E-mail: b.simon@accuracast.com
Website: http://www.accuracast.com
Directors: F. Divecha (Fin), J. Bergerou (MD)
Immediate Holding Company: ACCURACAST LIMITED
Registration no: 05050219 **Date established:** 2004
Turnover: Up to £250,000 **No.of Employees:** 1 - 10 **Product Groups:** 44

Date of Accounts	Jan 12	Jan 11	Feb 10
Sales Turnover	N/A	N/A	73
Working Capital	66	36	28
Fixed Assets	2	1	N/A
Current Assets	180	71	50

Accurist Watches

Asher House Blackburn Road, London, NW6 1AW
Tel: 020-7447 3900 **Fax:** 020-7447 3946
E-mail: sales@accurist.co.uk
Website: http://www.accurist.co.uk
Directors: A. Loftus (Dir), H. Hickson (Co Sec)
Managers: M. Hickson (Comptroller), N. Humphries (Tech Serv Mgr), P. Halliday
Immediate Holding Company: ACCURIST WATCHES LIMITED
Registration no: 00419400 **Date established:** 1946
Turnover: £10m - £20m **No.of Employees:** 21 - 50 **Product Groups:** 49

Date of Accounts	Mar 11	Mar 10	Mar 09
Sales Turnover	12m	10m	N/A
Pre Tax Profit/Loss	93	-881	-883
Working Capital	4m	5m	7m
Fixed Assets	75	122	2m
Current Assets	5m	6m	8m
Current Liabilities	467	531	352

Ace European Group

The Ace Building Leadenhall Street, London, EC3A 3BP
Tel: 0871-9719613 **Fax:** 020-7173 7800
E-mail: info@ace-ina.com
Website: http://www.aceeurope.com
Directors: A. Kendrick (Ch), A. Kendrick (MD), M. Russell (Gen Sec), P. Curtis (Dir), G. Schmalzriedt (Ch)
Immediate Holding Company: ACE EUROPEAN GROUP LIMITED
Registration no: 01112892 **Date established:** 1973
Turnover: Over £1,000m **No.of Employees:** 501 - 1000
Product Groups: 82

Date of Accounts	Dec 09	Dec 08	Dec 07
Pre Tax Profit/Loss	262m	3m	74m
Fixed Assets	2739m	2346m	1938m
Current Assets	923m	1048m	991m
Current Liabilities	779m	639m	520m

Ace Records Ltd

42-50 Steele Road, London, NW10 7AS
Tel: 020-8453 1311 **Fax:** 020-8961 8725
E-mail: sales@acerecords.co.uk
Website: http://www.acerecords.co.uk
Directors: R. Armstrong (Dir)
Ultimate Holding Company: ACE RECORDS LIMITED
Immediate Holding Company: ACE RECORDS LIMITED
Registration no: 01568303 **Date established:** 1981 **Turnover:** £2m - £5m
No.of Employees: 11 - 20 **Product Groups:** 28, 89

Date of Accounts	Mar 11	Mar 10	Mar 09
Sales Turnover	N/A	3m	N/A
Pre Tax Profit/Loss	N/A	181	N/A
Working Capital	-214	-188	-150
Fixed Assets	591	625	682
Current Assets	1m	1m	1m
Current Liabilities	N/A	89	N/A

Ace Systems Installations Ltd

103 Elsenham Street, London, SW18 5NY
Tel: 020-8874 8966 **Fax:** 020-8265 6050
E-mail: sales@acesystems.co.uk
Website: http://www.fire-alarms.uk.com
Directors: T. Evans (MD)
Immediate Holding Company: ALARMS, CONTROLS & ELECTRONIC SYSTEMS INSTALLATIONS LIMITED
Registration no: 01600772 **Date established:** 1981
No.of Employees: 1 - 10 **Product Groups:** 40, 52, 84

Date of Accounts	Dec 10	Dec 09	Dec 08
Working Capital	-51	-45	-46
Fixed Assets	15	18	10
Current Assets	39	55	56

Acquisitions Victorian Edwardian Fireplaces

24-26 Holmes Road, London, NW5 3AB
Tel: 020-7482 2949 **Fax:** 020-7267 4361
E-mail: sales@acquisitions.co.uk
Website: http://www.acquisitions.co.uk
Bank(s): Barclays, Strand, London, WC2R 0NX
Directors: J. Kennedy (MD)
Managers: D. Anthony (Sales Prom Mgr)
Ultimate Holding Company: KAK HOLDINGS LIMITED
Immediate Holding Company: ACQUISITIONS (FIREPLACES) LIMITED
Registration no: 01413462 **VAT No.:** GB 333 2702 89
Date established: 1979 **Turnover:** £2m - £5m **No.of Employees:** 11 - 20
Product Groups: 25, 33, 35, 49

Date of Accounts	May 11	May 10	May 09
Working Capital	257	172	431
Fixed Assets	349	352	283
Current Assets	475	632	892

Acre Lifts Ltd

2 Ladywell Road, London, SE13 7UW
Tel: 020-8690 6000 **Fax:** 020-8690 3000
E-mail: mail@acrelifts.com
Website: http://www.acrelifts.com
Directors: D. Wheeler (Fin), M. Bishop (Dir)
Managers: M. Vick
Immediate Holding Company: ACRE LIFTS LIMITED
Registration no: 02707590 **Date established:** 1992 **Turnover:** £5m - £10m
No.of Employees: 11 - 20 **Product Groups:** 35, 39, 45

Date of Accounts	Mar 12	Mar 11	Mar 10
Sales Turnover	6m	7m	6m
Pre Tax Profit/Loss	3	-248	121
Working Capital	-125	-150	96
Fixed Assets	7	10	13
Current Assets	1m	1m	2m
Current Liabilities	699	969	676

Action Shutters Ltd

6 The Commonwealth Buildings Woolwich Church Street, London, SE18 5NS
Tel: 020-8855 7700 **Fax:** 020-8855 7711
E-mail: sales@actionshutters.com
Website: http://www.actionshutters.com
Directors: D. Martin (MD), D. Martin (MD), L. Martin (Fin)
Immediate Holding Company: ACTION SHUTTERS LIMITED
Registration no: 02865323 **Date established:** 1993
Turnover: £500,000 - £1m **No.of Employees:** 11 - 20
Product Groups: 25, 34, 35, 36, 48, 66

Date of Accounts	Dec 11	Dec 10	Dec 09
Working Capital	-49	-33	-30
Fixed Assets	221	231	225
Current Assets	105	125	110

Active Lighting Ltd

14a St. Cross Street, London, EC1N 8XA
Tel: 020-7025 2010
Website: http://www.activelifeltd.co.uk
Directors: C. Clayton (Dir)
Registration no: 03080185 **Date established:** 1995
No.of Employees: 1 - 10 **Product Groups:** 37, 67

Acumedic Centre Ltd

101-105 Camden High Street, London, NW1 7JN
Tel: 020-7388 5783 **Fax:** 020-7387 5766
E-mail: courses@acumedic.com
Website: http://www.acumedic.com
Bank(s): National Westminster Bank Plc
Directors: D. Mei (Dir), M. Mei (MD)
Ultimate Holding Company: MEI GROUP LIMITED
Immediate Holding Company: ACUMEDIC LIMITED
Registration no: 01893173 **Date established:** 1985 **Turnover:** £2m - £5m
No.of Employees: 21 - 50 **Product Groups:** 28, 38

Date of Accounts	Mar 12	Mar 11	Mar 10
Working Capital	400	151	180
Fixed Assets	836	890	935
Current Assets	571	354	330

Acxiom Ltd

Dominican Court 17 Hatfields, London, SE1 8DJ
Tel: 020-7526 5100 **Fax:** 020-8213 5588
Website: http://www.acxiom.com
Bank(s): Barclays
Directors: R. Stanhope (Fin)
Managers: M. Mercer, B. Doyle (Chief Mgr), Bigwood, P. Kelly (Mktg Serv Mgr), B. Buttler (I.T. Exec)
Ultimate Holding Company: ACXIOM CORP. INC. (USA)
Immediate Holding Company: ACXIOM LIMITED
Registration no: 01182318 **Date established:** 1974
Turnover: £50m - £75m **No.of Employees:** 101 - 250
Product Groups: 44, 80, 81

Date of Accounts	Mar 11	Mar 10	Mar 09
Sales Turnover	50m	50m	55m
Pre Tax Profit/Loss	-2m	-2m	4m
Working Capital	-65	4m	16m
Fixed Assets	7m	4m	5m
Current Assets	21m	24m	35m
Current Liabilities	9m	9m	7m

Adam & Co plc

22 King Street, London, SW1Y 6QY
Tel: 020-7839 4615 **Fax:** 020-7839 5994
E-mail: london@adambank.com
Website: http://www.adambank.com
Bank(s): The Royal Bank of Scotland
Directors: R. Donaldson (Dir)
Ultimate Holding Company: THE ROYAL BANK OF SCOTLAND GROUP PUBLIC LIMITED COMPANY
Immediate Holding Company: CTL NOMINEES LIMITED
Registration no: 01916254 **Date established:** 1985
Turnover: Over £1,000m **No.of Employees:** 21 - 50 **Product Groups:** 80, 82

Jon Adam

Second Floor 184-192 Drummond Street, London, NW1 3HP
Tel: 020-7387 5384 **Fax:** 020-7383 4065
E-mail: reception@jonadam.co.uk
Website: http://www.jonadam.co.uk
Directors: R. Knight (Fin)
Immediate Holding Company: NATIONAL UNION OF STUDENTS (UNITED KINGDOM)
Registration no: 01061725 **Date established:** 2012
No.of Employees: 51 - 100 **Product Groups:** 24

Adamson Associates International Ltd

6th Floor 1 Canada Square, London, E14 5AB
Tel: 020-7418 2068 **Fax:** 020-7418 2517
E-mail: info@adamson-associates.com
Website: http://www.adamson-associates.com
Directors: M. Royston (Dir)
Ultimate Holding Company: SONGBIRD ESTATES PLC.
Immediate Holding Company: ADAMSON ASSOCIATES (INTERNATIONAL) LIMITED
Registration no: 03189540 **Date established:** 1996
No.of Employees: 21 - 50 **Product Groups:** 37, 65, 89

Date of Accounts	Mar 11	Mar 10	Mar 09
Sales Turnover	16m	17m	1m
Pre Tax Profit/Loss	808	582	-13
Working Capital	1m	531	60
Fixed Assets	57	36	46
Current Assets	2m	8m	554
Current Liabilities	1m	1m	416

Adamson & Partners Ltd

20 Abchurch Lane, London, EC4N 7BB
Tel: 020-7337 9890 **Fax:** 020-7623 7870
E-mail: stuart.adamson@adamsons.com
Website: http://www.adamsons.com
Bank(s): National Westminster Bank Plc
Directors: S. Adamson (MD), T. Morgan (Fin)
Immediate Holding Company: ADAMSON AND PARTNERS LIMITED
Registration no: 00968220 **VAT No.:** GB 418 0668 49
Date established: 1969 **Turnover:** £1m - £2m **No.of Employees:** 21 - 50
Product Groups: 80, 86

Date of Accounts	Dec 11	Dec 10	Dec 09
Working Capital	243	185	101
Fixed Assets	71	75	108
Current Assets	716	751	720

Adare International Ltd

Vantage House 1 Weir Road, London, SW19 8UX
Tel: 020-8946 7537 **Fax:** 020-8947 2740
Website: http://www.adare.com
Directors: A. Haines (I.T. Dir)
Managers: D. Minihane
Ultimate Holding Company: MAVISBANK LIMITED
Immediate Holding Company: ADARE INTERNATIONAL LIMITED
Registration no: 01610897 **Date established:** 1982 **Turnover:** £2m - £5m
No.of Employees: 11 - 20 **Product Groups:** 81

Date of Accounts	Oct 11	Oct 10	Oct 09
Sales Turnover	75m	63m	70m
Pre Tax Profit/Loss	2m	1m	2m
Working Capital	14m	12m	11m
Fixed Assets	2m	2m	1m
Current Assets	36m	35m	29m
Current Liabilities	7m	6m	4m

Addison Corporate Marketing

2 Cathedral Street, London, SE1 9DE
Tel: 020-7403 7444 **Fax:** 020-7403 1243
E-mail: info@addison.co.uk
Website: http://www.addison.co.uk
Bank(s): HSBC, London
Directors: P. Tomlinson (Fin), T. Robinson (Dir)
Ultimate Holding Company: WPP PLC (JERSEY)
Immediate Holding Company: ADDISON INVESTMENTS LIMITED
Registration no: 02819725 **Date established:** 1993 **Turnover:** £5m - £10m
No.of Employees: 21 - 50 **Product Groups:** 28

Date of Accounts	Dec 11	Dec 10	Dec 09
Pre Tax Profit/Loss	-2	-2	7
Working Capital	3m	3m	3m
Current Assets	3m	3m	3m
Current Liabilities	4	2	N/A

Addleshaw Goddard

Milton Gate 60 Chiswell Street, London, EC1Y 4AG
Tel: 020-7606 8855 **Fax:** 020-7606 4390
Website: http://www.addleshawgoddard.com
Bank(s): National Westminster, London
Directors: M. Jones (MD), M. Gaskin (Fin)
Managers: H. Ford (Personnel)
Immediate Holding Company: ADDLESHAW GODDARD LLP
Registration no: OC318149 **VAT No.:** GB 243 4682 60
Date established: 2006 **Turnover:** £125m - £250m
No.of Employees: 1001 - 1500 **Product Groups:** 80

Date of Accounts	Apr 11	Apr 10	Apr 09
Sales Turnover	161m	167m	173m
Pre Tax Profit/Loss	44m	55m	58m
Working Capital	54m	49m	44m
Fixed Assets	44m	48m	36m
Current Assets	83m	80m	73m
Current Liabilities	19m	18m	17m

Adel Rootstein

9 Beaumont Avenue, London, W14 9LP
Tel: 020-7381 1447 **Fax:** 020-7381 3263
E-mail: sales@adelrootstein.co.uk
Website: http://www.rootstein.com
Bank(s): Barclays
Directors: R. Conde (Co Sec)
Ultimate Holding Company: YOSHICHU LTD (JAPAN)
Immediate Holding Company: ADEL ROOTSTEIN LIMITED
Registration no: 00925820 **Date established:** 1968 **Turnover:** £2m - £5m
No.of Employees: 51 - 100 **Product Groups:** 49

see next page

Adel Rootstein - Cont'd

Date of Accounts	Mar 12	Mar 11	Mar 10
Sales Turnover	2m	2m	2m
Pre Tax Profit/Loss	197	458	331
Working Capital	1m	1m	727
Fixed Assets	105	101	82
Current Assets	2m	2m	2m
Current Liabilities	296	255	N/A

Adserve Computing Ltd

Blue Fin Building 110 Southwark Street, London, SE1 0TA
Tel: 020-7255 7400 **Fax:** 020-7255 7373
E-mail: sales@adserve.co.uk
Website: http://www.adserve.co.uk
Directors: C. Harris-Watts (Dir)
Ultimate Holding Company: DONOVAN DATA SYSTEMS INC. (USA)
Immediate Holding Company: ADSERVE COMPUTING LIMITED
Registration no: 01027404 **Date established:** 1971
Turnover: Up to £250,000 **No.of Employees:** 21 - 50 **Product Groups:** 44

Advanced Broadcast Services Ltd

Unit 11 Park Royal Metro Centre Britannia Way, London, NW10 7PA
Tel: 020-8838 6188 **Fax:** 020-8838 1173
E-mail: sass@abs.tv
Website: http://www.abs.tv
Directors: S. Jahani (MD)
Managers: R. Keith (Ops Mgr)
Immediate Holding Company: ADVANCED BROADCAST SERVICES LIMITED
Registration no: 03989811 **Date established:** 2000
No.of Employees: 11 - 20 **Product Groups:** 37, 79, 81, 89

Date of Accounts	Oct 11	Oct 10	Oct 09
Working Capital	12	-3	-250
Fixed Assets	4m	3m	3m
Current Assets	358	347	476

Advanced Design Technology Ltd

Dilke House 1 Malet Street, London, WC1E 7JN
Tel: 020-7299 1170 **Fax:** 020-7636 8028
E-mail: info@adtechnology.co.uk
Website: http://www.adtechnology.co.uk
Managers: L. Bossi (Develop Mgr)
Immediate Holding Company: ADVANCED DESIGN TECHNOLOGY LIMITED
Registration no: 03636794 **Date established:** 1998
Turnover: £500,000 - £1m **No.of Employees:** 1 - 10 **Product Groups:** 44, 84

Date of Accounts	Dec 11	Dec 10	Dec 09
Working Capital	426	364	375
Fixed Assets	257	249	231
Current Assets	991	813	666

Advantage Austria (Trade Commission United Kingdom)

45 Princes Gate, London, SW7 2QA
Tel: 020-7584 4411 **Fax:** 020-7584 7946
E-mail: london@advantageaustria.org/uk
Website: http://www.advantageaustria.org/uk
Managers: G. Karabaczek
No.of Employees: 1 - 10 **Product Groups:** 87

Advent Venture Partners

Eggington House 25-28 Buckingham Gate, London, SW1E 6LD
Tel: 020-7932 2100 **Fax:** 020-7828 1474
E-mail: info@adventventures.com
Website: http://www.adventventures.com
Bank(s): The Royal Bank of Scotland
Managers: L. Gabb (Fin Mgr)
Ultimate Holding Company: ADVENT VENTURE PARTNERS LLP
Immediate Holding Company: ADVENT LIMITED
Registration no: 02191603 **VAT No.:** GB 503 1389 77
Date established: 1987 **Turnover:** £2m - £5m **No.of Employees:** 11 - 20
Product Groups: 82

Date of Accounts	Mar 11	Mar 10	Mar 09
Sales Turnover	2m	3m	3m
Pre Tax Profit/Loss	579	-348	297
Working Capital	3m	2m	2m
Fixed Assets	222	290	365
Current Assets	3m	3m	3m
Current Liabilities	221	114	139

Aecom Global Group Ltd

Johnson Building 77 Hatton Garden, London, EC1N 8JS
Tel: 020-3009 2100 **Fax:** 020-7645 2099
E-mail: bill.hanway@aecom.com
Website: http://www.aecom.com
Directors: D. Farenheim (Fin), B. Challans (Mkt Research), T. Parncutt (Sales & Mktg)
Managers: A. Maiella (Personnel), N. Danks (I.T. Exec), B. Hanway
Ultimate Holding Company: AECOM TECHNOLOGY CORP (USA)
Immediate Holding Company: AECOM GLOBAL GROUP LIMITED
Registration no: 02492136 **Date established:** 1990
Turnover: Up to £250,000 **No.of Employees:** 101 - 250
Product Groups: 34, 51, 54, 80, 84

Date of Accounts	Sep 11	Oct 08	Oct 09
Sales Turnover	233	2m	727
Pre Tax Profit/Loss	-197	-570	-5m
Working Capital	-4m	2m	-4m
Fixed Assets	86	135	119
Current Assets	486	5m	3m
Current Liabilities	175	409	136

Aesa Access & Safety Solutions

104 Maltings Place 169 Tower Bridge Road, London, SE1 3LJ
Tel: 020-7357 0303 **Fax:** 020-7357 0703
E-mail: aesa.uk@aesanet.com
Website: http://www.aesanet.com
Managers: J. Watson (Sales Prom Mgr)
Registration no: 04985523 **Date established:** 2003 **Turnover:** £2m - £5m
No.of Employees: 1 - 10 **Product Groups:** 35, 45

Date of Accounts	Dec 07	Dec 06	Dec 05
Working Capital	-613	-522	-200
Fixed Assets	60	35	49
Current Assets	728	242	276
Current Liabilities	1341	765	476

Africa Travel

Premier House 150 Southampton Row, London, WC1B 5AL
Tel: 020-7387 1211 **Fax:** 020-7383 7512
E-mail: flights@africatravel.co.uk
Website: http://www.africatravel.co.uk
Managers: C. Satusin (Mgr)
Immediate Holding Company: AFRICA TRAVEL CENTRE LIMITED
Registration no: 03226628 **Date established:** 1996
No.of Employees: 1 - 10 **Product Groups:** 69

Age UK

York House 207-221 Pentonville Road, London, N1 9UZ
Tel: 020-8765 7200 **Fax:** 020-7278 1116
E-mail: info@acent.co.uk
Website: http://www.efa.org.uk
Managers: G. Morris (Mgr)
Ultimate Holding Company: AGE UK
Immediate Holding Company: AGE CONCERN LIMITED
Registration no: 05425966 **VAT No.:** GB 564 5598 00
Date established: 2005 **Turnover:** £125m - £250m
No.of Employees: 1 - 10 **Product Groups:** 80

Ahika-Design Ltd

Unit 13 2 Lansdowne Drive, London, E8 3EZ
Tel: 0870-4440650
E-mail: info@ahika-design.co.uk
Website: http://www.ahika-design.co.uk
Directors: J. Luther (Fin), I. Van Der Zalm (MD)
Managers: M. Luther (Accounts)
Registration no: 04753448 **Date established:** 2003
Turnover: £250,000 - £500,000 **No.of Employees:** 1 - 10
Product Groups: 81

Date of Accounts	May 07
Working Capital	-48
Fixed Assets	2
Current Assets	6
Current Liabilities	55

Ahli United Ltd

35 Portman Square, London, W1H 6LR
Tel: 020-7487 6500 **Fax:** 020-7487 6808
E-mail: info@ahliunited.com
Website: http://www.ahliunited.com
Managers: S. Hussey, M. Macdonald (Personnel), G. Dunnachie, P. Smith (Tech Serv Mgr)
Ultimate Holding Company: AHLI UNITED BANK B S C (BAHRAIN)
Immediate Holding Company: AHLI UNITED BANK (UK) PLC
Registration no: 00877859 **Date established:** 1966
No.of Employees: 51 - 100 **Product Groups:** 82

Aims Partnership plc

3 Park Road, London, NW1 6AS
Tel: 020-7616 6629 **Fax:** 020-7616 6634
E-mail: lara.frankel@asc.co.uk
Website: http://www.aims.co.uk
Managers: L. Frankel
Ultimate Holding Company: A S SECURITIES LIMITED
Immediate Holding Company: A I M S PARTNERSHIP PLC
Registration no: 02740695 **Date established:** 1992
Turnover: Up to £250,000 **No.of Employees:** 11 - 20 **Product Groups:** 82

Date of Accounts	Apr 11	Apr 10	Apr 09
Sales Turnover	1m	1m	1m
Pre Tax Profit/Loss	838	812	643
Working Capital	26	54	46
Current Assets	221	221	180
Current Liabilities	185	155	123

Ainscough Crane Hire Ltd

Roding Road, London, E6 6XD
Tel: 020-7473 8787 **Fax:** 020-7473 0157
E-mail: london.east@ainscough.co.uk
Website: http://www.ainscough.co.uk
Managers: C. Day (Depot Mgr), J. Mansfield (Mgr)
Ultimate Holding Company: BRADLEY HALL HOLDINGS LIMITED
Immediate Holding Company: AINSCOUGH CRANE HIRE LTD
Registration no: 03245223 **Date established:** 1996
Turnover: Up to £250,000 **No.of Employees:** 51 - 100
Product Groups: 83

Date of Accounts	May 11	May 10	May 09
Sales Turnover	98m	110m	129m
Pre Tax Profit/Loss	11m	19m	30m
Working Capital	16m	72m	48m
Fixed Assets	152m	150m	149m
Current Assets	24m	81m	60m
Current Liabilities	8m	8m	10m

Air Studios Lyndhurst Hall

Lyndhurst Hall Lyndhurst Road, London, NW3 5NG
Tel: 020-7794 0660 **Fax:** 020-7794 8518
E-mail: info@airstudios.com
Website: http://www.airstudios.com
Bank(s): National Westminster Bank Plc
Directors: R. Feather (Dir)
Immediate Holding Company: AIR STUDIOS (LYNDHURST) LIMITED
Registration no: 02534012 **Date established:** 1990 **Turnover:** £2m - £5m
No.of Employees: 21 - 50 **Product Groups:** 89

Date of Accounts	Dec 11	Dec 10	Dec 09
Working Capital	122	99	796
Fixed Assets	1m	2m	2m
Current Assets	1m	980	2m

Airmark

6 Becket Road, London, N18 3PN
Tel: 020-8807 7891 **Fax:** 020-8884 3898
E-mail: airmarkcom@aol.com
Directors: L. Mark (Ptnr), L. Markwijc (MD), M. Van-MarkWike (Prop)
VAT No.: GB 327 9014 58 **No.of Employees:** 1 - 10 **Product Groups:** 40

Airvent Ducting & Duct Fittings

Railway Arch 57 Cambridge Grove, London, W6 0LD
Tel: 020-8748 7913 **Fax:** 020-8741 5128
E-mail: airventducting@hotmail.co.uk
Directors: G. Gallagher (Prop)
Date established: 1975 **No.of Employees:** 1 - 10 **Product Groups:** 37, 40, 48

Alami International Ltd

7 Dace Road, London, E3 2NG
Tel: 020-8533 7800 **Fax:** 020-8533 0026
E-mail: sales@alami.co.uk
Website: http://www.alami.co.uk
Directors: B. Vora (Co Sec), S. Vora (Dir)
Immediate Holding Company: ALAMI INTERNATIONAL LIMITED
Registration no: 01149214 **Date established:** 1973 **Turnover:** £2m - £5m
No.of Employees: 11 - 20 **Product Groups:** 22, 63

Date of Accounts	Sep 11	Sep 10	Sep 09
Working Capital	-85	-234	-128
Fixed Assets	10m	8m	8m
Current Assets	722	662	684

Alan Pharmaceuticals

33 Greenwood Place, London, NW5 1LB
Tel: 020-7284 2887 **Fax:** 020-8346 5218
E-mail: alan@alanpharmaceuticals.com
Website: http://www.alanpharmaceuticals.com
Directors: M. Gore (Dir)
Immediate Holding Company: TRIMBOS TRAINING LIMITED
Registration no: 01110451 **Date established:** 2006
No.of Employees: 11 - 20 **Product Groups:** 63

Date of Accounts	Mar 11	Mar 10	Mar 08
Working Capital	19	9	20
Fixed Assets	1	1	1
Current Assets	45	24	51

Alandar Park

1 Guillemot Place Clarendon Road, London, N22 6XG
Tel: 020-8888 8833 **Fax:** 020-8888 4942
E-mail: barry@ellisbridals.co.uk
Website: http://www.ellisbridals.co.uk
Directors: J. Godfrey (Fin)
Managers: M. Windsor (Tech Serv Mgr), J. Ellis (Sales & Mktg Mg), B. Waterman (Mgr)
Immediate Holding Company: ALANDAR PARK LIMITED
Registration no: 02736978 **VAT No.:** GB 610 0161 18
Date established: 1992 **No.of Employees:** 21 - 50 **Product Groups:** 24

Date of Accounts	Mar 12	Mar 11	Mar 10
Working Capital	3m	2m	1m
Fixed Assets	57	27	28
Current Assets	4m	3m	2m

Albermarle Interim Management plc

Julco House, London, W1W 8QT
Tel: 020-7079 3737 **Fax:** 020-7631 1881
E-mail: alan.horn@albermarleinterim.com
Website: http://www.albemarle.co.uk
Directors: A. Horn (Dir), A. Hickmore (MD), A. Horn (Grp Chief Exec)
Ultimate Holding Company: Select Appointments (Holdings) Group of Companies
Registration no: 02343071 **VAT No.:** GB 649 3925 94
Turnover: £10m - £20m **No.of Employees:** 1 - 10 **Product Groups:** 80

Albrissi Interiors

1 Sloane Square, London, SW1W 8EE
Tel: 020-7730 6119 **Fax:** 020-7259 9113
E-mail: albrissiuk@aol.com
Website: http://www.albrissi.net
Directors: H. Mclaughlin (Dir)
Ultimate Holding Company: RUSSELL HOLDINGS (INVESTMENTS) LIMITED
Immediate Holding Company: CANARYSTATE LIMITED
Registration no: 00930238 **Date established:** 1994
No.of Employees: 1 - 10 **Product Groups:** 84

Date of Accounts	Mar 11	Mar 10	Mar 09
Working Capital	14	14	14
Current Assets	14	14	14

Alessi Ltd

22 Brook Street, London, W1K 5DF
Tel: 020-7518 9090 **Fax:** 020-7518 9080
E-mail: info@alessi.com
Website: http://www.alessi.com
Directors: S. Rossi (MD)
Immediate Holding Company: ALESSI LIMITED
Registration no: 05601989 **Date established:** 2005
No.of Employees: 11 - 20 **Product Groups:** 40, 52, 66

Alexander Forbes Risk Services Ltd

Lockton House 6 Bevis Marks, London, EC3A 7AF
Tel: 020-7933 0000 **Fax:** 020-7933 0915
Website: http://www.aforbes.co.uk
Directors: R. Gordan (Grp Chief Exec)
Immediate Holding Company: ALEXANDER FORBES SERVICES LIMITED
Registration no: 05888855 **VAT No.:** GB 449 6862 93
Date established: 2006 **Turnover:** £75m - £125m
No.of Employees: 1 - 10 **Product Groups:** 80

Alexandra Palace

Alexandra Palace Way, London, N22 7AY
Tel: 020-8365 2121 **Fax:** 020-8883 3999
E-mail: enquiries@alexandrapalace.com
Website: http://www.alexandrapalace.com
Bank(s): Co-op Bank
Managers: D. Wilson
Immediate Holding Company: ALEXANDRA PALACE TRADING LIMITED
Registration no: 03819988 **Date established:** 1999 **Turnover:** £2m - £5m
No.of Employees: 101 - 250 **Product Groups:** 69, 89

Date of Accounts	Mar 12	Mar 11	Mar 10
Sales Turnover	7m	5m	5m
Pre Tax Profit/Loss	55	-23	N/A
Working Capital	-210	297	-210
Fixed Assets	12	15	5
Current Assets	4m	2m	1m
Current Liabilities	4m	2m	1m

Alfred Dunhill Ltd

5-7 Mandeville Place, London, W1U 3AY
Tel: 08454-580779 **Fax:** 020-7838 8333
E-mail: customer.services@dunhill.com
Website: http://www.dunhill.com
Bank(s): Barclays
Managers: E. Starkey (Cust Serv Mgr)
Ultimate Holding Company: COMPAGNIE FINANCIERE RICHEMONT SA (SWITZERLAND)

Immediate Holding Company: ALFRED DUNHILL LIMITED
Registration no: 00191031 **VAT No.:** GB 238 4687 27
Date established: 2023 **No.of Employees:** 21 - 50 **Product Groups:** 22, 32, 49

Date of Accounts	Mar 11	Mar 10	Mar 09
Sales Turnover	100m	80m	85m
Pre Tax Profit/Loss	-15m	-12m	-8m
Working Capital	41m	52m	61m
Fixed Assets	12m	11m	8m
Current Assets	66m	66m	74m
Current Liabilities	9m	7m	6m

Alfresco Ltd
South Grove House South Grove, London, N6 6LP
Tel: 020-8348 6704 **Fax:** 020-8348 4939
E-mail: nobites@alfresco.uk.com
Website: http://www.alfrescoshop.com
Directors: M. Morris (Fin)
Immediate Holding Company: ALFRESCO LIMITED
Registration no: 03459812 **Date established:** 1997
Turnover: Up to £250,000 **No.of Employees:** 1 - 10 **Product Groups:** 31, 63

Date of Accounts	Sep 11	Sep 10	Sep 09
Sales Turnover	N/A	N/A	77
Pre Tax Profit/Loss	N/A	N/A	31
Working Capital	-40	-8	-13
Fixed Assets	14	10	10
Current Assets	38	29	19
Current Liabilities	N/A	N/A	3

The All England Lawn Tennis Club Championships Ltd
Church Road, London, SW19 5AE
Tel: 020-8946 2244 **Fax:** 020-8947 8752
E-mail: christine.tostevin@aeltc.com
Website: http://www.wimbledon.org
Managers: C. Tostevin
Immediate Holding Company: THE ALL ENGLAND LAWN TENNIS CLUB (CHAMPIONSHIPS) LIMITED
Registration no: 07546773 **Date established:** 2011 **Turnover:** £1m - £2m
No.of Employees: 101 - 250 **Product Groups:** 89

Allgood
297 Euston Road, London, NW1 3AQ
Tel: 020-7387 9951 **Fax:** 020-7383 7950
E-mail: info@allgood.co.uk
Website: http://www.allgood.co.uk
Bank(s): National Westminster Bank Plc
Managers: A. Field (Mktg Serv Mgr)
Ultimate Holding Company: ALLGOOD HOLDINGS LTD
Immediate Holding Company: ALLGOOD HARDWARE LIMITED
Registration no: 01341687 **VAT No.:** GB 232 1503 17
Date established: 1977 **Turnover:** £20m - £50m
No.of Employees: 21 - 50 **Product Groups:** 66

Date of Accounts	Nov 11	Nov 10	Nov 09
Sales Turnover	15m	17m	18m
Pre Tax Profit/Loss	234	425	-147
Working Capital	6m	6m	5m
Fixed Assets	612	374	570
Current Assets	8m	10m	8m
Current Liabilities	903	1m	1m

Allianz Insurance plc
Allianz Cornhill House 27 Leadenhall Street, London, EC3A 1AA
Tel: 020-7264 1530 **Fax:** 020-7929 3562
Website: http://www.allianz.co.uk
Bank(s): Lloyds TSB Bank plc
Directors: A. Terrence (MD), B. Baldock (Dir), G. Stantford (Fin), K. Lowe (Dir), C. Reeves (Dir)
Managers: J. Knowles (I.T. Exec), J. Robson (Mktg Serv Mgr), K. Rossi ()
Ultimate Holding Company: ALLIANZ SE (GERMANY)
Immediate Holding Company: W.G.WESTON,LIMITED
Registration no: 00084638 **Date established:** 2005
Turnover: £50m - £75m **No.of Employees:** 251 - 500 **Product Groups:** 82

Allied Cargo Express Ltd
384 Geffrye Street, London, E2 8HZ
Tel: 020-7729 2772 **Fax:** 020-7729 2333
Directors: C. Edney (Co Sec)
Immediate Holding Company: ALLIED CARGO EXPRESS LTD
Registration no: 02792110 **VAT No.:** GB 515 1190 81
Date established: 1993 **Turnover:** £1m - £2m **No.of Employees:** 1 - 10
Product Groups: 75, 76

Date of Accounts	Mar 12	Mar 11	Mar 10
Working Capital	27	23	39
Fixed Assets	5	4	5
Current Assets	126	84	102

Allied Manufacturing
Sarena House Grove Park Industrial Estate Grove Park, London, NW9 0EB
Tel: 020-8904 8844 **Fax:** 020-8200 9510
E-mail: stephen.joseph@kingswood-allied.co.uk
Website: http://www.kingswood-allied.co.uk
Directors: J. King (Dir), J. Joseph (Ch), S. Joseph (MD), D. Harris (Jt MD), S. Joseph (Dir)
Managers: S. McGuire (Sales Prom Mgr), P. Silverman (Personnel), M. Hayes (I.T. Exec)
Ultimate Holding Company: CROWN PRODUCTS (KENT) LIMITED
Immediate Holding Company: ALLIED MANUFACTURING COMPANY (LONDON) LIMITED
Registration no: 00414887 **VAT No.:** GB 581 7231 38
Date established: 1946 **Turnover:** £10m - £20m **No.of Employees:** 1 - 10
Product Groups: 26, 30, 48

Date of Accounts	Mar 11	Mar 10	Sep 09
Sales Turnover	24m	12m	27m
Pre Tax Profit/Loss	-448	-507	-981
Working Capital	1m	1m	1m
Fixed Assets	2m	3m	3m
Current Assets	7m	7m	7m
Current Liabilities	677	1m	1m

Allison International
7 Birchin Lane, London, EC3V 9BW
Tel: 020-7626 2266 **Fax:** 020-7626 2277
E-mail: mad@all.co.uk
Website: http://www.allisoninternational.com
Directors: M. Davies (Prop)
Immediate Holding Company: B.A.V.D.H. LIMITED
Registration no: 05648669 **Date established:** 2010 **Turnover:** £2m - £5m
No.of Employees: 1 - 10 **Product Groups:** 80

Date of Accounts	Apr 11	Apr 10	Apr 09
Working Capital	5m	3m	2m
Fixed Assets	209	172	4m
Current Assets	10m	7m	6m

Allsop Ltd
33 Wigmore Street, London, W1U 1BZ
Tel: 020-7437 6977 **Fax:** 0116-254 5140
E-mail: wayne.taylor@allsop.co.uk
Website: http://www.allsop.co.uk
Directors: W. Taylor (Fin)
Ultimate Holding Company: ALLSOP LLP
Immediate Holding Company: ALLSOP LIMITED
Registration no: 02158801 **Date established:** 1987
Turnover: £20m - £50m **No.of Employees:** 101 - 250
Product Groups: 52, 80, 82

Date of Accounts	Mar 11	Mar 10	Mar 09
Pre Tax Profit/Loss	-0	431	250
Fixed Assets	445	445	445
Current Assets	N/A	181	250
Current Liabilities	N/A	N/A	250

Alma Leather Ltd
12-14 Greatorex Street, London, E1 5NF
Tel: 020-7375 0343 **Fax:** 020-7375 2598
E-mail: info@almahome.co.uk
Website: http://www.almahome.co.uk
Bank(s): Allied Irish Bank
Directors: W. Greenhalgh (Fin), S. Khalique (MD)
Managers: S. Plant (Sales Prom Mgr)
Immediate Holding Company: ALMA LEATHER LIMITED
Registration no: 03668434 **VAT No.:** GB 726 2852 27
Date established: 1998 **Turnover:** £2m - £5m **No.of Employees:** 21 - 50
Product Groups: 22, 23, 24, 26, 27, 66

Date of Accounts	Dec 10	Dec 09	Dec 08
Working Capital	139	116	106
Current Assets	226	145	153

Alpha Bank London Ltd
66 Cannon Street, London, EC4N 6EP
Tel: 020-7332 6767 **Fax:** 020-7332 0010
E-mail: john.coxon@alpha.gr
Website: http://www.alpha.gr
Directors: J. Coxon (Fin)
Ultimate Holding Company: ALPHA BANK AE (GREECE)
Immediate Holding Company: ALPHA BANK LONDON NOMINEES LIMITED
Registration no: 00318931 **VAT No.:** GB 244 3555 66
Date established: 1936 **No.of Employees:** 51 - 100 **Product Groups:** 82

Alpha Designs
62 Hubert Road, London, E6 3EY
Tel: 020-8472 5422 **Fax:** 020-8470 3516
E-mail: alphadesignsuk@aol.com
Website: http://www.alpha-designs.com
Directors: W. Matejek (Prop)
Date established: 2002 **Turnover:** Up to £250,000
No.of Employees: 1 - 10 **Product Groups:** 44, 79

Alpha Gems UK Ltd
39 Greville Street, London, EC1N 8PJ
Tel: 020-7242 3748 **Fax:** 020-7813 3065
E-mail: alpha@haruni.freeserve.co.uk
Website: http://www.thegembank.com
Directors: R. Haruni (Dir), L. Jay Haruni (Fin)
Immediate Holding Company: ALPHA GEMS (UK) LIMITED
Registration no: 02453589 **VAT No.:** GB 524 9467 23
Date established: 1989 **Turnover:** Up to £250,000
No.of Employees: 1 - 10 **Product Groups:** 65

Date of Accounts	Sep 11	Sep 10	Sep 09
Sales Turnover	N/A	N/A	12
Pre Tax Profit/Loss	N/A	N/A	43
Working Capital	-319	-398	-453
Fixed Assets	N/A	1	1
Current Assets	69	25	34
Current Liabilities	N/A	N/A	1

Altima Ltd
4 Chase Road, London, NW10 6HZ
Tel: 020-8453 8740 **Fax:** 020-8965 8010
E-mail: sales@altima.co.uk
Website: http://www.altima.co.uk
Directors: D. Clarke (MD)
Immediate Holding Company: ALTIMA LTD
Registration no: 05222619 **Date established:** 2004 **Turnover:** £2m - £5m
No.of Employees: 1 - 10 **Product Groups:** 37

Date of Accounts	Sep 09	Sep 08	Sep 07
Working Capital	255	248	111
Fixed Assets	16	19	9
Current Assets	480	453	246

Alto Digital Networks Ltd
294-304 St James's Road, London, SE1 5JX
Tel: 020-7740 0700 **Fax:** 01268-561018
E-mail: info@altodigital.com
Website: http://www.altodigital.com
Managers: J. Dobbelaar (Sales Prom Mgr), T. Harrod (Sales Admin)
Ultimate Holding Company: ALTODIGITAL NETWORKS LIMITED
Immediate Holding Company: DATADENE LIMITED
Registration no: 01340660 **Date established:** 1977
Turnover: Up to £250,000 **No.of Employees:** 21 - 50 **Product Groups:** 44, 49, 52, 61

Date of Accounts	Mar 11	Mar 10	Sep 09
Sales Turnover	N/A	172	N/A
Pre Tax Profit/Loss	22	28	N/A
Working Capital	N/A	-22	1
Fixed Assets	N/A	N/A	96
Current Assets	N/A	N/A	213

Amanda Hutson Ltd
Studio 27 Townmead Business Centre, London, SW6 2SZ
Tel: 020-7371 9865
E-mail: design@hutsonbespoke.com
Website: http://www.amandahutson.com
Directors: P. Hutson (Dir)
Registration no: 06866612 **Date established:** 2009
Turnover: Up to £250,000 **No.of Employees:** 1 - 10 **Product Groups:** 61

Amazon Lighting Ltd
62 St Stephens Avenue, London, W12 8JD
Tel: 020-8743 3973
Website: http://www.amazonlighting.com
Directors: M. Khawaja (MD), S. Khawaja (Fin)
Immediate Holding Company: MAXILANCE LIMITED
Registration no: 04756006 **Date established:** 2003
No.of Employees: 1 - 10 **Product Groups:** 37, 67

Date of Accounts	Mar 12	Mar 11	Mar 10
Working Capital	12	23	13
Fixed Assets	1	2	2
Current Assets	15	23	17

Ambassadors Bloomsbury Hotel
12 Upper Woburn Place, London, WC1H 0HX
Tel: 020-7693 5400 **Fax:** 020-7388 9930
E-mail: reservations@ambassadors.co.uk
Website: http://www.ambassadors.co.uk
Managers: A. Apostolakos (Mgr), L. Pedro (Chief Mgr), S. Baker, T. Radha
Immediate Holding Company: GUIDEZONE LIMITED
Registration no: 01690203 **Date established:** 1983 **Turnover:** £2m - £5m
No.of Employees: 51 - 100 **Product Groups:** 69, 80

Date of Accounts	Dec 11	Dec 10	Dec 09
Sales Turnover	5m	5m	4m
Pre Tax Profit/Loss	2m	2m	940
Working Capital	336	632	606
Fixed Assets	6m	6m	5m
Current Assets	2m	2m	2m
Current Liabilities	1m	727	601

Ambican www.ambican.com
6 Commercial Way Abbey Road, London, NW10 7XF
Tel: 020-8965 8399 **Fax:** 020-8965 8990
E-mail: info@ambican.com
Website: http://www.ambican.com
Directors: D. Tanna (MD)
Immediate Holding Company: AMBICAN (UK) LTD
Registration no: 05803209 **Date established:** 2006 **Turnover:** £1m - £2m
No.of Employees: 1 - 10 **Product Groups:** 30

Date of Accounts	May 11	May 10	May 09
Working Capital	33	-21	-12
Fixed Assets	35	42	43
Current Assets	184	139	106

American Appraisal UK Ltd
Aldermary House 10-15 Queen Street, London, EC4N 1TX
Tel: 020-7778 0800 **Fax:** 020-7248 1453
E-mail: info@american-appraisal.co.uk
Website: http://www.american-appraisal.co.uk
Bank(s): Barclays
Directors: M. Weaver (MD), I. Gough (Dir)
Ultimate Holding Company: AMERICAN APPRAISAL ASSOCIATES INC (UNITED STATES)
Immediate Holding Company: AMERICAN APPRAISAL (UK) LIMITED
Registration no: 01549537 **VAT No.:** GB 365 3128 57
Date established: 1981 **Turnover:** £1m - £2m **No.of Employees:** 11 - 20
Product Groups: 61, 80, 82, 84

Date of Accounts	Mar 12	Mar 11	Mar 10
Working Capital	-2m	-2m	-2m
Fixed Assets	1m	1m	1m
Current Assets	1m	1m	613

American Carwash
68 York Way, London, N1 9AG
Tel: 020-7278 0600 **Fax:** 020-7278 8942
E-mail: admin@americancarwash.co.uk
Website: http://www.americancarwash.co.uk
Directors: D. Barnett (Fin)
Immediate Holding Company: AMERICAN CAR WASH COMPANY LIMITED(THE)
Registration no: 01672229 **VAT No.:** GB 396 4966 82
Date established: 1982 **Turnover:** £1m - £2m **No.of Employees:** 1 - 10
Product Groups: 39

Date of Accounts	Dec 11	Dec 10	Dec 09
Working Capital	178	195	186
Fixed Assets	109	91	101
Current Assets	599	419	375

American Express (Branch Office, Travel Division)
30 31 Haymarket, London, SW1Y 4EX
Tel: 08444-060044 **Fax:** 020-7484 9640
E-mail: louise.e.townsend@amexfranchise.co.uk
Website: http://www.americanexpress.com
Managers: L. Townsend
Immediate Holding Company: AMERICAN CENTURY INVESTMENT MANAGEMENT (UK) LIMITED
Registration no: FC011790 **VAT No.:** GB 190 1985 48
Date established: 2008 **No.of Employees:** 11 - 20 **Product Groups:** 69

Date of Accounts	Dec 07
Sales Turnover	492550
Pre Tax Profit/Loss	105930
Working Capital	111760
Current Assets	10244m
Current Liabilities	10132m
Total Share Capital	134670
ROCE% (Return on Capital Employed)	94.8

American Pie Ltd
197 Kings Cross Road, London, WC1X 9DB
Tel: 020-7278 9490 **Fax:** 020-7278 2447
E-mail: bacon@langservice.com
Website: http://www.americanization.com
Directors: J. Bacon (MD), A. Jbeili (Dir)
Ultimate Holding Company: Pholiota Limited
Registration no: 01278033 **VAT No.:** GB 629 8841 89
Date established: 2000 **Turnover:** £250,000 - £500,000
No.of Employees: 1 - 10 **Product Groups:** 80

Amherst Walkie Talkie Radio Centre
70 Kingsgate Road, London, NW6 4TE
Tel: 020-7328 9792 **Fax:** 020-7209 2704
E-mail: enquiries@walkie-talkie-radio.co.uk
Website: http://www.walkie-talkie-radio.co.uk
Directors: G. Toman (MD)
Immediate Holding Company: AMHERST ENTERPRISES LIMITED
Registration no: 02615762 **Date established:** 1991
Turnover: £500,000 - £1m **No.of Employees:** 1 - 10 **Product Groups:** 83

see next page

***Amherst Walkie Talkie Radio Centre** - Cont'd*

Date of Accounts	Jun 11	Jun 10	Jun 09
Sales Turnover	307	325	250
Pre Tax Profit/Loss	127	132	58
Working Capital	-140	-188	-217
Fixed Assets	3m	3m	3m
Current Assets	164	144	93
Current Liabilities	39	38	11

Amicus Mentor Ltd

837a High Road, London, N12 8PR
Tel: 020-8446 9139 **Fax:** 020-8446 9149
E-mail: contactus@amicusmentor.com
Website: http://www.amicusmentor.com
Directors: A. Mcnally (Dir), M. McNally (Fin)
Immediate Holding Company: AMICUS MENTOR LIMITED
Registration no: 03884330 **Date established:** 1999
No.of Employees: 1 - 10 **Product Groups:** 81

Date of Accounts	Nov 11	Nov 10	Nov 09
Working Capital	11	-5	1
Fixed Assets	5	6	8
Current Assets	258	424	571

Amipak Ltd

88 Cobbold Road, London, NW10 9SX
Tel: 020-8451 5099 **Fax:** 020-8451 5443
E-mail: sales@ampak.co.uk
Website: http://www.amipak.co.uk
Directors: P. Schwitzer (Dir)
Immediate Holding Company: AMIPAK LIMITED
Registration no: 03708621 **Date established:** 1999
No.of Employees: 1 - 10 **Product Groups:** 20, 27, 30

Date of Accounts	Feb 12	Feb 11	Feb 10
Working Capital	2m	1m	1m
Fixed Assets	585	432	310
Current Assets	3m	3m	2m

Amstore

Unit 13 Baden Place, London, SE1 1YW
Tel: 020-7940 6800 **Fax:** 020-7237 6097
E-mail: sales@amstore.co.uk
Website: http://www.amstore.co.uk
Directors: M. Bustamante (Dir)
Managers: P. Bela (Fin Mgr)
Registration no: 04234221 **No.of Employees:** 11 - 20
Product Groups: 28, 44, 48, 79, 81, 89

Andrew Dust Structural Engineers

39-41 North Road, London, N7 9DP
Tel: 020-7700 5533 **Fax:** 020-7700 1221
Website: http://www.andrewdust.co.uk
Directors: A. Dust (Prop)
Immediate Holding Company: ANDREW MANN LIMITED
Registration no: 00927714 **Date established:** 1968
No.of Employees: 1 - 10 **Product Groups:** 35

Date of Accounts	Nov 11	Nov 10	Nov 08
Working Capital	-22	-15	-8
Fixed Assets	1	2	2
Current Assets	33	33	11

Andrew Weir Shipping Ltd

Dexter House 2 Royal Mint Court, London, EC3N 4XX
Tel: 020-7575 6000 **Fax:** 020-7481 4784
E-mail: sxc@aws.co.uk
Website: http://www.aws.co.uk
Bank(s): Royal Bank of Scotland
Directors: S. Corkhill (MD), J. Carney (Fin)
Managers: G. Sullivan (Tech Serv Mgr)
Ultimate Holding Company: ANDREW WEIR & COMPANY LIMITED
Immediate Holding Company: ANDREW WEIR SHIPPING LIMITED
Registration no: SC005991 **VAT No.:** GB 243 2925 70
Date established: 2005 **Turnover:** £250m - £500m
No.of Employees: 21 - 50 **Product Groups:** 80

Date of Accounts	Dec 11	Dec 10	Dec 09
Sales Turnover	2m	2m	19m
Pre Tax Profit/Loss	3m	2m	-4m
Working Capital	3m	1m	-5m
Fixed Assets	5m	8m	15m
Current Assets	4m	2m	3m
Current Liabilities	522	418	8m

Angel Human Resources plc

2-4 Union Street, London, SE1 1SZ
Tel: 020-7940 2000 **Fax:** 020-7940 2018
E-mail: hq@angelhr.org
Website: http://www.angelhr.org
Directors: S. Crawford (Sales), R. Crawford (MD), C. Borhani Langroudi (Sales)
Managers: D. Merrison (Mgr)
Ultimate Holding Company: ANGEL HUMAN RESOURCES MANAGED SERVICES LIMITED
Immediate Holding Company: ANGEL HUMAN RESOURCES LIMITED
Registration no: 01848414 **Date established:** 1984
Turnover: £10m - £20m **No.of Employees:** 11 - 20 **Product Groups:** 80

Date of Accounts	Mar 11	Mar 10	Mar 09
Sales Turnover	14m	13m	16m
Pre Tax Profit/Loss	225	194	115
Working Capital	1m	1m	1m
Fixed Assets	124	121	163
Current Assets	4m	3m	3m
Current Liabilities	2m	2m	2m

Angel Trains Ltd

Portland House Stag Place, London, SW1E 5BH
Tel: 020-7592 0500 **Fax:** 020-7592 0520
E-mail: reception@angeltrains.co.uk
Website: http://www.angeltrains.co.uk
Bank(s): The Royal Bank of Scotland
Directors: C. Smith (Co Sec)
Managers: M. Brown, A. Craig (Personnel), A. Wren (Tech Serv Mgr), A. Lowe (Comptroller)
Ultimate Holding Company: WILLOW TOPCO LIMITED (JERSEY)
Immediate Holding Company: ANGEL TRAINS LIMITED
Registration no: 02912655 **Date established:** 1994
Turnover: £250m - £500m **No.of Employees:** 101 - 250
Product Groups: 51, 71

Date of Accounts	Dec 11	Dec 10	May 10
Sales Turnover	342m	194m	329m
Pre Tax Profit/Loss	132m	117m	118m
Working Capital	-143m	-136m	-105m
Fixed Assets	2092m	2205m	2195m
Current Assets	31m	33m	86m
Current Liabilities	85m	103m	121m

Angela Mortimer

37-38 Golden Square, London, W1F 9LA
Tel: 020-7287 7788 **Fax:** 020-7470 5578
E-mail: info@angelamortimer.com
Website: http://www.angelamortimer.com
Directors: J. Mortimer (Prop), D. Watson (Fin), D. Venus (Co Sec)
Managers: C. Hilton (Tech Serv Mgr)
Immediate Holding Company: ANGELA MORTIMER PLC
Registration no: 01205549 **Date established:** 1975
Turnover: £20m - £50m **No.of Employees:** 101 - 250 **Product Groups:** 80

Date of Accounts	Jun 11	Jun 10	Jun 09
Sales Turnover	27m	27m	30m
Pre Tax Profit/Loss	-394	68	-2m
Working Capital	1m	2m	2m
Fixed Assets	168	299	515
Current Assets	5m	6m	5m
Current Liabilities	4m	3m	3m

Anglo American Optical

210 Archway Road, London, N6 5AX
Tel: 020-8340 0888 **Fax:** 020-8340 1888
E-mail: mrt.aaoco@btconnect.com
Website: http://www.aaoco.com
Directors: T. Jenkin (MD)
Registration no: 03032196 **VAT No.:** GB 654 0500 67
Turnover: £1m - £2m **No.of Employees:** 1 - 10 **Product Groups:** 38

Date of Accounts	Jan 08	Jan 07	Jan 06
Sales Turnover	349	305	332
Pre Tax Profit/Loss	46	35	9
Working Capital	109	91	63
Fixed Assets	2	1	N/A
Current Assets	128	117	98
Current Liabilities	19	27	35
ROCE% (Return on Capital Employed)	41.2	38.1	13.7
ROT% (Return on Turnover)	13.2	11.4	2.6

Anglo American Sewing Machine

Unit 3 14a Burwell Road, London, E10 7QG
Tel: 020-8539 2220 **Fax:** 020-8539 2215
E-mail: anglosewing@aol.com
Website: http://www.anglosewing.co.uk
Directors: F. Shaffer (MD), P. Shaffer (MD), T. Shaffer (Jt MD), A. Shaffer (Dir)
Registration no: OC320336 **VAT No.:** GB 232 3573 83
Turnover: £1m - £2m **No.of Employees:** 1 - 10 **Product Groups:** 43

Date of Accounts	Aug 06	Sep 05	Sep 04
Working Capital	518	35	89
Fixed Assets	N/A	353	362
Current Assets	797	196	191
Current Liabilities	278	160	101
Total Share Capital	1	1	1

Anglo German Business & Finance Translation Services

25 Grand Avenue, London, N10 3BD
Tel: 020-8365 3778 **Fax:** 020-8365 3778
E-mail: sheelagh.neuling@btconnect.com
Website: http://www.neulingtranslations.co.uk
Directors: S. Neuling (Prop)
Date established: 1977 **No.of Employees:** 1 - 10 **Product Groups:** 80

Anglo Industrial Minerals Holdings Ltd

20 Carlton House Terrace, London, SW1Y 5AN
Tel: 020-7698 8888 **Fax:** 020-7430 8500
Website: http://www.angloamerican.co.uk
Directors: K. Hajjar (Dir), N. Jordan (Dir)
Ultimate Holding Company: ANGLO AMERICAN PLC
Immediate Holding Company: ANGLO INDUSTRIAL MINERALS HOLDINGS LTD.
Registration no: 02649815 **Date established:** 1991
Turnover: Over £1,000m **No.of Employees:** 1501 & over
Product Groups: 08, 11, 12, 27, 34, 66

Date of Accounts	Dec 10	Dec 09	Dec 08
Pre Tax Profit/Loss	2	13	11m
Working Capital	67m	66m	66m
Fixed Assets	223m	223m	223m
Current Assets	206m	206m	206m

Anglo Irish Bank Corpoation Ltd

10 Old Jewry, London, EC2R 8DN
Tel: 020-7710 7000 **Fax:** 020-7710 7050
E-mail: enquiries@angloirishbank.co.uk
Website: http://www.angloirishbank.co.uk
Managers: P. O"dwyer (Ops Mgr)
Ultimate Holding Company: IRISH BANK RESOLUTION CORPORATION LIMITED
Immediate Holding Company: ANGLO IRISH JCF 1 LLP
Registration no: OC341029 **Date established:** 2008
Turnover: Up to £250,000 **No.of Employees:** 251 - 500
Product Groups: 80, 82

Date of Accounts	Dec 11	Dec 10	Dec 09
Pre Tax Profit/Loss	2	6	6
Working Capital	264	262	262
Current Assets	264	262	262

Anglo-Romanian Bank Ltd

Centurion House 24 Monument Street, London, EC3R 8AJ
Tel: 020-7398 4200 **Fax:** 020-7628 1274
E-mail: info@anglorom.co.uk
Website: http://www.anglorom.co.uk
Bank(s): Barclays Bank plc
Directors: D. King (Co Sec), D. King (Chief Op Offcr), M. Radoi (MD), E. Gallivan (Co Sec)
Ultimate Holding Company: BANCA COMERCIALA ROMANA (ROMANIA)
Immediate Holding Company: ANGLO-ROMANIAN BANK LIMITED
Registration no: 01110826 **Date established:** 1973 **Turnover:** £2m - £5m
No.of Employees: 21 - 50 **Product Groups:** 82

Anodas Software Ltd

18 Mansell Street, London, E1 8AA
Tel: 020-7954 4260 **Fax:** 01444-401993
E-mail: info@anodas.com
Website: http://www.anodas.com
Directors: C. Mouly (MD), C. Venkataraman (Fin), C. Venkataraman (Fin)
Ultimate Holding Company: ZYLOG SYSTEMS LTD (INDIA)
Immediate Holding Company: ANODAS SOFTWARE LIMITED
Registration no: 03788673 **Date established:** 1999
Turnover: £500,000 - £1m **No.of Employees:** 11 - 20 **Product Groups:** 44

Date of Accounts	Mar 11	Mar 10	Mar 09
Working Capital	182	245	211
Fixed Assets	1	2	3
Current Assets	279	396	419

Ansaldo S T S UK Ltd

Bravington House Bravingtons Walk, London, N1 9AF
Tel: 020-7841 6850
Website: http://www.ansaldo-sts.co.uk
Directors: A. Harrsion (Prop), D. Colins (Dir)
Ultimate Holding Company: ANSALDO STS SPA (ITALY)
Immediate Holding Company: ANSALDO STS UK LIMITED
Registration no: 04825256 **Date established:** 2003
Turnover: £10m - £20m **No.of Employees:** 21 - 50 **Product Groups:** 37, 39, 52

Date of Accounts	Dec 10	Dec 09	Dec 08
Sales Turnover	12m	25m	24m
Pre Tax Profit/Loss	-5m	-649	-28
Working Capital	-4m	1m	3m
Fixed Assets	213	334	569
Current Assets	5m	10m	9m
Current Liabilities	2m	3m	3m

Anyword Ltd Anyword Sarl

Second Floor 6 London Street, London, W2 1HR
Tel: 0808-2342567
E-mail: laurence@anyword.co.uk
Website: http://anyword.co.uk
Managers: L. Freeman (Sales Prom Mgr)
Registration no: 06613369 **Date established:** 2004
No.of Employees: 1 - 10 **Product Groups:** 80

Apollo Sound

32 Ellerdale Road, London, NW3 6BB
Tel: 020-7435 5255 **Fax:** 020-7431 0621
Website: http://www.apollosound.co.uk
Directors: H. Herschmann (Prop)
Date established: 1959 **No.of Employees:** 1 - 10 **Product Groups:** 37, 38, 61

Aqua Legion UK Ltd

Suite 335 Kemp House 152-160 City Road London EC1V 2NX, London, EC1V 2NX
Tel: 020-8555 3797 **Fax:** 020-8555 3797
E-mail: enquiries@aqualegion.com
Website: http://www.aqualegion.com
Managers: D. Francis
Immediate Holding Company: AQUA LEGION (UK) LIMITED
Registration no: 05979183 **Date established:** 2006
No.of Employees: 1 - 10 **Product Groups:** 18, 32, 84

Date of Accounts	Oct 10	Oct 08	Oct 07
Working Capital	21	-14	12
Fixed Assets	1	1	1
Current Assets	21	5	12

Aquapac International Ltd

Unit 7 Bessemer Park 250 Milkwood Road, London, SE24 0HG
Tel: 020-7738 4466 **Fax:** 020-7738 6801
E-mail: info@aquapac.net
Website: http://www.aquapac.net
Directors: M. Malavasi (Dir)
Immediate Holding Company: AQUAPAC INTERNATIONAL LIMITED
Registration no: 01756654 **VAT No.:** GB 394 5437 19
Date established: 1983 **Turnover:** £1m - £2m **No.of Employees:** 11 - 20
Product Groups: 22

Date of Accounts	Sep 11	Sep 10	Sep 09
Working Capital	799	643	470
Fixed Assets	14	14	28
Current Assets	922	761	538

Aquascutum Pension Plan

Ibex House 42 Minories, London, EC3N 1DY
Tel: 020-7265 1553 **Fax:** 020-7675 9099
E-mail: customer.services@aquascutum.co.uk
Website: http://www.aquascutum.co.uk
Directors: D. Atkar (Co Sec), C. Carlisle (Fin), K. Nakamura (MD), R. Lindsay (MD), Y. Ueda (Dir)
Managers: L. Clemants (), G. Williams (Mktg Serv Mgr), J. Harper ()
Ultimate Holding Company: Broadwick Group Ltd
Immediate Holding Company: Aquascutum Group Ltd
Registration no: 01301292 **Date established:** 1979 **Turnover:** £5m - £10m
No.of Employees: 1 - 10 **Product Groups:** 63

Date of Accounts	Dec 06	Dec 05
Working Capital	-19140	-19420
Fixed Assets	2070	2070
Current Assets	300	20
Current Liabilities	19440	19440
Total Share Capital	4370	4370

Aradco VSI Ltd

Aradco House 128-134 Cleveland Street, London, W1T 6AB
Tel: 020-7692 7700 **Fax:** 020-7692 7711
E-mail: info@vsi.tv
Website: http://www.aradco.com
Directors: N. Dowd (Prop)
Immediate Holding Company: ARADCO VSI LIMITED
Registration no: 00645250 **Date established:** 1959 **Turnover:** £2m - £5m
No.of Employees: 51 - 100 **Product Groups:** 28, 80

Date of Accounts	Dec 11	Apr 11	Apr 10
Working Capital	310	265	294
Fixed Assets	60	63	76
Current Assets	728	718	819
Current Liabilities	164	260	N/A

ARAMARK Ltd

Millbank Tower 21-24 Millbank, London, SW1P 4QP
Tel: 0118-959 6761 **Fax:** 020-7623 7117
E-mail: info@aramark.co.uk
Website: http://www.aramark.co.uk
Directors: A. Main (Grp Chief Exec), N. Boston (Fin)
Ultimate Holding Company: ARAMARK HOLDINGS CORPORATION (USA)
Immediate Holding Company: ARAMARK LIMITED
Registration no: 00983951 **Date established:** 1970 **Turnover:** £1m - £2m
No.of Employees: 1 - 10 **Product Groups:** 40, 49, 61, 69, 84

Date of Accounts	Sep 11	Oct 08	Oct 09
Sales Turnover	341m	425m	410m
Pre Tax Profit/Loss	17m	9m	9m
Working Capital	56m	37m	41m
Fixed Assets	46m	60m	55m
Current Assets	107m	110m	126m
Current Liabilities	22m	18m	25m

Arc Recruitment
26 Mortimer Street, London, W1W 7RB
Tel: 020-7287 2525 **Fax:** 020-7287 9688
E-mail: arc@itjobs.co.uk
Website: http://www.arcrecruitment.com
Directors: J. Moore (Fin), T. Barton (MD)
Immediate Holding Company: ARC RECRUITMENT LIMITED
Registration no: 03407974 **Date established:** 1997
No.of Employees: 11 - 20 **Product Groups:** 80

Date of Accounts	Dec 11	Dec 10	Dec 09
Working Capital	63	164	59
Fixed Assets	2	2	2
Current Assets	379	1m	1m

Archco Rigidon Ltd
Denso House 33-35 Chapel Road, London, SE27 0TR
Tel: 020-8670 7511 **Fax:** 020-8761 2456
E-mail: johnburtonb@benso.net
Website: http://www.denso.net
Bank(s): Barclays, Grace Church St, London
Directors: C. Winn (MD)
Immediate Holding Company: WINN & COALES INTERNATIONAL LIMITED
Registration no: 02405829 **VAT No.:** GB 218 0172 94
Date established: 1989 **Turnover:** £2m - £5m **No.of Employees:** 51 - 100
Product Groups: 32

Archway Sheet Metal Works Ltd
1-3 Paxton Road, London, N17 0BP
Tel: 020-8365 0760 **Fax:** 020-8365 9670
E-mail: info@archwaysm.com
Website: http://www.archwaysm.com
Directors: J. Josif (Co Sec), A. Josif (MD)
Immediate Holding Company: ARCHWAY SHEET METAL WORKS LIMITED
Registration no: 01501004 **Date established:** 1980
No.of Employees: 21 - 50 **Product Groups:** 40, 67

Date of Accounts	Feb 12	Feb 11	Feb 10
Working Capital	87	148	131
Fixed Assets	901	935	877
Current Assets	842	809	715

Arcon Overseas Ltd
12 Relton Mews, London, SW7 1ET
Tel: 020-7225 1411 **Fax:** 020-7225 1811
E-mail: sales@arcon-london.co.uk
Website: http://www.cobbleusa.com
Directors: R. Shaw (Dir)
Managers: H. De Rijk (Sales Prom Mgr), J. Helps (Chief Acct)
Immediate Holding Company: ARCON OVERSEAS LIMITED
Registration no: 02874747 **VAT No.:** GB 645 7734 08
Date established: 1993 **Turnover:** £5m - £10m **No.of Employees:** 1 - 10
Product Groups: 61, 80

Date of Accounts	Dec 11	Dec 10	Dec 09
Sales Turnover	7m	5m	5m
Pre Tax Profit/Loss	181	165	89
Working Capital	1m	874	742
Fixed Assets	49	41	47
Current Assets	2m	3m	3m
Current Liabilities	983	631	536

Argent Group plc
5 Albany Courtyard, London, W1J 0HF
Tel: 020-7734 3721 **Fax:** 020-7734 4474
E-mail: reception@argentgroup.plc.uk
Website: http://www.argentgroup.plc.uk
Bank(s): The Royal Bank of Scotland
Directors: J. Prower (Fin), S. Alderson (Sales & Mktg), P. Hazell (Ch)
Managers: K. Sykes (Personnel), A. Ruck (Tech Serv Mgr)
Ultimate Holding Company: BT Pension Scheme
Immediate Holding Company: ARGENT GROUP PLC
Registration no: 02187385 **VAT No.:** GB 340 8042 **Date established:** 1987
Turnover: £10m - £20m **No.of Employees:** 51 - 100 **Product Groups:** 80

Date of Accounts	Dec 11	Dec 10	Dec 09
Sales Turnover	15m	14m	64m
Pre Tax Profit/Loss	7m	4m	-10m
Working Capital	70m	72m	58m
Fixed Assets	89m	88m	98m
Current Assets	77m	79m	129m
Current Liabilities	7m	7m	5m

Arkay Windows Ltd
573-575 Lordship Lane, London, N22 5LE
Tel: 020-8889 6821 **Fax:** 020-8888 0398
E-mail: info@arkaywindows.com
Website: http://www.arkaywindows.com
Directors: R. Radia (MD), R. Radia (MD)
Immediate Holding Company: ARKAY WINDOWS LIMITED
Registration no: 01238359 **Date established:** 1975 **Turnover:** £1m - £2m
No.of Employees: 21 - 50 **Product Groups:** 30, 52

Date of Accounts	Dec 11	Dec 10	Dec 09
Working Capital	264	154	74
Fixed Assets	911	952	1m
Current Assets	821	668	540

Arnold K L P
109 Wardour Street, London, W1F 0UN
Tel: 020-7478 3478 **Fax:** 020-7478 3578
Website: http://www.arnoldklp.com
Directors: H. Treacy (Dir)
Immediate Holding Company: SYNDICATEWORKS LIMITED
Registration no: 02942499 **VAT No.:** GB 539 2164 39
Date established: 2002 **Turnover:** £20m - £50m
No.of Employees: 51 - 100 **Product Groups:** 81

Date of Accounts	Dec 11	Dec 10	Dec 09
Sales Turnover	11m	14m	15m
Pre Tax Profit/Loss	1m	904	2m
Working Capital	2m	2m	2m
Fixed Assets	190	297	365
Current Assets	5m	5m	6m
Current Liabilities	1m	2m	3m

Bernard J Arnull & Co. Ltd
17-21 Sunbeam Road, London, NW10 6JP
Tel: 020-8965 6094 **Fax:** 020-8961 1585
E-mail: bernard.arnull@easynet.co.uk
Website: http://www.bernardarnull.co.uk
Directors: J. Arnull (MD), S. Arnull (Dir), T. Hely (Dir)
Immediate Holding Company: BERNARD J. ARNULL & CO. LIMITED
Registration no: 01385056 **VAT No.:** GB 229 0736 61
Date established: 1978 **Turnover:** £250,000 - £500,000
No.of Employees: 1 - 10 **Product Groups:** 33, 66

Around Wine
57 Chiltern Street, London, W1U 6ND
Tel: 020-7935 4679 **Fax:** 020-7935 0479
E-mail: info@aroundwine.co.uk
Website: http://www.aroundwine.co.uk
Directors: D. Primack (Dir)
Immediate Holding Company: EUROCAVE IMPORTERS LIMITED
Registration no: 02783016 **Date established:** 1993 **Turnover:** £1m - £2m
No.of Employees: 1 - 10 **Product Groups:** 26, 40, 41, 67

Date of Accounts	Dec 07	Dec 06	Mar 06
Working Capital	46	-22	-1
Fixed Assets	142	176	199
Current Assets	471	392	384
Current Liabilities	425	414	385
Total Share Capital	36	36	35

Arriva plc
16 Watsons Road, London, N22 7TZ
Tel: 020-8271 0101 **Fax:** 020-8271 0120
Website: http://www.arrivalondon.com
Directors: T. Milburn (Eng Serv), A. Sewell (Fin), J. Pycroft (Chief Op Offcr), M. Yexley (MD)
Managers: J. Traynor (Comm)
Immediate Holding Company: ARRIVA PLC
Registration no: 00347103 **Date established:** 1938
Turnover: £75m - £125m **No.of Employees:** 1 - 10 **Product Groups:** 72

Date of Accounts	Dec 10	Dec 09	Dec 08
Sales Turnover	N/A	3148m	3042m
Pre Tax Profit/Loss	-47m	122m	150m
Working Capital	290m	-313m	-392m
Fixed Assets	630m	2278m	2339m
Current Assets	480m	707m	640m
Current Liabilities	21m	739m	739m

Arrow Coated Products UK Ltd
Level 33 Cgc-33-01 Citigroup Tower 25 Canada Square, London, E14 5LB
Tel: 020-7038 8210 **Fax:** 020-7038 8310
E-mail: arrowuk@arrowcoated.com
Website: http://www.watersolublefilm.com
Immediate Holding Company: ARROW COATED PRODUCTS (UK) LIMITED
Registration no: 05187913 **Date established:** 2004
No.of Employees: 1 - 10 **Product Groups:** 30

Date of Accounts	Mar 12	Mar 11	Mar 10
Working Capital	1	3	5
Fixed Assets	10	10	14
Current Assets	57	56	59
Current Liabilities	52	N/A	N/A

Art Of Cast
Unit 14 Parkside Business Estate Rolt Street, London, SE8 5JB
Tel: 020-8694 1097 **Fax:** 020-8694 1097
E-mail: artofcast@aol.com
Website: http://www.artofcast.co.uk
Directors: A. Parnell (Ptnr)
Date established: 1991 **No.of Employees:** 1 - 10 **Product Groups:** 26, 35

Artemide GB Ltd
106 Great Russell Street, London, WC1B 3NB
Tel: 020-7631 5200 **Fax:** 020-7631 5222
E-mail: info@artemide.com
Website: http://www.artemide.com
Bank(s): HSBC Bank plc
Directors: A. Barbieri (MD)
Ultimate Holding Company: ARTEMIDE GROUP SPA (ITALY)
Immediate Holding Company: ARTEMIDE G.B. LIMITED
Registration no: 01514970 **VAT No.:** GB 237 6624 47
Date established: 1980 **Turnover:** £2m - £5m **No.of Employees:** 11 - 20
Product Groups: 37

Date of Accounts	Dec 11	Dec 10	Dec 09
Sales Turnover	4m	3m	2m
Pre Tax Profit/Loss	273	138	-253
Working Capital	336	55	-99
Fixed Assets	632	641	658
Current Assets	1m	836	627
Current Liabilities	367	517	109

Artemide GB
92 Great Portland Street, London, W1W 7NT
Tel: 020-7637 7238 **Fax:** 020-7291 9319
Immediate Holding Company: THE PRINCE'S REGENERATION TRUST
Date established: 2001 **No.of Employees:** 1 - 10 **Product Groups:** 37, 67

Arup (Head Office)
13 Fitzroy Steet, London, W1T 4BQ
Tel: 020-7755 3279 **Fax:** 020-7755 3716
E-mail: london@arup.com
Website: http://www.arup.com
Directors: J. Miles (Dir), M. Tweedie (Co Sec)
Ultimate Holding Company: ARUP GROUP LIMITED
Immediate Holding Company: ARUP LIMITED
Registration no: 02461313 **Date established:** 1990 **Turnover:** £2m - £5m
No.of Employees: 1 - 10 **Product Groups:** 40, 42, 44, 48, 52, 54, 72, 80, 81, 84, 85

Date of Accounts	Mar 11	Mar 10	Mar 09
Sales Turnover	3m	2m	N/A
Pre Tax Profit/Loss	582	416	N/A
Working Capital	819	-153	73
Fixed Assets	15m	16m	N/A
Current Assets	3m	497	73
Current Liabilities	538	610	N/A

Joseph Ash London
Glaucus Works Leven Road, London, E14 0LP
Tel: 020-7987 5070 **Fax:** 020-7515 7498
E-mail: london@josephash.co.uk
Website: http://www.josephash.co.uk
Directors: H. Everett (Co Sec), S. Hopkins (MD)
Ultimate Holding Company: ASH & LACY P.L.C.
Immediate Holding Company: JOSEPH ASH & SON LTD
Registration no: 00420672 **Turnover:** £2m - £5m
No.of Employees: 21 - 50 **Product Groups:** 48

Ash Norton Solicitors Ltd
7th Floor Westec House Westgate, London, W5 1YY
Tel: 020-8991 3330 **Fax:** 020-8991 3332
E-mail: priti@ashnorton-solicitors.com
Website: http://www.ashnorton-solicitors.com
Directors: P. Patel (MD), P. Patel (Fin)
Immediate Holding Company: ASH NORTON SOLICITORS LIMITED
Registration no: 05294310 **Date established:** 2004
Turnover: Up to £250,000 **No.of Employees:** 1 - 10 **Product Groups:** 80

Date of Accounts	Nov 10	Nov 09	Nov 08
Working Capital	13	17	36
Fixed Assets	1	1	3
Current Assets	21	34	71

Laura Ashley Ltd
Design Centre 27 Bagleys Lane, London, SW6 2QA
Tel: 020-7880 5100 **Fax:** 020-7880 5200
E-mail: sean.anglim@lauraashley.com
Website: http://www.lauraashley.com
Bank(s): HSBC Bank plc & The Bank of Nova Scotia & The Bank
Directors: S. Anglim (Dir)
Ultimate Holding Company: LAURA ASHLEY HOLDINGS PLC
Immediate Holding Company: LAURA ASHLEY LIMITED
Registration no: 00531301 **VAT No.:** GB 162 9742 43
Date established: 1954 **Turnover:** £250m - £500m
No.of Employees: 101 - 250 **Product Groups:** 23

Date of Accounts	Jan 09	Jan 10	Jan 11
Sales Turnover	254m	262m	279m
Pre Tax Profit/Loss	19m	21m	31m
Working Capital	16m	39m	69m
Fixed Assets	37m	34m	22m
Current Assets	239m	373m	248m
Current Liabilities	41m	129m	114m

Ashtead Plant Hire Ltd
37 Pomeroy Street, London, SE14 5BW
Tel: 020-7635 0123 **Fax:** 020-7635 0241
Website: http://www.aplant.com
Bank(s): Lloyds TSB Bank plc
Managers: C. Toll (Mgr)
Immediate Holding Company: ASHSTEAD GROUP P.L.C.
Registration no: 00444569 **VAT No.:** GB 217 5687 37
Turnover: £250m - £500m **No.of Employees:** 11 - 20
Product Groups: 72, 83

Ashursts LLP
5 Appold Street, London, EC2A 2HA
Tel: 020-7638 1111 **Fax:** 020-7638 1112
E-mail: info@ashurst.com
Website: http://www.ashursts.com
Directors: C. Geffen (Snr Part), N. Morland (Fin), N. Morland (Fin), P. Griffith (Pers), S. Hardman (Pers)
Managers: C. Sutcliffe, C. Sutcliffe, J. Stephenson (Purch Mgr), B. Pellicci
Immediate Holding Company: ASHURSTS LIMITED
Registration no: 02217139 **Date established:** 1988
No.of Employees: 1001 - 1500 **Product Groups:** 80

Aspire Beyond
2nd Floor 145-157 St John Street, London, EC1V 4PY
Tel: 0870-490 4296 **Fax:** 0870-706 4880
E-mail: info@aspirebeyond.co.uk
Website: http://www.aspirebeyond.co.uk
Directors: D. Simon (Dir)
Registration no: 05606328 **Date established:** 2005
Turnover: £250,000 - £500,000 **No.of Employees:** 1 - 10
Product Groups: 80

Asprey London Ltd
167 New Bond Street, London, W1S 4AY
Tel: 020-7493 6767 **Fax:** 020-7491 0384
E-mail: enquiries@asprey.com
Website: http://www.asprey.co.uk
Directors: P. De Santis (Fin)
Ultimate Holding Company: ASPREY INTERNATIONAL LTD (CAYMEN ISLANDS)
Immediate Holding Company: ASPREY LONDON LIMITED
Registration no: 01004355 **Date established:** 1971
Turnover: £10m - £20m **No.of Employees:** 1 - 10 **Product Groups:** 49

Date of Accounts	Mar 11	Mar 10	Mar 09
Sales Turnover	12m	13m	13m
Pre Tax Profit/Loss	34m	-6m	-663
Working Capital	12m	-23m	-17m
Fixed Assets	470	770	1m
Current Assets	24m	25m	29m
Current Liabilities	956	1m	1m

Assicurazioni Generali
100 Leman Street, London, E1 8AJ
Tel: 020-7265 6200 **Fax:** 020-7702 3745
E-mail: dominique_santini@generaliglobal.com
Website: http://www.generaliglobal.com
Managers: D. Santini
Ultimate Holding Company: ASSICURAZIONI GENERALI SPA
Immediate Holding Company: ASSICURAZIONI GENERALI-SOCIETA PER AZIONI
Registration no: FC005315 **VAT No.:** GB 244 2895 47
Date established: 1963 **No.of Employees:** 101 - 250 **Product Groups:** 82

Associated British Foods Plc
Weston Centre 10 Grosvenor Street, London, W1K 4QY
Tel: 020-7399 6500 **Fax:** 020-7399 6580
Website: http://www.abf.co.uk
Directors: J. Bason (Fin)
Managers: G. Weston
Ultimate Holding Company: WITTINGTON INVESTMENTS LIMITED
Immediate Holding Company: ASSOCIATED BRITISH FOODS PLC
Registration no: 00293262 **Date established:** 1934
Turnover: Over £1,000m **No.of Employees:** 51 - 100 **Product Groups:** 85

Date of Accounts	Sep 10	Sep 11	Sep 08
Sales Turnover	10167m	11065m	8235m
Pre Tax Profit/Loss	763m	757m	527m

see next page

Associated British Foods Plc - Cont'd

Working Capital	668m	621m	948m
Fixed Assets	6493m	7039m	5371m
Current Assets	2795m	3163m	2790m
Current Liabilities	998m	1025m	994m

Associated Newspapers

Northcliffe House 2 Derry Street, London, W8 5TT
Tel: 020-7938 6000 **Fax:** 020-7937 3214
E-mail: manchester@dailymail.co.uk
Website: http://www.associatednewspapers.co.uk
Directors: J. Welsh (Fin), S. Heath (Pers), S. Aukland (MD)
Managers: R. Agambar
Ultimate Holding Company: ROTHERMERE CONTINUATION LTD (BERMUDA)
Immediate Holding Company: ASSOCIATED NEWSPAPERS (U.S.A.) LIMITED
Registration no: 03016861 **Date established:** 1995
Turnover: £500m - £1,000m **No.of Employees:** 1501 & over
Product Groups: 28

Date of Accounts	Sep 08	Oct 09	Oct 10
Sales Turnover	834m	746m	726m
Pre Tax Profit/Loss	6m	-66m	91m
Working Capital	-45m	-95m	15m
Fixed Assets	382m	386m	361m
Current Assets	561m	700m	971m
Current Liabilities	137m	104m	115m

Associated Security Group Ltd

277 Wandsworth Bridge Road, London, SW6 2TX
Tel: 020-7731 0641 **Fax:** 020-8669 9890
E-mail: sales@associatedsecuritygroup.co.uk
Website: http://www.associatedsecuritygroup.co.uk
Bank(s): HSBC Bank plc
Directors: M. Challen (MD)
Immediate Holding Company: ASSOCIATED SECURITY GROUP LIMITED
Registration no: 01219795 **VAT No.:** GB 219 9820 34
Date established: 1975 **Turnover:** £1m - £2m **No.of Employees:** 11 - 20
Product Groups: 35, 36, 40

Date of Accounts	Sep 11	Sep 10	Sep 09
Working Capital	107	78	34
Fixed Assets	21	34	45
Current Assets	228	218	240

Association Of British Dispensing Opticians

199 Gloucester Terrace, London, W2 6LD
Tel: 020-7298 5100 **Fax:** 020-7298 5111
E-mail: info@fmo.co.uk
Website: http://www.fmo.co.uk
Managers: P. Kurma (Comptroller)
Immediate Holding Company: ASSOCIATION OF BRITISH DISPENSING OPTICIANS(THE)
Registration no: 02012484 **VAT No.:** GB 233 1172 08
Date established: 1986 **Turnover:** £2m - £5m **No.of Employees:** 1 - 10
Product Groups: 87

Date of Accounts	Dec 11	Dec 10	Dec 09
Sales Turnover	N/A	N/A	3m
Pre Tax Profit/Loss	N/A	N/A	-321
Working Capital	332	73	-251
Fixed Assets	944	955	988
Current Assets	683	498	525
Current Liabilities	N/A	N/A	171

Association Of Consulting Engineers

Alliance House 12 Caxton Street, London, SW1H 0QL
Tel: 020-7222 6557 **Fax:** 020-7222 0750
E-mail: consult@acenet.co.uk
Website: http://www.acenet.co.uk
Bank(s): Lloyds TSB Bank plc
Directors: N. Ogunshakin (Grp Chief Exec)
Managers: G. Bullett (Mktg Serv Mgr), J. Mayungbe (Fin Mgr)
Immediate Holding Company: ASSOCIATION FOR CONSULTANCY AND ENGINEERING
Registration no: 00132142 **VAT No.:** GB 238 8637 22
Date established: 2013 **Turnover:** £1m - £2m **No.of Employees:** 11 - 20
Product Groups: 80

Date of Accounts	Dec 11	Dec 10	Dec 09
Sales Turnover	2m	2m	2m
Pre Tax Profit/Loss	1	2	N/A
Working Capital	46	33	49
Fixed Assets	384	397	378
Current Assets	351	369	473
Current Liabilities	257	270	355

Association Of Teachers & Lecturers

7 Northumberland Street, London, WC2N 5RD
Tel: 020-7930 6441 **Fax:** 020-7930 1359
E-mail: info@atl.org.uk
Website: http://www.atl.org.uk
Directors: M. Bousted (Gen Sec), T. Nandhra (Fin)
Managers: V. Barlow (Mktg Serv Mgr), E. Ellis (Sales Admin), N. Landau (Personnel), S. Hines (Tech Serv Mgr)
Immediate Holding Company: THE ATL TRUST FUND LIMITED
Registration no: 06364897 **Date established:** 2007
No.of Employees: 51 - 100 **Product Groups:** 87

Date of Accounts	Sep 11	Sep 10	Sep 09
Sales Turnover	87	91	120
Pre Tax Profit/Loss	15	-31	113
Working Capital	39	16	44
Fixed Assets	2m	2m	2m
Current Assets	74	49	98
Current Liabilities	35	33	55

Assured Asset Finance Ltd

45 Charles Street Mayfair, London, W1J 5EH
Tel: 020-7079 1700 **Fax:** 01737-865342
E-mail: info@aafmail.com
Website: http://www.assuredassetfinance.com
Directors: A. Colombini (Prop)
Managers: S. Barris (Sales Prom Mgr)
Registration no: 05943979 **Date established:** 2006
No.of Employees: 1 - 10 **Product Groups:** 27, 33, 37, 42, 44, 82, 83, 89

Aston Communications

2 St Johns Buildings Friern Barnet Road, London, N11 3DP
Tel: 020-8361 8711 **Fax:** 020-8361 3633
E-mail: enquiry@aston-telex.com
Website: http://www.aston-telex.com
Directors: J. Burton (Prop)
Immediate Holding Company: ASTON COMMUNICATIONS LIMITED
Registration no: 02067450 **VAT No.:** GB 396 6858 75
Date established: 1986 **Turnover:** £250,000 - £500,000
No.of Employees: 1 - 10 **Product Groups:** 30

Aston Martin Sales Ltd

Brook House 113 Park Lane, London, W1K 7AJ
Tel: 020-7235 8888 **Fax:** 020- 76295376
Website: http://www.astonmartin.com
Directors: D. Hunsley (Fin), A. Griffin (MD)
Managers: C. Calabrese, A. Griffin (Mgr), A. Blake (District Mgr), Leonord-morgan (), G. Moran (Mktg Serv Mgr)
Immediate Holding Company: PENDRAGON P.L.C.
Registration no: 02163998 **VAT No.:** GB 508 0298 55
No.of Employees: 1 - 10 **Product Groups:** 39, 68

Astrazeneca Finance Ltd

15 Stanhope Gate, London, W1K 1LN
Tel: 020-7304 5000 **Fax:** 020-7304 5151
E-mail: justin.hoskins@astrazeneca.com
Website: http://www.astrazneca.co.uk
Directors: J. Hoskins (Co Sec)
Ultimate Holding Company: ASTRAZENECA PLC
Immediate Holding Company: ASTRAZENECA FINANCE LIMITED
Registration no: 02761796 **Date established:** 1992
Turnover: Up to £250,000 **No.of Employees:** 1 - 10 **Product Groups:** 63

Date of Accounts	Dec 10	Dec 09	Dec 08
Sales Turnover	N/A	N/A	3
Pre Tax Profit/Loss	N/A	N/A	3
Working Capital	65	65	65
Current Assets	65	65	81
Current Liabilities	N/A	N/A	16

Atco Development Ltd

42 Albemarle Street, London, W1S 4JH
Tel: 020-7491 3664 **Fax:** 020-7629 1120
E-mail: central@atcolondon.com
Website: http://www.fullers.co.uk
Managers: L. O'kirwan
Ultimate Holding Company: ATCO HOLDINGS LIMITED (CAYMAN ISLANDS)
Immediate Holding Company: ATCO DEVELOPMENT LIMITED
Registration no: 01353481 **VAT No.:** GB 242 4161 94
Date established: 1978 **Turnover:** Up to £250,000
No.of Employees: 1 - 10 **Product Groups:** 61

Date of Accounts	Dec 10	Dec 09	Dec 08
Sales Turnover	106	60	36
Pre Tax Profit/Loss	36	36	32
Working Capital	-50	-93	-136
Fixed Assets	3m	3m	3m
Current Assets	76	58	17
Current Liabilities	99	124	83

Atlantis European Ltd

1st Floor Brittania House 68-80 Hanbury Street, London, E1 5JL
Tel: 020-7377 8855 **Fax:** 020-7377 8850
E-mail: mail@atlantisart.co.uk
Website: http://www.atlantisart.co.uk
Bank(s): Barclays
Directors: M. Winthrop (MD)
Managers: G. Winthrop (Mgr), G. Winthrop (Mgr)
Immediate Holding Company: ATLANTIS EUROPEAN LIMITED
Registration no: 02690237 **VAT No.:** GB 609 8781 95
Date established: 1992 **Turnover:** £2m - £5m **No.of Employees:** 21 - 50
Product Groups: 27, 32, 35, 36, 49, 64

Date of Accounts	Mar 11	Mar 10	Mar 09
Sales Turnover	N/A	3m	3m
Pre Tax Profit/Loss	N/A	-228	13
Working Capital	251	53	283
Fixed Assets	3	5	9
Current Assets	790	832	798
Current Liabilities	N/A	327	102

Atos

4 Triton Square Regents Place, London, NW1 3HG
Tel: 020-7830 4447 **Fax:** 020-7830 4445
E-mail: ukwebenquiries@atosorigin.co.uk
Website: http://www.atosorigin.co.uk
Bank(s): HSBC Bank plc
Directors: S. Curl (Dir), A. Mccrae (Dir)
Ultimate Holding Company: ATOS ORIGIN SA (FRANCE)
Immediate Holding Company: ATOS UK IT LIMITED
Registration no: 02479330 **Date established:** 1990
Turnover: £20m - £50m **No.of Employees:** 51 - 100 **Product Groups:** 44

Atrium Underwriting Ltd

1 Lime Street, London, EC3M 7DQ
Tel: 020-7327 4877 **Fax:** 020-7327 4878
E-mail: robert.maguire@atrium-uw.com
Website: http://www.atrium-uw.com
Managers: A. Baddeley, P. Hargrave (Personnel), R. Maguire (Admin Off)
Ultimate Holding Company: ARIEL HOLDINGS LIMITED
Immediate Holding Company: ATRIUM UNDERWRITING GROUP LIMITED
Registration no: 02860390 **Date established:** 1993
Turnover: £10m - £20m **No.of Employees:** 101 - 250 **Product Groups:** 82

Date of Accounts	Dec 08
Pre Tax Profit/Loss	16m
Fixed Assets	276m
Current Assets	210m
Current Liabilities	425m

Aubrey David Solicitors

40 Manchester Street, London, W1U 7LL
Tel: 020-7224 4410 **Fax:** 020-7935 2410
E-mail: dfreedman@aubreydavid.com
Website: http://www.aubreydavid.com
Directors: D. Freedman (Ptnr)
Immediate Holding Company: DUE SOUTH SOLAR LIMITED
Registration no: 07236445 **Date established:** 2011
No.of Employees: 1 - 10 **Product Groups:** 80

Augustus Martin Ltd

8 St Andrews Way, London, E3 3PB
Tel: 020-7537 4200 **Fax:** 020-7537 2184
E-mail: enquiry@amartin.co.uk
Website: http://www.augustusmartin.com
Directors: B. Dix (MD), P. Aslet (Fin)
Immediate Holding Company: AUGUSTUS MARTIN HOLDINGS LIMITED
Registration no: 04344688 **Date established:** 2001
Turnover: £20m - £50m **No.of Employees:** 101 - 250
Product Groups: 28, 32, 49, 81

Austin Reed Group Ltd (London Office)

103-113 Regent Street, London, W1B 4HL
Tel: 020-7534 7777 **Fax:** 020-7534 7741
Website: http://www.austinreed.co.uk
Bank(s): National Westminster Bank Plc
Managers: I. Wallace (Fin Mgr), N. Hollingworth, O. Williamson, R. Tewson, A. Witter (Personnel), S. Ashmead
Immediate Holding Company: AUSTIN REED GROUP LIMITED
Registration no: 00164291 **Date established:** 2020
Turnover: £75m - £125m **No.of Employees:** 51 - 100 **Product Groups:** 61

Date of Accounts	Jan 11	Jan 10	Jan 09
Sales Turnover	121m	117m	110m
Pre Tax Profit/Loss	-2m	-485	1m
Working Capital	30m	30m	32m
Fixed Assets	16m	16m	15m
Current Assets	67m	59m	54m
Current Liabilities	18m	14m	7m

Autobar Group Ltd

East Wing 14th Floor, 389 Chiswick High Road, London, W4 4AJ
Tel: 020-8987 6500 **Fax:** 020-8987 6501
E-mail: sales@autobar.com
Website: http://www.autobar.com
Bank(s): Lloyds TSB Bank plc
Directors: A. Bristo (MD), A. Bristow (Grp Chief Exec), W. Mckay (Co Sec)
Managers: A. Marwood (Personnel)
Ultimate Holding Company: St. Martins Group Ltd
Immediate Holding Company: Autobar Group Ltd
Registration no: 00209116 **Turnover:** £125m - £250m
No.of Employees: 1501 & over **Product Groups:** 20, 27, 30, 32, 33, 40, 49, 62, 67, 83

Autocar Electrical Equipment Company Ltd

49-51 Tiverton Street, London, SE1 6NZ
Tel: 020-7403 4334 **Fax:** 020-7378 1270
E-mail: sales@autocar-electrical.com
Website: http://www.autocar-electrical.com
Managers: S. Pearce (Mgr)
Ultimate Holding Company: LUMENITION LIMITED
Immediate Holding Company: AUTOCAR ELECTRICAL EQUIPMENT CO LIMITED
Registration no: 02990627 **VAT No.:** GB 653 4681 23
Date established: 1994 **Turnover:** £1m - £2m **No.of Employees:** 1 - 10
Product Groups: 39

Date of Accounts	Dec 11	Dec 10	Dec 09
Working Capital	61	74	97
Fixed Assets	5	7	9
Current Assets	233	264	254

AV2 Hire Ltd

64 Millman Street, London, WC1N 3EF
Tel: 020-7831 8284 **Fax:** 020-7242 8430
E-mail: sales@av2hire.com
Website: http://www.av2hire.com
Managers: N. Swardt (Mgr)
Turnover: £250,000 - £500,000 **No.of Employees:** 1 - 10
Product Groups: 38

Date of Accounts	Aug 07	Aug 06
Working Capital	11	21
Fixed Assets	10	10
Current Assets	61	60
Current Liabilities	50	39

Avalon P R Ltd

4a Exmoor Street, London, W10 6BD
Tel: 020-7598 7222 **Fax:** 020-7598 7223
E-mail: enquiries@avalonuk.com
Website: http://www.avalonuk.com
Directors: R. Aslett (Dir), R. Allen Turner (Co Sec), J. Thotay (MD), J. Thoday (Dir)
Managers: D. George (Chief Acct), L. Tucker (Prod Mgr)
Ultimate Holding Company: NOLAVA HOLDINGS LIMITED
Immediate Holding Company: AVALON PUBLIC RELATIONS LIMITED
Registration no: 03353751 **Date established:** 1997 **Turnover:** £2m - £5m
No.of Employees: 1 - 10 **Product Groups:** 49, 80, 81

Date of Accounts	Jun 11	Jun 10	Jun 09
Sales Turnover	2m	N/A	N/A
Pre Tax Profit/Loss	179	N/A	N/A
Working Capital	695	565	278
Current Assets	2m	1m	2m
Current Liabilities	185	N/A	N/A

Avolites Ltd

Park Avenue, London, NW10 7XL
Tel: 020-8965 8522 **Fax:** 020-8965 0290
E-mail: richard@avolites.com
Website: http://www.avolites.com
Bank(s): National Westminster Bank Plc
Directors: R. Salzedo (MD), S. Warren (Sales), M. Varatharajan (Fin)
Managers: S. Matharu
Immediate Holding Company: AVOLITES LIMITED
Registration no: 02578003 **VAT No.:** GB 538 7704 14
Date established: 1991 **Turnover:** £5m - £10m **No.of Employees:** 21 - 50
Product Groups: 37

Date of Accounts	Apr 11	Apr 10	Apr 09
Sales Turnover	8m	5m	7m
Pre Tax Profit/Loss	1m	189	580
Working Capital	3m	2m	2m
Fixed Assets	2m	2m	2m
Current Assets	4m	3m	3m
Current Liabilities	207	114	292

Avon Scale Co. Ltd

1 Claremont Street, London, N18 2RP
Tel: 020-8807 2254 **Fax:** 020-8803 6653
E-mail: accounts@avonscale.freeserve.co.uk
Website: http://www.avonscale.co.uk
Directors: R. Smith (Co Sec)
Immediate Holding Company: AVON SCALE COMPANY LIMITED
Registration no: 02226425 **Date established:** 1988
Turnover: £250,000 - £500,000 **No.of Employees:** 1 - 10
Product Groups: 38

Date of Accounts	Feb 12	Feb 11	Feb 10
Working Capital	43	33	23
Fixed Assets	48	48	48

Current Assets	76	76	48

Avventura

18 Lindfield Road, London, W5 1QR
Tel: 020-8810 8020 **Fax:** 020-8997 5353
E-mail: avventura@btconnect.com
Website: http://www.avventura.co.uk
Directors: S. Hardwick (Dir)
Immediate Holding Company: AVVENTURA EVENT MANAGEMENT LIMITED
Registration no: 02841266 **VAT No.:** GB 284 1126 6
Date established: 1993 **Turnover:** £500,000 - £1m
No.of Employees: 1 - 10 **Product Groups:** 69, 80, 81, 86

Date of Accounts	Jul 11	Jul 10	Jul 07
Working Capital	-0	-0	-0

Axa Corporate Solutions

136-140 Fenchurch Street, London, EC3M 6BL
Tel: 020-7702 6600 **Fax:** 020-7702 6929
Website: http://www.axa-corporatesolutions.com
Managers: J. Morgan (Mgr)
Ultimate Holding Company: AXA IM PRIVATE EQUITY SA (FRANCE)
Immediate Holding Company: AXA CORPORATE SOLUTIONS SERVICES UK LIMITED
Registration no: 01020242 **Date established:** 1971
Turnover: £20m - £50m **No.of Employees:** 51 - 100 **Product Groups:** 82

Date of Accounts	Dec 11	Dec 10	Dec 09
Sales Turnover	23m	21m	19m
Pre Tax Profit/Loss	460	518	-569
Working Capital	2m	2m	2m
Fixed Assets	410	707	1m
Current Assets	14m	15m	18m
Current Liabilities	6m	5m	5m

Axa Framlington

7 Newgate Street,, London, EC1A 7NX
Tel: 020-7003 2233 **Fax:** 020-7330 6644
E-mail: ukpressoffice@axa-im.com
Website: http://www.axaframlington.com
Directors: N. Boulton (Dir), R. Bailey (Sales)
Ultimate Holding Company: AXA SA (FRANCE)
Immediate Holding Company: Axa Framlington Group Ltd
Registration no: 01556736 **Date established:** 1981 **Turnover:** £2m - £5m
No.of Employees: 51 - 100 **Product Groups:** 82, 88

Date of Accounts	Dec 07	Dec 06	Dec 05
Working Capital	3	3	3
Current Assets	3	3	3

Axa Framlington Group Ltd

155 Bishopsgate, London, EC2M 3FT
Tel: 020-7330 6400 **Fax:** 020-7330 6644
Website: http://www.axa.com
Bank(s): HSBC Bank plc
Directors: N. Boulton (Dir), R. Kytrianou (Grp Chief Exec)
Ultimate Holding Company: AXA SA (FRANCE)
Immediate Holding Company: Axa Framlington Group Ltd
Registration no: 01237167 **Date established:** 1975
Turnover: £20m - £50m **No.of Employees:** 101 - 250
Product Groups: 80, 82

Date of Accounts	Dec 09	Dec 08	Dec 07
Sales Turnover	9m	23m	N/A
Pre Tax Profit/Loss	9m	21m	20m
Working Capital	1m	8m	18m
Fixed Assets	16m	7m	9m
Current Assets	1m	26m	66m
Current Liabilities	13	9m	19m

Axflow

Orion Park Northfield Avenue, London, W13 9SJ
Tel: 020-8579 2111 **Fax:** 020-8579 7326
E-mail: info@axflow.co.uk
Website: http://www.axflow.co.uk
Bank(s): National Westminster Bank Plc
Directors: A. Peters (MD), M. Howard (Fin)
Managers: P. Basi (Tech Serv Mgr)
Ultimate Holding Company: AXEL JOHNSON INTERNATIONAL AB (SWEDEN)
Immediate Holding Company: AXFLOW LIMITED
Registration no: 04087125 **Date established:** 2000
Turnover: £10m - £20m **No.of Employees:** 11 - 20 **Product Groups:** 40, 41, 42, 43, 45, 46, 48, 66

Date of Accounts	Dec 11	Dec 10	Dec 09
Sales Turnover	12m	10m	10m
Pre Tax Profit/Loss	2m	1m	912
Working Capital	474	2m	1m
Fixed Assets	3m	819	946
Current Assets	5m	4m	4m
Current Liabilities	2m	1m	695

Axia FX Ltd

225 Angel House Marsh Wall, London, E14 9FW
Tel: 020-7093 7880 **Fax:** 0845-257 8259
E-mail: info@axiafx.com
Website: http://www.axiafx.com
Managers: M. Chambers (Comptroller), J. White (Mktg Serv Mgr)
Immediate Holding Company: AXIA FX LIMITED
Registration no: 05762951 **Date established:** 2006
Turnover: £250m - £500m **No.of Employees:** 21 - 50
Product Groups: 81, 82

Date of Accounts	Mar 12	Mar 11	Mar 10
Sales Turnover	359m	819m	507m
Pre Tax Profit/Loss	18	15	-49
Working Capital	173	143	142
Fixed Assets	31	42	35
Current Assets	9m	8m	39m
Current Liabilities	51	40	1m

Aziz Sharpquips

139 St Edmunds Road, London, N9 7PS
Tel: 020-8211 2400 **Fax:** 020-8328 3507
E-mail: ashikaziz@hotmail.co.uk
Website: http://www.sharpquips.co.uk
Directors: A. Aziz (Prop)
Managers: A. Aziz (Cust Serv Mgr)
Date established: 2008 **Turnover:** Up to £250,000
No.of Employees: 1 - 10 **Product Groups:** 41

Azizoff Co. Ltd

2 Beechfield Road, London, N4 1PE
Tel: 020-8809 6902 **Fax:** 020-8800 5795
E-mail: azizoffco@tiscali.net
Directors: J. Azizoff (Dir)
Immediate Holding Company: AZIZOFF LIMITED
Registration no: 03937167 **VAT No.:** GB 245 6517 53
Date established: 2000 **Turnover:** £250,000 - £500,000
No.of Employees: 1 - 10 **Product Groups:** 49

Date of Accounts	Dec 10	Dec 09	Dec 08
Working Capital	20	27	73
Fixed Assets	2	3	3
Current Assets	171	196	171

B B A Aviation plc

105 Wigmore Street, London, W1U 1QY
Tel: 020-7514 3999 **Fax:** 020-7408 2318
E-mail: info@bbaaviation.com
Website: http://www.bbaaviation.com
Bank(s): HSBC, Barclays.
Directors: Z. Stone (Co Sec)
Managers: M. Hoad
Ultimate Holding Company: REAL ESTATE VENTURE CAPITAL PARTNERS LLP
Immediate Holding Company: BBA AVIATION PLC
Registration no: 00053688 **Date established:** 1997
Turnover: Over £1,000m **No.of Employees:** 21 - 50 **Product Groups:** 71

Date of Accounts	Dec 09	Dec 08
Sales Turnover	1081m	1156m
Pre Tax Profit/Loss	60m	84m
Working Capital	137m	206m
Fixed Assets	929m	1067m
Current Assets	448m	551m
Current Liabilities	179m	223m

B B H

60 Kingly Street, London, W1B 5DS
Tel: 020-7734 1677 **Fax:** 020-7437 3666
E-mail: reception@bbh.co.uk
Website: http://www.bbh.co.uk
Bank(s): Barclays
Directors: N. Bogle (Ch), K. O'Shea (Co Sec)
Managers: D. Pearce (Comptroller)
Ultimate Holding Company: BBH HOLDINGS LIMITED
Immediate Holding Company: BBH COMMUNICATIONS LIMITED
Registration no: 02352341 **VAT No.:** GB 386 3359 18
Date established: 1989 **Turnover:** £125m - £250m
No.of Employees: 251 - 500 **Product Groups:** 81

Date of Accounts	Dec 11	Dec 10	Dec 09
Sales Turnover	148m	179m	171m
Pre Tax Profit/Loss	25m	20m	11m
Working Capital	25m	24m	16m
Fixed Assets	6m	8m	10m
Current Assets	80m	76m	71m
Current Liabilities	43m	42m	42m

B E S Investimento Bank

10 Paternoster Square, London, EC4M 7AL
Tel: 020-7246 0180 **Fax:** 020-7246 0190
E-mail: info@execution-noble.com
Website: http://www.besinvestimento.com
Managers: S. Jones, D. Keeka (Tech Serv Mgr), R. Earl (Chief Mgr)
Ultimate Holding Company: EXECUTION HOLDINGS LIMITED
Immediate Holding Company: CONNAUGHT NOMINEES LIMITED
Registration no: SC203624 **Date established:** 1981
Turnover: £10m - £20m **No.of Employees:** 251 - 500 **Product Groups:** 82

B E W Electrical Distributors Ltd

Unit 1 Kimber Centre 54 Kimber Road, London, SW18 4PP
Tel: 020-8874 7474 **Fax:** 020-8874 7200
E-mail: enquiries@bew-elec.co.uk
Website: http://www.bewdirect.co.uk
Directors: N. Godfrey (Fin)
Managers: D. Groves, L. Julian, S. Blowes (Tech Serv Mgr), P. Finnerty (District Mgr)
Immediate Holding Company: BEW ELECTRICAL DISTRIBUTORS LIMITED
Registration no: 01703444 **VAT No.:** GB 372 6658 24
Date established: 1983 **Turnover:** £20m - £50m
No.of Employees: 21 - 50 **Product Groups:** 77

Date of Accounts	Apr 11	Apr 10	Apr 09
Sales Turnover	28m	24m	26m
Pre Tax Profit/Loss	217	653	219
Working Capital	2m	2m	2m
Fixed Assets	2m	2m	2m
Current Assets	9m	8m	8m
Current Liabilities	2m	2m	2m

B & H Colour Change Ltd

212 St Anns Hill, London, SW18 2RU
Tel: 08454-584121 **Fax:** 0845-458 4131
E-mail: gilly@colourchange.com
Website: http://www.colourchange.com
Directors: R. Booth (MD)
Managers: K. Atkin (), K. Atkin, J. Skinner (Sales Prom Mgr), G. Beaumont (Mktg Serv Mgr)
Ultimate Holding Company: HALLCREST GROUP LIMITED
Immediate Holding Company: B&H COLOUR CHANGE LIMITED
Registration no: 04846379 **VAT No.:** GB 443 9893 06
Date established: 2003 **Turnover:** £1m - £2m **No.of Employees:** 1 - 10
Product Groups: 33

Date of Accounts	Jul 07	Jul 06	Jul 05
Working Capital	91	10	10
Current Assets	280	368	206

B & M Machine Tools

70 Silverthorne Road, London, SW8 3HE
Tel: 020-7720 9804 **Fax:** 020-7720 7276
E-mail: info@machinetoolsuk.com
Website: http://www.machinetoolsuk.com
Directors: B. Mcmillan (Ptnr)
Date established: 1977 **Turnover:** Up to £250,000
No.of Employees: 1 - 10 **Product Groups:** 46, 67

B & M Packaging

Unit 24 Uplands Business Park Blackhorse Lane, London, E17 5QJ
Tel: 020-8531 6611 **Fax:** 020-8531 6622
E-mail: aktasmehmet@hotmail.com
Directors: M. Aktas (MD)
Date established: 2002 **No.of Employees:** 1 - 10 **Product Groups:** 38, 42

B P plc

1 St James's Square, London, SW1Y 4PD
Tel: 020-7496 4000 **Fax:** 020-7496 4630
Website: http://www.bp.com
Directors: P. Sutherland (Ch), S. Gong (Dir), K. Seal (MD), H. Miles (Non Exec), C. Eng (Co Sec)
Managers: R. Wright
Ultimate Holding Company: BP P.L.C.
Immediate Holding Company: BP KOREA MARKETING LIMITED
Registration no: 00885307 **Date established:** 1966
Turnover: £10m - £20m **No.of Employees:** 1 - 10 **Product Groups:** 13, 31, 32, 51, 66

Date of Accounts	Dec 10	Dec 09	Dec 08
Sales Turnover	13m	13m	12m
Pre Tax Profit/Loss	168	310	3m
Working Capital	56m	56m	55m
Current Assets	57m	57m	57m
Current Liabilities	1m	2m	1m

B P I Ltd

County Hall Westminster Bridge Road, London, SE1 7JA
Tel: 020-7803 1300 **Fax:** 020-7803 1310
E-mail: general@bpi.co.uk
Website: http://www.bpi.co.uk
Managers: C. Lampard (Sales Admin)
Immediate Holding Company: BPI (BRITISH RECORDED MUSIC INDUSTRY) LIMITED
Registration no: 01132389 **Date established:** 1973
Turnover: £10m - £20m **No.of Employees:** 21 - 50 **Product Groups:** 87

Date of Accounts	Dec 11	Dec 10	Dec 09
Sales Turnover	13m	13m	14m
Pre Tax Profit/Loss	-52	47	96
Working Capital	1m	1m	1m
Fixed Assets	532	565	667
Current Assets	7m	6m	8m
Current Liabilities	4m	4m	6m

B P P Professional Education

B P P House Aldine Place, London, W12 8AA
Tel: 020-8740 2222 **Fax:** 020-8740 2239
E-mail: carl@bpp.com
Website: http://www.bpp.com
Directors: C. Ross Roberts (Fin), M. Daykin (Co Sec)
Managers: C. Lygo
Ultimate Holding Company: APOLLO GROUP INC (USA)
Immediate Holding Company: BPP CROYDON LIMITED
Registration no: 03422433 **Date established:** 1997
Turnover: £500,000 - £1m **No.of Employees:** 251 - 500
Product Groups: 28

Date of Accounts	Dec 08	Aug 11	Aug 10
Sales Turnover	2m	1m	2m
Pre Tax Profit/Loss	481	-325	-200
Working Capital	-1m	-2m	-2m
Fixed Assets	544	535	530
Current Assets	1m	2m	1m
Current Liabilities	250	132	468

B R C Reinforcements Ltd

Kierbeck Business Complex North Woolwich Road, London, E16 2BG
Tel: 020-7474 1800 **Fax:** 020-7474 8686
E-mail: sales@brc-uk.co.uk
Website: http://www.brc.ltd.uk
Directors: J. Thompson (MD)
Ultimate Holding Company: ACERTEC LTD
Immediate Holding Company: CAPRICORN FASHIONS (LONDON) LIMITED
Registration no: 00403085 **Date established:** 2010
Turnover: £50m - £75m **No.of Employees:** 1 - 10 **Product Groups:** 25, 29, 30, 31, 32, 33, 34, 35, 36, 45, 66

Date of Accounts	May 11
Sales Turnover	274
Pre Tax Profit/Loss	-3
Working Capital	-28
Fixed Assets	25
Current Assets	21

B S S (a division of BSS Group)

Unit 6-7 Industrial Estate Thomas Road, London, E14 7BN
Tel: 020-7531 3900 **Fax:** 020-7537 4849
E-mail: tony-maxwell@bssgroup.com
Website: http://www.bssgroup.com
Managers: L. Gray (Mgr)
Immediate Holding Company: BUSINESS SUPPORT SERVICES UK LTD
Registration no: 03106393 **Turnover:** £2m - £5m
No.of Employees: 11 - 20 **Product Groups:** 36

B S T O Ltd

65 Maygrove Road, London, NW6 2EH
Tel: 020-7624 0103 **Fax:** 020-7624 8979
E-mail: ios@ivanbsto.demon.co.uk
Website: http://www.bsto.demon.co.uk
Directors: I. Schwarz (MD)
Immediate Holding Company: BSTO LIMITED
Registration no: 00571360 **VAT No.:** GB 227 1715 76
Date established: 1956 **Turnover:** £500,000 - £1m
No.of Employees: 1 - 10 **Product Groups:** 61

Date of Accounts	Mar 08	Mar 07	Mar 06
Working Capital	97	95	81
Fixed Assets	15	15	11
Current Assets	242	251	226
Current Liabilities	144	155	145
Total Share Capital	100	100	100

B T G plc

5 Fleet Place, London, EC4M 7RD
Tel: 020-7575 0000 **Fax:** 020-7575 0010
E-mail: info@btgplc.com
Website: http://www.btgplc.com
Bank(s): National Westminster.
Managers: R. Soderstrom (Fin Mgr)
Ultimate Holding Company: BTG PLC
Immediate Holding Company: BTG INTERNATIONAL LIMITED
Registration no: 02664412 **VAT No.:** GB 473 5802 34
Date established: 1991 **Turnover:** £50m - £75m
No.of Employees: 51 - 100 **Product Groups:** 85

Date of Accounts	Mar 11	Mar 10	Mar 09
Sales Turnover	56m	50m	60m
Pre Tax Profit/Loss	25m	21m	7m
Working Capital	-81m	-97m	-122m
Fixed Assets	103m	104m	113m
Current Assets	52m	165m	156m
Current Liabilities	17m	16m	22m

B T Group plc
BT Centre 81 Newgate Street, London, EC1A 7AJ
Tel: 020-7356 5000 **Fax:** 020-7356 5520
E-mail: info@bt.com
Website: http://www.btplc.com
Managers: M. Korucu
Ultimate Holding Company: BT Group plc
Immediate Holding Company: BT GROUP PLC
Registration no: 04190816 **Date established:** 2001
Turnover: Over £1,000m **No.of Employees:** 1 - 10 **Product Groups:** 37, 79, 83

Date of Accounts	Mar 12	Mar 11	Mar 10
Sales Turnover	18897m	20076m	20859m
Pre Tax Profit/Loss	2445m	1717m	1007m
Working Capital	-4724m	-3100m	-4135m
Fixed Assets	19417m	19609m	22395m
Current Assets	4531m	3931m	6285m
Current Liabilities	3107m	3781m	6752m

Babcock International
33 Wigmore Street, London, W1U 1QX
Tel: 020-7355 5300 **Fax:** 020-7355 5360
E-mail: infrastructuredivision@babcock.co.uk
Website: http://www.babcock.co.uk
Managers: R. Rendell (Mgr), R. Rendall (Mgr)
Ultimate Holding Company: BABCOCK INTERNATIONAL GROUP PLC
Immediate Holding Company: BABCOCK INTERNATIONAL LIMITED
Registration no: 00065805 **Date established:** 2000
No.of Employees: 1 - 10 **Product Groups:** 35, 36, 39

Date of Accounts	Mar 11	Mar 10	Mar 08
Pre Tax Profit/Loss	2m	4m	9m
Working Capital	57m	54m	84m
Fixed Assets	23m	24m	22m
Current Assets	217m	181m	199m
Current Liabilities	10m	9m	15m

Babyrug
61 Pepys Road, London, SW20 8NL
Tel: 020-8944 8674
E-mail: info@babyrug.co.uk
Website: http://www.babyrug.co.uk
Directors: M. Nicheallaiva (Prop)
Turnover: Up to £250,000 **No.of Employees:** 1 - 10 **Product Groups:** 24, 49, 65

Bain & C O
40 Strand, London, WC2N 5RW
Tel: 020-7969 6000 **Fax:** 020-7969 6666
E-mail: info.london@bain.com
Website: http://www.bain.com
Directors: G. Smout (Fin), R. Buchanan (Snr Part), R. Siddle (Snr Part)
Managers: S. Smith
Ultimate Holding Company: BAIN & COMPANY INC (USA)
Immediate Holding Company: BAIN & COMPANY HOLDINGS LIMITED
Registration no: 03280380 **Date established:** 1996
Turnover: £250,000 - £500,000 **No.of Employees:** 251 - 500
Product Groups: 80, 81

Baker Hughes Inc
3rd Floor Building 5 Chiswick Park 566 Chiswick High Road, London, W4 5YF
Tel: 020-3320 4900 **Fax:** 020-7258 8001
Website: http://www.bakerhughes.com
Directors: P. Stokes (Co Sec)
Managers: M. Borras
Ultimate Holding Company: BAKER HUGHES INC (USA)
Immediate Holding Company: BAKER HUGHES LIMITED
Registration no: 01388658 **VAT No.:** GB 402 8037 87
Date established: 1978 **Turnover:** £500m - £1,000m
No.of Employees: 101 - 250 **Product Groups:** 48

Date of Accounts	Dec 11	Dec 10	Dec 09
Sales Turnover	591m	588m	590m
Pre Tax Profit/Loss	14m	60m	73m
Working Capital	114m	81m	33m
Fixed Assets	2226m	229m	236m
Current Assets	450m	370m	310m
Current Liabilities	37m	47m	N/A

Baker & Mckenzie Ltd
100 New Bridge Street, London, EC4V 6JA
Tel: 020-7919 1000 **Fax:** 020-7919 1999
E-mail: info@bakerinfo.com
Website: http://www.bakermckenzie.com
Directors: S. Hall (I.T. Dir), B. Landais (Mkt Research), C. Lynch (Pers), J. Hayhoe (Mkt Research), M. Carter (Fin), J. Rainbach (Fin), G. Senior (Dir), M. Blackburn (Pers)
Managers: C. Mooneybell
Immediate Holding Company: BAKER & MCKENZIE SERVICES LIMITED
Registration no: 02922570 **Date established:** 1994
Turnover: £20m - £50m **No.of Employees:** 501 - 1000
Product Groups: 80

Date of Accounts	Jun 11	Jun 10
Sales Turnover	36m	N/A
Pre Tax Profit/Loss	10	N/A
Working Capital	10	N/A
Current Assets	5m	207
Current Liabilities	5m	207

Baker Self Adhesive Materials
Unity Works Sutherland Road, London, E17 6BP
Tel: 020-8498 4900 **Fax:** 0800-0856992
E-mail: steve@bakerlabels.co.uk
Website: http://www.bakerlabels.co.uk
Bank(s): National Westminster Bank Plc
Directors: H. Baker (Ch), S. Baker (MD), S. Barker (Jt MD), S. Baker (Prop), M. Baker (Purch), A. Baker (Fin)
Managers: M. Bay (Mktg Serv Mgr)
Immediate Holding Company: BAKER SELF-ADHESIVE LABEL COMPANY LIMITED(THE)
Registration no: 01116854 **VAT No.:** GB 230 7578 65
Date established: 1973 **Turnover:** £2m - £5m **No.of Employees:** 21 - 50
Product Groups: 27

Date of Accounts	Aug 07	Aug 06
Working Capital	1686	1422
Fixed Assets	720	706
Current Assets	2479	2205
Current Liabilities	793	783
Total Share Capital	1	1

Baker Tilly
2 Bloomsbury Street, London, WC1B 3ST
Tel: 020-3201 8000 **Fax:** 020-3201 8001
E-mail: paul.beckett@bakertilly.co.uk
Website: http://www.bakertilly.co.uk
Directors: P. Beckett (Dir), C. Fish (Snr Part)
Managers: G. Hitchborn (Mktg Serv Mgr)
Ultimate Holding Company: BAKER TILLY UK HOLDINGS LIMITED
Immediate Holding Company: BAKER TILLY MANAGEMENT LIMITED
Registration no: 03077999 **Date established:** 1995
Turnover: £20m - £50m **No.of Employees:** 101 - 250 **Product Groups:** 80

Date of Accounts	Mar 11	Mar 10	Mar 09
Sales Turnover	39m	40m	79m
Pre Tax Profit/Loss	-47	318	822
Working Capital	-8m	-7m	-9m
Fixed Assets	13m	13m	14m
Current Assets	9m	8m	8m
Current Liabilities	16m	14m	16m

Balance Technology
33 Belgrave Road Wanstead, London, E11 3QW
Tel: 020-8989 0862 **Fax:** 020-8989 0862
E-mail: andy@balancetechnology.co.uk
Website: http://www.balancetechnology.co.uk
Directors: A. Tur (Prop)
Date established: 1987 **No.of Employees:** 1 - 10 **Product Groups:** 38, 42

Balkan & Black Sea Shipping Co. Ltd
Black Sea House 72 Wilson Street, London, EC2A 2DH
Tel: 020-7684 2800 **Fax:** 020-7684 2790
E-mail: chartering@bbss.uk.com
Website: http://www.bbss.uk.com
Directors: D. Haynes (Co Sec)
Ultimate Holding Company: KG MARITIME SHIPPING JSC (GERMANY)
Immediate Holding Company: BALKAN & BLACK SEA SHIPPING COMPANY LIMITED
Registration no: 00871726 **Date established:** 1966
Turnover: £250,000 - £500,000 **No.of Employees:** 1 - 10
Product Groups: 61, 74

Date of Accounts	Dec 11	Dec 10	Dec 09
Sales Turnover	537	397	2m
Pre Tax Profit/Loss	71	577	-1m
Working Capital	984	929	440
Fixed Assets	694	721	796
Current Assets	2m	2m	2m
Current Liabilities	651	370	159

Ball Bearing Centre Ltd
Unit 1 55-57 Park Royal Road, London, NW10 7LP
Tel: 020-8965 8833 **Fax:** 020-8965 7080
E-mail: ballbrgctr@btconnect.com
Directors: J. Blackmore (Fin)
Managers: L. Rammell (Mgr)
Immediate Holding Company: BALL BEARING CENTRE LTD
Registration no: 00707418 **Date established:** 1961
Turnover: £250,000 - £500,000 **No.of Employees:** 1 - 10
Product Groups: 30, 35, 37, 45

Date of Accounts	Oct 11	Oct 10	Oct 09
Working Capital	59	64	80
Fixed Assets	7	9	11
Current Assets	162	136	136

Balli Group plc
5 Stanhope Gate, London, W1K 1LQ
Tel: 020-7306 2000 **Fax:** 020-7491 9000
E-mail: davids@balli.co.uk
Website: http://www.balli.co.uk
Bank(s): Credit Suisse, Zurich
Directors: D. Spriddell (Fin)
Ultimate Holding Company: BALLI STIFTUNG (LIECHTENSTEIN)
Immediate Holding Company: BALLI GROUP PLC
Registration no: 02632984 **VAT No.:** GB 539 0006 67
Date established: 1991 **Turnover:** Over £1,000m
No.of Employees: 101 - 250 **Product Groups:** 34, 61

Date of Accounts	Dec 08
Sales Turnover	1320m
Pre Tax Profit/Loss	8500
Working Capital	90940
Fixed Assets	1640
Current Assets	246290
Current Liabilities	155350
Total Share Capital	49560
ROCE% (Return on Capital Employed)	9.2

Bally UK Sales Ltd
116 New Bond Street, London, W1S 1EN
Tel: 020-7491 7062 **Fax:** 020-7408 9888
E-mail: lhills@bally.ch
Website: http://www.bally.com
Managers: L. Hills (Mgr)
Ultimate Holding Company: JAB HOLDING (NETHERLANDS)
Immediate Holding Company: BALLY UK SALES LIMITED
Registration no: 00310156 **VAT No.:** GB 104 7115 13
Date established: 1936 **Turnover:** £5m - £10m **No.of Employees:** 1 - 10
Product Groups: 22, 61

Date of Accounts	Jan 09	Jan 10	Jan 11
Sales Turnover	10m	10m	8m
Pre Tax Profit/Loss	-594	-570	-640
Working Capital	-27m	-27m	-29m
Fixed Assets	737	732	557
Current Assets	5m	4m	4m
Current Liabilities	524	791	948

Balsa Trading ltd
2nd Floor 145-157 St. John Street, London, London, EC1V 4PY
Tel: 0207-1835300 **Fax:** 0207-1605266
E-mail: info@balsatrading.co.uk
Website: http://www.balsatrading.co.uk
Managers: C. von Buchwald (Sales Admin)
Registration no: 06267228 **Date established:** 2007
Turnover: £250,000 - £500,000 **No.of Employees:** 1 - 10
Product Groups: 49

Banco Do Brasil S A
105-108 Old Broad Street Forth Floor, London, EC2N 1ER
Tel: 020-7606 7101 **Fax:** 020-7606 2877
E-mail: londres@bb.com.br
Website: http://www.bb.com.br
Bank(s): Barclays, National Westminster
Directors: A. Calliari (Pres)
Immediate Holding Company: BANCO DO BRASIL S.A.
Registration no: FC006852 **No.of Employees:** 51 - 100
Product Groups: 82

Banco Espirito Santo
Swan House 33 Queen Street, London, EC4R 1ES
Tel: 020-7332 4300 **Fax:** 020-7332 4340
Website: http://www.bescl.co.uk
Managers: D. Tan (Mgr), D. Tan (Asst Gen Mgr)
Immediate Holding Company: PLUS MARKETS LIMITED
Registration no: 01437774 **VAT No.:** GB 245 7376 40
Date established: 2009 **No.of Employees:** 21 - 50 **Product Groups:** 82

Banham Security
233 Kensington High Street, London, W8 6SF
Tel: 020-7622 5151 **Fax:** 020-7498 2461
E-mail: sales@banham.com
Website: http://www.banham.com
Directors: T. Ward (Fin)
Ultimate Holding Company: BANHAMS PATENT LOCKS LIMITED
Immediate Holding Company: BANHAM SECURITY LIMITED
Registration no: 03047006 **VAT No.:** GB 238 8988 96
Date established: 1995 **Turnover:** £250,000 - £500,000
No.of Employees: 1 - 10 **Product Groups:** 36

Date of Accounts	Dec 11	Dec 10	Dec 09
Sales Turnover	260	261	253
Pre Tax Profit/Loss	193	134	-7
Working Capital	96	-959	89
Fixed Assets	9m	9m	9m
Current Assets	165	95	97
Current Liabilities	33	1m	8

Bank Of China UK Ltd
1 Lothbury, London, EC2R 7DB
Tel: 020-7282 8888 **Fax:** 020-7626 3892
E-mail: admin@bankofchina.com
Website: http://www.bankofchina.com/uk
Managers: L. Ong, W. Fang (Chief Mgr)
Ultimate Holding Company: CHINA INVESTMENT CORPORATION LTD (CHINA)
Immediate Holding Company: BANK OF CHINA (UK) LIMITED
Registration no: 06193060 **VAT No.:** GB 681 6405 28
Date established: 2007 **Turnover:** £125m - £250m
No.of Employees: 101 - 250 **Product Groups:** 82

Date of Accounts	Dec 11	Dec 10	Dec 09
Pre Tax Profit/Loss	-24m	20m	17m
Fixed Assets	161m	97m	283m
Current Assets	617m	639m	699m
Current Liabilities	565m	510m	770m

Bank Of Cyprus London Ltd
27-31 Charlotte Street, London, W1T 1RP
Tel: 020-7304 5800 **Fax:** 020-7436 6149
E-mail: admin@bankofcyprus.co.uk
Website: http://www.bankofcyprus.co.uk
Directors: I. Koumi (MD), I. Koumi (Dir)
Managers: D. Demetriou (Tech Serv Mgr), J. Richie (Personnel), H. Coe
Ultimate Holding Company: BANK OF CYPRUS PUBLIC COMPANY LIMITED
Immediate Holding Company: BANK OF CYPRUS UK LIMITED
Registration no: 04728421 **Date established:** 2003
Turnover: £250,000 - £500,000 **No.of Employees:** 251 - 500
Product Groups: 82

Date of Accounts	Dec 11	Dec 10	Dec 09
Working Capital	7m	9m	31
Fixed Assets	N/A	N/A	10m
Current Assets	8m	12m	3m

Bank Of Ireland Securities Services
Mary O Sullivan 36 Queen Street, London, EC4R 1BN
Tel: 020-7248 0919 **Fax:** 020-7489 9676
E-mail: buisness@boiuk.com
Website: http://www.bank-of-ireland.co.uk
Directors: W. Cotter (Dir), S. Neary (Co Sec)
Ultimate Holding Company: GOVERNOR AND COMPANY OF THE BANK OF IRELAND
Immediate Holding Company: BANK OF IRELAND SECURITIES SERVICES LIMITED
Registration no: FC019166 **Date established:** 1996
Turnover: £5m - £10m **No.of Employees:** 1 - 10 **Product Groups:** 82

Bank Leumi UK plc
20 Stratford Place, London, W1C 1BG
Tel: 020-7907 8000 **Fax:** 020-7907 8011
E-mail: nhillel@bankleumi.co.uk
Website: http://www.bankleumi.co.uk
Bank(s): Bank Leumi le Israel BM
Directors: S. Rothberg (Co Sec), L. Secretan (Chief Op Offcr)
Managers: L. White, N. Brigden, L. Walling (Personnel), M. Mayost (Mktg Serv Mgr)
Ultimate Holding Company: BANK LEUMI LE ISRAEL BM (ISRAEL)
Immediate Holding Company: LEUMI ABL LIMITED
Registration no: 00620951 **Date established:** 1959 **Turnover:** £5m - £10m
No.of Employees: 101 - 250 **Product Groups:** 82

Date of Accounts	Dec 11	Dec 10	Dec 09
Sales Turnover	9m	8m	8m
Pre Tax Profit/Loss	2m	2m	2m
Working Capital	3m	2m	1m
Fixed Assets	2m	1m	117
Current Assets	116m	96m	101m
Current Liabilities	5m	3m	4m

Bank Of Montreal Europe Ltd
95 Queen Victoria Street, London, EC4V 4HG
Tel: 020-7236 1010 **Fax:** 020-7664 8161
E-mail: gary.olivier@bmo.com
Website: http://www.bmo.com
Bank(s): Bank of England & Lloyds TSB Bank plc
Directors: G. Olivier (Dir)
Ultimate Holding Company: BANK OF MONTREAL
Immediate Holding Company: BANK OF MONTREAL CAPITAL MARKETS (HOLDINGS) LIMITED
Registration no: 01175125 **Date established:** 1974
Turnover: £20m - £50m **No.of Employees:** 101 - 250 **Product Groups:** 82

Date of Accounts	Oct 11	Oct 10	Oct 09
Sales Turnover	44m	37m	24m
Pre Tax Profit/Loss	2m	-499	-6m

Working Capital	70m	38m	-6m
Fixed Assets	21m	22m	23m
Current Assets	194m	156m	31m
Current Liabilities	105m	42m	35m

Bank Of Toyko Mitsubishi Ltd

Finsbury Circus House 14 Finsbury Circus, London, EC2M 7BT
Tel: 020-7588 1111 **Fax:** 020-7628 8241
E-mail: admin@btm.co.uk
Website: http://www.btm.co.uk
Directors: A. Tanaka (Dir), H. Eyre (Co Sec)
Ultimate Holding Company: MITSUBISHI UFJ FINANCIAL GROUP INC (JAPAN)
Immediate Holding Company: THE BANK OF TOKYO LTD, JAPAN
Registration no: 00924205 **Date established:** 1967
Turnover: £500,000 - £1m **No.of Employees:** 501 - 1000
Product Groups: 82

Banks Of America

5 Canada Square, London, E14 5AQ
Tel: 020-7174 4000 **Fax:** 020-7174 6128
Website: http://www.bankofamerica.com
Bank(s): Bank of America NA
Directors: G. Doherty (Dir)
Ultimate Holding Company: BANK OF AMERICA CORP (USA)
Immediate Holding Company: U.S. BANK TRUSTEES LIMITED
Registration no: 02379632 **VAT No.:** GB 578 0154 30
Date established: 1989 **Turnover:** £500,000 - £1m
No.of Employees: 501 - 1000 **Product Groups:** 82

Barber Wilson & Company Ltd

Crawley Road, London, N22 6AH
Tel: 020-8888 3461 **Fax:** 020-8888 2041
E-mail: sales@barwil.co.uk
Website: http://www.barwil.co.uk
Bank(s): Lloyds
Directors: S. Wilson (MD)
Immediate Holding Company: BARBER,WILSONS AND COMPANY LIMITED
Registration no: 00100285 **VAT No.:** GB 220 3688 85
Date established: 2008 **Turnover:** £2m - £5m **No.of Employees:** 21 - 50
Product Groups: 36

Date of Accounts	Oct 11	Oct 10	Oct 09
Working Capital	397	553	558
Fixed Assets	20	41	66
Current Assets	764	886	905

Barbican Supplies Ltd

26-30 Bernard Road, London, N15 4NE
Tel: 020-8808 4500 **Fax:** 020-8801 9297
E-mail: brian.higgins1@btinternet.com
Website: http://www.barbicansupplies.co.uk
Directors: B. Higgins (MD), K. Higgins (Fin)
Immediate Holding Company: BARBICAN SUPPLIES LTD.
Registration no: 02566915 **Date established:** 1990
No.of Employees: 21 - 50 **Product Groups:** 20

Date of Accounts	Dec 11	Dec 10	Dec 09
Working Capital	185	291	381
Fixed Assets	47	46	54
Current Assets	385	483	578

Barclays Bank plc

54 Lombard Street, London, EC3V 9EX
Tel: 0845-7555555 **Fax:** 020-7977 4574
Website: http://www.barclays.co.uk
Directors: S. Adams (Dir), M. MacAllan (I.T. Dir), D. Reid (Fin)
Managers: T. Bonham Carter
Immediate Holding Company: BARCLAYS BANK PLC
Registration no: 01026167 **Date established:** 1971
No.of Employees: 1 - 10 **Product Groups:** 82

Barking Dog Security Ltd

Riverside Business Centre Haldane Place, London, SW18 4UQ
Tel: 020-8874 3983
E-mail: andrew@cardean.co.uk
Website: http://www.barkingdogsecurity.co.uk
Directors: A. Cox (MD)
Immediate Holding Company: BARKING DOG SECURITY LTD
Registration no: 04366104 **Date established:** 2002
No.of Employees: 1 - 10 **Product Groups:** 37, 40

Date of Accounts	Feb 11	Feb 10	Feb 09
Working Capital	43	20	-3
Fixed Assets	8	10	3
Current Assets	97	54	38

Barley Mow Reprographics Ltd

10 Barley Mow Passage, London, W4 4PH
Tel: 020-8995 7042 **Fax:** 020-8747 8530
E-mail: enjayrepro@btinternet.com
Website: http://www.barleymowreprographics.co.uk
Directors: S. Wise (Dir), A. Wise (Fin)
Immediate Holding Company: BARLEY MOW REPROGRAPHICS LIMITED
Registration no: 05283369 **Date established:** 2004
Turnover: Up to £250,000 **No.of Employees:** 1 - 10 **Product Groups:** 80

Date of Accounts	Nov 10	Nov 09	Nov 08
Sales Turnover	N/A	229	213
Pre Tax Profit/Loss	N/A	13	-11
Working Capital	-1	29	17
Fixed Assets	9	14	19
Current Assets	57	80	57
Current Liabilities	N/A	39	29

Barlow Lyde & Gilbert

Beaufort House 15 St Botolph Street, London, EC3A 7DT
Tel: 020-7247 2277 **Fax:** 020-7643 8500
E-mail: akellyburns@blg.co.uk
Website: http://www.blg.co.uk
Directors: A. Kelly Burns (Fin), A. Kelly Burns (Co Sec), K. Michelle (Snr Part), I. Lauweris (I.T. Dir), R. Dedman (Snr Part)
Immediate Holding Company: BLG CLAIMS LLP
Registration no: OC344148 **Date established:** 2009
Turnover: £500,000 - £1m **No.of Employees:** 501 - 1000
Product Groups: 80, 82

Barnett Lawson Trimmings Ltd

16-17 Little Portland Street, London, W1W 8NE
Tel: 020-7636 8591 **Fax:** 02758-000669
E-mail: info@bltrimmings.com
Website: http://www.bltrimmings.com
Directors: C. Marx (Dir)
Immediate Holding Company: BARNETT, LAWSON (TRIMMINGS) LIMITED
Registration no: 02211489 **VAT No.:** GB 494 7316 13
Date established: 1988 **Turnover:** £500,000 - £1m
No.of Employees: 1 - 10 **Product Groups:** 23

Date of Accounts	May 11	May 10	May 09
Working Capital	114	107	107
Fixed Assets	7	8	8
Current Assets	229	212	204
Current Liabilities	59	N/A	N/A

Barron Warren & Redfern

19 South End, London, W8 5BU
Tel: 020-7937 0294 **Fax:** 020-7937 4786
E-mail: patags@baron-warren.co.uk
Website: http://www.bwr-ip.co.uk
Bank(s): Barclays
Directors: K. Warren (Ptnr), M. Stacey (Ptnr), S. Bankes (Ptnr)
VAT No.: GB 238 4965 43 **Turnover:** £2m - £5m **No.of Employees:** 21 - 50
Product Groups: 80

Barr Gazetas Ltd

Eastgate House 16-19 Eastcastle Street, London, W1W 8DA
Tel: 020-7636 5581 **Fax:** 020-7636 6865
E-mail: info@barrgazetas.com
Website: http://www.barrgazetas.com
Directors: A. Barr (MD), J. Barr (Fin)
Immediate Holding Company: BARR GAZETAS LIMITED
Registration no: 03948400 **Date established:** 2000 **Turnover:** £2m - £5m
No.of Employees: 11 - 20 **Product Groups:** 84

Date of Accounts	Mar 12	Mar 11	Mar 10
Working Capital	385	164	77
Fixed Assets	26	16	64
Current Assets	564	312	191

Barratt Homes Ltd

Central House 32-66 High Street, London, E15 2PF
Tel: 020-8522 5500 **Fax:** 020-8519 5536
E-mail: debbie.hadley@barratthomes.co.uk
Website: http://www.barratthomes.co.uk
Directors: A. Baird (MD), A. Collins (Fin), K. Sri Balakumaran (Co Sec)
Managers: K. Ajiboye (Personnel), L. George (Sales & Mktg Mg), J. Flaherty (Buyer)
Immediate Holding Company: BARRATT DEVELOPMENTS P L C
Registration no: 00528396 **Date established:** 1954
No.of Employees: 51 - 100 **Product Groups:** 80

Date of Accounts	Jun 09	Jun 08	Jun 07
Current Assets	9	9	N/A

Barrow Lane & Ballard Ltd

52-54 Southwark Street, London, SE1 1UR
Tel: 020-7015 1400 **Fax:** 020-7357 8905
E-mail: nick@barrow-lane.co.uk
Website: http://www.barrow-lane.co.uk
Bank(s): Mees Pierson
Directors: P. Sawbridge (Fin), M. Gulamali (Dir)
Managers: N. Thomas
Ultimate Holding Company: LOUDWATER MANAGEMENT LIMITED
Immediate Holding Company: BARROW,LANE & BALLARD LIMITED
Registration no: 00814563 **VAT No.:** GB 243 1411 09
Date established: 1964 **Turnover:** £50m - £75m
No.of Employees: 11 - 20 **Product Groups:** 02, 20

Date of Accounts	Mar 10	Mar 09	Sep 11
Sales Turnover	43m	42m	60m
Pre Tax Profit/Loss	896	609	422
Working Capital	3m	2m	2m
Fixed Assets	40	11	33
Current Assets	10m	8m	17m
Current Liabilities	350	357	209

Barry Bros

121-123 Praed Street, London, W2 1RL
Tel: 020-7262 9009 **Fax:** 020-7262 5005
E-mail: info@barrybros.com
Website: http://www.barrybros.com
Directors: O. Barry (Prop)
Registration no: 06199666 **VAT No.:** GB 240 1209 22
Date established: 2007 **Turnover:** £2m - £5m **No.of Employees:** 1 - 10
Product Groups: 26, 35, 36

Barry M Cosmetics

Unit 1 Bittacy Business Centre Bittacy Hill, London, NW7 1BA
Tel: 020-8349 2992 **Fax:** 020-8346 7773
E-mail: info@barrym.co.uk
Website: http://www.barrym.com
Bank(s): HSBC Bank plc
Directors: M. Mero (Co Sec), D. Mero (MD)
Managers: M. Appleby (Sales Admin), L. Taylor
Immediate Holding Company: BARRY M. COSMETICS LTD.
Registration no: 02520696 **VAT No.:** GB 544 6192 37
Date established: 1990 **Turnover:** £10m - £20m
No.of Employees: 51 - 100 **Product Groups:** 32

Date of Accounts	Aug 09	Aug 08	Feb 12
Sales Turnover	7m	N/A	15m
Pre Tax Profit/Loss	1m	1m	1m
Working Capital	2m	1m	3m
Fixed Assets	200	172	439
Current Assets	4m	3m	6m
Current Liabilities	1m	1m	2m

Barton Willmore Partnership

7 Soho Square, London, W1D 3QB
Tel: 020-7446 6888 **Fax:** 020-7446 6889
E-mail: iain.painting@bartonwillmore.co.uk
Website: http://www.bartonwillmore.co.uk
Directors: I. Painting (Ptnr)
Ultimate Holding Company: EXPEDIA INC (USA)
Immediate Holding Company: HOLIDAY LETTINGS LIMITED
Registration no: 02131349 **Date established:** 2004 **Turnover:** £5m - £10m
No.of Employees: 51 - 100 **Product Groups:** 84

Date of Accounts	Dec 10	Dec 09	Dec 08
Sales Turnover	7m	5m	3m
Pre Tax Profit/Loss	3m	1m	241
Working Capital	3m	685	-381
Fixed Assets	168	137	185
Current Assets	6m	3m	1m
Current Liabilities	3m	409	2m

Baruch Enterpises Ltd

Watkins House Pegamoid Road, London, N18 2NG
Tel: 020-8803 8899 **Fax:** 020-8965 5448
E-mail: info@baruch.co.uk
Website: http://www.baruch.co.uk
Directors: E. Baruch (MD), R. Baruch (Dir)
Ultimate Holding Company: BARUCH INVESTMENTS LIMITED
Immediate Holding Company: BARUCH ENTERPRISES LIMITED
Registration no: 02678218 **Date established:** 1992
Turnover: £10m - £20m **No.of Employees:** 11 - 20 **Product Groups:** 37

Date of Accounts	Apr 11	Apr 10	Apr 09
Sales Turnover	13m	12m	11m
Pre Tax Profit/Loss	333	389	136
Working Capital	1m	1m	1m
Fixed Assets	93	97	101
Current Assets	4m	4m	3m
Current Liabilities	332	152	168

Baselica Ltd (t/a Fine Italian Foods)

3 Somers Place, London, SW2 2AL
Tel: 020-8671 6622 **Fax:** 020-8678 6151
E-mail: enquiries@fineitalianfoods.co.uk
Website: http://www.fineitalianfoods.co.uk
Directors: R. Raj (Fin)
Managers: P. Tindal (Chief Mgr), S. Corsini (Tech Serv Mgr)
Immediate Holding Company: BASELICA LIMITED
Registration no: 01939525 **Date established:** 1985
Turnover: £20m - £50m **No.of Employees:** 11 - 20 **Product Groups:** 62

Date of Accounts	Dec 11	Mar 10	Mar 09
Sales Turnover	20m	20m	N/A
Pre Tax Profit/Loss	1m	1m	599
Working Capital	1m	2m	2m
Fixed Assets	51	59	66
Current Assets	5m	6m	4m
Current Liabilities	524	643	361

J Bashford & Associates

1 Stable Mews Dowanhill Road, London, SE6 1DS
Tel: 020-8698 1524 **Fax:** 020-8461 2217
E-mail: info@liftadvice.com
Website: http://www.liftadvice.com
Directors: J. Bashford (Snr Part)
Date established: 1995 **No.of Employees:** 1 - 10 **Product Groups:** 35, 39, 45

Bat Air Ltd

Quaker Street, London, E1 6SN
Tel: 020-7247 7355 **Fax:** 020- 73776274
E-mail: losefbattaglia@bat-air.com
Website: http://www.mgjservices.com
Directors: J. Battaglia (MD), P. Smith (Dir)
Managers: M. Jacobs (Mgr)
Registration no: 01307484 **No.of Employees:** 1 - 10 **Product Groups:** 76

Date of Accounts	Apr 06	Apr 05
Working Capital	3	3
Current Assets	3	3
Total Share Capital	5	5

J T Batchelor Ltd

9-10 Culford Mews, London, N1 4DZ
Tel: 020-7254 2962 **Fax:** 020-7254 0357
Directors: J. Patel (MD)
Immediate Holding Company: J.T. BATCHELOR LIMITED
Registration no: 01601240 **Date established:** 1981
Turnover: £500,000 - £1m **No.of Employees:** 1 - 10 **Product Groups:** 22, 35

Date of Accounts	Mar 11	Mar 10	Mar 09
Working Capital	306	279	277
Fixed Assets	73	79	86
Current Assets	653	574	484

Bathwise

265-271 Northfield Avenue, London, W5 4UA
Tel: 020-8840 9313 **Fax:** 020-8840 5313
E-mail: sales@bathwise.co.uk
Website: http://www.bathwise.uk.com
Directors: V. Bhimji (MD)
Immediate Holding Company: BATHWISE LIMITED
Registration no: 05967948 **Date established:** 2006
No.of Employees: 1 - 10 **Product Groups:** 26, 36

Date of Accounts	Oct 10	Oct 09	Oct 08
Sales Turnover	1m	1m	2m
Pre Tax Profit/Loss	-15	-24	-39
Working Capital	-237	-243	-240
Fixed Assets	52	73	94
Current Assets	329	331	296
Current Liabilities	186	192	217

H Bauer Publishing

Academic House 24-28 Oval Road, London, NW1 7DT
Tel: 020-7241 8000 **Fax:** 020-7241 8056
Website: http://www.bauer.co.uk
Managers: J. Joblin (Personnel), M. Beddard (Comptroller), J. Toni (Mktg Serv Mgr)
Ultimate Holding Company: HEINRICH BAUER VERLAG KG (GERMANY)
Immediate Holding Company: H.BAUER PUBLISHING LIMITED
Registration no: 02147090 **Date established:** 1987
Turnover: £125m - £250m **No.of Employees:** 101 - 250
Product Groups: 28

Date of Accounts	Dec 11	Dec 10	Dec 09
Working Capital	217	214	211
Current Assets	218	215	212

Bayswater Locks

240a Gloucester Terrace, London, W2 6HU
Tel: 020-7792 0558
E-mail: bayswaterlocks@aol.com
Website: http://www.bayswaterlocksmiths.co.uk
Directors: R. Clarke (Prop)
No.of Employees: 1 - 10 **Product Groups:** 52

B B Signs

Rear of 56 Aldermans Hill, London, N13 4PP
Tel: 020-8886 5034 **Fax:** 020-8447 8449
E-mail: bb-signs@btconnect.com
Website: http://www.bb-signs.co.uk

see next page

B B Signs - Cont'd

Directors: A. Clairmonte (Dir)
Immediate Holding Company: BB SIGNS LIMITED
Registration no: 04425661 **VAT No.:** GB 685 2275 11
Date established: 2002 **Turnover:** £250,000 - £500,000
No.of Employees: 1 - 10 **Product Groups:** 28, 37, 49

Date of Accounts	Aug 11	Aug 10	Aug 09
Working Capital	-22	-23	-24
Fixed Assets	14	18	24
Current Assets	27	23	31

BBC Worldwide Ltd

Woodlands 80 Wood Lane, London, W12 0TT
Tel: 020-8433 2000 **Fax:** 020-8749 0538
E-mail: bbcteam@servicehelpline.co.uk
Website: http://www.bbcworldwide.com
Directors: J. Stevenson (Co Sec), P. Phippen (Dir)
Immediate Holding Company: BBC Ventures Group Ltd
Registration no: 01420028 **Turnover:** £500m - £1,000m
No.of Employees: 1501 & over **Product Groups:** 89

Date of Accounts	Mar 08
Sales Turnover	641700
Pre Tax Profit/Loss	112500
Working Capital	7100
Fixed Assets	267600
Current Assets	278200
Current Liabilities	271100
Total Share Capital	200
ROCE% (Return on Capital Employed)	41.0

BCIS Ltd

12 Great George Street, London, SW1P 3AD
Tel: 020-7695 1500 **Fax:** 01202-742043
E-mail: mailorder@rics.org
Website: http://www.bcis.co.uk
Directors: A. Thompson (Dir), J. Martin (MD)
Managers: A. Thompson (Chief Mgr), D. Wood (Mktg Serv Mgr), I. Pegg (I.T. Exec)
Ultimate Holding Company: RICS HOLDINGS LIMITED
Immediate Holding Company: BCIS LIMITED
Registration no: 06318016 **Date established:** 2007
No.of Employees: 101 - 250 **Product Groups:** 80

Date of Accounts	Jul 11	Jul 10	Jul 09
Working Capital	N/A	-1	1
Fixed Assets	N/A	N/A	9
Current Assets	N/A	N/A	16

Bead Shop Retail Wholesale

21a Tower Street, London, WC2H 9NS
Tel: 020-7240 0931
E-mail: sales@beadworks.com
Website: http://www.beadshop.co.uk
Managers: A. Morar (Mgr)
Immediate Holding Company: THE BRITISH DERMATOLOGICAL NURSING GROUP
Registration no: 01052050 **VAT No.:** GB 235 2476 68
Date established: 2009 **Turnover:** £500,000 - £1m
No.of Employees: 1 - 10 **Product Groups:** 33, 35, 49

Beale & Co.

Garrick House 27-32 King Street, London, WC2E 8JD
Tel: 020-7240 3474 **Fax:** 020-7240 9111
E-mail: reception@beale-law.com
Website: http://www.beale-law.com
Directors: A. Smith (Snr Part)
Managers: J. Henderson (Fin Mgr), V. Petite (Mktg Serv Mgr), S. Gould (Tech Serv Mgr), A. Jones
Immediate Holding Company: BEALE AND COMPANY (BUSINESS SERVICES) LIMITED
Registration no: 03132256 **Date established:** 1995
Turnover: £10m - £20m **No.of Employees:** 51 - 100 **Product Groups:** 80

Beautiful Landscapes Ltd

55 Crondall court Pitfield streeet, Islington, London, N1 6JH
Tel: 07964-305410
E-mail: info@beautifullandsapes.co.uk
Website: http://www.beautifullandscapes.co.uk
Directors: P. Bradbury (Dir), G. Gutierrez (Dir)
Registration no: 6808463 **Date established:** 2009
No.of Employees: 1 - 10 **Product Groups:** 07

Date of Accounts	Feb 10
Sales Turnover	22
Working Capital	1
Current Assets	1

Bechtel Holdings Ltd

PO Box 739, London, W6 8DP
Tel: 020-8846 5111 **Fax:** 020-8846 6940
Website: http://www.bechtel.com
Bank(s): Barclays
Directors: K. Schafer (Co Sec), C. Dering (Dir)
Ultimate Holding Company: BECHTEL GROUP INC (USA)
Immediate Holding Company: BECHTEL LIMITED
Registration no: 00506133 **VAT No.:** GB 578 6513 95
Date established: 1952 **Turnover:** £125m - £250m
No.of Employees: 1001 - 1500 **Product Groups:** 18, 39, 51, 52, 54, 80, 84

Date of Accounts	Dec 11	Dec 10	Dec 09
Sales Turnover	144m	141m	135m
Pre Tax Profit/Loss	23m	8m	-1m
Working Capital	103m	105m	114m
Fixed Assets	5m	7m	9m
Current Assets	147m	144m	171m
Current Liabilities	36m	35m	47m

Beck Greener

Fulwood House 12 Fulwood Place, London, WC1V 6HR
Tel: 020-7242 2535 **Fax:** 020-7405 8113
E-mail: sales@beckgreener.com
Website: http://www.beckgreener.com
Bank(s): Barclays
Directors: J. Raynor (Ptnr)
Managers: E. Birgdale (Tech Serv Mgr), J. Speer (Personnel), M. Sloane
Ultimate Holding Company: DARBOURNE HOLDINGS LIMITED
Immediate Holding Company: FH SERVICES LIMITED
Registration no: 02185605 **VAT No.:** GB 333 2278 76
Date established: 2002 **Turnover:** Up to £250,000
No.of Employees: 21 - 50 **Product Groups:** 80, 87

Russell Bedford .

250 City Road, London, EC1V 2QQ
Tel: 020-7410 0339 **Fax:** 020-7490 5102
E-mail: info@russellbedford.com
Website: http://www.russellbedford.com
Bank(s): HSBC
Directors: K. Lebihan (Co Sec), K. Bedel (Mkt Research)
Immediate Holding Company: RUSSELL BEDFORD INTERNATIONAL
Registration no: 03331251 **Date established:** 1997
Turnover: Up to £250,000 **No.of Employees:** 51 - 100
Product Groups: 80

Date of Accounts	Jun 11	Jun 10	Jun 08
Working Capital	254	219	122
Fixed Assets	1	N/A	1
Current Assets	382	308	179

Beechwood Recruitment Ltd

221 High Street, London, W3 9BY
Tel: 020-8992 8647 **Fax:** 020-8992 5658
E-mail: mail@beechwoodrecruit.com
Website: http://www.beechwoodrecruit.com
Directors: G. Lowi (MD), C. Arnold (Fin)
Immediate Holding Company: BEECHWOOD RECRUITMENT LIMITED
Registration no: 01550997 **VAT No.:** GB 346 5947 19
Date established: 1981 **Turnover:** £500,000 - £1m
No.of Employees: 1 - 10 **Product Groups:** 80

Date of Accounts	Jun 11	Jun 10	Jun 09
Working Capital	324	314	75
Fixed Assets	169	179	717
Current Assets	337	333	189

Beggars Group Ltd

17 Alma Road, London, SW18 1AA
Tel: 020-8870 9912 **Fax:** 020-8871 1766
E-mail: postmaster@beggars.com
Website: http://www.beggars.com
Directors: N. Bolt (Fin), P. Redding (MD)
Managers: T. Collins (Tech Serv Mgr), R. Hartley (Purch Mgr), S. Green (Mktg Serv Mgr)
Immediate Holding Company: BEGGARS GROUP LIMITED
Registration no: 01414045 **VAT No.:** GB 340 1066 10
Date established: 1979 **Turnover:** £20m - £50m
No.of Employees: 51 - 100 **Product Groups:** 37

Date of Accounts	Dec 11	Dec 10	Dec 09
Sales Turnover	23m	25m	18m
Pre Tax Profit/Loss	23m	6m	4m
Working Capital	12m	3m	2m
Fixed Assets	18m	10m	10m
Current Assets	43m	12m	10m
Current Liabilities	25m	6m	5m

Bell Horswill Ltd

Unit 10 Saxon Business Centre Windsor Avenue, London, SW19 2RR
Tel: 020-8542 9955 **Fax:** 020-8542 9922
E-mail: ian@bellhorswill.co.uk
Website: http://www.bellhorswill.co.uk
Directors: G. Bell (MD), H. Bell (MD), J. Horswill (Tech Serv)
Immediate Holding Company: BELL HORSWILL ONE LTD
Registration no: 00796754 **VAT No.:** GB 243 1552 88
Date established: 1964 **No.of Employees:** 1 - 10 **Product Groups:** 77

Date of Accounts	Apr 08	Apr 07	Apr 06
Working Capital	391	409	423
Fixed Assets	15	15	19
Current Assets	468	459	487
Current Liabilities	77	50	64
Total Share Capital	1	1	1

Bell Pottinger Group

14 Curzon Street, London, W1J 5HN
Tel: 020-7495 4044 **Fax:** 020-7861 8506
E-mail: info@bell-pottinger.co.uk
Website: http://www.bell-pottinger.co.uk
Directors: M. Smith (Fin), P. Pottinger (Dir)
Managers: L. Francis, K. Fraser (Personnel)
Ultimate Holding Company: CHIME COMMUNICATIONS PLC
Immediate Holding Company: PELHAM BELL POTTINGER LIMITED
Registration no: 05196349 **Date established:** 2004
Turnover: £10m - £20m **No.of Employees:** 21 - 50 **Product Groups:** 81

Date of Accounts	Dec 11	Dec 10	Dec 09
Sales Turnover	12m	10m	5m
Pre Tax Profit/Loss	3m	2m	138
Working Capital	572	132	114
Fixed Assets	5m	5m	5m
Current Assets	4m	2m	1m
Current Liabilities	3m	2m	909

Bell Pottinger Public Affairs

Holborn Gate 330 High Holborn, London, WC1V 7QD
Tel: 020-7861 2400 **Fax:** 020-7861 2401
E-mail: info@bell-pottinger.co.uk
Website: http://www.bell-pottinger.co.uk
Directors: J. Leece (Fin)
Ultimate Holding Company: CHIME COMMUNICATIONS PLC
Immediate Holding Company: BELL POTTINGER PUBLIC AFFAIRS LIMITED
Registration no: 02488264 **Date established:** 1990 **Turnover:** £2m - £5m
No.of Employees: 101 - 250 **Product Groups:** 81, 84

Date of Accounts	Dec 11	Dec 10	Dec 09
Sales Turnover	4m	5m	4m
Pre Tax Profit/Loss	766	830	33
Working Capital	148	187	-18
Fixed Assets	29	21	32
Current Assets	1m	1m	1m
Current Liabilities	842	1m	650

Bells Control Equipment Ltd

49 Scrutton Street, London, EC2A 4XJ
Tel: 020-7729 1979 **Fax:** 020-7729 3731
E-mail: mcm@mcmbells.com
Website: http://www.mcmbells.com
Bank(s): Barclays
Directors: M. Murphy (MD), R. Rodwell (Fin)
Ultimate Holding Company: MCMILLAN HOLDINGS UK LIMITED
Immediate Holding Company: BELLS CONTROL EQUIPMENT LIMITED
Registration no: 00085951 **Date established:** 2027 **Turnover:** £5m - £10m
No.of Employees: 21 - 50 **Product Groups:** 37, 51

Date of Accounts	Jun 11	Jun 10	Jun 09
Sales Turnover	N/A	6m	4m
Pre Tax Profit/Loss	N/A	151	52
Working Capital	550	464	352
Current Assets	2m	4m	2m
Current Liabilities	N/A	46	8

Bemco Ltd

Bridgend Road, London, SW18 1TN
Tel: 020-8874 0404 **Fax:** 020-8877 0153
E-mail: bryan.barkes@bemco.co.uk
Website: http://www.bemco.co.uk
Bank(s): Lloyds TSB Bank plc
Directors: B. Barkes (Ch)
Immediate Holding Company: BEMCO LIMITED
Registration no: 04851594 **VAT No.:** GB 175 8013 58
Date established: 2003 **No.of Employees:** 11 - 20 **Product Groups:** 67

Date of Accounts	May 12	May 11	May 10
Working Capital	16	26	34
Fixed Assets	7	9	9
Current Assets	28	38	49

Ben Sherman Ltd

2 Eyre Street Hill, London, EC1R 5ET
Tel: 020-7812 5300 **Fax:** 020-7812 5301
E-mail: reception@bensherman.co.uk
Website: http://www.bensherman.com
Directors: J. Lanier (Dir), L. Gage (Co Sec), M. Lamont (Fin)
Ultimate Holding Company: OXFORD INDUSTRIES INC (USA)
Immediate Holding Company: BEN SHERMAN LIMITED
Registration no: 03998077 **VAT No.:** GB 575 5627 06
Date established: 2000 **No.of Employees:** 51 - 100 **Product Groups:** 24, 61

Date of Accounts	Jan 11	Jan 10	Jan 09
Pre Tax Profit/Loss	2m	2m	8m
Working Capital	4m	4m	4m
Fixed Assets	53m	53m	53m
Current Assets	44m	4m	4m
Current Liabilities	10	10	10

Bennison Fabrics

16 Holbein Place, London, SW1W 8NL
Tel: 020-7730 8076 **Fax:** 020-7823 4997
E-mail: sales@bennisonfabrics.com
Website: http://www.bennisonfabrics.com
Directors: G. Newberry (Fin)
Immediate Holding Company: BENNISON FABRICS LIMITED
Registration no: 01871290 **Date established:** 1984 **Turnover:** £1m - £2m
No.of Employees: 1 - 10 **Product Groups:** 23

Date of Accounts	May 11	May 10	May 09
Sales Turnover	1m	1m	1m
Pre Tax Profit/Loss	-83	-74	-149
Working Capital	661	741	811
Fixed Assets	340	343	348
Current Assets	800	862	980
Current Liabilities	17	19	15

The Beretta Gallery

36 St Jamess Street, London, SW1A 1JD
Tel: 020-7408 4411 **Fax:** 020-7491 8772
E-mail: pholden@gmk.co.uk
Managers: T. King (Mgr)
Registration no: OC300557 **Date established:** 2001
No.of Employees: 1 - 10 **Product Groups:** 36, 39, 40

Berkeley Insurance Ltd

Fibi House 24 Creechurch Lane, London, EC3A 5JX
Tel: 020-7623 4333 **Fax:** 020-7623 4555
E-mail: info@berkeleyinsurance.co.uk
Website: http://www.berkeley.co.uk
Directors: G. Huddart (Dir)
Ultimate Holding Company: BERKELEY (INSURANCE) HOLDINGS LIMITED
Immediate Holding Company: BERKELEY (INSURANCE) LIMITED
Registration no: 00736825 **Date established:** 1962
Turnover: Up to £250,000 **No.of Employees:** 1 - 10 **Product Groups:** 82

Date of Accounts	Oct 11	Oct 10	Oct 09
Sales Turnover	87	122	193
Pre Tax Profit/Loss	-19	19	58
Working Capital	65	81	76
Fixed Assets	N/A	N/A	1
Current Assets	182	160	181
Current Liabilities	113	64	50

Berry Bros & Rudd Ltd

3 St James's Street, London, SW1A 1EG
Tel: 020-7396 9600 **Fax:** 020-7396 9677
E-mail: simon.berry@bbr.com
Website: http://www.bbr.com
Directors: S. Berry (Ch)
Immediate Holding Company: BERRY BROS. & RUDD LIMITED
Registration no: 05490962 **Date established:** 2005
Turnover: £125m - £250m **No.of Employees:** 21 - 50 **Product Groups:** 62

Date of Accounts	Mar 12	Mar 11	Mar 10
Sales Turnover	165m	216m	293m
Pre Tax Profit/Loss	1m	28m	6m
Working Capital	77m	81m	57m
Fixed Assets	53m	53m	49m
Current Assets	112m	132m	143m
Current Liabilities	4m	7m	19m

Berrymans Lace Mawer

Salisbury House London Wall, London, EC2M 5QN
Tel: 020-7638 2811 **Fax:** 020-7920 0361
E-mail: info@blm-law.com
Website: http://www.blm-law.com
Directors: F. Lewitt (Fin), F. Lewitt (Fin), P. Taylor (Snr Part)
Managers: A. Taylor (Personnel), D. Greiff (Develop Mgr)
Immediate Holding Company: BERRYMANS LACE MAWER SERVICE COMPANY
Registration no: 02995501 **Date established:** 1994 **Turnover:** £5m - £10m
No.of Employees: 251 - 500 **Product Groups:** 80, 82

S J Berwin

222 Grays Inn Road, London, WC1X 8XF
Tel: 020-7111 2222 **Fax:** 020-7533 2000
E-mail: info@sjberwin.com
Website: http://www.sjberwin.com
Directors: R. Day (Snr Part), M. Giles (Fin)
Managers: S. Kosminsky, K. Chalmers (Personnel), T. Davis
Immediate Holding Company: SJ BERWIN LLP
Registration no: OC313176 **Date established:** 2005
Turnover: £125m - £250m **No.of Employees:** 501 - 1000
Product Groups: 80

Date of Accounts	Apr 11	Apr 10	Apr 09
Sales Turnover	176m	171m	184m
Pre Tax Profit/Loss	61m	56m	50m
Working Capital	53m	44m	53m
Fixed Assets	24m	27m	31m
Current Assets	85m	74m	85m
Current Liabilities	16m	13m	11m

Beta Lighting Ltd

19 Eton Garages Lambolle Place, London, NW3 4PE
Tel: 020-7794 3722 **Fax:** 020-7794 6001
Directors: D. Silver (MD)
No.of Employees: 1 - 10 **Product Groups:** 37, 67

Better Sound Ltd

31 Cathcart Street, London, NW5 3BJ
Tel: 020-7482 0177 **Fax:** 020-7482 2677
E-mail: admin@bettersound.co.uk
Website: http://www.bettersound.co.uk
Directors: C. Colomb (Tech Serv)
Immediate Holding Company: BETTER SOUND LIMITED
Registration no: 00726427 **VAT No.:** GB 232 1455 02
Date established: 1962 **Turnover:** £500,000 - £1m
No.of Employees: 1 - 10 **Product Groups:** 83

Date of Accounts	Jul 11	Jul 10	Jul 09
Working Capital	475	394	331
Fixed Assets	871	865	922
Current Assets	1m	687	605

Beyond Philosophy

180 Piccadilly, London, W1J 9HF
Tel: 020-7917 1717
E-mail: david.ive@beyondphilosophy.com
Website: http://www.beyondphilosophy.com
Directors: D. Ive (Fin)
Immediate Holding Company: DEABADH LIMITED
Date established: 2004 **No.of Employees:** 11 - 20 **Product Groups:** 81

BHS Ltd

Marylebone House 129-137 Marylebone Road, London, NW1 5QD
Tel: 08442-430000 **Fax:** 020-7723 1115
Website: http://www.bhs.co.uk
Directors: A. Goldman (Co Sec), P. Green (Prop)
Managers: G. Lund
Ultimate Holding Company: TAVETA INVESTMENTS LIMITED
Immediate Holding Company: BHS LIMITED
Registration no: 00229606 **Date established:** 2028
Turnover: £500m - £1,000m **No.of Employees:** 1501 & over
Product Groups: 61

Date of Accounts	Aug 09	Mar 08	Aug 10
Sales Turnover	1121m	850m	795m
Pre Tax Profit/Loss	-62m	21m	-7m
Working Capital	-88m	-41m	-96m
Fixed Assets	282m	315m	269m
Current Assets	129m	117m	102m
Current Liabilities	65m	61m	59m

Biachem Ltd

Boundary House 91-93 Charterhouse Street, London, EC1M 6HR
Tel: 020-7250 1905 **Fax:** 020-7250 1913
E-mail: sales@biachem.com
Website: http://www.biachem.com
Directors: G. Morris (Fin), R. Beaumont (MD), S. Raven (Sales & Mktg)
Ultimate Holding Company: BIACHEM GROUP LIMITED
Immediate Holding Company: BIACHEM LIMITED
Registration no: 01934652 **VAT No.:** GB 544 5810 42
Date established: 1985 **Turnover:** £5m - £10m **No.of Employees:** 1 - 10
Product Groups: 17, 31, 32

Date of Accounts	Nov 11	Nov 10	Nov 09
Sales Turnover	7m	7m	7m
Pre Tax Profit/Loss	794	478	550
Working Capital	2m	2m	1m
Fixed Assets	34	40	29
Current Assets	4m	3m	3m
Current Liabilities	391	243	290

Bianca UK Ltd

2nd Floor Ashley House 12 Great Portland Street, London, W1W 8QN
Tel: 020-7580 0085 **Fax:** 020-7436 3938
E-mail: info@bianca.de
Website: http://www.bianca.de
Managers: L. Desterre (Sales Prom Mgr), L. D'esterre, S. Jeram (Sales Admin)
Ultimate Holding Company: HUTTEN GMBH (GERMANY)
Immediate Holding Company: BIANCA (UK) PLC
Registration no: 03468300 **VAT No.:** GB 707 2981 24
Date established: 1997 **Turnover:** £1m - £2m **No.of Employees:** 1 - 10
Product Groups: 24

Date of Accounts	Mar 12	Mar 11	Mar 10
Sales Turnover	321	457	487
Pre Tax Profit/Loss	15	22	23
Working Capital	158	110	92
Fixed Assets	23	30	19
Current Assets	180	267	228
Current Liabilities	19	23	17

Biffa Waste Services Ltd

45 Pensbury Place, London, SW8 4TR
Tel: 020-7622 4511 **Fax:** 020-7622 2321
E-mail: peter.gridley@biffa.co.uk
Website: http://www.biffa.co.uk
Managers: P. Grindley (Mgr)
Immediate Holding Company: BIFFA WASTE SERVICES LIMITED
Registration no: 00946107 **Date established:** 1969
No.of Employees: 1 - 10 **Product Groups:** 32, 54

Date of Accounts	Mar 08	Mar 09	Apr 10
Sales Turnover	555m	574m	492m
Pre Tax Profit/Loss	23m	50m	30m
Working Capital	229m	271m	293m
Fixed Assets	371m	360m	378m
Current Assets	409m	534m	609m
Current Liabilities	50m	100m	115m

Big Group

91 Princedale Road, London, W11 4NS
Tel: 020-7229 8827 **Fax:** 020-7243 1462
E-mail: info@biggroup.co.uk
Website: http://www.biggroup.co.uk
Bank(s): Bank of Scotland
Directors: D. Hussey (Fin), E. Riseman (MD)
Managers: G. Hone (Tech Serv Mgr), J. Bulley, T. Dyton (Buyer)
Immediate Holding Company: THE BIG GROUP LIMITED
Registration no: 02520892 **Date established:** 1990 **Turnover:** £1m - £2m
No.of Employees: 21 - 50 **Product Groups:** 81, 89

Date of Accounts	Dec 11	Dec 10	Dec 09
Working Capital	552	346	-96
Fixed Assets	65	44	23
Current Assets	2m	1m	1m

Bipra Ltd

Northway House 1379 High Road, London, N20 9LP
Tel: 020-8445 3288
E-mail: info@bipra.com
Website: http://www.bipra.com
Managers: M. Patel (Mgr)
Immediate Holding Company: BIPRA LIMITED
Registration no: 06280600 **Date established:** 2007
Turnover: Up to £250,000 **No.of Employees:** 1 - 10 **Product Groups:** 67

Date of Accounts	Jun 12	Jun 11	Jun 10
Working Capital	4	-2	-6
Fixed Assets	5	2	2
Current Assets	169	34	2
Current Liabilities	N/A	N/A	1

Bird & Bird

15 Fetter Lane, London, EC4A 1JP
Tel: 020-7415 6000 **Fax:** 020-7415 6111
E-mail: info@twobirds.com
Website: http://www.twobirds.com
Directors: J. Nichols (Pers), J. Warren (Mkt Research)
Managers: D. Kerr, P. Colvin (Fin Mgr), K. Jacks (Tech Serv Mgr)
Ultimate Holding Company: BIRD & BIRD LLP
Immediate Holding Company: BIRD & BIRD (SERVICES) LIMITED
Registration no: 03717269 **VAT No.:** GB 232 2803 00
Date established: 1999 **Turnover:** £20m - £50m
No.of Employees: 251 - 500 **Product Groups:** 80

Date of Accounts	Apr 11	Apr 10	Apr 09
Sales Turnover	37m	28m	2m
Working Capital	-21	-21	-21
Current Assets	3m	2m	2m
Current Liabilities	3m	2m	2m

Biro UK

Unit 14 Atlas Business Centre Oxgate Lane, London, NW2 7HJ
Tel: 020-8450 8822 **Fax:** 020-8452 4433
Website: http://www.birouk.com
Directors: C. Caswell (Ptnr)
Date established: 1998 **No.of Employees:** 1 - 10 **Product Groups:** 20, 40, 41

Blackrock Global Real Estate Opportunity Fund UK Lp

33 King William Street, London, EC4R 9AS
Tel: 020-7743 3000 **Fax:** 020-7573 1561
E-mail: info@blackrock.com
Website: http://www.blackrock.co.uk
Directors: K. Watts (MD), N. Patel (Dir), N. Hall (Dir), A. Dyke (Co Sec)
Ultimate Holding Company: FP049941
Immediate Holding Company: BLACKROCK PENSIONS LIMITED
Registration no: 02348841 **Date established:** 1989
Turnover: £250m - £500m **No.of Employees:** 1 - 10 **Product Groups:** 82

Blade Rubber Stamps Ltd

12 Bury Place, London, WC1A 2JL
Tel: 020-7831 4123 **Fax:** 020-7831 4242
E-mail: sales@bladerubber.co.uk
Website: http://www.bladerubber.co.uk
Directors: K. Flack (Fin), F. Adams (Sales)
Immediate Holding Company: BLADE RUBBER STAMPS LTD
Registration no: 04369229 **Date established:** 2002
Turnover: £250,000 - £500,000 **No.of Employees:** 1 - 10
Product Groups: 30, 49, 64

Date of Accounts	Mar 12	Mar 11	Mar 10
Sales Turnover	531	486	412
Pre Tax Profit/Loss	104	79	71
Working Capital	118	97	56
Fixed Assets	34	12	17
Current Assets	175	157	130
Current Liabilities	42	48	36

Blakes Hotels

33 Roland Gardens, London, SW7 3PF
Tel: 020-7370 6701 **Fax:** 020-7373 0442
E-mail: marco@blakeshotels.com
Website: http://www.blakeshotels.com
Directors: S. Bendre (Fin), S. Bendre (Fin), C. Howard (Sales)
Managers: M. Cilia (Chief Mgr)
Ultimate Holding Company: BOSIES LTD
Immediate Holding Company: SOLAFA LTD
Registration no: 01221531 **Date established:** 2011 **Turnover:** £2m - £5m
No.of Employees: 51 - 100 **Product Groups:** 69

Blaze Heating

75 Milborough Crescent, London, SE12 0RP
Tel: 020-3149 3488
E-mail: info@blazeheating.co.uk
Website: http://www.blazeheating.co.uk
Directors: M. Fahri (Prop), Fahri (Prop)
Managers: M. Fahri (Eng)
No.of Employees: 1 - 10 **Product Groups:** 40, 52

Blenheim & Moorcroft

Unit 127 Lee Valley Technopark Ashley Road, London, N17 9LN
Tel: 020-8880 4091 **Fax:** 020- 88804113
E-mail: richard@blenheimandmoorcroft.com
Website: http://www.blenheimandmoorcroft.com
Directors: R. Akita (Dir)
Immediate Holding Company: BLENHEIM & MOORCROFT LTD
Registration no: 05419687 **Date established:** 2005
Turnover: Up to £250,000 **No.of Employees:** 1 - 10 **Product Groups:** 23, 40, 52, 61

Date of Accounts	Apr 11	Apr 10	Apr 09
Sales Turnover	199	258	224
Pre Tax Profit/Loss	-9	3	10
Working Capital	52	58	52
Fixed Assets	3	5	8
Current Assets	62	65	58
Current Liabilities	2	2	4

Bluntray

57-59 Lonsdale Road, London, NW6 6RA
Tel: 020-7624 8151 **Fax:** 020-7624 2533
Directors: K. Parry (Fin)
Immediate Holding Company: BLUNTRAY LIMITED
Registration no: 07984097 **Date established:** 2012
Turnover: £250,000 - £500,000 **No.of Employees:** 1 - 10
Product Groups: 48

Date of Accounts	Jun 05	Jun 04	Jun 03
Sales Turnover	278	255	251
Pre Tax Profit/Loss	22	2	-1
Working Capital	64	43	41
Fixed Assets	3	3	3
Current Assets	104	95	97
Current Liabilities	39	52	56

Blyth & Blyth Ltd

186 City Road, London, EC1V 2NT
Tel: 020-7017 3800 **Fax:** 020-7242 8184
E-mail: london@blythandblyth.co.uk
Website: http://www.blythandblyth.co.uk
Directors: M. Pile (MD)
Ultimate Holding Company: EMPRISE HOLDINGS LIMITED
Immediate Holding Company: EMPRISE TRUSTEES LIMITED
Registration no: SC103145 **Date established:** 1998
No.of Employees: 11 - 20 **Product Groups:** 80

Date of Accounts	Dec 11	Dec 10	Dec 09
Sales Turnover	91m	73m	65m
Pre Tax Profit/Loss	-5m	-3m	-3m
Working Capital	2m	4m	6m
Fixed Assets	38m	38m	38m
Current Assets	14m	15m	14m
Current Liabilities	8m	8m	5m

Bna International

Millbank Tower 21-24 Millbank, London, SW1P 4QP
Tel: 020-7559 4800 **Fax:** 020- 75594848
E-mail: sales@bnai.com
Website: http://www.bnai.com
Bank(s): Lloyds TSB Bank plc
Directors: A. Edmans (Dir)
Managers: N. Gallehawk (Mktg Serv Mgr), J. Oakes ()
Ultimate Holding Company: B N A INCORPORATED (U.S.A.)
Registration no: OC333858 **Date established:** 2007 **Turnover:** £2m - £5m
No.of Employees: 11 - 20 **Product Groups:** 28

Boc Gases Ltd

Stratford Hub Unit 4 4, Barbers Road, London, E15 2PH
Tel: 020-8555 1636
Website: http://www.boc.com
Managers: S. Jones (Mgr)
Ultimate Holding Company: LINDE AG (GERMANY)
Immediate Holding Company: BOC LIMITED
Registration no: 00337663 **Date established:** 1938
Turnover: £500m - £1,000m **No.of Employees:** 1 - 10
Product Groups: 18, 31, 66, 84

Date of Accounts	Dec 11	Dec 10	Dec 08
Sales Turnover	726m	691m	721m
Pre Tax Profit/Loss	122m	125m	67m
Working Capital	409m	278m	-219m
Fixed Assets	480m	492m	538m
Current Assets	724m	578m	371m
Current Liabilities	64m	68m	73m

Bond Street Translators Ltd

28 Old Brompton Road, London, SW7 3SS
Tel: 020-7493 2418 **Fax:** 020-7491 7971
E-mail: info@bond-st-translators.co.uk
Website: http://www.bond-st-translators.co.uk
Directors: N. Rackstraw (Prop)
Immediate Holding Company: LANGROP (ANSTEY) LIMITED
Registration no: 02455183 **VAT No.:** GB 242 0504 13
Date established: 1989 **Turnover:** Up to £250,000
No.of Employees: 1 - 10 **Product Groups:** 80

Bonhams Auctioneers

Montpelier Street, London, SW7 1HH
Tel: 020-7393 3900 **Fax:** 020-7393 3905
E-mail: chris.watson@bonhams.com
Website: http://www.bonhams.com
Directors: J. Knight (Prop)
Ultimate Holding Company: BONHAMS BROOKS PS&N LIMITED
Immediate Holding Company: BONHAMS UK LIMITED
Registration no: 05267980 **VAT No.:** GB 461 5036 68
Date established: 2004 **Turnover:** £20m - £50m
No.of Employees: 101 - 250 **Product Groups:** 65

Bonsoir Of London Ltd

45 Broadwick Street, London, W1F 9QW
Tel: 020-7439 2050 **Fax:** 020-7439 2215
E-mail: sophie@bonsoir-showroom.com
Website: http://www.bonsoirdirect.com
Managers: R. Bacon
Ultimate Holding Company: MAYTREES LTD (CHANNEL ISLANDS)
Immediate Holding Company: BONSOIR OF LONDON LIMITED
Registration no: 02958778 **Date established:** 1994 **Turnover:** £1m - £2m
No.of Employees: 11 - 20 **Product Groups:** 24

Date of Accounts	Dec 11	Dec 10	Dec 09
Sales Turnover	1m	2m	2m
Pre Tax Profit/Loss	747	2m	-3m
Working Capital	11m	10m	7m
Fixed Assets	5m	5m	5m
Current Assets	12m	10m	7m
Current Liabilities	132	194	178

Boodle Hatfield

89 New Bond Street, London, W1S 1DA
Tel: 020-7629 7411 **Fax:** 01865-798764
E-mail: sasmith@boodlehatfield.com
Website: http://www.boodlehatfield.com
Bank(s): Royal Bank of Scotland, Bond St, London W1
Directors: S. Laing (Ptnr)
Immediate Holding Company: THE YARDS GROUP EVENTING LIMITED
Registration no: 03955460 **VAT No.:** GB 238 4903 47
Date established: 2008 **Turnover:** £5m - £10m **No.of Employees:** 11 - 20
Product Groups: 80

Date of Accounts	Dec 07	Mar 11	Mar 10
Sales Turnover	N/A	5m	7m
Pre Tax Profit/Loss	-462	178	-284

see next page

Boodle Hatfield - Cont'd

Working Capital	-417	-2m	-561
Fixed Assets	N/A	200	N/A
Current Assets	811	554	1m
Current Liabilities	810	1m	1m

Boot Tree

1 Addison Bridge Place, London, W14 8XP
Tel: 020-7602 2866 **Fax:** 020-7602 2085
E-mail: robertlusk@boottree.co.uk
Website: http://www.birkinstock.co.uk
Directors: R. Lusk (Fin)
Immediate Holding Company: BOOT TREE LIMITED(THE)
Registration no: 01307584 **Date established:** 1977 **Turnover:** £1m - £2m
No.of Employees: 1 - 10 **Product Groups:** 61

Date of Accounts	Nov 11	Nov 10	Nov 09
Working Capital	-2m	-2m	-1m
Fixed Assets	439	497	565
Current Assets	2m	2m	2m

Booz & Co.

7 Savoy Court, London, WC2R 0JP
Tel: 020-7393 3333 **Fax:** 020-7393 0025
E-mail: london.reception@booz.com
Website: http://www.booz.com
Directors: A. Gemes (Fin), S. Banerjer (Prop)
Ultimate Holding Company: BOOZ & CO INC (UNITED STATES OF AMERICA)
Immediate Holding Company: BOOZ & COMPANY (U.K.) LTD.
Registration no: 01601493 **Date established:** 1981
Turnover: £20m - £50m **No.of Employees:** 101 - 250 **Product Groups:** 80

Date of Accounts	Mar 11	Mar 10	Mar 09
Sales Turnover	41m	40m	34m
Pre Tax Profit/Loss	-6m	-3m	-26m
Working Capital	7m	-16m	-14m
Fixed Assets	3m	4m	4m
Current Assets	25m	25m	36m
Current Liabilities	9m	10m	50m

Boss & Co. Ltd

16 Mount Street, London, W1K 2RH
Tel: 020-7493 1127 **Fax:** 020-7493 0711
E-mail: k.halsey@compoundsemi.co.uk
Website: http://www.bossguns.com
Directors: K. Halsey (MD)
Immediate Holding Company: BOSS & CO.LIMITED
Registration no: 00916700 **Date established:** 1967
No.of Employees: 1 - 10 **Product Groups:** 36, 39, 40

Date of Accounts	Jul 11	Jul 10	Jul 09
Working Capital	1m	1m	1m
Fixed Assets	2m	2m	2m
Current Assets	2m	2m	2m

Boston Consulting Group Ltd

20 Manchester Square, London, W1U 3PZ
Tel: 020-7753 5353 **Fax:** 020-7753 5750
E-mail: info@bcglondon.com
Website: http://www.bcg.com
Bank(s): National Westminster Bank Plc
Directors: L. Harris (Fin), A. Nicol (Co Sec), A. Maguire (MD)
Managers: K. Dhadwal (Tech Serv Mgr)
Ultimate Holding Company: THE BOSTON CONSULTING GROUP INC (USA)
Immediate Holding Company: BOSTON CONSULTING GROUP LIMITED (THE)
Registration no: 00958970 **Date established:** 1969
Turnover: £75m - £125m **No.of Employees:** 251 - 500
Product Groups: 80

Date of Accounts	Dec 11	Dec 10	Dec 09
Sales Turnover	N/A	92m	84m
Pre Tax Profit/Loss	-5m	20m	-215
Working Capital	-1m	12m	2m
Fixed Assets	26m	14m	16m
Current Assets	11m	67m	50m
Current Liabilities	3m	38m	23m

Boult Wade Tennant

Verulam Gardens 70 Gray's Inn Road, London, WC1X 8BT
Tel: 020-7430 7500 **Fax:** 020-7831 1768
E-mail: rcross@boult.com
Website: http://www.boult.com
Directors: R. Cross (Snr Part), F. Robb (Fin)
Immediate Holding Company: BOULT WADE TENNANT LIMITED
Registration no: 05408039 **Date established:** 2005
No.of Employees: 101 - 250 **Product Groups:** 44, 80

Bourjois Ltd

Princess House 50-60 Eastcastle Street, London, W1W 8EA
Tel: 020-7436 6110 **Fax:** 020-7436 5490
E-mail: claire.laurin@chanel.co.uk
Website: http://www.boujois.co.uk
Directors: M. Hamilton (Co Sec), C. Laurin (MD)
Ultimate Holding Company: CHANEL INTERNATIONAL BV (NETHERLANDS)
Immediate Holding Company: BOURJOIS LIMITED
Registration no: 00158193 **Date established:** 2019
Turnover: £10m - £20m **No.of Employees:** 21 - 50 **Product Groups:** 61, 63

Date of Accounts	Dec 11	Dec 10	Dec 09
Sales Turnover	18m	20m	19m
Pre Tax Profit/Loss	1m	505	950
Working Capital	7m	5m	6m
Fixed Assets	2m	3m	2m
Current Assets	19m	15m	13m
Current Liabilities	2m	3m	2m

Bramah Alarms

31 Oldbury Place, London, W1U 5PT
Tel: 020-7935 7147 **Fax:** 020-7935 2779
E-mail: lock.sales@bramah.co.uk
Website: http://www.bramah.co.uk
Directors: J. Bramah (Dir)
Immediate Holding Company: OLDBURY PLACE INVESTMENTS LIMITED
Registration no: 00289584 **VAT No.:** GB 308 5979 22
Date established: 1989 **Turnover:** £250,000 - £500,000
No.of Employees: 1 - 10 **Product Groups:** 36

Date of Accounts	Dec 11	Dec 10	Dec 09
Working Capital	1m	1m	1m
Fixed Assets	157	119	105
Current Assets	1m	1m	1m

Brampton Maintenance Manufacturing Services

4 Boughton Road, London, SE28 0AG
Tel: 020-8855 6779 **Fax:** 020-8855 0661
E-mail: sales@bramptons-ltd.co.uk
Website: http://www.bramptons-ltd.co.uk
Directors: S. Dowse (Co Sec)
Date established: 1989 **No.of Employees:** 11 - 20 **Product Groups:** 35, 39, 45

Brand Addition (4 Imprint)

Southbank Business Centre Ponton Road, London, SW8 5BL
Tel: 020-7393 0033 **Fax:** 020-7393 0080
E-mail: info@brandaddition.com
Website: http://www.brandaddition.com
Directors: A. Scull (Dir), S. Howlett (Comm)
Managers: A. Gorrie (Buyer)
Ultimate Holding Company: 4IMPRINT GROUP PLC
Immediate Holding Company: PRODUCT PLUS INTERNATIONAL LIMITED
Registration no: 01744913 **Date established:** 1983
Turnover: £10m - £20m **No.of Employees:** 21 - 50 **Product Groups:** 49, 81

Date of Accounts	Dec 11	Dec 08	Jan 10
Sales Turnover	N/A	14m	N/A
Pre Tax Profit/Loss	22	654	406
Working Capital	543	6m	6m
Fixed Assets	N/A	11	44
Current Assets	543	8m	8m
Current Liabilities	N/A	953	396

Brand Development Co.

50 Long Acre, London, WC2E 9JR
Tel: 020-7497 9727 **Fax:** 020-7497 3581
E-mail: info@brandevo.com
Directors: L. Morgan (Fin), P. Morgan (MD)
Immediate Holding Company: RESTAURANTS MANAGEMENT (UK) LIMITED
Registration no: 02764635 **Date established:** 2011
Turnover: Up to £250,000 **No.of Employees:** 1 - 10 **Product Groups:** 85

Date of Accounts	Dec 07	Dec 06	Dec 05
Sales Turnover	886	572	547
Pre Tax Profit/Loss	115	43	22
Working Capital	66	35	19
Fixed Assets	1	2	3
Current Assets	194	150	58
Current Liabilities	128	115	39
ROCE% (Return on Capital Employed)	171.1	119.6	97.9
ROT% (Return on Turnover)	13.0	7.6	4.0

Brassware Company

719 Green Lanes, London, N21 3RX
Tel: 020-8360 7771 **Fax:** 020-8360 8881
E-mail: sales@thebrasswarecompany.com
Website: http://www.thebrasswarecompany.com
Managers: S. Mulberry (Mgr)
Immediate Holding Company: THE BRASSWARE COMPANY LIMITED
Registration no: 07692708 **Date established:** 2011
No.of Employees: 1 - 10 **Product Groups:** 35, 36

Brazilian Chamber Of Commerce

32 Green Street, London, W1K 7AT
Tel: 020-7399 9281 **Fax:** 020-7499 0186
E-mail: brazilianchamber@brazilianchamber.org.uk
Website: http://brazilianchamber.org.uk
Directors: P. Heap (Grp Chief Exec)
Managers: E. Swan
VAT No.: GB 340 7432 78 **Date established:** 1942
Turnover: Up to £250,000 **No.of Employees:** 1 - 10 **Product Groups:** 80, 87

Brecker Grossmith Ltd

63 Wigmore Street, London, W1U 1BQ
Tel: 020-7486 3531 **Fax:** 020-7935 3074
E-mail: nicholas.duck@breckergrossmith.co.uk
Website: http://www.breckergrossmith.co.uk
Directors: S. Brecker (Fin), N. Duck (MD)
Immediate Holding Company: BRECKER GROSSMITH LIMITED
Registration no: 04387179 **Date established:** 2002
Turnover: £250,000 - £500,000 **No.of Employees:** 1 - 10
Product Groups: 80

Date of Accounts	Apr 12	Apr 11	Apr 10
Working Capital	125	115	87
Fixed Assets	2	3	3
Current Assets	249	899	1m

Bremer Landesbank Kreditanstalt Oldenburg-Girozentrale

71 Queen Victoria Street, London, EC4V 4NL
Tel: 020-7972 5400 **Fax:** 020-7972 5454
E-mail: info@nordlb.com
Website: http://www.bremerlb.co.uk
Directors: W. Schmidt (Dir)
Managers: C. Trestrer (Chief Mgr), A. Lee (Admin Off), C. Trestler (Chief Mgr)
Ultimate Holding Company: NORDDEUTSCHE LANDESBANK GIROCENTRALE (GERMANY)
Immediate Holding Company: BREMER LANDESBANK KREDITANSTALT OLDENBURG-GIROZENTRALE
Registration no: FC012745 **Date established:** 1985
No.of Employees: 1001 - 1500 **Product Groups:** 82

Brent Cross Office Furniture

Sayer House Oxgate Lane, London, NW2 7JN
Tel: 020-8208 2626 **Fax:** 020-8208 2012
E-mail: sales@brentxofficefurniture.co.uk
Website: http://www.brentxofficefurniture.co.uk
Directors: D. Van Der Zyl (Dir)
Immediate Holding Company: BRENT CROSS OFFICE FURNITURE LIMITED
Registration no: 03190946 **Date established:** 1996
Turnover: £250,000 - £500,000 **No.of Employees:** 1 - 10
Product Groups: 26, 36, 52, 67

Date of Accounts	May 11	May 10	May 09
Sales Turnover	306	N/A	N/A
Pre Tax Profit/Loss	-11	N/A	N/A
Working Capital	-58	-50	-19
Fixed Assets	16	19	22
Current Assets	50	65	58
Current Liabilities	10	N/A	N/A

Brent Plastics Ltd

Unit D Cobbold Estate Cobbold Road, London, NW10 9BP
Tel: 020-8451 0100 **Fax:** 020-8459 3226
E-mail: sales@brentplastics.co.uk
Website: http://www.brentplastics.co.uk
Bank(s): Lloyds TSB Bank plc
Directors: J. Young (Fin), F. Young (MD), F. Young (MD)
Immediate Holding Company: BRENT PLASTICS LIMITED
Registration no: 00883112 **Date established:** 1966 **Turnover:** £2m - £5m
No.of Employees: 21 - 50 **Product Groups:** 30, 42

Date of Accounts	Dec 11	Dec 10	Dec 09
Sales Turnover	N/A	3m	N/A
Pre Tax Profit/Loss	N/A	159	N/A
Working Capital	851	801	667
Fixed Assets	82	67	65
Current Assets	1m	1m	1m
Current Liabilities	N/A	101	N/A

Brentford & Ealing Radio Cars Ltd

South Ealing Station South Ealing Road, London, W5 4QB
Tel: 020-8840 6699 **Fax:** 020-8840 5580
Directors: J. Paul (MD)
Immediate Holding Company: BRENTFORD & EALING RADIO CARS LTD
Registration no: 04874206 **VAT No.:** GB 410 9438 69
Date established: 2003 **Turnover:** Up to £250,000
No.of Employees: 1 - 10 **Product Groups:** 39, 79

Date of Accounts	Aug 11	Aug 10	Aug 09
Working Capital	-8	-3	2
Fixed Assets	1	1	1
Current Assets	2	1	8

Brewin Dolphin Ltd

PO Box 804, London, EC1A 9BD
Tel: 020-7248 4400 **Fax:** 020-7236 2034
E-mail: online@brewin.co.uk
Website: http://www.brewin.co.uk
Directors: P. Brown (Mkt Research)
Ultimate Holding Company: BREWIN DOLPHIN HOLDINGS PLC
Immediate Holding Company: BREWIN DOLPHIN LIMITED
Registration no: 02135876 **Date established:** 1987
Turnover: £250m - £500m **No.of Employees:** 251 - 500
Product Groups: 82

Date of Accounts	Sep 11	Sep 08	Sep 09
Sales Turnover	274m	187m	212m
Pre Tax Profit/Loss	15m	25m	16m
Working Capital	45m	22m	33m
Fixed Assets	101m	123m	115m
Current Assets	339m	348m	516m
Current Liabilities	67m	76m	54m

The Bridal Chest

28 Well Hall Road, London, SE9 6SF
Tel: 020-8859 8822
E-mail: info@thebridalchest.com
Website: http://www.thebridalchest.com
Managers: A. Ekland (Mgr)
No.of Employees: 1 - 10 **Product Groups:** 23, 24, 63

Bridgeplex Ltd

1a Merivale Road, London, SW15 2NW
Tel: 020-8789 4063 **Fax:** 020-8785 4191
E-mail: soundcheck@btinternet.com
Website: http://www.fabritrak.co.uk
Directors: I. Lucas (Dir), J. Fellows (MD)
Immediate Holding Company: BRIDGEPLEX LIMITED
Registration no: 00981069 **Date established:** 1970
No.of Employees: 21 - 50 **Product Groups:** 33

Date of Accounts	Oct 11	Oct 10	Oct 09
Working Capital	1m	913	489
Fixed Assets	32	41	26
Current Assets	2m	2m	1m

Brighthouse Ltd

105 Powis Street, London, SE18 6JB
Tel: 020-8317 1331 **Fax:** 020-8317 9511
E-mail: customer.relations@brighthouse.co.uk
Website: http://www.brighthouse.co.uk
Managers: D. Simmons (Mgr)
Ultimate Holding Company: VISION CAPITAL PARTNERS VI B LP
Immediate Holding Company: BRIGHTHOUSE LIMITED
Registration no: 06073794 **Date established:** 2007
No.of Employees: 1 - 10 **Product Groups:** 36, 40

Date of Accounts	Mar 12	Mar 11	Mar 10
Sales Turnover	266m	228m	197m
Pre Tax Profit/Loss	29m	25m	20m
Working Capital	57m	49m	68m
Fixed Assets	171m	161m	123m
Current Assets	97m	87m	98m
Current Liabilities	29m	26m	22m

Brightside Print & Design

112 Union Street, London, SE1 0LH
Tel: 020-7960 5111
E-mail: mail@brightsideonline.com
Website: http://www.brightsideonline.com
Managers: L. Hobbs (Sales Prom Mgr)
Date established: 1991 **Turnover:** Up to £250,000
No.of Employees: 1 - 10 **Product Groups:** 28

Brintex Ltd

32 Vauxhall Bridge Road, London, SW1V 2SS
Tel: 020-7973 6401 **Fax:** 020-7233 5054
E-mail: m.taylor@hgluk.com
Website: http://www.brintex.com
Bank(s): HSBC Bank plc
Directors: B. Butler (Dir), J. Dowling (Fin), M. Taylor (Dir), P. Rees (Mkt Research), S. Service (Ptnr)
Managers: M. Mootoo (Personnel)
Ultimate Holding Company: HEMMING GROUP LIMITED
Immediate Holding Company: BRINTEX LIMITED
Registration no: 00946431 **VAT No.:** GB 342 0234 08
Date established: 1969 **Turnover:** £2m - £5m **No.of Employees:** 21 - 50
Product Groups: 81

Bristows

100 Victoria Embankment, London, EC4Y 0DH
Tel: 020-7400 8000 **Fax:** 020-7400 8050
E-mail: info@bristows.com
Website: http://www.bristows.com
Directors: J. Merchant (Ptnr), J. Merton (Fin)
Immediate Holding Company: BRISTOWS (LEGAL) LIMITED
Registration no: 03488038 **Date established:** 1998
Turnover: £10m - £20m **No.of Employees:** 101 - 250
Product Groups: 80, 87

Brit Insurance

55 Bishops Gate, London, EC2N 3AS
Tel: 020-7984 8700 **Fax:** 020-7984 8701
E-mail: dane.dovetil@britinsurance.com
Website: http://www.britinsurance.com
Directors: D. Douetil (Grp Chief Exec)
Ultimate Holding Company: BRIT INSURANCE HOLDINGS NV (NETHERLANDS)
Immediate Holding Company: BRIT INSURANCE LIMITED
Registration no: 02763688 **Date established:** 1992
Turnover: Over £1,000m **No.of Employees:** 501 - 1000
Product Groups: 82

Date of Accounts	Dec 11	Dec 10	Dec 09
Pre Tax Profit/Loss	30m	42m	58m
Fixed Assets	1326m	1160m	1290m
Current Assets	282m	713m	670m
Current Liabilities	120m	201m	126m

British American Tobacco plc

Globe House 4 Temple Place, London, WC2R 2PG
Tel: 020-7845 1000 **Fax:** 020-7240 0555
Website: http://www.bat.com
Directors: A. Porter (Dir), C. Andrew (Mkt Research), C. Steyn (Fin), J. Peterlessis (Ch), P. Adams (Grp Chief Exec), P. Taylor (Import)
Managers: J. Rembiszewski (Mktg Serv Mgr)
Immediate Holding Company: BRITISH AMERICAN TOBACCO P.L.C.
Registration no: 03407696 **Date established:** 1997
Turnover: Over £1,000m **No.of Employees:** 501 - 1000
Product Groups: 61

Date of Accounts	Dec 08	Dec 07
Sales Turnover	12122m	10018m
Pre Tax Profit/Loss	3684m	3078m
Working Capital	-159000	812000
Fixed Assets	18809m	13362m
Current Assets	8742m	5366m
Current Liabilities	8901m	4554m
Total Share Capital	506000	506000
ROCE% (Return on Capital Employed)	19.8	21.7
ROT% (Return on Turnover)	30.4	30.7

British Arab Commercial Bank Ltd

8-10 Manson House Place, London, EC4N 8BJ
Tel: 020-7648 7777 **Fax:** 020-7600 3318
E-mail: enquiries@bacb.co.uk
Website: http://www.bacb.co.uk
Bank(s): Midland
Managers: D. Crew (Personnel), S. Cook, N. Reeves (Tech Serv Mgr), J. Penn, C. Denby (Fin Mgr), M. Parr
Immediate Holding Company: BRITISH ARAB COMMERCIAL BANK PUBLIC LIMITED COMPANY
Registration no: 01047302 **Date established:** 1972
Turnover: Up to £250,000 **No.of Employees:** 101 - 250
Product Groups: 82

Date of Accounts	Dec 11	Dec 10	Dec 09
Pre Tax Profit/Loss	209	19m	5m
Fixed Assets	21m	11m	30m
Current Assets	2915m	3339m	3272m
Current Liabilities	2696m	3110m	3075m

British Bankers Association

Pinners Hall 105-108 Old Broad Street, London, EC2N 1EX
Tel: 020-7216 8800 **Fax:** 020-7216 8811
E-mail: info@bba.org.uk
Website: http://www.bba.org.uk
Managers: D. Morrison (Tech Serv Mgr), M. Prentice (Personnel), G. Ellis, D. Safo (Mktg Serv Mgr)
Immediate Holding Company: THE BANKERS BENEVOLENT FUND
Registration no: 00019366 **Date established:** 1984 **Turnover:** £2m - £5m
No.of Employees: 51 - 100 **Product Groups:** 87

Date of Accounts	Mar 12	Mar 11	Mar 10
Sales Turnover	108	110	115
Pre Tax Profit/Loss	-12	-6	-4
Working Capital	92	104	110
Current Assets	188	209	359
Current Liabilities	56	65	160

British Darts Organisation Ltd

2 Pages Lane, London, N10 1PS
Tel: 020-8883 5544 **Fax:** 020-8883 0109
Website: http://www.bdodarts.com
Directors: O. Croft (Fin)
Immediate Holding Company: BRITISH DARTS ORGANISATION LIMITED
Registration no: 01270325 **VAT No.:** GB 353 2008 91
Date established: 1976 **Turnover:** £500,000 - £1m
No.of Employees: 1 - 10 **Product Groups:** 81

Date of Accounts	May 12	May 11	May 10
Sales Turnover	705	778	868
Pre Tax Profit/Loss	-49	40	43
Working Capital	424	459	423
Fixed Assets	74	80	84
Current Assets	504	529	555
Current Liabilities	57	49	103

British Essential Oil Association Ltd

Flat 15 Exeter Mansions Exeter Road, London, NW2 3UG
Tel: 020-8450 3713 **Fax:** 020-8450 3197
E-mail: beoa@btinternet.com
Website: http://www.beoa.co.uk
Directors: M. Irvine (Co Sec), J. Wilson (Sales)
Immediate Holding Company: BRITISH ESSENTIAL OIL ASSOCIATION LIMITED(THE)
Registration no: 01357536 **Date established:** 1978
No.of Employees: 1 - 10 **Product Groups:** 31, 32, 87

Date of Accounts	Dec 11	Dec 10	Dec 09
Working Capital	27	25	24
Current Assets	32	26	26

British Land Co plc

York House 45 Seymour Street, London, W1H 7LX
Tel: 020-7486 4466 **Fax:** 020-7935 5552
E-mail: info@britishland.com
Website: http://www.britishland.com
Bank(s): National Westminster Bank Plc, Barclays Bank PLC & The Royal Bank of Scotland plc
Directors: N. Ekpo (Co Sec)
Managers: C. Grigg, S. Barzycki (Fin Mgr)
Ultimate Holding Company: BRITISH LAND COMPANY PUBLIC LIMITED COMPANY(THE)
Immediate Holding Company: BRITISH LAND PROPERTY MANAGEMENT LIMITED
Registration no: 02893197 **Date established:** 1994 **Turnover:** £2m - £5m
No.of Employees: 101 - 250 **Product Groups:** 80, 82

Date of Accounts	Mar 11	Mar 10	Mar 09
Sales Turnover	3m	3m	2m
Pre Tax Profit/Loss	462	145	284
Working Capital	2m	2m	2m
Current Assets	11m	4m	21m
Current Liabilities	874	186	180

British Monomarks

Monomark House 27 Old Gloucester Street, London, WC1N 3AX
Tel: 020-7419 5000 **Fax:** 020-7831 9489
E-mail: mail@monomark.co.uk
Website: http://www.britishmonomarks.co.uk
Managers: B. Brown (Mgr)
Immediate Holding Company: BRITISH MONOMARKS LIMITED
Registration no: 00674888 **Date established:** 1960
No.of Employees: 1 - 10 **Product Groups:** 44

Date of Accounts	Jun 11	Jun 10	Jun 09
Working Capital	18	12	15
Fixed Assets	22	22	22
Current Assets	223	248	258

British Museum Press Publications & Merchandise Ltd

38 Russell Square, London, WC1B 3QQ
Tel: 020-7323 1234 **Fax:** 020-7323 8616
E-mail: reception@britishmuseum.co.uk
Website: http://www.britishmuseum.org
Directors: B. Oldman (MD)
Ultimate Holding Company: THE BRITISH MUSEUM COMPANY LIMITED
Immediate Holding Company: BRITISH MUSEUM VENTURES LIMITED
Registration no: 01442912 **Date established:** 1979 **Turnover:** £2m - £5m
No.of Employees: 21 - 50 **Product Groups:** 28, 64

Date of Accounts	Mar 12	Mar 11	Mar 10
Sales Turnover	6m	5m	5m
Working Capital	1m	1m	1m
Current Assets	2m	2m	2m
Current Liabilities	977	N/A	N/A

British Plastics Federation

5-6 Bath Place, London, EC2A 3JE
Tel: 020-7457 5000 **Fax:** 020-7457 5038
E-mail: reception@bpf.co.uk
Website: http://www.bpf.co.uk
Bank(s): Barclays
Directors: A. Davey (Fin), P. Davies (Dir)
Managers: A. Ladner (Tech Serv Mgr), K. Hawksworth (Sales Prom Mgr)
Immediate Holding Company: BRITISH PLASTICS FEDERATION(THE)
Registration no: 00282883 **Date established:** 1933 **Turnover:** £1m - £2m
No.of Employees: 11 - 20 **Product Groups:** 84

Date of Accounts	Dec 11	Dec 10	Dec 09
Sales Turnover	2m	2m	2m
Pre Tax Profit/Loss	14	226	105
Working Capital	-322	-365	-536
Fixed Assets	2m	2m	2m
Current Assets	1m	808	558
Current Liabilities	1m	1m	985

British Promotional Merchandise Association

Arena House 66-68 Pentonville Road, London, N1 9HS
Tel: 020-7689 5555 **Fax:** 020-7837 5326
E-mail: gorden@bpma.co.uk
Website: http://www.bpma.co.uk
Bank(s): Barclays
Directors: E. Mutton (Dir), G. Glenister (Dir)
Managers: P. Mclellan (I.T. Exec)
Immediate Holding Company: Institute Of Sales Promotion Limited(The)
Registration no: 04546290 **VAT No.:** GB 303 8852 61
Date established: 2002 **Turnover:** £250,000 - £500,000
No.of Employees: 11 - 20 **Product Groups:** 24, 27, 28, 30, 31, 49, 81, 87

Date of Accounts	May 08	May 07	May 06
Working Capital	9	29	116
Fixed Assets	12	15	4
Current Assets	268	221	235
Current Liabilities	259	192	119

British Quality Foundation

32-34 Great Peter Street, London, SW1P 2QX
Tel: 020-7654 5000 **Fax:** 020-7654 5001
E-mail: mail@bqf.org.uk
Website: http://www.bqf.org.uk
Directors: J. Goasdoue (Grp Chief Exec), N. Friedlos (Fin)
Immediate Holding Company: THE BRITISH QUALITY FOUNDATION
Registration no: 02770257 **Date established:** 1992 **Turnover:** £1m - £2m
No.of Employees: 11 - 20 **Product Groups:** 80, 85, 87

Date of Accounts	Dec 11	Dec 10	Dec 09
Sales Turnover	1m	1m	1m
Pre Tax Profit/Loss	30	50	2
Working Capital	926	921	870
Fixed Assets	22	2	8
Current Assets	2m	2m	1m
Current Liabilities	591	472	394

British Worldwide Computers Ltd

Albany House 324/326 Regent Street, London, W1B 3HH
Tel: 0845-2255599 **Fax:** 07902-013224
E-mail: info@bwcomputers.co.uk
Website: http://www.bwcomputers.co.uk
Directors: M. Jackson (MD)
Immediate Holding Company: B W C Ltd
Registration no: 03281280 **Date established:** 2008
No.of Employees: 1 - 10 **Product Groups:** 44

Date of Accounts	Feb 08	Feb 07	Feb 06
Sales Turnover	115	94	85
Pre Tax Profit/Loss	N/A	N/A	-10
Working Capital	14	16	7
Fixed Assets	11	10	N/A
Current Assets	14	16	10
Current Liabilities	N/A	N/A	3
ROCE% (Return on Capital Employed)			-146.2
ROT% (Return on Turnover)			-12.2

British Worlwide Computers Ltd

Albany House 324/326 Regent Street, London, W1B 3HH
Tel: 0845-2255599
E-mail: info@bwcomputers.co.uk
Website: http://www.bwcomputers.co.uk
Directors: A. Blyth (Sales), M. Jackson (MD)
Immediate Holding Company: B W C Ltd
Registration no: 04698220 **Date established:** 2008
No.of Employees: 1 - 10 **Product Groups:** 44

Date of Accounts	Feb 08	Feb 07	Feb 06
Sales Turnover	115	94	85
Pre Tax Profit/Loss	N/A	N/A	-10
Working Capital	14	16	7
Fixed Assets	11	10	N/A
Current Assets	14	16	10
Current Liabilities	N/A	N/A	3
ROCE% (Return on Capital Employed)			-146.2
ROT% (Return on Turnover)			-12.2

British-American Chamber Of Commerce

75 Brook Street, London, W1K 4AD
Tel: 020-7290 9888 **Fax:** 020-7493 2394
E-mail: ogilligan-quinn@babinc.org
Website: http://www.babinc.org
Bank(s): National Westminster Bank Plc
Directors: T. Hall (Dir), P. Hunt (MD), A. Holmes (Dir)
Managers: M. Bulbeck (Mgr), S. Dolatshahi (Gen Contact)
Immediate Holding Company: British-American Chamber Of Commerce
Registration no: 00172178 **VAT No.:** GB 404 6052 89
Date established: 1921 **Turnover:** £2m - £5m **No.of Employees:** 21 - 50
Product Groups: 87

Brixton Ltd Partnership

50 Berkeley Street, London, W1J 8BX
Tel: 020-7399 4500 **Fax:** 020-7399 4550
Website: http://www.brixton.plc.uk
Directors: T. Wheeler (Grp Chief Exec), S. Owen (Dep Chief Exec), N. Fry (Non Exec), M. Moore (Dir), J. Rink (Non Exec), D. Scotland (Non Exec)
Managers: P. Dawson (Mgr), P. Reid (Mktg Serv Mgr)
Immediate Holding Company: BRIXTON PLC
Registration no: 00202342 **Date established:** 2006 **Turnover:** £2m - £5m
No.of Employees: 1 - 10 **Product Groups:** 80

Date of Accounts	Dec 07
Sales Turnover	82000
Pre Tax Profit/Loss	58200
Working Capital	-49000
Fixed Assets	2333m
Current Assets	32800
Current Liabilities	81800
Total Share Capital	67700
ROCE% (Return on Capital Employed)	2.5

Broadbean Technology

40 Marsh Wall, London, E14 9TP
Tel: 020-7536 1667 **Fax:** 020-7536 1668
E-mail: sales@broadbean.com
Website: http://www.broadbean.co.uk
Directors: D. Mccallion (Co Sec), D. McGuire (Ch & MD)
Managers: R. Essex (Sales Prom Mgr)
Immediate Holding Company: Associated Northcliffe Digital Group Ltd
Registration no: 04283360 **Date established:** 2007
Turnover: £10m - £20m **No.of Employees:** 1 - 10 **Product Groups:** 44

Date of Accounts	Dec 07	Dec 06	Dec 05
Working Capital	-13	-5	-8
Fixed Assets	192	43	13
Current Assets	973	551	117
Current Liabilities	986	555	125

Brody Trims Ltd

Unit 1 18 Gillender Street, London, E3 3JW
Tel: 020-7538 5666 **Fax:** 020-7510 1099
E-mail: sales@brody.co.uk
Website: http://www.brody.co.uk
Directors: G. Baptist (MD)
Immediate Holding Company: BRODY TRIMS LIMITED
Registration no: 06634987 **VAT No.:** GB 564 3518 34
Date established: 2008 **Turnover:** £2m - £5m **No.of Employees:** 11 - 20
Product Groups: 30

Date of Accounts	Dec 11	Dec 10	Dec 09
Working Capital	-42	-13	9
Fixed Assets	47	18	38
Current Assets	114	130	191

Brooks McRobbie Ltd (London Office)

43 St John Street, London, EC1M 4LX
Tel: 020-7490 0304 **Fax:** 020-7490 0307
E-mail: john.brooks2@ukonline.co.uk
Website: http://www.brooksmcrobbie.co.uk
Directors: F. Heaney (Fin), J. Brooks (MD)
Immediate Holding Company: BROOKS MCROBBIE LIMITED
Registration no: 01744365 **VAT No.:** GB 365 6544 28
Date established: 1983 **Turnover:** £20m - £50m **No.of Employees:** 1 - 10
Product Groups: 20, 61

Date of Accounts	Dec 11	Dec 10	Dec 09
Sales Turnover	37m	37m	29m
Pre Tax Profit/Loss	-125	-28	140
Working Capital	267	442	506
Fixed Assets	11	8	7
Current Assets	4m	4m	4m
Current Liabilities	194	78	247

Brooks Packaging Ltd

37-39 North Acton Road, London, NW10 6PF
Tel: 020-8961 2733 **Fax:** 020-8965 9841
E-mail: nick@brookspackaging.co.uk
Website: http://www.brookspackaging.co.uk
Bank(s): National Westminster
Directors: N. Horwood (MD)
Immediate Holding Company: BROOKS PACKAGING LIMITED
Registration no: 00908064 **VAT No.:** GB 232 2420 16
Date established: 1967 **Turnover:** £5m - £10m **No.of Employees:** 11 - 20
Product Groups: 27, 30

see next page

Brooks Packaging Ltd - Cont'd

Date of Accounts	Apr 11	Apr 10	Apr 09
Working Capital	2m	2m	2m
Fixed Assets	2m	2m	2m
Current Assets	3m	3m	2m

Sam Brown Furniture

Unit 9 Fountayne House Fountayne Road, London, N15 4QL
Tel: 07778-615980
E-mail: sam@sambrownfurniture.co.uk
Website: http://www.sambrownfurniture.co.uk
Directors: S. Brown (Prop)
Turnover: Up to £250,000 **No.of Employees:** 1 - 10 **Product Groups:** 25, 26, 30

Sandy Brown Associates

1 Coleridge Gardens, London, NW6 3QH
Tel: 020-7644 6500 **Fax:** 020-7644 6510
E-mail: post@sandybrown.com
Website: http://www.sandybrown.com
Bank(s): Lloyds, TSB
Directors: L. Haslam (Snr Part), R. Gailbraith (Snr Part), S. Stringer (Ptnr)
Immediate Holding Company: SANDY BROWN ASSOCIATES LIMITED LIABILITY PARTNERSHIP
Registration no: OC307504 **Date established:** 2004
Turnover: £500,000 - £1m **No.of Employees:** 11 - 20 **Product Groups:** 54

Browns Operating System Services Ltd

Brigade Works Cresswell Park, London, SE3 0TW
Tel: 020-8297 9797 **Fax:** 020-8318 3939
E-mail: mail@browns.co.uk
Website: http://www.brownsbox.com
Directors: A. Brown (Dir)
Immediate Holding Company: BROWN'S OPERATING SYSTEM SERVICES LIMITED
Registration no: 01383993 **VAT No.:** gb 121 4444 22
Date established: 1978 **Turnover:** £1m - £2m **No.of Employees:** 1 - 10
Product Groups: 44

Date of Accounts	Mar 11	Mar 10	Mar 09
Sales Turnover	250	184	302
Pre Tax Profit/Loss	-80	-148	-146
Working Capital	-174	-272	-157
Fixed Assets	N/A	22	33
Current Assets	113	99	132

Brownell Ltd

Unit 2 Abbey Road Industrial Estate Commercial Way Abbey Road, London, NW10 7XF
Tel: 020-8965 9281 **Fax:** 020-8965 3239
E-mail: info@brownell.co.uk
Website: http://www.brownell.co.uk
Bank(s): The Royal Bank of Scotland
Directors: M. Partridge (Dir)
Immediate Holding Company: BROWNELL LIMITED
Registration no: 04495331 **Date established:** 2002 **Turnover:** £1m - £2m
No.of Employees: 21 - 50 **Product Groups:** 32, 38, 40, 42

Date of Accounts	Dec 11	Dec 10	Dec 09
Working Capital	1m	1m	1m
Fixed Assets	221	201	185
Current Assets	2m	2m	2m

Browns S M S Ltd

23-27 South Molton Street, London, W1K 5RD
Tel: 020-7514 0000 **Fax:** 020-7408 1281
E-mail: buyingoffice@brownsfashion.com
Website: http://www.brownsfashions.com
Directors: S. Burnstein (Grp Chief Exec), S. Burstein (Grp Chief Exec), J. Burstine (MD), J. Burstein (MD)
Immediate Holding Company: BROWNS LIMITED
Registration no: 03975026 **Date established:** 2000
Turnover: £10m - £20m **No.of Employees:** 1 - 10 **Product Groups:** 61

Brumby Apparel

33 Fentons Avenue, London, E13 0AX
Tel: 07894-903085
E-mail: info@brumby.biz
Website: http://www.brumby.biz
Directors: Q. Abbas (Prop)
Date established: 1997 **Turnover:** Up to £250,000
No.of Employees: 1 - 10 **Product Groups:** 24

Brunner Machine Tools Ltd

6 Colville Road, London, W3 8BL
Tel: 020-8992 6011 **Fax:** 020-8992 7559
E-mail: sales@brunnermachine.co.uk
Website: http://www.brunnermachine.co.uk
Directors: M. Brunner (Fin), E. Brunner (MD)
Immediate Holding Company: BRUNNER MACHINE TOOLS LIMITED
Registration no: 00865656 **VAT No.:** GB 226 5626 61
Date established: 1965 **Turnover:** Up to £250,000
No.of Employees: 1 - 10 **Product Groups:** 26, 36, 46, 47

Date of Accounts	Dec 11	Dec 10	Dec 09
Working Capital	395	409	622
Fixed Assets	11	15	6
Current Assets	596	614	622
Current Liabilities	167	123	N/A

Bryan & Clark Ltd

Unit 2-3 Bowman Trading Estate Westmoreland Road, London, NW9 9RL
Tel: 020-8206 2200 **Fax:** 020-8960 7430
E-mail: sales@bryanandclark.co.uk
Website: http://www.bryanandclark.co.uk
Directors: D. Pattni (Dir)
Immediate Holding Company: BRYAN & CLARK LIMITED
Registration no: 02920449 **VAT No.:** GB 653 2274 46
Date established: 1994 **Turnover:** £500,000 - £1m
No.of Employees: 1 - 10 **Product Groups:** 63

Date of Accounts	Dec 11	Dec 10	Dec 09
Working Capital	104	93	88
Fixed Assets	416	421	421
Current Assets	600	491	461

Bryen & Langley Ltd

48-60 Footscray Road, London, SE9 2SU
Tel: 020-8850 7775 **Fax:** 020-8850 6772
E-mail: info@bryen-langley.com
Website: http://www.bryen-langley.com
Bank(s): Barclays, Piccadilly, Corporate Banking Centre
Directors: D. Wrighton (Comm)
Immediate Holding Company: BRYEN & LANGLEY LIMITED
Registration no: 03527466 **VAT No.:** GB 205 4214 12
Date established: 1998 **Turnover:** £20m - £50m
No.of Employees: 101 - 250 **Product Groups:** 25, 52, 84

Date of Accounts	Mar 12	Mar 11	Mar 10
Sales Turnover	31m	31m	37m
Pre Tax Profit/Loss	126	295	431
Working Capital	2m	2m	3m
Fixed Assets	2m	2m	189
Current Assets	10m	12m	14m
Current Liabilities	3m	4m	5m

BSI UK

389 Chiswick High Road, London, W4 4 AL
Tel: 020-8996 9001 **Fax:** 020-8996 7400
E-mail: tim.lewis@bsigroup.com
Website: http://www.bsigroup.com
Directors: S. Brease (Grp Chief Exec), D. John (Ch), M. Hannah (Fin)
Managers: N. Samme (Mktg Serv Mgr), T. Lewis (Tech Serv Mgr), K. Wright (Mgr), G. Grant (Mgr), D. Cole (I.T. Exec)
Ultimate Holding Company: BRITISH STANDARDS INSTITUTION
Immediate Holding Company: BSI LIMITED
Registration no: 03555107 **Date established:** 1998
Turnover: £50m - £75m **No.of Employees:** 501 - 1000
Product Groups: 85

Date of Accounts	Dec 11	Dec 10	Dec 09
Pre Tax Profit/Loss	2m	1m	1m
Working Capital	43m	42m	41m
Current Assets	43m	42m	42m
Current Liabilities	261	187	366

Buchanan

107 Cheapside, London, EC2V 6DN
Tel: 020-7466 5000 **Fax:** 020-7466 5001
E-mail: contact@buchanan.uk.com
Website: http://www.buchanan.uk.com
Bank(s): National Westminster Bank Plc
Directors: M. Edwards (Dir), G. Haque (Fin), W. Merchant (Tech Serv)
Managers: R. Oldworth
Ultimate Holding Company: WPP PLC (JERSEY)
Immediate Holding Company: BUCHANAN COMMUNICATIONS LIMITED
Registration no: 01499986 **VAT No.:** GB 245 7021 77
Date established: 1980 **Turnover:** £5m - £10m **No.of Employees:** 21 - 50
Product Groups: 81

Date of Accounts	Dec 11	Dec 10	Dec 09
Sales Turnover	7m	7m	7m
Pre Tax Profit/Loss	1m	1m	1m
Working Capital	893	2m	3m
Fixed Assets	743	25	103
Current Assets	3m	4m	4m
Current Liabilities	1m	1m	1m

Budd Shirt Makers Ltd

1a-3 Piccadilly Arcade, London, SW1Y 6NH
Tel: 020-7493 0139 **Fax:** 020-7491 7524
E-mail: mail@buddshirts.co.uk
Website: http://www.buddshirts.co.uk
Managers: A. Rowley (Mgr)
Ultimate Holding Company: H. HUNTSMAN & SONS LIMITED
Immediate Holding Company: BUDD (SHIRT MAKERS) LIMITED
Registration no: 00281295 **VAT No.:** GB 238 4544 49
Date established: 1933 **Turnover:** £250,000 - £500,000
No.of Employees: 1 - 10 **Product Groups:** 24

Date of Accounts	Dec 11	Dec 10	Jan 10
Working Capital	153	299	293
Fixed Assets	104	20	2
Current Assets	337	365	364

Buhler Sortex Ltd

Sortex Ltd 20 Atlantis Avenue, London, E16 2BF
Tel: 020-7055 7777 **Fax:** 020-7055 7700
E-mail: sales@buhlersortex.com
Website: http://www.buhlergroup.com
Bank(s): National Westminster Bank Plc & SG Hambros Bank and Trust Ltd
Directors: H. Kefayati (MD), N. Wilson (Fin)
Managers: M. Lee
Ultimate Holding Company: BUHLER HOLDING AG (SWITZERLAND)
Immediate Holding Company: BUHLER SORTEX LIMITED
Registration no: 00434274 **Date established:** 1947
Turnover: £50m - £75m **No.of Employees:** 101 - 250
Product Groups: 07, 37, 38, 41, 42, 67, 85

Date of Accounts	Dec 11	Dec 10	Dec 09
Sales Turnover	74m	85m	63m
Pre Tax Profit/Loss	20m	25m	16m
Working Capital	30m	25m	18m
Fixed Assets	729	13m	13m
Current Assets	44m	44m	36m
Current Liabilities	12m	14m	14m

The Building Centre Bookshop

26 Store Street, London, WC1E 7BT
Tel: 020-7692 4040 **Fax:** 020-7636 3628
E-mail: info@bcbookshop.co.uk
Website: http://www.buildingcentre.co.uk
Directors: M. Winter (Fin)
Managers: L. Forder
Ultimate Holding Company: BUILDING CENTRE GROUP LIMITED(THE)
Immediate Holding Company: THE BUILDING CENTRE BOOKSHOP LIMITED
Registration no: 01036915 **Date established:** 1972
Turnover: £250,000 - £500,000 **No.of Employees:** 1 - 10
Product Groups: 64, 69, 80, 81

Date of Accounts	Mar 11	Mar 10	Mar 09
Working Capital	-15	-15	-15
Current Assets	13	9	9
Current Liabilities	14	14	16

Bullen E V & Son Ltd

388-390 Lee High Road, London, SE12 8RW
Tel: 020-8318 0911 **Fax:** 020-8318 0014
E-mail: matt.bullen@evbullen.com
Website: http://www.evbullen.com
Directors: M. Bullen (MD), P. Bullen (MD), M. Bullen (Dir)
Managers: J. Collins (Sales Admin), M. Minch (I.T. Exec)
Registration no: 00653265 **VAT No.:** GB 205 4317 02
Date established: 1960 **Turnover:** £1m - £2m **No.of Employees:** 1 - 10
Product Groups: 37, 52, 84

Bulthaup Ltd (The Kitchen People Ltd)

37 Wigmore Street, London, W1U 1PP
Tel: 020-7495 3663 **Fax:** 020-7495 0139
E-mail: awrighton@bulthaup.co.uk
Website: http://www.bulthaup.co.uk
Directors: A. Wrighton (MD)
No.of Employees: 11 - 20 **Product Groups:** 26, 36, 63

Bupa

Bupa House 15-19 Bloomsbury Way, London, WC1A 2BA
Tel: 020-7656 2000 **Fax:** 020-7656 2701
Website: http://www.bupa.co.uk
Bank(s): HSBC Bank plc
Directors: V. Gooding (MD), S. Flanagan (Sales), R. King (Dir), P. Jacobs (Grp Chief Exec), B. Black (Fin), O. Black (Dir)
Immediate Holding Company: BRITISH UNITED PROVIDENT ASSOCIATION LIMITED(THE)
Registration no: 00432511 **Date established:** 1947
Turnover: Up to £250,000 **No.of Employees:** 501 - 1000
Product Groups: 82, 88

Burberry Ltd

21 New Bond Street, London, W1S 2RE
Tel: 020-3367 3000 **Fax:** 020-7839 2666
E-mail: marketing@burberry.com
Website: http://www.burberry.com
Directors: W. Chellingsworth (Chief Op Offcr)
Managers: D. Thursby (Chief Mgr)
Ultimate Holding Company: BURBERRY GROUP PLC
Immediate Holding Company: BURBERRY LIMITED
Registration no: 00162636 **Date established:** 2020 **Turnover:** £1m - £2m
No.of Employees: 1 - 10 **Product Groups:** 24

Date of Accounts	Mar 12	Mar 11	Mar 10
Sales Turnover	1099m	949m	733m
Pre Tax Profit/Loss	227m	196m	153m
Working Capital	717m	554m	348m
Fixed Assets	141m	121m	97m
Current Assets	1201m	933m	801m
Current Liabilities	134m	130m	99m

Burgopak

Thames House 18 Park Street, London, SE1 9EL
Tel: 020-7407 6291 **Fax:** 020-7407 6292
E-mail: infouk@burgopak.com
Website: http://www.burgopak.com
Directors: B. Wharton (Prop), T. Clarke (Sales), C. Bluett (MD), J. Canning (Co Sec), P. Heininger (Dir)
Managers: R. Ashurst (Mktg Serv Mgr)
Ultimate Holding Company: BURGOPAK HOLDINGS LIMITED
Immediate Holding Company: BURGOPAK LIMITED
Registration no: 04186315 **Date established:** 2001 **Turnover:** £2m - £5m
No.of Employees: 1 - 10 **Product Groups:** 27

Date of Accounts	May 10	May 09	May 08
Sales Turnover	5m	3m	4m
Pre Tax Profit/Loss	-827	-2m	-400
Working Capital	665	-2m	2m
Fixed Assets	4m	4m	2m
Current Assets	2m	921	3m
Current Liabilities	135	2m	227

F E Burman Ltd (Head Office)

20 Crimscott Street, London, SE1 5TF
Tel: 020-7206 1000 **Fax:** 020-7206 1040
E-mail: info@feburman.co.uk
Website: http://www.feburman.co.uk
Bank(s): Barclays
Directors: A. Onabanjo (Fin), M. Burman (MD)
Immediate Holding Company: F.E. BURMAN LIMITED
Registration no: 00598760 **VAT No.:** GB 350 7333 73
Date established: 1958 **Turnover:** £2m - £5m **No.of Employees:** 21 - 50
Product Groups: 81

Date of Accounts	Jun 11	Jun 10	Jun 09
Sales Turnover	3m	3m	3m
Pre Tax Profit/Loss	84	-11	-720
Working Capital	-632	-1m	-2m
Fixed Assets	273	1m	1m
Current Assets	589	742	626
Current Liabilities	872	2m	2m

Burness Corlett A division of The Oceanic Investment Corporation

19-21 Great Tower Street, London, EC3R 5AR
Tel: 020-7929 2299 **Fax:** 020-7929 4167
E-mail: enquiries@bctq.com
Website: http://www.bctq.com
Bank(s): The Royal Bank of Scotland
Directors: D. Smith (Mkt Research)
Managers: G. Armstrong (Mgr)
Ultimate Holding Company: FP047671
Immediate Holding Company: BURNESS CORLETT - THREE QUAYS LIMITED
Registration no: 00931996 **Date established:** 1968 **Turnover:** £5m - £10m
No.of Employees: 21 - 50 **Product Groups:** 81, 84

Date of Accounts	Mar 11	Mar 10	Mar 09
Sales Turnover	1m	7m	10m
Pre Tax Profit/Loss	-405	-553	-423
Working Capital	-2m	-2m	-1m
Fixed Assets	49	49	83
Current Assets	846	2m	2m
Current Liabilities	213	239	287

Buro Four Project Services Ltd

296-300 St John Street, London, EC1V 4PP
Tel: 020-7833 8663 **Fax:** 020-7833 8560
E-mail: sslade@burofour.co.uk
Website: http://www.burofour.co.uk
Bank(s): Barclays, Borehamwood, Herts
Directors: S. Slade (Fin), S. Slade (Co Sec), T. Taylor (Ch), J. Davies (Dir), D. Pelter (Dir), C. Birch (Dir), N. Biscoe (Dir)
Managers: R. Birchmore (Sales Prom Mgr)
Immediate Holding Company: BURO FOUR PROJECT SERVICES LIMITED
Registration no: 01911750 **VAT No.:** GB 426 6006 70
Date established: 1985 **Turnover:** £10m - £20m
No.of Employees: 51 - 100 **Product Groups:** 80

Date of Accounts	Jan 09	Jan 08	Nov 06
Sales Turnover	16m	17m	11m
Pre Tax Profit/Loss	795	993	436

Working Capital	3m	2m	1m
Fixed Assets	4m	3m	3m
Current Assets	7m	7m	5m
Current Liabilities	5m	5m	4m
Total Share Capital	1	1	1

Burson Marsteller

24-28 Bloomsbury Way, London, WC1A 2PX
Tel: 020-7831 2969 **Fax:** 020-7340 1033
E-mail: enquiries@bein.com
Website: http://www.bm.com
Directors: L. Richmond (Dir), A. Talbot (Fin), A. Watson (Ch), S. Townsend (Co Sec)
Ultimate Holding Company: WPP 2005 LIMITED
Immediate Holding Company: BURSON-MARSTELLER (UK) LIMITED
Registration no: 02183419 **Date established:** 1987
Turnover: £10m - £20m **No.of Employees:** 101 - 250 **Product Groups:** 81

Burton Saw International Ltd

Trading Estate Valmar Road, London, SE5 9NW
Tel: 020-7737 3577 **Fax:** 020-7733 2368
E-mail: burton.saw@virgin.net
Website: http://www.burtonsaw.co.uk
Directors: N. Day (Dir)
Immediate Holding Company: BURTON SAW INTERNATIONAL LIMITED
Registration no: 01242982 **VAT No.:** GB 356 8235 54
Date established: 1976 **Turnover:** £500,000 - £1m
No.of Employees: 1 - 10 **Product Groups:** 36, 41

Date of Accounts	Aug 11	Aug 10	Aug 09
Working Capital	368	294	273
Fixed Assets	11	20	14
Current Assets	451	426	315
Current Liabilities	N/A	3	6

Business & Decision Ltd

Broad Street House 55 Old Broad Street, London, EC2M 1RX
Tel: 020-7997 6060 **Fax:** 020-7997 6100
E-mail: info@businessdecision.co.uk
Website: http://www.businessdecision.co.uk
Directors: I. Huckall (MD)
Managers: J. Price (Sales Prom Mgr), A. Ruttens (Mktg Serv Mgr)
Registration no: 01643041 **VAT No.:** GB 358 9159 05
Turnover: £5m - £10m **No.of Employees:** 21 - 50 **Product Groups:** 44, 86

Business Design Centre Ltd

52 Upper Street, London, N1 0QH
Tel: 020-7359 3535 **Fax:** 020-7226 0590
E-mail: raya@businessdesigncentre.co.uk
Website: http://www.businessdesigncentre.co.uk
Bank(s): National Westminster Bank Plc
Directors: J. Mulee (Fin), J. Mullee (Co Sec), S. Margolis (Sales), D. Jones (MD)
Managers: C. King, K. Elson, S. Worland (Personnel)
Ultimate Holding Company: BDCG HOLDINGS LIMITED
Immediate Holding Company: BUSINESS DESIGN CENTRE LIMITED
Registration no: 01593648 **VAT No.:** GB 220 3321 32
Date established: 1981 **Turnover:** £10m - £20m
No.of Employees: 21 - 50 **Product Groups:** 69, 81

Date of Accounts	Mar 11	Mar 10	Mar 09
Sales Turnover	13m	15m	19m
Pre Tax Profit/Loss	6m	7m	7m
Working Capital	16m	15m	17m
Fixed Assets	75m	75m	76m
Current Assets	20m	19m	22m
Current Liabilities	2m	2m	2m

Business Monitor International

Senator House 85 Queen Victoria Street, London, EC4V 4AB
Tel: 020-7248 0468 **Fax:** 020-7248 0467
E-mail: info@businessmonitor.com
Website: http://www.businessmonitor.com
Bank(s): Barclays bank Fleet Street
Directors: S. Elgar (Mkt Research), W. Bond (Sales), K. Roberts (Fin)
Managers: J. Feroze, D. Milliard, A. Finch (Tech Serv Mgr)
Ultimate Holding Company: BMI 1 LIMITED
Immediate Holding Company: BUSINESS MONITOR INTERNATIONAL LIMITED
Registration no: 01763490 **VAT No.:** GB 386 1191 40
Date established: 1983 **Turnover:** £5m - £10m
No.of Employees: 101 - 250 **Product Groups:** 28

Date of Accounts	Jan 08
Sales Turnover	10m
Pre Tax Profit/Loss	2m
Working Capital	82
Fixed Assets	553
Current Assets	5m
Current Liabilities	4m

Business Systems Group UK

Simone Silverman BSG House, London, EC1V 2TT
Tel: 020-7880 8888 **Fax:** 020-7390 8500
E-mail: nick.gerard@bsg.co.uk
Website: http://www.bsg.co.uk
Directors: G. Reis (Fin), N. Gerard (Dir)
Immediate Holding Company: BUSINESS SYSTEMS GROUP (UK) LIMITED
Registration no: 06150507 **Date established:** 2007 **Turnover:** £1m - £2m
No.of Employees: 101 - 250 **Product Groups:** 80

Date of Accounts	Mar 12	Mar 11	Mar 10
Sales Turnover	1m	1m	1m
Pre Tax Profit/Loss	28	139	48
Working Capital	51	38	-84
Fixed Assets	18	7	2
Current Assets	377	651	628
Current Liabilities	316	586	705

Business To Business Exhibitions Ltd

377 Camden Road, London, N7 0SH
Tel: 020-7700 0008 **Fax:** 020-7700 0061
E-mail: info@btob.co.uk
Website: http://www.btob.co.uk
Directors: I. Heptonstall (MD)
Immediate Holding Company: BUSINESS TO BUSINESS EXHIBITIONS LIMITED
Registration no: 01510136 **Date established:** 1980 **Turnover:** £2m - £5m
No.of Employees: 11 - 20 **Product Groups:** 81

Date of Accounts	Aug 10	Aug 09	Aug 08
Sales Turnover	4m	3m	2m
Pre Tax Profit/Loss	263	251	217

Working Capital	270	99	87
Fixed Assets	22	28	57
Current Assets	818	824	732
Current Liabilities	367	543	542

Jason Buttons Ltd

Unit 40 Mahatma Gandhi Industrial Estate Milkwood Road, London, SE24 0JF
Tel: 020-7274 0724 **Fax:** 020-7737 0022
Directors: J. Elliott (MD), L. Pratt (Fin)
Immediate Holding Company: JASON BUTTONS LIMITED
Registration no: 01115029 **VAT No.:** GB 668 2354 11
Date established: 1973 **Turnover:** £500,000 - £1m
No.of Employees: 1 - 10 **Product Groups:** 25, 29, 30, 33, 35

Date of Accounts	Dec 10	Dec 09	Dec 06
Working Capital	48	43	36
Current Assets	75	61	62
Current Liabilities	N/A	N/A	7

Byblos Bank Europe

Suite 5 Berkeley Square House Berkeley Square, London, W1J 6BS
Tel: 020-7493 3537 **Fax:** 020-7493 1233
E-mail: gfadel@byblosbankeur.com
Website: http://www.byblosbank.com.lb
Bank(s): Barclays
Managers: G. Fadel (District Mgr)
Ultimate Holding Company: GAP INC (USA)
Immediate Holding Company: BYBLOS BANK EUROPE S.A.
Registration no: FC017059 **Date established:** 1976 **Turnover:** £1m - £2m
No.of Employees: 11 - 20 **Product Groups:** 87

C A C I

C A C I House Avonmore Road, London, W14 8TS
Tel: 020-7605 6000 **Fax:** 020-7603 5862
E-mail: admin@caci.co.uk
Website: http://www.caci.co.uk
Bank(s): National Westminster Bank Plc
Directors: I. Hobbs (Tech Serv), N. Robins-cherry (Fin), S. Walbank (Mkt Research), A. Post (Co Sec)
Managers: C. Tozzi (Sales Admin), M. Salisbury (Sales Prom Mgr), J. Brown (Personnel)
Ultimate Holding Company: CACI INTERNATIONAL INC (USA)
Immediate Holding Company: CACI LIMITED
Registration no: 01649776 **Date established:** 1982
Turnover: £50m - £75m **No.of Employees:** 101 - 250
Product Groups: 44, 81, 84

Date of Accounts	Jun 11	Jun 10	Jun 09
Sales Turnover	71m	69m	49m
Pre Tax Profit/Loss	5m	4m	3m
Working Capital	17m	15m	8m
Fixed Assets	33m	36m	22m
Current Assets	43m	40m	33m
Current Liabilities	19m	15m	14m

C & A Supplies Ltd

Bidder Street, London, E16 4ST
Tel: 020-7474 0474 **Fax:** 020-7474 5055
E-mail: charles@cabp.co.uk
Website: http://www.casupply.co.uk
Bank(s): National Westminster
Directors: C. Candlin (MD)
Immediate Holding Company: C & A SUPPLIES LIMITED
Registration no: 03895992 **VAT No.:** GB 248 0960 48
Date established: 1999 **No.of Employees:** 11 - 20 **Product Groups:** 30

Date of Accounts	Dec 11	Dec 10	Dec 09
Working Capital	1m	1m	1m
Fixed Assets	287	306	209
Current Assets	2m	2m	2m

C Brewer & Sons

Unit 31 Capitol Industrial Park Capitol Way, London, NW9 0EQ
Tel: 020-8905 9900 **Fax:** 020-8205 1772
E-mail: decorating@brewers.co.uk
Website: http://brewers.co.uk
Managers: C. Fulton (Mgr)
Immediate Holding Company: C.BREWER & SONS LIMITED
Registration no: 00203852 **VAT No.:** GB 198 1565 70
Date established: 1925 **No.of Employees:** 1 - 10 **Product Groups:** 61

C Brewer & Sons

327 Putney Bridge Road, London, SW15 2PG
Tel: 020-8780 1277 **Fax:** 020-8788 8285
Website: http://www.brewers.co.uk
Managers: G. Henry (District Mgr)
Immediate Holding Company: C.BREWER & SONS LIMITED
Registration no: 00203852 **VAT No.:** GB 203 1565 70
Date established: 1925 **No.of Employees:** 1 - 10 **Product Groups:** 27, 32

C Brewer & Sons Ltd

Unit 14 Chiltonian Industrial Estate Manor Lane, London, SE12 0TD
Tel: 020-8318 9511 **Fax:** 020-8463 0575
Website: http://www.brewers.co.uk
Bank(s): Barclays
Managers: W. Hughes
Immediate Holding Company: C.BREWER & SONS LIMITED
Registration no: 00203852 **Date established:** 2025
Turnover: £50m - £75m **No.of Employees:** 11 - 20 **Product Groups:** 27, 30, 32

Date of Accounts	Dec 11	Dec 10	Dec 09
Sales Turnover	126m	118m	114m
Pre Tax Profit/Loss	-778	4m	7m
Working Capital	16m	18m	21m
Fixed Assets	26m	22m	21m
Current Assets	37m	38m	34m
Current Liabilities	15m	16m	12m

C D F Cleaning Services Ltd

1c St Agnes Place, London, SE11 4AU
Tel: 020-7793 1746
E-mail: carlos@saqnet.co.uk
Website: http://www.freewebs.com/cdf_cleaning/index.htm
Directors: M. Puentes (Fin), C. Puentes (MD)
Immediate Holding Company: CDF CLEANING SERVICES LIMITED
Registration no: 04530600 **Date established:** 2002
No.of Employees: 1 - 10 **Product Groups:** 52

Date of Accounts	Sep 11	Sep 10	Sep 09
Working Capital	28	23	23
Fixed Assets	6	5	4
Current Assets	60	60	41

C & D Metalworks

20 Peacock Industrial Estate White Hart Lane, London, N17 8DT
Tel: 020-8808 1299 **Fax:** 020-8365 0199
E-mail: hidir_aslan@hotmail.co.uk
Website: http://www.cdmetal.co.uk
Managers: H. Aslan (Mgr)
Immediate Holding Company: C & D METALWORKS (UK) LIMITED
Registration no: 04280828 **Date established:** 2001
Turnover: £250,000 - £500,000 **No.of Employees:** 1 - 10
Product Groups: 26, 35, 48

Date of Accounts	Nov 10	Nov 09	Nov 08
Sales Turnover	398	272	361
Pre Tax Profit/Loss	18	18	13
Working Capital	100	87	71
Fixed Assets	21	20	22
Current Assets	322	319	293
Current Liabilities	53	51	51

C E S A Association (CESA)

Westminster Tower 3 Albert Embankment, London, SE1 7SL
Tel: 020-7793 3030 **Fax:** 020-7793 3031
E-mail: enquiries@cesa.org.uk
Website: http://www.cesa.org.uk
Directors: K. Warren (Dir)
Immediate Holding Company: CESA LIMITED
Registration no: 06620580 **Date established:** 2008
Turnover: £500,000 - £1m **No.of Employees:** 1 - 10 **Product Groups:** 87

Date of Accounts	Jun 11	Jun 10	Jun 09
Sales Turnover	605	552	426
Pre Tax Profit/Loss	22	47	-23
Working Capital	279	261	219
Fixed Assets	N/A	N/A	1
Current Assets	366	389	296
Current Liabilities	54	128	77

C F K LLP

33 Great Portland Street, London, W1W 8QG
Tel: 08700-533755 **Fax:** 020-7636 1727
E-mail: info@cfkllp.co.uk
Website: http://www.cfkllp.co.uk
Directors: I. Kitchener (Dir)
Immediate Holding Company: CONWAY FRASER LIMITED
Registration no: 03191720 **Date established:** 1996
Turnover: Up to £250,000 **No.of Employees:** 1 - 10 **Product Groups:** 80

Date of Accounts	Jun 11	Jun 10	Jun 09
Sales Turnover	217	250	157
Pre Tax Profit/Loss	2	-2	-40
Working Capital	-16	-17	-24
Fixed Assets	1	1	1
Current Assets	17	16	52
Current Liabilities	32	32	73

C Hoare & Co.

37 Fleet Street, London, EC4Y 1BT
Tel: 020-7353 4522 **Fax:** 020-7353 4521
E-mail: e-mail@hoaresbank.co.uk
Website: http://www.hoare.co.uk
Directors: D. Green (Co Sec)
Managers: J. Ayres (Comptroller), R. Winder (Tech Serv Mgr)
Immediate Holding Company: C. HOARE & CO.
Registration no: 00240822 **VAT No.:** GB 244 0783 68
Date established: 2029 **No.of Employees:** 251 - 500 **Product Groups:** 82

Date of Accounts	Mar 12	Mar 11	Mar 10
Pre Tax Profit/Loss	25m	22m	24m
Fixed Assets	533m	598m	781m
Current Assets	1748m	1400m	1387m
Current Liabilities	2091m	1841m	2030m

C I C

Veritas House 125 Finsbury Pavement, London, EC2A 1HX
Tel: 020-7454 5400 **Fax:** 020-7588 6038
E-mail: info@cic-banques.fr
Website: http://www.cic-banques.fr
Bank(s): National Westminster Bank Plc
Directors: P. Mais (Fin)
Ultimate Holding Company: BANQUE FEDERATIVE DE CREDIT MUTUEL
Immediate Holding Company: UNION EUROPEENNE (UK) LIMITED
Registration no: 02436956 **Date established:** 1989
No.of Employees: 21 - 50 **Product Groups:** 82

C I M A (Chartered Institute of Management Accountants)

26 Chapter Street, London, SW1P 4NP
Tel: 020-7663 5441 **Fax:** 020-7663 5442
E-mail: info@cimaglobal.com
Website: http://www.cimaglobal.com
Directors: P. Spence (Fin)
Managers: M. Mun (Tech Serv Mgr), F. Taylor (Personnel), R. Fennick
Ultimate Holding Company: CIMATEC GMBH (GERMANY)
Immediate Holding Company: CIMA PENSION AND ASSURANCE SCHEME TRUSTEE LIMITED
Registration no: 07586109 **Date established:** 2011
Turnover: Up to £250,000 **No.of Employees:** 101 - 250
Product Groups: 86, 87

Date of Accounts	Dec 10	Dec 09	Dec 08
Sales Turnover	219	901	725
Current Assets	N/A	96	91
Current Liabilities	N/A	96	91

C M S Cameron Mckenna

Mitre House 160 Aldersgate Street, London, EC1A 4DD
Tel: 020-7367 3000 **Fax:** 0117-934 9300
E-mail: info@cms-cmck.com
Website: http://www.cms-cmck.com
Directors: D. Tyler (Snr Part), J. Grieves (Co Sec)
Immediate Holding Company: CMS CAMERON MCKENNA LLP
Registration no: OC310335 **Date established:** 2004
Turnover: £125m - £250m **No.of Employees:** 501 - 1000
Product Groups: 80

Date of Accounts	Apr 11	Apr 10	Apr 09
Sales Turnover	216m	208m	240m
Pre Tax Profit/Loss	51m	49m	64m
Working Capital	75m	71m	86m
Fixed Assets	12m	12m	13m
Current Assets	130m	101m	118m
Current Liabilities	30m	21m	24m

C R U International Ltd (C R U Group)
31 Mount Pleasant, London, WC1X 0AD
Tel: 020-7903 2000 **Fax:** 020-7837 0976
E-mail: sales@crugroup.com
Website: http://www.crugroup.com
Bank(s): Drummonds
Managers: M. Wilson
Ultimate Holding Company: COMMODITIES RESEARCH UNIT INTERNATIONAL (HOLDINGS) LIMITED
Immediate Holding Company: CRU INTERNATIONAL LIMITED
Registration no: 00940750 **VAT No.:** GB 564 4113 55
Date established: 1968 **Turnover:** £20m - £50m
No.of Employees: 101 - 250 **Product Groups:** 80

Date of Accounts	Mar 11	Mar 10	Mar 09
Sales Turnover	21m	N/A	N/A
Pre Tax Profit/Loss	3m	1m	357
Working Capital	2m	1m	-498
Fixed Assets	1m	1m	2m
Current Assets	15m	10m	8m
Current Liabilities	11m	8m	7m

C S B Logistics Ltd
669 Woolwich Road, London, SE7 8LH
Tel: 020-8293 1282 **Fax:** 020-8293 1555
E-mail: sales@csblogistics.co.uk
Website: http://www.csblogistics.com
Directors: M. Barker (MD)
Immediate Holding Company: CSB LOGISTICS LIMITED
Registration no: 02381112 **VAT No.:** GB 547 7604 17
Date established: 1989 **Turnover:** £1m - £2m **No.of Employees:** 11 - 20
Product Groups: 45, 48, 66, 76, 77

Date of Accounts	Mar 11	Mar 10	Mar 09
Working Capital	24	97	94
Fixed Assets	8	15	30
Current Assets	123	258	229

C S M T
7 Kendal Parade Silver Street, London, N18 1ND
Tel: 020-8887 0562 **Fax:** 020-8807 2108
Website: http://www.csmt.co.uk
Directors: P. Wilkins (Ptnr), P. Munday (Ptnr)
Immediate Holding Company: CSMT LTD
Registration no: 08135538 **Date established:** 2012
No.of Employees: 1 - 10 **Product Groups:** 24, 39, 40, 86

C T L Components plc
Falcon House 19 Deer Park Road, London, SW19 3UX
Tel: 020-8545 8700 **Fax:** 020-8540 0034
E-mail: info@ctl-components.com
Website: http://www.ctl-components.com
Bank(s): Lloyds TSB Bank plc
Directors: A. Balabanovic (MD)
Managers: J. Puttock (Sales Eng), R. Griffiths
Ultimate Holding Company: CTL COMPONENTS GROUP PLC
Immediate Holding Company: C.T.L. COMPONENTS PLC
Registration no: 00743575 **VAT No.:** GB 468 6713 05
Date established: 1962 **Turnover:** £2m - £5m **No.of Employees:** 21 - 50
Product Groups: 28, 36, 37, 38, 48, 49, 67

Date of Accounts	Apr 11	Apr 10	Apr 09
Sales Turnover	2m	2m	2m
Pre Tax Profit/Loss	290	56	34
Working Capital	635	470	464
Fixed Assets	26	42	56
Current Assets	2m	1m	1m
Current Liabilities	422	306	366

C W W Engineers Supply Co. Ltd
7 Stanlake Mews, London, W12 7HA
Tel: 020-8743 0651 **Fax:** 020-8740 7731
E-mail: sales@cww.uk.net
Website: http://www.cww.uk.net
Directors: S. Conwell (Fin), N. Conwell (MD)
Immediate Holding Company: C.W.W.ENGINEERS SUPPLY COMPANY LIMITED
Registration no: 00500762 **Date established:** 1951
Turnover: £500,000 - £1m **No.of Employees:** 1 - 10 **Product Groups:** 30, 35, 36, 37, 66

Date of Accounts	Mar 11	Mar 10	Mar 09
Working Capital	33	100	214
Fixed Assets	54	66	80
Current Assets	153	201	345

Cable & Wireless Communications plc
3rd Floor 26 Red Lion Square, London, WC1R 4HQ
Tel: 020-7315 4000 **Fax:** 020-7315 5182
E-mail: tony.rice@cw.com
Website: http://www.cwc.com
Bank(s): The Royal Bank of Scotland
Directors: T. Pennington (Fin)
Managers: T. Rice
Immediate Holding Company: CABLE & WIRELESS COMMUNICATIONS PLC
Registration no: 07130199 **Date established:** 2010
Turnover: Over £1,000m **No.of Employees:** 51 - 100 **Product Groups:** 37

Date of Accounts	Mar 08
Pre Tax Profit/Loss	1140
Working Capital	9950
Current Assets	21830
Current Liabilities	11880
Total Share Capital	5000
ROCE% (Return on Capital Employed)	11.5

Cableduct Ltd
30 Selhurst Road, London, SE25 5QF
Tel: 020-8683 1126 **Fax:** 020-8689 7896
E-mail: info@cableductuk.com
Website: http://www.cableductuk.com
Bank(s): Barclays
Directors: C. Wrinch (MD), H. Wozniak (Sales)
Immediate Holding Company: CABLEDUCT LIMITED
Registration no: 00364046 **VAT No.:** GB 217 8706 49
Date established: 1940 **Turnover:** £500,000 - £1m
No.of Employees: 21 - 50 **Product Groups:** 37

Date of Accounts	Mar 12	Mar 11	Mar 10
Working Capital	1m	878	234
Fixed Assets	231	192	251
Current Assets	2m	1m	782

Cadex Ltd
Unit J209 Tower Bridge Business Complex 100 Clements Road, London, SE16 4DG
Tel: 020-7252 0000
Website: http://www.cadex.org
Directors: R. Davis (Fin)
Immediate Holding Company: CADEX LIMITED
Registration no: 03128279 **Date established:** 1995
No.of Employees: 1 - 10 **Product Groups:** 20, 40, 41

Date of Accounts	Apr 11	Apr 10	Apr 09
Working Capital	87	104	147
Current Assets	190	215	232

Caffe Nero Group Ltd
3 Neal Street, London, WC2H 9PU
Tel: 020-7520 5150 **Fax:** 020-7520 5198
E-mail: enquiries@caffenero.com
Website: http://www.caffenero.com
Managers: L. Hartigan (Sales Admin)
Ultimate Holding Company: SARATOGA LIMITED (ISLE OF MAN)
Immediate Holding Company: CAFFE NERO GROUP LIMITED
Registration no: 04129005 **Date established:** 2000
Turnover: £125m - £250m **No.of Employees:** 101 - 250
Product Groups: 69

Date of Accounts	May 11	May 10	May 09
Sales Turnover	166m	154m	142m
Pre Tax Profit/Loss	17m	17m	12m
Working Capital	44m	28m	9m
Fixed Assets	52m	50m	53m
Current Assets	78m	60m	35m
Current Liabilities	21m	19m	15m

Caledonia Investments plc
30 Buckingham Gate, London, SW1E 6NN
Tel: 020-7802 8080 **Fax:** 020-7802 8090
E-mail: enquiries@caledonia.com
Website: http://www.caledonia.com
Bank(s): Royal Bank of Scotland
Directors: G. Denison (Co Sec), J. Loudon (Ch), S. King (Fin)
Managers: P. Whiteley (Tech Serv Mgr), K. Burwood (Personnel)
Immediate Holding Company: CALEDONIA INVESTMENTS PLC
Registration no: 00235481 **VAT No.:** GB 564 5099 18
Date established: 2028 **Turnover:** £75m - £125m
No.of Employees: 51 - 100 **Product Groups:** 82

Date of Accounts	Mar 12	Mar 11	Mar 10
Sales Turnover	28m	206m	N/A
Pre Tax Profit/Loss	-96m	74m	299m
Working Capital	25m	77m	44m
Fixed Assets	1197m	1213m	1244m
Current Assets	79m	167m	80m
Current Liabilities	45m	83m	29m

Caledonian Cables Ltd
27 Old Gloucester Street, London, WC1N 3AX
Tel: 020-7419 5087 **Fax:** 020-7831 9489
E-mail: info@caledonian-cables.co.uk
Website: http://www.caledonian-cables.co.uk
Managers: J. Tam (Sales Prom)
Registration no: 06448812 **Date established:** 1978
Turnover: £500,000 - £1m **No.of Employees:** 21 - 50 **Product Groups:** 23

Callmonitor
207 Regent Street, London, W1B 4ND
Tel: 020-7292 9200 **Fax:** 0800-074 7458
E-mail: sales@satphone.co.uk
Website: http://www.satphone.co.uk
Directors: R. Offenbach (Dir)
Immediate Holding Company: CALLMONITOR LIMITED
Registration no: 03844878 **Date established:** 1999
No.of Employees: 1 - 10 **Product Groups:** 37, 39, 67

Date of Accounts	Mar 12	Mar 11	Mar 10
Working Capital	242	223	226
Fixed Assets	8	8	12
Current Assets	410	524	395

Campbell Reith Hill
Artillery House 11-19 Artillery Row, London, SW1P 1RT
Tel: 020-7340 1700 **Fax:** 0161-242 8939
E-mail: mikelawson@campbellreith.com
Website: http://www.campbellreith.com
Bank(s): Lloyds TSB Bank plc
Directors: M. Lawson (Ptnr), K. Yeoh (Co Sec)
Managers: G. Ross (Tech Serv Mgr), B. Price (Sales & Mktg Mg), J. Parker
Immediate Holding Company: CAMPBELL REITH HILL LIMITED LIABILITY PARTNERSHIP
Registration no: OC300082 **VAT No.:** GB 223 3711 01
Date established: 2001 **Turnover:** £5m - £10m **No.of Employees:** 21 - 50
Product Groups: 54, 84

Date of Accounts	Jul 11	Jul 10	Jul 09
Sales Turnover	8m	8m	10m
Pre Tax Profit/Loss	826	731	1m
Working Capital	1m	1m	2m
Fixed Assets	151	134	228
Current Assets	3m	3m	3m
Current Liabilities	983	589	1m

Camper & Nicholsons Mayfair Ltd
Fitzroy House 18-20 Grafton Street, London, W1S 4DZ
Tel: 020-7009 1950 **Fax:** 020-7629 2068
E-mail: info@lon.cnyachts.com
Website: http://www.camperandnicholsons.com
Directors: T. Walker (Sales)
Managers: K. Main (Sales Admin)
Ultimate Holding Company: RODRIGUEZ GROUP (FRANCE)
Immediate Holding Company: CAMPER & NICHOLSONS MAYFAIR LIMITED
Registration no: 00866955 **Date established:** 1965
Turnover: £250,000 - £500,000 **No.of Employees:** 1 - 10
Product Groups: 68

Date of Accounts	Sep 11	Sep 10	Sep 09
Sales Turnover	362	1m	1m
Pre Tax Profit/Loss	-505	-367	-169
Working Capital	-843	-362	-49
Fixed Assets	256	303	341
Current Assets	202	139	319
Current Liabilities	21	122	111

Canada - UK Chamber Of Commerce
38 Grosvenor Street, London, W1K 4DP
Tel: 020-7258 6578 **Fax:** 020-7258 6594
E-mail: info@canada-uk.org
Website: http://www.canada-uk.org.uk
Directors: N. Bacon (Dir)
Immediate Holding Company: CANADA-UNITED KINGDOM CHAMBER OF COMMERCE
Registration no: 00223529 **Date established:** 2027
Turnover: Up to £250,000 **No.of Employees:** 1 - 10 **Product Groups:** 82, 87

Date of Accounts	Dec 11	Dec 10	Dec 09
Sales Turnover	311	234	271
Pre Tax Profit/Loss	10	8	16
Working Capital	105	90	98
Fixed Assets	12	19	2
Current Assets	271	241	239
Current Liabilities	146	133	119

Canadian High Commission
1 Grosvenor Square, London, W1K 4AB
Tel: 020-7258 6600 **Fax:** 020- 72586333
Directors: M. Cappe (MD)
Managers: R. Conway (Mgr)
No.of Employees: 251 - 500 **Product Groups:** 80

Canary Wharf Holdings Ltd
One Canada Square Canary Wharf, London, E14 5AB
Tel: 020-7418 2000 **Fax:** 020-7418 2222
E-mail: admin@canarywharf.com
Website: http://www.sytnercitybmw.co.uk
Directors: J. Garwood (Co Sec), R. Lyons (Fin), G. Iacobesdu (MD), P. Anderson (Jt MD)
Managers: R. Lyons (Chief Acct), N. Whitmore (Mktg Serv Mgr), P. Stupps (I.T. Exec), M. Ashley-Brown (Legal)
Ultimate Holding Company: SONGBIRD ESTATES PLC.
Immediate Holding Company: CANARY WHARF HOLDINGS LIMITED
Registration no: 02798284 **Date established:** 1993
Turnover: £125m - £250m **No.of Employees:** 501 - 1000
Product Groups: 80

Date of Accounts	Dec 10	Dec 08	Dec 07
Pre Tax Profit/Loss	2m	2m	1m
Working Capital	2m	N/A	N/A
Current Assets	2m	N/A	N/A

Cancer Research Ventures Ltd
10 Cambridge Terrace Regents Park, London, NW1 4JL
Tel: 020-7224 1333 **Fax:** 020-7487 4310
Website: http://www.cancer.org.uk
Directors: H. Kumar (Dir), D. Scott (Co Sec)
Ultimate Holding Company: CANCER RESEARCH UK
Immediate Holding Company: CANCER RESEARCH VENTURES LIMITED
Registration no: 03521378 **Date established:** 1998 **Turnover:** £1m - £2m
No.of Employees: 11 - 20 **Product Groups:** 80

Date of Accounts	Mar 12	Mar 11	Mar 03
Sales Turnover	N/A	N/A	2m
Pre Tax Profit/Loss	N/A	N/A	-193
Working Capital	4m	4m	4m
Current Assets	4m	4m	4m

Candover Services Ltd
20 Old Bailey, London, EC4M 7LN
Tel: 020-7489 9848 **Fax:** 020-7248 5483
E-mail: info@candover.com
Website: http://www.candover.com
Directors: P. Price (Co Sec)
Managers: W. Wright
Ultimate Holding Company: CANDOVER INVESTMENTS PLC
Immediate Holding Company: ARLE CAPITAL PARTNERS LIMITED
Registration no: 01517104 **Date established:** 1980
Turnover: £10m - £20m **No.of Employees:** 1 - 10 **Product Groups:** 82

Date of Accounts	Dec 11	Dec 10	Dec 09
Sales Turnover	19m	19m	16m
Pre Tax Profit/Loss	8m	-6m	-6m
Working Capital	7m	40	-16m
Fixed Assets	20	10	40m
Current Assets	9m	2m	6m
Current Liabilities	614	855	3m

Canning
593-599 Fulham Road, London, SW6 5UA
Tel: 020-7381 7410 **Fax:** 020-7370 1056
E-mail: enquiry@canning.co.uk
Website: http://www.canning.co.uk
Bank(s): Barclays
Managers: S. Davies (Admin Off)
Immediate Holding Company: CANNING TRUSTEES LIMITED
Registration no: 05858839 **Date established:** 2006 **Turnover:** £2m - £5m
No.of Employees: 11 - 20 **Product Groups:** 86

Cannings Connolly
16 St Martin's Le Grand, London, EC1A 4EE
Tel: 020-7329 9000 **Fax:** 020-7329 5000
E-mail: jdifede@cclaw.co.uk
Website: http://www.cclaw.co.uk
Managers: J. Difede
Immediate Holding Company: GENERO2 GP LIMITED
Registration no: OC323888 **Date established:** 2009 **Turnover:** £2m - £5m
No.of Employees: 21 - 50 **Product Groups:** 80

Cannon Street Properties Ltd
16 Ashley Road, London, N17 9LJ
Tel: 020-8885 9430 **Fax:** 020-8885 9415
E-mail: ab@csjf.co.uk
Website: http://www.csjf.co.uk
Managers: A. Bleiberg (Chief Mgr)
Immediate Holding Company: CANNON STREET PROPERTIES LIMITED
Registration no: 02011306 **Date established:** 1986
Turnover: Up to £250,000 **No.of Employees:** 1 - 10 **Product Groups:** 23

Date of Accounts	Mar 11	Mar 10
Working Capital	-2	-5
Fixed Assets	4	5
Current Assets	5	6
Current Liabilities	1	11

Canonbury Services
The Smithfield Business Centre 5 St John's Lane, London, EC1M 4BH
Tel: 020-7549 1618 **Fax:** 020-7549 1619
E-mail: rw@canonbury-services.co.uk
Website: http://www.canonbury-services.co.uk

Directors: R. Widdicombe (MD)
Immediate Holding Company: MOONLIGHT MEDIA LIMITED
Registration no: 03530566 **Date established:** 1998
Turnover: £250,000 - £500,000 **No.of Employees:** 1 - 10
Product Groups: 44, 80

Date of Accounts	Mar 11	Mar 10	Mar 09
Working Capital	2	8	8
Fixed Assets	3	1	1
Current Assets	54	37	23
Current Liabilities	N/A	N/A	14

Cap Gemini UK plc
95 Wandsworth Road, London, SW8 2HG
Tel: 020-7735 0800 **Fax:** 020-7917 4666
Website: http://www.uk.capgemini.com
Bank(s): HSBC Bank plc
Directors: P. Spence (Grp Chief Exec)
Ultimate Holding Company: CAP GEMINI SA (FRANCE)
Immediate Holding Company: CAPGEMINI UK PLC
Registration no: 00943935 **Date established:** 1968
No.of Employees: 501 - 1000 **Product Groups:** 44, 84, 86

Date of Accounts	Dec 11	Dec 10	Dec 09
Sales Turnover	1643m	1647m	1661m
Pre Tax Profit/Loss	39m	59m	53m
Working Capital	257m	260m	245m
Fixed Assets	103m	88m	73m
Current Assets	802m	787m	767m
Current Liabilities	238m	207m	247m

Caparo Group Ltd
Caparo House 101-103 Baker Street, London, W1U 6LN
Tel: 020-7486 1417 **Fax:** 020-7224 4109
E-mail: sales@caparo.co.uk
Website: http://www.caparo.com
Bank(s): The Royal Bank of Scotland
Directors: P. Walker (Dir)
Immediate Holding Company: CAPARO GROUP LIMITED
Registration no: 01387694 **Date established:** 1978
Turnover: £250m - £500m **No.of Employees:** 11 - 20
Product Groups: 66, 82

Date of Accounts	Dec 11	Dec 10	Dec 09
Sales Turnover	454m	435m	571m
Pre Tax Profit/Loss	7m	-14m	-18m
Working Capital	9m	-5m	-89m
Fixed Assets	116m	113m	218m
Current Assets	138m	119m	152m
Current Liabilities	22m	25m	32m

Capio Nightingale Hospital
11-19 Lisson Grove, London, NW1 6SH
Tel: 020-7535 7700 **Fax:** 020-7724 6827
E-mail: head-office.reception@capiohealthcare.co.uk
Website: http://www.nightingaleshospitals.co.uk
Directors: M. Thomas (MD)
Managers: V. Moff (Mktg Serv Mgr), S. Gray (Comptroller), A. Hagger (Comptroller), C. Ball (Sales Admin), S. Fowkes (Tech Serv Mgr)
Ultimate Holding Company: CAPIO LUX TOP HOLDING SARL (LUXEMBOURG)
Immediate Holding Company: FLORENCE NIGHTINGALE HOSPITALS LIMITED
Registration no: 01431836 **Date established:** 1979 **Turnover:** £5m - £10m
No.of Employees: 101 - 250 **Product Groups:** 88

Date of Accounts	Dec 11	Dec 10	Dec 09
Sales Turnover	11m	11m	10m
Pre Tax Profit/Loss	300	6m	-3m
Working Capital	3m	1m	-6m
Fixed Assets	620	2m	4m
Current Assets	4m	2m	2m
Current Liabilities	313	394	391

Capisco
Unit 1 Period Works 1 Lammas Road, London, E10 7QT
Tel: 020-8532 8838 **Fax:** 020-7503 7201
E-mail: works@patination.com
Website: http://www.patination.com
Directors: A. Elton (MD)
Immediate Holding Company: CAPISCO LIMITED
Registration no: 02446894 **Date established:** 1989
No.of Employees: 1 - 10 **Product Groups:** 46, 48

Date of Accounts	Nov 10	Nov 09	Nov 08
Working Capital	-138	-50	-32
Fixed Assets	8	12	16
Current Assets	70	116	83

Capita Group plc
71 Victoria Street, London, SW1H 0XA
Tel: 020-7799 1525 **Fax:** 020-7799 1526
E-mail: lynn.chidwick@capita.co.uk
Website: http://www.capita.co.uk
Directors: I. Gates (I.T. Dir), J. Bacon (Pers), R. Aldridge (Ch), P. Doyle (Dir), P. Pindar (Grp Chief Exec), P. Kelly (Dir), J. Peel (Dir), G. Hurst (Fin), G. Hurst (Co Sec), D. Rigby (Dir), P. Braithwaite (Dir)
Immediate Holding Company: CAPITA PLC
Registration no: 02081330 **Date established:** 1986
Turnover: Over £1,000m **No.of Employees:** 101 - 250
Product Groups: 44, 80

Date of Accounts	Dec 07	Dec 06	Dec 05
Sales Turnover	2073m	1739m	1436m
Pre Tax Profit/Loss	228700	193200	153100
Working Capital	-194600	-129700	-117900
Fixed Assets	1033m	862500	783500
Current Assets	458100	404600	343800
Current Liabilities	652700	534300	461700
Total Share Capital	12600	12300	13400
ROCE% (Return on Capital Employed)	27.3	26.4	23.0
ROT% (Return on Turnover)	11.0	11.1	10.7

Capital Ceramics
899-901 Fulham Road, London, SW6 5HU
Tel: 020-7736 7468 **Fax:** 020-7736 7394
Managers: A. Kaluz (Mgr)
No.of Employees: 1 - 10 **Product Groups:** 30, 32, 36

Capital Coffee
Unit 5 Saxon Business Centre 41-59 Windsor Avenue, London, SW19 2RR
Tel: 020-8540 5000 **Fax:** 020-8543 4444
E-mail: sales@capitalcoffeeroasters.co.uk
Website: http://www.capitalcoffeeroasters.co.uk

Directors: L. Grey (Ptnr)
Immediate Holding Company: A LIMITED
Registration no: 05438136 **Date established:** 2005
No.of Employees: 1 - 10 **Product Groups:** 36, 41, 69

Capital Of London
105-107 Clarence Road, London, E5 8EE
Tel: 020-8986 4400 **Fax:** 020-8986 7900
E-mail: info@capitaloflondon.com
Website: http://www.capitaloflondon.com
Directors: E. Abid (Prop)
No.of Employees: 1 - 10 **Product Groups:** 28, 44

Capital Roofing Co. Ltd
193 Westcombe Hill Blackheath, London, SE3 7BB
Tel: 020-8858 5123 **Fax:** 020-8305 1202
E-mail: info@capital-roofing.co.uk
Website: http://www.capital-roofing.co.uk
Directors: T. Peck (MD)
Immediate Holding Company: CAPITAL ROOFING CO. LIMITED
Registration no: 01876577 **VAT No.:** GB 207 0885 70
Date established: 1985 **No.of Employees:** 21 - 50 **Product Groups:** 14, 31, 52

Date of Accounts	Sep 11	Sep 10	Sep 09
Working Capital	33	120	233
Fixed Assets	24	9	15
Current Assets	768	554	774

Capital Shopping Centres
40 Broadway, London, SW1H 0BU
Tel: 020-7887 4220 **Fax:** 020-7887 4225
Website: http://www.capcount.com
Bank(s): Barclays
Directors: S. Folger (Fin), R. Finch (Ch), P. Burgess (Ch), K. Chaldecott (MD)
Managers: M. Harworth (Sales Admin), K. Norris (Sales Admin), M. Harwood (Sales & Mktg Mg), J. Harwood (Sales & Mktg Mg), J. Watson (I.T. Exec), J. Hoare (Sales Admin)
Ultimate Holding Company: CAPITAL SHOPPING CENTRES GROUP PLC
Immediate Holding Company: CAPITAL SHOPPING CENTRES PLC
Registration no: 02893329 **Date established:** 1994
Turnover: £250m - £500m **No.of Employees:** 101 - 250
Product Groups: 80

Date of Accounts	Dec 10	Dec 09	Dec 08
Sales Turnover	390m	336m	223m
Pre Tax Profit/Loss	474m	-325m	-1551m
Working Capital	-970m	-1594m	-998m
Fixed Assets	4882m	4402m	4019m
Current Assets	161m	122m	125m
Current Liabilities	1085m	1640m	1084m

Captain Tolley Ltd
69 Valiant House Vicarage Cresent, London, SW11 3LX
Tel: 020-7924 2817 **Fax:** 020-7223 7025
E-mail: capt.tolleyltd@btinternet.com
Website: http://www.captaintolley.co.uk
Directors: P. Jordan (Dir)
Immediate Holding Company: CAPTAIN TOLLEY LIMITED
Registration no: 02068479 **VAT No.:** GB 448 8579 84
Date established: 1986 **Turnover:** Up to £250,000
No.of Employees: 1 - 10 **Product Groups:** 39, 84

Date of Accounts	Oct 11	Oct 10	Oct 09
Working Capital	-2	-1	7
Fixed Assets	1	1	2
Current Assets	16	9	12

Car Captain
Queen's Lodge 26 York Street, London, W1U 6PZ
Tel: 020-7099 1232 **Fax:** 07020-972030
E-mail: admin@carcaptain.com
Website: http://www.carcaptain.com
Directors: Y. Kriel (MD)
Immediate Holding Company: CARCAPTAIN LIMITED
Registration no: 07402502 **Date established:** 2010
No.of Employees: 1 - 10 **Product Groups:** 86

Date of Accounts	Mar 12
Working Capital	-5
Fixed Assets	5
Current Assets	16

Car Giant
44 Hythe Road, London, NW10 6RJ
Tel: 08444-824132 **Fax:** 020-8960 2659
E-mail: webgeneral@cargiants.co.uk
Website: http://www.cargiant.co.uk
Directors: J. Fordyke (Dir), M. Holohan (Fin), T. Mendes (MD), T. Mendis (MD)
Managers: D. Miller (Mktg Serv Mgr), S. Wast (Tech Serv Mgr)
Immediate Holding Company: CAR GIANT LIMITED
Registration no: 01407612 **VAT No.:** GB 442 1385 71
Date established: 1979 **Turnover:** £250m - £500m
No.of Employees: 501 - 1000 **Product Groups:** 68

Date of Accounts	Dec 11	Dec 10	Dec 09
Sales Turnover	295m	322m	274m
Pre Tax Profit/Loss	17m	13m	8m
Working Capital	38m	-14m	-11m
Fixed Assets	55m	67m	54m
Current Assets	53m	41m	47m
Current Liabilities	8m	43m	55m

Carat Group UK Ltd
43-49 Parker Street, London, WC2B 5PS
Tel: 020-7430 6300 **Fax:** 020-7430 6299
Website: http://www.carat.co.uk
Directors: N. Jones (Dir)
Immediate Holding Company: ZENPAY UK LIMITED
Registration no: 02496207 **Date established:** 2012
No.of Employees: 251 - 500 **Product Groups:** 81

Carbon Guerrilla
Floor 1 No. 4 New Burlington Street Mayfair, London, W1S 2JG
Tel: 020-7956 8698 **Fax:** 020-7712 1501
E-mail: Peter@carbonguerrilla.com
Website: http://www.carbonguerrilla.com
Managers: P. James (Mktg Serv Mgr)
Date established: 2010 **Turnover:** **No.of Employees:** 21 - 50
Product Groups: 54

Cardales
1 Lumley Street, London, W1K 6ND
Tel: 020-7629 6604 **Fax:** 020-7495 0150
E-mail: info@db.com
Website: http://www.cardales.co.uk
Bank(s): Bank of Scotland
Directors: R. Court (Co Sec)
Managers: S. Fields (Personnel), S. Fields (Personnel), S. Field (Sales Admin)
Ultimate Holding Company: GENERAL ACCIDENT P.L.C.
Immediate Holding Company: GENERAL ACCIDENT FINANCIAL SERVICES
Date established: 1946 **No.of Employees:** 11 - 20 **Product Groups:** 80, 81

Alexander Cardew Ltd (Head Office)
Unit 27 Chelsea Wharf 15 Lots Road, London, SW10 0QJ
Tel: 020-7235 3785 **Fax:** 020-7352 4635
E-mail: sales@cardew.com
Website: http://www.cardew.com
Directors: J. Vandeperre (Dir)
Immediate Holding Company: ALEXANDER CARDEW LIMITED
Registration no: 00357088 **VAT No.:** GB 443 9152 48
Date established: 1939 **Turnover:** £1m - £2m **No.of Employees:** 1 - 10
Product Groups: 27, 29, 30, 35, 36, 37, 38, 42, 45, 46, 51, 52, 61

Date of Accounts	Oct 11	Oct 10	Oct 09
Working Capital	224	230	241
Fixed Assets	24	24	24
Current Assets	247	462	339

Carefreecomputers.Com
29 University Road, London, SW19 2BU
Tel: 08450-940456
E-mail: info@carefreecomputers.com
Website: http://www.carefreecomputers.com
Directors: G. Earley (Prop), G. Earley (Tech Serv)
Immediate Holding Company: WHITECURVE LIMITED
Registration no: 05114054 **Date established:** 2004
Turnover: Up to £250,000 **No.of Employees:** 1 - 10 **Product Groups:** 44

Carfax Cards Ltd
76 Glentham Road, London, SW13 9JJ
Tel: 020-8748 1122 **Fax:** 020-8748 7110
E-mail: carfax.admin@business-cards.co.uk
Website: http://www.carfaxltd.co.uk
Directors: T. Jones (MD), A. Jones (Fin)
Managers: J. Bristow (Mktg Serv Mgr), L. Snell (Tech Serv Mgr)
Immediate Holding Company: CARFAX CARDS,LIMITED
Registration no: 00221533 **Date established:** 2027 **Turnover:** £1m - £2m
No.of Employees: 11 - 20 **Product Groups:** 28

Date of Accounts	Dec 11	Dec 10	Dec 09
Working Capital	49	-1	-69
Fixed Assets	235	253	275
Current Assets	271	261	171

Cargo Solutions International Ltd
Unit 116 Thames House 566 Cable Street, London, E1W 3HB
Tel: 020-7702 8555 **Fax:** 020-7702 8883
E-mail: info@cargosolutionsint.co.uk
Website: http://www.cargosolutionsint.co.uk
Directors: H. Begum (Fin), M. Ali (Sales)
Immediate Holding Company: CALLY STEEL FABRICATION LTD
Registration no: 05755414 **Date established:** 2001
Turnover: Up to £250,000 **No.of Employees:** 1 - 10 **Product Groups:** 72, 74, 75, 76, 80, 82

Date of Accounts	Dec 07	Dec 06
Working Capital	-22	-4
Fixed Assets	1	1
Current Assets	1	6
Current Liabilities	23	10

Carmel Olefins UK Ltd
215 West End Lane, London, NW6 1XJ
Tel: 020-7372 6833 **Fax:** 020-7625 9183
E-mail: terry@carmel-olefins.co.uk
Website: http://www.carmel-olefins.co.il
Managers: T. Harris (Sales Prom Mgr)
Immediate Holding Company: CARMEL OLEFINS (UK) LIMITED
Registration no: 02743529 **Date established:** 1992
Turnover: £250,000 - £500,000 **No.of Employees:** 1 - 10
Product Groups: 31

Date of Accounts	Dec 11	Dec 10	Dec 09
Working Capital	49	45	42
Current Assets	74	55	62

Carnegie Investment Bank
24 Chiswell Street, London, EC1Y 4UE
Tel: 020-7216 4000 **Fax:** 020-7417 9424
Website: http://www.carnegie.co.uk
Managers: M. Walker (Personnel), R. Burnett, J. Hurwalrth (I.T. Exec)
Ultimate Holding Company: KAUPTHING GROUP UK LIMITED
Immediate Holding Company: CARNEGIE LIMITED
Registration no: 02941368 **Date established:** 1994
Turnover: Up to £250,000 **No.of Employees:** 1 - 10 **Product Groups:** 82

Date of Accounts	Dec 11	Dec 10	Dec 03
Working Capital	26	26	26
Current Assets	30	30	30
Current Liabilities	4	4	4

The Carphone Warehouse plc
1 Portal Way, London, W3 6RS
Tel: 020-8896 5000 **Fax:** 020-8896 5005
E-mail: legal@cpw.co.uk
Website: http://www.carphonewarehouse.com
Managers: C. Dunston
Ultimate Holding Company: BEST BUY CO INC (USA)
Immediate Holding Company: THE CARPHONE WAREHOUSE LIMITED
Registration no: 02142673 **Date established:** 1987
Turnover: Over £1,000m **No.of Employees:** 1001 - 1500
Product Groups: 37

Date of Accounts	Mar 08	Apr 09	Apr 10
Sales Turnover	1440m	1643m	1583m
Pre Tax Profit/Loss	17m	-43m	62m
Working Capital	201m	260m	501m
Fixed Assets	283m	150m	253m
Current Assets	643m	859m	1041m
Current Liabilities	156m	141m	166m

Carpmaels & Ransford
1 Southampton Row, London, WC1B 5HA
Tel: 020-7242 8692 **Fax:** 020-7405 4166
E-mail: email@carpmaels.com
Website: http://www.carpmaels.com
Managers: L. Potgieter, A. Hermsen (Tech Serv Mgr), J. Getgood, J. Murphy (Mgr), L. Watts (Chief Acct)
Immediate Holding Company: CARPMAELS & RANSFORD SERVICES LIMITED
Registration no: 08077371 **Date established:** 2012
Turnover: £500,000 - £1m **No.of Employees:** 101 - 250
Product Groups: 80, 87

Cars for Stars Ltd
26 York Street, London, W1U 6PZ
Tel: 01474-362080 **Fax:** 0845-123 5238
E-mail: branch@carsforstars.co.uk
Website: http://www.carsforstars.net
Directors: S. Hughes (Prop)
Ultimate Holding Company: RECTITUDE LTD
Immediate Holding Company: CARS FOR STARS LIMITED
Registration no: 04747524 **Date established:** 2003
Turnover: £250,000 - £500,000 **No.of Employees:** 1 - 10
Product Groups: 72

Date of Accounts	Mar 11	Mar 10	Mar 09
Working Capital	8	-29	-50
Fixed Assets	25	34	93
Current Assets	75	2	5

Cashpoint Systems
26 Church Road, London, SE19 2ET
Tel: 020-8771 5777 **Fax:** 020-8653 9240
Website: http://www.cashpointsystems.co.uk
Directors: K. Sendall (Ptnr)
Date established: 1984 **No.of Employees:** 1 - 10 **Product Groups:** 38, 42

Casper Slieker
Unit 9 65-69 Lots Road, London, SW10 0RN
Tel: 020-7751 5577
E-mail: info@casperslieker.com
Website: http://www.casperslieker.com
Directors: C. Slieker (Prop)
Immediate Holding Company: CASPER SLIEKER LIMITED
Registration no: 06134116 **Date established:** 2007
Turnover: Up to £250,000 **No.of Employees:** 1 - 10 **Product Groups:** 37, 67

Date of Accounts	Mar 11	Mar 10	Mar 09
Sales Turnover	41	47	79
Pre Tax Profit/Loss	-12	-10	-1
Working Capital	-10	1	17
Fixed Assets	1	1	1
Current Assets	31	32	44
Current Liabilities	3	3	4

Castell Safety International Ltd
The Castell Building 217 Kingsbury Road, London, NW9 9PQ
Tel: 020-8200 1200 **Fax:** 020-8205 0055
E-mail: sales@castell.com
Website: http://www.castell.com
Bank(s): National Westminster Bank Plc
Directors: T. Whelan (MD), D. Hughes (Sales), R. McKerracher (Fin)
Managers: R. Mertin (Mktg Serv Mgr), M. Celler, M. Ahmed (Tech Serv Mgr)
Ultimate Holding Company: HALMA PUBLIC LIMITED COMPANY
Immediate Holding Company: CASTELL SAFETY INTERNATIONAL LIMITED
Registration no: 01514709 **VAT No.:** GB 649 9646 68
Date established: 1980 **Turnover:** £5m - £10m **No.of Employees:** 21 - 50
Product Groups: 26, 35, 36, 38, 40, 54, 67

Date of Accounts	Mar 12	Mar 09	Apr 10
Sales Turnover	10m	8m	7m
Pre Tax Profit/Loss	2m	1m	780
Working Capital	2m	2m	2m
Fixed Assets	3m	3m	3m
Current Assets	4m	3m	3m
Current Liabilities	411	288	232

Catercover Ltd
Vicarage House 58-60 Kensington Church Street, London, W8 4DB
Tel: 020-7368 3319
E-mail: sales@catercover.co.uk
Website: http://www.catercover.co.uk
Directors: J. Nicholas (Fin)
Immediate Holding Company: DRAYTONS PROPERTY LIMITED
Registration no: 02267625 **Date established:** 2010
Turnover: Up to £250,000 **No.of Employees:** 1 - 10 **Product Groups:** 20, 40, 41

Date of Accounts	Mar 08	Mar 07	Mar 06
Sales Turnover	133	147	245
Pre Tax Profit/Loss	1	-15	38
Working Capital	-13	-13	-1
Fixed Assets	1	7	11
Current Assets	6	31	41
Current Liabilities	19	44	42

Caterprint Ltd
30 High Street, London, N14 6EE
Tel: 020-8886 1600 **Fax:** 020-8886 1636
E-mail: sales@caterprint.co.uk
Website: http://www.caterprint.co.uk
Directors: L. Landsberg (MD)
Immediate Holding Company: CATERPRINT LIMITED
Registration no: 03161849 **Date established:** 1996
No.of Employees: 1 - 10 **Product Groups:** 81

Date of Accounts	Dec 11	Dec 10	Dec 09
Working Capital	-6	-4	-5
Fixed Assets	8	6	7
Current Assets	79	80	93

C A T I C Trading Development UK Ltd
Ironbridge House, London, NW1 8BD
Tel: 020-7586 3854 **Fax:** 020-7586 6799
E-mail: 380icuk@dtclict.com
Directors: W. Ping (Dir)
Ultimate Holding Company: CHINA NATIONAL AREO-TECHNOLOGY IMP & EXP
Immediate Holding Company: AVIC INTERNATIONAL CORPORATION (U.K.) LIMITED
Registration no: 02569831 **VAT No.:** GB 523 4301 88
Date established: 1990 **Turnover:** £1m - £2m **No.of Employees:** 1 - 10
Product Groups: 30, 33, 34, 35, 37, 38, 39, 48, 49, 63, 65, 67, 68, 89

Date of Accounts	Dec 11	Dec 10	Dec 09
Sales Turnover	24	N/A	N/A
Pre Tax Profit/Loss	-104	N/A	N/A
Working Capital	-48	55	14
Fixed Assets	5	6	8
Current Assets	215	83	86
Current Liabilities	7	N/A	N/A

Cavendish Group International Ltd
Commonwealth House New Oxford Street, London, WC1A 1NU
Tel: 020-3077 8700
E-mail: info@cavendishgroup.co.uk
Website: http://www.cavendishgroup.co.uk
Managers: M. Astill, T. Collins (Comptroller)
Immediate Holding Company: CAVENDISH GROUP INTERNATIONAL LIMITED
Registration no: 03617361 **Date established:** 1998
Turnover: £500,000 - £1m **No.of Employees:** 21 - 50
Product Groups: 28, 81

Date of Accounts	Dec 11	Dec 10	Dec 09
Working Capital	787	485	333
Fixed Assets	11	13	43
Current Assets	3m	2m	2m

Cedar Group
31-41 Worship Street, London, EC2A 2DX
Tel: 020-7065 7100
E-mail: mail@cedargroup.uk.com
Website: http://www.cedargroup.uk.com
Directors: P. Martin (Dir)
Registration no: 02200156 **Turnover:** £2m - £5m
No.of Employees: 11 - 20 **Product Groups:** 81

Cedar Tree Cases
7 Commonwealth Buildings Woolwich Church Street, London, SE18 5NS
Tel: 020-8855 5577 **Fax:** 020-8855 5599
Directors: J. Moffett (Prop)
No.of Employees: 1 - 10 **Product Groups:** 25, 35, 66, 76

Cembrit Ltd
57 Kellner Road, London, SE28 0AX
Tel: 020-8301 8900 **Fax:** 020-8301 8909
E-mail: sales@cembrit.co.uk
Website: http://www.cembrit.co.uk
Bank(s): Lloyds TSB Bank plc
Directors: P. Archer (Sales), D. Fair (Fin), M. Fisher (MD)
Managers: G. Ferris (Mktg Serv Mgr)
Ultimate Holding Company: FLSMIDTH & CO A/S (DENMARK)
Immediate Holding Company: CEMBRIT LIMITED
Registration no: 01968377 **VAT No.:** GB 277 7476 03
Date established: 1985 **Turnover:** £20m - £50m
No.of Employees: 21 - 50 **Product Groups:** 14

Date of Accounts	Dec 11	Dec 10	Dec 09
Sales Turnover	25m	25m	24m
Pre Tax Profit/Loss	44	322	112
Working Capital	2m	2m	3m
Fixed Assets	7	8	23
Current Assets	7m	7m	7m
Current Liabilities	1m	1m	873

Centre For Contemporary British History
King's College London Strand, London, WC2R 2LS
Tel: 020-7101 6090 **Fax:** 020-7101 6099
E-mail: tm@itma.org.uk
Website: http://www.ccbh.ac.uk
Directors: M. Tyler (Co Sec)
Immediate Holding Company: INSTITUTE OF CONSULTING LIMITED
Registration no: 00294396 **VAT No.:** GB 461 5184 53
Date established: 2006 **Turnover:** £500,000 - £1m
No.of Employees: 1 - 10 **Product Groups:** 87

Date of Accounts	Dec 08	Dec 07
Sales Turnover	969	926
Pre Tax Profit/Loss	-80	93
Working Capital	984	1054
Fixed Assets	49	50
Current Assets	1234	1224
Current Liabilities	250	170
ROCE% (Return on Capital Employed)	-7.7	8.5
ROT% (Return on Turnover)	-8.2	10.1

Centre For Economics & Business Research Ltd
4 Bath Street, London, EC1V 9DX
Tel: 020-7324 2850 **Fax:** 020-7234 2855
E-mail: enquiries@cebr.com
Website: http://www.cebr.com
Bank(s): The Royal Bank of Scotland
Directors: D. Mcwilliams (Dir)
Immediate Holding Company: CENTRE FOR ECONOMICS AND BUSINESS RESEARCH LIMITED
Registration no: 02592404 **VAT No.:** GB 523 3971 48
Date established: 1991 **Turnover:** £1m - £2m **No.of Employees:** 11 - 20
Product Groups: 80

Date of Accounts	May 12	May 11	May 10
Sales Turnover	2m	1m	1m
Pre Tax Profit/Loss	235	280	185
Working Capital	289	184	-7
Fixed Assets	389	393	409
Current Assets	864	552	541
Current Liabilities	504	310	372

CH Field Services Ltd
7 Albert Court Prince Consort Road, London, SW7 2BJ
Tel: 020-7589 1256 **Fax:** 020-7581 4112
E-mail: ck@charleskendall.com
Website: http://www.charleskendall.com
Bank(s): Barclays, 128 Moorgate, London EC2M 65X
Directors: G. Mitchell (Co Sec), J. Monkhouse (Fin), M. Kendall (MD), T. Bowen (Dir)
Ultimate Holding Company: Charles Kendall & Partners (Investments) Ltd
Immediate Holding Company: Charles Kendall Group Ltd
Registration no: 00501451 **Date established:** 1945
Turnover: Up to £250,000 **No.of Employees:** 21 - 50 **Product Groups:** 36, 39

Chadwick International
11th Floor Holborn Tower 137 High Holborn, London, WC1V 6PW
Tel: 020-7269 0920 **Fax:** 020-7269 0929
E-mail: chadwick@chadwick-international.com
Website: http://www.chadwick-international.com
Directors: A. Chadwick (Head)
Immediate Holding Company: CHADWICK INTERNATIONAL LIMITED
Registration no: 03445350 **Date established:** 1997
No.of Employees: 1 - 10 **Product Groups:** 84

Cham Ltd (Concentration Heat, & Momentum Ltd)
40 High Street Wimbledon, London, SW19 5AU
Tel: 020-8947 7651 **Fax:** 020-8879 3497
E-mail: ercj@cham.co.uk
Website: http://www.cham.co.uk
Bank(s): Lloyds TSB Bank plc
Directors: C. King (Fin), D. Spalding (MD)
Managers: P. Spalding (Sales Prom Mgr)
Immediate Holding Company: CHAM LIMITED
Registration no: 02262296 **Date established:** 1988 **Turnover:** £2m - £5m
No.of Employees: 11 - 20 **Product Groups:** 44, 54, 81

Chamber Engineering Ltd
35 Gondar Gardens, London, NW6 1EP
Tel: 020-7794 8100 **Fax:** 020-7443 9300
Website: http://www.chamberinternational.com
Directors: M. Lenny (MD)
Managers: P. Griffiths (Chief Mgr)
Immediate Holding Company: CHAMBER INTERNATIONAL LTD
Registration no: 04568239 **Date established:** 2002
No.of Employees: 1 - 10 **Product Groups:** 35

Date of Accounts	Oct 08	Oct 07	Oct 05
Working Capital	-22	-74	-0
Fixed Assets	2	1	1
Current Assets	148	117	57

The Chamber Of Shipping
Carthusian Court 12 Carthusian Street, London, EC1M 6EZ
Tel: 020-7417 2800 **Fax:** 020-7417 8877
E-mail: postmaster@british-shipping.org
Website: http://www.british-shipping.org
Managers: J. Lewis (Sales Admin)
Immediate Holding Company: THE CHAMBER OF SHIPPING LIMITED
Registration no: 02107383 **Date established:** 1987 **Turnover:** £2m - £5m
No.of Employees: 21 - 50 **Product Groups:** 87

Date of Accounts	Mar 11	Mar 10	Mar 09
Sales Turnover	3m	3m	3m
Pre Tax Profit/Loss	-745	45	-834
Working Capital	683	633	-633
Fixed Assets	7m	7m	6m
Current Assets	1m	1m	826
Current Liabilities	296	314	177

Chanel Ltd
Rotherwick House 19-21 Old Bond Street, London, W1S 4PX
Tel: 020-7493 3836 **Fax:** 020-7408 1557
E-mail: sales@chanel.co.uk
Website: http://www.chanel.com
Directors: K. Matthews (Dir)
Ultimate Holding Company: CHANEL INTERNATIONAL BV (NETHERLANDS)
Immediate Holding Company: CHANEL LIMITED
Registration no: 00203669 **Date established:** 2025
Turnover: £250m - £500m **No.of Employees:** 51 - 100
Product Groups: 24, 32, 63

Date of Accounts	Dec 11	Dec 10	Dec 09
Sales Turnover	339m	316m	274m
Pre Tax Profit/Loss	112m	103m	69m
Working Capital	101m	69m	79m
Fixed Assets	84m	71m	17m
Current Assets	182m	144m	156m
Current Liabilities	42m	40m	35m

Channel Four Television Co. Ltd
124-126 Horseferry Road, London, SW1P 2TX
Tel: 020-7396 4444 **Fax:** 020-7306 8347
E-mail: sales@channel4.co.uk
Website: http://www.channel4.com
Directors: G. Isherwood (Fin)
Ultimate Holding Company: CHANNEL FOUR TELEVISION CORPORATION
Immediate Holding Company: CHANNEL FOUR TELEVISION COMPANY LIMITED
Registration no: 01533774 **Date established:** 1980
No.of Employees: 501 - 1000 **Product Groups:** 37

Chantrey Ltd
51 Skylines, London, E14 9TS
Tel: 020-3327 3100 **Fax:** 020-7292 0595
E-mail: business@chantrey.co.uk
Website: http://www.chantrey.co.uk
Directors: P. Anthony (MD)
Managers: D. Millar (Mgr)
Immediate Holding Company: Mirvac UK Ltd
Registration no: 06872329 **VAT No.:** GB 645 4230 51
Date established: 2000 **Turnover:** £250,000 - £500,000
No.of Employees: 11 - 20 **Product Groups:** 52, 80, 82, 84, 89

Date of Accounts	Jun 08	Jun 07	Mar 06
Working Capital	-188	1052	2784
Fixed Assets	161	96	35
Current Assets	401	1532	4187
Current Liabilities	589	480	1404
Total Share Capital	500	500	500

Chaplin Benedicte & Co. Ltd
126 Aldersgate Street, London, EC1A 4JQ
Tel: 020-7490 7770 **Fax:** 020-7250 3109
E-mail: cbc@legal.com
Website: http://www.cbc-legal.com
Directors: L. Chaplin (MD), F. Suant (Fin)
Immediate Holding Company: CHAPLIN, BENEDICTE & CO LTD
Registration no: 03716018 **Date established:** 1999
Turnover: Up to £250,000 **No.of Employees:** 1 - 10 **Product Groups:** 80

Date of Accounts	Dec 10	Dec 09	Dec 08
Working Capital	7	7	7
Fixed Assets	1	2	2
Current Assets	9	11	10

David Charles Childrens Wear Ltd
1 Thane Works, London, N7 7NU
Tel: 020-7609 4797 **Fax:** 020-7609 9696
E-mail: davidcharles19@btconnect.com

Directors: A. Ansell (Fin), D. Graff (MD)
Immediate Holding Company: DAVID CHARLES CHILDRENS WEAR LIMITED
Registration no: 01006482 **Date established:** 1971
Turnover: £250,000 - £500,000 **No.of Employees:** 11 - 20
Product Groups: 24, 63

Date of Accounts	Apr 12	Apr 11	Apr 10
Working Capital	474	435	434
Fixed Assets	4	2	2
Current Assets	675	643	639

Charles Gee Group
Knightrider House 30-32 Knightrider Street, London, EC4V 5JT
Tel: 020-7815 3500 **Fax:** 020-7815 3506
E-mail: christopher.boden@geegroup.co.uk
Website: http://www.geegroup.co.uk
Bank(s): Royal Bank of Scotland, London EC3
Directors: C. Boden (Co Sec)
Immediate Holding Company: CHARLES GEE GROUP LTD.
Registration no: 07000093 **Date established:** 2009
Turnover: £20m - £50m **No.of Employees:** 51 - 100 **Product Groups:** 74, 76

Date of Accounts	Mar 11	Mar 10
Sales Turnover	41m	14m
Pre Tax Profit/Loss	618	199
Working Capital	-4m	-2m
Fixed Assets	8m	6m
Current Assets	12m	8m
Current Liabilities	10m	5m

Charles Kendall Group Ltd
7 Albert Court Prince Consort Road, London, SW7 2BJ
Tel: 020-7589 1256 **Fax:** 020-7581 5761
E-mail: john.kendall@charleskendall.com
Website: http://www.charleskendall.com
Bank(s): Barclays
Directors: G. Mitchell (Co Sec), I. Jenkins (Sales), J. Kendall (Ch)
Ultimate Holding Company: CHARLES KENDALL GROUP LIMITED
Immediate Holding Company: CHARLES KENDALL FREIGHT LIMITED
Registration no: 00540121 **VAT No.:** 238 4062 67 **Date established:** 1954
Turnover: £10m - £20m **No.of Employees:** 101 - 250 **Product Groups:** 76

Date of Accounts	Dec 10	Dec 09	Dec 07
Working Capital	93	93	93
Current Assets	93	93	93

Charmed Cards & Crafts
22 Somerville Road, London, SE20 7NA
Tel: 020-8659 0737
E-mail: sales@charmedcardsandcrafts.co.uk
Website: http://www.charmedcardsandcrafts.co.uk
Directors: K. Mortensen (Prop)
Turnover: Up to £250,000 **No.of Employees:** 1 - 10 **Product Groups:** 37, 64, 66

Chartered Institute Of Personnel & Development
151 The Broadway, London, SW19 1JQ
Tel: 020-8612 6200 **Fax:** 020-8612 6201
E-mail: cipd@cipd.co.uk
Website: http://www.cipd.co.uk
Directors: I. Saville (Fin), I. Pevreall (Tech Serv), J. Orme (Grp Chief Exec), L. Sajeant (Pers)
Managers: D. Stanley (Sales Admin), S. Upton (Sales & Mktg Mg)
Immediate Holding Company: INSTITUTE OF PERSONNEL AND DEVELOPMENT
Registration no: 02931892 **Date established:** 1994
Turnover: £20m - £50m **No.of Employees:** 251 - 500 **Product Groups:** 87

The Chartered Quality Institute
12 Grosvenor Crescent, London, SW1X 7EE
Tel: 020-7245 6722 **Fax:** 020-7245 6788
E-mail: enquiry@iqa.org
Website: http://www.thecqi.org
Bank(s): Lloyds TSB Bank plc
Directors: S. Feary (Dir), F. Steer (MD), I. Dunstan (Pres)
Managers: H. McBride (Accounts)
Registration no: 05120283 **VAT No.:** GB 240 2529 96
Date established: 1919 **Turnover:** £2m - £5m **No.of Employees:** 21 - 50
Product Groups: 85, 86, 87

Chemical Industries Association Ltd
Smith Square, London, SW1P 3HS
Tel: 020-7834 3399 **Fax:** 020-7834 4469
E-mail: enquiries@cia.org.uk
Website: http://www.cia.org.uk
Bank(s): National Westminster Bank Plc
Directors: C. Brooks (Co Sec)
Managers: L. Martin (Fin Mgr), G. McGuire, S. Marsh (Personnel)
Immediate Holding Company: CHEMICAL INDUSTRIES ASSOCIATION LIMITED
Registration no: 00860702 **VAT No.:** GB 235 5606 66
Date established: 1965 **Turnover:** £5m - £10m **No.of Employees:** 21 - 50
Product Groups: 87

Date of Accounts	Jun 11	Jun 10	Jun 09
Sales Turnover	5m	5m	6m
Pre Tax Profit/Loss	552	77	294
Working Capital	1m	980	1m
Fixed Assets	193	78	83
Current Assets	2m	2m	3m
Current Liabilities	770	716	2m

Chevron
1 Westferry Circus, London, E14 4HA
Tel: 020-7719 3000
Website: http://www.chevron.com
Bank(s): National Westminster Bank Plc
Directors: B. Zaza (Co Sec)
Ultimate Holding Company: CHEVRON CORPORATION (USA)
Immediate Holding Company: TEXACO LIMITED
Registration no: 05533507 **VAT No.:** GB 238 9240 44
Date established: 2005 **Turnover:** Over £1,000m
No.of Employees: 51 - 100 **Product Groups:** 31, 32, 66

Chile Copper Ltd
Birket House 27 Albemarle Street, London, W1S 4HZ
Tel: 020-7907 9600 **Fax:** 020-7907 9610
Website: http://www.codelcochile.com
Directors: G. Cuadra (Grp Chief Exec), G. Cuadra (Dir), R. Souper (Dir), R. Toro (Dir), C. Maule Oatway (Co Sec), H. Courtney (Co Sec)
Ultimate Holding Company: CORPORACION NACIONAL DEL COBRE DE CHILE (CHILE)
Immediate Holding Company: CHILE COPPER LIMITED
Registration no: 01006281 **Date established:** 1971 **Turnover:** £2m - £5m
No.of Employees: 1 - 10 **Product Groups:** 82

Date of Accounts	Dec 11	Dec 10	Dec 09
Sales Turnover	217	4m	2m
Pre Tax Profit/Loss	33	-132	-113
Working Capital	2m	2m	2m
Fixed Assets	624	176	N/A
Current Assets	2m	2m	2m
Current Liabilities	416	360	317

Chiller Box Ltd
Unit 6 Carbery Enterprise Park 36 White Hart Lane, London, N17 8DP
Tel: 0800-849 1188 **Fax:** 020-8364 3388
E-mail: salesadmin@chillerbox.com
Website: http://www.chillerbox.com
Directors: M. Pompouris (Dir)
Immediate Holding Company: CHILLER BOX LIMITED
Registration no: 05146918 **Date established:** 2004
No.of Employees: 1 - 10 **Product Groups:** 39, 67

Date of Accounts	Oct 11	Oct 10	Oct 09
Working Capital	-23	-26	-19
Fixed Assets	25	32	19
Current Assets	216	233	226

Chilli Sound Co UK
8 Albert Road, London, N4 3RW
Tel: 07973-500651 **Fax:** 01273-679416
E-mail: richard@chillisound.co.uk
Website: http://www.chillisound.co.uk
Directors: R. Whittam (Prop)
No.of Employees: 1 - 10 **Product Groups:** 37, 52, 83

China's Secret Teas
62 Charlesworth House Stanhope Gardens, London, SW7 5RD
Tel: 0121-228 0281
E-mail: info@chinasecret.co.uk
Website: http://www.chinasecret.co.uk
Directors: H. Tan (MD)
Registration no: 05695152 **Date established:** 2006
Turnover: Up to £250,000 **No.of Employees:** 1 - 10 **Product Groups:** 20

Chingford Dental Laboratories
118 Chingford Mount Road, London, E4 9AA
Tel: 020-8531 1212 **Fax:** 020-8926 2685
E-mail: derek@chingford-dental.co.uk
Website: http://www.chingford-dental.co.uk
Directors: A. Hayes (Co Sec), D. Clark (Prop)
Immediate Holding Company: CHINGFORD SERVICES LIMITED
Registration no: 03671090 **Date established:** 1998
Turnover: £500,000 - £1m **No.of Employees:** 1 - 10 **Product Groups:** 38, 67

Date of Accounts	Dec 11	Dec 10	Dec 09
Sales Turnover	524	490	436
Pre Tax Profit/Loss	73	111	98
Working Capital	74	58	43
Fixed Assets	44	48	55
Current Assets	202	158	106
Current Liabilities	11	18	9

Chivas Bros Holdings Ltd
Chivas House 72 Chancellors Road, London, W6 9RS
Tel: 020-8250 1000 **Fax:** 020-8250 1601
Website: http://www.chivas.com
Bank(s): The Royal Bank of Scotland
Directors: C. Porter (MD)
Managers: D. Payne (Chief Mgr)
Ultimate Holding Company: PERNOD RICARD SA (FRANCE)
Immediate Holding Company: CHIVAS BROTHERS (HOLDINGS) LIMITED
Registration no: 04248641 **Date established:** 2001
Turnover: £75m - £125m **No.of Employees:** 101 - 250
Product Groups: 21

Date of Accounts	Jun 11	Jun 10	Jun 09
Pre Tax Profit/Loss	-48m	787m	-4m
Working Capital	-1566m	123m	-454m
Fixed Assets	3448m	1314m	1293m
Current Assets	918m	539m	109m

Choice Hotels International
67-74 Saffron Hill, London, EC1N 8QX
Tel: 020-7061 9600 **Fax:** 020-7061 9601
E-mail: infouk@choicehotels.co.uk
Website: http://www.choicehotels.eu
Bank(s): National Westminster Bank Plc & The Royal Bank of Scotland plc
Managers: D. Berry
Ultimate Holding Company: MEDECINS SANS FRONTIERES (UK)
Immediate Holding Company: MEDECINS SANS FRONTIERES (UK)
Registration no: 02928751 **Date established:** 1993
Turnover: £50m - £75m **No.of Employees:** 21 - 50 **Product Groups:** 69

Date of Accounts	Dec 11	Dec 10	Dec 09
Sales Turnover	26m	27m	20m
Pre Tax Profit/Loss	783	495	430
Working Capital	5m	4m	3m
Fixed Assets	52	73	80
Current Assets	10m	7m	6m
Current Liabilities	5m	3m	3m

Chorion plc
Aldwych House 81 Aldwych, London, WC2B 4HN
Tel: 020-7061 3800 **Fax:** 020-7061 3801
E-mail: reception@chorion.co.uk
Website: http://www.chorion.co.uk
Bank(s): Coutts
Directors: P. Beale (Co Sec), T. Downing (Dir)
Ultimate Holding Company: PLANET ACQUISITIONS HOLDINGS LIMITED
Immediate Holding Company: CHORION LIMITED
Registration no: 04383538 **Date established:** 2002 **Turnover:** £1m - £2m
No.of Employees: 51 - 100 **Product Groups:** 28

Date of Accounts	Dec 07	Dec 06	Mar 10
Pre Tax Profit/Loss	6m	71	298
Working Capital	23m	17m	24m
Fixed Assets	7m	7m	7m
Current Assets	47m	39m	55m
Current Liabilities	6	5m	8

Chris Brock Photography
201a Fallsbrook Road, London, SW16 6DY
Tel: 07739-987791
E-mail: photo@chrisbrock.co.uk
Website: http://www.chrisbrock.co.uk
Directors: C. Brock (Prop)
Date established: 2007 **Turnover:** Up to £250,000
No.of Employees: 1 - 10 **Product Groups:** 81

Christie & Co. Ltd
Whitefriars House 6 Carmelite Street, London, EC4Y 0BS
Tel: 020-7227 0700 **Fax:** 020-7227 0701
E-mail: enquiries@christie.com
Website: http://www.christie.com
Bank(s): Barclays
Directors: C. Day (Dir), T. Moxon (Tech Serv), D. Prickett (Fin), K. Wheaton (Pers), D. Rugg (Dir)
Ultimate Holding Company: CHRISTIE GROUP PLC
Immediate Holding Company: CHRISTIE OWEN & DAVIES LIMITED
Registration no: 00453594 **VAT No.:** GB 358 5265 26
Date established: 1948 **Turnover:** £10m - £20m
No.of Employees: 21 - 50 **Product Groups:** 80

Date of Accounts	Dec 11	Dec 10	Dec 09
Sales Turnover	53m	49m	47m
Pre Tax Profit/Loss	237	939	-4m
Working Capital	-959	1m	-175
Fixed Assets	6m	6m	6m
Current Assets	12m	12m	12m
Current Liabilities	10m	7m	8m

Chrysalis Entertainments Ltd
13 Bramley Road, London, W10 6SP
Tel: 020-7465 6346 **Fax:** 020-7221 6455
E-mail: info@chrysalis.com
Website: http://www.cre.co.uk
Bank(s): National Westminster Bank Plc
Directors: J. Lasjells (Grp Chief Exec)
Immediate Holding Company: CHRYSALIS LIMITED
Registration no: 06344599 **Date established:** 2007
Turnover: £50m - £75m **No.of Employees:** 21 - 50 **Product Groups:** 37, 65

Date of Accounts	Dec 11	Sep 10	Sep 09
Sales Turnover	N/A	70m	63m
Pre Tax Profit/Loss	-7m	-4m	-4m
Working Capital	-21	14m	19m
Fixed Assets	88m	22m	11m
Current Assets	N/A	58m	58m
Current Liabilities	21	22m	16m

Chubb Fire & Security Ltd
Unit 233 Lee Valley Technopark Ashley Road, London, N17 9LN
Tel: 08448-791745 **Fax:** 020-7247 8193
E-mail: sales.tottenham@chubb.co.uk
Website: http://www.ies.uk.com
Bank(s): National Westminster Bank Plc
Managers: D. Bascombe (Comptroller), K. Brighton (District Mgr)
Ultimate Holding Company: UNITED TECHNOLOGIES CORP INC (USA)
Immediate Holding Company: CHUBB FIRE & SECURITY LIMITED
Registration no: 00524469 **VAT No.:** GB 609 0284 52
Date established: 1953 **No.of Employees:** 51 - 100 **Product Groups:** 40, 52

Date of Accounts	Dec 11	Dec 10	Dec 09
Sales Turnover	215m	121m	133m
Pre Tax Profit/Loss	-40m	9m	6m
Working Capital	44m	35m	27m
Fixed Assets	337m	234m	249m
Current Assets	148m	94m	94m
Current Liabilities	56m	44m	52m

Jane Churchill Ltd
19-23 Grosvenor Hill, London, W1K 3QD
Tel: 020-7318 6000 **Fax:** 020-7499 9910
E-mail: uksales@colefax.co.uk
Website: http://www.janechurchill.com
Managers: S. Smith
Registration no: 01520607 **VAT No.:** 446 2908 36
No.of Employees: 101 - 250 **Product Groups:** 23, 27

Date of Accounts	Apr 08	Apr 07	Apr 06
Sales Turnover	44380	40271	35917
Pre Tax Profit/Loss	3959	4030	1855
Working Capital	2685	1518	1548
Fixed Assets	1725	1913	1830
Current Assets	16367	14698	14074
Current Liabilities	13682	13180	12526
ROCE% (Return on Capital Employed)	89.8	117.5	54.9
ROT% (Return on Turnover)	8.9	10.0	5.2

Cieco Exploration & Production UK Ltd
River Plate House 7-11 Finsbury Circus, London, EC2M 7EA
Tel: 020-7920 0339 **Fax:** 020-7920 0063
Bank(s): Bank of Tokyo
Directors: S. Nakayana (MD)
Ultimate Holding Company: ITOCHU CORPORATION (JAPAN)
Immediate Holding Company: CIECO EXPLORATION AND PRODUCTION (UK) LIMITED
Registration no: 02669936 **Date established:** 1991
Turnover: £20m - £50m **No.of Employees:** 11 - 20 **Product Groups:** 13, 51

Date of Accounts	Dec 11	Dec 10	Dec 09
Sales Turnover	28m	25m	20m
Pre Tax Profit/Loss	19m	-3m	10m
Working Capital	29m	19m	27m
Fixed Assets	34m	32m	23m
Current Assets	34m	31m	34m
Current Liabilities	5m	13m	7m

The Cinema & Television Benevolent Fund
22 Golden Square, London, W1F 9AD
Tel: 020-7437 6567 **Fax:** 020-7437 7186
E-mail: charity@ctbf.co.uk
Website: http://www.ctbf.co.uk
Bank(s): National Westminster Bank Plc
Directors: P. Hore (Grp Chief Exec), D. Meade (Co Sec), D. Chalet (Grp Chief Exec), P. Hall (Dir), D. Murrell (Fin), B. Robertson (Grp Chief Exec), P. Hoare (Grp Chief Exec)
Managers: L. Filby (Mktg Serv Mgr)
Immediate Holding Company: THE CINEMA AND TELEVISION BENEVOLENT FUND
Registration no: 04816786 **Date established:** 2003 **Turnover:** £2m - £5m
No.of Employees: 11 - 20 **Product Groups:** 80

see next page

The Cinema & Television Benevolent Fund - Cont'd

Date of Accounts	Mar 11	Mar 10	Mar 09
Sales Turnover	4m	4m	4m
Pre Tax Profit/Loss	523	3m	-835
Working Capital	683	693	730
Fixed Assets	30m	30m	27m
Current Assets	1m	1m	1m
Current Liabilities	207	214	248

Cineworld Ltd

Power Road Studios Power Road, London, W4 5PY
Tel: 08448-157747 **Fax:** 020-8742 2998
E-mail: info@cineworld.co.uk
Website: http://www.cineworld.co.uk
Directors: S. Wiener (Grp Chief Exec), S. Burke (Dir), M. Thomson (Comm), S. Weiner (Grp Chief Exec)
Immediate Holding Company: CINEWORLD LIMITED
Registration no: 04081830 **Date established:** 2000
Turnover: £250m - £500m **No.of Employees:** 1 - 10 **Product Groups:** 89

Citigate Dewe Rogerson

3 London Wall Buildings London Wall, London, EC2M 5SY
Tel: 020-7638 9571 **Fax:** 020-7628 3444
E-mail: info@citigatedr.co.uk
Website: http://www.citigatedr.co.uk
Directors: P. Donovan (MD), L. Bessell-martin (Fin)
Managers: G. Ling (Personnel), L. Tillbury (Sales Admin), M. Roberts (Tech Serv Mgr)
Ultimate Holding Company: RIVINGTON STREET HOLDINGS (UK) LIMITED
Immediate Holding Company: BLUECURVE LIMITED
Registration no: 02662978 **Date established:** 2007 **Turnover:** £5m - £10m
No.of Employees: 101 - 250 **Product Groups:** 28, 44, 80, 81, 89

Date of Accounts	Aug 11	Aug 10	Aug 09
Sales Turnover	930	1m	325
Pre Tax Profit/Loss	109	202	74
Working Capital	450	319	92
Fixed Assets	17	38	59
Current Assets	1m	885	584
Current Liabilities	361	473	434

Citilites Ltd

397-399 Hornsey Road, London, N19 4DX
Tel: 020-7281 4141 **Fax:** 020-7281 0030
E-mail: danielsimons@citilites.co.uk
Website: http://www.citilites.co.uk
Directors: D. Simons (Sales), S. Swead (MD)
Immediate Holding Company: CITILITES LIMITED
Registration no: 01272357 **VAT No.:** GB 554 2558 34
Date established: 1976 **Turnover:** £10m - £20m
No.of Employees: 21 - 50 **Product Groups:** 63

Date of Accounts	Jan 12	Jan 11	Jan 10
Sales Turnover	9m	11m	11m
Pre Tax Profit/Loss	118	117	143
Working Capital	2m	2m	2m
Fixed Assets	131	114	406
Current Assets	3m	3m	3m
Current Liabilities	617	882	629

Citisoft

1 Fredericks Place, London, EC2R 8AE
Tel: 020-7776 1111 **Fax:** 020-7776 1122
E-mail: jonathan.clark@citisoft.com
Website: http://www.citisoft.com
Directors: J. Clark (Dir), J. Clark (Grp Chief Exec), M. Mitchell (Dir), D. King (Co Sec)
Ultimate Holding Company: SATYAM COMPUTER SERVICES LIMITED
Immediate Holding Company: CITISOFT PUBLIC LIMITED COMPANY
Registration no: 01968753 **Date established:** 1985 **Turnover:** £5m - £10m
No.of Employees: 21 - 50 **Product Groups:** 80

Date of Accounts	Mar 11	Mar 10	Mar 09
Sales Turnover	6m	5m	5m
Pre Tax Profit/Loss	253	49	-445
Working Capital	2m	2m	2m
Fixed Assets	25	45	65
Current Assets	4m	4m	3m
Current Liabilities	421	1m	269

City & Corporate Holdings Ltd

33 Cavendish Square, London, W1G 0PW
Tel: 020-7629 6180 **Fax:** 020-7647 5500
Website: http://www.gpe.co.uk
Directors: R. Peskin (Ch), T. Coultold (Grp Chief Exec)
Immediate Holding Company: CITY & CORPORATE HOLDINGS LIMITED
Registration no: 00633660 **Date established:** 1959
Turnover: £500,000 - £1m **No.of Employees:** 1 - 10 **Product Groups:** 82

Date of Accounts	Mar 08	Mar 07	Mar 06
Pre Tax Profit/Loss	6	78	-11
Working Capital	1286	1280	1163
Current Assets	1288	1288	1220
Current Liabilities	2	8	57
Total Share Capital	844	844	844
ROCE% (Return on Capital Employed)	0.5	6.1	-0.9

City Drains

27 Glebe Street, London, W4 2BD
Tel: 0800-007 5309 **Fax:** 020-8747 1209
E-mail: info@citydrains.com
Website: http://www.londonblockeddrain.co.uk
Directors: M. Santana (Prop)
Immediate Holding Company: ASHCAM PROPERTY SERVICES LIMITED
Date established: 2012 **Turnover:** Up to £250,000
No.of Employees: 1 - 10 **Product Groups:** 45

City Eyes Ltd

65 London Wall, London, EC2M 5TU
Tel: 020-7638 6192
E-mail: info@cityeyesopticians.com
Website: http://www.cityeyesopticians.com
Managers: C. Babumba (Mgr)
Immediate Holding Company: CITY EYES LTD
Registration no: 06389964 **Date established:** 2007
No.of Employees: 1 - 10 **Product Groups:** 38, 49, 63, 65

City Of London Courier Ltd

Unit A Digbyland Studios Digby Road, London, E9 6HX
Tel: 08450-600666 **Fax:** 08450-600888
E-mail: info@cityoflondoncourier.co.uk
Website: http://www.cityoflondoncourier.co.uk
Directors: M. Lyons (MD)
Managers: K. Chivers (Chief Acct), C. Lawford
Immediate Holding Company: CITY OF LONDON COURIER LIMITED
Registration no: 03576524 **VAT No.:** GB 718 7386 00
Date established: 1998 **Turnover:** £250,000 - £500,000
No.of Employees: 21 - 50 **Product Groups:** 79

Date of Accounts	Dec 11	Dec 10	Dec 09
Sales Turnover	272	323	366
Pre Tax Profit/Loss	4	-11	2
Working Capital	19	21	36
Fixed Assets	88	92	98
Current Assets	70	75	82
Current Liabilities	38	54	40

City Speakers International Ltd

Flat 3 Naylor Building East 15 Adler Street, London, E1 1HD
Tel: 020-7247 1193 **Fax:** 0845-257 0806
E-mail: info@cityspeakersinternational.co.uk
Website: http://www.cityspeakersinternational.co.uk
Directors: J. Lel (MD)
Immediate Holding Company: CITY SPEAKERS INTERNATIONAL LIMITED
Registration no: 05719703 **Date established:** 2006
Turnover: £250,000 - £500,000 **No.of Employees:** 1 - 10
Product Groups: 86

Date of Accounts	Mar 11	Mar 10	Mar 09
Working Capital	184	126	127
Fixed Assets	N/A	1	1
Current Assets	210	165	185

City Sprint

58-62 Scrutton Street, London, EC2A 4PH
Tel: 020-7880 1000 **Fax:** 020-7466 4901
E-mail: reception@citysprint.co.uk
Website: http://www.citysprint.co.uk
Directors: M. Timlett (Tech Serv), G. Keenan (Fin), J. Moore (Sales & Mktg)
Managers: K. Gerard (Personnel), P. Gallagher
Ultimate Holding Company: JAGAR LONDON HOLDINGS LIMITED
Immediate Holding Company: WESTONE PASSENGER TRANSPORT GROUP LIMITED
Registration no: 00432611 **VAT No.:** GB 539 3572 19
Date established: 2002 **Turnover:** £5m - £10m
No.of Employees: 51 - 100 **Product Groups:** 79

City & Guilds Of London Institute

1 Giltspur Street, London, EC1A 9DD
Tel: 020-7294 2468 **Fax:** 020-7294 2400
E-mail: info@city-and-guilds.co.uk
Website: http://www.city-and-guilds.co.uk
Bank(s): Royal Bank of Scotland P.L.C., 67 Lombard St, London EC3P 3DL
Directors: S. Saxton (Pers)
Managers: C. Huyton
Ultimate Holding Company: The City and Guilds of London Institute
Immediate Holding Company: CITY AND GUILDS INTERNATIONAL LIMITED
Registration no: 01894671 **Date established:** 1985 **Turnover:** £5m - £10m
No.of Employees: 1001 - 1500 **Product Groups:** 87

Date of Accounts	Sep 11	Sep 10	Sep 09
Sales Turnover	11m	10m	9m
Pre Tax Profit/Loss	580	427	42
Working Capital	4m	3m	1m
Fixed Assets	150	73	151
Current Assets	15m	12m	9m
Current Liabilities	366	149	619

Civil Aviation Authority

45-59 Kingsway, London, WC2B 6TE
Tel: 020-7379 7311 **Fax:** 020-7453 6028
E-mail: sales@caa.co.uk
Website: http://www.caa.co.uk
Bank(s): National Westminster Bank Plc
Directors: C. Jusnick (Fin), D. Townsend (Pers)
Managers: A. Haines
Immediate Holding Company: CAA INTERNATIONAL LIMITED
Registration no: 04104068 **Date established:** 2000 **Turnover:** £2m - £5m
No.of Employees: 101 - 250 **Product Groups:** 87

Date of Accounts	Mar 12	Mar 11	Mar 10
Sales Turnover	15m	15m	13m
Pre Tax Profit/Loss	2m	2m	1m
Working Capital	5m	3m	2m
Fixed Assets	68	135	116
Current Assets	7m	6m	4m
Current Liabilities	3m	3m	2m

CJA Recruitment Group Ltd

2 London Wall Buildings, London, EC2M 5UX
Tel: 020-7588 3588 **Fax:** 020-7256 8501
E-mail: jmm@cjagroup.com
Website: http://www.cjagroup.com
Bank(s): The Royal Bank of Scotland
Directors: K. Coss (Co Sec), J. Mcintyre (MD)
Immediate Holding Company: CJA GROUP LIMITED
Registration no: 04468103 **VAT No.:** GB 243 3220 06
Date established: 2002 **Turnover:** £1m - £2m **No.of Employees:** 11 - 20
Product Groups: 80

Date of Accounts	Sep 08	Sep 07	Sep 06
Working Capital	297	399	294
Fixed Assets	4	17	30
Current Assets	893	940	677
Current Liabilities	596	541	383
Total Share Capital	50	50	50

Clareville Communications

315-317 New Kings Road, London, SW6 4RF
Tel: 020-7736 4022 **Fax:** 020-7736 3504
E-mail: johnstarr@clareville.co.uk
Website: http://www.clareville.co.uk
Directors: J. Starr (Snr Part), P. Sumpster (Co Sec)
Immediate Holding Company: CLAREVILLE CONSULTANCY LIMITED
Registration no: 02334155 **Date established:** 1989 **Turnover:** £1m - £2m
No.of Employees: 11 - 20 **Product Groups:** 81

Clark Electrical Industries Ltd

North Crescent, London, E16 4TG
Tel: 020-7474 7404 **Fax:** 020-7473 1961
E-mail: daveburns@ceiltd.co.uk
Website: http://www.ceiltd.co.uk
Directors: D. Burns (MD), L. Ryan (Fin), W. Burns (Sales & Mktg)
Managers: C. Webb (Sales Admin)
Immediate Holding Company: CLARK ELECTRICAL INDUSTRIES LIMITED
Registration no: 01547876 **VAT No.:** GB 232 2300 26
Date established: 1981 **Turnover:** £1m - £2m **No.of Employees:** 11 - 20
Product Groups: 48, 67

Date of Accounts	Aug 11	Aug 10	Aug 09
Sales Turnover	2m	2m	2m
Pre Tax Profit/Loss	107	112	112
Working Capital	166	163	153
Fixed Assets	23	24	39
Current Assets	515	468	496
Current Liabilities	134	134	125

T Clarke plc

Stanhope House 116-117 Walworth Road, London, SE17 1JY
Tel: 020-7358 5000 **Fax:** 020-7701 6265
E-mail: martin.walton@tclarke.co.uk
Website: http://www.tclarke.co.uk
Bank(s): National Westminster Bank Plc
Directors: B. Defalco (MD), V. French (Co Sec), M. Walton (Co Sec), J. Daly (Co Sec), J. Daily (Co Sec)
Managers: J. Burrows (Mgr), A. Griffiths (I.T. Exec)
Ultimate Holding Company: T CLARKE PUBLIC LIMITED COMPANY
Immediate Holding Company: T CLARKE PUBLIC LIMITED COMPANY
Registration no: 00119351 **Date established:** 2011
Turnover: £125m - £250m **No.of Employees:** 51 - 100
Product Groups: 52

Date of Accounts	Dec 10	Dec 09	Dec 08
Sales Turnover	179m	178m	224m
Pre Tax Profit/Loss	6m	7m	13m
Working Capital	554	12m	12m
Fixed Assets	33m	19m	20m
Current Assets	44m	51m	60m
Current Liabilities	16m	18m	24m

Class Instrumentation Ltd

837 Garratt Lane, London, SW17 0PG
Tel: 020-8333 2288 **Fax:** 020-8944 0141
E-mail: info@classltd.com
Website: http://www.classltd.com
Directors: D. Richards (Fin)
Ultimate Holding Company: CAR LIGHT AND SOUND SYSTEMS LIMITED
Immediate Holding Company: CLASS INSTRUMENTATION LTD
Registration no: 03252796 **Date established:** 1996
Turnover: £500,000 - £1m **No.of Employees:** 1 - 10 **Product Groups:** 38

Date of Accounts	Mar 11	Mar 09	Mar 08
Working Capital	25	N/A	N/A
Fixed Assets	1	5	5
Current Assets	47	N/A	N/A

Classic Fine Foods Ltd

D24-D27 Fruit & Vegetable Market, London, SW8 5LL
Tel: 020-7627 9666 **Fax:** 020-7627 9696
E-mail: sales@classicfinefoods.co.uk
Website: http://www.grivan.co.uk
Directors: O. Batel (MD)
Managers: T. Allan (Fin Mgr)
Ultimate Holding Company: WESTERN UNITED INVESTMENT COMPANY LIMITED
Immediate Holding Company: CLASSIC FINE FOODS UK LIMITED
Registration no: 00207864 **Date established:** 2025 **Turnover:** £1m - £2m
No.of Employees: 11 - 20 **Product Groups:** 20, 62

Date of Accounts	Dec 11	Dec 10	Dec 09
Sales Turnover	11m	9m	7m
Pre Tax Profit/Loss	440	400	201
Working Capital	549	188	-71
Fixed Assets	380	344	203
Current Assets	4m	3m	3m
Current Liabilities	282	294	241

Clays Ltd

1 Tudor Street, London, EC4Y 0AH
Tel: 020-7928 8844 **Fax:** 020-7902 6436
E-mail: info@clays.co.uk
Website: http://www.st-ives.co.uk
Bank(s): National Westminster Bank Plc
Directors: M. Emley (Ch), T. Clarke (Dir)
Managers: K. Mobbs ()
Ultimate Holding Company: ST IVES PLC
Immediate Holding Company: CLAYS LTD.
Registration no: 00342498 **VAT No.:** GB 282 1136 80
Date established: 1938 **Turnover:** £75m - £125m
No.of Employees: 51 - 100 **Product Groups:** 28

Date of Accounts	Jul 09	Jul 10	Aug 07
Sales Turnover	81m	80m	81m
Pre Tax Profit/Loss	9m	13m	17m
Working Capital	18m	29m	32m
Fixed Assets	18m	11m	15m
Current Assets	32m	44m	44m
Current Liabilities	5m	6m	7m

Cleancare

33a Gautrey Road, London, SE15 2JE
Tel: 020-7639 0778 **Fax:** 020-7639 6169
E-mail: info@cleancareint.co.uk
Website: http://www.cleancareint.co.uk
Directors: C. Capocci (MD), R. Capocci (Dir)
Registration no: 01735707 **No.of Employees:** 1 - 10 **Product Groups:** 33, 40, 46, 52, 66

Clear Channel International Ltd

33 Golden Square, London, W1F 9JT
Tel: 020-7478 2200 **Fax:** 020-7287 9153
E-mail: sales@moorgroup.com
Website: http://www.clearchannel.co.uk
Directors: M. Mays (Dir)
Managers: J. Bevan
Ultimate Holding Company: CLEAR CHANNEL COMMUNICATIONS INC (USA)
Immediate Holding Company: CLEAR CHANNEL INTERNATIONAL LIMITED
Registration no: 00309019 **Date established:** 1936
Turnover: £20m - £50m **No.of Employees:** 101 - 250 **Product Groups:** 81

Date of Accounts	Dec 10	Dec 09	Dec 08
Pre Tax Profit/Loss	-2m	-3m	-85m
Working Capital	-4m	-3m	-19m
Fixed Assets	697m	697m	697m
Current Assets	5	7	8
Current Liabilities	N/A	N/A	427

Clear Graphics Ltd
17 Old Street, London, EC1V 9HF
Tel: 020-3058 1100 **Fax:** 020-8877 2678
E-mail: info@makeitclear.co.uk
Website: http://www.makeitclear.co.uk
Directors: J. Nicholl (MD)
Ultimate Holding Company: CLEAR GRAPHICS HOLDINGS LIMITED
Immediate Holding Company: CLEAR GRAPHICS LIMITED
Registration no: 02638544 **Date established:** 1991
No.of Employees: 11 - 20 **Product Groups:** 81

Date of Accounts	Feb 12	Feb 11	Feb 10
Working Capital	475	546	588
Fixed Assets	47	52	40
Current Assets	711	743	774

Clear View Ltd
Unit 7 The High Cross Centre, Fountayne Road, London, N15 4QN
Tel: 020-8801 0020 **Fax:** 020-8801 0021
E-mail: sales@clearview.ltd.uk
Website: http://www.clearview.ltd.uk
Directors: B. Sadgrove (Sales), P. Plaut (MD), P. Plaut (Prop)
Managers: B. Sedgrove (Sales Prom Mgr), P. Plaut (Mgr), S. Leverington (Sales Prom Mgr)
Registration no: 00327342 **VAT No.:** GB 440 0382 94
Turnover: £2m - £5m **No.of Employees:** 1 - 10 **Product Groups:** 20, 27, 28, 30

Date of Accounts	Mar 06
Working Capital	185
Fixed Assets	628
Current Assets	616
Current Liabilities	431
Total Share Capital	50

Cleveland Travel
92-94 Cleveland Street, London, W1T 6NW
Tel: 020-7813 6511 **Fax:** 020-7554 3599
E-mail: info@clevelandtravel.co.uk
Website: http://www.clevelandtravel.co.uk
Directors: G. Bayol (Dir)
Immediate Holding Company: CLEVELAND TRAVEL LIMITED
Registration no: 02797491 **Date established:** 1993
No.of Employees: 11 - 20 **Product Groups:** 61, 69, 81

Date of Accounts	Jun 11	Jun 10	Jun 09
Sales Turnover	N/A	11m	14m
Pre Tax Profit/Loss	N/A	80	47
Working Capital	332	307	261
Fixed Assets	50	66	83
Current Assets	2m	3m	2m
Current Liabilities	N/A	95	60

Clifford & Snell
Tom Cribb Road, London, SE28 0BH
Tel: 020-8854 6666 **Fax:** 020-8317 2400
E-mail: david.stelling@sarbe.com
Website: http://www.cliffordandsnell.com
Bank(s): National Westminster Bank Plc
Directors: T. Gage (Dir), D. Cairnie (Grp Chief Exec), J. Grant (Dir & Gen Mgr)
Managers: R. Tyler (Fin Mgr), R. Clayton, D. Stelling, M. Rody (Purch Mgr)
Immediate Holding Company: SARBE LIMITED
Registration no: 06952882 **VAT No.:** GB 626 3127 57
Date established: 2009 **Turnover:** £10m - £20m
No.of Employees: 51 - 100 **Product Groups:** 37, 40, 47

Clinical Computing
17-19 Bedford Street, London, WC2E 9HP
Tel: 020-3006 7536 **Fax:** 01473-694761
E-mail: sales@ccl.com
Website: http://www.ccl.com
Directors: H. Kitchner (MD), J. Marlovits (Fin)
Managers: E. Roper (Sales Prom Mgr), R. Harris
Immediate Holding Company: Clinical Computing plc
Registration no: 03017628 **VAT No.:** GB 225 3424 89
Date established: 1995 **Turnover:** £10m - £20m
No.of Employees: 21 - 50 **Product Groups:** 44

Date of Accounts	Dec 07
Sales Turnover	971
Pre Tax Profit/Loss	-884
Working Capital	-4159
Fixed Assets	294
Current Assets	519
Current Liabilities	4677
ROCE% (Return on Capital Employed)	22.9

Club Copying Co. Ltd
10-18 Sandgate Street, London, SE15 1LE
Tel: 020-7635 5252 **Fax:** 020-7635 5714
E-mail: jacquidalton@clubcopying.co.uk
Website: http://www.clubcopying.co.uk
Directors: T. Atkins (Dir)
Immediate Holding Company: CLUB COPYING CO. LIMITED
Registration no: 01524699 **Date established:** 1980 **Turnover:** £1m - £2m
No.of Employees: 11 - 20 **Product Groups:** 44

Date of Accounts	Dec 10	Dec 09	Dec 08
Sales Turnover	N/A	2m	N/A
Working Capital	153	-59	378
Fixed Assets	59	61	59
Current Assets	719	574	815
Current Liabilities	N/A	312	N/A

Clyde & Co
United Dominions House 51 Eastcheap, London, EC3M 1JP
Tel: 020-7623 1244 **Fax:** 01483-567330
E-mail: info@clydeco.com
Website: http://www.clydeco.com
Bank(s): National Westminster Bank Plc
Directors: M. Payton (MD)
Managers: L. Wilson (Sales Admin), C. Hill, C. Hill
Immediate Holding Company: CLYDE & CO (GREECE) LLP
Registration no: OC326540 **Date established:** 2007
Turnover: £125m - £250m **No.of Employees:** 251 - 500
Product Groups: 80

Date of Accounts	Apr 11	Apr 10	Apr 09
Working Capital	842	865	715
Fixed Assets	5	8	15
Current Assets	2m	1m	1m
Current Liabilities	643	491	672

Clydesdale Bank plc (Croydon District Commercial Centre)
B N Z House 89-91 Gresham Street, London, EC2V 7NQ
Tel: 08447-362616 **Fax:** 020-7710 2276
Website: http://www.clydesdalebank.co.uk
Managers: C. Smith (Mgr)
Immediate Holding Company: CLYDESDALE BANK PLC
Registration no: SC001111 **Date established:** 1982
No.of Employees: 11 - 20 **Product Groups:** 87

Date of Accounts	Sep 11	Sep 10	Sep 09
Pre Tax Profit/Loss	21m	49m	48m
Fixed Assets	7348m	8788m	9465m
Current Assets	39904m	34872m	32905m
Current Liabilities	44233m	41043m	40056m

Clydesdale Bank plc (Principal Branch - Piccadilly Circus, London)
35 Regent Street, London, SW1Y 4ND
Tel: 08447-362616 **Fax:** 020-7699 6428
Website: http://www.clydesdalebank.co.uk
Directors: J. Stewart (Grp Chief Exec), Sanderson of Bowden (Ch)
Immediate Holding Company: CLYDESDALE BANK PLC
Registration no: SC001111 **Date established:** 1982
No.of Employees: 11 - 20 **Product Groups:** 87

Date of Accounts	Sep 11	Sep 10	Sep 09
Pre Tax Profit/Loss	21m	49m	48m
Fixed Assets	7348m	8788m	9465m
Current Assets	39904m	34872m	32905m
Current Liabilities	44233m	41043m	40056m

The Co-Operative Financial Services
80 Cornhill Street, London, EC3V 3NJ
Tel: 020-7626 4953 **Fax:** 020-7626 0929
E-mail: enquiries@co-operativebank.co.uk
Website: http://www.cooperativebank.co.uk
Managers: C. Ayres (Mgr)
Immediate Holding Company: THE CO-OPERATIVE BANK PLC
Registration no: 00106416 **No.of Employees:** 1 - 10 **Product Groups:** 82

Cohn & Wolfe Ltd
Lynton House 7-12 Tavistock Square, London, WC1H 9LT
Tel: 020-7331 5300 **Fax:** 020-7331 9083
E-mail: helen_jones@uk.cohnwolfe.com
Website: http://www.cohnandwolfe.com
Managers: H. Dawson
Ultimate Holding Company: WPP PLC (JERSEY)
Immediate Holding Company: COHN & WOLFE LIMITED
Registration no: 00835128 **Date established:** 1965
No.of Employees: 11 - 20 **Product Groups:** 81

Date of Accounts	Dec 08
Working Capital	14
Current Assets	14

Cold Formed Products Ltd
24 St Mary's Road, London, E13 9AD
Tel: 020-8471 2727 **Fax:** 020-8470 1706
E-mail: andrewpalmer@cfp.biz
Website: http://www.cfp.biz
Bank(s): National Westminster Bank Plc
Directors: A. Palmer (MD), D. Binks (Dir)
Managers: J. Taylor (Sales Admin)
Immediate Holding Company: COLD FORMED PRODUCTS LIMITED
Registration no: 00571301 **VAT No.:** GB 248 0209 76
Date established: 1956 **Turnover:** £2m - £5m **No.of Employees:** 21 - 50
Product Groups: 29, 32, 34, 35, 36, 39, 48, 66, 68

Date of Accounts	Apr 12	Apr 11	Apr 10
Working Capital	99	-23	-80
Fixed Assets	1m	982	1m
Current Assets	1m	856	754

Colefax & Fowler Ltd
19-23 Grosvenor Hill, London, W1K 3QD
Tel: 020-7318 6000 **Fax:** 020-7499 9910
E-mail: enq@colefax.co.uk
Website: http://www.colefax.co.uk
Directors: D. Green (Grp Chief Exec), R. Barker (Fin)
Managers: G. Dennis, G. Dennis (Sales Prom Mgr)
Ultimate Holding Company: COLEFAX GROUP PLC
Immediate Holding Company: COLEFAX AND FOWLER LIMITED
Registration no: 01644809 **Date established:** 1982
Turnover: £20m - £50m **No.of Employees:** 51 - 100 **Product Groups:** 52, 84, 86

Date of Accounts	Apr 12	Apr 11	Apr 10
Sales Turnover	44m	42m	38m
Pre Tax Profit/Loss	2m	2m	1m
Working Capital	6m	4m	4m
Fixed Assets	1m	2m	1m
Current Assets	16m	16m	15m
Current Liabilities	2m	3m	2m

Coley Porter Bell Ltd
121-141 Westbourne Terrace, London, W2 6JR
Tel: 020-7824 7700 **Fax:** 020-7824 7701
E-mail: vicky.bullen@cpb.co.uk
Website: http://www.cpb.co.uk
Bank(s): HSBC Bank plc
Directors: A. Shafar (Co Sec)
Managers: V. Bullen
Ultimate Holding Company: WPP PLC (JERSEY)
Immediate Holding Company: COLEY PORTER BELL LIMITED
Registration no: 01393551 **VAT No.:** GB 242 7109 81
Date established: 1978 **Turnover:** £5m - £10m **No.of Employees:** 21 - 50
Product Groups: 80, 81, 85

Date of Accounts	Dec 11	Dec 10	Dec 09
Sales Turnover	6m	5m	5m
Pre Tax Profit/Loss	716	764	503
Working Capital	4m	3m	3m
Fixed Assets	132	163	38
Current Assets	5m	5m	3m
Current Liabilities	1m	922	834

Collaborative Solutions Ltd
57 Foulden Road, London, N16 7UU
Tel: 020-7254 0770 **Fax:** 020-7923 0021
Directors: C. Stephenson (Dir)
Immediate Holding Company: COLLABORATIVE SOLUTIONS LIMITED
Registration no: 02131517 **Date established:** 1987
Turnover: Up to £250,000 **No.of Employees:** 1 - 10 **Product Groups:** 44

Date of Accounts	Oct 11	Oct 10	Oct 09
Sales Turnover	3	N/A	7
Pre Tax Profit/Loss	-9	-12	-6
Working Capital	-76	-67	-55
Current Assets	1	1	1
Current Liabilities	N/A	N/A	2

Colliers International
9 Marylebone Lane, London, W1U 1HL
Tel: 020-7344 6666 **Fax:** 020-7344 6633
E-mail: marc.finney@colliers.com
Website: http://www.colliers.com
Managers: M. Finney
Immediate Holding Company: COLLIERS INTERNATIONAL PROPERTY CONSULTANTS LIMITED
Registration no: 07996509 **Date established:** 2012
Turnover: £75m - £125m **No.of Employees:** 11 - 20 **Product Groups:** 80, 82, 84

Colmac Plastic Fabricators
Unit C1 Up South Way Bounds Green Industrial Estate, London, N11 2UL
Tel: 020-8361 4807 **Fax:** 020-8361 4670
E-mail: info@colmacplastics.co.uk
Website: http://www.colmacplastics.co.uk
Directors: R. Mccreary (Ptnr)
Registration no: 02319913 **Date established:** 1968
Turnover: Up to £250,000 **No.of Employees:** 1 - 10 **Product Groups:** 48

Colorset Graphics Ltd
4 Black Swan Yard, London, SE1 3XW
Tel: 020-7234 0300
E-mail: frank@colorset.co.uk
Website: http://www.colorset.co.uk
Directors: F. Baptiste (MD)
Immediate Holding Company: COLORSET U.V.I LIMITED
Registration no: 06726565 **Date established:** 2008
No.of Employees: 11 - 20 **Product Groups:** 35, 49, 84

Colt Telecommunications Ltd
Beaufort House 15 St Botolph Street, London, EC3A 7QN
Tel: 020-7390 3900 **Fax:** 020-7390 3901
E-mail: sales@colt-telecom.com
Website: http://www.colt-telecom.com
Directors: R. Saphra (Dir), E. Chengapen (Co Sec)
Ultimate Holding Company: COLT GROUP SA (LUXEMBOURG)
Immediate Holding Company: COLT TECHNOLOGY SERVICES
Registration no: 02452736 **Date established:** 1989
Turnover: £250m - £500m **No.of Employees:** 501 - 1000
Product Groups: 37

Date of Accounts	Dec 11	Dec 10	Dec 09
Sales Turnover	318m	288m	276m
Pre Tax Profit/Loss	3m	3m	215
Working Capital	-107m	-132m	-332m
Fixed Assets	373m	375m	347m
Current Assets	116m	76m	66m
Current Liabilities	128m	128m	139m

Columbia Metals Ltd
Wingfield Mews Wingfield Street, London, SE15 4LH
Tel: 020-7732 1022 **Fax:** 020-7732 1029
E-mail: sales@columbiametals.co.uk
Website: http://www.columbiametals.co.uk
Directors: D. Stephenson (MD)
Immediate Holding Company: COLUMBIA METALS LIMITED
Registration no: 00700585 **VAT No.:** GB 235 5266 64
Date established: 1961 **Turnover:** £2m - £5m **No.of Employees:** 1 - 10
Product Groups: 34, 48

Date of Accounts	Oct 11	Oct 10	Oct 09
Working Capital	4m	4m	4m
Fixed Assets	396	416	452
Current Assets	5m	4m	4m

Colyer London
22-26 Vine Hill, London, EC1R 5LJ
Tel: 020-7837 8666 **Fax:** 020-7404 4762
E-mail: t.harding@colyer.co.uk
Website: http://www.colyer.co.uk
Bank(s): HSBC Bank plc
Directors: N. Southey (Dir)
Ultimate Holding Company: COLYER GROUP LIMITED
Immediate Holding Company: DIGITAL PRINT FACTORY LIMITED
Registration no: 03080181 **VAT No.:** GB 668 1721 15
Date established: 1995 **Turnover:** £1m - £2m **No.of Employees:** 21 - 50
Product Groups: 49, 81

Date of Accounts	Dec 11	Dec 10	Dec 09
Working Capital	-170	-12	-24
Fixed Assets	116	87	114
Current Assets	69	36	164
Current Liabilities	4	9	88

Combined Heat & Power Association
Grosvenor Gardens House 35-37 Grosvenor Gardens, London, SW1W 0BS
Tel: 020-7828 4077 **Fax:** 020-7828 0310
E-mail: info@chpa.co.uk
Website: http://www.chpa.co.uk
Directors: G. Meeks (Dir)
Immediate Holding Company: COMBINED HEAT AND POWER ASSOCIATION
Registration no: 00917116 **VAT No.:** GB 232 6793 54
Date established: 1967 **No.of Employees:** 1 - 10 **Product Groups:** 84, 87

Date of Accounts	Mar 11	Mar 10	Mar 09
Working Capital	369	303	307
Fixed Assets	13	15	15
Current Assets	490	439	473

Combined Trading Garments Ltd
77-79 Great Eastern Street, London, EC2A 3HU
Tel: 020-7739 0551 **Fax:** 020-7729 2556
Directors: C. Charbit (MD), D. Tanner (Fin)
Immediate Holding Company: COMBINED TRADING EXPORT LIMITED
Registration no: 00588173 **Date established:** 1957
Turnover: £500,000 - £1m **No.of Employees:** 1 - 10 **Product Groups:** 23

Date of Accounts	Dec 10	Dec 09	Dec 04
Working Capital	-43	-50	-6
Fixed Assets	1	N/A	N/A
Current Assets	14	12	15

E A Combs Ltd
Quantum House Station Estate Eastwood Close, London, E18 1BY
Tel: 020-8530 4216 **Fax:** 020-8530 1310
E-mail: stuart@eacombs.com
Website: http://www.eacombs.com
Bank(s): National Westminster, 134 Aldersgate St, London, EC1
Managers: S. Parsons (Mgr)
Immediate Holding Company: E.A. COMBS LIMITED
Registration no: 00583479 **VAT No.:** GB 232 2697 70
Date established: 1957 **Turnover:** £1m - £2m **No.of Employees:** 11 - 20
Product Groups: 65

Date of Accounts	Mar 12	Mar 11	Mar 10
Working Capital	1m	1m	1m
Fixed Assets	3	10	16
Current Assets	1m	1m	1m

Comex Import & Export Co. Ltd
Unit 11 Landmark Commercial Centre 19 Commercial Road, London, N18 1UB
Tel: 020-8807 1411 **Fax:** 020-8807 1055
E-mail: comex@comexuk.fsnet.co.uk
Website: http://www.comexuk.com
Directors: A. Ghelani (Fin), A. Ghelani (Dir)
Immediate Holding Company: COMEX IMPORT & EXPORT COMPANY LIMITED
Registration no: 01643947 **VAT No.:** GB 374 8009 39
Date established: 1982 **Turnover:** £1m - £2m **No.of Employees:** 1 - 10
Product Groups: 61

Date of Accounts	Dec 11	Dec 10	Dec 09
Sales Turnover	2m	2m	2m
Pre Tax Profit/Loss	50	45	44
Working Capital	272	260	257
Fixed Assets	389	392	395
Current Assets	2m	2m	1m
Current Liabilities	666	831	675

Commodore International Travel Ltd
117 Shaftesbury Avenue, London, WC2H 8JR
Tel: 020-7420 7300 **Fax:** 020-7420 7301
E-mail: info@commodore.co.uk
Website: http://www.commodore.co.uk
Directors: A. Mansour (MD), K. Patel (Fin)
Managers: L. Wong (Tech Serv Mgr)
Ultimate Holding Company: STATESMAN TRAVEL GROUP LIMITED
Immediate Holding Company: COMMODORE INTERNATIONAL TRAVEL LIMITED
Registration no: 01480303 **Date established:** 1980 **Turnover:** £2m - £5m
No.of Employees: 51 - 100 **Product Groups:** 69

Date of Accounts	Dec 11	Dec 10	Dec 09
Sales Turnover	3m	45m	43m
Pre Tax Profit/Loss	803	557	656
Working Capital	1m	2m	2m
Fixed Assets	16	2m	2m
Current Assets	4m	5m	5m
Current Liabilities	1m	1m	825

Como Holdings UK Ltd
2nd Floor Pemberton House, London, W8 5SL
Tel: 020-7368 8888 **Fax:** 020-7937 6757
Directors: B. Heng (Dir), V. Sodhy (Dir)
Ultimate Holding Company: ADOBE HOLDINGS LIMITED (GIBRALTAR)
Immediate Holding Company: HALKIN HOTEL LIMITED
Registration no: 02108865 **Date established:** 1987 **Turnover:** £5m - £10m
No.of Employees: 51 - 100 **Product Groups:** 24, 69

Date of Accounts	Dec 10	Dec 09	Dec 08
Sales Turnover	66m	68m	73m
Pre Tax Profit/Loss	-5m	-5m	-10m
Working Capital	-52m	-46m	-56m
Fixed Assets	44m	50m	55m
Current Assets	24m	24m	29m
Current Liabilities	18m	19m	20m

Companies House London Information Centre
21 Bloomsbury Street, London, WC1B 3XD
Tel: 03031-234500
E-mail: enquiries@companieshouse.gov.uk
Website: http://www.companieshouse.gov.uk
Directors: M. Pacey (Sales & Mktg), J. Holden (Grp Chief Exec)
Managers: S. Ball (Purch Mgr)
Immediate Holding Company: COMPANIES LIMITED
Registration no: 03358626 **Date established:** 1997
Turnover: Up to £250,000 **No.of Employees:** 1 - 10 **Product Groups:** 81, 82

Date of Accounts	Apr 11	Apr 10	Apr 09
Sales Turnover	21	58	98
Pre Tax Profit/Loss	-14	-3	1
Working Capital	-57	-44	-40
Fixed Assets	5	6	6
Current Assets	7	14	17
Current Liabilities	8	3	4

Complete Coffee Ltd
1 Kentish Buildings 125 Borough High Street, London, SE1 1NP
Tel: 020-7403 8787 **Fax:** 020-7403 5276
E-mail: breminer@completecoffee.com
Website: http://www.completecoffee.com
Bank(s): Natwest
Directors: I. Breminer (MD)
Ultimate Holding Company: ASSOCIATED COFFEE MERCHANTS (INTERNATIONAL) LIMITED
Immediate Holding Company: COMPLETE COFFEE FOUNDATION
Registration no: 05881229 **VAT No.:** GB 397 0017 48
Date established: 2006 **Turnover:** Up to £250,000
No.of Employees: 11 - 20 **Product Groups:** 20, 62

Date of Accounts	Mar 12	Mar 11	Mar 10
Sales Turnover	39m	41m	41m
Pre Tax Profit/Loss	280	204	214
Working Capital	2m	1m	1m
Fixed Assets	689	684	691
Current Assets	10m	12m	8m
Current Liabilities	189	316	189

Component Hire
28 Newman Street, London, W1T 1PR
Tel: 020-7631 4455
Website: http://www.centralrental.co.uk
Managers: G. Wasneeta (Mgr)
No.of Employees: 1 - 10 **Product Groups:** 37, 38, 44

Compre Services UK Ltd
110 Fenchurch Street, London, EC3M 5JT
Tel: 020-7816 4400 **Fax:** 020-7816 4401
E-mail: j.halls@compre-group.com
Website: http://www.compre-group.com
Bank(s): HSBC Aldgate Branch, London EC3M 5JD
Directors: T. Fitzgerald-O'Conner (Non Exec), P. Abbott (MD), N. Steer (Fin), M. Sinko (Ch), K. Davies (MD), J. Halls (MD)
Managers: D. Humphrey (Develop Mgr), D. Young
Immediate Holding Company: COMPRE SERVICES (UK) LIMITED
Registration no: 01176727 **VAT No.:** GB 244 8987 12
Date established: 1974 **Turnover:** £2m - £5m **No.of Employees:** 21 - 50
Product Groups: 80, 82

Computer Precision Ltd
185 Upper Street, London, N1 1RQ
Tel: 020-7359 9797 **Fax:** 020-7359 9507
E-mail: benny@cipi.co.uk
Website: http://www.cipi.co.uk
Directors: B. Jacobs (MD)
Immediate Holding Company: COMPUTER PRECISION LIMITED
Registration no: 01909505 **VAT No.:** GB 427 2691 43
Date established: 1985 **Turnover:** £250,000 - £500,000
No.of Employees: 1 - 10 **Product Groups:** 84

Date of Accounts	Sep 11	Sep 10	Sep 09
Working Capital	77	93	105
Fixed Assets	10	12	302
Current Assets	118	109	120

Concierge Direct Ltd
11 Presidents Drive Wapping London, London, E1W 2JH
Tel: 020-7488 4008 **Fax:** 020-7488 4008
E-mail: admin@bmyconcierge.com
Website: http://www.bmyconcierge.com
Directors: K. Wanless (Fin), B. Kemble (MD)
Immediate Holding Company: CONCIERGE DIRECT LIMITED
Registration no: 04154717 **Date established:** 2001
Turnover: Up to £250,000 **No.of Employees:** 1 - 10 **Product Groups:** 61, 84

Date of Accounts	Feb 08	Feb 11	Feb 09
Sales Turnover	46	N/A	17
Pre Tax Profit/Loss	3	N/A	1
Working Capital	22	9	26
Fixed Assets	4	N/A	2
Current Assets	24	12	28
Current Liabilities	N/A	3	1

Concorde Graphics Ltd
Unit 21 Chiltonian Industrial Estate Manor Lane, London, SE12 0TX
Tel: 020-8297 1115 **Fax:** 020-8297 9755
E-mail: sim.f@concordegraphics.co.uk
Website: http://www.concordegraphics.co.uk
Bank(s): National Westminster Bank Plc
Directors: I. Francis (Fin), S. Francis (MD)
Managers: J. Patterson (Tech Serv Mgr)
Ultimate Holding Company: CONCORDE GRAPHICS LIMITED
Immediate Holding Company: CONCORDE DIGITAL LTD.
Registration no: 03253189 **Date established:** 1996 **Turnover:** £2m - £5m
No.of Employees: 11 - 20 **Product Groups:** 23, 28, 44

Condor Cycles Ltd
49-53 Gray's Inn Road, London, WC1X 8PP
Tel: 020-7269 6820 **Fax:** 020-7269 6821
E-mail: info@condorcycles.com
Website: http://www.condorcycles.com
Bank(s): Barclays, Business Centre, Enfield, Middx, UK
Directors: G. Young (MD)
Ultimate Holding Company: ROSSER NOMINEES NO.3 LIMITED
Immediate Holding Company: CONDOR CYCLES LIMITED
Registration no: 05351196 **VAT No.:** GB 232 3275 91
Date established: 2005 **Turnover:** Up to £250,000
No.of Employees: 11 - 20 **Product Groups:** 22, 29, 33, 35, 37, 39, 68

Date of Accounts	Mar 11	Mar 10	Mar 09
Working Capital	1m	1m	1m
Fixed Assets	1m	2m	2m
Current Assets	2m	2m	2m
Current Liabilities	577	N/A	N/A

Confederation Of British Industry
103 New Oxford Street, London, WC1A 1DU
Tel: 020-7379 7400 **Fax:** 020-7240 1578
E-mail: enquiry.desk@cbi.org.uk
Website: http://www.cbi.org.uk
Directors: R. Lambert (D-G), T. Bird (MD), F. Hughes (Sales & Mktg), M. Hyde (Reg)
Immediate Holding Company: INDEPENDENT SECTOR COMPLAINTS ADJUDICATION SERVICE LIMITED
Registration no: RC000139 **Date established:** 2010
Turnover: Up to £250,000 **No.of Employees:** 11 - 20 **Product Groups:** 87

Date of Accounts	Apr 11	Apr 10
Working Capital	5	N/A
Current Assets	7	N/A

Connet UK Ltd.
Suite B, Harley street 29, London, W1G 9QR
Tel: 020-7193 7316 **Fax:** 020-7182 6892
E-mail: info@uk.company-on.net
Website: http://www.companyonnet.co.uk
Directors: J. Petkovic (Dir)
Registration no: 06694257 **Date established:** 2009
No.of Employees: 1 - 10 **Product Groups:** 44

Conocophillips Ltd
2 Portman Street, London, W1H 6DU
Tel: 020-7408 6138 **Fax:** 020-7408 6660
Website: http://www.conocophillips.com
Directors: M. Morrison (MD), R. Swallow (Co Sec)
Ultimate Holding Company: PHILLIPS 66 (USA)
Immediate Holding Company: PHILLIPS 66 LIMITED
Registration no: 00529086 **Date established:** 1954
Turnover: Over £1,000m **No.of Employees:** 101 - 250
Product Groups: 13, 51

Date of Accounts	Dec 11	Dec 10	Dec 09
Sales Turnover	27434m	21134m	15966m
Pre Tax Profit/Loss	233m	322m	351m
Working Capital	1127m	1008m	752m
Fixed Assets	669m	674m	647m
Current Assets	7544m	3285m	2228m
Current Liabilities	579m	831m	559m

Conran Design Group
35 Inverness Street, London, NW1 7HB
Tel: 020-7284 5200 **Fax:** 020-7566 4555
E-mail: info@conrandesigngroup.com
Website: http://www.conrandesigngroup.com
Directors: A. Ross (Co Sec)
Ultimate Holding Company: HAVAS SA (FRANCE)
Immediate Holding Company: GROUPTREE LIMITED
Registration no: 01002786 **VAT No.:** GB 524 2819 53
Date established: 1994 **Turnover:** £5m - £10m **No.of Employees:** 21 - 50
Product Groups: 80, 81, 84

Date of Accounts	Dec 11	Dec 10	Dec 09
Working Capital	90	77	108
Fixed Assets	14	15	20
Current Assets	202	151	181
Current Liabilities	100	N/A	N/A

Jasper Conran Ltd
1-7 Rostrevor Mews, London, SW6 5AZ
Tel: 020-7384 0800 **Fax:** 020-7384 0801
E-mail: info@jasperconran.com
Website: http://www.jasperconran.com
Directors: J. Conran (MD), R. Litler (Fin)
Managers: A. Nichol (Mktg Serv Mgr)
Immediate Holding Company: Jasper Conran Holdings Ltd
Registration no: 01331470 **VAT No.:** GB 235 1914 75
Date established: 1977 **Turnover:** £2m - £5m **No.of Employees:** 21 - 50
Product Groups: 30, 63, 72

Date of Accounts	Mar 08	Mar 07	Mar 06
Sales Turnover	4643	5545	5641
Pre Tax Profit/Loss	197	76	68
Working Capital	2841	688	585
Fixed Assets	76	126	189
Current Assets	6632	4615	4552
Current Liabilities	3791	3927	3967
Total Share Capital	462	462	462
ROCE% (Return on Capital Employed)	6.8	9.4	8.8
ROT% (Return on Turnover)	4.2	1.4	1.2

The Consultants
312 High Road Leyton, London, E10 5PW
Tel: 020-8556 6161 **Fax:** 020-8923 8883
Directors: T. Harriette (MD)
Date established: 2000 **No.of Employees:** 1 - 10 **Product Groups:** 35

Consulting Engineers' Co-Partnership London Ltd
1528 London Road, London, SW16 4EU
Tel: 020-8679 5621 **Fax:** 020-8679 7922
E-mail: mail@cecp.co.uk
Website: http://www.cecp.co.uk
Directors: T. Krakowska (MD)
Immediate Holding Company: CONSULTING ENGINEERS CO-PARTNERSHIP (LONDON) LIMITED
Registration no: 02514034 **VAT No.:** GB 743 6706 22
Date established: 1990 **Turnover:** £250,000 - £500,000
No.of Employees: 1 - 10 **Product Groups:** 84

Date of Accounts	Jun 11	Jun 10	Jun 09
Working Capital	7	5	2
Fixed Assets	2	3	2
Current Assets	16	13	6

Contactum Ltd
Victoria Works Edgware Road, London, NW2 6LF
Tel: 020-8452 6366 **Fax:** 020-8208 3340
E-mail: sales@contactum.co.uk
Website: http://www.contactum.co.uk
Bank(s): Royal Bank of Scotland
Directors: D. Katz (Fin), M. Dempsey (Sales), P. Fisher (MD)
Immediate Holding Company: CONTACTUM LIMITED
Registration no: 06835712 **Date established:** 2009 **Turnover:** £5m - £10m
No.of Employees: 101 - 250 **Product Groups:** 37

Date of Accounts	Dec 11	Dec 10	Dec 09
Sales Turnover	6m	6m	3m
Pre Tax Profit/Loss	-1m	-920	-223
Working Capital	62	795	2m
Fixed Assets	326	196	175
Current Assets	3m	3m	2m
Current Liabilities	3m	425	248

Contiki Travel UK Ltd
Royal National Hotel Bedford Way, London, WC1H 0DG
Tel: 020-7637 0802 **Fax:** 020-7637 2121
E-mail: basement.rep1@contiki.co.uk
Website: http://www.contiki.com
Directors: K. Bunney (Fin), D. Denton (Dir), P. Baker (MD)
Managers: P. Brooks (Mgr)
Ultimate Holding Company: TRAVEL CORPORATION LIMITED (BRITISH VIRGIN ISLANDS)
Immediate Holding Company: CONTIKI TRAVEL (U.K.) LIMITED
Registration no: 01336852 **Date established:** 1977
Turnover: £250,000 - £500,000 **No.of Employees:** 1 - 10
Product Groups: 69

Date of Accounts	Dec 11	Dec 10	Dec 09
Sales Turnover	2m	2m	3m
Pre Tax Profit/Loss	101	44	175
Working Capital	194	620	452
Fixed Assets	N/A	N/A	142
Current Assets	1m	1m	969
Current Liabilities	1m	131	451

Contracts Consultancy Ltd
162-164 Upper Richmond Road, London, SW15 2SL
Tel: 020-8333 4141 **Fax:** 020-8333 4151
E-mail: chris.maltby@cclglobal.com
Website: http://www.cclglobal.com
Bank(s): National Westminster Bank Plc
Directors: C. Maltby (Dir), M. Unsworth (Co Sec)
Managers: C. Van Zyl (Sales Admin)
Immediate Holding Company: CONTRACTS CONSULTANCY LIMITED
Registration no: 01600305 **VAT No.:** GB 318 2035 86
Date established: 1981 **Turnover:** £10m - £20m
No.of Employees: 11 - 20 **Product Groups:** 80

Date of Accounts	Dec 11	Dec 10	Dec 09
Sales Turnover	13m	12m	13m
Pre Tax Profit/Loss	389	456	493

Working Capital	1m	1m	1m
Fixed Assets	31	34	39
Current Assets	4m	3m	3m
Current Liabilities	2m	904	972

Controltech Services
63 Larkshall Road Chingford, London, E4 6PD
Tel: 020-3245 0016
E-mail: controltech@controltech-ltd.co.uk
Website: http://www.controltech-ltd.co.uk
Directors: C. Bailey (Fin)
Immediate Holding Company: CONTROLTECH SERVICES LIMITED
Registration no: 03426649 **Date established:** 1997
Turnover: Up to £250,000 **No.of Employees:** 1 - 10 **Product Groups:** 40, 84

Cook Hammond & Kell Ltd
Aztec House 397-405 Archway Road, Highgate, London, N6 4EY
Tel: 020-8347 3700 **Fax:** 020-8347 3701
E-mail: localgov@chk.co.uk
Website: http://www.chk.co.uk/contact/contact.htm
Directors: D. Rose (MD), P. Treadwell (MD), P. Treadwell (Sales & Mktg)
Managers: E. Newton (I.T. Exec), J. Hepburn (Admin Off), P. Dodge (Mgr)
Registration no: 00188894 **Turnover:** £500,000 - £1m
No.of Employees: 21 - 50 **Product Groups:** 28, 81

The Coolbox Hire Company
62 Eaton Park Road Palmers Green, London, N13 4EL
Tel: 020-3232 0055
E-mail: mail@thecoolboxhirecompany.co.uk
Website: http://www.thecoolboxhirecompany.co.uk
Product Groups: 21, 30, 40, 83

Coomsco
93a Vicarage Lane, London, E15 4HG
Tel: 020-8221 0345 **Fax:** 020-8534 4542
E-mail: mathan.coom@coomsco.com
Website: http://www.coomsco.com
Directors: M. Coomaraswamy (Prop)
No.of Employees: 1 - 10 **Product Groups:** 35

A J Cope & Son Ltd
11-12 The Oval, London, E2 9DU
Tel: 020-7729 2405 **Fax:** 020-7729 2657
E-mail: info@ajcope.co.uk
Website: http://www.ajcope.co.uk
Bank(s): HSBC
Directors: C. Cope (MD)
Managers: J. Evans, J. Williams (Tech Serv Mgr)
Immediate Holding Company: A.J. COPE & SON LIMITED
Registration no: 00601389 **VAT No.:** GB 628 4891 03
Date established: 1958 **Turnover:** £5m - £10m **No.of Employees:** 21 - 50
Product Groups: 24, 29, 30, 33

Date of Accounts	Mar 11	Mar 10	Mar 09
Working Capital	346	236	175
Fixed Assets	410	390	408
Current Assets	2m	2m	2m

Coppernob
Portland House 4 Great Portland Street, London, W1W 8QJ
Tel: 020-7436 3600 **Fax:** 020-7637 3232
E-mail: gifi@coppernob-fashion.com
Directors: A. Shah (MD), M. Newman (Dir)
Immediate Holding Company: COPPERNOB LIMITED
Registration no: 02649313 **Date established:** 1991
Turnover: £10m - £20m **No.of Employees:** 21 - 50 **Product Groups:** 63

Date of Accounts	May 08	May 09	May 10
Sales Turnover	15m	19m	18m
Pre Tax Profit/Loss	231	1m	146
Working Capital	681	2m	1m
Fixed Assets	78	54	68
Current Assets	5m	7m	5m
Current Liabilities	3m	3m	2m

Copyprint UK Ltd
West Block Westminster Business Square Durham Street, London, SE11 5JH
Tel: 020-7735 0956 **Fax:** 020-7793 0519
E-mail: flondon@copyprint.co.uk
Website: http://www.copyprint.co.uk
Directors: A. London (MD), F. London (Fin)
Immediate Holding Company: COPYPRINT UK LIMITED
Registration no: 00991016 **VAT No.:** GB 239 2775 34
Date established: 1970 **Turnover:** £1m - £2m **No.of Employees:** 11 - 20
Product Groups: 28, 80

Copyright Promotions Licensing Group plc
3 Shortlands, London, W6 8PP
Tel: 020-8563 6400 **Fax:** 020-8563 6465
E-mail: cprotheroe@cplg.com
Website: http://www.cplg.com
Bank(s): National Westminster Bank Plc
Directors: C. Protheroe (Dir), D. Levart (Fin)
Managers: J. Vercarre-shaw (Tech Serv Mgr), S. Vertigan (Sales Admin)
Ultimate Holding Company: COOKIE JAR ENTERTAINMENT INC (CANADA)
Immediate Holding Company: THE COPYRIGHT PROMOTIONS LICENSING GROUP LIMITED
Registration no: 02133747 **VAT No.:** GB 524 2529 62
Date established: 1987 **Turnover:** £2m - £5m **No.of Employees:** 21 - 50
Product Groups: 81

Date of Accounts	Aug 11	Aug 10	Aug 09
Sales Turnover	2m	1m	2m
Pre Tax Profit/Loss	136	-869	-57
Working Capital	-992	-1m	-339
Fixed Assets	905	926	984
Current Assets	2m	2m	3m
Current Liabilities	1m	2m	1m

Coram Family
49 Mecklenburgh Square, London, WC1N 2QA
Tel: 020-7520 0300 **Fax:** 020-7520 0301
E-mail: reception@coram.org.uk
Website: http://www.coram.org.uk
Managers: S. Massey, G. Farhadi, V. Singara (Fin Mgr), C. Kelly (Personnel)
Immediate Holding Company: CORAM TRADING LIMITED
Registration no: 07034159 **Date established:** 2009
Turnover: Up to £250,000 **No.of Employees:** 51 - 100
Product Groups: 80

Date of Accounts	Mar 12	Mar 11
Sales Turnover	268	130
Pre Tax Profit/Loss	-4	10
Working Capital	-22	-29
Fixed Assets	28	39
Current Assets	240	56
Current Liabilities	93	85

Cordings Ltd
19-20 Piccadilly, London, W1J 0LA
Tel: 020-7734 0830 **Fax:** 020-7494 2349
E-mail: shop@cordings.co.uk
Website: http://www.cordings.co.uk
Directors: N. Uloth (Dir)
Ultimate Holding Company: CORDINGS HOLDINGS LIMITED
Immediate Holding Company: CORDINGS LIMITED
Registration no: 02006137 **Date established:** 1986 **Turnover:** £1m - £2m
No.of Employees: 11 - 20 **Product Groups:** 61

Date of Accounts	Apr 11	Apr 10	Apr 09
Sales Turnover	N/A	2m	2m
Pre Tax Profit/Loss	N/A	17	112
Working Capital	235	176	206
Fixed Assets	12	16	16
Current Assets	1m	723	611
Current Liabilities	N/A	74	32

Core 1
663 High Road Leytonstone, London, E11 4RD
Tel: 020-8279 9189
E-mail: info@core1.co.uk
Website: http://www.core1.co.uk
Managers: Q. Ahmed (Eng)
Date established: 2002 **Turnover:** Up to £250,000
No.of Employees: 1 - 10 **Product Groups:** 44

Core Technical Solutions
169 St John's Hill, London, SW11 1TQ
Tel: 020-7738 2014
E-mail: jw@coretechnicalsolutions.co.uk
Website: http://www.coretechnicalsolutions.co.uk
Directors: J. Lover (Dir)
Date established: 1990 **No.of Employees:** 1 - 10 **Product Groups:** 44

Core Technology Systems UK Ltd
1 Alie Street, London, E1 8DE
Tel: 020-7626 0516 **Fax:** 020-7953 3600
E-mail: webenquiry@coregb.com
Website: http://www.coregb.com
Directors: E. Mcgann (Tech Serv), C. Callanan (Dir)
Managers: E. Callanan (Personnel), A. Shah (Comptroller)
Immediate Holding Company: CORE TECHNOLOGY SYSTEMS (U.K.) LIMITED
Registration no: 02502866 **Date established:** 1990 **Turnover:** £1m - £2m
No.of Employees: 21 - 50 **Product Groups:** 37, 44, 67, 80

Date of Accounts	Dec 11	Dec 10	Dec 09
Working Capital	115	211	223
Fixed Assets	38	25	12
Current Assets	778	749	451

Cornerstone Trading Partners Ltd
26 Salmons Road Edmonton London, London, N9 7JT
Tel: 020-8807 0870 **Fax:** 020-8882 8995
E-mail: info@cornerstonedesigns.co.uk
Website: http://www.cornerstonedesigns.co.uk
Directors: P. Theodorou (Fin), P. Leguen De Lacroix (MD)
Immediate Holding Company: CORNERSTONE PRESENTATIONS LIMITED
Registration no: 05101742 **Date established:** 2004
Turnover: Up to £250,000 **No.of Employees:** 1 - 10 **Product Groups:** 81

Date of Accounts	Mar 11	Mar 09	Mar 08
Working Capital	4	N/A	1
Current Assets	10	5	4

Corney & Barrow Ltd
1 Thomas More Street, London, E1W 1YZ
Tel: 020-7265 2400 **Fax:** 020-7265 2509
E-mail: wine@corneyandbarrow.com
Website: http://www.corneyandbarrow.com
Directors: A. Brett-Smith (MD), S. Wardnicholson (Chief Op Offcr), W. Sanderson (Fin)
Ultimate Holding Company: CORNEY AND BARROW GROUP LIMITED
Immediate Holding Company: CORNEY & BARROW BARS LIMITED
Registration no: 01820524 **Date established:** 1984
Turnover: £10m - £20m **No.of Employees:** 51 - 100 **Product Groups:** 21

Date of Accounts	Apr 11	Apr 10	Apr 09
Sales Turnover	17m	16m	16m
Pre Tax Profit/Loss	446	469	670
Working Capital	-2m	-1m	-357
Fixed Assets	8m	8m	9m
Current Assets	1m	1m	2m
Current Liabilities	1m	1m	2m

Coronation Export & Import
108 Aldersgate Street, London, EC1A 4JQ
Tel: 020-7253 6666 **Fax:** 020-7490 0669
E-mail: info@coronation-group.com
Directors: L. Lalwani (MD)
Ultimate Holding Company: BLANCO INVESTMENTS LTD (JERSEY)
Immediate Holding Company: CORONATION (EXPORT IMPORT) LIMITED
Registration no: 01160267 **VAT No.:** GB 244 7188 47
Date established: 1974 **No.of Employees:** 1 - 10 **Product Groups:** 61

Date of Accounts	Mar 08	Mar 11	Mar 10
Working Capital	-2m	-2m	-2m
Fixed Assets	31	39	45
Current Assets	503	836	612
Current Liabilities	N/A	N/A	2m

Corporate Edge
Lyric House 149 Hammersmith Road, London, W14 0QL
Tel: 020-7855 5885 **Fax:** 020-7858 5850
E-mail: hello@corporateedge.com
Website: http://www.corporateedge.com
Directors: A. Luff (MD)
Ultimate Holding Company: Lorica Group Ltd
Immediate Holding Company: CF PARTNERS SERVICES (UK) LIMITED
Registration no: 06827219 **Date established:** 2009 **Turnover:** £2m - £5m
No.of Employees: 11 - 20 **Product Groups:** 80, 81

Date of Accounts	Dec 11	Dec 10	Dec 09
Sales Turnover	4m	2m	3m
Pre Tax Profit/Loss	99	-598	625

Working Capital	113	137	739
Fixed Assets	323	30	26
Current Assets	837	2m	817
Current Liabilities	523	2m	3

Corporate I C T Ltd
Unit 31 Tileyard Studios Tileyard Road, London, N7 9AH
Tel: 020-7503 3000 **Fax:** 020-7503 3072
E-mail: info@corporategroup.co.uk
Website: http://www.corporategroup.co.uk
Bank(s): The Royal Bank of Scotland
Directors: P. Grant (Dir)
Managers: H. Kennar (Fin Mgr), G. Bishop (Tech Serv Mgr)
Registration no: 02438187 **Turnover:** £2m - £5m
No.of Employees: 21 - 50 **Product Groups:** 44, 64

Costain Ltd
Costain House 111 Westminster Bridge Road, London, SE1 7UE
Tel: 020-7705 8444 **Fax:** 020-7705 8599
Website: http://www.costain.com
Bank(s): Lloyds TSB Bank plc
Directors: T. Bickerstaff (Fin), G. Kraemer (Dir), B. Cashin (Sales & Mktg), A. Wyllie (Grp Chief Exec), A. Vaughan (Pers), J. Claire (I.T. Dir)
Managers: G. Read (Public Relation), J. Taylor (Mktg Serv Mgr), S. Hudson (Sales Admin), D. Taylor (I.T. Exec), S. Wells ()
Immediate Holding Company: COSTAIN PENSION SCHEME TRUSTEE LIMITED
Registration no: 05137385 **VAT No.:** GB 235 9835 31
Date established: 2004 **Turnover:** £500m - £1,000m
No.of Employees: 51 - 100 **Product Groups:** 14, 66, 67, 85, 87

Cotleigh Engineering
586-588 Green Lanes, London, N8 0RP
Tel: 020-8802 0111 **Fax:** 020-8809 5516
E-mail: recruitment@cotleigh.com
Website: http://www.cotleigh.com
Directors: R. Markham (MD)
Immediate Holding Company: COTLEIGH ENGINEERING CO. LIMITED
Registration no: 01555174 **Date established:** 1981 **Turnover:** £2m - £5m
No.of Employees: 1 - 10 **Product Groups:** 38, 42, 48, 51

Date of Accounts	Mar 11	Mar 10	Mar 09
Sales Turnover	3m	2m	3m
Pre Tax Profit/Loss	56	104	156
Working Capital	345	300	219
Fixed Assets	4	5	5
Current Assets	563	487	476
Current Liabilities	118	112	108

Coty UK Ltd
St Georges House 5 St Georges Road, London, SW19 4DR
Tel: 020-8971 1300 **Fax:** 020-8971 4101
E-mail: sales@coty.com
Website: http://www.coty.com
Bank(s): Lloyds TSB Bank plc
Directors: B. Riddick (Dir), T. Halton (Co Sec)
Ultimate Holding Company: DONATA HOLDING SE
Immediate Holding Company: COTY MANUFACTURING UK LIMITED
Registration no: 00428213 **Date established:** 1947
Turnover: £75m - £125m **No.of Employees:** 501 - 1000
Product Groups: 32

Date of Accounts	Jun 11	Jun 10	Jun 09
Sales Turnover	85m	79m	78m
Pre Tax Profit/Loss	2m	2m	4m
Working Capital	31m	32m	27m
Fixed Assets	42m	40m	42m
Current Assets	80m	74m	61m
Current Liabilities	32m	29m	24m

County Construction Chemicals Ltd
Unit 4 Chingford Industrial Centre Hall Lane, London, E4 8DJ
Tel: 020-8524 1931 **Fax:** 020-8529 0103
E-mail: info@countyconchem.co.uk
Website: http://www.countyconchem.co.uk
Directors: D. Boxall (Dir)
Immediate Holding Company: COUNTY CONSTRUCTION CHEMICALS LIMITED
Registration no: 03059024 **Date established:** 1995
No.of Employees: 11 - 20 **Product Groups:** 14, 23, 24, 25, 27, 29, 30, 31, 32, 33, 35, 36, 37, 42, 45, 46, 49, 52, 66

Date of Accounts	Mar 11	Mar 10	Mar 09
Working Capital	1m	971	926
Fixed Assets	400	412	508
Current Assets	2m	1m	2m

Court Catering Equipment Ltd
Unit 1-2 Acton Vale Industrial Park Cowley Road, London, W3 7XA
Tel: 020-8576 6500 **Fax:** 020-8746 1116
E-mail: info@courtcatering.co.uk
Website: http://www.courtcatering.co.uk
Directors: L. Howe (Fin), N. Howe (MD)
Immediate Holding Company: COURT CATERING EQUIPMENT LIMITED
Registration no: 01248264 **Date established:** 1976 **Turnover:** £2m - £5m
No.of Employees: 11 - 20 **Product Groups:** 24, 26, 40, 41, 48, 63, 66, 67, 69, 84

Date of Accounts	Apr 11	Apr 10	Apr 09
Working Capital	-42	-20	133
Fixed Assets	893	893	865
Current Assets	2m	2m	2m

Courtenay Stewart Ltd
3 Hanover Square, London, W1S 1HB
Tel: 0871-2227616 **Fax:** 0871-2227626
E-mail: sales@courtenayhr.com
Website: http://www.courtenayhr.co.uk
Directors: G. Jones (MD), J. Robson (MD)
Immediate Holding Company: ELMGROVE INVESTMENTS LIMITED
Registration no: 04463416 **Date established:** 2010 **Turnover:** £1m - £2m
No.of Employees: 1 - 10 **Product Groups:** 80, 86

Coverite Asphalters Ltd
Palace Gates Bridge Road, London, N22 7SP
Tel: 020-8888 7821 **Fax:** 020-8889 0731
Website: http://www.coverite.co.uk
Directors: A. Speroni (Dir), A. Speroni (MD), G. Jacobs (Fin), R. Speroni (Dir)
Immediate Holding Company: COVERITE (ASPHALTERS) LIMITED
Registration no: 02588401 **VAT No.:** GB 681 6228 24
Date established: 1991 **Turnover:** £5m - £10m **No.of Employees:** 1 - 10
Product Groups: 52

Craigie Stockwell Carpets
81 York Street, London, W1H 1QH
Tel: 020-7224 8380 **Fax:** 020-7224 8381
E-mail: craigiestockwell@aol.com
Website: http://www.craigiestockwellcarpets.com
Directors: J. Stockwell (MD), N. Stockwell (Fin)
Immediate Holding Company: TOFFEENOSE LIMITED
Registration no: 04971935 **Date established:** 2007
No.of Employees: 1 - 10 **Product Groups:** 23, 24, 25, 49, 63

Cramer Music Ltd
23 Garrick Street, London, WC2E 9RY
Tel: 020-7240 1612 **Fax:** 020-7240 2639
Website: http://www.cramermusic.co.uk
Directors: C. Dringer (Co Sec)
Immediate Holding Company: CRAMER MUSIC LIMITED
Registration no: 02631835 **VAT No.:** GB 577 3695 84
Date established: 1991 **Turnover:** £1m - £2m **No.of Employees:** 1 - 10
Product Groups: 28

Date of Accounts	Mar 11	Mar 10	Mar 09
Sales Turnover	1m	2m	2m
Pre Tax Profit/Loss	-71	25	50
Working Capital	274	336	315
Fixed Assets	10	15	16
Current Assets	487	578	555
Current Liabilities	103	55	58

Cravath Swaine & Moore LLP
Citypoint 1 Ropemaker Street, London, EC2Y 9HR
Tel: 020-7453 1000 **Fax:** 020-7860 1150
E-mail: cravath@cravath.com
Website: http://www.cravath.com
Bank(s): Chase Manhatton
Directors: W. Rogers (Snr Part)
Immediate Holding Company: CRAVATH SWAINE & MOORE (USA)
Date established: 1986 **No.of Employees:** 21 - 50 **Product Groups:** 80

create-a-blind.co.uk
arch no 624w The Tower Bridge Business Complex, 100 Clements Road, London, SE16 4DG
Tel: 020-7231 5331
E-mail: sales@create-a-blind.co.uk
Website: http://www.create-a-blind.co.uk
Product Groups: 25, 30, 63, 66

Crete Shipping
42 Battersea Rise, London, SW11 1EE
Tel: 020-7223 1244 **Fax:** 020-7924 3895
E-mail: sales@creteshipping.co.uk
Website: http://www.creteshipping.co.uk
Directors: S. Anroud (MD)
Date established: 1978 **No.of Employees:** 1 - 10 **Product Groups:** 76

Cripps Sears & Partners Ltd
Sardinia House 51-52 Lincoln's Inn Fields, London, WC2A 3LZ
Tel: 020-7440 8999 **Fax:** 020-7242 0515
E-mail: london@crippssears.com
Website: http://www.crippssears.com
Bank(s): National Westminster Bank Plc
Directors: C. Lane (Fin)
Immediate Holding Company: CRIPPS, SEARS & PARTNERS LIMITED
Registration no: 01641492 **VAT No.:** GB 235 3717 67
Date established: 1982 **Turnover:** £1m - £2m **No.of Employees:** 11 - 20
Product Groups: 80, 86

Date of Accounts	Sep 11	Sep 10	Sep 09
Working Capital	615	413	110
Fixed Assets	13	16	25
Current Assets	1m	757	796

Croco Worldwide Ltd
107 Power Road, London, W4 5PY
Tel: 020-8742 3636 **Fax:** 020-8995 1350
E-mail: sales@crocoworldwide.com
Website: http://www.crocoworldwide.com
Directors: T. Walls (Mkt Research), H. Eastwood (Fin)
Ultimate Holding Company: Galleon Holdings plc
Immediate Holding Company: CROCO WORLDWIDE LTD
Registration no: 04672015 **Date established:** 2003 **Turnover:** £2m - £5m
No.of Employees: 1 - 10 **Product Groups:** 81

Date of Accounts	Sep 11	Sep 10	Sep 09
Sales Turnover	2m	3m	5m
Pre Tax Profit/Loss	-81	-139	-158
Working Capital	191	181	282
Fixed Assets	32	85	140
Current Assets	2m	1m	1m
Current Liabilities	34	32	167

Crowtv Ltd
12 Wendell Road, London, W12 9RT
Tel: 020-8749 6071 **Fax:** 020-8740 0795
E-mail: mail@crowtv.com
Website: http://www.crowtv.com
Directors: M. Manning (Dir), P. Kingsley (MD), P. Kingsley (Co Sec), S. O'Connor (Non Exec), J. Buckley (MD)
Immediate Holding Company: CROWTV LIMITED
Registration no: 01355287 **Date established:** 1978
No.of Employees: 1 - 10 **Product Groups:** 89

Cryogenic Ltd
Unit 30 Acton Park Industrial Estate The Vale, London, W3 7QE
Tel: 020-8743 6049 **Fax:** 020-8749 5315
E-mail: sales@cryogenic.co.uk
Website: http://www.cryogenic.co.uk
Bank(s): National Westminster Bank Plc
Directors: Z. Omar (Dir), Z. Omar (Mkt Research), J. McKay (Co Sec), M. Owczarkowski (Dir), J. Good (Dir)
Managers: V. Gholian (Purch Mgr), N. Soori
Immediate Holding Company: CRYOGENIC LIMITED
Registration no: 02659543 **VAT No.:** GB 538 8881 84
Date established: 1991 **Turnover:** £5m - £10m
No.of Employees: 51 - 100 **Product Groups:** 38

Date of Accounts	Mar 12	Mar 11	Mar 10
Sales Turnover	8m	7m	5m
Pre Tax Profit/Loss	697	542	444
Working Capital	2m	1m	1m
Fixed Assets	874	859	622
Current Assets	6m	6m	5m
Current Liabilities	2m	2m	2m

Crystal Palace FC
Selhurst Park Stadium Holmesdale Road, London, SE25 6PU
Tel: 020-8768 6000 **Fax:** 020-8768 6106
E-mail: info@cpfc.co.uk
Website: http://www.cpfc.co.uk
Directors: P. Alexander (Grp Chief Exec), H. Jani (Fin)
Managers: K. Corner
Immediate Holding Company: CRYSTALPALACE FC FOUNDATION
Registration no: 06664142 **Date established:** 2008
Turnover: £10m - £20m **No.of Employees:** 21 - 50 **Product Groups:** 87

Date of Accounts	Jun 11	Jun 10
Sales Turnover	578	1m
Pre Tax Profit/Loss	-52	336
Working Capital	279	329
Fixed Assets	4	6
Current Assets	379	418
Current Liabilities	92	87

Cufflinks Dry Cleaners
PO Box 28386, London, N1 1QP
Tel: 020-7704 1851 **Fax:** 020-7354 8928
E-mail: bmzad@yahoo.co.uk
Website: http://www.cufflinkscompany.co.uk
Managers: B. Zadeh (Mgr)
Date established: 1992 **No.of Employees:** 1 - 10 **Product Groups:** 30, 35, 49

John Cullen
561 Kings Road, London, SW6 2EB
Tel: 020-7371 5400 **Fax:** 020-7371 7799
E-mail: design@johncullenlighting.co.uk
Website: http://www.johncullenlighting.co.uk
Directors: C. Brown (Dir)
Turnover: £10m - £20m **No.of Employees:** 11 - 20 **Product Groups:** 37, 38, 84

Culligan Bottled Water Group
Unit 74 Capitol Industrial Park Capitol Way, London, NW9 0EW
Tel: 020-8200 4646 **Fax:** 020-8201 3939
Managers: S. Sperring (Chief Mgr)
Ultimate Holding Company: UKO INTERNATIONAL LIMITED
Immediate Holding Company: AO EUROPEAN SERVICES LIMITED
Date established: 1957 **No.of Employees:** 21 - 50 **Product Groups:** 40, 66

Cuprichem Limited
20 Harcourt Street, London, W1H 4HG
Tel: 020-7193 4945 **Fax:** 020-7691 7857
E-mail: info@cuprichem.com
Website: http://www.cuprichem.com
Managers: E. Omay (Chief Mgr)
Registration no: 05940394 **Date established:** 2006 **Turnover:** £2m - £5m
No.of Employees: 11 - 20 **Product Groups:** 31, 42

Date of Accounts	Sep 08	Sep 07
Working Capital	29	-2
Current Assets	209	13

F G Curtis & Co Plc
Crownhall House Elm Grove, London, SW19 4HE
Tel: 020-8947 8178 **Fax:** 020-8944 1530
E-mail: info@curtispackaging.co.uk
Website: http://www.curtispackaging.co.uk
Directors: J. Williams (Dir)
Immediate Holding Company: F.G. CURTIS PLC
Registration no: 00367479 **Date established:** 1941 **Turnover:** £5m - £10m
No.of Employees: 21 - 50 **Product Groups:** 27, 30

Date of Accounts	Mar 12	Mar 11	Mar 10
Sales Turnover	6m	6m	5m
Pre Tax Profit/Loss	895	461	130
Working Capital	1m	809	555
Fixed Assets	361	487	511
Current Assets	3m	2m	2m
Current Liabilities	450	710	407

Cut-it Training Mavcom Ltd
262 Highbury New Park, London, N5 2LH
Tel: 0845-6446962 **Fax:** 020-7704 9918
E-mail: training@cut-it.tv
Website: http://www.cut-it.tv
Directors: T. Mavro (Ch)
Date established: 2007 **Turnover:** £500,000 - £1m
No.of Employees: 1 - 10 **Product Groups:** 86

Cybergate Internet Cafe
3 Leigh Street, London, WC1H 9EW
Tel: 020-7387 3210 **Fax:** 020-7387 1810
E-mail: cybergate@c-gate.com
Website: http://www.cybergateuk.com
Directors: J. Zadeh (MD), K. Wu (Prop)
Immediate Holding Company: ARMSTRONG CREDIT SERVICES LIMITED
Registration no: 07064226 **Date established:** 2009
Turnover: £250,000 - £500,000 **No.of Employees:** 1 - 10
Product Groups: 44, 52

Czarnikow Group Ltd
24 Chiswell Street, London, EC1Y 4SG
Tel: 020-7972 6600 **Fax:** 020-7972 6699
E-mail: czarnikow@czarnikow.com
Website: http://www.czarnikow.com
Managers: R. Cave
Ultimate Holding Company: C. CZARNIKOW LIMITED
Immediate Holding Company: CZARNIKOW GROUP LIMITED
Registration no: 02650590 **VAT No.:** GB 657 1325 36
Date established: 1991 **Turnover:** £50m - £75m
No.of Employees: 51 - 100 **Product Groups:** 62

Czech & Speake Ltd
244-254 Cambridge Heath Road, London, E2 9DA
Tel: 020-8983 7400 **Fax:** 020-8981 7232
E-mail: sales@czechspeake.com
Website: http://www.czechandspeake.com
Managers: B. Nishioka
Immediate Holding Company: CZECH & SPEAKE LIMITED
Registration no: 01447160 **VAT No.:** GB 731 2057 72
Date established: 1979 **Turnover:** £2m - £5m **No.of Employees:** 1 - 10
Product Groups: 33, 36

Date of Accounts	Dec 10	Dec 09	Dec 08
Working Capital	-20	-17	2
Current Assets	197	95	110

D K S H Great Britain Ltd
60-68 Wimbledon Hill Road, London, SW19 7PA
Tel: 020-8879 5500 **Fax:** 020-8879 5501
E-mail: marco.caspani@dksh.com
Website: http://www.dksh.com/uk
Bank(s): HSBC
Directors: C. Doyle (Fin), M. Caspani (Dir)
Managers: J. White
Ultimate Holding Company: DKSH HOLDINGS AG (SWITZERLAND)
Immediate Holding Company: DKSH GREAT BRITAIN LIMITED
Registration no: 00287620 **VAT No.:** GB 205 4956 65
Date established: 1934 **Turnover:** £10m - £20m
No.of Employees: 11 - 20 **Product Groups:** 20, 32

Date of Accounts	Dec 11	Dec 10	Dec 09
Sales Turnover	13m	12m	10m
Pre Tax Profit/Loss	-308	1	448
Working Capital	1m	1m	2m
Fixed Assets	114	165	212
Current Assets	8m	5m	3m
Current Liabilities	339	434	159

D & P Logistics UK Ltd
Saunders House 52-53 The Mall, London, W5 3TA
Tel: 020-3178 8313 **Fax:** 020-7022 8660
E-mail: info-uk@dp-logistics.com
Website: http://www.dp-logistics.com
Directors: R. Jedrzejewski (Dir)
Immediate Holding Company: D&P LOGISTICS UK LTD.
Registration no: 06460406 **Date established:** 2007
Turnover: Up to £250,000 **No.of Employees:** 1 - 10 **Product Groups:** 72, 76

Date of Accounts	Dec 10	Dec 09	Dec 08
Sales Turnover	997	92	27
Working Capital	-5	-117	-3
Fixed Assets	1	112	1
Current Assets	326	36	18

D R S Cases Ltd
Unit 17 Forest Business Park Argall Avenue, London, E10 7FB
Tel: 020-8520 7500 **Fax:** 020-8520 9385
Directors: J. Plumb (MD), J. Plumb (Dir)
Managers: S. Plumb (Sec)
Immediate Holding Company: D.R.S.CASES LIMITED
Registration no: 00824172 **Date established:** 1964
Turnover: £250,000 - £500,000 **No.of Employees:** 1 - 10
Product Groups: 76

Date of Accounts	Oct 10	Oct 09	Oct 08
Working Capital	154	183	206
Fixed Assets	7	9	10
Current Assets	192	216	254

D S Smith Ukraine
4-16 Artillery Row, London, SW1P 1RZ
Tel: 020-7932 5000 **Fax:** 020-7222 5003
E-mail: sales@kayplast.com
Website: http://www.dssmith.uk.com
Directors: A. Thorne (Dir), O. Stratton (Dir), A. Steele (Co Sec), A. Hichens (Ch)
Ultimate Holding Company: DS SMITH PLC
Immediate Holding Company: DS SMITH UKRAINE LIMITED
Registration no: 06352659 **VAT No.:** GB 563 0699 25
Date established: 2007 **Turnover:** £250,000 - £500,000
No.of Employees: 1 - 10 **Product Groups:** 27

Date of Accounts	Apr 11	Apr 10	Apr 09
Pre Tax Profit/Loss	8m	-638	-7m
Working Capital	320m	296m	302m
Fixed Assets	271m	271m	267m
Current Assets	323m	321m	323m
Current Liabilities	2m	3m	1m

D Y N Metal Ltd
25-29 Chase Road, London, NW10 6TA
Tel: 020-8961 0656 **Fax:** 020-8961 8820
E-mail: info@dynmetal.co.uk
Website: http://www.dynmetal.co.uk
Bank(s): Barclays
Directors: R. Glatter (Fin), S. Capper (MD)
Ultimate Holding Company: DYN-PAN INTERNATIONAL SA (LUXEMBOURG)
Immediate Holding Company: DYN-METAL LIMITED
Registration no: 00328977 **VAT No.:** GB 238 6940 31
Date established: 1937 **Turnover:** £2m - £5m **No.of Employees:** 21 - 50
Product Groups: 30, 34, 35

Date of Accounts	Dec 11	Dec 10	Dec 09
Working Capital	2m	2m	2m
Fixed Assets	1m	1m	1m
Current Assets	3m	3m	3m

D Young & Co.
120 Holborn, London, EC1N 2DY
Tel: 020-7269 8550 **Fax:** 020-7269 8555
E-mail: mail@dyoung.co.uk
Website: http://www.dyoung.com
Managers: P. Lorusso (Sales Admin)
Immediate Holding Company: D YOUNG & CO LLP
Registration no: OC352154 **VAT No.:** GB 232 7521 82
Date established: 2010 **Turnover:** £20m - £50m
No.of Employees: 21 - 50 **Product Groups:** 80

Date of Accounts	Mar 11
Sales Turnover	38m
Pre Tax Profit/Loss	10m
Working Capital	7m
Fixed Assets	754
Current Assets	10m
Current Liabilities	2m

Daa Directory Advertising Agency (Directory Advertising Agency)
Lloyds Avenue House 6 Lloyd's Avenue, London, EC3N 3AX
Tel: 020-7266 3020 **Fax:** 020-8332 1319
E-mail: information@daa.co.uk
Website: http://www.daa.co.uk
Directors: D. Woodcock (Dir), J. Frost (MD), B. Daw (MD), L. Thorley (Fin)
Immediate Holding Company: POLYGON INSURANCE COMPANY (U.K.) LIMITED
Registration no: 06491068 **Date established:** 1974
No.of Employees: 1 - 10 **Product Groups:** 81

Daas Organic Beer
35 Brompton Rd Knightsbridge, London, SW3 1DE
Tel: 020-3286 5958
E-mail: enquires@daasbeer.com
Website: http://www.daasbeer.com
Directors: A. Vandermoot (Export)
Date established: 2000 **No.of Employees:** 1 - 10 **Product Groups:** 21

Daily Mail & General Trust
Northcliffe House 2 Derry Street, London, W8 5TT
Tel: 020-7938 6000 **Fax:** 020-7937 3214
E-mail: nick.jennings@dmgt.co.uk
Website: http://www.assocnews.co.uk
Directors: N. Jennings (Co Sec)
Ultimate Holding Company: ROTHERMERE CONTINUATION LTD (BERMUDA)
Immediate Holding Company: DAILY MAIL AND GENERAL INVESTMENTS PLC
Registration no: 02251116 **Date established:** 1988 **Turnover:** £2m - £5m
No.of Employees: 501 - 1000 **Product Groups:** 28

Date of Accounts	Sep 08	Oct 09	Oct 10
Pre Tax Profit/Loss	-133m	-19m	13m
Working Capital	-42m	-281	546m
Fixed Assets	1m	600	94m
Current Assets	421m	592m	556m
Current Liabilities	50m	5m	3m

Daks
10 Old Bond Street, London, W1S 4PL
Tel: 020-7409 4000 **Fax:** 020-7499 4494
E-mail: enquiries@daks.co.uk
Website: http://www.daks.co.uk
Bank(s): Barclays
Directors: H. Miki (Pres), A. Larsen (Fin)
Managers: R. Fernandes (Personnel), J. Smith (Sales & Mktg Mg), J. Rob (Tech Serv Mgr)
Ultimate Holding Company: SANKYO SEIKO COMPANY LTD. (JAPAN)
Immediate Holding Company: DAKS SIMPSON GROUP PUBLIC LIMITED COMPANY
Registration no: 00275205 **VAT No.:** GB 238 5284 44
Date established: 1933 **Turnover:** £10m - £20m
No.of Employees: 21 - 50 **Product Groups:** 22, 24

Date of Accounts	Mar 12	Jan 11	Jan 10
Sales Turnover	20m	16m	15m
Pre Tax Profit/Loss	5m	5m	4m
Working Capital	17m	16m	12m
Fixed Assets	990	2m	2m
Current Assets	20m	17m	16m
Current Liabilities	1m	491	1m

Dalco International Ltd
166 Commercial Road, London, E1 2JY
Tel: 020-7790 9319 **Fax:** 020-7791 3174
E-mail: dalcoltd@aol.com
Directors: S. Shah (Sales), R. Shah (MD), A. Shah (Fin)
Immediate Holding Company: DALCO INTERNATIONAL LIMITED
Registration no: 01663664 **Date established:** 1982 **Turnover:** £1m - £2m
No.of Employees: 1 - 10 **Product Groups:** 63

Date of Accounts	Mar 11	Mar 10	Mar 09
Working Capital	1m	1m	1m
Fixed Assets	619	620	622
Current Assets	2m	2m	2m

Dalton Maag Ltd
9th Floor Blue Star House Stockwell Road, London, SW9 9SP
Tel: 020-7924 0633 **Fax:** 020-7738 6410
E-mail: info@daltonmaag.com
Website: http://www.daltonmaag.com
Directors: E. Dalton (Fin), B. Maag (MD)
Immediate Holding Company: DALTON MAAG LIMITED
Registration no: 03103619 **Date established:** 1995
Turnover: Up to £250,000 **No.of Employees:** 11 - 20 **Product Groups:** 28, 81

Date of Accounts	Sep 11	Sep 10	Sep 09
Working Capital	308	115	134
Fixed Assets	66	11	8
Current Assets	513	259	253

Damco Solutions
84 Uxbridge Road, London, W13 8RA
Tel: 020-8799 2800 **Fax:** 020-8090 6201
E-mail: info@damcogroup.co.uk
Website: http://www.damcogroup.co.uk
Directors: P. Raj (Mkt Research)
Managers: M. Gupta (Mgr)
Immediate Holding Company: DAMCO SOLUTIONS LTD
Registration no: 04155347 **Date established:** 2001
No.of Employees: 101 - 250 **Product Groups:** 38, 44

Date of Accounts	Mar 11	Mar 10	Mar 09
Working Capital	575	291	221
Fixed Assets	4	4	14
Current Assets	2m	905	563

Daniel Prince Ltd
24 Hatton Garden, London, EC1N 8BQ
Tel: 020-7831 4258 **Fax:** 020-8944 8418
E-mail: info@danielprince.co.uk
Website: http://www.danielprince.co.uk
Directors: D. Prince (Prop)
Immediate Holding Company: DANIEL PRINCE LIMITED
Registration no: 04730127 **Date established:** 2003
Turnover: £500,000 - £1m **No.of Employees:** 1 - 10 **Product Groups:** 34, 49, 65

Date of Accounts	Apr 11	Apr 10	Apr 08
Working Capital	23	24	-0
Fixed Assets	12	12	7
Current Assets	23	24	49

W J Daniel & Co. Ltd
132-138 Uxbridge Road, London, W13 8QS
Tel: 028-5676789 **Fax:** 020-8840 5705
E-mail: contact@danielstores.co.uk
Website: http://www.danielstores.co.uk
Directors: A. Widmer (Dir), A. Durkin (Dir), P. Daniel (Jt MD), P. Daviel (Dir), W. Daniel (Dir), T. Daniel (Dir)
Managers: B. Keegan (Mgr)
Registration no: 06194252 **Date established:** 2007
No.of Employees: 51 - 100 **Product Groups:** 61

Danone Ltd
International House 7 High Street, London, W5 5DW
Tel: 020-8799 5800 **Fax:** 020-8799 5801
Website: http://www.danone.co.uk
Directors: R. Jain (Co Sec)
Ultimate Holding Company: DANONE SA (FRANCE)
Immediate Holding Company: DANONE LIMITED
Registration no: 01769822 **Date established:** 1983
Turnover: £125m - £250m **No.of Employees:** 101 - 250
Product Groups: 21, 62

Date of Accounts	Dec 11	Dec 10	Dec 09
Sales Turnover	240m	239m	219m
Pre Tax Profit/Loss	28m	22m	22m
Working Capital	20m	13m	11m
Fixed Assets	19m	21m	23m
Current Assets	90m	83m	75m
Current Liabilities	60m	58m	52m

Danor Engineering Ltd
465 Hornsey Road, London, N19 4DR
Tel: 020-7281 0182 **Fax:** 020-7263 0154
E-mail: danor.uk@btinternet.com
Website: http://www.danor-engineering.co.uk
Directors: P. Donker Curtius (Dir)
Immediate Holding Company: DANOR ENGINEERING LIMITED
Registration no: 01423485 **Date established:** 1979
Turnover: Up to £250,000 **No.of Employees:** 1 - 10 **Product Groups:** 40

Date of Accounts	Dec 11	Dec 10	Dec 09
Sales Turnover	140	148	135
Pre Tax Profit/Loss	6	4	1
Working Capital	5	4	N/A
Fixed Assets	2	3	8
Current Assets	86	71	59
Current Liabilities	75	65	54

Daro Factors Ltd
80-84 Wallis Road, London, E9 5LW
Tel: 020-8510 4000 **Fax:** 020-8510 4001
E-mail: sales@daro.com
Website: http://www.daro.com
Bank(s): National Westminster Bank Plc
Directors: D. Stone (Dir), J. Stone (Tech Serv), R. Stone (Sales)
Managers: L. Creek, S. Jones (Personnel)
Immediate Holding Company: DARO FACTORS LIMITED
Registration no: 00485213 **VAT No.:** GB 249 6419 29
Date established: 1950 **Turnover:** Up to £250,000
No.of Employees: 51 - 100 **Product Groups:** 30, 35, 36, 48

Date of Accounts	Dec 11	Dec 10	Dec 09
Working Capital	264	206	161
Fixed Assets	3m	3m	3m
Current Assets	1m	1m	1m

Darton Longman & Todd Ltd
140-142 Wandsworth High Street, London, SW18 4JJ
Tel: 020-8875 0155 **Fax:** 020-8875 0133
E-mail: virginiah@darton-longman-todd.co.uk
Website: http://www.darton-longman-todd.co.uk
Directors: V. Hearn (Dir)
Immediate Holding Company: DARTON LONGMAN & TODD LIMITED
Registration no: 00633407 **VAT No.:** GB 238 6999 95
Date established: 1959 **Turnover:** £1m - £2m **No.of Employees:** 1 - 10
Product Groups: 28

Date of Accounts	Aug 11	Aug 10	Aug 09
Working Capital	-214	-137	-182
Fixed Assets	7	11	15
Current Assets	385	511	424

Darwin Press Ltd
77a Blackheath Road, London, SE10 8PD
Tel: 020-8691 1357 **Fax:** 020-8691 6556
E-mail: sales@darwinpress.co.uk
Website: http://www.darwinpress.co.uk
Directors: L. Brown (Dir), M. Brown (Co Sec)
Immediate Holding Company: DARWIN PRESS LIMITED
Registration no: 00990875 **Date established:** 1970
Turnover: £500,000 - £1m **No.of Employees:** 1 - 10 **Product Groups:** 28

Date of Accounts	Dec 11	Dec 10	Dec 09
Working Capital	221	98	122
Fixed Assets	681	764	814
Current Assets	840	699	795
Current Liabilities	N/A	10	N/A

Dashwood Finance Company
63 Coleman Street, London, EC2R 5BB
Tel: 020-7588 3215 **Fax:** 020-7588 4818
E-mail: dashwood.group@virgin.net
Directors: J. Stewart Smith (Fin), A. Aziz (Ch)
Immediate Holding Company: DASHWOOD FINANCE COMPANY LIMITED
Registration no: 00693394 **VAT No.:** GB 244 0714 87
Date established: 1961 **Turnover:** £1m - £2m **No.of Employees:** 11 - 20
Product Groups: 61, 80, 82

Date of Accounts	Sep 08	Sep 07	Sep 06
Working Capital	-383	-368	-400
Fixed Assets	3187	3188	3189
Current Assets	69	65	46
Current Liabilities	452	433	447
Total Share Capital	149	149	149

Data & Archival Damage Control Centre
4 Bridge Wharf 156 Caledonian Road, London, N1 9UU
Tel: 020-7837 8215 **Fax:** 020-7278 0221
E-mail: helene@dadcc.com
Website: http://www.dadcc.com
Directors: H. Donnelly (MD)
Immediate Holding Company: MILIKILO LTD
VAT No.: GB 466 3031 58 **Date established:** 2012
No.of Employees: 1 - 10 **Product Groups:** 28, 54, 80, 84

Data Know How
17 St Annes Court, London, W1F 0BQ
Tel: 020-7734 3532 **Fax:** 020-7734 1779
E-mail: info@dataknowhow.co.uk
Website: http://www.dataknowhow.co.uk
Directors: M. Pearce (MD)
Immediate Holding Company: FLUORESCENT PR LIMITED
Registration no: 05520374 **VAT No.:** GB 668 1401 33
Date established: 2005 **Turnover:** £2m - £5m **No.of Employees:** 1 - 10
Product Groups: 81

Date of Accounts	Jul 11	Jul 10	Jul 09
Working Capital	57	24	28
Fixed Assets	7	6	4
Current Assets	172	84	82

Data Recovery Lab
2a The Broadway Friern Barnet Road, London, N11 3DT
Tel: 020-7516 1077 **Fax:** 0207-117 4263
E-mail: info@datarecoverylab.co.uk
Website: http://www.datarecoverylab.co.uk
Directors: B. Ali (Dir)
Immediate Holding Company: D+ LTD.
Registration no: 02679956 **Date established:** 1992
Turnover: £500,000 - £1m **No.of Employees:** 11 - 20 **Product Groups:** 44

Date of Accounts	Jan 11	Jan 10	Jan 09
Working Capital	20	28	65
Fixed Assets	3	3	4
Current Assets	21	29	65

Datacash Ltd
International Buildings 71 Kingsway, London, WC2B 6ST
Tel: 020-7421 9280 **Fax:** 08707-274781
E-mail: info@datacash.com
Website: http://www.datacash.com
Directors: G. Breeze (Dir), K. Butcher (Fin), P. Burton (Fin), A. Dark (Grp Chief Exec)
Managers: D. Bailey, T. Garret (Gen Contact)
Ultimate Holding Company: DATACASH GROUP LIMITED
Immediate Holding Company: DATACASH LTD.
Registration no: 03430157 **Date established:** 1997
Turnover: £10m - £20m **No.of Employees:** 1 - 10 **Product Groups:** 44

Date of Accounts	Dec 11	Dec 10	Dec 09
Sales Turnover	15m	14m	13m
Pre Tax Profit/Loss	2m	5m	6m
Working Capital	11m	9m	5m
Fixed Assets	639	690	950
Current Assets	49m	33m	10m
Current Liabilities	3m	3m	5m

Datadial Ltd
8 Glenthorne Mews 115a Glenthorne Road, London, W6 0LJ
Tel: 020-8600 0500 **Fax:** 020-8600 0509
E-mail: info@datadial.net
Website: http://www.datadial.net
Directors: R. Faulkner (MD)
Immediate Holding Company: DATADIAL LIMITED
Registration no: 03509127 **Date established:** 1998
Turnover: Up to £250,000 **No.of Employees:** 11 - 20 **Product Groups:** 44

Date of Accounts	Feb 12	Feb 11	Feb 10
Working Capital	215	178	124
Fixed Assets	4	6	8
Current Assets	338	326	241

Datamonitor plc
Guardian House 119 Farringdon Road, London, EC1R 3DA
Tel: 020-7551 9000 **Fax:** 020-7675 7500
E-mail: lindsey.roberts@informa.com
Website: http://www.datamonitor.com
Managers: L. Roberts
Immediate Holding Company: ALLIED PROPERTIES LIMITED
Registration no: 02306113 **Date established:** 1980
Turnover: £250,000 - £500,000 **No.of Employees:** 251 - 500
Product Groups: 81

Helen David
22 South Grove, London, N6 6BB
Tel: 020-8440 7325 **Fax:** 020-7284 2530
Website: http://www.englisheccentrics.com
Directors: H. David (Dir), C. David (Co Sec)
No.of Employees: 1 - 10 **Product Groups:** 23

Davies Arnold Cooper
6-8 Bouverie Street, London, EC4Y 8DD
Tel: 020-7936 2222 **Fax:** 020-7936 2020
E-mail: reception@dacbeachcroft.com
Website: http://www.dacbeachcroft.com
Directors: D. Gowan (Snr Part), S. Howell (Chief Op Offcr)
Managers: N. Attree (Tech Serv Mgr)
Immediate Holding Company: DAVIES ARNOLD COOPER LIMITED
Registration no: 02710689 **VAT No.:** GB 243 3476 68
Date established: 1992 **No.of Employees:** 501 - 1000 **Product Groups:** 80

Date of Accounts	Mar 12	Mar 11	Mar 10
Current Assets	17	18	15
Current Liabilities	N/A	N/A	14

Davies Harvey & Murrell
236-237 Record Street, London, SE15 1TL
Tel: 020-7732 9988 **Fax:** 020-7732 5415
E-mail: mail@dhmpaper.com
Website: http://www.dhmpaper.com
Directors: J. Ovenden (Fin), N. Ovenden (Dir), P. Blakely (MD)
Managers: D. Little (Sales Prom Mgr)
Ultimate Holding Company: Davies Harvey & Murrell Group Ltd
Immediate Holding Company: DAVIES HARVEY AND MURRELL GROUP LIMITED
Registration no: 01674571 **VAT No.:** GB 243 5520 81
Date established: 1982 **Turnover:** £10m - £20m
No.of Employees: 21 - 50 **Product Groups:** 64, 66

Davstone Holdings Ltd
19-20 Grosvenor Street, London, W1K 4QH
Tel: 020-7493 9613 **Fax:** 020-7491 0692
Website: http://www.regalianplc.com
Directors: D. Darlington (Fin), D. Goldstone (MD), J. Goldstone (Sales), L. Goldstone (MD)
Immediate Holding Company: DAVSTONE (HOLDINGS) LIMITED
Registration no: 00661782 **Date established:** 1960
Turnover: £10m - £20m **No.of Employees:** 1 - 10 **Product Groups:** 52

Date of Accounts	Dec 10	Dec 09	Dec 08
Working Capital	-5m	-7m	-5m
Fixed Assets	5m	4m	3m
Current Assets	400	161	2m

D D B London Ltd
12 Bishops Bridge Road, London, W2 6AA
Tel: 020-7258 3979 **Fax:** 020-7724 2655
E-mail: kate.thomsen@ddblondon.com
Website: http://www.ddblondon.com

see next page

***D D B London Ltd** - Cont'd*

Directors: V. Malysh (Fin), S. Watson (Fin)
Managers: S. Burton (Tech Serv Mgr), K. Thomsen, F. Chafron (Personnel)
Ultimate Holding Company: OMNICOM GROUP INC (USA)
Immediate Holding Company: DDB UK LIMITED
Registration no: 00933578 **VAT No.:** GB 341 0358 93
Date established: 1968 **Turnover:** £50m - £75m
No.of Employees: 251 - 500 **Product Groups:** 81

Date of Accounts	Dec 11	Dec 10	Dec 09
Sales Turnover	56m	56m	50m
Pre Tax Profit/Loss	10m	11m	11m
Working Capital	11m	9m	4m
Fixed Assets	48m	43m	41m
Current Assets	62m	59m	48m
Current Liabilities	35m	33m	32m

Dean Associates
Carthew Road, London, W6 0DX
Tel: 01646-661646 **Fax:** 01646-661696
E-mail: dean.associates@dial.pipex.com
Directors: M. Pryce (Ptnr)
Immediate Holding Company: DEAN ASSOCIATES LIMITED
Registration no: 06173974 **VAT No.:** GB 411 4938 68
Date established: 2007 **Turnover:** Up to £250,000
No.of Employees: 1 - 10 **Product Groups:** 80

Deans Blinds & Awnings UK
4 Haslemere Industrial Estate Ravensbury Terrace, London, SW18 4SE
Tel: 020-8947 8931 **Fax:** 020-8947 8336
E-mail: info@deansblinds.co.uk
Website: http://www.deansblinds.co.uk
Bank(s): National Westminster Bank Plc
Managers: S. Cook (Mgr)
Immediate Holding Company: DEANS BLINDS AND AWNINGS UK LIMITED
Registration no: 00395298 **VAT No.:** GB 318 1427 74
Date established: 1945 **Turnover:** £1m - £2m **No.of Employees:** 11 - 20
Product Groups: 24, 30

Date of Accounts	Dec 11	Dec 10	Dec 09
Sales Turnover	N/A	2m	2m
Pre Tax Profit/Loss	N/A	30	N/A
Working Capital	145	120	111
Fixed Assets	43	62	57
Current Assets	399	471	456
Current Liabilities	N/A	79	64

Debenhams plc
1 Welbeck Street, London, W1G 0AA
Tel: 08445-616161 **Fax:** 020-7408 3366
E-mail: bournemouth@dibbens.co.uk
Website: http://www.dbenhams.com
Directors: M. Sharp (Grp Chief Exec), P. Eardley (Co Sec), R. Templeman (Grp Chief Exec)
Ultimate Holding Company: DEBENHAMS PLC
Immediate Holding Company: DEBENHAMS PRINCIPLES LIMITED
Registration no: 06860458 **Date established:** 2009
Turnover: Over £1,000m **No.of Employees:** 1 - 10 **Product Groups:** 61

Date of Accounts	Aug 10	Sep 11
Pre Tax Profit/Loss	-3	-5
Working Capital	2	3
Fixed Assets	46	41
Current Assets	2	3

Decra
Unit 34 Forest Business Park Argall Avenue, London, E10 7FB
Tel: 020-8520 4371 **Fax:** 020-8521 0605
E-mail: info@decraltd.co.uk
Website: http://www.decraltd.co.uk
Bank(s): Barclays, London
Directors: G. Matthews (MD)
Managers: C. Spencer (Sales Admin), J. English (Tech Serv Mgr)
Immediate Holding Company: DECRA LIMITED
Registration no: 00514476 **VAT No.:** GB 248 1820 59
Date established: 1952 **Turnover:** £2m - £5m **No.of Employees:** 51 - 100
Product Groups: 30, 48

Date of Accounts	Dec 11	Dec 10	Dec 09
Sales Turnover	4m	5m	5m
Pre Tax Profit/Loss	42	-83	-137
Working Capital	303	270	364
Fixed Assets	1m	2m	2m
Current Assets	2m	2m	2m
Current Liabilities	275	275	371

Deltalight
94 Webber Street, London, SE1 0QN
Tel: 08707-577087 **Fax:** 020-7729 9728
Website: http://www.deltalight.co.uk
Directors: I. Streeter (Sales), S. Barnes (Fin), V. Clifton (Mkt Research)
Managers: C. Olney (Sales Admin)
No.of Employees: 11 - 20 **Product Groups:** 37, 67

Deluxe Chauffeurs of London
Deluxe Office Crown House North Circular Road, London, NW10 7PN
Tel: 020-8907 8884
E-mail: info@deluxechauffeurs.com
Website: http://www.deluxechauffeurs.com
Managers: A. Istri (Mgr)
Immediate Holding Company: VIP LONDON CHAUFFEURS LTD
Date established: 2010 **Turnover:** £1m - £2m **No.of Employees:** 1 - 10
Product Groups: 72

Date of Accounts	Feb 12	Feb 11
Working Capital	-1	4
Fixed Assets	60	66
Current Assets	1	7

Deluxe Product
153-159 Bow Road, London, E3 2SE
Tel: 020-8980 3200
E-mail: paul@deluxeproduct.com
Website: http://www.deluxeproduct.com
Directors: P. Coleman (Dir), P. Colman (MD)
Immediate Holding Company: LONDON LOCKS LTD
Registration no: 03076465 **Date established:** 2004
Turnover: Up to £250,000 **No.of Employees:** 1 - 10 **Product Groups:** 26

Deminos HR
145 157 St John Street, London, EC1V 4PY
Tel: 020-7870 1090 **Fax:** 020-3292 1752
E-mail: neil.atkinson@deminos.co.uk
Website: http://www.deminos.co.uk
Directors: N. Atkinson (MD)
Immediate Holding Company: DEMINOS LTD
Registration no: 06376910 **Date established:** 2007
Turnover: £500,000 - £1m **No.of Employees:** 11 - 20
Product Groups: 44, 80

Dennis Publishing
30 Cleveland Street, London, W1T 4JD
Tel: 020-7907 6000 **Fax:** 020-7907 6020
E-mail: reception@dennis.co.uk
Website: http://www.dennis.co.uk
Managers: J. Tye
Ultimate Holding Company: DENNIS PUBLISHING (UK) LIMITED
Immediate Holding Company: DENNIS PUBLISHING (UK) LIMITED
Registration no: 03870844 **Date established:** 1999
Turnover: £50m - £75m **No.of Employees:** 251 - 500 **Product Groups:** 28

Date of Accounts	Dec 11	Dec 10	Dec 09
Sales Turnover	69m	64m	58m
Pre Tax Profit/Loss	4m	4m	2m
Working Capital	-3m	-6m	-7m
Fixed Assets	24m	26m	28m
Current Assets	23m	19m	16m
Current Liabilities	20m	19m	18m

Densitron Technologies plc Densitron Display Solutions
Cannon Street, London, EC4N 5BP
Tel: 020-7648 4200 **Fax:** 020-7648 4201
E-mail: sales@densitron.co.uk
Website: http://www.densitron.com
Bank(s): Barclays Bank Plc
Directors: C. Goodhall (Sales), T. Pearson (Fin)
Managers: C. Lugosi (Tech Serv Mgr)
Immediate Holding Company: DENSITRON TECHNOLOGIES PLC
Registration no: 01962726 **VAT No.:** GB 425 2820 700 001
Date established: 1985 **Turnover:** £10m - £20m
No.of Employees: 11 - 20 **Product Groups:** 37, 38, 39

Date of Accounts	Dec 11	Dec 10	Dec 09
Sales Turnover	23m	21m	15m
Pre Tax Profit/Loss	1m	-569	159
Working Capital	3m	7m	2m
Fixed Assets	1m	1m	6m
Current Assets	8m	13m	6m
Current Liabilities	3m	4m	2m

Denton Wilde Sapte
1 Fleet Place, London, EC4M 7WS
Tel: 020-7246 7000 **Fax:** 020-7246 7777
E-mail: howard.morris@dentonwildespate.com
Website: http://www.dentonwildesapte.com
Bank(s): National Westminster
Directors: S. Blakeley (Ptnr), M. Andrews (Ptnr), H. Morris (Grp Chief Exec)
Immediate Holding Company: SNR DENTON UK LLP
Registration no: OC322045 **VAT No.:** 243 7425 65 **Date established:** 2006
Turnover: £125m - £250m **No.of Employees:** 251 - 500
Product Groups: 82

Dentsu Sports Europe Ltd
Berger House 38 Berkeley Square, London, W1J 5AH
Tel: 020-7499 9124 **Fax:** 020-7493 7491
E-mail: reception@dentsu.co.uk
Website: http://www.dentsu.com
Directors: K. Miyakawa (Ch), Y. Amano (Dir), T. Ichikura (Dir), M. Otsuka (Asst MD), K. Nakamura (Asst MD), K. Kamigori (MD), K. Ogai (Dir)
Ultimate Holding Company: DENTSU INC (JAPAN)
Immediate Holding Company: DENTSU SPORTS EUROPE, LIMITED
Registration no: 06351498 **VAT No.:** GB 446 0192 63
Date established: 2007 **Turnover:** £1m - £2m **No.of Employees:** 1 - 10
Product Groups: 80, 81

Date of Accounts	Dec 11	Dec 10	Dec 09
Sales Turnover	3m	3m	2m
Pre Tax Profit/Loss	230	90	73
Working Capital	2m	1m	1m
Fixed Assets	24	25	22
Current Assets	3m	7m	9m
Current Liabilities	987	3m	4m

Department For Business Innovation & Skills
1 Victoria Street, London, SW1H 0ET
Tel: 020-7215 5000 **Fax:** 020-7222 2629
E-mail: enquiries@bis.gsi.gov.uk
Website: http://www.bis.gov.uk
Managers: P. Beardsley, M. Housden
Immediate Holding Company: UK SKILLS
Registration no: 02535199 **Date established:** 1990
No.of Employees: 1 - 10 **Product Groups:** 54, 80, 81, 86, 87

Derivatives Documentation Ltd
68 Lombard Street, London, EC3V 9LJ
Tel: 020-7060 1335 **Fax:** 01763-220902
E-mail: enquiries@derivsdocu.com
Website: http://www.derivsdocu.com
Directors: P. Harding (MD)
Registration no: 03223177 **Date established:** 1996
No.of Employees: 1 - 10 **Product Groups:** 86

Design Bridge Ltd
18 Clerkenwell Close, London, EC1R 0QN
Tel: 020-7814 9922 **Fax:** 020-7814 9024
E-mail: bill.goodenough@designbridge.com
Website: http://www.designbridge.com
Bank(s): Barclays
Directors: W. Goodenough (Ch), J. Bowers (Pers), M. Hawkins (Fin), N. Gray (Sales)
Managers: V. Levene (Sales Admin), J. Hughes (Tech Serv Mgr), S. Prentice
Immediate Holding Company: DESIGN BRIDGE LIMITED
Registration no: 02044752 **VAT No.:** GB 447 0501 70
Date established: 1986 **Turnover:** £20m - £50m
No.of Employees: 101 - 250 **Product Groups:** 81, 84

Date of Accounts	Dec 11	Dec 10	Dec 09
Sales Turnover	24m	21m	17m
Pre Tax Profit/Loss	690	1m	-11
Working Capital	6m	6m	5m
Fixed Assets	2m	2m	2m
Current Assets	11m	10m	9m
Current Liabilities	3m	3m	2m

Detail Plus
202b Upper Richmond Road West, London, SW14 8AN
Tel: 020-8878 1592 **Fax:** 020-8392 9995
E-mail: sales@detailplus.co.uk
Website: http://www.detailplus.co.uk
Directors: W. Osborne (Prop)
Date established: 1999 **No.of Employees:** 1 - 10 **Product Groups:** 35, 36

Deutscha Asset Management Ltd
PO Box 135, London, EC2A 2HE
Tel: 020-7545 6000 **Fax:** 020-7545 7700
Website: http://www.deam.co.uk
Directors: M. Phillips (MD)
Ultimate Holding Company: DEUTSCHE BANK AG (GERMANY)
Immediate Holding Company: DEUTSCHE ALTERNATIVE ASSET MANAGEMENT (UK) LIMITED
Registration no: 05233891 **Date established:** 1990
Turnover: £20m - £50m **No.of Employees:** 1 - 10 **Product Groups:** 80

Date of Accounts	Dec 11	Dec 10	Dec 09
Sales Turnover	N/A	N/A	4
Pre Tax Profit/Loss	-1	-639	112
Working Capital	N/A	5m	5m
Current Assets	N/A	5m	6m
Current Liabilities	N/A	N/A	31

Development Securities Investments plc
Portland House Bressenden Place, London, SW1E 5DS
Tel: 020-7828 4777 **Fax:** 020-7828 4999
E-mail: debbie.whetstone@devsecs.co.uk
Website: http://www.developmentsecurities.co.uk
Bank(s): Barclays
Directors: H. Ratsey (Co Sec)
Managers: D. Whetstone
Ultimate Holding Company: DEVELOPMENT SECURITIES PLC
Immediate Holding Company: DEVELOPMENT SECURITIES (INVESTMENTS) PLC
Registration no: 00701787 **Date established:** 1961
Turnover: £10m - £20m **No.of Employees:** 21 - 50 **Product Groups:** 80

Date of Accounts	Dec 10	Dec 09	Dec 08
Sales Turnover	14m	27m	140m
Pre Tax Profit/Loss	-4m	-7m	-28m
Working Capital	20m	34m	73m
Fixed Assets	73m	72m	75m
Current Assets	102m	115m	111m
Current Liabilities	9m	10m	18m

D F K International
Russell Square House 10-12 Russell Square, London, WC1B 5LF
Tel: 020-7436 6722 **Fax:** 020-7436 6606
E-mail: info@dfk.com
Website: http://www.dfk.com
Directors: M. Sharpe (Tech Serv), M. Sharp (Dir)
Immediate Holding Company: DFK INTERNATIONAL
Registration no: FC024704 **VAT No.:** GB 242 6465 64
Date established: 2003 **Turnover:** £20m - £50m **No.of Employees:** 1 - 10
Product Groups: 80

Date of Accounts	Jun 09	Jun 08	Jun 07
Sales Turnover	N/A	508	130
Pre Tax Profit/Loss	-17	16	1
Working Capital	-693	-455	-168
Fixed Assets	839	693	425
Current Assets	14	240	185
Current Liabilities	707	686	128

Dial A Flight
37-39 Queen Elizabeth Street, London, SE1 2BT
Tel: 020-7962 9966 **Fax:** 020-7334 7785
E-mail: reception@lotusgroup.co.uk
Website: http://www.dialaflight.co.uk
Directors: P. Stephens (MD), J. Phelps (Fin), C. Burrowes (Co Sec), G. Ross (Sales)
Managers: H. Chagger (Tech Serv Mgr)
Immediate Holding Company: DIAL-A-FLIGHT LIMITED
Registration no: 01641772 **Date established:** 1982
Turnover: £20m - £50m **No.of Employees:** 101 - 250 **Product Groups:** 69

Date of Accounts	Oct 09	Oct 08
Working Capital	20	20
Current Assets	20	20

Dial-A-Cab (ODRTS Ltd)
39-47 East Road, London, N1 6AH
Tel: 020-7253 5000 **Fax:** 020-7553 7294
E-mail: brianr@dialacab.co.uk
Website: http://www.dialacab.co.uk
Directors: B. Rice (Ch)
Immediate Holding Company: DIAL-A-CAB LIMITED
Registration no: 02865742 **VAT No.:** GB 239 2548 45
Date established: 1993 **Turnover:** £10m - £20m **No.of Employees:** 1 - 10
Product Groups: 72

Diamond & Gold Mining
Dunmore Point Gascoigne Place, London, E2 7LX
Tel: 020-7739 7853 **Fax:** 020-7613 0091
Directors: D. Ouereye (Prop)
Date established: 1997 **No.of Employees:** 1 - 10 **Product Groups:** 36

Diamond Manufacturers Ltd
90 Long Acre, London, WC2E 9RZ
Tel: 0800-5300541 **Fax:** 020-7242 2766
E-mail: service@diamondmanufacturers.co.uk
Website: http://www.diamondmanufacturers.co.uk
Directors: S. Madhurkar (Mkt Research)
Registration no: 06388524 **Date established:** 2007
Turnover: £10m - £20m **No.of Employees:** 21 - 50 **Product Groups:** 49

Diapo Ltd
Arch 356 Westgate Street, London, E8 3RL
Tel: 020-7923 0006
E-mail: info@diapo.co.uk
Website: http://www.diapo.co.uk
Directors: B. Urbarnoviez Abbey (Fin), N. Abbey (Dir)
Immediate Holding Company: DIAPO LTD.
Registration no: 04277059 **Date established:** 2001
No.of Employees: 1 - 10 **Product Groups:** 25, 30, 35, 52

Date of Accounts	Dec 11	Dec 10	Aug 09
Working Capital	-2	-1	5
Fixed Assets	15	19	20
Current Assets	76	91	191

Diatherm Vitrum Signum
Gresham Works Mornington Road, London, E4 7DR
Tel: 020-8524 9546 **Fax:** 020-8524 9546
E-mail: info@vitrumsignum.com
Website: http://www.vitrumsignum.com
Directors: D. Alexander Smith (Prop)
No.of Employees: 1 - 10 **Product Groups:** 40, 48

Diffusion Systems Ltd
43 Rosebank Road, London, W7 2EW
Tel: 020-8579 5231 **Fax:** 020-8566 1524
E-mail: sales@diffusion-systems.com
Website: http://www.diffusion-systems.com
Directors: W. Jones (MD)
Immediate Holding Company: DIFFUSION SYSTEMS LIMITED
Registration no: 01193966 **Date established:** 1974
Turnover: Up to £250,000 **No.of Employees:** 11 - 20 **Product Groups:** 38

Date of Accounts	Nov 11	Nov 10	Nov 09
Sales Turnover	270	191	170
Pre Tax Profit/Loss	70	34	35
Working Capital	15	-41	-46
Fixed Assets	318	319	322
Current Assets	106	57	44
Current Liabilities	53	67	11

Digital Applications International Ltd
Axtell House 24 Warwick Street, London, W1B 5NQ
Tel: 020-7292 7500 **Fax:** 020-7439 2077
E-mail: enquiries@dai.co.uk
Website: http://www.dai.co.uk
Directors: A. Kishiel (Ch), T. Kisiel (Fin)
Immediate Holding Company: DIGITAL APPLICATIONS INTERNATIONAL LIMITED
Registration no: 01008089 **Date established:** 1971
Turnover: £10m - £20m **No.of Employees:** 11 - 20 **Product Groups:** 42, 44, 45, 80, 84

Date of Accounts	Nov 11	Nov 10	Nov 09
Sales Turnover	16m	12m	13m
Pre Tax Profit/Loss	3m	2m	2m
Working Capital	8m	6m	8m
Fixed Assets	6m	6m	4m
Current Assets	11m	8m	11m
Current Liabilities	3m	2m	3m

Dimension Data Holdings Ltd
Sleet Place House 2 Sleet Place, London, EC4M 7RT
Tel: 020-7651 7000 **Fax:** 020-7651 7001
E-mail: info@uk.didata.com
Website: http://www.dimensiondata.com
Directors: P. Harrison (Dir), J. Duck (Fin)
Ultimate Holding Company: NIPPON TELEGRAPH & TELEPHONE CORP (JAPAN
Immediate Holding Company: DIMENSION DATA NETWORK SERVICES LIMITED
Registration no: 01505004 **Date established:** 1980
Turnover: £125m - £250m **No.of Employees:** 101 - 250
Product Groups: 44

Date of Accounts	Sep 11	Sep 10	Sep 09
Sales Turnover	162m	179m	156m
Pre Tax Profit/Loss	-7m	7m	-10m
Working Capital	15m	9m	13m
Fixed Assets	5m	16m	13m
Current Assets	71m	72m	68m
Current Liabilities	34m	40m	32m

Dineshco Textiles Ltd
134-136 Commercial Road, London, E1 1NL
Tel: 020-7480 6101 **Fax:** 020-7480 5752
E-mail: dtluk@btinternet.com
Directors: S. Agarwal (Dir)
Immediate Holding Company: DINESHCO TEXTILES LIMITED
Registration no: 02071362 **VAT No.:** GB 447 1245 57
Date established: 1986 **No.of Employees:** 1 - 10 **Product Groups:** 61

Date of Accounts	Jun 11	Jun 10	Jun 09
Working Capital	1m	933	773
Fixed Assets	28	32	37
Current Assets	2m	2m	1m
Current Liabilities	N/A	196	N/A

Direct Lift Services Ltd
21 Redstart Close, London, E6 5XB
Tel: 020-7473 5979 **Fax:** 020-7473 5989
E-mail: sales@directlift.com
Website: http://www.directliftservices.co.uk
Directors: A. Aviss (MD), P. Owen (Fin)
Immediate Holding Company: DIRECT LIFT SERVICES LIMITED
Registration no: 03423154 **Date established:** 1997
No.of Employees: 1 - 10 **Product Groups:** 35, 39, 45

Date of Accounts	Aug 11	Aug 10	Aug 09
Working Capital	3	6	55
Fixed Assets	3	1	3
Current Assets	148	148	159
Current Liabilities	84	N/A	N/A

The Disney Store Ltd
3 Queen Caroline Street, London, W6 9PE
Tel: 020-8222 1000 **Fax:** 020-8222 2795
Website: http://www.disney.co.uk
Directors: M. Reed (Dir)
Ultimate Holding Company: THE WALT DISNEY COMPANY (USA)
Immediate Holding Company: THE DISNEY STORE LIMITED
Registration no: 02523767 **Date established:** 1990
Turnover: £75m - £125m **No.of Employees:** 1 - 10 **Product Groups:** 81, 89

Date of Accounts	Sep 08	Oct 09	Oct 10
Sales Turnover	100m	100m	112m
Pre Tax Profit/Loss	3m	-11m	-2m
Working Capital	-10m	1m	-1m
Fixed Assets	13m	14m	19m
Current Assets	45m	50m	54m
Current Liabilities	13m	17m	17m

Display Graphics
Block J Unit 12 Tower Bridge Business Complex 100 Clements Road, London, SE16 4DG
Tel: 020-7231 8881 **Fax:** 020-7231 0025
E-mail: terry@display-graphics.co.uk
Website: http://www.display-graphics.co.uk
Directors: T. Greenwood (MD), T. Greenwood (Prop), T. Butterley (Ptnr)
Immediate Holding Company: XLNT RESULTS LIMITED
Registration no: 04436125 **Date established:** 2004
Turnover: £250,000 - £500,000 **No.of Employees:** 1 - 10
Product Groups: 23, 25, 26, 27, 28, 81

Diytravel Co UK Ltd
35 Kingsland Road, London, E2 8AA
Tel: 020-7183 7183
E-mail: ben@diytravel.co.uk
Website: http://www.diytravel.co.uk
Directors: B. Jackson (Dir)
Immediate Holding Company: DIY TRAVEL LIMITED
Registration no: 05201583 **Date established:** 2004
No.of Employees: 1 - 10 **Product Groups:** 69

Date of Accounts	Sep 11	Sep 10	Sep 09
Working Capital	-16	-18	-21
Fixed Assets	3	5	6
Current Assets	15	18	25

Docdata Ltd
4th Floor 20 Margaret Street, London, W1W8RS
Tel: 020-7580 2880 **Fax:** 020-7580 2926
E-mail: sales@docdatacommerce.co.uk
Website: http://www.docdata.co.uk
Bank(s): National Westminster Bank Plc
Directors: M. Von Geusau (Dir), A. Pitt (Fin), S. Toms (MD)
Managers: M. Tatman (Mktg Serv Mgr)
Ultimate Holding Company: DOCDATA NV (NETHERLANDS)
Immediate Holding Company: Ablex Audio Video Ltd
Registration no: 03020801 **VAT No.:** GB 650 9293 25
Date established: 1995 **Turnover:** £250,000 - £500,000
No.of Employees: 101 - 250 **Product Groups:** 44

Docklands Light Railway Ltd
PO Box 154, London, E14 0DX
Tel: 020-7363 9898 **Fax:** 020-7363 9708
E-mail: betty.waight@dlr.tfl.gov.uk
Website: http://www.dlr.co.uk
Bank(s): HSBC Bank plc
Managers: B. Waight (Sales Admin)
Ultimate Holding Company: TRANSPORT TRADING LIMITED
Immediate Holding Company: DOCKLANDS LIGHT RAILWAY LIMITED
Registration no: 02052677 **VAT No.:** GB 756 2770 08
Date established: 1986 **Turnover:** £75m - £125m
No.of Employees: 21 - 50 **Product Groups:** 39

Date of Accounts	Mar 12	Mar 11	Mar 10
Sales Turnover	104m	89m	80m
Pre Tax Profit/Loss	N/A	-616	N/A
Working Capital	-60m	-70m	-64m
Fixed Assets	1561m	1501m	1488m
Current Assets	9m	7m	32m
Current Liabilities	54m	49m	77m

Doctorcall
121 Harley Street, London, W1G 6AX
Tel: 08442-570345 **Fax:** 020-7589 5862
E-mail: info@doctorcall.co.uk
Website: http://www.doctorcall.co.uk
Directors: M. Edmondson (Fin)
Managers: C. Levinson
Immediate Holding Company: DOCTORCALL LIMITED
Registration no: 02352745 **Date established:** 1989
Turnover: £500,000 - £1m **No.of Employees:** 11 - 20 **Product Groups:** 88

Date of Accounts	Mar 11	Mar 10	Mar 09
Working Capital	87	121	33
Fixed Assets	24	44	52
Current Assets	599	642	453

Document S O S
9 Cambridge Street, London, SW1V 4PP
Tel: 020-7233 6006 **Fax:** 020-7233 6007
E-mail: help@documentsos.com
Website: http://www.documentsos.com
Managers: F. Francis (Sales Admin)
Immediate Holding Company: DOCUMENT SOS LIMITED
Registration no: 03350479 **Date established:** 1997
No.of Employees: 1 - 10 **Product Groups:** 54

Date of Accounts	Apr 11	Apr 10	Apr 09
Working Capital	289	300	345
Fixed Assets	6	6	8
Current Assets	310	329	408

Dod's Parliamentry Communications Ltd
Westminster Tower 3 Albert Embankment, London, SE1 7SP
Tel: 020-7091 7500 **Fax:** 020-7091 7505
E-mail: gerry.murray@dods.co.uk
Website: http://www.dods.co.uk
Bank(s): Lloyds
Directors: G. Murray (Grp Chief Exec), P. Currie (I.T. Dir), R. Hutchinson (MD), M. Farmery (Publishing)
Managers: G. Murray, J. Colquhoun (Mktg Serv Mgr), M. Beck (Sales Prom Mgr), R. Joyce (Publishing)
Ultimate Holding Company: SOLVALUB HOLDING AG (LIECHTENSTEIN)
Immediate Holding Company: SIP LIMITED
Registration no: 02185735 **Date established:** 1987
Turnover: £50m - £75m **No.of Employees:** 101 - 250 **Product Groups:** 28

M Doogan
5 Stadium Street, London, SW10 0PU
Tel: 020-7795 2233
Directors: M. Doogan (Ptnr), M. Doogan (Prop)
Date established: 1998 **No.of Employees:** 1 - 10 **Product Groups:** 35

Dora Wirth Languages Ltd
No2 32 Caxton Road, London, W12 8AJ
Tel: 020-7229 4552 **Fax:** 020-7727 0744
E-mail: info@dwlanguages.com
Website: http://www.dwlanguages.com
Directors: L. Wirth (Co Sec), S. Wirth (MD)
Immediate Holding Company: DORA WIRTH (LANGUAGES) LIMITED
Registration no: 00811383 **Date established:** 1964
Turnover: £500,000 - £1m **No.of Employees:** 1 - 10 **Product Groups:** 80

Date of Accounts	Sep 11	Sep 10	Sep 09
Working Capital	66	47	54
Fixed Assets	30	19	26
Current Assets	230	183	146

Double Gee Hair Fashions Ltd
Unit 12 Trojan Industrial Estate Cobbold Road, London, NW10 7ST
Tel: 020-8459 2046 **Fax:** 020-8459 0320
E-mail: doublegee35@aol.com
Directors: R. Kumar Gupta (Prop)
Immediate Holding Company: DOUBLE GEE HAIR FASHIONS LIMITED
Registration no: 00853073 **VAT No.:** GB 226 6506 66
Date established: 1965 **Turnover:** £500,000 - £1m
No.of Employees: 1 - 10 **Product Groups:** 23, 49, 63, 66

Date of Accounts	Jun 11	Jun 10	Jun 09
Working Capital	200	214	196
Fixed Assets	16	22	30
Current Assets	460	467	466

Dowding & Mills Southern Ltd
24-26 White Post Lane, London, E9 5EP
Tel: 020-8985 8351 **Fax:** 020-8985 9615
E-mail: lee.allen@dowdingandmills.com
Website: http://www.dowdingandmills.com
Directors: I. Harper (Pers)
Managers: L. Allen (Chief Mgr)
Ultimate Holding Company: SULZER AG (SWITZERLAND)
Immediate Holding Company: DOWDING & MILLS (SOUTHERN) LIMITED
Registration no: 00914189 **Date established:** 1967
No.of Employees: 21 - 50 **Product Groups:** 37, 44, 45, 48, 84, 85

Date of Accounts	Jun 10
Working Capital	5
Current Assets	5

Drake Medox Nursing
20 Regent Street, London, SW1Y 4PH
Tel: 0800-111 4335 **Fax:** 020-7495 1522
E-mail: reception@drakeintl.co.uk
Website: http://www.drakemedoxnursing.co.uk
Managers: M. Murphy (Mgr)
Ultimate Holding Company: CALADENA CORPORATION LTD(BAHAMAS)
Immediate Holding Company: DRAKE INTERNATIONAL LIMITED
Registration no: 01156185 **VAT No.:** GB 238 4834 40
Date established: 1974 **Turnover:** £20m - £50m **No.of Employees:** 1 - 10
Product Groups: 80

Date of Accounts	Sep 11	Sep 10	Sep 09
Sales Turnover	28m	26m	23m
Pre Tax Profit/Loss	-183	81	-2m
Working Capital	-14m	-14m	-14m
Fixed Assets	27	46	59
Current Assets	5m	4m	4m
Current Liabilities	2m	2m	1m

The Draycott Hotel
22-26 Cadogan Gardens, London, SW3 2RP
Tel: 020-7730 6466 **Fax:** 020-7730 0236
E-mail: sales@clivedentownhouse.co.uk
Website: http://www.draycotthotel.com
Managers: S. Smith (Personnel), P. Hawes (Sales & Mktg Mg), J. Hannah (Chief Mgr), A. Smith
Immediate Holding Company: THE DRAYCOTT HOTEL LLP
Registration no: OC303901 **Date established:** 2003
No.of Employees: 21 - 50 **Product Groups:** 69

Date of Accounts	Apr 12	Apr 11	Apr 10
Working Capital	-682	272	-166
Fixed Assets	7m	7m	7m
Current Assets	974	964	495

Dream Pharmaceuticals
176 Horn Lane, London, W3 6PJ
Tel: 020-8992 7000 **Fax:** 020-8992 7001
E-mail: info@dreampharma.com
Website: http://www.dreampharma.com
Directors: M. Alavi (Prop), F. Alavi (Co Sec)
Immediate Holding Company: DREAM PHARMA LTD
Registration no: 04637884 **Date established:** 2003
Turnover: £500,000 - £1m **No.of Employees:** 21 - 50 **Product Groups:** 31

Date of Accounts	Jan 12	Jan 11	Jan 10
Sales Turnover	N/A	N/A	844
Pre Tax Profit/Loss	N/A	N/A	94
Working Capital	521	413	337
Fixed Assets	3	7	9
Current Assets	581	413	363
Current Liabilities	52	N/A	21

Druces LLP
Salisbury House London Wall, London, EC2M 5PS
Tel: 020-7638 9271 **Fax:** 020-7628 7525
E-mail: info@druces.com
Website: http://www.druces.com
Directors: R. Campbell (Ch)
Immediate Holding Company: DRUCES & ATTLEE LIMITED
Registration no: 02191312 **Date established:** 1987
No.of Employees: 51 - 100 **Product Groups:** 80

Drum Distribution Services(UK) Ltd
Unit 3 Charles Street Silvertown, London, E16 2BY
Tel: 020-7511 2785 **Fax:** 020-7474 3975
E-mail: info@drumdistributionservicesltd.co.uk
Website: http://www.drumdistributionservicesltd.co.uk
Directors: R. O'neill (Dir)
Immediate Holding Company: The Drum Group Ltd
Registration no: 02094099 **Date established:** 2008
No.of Employees: 21 - 50 **Product Groups:** 35, 36, 45

Date of Accounts	Apr 10	Apr 09
Working Capital	-0	-3
Fixed Assets	19	24
Current Assets	82	90

Dryer & Hoffman Ltd
4 Lockwood Industrial Park Mill Mead Road, London, N17 9QP
Tel: 020-8365 1414 **Fax:** 020-8365 1457
E-mail: info@dryerandhoffmanltd.com
Website: http://www.dryerandhoffmanltd.com
Directors: M. Hoffman (Dir)
Immediate Holding Company: DRYER & HOFFMAN LIMITED
Registration no: 00530683 **VAT No.:** GB 232 2858 72
Date established: 1954 **Turnover:** £2m - £5m **No.of Employees:** 1 - 10
Product Groups: 63

Date of Accounts	Jan 12	Jan 11	Jan 10
Working Capital	210	282	227
Fixed Assets	785	683	703
Current Assets	639	770	791

Gerald Duckworth & Company Ltd
Cowcross Street, London, EC1M 6BF
Tel: 020-7490 7300 **Fax:** 020-7490 0080
E-mail: info@duckworth-publishers.co.uk
Website: http://www.ducknet.co.uk
Directors: D. Blake (Fin)
Managers: C. Halsey
Immediate Holding Company: GERALD DUCKWORTH & COMPANY LIMITED
Registration no: 04744342 **VAT No.:** GB 232 5658 65
Date established: 2003 **Turnover:** £1m - £2m **No.of Employees:** 1 - 10
Product Groups: 28, 64, 80

Date of Accounts	Dec 11	Dec 10	Dec 09
Sales Turnover	3m	1m	1m
Pre Tax Profit/Loss	-53	1m	70
Working Capital	61	1m	295
Fixed Assets	N/A	N/A	1
Current Assets	669	2m	937
Current Liabilities	476	478	505

Duncan Lawrie Ltd
1 Hobart Place, London, SW1W 0HU
Tel: 020-7245 1234 **Fax:** 020-7245 6276
E-mail: london@duncanlawrie.com
Website: http://www.duncanlawrie.com
Directors: M. Parden (MD), M. Pardon (MD)
Ultimate Holding Company: DUNCAN LAWRIE ASSET MANAGEMENT LIMITED
Immediate Holding Company: DOUGLAS DEAKIN YOUNG (TRUSTEE CORPORATION) LIMITED
Registration no: 01880585 **Date established:** 1985 **Turnover:** £2m - £5m
No.of Employees: 51 - 100 **Product Groups:** 82

Date of Accounts	Dec 10	Dec 09	Dec 07
Sales Turnover	N/A	2m	N/A
Pre Tax Profit/Loss	377	-818	2m
Working Capital	N/A	-110m	N/A
Fixed Assets	38m	133m	35m
Current Assets	98m	2m	246m
Current Liabilities	108m	112m	256m

Durmetal Ltd
Flat 13 Nash House Lupus Street, London, SW1V 3HQ
Tel: 020-7930 1508 **Fax:** 020-7931 0340
E-mail: sales@durmetal.com
Website: http://www.durmetal-uk.com
Directors: J. Durmetal (MD)
Immediate Holding Company: DURMETAL LIMITED
Registration no: 01873121 **Date established:** 1984
No.of Employees: 1 - 10 **Product Groups:** 46

Date of Accounts	Dec 11	Dec 10	Dec 09
Working Capital	-1m	-955	-906
Fixed Assets	1	2	2
Current Assets	58	283	307

Dyas
61 The Broadway, London, SW19 1QD
Tel: 020-8542 8518
Website: http://www.robertdyas.co.uk
Managers: J. Wright (Mgr), M. Arkwright (Mgr), D. Cole (Mgr)
No.of Employees: 1 - 10 **Product Groups:** 26, 35

E A Gibson Ship Brokers
16-20 Ely Place, London, EC1P 1HP
Tel: 020-7667 1000 **Fax:** 020-7831 8762
E-mail: tanker@eagibson.co.uk
Website: http://www.gibson.co.uk
Bank(s): Barclays
Directors: N. Richardson (MD)
Ultimate Holding Company: HUNTING PLC
Immediate Holding Company: E.A. GIBSON SHIPPING SERVICES LIMITED
Registration no: 02379540 **VAT No.:** GB 243 6918 47
Date established: 1989 **Turnover:** £20m - £50m
No.of Employees: 101 - 250 **Product Groups:** 68

E A Higginson & Co. Ltd
Unit 1 Carlisle Road, London, NW9 0HD
Tel: 020-8200 4848 **Fax:** 020-8200 8249
E-mail: sales@higginson.co.uk
Website: http://www.higginson.co.uk
Directors: E. Higginson (Prop)
Immediate Holding Company: E.A.HIGGINSON & CO LIMITED
Registration no: 00253389 **Date established:** 1931
No.of Employees: 21 - 50 **Product Groups:** 25, 35, 66

Date of Accounts	Apr 11	Apr 10	Apr 09
Working Capital	-103	8	120
Fixed Assets	124	109	66
Current Assets	121	165	336

E C A International
New Brook Building 16 Great Queen Street, London, WC2B 5DG
Tel: 020-7351 5000 **Fax:** 020-7351 9396
E-mail: alexander.graham@eca-international.com
Website: http://www.eca-international.com
Bank(s): National Westminster Bank Plc
Directors: A. Graham (Dir), R. Major (Admin)
Managers: F. Brazzill, S. Winterbottom (Mgr)
Ultimate Holding Company: EMPLOYMENT CONDITIONS ABROAD LIMITED
Immediate Holding Company: E.C.A. LIMITED
Registration no: 01529326 **Date established:** 1980 **Turnover:** £2m - £5m
No.of Employees: 51 - 100 **Product Groups:** 80, 82, 87

E C G D
Harbour Exchange Square, London, E14 9GE
Tel: 020-7512 7000 **Fax:** 020-7512 7649
E-mail: ian.dykstra@ecgd.gsi.gov.uk
Website: http://www.ecgd.gov.uk
Bank(s): Bank of England
Managers: I. Dykstra (Sales Admin)
Immediate Holding Company: M.H. TURNER (DEVELOPMENTS) LIMITED
Registration no: 05215929 **Date established:** 1987
Turnover: £50m - £75m **No.of Employees:** 101 - 250 **Product Groups:** 82

Date of Accounts	Apr 91	Apr 90	Apr 89
Current Assets	318	382	394

E C Harris llp
34 York Way, London, N1 9AB
Tel: 020-7812 2000 **Fax:** 020-7812 2001
E-mail: newbusiness@echarris.com
Website: http://www.echarris.com
Directors: G. Hill (Prop)
Ultimate Holding Company: ARCADIS NV (NETHERLANDS)
Immediate Holding Company: EC HARRIS GROUP LIMITED
Registration no: 02950545 **Date established:** 1994 **Turnover:** £2m - £5m
No.of Employees: 501 - 1000 **Product Groups:** 80

Date of Accounts	Dec 11	Apr 11	Apr 10
Pre Tax Profit/Loss	3	4	-8
Working Capital	448	445	441
Fixed Assets	6	6	7
Current Assets	9m	7m	13m
Current Liabilities	6	6	6

E C I A
Broadway House Tothill Street, London, SW1H 9NS
Tel: 020-7799 2000 **Fax:** 020-7233 1930
E-mail: michaelhockey@ecia.co.uk
Website: http://www.ecia.co.uk
Bank(s): Llyods TSB
Directors: M. Hockey (MD)
Immediate Holding Company: E.C.I.A. (INSURANCE SERVICES) LIMITED
Registration no: 04333180 **VAT No.:** GB 340 9423 69
Date established: 2001 **No.of Employees:** 11 - 20 **Product Groups:** 87

Date of Accounts	Dec 08	Dec 07	Dec 06
Working Capital	-1	-1	-1
Current Liabilities	1	1	1

E D F Energy
40 Grosvenor Place, London, SW1X 7EN
Tel: 020-7242 9050 **Fax:** 020-7331 3455
E-mail: vincent.derivaz@seeboardenergy.com
Website: http://www.edfenergy.com
Directors: V. De Rivaz (Grp Chief Exec)
Ultimate Holding Company: EDF ENERGIES NOUVELLES S.A (FRANCE)
Immediate Holding Company: EDF EN UK LIMITED
Registration no: 03606582 **VAT No.:** GB 523 0412 02
Date established: 1998 **Turnover:** £2m - £5m
No.of Employees: 1001 - 1500 **Product Groups:** 18

E Klein & Co.
122-126 Westferry Road, London, E14 3SG
Tel: 020-7987 1171 **Fax:** 020-7538 0477
Website: http://www.eklein.co.uk
Bank(s): Barclays Bank
Directors: J. Enright (Prop)
Immediate Holding Company: E.KLEIN LIMITED
Registration no: 00630760 **VAT No.:** GB 248 5853 24
Date established: 1959 **Turnover:** £2m - £5m **No.of Employees:** 11 - 20
Product Groups: 61

Date of Accounts	Sep 11	Sep 10	Sep 08
Working Capital	-0	-0	N/A

E M C Advertising Gifts Ltd
Derwent House 1064 High Road, London, N20 0YY
Tel: 08453-451064 **Fax:** 08453-451065
E-mail: simonkay@emcadgifts.co.uk
Website: http://www.emcadgifts.co.uk
Bank(s): National Westminster Bank Plc
Directors: S. Kay (MD), S. Friend (Co Sec)
Managers: N. Thomas (Personnel)
Immediate Holding Company: EMC ADVERTISING GIFTS LTD
Registration no: 07096477 **VAT No.:** GB 229 4545 48
Date established: 2009 **Turnover:** £2m - £5m **No.of Employees:** 11 - 20
Product Groups: 20, 21, 22, 23, 24, 25, 27, 28, 29, 30, 33, 35, 36, 37, 38, 43, 44, 49, 61, 62, 63, 64, 65, 67, 80, 81

Date of Accounts	Dec 11	Dec 10
Working Capital	58	121
Fixed Assets	97	107
Current Assets	245	326

E N I UK Ltd
10 Ebury Bridge Road, London, SW1W 8PZ
Tel: 020-7344 6000 **Fax:** 020-7344 6044
E-mail: daragh.fagan@eni-india.com
Website: http://www.eni.com
Directors: D. Fagan (Co Sec)
Immediate Holding Company: ENI UK LIMITED
Registration no: 00862823 **Date established:** 1965
Turnover: £500m - £1,000m **No.of Employees:** 101 - 250
Product Groups: 51

Date of Accounts	Dec 11	Dec 10	Dec 09
Sales Turnover	686m	536m	3090m
Pre Tax Profit/Loss	629m	556m	297m
Working Capital	5m	100m	71m
Fixed Assets	1418m	945m	1028m
Current Assets	624m	644m	654m
Current Liabilities	541m	538m	434m

E R Electrical
139 Mitcham Road, London, SW17 9PE
Tel: 020-8672 2625 **Fax:** 020-8672 2625
Website: http://www.erelectrical.co.uk
Directors: A. Hussain (Prop)
Immediate Holding Company: UK MEAL BOX LTD
Date established: 2011 **No.of Employees:** 1 - 10 **Product Groups:** 37, 67

E X X Projects
72 Rivington Street, London, EC2A 3AY
Tel: 020-7684 8200 **Fax:** 0845-630 1282
E-mail: exx@plax.co.uk
Website: http://www.plax.co.uk
Directors: G. Kang (Ptnr), C. Morgan (Ptnr)
Immediate Holding Company: YCN LTD
Registration no: 03871034 **VAT No.:** GB 340 2971 73
Date established: 1999 **Turnover:** Up to £250,000
No.of Employees: 1 - 10 **Product Groups:** 22, 30, 49

E Z Builders
Frithville Gardens, London, W12 7JN
Tel: 07905-230243
E-mail: info@ezbuilders.co.uk
Website: http://www.ezbuilders.co.uk
Directors: P. Petkov (MD)
Immediate Holding Company: EZ BUILDERS UK LIMITED
Registration no: 05806272 **Date established:** 2006
No.of Employees: 11 - 20 **Product Groups:** 25, 52

Date of Accounts	May 11	May 10	May 09
Working Capital	-19	-18	-18
Fixed Assets	N/A	N/A	1
Current Assets	1	2	2

Eagle Security Solutions Ltd
162 Trafalgar Road, London, SE10 9TZ
Tel: 020-8853 0580 **Fax:** 020-8854 9701
E-mail: info@eaglesecuritysolutions.co.uk
Website: http://www.eaglesecuritysolutions.co.uk
Managers: D. Agunbiade (Mgr)
Immediate Holding Company: EAGLE SECURITY SOLUTIONS LIMITED
Registration no: 04395406 **Date established:** 2002
No.of Employees: 1 - 10 **Product Groups:** 36, 37, 38, 40, 67, 81

Date of Accounts	Sep 11	Sep 10	Sep 09
Working Capital	34	36	45
Fixed Assets	42	41	48
Current Assets	57	60	83

Earlsfield Power Tools Ltd
533 Garratt Lane, London, SW18 4SR
Tel: 020-8879 0070 **Fax:** 020-8944 1926
E-mail: info@earlsfieldpowertools.co.uk
Website: http://www.earlsfieldpowertools.co.uk
Directors: W. Whitehouse (Fin), N. Bailey (MD)
Immediate Holding Company: EARLSFIELD POWER TOOLS LIMITED
Registration no: 03027088 **Date established:** 1995
No.of Employees: 1 - 10 **Product Groups:** 37

Date of Accounts	Apr 11	Apr 10	Apr 09
Working Capital	32	4	14
Fixed Assets	7	9	11
Current Assets	111	64	82

Ease Electrical Goods
Unit 2 1000 North Circular Road, London, NW2 7JP
Tel: 020-8452 1203 **Fax:** 020-8452 7819
E-mail: sales@ease.ltd.uk
Website: http://www.ease.ltd.uk
Managers: L. Dai (Mgr), L. DAI (Nat Sales Mgr)
Immediate Holding Company: E A S E LTD
Registration no: 03200056 **Date established:** 1996 **Turnover:** £1m - £2m
No.of Employees: 1 - 10 **Product Groups:** 30, 33, 35, 36, 37, 39, 40

Date of Accounts	Sep 10	Sep 09	Sep 08
Working Capital	159	169	202
Fixed Assets	10	13	24
Current Assets	584	572	748

East London School Of English
154-170 Cannon St Road, London, E1 2LH
Tel: 020-7265 8868 **Fax:** 020-7790 6696
E-mail: info@elsenglish.com
Website: http://www.elsenglish.com
Directors: M. Hues (Head)
Registration no: 06370709 **Date established:** 2007
Turnover: £250,000 - £500,000 **No.of Employees:** 11 - 20
Product Groups: 86

Easyart Ltd
32 Dover Street, London, W1X 3RA
Tel: 01825-891771 **Fax:** 020-7843 6871
E-mail: customercare@easyart.com
Website: http://www.easyart.com
Bank(s): HSBC, Wandsworth
Directors: S. Mathews (Grp Chief Exec)
Ultimate Holding Company: Easyart Holdings Ltd
Registration no: 03850720 **VAT No.:** GB 744 0456 43
Date established: 2002 **Turnover:** £2m - £5m **No.of Employees:** 11 - 20
Product Groups: 25, 28, 49, 64, 65, 77, 83, 89

Date of Accounts	Dec 07	Dec 06	Dec 05
Working Capital	44	21	-11
Fixed Assets	6	7	4
Current Assets	376	314	233
Current Liabilities	332	293	243
Total Share Capital	11	11	11

Economic Research & Advisory Services Ltd
4-6 Canfield Place, London, NW6 3BT
Tel: 020-7625 1455 **Fax:** 020-7625 1246
E-mail: info@erasuk.com
Website: http://www.erasuk.com
Directors: E. Fahy (Fin)
Immediate Holding Company: ECONOMIC RESEARCH AND ADVISORY SERVICES LTD
Registration no: 02101259 **VAT No.:** GB 454 2102 85
Date established: 1987 **Turnover:** £500,000 - £1m
No.of Employees: 1 - 10 **Product Groups:** 80

Date of Accounts	Jun 10	Jun 09	Jun 08
Working Capital	-2	-2	5
Fixed Assets	3	4	5
Current Assets	185	193	175

The Economist Overseas Holdings Ltd
25 St Jamess Street, London, SW1A 1HG
Tel: 020-7839 9104 **Fax:** 020-7839 2968
Website: http://www.economistshop.com
Directors: S. Abesser (Co Sec), N. Cadbury (Ch), J. Little (Pers), H. Alexander (MD), C. Stibbs (Dir), C. Collins (Dir), Y. Osman (Mkt Research), D. Hanger (Sales)
Managers: W. Emmott (Mgr)
Ultimate Holding Company: 00236383
Immediate Holding Company: THE ECONOMIST OVERSEAS (HOLDINGS) LIMITED
Registration no: 02147173 **VAT No.:** GB 340 4368 76
Date established: 1987 **Turnover:** £75m - £125m
No.of Employees: 1 - 10 **Product Groups:** 28

Ed - Solutions Direct Ltd
PO Box 36979, London, SE6 4WD
Tel: 020-8690 6995 **Fax:** 020-8690 8990
E-mail: info@ed-solutionsdirect.com
Website: http://www.ed-solutionsdirect.com
Directors: R. Anderson (MD), L. Anderson (Fin)
Immediate Holding Company: ED - SOLUTIONS DIRECT LTD
Registration no: 04807827 **Date established:** 2003
Turnover: Up to £250,000 **No.of Employees:** 1 - 10 **Product Groups:** 28

Date of Accounts	Aug 11	Aug 10	Aug 09
Working Capital	88	86	72
Current Assets	90	112	93

Edelman P R
Southside 105 Victoria Street, London, SW1E 6QT
Tel: 01273-722544 **Fax:** 020-3047 2507
E-mail: contactus@edelman.co.uk
Website: http://www.edelman.co.uk
Directors: J. Grassie (Tech Serv)
Immediate Holding Company: EDELMAN ASSOCIATES LIMITED
Registration no: 01720297 **VAT No.:** GB 238 6974 14
Date established: 1983 **Turnover:** £20m - £50m **No.of Employees:** 1 - 10
Product Groups: 81

Eden Plastics & Media Ltd
6 Prince Georges Road, London, SW19 2PX
Tel: 020-8646 5556 **Fax:** 020-8640 0475
E-mail: general@edenplastics.co.uk
Website: http://www.edenplastics.co.uk
Directors: J. Hookins (Prop)
Immediate Holding Company: EDEN PLASTICS & MEDIA LIMITED
Registration no: 02509705 **VAT No.:** GB 645 7300 41
Date established: 1990 **Turnover:** £1m - £2m **No.of Employees:** 1 - 10
Product Groups: 30

Date of Accounts	Jun 11	Jun 10	Jun 09
Working Capital	108	74	75
Fixed Assets	620	694	620
Current Assets	603	610	569

Egyptair
296 Regent Street, London, W1B 3PH
Tel: 020-7580 5477 **Fax:** 020-7637 4328
E-mail: habibaidrool@egyptair.com
Website: http://www.egyptair.com
Bank(s): Lloyds TSB Bank plc
Directors: H. Galal (Ch & MD), S. Mohamed (I.T. Dir)
Managers: E. Alsina (Sales Prom Mgr), H. Aidrool (Mgr), M. Hafny (Mktg Serv Mgr), M. Hamed (Chief Mgr), R. L'Aimable (Sales Prom Mgr)
Immediate Holding Company: EGYPT AIR
Registration no: FC005051 **VAT No.:** GB 233 6138 80
Date established: 1961 **Turnover:** Over £1,000m
No.of Employees: 11 - 20 **Product Groups:** 75

Elan Computing Ltd
Elan House 5-11 Fetter Lane, London, EC4A 1QX
Tel: 020-7830 1300 **Fax:** 020-7830 1333
E-mail: patricia.asemota@elanit.co.uk
Website: http://www.elan.co.uk
Directors: S. Burt (Sales), G. Nikodem (Co Sec), P. Asemota (Dir)
Managers: D. Vaughn (Tech Serv Mgr), R. Betson (Mktg Serv Mgr), S. Finley (Comptroller)
Ultimate Holding Company: MANPOWER INC (USA)
Immediate Holding Company: EXPERIS LIMITED
Registration no: 02114287 **Date established:** 1987
Turnover: £250m - £500m **No.of Employees:** 251 - 500
Product Groups: 80

Date of Accounts	Dec 11	Dec 10	Dec 09
Sales Turnover	325m	330m	341m
Pre Tax Profit/Loss	521	297	-2m
Working Capital	28m	27m	28m
Fixed Assets	3m	3m	2m
Current Assets	88m	104m	73m
Current Liabilities	6m	12m	8m

Eland Cables
Unit 120 Highgate Studio 53-79 Highgate Road, London, NW5 1TL
Tel: 020-7241 8787 **Fax:** 020-7241 8700
E-mail: sales@eland.co.uk
Website: http://www.eland.co.uk
Directors: J. Pelland (Fin)
Managers: K. Chapman (Comm), J. Burke, S. Machray (Mktg Serv Mgr)
Ultimate Holding Company: ELAND ELECTRICAL LIMITED
Immediate Holding Company: ELAND CABLES LIMITED
Registration no: 01229226 **Date established:** 1975
Turnover: £20m - £50m **No.of Employees:** 51 - 100 **Product Groups:** 23, 30, 32, 34, 35, 36, 37, 38, 39, 40, 41, 42, 44, 47, 48, 49, 63, 66, 67, 68

Date of Accounts	Dec 11	Dec 10	Dec 09
Sales Turnover	52m	45m	36m
Pre Tax Profit/Loss	1m	998	797
Working Capital	6m	6m	5m
Fixed Assets	3m	3m	3m
Current Assets	20m	20m	16m
Current Liabilities	2m	8m	5m

Elbee Traders
839 Harrow Road, London, NW10 5NH
Tel: 020-8969 9423 **Fax:** 020-8969 2611
E-mail: sales@elbee-traders.co.uk
Website: http://www.elbee-traders.co.uk
Directors: C. Gidoomal (Ptnr)
VAT No.: GB 228 2017 89 **Date established:** 1975
Turnover: Up to £250,000 **No.of Employees:** 1 - 10 **Product Groups:** 32, 49, 61, 65

Elborne Mitchell Solicitors
One America Square Crosswall, London, EC3N 2PR
Tel: 020-7320 9000 **Fax:** 020-7320 9111
E-mail: lawyers@elbornes.com
Website: http://www.elbornes.com
Directors: H. Vowles (Fin), H. Vowles (Fin), T. Brentnall (Snr Part)
Managers: J. Murray (I.T. Exec), V. Hinds (Personnel), V. Hinds (Personnel), R. Dinerstein (Tech Serv Mgr), B. Collins
Immediate Holding Company: ELBORNE MITCHELL LLP
Registration no: OC359822 **Date established:** 2010
Turnover: Up to £250,000 **No.of Employees:** 21 - 50 **Product Groups:** 80

Date of Accounts	Apr 12
Working Capital	970
Fixed Assets	27
Current Assets	2m

Elcorte Ingles London Ltd
43 Berners Street, London, W1T 3ND
Tel: 020-7580 6434 **Fax:** 020-7323 1562
E-mail: eci@london.es
Website: http://www.elcorteingleslondon.co.uk
Directors: D. Blanco (MD), D. Gonzalez (Dir), F. Lasaga (Dir), I. Alvarez (Dir)
Ultimate Holding Company: EL CORTE INGLES SA (SPAIN)
Immediate Holding Company: EL CORTE INGLES (LONDON) LIMITED
Registration no: 01174083 **VAT No.:** GB 241 0807 01
Date established: 1974 **Turnover:** £250,000 - £500,000
No.of Employees: 1 - 10 **Product Groups:** 61

Date of Accounts	Dec 07	Dec 06	Dec 05
Working Capital	147	143	142
Fixed Assets	N/A	2	N/A
Current Assets	165	162	168
Current Liabilities	19	19	26
Total Share Capital	50	50	50

Electrical Carbon UK Ltd
Reg'd Office: 788-790 Finchley Road, London, NW11 7TJ
Tel: 0114-2316454 **Fax:** 0114-2385464
E-mail: sales@ecarbonuk.com
Website: http://www.ecarbonuk.com
Directors: G. Brown (Sales)
Registration no: 7131928 **Date established:** 2010 **Turnover:**
No.of Employees: 1 - 10 **Product Groups:** 30, 33, 35, 37, 39

Electrician in London
Suite 596 28 Old Brompton Road, London, SW7 3SS
Tel: 0800-587 7035 **Fax:** 020-8373 0781
E-mail: electrician@electrician-in-london.co.uk
Website: http://www.electricianinlondon.co.uk
Directors: D. Gentle (Prop)
Immediate Holding Company: THE FLOWER COMPANY (UK) LTD
Date established: 2011 **No.of Employees:** 1 - 10 **Product Groups:** 37, 52, 84

Electrotex Sales Co.
86d Lillie Road, London, SW6 1TL
Tel: 020-7385 0836 **Fax:** 020-7381 8776
Directors: M. Iqbal (Prop)
No.of Employees: 1 - 10 **Product Groups:** 30, 37, 44, 52, 63

Elegant Patio Awnings Elegant Installations Ltd
2nd Floor 145-157 St John Street, London, EC1V 4PY
Tel: 020-7127 0005 **Fax:** 0871-7501963
E-mail: office@elegant-awnings.co.uk
Website: http://www.patio-awnings-uk.co.uk
Product Groups: 24, 35

Elite Tiles & Interiors Ltd
Elite House West Hendon Broadway, London, NW9 7BW
Tel: 020-8202 1806 **Fax:** 020-8202 8608
E-mail: info@elite-tiles.co.uk
Website: http://www.elite-tiles.co.uk
Directors: G. Weisz (MD), J. Myers (Pers)
Registration no: 01646306 **VAT No.:** GB 341 1493 82
Turnover: £2m - £5m **No.of Employees:** 21 - 50 **Product Groups:** 33, 49

Elizabeth Arden
87-91 Newman Street, London, W1T 3EY
Tel: 020-7574 2700 **Fax:** 020-7574 2727
E-mail: david.davies@elizabetharden.com
Website: http://www.elizabetharden.com
Directors: D. Davies (Dir)
Managers: M. McKellop (Tech Serv Mgr)
Immediate Holding Company: ELIZABETH ARDEN (UK) LTD
Registration no: 04126357 **Date established:** 2000
Turnover: £10m - £20m **No.of Employees:** 501 - 1000
Product Groups: 63

Date of Accounts	Jun 11	Jun 10	Jun 09
Sales Turnover	16m	15m	15m
Pre Tax Profit/Loss	685	638	808
Working Capital	2m	4m	3m
Fixed Assets	146	205	234
Current Assets	3m	5m	4m
Current Liabilities	1m	860	884

Elliot Leigh Property Management Ltd
Docklands Business Centre 10-16 Tiller Road, London, E14 8XP
Tel: 020-7000 3132 **Fax:** 020-7000 3142
E-mail: sales@etltd.co.uk
Website: http://www.elliotleigh.co.uk
Directors: E. Altman (Fin), L. Young (MD)
Immediate Holding Company: ELLIOT LEIGH PROPERTY MANAGEMENT LIMITED
Registration no: 04840441 **VAT No.:** GB 684 9854 57
Date established: 2003 **Turnover:** £500,000 - £1m
No.of Employees: 1 - 10 **Product Groups:** 12, 34, 35, 36, 48, 66

Date of Accounts	Sep 11	Sep 10	Sep 09
Working Capital	404	414	383
Fixed Assets	4m	4m	4m
Current Assets	1m	1m	1m

W A Ellis
174 Brompton Road, London, SW3 1HP
Tel: 020-7306 1600 **Fax:** 020-7589 8261
E-mail: lmorton@wa-ellis.co.uk
Website: http://www.waellis.co.uk
Directors: S. Smith (Co Sec), A. Coleman (Fin), L. Moreton (Snr Part), L. Morton (Snr Part)
Managers: C. Copland (Sales & Mktg Mg), K. Chong (Tech Serv Mgr), M. Doyle (Personnel)
Immediate Holding Company: W A ELLIS LLP
Registration no: OC321844 **Date established:** 2006
Turnover: £5m - £10m **No.of Employees:** 21 - 50 **Product Groups:** 40, 80, 82

Date of Accounts	Apr 11	Apr 10	Apr 09
Sales Turnover	6m	6m	5m
Pre Tax Profit/Loss	2m	2m	1m
Working Capital	2m	2m	3m
Fixed Assets	268	322	377
Current Assets	3m	3m	3m
Current Liabilities	634	681	434

Ellmax Electronics Ltd
Unit 29 Leyton Business Centre Etloe Road, London, E10 7BT
Tel: 020-8539 0136 **Fax:** 020-8539 7746
E-mail: ellmaxelec@aol.com
Website: http://www.ellmaxelec.com
Directors: E. Goodkin (MD), N. Kochan (Fin)
Immediate Holding Company: ELLMAX ELECTRONICS LIMITED
Registration no: 01714790 **VAT No.:** GB 371 0137 88
Date established: 1983 **Turnover:** £250,000 - £500,000
No.of Employees: 1 - 10 **Product Groups:** 28, 37

Date of Accounts	Mar 11	Mar 10	Mar 09
Working Capital	-5	3	-1
Fixed Assets	1	2	2
Current Assets	16	27	23

Elmcrest Diamond Drilling Ltd
4 Duncrievie Road, London, SE13 6TE
Tel: 020-8318 9923 **Fax:** 020-8318 1034
E-mail: office@elmcrest-diamond.co.uk
Website: http://www.elmcrest-diamond.co.uk
Directors: D. Royce (MD), P. Scott (MD)
Ultimate Holding Company: ELMCREST MANAGEMENT LIMITED
Immediate Holding Company: ELMCREST DIAMOND DRILLING LIMITED
Registration no: 01733014 **Date established:** 1983 **Turnover:** £2m - £5m
No.of Employees: 21 - 50 **Product Groups:** 36, 39, 45, 46, 47, 48, 51, 52, 66, 83

Date of Accounts	Jun 11	Jun 10	Jun 09
Working Capital	-24	1	1
Current Assets	1m	983	1m

Elmelin Ltd
1 Betts Mews, London, E17 8PQ
Tel: 020-8520 2248 **Fax:** 020-8521 2889
E-mail: info@elmelin.com
Website: http://www.elmelin.com
Bank(s): Bank of Scotland
Directors: S. Weiss (MD)
Managers: G. Watts (Works Gen Mgr)
Immediate Holding Company: ELMELIN LIMITED
Registration no: 01325770 **VAT No.:** GB 245 5656 44
Date established: 1977 **Turnover:** £1m - £2m **No.of Employees:** 11 - 20
Product Groups: 17, 30, 33, 37

Date of Accounts	Mar 12	Mar 11	Mar 10
Working Capital	1m	1m	593
Fixed Assets	13	8	10
Current Assets	2m	1m	808

Elsevier
32 Jamestown Road, London, NW1 7BY
Tel: 020-7424 4200 **Fax:** 020-7424 4431
E-mail: d.morton@elsevier.com
Website: http://www.elsevier.com
Directors: L. Lezenbroek (MD), S. Malik (Pers)
Managers: P. Warren (Fin Mgr)
Turnover: £2m - £5m **No.of Employees:** 101 - 250 **Product Groups:** 28, 64

Elsworth Sykes Ltd
75 Wells Street, London, W1T 3QH
Tel: 020-7580 5886 **Fax:** 020-7872 9547
E-mail: northern@esa-ltd.com
Website: http://www.esa-ltd.com
Bank(s): HSBC Bank plc
Directors: A. Roberts (Dir), C. Everitt (Dir), D. Collins (Dir), P. Little (Grp Chief Exec), R. Cranswick (Dir)
Ultimate Holding Company: ELSWORTH SYKES PARTNERSHIP LIMITED
Immediate Holding Company: ELSWORTH SYKES NORTHERN LIMITED
Registration no: 03145846 **Date established:** 1996
Turnover: Up to £250,000 **No.of Employees:** 21 - 50 **Product Groups:** 84

Eltham Welding Supplies Ltd
2-12 Parry Place, London, SE18 6AN
Tel: 020-8854 1226 **Fax:** 020-8854 2720
E-mail: sales.woolwich@elthamweldingsupplies.co.uk
Website: http://www.elthamweldingsupplies.co.uk
Directors: D. Simpson (MD), L. Simpson (Co Sec)
Immediate Holding Company: ELTHAM WELDING SUPPLIES LIMITED
Registration no: 02878440 **VAT No.:** GB 650 1442 74
Date established: 1993 **Turnover:** £2m - £5m **No.of Employees:** 11 - 20
Product Groups: 24, 30, 33, 34, 35, 36, 37, 38, 40, 46, 83

Date of Accounts	Dec 11	Dec 10	Dec 09
Working Capital	-13	-61	-69
Fixed Assets	401	412	451
Current Assets	564	489	574
Current Liabilities	N/A	N/A	220

Emap Ltd
Greater London House Hampstead Road, London, NW1 7EJ
Tel: 020-7728 5000 **Fax:** 01733-465353
E-mail: enquiries@emap.com
Website: http://www.emap.com
Bank(s): Barclays
Directors: E. Beale (MD)
Managers: C. Lesley (Publicity), N. Macken
Ultimate Holding Company: EDEN 2 & CIE SCA (LUXEMBOURG)
Immediate Holding Company: EMAP LIMITED
Registration no: 00537204 **Date established:** 1954 **Turnover:** £5m - £10m
No.of Employees: 1001 - 1500 **Product Groups:** 28

Date of Accounts	Dec 11	Dec 10	Dec 09
Sales Turnover	199m	195m	114m
Pre Tax Profit/Loss	24m	44m	-20m
Working Capital	-207m	-235m	-174m
Fixed Assets	368m	384m	392m
Current Assets	49m	53m	47m
Current Liabilities	92m	84m	74m

Emap Performance
Mappin House 4 Winsley Street, London, W1W 8HF
Tel: 020-7436 1515 **Fax:** 020-7323 0276
E-mail: mappin.reception@emap.com
Website: http://www.emap.com
Directors: M. Rich (Grp Chief Exec)
Ultimate Holding Company: EMAP P.L.C.
Immediate Holding Company: NETWORK TRAVEL SERVICES INT. LIMITED
Registration no: 02751163 **Date established:** 1992 **Turnover:** £2m - £5m
No.of Employees: 251 - 500 **Product Groups:** 28

Emko Consumer Products Ltd
19 Neville Court Abbey Road, London, NW8 9DD
Tel: 020-7289 3213 **Fax:** 020-7289 3213
E-mail: emehl@uk.co.uk
Directors: E. Mehl (Co Sec)
Immediate Holding Company: EMKO CONSUMER PRODUCTS LIMITED
Registration no: 01561034 **Date established:** 1981
Turnover: £250,000 - £500,000 **No.of Employees:** 1 - 10
Product Groups: 23, 24, 63

Date of Accounts	Apr 12	Apr 11	Apr 10
Sales Turnover	34	42	40
Pre Tax Profit/Loss	N/A	-5	N/A
Working Capital	1	1	6
Current Assets	223	179	147
Current Liabilities	221	177	3

Emko Products Ltd
59 Grove Avenue, London, N10 2AL
Tel: 020-8815 1832 **Fax:** 020-8365 3248
E-mail: emkouk@aol.com
Website: http://www.emko.co.uk
Directors: C. Kornhauser (Fin), H. Kornhauser (MD)
Immediate Holding Company: EMKO PRODUCTS LIMITED
Registration no: 00430783 **VAT No.:** GB 231 2717 96
Date established: 1947 **Turnover:** Up to £250,000
No.of Employees: 1 - 10 **Product Groups:** 23

Date of Accounts	Apr 12	Apr 11	Apr 10
Sales Turnover	36	27	2
Pre Tax Profit/Loss	10	4	N/A
Working Capital	142	134	130
Fixed Assets	1	1	1
Current Assets	240	228	223
Current Liabilities	98	91	93

Employers Federation Limited
Broadway House Tothill Street, London, SW1H 9NQ
Tel: 020-7222 7777 **Fax:** 020-7222 2782
E-mail: enquiries@eef.org.uk
Website: http://www.eef.org.uk
Directors: M. Temple (Dir)
Immediate Holding Company: Employers Federation Ltd
Registration no: 06396910 **Date established:** 2007
No.of Employees: 51 - 100 **Product Groups:** 87

Encyclopaedia Britannica UK Ltd
Unity Wharf 13 Mill Street, London, SE1 2BH
Tel: 020-7500 7800 **Fax:** 020-7500 7878
E-mail: enquiries@britannica.co.uk
Website: http://www.britannica.co.uk
Bank(s): HSBC Bank plc
Directors: E. Downey (Fin), L. Mansoor (MD)
Immediate Holding Company: ENCYCLOPAEDIA BRITANNICA (UK) LIMITED
Registration no: 03830890 **VAT No.:** GB 743 5639 16
Date established: 1999 **Turnover:** £2m - £5m **No.of Employees:** 21 - 50
Product Groups: 28, 64

Date of Accounts	Sep 11	Sep 10	Sep 09
Sales Turnover	4m	4m	4m
Pre Tax Profit/Loss	365	404	143
Working Capital	558	295	-12
Fixed Assets	46	36	51
Current Assets	2m	2m	1m
Current Liabilities	1m	1m	1m

Endemol
The Shepherds Building, London, W14 0EE
Tel: 08703-331700 **Fax:** 020-7436 7426
E-mail: info@endemoluk.com
Website: http://www.endemoluk.com
Directors: R. Johnston (Fin)
Ultimate Holding Company: GOLDMAN SACHS GROUP INC (USA)
Immediate Holding Company: ENDEMOL UK LIMITED
Registration no: 01692513 **Date established:** 1983
Turnover: £75m - £125m **No.of Employees:** 101 - 250
Product Groups: 28, 80

Date of Accounts	Dec 10	Dec 09	Dec 08
Sales Turnover	83m	168m	170m
Pre Tax Profit/Loss	95m	30m	28m
Working Capital	60m	109m	50m
Fixed Assets	49m	44m	12m
Current Assets	119m	205m	88m
Current Liabilities	20m	80m	35m

Energizer Ltd
93 Burleigh Gardens, London, N14 5AQ
Tel: 020-8882 8661 **Fax:** 020-8882 1938
Website: http://www.energizer.co.uk
Directors: A. Swan (Co Sec), M. Irvine (MD), P. Parmar (Co Sec)
Managers: S. Rogers (Mktg Serv Mgr)
Ultimate Holding Company: Energizer Investments UK Ltd
Immediate Holding Company: Energizer Holdings UK Company Ltd
Registration no: 03937798 **Turnover:** £10m - £20m
No.of Employees: 101 - 250 **Product Groups:** 33, 37

Energy Industries Council
Newcombe House 45 Notting Hill Gate, London, W11 3LQ
Tel: 020-7221 2043 **Fax:** 020-7221 8813
E-mail: sales@the-eic.com
Website: http://www.the-eic.com
Bank(s): National Westminster Bank Plc
Directors: I. Leitch (Comm), M. Stewart (Dir), O. Somerville-Jones (Grp Chief Exec)
Immediate Holding Company: ENERGY INDUSTRIES COUNCIL
Registration no: 00493459 **Date established:** 1951 **Turnover:** £5m - £10m
No.of Employees: 21 - 50 **Product Groups:** 30, 35, 36, 37, 38, 39, 40, 42, 45, 48, 51, 54, 67, 69, 84, 85, 87

Date of Accounts	Mar 10	Mar 09	Mar 08
Sales Turnover	6m	5m	5m
Pre Tax Profit/Loss	264	339	538
Working Capital	2m	2m	1m
Fixed Assets	388	134	89
Current Assets	5m	4m	4m
Current Liabilities	3m	2m	2m

Energy Networks Association Ltd
6th Floor Dean Bradley House 52 Horseferry Road, London, SW1P 2AF
Tel: 020-7706 5100 **Fax:** 020-7706 5101
E-mail: info@energynetworks.org
Website: http://www.energynetworks.org
Bank(s): National Westminster Bank Plc
Managers: M. Neagle
Immediate Holding Company: ENERGY NETWORKS ASSOCIATION LIMITED
Registration no: 04832301 **VAT No.:** GB 606 1845 51
Date established: 2003 **Turnover:** £5m - £10m **No.of Employees:** 21 - 50
Product Groups: 87

Date of Accounts	Dec 11	Dec 10	Dec 09
Working Capital	1m	705	445
Fixed Assets	206	287	374
Current Assets	2m	2m	1m

G English Electronics Ltd
Unit 8 Skeffington Street, London, SE18 6SR
Tel: 020-8855 0991 **Fax:** 020-8854 5563
E-mail: info@gelec.co.uk
Website: http://www.gelec.co.uk
Directors: D. English (MD)
Immediate Holding Company: G. ENGLISH ELECTRONICS LIMITED
Registration no: 01208319 **Date established:** 1975 **Turnover:** £2m - £5m
No.of Employees: 11 - 20 **Product Groups:** 29, 37, 40

Date of Accounts	Mar 11	Mar 10	Mar 09
Working Capital	649	414	439
Fixed Assets	733	756	790
Current Assets	2m	2m	2m

English & Overseas Wool Trading Co. Ltd
49-51 Central Street, London, EC1V 8AB
Tel: 020-7253 5241 **Fax:** 020-7250 1562
Directors: J. Hackenbroch (Fin)
Immediate Holding Company: ENGLISH & OVERSEAS WOOL TRADING CO. LIMITED
Registration no: 00310068 **Date established:** 1936
Turnover: Up to £250,000 **No.of Employees:** 1 - 10 **Product Groups:** 23, 61, 66

Date of Accounts	Dec 10	Dec 09	Dec 08
Working Capital	1	1	1
Fixed Assets	2	2	2
Current Assets	1	1	2
Current Liabilities	N/A	N/A	2

Enterprise Education Trust
1-2 Hatfields, London, SE1 9PG
Tel: 020-7620 0735 **Fax:** 020-7928 0578
E-mail: info@enterprise-education.org.uk
Website: http://www.enterprise-education.org.uk
Managers: D. Millar
Immediate Holding Company: ENTERPRISE EDUCATION TRUST
Registration no: 02647030 **Date established:** 1991
Turnover: £250,000 - £500,000 **No.of Employees:** 1 - 10
Product Groups: 86

Date of Accounts	Aug 11	Aug 10	Aug 09
Sales Turnover	384	717	1m
Pre Tax Profit/Loss	15	-114	-299
Working Capital	38	23	135
Fixed Assets	8	8	11
Current Assets	85	213	454
Current Liabilities	44	179	283

Entoch Meters and Metering Solutions
15 Cavendish Drive Edgware, London, HA8 7NR
Tel: 020-8732 4286 **Fax:** 020-8381 3803
E-mail: sales@entontechmeters.com
Website: http://www.entontechmeters.com
Product Groups: 38, 39

E-On UK P.L.C.
53 New Broad Street, London, EC2M 1JJ
Tel: 020-7256 6482 **Fax:** 020-7826 2890
E-mail: info@eon-uk.com
Website: http://www.eon-uk.com
Bank(s): HSBC Bank plc
Directors: P. Golby (Grp Chief Exec)
Registration no: 02366970 **VAT No.:** GB 559 0978 89
Date established: 1989 **Turnover:** Over £1,000m **Product Groups:** 18

Epr Architects Ltd
30 Millbank, London, SW1P 4DU
Tel: 020-7932 7600 **Fax:** 020-7932 7601
E-mail: architects@epr.co.uk
Website: http://www.epr.co.uk
Directors: D. Harnan (Fin), S. Lowther (MD)
Managers: D. Catling (Tech Serv Mgr), P. Mitchell (Mktg Serv Mgr)
Ultimate Holding Company: EPR ARCHITECTS GROUP LIMITED
Immediate Holding Company: EPR ARCHITECTS LIMITED
Registration no: 02257346 **Date established:** 1988 **Turnover:** £5m - £10m
No.of Employees: 51 - 100 **Product Groups:** 44, 49, 54, 84

Date of Accounts	Mar 12	Mar 11	Mar 10
Sales Turnover	8m	8m	8m
Pre Tax Profit/Loss	697	710	138
Working Capital	2m	2m	1m
Fixed Assets	198	222	351
Current Assets	6m	6m	7m
Current Liabilities	4m	3m	5m

Equifax plc
Capital House 25 Chapel Street, London, NW1 5DH
Tel: 08443-350550 **Fax:** 020-7723 7555
E-mail: info@equifax.co.uk
Website: http://www.equifax.co.uk
Directors: M. Shannon (MD)
Ultimate Holding Company: EQUIFAX INC (USA)
Immediate Holding Company: EQUIFAX LIMITED
Registration no: 02425920 **Date established:** 1989
Turnover: £50m - £75m **No.of Employees:** 1 - 10 **Product Groups:** 81, 82

Date of Accounts	Dec 11	Dec 10	Dec 09
Sales Turnover	74m	67m	66m
Pre Tax Profit/Loss	5m	4m	7m
Working Capital	8m	-6m	8m
Fixed Assets	11m	15m	18m
Current Assets	19m	20m	19m
Current Liabilities	10m	10m	9m

Erco Lighting Ltd
38 Dover Street, London, W1S 4NL
Tel: 020-7344 4900 **Fax:** 020-7409 1530
E-mail: info@erco.com
Website: http://www.erco.com
Directors: A. Stebbings (Co Sec), C. Tiernan (MD)
Managers: P. Taylor
Ultimate Holding Company: ERCO LEUCHTEN (GERMANY)
Immediate Holding Company: ERCO LIGHTING LIMITED
Registration no: 01408064 **Date established:** 1979 **Turnover:** £5m - £10m
No.of Employees: 21 - 50 **Product Groups:** 37

Date of Accounts	Dec 11	Dec 10	Dec 09
Sales Turnover	7m	7m	7m
Pre Tax Profit/Loss	263	229	188
Working Capital	1m	3m	2m
Fixed Assets	65	73	53
Current Assets	2m	4m	4m
Current Liabilities	895	854	800

Ergonom Ltd
Whittington House 19-30 Alfred Place, London, WC1E 7EA
Tel: 020-7323 2325 **Fax:** 020-7323 2032
E-mail: sales@ergonom.com
Website: http://www.ergonom.com
Directors: M. Vizzini (Fin)
Managers: L. Fuller (Sales Admin)
Ultimate Holding Company: MOLTENI SPA (ITALY)
Immediate Holding Company: ERGONOM LIMITED
Registration no: 00963271 **Date established:** 1969
Turnover: £10m - £20m **No.of Employees:** 11 - 20 **Product Groups:** 26, 67

Date of Accounts	Dec 11	Dec 10	Dec 09
Sales Turnover	19m	11m	10m
Pre Tax Profit/Loss	656	16	-11
Working Capital	52	-109	-162
Fixed Assets	1m	1m	1m
Current Assets	4m	4m	3m
Current Liabilities	904	596	405

Ernex Group
PO Box 53967, London, SW15 3UY
Tel: 020-7731 6707 **Fax:** 020-7731 6703
E-mail: ernex@colebrookclose.com
Directors: A. Fyne (Dir)
Turnover: £250,000 - £500,000 **No.of Employees:** 1 - 10
Product Groups: 24, 49, 81

Ernst & Young Global Ltd
Becket House 1 Lambeth Palace Road, London, SE1 7ER
Tel: 020-7951 2000 **Fax:** 020-7951 1345
E-mail: motty@uk.ey.com
Website: http://www.ey.com
Directors: J. Robertson (Dir), M. Otty (Snr Part), N. Blande (MD), N. Land (Snr Part), T. Howard (Dir)
Managers: S. Reed ()
Ultimate Holding Company: ERNST & YOUNG EUROPE LLP
Immediate Holding Company: ERNST & YOUNG SERVICES LIMITED
Registration no: 02812206 **Date established:** 1993
Turnover: £500m - £1,000m **No.of Employees:** 1501 & over
Product Groups: 80, 82, 86

Eskimo Ice
New Covent Garden Market Unit A 45-48 Nine Elms, London, SW8 5EE
Tel: 020-7720 4883 **Fax:** 020-7720 2731
E-mail: mishalle@eskimo-ice.co.uk
Website: http://www.eskimo-ice.co.uk
Directors: D. Glinert (Co Sec)
Managers: M. Deepchand (Mgr)
Immediate Holding Company: ESKIMO ICE LIMITED
Registration no: 02496217 **Date established:** 1990
No.of Employees: 1 - 10 **Product Groups:** 21, 32, 81

Espírito Santo Financial Group S.A.
33 Queen Street, London, EC4R 1ES
Tel: 020-7332 4350 **Fax:** 020-7332 4355
E-mail: fworsdell@esfg.com
Website: http://www.esfg.com
Directors: M. Villasblas (MD)
Managers: P. Worsdell ()
Immediate Holding Company: Espirito Santo Nominees Ltd
Registration no: 01437774 **Date established:** 1979
No.of Employees: 1 - 10 **Product Groups:** 82

Essex Engineering Works Wanstead Ltd
12 Nelson Road, London, E11 2AX
Tel: 020-8989 2012 **Fax:** 020-8530 1117
E-mail: enquiries@essexengineering.co.uk
Website: http://www.essexengineering.co.uk
Directors: K. Allen (MD)
Immediate Holding Company: ESSEX ENGINEERING WORKS (WANSTEAD) LIMITED
Registration no: 00545910 **Date established:** 1955 **Turnover:** £1m - £2m
No.of Employees: 11 - 20 **Product Groups:** 49

Date of Accounts	Mar 12	Mar 11	Mar 10
Working Capital	2m	2m	2m
Fixed Assets	170	164	169
Current Assets	2m	3m	3m

Essex Replica Castings Ltd
108-112 Westmoor Street, London, SE7 8NQ
Tel: 020-8858 6110 **Fax:** 020-8305 0907
E-mail: nick@jardineinternational.com
Website: http://www.jardane.co.uk
Directors: N. Townsend (Dir), A. Townsend (Fin)
Immediate Holding Company: ESSEX REPLICA CASTINGS (BASILDON) LTD.
Registration no: 02890331 **VAT No.:** GB 360 2637 71
Date established: 1994 **Turnover:** £500,000 - £1m
No.of Employees: 1 - 10 **Product Groups:** 34

Date of Accounts	Jan 11	Jan 10	Jan 09
Working Capital	39	68	62
Fixed Assets	22	12	12
Current Assets	155	161	155

Estee Lauder Co.
73 Grosvenor Street, London, W1K 3BQ
Tel: 020-7409 6700 **Fax:** 020-7409 6968
E-mail: enquiries@draytonfinch.com
Website: http://www.estee-lauder.co.uk
Directors: P. Nyberg (Fin), C. Good (MD)
Ultimate Holding Company: ESTEE LAUDER COMPANIES INC (USA)
Immediate Holding Company: ESTEE LAUDER INC (USA)
Registration no: 00659213 **Date established:** 1983
Turnover: £75m - £125m **No.of Employees:** 101 - 250
Product Groups: 32, 84

Eswa Ltd
32 Monkton Street, London, SE11 4TX
Tel: 020-7582 4300 **Fax:** 020-7735 1456
E-mail: info@eswa.co.uk
Website: http://www.eswa.co.uk
Directors: R. Scriven (Fin)
Immediate Holding Company: ESWA LIMITED
Registration no: 00630148 **Date established:** 1959
Turnover: £500,000 - £1m **No.of Employees:** 1 - 10 **Product Groups:** 37, 40

Date of Accounts	Dec 11	Dec 10	Dec 09
Working Capital	106	151	249
Fixed Assets	10	5	7
Current Assets	203	264	323

Etco International Commodities Ltd
Second Floor Cooper House 316 Regents Park Road, London, N3 2JX
Tel: 020-8371 8800 **Fax:** 020-8371 8850/51
E-mail: sales@etco.co.uk
Website: http://www.etco.co.uk
Bank(s): HSBC Bank P.L.C.
Directors: S. Pinkerton (Dir), I. O'Reilly (Dir)
Ultimate Holding Company: Telmar (Switzerland)
Immediate Holding Company: Telmar Holding SA (Switzerland)
Registration no: 01080084 **VAT No.:** GB 916 3323 40
Date established: 1974 **Turnover:** £2m - £5m **No.of Employees:** 11 - 20
Product Groups: 01, 07, 20, 34, 35, 38, 40, 41, 42, 61, 62, 67, 80, 82

Date of Accounts	Dec 11	Dec 10	Dec 09
Sales Turnover	5m	6m	4m
Pre Tax Profit/Loss	403	271	219
Working Capital	2m	2m	1m
Fixed Assets	6	3	N/A
Current Assets	2m	2m	2m
Current Liabilities	137	86	78

Euler Hermes
1 Canada Square, London, E14 5DX
Tel: 020-7512933 **Fax:** 020-7512 9186
E-mail: creditinfo@eulerhermes.com
Website: http://www.eulerhermes.com
Bank(s): Lloyds TSB Bank plc
Directors: R. Webster (Grp Chief Exec), P. Ward (Ch), J. Daly (Comm), F. Desnos (Grp Chief Exec), F. Desnos (Fin)
Managers: P. Flanagan, J. Swaby (Mktg Serv Mgr)
Immediate Holding Company: EULER HERMES MANAGEMENT UK LIMITED
Registration no: 03376459 **VAT No.:** GB 447 2904 38
Date established: 1997 **Turnover:** £50m - £75m
No.of Employees: 251 - 500 **Product Groups:** 82

Date of Accounts	Dec 07
Pre Tax Profit/Loss	18280
Fixed Assets	160750
Current Assets	88200
Current Liabilities	46810
Total Share Capital	21000
ROCE% (Return on Capital Employed)	9.0

Euro Bangla Catering & Domestic Equipment
458 Romford Road, London, E7 8DF
Tel: 020-8552 4388
Directors: M. Miya (Prop)
Date established: 1998 **No.of Employees:** 1 - 10 **Product Groups:** 20, 40, 41

Euro Label Printers
119-123 Hackford Road, London, SW9 0QT
Tel: 020-7582 9579 **Fax:** 01306-881900
E-mail: info@eurolabelprinters.com
Website: http://www.eurolabelprinters.com
Directors: J. Bayley (Dir)
Immediate Holding Company: EURO LABEL PRINTERS, LIMITED
Registration no: 01175435 **Date established:** 1974
Turnover: £250,000 - £500,000 **No.of Employees:** 1 - 10
Product Groups: 27, 28

Date of Accounts	Mar 11	Mar 10	Mar 09
Working Capital	39	65	7
Fixed Assets	172	84	95
Current Assets	224	174	95

Euro Marintechnic Services B V
1379 High Road Northway House, London, N20 9LP
Tel: 020-8982 0010 **Fax:** 020-8982 0008
Website: http://www.emts.nl
Directors: R. Molsbergen (Dir)
Managers: D. Osbourne (Mgr), K. Eggleton (Sales Prom Mgr)
Immediate Holding Company: EURO MARINTECHNIC SERVICES B.V.
Registration no: FC016114 **Date established:** 1991
Turnover: Up to £250,000 **No.of Employees:** 1 - 10 **Product Groups:** 67

Euro R S C G London
Cupola House 15 Alfred Place, London, WC1E 7EB
Tel: 020-7240 4111 **Fax:** 020-7467 9210
E-mail: enquiries@eurorscg.com
Website: http://www.eurorscglondon.co.uk
Bank(s): HSBC Bank plc
Directors: R. Lidstone (Grp Chief Exec)
Managers: A. Chapman (Chief Acct)
Ultimate Holding Company: HAVAS SA (FRANCE)
Immediate Holding Company: PARTNERS BDDH LIMITED
Registration no: 02066862 **VAT No.:** GB 645 1322 61
Date established: 1986 **Turnover:** £75m - £125m
No.of Employees: 251 - 500 **Product Groups:** 81

EuroDidact
27 Old Gloucester Street, London, WC1N 3AX
Tel: 07505-828983
E-mail: mail@eurodidact.co.uk
Website: http://www.eurodidact.co.uk
Directors: F. Andreasen (Admin)
Registration no: GB80503526 **Date established:** 1998
No.of Employees: 11 - 20 **Product Groups:** 64

Euromedica plc
3 Muirfield Crescent, London, E14 9SZ
Tel: 020-7536 7950 **Fax:** 020-7538 8362
E-mail: andy.macleod@euromedica.com
Website: http://www.euromedica.com
Directors: A. Macleod (MD)
Managers: R. Allin (Chief Acct)
Ultimate Holding Company: HEXAGON HUMAN CAPITAL PLC
Immediate Holding Company: EL REALISATIONS 2010 LIMITED
Registration no: 02129219 **VAT No.:** GB 417 8187 25
Date established: 1987 **Turnover:** £2m - £5m **No.of Employees:** 11 - 20
Product Groups: 80

Date of Accounts	Mar 08	Mar 07	Mar 06
Sales Turnover	2m	3m	3m
Pre Tax Profit/Loss	272	471	407
Working Capital	160	418	68
Fixed Assets	80	35	36
Current Assets	1m	1m	856
Current Liabilities	274	757	692

Europa Import Export Ltd
523 Porchester Gate Bayswater Road, London, W2 3HP
Tel: 020-7221 3449 **Fax:** 020-7221 7461
E-mail: eie@compuserve.com
Managers: A. Malik
Ultimate Holding Company: EUROCOM INVESTMENTS LIMITED
Immediate Holding Company: EUROPA IMPORT EXPORT LIMITED
Registration no: 02059651 **Date established:** 1986
Turnover: £125m - £250m **No.of Employees:** 1 - 10 **Product Groups:** 61

European Circuit Solutions Ltd
Impress House Mansell Road, London, W3 7QH
Tel: 020-8743 8880 **Fax:** 020-8740 4200
E-mail: sales@e2s.com
Website: http://www.ecsamplifiers.co.uk
Directors: B. Isard (Dir), N. Porter (Sales), P. Fay (MD)
Managers: M. Green (Fin Mgr)
Immediate Holding Company: EUROPEAN SAFETY SYSTEMS LIMITED
Registration no: 02763350 **Date established:** 1992
No.of Employees: 21 - 50 **Product Groups:** 37, 39, 40, 45, 67

Date of Accounts	Dec 11	Dec 10	Dec 09
Working Capital	3m	2m	1m
Fixed Assets	928	646	697
Current Assets	6m	4m	3m

European Colour plc
5 Edwardes Place, London, W8 6LR
Tel: 020-7603 7788 **Fax:** 020-7603 7667
E-mail: mail@ecplc.com
Website: http://www.ecpigments.com
Bank(s): National Westminster Bank Plc
Directors: G. Hughes (MD), P. Hall (MD), S. Smith (Dir)
Managers: D. Flint (I.T. Exec), G. Bristow (Site Co-ord), C. Thompson (Sales Admin)
Ultimate Holding Company: European Colour PLC
Immediate Holding Company: European Colour P.L.C.
Registration no: 00065706 **Date established:** 2007
Turnover: £20m - £50m **No.of Employees:** 21 - 50 **Product Groups:** 32

European Metal Recycling Ltd
29 Bidder, London, E16 4SZ
Tel: 020-7476 3104 **Fax:** 020-7474 5633
E-mail: ron.salt@emrltd.com
Website: http://www.emrgroup.com
Managers: R. Salt (Mgr)
Immediate Holding Company: EUROPEAN METAL RECYCLING LIMITED
Registration no: 02954623 **Date established:** 1994
Turnover: £10m - £20m **No.of Employees:** 21 - 50 **Product Groups:** 42, 66

Date of Accounts	Dec 11	Dec 10	Dec 09
Sales Turnover	3032m	2431m	1843m
Pre Tax Profit/Loss	116m	155m	91m
Working Capital	414m	371m	167m
Fixed Assets	518m	483m	480m
Current Assets	1027m	717m	557m
Current Liabilities	124m	118m	185m

European Metals Recycling Ltd
Thames Wharf Dock Road, London, E16 1AF
Tel: 020-7476 3100 **Fax:** 020-7511 0888
Website: http://www.elrltd.com
Directors: R. Garwood (Dir)
Managers: M. Ellis (Depot Mgr), R. Garwood (Mgr)
Immediate Holding Company: EUROPEAN METAL RECYCLING LIMITED
Registration no: 02954623 **Date established:** 1994
No.of Employees: 1 - 10 **Product Groups:** 42, 66

Eurosteel Products Ltd
Citypoint 1 Ropemaker Street, London, EC2Y 9ST
Tel: 020-7248 5473 **Fax:** 020-7248 3069
E-mail: paul.astels@eurosteelproducts.co.uk
Website: http://www.eurosteelproducts.co.uk
Bank(s): Barclays
Directors: P. Astels (MD)
Ultimate Holding Company: STEMCOR HOLDINGS LIMITED
Immediate Holding Company: EUROSTEEL PRODUCTS LIMITED
Registration no: 00759991 **Date established:** 1963
Turnover: £125m - £250m **No.of Employees:** 11 - 20 **Product Groups:** 61

Date of Accounts	Dec 11	Dec 10	Dec 09
Sales Turnover	167m	116m	91m
Pre Tax Profit/Loss	4m	4m	-807
Working Capital	5m	4m	1m
Fixed Assets	652	22	N/A
Current Assets	90m	83m	39m
Current Liabilities	5m	6m	2m

Eurosuits Ltd
631-637 Watford Way, London, NW7 3JR
Tel: 020-8906 3446 **Fax:** 020-8906 1775
E-mail: p.graham@eurosuits.co.uk
Website: http://www.eurosuits.co.uk
Directors: G. Graham (Fin), P. Graham (MD)
Immediate Holding Company: EUROSUITS LIMITED
Registration no: 01305899 **Date established:** 1977
Turnover: Up to £250,000 **No.of Employees:** 1 - 10 **Product Groups:** 61

Date of Accounts	Apr 11	Apr 10	Apr 09
Working Capital	175	143	132
Fixed Assets	1	2	3
Current Assets	222	168	170

Eurowelcome Latin Travel
19c Craven Road, London, W2 3BP
Tel: 020-7447 2750 **Fax:** 020-7447 0447
E-mail: robertor@eurowelcome.co.uk
Website: http://www.eurowelcome.co.uk
Bank(s): Barclays Bank. Hanover Square Corp Banking Group, 50 Pall Mall, London, SW1A 1SD
Directors: R. Pardal (MD), R. Pradal (MD)
Managers: F. Bensunsan
Immediate Holding Company: LATIN TRAVEL LIMITED
Registration no: 01066715 **VAT No.:** GB 404 3327 91
Date established: 1972 **Turnover:** £10m - £20m
No.of Employees: 21 - 50 **Product Groups:** 69

Date of Accounts	Dec 11	Dec 10	Dec 09
Sales Turnover	13m	10m	9m
Pre Tax Profit/Loss	669	392	459
Working Capital	2m	2m	2m
Fixed Assets	105	102	71
Current Assets	4m	3m	3m
Current Liabilities	611	468	445

Evans Gray & Hood Foods Ltd
10-14 Hewett Street, London, EC2A 3RL
Tel: 020-7247 2072 **Fax:** 020-7247 2784
E-mail: spices@kimpton.com
Website: http://www.kimpton.co.uk
Directors: B. Isaacs (Fin), M. Houghton (MD)
Managers: A. Rana (Sales Prom Mgr)
Immediate Holding Company: EVANS GRAY & HOOD FOODS LIMITED
Registration no: 03252489 **VAT No.:** GB 243 4559 59
Date established: 1996 **Turnover:** £1m - £2m **No.of Employees:** 1 - 10
Product Groups: 61

Date of Accounts	Sep 07	Sep 06	Sep 05
Sales Turnover	1786	N/A	N/A
Pre Tax Profit/Loss	36	N/A	N/A
Working Capital	-440	-468	-496
Current Assets	1150	985	839
Current Liabilities	1590	1453	1334
ROCE% (Return on Capital Employed)	-8.2		
ROT% (Return on Turnover)	2.0		

Paul Evans Design Associates Ltd
9 Dalmeny Road, London, N7 0HG
Tel: 020-7607 8002 **Fax:** 020-7700 1873
E-mail: paul.pedal@hotmail.co.uk
Directors: P. Evans (MD)
Immediate Holding Company: PAUL EVANS (DESIGN) ASSOCIATES LIMITED
Registration no: 01972371 **Date established:** 1985
Turnover: Up to £250,000 **No.of Employees:** 1 - 10 **Product Groups:** 84

Date of Accounts	Jun 11	Jun 10	Jun 09
Sales Turnover	29	33	33
Pre Tax Profit/Loss	-6	3	N/A
Working Capital	-27	-21	-25
Fixed Assets	3	4	5
Current Assets	5	8	11
Current Liabilities	20	16	22

Eventdomain.co.uk
100 Oxford St, London, W1D 1LL
Tel: 020-8597 6768
E-mail: admin@eventdomain.co.uk
Website: http://www.eventdomain.co.uk
Directors: C. Given (Dir)
Date established: 2005 **Turnover:** Up to £250,000
No.of Employees: 1 - 10 **Product Groups:** 44, 61

Eversheds
1 Wood Street, London, EC2V 7WS
Tel: 08454-979797 **Fax:** 020-7919 4919
E-mail: corneliusmedvei@eversheds.com
Website: http://www.eversheds.com
Directors: K. Flemings (Fin), C. Medvei (Ptnr)
Managers: M. Hopkinson, P. Caris (Tech Serv Mgr)
Immediate Holding Company: EVERSHEDS LLP
Registration no: OC304065 **Date established:** 2003
Turnover: £250m - £500m **No.of Employees:** 1001 - 1500
Product Groups: 80

Date of Accounts	Apr 11	Apr 10	Apr 09
Sales Turnover	355m	355m	366m
Pre Tax Profit/Loss	110m	105m	95m
Working Capital	113m	128m	119m
Fixed Assets	50m	54m	61m
Current Assets	201m	191m	180m
Current Liabilities	52m	52m	47m

Evertile Ltd
6 Moresby Road, London, E5 9LF
Tel: 020-8806 3167 **Fax:** 020-8806 7434
E-mail: sales@evertile.co.uk
Website: http://www.evertile.co.uk
Directors: S. Lew (Fin), M. Lew (MD)
Immediate Holding Company: EVERTILE LIMITED
Registration no: 01599895 **VAT No.:** GB 365 3238 50
Date established: 1981 **Turnover:** £250,000 - £500,000
No.of Employees: 1 - 10 **Product Groups:** 33

Date of Accounts	Jun 11	Jun 09	Jun 08
Working Capital	-43	-49	-72
Fixed Assets	3	4	5
Current Assets	238	223	227

Everymans Library Ltd
Northburgh House 10 Northburgh Street, London, EC1V 0AT
Tel: 020-7566 6350 **Fax:** 020-7490 3708
E-mail: books@everyman.uk.com
Website: http://www.randomhouse.com/classics
Directors: D. Campbell (MD)
Immediate Holding Company: SMART PHONE TECHNOLOGIES LIMITED
Registration no: 07189143 **Date established:** 2010 **Turnover:** £2m - £5m
No.of Employees: 1 - 10 **Product Groups:** 28

Evolution Voice & Data plc
36 Great St Helens, London, EC3A 6AP
Tel: 020-7628 2800 **Fax:** 020-7373 9514
E-mail: sales@evd-uk.com
Website: http://www.evd-uk.com
Directors: S. Osmand (Dir), J. Beale (Co Sec), M. Cosgrave (Dir)
Ultimate Holding Company: DUNCARY 79 LIMITED
Immediate Holding Company: EVOLUTION VOICE & DATA LIMITED
Registration no: 03918047 **Date established:** 2000
Turnover: Up to £250,000 **No.of Employees:** 11 - 20 **Product Groups:** 37, 79

Date of Accounts	Dec 10	Dec 09	Dec 08
Sales Turnover	21	2m	11m
Pre Tax Profit/Loss	-38	81	1m
Working Capital	1m	1m	1m
Fixed Assets	N/A	40	54
Current Assets	1m	2m	3m
Current Liabilities	10	19	1m

E-Volve Consulting
1 Poultry, London, EC2R 8JR
Tel: 020-7643 2219 **Fax:** 020-7643 2201
E-mail: acl@alderwick.com
Website: http://www.alderwick.com
Directors: J. Williams (MD), S. Bowie (MD)
Managers: L. Mak
Immediate Holding Company: JDHR SOLUTIONS LTD
Registration no: 00736898 **Date established:** 2002 **Turnover:** £1m - £2m
No.of Employees: 1 - 10 **Product Groups:** 80

see next page

E-Volve Consulting - Cont'd

Date of Accounts	Mar 11	Mar 10	Mar 09
Working Capital	-36	-33	-20
Fixed Assets	18	N/A	N/A
Current Assets	43	27	37

Excelsior Textiles Ltd
74 Wentworth Street, London, E1 7TF
Tel: 020-7377 9304 **Fax:** 020-7377 2743
E-mail: enquiries@excelsiortextiles.co.uk
Directors: T. Mahalla (MD), T. Mahalla (Dir)
Immediate Holding Company: EXCELSIOR TEXTILES LIMITED
Registration no: 01012731 **Date established:** 1971
No.of Employees: 1 - 10 **Product Groups:** 61

Date of Accounts	Jun 11	Jun 10	Jun 09
Working Capital	2m	2m	4m
Fixed Assets	1m	1m	1m
Current Assets	4m	3m	5m

Expand International GB Ltd (Expand International)
Unit 1 Saxon Business Centre Windsor Avenue, London, SW19 2RR
Tel: 020-8540 8800 **Fax:** 020-8540 0500
E-mail: info.uk@expandmedia.com
Website: http://www.expandmedia.com
Directors: M. Southey (MD)
Ultimate Holding Company: EXPAND INTERNATIONAL GROUP AB (SWEDEN)
Immediate Holding Company: EXPAND INTERNATIONAL (GB) LIMITED
Registration no: 03004510 **Date established:** 1994 **Turnover:** £1m - £2m
No.of Employees: 1 - 10 **Product Groups:** 26, 35, 49, 67

Date of Accounts	Dec 11	Dec 10	Dec 09
Sales Turnover	N/A	1m	872
Pre Tax Profit/Loss	N/A	51	15
Working Capital	325	289	247
Fixed Assets	N/A	N/A	3
Current Assets	550	655	383
Current Liabilities	N/A	358	123

Experian Q A S
George West House 2-3 Clapham Common North Side, London, SW4 0QL
Tel: 020-7498 7777 **Fax:** 020-7498 0303
E-mail: reception@qas.com
Website: http://www.qas.com
Managers: K. O'keffe
Ultimate Holding Company: EXPERIAN PLC (JERSEY)
Immediate Holding Company: QAS LIMITED
Registration no: 02582055 **Date established:** 1991
Turnover: £75m - £125m **No.of Employees:** 101 - 250
Product Groups: 81

Experience Communications Ltd
37 Golden Square, London, W1F 9LB
Tel: 020-7439 0105 **Fax:** 020-7543 4411
E-mail: anthony@exp-com.com
Website: http://www.exp-com.com
Directors: A. Clifton (Ptnr), A. Simmons (Dir), J. Winstanley (Co Sec), J. Whitmore (Ptnr)
Immediate Holding Company: EXPERIENCE COMMUNICATIONS LIMITED
Registration no: 04007561 **Date established:** 2000
Turnover: £75m - £125m **No.of Employees:** 1 - 10 **Product Groups:** 81

Expocentric
Bedford House 3 Bedford Street, London, WC2E 9HD
Tel: 020-7240 7567 **Fax:** 020-7379 4524
E-mail: c.carter@expocentric.co.uk
Website: http://www.expocentric.co.uk
Directors: M. Young (MD)
Managers: C. Carter (Mgr), M. Druzkowski (Mgr)
Immediate Holding Company: SLATER MICHAEL LLP
Date established: 2003 **Turnover:** £2m - £5m **No.of Employees:** 1 - 10
Product Groups: 44, 80

Express Export Services Ltd
Arlette House 143 Wardour Street, London, W1F 8WA
Tel: 020-7734 8356 **Fax:** 0800-034 1005
E-mail: expressexportservices@ukbusiness.com
Website: http://www.express-exports.co.uk
Directors: J. O'Hara (Fin), M. Craig (MD)
Managers: C. O' Hara (Nat Sales Mgr)
Registration no: 01172272 **Turnover:** £1m - £2m
No.of Employees: 1 - 10 **Product Groups:** 76, 79

Date of Accounts	Dec 07	Dec 06	Dec 05
Working Capital	34	24	16
Fixed Assets	7	9	11
Current Assets	232	191	192
Current Liabilities	198	167	176

Express Security Systems
88 Vallance Road, London, E1 5BW
Tel: 020-7377 6565 **Fax:** 020-7377 5656
E-mail: marketing@etsuk.co.uk
Website: http://www.etsuk.co.uk
Directors: S. Rahman (Dir)
Immediate Holding Company: NEW MOVE MANAGEMENT LIMITED
Registration no: 07026390 **Date established:** 2009
No.of Employees: 1 - 10 **Product Groups:** 37, 52, 67

Extraordinary Design
311 Chase Road, London, N14 6JS
Tel: 020-8886 9020
E-mail: info@extraordinarydesign.com
Website: http://www.extraordinarydesign.com
Directors: D. Maier (Prop)
Immediate Holding Company: DRAGON TEXTILES LIMITED
Registration no: 04961035 **Date established:** 2010
Turnover: Up to £250,000 **No.of Employees:** 1 - 10 **Product Groups:** 81

ExxonMobil Group
St. Catherine's House 2 Kingsway, London, WC2B 6HA
Tel: 020-7412 4000 **Fax:** 020-7412 4084
Website: http://www.exxonmobil.com
Directors: J. Boydell (Dir), L. Johnson (Ch)
Turnover: Up to £250,000 **No.of Employees:** 501 - 1000
Product Groups: 31, 66, 84

F & C Asset Management
8th Floor Exchange House, London, EC2A 2NY
Tel: 020-7628 8000 **Fax:** 020-7628 8188
Website: http://www.fandc.com
Directors: A. Grisay (Grp Chief Exec), R. Jenkins (Ch)
Managers: J. Yule, L. Lercq, S. Stevens
Ultimate Holding Company: F&C ASSET MANAGEMENT PLC
Immediate Holding Company: THE EUROPEAN INVESTMENT TRUST PLC
Registration no: 01055384 **Date established:** 1972 **Turnover:** £5m - £10m
No.of Employees: 501 - 1000 **Product Groups:** 80

F Q Trading Ltd
4a Mordaunt Road Harlesden London, London, NW10 8NU
Tel: 0870-760 6731
E-mail: salesmanager@fqtrading.com
Website: http://www.fqtrading.com
Directors: F. Rafiq (MD)
Registration no: 04783213 **Date established:** 2003
Turnover: Up to £250,000 **No.of Employees:** 1 - 10 **Product Groups:** 41

Date of Accounts	Jun 07	Jun 06
Sales Turnover	12	11
Pre Tax Profit/Loss	-3	2
Working Capital	-1	2
Fixed Assets	7	N/A
Current Assets	N/A	2
Current Liabilities	1	N/A
Total Share Capital	9	N/A
ROCE% (Return on Capital Employed)	-47.2	
ROT% (Return on Turnover)	-24.7	21.5

F S M Enterprises Ltd
2 Adams Close, London, NW9 8PT
Tel: 020-8200 7736 **Fax:** 020-8200 6112
E-mail: fmalik1541@aol.com
Directors: F. Malik (Dir)
Immediate Holding Company: F.S.M. ENTERPRISES LIMITED
Registration no: 01803038 **VAT No.:** GB 398 6929 66
Date established: 1984 **Turnover:** £250,000 - £500,000
No.of Employees: 1 - 10 **Product Groups:** 61, 80

Date of Accounts	Mar 12	Mar 11	Mar 10
Working Capital	9	19	18
Fixed Assets	1	1	1
Current Assets	57	91	79

F X Airport Services Ltd
5 The Pavement Worple Road, London, SW19 4DA
Tel: 020-8879 3334 **Fax:** 020-8241 6215
E-mail: info@fxairports.co.uk
Website: http://www.fxairports.co.uk
Directors: I. Kuhinko (Dir)
Immediate Holding Company: FX-AIRPORT SERVICES LTD
Registration no: 05772233 **Date established:** 2006
Turnover: Up to £250,000 **No.of Employees:** 1 - 10 **Product Groups:** 39, 72

Date of Accounts	Jun 11	Jun 10	Jun 09
Sales Turnover	19	26	14
Pre Tax Profit/Loss	N/A	1	1
Working Capital	1	N/A	N/A
Current Assets	1	N/A	N/A

Faber & Faber Publishing
Bloomsbury House 74-77 Great Russell Street, London, WC1B 3DA
Tel: 020-7927 3800 **Fax:** 020-7465 0034
E-mail: mailbox@faber.co.uk
Website: http://www.faber.co.uk
Bank(s): National Westminster Bank Plc
Managers: I. Bridges (I.T. Exec), N. Bright (Buyer), S. Page, W. Atkinson (Sales Prom Mgr)
Immediate Holding Company: FABER AND FABER LIMITED
Registration no: 00944703 **Date established:** 1968
Turnover: £10m - £20m **No.of Employees:** 51 - 100 **Product Groups:** 28

Date of Accounts	Mar 12	Mar 11	Mar 10
Sales Turnover	17m	19m	17m
Pre Tax Profit/Loss	502	767	575
Working Capital	7m	6m	6m
Fixed Assets	1m	1m	1m
Current Assets	15m	14m	14m
Current Liabilities	6m	6m	6m

Fabric Care Dry Cleaners
280a Brixton Hill, London, SW2 1HT
Tel: 020-8674 7192 **Fax:** 020-8674 7835
E-mail: kola.taiwo@fabric-care.co.uk
Website: http://www.fabric-care.co.uk
Directors: K. Taiwo (Prop)
Immediate Holding Company: FABRIC-CARE SERVICES LIMITED
Registration no: 07026622 **Date established:** 2009
Turnover: £250,000 - £500,000 **No.of Employees:** 1 - 10
Product Groups: 23

Fabrizio Fashions Ltd
138 Fonthill Road, London, N4 3HP
Tel: 020-7561 0102 **Fax:** 020-7561 0103
E-mail: barry.greenfield@fabrizio.co.uk
Website: http://www.fabrizio.co.uk
Directors: M. Fkordis (MD)
Immediate Holding Company: FABRIZIO FASHIONS LIMITED
Registration no: 02117739 **VAT No.:** GB 473 0357 54
Date established: 1987 **Turnover:** £2m - £5m **No.of Employees:** 1 - 10
Product Groups: 23, 24, 63

Date of Accounts	Jun 11	Jun 10	Jun 09
Working Capital	-3m	-2m	-2m
Fixed Assets	N/A	16	174
Current Assets	288	371	259

Fagerult Lighting Ltd
50 Southwark Street, London, SE1 1UN
Tel: 020-7403 4123 **Fax:** 020-7378 0906
E-mail: scott.allen@fagerhult.co.uk
Website: http://www.fagerhult.co.uk
Directors: K. Kampeskog (Sales)
Managers: S. Allen (Mktg Serv Mgr)
Ultimate Holding Company: BLUESCOPE STEEL LTD (AUSTRALIA)
Immediate Holding Company: BLUESCOPE STEEL INTERNATIONAL LIMITED
Registration no: 02407099 **Date established:** 1989
Turnover: £10m - £20m **No.of Employees:** 11 - 20 **Product Groups:** 33, 37

Date of Accounts	Jun 12	Jun 11	Jun 10
Sales Turnover	16m	29m	8m
Pre Tax Profit/Loss	4m	4m	2m
Working Capital	21m	18m	15m
Fixed Assets	N/A	7	15
Current Assets	26m	26m	21m
Current Liabilities	1m	2m	2m

Fairfax Coffee Ltd
2 Regency Parade Finchley Road, London, NW3 5EQ
Tel: 020-7722 7646 **Fax:** 020-7722 2333
E-mail: info@fairfaxcoffee.com
Website: http://www.fairfaxcoffee.com
Directors: R. Payman (MD)
Immediate Holding Company: FAIRFAX COFFEE LIMITED
Registration no: 00392387 **Date established:** 1945 **Turnover:** £1m - £2m
No.of Employees: 1 - 10 **Product Groups:** 63, 77

Date of Accounts	Dec 11	Dec 10	Dec 09
Working Capital	44	158	143
Fixed Assets	10	32	42
Current Assets	233	388	376

Faisal's Enterprises Ltd
98 Mitcham Road, London, SW17 9NG
Tel: 020-8767 5577 **Fax:** 020-8767 8269
E-mail: erick@faisals.co.uk
Directors: A. Gani (Fin), M. Gani (MD), Z. Ghani (MD), A. Gani (Dir), Z. Gani (MD)
Managers: J. Mussa (Mgr), J. Gathrad (Export Sales Mg), E. Washington (Sec), A. Gaffar (Sales Prom Mgr)
Immediate Holding Company: FAISAL'S ENTERPRISES LIMITED
Registration no: 01249115 **VAT No.:** GB 219 5779 25
Date established: 1976 **Turnover:** £5m - £10m **No.of Employees:** 1 - 10
Product Groups: 61

Date of Accounts	Mar 10	Mar 09	Mar 08
Working Capital	-9	49	28
Fixed Assets	105	105	101
Current Assets	543	720	706

Faith Footwear Holdings Ltd
42 48 Chase Road, London, NW10 6PX
Tel: 020-8838 1759 **Fax:** 020-8930 3499
Website: http://www.faith.co.uk
Directors: J. Faith (MD), M. Cox (Co Sec), R. Denning (MD), D. Schofield (Purch)
Managers: R. Ross (Mktg Serv Mgr)
Ultimate Holding Company: Faith Footwear Holdings Ltd
Registration no: 06743192 **Date established:** 2008
Turnover: £10m - £20m **No.of Employees:** 251 - 500 **Product Groups:** 61

Falcon Graphics
Unit 15 Astbury Business Park Station Pass, London, SE15 2JR
Tel: 020-7639 0492 **Fax:** 020-7639 0494
E-mail: sales@falcon-graphics.co.uk
Website: http://www.signssoutheast.co.uk
Directors: A. Wilson (MD)
Immediate Holding Company: PRADA CONTRACT SERVICES LIMITED
Date established: 2009 **No.of Employees:** 1 - 10 **Product Groups:** 27, 28, 30, 37, 40, 44, 49, 52, 67, 80, 81, 84

Date of Accounts	Aug 11	Aug 10	Aug 09
Working Capital	31	34	37
Fixed Assets	14	15	16
Current Assets	58	54	47

Fangeos Painting & Decorating Contractor
Crusader House 145-157 St John Street, London, EC1V 4PY
Tel: 020-7183 3016 **Fax:** 01268-682919
E-mail: info@fangeos.co.uk
Website: http://www.fangeos.co.uk
Directors: G. Fannin (Prop)
Immediate Holding Company: TANTTOO LTD
Registration no: 07280635 **Date established:** 2010 **Turnover:** £1m - £2m
No.of Employees: 11 - 20 **Product Groups:** 48, 52, 67, 81

Date of Accounts	Jun 11
Working Capital	-7
Current Assets	8

Far East Mercantile Company
7-8 Ritz Parade, London, W5 3RA
Tel: 020-8998 8885 **Fax:** 020-8566 8672
E-mail: mail@fareastuk.com
Website: http://www.fareastuk.com
Directors: J. Vhogwani (Fin), K. Bhojwani (MD)
Ultimate Holding Company: F M C HOLDINGS COMPANY LIMITED (BRITISH VIRGIN ISLANDS)
Immediate Holding Company: FAREAST MERCANTILE CO. LIMITED
Registration no: 00515372 **Date established:** 1953 **Turnover:** £2m - £5m
No.of Employees: 1 - 10 **Product Groups:** 61

Date of Accounts	Mar 11	Mar 10	Mar 09
Sales Turnover	N/A	N/A	2m
Pre Tax Profit/Loss	N/A	N/A	131
Working Capital	376	417	482
Fixed Assets	415	431	446
Current Assets	390	433	530
Current Liabilities	N/A	N/A	30

Farebrother Ellis
27 Breams Building, London, EC4A 1DZ
Tel: 020-7405 4545 **Fax:** 020-7404 4362
E-mail: asubbarow@farebrother.com
Website: http://www.farebrother.com
Bank(s): Bank of Scotland
Directors: A. Subba Row (Snr Part)
Immediate Holding Company: FAREBROTHER SERVICES LIMITED
Registration no: 03905446 **Date established:** 2000 **Turnover:** £1m - £2m
No.of Employees: 21 - 50 **Product Groups:** 80

Date of Accounts	Dec 11	Dec 10	Dec 09
Working Capital	-0	-0	-0
Current Assets	48	62	48

Farr Vintners Ltd
220 Queenstown Road, London, SW8 4LP
Tel: 020-7821 2000 **Fax:** 020-7821 2020
E-mail: sales@farrvintners.com
Website: http://www.farrvintners.com
Bank(s): Barclays
Directors: R. Patel (Fin), T. Doe (Dir)
Immediate Holding Company: FARR VINTNERS LIMITED
Registration no: 01393302 **VAT No.:** GB 232 0069 12
Date established: 1978 **Turnover:** £125m - £250m
No.of Employees: 21 - 50 **Product Groups:** 21

Date of Accounts	Oct 11	Oct 10	Oct 09
Sales Turnover	132m	100m	86m
Pre Tax Profit/Loss	15m	11m	10m
Working Capital	50m	67m	20m
Fixed Assets	109	163	217
Current Assets	134m	106m	37m
Current Liabilities	74m	21m	10m

Fashion Spinners
108 Commercial Road, London, E1 1NU
Tel: 020-7488 1133 **Fax:** 020-7481 4488
E-mail: fashion-spinners@hotmail.com
Directors: M. Gill (Prop)
VAT No.: GB 189 1035 52 **No.of Employees:** 1 - 10 **Product Groups:** 63

Fasken Martineau
17 Hanover Square, London, W4 5YA
Tel: 020-7917 8500 **Fax:** 020-7917 8555
E-mail: london@fasken.com
Website: http://www.fasken.com
Directors: G. Howes (Snr Part)
Immediate Holding Company: PROPHARMA PARTNERS LIMITED
Registration no: OC309059 **Date established:** 2000
No.of Employees: 101 - 250 **Product Groups:** 80

Date of Accounts	May 11	May 10
Working Capital	1	1
Current Assets	1	1

F C M Travel Solutions
Farringdon Point 29-35 Farringdon Road, London, EC1M 3JF
Tel: 020-7025 4545 **Fax:** 020-7025 4546
E-mail: keith.slater@fcmtravel.co.uk
Website: http://www.tq3.co.uk
Directors: A. Spence (MD)
Managers: K. Slater (Sales Admin), D. Freeman (Mgr), K. Slater (Mgr), M. Appleyard (Sales Admin)
Immediate Holding Company: PRINT YORKSHIRE LIMITED
Registration no: 06779079 **Date established:** 2008
Turnover: £500,000 - £1m **No.of Employees:** 51 - 100
Product Groups: 69

Fenton Holloway Ltd
199 Southwark Bridge Road, London, SE1 0HA
Tel: 020-7407 3668 **Fax:** 020-7407 3666
E-mail: mail@fentonholloway.com
Website: http://www.fentonholloway.com
Managers: C. Ward (Mgr)
Registration no: 03112034 **No.of Employees:** 1 - 10 **Product Groups:** 35

Ferco Intertrade (UK) Ltd
Alliance House 12 Caxton Street, London, SW1H 0QS
Tel: 020-7799 1000 **Fax:** 020-7799 1020
E-mail: mail@fercointertrade.com
Website: http://www.fercointertrade.com
Directors: A. Arda (Grp Chief Exec), I. Aral (Dir)
Immediate Holding Company: PTC Securities Ltd
Registration no: 02868379 **VAT No.:** GB 690 7093 15
Date established: 2008 **Turnover:** £500,000 - £1m
No.of Employees: 1 - 10 **Product Groups:** 80

Ferrari Catering Equipment
9 Orchard Lane, London, SW20 0SE
Tel: 020-8944 6564 **Fax:** 020-8944 6564
Directors: L. Ferrari (Prop)
Date established: 1993 **No.of Employees:** 1 - 10 **Product Groups:** 20, 40, 41

Fides Partners Ltd
12-20 Camomile Street, London, EC3A 7PT
Tel: 020-7256 3200
E-mail: vishal@fidespartners.co.uk
Website: http://www.fidespartners.co.uk
Managers: V. Ramanah (Chief Acct)
Immediate Holding Company: FIDES PARTNERS LIMITED
Registration no: 06190804 **Date established:** 2007
No.of Employees: 1 - 10 **Product Groups:** 80

Date of Accounts	Mar 10	Mar 09
Working Capital	2	N/A
Current Assets	3	N/A

Field Fisher Waterhouse LLP
PO Box 732, London, EC3N 2AA
Tel: 020-7861 4000 **Fax:** 020-7488 0084
E-mail: info@ffw.com
Website: http://www.ffwlaw.com
Directors: J. Fife (Sales & Mktg), S. Haynes (Fin), M. Evans (I.T. Dir)
Managers: I. Mark (Sales Admin), E. Elliot (Personnel)
Ultimate Holding Company: FIELD FISHER WATERHOUSE LLP
Immediate Holding Company: FIELD FISHER WATERHOUSE LIMITED
Registration no: 06377520 **Date established:** 2007
Turnover: £250,000 - £500,000 **No.of Employees:** 251 - 500
Product Groups: 80

Fieldmount Terrazzo Ltd
7-8 Liddell Road, London, NW6 2EW
Tel: 020-7624 8866 **Fax:** 020-7328 1836
E-mail: info@fieldmount.co.uk
Website: http://www.fieldmount.co.uk
Directors: S. Thomasson (Fin), V. Alfano (Contracts)
Ultimate Holding Company: NORTH LONDON HOLDINGS LIMITED
Immediate Holding Company: FIELDMOUNT (TERRAZZO) LIMITED
Registration no: 01733832 **VAT No.:** GB 341 4290 81
Date established: 1983 **Turnover:** £500,000 - £1m
No.of Employees: 1 - 10 **Product Groups:** 14, 33, 52

Date of Accounts	Feb 08	Feb 11	Feb 10
Working Capital	385	192	333
Fixed Assets	26	17	22
Current Assets	466	267	402

Filofax Stationary Suppliers
68 Neal Street, London, WC2H 9PF
Tel: 020-7836 1977 **Fax:** 020- 78364736
E-mail: shop@filofax.co.uk
Website: http://www.filofax.co.uk
Directors: B. Ferguson (Internat Sales), R. Laing (MD)
Managers: B. Russell Gonthier (Mgr), B. Russell-gonthier (Mgr)
Registration no: 01891062 **VAT No.:** GB 597 0522 19
Date established: 1993 **Turnover:** £250,000 - £500,000
No.of Employees: 1 - 10 **Product Groups:** 28

Date of Accounts	Jan 08
Sales Turnover	23660
Pre Tax Profit/Loss	5670
Working Capital	21340
Fixed Assets	2750
Current Assets	24150
Current Liabilities	2810
ROCE% (Return on Capital Employed)	23.5

The Financial Services Authority
25 The North Colonnade Canary Wharf, London, E14 5HS
Tel: 020-7066 1000 **Fax:** 020-7066 1099
E-mail: enquiries@fsa.gov.uk
Website: http://www.fsa.gov.uk
Directors: W. Raynes (Dir), D. Lipsey (Dir), L. Peach (Dir), C. Bowe (Dir), K. McBrien (Dir), J. Mitchell (Dir), T. Heiser (Dir), D. Mills (Dir), A. Daffern (Dir)
Immediate Holding Company: THE FINANCIAL SERVICES AUTHORITY
Registration no: 01920623 **Date established:** 1985
Turnover: £250m - £500m **No.of Employees:** 1501 & over
Product Groups: 82

Date of Accounts	Mar 12	Mar 11	Mar 10
Sales Turnover	N/A	464m	436m
Pre Tax Profit/Loss	36m	30m	51m
Working Capital	-99m	-118m	-101m
Fixed Assets	157m	155m	118m
Current Assets	103m	115m	45m
Current Liabilities	117m	134m	62m

Financial Times
1 Southwark Bridge, London, SE1 9HL
Tel: 020-7873 3000 **Fax:** 020-7407 5700
Website: http://www.ft.com
Bank(s): HSBC Bank plc
Directors: S. Henderson (Fin)
Managers: L. Barber
Ultimate Holding Company: PEARSON PLC
Immediate Holding Company: THE FINANCIAL TIMES (M-M UK) LIMITED
Registration no: 01398449 **Date established:** 1978
Turnover: £250m - £500m **No.of Employees:** 251 - 500
Product Groups: 28

Date of Accounts	Dec 10	Dec 09	Dec 08
Sales Turnover	9m	7m	7m
Pre Tax Profit/Loss	349	282	82
Working Capital	-3m	-3m	-3m
Fixed Assets	104	N/A	N/A
Current Assets	18	21	27
Current Liabilities	96	74	20

Fine Art Services Ltd
17 Enterprise Way, London, SW18 1EJ
Tel: 020-8870 6029 **Fax:** 020-8877 1477
E-mail: fine_art_services@yahoo.co.uk
Directors: J. Cox (Dir), J. Medway (Dir), J. Cox (MD)
Immediate Holding Company: FINE ART SERVICES LIMITED
Registration no: 01658023 **VAT No.:** GB 317 6023 79
Date established: 1982 **Turnover:** Up to £250,000
No.of Employees: 1 - 10 **Product Groups:** 76

Date of Accounts	Sep 11	Sep 10	Sep 09
Working Capital	750	148	155
Fixed Assets	N/A	30	39
Current Assets	929	216	199

Fine Interiors
Unit 34 Parkside Business Estate Rolt Street, London, SE8 5JB
Tel: 020-8692 3457 **Fax:** 020-8462 8808
E-mail: dennisrowden@aol.com
Directors: D. Rowden (Dir)
Immediate Holding Company: FINE INTERIORS LTD
Registration no: 06135081 **Date established:** 1985
No.of Employees: 1 - 10 **Product Groups:** 46, 48

Finers Stephens Innocent LLP
179-185 Great Portland Street, London, W1W 5LS
Tel: 020-7323 4000 **Fax:** 020-7580 7069
E-mail: marketing@fsilaw.com
Website: http://www.fsilaw.com
Directors: P. Millet (Snr Part), C. Sweeney (Pers), M. Rilli (Mkt Research)
Managers: P. Mitchell, C. Sweeney (Personnel), C. Adshead-grant (Mktg Serv Mgr), N. Boarland (Tech Serv Mgr)
Immediate Holding Company: FINERS STEPHENS INNOCENT SERVICES LIMITED
Registration no: 07573825 **Date established:** 2011
Turnover: £20m - £50m **No.of Employees:** 101 - 250 **Product Groups:** 80

Finnlines UK Ltd
8 Heron Quay, London, E14 4JB
Tel: 020-7519 7300 **Fax:** 020-7536 0255
E-mail: info@finnlines.co.uk
Website: http://www.finnlines.co.uk
Bank(s): National Westminster
Directors: S. Airas (Mkt Research), B. Rolfe (MD), D. Gabriel (I.T. Dir), A. Alapetri (Sales & Mktg)
Registration no: 02781256 **VAT No.:** GB 244 2927 60
Turnover: £2m - £5m **No.of Employees:** 11 - 20 **Product Groups:** 74

Fireguard Fire Extinguishers
215 Westcombe Hill, London, SE3 7DR
Tel: 020-8853 0088
E-mail: fireguard@btconnect.com
Website: http://www.fireguard.com
Directors: P. Brighty (Prop)
Date established: 1993 **No.of Employees:** 1 - 10 **Product Groups:** 38, 42

Fireguard safety equipment co ltd
2Nd Floor,145-157 St John Street, London, EC1V 4PY
Tel: 0845-0751042 **Fax:** 0845-0751043
E-mail: info@fireguard-uk.com
Website: http://www.fireguard-uk.com
Directors: A. Hussain (Export)
Registration no: 05717368 **Date established:** 2006 **Turnover:** £2m - £5m
No.of Employees: 21 - 50 **Product Groups:** 40

Firenzi Ltd
1a Tariff Road, London, N17 0DY
Tel: 020-8801 8016 **Fax:** 020-8801 8015
Directors: G. Whiting (MD)
Immediate Holding Company: FIRENZI ASPHALTE (DRAYTON PARK) LIMITED

Registration no: 00774190 **VAT No.:** GB 229 2846 44
Date established: 1963 **Turnover:** £500,000 - £1m
No.of Employees: 1 - 10 **Product Groups:** 17

Date of Accounts	Mar 11	Mar 10	Mar 08
Working Capital	2	2	2
Current Assets	2	2	2

First Capital North Ltd
Macmillan House Paddington Station, London, W2 1TY
Tel: 020-7298 7300 **Fax:** 020-7706 8789
E-mail: enquiries@firstgroup.com
Website: http://www.firstgroup.com
Directors: A. Jones (Dir), J. Dow (Co Sec)
Ultimate Holding Company: FIRSTGROUP PLC
Immediate Holding Company: FIRST CAPITAL NORTH LIMITED
Registration no: 02636481 **Date established:** 1991
Turnover: £20m - £50m **No.of Employees:** 21 - 50 **Product Groups:** 72

Date of Accounts	Mar 08	Mar 09	Mar 10
Sales Turnover	58m	60m	60m
Pre Tax Profit/Loss	2m	611	7m
Working Capital	-73	475	6m
Current Assets	16m	17m	9m
Current Liabilities	N/A	N/A	300

First State Investments
30 Cannon Street, London, EC4M 6YQ
Tel: 020-7332 6500 **Fax:** 020-7332 6501
E-mail: enquiries@firststate.co.uk
Website: http://www.firststate.co.uk
Directors: A. Smith (Co Sec)
Managers: J. Breyley (Comptroller), H. Wells (Personnel), K. Lakhani, G. Ferguson, G. Withers, E. Osborne-fardon, C. Adams (Sales Admin)
Ultimate Holding Company: COMMONWEALTH BANK OF AUSTRALIA
Immediate Holding Company: FIRST STATE INVESTMENTS (UK) LIMITED
Registration no: 02294743 **Date established:** 1988
Turnover: £125m - £250m **No.of Employees:** 51 - 100
Product Groups: 82

Date of Accounts	Jun 11	Jun 10	Jun 09
Sales Turnover	127m	86m	51m
Pre Tax Profit/Loss	1m	3m	638
Working Capital	5m	4m	2m
Current Assets	107m	83m	80m
Current Liabilities	10m	8m	5m

Fish Bros Group
114 High Street, London, E17 7JY
Tel: 020-8520 0293 **Fax:** 020-8509 2770
E-mail: susanneal@fishbrothersltd.co.uk
Website: http://www.charlesfish.co.uk
Directors: P. Coleman (MD)
Immediate Holding Company: FISH BROTHERS LIMITED
Registration no: 07100645 **Date established:** 2009
No.of Employees: 11 - 20 **Product Groups:** 61, 82

F K 3
Southbank House Black Prince Road, London, SE1 7SJ
Tel: 020-7463 2011
E-mail: info@fk3.biz
Website: http://www.fk3.biz
Directors: A. Crost (Dir)
Immediate Holding Company: GREEN POWER CONFERENCES LIMITED
Registration no: 04782620 **Date established:** 2008
Turnover: Up to £250,000 **No.of Employees:** 1 - 10 **Product Groups:** 81

Date of Accounts	Nov 08	Nov 07
Working Capital	2	25
Current Assets	11	39

Flamelog Ltd
6 Chingford Industrial Centre Hall Lane, London, E4 8DJ
Tel: 020-8529 5292 **Fax:** 020-8524 5340
E-mail: flamelogltd@btinternet.com
Website: http://www.flamelog.com
Directors: J. Bleach (MD)
Managers: P. WALLACE (Chief Acct)
Immediate Holding Company: FLAMELOG LIMITED
Registration no: 01378727 **Date established:** 1978
Turnover: £250,000 - £500,000 **No.of Employees:** 1 - 10
Product Groups: 40

Date of Accounts	Feb 08	Feb 07	Feb 06
Sales Turnover	299	338	346
Pre Tax Profit/Loss	-10	4	-15
Working Capital	23	43	37
Fixed Assets	18	8	10
Current Assets	52	83	87
Current Liabilities	29	40	50
ROCE% (Return on Capital Employed)	-25.3	8.2	-31.0
ROT% (Return on Turnover)	-3.5	1.2	-4.2

Flashpoint England Ltd
PO Box 726, London, NW11 7XQ
Tel: 020-7490 1444 **Fax:** 020-7253 4491
E-mail: sales@flashpoint.ws
Website: http://www.flashpoint.ws
Directors: N. Jones (Fin), M. Lyons (Dir)
Immediate Holding Company: FLASHPOINT INTERNATIONAL LIMITED
Registration no: 03525770 **Date established:** 1998
Turnover: Up to £250,000 **No.of Employees:** 1 - 10 **Product Groups:** 39

Date of Accounts	Sep 10	Sep 09	Sep 01
Sales Turnover	N/A	N/A	3
Working Capital	N/A	N/A	1
Fixed Assets	118	118	118
Current Assets	N/A	N/A	2

Fleetwick International
Senator House 2 Graham Road, London, NW4 3HF
Tel: 020-8202 1900 **Fax:** 020-8202 1818
E-mail: admin@fleetwick.com
Website: http://www.fleetwick.com
Managers: K. Kocik (Mgr)
Immediate Holding Company: FLEETWICK INTERNATIONAL LIMITED
Registration no: 01485842 **VAT No.:** GB 245 7822 43
Date established: 1980 **Turnover:** £2m - £5m **No.of Employees:** 1 - 10
Product Groups: 14, 20, 23, 24, 27, 29, 30, 31, 32, 33, 35, 36, 37, 39, 40, 41, 44, 61, 62, 63, 66, 67, 68

Date of Accounts	Sep 11	Sep 10	Sep 09
Sales Turnover	5m	4m	3m
Pre Tax Profit/Loss	77	173	128

see next page

Fleetwick International - Cont'd

Working Capital	261	259	215
Fixed Assets	12	14	17
Current Assets	1m	1m	1m
Current Liabilities	38	42	62

Fleurets

4 Roger Street, London, WC1N 2JX
Tel: 020-7280 4700 **Fax:** 020-7636 4750
E-mail: london@fleurets.com
Website: http://www.fleurets.com
Directors: C. Barger (Co Sec)
Managers: J. Footner
Ultimate Holding Company: FLEURETS HOLDINGS LIMITED
Immediate Holding Company: FLEURETS LIMITED
Registration no: 02223330 **Date established:** 1988 **Turnover:** £2m - £5m
No.of Employees: 21 - 50 **Product Groups:** 80

Date of Accounts	Sep 11	Sep 10	Sep 09
Sales Turnover	5m	5m	5m
Pre Tax Profit/Loss	-32	31	56
Working Capital	1m	1m	2m
Fixed Assets	248	313	305
Current Assets	2m	2m	2m
Current Liabilities	478	400	417

Flexal Springs UK Ltd

179 Park Avenue Park Royal, London, NW10 7XH
Tel: 020-8453 1178 **Fax:** 020-8961 9181
E-mail: flexalspringsuk@btconnect.com
Directors: G. DeSilva (MD), G. Desilva (Dir)
Managers: L. Linda (Sec)
Immediate Holding Company: FLEXAL SPRINGS UK LIMITED
Registration no: 05325736 **VAT No.:** GB 226 6765 42
Date established: 2005 **Turnover:** £500,000 - £1m
No.of Employees: 11 - 20 **Product Groups:** 35

Date of Accounts	Mar 11	Mar 10	Mar 09
Working Capital	57	61	53
Fixed Assets	191	215	241
Current Assets	222	186	223

Flo Rite Ltd

Unit 33-34 Brunswick Square White Hart Lane, London, N17 8DT
Tel: 020-8885 2320 **Fax:** 020-8885 1756
E-mail: floritespray@googlemail.com
Website: http://www.flo-rite.co.uk
Directors: G. Howard (Dir)
Immediate Holding Company: FLO-RITE LIMITED
Registration no: 00550022 **Date established:** 1955
No.of Employees: 1 - 10 **Product Groups:** 46, 48

Date of Accounts	Mar 11	Mar 10	Mar 08
Working Capital	5	5	7
Current Assets	9	9	11

The Flooring Group Ltd

3 South End Road, London, NW3 2PT
Tel: 020-7435 5678 **Fax:** 020-7433 1991
Website: http://www.theflooringgroup.co.uk
Directors: K. Hawkes (Fin), B. Hawkes (MD)
Ultimate Holding Company: THE ISLINGTON FLOORING CO LTD
Immediate Holding Company: THE FLOORING GROUP LIMITED
Registration no: 04116323 **Date established:** 2000
No.of Employees: 1 - 10 **Product Groups:** 23, 30, 33

Date of Accounts	Mar 11	Mar 10	Mar 09
Working Capital	-149	-158	-172
Fixed Assets	31	27	32
Current Assets	270	144	223

Geraldine Flower Publications (Trading As Geraldine Flower Publications)

71 Thornton Avenue, London, W4 1QF
Tel: 020-8747 8028 **Fax:** 020-8747 8054
Website: http://www.green-pages.co.uk
Directors: G. Flower (Grp Chief Exec), J. Vernon (Fin)
Immediate Holding Company: Geraldine Flower & Associates Ltd
Registration no: 02312710 **Date established:** 1988
Turnover: Up to £250,000 **No.of Employees:** 1 - 10 **Product Groups:** 28

FMI Limited

27 Queen Street, London, EC4R 1BB
Tel: 020-8498 2200 **Fax:** 0845-1210668
E-mail: sales@fmi.co.uk
Website: http://www.fmi.co.uk
Directors: N. Pawson (Ch)
Managers: N. Paulson (Mgr), P. Johnston (Chief Acct)
Immediate Holding Company: Fmi Ltd
Registration no: 01738299 **Date established:** 1983 **Turnover:** £2m - £5m
No.of Employees: 11 - 20 **Product Groups:** 44

Date of Accounts	Dec 08	Jun 07	Jun 06
Sales Turnover	4856	5180	4638
Pre Tax Profit/Loss	13	19	69
Working Capital	310	467	551
Fixed Assets	305	438	439
Current Assets	1092	1933	2015
Current Liabilities	781	1466	1465
Total Share Capital	30	30	30
ROCE% (Return on Capital Employed)	2.1	2.1	7.0
ROT% (Return on Turnover)	0.3	0.4	1.5

The Folio Society

44 Eagle Street, London, WC1R 4FS
Tel: 020-7573 3477 **Fax:** 020-7400 4242
Website: http://www.foliosociety.com
Managers: C. Heeney (Mgr)
Ultimate Holding Company: FOLIO HOLDINGS LIMITED
Immediate Holding Company: FOLIO SOCIETY LIMITED(THE)
Registration no: 01015675 **Date established:** 1971
Turnover: £20m - £50m **No.of Employees:** 51 - 100 **Product Groups:** 28, 61, 80

Date of Accounts	Aug 09	Aug 08	Aug 10
Sales Turnover	23m	31m	25m
Pre Tax Profit/Loss	1m	-2m	2m
Working Capital	5m	4m	7m
Fixed Assets	1m	2m	1m
Current Assets	9m	8m	11m
Current Liabilities	2m	3m	2m

Food & Drink Federation

6 Catherine Street, London, WC2B 5JJ
Tel: 020-7836 2460 **Fax:** 020-7379 5735
E-mail: reception@fdf.org.uk
Website: http://www.fdf.org.uk
Directors: J. Moseley (Pres), J. Baxter (I.T. Dir)
Managers: M. Singh (Tech Serv Mgr), A. Coleshill (Personnel)
Immediate Holding Company: FOOD AND DRINK FEDERATION(THE)
Registration no: 00210572 **VAT No.:** GB 240 0290 18
Date established: 2025 **Turnover:** £5m - £10m
No.of Employees: 51 - 100 **Product Groups:** 87

Date of Accounts	Dec 11	Dec 10	Dec 09
Sales Turnover	6m	6m	6m
Pre Tax Profit/Loss	145	267	163
Working Capital	-511	-658	-796
Fixed Assets	5m	5m	5m
Current Assets	4m	4m	3m
Current Liabilities	4m	4m	4m

The Foord Partnership

12 Paxton Place, London, SE27 9SS
Tel: 020-8761 5161 **Fax:** 020-7978 2189
Directors: B. Foord (Ptnr), B. Foord (Snr Part)
Managers: E. Rokaki (Personnel)
Turnover: £500,000 - £1m **No.of Employees:** 1 - 10 **Product Groups:** 52, 61, 80, 82

Foreign & Colonial Investment Trust

Exchange House Primrose Street, London, EC2A 2NY
Tel: 020-7628 8000 **Fax:** 020-7628 8188
E-mail: brokerline@fandc.com
Website: http://www.fandc.com
Directors: D. Logan (Fin), E. Bramson (Ch)
Managers: T. Fennell, J. Whyte, P. Cole (Personnel)
Immediate Holding Company: FOREIGN & COLONIAL INVESTMENT TRUST PLC
Registration no: 00012901 **Date established:** 1979
Turnover: £50m - £75m **No.of Employees:** 251 - 500 **Product Groups:** 82

Date of Accounts	Dec 11	Dec 10	Dec 09
Sales Turnover	58m	51m	53m
Pre Tax Profit/Loss	43m	37m	38m
Working Capital	-190m	-169m	-5m
Fixed Assets	2228m	2422m	2074m
Current Assets	6m	6m	4m
Current Liabilities	178m	105m	5m

Forest Hydraulics Ltd

19-20 Greenshield Industrial Estate Bradfield Road, London, E16 2AU
Tel: 020-7474 5738 **Fax:** 020-7474 5181
E-mail: steven.brown@virgin.net
Directors: R. Brown (Fin), S. Brown (MD)
Immediate Holding Company: FOREST HYDRAULICS LIMITED
Registration no: 03995822 **VAT No.:** GB 410 1462 15
Date established: 2000 **Turnover:** £1m - £2m **No.of Employees:** 11 - 20
Product Groups: 29, 30, 34

Date of Accounts	May 11	May 10	May 09
Working Capital	271	217	137
Fixed Assets	127	145	168
Current Assets	1m	1m	1m

Format Worldwide Ltd

26-26a Queens Parade Friern Barnet Road, London, N11 3DA
Tel: 020-8368 0222 **Fax:** 020-8368 0222
E-mail: osman.civici@formatworldwide.co.uk
Website: http://www.formatworldwide.com
Directors: B. Hussein (Dir)
Immediate Holding Company: CASPIAN CHILDREN FOUNDATION
Registration no: 05905645 **Date established:** 2010
Turnover: Up to £250,000 **No.of Employees:** 1 - 10 **Product Groups:** 12, 14, 20, 31, 33, 66

Forrester Ketley & Co.

Forrester House 52 Bounds Green Road, London, N11 2EY
Tel: 020-8889 6622 **Fax:** 020-8881 1088
E-mail: steven_wake@forresters.co.uk
Website: http://www.forresters.co.uk
Directors: S. Wake (Snr Part), C. Cook (Ptnr)
Immediate Holding Company: SEEKER WIRELESS LIMITED
Registration no: 04229509 **VAT No.:** GB 110 0242 58
Date established: 2006 **No.of Employees:** 21 - 50 **Product Groups:** 80

Forward Group plc

57 Buckland Road, London, E10 6QS
Tel: 020-8558 7110 **Fax:** 020-8558 5974
E-mail: info@forward-group.co.uk
Website: http://www.forward-group.co.uk
Managers: P. Davis (Mgr)
Immediate Holding Company: FORWARD GROUP PLC
Registration no: 04232158 **Date established:** 2001
Turnover: £250,000 - £500,000 **No.of Employees:** 1 - 10
Product Groups: 44, 64, 66, 67

Date of Accounts	Mar 12	Mar 11	Mar 10
Sales Turnover	234	347	378
Pre Tax Profit/Loss	-299	-102	-192
Working Capital	-4m	-4m	-4m
Fixed Assets	1	1	1
Current Assets	98	222	143
Current Liabilities	4m	4m	4m

Foster & Partners

Riverside Three 22 Hester Road, London, SW11 4AN
Tel: 020-7738 0455 **Fax:** 020-7738 1107
E-mail: info@fosterandpartners.com
Website: http://www.fosterandpartners.com
Directors: M. Majidi (Grp Chief Exec), K. Boon (Pers), M. Streets (Fin), G. Young (Tech Serv)
Managers: K. Burn (Personnel), K. Harris, I. Goodwin (I.T. Exec), A. Odonovan (Buyer), G. Markovitz (Mktg Serv Mgr), M. Wilson (Buyer)
Ultimate Holding Company: FOSTER + PARTNERS GROUP LIMITED
Immediate Holding Company: FOSTER HOLDINGS LIMITED
Registration no: 02518918 **Date established:** 1990
Turnover: £125m - £250m **No.of Employees:** 501 - 1000
Product Groups: 80

Date of Accounts	Apr 11	Apr 10	Apr 09
Pre Tax Profit/Loss	N/A	6m	-0
Working Capital	219	219	216
Fixed Assets	41	41	41
Current Assets	220	222	216

Fourth Passenger Ltd

29 Meridian Place, London, E14 9FE
Tel: 020-7100 3322
E-mail: mail@4puk.com
Website: http://www.4puk.com
Directors: A. Tegally (Mkt Research), F. Wood (Tech Serv)
Managers: E. Tessarin (Chief Mgr)
Registration no: 05446653 **Date established:** 2004
No.of Employees: 1 - 10 **Product Groups:** 89

Francis Chichester Ltd

9 St James's Place, London, SW1A 1PE
Tel: 020-7493 0931 **Fax:** 020-7409 1830
E-mail: sales@francischichester.com
Website: http://www.francischichester.co.uk
Directors: G. Chichester (MD)
Immediate Holding Company: FRANCIS CHICHESTER LIMITED
Registration no: 00574784 **Date established:** 1956
Turnover: Up to £250,000 **No.of Employees:** 1 - 10 **Product Groups:** 28

Date of Accounts	Mar 12	Mar 11	Mar 10
Sales Turnover	11	18	26
Pre Tax Profit/Loss	-7	-33	-5
Working Capital	2	-0	7
Fixed Assets	N/A	N/A	1
Current Assets	5	7	21
Current Liabilities	3	3	3

Frank Usher Group

66 Grosvenor Street, London, W1K 3JL
Tel: 020-7629 9696 **Fax:** 020-7629 6886
E-mail: avril.bell@frankusher.co.uk
Website: http://www.frankusher.co.uk
Directors: A. Bell (Sales)
Managers: G. Lee (Ops Mgr), A. Bell (Mgr)
Immediate Holding Company: DEGANWY QUAY LTD
Registration no: 03769991 **Date established:** 2001
Turnover: £10m - £20m **No.of Employees:** 1 - 10 **Product Groups:** 63

Franklin & Andrews

Sea Containers House 20 Upper Ground, London, SE1 9LZ
Tel: 020-7633 9966 **Fax:** 020-7928 2471
E-mail: michelle.swales@franklinandrews.com
Website: http://www.franklinandrews.com
Directors: G. Leonard (Ch), M. Blackburn (Dir), A. Williams (MD), M. Lynn (Co Sec), J. Mercer (Mkt Research), M. Swales (Mkt Research)
Ultimate Holding Company: Mott Macdonald Group Ltd
Immediate Holding Company: Franklin & Andrews Ltd
Registration no: 03164282 **VAT No.:** GB 243 4263 80
Turnover: £20m - £50m **No.of Employees:** 101 - 250
Product Groups: 80, 84

Fraser & Ellis

80-100 Gwynne Road, London, SW11 3UW
Tel: 020-7228 9999 **Fax:** 020-7228 7250
E-mail: sales@fraserellis.co.uk
Bank(s): National Westminster Bank Plc
Directors: P. Fraser (Prop)
Immediate Holding Company: FRASER & ELLIS LIMITED
Registration no: 00188957 **Date established:** 2023 **Turnover:** £1m - £2m
No.of Employees: 11 - 20 **Product Groups:** 36, 37, 48, 54, 66

Date of Accounts	Mar 12	Mar 11	Mar 10
Working Capital	2m	2m	2m
Fixed Assets	11	16	33
Current Assets	2m	2m	2m

Frazer Design Consultants Ltd

124 Fordwych Road, London, NW2 3PB
Tel: 020-8208 4426 **Fax:** 020-7328 6085
E-mail: info@frazerdesigners.com
Website: http://www.frazerdesigners.com
Directors: S. Frazer (Dir), S. Frazer (MD), J. Knight (Dir)
Immediate Holding Company: THE RAFT CONSULTANCY (UK): LIMITED LIABILITY PARTNERSHIP
Registration no: 01351077 **VAT No.:** GB 235 2548 69
Date established: 2006 **Turnover:** £250,000 - £500,000
No.of Employees: 1 - 10 **Product Groups:** 49

Date of Accounts	Mar 12	Mar 11	Mar 10
Sales Turnover	N/A	42	N/A
Pre Tax Profit/Loss	N/A	31	N/A
Working Capital	6	5	22
Fixed Assets	N/A	N/A	1
Current Assets	10	8	60
Current Liabilities	N/A	4	N/A

Freed Of London Ltd

62-64 Well Street, London, E9 7PX
Tel: 020-8510 4700 **Fax:** 020-8510 4750
E-mail: info@freedoflondon.com
Website: http://www.freedshop.com
Directors: K. Ash (Fin), M. Atkins (Co Sec), P. O'Neill (MD)
Managers: J. Kelly (Purch Mgr), S. Ozbey (Personnel), B. Seifert (Mktg Serv Mgr), M. Redhead (I.T. Exec)
Ultimate Holding Company: ONWARD HOLDINGS CO LTD (JAPAN)
Immediate Holding Company: FREED OF LONDON LIMITED
Registration no: 02693052 **Date established:** 1992 **Turnover:** £1m - £2m
No.of Employees: 51 - 100 **Product Groups:** 22

Date of Accounts	Dec 11	Dec 10	Dec 09
Sales Turnover	10m	11m	11m
Pre Tax Profit/Loss	354	461	-354
Working Capital	7m	6m	6m
Fixed Assets	793	974	990
Current Assets	7m	7m	7m
Current Liabilities	560	597	576

Freedown Food Co.

Unit 43 London Stone Business Estate Broughton Street, London, SW8 3QR
Tel: 020-7720 4520 **Fax:** 020-7720 2166
E-mail: info@freedownfood.co.uk
Website: http://www.freedownfood.co.uk
Directors: J. Bengue (MD)
Immediate Holding Company: THE FREEDOWN FOOD COMPANY LIMITED
Registration no: 03816255 **Date established:** 1999
Turnover: £250,000 - £500,000 **No.of Employees:** 1 - 10
Product Groups: 01, 20, 62

Date of Accounts	Mar 11	Mar 10
Working Capital	69	54
Fixed Assets	11	5
Current Assets	712	559
Current Liabilities	145	135

Anna French Ltd
36 Hinton Road, London, SE24 0HJ
Tel: 020-7737 6555 **Fax:** 020-7274 8193
E-mail: jonathan@annafrench.co.uk
Website: http://www.annafrench.co.uk
Directors: J. French (MD), S. French (Sales)
Immediate Holding Company: ANNA FRENCH LIMITED
Registration no: SC059316 **Date established:** 1976 **Turnover:** £1m - £2m
No.of Employees: 1 - 10 **Product Groups:** 23

Date of Accounts	Jun 11	Jun 10	Jun 09
Working Capital	137	193	198
Fixed Assets	N/A	N/A	3
Current Assets	152	232	254

French Lessons London
44 Kempshott Road, London, SW16 5LQ
Tel: 020-8133 4063
E-mail: tuition@lsfrench.com
Website: http://www.lsfrench.com
Directors: D. Belliot (Prop)
Date established: 2001 **No.of Employees:** 11 - 20 **Product Groups:** 86

Frenger International Ltd
Wilberforce House Station Road, London, NW4 4QE
Tel: 020-8202 4111 **Fax:** 020-8202 1804
E-mail: jnmermet@frenger.com
Website: http://www.frenger.com
Directors: B. Mermet (Fin), J. Mermet (MD)
Immediate Holding Company: FRENGER INTERNATIONAL LIMITED
Registration no: 01771512 **Date established:** 1983 **Turnover:** £1m - £2m
No.of Employees: 1 - 10 **Product Groups:** 80, 81, 85

Date of Accounts	Sep 11	Sep 10	Sep 09
Working Capital	301	242	236
Fixed Assets	16	15	32
Current Assets	863	614	580

Fresh Air Ltd
5 Horseshoe Close, London, NW2 7JJ
Tel: 020-8452 4266 **Fax:** 020-8452 2904
E-mail: studio@freshair.co.uk
Website: http://www.freshair.co.uk
Managers: C. Wagle (Fin Mgr), J. Morris, T. Hastick (Personnel)
Immediate Holding Company: FRESHAIR LIMITED
Registration no: 04905226 **Date established:** 2003 **Turnover:** £5m - £10m
No.of Employees: 51 - 100 **Product Groups:** 23

Date of Accounts	Jun 12	Jun 11	Jun 10
Sales Turnover	6m	8m	12m
Pre Tax Profit/Loss	13	-90	34
Working Capital	-169	84	198
Fixed Assets	2m	1m	1m
Current Assets	1m	3m	4m
Current Liabilities	347	920	1m

Fresh Cosmetics
92 Marylebone High Street, London, W1U 4RD
Tel: 020-7486 4100 **Fax:** 020-7935 0841
E-mail: london@fresh.com
Website: http://www.fresh.com
Managers: C. Odabasi (Mgr)
No.of Employees: 1 - 10 **Product Groups:** 32, 63

Friends Of The Earth
26-28 Underwood Street, London, N1 7JQ
Tel: 020-7490 1555 **Fax:** 020-7490 0881
E-mail: info@foe.co.uk
Website: http://www.foe.co.uk
Bank(s): Co-op
Directors: A. Atkins (Dir), C. Parsons (Fin)
Immediate Holding Company: FRIENDS OF THE EARTH LIMITED
Registration no: 01012357 **Date established:** 1971 **Turnover:** £2m - £5m
No.of Employees: 101 - 250 **Product Groups:** 80

Date of Accounts	May 11	May 10	May 09
Sales Turnover	3m	2m	3m
Pre Tax Profit/Loss	-7	-54	-62
Working Capital	1m	1m	1m
Fixed Assets	119	163	215
Current Assets	2m	2m	2m
Current Liabilities	331	307	333

Fuchs Lubritech International Ltd
8 Eley Road Eley Estate Edmonton, London, N18 3DB
Tel: 020-8345 5566 **Fax:** 020-8884 3255
E-mail: sales@fuchs-lubritech.co.uk
Website: http://www.fuchs-lubritech.co.uk
Directors: H. Vithlani (Fin)
Immediate Holding Company: FUCHS LUBRITECH INTERNATIONAL LIMITED
Registration no: 03998198 **VAT No.:** GB 220 5164 12
Date established: 2000 **Turnover:** £20m - £50m **No.of Employees:** 1 - 10
Product Groups: 20, 29, 30, 31, 32, 33, 36, 39, 42, 45, 46, 48, 66, 67, 68, 84

Date of Accounts	Dec 11	Dec 10	Dec 09
Pre Tax Profit/Loss	-2	248	-2
Working Capital	28	30	31
Fixed Assets	5m	5m	5m
Current Assets	43	42	42
Current Liabilities	14	12	11

Fullers Brewery Shop
Griffin Brewery Chiswick Lane South, London, W4 2QB
Tel: 020-8996 2085 **Fax:** 020-8995 0230
E-mail: comments@fullers.co.uk
Website: http://www.fullers.co.uk
Managers: D. Green (Mgr)
Immediate Holding Company: FULLER SMITH & TURNER PLC
Registration no: 00241882 **VAT No.:** GB 226 1480 83
Date established: 2029 **Turnover:** £125m - £250m
No.of Employees: 1 - 10 **Product Groups:** 21, 62

Date of Accounts	Mar 12	Mar 09	Mar 10
Sales Turnover	253m	210m	228m
Pre Tax Profit/Loss	29m	14m	27m
Working Capital	-19m	-24m	-101m
Fixed Assets	449m	357m	388m
Current Assets	33m	23m	25m
Current Liabilities	34m	26m	30m

Funky Venues Ltd
27B Tradescant Road, London, SW8 1XD
Tel: 020-7735 9263 **Fax:** 020-7735 5052
E-mail: info@funkyvenues.com
Website: http://www.funkyvenues.com
Directors: D. McGinnis (Grp Chief Exec)
Registration no: 05822724 **Date established:** 2006
No.of Employees: 1 - 10 **Product Groups:** 89

Fuss Wrought Ironwork
115 Station Passage, London, SE15 2JR
Tel: 020-7732 8115 **Fax:** 020- 77328664
Directors: P. Cromack (Prop)
Date established: 1995 **No.of Employees:** 1 - 10 **Product Groups:** 26, 35

The Futures Company (Head Office)
6 More London Place, London, SE1 2QY
Tel: 020-7955 1800 **Fax:** 020-7955 1900
E-mail: reception@tnsglobal.com
Website: http://www.thefuturescompany.com
Bank(s): HSBC
Directors: A. Furstenberg (Fin), A. Curry (Dir)
Managers: S. Tyler (Comptroller), L. Walkling (Personnel), C. Victor (Tech Serv Mgr), J. Childs
Ultimate Holding Company: WPP PLC (JERSEY)
Immediate Holding Company: HENLEY CENTRE HEADLIGHT VISION LTD
Registration no: 02083071 **VAT No.:** GB 397 2801 21
Date established: 1986 **Turnover:** £5m - £10m
No.of Employees: 51 - 100 **Product Groups:** 80, 81, 86

Date of Accounts	Dec 11	Dec 10	Dec 09
Sales Turnover	5m	7m	7m
Pre Tax Profit/Loss	-603	125	595
Working Capital	2m	2m	2m
Fixed Assets	139	238	203
Current Assets	3m	3m	4m
Current Liabilities	822	994	1m

G A M Ltd
12 St James Place, London, SW1A 1NX
Tel: 020-7493 9990 **Fax:** 020-7493 0715
E-mail: ahanges@gam.com
Website: http://www.gam.com
Directors: A. Hanges (Dir), A. Wills (Fin)
Ultimate Holding Company: GAM HOLDING LIMITED (SWITZERLAND)
Immediate Holding Company: GAM (U.K.) LIMITED
Registration no: 01664573 **Date established:** 1982
Turnover: £125m - £250m **No.of Employees:** 251 - 500
Product Groups: 82

Date of Accounts	Dec 11	Dec 10	Dec 09
Sales Turnover	216m	246m	185m
Pre Tax Profit/Loss	68m	59m	42m
Working Capital	60m	52m	59m
Fixed Assets	4m	12m	10m
Current Assets	136m	135m	120m
Current Liabilities	74m	80m	59m

G Baldwin & Co.
171-173 Walworth Road, London, SE17 1RW
Tel: 020-7703 5550 **Fax:** 020-7252 6264
E-mail: info@baldwins.co.uk
Website: http://www.baldwins.co.uk
Directors: S. Dagnell (Dir)
Immediate Holding Company: G BALDWIN & CO LTD
Registration no: 04639383 **Date established:** 2003
No.of Employees: 1 - 10 **Product Groups:** 31, 32

Date of Accounts	Mar 11	Mar 10	Mar 09
Working Capital	16	-5	23
Fixed Assets	147	167	190
Current Assets	277	235	292

G E Capital
201 Talgarth Road, London, W6 8BJ
Tel: 020-7302 6000 **Fax:** 020-7302 6800
Website: http://www.ge.com
Directors: C. Alexander (MD), Z. Citron (Dir)
Ultimate Holding Company: GENERAL ELECTRIC COMPANY (USA)
Immediate Holding Company: GE CAPITAL LIMITED
Registration no: 04053665 **Date established:** 2000 **Turnover:** £5m - £10m
No.of Employees: 501 - 1000 **Product Groups:** 82

Date of Accounts	Dec 11	Dec 10	Dec 09
Sales Turnover	5m	6m	10m
Pre Tax Profit/Loss	424	454	994
Working Capital	13m	28m	11m
Fixed Assets	11	16	21
Current Assets	30m	29m	30m
Current Liabilities	1m	2m	3m

G Gooch Engineers
Unit 1a Hotspur Industrial Estate West Road, London, N17 0XJ
Tel: 07860-541774 **Fax:** 020-8805 2996
E-mail: gerry@jgoochandsons.co.uk
Website: http://www.jgengineers.co.uk
Managers: G. Gooch (Mgr)
Immediate Holding Company: SOUTHBURY TYRES LTD
Registration no: 04137382 **VAT No.:** GB 589 8312 82
Date established: 2010 **Turnover:** Up to £250,000
No.of Employees: 1 - 10 **Product Groups:** 07, 48

Date of Accounts	Mar 08	Mar 07	Mar 06
Working Capital	1	11	15
Fixed Assets	1	N/A	N/A
Current Assets	24	30	30
Current Liabilities	23	20	15

Greater London Enterprise
Unit 10-12 The Circle Queen Elizabeth Street, London, SE1 2JE
Tel: 020-7403 0300 **Fax:** 020-7403 1742
E-mail: info@gle.co.uk
Website: http://www.gle.co.uk
Directors: M. Large (Grp Chief Exec)
Immediate Holding Company: GREATER LONDON ENTERPRISE LIMITED
Registration no: 01653116 **VAT No.:** GB 397 2680 07
Date established: 1982 **Turnover:** £20m - £50m
No.of Employees: 51 - 100 **Product Groups:** 80, 81

Date of Accounts	Mar 11	Mar 10	Mar 09
Sales Turnover	34m	45m	36m
Pre Tax Profit/Loss	-3m	997	-21m
Working Capital	7m	412	1m
Fixed Assets	35m	38m	37m
Current Assets	32m	38m	43m
Current Liabilities	23m	25m	22m

G M L International Ltd
Met Building 22 Percy Street, London, W1T 2BU
Tel: 020-7580 8588 **Fax:** 020-7580 8688
E-mail: info@gml.net
Website: http://www.gml.net
Directors: T. Stohner (MD)
Managers: C. Merrells (Tech Serv Mgr)
Ultimate Holding Company: GML (HOLDINGS) LTD.
Immediate Holding Company: G M L INTERNATIONAL LIMITED
Registration no: 01769934 **VAT No.:** GB 394 5843 08
Date established: 1983 **Turnover:** £20m - £50m
No.of Employees: 11 - 20 **Product Groups:** 82

Date of Accounts	Mar 11	Mar 10	Mar 09
Sales Turnover	31m	23m	1m
Pre Tax Profit/Loss	2m	127	117
Working Capital	4m	2m	2m
Fixed Assets	559	619	624
Current Assets	7m	10m	4m
Current Liabilities	3m	8m	2m

G M W Architects
PO Box 1613, London, W8 6SL
Tel: 020-7937 8020 **Fax:** 020-7937 5815
E-mail: terrybrown@gmw-architects.com
Website: http://www.gmw-architects.com
Managers: T. Brown (Mgr)
Immediate Holding Company: GMW ARCHITECTS LLP
Registration no: OC325769 **VAT No.:** GB 232 5277 77
Date established: 2007 **Turnover:** £5m - £10m
No.of Employees: 51 - 100 **Product Groups:** 84

G & P Autocare
41 Birkbeck Road, London, W3 6BQ
Tel: 020-8992 5031 **Fax:** 020-8992 5031
Directors: S. Burk (Prop)
Registration no: 00494423 **Date established:** 1996
No.of Employees: 1 - 10 **Product Groups:** 84

G V A Grimley Ltd
10 Stratton Street, London, W1J 8JR
Tel: 0870-9008990 **Fax:** 0131-469 6001
E-mail: enquiries@gvagrimley.co.uk
Website: http://www.gvagrimley.co.uk
Directors: D. Henson (Dir), M. Wetherstone (Ptnr), R. Bould (Ptnr), B. Barnett (Ch), D. Daniels (Co Sec)
Ultimate Holding Company: 06434650
Immediate Holding Company: GVA GRIMLEY LIMITED
Registration no: 06382509 **VAT No.:** GB 109 6324 476
Date established: 2007 **Turnover:** £50m - £75m
No.of Employees: 501 - 1000 **Product Groups:** 52, 80, 82, 84

G W London
1010 Harrow Road, London, NW10 5NS
Tel: 020-8968 0690 **Fax:** 020-8968 0692
E-mail: gwlondon@btconnect.com
Website: http://www.gwlondon.com
Directors: G. Walsh (Prop)
Immediate Holding Company: G WALSH LIMITED
Registration no: 05229129 **Date established:** 2004
No.of Employees: 1 - 10 **Product Groups:** 26

Date of Accounts	Jan 12	Jan 11	Jan 10
Working Capital	48	35	-19
Fixed Assets	2	2	3
Current Assets	111	112	86

Gab Robins UK Ltd
35 Great St Helen's, London, EC3A 6HB
Tel: 020-7200 3000 **Fax:** 020-7200 3001
E-mail: kieran-rigby@gabrobins.co.uk
Website: http://www.gabrobins.co.uk
Directors: K. Rigby (Grp Chief Exec), K. Rigby (MD), P. Bes (Dir), E. Tubb (Co Sec)
Ultimate Holding Company: GAB ROBINS HOLDINGS UK LTD
Immediate Holding Company: GAB ROBINS UK LIMITED
Registration no: 01304989 **VAT No.:** GB 244 1503 95
Date established: 1977 **Turnover:** £5m - £10m **No.of Employees:** 21 - 50
Product Groups: 82

Date of Accounts	Dec 10	Dec 09	Dec 08
Sales Turnover	52m	44m	39m
Pre Tax Profit/Loss	2m	486	-2m
Working Capital	5m	1m	140
Fixed Assets	3m	3m	2m
Current Assets	27m	21m	23m
Current Liabilities	11m	11m	12m

Gailarde Ltd
9 Mill Hill Industrial Estate Flower Lane, London, NW7 2HU
Tel: 020-8731 1313 **Fax:** 020-8731 1300
E-mail: office@gailarde.com
Website: http://www.gailarde.com
Bank(s): Bank of Scotland
Directors: C. Dauris (MD), P. Thomas (Sales)
Immediate Holding Company: GAILARDE LIMITED
Registration no: 01406026 **VAT No.:** GB 538 4410 46
Date established: 1978 **Turnover:** Up to £250,000
No.of Employees: 21 - 50 **Product Groups:** 24

Date of Accounts	Dec 09	Dec 08	Dec 07
Working Capital	673	568	666
Fixed Assets	189	238	199
Current Assets	2m	2m	1m

Galaxy Wholesalers Ltd
15-19 Benwell Road, London, N7 7BL
Tel: 020-7607 6560 **Fax:** 020-7700 3152
E-mail: info@galaxywholesalers.com
Website: http://www.galaxywholesalers.com
Directors: V. Patel (MD)
Immediate Holding Company: GALAXY WHOLESALERS LIMITED
Registration no: 02872447 **Date established:** 1993 **Turnover:** £2m - £5m
No.of Employees: 1 - 10 **Product Groups:** 35, 49, 61

Date of Accounts	Dec 11	Dec 10	Dec 09
Working Capital	843	840	822
Fixed Assets	38	46	42
Current Assets	1m	995	980

Galbraiths Ltd
Bridge Gate House 124-126 Borough High Street, London, SE1 1BL
Tel: 020-7378 6363 **Fax:** 020-7528 7201
E-mail: admin@galbraiths.co.uk
Website: http://www.galbraiths.co.uk
Directors: N. Rokison (MD)
Ultimate Holding Company: GALBRAITH HOLDINGS LIMITED
Immediate Holding Company: GALBRAITH HOLDINGS LIMITED
Registration no: 02171917 **Date established:** 1987
Turnover: £10m - £20m **No.of Employees:** 51 - 100 **Product Groups:** 74, 76, 82

Date of Accounts	Dec 11	Dec 10	Dec 09
Sales Turnover	9m	12m	12m
Pre Tax Profit/Loss	2m	2m	2m
Working Capital	-149	-285	-951
Fixed Assets	3m	3m	3m
Current Assets	4m	5m	3m
Current Liabilities	3m	4m	3m

Galpeg Ltd
70 Hampden Road, London, N10 2NX
Tel: 020-8444 4455 **Fax:** 020-8442 0357
E-mail: info@galpeg.com
Website: http://www.galpeg.com
Directors: L. Hiteshi (Fin), P. Green (MD)
Immediate Holding Company: GALPEG LIMITED
Registration no: 01233774 **VAT No.:** GB 231 3002 35
Date established: 1975 **Turnover:** £500,000 - £1m
No.of Employees: 1 - 10 **Product Groups:** 38, 49

Date of Accounts	Dec 11	Dec 10	Dec 09
Working Capital	590	134	171
Fixed Assets	566	1m	1m
Current Assets	661	185	215

Gardiner Security Ltd
Unit 13 Kingsbury Trading Estate Church Lane, London, NW9 8AU
Tel: 020-8905 9601
Website: http://www.gardinersecurity.co.uk
Immediate Holding Company: GARDINER SECURITY LIMITED
Registration no: 04124719 **Date established:** 2000
No.of Employees: 1 - 10 **Product Groups:** 37, 40

GB Engineering
Unit 35.4 35 White Hart Avenue, London, SE28 0GU
Tel: 020-8855 0395 **Fax:** 020-8855 0274
E-mail: pam@gbengineering.net
Website: http://www.gbengineering.net
Managers: P. Webb (Sales Admin)
Date established: 2000 **No.of Employees:** 11 - 20 **Product Groups:** 26, 35, 39, 45, 46

Gee & Garnham Ltd
1-6 Crescent Mews, London, N22 7GG
Tel: 020-8888 4982 **Fax:** 020-8881 1353
E-mail: gg@geeandgarnham.com
Website: http://www.geeandgarnham.com
Bank(s): Barclays P.L.C., London
Directors: P. Clague (Grp)
Immediate Holding Company: GEE & GARNHAM LIMITED
Registration no: 00522830 **VAT No.:** GB 220 9604 87
Date established: 1953 **Turnover:** £2m - £5m **No.of Employees:** 11 - 20
Product Groups: 39, 40, 42, 68

Date of Accounts	Sep 10	Sep 09	Sep 08
Sales Turnover	3m	3m	N/A
Pre Tax Profit/Loss	-364	268	N/A
Working Capital	2m	3m	3m
Fixed Assets	1m	1m	1m
Current Assets	3m	3m	4m
Current Liabilities	65	69	N/A

William Gee Ltd
William Gee House 520 522 Kingsland Road, London, E8 4AH
Tel: 020-7254 2451 **Fax:** 020-7249 8116
E-mail: wmgeetrims@aol.com
Website: http://www.williamgee.co.uk
Bank(s): Barclays
Directors: J. Graham (MD)
Ultimate Holding Company: WILLIAM GEE (HOLDINGS) LIMITED
Immediate Holding Company: WILLIAM GEE LIMITED
Registration no: 00205663 **VAT No.:** GB 220 3168 14
Date established: 2025 **Turnover:** £250,000 - £500,000
No.of Employees: 11 - 20 **Product Groups:** 23, 35, 63, 66

Gefco UK Ltd
376-378 Chiswick High Road, London, W4 5TF
Tel: 020-8742 2220 **Fax:** 020-8742 2066
E-mail: sales.uk@gefco.co.uk
Website: http://www.gefco.fr
Directors: G. McDonald (Co Sec), P. Cosse (Dir)
Ultimate Holding Company: PEUGEOT SA (FRANCE)
Immediate Holding Company: GEFCO U.K. LIMITED
Registration no: 01544410 **Date established:** 1981
Turnover: £75m - £125m **No.of Employees:** 11 - 20 **Product Groups:** 51, 61, 68, 72, 74, 76, 77, 82

Date of Accounts	Dec 10	Dec 09	Dec 08
Sales Turnover	115m	106m	138m
Pre Tax Profit/Loss	-3m	-11m	3m
Working Capital	5m	6m	13m
Fixed Assets	7m	7m	9m
Current Assets	32m	40m	35m
Current Liabilities	2m	6m	1m

Kurt Geiger Ltd
75 Bermondsey Street, London, SE1 3XF
Tel: 020-7546 1888 **Fax:** 020-7546 1880
E-mail: info@kurtgeiger.com
Website: http://www.kurtgeiger.com
Bank(s): HSBC Bank plc
Directors: D. Christilaw (Fin), R. Farrar Hockley (Purch)
Managers: L. Phillips, N. Wennington (Personnel), N. Turner, S. McClymont
Ultimate Holding Company: KG GROUP HOLDINGS LIMITED
Immediate Holding Company: KURT GEIGER LIMITED
Registration no: 00968046 **VAT No.:** GB 649 6916 80
Date established: 1969 **Turnover:** £125m - £250m
No.of Employees: 51 - 100 **Product Groups:** 63

Date of Accounts	Dec 11	Jan 09	Jan 10
Sales Turnover	183m	130m	151m
Pre Tax Profit/Loss	13m	8m	11m
Working Capital	7m	20m	25m
Fixed Assets	20m	8m	11m
Current Assets	87m	45m	55m
Current Liabilities	18m	7m	11m

The Gemmological Association Of Great Britain
27 Greville Street, London, EC1N 8TN
Tel: 020-7404 3334 **Fax:** 020-7404 8843
E-mail: info@gem-a.com
Website: http://www.gem-a.com
Bank(s): Barclays
Managers: J. Ogden
Immediate Holding Company: THE GEMMOLOGICAL ASSOCIATION OF GREAT BRITAIN
Registration no: 01945780 **VAT No.:** GB 417 8902 33
Date established: 1985 **Turnover:** £1m - £2m **No.of Employees:** 11 - 20
Product Groups: 86

Date of Accounts	Dec 11	Dec 10	Dec 09
Sales Turnover	2m	2m	1m
Pre Tax Profit/Loss	196	218	105
Working Capital	751	520	265
Fixed Assets	89	124	161
Current Assets	1m	973	713
Current Liabilities	507	399	286

General Catering Supplies Ltd
Tuborg House Mandrell Rd, London, SW2 5DL
Tel: 020-7733 7590 **Fax:** 020-7737 9201
E-mail: info@gcsgroup.co.uk
Website: http://www.gcsgroup.co.uk
Directors: S. Ahmed (Prop), A. Ahmed (MD), A. Ahmad (MD)
Managers: T. King (Mgr)
Registration no: 00950540 **Turnover:** £5m - £10m
No.of Employees: 21 - 50 **Product Groups:** 24, 26, 27, 30, 52, 63, 67, 81, 84

Date of Accounts	Apr 09	Apr 08	Apr 07
Sales Turnover	5m	6m	6m
Pre Tax Profit/Loss	-4	82	-19
Working Capital	941	982	914
Fixed Assets	154	218	299
Current Assets	2m	2m	3m
Current Liabilities	196	456	467

General Eyewear
Arch 67 The Stables Market Chalk Farm Road, London, NW1 8AH
Tel: 07790-102204 **Fax:** 020-7428 0123
E-mail: info@generaleyewear.com
Website: http://www.arckive.net
Directors: F. Laing (Prop)
Ultimate Holding Company: CAMDEN MARKET HOLDINGS CORPORATION (BVI)
Immediate Holding Company: CENTREPOINT MANAGEMENT LIMITED
Registration no: 03647458 **Date established:** 1998
No.of Employees: 1 - 10 **Product Groups:** 37, 38

Generali Portfolio Management
Aldermary House 15 Queen Street, London, EC4N 1TX
Tel: 020-7332 2080 **Fax:** 020-7332 2090
Website: http://www.bsi.ch
Managers: S. Turnbull
Ultimate Holding Company: ASSICURAZIONI GENERALL SPA(ITALY)
Immediate Holding Company: GENERALI PORTFOLIO MANAGEMENT (UK) LIMITED
Registration no: 03794233 **Date established:** 1999 **Turnover:** £1m - £2m
No.of Employees: 1 - 10 **Product Groups:** 82

Date of Accounts	Dec 11	Dec 10	Dec 09
Sales Turnover	2m	2m	2m
Pre Tax Profit/Loss	312	274	535
Working Capital	1m	863	775
Fixed Assets	5	7	19
Current Assets	1m	1m	1m
Current Liabilities	339	349	409

Genersys plc
37 Queen Anne Street, London, W1G 9JB
Tel: 020-7637 9708 **Fax:** 020-7636 3013
E-mail: info@genersys.com
Website: http://www.genersys.com
Directors: R. Kyriakides (Grp Chief Exec), A. Robins (Fin)
Managers: J. Dawson (Sales Prom Mgr), G. Hicks (Tech Serv Mgr)
Ultimate Holding Company: GENERSYS CORPORATION PLC
Immediate Holding Company: GENERSYS PLC
Registration no: 04173693 **Date established:** 2001
Turnover: £500,000 - £1m **No.of Employees:** 1 - 10 **Product Groups:** 37

Date of Accounts	Dec 11	Dec 10	Dec 09
Sales Turnover	859	901	2m
Pre Tax Profit/Loss	-103	-196	-422
Working Capital	255	295	-589
Fixed Assets	322	225	44
Current Assets	490	628	824
Current Liabilities	70	129	1m

George Corderoy & Co.
9 Marshalsea Road, London, SE1 1EP
Tel: 020-7015 1920 **Fax:** 020-7015 1930
E-mail: london@corderoy.com
Website: http://www.corderoy.com
Directors: A. Austin (Snr Part)
Immediate Holding Company: GEORGE CORDEROY LLP
Registration no: OC322621 **Date established:** 2006 **Turnover:** £2m - £5m
No.of Employees: 21 - 50 **Product Groups:** 80, 84

Gerald Eve LLP
72 Welbeck Street, London, W1G 0AY
Tel: 020-7493 3338 **Fax:** 020-7491 1825
E-mail: hbullock@geraldeve.com
Website: http://www.gerald.com
Bank(s): Barclays
Directors: H. Bullock (Snr Part), W. Stephen (Tech Serv), C. Campbell (Co Sec)
Immediate Holding Company: GERALD EVE LLP
Registration no: OC339470 **Date established:** 2008 **Turnover:** £1m - £2m
No.of Employees: 101 - 250 **Product Groups:** 80

Date of Accounts	Apr 11	Apr 10	Apr 09
Sales Turnover	34m	33m	34m
Pre Tax Profit/Loss	8m	7m	8m
Working Capital	9m	8m	8m
Fixed Assets	2m	1m	2m
Current Assets	16m	14m	13m
Current Liabilities	6m	6m	5m

Getaway Executive Travel Ltd
192-198 Vauxhall Bridge Road, London, SW1 1DX
Tel: 0845-180 7820 **Fax:** 020-7973 0014
E-mail: travel@getaway.co.uk
Directors: C. Marlow (Fin), M. De Laszlo (MD)
Immediate Holding Company: DDA BLUEPRINT PUBLIC RELATIONS LTD
Registration no: 00906605 **VAT No.:** GB 217 9574 35
Date established: 2011 **Turnover:** £2m - £5m **No.of Employees:** 1 - 10
Product Groups: 69

Date of Accounts	Sep 11	Sep 10
Working Capital	-200	-200
Fixed Assets	2m	2m

Gibson Dunn & Crutcher
Telephone House 2-4 Temple Avenue, London, EC4Y 0HB
Tel: 020-7071 4000 **Fax:** 020-7071 4244
E-mail: epalmer@gibsondunn.com
Website: http://www.gibsondunn.com
Managers: A. Patricot
Immediate Holding Company: GIBSON, DUNN & CRUTCHER TRUSTEES LIMITED
Registration no: 04432206 **Date established:** 2002
No.of Employees: 51 - 100 **Product Groups:** 80

Gillhams
47 Fleet Street, London, EC4Y 1BJ
Tel: 020-7353 2732 **Fax:** 020-7353 2733
E-mail: solicitors@gillhams.com
Website: http://www.gillhams.com
Directors: L. Ellis (Ptnr)
Immediate Holding Company: GILLHAMS SOLICITORS LLP
Registration no: OC334863 **Date established:** 2008
No.of Employees: 1 - 10 **Product Groups:** 80

Gilmark Electro
The Print House 18 Ashwin Street, London, E8 3DL
Tel: 020-8123 1139
E-mail: sales@wattbits.com
Website: http://www.gilmark.co.uk
Directors: T. Giles (Sales)
Date established: 2008 **No.of Employees:** 1 - 10 **Product Groups:** 67

Gilmex International Ltd
Unit 40 The I O Centre Armstrong Road, London, SE18 6RS
Tel: 020-8331 4130 **Fax:** 020-8463 0565
E-mail: sales@gilmex.com
Website: http://www.bindingbazaar.com
Bank(s): National Westminster Bank Plc & Barclays Bank PLC
Directors: S. Gill (MD)
Managers: L. Nicoll (Comptroller)
Immediate Holding Company: GILMEX INTERNATIONAL LIMITED
Registration no: 00399820 **VAT No.:** GB 235 7098 49
Date established: 1945 **Turnover:** £2m - £5m **No.of Employees:** 21 - 50
Product Groups: 28, 30, 35, 44, 49, 67

Date of Accounts	Mar 11	Mar 10	Mar 09
Working Capital	576	459	658
Fixed Assets	248	183	133
Current Assets	1m	1m	1m

Gina Shoes Ltd
104-106 Brantwood Droad, London, N17 0XW
Tel: 020-8885 7500 **Fax:** 020-7249 1984
E-mail: sales@gina.com
Website: http://www.gina.com
Directors: A. Kurdash (MD)
Managers: A. Kurdash (Sales & Mktg Mg), A. Kurdash (Tech Serv Mgr)
Ultimate Holding Company: THE GINA GROUP PLC
Immediate Holding Company: GINA SHOES LIMITED
Registration no: 00528524 **VAT No.:** GB 220 7457 84
Date established: 1954 **Turnover:** £5m - £10m
No.of Employees: 51 - 100 **Product Groups:** 22

Date of Accounts	Mar 12	Mar 11	Mar 10
Sales Turnover	7m	8m	7m
Pre Tax Profit/Loss	476	582	118
Working Capital	2m	2m	2m
Fixed Assets	2m	863	573
Current Assets	4m	4m	4m
Current Liabilities	454	711	573

Glass & Glazing Federation
54 Ayres Street, London, SE1 1EU
Tel: 020-7939 9100 **Fax:** 020-7357 7458
E-mail: info@ggf.org.uk
Website: http://www.ggf.org.uk
Bank(s): HSBC Bank plc
Directors: E. Hardacre (Fin), N. Rees (Grp Chief Exec), R. Aitken (Fin)
Managers: J. Lee
Immediate Holding Company: GLASS AND GLAZING FEDERATION
Registration no: 04063012 **VAT No.:** GB 241 8419 67
Date established: 2000 **Turnover:** £5m - £10m **No.of Employees:** 21 - 50
Product Groups: 33, 35

Date of Accounts	Dec 11	Dec 10	Dec 09
Sales Turnover	7m	7m	7m
Pre Tax Profit/Loss	618	1m	2m
Working Capital	6m	6m	5m
Fixed Assets	4m	4m	4m
Current Assets	9m	9m	7m
Current Liabilities	3m	3m	2m

Gleave & Co.
111-113 St John Street, London, EC1V 4JA
Tel: 020-7253 1345 **Fax:** 020-7253 0447
E-mail: sales@gleaveandco.com
Website: http://www.gleaveandco.com
Directors: G. Gleave (Prop)
No.of Employees: 1 - 10 **Product Groups:** 47

Gleeds
95 New Cavendish Street, London, W1W 6XF
Tel: 020-7631 7000 **Fax:** 020-7631 7001
E-mail: london@gleeds.co.uk
Website: http://www.gleeds.com

Directors: R. Speer (Ch)
Ultimate Holding Company: GLEEDS HOLDINGS LIMITED
Immediate Holding Company: GLEEDS UK LIMITED
Registration no: 06473135 **Date established:** 2008
Turnover: £500,000 - £1m **No.of Employees:** 101 - 250
Product Groups: 80, 84

Glentree Estates

698 Finchley Road, London, NW11 7NE
Tel: 020-8209 1144 **Fax:** 020-8209 0307
E-mail: rentals@glentree.co.uk
Website: http://www.glentree.co.uk
Managers: J. Gee (Sales Prom Mgr)
Immediate Holding Company: GLENTREE ESTATES LIMITED
Registration no: 01259568 **Date established:** 1976 **Turnover:** £2m - £5m
No.of Employees: 1 - 10 **Product Groups:** 80

Date of Accounts	Sep 11	Sep 10	Sep 09
Working Capital	4m	3m	2m
Fixed Assets	430	435	387
Current Assets	5m	5m	4m

Global Aerospace Underwriting Managers Ltd

Fitzwilliam House 10 St Mary Axe, London, EC3A 8EQ
Tel: 020-7369 2244 **Fax:** 020-7369 2840
E-mail: info@practicallaw.com
Website: http://www.global-aero.com
Bank(s): Coutts, London
Directors: A. Mednuik (MD), D. Boyle (Ch)
Immediate Holding Company: GLOBAL AEROSPACE UNDERWRITING MANAGERS LIMITED
Registration no: 02512067 **Date established:** 1990
Turnover: £50m - £75m **No.of Employees:** 101 - 250 **Product Groups:** 82

Date of Accounts	Dec 10	Dec 09	Dec 08
Sales Turnover	68m	61m	68m
Pre Tax Profit/Loss	12m	7m	7m
Working Capital	21m	18m	24m
Fixed Assets	80m	77m	82m
Current Assets	35m	33m	51m
Current Liabilities	15m	14m	2m

Global Industries Ltd

8 Leopold Road, London, W5 3PB
Tel: 020-8992 8497 **Fax:** 020-8992 2917
E-mail: angela.keshishian@importcarsearch.com
Website: http://www.global-ind.com
Directors: A. Keshishian (MD)
Immediate Holding Company: GLOBAL INDUSTRIES LIMITED
Registration no: 00416337 **VAT No.:** GB 495 4192 14
Date established: 1946 **Turnover:** £5m - £10m **No.of Employees:** 1 - 10
Product Groups: 35, 37, 39, 61, 68

Date of Accounts	Dec 11	Dec 10	Dec 09
Sales Turnover	7m	N/A	N/A
Pre Tax Profit/Loss	401	N/A	N/A
Working Capital	68	-8	-157
Fixed Assets	2m	2m	2m
Current Assets	1m	927	759
Current Liabilities	462	N/A	N/A

Global Radio

30 Leicester Square, London, WC2H 7LA
Tel: 020-7766 6001 **Fax:** 020-7766 6111
E-mail: info@thisisglobal.com
Website: http://www.thisisglobal.com
Directors: L. Waterman (Pers), D. Holroyd (Tech Serv), M. Connole (Fin)
Managers: A. Tabor
Ultimate Holding Company: THIS IS GLOBAL LIMITED
Immediate Holding Company: GLOBAL RADIO UK LIMITED
Registration no: 06288359 **Date established:** 2007
No.of Employees: 251 - 500 **Product Groups:** 79

Date of Accounts	Mar 12	Mar 11	Mar 10
Sales Turnover	21m	18m	16m
Pre Tax Profit/Loss	14m	12m	11m
Working Capital	114m	104m	96m
Fixed Assets	171m	171m	171m
Current Assets	114m	104m	96m

Go Interiors

3 Elizabeth Trading Estate Juno Way, London, SE14 5RW
Tel: 020-8469 3716 **Fax:** 020-8469 0037
E-mail: sales@gointeriors.co.uk
Managers: F. Rowe (Mgr), D. Moore (Mgr)
Date established: 2003 **No.of Employees:** 1 - 10 **Product Groups:** 35, 52

Golden Plan Ltd

Second Floor Linen Hall 162-168 Regent Street, London, W1B 5TB
Tel: 020-7434 2066 **Fax:** 020-7287 2329
Directors: J. Miller (MD), J. Miller (Dir)
Immediate Holding Company: GOLDEN PLAN LIMITED
Registration no: 01095171 **VAT No.:** GB 340 9594 42
Date established: 1973 **Turnover:** £250,000 - £500,000
No.of Employees: 1 - 10 **Product Groups:** 49

Date of Accounts	Jun 08	Jun 07	Jun 06
Working Capital	-192	-109	-94
Fixed Assets	1	2	3
Current Assets	41	104	85
Current Liabilities	232	213	179

Goldenberg Real Estate LLP

Fifth Floor Linen Hall 162-168 Regent Street, London, W1B 5TF
Tel: 020-7491 4101 **Fax:** 020-7491 0809
E-mail: reception@goldenberg.co.uk
Website: http://www.goldenberg.co.uk
Directors: B. Goldenberg (Snr Part)
Immediate Holding Company: GOLDENBERG REAL ESTATE LLP
Registration no: OC344568 **Date established:** 2009
Turnover: Up to £250,000 **No.of Employees:** 1 - 10 **Product Groups:** 80

Date of Accounts	Mar 11	Apr 10
Sales Turnover	N/A	76
Pre Tax Profit/Loss	N/A	25
Working Capital	-1	-6
Fixed Assets	1	N/A
Current Assets	34	18
Current Liabilities	N/A	24

Goldsmiths Jewellers Ltd

186-190 Bishopsgate, London, EC2M 4NL
Tel: 020-7283 6622 **Fax:** 020-7623 3696
Website: http://www.goldsmiths.co.uk
Directors: C. D'costa (MD)
Managers: P. Warrington (Mgr), R. Metcalf (Mgr), M. McCabe (Mgr), J. Herman (Admin Off)
Immediate Holding Company: GOLDSMITHS (JEWELLERS) LIMITED
Registration no: 02117655 **Date established:** 1987
No.of Employees: 11 - 20 **Product Groups:** 49

Date of Accounts	Feb 08
Sales Turnover	2158
Pre Tax Profit/Loss	280
Working Capital	798
Current Assets	873
Current Liabilities	75
ROCE% (Return on Capital Employed)	35.1

Richard S Goldstein

96a Mount Street, London, W1K 2SZ
Tel: 020-7499 8200 **Fax:** 020-7499 8300
E-mail: info@goldsteinvisa.com
Website: http://www.goldsteinvisa.com
Directors: R. Goldstein (Prop)
Managers: R. Goldstein
Registration no: 05333267 **Date established:** 2005
No.of Employees: 1 - 10 **Product Groups:** 80

Golly Slater Group Ltd

12 Margaret Street, London, W1W 8JQ
Tel: 020-7255 6400 **Fax:** 020-7379 4166
E-mail: lreception@golleyslater.co.uk
Website: http://www.gollyslater.co.uk
Directors: C. Lovell (MD), S. Henderson (Dir)
Ultimate Holding Company: TGTHR GROUP LIMITED
Immediate Holding Company: GOLLEY SLATER GROUP LIMITED
Registration no: 00584047 **Date established:** 1957
Turnover: £20m - £50m **No.of Employees:** 51 - 100 **Product Groups:** 81

Date of Accounts	Mar 08	Nov 06	Nov 05
Working Capital	7	7	7
Current Assets	7	11	10
Current Liabilities	N/A	4	4

Good Relations Ltd

Hobern Gate 26 South Hampton Buildings, London, WC2A 1PQ
Tel: 020-7861 3030 **Fax:** 020-7861 3200
E-mail: afossey@goodrelations.co.uk
Website: http://www.goodrelations.co.uk
Directors: J. Leece (Fin), A. Fossey (Ch)
Ultimate Holding Company: CHIME COMMUNICATIONS PLC
Immediate Holding Company: GOOD RELATIONS LIMITED
Registration no: 00697060 **VAT No.:** GB 480 8429 26
Date established: 1961 **Turnover:** £5m - £10m **No.of Employees:** 21 - 50
Product Groups: 81

Date of Accounts	Dec 11	Dec 10	Dec 09
Sales Turnover	8m	8m	7m
Pre Tax Profit/Loss	946	767	923
Working Capital	-2m	-1m	-1m
Fixed Assets	2m	2m	2m
Current Assets	2m	2m	2m
Current Liabilities	1m	801	1m

Goodman Derrick LLP

10 St Bride Street, London, EC4A 4AD
Tel: 020-7404 0606 **Fax:** 020-7831 6407
E-mail: law@gdlaw.co.uk
Website: http://www.gdlaw.co.uk
Bank(s): National Westminster
Directors: T. Langton (Snr Part)
Immediate Holding Company: GOODMAN DERRICK LLP
Registration no: OC321066 **Date established:** 2006
Turnover: £5m - £10m **No.of Employees:** 51 - 100 **Product Groups:** 80

Date of Accounts	Apr 11	Apr 10	Apr 09
Sales Turnover	10m	9m	8m
Pre Tax Profit/Loss	4m	4m	2m
Working Capital	6m	4m	3m
Fixed Assets	102	260	452
Current Assets	7m	5m	4m
Current Liabilities	1m	592	N/A

Goodmans Garage Ltd

Pensbury Place, London, SW8 4TP
Tel: 020-7498 6478 **Fax:** 020-7498 3842
E-mail: info@goodmansgarage.co.uk
Website: http://www.goodmansgarage.co.uk
Directors: C. Parry (MD)
Immediate Holding Company: C.GOODMAN & SONS,LIMITED
Registration no: 00274609 **VAT No.:** GB 235 5430 77
Date established: 1933 **Turnover:** £500,000 - £1m
No.of Employees: 1 - 10 **Product Groups:** 39

Gover Horowitz & Blunt Ltd

Grosvenor Gardens House 35-37 Grosvenor Gardens, London, SW1W 0BS
Tel: 020-7630 7777 **Fax:** 020-7828 3867
E-mail: sh@ghb.co.uk
Website: http://www.ghb.co.uk
Directors: C. Gasser (Co Sec), S. Horowitz (Dir)
Immediate Holding Company: GOVER, HOROWITZ AND BLUNT LIMITED
Registration no: 00661715 **Date established:** 1960 **Turnover:** £5m - £10m
No.of Employees: 1 - 10 **Product Groups:** 82

Date of Accounts	Jun 11	Jun 10	Jun 09
Working Capital	1m	894	995
Fixed Assets	25	24	10
Current Assets	3m	3m	3m

Graff Diamonds London Ltd

29 Albemarle Street, London, W1S 4JA
Tel: 020-7290 6760 **Fax:** 020-7581 3415
E-mail: enquiries@graffdiamonds.com
Website: http://www.graffdiamonds.com
Directors: L. Graff (MD)
Ultimate Holding Company: GRAFF DIAMONDS HOLDINGS LTD (BRITISH VIRGIN ISLANDS)
Immediate Holding Company: GRAFF DIAMONDS (JAPAN) LIMITED
Registration no: 03838146 **Date established:** 1999
Turnover: £500m - £1,000m **No.of Employees:** 51 - 100
Product Groups: 49

Date of Accounts	Dec 07	Dec 06	Dec 05
Sales Turnover	6m	803	N/A
Pre Tax Profit/Loss	-1m	-760	N/A
Working Capital	2m	1m	N/A
Fixed Assets	345	34	N/A
Current Assets	3m	1m	N/A
Current Liabilities	781	101	N/A
Total Share Capital	196	N/A	N/A

Grafton Recruitment Ltd

2 Upper Tachbrook Street, London, SW1V 1SH
Tel: 020-7828 0809 **Fax:** 020-7828 0962
E-mail: idarmstetter@grafton-group.com
Website: http://www.grafton-group.com
Managers: A. Samu (Develop Mgr), A. Siechowicz, S. Parry, D. Klein
Ultimate Holding Company: GRAFTON RECRUITMENT INTERNATIONAL LIMITED
Immediate Holding Company: GRAFTON RECRUITMENT LIMITED
Registration no: 01873249 **Date established:** 1984
No.of Employees: 1 - 10 **Product Groups:** 80

Date of Accounts	Mar 11	Mar 10	Mar 09
Sales Turnover	56m	52m	75m
Pre Tax Profit/Loss	-2m	-902	-3m
Working Capital	-2m	-782	-85
Fixed Assets	3m	4m	4m
Current Assets	16m	15m	14m
Current Liabilities	14m	11m	7m

Grant Thornton Ltd

22 Melton Street, London, NW1 2EP
Tel: 020-7383 5100 **Fax:** 020-7383 4715
E-mail: scott.c.barnes@gtuk.com
Website: http://www.grant-thornton.co.uk
Bank(s): National Westminster Bank Plc
Managers: S. Barnes
Ultimate Holding Company: GRANT THORNTON UK LLP
Immediate Holding Company: GRANT THORNTON LIMITED
Registration no: 02917818 **Date established:** 1994
Turnover: £50m - £75m **No.of Employees:** 501 - 1000
Product Groups: 72, 80, 82, 86

Gratte Brothers Ltd

2 Regents Wharf All Saints Street, London, N1 9RL
Tel: 020-7837 6433 **Fax:** 020-7837 6779
E-mail: info@gratte.com
Website: http://www.gratte.com
Bank(s): AIB Group
Directors: A. Hills (Mkt Research), D. Southern (Sales), I. Bass (Fin), I. Gratte (MD), S. Jellis (Pers)
Managers: T. Snowling (Purch Mgr), M. Mahoney (Tech Serv Mgr)
Ultimate Holding Company: GRATTE BROTHERS GROUP LIMITED
Immediate Holding Company: GRATTE BROTHERS LIMITED
Registration no: 00411138 **VAT No.:** GB 232 3603 03
Date established: 1946 **Turnover:** £50m - £75m
No.of Employees: 251 - 500 **Product Groups:** 48, 52, 84

Date of Accounts	Mar 11	Mar 10	Mar 09
Sales Turnover	53m	42m	55m
Pre Tax Profit/Loss	219	182	132
Working Capital	681	914	88
Fixed Assets	2m	2m	2m
Current Assets	29m	19m	13m
Current Liabilities	9m	7m	3m

Great Portland Estates plc

33 Cavendish Square, London, W1G 0PW
Tel: 020-7647 3000 **Fax:** 020-7016 5500
E-mail: toby.courtauld@gpe.co.uk
Website: http://www.gpe.co.uk
Directors: N. Sanderson (Fin), T. Courtauld (Grp Chief Exec)
Managers: R. Moran (Tech Serv Mgr)
Immediate Holding Company: GREAT PORTLAND ESTATES P L C
Registration no: 00596137 **VAT No.:** GB 233 3690 73
Date established: 1957 **Turnover:** £20m - £50m
No.of Employees: 51 - 100 **Product Groups:** 80

Date of Accounts	Mar 12	Mar 11	Mar 10
Sales Turnover	58m	74m	55m
Pre Tax Profit/Loss	155m	261m	157m
Working Capital	-129m	-7m	49m
Fixed Assets	1906m	1501m	1109m
Current Assets	58m	25m	79m
Current Liabilities	187m	20m	20m

Greater London Fund For Blind

12 Whitehorse Mews 37 Westminster Bridge Road, London, SE1 7QD
Tel: 020-7620 2066 **Fax:** 020-7620 2016
E-mail: info@glfb.org.uk
Website: http://www.glfb.org.uk
Directors: R. Edwards (Grp Chief Exec)
Immediate Holding Company: GREATER LONDON FUND FOR THE BLIND
Registration no: 03693002 **Date established:** 1999 **Turnover:** £2m - £5m
No.of Employees: 11 - 20 **Product Groups:** 80

Date of Accounts	Mar 12	Mar 11	Mar 10
Sales Turnover	3m	3m	3m
Pre Tax Profit/Loss	-170	339	136
Working Capital	3m	3m	2m
Fixed Assets	400	442	430
Current Assets	3m	3m	3m
Current Liabilities	624	576	685

Green Island (UK) Ltd

Stirling House 107 Stirling Road, London, N22 5BN
Tel: 020-8881 8686 **Fax:** 020-8881 8688
E-mail: info@greenislandrum.com
Website: http://www.greenislandrum.com
Registration no: 05334494 **No.of Employees:** 1 - 10 **Product Groups:** 21

Date of Accounts	Dec 08	Dec 07	Dec 06
Working Capital	-76	-59	-23
Fixed Assets	4	N/A	N/A
Current Assets	150	116	100

Green & White Ltd

112 Fortune Green Road, London, NW6 1DH
Tel: 020-7794 7783 **Fax:** 020-7433 1143
E-mail: jon@greenandwhite.co.uk
Website: http://www.greenandwhite.co.uk
Directors: J. Sass (MD), G. Sass (Fin)
Immediate Holding Company: GREEN & WHITE LIMITED
Registration no: 01917387 **Date established:** 1985
No.of Employees: 1 - 10 **Product Groups:** 40, 54, 83

Date of Accounts	Oct 11	Oct 10	Oct 09
Working Capital	40	57	61
Fixed Assets	61	63	64

see next page

Green & White Ltd - Cont'd

Current Assets	211	247	243

Green's Restaurant

36 Duke Street St James, London, SW1Y 6DF
Tel: 020-7930 4566 **Fax:** 020-7930 2958
E-mail: lld@greens.org.uk
Website: http://www.greens.org.uk
Directors: D. Vickerstaff (Dir)
Managers: M. Harris (Chief Mgr), L. Lucas Dufour (Mgr), L. Lucas-dufour (Mgr)
Immediate Holding Company: GREEN'S (ST JAMES'S) LIMITED
Registration no: 03581138 **Date established:** 1998 **Turnover:** £1m - £2m
No.of Employees: 21 - 50 **Product Groups:** 69

Date of Accounts	Mar 11	Mar 10	Mar 09
Working Capital	-3	-13	-11
Current Assets	17	N/A	3

Greenclean Ltd

32 Philip Lane, London, N15 4JB
Tel: 020-8808 3712 **Fax:** 020-8365 0996
E-mail: enquiries@greenclean.ltd.uk
Website: http://www.greenclean.ltd.uk
Bank(s): Barclays
Directors: G. Green (MD), J. Davis (Sales), J. Green (Fin)
Immediate Holding Company: GREENCLEAN LIMITED
Registration no: 01357609 **VAT No.:** GB 292 3909 34
Date established: 1978 **No.of Employees:** 11 - 20 **Product Groups:** 52

Date of Accounts	Mar 11	Mar 10	Mar 09
Working Capital	183	172	222
Fixed Assets	6	8	29
Current Assets	291	279	317

Greencore

4-6 Willen Field Road, London, NW10 7AQ
Tel: 020-8965 9807 **Fax:** 020-8963 0967
E-mail: antony.adu@greencore.com
Website: http://www.greencore.com
Bank(s): National Westminster Bank Plc
Managers: A. Adu (Mgr)
Immediate Holding Company: HAZELWOOD FOODS P.L.C.
Registration no: 00989693 **Turnover:** £250m - £500m
No.of Employees: 51 - 100 **Product Groups:** 20

Greenjackets Roofing Services Ltd

61 The Waterside Trading Centre Trumpers Way, London, W7 2QD
Tel: 020-8571 6555 **Fax:** 020-8571 6633
E-mail: sales@greenjackets.co.uk
Website: http://www.greenjackets.co.uk
Directors: N. Chapman (MD)
Immediate Holding Company: THE GREENJACKETS ROOFING SERVICES LIMITED
Registration no: 02690319 **Date established:** 1992
Turnover: £250,000 - £500,000 **No.of Employees:** 11 - 20
Product Groups: 52

Date of Accounts	Apr 12	Apr 11	Apr 10
Working Capital	787	471	670
Fixed Assets	524	487	453
Current Assets	2m	2m	2m

Greenwich Design Associates Ltd

David Mews 11a Greenwich South Street, London, SE10 8NJ
Tel: 020-8853 3028 **Fax:** 020-8858 2128
E-mail: simon@greenwich-design.co.uk
Website: http://www.greenwich-design.co.uk
Directors: S. Wright (MD)
Immediate Holding Company: W.H.M. DESIGN LIMITED
Registration no: 01001210 **Date established:** 1971
Turnover: £500,000 - £1m **No.of Employees:** 11 - 20
Product Groups: 28, 44, 49, 81, 84

Date of Accounts	Apr 11	Apr 10	Apr 09
Working Capital	70	35	-234
Fixed Assets	729	746	677
Current Assets	293	203	531

Greenwich Forge Ltd

62 Guildford Grove, London, SE10 8JT
Tel: 020-8691 6595 **Fax:** 020-8692 0089
E-mail: contact@greenwichforge.co.uk
Directors: S. Oneill (MD)
Immediate Holding Company: GREENWICH FORGE LIMITED
Registration no: 04307415 **Date established:** 2001
Turnover: Up to £250,000 **No.of Employees:** 1 - 10 **Product Groups:** 26, 35

Date of Accounts	Mar 11	Mar 10	Mar 04
Sales Turnover	N/A	N/A	53
Working Capital	2	2	1
Fixed Assets	1	1	2
Current Assets	4	3	6
Current Liabilities	N/A	N/A	5

Gresham Wood Technical Furniture

Unit 7b Quadrant Business Centre 135 Salusbury Road, London, NW6 6RJ
Tel: 020-7624 0133 **Fax:** 01279-814627
E-mail: sales@greshamwood.com
Website: http://www.greshamwood.com
Directors: C. Chappell (Fin)
Managers: B. Roberts (Mgr)
Immediate Holding Company: GRESHAM WOOD INDUSTRIES LIMITED
Registration no: 01130229 **VAT No.:** GB 214 4057 01
Date established: 1973 **Turnover:** £500,000 - £1m
No.of Employees: 1 - 10 **Product Groups:** 35, 37, 40

Date of Accounts	Oct 11	Oct 10	Oct 09
Working Capital	258	377	259
Fixed Assets	2m	2m	2m
Current Assets	388	527	406

Grosvenor Gallery

21 Ryder Street, London, SW1Y 6PX
Tel: 020-7484 7979 **Fax:** 020-7484 7980
E-mail: art@grosvenorgallery.com
Website: http://www.grosvenorgallery.com
Directors: G. Perman (MD)
Date established: 1992 **No.of Employees:** 1 - 10 **Product Groups:** 89

Grosvenor Workspace Solutions

3 new burlington street mayfair, London, W1S 2JF
Tel: 020-7851 4000 **Fax:** 020-7434 1681
E-mail: info@grosvenor.uk.com
Website: http://www.grosvenor.uk.com
Directors: T. Alexander (MD), T. Freitas (Sales & Mktg)
Managers: J. McKenzie (Sales Admin)
Registration no: 06450358 **VAT No.:** GB 688 3540 92
Date established: 2009 **Turnover:** £1m - £2m **No.of Employees:** 1 - 10
Product Groups: 84

Date of Accounts	Jun 06
Working Capital	67
Fixed Assets	25
Current Assets	208
Current Liabilities	141
Total Share Capital	1

GS1 UK ltd (EPCjobs Ltd)

Staple Court Staple Inn, London, WC1V 7QH
Tel: 020-7092 3500 **Fax:** 020-7681 2290
E-mail: info@gs1uk.org
Website: http://www.gs1uk.org
Directors: S. Oades (Grp Chief Exec)
Managers: T. Beston (Mktg Serv Mgr), M. Fox (Fin Mgr), S. Williams (Tech Serv Mgr), A. Hussain (Personnel)
Immediate Holding Company: GS1 UK LIMITED
Registration no: 01256140 **Date established:** 1976 **Turnover:** £5m - £10m
No.of Employees: 21 - 50 **Product Groups:** 80

Date of Accounts	Jun 11	Jun 10	Jun 09
Sales Turnover	7m	7m	7m
Pre Tax Profit/Loss	-197	2	411
Working Capital	605	947	1m
Fixed Assets	2m	1m	943
Current Assets	8m	7m	8m
Current Liabilities	7m	6m	6m

Guerlain Ltd

U K House 180 Oxford Street, London, W1D 1AB
Tel: 020-7563 7555 **Fax:** 020-7563 7500
E-mail: sales@guerlain.fr
Website: http://www.guerlain.com
Bank(s): Barclays
Directors: E. Noyer (MD), C. Wygas (Fin), C. Vileghe (Fin)
Managers: S. Euzen, A. Hichens (Tech Serv Mgr)
Ultimate Holding Company: LVMH MOET HENNESSY LOUIS VUTTON SA (FRANCE)
Immediate Holding Company: GUERLAIN LIMITED
Registration no: 00317311 **VAT No.:** GB 222 4555 87
Date established: 1936 **Turnover:** £10m - £20m
No.of Employees: 21 - 50 **Product Groups:** 32

Date of Accounts	Dec 11	Dec 10	Dec 09
Sales Turnover	12m	11m	11m
Pre Tax Profit/Loss	-934	632	765
Working Capital	3m	4m	3m
Fixed Assets	586	379	285
Current Assets	7m	7m	6m
Current Liabilities	2m	1m	1m

Guinness World Records

184-192 Drummond Street, London, NW1 3HP
Tel: 020-7891 4567 **Fax:** 020-7891 4501
E-mail: enquiries@guinnessworldrecords.com
Website: http://www.guinnessworldrecords.com
Directors: A. Richards (MD), A. Richards (MD)
Managers: K. Garett (Personnel)
Ultimate Holding Company: APAX PARTNERS UK LTD
Immediate Holding Company: GUINNESS WORLD RECORDS LIMITED
Registration no: 00541295 **Date established:** 1954
Turnover: £10m - £20m **No.of Employees:** 21 - 50 **Product Groups:** 28

Date of Accounts	Dec 11	Dec 10	Dec 09
Sales Turnover	19m	19m	21
Pre Tax Profit/Loss	7m	9m	8
Working Capital	9m	8m	9
Fixed Assets	177	231	N/A
Current Assets	14m	14m	15
Current Liabilities	4m	3m	5

J P Guivier & Co. Ltd

99 Mortimer Street, London, W1W 7SX
Tel: 020-7580 2560 **Fax:** 020-7436 1461
E-mail: sales@guivier.com
Website: http://www.guivier.com
Directors: R. Hamilton (MD)
Immediate Holding Company: J.P.GUIVIER & CO.LIMITED
Registration no: 00514437 **Date established:** 1952
No.of Employees: 1 - 10 **Product Groups:** 65

Date of Accounts	Dec 11	Dec 10	Dec 09
Working Capital	382	433	412
Fixed Assets	4	2	2
Current Assets	479	576	555

Gulf International Bank

1 Knightsbridge, London, SW1X 7XS
Tel: 020-7259 3456 **Fax:** 020-7259 6060
E-mail: matthew.snyder@gibuk.com
Website: http://www.gibonline.com
Bank(s): National Westminster
Directors: T. Billington (Co Sec)
Managers: M. Snyder
Immediate Holding Company: GULF INTERNATIONAL BANK (UK) LIMITED
Registration no: 01223938 **Date established:** 1975
Turnover: Over £1,000m **No.of Employees:** 51 - 100 **Product Groups:** 82

Date of Accounts	Dec 07
Pre Tax Profit/Loss	-79m
Fixed Assets	25m
Current Assets	4804m
Current Liabilities	4589m

GV Global Marketing

7 Eden Way, London, E3 2JD
Tel: 020-89817578
E-mail: info@gigavine.com
Website: http://www.gigavine.com
Managers: T. Ghali (Accounts)
Date established: 2002 **Turnover:** £250,000 - £500,000
No.of Employees: 21 - 50 **Product Groups:** 44

H & B Food Provisions Ltd

44/54 Stewarts Road, London, SW8 4DF
Tel: 020-7819 6000 **Fax:** 020-7622 0696
E-mail: enquiries@hb-foods.co.uk
Website: http://www.hbfoodprovisions.co.uk
Directors: S. Yorke (Sales)
Managers: K. Causton (Personnel)
Immediate Holding Company: Novel Realisations Ltd
Registration no: 01619681 **Date established:** 1979
Turnover: £20m - £50m **No.of Employees:** 101 - 250
Product Groups: 41, 62

Date of Accounts	Sep 07	Sep 06	Sep 05
Sales Turnover	40803	35171	32628
Pre Tax Profit/Loss	5742	2570	2004
Working Capital	4861	2469	429
Fixed Assets	10873	6625	6856
Current Assets	20927	8198	6178
Current Liabilities	16066	5729	5749
Total Share Capital	20	20	20
ROCE% (Return on Capital Employed)	36.5	28.3	27.5
ROT% (Return on Turnover)	14.1	7.3	6.1

H E Olby & Co. Ltd

299-313 Lewisham High Street PO Box 293, London, SE13 6NW
Tel: 020-8690 3401 **Fax:** 020-8690 1408
E-mail: info@heolby.co.uk
Website: http://www.vergin.net
Directors: G. Olby (Dir), H. Olby (Prop)
Immediate Holding Company: H.E.OLBY & CO.LIMITED
Registration no: 00538335 **VAT No.:** GB 205 5445 85
Date established: 1954 **Turnover:** £1m - £2m **No.of Employees:** 11 - 20
Product Groups: 66

Date of Accounts	Dec 11	Dec 10	Dec 09
Sales Turnover	2m	2m	2m
Pre Tax Profit/Loss	-14	78	59
Working Capital	935	1m	1m
Fixed Assets	2m	2m	1m
Current Assets	1m	1m	1m
Current Liabilities	54	68	81

H H B Communications Ltd

73-75 Scrubs Lane, London, NW10 6QU
Tel: 020-8962 5000 **Fax:** 020-8962 5050
E-mail: richard.kershaw@hhb.co.uk
Website: http://www.hhb.com
Directors: J. Rainey (Fin), R. Kershaw (Dir), S. Angel (Mkt Research)
Immediate Holding Company: H H B COMMUNICATIONS LIMITED
Registration no: 02316548 **Date established:** 1988
Turnover: £10m - £20m **No.of Employees:** 21 - 50 **Product Groups:** 37

Date of Accounts	Jan 12	Jan 11	Jan 10
Sales Turnover	15m	14m	13m
Pre Tax Profit/Loss	399	342	222
Working Capital	2m	2m	2m
Fixed Assets	1m	1m	1m
Current Assets	4m	3m	3m
Current Liabilities	563	675	507

H H & S

Regal Place, London, SW6 2HD
Tel: 020-7751 8585 **Fax:** 020-7751 8586
E-mail: mikeh@hhs.co.uk
Website: http://www.hhs.co.uk
Directors: M. Halstead (MD)
Ultimate Holding Company: H H & S GROUP LIMITED
Immediate Holding Company: H H & S LIMITED
Registration no: 02054504 **Date established:** 1986
No.of Employees: 11 - 20 **Product Groups:** 81

Date of Accounts	Dec 11	Dec 10	Dec 09
Working Capital	-16	-16	-16
Fixed Assets	11	11	11
Current Assets	22	22	22
Current Liabilities	38	N/A	N/A

H P D Software Ltd

176 Upper Richmond Road, London, SW15 2SH
Tel: 020-8780 6800 **Fax:** 020-8780 6801
E-mail: sales@hpdsoftware.com
Website: http://www.hpd.co.uk
Directors: A. Price (Co Sec), T. Davison (MD), K. Clarke (Fin), A. Davison (MD), G. Turley (Fin)
Managers: L. Low (Personnel), D. Lewis (Sales Prom Mgr), P. Bennett (I.T. Exec)
Immediate Holding Company: HPD LIMITED
Registration no: 03927052 **Date established:** 2000 **Turnover:** £1m - £2m
No.of Employees: 51 - 100 **Product Groups:** 44

Date of Accounts	Oct 09	Oct 08	Oct 07
Sales Turnover	6m	N/A	N/A
Pre Tax Profit/Loss	156	317	155
Working Capital	2m	2m	2m
Fixed Assets	211	262	326
Current Assets	4m	4m	3m
Current Liabilities	1m	1m	1m

H S French Flint Ltd

Unit 4g4 The Leather Market Weston Street, London, SE1 3ER
Tel: 020-7620 3200 **Fax:** 020-7401 7363
E-mail: sales@frenchflint.co.uk
Website: http://www.frenchflint.com
Directors: P. Harrison (Dir)
Immediate Holding Company: H.S. FRENCH FLINT LIMITED
Registration no: 05472551 **Date established:** 2005
No.of Employees: 1 - 10 **Product Groups:** 30, 33, 49, 61, 65, 66

Date of Accounts	Jun 11	Jun 10	Jun 09
Working Capital	44	31	15
Fixed Assets	58	63	33
Current Assets	941	487	451

H V Sier Ltd

Unit 5-6 Meridian Trading Estate Bugsby's Way, London, SE7 7SJ
Tel: 020-8331 2070 **Fax:** 020-8331 2071
E-mail: sales@hvsier.co.uk
Website: http://www.hvsier.co.uk
Directors: M. Rolfe (MD)
Immediate Holding Company: H.V.SIER LIMITED
Registration no: 00392724 **Date established:** 1945 **Turnover:** £1m - £2m
No.of Employees: 11 - 20 **Product Groups:** 66

Date of Accounts	Dec 11	Dec 10	Dec 09
Working Capital	468	458	495
Fixed Assets	N/A	5	5
Current Assets	1m	1m	932

H W Cooper
1 Farnham Royal, London, SE11 5RQ
Tel: 020-7582 1874 **Fax:** 020-7582 2386
E-mail: hwcooper@hotmail.com
Directors: B. Pearce (MD)
Managers: G. Morris (Chief Mgr), M. Berwick (District Mgr)
Ultimate Holding Company: Bird & Co. (London) Ltd
Registration no: 00679053 **VAT No.:** GB 235 5782 46
Date established: 1995 **Turnover:** Up to £250,000
No.of Employees: 1 - 10 **Product Groups:** 30

Hachette UK Ltd
338 Euston Road, London, NW1 3BH
Tel: 020-7873 6000 **Fax:** 020-7873 6024
Website: http://www.hachette.co.uk
Directors: T. Hely-Hutchinson (Grp Chief Exec)
Ultimate Holding Company: LAGARDERE SCA (FRANCE)
Immediate Holding Company: THE WATTS PUBLISHING GROUP LIMITED
Registration no: 03911258 **VAT No.:** GB 205 5053 05
Date established: 2000 **Turnover:** £10m - £20m
No.of Employees: 501 - 1000 **Product Groups:** 28, 64

Date of Accounts	Dec 11	Dec 10	Dec 09
Sales Turnover	15m	17m	18m
Pre Tax Profit/Loss	941	3m	3m
Working Capital	30m	29m	27m
Fixed Assets	1m	2m	2m
Current Assets	32m	32m	30m
Current Liabilities	1m	954	1m

Hague Dental Supplies Ltd
The Trident Business Centre 89 Bickersteth Road, London, SW17 9SH
Tel: 0800-298 5003
E-mail: info@haguedental.com
Website: http://www.haguedental.com
Directors: K. Hague (Mkt Research)
Immediate Holding Company: HAGUE DENTAL SUPPLIES LIMITED
Registration no: 03667772 **Date established:** 1998
No.of Employees: 11 - 20 **Product Groups:** 26, 38, 40, 67

Date of Accounts	Oct 11	Oct 10	Oct 09
Sales Turnover	N/A	2m	1m
Pre Tax Profit/Loss	N/A	120	120
Working Capital	-2	145	103
Fixed Assets	314	227	236
Current Assets	399	269	261
Current Liabilities	N/A	119	158

Hainenko Ltd
284 Chase Road, London, N14 6HF
Tel: 020-8882 8734 **Fax:** 020-8882 7749
E-mail: h.laubis@hainenko.com
Website: http://www.hainenko.com
Bank(s): National Westminster Bank Plc
Directors: D. Ashpole (MD)
Immediate Holding Company: HAINENKO LIMITED
Registration no: 01096654 **VAT No.:** GB 230 5354 00
Date established: 1973 **Turnover:** £10m - £20m
No.of Employees: 11 - 20 **Product Groups:** 64

Date of Accounts	Aug 11	Aug 10	Aug 09
Sales Turnover	13m	13m	11m
Pre Tax Profit/Loss	478	300	300
Working Capital	2m	2m	2m
Fixed Assets	321	345	333
Current Assets	13m	6m	6m
Current Liabilities	2m	1m	3m

Hairco Ltd
23 Dollis Hill Estate 105 Brook Road, London, NW2 7BZ
Tel: 020-8830 7344 **Fax:** 020-8830 7355
Directors: A. Heckscher (Dir)
Managers: A. Edwards (Mgr), R. Pelton (Accounts)
Immediate Holding Company: HAIRCO LIMITED
Registration no: 00292542 **VAT No.:** GB 243 5613 74
Date established: 1934 **Turnover:** Up to £250,000
No.of Employees: 1 - 10 **Product Groups:** 23, 49, 66

Date of Accounts	Dec 07	Dec 06	Dec 05
Sales Turnover	55	46	26
Pre Tax Profit/Loss	15	N/A	8
Working Capital	121	113	117
Fixed Assets	10	8	8
Current Assets	188	166	151
Current Liabilities	67	53	34
Total Share Capital	50	50	50
ROCE% (Return on Capital Employed)	11.3		6.6
ROT% (Return on Turnover)	27.1		31.8

Halcrow Group Ltd
Elms House 43 Brook Green, London, W6 7EF
Tel: 020-3479 8000 **Fax:** 020-7603 0095
E-mail: info@halcrow.com
Website: http://www.halcrow.com
Directors: T. Allum (Ch), W. Che (Fin), P. Gammie (Fin), P. Gammie (MD), D. Kerr (Dir), C. Fleming (Dir), A. Saffer (Fin), A. Burns (Co Sec), A. Allam (Ch)
Managers: G. Whittaker (Commun Mgr), G. Whitaker (Commun Mgr)
Ultimate Holding Company: 01674044
Immediate Holding Company: HALCROW GROUP LIMITED
Registration no: 03415971 **Date established:** 1997
Turnover: £250,000 - £500,000 **No.of Employees:** 501 - 1000
Product Groups: 80, 84

Robert Hale Ltd
Clerkenwell House 45-47 Clerkenwell Green, London, EC1R 0HT
Tel: 020-7251 2661 **Fax:** 020-7490 4958
E-mail: enquire@halebooks.com
Website: http://www.halebooks.com
Directors: R. Kynaston (Fin)
Immediate Holding Company: ROBERT HALE LIMITED
Registration no: 01263060 **Date established:** 1976
Turnover: Up to £250,000 **No.of Employees:** 11 - 20 **Product Groups:** 28

Date of Accounts	Jun 11	Jun 10	Jun 09
Working Capital	987	1m	1m
Fixed Assets	484	495	448
Current Assets	1m	1m	1m

Hallmark Blinds Ltd
173 Caledonian Road, London, N1 0SL
Tel: 020-7837 0964 **Fax:** 020-7833 1693
E-mail: info@hallmarkblinds.co.uk
Website: http://www.hallmarkblinds.co.uk
Directors: D. Bush (Dir)
Immediate Holding Company: HALLMARK BLINDS LIMITED
Registration no: 01645708 **VAT No.:** GB 233 2532 80
Date established: 1982 **Turnover:** Up to £250,000
No.of Employees: 1 - 10 **Product Groups:** 25, 35, 36, 52

Date of Accounts	Dec 11	Dec 10	Dec 09
Sales Turnover	274	227	205
Pre Tax Profit/Loss	10	5	2
Working Capital	4	-3	-7
Fixed Assets	N/A	1	1
Current Assets	125	119	102
Current Liabilities	33	32	32

Hallmark Ip Ltd
1 Pemberton Row, London, EC4A 3BG
Tel: 020-3102 9000 **Fax:** 020-3102 9001
E-mail: info@hallmark-ip.com
Website: http://www.hallmark-ip.com
Bank(s): Midland
Directors: M. Stannard (MD)
Managers: K. McRoe
Ultimate Holding Company: NUCLEUS LIMITED
Immediate Holding Company: HALLMARK I P LIMITED
Registration no: 03734748 **Date established:** 1999 **Turnover:** £2m - £5m
No.of Employees: 21 - 50 **Product Groups:** 80

Date of Accounts	Dec 11	Dec 10	Dec 09
Sales Turnover	4m	3m	3m
Pre Tax Profit/Loss	301	88	-134
Working Capital	2m	1m	1m
Fixed Assets	32	39	68
Current Assets	3m	3m	3m
Current Liabilities	301	207	181

Hambalt Ltd
101 Hambalt Road, London, SW4 9EL
Tel: 020-8772 1044 **Fax:** 020-8772 1530
E-mail: sales@hambalt.com
Website: http://www.hambalt.com
Directors: R. Ronald (Fin), E. Ronald (MD)
Immediate Holding Company: HAMBALT LTD
Registration no: 04599313 **Date established:** 2002
No.of Employees: 1 - 10 **Product Groups:** 80

Date of Accounts	Oct 11	Oct 10	Oct 09
Working Capital	11	N/A	22
Current Assets	164	42	68

Hammerson plc
10 Grosvenor Street, London, W1K 4BJ
Tel: 020-7887 1000 **Fax:** 020-7887 1010
E-mail: info@hammerson.com
Website: http://www.hammerson.com
Directors: S. Haydon (Co Sec), T. Drakesmith (Fin)
Ultimate Holding Company: HAMMERSON PLC
Immediate Holding Company: HAMMERSON GROUP MANAGEMENT LIMITED
Registration no: 00574728 **Date established:** 1956
Turnover: £20m - £50m **No.of Employees:** 101 - 250 **Product Groups:** 80

Date of Accounts	Dec 11	Dec 10	Dec 09
Sales Turnover	44m	40m	38m
Pre Tax Profit/Loss	5m	4m	4m
Working Capital	37m	34m	32m
Fixed Assets	4m	4m	4m
Current Assets	49m	51m	43m
Current Liabilities	9m	9m	8m

Hammonds Furniture Ltd
Butler House 177-178 Tottenham Court Road, London, W1T 7NY
Tel: 020-7255 2166
Website: http://www.hammonds-uk.com
Managers: E. Cross (Mgr)
Ultimate Holding Company: HFG HOLDINGS LIMITED
Immediate Holding Company: HAMMONDS FURNITURE LIMITED
Registration no: 01320508 **Date established:** 1977
No.of Employees: 1 - 10 **Product Groups:** 35, 36

Date of Accounts	Jun 11	Jun 10	Jun 09
Sales Turnover	61m	60m	55m
Pre Tax Profit/Loss	551	1m	416
Working Capital	6m	8m	6m
Fixed Assets	5m	5m	6m
Current Assets	17m	18m	16m
Current Liabilities	2m	2m	2m

Hancocks
52-53 Burlington Arcade, London, W1J 0HH
Tel: 020-7493 8904 **Fax:** 020-7493 8905
E-mail: info@hancocks-london.com
Website: http://www.hancocks-london.com
Directors: S. Burton (Ch)
Managers: P. Gibbard (Mktg Serv Mgr)
Ultimate Holding Company: YOUNG & STEPHENS LIMITED
Immediate Holding Company: HANCOCKS & CO.(JEWELLERS) LIMITED
Registration no: 00319323 **VAT No.:** GB 238 8413 44
Date established: 1936 **Turnover:** £10m - £20m **No.of Employees:** 1 - 10
Product Groups: 49, 65

Date of Accounts	Dec 11	Dec 10	Dec 09
Sales Turnover	15m	11m	10m
Pre Tax Profit/Loss	640	518	116
Working Capital	5m	4m	4m
Fixed Assets	72	69	71
Current Assets	10m	9m	6m
Current Liabilities	1m	2m	406

Handlesbanken
Trinity Tower 9 Thomas More Street, London, E1W 1WY
Tel: 020-7578 8000 **Fax:** 020-7578 8300
Website: http://www.handelsbanken.co.uk
Managers: A. Bouvin
Immediate Holding Company: SVENSKA PROPERTY NOMINEES LIMITED
Registration no: 00000589 **Date established:** 1988
No.of Employees: 501 - 1000 **Product Groups:** 82

Hanover Saffron Ltd
29 Saffron Hill, London, EC1N 8FH
Tel: 020-7404 4302 **Fax:** 020-7831 6080
E-mail: mailbox@hanoversaffron.co.uk
Website: http://www.hanoversaffron.co.uk
Directors: C. Shakebrew (MD)
Immediate Holding Company: HANOVER SAFFRON LIMITED
Registration no: 02771072 **Date established:** 1992
Turnover: £500,000 - £1m **No.of Employees:** 1 - 10 **Product Groups:** 81

Date of Accounts	Mar 12	Mar 11	Mar 10
Sales Turnover	916	959	902
Pre Tax Profit/Loss	82	105	122
Working Capital	220	202	172
Fixed Assets	57	58	54
Current Assets	339	294	228
Current Liabilities	84	73	46

Hansa Capital Partners LLP
50 Curzon Street, London, W1J 7UW
Tel: 020-7647 5750 **Fax:** 020-7647 5770
E-mail: info@hansacap.com
Website: http://www.hansagrp.com
Directors: W. Salomon (Snr Part)
Immediate Holding Company: HANSA CAPITAL PARTNERS LLP
Registration no: OC309528 **Date established:** 2004
Turnover: £5m - £10m **No.of Employees:** 11 - 20 **Product Groups:** 82

Date of Accounts	Mar 12	Mar 11	Mar 10
Sales Turnover	4m	4m	3m
Pre Tax Profit/Loss	2m	2m	2m
Working Capital	2m	2m	2m
Fixed Assets	65	116	85
Current Assets	2m	2m	3m
Current Liabilities	313	271	754

Hanson Green
110 Park Street, London, W1K 6NX
Tel: 020-7493 0837 **Fax:** 020-7355 1436
E-mail: info@hansongreen.co.uk
Website: http://www.hansongreen.co.uk
Bank(s): Natwest
Directors: N. Guilder (Co Sec), P. Waine (Dir)
Ultimate Holding Company: NOVA GENERAL PARTNER (GUERNSEY) lIMITED
Immediate Holding Company: HANSON GREEN GROSVENOR LIMITED
Registration no: 02892469 **VAT No.:** GB 629 1734 28
Date established: 1994 **Turnover:** £1m - £2m **No.of Employees:** 21 - 50
Product Groups: 80

Date of Accounts	Jun 11	Jun 10	Jun 09
Sales Turnover	N/A	2m	2m
Pre Tax Profit/Loss	N/A	543	510
Working Capital	272	272	2m
Fixed Assets	N/A	N/A	31
Current Assets	272	272	2m
Current Liabilities	N/A	N/A	231

Hantarex International Ltd
34 Salisbury Street, London, NW8 8QE
Tel: 020-8778 1414 **Fax:** 020-8659 9348
E-mail: sales@hantarex.com
Website: http://www.hantarex.com
Directors: E. Cohen (MD)
Immediate Holding Company: HANTAREX INTERNATIONAL LIMITED
Registration no: 04719953 **VAT No.:** GB 237 3325 72
Date established: 2003 **Turnover:** £1m - £2m **No.of Employees:** 1 - 10
Product Groups: 37, 44

Date of Accounts	Apr 11	Apr 10	Apr 09
Working Capital	266	476	436
Fixed Assets	62	25	31
Current Assets	344	514	494

Hardy Amies London Ltd
14 Savile Row, London, W1S 3JN
Tel: 020-7734 2436 **Fax:** 020-7439 7116
E-mail: reception@hardyamies.com
Website: http://www.hardyamies.com
Managers: A. Smith (Mgr)
Ultimate Holding Company: KING LUN HOLDINGS LTD (BRITISH VIRGIN IS
Immediate Holding Company: HARDY AMIES LONDON LIMITED
Registration no: 06731666 **Date established:** 2008 **Turnover:** £1m - £2m
No.of Employees: 1 - 10 **Product Groups:** 24

Date of Accounts	Dec 11	Dec 10	Dec 09
Sales Turnover	1m	1m	1m
Pre Tax Profit/Loss	-2m	-821	-213
Working Capital	-108	-123	-636
Fixed Assets	52	204	409
Current Assets	924	616	360
Current Liabilities	605	534	355

Harmsworth Quays Printing Ltd
1 Surrey Quays Road, London, SE16 7ND
Tel: 020-7634 7780 **Fax:** 020-7237 8844
Website: http://www.dailymail.co.uk
Directors: K. Duncan (Fin), J. Bird (MD)
Managers: C. Klaskowska (Accounts), D. Hemmings (I.T. Exec)
Ultimate Holding Company: DAILY MAIL AND GENERAL TRUST P L C
Immediate Holding Company: HARMSWORTH QUAYS PRINTING LIMITED
Registration no: 02208582 **Date established:** 1987
Turnover: £75m - £125m **No.of Employees:** 251 - 500
Product Groups: 44

Date of Accounts	Sep 08	Oct 09	Oct 10
Sales Turnover	130m	135m	130m
Pre Tax Profit/Loss	-17m	-19m	-3m
Working Capital	-162m	-184m	-179m
Fixed Assets	162m	154m	145m
Current Assets	259m	33m	40m
Current Liabilities	4m	7m	6m

Harpercollins Publishers Ophelia House
Elsinore House 77 Fulham Palace Road, London, W6 8JB
Tel: 020-8741 7070 **Fax:** 020-7792 3176
E-mail: victoria.barnsley@harpercollins.co.uk
Website: http://www.harpercollins.co.uk
Bank(s): Lloyds TSB Bank plc
Managers: O. Sobczak
Ultimate Holding Company: NEWS CORP (USA)
Immediate Holding Company: HARPERCOLLINS (UK)
Registration no: 02380447 **VAT No.:** GB 259 6397 06
Date established: 1989 **Turnover:** £75m - £125m
No.of Employees: 251 - 500 **Product Groups:** 28, 64

Date of Accounts	Jun 11	Jun 10	Jun 09
Pre Tax Profit/Loss	-2m	-3m	-9m
Working Capital	-1064m	-1062m	-1060m
Fixed Assets	749m	749m	749m
Current Liabilities	86	86	86

Harris & Porter
49 Whitehall, London, SW1A 2BX
Tel: 020-7839 6064 **Fax:** 020-7839 3876
E-mail: jill.chapmam@harrisandporter.co.uk
Website: http://www.harrisandporter.co.uk
Bank(s): National Westminster Bank Plc
Managers: J. Chapman (Sales Admin)
Immediate Holding Company: HARRIS & PORTER LIMITED
Registration no: 02919377 **VAT No.:** GB 238 9596 05
Date established: 1994 **Turnover:** £1m - £2m **No.of Employees:** 11 - 20
Product Groups: 84

Harrow Tool Co. Ltd
853-857 Harrow Road, London, NW10 5NH
Tel: 020-8969 8237 **Fax:** 020-8968 6121
E-mail: sales@harrowtool.co.uk
Website: http://www.harrowtool.co.uk
Bank(s): National Westminster Bank Plc
Directors: K. Rogers (Dir), P. Ridgeway (MD), P. Ridgeway (Dir)
Immediate Holding Company: HARROW TOOL CO. LIMITED
Registration no: 00841815 **VAT No.:** GB 226 8575 37
Date established: 1965 **Turnover:** £2m - £5m **No.of Employees:** 11 - 20
Product Groups: 35, 37

Date of Accounts	Apr 08	Apr 07	Apr 06
Working Capital	584	563	530
Fixed Assets	293	320	354
Current Assets	1194	1020	931
Current Liabilities	610	457	401
Total Share Capital	1	1	1

Hart Brown Solicitors
58 High St Wimbledon, London, SW19 5EE
Tel: 020-8947 8171 **Fax:** 020-8879 7352
E-mail: info@hartbrown.co.uk
Website: http://www.hartbrown.co.uk
Directors: B. Brueggemann (Ptnr)
Immediate Holding Company: HART BROWN SOLICITORS LIMITED
Registration no: 04215370 **Date established:** 2001
No.of Employees: 1 - 10 **Product Groups:** 80

Hartnell Taylor Cook
12-13 Conduit Street, London, W1S 2XH
Tel: 020-7491 7323 **Fax:** 020-7491 3032
E-mail: info@htc.uk.com
Website: http://www.htc.uk.com
Directors: L. Clark (Tech Serv)
Managers: S. Howell (Mgr)
Immediate Holding Company: HARTNELL LIMITED
Registration no: 02070119 **Date established:** 1986
No.of Employees: 11 - 20 **Product Groups:** 80

Harton Services Ltd
Unit 6 Thistlebrook Industrial Estate Eynsham Drive, London, SE2 9RB
Tel: 020-8310 0421 **Fax:** 020-8310 6785
E-mail: info@hartons.co.uk
Website: http://www.hartons.co.uk
Bank(s): HSBC Bank plc
Directors: R. Newell (MD)
Immediate Holding Company: HARTON SERVICES LIMITED
Registration no: 03371021 **Date established:** 1997 **Turnover:** £1m - £2m
No.of Employees: 11 - 20 **Product Groups:** 40, 66, 84

Date of Accounts	Jun 12	Jun 11	Jun 10
Working Capital	400	332	248
Fixed Assets	19	20	9
Current Assets	778	556	642

Harvie & Hudson Ltd
96 Jermyn Street, London, SW1Y 6JE
Tel: 020-7839 3578 **Fax:** 020-7839 7020
E-mail: matthew@harvieandhudson.com
Website: http://www.harvieandhudson.com
Directors: D. Hudson (Ptnr), R. Harvie (Ptnr)
Managers: M. Beadle (Chief Mgr), L. Beaumont (Tech Serv Mgr)
Immediate Holding Company: HARVIE AND HUDSON LIMITED
Registration no: 00551660 **VAT No.:** GB 238 4448 45
Date established: 1955 **Turnover:** £500,000 - £1m
No.of Employees: 11 - 20 **Product Groups:** 24, 63

Date of Accounts	Aug 11	Aug 10	Aug 09
Working Capital	202	49	304
Fixed Assets	254	284	36
Current Assets	881	986	686

Haskoning (UK) Ltd
4 Deans Yard, London, SW1P 3NL
Tel: 020-7222 2115 **Fax:** 020-7222 2659
E-mail: info@london.royalhaskoning.com
Website: http://www.royalhaskoning.co.uk
Directors: J. Barker (Dir), R. Hennessy (Dir), R. Henton (Dir)
Managers: S. Branch (Sales Admin)
Immediate Holding Company: Haskoning UK Ltd
Registration no: 01336844 **Turnover:** £10m - £20m
No.of Employees: 21 - 50 **Product Groups:** 54

Hatch Associates
Portland House Stag Place, London, SW1E 5AG
Tel: 020-7906 5100 **Fax:** 020-7233 1908
E-mail: john.tummers@waddington-associates.com
Website: http://www.hatch.ca
Bank(s): Barclays
Directors: J. Tummers (Fin), R. Wyer (Fin)
Managers: D. Reid (Tech Serv Mgr), S. Plumb, Z. Islam (Personnel)
Ultimate Holding Company: HATCHCOS HOLDINGS INTERNATIONAL INC (CANADA)
Immediate Holding Company: HATCH ASSOCIATES LIMITED
Registration no: 02425546 **Date established:** 1989
Turnover: £10m - £20m **No.of Employees:** 21 - 50 **Product Groups:** 80, 81, 82, 86

Date of Accounts	Sep 11	Sep 10	Sep 09
Sales Turnover	12m	16m	26m
Pre Tax Profit/Loss	-911	628	1m
Working Capital	4m	4m	13m
Fixed Assets	1m	2m	2m
Current Assets	8m	9m	22m
Current Liabilities	1m	2m	2m

Hatfields Machine Tools Ltd
12 Boughton Road, London, SE28 0AG
Tel: 020-8644 6661 **Fax:** 020-8644 4233
E-mail: len.martin@hatmac.co.uk
Website: http://www.hatmac.com
Directors: L. Martin (MD)
Immediate Holding Company: HATFIELD SHEET METAL COMPANY LIMITED
Registration no: 03109983 **VAT No.:** GB 318 0135 92
Date established: 1995 **Turnover:** £2m - £5m **No.of Employees:** 1 - 10
Product Groups: 67

Date of Accounts	Sep 11	Sep 10	Sep 09
Working Capital	-511	-795	-713
Fixed Assets	345	701	701
Current Assets	363	51	147

Hatton Metalcraft Ltd
Unit 1 12 Trading Estate Road, London, NW10 7LU
Tel: 020-8961 6378 **Fax:** 020-8965 3319
E-mail: enquiries@hattonmetalcraft.co.uk
Website: http://www.hattonmetalcraft.co.uk
Directors: B. Tregunna (Fin)
Immediate Holding Company: HATTON METALCRAFT LTD
Registration no: 04145841 **Date established:** 2001
No.of Employees: 1 - 10 **Product Groups:** 26, 35

Date of Accounts	Jan 11	Jan 10	Jan 09
Working Capital	98	89	87
Fixed Assets	22	17	7
Current Assets	113	102	100

Hava Shapiro 1878 Ltd
Stratford Workshops Burford Road, London, E15 2SP
Tel: 020-8555 9607
E-mail: info@technicalsupermarket.com
Website: http://www.technicalsupermarket.com
Directors: M. Aksenov (Prop)
Managers: A. Isaev (Sales Prom Mgr)
Immediate Holding Company: Hava Shapiro 1878 Ltd
Registration no: 05224080 **Date established:** 2004
Turnover: Up to £250,000 **No.of Employees:** 1 - 10 **Product Groups:** 38, 46

Date of Accounts	Sep 07	Sep 06
Sales Turnover	52	30
Pre Tax Profit/Loss	15	-14
Working Capital	-15	-30
Fixed Assets	4	4
Current Assets	N/A	2
Current Liabilities	15	32
ROCE% (Return on Capital Employed)	-129.4	53.8
ROT% (Return on Turnover)	28.5	-45.9

Hay Group
33 Grosvenor Place, London, SW1X 7HG
Tel: 020-7856 7000 **Fax:** 020-7856 7100
E-mail: info@haygroup.com
Website: http://www.haygroup.com
Directors: N. Boulter (MD)
Managers: M. Hayden (Fin Mgr), P. Bharj, J. Wright, S. Molloy (Personnel)
Ultimate Holding Company: HAY GROUP (BERMUDA) LTD (BERMUDA)
Immediate Holding Company: HAY GROUP INTERMEDIARY LIMITED
Registration no: 01314816 **Date established:** 1977
Turnover: £500,000 - £1m **No.of Employees:** 101 - 250
Product Groups: 80

Date of Accounts	Sep 10	Sep 09	Sep 08
Fixed Assets	3m	3m	3m

Heal's
The Heal's Building 196 Tottenham Court Road, London, W1T 7LQ
Tel: 020-7636 1666 **Fax:** 020-7637 5582
E-mail: enquiries@heals.co.uk
Website: http://www.heals.co.uk
Managers: G. Jackson (District Mgr)
Ultimate Holding Company: WITTINGTON INVESTMENTS LIMITED
Immediate Holding Company: HEAL'S PLC
Registration no: 02486613 **VAT No.:** GB 524 3006 89
Date established: 1990 **Turnover:** £20m - £50m
No.of Employees: 51 - 100 **Product Groups:** 87

Date of Accounts	Sep 10	Sep 11	Sep 08
Sales Turnover	30m	27m	32m
Pre Tax Profit/Loss	-4m	-3m	-3m
Working Capital	3m	2m	2m
Fixed Assets	3m	3m	4m
Current Assets	7m	7m	8m
Current Liabilities	3m	4m	5m

Health Protection Agency
Colindale, London, NW9 5DF
Tel: 020-8200 4400 **Fax:** 020-8200 8130
E-mail: maria.zambon@hpa.org.uk
Website: http://www.hpa.org.uk
Directors: D. Conway (Mkt Research), M. Catchpole (Dir)
Managers: L. Balby (Purch Mgr), P. Fox (Tech Serv Mgr), R. A'court (Mktg Serv Mgr), S. Rasper (Fin Mgr), M. Kephalas (Personnel)
No.of Employees: 501 - 1000 **Product Groups:** 38, 85, 88

Heath Lambert
133 Houndsditch, london, EC3A 7AH
Tel: 020-7234 4000 **Fax:** 020-7234 4111
E-mail: nthomas@heathlambert.com
Website: http://www.heathlambert.co.uk
Directors: N. Thomas (MD)
Ultimate Holding Company: HLG HOLDINGS LIMITED
Immediate Holding Company: HEATH LAMBERT GROUP LIMITED
Registration no: 05347036 **Date established:** 2005
Turnover: £125m - £250m **No.of Employees:** 1 - 10 **Product Groups:** 82

Date of Accounts	Dec 10	Dec 09	Dec 07
Sales Turnover	N/A	N/A	114m
Pre Tax Profit/Loss	N/A	N/A	24m
Working Capital	N/A	N/A	68m
Fixed Assets	N/A	N/A	14m
Current Assets	N/A	N/A	376m
Current Liabilities	N/A	N/A	308m

Helical Bar plc
11-15 Farm Street, London, W1J 5RS
Tel: 020-7629 0113 **Fax:** 020-7408 1666
E-mail: slade@helical.co.uk
Website: http://www.helical.co.uk
Bank(s): Barclays
Directors: G. Kaye (Dir), J. Southwell (Ch), M. Slade (MD), N. Mcnair Scott (Fin), T. Murphy (Co Sec)
Immediate Holding Company: HELICAL BAR (WALES) LIMITED
Registration no: 01938061 **Date established:** 1985
Turnover: Up to £250,000 **No.of Employees:** 21 - 50 **Product Groups:** 80

Date of Accounts	Mar 08	Mar 07	Mar 06
Pre Tax Profit/Loss	-38	822	562
Working Capital	N/A	N/A	-218
Current Liabilities	N/A	N/A	218

Helifix Ltd
21 Warple Way, London, W3 0RX
Tel: 020-8735 5200 **Fax:** 020-8735 5201
E-mail: robert.paterson@helifix.co.uk
Website: http://www.helifix.co.uk
Bank(s): National Westminster Bank Plc
Directors: N. Patel (Fin), R. Patterson (MD)
Ultimate Holding Company: SEALWOOD GROUP LIMITED
Immediate Holding Company: HELIFIX LIMITED
Registration no: 01798945 **Date established:** 1984 **Turnover:** £2m - £5m
No.of Employees: 21 - 50 **Product Groups:** 35

Date of Accounts	Dec 11	Dec 10	Dec 09
Working Capital	1m	766	407
Fixed Assets	79	83	116
Current Assets	2m	2m	2m

Helix Forge Ltd
25 Winthorpe Road, London, SW15 2LW
Tel: 020-8788 9583
Website: http://www.helixforge.co.uk
Directors: J. Head (MD)
Immediate Holding Company: HELIX FORGE LIMITED
Registration no: 03379414 **Date established:** 1997
No.of Employees: 1 - 10 **Product Groups:** 25, 35, 48

Help 4 I T Ltd
61 Queen Street, London, EC4R 1AE
Tel: 020-7653 9780 **Fax:** 0845-257 4449
E-mail: info@help4it.co.uk
Website: http://www.help4it.co.uk
Directors: J. Hudson (MD)
Managers: S. Patel, T. Finnis (Tech Serv Mgr)
Immediate Holding Company: HELP4IT LIMITED
Registration no: 05336413 **Date established:** 2005 **Turnover:** £1m - £2m
No.of Employees: 21 - 50 **Product Groups:** 44, 84

Date of Accounts	Mar 12	Mar 11	Mar 10
Working Capital	88	82	106
Fixed Assets	26	7	7
Current Assets	299	258	311

Hemming Group
32 Vauxhall Bridge Road, London, SW1V 2SS
Tel: 020-7973 6400 **Fax:** 020-7233 5052
E-mail: info@hgluk.com
Website: http://www.hgluk.com
Bank(s): HSBC Bank plc
Directors: G. Bond (MD)
Immediate Holding Company: HEMMING GROUP LIMITED
Registration no: 00490200 **Date established:** 1951
Turnover: £10m - £20m **No.of Employees:** 51 - 100 **Product Groups:** 28

Date of Accounts	Jun 11	Jun 10	Jun 09
Sales Turnover	16	19m	20m
Pre Tax Profit/Loss	-1	146	-699
Working Capital	5	6m	5m
Fixed Assets	11	11m	13m
Current Assets	9	10m	11m
Current Liabilities	3	3m	6m

Henderson Global Investers
201 Bishopsgate, London, EC2M 3AE
Tel: 020-7818 1818 **Fax:** 020-7818 1819
E-mail: facilities@henderson.com
Website: http://www.henderson.com
Directors: S. Garrood (Fin), A. Boorman (Pers), A. Rydon (Tech Serv), R. Colvill (Fin)
Managers: C. Davies (Mktg Serv Mgr), N. Bromley, A. Formica
Ultimate Holding Company: HENDERSON GROUP PLC (JERSEY)
Immediate Holding Company: HENDERSON GLOBAL INVESTORS LIMITED
Registration no: 00906355 **Date established:** 1967
Turnover: £125m - £250m **No.of Employees:** 501 - 1000
Product Groups: 82

Date of Accounts	Dec 11	Dec 10	Dec 09
Sales Turnover	145m	126m	95m
Pre Tax Profit/Loss	-20m	34m	46m
Working Capital	63m	113m	75m
Fixed Assets	4m	4m	6m
Current Assets	397m	363m	242m
Current Liabilities	93m	82m	62m

Henry's Electronics Ltd
404-406 Edgware Road, London, W2 1ED
Tel: 020-7258 1831 **Fax:** 020-7724 0322
E-mail: sales@henrys.co.uk
Website: http://www.henrys.co.uk
Directors: M. French (Dir)
Immediate Holding Company: HENRY'S ELECTRONICS LIMITED
Registration no: 01276917 **Date established:** 1976
No.of Employees: 1 - 10 **Product Groups:** 40, 67

Date of Accounts	Feb 12	Feb 11	Feb 10
Working Capital	311	393	405
Fixed Assets	1	2	11
Current Assets	414	492	607

Heritage Chocolates Ltd
1 - 21 Tower Heritage Centre Carew Street, London, SE5 9DF
Tel: 020-7733 7268 **Fax:** 020-7274 0151
E-mail: info@heritagechocolates.com
Website: http://www.heritagechocolates.com
Bank(s): HSBC, Greenwich High Rd
Directors: R. Sugdon (MD)
Managers: C. Lewis (Sales Prom Mgr), J. Poole (Sales Admin)
Ultimate Holding Company: The Tower Mint
Registration no: 03638990 **VAT No.:** GB 548 0743 32
Turnover: £2m - £5m **No.of Employees:** 11 - 20 **Product Groups:** 20, 49, 65

Heron Cardiff Properties Ltd
19 Marylebone Road, London, NW1 5JP
Tel: 020-7486 4477 **Fax:** 020-7486 3349
E-mail: l.zeltser@heron.co.uk
Website: http://www.heron.co.uk
Directors: G. Ronson (MD), G. Ronson (Grp Chief Exec), L. Zelster (Co Sec), L. Zeltser (Co Sec), A. Goldman (Dir), L. Ronson (Mkt Research)
Ultimate Holding Company: HERON INTERNATIONAL LTD (CAYMAN ISLANDS)

Immediate Holding Company: HERON CORPORATION
Registration no: 00828750 **Date established:** 1964
Turnover: Up to £250,000 **No.of Employees:** 21 - 50 **Product Groups:** 80

Hewitt & May (Shirtmakers) Ltd

Unit G32b Waterfront Studios 1 Dock Road, London, E16 1AG
Tel: 020-7511 6829 **Fax:** 0870-471 1421
E-mail: info@hewittandmay.com
Website: http://www.hewittandmay.co.uk
Managers: H. D'Hoore (Chief Acct)
Immediate Holding Company: HEWITT & MAY (SHIRTMAKERS) LIMITED
Registration no: 05500898 **Date established:** 2005
Turnover: £500,000 - £1m **No.of Employees:** 1 - 10 **Product Groups:** 24, 63

Date of Accounts	Jul 09	Jul 08	Jul 07
Working Capital	-39	-26	13
Fixed Assets	2	2	3
Current Assets	13	37	56

Hexagon Of Highgate Ltd

82-92 Great North Road, London, N2 0NL
Tel: 020-8444 1111 **Fax:** 020-8444 1011
E-mail: helen.cowie@hexagonbmw.co.uk
Website: http://www.hexagonbmw.co.uk
Directors: H. Cowie (Co Sec)
Managers: N. Levy (Personnel), S. Cox (Mktg Serv Mgr), S. Potter, D. Patel, M. Clarke (Tech Serv Mgr)
Immediate Holding Company: HEXAGON OF HIGHGATE LIMITED
Registration no: 00819349 **Date established:** 1964
Turnover: £50m - £75m **No.of Employees:** 101 - 250 **Product Groups:** 68

Date of Accounts	Dec 11	Dec 10	Dec 09
Sales Turnover	77m	69m	63m
Pre Tax Profit/Loss	855	2m	2m
Working Capital	10m	9m	9m
Fixed Assets	12m	12m	12m
Current Assets	18m	17m	16m
Current Liabilities	4m	3m	3m

High Profile Investment Ltd

61 Aberfeldy House Brandon Estate John Ruskin Street, London, SE5 0XH
Tel: 07930-134773 **Fax:** 01304-332830
E-mail: narcissenabo@hotmail.com
Directors: J. Nabo (MD), C. Koukougnon (Fin)
Immediate Holding Company: F.P.D. AVIATION SERVICES LIMITED
Registration no: 05239107 **Date established:** 2009
No.of Employees: 1 - 10 **Product Groups:** 62

High-Point Rendel Ltd

61 Southwark Street, London, SE1 1SA
Tel: 020-7654 0400 **Fax:** 020-7261 0588
E-mail: london@hprworld.com
Website: http://www.hprworld.com
Bank(s): Barclays
Directors: K. Hingley (Grp Chief Exec), R. Preece (Fin)
Ultimate Holding Company: HPR HOLDINGS LIMITED
Immediate Holding Company: HIGH-POINT RENDEL LIMITED
Registration no: 01898695 **VAT No.:** GB 352 3461 72
Date established: 1985 **Turnover:** £20m - £50m
No.of Employees: 51 - 100 **Product Groups:** 54, 80, 81, 82, 84, 85

Date of Accounts	Jul 11	Jul 10	Jul 09
Sales Turnover	14m	20m	23m
Pre Tax Profit/Loss	959	1m	1m
Working Capital	3m	4m	3m
Fixed Assets	165	257	164
Current Assets	5m	6m	6m
Current Liabilities	1m	2m	2m

Hill Dickinson Ltd

Irongate House 22-30 Dukes Place, London, EC3A 7HX
Tel: 020-7283 9033 **Fax:** 020-7283 1144
E-mail: tony.wilson@hilldickinson.com
Website: http://www.hilldickinson.co.uk
Directors: T. Wilson (Ptnr)
Immediate Holding Company: HILL DICKINSON SERVICES (LONDON) LIMITED
Registration no: 02801145 **VAT No.:** GB 524 7063 57
Date established: 1993 **Turnover:** £250,000 - £500,000
No.of Employees: 251 - 500 **Product Groups:** 80

Hilton International Eye Wear Ltd

21 Sapcote Trading Centre 374 High Road, London, NW10 2DH
Tel: 020-8451 7800 **Fax:** 020-8451 6357
E-mail: sales@hilton-eyewear.com
Website: http://www.hilton-eyewear.com
Directors: D. Shah (MD)
Immediate Holding Company: HILTON INTERNATIONAL EYEWEAR LIMITED
Registration no: 01955329 **VAT No.:** GB 441 9058 52
Date established: 1985 **Turnover:** £2m - £5m **No.of Employees:** 1 - 10
Product Groups: 33, 65

Date of Accounts	Mar 11	Mar 10	Mar 09
Working Capital	963	697	543
Fixed Assets	335	130	64
Current Assets	2m	2m	1m

Hire Information Technology Ltd

Clerkenwell House 67 Clerkenwell Road, Finsbury, London, EC1R 5BL
Tel: 020-7421 3333 **Fax:** 020-7430 1602
E-mail: rentals@hireit.co.uk
Website: http://www.hireit.co.uk
Directors: D. Franklin (MD), M. Ursel (Sales), P. Surry (Co Sec)
Managers: D. Truswell (Sales Prom Mgr), M. Elkins (Purch Mgr)
Ultimate Holding Company: 2e2 Holdings Ltd
Immediate Holding Company: Hamilton Services Group Ltd
Registration no: 02585601 **Date established:** 2003 **Turnover:** £5m - £10m
No.of Employees: 21 - 50 **Product Groups:** 83

Date of Accounts	Dec 07	Jun 06
Sales Turnover	N/A	5607
Pre Tax Profit/Loss	1880	-792
Working Capital	3115	2196
Fixed Assets	961	N/A
Current Assets	3115	4390
Current Liabilities	N/A	2194
Total Share Capital	100	100
ROCE% (Return on Capital Employed)		-36.1
ROT% (Return on Turnover)		-14.1

Hirsh Diamonds

10 Hatton Garden, London, EC1N 8AH
Tel: 020-7404 4392 **Fax:** 020-7430 0107
E-mail: enquiries@hirsh.co.uk
Website: http://www.hirsh.co.uk
Directors: A. Hirsh (MD)
Immediate Holding Company: HIRSH LIMITED
Registration no: 01495932 **VAT No.:** GB 342 1529 81
Date established: 1980 **Turnover:** Up to £250,000
No.of Employees: 1 - 10 **Product Groups:** 49, 65

Date of Accounts	Jan 12	Jan 11	Jan 10
Working Capital	2m	2m	1m
Fixed Assets	161	195	240
Current Assets	3m	3m	2m

His Contracts Ltd

24-28 Pritchards Road, London, E2 9AP
Tel: 020-7739 1455 **Fax:** 020-7729 9438
E-mail: info@hiscontracts.co.uk
Website: http://www.hiscontracts.co.uk
Directors: E. Mills (Dir)
Immediate Holding Company: STAIRCASE SAFETY SERVICES (LONDON) LIMITED
Registration no: 04988829 **Date established:** 2003 **Turnover:** £1m - £2m
No.of Employees: 1 - 10 **Product Groups:** 23, 52

Hobart UK

51 The Bourne, London, N14 6RT
Tel: 08448-887777 **Fax:** 020-8886 0450
E-mail: chris.birch@hobartuk.com
Website: http://www.hobartuk.com
Bank(s): Barclays
Directors: I. Garner (MD), D. Riley (Dir)
Managers: R. Rajah, C. Birch (Mktg Serv Mgr), A. Griggs (Sales Admin), P. Lythell, K. Khajuria (Mgr), C. Williams (Cust Serv Mgr)
Ultimate Holding Company: ILLINOIS TOOL WORKS INC
Immediate Holding Company: WAVEBEST LTD
Registration no: 00158412 **VAT No.:** GB 370 7227 58
Turnover: £50m - £75m **No.of Employees:** 21 - 50 **Product Groups:** 40, 41, 48

Hobbs Ltd

Milton Gate 60 Chiswell Street, London, EC1Y 4AG
Tel: 0845-3133130 **Fax:** 020-34402 198
E-mail: customerservices@hobbs.co.uk
Website: http://www.hobbs.co.uk
Directors: N. Samuel (MD)
Managers: S. Fawcett, A. Chowdhury (Personnel), M. Spearing, A. Goh (Mktg Serv Mgr), E. Osbourne (I.T. Exec)
Ultimate Holding Company: Hobbs Holdings No.1 Ltd
Immediate Holding Company: Peace & Quiet Ltd
Registration no: 01577740 **Turnover:** £75m - £125m
No.of Employees: 51 - 100 **Product Groups:** 24

Hobsons Publishing plc

44 Featherstone Street, London, EC1Y 8RN
Tel: 020-7250 6600 **Fax:** 020-7958 5001
E-mail: info@hobsons.com
Website: http://www.hobsons.com
Directors: S. Johnson (Dir), K. Nicholl (Comm)
Managers: A. Webster, H. Virdi (Tech Serv Mgr), M. Clarke (Mktg Serv Mgr), V. Thatcher (Personnel)
Ultimate Holding Company: ROTHERMERE CONTINUATION LTD (BERMUDA)
Immediate Holding Company: HOBSONS PLC
Registration no: 00640846 **VAT No.:** GB 299 7100 95
Date established: 1959 **Turnover:** £2m - £5m **No.of Employees:** 21 - 50
Product Groups: 28, 64

Date of Accounts	Sep 11	Sep 10	Sep 09
Sales Turnover	4m	3m	3m
Pre Tax Profit/Loss	209	11	-342
Working Capital	38m	38m	38m
Fixed Assets	2m	2m	2m
Current Assets	43m	43m	41m
Current Liabilities	1m	1m	967

Hocaps Ltd

7 Eccleston Street, London, SW1W 9LX
Tel: 020-7730 8883 **Fax:** 020-7730 8885
E-mail: mail@hocaps.com
Website: http://www.hocaps.com
Directors: R. Wasef (MD)
Immediate Holding Company: HOCAPS LIMITED
Registration no: 03026633 **Date established:** 1995
No.of Employees: 1 - 10 **Product Groups:** 80

Date of Accounts	Feb 12	Feb 11	Feb 10
Working Capital	18	-3	-4
Fixed Assets	3	3	4
Current Assets	77	57	88

Hoggett Bowers Interim Management Ltd

48-49 Chancery Lane, London, WC2A 1JF
Tel: 020-7964 9100 **Fax:** 020-7964 9101
E-mail: imoss@hoggett-bowers.com
Website: http://www.hoggett-bowers.com
Directors: I. Moss (Fin)
Ultimate Holding Company: PSD GROUP LIMITED
Immediate Holding Company: HOGGETT BOWERS INTERIM MANAGEMENT LIMITED
Registration no: 02566143 **Date established:** 1990 **Turnover:** £2m - £5m
No.of Employees: 21 - 50 **Product Groups:** 80, 86

Date of Accounts	Dec 11	Dec 10	Dec 09
Sales Turnover	4m	3m	3m
Pre Tax Profit/Loss	244	66	89
Working Capital	209	21	648
Current Assets	716	195	812
Current Liabilities	259	18	29

Holborn Direct Mail

Capacity House 2-6 Rothsay Street, London, SE1 4UD
Tel: 020-7407 6444 **Fax:** 020-7357 6065
E-mail: sales@holborndirectmail.co.uk
Website: http://www.holborndirectmail.co.uk
Directors: S. Sharp (MD)
Immediate Holding Company: BURONIAN LIMITED
Registration no: 01101274 **VAT No.:** GB 235 6791 40
Date established: 1973 **Turnover:** £250,000 - £500,000
No.of Employees: 1 - 10 **Product Groups:** 44, 81

Date of Accounts	Mar 12	Mar 11	Mar 10
Working Capital	-32	13	154
Fixed Assets	704	709	714
Current Assets	101	40	187

Holbud Ltd

66 Leman Street, London, E1 8EU
Tel: 020-7488 4901 **Fax:** 020-7265 0654
E-mail: david@holbud.co.uk
Website: http://www.holbud.co.uk
Bank(s): National Westminster Bank Plc
Directors: D. Rowe (Fin)
Immediate Holding Company: HOLBUD LIMITED
Registration no: 01328840 **VAT No.:** GB 524 7635 38
Date established: 1977 **Turnover:** £250m - £500m
No.of Employees: 21 - 50 **Product Groups:** 82

Date of Accounts	Oct 11	Oct 10	Oct 09
Sales Turnover	421m	524m	650m
Pre Tax Profit/Loss	2m	4m	3m
Working Capital	16m	11m	8m
Fixed Assets	25m	29m	28m
Current Assets	147m	103m	105m
Current Liabilities	3m	7m	3m

Holland & Holland Holdings Ltd

33 Bruton Street, London, W1J 6HH
Tel: 020-7499 4411 **Fax:** 020-7499 4544
E-mail: reception@hollandandholland.com
Website: http://www.hollandandholland.com
Bank(s): Royal Bank of Scotland, London
Directors: B. Frost (Co Sec), S. Wilson (MD)
Managers: A. Ambrose (Mgr), D. Maloni (I.T. Exec), L. Dean (Personnel)
Ultimate Holding Company: CHANEL INTERNATIONAL BV (NETHERLANDS)
Immediate Holding Company: HOLLAND & HOLLAND HOLDINGS LIMITED
Registration no: 00597891 **VAT No.:** GB 238 4748 33
Date established: 1958 **Turnover:** £5m - £10m **No.of Employees:** 21 - 50
Product Groups: 24, 36, 63, 84

Date of Accounts	Dec 10	Dec 09	Dec 06

Hollander Hyams Ltd

9 Berners Place, London, W1T 3HH
Tel: 020-7636 1562 **Fax:** 020-7636 1564
E-mail: sales@hollanderhyams.com
Website: http://www.hollanderhyams.com
Bank(s): Barclays, London
Directors: H. Rabinowicz (MD), J. Lind (Fin), D. Feld (Dir), D. Feld (Sales), J. Lind (Co Sec)
Managers: D. Feld (Mgr), K. Impiazzi (Shipping Mgr)
Immediate Holding Company: HOLLANDER HYAMS LIMITED
Registration no: 00396137 **VAT No.:** GB 232 3645 84
Date established: 1945 **Turnover:** £5m - £10m **No.of Employees:** 21 - 50
Product Groups: 66

Date of Accounts	Feb 08	Feb 11	Feb 10
Sales Turnover	N/A	8m	7m
Pre Tax Profit/Loss	38	28	14
Working Capital	1m	2m	1m
Fixed Assets	592	750	551
Current Assets	3m	4m	3m
Current Liabilities	166	121	157

Holman & Williams Packaging Ltd

Wimbledon Art Studios 10 Riverside Yard, London, SW17 0BB
Tel: 020-8944 5151 **Fax:** 020-8944 5162
E-mail: enquiries@hwpackaging.co.uk
Website: http://www.hwpackaging.co.uk
Directors: D. Smith (MD)
Ultimate Holding Company: HOLMAN INDUSTRIES LIMITED
Immediate Holding Company: HOLMAN & WILLIAMS (PACKAGING) LIMITED
Registration no: 03324685 **Date established:** 1997 **Turnover:** £1m - £2m
No.of Employees: 1 - 10 **Product Groups:** 27

Date of Accounts	Mar 11	Mar 10	Mar 09
Working Capital	347	264	222
Fixed Assets	7	9	11
Current Assets	587	653	540

Hong Kong Trade Development Council

16 Upper Grosvenor Street, London, W1K 7PL
Tel: 020-7616 9500 **Fax:** 020-7616 9520
E-mail: london.office@tdc.org.hk
Website: http://www.hktdc.com
Directors: D. Marsden (Dir)
Immediate Holding Company: HONG KONG TRADE DEVELOPMENT COUNCIL
Registration no: FC007489 **Date established:** 1972
Turnover: Over £1,000m **No.of Employees:** 1 - 10 **Product Groups:** 80

Hornsey Metal Works

410 Hornsey Road, London, N19 4EB
Tel: 020-7281 6740 **Fax:** 020-7281 6740
E-mail: bajanwes@hotmail.co.uk
Directors: W. Brown (Prop)
No.of Employees: 1 - 10 **Product Groups:** 26, 35

Horton International

1 Palace Street, London, SW1E 5HX
Tel: 020-7630 0200 **Fax:** 020-7630 0322
E-mail: london@horton-intl.co.uk
Website: http://www.horton-intl.co.uk
Directors: C. Taylor (MD)
Immediate Holding Company: HORTON GROUP INTERNATIONAL LIMITED
Registration no: 02855609 **VAT No.:** GB 110 0384 38
Date established: 1993 **Turnover:** £250,000 - £500,000
No.of Employees: 1 - 10 **Product Groups:** 80

Date of Accounts	Mar 11	Mar 10	Mar 09
Working Capital	48	24	11
Current Assets	319	175	215
Current Liabilities	184	109	171

Hospitality Sales Solutions Ltd

20 Lexham House 45 53 Lexham Gardens, London, W8 5JT
Tel: 020-3287 6483 **Fax:** 020-7806 8185
E-mail: info@hospitalitysalessolutions.co.uk
Website: http://www.hospitalitysalessolutions.co.uk
Directors: V. Purushothaman (Dir)
Registration no: 06252970 **Date established:** 2007
No.of Employees: 1 - 10 **Product Groups:** 84

Hospitality Trading Ltd (H C I M A)

191 Trinity Road, London, SW17 7HN
Tel: 020-8672 4251 **Fax:** 020-8682 1707
E-mail: commdept@hcima.co.uk
Website: http://www.hcima.org.uk
Directors: P. Rossiter (Grp Chief Exec), A. Corrigan (Co Sec)
Ultimate Holding Company: INSTITUTE OF HOSPITALITY
Immediate Holding Company: HOSPITALITY QUALITY SERVICES (HQS) LIMITED
Registration no: 02706545 **VAT No.:** GB 218 6595 36
Date established: 1992 **Turnover:** Up to £250,000
No.of Employees: 1 - 10 **Product Groups:** 86, 87

Date of Accounts	Dec 11	Dec 10	Dec 09
Sales Turnover	54	38	30
Working Capital	15	15	15
Current Assets	15	19	17
Current Liabilities	N/A	4	2

Hotbray Ltd

16 Jubilee Way, London, SW19 3GZ
Tel: 020-8545 0011 **Fax:** 020-8545 0020
E-mail: info@hotbray.co.uk
Website: http://www.hotbray.co.uk
Bank(s): National Westminster Bank Plc
Directors: B. Johnson (MD)
Managers: R. Pope (Tech Serv Mgr)
Ultimate Holding Company: HALCYON ENTERPRISES INC (PANAMA)
Immediate Holding Company: HOTBRAY LIMITED
Registration no: 01053848 **VAT No.:** GB 237 0574 66
Date established: 1972 **Turnover:** £20m - £50m
No.of Employees: 21 - 50 **Product Groups:** 29, 35, 36, 37, 39, 40, 41, 45, 61, 67, 68

Date of Accounts	Apr 12	Apr 11	Apr 10
Sales Turnover	32m	36m	29m
Pre Tax Profit/Loss	2m	3m	1m
Working Capital	12m	10m	8m
Fixed Assets	110	117	79
Current Assets	15m	15m	12m
Current Liabilities	571	1m	531

Hotcourses

150-152 King Street, London, W6 0QU
Tel: 020-8600 5300
E-mail: sales@hotcourses.com
Website: http://www.hotcourses.com
Managers: P. Redman (Mktg Serv Mgr), P. Lai (Sales Admin), A. Gaveridge (Personnel)
Immediate Holding Company: HOTCOURSES LTD
Registration no: 02471319 **Date established:** 1990
Turnover: £10m - £20m **No.of Employees:** 51 - 100 **Product Groups:** 28

Date of Accounts	Dec 10	Dec 09	Dec 08
Sales Turnover	10m	10m	10m
Pre Tax Profit/Loss	3m	2m	2m
Working Capital	4m	2m	2m
Fixed Assets	264	2m	2m
Current Assets	12m	11m	10m
Current Liabilities	7m	8m	7m

Hotel Ibis Greenwich

30 Stockwell Street, London, SE10 9JN
Tel: 020-8305 1177 **Fax:** 020-8858 7139
E-mail: h0975@accor-hotels.com
Website: http://www.ibishotel.com
Managers: M. Dgasser (Mgr)
Immediate Holding Company: SO ORGANIC (UK) LIMITED
Registration no: 06512463 **Date established:** 2008
No.of Employees: 11 - 20 **Product Groups:** 69

Hotel Inspector

56 Gloucester Road, London, SW7 4UB
Tel: 0207-1172760
E-mail: sales@hotelinspector.us
Website: http://www.hotelinspector.org.uk
Managers: C. Bowen (Sales Admin)
Date established: 1999 **Turnover:** **No.of Employees:** 51 - 100
Product Groups: 69

Hotel Lilly

23-33 Lillie Road, London, SW6 1UG
Tel: 020-7381 1881 **Fax:** 020-7381 8695
E-mail: hotellily@aol.com
Website: http://www.hotellilly.com
Managers: M. O'Donoghue (Mgr), M. Odonoghue (Chief Mgr)
Immediate Holding Company: SUNHOPE LIMITED
Registration no: 02754947 **Date established:** 1992
Turnover: £500,000 - £1m **No.of Employees:** 11 - 20 **Product Groups:** 69

Date of Accounts	Mar 11	Mar 10	Mar 09
Working Capital	-569	-608	-474
Fixed Assets	2m	2m	2m
Current Assets	69	58	207

Houlder Ltd

59 Lafone Street, London, SE1 2LX
Tel: 020-7357 7317 **Fax:** 020-7403 8201
E-mail: barry.farrelly@houlderltd.com
Website: http://www.houlderltd.com
Bank(s): The Royal Bank of Scotland
Directors: B. Farrelly (Fin)
Ultimate Holding Company: HOULDER BIDCO LIMITED
Immediate Holding Company: HOULDER LIMITED
Registration no: 04400298 **Date established:** 2002 **Turnover:** £5m - £10m
No.of Employees: 21 - 50 **Product Groups:** 84

Date of Accounts	Dec 11	Dec 10	Dec 09
Sales Turnover	9m	11m	9m
Pre Tax Profit/Loss	249	591	385
Working Capital	1m	2m	2m
Fixed Assets	744	498	97
Current Assets	4m	5m	4m
Current Liabilities	2m	3m	2m

Houlder Group

Michaels House 10-12 Alie Street, London, E1 8DE
Tel: 020-7980 3800 **Fax:** 020-7980 3814
E-mail: general@houlder.co.uk
Website: http://www.houlder.co.uk
Bank(s): The Royal Bank of Scotland
Managers: A. Cross (Sales Admin)
Ultimate Holding Company: CHINA MERCHANTS HOLDINGS (UK) LIMITED
Immediate Holding Company: HOULDER GROUP LIMITED
Registration no: 02618499 **Date established:** 1991 **Turnover:** £5m - £10m
No.of Employees: 51 - 100 **Product Groups:** 82

Date of Accounts	Dec 11	Dec 10	Dec 09
Pre Tax Profit/Loss	-96	-155	-206
Working Capital	-1m	-748	-360
Fixed Assets	7m	7m	6m
Current Assets	23	23	102
Current Liabilities	26	19	11

Howarth Of London

31-37 Chiltern Street, London, W1U 7PN
Tel: 020-7935 2407 **Fax:** 020-7224 2564
E-mail: sales@howarth.uk.com
Website: http://www.howarth.uk.com
Bank(s): HSBC
Directors: J. Walsworth (MD), N. Clark (MD), N. Clarke (Sales)
Immediate Holding Company: HOWARTH OF LONDON LIMITED
Registration no: 00492396 **VAT No.:** GB 233 9902 54
Date established: 1951 **Turnover:** £5m - £10m **No.of Employees:** 11 - 20
Product Groups: 65

Date of Accounts	Jun 11	Jun 10	Jun 09
Sales Turnover	N/A	5m	4m
Pre Tax Profit/Loss	N/A	519	309
Working Capital	2m	2m	1m
Fixed Assets	54	81	99
Current Assets	3m	3m	3m
Current Liabilities	N/A	694	562

Howgate Sable

33 St James's Square, London, SW1Y 4JS
Tel: 020-7495 1234 **Fax:** 020-7317 0920
E-mail: london@howgate-sable.com
Website: http://www.howgate-sable.com
Directors: S. Banks (Snr Part)
Managers: A. Sharman (Fin Mgr)
Ultimate Holding Company: ALMAR PLC
Immediate Holding Company: TIME PRODUCTS LUXURY LIMITED
Registration no: 00562974 **Date established:** 1956 **Turnover:** £2m - £5m
No.of Employees: 11 - 20 **Product Groups:** 80

James Hoyle & Son

48-50 Andrews Road, London, E8 4RL
Tel: 020-7254 2335 **Fax:** 020-7254 8811
E-mail: jameshoyle@btclick.com
Website: http://www.ironheritage.co.uk
Directors: A. Hoyle (MD)
Immediate Holding Company: JAMES HOYLE & SON LTD
Registration no: 05440821 **Turnover:** £250,000 - £500,000
No.of Employees: 1 - 10 **Product Groups:** 34

HSBC Bank plc

8-14 Canada Square, London, E14 5HQ
Tel: 08457-404404 **Fax:** 020-7991 4888
E-mail: douglas.flint@ntlworld.com
Website: http://www.hsbc.co.uk
Directors: D. Flint (Ch)
Ultimate Holding Company: HSBC HOLDINGS PLC
Immediate Holding Company: HSBC BANK PLC
Registration no: 00014259 **Date established:** 1980
No.of Employees: 1501 & over **Product Groups:** 80, 82

Date of Accounts	Dec 11	Dec 10	Dec 09
Pre Tax Profit/Loss	3111m	4011m	4014m
Fixed Assets	298852m	260368m	118419m
Current Assets	29118m	38126m	33509m
Current Liabilities	785282m	758251m	716175m

HSS Hire

45 Barking Road Canning Town, London, E16 4HB
Tel: 020-7474 7040 **Fax:** 020-7474 7080
Website: http://www.hss.com
Managers: J. Hardy (Mgr)
Immediate Holding Company: VULCAN SERVICE & SUPPLY COMPANY LIMITED
Registration no: 03080799 **Date established:** 1995
No.of Employees: 1 - 10 **Product Groups:** 36, 37

Date of Accounts	Jul 08	Jul 07	Jul 06
Working Capital	1	464	-4
Fixed Assets	2m	405	179
Current Assets	650	2m	300
Current Liabilities	N/A	219	N/A

Hugall Services Ltd

Unit 16 250 Milkwood Road, London, SE24 0HG
Tel: 020-7738 6104 **Fax:** 020-7738 3994
E-mail: robin@hugallservices.co.uk
Website: http://www.hugallservices.co.uk
Directors: R. Usher (MD), P. Martin (Fin)
Immediate Holding Company: HUGALL SERVICES LIMITED
Registration no: 03129062 **Date established:** 1995
No.of Employees: 11 - 20 **Product Groups:** 20, 22, 24, 27, 30, 32, 33, 35, 36, 37, 38, 40, 41, 42, 44, 45, 48, 62, 63, 64, 66, 67, 69, 83

Date of Accounts	Sep 11	Sep 10	Sep 09
Working Capital	569	642	578
Fixed Assets	412	28	33
Current Assets	950	1m	939

Hull Blyth & Co. Ltd

2 Coldbath Square, London, EC1R 5HL
Tel: 020-7696 9688 **Fax:** 020-7696 9686
E-mail: caven.hammock@hull-blyth.com
Website: http://www.hull-blyth.com
Managers: S. Choo (Fin Mgr)
Immediate Holding Company: ABSOLUTE RETURN CAPITAL MANAGEMENT LTD
Registration no: 07022066 **Date established:** 2008
No.of Employees: 1 - 10 **Product Groups:** 76

Date of Accounts	Mar 11	Mar 10	Mar 09
Working Capital	158	10	46
Fixed Assets	27	42	37
Current Assets	214	151	84
Current Liabilities	32	84	9

Human Factors International

Warnford Court 29 Throgmorton Street, London, EC2N 2AT
Tel: 020-7831 3123 **Fax:** 020-7831 8643
E-mail: enquiries@hfi.com
Website: http://www.hfi.com
Directors: A. Atkinson (Ch)
Immediate Holding Company: ALTERNATE FUTURES LIMITED
Registration no: 01303391 **Date established:** 2010
Turnover: £500,000 - £1m **No.of Employees:** 11 - 20 **Product Groups:** 80

Date of Accounts	Jun 11	Jun 10	Jun 09
Pre Tax Profit/Loss	-0	-0	-0
Working Capital	-9	-9	-0
Fixed Assets	9	9	N/A

Hunter & Partners Group Ltd

26-28 Hammersmith Grove, London, W6 7HU
Tel: 020-8237 8200 **Fax:** 020-8741 2814
E-mail: mail@hunters.co.uk
Website: http://www.hunters.co.uk
Directors: I. Hurlstone (Co Sec)
Managers: S. Hurlstone (Tech Serv Mgr), A. Jourdren (Personnel)
Immediate Holding Company: HUNTER & PARTNERS GROUP LIMITED
Registration no: 02288274 **VAT No.:** GB 241 8070 83
Date established: 1988 **Turnover:** £5m - £10m
No.of Employees: 101 - 250 **Product Groups:** 84

Date of Accounts	Dec 11	Dec 10	Dec 09
Sales Turnover	7m	8m	9m
Pre Tax Profit/Loss	312	741	-195
Working Capital	3m	3m	2m
Fixed Assets	472	780	1m
Current Assets	6m	5m	5m
Current Liabilities	2m	2m	2m

Hunter Penrose Supplies Ltd

32 Southwark Street, London, SE1 1TU
Tel: 020-7407 5051 **Fax:** 020-7378 1800
E-mail: info@hunterpenrose.co.uk
Website: http://www.hunterpenrose.co.uk
Directors: J. Sewell (MD)
Immediate Holding Company: HUNTER PENROSE SUPPLIES LIMITED
Registration no: 01693963 **VAT No.:** GB 380 6590 37
Date established: 1983 **Turnover:** £1m - £2m **No.of Employees:** 1 - 10
Product Groups: 27, 28, 32, 38, 44

Date of Accounts	Mar 11	Mar 10	Mar 09
Working Capital	164	156	141
Fixed Assets	3	6	11
Current Assets	785	906	963
Current Liabilities	N/A	133	N/A

Hunter Plastics

Nathan Way Woolwich, London, SE28 0AE
Tel: 020-8855 9851 **Fax:** 020-8317 7764
E-mail: bill.wallace@hunterplastics.co.uk
Website: http://www.hunterplastics.co.uk
Bank(s): National Westminster Bank Plc
Directors: W. Wallace (Fin)
Managers: S. Dunkley, P. Smith (Sales Prom Mgr), S. Bolton (Mktg Serv Mgr), K. Sturrock (Comptroller)
Ultimate Holding Company: ALIAXIS SA (BELGIUM)
Immediate Holding Company: MARLEY PLASTICS LTD
Registration no: 00478797 **VAT No.:** GB 586 5473 91
Date established: 1991 **Turnover:** £20m - £50m
No.of Employees: 51 - 100 **Product Groups:** 30, 66

Date of Accounts	Dec 07	Dec 06	Dec 05
Sales Turnover	34512	32531	29868
Pre Tax Profit/Loss	2140	1814	2014
Working Capital	4734	4339	706
Fixed Assets	9286	11179	8873
Current Assets	9306	9273	6688
Current Liabilities	4572	4934	5982
Total Share Capital	7000	7000	7000
ROCE% (Return on Capital Employed)	15.3	11.7	21.0
ROT% (Return on Turnover)	6.2	5.6	6.7

Hunters & Frankau Ltd

Hurlingham Business Park Sulivan Road, London, SW6 3DU
Tel: 020-7471 8400 **Fax:** 020-7371 0374
E-mail: p.hambidge@cigars.co.uk
Website: http://www.cigars.co.uk
Directors: P. Hambidge (Fin)
Managers: S. Croley
Ultimate Holding Company: HUNTERS & FRANKAU GROUP LIMITED
Immediate Holding Company: J. FRANKAU & COMPANY LIMITED
Registration no: 00084385 **Date established:** 2005
Turnover: £20m - £50m **No.of Employees:** 21 - 50 **Product Groups:** 20

Date of Accounts	Dec 11	Dec 10	Dec 09
Pre Tax Profit/Loss	1m	1m	1m
Fixed Assets	323	323	323

Hunting Plc

3 Cockspur Street, London, SW1Y 5BQ
Tel: 020-7321 0123 **Fax:** 020-7839 2072
E-mail: pr@hunting.plc.uk
Website: http://www.huntingplc.com
Bank(s): Lloyds TSB Bank plc
Directors: D. Proctor (Grp Chief Exec), D. Clark (Fin)
Managers: D. Hunting
Immediate Holding Company: HUNTING PLC
Registration no: 00974568 **Date established:** 1970
Turnover: £500m - £1,000m **No.of Employees:** 11 - 20
Product Groups: 24, 32, 38, 39, 40, 42, 84

Date of Accounts	Dec 11	Dec 10	Dec 09
Sales Turnover	609m	462m	360m
Pre Tax Profit/Loss	39m	39m	39m
Working Capital	232m	286m	363m
Fixed Assets	802m	353m	238m
Current Assets	491m	506m	580m
Current Liabilities	160m	123m	134m

Huntress

Imperial House 15 Kingsway, London, WC2B 6UD
Tel: 020-7759 9000 **Fax:** 020-7774 1301
E-mail: info@huntress.co.uk
Website: http://www.huntress.co.uk
Directors: G. Laurence (Dir)
Ultimate Holding Company: HUNTRESS GROUP LIMITED
Immediate Holding Company: HUNTRESS SEARCH LIMITED
Registration no: 04041477 **Date established:** 2000
Turnover: £50m - £75m **No.of Employees:** 101 - 250 **Product Groups:** 80

Date of Accounts	Dec 11	Dec 10	Dec 09
Sales Turnover	61m	60m	61m
Pre Tax Profit/Loss	2m	858	-506
Working Capital	4m	4m	5m
Fixed Assets	498	715	886
Current Assets	11m	11m	11m
Current Liabilities	6m	6m	4m

H Huntsman & Sons Ltd
11 Savile Row, London, W1S 3PS
Tel: 020-7734 7441 **Fax:** 020-7287 2937
E-mail: sales@h-huntsman.com
Website: http://www.h-huntsman.com
Directors: P. Smith (Sales & Mktg), G. Scotton (Co Sec)
Managers: P. Smith (Chief Mgr), C. Mcgrovern (Chief Acct), C. McGrovern (Chief Acct)
Immediate Holding Company: H. HUNTSMAN & SONS LIMITED
Registration no: 05313942 **Date established:** 2004 **Turnover:** £2m - £5m
No.of Employees: 21 - 50 **Product Groups:** 24

Date of Accounts	Dec 11	Dec 10	Dec 09
Working Capital	752	686	790
Fixed Assets	351	355	18
Current Assets	2m	2m	2m
Current Liabilities	N/A	6	9

A F Hussey London Ltd
Unit B10 Down Bounds Green Industrial Estate Ringway, London, N11 2UD
Tel: 020-8368 3680 **Fax:** 020-8361 2992
E-mail: sales@afhussey.co.uk
Website: http://www.afhussey.co.uk
Directors: V. Beckwith (Co Sec), B. Harmsworth (MD)
Immediate Holding Company: A.F.HUSSEY(LONDON)LIMITED
Registration no: 00757948 **VAT No.:** GB 229 3298 44
Date established: 1963 **Turnover:** £250,000 - £500,000
No.of Employees: 1 - 10 **Product Groups:** 48

Date of Accounts	May 11	May 10	May 09
Working Capital	33	58	78
Current Assets	84	111	140

Hyder Consulting Ltd
29 Bressenden Place, London, SW1E 5DZ
Tel: 020-3014 9000 **Fax:** 020-7316 6125
E-mail: graham.reid@hyderconsulting.com
Website: http://www.hyder-consulting.com
Directors: G. Reid (MD)
Managers: C. Pullen (Purch Mgr), M. Melville (Personnel), S. Hay (Tech Serv Mgr), R. Down (Fin Mgr), S. Okeefe (Mktg Serv Mgr)
Ultimate Holding Company: HYDER CONSULTING PLC
Immediate Holding Company: HYDER CONSULTING PLC
Registration no: 00768087 **Date established:** 1963
Turnover: £125m - £250m **No.of Employees:** 101 - 250
Product Groups: 34, 42, 54, 80, 81, 84, 85

Date of Accounts	Mar 11	Mar 10	Mar 09
Sales Turnover	290m	309m	319m
Pre Tax Profit/Loss	18m	13m	3m
Working Capital	60m	56m	51m
Fixed Assets	57m	64m	72m
Current Assets	135m	138m	158m
Current Liabilities	61m	67m	91m

I A L Consultants
C P House 97-107 Uxbridge Road, London, W5 5TL
Tel: 020-8832 7780 **Fax:** 020-8566 4931
E-mail: enquiries@brggroup.com
Website: http://www.brg.co.uk
Bank(s): HSBC Bank plc
Directors: J. Berents (MD)
Managers: J. Wildey (Personnel), K. Owusu (Tech Serv Mgr)
Ultimate Holding Company: BUSINESS RESEARCH GROUP LIMITED
Immediate Holding Company: CONSULT GB LIMITED
Registration no: 02098164 **VAT No.:** GB 538 8388 90
Date established: 1987 **Turnover:** £1m - £2m **No.of Employees:** 21 - 50
Product Groups: 81

Date of Accounts	Dec 11	Dec 10	Dec 09
Working Capital	10	10	10
Current Assets	10	10	10

I A M Drive & Survive
510 Chiswick High Road, London, W4 5RG
Tel: 08453-108311 **Fax:** (020)-8996 9701
E-mail: jane.kite@iamdriveandsurvive.co.uk
Website: http://www.iamdriveandsurvive.co.uk
Directors: P. Doughty (Chief Op Offcr), N. Hawley (Sales)
Managers: M. Stonard, M. Jones (Tech Serv Mgr), D. Batten, S. Bowden (Personnel), B. Cooper (Mktg Serv Mgr)
Ultimate Holding Company: INSTITUTE OF ADVANCED MOTORISTS LIMITED(THE)
Immediate Holding Company: IAM DRIVE & SURVIVE LIMITED
Registration no: 02019635 **Date established:** 1986 **Turnover:** £1m - £2m
No.of Employees: 21 - 50 **Product Groups:** 86

Date of Accounts	Mar 11	Mar 10	Mar 09
Sales Turnover	2m	2m	2m
Pre Tax Profit/Loss	-586	-857	-600
Working Capital	-2m	-1m	-464
Fixed Assets	6	11	2
Current Assets	365	738	843
Current Liabilities	254	295	108

I M O Electronics Ltd
Unit 15 1000 North Circular Road, London, NW2 7JP
Tel: 020-8452 6444 **Fax:** 020-8450 2274
E-mail: sales@imopc.com
Website: http://www.imopc.com
Bank(s): Lloyds TSB Bank plc
Directors: T. Ballard (Fin)
Managers: F. Furlotto, J. Vincent (Personnel), A. Keohane (Tech Serv Mgr)
Immediate Holding Company: I.M.O. ELECTRONICS LIMITED
Registration no: 01240559 **Date established:** 1976
Turnover: £10m - £20m **No.of Employees:** 51 - 100 **Product Groups:** 37, 38, 49

Date of Accounts	Apr 11	Apr 10	Apr 09
Working Capital	3m	3m	3m
Current Assets	3m	3m	3m

I Nemetnejad Ltd
403-405 Edgware Road, London, NW2 6LN
Tel: 020-8830 5511 **Fax:** 020-8530 5522
E-mail: info@inemetnejad.com
Website: http://www.inemetnejad.com
Directors: A. Nemetnejad (Prop), J. Nemetnejad (MD)
Immediate Holding Company: I. NEMETNEJAD LIMITED
Registration no: 03902087 **VAT No.:** GB 243 4668 54
Date established: 2000 **Turnover:** Up to £250,000
No.of Employees: 1 - 10 **Product Groups:** 63

I P C Media Ltd
Blue Fin Building 110 Southwark Street, London, SE1 0SU
Tel: 0800-731 0616
E-mail: press_office@ipc.media.com
Website: http://www.horseandhound.co.uk
Managers: R. Sidoli
Ultimate Holding Company: TIME WARNER INC (USA)
Immediate Holding Company: IPC MEDIA LIMITED
Registration no: 00053626 **VAT No.:** GB 646 1506 45
Date established: 1997 **Turnover:** £250m - £500m
No.of Employees: 51 - 100 **Product Groups:** 28

I S B A
Langham House 1b Portland Place, London, W1B 1PN
Tel: 020-7291 9020 **Fax:** 020-7291 9030
E-mail: info@isba.org.uk
Website: http://www.isba.org.uk
Bank(s): The Royal Bank of Scotland
Directors: J. Earnshaw (MD), C. Perrett (Co Sec), J. Marlow (Dir)
Managers: A. Collins
Immediate Holding Company: ALPHA REAL CAPITAL LLP
Registration no: 00068497 **VAT No.:** GB 238 6785 17
Date established: 2005 **Turnover:** £5m - £10m **No.of Employees:** 21 - 50
Product Groups: 87

Date of Accounts	Mar 11	Mar 10	Mar 09
Sales Turnover	2m	2m	2m
Pre Tax Profit/Loss	15	-32	51
Working Capital	579	547	538
Fixed Assets	90	94	116
Current Assets	3m	3m	2m
Current Liabilities	2m	2m	2m

I T E Group plc (Mining & Metals Exhibitions)
105 Salusbury Road, London, NW6 6RG
Tel: 020-7596 5000 **Fax:** 020-7596 5111
E-mail: enquiry@ite-exhibitions.com
Website: http://www.ite-exhibitions.com
Directors: E. Tompkins (Grp Chief Exec), I. Tomkins (Fin)
Managers: K. Mellidiyev (Mgr), O. Netchaev, N. Sanderson (Mktg Serv Mgr)
Immediate Holding Company: Ite Group plc
Registration no: 01927339 **Date established:** 1985
Turnover: £75m - £125m **No.of Employees:** 251 - 500
Product Groups: 81

I T S C Ltd
9 Northfields Prospect Northfields, London, SW18 1PE
Tel: 020-8874 7282 **Fax:** 020-8874 7539
E-mail: info@itscltd.com
Website: http://www.itscltd.com
Directors: N. Ahmed (Dir)
Managers: A. Goodson (Sales Admin)
Immediate Holding Company: I.T.S.C. LIMITED
Registration no: 02321497 **VAT No.:** GB 493 7814 03
Date established: 1988 **Turnover:** £500,000 - £1m
No.of Employees: 1 - 10 **Product Groups:** 51

Date of Accounts	Dec 10	Dec 09	Dec 08
Working Capital	494	363	271
Fixed Assets	305	316	328
Current Assets	799	736	1m

I T V Breakfast
The London Television Centre 58-72 Upper Ground, London, SE1 9TT
Tel: 020-7827 7000 **Fax:** 020-7827 7001
E-mail: david.kermode@itv.com
Website: http://www.itv.com
Directors: G. Morrison (Co Sec)
Managers: D. Kermode
Ultimate Holding Company: ITV PLC
Immediate Holding Company: ITV BREAKFAST LIMITED
Registration no: 02578005 **Date established:** 1991
Turnover: £50m - £75m **No.of Employees:** 251 - 500 **Product Groups:** 89

Date of Accounts	Dec 11	Dec 10	Dec 09
Sales Turnover	56m	71m	68m
Pre Tax Profit/Loss	13m	14m	14m
Working Capital	54m	39m	23m
Fixed Assets	728	2m	4m
Current Assets	91m	87m	35m
Current Liabilities	4m	12m	11m

Iberia Airlines
Iberia House 10 Hammersmith Broadway, London, W6 7AL
Tel: 08706-090500 **Fax:** 020-8222 8983
E-mail: sales@iberiaairlines.co.uk
Website: http://www.iberiaairlines.co.uk
Managers: A. Baldemoors (Mgr)
VAT No.: GB 239 2896 22 **Date established:** 2001
No.of Employees: 51 - 100 **Product Groups:** 75

Icon Digital Communications Ltd
United House North Road, London, N7 9DP
Tel: 020-7609 8001 **Fax:** 020-7700 3429
E-mail: info@iconcomms.co.uk
Website: http://www.iconprintsolutions.co.uk
Directors: D. Cooper (Co Sec), F. Allen (Dir)
Immediate Holding Company: ICON DIGITAL COMMUNICATIONS LIMITED
Registration no: 03787234 **Date established:** 1999 **Turnover:** £1m - £2m
No.of Employees: 1 - 10 **Product Groups:** 28, 32, 80

Date of Accounts	Jul 11	Jul 10	Jul 09
Working Capital	-5	6	24
Current Assets	92	152	162

Ideal Catering Equipment
Unit 2 12 Horn Lane, London, SE10 0RT
Tel: 020-8269 2866
E-mail: john@ideal-catering.co.uk
Website: http://www.ideal-catering.co.uk
Directors: R. Vosper (Dir)
Date established: 2003 **No.of Employees:** 1 - 10 **Product Groups:** 20, 40, 41

Ideo Ltd
144a Clerkenwell Road, London, EC1R 5DF
Tel: 020-7713 2600 **Fax:** 020-7713 2601
E-mail: lclarke@ideo.com
Website: http://www.ideo.com
Directors: J. Styles (Pers), D. McDowell (Tech Serv), D. Ziel (Fin)
Managers: L. Clarke (Sales Admin)
Immediate Holding Company: IDEO PRODUCT DEVELOPMENT INC.
Registration no: FC016145 **Date established:** 1991
No.of Employees: 21 - 50 **Product Groups:** 44, 84, 85

Ifa Promotion Ltd
117 Farringdon Road, London, EC1R 3BX
Tel: 0330-303 0025
E-mail: contact@unbiased.co.uk
Website: http://www.unbiased.co.uk
Directors: D. Elms (Grp Chief Exec)
Registration no: SC114606 **Date established:** 2003 **Turnover:** £2m - £5m
No.of Employees: 1 - 10 **Product Groups:** 81

Date of Accounts	Sep 08	Sep 07	Sep 06
Sales Turnover	2883	2839	2825
Pre Tax Profit/Loss	-15	23	92
Working Capital	674	693	673
Fixed Assets	25	21	18
Current Assets	1597	1820	1746
Current Liabilities	923	1126	1073
ROCE% (Return on Capital Employed)	-2.2	3.2	13.3
ROT% (Return on Turnover)	-0.5	0.8	3.3

Ikea Ltd
255 North Circular Road, London, NW10 0JQ
Tel: 020-8233 2300 **Fax:** 020-8451 2813
Website: http://www.ikea.co.uk
Managers: C. Wallace (Tech Serv Mgr), I. Duffy
Ultimate Holding Company: INGKA HOLDING BV (NETHERLANDS)
Immediate Holding Company: IKEA LIMITED
Registration no: 01986283 **Date established:** 1986
Turnover: Over £1,000m **No.of Employees:** 101 - 250
Product Groups: 26, 61

Date of Accounts	Aug 11	Aug 10	Aug 09
Sales Turnover	1191m	1239m	1230m
Pre Tax Profit/Loss	24m	36m	17m
Working Capital	-232m	-236m	-179m
Fixed Assets	705m	745m	734m
Current Assets	135m	145m	113m
Current Liabilities	72m	60m	42m

Ilab Reliance Media Orks UK Ltd
55 Poland Street, London, W1F 7NN
Tel: 020-3463 2420
E-mail: nigel@ilabuk.co.uk
Website: http://www.ilabuk.co.uk
Directors: N. Horn (Grp Chief Exec)
Managers: N. Horn
No.of Employees: 1 - 10 **Product Groups:** 37, 42, 89

Image Connect
9 Linacre Road, London, NW2 5BD
Tel: 07932-744204
E-mail: info@imageconnect.co.uk
Website: http://www.imageconnect.co.uk
Directors: V. Hodge (Prop)
Date established: 2009 **No.of Employees:** 1 - 10 **Product Groups:** 44, 81

Imagefarm Ltd
175 Brent Crescent, London, NW10 7XR
Tel: 020-8963 1277 **Fax:** 020-8961 2404
Website: http://www.imagefarm.co.uk
Bank(s): HSBC Bank plc
Directors: Y. Rassam (Dir)
Immediate Holding Company: IMAGEFARM LIMITED
Registration no: 02325450 **VAT No.:** GB 523 1151 96
Date established: 1988 **Turnover:** £2m - £5m **No.of Employees:** 21 - 50
Product Groups: 20, 62

Date of Accounts	Mar 11	Mar 10	Mar 09
Working Capital	245	508	683
Fixed Assets	2m	2m	2m
Current Assets	792	979	941

Imparta Ltd
14-16 Peterborough Road, London, SW6 3BN
Tel: 020-7610 8800 **Fax:** 020-7610 8801
E-mail: richard.barkey@imparta.com
Website: http://www.imparta.com
Directors: R. Barham (Dir), R. Barkey (Grp Chief Exec)
Managers: J. Heaford, R. Nixon (Fin Mgr), M. Abell
Immediate Holding Company: IMPARTA LIMITED
Registration no: 03370400 **Date established:** 1997 **Turnover:** £5m - £10m
No.of Employees: 21 - 50 **Product Groups:** 86

Date of Accounts	Dec 11	Dec 10	Dec 09
Sales Turnover	9m	7m	5m
Pre Tax Profit/Loss	1m	311	324
Working Capital	3m	2m	2m
Fixed Assets	623	535	615
Current Assets	4m	3m	3m
Current Liabilities	1m	1m	960

Imperial College Gym
7 Princes Gardens Imperial College, London, SW7 2AZ
Tel: 020-7594 6660 **Fax:** 020-7589 3553
E-mail: sales@imperial.ac.uk
Website: http://www.imperial.ac.uk/sports/ethos
Bank(s): National Westminster Bank Plc
Managers: J. Cottrill (Mgr), I. Reed (Mgr)
Ultimate Holding Company: IMPERIAL COLLEGE OF SCIENCE TECHNOLOGY AND MEDICINE
Immediate Holding Company: IMPERIAL COLLEGE LONDON LIMITED
Registration no: 04465125 **Date established:** 2002 **Turnover:** £5m - £10m
No.of Employees: 21 - 50 **Product Groups:** 86

Imperial Society Of Teachers Of Dancing
Imperial House 22-26 Paul Street, London, EC2A 4QE
Tel: 020-7377 1577 **Fax:** 020-7247 8979
E-mail: sales@istd.org
Website: http://www.istd.org
Directors: G. Owen James (Ch)
Managers: C. New (Sales Admin), P. Donnelly (Tech Serv Mgr), S. Clarke (Mktg Serv Mgr), J. French (Comptroller), D. James (Personnel)
Immediate Holding Company: IMPERIAL SOCIETY OF TEACHERS OF DANCING(THE)
Registration no: 00392978 **Date established:** 1945 **Turnover:** £5m - £10m
No.of Employees: 21 - 50 **Product Groups:** 86

see next page

Imperial Society Of Teachers Of Dancing - Cont'd

Date of Accounts	Dec 11	Dec 10	Dec 09
Sales Turnover	6m	6m	6m
Pre Tax Profit/Loss	-22	-229	156
Working Capital	410	240	713
Fixed Assets	5m	5m	5m
Current Assets	1m	1m	2m
Current Liabilities	756	705	762

Imprint Design Ltd

122 Elmhurst Mansions Edgeley Road, London, SW4 6EX
Tel: 020-7627 4838
E-mail: info@imprint-design.co.uk
Website: http://www.imprint-design.co.uk
Directors: S. Rawlins Kimloch (Dir), A. Dionysiou (MD)
Immediate Holding Company: IMPRINT DESIGN LIMITED
Registration no: 06342881 **Date established:** 2007
No.of Employees: 1 - 10 **Product Groups:** 81

Date of Accounts	Aug 11	Aug 10	Aug 09
Working Capital	6	2	6
Fixed Assets	2	2	1
Current Assets	28	23	11

Improvement Development Agency

76-86 Turnmill Street, London, EC1M 5LG
Tel: 020-7296 6600 **Fax:** 020-7296 6666
E-mail: rob.whiteman@local.gov.uk
Website: http://www.idea.gov.uk
Bank(s): HSBC
Directors: L. De Groot (MD), D. Groot (Grp Chief Exec), T. Farser (Fin), R. Whiteman (MD), P. Roberts (MD)
Managers: J. Rogerson (Personnel), J. Rogerson, P. Bailey (Sales & Mktg Mg), K. Trim (I.T. Exec), C. Trim (I.T. Exec)
Immediate Holding Company: LAND DATA COMMUNITY INTEREST COMPANY
Registration no: OC346845 **VAT No.:** GB 540 3855 54
Date established: 2005 **No.of Employees:** 51 - 100 **Product Groups:** 80

Date of Accounts	Mar 11	Mar 10	Mar 09
Sales Turnover	48m	51m	50m
Pre Tax Profit/Loss	10m	391	-1m
Working Capital	3m	5m	5m
Fixed Assets	5m	93	109
Current Assets	16m	17m	17m
Current Liabilities	11m	10m	9m

In Practice Systems Ltd

Bread Factory 1a Broughton Street, London, SW8 3QJ
Tel: 020-7501 7000 **Fax:** 020-7501 7100
E-mail: max.brighton@inps.co.uk
Website: http://www.inps.co.uk
Bank(s): Bank of Scotland
Directors: T. Mihayza (Fin), P. Hiscock (Chief Op Offcr), M. Brighton (Fin), M. Brighton (MD), D. Hinkson (Mkt Research)
Managers: D. Westbrook (Personnel)
Ultimate Holding Company: CEGEDIM SA (FRANCE)
Immediate Holding Company: IN PRACTICE SYSTEMS LIMITED
Registration no: 01788577 **VAT No.:** GB 735 8987 70
Date established: 1984 **Turnover:** £20m - £50m
No.of Employees: 101 - 250 **Product Groups:** 84

Date of Accounts	Dec 10	Dec 09	Dec 08
Sales Turnover	31m	33m	32m
Pre Tax Profit/Loss	-7m	6m	5m
Working Capital	22m	30m	26m
Fixed Assets	2m	1m	1m
Current Assets	38m	40m	36m
Current Liabilities	4m	4m	7m

In Tuition House

210 Borough High Street, London, SE1 1JX
Tel: 020-7403 7050 **Fax:** 020-7403 2861
E-mail: info@intuition.co.uk
Website: http://www.roomhire.biz
Directors: L. Hassan (MD), A. Hassan (MD)
Ultimate Holding Company: CHILDHOOD FIRST
Immediate Holding Company: CHILDHOOD FIRST (SOUTH) LIMITED
Registration no: 05758444 **Date established:** 1998 **Turnover:** £1m - £2m
No.of Employees: 1 - 10 **Product Groups:** 44

Date of Accounts	Mar 12	Mar 11	Mar 10
Sales Turnover	2m	1m	2m
Pre Tax Profit/Loss	197	18	183
Working Capital	554	373	355
Fixed Assets	17	N/A	N/A
Current Assets	961	652	620
Current Liabilities	408	279	265

Incair Ltd

62 Garman Road Tottenham, London, N17 0UT
Tel: 020-8801 9400 **Fax:** 020-8801 9405
E-mail: info@incair.co.uk
Website: http://www.incair.co.uk
Directors: I. Yavuz (Fin), G. Kucuk (MD)
Immediate Holding Company: INCAIR (UK) LIMITED
Registration no: 04514726 **Date established:** 2002
Turnover: £250,000 - £500,000 **No.of Employees:** 1 - 10
Product Groups: 77

Date of Accounts	Dec 09	Dec 08	Dec 07
Sales Turnover	379	334	494
Pre Tax Profit/Loss	73	33	100
Working Capital	104	39	-1
Fixed Assets	88	97	112
Current Assets	127	61	60
Current Liabilities	21	10	28

Ince & Co

International House 1 St Katharines Way, London, E1W 1AY
Tel: 020-7481 0018 **Fax:** 020-7623 3225
E-mail: david.steward@ince.co.uk
Website: http://www.incelaw.com
Directors: A. Chan (Ptnr), C. Kidd (Ptnr), P. Rogan (Snr Part), T. Suchy (Ptnr), L. Krenca (Dir), A. George (Ptnr)
Managers: F. White (I.T. Exec)
Immediate Holding Company: INCE (HERITAGE PARTNERS) LIMITED
Registration no: 02429258 **VAT No.:** GB 243 8873 33
Date established: 1989 **No.of Employees:** 251 - 500 **Product Groups:** 80

Date of Accounts	Apr 05	Apr 04	Apr 03
Working Capital	24	24	24
Current Assets	24	24	26
Current Liabilities	N/A	N/A	2

Indepen Consulting Ltd

Diespeker Wharf 38 Graham Street, London, N1 8JX
Tel: 020-7226 6336 **Fax:** 020-7704 0872
E-mail: johnhargreaves@indepen.co.uk
Website: http://www.indepen.co.uk
Bank(s): Barclays
Directors: J. Hargreaves (Dir), N. Chesson (Co Sec), A. Bishop (MD)
Managers: L. Groundsell (Sales Admin)
Immediate Holding Company: P.T.E. PROPERTY LIMITED
Registration no: 02474302 **VAT No.:** GB 577 4112 32
Date established: 2000 **Turnover:** £1m - £2m **No.of Employees:** 11 - 20
Product Groups: 80

Date of Accounts	May 11	May 10	May 09
Sales Turnover	235	100	160
Pre Tax Profit/Loss	386	1m	154
Working Capital	1	473	395
Fixed Assets	1	1	1
Current Assets	362	496	510
Current Liabilities	358	21	113

The Independent

2 Derry Street, London, W8 5HF
Tel: 020-7005 2000 **Fax:** 020-7005 2999
E-mail: krolfe@img-uk.demon.co.uk
Website: http://www.independant.co.uk
Directors: M. Danks (Adv), P. Goodwin (Fin), D. Bracken (Co Sec), B. McCann (Pers), A. Brown (Chief Op Offcr), B. Hopkins (MD)
Managers: P. Little
Ultimate Holding Company: INDEPENDENT NEWS & MEDIA PUBLIC LIMITED COMPANY
Immediate Holding Company: INDEPENDENT NEWS AND MEDIA LTD
Registration no: 01908967 **Date established:** 1985
Turnover: £20m - £50m **No.of Employees:** 1001 - 1500
Product Groups: 28

Date of Accounts	Dec 11	Dec 10	Dec 08
Sales Turnover	46m	71m	143m
Pre Tax Profit/Loss	-52m	-46m	-108m
Working Capital	25m	-141m	-104m
Fixed Assets	137m	197m	278m
Current Assets	35m	28m	46m
Current Liabilities	6m	10m	11m

Independent Radio News Ltd

Mappin House 4 Winsley Street, London, W1W 8HF
Tel: 020-7182 8591 **Fax:** 020-7182 8594
E-mail: news@irn.co.uk
Website: http://www.irnco.uk
Directors: T. Molloy (MD)
Immediate Holding Company: INDEPENDENT RADIO NEWS LIMITED
Registration no: 01112963 **Date established:** 1973
Turnover: £10m - £20m **No.of Employees:** 1 - 10 **Product Groups:** 89

Date of Accounts	Mar 12	Mar 11	Sep 09
Sales Turnover	15m	20m	13m
Pre Tax Profit/Loss	3m	5m	3m
Working Capital	2m	3m	3m
Fixed Assets	40	73	159
Current Assets	5m	8m	7m
Current Liabilities	3m	5m	4m

Indian Ocean Trading Co.

155-163 Balham Hill, London, SW12 9DJ
Tel: 020-8675 4808 **Fax:** 020-8675 4652
E-mail: j.hobbs@indian-ocean.co.uk
Website: http://www.indian-ocean.co.uk
Bank(s): HSBC Bank plc
Directors: D. Gondalia (Fin), J. Hobbs (MD)
Managers: H. Hobbs (Public Relation)
Ultimate Holding Company: INDIAN OCEAN TRADING COMPANY (UK) LIMITED
Immediate Holding Company: INDIAN OCEAN TRADING COMPANY LIMITED
Registration no: 03290687 **VAT No.:** GB 562 0268 58
Date established: 1996 **Turnover:** £2m - £5m **No.of Employees:** 11 - 20
Product Groups: 24, 26

Date of Accounts	Dec 11	Dec 10	Dec 09
Working Capital	634	733	248
Fixed Assets	98	49	68
Current Assets	995	1m	867

Indusmond Diamond Tools Ltd

9 Dawson Place, London, W2 4TD
Tel: 020-7706 7640 **Fax:** 020-7727 5268
Website: http://www.indusmond.com
Directors: A. Greengross (MD)
Immediate Holding Company: INDUSMOND (DIAMOND TOOLS) LIMITED
Registration no: 00355927 **VAT No.:** GB 233 3317 35
Date established: 1939 **Turnover:** £500,000 - £1m
No.of Employees: 1 - 10 **Product Groups:** 33, 36, 46

Date of Accounts	Jun 11	Jun 10	Jun 09
Working Capital	811	782	699
Fixed Assets	4	5	6
Current Assets	880	889	791

Industrial Blowers Services Ltd

Unit 6 River Brent Business Park Trumpers Way, London, W7 2QA
Tel: 020-8571 3988 **Fax:** 020-8571 3955
E-mail: sales@ibsblowers.com
Website: http://www.ibsblowers.com
Bank(s): Lloyds TSB Bank plc
Directors: A. Matthews (Fin), G. Matthews (MD)
Managers: T. Reed (Tech Serv Mgr)
Immediate Holding Company: INDUSTRIAL BLOWER SERVICES LIMITED
Registration no: 03830545 **Date established:** 1999
Turnover: £500,000 - £1m **No.of Employees:** 11 - 20
Product Groups: 30, 40, 41, 43, 45, 48

Date of Accounts	Mar 11	Mar 10	Mar 09
Working Capital	241	194	84
Fixed Assets	300	224	242
Current Assets	865	910	928

Industrial Exports Ltd

Suite 2 Ambika House 9a Portland Place, London, W1B 1PR
Tel: 020-7637 0283 **Fax:** 020-7580 6105
Website: http://www.nscindex.com
Directors: A. Mcghee (Fin), A. Mcghee (Co Sec)
Managers: J. Osman (Sales Admin)
Immediate Holding Company: INDUSTRIAL EXPORTS LIMITED
Registration no: 00381921 **Date established:** 1943
Turnover: Up to £250,000 **No.of Employees:** 1 - 10 **Product Groups:** 80

Date of Accounts	Mar 11	Mar 10	Mar 08
Working Capital	-2m	-1m	-1m
Fixed Assets	1	1	1
Current Assets	181	150	94

Industrial Pipe Freezing Services Ltd (incorporating Bishop Pipe Freezing Services)

8 The Coles Shop, London, SW19 2RD
Tel: 020-8543 9390 **Fax:** 020-8543 8748
E-mail: steve@ipsgroup.net
Website: http://www.ipsgroup.net
Directors: S. Turner (MD)
Ultimate Holding Company: SST HOLDINGS LIMITED
Immediate Holding Company: INDUSTRIAL PIPEFREEZING SERVICES LIMITED
Registration no: 01741938 **Date established:** 1983
Turnover: £250,000 - £500,000 **No.of Employees:** 1 - 10
Product Groups: 84

Date of Accounts	Dec 11	Dec 10	Dec 09
Working Capital	744	885	777
Fixed Assets	58	37	25
Current Assets	1m	1m	1m

Infiniti Research Ltd

33 Cavendish Square, London, W1G 0PW
Tel: 020-7031 0968 **Fax:** 0845-280 2825
E-mail: mahesh@infiniti-research.com
Website: http://www.infiniti-research.com
Directors: M. Santanan (Pres)
Immediate Holding Company: INFINITI RESEARCH LTD
Registration no: 04922062 **Date established:** 2003
No.of Employees: 1 - 10 **Product Groups:** 80

Date of Accounts	Oct 11	Oct 10	Oct 09
Working Capital	365	301	172
Fixed Assets	3	3	3
Current Assets	418	334	188

Infocat Ltd

Riverside House 27-29 Vauxhall Grove, London, SW8 1SY
Tel: 020-7735 7711 **Fax:** 020-7735 8811
E-mail: info@infocat.co.uk
Website: http://www.infocat.co.uk
Directors: S. Waters (Co Sec)
Immediate Holding Company: INFOCAT LIMITED
Registration no: 02843261 **Date established:** 1993 **Turnover:** £1m - £2m
No.of Employees: 1 - 10 **Product Groups:** 80

Date of Accounts	Dec 10	Dec 09	Dec 08
Sales Turnover	N/A	1m	793
Pre Tax Profit/Loss	N/A	10	-91
Working Capital	99	168	157
Fixed Assets	16	6	7
Current Assets	665	760	660
Current Liabilities	N/A	504	404

Inform Plastics Ltd

Unit 6 Block 2 Woolwich Dockyard Industrial Estate Woolwich Church Street, London, SE18 5PQ
Tel: 020-8317 7095 **Fax:** 020-8316 6720
E-mail: info@informplastics.com
Website: http://www.informplastics.com
Directors: L. Daniel (Fin), R. Daniel (MD)
Immediate Holding Company: INFORM PLASTICS LIMITED
Registration no: 01638100 **Date established:** 1982
Turnover: £250,000 - £500,000 **No.of Employees:** 1 - 10
Product Groups: 28, 30

Date of Accounts	May 11	May 10	May 09
Working Capital	-22	20	8
Fixed Assets	29	47	64
Current Assets	93	142	156

Ingleby Trice

11 Old Jewry, London, EC2R 8DU
Tel: 020-7606 7461 **Fax:** 020-7726 2578
E-mail: enquiries@inglebytrice.co.uk
Website: http://www.inglebytrice.co.uk
Directors: C. Ingleby (Ptnr)
Immediate Holding Company: INGLEBY TRICE LLP
Registration no: OC362585 **Date established:** 2011
No.of Employees: 1 - 10 **Product Groups:** 80

Initial Cleaning Services

13-27 Brunswick Place, London, N1 6DX
Tel: 020-7466 7777 **Fax:** 020-7466 7778
E-mail: contactus@initialcleaning.co.uk
Website: http://www.initialcleaning.co.uk
Bank(s): HSBC Bank plc
Managers: M. Wells (Mgr)
Ultimate Holding Company: RENTOKIL INITIAL PLC
Immediate Holding Company: RENTOKIL INITIAL FACILITIES SERVICES (UK) LIMITED
Registration no: 02329448 **VAT No.:** GB 625 9496 02
Date established: 1988 **Turnover:** £75m - £125m
No.of Employees: 51 - 100 **Product Groups:** 52

Date of Accounts	Dec 11	Dec 10	Dec 09
Sales Turnover	206m	199m	191m
Pre Tax Profit/Loss	5m	2m	648
Working Capital	-23m	-22m	-14m
Fixed Assets	63m	54m	37m
Current Assets	122m	47m	59m
Current Liabilities	33m	28m	20m

Inmarsat Global Ltd

99 City Road, London, EC1Y 1AX
Tel: 020-7728 1000 **Fax:** 020-7728 1044
E-mail: customer_care@inmarsat.com
Website: http://www.inmarsat.com
Directors: C. Medlock (Grp Chief Exec), R. Medlock (Fin)
Ultimate Holding Company: INMARSAT PLC
Immediate Holding Company: INMARSAT GLOBAL LIMITED
Registration no: 03675885 **Date established:** 1998
Turnover: £500m - £1,000m **No.of Employees:** 251 - 500
Product Groups: 37

Date of Accounts	Dec 08	Dec 07	Dec 06
Sales Turnover	625m	555m	499m
Pre Tax Profit/Loss	251m	208m	149m

Working Capital	322m	846m	99m
Fixed Assets	1224m	545m	1343m
Current Assets	589m	1020m	288m
Current Liabilities	267m	174m	189m
Total Share Capital	162m	162m	162m

Inner City Lifts

42 Rutherglen Road, London, SE2 0XU
Tel: 020-8310 6071 **Fax:** 020-8310 6071
Directors: G. Clark (Ptnr)
Immediate Holding Company: RETAIL LIFT SPECIALISTS LIMITED
Registration no: 06517318 **Date established:** 2011
No.of Employees: 1 - 10 **Product Groups:** 35, 39, 45

Innovative Marketing International Ltd

21 Dorset Square, London, NW1 6QG
Tel: 020-7723 7228 **Fax:** 020-7723 1192
E-mail: jalyons@innovativemarketing.co.uk
Website: http://www.innovativemarketing.co.uk
Directors: J. Lyons (MD)
Immediate Holding Company: INNOVATIVE MARKETING INTERNATIONAL LIMITED
Registration no: 01082967 **Date established:** 1972 **Turnover:** £5m - £10m
No.of Employees: 1 - 10 **Product Groups:** 49, 80

Date of Accounts	Dec 11	Dec 10	Dec 09
Working Capital	536	561	875
Fixed Assets	157	144	158
Current Assets	959	1m	1m

Inprojex International UK Ltd

58 Uxbridge Road, London, W5 2ST
Tel: 020-8567 9680 **Fax:** 020-8579 5241
E-mail: inprojex@inprojex.co.uk
Website: http://www.inprojex.co.uk
Directors: B. Abbou (Mkt Research), G. Rime (Dir)
Ultimate Holding Company: INPROJEX ESTABLISHMENT IND PROJECTS & EXPORT PROMOTION
Immediate Holding Company: INPROJEX INTERNATIONAL (U.K.) LIMITED
Registration no: 01200465 **VAT No.:** GB 340 0452 10
Date established: 1975 **Turnover:** £2m - £5m **No.of Employees:** 1 - 10
Product Groups: 61

Date of Accounts	Mar 12	Mar 11	Mar 10
Sales Turnover	2m	2m	4m
Pre Tax Profit/Loss	88	125	174
Working Capital	762	670	557
Fixed Assets	9	12	N/A
Current Assets	948	1m	1m
Current Liabilities	115	419	505

Insitive Media

32-34 Broadwick Street, London, W1F 8JB
Tel: 020-7316 9000 **Fax:** 020-7316 9003
Website: http://www.vnunet.com
Directors: J. Campbell Harris (Fin)
Managers: L. Fraser (Personnel), M. Bush, M. Kennedy (Tech Serv Mgr), T. Weller, A. Ryan (Sales Admin), A. Knight (Sales Prom Mgr)
Ultimate Holding Company: VNU PRESS GROUP
Immediate Holding Company: VNU BUSINESS PUBLICATIONS B.V. (HOLLAND)
Registration no: 01513633 **No.of Employees:** 251 - 500
Product Groups: 28

Institute of Directors (IoD)

123 Pall Mall, London, SW1Y 5EA
Tel: 020-7839 1233 **Fax:** 020-7930 1949
Website: http://www.iod.com
Directors: A. Main-Wilson (Chief Op Offcr)
Immediate Holding Company: DIRECTOR PUBLICATIONS LIMITED(THE)
Registration no: RC000252 **Date established:** 1906 **Product Groups:** 69, 80, 86, 87

Institute Of Marine Engineering Science & Technology

Aldgate House 33 Aldgate High Street, London, EC3N 1EN
Tel: 020-7382 2600 **Fax:** 020-7382 2670
E-mail: reception@imarest.org.uk
Website: http://www.imarest.org.uk
Bank(s): Barclays
Managers: F. Morris
Immediate Holding Company: MARINE INFORMATION ALLIANCE LIMITED
Registration no: FP007155 **Date established:** 2002
Turnover: Up to £250,000 **No.of Employees:** 21 - 50 **Product Groups:** 87

Institute Of Physics

76 Portland Place, London, W1B 1NT
Tel: 020-7470 4800 **Fax:** 020-7470 4848
E-mail: kate.meehan@iop.org
Website: http://www.iop.org
Bank(s): Lloyds, 79-81 Brompton Rd, London SW3 1DD
Directors: S. Fox (Fin), P. Main (Dir)
Managers: L. Ward (Sales Admin), C. Irvine (Personnel), L. Ward (Sales Admin), D. Halton (Personnel), J. Bergman, J. Bergman, K. Meehan, P. Hardaker, M. Bray
Immediate Holding Company: THE INSTITUTE OF KNOWLEDGE TRANSFER
Registration no: 05312703 **Date established:** 2004
Turnover: Up to £250,000 **No.of Employees:** 51 - 100
Product Groups: 80, 87

Date of Accounts	Dec 11	Dec 10	Dec 09
Sales Turnover	51	49	141
Working Capital	-0	-0	-0
Current Assets	73	94	44
Current Liabilities	30	53	11

Institute Of Practitioners In Advertising Ltd

44 Belgrave Square, London, SW1X 8QS
Tel: 020-7235 7020 **Fax:** 020-7245 9904
E-mail: info@ipa.co.uk
Website: http://www.ipa.co.uk
Managers: P. Bainsfair
Immediate Holding Company: INSTITUTE OF PRACTITIONERS IN ADVERTISING(THE)
Registration no: 00221167 **VAT No.:** GB 239 2269 49
Date established: 2027 **Turnover:** £10m - £20m
No.of Employees: 51 - 100 **Product Groups:** 81

Date of Accounts	Dec 11	Dec 10	Dec 09
Sales Turnover	11m	11m	10m
Pre Tax Profit/Loss	91	96	54

Working Capital	681	563	286
Fixed Assets	2m	2m	2m
Current Assets	4m	4m	3m
Current Liabilities	2m	2m	2m

Institution Of Engineering & Technology

2 Savoy Place, London, WC2R 0BL
Tel: 020-7240 1871 **Fax:** 020-7240 7735
E-mail: postmaster@theiet.org
Website: http://www.theiet.org
Bank(s): Barclays
Managers: S. Spencer (Sales Admin)
Ultimate Holding Company: THE INSTITUTION OF ELECTRICAL ENGINEERS
Immediate Holding Company: THE INSTITUTION OF ENGINEERING AND TECHNOLOGY BENEVOLENT FUND
Registration no: 00441284 **Date established:** 1947 **Turnover:** £1m - £2m
No.of Employees: 101 - 250 **Product Groups:** 84, 87

Date of Accounts	Dec 11	Dec 10	Dec 09
Sales Turnover	9m	9m	11m
Pre Tax Profit/Loss	5	21	23
Working Capital	334	274	214
Fixed Assets	360	420	480
Current Assets	2m	2m	2m
Current Liabilities	59	31	54

Instyle Direct Ltd

28 Salter Street, London, NW10 6UN
Tel: 020-8964 1966 **Fax:** 020-8960 7479
E-mail: info@instyledirect.co.uk
Website: http://www.instyledirect.co.uk
Directors: V. Mehmra (Fin), M. Mehra (Dir)
Immediate Holding Company: IN-STYLE DIRECT LIMITED
Registration no: 05147362 **Date established:** 2004
No.of Employees: 21 - 50 **Product Groups:** 52

Date of Accounts	Mar 11	Mar 10	Mar 09
Working Capital	-102	18	7
Fixed Assets	17	23	15
Current Assets	774	703	640
Current Liabilities	N/A	127	123

Integral Memory plc

Unit 6-8 Iron Bridge Close Great Central Way, London, NW10 0UF
Tel: 020-8451 8700 **Fax:** 020-8459 6301
E-mail: admin@integralmemory.com
Website: http://www.integralmemoryplc.com
Directors: S. Kotecha (MD), S. Katecha (Dir), G. Yates (Fin)
Managers: S. Kotecha
Ultimate Holding Company: LINDEN INVESTMENTS LTD (GUERNSEY)
Immediate Holding Company: INTEGRAL MEMORY PLC
Registration no: 02480354 **VAT No.:** GB 427 7709 76
Date established: 1990 **Turnover:** £50m - £75m
No.of Employees: 101 - 250 **Product Groups:** 37, 67

Date of Accounts	Sep 11	Sep 10	Sep 09
Sales Turnover	60m	93m	73m
Pre Tax Profit/Loss	84	2m	4m
Working Capital	15m	14m	14m
Fixed Assets	3m	3m	4m
Current Assets	26m	29m	39m
Current Liabilities	7m	1m	9m

Intellect

Russell Square House 10-12 Russell Square, London, WC1B 5EE
Tel: 020-7331 2000 **Fax:** 020-7331 2040
E-mail: info@intellectuk.org
Website: http://www.intellectuk.org
Directors: J. Higgins (Grp Chief Exec)
Managers: A. Langford, R. Millard, M. Cutt (Personnel), A. Farrell
Ultimate Holding Company: INFORMATION TECHNOLOGY TELECOMMUNICATIONS AND ELECTRONICS ASSOCIATION
Immediate Holding Company: INTELLECT ENTERPRISES LIMITED
Registration no: 04396105 **Date established:** 2002 **Turnover:** £5m - £10m
No.of Employees: 51 - 100 **Product Groups:** 37, 87

Date of Accounts	Dec 11	Dec 10	Dec 09
Sales Turnover	N/A	N/A	7m
Pre Tax Profit/Loss	N/A	N/A	273
Working Capital	57	15	1m
Fixed Assets	N/A	N/A	500
Current Assets	97	46	4m
Current Liabilities	N/A	31	2m

Inter Ina Ltd

112 Jermyn Street, London, SW1Y 6LS
Tel: 020-7925 0125 **Fax:** 020-7925 0418
Website: http://www.inter-ina.co.uk
Directors: D. Blagovic (MD), D. Blogovic (MD), D. Popovic (Fin)
Managers: S. Green (Comptroller), T. Ansell (Sales Admin)
Ultimate Holding Company: INA INDUSTRIJA NAFTE DD (CROATIA)
Immediate Holding Company: INTER INA LIMITED
Registration no: 01466591 **Date established:** 1979
Turnover: Over £1,000m **No.of Employees:** 1 - 10 **Product Groups:** 31, 61

Date of Accounts	Dec 08	Dec 07	Dec 06
Sales Turnover	2359m	2244m	1226m
Pre Tax Profit/Loss	1m	2m	2m
Working Capital	20m	19m	18m
Fixed Assets	60	50	60
Current Assets	367m	543m	365m
Current Liabilities	347m	524m	347m
Total Share Capital	4m	4m	4m

Interactive Data

Fitzroy House, London, EC2A 4DL
Tel: 020-7825 8000 **Fax:** 020-7251 2725
E-mail: investorrelations@interactivedata.com
Website: http://www.interactivedata.com
Bank(s): Royal Bank of Scotland, 67 Lombard St, EC3
Directors: K. Bossey (Fin)
Managers: L. Butler (Mktg Serv Mgr)
Ultimate Holding Company: IGLOO HOLDINGS CORPORATION (USA)
Immediate Holding Company: INTERACTIVE DATA (EUROPE) LIMITED
Registration no: 00949387 **Date established:** 1969
Turnover: £75m - £125m **No.of Employees:** 251 - 500
Product Groups: 81

Date of Accounts	Dec 11	Dec 10	Dec 09
Sales Turnover	90m	85m	87m
Pre Tax Profit/Loss	15m	-57m	19m
Working Capital	48m	33m	17m
Fixed Assets	47m	47m	47m
Current Assets	63m	52m	43m
Current Liabilities	8m	11m	16m

Interbrand

85 Strand, London, WC2R 0DW
Tel: 020-7554 1000 **Fax:** 020-7554 1001
E-mail: reception@interbrand.com
Website: http://www.interbrand.com
Bank(s): Barclays
Directors: G. Cox (Develop), G. Hales (Grp Chief Exec)
Managers: M. Dent (Tech Serv Mgr), M. Love (Personnel)
Immediate Holding Company: IQ PARTNERS LIMITED
Registration no: 05959220 **VAT No.:** GB 380 6120 74
Date established: 2006 **Turnover:** Up to £250,000
No.of Employees: 101 - 250 **Product Groups:** 80, 81

Date of Accounts	Dec 11	Dec 10	Dec 09
Sales Turnover	N/A	N/A	84
Pre Tax Profit/Loss	N/A	N/A	25
Working Capital	36	-10	1
Fixed Assets	3	3	N/A
Current Assets	136	43	20
Current Liabilities	N/A	N/A	18

Interlingua Services Hungarian

PO Box 48595, London, NW4 9DR
Tel: 020-8202 8688
E-mail: info@interlinguaservices.com
Website: http://www.interlinguaservices.com
Directors: T. Domotor (Prop)
Date established: 2007 **No.of Employees:** 1 - 10 **Product Groups:** 80

International Lift Equipment Ltd

17 Hickman Avenue, London, E4 9JG
Tel: 020-8527 9669 **Fax:** 020-8531 0936
E-mail: nancy.lycett@interlift.co.uk
Website: http://www.interlift.co.uk
Bank(s): Lloyds
Directors: N. Lycett (MD)
Ultimate Holding Company: ILE HOLDINGS LIMITED
Immediate Holding Company: INTERNATIONAL LIFT EQUIPMENT LTD
Registration no: 01236448 **Date established:** 1975
Turnover: £10m - £20m **No.of Employees:** 21 - 50 **Product Groups:** 37, 45

Date of Accounts	Sep 11	Sep 10	Sep 09
Sales Turnover	13m	14m	15m
Pre Tax Profit/Loss	70	106	10
Working Capital	2m	2m	2m
Fixed Assets	1m	1m	1m
Current Assets	6m	5m	6m
Current Liabilities	528	538	435

International Precision Casting Supplies Ltd

14 Hatton Wall, London, EC1N 8JH
Tel: 020-7831 3111
E-mail: mhattersley@ipcs-uk.com
Website: http://www.ipcs-uk.com
Directors: M. Hattersley (Dir)
Ultimate Holding Company: HATTON DESIGNS OF LONDON LIMITED
Immediate Holding Company: INTERNATIONAL PRECISION CASTING SUPPLIES LIMITED
Registration no: 03576088 **Date established:** 1998
No.of Employees: 1 - 10 **Product Groups:** 31, 32, 33

Date of Accounts	Jul 11	Jul 10	Jul 09
Working Capital	503	408	327
Fixed Assets	62	87	112
Current Assets	2m	1m	1m

International Press Cutting Bureau

224-236 Walworth Road, London, SE17 1JE
Tel: 020-7708 2113 **Fax:** 020-7701 4489
E-mail: info@ipcb.co.uk
Website: http://www.ipcb.co.uk
Bank(s): HSBC Bank plc
Directors: R. Podro (Grp Chief Exec)
Immediate Holding Company: LIFETIME TRUST LTD
Registration no: 02118525 **VAT No.:** GB 239 0197 58
Date established: 2004 **Turnover:** £2m - £5m
No.of Employees: 101 - 250 **Product Groups:** 81

International Graphic Press Ltd

52a Borough High Street, London, SE1 1XN
Tel: 020-7403 4589 **Fax:** 020-7403 4590
E-mail: info@igpmedia.com
Website: http://www.igpmedia.com
Directors: C. Cullingford (MD)
Immediate Holding Company: INTERNATIONAL GRAPHIC PRESS LIMITED
Registration no: 00237259 **Date established:** 2029 **Turnover:** £2m - £5m
No.of Employees: 1 - 10 **Product Groups:** 81

Date of Accounts	Mar 11	Mar 10	Mar 09
Working Capital	-15	-10	1
Fixed Assets	1	1	N/A
Current Assets	153	69	103

International Lead Association

17a Welbeck Way, London, W1G 9YJ
Tel: 020-7935 6146 **Fax:** 020-7493 1555
E-mail: enq@ila-lead.org
Website: http://www.ila-lead.org
Directors: A. Bush (MD), D. Wilson (Dir)
Managers: M. McDermott
Immediate Holding Company: INTERNATIONAL LEAD ASSOCIATION
Registration no: 06391803 **Date established:** 2007 **Turnover:** £1m - £2m
No.of Employees: 1 - 10 **Product Groups:** 87

Date of Accounts	Dec 10	Dec 09	Dec 08
Sales Turnover	2m	2m	2m
Pre Tax Profit/Loss	55	70	114
Working Capital	231	179	112
Current Assets	534	375	408
Current Liabilities	284	196	292

International Power plc

Senator House 85 Queen Victoria Street, London, EC4V 4DP
Tel: 020-7320 8600 **Fax:** 020-7320 8700
E-mail: philip.cox@ipplc.com
Website: http://www.ipplc.com
Directors: P. Cox (Grp Chief Exec)
Managers: M. Williamson (Comptroller)
Immediate Holding Company: INTERNATIONAL POWER AUSTRALIA HOLDINGS (1) LIMITED

see next page

International Power plc - Cont'd

Registration no: 04790836 **Date established:** 2003
No.of Employees: 251 - 500 **Product Groups:** 18

International Company Profile

6-14 Underwood Street, London, N1 7JQ
Tel: 020-7490 0049 **Fax:** 020-7566 8319
E-mail: transactions@wlrstore.com
Website: http://www.icpcredit.com
Bank(s): The Royal Bank of Scotland
Directors: B. Gilbert (Grp Chief Exec), P. Lunn (MD)
Managers: T. Underwood (Admin Off)
Ultimate Holding Company: WILMINGTON GROUP PLC
Immediate Holding Company: CENTRAL LAW TRAINING LIMITED
Registration no: 03368442 **Date established:** 1998
Turnover: £50m - £75m **No.of Employees:** 51 - 100 **Product Groups:** 81, 82

International Underwriting Association

3 Minster Court, London, EC3R 7DD
Tel: 020-7617 4444 **Fax:** 020-7617 4440
E-mail: info@rua.co.uk
Website: http://www.rua.co.uk
Managers: D. Matcham, J. Lane (Fin Mgr)
Immediate Holding Company: INTERNATIONAL UNDERWRITING ASSOCIATION OF LONDON LIMITED
Registration no: 01244052 **Date established:** 1976 **Turnover:** £2m - £5m
No.of Employees: 21 - 50 **Product Groups:** 87

Date of Accounts	Dec 11	Dec 10	Dec 09
Sales Turnover	3m	3m	3m
Pre Tax Profit/Loss	1m	961	448
Working Capital	8m	7m	6m
Fixed Assets	2m	2m	2m
Current Assets	9m	8m	8m
Current Liabilities	421	890	2m

Intersect Recruitment Ltd

175-185 Gray's Inn Road, London, WC1X 8UE
Tel: 020-7812 0632 **Fax:** 020-7812 0650
E-mail: info@intersectuk.com
Website: http://www.intersectuk.com
Directors: J. Dunkley (Dir)
Managers: C. Evans (Mktg Serv Mgr)
Immediate Holding Company: INTERSECT RECRUITMENT LTD
Registration no: 05288909 **Date established:** 2004
No.of Employees: 11 - 20 **Product Groups:** 80

Date of Accounts	Mar 12	Mar 11	Mar 10
Working Capital	67	135	158
Fixed Assets	N/A	N/A	3
Current Assets	68	144	208
Current Liabilities	N/A	9	N/A

Intertech Plastics Ltd

17 Raven Road, London, E18 1HB
Tel: 020-8504 2334 **Fax:** 020-8504 2335
E-mail: gordon@intertechplastic.demon.co.uk
Directors: G. Brown (MD), G. Brown (Dir), L. Brown (Fin)
Immediate Holding Company: INTERTECH PLASTICS LIMITED
Registration no: 02810074 **VAT No.:** GB 626 0282 60
Date established: 1993 **Turnover:** £500,000 - £1m
No.of Employees: 1 - 10 **Product Groups:** 26, 30, 33

Date of Accounts	Apr 11	Feb 10	Feb 09
Working Capital	92	92	95
Fixed Assets	9	12	15
Current Assets	186	162	156

Intourist Ltd

7 Wellington Terrace, London, W2 4LW
Tel: 020-7727 4100 **Fax:** 020-7727 8090
E-mail: info@intourist.co.uk
Website: http://www.intouristuk.com
Managers: F. Moumei (District Mgr)
Ultimate Holding Company: JOINT STOCK FINANCIAL CORP SISTEMA (RUSSIA)
Immediate Holding Company: INTOURIST LIMITED
Registration no: 03986319 **Date established:** 2000 **Turnover:** £1m - £2m
No.of Employees: 1 - 10 **Product Groups:** 69

Date of Accounts	Dec 11	Dec 10	Dec 09
Sales Turnover	N/A	N/A	2m
Pre Tax Profit/Loss	N/A	N/A	-20
Working Capital	182	273	320
Fixed Assets	31	20	8
Current Assets	950	1m	867
Current Liabilities	N/A	N/A	246

Invensys PLC

3rd Floor 40 Grosvenor Place, London, SW1X 7AW
Tel: 020-3155 1200 **Fax:** 020-7834 3879
E-mail: reception@invensys.com
Website: http://www.invensys.com
Bank(s): The Royal Bank of Scotland
Directors: U. Henriksson (Dir), R. Spencer (Dir)
Ultimate Holding Company: INVENSYS PLC
Immediate Holding Company: INVENSYS PLC
Registration no: 00166023 **Date established:** 1982
Turnover: Over £1,000m **No.of Employees:** 1501 & over
Product Groups: 44, 84

Date of Accounts	Mar 12	Mar 11	Mar 10
Sales Turnover	2539m	2486m	2243m
Pre Tax Profit/Loss	140m	222m	179m
Working Capital	348m	418m	435m
Fixed Assets	791m	756m	762m
Current Assets	1204m	1284m	1228m
Current Liabilities	582m	585m	522m

Invest In France Agency

Sixth Floor Haymarket House, 28/29 Haymarket, London, SW1Y 4SP
Tel: 020-7024 3672 **Fax:** 020-7024 3635
E-mail: info@investinfrance.org
Website: http://www.invest-in-france.org
Directors: P. Ydergniaux (Dir)
Registration no: 04383394 **Date established:** 2002
Turnover: £10m - £20m **No.of Employees:** 1 - 10 **Product Groups:** 82

Investec Bank

2 Gresham Street, London, EC2V 7QP
Tel: 020-7597 4000 **Fax:** 020-7597 4070
E-mail: info@investec.com
Website: http://www.investec.co.uk
Directors: B. Kantor (Grp MD), D. Miller (Co Sec)
Ultimate Holding Company: INVESTEC PLC
Immediate Holding Company: INVESTEC 1 LIMITED
Registration no: 00119609 **VAT No.:** GB 564 6389 04
Date established: 2012 **Turnover:** £20m - £50m
No.of Employees: 251 - 500 **Product Groups:** 82

Date of Accounts	Mar 12	Mar 11	Mar 10
Pre Tax Profit/Loss	53m	82m	19m
Working Capital	-1064m	-1043m	-446m
Fixed Assets	2307m	2082m	1796m
Current Assets	87m	107m	800m
Current Liabilities	26m	46m	81m

Ipsos Mori

Market & Opinion Research International, London, SE1 1FY
Tel: 020-7347 3000 **Fax:** 020-7347 3800
E-mail: info@ipsos.com
Website: http://www.ipsos.com
Directors: C. Wingfield (Pers)
Managers: D. Koveof (Tech Serv Mgr), D. Holliss (Comptroller), B. Page
Ultimate Holding Company: IPSOS SA (FRANCE)
Immediate Holding Company: MORI LIMITED
Registration no: 03904207 **VAT No.:** GB 584 2089 22
Date established: 2000 **Turnover:** £75m - £125m
No.of Employees: 251 - 500 **Product Groups:** 81, 82

Date of Accounts	Dec 11	Dec 10	Dec 09
Pre Tax Profit/Loss	-0	-0	1m
Working Capital	-24m	-24m	-24m
Fixed Assets	29m	29m	29m
Current Assets	6m	6m	6m

Iron Mountain Ltd

Cottons Centre Hays Lane, London, SE1 2TT
Tel: 020-7939 1500 **Fax:** 020-7939 1501
Website: http://www.ironmountain.co.uk
Bank(s): National Westminster
Directors: A. Pevy (Jt MD), R. Hamlin (MD)
Ultimate Holding Company: IRON MOUNTAIN INC (USA)
Immediate Holding Company: IRON MOUNTAIN LIMITED
Registration no: 02236749 **Date established:** 1988
Turnover: £125m - £250m **No.of Employees:** 11 - 20 **Product Groups:** 77

Date of Accounts	Apr 11	Apr 10	Apr 09
Working Capital	-274	-245	-239
Fixed Assets	128	109	113
Current Assets	14	48	133

Irwin Mitchell Solicitors (The Debt Recovery Division of Irwin Mitchell Solicitors)

150 Holborn, London, EC1N 2NS
Tel: 020-7404 3600 **Fax:** 020-7404 0208
E-mail: sales@imonline.co.uk
Website: http://www.imonline.co.uk
Directors: H. Robertson (Ptnr), P. Devine (Ptnr)
Managers: A. Lunn (Sales Admin)
No.of Employees: 1 - 10 **Product Groups:** 80, 82

Iss Eaton

59-66 Greenfield Road, London, E1 1EJ
Tel: 08449-361255 **Fax:** 020-7375 3032
E-mail: maria.farrell@uk.issworld.com
Website: http://www.issworld.co.uk
Managers: L. Green
Immediate Holding Company: LONDON SCHOOL OF COMMERCE & IT LIMITED
Date established: 2008 **No.of Employees:** 1 - 10 **Product Groups:** 37, 69, 83

Date of Accounts	Mar 11	Mar 10	Mar 09
Sales Turnover	637	800	N/A
Pre Tax Profit/Loss	-39	54	N/A
Working Capital	-182	227	-14
Fixed Assets	113	156	24
Current Assets	96	283	31
Current Liabilities	13	39	N/A

It Job Board

41-44 Great Windmill Street, London, W1D 7NB
Tel: 020-7292 3899 **Fax:** 020-7292 3898
E-mail: r.macdonald@theitjobboard.com
Website: http://www.theitjobsboard.co.uk
Managers: R. Macdonald
Immediate Holding Company: 1000HEADS LIMITED
Registration no: 04056153 **Date established:** 2000 **Turnover:** £2m - £5m
No.of Employees: 1 - 10 **Product Groups:** 80

Date of Accounts	Dec 11	Dec 10	Dec 09
Working Capital	9	-8	-28
Current Assets	48	51	13

It's Done

4 New Wave House Humber Road, London, NW2 6DW
Tel: 08450-605566 **Fax:** 020-8201 8594
E-mail: info@itsdone.info
Website: http://www.itsdone.info
Directors: W. Zajat (Tech Serv)
Immediate Holding Company: BEHISTUN LTD
Date established: 2009 **No.of Employees:** 1 - 10 **Product Groups:** 44

Item Ltd

Kingsway House 103 KingswayCamden, London, WC2B 6QX
Tel: 020-7405 4767 **Fax:** 020-7405 4768
E-mail: comms@item.co.uk
Website: http://www.item.co.uk
Directors: A. Crossley (MD), V. Houghton (Fin)
Registration no: 01184697 **Date established:** 2002 **Turnover:** £2m - £5m
No.of Employees: 21 - 50 **Product Groups:** 28, 86

Itochu Europe plc

76 Shoe Lane, London, EC4A 3JB
Tel: 020-7827 0822 **Fax:** 020-7583 1847
E-mail: enquiry@itochu.co.uk
Website: http://www.itochu.eu.com
Managers: A. Butler (Personnel)
Ultimate Holding Company: ITOCHU CORPORATION (JAPAN)
Immediate Holding Company: ITOCHU EUROPE PLC
Registration no: 02098168 **VAT No.:** GB 564 4590 21
Date established: 1987 **Turnover:** £500m - £1,000m
No.of Employees: 101 - 250 **Product Groups:** 61, 80

Date of Accounts	Dec 10	Dec 09	Dec 08
Sales Turnover	987m	890m	779m
Pre Tax Profit/Loss	15m	5m	8m
Working Capital	58m	37m	41m
Fixed Assets	110m	97m	92m
Current Assets	391m	334m	350m
Current Liabilities	185m	131m	79m

Ivory & Ledoux Ltd

201 Haverstock Hill, London, NW3 4QG
Tel: 020-7887 0770 **Fax:** 020-7436 4877
E-mail: enquiries@ivory-ledoux.co.uk
Website: http://www.ivory-ledoux.co.uk
Directors: B. Ben Ari (Fin), B. Ben-ari (Fin)
Managers: K. Graham (Purch Mgr), S. Freeman (Sales Admin)
Ultimate Holding Company: IVORY & LEDOUX HOLDINGS LIMITED
Immediate Holding Company: IVORY & LEDOUX LIMITED
Registration no: 00529807 **Date established:** 1954
Turnover: £20m - £50m **No.of Employees:** 11 - 20 **Product Groups:** 20

Date of Accounts	Dec 11	Dec 10	Dec 09
Sales Turnover	40m	30m	46m
Pre Tax Profit/Loss	596	585	849
Working Capital	3m	2m	3m
Fixed Assets	41	77	152
Current Assets	10m	9m	12m
Current Liabilities	300	321	954

J & B Art Metal

4-6 Stoney Lane, London, SE19 3BD
Tel: 020-8771 9622 **Fax:** 020-8771 9622
Directors: S. Maw (Prop)
Immediate Holding Company: ST. BERNARD MANAGEMENT LIMITED
Registration no: 04516323 **Date established:** 1998
No.of Employees: 1 - 10 **Product Groups:** 26, 35

J C Decaux UK Ltd

Summit House 27 Sale Place, London, W2 1YR
Tel: 020-7298 8000 **Fax:** 020-7298 8190
E-mail: sales@jcdecaux.co.uk
Website: http://www.jcdecaux.co.uk
Bank(s): National Westminster Bank, Liverpool City Office
Directors: J. Male (MD)
Ultimate Holding Company: JC DECAUX SA (FRANCE)
Immediate Holding Company: JCDECAUX UK LIMITED
Registration no: 01679670 **VAT No.:** GB 164 4268 58
Date established: 1982 **Turnover:** Up to £250,000
No.of Employees: 101 - 250 **Product Groups:** 81

Date of Accounts	Dec 11	Dec 10	Dec 09
Sales Turnover	257m	251m	179m
Pre Tax Profit/Loss	21m	20m	6m
Working Capital	30m	19m	12m
Fixed Assets	79m	81m	84m
Current Assets	112m	107m	71m
Current Liabilities	69m	73m	46m

J Floris Ltd

89 Jermyn Street, London, SW1Y 6JH
Tel: 020-7930 2885 **Fax:** 020-7930 1402
E-mail: fragrance@florislondon.com
Website: http://www.florislondon.com
Directors: J. Bodenham (Dir), A. Brunt (MD)
Managers: W. Tewson (Sales Admin)
Immediate Holding Company: J.FLORIS LIMITED
Registration no: 00451581 **Date established:** 1948
Turnover: £10m - £20m **No.of Employees:** 11 - 20 **Product Groups:** 32, 49, 63

Date of Accounts	Jan 10	Jan 09	Jan 08
Sales Turnover	N/A	4m	N/A
Pre Tax Profit/Loss	N/A	139	-430
Working Capital	2m	2m	2m
Fixed Assets	156	704	835
Current Assets	3m	4m	6m
Current Liabilities	N/A	516	554

J & J B Traders Ltd

Hamilton House 1 Temple Avenue, London, EC4Y 0HA
Tel: 020-7353 2123 **Fax:** 020-7583 8823
E-mail: jjbtl@btinternet.com
Website: http://www.btinternet.com
Directors: R. Baher (Fin), J. Baher (Dir)
Immediate Holding Company: J. & J. B. TRADERS LIMITED
Registration no: 01192912 **VAT No.:** GB 150 0594 96
Date established: 1974 **Turnover:** Up to £250,000
No.of Employees: 1 - 10 **Product Groups:** 61

Date of Accounts	Jun 11	Jun 10	Jun 07
Working Capital	2m	2m	1m
Fixed Assets	43	28	25
Current Assets	2m	2m	2m

J K X Oil & Gas plc

6 Cavendish Square, London, W1G 0PD
Tel: 020-7323 4464 **Fax:** 020-7323 5258
E-mail: bruce.burrows@jkx.co.uk
Website: http://www.jkx.co.uk
Directors: B. Burrows (Fin)
Immediate Holding Company: JKX OIL & GAS PLC
Registration no: 03050645 **Date established:** 1995
Turnover: £125m - £250m **No.of Employees:** 1 - 10 **Product Groups:** 51

J Mccafferty Architectural Metalwork

Unit 7 Rainbow Industrial Park Station Approach, London, SW20 0JY
Tel: 020-8944 8687
Directors: J. Mccafferty (Prop)
Date established: 1995 **No.of Employees:** 1 - 10 **Product Groups:** 26, 35

J Murphy & Sons

Hiview House Highgate Road, London, NW5 1TN
Tel: 020-7267 4366 **Fax:** 020-7482 3107
E-mail: info@murphygroup.co.uk
Website: http://www.murphygroup.co.uk
Bank(s): National Westminster Bank Plc
Directors: J. Stack (MD), T. Cassidy (Fin)
Ultimate Holding Company: MARYLAND LIMITED (ISLE OF MAN)
Immediate Holding Company: MURPHY PIPELINES LIMITED
Registration no: 00861600 **Date established:** 1965
Turnover: £50m - £75m **No.of Employees:** 501 - 1000
Product Groups: 51, 52

Date of Accounts	Dec 11	Dec 10	Dec 09
Sales Turnover	485m	401m	408m
Pre Tax Profit/Loss	26m	23m	25m

Working Capital	94m	142m	125m
Fixed Assets	94m	36m	37m
Current Assets	205m	210m	192m
Current Liabilities	65m	31m	30m

J P Morgan

155 Bishops Gate, London, EC2N 3TZ
Tel: 020-7742 4000 **Fax:** 020-7847 1235
E-mail: info@sempra.com
Website: http://www.jpmorgan.com
Directors: R. Beitler (Fin), W. Winget (MD)
Ultimate Holding Company: JP MORGAN CHASE & CO (USA)
Immediate Holding Company: J.P. MORGAN ENERGY EUROPE LTD.
Registration no: 03704235 **Date established:** 1999
Turnover: £75m - £125m **No.of Employees:** 251 - 500
Product Groups: 82

Date of Accounts	Dec 09	Dec 08	Dec 07
Sales Turnover	540m	376m	400m
Pre Tax Profit/Loss	331m	145m	136m
Working Capital	329m	258m	237m
Fixed Assets	23m	35m	41m
Current Assets	1027m	644m	915m
Current Liabilities	626m	358m	565m

J P Morgan Funding Corp

60 Victoria Embankment, London, EC4Y 0JP
Tel: 020-7600 2300
E-mail: info@jpmorgan.com
Website: http://www.jpmorgan.com
Directors: I. Lyall (Dir), E. Darko (Dep Pres), G. Meadows (Dir)
Ultimate Holding Company: JP MORGAN CHASE & CO (USA)
Registration no: 01420459 **Date established:** 1986
Turnover: £20m - £50m **No.of Employees:** 1 - 10 **Product Groups:** 82

Date of Accounts	Dec 07	Mar 07
Pre Tax Profit/Loss	-670	380
Working Capital	1600	1600
Fixed Assets	520	N/A
Current Assets	1610	1600
Total Share Capital	1600	1600

J & S Franklin Holdings & Management Services Ltd

Franklin House 151 Strand, London, WC2R 1HL
Tel: 020-7836 5746 **Fax:** 020-7836 2784
E-mail: defence@franklin.co.uk
Website: http://www.franklin.co.uk
Directors: M. Ladell (Co Sec), S. Franklin (MD)
Ultimate Holding Company: J. & S. FRANKLIN (HOLDINGS AND MANAGEMENT SERVICES) LIMITED
Immediate Holding Company: J. & S. FRANKLIN (HOLDINGS AND MANAGEMENT SERVICES) LIMITED
Registration no: 00428935 **VAT No.:** GB 345 6191 49
Date established: 1947 **Turnover:** £5m - £10m **No.of Employees:** 11 - 20
Product Groups: 24

Date of Accounts	Mar 11	Mar 10	Mar 09
Sales Turnover	9m	9m	10m
Pre Tax Profit/Loss	62	-26	-65
Working Capital	1m	1m	1m
Fixed Assets	6m	6m	5m
Current Assets	3m	3m	3m
Current Liabilities	249	754	255

J & S Services

Mortlake, London, SW14 7ET
Tel: 020-8878 3998 **Fax:** 020- 88783998
Directors: F. Hutson (Prop)
Date established: 2002 **No.of Employees:** 1 - 10 **Product Groups:** 35

J V C Forex UK Ltd

JVC House JVC Business Park, London, NW2 7BA
Tel: 020-8450 3282 **Fax:** 020-8208 4385
Website: http://www.jvc.co.uk
Bank(s): Lloyds TSB Bank plc
Managers: C. Morgan
Ultimate Holding Company: VICTOR COMPANY OF JAPAN LTD (JAPAN)
Immediate Holding Company: JVC EUROPE LIMITED
Registration no: 03537298 **Date established:** 1998
Turnover: £250,000 - £500,000 **No.of Employees:** 51 - 100
Product Groups: 37

Date of Accounts	Mar 11	Mar 10	Mar 09
Sales Turnover	51m	77m	123m
Pre Tax Profit/Loss	-6m	-30m	-35m
Working Capital	-6m	-35m	-29m
Fixed Assets	21m	54m	27m
Current Assets	61m	55m	65m
Current Liabilities	1m	4m	7m

J W T

1 Knightsbridge Green, London, SW1X 7NW
Tel: 020-7656 7000 **Fax:** 020-7656 7010
E-mail: peter.womersley@jwt.com
Website: http://www.jwt.co.uk
Bank(s): National Westminster Bank Plc & Morgan Guaranty In
Directors: R. Wigley (Pers), D. Walker (Fin), E. McSween (Tech Serv)
Managers: J. Petyan
Ultimate Holding Company: WPP 2005 LIMITED
Immediate Holding Company: J. WALTER THOMPSON COMPANY (MANCHESTER) LIMITED
Registration no: 00830818 **Date established:** 1964
Turnover: £500m - £1,000m **No.of Employees:** 501 - 1000
Product Groups: 81

Date of Accounts	Dec 11	Dec 10	Dec 09
Pre Tax Profit/Loss	13m	43m	270
Working Capital	32m	19m	19m
Fixed Assets	65m	65m	65m
Current Assets	32m	19m	19m
Current Liabilities	140	140	140

Jacaranda Productions Ltd

J House 6 Studland Street, London, W6 0JS
Tel: 020-8741 9088 **Fax:** 020-8748 5670
E-mail: info@jacaranda.co.uk
Website: http://www.jacaranda.co.uk
Directors: G. Wheatley (Co Sec), K. Eyre (MD)
Immediate Holding Company: JACARANDA PRODUCTIONS LIMITED
Registration no: 03083442 **Date established:** 1995 **Turnover:** £2m - £5m
No.of Employees: 1 - 10 **Product Groups:** 89

Date of Accounts	Feb 11	Feb 10	Feb 09
Working Capital	-187	-224	84
Fixed Assets	704	753	807
Current Assets	176	238	540

Jackson Lift Group

Units 3-19 Ropery Business Park, London, SE7 7RX
Tel: 020-8293 4176 **Fax:** 020-8305 0274
E-mail: gjackson@jacksonlifts.com
Website: http://www.jacksonlift.com
Bank(s): Barclays, London
Directors: G. Jackson (Prop)
Managers: J. Clarke (Tech Serv Mgr), J. Cruse (Comptroller), P. Rudd (Mktg Serv Mgr), A. Sawyer (Personnel)
Immediate Holding Company: JACKSON LIFTS LIMITED
Registration no: 03574502 **VAT No.:** GB 506 6026 70
Date established: 1998 **Turnover:** £10m - £20m
No.of Employees: 251 - 500 **Product Groups:** 45, 48

Jacksons Art Supplies

Farleigh Place, London, N16 7SX
Tel: 020-7254 0077 **Fax:** 020-7254 0088
E-mail: sales@jacksonsart.co.uk
Website: http://www.jacksonsart.co.uk
Managers: G. Thompson (Mgr)
Immediate Holding Company: UPFRONT THEATRE ALLIANCE LIMITED
Date established: 2012 **No.of Employees:** 11 - 20 **Product Groups:** 32, 49, 64

Jaeger Ladieswear

57 Broadwick Street, London, W1F 9QS
Tel: 020-7200 4000 **Fax:** 020-7200 4001
E-mail: andrew.mackenzie@jaeger.co.uk
Website: http://www.jaeger.co.uk
Bank(s): National Westminster Bank Plc
Directors: A. Mackenzie (Dir), G. Edgerton (Fin), L. Bucke (Purch)
Managers: A. Wootley, L. Lockheart (Personnel)
Ultimate Holding Company: GUSTAV (REALISATIONS) LIMITED
Immediate Holding Company: JAEGER LONDON LIMITED
Registration no: 06587828 **VAT No.:** GB 238 7871 19
Date established: 2008 **Turnover:** Up to £250,000
No.of Employees: 101 - 250 **Product Groups:** 24

Date of Accounts	Feb 11	Feb 10	Feb 09
Sales Turnover	133	130	N/A
Pre Tax Profit/Loss	-20m	N/A	N/A
Working Capital	-5m	-5m	-5
Fixed Assets	40m	60m	60
Current Assets	437	304	N/A

Jakar International Ltd

Hillside House 2-6 Friern Park, London, N12 9BX
Tel: 020-8445 6376 **Fax:** 020-8445 2714
E-mail: info@jakar.co.uk
Website: http://www.jakar.co.uk
Bank(s): HSBC Bank plc
Directors: P. Sacki (Sales)
Immediate Holding Company: JAKAR INTERNATIONAL LIMITED
Registration no: 00495767 **VAT No.:** GB 229 3732 54
Date established: 1951 **Turnover:** £1m - £2m **No.of Employees:** 11 - 20
Product Groups: 64

Date of Accounts	Dec 11	Dec 10	Dec 09
Working Capital	520	512	482
Fixed Assets	45	53	38
Current Assets	737	675	614

James Finlay Limited

Swire House 59 Buckingham Gate, London, SW1E 6AJ
Tel: 020-7802 3230 **Fax:** 020-7834 0587
E-mail: sec@finlays.co.uk
Website: http://www.finlays.net
Bank(s): National Westminster Bank Plc
Directors: D. Gilmour (Co Sec), P. Henson (Fin)
Registration no: SC007139 **VAT No.:** 309 1093 75
Turnover: £125m - £250m **No.of Employees:** 21 - 50
Product Groups: 20, 62

Jarroy Importers Ltd (t/a jarroy of london)

Unit 8 Heron Industrial Estate Barbers Road, London, E15 2PE
Tel: 020-8519 7780 **Fax:** 020-8519 7265
E-mail: info@jarroy.com
Website: http://www.jarroy.com
Bank(s): National Westminster Bank Plc
Directors: G. Goldstein (MD), G. Goldstein (Dir), A. Bush (Dir), J. Goldstein (Dir)
Managers: K. Worby
Immediate Holding Company: HISTWAIN LIMITED
Registration no: 01419493 **VAT No.:** GB 333 2899 44
Date established: 1980 **Turnover:** £1m - £2m **No.of Employees:** 11 - 20
Product Groups: 24, 32, 49, 83

Date of Accounts	Jun 07	Jun 06
Working Capital	-169	-80
Current Assets	31	155
Current Liabilities	200	235
Total Share Capital	10	10

Jayex Technology Ltd

Unit 13 Sovereign Park Coronation Road, London, NW10 7QP
Tel: 020-8838 6222 **Fax:** 020-8838 3222
E-mail: sales@jayex.com
Website: http://www.jayex.com
Directors: S. Jain (Co Sec)
Ultimate Holding Company: JAYEX GROUP LIMITED
Immediate Holding Company: JAYEX TECHNOLOGY LIMITED
Registration no: 05569302 **VAT No.:** GB 228 7777 18
Date established: 2005 **Turnover:** £2m - £5m **No.of Employees:** 21 - 50
Product Groups: 37

Date of Accounts	Sep 11	Sep 10	Sep 09
Sales Turnover	3m	3m	4m
Pre Tax Profit/Loss	337	306	769
Working Capital	1m	1m	1m
Fixed Assets	40	39	43
Current Assets	2m	2m	2m
Current Liabilities	311	419	664

Jeeves Of Belgravia

94 High St Wimbledon, London, SW19 5EG
Tel: 020-8946 0665 **Fax:** 020-8809 7833
E-mail: a@jeevesofbelgravia.co.uk
Website: http://www.jeevesofbelgravia.co.uk
Managers: D. Castillejo (Mgr)
Immediate Holding Company: STACK EVENTS LTD
Registration no: 01331370 **Date established:** 2007 **Turnover:** £2m - £5m
No.of Employees: 1 - 10 **Product Groups:** 23

Date of Accounts	Dec 08	Dec 07
Sales Turnover	3903	3743
Pre Tax Profit/Loss	264	-1254
Working Capital	227	192
Fixed Assets	230	243
Current Assets	693	692
Current Liabilities	466	500
Total Share Capital	29	29
ROCE% (Return on Capital Employed)	57.8	-288.3
ROT% (Return on Turnover)	6.8	-33.5

W S Jenkins & Co. Ltd

Tariff Road, London, N17 0EN
Tel: 020-8808 2336 **Fax:** 020-8365 1534
E-mail: sales@wsjenkins.co.uk
Website: http://www.wsjenkins.co.uk
Directors: P. Humphrey (Dir)
Immediate Holding Company: W.S.JENKINS & COMPANY LIMITED
Registration no: 00259600 **VAT No.:** GB 220 4691 91
Date established: 1931 **Turnover:** £500,000 - £1m
No.of Employees: 1 - 10 **Product Groups:** 48

Date of Accounts	Sep 11	Sep 10	Sep 09
Working Capital	23	55	54
Fixed Assets	38	38	25
Current Assets	239	254	237

Jewson Ltd

Trussley Road, London, W6 7PS
Tel: 020-8741 1021 **Fax:** 020-8741 5259
Website: http://www.jewson.co.uk
Directors: P. Hindle (MD)
Managers: M. Szit., G. Kelley (District Mgr), D. Mason (District Mgr), G. Kelly (District Mgr)
Ultimate Holding Company: COMPAGNIE DE SAINT GOBAIN (FRANCE)
Immediate Holding Company: JEWSON LIMITED
Registration no: 00348407 **VAT No.:** GB 394 1212 63
Date established: 1939 **Turnover:** £2m - £5m **No.of Employees:** 21 - 50
Product Groups: 66

Date of Accounts	Dec 11	Dec 10	Dec 09
Sales Turnover	1606m	1547m	1485m
Pre Tax Profit/Loss	18m	100m	45m
Working Capital	-345m	-250m	-349m
Fixed Assets	496m	387m	461m
Current Assets	657m	1005m	1320m
Current Liabilities	66m	120m	64m

Jewson Ltd

11 Tottenham Lane, London, N8 9DP
Tel: 020-8340 9445 **Fax:** 020-8348 6614
Website: http://www.jewson.co.uk
Directors: P. Hindle (MD)
Managers: J. Lall (Sales Prom Mgr), T. Dyke (District Mgr)
Ultimate Holding Company: COMPAGNIE DE SAINT GOBAIN (FRANCE)
Immediate Holding Company: JEWSON LIMITED
Registration no: 00348407 **VAT No.:** GB 497 7184 83
Date established: 1939 **Turnover:** £2m - £5m **No.of Employees:** 1 - 10
Product Groups: 66

Date of Accounts	Dec 11	Dec 10	Dec 09
Sales Turnover	1606m	1547m	1485m
Pre Tax Profit/Loss	18m	100m	45m
Working Capital	-345m	-250m	-349m
Fixed Assets	496m	387m	461m
Current Assets	657m	1005m	1320m
Current Liabilities	66m	120m	64m

Jewson Ltd

6-12 Kennington Lane, London, SE11 4LT
Tel: 020-7735 1251 **Fax:** 020-7587 1702
E-mail: stephen.parratt@jewson.co.uk
Website: http://www.jewson.co.uk
Managers: R. Patel (Mgr)
Ultimate Holding Company: COMPAGNIE DE SAINT GOBAIN (FRANCE)
Immediate Holding Company: JEWSON LIMITED
Registration no: 00348407 **VAT No.:** GB 394 1212 63
Date established: 1939 **Turnover:** £2m - £5m **No.of Employees:** 11 - 20
Product Groups: 66

Date of Accounts	Dec 11	Dec 10	Dec 09
Sales Turnover	1606m	1547m	1485m
Pre Tax Profit/Loss	18m	100m	45m
Working Capital	-345m	-250m	-349m
Fixed Assets	496m	387m	461m
Current Assets	657m	1005m	1320m
Current Liabilities	66m	120m	64m

Jewson Ltd

Ilderton Wharf Rollins Street, London, SE15 1EP
Tel: 020-7732 3551 **Fax:** 020-7358 1058
E-mail: richard.oneill@jewson.co.uk
Website: http://www.hirepoint.co.uk
Managers: R. O'neill (District Mgr)
Ultimate Holding Company: COMPAGNIE DE SAINT GOBAIN (FRANCE)
Immediate Holding Company: JEWSON LIMITED
Registration no: 00348407 **VAT No.:** GB 394 1212 63
Date established: 1939 **Turnover:** £2m - £5m **No.of Employees:** 11 - 20
Product Groups: 66

Date of Accounts	Dec 11	Dec 10	Dec 09
Sales Turnover	1606m	1547m	1485m
Pre Tax Profit/Loss	18m	100m	45m
Working Capital	-345m	-250m	-349m
Fixed Assets	496m	387m	461m
Current Assets	657m	1005m	1320m
Current Liabilities	66m	120m	64m

John Ayling & Associates

27 Soho Square, London, W1D 3QR
Tel: 020-7439 6070 **Fax:** 020-7437 8473
E-mail: jayling@jaa-media.co.uk
Website: http://www.jaa-media.co.uk
Bank(s): Lloyds TSB Bank plc
Directors: A. Hickey (Fin), J. Ayling (MD)
Managers: A. Singh (Tech Serv Mgr)
Immediate Holding Company: JOHN AYLING AND ASSOCIATES LIMITED
Registration no: 01364599 **VAT No.:** GB 235 3634 71
Date established: 1978 **Turnover:** £50m - £75m
No.of Employees: 21 - 50 **Product Groups:** 81

Date of Accounts	Dec 11	Dec 10	Dec 09
Sales Turnover	60m	47m	48m
Pre Tax Profit/Loss	455	281	146

see next page

***John Ayling & Associates** - Cont'd*

Working Capital	3m	3m	3m
Fixed Assets	90	98	93
Current Assets	14m	15m	14m
Current Liabilities	978	1m	822

John Brown Publishing
136-142 Bramley Road, London, W10 6SR
Tel: 020-7565 3000 **Fax:** 020-7565 3050
E-mail: info@johnbrownmedia.com
Website: http://www.johnbrownmedia.co.uk
Directors: S. Mandil (Pers), A. Hirsch (Grp Chief Exec), T. Gleeson (Co Sec)
Managers: B. Davison (Tech Serv Mgr), M. Stanton, M. Sharman, R. Sacre (I.T. Exec), R. Biagioni, H. Watson (Personnel)
Ultimate Holding Company: BRIDGEPOINT CAPITAL LIMITED (BELGIUM)
Immediate Holding Company: CITRUS PUBLISHING LIMITED
Registration no: 01049793 **Date established:** 1972
Turnover: £10m - £20m **No.of Employees:** 101 - 250 **Product Groups:** 28

John D Wood
19 Berkeley Street, London, W1J 8ED
Tel: 020-7629 9050 **Fax:** 020-7493 4749
E-mail: property@johndwood.com
Website: http://www.johndwood.com
Directors: J. Charles (Dir), R. Bloom (Grp Chief Exec)
Immediate Holding Company: JOHN D WOOD & CO. (RESIDENTIAL & AGRICULTURAL) LIMITED
Registration no: 02349482 **Date established:** 1989
No.of Employees: 1 - 10 **Product Groups:** 80, 84

John Myland Ltd
26-34 Rothschild Street, London, SE27 0HQ
Tel: 020-8670 9161 **Fax:** 020-8761 5700
E-mail: sales@mylands.co.uk
Website: http://www.mylands.co.uk
Bank(s): Lloyds TSB Bank plc
Directors: M. Myland (Dir), J. Myland (MD), D. Myland (Dir)
Registration no: 00232215 **VAT No.:** GB 217 9787 18
Date established: 1972 **Turnover:** £2m - £5m **No.of Employees:** 21 - 50
Product Groups: 32

Johnson Matthey Plc
5th Floor 25 Farringdon Street, London, EC4A 4AB
Tel: 020-7269 8400 **Fax:** 020-7269 8422
E-mail: godwini@matthey.com
Website: http://www.matthey.com
Directors: S. Farrant (Co Sec), R. Macleod (Fin)
Managers: J. Adams (Personnel), P. Axworthy (Tech Serv Mgr), I. Godwin, N. Carson
Ultimate Holding Company: JOHNSON MATTHEY PLC
Immediate Holding Company: JOHNSON MATTHEY (CM) LIMITED
Registration no: 02885614 **VAT No.:** GB 232 6241 93
Date established: 1994 **Turnover:** Over £1,000m
No.of Employees: 51 - 100 **Product Groups:** 31, 32, 34, 35, 36, 38, 42, 48

Date of Accounts	Mar 12	Mar 11	Mar 10
Pre Tax Profit/Loss	2m	1m	2m
Working Capital	331m	330m	330m
Current Assets	331m	331m	331m
Current Liabilities	N/A	N/A	500

Johnson Walker Ltd
64 Burlington Arcade, London, W1J 0QT
Tel: 020-7629 2615 **Fax:** 020-7409 0709
E-mail: info@johnson-walker.com
Website: http://www.johnson-walker.com
Directors: R. Gill (MD)
Immediate Holding Company: JOHNSON WALKER LIMITED
Registration no: 02411511 **Date established:** 1989
Turnover: £500,000 - £1m **No.of Employees:** 1 - 10 **Product Groups:** 24, 34, 49, 61, 65, 85

Date of Accounts	Sep 11	Sep 10	Sep 09
Working Capital	429	253	86
Fixed Assets	59	68	79
Current Assets	838	829	546

Jonathan Berney Chartered Surveyors
35 Bruton Street Mayfair, London, W1J 6QY
Tel: 0871-218 3771 **Fax:** 0704-090 0561
E-mail: headoffice@jonathanberney.co.uk
Website: http://www.jonathanberney.co.uk
Directors: J. Berney (Ptnr)
Registration no: 07412878 **Date established:** 1955
Turnover: Over £1,000m **No.of Employees:** 1501 & over
Product Groups: 14, 33, 80, 82

Jones Lang LaSalle (West End Office)
22 Hanover Square, London, W1S 1JA
Tel: 020-7493 6040 **Fax:** 020-7408 0220
E-mail: jason.stone@eu.jll.com
Website: http://www.joneslanglasalle.com
Bank(s): National Westminster Bank Plc
Directors: R. Webster (Dir), N. Taylor (Fin), A. Gould (Grp Chief Exec)
Managers: C. Tyler-Lowe (Mktg Serv Mgr), J. Stone
Ultimate Holding Company: JONES LANG LASALLE INC (USA)
Immediate Holding Company: JONES LANG LASALLE EUROPEAN SERVICES LIMITED
Registration no: 02176622 **Date established:** 1987 **Turnover:** £5m - £10m
No.of Employees: 501 - 1000 **Product Groups:** 80, 82, 84

Date of Accounts	Dec 10
Sales Turnover	6m
Pre Tax Profit/Loss	-191
Working Capital	809
Current Assets	2m
Current Liabilities	751

Jones Lang Lasalle
10 Gresham Street, London, EC2V 7JD
Tel: 020-7248 6040 **Fax:** 020-7408 0220
E-mail: richard.webster@eu.jll.com
Website: http://www.joneslanglasalle.co.uk
Directors: R. Howling (Fin), P. Connolly (Pers), N. Taylor (Co Sec)
Managers: R. Webster, H. Sanderson (Buyer), D. Allen, T. Salter (Personnel)
Ultimate Holding Company: JONES LANG LASALLE INC (USA)
Immediate Holding Company: JONES LANG LASALLE RESOURCES LIMITED
Registration no: 01231849 **Date established:** 1975
Turnover: £20m - £50m **No.of Employees:** 101 - 250
Product Groups: 80, 82

Date of Accounts	Dec 11	Dec 10	Dec 09
Sales Turnover	25m	25m	24m
Current Assets	10m	9m	8m
Current Liabilities	9m	8m	5m

Simon Jones Superfreight Ltd
Unit 15 Vale Industrial Park 170 Rowan Road, London, SW16 5BN
Tel: 020-7924 3933 **Fax:** 020-7223 1293
E-mail: traceyjones@superfreight.co.uk
Website: http://www.sjsltd.co.uk
Bank(s): Barclays
Directors: T. Jones (Dir)
Immediate Holding Company: SIMON JONES SUPERFREIGHT LIMITED
Registration no: 03292664 **Date established:** 1996
Turnover: £500,000 - £1m **No.of Employees:** 11 - 20 **Product Groups:** 76

Date of Accounts	Dec 11	Dec 10	Dec 09
Working Capital	103	-31	68
Fixed Assets	1m	661	131
Current Assets	635	584	343

Jordan International Bank plc
103 Mount Street, London, W1K 2AP
Tel: 020-7493 7528 **Fax:** 020- 73554359
E-mail: mort@jordanbank.co.uk
Website: http://www.jordanbank.co.uk
Bank(s): HSBC Bank plc
Directors: Z. Fariz (Ch), Y. Mufti (Dir), Z. Khouri (Dep Ch), D. Gates (MD), J. Story (Co Sec), M. Mirghavameddin (Grp Chief Exec), W. Azar (Dir), R. Muasher (Dir), N. Barakat (Dir), M. Marto (Ch), M. Hadid (Grp Chief Exec), A. Dweik (Dep Ch), B. Jardaneh (Dir), R. Saifiti (Dir), H. Qadi (Dir), M. Saliba (Dir), M. Tahboub (Dir), M. Al-Asmar (Dir), N. Al-Shaka (Dir), O. Talhouni (Dir), F. Abul-Enein (Dir)
Managers: J. Bell (I.T. Exec)
Immediate Holding Company: JORDAN INTERNATIONAL BANK PLC
Registration no: 01814093 **VAT No.:** GB 397 1529 16
Date established: 1984 **Turnover:** £10m - £20m
No.of Employees: 21 - 50 **Product Groups:** 82

Date of Accounts	Dec 10	Dec 09	Dec 08
Pre Tax Profit/Loss	-5m	-9m	-9m
Fixed Assets	126m	72m	85m
Current Assets	82m	125m	134m
Current Liabilities	174m	175m	190m

Joseph & Co
The Piper Centre 50 Carnwath Road, London, SW6 3JX
Tel: 020-7736 2522 **Fax:** 020-7736 1644
E-mail: andrew.franklin@joseph.co.uk
Website: http://www.joseph.co.uk
Directors: A. Franklin (Fin), M. Forrester (MD), Z. Withers (Fin)
Managers: J. Ettedgui (I.T. Exec)
Ultimate Holding Company: ONWARD HOLDINGS CO LTD (JAPAN)
Immediate Holding Company: JOSEPH LIMITED
Registration no: 01068214 **Date established:** 1972
Turnover: £50m - £75m **No.of Employees:** 251 - 500
Product Groups: 61, 81

Date of Accounts	Nov 09	Nov 08	Nov 07
Sales Turnover	57m	51m	54m
Pre Tax Profit/Loss	4m	4m	6m
Working Capital	14m	12m	6m
Fixed Assets	16m	15m	15m
Current Assets	30m	22m	16m
Current Liabilities	5m	4m	5m

Jubilee Printers
430 Edgware Road, London, W2 1EG
Tel: 020-7724 1094 **Fax:** 020-7706 0518
E-mail: info@jubileeprinters.co.uk
Website: http://www.jubileeprinters.co.uk
Managers: A. Kara (Mgr)
Immediate Holding Company: V.N.C. TRANSPORT SERVICES LIMITED
Registration no: 01843235 **Date established:** 1984
Turnover: £250,000 - £500,000 **No.of Employees:** 1 - 10
Product Groups: 27, 28

Juggletime Ltd
Po Box 54240, London, W14 8HG
Tel: 020-8144 6456
E-mail: info@juggletime.com
Website: http://www.juggletime.com
Directors: E. Montasell (Mkt Research)
Registration no: 05560692 **Date established:** 2005
Turnover: Up to £250,000 **No.of Employees:** 1 - 10 **Product Groups:** 83

Date of Accounts	Jan 08
Working Capital	-8
Current Liabilities	8

Julius Baer
64 St Jamess Street, London, SW1A 1NF
Tel: 020-3205 1600 **Fax:** 020-7629 5931
Website: http://www.juliusbaer.com
Directors: P. Mathews (Prop)
Ultimate Holding Company: JULIUS BAER HOLDING LIMITED (SWITZERLAND)
Immediate Holding Company: JULIUS BAER INTERNATIONAL LIMITED
Registration no: 01120330 **Date established:** 1973
Turnover: £10m - £20m **No.of Employees:** 1 - 10 **Product Groups:** 82

Date of Accounts	Dec 11	Dec 10	Dec 09
Sales Turnover	12m	7m	4m
Pre Tax Profit/Loss	4m	-756	-3m
Working Capital	7m	4m	4m
Fixed Assets	187	257	344
Current Assets	9m	6m	6m
Current Liabilities	2m	2m	1m

Juno Installations Ltd
8 Carlton Park Avenue, London, SW20 8BL
Tel: 020-8543 1697 **Fax:** 020-8543 1697
E-mail: harle8@aol.com
Website: http://www.new-windows.biz
Directors: D. Harle (MD), D. Harle (Dir)
Managers: A. Harle (Sales Prom Mgr)
Immediate Holding Company: JUNO INSTALLATIONS LIMITED
Registration no: 06295960 **VAT No.:** GB 391 4399 24
Date established: 2007 **Turnover:** £500,000 - £1m
No.of Employees: 1 - 10 **Product Groups:** 30, 35, 36

Jupiter Assett Management plc
1 Grosvenor Place, London, SW1X 7JJ
Tel: 020-7412 0703 **Fax:** 020-7581 3857
E-mail: reception@jupiter-group.co.uk
Website: http://www.jupiteronline.co.uk
Directors: P. Johnson (Fin), E. Burnham Carter (Prop)
Managers: C. Crawford (Sales & Mktg Mg), J. Gray (Personnel), S. Marriner (Buyer), D. Ingles (Tech Serv Mgr)
Ultimate Holding Company: JUPITER FUND MANAGEMENT PLC
Immediate Holding Company: JUPITER ASSET MANAGEMENT LIMITED
Registration no: 02036243 **Date established:** 1986
Turnover: £125m - £250m **No.of Employees:** 251 - 500
Product Groups: 80, 82

Date of Accounts	Dec 11	Dec 10	Dec 09
Sales Turnover	139m	115m	88m
Pre Tax Profit/Loss	111m	117m	80m
Working Capital	47m	73m	80m
Fixed Assets	4m	3m	3m
Current Assets	101m	113m	112m
Current Liabilities	45m	30m	22m

Jupiter Display Ltd
City Pavillion 33 Britton Street, London, EC1M 5UG
Tel: 08707-509200 **Fax:** 0870-750 9250
E-mail: sales@jupitardisplay.com
Website: http://www.jupiterdisplay.com
Directors: B. Moss (MD), M. Mitchell (Sales), C. Reed (Dir), R. Ward (Sales), G. Page (Chief Op Offcr)
Managers: R. Ward (Sales Prom Mgr), R. Kelly (Mktg Serv Mgr), J. Boniface (I.T. Exec)
Immediate Holding Company: MEDIASHORE LIMITED
Registration no: 04122759 **Date established:** 2000 **Turnover:** £5m - £10m
No.of Employees: 101 - 250 **Product Groups:** 26, 30, 49, 81

Just Jamie & the Paulrich Ltd
Unit 1 City North, Fonthill Road, London, N4 3HN
Tel: 020-7561 4500 **Fax:** 020-7561 4501
E-mail: martin@justjamie.com
Directors: M. Benton (Dir), R. Godfrey (MD)
Managers: D. Shield (Sales Prom Mgr)
Ultimate Holding Company: J5 Ltd
Immediate Holding Company: Just Jamie Holdings Ltd
Registration no: 01363111 **Date established:** 1978
Turnover: £20m - £50m **No.of Employees:** 21 - 50 **Product Groups:** 24

Justerini & Brooks Ltd
61 St Jamess Street, London, SW1A 1LZ
Tel: 020-7484 6400 **Fax:** 020-7484 6499
E-mail: justorders@justerinis.com
Website: http://www.justerinis.com
Managers: L. Holliday (Mgr)
Ultimate Holding Company: DIAGEO PLC
Immediate Holding Company: JUSTERINI & BROOKS,LIMITED
Registration no: 00068576 **Date established:** 2000
Turnover: £75m - £125m **No.of Employees:** 11 - 20 **Product Groups:** 21, 62

Date of Accounts	Jun 11	Jun 10	Jun 09
Sales Turnover	95m	71m	62m
Pre Tax Profit/Loss	2m	6m	-4m
Working Capital	342m	470m	664m
Fixed Assets	1208m	1242m	1241m
Current Assets	366m	493m	699m
Current Liabilities	3m	3m	2m

Justina Of London Ltd
6 Lockwood Industrial Park Mill Mead Road, London, N17 9QP
Tel: 020-8801 3663 **Fax:** 020-8808 4578
E-mail: michael@justinaoflondon.biz
Website: http://www.justinaoflondon.biz
Directors: M. Barnett (Sales)
Ultimate Holding Company: JUSTINA HOLDINGS LIMITED
Immediate Holding Company: JUSTINA OF LONDON LIMITED
Registration no: 00939575 **Date established:** 1968 **Turnover:** £1m - £2m
No.of Employees: 21 - 50 **Product Groups:** 63

Date of Accounts	Apr 11	Apr 10	Apr 09
Working Capital	1m	880	839
Fixed Assets	2	25	53
Current Assets	3m	3m	2m

Justis Publishing Ltd
20 Kentish Town Road, London, NW1 9NR
Tel: 020-7284 8060 **Fax:** 020-7267 1133
E-mail: sales@justis.com
Website: http://www.justis.com
Directors: M. Green (Develop), M. Gerami (MD), D. Cristelow (Comm), R. Williamson (MD)
Managers: B. Oye (Sales Admin), N. Wood (I.T. Exec), J. Daymond (Sales Prom Mgr)
Ultimate Holding Company: CONTEXT LIMITED
Immediate Holding Company: JUSTIS PUBLISHING LIMITED
Registration no: SC095752 **VAT No.:** GB 544 5844 25
Date established: 1985 **Turnover:** Up to £250,000
No.of Employees: 21 - 50 **Product Groups:** 44

Date of Accounts	Dec 10	Dec 09	Dec 08
Working Capital	3m	3m	3m
Fixed Assets	335	138	47
Current Assets	5m	5m	5m

JVC Professional Europe Ltd
JVC House Jvc Business Park, 12 Priestley Way, London, NW2 7BA
Tel: 020-8208 6200 **Fax:** 020-8208 6260
E-mail: sales@jvcpro.co.uk
Website: http://www.jvcproeurope.com
Directors: K. Yoshikawa (MD)
Managers: B. Steventon (Sales Off Mgr), C. Roth (I.T. Exec), J. Waters, N. Fletcher (Mktg Serv Mgr)
Ultimate Holding Company: Matsushita Electric Industrial Co. (Japan)
Immediate Holding Company: JVC PROFESSIONAL EUROPE LIMITED
Registration no: 02249910 **VAT No.:** GB 505 2324 88
Date established: 1988 **Turnover:** £50m - £75m **No.of Employees:** 1 - 10
Product Groups: 37, 38

Date of Accounts	Mar 08	Mar 07	Mar 06
Sales Turnover	80m	82m	79m
Pre Tax Profit/Loss	630	1m	-2m
Working Capital	4m	4m	3m
Fixed Assets	1m	2m	2m
Current Assets	27m	26m	27m
Current Liabilities	23m	22m	25m
Total Share Capital	5m	5m	5m

K B Natural Foods Ltd
7d Standard Road, London, NW10 6EX
Tel: 020-8453 1988 **Fax:** 020-8961 6998
E-mail: kbnaturalfoods@hotmail.com

Directors: S. Ahmed (Dir), N. Ahmed (MD)
Immediate Holding Company: K B NATURAL FOODS LIMITED
Registration no: 04481223 **Date established:** 2002
No.of Employees: 1 - 10 **Product Groups:** 62

Date of Accounts	Oct 11	Oct 10	Oct 09
Working Capital	-31	-29	-37
Fixed Assets	69	100	136
Current Assets	113	105	118

K C Engineering

Rear of 89 Upper Brockley Road, London, SE4 1TF
Tel: 020-8691 0219 **Fax:** 020-8691 0219
Managers: A. Turner (Mgr)
Turnover: Up to £250,000 **No.of Employees:** 1 - 10 **Product Groups:** 48

K Com

2nd & 3rd Floor 4 Crown Place, London, EC2A 4BT
Tel: 020-7422 8700 **Fax:** 0121-779 7222
E-mail: info@kcom.com
Website: http://www.kcom.com
Bank(s): Barclays
Directors: B. Halbert (MD)
Managers: T. Aguilar (Mgr), R. Logan (Sales Prom Mgr), Y. Dainton (Mktg Serv Mgr)
Ultimate Holding Company: KINGSTON COMMUNICATION
Registration no: 02150618 **VAT No.:** GB 198 9556 80
No.of Employees: 51 - 100 **Product Groups:** 37, 38, 44, 48, 52, 67, 79, 80, 81, 84, 86

K P M Taxi Advertising Direct Ltd

Hemming House Hemming Street, London, E1 5BL
Tel: 020-7377 2182 **Fax:** 020-7377 2410
E-mail: info@kpmuktaxis.com
Website: http://www.kpmuktaxis.com
Directors: K. Marder (Dir), M. Troullis (Dir), P. Dacosta (MD)
Ultimate Holding Company: ECO CITY VEHICLES PLC
Immediate Holding Company: KPM-UK TAXIS PLC
Registration no: 02164842 **Date established:** 1987
Turnover: £20m - £50m **No.of Employees:** 1 - 10 **Product Groups:** 39

Date of Accounts	Dec 11	Dec 10	Dec 09
Sales Turnover	20m	25m	25m
Pre Tax Profit/Loss	-1m	86	-1m
Working Capital	-3m	-3m	-4m
Fixed Assets	177	368	2m
Current Assets	7m	10m	5m
Current Liabilities	5m	741	5m

K & S Packaging

33-37 Garman Road, London, N17 0UL
Tel: 020-8885 6677 **Fax:** 020-8885 6678
E-mail: info@kspackaging.com
Website: http://www.kspackaging.com
Directors: M. Zaisotlu (MD)
Immediate Holding Company: CLEAN SUPPLY LIMITED
Registration no: 06957713 **Date established:** 2009
Turnover: Up to £250,000 **No.of Employees:** 1 - 10 **Product Groups:** 30, 42

Date of Accounts	Mar 11	Mar 10
Working Capital	433	173
Fixed Assets	42	N/A
Current Assets	880	566
Current Liabilities	85	57

Kadence International Ltd

Carlton House 27a Carlton Drive, London, SW15 2BS
Tel: 020-8246 5400 **Fax:** 020-8246 5401
E-mail: lmcglaughlin@kadence.com
Website: http://www.kadence.com
Managers: A. Tandolfo (Tech Serv Mgr), S. Everard, L. McGlaughlin (Sales Admin)
Immediate Holding Company: KADENCE INTERNATIONAL LIMITED
Registration no: 02646756 **VAT No.:** GB 672 4171 38
Date established: 1991 **No.of Employees:** 21 - 50 **Product Groups:** 81

Date of Accounts	Jun 11	Jun 10	Jun 09
Working Capital	362	375	333
Fixed Assets	186	93	95
Current Assets	794	892	845

Kajima Design Europe Ltd

55 Baker Street, London, W1U 8EW
Tel: 020-3075 1800 **Fax:** 020-3075 1899
E-mail: enquiries@kajima.co.uk
Website: http://www.kajima.co.uk
Directors: D. Evans (MD), D. Evens (MD), E. Evans (MD), F. Shibaski (Pres), R. Marshall (Develop), T. Quinn (Dir)
Managers: K. Endo (I.T. Exec), W. Martin (Personnel)
Ultimate Holding Company: KAJIMA CORPORATION (JAPAN)
Immediate Holding Company: Kajima Europe U.K. Holding Ltd
Registration no: 02684226 **Date established:** 1992
Turnover: Up to £250,000 **No.of Employees:** 1 - 10 **Product Groups:** 80

Date of Accounts	Dec 09	Dec 08	Dec 07
Sales Turnover	N/A	18	289
Pre Tax Profit/Loss	10	-664	-649
Working Capital	-6m	-6m	-5m
Current Assets	945	1m	2m
Current Liabilities	5	5	102

Kaloric Heater Co. Ltd

31-33 Beethoven Street, London, W10 4LJ
Tel: 020-8969 1367 **Fax:** 020-8968 8913
E-mail: admin@kaloricheater.co.uk
Website: http://www.kaloricheater.co.uk
Directors: R. Lossos (MD), H. Lossos (Co Sec)
Immediate Holding Company: KALORIC HEATER CO. LIMITED
Registration no: 00841148 **Date established:** 1965
Turnover: £250,000 - £500,000 **No.of Employees:** 11 - 20
Product Groups: 33, 37, 40, 68, 84

Date of Accounts	Mar 11	Mar 10	Mar 09
Working Capital	-160	-148	-161
Fixed Assets	189	190	192
Current Assets	59	38	31

Kandor Model Makers Ltd

1 Berry Place Sebastion Street, London, EC1V 0HE
Tel: 020-7251 6366 **Fax:** 020-7608 3356
E-mail: mf.kandoroffice@btconnect.com
Website: http://www.kandormodels.com
Bank(s): Barclays
Directors: M. Finnesy (MD)
Immediate Holding Company: KANDOR MODELMAKERS LIMITED
Registration no: 01552918 **VAT No.:** GB 447 0882 32
Date established: 1981 **Turnover:** £500,000 - £1m
No.of Employees: 11 - 20 **Product Groups:** 81

Date of Accounts	Jun 11	Jun 10	Jun 09
Working Capital	822	719	726
Fixed Assets	60	104	148
Current Assets	1m	942	991

Kansara's - Exclusive Luxury Chocolates

15 Pear Close, London, NW9 0LJ
Tel: 020-8205 7921 **Fax:** 020-8205 7176
E-mail: info@kansaras.co.uk
Website: http://www.kansaras.co.uk
Registration no: 04373110 **Product Groups:** 20, 24, 63, 64

Karimjee Jivanjee & Co UK Ltd

Suite 41-44 Temple Chambers 3-7 Temple Avenue, London, EC4Y 0DA
Tel: 020-7583 3768 **Fax:** 020-7583 3916
E-mail: carol@karimjee.com
Website: http://www.karimjee.com
Directors: S. Karimjee (Co Sec), M. Currimjee (Dir), L. Karimjee (MD)
Immediate Holding Company: KARIMJEE JIVANJEE & CO.(U.K.)LIMITED
Registration no: 00701022 **Date established:** 1961 **Turnover:** £2m - £5m
No.of Employees: 1 - 10 **Product Groups:** 61

Date of Accounts	Dec 07	Dec 06	Dec 05
Sales Turnover	4959	5545	5184
Pre Tax Profit/Loss	-49	-141	50
Working Capital	348	362	359
Fixed Assets	17	19	40
Current Assets	3332	3687	2398
Current Liabilities	2984	3325	2039
Total Share Capital	199	199	199
ROCE% (Return on Capital Employed)	-13.4	-36.9	12.4
ROT% (Return on Turnover)	-1.0	-2.5	1.0

S Karir & Sons Ltd

2 Brick Lane, London, E1 6RF
Tel: 020-7247 7762 **Fax:** 020-7375 0980
E-mail: info@skarir.com
Directors: R. Karir (MD)
Immediate Holding Company: S. KARIR & SONS LIMITED
Registration no: 01359801 **VAT No.:** GB 249 8633 17
Date established: 1978 **Turnover:** £2m - £5m **No.of Employees:** 1 - 10
Product Groups: 63

Date of Accounts	May 11	May 10	May 09
Working Capital	662	585	540
Fixed Assets	34	43	4
Current Assets	2m	1m	1m

Kashket & Partners Ltd

35 Hoxton Square, London, N1 6NN
Tel: 020-8365 9350 **Fax:** 020-7729 0107
Website: http://www.kashket.net
Bank(s): National Westminster Bank Plc
Directors: P. Choi (Co Sec), R. Kashket (Dir)
Managers: M. Kashket (Safety)
Immediate Holding Company: KASHKET & PARTNERS LIMITED
Registration no: 00690853 **VAT No.:** GB 232 6847 57
Date established: 1961 **Turnover:** £500,000 - £1m
No.of Employees: 21 - 50 **Product Groups:** 24

Date of Accounts	Sep 10	Sep 09	Sep 08
Working Capital	505	148	-56
Fixed Assets	212	270	358
Current Assets	2m	1m	973

C J Kaye

22 Rheidol Mews, London, N1 8NU
Tel: 020-7226 5827 **Fax:** 020-7226 5827
E-mail: c.j.kaye@sky.com
Website: http://www.steel-fabricating.co.uk
Directors: B. Kaye (Ptnr)
Date established: 1969 **No.of Employees:** 1 - 10 **Product Groups:** 35

A T Kearney Ltd

Lansdowne House Berkeley Square, London, W1J 6ER
Tel: 020-7468 8000 **Fax:** 020-7468 8001
E-mail: london.reception@atkearney.com
Website: http://www.atkearney.com
Bank(s): Lloyds TSB Bank plc
Directors: S. Bevan (Pers), J. Dyall (Fin), S. Bevan (Pers)
Ultimate Holding Company: A.T. KEARNEY HOLDINGS LIMITED
Immediate Holding Company: A.T.KEARNEY LIMITED
Registration no: 00944763 **Date established:** 1968
Turnover: £20m - £50m **No.of Employees:** 101 - 250 **Product Groups:** 80

Date of Accounts	Dec 11	Dec 10	Dec 09
Sales Turnover	42m	43m	41m
Pre Tax Profit/Loss	-9m	1m	123
Working Capital	12m	17m	17m
Fixed Assets	918	998	723
Current Assets	36m	41m	38m
Current Liabilities	14m	15m	10m

Kedge & Quince

45 Wimpole Street, London, W1G 8SB
Tel: 020-7935 0136 **Fax:** 020-7224 5371
E-mail: kandq@cavendishimaging.com
Directors: M. Kedge (Ptnr)
Immediate Holding Company: PRECISION ORTHOPAEDICS LIMITED
Date established: 2011 **No.of Employees:** 1 - 10 **Product Groups:** 38, 67

Date of Accounts	Jul 11	Jul 10
Working Capital	-0	13
Fixed Assets	19	19
Current Assets	99	99

Kee Systems Ltd

11 Thornsett Road, London, SW18 4EW
Tel: 020-8874 6566 **Fax:** 020-8874 5726
E-mail: sales@keesystems.com
Website: http://www.keesystems.com
Managers: J. Glenwright (Sales Admin)
Ultimate Holding Company: KEE SAFETY GROUP LIMITED
Immediate Holding Company: KEE SYSTEMS LIMITED
Registration no: 02391277 **Date established:** 1989 **Turnover:** £1m - £2m
No.of Employees: 1 - 10 **Product Groups:** 36, 40

Date of Accounts	Dec 11	Dec 10	Dec 09
Working Capital	510	545	432
Fixed Assets	62	24	42
Current Assets	686	668	538

Kenkko Commodities plc

Kenkko House 8 Heriot Road, London, NW4 2DG
Tel: 020-8202 6600 **Fax:** 020-8202 5500
E-mail: orli@kenkko.com
Website: http://www.kenkko.com
Bank(s): Bank Leumi
Managers: O. Lang (Chief Mgr)
Immediate Holding Company: KENKKO COMMODITIES PLC
Registration no: 03794543 **VAT No.:** GB 743 7871 02
Date established: 1999 **Turnover:** £20m - £50m
No.of Employees: 11 - 20 **Product Groups:** 02, 20, 62

Date of Accounts	Oct 07
Sales Turnover	45m
Pre Tax Profit/Loss	-18
Working Capital	963
Fixed Assets	37
Current Assets	7m
Current Liabilities	355

Kenwood Travel Ltd

84 Great Eastern Street, London, EC2A 3JL
Tel: 020-7749 9220 **Fax:** 020-7749 7290
E-mail: info@kenwoodtravel.com
Website: http://www.kenwoodtravel.com
Directors: G. Koumi (MD)
Managers: L. Jordan (Mgr)
Immediate Holding Company: KENWOOD TRAVEL LIMITED
Registration no: 01300261 **VAT No.:** GB 606 0201 03
Date established: 1977 **Turnover:** £20m - £50m
No.of Employees: 11 - 20 **Product Groups:** 69

Date of Accounts	Mar 12	Mar 11	Mar 10
Sales Turnover	31m	21m	12m
Pre Tax Profit/Loss	390	237	143
Working Capital	1m	755	677
Fixed Assets	101	95	44
Current Assets	7m	5m	3m
Current Liabilities	158	141	89

Kerr Multilingual

41-42 Haven Green, London, W5 2NX
Tel: 020-8810 7839 **Fax:** 020-8998 0388
E-mail: info@kerr-recruitment.co.uk
Website: http://www.kerr-recruitment.co.uk
Directors: J. Enteghami Coulon (Dir)
Registration no: 02668058 **No.of Employees:** 1 - 10 **Product Groups:** 80

Kesslers International Ltd

11 Rick Roberts Way, London, E15 2NF
Tel: 020-8522 3000 **Fax:** 020-8522 3129
E-mail: john.anderson@kesslers.com
Website: http://www.kesslers.com
Bank(s): Barclays
Directors: A. Watson (Grp Chief Exec), G. Kessler (Dir), J. Anderson (Grp Chief Exec), W. Cochrane (Fin), W. Kessler (Ch), W. Cochrane (Dir)
Managers: C. Kessler (Sales Prom Mgr)
Immediate Holding Company: KESSLERS INTERNATIONAL LIMITED
Registration no: 01885833 **VAT No.:** GB 609 9859 79
Date established: 1985 **Turnover:** £10m - £20m
No.of Employees: 251 - 500 **Product Groups:** 26, 30, 49

Date of Accounts	Dec 07
Sales Turnover	21100
Pre Tax Profit/Loss	320
Working Capital	2270
Fixed Assets	14130
Current Assets	16580
Current Liabilities	14310
Total Share Capital	900
ROCE% (Return on Capital Employed)	2.0

Ketchum Pleon

35-41 Folgate Street, London, E1 6BX
Tel: 020-7611 3500 **Fax:** 020-7611 3501
E-mail: david.gallagher@ketchum.com
Website: http://www.ketchum.com
Directors: G. Cooper (Fin)
Managers: K. Mellows (Personnel), A. Lee, C. Malah (Tech Serv Mgr)
Ultimate Holding Company: OMNICOM GROUP INC (USA)
Immediate Holding Company: KETCHUM PLEON LIMITED
Registration no: 01733060 **Date established:** 1983
Turnover: £10m - £20m **No.of Employees:** 101 - 250 **Product Groups:** 81

Date of Accounts	Dec 11	Dec 10	Dec 09
Sales Turnover	19m	17m	17m
Pre Tax Profit/Loss	4m	3m	2m
Working Capital	3m	3m	3m
Fixed Assets	615	755	882
Current Assets	18m	17m	16m
Current Liabilities	7m	6m	4m

Ketech Systems Ltd

124-128 City Road, London, EC1V 2NJ
Tel: 0115-900 5600 **Fax:** 0115-900 5601
E-mail: info@ketech.com
Website: http://www.ketech.com
Bank(s): National Westminster Bank Plc
Directors: H. Haynes (Pers)
Managers: T. Shaw (Buyer), S. Berg, K. Dimarline, G. Dudey (Tech Serv Mgr)
Ultimate Holding Company: KETECH GROUP LTD
Immediate Holding Company: KETECH SYSTEMS LIMITED
Registration no: 05064341 **Date established:** 2004 **Turnover:** £5m - £10m
No.of Employees: 101 - 250 **Product Groups:** 37, 38

Date of Accounts	Aug 11	Aug 10	Aug 09
Sales Turnover	7m	6m	6m
Pre Tax Profit/Loss	26	694	-748
Working Capital	452	619	-673
Fixed Assets	56	N/A	28
Current Assets	2m	2m	2m
Current Liabilities	500	421	2m

Key Catering plc

Thames House Eastbury Road, London, E6 6GP
Tel: 020-7511 4100 **Fax:** 020-7511 0417
E-mail: ray.stacey@keycatering.co.uk
Website: http://www.keycatering.co.uk
Bank(s): National Westminster Bank Plc

see next page

Key Catering plc - *Cont'd*

Directors: K. Stacey (Mkt Research), R. Stacey (MD)
Ultimate Holding Company: KEY CATERING HOLDINGS LIMITED
Immediate Holding Company: KEY CATERING PLC
Registration no: 01235023 **VAT No.:** GB 221 9777 50
Date established: 1975 **Turnover:** £10m - £20m
No.of Employees: 101 - 250 **Product Groups:** 49, 67

Date of Accounts	May 11	May 10	Nov 08
Sales Turnover	16m	27m	21m
Pre Tax Profit/Loss	23	-2m	-307
Working Capital	505	530	3m
Fixed Assets	6m	6m	6m
Current Assets	5m	5m	7m
Current Liabilities	1m	250	435

Keysigns Signs & Nameplates

21 Woodside Green, London, SE25 5EY
Tel: 020-8676 1110 **Fax:** 020- 86565588
E-mail: janice.collins@btopenworld.com
Directors: J. Collins (Prop)
Date established: 2003 **No.of Employees:** 1 - 10 **Product Groups:** 30, 39, 40

Keystone

272-276 Pentonville Road, London, N1 9JY
Tel: 020-7837 6444 **Fax:** 020-7833 7783
E-mail: francis@keystone-recruitment.co.uk
Website: http://www.keystone-house.com
Directors: R. Norris (MD)
Managers: A. Mears (Mgr)
Immediate Holding Company: C & C RECYCLING LIMITED
Registration no: 01035412 **Date established:** 1996 **Turnover:** £2m - £5m
No.of Employees: 1 - 10 **Product Groups:** 80

Keyworks Locksmiths Services

20 Byegrove Road, London, SW19 2AY
Tel: 07812-008629
E-mail: admin@keyworkslocksmithing.uktc.com
Website: http://www.locksmiths-london.org.uk
Directors: S. Western (Prop)
Date established: 2005 **Turnover:** Up to £250,000
No.of Employees: 1 - 10 **Product Groups:** 52

Khiara International Agencies Ltd

29 Poland Street, London, W1F 8QR
Tel: 020-7437 2171 **Fax:** 020-7437 0534
E-mail: donald.mascarenhas@khiara.com
Website: http://www.khiara.com
Directors: D. Mascarenhas (Dir)
Immediate Holding Company: KHIARA TRADING CO. LTD
Registration no: 05107216 **VAT No.:** GB 242 9624 55
Date established: 2004 **Turnover:** £1m - £2m **No.of Employees:** 1 - 10
Product Groups: 61

Kiddy & Partners Llp

Ariel House 74a Charlotte Street, London, W1T 4QH
Tel: 020-7486 6867 **Fax:** 020-7486 6863
E-mail: info@kpl.co.uk
Website: http://www.kiddyandpartners.com
Directors: S. Brittain (Dir)
Immediate Holding Company: KIDDY AND PARTNERS LLP
Registration no: OC325582 **VAT No.:** GB 567 7875 69
Date established: 2007 **Turnover:** Up to £250,000
No.of Employees: 1 - 10 **Product Groups:** 86

Date of Accounts	Feb 12	Feb 11	Feb 10
Working Capital	619	1m	1m
Fixed Assets	28	47	6
Current Assets	1m	1m	1m

Kimbo UK Ltd

10 Barley Mow Passage, London, W4 4PH
Tel: 020-8743 8959 **Fax:** 020-8743 4929
E-mail: sales@kimbo.co.uk
Website: http://www.kimbo.co.uk
Directors: A. Mckenzie (MD)
Immediate Holding Company: KIMBO UK LTD.
Registration no: 02603850 **VAT No.:** GB 538 7957 82
Date established: 1991 **Turnover:** £2m - £5m **No.of Employees:** 1 - 10
Product Groups: 20, 62

Date of Accounts	Dec 11	Dec 10	Dec 09
Working Capital	245	441	-841
Fixed Assets	109	108	109
Current Assets	451	597	576

King Builders

Golders Way, London, NW11 8JX
Tel: 0800-1182206 **Fax:** 020-8731 6678
E-mail: info@kingbuilders.com
Website: http://www.kingbuilders.co.uk
Managers: S. Haiamlam (Mgr), J. Balance (Consultant)
Registration no: 05585011 **Date established:** 1998 **Turnover:** £2m - £5m
No.of Employees: 21 - 50 **Product Groups:** 25

King Sturge LLP

30 Warwick Street, London, W1B 5NH
Tel: 020-7493 4933 **Fax:** 020-7087 5555
E-mail: contactus@kingsturge.com
Website: http://www.kingsturge.co.uk
Bank(s): Lloyds TSB Bank plc
Directors: C. Hall (Ptnr), C. Island (Snr Part), P. Bache (MD)
Immediate Holding Company: WARWICK STREET (KS) LLP
Registration no: OC311501 **Date established:** 2005
Turnover: £75m - £125m **No.of Employees:** 251 - 500
Product Groups: 61, 80, 82

Kinleigh Folkard & Hayward Ltd

298 Upper Street, London, N1 2TU
Tel: 020-3441 3419 **Fax:** 020-7354 9725
E-mail: sis@kfh.co.uk
Website: http://www.kfh.co.uk
Directors: L. Watts (MD), A. Townend (Fin)
Managers: T. Steer (District Mgr), T. Steer (Mgr), T. Statham (Mgr)
Ultimate Holding Company: KINLEIGH LIMITED
Immediate Holding Company: KINLEIGH FOLKARD & HAYWARD LIMITED
Registration no: 02965708 **Date established:** 1994
Turnover: £10m - £20m **No.of Employees:** 11 - 20 **Product Groups:** 80

Date of Accounts	Dec 10	Dec 09	Mar 09
Sales Turnover	3m	2m	3m
Pre Tax Profit/Loss	-8	126	-895
Working Capital	-1m	-1m	-1m
Fixed Assets	36	40	51
Current Assets	503	326	495
Current Liabilities	593	603	713

Kinnerton Confectionery Co. Ltd

53-79 Highgate Road, London, NW5 1TL
Tel: 020-7284 9500 **Fax:** 020-7248 9501
E-mail: info@kinnerton.com
Website: http://www.kinnerton.com
Directors: D. Clack (Dir), R. Wyatt (Mkt Research), M. Clark (Fin)
Managers: M. Davies (Tech Serv Mgr), B. Davis, D. Hunter (Personnel)
Ultimate Holding Company: ZETAR PLC
Immediate Holding Company: KINNERTON (CONFECTIONERY) CO. LIMITED
Registration no: 01401107 **Date established:** 1978
Turnover: £50m - £75m **No.of Employees:** 501 - 1000
Product Groups: 20

Date of Accounts	Apr 11	Apr 12	May 09
Sales Turnover	71m	70m	59m
Pre Tax Profit/Loss	5m	3m	2m
Working Capital	-8m	-8m	-9m
Fixed Assets	19m	20m	16m
Current Assets	22m	18m	24m
Current Liabilities	10m	5m	7m

Kiril Mischeff Ltd

Broadwall House 21 Broadwall, London, SE1 9PL
Tel: 020-8946 2852 **Fax:** 020-7261 9085
Website: http://www.kiril-mischeff.com
Directors: A. Dent (MD)
Ultimate Holding Company: KIRIL MISCHEFF (TRADING) LIMITED
Immediate Holding Company: KIRIL MISCHEFF LIMITED
Registration no: 00250446 **VAT No.:** GB 235 6543 59
Date established: 1930 **Turnover:** £75m - £125m
No.of Employees: 51 - 100 **Product Groups:** 61

Date of Accounts	Sep 11	Sep 10	Sep 09
Sales Turnover	97m	87m	86m
Pre Tax Profit/Loss	586	717	466
Working Capital	2m	2m	965
Fixed Assets	3m	3m	3m
Current Assets	24m	19m	18m
Current Liabilities	4m	5m	3m

Kirill photography

Flat 2A Enterprise House, Tudor Grove, London, E9 7QL
Tel: 07514-270 904
E-mail: mail@kirill.co.uk
Website: http://www.kirill.co.uk
Registration no: 07488174 **Product Groups:** 28, 38, 64, 65, 81

Kirkby Computing Services Ltd

68 Horn Lane Acton, London, W3 6NT
Tel: 07976-852553
E-mail: kirkby@kirkbycomputing.co.uk
Directors: G. McAllister (Co Sec), G. Mcallister (Dir)
Immediate Holding Company: KIRKBY COMPUTING SERVICES LIMITED
Registration no: 02558427 **Date established:** 1990
No.of Employees: 1 - 10 **Product Groups:** 44, 81

Date of Accounts	Nov 11	Nov 10	Nov 09
Working Capital	123	107	106
Fixed Assets	N/A	N/A	1
Current Assets	155	135	133

Kitchen La Frenais Morgan

Langham House 302-308 Regent Street, London, W1B 3AT
Tel: 020-7317 3700 **Fax:** 020-7499 2476
E-mail: dsmith@klmproperty.co.uk
Website: http://www.klmproperty.co.uk
Directors: N. Morgan (Ptnr)
Managers: D. Smith (Mgr)
Immediate Holding Company: KITCHEN LA FRENAIS MORGAN LLP
Registration no: OC305406 **Date established:** 2003 **Turnover:** £2m - £5m
No.of Employees: 11 - 20 **Product Groups:** 80

Date of Accounts	Apr 11	Apr 10	Apr 09
Sales Turnover	N/A	N/A	2m
Pre Tax Profit/Loss	N/A	N/A	996
Working Capital	3m	2m	2m
Fixed Assets	190	129	137
Current Assets	3m	2m	2m
Current Liabilities	N/A	N/A	34

The Knife Sharpening Company

5 Henryson Road, London, SE4 1HL
Tel: 020-8690 5163 **Fax:** 020-8690 5163
E-mail: info@knifesharpeningcompany.com
Website: http://www.knifesharpeningcompany.com
Directors: C. Beltrami (Prop)
Date established: 1953 **Turnover:** £250,000 - £500,000
No.of Employees: 1 - 10 **Product Groups:** 48

Knight Frank

55 Baker Street, London, W1U 8AN
Tel: 020-7629 8171 **Fax:** 020-7493 4114
E-mail: hotels@knightfrank.com
Website: http://www.knightfrank.com
Directors: N. Thomlinson (Snr Part)
Ultimate Holding Company: KNIGHT FRANK LLP
Immediate Holding Company: KNIGHT FRANK (SP) LLP
Registration no: OC343254 **VAT No.:** GB 238 5156 53
Date established: 2009 **Turnover:** £250m - £500m
No.of Employees: 501 - 1000 **Product Groups:** 80, 82, 84

Knowledgewire Systems

4 Grosvenor Place, London, SW1X 7HJ
Tel: 0845-0945669 **Fax:** 020-7823 2602
E-mail: info@knowledgewire.co.uk
Website: http://www.KnowledgeWire.co.uk
Managers: P. Nsiah (Mktg Serv Mgr)
Registration no: 05173579 **Date established:** 2004
Turnover: £250,000 - £500,000 **No.of Employees:** 1 - 10
Product Groups: 44, 80

Kogan Page Ltd

120 Pentonville Road, London, N1 9JN
Tel: 020-7278 0433 **Fax:** 020-7837 6348
E-mail: hkogan@koganpage.com
Website: http://www.koganpage.com
Bank(s): Barclays, The Strand, London WC2
Directors: M. Briars (Fin), H. Kogan (MD)
Managers: C. Frazer (Mktg Serv Mgr)
Ultimate Holding Company: KOGAN PAGE LIMITED
Immediate Holding Company: KOGAN PAGE COMMUNICATIONS LIMITED
Registration no: 04339913 **VAT No.:** GB 417 8457 28
Date established: 2001 **Turnover:** £250,000 - £500,000
No.of Employees: 21 - 50 **Product Groups:** 28, 64

Date of Accounts	Jun 11	Jun 10	Jun 09
Sales Turnover	333	992	1m
Pre Tax Profit/Loss	-148	-50	21
Working Capital	-133	15	54
Current Assets	276	553	679
Current Liabilities	236	187	317

Kone Lifts Ltd

Unit 1 Gemini Business Park South Crescent, London, E16 4TL
Tel: 020-7474 0150 **Fax:** 020-7474 0102
Website: http://www.kone.com
Directors: K. Dwyer (Pers), S. Rich (Tech Serv), G. Loty (Fin), S. Dow (Mkt Research)
Managers: M. Rainford (Purch Mgr)
No.of Employees: 21 - 50 **Product Groups:** 35, 39, 45

Korea Trade

Brettenham House Lancaster Place, London, WC2E 7EN
Tel: 020-7520 5300 **Fax:** 020-7240 2367
E-mail: kotra@kotra.co.uk
Website: http://www.kotra.co.uk
Managers: J. Jeng
Immediate Holding Company: ECI PARTNERS LLP
Registration no: 02384442 **Date established:** 2002
No.of Employees: 11 - 20 **Product Groups:** 87

Date of Accounts	Dec 11	Dec 10	Dec 09
Sales Turnover	1m	4m	N/A
Pre Tax Profit/Loss	1m	4m	4m
Working Capital	-4m	-4m	-5m
Fixed Assets	5m	5m	5m
Current Assets	104	349	98
Current Liabilities	92	94	92

KT Technology

5 Percy Street Office 4, London, W1T 1BG
Tel: 020-7193 2740
E-mail: sales@kioskterminals.co.uk
Website: http://www.kioskterminals.co.uk
Managers: K. Larsen (Chief Mgr)
Date established: 2005 **Turnover:** £1m - £2m **No.of Employees:** 1 - 10
Product Groups: 35

Kvadrat Ltd

10, Shepherdess Walk, London, N1 7LB
Tel: 020-7324 5555 **Fax:** 020-7324 5544
E-mail: uk@kvadrat.org
Website: http://www.kvadrat.dk
Directors: N. Kemp (MD)
Ultimate Holding Company: KVADRAT HOLDINGS AS (DENMARK)
Registration no: 02084887 **Date established:** 2003 **Turnover:** £1m - £2m
No.of Employees: 11 - 20 **Product Groups:** 61

Date of Accounts	Dec 09	Dec 08	Dec 07
Sales Turnover	N/A	5m	5m
Pre Tax Profit/Loss	N/A	326	402
Working Capital	332	434	477
Fixed Assets	64	N/A	N/A
Current Assets	1m	951	947
Current Liabilities	N/A	325	263

Kysen P R

22 Long Acre Covent Garden, London, WC2E 9LY
Tel: 020-7323 3230 **Fax:** 020-7436 9103
E-mail: info@kysen.com
Website: http://www.kysenpr.co.uk
Directors: C. Rodway (MD)
Ultimate Holding Company: HEATH STREET LIMITED
Immediate Holding Company: REDBUS RETAIL ADVERTISING LIMITED
Registration no: 03755589 **Date established:** 2009
Turnover: £500,000 - £1m **No.of Employees:** 1 - 10 **Product Groups:** 81

L C H Clearnet Group Ltd

Aldgate House 33 Aldgate High Street, London, EC3N 1EA
Tel: 020-7426 7000 **Fax:** 020-7426 7011
E-mail: roger.liddell@lchclearnet.com
Website: http://www.lchclearnet.com
Bank(s): HSBC
Directors: S. Ward (Co Sec)
Managers: R. Liddell
Immediate Holding Company: LCH.CLEARNET GROUP LIMITED
Registration no: 04743602 **Date established:** 2003
Turnover: £250m - £500m **No.of Employees:** 501 - 1000
Product Groups: 87

Date of Accounts	Dec 08	Dec 07	Dec 06
Sales Turnover	570m	500m	790m
Pre Tax Profit/Loss	300m	260m	180m
Working Capital	1910m	1950m	2170m
Fixed Assets	560m	540m	560m
Current Liabilities	354630m	292970m	271380m
Total Share Capital	70m	80m	100m

L.N. E-Consulting Ltd

Flat 12 16 Carlton Drive, Putney, London, SW15 2BDÂ
Tel: 07939-325816
E-mail: info@webservicesconsultancy.com
Website: http://www.webservicesconsultancy.com
Directors: L. Nicoletta (Admin)
Registration no: 07239206 **Date established:** 2010 **Turnover:**
No.of Employees: Unknown **Product Groups:** 44, 86

La Maison des Sorbets Foods Ltd

Unit 10 Gateway Industrial Estate Hythe Road, London, NW10 6RJ
Tel: 020-8968 0707 **Fax:** 020-8960 1332
E-mail: sales@lmdsfoods.com
Website: http://www.lamaisondessorbets.com

Directors: T. Hilder (Dir)
Ultimate Holding Company: ACTFARM LIMITED
Immediate Holding Company: LA MAISON DES SORBETS FOODS LIMITED
Registration no: 02940485 **Date established:** 1994
Turnover: £500,000 - £1m **No.of Employees:** 21 - 50 **Product Groups:** 20

Date of Accounts	Jul 11	Jul 10	Jul 09
Sales Turnover	N/A	902	1m
Pre Tax Profit/Loss	N/A	18	-99
Working Capital	52	99	87
Fixed Assets	52	72	94
Current Assets	226	222	215
Current Liabilities	N/A	72	56

La Porcellana Tableware International Ltd

1 Somers Place, London, SW2 2AL
Tel: 020-8671 5959 **Fax:** 020-8671 5956
E-mail: info@laporcellana.co.uk
Website: http://www.laporcellana.co.uk
Directors: P. Costa (MD)
Immediate Holding Company: LA PORCELLANA LIMITED
Registration no: 01465935 **Date established:** 1979 **Turnover:** £2m - £5m
No.of Employees: 11 - 20 **Product Groups:** 33, 36, 40, 49, 62, 63, 65, 67

Date of Accounts	Mar 11	Mar 10	Mar 09
Working Capital	392	265	240
Fixed Assets	26	31	38
Current Assets	666	655	593

Ladybird Books Ltd

80 Strand, London, WC2R 0RL
Tel: 0845-313 4444 **Fax:** 020-8757 4099
E-mail: ladybird@uk.penguingroup.com
Website: http://www.ladybird.co.uk
Bank(s): HSBC Bank plc
Directors: P. Mayer (Ch), A. Forbes Watson (Ch), W. Howarth (Fin)
Managers: D. Collington (Purch Mgr), C. Sanderson (Sales Prom Mgr)
Ultimate Holding Company: Pearson P.L.C.
Immediate Holding Company: Penguin Books
Registration no: 00200130 **VAT No.:** GB 114 0688 91
Turnover: £10m - £20m **Product Groups:** 28, 64

Date of Accounts	Dec 09	Dec 08	Dec 07
Sales Turnover	12m	10m	10m
Pre Tax Profit/Loss	1m	-794	92
Working Capital	-4m	-5m	-5m
Fixed Assets	N/A	N/A	233
Current Assets	2m	2m	4m
Current Liabilities	70	N/A	N/A

Lalou Ltd

Gas Works The Depot Unit C3, London, SW6 2AD
Tel: 020-7736 0030
Website: http://www.la-lou.com
Directors: T. Von Sethe (Fin)
Immediate Holding Company: LALOU LIMITED
Registration no: 06250598 **Date established:** 2007
No.of Employees: 1 - 10 **Product Groups:** 37, 67

Date of Accounts	May 11	May 10	May 09
Working Capital	120	68	70
Fixed Assets	1	1	2
Current Assets	120	70	110
Current Liabilities	1	2	10

M Lamb Fixing

Railway Arch 58 Cambridge Grove, London, W6 0LD
Tel: 020-8748 8983
Directors: M. Lamb (Prop)
Date established: 1977 **No.of Employees:** 1 - 10 **Product Groups:** 26, 35

Lambeth Scientific Services Ltd

Rear of 26 Wanless Road, London, SE24 0HW
Tel: 020-7737 1111 **Fax:** 020-7926 8882
E-mail: info@scientificservices.co.uk
Website: http://www.scientificservices.co.uk
Directors: K. Sallows (Co Sec), C. Samasuwo (Dir)
Immediate Holding Company: LAMBETH SCIENTIFIC SERVICES LIMITED
Registration no: 03493325 **Date established:** 1998
Turnover: £250,000 - £500,000 **No.of Employees:** 1 - 10
Product Groups: 54

Date of Accounts	Dec 11	Dec 10	Dec 09
Working Capital	11	2	13
Fixed Assets	14	5	2
Current Assets	75	53	68

Land Securities Business Services Ltd

5 Strand, London, WC2N 5HR
Tel: 020-7024 5000 **Fax:** 020-792 0202
E-mail: landsecurities@landsecurities.com
Website: http://www.landsecurities.com
Bank(s): Lloyds TSB Bank plc
Directors: P. Dudgeon (Co Sec), F. Solway (Grp Chief Exec)
Managers: T. Foulk (Mktg Serv Mgr), N. Foster (I.T. Exec)
Immediate Holding Company: LAND SECURITIES BUSINESS SERVICES LIMITED
Registration no: 04936226 **Date established:** 2003
Turnover: £500m - £1,000m **No.of Employees:** 251 - 500
Product Groups: 80

Land Security

5 Strand, London, WC2N 5AS
Tel: 020-7413 9000 **Fax:** 020-7925 0202
E-mail: investor.relations@landsecurities.com
Website: http://www.landsecurity.com
Directors: M. Greenslade (Fin)
Managers: J. Titford (Personnel), P. Gombera, F. Solway, C. O'Donnell, C. Thomas
Ultimate Holding Company: LAND SECURITIES GROUP PLC
Immediate Holding Company: LAND SECURITIES (INSURANCE SERVICES) LIMITED
Registration no: 00551412 **VAT No.:** GB 243 1537 84
Date established: 2001 **Turnover:** Up to £250,000
No.of Employees: 251 - 500 **Product Groups:** 82, 85

Date of Accounts	Mar 06	Mar 05	Mar 04
Working Capital	10	N/A	N/A
Current Assets	10	N/A	N/A

Landauer Ltd

25 Beaufort Court Admirals Way, London, E14 9XL
Tel: 020-7538 5383 **Fax:** 020-7538 2007
E-mail: trading@landauerseafood.com
Website: http://www.landauergroup.co.uk
Bank(s): Brown Shipley & Co. Ltd
Directors: S. Ryle (MD), A. Georgiou (Fin), S. Brown (Dir)
Managers: D. Lipman-collins (Personnel)
Ultimate Holding Company: WESTINDIA AB (SWEDEN)
Immediate Holding Company: LANDAUER LIMITED
Registration no: 01714846 **VAT No.:** GB 549 2601 36
Date established: 1983 **Turnover:** £75m - £125m
No.of Employees: 11 - 20 **Product Groups:** 02, 09, 20, 23, 32, 62, 66

Date of Accounts	Dec 11	Dec 10	Dec 09
Sales Turnover	101m	86m	76m
Pre Tax Profit/Loss	1m	2m	1m
Working Capital	6m	6m	6m
Fixed Assets	772	796	807
Current Assets	34m	32m	22m
Current Liabilities	2m	2m	2m

Landor Associates

Level 7 2 More London Riverside, London, SE1 2AP
Tel: 020-7880 8000 **Fax:** 020-7880 8001
E-mail: london.reception@landor.com
Website: http://www.landor.com
Directors: C. Sweetland (Dir), T. Bihl (Fin)
Managers: A. Derbyshire (Personnel)
Ultimate Holding Company: WPP 2008 LIMITED
Immediate Holding Company: LANDOR ASSOCIATES EUROPE LTD
Registration no: 01797828 **Date established:** 1984
No.of Employees: 51 - 100 **Product Groups:** 84

Langford & Hill Ltd

Unit 17 Kings Exchange Tileyard Road, London, N7 9AH
Tel: 020-7619 0527 **Fax:** 020-7619 9856
E-mail: keith@langfordhill.co.uk
Website: http://www.langfordandhill.com
Bank(s): Robert Fleming & Co. Ltd
Directors: K. Lockwood (Fin)
Managers: D. Harrison (I.T. Exec), J. Newton (Sales Prom Mgr), K. Lockwood (Chief Mgr)
Immediate Holding Company: LANGFORD AND HILL LIMITED
Registration no: 00513989 **VAT No.:** GB 239 8620 33
Date established: 1952 **Turnover:** £1m - £2m **No.of Employees:** 11 - 20
Product Groups: 64, 67

Date of Accounts	Feb 08	Feb 07	Feb 06
Working Capital	573	568	584
Fixed Assets	3	6	7
Current Assets	838	860	876
Current Liabilities	265	292	292
Total Share Capital	180	180	180

Language Direct

90 Matlock Road, London, E10 6DJ
Tel: 020-8539 5142 **Fax:** 020-8539 9588
E-mail: info@languagedirect.org
Website: http://www.languagedirect.org
Managers: H. James (Mgr)
Date established: 1998 **No.of Employees:** 1 - 10 **Product Groups:** 80

Laryngograph Ltd

Laryngograph Limited 1 Foundry Mews, Tolmers Square, London, NW1 2PR
Tel: 020-7387 7793 **Fax:** 020-7383 2039
E-mail: sales@laryngograph.com
Website: http://www.laryngograph.com
Directors: A. Fourcin (MD)
Managers: X. Hu (Snr Eng)
Immediate Holding Company: LARYNGOGRAPH LIMITED
Registration no: 01135704 **VAT No.:** GB 209 0804 84
Date established: 1973 **Turnover:** Up to £250,000
No.of Employees: 1 - 10 **Product Groups:** 28, 37, 38, 88

Date of Accounts	Dec 11	Dec 10	Dec 09
Sales Turnover	233	294	283
Pre Tax Profit/Loss	-22	6	-4
Working Capital	423	441	435
Fixed Assets	3	1	1
Current Assets	430	447	442
Current Liabilities	3	5	3

Laser Kilns Ltd

Unit C9 Angel Road Works Advent Way, London, N18 3AH
Tel: 020-8803 1016 **Fax:** 020-8807 2888
E-mail: info@laser-kiln.co.uk
Website: http://www.laser-kilns.co.uk
Directors: S. Burton (Co Sec), R. Jackson (Dir), R. Jackson (MD)
Immediate Holding Company: LASER KILNS LIMITED
Registration no: 01542719 **Date established:** 1981
Turnover: £250,000 - £500,000 **No.of Employees:** 1 - 10
Product Groups: 38, 40, 45

Date of Accounts	Jan 09	Jan 08	Jan 07
Working Capital	299	295	281
Fixed Assets	105	108	111
Current Assets	380	344	429
Current Liabilities	81	49	148

Laser Life plc

Excelda House 15 Tennis Street, London, SE1 1YD
Tel: 020-7403 6866 **Fax:** 01638-560305
E-mail: sales@laserlife.co.uk
Website: http://www.laserlife.co.uk
Directors: R. Parncutt (MD), C. Hancock (Fin), C. Mather (MD)
Managers: C. Brown, R. Bauer (Tech Serv Mgr), R. Baubr (I.T. Exec), M. Martin, N. Crayer (Personnel), P. Skinner
Ultimate Holding Company: LAZERTRONIC HOLDINGS LTD (GIBRALTER)
Immediate Holding Company: VITESSE PLC
Registration no: 02960035 **Date established:** 1994
No.of Employees: 11 - 20 **Product Groups:** 44

Latch & Batchelor Ltd

104 Clarence Road, London, E12 5BH
Tel: 020-8478 8000 **Fax:** 020-8514 8525
E-mail: slongden@latchandbatchelor.co.uk
Website: http://www.latchandbatchelor.co.uk
Managers: S. Longden (Mgr)
Ultimate Holding Company: LATCH & BATCHELOR (HOLDINGS) LIMITED
Immediate Holding Company: LATCH & BATCHELOR LIMITED
Registration no: 00541289 **Date established:** 1954
No.of Employees: 1 - 10 **Product Groups:** 35, 39, 45

Date of Accounts	Dec 10	Dec 07	Dec 08
Working Capital	524	521	394
Fixed Assets	17	90	234
Current Assets	2m	2m	2m

Lavery Rowe Advertising Ltd

69-71 Newington Causeway, London, SE1 6BD
Tel: 020-7378 1780 **Fax:** 020-7407 4612
E-mail: sales@laveryrowe.co.uk
Website: http://www.laveryrowe.com
Directors: N. Rowe (MD)
Immediate Holding Company: LAVERY ROWE ADVERTISING LIMITED
Registration no: 01481734 **Date established:** 1980
Turnover: £10m - £20m **No.of Employees:** 21 - 50 **Product Groups:** 81

Date of Accounts	Dec 11	Dec 10	Dec 09
Sales Turnover	16m	19m	13m
Pre Tax Profit/Loss	352	243	78
Working Capital	302	376	268
Fixed Assets	638	651	632
Current Assets	3m	4m	3m
Current Liabilities	210	287	112

Law Debenture Corporation

100 Wood Street, London, EC2V 7EX
Tel: 020-7606 5451 **Fax:** 020-7606 0643
E-mail: general@lawdeb.co.uk
Website: http://www.lawdeb.co.uk
Directors: C. Banszky (Grp Chief Exec)
Immediate Holding Company: LAW DEBENTURE CORPORATION PLC(THE)
Registration no: 00030397 **VAT No.:** GB 244 0063 05
Date established: 1989 **Turnover:** £20m - £50m
No.of Employees: 51 - 100 **Product Groups:** 80, 82

Date of Accounts	Dec 11	Dec 10	Dec 09
Sales Turnover	46m	43m	47m
Pre Tax Profit/Loss	-2m	86m	91m
Working Capital	12m	13m	13m
Fixed Assets	427m	445m	377m
Current Assets	29m	31m	27m
Current Liabilities	6m	17m	6m

Lawrence Graham Solicitors

4 More London Riverside, London, SE1 2AU
Tel: 020-7379 0000 **Fax:** 020-7379 6854
E-mail: info@lg-legal.com
Website: http://www.lg-legal.com
Directors: A. Wittes (Snr Part), K. Rae (Fin)
Ultimate Holding Company: LAWRENCE GRAHAM LLP
Immediate Holding Company: LAWRENCE GRAHAM TRUST CORPORATION
Registration no: 02209819 **Date established:** 1988
Turnover: Up to £250,000 **No.of Employees:** 501 - 1000
Product Groups: 80

Date of Accounts	Apr 94	Apr 93	Apr 92
Working Capital	100	100	N/A
Current Assets	100	100	100

Lawsons Whetstone Ltd

1208 High Road, London, N20 0LL
Tel: 020-8446 1321 **Fax:** 020-8446 2509
E-mail: info@lawsons.co.uk
Website: http://www.lawsons.co.uk
Bank(s): Barclays
Managers: M. Salmon (District Mgr)
Immediate Holding Company: LAWSONS (WHETSTONE) LIMITED
Registration no: 02790259 **VAT No.:** GB 626 4271 45
Date established: 1993 **Turnover:** £5m - £10m **No.of Employees:** 21 - 50
Product Groups: 25, 35, 52, 66

Date of Accounts	Jun 12	Jun 11	Jun 10
Sales Turnover	51m	48m	41m
Pre Tax Profit/Loss	4m	3m	2m
Working Capital	7m	8m	2m
Fixed Assets	4m	3m	6m
Current Assets	16m	16m	11m
Current Liabilities	2m	2m	2m

Laytons Wine Merchants Ltd

7 9 Elliotts Place, London, N1 8HX
Tel: 020-7288 8888 **Fax:** 020-7359 2616
E-mail: tradesales@laytons.co.uk
Website: http://www.laytons.co.uk
Managers: T. Turner
Ultimate Holding Company: JEROBOAMS LIMITED
Immediate Holding Company: LAYTONS WINE MERCHANTS LIMITED
Registration no: 03315645 **VAT No.:** GB 696 6477 63
Date established: 1997 **Turnover:** £5m - £10m **No.of Employees:** 21 - 50
Product Groups: 21, 62

Date of Accounts	Mar 12	Mar 11	Mar 10
Sales Turnover	8m	8m	9m
Pre Tax Profit/Loss	115	165	379
Working Capital	-763	-913	-1m
Fixed Assets	360	396	432
Current Assets	2m	2m	3m
Current Liabilities	98	75	377

Le Mirage London Ltd

Unit 2 Glenville Mews Kimber Road Wandsworth, London, SW18 4NJ
Tel: 020-8870 2777 **Fax:** 020-8874 8181
E-mail: lemirageuk@btconnect.com
Website: http://www.lemiragecateringequip.co.uk
Directors: S. Amini (Prop)
Immediate Holding Company: LE MIRAGE (LONDON) LIMITED
Registration no: 06717534 **Date established:** 2008
No.of Employees: 1 - 10 **Product Groups:** 20, 40, 41

Date of Accounts	Oct 11	Oct 10	Oct 09
Working Capital	-17	-11	-4
Fixed Assets	17	9	12
Current Assets	128	91	103

Leadership Development Ltd

495 Fulham Road, London, SW6 1HH
Tel: 020-7381 6233 **Fax:** 020-7381 6917
E-mail: learning@ldl.co.uk
Website: http://www.ldl.co.uk
Directors: R. Fielder (Dir)
Ultimate Holding Company: LEADERSHIP DEVELOPMENT HOLDINGS LIMITED
Immediate Holding Company: LEADERSHIP DEVELOPMENT LIMITED
Registration no: 01411136 **Date established:** 1979 **Turnover:** £1m - £2m
No.of Employees: 21 - 50 **Product Groups:** 86

Date of Accounts	Dec 11	Dec 10	Dec 09
Sales Turnover	2m	2m	2m
Pre Tax Profit/Loss	-41	-101	-173

see next page

Leadership Development Ltd - Cont'd

Working Capital	535	579	878
Fixed Assets	45	45	66
Current Assets	1m	1m	1m
Current Liabilities	437	447	478

Leaper & Co.

8 Broadbent Close 20-22 Highgate High Street, London, N6 5JW
Tel: 020-8348 0035 **Fax:** 020-8348 4088
E-mail: leaperco@btconnect.com
Website: http://www.datadesk.co.uk
Directors: J. Leaper (Prop)
Immediate Holding Company: LEAPER & CO. LTD.
Registration no: 03287914 **Date established:** 1996
No.of Employees: 1 - 10 **Product Groups:** 35

Date of Accounts	Mar 12	Mar 11	Mar 10
Working Capital	-52	-49	-58
Fixed Assets	62	62	73
Current Assets	27	24	60

Leathams Ltd

227-255 Ilderton Road, London, SE15 1NS
Tel: 020-7635 4000 **Fax:** 020-7635 4040
E-mail: customerservice@merchant-gourmet.com
Website: http://www.leathams.co.uk
Directors: C. Moxham (Dir), D. Dunmore (Fin), T. Faulkner (Ch), A. Cherry (Purch)
Ultimate Holding Company: LEATHAMS HOLDINGS LTD
Immediate Holding Company: LEATHAMS LIMITED
Registration no: 01689381 **Date established:** 1982
Turnover: £50m - £75m **No.of Employees:** 101 - 250
Product Groups: 20, 61, 62, 69, 82

Date of Accounts	Apr 11	Apr 10	Apr 09
Sales Turnover	54m	49m	51m
Pre Tax Profit/Loss	3m	3m	3m
Working Capital	10m	7m	6m
Fixed Assets	4m	4m	4m
Current Assets	21m	17m	15m
Current Liabilities	6m	5m	5m

Ledrop Exports Ltd

251 Brompton Road, London, SW3 2EP
Tel: 020-7581 3188 **Fax:** 020-7589 9611
E-mail: mail@ledropexports.co.uk
Managers: H. Clift (Mgr)
Immediate Holding Company: LEDROP EXPORTS LIMITED
Registration no: 01228092 **Date established:** 1975 **Turnover:** £2m - £5m
No.of Employees: 1 - 10 **Product Groups:** 21, 61

Date of Accounts	Jul 11	Jul 10	Jul 09
Working Capital	1m	1m	1m
Fixed Assets	12	55	51
Current Assets	3m	2m	3m

Legal & General Group P.L.C. (Head Office) (Holding Company)

Temple Court 11 Queen Victoria Street, London, EC4N 4TP
Tel: 020-7528 6200 **Fax:** 020-7528 6222
Website: http://www.legalandgeneral.com
Directors: D. Prosser (Grp Chief Exec), G. Laming (Grp Sales), T. Breedon (Grp), E. Mclane (Pers)
Registration no: 01417162 **Turnover:** £75m - £125m
No.of Employees: 11 - 20 **Product Groups:** 44, 80, 82

Lejaby

28 Poland Street, London, W1F 8QW
Tel: 020-7478 4340 **Fax:** 020-7478 4350
E-mail: kmorgan@lejaby.com
Website: http://www.lejaby.com
Bank(s): National Westminster, 3 Thurland Street
Directors: P. Tavener (Sales)
Managers: B. Leca (Sales Prom Mgr), K. Morgan
Ultimate Holding Company: WARNERCO (U.S.A.)
Immediate Holding Company: WARNER EUROPE LTD
Registration no: 00005449 **No.of Employees:** 11 - 20 **Product Groups:** 63

Lendon Containers Ltd

60 Webb's Road, London, SW11 6SE
Tel: 020-7350 1940 **Fax:** 020-7350 1962
E-mail: enquiries@lcltd.co.uk
Website: http://www.lcltd.co.uk
Directors: L. Meaby (MD)
Immediate Holding Company: LENDON CONTAINERS LIMITED
Registration no: 03665325 **Date established:** 1998
Turnover: £500,000 - £1m **No.of Employees:** 1 - 10 **Product Groups:** 45, 48, 76

Date of Accounts	Mar 11	Mar 10	Mar 09
Sales Turnover	884	1m	1m
Pre Tax Profit/Loss	103	113	209
Working Capital	661	704	602
Fixed Assets	187	190	408
Current Assets	829	904	802
Current Liabilities	76	127	106

Lenlyn Ltd

47-48 Piccadilly, London, W1J 0LR
Tel: 020-7292 5400 **Fax:** 020-7287 4311
Website: http://www.iceplc.com
Directors: A. White (Co Sec), F. Tejani (MD), H. Tejani (Dir)
Ultimate Holding Company: LENLYN HOLDINGS PLC
Immediate Holding Company: LENLYN LIMITED
Registration no: 01140115 **Date established:** 1973
Turnover: £500m - £1,000m **No.of Employees:** 1 - 10
Product Groups: 81

Date of Accounts	Feb 12	Feb 11	Feb 10
Sales Turnover	82m	76m	87m
Pre Tax Profit/Loss	2m	2m	1m
Working Capital	2m	5m	11m
Fixed Assets	411	552	670
Current Assets	7m	6m	12m
Current Liabilities	407	446	326

The Letter Factory

48d Percy Road, London, N12 8BU
Tel: 020-8445 1616 **Fax:** 020-8445 1388
E-mail: christine.power@theletterfactory.co.uk
Website: http://www.theletterfactory.co.uk
Directors: C. Power (Prop), M. Summers (Prop)
VAT No.: GB 231 5685 68 **Date established:** 1976
Turnover: Up to £250,000 **No.of Employees:** 1 - 10 **Product Groups:** 80, 81

Leventis Overseas Ltd

West Africa House Ashbourne Road, Hanger Lane, London, W5 3QR
Tel: 020-8997 6651 **Fax:** 020-8997 2621
E-mail: foundation@leventis-overseas.com
Website: http://www.leventis-overseas.com
Bank(s): Barclays, 54 Lombard St, London EC3V 9EX
Directors: A. Adetona (Fin)
Managers: M. Tilling (Ops Mgr), R. Boddy (Chief Mgr), A. Courtnell (Purch Mgr), J. Cunningham
Immediate Holding Company: A.G.LEVENTIS (NIGERIA) PLC.
Registration no: FC004809 **VAT No.:** GB 226 6462 60
Date established: 1958 **Turnover:** Over £1,000m
No.of Employees: 11 - 20 **Product Groups:** 61, 62

Levy Gems Ltd

Minerva House 26-27 Hatton Garden, London, EC1N 8BR
Tel: 020-7242 4547 **Fax:** 020-7831 0102
E-mail: info@levygems.co.uk
Directors: D. Levy (Dir)
Immediate Holding Company: LEVY GEMS LIMITED
Registration no: 06452874 **VAT No.:** GB 233 0178 01
Date established: 2007 **Turnover:** £1m - £2m **No.of Employees:** 1 - 10
Product Groups: 49, 65

Date of Accounts	Mar 11	Mar 10	Mar 09
Working Capital	315	217	43
Fixed Assets	71	87	102
Current Assets	999	804	469

Lewis Direct Mail Ltd

433 Caledonian Road, London, N7 9BG
Tel: 020-7607 6505 **Fax:** 020-7607 0932
E-mail: eloane@ldm.co.uk
Website: http://www.ldm.co.uk
Bank(s): Lloyds TSB Bank plc
Directors: J. Phillips (MD), E. Loane (Prop), J. Philips (MD)
Managers: D. Foster (Chief Mgr)
Immediate Holding Company: LEWIS DIRECT MAIL MARKETING LIMITED
Registration no: 02256732 **VAT No.:** GB 505 9722 41
Date established: 1988 **Turnover:** £2m - £5m **No.of Employees:** 21 - 50
Product Groups: 28, 44, 81

R G Lewis Ltd

29 Southampton Row, London, WC1B 5HL
Tel: 020-7242 2916 **Fax:** 020-7831 4062
E-mail: sales@rglewis.co.uk
Website: http://www.rglewis.co.uk
Directors: L. Lyons (MD)
Immediate Holding Company: R.G.LEWIS LIMITED
Registration no: 01763557 **Date established:** 1983
Turnover: £250,000 - £500,000 **No.of Employees:** 1 - 10
Product Groups: 81

Date of Accounts	Jul 11	Jul 10	Jul 09
Working Capital	454	373	269
Fixed Assets	3	1	3
Current Assets	791	700	564

Lexis Nexis Martindale Hubbell

Halsbury House 35 Chancery Lane, London, WC2A 1EL
Tel: 020-7347 3700 **Fax:** 020-7911 1921
Website: http://www.martindale.com
Directors: R. Eastmond (Pers), D. Benson (Dir), E. Cassar (Fin), H. Mumford (MD)
Managers: M. Casimir
Ultimate Holding Company: REED ELSEVIER GROUP PLC
Immediate Holding Company: BUTTERWORTHS LIMITED
Registration no: 07416642 **Date established:** 1993
Turnover: £125m - £250m **No.of Employees:** 11 - 20 **Product Groups:** 80

Libran Laminations Ltd

The Finishing Factory Unit 4 156 Coles Green Road, London, NW2 7HW
Tel: 020-8452 2006 **Fax:** 020-8452 4456
E-mail: info@libranlaminations.co.uk
Website: http://www.libranlaminations.co.uk
Directors: R. Sadur (Fin), S. Hutson (MD)
Immediate Holding Company: LIBRAN LAMINATIONS LIMITED
Registration no: 02980212 **Date established:** 1994
Turnover: £250,000 - £500,000 **No.of Employees:** 1 - 10
Product Groups: 28, 30, 44, 49

Date of Accounts	Oct 11	Oct 10	Oct 08
Working Capital	25	43	95
Fixed Assets	127	127	127
Current Assets	38	58	189

Life Line Personnel

2 Arundel Street, London, WC2R 3DA
Tel: 020-7637 3737 **Fax:** 020-7637 7337
E-mail: info@lifeline-personnel.com
Website: http://www.lifeline-personnel.com
Directors: K. Freeston (Fin)
Ultimate Holding Company: LIFELINE RECRUITMENT SOLUTIONS LIMITED
Immediate Holding Company: LIFELINE PERSONNEL LIMITED
Registration no: 02411288 **Date established:** 1989 **Turnover:** £1m - £2m
No.of Employees: 1 - 10 **Product Groups:** 80

Date of Accounts	Aug 11	Aug 10	Aug 09
Sales Turnover	2m	N/A	N/A
Pre Tax Profit/Loss	-120	N/A	N/A
Working Capital	39	145	120
Fixed Assets	16	29	36
Current Assets	502	750	951
Current Liabilities	27	N/A	N/A

Lifestyle Management

58a Wimpole Street, London, W1G 8YR
Tel: 020-7935 1965
E-mail: info@alixneedham.com
Website: http://www.alixneedham.com
Managers: A. Needham (Chief Acct)
Immediate Holding Company: CHIJI GLOBAL INVESTMENT LIMITED
Date established: 2009 **No.of Employees:** 1 - 10 **Product Groups:** 28

Light & Design Associates

The Leather Market Weston Street, London, SE1 3ER
Tel: 020-7403 4700 **Fax:** 020-7403 4707
E-mail: design@lightanddesign.co.uk
Website: http://www.lightanddesign.co.uk
Directors: L. Prince (Ptnr)
Immediate Holding Company: LIGHT & DESIGN ASSOCIATES LIMITED
Registration no: 06538082 **Date established:** 2008
Turnover: Up to £250,000 **No.of Employees:** 1 - 10 **Product Groups:** 37, 67, 84

Date of Accounts	Mar 11	Mar 10	Mar 09
Working Capital	-30	-21	-73
Fixed Assets	35	54	74
Current Assets	159	144	152

Light Engineering

64 Eden Road, London, E17 9JY
Tel: 020-8520 2336 **Fax:** 020-8509 1332
E-mail: sales@light-engineering.com
Website: http://www.light-engineering.com
Directors: C. Wilding (MD), I. Price-Smith (MD), J. Wildman (Fin), P. Manning (MD)
Immediate Holding Company: HIGHLIGHT LIMITED
Registration no: 01522363 **VAT No.:** 223 1514 13 **Date established:** 1980
Turnover: £500,000 - £1m **No.of Employees:** 1 - 10 **Product Groups:** 37, 38

H Lilley & Co. Ltd

70 Footscray Road, London, SE9 2SU
Tel: 020-8850 7179 **Fax:** 020-8850 8365
E-mail: enquiries@hlilley.co.uk
Website: http://www.hlilley.co.uk
Managers: S. Bartlett (Mgr)
Immediate Holding Company: H. LILLEY & COMPANY LIMITED
Registration no: 00651509 **VAT No.:** GB 205 9029 79
Date established: 1960 **Turnover:** £1m - £2m **No.of Employees:** 1 - 10
Product Groups: 37

Date of Accounts	Apr 11	Apr 10	Apr 09
Working Capital	254	243	238
Fixed Assets	14	17	19
Current Assets	676	713	718

Lillywhites

24-36 Regent Street, London, SW1Y 4QF
Tel: 08443-325602 **Fax:** 020-7930 2330
Website: http://www.lillywhites.com
Directors: F. Funcke (MD), P. McDonald (Fin)
Ultimate Holding Company: MASH HOLDINGS LIMITED
Immediate Holding Company: LILLYWHITES LIMITED
Registration no: 00290939 **Date established:** 1934
No.of Employees: 51 - 100 **Product Groups:** 49, 65

Date of Accounts	Apr 08	Apr 09	Apr 10
Sales Turnover	38m	44m	36m
Pre Tax Profit/Loss	6m	7m	4m
Working Capital	28m	32m	35m
Fixed Assets	11m	11m	11m
Current Assets	37m	41m	36m
Current Liabilities	2m	2m	59

Lindab Ltd

98 Roding Road, London, E6 6LS
Tel: 020-7474 5102
Website: http://www.lindab.co.uk
Managers: T. Smith (Mgr), C. Dormer (Mgr)
Ultimate Holding Company: FP009344
Immediate Holding Company: LINDAB LIMITED
Registration no: 01641399 **Date established:** 1982
No.of Employees: 1 - 10 **Product Groups:** 37, 40, 48

Lindner Schmidlin Facades Ltd

Unit 1 Ashleigh Commercial Westmoor Street, London, SE7 8NQ
Tel: 020-8858 9128
E-mail: rod.graves@lindner-group.com
Website: http://www.lindnerschmidlin.com
Managers: R. Graves (Mgr)
Ultimate Holding Company: Lindner Holding Kga (Germany)
Registration no: 05759393 **Date established:** 2006
Turnover: £20m - £50m **No.of Employees:** 1 - 10 **Product Groups:** 33, 37, 45

Linton Fuel Oils Ltd

11a Osiers Road, London, SW18 1NR
Tel: 020-8874 6583 **Fax:** 020-8877 1043
E-mail: sales@lintonfueloils.com
Website: http://www.lintonfueloils.com
Directors: N. Flynn (MD)
Managers: R. Mortimer (Mktg Serv Mgr), D. Myers (Fin Mgr), N. Patel (Tech Serv Mgr)
Immediate Holding Company: LINTON FUEL OILS LIMITED
Registration no: 01649977 **Date established:** 1982
Turnover: £75m - £125m **No.of Employees:** 21 - 50 **Product Groups:** 31, 66

Date of Accounts	May 11	May 10	May 09
Sales Turnover	109m	85m	84m
Pre Tax Profit/Loss	551	384	304
Working Capital	2m	2m	2m
Fixed Assets	3m	2m	3m
Current Assets	13m	12m	8m
Current Liabilities	1m	1m	968

The Little Brown Book Group

Unilever House 100 Victoria Embankment, London, EC4Y 0DY
Tel: 020-7911 8000 **Fax:** 020-7911 8100
E-mail: info@littlebrown.co.uk
Website: http://www.littlebrown.co.uk
Bank(s): Barclays
Directors: R. Manser (Sales), A. Woodhall (Pers), E. Jane-taylor (Fin), U. Mackenzie (Grp Chief Exec)
Managers: T. Ashton (Tech Serv Mgr)
Ultimate Holding Company: LAGARDERE SCA (FRANCE)
Immediate Holding Company: LITTLE, BROWN BOOK GROUP LIMITED
Registration no: 02304585 **Date established:** 1988
Turnover: £50m - £75m **No.of Employees:** 101 - 250 **Product Groups:** 28

Date of Accounts	Dec 11	Dec 10	Dec 09
Sales Turnover	55m	68m	90m
Pre Tax Profit/Loss	6m	12m	23m
Working Capital	16m	27m	18m
Fixed Assets	10m	10m	11m
Current Assets	44m	53m	45m
Current Liabilities	18m	18m	18m

Livebookings Ltd

5th Floor Elizabeth House, 39 York Road, London, SE1 7NQ
Tel: 020-7199 4300 **Fax:** 020-7199 4301
E-mail: info@livebookings.co.uk
Website: http://www.livebookings.com
Immediate Holding Company: Livebookings Holdings Ltd
Registration no: 04494036 **Date established:** 2002
No.of Employees: 1 - 10 **Product Groups:** 69, 79

Date of Accounts	Dec 09	Dec 08	Dec 07
Working Capital	122	-25	545
Fixed Assets	25	46	29
Current Assets	1m	549	864
Current Liabilities	168	345	178

Living Architects Ltd (Architects)

14 The Linen House 253 Kilburn Lane, London, W10 4BQ
Tel: 020-8962 6660 **Fax:** 020-8962 6661
E-mail: alda@living-architects.com
Website: http://www.living-architects.com
Bank(s): Barclays
Directors: C. Alda (Dir)
Immediate Holding Company: LIVING ARCHITECTS LIMITED
Registration no: 04055337 **Date established:** 2000
Turnover: £500,000 - £1m **No.of Employees:** 11 - 20 **Product Groups:** 84

Date of Accounts	Nov 11	Nov 10	Nov 09
Working Capital	175	304	486
Fixed Assets	41	598	597
Current Assets	241	436	646

Livingstone Guarantee plc

15 Adam Street, London, WC2N 6RJ
Tel: 020-7484 4700 **Fax:** 020-7839 6912
E-mail: harvinder.palmatharu@livguarantee.com
Website: http://www.livingstonepartners.com
Bank(s): Barclays
Directors: H. Matharu (Fin)
Managers: K. Fendick (Sales Admin), A. Wilson
Immediate Holding Company: LIVINGSTONE GUARANTEE SERVICES PLC
Registration no: 04695324 **VAT No.:** GB 386 4374 17
Date established: 2003 **Turnover:** £5m - £10m **No.of Employees:** 21 - 50
Product Groups: 80, 82

Date of Accounts	Mar 12	Mar 11	Mar 10
Sales Turnover	8m	5m	4m
Pre Tax Profit/Loss	5m	3m	2m
Working Capital	2m	2m	2m
Fixed Assets	66	68	65
Current Assets	3m	2m	2m
Current Liabilities	220	249	164

Lloyds British Testing Ltd

Unit 7 Thistlebrook Industrial Estate Eynsham Drive, London, SE2 9RB
Tel: 020-8320 4300 **Fax:** 020-8311 1179
E-mail: info@lloydsgroup.co.uk
Website: http://www.lloydsgroup.co.uk
Managers: D. Holmes (Depot Mgr)
Ultimate Holding Company: LLOYDS BRITISH GROUP LIMITED
Immediate Holding Company: LLOYDS BRITISH TESTING LIMITED
Registration no: 04444099 **Date established:** 2002
No.of Employees: 1 - 10 **Product Groups:** 35, 39, 45

Date of Accounts	Dec 11	Dec 10	Dec 09
Sales Turnover	16m	15m	15m
Pre Tax Profit/Loss	86	75	142
Working Capital	3m	3m	3m
Fixed Assets	2m	2m	2m
Current Assets	9m	8m	9m
Current Liabilities	6m	3m	4m

John Lobb Ltd

9 St James Street, London, SW1A 1EF
Tel: 020-7930 3664 **Fax:** 020-7930 2811
E-mail: info@johnlobbltd.co.uk
Website: http://www.johnlobbltd.co.uk
Directors: J. Lobb (MD), W. Lobb (Dir)
Immediate Holding Company: JOHN LOBB LIMITED
Registration no: 01072595 **Date established:** 1972 **Turnover:** £1m - £2m
No.of Employees: 11 - 20 **Product Groups:** 22

Date of Accounts	Apr 11	Apr 10	Apr 09
Working Capital	263	311	368
Fixed Assets	14	17	20
Current Assets	2m	1m	1m

L'Occitane

8 Alpine Way, London, E6 6LA
Tel: 020-7055 3550 **Fax:** 020-7511 8300
Ultimate Holding Company: L'Occitane International Sa (Luxembourg)
Registration no: 03278335 **Date established:** 1996
Turnover: £10m - £20m **No.of Employees:** 11 - 20 **Product Groups:** 32, 63

Lock Door & Shutters

Unit 12 Nathan Way, London, SE28 0AQ
Tel: 01322-554538 **Fax:** 020-8311 1222
E-mail: lockdoorshutters@btconnect.com
Directors: K. Burke (MD)
Immediate Holding Company: LOCK DOOR AND SHUTTERS LTD
Registration no: 03544552 **Date established:** 1998
Turnover: Up to £250,000 **No.of Employees:** 1 - 10 **Product Groups:** 26, 35

Date of Accounts	Mar 11	Mar 10	Mar 09
Sales Turnover	3	193	234
Pre Tax Profit/Loss	N/A	3	14
Working Capital	52	68	61
Fixed Assets	9	12	16
Current Assets	81	106	93
Current Liabilities	N/A	5	11

Lockers for School

Daws House, 33-35 Daws Lane, London, NW7 4SD
Tel: 020-8906 6797 **Fax:** 0870-4280166
E-mail: info@lockersfor.com
Website: http://www.lockersforschool.com
No.of Employees: 1 - 10 **Product Groups:** 26

O W Loeb & Co. Ltd

3 Archie Street, London, SE1 3JT
Tel: 020-7234 0385 **Fax:** 020-7357 0440
E-mail: chrisdavey@owloeb.com
Website: http://www.owloeb.com
Directors: C. Davey (MD), P. Barry (Co Sec)
Immediate Holding Company: O.W.LOEB & CO LIMITED
Registration no: 00337474 **Date established:** 1938 **Turnover:** £2m - £5m
No.of Employees: 1 - 10 **Product Groups:** 62

Date of Accounts	Mar 12	Mar 11	Mar 10
Sales Turnover	5m	4m	4m
Pre Tax Profit/Loss	384	297	276
Working Capital	1m	1m	1m
Fixed Assets	501	627	626
Current Assets	5m	4m	3m
Current Liabilities	427	2m	255

Logbook Loans Ltd

Bridge Studio 34a Deodar Road, London, SW15 2NN
Tel: 08448-716665 **Fax:** 0870-033 9964
E-mail: iain.shearer@logbookloans.co.uk
Website: http://www.logbookloans.co.uk
Directors: M. Heap (Grp Chief Exec), A. Duckworth (MD)
Immediate Holding Company: LBL REALISATIONS LIMITED
Registration no: 03636230 **Date established:** 1998 **Turnover:** £1m - £2m
No.of Employees: 51 - 100 **Product Groups:** 82

Date of Accounts	Aug 10	Aug 09	Aug 08
Working Capital	171	165	122
Fixed Assets	14	20	17
Current Assets	1m	1m	1m

Logic Programming Associates Ltd

Studio 30 Royal Victoria Patriotic Building John Archer Way, London, SW18 3SX
Tel: 020-8871 2016 **Fax:** 020-8874 0449
E-mail: info@lpa.co.uk
Website: http://www.ita.co.uk
Directors: C. Spenser (Mkt Research)
Immediate Holding Company: LOGIC PROGRAMMING ASSOCIATES LIMITED
Registration no: 01514958 **VAT No.:** GB 237 7284 40
Date established: 1980 **Turnover:** £250,000 - £500,000
No.of Employees: 1 - 10 **Product Groups:** 44

Date of Accounts	May 11	May 10	May 09
Working Capital	23	19	18
Current Assets	36	41	42

Lomart Ltd

Unit 14 Mowlem Trading Estate Leeside Road, London, N17 0QJ
Tel: 020-8493 8383 **Fax:** 020-8493 8363
E-mail: info@lomart.co.uk
Website: http://www.liftmate.co.uk
Directors: P. Votapek (Dir)
Immediate Holding Company: LOMART LIMITED
Registration no: 02614912 **Date established:** 1991 **Turnover:** £1m - £2m
No.of Employees: 1 - 10 **Product Groups:** 35, 39, 45

Date of Accounts	Dec 11	Dec 10	Dec 09
Sales Turnover	2m	2m	1m
Pre Tax Profit/Loss	143	154	69
Working Capital	511	400	338
Fixed Assets	19	16	10
Current Assets	803	589	512
Current Liabilities	81	62	50

Lombard Risk

India House 45 Curlew Street, London, SE1 2ND
Tel: 020-7403 2188 **Fax:** 020-7403 4425
E-mail: info@stbsystems.com
Website: http://www.stbsystems.com
Bank(s): HSBC
Directors: A. Brown (Dir), C. Phillips (Dir), K. Butcher (Co Sec), M. Thomas (Dir)
Immediate Holding Company: LOMBARD RISK COMPLIANCE LIMITED
Registration no: 02342639 **VAT No.:** GB 722 3155 68
Date established: 1989 **Turnover:** £2m - £5m **No.of Employees:** 51 - 100
Product Groups: 44

London City Airport Ltd

Royal Docks, London, E16 2PX
Tel: 020-7646 0000 **Fax:** 020-7511 1040
E-mail: richard.gooding@londoncityairport.com
Website: http://www.londoncityairport.com
Directors: D. Thomson (Fin), R. Gooding (MD), R. Gooding (Grp Chief Exec)
Managers: G. Wright (Personnel), L. Hopkins (Sales & Mktg Mg), J. Squires (Sales Admin), T. Handley (Sales & Mktg Mg), P. Larner (Sales Admin), D. Shkula (Tech Serv Mgr), G. O'Connor (Purch Mgr)
Ultimate Holding Company: CLOVER EQUITY CO LIMITED (JERSEY)
Immediate Holding Company: LONDON CITY AIRPORT LIMITED
Registration no: 01963361 **Date established:** 1985
Turnover: £50m - £75m **No.of Employees:** 1501 & over
Product Groups: 75

Date of Accounts	Dec 10	Dec 09	Dec 08
Sales Turnover	67m	68m	70m
Pre Tax Profit/Loss	17m	20m	44m
Working Capital	55m	60m	138m
Fixed Assets	25m	19m	12m
Current Assets	190m	195m	263m
Current Liabilities	9m	13m	102m

London City Mission

175 Tower Bridge Road, London, SE1 2AH
Tel: 020-7407 7585 **Fax:** 020-7403 6711
E-mail: enquiries@lcm.org.uk
Website: http://www.lcm.org.uk
Bank(s): Barclays
Directors: J. Nicholls (Grp Chief Exec)
Immediate Holding Company: THE LONDON CITY MISSION
Registration no: 04284615 **VAT No.:** GB 237 0387 65
Date established: 2001 **Turnover:** £5m - £10m **No.of Employees:** 21 - 50
Product Groups: 28

Date of Accounts	Dec 11	Dec 10	Dec 09
Sales Turnover	6m	7m	7m
Pre Tax Profit/Loss	-778	2m	51
Working Capital	416	576	389
Fixed Assets	35m	34m	33m
Current Assets	520	737	483
Current Liabilities	31	161	94

London Clubs

10 Brick Street, London, W1J 7HQ
Tel: 020-7518 0000 **Fax:** 020-7495 6919
E-mail: rramm@london-clubs.co.uk
Website: http://www.lciclubs.com
Directors: R. Ramm (MD), M. Rothwell (Fin)
Managers: C. Rayer (Tech Serv Mgr), I. Woodward (Personnel), J. Spitall (Mktg Serv Mgr)
Ultimate Holding Company: HARRAH'S ENTERTAINMENT INC
Immediate Holding Company: LONDON CLUBS LIMITED
Registration no: 00860214 **Date established:** 1965 **Turnover:** £1m - £2m
No.of Employees: 51 - 100 **Product Groups:** 89

Date of Accounts	Dec 08
Working Capital	-38
Fixed Assets	63
Current Assets	25

London College Of Communications

Elephant & Castle, London, SE1 6SB
Tel: 020-7514 6569 **Fax:** 020-7514 7313
E-mail: info@lcc.arts.ac.uk
Website: http://www.lcc.arts.ac.uk
Managers: T. Keane
Immediate Holding Company: LONDON INSTITUTE
No.of Employees: 51 - 100 **Product Groups:** 86

London & Devonshire Trust Ltd

Heathcoat House 20 Savile Row, London, W1S 3PR
Tel: 020-7439 0246 **Fax:** 020-7734 2561
E-mail: cpm@cpm.uk
Website: http://www.londonanddevonshire.com
Directors: D. Stephenson (Dir)
Immediate Holding Company: TRILOGIE CORPORATE REAL ESTATE LIMITED
Registration no: 01263589 **Date established:** 1976 **Turnover:** £2m - £5m
No.of Employees: 1 - 10 **Product Groups:** 52, 80

Date of Accounts	Dec 11	Dec 10	Dec 09
Sales Turnover	3m	3m	3m
Pre Tax Profit/Loss	58	168	257
Working Capital	332	423	486
Fixed Assets	3m	3m	3m
Current Assets	1m	1m	1m
Current Liabilities	391	485	566

London Economics

71-75 Shelton Street, London, WC2H 9JQ
Tel: 020-7866 8185 **Fax:** 020-7866 8186
E-mail: info@londecon.co.uk
Website: http://www.londecon.co.uk
Managers: P. Muller (Mgr)
Immediate Holding Company: LONDON ECONOMICS LIMITED
Registration no: 04083204 **Date established:** 2000 **Turnover:** £2m - £5m
No.of Employees: 11 - 20 **Product Groups:** 80

Date of Accounts	Aug 11	Aug 10	Aug 09
Sales Turnover	3m	N/A	N/A
Pre Tax Profit/Loss	137	N/A	N/A
Working Capital	821	818	900
Fixed Assets	54	80	80
Current Assets	2m	1m	2m
Current Liabilities	N/A	224	64

The London Fan Co. Ltd

75-81 Stirling Road, London, W3 8DJ
Tel: 020-8992 6923 **Fax:** 020-8992 6928
E-mail: sales@londonfan.co.uk
Website: http://www.londonfan.co.uk
Bank(s): Barclays
Directors: A. Webber (Dir)
Ultimate Holding Company: HORVAL HOLDINGS LIMITED
Immediate Holding Company: LONDON FAN COMPANY LIMITED (THE)
Registration no: 00227801 **VAT No.:** GB 226 6021 90
Date established: 2028 **Turnover:** £2m - £5m **No.of Employees:** 21 - 50
Product Groups: 30, 40, 41, 66

Date of Accounts	Mar 11	Mar 10	Mar 09
Working Capital	-1m	-885	-598
Fixed Assets	82	106	104
Current Assets	963	955	1m

London Freight Forwarders

Unit 72 Wimbledon Stadium Business Centre Riverside Road, London, SW17 0BA
Tel: 020-8947 6767 **Fax:** 020-8944 1414
E-mail: info@london-freight.co.uk
Website: http://www.london-freight.co.uk
Directors: M. Haider (Dir), S. Jafri (Co Sec)
Immediate Holding Company: AVROHILL LIMITED
Date established: 1973 **Turnover:** £1m - £2m **No.of Employees:** 11 - 20
Product Groups: 61, 74

London Languages Ltd

44 Alderney Street, London, SW1V 4EU
Tel: 020-7233 8205 **Fax:** 020-7233 8206
E-mail: mail@londonlanguages.com
Website: http://www.londonlanguages.com
Directors: A. James (MD), J. Kite (Co Sec)
Immediate Holding Company: LONDON LANGUAGES LIMITED
Registration no: 02408485 **Date established:** 1989 **Turnover:** £2m - £5m
No.of Employees: 1 - 10 **Product Groups:** 80, 86

Date of Accounts	Mar 11	Mar 10	Mar 09
Working Capital	80	76	83
Fixed Assets	2	11	13
Current Assets	164	169	216

London Lights

194 Upper Richmond Road West, London, SW14 8AN
Tel: 020-8878 1955
No.of Employees: 1 - 10 **Product Groups:** 37, 67

London Metals Ltd

10 Graham Street, London, N1 8GB
Tel: 020-7354 5450 **Fax:** 020-7359 5064
E-mail: trading@londonmetals.co.uk
Website: http://www.londonmetals.co.uk
Directors: D. Dehaas (Ch)
Ultimate Holding Company: LONDON METALS HOLDINGS LIMITED
Immediate Holding Company: LONDON METALS LIMITED
Registration no: 01494995 **VAT No.:** GB 346 4308 58
Date established: 1980 **Turnover:** £20m - £50m **No.of Employees:** 1 - 10
Product Groups: 34, 66

Date of Accounts	Dec 11	Dec 10	Dec 09
Sales Turnover	37m	34m	25m
Pre Tax Profit/Loss	471	707	934
Working Capital	4m	3m	3m
Fixed Assets	855	895	837
Current Assets	7m	8m	6m
Current Liabilities	343	434	450

London Piling
62 Aboyne Road, London, NW10 0HA
Tel: 07751-661682
E-mail: info@pilinglondon.co.uk
Website: http://www.pilinglondon.co.uk
Directors: J. O'Sullivan (Dir)
Date established: 2007 **No.of Employees:** 1 - 10 **Product Groups:** 51

London Stock Exchange plc
The London Stock Exchange 10 Paternoster Square, London, EC4M 7LS
Tel: 020-7797 1000
E-mail: enquiries@londonstockexchange.com
Website: http://www.londonstockexchange.com
Directors: L. Condron (Co Sec)
Ultimate Holding Company: LONDON STOCK EXCHANGE GROUP PLC
Immediate Holding Company: LONDON STOCK EXCHANGE PLC
Registration no: 02075721 **VAT No.:** GB 524 9224 49
Date established: 1986 **Turnover:** £250m - £500m
No.of Employees: 501 - 1000 **Product Groups:** 82

Date of Accounts	Mar 12	Mar 11	Mar 10
Sales Turnover	301m	317m	323m
Pre Tax Profit/Loss	167m	176m	141m
Working Capital	180m	161m	243m
Fixed Assets	199m	244m	115m
Current Assets	377m	355m	345m
Current Liabilities	90m	120m	98m

London Waste Technology Ltd
165 Kensington High Street, London, W8 6SH
Tel: 020-7937 6262 **Fax:** 020-7937 4848
E-mail: info@lwtechnology.co.uk
Website: http://www.lwtechnology.co.uk
Directors: C. Magee (Fin)
Immediate Holding Company: LONDON WASTE TECHNOLOGY LIMITED
Registration no: 04116457 **Date established:** 2000
Turnover: £500,000 - £1m **No.of Employees:** 1 - 10 **Product Groups:** 38, 42

Date of Accounts	Feb 12	Feb 11	Feb 10
Sales Turnover	N/A	606	592
Pre Tax Profit/Loss	N/A	261	176
Working Capital	-2	-1	9
Fixed Assets	50	52	37
Current Assets	163	154	112
Current Liabilities	N/A	85	70

Lonewolf B2b Tele Marketing
31 Southampton Row, London, WC1B 5HA
Tel: 020-3397 3559
E-mail: nigel@lwolf.co.uk
Website: http://www.lwolf.co.uk
Directors: N. Morgan (Prop)
Immediate Holding Company: SIGNATURE RECRUITMENT LTD
Date established: 2010 **Turnover:** **No.of Employees:** 1 - 10
Product Groups: 81

Date of Accounts	Sep 11	Sep 10	Sep 09
Working Capital	22	30	6
Current Assets	118	89	29

Lonmin plc
4 Grosvenor Place, London, SW1X 7YL
Tel: 020-7201 6000 **Fax:** 020-7201 6100
E-mail: info@lonmin.com
Website: http://www.lonmin.com
Directors: I. Farmer (Grp Chief Exec), S. Maxwell (Pers)
Managers: A. Ferguson (Fin Mgr), J. Beetge (Tech Serv Mgr)
Immediate Holding Company: LONMIN PUBLIC LIMITED COMPANY
Registration no: 00103002 **Date established:** 2009
Turnover: Over £1,000m **No.of Employees:** 1 - 10 **Product Groups:** 51

Date of Accounts	Sep 07	Sep 06
Sales Turnover	1941m	1855m
Pre Tax Profit/Loss	705000	633000
Working Capital	200000	279000
Fixed Assets	3174m	2140m
Current Assets	764000	601000
Current Liabilities	564000	322000
Total Share Capital	156000	143000
ROCE% (Return on Capital Employed)	20.9	26.2
ROT% (Return on Turnover)	36.3	34.1

Lonsto Insternational Ltd
Lonsto House 276 Chase Road, London, N14 6HA
Tel: 020-8882 8575 **Fax:** 020-8886 6676
E-mail: py@lonsto.co.uk
Website: http://www.lonsto.co.uk
Bank(s): Barclays
Directors: R. Dudding (MD), T. O'Donovan (Dir), P. Yeoland (Chief Op Offcr), J. Ancell (Dir)
Managers: P. Yeolland (Tech Serv Mgr), G. Papathomas (Sales Prom Mgr)
Immediate Holding Company: TICKETSYSTEMS LIMITED
Registration no: 03995815 **VAT No.:** GB 229 1396 66
Date established: 2000 **Turnover:** £500,000 - £1m
No.of Employees: 21 - 50 **Product Groups:** 40, 44

Date of Accounts	Mar 11	Mar 10	Mar 09
Sales Turnover	643	741	913
Pre Tax Profit/Loss	-190	-145	-23
Working Capital	221	354	446
Fixed Assets	18	18	27
Current Assets	1m	1m	1m
Current Liabilities	910	682	490

Lorien Resourcing Ltd
Bankside House 107-112 Leadenhall Street, London, EC3A 4AF
Tel: 020-7654 1000 **Fax:** 020-7654 1066
E-mail: info@lorien.co.uk
Website: http://www.lorien.co.uk
Bank(s): Lloyds TSB Bank plc
Directors: D. O'neill (Dir)
Ultimate Holding Company: LORIEN LIMITED
Immediate Holding Company: LORIEN RESOURCING LIMITED
Registration no: 01333388 **Date established:** 1977
Turnover: £75m - £125m **No.of Employees:** 51 - 100
Product Groups: 80, 81, 86

Date of Accounts	Jan 12	Jan 11	Jan 10
Sales Turnover	203m	204m	165m
Pre Tax Profit/Loss	3m	3m	2m
Working Capital	4m	4m	3m
Fixed Assets	466	731	964
Current Assets	48m	56m	47m
Current Liabilities	24m	29m	26m

Lorraine Electronics Surveillance
716 Lea Bridge Road, London, E10 6AW
Tel: 020-8558 4226 **Fax:** 020-8558 1338
E-mail: info@lorraine.co.uk
Website: http://www.lorraine.co.uk
Directors: R. Bhan (Prop), J. O'Neil (Fin)
Ultimate Holding Company: DATAGLEN LIMITED
Immediate Holding Company: LORRAINE ELECTRONICS LIMITED
Registration no: 02924581 **VAT No.:** GB 549 3465 13
Date established: 1994 **Turnover:** £1m - £2m **No.of Employees:** 1 - 10
Product Groups: 40

Date of Accounts	Dec 11	Dec 10	Dec 09
Working Capital	1	1	1
Current Assets	1	1	1

Low Profile
B D C House 590-598 Green Lanes, London, N8 0RA
Tel: 020-8800 8083 **Fax:** 020-8809 0567
E-mail: mustafa.suleyman@low-profile.com
Website: http://www.low-profile.com
Directors: M. Suleyman (MD)
Ultimate Holding Company: LOW PROFILE HOLDINGS LIMITED
Immediate Holding Company: LOW PROFILE COLLECTIONS LIMITED
Registration no: 04112054 **Date established:** 2000
No.of Employees: 11 - 20 **Product Groups:** 63

Date of Accounts	Dec 10	Dec 09	Dec 06
Working Capital	10	10	10
Current Assets	10	10	10

LUCID PRODUCTIONS
Hollybush Place, London, E2 9QX
Tel: 020-7739 0240 **Fax:** 020-7739 0240
E-mail: info@clubdecor.co.uk
Website: http://www.clubdecor.co.uk
Directors: C. Branson (Prop)
Registration no: 744204946 **Date established:** 1999
Turnover: Up to £250,000 **No.of Employees:** 1 - 10 **Product Groups:** 29, 83

Luso Electronic Products Ltd (Power Transmission Division)
794 Salisbury House, London, EC2M 5QQ
Tel: 020-7606 0752 **Fax:** 020-7638 7674
E-mail: yvonne.o@lusoelectronics.com
Website: http://www.lusoelectronics.com
Directors: G. Zelkha (Dir)
Immediate Holding Company: LUSO ELECTRONIC PRODUCTS LIMITED
Registration no: 00895822 **VAT No.:** GB 243 1602 02
Date established: 1967 **Turnover:** £10m - £20m **No.of Employees:** 1 - 10
Product Groups: 67

Date of Accounts	Dec 11	Dec 10	Dec 09
Sales Turnover	11m	10m	N/A
Pre Tax Profit/Loss	570	160	N/A
Working Capital	1m	876	777
Fixed Assets	32	56	25
Current Assets	4m	4m	4m
Current Liabilities	698	1m	N/A

M E C
1 Paris Garden, London, SE1 8NU
Tel: 020-7803 2000 **Fax:** 020-7803 2502
E-mail: tom.george@mecglobal.com
Website: http://www.mecglobal.co.uk
Bank(s): National Westminster Bank Plc
Directors: D. Bryan (Fin), M. Tiley-hill (Fin)
Managers: B. Zawlotki (Tech Serv Mgr), S. Hatch, J. Healy (Personnel)
Ultimate Holding Company: WPP PLC (JERSEY)
Immediate Holding Company: OUTRIDER LIMITED
Registration no: 03353280 **Date established:** 1997
Turnover: £125m - £250m **No.of Employees:** 251 - 500
Product Groups: 81

Date of Accounts	Dec 11	Dec 10	Dec 09
Sales Turnover	147m	108m	78m
Pre Tax Profit/Loss	5m	4m	2m
Working Capital	5m	657	-4m
Fixed Assets	6m	6m	6m
Current Assets	66m	47m	29m
Current Liabilities	6m	5m	3m

M F H Helicopters Ltd
1 Green Street, London, W1K 6RG
Tel: 020-7499 2233 **Fax:** 020-7499 2233
E-mail: info@mfhhelicopters.co.uk
Website: http://www.mfhhelicopters.co.uk
Directors: N. Hawkings-Byass (MD)
Immediate Holding Company: MFH HELICOPTERS LTD
Registration no: 02204219 **Date established:** 1987
No.of Employees: 1 - 10 **Product Groups:** 46, 48

Date of Accounts	Mar 11	Mar 10	Mar 09
Working Capital	-444	-610	-695
Fixed Assets	150	169	290
Current Assets	219	30	54

M & G Group plc
Governors House 5 Laurence Pountney Hill, London, EC4R 0HH
Tel: 020-7626 4588 **Fax:** 020-7623 8615
E-mail: info@mandg.co.uk
Website: http://www.mandg.co.uk
Bank(s): National Westminster Bank Plc
Directors: W. Nott (Dir), G. Macdowall (Fin)
Ultimate Holding Company: PRUDENTIAL PUBLIC LIMITED COMPANY
Immediate Holding Company: M & G GROUP LIMITED
Registration no: 00633480 **Date established:** 1959
Turnover: Up to £250,000 **No.of Employees:** 501 - 1000
Product Groups: 82

Date of Accounts	Dec 11	Dec 10	Dec 09
Sales Turnover	6	8	8
Pre Tax Profit/Loss	213m	150m	94m
Working Capital	-33m	-32m	-32m
Fixed Assets	39m	39m	39m
Current Assets	148	135	101
Current Liabilities	4	10	154

M M & M Ltd
102 Seymour Place, London, W1H 1NF
Tel: 020-7724 5117 **Fax:** 020-7724 5087
E-mail: mmm@mmmltd.com
Website: http://www.mmmltd.com
Directors: A. Shirazi (Dir), E. Shirazi (Dir), Z. Shirazi (Dir)
Immediate Holding Company: M, M & M Ltd
Registration no: 02129164 **VAT No.:** GB 494 6400 29
Date established: 1987 **Turnover:** £500,000 - £1m
No.of Employees: 1 - 10 **Product Groups:** 44, 61

Date of Accounts	Mar 08	Mar 07	Mar 06
Working Capital	-424	-489	-430
Fixed Assets	10	N/A	N/A
Current Assets	107	76	84
Current Liabilities	531	565	514
Total Share Capital	50	50	50

M P Electrical Ltd
4 Barking Road, London, E6 3BP
Tel: 020-8472 5356 **Fax:** 020-8552 3086
E-mail: ash@4lights.co.uk
Website: http://www.4lights.co.uk
Managers: A. Patel (Mgr)
Immediate Holding Company: M.P.ELECTRICAL LIMITED
Registration no: 00582319 **Date established:** 1957
No.of Employees: 1 - 10 **Product Groups:** 37, 67

Date of Accounts	Apr 11	Apr 10	Apr 09
Working Capital	152	152	164
Fixed Assets	229	222	223
Current Assets	241	243	251

Maas International Ltd
Unit C Twelvetrees Crescent, London, E3 3JG
Tel: 020-7068 7500 **Fax:** 020-7068 7577
E-mail: sales@maas.nl
Website: http://www.massint.co.uk
Directors: M. Stone (MD), N. Scarfe (MD)
Ultimate Holding Company: MAAS INTERNATIONAL EUROPE BV (NETHERLANDS)
Immediate Holding Company: MAAS INTERNATIONAL LIMITED
Registration no: 02388146 **Date established:** 1989
Turnover: £10m - £20m **No.of Employees:** 51 - 100 **Product Groups:** 38, 42

Date of Accounts	Dec 11	Dec 10	Dec 09
Sales Turnover	11m	8m	6m
Pre Tax Profit/Loss	-7m	-1m	183
Working Capital	-9m	-3m	-5m
Fixed Assets	13m	12m	5m
Current Assets	8m	9m	3m
Current Liabilities	3m	4m	342

Mac Millan
Studio 28, DRCA Business Centre Charlotte Despard Avenue, Battersea, London, SW11 5HD
Tel: 020-7498 3787 **Fax:** 0207-731 8622
E-mail: info@mac-millan.com
Website: http://www.mac-millan.com
Directors: J. Mcmillan (MD)
Managers: S. Robertson
Registration no: 00785999 **Product Groups:** 23, 24, 63

Macandrews & Co.
75 King William Street, London, EC4N 7BE
Tel: 020-7220 6100
E-mail: info@macandrews.com
Website: http://www.macandrews.com
Directors: G. Smith (MD)
Ultimate Holding Company: CMA CGM SA (FRANCE)
Immediate Holding Company: MACANDREWS & COMPANY LIMITED
Registration no: 00334790 **Date established:** 1937
Turnover: £75m - £125m **No.of Employees:** 21 - 50 **Product Groups:** 45, 67, 76

Date of Accounts	Dec 10	Dec 09	Dec 08
Sales Turnover	111m	89m	91m
Pre Tax Profit/Loss	7m	10m	-7m
Working Capital	21m	14m	3m
Fixed Assets	5m	5m	6m
Current Assets	47m	41m	24m
Current Liabilities	11m	17m	15m

Macarthur & Co.
60 Lombard Street, London, EC3V 9EA
Tel: 020-7464 8644 **Fax:** 020- 74648686
E-mail: peter.may@macarthur.uk.com
Website: http://www.macarthur.com
Directors: P. May (Ch)
Immediate Holding Company: WAYMARK FINANCIAL LIMITED
Registration no: 01760823 **Date established:** 2011
Turnover: £500,000 - £1m **No.of Employees:** 1 - 10 **Product Groups:** 80, 82

Date of Accounts	Dec 11	Jan 11	Jan 10
Pre Tax Profit/Loss	N/A	-4m	-314
Working Capital	131	131	-41
Fixed Assets	N/A	N/A	669
Current Assets	135	199	103
Current Liabilities	4	N/A	144

Macfarlanes
20 Cursitor Street, London, EC4A 1LT
Tel: 020-7831 9222 **Fax:** 020-7831 9607
E-mail: bibi.ally@macfarlanes.com
Website: http://www.macfarlanes.com
Directors: R. Gibbons (Fin), R. Gibbons (Fin), B. Ally (Co Sec)
Managers: E. Gilbert (Mgr), M. Millen (Tech Serv Mgr), R. Hind (Personnel)
Ultimate Holding Company: MACFARLANES LLP
Immediate Holding Company: MACFARLANES LIMITED
Registration no: 02292048 **Date established:** 1988
Turnover: £20m - £50m **No.of Employees:** 251 - 500 **Product Groups:** 80

Machine Mart Ltd
503 Lea Bridge Road, London, E10 7EB
Tel: 020-8558 8284 **Fax:** 020-8558 9405
Website: http://www.machinemart.co.uk
Immediate Holding Company: MACHINE MART LIMITED
Registration no: 01555925 **Date established:** 1981
Turnover: £50m - £75m **No.of Employees:** 1 - 10 **Product Groups:** 40

Date of Accounts	May 11	May 10	May 09
Sales Turnover	67m	64m	56m
Pre Tax Profit/Loss	11m	11m	9m
Working Capital	61m	53m	27m
Fixed Assets	4m	5m	5m
Current Assets	68m	59m	51m
Current Liabilities	3m	3m	21m

Mckinsey & Company
1 Jermyn Street, London, SW1Y 4UH
Tel: 020-7839 8040 **Fax:** 020-7339 5000
Website: http://www.mckinsey.com
Directors: D. Casserley (MD), G. Stud (Fin)
Immediate Holding Company: MCKINSEY & COMPANY INC. (UK) PENSION TRUSTEES LIMITED
Registration no: 06384346 **Date established:** 2007
No.of Employees: 501 - 1000 **Product Groups:** 80

Macksons London Ltd
270 Kilburn High Road, London, NW6 2BY
Tel: 020-7624 7133 **Fax:** 020-7625 6091
E-mail: enquiries@macksons.co.uk
Directors: A. Macci (MD), H. Macci (Grp Chief Exec), M. Maccci (Co Sec), M. Macci (Fin)
Managers: A. Amin (Chief Mgr)
Immediate Holding Company: MACKSONS (LONDON) LIMITED
Registration no: 01887760 **VAT No.:** GB 227 1043 02
Date established: 1985 **Turnover:** Up to £250,000
No.of Employees: 1 - 10 **Product Groups:** 61

Date of Accounts	Mar 11	Mar 10	Mar 08
Working Capital	369	568	744
Fixed Assets	N/A	N/A	1
Current Assets	633	710	1m

Maclaye Marie Spens
1 London Wall, London, EC2Y 5EZ
Tel: 020-7248 9529
Website: http://www.maclayemariespens.co.uk
Directors: J. Brooks (Ptnr)
Immediate Holding Company: THE CITY LAW PARTNERSHIP LIMITED
Registration no: 03047480 **Date established:** 1995
No.of Employees: 1 - 10 **Product Groups:** 80

Nick Maclean Civil & Structural Engineers
8a Chamberlain Street, London, NW1 8XB
Tel: 020-7722 7525 **Fax:** 020-7722 9711
E-mail: office@nickmaclean.co.uk
Website: http://www.nickmaclean.co.uk
Directors: N. Maclean (Prop)
Date established: 1984 **No.of Employees:** 1 - 10 **Product Groups:** 35

Maclellan International Ltd (Integrated Cleaning & Support Services Ltd)
4 Bromells Road, London, SW4 0BG
Tel: 020-7498 0220 **Fax:** 020- 74983191
Bank(s): Barclays
Directors: S. Hughey (Chief Op Offcr)
Managers: L. Riser (Mgr)
Ultimate Holding Company: INTERSERVE PLC
Immediate Holding Company: MACLELLAN INTERNATIONAL LIMITED
Registration no: 03688689 **Date established:** 1998
Turnover: £20m - £50m **No.of Employees:** 11 - 20 **Product Groups:** 52

Date of Accounts	Dec 10	Dec 09	Dec 08
Sales Turnover	74m	102m	138m
Pre Tax Profit/Loss	3m	815	4m
Working Capital	10m	3m	-19m
Fixed Assets	216	226	20m
Current Assets	49m	90m	77m
Current Liabilities	6m	7m	11m

Macob Systems Ltd
406 West Green Road, London, N15 3PX
Tel: 020-8881 3050 **Fax:** 020-8889 6010
E-mail: info@macobsystems.co.uk
Website: http://www.macobsystems.co.uk
Directors: J. Oza (MD)
Immediate Holding Company: MACOB SYSTEMS LIMITED
Registration no: 01993318 **Date established:** 1986 **Turnover:** £2m - £5m
No.of Employees: 1 - 10 **Product Groups:** 44

Date of Accounts	Jun 11	Jun 10	Jun 09
Working Capital	-105	-107	-115
Fixed Assets	320	320	320
Current Assets	11	6	11

Macsteel International UK Ltd
1 Connaught Place, London, W2 2ET
Tel: 020-7971 5678 **Fax:** 020-7531 9187
E-mail: sales@miuk.co.uk
Website: http://www.miuk.co.uk
Directors: T. Wharton (Co Sec), J. Gerber (Dir)
Immediate Holding Company: MACSTEEL INTERNATIONAL U.K. LIMITED
Registration no: 03173529 **VAT No.:** GB 243 6921 58
Date established: 1996 **Turnover:** £250m - £500m
No.of Employees: 1 - 10 **Product Groups:** 61

Date of Accounts	Dec 07	Dec 06
Sales Turnover	742310	598880
Pre Tax Profit/Loss	4130	6250
Working Capital	28980	26050
Fixed Assets	230	400
Current Assets	213280	134510
Current Liabilities	184300	108460
Total Share Capital	13900	13900
ROCE% (Return on Capital Employed)	14.1	23.6
ROT% (Return on Turnover)	0.6	1.0

The Maersk Company UK Ltd
Maersk House Brayham Street, London, E1 8EP
Tel: 020-7712 5000 **Fax:** 020-7712 5120
E-mail: info@kerr-mcgee.com
Website: http://www.maersk.com
Bank(s): Citybank N A
Managers: T. Cornick
Ultimate Holding Company: AP MOLLER MAERSK A/S (DENMARK)
Immediate Holding Company: MAERSK COMPANY LIMITED(THE)
Registration no: 00493147 **Date established:** 1951
Turnover: £125m - £250m **No.of Employees:** 101 - 250
Product Groups: 39, 74, 76, 82

Maintel Holdings Ltd
61 Webber Street, London, SE1 0RF
Tel: 08448-711122
E-mail: info@maintel.co.uk
Website: http://www.maintel.co.uk
Bank(s): National Westminster Bank Plc
Directors: W. Todd (Co Sec), A. Mccaffery (MD)
Managers: H. Hope (Mktg Serv Mgr), A. Monk (Tech Serv Mgr), D. Davies (Personnel)
Immediate Holding Company: MAINTEL HOLDINGS PLC
Registration no: 03181729 **VAT No.:** GB 690 6618 10
Date established: 1996 **Turnover:** £20m - £50m
No.of Employees: 101 - 250 **Product Groups:** 44, 67

Date of Accounts	Dec 11	Dec 10	Dec 09
Sales Turnover	26m	22m	19m
Pre Tax Profit/Loss	3m	3m	2m
Working Capital	-1m	-316	731
Fixed Assets	5m	2m	1m
Current Assets	8m	7m	6m
Current Liabilities	8m	6m	5m

Maisonneuve & Co.
29 Newman Street, London, W1T 1PS
Tel: 020-7636 9686 **Fax:** 020-7436 0770
E-mail: enq@maisonneuve.co.uk
Website: http://www.maisonneuve.co.uk
Directors: H. Petitjean (Prop)
Immediate Holding Company: MAISONNEUVE & CO. LIMITED
Registration no: 00212610 **Date established:** 2026
Turnover: £250,000 - £500,000 **No.of Employees:** 1 - 10
Product Groups: 63

Mak Automotive Company
38 Cumberland Avenue Mak House, London, NW10 7RQ
Tel: 020-8838 3080 **Fax:** 020-8838 3081
E-mail: mail@makautomotive.co.uk
Website: http://www.makautomotive.co.uk
Directors: M. Khurana (Dir)
Immediate Holding Company: MAK BEARINGS LTD.
Registration no: 05273403 **Date established:** 2004
No.of Employees: 1 - 10 **Product Groups:** 35, 66

Mall Galleries
17 Carlton House Terrace, London, SW1Y 5BD
Tel: 020-7930 6844 **Fax:** 020-7839 7830
E-mail: info@mallgalleries.com
Website: http://www.mallgalleries.org.uk
Managers: J. Deston (Mgr)
Immediate Holding Company: MALL GALLERIES TRADING LIMITED
Registration no: 06315430 **VAT No.:** GB 240 4847 72
Date established: 2007 **Turnover:** Up to £250,000
No.of Employees: 1 - 10 **Product Groups:** 69

Date of Accounts	Dec 11	Dec 10	Dec 09
Sales Turnover	117	115	102
Pre Tax Profit/Loss	N/A	1	N/A
Current Assets	136	93	78
Current Liabilities	13	3	27

Mallett Public Ltd Company
141 New Bond Street, London, W1S 2BS
Tel: 020-7499 7411 **Fax:** 020-7495 3179
E-mail: info@mallettantiques.com
Website: http://www.mallettantiques.com
Directors: M. Smyth Osbourne (Co Sec), M. Smyth-osbourne (Co Sec), T. Woodham Smith (Dir)
Ultimate Holding Company: MALLETT PUBLIC LIMITED COMPANY
Immediate Holding Company: MALLETT PUBLIC LIMITED COMPANY
Registration no: 01838233 **Date established:** 1984
Turnover: £10m - £20m **No.of Employees:** 21 - 50 **Product Groups:** 65

Date of Accounts	Dec 11	Dec 10	Dec 09
Sales Turnover	13m	13m	14m
Pre Tax Profit/Loss	508	-1m	-2m
Working Capital	12m	12m	14m
Fixed Assets	5m	4m	7m
Current Assets	18m	18m	17m
Current Liabilities	2m	816	732

Management One - Retail Specialists
12 Aycliffe Road, London, W12 0LL
Tel: 020-8576 6233
E-mail: retail@globalfashionmanagement.com
Website: http://www.globalfashionmanagement.com/retail.htm
Directors: T. Bayle (Prop)
No.of Employees: 1 - 10 **Product Groups:** 24, 63, 86

Manderstam International Group Ltd
10 Greycoat Place, London, SW1P 1SB
Tel: 020-7730 9224 **Fax:** 020-7823 3056
E-mail: peterlumley@manderstam.com
Website: http://www.manderstam.com
Bank(s): National Westminster
Directors: P. Lumley (MD)
Immediate Holding Company: MAJEKODUNMI VENTURES LIMITED
Registration no: 02584799 **Date established:** 1991 **Turnover:** £2m - £5m
No.of Employees: 11 - 20 **Product Groups:** 84

Date of Accounts	Feb 07	Feb 06
Working Capital	119	11
Fixed Assets	53	N/A
Current Assets	259	45
Current Liabilities	140	34

Mango Surf (City Telecom Ltd)
C E T House 36 Golders Gardens, London, NW11 9BU
Tel: 020-8266 2800 **Fax:** 08700-118330
E-mail: support@citytelecom.co.uk
Website: http://www.mangosurf.net
Directors: N. Hamburger (Dir)
Date established: 1994 **No.of Employees:** 1 - 10 **Product Groups:** 37, 44, 79, 81

Manning Gottlieb Media Ltd
Seymour Mews House 26-37 Seymour Mews, London, W1H 6BN
Tel: 020-7470 5300 **Fax:** 020-7412 0244
E-mail: reception@mgomd.com
Website: http://www.mgomd.com
Directors: S. Loney (Fin)
Managers: B. Clifton (Tech Serv Mgr)
Immediate Holding Company: MANNING GOTTLIEB OMD
Registration no: 02477134 **Date established:** 1990
No.of Employees: 101 - 250 **Product Groups:** 81

Manuplastics Ltd
13-15 Lombard Road, London, SW19 3TZ
Tel: 020-8542 3421 **Fax:** 020-8540 0594
E-mail: sales@manuplastics.co.uk
Website: http://www.manuplastics.co.uk
Bank(s): Barclays, Richmond
Directors: A. Bray (Sales), D. Wearn (MD), S. Haley (Comm)
Managers: D. O'Grady (Works Gen Mgr)
Immediate Holding Company: MANUPLASTICS LIMITED
Registration no: 00281845 **VAT No.:** GB 512 9626 54
Date established: 1933 **Turnover:** £5m - £10m
No.of Employees: 51 - 100 **Product Groups:** 30

Date of Accounts	Jun 11	Jun 10	Jun 09
Sales Turnover	8m	7m	7m
Pre Tax Profit/Loss	863	852	304
Working Capital	2m	2m	1m
Fixed Assets	7m	7m	7m
Current Assets	4m	3m	2m
Current Liabilities	898	723	456

Map Trading Ltd
2 Abbey Road, London, NW10 7BS
Tel: 020-8965 0193 **Fax:** 020-8963 1184
E-mail: post@whitepearl.co.uk
Website: http://www.whitepearl.co.uk
Directors: A. Bhatti (Dir), M. Chowdry (MD)
Ultimate Holding Company: BESTWAY (HOLDINGS) LIMITED
Immediate Holding Company: MAP TRADING LIMITED
Registration no: 01826942 **Date established:** 1984
Turnover: £10m - £20m **No.of Employees:** 11 - 20 **Product Groups:** 20, 61, 62, 84

Date of Accounts	Jun 11	Jun 10	Jun 09
Sales Turnover	16m	13m	15m
Pre Tax Profit/Loss	88	108	321
Working Capital	3m	3m	3m
Fixed Assets	414	341	389
Current Assets	6m	5m	5m
Current Liabilities	188	138	122

Maplin Electronics Ltd
21-23 High Road, London, N22 6BH
Tel: 08432-277325 **Fax:** 020-8881 2165
E-mail: customercare@maplin.co.uk
Website: http://www.maplin.co.uk
Managers: C. Peara (Mgr)
Ultimate Holding Company: MONTAGU PRIVATE EQUITY LLP
Immediate Holding Company: MAPLIN ELECTRONICS LIMITED
Registration no: 01264385 **Date established:** 1976
Turnover: £125m - £250m **No.of Employees:** 1 - 10 **Product Groups:** 37, 61

Date of Accounts	Dec 11	Dec 08	Dec 09
Sales Turnover	205m	204m	204m
Pre Tax Profit/Loss	25m	32m	35m
Working Capital	118m	49m	75m
Fixed Assets	27m	28m	28m
Current Assets	207m	108m	142m
Current Liabilities	78m	51m	59m

Maplin Electronics Ltd
218-219 Tottenham Court Road, London, W1T 7PX
Tel: 08432-277353
Website: http://www.maplin.co.uk
Managers: C. Perera (Mgr)
Ultimate Holding Company: MONTAGU PRIVATE EQUITY LLP
Immediate Holding Company: MAPLIN ELECTRONICS LIMITED
Registration no: 01264385 **Date established:** 1976
Turnover: £125m - £250m **No.of Employees:** 11 - 20
Product Groups: 37, 61

Date of Accounts	Dec 11	Dec 08	Dec 09
Sales Turnover	205m	204m	204m
Pre Tax Profit/Loss	25m	32m	35m
Working Capital	118m	49m	75m
Fixed Assets	27m	28m	28m
Current Assets	207m	108m	142m
Current Liabilities	78m	51m	59m

Maplin Electronics Ltd
Westhorne Avenue, London, SE9 5LT
Tel: 020-8850 4250 **Fax:** 020-8850 6971
Website: http://www.maplin.co.uk
Managers: D. Matthews (Mgr)
Ultimate Holding Company: Maplin Electronics Group (Holdings) Ltd
Immediate Holding Company: Maplin Electronics (Holdings) Ltd
Registration no: 01264385 **Date established:** 1976
Turnover: £125m - £250m **No.of Employees:** 1 - 10 **Product Groups:** 37, 61

Maplin Electronics Ltd
107-113 Stanstead Road, London, SE23 1HH
Tel: 08432-277311 **Fax:** 020-8291 9107
E-mail: customercare@maplin.co.uk
Website: http://www.maplin.co.uk
Managers: P. Johnson (Reg Mgr)
Ultimate Holding Company: MONTAGU PRIVATE EQUITY LLP
Immediate Holding Company: MAPLIN ELECTRONICS LIMITED
Registration no: 01264385 **Date established:** 1976
Turnover: £125m - £250m **No.of Employees:** 1 - 10 **Product Groups:** 37, 61

Date of Accounts	Dec 11	Dec 08	Dec 09
Sales Turnover	205m	204m	204m
Pre Tax Profit/Loss	25m	32m	35m
Working Capital	118m	49m	75m
Fixed Assets	27m	28m	28m
Current Assets	207m	108m	142m
Current Liabilities	78m	51m	59m

Maplin Electronics Ltd
120-124 King Street, London, W6 0QU
Tel: 08432-277343 **Fax:** 020-8741 5362
E-mail: customercare@maplin.co.uk
Website: http://www.maplin.co.uk
Managers: E. Hilton (Mgr)
Ultimate Holding Company: MONTAGU PRIVATE EQUITY LLP
Immediate Holding Company: MAPLIN ELECTRONICS LIMITED
Registration no: 01264385 **Date established:** 1976
Turnover: £125m - £250m **No.of Employees:** 11 - 20
Product Groups: 37, 61

Date of Accounts	Dec 11	Dec 08	Dec 09
Sales Turnover	205m	204m	204m
Pre Tax Profit/Loss	25m	32m	35m
Working Capital	118m	49m	75m
Fixed Assets	27m	28m	28m
Current Assets	207m	108m	142m
Current Liabilities	78m	51m	59m

Maplin Electronics Ltd
52 - 54 High Holborn, London, WC1V 6RL
Tel: 08432-277336 **Fax:** 020-7242 8165
E-mail: customercare@maplin.co.uk
Website: http://www.maplin.co.uk
Managers: D. Turnbull (District Mgr)
Ultimate Holding Company: MONTAGU PRIVATE EQUITY LLP
Immediate Holding Company: MAPLIN ELECTRONICS LIMITED
Registration no: 01264385 **Date established:** 1976
Turnover: £125m - £250m **No.of Employees:** 1 - 10 **Product Groups:** 37, 61

Date of Accounts	Dec 11	Dec 08	Dec 09
Sales Turnover	205m	204m	204m
Pre Tax Profit/Loss	25m	32m	35m
Working Capital	118m	49m	75m
Fixed Assets	27m	28m	28m
Current Assets	207m	108m	142m
Current Liabilities	78m	51m	59m

Maplin Electronics Ltd
186 Edgware Road, London, W2 2DS
Tel: 08432-277330 **Fax:** 020-7224 9254
E-mail: customercare@maplin.co.uk
Website: http://www.maplin.co.uk
Managers: A. Mizzar (Mgr)
Ultimate Holding Company: MONTAGU PRIVATE EQUITY LLP
Immediate Holding Company: MAPLIN ELECTRONICS LIMITED
Registration no: 01264385 **Date established:** 1976
Turnover: £125m - £250m **No.of Employees:** 1 - 10 **Product Groups:** 37, 61

Date of Accounts	Dec 11	Dec 08	Dec 09
Sales Turnover	205m	204m	204m
Pre Tax Profit/Loss	25m	32m	35m
Working Capital	118m	49m	75m
Fixed Assets	27m	28m	28m
Current Assets	207m	108m	142m
Current Liabilities	78m	51m	59m

Maplin Electronics Ltd
104-106 Broadway, London, E15 1NG
Tel: 08432-277326 **Fax:** 020-8534 9359
E-mail: customercare@maplin.co.uk
Website: http://www.maplin.co.uk
Managers: E. Hilton (Mgr)
Ultimate Holding Company: MONTAGU PRIVATE EQUITY LLP
Immediate Holding Company: MAPLIN ELECTRONICS LIMITED
Registration no: 01264385 **Date established:** 1976
Turnover: £125m - £250m **No.of Employees:** 1 - 10 **Product Groups:** 37, 61

Date of Accounts	Dec 11	Dec 08	Dec 09
Sales Turnover	205m	204m	204m
Pre Tax Profit/Loss	25m	32m	35m
Working Capital	118m	49m	75m
Fixed Assets	27m	28m	28m
Current Assets	207m	108m	142m
Current Liabilities	78m	51m	59m

Marathon Service GB Ltd
Capital House 25 Chapel Street, London, NW1 5DQ
Tel: 020-7298 2500 **Fax:** 020-7298 2501
E-mail: mash@marathonoil.com
Website: http://www.marathonoil.com
Bank(s): Citibank
Directors: J. Reid (Fin), S. Macdonald (Pers), M. Ash (Dir), P. Cartwright (Co Sec)
Managers: D. Macleod (Purch Mgr), E. White (Mktg Serv Mgr)
Ultimate Holding Company: MARATHON PETROLEUM (USA)
Immediate Holding Company: MARATHON SERVICE (G.B.) LIMITED
Registration no: 01293052 **Date established:** 1976
Turnover: £50m - £75m **No.of Employees:** 21 - 50 **Product Groups:** 13, 51

Date of Accounts	Dec 11	Dec 10	Dec 09
Sales Turnover	60m	58m	62m
Pre Tax Profit/Loss	N/A	3m	4m
Working Capital	3m	920	633
Current Assets	6m	4m	3m
Current Liabilities	2m	3m	2m

Marco Specialist Interiors
14 Boughton Road, London, SE28 0AG
Tel: 020-8331 0066 **Fax:** 020-8317 3161
E-mail: info@marcointeriors.co.uk
Website: http://www.marcointeriors.co.uk
Directors: C. Scott (Ptnr)
Immediate Holding Company: MARCO SPECIALIST INTERIORS LIMITED
Registration no: 05536025 **Date established:** 2005
No.of Employees: 1 - 10 **Product Groups:** 35, 39, 45

Date of Accounts	Mar 11	Mar 10	Mar 09
Working Capital	152	182	138
Fixed Assets	170	200	227
Current Assets	340	382	414

Marek Mularczyk
40 Beacon Gate, London, SE14 5UB
Tel: 0770-9564 098
E-mail: info@marekmularczyk.com
Website: http://www.marekmularczyk.com
Directors: M. Mularczyk (Dir)
Date established: 2008 **No.of Employees:** 1 - 10 **Product Groups:** 44, 86

Marine Safety Services Ltd
19-21 Great Tower Street, London, EC3R 5AR
Tel: 020-7929 2029 **Fax:** 020-7929 1655
E-mail: enquiries@bctq.com
Website: http://www.bctq.com
Bank(s): Royal Bank of Scotland P.L.C.
Directors: M. Bryce (Dir)
Immediate Holding Company: BURNESS CORLETT THREE QUAYS SURVEY & SAFETY SERVICES LIMITED
Registration no: 05131184 **VAT No.:** GB 672 8575 91
Date established: 2004 **Turnover:** £1m - £2m **No.of Employees:** 21 - 50
Product Groups: 86

Mark Cansick & Co.
44a Highgate High Street, London, N6 5JE
Tel: 020-8340 0094 **Fax:** 020-8340 0096
E-mail: markcansick@btconnect.com
Directors: C. Cansick (MD)
Immediate Holding Company: EXPORT MANAGEMENT SERVICES LIMITED
Registration no: 00676132 **VAT No.:** GB 231 3500 19
Date established: 1960 **Turnover:** £1m - £2m **No.of Employees:** 1 - 10
Product Groups: 61

Date of Accounts	May 11	May 10	May 09
Working Capital	223	234	244
Fixed Assets	29	24	15
Current Assets	299	330	307
Current Liabilities	32	28	20

MarketForce (UK) Ltd
Blue Fin Building 110 Southwark Street, London, SE1 0SU
Tel: 020-7633 3300 **Fax:** 020-3148 8105
E-mail: salesinnovation@marketforce.co.uk
Website: http://www.marketforce.co.uk
Directors: D. Stam (MD)
Immediate Holding Company: Ipc Media Ltd
Registration no: 00499150 **Turnover:** £10m - £20m
No.of Employees: 101 - 250 **Product Groups:** 28

Marketing Dynamics Ltd
55 Lancaster Grove, London, NW3 4HD
Tel: 020-7433 3555 **Fax:** 020-7433 3560
E-mail: info@marketingdynamics.co.uk
Website: http://www.marketingdynamics.co.uk
Directors: A. Melkman (MD)
Immediate Holding Company: MARKETING DYNAMICS LIMITED
Registration no: 01419712 **Date established:** 1979
Turnover: Up to £250,000 **No.of Employees:** 1 - 10 **Product Groups:** 80

Date of Accounts	Jun 08	Jun 07	Jun 06
Sales Turnover	11	39	74
Pre Tax Profit/Loss	2	14	52
Working Capital	13	11	5
Fixed Assets	3	3	3
Current Assets	46	37	16
Current Liabilities	28	26	10

Markforce
Emperor House 35 Vine Street, London, EC3N 2PX
Tel: 020-7554 1800 **Fax:** 020-7554 1801
Website: http://www.markforce.com
Ultimate Holding Company: FIELD FISHER WATERHOUSE LLP
Immediate Holding Company: A. & H. NOMINEES LIMITED
Registration no: 01813296 **Date established:** 1967 **Turnover:** £1m - £2m
No.of Employees: 1 - 10 **Product Groups:** 80

Date of Accounts	Dec 11	Dec 10	Dec 09
Sales Turnover	29	29	30
Pre Tax Profit/Loss	3	4	-3
Working Capital	-56	-58	-63
Current Assets	19	14	9
Current Liabilities	6	4	3

Marking Products Ltd
16 Mitcham Lane Streatham, London, SW16 6NN
Tel: 020-8769 8676 **Fax:** 020-8677 1088
E-mail: enquiries@markingproducts.co.uk
Website: http://www.markingproducts.co.uk
Directors: G. Baxter (MD)
Immediate Holding Company: MARKING PRODUCTS LIMITED
Registration no: 00914200 **Date established:** 1967
No.of Employees: 1 - 10 **Product Groups:** 37

Date of Accounts	Dec 11	Dec 10	Dec 09
Working Capital	-31	-30	-31
Fixed Assets	4	N/A	N/A
Current Assets	4	4	6
Current Liabilities	N/A	N/A	37

Marking Solutions Ltd
16 Hurst Avenue, London, E4 8DW
Tel: 020-8529 7479
E-mail: contact@marking-solutions.co.uk
Website: http://www.marking-solutions.co.uk
Directors: G. Vaitekunas (Dir), G. Gabalyte (Fin)
Registration no: 05992484 **Date established:** 2006
No.of Employees: 1 - 10 **Product Groups:** 42, 48, 81

Date of Accounts	Nov 08	Nov 07
Working Capital	-46	-43
Fixed Assets	35	40
Current Assets	3	11
Current Liabilities	50	54

Marks & Clerk LLP
19 Long Acre, London, WC2E 9RA
Tel: 020-7420 0000 **Fax:** 020-7836 3339
E-mail: rwaldren@marks-clerk.com
Website: http://www.marks-clerk.com
Directors: R. Waleren (Snr Part), K. Hodkinson (Fin)
Managers: P. Tallant, A. Hancock (Fin Mgr)
Immediate Holding Company: MARKS & CLERK LEASES
Registration no: 00929922 **Date established:** 1968
Turnover: £50m - £75m **No.of Employees:** 101 - 250 **Product Groups:** 80

Marsh Ltd
1 Tower Place West, London, EC3R 5BU
Tel: 020-7357 1000 **Fax:** 020-7929 2705
E-mail: marcus.rennick@marsh.com
Website: http://www.marsh.co.uk
Directors: A. Cormack (Co Sec)
Ultimate Holding Company: MARSH & MCLENNAN COMPANIES INC (U.S.A)
Immediate Holding Company: BOWRING MARSH LIMITED
Registration no: 05163005 **Date established:** 2004
Turnover: Over £1,000m **No.of Employees:** 1 - 10 **Product Groups:** 80, 82, 86, 87

Date of Accounts	Dec 11	Dec 10	Dec 09
Sales Turnover	670m	567m	528m
Pre Tax Profit/Loss	157m	139m	91m
Working Capital	632m	710m	616m
Fixed Assets	232m	271m	287m
Current Assets	5216m	5018m	4982m
Current Liabilities	4144m	3822m	3971m

The Marsh Agency Ltd
50 Albemarle Street, London, W1S 4BD
Tel: 020-7493 4361 **Fax:** 020-7495 8961
E-mail: paterson@patersonmarsh.co.uk
Website: http://www.marsh-agency.co.uk
Directors: M. Paterson (Dir)
Immediate Holding Company: Mark Paterson & Associates
Registration no: 04038927 **No.of Employees:** 1 - 10 **Product Groups:** 87

Date of Accounts	Mar 07	Mar 06
Working Capital	1	1

Marshall Cavendish Ltd
5th Floor 32/38 Saffron Hill, London, EC1N 8FH
Tel: 020-7421 8120 **Fax:** 020-7421 8121
E-mail: info@marshallcavendish.co.uk
Website: http://www.marshallcavendish.co.uk
Directors: A. Cheong (Dir), D. Chow (Dir), K. Hooi (Grp Chief Exec), K. Lim (Ch)
Managers: S. Dyer
Ultimate Holding Company: Times Publishing Ltd, Singapore
Immediate Holding Company: Times Publishing Limited
Registration no: 00908793 **VAT No.:** GB 241 5267 79
Date established: 1944 **Turnover:** £10m - £20m
No.of Employees: 51 - 100 **Product Groups:** 28, 64

Date of Accounts	Sep 07	Sep 06	Sep 05
Pre Tax Profit/Loss	-90	1700	-1210
Working Capital	90	90	-1610
Current Assets	N/A	90	4660
Current Liabilities	N/A	N/A	6270
Total Share Capital	5010	5010	5010
ROCE% (Return on Capital Employed)			75.2

E W Marshall Ltd
79 Enid Street, London, SE16 3RA
Tel: 020-7394 0900 **Fax:** 020-7394 0827
E-mail: info@ewmarshall.com
Website: http://www.ewmarshall.com
Directors: J. Wynne (MD)
Immediate Holding Company: E.W. MARSHALL LIMITED
Registration no: 04683555 **VAT No.:** GB 232 8276 64
Date established: 2003 **Turnover:** £250,000 - £500,000
No.of Employees: 1 - 10 **Product Groups:** 26, 49, 67

Date of Accounts	Mar 11	Mar 10	Mar 09
Sales Turnover	N/A	N/A	494
Pre Tax Profit/Loss	N/A	N/A	14
Working Capital	44	41	67
Fixed Assets	2	3	4
Current Assets	95	104	142
Current Liabilities	29	N/A	11

Marshall Tufflex Ltd
101c-101d Blackhorse Lane, London, E17 6DJ
Tel: 08702-403200 **Fax:** 020-8527 5527
E-mail: sales@marshall-tufflex.com
Website: http://www.marshall-tufflex.com
Directors: J. Fletcher (Dir)
Managers: J. Lin (Buyer)
Immediate Holding Company: MARSHALL-TUFFLEX LIMITED
Registration no: 01007764 **Date established:** 1971
No.of Employees: 51 - 100 **Product Groups:** 36, 40

Date of Accounts	May 11	May 10	May 09
Working Capital	25	36	86
Current Assets	184	58	230

Marwood Group Ltd
72 Roding Road London Industrial Park, London, E6 6JG
Tel: 020-7540 2500 **Fax:** 020-7540 2521
E-mail: london@marwoodgroup.co.uk
Website: http://www.marwoodgroup.co.uk
Bank(s): Barclays
Directors: C. Martin (Ch)
Immediate Holding Company: MARWOOD GROUP LIMITED
Registration no: 01422430 **VAT No.:** GB 250 1003 35
Date established: 1979 **Turnover:** £2m - £5m **No.of Employees:** 21 - 50
Product Groups: 51

Date of Accounts	Dec 11	Dec 10	Dec 09
Sales Turnover	17m	15m	13m
Pre Tax Profit/Loss	2m	374	488
Working Capital	5m	4m	4m
Fixed Assets	2m	2m	2m
Current Assets	10m	8m	8m
Current Liabilities	1m	946	398

Wilson Mason & Partners (Chartered Architects & Landscape Consultants)
3 Chandos Street, London, W1G 9JU
Tel: 020-7637 1501 **Fax:** 020-7631 0325
E-mail: london@wilsonmason.co.uk
Website: http://www.wilsonmason.co.uk
Bank(s): Royal Bank of Scotland
Directors: P. Etches (Snr Part), R. Ward (Ptnr)
Managers: R. Peters (Tech Serv Mgr), S. Cox (Sales Admin), P. Fung
VAT No.: 233 3968 54 **Turnover:** £2m - £5m **No.of Employees:** 21 - 50
Product Groups: 07, 52, 84

Matglen Ltd
90 Seymour Avenue, London, N17 9ED
Tel: 020-8801 7799 **Fax:** 020-8801 7985
E-mail: sales@matglen.demon.co.uk
Directors: G. Musthan (Fin), S. Musthan (MD)
Immediate Holding Company: MATGLEN LIMITED
Registration no: 00933899 **VAT No.:** GB 230 3120 35
Date established: 1968 **Turnover:** £500,000 - £1m
No.of Employees: 1 - 10 **Product Groups:** 37, 47

Date of Accounts	Dec 11	Dec 10	Dec 09
Working Capital	51	107	143
Current Assets	77	107	230

Matheson & Co. Ltd
Scottish Provident Building 3 Lombard Street, London, EC3V 9AQ
Tel: 020-7816 8100 **Fax:** 020-7816 8182
E-mail: enquiries@matheson.co.uk
Website: http://www.matheson.co.uk
Directors: P. Hawkins (Fin)
Managers: D. Mulligan (Tech Serv Mgr)
Ultimate Holding Company: JARDINE MATHESON HOLDINGS LTD (BERMUDA)
Immediate Holding Company: MATHESON & CO.,LIMITED
Registration no: 00100295 **Date established:** 2008 **Turnover:** £2m - £5m
No.of Employees: 21 - 50 **Product Groups:** 82

Date of Accounts	Dec 11	Dec 10	Dec 09
Sales Turnover	2m	2m	2m
Pre Tax Profit/Loss	2m	-206	780
Working Capital	59m	62m	64m
Fixed Assets	424	367	328
Current Assets	59m	62m	64m
Current Liabilities	149	190	201

Mathmos Ltd
96 Kingsland Road, London, E2 8DP
Tel: 020-7549 2700 **Fax:** 020-7549 2715
E-mail: michael@mathmos.com
Website: http://www.mathmos.com
Directors: C. Granger (MD)
Managers: M. Beat (Sales & Mktg Mg), M. Beatt (Mgr)
Immediate Holding Company: MATHMOS LIMITED
Registration no: 02526274 **VAT No.:** GB 579 8364 70
Date established: 1990 **Turnover:** £1m - £2m **No.of Employees:** 1 - 10
Product Groups: 37

Maurice Phillips Contractsagua Fabrics
Hyde House The Hyde, London, NW9 6LH
Tel: 020-8205 0050 **Fax:** 020-8205 0660
E-mail: sales@aguafabrics.com
Website: http://www.aguafabrics.com
Directors: G. Ralton (Fin), S. Ralton (Dir)
Immediate Holding Company: MAURICE PHILLIPS CONTRACTS LIMITED
Registration no: 04470178 **Date established:** 2002
Turnover: Up to £250,000 **No.of Employees:** 1 - 10 **Product Groups:** 23

Maxwell Stamp Group plc
Abbots Court 34 Farringdon Lane, London, EC1R 3AX
Tel: 020-7251 0147 **Fax:** 020-7251 0140
E-mail: london@maxwellstamp.com
Website: http://www.maxwellstamp.com
Bank(s): Bank of Scotland, EC2
Directors: A. Osborne (Dir), S. Cole (Co Sec)
Immediate Holding Company: MAXWELL STAMP GROUP PLC
Registration no: 01998904 **VAT No.:** GB 648 9832 77
Date established: 1986 **Turnover:** £20m - £50m
No.of Employees: 21 - 50 **Product Groups:** 80, 82

Date of Accounts	Mar 12	Mar 11	Mar 10
Sales Turnover	24m	21m	17m
Pre Tax Profit/Loss	902	2m	624
Working Capital	4m	4m	2m
Fixed Assets	3m	3m	3m
Current Assets	9m	10m	7m
Current Liabilities	3m	4m	2m

Mcdonald Brown & Facilities Ltd
7 Eastbury Road, London, E6 6LP
Tel: 020-7511 8899 **Fax:** 020-7473 1133
E-mail: gdm@mcdonaldbrownltd.co.uk
Website: http://www.mcdonaldbrownltd.co.uk
Bank(s): Barclays
Directors: J. Bones (Dir), G. Mcdonald (MD)
Ultimate Holding Company: MCDONALD INSULATION AND MAINTENANCE LIMITED
Immediate Holding Company: MCDONALD BROWN LIMITED
Registration no: 01253816 **VAT No.:** GB 506 4652 55
Date established: 1976 **No.of Employees:** 21 - 50 **Product Groups:** 48

Date of Accounts	Mar 12	Nov 10	Nov 09
Working Capital	514	501	590
Fixed Assets	36	30	46
Current Assets	2m	2m	2m

Mcdonald's Head Office
11-59 High Road, London, N2 8AW
Tel: 08705-244622 **Fax:** 020-8700 7050
E-mail: steve.easterbrook@uk.mcd.com
Website: http://www.mcdonald-engineers.com
Directors: L. Morgan (Mkt Research), D. Burnside (Fin), S. Easterbrook (Dir), S. Easterbrook (Grp Chief Exec), J. Hilton Johnson (Co Sec)
Immediate Holding Company: MCDONALD'S RESTAURANTS PENSIONS TRUSTEE LIMITED
Registration no: 07052614 **Date established:** 2009
Turnover: £50m - £75m **No.of Employees:** 1 - 10 **Product Groups:** 69

Date of Accounts	Dec 09	Dec 08	Dec 07
Sales Turnover	1130m	1076m	1070m
Pre Tax Profit/Loss	114m	78m	40m
Working Capital	-365m	-463m	-524m
Fixed Assets	704m	718m	733m
Current Assets	64m	106m	107m
Current Liabilities	102m	89m	92m

Mckinlay Electrical Ltd
62 Weir Road, London, SW19 8UG
Tel: 020-8879 1141 **Fax:** 020- 89463047
E-mail: mckinlayelec@aol.com
Website: http://www.mckinlayelectrical.co.uk
Directors: M. Sharman (Fin), M. Bourne (MD)
Managers: D. Kimber (Sales Prom Mgr)
Immediate Holding Company: MCKINLAY ELECTRICAL MANUFACTURING CO LIMITED
Registration no: 00337471 **Date established:** 1938
Turnover: £500,000 - £1m **No.of Employees:** 11 - 20
Product Groups: 29, 30, 31, 37, 42, 46, 47, 48

Date of Accounts	Sep 10	Sep 09	Sep 08
Working Capital	694	536	695
Fixed Assets	316	324	337
Current Assets	795	561	774

Mckinnes Cook
31 Lisson Grove, London, NW1 6UB
Tel: 020-7258 0600 **Fax:** 020-7723 7005
Directors: D. Cook (Ptnr), J. Cook (Prop)
Immediate Holding Company: MCINNES COOK (2008) LIMITED
Date established: 2008 **No.of Employees:** 1 - 10 **Product Groups:** 37, 67

Mead Grove Export Ltd
25 Curzon Street, London, W1J 7TG
Tel: 020-7629 5886 **Fax:** 020-7408 0849
E-mail: info@meadoil.com
Website: http://www.meadgrove.com
Directors: A. Hassan (Dir)
Immediate Holding Company: MEADGROVE EXPORTS LIMITED
Registration no: 02800355 **VAT No.:** 626 5257 34 **Date established:** 1993
Turnover: £250,000 - £500,000 **No.of Employees:** 1 - 10
Product Groups: 61

Date of Accounts	Apr 11	Apr 10	Apr 09
Sales Turnover	783	438	343
Pre Tax Profit/Loss	158	-231	514
Working Capital	-150	-282	-285
Fixed Assets	2m	2m	2m
Current Assets	2m	2m	1m
Current Liabilities	60	179	344

Medema Ltd
329-339 Putney Bridge Road, London, SW15 2PG
Tel: 020-8780 0338 **Fax:** 020-8785 3409
E-mail: sales@medema.co.uk
Website: http://www.medema.co.uk
Managers: A. Her
Immediate Holding Company: MEDEMA LIMITED
Registration no: 05630680 **Date established:** 2005
Turnover: £500,000 - £1m **No.of Employees:** 1 - 10 **Product Groups:** 61

Date of Accounts	Nov 07	Nov 06
Working Capital	-5	-22
Fixed Assets	25	28
Current Assets	27	3

Media Brands Ltd
42-48 St John's Square, London, EC1M 4EA
Tel: 020-7663 7000 **Fax:** 020-7663 7001
E-mail: alex.altman@uk.initiative.com
Website: http://www.initiative.com
Directors: D. Bletsco (Fin), L. Bean (Fin)
Managers: A. Altman
Ultimate Holding Company: INTERPUBLIC GROUP OF COMPANIES INC (USA)
Immediate Holding Company: MEDIABRANDS LIMITED
Registration no: 00773961 **Date established:** 1963
Turnover: £20m - £50m **No.of Employees:** 101 - 250 **Product Groups:** 81

Date of Accounts	Dec 11	Dec 10	Dec 09
Sales Turnover	21m	21m	21m
Pre Tax Profit/Loss	1m	4m	4m
Working Capital	16m	15m	11m
Fixed Assets	4m	5m	6m
Current Assets	82m	94m	89m
Current Liabilities	11m	10m	11m

Media Campaign Ltd
20 Orange Street, London, WC2H 7EF
Tel: 020-7389 0800 **Fax:** 020-7839 6997
E-mail: sales@mediacampaign.co.uk
Website: http://www.mediacampaign.co.uk
Bank(s): The Royal Bank of Scotland
Directors: V. Mistry (Fin), A. Richmond (Comm)
Managers: S. Watts (Sales Admin)
Immediate Holding Company: MEDIA CAMPAIGN HOLDINGS LIMITED
Registration no: 02900407 **VAT No.:** GB 241 4592 73
Date established: 1994 **Turnover:** £20m - £50m
No.of Employees: 21 - 50 **Product Groups:** 81

Date of Accounts	Jan 12	Jan 11	Jan 10
Pre Tax Profit/Loss	N/A	N/A	-26
Working Capital	-9	-9	-9
Current Assets	5	5	5

Media Com
124 Theobalds Road, London, WC1X 8RX
Tel: 020-7158 5000 **Fax:** 020-7158 5999
E-mail: reception@mediacomuk.com
Website: http://www.mediacom.com
Managers: S. Allan
Ultimate Holding Company: WPP PLC (JERSEY)
Immediate Holding Company: MEDIACOM HOLDINGS LIMITED
Registration no: 03525784 **Date established:** 1998
Turnover: £75m - £125m **No.of Employees:** 501 - 1000
Product Groups: 81

Date of Accounts	Dec 11	Dec 10	Dec 09
Pre Tax Profit/Loss	25m	15m	25m
Working Capital	1m	967	967
Fixed Assets	37m	37m	37m
Current Assets	44m	19m	49m

Mediatech Av
Innovation House 17- 27 Stirling Road Acton London, London, W3 8DJ
Tel: 020-8903 4372 **Fax:** 020-8752 3940
E-mail: robertj@mediatechav.co.uk
Website: http://www.mediatechav.com
Directors: C. Gould (Dir)
Immediate Holding Company: MEDIATECH A. V. LIMITED
Registration no: 03058554 **VAT No.:** GB 657 2977 85
Date established: 1995 **Turnover:** £1m - £2m **No.of Employees:** 1 - 10
Product Groups: 37, 69

Date of Accounts	Apr 11	Apr 10	Apr 09
Working Capital	31	42	60
Fixed Assets	5	1	7
Current Assets	113	114	201

Medicell International Ltd
239 Liverpool Road, London, N1 1LX
Tel: 020-7607 2295 **Fax:** 020-7700 4156
E-mail: info@medicell.co.uk
Website: http://www.medicell.co.uk
Directors: R. Soolia (Fin)
Immediate Holding Company: MEDICELL INTERNATIONAL LIMITED
Registration no: 01156576 **VAT No.:** GB 244 5595 44
Date established: 1974 **Turnover:** £250,000 - £500,000
No.of Employees: 1 - 10 **Product Groups:** 42

Date of Accounts	Dec 11	Dec 10	Dec 09
Sales Turnover	318	320	323
Pre Tax Profit/Loss	2	9	N/A
Working Capital	N/A	-1	8
Fixed Assets	3	4	4
Current Assets	146	151	143
Current Liabilities	34	62	32

The Medici Galleries
19 - 23 White Lion street Islington, London, N1 9PD
Tel: 020-7713 8800 **Fax:** 020-7837 7579
E-mail: info@medici.co.uk
Website: http://www.medici.co.uk
Bank(s): Barclays, London
Directors: G. Derby (Grp Chief Exec), J. Marsh (Sales), D. Hardstaff (MD), A. Trinity (Dir)
Managers: C. Mitchell (Mgr)
Immediate Holding Company: Medici Society,Limited(The)
Registration no: 00098457 **VAT No.:** GB 342 0169 90
Date established: 2008 **Turnover:** £2m - £5m **No.of Employees:** 51 - 100
Product Groups: 27, 28

Date of Accounts	Mar 07	Mar 06
Sales Turnover	N/A	4954
Pre Tax Profit/Loss	N/A	-307

Working Capital	459	1642
Fixed Assets	485	638
Current Assets	1683	2293
Current Liabilities	1224	651
Total Share Capital	32	33
ROCE% (Return on Capital Employed)		-13.5
ROT% (Return on Turnover)		-6.2

Medicina (UK) Ltd
145-147 St John Street, London, EC1V 4PY
Tel: 020-8205 2369 **Fax:** 020-8205 2346
E-mail: info@medicina-uk.com
Website: http://www.naturalrussia.com
Directors: G. St George (Comm)
Registration no: 05359901 **Date established:** 2005
Turnover: Up to £250,000 **No.of Employees:** 1 - 10 **Product Groups:** 32

Date of Accounts	Feb 07
Sales Turnover	1
Current Assets	2
Current Liabilities	2

Mediequip Assistive Technology
Unit 5a Oakwood Business Park Standard Road, London, NW10 6EX
Tel: 020-8965 1031 **Fax:** 020-8965 1039
Website: http://www.mediquip-uk.com
Managers: P. Harji (Mgr)
No.of Employees: 21 - 50 **Product Groups:** 38, 67

Medlock Electrical Distributors
15-16 Heckford St Business Centre Heckford Street, London, E1W 3HS
Tel: 020-7265 8836 **Fax:** 020-7265 8733
E-mail: david.walls@medlocks.co.uk
Website: http://www.medlocks.co.uk
Managers: D. Walls (District Mgr)
Immediate Holding Company: MEDLOCK ELECTRIC LIMITED
Registration no: 01332367 **Date established:** 1977
No.of Employees: 1 - 10 **Product Groups:** 36, 40

Medlock Electrical Distributors
605-609 Green Lanes, London, N8 0RE
Tel: 020-8348 5191
E-mail: peter.moore@medlocks.co.uk
Website: http://www.medlocks.co.uk
Managers: P. Moore (District Mgr), T. Mills (Personnel)
Immediate Holding Company: MEDLOCK ELECTRIC LIMITED
Registration no: 01332367 **Date established:** 1977
No.of Employees: 21 - 50 **Product Groups:** 37, 67

Melanie Potro
Unit 53 Craft Central 33-35 St John's Square, London, EC1M 4DS
Tel: 020-7490 8634 **Fax:** 020-7490 8634
E-mail: bride@melaniepotro.com
Website: http://www.melaniepotro.com
Directors: M. Potro (Prop)
Registration no: 06416909 **Date established:** 2007
Turnover: Up to £250,000 **No.of Employees:** 1 - 10 **Product Groups:** 24

Mellersh & Harding
32 St James's Street, London, SW1A 1HD
Tel: 020-7522 8500 **Fax:** 020-7522 8501
E-mail: info@mellersh.co.uk
Website: http://www.mellersh.co.uk
Bank(s): National Westminster Bank Plc
Directors: D. Mundy (Dir)
Ultimate Holding Company: CITIGROUP INC (USA)
Registration no: 02386153 **Date established:** 1989 **Turnover:** £2m - £5m
No.of Employees: 11 - 20 **Product Groups:** 80, 82, 84

Date of Accounts	Mar 07	Mar 06
Working Capital	135	43
Fixed Assets	83	221
Current Assets	547	469
Current Liabilities	411	426
Total Share Capital	10	10

Membery London
1 Church Road, London, SW13 9HE
Tel: 020-8876 8075 **Fax:** 020-8392 1229
E-mail: sallymembery@yahoo.co.uk
Website: http://www.memberylondon.com
Directors: S. Membery (Ptnr)
Managers: M. Hill (Chief Buyer)
Immediate Holding Company: MEMBERY LIMITED
Registration no: 07351369 **Date established:** 2010
No.of Employees: 1 - 10 **Product Groups:** 63

Date of Accounts	Aug 11
Working Capital	-8
Fixed Assets	5
Current Assets	49

Mercer
1 Tower Place West, London, EC3R 5BU
Tel: 020-7626 6000 **Fax:** 020-7222 6140
Website: http://www.mercer.com
Directors: D. O'Regan (Ch)
Ultimate Holding Company: MARSH & MCLENNAN COMPANIES INC (U.S.A)
Immediate Holding Company: MERCER LIMITED
Registration no: 00984275 **VAT No.:** GB 662 7175 22
Date established: 1970 **Turnover:** £250m - £500m
No.of Employees: 101 - 250 **Product Groups:** 82

Date of Accounts	Dec 11	Dec 10	Dec 09
Sales Turnover	331m	319m	329m
Pre Tax Profit/Loss	77m	73m	73m
Working Capital	424m	370m	331m
Fixed Assets	15m	43m	20m
Current Assets	487m	426m	389m
Current Liabilities	51m	48m	46m

Mercuri Urval ltd
35 Portman Square, London, W1H 6LR
Tel: 020-7467 3730 **Fax:** 020-7467 3738
E-mail: stephen.finley@mercuriurval.com
Website: http://www.mercuriurval.co.uk
Directors: T. Rayner (Fin), S. Finley (MD)
Ultimate Holding Company: MERCURI URVAL INTERNATIONAL AB (SWEDEN)
Immediate Holding Company: MERCURI URVAL LIMITED
Registration no: 01170240 **Date established:** 1974 **Turnover:** £2m - £5m
No.of Employees: 21 - 50 **Product Groups:** 80

see next page

Mercuri Urval ltd - Cont'd

Date of Accounts	Dec 11	Dec 10	Dec 09
Sales Turnover	4m	3m	3m
Pre Tax Profit/Loss	252	126	-536
Working Capital	911	790	668
Fixed Assets	7	27	56
Current Assets	2m	2m	2m
Current Liabilities	717	594	324

Mercury Records

1 Sussex Place, London, W6 9EA
Tel: 020-8910 5333
Website: http://www.umusic.co.uk
Directors: M. Howle (Co Sec)
Ultimate Holding Company: VIVENDI SA (FRANCE)
Immediate Holding Company: BRAVADO INTERNATIONAL GROUP LIMITED
Registration no: 00586873 **Date established:** 1992
Turnover: £75m - £125m **No.of Employees:** 1 - 10 **Product Groups:** 28, 37

Date of Accounts	Dec 09	Dec 08	Dec 07
Sales Turnover	85m	76m	80m
Working Capital	7m	6m	4m
Current Assets	48m	52m	42m
Current Liabilities	10m	42m	34m

Merlyn Court Hotel Bed & Breakfast

2 Barkston Gardens, London, SW5 0EN
Tel: 020-7370 1640
E-mail: london@merlyncourthotel.com
Website: http://www.merlyncourthotel.com
Date established: 1947 **No.of Employees:** 21 - 50 **Product Groups:** 69

Merrill Lynch Commodities Europe Holdings Ltd

Merrill Lynch Financial Centre 2 King Edward Street, London, EC1A 1HP
Tel: 020-7628 1000
Website: http://www.ml.com
Directors: D. Thomson (Fin)
Ultimate Holding Company: BANK OF AMERICA CORP (USA)
Immediate Holding Company: MERRILL LYNCH COMMODITIES (EUROPE) HOLDINGS LIMITED
Registration no: 05194611 **VAT No.:** GB 245 1224 93
Date established: 2004 **Turnover:** £2m - £5m
No.of Employees: 101 - 250 **Product Groups:** 80, 82

Date of Accounts	Dec 09	Dec 08	Dec 07
Sales Turnover	167m	183m	3396m
Pre Tax Profit/Loss	-5m	-11183m	-7188m
Working Capital	-78m	-144m	12562m
Fixed Assets	6636m	6690m	657m
Current Assets	727m	695m	N/A
Current Liabilities	805m	839m	274956m

Metafour UK Ltd

2 Berghem Mews Blythe Road, London, W14 0HN
Tel: 020-7912 2000
E-mail: sales@metafour.com
Website: http://www.metafour.com
Bank(s): Barclays
Directors: M. Rogers (MD)
Immediate Holding Company: METAFOUR UK LIMITED
Registration no: 01528556 **Date established:** 1980 **Turnover:** £1m - £2m
No.of Employees: 11 - 20 **Product Groups:** 84

Date of Accounts	Jun 11	Jun 10	Jun 09
Sales Turnover	1m	1m	1m
Pre Tax Profit/Loss	204	98	52
Working Capital	399	194	95
Fixed Assets	N/A	1	1
Current Assets	655	403	327
Current Liabilities	229	184	165

Metal Bulletin plc

71-73 Carter Lane, London, EC4V 5EQ
Tel: 020-7779 8888 **Fax:** 020-8337 8943
E-mail: info@metalbulletin.com
Website: http://www.metalbulletinstore.com
Bank(s): HSBC
Directors: C. Jones (Fin)
Ultimate Holding Company: ROTHERMERE CONTINUATION LTD (BERMUDA)
Immediate Holding Company: METAL BULLETIN LIMITED
Registration no: 00142215 **VAT No.:** GB 232 4922 79
Date established: 2015 **Turnover:** £20m - £50m
No.of Employees: 21 - 50 **Product Groups:** 28, 64

Date of Accounts	Sep 11	Sep 10	Sep 09
Sales Turnover	25m	23m	21m
Pre Tax Profit/Loss	309m	29m	16m
Working Capital	3m	17m	7m
Fixed Assets	N/A	12m	12m
Current Assets	33m	29m	19m
Current Liabilities	14m	12m	10m

Metal Enterprises & Co. Ltd

150 Buckingham Palace Road, London, SW1W 9TR
Tel: 020-7730 6134 **Fax:** 020-7730 0740
E-mail: info@metent.com
Website: http://www.metent.com
Bank(s): Midland
Directors: T. Warren (MD), A. Besser (Fin)
Immediate Holding Company: METAL ENTERPRISES & CO LIMITED
Registration no: 03855758 **Date established:** 1999
Turnover: £10m - £20m **No.of Employees:** 11 - 20 **Product Groups:** 66

Date of Accounts	Dec 11	Dec 10	Dec 09
Sales Turnover	13m	15m	9m
Pre Tax Profit/Loss	145	111	85
Working Capital	2m	2m	2m
Fixed Assets	45	51	47
Current Assets	9m	10m	9m
Current Liabilities	548	156	156

Metalcraft Tottenham Ltd

6-40 Durnford Street, London, N15 5NQ
Tel: 020-8802 1715 **Fax:** 020-8802 1258
E-mail: sales@makingmetalwork.com
Website: http://www.makingmetalwork.com
Directors: D. Sugarman (Dir), A. Sugarman (Fin)
Immediate Holding Company: METALCRAFT (TOTTENHAM) LIMITED
Registration no: 01269074 **Date established:** 1976 **Turnover:** £1m - £2m
No.of Employees: 1 - 10 **Product Groups:** 26, 35

Date of Accounts	Jun 11	Jun 10	Jun 09
Sales Turnover	1m	1m	N/A
Pre Tax Profit/Loss	274	204	N/A
Working Capital	223	164	246
Fixed Assets	79	64	78
Current Assets	570	757	589

Metdist Enterprises Ltd

80 Cannon Street, London, EC4N 6EJ
Tel: 020-7280 0000 **Fax:** 020-7606 6650
E-mail: enquiries@metdist.com
Website: http://www.metdist.com
Managers: F. Sawyer (Sales Admin)
Ultimate Holding Company: MINMETCO LIMITED
Immediate Holding Company: METDIST LIMITED
Registration no: 00973341 **Date established:** 1970
Turnover: £500m - £1,000m **No.of Employees:** 11 - 20
Product Groups: 66

Date of Accounts	Mar 08	Mar 07	Mar 06
Sales Turnover	717170	578250	433030
Pre Tax Profit/Loss	1860	1580	1340
Working Capital	62700	61140	59860
Fixed Assets	1220	1590	1810
Current Assets	127770	98970	110730
Current Liabilities	65070	37830	50870
Total Share Capital	2850	2850	2850
ROCE% (Return on Capital Employed)	2.9	2.5	2.2
ROT% (Return on Turnover)	0.3	0.3	0.3

Metra Martech Ltd

7 Chiswick High Road, London, W4 2ND
Tel: 020-8742 7888 **Fax:** 020-8742 8558
E-mail: research@metra-martech.com
Website: http://www.metra-martech.com
Bank(s): Lloyds TSB Bank plc
Directors: P. Gorle (MD)
Managers: P. Borman (Fin Mgr)
Ultimate Holding Company: M M DUBOIS LIMITED
Immediate Holding Company: METRA MARTECH LIMITED
Registration no: 02196706 **VAT No.:** GB 503 3063 00
Date established: 1987 **Turnover:** £1m - £2m **No.of Employees:** 11 - 20
Product Groups: 54, 80, 81, 84, 85, 86

Date of Accounts	Jun 11	Jun 10	Jun 09
Working Capital	28	12	-12
Fixed Assets	1	1	2
Current Assets	45	37	10

Metro Lifts Ltd

3 Kings Bench Walk Temple, London, EC4Y 7DQ
Tel: 020-7353 1831 **Fax:** 020-8363 4505
Managers: J. Eddicott (Mgr), T. Eddicott (Mgr)
Immediate Holding Company: METRO LIFTS LIMITED
Registration no: 01349530 **Date established:** 1978
No.of Employees: 11 - 20 **Product Groups:** 35, 39, 45

Date of Accounts	Jan 11	Jan 10	Jan 09
Working Capital	8	-25	-34
Fixed Assets	145	162	184
Current Assets	354	253	299

Metro Textiles Ltd

35a Walm Lane, London, NW2 5SH
Tel: 020-8459 3756 **Fax:** 020-8451 4410
Website: http://www.metrotextiles.co.uk
Directors: S. Shalom (MD), A. Shalom (Fin)
Immediate Holding Company: METRO TEXTILES CORNER LIMITED
Registration no: 01837300 **Date established:** 1984
No.of Employees: 1 - 10 **Product Groups:** 24

Date of Accounts	Jul 11	Jul 10	Jul 09
Working Capital	1m	2m	2m
Fixed Assets	1m	1m	1m
Current Assets	2m	2m	3m
Current Liabilities	N/A	110	110

Metroline Travel Ltd

ComfortDelGro House 3rd Floor, 329 Edgware Road, Cricklewood, London, NW2 6JP
Tel: 0845-300 7000 **Fax:** 020-7027 9914
E-mail: customerservices@tfl-buses.co.uk
Website: http://www.metroline.co.uk
Bank(s): National Westminster, London
Directors: K. Lee (Dir), H. Lim (Grp Chief Exec), J. Singh (Grp Chief Exec)
Managers: N. Patel (I.T. Exec), O. Nevin (Personnel)
Ultimate Holding Company: COMFORTDELGRO CORPORATION LIMITED (SINGAPORE)
Registration no: 02328401 **VAT No.:** GB 649 3410 30
Date established: 1988 **Turnover:** £125m - £250m
No.of Employees: 1501 & over **Product Groups:** 39, 72

Date of Accounts	Dec 09	Dec 08	Dec 07
Sales Turnover	223m	214m	208m
Pre Tax Profit/Loss	14m	6m	17m
Working Capital	-3m	-11m	-4m
Fixed Assets	111m	108m	99m
Current Assets	58m	40m	41m
Current Liabilities	24m	19m	15m

Metwin Ltd

104 Chingford Mount Road, London, E4 9AA
Tel: 020-8523 2081 **Fax:** 020-8531 8313
E-mail: sales@metwin.co.uk
Website: http://www.metwin.co.uk
Bank(s): HSBC
Directors: F. Anderson (MD)
Immediate Holding Company: METWIN LIMITED
Registration no: 00605746 **VAT No.:** GB 233 1802 01
Date established: 1958 **No.of Employees:** 11 - 20 **Product Groups:** 35

Date of Accounts	Jun 11	Jun 10	Jun 09
Working Capital	594	702	720
Fixed Assets	29	37	51
Current Assets	1m	915	970

Michael Page International plc

Victoria House Southampton Row, London, WC1B 4JB
Tel: 020-7831 2000 **Fax:** 020-7404 5557
E-mail: stepheningham@michealpage.com
Website: http://www.michaelpage.com
Directors: S. Puckett (Fin)
Ultimate Holding Company: MICHAEL PAGE INTERNATIONAL PLC
Immediate Holding Company: MICHAEL PAGE LIMITED
Registration no: 01609138 **Date established:** 1982
Turnover: £500m - £1,000m **No.of Employees:** 101 - 250
Product Groups: 80

Date of Accounts	Dec 10	Dec 09	Dec 08
Working Capital	2	2	2
Current Assets	8m	8m	8m

Michelle Antoinette

Cosgrove Close Winchmore Hill, London, N21 3BG
Tel: 07908-898441
E-mail: michelleantoinettes@ymail.com
Website: http://www.michelleantoinette.co.uk
Directors: M. Antoinette (Dir)
Date established: 2002 **No.of Employees:** 1 - 10 **Product Groups:** 32

Micro Globe

3 Galen Place, London, WC1A 2JR
Tel: 020-7240 6774 **Fax:** 020-7419 4729
E-mail: submit@microglobe.co.uk
Website: http://www.microglobe.co.uk
Directors: A. Amin (Prop)
No.of Employees: 1 - 10 **Product Groups:** 38

Microphonic Ltd

Silvertown viaduct Royal Docks, London, E16 1AG
Tel: 020-3039 2979
E-mail: info@microphonic.biz
Website: http://www.microphonic.biz
Directors: C. Bird (MD)
Registration no: 04731775 **Date established:** 1903
No.of Employees: 1 - 10 **Product Groups:** 37, 67

Micro-Reg Carousels

31 Hawthorn Grove, London, SE20 8LS
Tel: 020-8659 9362
E-mail: bill_folley@tiscali.co.uk
Directors: B. Folley (Prop)
Date established: 2007 **No.of Employees:** 1 - 10 **Product Groups:** 44

Middlesex County Cricket Club

Lords Cricket Ground St Johns Wood Road, London, NW8 8QN
Tel: 020-7289 1300 **Fax:** 020-7289 5831
E-mail: enquiries@middlesexccc.com
Website: http://www.middlesexccc.com
Directors: V. Codrington (Grp Chief Exec)
Immediate Holding Company: MIDDLESEX CRICKET BOARD LIMITED
Registration no: 07490363 **Date established:** 2011
Turnover: Up to £250,000 **No.of Employees:** 1 - 10 **Product Groups:** 89

Date of Accounts	Dec 11
Sales Turnover	627
Pre Tax Profit/Loss	29
Working Capital	61
Fixed Assets	2
Current Assets	622
Current Liabilities	562

Middlesex Reboring Co. Ltd

Lawrence Street Mill Hill, London, NW7 4JH
Tel: 020-8959 2567 **Fax:** 020-8959 7579
E-mail: office@middxrebore.co.uk
Website: http://www.middlesexreboringcoltd.co.uk
Directors: A. Flower (Dir)
Immediate Holding Company: MIDDLESEX RE-BORING COMPANY LIMITED
Registration no: 02861880 **Date established:** 1993
No.of Employees: 1 - 10 **Product Groups:** 35, 36, 39

Date of Accounts	Oct 11	Oct 10	Oct 09
Working Capital	16	4	8
Fixed Assets	18	12	14
Current Assets	69	51	41

Miller Insurance Services Ltd

Dawson House 5 Jewry Street, London, EC3N 2PJ
Tel: 020-7488 2345 **Fax:** 020-7265 1423
E-mail: sam.bheda@miller-insurance.com
Website: http://www.miller-insurance.com
Bank(s): Royal Bank Of Scotland
Directors: E. Johnson (Co Sec)
Managers: S. Bheda
Ultimate Holding Company: MILLER INSURANCE SERVICES LLP
Immediate Holding Company: MILLER INSURANCE HOLDINGS LIMITED
Registration no: 00830141 **Date established:** 1964
Turnover: £75m - £125m **No.of Employees:** 251 - 500
Product Groups: 82

Date of Accounts	Apr 12	Apr 11	Apr 10
Sales Turnover	97m	84m	77m
Pre Tax Profit/Loss	19m	8m	7m
Working Capital	31m	38m	37m
Fixed Assets	5m	3m	3m
Current Assets	660m	570m	649m
Current Liabilities	44m	33m	27m

Millers Catering Equipment Ltd

Unit 2 College Fields Business Centre Prince Georges Road, London, SW19 2PT
Tel: 020-8687 5390 **Fax:** 020-8687 5399
E-mail: info@millerscatering.co.uk
Website: http://www.millerscatering.co.uk
Directors: A. Winslade (MD)
Registration no: 00507326 **Turnover:** £1m - £2m
No.of Employees: 1 - 10 **Product Groups:** 20, 40, 41

Mineral Products Association

Gillingham House 38-44 Gillingham Street, London, SW1V 1HU
Tel: 020-7963 8000 **Fax:** 020-7963 8001
E-mail: info@mineralproducts.org
Website: http://www.mineralproducts.org
Bank(s): National Westminster Bank Plc
Directors: R. Riley (Fin), N. Jackson (Grp Chief Exec)
Managers: J. McLaughlin (Commun Mgr)
Immediate Holding Company: MINERAL PRODUCTS ASSOCIATION LIMITED
Registration no: 01634996 **Date established:** 1982 **Turnover:** £5m - £10m
No.of Employees: 21 - 50 **Product Groups:** 14, 17, 33, 45, 87

Date of Accounts	Dec 11	Dec 10	Dec 09
Sales Turnover	7m	7m	9m
Pre Tax Profit/Loss	433	239	44
Working Capital	1m	1m	918
Fixed Assets	19	338	2m
Current Assets	6m	6m	3m
Current Liabilities	4m	4m	2m

Mingo Sewing Machines
1 Fonthill Road, London, N4 3HY
Tel: 020-7561 1066 **Fax:** 020-7561 1066
Directors: P. Mingides (Prop)
Date established: 1994 **No.of Employees:** 1 - 10 **Product Groups:** 43

Mintel Group Ltd
18-19 Long Lane, London, EC1A 9PL
Tel: 020-7606 4533 **Fax:** 020-7606 5932
E-mail: info@mintel.com
Website: http://www.mintel.com
Directors: J. Weeks (Ch)
Immediate Holding Company: MINTEL INTERNATIONAL GROUP LIMITED
Registration no: 04186586 **Date established:** 2001
Turnover: £10m - £20m **No.of Employees:** 251 - 500 **Product Groups:** 81

Mirrorpix
1 Canada Square, London, E14 5AP
Tel: 020-7293 3700 **Fax:** 01923-815015
E-mail: desk@mirrorpix.com
Website: http://www.mirrorpix.com
Managers: F. Mckenna
Ultimate Holding Company: TRINITY MIRROR PLC
Immediate Holding Company: RIPPLEFFECT STUDIO LTD
Registration no: 02542560 **Date established:** 1999
No.of Employees: 1 - 10 **Product Groups:** 28

Date of Accounts	Dec 08	Jan 10	Jan 11
Sales Turnover	3m	4m	4m
Pre Tax Profit/Loss	236	275	614
Working Capital	559	752	1m
Fixed Assets	35	29	23
Current Assets	1m	2m	2m
Current Liabilities	792	496	548

Mishcon De Reya
Summit House 12 Red Lion Square, London, WC1R 4QD
Tel: 020-7440 7000 **Fax:** 020-7404 5982
E-mail: contactus@mishcon.com
Website: http://www.mishcon.com
Directors: K. Gold (Snr Part)
Immediate Holding Company: MISHCON DE REYA (HOLDINGS) LLP
Registration no: OC351102 **Date established:** 2009
Turnover: £10m - £20m **No.of Employees:** 251 - 500 **Product Groups:** 80

Date of Accounts	Apr 11
Pre Tax Profit/Loss	-84
Working Capital	2m
Current Assets	3m
Current Liabilities	311

Mister Steel Ltd
Stewarts Lane Depot Dickens Street, London, SW8 3EP
Tel: 020-7738 8858 **Fax:** 020-7738 8893
E-mail: info@mistersteel.co.uk
Website: http://www.mistersteel.co.uk
Directors: K. Stewart (Dir)
Immediate Holding Company: MISTER STEEL LIMITED
Registration no: 02552312 **VAT No.:** GB 548 0255 45
Date established: 1990 **Turnover:** Up to £250,000
No.of Employees: 1 - 10 **Product Groups:** 35, 66

Date of Accounts	Dec 11	Dec 10	Dec 09
Working Capital	63	75	96
Fixed Assets	113	51	60
Current Assets	204	179	215

Misys plc
1 Kingdom Street, London, W2 6BL
Tel: 020-3320 5000 **Fax:** 020-3320 1771
E-mail: info@misys.com
Website: http://www.misys.com
Directors: N. Farrimond (Fin), P. Davies (Tech Serv)
Managers: E. Hill-Wood, A. Mills (Personnel), M. Pearcey, A. Buckley
Ultimate Holding Company: MISYS PLC
Immediate Holding Company: MISYS LIMITED
Registration no: 01360027 **Date established:** 1978
Turnover: £250m - £500m **No.of Employees:** 501 - 1000
Product Groups: 44

Date of Accounts	May 11	May 10	May 09
Sales Turnover	370m	782m	692m
Pre Tax Profit/Loss	32m	105m	94m
Working Capital	-54m	19m	-8m
Fixed Assets	573m	604m	567m
Current Assets	192m	414m	295m
Current Liabilities	215m	321m	279m

Mito Construction & Engineering Ltd
Adams Wharf 19 Yeoman Street, London, SE8 5DT
Tel: 020-7231 0918 **Fax:** 020-7231 6307
E-mail: mitocons@aol.com
Bank(s): Lloyds, Twickenham
Directors: B. Gill (Fin), M. Hollings (MD)
Immediate Holding Company: MITO CONSTRUCTION & ENGINEERING LIMITED
Registration no: 01234885 **VAT No.:** GB 609 1445 49
Date established: 1975 **Turnover:** £1m - £2m **No.of Employees:** 11 - 20
Product Groups: 28, 35, 36

Date of Accounts	Dec 10	Dec 08	Dec 07
Working Capital	-62	-43	-54
Current Assets	51	64	39

Mitre Sports International Ltd
Pentland Centre Squires Lane, Finchley, London, N3 2QL
Tel: 020-8346 2600 **Fax:** 020-8970 2887
E-mail: enquiries@mitre.com
Website: http://www.mitre.com
Bank(s): Barclays, London
Directors: D. Hyslop (Sales), G. Hibbert (MD), P. Dundon (Dir), R. Holmes (MD), I. Tolman (Sales)
Managers: D. Anderson (Prod Mgr), D. Blackburn (Quality Control), M. Winterbottom (Export Sales Mg), S. Reynolds (Publicity), T. Lloyd (Transport), P. Bell (Mktg Serv Mgr), G. Davison (Import Mgr), R. Armitage
Immediate Holding Company: Pentland Group P.L.C.
Registration no: 02688851 **VAT No.:** GB 231 0451 21
Turnover: £50m - £75m **No.of Employees:** 21 - 50 **Product Groups:** 22, 49

Mitre Welding Products Ltd
Unit B6 Angel Road Works Advent Way, London, N18 3AH
Tel: 020-8803 0726 **Fax:** 020-8807 7690
E-mail: kathleen.arnold@mitrewelding.co.uk
Website: http://www.mitrewelding.co.uk
Directors: G. Arnold (MD), K. Arnold (MD)
Immediate Holding Company: MITRE WELDING PRODUCTS LIMITED
Registration no: 01094864 **VAT No.:** GB 214 2656 86
Date established: 1973 **Turnover:** Up to £250,000
No.of Employees: 1 - 10 **Product Groups:** 40, 46

Date of Accounts	Oct 11	Oct 10	Oct 09
Sales Turnover	124	107	N/A
Pre Tax Profit/Loss	17	3	-11
Working Capital	4	-9	-13
Fixed Assets	9	10	11
Current Assets	64	62	62
Current Liabilities	8	8	6

Mitsui & Co. Ltd
24 King William Street, London, EC4R 9AJ
Tel: 020-7822 0321 **Fax:** 020-7236 2130
E-mail: info@mitsui.co.uk
Website: http://www.mitsui.com
Directors: T. Ando (Co Sec), T. Kitahara (Dir)
Managers: Y. Okinaga (Personnel), M. Ito (Comptroller)
Ultimate Holding Company: MITSUI & CO LIMITED (JAPAN)
Immediate Holding Company: MITSUI & CO. EUROPE PLC
Registration no: 02204039 **Date established:** 1987
Turnover: £75m - £125m **No.of Employees:** 101 - 250
Product Groups: 82

Date of Accounts	Mar 12	Mar 11	Mar 10
Sales Turnover	103m	127m	91m
Pre Tax Profit/Loss	-14m	162	-8m
Working Capital	-56m	-48m	-64m
Fixed Assets	158m	126m	156m
Current Assets	237m	263m	190m
Current Liabilities	69m	57m	154m

Mizuho Corporate Bank
River Plate House 7-11 Finsbury Circus, London, EC2M 7DH
Tel: 020-7012 4000 **Fax:** 020-7012 4500
E-mail: seiichiro.sato@mhcb.co.uk
Website: http://www.mizuhocbk.com
Directors: S. Sato (MD)
Ultimate Holding Company: MIZUHO FINANCIAL GROUP INC (JAPAN)
Registration no: 02691499 **VAT No.:** 524 676 432 **Date established:** 1992
Turnover: £125m - £250m **No.of Employees:** 251 - 500
Product Groups: 82

Mobilis Mobile Systems
Swan Centre 9 Fishers Lane, London, W4 1RX
Tel: 020-8747 8222
E-mail: info@mobiliscase.com
Website: http://www.mobiliscase.com
Directors: B. Jeanneau (Fin)
Immediate Holding Company: MOBILIS MOBILE SYSTEMS LIMITED
Registration no: 04492719 **Date established:** 2002
No.of Employees: 1 - 10 **Product Groups:** 22, 26, 37

Date of Accounts	Mar 11	Mar 09	Mar 08
Working Capital	41	-358	-199
Current Assets	169	78	180

Mobility One Ltd
145-157, St Johns Street, London, EC1V 4PY
Tel: 0800-404 7067
E-mail: james@mobilityone.co.uk
Website: http://www.mobilityone.co.uk
Registration no: 06090650 **Turnover:** £250,000 - £500,000
No.of Employees: 1 - 10 **Product Groups:** 39, 45, 67, 85

Models One Ltd
12 Macklin Street, London, WC2B 5SZ
Tel: 020-7025 4910 **Fax:** 020-7025 4921
E-mail: info@models1.co.uk
Website: http://www.models1.co.uk
Directors: K. Diamond (MD), P. Negi (Fin)
Managers: N. Frost (Tech Serv Mgr)
Ultimate Holding Company: ONE WORLDWIDE LIMITED
Immediate Holding Company: MODELS ONE LIMITED
Registration no: 03678510 **Date established:** 1998
No.of Employees: 21 - 50 **Product Groups:** 89

Date of Accounts	Dec 11	Dec 10	Dec 09
Working Capital	580	427	748
Fixed Assets	1m	1m	2m
Current Assets	1m	2m	2m

G Modiano
55 Old Broad Street, London, EC2M 1RX
Tel: 020-7012 0000 **Fax:** 020-7374 6468
E-mail: giuseppe@gmodiano.com
Website: http://www.gmodiano.com
Directors: G. Modiano (MD), J. Aarvold (Grp Chief Exec), L. Modiano (Sales)
Managers: T. Addams (I.T. Exec)
Immediate Holding Company: G. MODIANO LIMITED
Registration no: 00872284 **VAT No.:** GB 243 7889 23
Date established: 1966 **Turnover:** £75m - £125m
No.of Employees: 11 - 20 **Product Groups:** 66

Date of Accounts	Mar 10	Mar 09	Mar 08
Sales Turnover	85m	83m	136m
Pre Tax Profit/Loss	10m	-7m	7m
Working Capital	35m	23m	33m
Fixed Assets	26m	29m	24m
Current Assets	63m	67m	96m
Current Liabilities	9m	4m	8m

Modis International Ltd
5th Floor 33 Queen Street, London, EC4R 1BR
Tel: 020-7038 6400 **Fax:** 020-7038 6401
E-mail: info@modis.co.uk
Website: http://www.modis.co.uk
Directors: R. Dungworth (Dir)
Ultimate Holding Company: ADECCO SA (SWITZERLAND)
Immediate Holding Company: MODIS INTERNATIONAL LIMITED
Registration no: 01625479 **Date established:** 1982
Turnover: £250m - £500m **No.of Employees:** 51 - 100
Product Groups: 80, 81, 84, 85

Date of Accounts	Dec 11	Dec 10	Dec 08
Sales Turnover	85m	67m	118m
Pre Tax Profit/Loss	-2m	3m	2m

Working Capital	16m	17m	18m
Fixed Assets	704	2m	3m
Current Assets	23m	23m	28m
Current Liabilities	5m	6m	8m

Moet Hennessy UK Ltd
13 Grosvenor Crescent, London, SW1X 7EE
Tel: 020-7235 9411 **Fax:** 020-7235 8667
Website: http://www.moet.co.uk
Directors: J. Stewart (Dir), J. Cockeram (MD), D. Bell (Fin), D. Cunningham (Mkt Research)
Ultimate Holding Company: LVMH MOET HENNESSY LOUIS VUTTON SA (FRANCE)
Immediate Holding Company: MOET HENNESSY U.K. LIMITED
Registration no: 00371236 **Date established:** 1941
Turnover: £125m - £250m **No.of Employees:** 101 - 250
Product Groups: 21

Date of Accounts	Dec 10	Dec 09	Dec 08
Sales Turnover	152m	142m	169m
Pre Tax Profit/Loss	15m	13m	16m
Working Capital	16m	14m	15m
Fixed Assets	597	673	755
Current Assets	70m	66m	72m
Current Liabilities	23m	22m	20m

Molton Brown Ltd
The Terrace Camden Wharf 28 Jamestown Road, London, NW1 7AP
Tel: 020-7428 2400 **Fax:** 020-7428 2401
E-mail: info@moltonbrown.com
Website: http://www.moltonbrown.co.uk
Bank(s): Midland
Directors: A. Nelson-Bennett (Pres)
Managers: P. Currie
Ultimate Holding Company: KAO CORPORATION (JAPAN)
Immediate Holding Company: MOLTON BROWN LIMITED
Registration no: 02414997 **Date established:** 1989
Turnover: £50m - £75m **No.of Employees:** 51 - 100 **Product Groups:** 32

Date of Accounts	Dec 11	Dec 10	Dec 09
Sales Turnover	57m	57m	58m
Pre Tax Profit/Loss	2m	6m	4m
Working Capital	42m	40m	36m
Fixed Assets	6m	6m	7m
Current Assets	53m	54m	49m
Current Liabilities	5m	5m	6m

Molton Brown Emporium
58 South Molton Street, London, W1K 5SL
Tel: 0870-2243900 **Fax:** 0870-2243900
Website: http://www.moltonbrown.com
Managers: K. Canestra (Mgr)
Ultimate Holding Company: FP004132
Immediate Holding Company: MOLTON BROWN LIMITED
Registration no: 02414997 **Date established:** 1989
No.of Employees: 1 - 10 **Product Groups:** 32, 63

Mona Lisa Of London plc
Zenith House 69 Lawrence Road, London, N15 4EY
Tel: 020-8800 7747 **Fax:** 020-8802 7807
E-mail: info@monalisaplc.co.uk
Bank(s): HSBC
Directors: M. Matthew (MD), G. Nye-matthew (Dir)
Managers: E. Lang (Sales Admin), S. Barnes (Sales Prom Mgr)
Immediate Holding Company: MONA LISA OF LONDON PLC
Registration no: 02261472 **VAT No.:** 524 1744 63 **Date established:** 1988
Turnover: £2m - £5m **No.of Employees:** 11 - 20 **Product Groups:** 24

Date of Accounts	Dec 11	Dec 10	Dec 09
Sales Turnover	4m	4m	3m
Pre Tax Profit/Loss	68	45	20
Working Capital	380	303	261
Fixed Assets	18	39	49
Current Assets	1m	850	457
Current Liabilities	59	82	56

Monad Precision Engineering Ltd
Montague House 615-621 Kingston Road, London, SW20 8SA
Tel: 020-8543 1701 **Fax:** 020-8443 2458
E-mail: admin@monadltd.com
Website: http://www.monadltd.com
Directors: S. Reeder (MD)
Immediate Holding Company: MONAD PRECISION ENGINEERING LIMITED
Registration no: 01204208 **Date established:** 1975 **Turnover:** £1m - £2m
No.of Employees: 11 - 20 **Product Groups:** 38, 42

Date of Accounts	Mar 12	Mar 11	Mar 10
Sales Turnover	2m	2m	2m
Pre Tax Profit/Loss	-11	142	276
Working Capital	550	575	532
Fixed Assets	194	192	145
Current Assets	735	1m	702
Current Liabilities	64	96	94

Montagu Evans
Red Wolf House 5-10 Bolton Street, London, W1J 8BA
Tel: 020-7493 4002 **Fax:** 020-7312 7547
E-mail: susan.wilson@montagu-evans.co.uk
Website: http://www.montagu-evans.co.uk
Directors: S. Wilson (Fin)
Managers: K. Neal (Tech Serv Mgr)
Immediate Holding Company: MONTAGU EVANS LLP
Registration no: OC312072 **Date established:** 2005
Turnover: £10m - £20m **No.of Employees:** 101 - 250 **Product Groups:** 80

Date of Accounts	Mar 11	Mar 10	Mar 09
Sales Turnover	28m	28m	26m
Pre Tax Profit/Loss	15m	16m	13m
Working Capital	7m	10m	5m
Fixed Assets	756	813	1m
Current Assets	11m	14m	10m
Current Liabilities	4m	4m	4m

Montgomery Exhibitions
9 Manchester Square, London, W1U 3PL
Tel: 020-7886 3000 **Fax:** 020-7886 3001
E-mail: enquiries@montex.co.uk
Website: http://www.montex.co.uk
Bank(s): Barcleys
Directors: C. Newton (MD), I. Angus (Ch)
Ultimate Holding Company: ANGUS MONTGOMERY LIMITED
Immediate Holding Company: MONTGOMERY INDIA LIMITED
Registration no: 06243159 **Date established:** 2007 **Turnover:** £5m - £10m
No.of Employees: 21 - 50 **Product Groups:** 81

see next page

Montgomery Exhibitions - Cont'd

Date of Accounts	Jun 10	Jun 09	Jun 08
Pre Tax Profit/Loss	N/A	-329	-17
Working Capital	-310	-346	-124
Fixed Assets	N/A	1	108
Current Assets	N/A	N/A	2
Current Liabilities	N/A	62	25

Moorevale Ltd
45 Clarges Street, London, W1J 7EP
Tel: 020-7399 2300 **Fax:** 020-7399 2309
E-mail: mikeprobert@moorevale.com
Website: http://www.moorevale.com
Directors: M. Probert (Grp Chief Exec)
Ultimate Holding Company: MOOREVALE INVESTMENTS LIMITED
Immediate Holding Company: MOOREVALE INVESTMENTS (NEW PREMIER HOUSE) LIMITED
Registration no: 05811879 **Date established:** 2006
Turnover: Up to £250,000 **No.of Employees:** 1 - 10 **Product Groups:** 82

Date of Accounts	Sep 11	Sep 10	Sep 09
Pre Tax Profit/Loss	N/A	N/A	-1

Louis Moreau The Quilters Ltd
Unit 5 United House 11 Tariff Road, London, N17 0DY
Tel: 020-8808 1337 **Fax:** 020-8365 0547
E-mail: moreau@smeuk.com
Website: http://www.louismoreau.co.uk
Directors: V. Rutter (MD)
Immediate Holding Company: LOUIS MOREAU (THE QUILTERS) LIMITED
Registration no: 03463701 **VAT No.:** GB 220 6939 71
Date established: 1997 **Turnover:** Up to £250,000
No.of Employees: 1 - 10 **Product Groups:** 24, 63

Date of Accounts	Mar 11	Mar 10	Mar 09
Sales Turnover	133	N/A	136
Pre Tax Profit/Loss	-6	N/A	8
Working Capital	-37	-26	-15
Fixed Assets	16	3	N/A
Current Assets	30	22	27
Current Liabilities	65	49	N/A

Morgan Walker
115 Chancery Lane, London, WC2A 1PR
Tel: 020-7831 8333 **Fax:** 020-7831 9638
E-mail: ashok@morganwalker.co.uk
Website: http://www.morganwalker.co.uk
Directors: A. Sancheti (Snr Part)
Immediate Holding Company: MORGAN WALKER SOLICITORS LLP
Registration no: OC312540 **Date established:** 2005
Turnover: £250,000 - £500,000 **No.of Employees:** 1 - 10
Product Groups: 80

Date of Accounts	Apr 06	Apr 09	Apr 08
Sales Turnover	843	493	588
Pre Tax Profit/Loss	77	110	114
Working Capital	-117	66	-142
Fixed Assets	6	16	20
Current Assets	86	66	N/A
Current Liabilities	48	N/A	143

Mortimer Springs Ltd
166-168 Villiers Road, London, NW2 5PU
Tel: 020-8459 1420 **Fax:** 020-8451 7614
E-mail: sales@mortimersprings.com
Website: http://www.mortimersprings.com
Directors: S. Coleman (Fin), S. Coleman (MD)
Immediate Holding Company: MORTIMER SPRINGS LIMITED
Registration no: 01632204 **VAT No.:** GB 587 1453 14
Date established: 1982 **No.of Employees:** 1 - 10 **Product Groups:** 35, 36, 41, 48, 66

Date of Accounts	Oct 10	Oct 09	Oct 08
Working Capital	55	46	72
Fixed Assets	13	15	17
Current Assets	243	217	193

Mostyns Ltd
32 High Street, London, W5 5DB
Tel: 020-8840 8110 **Fax:** 020-8840 8110
Website: http://www.mostyns.co.uk
Directors: C. Cartwright (Ptnr)
Ultimate Holding Company: MGL REALISATIONS LIMITED
Immediate Holding Company: MOST REALISATIONS LIMITED
Registration no: 02343900 **Date established:** 1989 **Turnover:** £5m - £10m
No.of Employees: 1 - 10 **Product Groups:** 23, 24, 63

Date of Accounts	Feb 10	Feb 09	Feb 11
Sales Turnover	8m	8m	7m
Pre Tax Profit/Loss	79	-92	9
Working Capital	465	261	412
Fixed Assets	568	569	514
Current Assets	2m	2m	2m
Current Liabilities	768	537	732

Motability Operations
22 Southwark Bridge Road, London, SE1 9HB
Tel: 08454-564566 **Fax:** 020-7928 1818
Website: http://www.motability.co.uk
Directors: D. Gilman (Fin), A. Downey (Pers)
Managers: E. Courtney
Ultimate Holding Company: MOTABILITY OPERATIONS GROUP PLC
Immediate Holding Company: MOTABILITY OPERATIONS LIMITED
Registration no: 01373876 **Date established:** 1978
Turnover: Over £1,000m **No.of Employees:** 1 - 10 **Product Groups:** 82

Date of Accounts	Sep 11	Sep 10	Sep 09
Sales Turnover	1621m	1462m	1354m
Pre Tax Profit/Loss	2m	2m	2m
Working Capital	511	4m	-343
Fixed Assets	12m	9m	12m
Current Assets	242m	228m	172m
Current Liabilities	151m	66m	81m

Motorgear Gearboxes Ltd
143 Coppermill Lane, London, E17 7HD
Tel: 020-8520 5181 **Fax:** 020-8520 5181
E-mail: sales@motorgearltd.com
Website: http://www.motorgearltd.com
Directors: N. Fasil (MD)
Immediate Holding Company: MOTOR GEAR LIMITED
Registration no: 04602974 **Date established:** 2002
Turnover: Up to £250,000 **No.of Employees:** 1 - 10 **Product Groups:** 39

Date of Accounts	Nov 11	Nov 10	Nov 09
Working Capital	33	34	31
Fixed Assets	17	15	17
Current Assets	34	35	32

Mouse Training
7th Floor Crystal Gate 28-30 Worship Street, London, EC2A 2AH
Tel: 020-7920 9500 **Fax:** 020-7920 9502
E-mail: info@mousetraining.co.uk
Website: http://www.mousetraining.co.uk
Directors: J. Caulfield (Dir)
Immediate Holding Company: THE MOUSE TRAINING COMPANY LIMITED
Registration no: 06102197 **Date established:** 2007
Turnover: £500,000 - £1m **No.of Employees:** 1 - 10 **Product Groups:** 86

Moving Picture Co. Ltd
127 Wardour Street, London, W1F 0NL
Tel: 020-7434 3100 **Fax:** 020-7437 3951
E-mail: mailbox@moving-picture.com
Website: http://www.moving-picture.com
Directors: A. Camilleri (Dir)
Ultimate Holding Company: TECHNICOLOR SA (FRANCE)
Immediate Holding Company: MOVING PICTURE COMPANY LIMITED (THE)
Registration no: 01191228 **Date established:** 1974
Turnover: £50m - £75m **No.of Employees:** 251 - 500 **Product Groups:** 89

Date of Accounts	Dec 11	Dec 10	Dec 09
Sales Turnover	75m	64m	41m
Pre Tax Profit/Loss	17m	16m	553
Working Capital	27m	18m	3m
Fixed Assets	7m	4m	4m
Current Assets	60m	38m	16m
Current Liabilities	26m	18m	11m

Muirhead Aerospace
Oakfield Road, London, SE20 8EW
Tel: 020-8659 9090 **Fax:** 020-8659 9906
E-mail: sales@muirheadaerospace.com
Website: http://www.muirheadaerospace.com
Bank(s): Barclays
Directors: K. Sena (Co Sec), S. Wells (Dir), M. Wornett (Fin)
Managers: S. Fowler (Personnel), M. Plimmer (Tech Serv Mgr)
Ultimate Holding Company: AMETEK INC (USA)
Immediate Holding Company: MUIRHEAD AEROSPACE LIMITED
Registration no: 00560015 **VAT No.:** GB 740 5950 34
Date established: 1956 **Turnover:** £10m - £20m
No.of Employees: 251 - 500 **Product Groups:** 37, 38, 39, 67

Date of Accounts	Dec 11	Dec 10	Dec 09
Sales Turnover	11m	11m	31m
Pre Tax Profit/Loss	2m	3m	16m
Working Capital	22m	21m	22m
Fixed Assets	5m	5m	5m
Current Assets	24m	23m	24m
Current Liabilities	945	864	1m

Mulberry
41-42 New Bond Street, London, W1S 2RY
Tel: 020-7491 3900 **Fax:** 020-7495 2838
E-mail: enquiries@mulberryengland.co.uk
Website: http://www.mulberry.com
Directors: L. Montague (Ch)
Managers: A. Fawkz (Mgr), S. Burt (Chief Mgr), A. Sojren (Mgr)
VAT No.: GB 452 8911 34 **Date established:** 1995
Turnover: £500,000 - £1m **No.of Employees:** 11 - 20
Product Groups: 22, 24

MuLondon - Natural Organic Skincare
64c Evelyn Street Ref-118, London, SE8 5DD
Tel: 020-3582 6035
E-mail: info@mulondon.com
Website: http://www.mulondon.com
Managers: A. Sorbi (Mgr)
Date established: 2008 **No.of Employees:** 1 - 10 **Product Groups:** 31, 32, 88

Multi Corporation International Ltd
100 Harlesden Road, London, NW10 2BD
Tel: 020-8451 2411 **Fax:** 020-8451 2413
E-mail: henrysehayek@multi-corporation.com
Website: http://www.multi-corporation.com
Directors: H. Sehayek (MD)
Immediate Holding Company: MULTI-CORPORATION INTERNATIONAL LIMITED
Registration no: 01534307 **VAT No.:** GB 340 5754 66
Date established: 1980 **Turnover:** Up to £250,000
No.of Employees: 1 - 10 **Product Groups:** 36, 37, 38, 40, 45, 61, 66, 85

Date of Accounts	Mar 12	Mar 11	Mar 10
Sales Turnover	N/A	83	91
Pre Tax Profit/Loss	N/A	31	87
Working Capital	613	729	705
Fixed Assets	1	1	3
Current Assets	2m	1m	2m
Current Liabilities	N/A	21	33

Multiload Technology
2 Rosemont Road, London, NW3 6NE
Tel: 020-7794 9152 **Fax:** 020-7794 9257
E-mail: mail@multiload.co.uk
Website: http://www.multiload.co.uk
Directors: B. Cuthbertson (MD), P. Vincent (Fin)
Immediate Holding Company: MULTILOAD TECHNOLOGY LIMITED
Registration no: 04477105 **VAT No.:** GB 539 0104 67
Date established: 2002 **Turnover:** £500,000 - £1m
No.of Employees: 1 - 10 **Product Groups:** 67

Date of Accounts	Dec 11	Dec 10	Dec 09
Working Capital	49	71	-30
Fixed Assets	26	22	18
Current Assets	142	155	39

Multiuniversal, Ltd Advertising, des
London, London, W1B 3HH
Tel: 00000-000000
E-mail: brunodomingues@hotmail.com
Website: http://www.multiuniversal.com
Directors: B. Domingues (Dir)
No.of Employees: 11 - 20 **Product Groups:** 44, 81

Munro-Faure
11 Maddox Street, London, W1S 2QF
Tel: 020-7408 1035 **Fax:** 020-7408 1048
E-mail: general@munro-4.fsnet.co.uk
Directors: J. Munro Faure (Head)
Immediate Holding Company: BOLTONS INVESTMENTS LTD
Date established: 2006 **Turnover:** Up to £250,000
No.of Employees: 1 - 10 **Product Groups:** 80

Date of Accounts	Mar 11	Mar 10	Sep 08
Working Capital	-66	-71	-3
Fixed Assets	7	7	3
Current Assets	217	420	397

Murder One
71-73 Charing Cross Road, London, WC2H 0ND
Tel: 020-7734 3483 **Fax:** 020-7734 3429
E-mail: murderone.mail@virgin.net
Website: http://www.murderone.co.uk
Directors: M. Jakubowski (MD), N. Landau (Dir)
Immediate Holding Company: Murder One Ltd
Registration no: 02246009 **VAT No.:** GB 512 6407 75
Turnover: £1m - £2m **No.of Employees:** 1 - 10 **Product Groups:** 64

Date of Accounts	Dec 07	Dec 06	Dec 05
Working Capital	201	205	254
Fixed Assets	130	149	153
Current Assets	308	296	372
Current Liabilities	107	91	118
Total Share Capital	1	1	1

Murphy Ltd
Ashley House Ashley Road, London, N17 9LZ
Tel: 020-8885 3545 **Fax:** 020-8801 1126
E-mail: enq@murphy.ltd.uk
Website: http://www.murphy.ltd.uk
Directors: K. Tims (Fin), P. Salmon (MD), S. Rudd (Tech Serv), D. Stedman (Pers)
Managers: M. Goodger
Ultimate Holding Company: GREENANE LTD (ISLE OF MAN)
Immediate Holding Company: MURPHY LIMITED
Registration no: 01916346 **VAT No.:** GB 233 5864 56
Date established: 1985 **Turnover:** £50m - £75m
No.of Employees: 501 - 1000 **Product Groups:** 52

Date of Accounts	Aug 11	Aug 10	Aug 09
Sales Turnover	63m	58m	72m
Pre Tax Profit/Loss	580	8m	544
Working Capital	7m	9m	3m
Fixed Assets	3m	3m	3m
Current Assets	19m	26m	25m
Current Liabilities	2m	5m	3m

B Murphy
2 Avenue Mews, London, N10 3NP
Tel: 020-8883 4555 **Fax:** 020-8883 3363
E-mail: hathersichroger@hotmail.com
Directors: M. McNicholas (Ptnr)
Immediate Holding Company: B. MURPHY UK LIMITED
Registration no: 03762652 **VAT No.:** GB 672 3827 18
Date established: 1999 **Turnover:** Up to £250,000
No.of Employees: 1 - 10 **Product Groups:** 66

Mute A & R
1 Albion Place, London, W6 0QT
Tel: 020-8964 2001 **Fax:** 020-8968 4977
E-mail: sales@mute.com
Website: http://mutedotcom.wordpress.com
Directors: A. Chadd (Dir)
Managers: C. Leighton-Bennett (Mgr)
Ultimate Holding Company: Emi Group Ltd
Immediate Holding Company: Mute Ltd
Registration no: 01766113 **Turnover:** Up to £250,000
No.of Employees: 51 - 100 **Product Groups:** 61, 65

Date of Accounts	Mar 08	Mar 07
Sales Turnover	8240	13710
Pre Tax Profit/Loss	-3730	-5090
Working Capital	6270	-15110
Fixed Assets	N/A	110
Current Assets	14530	17690
Current Liabilities	8260	32800
Total Share Capital	25000	N/A
ROCE% (Return on Capital Employed)	-59.5	33.9
ROT% (Return on Turnover)	-45.3	-37.1

S & M Myers Ltd
126 Ballards Lane, London, N3 2PA
Tel: 020-8444 3457 **Fax:** 020-7609 2457
E-mail: myerscarpets@hotmail.co.uk
Website: http://www.myerscarpets.co.uk
Directors: A. Myers (Ptnr)
Immediate Holding Company: S.& M.MYERS,LIMITED
Registration no: 00149273 **Date established:** 2017
No.of Employees: 1 - 10 **Product Groups:** 23, 24, 30, 39

Date of Accounts	Dec 11	Dec 10	Dec 09
Working Capital	1m	74	94
Fixed Assets	1m	822	824
Current Assets	2m	247	171

Myrene Signs Ltd
Unit 4d Standard Indl-Est Henley Road, London, E16 2ES
Tel: 01702-558655 **Fax:** 01702-557994
Website: http://www.myrene-signs.com
Directors: A. Spray (Fin), N. Spray (Dir), N. Spray (MD)
Immediate Holding Company: MYRENE SIGNS LIMITED
Registration no: 03041076 **Date established:** 1995
No.of Employees: 1 - 10 **Product Groups:** 28, 30, 39, 80

N O P Research Group Ltd
Ludgate House 245 Blackfriars Road, London, SE1 9UL
Tel: 020-7890 9000 **Fax:** 020-7890 9001
E-mail: ukinfo@gfk.com
Website: http://www.gfknop.com
Directors: I. Stocker (Dir), S. Chadwick (Grp Chief Exec)
Managers: P. Macfarlane
Ultimate Holding Company: GFK AG (GERMANY)
Immediate Holding Company: GFK NOP FIELD INTERVIEWING SERVICES LIMITED
Registration no: 00471008 **VAT No.:** GB 680 9514 14
Date established: 1995 **Turnover:** £250,000 - £500,000
No.of Employees: 501 - 1000 **Product Groups:** 80, 81, 86

Date of Accounts	Dec 07	Dec 06	Dec 05
Sales Turnover	88630	90690	85010
Pre Tax Profit/Loss	2980	-320	-7860

Working Capital	30550	27090	17240
Fixed Assets	3710	3810	3720
Current Assets	62800	53440	56330
Current Liabilities	32250	26350	39090
Total Share Capital	44000	44000	44000
ROCE% (Return on Capital Employed)	8.7	-1.0	-37.5
ROT% (Return on Turnover)	3.4	-0.4	-9.2

N P Mander

St Peters Square, London, E2 7AF
Tel: 020-7739 4747 **Fax:** 020-7729 4718
E-mail: manderuk@mander-organs.com
Website: http://www.mander-organs.com
Bank(s): Barclays
Directors: M. Mian (Co Sec), J. Mander (Prop)
Ultimate Holding Company: N.P. MANDER HOLDINGS LIMITED
Immediate Holding Company: N.P.MANDER LIMITED
Registration no: 00450367 **VAT No.:** GB 232 8142 85
Date established: 1948 **Turnover:** £1m - £2m **No.of Employees:** 11 - 20
Product Groups: 49

Date of Accounts	Aug 11	Aug 10	Aug 09
Working Capital	223	162	146
Fixed Assets	22	30	40
Current Assets	902	799	628

N & P Thermo Plastic Moulders Acton Ltd

69-73 Stirling Road, London, W3 8DJ
Tel: 020-8992 8258 **Fax:** 020-8993 0860
Bank(s): Barclays
Directors: K. Press (Fin), D. Press (Dir)
Immediate Holding Company: N & P THERMO-PLASTIC MOULDERS (ACTON) LIMITED
Registration no: 01735898 **VAT No.:** GB 398 5331 11
Date established: 1983 **Turnover:** £1m - £2m **No.of Employees:** 11 - 20
Product Groups: 30

Date of Accounts	Aug 11	Aug 10	Aug 09
Working Capital	486	613	654
Fixed Assets	2	5	13
Current Assets	524	644	690

N S B Casements Ltd

3 Steele Road, London, NW10 7AR
Tel: 020-8961 3090 **Fax:** 020-8961 3050
E-mail: info@nsbcasements.co.uk
Directors: D. Northam (MD), G. Northam (Co Sec)
Immediate Holding Company: N S B CASEMENTS LIMITED
Registration no: 02893532 **Date established:** 1994
Turnover: Up to £250,000 **No.of Employees:** 1 - 10 **Product Groups:** 26, 35

Date of Accounts	Jun 11	Jun 10	Jun 09
Working Capital	59	58	120
Fixed Assets	17	20	35
Current Assets	188	213	255

N S G Export Ltd

40 The Mall, London, W5 3TJ
Tel: 020-8840 2323 **Fax:** 020-8840 0268
E-mail: sales@nsgexports.com
Website: http://www.nsgexports.com
Directors: P. Hobson (MD)
Immediate Holding Company: N. S. G. EXPORTS LIMITED
Registration no: 01022688 **VAT No.:** GB 172 8656 34
Date established: 1971 **Turnover:** £2m - £5m **No.of Employees:** 1 - 10
Product Groups: 61

Date of Accounts	Aug 11	Aug 10	Aug 09
Working Capital	-251	-5	474
Fixed Assets	2m	2m	1m
Current Assets	2m	2m	3m

Nabarro LLP

Lacon House 84 Theobalds Road, London, WC1X 8RW
Tel: 020-7524 6000 **Fax:** 020-7524 6524
E-mail: simon.johnston@nabarro.com
Website: http://www.nabarro.com
Directors: A. Powell (Tech Serv), C. Furness-smith (Fin), S. Johnston (Dir), S. Murdoch (Pers)
Managers: C. Jones, K. Richardson
Ultimate Holding Company: NABARRO NATHANSON (PARTNERSHIP)
Immediate Holding Company: NABCO 1 LIMITED
Registration no: 02122392 **Date established:** 1987
Turnover: £10m - £20m **No.of Employees:** 501 - 1000
Product Groups: 80

Nares International Ltd

61 Broadway, London, E15 4BQ
Tel: 020-8555 7441 **Fax:** 020-8519 5400
E-mail: nares@aol.com
Website: http://www.nares.co.uk
Directors: J. Holmes (MD), K. Holmes (Fin)
Immediate Holding Company: NARES INTERNATIONAL LIMITED
Registration no: 02878768 **VAT No.:** GB 629 7028 21
Date established: 1993 **Turnover:** £250,000 - £500,000
No.of Employees: 1 - 10 **Product Groups:** 76

Date of Accounts	Sep 07	Sep 06
Sales Turnover	1020	991
Pre Tax Profit/Loss	22	75
Working Capital	78	65
Fixed Assets	1	2
Current Assets	221	346
Current Liabilities	143	281
ROCE% (Return on Capital Employed)	27.5	111.6
ROT% (Return on Turnover)	2.1	7.6

National Australia Bank

88 Wood Street, London, EC2V 7QQ
Tel: 020-7710 2100 **Fax:** 020-7710 1353
Website: http://www.nab.com.au
Bank(s): Lloyds
Managers: B. Ramoss (Mgr)
Ultimate Holding Company: NABARRO NATHANSON (PARTNERSHIP)
Immediate Holding Company: NATIONAL AUSTRALIA FINANCE (VESSEL LEASING NO.6) LIMITED
Registration no: 06622181 **Date established:** 2008 **Turnover:** £5m - £10m
No.of Employees: 251 - 500 **Product Groups:** 82

National Car Parks Ltd

21 Bryanston Street, London, W1H 7AB
Tel: 020-7629 6702 **Fax:** 020-7491 3577
E-mail: info@ncp.co.uk
Website: http://www.ncp.co.uk
Directors: R. McNorton (Grp Chief Exec)
Managers: A. Mcfarlane (Mgr)
Ultimate Holding Company: MACQUARIE EUROPEAN INFRASTRUCTURE FUND II (GUERNSEY)
Immediate Holding Company: NATIONAL CAR PARKS LIMITED
Registration no: 00253240 **VAT No.:** GB 239 0546 59
Date established: 1931 **Turnover:** £250m - £500m
No.of Employees: 1 - 10 **Product Groups:** 80

Date of Accounts	Mar 08	Mar 09	Mar 10
Sales Turnover	316m	225m	229m
Pre Tax Profit/Loss	68m	8m	11m
Working Capital	92m	95m	106m
Fixed Assets	74m	82m	76m
Current Assets	635m	651m	666m
Current Liabilities	532m	81m	70m

National Care Association

45-49 Leather Lane, London, EC1N 7TJ
Tel: 020-7831 7090 **Fax:** 020-7831 7040
E-mail: claire@nca.gb.com
Website: http://www.nationalcareassociation.org.uk
Directors: S. Scott (Grp Chief Exec)
Immediate Holding Company: NATIONAL CARE ASSOCIATION
Registration no: 02537672 **Date established:** 1990
Turnover: £250,000 - £500,000 **No.of Employees:** 1 - 10
Product Groups: 87

Date of Accounts	Dec 10	Dec 09	Dec 08
Sales Turnover	409	418	420
Pre Tax Profit/Loss	-13	-32	11
Working Capital	171	16	54
Fixed Assets	15	16	11
Current Assets	171	239	203
Current Liabilities	N/A	112	109

National Grid plc

David Charles Forward 1-3 Strand, London, WC2N 5EH
Tel: 020-7004 3000 **Fax:** 020-7004 3004
E-mail: david.forward@ngrid.com
Website: http://www.nationalgrid.com
Directors: M. Westcott (Pers), C. Waters (Fin), D. Forward (Co Sec)
Managers: D. Lister
Ultimate Holding Company: NATIONAL GRID PLC
Immediate Holding Company: NATIONAL GRID (IOM) UK LIMITED
Registration no: FC023647 **Date established:** 2002
Turnover: £20m - £50m **No.of Employees:** 101 - 250 **Product Groups:** 38

Date of Accounts	Mar 11	Mar 10	Mar 09
Working Capital	18m	18m	18m
Current Assets	18m	18m	18m

National Magazine Company Ltd

72 Broadwick Street, London, W1F 9EP
Tel: 020-7439 5000 **Fax:** 020-7437 6886
Website: http://www.natmags.co.uk
Bank(s): The Royal Bank of Scotland
Managers: R. Miskin
Ultimate Holding Company: LAGARDERE SCA (FRANCE)
Immediate Holding Company: HEARST MAGAZINES UK 2012-1 LIMITED
Registration no: 00112955 **Date established:** 2002 **Turnover:** £2m - £5m
No.of Employees: 501 - 1000 **Product Groups:** 28

Date of Accounts	Dec 10	Dec 09	Dec 08
Sales Turnover	2m	1m	697
Pre Tax Profit/Loss	197	-251	45
Working Capital	67	-67	109
Fixed Assets	81	74	83
Current Assets	596	383	729
Current Liabilities	338	148	176

National Map Centre

22-24 Caxton Street, London, SW1H 0QU
Tel: 020-7222 2466 **Fax:** 020-7222 2619
E-mail: peter@mapsnmc.co.uk
Website: http://www.mapstore.co.uk
Directors: J. Hellings (Jt MD), A. Morgan (Jt MD)
Managers: P. Treadwell (Sales & Mktg Mg), C. Mapley (I.T. Exec), K. Ferries (Chief Mgr), P. Clarke (Chief Mgr)
Immediate Holding Company: Cook Hammond & Kell Ltd
VAT No.: GB 344 8899 01 **Date established:** 1966
No.of Employees: 1 - 10 **Product Groups:** 28

National Readership Surveys

40-42 Parker Street Covent Garden, London, WC2B 5PQ
Tel: 020-7242 8111 **Fax:** 020-7632 2916
E-mail: info@nrs.co.uk
Website: http://www.nrs.co.uk
Directors: S. Marquis (Ch)
Managers: S. Forde (Sales Admin)
Immediate Holding Company: NATIONAL READERSHIP SURVEYS LIMITED
Registration no: 02675544 **VAT No.:** GB 605 8967 08
Date established: 1991 **Turnover:** £2m - £5m **No.of Employees:** 1 - 10
Product Groups: 81

Date of Accounts	Dec 11	Dec 10	Dec 09
Sales Turnover	4m	4m	4m
Pre Tax Profit/Loss	108	96	86
Working Capital	673	590	516
Fixed Assets	11	9	9
Current Assets	1m	1m	1m
Current Liabilities	643	730	665

National Security Systems Group

29 Ferndale Road, London, E7 8JX
Tel: 0800-083 6400 **Fax:** 020-8281 7776
E-mail: sales@nssg.co.uk
Website: http://www.nssg.co.uk
Directors: D. Narran (Prop)
Immediate Holding Company: NSS SECURITY SYSTEMS LIMITED
Registration no: 07800341 **Date established:** 2011
No.of Employees: 1 - 10 **Product Groups:** 36, 40, 52, 67

National Union Of Rail Maritime & Transport Worker

39 Chalton Street, London, NW1 1JD
Tel: 020-7387 4771 **Fax:** 020-7387 4123
E-mail: info@rmt.org.uk
Website: http://www.rmt.org.uk
Directors: B. Crow (Gen Sec)
Managers: B. Denny (Mktg Serv Mgr), S. Perkins (Property Mgr), D. Craig (Personnel), V. Bryce (Fin Mgr)
Immediate Holding Company: THE NATIONAL UNION OF RAIL, MARITIME AND TRANSPORT WORKERS PENSION SCH
Registration no: 01008371 **Date established:** 1971
Turnover: Up to £250,000 **No.of Employees:** 21 - 50 **Product Groups:** 87

Date of Accounts	Dec 11	Dec 10	Dec 09
Sales Turnover	1	1	1
Current Assets	1	1	1
Current Liabilities	1	1	1

Naturefusion Stone Products

647 Portslade Road, London, SW8 3DH
Tel: 020-7627 5577 **Fax:** 020-7627 5588
E-mail: info@nature-fusion.com
Website: http://www.nature-fusion.com
Directors: M. Lubkowski (Co Sec), M. Sasmaz (Prop), B. James (Ptnr)
Immediate Holding Company: NATURE FUSION LIMITED
Registration no: 05939535 **Date established:** 2006
Turnover: £500,000 - £1m **No.of Employees:** 1 - 10 **Product Groups:** 14

Geo W Neale Ltd

Victoria Road, London, NW10 6NG
Tel: 020-8965 1336 **Fax:** 020-8965 1725
E-mail: william@gwneale.fsnet.co.uk
Website: http://www.gwneale.co.uk
Directors: W. Sharpley (MD)
Immediate Holding Company: GEO.W.NEALE LIMITED
Registration no: 00180537 **Date established:** 2022 **Turnover:** £2m - £5m
No.of Employees: 21 - 50 **Product Groups:** 32, 34

Date of Accounts	Oct 11	Oct 10	Oct 09
Working Capital	1m	1m	1000
Fixed Assets	41	47	45
Current Assets	2m	2m	2m

Neat Concepts Ltd

F25 Hastingwood Trading Estate 35 Harbet Road, London, N18 3HU
Tel: 020-8807 5805 **Fax:** 020-8884 4963
E-mail: info@neatconcepts.com
Website: http://www.neatconcepts.com
Bank(s): HSBC Bank plc
Directors: C. Obrien (MD), C. O'Brien (MD)
Immediate Holding Company: NEAT CONCEPTS LIMITED
Registration no: 01823727 **VAT No.:** GB 396 5919 86
Date established: 1984 **Turnover:** £500,000 - £1m
No.of Employees: 21 - 50 **Product Groups:** 25, 26

Date of Accounts	Sep 11	Sep 10	Sep 09
Working Capital	37	-36	-35
Fixed Assets	276	341	411
Current Assets	433	521	463

Nec Europe Ltd

N E C House 1 Victoria Road, London, W3 6BL
Tel: 020-8993 8111 **Fax:** 020-8992 7161
E-mail: sales@neceurope.com
Website: http://www.nec.com
Bank(s): Barclays & Sumitomo
Directors: T. Mineno (Dir), T. Fujioka (Co Sec)
Ultimate Holding Company: NEC CORPORATION (JAPAN)
Immediate Holding Company: NEC EUROPE LTD
Registration no: 02832014 **VAT No.:** GB 234 1804 88
Date established: 1993 **Turnover:** £50m - £75m
No.of Employees: 101 - 250 **Product Groups:** 37, 44

neighbo

140 Brompton Road, London, SW3 1HY
Tel: 020-8144 9196
E-mail: hello@neighbo.com
Website: http://neighbo.com
Directors: P. Fox (MD)
Date established: 2006 **No.of Employees:** 11 - 20 **Product Groups:** 44

Nemat

Unit 10 Cromwell Industrial Estate Staffa Road, London, E10 7QZ
Tel: 0781-345 1614 **Fax:** 020-8531 1717
E-mail: sales@nemat.co.uk
Website: http://www.nemat.co.uk
Directors: E. Patel (Prop)
Immediate Holding Company: NE'MAT FOODS LIMITED
Registration no: 07191294 **Date established:** 2010
No.of Employees: 1 - 10 **Product Groups:** 20

Date of Accounts	Mar 11
Working Capital	-16
Fixed Assets	58
Current Assets	28

Ness Furniture Ltd

17 Metro Centre, London, NW10 7PR
Tel: 020-8965 8850
Website: http://www.nessfurniture.co.uk
Directors: J. Williams (MD), R. Sugden (Co Sec)
Ultimate Holding Company: 01794322
Immediate Holding Company: NESS FURNITURE LIMITED
Registration no: 00402191 **Date established:** 1945
Turnover: £10m - £20m **No.of Employees:** 101 - 250
Product Groups: 26, 36, 49

Netvoyager Technology Limited

81 Oxford Street, London, W1D 2EU
Tel: 020-7903 5172 **Fax:** 020-3397 1330
E-mail: sales@netvoyager.co.uk
Website: http://www.netvoyager.co.uk
Directors: J. Aboulzelof (Fin), J. Zelof (MD)
Managers: M. Lang
Immediate Holding Company: Netvoyager plc
Registration no: 04058296 **Date established:** 2000
Turnover: £250,000 - £500,000 **No.of Employees:** 1 - 10
Product Groups: 44

Date of Accounts	Jun 08	Jun 07	Jun 06
Sales Turnover	367	415	252
Pre Tax Profit/Loss	57	-164	-95
Working Capital	-371	-534	-343
Fixed Assets	N/A	N/A	1
Current Assets	199	138	114
Current Liabilities	570	672	457
Total Share Capital	139	139	139
ROCE% (Return on Capital Employed)	-15.3	30.7	27.8
ROT% (Return on Turnover)	15.4	-39.5	-37.7

Netvue

Kingsdowne Court 10 The Common, London, W5 3TT
Tel: 020-8567 2201
E-mail: info@netvue.co.uk
Website: http://www.netvue.co.uk
Directors: J. Rackowe (MD)
Immediate Holding Company: NETVUE LTD
Registration no: 05619979 **Date established:** 2005
Turnover: Up to £250,000 **No.of Employees:** 1 - 10 **Product Groups:** 84

Date of Accounts	Mar 11	Mar 10	Mar 08
Sales Turnover	N/A	N/A	159
Pre Tax Profit/Loss	N/A	N/A	62
Working Capital	3	3	16
Current Assets	13	5	60
Current Liabilities	N/A	2	N/A

Nevica Ltd

8 Scrubs Lane, London, NW10 6RB
Tel: 020-8968 2300 **Fax:** 020-8968 2330
E-mail: sales@nevicakilly.com
Website: http://www.nevica.com
Directors: J. Crowson (MD), P. Goldstein (MD)
Managers: N. Howes (Mktg Serv Mgr)
Ultimate Holding Company: NTS INVESTMENTS LIMITED
Immediate Holding Company: NEVICA LIMITED
Registration no: 01372840 **Date established:** 1978
No.of Employees: 11 - 20 **Product Groups:** 24

Date of Accounts	Dec 10	Dec 09	Dec 08
Working Capital	2m	1m	1m
Fixed Assets	68	113	124
Current Assets	3m	3m	2m

New Brand Vision

26 Curtain Road, London, EC2A 3NY
Tel: 08451-232900
E-mail: team@newbrandvision.com
Website: http://www.newbrandvision.com
Managers: C. O'Mahony (Mgr)
Registration no: 05313469 **Date established:** 2004
No.of Employees: 11 - 20 **Product Groups:** 81

New Zealand Farmers Ltd

140-142 St John Street, London, EC1V 4UB
Tel: 020-7566 5000 **Fax:** 020-7490 2552
E-mail: robbies@nzfarmers.co.uk
Website: http://www.nzfarmers.co.uk
Bank(s): Bank of Scotland
Directors: B. Johnston (MD), M. Horn (Fin)
Ultimate Holding Company: ALLIANCE GROUP LTD (NEW ZEALAND)
Immediate Holding Company: NEW ZEALAND FARMERS LIMITED
Registration no: 01256992 **VAT No.:** GB 342 0225 09
Date established: 1976 **Turnover:** £75m - £125m
No.of Employees: 11 - 20 **Product Groups:** 61

Date of Accounts	Sep 08	Oct 09	Oct 10
Sales Turnover	78m	105m	113m
Pre Tax Profit/Loss	1m	1m	2m
Working Capital	8m	9m	10m
Fixed Assets	75	46	68
Current Assets	13m	16m	15m
Current Liabilities	1m	1m	1m

G C Newbury & Co. Ltd

Walmar House 296 Regent Street, London, W1B 3HR
Tel: 020-7255 2303 **Fax:** 020-7255 1453
E-mail: rm@gcnewbury.co.uk
Website: http://www.gcnewbury.co.uk
Directors: A. Musry (Fin), R. Musry (MD)
Ultimate Holding Company: WRENGATE HOLDINGS LIMITED
Immediate Holding Company: G C NEWBURY AND COMPANY LIMITED
Registration no: 00928560 **VAT No.:** GB 238 4505 59
Date established: 1968 **No.of Employees:** 1 - 10 **Product Groups:** 61

Date of Accounts	Apr 11	Apr 10	Apr 09
Working Capital	2m	2m	2m
Fixed Assets	N/A	17	22
Current Assets	2m	2m	3m

The Newcomen Society

Exhibition Road, London, SW7 2DD
Tel: 020-7371 4445 **Fax:** 020-7371 4445
E-mail: office@newcomen.com
Website: http://www.newcomen.com
Directors: T. Criton (Grp Chief Exec)
Immediate Holding Company: NEWCOMEN SOCIETY FOR THE STUDY OF THE HISTORY OF ENGINEERING AND TECHN
Registration no: 00691545 **VAT No.:** GB 242 7979 28
Date established: 1961 **Turnover:** Up to £250,000
No.of Employees: 1 - 10 **Product Groups:** 87

Date of Accounts	Jun 11	Jun 10	Jun 09
Sales Turnover	82	56	69
Pre Tax Profit/Loss	-41	-5	19
Working Capital	74	118	123
Fixed Assets	35	31	30
Current Assets	104	136	140
Current Liabilities	21	18	16

Newman Martin & Buchan LLP

NMB House 17 Bevis Marks, London, EC3A 7LN
Tel: 020-7648 8800 **Fax:** 020-7283 8703
E-mail: reception@nmbinsurance.com
Website: http://www.nmbinsurance.com
Bank(s): Barclays, Royal Bank Of Scotland
Directors: C. Sims (MD)
Ultimate Holding Company: NMB HOLDINGS (1987) LIMITED
Immediate Holding Company: NEWMAN MARTIN AND BUCHAN (1987) LIMITED
Registration no: 02088841 **Date established:** 1987 **Turnover:** £2m - £5m
No.of Employees: 101 - 250 **Product Groups:** 82

Date of Accounts	May 09	Mar 12	Mar 11
Sales Turnover	15m	4m	N/A
Pre Tax Profit/Loss	2m	4m	3m
Working Capital	2m	2m	2m
Fixed Assets	3m	3m	3m
Current Assets	2m	4m	3m
Current Liabilities	67	2m	950

Newport Industries

Merlin House Belmont Terrace, London, W4 5UG
Tel: 020-8742 0333 **Fax:** 020-8742 0444
E-mail: sales@newport-industries.com
Website: http://www.newport-industries.com

Directors: R. Patel (MD)
Registration no: 3407212 **Date established:** 1997 **Turnover:** £5m - £10m
No.of Employees: 11 - 20 **Product Groups:** 32, 66

Date of Accounts	Dec 07	Dec 06	Dec 05
Sales Turnover	N/A	5262	5131
Pre Tax Profit/Loss	N/A	76	129
Working Capital	-71	83	21
Fixed Assets	124	89	77
Current Assets	3597	1674	1319
Current Liabilities	3668	1591	1298
Total Share Capital	1	1	1
ROCE% (Return on Capital Employed)		44.0	131.6
ROT% (Return on Turnover)		1.4	2.5

News International

3 Thomas Moor Square, London, E98 1XY
Tel: 020-7782 6000 **Fax:** 020-7781 0517
E-mail: enquiries@newscore.com
Website: http://www.newscourt.com
Directors: L. Hinton (Grp Chief Exec), L. O'Neil (I.T. Dir), K. Murdoch (Ch)
Ultimate Holding Company: NEWS HOLDINGS LIMITED
Immediate Holding Company: TIMES LIMITED(THE)
Registration no: 00931844 **Date established:** 1968 **Turnover:** £5m - £10m
No.of Employees: 1 - 10 **Product Groups:** 28

Date of Accounts	Jun 08	Jun 09	Jun 10
Sales Turnover	124m	35m	35m
Pre Tax Profit/Loss	3m	699	-3m
Working Capital	-312m	-306m	-293m
Fixed Assets	575m	571m	554m
Current Assets	235m	270m	314m
Current Liabilities	30m	7m	2m

John Newton & Sons

68 Lombard Street, London, EC3V 9LJ
Tel: 020-7626 6068 **Fax:** 020-7283 3878
E-mail: johnnewtonsons@btinternet.com
Website: http://johnnewtonnotaries.co.uk
Directors: B. Hooke (Prop)
Immediate Holding Company: FIDENSYS CAPITAL LIMITED
Registration no: OC346590 **VAT No.:** GB 244 3196 68
Date established: 2009 **No.of Employees:** 1 - 10 **Product Groups:** 80

Noetica Ltd

7-11 St John's Hill, London, SW11 1TN
Tel: 020-7326 8500 **Fax:** 020-7801 9515
E-mail: sales@noetica.com
Website: http://www.Noetica.com
Bank(s): Lloyds TSB Bank plc
Directors: D. Singer (MD), L. Gordon (Fin)
Managers: C. Belcher (Sales Prom Mgr)
Ultimate Holding Company: Scandex Parent Ltd
Immediate Holding Company: NOETICA LIMITED
Registration no: 03319396 **VAT No.:** GB 544 5844 25
Date established: 1997 **Turnover:** £5m - £10m **No.of Employees:** 11 - 20
Product Groups: 67

Date of Accounts	Mar 08	Mar 07	Mar 06
Sales Turnover	N/A	1485	1039
Pre Tax Profit/Loss	N/A	-327	-425
Working Capital	57	432	42
Fixed Assets	66	37	38
Current Assets	411	739	399
Current Liabilities	354	307	356
Total Share Capital	10	10	10
ROCE% (Return on Capital Employed)		-69.6	-530.0
ROT% (Return on Turnover)		-22.0	-40.9

Nordic Style Ltd

109 Lots Road, London, SW10 0RN
Tel: 020-7351 1755 **Fax:** 020-7351 4966
E-mail: sales@nordicstyle.com
Website: http://www.nordicstyle.com
Directors: M. Essex (MD)
Immediate Holding Company: NORDIC STYLE LIMITED
Registration no: 03341373 **Date established:** 1997
Turnover: £500,000 - £1m **No.of Employees:** 1 - 10 **Product Groups:** 63

Date of Accounts	Mar 11	Mar 10
Working Capital	164	-11
Fixed Assets	66	9
Current Assets	296	83

Norland Managed Services Ltd

City Bridge House 57 Southwark Street, London, SE1 1RU
Tel: 020-7645 3750 **Fax:** 020-7871 9101
E-mail: info@norlandmanagedservices.co.uk
Website: http://www.norlandmanagedservices.co.uk
Directors: I. Entwisle (MD), R. Henderson (Dir)
Ultimate Holding Company: WILLIAM INVESTMENTS LIMITED
Immediate Holding Company: NORLAND MANAGED SERVICES LIMITED
Registration no: 01799580 **VAT No.:** GB 394 8397 87
Date established: 1984 **Turnover:** £250m - £500m
No.of Employees: 1 - 10 **Product Groups:** 52

Date of Accounts	Mar 12	Apr 09	Apr 10
Sales Turnover	312m	190m	210m
Pre Tax Profit/Loss	10m	8m	6m
Working Capital	25m	17m	21m
Fixed Assets	2m	2m	2m
Current Assets	96m	52m	66m
Current Liabilities	49m	22m	29m

Norman Linton Ltd

Linton House 39-51 Highgate Road, London, NW5 1RT
Tel: 020-7428 7700 **Fax:** 020-7267 0928
E-mail: brian@normanlinton.co.uk
Website: http://www.lintonoffices.co.uk
Managers: B. Fenn (Mgr)
Immediate Holding Company: NORMAN LINTON (HOLDINGS) LIMITED
Registration no: 00392482 **VAT No.:** GB 544 7756 12
Date established: 1945 **Turnover:** £1m - £2m **No.of Employees:** 1 - 10
Product Groups: 80

Date of Accounts	Mar 11	Mar 10	Mar 09
Sales Turnover	1m	1m	1m
Pre Tax Profit/Loss	2	90	192
Working Capital	2m	2m	3m
Fixed Assets	19m	19m	17m
Current Assets	5m	4m	4m
Current Liabilities	2m	2m	1m

Northcliffe Media Ltd

Northcliffe House 2 Derry Street, London, W8 5TT
Tel: 020-7400 1401 **Fax:** 020-7400 1518
E-mail: michael.pelosi@northcliffemedia.co.uk
Website: http://www.northcliffemedia.co.uk
Directors: S. Heath (Pers), S. Auckland (MD), R. Addison (Fin)
Managers: K. Carrick, K. Wall (Mktg Serv Mgr)
Ultimate Holding Company: ROTHERMERE CONTINUATION LTD (BERMUDA)
Immediate Holding Company: NORTHCLIFFE MEDIA LIMITED
Registration no: 03403993 **VAT No.:** GB 749 7046 94
Date established: 1997 **Turnover:** £75m - £125m
No.of Employees: 1 - 10 **Product Groups:** 28

Date of Accounts	Oct 10	Oct 09	Oct 11
Sales Turnover	15m	17m	13m
Pre Tax Profit/Loss	-985	-3m	-3m
Working Capital	-4m	9m	10m
Fixed Assets	3m	3m	94m
Current Assets	20m	23m	50m
Current Liabilities	12m	1m	22m

NorthgateArinso

41 Kingsway, London, WC2B 6TP
Tel: 020-7257 6413 **Fax:** 01244-399666
E-mail: hrsolutions@northgatearinso.com
Website: http://www.northgatearinso.com
Directors: C. Stone (MD), N. Hogen (Sales)
Managers: A. Layton (Grp Mgr), M. Rice (I.T. Exec)
No.of Employees: 21 - 50 **Product Groups:** 80

Northrop Grumman

Clareville House 26 Oxendon Street, London, SW1Y 4EL
Tel: 020-7930 4173 **Fax:** 020-7930 7418
Website: http://www.northropgrumman.co.uk
Bank(s): HSBC, Clerkenwell Branch
Directors: W. Von Kumberg (Legal)
Managers: N. Quinn, K. Beedle
Ultimate Holding Company: NORTHROP GRUMMAN CORPORATION (USA)
Immediate Holding Company: NORTHROP GRUMMAN UK LIMITED
Registration no: 05989428 **Date established:** 2006
Turnover: £250m - £500m **No.of Employees:** 11 - 20
Product Groups: 37, 48

Date of Accounts	Dec 11	Dec 10	Dec 09
Pre Tax Profit/Loss	-7	-6	-6
Working Capital	2	9	15
Current Assets	12	18	24
Current Liabilities	10	9	9

Northwood Spares & Accessories Ltd

87 Newington Causeway, London, SE1 6DH
Tel: 020-7407 9681 **Fax:** 020-7940 0820
E-mail: northwoodsltd@netscapeonline.co.uk
Website: http://www.northwoods-ltd.com
Bank(s): HSBC Bank plc
Directors: M. Northwood (MD)
Managers: J. Green (Sales Prom Mgr)
Immediate Holding Company: NORTHWOOD SPARES AND ACCESSORIES LIMITED
Registration no: 00271467 **VAT No.:** GB 238 2235 72
Date established: 1932 **Turnover:** £1m - £2m **No.of Employees:** 11 - 20
Product Groups: 61

Date of Accounts	Mar 09	Mar 08	Mar 07
Working Capital	586	581	550
Fixed Assets	128	135	143
Current Assets	1m	1m	1m

Norton Folgate F G plc

13 Crown Place, London, EC2A 4BT
Tel: 020-7965 4777 **Fax:** 01992-537733
E-mail: robertkeep@nortonfolgate.co.uk
Website: http://www.nortonfolgate.co.uk
Directors: R. Keep (MD)
Immediate Holding Company: NORTON FOLGATE FG PLC
Registration no: 03940795 **Date established:** 2000
Turnover: £250,000 - £500,000 **No.of Employees:** 1 - 10
Product Groups: 82

Norton Rose

3 More London Riverside, London, SE1 2AQ
Tel: 020-7283 6000 **Fax:** 020-7283 6500
E-mail: peter.martyr@nortonrose.com
Website: http://www.nortonrose.com
Directors: D. Chalmers (Fin), J. Roberts (Tech Serv)
Managers: A. McEachern, D. Simons, K. Mortell, P. Martyr, S. Thomas, L. Shumiloff
Immediate Holding Company: NORTON ROSE LIMITED
Registration no: 02230419 **Date established:** 1988
No.of Employees: 501 - 1000 **Product Groups:** 80

Novotel Lounge & West

1 Shortlands, London, W6 8DR
Tel: 020-8741 1555 **Fax:** 020-8741 2120
E-mail: h0737@accor-hotels.com
Website: http://www.novotellondonwest.co.uk
Managers: M. Sloan
Ultimate Holding Company: ACCOR SA (FRANCE)
Immediate Holding Company: NOVOTEL HOTEL EDINBURGH LIMITED
Registration no: 05308137 **Date established:** 2004 **Turnover:** £1m - £2m
No.of Employees: 101 - 250 **Product Groups:** 69

Date of Accounts	Dec 11	Dec 10	Dec 09
Sales Turnover	1m	1m	1m
Pre Tax Profit/Loss	1	N/A	N/A
Working Capital	1	N/A	N/A
Current Assets	332	316	316
Current Liabilities	330	316	316

Nursery Window Ltd

83 Walton Street, London, SW3 2HP
Tel: 020-7581 3358 **Fax:** 020-7823 8839
E-mail: info@nurserywindow.co.uk
Website: http://www.nurserywindow.co.uk
Directors: A. Kleiner (Prop)
Immediate Holding Company: THE NURSERY WINDOW LIMITED
Registration no: 01894487 **VAT No.:** GB 394 7767 85
Date established: 1985 **Turnover:** £250,000 - £500,000
No.of Employees: 1 - 10 **Product Groups:** 26

Date of Accounts	Mar 11	Mar 10	Mar 09
Working Capital	327	259	247
Fixed Assets	43	10	12

Current Assets	536	331	307

O A Steel Fabrication
211 Railway Arches Trussley Road, London, W6 7PP
Tel: 020-8743 4579 **Fax:** 020-8743 4579
E-mail: oasteeljohn@live.co.uk
Directors: J. Avakyan (Prop)
Date established: 1984 **No.of Employees:** 1 - 10 **Product Groups:** 35

O M C Plan Stairways Ltd
58 Wood Lane, London, W12 7RZ
Tel: 07825-339453
Website: http://www.omcengineering.com
Managers: B. Comerfrod (Comm)
Ultimate Holding Company: OMC TECHNOLOGIES LIMITED
Immediate Holding Company: OMC PLAN STAIRWAYS LIMITED
Registration no: 04821901 **Date established:** 2003
No.of Employees: 21 - 50 **Product Groups:** 33, 35

Date of Accounts	Dec 10	Dec 09	Dec 08
Pre Tax Profit/Loss	N/A	14	127
Working Capital	-160	-174	-227
Fixed Assets	33	58	96
Current Assets	2m	2m	2m
Current Liabilities	N/A	138	1m

O M V UK Ltd
Ryder Court 14 Ryder Street, London, SW1Y 6QB
Tel: 020-7333 1600 **Fax:** 020-7333 1610
E-mail: info@omv.com
Website: http://www.omv.com
Directors: W. Herzog (Fin), W. Remp (Dir)
Ultimate Holding Company: OMV AKIENGESELLSCHAFT (AUSTRIA)
Immediate Holding Company: OMV (U.K.) LIMITED
Registration no: 01504603 **Date established:** 1980
Turnover: £75m - £125m **No.of Employees:** 21 - 50 **Product Groups:** 84

Date of Accounts	Sep 08	Dec 07	Dec 06
Sales Turnover	222m	239m	241m
Pre Tax Profit/Loss	110m	89m	130m
Working Capital	436m	433m	442m
Fixed Assets	313m	312m	277m
Current Assets	462m	474m	486m
Current Liabilities	27m	41m	44m
Total Share Capital	164m	164m	164m

O P B Paper Sales Ltd
26-28 Sidney Road Stockwell, London, SW9 0TS
Tel: 020-7737 3131 **Fax:** 020-7738 7052
E-mail: anil.bhola@opb-paper.co.uk
Directors: A. Bhola (MD)
Immediate Holding Company: O.P.B. PAPER SALES LIMITED
Registration no: 01173902 **VAT No.:** GB 236 7295 41
Date established: 1974 **Turnover:** £500,000 - £1m
No.of Employees: 1 - 10 **Product Groups:** 64, 66

Date of Accounts	Jun 11	Jun 10	Jun 09
Working Capital	762	1m	1m
Fixed Assets	169	177	180
Current Assets	1m	1m	2m

Obelisk Music
32 Ellerdale Road, London, NW3 6BB
Tel: 020-7813 2253 **Fax:** 020-7431 0621
E-mail: heinzherschmann@yahoo.co.uk
Website: http://www.apollosound.com
Directors: H. Herschmann (Prop)
Date established: 1959 **Turnover:** £250,000 - £500,000
No.of Employees: 1 - 10 **Product Groups:** 28

Office Team
7 Spa Road Bermondsey, London, SE16 3QQ
Tel: 020-7556 3345 **Fax:** 020-7231 9810
E-mail: angie.deverell@officeteam.co.uk
Website: http://www.officeteam.co.uk
Managers: A. Deverell (Cust Serv Mgr)
Ultimate Holding Company: AAC CAPITAL PARTNERS HOLDING BV (NETHERLANDS)
Immediate Holding Company: TAVISH LIMITED
Registration no: 05095978 **Date established:** 2008
No.of Employees: 11 - 20 **Product Groups:** 27

Date of Accounts	Apr 11	Apr 10	Apr 09
Sales Turnover	3m	N/A	N/A
Pre Tax Profit/Loss	286	N/A	N/A
Working Capital	219	5	N/A
Current Assets	352	42	N/A
Current Liabilities	78	3	N/A

Ogilvy Advertising
10 Cabot Square, London, E14 4QB
Tel: 020-7345 3000 **Fax:** 020-7345 9000
E-mail: paul.o'donnell@ogilvy.com
Website: http://www.ogilvy.com
Directors: P. O Donnell (Grp Ch), P. Jackson (Grp Chief Exec), L. Collinet (Dir)
Immediate Holding Company: QCI ASSESSMENT LIMITED
Registration no: 03577489 **VAT No.:** GB 239 0618 60
Date established: 1998 **Turnover:** Up to £250,000
No.of Employees: 251 - 500 **Product Groups:** 81

Date of Accounts	Dec 07	Dec 06
Sales Turnover	175790	156150
Pre Tax Profit/Loss	18130	14270
Working Capital	251720	234090
Fixed Assets	25970	26540
Current Assets	301170	279320
Current Liabilities	49450	45230
Total Share Capital	124200	124200
ROCE% (Return on Capital Employed)	6.5	5.5
ROT% (Return on Turnover)	10.3	9.1

Oil & Gas UK Ltd
Portland House Bressenden Place, London, SW1E 5BH
Tel: 020-7802 2400 **Fax:** 020-7802 2401
E-mail: info@oilandgasuk.co.uk
Website: http://oilandgasuk.co.uk
Managers: S. Fraser (Public Relation), G. Elgie
Ultimate Holding Company: WILLOW TOPCO LIMITED (JERSEY)
Immediate Holding Company: OIL & GAS UK LIMITED
Registration no: 06255457 **VAT No.:** GB 241 4219 95
Date established: 2007 **Turnover:** £5m - £10m **No.of Employees:** 21 - 50
Product Groups: 87

Date of Accounts	May 10	May 09	May 08
Working Capital	-3	-3	-1
Fixed Assets	N/A	N/A	1
Current Liabilities	3	N/A	N/A

Oiluk
145-157 St John Street, London, EC1V 4PY
Tel: 029-2057 5515 **Fax:** 029-2057 5595
E-mail: info@oiluk.net
Website: http://www.oiluk.net
Managers: P. Williams (Mgr)
Date established: 2006 **Turnover:** Up to £250,000
No.of Employees: 1 - 10 **Product Groups:** 31

Old Mutual Asset Managers UK
2 Lambeth Hill, London, EC4V 4AD
Tel: 020-7332 7500 **Fax:** 020-7332 7550
E-mail: info@omam.co.uk
Website: http://www.oldmutual.com
Directors: J. Ainsworth (Grp Chief Exec), P. Baxter (Dir), P. Nathan (Fin)
Ultimate Holding Company: OLD MUTUAL PUBLIC LIMITED COMPANY
Immediate Holding Company: OLD MUTUAL ASSET MANAGERS (UK) LIMITED
Registration no: 02949554 **Date established:** 1994
Turnover: £20m - £50m **No.of Employees:** 101 - 250 **Product Groups:** 82

Date of Accounts	Dec 11	Dec 10	Dec 09
Sales Turnover	21m	22m	20m
Pre Tax Profit/Loss	847	3m	458
Working Capital	19m	20m	17m
Fixed Assets	3m	3m	5m
Current Assets	37m	36m	36m
Current Liabilities	12m	15m	17m

Bruce Oldfield Ltd
27 Beauchamp Place, London, SW3 1NJ
Tel: 020-7584 1363 **Fax:** 020-7761 0351
E-mail: hq@bruceoldfield.com
Website: http://www.bruceoldfield.com
Directors: B. Oldfield (MD), G. Alexander Sinclair (Co Sec)
Immediate Holding Company: BRUCE OLDFIELD LIMITED
Registration no: 03098318 **Date established:** 1995
Turnover: £500,000 - £1m **No.of Employees:** 1 - 10 **Product Groups:** 81

Date of Accounts	Oct 11	Oct 10	Nov 09
Working Capital	89	86	128
Fixed Assets	42	40	46
Current Assets	492	479	362

Oliver Goldsmiths Sunglasses
15 All Saints Road, London, W11 1HA
Tel: 0845-053 3440 **Fax:** 0870-754 1899
E-mail: info@olivergoldsmith.com
Website: http://www.olivergoldsmith.com
Directors: C. Gold (MD)
Immediate Holding Company: NETHERWOOD STUDIOS LTD
Registration no: 06691278 **Date established:** 2008
No.of Employees: 1 - 10 **Product Groups:** 24, 33, 49, 63

Omdesign London Ltd
4 Montrose Court Finchley Road, London, NW11 6AG
Tel: 020-8731 9230
E-mail: contact@omdesign.co.uk
Website: http://www.omdesign.co.uk
Directors: M. Matias (Dir)
Immediate Holding Company: OMDESIGN LONDON LIMITED
Registration no: 06631877 **Date established:** 2008
Turnover: Up to £250,000 **No.of Employees:** 1 - 10 **Product Groups:** 44

Date of Accounts	Mar 11	Mar 10
Working Capital	9	N/A
Current Assets	12	N/A

On Sight Ltd
14-15 Berners Street, London, W1T 3LJ
Tel: 020-7637 0888 **Fax:** 020-7637 0444
E-mail: simon@onsight.co.uk
Website: http://www.onsight.co.uk
Directors: S. Craddock (MD), S. Panessar (Fin), J. Craddock (Fin)
Managers: A. Shelley (Mktg Serv Mgr), P. Jessop (Personnel), R. Tester (Tech Serv Mgr)
Ultimate Holding Company: ON SIGHT HOLDINGS LIMITED
Immediate Holding Company: ON SIGHT LIMITED
Registration no: 02410150 **Date established:** 1989
No.of Employees: 21 - 50 **Product Groups:** 37, 83

Date of Accounts	Jul 11	Jul 10	Jul 09
Working Capital	-1m	-765	-319
Fixed Assets	6m	4m	4m
Current Assets	1m	750	1m

1 Onion Ltd
53 Balham Grove, London, SW12 8AZ
Tel: 020-8675 8631
E-mail: enquiry@1onion.com
Website: http://www.1onion.com
Directors: N. Cesareo (Dir), J. Fraser (Dir)
Registration no: 03354877 **No.of Employees:** 1 - 10 **Product Groups:** 80

Date of Accounts	Mar 08	Mar 07	Mar 06
Working Capital	5	6	7
Fixed Assets	3	1	1
Current Assets	13	72	41
Current Liabilities	9	67	34

Oneida International Ltd
106 Brent Terrace, London, NW2 1BZ
Tel: 020-8450 8900 **Fax:** 020-8450 9985
E-mail: james.joseph@oneida.co.uk
Website: http://www.oneida.co.uk
Directors: M. Weston (MD), S. Spetch (Tech Serv), M. Scott (Fin), J. Joseph (Dir)
Managers: M. Sukhdeo (Personnel), E. Hayward (Sales Prom Mgr), L. Hoyle (Mktg Serv Mgr)
Ultimate Holding Company: ONEIDA LIMITED
Immediate Holding Company: ONEIDA INTERNATIONAL LIMITED
Registration no: 00995820 **Date established:** 1970
Turnover: £10m - £20m **No.of Employees:** 101 - 250 **Product Groups:** 49

Date of Accounts	Dec 11	Dec 10	Dec 09
Sales Turnover	12m	13m	11m
Pre Tax Profit/Loss	225	206	-1m
Working Capital	4m	3m	3m
Fixed Assets	150	258	317
Current Assets	6m	5m	5m
Current Liabilities	984	839	1m

Optim Contracts
The Hop Exchange 24 Southwark Street, London, SE1 1TY
Tel: 020-7940 2700 **Fax:** 020-7378 0580
E-mail: info@optimgroup.co.uk
Website: http://www.optimgroup.co.uk
Directors: B. Birrane (MD)
Immediate Holding Company: CAPITAL BUSINESS VENTURES LTD
Registration no: 03826851 **Date established:** 2007
Turnover: £10m - £20m **No.of Employees:** 1 - 10 **Product Groups:** 48, 52, 71, 81

Optimize Search Marketing
25 Crescent Road, London, SW20 8HA
Tel: 020-8879 3180 **Fax:** 07930-479217
Website: http://www.optimize.co.uk
Directors: M. Rogers (MD)
Turnover: £1m - £2m **No.of Employees:** 1 - 10 **Product Groups:** 44, 79, 81

Opus Consultancy Service (An Organisation for Promoting Understanding of Society)
26 Fernhurst Road, London, SW6 7JW
Tel: 020-7736 3844 **Fax:** 020-7736 3844
E-mail: director@opus.org.uk
Website: http://www.opus.org.uk
Directors: L. Stapley (Dir)
Immediate Holding Company: OPUS - AN ORGANISATION FOR PROMOTING UNDERSTANDING OF SOCIETY
Registration no: 01514106 **Date established:** 1980
Turnover: Up to £250,000 **No.of Employees:** 1 - 10 **Product Groups:** 80

Date of Accounts	Mar 12	Mar 11	Mar 10
Sales Turnover	111	104	98
Pre Tax Profit/Loss	7	-3	-2
Working Capital	46	39	42
Current Assets	46	42	45

Orion Forklift & Plant
94 Alleyn Road, London, SE21 8AH
Tel: 020-8766 7223 **Fax:** 020-8761 0223
E-mail: enquiries@orionforklift.com
Directors: I. Cox (Prop)
Registration no: 04406670 **Date established:** 2002
No.of Employees: 1 - 10 **Product Groups:** 35, 39, 45

Orion Publishing Group Ltd
Orion House 5 Upper St Martins Lane, London, WC2H 9EA
Tel: 020-7240 3444 **Fax:** 020-7240 4822
E-mail: peter.roche@orionbooks.co.uk
Website: http://www.orionbooks.co.uk
Directors: D. Manderson (Sales), P. Roche (Grp Chief Exec), P. De Cacqueray (Fin)
Ultimate Holding Company: LAGARDERE SCA (FRANCE)
Immediate Holding Company: THE ORION PUBLISHING GROUP LIMITED
Registration no: 02663988 **Date established:** 1991
Turnover: £50m - £75m **No.of Employees:** 101 - 250 **Product Groups:** 28

Date of Accounts	Dec 11	Dec 10	Dec 09
Sales Turnover	64m	66m	68m
Pre Tax Profit/Loss	-384	4m	2m
Working Capital	20m	23m	22m
Fixed Assets	4m	4m	5m
Current Assets	42m	50m	49m
Current Liabilities	15m	18m	18m

Orman Risk Analysts
10 Albert Bridge Road, London, SW11 4PY
Tel: 020-7622 8645 **Fax:** 020-7498 0346
E-mail: geraldorman@btconnect.com
Website: http://www.contrac-texpert.com
Directors: G. Orman (Dir), G. Orman (MD)
Date established: 1993 **Turnover:** Up to £250,000
No.of Employees: 1 - 10 **Product Groups:** 80, 82

Other Media
1 Newhams Row, London, SE1 3UZ
Tel: 020-7089 5959 **Fax:** 020-7089 5960
E-mail: info@othermedia.com
Website: http://www.othermedia.com
Directors: G. Crabb (MD)
Immediate Holding Company: THE OTHER MEDIA LIMITED
Registration no: 03468671 **Date established:** 1997 **Turnover:** £1m - £2m
No.of Employees: 21 - 50 **Product Groups:** 44, 80

Date of Accounts	Apr 11	Apr 10	Apr 09
Working Capital	104	92	181
Fixed Assets	134	107	106
Current Assets	704	971	697

Otis Ltd
187 Twyford Abbey Road, London, NW10 7DG
Tel: 020-8955 3000 **Fax:** 020-8955 3001
E-mail: lindsay.harvey@otis.com
Website: http://www.otis.com
Bank(s): Royal Bank of Scotland, London
Directors: L. Harvey (MD)
Ultimate Holding Company: UNITED TECHNOLOGIES CORP INC (USA)
Immediate Holding Company: OTIS LIMITED
Registration no: 00147366 **Date established:** 2017
Turnover: £125m - £250m **No.of Employees:** 1501 & over
Product Groups: 45

Date of Accounts	Nov 11	Nov 10	Nov 09
Sales Turnover	186m	200m	237m
Pre Tax Profit/Loss	35m	48m	37m
Working Capital	199m	179m	153m
Fixed Assets	233m	233m	208m
Current Assets	254m	241m	217m
Current Liabilities	39m	43m	49m

Out Takes Ltd
Unit B207 Faircharm Trading Estate Creekside, London, SE8 3DX
Tel: 020-8293 9888 **Fax:** 020-8293 9881
E-mail: info@outtakes.co.uk
Website: http://www.outtakes.co.uk
Directors: D. Brown (MD)
Immediate Holding Company: OUT TAKES LIMITED
Registration no: 02897614 **Date established:** 1994
No.of Employees: 1 - 10 **Product Groups:** 89

see next page

Out Takes Ltd - Cont'd

Date of Accounts	Jul 11	Jul 10	Jul 09
Working Capital	24	21	7
Fixed Assets	173	134	13
Current Assets	69	52	42

Outmere Direct Mail Ltd

Unit 5-6 Wellington Road, London, SW19 8EX
Tel: 020-8947 7577 **Fax:** 020-8944 9736
E-mail: nick@outmere.co.uk
Website: http://www.outmere.co.uk
Directors: N. Blanchard (Dir), A. Blanchard (Co Sec)
Immediate Holding Company: OUTMERE DIRECT MAIL LIMITED
Registration no: 01408547 **Date established:** 1979
No.of Employees: 11 - 20 **Product Groups:** 81

Date of Accounts	Oct 11	Oct 10	Oct 09
Working Capital	-11	-15	5
Fixed Assets	21	23	27
Current Assets	144	104	102

Outstanding Branding

Unit 12 11 The Leather Market Weston Street, London, SE1 3ER
Tel: 020-3142 6700 **Fax:** 020-3031 1355
E-mail: info@outstandingbranding.com
Website: http://www.outstandingbranding.com
Directors: A. Thorne (Sales)
Immediate Holding Company: OUTSTANDING BRANDING LIMITED
Registration no: 06938008 **Date established:** 2009
No.of Employees: 1 - 10 **Product Groups:** 24, 49

Date of Accounts	Jun 11	Jun 10
Working Capital	29	15
Fixed Assets	4	N/A
Current Assets	183	116

Oxford House College

30 Oxford Street, London, W1D 1AU
Tel: 020-7580 9785 **Fax:** 020-7323 4582
E-mail: info@oxfordhousegroup.com
Website: http://www.oxfordhousecollege.co.uk
Bank(s): The Royal Bank of Scotland
Directors: T. Matthews (Head)
Immediate Holding Company: PIZO CATERING LTD
Registration no: 02763508 **VAT No.:** GB 625 9189 11
Date established: 2011 **Turnover:** £2m - £5m **No.of Employees:** 21 - 50
Product Groups: 86

Date of Accounts	Dec 07
Sales Turnover	685
Pre Tax Profit/Loss	-671
Working Capital	-1486
Fixed Assets	38
Current Assets	125
Current Liabilities	1611
ROCE% (Return on Capital Employed)	46.3

Oxypas

Unit 6 Corben Mews Clyston Street, London, SW8 4TA
Tel: 0845-8812262 **Fax:** 0845-8812261
E-mail: order@oxypas.com
Website: http://en.oxypas.com
Directors: R. QUILLIOT (Dir)
Registration no: 5618745 **Date established:** 1994 **Turnover:** £2m - £5m
No.of Employees: 51 - 100 **Product Groups:** 22, 24

P A Consulting Group

Level 4 123 Buckingham Palace Road, London, SW1W 9SR
Tel: 020-7333 5865 **Fax:** 020-7333 5050
E-mail: info@paconsulting.com
Website: http://www.paconsulting.com
Directors: J. Moynihan (Grp Chief Exec), K. Janjuah (Fin), K. Janjuah (Dir), L. Todd (Co Sec)
Immediate Holding Company: PA CONSULTING GROUP LIMITED
Registration no: 06555894 **Date established:** 2008
Turnover: £250m - £500m **No.of Employees:** 1501 & over
Product Groups: 44, 80, 81, 84, 85, 86

Date of Accounts	Dec 11	Dec 10	Dec 09
Sales Turnover	336m	328m	370m
Pre Tax Profit/Loss	27m	31m	55m
Working Capital	179m	190m	191m
Fixed Assets	45m	44m	52m
Current Assets	279m	284m	335m
Current Liabilities	97m	90m	143m

P A G Ltd

565 Kingston Road, London, SW20 8SA
Tel: 020-8543 3131 **Fax:** 020-8540 4797
E-mail: sales@paguk.com
Website: http://www.paguk.com
Bank(s): Svenska Handelsbanken
Directors: N. Gardner (Sales), D. Hardy (Co Sec), J. Lavender (Dir)
Managers: S. Emmett (Publicity), R. Coulthard (Comptroller), P. Lavender (I.T. Exec)
Immediate Holding Company: PAG LIMITED
Registration no: 01294856 **Date established:** 1977 **Turnover:** £2m - £5m
No.of Employees: 11 - 20 **Product Groups:** 37

Date of Accounts	Jan 12	Jan 11	Jan 10
Working Capital	382	350	494
Fixed Assets	1m	1m	1m
Current Assets	816	901	914

P E C O

250 Grand Drive, London, SW20 9NE
Tel: 020-8543 1030 **Fax:** 020-8543 0067
Website: http://www.pecoltd.co.uk
Directors: D. Paul (MD)
Managers: P. Leiberman (Chief Mgr)
Immediate Holding Company: Paul Electrical Co Ltd
VAT No.: GB 215 9128 70 **No.of Employees:** 1 - 10 **Product Groups:** 84

P H D Media Ltd

5 North Crescent Chenies Street, London, WC1E 7PH
Tel: 020-7436 2005 **Fax:** 020-7446 7100
E-mail: info@newphd.co.uk
Website: http://www.phd.co.uk
Directors: K. King (Pers), D. Rubens (Dir), I. Paterson (Fin)
Managers: E. Hudghton
Ultimate Holding Company: OMNICORN GROUP INC (USA)
Immediate Holding Company: PHD MEDIA LIMITED
Registration no: 02423952 **Date established:** 1989
Turnover: £250m - £500m **No.of Employees:** 101 - 250
Product Groups: 81

Date of Accounts	Dec 11	Dec 10	Dec 09
Sales Turnover	380m	21m	259m
Pre Tax Profit/Loss	6m	6m	5m
Working Capital	6m	5m	4m
Fixed Assets	1m	1m	1m
Current Assets	113m	122m	92m
Current Liabilities	11m	7m	4m

P I P Electrics

Exchange Tower 1 Harbour Exchange Square, London, E14 9GE
Tel: 01268-541651 **Fax:** 01268-541625
E-mail: candlerr@pipelectrics.com
Website: http://www.pipelectrics.com
Directors: G. Pasco (MD), S. Brewer (Contracts), S. Brewer (Dir)
Managers: R. Candler (Comptroller)
Immediate Holding Company: P.I.P. ELECTRICS LIMITED
Registration no: 00968629 **VAT No.:** GB 244 2109 94
Date established: 1969 **Turnover:** £10m - £20m
No.of Employees: 21 - 50 **Product Groups:** 52

Date of Accounts	Dec 10	Dec 09	Dec 08
Sales Turnover	16m	13m	26m
Pre Tax Profit/Loss	89	94	557
Working Capital	6m	6m	6m
Fixed Assets	952	1m	1m
Current Assets	8m	8m	10m
Current Liabilities	1m	1m	3m

P O S Services

14-15 D'Arblay Street, London, W1F 8DZ
Tel: 020-7437 5000 **Fax:** 08703-307401
E-mail: enquiry@posservices.com
Website: http://www.posservices.com
Directors: H. Diamond (MD)
Immediate Holding Company: THE MINIMART LTD
Registration no: 04825209 **Date established:** 2003 **Turnover:** £1m - £2m
No.of Employees: 11 - 20 **Product Groups:** 81

Date of Accounts	Mar 11	Mar 10	Mar 09
Sales Turnover	N/A	812	1m
Pre Tax Profit/Loss	N/A	119	144
Working Capital	621	497	502
Fixed Assets	29	23	23
Current Assets	895	667	632
Current Liabilities	N/A	138	49

P & O Steam Navigation Co

Peninsular House 79 Pall Mall, London, SW1Y 5EJ
Tel: 020-7930 4343 **Fax:** 020-7930 8572
E-mail: groupinformation@p-and-o.com
Website: http://www.pogroup.com
Directors: B. MacPhail (MD), R. Gradon (Dir), P. Walker (Fin), N. Luff (Fin), M. Graydem (Co Sec)
Managers: M. Sil (I.T. Exec), C. Rogers, J. Fisher (Personnel)
Ultimate Holding Company: CIT GROUP INC. (USA)
Immediate Holding Company: CIT BANK LIMITED
Registration no: ZC000073 **VAT No.:** GB 243 4566 62
Date established: 1996 **Turnover:** Over £1,000m
No.of Employees: 101 - 250 **Product Groups:** 71, 72, 74, 77

Date of Accounts	Dec 08	Dec 07	Dec 06
Pre Tax Profit/Loss	-13m	8m	2m
Fixed Assets	47	2m	2m
Current Assets	613m	562m	448m
Current Liabilities	443m	100m	65m

P P S Rotaprint Ltd

Unit 720 Tudor Estate Abbey Road, London, NW10 7UN
Tel: 020-8951 9500 **Fax:** 020-8963 1940
E-mail: sales@rotaprint.com
Website: http://www.wwpps.com
Directors: I. Mercer (Dir), I. Mirza (Jt MD), R. Mirza (Jt MD)
Managers: L. Matthews (Sales Prom Mgr), B. Wilson
Immediate Holding Company: OMNITEK LTD
Registration no: 04518364 **Date established:** 2011 **Turnover:** £5m - £10m
No.of Employees: 1 - 10 **Product Groups:** 44

P S A Transport Ltd

16 Devonshire Street, London, W1G 7AF
Tel: 020-7637 3271 **Fax:** 020-7255 2229
E-mail: sales@psatransport.co.uk
Website: http://www.psatransport.co.uk
Directors: J. Gerguri (Co Sec), M. Mojsa (MD)
Managers: I. McCormick
Ultimate Holding Company: C HARTWIG GDYNIA SA (POLAND)
Immediate Holding Company: EON ENTERPRISES LIMITED
Registration no: 00358578 **VAT No.:** GB 243 6230 85
Date established: 2008 **Turnover:** £1m - £2m **No.of Employees:** 1 - 10
Product Groups: 76

Date of Accounts	Dec 08	Dec 07	Dec 06
Pre Tax Profit/Loss	N/A	N/A	3
Working Capital	341	461	459
Fixed Assets	268	279	321
Current Assets	738	1085	1103
Current Liabilities	397	624	644
Total Share Capital	100	100	100
ROCE% (Return on Capital Employed)			0.4

P S D Group Ltd

28-31 Essex Street, London, WC2R 3AT
Tel: 020-7970 9700 **Fax:** 020-7353 6127
E-mail: london@psdgroup.com
Website: http://www.psdgroup.com
Directors: I. Moss (Fin)
Managers: P. Thompson (Tech Serv Mgr), A. French (Personnel), Z. Child (Mktg Serv Mgr)
Ultimate Holding Company: OFFERCO LIMITED
Immediate Holding Company: OPD GROUP LIMITED
Registration no: 03201382 **Date established:** 1996
Turnover: Up to £250,000 **No.of Employees:** 501 - 1000
Product Groups: 80

Date of Accounts	Dec 11	Dec 10	Dec 09
Sales Turnover	60	43	49m
Pre Tax Profit/Loss	2m	8m	-2m
Working Capital	16m	15m	8m
Fixed Assets	9m	9m	31m
Current Assets	17m	15m	13m
Current Liabilities	82	56	4m

P S G Group Ltd

Polymex House 49-53 Glengall Road, London, SE15 6NF
Tel: 020-7740 9740 **Fax:** 020-7277 5654
E-mail: sales@psggroup.co.uk
Website: http://www.psggroup.co.uk
Bank(s): National Westminster Bank Plc
Directors: T. Quazi (Dir), Y. Feussner (Dir), L. Gardezi (Dir)
Immediate Holding Company: PSG GROUP LIMITED
Registration no: 02260957 **VAT No.:** GB 233 0574 90
Date established: 1988 **Turnover:** £500,000 - £1m
No.of Employees: 21 - 50 **Product Groups:** 22, 23, 25, 27, 28, 29, 30, 33, 35, 36, 37, 39, 40, 41, 42, 44, 49, 66, 68

Date of Accounts	Sep 11	Sep 10	Sep 09
Working Capital	256	495	452
Fixed Assets	524	308	198
Current Assets	2m	3m	2m

P S G Solutions plc

133 Ebury Street, London, SW1W 9QU
Tel: 020-7881 0800 **Fax:** 020-7881 0707
E-mail: info@psgsols.com
Website: http://www.psgsols.com
Directors: J. Holme (Fin), J. Mervis (Ch)
Managers: J. Lim, J. Warwick
Immediate Holding Company: SECURITY RESEARCH GROUP PLC
Registration no: 03170812 **Date established:** 1996
Turnover: £10m - £20m **No.of Employees:** 1 - 10 **Product Groups:** 80

Date of Accounts	Mar 12	Mar 11	Mar 10
Sales Turnover	37m	11m	11m
Pre Tax Profit/Loss	8m	1m	-3m
Working Capital	12m	6m	5m
Fixed Assets	7m	11m	10m
Current Assets	26m	8m	7m
Current Liabilities	9m	2m	1m

Pa Finlay & Company Ltd

8 Gemini Business Park Hornet Way, London, E6 7FF
Tel: 020-7540 6450 **Fax:** 020-8534 7652
E-mail: hugh.finlay@pa-finlay.co.uk
Website: http://www.pa-finlay.co.uk
Bank(s): National Westminster
Directors: P. Finlay (Dir), C. Athienitou (Co Sec), M. Finlay (MD), H. Finlay (MD)
Immediate Holding Company: P.A. FINLAY & COMPANY LIMITED
Registration no: 00988222 **Date established:** 1970 **Turnover:** £2m - £5m
No.of Employees: 21 - 50 **Product Groups:** 52

Date of Accounts	Dec 07	Aug 06
Sales Turnover	8553	6844
Pre Tax Profit/Loss	604	-141
Working Capital	1749	1319
Fixed Assets	849	708
Current Assets	3531	3555
Current Liabilities	1782	2236
Total Share Capital	10	10
ROCE% (Return on Capital Employed)	23.2	-7.0
ROT% (Return on Turnover)	7.1	-2.1

Pa News Ltd

292 Vauxhall Bridge Road, London, SW1V 1AE
Tel: 08701-203200 **Fax:** 020-7963 7192
E-mail: sales@pressassociation.com
Website: http://www.pressassociation.com
Managers: A. Scott
Immediate Holding Company: PA NEWS LIMITED
Registration no: 05385891 **Date established:** 2005
Turnover: £20m - £50m **No.of Employees:** 251 - 500 **Product Groups:** 81

Pads Ltd

The Coach House 3a Woodchuch Road, London, NW6 3PL
Tel: 020-7372 2456 **Fax:** 020-7372 2458
E-mail: timflkn@btconnect.com
Website: http://www.pads-creative.co.uk
Directors: I. Lancer (Dir), T. Faulkner (MD)
Registration no: 02210233 **VAT No.:** GB 495 3555 09
Date established: 1980 **Turnover:** Up to £250,000
No.of Employees: 1 - 10 **Product Groups:** 81

Date of Accounts	Sep 08	Sep 07
Working Capital	14	23
Fixed Assets	N/A	4
Current Assets	18	30
Current Liabilities	3	7
Total Share Capital	4	4

Paintworks Ltd

240 Camberwell Road, London, SE5 0DP
Tel: 020-7708 1100 **Fax:** 020-7708 2200
E-mail: julian@paintworks.uk.com
Website: http://www.paintworks.uk.com
Directors: J. Rowley (MD)
Immediate Holding Company: PAINTWORKS LIMITED
Registration no: 01827340 **Date established:** 1984
No.of Employees: 1 - 10 **Product Groups:** 46, 48

Date of Accounts	Jun 11	Jun 10	Jun 09
Working Capital	218	204	152
Fixed Assets	168	174	181
Current Assets	272	261	204

Pakistan International Airlines

1-15 King Street, London, W6 9HR
Tel: 020-8741 8066 **Fax:** 020-8741 9376
E-mail: longrpk@piac.com.pk
Website: http://www.piac.com.pk
Bank(s): National Westminster, Piccadilly
Managers: F. Masood (Mktg Serv Mgr), I. Choudry (Personnel), S. Ansari (Admin Off)
Registration no: FC004532 **Date established:** 1954
Turnover: £20m - £50m **No.of Employees:** 21 - 50 **Product Groups:** 75

Palco Industries Ltd

Palco House 11 Beavor Lane, London, W6 9AR
Tel: 020-8741 1222 **Fax:** 020-8741 9116
Website: http://www.palco.co.uk
Managers: J. Still (Admin Off)
Immediate Holding Company: PALCO INDUSTRIES LIMITED
Registration no: 03208516 **Date established:** 1996 **Turnover:** £5m - £10m
No.of Employees: 21 - 50 **Product Groups:** 23, 28

Date of Accounts	Mar 11	Mar 10	Mar 09
Working Capital	170	50	-0
Current Assets	840	684	25
Current Liabilities	N/A	N/A	25

Palebeck Telecomms

9 Little Portland Street, London, W1W 7JF
Tel: 020-7580 7226 **Fax:** 020-7580 3115
E-mail: info@pttl.co.uk
Website: http://www.palebeck.co.uk

Directors: K. McNeill (Fin), D. Cook (MD)
Immediate Holding Company: PALEBECK TELECOMMUNICATIONS TECHNOLOGY LIMITED
Registration no: 01681218 **Date established:** 1982 **Turnover:** £1m - £2m
No.of Employees: 1 - 10 **Product Groups:** 52, 84

Date of Accounts	Dec 11	Dec 10	Dec 09
Working Capital	72	59	40
Fixed Assets	7	9	13
Current Assets	314	388	435

Panduit Europe Ltd

West World Westgate, London, W5 1UD
Tel: 020-8601 7200 **Fax:** 020-8601 7319
E-mail: info@panduit.com
Website: http://www.panduit.com
Managers: L. Bojarski
Immediate Holding Company: PANDUIT EUROPE LTD.
Registration no: 03287919 **Date established:** 1996
Turnover: £20m - £50m **No.of Employees:** 51 - 100 **Product Groups:** 37, 44

Date of Accounts	Dec 07	Dec 06	Dec 05
Pre Tax Profit/Loss	691	975	504
Working Capital	1280	1241	1054
Fixed Assets	923	576	478
Current Assets	21931	12793	4077
Current Liabilities	20651	11552	3023
Total Share Capital	612	612	612
ROCE% (Return on Capital Employed)	31.3	53.7	32.9

Panfoods Co. Ltd

16 St Clare Street, London, EC3N 1LQ
Tel: 020-7680 1828 **Fax:** 020-7680 1646
E-mail: pan_admin@iguacu.co.uk
Website: http://www.iguacu.com.br
Directors: J. Gallagher (MD), R. Davis (Fin)
Ultimate Holding Company: MARUBENI CORPORATION (JAPAN)
Immediate Holding Company: PANFOODS CO., LIMITED
Registration no: 01961948 **Date established:** 1985
Turnover: £125m - £250m **No.of Employees:** 11 - 20 **Product Groups:** 62

Date of Accounts	Dec 08
Sales Turnover	245990
Pre Tax Profit/Loss	8080
Working Capital	15870
Fixed Assets	25370
Current Assets	52390
Current Liabilities	36520
Total Share Capital	2780
ROCE% (Return on Capital Employed)	19.6

Panorama Antennas Ltd

61 Frogmore, London, SW18 1HF
Tel: 020-8877 4444 **Fax:** 020-8877 4477
E-mail: enquiry@panorama.co.uk
Website: http://www.panorama.co.uk
Bank(s): Barclays
Directors: C. Jesman (Prop)
Managers: A. Palmer (Purch Mgr), A. Corden (Tech Serv Mgr), D. Dickens (Chief Acct)
Immediate Holding Company: PANORAMA ANTENNAS LIMITED
Registration no: 01203531 **VAT No.:** GB 217 2160 00
Date established: 1975 **Turnover:** £5m - £10m **No.of Employees:** 21 - 50
Product Groups: 37

Date of Accounts	Mar 11	Mar 10	Mar 09
Working Capital	2m	1m	1m
Fixed Assets	511	390	435
Current Assets	3m	2m	2m

Pantheon Ventures Ltd

Norfolk House 31 St James's Square, London, SW1Y 4JR
Tel: 020-7484 6200 **Fax:** 020-7484 6201
E-mail: ckennedy@pantheonventures.com
Website: http://www.pantheonventures.com
Directors: C. Huwendiek (Head), J. Morgan (Co Sec), R. Bailey (Head), C. Kennedy (Dir)
Managers: M. Ellenbroek
Ultimate Holding Company: NORTHWESTERN MUTUAL LIFE INSURANCE CO (USA)
Immediate Holding Company: PANTHEON VENTURES LIMITED
Registration no: 02052746 **Date established:** 1986
Turnover: £50m - £75m **No.of Employees:** 51 - 100 **Product Groups:** 82

Date of Accounts	Dec 08
Sales Turnover	52m
Pre Tax Profit/Loss	35m
Working Capital	38m
Fixed Assets	758
Current Assets	67m
Current Liabilities	24m

Paper Flow Ltd

Unit 5-6 Meridian Trading Estate Bugsby's Way, London, SE7 7SJ
Tel: 020-8331 2000 **Fax:** 020-8331 2001
E-mail: sales@paperflowonline.com
Website: http://www.useonesource.com
Bank(s): HSBC
Directors: M. Rolfe (MD)
Immediate Holding Company: PAPERFLOW LTD
Registration no: 01268438 **VAT No.:** 249 5609 29 **Date established:** 1976
Turnover: £2m - £5m **No.of Employees:** 11 - 20 **Product Groups:** 27, 32, 44, 64, 77

Date of Accounts	Dec 11	Dec 10	Dec 09
Working Capital	178	144	197
Fixed Assets	222	255	287
Current Assets	896	819	820

Paperchase

213-215 Tottenham Court Road, London, W1T 7PN
Tel: 020-7467 6200 **Fax:** 020-7636 1322
E-mail: timothy@paperchase.co.uk
Website: http://www.paperchase.co.uk
Directors: T. Melgund (MD), D. Bateman (Fin), D. Bateman (Co Sec), R. Warden (Mkt Research), T. Melgund (Dir)
Managers: N. Tupper (I.T. Exec), D. Zand (Mgr), N. Wilton (Personnel)
Immediate Holding Company: PAPERCHASE PRODUCTS LIMITED
Registration no: 03185938 **Date established:** 1996
Turnover: £50m - £75m **No.of Employees:** 251 - 500 **Product Groups:** 61

Paperhat Consulting Ltd

44A Curlew Street, London, SE1 2ND
Tel: 020-7089 0360 **Fax:** 020-7407 5880
E-mail: info@paperhat.co.uk
Website: http://www.paperhat.co.uk
Directors: T. Peppiatt (Grp Chief Exec), R. Perrio (Fin)
Managers: N. Hendrick (Personnel), R. Telford (Tech Serv Mgr), C. Owens, M. Henson (Sales & Mktg Mg)
Immediate Holding Company: PAPERHAT COMMUNICATIONS LIMITED
Registration no: 03126476 **Date established:** 1995 **Turnover:** £5m - £10m
No.of Employees: 21 - 50 **Product Groups:** 81

Date of Accounts	Feb 08	Feb 11	Feb 10
Sales Turnover	19m	8m	13m
Pre Tax Profit/Loss	556	391	-780
Working Capital	-446	-550	-999
Fixed Assets	4m	2m	2m
Current Assets	5m	3m	3m
Current Liabilities	1m	2m	1m

Paramarq Ltd

18 b Charles Street Mayfair, London, W1J 5DU
Tel: 020-7667 6350 **Fax:** 020-7667 6550
E-mail: info@paramarq.com
Website: http://www.paramarq.com
Immediate Holding Company: PARAMARQ LIMITED
Registration no: 04958391 **Date established:** 2003
No.of Employees: 1 - 10 **Product Groups:** 81

Date of Accounts	Mar 08
Working Capital	-1
Fixed Assets	1
Current Assets	12
Current Liabilities	13

Paramount Pest Control Ltd

Flat 28 Charlwood House Vauxhall Bridge Road, London, SW1V 2SY
Tel: 020-7821 1155 **Fax:** 020- 85784133
E-mail: anita.cockburn@btconnect.com
Website: http://www.paramountpestcontrol.co.uk
Directors: A. Cockburn (Comm), A. Cockburn (Prop)
Immediate Holding Company: PARAMOUNT PEST CONTROL LIMITED
Registration no: 06591139 **Date established:** 2008 **Turnover:** £2m - £5m
No.of Employees: 1 - 10 **Product Groups:** 54

Date of Accounts	Mar 11	Mar 10	Mar 09
Working Capital	-39	-32	-40
Fixed Assets	39	40	45
Current Assets	45	21	20
Current Liabilities	64	N/A	N/A

Parkheath

8a Canfield Gardens, London, NW6 3BS
Tel: 020-7625 4567 **Fax:** 020-7327 2033
E-mail: info@parkheath.com
Website: http://www.parkheath.com
Managers: J. Curtis (Sales Admin)
Registration no: 02695933 **VAT No.:** GB 587 1580 07
Date established: 1985 **No.of Employees:** 1 - 10 **Product Groups:** 80

Parmar Udai & Co.

29 New Way Road, London, NW9 6PL
Tel: 020-8931 0504
E-mail: udai@udaiparmar.co.uk
Website: http://www.udaiparmar.co.uk
Directors: U. Parmar (Prop)
Immediate Holding Company: UDAI PARMAR & CO LTD
Registration no: 04624209 **Date established:** 2002
No.of Employees: 1 - 10 **Product Groups:** 80

Date of Accounts	Apr 11	Apr 10	Apr 09
Working Capital	-30	-27	-27
Fixed Assets	38	42	45
Current Assets	10	11	11

Pastle Sollutions Ltd

51 Woodend Road, London, E17 4JS
Tel: 020-8523 5831 **Fax:** 07970-715118
E-mail: paul.leader@pastle.co.uk
Website: http://www.pastle.co.uk
Directors: P. Leader (Dir)
Immediate Holding Company: PASTLE SOLUTIONS LIMITED
Registration no: 02642650 **Date established:** 1991
Turnover: Up to £250,000 **No.of Employees:** 1 - 10 **Product Groups:** 44, 86

Date of Accounts	Feb 12	Feb 11	Feb 09
Working Capital	3	3	4
Current Assets	8	7	8

Pat Freight Ltd

119 Turnpike Lane, London, N8 0DU
Tel: 020-8340 4395 **Fax:** 020-8348 8036
E-mail: enquiries@patfreight.co.uk
Website: http://www.patfreight.co.uk
Directors: M. Kokkinou (Dir)
Immediate Holding Company: PAT FREIGHT LIMITED
Registration no: 05579844 **VAT No.:** GB 691 1218 45
Date established: 2005 **Turnover:** £250,000 - £500,000
No.of Employees: 1 - 10 **Product Groups:** 76

Date of Accounts	Dec 11	Dec 10	Dec 09
Working Capital	-100	-115	-122
Fixed Assets	65	76	87
Current Assets	21	12	24

Patman

33 Fitzgeorge Avenue, London, W14 0SZ
Tel: 020-7603 9214 **Fax:** 020-7603 5366
E-mail: tom@patman.info
Website: http://www.patman.info
Directors: T. Phillips (Prop)
No.of Employees: 1 - 10 **Product Groups:** 38, 44, 85

Patriarche Wine Agencies

4 Rickett Street, London, SW6 1RU
Tel: 020-7381 4016 **Fax:** 020-7381 2023
E-mail: sales@patriarchewines.com
Website: http://www.patriarchewines.com
Managers: K. Isaac (Chief Mgr)
Immediate Holding Company: HESPERUS PRESS LIMITED
Registration no: 04294909 **Date established:** 2001
No.of Employees: 1 - 10 **Product Groups:** 61

Date of Accounts	Dec 10	Dec 09	Dec 08
Working Capital	-265	-60	161
Fixed Assets	1	2	2
Current Assets	180	234	350

Paula Designs Ltd

Unit 1 Hurlingham Business Park, London, SW6 3DU
Tel: 020-7384 6200 **Fax:** 020-7384 6262
E-mail: valerie@pauladesigns.co.uk
Website: http://www.pauladesigns.co.uk
Managers: V. Williams (Mgr)
Immediate Holding Company: PAULA DESIGNS LIMITED
Registration no: 05058395 **Date established:** 2004 **Turnover:** £5m - £10m
No.of Employees: 21 - 50 **Product Groups:** 33, 49

Date of Accounts	Dec 11	Dec 10	Dec 09
Sales Turnover	N/A	5m	6m
Pre Tax Profit/Loss	N/A	76	409
Working Capital	-246	-33	97
Fixed Assets	71	88	89
Current Assets	1m	905	935
Current Liabilities	120	440	430

Pax Guns Ltd

166 Archway Road, London, N6 5BB
Tel: 020-8340 3039 **Fax:** 020-8340 3039
Website: http://www.paxguns.co.uk
Directors: H. Earl (Dir)
Immediate Holding Company: PAX GUNS LIMITED
Registration no: 00935529 **Date established:** 1968
No.of Employees: 1 - 10 **Product Groups:** 36, 39, 40

Date of Accounts	Sep 11	Sep 10	Sep 09
Working Capital	291	267	242
Fixed Assets	257	265	267
Current Assets	377	344	315

Pearl & Coutts Ltd

9 White Lion Street, London, N1 9PD
Tel: 020-7843 3788 **Fax:** 020-7843 3799
E-mail: commercial@pearl-coutts.co.uk
Website: http://www.pearl-coutts.co.uk
Directors: M. Goldberger (MD)
Managers: G. Patel (Chief Acct)
Immediate Holding Company: PEARL & COUTTS LIMITED
Registration no: 00846950 **Date established:** 1965 **Turnover:** £2m - £5m
No.of Employees: 51 - 100 **Product Groups:** 80

Date of Accounts	Sep 09
Working Capital	4
Current Assets	4

Pearlco Infra-Red Ltd

11 Hanger Lane, London, W5 3HH
Tel: 020-8896 0550 **Fax:** 020-8896 0770
Directors: R. Newman (Fin)
Immediate Holding Company: PEARLCO INFRA-RED LIMITED
Registration no: 08076758 **Date established:** 2012
No.of Employees: 1 - 10 **Product Groups:** 40

Pearson Panke Ltd

1-3 Hale Grove Gardens, London, NW7 3LR
Tel: 020-8959 3232 **Fax:** 020-8959 5613
E-mail: stephen.panke@pearsonpanke.demon.co.uk
Website: http://www.pearsonpanke.co.uk
Directors: S. Panke (MD)
Immediate Holding Company: PEARSON PANKE EQUIPMENT LIMITED
Registration no: 01602861 **VAT No.:** GB 586 9411 93
Date established: 1981 **Turnover:** £2m - £5m **No.of Employees:** 1 - 10
Product Groups: 46

Date of Accounts	Sep 11	Sep 10	Sep 09
Working Capital	55	55	55
Current Assets	830	830	830

Norman Pendred & Co. Ltd

Unit B1 Broomsleigh Business Park Worsley Bridge Road, London, SE26 5BN
Tel: 020-8461 1155 **Fax:** 020-8461 1166
E-mail: info@pendred.com
Website: http://www.pendred.com
Directors: P. Pendred (Fin), C. Pendred (MD)
Immediate Holding Company: NORMAN PENDRED & COMPANY LIMITED
Registration no: 00495729 **VAT No.:** GB 205 5350 96
Date established: 1951 **Turnover:** £1m - £2m **No.of Employees:** 11 - 20
Product Groups: 28, 30

Date of Accounts	Nov 11	Nov 10	Nov 09
Working Capital	399	326	286
Fixed Assets	223	200	181
Current Assets	752	668	522

Penguin Books Ltd

80 Strand, London, WC2R 0RL
Tel: 020-7010 3000 **Fax:** 020-7010 6060
E-mail: helena.peacock@penguin.co.uk
Website: http://www.penguin.com
Bank(s): National Westminster Bank Plc
Directors: A. Welham (Asst MD), B. Landers (Fin), H. Peacock (Co Sec), H. Fraser (Dir)
Managers: J. Makinson
Ultimate Holding Company: Pearson plc
Immediate Holding Company: PENGUIN BOOKS LIMITED
Registration no: 00861590 **VAT No.:** GB 222 3251 15
Date established: 1965 **Turnover:** £125m - £250m
No.of Employees: 1501 & over **Product Groups:** 28, 64, 80

Date of Accounts	Dec 09	Dec 08	Dec 07
Sales Turnover	138m	136m	134m
Pre Tax Profit/Loss	-11m	35m	-14m
Working Capital	73m	79m	-15m
Fixed Assets	44m	46m	48m
Current Assets	192m	230m	174m
Current Liabilities	34m	23m	21m

Penna plc

Regent Arcade House 19-25 Argyll Street, London, W1F 7TS
Tel: 020-7663 6633 **Fax:** 020-7663 7321
E-mail: londonwest@e-penna.com
Website: http://www.e-penna.com
Directors: I. Saville (Dir), J. Hunt (MD), P. Hills (Dir)
Managers: O. Magee (Mktg Serv Mgr)
Immediate Holding Company: PENNA PLC
Registration no: 01918150 **Date established:** 1985
Turnover: £20m - £50m **No.of Employees:** 11 - 20 **Product Groups:** 80

Penningtons

33 Gutter Lane, London, EC2V 8AR
Tel: 020-7457 3000 **Fax:** 020-7457 3240
E-mail: david.raine@penningtons.co.uk
Website: http://www.penningtons.co.uk
Managers: D. Raine
Immediate Holding Company: PENNINGTONS (LEGAL SERVICES) LIMITED
Registration no: 02273106 **VAT No.:** GB 211 6498 76
Date established: 1988 **Turnover:** £20m - £50m
No.of Employees: 51 - 100 **Product Groups:** 80

Date of Accounts	Apr 11	Apr 10	Apr 09
Sales Turnover	24m	22m	22m
Pre Tax Profit/Loss	8m	7m	5m
Working Capital	8m	7m	5m
Fixed Assets	3m	4m	5m
Current Assets	16m	14m	14m
Current Liabilities	3m	2m	4m

Pentagram Design

11 Needham Road, London, W11 2RP
Tel: 020-7229 3477 **Fax:** 020-7727 9932
E-mail: hyland@pentagram.co.uk
Website: http://www.pentragram.com
Bank(s): Barclays
Directors: A. Hyland (Ptnr)
Managers: C. Knucey, J. Wyatt (Personnel), T. Foster (Mktg Serv Mgr)
Ultimate Holding Company: PENTAGRAM DESIGN AG (SWITZERLAND)
Immediate Holding Company: PENTAGRAM DESIGN LIMITED
Registration no: 01599748 **VAT No.:** GB 241 3877 62
Date established: 1981 **Turnover:** £5m - £10m **No.of Employees:** 21 - 50
Product Groups: 80, 81, 84

Date of Accounts	Sep 11	Sep 10	Sep 09
Sales Turnover	6m	7m	7m
Pre Tax Profit/Loss	52	163	62
Working Capital	1m	1m	1m
Fixed Assets	133	116	152
Current Assets	3m	3m	3m
Current Liabilities	1m	483	952

Pentland Group plc

8 Manchester Square, London, W1U 3PH
Tel: 020-7535 3800 **Fax:** 020-7535 3837
E-mail: sales@pentlandwholesale.co.uk
Website: http://www.pentlandwholesale.co.uk
Bank(s): National Westminster
Directors: P. Campbell (Co Sec)
Managers: T. Hockings
Immediate Holding Company: PENTLAND GROUP PLC
Registration no: 00793577 **Date established:** 1964
Turnover: Over £1,000m **No.of Employees:** 1501 & over
Product Groups: 22, 61

Date of Accounts	Dec 11	Dec 10	Dec 09
Sales Turnover	1523m	1299m	1135m
Pre Tax Profit/Loss	114m	97m	66m
Working Capital	189m	181m	142m
Fixed Assets	393m	332m	315m
Current Assets	468m	435m	456m
Current Liabilities	164m	141m	136m

Pepe Jeans London

99C Talbot Road, London, W11 2AT
Tel: 020-7313 3800 **Fax:** 020-7313 3803
E-mail: nsoneji@pepejeans.co.uk
Website: http://www.pepejeans.com
Directors: N. Soneji (MD)
Ultimate Holding Company: PEPE JEANS SL (SPAIN)
Immediate Holding Company: PEPE JEANS LONDON LIMITED
Registration no: 02640488 **Date established:** 1991 **Turnover:** £2m - £5m
No.of Employees: 1 - 10 **Product Groups:** 24, 63

Date of Accounts	Mar 11	Mar 10	Mar 09
Sales Turnover	4m	6m	7m
Pre Tax Profit/Loss	-2m	-2m	-2m
Working Capital	867	233	-1m
Fixed Assets	1m	1m	2m
Current Assets	4m	3m	4m
Current Liabilities	2m	2m	2m

Percy Short & Cuthbert

402 Holloway Road, London, N7 6PZ
Tel: 020-7700 0265 **Fax:** 020-7607 2489
E-mail: stephen@percyshort.co.uk
Website: http://www.percyshort.co.uk
Directors: S. Friday (Snr Part)
Immediate Holding Company: SPEXX.NET ENTERPRISES LIMITED
Registration no: 05750692 **Date established:** 2001
No.of Employees: 11 - 20 **Product Groups:** 80

R Perkins & Sons

201 London Central Markets, London, EC1A 9LH
Tel: 020-7329 4612 **Fax:** 020-7329 4192
E-mail: info@rperkins.co.uk
Website: http://www.rperkins.co.uk
Directors: K. Perkins (MD)
No.of Employees: 11 - 20 **Product Groups:** 39, 40, 52

Stuart Peters Ltd

184-192 Drummond Street, London, NW1 3HP
Tel: 020-7554 8440 **Fax:** 020-7383 5425
E-mail: esspee@speters.co.uk
Website: http://www.speters.co.uk
Directors: J. Peters (MD)
Ultimate Holding Company: STUART PETERS (HOLDINGS) LIMITED
Immediate Holding Company: STUART PETERS LIMITED
Registration no: 01617684 **Date established:** 1982
No.of Employees: 1 - 10 **Product Groups:** 63

Date of Accounts	Jun 11	Jun 10	Jun 09
Sales Turnover	9m	9m	N/A
Pre Tax Profit/Loss	398	854	251
Working Capital	2m	2m	3m
Current Assets	5m	6m	7m
Current Liabilities	2m	805	679

Phaidon Press Ltd

18 Regents Wharf All Saints Street, London, N1 9PA
Tel: 020-7843 1000 **Fax:** 020-7843 1010
E-mail: enquiries@phaidon.com
Website: http://www.phaidon.com
Bank(s): Royal Bank Of Scotland
Directors: A. Price (Ch), J. Booth Clibborn (Sales), J. Feinmesser (Co Sec)
Ultimate Holding Company: PHAIDON LTD (BVI)
Immediate Holding Company: PHAIDON PRESS LIMITED
Registration no: 02525791 **VAT No.:** GB 537 3492 29
Date established: 1990 **Turnover:** £20m - £50m
No.of Employees: 51 - 100 **Product Groups:** 28

Date of Accounts	Jun 12	Jun 11	Jun 10
Sales Turnover	24m	23m	19m
Pre Tax Profit/Loss	939	411	-149
Working Capital	9m	4m	8m
Fixed Assets	770	798	841
Current Assets	18m	18m	15m
Current Liabilities	3m	7m	2m

Frederick Phelps Ltd

34 Conway Road Southgate London, London, N14 7BA
Tel: 020-8482 3887 **Fax:** 020-8882 2006
E-mail: office@phelpsviolins.com
Website: http://www.phelpsviolins.com
Directors: M. Strnad (MD)
Immediate Holding Company: FREDERICK PHELPS LIMITED
Registration no: 04646599 **Date established:** 2003
Turnover: £250,000 - £500,000 **No.of Employees:** 1 - 10
Product Groups: 61

Date of Accounts	Mar 11	Mar 10	Mar 09
Working Capital	-4	-18	67
Fixed Assets	14	19	25
Current Assets	181	182	249

S J Phillips Ltd

139 New Bond Street, London, W1S 2TL
Tel: 020-7629 6261 **Fax:** 020-7495 6180
E-mail: enquiries@sjphillips.com
Website: http://www.sjphillips.com
Directors: N. Norton (Ch)
Immediate Holding Company: S.J.PHILLIPS LIMITED
Registration no: 00711442 **VAT No.:** GB 239 1734 53
Date established: 1961 **Turnover:** £20m - £50m
No.of Employees: 11 - 20 **Product Groups:** 61

Date of Accounts	Dec 11	Dec 10	Dec 09
Sales Turnover	38m	38m	29m
Pre Tax Profit/Loss	5m	4m	3m
Working Capital	53m	51m	49m
Fixed Assets	21m	20m	19m
Current Assets	63m	63m	60m
Current Liabilities	4m	4m	4m

Phils Wholesale Ltd

Unit 1 Horseshoe Close, London, NW2 7JJ
Tel: 020-8830 8830 **Fax:** 020-8830 8833
E-mail: mark@trimarksnet.co.uk
Managers: K. Baldwin (Mgr)
Immediate Holding Company: PHILS (WHOLESALE) LIMITED
Registration no: 00772655 **VAT No.:** GB 226 8684 32
Date established: 1963 **Turnover:** £250,000 - £500,000
No.of Employees: 1 - 10 **Product Groups:** 61

Date of Accounts	Aug 12	Aug 11	Aug 10
Working Capital	2m	2m	2m
Fixed Assets	13	49	86
Current Assets	2m	2m	2m

Phoenix Electrical Ltd

Cityside House 40 Adler Street, London, E1 1EE
Tel: 020-7422 1900 **Fax:** 020-7422 1999
E-mail: enquiry@phoenixelectrical.co.uk
Website: http://www.phoenixelectrical.co.uk
Bank(s): HSBC
Directors: L. Compton (MD)
Ultimate Holding Company: LANSTON LIMITED
Immediate Holding Company: PHOENIX ELECTRICAL CO (UK) LTD.
Registration no: 05385052 **Date established:** 2005
Turnover: £20m - £50m **No.of Employees:** 21 - 50 **Product Groups:** 52

Date of Accounts	Mar 08	Sep 11	Sep 10
Working Capital	N/A	-115	-115
Fixed Assets	N/A	N/A	24

Phione Ltd

Unit 1 The Rubicon, London, SE10 9QB
Tel: 020-8853 7595 **Fax:** 020-8293 7123
E-mail: info@phione.co.uk
Website: http://www.phione.co.uk
Directors: M. Burrow (MD)
Immediate Holding Company: PHIONE LIMITED
Registration no: 05679130 **Date established:** 2006 **Turnover:** £1m - £2m
No.of Employees: 1 - 10 **Product Groups:** 34, 36

Date of Accounts	Dec 11	Dec 10	Dec 09
Working Capital	117	91	30
Fixed Assets	1	N/A	N/A
Current Assets	197	219	69

Pi Global

1 Colville Mews, London, W11 2AR
Tel: 020-7908 0808 **Fax:** 020-7908 0809
E-mail: hello@piglobal.com
Website: http://www.piglobal.com
Bank(s): HSBC Bank plc
Directors: S. Kelsey (Dir), C. Griffin (MD)
Ultimate Holding Company: PACKAGING INNOVATION LIMITED
Immediate Holding Company: PI GLOBAL LIMITED
Registration no: 02688990 **Date established:** 1992
Turnover: Up to £250,000 **No.of Employees:** 21 - 50 **Product Groups:** 84, 85

Date of Accounts	Mar 11	Mar 10
Working Capital	-77	-77
Current Liabilities	77	N/A

Pickfords Ltd

Unit 10 Laxcon Close, London, NW10 0TG
Tel: 020-3188 2655 **Fax:** 020-8219 8516
Website: http://www.pickfords.com
Bank(s): Midland
Directors: D. Barrass (MD)
Managers: J. Weeks (I.T. Exec), F. Hopping (Chief Mgr), L. Schofield (Mktg Serv Mgr), N. Rajput (Accounts), S. Morris (Sales Prom Mgr)
Ultimate Holding Company: PICOT LIMITED (JERSEY)
Immediate Holding Company: PICKFORDS LIMITED
Registration no: 05025126 **VAT No.:** GB 414 9205 68
Date established: 2004 **Turnover:** £250,000 - £500,000
No.of Employees: 11 - 20 **Product Groups:** 26, 72

Pilat Europe Ltd

29 Hendon Lane, London, N3 1PZ
Tel: 020-8343 3433 **Fax:** 020-8343 4656
E-mail: admin@pilat.com
Website: http://www.pilat.com
Directors: S. Shah (Co Sec)
Managers: M. Smith, N. Armitago (I.T. Exec), R. Edwards (Sales & Mktg Mg), R. Ryan (Sales Admin)
Ultimate Holding Company: PILAT TECHNOLOGIES INTERNATIONAL LTD (ISRAEL)
Immediate Holding Company: PILAT EUROPE LIMITED
Registration no: 04207292 **Date established:** 2001
No.of Employees: 21 - 50 **Product Groups:** 80

Date of Accounts	Dec 11	Dec 10	Dec 09
Sales Turnover	2m	2m	2m
Pre Tax Profit/Loss	-538	-89	-126
Working Capital	-69	359	419
Fixed Assets	21	29	38
Current Assets	441	945	1m
Current Liabilities	316	484	557

Pims Associates

15-16 Basinghall Street, London, EC2V 5BR
Tel: 020-3161 4000 **Fax:** 020-7776 2828
E-mail: info@malikpims.com
Website: http://www.malikpims.com
Managers: J. Morrison (Sales Admin)
Ultimate Holding Company: MALIK MANAGEMENT ZENTRUM ST GALLEN AG (SWITZERLAND)
Immediate Holding Company: PIMS ASSOCIATES LIMITED
Registration no: 02429278 **VAT No.:** GB 497 5318 01
Date established: 1989 **Turnover:** £1m - £2m **No.of Employees:** 1 - 10
Product Groups: 80

Date of Accounts	Dec 11	Dec 10	Dec 09
Working Capital	-292	-506	-535
Fixed Assets	32	7	9
Current Assets	219	332	193

Pinsent Masons

Woodbridge House 30 Aylesbury Street, London, EC1R 0ER
Tel: 020-7490 4000 **Fax:** 020-7490 2545
E-mail: chris.mullen@pinsentmasons.com
Website: http://www.pinsentmasons.com
Directors: C. Mullen (Snr Part)
Managers: J. Eblett (I.T. Exec)
Ultimate Holding Company: MINOAN GROUP PLC
Immediate Holding Company: LOYALWARD LIMITED
Registration no: 04329960 **Date established:** 1991 **Turnover:** £5m - £10m
No.of Employees: 1501 & over **Product Groups:** 80

Pinsent Mason

30 Crown Place, London, EC2A 4ES
Tel: 020-7418 7000 **Fax:** 0113-244 8000
E-mail: enquiries@pinsentmasons.com
Website: http://www.pinsentmason.com
Directors: C. Mullen (Snr Part)
Managers: D. Ryan, C. Turnbull (Mktg Serv Mgr)
Immediate Holding Company: PINSENTS LIMITED
Registration no: 03027484 **Date established:** 1995
Turnover: £125m - £250m **No.of Employees:** 101 - 250
Product Groups: 80

Pintorex Ltd

Unit 16 Compass West Estate 33 West Road, London, N17 0XL
Tel: 020-8808 0882 **Fax:** 020-8801 9846
E-mail: pintorex@pintorex.co.uk
Website: http://www.pintorex.com
Directors: M. Semsarilar (Fin)
Immediate Holding Company: PINTOREX LIMITED
Registration no: 01316399 **Date established:** 1977 **Turnover:** £1m - £2m
No.of Employees: 1 - 10 **Product Groups:** 61

Date of Accounts	Dec 11	Dec 10	Dec 09
Working Capital	376	427	491
Fixed Assets	149	112	138
Current Assets	957	1m	1m

Pipminster Ltd

1 Queens Road, London, N11 2QJ
Tel: 020-8881 1888 **Fax:** 020-8888 8153
E-mail: info@pipminster.co.uk
Website: http://www.pipminster.com
Directors: A. Aspis (MD)
Immediate Holding Company: PIPMINSTER LIMITED
Registration no: 01582693 **Date established:** 1981
Turnover: £500,000 - £1m **No.of Employees:** 1 - 10 **Product Groups:** 23, 24

Date of Accounts	Aug 09	Aug 08	Aug 07
Working Capital	68	87	107
Fixed Assets	1	2	3
Current Assets	77	97	117

Pipposoft Financial Services

40 Dunford Road,, London, N7 6EL
Tel: 020-3239 9484
E-mail: info@pipposoft.co.uk
Website: http://www.pipposoft.co.uk
Managers: R. Anscomb (Accounts)
Immediate Holding Company: Pipposoft Financial Services Ltd
Registration no: 04726043 **Turnover:** Up to £250,000
No.of Employees: 1 - 10 **Product Groups:** 80, 86

Pitney Bowes Office Direct New Business Aquisitions

New City Court 20 St Thomas Street, London, SE1 9RS
Tel: 020-7200 5410 **Fax:** 020-7200 5432
E-mail: hassan.dayem@pb.com
Website: http://www.pitneybowes.com
Directors: J. Sehmi (Dir)
Managers: H. Dayem (Sales Prom Mgr)
Registration no: OC320522 **Date established:** 2006 **Turnover:** £1m - £2m
No.of Employees: 51 - 100 **Product Groups:** 37, 44, 67, 81

Pneumatic Tool Services Ltd

8 Riverside Business Park 16 Lyon Road, London, SW19 2RL
Tel: 020-8543 8575 **Fax:** 020- 85450091
Website: http://www.pneumatictoolservices.co.uk

Directors: N. Waters (Dir)
Immediate Holding Company: PNEUMATIC TOOL SERVICES LIMITED
Registration no: 02499401 Date established: 1990
Turnover: £250,000 - £500,000 No.of Employees: 1 - 10
Product Groups: 37

Date of Accounts	Oct 10	Oct 09	Mar 12
Sales Turnover	N/A	305	N/A
Working Capital	6	9	14
Fixed Assets	10	2	20
Current Assets	57	35	59

Pollard Thomas Edwards
Diespeker Wharf 38 Graham Street, London, N1 8JX
Tel: 020-7336 7777 Fax: 0151-703 2229
E-mail: ptea@ptea.demon.co.uk
Website: http://www.ptea.co.uk
Bank(s): National Westminster Bank Plc
Managers: G. Gullberg (Chief Mgr), P. Lee
Immediate Holding Company: POLLARD, THOMAS & EDWARDS LIMITED
Registration no: 01938992 VAT No.: GB 440 6281 70
Date established: 1985 Turnover: £5m - £10m
No.of Employees: 51 - 100 Product Groups: 84

Date of Accounts	Nov 11	Nov 10	Nov 09
Sales Turnover	N/A	N/A	5m
Pre Tax Profit/Loss	N/A	N/A	23
Working Capital	304	225	191
Fixed Assets	125	97	113
Current Assets	2m	2m	2m
Current Liabilities	N/A	N/A	1m

Polydiam Industries
70-80 Markfield Road, London, N15 4QF
Tel: 020-8493 1060 Fax: 020-8885 5711
E-mail: sales@rubberstamp.co.uk
Website: http://www.polydiam.com
Directors: P. Kapadia (Prop)
Immediate Holding Company: POLYDIAM INDUSTRIES LIMITED
Registration no: 01669976 VAT No.: GB 387 0011 67
Date established: 1982 Turnover: £1m - £2m No.of Employees: 11 - 20
Product Groups: 27, 28, 29, 30, 32, 40, 42, 43, 44, 46, 47, 48, 49, 64, 67, 84

Date of Accounts	Dec 11	Dec 10	Dec 09
Working Capital	140	144	128
Fixed Assets	23	38	36
Current Assets	262	267	262

Polymail Ltd
7 Holland Road, London, NW10 5AH
Tel: 020-8964 8566 Fax: 020-8968 5602
E-mail: info@polymail.co.uk
Website: http://www.polymail.co.uk
Directors: J. Marchadour (MD), J. Marchadour (Fin)
Immediate Holding Company: POLYMAIL LIMITED
Registration no: 03982962 Date established: 2000
Turnover: £500,000 - £1m No.of Employees: 1 - 10 Product Groups: 28, 44, 81

Date of Accounts	Jul 11	Jul 10	Jul 09
Working Capital	-16	-14	-13
Fixed Assets	13	13	14
Current Assets	13	23	28

Porfan Metal Work Ltd
Unit 8 Enterprise Way, London, NW10 6UG
Tel: 020-8969 0051 Fax: 020-8969 0051
Website: http://www.railingandgates.com
Directors: M. Moaresfi (Dir)
Immediate Holding Company: PORFAN METALWORK LTD
Registration no: 07140779 Date established: 2010
No.of Employees: 1 - 10 Product Groups: 35, 48

Portobello Press Ltd
69-71 Scrubs Lane, London, NW10 6QU
Tel: 020-8960 6796 Fax: 020-8960 2708
E-mail: sales@portobellopress.co.uk
Website: http://www.portobellopress.co.uk
Bank(s): Barclays
Directors: M. Green (Sales), I. Storey (Dir)
Ultimate Holding Company: PORTOBELLO PRESS HOLDINGS LIMITED
Immediate Holding Company: PORTOBELLO PRESS LIMITED
Registration no: 01693172 Date established: 1983 Turnover: £2m - £5m
No.of Employees: 21 - 50 Product Groups: 28

Date of Accounts	Jun 11	Jun 10	Jun 09
Working Capital	736	696	546
Fixed Assets	765	632	739
Current Assets	2m	2m	2m

Portugalia Wines UK
4-7 Whitby Avenue, London, NW10 7SF
Tel: 020-8965 8970 Fax: 020-8965 8971
E-mail: sales@portugaliawines.co.uk
Website: http://www.portugaliawines.co.uk
Immediate Holding Company: PORTUGALIA WINES (UK) LIMITED
Registration no: 02910821 Date established: 1994
No.of Employees: 1 - 10 Product Groups: 61

Date of Accounts	Mar 11	Mar 10	Mar 09
Working Capital	597	584	401
Fixed Assets	51	35	40
Current Assets	1m	1m	915

The Post Factory
Ground Floor 29-33 The Colonnade, London, WC1N 1JA
Tel: 020-7183 1600 Fax: 020-7727 8509
E-mail: info@postfactory.co.uk
Website: http://www.postfactory.co.uk
Directors: J. Milner-Symth (MD)
Managers: S. Jinnah (Sales Admin)
No.of Employees: 1 - 10 Product Groups: 37, 89

Postal & Courier Etc Ltd
58 Chetwynd Road, London, NW5 1DJ
Tel: 03335-772031 Fax: 03335-772032
E-mail: info@postalandcourieretc.co.uk
Website: http://www.postalandcourieretc.co.uk
Managers: N. Uddin (Mgr)
Immediate Holding Company: POSTAL & COURIER ETC LIMITED
Registration no: 05906096 Date established: 2006
No.of Employees: 1 - 10 Product Groups: 79

Date of Accounts	Jul 08	Jun 11	Jun 10
Working Capital	2	4	8
Fixed Assets	4	10	9
Current Assets	12	13	20

Power Steering Specialists (Head Office)
Unit 1 Brocklebank Industrial Estate Brocklebank Road, London, SE7 7SX
Tel: 020-8858 0168 Fax: 020-8858 7595
E-mail: info@powersteeringspecialist.co.uk
Website: http://www.powersteering.co.uk
Directors: A. Traquair (Ptnr)
VAT No.: GB 474 7351 25 No.of Employees: 1 - 10 Product Groups: 39

Powerail Ltd
High Road Finchley, London, N12 8PT
Tel: 020-8446 0350 Fax: 020-8446 7054
E-mail: enquiries@poweraillltd.com
Website: http://www.poweraillltd.com
Directors: N. Dale (Dir)
Immediate Holding Company: POWERAIL LIMITED
Registration no: 00944499 Date established: 1968
Turnover: Up to £250,000 No.of Employees: 1 - 10 Product Groups: 84

Date of Accounts	Dec 11	Dec 10	Dec 09
Working Capital	245	252	224
Fixed Assets	113	93	118
Current Assets	741	664	670

Powerpoint
72 Green Street, London, E7 8JG
Tel: 020-8821 9786 Fax: 020- 88219786
Directors: K. Bobby (Prop)
Registration no: 06688726 Date established: 2006
Turnover: £250,000 - £500,000 No.of Employees: 1 - 10
Product Groups: 36, 37, 40, 43

Precision Micro Drive Ltd
Canterbury Court 1-3 Brixton Road, London, SW9 6DE
Tel: 01932-252482 Fax: 01932-325353
E-mail: tom@pmdri.com
Website: http://www.precisionmicrodrive.com
Directors: T. Arundel (Dir)
Immediate Holding Company: PRECISION MICRODRIVES LTD.
Registration no: 05114621 Date established: 2004
Turnover: Up to £250,000 No.of Employees: 11 - 20 Product Groups: 35, 37, 38, 39, 45, 49, 67, 81, 84

Date of Accounts	Dec 11	Dec 10	Dec 09
Working Capital	59	24	16
Fixed Assets	5	6	5
Current Assets	95	64	84

Preferred Developments Ltd
Dgm House, 44 Millway Mill Hill, London, NW7 3RA
Tel: 020-8201 1752 Fax: 020-8906 4747
E-mail: david_godfrey@msn.com
Website: http://www.c-instore.com
Directors: D. Godfrey (MD)
Registration no: 01618289 No.of Employees: 1 - 10 Product Groups: 79, 80, 81, 84, 86

Premier Oil plc
23 Lower Belgrave Street, London, SW1W 0NR
Tel: 020-7730 1111 Fax: 020-7730 4696
E-mail: premier@premier-oil.com
Website: http://www.premier-oil.com
Directors: A. Booth (Grp Chief Exec), T. Durrant (Fin)
Ultimate Holding Company: PREMIER OIL PLC
Immediate Holding Company: ENCORE OIL LIMITED
Registration no: 03328217 VAT No.: GB 242 4053 00
Date established: 1997 Turnover: £20m - £50m No.of Employees: 1 - 10
Product Groups: 13, 51

Date of Accounts	Dec 11	Jun 11	Jun 10
Pre Tax Profit/Loss	-26m	-3m	10m
Working Capital	-516	16m	46m
Fixed Assets	36m	42m	15m
Current Assets	23m	20m	49m
Current Liabilities	22m	4m	3m

President Blinds Ltd
13 Forest Hill Business Centre 2 Clyde Va, London, SE23 3JF
Tel: 020-8699 8885 Fax: 020-8699 8005
E-mail: info@presidentblinds.com
Website: http://www.flyscreens-uk.co.uk
Managers: H. Phillips (Mgr)
Immediate Holding Company: PRESIDENT BLINDS LIMITED
Registration no: 02582742 Date established: 1991
Turnover: £250,000 - £500,000 No.of Employees: 1 - 10
Product Groups: 07, 30, 41

Date of Accounts	Dec 11	Dec 10	Dec 09
Working Capital	35	34	56
Fixed Assets	5	7	8
Current Assets	87	96	119

Presight Marketing Consultants
4 Addison Avenue, London, W11 4QR
Tel: 020-7603 6553 Fax: 020-7602 8089
E-mail: sales@presight.co.uk
Website: http://www.presight.co.uk
Directors: A. Douglas (Jt MD), R. Wisdom (Ptnr)
Date established: 1974 Turnover: Up to £250,000
No.of Employees: 1 - 10 Product Groups: 80, 81, 84

Prestige Procurement Ltd
St John Street, London, EC1V 4PY
Tel: 0844-8843337 Fax: 0844-357 6811
E-mail: adesogi.adewusi@prestigeprocurement.com
Website: http://www.prestigeprocurement.com
Directors: A. Adewusi (Dir)
Immediate Holding Company: PRESTIGE EXCLUSIVE LIFESTYLE LIMITED
Registration no: 06979719 Date established: 2009
No.of Employees: 1 - 10 Product Groups: 61

Date of Accounts	Nov 08	Nov 07	Nov 06
Working Capital	N/A	1	-7
Current Assets	40	15	1

Pricewaterhousecoopers LLP
1 Embankment Place, London, WC2N 6RH
Tel: 020-7583 5000 Fax: 020-7822 4652
E-mail: info@pcwglobal.com
Website: http://www.pwc.com
Directors: K. Poynter (Snr Part)
Managers: A. Breanach, M. Donnellan (Mktg Serv Mgr)
Immediate Holding Company: PRICEWATERHOUSECOOPERS LLP
Registration no: OC303525 Date established: 2002
Turnover: Over £1,000m No.of Employees: 251 - 500
Product Groups: 80

Date of Accounts	Jun 11	Jun 10	Jun 09
Sales Turnover	2461m	2331m	2248m
Pre Tax Profit/Loss	667m	665m	688m
Working Capital	405m	492m	488m
Fixed Assets	375m	274m	204m
Current Assets	980m	1038m	951m
Current Liabilities	495m	477m	416m

Prima Baby Magazine
33 Broadwick Street, London, W1F 9EP
Tel: 020-7312 3852 Fax: 020-7437 6886
E-mail: elaine.griffiths@natmags.co.uk
Website: http://www.babyexpert.com
Managers: E. Griffiths
Ultimate Holding Company: HEARST CORPORATION (USA)
Immediate Holding Company: NETDOCTOR LIMITED
Date established: 2005 No.of Employees: 21 - 50 Product Groups: 24, 31, 61

Primary Industries Ltd
4 Harley Street, London, W1G 9PB
Tel: 020-7483 6940 Fax: 020-7483 6941
E-mail: info@primaryuk.co.uk
Website: http://www.primaryuk.co.uk
Directors: P. Saiman (Dir)
Ultimate Holding Company: KETTERING HOLDINGS LTD (GIBRALTAR)
Immediate Holding Company: PRIMARY INDUSTRIES (UK) LIMITED
Registration no: 02702620 Date established: 1992
Turnover: Over £1,000m No.of Employees: 1 - 10 Product Groups: 61

Date of Accounts	Dec 07
Sales Turnover	42m
Pre Tax Profit/Loss	2m
Working Capital	5m
Fixed Assets	62
Current Assets	13m
Current Liabilities	576

Primatel Products Ltd
5 Norbury Trading Estate Craignish Avenue, London, SW16 4RW
Tel: 020-8679 4428 Fax: 020-8679 4420
E-mail: enquiries@primatel.co.uk
Website: http://www.primatel.co.uk
Bank(s): Lloyds TSB Bank plc
Directors: K. Hickey (MD), P. Low (Fin)
Immediate Holding Company: PRIMATEL PRODUCTS LIMITED
Registration no: 01434326 VAT No.: GB 602 8512 67
Date established: 1979 Turnover: £500,000 - £1m
No.of Employees: 11 - 20 Product Groups: 27

Date of Accounts	Jul 11	Jul 10	Jul 09
Sales Turnover	N/A	N/A	551
Pre Tax Profit/Loss	N/A	N/A	24
Working Capital	53	60	89
Fixed Assets	62	64	67
Current Assets	143	137	141
Current Liabilities	N/A	N/A	32

Primesight London Ltd
Metropolis House 22 Percy Street, London, W1T 2BU
Tel: 020-7908 4300 Fax: 020-7882 1212
E-mail: zoew@primesight.co.uk
Website: http://www.primesight.co.uk
Directors: N. Patel (MD)
Ultimate Holding Company: BELL HOLDCO LIMITED
Immediate Holding Company: PRIMESIGHT LIMITED
Registration no: 01847728 Date established: 1984
Turnover: £20m - £50m No.of Employees: 101 - 250 Product Groups: 81

Date of Accounts	Dec 11	Dec 10	Dec 09
Sales Turnover	47m	51m	31m
Pre Tax Profit/Loss	690	428	4m
Working Capital	2m	76	8m
Fixed Assets	13m	13m	14m
Current Assets	17m	17m	18m
Current Liabilities	12m	14m	10m

Prior Clave
129-131 Nathan Way West Thamesmead Business Park, London, SE28 0AB
Tel: 020-8316 6620 Fax: 020-8855 9374
E-mail: tonycollins@priorclave.co.uk
Website: http://www.priorclave.co.uk
Bank(s): Barclays
Directors: K. Prior (Dir), T. Collins (MD)
Managers: N. Dabagoglu (Buyer)
Immediate Holding Company: PRIOR CLAVE LIMITED
Registration no: 02221879 VAT No.: GB 586 4317 13
Date established: 1988 Turnover: £2m - £5m No.of Employees: 21 - 50
Product Groups: 35, 38, 40, 42

Date of Accounts	Mar 11	Mar 10	Mar 09
Working Capital	542	419	301
Fixed Assets	436	414	436
Current Assets	1m	1m	1m

Prizeflex Ltd
3 Cygnus Business Centre Dalmeyer Road, London, NW10 2XA
Tel: 020-8451 7071 Fax: 020-8459 8979
E-mail: nishel@prizeflex.co.uk
Website: http://www.prizeflex.co.uk
Directors: N. Surana (Dir)
Immediate Holding Company: PRIZEFLEX LIMITED
Registration no: 02135464 VAT No.: GB 493 4401 43
Date established: 1987 Turnover: £20m - £50m No.of Employees: 1 - 10
Product Groups: 63

Date of Accounts	Jun 11	Jun 10	Jun 09
Sales Turnover	22m	31m	18m
Pre Tax Profit/Loss	113	368	477
Working Capital	641	646	539
Fixed Assets	166	170	172
Current Assets	5m	4m	4m
Current Liabilities	385	253	491

Pro Motion Hire
181 Hercules Road, London, SE1 7LD
Tel: 020-7735 9988 **Fax:** 020-7735 6656
E-mail: hire@promotionhire.co.uk
Website: http://www.promotionhire.co.uk
Directors: D. Martin (Jt MD), D. Martin (Dir), M. Standish (Jt MD)
Turnover: Up to £250,000 **No.of Employees:** 1 - 10 **Product Groups:** 37, 83

Product First Ltd
10 Barley Mow Passage Chiswick, London, W4 4PH
Tel: 020-8994 6477 **Fax:** 020-8742 1886
E-mail: info@productfirst.co.uk
Website: http://www.productfirst.co.uk
Directors: D. Scothron (Dir), G. Thomson (Dir), J. Boult (Dir)
Managers: N. Chater (Sales Admin)
Registration no: 02074911 **VAT No.:** GB 453 0615 72
Date established: 1986 **Turnover:** Up to £250,000
No.of Employees: 1 - 10 **Product Groups:** 44, 80, 81, 84, 85

Date of Accounts	Dec 09	Dec 08	Dec 07
Sales Turnover	19	22	37
Pre Tax Profit/Loss	N/A	4	-16
Working Capital	11	11	8
Current Assets	13	17	11
Current Liabilities	N/A	2	4

Product Innovation Ltd
39 St Gabriels Road, London, NW2 4DT
Tel: 020-8452 3968 **Fax:** 020-8452 5665
E-mail: enquiries@productinnovation.com
Website: http://www.productinnovation.com
Directors: P. Frank (Dir)
Immediate Holding Company: Product Innovation Ltd
Registration no: 02269650 **VAT No.:** GB 524 0193 79
Date established: 2007 **Turnover:** £250,000 - £500,000
No.of Employees: 1 - 10 **Product Groups:** 81, 85

Date of Accounts	Feb 09	Feb 08	Feb 07
Working Capital	79	84	93
Fixed Assets	4	5	7
Current Assets	103	95	122
Current Liabilities	24	11	28

Project Building Company Ltd (t/a Gadmon Industries)
Kofo House 57 Glengall Road, London, SE15 6NF
Tel: 020-7277 8878 **Fax:** 020-7277 9476
E-mail: leke@gadmon.com
Website: http://www.gadmon.com
Directors: L. Payne (Co Sec)
Immediate Holding Company: PROJECT BUILDING COMPANY LIMITED
Registration no: 02535559 **VAT No.:** GB 102 1973 09
Date established: 1990 **No.of Employees:** 11 - 20 **Product Groups:** 25, 35, 39, 41, 45

Date of Accounts	Jul 11	Jul 10	Jul 09
Working Capital	480	533	563
Fixed Assets	134	137	134
Current Assets	711	723	881
Current Liabilities	5	22	46

Project Profile
1 Butlers & Colonial Wharf, London, SE1 2PX
Tel: 020-7407 7200
E-mail: production@projectprofile.com
Website: http://www.projectprofile.com
Directors: M. Green (Dir)
Registration no: 01880794 **Date established:** 1983
No.of Employees: 1 - 10 **Product Groups:** 81

Promat Gifts Ltd
78 York Street, London, W1H 1DP
Tel: 020-7692 4940 **Fax:** 020-7284 1090
E-mail: gary.kahn@promatgifts.co.uk
Website: http://www.promatgifts.co.uk
Directors: G. Kahn (Fin)
Immediate Holding Company: PROMAT GIFTS LIMITED
Registration no: 02591561 **VAT No.:** GB 586 9079 75
Date established: 1991 **Turnover:** Up to £250,000
No.of Employees: 1 - 10 **Product Groups:** 49

Date of Accounts	Mar 11	Mar 10	Mar 09
Working Capital	43	46	51
Fixed Assets	1	1	1
Current Assets	58	51	59

Promo2u Ltd
First Floor
4 Kings Road
North Chingford, London, E4 7 EY
Tel: 0203-640 7670
E-mail: sales@promo2u.com
Website: http://www.promo2u.com
Directors: D. Cowell (MD)
Immediate Holding Company: PROMO2U LIMITED
Registration no: 04060322 **Date established:** 2000
Turnover: Up to £250,000 **No.of Employees:** 1 - 10 **Product Groups:** 22, 24, 49, 81

Date of Accounts	Oct 10	Oct 09	Oct 08
Sales Turnover	112	N/A	N/A
Working Capital	24	2	4
Fixed Assets	1	1	2
Current Assets	24	47	60

Promotional Marketing Publishing Ltd
70 Margaret Street, London, W1W 8SS
Tel: 020-7291 7740 **Fax:** 020-7291 7731
E-mail: info@promomarketing.info
Website: http://www.promomarketing.info
Managers: M. Croft
Immediate Holding Company: SALES PROMOTION PUBLISHING LIMITED
Registration no: 06318298 **VAT No.:** GB 234 0739 78
Date established: 2007 **Turnover:** £1m - £2m **No.of Employees:** 1 - 10
Product Groups: 80, 87

Date of Accounts	Sep 11	Sep 10	Sep 09
Working Capital	-2	2	-9
Fixed Assets	7	12	15
Current Assets	98	84	60

Protector Alarms UK Ltd
20-22 Gipsy Hill, London, SE19 1NL
Tel: 020-8761 3771 **Fax:** 020-8670 9441
E-mail: sales@protectoralarms.com
Website: http://www.protectoralarms.com
Directors: A. Szpunar (MD)
Immediate Holding Company: PROTECTOR ALARMS UK LIMITED
Registration no: 03736892 **VAT No.:** GB 735 4915 18
Date established: 1999 **No.of Employees:** 1 - 10 **Product Groups:** 37, 38, 40

Date of Accounts	Mar 12	Mar 11	Mar 10
Working Capital	10	22	29
Fixed Assets	N/A	N/A	1
Current Assets	97	105	110

Proteus Investigations
Holborn Gate 330 High Holborn, London, WC1V 7QT
Tel: 020-7203 8444 **Fax:** 020-7203 8443
E-mail: info@proteusinvestigations.com
Website: http://www.proteusinvestigations.co.uk
Managers: K. Mitchell (Chief Mgr)
Immediate Holding Company: ZANUKLE LIMITED
Date established: 2009 **No.of Employees:** 1 - 10 **Product Groups:** 80

Date of Accounts	Sep 11	Sep 10	Sep 09
Working Capital	349	275	191
Fixed Assets	4	3	1
Current Assets	484	390	201

Prototype 21
23 Liddell Road, London, NW6 2EW
Tel: 020-7624 3278 **Fax:** 020-7372 6841
E-mail: john@p21.co.uk
Website: http://www.p21.co.uk
Managers: J. Boak (Mgr)
No.of Employees: 1 - 10 **Product Groups:** 24, 44, 84

Prudential
Governors House Laurence Pountney Hill, London, EC4R 0HH
Tel: 020-7220 7588 **Fax:** 020-7548 3725
E-mail: info@swanshopping.com
Website: http://www.pru.co.uk
Directors: N. Fitzgerald (Non Exec), D. Gillmore (Non Exec), R. Hurn (Ch), Davis (Grp Chief Exec), M. Abrahams (Dep Ch), K. Bedell-Pearce (Dir), J. Bloomer (Grp Chief Exec), D. Higgs (Dir), Jacomb (Ch)
Immediate Holding Company: PRUDENTIAL PUBLIC LIMITED COMPANY
Registration no: 01397169 **Date established:** 1978
Turnover: £250m - £500m **No.of Employees:** 1 - 10 **Product Groups:** 82

Date of Accounts	Dec 11	Dec 10	Dec 09
Pre Tax Profit/Loss	1943m	2072m	1564m
Fixed Assets	260430m	246260m	214678m
Current Assets	13150m	14546m	13076m
Current Liabilities	257014m	244529m	214022m

Public Relations Consultants Association Ltd
17-23 Willow Place, London, SW1P 1JH
Tel: 020-7233 6026 **Fax:** 020-7828 4797
E-mail: info@prca.org.uk
Website: http://www.prca.org.uk
Directors: F. Ingham (Dir)
Immediate Holding Company: PUBLIC RELATIONS CONSULTANTS ASSOCIATION LIMITED
Registration no: 00965517 **Date established:** 1969 **Turnover:** £1m - £2m
No.of Employees: 11 - 20 **Product Groups:** 81, 87

Date of Accounts	Dec 07	Mar 11	Mar 10
Sales Turnover	728	1m	1m
Pre Tax Profit/Loss	74	35	-3
Working Capital	285	389	350
Fixed Assets	68	14	28
Current Assets	361	1m	1m
Current Liabilities	52	813	693

Publicis Chemistry
82 Baker Street, London, W1U 6AE
Tel: 020-7935 4426 **Fax:** 020-7487 5351
E-mail: info@publicis-networks.com
Website: http://www.publicis.co.uk
Bank(s): National Westminster
Directors: M. Gonzalez Gomez (Co Sec), J. Foo (MD)
Ultimate Holding Company: PUBLICIS GROUPE SA (FRANCE)
Immediate Holding Company: PUBLICIS LIMITED
Registration no: 01046052 **Date established:** 1972
Turnover: £75m - £125m **No.of Employees:** 251 - 500
Product Groups: 81

Date of Accounts	Dec 11	Dec 10	Dec 09
Sales Turnover	120m	77m	62m
Pre Tax Profit/Loss	7m	5m	2m
Working Capital	18m	17m	15m
Fixed Assets	488	599	701
Current Assets	52m	57m	45m
Current Liabilities	24m	28m	18m

Purefix Ltd
2 St Johns Parade Mattock Lane, London, W13 9LL
Tel: 020-8567 6888 **Fax:** 020-8567 8500
E-mail: purefix@btconnect.com
Directors: T. Regan (Dir)
Immediate Holding Company: PUREFIX LIMITED
Registration no: 03672931 **Date established:** 1998
Turnover: Up to £250,000 **No.of Employees:** 1 - 10 **Product Groups:** 35

Date of Accounts	Dec 10	Dec 09	Dec 08
Sales Turnover	61	91	114
Pre Tax Profit/Loss	N/A	1	20
Working Capital	N/A	3	16
Current Assets	29	29	33
Current Liabilities	5	4	6

Purlfrost Ltd
Vision Kendal Avenue, London, W3 0AF
Tel: 020-8992 4024 **Fax:** 0871-733 4587
E-mail: info@purlfrost.com
Website: http://www.purlfrost.com
Directors: E. Baumard (Dir)
Immediate Holding Company: PURLFROST LIMITED
Registration no: 04770280 **Date established:** 2003
No.of Employees: 1 - 10 **Product Groups:** 64

Date of Accounts	May 11	May 10	May 09
Sales Turnover	N/A	593	600
Pre Tax Profit/Loss	N/A	126	164

Working Capital	56	21	20
Fixed Assets	38	27	29
Current Assets	152	95	101
Current Liabilities	N/A	62	78

Purpose Powder Coatings Ltd
18 Manor Grove, London, SE15 1SX
Tel: 020-7639 2511 **Fax:** 020-7277 5942
E-mail: sales@purposepowdercoatings.com
Website: http://www.purposepowdercoatings.com
Bank(s): National Westminster
Directors: G. Peck (Fin)
Immediate Holding Company: PURPOSE POWDER COATINGS LIMITED
Registration no: 00352108 **VAT No.:** GB 235 5200 94
Date established: 1939 **No.of Employees:** 11 - 20 **Product Groups:** 32, 48

Date of Accounts	Mar 11	Mar 10	Mar 09
Working Capital	432	258	219
Fixed Assets	136	148	139
Current Assets	722	486	828

Pye London Ltd
Unit 7 Hookers Road, London, E17 6DP
Tel: 020-8531 3334 **Fax:** 020-8531 3336
E-mail: john@pyelondon.co.uk
Website: http://www.pyelondon.com
Directors: J. Gausden (MD)
Immediate Holding Company: PYE LONDON LIMITED
Registration no: 01064175 **VAT No.:** GB 232 9818 49
Date established: 1972 **Turnover:** £250,000 - £500,000
No.of Employees: 1 - 10 **Product Groups:** 46

Date of Accounts	Nov 11	Nov 10	Nov 09
Working Capital	401	322	266
Fixed Assets	55	44	39
Current Assets	668	544	419

Pyricon Ltd
PO Box 4641, London, SE11 4XX
Tel: 020-7735 8777 **Fax:** 020-7735 8778
Directors: N. Goulding (Dir)
Immediate Holding Company: PYRICON LIMITED
Registration no: 02064845 **Date established:** 1986 **Turnover:** £1m - £2m
No.of Employees: 1 - 10 **Product Groups:** 23, 30

Date of Accounts	Oct 11	Oct 10	Oct 09
Sales Turnover	33	36	44
Pre Tax Profit/Loss	-6	7	2
Working Capital	-2	2	-3
Fixed Assets	7	7	7
Current Assets	15	16	11
Current Liabilities	4	4	2

Quadrant Harmon
Morley House 320 Regent Street, London, W1B 3BD
Tel: 020-7637 2770 **Fax:** 020-7637 2770
E-mail: info@quadrantharmon.co.uk
Website: http://www.quadrantharmon.co.uk
Directors: S. Harmon (MD)
Immediate Holding Company: GRANDCASTLE LIMITED
Registration no: 01069099 **Date established:** 1972
Turnover: £250,000 - £500,000 **No.of Employees:** 1 - 10
Product Groups: 35

Quality First International
11 Burford Road, London, E15 2ST
Tel: 020-8221 2361 **Fax:** 020-8221 9192
E-mail: haroon@qualityfirstint.com
Website: http://www.qualityfirstint.com
Managers: H. Atchia (Mgr)
Immediate Holding Company: LIFECARE QUALIFICATIONS LIMITED
Registration no: 07222766 **Date established:** 2010
No.of Employees: 1 - 10 **Product Groups:** 38, 67

Quality Monitoring Instruments Q M I
224 Iverson Road Unit 5 Hampstead West, London, NW6 2HL
Tel: 020-7328 3121 **Fax:** 020-7328 5888
E-mail: josh@oilmist.com
Website: http://www.oilmist.com
Directors: J. Smith (MD)
Ultimate Holding Company: JAMES HUGH GROUP LIMITED
Immediate Holding Company: JAMES HUGH GROUP LIMITED
Registration no: 00679021 **Date established:** 1960 **Turnover:** £1m - £2m
No.of Employees: 1 - 10 **Product Groups:** 39

Date of Accounts	May 11	May 10	May 09
Working Capital	77	72	71
Fixed Assets	10	10	10
Current Assets	119	127	125

Question Mark Computing Ltd
4Th Floor Hill House Highgate Hill, London, N19 5NA
Tel: 020-7263 7575 **Fax:** 020-7263 7555
E-mail: info@qmark.co.uk
Website: http://www.questionmark.com/uk
Directors: J. Kleeman (MD)
Managers: E. Knopp (I.T. Exec), K. Williams (Sales Prom Mgr)
Immediate Holding Company: Questionmark Computing Ltd
Registration no: 02278553 **Date established:** 1988 **Turnover:** £1m - £2m
No.of Employees: 21 - 50 **Product Groups:** 84

Date of Accounts	Apr 10	Apr 09	Apr 08
Sales Turnover	8m	N/A	N/A
Pre Tax Profit/Loss	142	N/A	N/A
Working Capital	-211	192	-0
Fixed Assets	311	357	376
Current Assets	3m	1m	774
Current Liabilities	3m	N/A	N/A

R G C Jenkins & Co.
26 Caxton Street, London, SW1H 0RJ
Tel: 020-7931 7141 **Fax:** 020-7222 4660
E-mail: info@jenkins.eu
Website: http://www.jenkins.eu
Directors: S. James (Ptnr), D. Barber (Fin)
Managers: L. Robinson, J. Mevlin (Fin Mgr), S. Chohan (Tech Serv Mgr), M. Leech (Personnel), J. Pratt (Develop Mgr), J. Sumar (I.T. Exec)
Registration no: 00201373 **Turnover:** £500,000 - £1m
No.of Employees: 51 - 100 **Product Groups:** 80

R I C S
12 Great George Street, London, SW1P 3AD
Tel: 020-7222 7000 **Fax:** 020-7334 3811
E-mail: contact@rics.org
Website: http://www.rics.org

Bank(s): National Westminster Bank Plc
Directors: M. Mcdermott (Sales & Mktg)
Immediate Holding Company: RICS HOLDINGS LIMITED
Registration no: 04492677 **Date established:** 2002 **Turnover:** £5m - £10m
No.of Employees: 501 - 1000 **Product Groups:** 08, 51, 80, 82, 84, 85, 87

Date of Accounts	Jul 11	Jul 10	Jul 09
Sales Turnover	6m	4m	5m
Pre Tax Profit/Loss	522	696	-488
Working Capital	-14m	-18m	-19m
Fixed Assets	23m	25m	22m
Current Assets	2m	1m	1m
Current Liabilities	929	722	828

R Interiors

2 Michael Road, London, SW6 2AD
Tel: 020-7384 9284 **Fax:** 020-7731 8216
E-mail: info@rinteriors.net
Website: http://www.rinteriors.net
Directors: R. Beckett (Dir)
Immediate Holding Company: FIONA BARRATT INTERIORS LIMITED
Registration no: 05765715 **Date established:** 2006
Turnover: Up to £250,000 **No.of Employees:** 1 - 10 **Product Groups:** 33

Date of Accounts	Sep 11	Sep 10	Apr 09
Working Capital	111	68	31
Fixed Assets	13	2	1
Current Assets	325	365	361

R J L

24 Victoria Drive, London, SW19 6AE
Tel: 020-8789 7749
Directors: R. Laight (Prop)
Immediate Holding Company: R.J.L. LTD
Registration no: 01632059 **Date established:** 1997
No.of Employees: 1 - 10 **Product Groups:** 37, 40, 48

R M J M London Ltd

42 Elcho Street, London, SW11 4AU
Tel: 020-7801 4900 **Fax:** 020-7801 4901
E-mail: london@rmjm.com
Website: http://www.rmjm.com
Bank(s): Bank of Scotland
Directors: S. Lorry (MD), P. Morrison (MD)
Immediate Holding Company: RMJM LONDON LIMITED
Registration no: 01764290 **VAT No.:** GB 502 4272 89
Date established: 1983 **Turnover:** £10m - £20m
No.of Employees: 21 - 50 **Product Groups:** 84

R R C Business Training Ltd

Tuition House 27-37 St Georges Road, London, SW19 4DS
Tel: 020-8944 3100 **Fax:** 020-8944 7099
E-mail: sales@rrc.co.uk
Website: http://www.rrc.co.uk
Bank(s): National Westminster
Directors: G. Fallaize (MD)
Immediate Holding Company: THE RAPID RESULTS COLLEGE
Registration no: 04126693 **VAT No.:** GB 628 4798 90
Date established: 2000 **Turnover:** £1m - £2m **No.of Employees:** 11 - 20
Product Groups: 86

R S A Direct

Boundary House Boston Road, London, W7 2QE
Tel: 020-8434 3680 **Fax:** 020-8434 3449
E-mail: info@rsadirect.com
Website: http://www.rsadirect.com
Directors: R. Smith (MD)
Immediate Holding Company: OPENSTART LIMITED
Registration no: 04615365 **Date established:** 2001
Turnover: £250,000 - £500,000 **No.of Employees:** 1 - 10
Product Groups: 81

Date of Accounts	Nov 11	Nov 10	Nov 09
Working Capital	-44	-35	-44
Fixed Assets	70	70	42
Current Assets	36	9	20
Current Liabilities	N/A	23	N/A

R S Components Ltd

1 Maverton Road, London, E3 2JE
Tel: 020-8983 3233 **Fax:** 020-8981 4937
E-mail: rsint@rs-components.com
Website: http://www.rswww.com
Managers: T. Barron (Mgr)
Ultimate Holding Company: ELECTROCOMPONENTS PUBLIC LIMITED COMPANY
Immediate Holding Company: RS COMPONENTS LIMITED
Registration no: 01002091 **Date established:** 1971
Turnover: £500m - £1,000m **No.of Employees:** 1 - 10
Product Groups: 67

Date of Accounts	Mar 11	Mar 10	Mar 09
Sales Turnover	579m	486m	494m
Pre Tax Profit/Loss	41m	26m	55m
Working Capital	19m	-6m	10m
Fixed Assets	89m	77m	83m
Current Assets	229m	177m	145m
Current Liabilities	33m	32m	30m

Racetech

88 Bushey Road Raynes Park, London, SW20 0JH
Tel: 020-8947 3333 **Fax:** 020-8879 7354
E-mail: admin@racetech.co.uk
Website: http://www.racetech.co.uk
Directors: S. Harris (MD)
Managers: M. Gooch ()
Ultimate Holding Company: Racecourse Association
Registration no: 03288138 **No.of Employees:** 21 - 50 **Product Groups:** 49

Radio Centre

77 Shaftesbury Avenue, London, W1D 5DU
Tel: 020-7306 2500 **Fax:** 020-7306 2505
E-mail: info@rab.co.uk
Website: http://www.radiocentre.org
Directors: A. Ingram (Fin), D. McArthur (Dir)
Immediate Holding Company: RADIOCENTRE LIMITED
Registration no: 02669040 **Date established:** 1991
Turnover: Up to £250,000 **No.of Employees:** 11 - 20 **Product Groups:** 87

Date of Accounts	Sep 11	Sep 10	Sep 09
Working Capital	92	39	330
Fixed Assets	45	87	102
Current Assets	1m	2m	3m

Radio Taxis London Ltd

Mountview House Lennox Road, London, N4 3TX
Tel: 020-8640 0400 **Fax:** 020-7281 5709
E-mail: fiona.gavin@radiotaxis.co.uk
Website: http://www.radiotaxis.co.uk
Bank(s): Lloyds TSB
Managers: F. Gavin (Mgr)
Immediate Holding Company: RADIO TAXIS GROUP LIMITED
Registration no: 05155416 **VAT No.:** GB 221 2625 11
Date established: 2004 **Turnover:** £20m - £50m
No.of Employees: 21 - 50 **Product Groups:** 72

Date of Accounts	Nov 11	Nov 10	Nov 09
Sales Turnover	38m	36m	34m
Pre Tax Profit/Loss	15	-73	-982
Working Capital	-2m	-2m	-2m
Fixed Assets	4m	3m	3m
Current Assets	7m	6m	7m
Current Liabilities	3m	3m	3m

Rainbow Cleaning Group Rainbow Group

Unit 8 Camberwell Trading Estate 117-119 Denmark Road, London, SE5 9LB
Tel: 020-7501 9999 **Fax:** 020-7501 9988
E-mail: info@rainbow-cleaning.co.uk
Website: http://www.allianceuk.com
Directors: A. Fernandes (Fin), P. Fernandes (MD)
Immediate Holding Company: RAINBOW CLEANING LTD
Registration no: 04397335 **Date established:** 2002
Turnover: Over £1,000m **No.of Employees:** 21 - 50 **Product Groups:** 32, 44, 52, 66

Date of Accounts	Mar 11	Mar 10	Mar 09
Working Capital	491	493	324
Fixed Assets	1m	1m	1m
Current Assets	1m	993	871

Raindrop Information Systems Ltd

Queens House 55-56 Lincoln's Inn Fields, London, WC2A 3LJ
Tel: 020-7269 8500 **Fax:** 020-7269 8501
E-mail: info@raindrop.co.uk
Website: http://www.manhattansoftware.co.uk
Directors: S. Vatidis (MD), S. Vatidis (MD)
Managers: J. Donnelly (Tech Serv Mgr), Y. Wiseman (Chief Acct), B. Gardner (Mktg Serv Mgr)
Immediate Holding Company: RAINDROP INFORMATION SYSTEMS LTD
Registration no: 02488556 **Date established:** 1990 **Turnover:** £5m - £10m
No.of Employees: 51 - 100 **Product Groups:** 28, 44

Date of Accounts	Apr 11	Apr 10	Apr 09
Sales Turnover	6m	5m	N/A
Pre Tax Profit/Loss	265	416	N/A
Working Capital	2m	1m	966
Fixed Assets	2m	2m	2m
Current Assets	4m	4m	4m
Current Liabilities	962	1m	N/A

Ramboll

60 Newman Street, London, W1T 3DA
Tel: 020-7631 5291 **Fax:** 020-7809 1801
E-mail: charles.mcbeath@rambollwhitbybird.com
Website: http://www.ramble.co.uk
Directors: C. McBeath (Dir)
Ultimate Holding Company: RAMBOLL GRUPPEN A/S (DENMARK)
Immediate Holding Company: RAMBOLL UK LIMITED
Registration no: 03659970 **Date established:** 1998
Turnover: £20m - £50m **No.of Employees:** 251 - 500 **Product Groups:** 35

Date of Accounts	Dec 11	Dec 10	Dec 09
Sales Turnover	59m	35	N/A
Pre Tax Profit/Loss	-304	N/A	N/A
Working Capital	12m	7	N/A
Fixed Assets	14m	2	N/A
Current Assets	29m	21	N/A
Current Liabilities	12m	10	N/A

Ramostyle Ltd

21 Noel Street, London, W1F 8GP
Tel: 020-7437 1127 **Fax:** 020-7287 0971
Directors: P. Dias (MD)
Immediate Holding Company: RAMOSTYLE LIMITED
Registration no: 01791571 **VAT No.:** GB 404 4534 81
Date established: 1984 **Turnover:** £500,000 - £1m
No.of Employees: 1 - 10 **Product Groups:** 63

Date of Accounts	Apr 12	Apr 11	Apr 10
Working Capital	-78	-64	-27
Fixed Assets	N/A	7	9
Current Assets	90	204	305

Random House UK Ltd

20 Vauxhall Bridge Road, London, SW1V 2SA
Tel: 020-7840 8400 **Fax:** 020-7233 8791
Website: http://www.randomhouse.co.uk
Managers: M. Gardener, K. Keegan
Ultimate Holding Company: BERTELSMANN AG (GERMANY)
Immediate Holding Company: RANDOM HOUSE PROPERTIES LIMITED
Registration no: 00209350 **Date established:** 2025
Turnover: £125m - £250m **No.of Employees:** 251 - 500
Product Groups: 28, 64

Range Choice

Unit 24-25 Lake Business Centre Tariff Road, London, N17 0YX
Tel: 020-8808 5757 **Fax:** 020-8808 3232
E-mail: rangechoice@hotmail.com
Directors: D. Cavit (Prop)
Immediate Holding Company: DAMDAM NORTH LTD
Registration no: 5305797 **Date established:** 2009
No.of Employees: 1 - 10 **Product Groups:** 24

Rankins Glass Company Ltd

24-34 Pearson Street, London, E2 8JD
Tel: 020-7729 4200 **Fax:** 020-7729 7135
E-mail: sales@rankinsglass.co.uk
Website: http://www.rankinsglass.co.uk
Directors: P. Rankin (MD)
Managers: M. Irving (Buyer), P. Osman (Sales Prom Mgr), J. Buhari (Personnel), O. Mendy (Chief Acct)
Immediate Holding Company: RANKINS (GLASS) COMPANY LIMITED
Registration no: 00445545 **Date established:** 1947 **Turnover:** £2m - £5m
No.of Employees: 21 - 50 **Product Groups:** 14, 33, 52

Date of Accounts	Dec 10	Dec 09	Dec 08
Working Capital	297	429	582
Fixed Assets	342	423	447
Current Assets	1m	1m	1m
Current Liabilities	274	138	304

Rapleys LLP

51 Great Marlborough Street, London, W1F 7JT
Tel: 08707-776292 **Fax:** 01480-433070
E-mail: info@rapleys.co.uk
Website: http://www.rapleys.co.uk
Directors: J. Banks (Snr Part), R. Bishop (Ptnr)
Managers: C. Young, S. Glover, S. Colman
Immediate Holding Company: HELISPRINT LIMITED
Registration no: 07178727 **Date established:** 2011 **Turnover:** £5m - £10m
No.of Employees: 21 - 50 **Product Groups:** 80, 84

Date of Accounts	Dec 10
Working Capital	-334
Fixed Assets	209
Current Assets	607

Ratcliffe Groves Partnership (Ratcliffe Groves Partnership)

4 Tavistock Place, London, WC1H 9RA
Tel: 020-7600 6666 **Fax:** 020-7397 2525
E-mail: london@rgp.uk.com
Website: http://www.rgp.uk.com
Directors: A. Summers (MD), C. Horner (MD)
Managers: M. Couch (Mktg Serv Mgr)
Immediate Holding Company: BRITISH BEER & PUB ASSOCIATION
Registration no: 07159396 **Date established:** 1974
No.of Employees: 1 - 10 **Product Groups:** 84

RAWvideo Ltd RAWaudio Ltd

4 Paddington Street, London, W1U 5QE
Tel: 020-7935 9696 **Fax:** 0871-2462704
E-mail: info@rawvideo.co.uk
Website: http://rawvideo.co.uk
Directors: R. Wilkins (Dir)
Registration no: 07380998 **Date established:** 2008
Turnover: Up to £250,000 **No.of Employees:** 1 - 10 **Product Groups:** 37

Ray Ward

12 Cadogan Place, London, SW1X 9PU
Tel: 020-7235 2550 **Fax:** 020-7259 6359
E-mail: customerservices@rayward.co.uk
Website: http://www.rayward.co.uk
Directors: J. Ward (Dir)
Immediate Holding Company: WEST LONDON SHOOTING GROUNDS LIMITED
Registration no: 03196132 **Date established:** 1996
Turnover: £500,000 - £1m **No.of Employees:** 1 - 10 **Product Groups:** 36, 39, 40

W A Read & Sons Ltd

554 Green Street, London, E13 9DA
Tel: 020-8472 0825 **Fax:** 020-8470 1244
Website: http://www.kellysearch.com/partners/waread.asp
Directors: S. Mayers (Dir)
Immediate Holding Company: W.A. READ & SONS LIMITED
Registration no: 01415349 **Date established:** 1979
No.of Employees: 11 - 20 **Product Groups:** 49

Date of Accounts	Mar 12	Mar 11	Mar 10
Working Capital	11	-30	-34
Fixed Assets	10	10	11
Current Assets	131	107	97

Recruitment & Employment Confederation

15 Welbeck Street, London, W1G 9XT
Tel: 020-7009 2140 **Fax:** 020-7255 2878
E-mail: info@rec.uk.com
Website: http://www.rec.uk.com
Bank(s): Barclays
Managers: K. Green, D. Valance (Admin Off)
Immediate Holding Company: THE RECRUITMENT AND EMPLOYMENT CONFEDERATION
Registration no: 03895053 **VAT No.:** 235 0903 85 **Date established:** 1999
Turnover: £5m - £10m **No.of Employees:** 51 - 100 **Product Groups:** 87

Date of Accounts	Dec 11	Dec 10	Dec 09
Sales Turnover	6m	6m	5m
Pre Tax Profit/Loss	317	51	-574
Working Capital	781	452	377
Fixed Assets	167	168	178
Current Assets	2m	2m	2m
Current Liabilities	1m	1m	1m

Red Ant Design Ltd

18 Charlotte Road, London, EC2A 3PB
Tel: 0845-4593333 **Fax:** 01622-664888
E-mail: info@redantdesign.com
Website: http://www.redantdesign.com
Directors: D. Mortimer (MD)
Immediate Holding Company: Red Ant Design Ltd
Registration no: 07282011 **Date established:** 2009
No.of Employees: 21 - 50 **Product Groups:** 44, 81

Date of Accounts	Sep 08	Sep 07	Sep 06
Working Capital	41	76	80
Fixed Assets	127	80	52
Current Assets	318	241	127
Current Liabilities	277	165	47

Red Chilli Structured Finance

Minories House 2 - 5 Minories, London, EC3N 1BJ
Tel: 020-7780 6500 **Fax:** 020-7780 6501
E-mail: info@redchilli.com
Website: http://www.redchilli.com
Managers: S. Page (Chief Acct)
Registration no: OC332330 **Date established:** 2008
No.of Employees: 21 - 50 **Product Groups:** 82

Redhouse Lane Communications

14-15 Bedford Square, London, WC1B 3JA
Tel: 020-7462 2600 **Fax:** 020-7462 2601
E-mail: reception@redhouselane.com
Website: http://www.redhouselane.com
Directors: M. Drewman (Fin), K. Woods (Sales)
Managers: A. Menzies (Sales Admin), I. Samuels (Mktg Serv Mgr)
Immediate Holding Company: REDHOUSE LANE COMMUNICATIONS LIMITED
Registration no: 02320395 **VAT No.:** GB 494 3316 28
Date established: 1988 **Turnover:** £1m - £2m **No.of Employees:** 21 - 50
Product Groups: 44, 81, 89

see next page

Redhouse Lane Communications - Cont'd

Date of Accounts	Feb 08	Feb 11	Feb 10
Working Capital	1m	914	1m
Fixed Assets	90	62	81
Current Assets	2m	2m	2m

Redsea Refridgeration & Catering Equipment
44 Myrdle Street, London, E1 1EU
Tel: 020-7377 0100 **Fax:** 020-7377 0100
Directors: E. Mehmet (Prop)
Date established: 2006 **No.of Employees:** 1 - 10 **Product Groups:** 20, 40, 41

Martin Redston Associates
6 Hale Lane, London, NW7 3NX
Tel: 020-8959 1666 **Fax:** 020-8906 8503
E-mail: mredston@compuserve.com
Directors: M. Redston (Prop)
Registration no: 02016943 **Date established:** 1986
No.of Employees: 1 - 10 **Product Groups:** 35

Reed
112-120 Coombe Lane, London, SW20 0BA
Tel: 020-8288 5065 **Fax:** 020-8831 7571
E-mail: twickenham.employment@reed.co.uk
Website: http://www.reed.co.uk
Directors: E. Hickman (MD), J. Reed (Grp Chief Exec)
Managers: S. Clarke (Chief Mgr)
Ultimate Holding Company: REED GLOBAL LTD (MALTA)
Immediate Holding Company: REED EMPLOYMENT LIMITED
Registration no: 00669854 **Date established:** 1960
Turnover: £250m - £500m **No.of Employees:** 1 - 10 **Product Groups:** 80

Date of Accounts	Jun 11	Jun 10	Dec 07
Sales Turnover	618	450	287m
Pre Tax Profit/Loss	-2m	310	8m
Working Capital	23m	28m	28m
Fixed Assets	31	36	5m
Current Assets	28m	30m	74m
Current Liabilities	37	29	21m

Reed Accountancy Services
Broadway Chambers Hammersmith Broadway, London, W6 7AF
Tel: 020-8748 9707 **Fax:** 020-8846 9225
E-mail: rap.hammersmith@reed.co.uk
Website: http://www.reed.co.uk
Managers: S. Draper (Mgr)
Ultimate Holding Company: REED GLOBAL LTD (MALTA)
Immediate Holding Company: REED EMPLOYMENT LIMITED
Registration no: 00669854 **Date established:** 1960 **Turnover:** £5m - £10m
No.of Employees: 1 - 10 **Product Groups:** 80

Date of Accounts	Jun 11	Jun 10	Dec 07
Sales Turnover	618	450	287m
Pre Tax Profit/Loss	-2m	310	8m
Working Capital	23m	28m	28m
Fixed Assets	31	36	5m
Current Assets	28m	30m	74m
Current Liabilities	37	29	21m

Reed Elsevier Group plc
Grand Buildings 1-3 Strand, London, WC2N 5JR
Tel: 020-7930 7077 **Fax:** 020-7166 5799
E-mail: london@reedelsevier.com
Website: http://www.reedelsevier.com
Bank(s): Natwest
Directors: M. Armour (Fin), S. Cowden (Co Sec)
Immediate Holding Company: REED ELSEVIER GROUP PLC
Registration no: 02746616 **Date established:** 1992
Turnover: Over £1,000m **No.of Employees:** 101 - 250
Product Groups: 28, 80

Date of Accounts	Dec 11	Dec 10	Dec 09
Sales Turnover	5934m	5992m	6011m
Pre Tax Profit/Loss	603m	377m	38m
Working Capital	-4589m	-3937m	-4721m
Fixed Assets	8911m	8583m	8752m
Current Assets	2997m	3581m	3110m
Current Liabilities	7285m	5995m	7735m

Reed Employment Ltd
52 Welbeck Street, London, W1G 9XP
Tel: 020-7467 4690 **Fax:** 020-7467 4691
E-mail: n.parkinson@reed.co.uk
Website: http://www.reedglobal.com
Directors: J. Reed (Prop)
Managers: N. Parkinson (Mgr), M. Miles (Mgr), C. Willsher (Comm)
Immediate Holding Company: REED EMPLOYMENT LIMITED
Registration no: 00669854 **Date established:** 1960 **Turnover:** £1m - £2m
No.of Employees: 1 - 10 **Product Groups:** 80

Reed Employment Ltd
376 Holloway Road, London, N7 6PN
Tel: 020-7607 8763 **Fax:** 020-7607 5460
E-mail: matt.heather@reedglobal.com
Website: http://www.reed.co.uk
Directors: J. Reed (MD)
Managers: C. Galagher (Mgr), M. Heather (Mgr)
Ultimate Holding Company: REED GLOBAL LTD (MALTA)
Immediate Holding Company: REED EMPLOYMENT LIMITED
Registration no: 00669854 **Date established:** 1960
Turnover: £75m - £125m **No.of Employees:** 1 - 10 **Product Groups:** 80

Date of Accounts	Jun 11	Jun 10	Dec 07
Sales Turnover	618	450	287m
Pre Tax Profit/Loss	-2m	310	8m
Working Capital	23m	28m	28m
Fixed Assets	31	36	5m
Current Assets	28m	30m	74m
Current Liabilities	37	29	21m

Reed Employment Ltd
69 King Street, London, W6 9HW
Tel: 020-8748 9733 **Fax:** 020-8748 9765
E-mail: alexandra.martin@reedglobal.com
Website: http://www.reed.co.uk
Managers: A. Martin (Comm)
Ultimate Holding Company: REED GLOBAL LTD (MALTA)
Immediate Holding Company: REED EMPLOYMENT LIMITED
Registration no: 00669854 **Date established:** 1960
Turnover: £75m - £125m **No.of Employees:** 11 - 20 **Product Groups:** 80

Date of Accounts	Jun 11	Jun 10	Dec 07
Sales Turnover	618	450	287m
Pre Tax Profit/Loss	-2m	310	8m
Working Capital	23m	28m	28m
Fixed Assets	31	36	5m
Current Assets	28m	30m	74m
Current Liabilities	37	29	21m

Reed Employment Ltd
50 Broadway, London, E15 1NG
Tel: 020-8555 0313 **Fax:** 020-8519 8784
E-mail: christine.lambert@reedglobal.com
Website: http://www.reed.co.uk
Managers: C. Lambert (Mgr)
Ultimate Holding Company: REED GLOBAL LTD (MALTA)
Immediate Holding Company: REED EMPLOYMENT LIMITED
Registration no: 00669854 **Date established:** 1960
Turnover: £75m - £125m **No.of Employees:** 1 - 10 **Product Groups:** 80

Date of Accounts	Jun 11	Jun 10	Dec 07
Sales Turnover	618	450	287m
Pre Tax Profit/Loss	-2m	310	8m
Working Capital	23m	28m	28m
Fixed Assets	31	36	5m
Current Assets	28m	30m	74m
Current Liabilities	37	29	21m

Reed Employment Ltd
143 Victoria Street, London, SW1E 5NH
Tel: 020-7821 8078 **Fax:** 020-7821 5593
Website: http://www.reed.co.uk
Managers: S. Slater (Consultant)
Ultimate Holding Company: REED GLOBAL LTD (MALTA)
Immediate Holding Company: REED EMPLOYMENT LIMITED
Registration no: 00669854 **Date established:** 1960
No.of Employees: 1 - 10 **Product Groups:** 80

Date of Accounts	Jun 11	Jun 10	Dec 07
Sales Turnover	618	450	287m
Pre Tax Profit/Loss	-2m	310	8m
Working Capital	23m	28m	28m
Fixed Assets	31	36	5m
Current Assets	28m	30m	74m
Current Liabilities	37	29	21m

Reed Employment Ltd
28 Putney High Street, London, SW15 1SQ
Tel: 020-8246 4030 **Fax:** 020-8246 4033
E-mail: tom.pickard@reed.co.uk
Website: http://www.reed.co.uk
Directors: J. Reed (Grp Chief Exec)
Managers: T. Pickard (Mgr)
Ultimate Holding Company: REED GLOBAL LTD (MALTA)
Immediate Holding Company: REED EMPLOYMENT LIMITED
Registration no: 00669854 **Date established:** 1960
Turnover: £250m - £500m **No.of Employees:** 1 - 10 **Product Groups:** 80

Date of Accounts	Jun 11	Jun 10	Dec 07
Sales Turnover	618	450	287m
Pre Tax Profit/Loss	-2m	310	8m
Working Capital	23m	28m	28m
Fixed Assets	31	36	5m
Current Assets	28m	30m	74m
Current Liabilities	37	29	21m

Reed Employment Ltd
9 Wimbledon Bridge, London, SW19 7NW
Tel: 020-8944 3002 **Fax:** 020-8944 3001
Website: http://www.reed.co.uk
Directors: J. Reed (MD)
Managers: S. Hathaway (Mgr), S. Stradlings (Comm), N. Cole (Consultant), S. Radford (Mgr)
Ultimate Holding Company: Reed Executive P.L.C.
Immediate Holding Company: REED EMPLOYMENT LIMITED
Registration no: 00669854 **Date established:** 1960
Turnover: £125m - £250m **No.of Employees:** 1 - 10 **Product Groups:** 80

Reed Employment Ltd
44 Denmark Hill, London, SE5 8RZ
Tel: 020-7733 2173 **Fax:** 020-7326 7500
Website: http://www.reed.co.uk
Managers: E. Ellison (District Mgr)
Ultimate Holding Company: REED GLOBAL LTD (MALTA)
Immediate Holding Company: REED EMPLOYMENT LIMITED
Registration no: 00669854 **Date established:** 1960
Turnover: £75m - £125m **No.of Employees:** 1 - 10 **Product Groups:** 80

Date of Accounts	Jun 11	Jun 10	Dec 07
Sales Turnover	618	450	287m
Pre Tax Profit/Loss	-2m	310	8m
Working Capital	23m	28m	28m
Fixed Assets	31	36	5m
Current Assets	28m	30m	74m
Current Liabilities	37	29	21m

Reed Specialist Recruitment
380 Chiswick High Road, London, W4 5TF
Tel: 020-8994 0106 **Fax:** 020-8994 8095
Website: http://www.reed.co.uk
Managers: R. Woulfe (Comm), H. Lorigan (District Mgr)
Ultimate Holding Company: REED GLOBAL LTD (MALTA)
Immediate Holding Company: REED EMPLOYMENT LIMITED
Registration no: 00669854 **Date established:** 1960
Turnover: £75m - £125m **No.of Employees:** 1 - 10 **Product Groups:** 80

Date of Accounts	Jun 11	Jun 10	Dec 07
Sales Turnover	618	450	287m
Pre Tax Profit/Loss	-2m	310	8m
Working Capital	23m	28m	28m
Fixed Assets	31	36	5m
Current Assets	28m	30m	74m
Current Liabilities	37	29	21m

Reed Hospitality
189 Victoria Street, London, SW1E 5NE
Tel: 020-7828 5292 **Fax:** 020-7828 1230
E-mail: bill@reed.co.uk
Website: http://www.reed.co.uk
Bank(s): Barclays
Managers: B. Dawes (Mgr)
Immediate Holding Company: REED PERSONNEL
Date established: 1989 **No.of Employees:** 11 - 20 **Product Groups:** 80

Reed Nurse
Copenhagen House 5-10 Bury Street, London, EC3A 5AT
Tel: 020-7221 0672 **Fax:** 020-7313 6901
Website: http://www.reedglobal.com
Managers: M. Mbelu (District Mgr)
Ultimate Holding Company: REED EXECUTIVE LIMITED
Immediate Holding Company: REED NURSE LIMITED
Registration no: 01495718 **Date established:** 1980
No.of Employees: 11 - 20 **Product Groups:** 80

Reed Smith
The Broadgate Tower 20 Primrose Street, London, EC2A 2RS
Tel: 020-3116 3000 **Fax:** 020-7247 5091
E-mail: rparker@reedsmith.com
Website: http://www.reedsmith.com
Directors: R. Parker (Snr Part)
Immediate Holding Company: RICHARDS BUTLER LIMITED
Registration no: 02277157 **VAT No.:** GB 235 4555 62
Date established: 1988 **Turnover:** £2m - £5m
No.of Employees: 251 - 500 **Product Groups:** 80

Reed Social Care
68 Lewisham High Street, London, SE13 5JH
Tel: 020-8297 1297 **Fax:** 020-8852 0856
E-mail: sheron.aspinall@reedhealth.com
Website: http://www.reedhealth.com
Managers: C. Noden (Mgr)
Ultimate Holding Company: FINEM LTD
Immediate Holding Company: REED PROPERTY LTD
Registration no: 01495718 **No.of Employees:** 1 - 10 **Product Groups:** 80

Reed Specialist Ltd
5 High Holborn, London, WC1V 6DR
Tel: 020-7405 6525 **Fax:** 020-7405 7284
Website: http://www.reedglobal.com
Directors: J. Reed (MD)
Managers: M. Hellery (Mgr), N. Kennedy (Mgr), K. Kirk (Mgr), L. Carter (District Mgr)
Ultimate Holding Company: REED GLOBAL LTD (MALTA)
Registration no: 00669854 **Date established:** 1985
Turnover: £75m - £125m **No.of Employees:** 1 - 10 **Product Groups:** 80

Reed Specialist Recruitment
94 Baker Street, London, W1U 6FZ
Tel: 020-7224 2820 **Fax:** 020-7935 1265
Website: http://www.reed.co.uk
Directors: J. Reed (MD)
Managers: C. Skipper (District Mgr)
Ultimate Holding Company: REED GLOBAL LTD (MALTA)
Immediate Holding Company: REED EMPLOYMENT LIMITED
Registration no: 00669854 **Date established:** 1960
Turnover: £500,000 - £1m **No.of Employees:** 1 - 10 **Product Groups:** 80

Date of Accounts	Jun 11	Jun 10	Jun 09
Sales Turnover	761m	650m	N/A
Pre Tax Profit/Loss	758	9m	N/A
Working Capital	-6m	-9m	-16m
Fixed Assets	15m	17m	18m
Current Assets	108m	96m	158m
Current Liabilities	60m	62m	52m

Reed Specialist Recruitment
141 Camden High Street, London, NW1 7JR
Tel: 020-7267 4091 **Fax:** 020-7428 6500
Website: http://www.reed.co.uk
Managers: M. Saunders (Mgr)
Ultimate Holding Company: REED GLOBAL LTD (MALTA)
Immediate Holding Company: REED EMPLOYMENT LIMITED
Registration no: 00669854 **Date established:** 1960
Turnover: £75m - £125m **No.of Employees:** 1 - 10 **Product Groups:** 80

Date of Accounts	Jun 11	Jun 10	Dec 07
Sales Turnover	618	450	287m
Pre Tax Profit/Loss	-2m	310	8m
Working Capital	23m	28m	28m
Fixed Assets	31	36	5m
Current Assets	28m	30m	74m
Current Liabilities	37	29	21m

Reed Specialist Recruitment
26 The Broadway, London, W5 2NP
Tel: 020-8326 3900 **Fax:** 020-8326 3901
Website: http://www.reed.co.uk
Managers: P. Brady (District Mgr)
Ultimate Holding Company: REED GLOBAL LTD (MALTA)
Immediate Holding Company: REED EMPLOYMENT LIMITED
Registration no: 00669854 **Date established:** 1960 **Turnover:** £1m - £2m
No.of Employees: 1 - 10 **Product Groups:** 80

Date of Accounts	Jun 11	Jun 10	Dec 07
Sales Turnover	618	450	287m
Pre Tax Profit/Loss	-2m	310	8m
Working Capital	23m	28m	28m
Fixed Assets	31	36	5m
Current Assets	28m	30m	74m
Current Liabilities	37	29	21m

Ann Reeves & Co. Ltd
78 Great Titchfield Street, London, W1W 7QS
Tel: 020-7637 7965 **Fax:** 020-7637 9272
E-mail: peter@annreeves.com
Website: http://www.annreeves.com
Directors: P. Billows (Fin), S. Goldschmidt (Sales), A. Goldschmidt (Co Sec)
Ultimate Holding Company: ANN REEVES HOLDINGS LIMITED
Immediate Holding Company: ANN REEVES & COMPANY LIMITED
Registration no: 01014866 **Date established:** 1971
Turnover: £10m - £20m **No.of Employees:** 21 - 50 **Product Groups:** 24

Date of Accounts	Mar 11	Mar 10	Mar 09
Sales Turnover	14m	14m	15m
Pre Tax Profit/Loss	329	488	395
Working Capital	1m	885	644
Fixed Assets	41	54	74
Current Assets	4m	4m	4m
Current Liabilities	784	901	351

Reeves Lund And Company Limited
The Courtyard 55 Charterhouse Street, London, EC1M 6HA
Tel: 020-7739 8888 **Fax:** 020-7490 4488
E-mail: sales@reeveslund.com
Website: http://www.reeveslund.com
Directors: P. Harper Hill (Sales), P. Hobb-Hill (Sales), P. Lund (MD), W. Morgan (Fin)

Immediate Holding Company: Reeves Lund & Company Ltd
Registration no: 02035650 **VAT No.:** GB 524 8012 69
Date established: 1986 **Turnover:** £1m - £2m **No.of Employees:** 1 - 10
Product Groups: 37, 46, 79, 84

Date of Accounts	Mar 08	Mar 07	Mar 06
Sales Turnover	N/A	N/A	1144
Pre Tax Profit/Loss	N/A	N/A	1
Working Capital	-141	-214	-151
Fixed Assets	42	52	93
Current Assets	218	238	390
Current Liabilities	359	452	541
Total Share Capital	1	1	1
ROCE% (Return on Capital Employed)			-1.1
ROT% (Return on Turnover)			0.1

Regal House International Ltd
1102 High Road, London, N20 0QX
Tel: 020-8446 7300 **Fax:** 020-8446 7448
E-mail: regalds1@btconnect.com
Directors: P. Sivanandam (Fin), D. Simons (Dir)
Immediate Holding Company: REGAL HOUSE INTERNATIONAL LIMITED
Registration no: 05777575 **VAT No.:** GB 229 8296 23
Date established: 2006 **Turnover:** £1m - £2m **No.of Employees:** 1 - 10
Product Groups: 33, 65

Date of Accounts	Mar 12	Mar 11	Mar 10
Working Capital	1	7	4
Fixed Assets	1	1	1
Current Assets	102	110	104

J Reid Pianos
184 St Anns Road, London, N15 5RP
Tel: 020-8800 6907 **Fax:** 020-8809 0767
E-mail: sales@jreidpianos.co.uk
Website: http://www.jreidpianos.co.uk
Directors: J. Gregory (Ptnr)
Immediate Holding Company: J. REID PIANO HIRE LIMITED
Registration no: 01993360 **VAT No.:** GB 327 7061 59
Date established: 1986 **Turnover:** £500,000 - £1m
No.of Employees: 1 - 10 **Product Groups:** 49

Date of Accounts	Mar 11	Mar 10	Mar 07
Sales Turnover	N/A	N/A	550
Pre Tax Profit/Loss	N/A	N/A	150
Working Capital	825	793	570
Fixed Assets	18	28	44
Current Assets	1m	998	773
Current Liabilities	169	177	112

Reiss Retail Ltd
114 Kings Road, London, SW3 4TX
Tel: 020-7225 4910 **Fax:** 020-7225 4901
E-mail: reception@reiss.co.uk
Website: http://www.reiss.co.uk
Managers: C. Flowe (Mgr)
Ultimate Holding Company: REISS (HOLDINGS) LIMITED
Immediate Holding Company: REISS (RETAIL) LIMITED
Registration no: 02487563 **VAT No.:** 563 0523 62 **Date established:** 1990
Turnover: £5m - £10m **No.of Employees:** 1 - 10 **Product Groups:** 63

Date of Accounts	Jan 11	Jan 10	Jan 09
Sales Turnover	7m	7m	7m
Pre Tax Profit/Loss	-4m	-5m	-3m
Working Capital	1m	902	1m
Fixed Assets	3m	4m	7m
Current Assets	2m	2m	2m
Current Liabilities	490	633	613

Reliance GeneMedix plc
8Th Floor 105 Wigmore Street, London, W1U 1QY
Tel: 01638-663320 **Fax:** 01638-663411
E-mail: enquiries@genemedix.com
Website: http://www.genemedix.com
Directors: A. Dayal (Dir), J. Attfield (Grp Chief Exec)
Ultimate Holding Company: Equiniti Holdings Ltd
Immediate Holding Company: SLC Registrars Ltd
Registration no: 03467317 **No.of Employees:** 21 - 50 **Product Groups:** 31

Date of Accounts	Mar 08	Mar 07	Nov 05
Pre Tax Profit/Loss	-5236	-5928	-5460
Working Capital	1439	9293	273
Fixed Assets	5016	3301	6578
Current Assets	4176	11080	2511
Current Liabilities	2737	1787	2238
Total Share Capital	15572	15572	3716
ROCE% (Return on Capital Employed)	-81.1	-47.1	-79.7

Reliance Security Group Limited
Tayside House 31 Pepper Street, London, E14 9RP
Tel: 0870-6068999 **Fax:** 020-7987 3142
E-mail: info@reliancesecurity.co.uk
Website: http://www.reliancesecurity.co.uk
Directors: K. Allison (Ch)
Managers: L. Nelson (Chief Mgr)
Ultimate Holding Company: Barclays plc
Immediate Holding Company: Reliance Security Group Ltd
Registration no: 01473721 **Date established:** 2006
Turnover: £10m - £20m **No.of Employees:** 11 - 20 **Product Groups:** 81

Reliance Security Group Ltd (Central London)
Surety House 81 Chester Square, London, SW1W 9DP
Tel: 020-7730 9716 **Fax:** 020-7837 1113
E-mail: brian.kingham@reliancegroup.co.uk
Website: http://www.reliancegroup.co.uk
Directors: B. Kingham (Prop)
Ultimate Holding Company: RELIANCE TRUST LIMITED
Immediate Holding Company: RELIANCE SECURITY GROUP LIMITED
Registration no: 01473721 **Date established:** 1980
Turnover: Over £1,000m **No.of Employees:** 1 - 10 **Product Groups:** 81

Date of Accounts	Apr 11	Apr 10	Apr 08
Sales Turnover	250m	N/A	382m
Pre Tax Profit/Loss	41m	-1m	14m
Working Capital	86m	14m	37m
Fixed Assets	10m	8m	9m
Current Assets	131m	56m	98m
Current Liabilities	35m	2m	54m

Reliance Security Services Ltd
151 Tower Bridge Road, London, SE1 3LW
Tel: 020-7939 8400 **Fax:** 020-7222 9415
E-mail: info@reliancesecurity.co.uk
Website: http://www.reliancesecurity.co.uk
Managers: M. Gilbert (District Mgr)
Ultimate Holding Company: RELIANCE CORPORATION LIMITED
Immediate Holding Company: RELIANCE PROPERTY HOLDINGS LIMITED
Registration no: 01033997 **Date established:** 1971 **Turnover:** £5m - £10m
No.of Employees: 21 - 50 **Product Groups:** 81

Reliance Veneer Co. Ltd
Craven Walk Stamford Hill, London, N16 6DE
Tel: 020-8802 2361 **Fax:** 020-8802 2368
E-mail: michael@relianceveneer.co.uk
Website: http://www.relianceveneer.co.uk
Bank(s): Bank of Scotland, London
Directors: M. Steinberg (MD)
Managers: D. Harrison (Fin Mgr)
Ultimate Holding Company: RIVER LEA HOLDING COMPANY LIMITED
Immediate Holding Company: RELIANCE VENEER COMPANY LIMITED
Registration no: 00483044 **VAT No.:** GB 220 3009 34
Date established: 1950 **Turnover:** £2m - £5m **No.of Employees:** 21 - 50
Product Groups: 25

Date of Accounts	Aug 11	Aug 10	Aug 09
Working Capital	3m	3m	2m
Fixed Assets	512	599	640
Current Assets	4m	4m	4m

Reliant Engineers Ltd
32 Stephenson Street, London, E16 4SA
Tel: 020-7511 3010 **Fax:** 020-7474 0142
Website: http://www.reliantengineers.com
Directors: N. Collins (Fin), H. Collins (MD)
Immediate Holding Company: RELIANT ENGINEERS LIMITED
Registration no: 01683707 **Date established:** 1982
No.of Employees: 1 - 10 **Product Groups:** 46

Date of Accounts	Apr 11	Apr 10	Apr 09
Working Capital	-41	-44	-57
Fixed Assets	284	286	289
Current Assets	43	68	62

Remploy Ltd
2 Portal Way, London, W3 6RT
Tel: 020-8992 8614 **Fax:** 020-8993 8871
E-mail: george.hoskins@remploy.co.uk
Website: http://www.remploy.co.uk
Bank(s): National Westminster Bank Plc
Managers: G. Hoskins (Mgr)
Immediate Holding Company: REMPLOY PENSION SCHEME TRUSTEES LIMITED
Registration no: 07588018 **VAT No.:** GB 226 5029 79
Date established: 2011 **Turnover:** £125m - £250m
No.of Employees: 51 - 100 **Product Groups:** 37, 48, 84

Date of Accounts	Mar 12
Working Capital	497m
Current Assets	497m

REMTV AGENCY LTd
Second Floor 6, LONDON STREET, London, W2 1HR
Tel: 020-7060 0859 **Fax:** 0207-0601409
E-mail: ibiza@remtv.org
Website: http://www.remtv.org
Directors: C. René (Dir), B. Joëlle (Dir)
Registration no: 6544201 **Date established:** 2008
Turnover: Up to £250,000 **No.of Employees:** 1 - 10 **Product Groups:** 44, 81

Renair Ltd
11-15 Chase Road, London, NW10 6PT
Tel: 020-8965 3001 **Fax:** 020-8965 5773
E-mail: sales@renair.co.uk
Website: http://www.renair.co.uk
Bank(s): Barclays
Managers: J. Futter (Mgr)
Immediate Holding Company: RENAIR LIMITED
Registration no: 00913542 **VAT No.:** GB 532 3919 49
Date established: 1967 **Turnover:** £500,000 - £1m
No.of Employees: 11 - 20 **Product Groups:** 37

Date of Accounts	Dec 11	Dec 10	Dec 09
Working Capital	31	29	26
Fixed Assets	14	15	15
Current Assets	45	45	39

Renaix Ltd
Mr Paul Anthony Jarrett 5a Underwood Street, London, N1 7LY
Tel: 020-7553 6320 **Fax:** 020-7553 6321
E-mail: info@renaix.com
Website: http://www.renaix.com
Directors: P. Jarrett (MD)
Immediate Holding Company: RENAIX LIMITED
Registration no: FC021275 **Date established:** 1998
No.of Employees: 1 - 10 **Product Groups:** 80

Date of Accounts	Dec 07	Dec 06	Dec 05
Working Capital	28	35	-1
Fixed Assets	491	511	534
Current Assets	414	441	326
Current Liabilities	386	406	327
Total Share Capital	1	1	1

Rentrifone Ltd
776a Finchley Road, London, NW11 7TH
Tel: 020-8455 3304 **Fax:** 020-8609 0627
E-mail: sales@rentrifone.com
Website: http://www.rentrifone.com
Directors: M. Srewin (Fin)
Immediate Holding Company: RENTRIFONE LIMITED
Registration no: 01765843 **VAT No.:** GB 421 4264 88
Date established: 1983 **Turnover:** Up to £250,000
No.of Employees: 11 - 20 **Product Groups:** 35, 37, 40

Date of Accounts	Mar 11	Mar 10	Mar 09
Working Capital	20	77	-27
Fixed Assets	1m	1m	1m
Current Assets	861	933	678

Renubath Services London
246 Lillie Road, London, SW6 7QA
Tel: 020-7381 8337 **Fax:** 020-7381 8907
E-mail: london@renubath.co.uk
Website: http://www.renubath.co.uk
Directors: R. Jones (MD)
Date established: 1988 **No.of Employees:** 1 - 10 **Product Groups:** 46, 48

Research For Today Ltd
77 Gunnersbury Avenue, London, W5 4LP
Tel: 020-8992 4877 **Fax:** 020-8993 5818
E-mail: simalto@researchfortoday.com
Directors: J. Green (MD)
Immediate Holding Company: RESEARCH FOR TODAY LIMITED
Registration no: 01743550 **Date established:** 1983
Turnover: £500,000 - £1m **No.of Employees:** 1 - 10 **Product Groups:** 81

Date of Accounts	Jul 11	Jul 10	Jul 08
Working Capital	17	22	14
Current Assets	32	50	125

Research International Group Ltd
6-7 Grosvenor Place, London, SW1X 7SH
Tel: 020-7656 5500 **Fax:** 020-7235 0202
E-mail: j.bower@research-int.com
Website: http://www.research-int.com
Directors: S. Blackall (Vice Ch), C. Evans (Grp Chief Exec), L. Davison (Mkt Research), J. Bond (Grp Chief Exec)
Managers: C. Backingham (Chief Mgr), D. Phillips (Sales Prom Mgr), M. O'Reilley (I.T. Exec)
Ultimate Holding Company: WPP 2008 Ltd
Immediate Holding Company: Ogilvy & Mather Group (Holdings) Ltd
Registration no: 00103490 **VAT No.:** GB 243 3351 88
Date established: 1909 **No.of Employees:** 1 - 10 **Product Groups:** 81

Date of Accounts	Dec 07	Dec 06	Dec 05
Pre Tax Profit/Loss	1090	860	890
Working Capital	24860	23770	22910
Current Assets	24860	23770	22910
Total Share Capital	5220	5220	5220

ReSpace Acoustics Ltd
19 Stansfield Road Brixton, London, SW9 9RY
Tel: 0844-8844011 **Fax:** 0844-8844019
E-mail: yebullen@gmail.com
Website: http://www.respace-acoustics.co.uk
Directors: M. Bullen (Prop)
Date established: 2009 **Turnover:** **No.of Employees:** 11 - 20
Product Groups: 30, 35, 40, 52

Rexam Holding plc
Third Floor 4 Millbank, London, SW1P 3XR
Tel: 020-7227 4100 **Fax:** 020-7227 4109
E-mail: stuart.bull@rexam.com
Website: http://www.rexam.com
Directors: D. Robbie (Fin), L. Emilson (Grp Chief Exec), R. Borjesson (Ch), S. Bull (Dir), V. Walle (Grp Chief Exec), D. Gibson (Co Sec)
Managers: M. Halvang (Mktg Serv Mgr), S. Ince (I.T. Exec), S. Trowbridge (Personnel)
Immediate Holding Company: BOWATERS CANADIAN HOLDINGS LIMITED
Registration no: 01000603 **VAT No.:** GB 238 5870 31
Date established: 1971 **Turnover:** Over £1,000m
No.of Employees: 51 - 100 **Product Groups:** 30, 31, 35

Reynards UK Ltd
14-16 Whitby Avenue, London, NW10 7SF
Tel: 020-8965 8161 **Fax:** 020-8965 4585
E-mail: rperkins@reynards.com
Website: http://www.reynards.com
Directors: R. Perkins (MD)
Immediate Holding Company: REYNARDS (LONDON) LIMITED
Registration no: 01519005 **Date established:** 1980 **Turnover:** £2m - £5m
No.of Employees: 1 - 10 **Product Groups:** 25, 27, 30, 35, 41

Richard Caplan Photographic Ltd
25 Bury Street, London, SW1Y 6AL
Tel: 020-7807 9990 **Fax:** 020-7807 9991
E-mail: leica@richardcaplan.co.uk
Website: http://www.richardcaplan.co.uk
Directors: R. Caplan (MD)
Immediate Holding Company: RICHARD CAPLAN PHOTOGRAPHIC LIMITED
Registration no: 04557725 **Date established:** 2002
No.of Employees: 1 - 10 **Product Groups:** 37, 38, 65

Date of Accounts	Dec 11	Dec 10	Dec 09
Working Capital	321	202	178
Fixed Assets	10	12	20
Current Assets	431	329	412

Richard Taylor Designs Ltd
Studio One Fairbank Studios 140 Lots Road, London, SW10 0NS
Tel: 020-7351 2567 **Fax:** 020-7349 8749
E-mail: enquiries@richardtaylordesigns.co.uk
Website: http://www.richardtaylordesigns.co.uk
Directors: R. Taylor (MD), J. Pittman (Fin)
Immediate Holding Company: RICHARD TAYLOR DESIGNS LIMITED
Registration no: 03426892 **Date established:** 1997
No.of Employees: 1 - 10 **Product Groups:** 37, 67

Date of Accounts	Apr 12	Apr 11	Apr 10
Working Capital	12	13	6
Fixed Assets	8	6	8
Current Assets	267	202	142

Richards Butler
Beaufort House 15 St. Botolph Street, London, EC3A 7EE
Tel: 020-7247 6555 **Fax:** 020-7247 5091
E-mail: law@richardsbutler.com
Website: http://www.richardsbutler.com
Bank(s): Lloyds TSB, Threadneedle Street
Directors: R. Parker (MD)
Immediate Holding Company: Richards Butler Ltd
Registration no: 02277157 **VAT No.:** GB 243 9826 37
Date established: 2006 **No.of Employees:** 501 - 1000 **Product Groups:** 80

Richmond Towers Communications Ltd
26 Fitzroy Square, London, W1T 6BT
Tel: 020-7388 7421 **Fax:** 020-7388 7761
E-mail: info@rt-com.com
Website: http://www.rt-com.com
Bank(s): Bank of Scotland
Directors: M. Nieman (Ch), V. Furzer (Dir), R. Metcalfe (Prop), B. Morris (Fin), R. Metcalfe (Dir), R. Jupe (Grp Chief Exec), I. Jesnick (MD)
Registration no: 05452146 **Date established:** 1935 **Turnover:** £2m - £5m
No.of Employees: 21 - 50 **Product Groups:** 80, 81

Date of Accounts	Jun 09	Jun 08	Jun 07
Working Capital	-1m	-794	-451
Fixed Assets	1m	1m	1m
Current Assets	311	580	628

Ridat
674 Finchley Road, London, NW11 7NP
Tel: 020-8458 6485 **Fax:** 020-8455 5056
E-mail: sales@ridat.com
Website: http://www.ridat.com
Managers: D. Sen Gupta (Mgr)
Immediate Holding Company: TECHNOBEAM LTD
Date established: 1985 **Turnover:** £500,000 - £1m
No.of Employees: 1 - 10 **Product Groups:** 30, 42, 48

Rigging Services
3 Mills Studios Three Mill Lane, London, E3 3DU
Tel: 020-8215 1240 **Fax:** 020-8215 1243
E-mail: london@riggingservices.co.uk
Website: http://www.riggingservices.co.uk
Directors: P. Fulcher (MD)
Immediate Holding Company: RIGGING SERVICES TRAINING AND CONSULTANCY LTD
Registration no: 07422466 **Date established:** 2010
Turnover: £20m - £50m **No.of Employees:** 1 - 10 **Product Groups:** 35, 37, 38, 39, 45, 48, 83

Rinku Group plc
622 Western Avenue, London, W3 0TF
Tel: 020-8896 9922 **Fax:** 020-8896 9977
E-mail: mail@rinku.co.uk
Website: http://www.rinku.co.uk
Bank(s): Midland
Directors: R. Loomba (Ch)
Managers: R. Sivarajah (Comptroller), U. Sharma (Tech Serv Mgr)
Immediate Holding Company: TIGI-WEAR LIMITED
Registration no: 01493479 **VAT No.:** GB 404 4141 03
Date established: 1980 **Turnover:** £10m - £20m
No.of Employees: 21 - 50 **Product Groups:** 24

Date of Accounts	Jun 11	Jun 10	Jun 09
Sales Turnover	11m	11m	12m
Pre Tax Profit/Loss	75	1m	786
Working Capital	1m	1m	932
Fixed Assets	642	706	754
Current Assets	3m	4m	5m
Current Liabilities	446	374	2m

Rio Tinto Vostok Ltd
2 Eastbourne Terrace, London, W2 6LG
Tel: 020-7781 2000 **Fax:** 020-7781 1800
E-mail: questions@riotinto.com
Website: http://www.riotinto.com
Bank(s): Royal Bank of Scotland, London
Directors: M. Greaves (Dir), P. Nadjar (MD)
Managers: S. Yalias (Admin Off), S. Buccleuch (I.T. Exec), I. Bell (Nat Sales Mgr), J. Skelton (Cust Serv Mgr), P. Archer (Chief Mgr)
Ultimate Holding Company: BNP PARIBAS S.A. (FRANCE)
Immediate Holding Company: RIO TINTO PLC
Registration no: 00719885 **VAT No.:** GB 338 2142 26
Date established: 1962 **Turnover:** £20m - £50m
No.of Employees: 251 - 500 **Product Groups:** 34, 46

Rit Capital Partners Associates Ltd
27 St James's Place, London, SW1A 1NR
Tel: 020-7493 8111 **Fax:** 020-7493 5765
E-mail: d_budge@ritcap.co.uk
Website: http://www.ritcap.co.uk
Directors: D. Budge (Dir)
Ultimate Holding Company: RIT CAPITAL PARTNERS PLC
Immediate Holding Company: RIT CAPITAL PARTNERS ASSOCIATES LIMITED
Registration no: 02384566 **Date established:** 1989
Turnover: £500,000 - £1m **No.of Employees:** 21 - 50 **Product Groups:** 82

Date of Accounts	Mar 12	Mar 11	Mar 10
Pre Tax Profit/Loss	63	469	15
Working Capital	4m	14m	14m
Fixed Assets	4m	4m	4m
Current Assets	9m	19m	19m
Current Liabilities	132	16	62

Rita Fancy Goods Ltd
4-6 Gravel Lane, London, E1 7AW
Tel: 020-7247 4616 **Fax:** 020-7377 6040
E-mail: ritaltd@btinternet.com
Website: http://www.ritadirect.com
Directors: T. Mirpuri (MD)
Immediate Holding Company: RITA FANCY GOODS LIMITED
Registration no: 00961593 **VAT No.:** GB 244 0126 07
Date established: 1969 **Turnover:** £250,000 - £500,000
No.of Employees: 1 - 10 **Product Groups:** 65

Date of Accounts	Mar 11	Mar 10	Mar 09
Working Capital	378	369	366
Fixed Assets	501	503	506
Current Assets	983	972	1m

Rite Fast Ltd
Units B & C 14 Lombard Road, London, SW19 3TZ
Tel: 020-8542 0909 **Fax:** 020-8542 0330
E-mail: davidleon@ritefast.co.uk
Website: http://www.ritefast.com
Directors: E. Presley (Fin), D. Leon (MD)
Immediate Holding Company: RITEFAST LTD
Registration no: 04712257 **VAT No.:** GB 344 8435 43
Date established: 2003 **Turnover:** Up to £250,000
No.of Employees: 11 - 20 **Product Groups:** 35, 66

Date of Accounts	Mar 11	Mar 10	Mar 09
Working Capital	215	160	274
Fixed Assets	224	377	389
Current Assets	639	485	745

The Ritz Hotel
150 Piccadilly, London, W1J 9BR
Tel: 020-7493 8181 **Fax:** 020- 74932687
E-mail: alove@theritzlondon.com
Website: http://www.theritzlondon.com
Directors: A. Love (Ch), S. Vauxhall (MD), A. Love (Dep Ch)
Managers: S. Boxall (Hotel Mgr)
Ultimate Holding Company: ELLERMAN INVESTMENTS LIMITED
Immediate Holding Company: RITZ HOTEL (LONDON) LIMITED(THE)
Registration no: 00064203 **Date established:** 1999
Turnover: £20m - £50m **No.of Employees:** 251 - 500 **Product Groups:** 69

Date of Accounts	Dec 10	Dec 09	Dec 08
Sales Turnover	31m	28m	30m
Pre Tax Profit/Loss	7m	5m	-3m
Working Capital	24m	18m	13m
Fixed Assets	143m	143m	143m
Current Assets	30m	24m	19m
Current Liabilities	2m	2m	3m

Ritz Recruitment Ltd
133 Middlesex Street, London, E1 7JF
Tel: 020-7929 5850 **Fax:** 020-7491 2972
E-mail: info@ritzrec.com
Website: http://www.ritzrec.com
Directors: C. Hush (MD)
Immediate Holding Company: RITZ RECRUITMENT LIMITED
Registration no: 01866661 **Date established:** 1984 **Turnover:** £5m - £10m
No.of Employees: 1 - 10 **Product Groups:** 80

Date of Accounts	Dec 11	Dec 10	Dec 09
Working Capital	288	314	-389
Fixed Assets	68	69	66
Current Assets	609	604	480

Rnid
19-23 Featherstone Street, London, EC1Y 8SL
Tel: 08088-080123 **Fax:** 020-7296 8199
E-mail: informationline@rnid.org.uk
Website: http://www.rnid.org.uk
Bank(s): Natwest
Directors: J. Low (Grp Chief Exec)
Ultimate Holding Company: THE ROYAL NATIONAL INSTITUTE FOR DEAF PEOPLE
Immediate Holding Company: R.N.I.D. ACTIVITIES LIMITED
Registration no: 00913439 **Date established:** 1967
Turnover: Up to £250,000 **No.of Employees:** 101 - 250
Product Groups: 80

Date of Accounts	Mar 12	Mar 11	Mar 10
Sales Turnover	241	79	286
Current Assets	252	21	244
Current Liabilities	150	20	5

C Roberson & Co. Ltd
1a Hercules Street, London, N7 6AT
Tel: 020-7272 0567 **Fax:** 020-7263 0212
E-mail: info@robco.co.uk
Website: http://www.robco.co.uk
Directors: N. Walt (MD), H. Walt (Fin)
Immediate Holding Company: C. ROBERSON & CO. LIMITED
Registration no: 01935264 **Date established:** 1985
Turnover: £250,000 - £500,000 **No.of Employees:** 1 - 10
Product Groups: 27, 32, 36, 48, 49, 64, 66

Date of Accounts	Mar 11	Mar 10	Mar 09
Working Capital	137	104	96
Fixed Assets	6	7	6
Current Assets	287	231	393

Robert W Baird Group Ltd
Mint House 77 Mansell Street, London, E1 8AF
Tel: 020-7488 1212 **Fax:** 020-7481 3911
Website: http://www.rwbaird.com
Directors: J. Fordhan (MD)
Ultimate Holding Company: BAIRD HOLDING COMPANY (USA)
Immediate Holding Company: ROBERT W. BAIRD GROUP LIMITED
Registration no: 00863502 **Date established:** 1965
Turnover: £20m - £50m **No.of Employees:** 101 - 250 **Product Groups:** 82

Date of Accounts	Dec 11	Dec 10	Dec 09
Sales Turnover	36m	35m	22m
Pre Tax Profit/Loss	9m	12m	3m
Working Capital	29m	26m	18m
Fixed Assets	3m	3m	3m
Current Assets	48m	42m	26m
Current Liabilities	15m	16m	8m

Patricia Roberts Knitting Ltd
60 Kinnerton Street, London, SW1X 8ES
Tel: 020-7235 4742 **Fax:** 020-7235 6517
E-mail: shop@patriciaroberts.co.uk
Directors: P. Roberts (MD)
Immediate Holding Company: P.R.K. LTD.
Registration no: 01567269 **VAT No.:** GB 340 9236 68
Date established: 1981 **Turnover:** Up to £250,000
No.of Employees: 1 - 10 **Product Groups:** 24, 43

Date of Accounts	Sep 11	Sep 10	Sep 09
Sales Turnover	N/A	1	58
Working Capital	33	-13	-16
Fixed Assets	76	75	75
Current Assets	63	71	69

Robinson Low Francis
Marylebone House 52-54 St John Street, London, EC1M 4HF
Tel: 020-7566 8400 **Fax:** 020-7250 0054
E-mail: london@rlf.co.uk
Website: http://www.rlf.co.uk
Directors: S. Barker (Ch)
Immediate Holding Company: ROBINSON LOW FRANCIS LLP
Registration no: OC309255 **VAT No.:** GB 235 5697 37
Date established: 2004 **Turnover:** £5m - £10m **No.of Employees:** 21 - 50
Product Groups: 80

Date of Accounts	May 11	May 10	May 09
Sales Turnover	10m	10m	12m
Pre Tax Profit/Loss	969	2m	2m
Working Capital	4m	4m	4m
Fixed Assets	473	534	537
Current Assets	5m	5m	5m
Current Liabilities	1m	684	664

Robson & Francis Rewinds Ltd
Unit 2 Hardess Street Industrial Estate Hardess Street, London, SE24 0HN
Tel: 020-7733 2353
E-mail: info@robsonandfrancisrewinds.co.uk
Website: http://www.robsonandfrancisrewinds.co.uk
Directors: M. Robson (MD)
Immediate Holding Company: ROBSON & FRANCIS REWINDS LIMITED
Registration no: 03376788 **VAT No.:** GB 696 8462 66
Date established: 1997 **Turnover:** £250,000 - £500,000
No.of Employees: 1 - 10 **Product Groups:** 37, 48

Date of Accounts	May 11	May 10	May 09
Working Capital	23	20	19
Fixed Assets	2	3	4
Current Assets	96	98	99

Rocket Badge
1 Torriano Mews, London, NW5 2RZ
Tel: 0800-177 7902 **Fax:** 020-7424 4041
E-mail: dlyons@lyonsgroup.co.uk
Website: http://www.rocketbadge.co.uk
Directors: D. Lyons (Prop)
Immediate Holding Company: ROCKET BADGE COMPANY LIMITED
Registration no: 02699509 **Date established:** 1992
Turnover: £500,000 - £1m **No.of Employees:** 21 - 50
Product Groups: 35, 49

E R A Rodman Bros Ltd
20 Lower Park Road, London, N11 1QD
Tel: 020-8361 8553 **Fax:** 020-8245 6389
E-mail: erarodmanbros@aol.com
Website: http://www.erarodmanbros.co.uk
Directors: K. Rodman (MD)
Immediate Holding Company: E.R.A. RODMAN BROS. LIMITED
Registration no: 01198838 **Date established:** 1975
Turnover: Up to £250,000 **No.of Employees:** 1 - 10 **Product Groups:** 46, 48

Date of Accounts	Aug 11	Aug 10	Aug 09
Working Capital	122	88	71
Fixed Assets	33	37	46
Current Assets	228	192	137

Rolex
19 St James's Square, London, SW1Y 4JE
Tel: 020-7024 7300 **Fax:** 020-7024 7317
E-mail: graham.richards@rolex.com
Website: http://www.rolex.com
Directors: G. Richards (MD)
Ultimate Holding Company: ROLEX HOLDING (SWITZERLAND)
Immediate Holding Company: ROLEX WATCH COMPANY,LIMITED(THE)
Registration no: 00142138 **Date established:** 2015
Turnover: £75m - £125m **No.of Employees:** 101 - 250
Product Groups: 49

Date of Accounts	Dec 11	Dec 10	Dec 09
Sales Turnover	133m	109m	98m
Pre Tax Profit/Loss	5m	2m	6m
Working Capital	37m	32m	40m
Fixed Assets	36m	37m	28m
Current Assets	66m	47m	53m
Current Liabilities	5m	6m	4m

Rolls-Royce plc
65 Buckingham Gate, London, SW1E 6AT
Tel: 020-7222 9020 **Fax:** 020-7227 9170
E-mail: info@nelincs.gov.uk
Website: http://www.rolls-royce.com
Bank(s): National Westminster Bank Plc
Directors: A. Shilston (Fin), J. Rishton (Grp Chief Exec), M. Morris (Fin)
Ultimate Holding Company: ROLLS-ROYCE HOLDINGS PLC
Immediate Holding Company: ROLLS-ROYCE PLC
Registration no: 01003142 **Date established:** 1971
Turnover: Over £1,000m **No.of Employees:** 1501 & over
Product Groups: 18, 22, 23, 24, 25, 26, 27, 28, 29, 30, 31, 32, 33, 34, 35, 36, 37, 38, 39, 40, 42, 44, 45, 46, 48, 49, 52, 54, 62, 66, 67, 68, 71, 75, 82, 84, 85, 86, 89

Date of Accounts	Dec 11	Dec 10	Dec 09
Sales Turnover	11124m	11085m	10414m
Pre Tax Profit/Loss	1106m	703m	2957m
Working Capital	1558m	2484m	3144m
Fixed Assets	8108m	6410m	6048m
Current Assets	8510m	9823m	9443m
Current Liabilities	5864m	6189m	5430m

Roneford Catering Equipment
192 Philip Lane, London, N15 4HH
Tel: 020-8801 8729 **Fax:** 020-8801 5516
E-mail: sales@ronefordcatering.co.uk
Website: http://www.ronefordcatering.co.uk
Directors: K. Iliadis (Prop)
Turnover: £250,000 - £500,000 **No.of Employees:** 1 - 10
Product Groups: 33, 36, 40, 49, 62, 65, 67, 83

Rooff Ltd
Rooff House Cooks Road, London, E15 2PN
Tel: 020-8534 9797 **Fax:** 020-8534 0789
E-mail: enquiries@rooff.co.uk
Website: http://www.rooff.co.uk
Bank(s): National Westminster
Directors: A. Horn (Dir), J. Pearson (Fin), M. Horn (MD)
Managers: J. Cole (Accounts), R. Cross (I.T. Exec)
Immediate Holding Company: ROOFF HOLDINGS LIMITED
Registration no: 03677170 **VAT No.:** GB 248 5014 66
Date established: 1998 **Turnover:** £20m - £50m
No.of Employees: 51 - 100 **Product Groups:** 52

Rooks Rider
19-21 Clerkenwell Close, London, EC1R 0RR
Tel: 020-7689 7000 **Fax:** 020-7689 7001
E-mail: lawyers@rooksrider.co.uk
Website: http://www.rooksrider.co.uk
Bank(s): HSBC
Directors: C. Cooke (Snr Part)
Managers: L. Wall (Fin Mgr), D. Bailey (Tech Serv Mgr), D. Clements (Personnel)
Immediate Holding Company: ROOKS RIDER LEGAL LLP
Registration no: OC367630 **Date established:** 2011
No.of Employees: 21 - 50 **Product Groups:** 80

Root 6 Ltd
4 Wardour Mews, London, W1F 8AJ
Tel: 020-7437 6052 **Fax:** 08700-940783
Website: http://www.root6.com
Directors: J. Harris (MD), P. Sherrell (MD)
Immediate Holding Company: ROOT 6 LIMITED
Registration no: 03433253 **Date established:** 1997
No.of Employees: 21 - 50 **Product Groups:** 26, 37, 44

Date of Accounts	Oct 11	Oct 10	Oct 09
Working Capital	397	345	403
Fixed Assets	188	179	105
Current Assets	2m	2m	1m

Rope & Marine Services Ltd
31 Yorkshire Road, London, E14 7LR
Tel: 020-7790 2261 **Fax:** 020-7790 2750
E-mail: jean@ropemar.co.uk
Website: http://www.ropemar.co.uk

Bank(s): Lloyds
Directors: J. Edwards (Co Sec)
Ultimate Holding Company: ROPE & MARINE SERVICES LIMITED
Immediate Holding Company: ROPE & MARINE LIMITED
Registration no: 00456152 **VAT No.:** GB 248 6813 31
Date established: 1948 **Turnover:** £2m - £5m **No.of Employees:** 21 - 50
Product Groups: 45, 48

Date of Accounts	Dec 11	Dec 10	Dec 09
Working Capital	200	200	761
Fixed Assets	N/A	N/A	61
Current Assets	200	200	1m

Rosenstiels
33-35 Markham Street, London, SW3 3NR
Tel: 020-7352 3551 **Fax:** 020-7351 5300
E-mail: martin.vernon@felixr.com
Website: http://www.felixr.com
Directors: M. Vernon (Fin)
Immediate Holding Company: 20/21 FINE ART LIMITED
Registration no: 00581275 **VAT No.:** GB 215 9300 84
Date established: 1989 **Turnover:** £2m - £5m **No.of Employees:** 11 - 20
Product Groups: 49, 64

Roshe Power Ltd
Unit F13 Hastingwood Trading Estate 35 Harbet Road, London, N18 3HU
Tel: 020-8884 4980 **Fax:** 020-8884 4970
E-mail: sales@roshepower.co.uk
Website: http://www.roshepower.co.uk
Directors: S. Akdogan (MD), D. Akdogan (Fin)
Managers: S. Adams (I.T. Exec)
Immediate Holding Company: ROSHE POWER LIMITED
Registration no: 02617290 **VAT No.:** GB 629 9712 95
Date established: 1991 **Turnover:** £500,000 - £1m
No.of Employees: 11 - 20 **Product Groups:** 37

Date of Accounts	Dec 10	Dec 09	Dec 08
Working Capital	1m	2m	1m
Fixed Assets	28	33	39
Current Assets	2m	2m	2m

Roth Associates
83-87 Crawford Street, London, W1H 2HB
Tel: 020-7499 5051 **Fax:** 020-7499 5055
E-mail: info@rothassociates.co.uk
Website: http://www.rothassociates.co.uk
Directors: S. Roth (Prop)
Immediate Holding Company: SPOTLIGHT TRAVEL LTD
Registration no: 02488166 **Date established:** 2010
Turnover: £500,000 - £1m **No.of Employees:** 11 - 20 **Product Groups:** 80

Rotoplas Ltd
Stormont Road Battersea, London, SW11 5EN
Tel: 020-7228 6633 **Fax:** 020-7228 4864
E-mail: mail@rotoplas.net
Website: http://www.rotoplas.net
Bank(s): Barclays
Directors: M. Robson (MD)
Immediate Holding Company: ROTOPLAS LIMITED
Registration no: 00632962 **VAT No.:** GB 235 8602 59
Date established: 1959 **Turnover:** £1m - £2m **No.of Employees:** 11 - 20
Product Groups: 48

Date of Accounts	Jul 12	Jul 11	Jul 10
Working Capital	330	339	267
Fixed Assets	193	209	211
Current Assets	386	428	392

Rough Guides
80 Strand, London, WC2R 0RL
Tel: 020-7010 3000 **Fax:** 020-7010 6060
E-mail: mail@roughguides.com
Website: http://www.roughguides.com
Managers: L. Vipond
Ultimate Holding Company: PEARSON PLC
Immediate Holding Company: ROUGH GUIDES LIMITED(THE)
Registration no: 01969090 **Date established:** 1985 **Turnover:** £5m - £10m
No.of Employees: 251 - 500 **Product Groups:** 28

Date of Accounts	Dec 11	Dec 10	Dec 09
Sales Turnover	7m	8m	8m
Pre Tax Profit/Loss	-1m	-999	-523
Working Capital	-11m	-10m	-9m
Current Assets	950	772	2m
Current Liabilities	1m	2m	N/A

Rough Trade Management
66 Golborne Road, London, W10 5PS
Tel: 020-8875 5194 **Fax:** 020-8968 6715
E-mail: info@roughtraderecords.com
Website: http://www.roughtraderecords.com
Directors: J. Lee (Dir), E. Dick (Co Sec)
Registration no: 06093194 **No.of Employees:** 11 - 20 **Product Groups:** 65

Royal Aeronautical Society
4 Hamilton Place, London, W1J 7BQ
Tel: 020-7670 4300 **Fax:** 020-7670 4309
E-mail: sales@raes.org.uk
Website: http://www.aerosociety.com
Directors: S. Luxmoore (Grp Chief Exec)
Managers: F. Smith (Mktg Serv Mgr), J. Byrne (Sales Admin), T. Home (Fin Mgr)
Immediate Holding Company: LAUNCHPAD FOR LEARNING LIMITED
Registration no: 06589616 **Date established:** 2008
No.of Employees: 21 - 50 **Product Groups:** 69, 81

Royal Bank Of Canada
Thames Court 1 Queenhithe, London, EC4V 3RL
Tel: 020-7653 4000 **Fax:** 020-7329 6144
E-mail: andrew.foster@royalbank.com
Website: http://www.rbc.com
Bank(s): National Westminster
Directors: A. Foster (Dep Ch), J. Wright (Co Sec)
Ultimate Holding Company: ROYAL BANK OF CANADA (CANADA)
Immediate Holding Company: RBC EUROPE LIMITED
Registration no: 00995939 **Date established:** 1970
No.of Employees: 1001 - 1500 **Product Groups:** 82

Date of Accounts	Oct 11	Oct 10	Oct 09
Pre Tax Profit/Loss	-133m	35m	479m
Fixed Assets	16813m	1270m	621m
Current Assets	17276m	40110m	31781m
Current Liabilities	32794m	39991m	31037m

Royal Horticultural Halls & Conference Centre
80 Vincent Square, London, SW1P 2PE
Tel: 08453-704606 **Fax:** 020-7834 2072
E-mail: horthalls@rhs.org.uk
Website: http://www.horticultural-halls.co.uk
Directors: E. Sells (Fin)
Managers: O. Oxlade
Ultimate Holding Company: ROYAL HORTICULTURAL SOCIETY , THE
Immediate Holding Company: HORTICULTURAL HALLS LIMITED
Registration no: 02074555 **VAT No.:** GB 461 5327 57
Date established: 1986 **Turnover:** £500,000 - £1m
No.of Employees: 11 - 20 **Product Groups:** 69, 83

Date of Accounts	Jan 11	Jan 09	Jan 08
Sales Turnover	N/A	914	3m
Pre Tax Profit/Loss	N/A	101	26
Working Capital	10	10	-294
Fixed Assets	N/A	N/A	253
Current Assets	10	10	1m
Current Liabilities	N/A	N/A	1m

Royal Institute of British Architects
66 Portland Place, London, W1B 1AD
Tel: 020-7580 5533 **Fax:** 020-7255 1541
E-mail: info@inst.riba.org
Website: http://www.architecture.com
Directors: R. Hastilow (Grp Chief Exec)
Ultimate Holding Company: UNITED BUSINESS MEDIA LIMITED (JERSEY)
Immediate Holding Company: OLD JOURNALS LIMITED
Registration no: FP012292 **VAT No.:** GB 232 3518 91
Date established: 1992 **Turnover:** £5m - £10m **No.of Employees:** 1 - 10
Product Groups: 84

Royal Institution Of Naval Architects
10 Upper Belgrave Street, London, SW1X 8BQ
Tel: 020-7235 4622 **Fax:** 020-7259 5912
E-mail: hq@rina.org.uk
Website: http://www.rina.org.uk
Directors: T. Blakeley (Grp Chief Exec)
Managers: L. Whelan, G. Mitchell
Ultimate Holding Company: THE ROYAL INSTITUTION OF NAVAL ARCHITECTS
Immediate Holding Company: RINA LIMITED
Registration no: 02307296 **Date established:** 1988 **Turnover:** £1m - £2m
No.of Employees: 21 - 50 **Product Groups:** 87

Royal Selangor Ltd
21 Eastbury Road, London, E6 6LP
Tel: 020-7474 5511 **Fax:** 020-7474 5522
E-mail: marketing@royalselangor.co.uk
Website: http://www.royalselangor.com
Directors: P. Coleman (MD)
Immediate Holding Company: ROYAL SELANGOR PEWTER (U K) LIMITED
Registration no: 00417847 **Date established:** 1946 **Turnover:** £2m - £5m
No.of Employees: 1 - 10 **Product Groups:** 49

Date of Accounts	Jun 11	Jun 10	Jun 09
Working Capital	-105	-69	-26
Fixed Assets	57	41	71
Current Assets	906	786	847

Royal Society Of Chemistry
Burlington House Piccadilly, London, W1J 0BA
Tel: 020-7437 8656 **Fax:** 020-7437 8883
E-mail: beaumontw@rsc.org
Website: http://www.rsc.org
Directors: W. Beaumont (Fin)
Ultimate Holding Company: ROYAL SOCIETY OF CHEMISTRY
Immediate Holding Company: CHEMISTRY LIMITED
Registration no: FP051709 **Date established:** 1999 **Turnover:** £1m - £2m
No.of Employees: 21 - 50 **Product Groups:** 28

Date of Accounts	Dec 11	Dec 10	Dec 09
Sales Turnover	N/A	N/A	5
Pre Tax Profit/Loss	N/A	-3	N/A
Working Capital	-1	-1	2
Current Assets	N/A	N/A	114
Current Liabilities	N/A	N/A	5

The Royal Society For Public Health
Market Towers Nine Elms Lane, London, SW8 5NQ
Tel: 020-3177 1600 **Fax:** 020-3177 1601
E-mail: info@rsph.org.uk
Website: http://www.rsph.org.uk
Bank(s): Lloyds
Directors: H. Lawson (MD), N. Carter (Grp Chief Exec), E. Jason (Pers), S. Royston (Grp Chief Exec)
Managers: A. Jason (Mgr), A. Luke (I.T. Exec), A. Walton (Personnel), K. Naameh (Mktg Serv Mgr)
Immediate Holding Company: ROYAL SOCIETY FOR THE PROMOTION OF HEALTH(THE)
Registration no: 00027293 **VAT No.:** GB 240 6432 10
Date established: 1988 **Turnover:** £1m - £2m **No.of Employees:** 21 - 50
Product Groups: 87

Date of Accounts	Dec 07	Dec 06	Dec 05
Sales Turnover	1390	1376	1188
Pre Tax Profit/Loss	911	92	92
Working Capital	156	113	70
Fixed Assets	3169	2302	2155
Current Assets	433	311	236
Current Liabilities	277	198	165
ROCE% (Return on Capital Employed)	27.4	3.8	4.1
ROT% (Return on Turnover)	65.5	6.7	7.7

Rsi
69 Manor Park Road, London, NW10 4JX
Tel: 020-8965 2510 **Fax:** 020-8963 0662
E-mail: sales@ariane-int.com
Website: http://www.rsi-cycles.com
Directors: A. Wallace (Co Sec), P. Merody (Dir)
Immediate Holding Company: EVIAN (HOLDINGS) LIMITED
Registration no: 00614485 **Date established:** 1958 **Turnover:** £1m - £2m
No.of Employees: 1 - 10 **Product Groups:** 68

RTD Systems Limited (t/a Octanorm UK)
10 Lyon Road South Wimbledon, London, SW19 2RL
Tel: 020-8545 2945 **Fax:** 020-8545 2955
E-mail: solutions@rtdsystems.co.uk
Website: http://www.rtdisplay.co.uk
Bank(s): HSBC

Directors: R. Armitage (MD)
Managers: S. Pritchard (Mktg Serv Mgr), L. White (Sales Admin), E. White (Sales Prom Mgr), R. Parkinson (Accounts)
Registration no: 00938000 **VAT No.:** GB 239 3372 51
Date established: 1968 **Turnover:** £2m - £5m **No.of Employees:** 21 - 50
Product Groups: 26

Rugby Estates plc
4 Farm Street, London, W1J 5RD
Tel: 020-7016 0050 **Fax:** 020-7016 0080
E-mail: reception@rugbyestates.plc.uk
Website: http://www.rugbyestates.plc.uk
Directors: D. Tye (Ch)
Ultimate Holding Company: RUGBY ESTATES PLC.
Immediate Holding Company: RUGBY ESTATES PLC.
Registration no: 02548935 **Date established:** 1990
Turnover: £10m - £20m **No.of Employees:** 11 - 20 **Product Groups:** 80

Date of Accounts	Jan 11	Jan 10	Jan 09
Sales Turnover	23m	14m	10m
Pre Tax Profit/Loss	2m	184	-16m
Working Capital	20m	43m	55m
Fixed Assets	3m	6m	5m
Current Assets	24m	45m	57m
Current Liabilities	4m	3m	3m

Ruhi Enterprises Ltd
Unit 13 Iron Bridge Close Great Central Way, London, NW10 0UF
Tel: 020-8451 7676 **Fax:** 020-8459 7555
E-mail: malika.ruhi@btinternet.com
Directors: H. Popat (Dir), S. Aardoran (Fin)
Immediate Holding Company: RUHI ENTERPRISES LIMITED
Registration no: 02173471 **Date established:** 1987
Turnover: Up to £250,000 **No.of Employees:** 1 - 10 **Product Groups:** 61

Date of Accounts	Feb 08	Feb 11	Feb 10
Working Capital	593	135	414
Fixed Assets	15	7	8
Current Assets	1m	711	872

Rupert Magnus Trading Co. Ltd
160 Dukes Road, London, W3 0SL
Tel: 020-8993 2231 **Fax:** 020-8993 4445
E-mail: bernardcrist@ukonline.co.uk
Website: http://www.rupertmagnus.co.uk
Directors: E. Magnus (Sales), R. Newman (Dir)
Ultimate Holding Company: PASTA REALE LIMITED
Immediate Holding Company: MAGNUS CREATIVE LIMITED
Registration no: 01106465 **Date established:** 1973
No.of Employees: 1 - 10 **Product Groups:** 27

Date of Accounts	Apr 11	Apr 10	Apr 09
Working Capital	-10	-8	4
Fixed Assets	1m	1m	1m
Current Assets	6	7	20

Rush Couriers
67 Wells Street, London, W1T 3PZ
Tel: 020-7629 2929 **Fax:** 020-7323 2376
E-mail: info@rushcouriers.co.uk
Website: http://www.rushcouriers.co.uk
Managers: L. Gamble (Mgr)
Ultimate Holding Company: FACTORFAST LIMITED
Immediate Holding Company: RUSH COURIER SERVICES LIMITED
Registration no: 02619179 **Date established:** 1991
No.of Employees: 1 - 10 **Product Groups:** 79

Date of Accounts	Jun 11	Jun 10	Jun 09
Working Capital	195	179	-276
Fixed Assets	729	667	2m
Current Assets	1m	797	1m

Russell & Chapple Ltd
68 Drury Lane, London, WC2B 5SP
Tel: 020-7836 7521 **Fax:** 020-7497 0554
E-mail: info@randc.net
Website: http://www.randc.net
Directors: N. Walt (MD)
Immediate Holding Company: RUSSELL & CHAPPLE LIMITED
Registration no: 03873005 **VAT No.:** GB 232 9175 65
Date established: 1999 **Turnover:** £1m - £2m **No.of Employees:** 1 - 10
Product Groups: 23, 24, 64

Date of Accounts	Mar 11	Mar 10	Mar 09
Pre Tax Profit/Loss	N/A	-97	N/A
Working Capital	N/A	N/A	97
Current Assets	N/A	N/A	97

S E A UK Ltd
Unit 1-4 Grange Mews The Grangeway, London, N21 2HG
Tel: 020-8360 8022 **Fax:** 020-8364 2516
E-mail: samlarkins@supanet.com
Website: http://www.seaukltd.co.uk
Managers: S. Larkins (Mgr)
Immediate Holding Company: S.E.A. (U.K.) LIMITED
Registration no: 02689035 **Date established:** 1992
Turnover: Up to £250,000 **No.of Employees:** 1 - 10 **Product Groups:** 36, 40

Date of Accounts	Mar 12	Mar 11	Mar 10
Working Capital	201	251	244
Fixed Assets	165	1	1
Current Assets	427	406	418

S H & E Ltd
Sardinia House 51-52 Lincoln's Inn Fields, London, WC2A 3LZ
Tel: 020-7242 9333 **Fax:** 020-7242 9334
E-mail: london@sh-e.com
Website: http://www.sh-e.com
Directors: A. Stewart (Co Sec), A. Carlisle (MD)
Ultimate Holding Company: SIMAT HELLIESEN & EICHNER INC (USA)
Immediate Holding Company: ICF SH&E LIMITED
Registration no: 03131624 **VAT No.:** GB 644 6681 14
Date established: 1995 **Turnover:** £2m - £5m **No.of Employees:** 11 - 20
Product Groups: 84

Date of Accounts	Dec 11	Dec 10	Dec 09
Sales Turnover	2m	N/A	N/A
Pre Tax Profit/Loss	218	N/A	N/A
Working Capital	1m	1m	1m
Fixed Assets	519	189	192
Current Assets	2m	2m	2m
Current Liabilities	45	N/A	N/A

S K Metal Works Ltd
16 Dartmouth Park Hill, London, NW5 1HL
Tel: 020-7263 1575 **Fax:** 020-7263 1575
Directors: S. Brown (Fin)
Immediate Holding Company: KITCHEN TRADE WAREHOUSE LIMITED
Registration no: 02260598 **Date established:** 1983
Turnover: Up to £250,000 **No.of Employees:** 1 - 10 **Product Groups:** 26, 35

Date of Accounts	Sep 10	Sep 09	Sep 08
Working Capital	-56	-53	-53
Fixed Assets	1	1	N/A
Current Assets	3	11	8

S M M T Ltd
71 Great Peter Street, London, SW1P 2BN
Tel: 020-7235 7000 **Fax:** 020-7235 7112
E-mail: sales@smmt.co.uk
Website: http://www.smmt.co.uk
Bank(s): National Westminster Bank Plc
Directors: N. Stein (Ch), P. Christian (Fin)
Managers: V. Phul (Tech Serv Mgr), K. Milbourn (Personnel)
Immediate Holding Company: SOCIETY OF MOTOR MANUFACTURERS AND TRADERS LIMITED(THE)
Registration no: 00074359 **Date established:** 2002
Turnover: £10m - £20m **No.of Employees:** 51 - 100 **Product Groups:** 72, 87

Date of Accounts	Dec 11	Dec 10	Dec 09
Sales Turnover	15m	18m	18m
Pre Tax Profit/Loss	33m	-556	1m
Working Capital	8m	-7m	815
Fixed Assets	20m	13m	5m
Current Assets	15m	13m	5m
Current Liabilities	5m	15m	3m

S O S Catering Equipment Engineering Ltd
204-208 Billet Road, London, E17 5DX
Tel: 020-8531 8543 **Fax:** 020-8531 6587
E-mail: info@soscateringequipment.co.uk
Website: http://www.soscateringequipment.co.uk
Directors: M. Papanicola (Fin)
Immediate Holding Company: S.O.S. CATERING EQUIPMENT AND ENGINEERING LIMITED
Registration no: 04129990 **Date established:** 2000
No.of Employees: 1 - 10 **Product Groups:** 20, 40, 41

Date of Accounts	Dec 11	Dec 10	Dec 09
Sales Turnover	N/A	N/A	832
Pre Tax Profit/Loss	N/A	N/A	81
Working Capital	129	163	179
Fixed Assets	22	33	47
Current Assets	226	263	287
Current Liabilities	N/A	N/A	43

S & P Ltd
30 Kingsway, London, WC2B 6EX
Tel: 020-7831 8877 **Fax:** 020-7831 4477
E-mail: answers@s-parchitects.com
Website: http://www.s-parchitects.com
Bank(s): National Westminster
Managers: K. Ashton
Immediate Holding Company: S & P LIMITED
Registration no: 02599394 **Date established:** 1991 **Turnover:** £5m - £10m
No.of Employees: 21 - 50 **Product Groups:** 84

Date of Accounts	Sep 11	Sep 10	Sep 09
Sales Turnover	N/A	5m	6m
Pre Tax Profit/Loss	N/A	257	309
Working Capital	88	241	37
Fixed Assets	197	207	310
Current Assets	2m	2m	3m
Current Liabilities	N/A	756	1m

S T A Travel
Priory House 6 Wrights Lane, London, W8 6TA
Tel: 020-7361 6202 **Fax:** 020-7368 0075
E-mail: info@statravel.co.uk
Website: http://www.statravel.co.uk
Directors: P. Maine (Fin), P. Liney (Dir)
Ultimate Holding Company: DIETHELM KELLER HOLDING LTD (SWITZERLAND)
Immediate Holding Company: STA TRAVEL LIMITED
Registration no: 01263330 **Date established:** 1976
Turnover: £20m - £50m **No.of Employees:** 251 - 500 **Product Groups:** 69

Date of Accounts	Dec 11	Dec 10	Dec 09
Sales Turnover	23m	24m	24m
Pre Tax Profit/Loss	276	2m	3m
Working Capital	9m	8m	9m
Fixed Assets	2m	2m	2m
Current Assets	20m	20m	23m
Current Liabilities	2m	2m	4m

S T T International Ltd
724 Holloway Road, London, N19 3JD
Tel: 020-7263 0456 **Fax:** 020-7263 1044
E-mail: stt@stt-int.com
Website: http://www.stt-int.com
Directors: M. Eratalar (Fin), S. Taylan (Dir)
Immediate Holding Company: S.T.T. INTERNATIONAL LIMITED
Registration no: 01772732 **VAT No.:** GB 396 5126 24
Date established: 1983 **Turnover:** £2m - £5m **No.of Employees:** 1 - 10
Product Groups: 37

Date of Accounts	Mar 12	Mar 11	Mar 10
Sales Turnover	N/A	2m	2m
Pre Tax Profit/Loss	N/A	57	47
Working Capital	105	156	151
Fixed Assets	14	11	15
Current Assets	895	783	774
Current Liabilities	N/A	31	25

Sabri Technologies
145-157 St John Street, London, EC1V 4PY
Tel: 020-7993 5333 **Fax:** 020-7993 5287
E-mail: sabahat.sabri@sabritech.com
Website: http://www.sabritech.com
Managers: S. Sabri (Mktg Serv Mgr), S. Yavari (Mktg Serv Mgr)
Immediate Holding Company: CODESOLO TECHNOLOGIES LTD
Registration no: 07351997 **Date established:** 2010 **Turnover:** £1m - £2m
No.of Employees: 21 - 50 **Product Groups:** 38, 44

Safe Health Surgical
372a Grove Green Road, London, E11 4AP
Tel: 07972-735884
E-mail: saqib.rauf@safehealthsurgical.com
Website: http://www.safehealthsurgical.com
Directors: S. Rauf (Prop)
Immediate Holding Company: IMAAN GLOBAL LIMITED
Date established: 2011 **Turnover:** Up to £250,000
No.of Employees: 1 - 10 **Product Groups:** 38, 67

Safer Staff Training & Recruitment Ltd
The American Church Building 79a Tottenham Court Road, London, W1T 4TD
Tel: 020-7637 7959 **Fax:** 01676- 529106
E-mail: training@sstar.co.uk
Website: http://www.sstar.co.uk
Directors: J. Walker (Dir), J. Walker (Fin), V. Walker (MD), V. Walker (Dir)
Immediate Holding Company: SAFER STAFF TRAINING & RECRUITMENT LIMITED
Registration no: 03539784 **Date established:** 1998
Turnover: Up to £250,000 **No.of Employees:** 21 - 50 **Product Groups:** 86

Date of Accounts	Sep 10	Sep 09	Sep 08
Sales Turnover	104	133	130
Pre Tax Profit/Loss	13	29	16
Working Capital	31	37	19
Fixed Assets	5	1	N/A
Current Assets	51	55	38
Current Liabilities	9	6	3

Safety First Aid Group
Unit 15-17 Garrick Industrial Centre Irving Way, London, NW9 6AQ
Tel: 020-8366 0042 **Fax:** 0800-281655
E-mail: sales@sfag.co.uk
Website: http://www.safetyfirstaid.co.uk
Bank(s): National Westminster
Managers: E. Fox (Mktg Serv Mgr)
Immediate Holding Company: SAFETY FIRST AID GROUP LIMITED
Registration no: 03999398 **Date established:** 1959 **Turnover:** £5m - £10m
No.of Employees: 51 - 100 **Product Groups:** 38, 46, 86

Date of Accounts	Dec 10	Dec 09	Mar 09
Sales Turnover	6m	6m	7m
Pre Tax Profit/Loss	264	335	406
Working Capital	338	248	98
Fixed Assets	379	487	997
Current Assets	1m	1m	1m
Current Liabilities	337	309	275

Sainsbury's
33 Holborn, London, EC1N 2HT
Tel: 020-7695 6000 **Fax:** 020-7695 7610
E-mail: imelda.walsh@sainsburys.co.uk
Website: http://www.sainsbury.co.uk
Directors: R. Fraser (Tech Serv), J. Rogers (Fin), D. Shapland (Fin), I. Walsh (Dir)
Managers: H. Webb
Ultimate Holding Company: J SAINSBURY PLC
Immediate Holding Company: SAINSBURY'S SUPERMARKETS LTD
Registration no: 03261722 **VAT No.:** GB 660 4548 36
Date established: 1996 **Turnover:** Over £1,000m
No.of Employees: 1501 & over **Product Groups:** 61

Date of Accounts	Mar 09	Mar 10	Mar 11
Sales Turnover	18910m	19962m	21100m
Pre Tax Profit/Loss	548m	562m	775m
Working Capital	-2015m	-2244m	-2393m
Fixed Assets	6230m	6787m	7186m
Current Assets	1316m	1140m	1560m
Current Liabilities	986m	770m	852m

St George International Ltd
Kenilworth House 79-80 Margaret Street, London, W1W 8TA
Tel: 020-7299 1700 **Fax:** 020-7299 1711
E-mail: info@stgeorges.co.uk
Website: http://www.stgeorges.co.uk
Directors: M. Wagner (Dir)
Immediate Holding Company: MCLURE JAMES LLP
Registration no: 00800021 **VAT No.:** GB 233 3099 79
Date established: 2004 **Turnover:** £250,000 - £500,000
No.of Employees: 11 - 20 **Product Groups:** 86

Date of Accounts	Nov 11	Nov 10	Nov 09
Sales Turnover	N/A	221	90
Pre Tax Profit/Loss	N/A	191	60
Working Capital	30	15	8
Fixed Assets	3	4	4
Current Assets	53	26	19
Current Liabilities	N/A	8	9

St Ives Holdings Ltd
St Ives House Lavington Street, London, SE1 0NX
Tel: 020-7928 8844 **Fax:** 020-7928 9838
E-mail: philip.harris@st-ives.com
Website: http://www.st-ives.co.uk
Directors: P. Harris (MD), S. Hart (MD)
Ultimate Holding Company: 01552113
Immediate Holding Company: ST IVES HOLDINGS LIMITED
Registration no: 00190460 **VAT No.:** GB 583 9953 75
Date established: 1923 **Turnover:** £250m - £500m
No.of Employees: 1 - 10 **Product Groups:** 27, 28

Sal UK Ltd
Unit 11-12 Blackheath Business Estate Blackheath Hill, London, SE10 8BA
Tel: 020-8694 1294 **Fax:** 020-8691 1927
E-mail: saluk@dial.pipex.com
Directors: E. Lolavar (MD), S. Lolavar (Fin)
Immediate Holding Company: S.A.L. (U.K.) LIMITED
Registration no: 01950057 **VAT No.:** GB 324 0869 64
Date established: 1985 **Turnover:** £1m - £2m **No.of Employees:** 1 - 10
Product Groups: 64

Date of Accounts	May 11	May 10	May 09
Working Capital	-33	-41	-45
Fixed Assets	115	116	119
Current Assets	558	643	321

Sallmanns UK Ltd (International Property Consultants)
3-4 John Princes Street, London, W1G 0JL
Tel: 020-7409 2222 **Fax:** 020-7895 1375
E-mail: info@sallmanns.co.uk
Website: http://www.sallmanns.co.uk
Directors: J. Beattie (Prop)
Immediate Holding Company: SALLMANNS (UK) LIMITED
Registration no: 02600845 **VAT No.:** GB 562 9201 45
Date established: 1991 **Turnover:** Up to £250,000
No.of Employees: 1 - 10 **Product Groups:** 80

Date of Accounts	Jun 11	Jun 10	Jun 09
Working Capital	9	15	12
Fixed Assets	10	13	8
Current Assets	27	34	28

Salt & Son Ltd
639 Garratt Lane, London, SW18 4SX
Tel: 020-8946 9950 **Fax:** 020-8947 9406
Website: http://www.salts.co.uk
Managers: K. Fox (Mgr)
Ultimate Holding Company: SALTS HEALTHCARE LIMITED
Immediate Holding Company: SALT & SON LIMITED
Registration no: 01228010 **Date established:** 1975
No.of Employees: 1 - 10 **Product Groups:** 32, 38, 61, 87

Samac Steel Supplies plc
11-21 Paul Street, London, EC2A 4JU
Tel: 020-7614 5651 **Fax:** 020-8900 2373
E-mail: samac@stemcor.com
Website: http://www.samac.com
Directors: D. Paul (Fin)
Managers: M. Broom (Comptroller), S. Glaysher, J. Blake (Personnel), B. Patterson, H. Wall (Purch Mgr)
Ultimate Holding Company: STEMCOR HOLDINGS LIMITED
Immediate Holding Company: SAMAC STEEL SUPPLIES PLC
Registration no: 02278492 **VAT No.:** GB 581 8081 26
Date established: 1988 **Turnover:** £75m - £125m
No.of Employees: 11 - 20 **Product Groups:** 66

Date of Accounts	Dec 11	Dec 10	Dec 09
Sales Turnover	102m	74m	56m
Pre Tax Profit/Loss	2m	2m	808
Working Capital	4m	3m	1m
Fixed Assets	18	60	72
Current Assets	57m	48m	35m
Current Liabilities	2m	2m	1m

M A Samad
105 Eade Road, London, N4 1TJ
Tel: 020-8802 2929 **Fax:** 020-8802 2777
E-mail: office@samad.biz
Directors: M. Samad (Prop)
Immediate Holding Company: AHWAZIAN LIMITED
Registration no: 02677306 **Date established:** 1992
Turnover: £250,000 - £500,000 **No.of Employees:** 1 - 10
Product Groups: 63

Date of Accounts	Jun 11	Jun 10	Jun 09
Sales Turnover	304	318	459
Pre Tax Profit/Loss	2	2	11
Working Capital	316	332	344
Fixed Assets	47	49	51
Current Assets	671	720	806
Current Liabilities	6	18	27

Same Day Company Services
9 Perseverance Works Kingsland Road, London, E2 8DD
Tel: 020-7613 8161 **Fax:** 020-7613 8162
E-mail: info@samedaycompany.co.uk
Website: http://www.samedaycompany.co.uk
Directors: J. Warne (Fin)
Immediate Holding Company: SAME-DAY COMPANY SERVICES LIMITED
Registration no: 01347553 **VAT No.:** GB 245 2010 10
Date established: 1978 **Turnover:** Up to £250,000
No.of Employees: 1 - 10 **Product Groups:** 80, 81, 82

Date of Accounts	Mar 11	Mar 10	Mar 09
Working Capital	1	1	-18
Fixed Assets	7	9	10
Current Assets	57	56	33

Sams Blinds
846 Green Lanes Winchmore Hill, London, N21 2RT
Tel: 020-8360 2888 **Fax:** 020-8372 0786
E-mail: samsblinds@msn.com
Website: http://www.samsblinds.co.uk
Directors: S. Al Memani (Prop)
No.of Employees: 1 - 10 **Product Groups:** 23, 24, 63, 66

Sardi Designs Ltd
34 Clifton Road, London, NW10 4RB
Tel: 020-8961 1334 **Fax:** 020-8961 1334
E-mail: marketing@sardi.co.uk
Website: http://www.sardi.co.uk
Directors: S. Skrabski (MD)
Immediate Holding Company: SARDI DESIGNS LIMITED
Registration no: 02288140 **Date established:** 1988
No.of Employees: 1 - 10 **Product Groups:** 49

Date of Accounts	Nov 10	Nov 09	Nov 08
Working Capital	-0	-1	-0
Fixed Assets	1	1	1
Current Assets	33	31	28

Satellite Sports Services Ltd
Satellite House 17 Corsham Street, London, N1 6DR
Tel: 020-7696 8700 **Fax:** 020-7251 3737
Website: http://www.sis.tv
Directors: D. Holdgate (Grp Chief Exec), K. Smith (Co Sec)
Ultimate Holding Company: SATELLITE INFORMATION SERVICES (HOLDINGS) LIMITED
Immediate Holding Company: SATELLITE INFORMATION SERVICES LIMITED
Registration no: 04243307 **Date established:** 2001
Turnover: £125m - £250m **No.of Employees:** 251 - 500
Product Groups: 79

Date of Accounts	Mar 12	Mar 11	Mar 10
Sales Turnover	189m	169m	161m
Pre Tax Profit/Loss	29m	24m	27m
Working Capital	-25m	9m	-3m
Fixed Assets	111m	72m	71m
Current Assets	75m	86m	71m
Current Liabilities	48m	35m	35m

Satsuma Consultancy Ltd
Suite 9 St Lukes Enterprise Centre 85 Tarling Road, London, E16 1HN
Tel: 020-7366 6311 **Fax:** 020- 75119500
E-mail: g.ohajah@satsumaconsultancy.co.uk
Website: http://www.satsumaconsultancy.co.uk

Directors: G. Ohajah (MD), H. Singh (Fin)
Immediate Holding Company: SATSUMA CONSULTANCY LTD
Registration no: 04097282 **Date established:** 2000
No.of Employees: 1 - 10 **Product Groups:** 81

Date of Accounts	Mar 07	Mar 06
Working Capital	3	15
Fixed Assets	1	1
Current Assets	13	42
Current Liabilities	10	27

Saunderson House

1 Long Lane, London, EC1A 9HF
Tel: 020-7315 6500 **Fax:** 020-7315 6550
E-mail: shl@sanderson-house.co.uk
Website: http://www.saunderson-house.co.uk
Bank(s): Barclays
Directors: N. Fletcher (MD), D. Saunderson (MD)
Ultimate Holding Company: I F G GROUP PUBLIC LIMITED COMPANY
Immediate Holding Company: SAUNDERSON HOUSE LIMITED
Registration no: 00940473 **VAT No.:** GB 675 1715 21
Date established: 1968 **Turnover:** £10m - £20m
No.of Employees: 101 - 250 **Product Groups:** 80, 82

Date of Accounts	Dec 11	Dec 10	Dec 09
Sales Turnover	19m	18m	16m
Pre Tax Profit/Loss	4m	3m	3m
Working Capital	2m	2m	2m
Fixed Assets	490	493	382
Current Assets	10m	10m	10m
Current Liabilities	8m	7m	7m

Savile Row Shirt Co.

Savile House 14 Coach & Horses Yard, London, W1S 2EJ
Tel: 020-7432 9500 **Fax:** 020-7432 9501
E-mail: info@savile-row.co.uk
Website: http://www.savilerowco.com
Managers: D. Canady
Ultimate Holding Company: NIKID HOLDINGS LTD
Immediate Holding Company: NIKID DESIGN LIMITED
Registration no: 06356360 **Date established:** 2002
No.of Employees: 1 - 10 **Product Groups:** 24, 63

Saville & Co.

1 Carey Lane, London, EC2V 8AE
Tel: 020-7920 0000 **Fax:** 020-7920 0088
E-mail: mail@savillenotaries.com
Website: http://www.savillenotaries.com
Directors: R. Saville (Snr Part)
Managers: K. Morrison
Immediate Holding Company: THE OCTAVE HOUSE FREEHOLD COMPANY LTD
Registration no: 02450886 **VAT No.:** GB 644 9714 10
Date established: 2012 **Turnover:** Up to £250,000
No.of Employees: 21 - 50 **Product Groups:** 28, 80

Date of Accounts	Mar 12	Mar 11	Mar 10
Sales Turnover	4m	4m	6m
Pre Tax Profit/Loss	-2m	-2m	-602
Working Capital	4m	4m	6m
Fixed Assets	43	39	81
Current Assets	6m	6m	10m
Current Liabilities	784	1m	3m

SCA Group Ltd

7 Chiswick High Road, London, W4 2ND
Tel: 020-8995 2914 **Fax:** 020-8995 2875
E-mail: mail@sca-group.co.uk
Website: http://www.sca-group.co.uk
Directors: J. Donnelly (MD)
Registration no: 03896934 **Date established:** 1989 **Turnover:** £5m - £10m
No.of Employees: 1 - 10 **Product Groups:** 44

Scanna MSC

International House 223 Regent Street, London, W1B 2EB
Tel: 020-7355 3555 **Fax:** 020-7355 3556
E-mail: info@scanna-msc.com
Website: http://www.scanna-msc.com
Directors: N. Cummings (Dir)
Immediate Holding Company: SCANNA MSC LIMITED
Registration no: 02151037 **Date established:** 1987 **Turnover:** £2m - £5m
No.of Employees: 1 - 10 **Product Groups:** 44

Date of Accounts	Mar 11	Mar 10	Mar 09
Working Capital	2m	2m	1m
Fixed Assets	81	103	77
Current Assets	4m	4m	6m

Schawk

St Marks House Shepherdess Walk, London, N1 7LH
Tel: 020-7861 7777 **Fax:** 020-7871 7777
E-mail: fred.goff@schawk.com
Website: http://www.schawk.com
Bank(s): National Westminster
Managers: F. Goff (Sales Admin)
Ultimate Holding Company: SCHAWK INC (USA)
Immediate Holding Company: SCHAWK UK LIMITED
Registration no: 03462552 **Date established:** 1997
Turnover: £20m - £50m **No.of Employees:** 51 - 100 **Product Groups:** 28, 44, 81, 89

Date of Accounts	Dec 11	Dec 10	Dec 09
Sales Turnover	36m	33m	31m
Pre Tax Profit/Loss	1m	2m	858
Working Capital	-2m	-3m	-4m
Fixed Assets	9m	9m	6m
Current Assets	13m	12m	8m
Current Liabilities	3m	4m	3m

Schneider Electric Ltd

120 New Cavendish Street, London, W1W 6XX
Tel: 020-3107 1610 **Fax:** 020-7462 3901
E-mail: nicola.rahilly@schneider-electric.com
Website: http://www.schneider-electric.com
Bank(s): HSBC
Directors: S. Thorogood (MD)
Managers: N. Rahilly
Ultimate Holding Company: SCHNEIDER ELECTRIC SA (FRANCE)
Immediate Holding Company: SCHNEIDER ELECTRIC LIMITED
Registration no: 01407228 **VAT No.:** 616 6593 20 **Date established:** 1978
Turnover: £75m - £125m **No.of Employees:** 21 - 50 **Product Groups:** 54

Date of Accounts	Dec 11	Dec 10	Dec 09
Sales Turnover	444m	407m	357m
Pre Tax Profit/Loss	28m	37m	38m
Working Capital	188m	164m	124m
Fixed Assets	35m	32m	20m
Current Assets	314m	263m	219m
Current Liabilities	48m	39m	34m

Schroders

Garrard House 31-45 Gresham Street, London, EC2V 7QA
Tel: 020-7658 6000 **Fax:** 020-7658 3950
E-mail: michael.dobson@schroders.com
Website: http://www.schroders.co.uk
Directors: H. Ashdown (Co Sec)
Managers: K. Parry, M. Dobson, J. Cardew
Ultimate Holding Company: SCHRODERS PLC
Immediate Holding Company: SCHRODER VENTURES INVESTMENT ADVISERS LIMITED
Registration no: 02228193 **Date established:** 1988
Turnover: Up to £250,000 **No.of Employees:** 101 - 250
Product Groups: 82

Date of Accounts	Dec 11	Dec 10	Dec 09
Sales Turnover	13	20	30
Working Capital	14	14	14
Current Assets	35	34	46
Current Liabilities	13	20	24

Schuco International

Business Design Centre 52 Upper Street, London, N1 0QH
Tel: 020-7704 0701 **Fax:** 020-7288 2783
E-mail: solutions@schuco.com
Website: http://www.schuco.com
Managers: S. Post (Mgr)
Ultimate Holding Company: THE KYTE GROUP LIMITED
Immediate Holding Company: KYTE - COLE LLP
Registration no: 02433198 **Date established:** 2009
Turnover: Up to £250,000 **No.of Employees:** 1 - 10 **Product Groups:** 46

Date of Accounts	Apr 11	Apr 10
Sales Turnover	N/A	51
Pre Tax Profit/Loss	N/A	51
Working Capital	3	6
Current Assets	5	6

Schumi Hairdressers

18 Britten Street, London, SW3 3TU
Tel: 020-7352 6504 **Fax:** 020-7581 3245
Directors: G. Schumi (Prop), H. Schumi (MD)
No.of Employees: 1 - 10 **Product Groups:** 61

Sciteb Ltd

1 Heddon Street, London, W1B 4BD
Tel: 020-7381 1481 **Fax:** 020-7499 9253
E-mail: christine.beale@sciteb.com
Website: http://www.sciteb.com
Directors: C. Beale (Dir)
Immediate Holding Company: SCITEB LTD.
Registration no: 02255620 **VAT No.:** GB 493 9738 80
Date established: 1988 **Turnover:** £250,000 - £500,000
No.of Employees: 1 - 10 **Product Groups:** 80

Date of Accounts	Mar 12	Mar 11	Mar 10
Sales Turnover	1m	944	429
Pre Tax Profit/Loss	95	235	208
Working Capital	109	141	5
Fixed Assets	40	9	11
Current Assets	220	325	190
Current Liabilities	98	179	185

Scope

4a Weale Road, London, E4 6JL
Tel: 020-8524 1151 **Fax:** 020-8559 3487
E-mail: rodger.hughes@scope.org.uk
Website: http://www.scope.org.uk
Bank(s): HSBC
Managers: R. Hughes (Serv Mgr)
Immediate Holding Company: SCOPE
Registration no: 00520866 **Date established:** 1953
Turnover: £250,000 - £500,000 **No.of Employees:** 11 - 20
Product Groups: 37

Date of Accounts	Mar 11	Mar 10	Mar 09
Sales Turnover	104m	102m	98m
Pre Tax Profit/Loss	5m	5m	-4m
Working Capital	10m	6m	-2m
Fixed Assets	29m	26m	25m
Current Assets	21m	15m	7m
Current Liabilities	10m	7m	7m

Screen Coatings Ltd

11 Carlton Road, London, W5 2AW
Tel: 020-8997 1694
E-mail: sales@screencoloursystems.co.uk
Website: http://www.screencoloursystems.co.uk
Directors: C. French (MD)
Immediate Holding Company: SCREEN COATINGS LIMITED
Registration no: 02382735 **Date established:** 1989
No.of Employees: 1 - 10 **Product Groups:** 32, 44

Date of Accounts	Sep 11	Sep 10	Sep 09
Working Capital	275	231	170
Fixed Assets	3	4	4
Current Assets	343	313	318

Scudder Investments

St Mary Axe House St Mary Axe, London, EC3A 8BA
Tel: 020-7464 5799 **Fax:** 020-7464 5050
Website: http://www.threadneedle.co.uk
Directors: G. Beech (Sales), S. Davies (MD)
Immediate Holding Company: CHEMICAL COMPOUNDS LIMITED
Date established: 1946 **No.of Employees:** 1 - 10 **Product Groups:** 82

Sdi Media UK Ltd

Cambridge House 100 Cambridge Grove, London, W6 0LE
Tel: 020-8237 7900 **Fax:** 020-8237 7950
E-mail: luc.tomasino@sdi-media.com
Website: http://www.sdimedia.com
Directors: S. Hopkins (Dir)
Ultimate Holding Company: BNP PARIBAS S.A. (FRANCE)
Immediate Holding Company: SDI MEDIA LIMITED
Registration no: 05161289 **Date established:** 2004
No.of Employees: 11 - 20 **Product Groups:** 89

Date of Accounts	Dec 11	Dec 10	Dec 09
Pre Tax Profit/Loss	-572	533	442
Working Capital	-5m	-5m	-6m
Fixed Assets	10m	10m	10m
Current Assets	3m	3m	2m
Current Liabilities	13	13	13

Sea Containers

Sea Containers House 20 Upper Ground, London, SE1 9LZ
Tel: 020-7805 5000 **Fax:** 020-7805 5900
E-mail: info@seacontainers.com
Website: http://www.seacontainers.com
Directors: A. Dalton (Dir), K. Crossan (Co Sec)
Ultimate Holding Company: SEA CONTAINERS LTD (BERMUDA)
Immediate Holding Company: SEA CONTAINERS FERRIES LIMITED
Registration no: 02404064 **Date established:** 1989 **Turnover:** £2m - £5m
No.of Employees: 1 - 10 **Product Groups:** 45, 71

Date of Accounts	Dec 05	Dec 04	Dec 03
Working Capital	N/A	-19m	N/A

Sealandair Transport Co

101 Stephenson Street, London, E16 4SA
Tel: 020-7511 2288 **Fax:** 020-7511 1466
E-mail: frt@sealandair.com
Website: http://www.sealandair.com
Bank(s): Barclays Bank
Directors: J. Yannaghas (Grp Chief Exec)
Managers: S. Wise (Chief Mgr), M. Mastrominas (Consultant)
Immediate Holding Company: SEALANDAIR TRANSPORT COMPANY LIMITED
Registration no: 02871503 **VAT No.:** 207 5647 61 **Date established:** 1993
Turnover: £2m - £5m **No.of Employees:** 11 - 20 **Product Groups:** 72, 76

Seatem

Seatem House 39 Moreland Street, London, EC1V 8BB
Tel: 020-7014 8450 **Fax:** 020-7014 8451
E-mail: commercial@seatem.com
Website: http://www.applausegroups.com
Directors: D. Parkhill (Grp Chief Exec)
Ultimate Holding Company: SEATEM GROUP HOLDINGS LTD (BVI)
Immediate Holding Company: SEATEM GROUP (UK) LIMITED
Registration no: 03880714 **VAT No.:** GB 404 6378 59
Date established: 1999 **Turnover:** £50m - £75m
No.of Employees: 51 - 100 **Product Groups:** 44

Date of Accounts	Dec 07	Dec 06	Dec 05
Sales Turnover	70m	50m	58m
Pre Tax Profit/Loss	-141	-1m	-3m
Working Capital	-5m	-13m	-12m
Fixed Assets	10m	9m	10m
Current Assets	15m	12m	11m
Current Liabilities	4m	13m	11m

Seawork UK Ltd

43 Langdon Park Road, london, N6 5PT
Tel: 7810447618 **Fax:** 208-34160555
E-mail: john@seawork.biz
Directors: J. Sauer (Ptnr)
Registration no: 664 1210 **Date established:** 2008 **Turnover:**
No.of Employees: 1 - 10 **Product Groups:** 09

Second Nature Ltd

10 Malton Road, London, W10 5UP
Tel: 020-8960 0212 **Fax:** 020-8960 8700
E-mail: trevor.schragger@secondnature.co.uk
Website: http://www.secondnature.co.uk
Directors: R. Schragger (Mkt Research), T. Schragger (MD)
Managers: M. Skelcey (Prod Mgr)
Immediate Holding Company: SECOND NATURE LIMITED
Registration no: 01594736 **Date established:** 1981 **Turnover:** £5m - £10m
No.of Employees: 11 - 20 **Product Groups:** 27

Date of Accounts	Dec 10	Dec 09	Dec 08
Sales Turnover	7m	7m	N/A
Pre Tax Profit/Loss	91	-58	52
Working Capital	887	838	900
Fixed Assets	2	13	51
Current Assets	3m	3m	3m
Current Liabilities	269	139	271

Secure A Site UK Ltd

168 Church Lane, London, NW9 8SP
Tel: 08455-550999 **Fax:** 08451-304592
E-mail: sales@scaffoldalarms.com
Website: http://www.scaffoldalarms.com
Directors: S. Christie (MD)
Immediate Holding Company: SECURE-A-SITE (UK) LTD
Registration no: 03254887 **Date established:** 1996
Turnover: Up to £250,000 **No.of Employees:** 1 - 10 **Product Groups:** 40

Date of Accounts	Mar 11	Mar 10	Mar 09
Sales Turnover	N/A	N/A	207
Pre Tax Profit/Loss	N/A	N/A	42
Working Capital	-18	-23	-33
Fixed Assets	23	26	34
Current Assets	104	77	56
Current Liabilities	N/A	N/A	50

Securewais UK Ltd

Group House 703 High Road, London, N12 0BT
Tel: 020-8446 9041 **Fax:** 020-8446 9131
Directors: R. Fredman (Dir)
Immediate Holding Company: SECURE WAIS (UK) LIMITED
Registration no: 02839363 **Date established:** 1993 **Turnover:** £2m - £5m
No.of Employees: 11 - 20 **Product Groups:** 37, 40, 81

Date of Accounts	Feb 12	Feb 11	Feb 10
Sales Turnover	2m	2m	2m
Pre Tax Profit/Loss	258	186	237
Working Capital	458	321	503
Fixed Assets	25	30	23
Current Assets	1m	768	1m
Current Liabilities	393	342	421

Securit World Ltd

Spectrum House Hillview Gardens, London, NW4 2JQ
Tel: 020-8266 3300 **Fax:** 020-8203 1027
E-mail: ed.heyden@securitworld.com
Website: http://www.securitworld.com
Bank(s): National Westminster Bank Plc
Directors: R. Wylie (Sales), P. James (Fin), S. Woodcock (Mkt Research), E. Heyden (Dir)
Managers: S. Jones (Personnel), R. Snow (Comptroller), D. Martinez (Tech Serv Mgr)

see next page

Securit World Ltd - Cont'd

Immediate Holding Company: SECURIT WORLD LIMITED
Registration no: 00691451 **Date established:** 1961
Turnover: £10m - £20m **No.of Employees:** 21 - 50 **Product Groups:** 44

Date of Accounts	Apr 11	Apr 10	Apr 09
Sales Turnover	11m	9m	8m
Pre Tax Profit/Loss	1m	679	285
Working Capital	1m	1m	1m
Fixed Assets	2m	2m	3m
Current Assets	3m	3m	2m
Current Liabilities	528	454	225

Security Drivers International

211 Piccadilly, London, W1J 9HF
Tel: 020-3468 5606 **Fax:** 020-7106 6719
E-mail: info@securitydrivers.com
Website: http://www.securitydrivers.com
Registration no: 06910499 **VAT No.:** GB 773 7042 20
Date established: 2009 **Turnover:** £250,000 - £500,000
No.of Employees: 1 - 10 **Product Groups:** 37, 40, 44, 45, 80, 81, 86

Selkent Industrial

12 Willow Way, London, SE26 4QP
Tel: 020-8699 6777 **Fax:** 020-8699 6709
E-mail: sales@selkent.net
Website: http://www.selkent.net
Bank(s): Royal Bank of Scotland
Managers: J. Bushnell (Mgr)
VAT No.: 358 3846 16 **Turnover:** £500,000 - £1m
No.of Employees: 11 - 20 **Product Groups:** 35, 66

Sequana Maritime Ltd

200 Court Road, London, SE9 4EW
Tel: 020-8299 7700 **Fax:** 020-8857 2886
E-mail: info@sequana.co.uk
Website: http://www.sequana.co.uk
Bank(s): Midland
Directors: A. Coleman (Dir), M. Coleman (MD)
Immediate Holding Company: SEQUANA MARITIME LIMITED
Registration no: 01048185 **VAT No.:** 218 5357 57 **Date established:** 1972
Turnover: £1m - £2m **No.of Employees:** 11 - 20 **Product Groups:** 74, 76

Date of Accounts	Dec 10	Dec 09	Dec 08
Sales Turnover	2m	57m	88m
Pre Tax Profit/Loss	100	-6m	2m
Working Capital	3m	3m	3m
Fixed Assets	7m	7m	15m
Current Assets	4m	5m	4m
Current Liabilities	105	234	370

Service Point UK Ltd

192-198 Vauxhall Bridge Road, London, SW1V 1DX
Tel: 020-7520 0200 **Fax:** 020-7837 5497
E-mail: infouk@servicepointuk.com
Website: http://www.servicepointuk.com
Directors: M. Buzzi (Dir), D. O Regan (Fin)
Managers: M. Baldwin (District Mgr), N. Dicosta (Purch Mgr)
Ultimate Holding Company: FP047764
Immediate Holding Company: SERVICE POINT UK LIMITED
Registration no: 01093958 **Date established:** 1973
Turnover: £50m - £75m **No.of Employees:** 1 - 10 **Product Groups:** 80

Sextons

Unit 9 Ferrier Industrial Estate Ferrier Street, London, SW18 1SW
Tel: 020-8877 1148 **Fax:** 020-8870 7727
E-mail: sales@sextonslondon.co.uk
Website: http://www.sextonslondon.co.uk
Directors: J. Patel (Dir)
Ultimate Holding Company: SEXTONS GROUP LTD
Registration no: 05949127 **Turnover:** £50m - £75m
No.of Employees: 1 - 10 **Product Groups:** 37

Seymour Distribution Ltd

Suites P & Q 2 East Poultry Avenue, London, EC1A 9PT
Tel: 020-7429 4000 **Fax:** 020-7429 4001
E-mail: info@seymour.co.uk
Website: http://www.seymour.co.uk
Bank(s): Barclays
Directors: T. O'sullivan (MD), M. Lambert (Fin)
Managers: S. Boyle, F. Winchester (Personnel), P. Hampel, M. Halling (Tech Serv Mgr), M. Winsor (Mktg Serv Mgr)
Immediate Holding Company: SEYMOUR DISTRIBUTION LIMITED
Registration no: 02954685 **VAT No.:** GB 668 2192 11
Date established: 1994 **No.of Employees:** 101 - 250 **Product Groups:** 64

Date of Accounts	Dec 11	Dec 10	Dec 09
Sales Turnover	125m	127m	128m
Pre Tax Profit/Loss	993	1m	2m
Working Capital	-544	-571	-169
Fixed Assets	1m	2m	2m
Current Assets	20m	20m	17m
Current Liabilities	1m	1m	1m

Shades Window Couture

54 Larkshall Road, London, E4 6PD
Tel: 020-8498 5818
E-mail: info@shadeswindowcouture.co.uk
Website: http://www.shadeswindowcouture.co.uk
Directors: S. Willsdon (Prop)
Immediate Holding Company: PARKWAY ELECTRICAL SUPPLIES LIMITED
Date established: 2007 **No.of Employees:** 1 - 10 **Product Groups:** 25, 30, 35

Date of Accounts	Aug 12	Aug 11	Aug 10
Working Capital	-43	-65	-16
Current Assets	116	45	91

Shell Gas Direct

Grand Building 1-3 Strand, London, WC2N 5EJ
Tel: 020-7257 3000 **Fax:** 020-7257 0101
E-mail: sgd-enquiries@shell.com
Website: http://www.shell.co.uk
Managers: G. Vam't Hoff
Immediate Holding Company: SHELL UK P.L.C.
Registration no: 02405635 **Turnover:** £75m - £125m
No.of Employees: 21 - 50 **Product Groups:** 13, 18, 31

Shell UK Ltd

Shell Centre, London, SE1 7NA
Tel: 020-7934 1234 **Fax:** 0161-848 0528
E-mail: info@shell.com
Website: http://www.shell.com
Bank(s): Lloyds Bank
Managers: P. Hinles (Chief Mgr), P. Hindley (Mgr)
Ultimate Holding Company: Royal Dutch Shell plc
Immediate Holding Company: Shell Distributor (Holdings) Ltd
Registration no: 00140141 **Date established:** 1979
No.of Employees: 21 - 50 **Product Groups:** 66

Shepherd Epstein Hunter

Pheonix Yard 65 King's Cross Road, London, WC1X 9LW
Tel: 020-7841 7500 **Fax:** 020-7841 7575
E-mail: alainhead@seh.co.uk
Website: http://www.seh.co.uk
Bank(s): National Westminster P.L.C., Oxford Circus
Directors: A. Mitra (Fin), R. Hughes (Dir), H. Bird (Dir), A. Head (Prop), S. Pidwill (Dir), J. Thacker (Ch), A. Head (Dir)
Immediate Holding Company: SHEPHEARD EPSTEIN &HUNTER PUBLIC LIMITED COMPANY
Registration no: 01330885 **VAT No.:** GB 702 2750 73
Date established: 1977 **Turnover:** £1m - £2m **No.of Employees:** 21 - 50
Product Groups: 84

Sheppard Robson Architects

77 Parkway, London, NW1 7PU
Tel: 020-7504 1700 **Fax:** 020-7504 1701
E-mail: malcolm.mcgowan@sheppardrobson.com
Website: http://www.sheppardrobson.com
Bank(s): Lloyds TSB Bank plc
Directors: M. Mcgowan (Snr Part), J. Barker (Fin)
Managers: S. Viveash (Tech Serv Mgr), N. Clarke
Immediate Holding Company: SHEPPARD ROBSON LIMITED
Registration no: 03232209 **VAT No.:** GB 232 8576 52
Date established: 1996 **Turnover:** £1m - £2m
No.of Employees: 101 - 250 **Product Groups:** 52, 84

Date of Accounts	Mar 11	Mar 10	Apr 09
Sales Turnover	2m	677	1m
Pre Tax Profit/Loss	20	9	29
Working Capital	50	30	21
Current Assets	765	185	32
Current Liabilities	695	153	10

Shesto Ltd

2 Sapcote Trading Centre 374 High Road, London, NW10 2DH
Tel: 020-8451 6188 **Fax:** 020-8451 5450
E-mail: info@shesto.com
Website: http://www.shesto.com
Directors: R. Shestopal (MD)
Immediate Holding Company: SHESTO LIMITED
Registration no: 00428331 **VAT No.:** GB 244 6441 66
Date established: 1947 **Turnover:** £2m - £5m **No.of Employees:** 1 - 10
Product Groups: 47

Date of Accounts	Dec 11	Dec 10	Dec 09
Working Capital	618	475	472
Fixed Assets	24	20	25
Current Assets	1m	2m	1m

Shi Cashmere

30 Lowndes Street, London, SW1X 9HX
Tel: 020-7235 3829 **Fax:** 020-7245 0944
E-mail: shi@shicashmere.com
Website: http://www.shicashmere.com
Directors: S. Nazemi (Dir)
Immediate Holding Company: SHI LONDON LIMITED
Registration no: 06391909 **VAT No.:** GB 697 1222 18
Date established: 2007 **No.of Employees:** 1 - 10 **Product Groups:** 63, 66

Date of Accounts	Dec 11	Dec 10	Dec 09
Working Capital	60	51	50
Fixed Assets	1	1	1
Current Assets	116	92	104

Shilton plc

90 Peterborough Road, London, SW6 3HH
Tel: 020-7736 7771 **Fax:** 020-7731 7683
E-mail: info@janeshilton.co.uk
Website: http://www.janeshilton.co.uk
Directors: A. Shilton (Sales), D. Shilton (MD), S. Smith (Fin)
Managers: J. Foster (Personnel)
Ultimate Holding Company: SHILTON GROUP HOLDINGS LIMITED
Immediate Holding Company: SHILTON PROPERTIES LIMITED
Registration no: 03499054 **VAT No.:** GB 227 1492 70
Date established: 1998 **Turnover:** £250,000 - £500,000
No.of Employees: 11 - 20 **Product Groups:** 22

Date of Accounts	Jun 11	Jun 10	Jun 09
Sales Turnover	398	521	533
Pre Tax Profit/Loss	15	204	100
Working Capital	-17	4m	3m
Fixed Assets	3m	3m	4m
Current Assets	50	4m	4m
Current Liabilities	44	62	61

Shooters Ltd

Unit 10 Eurolink Business Centre 49 Effra Road, London, SW2 1BZ
Tel: 020-7737 6651
E-mail: info@shootersltd.com
Website: http://www.shootersltd.com
Directors: A. Parker (Co Sec)
Immediate Holding Company: SHOOTERS LIMITED
Registration no: 03713448 **Date established:** 1999
No.of Employees: 1 - 10 **Product Groups:** 35, 37, 89

Date of Accounts	Mar 12	Mar 11	Mar 10
Working Capital	-19	-31	-47
Fixed Assets	47	49	57
Current Assets	40	36	45

Short Stories of London Ltd

31 The Hale, London, N17 9JZ
Tel: 020-8801 4098 **Fax:** 020-8365 0012
Directors: T. Sonmez (Dir)
Immediate Holding Company: SHORT STORIES OF LONDON LIMITED
Registration no: 02567608 **Date established:** 1990
Turnover: £500,000 - £1m **No.of Employees:** 1 - 10 **Product Groups:** 63

Date of Accounts	Mar 08	Mar 07	Mar 06
Working Capital	251	290	340
Fixed Assets	7	4	5
Current Assets	330	350	424
Current Liabilities	78	60	84

Sibilo UK Ltd

Communications House 26 York Street, London, W1U 6PZ
Tel: 0800-7566777 **Fax:** 0800-7566743
E-mail: info@sibilo.co.uk
Website: http://www.sibilo.co.uk
Directors: E. Caglar (MD), M. Bersani (Fin)
Registration no: 04350482 **Turnover:** Up to £250,000
No.of Employees: 1 - 10 **Product Groups:** 44

Date of Accounts	Mar 07
Working Capital	-12
Fixed Assets	500
Current Assets	15
Current Liabilities	27

Siebert Head Ltd

35-39 Old Street, London, EC1V 9HX
Tel: 020-7689 9090 **Fax:** 020-7689 9080
E-mail: melina.shah@sieberthead.com
Website: http://www.sieberthead.com
Bank(s): Barclays
Directors: J. Parsons (MD), S. Gidda (Sales & Mktg), S. Gidda (Dir), M. Shah (Co Sec)
Ultimate Holding Company: ENFRANCHISE NINETY THREE LIMITED
Immediate Holding Company: SIEBERT HEAD LIMITED
Registration no: 01041265 **Date established:** 1972 **Turnover:** £2m - £5m
No.of Employees: 11 - 20 **Product Groups:** 84

Date of Accounts	Dec 08	Dec 07	Mar 11
Working Capital	6	234	-138
Fixed Assets	132	188	29
Current Assets	628	773	412

Signware Sign Writers

9 Blackheath Hill, London, SE10 8PB
Tel: 020-8694 9055 **Fax:** 020-8694 8946
E-mail: shop@signware.co.uk
Website: http://www.signwriters.co.uk
Directors: R. Mbogga (Prop)
Immediate Holding Company: WIGHT SCIENTIFIC
VAT No.: GB 109 1594 72 **Turnover:** £250,000 - £500,000
No.of Employees: 1 - 10 **Product Groups:** 37, 40, 45, 49

Silhouette UK Ltd

2 Bath Road Chiswick, London, W4 1LW
Tel: 020-8987 8899 **Fax:** 020-8987 2430
E-mail: office@uk.silhouette.com
Website: http://www.silhouette.com
Directors: D. Chalmers (MD), S. Robinson (Fin)
Managers: J. Lanaway (Mktg Serv Mgr)
Ultimate Holding Company: SILHOUETTE INTERNATIONAL SCHMIED AG (AUSTRIA)
Immediate Holding Company: SILHOUETTE U.K. LIMITED
Registration no: 01459046 **Date established:** 1979 **Turnover:** £5m - £10m
No.of Employees: 21 - 50 **Product Groups:** 65

Date of Accounts	Jan 12	Jan 11	Jan 10
Sales Turnover	N/A	6m	7m
Pre Tax Profit/Loss	N/A	-164	85
Working Capital	-1m	-1m	-999
Fixed Assets	2m	2m	2m
Current Assets	1m	1m	2m
Current Liabilities	N/A	430	593

Silloutte UK Ltd

333 High Road, London, N22 8JA
Tel: 020-8889 9371
Directors: D. Mclaren (Dir)
No.of Employees: 11 - 20 **Product Groups:** 37, 38, 65

Silverline Windows Ltd

1a Clarence Road Bounds Green, London, N22 8PG
Tel: 020-8881 6702 **Fax:** 020-8881 6782
E-mail: info@silverlinewindows.co.uk
Managers: J. Michael (Product)
Immediate Holding Company: SILVERLINE WINDOWS LIMITED
Registration no: 01567550 **Date established:** 1981
No.of Employees: 1 - 10 **Product Groups:** 26, 35

Date of Accounts	Jul 11	Jul 10	Jul 09
Working Capital	-6	-7	-9
Fixed Assets	8	8	10
Current Assets	69	73	84

Silverts Ltd

116-120 Goswell Road, London, EC1V 7DP
Tel: 020-7253 5766 **Fax:** 020-7608 2230
E-mail: sales@silverts.co.uk
Website: http://www.silverts.co.uk
Directors: D. Silvert (Dir), P. Silvert (MD)
Managers: D. Conway (Chief Acct), M. Stadler (Sales & Mktg Mg)
Immediate Holding Company: A.M.S. Investments Ltd
Registration no: 00240050 **Turnover:** £5m - £10m
No.of Employees: 11 - 20 **Product Groups:** 24

Date of Accounts	Mar 08	Mar 07	Mar 06
Pre Tax Profit/Loss	N/A	N/A	171
Working Capital	1815	1864	2026
Fixed Assets	595	607	622
Current Assets	5368	5314	5109
Current Liabilities	3553	3450	3083
Total Share Capital	28	28	28
ROCE% (Return on Capital Employed)			6.4

Simmons & Simmons Ltd

Citypoint 1 Ropemaker Street, London, EC2Y 9SS
Tel: 020-7628 2020 **Fax:** 020-7628 2070
E-mail: marketing@simmons-simmons.com
Website: http://www.simmons-simmons.com
Directors: C. Passmore (Snr Part), D. Dickinson (Snr Part)
Immediate Holding Company: SIMMONS & SIMMONS (NO.1) LIMITED
Registration no: 02092142 **Date established:** 1987
No.of Employees: 501 - 1000 **Product Groups:** 80

Simmy Ceramics

Sayer House Oxgate Lane, London, NW2 7JN
Tel: 0843-2897326 **Fax:** 020-8450 1140
E-mail: sales@simmyceramics.com
Website: http://www.simmyceramics.com
Directors: H. Umradia (Dir), S. Moore (MD), S. More (MD), S. Mann (Co Sec)
Registration no: 03936228 **VAT No.:** GB 751 9778 84
Date established: 1992 **Turnover:** £500,000 - £1m
No.of Employees: 1 - 10 **Product Groups:** 26, 33, 48

Simon Morris Associates Limited
Studio 5 Ravensquay, Cray Avenue, London, BR5 4BQ
Tel: 0845-6121831 **Fax:** 0845-6121832
E-mail: enq@madesignstudios.com
Website: http://www.madesignstudios.com
Directors: S. Morris (Design)
Managers: T. Deschepper (Sales Prom Mgr), M. Dewitte
Registration no 04941994 **No.of Employees:** 11 - 20 **Product Groups:** 52

D J Simons & Sons Ltd
122-150 Hackney Road, London, E2 7QL
Tel: 020-7739 3744 **Fax:** 020-7739 4452
E-mail: sales@djsimons.co.uk
Website: http://www.djsimons.co.uk
Directors: D. Simons (Dir), S. Simons (Dir)
Immediate Holding Company: D. & J. SIMONS & SONS LIMITED
Registration no: 01222521 **VAT No.:** 549 3314 34 **Date established:** 1975
Turnover: £5m - £10m **No.of Employees:** 251 - 500 **Product Groups:** 25, 27, 36, 64

Date of Accounts	Oct 11	Oct 10	Oct 09
Sales Turnover	9m	9m	9m
Pre Tax Profit/Loss	278	296	21
Working Capital	3m	3m	4m
Fixed Assets	10m	9m	9m
Current Assets	8m	8m	9m
Current Liabilities	2m	3m	2m

Simplex
PO Box 33903, London, NW9 6ER
Tel: 020-8200 9991 **Fax:** 020-8200 6598
E-mail: alan@simplex.org.uk
Website: http://www.simplex.org.uk
Directors: A. Sinclair (Prop)
Turnover: Up to £250,000 **No.of Employees:** 1 - 10 **Product Groups:** 35, 49

Simply Cigars
25 Tabor Road, London, W6 0BN
Tel: 020-8834 7123 **Fax:** 020-8834 7123
E-mail: sales@simplycigar.co.uk
Website: http://www.simplycigar.co.uk
Directors: S. Speller (Dir)
Registration no: 04727332 **Date established:** 2001
Turnover: £250,000 - £500,000 **No.of Employees:** 1 - 10
Product Groups: 20, 32, 49

Simportex Ltd
452a Finchley Road, London, NW11 8DG
Tel: 020-8457 8770 **Fax:** 020-8457 7484
E-mail: sales@simportex.com
Website: http://www.simportex.com
Directors: A. Singhania (Dir)
Immediate Holding Company: SIMPORTEX LIMITED
Registration no: 00826063 **VAT No.:** GB 244 0737 75
Date established: 1964 **Turnover:** £75m - £125m
No.of Employees: 1 - 10 **Product Groups:** 61

Date of Accounts	Dec 11	Dec 10	Dec 09
Working Capital	280	429	681
Fixed Assets	335	333	336
Current Assets	350	475	736

Simpsons In The Strand
100 Strand, London, WC2R 0EW
Tel: 020-7836 9112 **Fax:** 020-7836 1381
E-mail: info@simpsonsinthestrand.co.uk
Website: http://www.simpsonsinthestrand.co.uk
Managers: S. Busby (Mgr)
Immediate Holding Company: THE SAVOY GROUP
Registration no: 00348446 **VAT No.:** GB 238 7315 49
Turnover: £50m - £75m **No.of Employees:** 21 - 50 **Product Groups:** 69

Sinclair I S Pharma
Whitfield Court 30-32 Whitfield Street, London, W1T 2RQ
Tel: 020-7467 6920 **Fax:** 020-7467 6930
E-mail: info@sinclairpharma.com
Website: http://www.sinclairpharma.com
Managers: J. Terry (Sales Admin)
Ultimate Holding Company: SINCLAIR IS PHARMA PLC
Immediate Holding Company: SINCLAIR PHARMACEUTICALS LIMITED
Registration no: 01007146 **VAT No.:** GB 779 4089 70
Date established: 1971 **Turnover:** £10m - £20m
No.of Employees: 21 - 50 **Product Groups:** 63

Date of Accounts	Jun 11	Jun 10	Jun 09
Sales Turnover	11m	10m	13m
Pre Tax Profit/Loss	-5m	-9m	2m
Working Capital	3m	972	-92
Fixed Assets	17m	17m	8m
Current Assets	8m	5m	4m
Current Liabilities	2m	1m	2m

Single Market Events Cosumer Exhibitions
9 Manchester Square, London, W1U 3PL
Tel: 020-7886 3112 **Fax:** 020-8940 1685
E-mail: info@single-market.co.uk
Website: http://www.single-market.co.uk
Directors: K. Moles (Prop), T. Etchells (MD)
Ultimate Holding Company: ANGUS MONTGOMERY LIMITED
Immediate Holding Company: SINGLE MARKET EVENTS LIMITED
Registration no: 02515823 **Date established:** 1990 **Turnover:** £2m - £5m
No.of Employees: 11 - 20 **Product Groups:** 80, 81

Date of Accounts	Jun 11	Jun 10	Jun 09
Working Capital	-422	-482	9
Fixed Assets	N/A	117	69
Current Assets	291	554	667

Skandinaviska Enskilda Banken
Scandinavian House 2-6 Cannon Street, London, EC4M 6XX
Tel: 020-7246 4000 **Fax:** 020-7588 0929
E-mail: kathryn.berry@seb.co.uk
Website: http://www.seb.co.uk
Directors: K. Berry (Fin)
Ultimate Holding Company: SKANDINAVISKA ENSKILDA BANKEN AB (PUBL)
Immediate Holding Company: SKANDINAVISKA ENSKILDA LIMITED
Registration no: 01618680 **Date established:** 1982
No.of Employees: 101 - 250 **Product Groups:** 82, 87

Date of Accounts	Dec 11	Dec 10	Dec 09
Pre Tax Profit/Loss	66	121	7m
Working Capital	16m	25m	35m
Fixed Assets	35m	29m	26m
Current Assets	19m	25m	35m
Current Liabilities	3m	617	141

Ski Club Of Great Britain
57-63 Church Road, London, SW19 5SB
Tel: 020-8410 2000 **Fax:** 020-8410 2001
E-mail: maggie.colpus@skiclub.co.uk
Website: http://www.skiclub.co.uk
Bank(s): National Westminster
Directors: C. Stewart Taylor (Grp Chief Exec)
Managers: P. White (Tech Serv Mgr)
Immediate Holding Company: SKI CLUB OF GREAT BRITAIN LIMITED
Registration no: 04312167 **VAT No.:** 239 3665 36 **Date established:** 2001
Turnover: £2m - £5m **No.of Employees:** 21 - 50 **Product Groups:** 69

Date of Accounts	Apr 11	Apr 10	Apr 09
Sales Turnover	4m	4m	4m
Pre Tax Profit/Loss	-3	126	83
Working Capital	522	541	410
Fixed Assets	2m	2m	2m
Current Assets	2m	2m	2m
Current Liabilities	954	968	1m

Skills Venture Limited
2 Braddyll Street, London, SE10 9AE
Tel: 020-7871 4485
E-mail: enquiries@skillsventure.com
Website: http://www.skillsventure.com
Directors: R. Breare (Dir), W. Snell (Dir)
Registration no: 06304882 **Date established:** 2007
Turnover: Up to £250,000 **No.of Employees:** 1 - 10 **Product Groups:** 86

Slade & Kempton
1 New Brent Street, London, NW4 2DF
Tel: 020-8202 9000 **Fax:** 020-8202 1500
E-mail: sales@slade-kempton.com
Website: http://www.slades-kempton.com
Directors: R. Kanzen (MD)
Immediate Holding Company: CUSTOMCHAIN LTD
Registration no: 05879176 **VAT No.:** GB 697 1337 01
Date established: 2006 **Turnover:** £1m - £2m **No.of Employees:** 1 - 10
Product Groups: 49

Slaughter & May
One Bunhill Row, London, EC1Y 8YY
Tel: 020-7600 1200 **Fax:** 020-7090 5000
Website: http://www.slaughterandmay.com
Directors: J. Jones (Fin)
Managers: C. Barrett
Ultimate Holding Company: SLAUGHTER AND MAY LIMITED
Immediate Holding Company: SLAUGHTER AND MAY LIMITED
Registration no: 02228255 **Date established:** 1988
Turnover: £50m - £75m **No.of Employees:** 1501 & over
Product Groups: 80

Slick Willies Ltd
12 Gloucester Road, London, SW7 4RB
Tel: 020-7225 0004 **Fax:** 020-7591 0918
E-mail: info@slickwillies.co.uk
Website: http://www.slickwillies.co.uk
Directors: R. Porter (MD)
Immediate Holding Company: SLICK WILLIES LIMITED
Registration no: 03527557 **VAT No.:** GB 714 0278 62
Date established: 1998 **Turnover:** £2m - £5m **No.of Employees:** 1 - 10
Product Groups: 22, 49

Date of Accounts	Mar 11	Mar 10	Mar 09
Working Capital	-169	-178	-163
Fixed Assets	4	5	7
Current Assets	79	41	54

SMA Design Limited
Studio 5 Ravensquay Business Centre, Cray Avenue, London, BR5 4BQ
Tel: 0845-6121831 **Fax:** 0845-6121832
E-mail: enq@madesignstudios.com
Website: http://www.smadesign.org
Directors: S. Morris (MD)
Managers: K. Maine (Sales Prom Mgr), T. De Schepper (Mktg Serv Mgr), E. Williams (Sales Prom Mgr)
Registration no: 06814901 **Turnover:** £250,000 - £500,000
No.of Employees: 11 - 20 **Product Groups:** 81

Small Back Room
88 Camberwell Road, London, SE5 0EG
Tel: 020-7701 4227 **Fax:** 020-7703 3474
E-mail: info@smallbackroom.co.uk
Website: http://www.smallbackroom.com
Directors: I. Tasney (Dir)
Ultimate Holding Company: SBR DESIGN CONSULTANTS LTD
Registration no: 02608804 **Date established:** 1985 **Turnover:** £2m - £5m
No.of Employees: 21 - 50 **Product Groups:** 80, 81

Small Products
20 St Andrews Way Bow, London, E3 3PA
Tel: 020-7537 4222 **Fax:** 020-7538 3957
E-mail: sales@smallproducts.co.uk
Website: http://www.smallproducts.co.uk
Bank(s): Lloyds
Directors: B. Dix (Co Sec), D. Patel (Dir)
Immediate Holding Company: SMALL PRODUCTS LIMITED
Registration no: 01645227 **VAT No.:** 365 3963 23 **Date established:** 1982
Turnover: £1m - £2m **No.of Employees:** 11 - 20 **Product Groups:** 32

Date of Accounts	Jun 11	Jun 10	Jun 09
Working Capital	415	682	886
Fixed Assets	31	40	51
Current Assets	1m	1m	2m

John Smedley Ltd
24 Brook Street, London, W1K 5DG
Tel: 020-7495 2222 **Fax:** 020-7629 5481
E-mail: sales@johnsmedley.co.uk
Website: http://www.johnsmedley.com
Managers: C. Masson (Mgr)
Immediate Holding Company: JOHN SMEDLEY LIMITED
Registration no: 00040000 **VAT No.:** GB 125 6154 85
Date established: 1993 **No.of Employees:** 1 - 10 **Product Groups:** 24

Date of Accounts	Dec 10	Dec 09	Dec 08
Sales Turnover	16m	15m	15m
Pre Tax Profit/Loss	-2m	32	988
Working Capital	5m	7m	8m
Fixed Assets	2m	2m	2m
Current Assets	7m	9m	11m
Current Liabilities	2m	2m	2m

Herbert Smith
Exchange House 12 Primrose Street, London, EC2A 2HS
Tel: 020-7374 8000 **Fax:** 020-7374 0888
E-mail: jonathan.scott@herbertsmith.com
Website: http://www.herbertsmith.com
Bank(s): Coutts & Co
Directors: J. Scott (Snr Part)
Managers: D. Norris, R. Boardman, H. Tyler
Immediate Holding Company: HERBERT SMITH LIMITED
Registration no: 05447853 **VAT No.:** GB 243 3423 89
Date established: 2005 **Turnover:** £250m - £500m
No.of Employees: 1501 & over **Product Groups:** 80

Smith & Nephew plc
15 Adam Street, London, WC2N 6LA
Tel: 020-7401 7646 **Fax:** 020-7960 2350
E-mail: dave.illingworth@smith-nephew.com
Website: http://www.smith-nephew.com
Directors: L. Pendle (Pers)
Managers: A. Hennah (Comptroller), O. Bohoun
Ultimate Holding Company: SMITH & NEPHEW PLC
Immediate Holding Company: SMITH & NEPHEW (OVERSEAS) LIMITED
Registration no: 00681251 **Date established:** 1961
Turnover: £20m - £50m **No.of Employees:** 51 - 100 **Product Groups:** 24, 30, 31, 37, 38, 44, 61

Date of Accounts	Dec 07	Dec 06	Dec 05
Sales Turnover	3369m	2779m	1407m
Pre Tax Profit/Loss	469000	550000	240000
Working Capital	-366000	829000	348000
Fixed Assets	2545m	1586m	817000
Current Assets	1905m	1645m	937000
Current Liabilities	2271m	816000	589000
Total Share Capital	190000	189000	115000
ROCE% (Return on Capital Employed)	21.5	22.8	20.6
ROT% (Return on Turnover)	13.9	19.8	17.1

Smiths Group plc
765 Finchley Road Childs Hill, London, NW11 8DS
Tel: 020-8457 8403 **Fax:** 020-8458 0680
E-mail: plc@smiths-group.com
Website: http://www.smiths-group.com
Directors: G. Hardcastle (Dir), K. Orrel-Jones (Ch), N. Burdett (Co Sec), P. Jackson (Grp Chief Exec), R. Ellis (Dir)
Ultimate Holding Company: SMITHS GROUP PLC
Immediate Holding Company: T I GROUP LIMITED
Registration no: 00059990 **Date established:** 1998
Turnover: £250m - £500m **No.of Employees:** 1 - 10 **Product Groups:** 37

Date of Accounts	Jul 08	Jul 07
Sales Turnover	2321m	2161m
Pre Tax Profit/Loss	319300	256000
Working Capital	267500	137900
Fixed Assets	1849m	1769m
Current Assets	1085m	1009m
Current Liabilities	817200	871300
Total Share Capital	145500	144600
ROCE% (Return on Capital Employed)	15.1	13.4
ROT% (Return on Turnover)	13.8	11.8

Smiths Metal Centres Ltd
42-56 Tottenham Road, London, N1 4BZ
Tel: 020-7241 2430 **Fax:** 020-7254 9608
E-mail: roffea@smithmetal.com
Website: http://www.smithmetal.com
Managers: A. Roffe (Mgr)
Ultimate Holding Company: HENLEY MANAGEMENT COMPANY (USA)
Immediate Holding Company: SMITHS METAL CENTRES LIMITED
Registration no: 03485838 **VAT No.:** GB 340 1992 70
Date established: 1997 **Turnover:** £50m - £75m **No.of Employees:** 1 - 10
Product Groups: 34, 49, 66

Date of Accounts	Dec 11	May 10	May 09
Sales Turnover	45m	46m	49m
Pre Tax Profit/Loss	2m	830	629
Working Capital	7m	12m	13m
Fixed Assets	1m	1m	2m
Current Assets	28m	23m	21m
Current Liabilities	4m	2m	2m

Smooth Radio
26-27 Castlereagh Street, London, W1H 5DL
Tel: 020-7706 4100 **Fax:** 020-7723 9742
E-mail: info@smoothradio.com
Website: http://www.smoothradio.com
Managers: S. Taylor, A. Tingey, C. Roberts (Sales Prom Mgr)
Ultimate Holding Company: THE SCOTT TRUST LIMITED
Immediate Holding Company: SMOOTH RADIO INVESTMENTS LIMITED
Registration no: 02585798 **Date established:** 1991 **Turnover:** £2m - £5m
No.of Employees: 21 - 50 **Product Groups:** 79

Date of Accounts	Mar 11	Mar 10	Mar 09
Working Capital	N/A	-1m	-1m
Fixed Assets	4m	4m	4m
Current Liabilities	N/A	5	5

Snappy Snaps Franchises Ltd
12 Glenthorne Mews, London, W6 0LJ
Tel: 020-8741 7474 **Fax:** 020-8748 3849
E-mail: ann@snappysnaps.co.uk
Website: http://www.snappysnaps.co.uk
Directors: D. Kennedy (Dir), R. Simpson (Dir), T. Macandrews (Fin)
Ultimate Holding Company: 02769377
Immediate Holding Company: SNAPPY SNAPS FRANCHISES LIMITED
Registration no: 02632020 **Date established:** 1991
Turnover: £10m - £20m **No.of Employees:** 21 - 50 **Product Groups:** 81

Date of Accounts	Mar 10	Mar 09	Mar 08
Working Capital	-5m	-3m	-1m
Fixed Assets	3m	5m	5m
Current Assets	1m	1m	2m

Sneath Group Holdings Ltd
13 Solebay Street, London, E1 4PN
Tel: 020-7790 7900 **Fax:** 020-7265 8090
E-mail: enquiries@sneath.co.uk
Website: http://www.sneath.co.uk

see next page

Sneath Group Holdings Ltd - Cont'd

Directors: J. Veness (MD)
Immediate Holding Company: SNEATH GROUP (HOLDINGS) LIMITED
Registration no: 00241987 **VAT No.:** GB 248 1947 35
Date established: 2029 **Turnover:** £250,000 - £500,000
No.of Employees: 21 - 50 **Product Groups:** 52, 67, 85

Date of Accounts	Dec 11	Dec 10	Dec 09
Sales Turnover	413	331	446
Pre Tax Profit/Loss	774	14	13
Working Capital	597	303	291
Fixed Assets	51	71	70
Current Assets	2m	1m	1m
Current Liabilities	640	80	76

Socks By Us Limited

329 Archway Road Highgate, London, N6 5AA
Tel: 020-8347 9903 **Fax:** 0208-386 26 81
E-mail: info@socksbyus.com
Website: http://www.socksbyus.com
Registration no: 06833071 **Turnover:** Up to £250,000
No.of Employees: 1 - 10 **Product Groups:** 22, 24, 63

Sofa & Chair Co.

4-5 Roslin Road, London, W3 8DH
Tel: 020-8993 4415 **Fax:** 020-8993 1863
E-mail: info@thesofaandchair.co.uk
Website: http://www.thesofaandchair.co.uk
Directors: K. Ahmad (Prop)
Managers: N. Eacott (Mktg Serv Mgr)
Immediate Holding Company: RONO LONDON LIMITED
Date established: 2011 **No.of Employees:** 21 - 50 **Product Groups:** 49, 61, 63, 67

Date of Accounts	Mar 08	Mar 07
Working Capital	-95	-16
Fixed Assets	160	138
Current Assets	296	297
Current Liabilities	391	312

Solar Century

91-94 Lower Marsh, London, SE1 7AB
Tel: 020-7803 0100 **Fax:** 020-7803 0101
E-mail: enquiries@solarcentury.com
Website: http://www.solarcentury.co.uk
Directors: D. Newman (MD), N. Terry (Fin)
Managers: S. Godfry (Tech Serv Mgr), H. Roper (Personnel), K. Coubrough (Sales Admin)
Ultimate Holding Company: SOLAR CENTURY HOLDINGS LIMITED
Immediate Holding Company: SOLAR CENTURY HOLDINGS LIMITED
Registration no: 03570325 **Date established:** 1998
Turnover: £50m - £75m **No.of Employees:** 51 - 100 **Product Groups:** 37, 52, 67

Date of Accounts	Mar 12	Mar 11	Mar 10
Sales Turnover	62m	50m	35m
Pre Tax Profit/Loss	789	940	-1m
Working Capital	14m	13m	11m
Fixed Assets	2m	2m	1m
Current Assets	26m	26m	25m
Current Liabilities	7m	6m	5m

Solar Marine Services Ltd

4 Barratt Industrial Park Gillender Street, London, E3 3JX
Tel: 020-7987 2244 **Fax:** 020-7987 0242
E-mail: solarmarine@hotmail.com
Directors: A. Laverick (Co Sec), J. Archer (MD)
Immediate Holding Company: SOLAR MARINE SERVICES LIMITED
Registration no: 04338948 **VAT No.:** 245 5461 59 **Date established:** 2001
Turnover: £1m - £2m **No.of Employees:** 1 - 10 **Product Groups:** 76

Date of Accounts	Dec 11	Dec 10	Dec 09
Working Capital	1	2	2
Fixed Assets	1	1	3
Current Assets	79	106	121

Soleseek Limited

9 Bickels Yard 151-153 Bermondsey Street, London, SE1 3HA
Tel: 020-8346 4743
E-mail: jb@soleseek.co.uk
Website: http://www.soleseek.co.uk
Directors: J. Brolly (Dir)
Registration no: 06746137 **Date established:** 2008
Turnover: Up to £250,000 **No.of Employees:** 1 - 10 **Product Groups:** 81

Sonata Ltd

17-20 Parr Street, London, N1 7ET
Tel: 020-7253 4221 **Fax:** 020-7251 2984
E-mail: ca@sonata.co.uk
Website: http://www.sonata.co.uk
Managers: C. Alleyne (Prod Mgr)
Immediate Holding Company: SONATA LIMITED
Registration no: 01319735 **Date established:** 1977 **Turnover:** £2m - £5m
No.of Employees: 1 - 10 **Product Groups:** 81

Date of Accounts	Dec 11	Dec 10	Dec 09
Working Capital	245	269	290
Fixed Assets	2	3	4
Current Assets	321	360	328

Songmaker Ltd

Suite 296 2 Lansdowne Row, Mayfair, London, W1J 6HL
Tel: 0871-7505555
E-mail: enquiries@songmaker.co.uk
Website: http://www.songmaker.co.uk
Directors: C. Powell (Co Sec)
Managers: M. Parsons (Sec)
Registration no: 07402276 **Date established:** 2001
No.of Employees: 21 - 50 **Product Groups:** 37

Date of Accounts	Mar 08	Mar 07	Mar 06
Working Capital	-30	-45	-49
Fixed Assets	N/A	1	5
Current Assets	2	2	5
Current Liabilities	32	46	54

Sonic Solutions

22 Warwick Street, London, W1B 5NF
Tel: 020-7437 1100 **Fax:** 020-7437 1151
E-mail: info@fonic.com
Website: http://www.sonic.com
Directors: R. Linecar (Dir)
No.of Employees: 251 - 500 **Product Groups:** 37, 44, 65, 67

Sony BMG Music Entertainment

9 Derry Street, London, W8 5HY
Tel: 020-7361 8000 **Fax:** 020-7371 9298
Website: http://www.sonymusic.com
Managers: D. Morris
Ultimate Holding Company: SONY CORPORATION (JAPAN)
Immediate Holding Company: SONY MUSIC ENTERTAINMENT UK HOLDINGS LIMITED
Registration no: 03185450 **Date established:** 1996 **Turnover:** £5m - £10m
No.of Employees: 1 - 10 **Product Groups:** 87

Date of Accounts	Dec 07	Mar 11	Mar 10
Pre Tax Profit/Loss	-31m	-10m	-11m
Working Capital	-63m	-472m	-165m
Fixed Assets	551m	575m	551m
Current Assets	118m	25m	22m

Sothebys

34-35 New Bond Street, London, W1A 2AA
Tel: 020-7293 5000 **Fax:** 020-7293 5989
E-mail: info@sothebys.com
Website: http://www.sothebys.com
Directors: G. Bailey (MD), J. Weller (Property), T. Christopherson (Co Sec)
Ultimate Holding Company: SOTHEBY'S HOLDINGS INC (USA).
Immediate Holding Company: SOTHEBY'S
Registration no: 00874867 **VAT No.:** GB 512 5492 63
Date established: 1966 **Turnover:** £75m - £125m
No.of Employees: 1 - 10 **Product Groups:** 65

Date of Accounts	Dec 09	Dec 08	Dec 07
Sales Turnover	94m	190m	190m
Pre Tax Profit/Loss	3m	38m	47m
Working Capital	71m	70m	51m
Fixed Assets	36m	37m	36m
Current Assets	157m	208m	209m
Current Liabilities	13m	125m	147m

South London Press

2-4 Leigham Court Road, London, SW16 2PD
Tel: 020-8769 4444 **Fax:** 020-8664 7213
E-mail: peter.edwards@slp.co.uk
Website: http://www.southlondononline.co.uk
Directors: P. Edwards (Publishing)
Managers: J. Curtis (Tech Serv Mgr), S. Clarke (Cr Control), C. Nolan (Sales Admin)
Ultimate Holding Company: ARGUS PRESS LTD
Immediate Holding Company: TRINITY SOUTHERN NEWSPAPER GROUP
Registration no: 02246797 **No.of Employees:** 101 - 250
Product Groups: 28

South London Video

70 Stewarts Road, London, SW8 4DE
Tel: 020-7720 6464 **Fax:** 020-7622 3666
E-mail: sales@slvision.co.uk
Website: http://www.slvision.co.uk
Directors: F. Dow (Ptnr)
Immediate Holding Company: STRONG PRODUCTIONS LIMITED
Date established: 2008 **No.of Employees:** 1 - 10 **Product Groups:** 37, 83

Southern Engine Services Ltd

Unit 28 Ropery Business Park Anchor & Hope Lane, London, SE7 7RX
Tel: 020-8858 8539 **Fax:** 020-8858 8530
Directors: A. Page (Dir)
Immediate Holding Company: SOUTHERN ENGINE SERVICES LIMITED
Registration no: 05550245 **Date established:** 2005
No.of Employees: 1 - 10 **Product Groups:** 35, 36, 39

Date of Accounts	Aug 11	Aug 10	Aug 09
Sales Turnover	342	254	268
Pre Tax Profit/Loss	50	48	40
Working Capital	-42	-38	-40
Fixed Assets	44	44	50
Current Assets	2	2	7
Current Liabilities	37	34	47

Space Savers Plus

326 High Road, London, N2 9AD
Tel: 020-8442 0707
Directors: A. Antoinette (Prop)
Date established: 2002 **No.of Employees:** 1 - 10 **Product Groups:** 35

Specialist Building Products Ltd

571 Finchley Road, London, NW3 7BN
Tel: 020-8458 8212 **Fax:** 020-8458 4116
E-mail: sbpchemicals@hotmail.com
Managers: A. Williams (Mgr)
Immediate Holding Company: FABRIC FLAVOURS LIMITED
Registration no: 06838011 **Date established:** 2005
No.of Employees: 11 - 20 **Product Groups:** 02, 07, 09, 11, 12, 13, 14, 16, 17, 20, 21, 23, 24, 25, 26, 27, 28, 29, 30, 31, 32, 33, 34, 35, 36, 37, 38, 39, 40, 41, 42, 48, 49, 51, 52, 62, 63, 66, 80, 81, 84, 85

Date of Accounts	Jan 11	Jan 10	Jan 09
Working Capital	22	15	18
Current Assets	23	18	19

Speedy Asset Services Ltd

41-45 Minerva Road, London, NW10 6HJ
Tel: 020-8961 9991 **Fax:** 020-8961 9891
E-mail: london-west-lifting@speedydepots.co.uk
Website: http://www.speedyservices.com
Managers: P. Israel (Chief Mgr)
Ultimate Holding Company: SPEEDY HIRE PLC
Immediate Holding Company: SPEEDY ASSET SERVICES LIMITED
Registration no: 06847930 **Date established:** 2009
No.of Employees: 21 - 50 **Product Groups:** 35

Date of Accounts	Mar 11	Mar 10	Mar 09
Working Capital	551	514	490
Fixed Assets	316	339	353
Current Assets	2m	2m	2m

Speedy Lifting (Speedy Group)

West Thamesmead Business Park Kellner Road, Thamesmead, London, SE28 0AX
Tel: 020-8854 6248 **Fax:** 020-8316 0501
E-mail: 0817.souththames@speedyhire.com
Website: http://www.speedyservices.com
Managers: R. English (Gen Contact)
Ultimate Holding Company: L.G.H. Group Ltd
Immediate Holding Company: L G H Group Ltd
Registration no: 04529136 **Turnover:** £20m - £50m
No.of Employees: 11 - 20 **Product Groups:** 45, 48, 83

Spencer Stuart & Associates Ltd

Bain House 16 Connaught Place, London, W2 2ED
Tel: 020-7298 3333 **Fax:** 020-7298 3388
E-mail: kwinter@spencerstuart.com
Website: http://www.spencerstuart.com
Directors: K. Winter (Fin)
Managers: A. Rolfe (Mktg Serv Mgr), M. Andrus
Ultimate Holding Company: SPENCER STUART MANAGEMENT CONSULTANTNETHERLANDS ANTILLE
Immediate Holding Company: SPENCER STUART & ASSOCIATES LIMITED
Registration no: 00703962 **VAT No.:** GB 239 6699 04
Date established: 1961 **Turnover:** £20m - £50m
No.of Employees: 101 - 250 **Product Groups:** 80

Date of Accounts	Sep 11	Sep 10	Sep 09
Sales Turnover	35m	33m	30m
Pre Tax Profit/Loss	602	496	284
Working Capital	4m	5m	3m
Fixed Assets	6m	7m	9m
Current Assets	21m	20m	14m
Current Liabilities	13m	12m	10m

Sphinx Jewels Ltd

111 Power Road, London, W4 5PY
Tel: 020-8995 8045 **Fax:** 020-8995 3979
E-mail: keith@sphinxandfeminajewels.co.uk
Website: http://www.sphinx.com
Directors: K. Palmer (Dir)
Immediate Holding Company: PENN CONTRACTING LIMITED
Registration no: 04340580 **VAT No.:** GB 227 0019 04
Date established: 1992 **Turnover:** £2m - £5m **No.of Employees:** 1 - 10
Product Groups: 30, 49

Date of Accounts	Dec 07	Dec 06	Dec 05
Working Capital	281	305	295
Current Assets	423	424	450
Current Liabilities	142	119	155

Spice Design Consultants Ltd

Hop Studios 2 Jamaica Road, London, SE1 2BX
Tel: 020-7252 0808 **Fax:** 020-7237 7199
E-mail: rog@spicehop.com
Website: http://www.spicehop.com
Directors: R. Butler (MD)
Immediate Holding Company: SPICE DESIGN CONSULTANTS LTD.
Registration no: 02866005 **Date established:** 1993
Turnover: Up to £250,000 **No.of Employees:** 1 - 10 **Product Groups:** 37, 44, 52, 81

Date of Accounts	Sep 11	Sep 10	Sep 09
Sales Turnover	N/A	N/A	130
Pre Tax Profit/Loss	N/A	N/A	-28
Working Capital	20	23	20
Fixed Assets	2	N/A	1
Current Assets	26	33	31
Current Liabilities	N/A	N/A	11

Spink & Son Ltd

69 Southampton Row, London, WC1B 4ET
Tel: 020-7563 4000 **Fax:** 020-7563 4066
E-mail: info@spink.com
Website: http://www.spink-online.com
Bank(s): Royal Bank of Scotland, London
Directors: A. Bennet (Fin), A. Spink (Dir)
Managers: L. Cones (Personnel), B. Qarauli (Tech Serv Mgr), S. Maylor (Mktg Serv Mgr)
Immediate Holding Company: SPINK AND SON LIMITED
Registration no: 04369748 **VAT No.:** GB 650 0414 84
Date established: 2002 **Turnover:** £20m - £50m
No.of Employees: 21 - 50 **Product Groups:** 49, 65

Date of Accounts	Jan 12	Jan 11	Jan 10
Sales Turnover	21m	22m	19m
Pre Tax Profit/Loss	983	1m	180
Working Capital	4m	4m	3m
Fixed Assets	1m	2m	3m
Current Assets	19m	18m	18m
Current Liabilities	5m	4m	3m

Sport England Funding Page

3rd Floor Victoria House Bloomsbury Square, London, WC1B 4SE
Tel: 08458-508508 **Fax:** 020-7383 5740
E-mail: kate.dale@sportengland.org
Website: http://www.sportengland.org
Managers: L. Brown (Purch Mgr), P. Schwar, K. Dale
Date established: 1972 **No.of Employees:** 101 - 250 **Product Groups:** 87

Spotlight Casting Directories & Contacts

7 Leicester Place, London, WC2H 7RJ
Tel: 020-7437 7631 **Fax:** 020-7437 5881
E-mail: enquiries@spotlight.com
Website: http://www.spotlight.com
Directors: B. Seal (Ptnr)
Managers: M. Peach (Personnel), N. Fokeerchand, L. Albery, P. Goldsmith
Immediate Holding Company: HAMILTON VERNON
Registration no: 07172054 **Date established:** 2010
Turnover: £500,000 - £1m **No.of Employees:** 21 - 50 **Product Groups:** 28

Spring Group (t/a Best Inetrnational)

Hasslet House 4 Bouverie Street, London, EC4Y 8AX
Tel: 020-7300 9000 **Fax:** 020-7300 9090
E-mail: info@spring.com
Website: http://www.glotel.com
Bank(s): National Westminster Bank Plc
Directors: N. Martin (Fin), G. Jones (Pers)
Managers: M. Clark (Tech Serv Mgr), T. Briant (Purch Mgr), G. Vale (Mktg Serv Mgr), S. O Connell (Sales Prom Mgr)
Ultimate Holding Company: ADECCO SA (SWITZERLAND)
Immediate Holding Company: SPRING GROUP LIMITED
Registration no: 00590054 **Date established:** 1957
Turnover: £500m - £1,000m **No.of Employees:** 51 - 100
Product Groups: 80

Date of Accounts	Dec 11	Dec 10	Dec 09
Pre Tax Profit/Loss	29m	876	-6m
Working Capital	10m	18m	19m
Fixed Assets	120m	83m	82m
Current Assets	54m	58m	66m
Current Liabilities	167	3m	3m

Ivor Spry & Co. Ltd

2 Knights Hill Square, London, SE27 0HH
Tel: 020-8761 1813
E-mail: sales@spry.co.uk
Website: http://www.spry.co.uk

Directors: M. King (MD)
Immediate Holding Company: IVOR SPRY & CO. LIMITED
Registration no: 00552369 **VAT No.:** GB 226 5768 41
Date established: 1955 **Turnover:** £500,000 - £1m
No.of Employees: 1 - 10 **Product Groups:** 30, 35, 36, 49, 66

Date of Accounts	May 11	May 10	May 09
Working Capital	65	42	48
Fixed Assets	11	15	20
Current Assets	103	93	94

Spud U Like
9 Central Business Centre Great Central Way, London, NW10 0UR
Tel: 020-8830 2424 **Fax:** 020-8830 2427
E-mail: headoffice@spudulike.com
Website: http://www.spudulike.com
Directors: J. Krebs (Dir), G. Crabbs (Dir), J. Krebs (Admin), A. Schlesinger (MD), A. Roberts (Fin)
Ultimate Holding Company: SPUDULIKE GROUP LTD
Immediate Holding Company: SPUD-U-LIKE HOLDINGS LIMITED
Registration no: 01845632 **Date established:** 1984
Turnover: £10m - £20m **No.of Employees:** 11 - 20 **Product Groups:** 20

Date of Accounts	Dec 10	Dec 09	Dec 08
Pre Tax Profit/Loss	N/A	501	2m
Working Capital	-112	-112	-13
Fixed Assets	501	501	501

Spy Equipment
Langham House 302-308 Regent Street, London, W1B 3AT
Tel: 0701-740 0850
Website: http://www.spyshop.ltd.uk
Directors: C. Brightman (Ptnr)
Immediate Holding Company: SEAVINE LIMITED
Date established: 1995 **No.of Employees:** 1 - 10 **Product Groups:** 37, 44, 49

Date of Accounts	Aug 11	Aug 10	Aug 09
Working Capital	581	109	77
Fixed Assets	320	925	845
Current Assets	595	156	126

Square Enix Ltd
Wimbledon Bridge House 1 Hartfield Road, London, SW19 3RU
Tel: 020-8636 3000 **Fax:** 020-8636 3001
E-mail: philr@eidos.co.uk
Website: http://www.square-enix.com
Managers: P. Rogers
Ultimate Holding Company: SQUARE ENIX HOLDINGS CO LTD (JAPAN)
Immediate Holding Company: SQUARE ENIX LIMITED
Registration no: 01804186 **Date established:** 1984
Turnover: £50m - £75m **No.of Employees:** 251 - 500 **Product Groups:** 28

Date of Accounts	Mar 11	Mar 10	Mar 09
Sales Turnover	56m	95m	67m
Pre Tax Profit/Loss	-11m	-38m	-25m
Working Capital	-209m	-198m	-143m
Fixed Assets	51m	50m	34m
Current Assets	99m	133m	96m
Current Liabilities	11m	21m	9m

Squeezyball Merchandising Ltd
2 The Linen House 253 Kilburn Lane, London, W10 4BQ
Tel: 020-8960 9013 **Fax:** 020-8960 6077
E-mail: sales@squeezyball.com
Website: http://www.squeezyball.com
Managers: D. Jones (Mgr), V. Jones (Mgr)
Immediate Holding Company: SQUEEZYBALL MERCHANDISING LTD
Registration no: 05249288 **VAT No.:** GB 736 3154 39
Date established: 2004 **Turnover:** £250,000 - £500,000
No.of Employees: 1 - 10 **Product Groups:** 44, 49, 65, 81

Date of Accounts	Oct 11	Oct 10	Oct 09
Sales Turnover	345	410	261
Pre Tax Profit/Loss	9	36	28
Working Capital	19	7	11
Fixed Assets	2	3	3
Current Assets	56	61	43
Current Liabilities	26	39	10

St Ermin's Hotel
2 Caxton Street, London, SW1H 0QW
Tel: (020)-7227 7774
E-mail: rpayne@sterminshotel.co.uk
Website: http://www.sterminshotellondon.co.uk
Product Groups: 69

Stafflink UK Ltd
138 Lower Road, London, SE16 2UG
Tel: 020-7252 2212 **Fax:** 020-7252 2901
E-mail: info@staff-link.co.uk
Website: http://www.staff-link.co.uk
Directors: T. Goodluck (MD)
Managers: I. Goodluck (Mktg Serv Mgr), C. Francois (Consultant)
Immediate Holding Company: DIAMONDCREST SERVICES (UK) LIMITED
Registration no: 07236349 **Date established:** 2010
No.of Employees: 1 - 10 **Product Groups:** 80, 81

Stainer & Bell Ltd
PO Box 110, London, N3 1DZ
Tel: 020-8343 3303 **Fax:** 020-8343 3024
E-mail: post@stainer.co.uk
Website: http://www.stainer.co.uk
Directors: C. Wakefield (Co Sec), A. Kearns (Dir)
Immediate Holding Company: STAINER & BELL LIMITED
Registration no: 00095905 **VAT No.:** GB 230 1613 22
Date established: 2007 **Turnover:** £500,000 - £1m
No.of Employees: 1 - 10 **Product Groups:** 28

Date of Accounts	Dec 11	Dec 10	Dec 09
Sales Turnover	783	813	793
Pre Tax Profit/Loss	23	59	524
Working Capital	1m	1m	1m
Fixed Assets	1m	1m	1m
Current Assets	2m	2m	2m
Current Liabilities	45	51	61

Standard Bank London Ltd
5th Floor Cannon Bridge House 25 Dowgate Hill, London, EC4R 2SB
Tel: 020-7815 3000 **Fax:** 020-7815 3099
E-mail: helpdesk@sitescope.co.uk
Website: http://www.standardbank.co.za
Bank(s): Barclays
Directors: D. Cooper (Ch), J. Maree (Dep Ch), R. Liegh (Grp Chief Exec), S. Smollett (Co Sec), S. Smollett (Fin)
Managers: D. Dugmore (Chief Acct), J. Garraway (Mktg Serv Mgr)
Ultimate Holding Company: STANDARD BANK GROUP LTD (SOUTH AFRICA)
Immediate Holding Company: STANDARD BANK PLC
Registration no: 02130447 **VAT No.:** GB 625 8615 25
Date established: 1987 **Turnover:** £20m - £50m
No.of Employees: 1001 - 1500 **Product Groups:** 82

Stanhope plc
31 St James Square, London, SW1Y 4JJ
Tel: 020-7170 1700 **Fax:** 020-7170 1701
E-mail: david.camp@stanhopeplc.com
Website: http://www.stanhopeplc.com
Directors: D. Camp (Grp Chief Exec), C. Pagan (Fin)
Managers: K. Young (Sales Admin)
Ultimate Holding Company: STANHOPE GROUP HOLDINGS LIMITED
Immediate Holding Company: STANHOPE GATE DEVELOPMENTS LIMITED
Registration no: 03797624 **Date established:** 1999 **Turnover:** £2m - £5m
No.of Employees: 21 - 50 **Product Groups:** 80

Date of Accounts	Dec 11	Dec 10	Dec 09
Sales Turnover	2m	4m	2m
Pre Tax Profit/Loss	128	903	369
Working Capital	423	633	-115
Fixed Assets	34	93	264
Current Assets	896	1m	744
Current Liabilities	161	437	671

Stanley Gibbons Ltd
399 Strand, London, WC2R 0LX
Tel: 020-7836 8444 **Fax:** 020-7836 7342
E-mail: sales@stanleygibbons.co.uk
Website: http://www.stanleygibbons.com
Directors: M. Henley (Fin)
Managers: L. Carden (Tech Serv Mgr), G. Sellers (Personnel), A. Sullivan (Purch Mgr), A. Hanrahan (Mktg Serv Mgr), R. Purkis (Admin Off)
Ultimate Holding Company: THE STANLEY GIBBONS GROUP PLC (JERSEY)
Immediate Holding Company: STANLEY GIBBONS HOLDINGS PLC
Registration no: 01124806 **Date established:** 1973
Turnover: £10m - £20m **No.of Employees:** 101 - 250
Product Groups: 27, 28, 61, 65

Date of Accounts	Dec 11	Dec 10	Dec 09
Sales Turnover	17m	14m	13m
Pre Tax Profit/Loss	1m	2m	2m
Working Capital	8m	9m	11m
Fixed Assets	3m	3m	1m
Current Assets	23m	21m	18m
Current Liabilities	694	944	1m

Stanwell Office Furniture
23 Muswell Avenue, London, N10 2EB
Tel: 020-8883 1039 **Fax:** 020-8444 3988
E-mail: info@stanwellofficefurniture.co.uk
Website: http://www.stanwellofficefurniture.co.uk
Directors: P. Negus (Dir)
Immediate Holding Company: STANWELL OFFICE FURNITURE LIMITED
Registration no: 04661507 **Date established:** 2003
Turnover: Up to £250,000 **No.of Employees:** 1 - 10 **Product Groups:** 26, 49

Date of Accounts	Mar 11	Mar 10	Mar 09
Working Capital	1	1	11
Fixed Assets	1	1	N/A
Current Assets	41	128	20

Star Capital Partners
6th Floor 33 Cavendish Square, London, W1G 0PW
Tel: 020-7016 8500 **Fax:** 020-7016 5500
E-mail: mail@star-capital.com
Website: http://www.star-capital.com
Directors: M. Williams (Fin)
Managers: E. Warner (Sales Admin)
Immediate Holding Company: STAR CAPITAL PARTNERS INVESTMENTS LLP
Registration no: OC326138 **Date established:** 2007
Turnover: £500,000 - £1m **No.of Employees:** 11 - 20 **Product Groups:** 80

Date of Accounts	Dec 11	Dec 10	Dec 09
Sales Turnover	576	587	143
Pre Tax Profit/Loss	474	762	135
Working Capital	2m	2m	2m
Fixed Assets	7m	7m	7m
Current Assets	2m	2m	2m
Current Liabilities	13	8	9

State Street Bank & Trust Co. Ltd
20 Churchill Place, London, E14 5HJ
Tel: 020-3395 2500 **Fax:** 020-7864 7344
Website: http://www.statestreet.com
Directors: J. Conway (MD)
Ultimate Holding Company: STATE STREET CORP (USA)
Immediate Holding Company: STATE STREET BANK EUROPE LIMITED
Registration no: 03413759 **Date established:** 1997
Turnover: £500,000 - £1m **No.of Employees:** 1501 & over
Product Groups: 80, 82

Date of Accounts	Dec 11	Dec 10
Sales Turnover	3m	95m
Pre Tax Profit/Loss	1m	48m
Working Capital	-97m	251m
Fixed Assets	228m	5m
Current Assets	125m	321m
Current Liabilities	222m	2m

Steeltec Wrought Ironwork
7 The Village, London, SE7 8UG
Tel: 020-8293 1166 **Fax:** 020-8465 5749
Directors: R. Wilkinson (Prop)
Date established: 1997 **No.of Employees:** 1 - 10 **Product Groups:** 26, 35

Stephenson Harwood
1 Finsbury Circus, London, EC2M 7SH
Tel: 020-7329 4422 **Fax:** 020-7329 7100
E-mail: info@shlegal.com
Website: http://www.shlegal.com
Directors: A. Sutch (Dir), D. Cohen (Fin), S. Gadhia (Grp Chief Exec)
Immediate Holding Company: STEPHENSON HARWOOD SERVICES LIMITED
Registration no: 02900722 **Date established:** 1994
Turnover: £20m - £50m **No.of Employees:** 501 - 1000
Product Groups: 80

Date of Accounts	Apr 11	Apr 10	Apr 09
Sales Turnover	26m	23m	23m
Pre Tax Profit/Loss	1m	907	1m
Working Capital	-108	-127	-146
Fixed Assets	13	31	50
Current Assets	4m	5m	4m
Current Liabilities	4m	5m	5m

Stiles Harold Williams Ltd
6 Babmaes Street, London, SW1Y 6HD
Tel: 020-7389 1500 **Fax:** 020-7389 1515
E-mail: london@shw.co.uk
Website: http://www.shw.co.uk
Directors: C. Williams (Tech Serv), H. Murton (Dir), R. Pollard (Fin)
Immediate Holding Company: STILES HAROLD WILLIAMS LIMITED
Registration no: 03311644 **VAT No.:** GB 692 7716 90
Date established: 1997 **Turnover:** £5m - £10m **No.of Employees:** 11 - 20
Product Groups: 80, 84

Date of Accounts	Apr 11	Apr 10	Apr 09
Sales Turnover	9m	9m	9m
Pre Tax Profit/Loss	478	590	168
Working Capital	2m	1m	1m
Fixed Assets	984	934	1m
Current Assets	4m	3m	3m
Current Liabilities	2m	2m	1m

Stirling Medical & Scientific Ltd
33-39 Beadnell Road, London, SE23 1AA
Tel: 020-8699 8993 **Fax:** 020-8291 7065
E-mail: sales@stirlingmedical.org
Website: http://www.stirlingmedical.org
Directors: P. Glass (Dir)
Immediate Holding Company: STIRLING MEDICAL & SCIENTIFIC LTD
Registration no: 07726465 **Date established:** 2011
Turnover: £250,000 - £500,000 **No.of Employees:** 1 - 10
Product Groups: 26, 30, 33, 36, 49, 67

Stone Fasteners Ltd
669a Woolwich Road, London, SE7 8SL
Tel: 020-8293 5080 **Fax:** 020-8293 4935
E-mail: info@stonefasteners.com
Website: http://www.stonefasteners.com
Directors: C. Darcy (Fin), S. Morgan (MD)
Ultimate Holding Company: LANGHAM INDUSTRIES LIMITED
Immediate Holding Company: STONE FASTENERS LIMITED
Registration no: 01627558 **VAT No.:** GB 358 4666 13
Date established: 1982 **Turnover:** £500,000 - £1m
No.of Employees: 1 - 10 **Product Groups:** 35

Date of Accounts	Dec 11	Dec 10	Dec 09
Sales Turnover	794	695	742
Pre Tax Profit/Loss	3	-136	-100
Working Capital	79	12	115
Fixed Assets	154	186	193
Current Assets	732	614	680
Current Liabilities	62	37	81

Stone Foundries Ltd
669a Woolwich Road, London, SE7 8SL
Tel: 020-8853 4648 **Fax:** 020-8305 1934
E-mail: sales@stonefoundries.com
Website: http://www.stonefoundries.com
Bank(s): Lloyds TSB
Directors: A. Alderton (MD), C. Darcy (Fin)
Managers: J. Staines (Prod Mgr), L. Duffy (Sales Prom Mgr)
Ultimate Holding Company: LANGHAM INDUSTRIES LIMITED
Immediate Holding Company: STONE FOUNDRIES LIMITED
Registration no: 01627562 **VAT No.:** GB 358 4665 15
Date established: 1982 **Turnover:** £5m - £10m
No.of Employees: 101 - 250 **Product Groups:** 34

Date of Accounts	Dec 11	Dec 10	Dec 09
Sales Turnover	7m	5m	5m
Pre Tax Profit/Loss	148	-371	-445
Working Capital	3m	2m	3m
Fixed Assets	1m	1m	1m
Current Assets	4m	4m	3m
Current Liabilities	658	577	202

Stone House Tiles Ltd
12 Ossory Road, London, SE1 5AN
Tel: 020-7237 5375 **Fax:** 020-7231 7597
E-mail: info@stonehousetiles.co.uk
Website: http://www.stonehousetiles.co.uk
Directors: G. Ruiz Urda (Dir), G. Ruiz (Dir), G. Urda (Fin), S. Errill (Dir), S. Errills (MD)
Managers: D. Crosser (Sales Prom)
Immediate Holding Company: STONEHOUSE TILES (LONDON) LIMITED
Registration no: 04626261 **Date established:** 2002
No.of Employees: 1 - 10 **Product Groups:** 14, 33, 49, 66

Stoneleigh Engineering
Unit 10 Lansdowne Workshops Lansdowne Mews, London, SE7 8AZ
Tel: 020-8305 0792 **Fax:** 020-8858 6665
Directors: R. Hudd (Ptnr)
Immediate Holding Company: STONELEIGH ENGINEERING SERVICES LTD.
Registration no: 02214241 **Date established:** 1988
Turnover: £250,000 - £500,000 **No.of Employees:** 1 - 10
Product Groups: 48, 66

Storm
5 Jubilee Place, London, SW3 3TD
Tel: 020-7368 9900 **Fax:** 020-7376 5145
E-mail: info@stormmodels.com
Website: http://www.stormmodels.com
Directors: S. Doukas (MD), S. Chambers (Fin)
Managers: M. Gokool (Tech Serv Mgr)
Ultimate Holding Company: CKX INC (USA)
Immediate Holding Company: STORM MODEL MANAGEMENT LIMITED
Registration no: 02138622 **Date established:** 1987 **Turnover:** £2m - £5m
No.of Employees: 21 - 50 **Product Groups:** 89

Date of Accounts	Dec 11	Dec 10	Dec 09
Sales Turnover	4m	3m	2m
Pre Tax Profit/Loss	562	588	136
Working Capital	223	667	245
Fixed Assets	139	76	84
Current Assets	2m	3m	2m
Current Liabilities	2m	2m	1m

Strand
44 Southside Clapham Common, London, SW4 9BU
Tel: 0844-9670720 **Fax:** 020-78018544
E-mail: enquiries@strandclean.co.uk
Website: http://www.strandclean.co.uk
Immediate Holding Company: O.C.S. Group Ltd
Registration no: 00628031 **Turnover:** £20m - £50m
No.of Employees: 51 - 100 **Product Groups:** 52

Strap Trap
Stanmore Road, London, E11 3BU
Tel: 020-8530 3484
E-mail: info@straptrap.co.uk
Website: http://www.straptrap.co.uk
Directors: H. Varley (Prop)
Date established: 2004 **Turnover:** Up to £250,000
No.of Employees: 1 - 10 **Product Groups:** 30, 35, 63

The Strategic Enterprise Group Ltd
7 Douglas Little Strand, London, NW9 5NS
Tel: 020-8200 0078 **Fax:** 020-8200 0334
E-mail: office@strategic-enterprise.com
Website: http://www.sankosa.co.uk
Directors: B. Horsford (Ch)
Managers: S. Johnson, K. Wallace (Purch Mgr), F. Horford (Sales & Mktg Mg)
Immediate Holding Company: THE STRATEGIC ENTERPRISE GROUP LIMITED
Registration no: 04440936 **Date established:** 2002
No.of Employees: 21 - 50 **Product Groups:** 80

Date of Accounts	May 11	May 10	May 03
Working Capital	33	33	1m
Current Assets	33	33	1m

Stratford Wire Works
2 Rowse Close, London, E15 2HX
Tel: 020-8534 1950 **Fax:** 01245-223869
E-mail: info@stratfordwireworks.co.uk
Website: http://www.stratfordwireworks.co.uk
Directors: S. Crampton (Ptnr)
Date established: 1927 **No.of Employees:** 1 - 10 **Product Groups:** 26, 35

Stream Environmental Solutions
145-157 St John Street, London, EC1V 4PY
Tel: 0870-7587801 **Fax:** 020-7117 1636
E-mail: info@fwd-solutions.co.uk
Website: http://www.elementalpr.co.uk
Directors: E. Tappenden (Dir)
Immediate Holding Company: IRON LTD
Registration no: 07351677 **Date established:** 2010
No.of Employees: 1 - 10 **Product Groups:** 80, 81

Stream UK Media Services
1 Water Lane, London, NW1 8NZ
Tel: 020-7482 4574 **Fax:** 020-7419 1819
E-mail: info@streamuk.com
Website: http://www.streamuk.com
Directors: D. Burbidge (Co Sec), J. Bray (Dir)
Immediate Holding Company: STREAM UK MEDIA SERVICES LIMITED
Registration no: 04206916 **Date established:** 2001
No.of Employees: 21 - 50 **Product Groups:** 44, 79

Date of Accounts	Mar 11	Mar 10	Mar 09
Working Capital	466	374	452
Fixed Assets	90	48	41
Current Assets	639	555	599

Streamline Surgical LLP
84-88 Pinner Road Harrow, London, HA1 4HZ
Tel: 0800-157 7033 **Fax:** 01243-831655
E-mail: info@streamline-surgical.com
Website: http://www.streamline-surgical.com
Directors: G. Slater (Ptnr), S. Somers (Ptnr), S. Toh (Ptnr)
Managers: C. Bigg (Sec)
Registration no: OC322779 **Date established:** 2006
No.of Employees: 1 - 10 **Product Groups:** 88

Strickland Mobile Marine Engines
94 Devonport Road, London, W12 8NU
Tel: 020-8746 0766
Directors: S. Strickland (Prop)
Registration no: 07214627 **Date established:** 1910
No.of Employees: 1 - 10 **Product Groups:** 35, 36, 39

Strom International Ltd
Unit B3 Connaught Business Centre Edgware Road, London, NW9 6JL
Tel: 020-8205 9697 **Fax:** 020-8905 8189
E-mail: sales@strom.co.uk
Directors: E. Strom (Fin), A. Strom (MD)
Immediate Holding Company: STROM INTERNATIONAL LIMITED
Registration no: 03508601 **VAT No.:** GB 713 8343 43
Date established: 1998 **Turnover:** £1m - £2m **No.of Employees:** 1 - 10
Product Groups: 24, 61

Date of Accounts	Feb 11	Feb 10	Feb 09
Working Capital	-14	42	4
Fixed Assets	10	12	8
Current Assets	333	411	303

Strong Packing Cases Ltd
Violet Road, London, E3 3QQ
Tel: 020-7987 7113 **Fax:** 020-7987 9060
E-mail: stephen@strongcases.com
Website: http://www.strongcases.com
Directors: H. Strong (Co Sec)
Ultimate Holding Company: STRONG HOLDINGS P.L.C.
Immediate Holding Company: STRONG HOLDINGS LTD
Registration no: 00411613 **VAT No.:** GB 549 0855 15
Turnover: £1m - £2m **No.of Employees:** 11 - 20 **Product Groups:** 25

Date of Accounts	May 06
Sales Turnover	1706
Pre Tax Profit/Loss	18
Working Capital	967
Fixed Assets	335
Current Assets	1241
Current Liabilities	274
Total Share Capital	50
ROCE% (Return on Capital Employed)	1.4

Studio Boardman
143 Talgarth Road, London, W14 9DA
Tel: 0845-258 1111 **Fax:** 07092-885152
E-mail: emma@studioboardman.com
Website: http://www.studioboardman.com
Managers: E. Boardman (Mgr)
Immediate Holding Company: ABCD LTD
Registration no: 05590876 **Date established:** 2005
No.of Employees: 1 - 10 **Product Groups:** 89

Studio Spares Ltd
964 North Circular Road, London, NW2 7JR
Tel: 020-8208 9930 **Fax:** 0800-731 3767
E-mail: sales@studiospares.com
Website: http://www.studiospares.com
Directors: B. Lamden (Dir)
Immediate Holding Company: STUDIOSPARES LIMITED
Registration no: 01699152 **Date established:** 1983 **Turnover:** £2m - £5m
No.of Employees: 21 - 50 **Product Groups:** 37

Date of Accounts	Feb 12	Feb 11	Feb 10
Working Capital	658	641	623
Fixed Assets	2m	2m	2m
Current Assets	995	915	906

Sturtivant & Co.
56 Queen Anne Street, London, W1G 8LA
Tel: 020-7486 9524 **Fax:** 020-7224 3164
E-mail: visas@sturtivant.co.uk
Website: http://www.sturtivant.co.uk
Directors: K. Sturtivant (Snr Part)
Immediate Holding Company: KENETH PETERS & COMPANY LIMITED
Date established: 1990 **No.of Employees:** 1 - 10 **Product Groups:** 80

Date of Accounts	Feb 12	Feb 11
Working Capital	75	44
Fixed Assets	7	10
Current Assets	282	47

Stylex
49 Berwick Street, London, W1F 8SH
Tel: 020-7437 2428 **Fax:** 020-7437 0649
E-mail: sales@style-x.co.uk
Website: http://www.style-x.co.uk
Directors: S. Shah (Snr Part), S. Shah (Ptnr), M. Shah (Ptnr), P. Shah (Ptnr)
VAT No.: GB 241 9519 58 **Date established:** 1977 **Turnover:** £1m - £2m
No.of Employees: 1 - 10 **Product Groups:** 24, 35

Sudler & Hennessey
Middlesex House 34 Cleveland Street, London, W1T 4JE
Tel: 020-7307 7801 **Fax:** 020-7307 7811
E-mail: brian.kelly@sudler.com
Website: http://www.sudler.com
Directors: B. Kelly (MD), B. Kelly (Prop)
Ultimate Holding Company: Young & Rubicam Development (Holdings) Ltd
Immediate Holding Company: SUDLER & HENNESSEY LIMITED
Registration no: 01401175 **Date established:** 1978
Turnover: £10m - £20m **No.of Employees:** 11 - 20 **Product Groups:** 87

Sugiarto Electroplaters Ltd
194 Hackney Road, London, E2 7QL
Tel: 020-7739 5011 **Fax:** 020-7739 6441
Directors: S. Herman (Prop)
Immediate Holding Company: SUGIARTO ELECTROPLATERS LIMITED
Registration no: 01980945 **Date established:** 1986
No.of Employees: 1 - 10 **Product Groups:** 46, 48

Date of Accounts	Jan 11	Jan 09	Jan 08
Working Capital	-25	4	N/A
Fixed Assets	N/A	N/A	2
Current Assets	36	36	28

Sumitomo Corporation Europe Holding Ltd
Vintners Place 68 Upper Thames Street, London, EC4V 3BJ
Tel: 020-7246 3600 **Fax:** 020-7246 3925
E-mail: info@sumitomocorp.co.uk
Website: http://www.sumitomocorp.co.uk
Directors: S. Sasaki (Dir)
Ultimate Holding Company: SUMITOMO CORPORATION (JAPAN)
Immediate Holding Company: SUMITOMO CORPORATION EUROPE HOLDING LIMITED
Registration no: 03285604 **VAT No.:** GB 769 0075 11
Date established: 1996 **Turnover:** £250m - £500m
No.of Employees: 101 - 250 **Product Groups:** 61

Date of Accounts	Mar 09	Mar 08	Mar 07
Sales Turnover	550m	466m	384m
Pre Tax Profit/Loss	141m	106m	71m
Working Capital	709m	-12m	-11m
Fixed Assets	280m	291m	187m
Current Assets	3001m	998m	724m
Current Liabilities	2291m	1010m	735m
Total Share Capital	215m	79m	79m

Sumitomo Trust & Banking Co. Ltd
155 Bishopsgate, London, EC2M 3XU
Tel: 020-7945 7000 **Fax:** 020-7945 7177
E-mail: sales@sumitomotrust.co.jp
Website: http://www.sumitomotrust.co.jp
Managers: H. Evans (Mgr), R. Seymour (Fin Mgr), J. Shipp, D. Grealy (Personnel), C. Dowson (Tech Serv Mgr), M. Jenkins (Mgr), D. Grealy (Personnel)
Immediate Holding Company: SUMITOMO MITSUI TRUST BANK, LIMITED
Registration no: FC008329 **VAT No.:** GB 244 8126 64
Date established: 1971 **Turnover:** £250,000 - £500,000
No.of Employees: 51 - 100 **Product Groups:** 82

Summit
54c Railway Arches North Woolwich Road, London, E16 2AA
Tel: 020-7474 5552
Website: http://www.summitdeafaids.co.uk
Managers: S. Georgiou (Mgr)
Immediate Holding Company: AVSUM LIMITED
Date established: 2009 **No.of Employees:** 1 - 10 **Product Groups:** 37, 38, 40, 49

Sun Capital Partners
4th Floor Watson House 54 Baker Street, London, W1U 7BU
Tel: 020-7725 0800 **Fax:** 020-7725 0808
E-mail: info@suncap.co.uk
Website: http://www.suncap.co.uk
Directors: A. Bradshaw (Fin)
Managers: A. Pandore (Tech Serv Mgr)
Ultimate Holding Company: SUN CAPITAL PARTNERS LIMITED
Immediate Holding Company: SUN CAPITAL LIMITED
Registration no: 04257139 **Date established:** 2001
No.of Employees: 11 - 20 **Product Groups:** 82

Sun 99 Ltd
365 Euston Road, London, NW1 3AR
Tel: 020-7874 6900 **Fax:** 020-7874 6919
E-mail: info@stormwatches.com
Website: http://www.stormwatches.com
Managers: C. Shearwood (Sales Prom)
Immediate Holding Company: SUN 99 LIMITED
Registration no: 01914818 **Date established:** 1985 **Turnover:** £5m - £10m
No.of Employees: 21 - 50 **Product Groups:** 65

Date of Accounts	Mar 11	Mar 10	Mar 09
Sales Turnover	6m	7m	N/A
Pre Tax Profit/Loss	52	376	-806
Working Capital	509	572	772
Fixed Assets	8m	8m	8m
Current Assets	5m	8m	8m
Current Liabilities	3m	3m	2m

Sungard
25 Canada Square, London, E14 5LQ
Tel: 020-8081 2000 **Fax:** 020-7623 8899
E-mail: info@reech.com
Website: http://www.sungard.com
Directors: H. Wallis (Co Sec)
Ultimate Holding Company: SUNGARD DATA SYSTEMS INC (USA)
Immediate Holding Company: REECH CAPITAL LIMITED
Registration no: 03649490 **Date established:** 1998 **Turnover:** £5m - £10m
No.of Employees: 501 - 1000 **Product Groups:** 44

Date of Accounts	Dec 11	Dec 10	Dec 09
Sales Turnover	5m	6m	6m
Pre Tax Profit/Loss	2m	986	259
Working Capital	2m	-42	-913
Fixed Assets	68	193	335
Current Assets	3m	2m	4m
Current Liabilities	1m	1m	1m

Sunley Holdings plc
20 Berkeley Square, London, W1J 6LH
Tel: 020-7499 8842 **Fax:** 020-7499 8832
E-mail: johns@sunley.co.uk
Website: http://www.sunley.co.uk
Bank(s): Clysdale
Directors: J. Sunley (MD)
Managers: L. Stradling (Comptroller)
Immediate Holding Company: SUNLEY PROPERTY LLP
Registration no: OC350451 **VAT No.:** GB 335 8803 41
Date established: 2009 **Turnover:** Up to £250,000
No.of Employees: 11 - 20 **Product Groups:** 80, 82, 84

Date of Accounts	Mar 12	Mar 11
Pre Tax Profit/Loss	N/A	1
Working Capital	5	-4
Fixed Assets	1m	1m
Current Assets	89	36
Current Liabilities	3	40

Super Stork I P T Ltd
Carlisle Road, London, NW9 0HD
Tel: 020-8200 1144 **Fax:** 020-8200 4385
E-mail: sales1@superstork.co.uk
Website: http://www.superstork.co.uk
Directors: J. Ransom (Co Sec), M. Dinca (MD), M. Theobald (MD), M. Theobald (Co Sec)
Managers: M. Bull (Serv Mgr)
Ultimate Holding Company: RPS HOLDING SARL (LUXEMBOURG)
Immediate Holding Company: SUPER STORK (INDUSTRIAL POWER TOOLS) LIMITED
Registration no: 00676499 **VAT No.:** GB 226 9954 24
Date established: 1960 **Turnover:** £1m - £2m **No.of Employees:** 1 - 10
Product Groups: 37, 40, 54

Date of Accounts	Dec 08	Dec 07	Dec 06
Sales Turnover	N/A	1m	1m
Pre Tax Profit/Loss	N/A	-199	-53
Working Capital	34	236	436
Fixed Assets	29	38	42
Current Assets	616	671	751
Current Liabilities	N/A	62	72

Supplies House Ltd
Unit 21 Interchange East Business Park Grosvenor Way, London, E5 9ND
Tel: 020-8806 8666 **Fax:** 020-8806 8686
E-mail: sales@supplieshouse.com
Website: http://www.supplieshouse.com
Bank(s): Barclays
Directors: B. Chapman (MD), C. Chapman (Dir), W. Martin (Fin)
Immediate Holding Company: SUPPLIES HOUSE LIMITED(THE)
Registration no: 01889752 **VAT No.:** GB 524 8516 41
Date established: 1985 **Turnover:** £2m - £5m **No.of Employees:** 11 - 20
Product Groups: 27, 63

Date of Accounts	Sep 11	Sep 10	Sep 09
Working Capital	-20	-86	-74
Fixed Assets	135	135	145
Current Assets	1m	1m	1m

Swada London
High Street, London, E15 2PP
Tel: 020-8534 7171 **Fax:** 020-8519 2818
E-mail: info@swada.co.uk
Website: http://www.swada.co.uk
Bank(s): Clydesdale
Directors: C. Dane (MD), P. Ryan (Dir)
Managers: R. Rosen (Sales Prom Mgr)
Ultimate Holding Company: Dane & Co. Ltd
Registration no: 00491985 **Date established:** 1990 **Turnover:** £5m - £10m
No.of Employees: 51 - 100 **Product Groups:** 32

Swift Line Engineering Ltd
Unit 5 Wellesley Court Apsley Way, London, NW2 7HF
Tel: 020-8452 4080
E-mail: info@swiftline.co.uk
Website: http://www.swiftline.co.uk
Directors: P. McLoughlin (Fin), K. Mcloughlin (MD)
Immediate Holding Company: SWIFTLINE ENGINEERING LIMITED
Registration no: 04190648 **Date established:** 2001
No.of Employees: 21 - 50 **Product Groups:** 37, 52, 84, 85

Date of Accounts	Mar 12	Mar 11	Mar 10
Working Capital	800	3m	115
Fixed Assets	104	84	88
Current Assets	3m	3m	1m

Swindens Patents Ltd
Suite 404, Albany House 324 Regent Street, London, W1B 3HH
Tel: 020-7580 6491 **Fax:** 020-7580 4729
E-mail: am@swindens-vices.co.uk
Website: http://www.swindens-vices.co.uk
Directors: D. Marangos (Co Sec), A. Marangos (MD)
Ultimate Holding Company: Swindens Patents Ltd
Registration no: 00226501 **VAT No.:** GB 235 9907 32
Turnover: £500,000 - £1m **No.of Employees:** 1 - 10 **Product Groups:** 36, 45, 46, 47, 66, 67

Swiss Re Services Ltd
30 St Mary Axe, London, EC3A 8EP
Tel: 020-7933 3000 **Fax:** 020-7933 5000
Website: http://www.swissre.com
Bank(s): Citibank International plc
Directors: M. Albers (MD), E. Zimmermann (Dir)
Ultimate Holding Company: SWISS REINSURANCE CO (SWITZERLAND).
Immediate Holding Company: SWISS RE GB LIMITED
Registration no: 01867359 **VAT No.:** GB 244 7975 24
Date established: 1984 **Turnover:** £500,000 - £1m
No.of Employees: 1001 - 1500 **Product Groups:** 82

Date of Accounts	Dec 11	Dec 10	Dec 09
Pre Tax Profit/Loss	265m	50m	77m
Working Capital	25m	7m	255m
Fixed Assets	215m	1236m	1256m
Current Assets	79m	73m	318m
Current Liabilities	50m	N/A	10m

Swiss Risk
19-21 Great Tower Street, London, EC3R 5AR
Tel: 020-7815 5200 **Fax:** 020-7815 5201
E-mail: info@swissrisk.com
Website: http://www.swissrisk.com
Directors: G. Owen (MD), P. Marshall (Grp Chief Exec)
Managers: J. Blon (Mktg Serv Mgr), P. Marshall
Ultimate Holding Company: CSK Corporation (Japan)
Immediate Holding Company: GRACECHURCH BLOODSTOCK LIMITED
Registration no: 04040258 **Date established:** 2000
Turnover: Up to £250,000 **No.of Employees:** 1 - 10 **Product Groups:** 44

System Logistics Limited
3 More London Riverside, London, SE1 2RE
Tel: 020-7770 6388 **Fax:** 020-7770 6389
E-mail: info@systemlogistics.com
Website: http://www.systemlogistics.com
Managers: G. Boner (Sales Prom Mgr)
Immediate Holding Company: DIAMOND PHOENIX, LTD.
Registration no: 05689171 **Date established:** 2000
Turnover: £20m - £50m **No.of Employees:** 1 - 10 **Product Groups:** 44, 45, 84

T B A P.L.C.
174-178 North Gower Street, London, NW1 2NB
Tel: 020-7554 9900 **Fax:** 020-7387 9004
E-mail: info@tbaplc.co.uk
Website: http://www.tbaplc.co.uk
Directors: G. Horner (MD), T. Ball MBE (Ch)
Registration no: 04455142 **VAT No.:** GB 749 6519 82
Turnover: £2m - £5m **No.of Employees:** 1 - 10 **Product Groups:** 80, 81

T B W A London
76-80 Whitfield Street, London, W1T 4EZ
Tel: 020-7573 6666 **Fax:** 020-7573 6728
E-mail: human.resources@tbwa-london.com
Website: http://www.tbwa-london.com
Directors: R. Harwood-Matthews (Pres)
Ultimate Holding Company: OMNICOM GROUP INC (USA)
Immediate Holding Company: TBWAONDON LIMITED
Registration no: 01367372 **Date established:** 1978
Turnover: £20m - £50m **No.of Employees:** 101 - 250 **Product Groups:** 81

Date of Accounts	Dec 11	Dec 10	Dec 09
Sales Turnover	25m	95m	18m
Pre Tax Profit/Loss	2m	2m	-301
Working Capital	2m	3m	-162
Fixed Assets	6m	8m	9m
Current Assets	52m	45m	27m
Current Liabilities	8m	6m	7m

T & F Informa Two Ltd
Mortimer House 37-41 Mortimer Street, London, W1T 3JH
Tel: 020-7436 0585 **Fax:** 020-7631 3214
Website: http://www.informayachtgroup.com
Directors: D. Gilbertson (MD), S. Kemp (Mkt Research), S. Osborne (I.T. Dir), P. Rigby (Grp Chief Exec), P. Rigby (Ch), J. Burton (Co Sec), J. Pleasance (Dir)
Ultimate Holding Company: INFORMA PLC (JERSEY)
Immediate Holding Company: T & F INFORMA TWO LIMITED
Registration no: 05232106 **Date established:** 2004
Turnover: Over £1,000m **No.of Employees:** 1 - 10 **Product Groups:** 80

Date of Accounts	Dec 11	Dec 10	Dec 09
Pre Tax Profit/Loss	-979	-548	-1m
Working Capital	-30m	-30m	-29m
Fixed Assets	244m	244m	244m
Current Assets	604	324	N/A

T & J Sprayers Ltd
Unit 15s Silvermere Drive Stonehill Business Park, London, N18 3QH
Tel: 020-8807 9511 **Fax:** 020-8807 9576
E-mail: colinm820@aol.com
Directors: C. Madden (Dir)
Immediate Holding Company: T & J SPRAYERS LIMITED
Registration no: 04582433 **Date established:** 2002
No.of Employees: 1 - 10 **Product Groups:** 46, 48

Date of Accounts	Sep 11	Sep 10	Sep 09
Working Capital	24	43	45
Fixed Assets	13	20	2
Current Assets	53	99	66

T M P Worldwide Ltd
53-64 Chancery Lane Chancery House, London, WC2A 1QY
Tel: 020-7406 5000 **Fax:** 020-7406 5001
E-mail: admin@tmpw.co.uk
Website: http://www.tmp.com
Directors: A. Wilkinson (MD)
Managers: J. Porter, N. Vipan (I.T. Exec)
Registration no: 00554092 **Turnover:** £20m - £50m
No.of Employees: 1 - 10 **Product Groups:** 80

T P Bennett Partnership
1 America Street, London, SE1 0NE
Tel: 020-7208 2008 **Fax:** 020-7208 2020
E-mail: richard.beastall@tpbennett.co.uk
Website: http://www.tpbennett.com
Bank(s): National Westminster Bank Plc
Directors: G. Smith (Dir), L. Zealley (Sales & Mktg), R. Beastall (Dir), D. Homes (Dir), R. Beastall (MD)
Ultimate Holding Company: CARGIL MANAGEMENT SERVICES LIMITED
Immediate Holding Company: BERNARD ENGLE ARCHITECTS & PLANNERS LIMITED
Registration no: 02750457 **VAT No.:** GB 232 1488 84
Date established: 1992 **Turnover:** £5m - £10m
No.of Employees: 101 - 250 **Product Groups:** 54, 84

T4 Alvern Media Ltd
3rd Floor 1 Warwick Row, London, SW1E 5ER
Tel: 020-7233 9777 **Fax:** 01225-329388
E-mail: info@t4media.co.uk
Website: http://www.t4media.co.uk
Bank(s): Lloyds
Managers: D. James (Sales Admin), J. Willett (Fin Mgr)
Ultimate Holding Company: T4 HOLDINGS LIMITED
Immediate Holding Company: ALVERN MEDIA LTD.
Registration no: 02985892 **VAT No.:** GB 237 6265 49
Date established: 1994 **Turnover:** £250,000 - £500,000
No.of Employees: 21 - 50 **Product Groups:** 86

Date of Accounts	Dec 11	Dec 10	Dec 09
Working Capital	2m	2m	1m
Fixed Assets	68	61	17
Current Assets	4m	3m	3m

Tal Talent
Colechurch House London Bridge Walk, London, SE1 2SS
Tel: 020-7378 7470 **Fax:** 020-7403 6729
E-mail: info@taltalent.com
Website: http://www.taltalent.com
Managers: J. Hill
Immediate Holding Company: W.G.I. SPORTS & LEISURE LIMITED
Registration no: 02561472 **VAT No.:** GB 574 1339 37
Date established: 1997 **Turnover:** Up to £250,000
No.of Employees: 1 - 10 **Product Groups:** 80

Talash Group
286-288 Streatham High Road, London, SW16 6HE
Tel: 020-8769 2998 **Fax:** 020-8769 2998
Directors: S. Kathuria (Prop)
Immediate Holding Company: TALASH LIMITED
Registration no: 06343753 **Date established:** 2007
No.of Employees: 1 - 10 **Product Groups:** 43

Date of Accounts	Oct 10	Oct 09	Oct 08
Working Capital	-139	-177	-127
Fixed Assets	3m	3m	4m
Current Assets	166	86	78

Talbot Designs Ltd
225 Long Lane Finchley, London, N3 2RL
Tel: 020-8346 8515 **Fax:** 020-8349 0294
E-mail: sales@talbotdesigns.co.uk
Website: http://www.talbotdesigns.co.uk
Bank(s): Bank of Ireland
Directors: R. Woolff (MD), A. Woolff (Co Sec), C. Woolff (Dir)
Immediate Holding Company: TALBOT DESIGNS LIMITED
Registration no: 00659101 **VAT No.:** GB 232 0655 96
Date established: 1960 **Turnover:** £1m - £2m **No.of Employees:** 21 - 50
Product Groups: 26, 30, 40, 41, 49, 66, 81

Date of Accounts	Mar 11	Mar 10	Mar 09
Working Capital	-68	-45	-9
Fixed Assets	40	70	67
Current Assets	278	256	318

Talentmark Ltd
King House 5-11 Westbourne Grove, London, W2 4UA
Tel: 020-7229 2266 **Fax:** 020-7229 3549
E-mail: william.neilson@talentmark.com
Website: http://www.talentmark.com
Directors: A. Chandler (MD), W. Nealson (MD), S. Brown (Co Sec)
Managers: W. Neilson (Mgr)
Immediate Holding Company: TALENTMARK LIMITED
Registration no: 01004708 **VAT No.:** GB 238 5024 70
Date established: 1971 **Turnover:** £1m - £2m **No.of Employees:** 1 - 10
Product Groups: 80

Date of Accounts	Jun 07	Jun 06
Working Capital	205	179
Fixed Assets	62	58
Current Assets	574	429
Current Liabilities	369	250
Total Share Capital	140	140

Talk Talk
11 Evesham Street, London, W11 4AR
Tel: 0800-049 5969 **Fax:** 020-3417 1001
E-mail: pressoffice@talktalkgroup.com
Website: http://https://sales.talktalk.co.uk/product/broadband
Managers: A. Bradbury
Ultimate Holding Company: TALKTALK TELECOM GROUP PLC
Immediate Holding Company: TALKTALK CORPORATE LIMITED
Registration no: 06755322 **VAT No.:** GB 636 1333 57
Date established: 2008 **Turnover:** £250,000 - £500,000
No.of Employees: 1 - 10 **Product Groups:** 37, 48, 84, 85

Date of Accounts	Mar 12	Mar 11	Mar 09
Sales Turnover	1m	N/A	1385m
Pre Tax Profit/Loss	158m	-617m	-72m
Working Capital	741m	580m	-210m
Fixed Assets	238m	239m	1751m
Current Assets	753m	631m	147m
Current Liabilities	2m	5m	247m

Talon Coffee Services Ltd
16a Morris Avenue, London, E12 6EW
Tel: 020-8514 2023 **Fax:** 020-8553 9690
E-mail: sales@talon-direct.com
Website: http://www.talon-direct.com
Directors: S. Hoy (MD)
Registration no: 04680966 **Date established:** 2003
Turnover: Up to £250,000 **No.of Employees:** 1 - 10 **Product Groups:** 40

Tapdie
445 West Green Road South Tottenham, London, N15 3PL
Tel: 020-8888 1865 **Fax:** 020-8888 4613
E-mail: sales@tapdie.com
Website: http://www.tapdie.com
Managers: Z. Shaw (Sales Admin)
Registration no: 03759867 **Date established:** 1978
No.of Employees: 1 - 10 **Product Groups:** 47

Tara Antiques
6 Church Street, London, NW8 8ED
Tel: 020-7724 2405 **Fax:** 020-7723 7415
E-mail: info@churchstreetantiques.net
Website: http://www.churchstreetantiques.net
Directors: D. Hudson (Ptnr)
Immediate Holding Company: ANTIQUE HYPERMARKET LIMITED
Registration no: 00884258 **Date established:** 1966
No.of Employees: 1 - 10 **Product Groups:** 25, 26, 33, 61, 65

Tara Fabrications Ltd
22a Blenheim Grove, London, SE15 4QS
Tel: 020-7732 8100 **Fax:** 020-7252 8020
E-mail: tarafabrications@btconnect.com
Website: http://www.tarafabrications.co.uk
Directors: S. Parsons (Dir)
No.of Employees: 1 - 10 **Product Groups:** 35

Target Arms
PO Box 58881, London, SE15 9BS
Tel: 020-7635 5086 **Fax:** 020-8693 4211
E-mail: webmaster@target-arms.co.uk
Website: http://www.target-arms.co.uk
Directors: D. Targett (Ptnr)
Date established: 1987 **No.of Employees:** 1 - 10 **Product Groups:** 36, 39, 40

Task International Ltd
156-158 Victoria Street, London, SW1E 5LB
Tel: 0114-270 2498 **Fax:** 020-7932 9461
E-mail: security@task-int.com
Website: http://www.task-int.com
Bank(s): HSBC Bank plc
Directors: R. Dyson (Fin)
Immediate Holding Company: TASK INTERNATIONAL LTD
Registration no: 03085665 **VAT No.:** GB 562 1900 59
Date established: 1995 **No.of Employees:** 11 - 20 **Product Groups:** 80, 81, 86

Date of Accounts	Apr 11	Apr 10	Apr 09
Working Capital	45	-39	6
Fixed Assets	1	3	3
Current Assets	68	191	90

Tastes Catering
23 Crimscott Street, London, SE1 5TE
Tel: 020-7232 2325 **Fax:** 020-7232 0458
E-mail: kinga@tastescatering.co.uk
Website: http://www.tastescatering.co.uk
Directors: L. Sutherland (Fin)
Managers: K. Adamczuk (Ops Mgr), I. Kibby
Immediate Holding Company: TASTES CATERING LIMITED
Registration no: 02938553 **Date established:** 1994
Turnover: £500,000 - £1m **No.of Employees:** 1 - 10 **Product Groups:** 69, 89

Date of Accounts	Mar 12	Mar 11	Mar 10
Working Capital	-33	-21	-23
Fixed Assets	46	51	40
Current Assets	101	243	141

Tata Steel
30 Millbank, London, SW1P 4WY
Tel: 020-7975 8000 **Fax:** 020-7717 4455
E-mail: feedback@tatasteel.com
Website: http://www.tatasteel.com
Managers: K. Ohere (Comptroller), M. McCombe (Purch Mgr), G. Lucas (Chief Mgr), G. Davis (Personnel), R. Lockhart (Chief Mgr)
Ultimate Holding Company: TATA STEEL LIMITED (INDIA)
Immediate Holding Company: TATA STEEL UK HOLDINGS LIMITED
Registration no: 05887351 **VAT No.:** GB 238 7122 60
Date established: 2006 **Turnover:** Over £1,000m
No.of Employees: 101 - 250 **Product Groups:** 30, 66

Date of Accounts	Mar 08	Mar 09	Apr 10
Sales Turnover	419m	494m	162m
Pre Tax Profit/Loss	3m	-5m	612
Working Capital	17m	14m	14m
Current Assets	46m	27m	47m
Current Liabilities	2m	6m	3m

Tate & Lyle Public Ltd Company
Sugar Quay Lower Thames Street, London, EC3R 6DQ
Tel: 020-7626 6525 **Fax:** 020-7623 5213
E-mail: robert.gibber@tateandlyle.com
Website: http://www.tateandlyle.com
Bank(s): HSBC, Greenwich High Road, SE10
Directors: L. Gilbert (Co Sec), R. Gibber (Co Sec), R. Delbridge (Dir), R. Gibber (Dir), J. Beal (Co Sec), I. Ferguson (MD), D. Ward (Chief Op Offcr), R. Burden (MD)
Managers: M. Stanton (Personnel), L. Dorran, S. Pelc, M. McGuire (Sales Prom Mgr), C. Pycraft (Purch Mgr)
Ultimate Holding Company: Tate Lyle P.L.C.
Immediate Holding Company: TATE & LYLE PUBLIC LIMITED COMPANY
Registration no: 00076535 **Date established:** 2003
Turnover: Over £1,000m **No.of Employees:** 1501 & over
Product Groups: 20, 31, 32

Taylor Wessing LLP
5 New Street Square, London, EC4A 3TW
Tel: 020-7300 7000 **Fax:** 020-7300 7001
E-mail: london@taylorwessing.com
Website: http://www.taylorwessing.com
Bank(s): National Westminster
Directors: S. Walters (Tech Serv), T. Eyles (Ptnr), C. Rawes (Pers), C. Beckett (Fin)

see next page

Taylor Wessing LLP - *Cont'd*
Immediate Holding Company: TAYLOR WESSING (LONDON) LIMITED
Registration no: 04515549 **Date established:** 2002
Turnover: £50m - £75m **No.of Employees:** 501 - 1000
Product Groups: 80

Team Saatchi
23 Howland Street, London, W1T 4AY
Tel: 020-7436 6636 **Fax:** 020-7462 7756
Website: http://www.teamsaatchi.co.uk
Directors: S. Hooper (MD)
Immediate Holding Company: MMS UK HOLDINGS LTD
Registration no: 02415224 **VAT No.:** GB 276 7319 25
Turnover: £10m - £20m **No.of Employees:** 21 - 50 **Product Groups:** 81

Date of Accounts	Dec 11	Dec 10	Dec 09
Working Capital	28	33	51
Fixed Assets	122	66	39
Current Assets	197	180	193

Techmaco
88 Station Road, London, N22 7SY
Tel: 020-8882 7852 **Fax:** 020-8882 6534
E-mail: techmaco@msn.com
Directors: K. Chowdhury (MD)
VAT No.: GB 735 4012 80 **Turnover:** Up to £250,000
No.of Employees: 1 - 10 **Product Groups:** 61

Technical Publications Service Ltd
5 Vines Avenue, London, N3 2QD
Tel: 020-8349 1757 **Fax:** 020-8343 1218
E-mail: info@tractor-manuals.com
Website: http://www.tractor-manuals.com
Directors: A. Galatopoulos (MD), K. Galatopoulos (Fin)
Immediate Holding Company: TECHNICAL PUBLICATIONS SERVICE LIMITED
Registration no: 01680906 **Date established:** 1982
Turnover: Up to £250,000 **No.of Employees:** 1 - 10 **Product Groups:** 67

Date of Accounts	Mar 11	Mar 10	Mar 06
Working Capital	162	186	108
Fixed Assets	1	1	1
Current Assets	285	295	186

Techniker Structural Engineers
13-19 Vine Hill, London, EC1R 5DW
Tel: 020-7360 4300 **Fax:** 020-7360 4301
E-mail: mail@techniker.co.uk
Website: http://www.techniker.co.uk
Directors: M. Wells (Prop)
Immediate Holding Company: TECHNIKER LIMITED
Registration no: 02783793 **Date established:** 1993
No.of Employees: 1 - 10 **Product Groups:** 35

Date of Accounts	Jan 11	Jan 10	Jan 09
Working Capital	-40	101	119
Fixed Assets	57	72	61
Current Assets	527	645	406

Ted Baker Ltd
6a St Pancras Way, London, NW1 0TB
Tel: 020-7255 4800 **Fax:** 020-7387 0106
E-mail: charles.anderson@tedbaker.com
Website: http://www.tedbaker.com
Directors: L. Page (Fin), C. Anderson (Fin)
Managers: C. Smith, D. Steer, J. Wahla
Immediate Holding Company: TED BAKER PLC
Registration no: 03393836 **VAT No.:** GB 697 0864 80
Date established: 1997 **Turnover:** £125m - £250m
No.of Employees: 251 - 500 **Product Groups:** 24

Date of Accounts	Jan 09	Jan 10	Jan 11
Sales Turnover	153m	164m	188m
Pre Tax Profit/Loss	18m	20m	24m
Working Capital	31m	39m	45m
Fixed Assets	31m	29m	33m
Current Assets	65m	67m	84m
Current Liabilities	17m	18m	20m

TEK International
7 Altior Court Shepherds Hill, London, N6 5RJ
Tel: 0203-0087221 **Fax:** 0203-0087222
E-mail: info@tekinternational.co.uk
Website: http://www.tekinternational.co.uk
Managers: J. Deacon (Mgr)
Registration no: 6981212 **Date established:** 2009 **Turnover:**
No.of Employees: 1 - 10 **Product Groups:** 80

Tektura plc
Harbour Exchange Square, London, E14 9JE
Tel: 020-7536 3300 **Fax:** 020-7536 3322
E-mail: enquiries@tektura.com
Website: http://www.tektura.com
Directors: N. Hooper (MD)
Ultimate Holding Company: BN INTERNATIONAL HOLDING BV (NETHERLANDS)
Immediate Holding Company: TEKTURA PUBLIC LIMITED COMPANY
Registration no: 00786933 **Date established:** 1964 **Turnover:** £5m - £10m
No.of Employees: 11 - 20 **Product Groups:** 23, 27, 30, 32

Date of Accounts	Dec 11	Dec 10	Dec 09
Sales Turnover	8m	7m	6m
Pre Tax Profit/Loss	731	155	4
Working Capital	602	572	582
Fixed Assets	41	59	88
Current Assets	3m	2m	2m
Current Liabilities	1m	716	499

Telco Lifts
5 Culmore Business Centre Culmore Road, London, SE15 2RQ
Tel: 020-7635 5851 **Fax:** 020-7639 1065
Website: http://www.telcolifts.co.uk
Directors: M. O'connor (Ptnr)
Date established: 1982 **No.of Employees:** 1 - 10 **Product Groups:** 35, 39, 45

Telehouse International
Coriander Avenue, London, E14 2AA
Tel: 020-7512 0550 **Fax:** 020-7512 0033
E-mail: info@uk.telehouse.net
Website: http://www.telehouse.net
Directors: S. Hara (Co Sec), T. Mitsui (MD)
Ultimate Holding Company: KDDI CORPORATION (JAPAN)
Immediate Holding Company: TELEHOUSE HOLDINGS LIMITED
Registration no: 02814979 **Date established:** 1993
Turnover: £75m - £125m **No.of Employees:** 101 - 250
Product Groups: 54

Date of Accounts	Dec 11	Dec 10	Dec 09
Sales Turnover	90m	79m	68m
Pre Tax Profit/Loss	27m	25m	21m
Working Capital	-29m	-23m	-21m
Fixed Assets	254m	243m	231m
Current Assets	40m	34m	40m
Current Liabilities	48m	43m	40m

Tempest Consultancy Ltd
Central House 1 Ballards Lane, Finchley Central, London, N3 1LQ
Tel: 020-3286 1298
E-mail: enquiries@tempestconsult.co.uk
Website: http://www.tempestconsult.co.uk
Directors: F. Odekeye (Dir)
Registration no: 06544139 **Date established:** 2008
No.of Employees: 1 - 10 **Product Groups:** 80, 86

Temple Lifts
329 Baring Road, London, SE12 0DZ
Tel: 020-8851 8900 **Fax:** 0116-269 7666
E-mail: enquiries@templelifts.com
Website: http://www.templelifts.com
Managers: S. Hamlin (Chief Mgr)
Ultimate Holding Company: TEMPLE LIFTS GROUP 2010 LIMITED
Immediate Holding Company: TEMPLE LIFTS LIMITED
Registration no: 02388497 **Date established:** 1989
Turnover: £10m - £20m **No.of Employees:** 11 - 20 **Product Groups:** 35, 39, 45

Date of Accounts	Dec 11	Dec 10	Dec 09
Sales Turnover	10m	12m	13m
Pre Tax Profit/Loss	294	636	879
Working Capital	1m	905	487
Fixed Assets	380	388	409
Current Assets	3m	3m	3m
Current Liabilities	1m	2m	1m

Temple Wines Ltd (Rajni Kataria & Madhu Kataria)
472 Church Lane, London, NW9 8UA
Tel: 020-8905 9484 **Fax:** 020-8200 8393
E-mail: neal.nalin@bt.com
Directors: K. Raj (MD)
Immediate Holding Company: TEMPLE WINES (CASH & CARRY) LTD
Registration no: 02649717 **No.of Employees:** 1 - 10 **Product Groups:** 21, 62

Terrell Ltd
30 Snowsfields, London, SE1 3SU
Tel: 020-7403 6111 **Fax:** 020-7378 0378
E-mail: sales@terrellinternational.co.uk
Website: http://www.terrellinternational.co.uk
Directors: D. Conroy (MD), A. Allart (Co Sec)
Immediate Holding Company: TERRELL LIMITED
Registration no: 03558113 **Date established:** 1998
Turnover: £500,000 - £1m **No.of Employees:** 1 - 10 **Product Groups:** 35

Date of Accounts	Sep 11	Sep 10	Sep 09
Sales Turnover	688	908	929
Pre Tax Profit/Loss	36	-31	-56
Working Capital	128	90	151
Fixed Assets	24	27	32
Current Assets	333	408	669
Current Liabilities	73	203	322

The Tgi Group Ltd
81 Carter Lane, London, EC4V 5EP
Tel: 020-7246 0204 **Fax:** 020-7236 0997
Website: http://www.pgi-uk.com
Directors: S. Wayne (Grp Chief Exec), S. Hobhouse (Dir)
Managers: G. Donovan (Sec)
Immediate Holding Company: PGI GROUP LIMITED
Registration no: 01338135 **VAT No.:** 380 4497 37 **Date established:** 1977
Turnover: £1m - £2m **No.of Employees:** 1 - 10 **Product Groups:** 62

Date of Accounts	Dec 09	Dec 08	Dec 07
Sales Turnover	29m	23m	18m
Pre Tax Profit/Loss	6m	-2m	4m
Working Capital	3m	893	458
Fixed Assets	32m	32m	28m
Current Assets	13m	9m	6m
Current Liabilities	3m	2m	2m

Thales Avionics Ltd
88 Bushey Road, London, SW20 0JW
Tel: 020-8946 8011 **Fax:** 020-8946 3014
Website: http://www.thales-avionics.com
Bank(s): National Westminster, 15 Bishopsgate
Directors: P. Cahn (MD), M. Seabrook (Co Sec), D. Ranque (Ch), R. Deacon (MD)
Managers: K. Dods (Personnel), J. Mountfield (Mktg Serv Mgr)
Immediate Holding Company: THALES AVIONICS LIMITED
Registration no: 00523160 **Date established:** 1953
Turnover: £75m - £125m **No.of Employees:** 251 - 500
Product Groups: 37, 39, 67

Date of Accounts	Dec 07
Sales Turnover	66200
Pre Tax Profit/Loss	7360
Working Capital	-10800
Fixed Assets	42220
Current Assets	28990
Current Liabilities	39790
Total Share Capital	9350
ROCE% (Return on Capital Employed)	23.4

The Ex Mill Envelope & Paper Co. Ltd
5-9 City Garden Row, London, N1 8DW
Tel: 020-7253 8312 **Fax:** 020-7251 5336
E-mail: sales@exmill.co.uk
Website: http://www.exmill.co.uk
Directors: H. Moszkowicz (MD)
Immediate Holding Company: THE EX MILL ENVELOPE AND PAPER COMPANY LIMITED
Registration no: 00716867 **Date established:** 1962
Turnover: Up to £250,000 **No.of Employees:** 1 - 10 **Product Groups:** 27, 64, 66

Date of Accounts	Feb 12	Feb 11	Feb 10
Working Capital	1m	1m	1m
Fixed Assets	3m	3m	3m
Current Assets	1m	1m	1m

The Lancet
32 Jamestown Road, London, NW1 7BY
Tel: 020-7424 4910 **Fax:** 020-7424 4912
Website: http://www.lancet.com
Directors: R. Horton (MD)
Ultimate Holding Company: ELSEVIER SCIENCE BV
Immediate Holding Company: ELSEVIER SCIENCE LIMITED
No.of Employees: 1 - 10 **Product Groups:** 28, 64

The National Gallery
St Vincent House 30 Orange Street, London, WC2H 7HH
Tel: 020-7747 5800 **Fax:** 020-7747 5951
E-mail: admin@nationalgallery.co.uk
Website: http://www.nationalgallery.co.uk
Directors: J. Molloy (MD)
Managers: R. Cross (I.T. Exec), J. Warne
Immediate Holding Company: NATIONAL GALLERY COMPANY LIMITED
Registration no: 02280277 **Date established:** 1988 **Turnover:** £5m - £10m
No.of Employees: 1 - 10 **Product Groups:** 28, 82

The Old Southern Forge Ltd
Southern Rail Stables St James Road, London, SE1 5JX
Tel: 020-7237 8825 **Fax:** 020-7237 8700
E-mail: sally@theoldsouthernforge.co.uk
Directors: S. Maher (Co Sec)
Immediate Holding Company: THE OLD SOUTHERN FORGE LIMITED
Registration no: 02692501 **Date established:** 1992
Turnover: £500,000 - £1m **No.of Employees:** 1 - 10 **Product Groups:** 26, 35

Date of Accounts	Sep 11	Sep 10	Sep 09
Working Capital	-3	26	15
Fixed Assets	34	42	53
Current Assets	379	402	230

The P R Organisation (Personnel Relations Ltd)
Burlington House 64 Chiswick High Road, London, W4 1SY
Tel: 020-8995 4343 **Fax:** 020-8995 2349
E-mail: robin@personnelrelations.co.uk
Website: http://www.personnelrelations.com
Directors: R. Broadway (MD), P. Rendall (Fin)
Immediate Holding Company: PERSONNEL RELATIONS LIMITED
Registration no: 02716392 **VAT No.:** 222 7399 60 **Date established:** 1963
Turnover: Up to £250,000 **No.of Employees:** 1 - 10 **Product Groups:** 28, 81, 86

Date of Accounts	Dec 10	Dec 09	Dec 08
Sales Turnover	N/A	43	63
Pre Tax Profit/Loss	N/A	-25	-7
Working Capital	-560	-555	-542
Fixed Assets	627	631	636
Current Assets	18	14	21
Current Liabilities	N/A	563	558

The Paper Co.
Unit 2 Bricklayers Arms Distribution Centre Mandela Way, London, SE1 5SP
Tel: 020-7740 2244 **Fax:** 01625-511144
E-mail: info@m6papers.co.uk
Website: http://www.paperco.co.uk
Bank(s): Barclays
Directors: M. Allen (Reg)
Ultimate Holding Company: PAPERLINX LIMITED (AUSTRALIA)
Immediate Holding Company: THE PAPER COMPANY LIMITED
Registration no: 01995271 **VAT No.:** GB 611 5600 84
Date established: 1986 **Turnover:** £250m - £500m
No.of Employees: 11 - 20 **Product Groups:** 66

Date of Accounts	Jun 11	Jun 10	Jun 09
Sales Turnover	297m	288m	320m
Pre Tax Profit/Loss	1m	2m	2m
Working Capital	107m	103m	100m
Fixed Assets	4m	6m	8m
Current Assets	164m	163m	165m
Current Liabilities	20m	14m	17m

The Tool & Gauge Co.
200e Iverson Road, London, NW6 2HL
Tel: 020-7372 1973 **Fax:** 020-7813 3345
E-mail: thetoolngaugeco@aol.com
Website: http://www.thetoolandgauge.com
Directors: A. Shah (Prop)
No.of Employees: 1 - 10 **Product Groups:** 35, 36

The Who Cares Trust
Kemp House 152-160 City Road, London, EC1V 2NP
Tel: 020-7251 3117 **Fax:** 020-7251 3123
E-mail: mailbox@thewhocarestrust.org.uk
Website: http://www.thewhocarestrust.org.uk
Directors: A. Sandison (Fin), N. Finlayson (Grp Chief Exec)
Immediate Holding Company: THE WHO CARES? TRUST
Registration no: 02700693 **VAT No.:** GB 577 8530 91
Date established: 1992 **Turnover:** £500,000 - £1m
No.of Employees: 1 - 10 **Product Groups:** 80

Date of Accounts	Mar 12	Mar 11	Mar 10
Sales Turnover	956	542	N/A
Pre Tax Profit/Loss	383	-31	N/A
Working Capital	625	298	616
Fixed Assets	259	204	7
Current Assets	703	399	623
Current Liabilities	56	92	N/A

Theo Fennell plc
169 Fulham Road, London, SW3 6SP
Tel: 020-7591 5000 **Fax:** 020-7591 5001
E-mail: gavin.saunders@theofennell.com
Website: http://www.theofennell.com
Directors: G. Saunders (Fin)
Managers: E. Perry
Immediate Holding Company: THEO FENNELL PLC
Registration no: 01955534 **Date established:** 1985
Turnover: £10m - £20m **No.of Employees:** 51 - 100 **Product Groups:** 49

Date of Accounts	Mar 12	Mar 11	Mar 10
Sales Turnover	12m	12m	13m
Pre Tax Profit/Loss	-2m	-547	-350

Working Capital	5m	7m	6m
Fixed Assets	705	871	430
Current Assets	9m	10m	9m
Current Liabilities	1m	557	609

Thin Layer Components & Devices Ltd
Unit 11 21 Wren Street, London, WC1X 0HF
Tel: 020-7278 5196 **Fax:** 020-7278 5196
E-mail: tlcdltd@btinternet.com
Directors: M. Ambersley (Fin), M. Ambersley (MD)
Immediate Holding Company: THIN LAYER COMPONENTS & DEVICES LIMITED
Registration no: 01648179 **VAT No.:** GB 380 5181 59
Date established: 1982 **Turnover:** Up to £250,000
No.of Employees: 1 - 10 **Product Groups:** 38, 40, 48

Date of Accounts	Dec 11	Dec 10	Dec 09
Working Capital	-17	-24	-15
Fixed Assets	N/A	1	1
Current Assets	21	19	12

Think Mortgage Solutions
Unit 1 Mercer Building 1 New Inn Yard, London, EC2A 3EE
Tel: 020-7729 9989 **Fax:** 020-7729 4099
E-mail: info@herbline.co.uk
Website: http://www.herbline.com
Directors: R. Dass (Dir)
Immediate Holding Company: REDBIRD FINANCIAL SERVICES LTD
Registration no: 06240339 **Date established:** 2007
Turnover: Up to £250,000 **No.of Employees:** 1 - 10 **Product Groups:** 32, 61, 63, 84, 85

Date of Accounts	Jul 08
Working Capital	-6
Fixed Assets	3
Current Assets	11

Third Eye Services
104 Mount View Road, London, N4 4JX
Tel: 0872-1154155 **Fax:** 0872-1154155
E-mail: sales@thirdeyeservices.co.uk
Website: http://www.thirdeyeservices.co.uk
Directors: M. Ponting (Dir)
Registration no: 04252593 **Date established:** 2001
No.of Employees: 1 - 10 **Product Groups:** 44

Thistle Kensington Park Hotel
16 De Vere Gardens, London, W8 5AG
Tel: 0871-9960141 **Fax:** 020-7937 7616
Website: http://www.thistlehotels.com
Managers: M. Mckay (Chief Mgr)
Ultimate Holding Company: Thistle Hotels
Registration no: 02960704 **VAT No.:** GB 243 2841 76
Turnover: £5m - £10m **No.of Employees:** 1 - 10 **Product Groups:** 69

Thomas Cooper
Ibex House 42-47 Minories, London, EC3N 1HA
Tel: 020-7481 8851 **Fax:** 020-7480 6097
E-mail: stephen.swabey@thomascooperlaw.com
Website: http://www.thomascooperlaw.com
Bank(s): Barclays
Directors: S. Swabey (Snr Part), T. Goode (Snr Part)
Managers: K. Tapley (Personnel), Y. Alie (Mktg Serv Mgr)
Immediate Holding Company: THOMAS COOPER
Registration no: 03681368 **VAT No.:** GB 243 7765 41
Date established: 1998 **No.of Employees:** 51 - 100 **Product Groups:** 80

Date of Accounts	Dec 08	Dec 07	Dec 06
Working Capital	456	235	188
Current Assets	492	249	193

Thomas Fattorini Ltd (London)
150 Minories, London, EC3N 1LS
Tel: 020-7264 2171 **Fax:** 020-7264 2172
E-mail: sales@fattorini.co.uk
Website: http://www.fattorini.co.uk
Directors: G. Fattorini (MD), T. Fattorini (Sales)
Ultimate Holding Company: FORESTRE (HOLDINGS) LIMITED
Immediate Holding Company: AGROFOREST RISK MANAGEMENT LIMITED
Registration no: 00153351 **VAT No.:** GB 343 4128 78
Date established: 1950 **Turnover:** £2m - £5m **No.of Employees:** 1 - 10
Product Groups: 23, 24, 25, 27, 28, 30, 32, 33, 35, 36, 40, 41, 46, 49, 63, 65

Date of Accounts	Dec 11	Dec 10	Dec 09
Sales Turnover	10m	N/A	N/A
Pre Tax Profit/Loss	1m	N/A	N/A
Working Capital	3m	3m	2m
Fixed Assets	734	429	386
Current Assets	5m	5m	3m
Current Liabilities	795	N/A	N/A

Thompson Clive & Partners Ltd
24 Old Bond Street, London, W1S 4AW
Tel: 020-7535 4900 **Fax:** 020-7493 9172
E-mail: colin@tcvc.com
Website: http://www.tcvc.com
Directors: C. Clive (Dir)
Immediate Holding Company: THOMPSON CLIVE & PARTNERS LIMITED
Registration no: 01342042 **VAT No.:** 242 5234 88 **Date established:** 1977
Turnover: £500,000 - £1m **No.of Employees:** 1 - 10 **Product Groups:** 82

Date of Accounts	Mar 12	Mar 11	Mar 10
Sales Turnover	N/A	N/A	21
Pre Tax Profit/Loss	-139	-389	-208
Working Capital	807	945	1m
Fixed Assets	N/A	1	193
Current Assets	812	956	1m
Current Liabilities	5	10	20

Thomson Reuters
Aldgate House 33 Aldgate High Street, London, EC3N 1DL
Tel: 020-7369 7000 **Fax:** 020-7369 7240
E-mail: info@tfsd.com
Website: http://www.thomsonreuters.com
Directors: N. Harding (Dir), E. Maclean (Co Sec)
Managers: T. Blackmore (Tech Serv Mgr), N. Smith
Ultimate Holding Company: THOMSON INVESTMENTS LTD (CANADA)
Immediate Holding Company: THOMSON FINANCIAL LIMITED
Registration no: 02012235 **Date established:** 1986
Turnover: £250m - £500m **No.of Employees:** 1001 - 1500
Product Groups: 80

Date of Accounts	Dec 11	Dec 10	Dec 09
Pre Tax Profit/Loss	N/A	N/A	230m
Working Capital	384m	384m	384m
Fixed Assets	16m	16m	16m
Current Assets	458m	458m	458m

A.A. Thornton & Co.
235 High Holborn, London, WC1V 7LE
Tel: 020-7405 4044 **Fax:** 020-7405 3580
E-mail: aat@aathornton.com
Website: http://www.aathornton.com
Managers: J. Barnes (Sales Prom Mgr)
Registration no: 05415161 **VAT No.:** 232 9300 88
Turnover: £500,000 - £1m **No.of Employees:** 51 - 100
Product Groups: 80

Bernard Thorp & Co. Ltd
53 Chelsea Manor Street, London, SW3 5RZ
Tel: 020-7352 5745 **Fax:** 020-7376 3640
E-mail: sales@bernardthorp.com
Website: http://www.bernardthorp.co.uk
Bank(s): Lloyds TSB Bank plc
Directors: G. Kinsella (MD)
Immediate Holding Company: BERNARD THORP & CO LIMITED
Registration no: 01445698 **Date established:** 1979 **Turnover:** £2m - £5m
No.of Employees: 11 - 20 **Product Groups:** 23, 52

Date of Accounts	Dec 11	Jun 10	Jun 09
Working Capital	-162	2	-67
Fixed Assets	8	93	94
Current Assets	224	186	287

Thread Needle
60 St Mary Axe, London, EC3A 8JQ
Tel: 020-7464 5000 **Fax:** 020-7626 1266
E-mail: alan.kaye@threadneedle.co.uk
Website: http://www.threadneedle.com
Directors: A. Kaye (Co Sec), T. Gillbanks (Fin)
Ultimate Holding Company: AMERIPRISE FINANCIAL INC (USA)
Immediate Holding Company: THREADNEEDLE ASSET MANAGEMENT LIMITED
Registration no: 00573204 **Date established:** 1956
Turnover: £20m - £50m **No.of Employees:** 251 - 500 **Product Groups:** 82

Date of Accounts	Dec 11	Dec 10	Dec 09
Sales Turnover	50m	46m	36m
Pre Tax Profit/Loss	4m	4m	-19m
Working Capital	24m	24m	24m
Current Assets	88m	61m	49m
Current Liabilities	23m	20m	13m

Richard Threadgill Associates
Unit 5g Union Court 20 Union Road, London, SW4 6JP
Tel: 020-7207 1710 **Fax:** 020-7622 2734
E-mail: richard@richardthreadgillassociates.co.uk
Website: http://www.richardthreadgillassociates.co.uk
Directors: R. Threadgill (Prop)
Registration no: OC303787 **Date established:** 2003
Turnover: Up to £250,000 **No.of Employees:** 11 - 20 **Product Groups:** 49, 52

321 Systems Ltd
6 Maryon Mews, London, NW3 2PU
Tel: 020-7794 3236 **Fax:** 020-7431 3213
E-mail: laurencep@dial.pipex.com
Website: http://www.321systems.com
Directors: L. Payne (Dir)
Immediate Holding Company: 321 SYSTEMS LIMITED
Registration no: 02518782 **VAT No.:** GB 538 6218 28
Date established: 1990 **No.of Employees:** 1 - 10 **Product Groups:** 44, 80, 84

Date of Accounts	Aug 11	Aug 10	Aug 09
Working Capital	17	16	17
Current Assets	18	17	18

Tickbox Systems Ltd
St Martins House 16 St Martins Le Grand, London, EC1A 4EN
Tel: 020-7397 8490 **Fax:** 0871-288 4087
E-mail: contact@tickboxdb.com
Website: http://www.tickboxsystems.com
Directors: P. Curtis (Dir)
Immediate Holding Company: TICKBOX SYSTEMS LTD
Registration no: 03523377 **Date established:** 1998
Turnover: Up to £250,000 **No.of Employees:** 1 - 10 **Product Groups:** 44

Date of Accounts	Mar 11	Mar 10	Mar 09
Working Capital	21	6	15
Fixed Assets	2	1	2
Current Assets	59	69	62

Tie Rack Ltd
Unit 36 Waterloo Station, London, SE1 7LY
Tel: 020-7928 5461
Managers: N. Rotella (Mgr)
Ultimate Holding Company: TIE RACK RETAIL GROUP LIMITED
Immediate Holding Company: TIE RACK LIMITED
Registration no: 01524977 **Date established:** 1980 **Turnover:** £1m - £2m
No.of Employees: 11 - 20 **Product Groups:** 24, 38

Date of Accounts	Jan 12	Jan 11	Jan 10
Sales Turnover	1m	944	1m
Pre Tax Profit/Loss	787	-84	-1m
Working Capital	10m	8m	8m
Fixed Assets	8m	8m	8m
Current Assets	22m	22m	22m
Current Liabilities	215	493	669

Tigerfish Design Ltd
27 Disbrowe Road, London, W6 8QG
Tel: 020-7385 2890
No.of Employees: 1 - 10 **Product Groups:** 37, 67

Time Life International Ltd
Brettenham House Lancaster Place, London, WC2E 7TL
Tel: 020-7499 4080 **Fax:** 020-7322 1147
E-mail: info@time.com
Website: http://www.time.com
Bank(s): Barclays, National Westminster
Directors: R. King (I.T. Dir)
Managers: P. Murphey (Sales Admin)
Immediate Holding Company: Time Warner Inc
Registration no: 00317127 **VAT No.:** GB 239 5356 39
Turnover: £1m - £2m **No.of Employees:** 101 - 250 **Product Groups:** 80

Time Out Group
Universal House 251 Tottenham Court Road, London, W1T 7AB
Tel: 020-7813 3000 **Fax:** 020-7813 6001
E-mail: editorial@timeout.com
Website: http://www.timeout.com
Directors: C. Sims (Sales & Mktg), P. Buckley (Pers), P. Rakkar (Fin)
Managers: A. Van Der Wal, S. Chappell, E. Jackson (Sales Admin)
Ultimate Holding Company: TIME OUT GROUP HC LIMITED
Immediate Holding Company: TIME OUT GUIDES LIMITED
Registration no: 03210982 **Date established:** 1996 **Turnover:** £2m - £5m
No.of Employees: 101 - 250 **Product Groups:** 28

Date of Accounts	Dec 11	Dec 10	Dec 09
Sales Turnover	2m	3m	4m
Pre Tax Profit/Loss	-1m	28	-1m
Working Capital	2m	2m	995
Fixed Assets	26	N/A	N/A
Current Assets	3m	3m	3m
Current Liabilities	552	483	1m

Time Products UK Ltd
23 Grosvenor Street, London, W1K 4QL
Tel: 020-7416 4160 **Fax:** 020- 74164161
Website: http://www.timeproducts.co.uk
Directors: D. Merriman (MD), W. Colville (Co Sec)
Ultimate Holding Company: ALMAR PLC
Immediate Holding Company: TIME PRODUCTS (UK) LIMITED
Registration no: 00746690 **VAT No.:** GB 234 6217 78
Date established: 1963 **Turnover:** £20m - £50m
No.of Employees: 101 - 250 **Product Groups:** 65

Date of Accounts	Jan 12	Jan 11	Jan 10
Sales Turnover	31m	27m	26m
Pre Tax Profit/Loss	6m	4m	5m
Working Capital	7m	7m	7m
Fixed Assets	1m	1m	1m
Current Assets	23m	21m	22m
Current Liabilities	6m	5m	6m

The Times Newspaper Classified
1 Virginia Street, London, E98 1XY
Tel: 020-7782 4000
E-mail: home.news@thetimes.co.uk
Website: http://www.timesonline.co.uk
Directors: C. Stone (Co Sec), L. Hinton (Dir)
Ultimate Holding Company: NEWS CORP (USA)
Immediate Holding Company: TIMES NEWSPAPERS LIMITED
Registration no: 00894646 **Date established:** 1966
Turnover: £250m - £500m **No.of Employees:** 1 - 10 **Product Groups:** 28, 64

Date of Accounts	Jun 08	Jun 09	Jun 10
Sales Turnover	445m	386m	393m
Pre Tax Profit/Loss	-50m	-88m	-45m
Working Capital	-261m	-348m	-394m
Fixed Assets	1m	1m	3m
Current Assets	462m	400m	399m
Current Liabilities	18m	15m	22m

Timeslice Ltd
William Gaitskill House 23 Paradise Street, London, SE16 4QD
Tel: 020-7231 0073 **Fax:** 020-7237 9806
E-mail: sales@timeslice.co.uk
Website: http://www.timeslice.co.uk
Directors: I. Khair (Prop), L. Guiver (Co Sec)
Managers: E. Morgan (Sales & Mktg Mg), M. Jackson (Sales Admin)
Immediate Holding Company: TIMESLICE LIMITED
Registration no: 00745445 **Date established:** 1962
Turnover: £500,000 - £1m **No.of Employees:** 21 - 50 **Product Groups:** 44

Date of Accounts	Dec 11	Dec 10	Dec 09
Working Capital	104	155	931
Fixed Assets	150	144	N/A
Current Assets	190	170	954

Tipmaster Ltd
Rigg Approach Lea Bridge Road, London, E10 7QN
Tel: 020-8539 0611 **Fax:** 020-8539 9462
E-mail: sales@tipmaster.co.uk
Website: http://www.tipmaster.co.uk
Directors: M. Terry (Dir)
Ultimate Holding Company: CROWNFIELD HOLDINGS LIMITED
Immediate Holding Company: TIPMASTER LIMITED
Registration no: 00902520 **Date established:** 1967 **Turnover:** £2m - £5m
No.of Employees: 21 - 50 **Product Groups:** 39, 45

Date of Accounts	Dec 11	Dec 10	Dec 09
Working Capital	338	642	572
Fixed Assets	318	263	271
Current Assets	1m	1m	1m

TNS UK Ltd
TNS Research International 222 Gray's Inn Road, London, WC1X 8HB
Tel: 020-7160 5500 **Fax:** 01903-534430
E-mail: enquiries@tns-global.com
Website: http://www.tns-global.com
Bank(s): Lloyds
Directors: D. Wading (Sales), D. Waiding (Dir), M. Peckham (Dir), J. Hickling (MD)
Immediate Holding Company: The Press Association Co.
Registration no: 03073845 **Date established:** 1997
Turnover: £500,000 - £1m **No.of Employees:** 21 - 50 **Product Groups:** 79

Toast Ltd
10 Frith Street, London, W1D 3JF
Tel: 020-7437 0506 **Fax:** 020-7439 8852
E-mail: michael@toasttv.co.uk
Website: http://www.toasttv.co.uk
Directors: F. Warren (Dir)
Immediate Holding Company: TOAST LTD
Registration no: 06571310 **Date established:** 2008
Turnover: Up to £250,000 **No.of Employees:** 1 - 10 **Product Groups:** 37, 84, 86, 89

Date of Accounts	Apr 11	Apr 10	Apr 09
Working Capital	-23	121	-205
Fixed Assets	252	226	453
Current Assets	1	251	525

Together Ltd
26-28 Conway Street, London, W1T 6BH
Tel: 020-7209 2222 **Fax:** 020-7916 2277
E-mail: hello@together.co.uk
Website: http://www.together.co.uk

see next page

Together Ltd - Cont'd

Directors: L. Gladdish (Co Sec)
Ultimate Holding Company: OTTO AKTIENGESELLSCHAFT FUR BETEILIGUNGEN (GERMANY)
Immediate Holding Company: TOGETHER LIMITED
Registration no: 01818712 **Date established:** 1984 **Turnover:** £2m - £5m
No.of Employees: 11 - 20 **Product Groups:** 24, 61

Date of Accounts	Feb 12	Feb 11	Feb 10
Sales Turnover	2m	2m	3m
Pre Tax Profit/Loss	-779	-2m	-1m
Working Capital	-4m	-3m	-1m
Fixed Assets	42	66	95
Current Assets	2m	3m	3m
Current Liabilities	5m	5m	4m

Tonertex Foils Ltd

PO Box 3746, London, N2 9DE
Tel: 020-8444 1992 **Fax:** 020-8883 0845
E-mail: michelle@tonertex.com
Website: http://www.tonertex.com
Directors: M. Huberman (MD)
Immediate Holding Company: TONERTEX FOILS LIMITED
Registration no: 03522472 **Date established:** 1998
No.of Employees: 1 - 10 **Product Groups:** 34, 49, 81

Date of Accounts	Mar 11	Mar 10	Mar 09
Working Capital	30	1	1
Fixed Assets	11	12	14
Current Assets	90	57	53

Tool Services Ltd

14 The Swan Centre Rosemary Road, London, SW17 0AR
Tel: 020-8944 7222 **Fax:** 020-8944 7222
E-mail: info@toolservices.co.uk
Website: http://www.toolservices.co.uk
Directors: C. Dann (Dir)
Immediate Holding Company: TOOL SERVICES LIMITED
Registration no: 02999262 **Date established:** 1994
Turnover: £250,000 - £500,000 **No.of Employees:** 1 - 10
Product Groups: 37, 41, 48, 83

Date of Accounts	Dec 11	Dec 10	Dec 09
Working Capital	55	58	63
Fixed Assets	N/A	N/A	16
Current Assets	106	120	137

Top Shop / Top Man Ltd

Great Castle Street, London, W1W 8LG
Tel: 020-7636 7700 **Fax:** 020-7927 0072
Website: http://www.topshop.com
Managers: S. Harpers (Mgr)
Ultimate Holding Company: TAVETA INVESTMENTS LIMITED
Immediate Holding Company: TOP SHOP/TOP MAN LIMITED
Registration no: 02317752 **VAT No.:** GB 169 0943 36
Date established: 1988 **Turnover:** £50m - £75m **No.of Employees:** 1 - 10
Product Groups: 61

Date of Accounts	Aug 08	Aug 09	Aug 10
Sales Turnover	672	704	733
Pre Tax Profit/Loss	672	704	733
Working Capital	2m	2m	3m
Current Assets	2m	2m	3m

Topical Time Ltd

5 Bleeding Heart Yard, London, EC1N 8SJ
Tel: 020-7405 2439 **Fax:** 020-7831 4254
E-mail: topicaltime@btconnect.com
Directors: H. Kaye (MD), L. Kaye (MD)
Immediate Holding Company: TOPICAL TIME LIMITED
Registration no: 01656282 **Date established:** 1982
Turnover: £500,000 - £1m **No.of Employees:** 1 - 10 **Product Groups:** 48, 49, 65

Date of Accounts	Aug 11	Aug 10	Aug 08
Working Capital	171	166	149
Fixed Assets	4	3	5
Current Assets	243	252	268

Total Systems plc

394 City Road, London, EC1V 2QA
Tel: 020-7294 4888 **Fax:** 020-7294 4999
E-mail: info@totalsystems.co.uk
Website: http://www.totalsystems.co.uk
Bank(s): Lloyds TSB Bank plc
Directors: A. Weber (I.T. Dir), C. Dutton (Chief Op Offcr), T. Bourne (MD)
Immediate Holding Company: TOTAL SYSTEMS PLC
Registration no: 01024277 **VAT No.:** GB 235 1889 48
Date established: 1971 **Turnover:** £2m - £5m **No.of Employees:** 21 - 50
Product Groups: 44

Date of Accounts	Mar 12	Mar 11	Mar 10
Sales Turnover	2m	3m	4m
Pre Tax Profit/Loss	-1m	-278	439
Working Capital	3m	4m	4m
Fixed Assets	687	759	822
Current Assets	3m	4m	5m
Current Liabilities	526	562	1m

Totally Typing Ltd

PO Box 26995, London, SE21 8XZ
Tel: 020-8761 5045
E-mail: joanne@totallytyping.com
Website: http://www.totallytyping.com
Directors: J. Jarrett (MD)
Immediate Holding Company: TOTALLY TYPING LIMITED
Registration no: 05872173 **Date established:** 2006
Turnover: Up to £250,000 **No.of Employees:** 1 - 10 **Product Groups:** 80

Tower Hill Merchants plc

92-94 Tooley Street, London, SE1 2TH
Tel: 020-7407 8161 **Fax:** 020-7407 2949
E-mail: michael.o'connell@towerhillmerchants.co.uk
Website: http://www.towerhillmerchants.co.uk
Directors: M. O'connell (Fin)
Immediate Holding Company: TOWER HILL MERCHANTS PLC
Registration no: 02427432 **VAT No.:** GB 547 8025 28
Date established: 1989 **Turnover:** £10m - £20m **No.of Employees:** 1 - 10
Product Groups: 61

Date of Accounts	Sep 11	Sep 10	Sep 09
Sales Turnover	18m	16m	13m
Pre Tax Profit/Loss	611	650	563
Working Capital	2m	1m	1m
Fixed Assets	66	69	59
Current Assets	4m	3m	3m
Current Liabilities	509	533	534

Tower Mint Ltd

1-21 Carew Street, London, SE5 9DF
Tel: 020-7733 7268 **Fax:** 020-7274 0151
E-mail: info@towermint.co.uk
Website: http://www.towermint.com
Directors: A. Wells (Co Sec), C. Browning (MD), C. Browning (Dir)
Immediate Holding Company: TOWER MINT LIMITED
Registration no: 01276974 **Date established:** 1976 **Turnover:** £1m - £2m
No.of Employees: 11 - 20 **Product Groups:** 49, 65

Date of Accounts	Dec 11	Dec 10	Dec 09
Working Capital	499	376	293
Fixed Assets	172	191	239
Current Assets	1m	965	866

TR Property Investment Trust P.L.C.

51 Berkeley Square, London, W1J 5BB
Tel: 020-7360 1200 **Fax:** 020-7360 1300
E-mail: enquiries@trproperty.co.uk
Website: http://www.trproperty.com
Directors: A. Goobey (Non Exec), R. Stone (Non Exec), P. Salsbury (Non Exec)
Registration no: 00084492 **No.of Employees:** 501 - 1000
Product Groups: 80, 82

Trac Office Contracts

Thornton House Thornton Road, London, SW19 4NG
Tel: 020-8405 6446 **Fax:** 020-8405 6448
E-mail: info@trac2000.co.uk
Website: http://www.trac2000.co.uk
Directors: T. Lardner Burke (Dir), V. Lardner Burke (Co Sec)
Immediate Holding Company: TRAC OFFICE CONTRACTS LIMITED
Registration no: 01130113 **VAT No.:** GB 232 1652 00
Date established: 1973 **Turnover:** £1m - £2m **No.of Employees:** 1 - 10
Product Groups: 67

Date of Accounts	Sep 11	Sep 10	Sep 09
Working Capital	-155	-189	-190
Fixed Assets	283	284	285
Current Assets	329	54	13

Trade Link London Ltd

31 Wessex Gardens, London, NW11 9RS
Tel: 020-8905 5818 **Fax:** 020-8455 2987
E-mail: info@saffrondirect.com
Website: http://www.saffrondirect.com
Directors: R. Doshi (MD)
Immediate Holding Company: TRADELINK (LONDON) LIMITED
Registration no: 02017996 **Date established:** 1986
Turnover: Up to £250,000 **No.of Employees:** 1 - 10 **Product Groups:** 20, 62

Date of Accounts	Oct 11	Oct 10	Oct 09
Working Capital	-2	6	16
Fixed Assets	2	2	2
Current Assets	46	30	41

Trailfinders

194 Kensington High Street, London, W8 7RG
Tel: 020-7938 3939 **Fax:** 020-7937 0555
E-mail: adamw@trailfinders.com
Website: http://www.trailfinders.co.uk
Directors: N. Davies (Dir)
Managers: A. Waldosk
Ultimate Holding Company: TRAILFINDERS GROUP LIMITED
Immediate Holding Company: TRAILFINDERS LIMITED
Registration no: 01004502 **Date established:** 1971
Turnover: £250m - £500m **No.of Employees:** 251 - 500
Product Groups: 69

Date of Accounts	Feb 08	Feb 11	Feb 10
Sales Turnover	510m	533m	483m
Pre Tax Profit/Loss	14m	20m	12m
Working Capital	69m	75m	68m
Fixed Assets	44m	57m	53m
Current Assets	202m	207m	206m
Current Liabilities	10m	14m	12m

Trans Perfect Translations Ltd

120 Fenchurch Street, London, EC3M 5BA
Tel: 020-7398 8201 **Fax:** 020-7398 8202
E-mail: london@transperfect.com
Website: http://www.transperfect.com
Directors: A. O'sullavan (Pres)
Immediate Holding Company: TRANSPERFECT TRANSLATIONS LIMITED
Registration no: 04195126 **Date established:** 2001
No.of Employees: 51 - 100 **Product Groups:** 38, 44, 80

Date of Accounts	Dec 11	Dec 10	Dec 09
Sales Turnover	10m	7m	N/A
Pre Tax Profit/Loss	1m	627	455
Working Capital	4m	3m	3m
Fixed Assets	42	48	27
Current Assets	5m	4m	3m
Current Liabilities	1m	1m	519

Transcript Divas

43 St. John S Road, London, E17 4JG
Tel: 020-7558 8846
E-mail: sales@transcriptdivas.co.uk
Website: http://transcriptdivas.co.uk
Managers: L. Watson (Develop Mgr)
Date established: 2005 **Turnover:** Up to £250,000
No.of Employees: 21 - 50 **Product Groups:** 80

Transport For London

55 Broadway, London, SW1H 0BD
Tel: 020-7222 5600 **Fax:** 020-7222 5719
E-mail: info@thetube.com
Website: http://www.tfl.gov.uk
Directors: A. Mcgill (Dir)
Managers: P. Mason
Ultimate Holding Company: TRANSPORT TRADING LIMITED
Immediate Holding Company: TRANSPORT FOR LONDON FINANCE LIMITED
Registration no: 04058343 **VAT No.:** GB 238 7244 46
Date established: 2008 **Turnover:** £2m - £5m **No.of Employees:** 1 - 10
Product Groups: 72

Date of Accounts	Mar 12	Mar 11	Mar 10
Sales Turnover	62m	N/A	N/A
Pre Tax Profit/Loss	51	N/A	N/A
Working Capital	-43m	-2m	N/A
Fixed Assets	357m	5m	N/A
Current Assets	2m	N/A	N/A
Current Liabilities	9m	2m	N/A

Travco LLP

92 Paul Street, London, EC2A 4UX
Tel: 020-7739 3333 **Fax:** 020-7739 2233
E-mail: mallan@travco.co.uk
Website: http://www.travco.co.uk
Directors: R. Allan (Dir), M. Allan (Dir), J. Fielder (Fin)
Managers: R. Shaikh (Tech Serv Mgr), D. Careswell (Personnel)
Immediate Holding Company: TRAVCO INTERNATIONAL LIMITED
Registration no: 02216088 **Date established:** 1988
Turnover: £75m - £125m **No.of Employees:** 101 - 250
Product Groups: 69

Date of Accounts	Feb 08	Feb 11	Feb 10
Sales Turnover	75m	N/A	N/A
Pre Tax Profit/Loss	529	N/A	4m
Working Capital	-2m	-259	-1m
Fixed Assets	4m	8m	6m
Current Assets	11m	56	87
Current Liabilities	2m	N/A	1m

Travel Info Systems

20 Kentish Town Road, London, NW1 9BB
Tel: 020-7428 1288 **Fax:** 020-7267 2745
E-mail: enquiries@travelinfosystems.com
Website: http://www.travelinfosystems.com
Managers: I. Spring (Mgr)
Ultimate Holding Company: SCANDEX PARENT LIMITED
Immediate Holding Company: TRAVEL INFORMATION SYSTEMS LIMITED
Registration no: 01157567 **Date established:** 1974
Turnover: £250,000 - £500,000 **No.of Employees:** 1 - 10
Product Groups: 44

Date of Accounts	Mar 11	Mar 10	Mar 09
Working Capital	1m	1m	1m
Current Assets	2m	1m	1m

Travelex Group Ltd

65 Kingsway, London, WC2B 6TD
Tel: 020-7400 4000 **Fax:** 020-7400 4001
E-mail: sylvain.pignet@travelex.com
Website: http://www.travelex.com
Managers: S. Pignet (Mgr)
Ultimate Holding Company: TRAVELEX HOLDINGS LIMITED
Immediate Holding Company: TRAVELEX UK LIMITED
Registration no: 01985596 **VAT No.:** GB 466 2627 30
Date established: 1986 **Turnover:** £75m - £125m
No.of Employees: 101 - 250 **Product Groups:** 82

Date of Accounts	Dec 11	Dec 10	Dec 09
Sales Turnover	99m	89m	85m
Pre Tax Profit/Loss	12m	11m	2m
Working Capital	17m	8m	208
Fixed Assets	6m	5m	6m
Current Assets	46m	36m	39m
Current Liabilities	16m	18m	11m

Travers Smith Ltd

10 Snow Hill, London, EC1A 2AL
Tel: 020-7248 9133 **Fax:** 020-7236 3728
E-mail: david.thomas@traverssmith.com
Website: http://www.traverssmith.com
Directors: D. Thomas (Co Sec)
Managers: D. Alexander, A. Cant (Tech Serv Mgr), K. McLoughan
Ultimate Holding Company: TRAVERS SMITH LLP
Immediate Holding Company: TRAVERS SMITH SECRETARIES LIMITED
Registration no: 02132094 **Date established:** 1987
Turnover: £20m - £50m **No.of Employees:** 251 - 500 **Product Groups:** 80

Travis Perkins plc

61 Pimlico Road, London, SW1W 8NF
Tel: 020-7730 6622 **Fax:** 020-7730 6012
E-mail: pimlico@travisperkins.co.uk
Website: http://www.travisperkins.co.uk
Managers: M. Roberts (District Mgr)
Immediate Holding Company: TRAVIS PERKINS PLC
Registration no: 00824821 **Date established:** 1964
Turnover: Up to £250,000 **No.of Employees:** 101 - 250
Product Groups: 66

Date of Accounts	Dec 11	Dec 10	Dec 09
Sales Turnover	4779m	3153m	2931m
Pre Tax Profit/Loss	270m	197m	213m
Working Capital	133m	159m	248m
Fixed Assets	2771m	2749m	2108m
Current Assets	1421m	1329m	1035m
Current Liabilities	473m	412m	109m

Travis Perkins plc

Grahame Park Way, London, NW9 5QY
Tel: 020-8200 6622 **Fax:** 020-8905 9400
Website: http://www.travisperkins.co.uk
Directors: G. Cooper (MD)
Immediate Holding Company: TRAVIS PERKINS PLC
Registration no: 00824821 **VAT No.:** GB 235 1108 05
Date established: 1964 **Turnover:** £5m - £10m **No.of Employees:** 1 - 10
Product Groups: 66, 67

Date of Accounts	Dec 11	Dec 10	Dec 09
Sales Turnover	4779m	3153m	2931m
Pre Tax Profit/Loss	270m	197m	213m
Working Capital	133m	159m	248m
Fixed Assets	2771m	2749m	2108m
Current Assets	1421m	1329m	1035m
Current Liabilities	473m	412m	109m

Trescher Fabrications Ltd

Rail Arch 2 Bermondsey Trading Estate Rotherhithe New Road, London, SE16 3LL
Tel: 020-7231 8692 **Fax:** 020-7252 3303
E-mail: info@trescherfabrications.co.uk
Website: http://www.trescherfabrications.co.uk
Directors: C. Mee (Ch)
Immediate Holding Company: TRESCHER FABRICATIONS LIMITED
Registration no: 01530563 **Date established:** 1980
No.of Employees: 1 - 10 **Product Groups:** 26, 35

Date of Accounts	Jan 11	Jan 10	Jan 09
Working Capital	-5	-7	15
Fixed Assets	10	11	13
Current Assets	102	69	115
Current Liabilities	N/A	6	N/A

Tri Hospitality Consulting Ltd
88 Baker Street, London, W1U 6TQ
Tel: 020-7486 5191 **Fax:** 020-7486 1189
E-mail: info@trihc.com
Website: http://www.trihc.com
Bank(s): Natwest
Managers: I. Idafar (Chief Acct)
Immediate Holding Company: TRI HOSPITALITY CONSULTING LIMITED
Registration no: 03476003 **VAT No.:** GB 707 4065 48
Date established: 1997 **Turnover:** £5m - £10m **No.of Employees:** 11 - 20
Product Groups: 84

Date of Accounts	Apr 11	Apr 10	Apr 09
Working Capital	77	-62	-30
Fixed Assets	121	179	266
Current Assets	353	675	7m
Current Liabilities	N/A	N/A	7m

The Triangle
1-3 Ferme Park Road, London, N4 4DS
Tel: 020-8292 0516 **Fax:** 020-8292 0516
E-mail: info@thetrianglerestaurant.co.uk
Website: http://www.thetrianglerestaurant.co.uk
Directors: A. Begdouri (Prop)
No.of Employees: 1 - 10 **Product Groups:** 40, 67, 84

Tribeca Knowledge
40 Southwick Street, London, W2 1JQ
Tel: 020-7402 3133 **Fax:** 020-7402 3933
E-mail: amoa@tribecanewmedia.com
Website: http://www.tribecamedia.com
Directors: S. Moran (MD)
Date established: 1989 **Turnover:** £500,000 - £1m
No.of Employees: 1 - 10 **Product Groups:** 81, 89

Trinity Mirror Digital Recruitment
1 Canada Square, London, E14 5AP
Tel: 08454-680568 **Fax:** 024-7650 0584
Website: http://www.tmdr.com
Directors: D. Faltner (MD)
Managers: A. Flynn (Mktg Serv Mgr), M. Wyman (I.T. Exec)
Ultimate Holding Company: TRINITY MIRROR PLC
Immediate Holding Company: TRINITY MIRROR DIGITAL RECRUITMENT LIMITED
Registration no: 01904765 **Date established:** 1985
Turnover: £10m - £20m **No.of Employees:** 101 - 250 **Product Groups:** 28

Date of Accounts	Dec 07	Dec 08	Jan 10
Sales Turnover	2m	14m	9m
Pre Tax Profit/Loss	-167	40m	480
Working Capital	-10m	-7m	-5m
Fixed Assets	360	293	138
Current Assets	3m	13m	14m
Current Liabilities	899	3m	2m

Triple Tee London Ltd
51 Manston Adams Road, London, N17 6HU
Tel: 020-8880 9117 **Fax:** 020-8704 0106
E-mail: shohel69@yahoo.com
Website: http://www.tripleteelondonltd.com
Immediate Holding Company: TRIPLE TEE (LONDON) LIMITED
Registration no: 07038802 **Date established:** 2009
No.of Employees: 1 - 10 **Product Groups:** 23, 24, 63, 84

Triton Chemical Manufacturing Co. Ltd
Unit 5 Lyndean Industrial Estate, London, SE2 9SG
Tel: 020-8310 3929 **Fax:** 020-8312 0349
E-mail: ian@triton-chemicals.com
Website: http://www.triton-chemicals.com
Bank(s): Barclays
Directors: A. Woollard (Factory), I. Taylor (Dir), N. Taylor (Sales & Mktg)
Managers: B. Talyor (Admin Off)
Immediate Holding Company: TRITON CHEMICAL MANUFACTURING CO. LIMITED
Registration no: 01291832 **Date established:** 1976 **Turnover:** £2m - £5m
No.of Employees: 11 - 20 **Product Groups:** 32

Date of Accounts	Oct 07	Apr 11	Apr 10
Working Capital	245	-43	101
Fixed Assets	156	216	127
Current Assets	1m	1m	1m

Trowers & Hamlins
Sceptre Court 40 Tower Hill, London, EC3N 4DX
Tel: 020-7423 8000 **Fax:** 01392-221047
E-mail: jadlington@trowers.com
Website: http://www.trowers.com
Directors: J. Adlington (Snr Part)
Ultimate Holding Company: GI PARTNERS FUND II LP (USA)
Immediate Holding Company: CAMBIAN HEALTHCARE LIMITED
Registration no: 02661113 **Date established:** 2000
No.of Employees: 251 - 500 **Product Groups:** 80

Date of Accounts	Mar 11	Mar 10	Mar 09
Working Capital	1m	1m	2m
Fixed Assets	5	6	12
Current Assets	2m	2m	2m

Truebell plc
Truebell House 5b Lombard Road, London, SW19 3TZ
Tel: 020-8543 8111 **Fax:** 020-8543 9607
E-mail: harriet@eloise.co.uk
Website: http://www.edenhouseonline.co.uk
Bank(s): HSBC
Directors: L. Eden (MD), H. De-Wolff (MD), P. Scott Francis (Dir)
Immediate Holding Company: TRUEBELL LIMITED
Registration no: 01291834 **Date established:** 1976
Turnover: Up to £250,000 **No.of Employees:** 11 - 20 **Product Groups:** 61

Date of Accounts	Dec 10	Dec 09	Dec 08
Sales Turnover	221	882	5m
Pre Tax Profit/Loss	-112	-208	-139
Working Capital	483	641	694
Fixed Assets	45	60	300
Current Assets	562	761	2m
Current Liabilities	38	101	878

T-shirt Printing London
8 LEXHAM GARDENS KENSINGTON, London, W8 6JQ
Tel: 08448-844992
E-mail: info@tshirtprintinglondon.com
Website: http://www.tshirtprintinglondon.com/
No.of Employees: 1 - 10 **Product Groups:** 23, 24, 63

Turnbull & Asser Ltd
71-72 Jermyn Street, London, SW1Y 6PF
Tel: 020-7808 3000 **Fax:** 020-7808 3001
E-mail: info@turnbullandasser.co.uk
Website: http://www.turnbullandasser.co.uk
Directors: S. Miller (MD)
Managers: C. Holmess (Sales Admin)
Immediate Holding Company: TURNBULL & ASSER LIMITED
Registration no: 01066321 **Date established:** 1972
No.of Employees: 21 - 50 **Product Groups:** 24, 63

Date of Accounts	Jan 09	Jan 10	Jan 11
Sales Turnover	N/A	9m	10m
Pre Tax Profit/Loss	-23	284	1m
Working Capital	2m	2m	3m
Fixed Assets	4m	4m	4m
Current Assets	3m	4m	4m
Current Liabilities	948	1m	1m

Turner Morum LLP
Faulkner House 32-33 Cowcross Street, London, EC1M 6DF
Tel: 020-7490 5505 **Fax:** 020-7490 5504
E-mail: icharman@turner-morum.co.uk
Website: http://www.turner-morum.co.uk
Directors: I. Charman (Fin)
Immediate Holding Company: TURNER MORUM ROADSIDE LIMITED
Registration no: 03784711 **Date established:** 1999
Turnover: £250,000 - £500,000 **No.of Employees:** 1 - 10
Product Groups: 80

Date of Accounts	Apr 11	Apr 10	Apr 09
Pre Tax Profit/Loss	N/A	-1	-1
Working Capital	6	7	7
Current Assets	8	8	8
Current Liabilities	N/A	1	1

Turnstone Group Ltd
9 St Clare Street, London, EC3N 1LQ
Tel: 020-7954 4329 **Fax:** 020-7954 4362
E-mail: sbond@turnstonegroup.co.uk
Website: http://www.turnstonegroup.co.uk
Directors: S. Bond (MD)
Registration no: 06467588 **No.of Employees:** 1 - 10 **Product Groups:** 44, 80, 82

Turnstone Services Ltd
3 Temple Avenue, London, EC4Y 0HP
Tel: 020-7936 4373 **Fax:** 0207-936 9100
E-mail: david.brook@turnstoneservices.com
Website: http://www.turnstoneservices.com
Directors: D. Brook (Dir)
Immediate Holding Company: TURNSTONE SERVICES LTD
Registration no: 05796176 **Date established:** 2006
Turnover: £250,000 - £500,000 **No.of Employees:** 1 - 10
Product Groups: 44, 80, 81

Date of Accounts	Apr 11	Apr 10	Apr 09
Working Capital	-2	14	21
Fixed Assets	3	6	2
Current Assets	150	91	65

20th Century Fox Film Co. Ltd
31-32 Soho Square, London, W1D 3AP
Tel: 020-7437 7766 **Fax:** 020-7753 0013
E-mail: paul.higginson@fox.com
Website: http://www.fox.co.uk
Directors: D. Tomoszko (Sales), P. Higginson (Fin)
Ultimate Holding Company: NEWS CORP (USA)
Immediate Holding Company: TWENTIETH CENTURY FOX HOME ENTERTAINMENT LIMITED
Registration no: 01633880 **Date established:** 1982
Turnover: £125m - £250m **No.of Employees:** 1 - 10 **Product Groups:** 65, 83

Date of Accounts	May 11	May 10	May 09
Sales Turnover	152m	207m	174m
Pre Tax Profit/Loss	10m	5m	17m
Working Capital	34m	89m	89m
Fixed Assets	757	228	298
Current Assets	94m	168m	223m
Current Liabilities	37m	52m	48m

Twins Catering Equipment Ltd
191e Uxbridge Road Shepherds Bush, London, W12 9RA
Tel: 020-8749 6634 **Fax:** 020-8762 0883
E-mail: twinscatering@googlemail.com
Website: http://www.twinscatering.co.uk
Directors: T. Liberos (Prop)
Immediate Holding Company: TWINS CATERING EQUIPMENT LTD
Registration no: 04951448 **Date established:** 2003
No.of Employees: 1 - 10 **Product Groups:** 20, 40, 41

Date of Accounts	Mar 11	Mar 10	Mar 09
Working Capital	2	19	11
Fixed Assets	3	4	4
Current Assets	12	33	16

Typing Overload Ltd
47 Chancery Lane, London, WC2A 1RH
Tel: 020-7404 5464 **Fax:** 020-7831 0878
Website: http://www.typingoverload.com
Directors: O. Tickner (Dir)
Immediate Holding Company: TYPING OVERLOAD LIMITED
Registration no: 01271791 **Date established:** 1976
No.of Employees: 1 - 10 **Product Groups:** 80

Date of Accounts	Nov 08	Nov 07	Nov 06
Working Capital	11	36	18
Fixed Assets	14	14	13
Current Assets	29	56	32

U B S Global Assett Managment
21 Lombard Street, London, EC3V 9AH
Tel: 020-7901 5000 **Fax:** 020-7929 0487
E-mail: info@ubs.com
Website: http://www.ubs.com
Directors: J. Fraser (Grp Chief Exec)
Ultimate Holding Company: UBS AG (SWITZERLAND)
Immediate Holding Company: UBS GLOBAL ASSET MANAGEMENT HOLDING (NO.2) LTD
Registration no: 03528371 **Date established:** 1998
Turnover: £75m - £125m **No.of Employees:** 501 - 1000
Product Groups: 82

Date of Accounts	Dec 11	Dec 10	Dec 09
Sales Turnover	121m	108m	102m
Pre Tax Profit/Loss	-10m	-40m	-23m
Working Capital	101m	93m	67m
Fixed Assets	3m	4m	6m
Current Assets	6562m	7056m	7749m
Current Liabilities	6447m	6952m	7670m

U O E UK Ltd East Finchley
120 High Road, London, N2 9ED
Tel: 08456-434344 **Fax:** 020-8883 2790
E-mail: sales@uoe.co.uk
Website: http://www.uoe.co.uk
Bank(s): Lloyds TSB Bank plc
Managers: E. Jacobs (Ops Mgr)
Ultimate Holding Company: ONJOY LTD
Immediate Holding Company: BRITSALES LIMITED
Registration no: 01537002 **VAT No.:** GB 304 2923 88
Date established: 1981 **Turnover:** £1m - £2m **No.of Employees:** 11 - 20
Product Groups: 64

Date of Accounts	Apr 11	Apr 10	Apr 09
Working Capital	4	-37	-25
Fixed Assets	1	4	7
Current Assets	167	72	51

U-Pol Ltd
1 Totteridge Lane, London, N20 0EY
Tel: 020-8492 5900 **Fax:** 020-8492 5999
E-mail: sales@u-pol.com
Website: http://www.u-pol.com
Bank(s): Midland
Managers: P. May
Ultimate Holding Company: GRAPHITE CAPITAL MANAGEMENT LLP
Immediate Holding Company: U-POL LIMITED
Registration no: 00464919 **VAT No.:** GB 232 4496 70
Date established: 1949 **Turnover:** £20m - £50m
No.of Employees: 11 - 20 **Product Groups:** 32

Date of Accounts	Dec 11	Dec 10	Dec 09
Sales Turnover	50m	47m	40m
Pre Tax Profit/Loss	10m	10m	10m
Working Capital	70m	88m	77m
Fixed Assets	4m	4m	4m
Current Assets	79m	96m	83m
Current Liabilities	2m	2m	2m

Udny Edgar & Co. Ltd
314 Balham High Road, London, SW17 7AA
Tel: 020-8767 8181 **Fax:** 020-8767 7709
Directors: R. Young (Dir), A. Warner (Dir)
Registration no: 00179522 **Turnover:** £250,000 - £500,000
No.of Employees: 1 - 10 **Product Groups:** 49

UK Petroleum Industry Association Ltd
Quality House Quality Court, London, WC2A 1HP
Tel: 020-7269 7600 **Fax:** 020-7379 3102
E-mail: info@ukpia.com
Website: http://www.ukpia.com
Managers: C. Hunt
Immediate Holding Company: UNITED KINGDOM PETROLEUM INDUSTRY ASSOCIATION LIMITED
Registration no: 01404376 **VAT No.:** 242 9439 50 **Date established:** 1978
Turnover: £500,000 - £1m **No.of Employees:** 1 - 10 **Product Groups:** 87

Date of Accounts	Dec 11	Dec 10	Dec 09
Working Capital	-28	-26	-34
Fixed Assets	37	26	34
Current Assets	723	666	774

UK Tyre Exporters Ltd
131 Scrubs Lane, London, NW10 6QU
Tel: 020-8960 6222 **Fax:** 020-8960 7863
E-mail: uktyres108@aol.com
Website: http://www.uktyres.co.uk
Directors: R. Hannington (Jt MD), D. Hannington (Jt MD)
Managers: D. Hannington (Mgr)
Immediate Holding Company: UNITED KINGDOM TYRE EXPORTERS LIMITED
Registration no: 00977770 **Date established:** 1970 **Turnover:** £1m - £2m
No.of Employees: 1 - 10 **Product Groups:** 29, 68

Date of Accounts	Apr 11	Apr 10	Apr 09
Working Capital	733	682	567
Fixed Assets	3m	3m	3m
Current Assets	1m	1m	1m

UK Work Permits Ltd
St Martins House 1 Lyric Square, London, W6 0NB
Tel: 08452-264030 **Fax:** 08452-264033
E-mail: info@uk-wp.com
Website: http://www.uk-wp.com
Directors: L. De Costa (MD), P. Taylor (Dir), P. Taylor (MD), K. Farmer (Dir)
Immediate Holding Company: UK WORK PERMITS LIMITED
Registration no: 04916251 **Date established:** 2003
No.of Employees: 1 - 10 **Product Groups:** 80

Date of Accounts	Mar 11	Sep 10	Sep 09
Sales Turnover	257	N/A	N/A
Pre Tax Profit/Loss	96	N/A	N/A
Working Capital	42	38	5
Fixed Assets	6	7	9
Current Assets	204	122	109
Current Liabilities	160	N/A	N/A

UK2 Limited
29th Floor 1 Canada Square, Canary Wharf, London, E14 5DY
Tel: 0905-1680086 **Fax:** 0845-2705570
E-mail: info-@uk2.net
Website: http://www.uk2.net
Directors: T. Smith (Dir)
Registration no: 03550739 **Date established:** 2008
No.of Employees: 1 - 10 **Product Groups:** 44

Ulkutay & Co.
90 Long Acre, London, WC2E 9RZ
Tel: 020-8849 3000 **Fax:** 020-7849 3200
E-mail: tulin@ulkutay.com
Website: http://www.ulkutay.com
Directors: N. Ulkutay (Dir)
Immediate Holding Company: GOLD ACCOUNTANTS (UK) LIMITED
Registration no: 02006796 **Date established:** 2011
No.of Employees: 1 - 10 **Product Groups:** 81, 89

Date of Accounts	Dec 11	Dec 10	Dec 09
Working Capital	135	129	98
Current Assets	425	430	193

Ultrasis
Fifth Floor Winchester House 259-269 Old Marylebone Road, London, NW1 5RA
Tel: 020-7535 2050 **Fax:** 020-7535 2070
E-mail: ultrasis@ultrasis.com
Website: http://www.ultrasis.com
Managers: N. Brabbins
Ultimate Holding Company: ULTRASIS PLC
Immediate Holding Company: ULTRASIS UK LIMITED
Registration no: 02425966 **Date established:** 1989 **Turnover:** £2m - £5m
No.of Employees: 11 - 20 **Product Groups:** 44

Date of Accounts	Jul 11	Jul 10	Jul 09
Sales Turnover	3m	3m	4m
Pre Tax Profit/Loss	-2m	1m	730
Working Capital	696	2m	2m
Fixed Assets	2m	2m	3m
Current Assets	2m	3m	4m
Current Liabilities	1m	1m	3m

Underwater Security Consultants Ltd
6 Bell Yard, London, WC2A 2JR
Tel: 020-7240 1314 **Fax:** 020-7240 2663
E-mail: admin@mandusc.com
Website: http://www.mandusc.com
Directors: B. Still (MD), B. Still (Fin), D. Szulc (Co Sec), G. Cosnahon (Grp Chief Exec), G. Shaw (MD)
Managers: R. Mortimer (Mgr)
Immediate Holding Company: UNDERWATER SECURITY CONSULTANTS LIMITED
Registration no: 01184587 **Date established:** 1974
Turnover: £20m - £50m **No.of Employees:** 21 - 50 **Product Groups:** 81

Date of Accounts	Dec 09	Dec 08	Dec 07
Sales Turnover	24m	N/A	N/A
Pre Tax Profit/Loss	4m	N/A	N/A
Working Capital	2m	116	-45
Fixed Assets	495	281	45
Current Assets	5m	3m	339
Current Liabilities	2m	N/A	N/A

Unilever plc
PO Box 68, London, EC4P 4BQ
Tel: 020-7822 5252 **Fax:** 020-7822 5898
E-mail: press-office.london@unilever.com
Website: http://www.unilever.com
Bank(s): National Westminster Bank Plc
Directors: G. Neath (Dir)
Ultimate Holding Company: UNILEVER PLC
Immediate Holding Company: UNILEVER U.K. HOLDINGS LIMITED
Registration no: 00017049 **Date established:** 1982
Turnover: Over £1,000m **No.of Employees:** 101 - 250
Product Groups: 20, 21, 31, 32, 63, 66

Date of Accounts	Dec 11	Dec 10	Dec 09
Sales Turnover	704m	699m	647m
Pre Tax Profit/Loss	244m	76m	-36m
Working Capital	3643m	3869m	3111m
Fixed Assets	340m	333m	325m
Current Assets	9846m	4104m	3359m
Current Liabilities	194m	203m	161m

Union Bank UK plc
14-18 Copthall Avenue, London, EC2R 7BN
Tel: 020-7600 0751 **Fax:** 020-7638 7642
E-mail: info@ubnl.co.uk
Website: http://unionbankuk.com
Managers: K. Ali (District Mgr)
Ultimate Holding Company: UNION BANK OF NIGERIA PLC (NIGERIA)
Immediate Holding Company: UNION BANK OF NIGERIA PLC
Registration no: FC012171 **Date established:** 1983
No.of Employees: 51 - 100 **Product Groups:** 82

Union Coffee Roasters
Unit 2 South Crescent, London, E16 4TL
Tel: 020-7474 8990 **Fax:** 020-7511 2786
E-mail: admin@unionroasted.com
Website: http://www.unionroasted.com
Directors: J. Torz (MD)
No.of Employees: 21 - 50 **Product Groups:** 20, 36, 41, 62

Unique Languages
532a Kingston Road, London, SW20 8DT
Tel: 020-3566 0145
E-mail: info@uniquelanguages.com
Website: http://www.uniquelanguages.com
Directors: M. Davies (MD)
Immediate Holding Company: WEST WIMBLEDON PHYSIOTHERAPY CLINIC LIMITED
Date established: 2008 **Turnover:** Up to £250,000
No.of Employees: 1 - 10 **Product Groups:** 86

Date of Accounts	Jun 09
Working Capital	-90
Fixed Assets	78
Current Assets	17

Unistay London
99 Gerda Road, London, SE9 3SH
Tel: 020-8859 5777 **Fax:** 020-8859 5777
Directors: J. May (Prop)
Date established: 1984 **No.of Employees:** 1 - 10 **Product Groups:** 38, 42

Unite The Union
35 King Street, London, WC2E 8JG
Tel: 020-7420 8900 **Fax:** 020-7420 8998
Website: http://www.unitetheunion.com
Directors: R. Gomez (Grp Chief Exec), C. Grant (Fin), D. Simpson (MD)
Managers: C. Joy (I.T. Exec), N. Brown (Mktg Serv Mgr)
Immediate Holding Company: AMICUS LIMITED
Registration no: 04354778 **Date established:** 2002
No.of Employees: 1 - 10 **Product Groups:** 86

Date of Accounts	Dec 10	Dec 09	Dec 08
Sales Turnover	9m	9m	9m
Pre Tax Profit/Loss	1m	814	1m
Working Capital	3m	2m	2m
Fixed Assets	260	217	169
Current Assets	5m	3m	3m
Current Liabilities	2m	965	1m

United Factories Ltd
Unit 2 Fortune Way Triangle Business Centre, London, NW10 6UF
Tel: 020-8960 9080 **Fax:** 020- 89609511
Directors: D. Vida (Dir)
No.of Employees: 1 - 10 **Product Groups:** 20, 40, 41

Univar
Unit 26 The I O Centre Armstrong Road, London, SE18 6RS
Tel: 020-8312 7200 **Fax:** 020-8305 1401
E-mail: uscmsales@univareurope.com
Website: http://www.univar.com
Bank(s): Barclays, PO Box 40, Knightsbridge, London SW3 1QB
Directors: D. Rothwell (Co Sec)
Managers: D. Reed (Sales Prom Mgr)
Ultimate Holding Company: ULIXES HOLDING BV (THE NETHERLANDS)
Immediate Holding Company: UNIVAR SPECIALTY CONSUMABLES LIMITED
Registration no: 00994213 **Date established:** 1970
Turnover: £20m - £50m **No.of Employees:** 11 - 20 **Product Groups:** 23, 27, 30

Date of Accounts	Dec 11	Dec 10	Dec 09
Sales Turnover	26m	28m	5m
Pre Tax Profit/Loss	36	324	112
Working Capital	6m	7m	4m
Fixed Assets	2m	3m	181
Current Assets	10m	10m	5m
Current Liabilities	495	245	339

Universal Display Fittings
Network Hub 300 Kensal Road, London, W10 5BE
Tel: 020-8206 5010 **Fax:** 020-8969 4215
E-mail: info@universaldisplay.co.uk
Website: http://www.universaldisplay.co.uk
Managers: J. Berlin (Mgr)
Immediate Holding Company: UNIVERSAL DISPLAY FITTINGS CO. LIMITED
Registration no: 00498143 **VAT No.:** GB 232 5863 64
Date established: 1951 **Turnover:** £2m - £5m **No.of Employees:** 1 - 10
Product Groups: 49, 65

Date of Accounts	Dec 11	Dec 10	Dec 09
Working Capital	772	426	195
Fixed Assets	156	156	159
Current Assets	1m	851	547

Universal Impex Ltd
2 Albert Place, London, N3 1QB
Tel: 020-8349 4666 **Fax:** 020-8343 4315
E-mail: info@unitechouse.com
Website: http://www.unitechouse.com
Managers: M. Valijee
Immediate Holding Company: UNIVERSAL IMPEX LIMITED
Registration no: 00948957 **VAT No.:** GB 244 3286 67
Date established: 1969 **Turnover:** £500,000 - £1m
No.of Employees: 1 - 10 **Product Groups:** 61

Date of Accounts	Dec 11	Dec 10	Dec 09
Working Capital	2m	1m	1m
Fixed Assets	40	53	59
Current Assets	6m	6m	5m

Universal Island Music Ltd
364-366 Kensington High Street, London, W14 8NS
Tel: 020-7471 5300 **Fax:** 020-7471 5001
E-mail: contact@umusic.com
Website: http://www.umusic.co.uk
Directors: N. Gitfield (MD), N. Gatfield (MD), J. White (Fin)
Managers: M. Albert (Mgr)
Ultimate Holding Company: VIVENDI SA (FRANCE)
Immediate Holding Company: UNIVERSAL/ISLAND MUSIC LIMITED
Registration no: 00761597 **VAT No.:** GB 246 2974 39
Date established: 1963 **Turnover:** £2m - £5m **No.of Employees:** 1 - 10
Product Groups: 28

Date of Accounts	Dec 11	Dec 10	Dec 09
Sales Turnover	4m	4m	5m
Pre Tax Profit/Loss	2m	1m	1m
Working Capital	24m	22m	21m
Current Assets	63m	59m	55m
Current Liabilities	N/A	50	84

Universal Pictures (Polygram Film International)
Oxford House 76 Oxford Street, London, W1D 1BS
Tel: 020-7307 1300 **Fax:** 020-7307 1301
E-mail: reception76@mvcuni.com
Website: http://www.nbcuni.com
Bank(s): National Westminster
Directors: M. Laithwaite (Dir), A. Mansfield (Fin), J. Tandy (Dir), S. Till (Dir)
Managers: S. Meaney (Sales Admin)
Ultimate Holding Company: GENERAL ELECTRIC COMPANY (USA)
Immediate Holding Company: UNIVERSAL PICTURES INTERNATIONAL NO.2 LIMITED
Registration no: 02918913 **Date established:** 1994
Turnover: Up to £250,000 **No.of Employees:** 251 - 500
Product Groups: 89

University Of London
Senate House Malet Street, London, WC1E 7HU
Tel: 020-7862 8000 **Fax:** 020-7862 8032
E-mail: enquiries@london.ac.uk
Website: http://www.london.ac.uk
Directors: R. Cryer (Fin), K. Frost (Pers)
Immediate Holding Company: SOCIETY FOR THE PROMOTION OF ROMAN STUDIES(THE)
Registration no: 03214601 **Date established:** 2011 **Turnover:** £2m - £5m
No.of Employees: 251 - 500 **Product Groups:** 86

Updata plc
Updata House Podmore Road, London, SW18 1AJ
Tel: 020-8874 4747 **Fax:** 020-8874 3931
E-mail: david@updata.co.uk
Website: http://www.updata.co.uk
Bank(s): National Westminster Bank Plc
Directors: D. Linton (MD), P. Shaw (Co Sec)
Managers: S. Mullins (Comptroller)
Immediate Holding Company: UPDATA LIMITED
Registration no: 02095011 **VAT No.:** GB 596 1677 88
Date established: 1987 **Turnover:** £1m - £2m **No.of Employees:** 11 - 20
Product Groups: 44

Date of Accounts	Mar 08	Mar 07	Mar 06
Sales Turnover	1192	912	827
Pre Tax Profit/Loss	212	102	110
Working Capital	52	-157	-261
Fixed Assets	8	5	3
Current Assets	440	277	124
Current Liabilities	388	434	386
Total Share Capital	80	80	80
ROCE% (Return on Capital Employed)	352.0	-67.3	-42.7
ROT% (Return on Turnover)	17.8	11.2	13.4

Urban Initiatives Ltd
Adam House 1 Fitzroy Square, London, W1T 5HE
Tel: 020-7380 4545 **Fax:** 020-7380 4546
E-mail: k.campbell@urbaninitiatives.co.uk
Website: http://www.urbaninitiatives.co.uk
Bank(s): HSBC
Directors: K. Campbell (MD)
Managers: M. Wilshere (Fin Mgr)
Ultimate Holding Company: URBAN SPECTRUM LIMITED
Immediate Holding Company: URBAN INITIATIVES LTD
Registration no: 03985967 **VAT No.:** GB 756 5504 14
Date established: 2000 **No.of Employees:** 11 - 20 **Product Groups:** 84

Date of Accounts	Apr 11	Apr 10	Apr 09
Working Capital	526	481	374
Fixed Assets	258	319	382
Current Assets	2m	2m	2m

Urolite Ltd
4 Northwold Road, London, N16 7HR
Tel: 020-7241 6093 **Fax:** 020-7923 3592
E-mail: info@urolite.co.uk
Website: http://www.urolite.co.uk
Directors: A. Fleeting (Dir)
Immediate Holding Company: UROLITE LIMITED
Registration no: 02700834 **Date established:** 1992
Turnover: Up to £250,000 **No.of Employees:** 1 - 10 **Product Groups:** 26, 35

Date of Accounts	Jan 11	Jan 10	Jan 09
Working Capital	43	38	-3
Fixed Assets	1	1	2
Current Assets	66	65	63

Usborne Publishing
83-85 Saffron Hill, London, EC1N 8RT
Tel: 020-7430 2800 **Fax:** 020-7430 1562
E-mail: mail@usborne.com
Website: http://www.usborne.com
Managers: R. Jones (Chief Mgr)
Ultimate Holding Company: USBORNE PUBLISHING LIMITED
Immediate Holding Company: USBORNE BOOKS AT HOME LIMITED
Registration no: 02774498 **Date established:** 1992
Turnover: £20m - £50m **No.of Employees:** 101 - 250 **Product Groups:** 28

Utopia Records Ltd
Utopia Village Chalcot Road, London, NW1 8LH
Tel: 020-7586 3434 **Fax:** 020-7586 3438
Directors: J. Wainman (MD)
Immediate Holding Company: UTOPIA RECORDS LIMITED
Registration no: 01116044 **Date established:** 1973
No.of Employees: 1 - 10 **Product Groups:** 65

Date of Accounts	Mar 11	Mar 10	Mar 09
Working Capital	-2m	-2m	-2m
Fixed Assets	9	13	16
Current Assets	700	571	427

V & A Enterprises Ltd
160 Brompton Road, London, SW3 1HW
Tel: 020-7942 2966 **Fax:** 020-7942 2967
Website: http://www.vandashop.co.uk
Bank(s): Coutts & Co
Directors: I. Blatchford (Fin), R. Fitch (Ch)
Managers: S. Sedier
Immediate Holding Company: V&A ENTERPRISES LIMITED
Registration no: 01955898 **VAT No.:** GB 444 0850 63
Date established: 1985 **Turnover:** £10m - £20m
No.of Employees: 101 - 250 **Product Groups:** 89

Date of Accounts	Mar 12	Mar 11	Mar 10
Sales Turnover	12m	13m	11m
Working Capital	881	752	980
Fixed Assets	322	451	222
Current Assets	5m	5m	4m
Current Liabilities	602	3m	685

V D C Trading Ltd
V D C House 4 Brandon Road, London, N7 9AA
Tel: 020-7700 2777
E-mail: sales@vdctrading.com
Website: http://www.vdctrading.com
Directors: C. D'aguiar (Comm), N. Holden (MD)
Managers: L. Mole, I. Vondrasova (Fin Mgr), M. Alexiou (Purch Mgr)
Immediate Holding Company: VDC TRADING LIMITED
Registration no: 02708733 **Date established:** 1992
No.of Employees: 21 - 50 **Product Groups:** 30, 36, 37

Date of Accounts	Dec 11	Dec 10	Dec 09
Working Capital	867	1m	966
Fixed Assets	228	278	274
Current Assets	2m	2m	2m

V Ships Capital
63 Queen Victoria Street, London, EC4N 4UA
Tel: 020-7489 0088 **Fax:** 020-7489 0529
E-mail: contact@vships.com
Website: http://www.vships.com
Bank(s): Citibank, National Westminster
Managers: E. Kellman (Sales Admin), R. Barford (Fin Mgr), M. Rossco (Chief Mgr)

Ultimate Holding Company: V GROUP LTD (ISLE OF MAN)
Immediate Holding Company: V.SHIPS PLC
Registration no: 00209897 **VAT No.:** GB 244 0496 71
Date established: 2025 **Turnover:** £2m - £5m **No.of Employees:** 21 - 50
Product Groups: 74

Date of Accounts	Dec 11	Dec 10
Sales Turnover	3m	4m
Pre Tax Profit/Loss	148	-596
Working Capital	-5m	-6m
Fixed Assets	299	956
Current Assets	3m	8m
Current Liabilities	1m	4m

Vacherin Ltd
16-18 Hatton Garden, London, EC1N 8AT
Tel: 020-7404 2277 **Fax:** 020-7404 8833
E-mail: mark.philpott@vacherin.com
Website: http://www.vacherin.com
Directors: M. Philpott (MD), C. Hetherington (Fin)
Immediate Holding Company: VACHERIN LIMITED
Registration no: 04516461 **Date established:** 2002 **Turnover:** £5m - £10m
No.of Employees: 11 - 20 **Product Groups:** 69, 83

Date of Accounts	Aug 11	Aug 10	Aug 09
Sales Turnover	10m	9m	N/A
Pre Tax Profit/Loss	189	68	N/A
Working Capital	124	-2	-107
Fixed Assets	52	70	81
Current Assets	2m	1m	961
Current Liabilities	650	607	N/A

Vacuum Coatings Ltd
66 Barrett Road, London, E17 9ET
Tel: 020-8520 5353 **Fax:** 020-8520 5353
E-mail: enquiries@scientificmirrors.co.uk
Website: http://www.scientificmirrors.co.uk
Directors: T. Pierce (Prop)
Immediate Holding Company: VACUUM COATINGS LIMITED
Registration no: 00513551 **VAT No.:** GB 220 8762 74
Date established: 1952 **Turnover:** Up to £250,000
No.of Employees: 1 - 10 **Product Groups:** 33, 38, 48, 67

Date of Accounts	Feb 11	Feb 10	Feb 09
Working Capital	22	12	19
Fixed Assets	5	6	5
Current Assets	38	27	36
Current Liabilities	12	N/A	N/A

Vale Europe Ltd
Bashley Road, London, NW10 6SN
Tel: 020-8453 9224 **Fax:** 020-8453 0307
E-mail: ian.guille@valeinco.com
Website: http://www.vale.com
Bank(s): National Westminster Bank Plc
Managers: M. Cox (Chief Mgr)
Ultimate Holding Company: CVRD (BRAZIL)
Immediate Holding Company: VALE EUROPE LIMITED
Registration no: 00137114 **VAT No.:** GB 123 1895 80
Date established: 2014 **Turnover:** £250m - £500m
No.of Employees: 101 - 250 **Product Groups:** 34

Date of Accounts	Dec 11	Dec 10	Dec 09
Sales Turnover	378m	322m	380m
Pre Tax Profit/Loss	23m	11m	20m
Working Capital	40m	34m	46m
Fixed Assets	32m	27m	23m
Current Assets	82m	109m	92m
Current Liabilities	36m	9m	34m

Vandome & Hart Ltd
Unit 27 New Lydenburg Commercial Estate New Lydenburg Street, London, SE7 8NF
Tel: 020-8269 0279 **Fax:** 020-8269 0289
E-mail: suzannedickinson@vandomeandhart.co.uk
Website: http://www.vandomeandhart.co.uk
Directors: R. Taylor (Dir)
Ultimate Holding Company: VANDOME & HART HOLDINGS LIMITED
Immediate Holding Company: VANDOME & HART LIMITED
Registration no: 00081007 **VAT No.:** 233 6389 55 **Date established:** 2004
Turnover: £1m - £2m **No.of Employees:** 1 - 10 **Product Groups:** 38, 41

Date of Accounts	Jan 12	Jan 11	Jan 10
Working Capital	46	24	27
Fixed Assets	31	51	48
Current Assets	236	232	253

Vaughan Ltd
Unit 17 & 23 Carnwath Road Industrial Estate, London, SW6 3HR
Tel: 020-7610 6544 **Fax:** 020-7610 9230
Directors: M. Vaughan (MD)
Immediate Holding Company: VAUGHAN LIMITED
Registration no: 02889411 **Date established:** 1994
Turnover: £10m - £20m **No.of Employees:** 11 - 20 **Product Groups:** 37, 67

Date of Accounts	Apr 11	Apr 10	Apr 09
Sales Turnover	13m	13m	17m
Pre Tax Profit/Loss	1m	2m	225
Working Capital	5m	4m	5m
Fixed Assets	195	170	264
Current Assets	7m	6m	8m
Current Liabilities	1m	2m	2m

Veevers Carter Flowers Ltd
Unit B3-B4 Trading Estate Galleywall Road, London, SE16 3PB
Tel: 020-7237 8800 **Fax:** 020-7237 7788
E-mail: info@veeverscarter.co.uk
Website: http://www.veeverscarter.co.uk
Directors: M. Veevers Carter (MD), B. Bastow (Fin)
Immediate Holding Company: VEEVERS-CARTER FLOWERS LIMITED
Registration no: 01954293 **Date established:** 1985
Turnover: Up to £250,000 **No.of Employees:** 1 - 10 **Product Groups:** 62, 63, 65

Date of Accounts	Mar 11	Mar 10	Mar 09
Working Capital	-17	-50	-19
Fixed Assets	66	54	66
Current Assets	278	251	256

Venus Enterprises Ltd
The Chandlery 50 Westminster Bridge Road, London, SE1 7QY
Tel: 020-7620 2252 **Fax:** 020-7407 9933
E-mail: spices@venusenterprises.co.uk
Website: http://www.venusenterprises.co.uk
Directors: P. Mehta (Dir)
Immediate Holding Company: VENUS ENTERPRISES LIMITED
Registration no: 00994910 **Date established:** 1970
Turnover: Up to £250,000 **No.of Employees:** 1 - 10 **Product Groups:** 20, 62

Date of Accounts	Dec 11	Dec 10	Dec 09
Working Capital	485	354	272
Fixed Assets	13	33	32
Current Assets	992	1m	913

Veolia Enviromental Services plc
Veolia House 154a Pentonville Road, London, N1 9PE
Tel: 020-7812 5000 **Fax:** 020-7812 5026
E-mail: edward.demaslatrie@veolia.co.uk
Website: http://www.onyxgroup.co.uk
Directors: J. Domonique (Grp Chief Exec)
Managers: M. Tipson (Mktg Serv Mgr), A. Houghton (Accounts), D. Ashcroft (Mgr)
Immediate Holding Company: VEOLIA ENVIRONMENTAL SERVICES (UK) PLC
Registration no: 02215767 **VAT No.:** GB 352 1129 90
Date established: 1988 **Turnover:** Over £1,000m **No.of Employees:** 1 - 10
Product Groups: 54

Veolia Water Solutions & Technologies
37-41 Old Queen Street, London, SW1H 9JA
Tel: 020-7393 2700 **Fax:** 020-7393 2749
Website: http://www.veoliawaterst.com
Directors: H. Proglio (Pres), J. Contamine (Grp Chief Exec), J. Banon (MD)
Ultimate Holding Company: VEOLIA ENVIRONNEMENT SA (FRANCE)
Immediate Holding Company: Vivendi (France)
Registration no: 02664833 **Date established:** 1987
Turnover: £20m - £50m **No.of Employees:** 21 - 50 **Product Groups:** 18, 51

Vestey Group Ltd
16 St Johns Lane, London, EC1M 4AF
Tel: 020-7248 1212 **Fax:** 020-7350 3159
E-mail: enquiries@angliss-international.com
Website: http://www.vesteyfoods.com
Directors: J. Collins (Ch)
Managers: L. Pearson (Sec)
Immediate Holding Company: VESTEY GROUP LIMITED
Registration no: 04494323 **Date established:** 2002
No.of Employees: 21 - 50 **Product Groups:** 39

Date of Accounts	Dec 09	Dec 08	Dec 07
Pre Tax Profit/Loss	-1m	972	388
Working Capital	2m	3m	3m
Fixed Assets	78m	78m	78m
Current Assets	3m	4m	3m
Current Liabilities	149	92	223

Videk Ltd
Kingsbury Works Kingsbury Road, London, NW9 8RW
Tel: 020-8200 1122 **Fax:** 020-8200 6494
E-mail: sales@videk.co.uk
Website: http://www.videk.co.uk
Bank(s): Barclays
Directors: R. Bracey (Mkt Research), M. Wilson (MD)
Immediate Holding Company: VIDEK LIMITED
Registration no: 01406928 **VAT No.:** GB 228 8395 27
Date established: 1978 **Turnover:** £2m - £5m **No.of Employees:** 21 - 50
Product Groups: 37

Date of Accounts	Dec 11	Dec 10	Dec 09
Working Capital	1m	1m	1m
Fixed Assets	36	44	49
Current Assets	2m	2m	2m

Video Arts Group Ltd
Elsinore House 77 Fulham Palace Road, London, W6 8JA
Tel: 020-7400 4800 **Fax:** 020-7400 4900
E-mail: maddison@videoarts.co.uk
Website: http://www.videoarts.com
Directors: M. Addison (Dir), J. Griffiths Jones (Co Sec)
Ultimate Holding Company: DMWSL 660 LIMITED
Immediate Holding Company: VIDEO ARTS LIMITED
Registration no: 01007689 **VAT No.:** GB 440 6447 62
Date established: 1971 **Turnover:** £2m - £5m **No.of Employees:** 11 - 20
Product Groups: 28, 86, 89

Date of Accounts	Sep 11	Sep 10	Sep 09
Sales Turnover	2m	3m	3m
Pre Tax Profit/Loss	-240	-340	4
Working Capital	-460	-601	-668
Fixed Assets	215	614	1m
Current Assets	1m	878	1m
Current Liabilities	612	588	886

Viewpulse Ltd
Flat 26 Tarranbrae Willesden Lane, London, NW6 7PL
Tel: 020-7372 7595 **Fax:** 020-7372 4067
Managers: S. Raja (Mgr)
Immediate Holding Company: VIEWPULSE LIMITED
Registration no: 02664343 **Date established:** 1991
Turnover: £500,000 - £1m **No.of Employees:** 1 - 10 **Product Groups:** 61

Date of Accounts	Nov 11	Nov 10	Nov 09
Working Capital	-45	-33	19
Current Assets	105	184	257

vince fraser illustration
22 Litchfield Avenue Stratford, London, E15 4LN
Tel: 07729-328750
E-mail: vince@vincefraser.com
Website: http://www.vincefraser.com
Directors: V. Fraser (Prop)
Date established: 1998 **Turnover:** Up to £250,000
No.of Employees: 1 - 10 **Product Groups:** 44

Virt X Exchange Ltd
1 Canada Square, London, E14 5AA
Tel: 020-7074 4444 **Fax:** 020-7074 4433
E-mail: sia-rec@virt-x.com
Website: http://www.virt-x.com
Directors: P. Keller (Grp Chief Exec), M. Blair (Dir), R. Francioni (Non Exec), S. Ermotti (Non Exec), S. Sharma (Non Exec), W. Berchtold (Non Exec), B. Steil (Non Exec), P. Nobel (Non Exec), A. Hodson (Non Exec), L. Hodgkinson (Grp Chief Exec), J. De Saussure (Non Exec), J. Gollan (Dir)
Managers: P. Stevens
Immediate Holding Company: SWX EUROPE LIMITED
Registration no: 04199482 **Date established:** 2001
Turnover: £75m - £125m **No.of Employees:** 21 - 50 **Product Groups:** 82

Visa Bureau
15 Harwood Road, London, SW6 4QP
Tel: 020-7731 9000 **Fax:** 020-7731 9011
E-mail: guy.bradley@visabureau.com
Website: http://www.visabureau.com
Directors: G. Bradley (MD)
Immediate Holding Company: CREDENTIAL INTERNATIONAL HOLDINGS LTD
Registration no: 03306890 **Date established:** 1997
No.of Employees: 21 - 50 **Product Groups:** 80

Date of Accounts	Jun 12	Jun 11	Jun 10
Working Capital	53	47	42
Fixed Assets	6	8	9
Current Assets	78	74	82

Vita Group
Times Place 45 Pall Mall, London, SW1Y 5JG
Tel: 07740-770424 **Fax:** 01625-574075
E-mail: info@thevitagroup.com
Website: http://www.kay-metzeler.co.uk
Bank(s): Lloyds TSB Bank plc
Directors: A. Marland (MD), D. Reeve (Fin), G. Maundrell (Dir), J. Oliver (Dir), T. France (MD)
Managers: M. Pritchard (Computer Mgr), L. Whittle (Personnel)
Ultimate Holding Company: British Vita UK Ltd
Immediate Holding Company: British Vita Unlimited
Registration no: 00621497 **VAT No.:** GB 606 3424 65
Turnover: £75m - £125m **No.of Employees:** 251 - 500
Product Groups: 30

Vitabiotics Health Foods
1 Apsley Way, London, NW2 7HF
Tel: 020-8955 2600 **Fax:** 020-8955 2601
E-mail: customerservices@vitabiotics.com
Website: http://www.vitabiotics.com
Bank(s): National Westminster
Directors: H. Singh (Fin), R. Taylor (MD)
Ultimate Holding Company: VITABIOTICS GROUP HOLDINGS LIMITED (B.V.I)
Immediate Holding Company: VITABIOTICS LIMITED
Registration no: 01012146 **VAT No.:** GB 228 5983 25
Date established: 1971 **Turnover:** £50m - £75m
No.of Employees: 21 - 50 **Product Groups:** 17, 31

Date of Accounts	Dec 10	Dec 09	Dec 08
Sales Turnover	55m	49m	39m
Pre Tax Profit/Loss	10m	8m	10m
Working Capital	22m	19m	14m
Fixed Assets	7m	7m	7m
Current Assets	27m	24m	18m
Current Liabilities	636	874	1m

Vivat Direct Limited ((t/a Reader's Digest)
157 Edgware Road, London, W2 2HR
Tel: 020-7053 4500 **Fax:** 020-7715 8181
E-mail: info@readersdigest.co.uk
Website: http://www.readersdigest.co.uk
Bank(s): Barclays; National Westminster
Directors: A. Lynam-Smith (MD), A. Wilton (Mkt Research), D. Cocknell (I.T. Dir), J. Compson (Dir), M. Pasteiner (Dir), P. Brady (Fin), R. Clayton (I.T. Dir), B. Cacton (Pers), B. Patton (Pers), V. Scott (Sales)
Managers: S. Ross-Bryan (Sales Admin), S. Lugthart (Mktg Serv Mgr)
Ultimate Holding Company: RIPPLEWOOD HOLDINGS LLC (USA)
Immediate Holding Company: Rda Realisations 2010 Ltd
Registration no: 04013634 **Date established:** 1992 **Turnover:** £5m - £10m
No.of Employees: 251 - 500 **Product Groups:** 28

Vizeum
10 Triton Street, London, NW1 3BF
Tel: 020-7379 9000 **Fax:** 020-7497 1177
E-mail: rpfacilities@aemedia.com
Website: http://www.vizeum.co.uk
Managers: S. Marott
Ultimate Holding Company: AEGIS GROUP PLC
Immediate Holding Company: VIZEUM UK LIMITED
Registration no: 02394574 **Date established:** 1989
Turnover: £250,000 - £500,000 **No.of Employees:** 101 - 250
Product Groups: 81

Date of Accounts	Dec 10	Dec 09	Dec 08
Sales Turnover	N/A	N/A	217
Working Capital	-9m	-9m	-9m
Current Liabilities	9m	9m	N/A

VMI Consultancy
20 Prince Of Wales Drive, London, SW11 4SF
Tel: 020-3051 3358
E-mail: info@vmi-uk.com
Website: http://www.vmiconsultancy.com/
Registration no: 05974567 **Date established:** 2008
No.of Employees: 1 - 10 **Product Groups:** 44

Voiplex
5 Astwood Mews, London, SW7 4DE
Tel: 020-7100 8071
E-mail: info@voiplex.co.uk
Website: http://www.voiplex.co.uk
Managers: T. Pratt (Nat Sales Mgr)
Date established: 2002 **No.of Employees:** 1 - 10 **Product Groups:** 37, 79

Volex Group Ltd
10 Eastbourne Terrace, London, W2 6LG
Tel: 020-3370 8830 **Fax:** 01925-830141
E-mail: wtate@volex-group.com
Website: http://www.volex.com
Bank(s): Barclays, City Branch, Manchester
Directors: A. Cherry (Fin), I. Anderson (Tech Serv), P. Mather (Pers), W. Tate (Fin)
Ultimate Holding Company: VOLEX PLC
Immediate Holding Company: VOLEX PLC
Registration no: 00158956 **VAT No.:** GB 145 1018 07
Date established: 2019 **Turnover:** £250m - £500m
No.of Employees: 11 - 20 **Product Groups:** 37

Date of Accounts	Apr 09	Apr 10
Sales Turnover	265m	229m
Pre Tax Profit/Loss	4m	5m
Working Capital	34m	34m
Fixed Assets	11m	11m
Current Assets	101m	106m
Current Liabilities	24m	27m

Vulcan Gates

77 Mostyn Road, London, SW19 3LW
Tel: 020-8288 1828
E-mail: nigel@vulcangates.co.uk
Website: http://www.vulcangates.co.uk
Directors: N. Barclay (Prop)
No.of Employees: 1 - 10 **Product Groups:** 26, 35

W F Wade W F Electrical

Garrick Industrial Centre Irving Way, London, NW9 6AQ
Tel: 020-8203 0055 **Fax:** 020-8203 6570
Website: http://www.wf-online.com
Directors: S. Hayne (Div), T. Judge (MD)
Managers: L. Woolaway (District Mgr)
Immediate Holding Company: Wholesale Fittings Group
VAT No.: GB 430 5213 02 **Date established:** 1900
No.of Employees: 1 - 10 **Product Groups:** 67

W G Ford Ventilating Ltd

25 Poyser Street, London, E2 9RE
Tel: 020-7739 7779 **Fax:** 020-7739 3307
E-mail: sylvia.ford@wgford.co.uk
Website: http://www.wgford.co.uk
Directors: S. Ford (Fin)
Immediate Holding Company: W. G. FORD (VENTILATING) LIMITED
Registration no: 01281702 **Date established:** 1976
Turnover: Up to £250,000 **No.of Employees:** 1 - 10 **Product Groups:** 40, 48

Date of Accounts	Mar 11	Mar 10	Mar 09
Working Capital	49	35	8
Fixed Assets	14	28	32
Current Assets	257	244	175

W Mannering London Ltd

7 Bellingham Trading Estate Randlesdown Road, London, SE6 3BT
Tel: 020-8461 4400 **Fax:** 020-8695 8784
E-mail: sales@mannering-rubber.co.uk
Website: http://www.mannering-rubber.co.uk
Directors: D. Cole (Fin), A. Pays (MD)
Immediate Holding Company: W. MANNERING (LONDON) LIMITED
Registration no: 03459745 **VAT No.:** GB 707 0293 55
Date established: 1997 **Turnover:** £250,000 - £500,000
No.of Employees: 1 - 10 **Product Groups:** 22, 23, 24, 25, 26, 27, 29, 30, 31, 35, 36, 39, 41, 48, 63, 66

Date of Accounts	Dec 11	Dec 10	Dec 09
Working Capital	1	43	43
Fixed Assets	20	N/A	N/A
Current Assets	53	85	100

W S P Group plc

WSP House 70 Chancery Lane, London, WC2A 1AF
Tel: 020-7314 5000 **Fax:** 020-7314 5111
E-mail: info@wspgroup.com
Website: http://www.wspgroup.com
Bank(s): Barclays
Managers: N. Evans (Admin Off)
Ultimate Holding Company: WSP GROUP PLC
Immediate Holding Company: WSP GROUP HOLDINGS LIMITED
Registration no: 07773599 **Date established:** 2011
Turnover: £125m - £250m **No.of Employees:** 251 - 500
Product Groups: 81, 84

Waltons & Morse LLP

77 Gracechurch Street, London, EC3V 0DL
Tel: 020-7623 4255 **Fax:** 020-7626 4153
E-mail: waltons@wamlaw.co.uk
Website: http://www.waltonsandmorse.com
Bank(s): National Westminster
Directors: D. Perry (Ptnr)
Immediate Holding Company: WALTONS & MORSE LLP
Registration no: OC322825 **VAT No.:** GB 102 1434 39
Date established: 2006 **Turnover:** £2m - £5m **No.of Employees:** 21 - 50
Product Groups: 80

Date of Accounts	Apr 11	Apr 10	Apr 09
Working Capital	4m	3m	3m
Fixed Assets	293	358	481
Current Assets	5m	4m	3m

Ward Cole

2 Archer Street, London, W1D 7AW
Tel: 020-7494 3224 **Fax:** 020-7290 4741
E-mail: david@wardcole.co.uk
Website: http://www.wardcole.co.uk
Managers: D. Pickering (Reg Mgr)
Immediate Holding Company: MEDIA JUNCTION PROMOTIONS LIMITED
Date established: 2011 **No.of Employees:** 1 - 10 **Product Groups:** 35

Date of Accounts	Jun 11	Jun 10	Jun 09
Working Capital	-103	16	49
Fixed Assets	175	81	39
Current Assets	951	605	748

Ward Divecha Ltd

29 Welbeck Street, London, W1G 8DA
Tel: 020-7486 9893 **Fax:** 020-7487 5557
E-mail: info@warddivecha.co.uk
Website: http://www.warddivecha.co.uk
Directors: A. Divecha (Dir)
Immediate Holding Company: WARD DIVECHA LIMITED
Registration no: 03908945 **Date established:** 2000
No.of Employees: 11 - 20 **Product Groups:** 80

Date of Accounts	Dec 11	Dec 10	Dec 09
Working Capital	-286	-291	-140
Fixed Assets	735	734	569
Current Assets	45	106	305

A Warne & Co. Ltd

Unit 11 Nelson Trade Park The Path, London, SW19 3BL
Tel: 020-8543 3045 **Fax:** 020-8543 6089
E-mail: info@awarne.com
Website: http://www.awarne.com
Bank(s): Lloyds TSB Bank plc
Directors: S. Moore (Fin), J. Moore (MD)
Immediate Holding Company: A.WARNE & COMPANY LIMITED
Registration no: 00350961 **VAT No.:** GB 235 6453 63
Date established: 1939 **Turnover:** £2m - £5m **No.of Employees:** 21 - 50
Product Groups: 64, 66

Date of Accounts	Mar 11	Mar 10	Mar 09
Working Capital	952	613	660
Fixed Assets	250	302	257
Current Assets	2m	1m	1m

Warner Bros. International Television Production

Warner House 98 Theobalds Road, London, WC1X 8WB
Tel: 020-7984 5200 **Fax:** 020-7984 5001
Website: http://www.warnerbros.com
Directors: C. Lima (Dir)
Managers: A. Douglas
Immediate Holding Company: Time Warner Inc
Registration no: 00259661 **Turnover:** £75m - £125m
No.of Employees: 501 - 1000 **Product Groups:** 89

Date of Accounts	Dec 09	Dec 08	Dec 07
Pre Tax Profit/Loss	-2	4	1
Working Capital	42	44	40
Current Assets	45	130	124

Warwick Evans Optical Co. Ltd

22 Palace Road, London, N11 2PS
Tel: 020-8888 0051 **Fax:** 020-8888 9055
E-mail: sales@keystonevision.com
Website: http://www.keystonevision.com
Directors: K. Shah (MD)
Ultimate Holding Company: TARGETSTOCK LIMITED
Immediate Holding Company: WARWICK-EVANS OPTICAL COMPANY LIMITED
Registration no: 00430194 **VAT No.:** GB 229 5311 68
Date established: 1947 **Turnover:** £250,000 - £500,000
No.of Employees: 1 - 10 **Product Groups:** 38

Date of Accounts	Mar 12	Mar 11	Mar 10
Working Capital	812	854	914
Fixed Assets	12	14	19
Current Assets	824	895	959

Washington E & C

20 Bedford Square, London, WC1B 3HH
Tel: 020-7580 2623 **Fax:** 020-7908 4911
E-mail: info.uk@wgint.com
Website: http://www.wgint.com
Managers: A. Halstead ()
Ultimate Holding Company: RAYTHEON INC (U.S.A.)
Immediate Holding Company: RAYTHEON ENGINEERS & CONSTRUCTORS
Registration no: 04444814 **VAT No.:** GB 238 4364 51
Turnover: £10m - £20m **No.of Employees:** 1 - 10 **Product Groups:** 42, 81, 84

Date of Accounts	Mar 11	Mar 10	Mar 09
Working Capital	-87	360	126
Fixed Assets	184	214	21
Current Assets	189	559	151

Waterlow Legal & Regulatory

Paulton House 8 Shepherdess Walk, London, N1 7LB
Tel: 020-7490 0049 **Fax:** 020-7253 1308
E-mail: sales@wilmington.co.uk
Website: http://www.waterlow.com
Managers: N. Smith
Ultimate Holding Company: WHITEWATER HOLDINGS LIMITED
Immediate Holding Company: OUR LASTING TRIBUTE LIMITED
Date established: 2003 **No.of Employees:** 51 - 100 **Product Groups:** 28, 81

Date of Accounts	Jun 11	Jun 10	Jun 09
Pre Tax Profit/Loss	37	37	37
Working Capital	-252	-352	-252
Fixed Assets	370	370	370
Current Liabilities	N/A	100	N/A

Watkins Gray International

Colechurch House 1 London Bridge Walk, London, SE1 2SX
Tel: 020-7940 8400 **Fax:** 020-7940 8444
E-mail: mail@wgi.co.uk
Website: http://www.wgi.co.uk
Bank(s): Barclays
Directors: A. Walker (Snr Part), R. Storey (Tech Serv), R. Caddock (Ptnr), S. Kahlow (Fin)
Immediate Holding Company: WATKINS GRAY INTERNATIONAL LLP
Registration no: OC301851 **VAT No.:** GB 697 1549 83
Date established: 2002 **Turnover:** £2m - £5m **No.of Employees:** 51 - 100
Product Groups: 84

Date of Accounts	Mar 11	Mar 10	Mar 09
Sales Turnover	4m	4m	5m
Pre Tax Profit/Loss	511	646	665
Working Capital	569	456	284
Fixed Assets	101	159	231
Current Assets	2m	2m	2m
Current Liabilities	1m	1m	1m

Watpower International Ltd

PO Box 1389, London, W5 1JJ
Tel: 020-8810 9148 **Fax:** 020-8810 5509
E-mail: susan@watpower.co.uk
Website: http://www.watpower.co.uk
Directors: B. Watkins (MD), S. Watkins (MD)
Immediate Holding Company: WATPOWER INTERNATIONAL LTD
Registration no: 01370895 **VAT No.:** GB 228 8821 36
Date established: 1978 **Turnover:** Up to £250,000
No.of Employees: 1 - 10 **Product Groups:** 37, 61

Date of Accounts	Mar 08
Sales Turnover	29
Pre Tax Profit/Loss	5
Working Capital	-9
Current Assets	22
Current Liabilities	31
Total Share Capital	10
ROCE% (Return on Capital Employed)	-62.7

A P Watson Ltd

80 Highbury Park, London, N5 2XE
Tel: 020-7226 2303 **Fax:** 020-7354 8372
E-mail: enquiries@apwatsonltd.co.uk
Website: http://www.apwatsonltd.co.uk
Directors: R. Watson (Fin), A. Watson (MD)
Immediate Holding Company: A P WATSON LIMITED
Registration no: 01182569 **Date established:** 1974
Turnover: £250,000 - £500,000 **No.of Employees:** 1 - 10
Product Groups: 24, 26

Date of Accounts	Mar 12	Mar 11	Mar 10
Sales Turnover	256	186	155
Pre Tax Profit/Loss	33	44	5
Working Capital	204	187	159
Fixed Assets	325	326	328
Current Assets	239	219	184
Current Liabilities	20	12	15

Watson Diesel Ltd

Ronian Works Elm Grove, London, SW19 4HE
Tel: 020-8879 3854 **Fax:** 08704-441386
E-mail: sales@watsondiesel.com
Website: http://www.watsondiesel.com
Directors: I. Watson (MD)
Immediate Holding Company: WATSON (DIESEL) LIMITED
Registration no: 00897911 **VAT No.:** GB 216 2668 67
Date established: 1967 **Turnover:** £500,000 - £1m
No.of Employees: 1 - 10 **Product Groups:** 39, 40, 48

Date of Accounts	Mar 11	Mar 10	Mar 09
Sales Turnover	790	853	994
Pre Tax Profit/Loss	31	17	-20
Working Capital	-274	-299	-310
Fixed Assets	167	180	193
Current Assets	241	227	254
Current Liabilities	99	68	47

Watson & Lewis Ltd

5 Cullen Way, London, NW10 6JZ
Tel: 020-8961 3000 **Fax:** 020-8965 1990
Website: http://www.watsonandlewis.co.uk
Directors: J. Stelm (Dir)
Immediate Holding Company: WATSON & LEWIS LIMITED
Registration no: 00319734 **Date established:** 1936
Turnover: £250,000 - £500,000 **No.of Employees:** 1 - 10
Product Groups: 48

Date of Accounts	Jun 11	Jun 10	Jun 09
Working Capital	-4	-2	15
Fixed Assets	3	3	14
Current Assets	13	30	33

Watts Group plc

1 Great Tower Street, London, EC3R 5AA
Tel: 020-7280 8000 **Fax:** 020-7280 8001
E-mail: london@watts.co.uk
Website: http://www.watts.co.uk
Bank(s): Lloyds TSB Bank plc
Directors: D. Dorrington (Dir)
Immediate Holding Company: WATTS GROUP PLC
Registration no: 05728557 **VAT No.:** GB 205 9609 61
Date established: 2006 **Turnover:** £10m - £20m
No.of Employees: 51 - 100 **Product Groups:** 80, 84

Date of Accounts	Apr 11	Apr 10	Apr 12
Sales Turnover	14m	15m	13m
Pre Tax Profit/Loss	-581	-2m	967
Working Capital	-440	9	87
Fixed Assets	268	375	204
Current Assets	5m	6m	4m
Current Liabilities	2m	2m	2m

Wave Enterprises Lighting Manufacturer Ltd

Unit 7 Brent New Enterprise Centre Cobbold Road, London, NW10 9SF
Tel: 020-8428 6895
E-mail: m.hirani@wavelighting.co.uk
Directors: M. Hirani (Dir)
No.of Employees: 1 - 10 **Product Groups:** 37, 67

Wayne Maxwell Design

Unit 6 Resolution Way, Deptford, London, SE8 4NT
Tel: 020-8691 3000
E-mail: designs@waynemaxwell.com
Website: http://www.waynemaxwell.com
Directors: G. Maxwell (Dir)
Date established: 2005 **No.of Employees:** 1 - 10 **Product Groups:** 61

Wine Box Co. Ltd

Unit 11 Ellerslie Square Lyham Road, London, SW2 5DZ
Tel: 020-7737 4040 **Fax:** 020-7737 4422
E-mail: sales@thewbc.co.uk
Website: http://www.winebox.co.uk
Directors: A. Wilson (Dir)
Immediate Holding Company: Wine Box Company Ltd
Registration no: 02384680 **Date established:** 1989 **Turnover:** £5m - £10m
No.of Employees: 11 - 20 **Product Groups:** 38, 42

WCRS

5 Golden Square, London, W1F 9BS
Tel: 020-7806 5000 **Fax:** 020-7806 5099
E-mail: r.wight@wcrs.co.uk
Website: http://www.wars.com
Bank(s): HSBC
Directors: R. Wight (Dir), S. Woodford (Grp Chief Exec), W. Orr (MD)
Managers: S. Chalisey (I.T. Exec)
Ultimate Holding Company: 05015446
Immediate Holding Company: WCRS&CO LIMITED
Registration no: 01737774 **VAT No.:** GB 417 6776 22
Date established: 1983 **Turnover:** £20m - £50m
No.of Employees: 101 - 250 **Product Groups:** 81

Weather Call

Avalon House 57-63 Scrutton Street, London, EC2A 4PJ
Tel: 020-7613 6000 **Fax:** 020-7613 5005
E-mail: weathercall@itouch.co.uk
Website: http://www.itouch.co.uk
Directors: D. Mcpherson (Co Sec), I. Russell (Dir)
Managers: H. Turnbull (Mgr)
Ultimate Holding Company: FREEVER SA (FRANCE)
Immediate Holding Company: BUONGIORNO UK LIMITED
Registration no: 04101267 **Date established:** 2000
Turnover: £10m - £20m **No.of Employees:** 51 - 100 **Product Groups:** 81, 82

Date of Accounts	Mar 08
Sales Turnover	576200
Pre Tax Profit/Loss	-4740
Working Capital	-11560
Fixed Assets	507270
Current Assets	199870
Current Liabilities	211430
Total Share Capital	31960
ROCE% (Return on Capital Employed)	-1.0

Wedgewood Travel Ltd (a division of Waterford Wedgwood P.L.C.)
7 Prescot Street, London, E1 8AY
Tel: 020-7265 7000 **Fax:** 020-7265 7070
E-mail: alda@wedgewood.co.uk
Website: http://www.wedgewood.co.uk
Bank(s): National Westminster Bank Plc
Directors: A. Ford (MD)
Immediate Holding Company: WEDGEWOOD TRAVEL LIMITED
Registration no: 01458614 **Date established:** 1979
Turnover: Up to £250,000 **No.of Employees:** 21 - 50 **Product Groups:** 14, 24, 33, 36, 49, 63, 65

Date of Accounts	Dec 11	Dec 10	Dec 09
Working Capital	714	220	127
Fixed Assets	34	35	10
Current Assets	2m	1m	1m

George Weidenfeld & Nicolson Ltd
Orion House 5 Upper St Martins Lane, London, WC2H 9EA
Tel: 020-7240 3444 **Fax:** 020-7240 4822
Website: http://www.orionbooks.co.uk
Directors: P. Roche (Grp Chief Exec)
Immediate Holding Company: The Orion Publishing Group Ltd
Registration no: 00472173 **VAT No.:** GB 235 9971 23
Turnover: £10m - £20m **No.of Employees:** 101 - 250
Product Groups: 28, 64

Date of Accounts	Dec 99	Dec 98	Dec 95
Working Capital	-212	-212	-212
Current Assets	4	4	4

Weldatube Mechanical Services Ltd
187 Edward Place, London, SE8 5HD
Tel: 020-8691 5875 **Fax:** 020-8469 2631
E-mail: keepingcool@btopenworld.com
Website: http://www.keepingcool.co.uk
Directors: E. Smith (MD), L. Smith (Fin)
Immediate Holding Company: WELDATUBE MECHANICAL SERVICES LIMITED
Registration no: 03394870 **Date established:** 1997
Turnover: £500,000 - £1m **No.of Employees:** 1 - 10 **Product Groups:** 36, 40, 44, 48, 52, 84

Date of Accounts	Sep 11	Sep 10	Sep 09
Working Capital	145	182	197
Fixed Assets	24	8	14
Current Assets	286	331	472

Welding Marine & General Engineers
Pipers Wharf 79 Banning Street, London, SE10 0NT
Tel: 020-8305 1993 **Fax:** 020-8305 1992
Website: http://www.thamescraft.com
Directors: P. Deverell (Prop)
Immediate Holding Company: WELDING MARINE (GREENWICH) LIMITED
Registration no: 03184479 **Date established:** 1996
No.of Employees: 11 - 20 **Product Groups:** 35, 36, 39

Wereldhave Property Management
39 Sloane Street, London, SW1X 9WR
Tel: 020-7235 2080 **Fax:** 020-7245 9962
E-mail: sales@wereldhave.com
Website: http://www.wereldhave.com
Bank(s): Barclays
Directors: A. Turton (MD), B. Crook (Fin), J. Laker (MD), R. Smart (Fin)
Ultimate Holding Company: WERELDHAVE NV (HOLLAND)
Immediate Holding Company: WERELDHAVE PROPERTY CORPORATION PLC
Registration no: 00295909 **VAT No.:** GB 239 4101 77
Date established: 1935 **Turnover:** £5m - £10m **No.of Employees:** 11 - 20
Product Groups: 80

Date of Accounts	Dec 11	Dec 10	Dec 09
Sales Turnover	8m	9m	9m
Pre Tax Profit/Loss	9m	10m	-3m
Working Capital	-7m	9m	81m
Fixed Assets	163m	165m	83m
Current Assets	3m	18m	91m
Current Liabilities	4m	4m	4m

Lucy Wernick & Associates
11 Bowling Green Lane, London, EC1R 0BG
Tel: 020-7580 8644 **Fax:** 020-7580 8744
E-mail: sales@lwfa.co.uk
Website: http://www.lwfa.co.uk
Directors: K. Cheney (Dir), L. Wernick (Prop)
Ultimate Holding Company: LUCY WERNICK HOLDINGS LIMITED
Immediate Holding Company: LUCY WERNICK & ASSOCIATES LIMITED
Registration no: 02814743 **Date established:** 1993 **Turnover:** £5m - £10m
No.of Employees: 1 - 10 **Product Groups:** 38, 42

Date of Accounts	May 12	May 11	May 10
Sales Turnover	9m	9m	11m
Pre Tax Profit/Loss	1m	1m	2m
Working Capital	221	229	245
Fixed Assets	17	20	19
Current Assets	933	979	4m
Current Liabilities	139	314	451

West Hill
4 Highgate West Hill, London, N6 6JS
Tel: 020-8341 5332 **Fax:** 020-7485 7957
E-mail: sales@westhill.info
Website: http://www.westhill.info
Directors: J. Dewan (Prop)
Registration no: 02974795 **Date established:** 1994
No.of Employees: 1 - 10 **Product Groups:** 80

West Leigh Ltd
11-13 Spa Road, London, SE16 3RB
Tel: 020-7232 0030 **Fax:** 020-7232 1763
E-mail: info@west-leigh.co.uk
Website: http://www.west-leigh.co.uk
Bank(s): HSBC Bank plc
Directors: D. Grew (Dir)
Managers: P. Cox (Comm), A. Hart (Sales Prom Mgr)
Immediate Holding Company: WEST LEIGH LIMITED
Registration no: 00384694 **VAT No.:** GB 662 8441 22
Date established: 1944 **Turnover:** £5m - £10m
No.of Employees: 51 - 100 **Product Groups:** 35, 36, 40

Date of Accounts	Mar 12	Mar 11	Mar 10
Sales Turnover	5m	5m	6m
Pre Tax Profit/Loss	22	273	491
Working Capital	2m	2m	2m
Fixed Assets	1m	1m	1m
Current Assets	3m	3m	3m
Current Liabilities	355	415	535

Westferry Printers
235 Westferry Road, London, E14 8NX
Tel: 020-7538 3100 **Fax:** 020-7538 4844
E-mail: davidb@westferry.co.uk
Website: http://www.westferry.co.uk
Bank(s): National Westminster
Managers: D. Broadhurst (Mgr)
Immediate Holding Company: WEST FERRY PRINTERS LIMITED
Registration no: 01997219 **Date established:** 1986
Turnover: £20m - £50m **No.of Employees:** 51 - 100 **Product Groups:** 28

Date of Accounts	Dec 11	Dec 10	Dec 09
Sales Turnover	25m	27m	39m
Pre Tax Profit/Loss	3m	3m	8m
Working Capital	-11m	7m	7m
Fixed Assets	23m	1m	1m
Current Assets	10m	20m	20m
Current Liabilities	11m	12m	11m

Westone Products Ltd
8 Hampstead Gate 1a Frognal, London, NW3 6AL
Tel: 020-7431 9001 **Fax:** 020-7431 9002
Website: http://www.synpart.com
Bank(s): HSBC
Directors: M. Levenstein (Grp Chief Exec), A. Richardson (Grp Chief Exec), T. Richardson (MD)
Managers: J. Rifkin (Personnel), D. Joseph (Purch Mgr), D. Aston (I.T. Exec), D. Blackwell (Sales & Mktg Mg)
Ultimate Holding Company: FP053614
Immediate Holding Company: SYNPART LIMITED
Registration no: 01002537 **VAT No.:** GB 233 7572 59
Date established: 1971 **Turnover:** £10m - £20m
No.of Employees: 11 - 20 **Product Groups:** 63

Date of Accounts	Dec 07	Dec 06	Dec 05
Sales Turnover	12245	12020	13448
Pre Tax Profit/Loss	707	688	279
Working Capital	544	1326	1511
Fixed Assets	2997	277	355
Current Assets	5203	4555	4698
Current Liabilities	4659	3229	3187
Total Share Capital	2	2	2
ROCE% (Return on Capital Employed)	20.0	42.9	15.0
ROT% (Return on Turnover)	5.8	5.7	2.1

Westwood International Ltd
6 The Office Village Romford Road, London, E15 4EA
Tel: 020-8503 0901 **Fax:** 020-8503 1397
E-mail: info@westwoodinternational.co.uk
Website: http://www.westwoodinternational.co.uk
Directors: K. Joseph (MD)
Immediate Holding Company: WESTWOOD INTERNATIONAL LIMITED
Registration no: 02496384 **VAT No.:** GB 549 1206 47
Date established: 1990 **No.of Employees:** 1 - 10 **Product Groups:** 22, 23, 24, 30, 32, 35, 36, 37, 38, 39, 40, 44, 49, 52, 63, 67, 68, 84

Date of Accounts	Dec 11	Dec 10	Dec 09
Working Capital	61	162	-76
Fixed Assets	4	6	5
Current Assets	148	222	308

Wexas Travel (t/a Wexas International)
47-49 Brompton Road, London, SW3 1DE
Tel: 08458-386262 **Fax:** 020-7589 8418
E-mail: travel@wexas.com
Website: http://www.wexas.com
Directors: T. Cook (Fin)
Managers: S. Lloyd (Mgr)
Immediate Holding Company: WEXAS LIMITED
Registration no: 01820489 **Date established:** 1984
Turnover: £20m - £50m **No.of Employees:** 51 - 100 **Product Groups:** 69

Date of Accounts	Dec 11	Dec 10	Dec 09
Sales Turnover	21m	26m	22m
Pre Tax Profit/Loss	51	217	253
Working Capital	-2m	-2m	-185
Fixed Assets	9m	7m	5m
Current Assets	3m	2m	3m
Current Liabilities	502	892	492

Which Magazine
2 Marylebone Road, London, NW1 4DF
Tel: 020-7770 7000 **Fax:** 020-7770 7600
E-mail: pvs@which.co.uk
Website: http://www.which.co.uk
Directors: A. Reading (Co Sec), P. Vicary Smith (Grp Chief Exec)
Ultimate Holding Company: CONSUMERS ASSOCIATION
Immediate Holding Company: WHICH? LIMITED
Registration no: 00677665 **Date established:** 1960
Turnover: £50m - £75m **No.of Employees:** 251 - 500 **Product Groups:** 28

Date of Accounts	Jun 11	Jun 10	Jun 09
Sales Turnover	74m	70m	66m
Pre Tax Profit/Loss	-1m	-309	-886
Working Capital	-3m	379	-44
Fixed Assets	7m	5m	423
Current Assets	14m	13m	12m
Current Liabilities	5m	5m	5m

Whistles Ltd
12 St Christophers Place, London, W1U 1NH
Tel: 020-7487 4484 **Fax:** 020-7486 2043
E-mail: info@whistles.co.uk
Website: http://www.whistles.co.uk
Bank(s): Lloyds
Managers: A. Pointer (Mgr)
Ultimate Holding Company: WHISTLES HOLDINGS LIMITED
Immediate Holding Company: WHISTLES LIMITED
Registration no: 01514754 **Date established:** 1980
No.of Employees: 11 - 20 **Product Groups:** 63

Date of Accounts	Jan 09	Jan 10	Jan 11
Sales Turnover	33m	33m	38m
Pre Tax Profit/Loss	-3m	-3m	-700
Working Capital	-600	-2m	-3m
Fixed Assets	7m	6m	6m
Current Assets	8m	6m	6m
Current Liabilities	2m	2m	3m

White & Case
5 Old Broad Street, London, EC2N 1DW
Tel: 020-7532 1000 **Fax:** 020-7532 1001
E-mail: jmartin@whitecase.com
Website: http://www.whitecase.com
Managers: J. Martin (Mgr)
Immediate Holding Company: WHITE & CASE (INTERNATIONAL) LLP
Registration no: OC333623 **Date established:** 2007 **Turnover:** £2m - £5m
No.of Employees: 251 - 500 **Product Groups:** 80

Ron White Fixing www.repairyourwindow.co.uk
Unit 25 571 Finchley Road, London, NW3 7BN
Tel: 0800-107 5113 **Fax:** 020-785 6855
E-mail: ronwhitefixing@ntlworld.com
Website: http://www.repairyourwindow.co.uk
Directors: R. White (Prop)
Immediate Holding Company: FABRIC FLAVOURS LIMITED
Registration no: 03464719 **Date established:** 2005
No.of Employees: 1 - 10 **Product Groups:** 35, 39, 52, 66

Date of Accounts	Jan 11	Jan 10	Jan 09
Working Capital	22	15	18
Current Assets	23	18	19

Whitechapel Bell Foundry Ltd
34 Whitechapel Road, London, E1 1DY
Tel: 020-7247 2599 **Fax:** 020-7375 1979
E-mail: sales@whitechapelbellfoundry.co.uk
Website: http://www.whitechapelbellfoundry.co.uk
Bank(s): Barclays
Directors: K. Hughes (Dir), A. Hughes (Dir)
Immediate Holding Company: WHITECHAPEL BELL FOUNDRY LIMITED
Registration no: 00938186 **VAT No.:** GB 243 1770 78
Date established: 1968 **Turnover:** £1m - £2m **No.of Employees:** 21 - 50
Product Groups: 39, 40, 49

Date of Accounts	Sep 11	Sep 10	Sep 09
Working Capital	205	180	167
Fixed Assets	183	190	169
Current Assets	481	494	487

Whitehead Man G K R & Associates
Queensbury House 3 Old Burlington Street, London, W1S 3AE
Tel: 020-7534 0000 **Fax:** 020-7290 2050
E-mail: mail@wmann.com
Website: http://www.wman.com
Bank(s): HSBC Bank plc
Directors: B. Burwash (Dir), C. Burrows (Dir), J. Hyde (Dir), P. Turner (MD), R. Andrews (I.T. Dir)
Managers: M. Greenfield (Mktg Serv Mgr)
Immediate Holding Company: G K R Group Ltd
Registration no: 01288875 **Date established:** 1972 **Turnover:** £5m - £10m
No.of Employees: 101 - 250 **Product Groups:** 80

Whitmore Security
Unit 119 Tudorleaf Business Centre 2-8 Fountayne Road, London, N15 4QL
Tel: 020-8885 2099 **Fax:** 020-8808 3932
E-mail: info@whitmoresecurityltd.com
Website: http://www.whitmoresecurityltd.com
Directors: A. Odimegwu (Dir), K. Okakpu (Fin)
Immediate Holding Company: WHITMORE SECURITY LIMITED
Registration no: 06100711 **Date established:** 2007
Turnover: Up to £250,000 **No.of Employees:** 1 - 10 **Product Groups:** 81

Date of Accounts	Feb 08	Feb 11	Feb 10
Sales Turnover	132	N/A	N/A
Pre Tax Profit/Loss	15	N/A	N/A
Working Capital	14	68	58
Fixed Assets	3	9	11
Current Assets	17	82	74
Current Liabilities	3	N/A	N/A

Whittingdales Solicitors
Chancery House 53-64 Chancery Lane, London, WC2A 1QU
Tel: 020-7831 5591 **Fax:** 020-7430 0448
E-mail: m.whittingdale@whittingdales.co.uk
Website: http://www.whittingdales.co.uk
Directors: M. Whittingdale (Snr Part)
Immediate Holding Company: ROMANIAN TRADE SERVICES LIMITED
Registration no: 06570828 **Date established:** 2008
No.of Employees: 1 - 10 **Product Groups:** 80

Whitton Precision Ltd
Bridge Works 206 Durnsford Road, London, SW19 8DR
Tel: 020-8946 6431 **Fax:** 020-8947 1292
E-mail: whittonprecision@btconnet.com
Website: http://www.whittonprecision.co.uk
Directors: J. Aldridge (MD)
Immediate Holding Company: WHITTON PRECISION LIMITED
Registration no: 00523846 **VAT No.:** GB 215 9838 39
Date established: 1953 **Turnover:** £250,000 - £500,000
No.of Employees: 1 - 10 **Product Groups:** 35, 46, 66

Date of Accounts	Mar 11	Mar 10	Mar 09
Sales Turnover	N/A	N/A	315
Pre Tax Profit/Loss	N/A	N/A	3
Working Capital	420	417	421
Fixed Assets	89	93	98
Current Assets	467	466	470
Current Liabilities	N/A	N/A	19

Whyte Chemicals Ltd
Marlborough House 298 Regents Park Road, London, N3 2UA
Tel: 020-8346 5946 **Fax:** 020-8349 4589
E-mail: info@whytechemicals.co.uk
Website: http://www.whytechemicals.co.uk
Directors: B. Rattan (Fin), P. Bloom (Fin), A. Taylor (Dir)
Managers: G. Hughes (Tech Serv Mgr), S. Clifton (Personnel)
Ultimate Holding Company: WHYTE GROUP LIMITED
Immediate Holding Company: WHYTE GROUP LIMITED
Registration no: 01286190 **VAT No.:** GB 231 5179 83
Date established: 1976 **Turnover:** £75m - £125m
No.of Employees: 101 - 250 **Product Groups:** 66

Date of Accounts	Dec 10	Dec 09	Dec 08
Sales Turnover	103m	94m	124m
Pre Tax Profit/Loss	-2m	665	824
Working Capital	2m	2m	1m
Fixed Assets	10m	10m	9m
Current Assets	38m	34m	29m
Current Liabilities	22m	5m	5m

Wigglesworth & Co. Ltd

Nutmeg House 60 Gainsford Street, London, SE1 2NY
Tel: 020-7940 6000 **Fax:** 020-7403 3232
E-mail: pbrazier@wigco.co.uk
Website: http://www.wigglesworthfibres.com
Bank(s): The Royal Bank of Scotland
Directors: P. Brazier (MD)
Ultimate Holding Company: ROBINOW LIMITED
Immediate Holding Company: WIGGLESWORTH & CO. LIMITED
Registration no: 03973490 **VAT No.:** GB 707 5230 54
Date established: 2000 **Turnover:** £20m - £50m
No.of Employees: 11 - 20 **Product Groups:** 23, 24, 66

Date of Accounts	May 12	May 11	May 10
Sales Turnover	42m	36m	24m
Pre Tax Profit/Loss	1m	1m	468
Working Capital	3m	3m	3m
Fixed Assets	777	851	360
Current Assets	9m	8m	5m
Current Liabilities	1m	1m	458

Wightman Metals

Rear of Block D Ringway Bounds Green Industrial Estate, London, N11 2UD
Tel: 020-8368 1660 **Fax:** 020-8368 9570
Website: http://www.wightmanmetals.co.uk
Directors: V. Gavin (Ptnr)
VAT No.: GB 229 8549 20 **Turnover:** £250,000 - £500,000
No.of Employees: 1 - 10 **Product Groups:** 66

R H Wilkins Ltd

59 Leather Lane, London, EC1N 7TJ
Tel: 020-7405 5187 **Fax:** 020-7831 2805
E-mail: sales@rhwilkins.co.uk
Website: http://www.rhwilkins.co.uk
Bank(s): Barclays
Directors: E. Smith (MD)
Immediate Holding Company: R.H. WILKINS (ENGRAVERS) LIMITED
Registration no: 04441124 **Date established:** 2002
Turnover: £500,000 - £1m **No.of Employees:** 11 - 20 **Product Groups:** 28

Date of Accounts	Aug 11	Aug 10	Aug 09
Working Capital	157	167	157
Fixed Assets	5	9	7
Current Assets	263	301	243

William Evans

67a St James's Street, London, SW1A 1PH
Tel: 020-7493 0415 **Fax:** 020-7499 5515
E-mail: sales@williamevans.com
Website: http://www.williamevans.com
Directors: D. Cavenagh (Sales), N. Hadan-Taton (Dir)
Ultimate Holding Company: WILLIAM EVANS HOLDINGS LIMITED
Immediate Holding Company: WILLIAM EVANS HOLDINGS LIMITED
Registration no: 02549604 **Date established:** 1990 **Turnover:** £2m - £5m
No.of Employees: 1 - 10 **Product Groups:** 36, 39, 40

Date of Accounts	Mar 11	Mar 10	Mar 09
Pre Tax Profit/Loss	N/A	N/A	-0
Working Capital	-0	N/A	-3
Fixed Assets	750	750	750
Current Assets	-0	N/A	-0

William Hill

Greenside House 50 Station Road, London, N22 7TP
Tel: 020-8918 3600 **Fax:** 020-8918 3726
E-mail: name@williamhill.co.uk
Website: http://www.williamhillplc.com
Directors: D. Russell (Pers), D. Read (Co Sec)
Managers: N. Cooper, M. Oakes, C. Bower
Ultimate Holding Company: WILLIAM HILL PLC
Immediate Holding Company: CAMEC LIMITED
Registration no: 00308820 **Date established:** 1936
Turnover: £500m - £1,000m **No.of Employees:** 101 - 250
Product Groups: 89

Date of Accounts	Dec 08	Dec 09	Dec 10
Working Capital	46m	46m	46m
Current Assets	46m	46m	46m

William & Son

10 Mount Street, London, W1K 2TY
Tel: 020-7493 8385 **Fax:** 020-7493 8386
E-mail: info@williamandson.com
Website: http://www.williamandson.com
Directors: W. Asprey (Prop), J. Hicks (Fin)
Date established: 1999 **No.of Employees:** 21 - 50 **Product Groups:** 36, 39, 40

Wills Associates Ltd

10 Greenham Road, London, N10 1LP
Tel: 020-7251 6611 **Fax:** 020-8374 3549
E-mail: tony@wills-watson.co.uk
Website: http://www.wills-watson.co.uk
Directors: T. Wills (Snr Part), L. Strickland (Fin), A. Wills (MD)
Immediate Holding Company: WILLS ASSOCIATES DESIGN CONSULTANTS LTD
Registration no: 04455990 **VAT No.:** GB 657 1421 40
Date established: 2002 **Turnover:** Up to £250,000
No.of Employees: 1 - 10 **Product Groups:** 26, 35, 67, 84

Date of Accounts	Mar 11	Mar 10	Mar 09
Working Capital	11	10	22
Fixed Assets	6	5	3
Current Assets	63	23	43

Wilson Electric Battersea Ltd

12-18 Radstock Street, London, SW11 4AT
Tel: 020-7228 3343 **Fax:** 020-7924 1887
E-mail: info@wilsonelectric.co.uk
Website: http://www.wilsonelectric.co.uk
Bank(s): National Westminster
Directors: J. Plumbridge (Fin), G. Brooker (MD), D. Taylor (Serv)
Managers: C. Brooker (Sales Admin)
Immediate Holding Company: WILSON ELECTRIC (BATTERSEA) LIMITED
Registration no: 00491289 **Date established:** 1951
Turnover: £500,000 - £1m **No.of Employees:** 21 - 50 **Product Groups:** 52

Date of Accounts	Jan 11	Jan 10	Jan 09
Working Capital	228	234	230
Fixed Assets	309	322	306
Current Assets	671	800	902

Wilson Sloane Street Ltd

116-120 Coldharbour Lane Camberwell, London, SE5 9PZ
Tel: 020-7733 2500 **Fax:** 020-7738 7937
E-mail: sales@wilsonmeats.com
Website: http://www.wilsonmeats.com
Directors: S. Wilson (MD), D. Wilson (Co Sec)
Immediate Holding Company: WILSON (SLOANE STREET) LIMITED
Registration no: 00553809 **Date established:** 1955
Turnover: £250,000 - £500,000 **No.of Employees:** 1 - 10
Product Groups: 20, 62

Date of Accounts	May 09	May 08	Nov 06
Working Capital	-28	144	178
Fixed Assets	N/A	26	2m
Current Assets	193	480	723

Wim Hemmink

106 Crawford Street, London, W1H 2HY
Tel: 020-7935 1755 **Fax:** 020-7224 0573
E-mail: wimhemmink@btinternet.com
Directors: J. Hegron (Fin), W. Hemmink (MD)
Immediate Holding Company: WIM HEMMINK LIMITED
Registration no: 01872962 **Date established:** 1984
Turnover: £500,000 - £1m **No.of Employees:** 1 - 10 **Product Groups:** 63

Date of Accounts	Dec 11	Dec 10	Dec 08
Working Capital	-17	-18	-19
Fixed Assets	83	83	83
Current Assets	32	25	21

Wimbledon Sash Weight

4 Riverside Business Park Lyon Road, London, SW19 2RL
Tel: 020-8417 1112 **Fax:** 020-8417 1117
E-mail: wimbledonsash@aol.com
Website: http://www.wimbledonsash.co.uk
Directors: C. Smith (Prop), P. Sullivan (Prop)
Date established: 2004 **No.of Employees:** 1 - 10 **Product Groups:** 36, 38, 39, 67

Wimbledon Sewing Machine Co. Ltd

292-312 Balham High Road, London, SW17 7AA
Tel: 020-8767 4724 **Fax:** 020-8767 4726
E-mail: wimbledonsewingmachinecoltd@btinternet.com
Website: http://www.wimsew.com
Bank(s): Midland
Directors: R. Rushton (Prop), R. Rushton (Prop)
Immediate Holding Company: WIMBLEDON SEWING MACHINE CO.LIMITED
Registration no: 00641468 **VAT No.:** GB 216 5581 64
Date established: 1959 **Turnover:** £1m - £2m **No.of Employees:** 11 - 20
Product Groups: 67

Date of Accounts	Apr 11	Apr 10	Apr 09
Working Capital	53	18	43
Fixed Assets	1m	2m	1m
Current Assets	286	291	277

Wimbledon Signs

Unit 3 1a Cowper Road, London, SW19 1AA
Tel: 020-8543 8178 **Fax:** 020-8543 2687
E-mail: sales@wimbledonsigns.co.uk
Website: http://www.wimbledonsigns.co.uk
Directors: K. Osborne (Ptnr)
No.of Employees: 1 - 10 **Product Groups:** 28, 40

Wine Box Co Ltd

Unit 11 Ellerslie Square Lyham Road, London, SW2 5DZ
Tel: 020-7737 1100 **Fax:** 020-7737 4422
E-mail: sales@wbccreativepackaging.co.uk
Website: http://www.wbccreativepackaging.co.uk
Directors: D. Aston (Dir)
Immediate Holding Company: Wine & Spirit Packaging Company Ltd
Registration no: 02384680 **No.of Employees:** 21 - 50
Product Groups: 38, 42

Wine For Spice Ltd

3 Park Steps St Georges Fields, London, W2 2YQ
Tel: 020-7724 4606 **Fax:** 08701-320055
E-mail: we@dc3.co.uk
Website: http://www.dc3.co.uk
Directors: M. Martinez Zurita (Fin), W. Edwardes (MD)
Immediate Holding Company: WINE FOR SPICE LIMITED
Registration no: 04756397 **Date established:** 2003
Turnover: Up to £250,000 **No.of Employees:** 1 - 10 **Product Groups:** 61

Date of Accounts	May 10	May 09	May 08
Sales Turnover	3	3	10
Pre Tax Profit/Loss	-4	-5	-9
Working Capital	-84	-80	-74
Fixed Assets	1	1	1
Current Assets	1	1	1

Winged Bull Aviation Ltd

5 Norway House Trafalgar Square, London, SW1Y 5BN
Tel: 0870-8503395 **Fax:** 0870-8503396
E-mail: fly@bullwings.com
Website: http://www.bullwings.co.uk
Directors: E. Al-Kirkhy (MD)
Date established: 2005 **Turnover:** £2m - £5m **No.of Employees:** 11 - 20
Product Groups: 75

Winn & Coales Denso Ltd

Denso House 33-35 Chapel Road, London, SE27 0TR
Tel: 020-8670 7511 **Fax:** 020-8761 2456
E-mail: mail@denso.net
Website: http://www.denso.net
Bank(s): Barclays
Directors: C. Winn (MD), S. Ahearne (Co Sec)
Ultimate Holding Company: WINN & COALES INTERNATIONAL LIMITED
Immediate Holding Company: WINN & COALES (DENSO) LIMITED
Registration no: 01372246 **VAT No.:** 218 0172 94 **Date established:** 1978
Turnover: £10m - £20m **No.of Employees:** 51 - 100 **Product Groups:** 27, 29, 31, 32

Date of Accounts	Jun 11	Jun 10	Jun 09
Sales Turnover	11m	9m	9m
Pre Tax Profit/Loss	687	883	742
Working Capital	790	2m	2m
Fixed Assets	453	191	239
Current Assets	4m	4m	3m
Current Liabilities	758	1m	258

Witcomb Cycles (t/a Witcomb Cycles)

25 Tanners Hill, London, SE8 4PJ
Tel: 020-8692 1734 **Fax:** 020-8692 1734
E-mail: joymartin@deloittecompanyuk.com
Website: http://www.witcombcycles.com
Directors: J. Martin (Fin), B. Witcomb (MD)
Immediate Holding Company: Witcomb Trading Co. Ltd
Registration no: 00565140 **Date established:** 1956
Turnover: Up to £250,000 **No.of Employees:** 1 - 10 **Product Groups:** 39, 68

Date of Accounts	Dec 07	Dec 06	Dec 05
Sales Turnover	71	64	54
Pre Tax Profit/Loss	1	6	3
Working Capital	-19	-21	-25
Fixed Assets	101	106	104
Current Assets	39	39	29
Current Liabilities	57	60	55
Total Share Capital	2	2	2
ROCE% (Return on Capital Employed)	1.1	6.5	3.4
ROT% (Return on Turnover)	1.3	8.6	4.9

Withers & Rogers LLP

Goldings House 2 Hays Lane, London, SE1 2HW
Tel: 020-7663 3500 **Fax:** 020-7663 3550
E-mail: ndougan@withersrogers.com
Website: http://www.withersrogers.com
Directors: R. Bunn (Dir), N. Dougan (Dir)
Managers: M. Blatchford (Chief Acct), A. Clyne (Gen Contact), S. Greaves (Personnel), D. Montagu-Fryer (Personnel)
Ultimate Holding Company: WITHERS & ROGERS GROUP LLP
Immediate Holding Company: WITHERS & ROGERS LLP
Registration no: OC310992 **Date established:** 2005
Turnover: £10m - £20m **No.of Employees:** 21 - 50 **Product Groups:** 80

Date of Accounts	Mar 11	Mar 10	Mar 09
Sales Turnover	22m	19m	N/A
Pre Tax Profit/Loss	3m	2m	1m
Working Capital	4m	3m	3m
Current Assets	7m	5m	5m
Current Liabilities	600	426	507

Wogen Resources

4 The Sanctuary Westminster, London, SW1P 3JS
Tel: 020-7222 3521 **Fax:** 020-7222 5862
E-mail: sales@wogen.com
Website: http://www.wogen.com
Directors: N. Poulter (Co Sec), A. Greenwood (Fin), C. Williams (MD), C. Williams (Ch), D. Hunter (Dir)
Managers: A. Gordon ()
Immediate Holding Company: WOGEN RESOURCES LIMITED
Registration no: 02071596 **VAT No.:** GB 461 5852 38
Date established: 1986 **Turnover:** £125m - £250m
No.of Employees: 21 - 50 **Product Groups:** 61

Date of Accounts	Sep 09	Sep 08	Sep 07
Sales Turnover	99m	178m	181m
Pre Tax Profit/Loss	1m	-3m	5m
Working Capital	13m	12m	14m
Current Assets	34m	59m	55m
Current Liabilities	606	2m	2m

Wolff Olins Brand Consultants

10 Regents Wharf All Saints Street, London, N1 9RL
Tel: 020-7713 7733 **Fax:** 020-7713 0217
E-mail: ije.nwokorie@wolffolins.com
Website: http://www.wolff-olins.com
Bank(s): National Westminster
Directors: I. Nwokorie (MD), J. Williamson (Sales & Mktg), S. Dent (Fin), S. Bray (Co Sec)
Managers: S. King, E. O'Connor (Personnel), R. Bentley (Sales & Mktg Mg), T. Parfitt (I.T. Exec)
Ultimate Holding Company: OMNICOM GROUP INC (USA)
Immediate Holding Company: WOLFF OLINS LIMITED
Registration no: 01945130 **VAT No.:** GB 380 5699 20
Date established: 1985 **Turnover:** £10m - £20m
No.of Employees: 101 - 250 **Product Groups:** 52, 81, 85

Date of Accounts	Dec 11	Dec 10	Dec 09
Sales Turnover	13m	9m	9m
Pre Tax Profit/Loss	1m	1m	427
Working Capital	5m	5m	4m
Fixed Assets	236	245	362
Current Assets	7m	7m	5m
Current Liabilities	2m	2m	783

Wolters Kluwer Health

250 Waterloo Road, London, SE1 8RD
Tel: 020-7981 0600 **Fax:** 020-7981 0601
E-mail: europe@ovid.com
Website: http://www.wolterskluwer.com
Managers: F. Virmani
Ultimate Holding Company: WOLTERS KLUWER NV (NETHERLANDS)
Immediate Holding Company: SILVERPLATTER INTERNATIONAL NV (NETHERLANDS)
Registration no: 02509986 **Date established:** 1972
Turnover: £250,000 - £500,000 **No.of Employees:** 101 - 250
Product Groups: 28, 64, 80, 81

Date of Accounts	Dec 11	Dec 10	Dec 09
Sales Turnover	3m	3m	2m
Pre Tax Profit/Loss	7	41	15
Working Capital	166	151	89
Fixed Assets	38	47	80
Current Assets	1m	2m	857
Current Liabilities	931	1m	676

Wood Fired Ovens By Jamie Oliver

19-21 Nile Street, London, N1 7LL
Tel: 020-3375 5399 **Fax:** 01772-619572
E-mail: info@jamieoliverovens.com
Website: http://www.orchardovens.co.uk
Directors: S. Cochrane (MD)
Ultimate Holding Company: JAMIE OLIVER HOLDINGS LIMITED
Immediate Holding Company: JAMIE OLIVER LIMITED
Registration no: 03822122 **Date established:** 1999
Turnover: £10m - £20m **No.of Employees:** 1 - 10 **Product Groups:** 20, 40, 41

Date of Accounts	Dec 11	Dec 10	Dec 09
Sales Turnover	14m	14m	11m
Pre Tax Profit/Loss	7	6m	5m
Working Capital	14m	15m	10m
Fixed Assets	959	1m	793
Current Assets	25m	23m	15m
Current Liabilities	5m	4m	4m

Wordflow Ltd
11-19 Vyner Street, London, E2 9DG
Tel: 08456-092450 **Fax:** 020-7377 2942
E-mail: sales@wordflow.co.uk
Website: http://www.wordflow.co.uk
Bank(s): National Westminster
Directors: P. Everest (MD), P. Everiss (MD), S. Ubhi (Sales & Mktg)
Managers: P. Butterfield (Tech Serv Mgr)
Immediate Holding Company: WORDFLOW LIMITED
Registration no: 03297987 **VAT No.:** GB 346 5013 72
Date established: 1996 **Turnover:** £5m - £10m **No.of Employees:** 21 - 50
Product Groups: 44

Date of Accounts	May 11	May 10	May 09
Sales Turnover	5m	6m	6m
Pre Tax Profit/Loss	99	20	-28
Working Capital	43	-25	96
Fixed Assets	803	514	389
Current Assets	966	1m	1m
Current Liabilities	271	348	311

Workingvoices Ltd
Flat 7 Parr Place 23-27 Chiswick High Road, London, W4 2ET
Tel: 0800-3892639
E-mail: info@workingvoices.com
Website: http://www.workingvoices.com
Directors: N. Smallman (Dir)
Managers: T. Parish
Immediate Holding Company: Working Voices Ltd
Registration no: 04018115 **Date established:** 2000
No.of Employees: 21 - 50 **Product Groups:** 28

Date of Accounts	Jun 08	Jun 07	Jun 06
Working Capital	75	7	-86
Fixed Assets	383	408	433
Current Assets	208	117	102
Current Liabilities	132	110	188

Works Design Ltd
7 Homeleigh Road, London, SE15 3EE
Tel: 07815-636003 **Fax:** 020-7820 8502
E-mail: enquiries@worksdesign.co.uk
Website: http://www.worksdesign.co.uk
Directors: A. Tytherleigh (Dir), I. Gravatt (Dir)
Registration no: 03958230 **Date established:** 2000
Turnover: Up to £250,000 **No.of Employees:** 1 - 10 **Product Groups:** 48, 84, 85

Date of Accounts	Mar 10	Mar 09	Mar 08
Working Capital	N/A	1	1
Current Assets	15	27	32

Workspace Group
Magenta House 85 Whitechapel Road, London, E1 1DU
Tel: 020-7247 7614 **Fax:** 020-7247 0157
E-mail: harry.platt@workspacegroup.co.uk
Website: http://www.workspacegroup.co.uk
Directors: A. Whalley (Co Sec), H. Platt (Dir), H. Platt (Grp Chief Exec)
Ultimate Holding Company: WORKSPACE GROUP PLC
Immediate Holding Company: WORKSPACE 2 LIMITED
Registration no: 02469485 **Date established:** 1990
Turnover: £50m - £75m **No.of Employees:** 51 - 100 **Product Groups:** 54

Work2Research
136c Mill Lane West Hampstead, London, NW6 1TG
Tel: 020-7433 8375
E-mail: info@work2research.com
Website: http://www.work2research.com
Product Groups: 80

World Courier UK Ltd
Sea Containers House 20 Upper Ground, London, SE1 9PD
Tel: 020-7717 1400 **Fax:** 020-7928 7105
E-mail: sales@worldcourier.com
Website: http://www.worldcourier.com
Bank(s): National Westminster Bank Plc
Directors: J. Townsend (Fin), J. Butler (MD)
Managers: M. Hohne (Personnel), M. Day (Tech Serv Mgr), M. Bishop
Ultimate Holding Company: WORLD COURIER GROUP INC (USA)
Immediate Holding Company: WORLD COURIER (U.K.) LIMITED
Registration no: 01194193 **VAT No.:** GB 245 0290 85
Date established: 1974 **Turnover:** £20m - £50m
No.of Employees: 101 - 250 **Product Groups:** 71, 72, 75, 79, 84

Date of Accounts	Dec 11	Dec 10	Dec 09
Sales Turnover	33m	32m	42m
Pre Tax Profit/Loss	5m	428	1m
Working Capital	5m	5m	7m
Fixed Assets	20m	20m	313
Current Assets	7m	8m	14m
Current Liabilities	1m	1m	1m

World First
Regent House 16-18 Lombard Road, London, SW11 3RB
Tel: 020-7801 9050 **Fax:** 020-7924 6535
E-mail: elisabeth.dobson@worldfirst.com
Website: http://www.worldfirst.com
Managers: E. Dobson (Mgr)
Immediate Holding Company: WORLD FIRST UK LIMITED
Registration no: 05022388 **Date established:** 2004
Turnover: Over £1,000m **No.of Employees:** 51 - 100 **Product Groups:** 82

Date of Accounts	Jan 12	Jan 11	Jan 10
Sales Turnover	2962m	1851m	958m
Pre Tax Profit/Loss	4m	4m	2m
Working Capital	6m	4m	3m
Fixed Assets	87	116	67
Current Assets	37m	25m	18m
Current Liabilities	31m	N/A	15m

World Language Consultants Ltd
88 Bermondsey Street, London, SE1 3UB
Tel: 020-7357 6981 **Fax:** 020-7357 7755
E-mail: worldlanguages@btconnect.com
Website: http://www.world-language.com
Managers: J. Soto
Immediate Holding Company: WORLD LANGUAGE CONSULTANTS LIMITED
Registration no: 02056622 **VAT No.:** GB 434 9737 21
Date established: 1986 **Turnover:** £250,000 - £500,000
No.of Employees: 21 - 50 **Product Groups:** 80, 86

Date of Accounts	Sep 11	Sep 10	Sep 09
Sales Turnover	327	216	286
Pre Tax Profit/Loss	65	9	56
Working Capital	-74	-140	-150
Fixed Assets	4	4	5
Current Assets	117	67	85
Current Liabilities	186	204	50

World Productions Ltd
Lasenby House 32 Kingly Street, London, W1B 5QQ
Tel: 020-3179 1800 **Fax:** 020-3179 1801
E-mail: roderick@world-productions.com
Website: http://www.world-productions.com
Directors: R. Seligman (MD)
Immediate Holding Company: WORLD PRODUCTIONS LIMITED
Registration no: 02483078 **Date established:** 1990
Turnover: £500,000 - £1m **No.of Employees:** 1 - 10 **Product Groups:** 79

Date of Accounts	Dec 11	Dec 10	Dec 09
Sales Turnover	1m	839	1m
Pre Tax Profit/Loss	-38	-426	-959
Working Capital	943	983	1m
Fixed Assets	3	2	3
Current Assets	1m	1m	2m
Current Liabilities	125	223	506

World Wide International Television Ltd
2125 St Anne's Court, London, W1F 0BJ
Tel: 020-7434 1121 **Fax:** 020-7734 0619
E-mail: pics@worldwidegroup.ltd.uk
Website: http://www.worldwidegroup.ltd.uk
Directors: R. King (Dir)
Managers: C. Courtenay-Taylor (Public Relation), D. Ross (Accounts)
Ultimate Holding Company: WESTERN ST ANNE'S LIMITED
Immediate Holding Company: WORLD WIDE INTERNATIONAL TELEVISION LIMITED
Registration no: 02151130 **Date established:** 1987 **Turnover:** £2m - £5m
No.of Employees: 1 - 10 **Product Groups:** 89

Date of Accounts	Dec 03
Working Capital	5
Current Assets	5

World's End Couriers Ltd
Unit 6b Farm Lane Trading Estate 101 Farm Lane, London, SW6 1QJ
Tel: 020-7381 8991 **Fax:** 020- 73854468
E-mail: info@worldsendcouriers.co.uk
Website: http://www.wecouriers.co.uk
Directors: P. England (Prop), J. Popham (MD)
Managers: D. Norman (Sales Prom Mgr), V. Doe (Sales Admin)
Immediate Holding Company: WORLD'S END COURIERS LTD
Registration no: 06316873 **Date established:** 2007
Turnover: Up to £250,000 **No.of Employees:** 1 - 10 **Product Groups:** 72, 79

Date of Accounts	Apr 11	Apr 10	Apr 09
Sales Turnover	N/A	N/A	311
Pre Tax Profit/Loss	N/A	N/A	-5
Working Capital	18	-1	-29
Fixed Assets	41	61	81
Current Assets	96	135	103
Current Liabilities	N/A	N/A	118

Worldwide Dispensers
Unit 17-19 Merton Industrial Park Lee Road, London, SW19 3WD
Tel: 020-8545 7500 **Fax:** 020-8545 7502
E-mail: marketing@dsswd.com
Website: http://www.worldwidedispensers.com
Bank(s): National Westminster Bank Plc
Directors: A. Steele (Co Sec), B. Rothwell (Fin)
Managers: J. Newbury (Tech Serv Mgr), A. Bachelet (Cust Serv Mgr), J. Lodder
Ultimate Holding Company: DS SMITH (HOLDINGS) P.L.C.
Immediate Holding Company: DAVID S. SMITH (HOLDINGS) P.L.C.
Registration no: 00501594 **VAT No.:** GB 521 8863 38
Date established: 1956 **Turnover:** £10m - £20m
No.of Employees: 51 - 100 **Product Groups:** 30, 66

Wovenground
2-3 Treadway Street Unit 7 Tanners Yard, London, E2 6QW
Tel: 020-7033 3731
E-mail: service@wovenground.com
Website: http://www.wovenground.com
Turnover: £500,000 - £1m **No.of Employees:** 1 - 10 **Product Groups:** 23, 24, 39, 63

Wrapology Ltd
Unit 22 Victoria Industrial Estate Victoria Road, London, W3 6UU
Tel: 08708-503887 **Fax:** 020-8992 5574
E-mail: sales@wrapology-international.com
Website: http://www.giftpackaging.com
Directors: A. Bosanquet (Prop)
Immediate Holding Company: WRAPOLOGY LIMITED
Registration no: 04190700 **Date established:** 2001
No.of Employees: 11 - 20 **Product Groups:** 20, 30

Date of Accounts	Dec 11	Dec 10	Dec 09
Working Capital	1	65	14
Fixed Assets	39	19	23
Current Assets	225	324	379

Wray
600 Kings Road, London, SW6 2YW
Tel: 020-7751 8650 **Fax:** 020-7751 8699
E-mail: christopher.wray@christopherwray.com
Website: http://www.christopherwray.com
Directors: C. Wray (Prop), J. Wray (Dir)
Immediate Holding Company: WRAY & SON LIMITED
Registration no: 04154725 **Date established:** 2001
No.of Employees: 51 - 100 **Product Groups:** 37, 67

Date of Accounts	Mar 06	Mar 05	Mar 04
Sales Turnover	220	195	194
Pre Tax Profit/Loss	19	11	4
Working Capital	-69	-82	-100
Fixed Assets	114	112	125
Current Assets	25	20	24
Current Liabilities	19	16	15

Jonathan Wren & Co. Ltd
34 London Wall, London, EC2M 5RU
Tel: 020-7309 3550 **Fax:** 020-7626 1242
E-mail: career@jwren.com
Website: http://www.jwren.com
Directors: S. McCracken (Fin)
Ultimate Holding Company: COMPUTER PEOPLE
Immediate Holding Company: AJILON
Registration no: 00935596 **Turnover:** £10m - £20m
No.of Employees: 51 - 100 **Product Groups:** 80

Denis Wright Ltd
1 Purley Place, London, N1 1QA
Tel: 020-7226 2628 **Fax:** 020-7226 6890
E-mail: john.wright@denis-wright.com
Website: http://www.denis-wright.com
Bank(s): National Westminster Bank Plc
Directors: J. Wright (MD), A. Wright (Co Sec)
Immediate Holding Company: DENIS WRIGHT LIMITED
Registration no: 00370358 **VAT No.:** GB 233 4175 84
Date established: 1941 **Turnover:** £2m - £5m **No.of Employees:** 21 - 50
Product Groups: 27, 28, 36

Date of Accounts	Dec 11	Dec 10	Dec 09
Working Capital	-215	-200	-100
Fixed Assets	119	136	141
Current Assets	387	480	521

Wrightson Wood Associates Ltd
Radiant House 36-38 Mortimer Street, London, W1W 7RG
Tel: 020-7323 9861 **Fax:** 020-7323 9862
E-mail: info@wrightsonwood.com
Website: http://www.wrightsonwood.com
Directors: R. Fermon (Dir), J. Henderson (Dir), J. Issacs (MD)
Managers: M. Smith (Admin Off), M. Smith
Ultimate Holding Company: Gryphon Co.
Immediate Holding Company: CARRITT BATTESON LLP
Registration no: 03885865 **VAT No.:** GB 567 6522 10
Date established: 2009 **Turnover:** Up to £250,000
No.of Employees: 1 - 10 **Product Groups:** 80

Date of Accounts	Oct 07	Oct 06	Oct 05
Working Capital	24	22	33
Current Assets	53	74	86
Current Liabilities	29	51	53

www.tap-die.com
445 West Green Road, London, N15 3PL
Tel: 020-8888 1865 **Fax:** 020-8888 4613
E-mail: sales@tap-die.com
Website: http://www.tap-die.com
Date established: 1978 **No.of Employees:** 1 - 10 **Product Groups:** 36, 45, 47, 66

X L World
15 Hanover Square, London, W1S 1HS
Tel: 020-7099 2892 **Fax:** 020-7043 1857
E-mail: anelia.trifu@xlworld.eu
Website: http://www.xlworld.eu
Managers: D. Cavallini (Chief Mgr), A. Trifu (), A. Trifu (Accounts)
Immediate Holding Company: BLUE FLARE POWER (SL) LIMITED
Registration no: 04200614 **Date established:** 2011
Turnover: Up to £250,000 **No.of Employees:** 501 - 1000
Product Groups: 37, 44, 79, 80, 81, 86

Date of Accounts	Dec 07	Dec 06	Dec 05
Sales Turnover	146	56	29
Pre Tax Profit/Loss	89	37	14
Working Capital	413	166	141
Current Assets	1847	1028	384
Current Liabilities	1434	861	243
Total Share Capital	143	143	143
ROCE% (Return on Capital Employed)	21.6	22.0	10.2
ROT% (Return on Turnover)	60.9	65.3	49.8

Xchanging plc
34 Leadenhall Street, London, EC3A 1AX
Tel: 01303-850111 **Fax:** 01303-252858
E-mail: info@xchanging.com
Website: http://www.xchanging.com
Directors: C. Hair (Pers), D. Fisher (Fin), M. Pell (MD)
Immediate Holding Company: XCHANGING PLC
Registration no: 05819018 **Date established:** 2006
No.of Employees: 101 - 250 **Product Groups:** 82

Date of Accounts	Dec 11	Dec 10	Dec 09
Sales Turnover	651m	781m	750m
Pre Tax Profit/Loss	-3m	-60m	19m
Working Capital	17m	-11m	-2m
Fixed Assets	294m	339m	421m
Current Assets	229m	241m	214m
Current Liabilities	177m	188m	184m

Xpert Cleaning UK Ltd
Ground Floor 132 Brownlow Road, London, N11 2BP
Tel: 08456-029509 **Fax:** 020-8881 3058
E-mail: office@xpertcleaning.co.uk
Website: http://www.xpertcleaning.co.uk
Directors: S. Hatt (MD)
Immediate Holding Company: XPERT CLEANING (UK) LIMITED
Registration no: 06470950 **Date established:** 2008
No.of Employees: 1 - 10 **Product Groups:** 80

Date of Accounts	Mar 11	Mar 10
Working Capital	-11	-11
Current Assets	12	22

Xpressions (Cardwalla.com)
South Woodford, London, E18
Tel: 020-8279 3300
E-mail: contact@weddingcards.biz
Website: http://www.weddingcards.biz
Directors: H. Fingh (Prop)
Turnover: Up to £250,000 **No.of Employees:** 1 - 10 **Product Groups:** 28, 37, 64, 65, 81

Y P International Ltd
1 Basing Hill, London, NW11 8TE
Tel: 020-8458 0126 **Fax:** 020-8209 0591
E-mail: ypihe@talk21.com
Website: http://www.ypinternational.co.uk
Directors: E. Polushko (Dir)
Immediate Holding Company: Y.P. INTERNATIONAL LIMITED
Registration no: 01874487 **Date established:** 1984
Turnover: Up to £250,000 **No.of Employees:** 1 - 10 **Product Groups:** 38, 42

Date of Accounts	Mar 12	Mar 11	Mar 10
Working Capital	-23	-50	-28
Fixed Assets	7	8	10
Current Assets	46	7	4

Y S C
50 Floral Street, London, WC2E 9DA
Tel: 020-7520 5555 **Fax:** 020-7976 2201
E-mail: enquiries@ysc.com
Website: http://www.ysc.com
Directors: B. Latham (Fin), R. Sharrock (Co Sec)
Immediate Holding Company: YSC INTERNATIONAL LIMITED
Registration no: 05851314 **VAT No.:** GB 540 1410 05
Date established: 2006 **Turnover:** £1m - £2m **No.of Employees:** 51 - 100
Product Groups: 80

Ying Trading Ltd
24 Landseer Road, London, N19 4JZ
Tel: 020-7281 2478 **Fax:** 020-7686 4042
E-mail: info@yingtrading.com
Website: http://www.yingtrading.com
Directors: G. Wang (Dir)
Registration no: 04446331 **Date established:** 2002
No.of Employees: 1 - 10 **Product Groups:** 20, 40, 41

Date of Accounts	May 09	May 08	May 07
Working Capital	41	32	21
Fixed Assets	N/A	N/A	1
Current Assets	187	163	95

Yoga Model London Limited
1, ajax avenue, london, NW9 5EY
Tel: 07961-882895 **Fax:** 020-7979 0093
E-mail: sales@yogamodel.co.uk
Website: http://www.yogamodel.co.uk
Managers: R. Bastos (Sales Prom Mgr), F. Santos (Chief Mgr)
Registration no: 04847970 **Date established:** 2003
Turnover: Up to £250,000 **No.of Employees:** 1 - 10 **Product Groups:** 24

Yougovcentaur
50 Poland Street, London, W1F 7AX
Tel: 020-7970 4000 **Fax:** 020-7970 4398
E-mail: ian.roberts@centaur.co.uk
Website: http://www.centaur.co.uk
Directors: I. Roberts (Co Sec)
Immediate Holding Company: YOUGOVCENTAUR TWO LIMITED
Registration no: 06100272 **Date established:** 2007 **Turnover:** £1m - £2m
No.of Employees: 1 - 10 **Product Groups:** 28

Date of Accounts	Jun 11	Jun 10	Jun 09
Working Capital	-49	-49	-49
Current Liabilities	49	49	49

Young & Co Brewery plc
26 Osiers Road Wandsworth High Street, London, SW18 1NH
Tel: 020-8875 7000 **Fax:** 020-8875 7100
E-mail: sales@youngs.co.uk
Website: http://www.young.co.uk
Bank(s): National Westminster
Directors: S. Goodyear (Grp Chief Exec), T. Sligo Young (Tech Serv), P. Whitehead (Fin)
Managers: G. McLaren (Mktg Serv Mgr)
Immediate Holding Company: YOUNG & CO'S BREWERY PLC
Registration no: 00032762 **VAT No.:** 216 0835 84 **Date established:** 1990
Turnover: £125m - £250m **No.of Employees:** 51 - 100
Product Groups: 21, 62, 69

Date of Accounts	Mar 10	Mar 09	Apr 11
Sales Turnover	128m	126m	143m
Pre Tax Profit/Loss	18m	4m	15m
Working Capital	-12m	-12m	-21m
Fixed Assets	283m	285m	357m
Current Assets	8m	9m	9m
Current Liabilities	17m	17m	26m

Young & Rubicam Europe Ltd
Greater London House Hampstead Road, London, NW1 7QP
Tel: 020-7611 6568 **Fax:** 020-7611 6570
E-mail: maria-critcher@yr.com
Website: http://www.rkcyr.com
Bank(s): National Westminster
Directors: H. Mazur (Co Sec), D. Gradwell (Fin)
Managers: M. Roalfe, S. Peace (Mktg Serv Mgr), P. Bhudia (Tech Serv Mgr), C. St John (Personnel)
Ultimate Holding Company: WPP PLC (JERSEY)
Immediate Holding Company: YOUNG & RUBICAM EUROPE LIMITED
Registration no: 01525238 **Date established:** 1980
Turnover: £50m - £75m **No.of Employees:** 101 - 250 **Product Groups:** 81

Date of Accounts	Dec 11	Dec 10	Dec 09
Sales Turnover	77m	74m	47m
Pre Tax Profit/Loss	-607	197	890
Working Capital	21m	22m	21m
Fixed Assets	278	284	345
Current Assets	42m	44m	40m
Current Liabilities	5m	5m	7m

Your Key To Spain
83 Baker Street, London, W1U 6AG
Tel: 0121-363 9374
E-mail: brittney.jackeline@mail.com
Website: http://www.yourkeytospain.co.uk
Date established: 2006 **Turnover:** Up to £250,000
No.of Employees: 1 - 10 **Product Groups:** 80

Yusen Logistics (Europe)
Citypoint 1 Ropemaker Street, London, EC2Y 9NY
Tel: 020-7090 2300 **Fax:** 01623-518612
E-mail: nvoexpao@hk.yusen-logistics.com
Website: http://www.eur.yusen-logistics.com
Directors: I. Veitch (MD), K. Wicks (Co Sec)
Managers: K. Higgs (), M. Storey (Sales Prom Mgr), D. Hardy (Comptroller), J. Thackery (Personnel), S. Mercer (Personnel)
Ultimate Holding Company: Nippon Yusen Kabushiki Kaisha(Japan)
Immediate Holding Company: Nyk Group Europe Ltd
Registration no: FC030087 **VAT No.:** 593 4111 44 **Date established:** 2004
Turnover: £20m - £50m **No.of Employees:** 1 - 10 **Product Groups:** 76

Zam Zam International Fragrances
Unit 137 Tritton Industrial Estate 62 Tritton Road, London, SE21 8DE
Tel: 020-8761 4412 **Fax:** 020-8655 7062
E-mail: zamzamincense@yahoo.com
Website: http://www.thezamzamcompany.com
Directors: N. Ghedda (Ptnr)
Turnover: Up to £250,000 **No.of Employees:** 1 - 10 **Product Groups:** 49

Zamo Household Products Ltd
27 White Post Lane, London, E9 5EN
Tel: 020-8525 1177 **Fax:** 020-8533 4013
E-mail: zamoproducts@aol.com
Website: http://www.zamohouseholdproductsltd.co.uk
Directors: T. Rhodes (MD)
Immediate Holding Company: ZAMO HOUSEHOLD PRODUCTS LIMITED
Registration no: 03098901 **Date established:** 1995
Turnover: Up to £250,000 **No.of Employees:** 1 - 10 **Product Groups:** 32, 42

Date of Accounts	Sep 11	Sep 10	Sep 09
Working Capital	82	78	59
Fixed Assets	32	32	39
Current Assets	145	143	135

Zarka Marble Ltd
43 Belsize Lane, London, NW3 5AU
Tel: 020-7431 3042 **Fax:** 020-7431 3879
E-mail: colin@zarkamarble.co.uk
Website: http://www.zarkamarble.co.uk
Directors: C. Wilkins (Sales), V. Schofield (Co Sec)
Managers: M. Nix (Mktg Serv Mgr)
Immediate Holding Company: ZARKA MARBLE LIMITED
Registration no: 01733887 **Date established:** 1983
Turnover: Up to £250,000 **No.of Employees:** 1 - 10 **Product Groups:** 33

Zeag UK Ltd
Zeag House 17 Deer Park Road, London, SW19 3XJ
Tel: 0800-6524111 **Fax:** 020-8443 5344
E-mail: paul.woods@zeaguk.com
Website: http://www.zeaguk.com
Bank(s): Lloyds
Directors: B. Boland (MD), C. Scott (Grp Chief Exec), D. Jones (MD), P. Woods (MD), J. Fosgatt (Eng Serv)
Managers: D. Urry (I.T. Exec), M. Bouther-Belch (Mktg Serv Mgr)
Immediate Holding Company: HALLARK LIMITED
Registration no: 00907240 **VAT No.:** 239 9422 32 **Date established:** 1967
Turnover: £5m - £10m **No.of Employees:** 11 - 20 **Product Groups:** 40

Date of Accounts	Dec 09	Dec 08	Dec 07
Sales Turnover	7m	6m	8m
Pre Tax Profit/Loss	-187	-607	259
Working Capital	3m	3m	2m
Fixed Assets	539	540	532
Current Assets	5m	5m	5m
Current Liabilities	1m	648	833

Zeal Clean Supplies Ltd
8 Deer Park Road, London, SW19 3UU
Tel: 020-8254 8800 **Fax:** 020-8254 0930
E-mail: enquiries@zealpackaging.com
Website: http://www.zealcleansupplies.co.uk
Bank(s): National Westminster
Directors: J. Coles (Fin), H. More Gordon (MD)
Ultimate Holding Company: COLES HOLDINGS LTD
Immediate Holding Company: ZEAL CLEAN SUPPLIES LTD
Registration no: 03091576 **VAT No.:** GB 561 9244 33
Date established: 1995 **Turnover:** £1m - £2m **No.of Employees:** 21 - 50
Product Groups: 38

Date of Accounts	Dec 11	Dec 10	Dec 09
Sales Turnover	2m	2m	1m
Pre Tax Profit/Loss	129	128	-55
Working Capital	276	141	-26
Fixed Assets	166	205	256
Current Assets	606	365	425
Current Liabilities	111	160	171

Zenith Media Ltd
Bridge House 63-65 North Wharf Road, London, W2 1LA
Tel: 020-7224 8500 **Fax:** 020-7706 2650
E-mail: info@zenithmedia.com
Website: http://www.zenithmedia.se
Directors: A. Young (Prop)
Immediate Holding Company: PADDINGTON BUSINESS IMPROVEMENT DISTRICT LIMITED
Registration no: 04193693 **VAT No.:** GB 577 3553 07
Date established: 2005 **Turnover:** £500,000 - £1m
No.of Employees: 1 - 10 **Product Groups:** 81

Date of Accounts	Mar 11	Mar 10	Mar 09
Sales Turnover	568	503	491
Pre Tax Profit/Loss	23	75	-111
Working Capital	190	161	98
Fixed Assets	6	12	N/A
Current Assets	331	278	355
Current Liabilities	129	104	108

0800 Promote
14 Hendon Lane, London, N3 1TR
Tel: 020-8371 8222 **Fax:** 020-8371 8220
E-mail: sales@0800promote.com
Website: http://www.0800promote.com
Directors: S. Harris (Dir), A. Carroll (Co Sec), L. Harris (MD)
Immediate Holding Company: 0800 PROMOTE (UK) LTD
Registration no: 07355359 **VAT No.:** GB 587 0072 31
Date established: 2010 **Turnover:** £250,000 - £500,000
No.of Employees: 1 - 10 **Product Groups:** 24, 30, 35, 49

Date of Accounts	May 08	May 07	May 06
Working Capital	-165	-148	-121
Fixed Assets	10	N/A	3
Current Assets	51	47	68
Current Liabilities	216	195	189

The Zetter
86-88 Clerkenwell Road, London, EC1M 5RJ
Tel: 020-7324 4444 **Fax:** 020-7324 4445
E-mail: info@thezetter.com
Website: http://www.thezetter.com
Bank(s): HSBC
Managers: G. Kiszler
Immediate Holding Company: BISTROT BRUNO LOUBET LLP
Registration no: OC350820 **Date established:** 2009
Turnover: £20m - £50m **No.of Employees:** 21 - 50 **Product Groups:** 89

Date of Accounts	Mar 11	Mar 10
Sales Turnover	N/A	22
Pre Tax Profit/Loss	N/A	-0
Working Capital	24	4
Current Assets	47	22
Current Liabilities	N/A	18

Zimo Communications
26 York Street, London, W1U 6PZ
Tel: 0800-321 3000
E-mail: sales@ewcoms.com
Website: http://www.zimo.co.uk
Directors: K. James (Grp Chief Exec)
Immediate Holding Company: ZIMO COMMUNICATIONS LIMITED
Registration no: 05374218 **Date established:** 2005
Turnover: Up to £250,000 **No.of Employees:** 11 - 20 **Product Groups:** 79

Date of Accounts	Jan 11	Jan 10	Jan 09
Working Capital	212	214	-11
Fixed Assets	40	49	68
Current Assets	394	384	176

Zippo UK Ltd
Unit 27 Grand Union Centre West Row, London, W10 5AS
Tel: 020-8964 0666 **Fax:** 020-8968 0400
E-mail: sales@zippo-uk.co.uk
Website: http://www.zippo.co.uk
Directors: J. Sweeney (Co Sec)
Immediate Holding Company: ZIPPO UK LIMITED
Registration no: 00545691 **Date established:** 1955 **Turnover:** £2m - £5m
No.of Employees: 1 - 10 **Product Groups:** 35, 49

Date of Accounts	Dec 11	Dec 10	Dec 09
Working Capital	1m	1m	1m
Fixed Assets	16	16	17
Current Assets	2m	2m	1m

MERSEYSIDE

Birkenhead

A & I (Peco) Acoustics Ltd
100 Sandford Street, Birkenhead, CH41 1AZ
Tel: 0151-647 9015 **Fax:** 0151- 6661805
E-mail: sales@peco.co.uk
Website: http://www.peco.co.uk
Directors: S. Smith (MD), J. Darlington (Sales & Mktg), M. Smith (Dir & Buyer)
Immediate Holding Company: CYBRAND LIMITED
Registration no: 06661853 **Date established:** 2008
Turnover: £250,000 - £500,000 **No.of Employees:** 21 - 50
Product Groups: 39, 40

Date of Accounts	Jul 11	Jul 10	Jul 09
Working Capital	-15	-13	-5
Fixed Assets	17	17	21
Current Assets	129	83	66

Air Sea Containers
318 New Chester Road, Birkenhead, CH42 1LE
Tel: 0151-645 0636 **Fax:** 0151-644 9268
E-mail: kstaniford@air-sea.co.uk
Website: http://www.air-sea.co.uk
Directors: K. Staniford (Dir), D. Staniford (MD), A. Staniford (Fin)
Immediate Holding Company: AIRSEA CONTAINERS LIMITED
Registration no: 01550861 **VAT No.:** GB 320 1946 91
Date established: 1981 **No.of Employees:** 1 - 10 **Product Groups:** 76

Date of Accounts	Jul 08	Jul 07	Jul 06
Working Capital	1m	1m	988
Fixed Assets	866	899	909
Current Assets	2m	2m	2m
Current Liabilities	441	434	579
Total Share Capital	1	1	1

Apex Enterprises
Kern House Corporation Road, Birkenhead, CH41 1HB
Tel: 0151-647 9323 **Fax:** 0151-605 0655
E-mail: j.t.kern@btinternet.com
Website: http://www.o2.co.uk
Bank(s): Yorkshire Bank PLC
Directors: J. Kern (MD), E. Kern (Fin)
Ultimate Holding Company: W. & J. KERN LIMITED
Immediate Holding Company: W & J KERN (PROPERTIES) LIMITED
Registration no: 01211529 **VAT No.:** GB 166 3502 69
Date established: 1975 **Turnover:** Up to £250,000
No.of Employees: 11 - 20 **Product Groups:** 25, 35, 36

Date of Accounts	Dec 99	Dec 98	Dec 96
Sales Turnover	N/A	N/A	5
Pre Tax Profit/Loss	-2	-3	3
Working Capital	257	264	275
Fixed Assets	153	153	153
Current Assets	279	285	296
Current Liabilities	15	16	15

Autopaint Wirral
Unit 10 Quarrybank Street, Birkenhead, CH41 2XJ
Tel: 0151-652 2302
Website: http://www.classiccarpaints.com
Managers: S. Johnson (Mgr)
No.of Employees: 1 - 10 **Product Groups:** 32, 39

Beaufort Air Sea Equipment Ltd
Beaufort Road, Birkenhead, CH41 1HQ
Tel: 0151-652 9151 **Fax:** 0151-653 6639
E-mail: cgreen@rfdbeaufort.com
Website: http://www.rfdbeaufort.com
Bank(s): National Westminster Bank Plc
Directors: D. Griffiths (Sales), A. Moses (Plant), J. Earp (Fin), W. Mcchesney (Dir)
Ultimate Holding Company: SGL Ltd
Immediate Holding Company: Survitec Group Ltd
Registration no: 00509588 **VAT No.:** GB 159 6596 08
Date established: 1952 **No.of Employees:** 251 - 500 **Product Groups:** 24, 29, 39, 40

Clearground Ltd
67c Corporation Road, Birkenhead, CH41 3NG
Tel: 0151-652 8010 **Fax:** 0151-652 8050
E-mail: info@clearground.co.uk
Website: http://www.clearground.co.uk
Directors: C. Piercy (Co Sec)
Immediate Holding Company: CLEARGROUND LIMITED
Registration no: 04887730 **Date established:** 2003
Turnover: £500,000 - £1m **No.of Employees:** 11 - 20 **Product Groups:** 80

Date of Accounts	Sep 11	Sep 10	Sep 09
Sales Turnover	N/A	N/A	679
Pre Tax Profit/Loss	N/A	N/A	116
Working Capital	93	108	77
Fixed Assets	135	93	78
Current Assets	248	228	168
Current Liabilities	N/A	N/A	40

Connell Consulting Engineers Ltd
315 Old Chester Road, Birkenhead, CH42 3XQ
Tel: 0151-334 3606
E-mail: connellconsulting@btinternet.com
Website: http://www.connellconsulting.co.uk
Directors: P. Connell (MD)
Immediate Holding Company: CONNELL CONSULTING ENGINEERS LIMITED
Registration no: 07583256 **Date established:** 2011
No.of Employees: 1 - 10 **Product Groups:** 35

Cowen Signs
65-69 Old Chester Road, Birkenhead, CH41 9AW
Tel: 0151-647 8081 **Fax:** 0151- 6661087
E-mail: daveritson@cowensigns.com
Website: http://www.cowensigns.com
Directors: P. Peers (MD), P. Peers (Prop)
Immediate Holding Company: E P COWEN & COMPANY LIMITED
Registration no: 01115291 **Date established:** 1973
Turnover: £250,000 - £500,000 **No.of Employees:** 11 - 20
Product Groups: 28, 30, 40

Date of Accounts	Mar 11	Mar 10	Mar 09
Working Capital	59	104	150
Fixed Assets	267	188	205
Current Assets	225	223	268

Denholm Handling Ltd
Vittoria Complex Vittoria Dock Duke Street, Birkenhead, CH41 1EY
Tel: 0151-653 9789 **Fax:** 0151-653 5635
E-mail: john.cain@denholm-handling.co.uk
Website: http://www.denholm-group.co.uk
Managers: J. Cain (Ops Mgr)
Ultimate Holding Company: J. & J. DENHOLM LIMITED
Immediate Holding Company: DENHOLM HANDLING LIMITED
Registration no: SC213584 **Date established:** 2000
Turnover: £20m - £50m **No.of Employees:** 1 - 10 **Product Groups:** 72, 74

Date of Accounts	Dec 11	Dec 10	Dec 09
Sales Turnover	4m	4m	3m
Pre Tax Profit/Loss	216	825	-220
Working Capital	495	440	-117
Fixed Assets	399	233	288
Current Assets	1m	1m	1m
Current Liabilities	135	323	795

Eagle Manufacturing
Lincoln Street, Birkenhead, CH41 1HE
Tel: 0151-670 1991 **Fax:** 0151-670 4100
E-mail: colinshimmin@btconnect.com
Directors: F. Shimmin (Fin), C. Shimmin (MD)
Immediate Holding Company: EAGLE MANUFACTURING LIMITED
Registration no: 04209425 **Date established:** 2001
No.of Employees: 1 - 10 **Product Groups:** 46

Date of Accounts	Apr 11	Apr 10	Apr 09
Working Capital	205	158	160
Fixed Assets	45	55	60
Current Assets	330	271	269

Eye 2 Eye Gartshore Optical Centre
231 Grange Road, Birkenhead, L41 2YX
Tel: 0151-647 3048 **Fax:** 0151-666 2174
Website: http://www.eye2eyeshop.com
Directors: G. Gartshore (Prop)
Date established: 1989 **Turnover:** £1m - £2m **No.of Employees:** 11 - 20
Product Groups: 61

Faiveley Transport
Morpeth Wharf, Birkenhead, CH41 1LF
Tel: 0151-649 5000 **Fax:** 0151-649 5001
E-mail: ian.dolman@faiveleytransport.com
Website: http://www.faiveleytransport.com
Bank(s): SEB, 2 Cannon Street, London EC4M 6XX
Directors: I. Dolman (MD)
Ultimate Holding Company: FAIVELEY SA (FRANCE)
Immediate Holding Company: FAIVELEY TRANSPORT BIRKENHEAD LIMITED
Registration no: 01841352 **VAT No.:** GB 360 4266 70
Date established: 1984 **Turnover:** £20m - £50m
No.of Employees: 101 - 250 **Product Groups:** 39

Date of Accounts	Mar 11	Mar 10	Mar 09
Sales Turnover	27m	29m	35m
Pre Tax Profit/Loss	2m	3m	2m
Working Capital	13m	12m	11m
Fixed Assets	5m	5m	5m
Current Assets	20m	19m	20m
Current Liabilities	2m	2m	3m

Graham
133-141 Chester Street, Birkenhead, CH41 5HY
Tel: 0151-647 7070 **Fax:** 01704-501930
E-mail: richard.nightingale@graham-group.co.uk
Website: http://www.graham-group.co.uk
Managers: R. Nightingale (Mgr)
Immediate Holding Company: DAVID GRAHAM VEHICLE REPAIRS LTD
Registration no: SC254141 **No.of Employees:** 11 - 20
Product Groups: 63, 66

Greyhound Chromotography & Allied Chemicals
6 Kelvin Park Dock Road, Birkenhead, CH41 1LT
Tel: 0151-649 4000 **Fax:** 0151-649 4001
E-mail: sales@greyhoundchrom.com
Website: http://www.greyhoundchrom.com
Directors: P. Massie (MD)
No.of Employees: 1 - 10 **Product Groups:** 28, 31, 38, 40, 42

Hamilton Engineering Ltd
69 Corporation Road, Birkenhead, CH41 3NG
Tel: 0151-647 6444 **Fax:** 0151-666 1065
E-mail: john@hamiltonengineering.fsnet.co.uk
Website: http://www.hamiltonengineering.fsnet.co.uk
Directors: J. Hamilton (MD)
Immediate Holding Company: HAMILTON ENGINEERING LIMITED
Registration no: 05741835 **VAT No.:** GB 625 0891 41
Date established: 2006 **Turnover:** Up to £250,000
No.of Employees: 1 - 10 **Product Groups:** 48

Date of Accounts	Mar 12	Mar 11	Mar 10
Working Capital	20	1	-13
Fixed Assets	11	12	13
Current Assets	102	111	66

Hammer & Tongs
Unit 12 SMM Business Park Dock Road, Birkenhead, CH41 1DT
Tel: 0151-653 6530 **Fax:** 0151-201 7153
Directors: A. Riley (Prop)
Immediate Holding Company: JBA LIVE LIMITED
Registration no: 00058613 **Date established:** 2009 **Turnover:** £1m - £2m
No.of Employees: 1 - 10 **Product Groups:** 26, 35

I E B S Ltd Electrical and Building Contractors
Unit 7 Roslyn Street, Birkenhead, CH41 9AH
Tel: 0151-647 4331 **Fax:** 0151-647 2142
E-mail: mail@iebsltd.co.uk
Website: http://www.iebsltd.co.uk
Directors: C. Price (MD)
Immediate Holding Company: INDUSTRIAL ELECTRICAL AND BUILDING SERVICES LIMITED
Registration no: 04510936 **VAT No.:** 320 2168 11 **Date established:** 2002
Turnover: £1m - £2m **No.of Employees:** 1 - 10 **Product Groups:** 52

Date of Accounts	Jul 11	Jul 10	Jul 09
Working Capital	-76	-45	1
Fixed Assets	27	25	26
Current Assets	154	115	181

Jewson Ltd
300 Price Street, Birkenhead, CH41 3PX
Tel: 0151-647 7421 **Fax:** 0151-647 3381
E-mail: helen.cowle@jewson.co.uk
Website: http://www.jewson.co.uk
Managers: H. Cowle (Mgr)
Ultimate Holding Company: COMPAGNIE DE SAINT GOBAIN (FRANCE)
Immediate Holding Company: JEWSON LIMITED
Registration no: 00348407 **Date established:** 1939
Turnover: £500m - £1,000m **No.of Employees:** 11 - 20
Product Groups: 66

Date of Accounts	Dec 11	Dec 10	Dec 09
Sales Turnover	1606m	1547m	1485m
Pre Tax Profit/Loss	18m	100m	45m

see next page

Jewson Ltd - *Cont'd*

Working Capital	-345m	-250m	-349m
Fixed Assets	496m	387m	461m
Current Assets	657m	1005m	1320m
Current Liabilities	66m	120m	64m

M R Engineering Group Ltd
107-125 Bridge Street, Birkenhead, CH41 1BD
Tel: 0151-647 9997 **Fax:** 0151-647 9994
E-mail: admin@mrengineering.co.uk
Website: http://www.mrengineering.co.uk
Directors: D. Smith (Fin), B. Norcott (MD)
Managers: D. Rudge (Sales Prom Mgr), A. Barker (Mktg Serv Mgr), L. Barron (Purch Mgr)
Immediate Holding Company: MERSEY REWINDS LIMITED
Registration no: 01440274 **Date established:** 1979 **Turnover:** £5m - £10m
No.of Employees: 51 - 100 **Product Groups:** 35, 48, 66, 67

Date of Accounts	Jul 10	Jul 09	Jul 08
Working Capital	147	93	23
Fixed Assets	402	414	515
Current Assets	2m	1m	2m

Manzan Electronics
60 Church Road Tranmere, Birkenhead, CH42 0LH
Tel: 0151-651 1121 **Fax:** 0151-651121
E-mail: manzanelectronics@yahoo.co.uk
Website: http://www.fredsharpeelectronics.co.uk
Directors: F. Sharpe (Dir)
Managers: D. Dougherty (Sales Prom Mgr), J. Dougherty (Tech Serv Mgr)
No.of Employees: 1 - 10 **Product Groups:** 37, 67, 79

Marine Turbo Engineering Ltd
Abbey House 2 Abbey Street, Birkenhead, CH41 5JU
Tel: 0151-647 8141 **Fax:** 0151-666 2143
E-mail: reception@marineturbo.co.uk
Website: http://www.marineturbo.co.uk
Directors: R. Purchase (Dir), J. Dean (Fin)
Managers: L. Beswick (Chief Acct), D. Favager
Immediate Holding Company: MARINE TURBO ENGINEERING LIMITED
Registration no: 00980787 **Date established:** 1970
No.of Employees: 21 - 50 **Product Groups:** 35, 36, 39

Date of Accounts	Jul 10	Jul 09	Jul 08
Working Capital	637	611	597
Fixed Assets	323	324	291
Current Assets	1m	1m	1m

Mersey Can Ltd
12-14 Ebenezer Street, Birkenhead, CH42 1NH
Tel: 0151-645 8511 **Fax:** 0151-644 6749
Directors: T. Lomas (MD)
Immediate Holding Company: MERSEY CAN LIMITED
Registration no: 02677790 **Date established:** 1992
No.of Employees: 11 - 20 **Product Groups:** 35, 45

Date of Accounts	Dec 11	Dec 10	Dec 09
Working Capital	758	924	445
Fixed Assets	762	718	723
Current Assets	2m	2m	2m

Mersey Equipment Co. Ltd
Arc House 82-90 Taylor Street, Birkenhead, CH41 1BQ
Tel: 0151-647 9751 **Fax:** 0151-647 3343
E-mail: graye@fsmail.net
Website: http://www.merseyequipment.com
Directors: G. Exley (Dir)
Immediate Holding Company: MERSEY EQUIPMENT COMPANY LIMITED
Registration no: 01185922 **VAT No.:** GB 164 1620 85
Date established: 1974 **Turnover:** £1m - £2m **No.of Employees:** 1 - 10
Product Groups: 24, 30, 33, 34, 35, 36, 37, 38, 40, 46

Date of Accounts	Feb 12	Feb 11	Feb 10
Working Capital	134	97	83
Fixed Assets	9	11	7
Current Assets	548	489	428

Merseyside Metal Services
36 Lord Street, Birkenhead, CH41 1BJ
Tel: 0151-650 1600 **Fax:** 0151-647 6157
E-mail: sales@merseymetals.co.uk
Website: http://www.merseymetals.co.uk
Directors: D. Thompson (MD)
Managers: J. Dilaney (Sales Prom Mgr), D. Thompson (I.T. Exec), D. Greenall (Purch Mgr)
Immediate Holding Company: MERSEYSIDE METAL SERVICES LIMITED
Registration no: 01832058 **Date established:** 1984 **Turnover:** £2m - £5m
No.of Employees: 11 - 20 **Product Groups:** 30, 31, 34, 36, 48, 66

Date of Accounts	Sep 11	Sep 10	Sep 09
Working Capital	592	555	1m
Fixed Assets	326	335	378
Current Assets	1m	1m	2m

One Call Many Solutions
29 Woodchurch Lane, Birkenhead, CH42 9PJ
Tel: 0151-670 1212 **Fax:** 0151-670 5179
E-mail: mail@onecallmanysolutions.co.uk
Website: http://www.onecallmanysolutions.co.uk
Managers: T. Doyle (Mgr)
Immediate Holding Company: MILBANK LIMITED
Registration no: 05429297 **Date established:** 1986
Turnover: £250,000 - £500,000 **No.of Employees:** 1 - 10
Product Groups: 81

Date of Accounts	Dec 10	Dec 09	Dec 08
Working Capital	-111	-125	-90
Fixed Assets	252	200	200
Current Assets	84	5	8

Oxton Engineering Co. Ltd
9 Pilgrim Street, Birkenhead, CH41 5EH
Tel: 0151-666 1352 **Fax:** 0151-666 2260
E-mail: phil@oxton-engineering.co.uk
Website: http://www.oxton-engineering.co.uk
Directors: P. McWilliam (Fin)
Ultimate Holding Company: OXTON ENGINEERING (2006) LIMITED
Immediate Holding Company: OXTON ENGINEERING COMPANY LIMITED
Registration no: 01426174 **VAT No.:** GB 166 7258 34
Date established: 1979 **Turnover:** £500,000 - £1m
No.of Employees: 21 - 50 **Product Groups:** 48

Date of Accounts	Sep 11	Sep 10	Sep 09
Working Capital	713	503	386
Fixed Assets	228	176	197
Current Assets	1m	770	650

Park Group plc
1 Valley Road, Birkenhead, CH41 7ED
Tel: 0151-653 1700 **Fax:** 0151-653 5416
E-mail: peter.johnson@parkgroup.co.uk
Website: http://www.parkdirect.co.uk
Bank(s): National Westminster
Directors: C. Houghton (MD), P. Johnson (Dir), M. Stewart (Fin)
Managers: D. Lucius (Mktg Serv Mgr)
Immediate Holding Company: PARK GROUP PLC
Registration no: 01711939 **VAT No.:** GB 165 9070 48
Date established: 1983 **Turnover:** £250m - £500m
No.of Employees: 251 - 500 **Product Groups:** 81

Plastok Associates Ltd
79 Market Street, Birkenhead, CH41 6AN
Tel: 0151-666 2056 **Fax:** 0151-650 0073
E-mail: david.sanders@plastok.co.uk
Website: http://www.plastok.co.uk
Directors: R. Marchetti (Fin), K. Lovatt (Dir), F. Sanders (Sales)
Managers: J. Lovatt, F. Sanders, D. Sanders (Mgr), D. Sanders
Ultimate Holding Company: PLASTOK SEPARATION SYSTEMS LIMITED
Immediate Holding Company: PLASTOK ASSOCIATES LIMITED
Registration no: 01383703 **Date established:** 1978 **Turnover:** £1m - £2m
No.of Employees: 1 - 10 **Product Groups:** 14, 23, 24, 25, 27, 29, 30, 32, 33, 34, 35, 36, 37, 38, 40, 41, 42, 43, 45, 48, 63, 66, 67, 85

Date of Accounts	Dec 11	Dec 10	Dec 09
Working Capital	233	201	165
Fixed Assets	76	55	41
Current Assets	347	303	280

Postal Supplies Direct
UNIT C, MARITIME BUSINESS PARK SOVEREIGN WAY, DOCK ROAD, Birkenhead, CH41 1DL
Tel: 0800-7838587 **Fax:** 01752-606999
Website: http://www.postalsuppliesdirect.com
Managers: C. White (Mgr)
Registration no: 04167111 **Date established:** 2001
No.of Employees: 1 - 10 **Product Groups:** 38, 42

Samelco Automation Systems Ltd
Unit 5 The Odyssey Centre Corporation Road, Birkenhead, CH41 1LB
Tel: 0151-647 2123
E-mail: general@samelco.com
Website: http://www.samelco.com
Directors: M. Walton (Dir)
Immediate Holding Company: SAMELCO AUTOMATION SYSTEMS LIMITED
Registration no: 04424756 **Date established:** 2002
Turnover: £500,000 - £1m **No.of Employees:** 1 - 10 **Product Groups:** 37, 38, 44, 45, 67, 84

Date of Accounts	Apr 11	Apr 10	Apr 09
Working Capital	70	36	49
Fixed Assets	21	20	11
Current Assets	152	66	79

Stone Marine Propulsion Ltd
Dock Road, Birkenhead, CH41 1DT
Tel: 0151-652 2372 **Fax:** 0151-652 2377
E-mail: sales@smpropulsion.com
Website: http://www.smpropulsion.com
Directors: A. Deves (Co Sec)
Managers: K. Roper (Projects)
Ultimate Holding Company: LANGHAM INDUSTRIES LIMITED
Immediate Holding Company: STONE MARINE PROPULSION LIMITED
Registration no: 00147133 **Date established:** 2017 **Turnover:** £1m - £2m
No.of Employees: 1 - 10 **Product Groups:** 39

Date of Accounts	Dec 11	Dec 10	Dec 09
Sales Turnover	1m	2m	2m
Pre Tax Profit/Loss	513	404	152
Working Capital	550	191	-63
Fixed Assets	19	1	2
Current Assets	1m	1m	784
Current Liabilities	309	399	192

Tamark Engineering Ltd
924 Borough Road, Birkenhead, CH42 6QW
Tel: 0151-201 7907 **Fax:** 0151-334 7407
E-mail: sales@tamarkengineering.co.uk
Website: http://www.tamarkengineering.co.uk
Directors: M. Brown (MD), R. Brown (MD), T. Brown (Fin)
Registration no: 05269531 **Date established:** 2004
Turnover: Up to £250,000 **No.of Employees:** 1 - 10 **Product Groups:** 37

Date of Accounts	Oct 06	Oct 05
Working Capital	-2	-2
Fixed Assets	3	3
Current Assets	2	5
Current Liabilities	5	6

Valvoline Oil Co.
Dock Road, Birkenhead, CH41 1DR
Tel: 0151-652 1551 **Fax:** 0151-653 8900
E-mail: sales@valvoline.com
Website: http://www.valvolineuk.com
Directors: G. Probert (MD)
Ultimate Holding Company: ASHLAND OIL INC (USA)
Immediate Holding Company: VALVOLINE INC (USA)
Registration no: 00570490 **Date established:** 1953 **Turnover:** £2m - £5m
No.of Employees: 1 - 10 **Product Groups:** 31, 32, 66

Vision Card
Unit 4 Wirral Business Centre Dock Road, Birkenhead, CH41 1JW
Tel: 0151-630 5006 **Fax:** 0151-630 5006
E-mail: admin@vision-card.co.uk
Website: http://www.vision-card.co.uk
Managers: M. Macartney (Mgr)
Immediate Holding Company: AUTEC (VACUUM COOLERS) LIMITED
Registration no: 06928387 **Date established:** 2009
Turnover: Up to £250,000 **No.of Employees:** 1 - 10 **Product Groups:** 28, 30, 35, 36, 40, 49, 64

Wirral Catering Equipment Ltd
46 Fairfax Road, Birkenhead, CH41 9EJ
Tel: 0151-666 2820 **Fax:** 0151-647 4077
E-mail: info@wirralcatering.co.uk
Website: http://www.wirralcatering.co.uk
Directors: A. Heraghty (MD)
Immediate Holding Company: WIRRAL CATERING EQUIPMENT LIMITED
Registration no: 05016270 **Date established:** 2004
No.of Employees: 1 - 10 **Product Groups:** 20, 40, 41

Date of Accounts	Apr 09	Apr 08	Apr 06
Working Capital	16	31	14
Fixed Assets	N/A	N/A	1
Current Assets	29	51	21

Bootle

Battery Specialist N W Ltd
244 Derby Road, Bootle, L20 8LJ
Tel: 0151-933 4646 **Fax:** 0151-933 4848
E-mail: enquiries@batteryspecialistnw.gbr.cc
Website: http://www.battery2u.co.uk
Directors: K. Rooney (MD)
Immediate Holding Company: BATTERY SPECIALIST NORTH WEST LIMITED
Registration no: 03934720 **Date established:** 2000
No.of Employees: 1 - 10 **Product Groups:** 37, 68

Date of Accounts	Mar 08	Mar 07	Mar 06
Sales Turnover	N/A	N/A	358
Pre Tax Profit/Loss	N/A	N/A	66
Working Capital	60	44	43
Fixed Assets	7	12	15
Current Assets	143	135	135
Current Liabilities	82	91	92
ROCE% (Return on Capital Employed)			113.2
ROT% (Return on Turnover)			18.5

Bootle Containers Ltd
72 St Johns Road, Bootle, L20 8BH
Tel: 0151-922 0610 **Fax:** 0151-944 1280
E-mail: paul.thompson@bootlecontainers.co.uk
Website: http://www.bootlecontainers.co.uk
Bank(s): National Westminster Bank Plc
Directors: L. Richards (Ch), P. Thompson (Dir)
Managers: J. Callan (Sales Prom Mgr)
Ultimate Holding Company: WINLIE HOLDINGS LIMITED
Immediate Holding Company: BOOTLE CONTAINERS LIMITED
Registration no: 01299127 **Date established:** 1977 **Turnover:** £1m - £2m
No.of Employees: 21 - 50 **Product Groups:** 35, 45, 48, 72, 74

Date of Accounts	May 11	May 10	May 09
Working Capital	473	268	497
Fixed Assets	2m	2m	1m
Current Assets	1m	1m	1m

Bruce & Hyslop Brucast Ltd
1 Well Lane, Bootle, L20 3BS
Tel: 0151-922 2404 **Fax:** 0151-922 5994
E-mail: mail@bruceandhyslop.com
Website: http://www.bruceandhyslop.com
Directors: C. Appleton (MD)
Immediate Holding Company: BRUCE AND HYSLOP (BRUCAST) LIMITED
Registration no: 02809316 **Date established:** 1993
Turnover: £250,000 - £500,000 **No.of Employees:** 1 - 10
Product Groups: 26, 34, 35, 36, 49, 66, 68

Date of Accounts	Mar 11	Mar 10	Mar 09
Working Capital	-64	-42	-17
Fixed Assets	11	7	9
Current Assets	49	103	87

Carter Synergy (Northern Division)
111-115 Marsh Lane, Bootle, L20 4JD
Tel: 0151-922 2342 **Fax:** 0151-922 4004
E-mail: rob.orbell@cartersynergy.com
Website: http://www.crrs.co.uk
Bank(s): Barclays
Directors: P. Madley (Fin), A. Bews (Pers)
Managers: D. Wiltshore (Tech Serv Mgr), N. Farrell (Reg Mgr)
Ultimate Holding Company: LONGDON ESTATES LIMITED
Immediate Holding Company: CARTER SYNERGY LIMITED
Registration no: 00176807 **VAT No.:** GB 109 7690 46
Date established: 2021 **Turnover:** £20m - £50m
No.of Employees: 101 - 250 **Product Groups:** 29, 40, 41, 48, 52

Date of Accounts	Dec 11	Dec 10	Dec 09
Sales Turnover	45m	42m	44m
Pre Tax Profit/Loss	492	154	657
Working Capital	6m	6m	6m
Fixed Assets	2m	2m	727
Current Assets	15m	19m	15m
Current Liabilities	2m	3m	2m

F Charnock
Crosby House 4-5 Church Street, Bootle, L20 1AF
Tel: 0151-933 0444
E-mail: f.charnock@btconnect.com
Directors: F. Charnock (Prop)
No.of Employees: 1 - 10 **Product Groups:** 35

Cole Metal Products Ltd
71 Strand Road, Bootle, L20 4BB
Tel: 0151-933 8588 **Fax:** 0151-933 0504
E-mail: sales@colemetal.co.uk
Website: http://www.colemetal.co.uk
Bank(s): Barclays
Directors: J. Mccarron (MD)
Immediate Holding Company: COLE METAL PRODUCTS LIMITED
Registration no: 01385929 **Date established:** 1978
Turnover: £500,000 - £1m **No.of Employees:** 11 - 20
Product Groups: 30, 35, 36, 46, 48, 67, 84

Date of Accounts	Sep 11	Sep 10	Sep 09
Working Capital	97	76	66
Fixed Assets	14	10	14
Current Assets	356	237	213

Combined Catering Services
73 Brewster Street, Bootle, L20 9NG
Tel: 0151-922 4454 **Fax:** 0151- 9225005
E-mail: office@combinedcatering.com
Website: http://www.combinedcatering.com
Directors: A. Emerson (Dir), P. Gittins (MD)
Managers: A. Emerson (Mgr), M. Brown (Purch Mgr), N. Johnson (Sales Prom Mgr)

Turnover: £250,000 - £500,000 **No.of Employees:** 21 - 50
Product Groups: 20, 24, 26, 27, 30, 32, 33, 35, 36, 37, 38, 40, 41, 42, 48, 52, 62, 63, 64, 66, 67, 69, 84, 89

Date of Accounts	Jan 08	Jan 07	Jan 06
Working Capital	159	106	66
Fixed Assets	104	45	64
Current Assets	517	431	274
Current Liabilities	358	326	208
Total Share Capital	1	1	1

Cumberland Cathodic Protection
4 Strand View Liverpool Intermodal Freeport Terminal, Bootle, L20 1HA
Tel: 0151-922 3041 **Fax:** 0151-922 4605
E-mail: sales@cumberlandcp.com
Website: http://www.cumberlandcp.com
Directors: A. Roache (Co Sec), B. Billington (Dir), P. Smith (MD)
Immediate Holding Company: CUMBERLAND GROUP HOLDINGS LTD
Registration no: 02014322 **Date established:** 1912 **Turnover:** £1m - £2m
No.of Employees: 1 - 10 **Product Groups:** 35, 37, 39, 52, 85

Davies Products Liverpool Ltd
Alsol House Laburnum Place, Bootle, L20 3NE
Tel: 0151-922 4246 **Fax:** 0151-944 1901
E-mail: sales@daviesproducts.co.uk
Website: http://www.daviesproducts.co.uk
Directors: A. Davies (Sales), G. Davies (Dir)
Immediate Holding Company: DAVIES PRODUCTS (LIVERPOOL) LIMITED
Registration no: 00440295 **Date established:** 1947
Turnover: £10m - £20m **No.of Employees:** 11 - 20 **Product Groups:** 27, 30, 32, 33, 37, 49, 65

Date of Accounts	Dec 11	Dec 10	Dec 09
Working Capital	931	928	934
Fixed Assets	420	429	439
Current Assets	1m	1m	1m

E D F Man
Hornby Dock Regent Road, Bootle, L20 1EF
Tel: 0151-922 2803 **Fax:** 0151-944 3919
E-mail: phil.higgins@edfman.com
Website: http://www.edfman.com
Directors: P. Holder (Prop)
Immediate Holding Company: ADVANCED LIQUID FEEDS LLP
Date established: 2004 **No.of Employees:** 11 - 20 **Product Groups:** 20

E M H International Ltd
Kingfisher Business Park Hawthorne Road, Bootle, L20 6PF
Tel: 0151-933 6373 **Fax:** 0151-922 5327
E-mail: davidr@emh-international.com
Website: http://www.emh-international.com
Bank(s): Lloyds TSB Bank plc
Directors: D. Russell (MD), D. Russell (Dir), S. Russell (Sales & Mktg)
Managers: S. Brown (District Mgr), T. Swale (I.T. Exec)
Immediate Holding Company: E.M.H. INTERNATIONAL LIMITED
Registration no: 01411544 **Date established:** 1979 **Turnover:** £5m - £10m
No.of Employees: 51 - 100 **Product Groups:** 48

Date of Accounts	Jun 10	Jun 09	Jun 08
Sales Turnover	7m	7m	815
Pre Tax Profit/Loss	-374	26	17
Working Capital	-761	-462	-490
Fixed Assets	2m	2m	3m
Current Assets	3m	3m	4m
Current Liabilities	517	680	679

Engineering Plastic Services
23a Eliot Street, Bootle, L20 4PD
Tel: 0151-922 3243 **Fax:** 0151-922 6306
Directors: M. Wynne (Ptnr)
Turnover: Up to £250,000 **No.of Employees:** 1 - 10 **Product Groups:** 30, 32

Fleming Fabrications North West Ltd
12 Berry Street, Bootle, L20 8AT
Tel: 0151-922 5554 **Fax:** 0151-922 5554
Directors: I. Fleming (Dir)
Immediate Holding Company: FLEMING FABRICATIONS NW LTD
Registration no: 07130182 **Date established:** 2010
No.of Employees: 1 - 10 **Product Groups:** 35

Date of Accounts	Jan 11
Working Capital	-43
Fixed Assets	50
Current Assets	25

Hardy UK Ltd
175 Fernhill Road, Bootle, L20 9DU
Tel: 0151-922 2291 **Fax:** 0151-933 4164
E-mail: hardyuk@aol.com
Website: http://www.hardy-group.com
Bank(s): Barclays, Liverpool
Directors: D. Smith (MD), R. Martindale (Co Sec)
Ultimate Holding Company: L HARDY CO (USA)
Immediate Holding Company: HARDY - U.K. LIMITED
Registration no: 02534664 **VAT No.:** GB 548 5963 90
Date established: 1990 **Turnover:** £1m - £2m **No.of Employees:** 11 - 20
Product Groups: 43

Date of Accounts	Oct 11	Oct 10	Oct 09
Working Capital	552	791	622
Fixed Assets	83	93	97
Current Assets	1m	1m	1m
Current Liabilities	N/A	N/A	8

Hughes Sub Surface Engineering Ltd
Marine House 40 Rimrose Road, Bootle, L20 4TX
Tel: 0151-922 2023 **Fax:** 0151-922 2022
E-mail: info@hsse.co.uk
Website: http://www.hsse.co.uk
Directors: I. Hughes (MD)
Immediate Holding Company: HUGHES SUB SURFACE ENGINEERING LIMITED
Registration no: 05699029 **Date established:** 2006
No.of Employees: 11 - 20 **Product Groups:** 29, 36, 37, 38, 39, 40, 42, 45, 47, 48, 49, 51, 52, 54, 65, 67, 68, 71, 81, 84, 85

Date of Accounts	Feb 12	Feb 11	Feb 10
Working Capital	229	265	258
Fixed Assets	433	137	127
Current Assets	604	547	522

Josef Kihlberg UK
The Bridgewater Complex 36 Canal Street, Bootle, L20 8AH
Tel: 0151-550 0085 **Fax:** 0151-479 3012
E-mail: sam.sharples@kihlberg.co.uk
Website: http://www.kihlberg.co.uk
Managers: S. Sharples (Mgr)
Immediate Holding Company: ABLE CARE SERVICES (NORTHERN) LIMITED
Registration no: 03413217 **VAT No.:** GB 652 6818 18
Date established: 2009 **Turnover:** £1m - £2m **No.of Employees:** 1 - 10
Product Groups: 35, 40, 42, 47

Date of Accounts	Nov 07	Nov 06	Dec 05
Sales Turnover	1716	1331	N/A
Pre Tax Profit/Loss	227	44	N/A
Working Capital	654	490	455
Fixed Assets	N/A	N/A	3
Current Assets	925	713	567
Current Liabilities	271	223	112
Total Share Capital	100	100	100
ROCE% (Return on Capital Employed)	34.7	9.0	
ROT% (Return on Turnover)	13.2	3.3	

Kick Audio Visual
Unit 4 The Box Works Heysham Road, Bootle, L30 6UR
Tel: 0151-430 7000
E-mail: info@kickpa.co.uk
Website: http://www.kickpa.co.uk
Managers: P. Jeffery (Mgr)
Date established: 1990 **No.of Employees:** 1 - 10 **Product Groups:** 83

W J Leech & Sons Ltd
275 Derby Road, Bootle, L20 8PL
Tel: 0151-933 9334 **Fax:** 0151-933 5005
E-mail: alan.leech@wjleech.com
Website: http://www.wjleech.com
Bank(s): National Westminster, Victoria St
Directors: A. Leech (Ch), D. Leech (MD)
Managers: R. Dodd (Chief Acct), L. Gregory (Sales Admin), W. Martland, D. Stroh (Develop Mgr)
Immediate Holding Company: W.J.LEECH & SONS LIMITED
Registration no: 00485220 **VAT No.:** GB 387 3891 93
Date established: 1950 **Turnover:** £2m - £5m **No.of Employees:** 21 - 50
Product Groups: 23, 24, 39, 45

Date of Accounts	Jun 11	Jun 10	Jun 09
Working Capital	144	67	107
Fixed Assets	356	394	431
Current Assets	980	893	796

Liverpool Steel Services
Seymour Street Millers Bridge Industrial Estate, Bootle, L20 1EE
Tel: 0151-922 4265 **Fax:** 0151-922 0400
E-mail: sales@bmsteel.co.uk
Website: http://www.bmsteel.co.uk
Managers: C. Donnelly (Mgr)
Ultimate Holding Company: BARCLAY MATTIESON LTD
Registration no: 02109635 **VAT No.:** GB 723 9322 39
Date established: 1987 **No.of Employees:** 1 - 10 **Product Groups:** 34

Lloyd & Jones Engineering
PO Box 29, Bootle, L20 1EJ
Tel: 0151-630 2443 **Fax:** 0151-922 5418
E-mail: marine@lloyd-jones.com
Website: http://www.lloyd-jones.com
Bank(s): HSBC Bank plc
Managers: G. Deakin (Sales Prom Mgr)
Ultimate Holding Company: LLOYD & JONES ENGINEERS (HOLDINGS) LIMITED
Immediate Holding Company: LLOYD & JONES ENGINEERS LIMITED
Registration no: 01751835 **VAT No.:** GB 387 2423 34
Date established: 1983 **Turnover:** £10m - £20m
No.of Employees: 21 - 50 **Product Groups:** 36, 37, 66, 67

Date of Accounts	Oct 11	Oct 10	Oct 09
Sales Turnover	13m	13m	13m
Pre Tax Profit/Loss	656	282	185
Working Capital	2m	1m	1m
Fixed Assets	2m	3m	3m
Current Assets	5m	5m	4m
Current Liabilities	1m	1m	1m

M G Ceilings & Linings Limited
2 Dacre Street, Bootle, L30 1NY
Tel: 0844-873 1800 **Fax:** 0844-8731795
E-mail: info@mgceilings.co.uk
Website: http://www.mggroupinteriors.com
Directors: A. Pitt (MD), C. Adshead (Fin)
Immediate Holding Company: M G Ceilings & Linings Ltd
Registration no: 01947540 **Date established:** 1985 **Turnover:** £5m - £10m
No.of Employees: 11 - 20 **Product Groups:** 30, 35, 52

The Mast Group Ltd
Mast House Derby Road, Bootle, L20 1EA
Tel: 0151-933 7277 **Fax:** 0151-944 1332
E-mail: sales@mastgrp.com
Website: http://www.mastgrp.com
Bank(s): National Westminster Bank Plc
Directors: J. Lomas (Fin), C. Oliver (MD)
Managers: S. Gaskell, L. Stubbon (Personnel), H. Rose, J. Lyndsey (Mktg Serv Mgr)
Ultimate Holding Company: MAST GROUP LIMITED
Immediate Holding Company: MERCURY INVESTMENTS (UK) LIMITED
Registration no: 02888176 **VAT No.:** GB 387 2953 05
Date established: 1994 **Turnover:** £5m - £10m
No.of Employees: 51 - 100 **Product Groups:** 31, 42

Date of Accounts	Sep 10	Sep 09	Sep 06
Pre Tax Profit/Loss	N/A	N/A	-0
Working Capital	-117	-117	-117
Fixed Assets	102	102	102

Metal Cleaning Ltd
2-10 St Johns Road, Bootle, L20 8BH
Tel: 0151-922 3033 **Fax:** 0151-944 1450
E-mail: scott@metalcleaningltd.com
Website: http://www.metalcleaningltd.com
Directors: G. Owen (MD), B. Owen (Jt MD), S. Owen (Jt MD), S. Owen (Sales)
Managers: D. Howells (Fin Mgr)
Immediate Holding Company: METAL CLEANING LIMITED
Registration no: 01038340 **VAT No.:** GB 163 4172 77
Date established: 1972 **Turnover:** £500,000 - £1m
No.of Employees: 1 - 10 **Product Groups:** 48

Date of Accounts	Dec 10	Dec 09	Dec 08
Working Capital	-150	-155	-67
Fixed Assets	320	144	151
Current Assets	39	70	340

Peoples Liverpool Ltd
Trinity Park Orrell Lane, Bootle, L20 6PD
Tel: 0151-922 8481 **Fax:** 0151-922 0023
Website: http://www.peoplescars.co.uk
Directors: B. Gilea (Dir)
Managers: J. Waterhouse
Ultimate Holding Company: PEOPLES LIMITED
Immediate Holding Company: PEOPLES LIVERPOOL LIMITED
Registration no: SC112752 **Date established:** 1988
Turnover: £50m - £75m **No.of Employees:** 101 - 250 **Product Groups:** 68

Date of Accounts	Jul 08	Jul 07
Sales Turnover	102540	101210
Pre Tax Profit/Loss	230	540
Working Capital	160	-60
Fixed Assets	6950	7180
Current Assets	34010	30420
Current Liabilities	33850	30480
ROCE% (Return on Capital Employed)	3.2	7.6
ROT% (Return on Turnover)	0.2	0.5

Peter Marsh Packaging Ltd
47 Canal Street, Bootle, L20 8AE
Tel: 0151-922 1971 **Fax:** 0151-922 3804
E-mail: info@petermarsh.co.uk
Website: http://www.petermarsh.co.uk
Directors: P. Marsh (MD)
Ultimate Holding Company: PETER MARSH & SONS,LIMITED
Immediate Holding Company: PETER MARSH PACKAGING LIMITED
Registration no: 00104503 **Date established:** 2009
No.of Employees: 51 - 100 **Product Groups:** 76

Date of Accounts	Dec 11	Dec 10	Dec 09
Working Capital	851	636	535
Fixed Assets	166	209	249
Current Assets	1m	940	823
Current Liabilities	N/A	N/A	242

Phoenix Safe Company Ltd
Apex House 1 Orrell Mount, Bootle, L20 6NS
Tel: 0151-944 6444 **Fax:** 0151-944 6445
E-mail: john.thompson@phoenixsafe.co.uk
Website: http://www.phoenixsafe.com
Directors: D. Thompson (Sales), J. Thompson (MD)
Managers: A. Evans (Comptroller), J. Mackenzie (Buyer)
Immediate Holding Company: PHOENIX SAFE COMPANY LIMITED(THE)
Registration no: 02040124 **Date established:** 1986 **Turnover:** £5m - £10m
No.of Employees: 21 - 50 **Product Groups:** 33, 36, 41, 66, 67, 81

Date of Accounts	Dec 10	Dec 09	Jun 08
Sales Turnover	8m	11m	N/A
Pre Tax Profit/Loss	320	494	161
Working Capital	1m	1m	1m
Fixed Assets	156	127	129
Current Assets	3m	3m	3m
Current Liabilities	534	646	136

Pro-Temp Air Conditioning Ltd
17 Farriers Way Liverpool, Bootle, L30 4XL
Tel: 0151-523 3086 **Fax:** 0151-523 3072
E-mail: enquiries@pro-temp.co.uk
Website: http://www.pro-temp.co.uk
Directors: T. Hetherington (Dir)
Immediate Holding Company: PRO-TEMP AIR CONDITIONING LIMITED
Registration no: 05251252 **Date established:** 2004
No.of Employees: 1 - 10 **Product Groups:** 40, 66

Date of Accounts	Mar 11	Mar 10	Mar 09
Working Capital	33	30	19
Fixed Assets	108	114	133
Current Assets	726	391	383

Robinson Willey
Trinity Park Orrell Lane, Bootle, L20 6PB
Tel: 0151-530 1900 **Fax:** 0151-228 6661
E-mail: colinpemberton@robinson-willey.com
Website: http://www.robinson-willey.co.uk
Bank(s): Barclays
Directors: J. Colpitts (Fin), C. Pemberton (MD), C. Pemberton (Sales & Mktg)
Managers: B. Blythe (Comm), T. Falshaw (Mktg Serv Mgr), M. Giaquinto (Export Sales Mg), G. Lawson (Sales Prom Mgr), P. Scott (Accounts), K. Brimble (Accounts), J. Carter (Sales Prom Mgr), C. Hall (Purch Mgr)
Immediate Holding Company: CARVER P.L.C.
Registration no: 00245145 **Date established:** 1860
Turnover: £10m - £20m **No.of Employees:** 21 - 50 **Product Groups:** 40

Date of Accounts	Jul 07	Jul 06	Jul 05
Sales Turnover	12m	13m	13m
Pre Tax Profit/Loss	-860	-190	40
Working Capital	3m	3m	4m
Fixed Assets	760	650	1m
Current Assets	8m	6m	7m
Current Liabilities	5m	3m	3m
Total Share Capital	500	500	500

S Norton
Bankfield Site Regent Road, Bootle, L20 8RQ
Tel: 0151-955 3300 **Fax:** 0151-955 3399
E-mail: matthew.harry@s-norton.com
Website: http://www.s-norton.com
Directors: M. Harry (Dir)
Immediate Holding Company: S. NORTON & CO LIMITED
Registration no: 01859428 **Date established:** 1984
Turnover: £250m - £500m **No.of Employees:** 101 - 250
Product Groups: 30, 34, 42, 61, 66

Date of Accounts	Dec 11	Dec 10	Dec 09
Sales Turnover	352m	303m	146m
Pre Tax Profit/Loss	16m	40m	3m
Working Capital	74m	64m	42m
Fixed Assets	26m	25m	19m
Current Assets	105m	96m	68m
Current Liabilities	4m	12m	2m

Scimitar Steels Ltd
Admiral Works 3 Benbow Street, Bootle, L20 1EP
Tel: 0151-922 4050 **Fax:** 0151-922 1191
E-mail: scimitarsteels@timewarpuk.net
Bank(s): National Westminster

see next page

Scimitar Steels Ltd - Cont'd

Directors: J. Hope (Sales), A. Richards (Co Sec)
Immediate Holding Company: SCIMITAR STEELS (LIVERPOOL) LTD
Registration no: 03693965 **VAT No.:** GB 719 7367 95
Date established: 1999 **Turnover:** £2m - £5m **No.of Employees:** 11 - 20
Product Groups: 66

Date of Accounts	Jan 12	Jan 11	Jan 10
Working Capital	599	597	606
Fixed Assets	866	816	758
Current Assets	1m	1m	964

Skinners Cooperage
9 Canal Street, Bootle, L20 8AB
Tel: 0151-922 8732
E-mail: skinnerscoopers@aol.com
Website: http://www.barrels.org.uk
Directors: L. Skinner (Prop)
Date established: 1972 **No.of Employees:** 1 - 10 **Product Groups:** 35, 36, 45

Ellesmere Port

Alco Earth Braids
Unit2 Rossmoor Terrace Factory Rossfield Road, Ellesmere Port, CH65 3BS
Tel: 0151-355 3696 **Fax:** 0151-357 2262
E-mail: sales@alcoltd.com
Website: http://www.alcoltd.com
Directors: D. Allum (Prop)
Immediate Holding Company: HYDROFLEX LIMITED
Registration no: 05556547 **Date established:** 2010
No.of Employees: 1 - 10 **Product Groups:** 37, 67

Alco Manufacturing Ltd
Unit 2 Rossmoor Terrace Factory Rossfield Road, Ellesmere Port, CH65 3BS
Tel: 0151-355 3696 **Fax:** 0151-357 2262
E-mail: sales@alcoltd.com
Website: http://www.alcoltd.com
Directors: D. Allen (Prop)
Immediate Holding Company: ALCO MANUFACTURING LIMITED
Registration no: 04938901 **Date established:** 2003
No.of Employees: 1 - 10 **Product Groups:** 23, 30, 35, 37, 39, 67

Date of Accounts	Nov 11	Nov 10	Nov 09
Working Capital	337	252	426
Fixed Assets	195	195	31
Current Assets	517	339	575

Arco Ellesmere Port Ltd
Hooton Road Hooton, Ellesmere Port, CH66 7PA
Tel: 0151-327 6666 **Fax:** 0151- 3277930
Website: http://www.arco.co.uk
Directors: N. Hildyard (Fin)
Managers: G. Cartwright (District Mgr), N. Lightford (Sales Prom Mgr), N. Lightford (Asst Gen Mgr), L. Hardie (District Mgr), L. Hardy (District Mgr)
Immediate Holding Company: ARCO LTD
Registration no: 00133804 **Turnover:** £5m - £10m
No.of Employees: 21 - 50 **Product Groups:** 24, 29, 30, 40

Barbour - A B I
Hinderson Point, Ellesmere Port, CH65 9HQ
Tel: 0151-353 3500 **Fax:** 0151-353 3637
E-mail: info@barbour-abi.com
Website: http://www.barbour-abi.com
Directors: S. Mahoney (Dir)
Managers: J. Moorhead (Research & Deve)
Immediate Holding Company: CMP INFORMATION (2004) LTD
Registration no: 02385277 **Date established:** 1930
No.of Employees: 101 - 250 **Product Groups:** 80

Be-Plas Hygienic Walls & Ceilings Ltd
Unit 2 Junction 8 Business Park Rosscliffe Road, Ellesmere Port, CH65 3AS
Tel: 0800-413758 **Fax:** 0151-334 9399
E-mail: rob.shaw@beplas.com
Website: http://www.beplas.com
Directors: R. Shaw (Dir)
Immediate Holding Company: BE-PLAS HYGIENIC WALLS & CEILINGS LTD
Registration no: 06762745 **Date established:** 2008
No.of Employees: 1 - 10 **Product Groups:** 30

Date of Accounts	Dec 11	Dec 10	Dec 09
Working Capital	20	12	17
Fixed Assets	53	48	47
Current Assets	381	293	195

Buck & Hickman Ltd
Rosswood Road, Ellesmere Port, CH65 3BU
Tel: 0151-356 1481 **Fax:** 0151-357 2019
E-mail: ellesmere@buckandhickman.com
Website: http://www.buckandhickman.com
Managers: T. Ravenscroft (District Mgr)
Ultimate Holding Company: TRAVIS PERKINS PLC
Immediate Holding Company: BOSTON (2011) LIMITED
Registration no: 06028304 **Date established:** 2006
No.of Employees: 1 - 10 **Product Groups:** 23, 24, 29, 30, 33, 36, 37, 41, 46

Date of Accounts	Dec 10	Mar 10	Mar 09
Working Capital	6m	6m	6m
Current Assets	27m	27m	27m

Business Information Service
Ellesmere Port Library Civic Way, Ellesmere Port, CH65 0BG
Tel: 0151-337 4693 **Fax:** 0151-335 4689
E-mail: sue.eddison@cheshiresharedservices.gov.uk
Website: http://www.cheshirewestandchester.gov.uk/bis
Managers: S. Eddison
Date established: 1979 **No.of Employees:** 1 - 10 **Product Groups:** 81, 87

Cape Industrial Services Ltd
Cabot Carbon Lees Lane, Ellesmere Port, CH65 4HT
Tel: 0151-356 5591
Ultimate Holding Company: Cape PLC
Immediate Holding Company: CAPE INDUSTRIAL SERVICES LIMITED
Registration no: 03337119 **Date established:** 1997
Turnover: £250m - £500m **No.of Employees:** 1 - 10 **Product Groups:** 29, 52, 54

Complete Handling Northern Ltd
Complete House Ross Road, Ellesmere Port, CH65 3AW
Tel: 0151-357 1000 **Fax:** 0151-357 1999
E-mail: mat.b@chlnorthern.co.uk
Website: http://www.completehandling-mitsubishi.com
Directors: M. Byron (Sales)
Immediate Holding Company: COMPLETE HANDLING (NORTHERN) LIMITED
Registration no: 04128683 **Date established:** 2000
No.of Employees: 11 - 20 **Product Groups:** 35, 39, 45

Date of Accounts	Dec 11	Dec 10	Dec 09
Working Capital	-13	4	-24
Fixed Assets	172	170	135
Current Assets	291	381	321

Convoy E P Ltd
North Road, Ellesmere Port, CH65 1AL
Tel: 0151-357 1966 **Fax:** 0151-357 1966
Directors: J. Calvert (Dir)
Managers: G. Armstrong (Mgr)
Immediate Holding Company: CONVOY (EP) LIMITED
Registration no: 06441706 **Date established:** 2007
No.of Employees: 11 - 20 **Product Groups:** 35

Date of Accounts	Jan 11	Jan 10	Jan 09
Sales Turnover	N/A	N/A	950
Pre Tax Profit/Loss	N/A	N/A	286
Working Capital	20	113	35
Fixed Assets	18	23	28
Current Assets	97	265	203
Current Liabilities	N/A	N/A	114

Cook Compression Ltd
4 Burnell Road, Ellesmere Port, CH65 5EX
Tel: 0151-355 5937 **Fax:** 0151-357 1098
E-mail: salesuk@cookcompression.com
Website: http://www.cookcompression.com
Bank(s): Lloyds TSB Bank plc
Directors: D. Heaton (Sales), D. Lewis (MD)
Managers: T. Greenland, J. Johnson (Comptroller)
Ultimate Holding Company: DOVER CORPORATION (U.S.A.)
Immediate Holding Company: COOK COMPRESSION LIMITED
Registration no: 01994524 **VAT No.:** GB 428 9408 23
Date established: 1986 **Turnover:** £5m - £10m
No.of Employees: 51 - 100 **Product Groups:** 40, 48

Date of Accounts	Dec 11	Dec 10	Dec 09
Sales Turnover	10m	9m	6m
Pre Tax Profit/Loss	2m	1m	734
Working Capital	5m	4m	3m
Fixed Assets	1m	1m	1m
Current Assets	7m	6m	4m
Current Liabilities	1m	823	554

DSM UK Ltd
Cloister Way Bridges Road, Ellesmere Port, CH65 4EL
Tel: 0151-348 8800 **Fax:** 01527-590555
E-mail: sales@dsm.com
Website: http://www.dsm.com
Bank(s): Lloyds TSB Bank plc
Directors: C. Woudenberg (Fin), P. Lowe (Co Sec)
Managers: D. Westaway (Mktg Serv Mgr), I. Rollings (Sales Admin), J. Bailey (Sales Prom Mgr), M. Wilkinson (Contrlr)
Ultimate Holding Company: D S M N.V. (The Netherlands)
Immediate Holding Company: D S M Resins B.V. (The Netherlands)
Registration no: 05339239 **Date established:** 1973
Turnover: £10m - £20m **No.of Employees:** 21 - 50 **Product Groups:** 31, 32

Date of Accounts	Jun 05	Feb 04
Working Capital	-11	-11
Current Assets	N/A	1
Current Liabilities	11	12

Emdee Training
11 Melrose Drive Great Sutton, Ellesmere Port, CH66 2YH
Tel: 0151-201 7196 **Fax:** 0151-201 7196
E-mail: flt.training@homecall.co.uk
Website: http://www.homecall.co.uk
Directors: M. Dudley (Prop)
Date established: 1999 **No.of Employees:** 1 - 10 **Product Groups:** 35, 39, 45

Glazewall Installation North West
Roften House North Road, Ellesmere Port, CH65 1AB
Tel: 0151-356 5588 **Fax:** 0151-355 9155
Directors: J. Williams (Fin), K. Sleeman (Dir)
Immediate Holding Company: GLAZEWALL INSTALLATION LIMITED
Registration no: 04406357 **Date established:** 2002
Turnover: £500,000 - £1m **No.of Employees:** 1 - 10 **Product Groups:** 26, 35

Date of Accounts	Mar 04	Mar 03
Sales Turnover	514	573
Pre Tax Profit/Loss	149	114
Working Capital	-28	-59
Fixed Assets	58	70
Current Assets	70	99
Current Liabilities	89	113

Greif UK Ltd
Merseyside Works Oil Sites Road, Ellesmere Port, CH65 4EZ
Tel: 0151-373 2000 **Fax:** 0151-373 2072
E-mail: info.uk@greif.com
Website: http://www.greif.com
Bank(s): Hill Samuel
Directors: D. Tillotson (Fin), Y. Martin (Sales & Mktg), G. Duerden (MD)
Managers: L. Willson (Sales Admin), J. Hughes (Sales Admin)
Ultimate Holding Company: GREIF INC (USA)
Immediate Holding Company: GREIF UK LTD
Registration no: 06633687 **Date established:** 2008 **Turnover:** £2m - £5m
No.of Employees: 51 - 100 **Product Groups:** 30, 35

Date of Accounts	Oct 11	Oct 10	Oct 09
Sales Turnover	55m	53m	47m
Pre Tax Profit/Loss	4m	-635	-7m
Working Capital	-4m	-7m	-11m
Fixed Assets	69m	74m	75m
Current Assets	14m	13m	11m
Current Liabilities	3m	3m	5m

H P F Energy Services Ltd
5 Hoyer Industrial Estate Bridges Road, Ellesmere Port, CH65 4LB
Tel: 0151-357 3322 **Fax:** 0151-357 1334
E-mail: ellesmere@hpf-energy.com
Website: http://www.hpf-energy.com
Directors: E. Murphy (Dir)
Immediate Holding Company: MARLA TUBE FITTING LTD
Turnover: £20m - £50m **No.of Employees:** 11 - 20 **Product Groups:** 36

Inspection Consultant Ltd
Unit 1 Terrace Factory Rossfield Road, Ellesmere Port, CH65 3BS
Tel: 0151-357 2212 **Fax:** 0151-357 4181
E-mail: mail@incon.co.uk
Website: http://www.incon.co.uk
Directors: D. Witfield (MD), M. Gouldson (Fin)
No.of Employees: 1 - 10 **Product Groups:** 37, 38, 48, 51, 85

Date of Accounts	Apr 08	Apr 07	Apr 06
Working Capital	61	-36	-63
Fixed Assets	444	413	293
Current Assets	790	466	310
Current Liabilities	728	502	373

Inspection Consultants Ltd
1 Terrace Factory Rossfield Road, Ellesmere Port, CH65 3BS
Tel: 0151-357 2212 **Fax:** 0151-357 4181
E-mail: mail@incon.co.uk
Website: http://www.incon.co.uk
Directors: M. Gouldson (Co Sec)
Immediate Holding Company: Ultra Tec Ndt Services Ltd
Registration no: 05700569 **Date established:** 2006
No.of Employees: 11 - 20 **Product Groups:** 38, 48, 85

International Pheromone Systems Ltd
Units 10-15 Meadow Lane Industrial Estate, Ellesmere Port, CH65 4TY
Tel: 0151-357 2655 **Fax:** 0151-355 0299
E-mail: dave@internationalpheromone.co.uk
Website: http://www.internationalpheromone.co.uk
Directors: D. Hartley (MD)
Immediate Holding Company: INTERNATIONAL PHEROMONE SYSTEMS LIMITED
Registration no: 01824905 **VAT No.:** GB 414 5630 73
Date established: 1984 **Turnover:** £250,000 - £500,000
No.of Employees: 1 - 10 **Product Groups:** 32

Date of Accounts	Dec 11	Dec 10	Dec 08
Working Capital	367	290	279
Fixed Assets	16	16	15
Current Assets	565	317	287

Laker Vent Engineering Ltd
Lakers House North Road, Ellesmere Port, CH65 1BA
Tel: 0151-355 9293 **Fax:** 0151-357 1893
E-mail: sales@lakervent.co.uk
Website: http://www.lakervent.co.uk
Directors: J. Ashe (Fin), M. Ventre (Dir), R. Ventre (MD)
Managers: S. Kennedy (Purch Mgr), H. Jones (Personnel)
Ultimate Holding Company: LV ENGINEERING LIMITED
Immediate Holding Company: LAKER VENT ENGINEERING LIMITED
Registration no: 02001095 **Date established:** 1986
Turnover: £10m - £20m **No.of Employees:** 101 - 250
Product Groups: 35, 36, 37, 39, 40, 41, 46, 48, 51, 52, 54, 80

Date of Accounts	Mar 10	Mar 09	Apr 11
Sales Turnover	11m	9m	10m
Pre Tax Profit/Loss	141	147	125
Working Capital	152	59	277
Fixed Assets	651	724	587
Current Assets	3m	2m	2m
Current Liabilities	2m	2m	948

Maineport Ltd
8 Terrace Factory Rossfield Road, Ellesmere Port, CH65 3BS
Tel: 0151-355 0111 **Fax:** 0151-356 1093
E-mail: sales@uecnet.co.uk
Website: http://www.maineport.com
Bank(s): Barclays
Directors: J. Wilson (MD), N. Philpott (Fin), N. Philpott (Comm), N. Philpot (Dir), R. Moorehead (Sales), D. Kinvig (Dir)
Managers: B. Moore (Buyer), M. Formston (Chief Acct)
Immediate Holding Company: MAINEPORT LTD
Registration no: 03966675 **VAT No.:** GB 482 5633 30
Date established: 2000 **Turnover:** £5m - £10m **No.of Employees:** 21 - 50
Product Groups: 26, 35, 36

Mersey Weigh Ltd
Unit 49 Canal Bridge Enterprise Centre Meadow Lane, Ellesmere Port, CH65 4EH
Tel: 0151-356 5274 **Fax:** 0151-356 5274
E-mail: info@merseyweigh.co.uk
Website: http://www.merseyweigh.co.uk
Directors: A. Dover (Dir)
Immediate Holding Company: MERSEY WEIGH LTD
Registration no: 04349385 **Date established:** 2002
Turnover: Up to £250,000 **No.of Employees:** 1 - 10 **Product Groups:** 38, 42

Date of Accounts	Dec 11	Dec 10	Dec 09
Sales Turnover	181	147	166
Pre Tax Profit/Loss	53	49	54
Working Capital	14	12	8
Fixed Assets	7	7	3
Current Assets	48	45	45
Current Liabilities	31	15	20

Odlings M C R Ltd
Rosscliffe Road Junction 8 Business Centre, Ellesmere Port, CH65 3AS
Tel: 0151-355 0261 **Fax:** 0151-356 4423
E-mail: sales@odlingsmcr.co.uk
Website: http://www.odlingsmcr.co.uk
Bank(s): Barclays
Directors: A. White (Fin)
Managers: S. Clark (Chief Mgr)
Ultimate Holding Company: BRIDGWATER BROS.HOLDINGS LIMITED
Immediate Holding Company: ODLINGS MCR LIMITED
Registration no: 00890658 **VAT No.:** GB 441 5147 73
Date established: 1966 **Turnover:** £1m - £2m **No.of Employees:** 11 - 20
Product Groups: 46

Date of Accounts	Sep 11	Sep 10	Sep 09
Sales Turnover	N/A	1m	1m
Pre Tax Profit/Loss	N/A	168	95
Working Capital	356	314	274
Fixed Assets	13	10	10
Current Assets	576	548	444
Current Liabilities	N/A	111	61

P S I Industrial Supplies Ltd
Unit 55-56 Canal Bridge Enterprise Centre Meadow Lane, Ellesmere Port, CH65 4EH
Tel: 0151-356 8088 **Fax:** 0151-356 8099
E-mail: nigel00thomas@aol.com
Website: http://www.pneumaticssteaminstrumentationltd.co.uk
Directors: M. Thomas (Fin), N. Thomas (MD)
Immediate Holding Company: PSI INDUSTRIAL SUPPLIES LIMITED
Registration no: 03476540 **VAT No.:** 595 7206 06 **Date established:** 1997
Turnover: £500,000 - £1m **No.of Employees:** 1 - 10 **Product Groups:** 38, 40, 46

Date of Accounts	Dec 11	Dec 10	Dec 09
Working Capital	138	97	77
Fixed Assets	16	5	6
Current Assets	234	179	165

panache interiors
Crowthorns School Lane, Childer Thornton, Ellesmere Port, CH66 5PL
Tel: 0151-339 7134 **Fax:** 0151-339 7134
E-mail: rachelhunt@iloveinteriordesign.co.uk
Website: http://www.iloveinteriordesign.co.uk
Directors: R. Hunt (Prop)
Immediate Holding Company: ANGLO SWISS OIL LIMITED
Registration no: 07146926 **Date established:** 2010
Turnover: Up to £250,000 **No.of Employees:** 1 - 10 **Product Groups:** 84

Pipeline Equipment Supply
Unit 8 Meadow Lane Industrial Park, Ellesmere Port, CH65 4TY
Tel: 0151-357 1524 **Fax:** 0151-357 1958
E-mail: pesnwltd@aol.com
Directors: P. Chalton (MD)
Registration no: 02195646 **VAT No.:** GB 712 2491 64
Date established: 1987 **Turnover:** £500,000 - £1m
No.of Employees: 1 - 10 **Product Groups:** 30, 36

Protocol Skills
Aldford House Lloyd Drive, Ellesmere Port, CH65 9HQ
Tel: 08450-719011 **Fax:** 01709-874817
E-mail: info@protocol-skills.co.uk
Website: http://www.protocol.co.uk
Directors: J. O'Boyle (Reg)
Ultimate Holding Company: PROTOCOL ASSOCIATES NV (BELGIUM)
Immediate Holding Company: PROTOCOL TRAINING LIMITED
Registration no: 03826857 **Date established:** 1999
Turnover: £20m - £50m **No.of Employees:** 11 - 20 **Product Groups:** 80

Date of Accounts	Jul 10	Jul 09	Jul 08
Sales Turnover	32m	38m	32m
Pre Tax Profit/Loss	-6m	-7m	-2m
Working Capital	5m	6m	5m
Fixed Assets	40m	43m	44m
Current Assets	9m	9m	10m
Current Liabilities	4m	3m	5m

Roften Galvanising Ltd
North Road, Ellesmere Port, CH65 1AB
Tel: 0151-355 4257 **Fax:** 0151-355 0753
E-mail: accounts@roften.com
Website: http://www.roften.com
Directors: A. Humphreys (Dir)
Managers: G. Stockton (Personnel)
Immediate Holding Company: ROFTEN GALVANIZING LIMITED
Registration no: 01290735 **Date established:** 1976 **Turnover:** £2m - £5m
No.of Employees: 51 - 100 **Product Groups:** 46

Date of Accounts	Oct 11	Oct 10	Oct 09
Working Capital	1m	1m	1m
Fixed Assets	3m	3m	3m
Current Assets	2m	2m	2m

Rossendale Group Of Lifting Gear Co. Ltd
Portside North, Ellesmere Port, CH65 2HQ
Tel: 0151-355 5091 **Fax:** 01706-830490
E-mail: sales@rossendalegroup.co.uk
Website: http://www.rossendalegroup.co.uk
Bank(s): HSBC
Directors: J. Bamford (Sales), S. Bamford (MD)
Managers: B. Diggle (Sales Prom Mgr), S. Davis (Purch Mgr), M. Bamford (Personnel)
Immediate Holding Company: ROSSENDALE GROUP LIMITED
Registration no: 00463320 **VAT No.:** GB 457 9798 66
Date established: 1949 **Turnover:** £2m - £5m **No.of Employees:** 51 - 100
Product Groups: 45

Date of Accounts	Mar 12	Mar 11	Mar 10
Working Capital	686	384	490
Fixed Assets	455	513	635
Current Assets	1m	1m	1m

S G S UK Ltd
Rossmore Business Park Inward Way, Ellesmere Port, CH65 3EN
Tel: 0151-350 6666 **Fax:** 0151-350 6600
E-mail: ukenquiries@sgs.com
Website: http://www.sgs.com
Managers: T. Dubbins (Sales & Mktg Mg)
Ultimate Holding Company: SGS SA (SWITZERLAND)
Immediate Holding Company: SGS UNITED KINGDOM LIMITED
Registration no: 01193985 **Date established:** 1974
Turnover: £10m - £20m **No.of Employees:** 101 - 250
Product Groups: 51, 80, 82, 84, 85

Date of Accounts	Dec 11	Dec 10	Dec 09
Sales Turnover	101m	90m	97m
Pre Tax Profit/Loss	19m	7m	10m
Working Capital	8m	8m	12m
Fixed Assets	32m	27m	22m
Current Assets	34m	29m	35m
Current Liabilities	20m	18m	14m

Sealex Ltd
Poole Hall Industrial Estate, Ellesmere Port, CH66 1ST
Tel: 0151-357 1551 **Fax:** 0151-357 1734
E-mail: sales@sealexgroup.com
Website: http://www.sealexgroup.com
Directors: I. Marray (Sales), P. Marray (MD), S. Clarkson (Sales)
Managers: J. Griffin
Immediate Holding Company: SEALEX LIMITED
Registration no: 01657257 **Date established:** 1982 **Turnover:** £2m - £5m
No.of Employees: 11 - 20 **Product Groups:** 38, 42

Date of Accounts	Dec 11	Sep 10	Sep 09
Sales Turnover	3m	N/A	N/A
Pre Tax Profit/Loss	305	N/A	N/A
Working Capital	645	369	277
Fixed Assets	118	408	407
Current Assets	1m	935	666
Current Liabilities	192	N/A	N/A

Stanfast Products Ltd
North Road, Ellesmere Port, CH65 1AB
Tel: 0151-355 5577 **Fax:** 0151-355 6300
E-mail: stanfast@talk21.com
Directors: A. Humphreys (MD)
Ultimate Holding Company: ALEXANDER ECCLES LIMITED
Immediate Holding Company: CHESHIRE SCIENTIFIC LTD.
Registration no: 00948016 **VAT No.:** GB 338 4181 51
Date established: 2002 **Turnover:** Up to £250,000
No.of Employees: 1 - 10 **Product Groups:** 34, 35, 42

Date of Accounts	Oct 07	Oct 06	Oct 05
Working Capital	6	6	363
Fixed Assets	N/A	N/A	600
Current Assets	6	6	410
Current Liabilities	N/A	N/A	48
Total Share Capital	6	6	6

Vauxhall Motors Ltd
North Road, Ellesmere Port, CH65 1AL
Tel: 0151-355 3777 **Fax:** 0151-350 2911
Website: http://www.vauxhall.co.uk
Bank(s): Barclays, Lloyds TSB, National
Managers: J. Cartwright (Tech Serv Mgr), P. Croxford (Fin Mgr), B. Thomas (Personnel), T. Francavilla (Plant)
Immediate Holding Company: VAUXHALL MOTORS LIMITED
Registration no: 06356274 **Date established:** 2007
Turnover: Over £1,000m **No.of Employees:** 1501 & over
Product Groups: 39

Vernolab Laboratories
PO Box 14, Ellesmere Port, CH65 4ES
Tel: 0151-348 6800 **Fax:** 0151-348 6829
E-mail: sales@vernolab.com
Website: http://www.vernolab.com
Directors: P. Parkinson (MD)
Managers: J. Hinde (Mgr)
Registration no: 06454460 **Date established:** 2007 **Turnover:** £2m - £5m
No.of Employees: 21 - 50 **Product Groups:** 38, 84, 85

Wrought In The Port
1 Westminster Industrial Park Rossfield Road, Ellesmere Port, CH65 3DU
Tel: 0151-327 7450 **Fax:** 0151-356 3223
E-mail: handmadeironwork@ntlworld.com
Website: http://www.wrought-in-the-port.co.uk
Directors: K. Goodaham (Prop), K. Gooderham (Prop)
Date established: 2001 **No.of Employees:** 1 - 10 **Product Groups:** 26, 35

Liverpool

A Algeo Ltd
Unit 14 Sheridan House Speke Hall Road, Liverpool, L24 9HB
Tel: 0151-448 1228 **Fax:** 0151-448 1008
E-mail: sales@algeos.com
Website: http://www.algeos.com
Bank(s): National Westminster
Directors: B. Howard (Fin)
Managers: C. Rutter (Tech Serv Mgr), K. Knowle (Purch Mgr), E. Halliday (Ops Mgr), M. Cameron (Sales & Mktg Mg)
Immediate Holding Company: A.ALGEO LIMITED
Registration no: 00437100 **VAT No.:** GB 164 8125 60
Date established: 1947 **Turnover:** £10m - £20m
No.of Employees: 51 - 100 **Product Groups:** 29, 30, 38

Date of Accounts	Aug 11	Aug 10	Aug 09
Sales Turnover	10m	N/A	N/A
Pre Tax Profit/Loss	323	N/A	N/A
Working Capital	1m	847	587
Fixed Assets	707	684	794
Current Assets	4m	3m	2m
Current Liabilities	1m	N/A	387

A E B Precision
2 Cusson Road Knowsley Industrial Park, Liverpool, L33 7BY
Tel: 0151-546 3240 **Fax:** 0151-546 3206
E-mail: tony.butler@aebprecision.co.uk
Website: http://www.aebprecision.co.uk
Directors: T. Butler (Ptnr), J. Butler (Ptnr)
Immediate Holding Company: AEB PRECISION LLP
Registration no: OC301100 **Date established:** 2001
No.of Employees: 21 - 50 **Product Groups:** 46

Date of Accounts	Apr 10	Apr 09
Working Capital	35	189
Fixed Assets	N/A	24
Current Assets	35	293
Current Liabilities	N/A	5

Aalco Metals
201-207 Great Howard Street, Liverpool, L5 9ZH
Tel: 0151-207 3551 **Fax:** 0151-207 2657
E-mail: liverpool@aalco.co.uk
Website: http://www.aalco.co.uk
Bank(s): National Westminster Bank Plc
Managers: J. Simms (Chief Mgr), K. Niblock (), S. Spencer ()
Ultimate Holding Company: UK STEELSTOCK LTD
Immediate Holding Company: AMARI METALS LTD
Registration no: 03551533 **Date established:** 1991
Turnover: £125m - £250m **No.of Employees:** 21 - 50
Product Groups: 34, 35, 36, 66

Adsteam Towedge Ltd
South Bramley-Moore Dock Regent Road, Liverpool, L3 0AP
Tel: 0151-207 6652 **Fax:** 0151-207 9703
E-mail: info@liverpool.adsteam.co.uk
Website: http://www.svitzer.com
Directors: I. Aitchison (Mkt Research), J. Muller (MD), J. Thorton (Mkt Research), S. Eastwood (Grp Chief Exec)
Managers: D. Waterhouse (Mgr)
Registration no: 00024907 **Turnover:** £2m - £5m
No.of Employees: 1 - 10 **Product Groups:** 71, 74

Gordon Alison Ltd
16 Jordan Street, Liverpool, L1 0BP
Tel: 0151-709 4687 **Fax:** 0151-709 4723
E-mail: info@gordonalisonltd.com
Website: http://www.gordonalisonltd.com
Directors: S. Thomson (MD)
Ultimate Holding Company: BULLMAN HOLDINGS LIMITED
Immediate Holding Company: GORDON ALISON LIMITED
Registration no: 03615549 **VAT No.:** GB 647 2999 82
Date established: 1998 **Turnover:** £500,000 - £1m
No.of Employees: 1 - 10 **Product Groups:** 39

Date of Accounts	Dec 11	Dec 10	Dec 09
Working Capital	22	19	-4
Fixed Assets	1	1	2
Current Assets	250	238	207

Alpha Machine Tool Company
Unit 5 Arbour Place Kirkby, Liverpool, L33 7XG
Tel: 0151-547 1062 **Fax:** 0151-547 1063
E-mail: sales@alphamachinetools.co.uk
Website: http://www.alphamachinetools.co.uk
Directors: A. Clarks (Dir)
Immediate Holding Company: ALPHA MACHINE TOOLS COMPANY LIMITED
Registration no: 06607960 **Date established:** 2008
No.of Employees: 1 - 10 **Product Groups:** 46

Date of Accounts	Aug 11	Aug 10	Aug 09
Working Capital	121	-2	-15
Fixed Assets	10	14	19
Current Assets	309	276	272

Alpha Polymers Ltd
1-7 Costain Street, Liverpool, L20 8QJ
Tel: 0151-933 3020 **Fax:** 0151-944 1494
E-mail: info@alpha-polymers.com
Website: http://www.alpha-polymers.com
Directors: L. Kirby (Fin)
Immediate Holding Company: ALPHA POLYMERS LIMITED
Registration no: 01543079 **VAT No.:** GB 325 1445 83
Date established: 1981 **Turnover:** £500,000 - £1m
No.of Employees: 1 - 10 **Product Groups:** 30

Date of Accounts	Dec 11	Dec 10	Dec 09
Working Capital	-44	-36	-66
Fixed Assets	84	84	77
Current Assets	362	313	223

Andrews Sykes Hire Ltd
Sandy Road, Liverpool, L21 1AF
Tel: 0151-920 8200 **Fax:** 0151-949 0911
E-mail: info@andrews-sykes.com
Website: http://www.andrews-sykes.com
Managers: E. Jones (Mgr)
Immediate Holding Company: ANDREWS SYKES HIRE LIMITED
Registration no: 02985657 **VAT No.:** GB 100 4295 24
Date established: 1994 **No.of Employees:** 1 - 10 **Product Groups:** 37, 38, 39, 40, 52

Date of Accounts	Dec 11	Dec 10	Dec 09
Sales Turnover	35m	36m	34m
Pre Tax Profit/Loss	10m	10m	8m
Working Capital	8m	6m	2m
Fixed Assets	7m	7m	9m
Current Assets	33m	35m	35m
Current Liabilities	7m	7m	5m

Anson Systems Ltd (a division of G M Business Print & Systems Ltd)
Unit 11 Glacier Buildings Harrington Road, Brunswick Business Park, Liverpool, L3 4BH
Tel: 0151-709 0676 **Fax:** 0151-709 0678
E-mail: sales@gmbusinessprint.co.uk
Website: http://www.gmbusinessprint.co.uk
Directors: R. Board (MD)
Registration no: 00204615 **Turnover:** £1m - £2m
No.of Employees: 1 - 10 **Product Groups:** 49

Armourguard
87 Fulwood Road, Liverpool, L17 9PY
Tel: 0151-727 4901
Website: http://www.armourguard.co.uk
Directors: D. Paterson (Prop)
Date established: 1991 **No.of Employees:** 1 - 10 **Product Groups:** 26, 35

Arriva North West
73 Ormskirk Road, Liverpool, L9 5AE
Tel: 0151-522 2800 **Fax:** 0151-522 2811
E-mail: stonep@arrivanw.co.uk
Website: http://www.arrivabus.co.uk
Directors: S. Mills (Fin), P. Stone (MD), D. Turner (Co Sec), A. Hughes (Pers)
Managers: P. Murphy (Buyer), D. Mercer, E. Kennett
Ultimate Holding Company: ARRIVA PLC
Immediate Holding Company: ARRIVA (2007) LTD
Registration no: 02127702 **Turnover:** £20m - £50m
No.of Employees: 21 - 50 **Product Groups:** 72

Aston & Fincher Ltd
3 Trafalgar Way Erskine Industrial Estate, Liverpool, L6 1NA
Tel: 0151-263 8811 **Fax:** 0151-263 8855
E-mail: info@astonandfincher.co.uk
Website: http://www.astonandfincher.co.uk
Managers: D. Doyal (Mgr)
Immediate Holding Company: ASTON & FINCHER LIMITED
Registration no: 00970902 **Date established:** 1970 **Turnover:** £2m - £5m
No.of Employees: 1 - 10 **Product Groups:** 30, 36, 40

Date of Accounts	Dec 11	Dec 10	Dec 09
Sales Turnover	34m	29m	27m
Pre Tax Profit/Loss	981	1m	422
Working Capital	4m	3m	3m
Fixed Assets	4m	4m	4m
Current Assets	8m	8m	6m
Current Liabilities	2m	2m	2m

Atlanta Shutters
154 Dinas Lane, Liverpool, L36 2NT
Tel: 0151-480 1106
Website: http://www.atlantashutters.co.uk
Directors: P. Kirby (Dir), N. Kirby (Dir)
No.of Employees: 1 - 10 **Product Groups:** 26, 35

Aughton Automation Ltd
115 Evans Road Venture Point Business Park, Liverpool, L24 9PB
Tel: 01928-689700 **Fax:** 01928-589601
E-mail: brian.duffy@aughtonuk.com
Website: http://www.aughton.co.uk
Bank(s): The Royal Bank of Scotland plc
Directors: B. Duffy (MD)
Ultimate Holding Company: ELLINGTON HOLDINGS LIMITED
Immediate Holding Company: AUGHTON AUTOMATION LIMITED
Registration no: 03872570 **VAT No.:** GB 732 4520 59
Date established: 1999 **Turnover:** £5m - £10m **No.of Employees:** 11 - 20
Product Groups: 37, 38, 48, 67, 82, 83, 85

Date of Accounts	Sep 11	Sep 10	Sep 09
Sales Turnover	8m	7m	8m
Pre Tax Profit/Loss	339	-107	260
Working Capital	895	663	1m
Fixed Assets	880	914	114
Current Assets	2m	2m	2m
Current Liabilities	789	856	528

Austin Smith Lord LLP
Port of Liverpool Building Pier Head, Liverpool, L3 1BY
Tel: 0151-227 1083 **Fax:** 020-7843 6166
E-mail: liverpool@austinsmithlord.com
Website: http://www.austinsmithlord.com
Directors: A. Sunderland (Ptnr), C. Pritchett (Ptnr)
Immediate Holding Company: AUSTIN-SMITH:LORD LLP
Registration no: OC315362 **Date established:** 2005
Turnover: £10m - £20m **No.of Employees:** 21 - 50 **Product Groups:** 84

Auto Interiors
56 Norfolk Street, Liverpool, L1 0BE
Tel: 0151-708 8881 **Fax:** 0151- 7086002
E-mail: birchmotors@yahoo.co.uk
Website: http://www.birch4x4-uk.com
Directors: W. Birch (Ptnr), J. Birch (Ptnr)
Managers: J. Birch (Sales Prom Mgr)
Date established: 1976 **Turnover:** £2m - £5m **No.of Employees:** 1 - 10
Product Groups: 23, 29, 39

Axcess UK Ltd
8 Manor House Close Maghull, Liverpool, L31 7BX
Tel: 0151-222 1016 **Fax:** 0151-526 8093
E-mail: gary@axcessuk.co.uk
Website: http://axcessuk.co.uk
Directors: G. Newall (MD)
No.of Employees: 1 - 10 **Product Groups:** 36, 40, 52

R Baker Electrical Ltd
Evans Road, Liverpool, L24 9PB
Tel: 0151-486 6760 **Fax:** 0151-448 1225
E-mail: mail@rbaker.co.uk
Website: http://www.rbaker.co.uk
Bank(s): HSBC Bank plc
Directors: R. Baker (MD)
Immediate Holding Company: R BAKER (ELECTRICAL) LIMITED
Registration no: 01650221 **VAT No.:** GB 320 2771 95
Date established: 1982 **Turnover:** £500,000 - £1m
No.of Employees: 11 - 20 **Product Groups:** 35, 37, 38

Date of Accounts	Dec 11	Dec 10	Dec 09
Working Capital	488	409	183
Fixed Assets	409	421	436
Current Assets	713	628	448

Barlass Engineering Ltd
59 Shaw Street, Liverpool, L6 1HL
Tel: 0151-298 2528
E-mail: info@barlassshutters.fsnet.co.uk
Managers: P. Gibson (Mgr)
Ultimate Holding Company: RAYMED TRADING LIMITED
Immediate Holding Company: BARLASS ENGINEERING LIMITED
Registration no: 00723197 **Date established:** 1962
No.of Employees: 11 - 20 **Product Groups:** 35

Date of Accounts	Feb 08	Feb 09	Feb 07
Working Capital	28	-29	13
Fixed Assets	14	15	28
Current Assets	192	120	191

Len Beaman Ltd
Wilson Road, Liverpool, L36 6JQ
Tel: 0151-480 8288 **Fax:** 0151-449 3033
E-mail: sales@beaman.co.uk
Website: http://www.beaman.co.uk
Directors: C. Speck (Dir)
Immediate Holding Company: LEN BEAMAN LIMITED
Registration no: 02061033 **VAT No.:** GB 151 6727 67
Date established: 1986 **No.of Employees:** 1 - 10 **Product Groups:** 26, 29

Date of Accounts	Dec 11	Dec 10	Dec 09
Working Capital	246	304	401
Fixed Assets	294	302	310
Current Assets	366	445	562

Len Beaman Ltd
65 Liverpool Road Formby, Liverpool, L37 6BU
Tel: 01704-834777 **Fax:** 01704-834888
E-mail: sales@beaman.co.uk
Website: http://www.beaman.co.uk
Managers: S. Lee (Mgr)
Immediate Holding Company: LEN BEAMAN LIMITED
Registration no: 02061033 **VAT No.:** GB 151 6727 67
Date established: 1986 **No.of Employees:** 1 - 10 **Product Groups:** 26

Date of Accounts	Dec 11	Dec 10	Dec 09
Working Capital	246	304	401
Fixed Assets	294	302	310
Current Assets	366	445	562

Becker Industrial Coatings Ltd
Goodlass Road, Liverpool, L24 9HJ
Tel: 0151-448 1010 **Fax:** 0151-448 2589
E-mail: reception@beckers-bic.com
Website: http://www.beckers-bic.com
Directors: T. Ellis (Fin), P. Thomas (MD)
Managers: P. Booth (Purch Mgr), L. St Clair (Sales Prom Mgr), J. Russel (Tech Serv Mgr)
Ultimate Holding Company: LINDEN GRUPPEN AB (SWEDEN)
Immediate Holding Company: BECKER INDUSTRIAL COATINGS LIMITED
Registration no: 00680990 **Date established:** 1961
Turnover: £20m - £50m **No.of Employees:** 101 - 250
Product Groups: 32, 48, 66, 76

Date of Accounts	Dec 11	Dec 10	Dec 09
Sales Turnover	32m	29m	20m
Pre Tax Profit/Loss	135	227	-2m
Working Capital	4m	3m	4m
Fixed Assets	4m	5m	5m
Current Assets	14m	13m	10m
Current Liabilities	1m	2m	1m

Belmont Tyres Liverpoollimited
21 Belmont Road Anfield, Liverpool, L6 5BG
Tel: 0151-260 1144
E-mail: lindsaywilliams.suew@blueyonder.co.uk
Website: http://www.belmont-tyres.com
Directors: M. Williams (Prop)
No.of Employees: 1 - 10 **Product Groups:** 29, 68

Bennett Safetywear
11 Mersey Road Crosby, Liverpool, L23 3AF
Tel: 0151-924 3996 **Fax:** 0151-924 6548
E-mail: sales@bennettsafetywear.co.uk
Website: http://www.bennettsafetywear.co.uk
Bank(s): National Westminster Bank Plc
Directors: D. Bennett (Dir), G. Griffin (Fin)
Immediate Holding Company: BENNETT SAFETYWEAR LIMITED
Registration no: 00367257 **VAT No.:** GB 163 3623 75
Date established: 1941 **Turnover:** £2m - £5m **No.of Employees:** 21 - 50
Product Groups: 24, 29, 40, 63, 67

Date of Accounts	Mar 12	Mar 11	Mar 10
Working Capital	658	539	490
Fixed Assets	240	232	249
Current Assets	809	824	818

Benross Marketing Ltd
Benross House Speke Hall Road, Liverpool, L24 9WD
Tel: 0151-448 1200 **Fax:** 0151-448 1221
E-mail: anil@benross.com
Website: http://www.benross.com
Directors: A. Juneja (MD), M. Dev (Fin)
Immediate Holding Company: BENROSS MARKETING LIMITED
Registration no: 03037336 **Date established:** 1995
No.of Employees: 21 - 50 **Product Groups:** 61

Date of Accounts	Mar 12	Mar 11	Mar 10
Pre Tax Profit/Loss	620	599	1m
Working Capital	4m	4m	3m
Fixed Assets	34	40	9
Current Assets	10m	6m	6m
Current Liabilities	2m	1m	588

Berrymans Lace Mawer LLP
Castle Chambers 43 Castle Street, Liverpool, L2 9SU
Tel: 0151-236 2002 **Fax:** 0151-236 2585
E-mail: postbox@blm-law.com
Website: http://www.blm-law.com
Directors: D. Evans (Snr Part)
Managers: N. Brenner (Tech Serv Mgr), L. Coppell (Mktg Serv Mgr), J. Fawcett (Sales Admin)
Immediate Holding Company: BERRYMANS LIMITED
Registration no: 02765393 **VAT No.:** GB **Date established:** 1992
Turnover: £10m - £20m **No.of Employees:** 101 - 250 **Product Groups:** 80

Bibby Lion Group
105 Duke Street, Liverpool, L1 5JQ
Tel: 0151-708 8000 **Fax:** 0151-794 1001
E-mail: iain.speak@bibbydist.co.uk
Website: http://www.bibbydist.co.uk
Directors: M. Howard (Pers), P. O'Keefe (Chief Op Offcr), M. Bibby (Grp MD), T. De Pencier (MD), I. Downing (Fin), M. Bibby (Ch), I. Speak (Comm)
Managers: M. Hansard (Chief Mgr), R. Hare (Sales Admin), R. Lee (I.T. Exec), A. Hooper, J. Beech (Develop Mgr)
Immediate Holding Company: BIBBY FACTORS LIMITED
Registration no: 00584342 **VAT No.:** GB 163 5970 44
Date established: 1957 **Turnover:** £5m - £10m **No.of Employees:** 21 - 50
Product Groups: 72, 74, 76, 77, 84

Biodeg Chemical Co. Ltd
Edwards Lane, Liverpool, L24 9HW
Tel: 0151-486 1873 **Fax:** 0151-448 1433
E-mail: sales@biodeg.co.uk
Website: http://www.biodeg.co.uk
Directors: L. Foster (Co Sec), M. Laws (MD)
Immediate Holding Company: BIODEG CHEMICAL CO LIMITED
Registration no: 02414239 **Date established:** 1989
Turnover: £500,000 - £1m **No.of Employees:** 21 - 50
Product Groups: 30, 32, 67, 68

Date of Accounts	Mar 12	Mar 11	Mar 10
Sales Turnover	N/A	879	646
Pre Tax Profit/Loss	N/A	58	-34
Working Capital	107	93	-32
Fixed Assets	455	456	495
Current Assets	294	271	203
Current Liabilities	N/A	N/A	50

Blue Fountain Systems Ltd
Liverpool Science Park Innovation Centre 2, 146 Brownlow Hill, Liverpool, L3 5RF
Tel: 0845-6436777 **Fax:** 0845-6436 778
E-mail: sales@bluefountain.com
Website: http://www.bluefountain.com
Managers: R. Leatham (Mktg Serv Mgr)
Registration no: 03216139 **Turnover:** £2m - £5m
No.of Employees: 21 - 50 **Product Groups:** 40, 44, 80

Bold Transmission Parts Ltd
Webber Road Knowsley Industrial Park, Liverpool, L33 7SW
Tel: 0151-548 2303 **Fax:** 0151-549 1117
E-mail: sales@engineerskeys.co.uk
Website: http://www.engineerskeys.co.uk
Managers: C. Low (Mgr)
Immediate Holding Company: BOLD TRANSMISSION PARTS (SALES) LIMITED
Registration no: 04042449 **Date established:** 2000
Turnover: £250,000 - £500,000 **No.of Employees:** 1 - 10
Product Groups: 35, 48

Date of Accounts	Oct 11	Oct 10	Oct 09
Working Capital	36	23	6
Fixed Assets	54	62	70
Current Assets	93	86	61

Boodles
Boodles House 35 Lord Street, Liverpool, L2 9SQ
Tel: 0151-227 2525 **Fax:** 0151-255 1070
E-mail: nicholaswainwright@boodles.com
Website: http://www.boodles.com
Directors: N. Wainwright (Dir), M. Wainwright (Fin)
Immediate Holding Company: BOODLE & DUNTHORNE LIMITED
Registration no: 00472968 **Date established:** 1949
Turnover: £20m - £50m **No.of Employees:** 21 - 50 **Product Groups:** 61

Date of Accounts	Feb 12	Feb 11	Feb 10
Sales Turnover	48m	42m	37m
Pre Tax Profit/Loss	6m	5m	4m
Working Capital	31m	27m	24m
Fixed Assets	2m	1m	2m
Current Assets	36m	34m	29m
Current Liabilities	4m	4m	3m

Boxes & Packaging
1 Dolomite Avenue, Liverpool, L24 9BG
Tel: 0151-486 1324 **Fax:** 0151-486 1847
Website: http://www.boxesandpackaging.co.uk
Directors: S. Weig (MD)
Managers: B. Southan (Chief Acct), R. Byrne (Sales Prom Mgr), C. Bowan (Admin Off)
Ultimate Holding Company: MONDI PLC
Immediate Holding Company: MONDI PACKAGING UK HOLDINGS LTD
Registration no: 03051244 **VAT No.:** GB 338 2934 38
No.of Employees: 51 - 100 **Product Groups:** 27

Brayton Snooker Cues Ltd
PO Box 205, Liverpool, L25 0WB
Tel: 07006-300147 **Fax:** 0844-443 1474
E-mail: sales@braytoncues.co.uk
Website: http://www.braytoncues.co.uk
Directors: J. Smith (MD)
No.of Employees: 1 - 10 **Product Groups:** 24, 49, 63

The Bullen Healthcare Group Ltd
85-87 Kempston Street, Liverpool, L3 8HE
Tel: 0151-207 6995 **Fax:** 0151-207 3804
E-mail: info@bullens.com
Website: http://www.bullens.com
Bank(s): Midland
Directors: L. Marsden (Pers), I. Burton (Fin)
Managers: J. Ennion (Tech Serv Mgr), A. Demick (Mktg Serv Mgr)
Immediate Holding Company: THE BULLEN HEALTHCARE GROUP LIMITED
Registration no: 03137456 **VAT No.:** GB 163 4403 84
Date established: 1995 **Turnover:** £2m - £5m **No.of Employees:** 51 - 100
Product Groups: 30

Date of Accounts	Mar 11	Mar 10	Mar 09
Sales Turnover	16m	14m	N/A
Pre Tax Profit/Loss	459	416	1
Working Capital	401	169	-305
Fixed Assets	1m	999	791
Current Assets	5m	4m	399
Current Liabilities	3m	2m	86

Busi & Stephenson Ltd
101 Bold Street, Liverpool, L1 4HL
Tel: 0151-709 8998 **Fax:** 0151-709 8919
E-mail: enquiries@busistephenson.com
Directors: J. Roberts (MD)
Managers: J. Johnson (Chief Buyer), W. Gilham (Fin Mgr)
Ultimate Holding Company: JAVANA INVESTMENTS (GUERNSEY) LTD (GUERNSEY)
Immediate Holding Company: BUSI AND STEPHENSON LIMITED
Registration no: 00158661 **VAT No.:** GB 163 4860 56
Date established: 2019 **Turnover:** £20m - £50m **No.of Employees:** 1 - 10
Product Groups: 61

Date of Accounts	Aug 11	Aug 10	Aug 09
Sales Turnover	25m	18m	22m
Pre Tax Profit/Loss	158	33	13
Working Capital	958	707	706
Fixed Assets	931	1m	1m
Current Assets	5m	6m	7m
Current Liabilities	127	91	115

C B C International (t/a Debtsave Eurotrade)
7th Floor - Silkhouse Court Tithebarn Street, Liverpool, L2 2LZ
Tel: 0151-515 3014 **Fax:** 0151-515 3015
E-mail: enquiries@cbc-international.co.uk
Website: http://www.cbc-international.co.uk
Directors: R. Caligari (Dir)
Immediate Holding Company: DRB LEGAL LIMITED
Registration no: 06764631 **VAT No.:** GB 719 4774 00
Date established: 2011 **Turnover:** Up to £250,000
No.of Employees: 1 - 10 **Product Groups:** 80, 81, 82

Date of Accounts	Mar 11	Mar 10	Mar 08
Working Capital	26	18	-22
Current Assets	28	20	N/A

C D P Print Management
74-82 Rose Lane, Liverpool, L18 8EE
Tel: 0151-724 7000 **Fax:** 0151-724 6478
E-mail: info@cdp.co.uk
Website: http://www.cdp.co.uk
Bank(s): National Westminster Bank Plc
Directors: M. Scanlon (MD), P. Bracken (Fin), T. Fitzgerald (Develop)
Managers: P. Scanlon
Immediate Holding Company: CDP PRINT MANAGEMENT LIMITED
Registration no: 02820094 **Date established:** 1993 **Turnover:** £5m - £10m
No.of Employees: 21 - 50 **Product Groups:** 27, 77, 80, 81

C & G Finishes
274b Smithdown Road, Liverpool, L15 5AH
Tel: 0151-734 3088 **Fax:** 0151-734 3088
Managers: G. Williams (Mgr)
Date established: 1955 **No.of Employees:** 1 - 10 **Product Groups:** 46, 48

Robert Cain Brewery (The Robert Cain Brewery)
Stanhope Street, Liverpool, L8 5XJ
Tel: 0151-709 8734 **Fax:** 0151-708 8395
E-mail: info@cains.co.uk
Website: http://www.cains.co.uk
Bank(s): National Westminster

Directors: S. Dusanj (MD), S. Dunsanj (Jt MD), A. Dusanj (Prop)
Managers: D. Nijs
Immediate Holding Company: WAYHILL INVESTMENTS LIMITED
Registration no: 04397202 **VAT No.:** GB 548 5204 37
Date established: 1994 **Turnover:** £20m - £50m
No.of Employees: 51 - 100 **Product Groups:** 21

Date of Accounts	Sep 10	Sep 09
Sales Turnover	25m	19m
Pre Tax Profit/Loss	-896	-2m
Working Capital	-3m	-2m
Fixed Assets	286	272
Current Assets	3m	2m
Current Liabilities	4m	4m

Carbide Services

2a-2b Church Road Stanley, Liverpool, L13 2BA
Tel: 0151-220 6122 **Fax:** 0151-220 6122
Website: http://www.carbideservices.co.uk
Directors: E. Lowrey (MD)
Date established: 1989 **No.of Employees:** 1 - 10 **Product Groups:** 36

Cargill Cotton

12 Princes Parade, Liverpool, L3 1BG
Tel: 0151-242 7500 **Fax:** 01932-576256
E-mail: paul_kinney@cargill.com
Website: http://www.cargillcotton.com
Bank(s): Barclays
Directors: P. Kinney (Dir)
Managers: J. Roth
Immediate Holding Company: LIVERPOOL CITY REGION LOCAL ENTERPRISE PARTNERSHIP
Registration no: 05046062 **Date established:** 1992
Turnover: £250m - £500m **No.of Employees:** 21 - 50
Product Groups: 66, 82

Cargopak UK Ltd

Draw Well Road Knowsley Industrial Park, Liverpool, L33 7BJ
Tel: 07980-558561 **Fax:** 0151-546 7080
E-mail: sales@cargopak.co.uk
Website: http://www.cargopak.co.uk
Directors: S. Loughlin (Fin)
Immediate Holding Company: CARGO PAK (U.K.) LIMITED
Registration no: 03945833 **Date established:** 2000
No.of Employees: 1 - 10 **Product Groups:** 35, 39, 45

Date of Accounts	Jul 07	Jul 06
Working Capital	94	70
Fixed Assets	41	43
Current Assets	106	99
Current Liabilities	11	30
Total Share Capital	1	1

Cater Bake UK Ltd

Unit A1 Senator Point South Boundary Road, Knowsley Industrial Park, Liverpool, L33 7RR
Tel: 0151-548 5818 **Fax:** 0151-548 5835
E-mail: info@cater-bake.co.uk
Website: http://www.cater-bake.co.uk
Directors: M. Hutchings (MD)
Immediate Holding Company: CATER-BAKE UK LIMITED
Registration no: 04347302 **Date established:** 2002
Turnover: £250,000 - £500,000 **No.of Employees:** 1 - 10
Product Groups: 40, 41, 66, 67

Date of Accounts	Mar 12	Mar 11	Mar 10
Working Capital	761	737	738
Fixed Assets	96	112	120
Current Assets	902	891	882
Current Liabilities	104	N/A	N/A

Catertech

1a Windermere Street, Liverpool, L5 6RA
Tel: 0151-260 1661 **Fax:** 0151-260 1661
E-mail: sales@catertech.biz
Website: http://www.catertech.biz
Directors: A. Dunne (Prop)
Immediate Holding Company: CATERTECH SERVICES LIMITED
Registration no: 03092136 **Date established:** 1995
No.of Employees: 1 - 10 **Product Groups:** 20, 40, 41

Cavern City Tours Ltd

Century Buildings 31 North John Street, Liverpool, L2 6RG
Tel: 0151-236 9091 **Fax:** 0151-236 8081
E-mail: david@thecavernliverpool.com
Website: http://www.mathewstreetfestival.com
Directors: D. Jones (Dir)
Immediate Holding Company: CAVERN CITY TOURS LIMITED
Registration no: 01744312 **Date established:** 1983
Turnover: Up to £250,000 **No.of Employees:** 1 - 10 **Product Groups:** 69

Date of Accounts	Sep 11	Sep 10	Sep 09
Working Capital	-587	-423	-534
Fixed Assets	2m	2m	2m
Current Assets	464	414	265

Centriforce Products Ltd

14-16 Derby Road Kirkdale, Liverpool, L20 8EE
Tel: 0151-207 8100 **Fax:** 0151-298 1319
E-mail: sales@centriforce.com
Website: http://www.centriforce.com
Bank(s): HSBC Bank plc
Directors: M. Lloyd (Fin), S. Carroll (MD)
Managers: D. Leppert (Personnel), D. Williams (Tech Serv Mgr), S. Wallace (Buyer)
Immediate Holding Company: CHISHOLM PLASTICS LIMITED
Registration no: 02459585 **Date established:** 1990 **Turnover:** £5m - £10m
No.of Employees: 51 - 100 **Product Groups:** 30, 31, 33, 37, 41, 42, 66

Challenge Forge Ltd

5 Birchall Street, Liverpool, L20 8PD
Tel: 0151-933 0094 **Fax:** 0151-933 0094
E-mail: challenge.forge@btconnect.com
Directors: M. Bates (Fin), C. Bates (MD)
Immediate Holding Company: CHALLENGE FORGE LIMITED
Registration no: 04911029 **Date established:** 2003
No.of Employees: 1 - 10 **Product Groups:** 26, 35

Date of Accounts	Sep 11	Sep 10	Sep 09
Working Capital	149	213	133
Fixed Assets	39	49	58
Current Assets	208	299	206

E A Clare & Son Ltd

46-48 St Anne Street, Liverpool, L3 3DW
Tel: 0151-482 2700 **Fax:** 0151-298 1134
E-mail: thurston@eaclare.co.uk
Website: http://www.eaclare.co.uk
Bank(s): Barclays
Directors: P. Eggington (Fin), P. Clare (MD), T. Brophy (Works), N. Clare (MD), P. Crail (Sales), G. Padmore (Dir), C. Felton (Dir), P. Crail (Dir), P. Clare (Prop)
Immediate Holding Company: E.A. CLARE & SON LIMITED
Registration no: 01189168 **VAT No.:** GB 166 0283 70
Date established: 1974 **Turnover:** £2m - £5m **No.of Employees:** 51 - 100
Product Groups: 49

Date of Accounts	Mar 08	Mar 07	Mar 06
Working Capital	1717	1683	1558
Fixed Assets	1092	1020	1038
Current Assets	2105	2161	2040
Current Liabilities	389	478	482
Total Share Capital	181	181	181

R S Clare & Co. Ltd

8 Stanhope Street, Liverpool, L8 5RQ
Tel: 0151-709 2902 **Fax:** 0151-709 0518
E-mail: sales@rsclare.com
Website: http://www.rsclare.com
Bank(s): Barclays, Liverpool
Directors: N. Biddle (Dir), G. Chapple (Co Sec)
Immediate Holding Company: R.S.CLARE & CO.,LIMITED
Registration no: 00072349 **Date established:** 2002
Turnover: £20m - £50m **No.of Employees:** 101 - 250
Product Groups: 31, 32, 33, 38, 66, 68

Date of Accounts	Dec 11	Dec 10	Dec 09
Sales Turnover	23m	18m	17m
Pre Tax Profit/Loss	2m	1m	2m
Working Capital	4m	3m	3m
Fixed Assets	5m	4m	4m
Current Assets	8m	6m	5m
Current Liabilities	1m	777	995

CNW Architectural

Unit 1 The Bond, Hammond Road Knowsley Industrial Park, Knowsley, Liverpool, L33 7UL
Tel: 0151-547 7880 **Fax:** 0151-546 2248
E-mail: sales@cnwa.co.uk
Website: http://www.cnwa.co.uk
Bank(s): Barclays, Bootle
Directors: J. Rutter (Jt MD), P. Clarke (Jt MD)
Immediate Holding Company: Coatings (North West) Ltd
Registration no: 07146043 **VAT No.:** GB 324 9307 61
Turnover: £1m - £2m **No.of Employees:** 11 - 20 **Product Groups:** 48

Date of Accounts	Sep 08	Sep 07	Sep 06
Working Capital	-112	333	299
Fixed Assets	366	202	201
Current Assets	1028	1038	991
Current Liabilities	1140	705	692

Collage Marketing

The Gate 600 Princess Drive, Liverpool, L14 9NQ
Tel: 0151-443 5887 **Fax:** 0151-443 5884
E-mail: info@collagemarketing.co.uk
Website: http://www.collagemarketing.co.uk
Directors: D. Lucy (Co Sec), M. O'Mara (Dir)
Immediate Holding Company: COLLAGE MARKETING LIMITED
Registration no: 06179714 **Date established:** 2007
Turnover: £250,000 - £500,000 **No.of Employees:** 1 - 10
Product Groups: 81

Date of Accounts	Mar 11	Mar 10	Mar 09
Sales Turnover	N/A	251	N/A
Pre Tax Profit/Loss	N/A	11	N/A
Working Capital	32	81	69
Fixed Assets	7	13	17
Current Assets	46	131	115
Current Liabilities	N/A	41	N/A

Colloids Ltd

Kirkby Bank Road Knowsley Industrial Park, Liverpool, L33 7SY
Tel: 0151-546 9222 **Fax:** 0151-549 0489
E-mail: sales@colloids.co.uk
Website: http://www.colloids.co.uk
Directors: J. Ashelby (Fin), R. Lidesey (MD), J. Bagnall (Mkt Research)
Managers: F. Johnson (Tech Serv Mgr), P. Scales (Export Sales Mg), L. Whittingham
Immediate Holding Company: COLLOIDS LIMITED
Registration no: 05058123 **VAT No.:** GB 153 1880 72
Date established: 2004 **Turnover:** £20m - £50m
No.of Employees: 51 - 100 **Product Groups:** 30, 31, 32

Date of Accounts	Dec 11	Dec 10	Dec 09
Sales Turnover	29m	26m	16m
Pre Tax Profit/Loss	1m	1m	257
Working Capital	1m	693	-458
Fixed Assets	4m	2m	2m
Current Assets	9m	10m	6m
Current Liabilities	920	787	1m

Comtreat Ltd

Unit 105 North Mersey Business Centre Woodward Road, Knowsley Industrial Park, Liverpool, L33 7UY
Tel: 0151-477 1123 **Fax:** 0151-549 2600
E-mail: i.winstanley@comtreat.co.uk
Website: http://www.comtreat.co.uk
Directors: C. Winstanley (Fin), I. Winstanley (MD)
Immediate Holding Company: COMTREAT LIMITED
Registration no: 04102146 **Date established:** 2000
Turnover: Up to £250,000 **No.of Employees:** 1 - 10 **Product Groups:** 52, 83

Date of Accounts	Dec 11	Dec 10	Dec 09
Working Capital	-10	-11	4
Fixed Assets	24	36	33
Current Assets	36	34	40

Connell Consulting Engineers

Victoria House 25 Victoria Street, Liverpool, L1 6BD
Tel: 0151-236 2900
Website: http://www.connellconsulting.co.uk
Directors: P. Connell (Prop)
Immediate Holding Company: CONNELL CONSULTING ENGINEERS LIMITED
Registration no: 07583256 **Date established:** 2011
No.of Employees: 1 - 10 **Product Groups:** 35

Cubis Industries Ltd

Units 3-5 Yardley Road Knowsley Industrial Park, Liverpool, L33 7SS
Tel: 0151-548 7900 **Fax:** 0151-548 7184
E-mail: info@cubisindustries.com
Website: http://www.cubisindustries.com
Directors: A. Wright (MD), G. Pringle (Co Sec)
Managers: K. Anten, S. McGuire (Personnel)
Ultimate Holding Company: BRABCO 620 LIMITED
Immediate Holding Company: C4 INDUSTRIES LIMITED
Registration no: 04463234 **Date established:** 2002 **Turnover:** £2m - £5m
No.of Employees: 51 - 100 **Product Groups:** 33

Date of Accounts	Dec 11	Dec 10	Dec 09
Sales Turnover	N/A	N/A	2m
Pre Tax Profit/Loss	N/A	N/A	190
Working Capital	1m	1m	1m
Current Assets	1m	1m	1m

Curtins Consulting Engineers Ltd

Curtins House 6 Columbus Quay Riverside Drive, Liverpool, L3 4DB
Tel: 0151-726 2000 **Fax:** 0151-726 2001
E-mail: liverpool@curtins.com
Website: http://www.curtins.com
Directors: R. Melling (Grp Chief Exec), S. Howard (Fin), P. Osborne (Sales & Mktg)
Managers: P. Jackson (Personnel), J. Rice, S. Peters (Tech Serv Mgr)
Ultimate Holding Company: CURTINS GROUP LIMITED
Immediate Holding Company: CURTINS CONSULTING LIMITED
Registration no: 02054159 **VAT No.:** GB 163 4362 72
Date established: 1986 **Turnover:** £10m - £20m
No.of Employees: 21 - 50 **Product Groups:** 84

Date of Accounts	Dec 11	Dec 10	Dec 09
Sales Turnover	11m	12m	12m
Pre Tax Profit/Loss	222	385	770
Working Capital	1m	1m	1m
Fixed Assets	254	263	261
Current Assets	4m	5m	5m
Current Liabilities	2m	3m	4m

D P M UK Ltd

Port of Liverpool Building 2nd Floor Pier Head, Liverpool, L3 1BY
Tel: 0151-236 2776 **Fax:** 0151-236 4577
E-mail: anthony.taylor@dpm.co.uk
Website: http://www.dpm.co.uk
Managers: D. Hoare (Fin Mgr), P. Charlton (Sales Admin)
Ultimate Holding Company: HARRISON MARITIME (HOLDINGS) LIMITED
Immediate Holding Company: DPM (UK) LTD
Registration no: 01873849 **Date established:** 1984 **Turnover:** £2m - £5m
No.of Employees: 11 - 20 **Product Groups:** 28, 64

Date of Accounts	Dec 11	Dec 10	Dec 09
Sales Turnover	6m	5m	5m
Pre Tax Profit/Loss	1m	771	676
Working Capital	3m	1m	2m
Fixed Assets	62	65	73
Current Assets	4m	2m	2m
Current Liabilities	203	101	79

Dales Of Liverpool Ltd

325 Prescot Road Old Swan, Liverpool, L13 3AT
Tel: 0151-220 4341 **Fax:** 0151-254 2626
Directors: L. Harrison (Dir)
Managers: A. Kubina (Purch Mgr)
Immediate Holding Company: LENSONTONE LIMITED
Registration no: 04459343 **VAT No.:** GB 165 7077 44
Date established: 1976 **No.of Employees:** 11 - 20 **Product Groups:** 62

Date of Accounts	Jan 11	Jan 10	Jan 09
Working Capital	-34	-42	-49
Fixed Assets	1	1	4
Current Assets	161	224	210

John Davies 2001 Ltd

61 Waterloo Road, Liverpool, L3 7BE
Tel: 0151-227 5728 **Fax:** 0151- 2550652
E-mail: sales@johndavies.co.uk
Website: http://www.johndavies.co.uk
Directors: E. Smith (Dir), A. Smith (MD), A. Smith (Fin)
Managers: A. Robertson (Mktg Serv Mgr)
Immediate Holding Company: JOHN DAVIES (2001) LTD
Registration no: 04293566 **VAT No.:** GB 163 4482 62
Turnover: £250,000 - £500,000 **No.of Employees:** 1 - 10
Product Groups: 67, 83

Date of Accounts	Feb 08	Feb 07	Feb 06
Working Capital	-43	-22	-2
Fixed Assets	20	26	31
Current Assets	104	153	199
Current Liabilities	147	175	202

Davies Turner & Co. Ltd

9-10 Brickfields Trading Estate, Liverpool, L36 6HY
Tel: 0151-480 8118 **Fax:** 0151-480 6292
E-mail: peterellison@daviesturner.co.uk
Website: http://www.daviesturnerpacking.co.uk
Managers: P. Ellison (District Mgr)
Ultimate Holding Company: DAVIES TURNER HOLDINGS PLC
Immediate Holding Company: DAVIES TURNER & CO. LIMITED
Registration no: 04345197 **Date established:** 2001
No.of Employees: 1 - 10 **Product Groups:** 25, 72, 74, 76, 82

Date of Accounts	Mar 12	Mar 11	Mar 10
Sales Turnover	97m	100m	84m
Pre Tax Profit/Loss	2m	2m	1m
Working Capital	3m	8m	7m
Fixed Assets	2m	1m	2m
Current Assets	20m	24m	22m
Current Liabilities	3m	4m	3m

Delphi Electronics

The Delphi Building Moorgate Road, Knowsley Industrial Park, Liverpool, L33 7XL
Tel: 0151-546 2720 **Fax:** 0151-549 3547
E-mail: alanleyland@delphi.com
Website: http://www.delphi.com
Bank(s): National Westminster
Managers: C. Boddy (Tech Serv Mgr), M. Butterworth (Personnel), P. Roberts (Mgr), L. Kelly (Fin Mgr)
Immediate Holding Company: A 2 B CAR HIRE (NW) LIMITED
Registration no: 06976024 **Date established:** 2009
No.of Employees: 21 - 50 **Product Groups:** 38, 39

Date of Accounts	Jul 11	Jul 10
Sales Turnover	N/A	40
Working Capital	N/A	6
Current Assets	N/A	11

Denholm Rees & O'Donnell Ltd
116 Albany Road Walton, Liverpool, L9 0HB
Tel: 0151-525 1663 **Fax:** 0151-525 7416
E-mail: sales@denholms.co.uk
Website: http://www.denholms.co.uk
Bank(s): HSBC Bank plc
Directors: A. Hayes (MD), S. Roberts (Fin)
Immediate Holding Company: DENHOLM REES & O DONNELL LIMITED
Registration no: 00257758 **Date established:** 1931 **Turnover:** £5m - £10m
No.of Employees: 51 - 100 **Product Groups:** 48

Date of Accounts	Jun 11	Jun 10	Jun 09
Sales Turnover	6m	4m	4m
Pre Tax Profit/Loss	610	117	285
Working Capital	940	543	916
Fixed Assets	2m	2m	2m
Current Assets	3m	2m	2m
Current Liabilities	682	287	338

Henry Diaper & Co. Ltd
PO Box 25, Liverpool, L33 7SD
Tel: 0151-546 2797 **Fax:** 0151-548 2910
E-mail: kevin.williams@diaper.co.uk
Website: http://www.henrydiaper.co.uk
Bank(s): Barclays, Liverpool
Directors: K. Williams (Dir)
Immediate Holding Company: HENRY DIAPER & CO. LIMITED
Registration no: 00491378 **VAT No.:** GB 163 3564 65
Date established: 1951 **Turnover:** £2m - £5m **No.of Employees:** 21 - 50
Product Groups: 76, 77

Date of Accounts	Mar 12	Mar 11	Mar 10
Sales Turnover	5m	N/A	N/A
Pre Tax Profit/Loss	187	N/A	N/A
Working Capital	503	540	1m
Fixed Assets	1m	1m	1m
Current Assets	1m	2m	2m
Current Liabilities	590	N/A	N/A

Dibro Ltd
Unit 2 Valentines Building Aintree Racecourse Business Park, Aintree Racecourse Retail & Bus Pk, Liverpool, L9 5AY
Tel: 0151-525 0365 **Fax:** 0151-525 0342
E-mail: tom@dibro.com
Website: http://www.dibro.com
Directors: T. Dickinson (MD)
Managers: P. Pritchard (Sales Admin)
Immediate Holding Company: DIBRO LIMITED
Registration no: 00515338 **Date established:** 1953 **Turnover:** £1m - £2m
No.of Employees: 1 - 10 **Product Groups:** 30, 33, 48, 49, 66

Date of Accounts	Dec 11	Dec 10	Dec 09
Working Capital	136	181	283
Fixed Assets	312	309	145
Current Assets	288	367	373

Document Direct
The Plaza 100 Old Hall Street, Liverpool, L3 9QJ
Tel: 0151-227 9150 **Fax:** 0151-227 1734
E-mail: info@documentdirect.co.uk
Website: http://www.documentdirect.co.uk
Directors: M. Best (Fin)
Immediate Holding Company: DOCUMENT DIRECT LIMITED
Registration no: 05584808 **Date established:** 2005
Turnover: £50m - £75m **No.of Employees:** 51 - 100 **Product Groups:** 80

Date of Accounts	Dec 11	Dec 10	Dec 09
Working Capital	88	41	-11
Fixed Assets	30	3	5
Current Assets	146	57	26

Downland Bedding Co. Ltd
23 Blackstock Street, Liverpool, L3 6ER
Tel: 0151-236 7166 **Fax:** 0151-236 0062
E-mail: graham@downlandbedding.co.uk
Website: http://www.downlandbedding.co.uk
Bank(s): HSBC City Branch, 4 Dale Street, Liverpool L69 2BZ
Directors: P. Draper (Purch), G. Smith (MD)
Managers: M. Roche (Sales Admin)
Immediate Holding Company: DOWNLAND BEDDING COMPANY LIMITED(THE)
Registration no: 00419883 **VAT No.:** GB 163 7847 33
Date established: 1946 **Turnover:** £2m - £5m **No.of Employees:** 51 - 100
Product Groups: 24, 26, 43

Date of Accounts	Apr 11	Apr 10	Apr 09
Working Capital	1m	1m	849
Fixed Assets	189	165	162
Current Assets	3m	2m	2m

Drakes Pride Bowls Co.
128 Richmond Row, Liverpool, L3 3BL
Tel: 0151-298 1355 **Fax:** 0151-298 2988
E-mail: drakespride@eaclare.co.uk
Website: http://www.drakespride.co.uk
Directors: P. Givens (Sales), M. Eggington (MD)
Managers: E. Givens (Mgr)
Ultimate Holding Company: THE E.A. CLARE & SON LTD GROUP
Registration no: 01187245 **Date established:** 1974
No.of Employees: 21 - 50 **Product Groups:** 49

E Tech Componants
4 Carraway Road Gilmoss Industrial Estate, Liverpool, L11 0EE
Tel: 0151-547 2666 **Fax:** 0151-547 1444
E-mail: sales@e-tech-components.co.uk
Website: http://www.elpress-uk.com
Directors: C. Montgomery (Dir), C. Montgonery (MD)
Managers: P. Forrester (Mgr)
Immediate Holding Company: E-Tech Components UK Ltd
Registration no: 05076040 **Date established:** 2004
No.of Employees: 1 - 10 **Product Groups:** 37

E V C UK Ltd
102 Vauxhall Road, Liverpool, L3 6EZ
Tel: 0151-255 0935 **Fax:** 0151-236 2767
E-mail: info@evcuk.com
Website: http://www.evcuk.com
Directors: L. Forrester (Dir), P. McNeil (Co Sec)
Immediate Holding Company: EVC-UK LTD
Registration no: 07197754 **Date established:** 2010
No.of Employees: 21 - 50 **Product Groups:** 37, 67

Eastwood & Dickinson Ltd
Mayflower Works Gladstone Road, Seaforth, Liverpool, L21 1DE
Tel: 0151-928 2316 **Fax:** 0151-474 6224
E-mail: info@eastwood-dickinson.co.uk
Website: http://www.eastwood-dickinson.co.uk
Directors: C. Paton (MD)
Immediate Holding Company: EASTWOOD AND DICKINSON LIMITED
Registration no: 00666010 **VAT No.:** GB 548 7649 86
Date established: 1960 **Turnover:** £250,000 - £500,000
No.of Employees: 1 - 10 **Product Groups:** 35, 45

Date of Accounts	Oct 11	Oct 10	Oct 09
Working Capital	103	125	127
Fixed Assets	12	14	16
Current Assets	135	181	187

Ekaton Ltd
Jubilee House Altcar Road Formby, Liverpool, L37 8DL
Tel: 01704-870107 **Fax:** 01704-831269
E-mail: sales@ekaton.ltd.uk
Website: http://www.ekaton.ltd.uk
Directors: C. Mackay (Prop)
Immediate Holding Company: EKATON LIMITED
Registration no: 05820157 **VAT No.:** GB 165 9376 24
Date established: 2006 **No.of Employees:** 1 - 10 **Product Groups:** 33, 34, 35, 37, 67

Date of Accounts	Jun 11	Jun 10	Jun 09
Working Capital	318	268	258
Fixed Assets	42	56	80
Current Assets	398	347	437

Electricians Direct
Unit 4 Carraway Road Gillmoss Industrial Estate Croxteth, Liverpool, L11 0EE
Tel: 0151-547 2666 **Fax:** 0151-547 1444
E-mail: offers@electricians-direct.co.uk
Website: http://www.electricians-direct.com
Directors: P. Forester (Dir), A. Doubleday (Dir), S. Hayes (Sales), C. Montgomery (MD)
Date established: 2009 **No.of Employees:** 1 - 10 **Product Groups:** 24, 36, 40

Eli Lilly Ltd
Fleming Road Speke, Liverpool, L24 9LN
Tel: 0151-486 3939 **Fax:** 0151-486 8740
Website: http://www.lilly.co.uk
Directors: D. Urbanek (Dir)
VAT No.: GB 232 7037 87 **No.of Employees:** 251 - 500
Product Groups: 31

Environmental Cleaning Technologies Ltd
Unit 65 North Mersey Business Centre Woodward Road, Knowsley Industrial Park, Liverpool, L33 7UY
Tel: 0151-548 4015 **Fax:** 0151-548 4122
E-mail: sales@ect-ltd.co.uk
Website: http://www.ect-ltd.co.uk
Directors: S. Pearse (Dir)
Immediate Holding Company: ENVIRONMENTAL CLEANING TECHNOLOGIES LTD
Registration no: 02939253 **VAT No.:** GB 643 7173 34
Date established: 1994 **Turnover:** £250,000 - £500,000
No.of Employees: 1 - 10 **Product Groups:** 46

Date of Accounts	Jun 11	Jun 10	Jun 09
Working Capital	-14	-19	-20
Fixed Assets	1	2	2
Current Assets	10	1	9

Erik's Electro Mechanical Services (Liverpool Electro Mechanical)
Brookfield Drive, Liverpool, L9 7AN
Tel: 0151-524 3358 **Fax:** 0151-524 0215
E-mail: liverpool.repair@eriks.co.uk
Website: http://www.eriks.co.uk
Managers: M. Griffiths (Mgr)
Ultimate Holding Company: BLUNDELL & RIMMER GROUP LIMITED
Immediate Holding Company: BLUNDELL & RIMMER (ENGINEERING) LIMITED
Date established: 1976 **Turnover:** £250,000 - £500,000
No.of Employees: 11 - 20 **Product Groups:** 35

Date of Accounts	Sep 90	Sep 89	Sep 88
Working Capital	-62	-62	-62

ERIKS Industrial Services Limited (Aintree Industrial Electronic)
Industrial Electronic Service Centre, Unit 2b Beechers Dirve Aintree Racecourse & Retail Business Park, Aintree, Liverpool, L9 5AY
Tel: 0151-525 4025 **Fax:** 0151-525 4048
E-mail: aintree.electronic@eriks.co.uk
Website: http://www.eriks.co.uk
Managers: A. Thomas
Registration no: 03142338 **Date established:** 1998
No.of Employees: 11 - 20 **Product Groups:** 48

Ernst & Young Ltd
20 Chapel Street, Liverpool, L3 9AG
Tel: 0151-210 4200 **Fax:** 0151-210 4201
E-mail: bflynn@uk.ey.com
Website: http://www.ey.com
Directors: T. Leary (Ptnr)
Managers: J. Mellor (I.T. Exec), B. Flynn (Mgr)
Ultimate Holding Company: ERNST & YOUNG EUROPE LLP
Immediate Holding Company: ERNST & YOUNG LIMITED
Registration no: 05458987 **Date established:** 2005 **Turnover:** £2m - £5m
No.of Employees: 21 - 50 **Product Groups:** 80

Date of Accounts	Jun 08	Jul 09	Jul 10
Sales Turnover	217	2m	4m
Pre Tax Profit/Loss	N/A	529	649
Working Capital	N/A	155	303
Fixed Assets	N/A	N/A	21
Current Assets	500	2m	2m
Current Liabilities	500	902	679

Essex UK Ltd
Ellis Ashton Street, Liverpool, L36 6BW
Tel: 0151-443 6000 **Fax:** 0151-443 6025
Website: http://www.essexgroup.co.uk
Directors: T. Gilleland (Co Sec)
Managers: C. Basinger (Comm), J. Merrills (Buyer), J. Pye (Accounts), J. Swindell (Chief Mgr)
Ultimate Holding Company: THE ALPINE GROUP INC (USA)
Immediate Holding Company: ESSEX UK LIMITED
Registration no: 03512877 **VAT No.:** GB 232 5797 512 233
Date established: 1998 **Turnover:** £10m - £20m **No.of Employees:** 1 - 10
Product Groups: 35, 37

Date of Accounts	Dec 10	Dec 09	Dec 08
Sales Turnover	34m	19m	28m
Pre Tax Profit/Loss	-869	-1m	-659
Working Capital	-5	878	2m
Fixed Assets	1m	1m	1m
Current Assets	12m	7m	6m
Current Liabilities	1m	329	238

Euroliters Ltd
Hornhouse Lane Knowsley Industrial Park, Liverpool, L33 7YQ
Tel: 0151-549 2122 **Fax:** 0151-548 4008
E-mail: jeff@euroliters.co.uk
Website: http://www.euroliters.com
Directors: L. Herbert (Co Sec), J. Harrison (MD)
Immediate Holding Company: EUROLITERS LIMITED
Registration no: 02633010 **Date established:** 1991
Turnover: £500,000 - £1m **No.of Employees:** 21 - 50 **Product Groups:** 32

Date of Accounts	Jun 11	Jun 10	Jun 09
Working Capital	2m	1m	1m
Fixed Assets	312	305	256
Current Assets	3m	2m	2m

Eyre & Elliston Ltd
49-57 Bridgewater Street, Liverpool, L1 0AU
Tel: 0151-709 3154 **Fax:** 0151-709 6775
E-mail: liverpool@eyreandellitson.co.uk
Website: http://www.eyreandelliston.co.uk
Managers: M. Hope (Mgr)
Immediate Holding Company: EYRE & ELLISTON LIMITED
Registration no: 00363429 **Date established:** 1940 **Turnover:** £2m - £5m
No.of Employees: 1 - 10 **Product Groups:** 77

Fabs 4 Ltd
Arbour Works Arbour Lane, Liverpool, L33 7XB
Tel: 0151-547 4822
E-mail: enquiries@fabs4ltd.com
Website: http://www.fabs4ltd.com
Directors: S. Love (MD)
Immediate Holding Company: FABS 4 LIMITED
Registration no: 05297598 **Date established:** 2004
No.of Employees: 1 - 10 **Product Groups:** 35

Date of Accounts	Dec 11	Dec 10	Dec 09
Working Capital	-176	-181	-187
Fixed Assets	86	102	133
Current Assets	493	457	487

Facelift GB
8 Boundary Street, Liverpool, L5 9UF
Tel: 0151-207 2071 **Fax:** 0151-207 2073
E-mail: liverpool@facelift.co.uk
Website: http://www.facelift.co.uk
Directors: P. Boyce (MD)
Managers: E. Smith (Depot Mgr)
Immediate Holding Company: BOYCE AND DAUGHTERS LIMITED
Registration no: 04455449 **Date established:** 1983
No.of Employees: 11 - 20 **Product Groups:** 45, 67, 83

Date of Accounts	Apr 11	Apr 10	Apr 09
Working Capital	-245	-231	-209
Fixed Assets	771	731	682
Current Assets	43	36	22

Fieldway Supplies Ltd
Unit 12 Block E Paramount Business Park Wilson Road, Liverpool, L36 6AW
Tel: 0151-480 9909 **Fax:** 0151-480 9902
E-mail: brian@fieldwaysupplies.com
Website: http://www.fieldway.co.uk
Directors: B. Murphy (MD)
Immediate Holding Company: FIELDWAY SUPPLIES LIMITED
Registration no: 05743944 **Date established:** 2006
Turnover: Up to £250,000 **No.of Employees:** 11 - 20 **Product Groups:** 30, 37, 39, 49

Date of Accounts	Mar 12	Mar 11	Mar 10
Working Capital	108	-104	-185
Fixed Assets	239	237	234
Current Assets	475	172	75

Fireplace Interior Studio
149-151 Linacre Road, Liverpool, L21 8JP
Tel: 0151-933 0783 **Fax:** 0151-933 0783
E-mail: discountcentreuk@yahoo.co.uk
Website: http://www.fireplacesuk.org.uk
Directors: M. Mccarthy (Prop)
Immediate Holding Company: FIREPLACE INTERIOR STUDIO LTD
Registration no: 06481435 **Date established:** 2008
No.of Employees: 1 - 10 **Product Groups:** 33

Date of Accounts	Jan 12	Jan 11	Jan 10
Working Capital	-2	N/A	-3
Fixed Assets	4	5	6
Current Assets	11	10	11

Flexicon UK Ltd
1 Larch Lea, Liverpool, L6 5BN
Tel: 0151-260 6141 **Fax:** 0151-260 4477
E-mail: info@flexicon.org.uk
Website: http://www.flexicon.org.uk
Directors: N. Carmichael (Prop)
Immediate Holding Company: FLEXICON UK LIMITED
Registration no: 06497490 **Date established:** 2008
Turnover: £250,000 - £500,000 **No.of Employees:** 1 - 10
Product Groups: 22, 29, 39, 40, 45, 46

Date of Accounts	Mar 12	Mar 11	Mar 10
Working Capital	-30	-91	-206
Fixed Assets	185	215	244
Current Assets	159	147	115

Fluid Power Services Ltd
71-73 Regent Road Kirkdale, Liverpool, L5 9SY
Tel: 0151-207 8370 **Fax:** 0151-298 2226
E-mail: info@fluidpowerservices.co.uk
Website: http://www.fluidpowerservices.co.uk
Bank(s): HSBC Bank plc

Directors: A. Palmer (MD)
Immediate Holding Company: FLUID POWER SERVICES LIMITED
Registration no: 02553333 **VAT No.:** GB 482 6445 26
Date established: 1990 **Turnover:** £1m - £2m **No.of Employees:** 11 - 20
Product Groups: 29, 40

Date of Accounts	Oct 11	Oct 10	Oct 09
Sales Turnover	N/A	N/A	2m
Pre Tax Profit/Loss	N/A	N/A	52
Working Capital	465	415	419
Fixed Assets	156	140	141
Current Assets	747	837	763
Current Liabilities	N/A	N/A	13

Forresters Pressure Washer Services Ltd

12 Courtyard Works Newstet Road, Knowsley Industrial Park, Liverpool, L33 7TJ
Tel: 0151-549 2003 **Fax:** 0151-546 4009
E-mail: peter_forrester@btinternet.com
Website: http://www.kellysearch.com/partners/forresterspressurewash.asp
Managers: P. Forrester (Mgr)
Immediate Holding Company: F. P. W. S. LIMITED
Registration no: 02044660 **Date established:** 1986
Turnover: Up to £250,000 **No.of Employees:** 1 - 10 **Product Groups:** 31, 40, 47, 52, 71, 83

Date of Accounts	Aug 11	Aug 10	Aug 09
Sales Turnover	159	125	109
Pre Tax Profit/Loss	17	2	-1
Working Capital	80	67	65
Fixed Assets	18	18	18
Current Assets	130	130	107
Current Liabilities	6	1	1

Fuse Co

49 Brasenose Road, Liverpool, L20 8HL
Tel: 0151-933 1143 **Fax:** 0151-933 1043
E-mail: b.starr@thefuseco.co.uk
Website: http://www.thefuseco.co.uk
Managers: B. Starr (Mgr)
Date established: 2000 **No.of Employees:** 1 - 10 **Product Groups:** 36, 40

G A P Personnel

32 Bixteth Street, Liverpool, L3 9UH
Tel: 0151-236 9231 **Fax:** 0151-227 4048
E-mail: daniel.hogan@gap-personnel.com
Website: http://www.gap-personnel.com
Directors: P. Mayberry (Mkt Research)
Managers: S. Helms (Mgr)
Immediate Holding Company: GAP PERSONNEL LIMITED
Registration no: 06896029 **Date established:** 2009
No.of Employees: 1 - 10 **Product Groups:** 30, 80

Date of Accounts	Dec 07	Dec 06	Dec 05
Working Capital	-18	-18	-18
Current Assets	30	30	30
Current Liabilities	48	48	48

G M Business Print & Systems Ltd

Unit 11 Glacier Buildings, Brunswick Business Park, Liverpool, L3 4BH
Tel: 0151-709 0676 **Fax:** 0151-709 0678
E-mail: nigelboard@gmbusinessprint.co.uk
Website: http://www.gmbusinessprint.co.uk
Bank(s): Lloyds TSB Bank plc
Directors: N. Board (Dir)
Immediate Holding Company: G.M. BUSINESS PRINT AND SYSTEMS LIMITED
Registration no: 00204615 **VAT No.:** GB 163 5852 50
Date established: 2025 **Turnover:** £2m - £5m **No.of Employees:** 11 - 20
Product Groups: 44, 49, 64

Date of Accounts	Dec 10	Dec 09	Dec 08
Working Capital	235	235	125
Fixed Assets	22	34	60
Current Assets	634	565	574

Gallagher Heath Insurance Services Ltd

Orleans House Edmund Street, Liverpool, L3 9NG
Tel: 0151-227 4321 **Fax:** 0151-227 4322
E-mail: gjones@heathlambert.com
Website: http://www.heathlambert.com
Directors: G. Jones (MD)
Immediate Holding Company: BASKERVYLE HOMES LLP
Registration no: 00308512 **Date established:** 2008
Turnover: £125m - £250m **No.of Employees:** 1 - 10 **Product Groups:** 80, 82

Date of Accounts	Dec 10	Dec 09	Dec 07
Sales Turnover	N/A	N/A	114m
Pre Tax Profit/Loss	N/A	N/A	24m
Working Capital	N/A	N/A	68m
Fixed Assets	N/A	N/A	14m
Current Assets	N/A	N/A	376m
Current Liabilities	N/A	N/A	308m

Gateacre Press Ltd

260 Picton Road Wavertree, Liverpool, L15 4LP
Tel: 0151-734 3038 **Fax:** 0151-734 2860
E-mail: info@onthebell.co.uk
Website: http://www.inattendance.co.uk
Directors: Z. Billal (Fin), C. Elliott (Prop)
Immediate Holding Company: GATEACRE PRESS LIMITED
Registration no: 02485714 **VAT No.:** GB 548 8662 89
Date established: 1990 **Turnover:** £1m - £2m **No.of Employees:** 11 - 20
Product Groups: 28

Date of Accounts	Oct 11	Oct 10	Oct 09
Working Capital	-13	21	31
Fixed Assets	40	40	43
Current Assets	192	40	51

Gencoa Ltd

Physics Road, Liverpool, L24 9HP
Tel: 0151-486 4466 **Fax:** 0151-486 4488
E-mail: sales@gencoa.com
Website: http://www.gencoa.com
Bank(s): National Westminster
Directors: J. Nethercote (Fin)
Managers: A. Mcguinness (Admin Off), A. Park (Buyer), D. Monaghan (Mktg Serv Mgr), S. Smith (Personnel)
Immediate Holding Company: GENCOA LIMITED
Registration no: 02956450 **Date established:** 1994
Turnover: £500,000 - £1m **No.of Employees:** 21 - 50
Product Groups: 32, 37, 40

Date of Accounts	Mar 11	Mar 10	Mar 09
Working Capital	852	49	-32
Fixed Assets	97	112	121
Current Assets	3m	763	685

Global Computer Training Ltd

34 Mere Cliff Stockbridge Village, Liverpool, L28 5RF
Tel: 0151-443 0160
Directors: E. Dorrian (Fin), G. McEntaggart (MD)
Turnover: £250,000 - £500,000 **No.of Employees:** 1 - 10
Product Groups: 86

Grampian Motors

Musker Street, Liverpool, L23 0UB
Tel: 0151-931 5009 **Fax:** 0151-931 4959
E-mail: sales@mi-taka.com
Managers: J. Nicholson (Mgr)
No.of Employees: 21 - 50 **Product Groups:** 39, 40, 68

H F S Engineering Services

Southern Gateway Speke, Liverpool, L24 9JD
Tel: 0151-486 0923 **Fax:** 0845-017 1102
E-mail: enquiries@hfs-info.com
Website: http://www.hfsengineering.co.uk
Directors: S. Story (Dir)
Immediate Holding Company: HFS ENGINEERING SERVICES LIMITED
Registration no: 06070508 **Date established:** 2007
No.of Employees: 1 - 10 **Product Groups:** 38, 81, 84, 85, 86

Date of Accounts	Dec 11	Dec 10	Dec 09
Working Capital	-16	-14	-11
Fixed Assets	55	63	23
Current Assets	32	25	5

Thomas Hardie Commercials Ltd

Newstet Road Knowsley Industrial Park North, Knowsley Industrial Park, Liverpool, L33 7TJ
Tel: 0151-549 3000 **Fax:** 0151-549 3070
E-mail: info@thardie.co.uk
Website: http://www.thardie.co.uk
Bank(s): Royal Bank of Scotland
Directors: M. Woosnam (MD), S. Kenyon (Fin)
Managers: G. Harper (Tech Serv Mgr), J. Gimblett (Personnel)
Ultimate Holding Company: THOMAS HARDIE TRUCK & BUS LIMITED
Immediate Holding Company: THOMAS HARDIE COMMERCIALS LIMITED
Registration no: 01879630 **VAT No.:** GB 643 8617 19
Date established: 1985 **Turnover:** £50m - £75m
No.of Employees: 251 - 500 **Product Groups:** 68

Date of Accounts	Dec 11	Dec 10	Dec 09
Sales Turnover	74m	57m	62m
Pre Tax Profit/Loss	492	970	-415
Working Capital	2m	3m	4m
Fixed Assets	6m	5m	5m
Current Assets	17m	16m	14m
Current Liabilities	2m	2m	3m

Harrison Advanced Rods (Suremag Ltd)

201 Summers Road Brunswick Business Park, Liverpool, L3 4BL
Tel: 0151-709 5981 **Fax:** 0151-709 6096
E-mail: dr.s.harrison@harrisonrods.co.uk
Website: http://www.harrisonrods.co.uk
Directors: S. Harrison (Prop)
Immediate Holding Company: SUREMAG LIMITED
Registration no: 02329709 **Date established:** 1988
No.of Employees: 1 - 10 **Product Groups:** 30, 33, 49

Date of Accounts	Dec 11	Dec 10	Dec 09
Working Capital	149	137	133
Fixed Assets	23	26	26
Current Assets	222	239	244

Higson Edwards Steel Stock Ltd

9 Boundary Street, Liverpool, L5 9XR
Tel: 0151-207 6000 **Fax:** 0151-482 2914
E-mail: sales@higsonedwards.co.uk
Website: http://www.higsonedwards.co.uk
Bank(s): Barclays
Directors: S. Ross (MD)
Managers: N. Walsh (Sales Prom Mgr)
Immediate Holding Company: HIGSON EDWARDS (STEELSTOCK) LIMITED
Registration no: 01768764 **VAT No.:** GB 387 2461 26
Date established: 1983 **Turnover:** £2m - £5m **No.of Employees:** 11 - 20
Product Groups: 66

Date of Accounts	Dec 11	Dec 10	Dec 09
Working Capital	378	358	369
Fixed Assets	744	761	752
Current Assets	1m	983	806

Hobs Reprographics plc

8 Castle Street, Liverpool, L2 0NE
Tel: 0151-709 0261 **Fax:** 0151-709 4769
E-mail: kjob@hobsrepro.com
Website: http://www.hobsrepro.com
Bank(s): HSBC Bank plc
Directors: K. O'brien (Dir)
Managers: C. Johnson (Chief Acct)
Ultimate Holding Company: OBETT HOLDINGS LIMITED
Immediate Holding Company: HOBS REPROGRAPHICS PLC
Registration no: 00511368 **VAT No.:** GB 482 9618 06
Date established: 1952 **Turnover:** £10m - £20m
No.of Employees: 11 - 20 **Product Groups:** 64, 81

HSS Hire

187 Picton Road Wavertree, Liverpool, L15 4LG
Tel: 0151-733 1411 **Fax:** 0151-734 0831
Website: http://www.hss.com
Managers: A. White (District Mgr)
Immediate Holding Company: VULCAN SERVICE & SUPPLY COMPANY LIMITED
Registration no: 03080799 **Date established:** 1995
No.of Employees: 1 - 10 **Product Groups:** 46

Date of Accounts	Jul 08	Jul 07	Jul 06
Working Capital	1	464	-4
Fixed Assets	2m	405	179
Current Assets	650	2m	300
Current Liabilities	N/A	219	N/A

Huskisson Ltd

118 Brasenose Road, Liverpool, L20 8HT
Tel: 0151-922 2761 **Fax:** 0151-922 2762
E-mail: admin@huskissonltd.co.uk
Website: http://www.huskissonltd.co.uk
Directors: B. Davies (MD)
Immediate Holding Company: HUSKISSON LIMITED
Registration no: 01422826 **Date established:** 1979
No.of Employees: 1 - 10 **Product Groups:** 36, 39, 41, 43, 45, 46, 47, 67, 72, 83

Date of Accounts	Oct 11	Oct 10	Oct 09
Working Capital	476	485	475
Fixed Assets	310	300	265
Current Assets	728	673	770

Hydraulic Engineering Services Ltd

22 Dublin Street, Liverpool, L3 7DT
Tel: 0151-207 3339 **Fax:** 0151-207 7634
E-mail: sales@hesliverpool.co.uk
Website: http://www.hesliverpool.co.uk
Directors: I. Cantrill (Dir)
Immediate Holding Company: HYDRAULIC ENGINEERING SERVICES LIMITED
Registration no: NI027224 **VAT No.:** GB 678 2010 36
Date established: 1993 **Turnover:** £250,000 - £500,000
No.of Employees: 1 - 10 **Product Groups:** 25, 29, 30, 32, 33, 35, 36, 40

Date of Accounts	Feb 11	Feb 10	Feb 08
Working Capital	4	5	24
Fixed Assets	74	76	81
Current Assets	24	24	34
Current Liabilities	N/A	18	N/A

Immediate Transportation Co. Ltd

Ground Floor St Nicholas House Old Churchyard, Liverpool, L2 8TX
Tel: 0151-227 4521 **Fax:** 0151-236 8036
E-mail: liverpool@itcoltd.com
Website: http://www.immediatetransport.com
Directors: G. Brady (Dir)
Immediate Holding Company: WALTONS INSURANCE BROKERS LIMITED
Registration no: 03671217 **Date established:** 1998 **Turnover:** £5m - £10m
No.of Employees: 1 - 10 **Product Groups:** 76

Date of Accounts	Nov 11	Nov 10	Nov 09
Working Capital	-15	-10	41
Fixed Assets	29	40	39
Current Assets	237	209	376
Current Liabilities	164	120	200

Impact Control Systems Ltd

9 Tapton Way, Liverpool, L13 1DA
Tel: 0151-254 2658 **Fax:** 0151-254 2659
E-mail: sales@impactcontrols.co.uk
Website: http://www.impactcontrols.co.uk
Directors: G. Price (MD)
Immediate Holding Company: IMPACT CONTROL SYSTEMS LIMITED
Registration no: 02654941 **Date established:** 1991
No.of Employees: 11 - 20 **Product Groups:** 38, 42, 52, 67, 84

Date of Accounts	Dec 11	Dec 10	Dec 09
Sales Turnover	N/A	5m	5m
Pre Tax Profit/Loss	N/A	305	389
Working Capital	329	289	386
Fixed Assets	35	28	14
Current Assets	2m	2m	1m
Current Liabilities	N/A	191	185

Industrial & Rubber Supplies Ltd

184 Smithdown Road, Liverpool, L15 3JR
Tel: 0151-733 7859 **Fax:** 0151-733 4980
E-mail: indrub@talk21.com
Directors: A. Clark (MD), D. Clark (Fin)
Immediate Holding Company: INDUSTRIAL & RUBBER (SUPPLIES) LIMITED
Registration no: 00731124 **VAT No.:** GB 163 7560 53
Date established: 1962 **Turnover:** Up to £250,000
No.of Employees: 1 - 10 **Product Groups:** 30, 37

Date of Accounts	Jul 07	Jul 06
Sales Turnover	217	1994
Pre Tax Profit/Loss	4	-11
Working Capital	12	8
Current Assets	55	46
Current Liabilities	44	38
Total Share Capital	5	5
ROCE% (Return on Capital Employed)	30.3	-134.9
ROT% (Return on Turnover)	1.7	-0.6

Industrial Cleaning Supplies Liverpool Ltd

Hygiene House 7-29 Brasenose Road, Liverpool, L20 8HL
Tel: 0151-922 2000 **Fax:** 0151-922 3733
E-mail: office@icsliverpool.co.uk
Website: http://www.icsliverpool.co.uk
Bank(s): Barclays
Directors: M. Dodgson (MD)
Immediate Holding Company: INDUSTRIAL CLEANING SUPPLIES(LIVERPOOL)LIMITED
Registration no: 00859411 **VAT No.:** GB 163 6738 42
Date established: 1965 **Turnover:** £2m - £5m **No.of Employees:** 11 - 20
Product Groups: 40, 45, 66

Date of Accounts	Apr 12	Apr 11	Apr 10
Working Capital	263	228	513
Fixed Assets	642	661	679
Current Assets	713	748	797

Instem LSS

Stanley Hall Edmund Street, Liverpool, L3 9NG
Tel: 0151-224 7700 **Fax:** 01785-825625
E-mail: info@instem.com
Website: http://www.instem.com
Directors: J. Mclouchlan (Fin), P. Reason (MD)
Managers: J. McNamee (Mktg Serv Mgr), H. Powell (I.T. Exec), H. Prosser (Personnel), N. Donaldson (Sales Prom)
Immediate Holding Company: ART AIM DESIGNS LIMITED
Registration no: 02722687 **Date established:** 1992 **Turnover:** £2m - £5m
No.of Employees: 51 - 100 **Product Groups:** 44

Date of Accounts	Jan 12	Jan 11	Jan 07
Working Capital	115	119	128
Fixed Assets	6	8	24
Current Assets	167	160	183

Instruments To Industry Ltd

Woodward Road Knowsley Industrial Park North, Knowsley Industrial Park, Liverpool, L33 7UZ
Tel: 0151-546 4943 **Fax:** 0151-548 6262
E-mail: sales@itiuk.com
Website: http://www.itiuk.com

see next page

Instruments To Industry Ltd - Cont'd

Directors: A. Halford (Co Sec), J. Murray (MD)
Ultimate Holding Company: PRECISION 21 LIMITED
Immediate Holding Company: INSTRUMENTS TO INDUSTRY LIMITED
Registration no: 02076612 **Date established:** 1986
Turnover: £500,000 - £1m **No.of Employees:** 11 - 20 **Product Groups:** 38

Date of Accounts	Nov 11	Nov 10	Nov 09
Working Capital	54	38	13
Fixed Assets	106	109	102
Current Assets	348	368	289

Intaglobe Ltd

52-56 Islington, Liverpool, L3 8LG
Tel: 0151-207 4102 **Fax:** 0151-298 1902
Directors: D. Batty (MD)
Immediate Holding Company: INTAGLOBE LIMITED
Registration no: 01819830 **Date established:** 1984
No.of Employees: 1 - 10 **Product Groups:** 22, 24, 49

Date of Accounts	Jun 11	Jun 09	Jun 08
Working Capital	-4	16	86
Fixed Assets	1	N/A	N/A
Current Assets	67	89	170

Interfit Ltd

Unit 7 Brickfields, Liverpool, L36 6HY
Tel: 0151-481 4500 **Fax:** 0151- 4814501
Website: http://www.interfit-uk.com
Directors: D. Pearson (MD), P. Perry (Sales), P. Morey (Dir)
Managers: T. Gallagher (Sales Prom Mgr), S. Evans (District Mgr)
Ultimate Holding Company: TRELLEBORG AB (SWEDEN)
Immediate Holding Company: INTERFIT LIMITED
Registration no: 04340401 **Date established:** 2001
Turnover: £75m - £125m **No.of Employees:** 1 - 10 **Product Groups:** 29, 68

Date of Accounts	Dec 10	Dec 09	Dec 08
Sales Turnover	10m	12m	14m
Pre Tax Profit/Loss	906	60	28
Working Capital	446	-398	-625
Fixed Assets	597	551	719
Current Assets	4m	5m	4m
Current Liabilities	541	565	610

Ioma Clothing Co. Ltd

Woodend Avenue Speke, Liverpool, L24 9WF
Tel: 0151-448 9000 **Fax:** 0151-448 9009
E-mail: sales@iomaclothing.co.uk
Website: http://www.iomaclothing.co.uk
Bank(s): National Westminster Bank Plc
Directors: A. Thomas (Sales & Mktg), C. Burton (Comm), E. Levinson (MD)
Managers: E. Bowden (Buyer)
Immediate Holding Company: IOMA CLOTHING COMPANY LIMITED
Registration no: 00505191 **VAT No.:** GB 163 4209 80
Date established: 1952 **Turnover:** £2m - £5m **No.of Employees:** 21 - 50
Product Groups: 24, 49, 63

Date of Accounts	Dec 11	Dec 10	Dec 09
Working Capital	574	460	411
Fixed Assets	903	918	915
Current Assets	962	982	792

Iride Global Ltd

Iride House 168 Woolfall Heath Avenue, Liverpool, L36 3TR
Tel: 0151-480 2233 **Fax:** 0151-480 2233
E-mail: info@irideglobal.com
Website: http://www.irideglobal.com
Directors: F. Auriemma (Dir)
Immediate Holding Company: IRIDE GLOBAL LIMITED
Registration no: 04710292 **Date established:** 2003
Turnover: £500,000 - £1m **No.of Employees:** 1 - 10 **Product Groups:** 61, 76, 81, 82

Date of Accounts	Mar 09	Apr 11	Apr 10
Working Capital	8	146	12
Fixed Assets	14	12	16
Current Assets	93	146	96

J B Treasure & Co. Ltd

36 Vauxhall Road, Liverpool, L3 6DN
Tel: 0151-236 8314 **Fax:** 0151-236 2804
E-mail: treasurejb@aol.com
Website: http://www.jbtreasure.co.uk
Bank(s): H S B C, Dale St
Directors: S. Elliott (Fin)
Ultimate Holding Company: THOUGHTFUL GLANCE LIMITED
Immediate Holding Company: J.B.TREASURE AND COMPANY,LIMITED
Registration no: 00136602 **VAT No.:** GB 164 0423 92
Date established: 2014 **Turnover:** £1m - £2m **No.of Employees:** 11 - 20
Product Groups: 33, 38, 48

Date of Accounts	Mar 11	Mar 10	Mar 09
Working Capital	109	136	1m
Fixed Assets	291	324	350
Current Assets	270	307	1m

J E T Industrial Services

13 Rosemary Lane, Liverpool, L37 3HA
Tel: 01704-872972 **Fax:** 01704-833986
E-mail: jetind@blueyonder.co.uk
Website: http://www.toyo-mm.co.jp
Directors: J. Thomas (Prop)
Date established: 1986 **Turnover:** £250,000 - £500,000
No.of Employees: 1 - 10 **Product Groups:** 42, 46, 48, 67, 85

The Jacobs Bakery Ltd

Long Lane Aintree, Walton, Liverpool, L9 7BQ
Tel: 0151-525 3661 **Fax:** 0151-530 3444
E-mail: info@danone.co.uk
Website: http://www.unitedbiscuits.co.uk
Bank(s): National Westminster Bank Plc
Directors: L. Kinsley (Prop)
Ultimate Holding Company: UNITED BISCUITS LUXCO SCA (LUXEMBOURG)
Immediate Holding Company: THE JACOB'S BAKERY LIMITED
Registration no: 02322741 **VAT No.:** GB 533 3362 66
Date established: 1988 **Turnover:** £125m - £250m
No.of Employees: 501 - 1000 **Product Groups:** 20

Date of Accounts	Jan 09	Jan 10
Working Capital	33	33m
Current Assets	33	33m

Joloda Hydraroll Ltd

51 Speke Road Garston, Liverpool, L19 2NY
Tel: 0151-427 8954 **Fax:** 0151-427 1393
E-mail: info@joloda.com
Website: http://www.joloda.com
Bank(s): Bank of Scotland
Directors: W. Kordel (MD)
Immediate Holding Company: HYDRAROLL LIMITED
Registration no: 04432156 **Date established:** 2002 **Turnover:** £5m - £10m
No.of Employees: 51 - 100 **Product Groups:** 39, 45

A T Juniper Liverpool Ltd

Marshalls Works 5-17 Bleasdale Road, Liverpool, L18 5JB
Tel: 0151-733 1553 **Fax:** 0151-734 3166
E-mail: sales@juniper-liverpool.com
Website: http://www.juniper-liverpool.com
Bank(s): HSBC Bank plc
Directors: C. Marshall (Dir)
Managers: C. Stapleton (Chief Acct), P. Burbridge (Mktg Serv Mgr)
Immediate Holding Company: A.T. JUNIPER (LIVERPOOL) LIMITED
Registration no: 01406834 **VAT No.:** GB 319 7308 46
Date established: 1978 **Turnover:** £250,000 - £500,000
No.of Employees: 11 - 20 **Product Groups:** 39

Date of Accounts	Dec 11	Dec 10	Dec 09
Working Capital	2m	1m	914
Fixed Assets	74	118	98
Current Assets	2m	1m	1m

K M C Packaging & Products Ltd

Unit 10 High Grove Business Centre Knowsley Industrial Park, Liverpool, L33 7SE
Tel: 0151-548 6111
E-mail: sales@kmcpackaging.co.uk
Website: http://www.kmcpackaging.co.uk
Directors: M. Jefferies (MD)
Immediate Holding Company: VPFS NATIONWIDE LIMITED
Registration no: 06450417 **Date established:** 2011
Turnover: Up to £250,000 **No.of Employees:** 1 - 10 **Product Groups:** 27, 30, 66

Kenland Overseas Ltd

31 Roby Road Huyton, Liverpool, L36 4HA
Tel: 0151-443 0101 **Fax:** 0151-443 0111
E-mail: sales@kenlan.co.uk
Website: http://www.kenlan.co.uk
Directors: A. Mclaren (Dir)
Immediate Holding Company: KENLAN TRADING LIMITED
Registration no: 02425944 **Date established:** 1989
Turnover: £250,000 - £500,000 **No.of Employees:** 1 - 10
Product Groups: 45, 48, 67, 75, 76

Date of Accounts	Apr 08	Apr 07	Apr 06
Sales Turnover	455	497	579
Pre Tax Profit/Loss	33	-77	5
Working Capital	21	14	87
Fixed Assets	31	35	39
Current Assets	126	183	226
Current Liabilities	8	10	8

Kent & Co Twines Ltd

Long Lane Walton, Liverpool, L9 7DE
Tel: 0151-525 1601 **Fax:** 0151-523 1410
E-mail: kenttwines@aol.com
Bank(s): Barclays
Directors: M. Hall (MD), C. Mortis (MD)
Immediate Holding Company: KENT & COMPANY (TWINES) LIMITED
Registration no: 00221303 **VAT No.:** GB 163 4260 80
Date established: 2027 **Turnover:** £1m - £2m **No.of Employees:** 11 - 20
Product Groups: 23, 63

Date of Accounts	Sep 11	Sep 10	Sep 09
Working Capital	687	682	482
Fixed Assets	26	25	26
Current Assets	687	682	699

Kier Group plc

Windward Drive Estuary Business Park, Speke, Liverpool, L24 8QR
Tel: 0151-448 5200 **Fax:** 0151-448 5210
E-mail: kn.liverpool@kier.co.uk
Website: http://www.kier.co.uk
Bank(s): National Westminster
Directors: J. French (Ch), L. Wilkinson (MD), M. Ashton (Dir)
Managers: D. Johnston (Mktg Serv Mgr), M. Green (Purch Mgr)
Immediate Holding Company: Kier Group P.L.C.
Registration no: 02708030 **Turnover:** £20m - £50m
No.of Employees: 101 - 250 **Product Groups:** 51

King Components Ltd

4 Atherton Road, Liverpool, L9 7EL
Tel: 0151-524 2744 **Fax:** 0151-523 3330
E-mail: enquiries@kingcomponents.co.uk
Website: http://www.kingcomponents.co.uk
Directors: R. King (Fin)
Immediate Holding Company: KING COMPONENTS LIMITED
Registration no: 03750873 **Date established:** 1999
No.of Employees: 1 - 10 **Product Groups:** 40, 68

Date of Accounts	Mar 12	Mar 11	Mar 10
Working Capital	20	-12	-12
Fixed Assets	36	34	18
Current Assets	383	389	351

Kirkby Jig & Tool Co. Ltd

Bradman Road Knowsley Industrial Park, Liverpool, L33 7UR
Tel: 0151-546 2681
Website: http://www.kirkby-jig-tool.co.uk
Directors: K. Roche (MD)
Immediate Holding Company: KIRKBY JIG & TOOL COMPANY LIMITED
Registration no: 00547457 **Date established:** 1955
Turnover: £500,000 - £1m **No.of Employees:** 1 - 10 **Product Groups:** 46, 48

Date of Accounts	Dec 11	Dec 10	Dec 09
Working Capital	40	43	42
Fixed Assets	176	160	168
Current Assets	125	102	101

T.P. (Kirkby) Ltd

57 Admin Road Knowsley Industrial Park, Liverpool, L33 7TX
Tel: 0151-546 6232 **Fax:** 0151-549 1477
E-mail: sales@tpfay.co.uk
Website: http://www.tpfay.co.uk
Registration no: 01380853 **VAT No.:** GB 166 3265 57
Date established: 1976 **No.of Employees:** 1 - 10 **Product Groups:** 37, 38, 40, 67

Knowsley Instrument Services Ltd

Lodge Works Ashcroft Road, Knowsley Industrial Park, Liverpool, L33 7TW
Tel: 0151-548 8099 **Fax:** 0151-548 6599
E-mail: sales@kis-liverpool.co.uk
Website: http://www.kis-liverpool.co.uk
Bank(s): HSBC Bank plc
Directors: D. Sumpter (Dir)
Managers: S. Fowell (Ops Mgr), A. Malaki (Buyer), M. Houlton (Chief Mgr)
Immediate Holding Company: Enovegen (UK) Ltd
Registration no: 01774757 **VAT No.:** GB 387 2511 37
Date established: 1983 **Turnover:** £1m - £2m **No.of Employees:** 11 - 20
Product Groups: 38

Date of Accounts	Dec 11	Dec 10	Dec 09
Working Capital	-12	48	107
Fixed Assets	324	326	334
Current Assets	205	247	215

Knowsley Metals

13c Newstet Road Knowsley Industrial Park, Liverpool, L33 7TJ
Tel: 0151-546 3786 **Fax:** 0151-549 2776
Directors: D. Bailey (Dir)
Date established: 1982 **No.of Employees:** 1 - 10 **Product Groups:** 35

Knowsley Roller Shutters

Unit 3 Cusson Road, Knowsley Industrial Park, Liverpool, L33 7BY
Tel: 0151-546 1385 **Fax:** 0151-546 1385
E-mail: adavies.krs@btconnect.com
Website: http://www.knowsleyrollershutters.co.uk
Directors: A. Davies (Ptnr)
Date established: 1992 **No.of Employees:** 1 - 10 **Product Groups:** 26, 35

Kuehne & Nagel UK Ltd

Port of Liverpool Building Pier Head, Liverpool, L3 1BY
Tel: 0151-243 5000 **Fax:** 0151-243 5001
E-mail: morreen.owens@kuehne-nagel.com
Website: http://www.kuehne-nagel.com
Managers: B. Owens (District Mgr)
Ultimate Holding Company: KUEHNE & NAGEL INTERNATIONAL AG (SWITZERLAND)
Immediate Holding Company: KUEHNE + NAGEL (UK) LIMITED
Registration no: 01463105 **VAT No.:** GB 584 6403 22
Date established: 1979 **Turnover:** £500,000 - £1m
No.of Employees: 21 - 50 **Product Groups:** 76

Date of Accounts	Dec 11	Dec 10	Dec 09
Sales Turnover	958m	948m	833m
Pre Tax Profit/Loss	22m	27m	15m
Working Capital	20m	18m	16m
Fixed Assets	17m	12m	18m
Current Assets	175m	177m	148m
Current Liabilities	68m	73m	74m

L E C Liverpool Ltd

L E C House Picton Road, Wavertree, Liverpool, L15 4LH
Tel: 0151-734 1411 **Fax:** 0151-734 4054
E-mail: sales@insette.com
Website: http://www.insette.com
Bank(s): Nat West
Directors: L. Blackhurst (Co Sec), S. Daly (MD), S. Daly (MD)
Managers: B. Lewis, D. Dwyer (Sales Admin)
Immediate Holding Company: L.E.C.(L POOL) LIMITED
Registration no: 01256061 **VAT No.:** GB 166 3941 43
Date established: 1976 **Turnover:** £5m - £10m **No.of Employees:** 21 - 50
Product Groups: 32, 35

Date of Accounts	Mar 11	Mar 10	Mar 09
Sales Turnover	9m	9m	N/A
Pre Tax Profit/Loss	-44	924	105
Working Capital	836	1m	731
Fixed Assets	2m	2m	2m
Current Assets	3m	3m	3m
Current Liabilities	841	754	1m

L G S A Marine

67-83 Mariners House Queens Dock Commercial Centre Norfolk S, Liverpool, L1 0BG
Tel: 0151-707 2233 **Fax:** 0151-707 2170
E-mail: liverpool@lgsamarine.co.uk
Website: http://www.lgsamarine.co.uk
Managers: A. Gelling (Mgr)
Immediate Holding Company: NEPTUNE SHIPPING (NORTHERN) LIMITED
Registration no: 00015147 **VAT No.:** GB 164 6020 84
Date established: 1991 **Turnover:** £500,000 - £1m
No.of Employees: 1 - 10 **Product Groups:** 74

Date of Accounts	Feb 11	Feb 10	Feb 09
Working Capital	-12	-16	-9
Fixed Assets	32	43	18
Current Assets	113	128	104

L K Valves & Controls Ltd

Unit 6 Arbour Place Arbour Lane, Kirkby, Liverpool, L33 7XG
Tel: 0151-548 3300 **Fax:** 0151-548 3311
E-mail: sales@lkvalvesandcontrols.co.uk
Website: http://www.lkvalvesandcontrols.co.uk
Directors: A. Wareing (Co Sec), C. Evans (Dir)
Immediate Holding Company: LK VALVES & CONTROLS LIMITED
Registration no: 04395646 **Date established:** 2002
No.of Employees: 1 - 10 **Product Groups:** 36, 37, 38

Date of Accounts	Mar 12	Mar 11	Mar 10
Working Capital	601	531	597
Fixed Assets	7	6	12
Current Assets	987	876	922

La Furnitura, Ltd.

Formations House 42, Crosby Road North Crosby, Liverpool, L22 4QQ
Tel: 020-8123 7263 **Fax:** 020-8181 7869
E-mail: info@lafurnitura.com
Website: http://lafurnitura.com
Directors: L. Skonnord (Dir)
Managers: T. Indriaty (Admin Off)
Registration no: 06134907 **Date established:** 2006
No.of Employees: 1 - 10 **Product Groups:** 26, 63

Landlife Ltd
Court Hey Park, Liverpool, L16 3NA
Tel: 0151-737 1819 **Fax:** 0151-737 1820
E-mail: jpell@landlife.org.uk
Website: http://www.landlife.org.uk
Managers: G. Watson (Fin Mgr), J. Pell (Mktg Serv Mgr)
Immediate Holding Company: LANDLIFE
Registration no: 01838004 **VAT No.:** GB 548 4057 29
Date established: 1984 **Turnover:** £500,000 - £1m
No.of Employees: 1 - 10 **Product Groups:** 62

Date of Accounts	Mar 11	Mar 10	Mar 09
Sales Turnover	606	768	831
Pre Tax Profit/Loss	-28	-92	-65
Working Capital	232	211	239
Fixed Assets	2m	2m	2m
Current Assets	308	276	320
Current Liabilities	41	22	23

L C W
56 Norfolk Street, Liverpool, L1 0BE
Tel: 0151-709 7034 **Fax:** 0151-708 6022
Website: http://www.lcw-underlay.co.uk
Directors: J. Birch (MD), J. Birch (Prop), S. Birch (Dir)
No.of Employees: 1 - 10 **Product Groups:** 23, 29, 40, 63

Leeming Murphy Fabrications Ltd
Bankhall Works Juniper Street, Liverpool, L20 8EL
Tel: 0151-922 7019 **Fax:** 0151-922 0795
Directors: A. Leeming (Ptnr), C. Murphy (Fin)
Immediate Holding Company: LEEMING MURPHY PROPERTIES LIMITED
Registration no: 01871803 **VAT No.:** GB 548 6205 30
Date established: 1984 **Turnover:** £250,000 - £500,000
No.of Employees: 1 - 10 **Product Groups:** 39

Date of Accounts	Sep 11	Sep 10	Sep 09
Working Capital	18	7	8
Fixed Assets	252	296	130
Current Assets	45	38	28

Lewis & Raby Ltd
Birchill Road Knowsley Industrial Park, Liverpool, L33 7TG
Tel: 0151-546 2882 **Fax:** 0151-546 7877
E-mail: enquiries@lewisandraby.co.uk
Website: http://www.lewisandraby.co.uk
Bank(s): Lloyds, Huyton
Directors: T. Raby (MD)
Managers: M. Harrison
Immediate Holding Company: LEWIS & RABY (ENGINEERS) LIMITED
Registration no: 00724914 **VAT No.:** GB 163 4297 57
Date established: 1962 **Turnover:** £2m - £5m **No.of Employees:** 21 - 50
Product Groups: 40, 42, 45

Date of Accounts	Sep 11	Sep 10	Sep 09
Working Capital	774	595	538
Fixed Assets	462	400	453
Current Assets	1m	1m	1m

Leyholdings Export & Import Agents
64 Bridgewater Street, Liverpool, L1 0AY
Tel: 0151-709 2576 **Fax:** 0151-709 0731
E-mail: sales@leyholdings.com
Website: http://www.leyholdings.com
Bank(s): National Westminster Bank Plc
Directors: M. Wealleans (Dir), M. Whealleans (Jt MD), S. Thurgood (Fin), S. Fairgood (Jt MD)
Managers: K. Tremarco (Accounts)
Immediate Holding Company: LEY HOLDINGS LIMITED
Registration no: 04191494 **VAT No.:** GB 164 0028 01
Date established: 2001 **Turnover:** £500,000 - £1m
No.of Employees: 11 - 20 **Product Groups:** 29

Date of Accounts	Jun 11	Jun 10	Jun 09
Working Capital	-922	-1m	-1m
Fixed Assets	1m	1m	2m
Current Assets	N/A	8	10

Littlewoods Home Shopping Orders & Enquiries
Skyways House Speke Road, Speke, Liverpool, L70 1AB
Tel: 08448-228000 **Fax:** 0870-263 1701
Website: http://www.littlewoods.com
Directors: P. Jones (Ch)
Ultimate Holding Company: LW CORPORATION LIMITED (JERSEY)
Immediate Holding Company: LITTLEWOODS LIMITED
Registration no: 00262152 **VAT No.:** GB 163 7696 28
Date established: 1932 **Turnover:** Up to £250,000
No.of Employees: 1 - 10 **Product Groups:** 63, 65, 66

Date of Accounts	Jun 11	Apr 10	Apr 09
Sales Turnover	N/A	N/A	1m
Working Capital	-758m	-638m	-568m
Fixed Assets	1208m	1089m	1019m

Liver Grease Oil & Chemical Company Ltd
11 Norfolk Street, Liverpool, L1 0BE
Tel: 0151-709 7494 **Fax:** 0151-709 3774
E-mail: info@livergrease.co.uk
Website: http://www.livergrease.co.uk
Directors: C. Wylie (MD)
Immediate Holding Company: LIVER GREASE OIL AND CHEMICAL COMPANY LIMITED
Registration no: 00093470 **Date established:** 1809
Turnover: Up to £250,000 **No.of Employees:** 1 - 10 **Product Groups:** 23, 31, 42

Date of Accounts	Sep 11	Sep 10	Sep 09
Working Capital	39	32	23
Fixed Assets	11	11	12
Current Assets	46	54	47

Liverpool Chamber Of Commerce
1 Old Hall Street, Liverpool, L3 9HG
Tel: 0151-227 1234 **Fax:** 0151-236 0121
E-mail: jack.stopforth@liverpoolchamber.org.uk
Website: http://www.liverpoolchamber.org.uk
Directors: J. Stopforth (Grp Chief Exec)
Immediate Holding Company: LIVERPOOL CHAMBER OF COMMERCE C.I.C.
Registration no: 07159767 **Date established:** 2010 **Turnover:** £1m - £2m
No.of Employees: 21 - 50 **Product Groups:** 80

Date of Accounts	Mar 11
Sales Turnover	7m
Pre Tax Profit/Loss	283
Working Capital	136
Fixed Assets	577
Current Assets	2m
Current Liabilities	1m

Liverpool Daily Post & Echo
PO Box 48, Liverpool, L69 3EB
Tel: 0151-227 2000 **Fax:** 0151-236 4682
E-mail: hr@liverpool.com
Website: http://www.icliverpool.co.uk
Directors: R. Grant (Pers), W. Butcher (MD), R. Grant (Pers), L. Ball (Fin), A. McGreevey (Fin), M. Eld (Mkt Research)
Managers: L. Jato (I.T. Exec), C. Wood, D. McKenzie (Tech Serv Mgr)
Ultimate Holding Company: TRINITY INTERNATIONAL HOLDINGS PLC
Immediate Holding Company: TRINITY INTERNATIONAL HOLDINGS P.L.C.
Registration no: 00127699 **Turnover:** £10m - £20m
No.of Employees: 251 - 500 **Product Groups:** 28

Liverpool Football Club Ticket Bookings
Anfield Road, Liverpool, L4 0TH
Tel: 08431-705555 **Fax:** 0151-260 8813
Website: http://www.liverpoolfc.tv
Directors: I. Ayre (MD)
Ultimate Holding Company: KOP INVESTMENTS LLC (USA)
Immediate Holding Company: THE LIVERPOOL FOOTBALL CLUB AND ATHLETIC GROUNDS LIMITED
Registration no: 00035668 **Date established:** 1992
Turnover: £125m - £250m **No.of Employees:** 1 - 10 **Product Groups:** 87

Date of Accounts	Jul 11	Jul 10	Jul 09
Sales Turnover	184m	185m	177m
Pre Tax Profit/Loss	-49m	-20m	-16m
Working Capital	-116m	-166m	-167m
Fixed Assets	205m	191m	211m
Current Assets	69m	61m	60m
Current Liabilities	66m	58m	54m

Liverpool Roller Shutters Ltd
36 Bedford Road, Liverpool, L4 5PU
Tel: 0151-525 5555
E-mail: dave.lambert@liverpoolshutter.f9.co.uk
Website: http://www.liverpoolrollershutters.co.uk
Directors: D. Lambert (MD)
Immediate Holding Company: LIVERPOOL ROLLER SHUTTERS LIMITED
Registration no: 04385912 **Date established:** 2002
No.of Employees: 1 - 10 **Product Groups:** 26, 35

Date of Accounts	Mar 12	Mar 11	Mar 10
Working Capital	-3	-0	2
Fixed Assets	7	8	11
Current Assets	47	50	46

Locker Freight Ltd
Hale View Road, Liverpool, L36 6DD
Tel: 0151-480 8922 **Fax:** 0151-480 3744
E-mail: general@locker-freight.co.uk
Website: http://www.locker-freight.co.uk
Bank(s): Lloyds TSB
Directors: S. Locker (Prop)
Ultimate Holding Company: LOCKER FREIGHT (HOLDINGS) LIMITED
Immediate Holding Company: LOCKER FREIGHT (HOLDINGS) LIMITED
Registration no: 06777103 **VAT No.:** GB 164 4969 28
Date established: 2008 **No.of Employees:** 21 - 50 **Product Groups:** 76

Date of Accounts	Feb 11	Feb 10
Working Capital	68	73
Fixed Assets	933	952
Current Assets	174	118

M A K Drums & Containers
Unit 16 Garston Industrial Estate Blackburne Street, Liverpool, L19 8JB
Tel: 0151-494 3331 **Fax:** 0151-494 9580
E-mail: sales@makdrums.co.uk
Website: http://www.makdrums.co.uk
Directors: P. Kewley (Prop)
Date established: 2000 **No.of Employees:** 1 - 10 **Product Groups:** 35, 36, 45

M P E Ltd
Hammond Road Knowsley Industrial Park, Liverpool, L33 7UL
Tel: 0151-632 9100 **Fax:** 0151-632 9112
E-mail: sales@mpe.co.uk
Website: http://www.mpe.co.uk
Bank(s): Barclays
Directors: A. Nalborczyk (Tech Serv), D. Seabury (MD)
Managers: J. Bayliss (Fin Mgr), P. Currie
Immediate Holding Company: MPE LIMITED
Registration no: 03291415 **VAT No.:** GB 325 2428 78
Date established: 1996 **Turnover:** £2m - £5m **No.of Employees:** 21 - 50
Product Groups: 37, 42

Date of Accounts	Jan 12	Jan 11	Jan 10
Working Capital	529	294	374
Fixed Assets	78	65	70
Current Assets	1m	899	1m

A F & D Mackay Ltd
29-35 Moor Lane Crosby, Liverpool, L23 2SF
Tel: 0151-924 2224 **Fax:** 0151-931 4956
E-mail: sales@afdmackay.co.uk
Website: http://www.afdmackay.co.uk
Directors: W. Boulton (Dir), B. Ormrod (Fin), M. Bolton (MD)
Managers: P. Radcliff (I.T. Exec), B. Ormrod (Fin Mgr)
Ultimate Holding Company: HIDEJET LIMITED
Immediate Holding Company: A.F. & D. MACKAY LIMITED
Registration no: 00194663 **VAT No.:** GB 163 5004 93
Date established: 1923 **Turnover:** £5m - £10m **No.of Employees:** 1 - 10
Product Groups: 66, 76

Date of Accounts	Apr 11	Apr 10	Apr 09
Sales Turnover	8m	9m	N/A
Pre Tax Profit/Loss	-44	6	N/A
Working Capital	478	532	527
Fixed Assets	38	26	37
Current Assets	1m	1m	2m
Current Liabilities	31	37	N/A

Maersk Line
The Plaza 100 Old Hall Street, Liverpool, L3 9QJ
Tel: 0844-264 1263 **Fax:** 0844-264 1259
E-mail: gbrsalins@maersk.com
Website: http://www.maerskline.com
Directors: I. Kruse (Dir), J. Baker (Dir)
Ultimate Holding Company: A P Moller Group
Immediate Holding Company: The Maersk Co. Ltd
Registration no: 00493147 **VAT No.:** GB 646 0823 38
Date established: 1951 **Turnover:** £125m - £250m
No.of Employees: 101 - 250 **Product Groups:** 72, 74, 76

Maplin Electronics Ltd
355 Edge Lane Fairfield, Liverpool, L7 9LG
Tel: 08432-277317 **Fax:** 0151-230 0365
E-mail: customercare@maplin.co.uk
Website: http://www.maplin.co.uk
Managers: G. Powell (Mgr)
Ultimate Holding Company: MONTAGU PRIVATE EQUITY LLP
Immediate Holding Company: MAPLIN ELECTRONICS LIMITED
Registration no: 01264385 **Date established:** 1976
Turnover: £125m - £250m **No.of Employees:** 1 - 10 **Product Groups:** 37, 61

Date of Accounts	Dec 11	Dec 08	Dec 09
Sales Turnover	205m	204m	204m
Pre Tax Profit/Loss	25m	32m	35m
Working Capital	118m	49m	75m
Fixed Assets	27m	28m	28m
Current Assets	207m	108m	142m
Current Liabilities	78m	51m	59m

Marine Specialised Technology Ltd
Unit 2 Atlantic Way, Brunswick Business Park, Liverpool, L3 4BE
Tel: 0151-708 4112 **Fax:** 0151-708 4113
E-mail: sales@mstltd.com
Website: http://www.mstltd.com
Directors: B. Kerfoot (MD), P. Hilbert (Sales), P. Hilbert (Sales)
Managers: S. Blake (Purch Mgr), J. Pownall
Immediate Holding Company: MARINE SPECIALISED TECHNOLOGY LIMITED
Registration no: 04390226 **Date established:** 2002 **Turnover:** £5m - £10m
No.of Employees: 21 - 50 **Product Groups:** 29, 39

Date of Accounts	Sep 11	Sep 10	Sep 09
Sales Turnover	5m	5m	4m
Pre Tax Profit/Loss	459	311	122
Working Capital	71	73	228
Fixed Assets	966	919	703
Current Assets	6m	4m	3m
Current Liabilities	3m	646	803

Martin Electrical Services
11 Courthope Road, Liverpool, L4 9UN
Tel: 0151-286 3064 **Fax:** 0151-286 3064
E-mail: info@martinelectrical.co.uk
Website: http://www.martinelectrical.co.uk
Directors: M. Donegan (Prop)
No.of Employees: 1 - 10 **Product Groups:** 40, 52, 67

Massey Coldbeck Ltd
Stockpit Road Knowsley Industrial Park, Liverpool, L33 7TQ
Tel: 0151-546 9118 **Fax:** 0151-546 9234
E-mail: masseycoldbeck@btconnect.com
Website: http://www.massey-coldbeck.co.uk
Bank(s): Natwest
Managers: S. Meath, S. Morton (Chief Mgr)
Ultimate Holding Company: OSS GROUP LIMITED
Immediate Holding Company: MASSEY COLDBECK LIMITED
Registration no: 01512716 **VAT No.:** 165 9569 13 **Date established:** 1980
Turnover: £1m - £2m **No.of Employees:** 21 - 50 **Product Groups:** 48

Date of Accounts	Mar 11	Mar 10	Mar 09
Working Capital	632	524	520
Fixed Assets	99	128	163
Current Assets	1m	1m	1m

Maximum Lift Trucks Ltd
Unit 7 Capitol Trading Park Kirkby Bank Road, Knowsley Industrial Park, Liverpool, L33 7SY
Tel: 0151-546 9000 **Fax:** 0151-546 0909
Website: http://www.maxlift-trucks.co.uk
Directors: P. Turner (MD), R. Wilson (Fin)
Immediate Holding Company: MAXIMUM LIFT TRUCKS LIMITED
Registration no: 04153605 **Date established:** 2001
No.of Employees: 1 - 10 **Product Groups:** 35, 39, 45

Date of Accounts	Feb 08	Feb 11	Feb 10
Working Capital	-33	-11	-34
Fixed Assets	79	52	64
Current Assets	91	90	75
Current Liabilities	37	28	31

Meade King Robinson & Company Ltd
Office Suite 10 Tower Building 22 Water Street, Liverpool, L3 1BL
Tel: 0151-236 3191 **Fax:** 0151-236 4431
E-mail: sales@mkr.co.uk
Website: http://www.mkr.co.uk
Bank(s): Barclays
Directors: P. Tarleton (MD)
Immediate Holding Company: MEADE-KING,ROBINSON & COMPANY LIMITED
Registration no: 00146176 **Date established:** 2017
Turnover: £50m - £75m **No.of Employees:** 21 - 50 **Product Groups:** 66

Date of Accounts	Mar 12	Mar 11	Mar 10
Sales Turnover	60m	47m	29m
Pre Tax Profit/Loss	1m	928	991
Working Capital	3m	2m	2m
Fixed Assets	1m	1m	238
Current Assets	16m	15m	9m
Current Liabilities	6m	4m	3m

Meadows Fabrications
31a Sefton Lane Industrial Estate, Liverpool, L31 8BX
Tel: 0151-527 2712 **Fax:** 0151-527 2712
Directors: T. Watts (Prop)
Date established: 1992 **No.of Employees:** 1 - 10 **Product Groups:** 35

Mersey Docks & Harbour Co.
Maritime Centre Port of Liverpool, Liverpool, L21 1LA
Tel: 0151-949 6000 **Fax:** 0151-949 6338
E-mail: eric.leatherbarrow@merseydocks.co.uk
Website: http://www.merseydocks.co.uk
Directors: N. Lees (Co Sec), G. Hodgson (MD)
Managers: H. Sloane (Personnel), D. Leeson (Tech Serv Mgr), P. Sumner
Ultimate Holding Company: TOKENHOUSE LIMITED (ISLE OF MAN)
Immediate Holding Company: MERSEY DOCKS PROPERTY HOLDINGS LIMITED

see next page

Mersey Docks & Harbour Co. - Cont'd
Registration no: 02184084 **Date established:** 1987 **Turnover:** £1m - £2m
No.of Employees: 251 - 500 **Product Groups:** 35, 69, 71, 74, 77, 84

Date of Accounts	Mar 11	Mar 10	Mar 09
Sales Turnover	1m	2m	2m
Pre Tax Profit/Loss	487	2m	82m
Working Capital	43m	42m	40m
Fixed Assets	79m	81m	80m
Current Assets	61m	60m	59m
Current Liabilities	702	702	158

Mersey Forge
3-5 Seaforth Vale West, Liverpool, L21 3TP
Tel: 0151-293 3738 **Fax:** 0151-293 3738
Directors: S. Everington (Prop)
Immediate Holding Company: MERSEY FORGE LTD
Registration no: 06422456 **Date established:** 2007
No.of Employees: 1 - 10 **Product Groups:** 26, 35

Date of Accounts	Mar 12	Mar 11	Mar 10
Working Capital	54	49	6
Fixed Assets	11	15	20
Current Assets	76	87	61

Merseyrail Electrics
Rail House, Liverpool, L1 1JF
Tel: 0151-702 2071 **Fax:** 0151-702 2413
E-mail: mspaargaren@merseyrail.org
Website: http://www.merseyrail.org
Directors: M. Spaargaren (MD)
Immediate Holding Company: MERSEYRAIL ELECTRICS 2002 LIMITED
Registration no: 04356933 **Date established:** 2002
Turnover: £125m - £250m **No.of Employees:** 1 - 10 **Product Groups:** 72

Date of Accounts	Jan 10	Jan 11	Jan 12
Sales Turnover	124m	126m	132m
Pre Tax Profit/Loss	10m	11m	12m
Working Capital	-1m	-1m	-1m
Fixed Assets	11m	11m	11m
Current Assets	21m	21m	24m
Current Liabilities	9m	10m	14m

Merseyside Compressor Services Ltd
3 Atherton Road, Liverpool, L9 7EL
Tel: 0151-523 2160 **Fax:** 0151-523 2413
E-mail: mikefoley.mcs@tiscali.co.uk
Directors: M. Foley (MD)
Immediate Holding Company: MERSEYSIDE COMPRESSOR SERVICES LIMITED
Registration no: 03686505 **Date established:** 1998
No.of Employees: 1 - 10 **Product Groups:** 38, 40, 48, 67, 83

Date of Accounts	Jan 12	Jan 11	Jan 10
Working Capital	35	-5	-76
Fixed Assets	6	10	91
Current Assets	147	113	72

Merseyside Galvanising Ltd (Wedge Group Galvanizing)
Unit 10 Weaver Industrial Estate Blackburne Street, Liverpool, L19 8JA
Tel: 0151-427 1449 **Fax:** 0151-427 2690
E-mail: merseyside@wedge-galv.co.uk
Website: http://www.wedge-galv.co.uk
Bank(s): National Westminster Bank Plc
Directors: D. Lynam (Dir)
Ultimate Holding Company: B.E. WEDGE HOLDINGS LIMITED
Immediate Holding Company: MERSEYSIDE GALVANIZING LIMITED
Registration no: 01556126 **Date established:** 1981
No.of Employees: 21 - 50 **Product Groups:** 48

Date of Accounts	Mar 11	Mar 10	Mar 09
Pre Tax Profit/Loss	12	12	12
Current Assets	3	3	2
Current Liabilities	3	3	2

Merseyside Ornamental Forge Ltd
62 Upper Warwick Street, Liverpool, L8 5TP
Tel: 0151-709 5885 **Fax:** 0151-709 5885
Directors: B. Smith (Fin)
Immediate Holding Company: MERSEYSIDE ORNAMENTAL FORGE LIMITED
Registration no: 04468896 **Date established:** 2002
No.of Employees: 1 - 10 **Product Groups:** 26, 35

Date of Accounts	Jun 11	Jun 10	Jun 09
Working Capital	-12	-14	-15
Fixed Assets	17	23	18
Current Assets	27	42	32

Merseytravel
24 Hatton Garden, Liverpool, L3 2AN
Tel: 0151-227 5181 **Fax:** 0151-236 2457
Website: http://www.merseyferries.co.uk
Directors: N. Scales (MD), L. Outram (Co Sec), L. Outram (Fin), J. Barcley (Fin)
Ultimate Holding Company: MERSEYSIDE PASSENGER TRANSPORT SERVICES LIMITED
Immediate Holding Company: MERSEYTRAVEL LIMITED
Registration no: 02027686 **Date established:** 1986
Turnover: £10m - £20m **No.of Employees:** 251 - 500
Product Groups: 74, 81

Merseyside Satellite Consultants Ltd
Antenna House Atherton Road, Liverpool, L9 7EL
Tel: 0151-521 8000 **Fax:** 0151-525 3008
E-mail: sales@merseysat.co.uk
Website: http://www.merseysat.co.uk
Directors: P. Flaherty (Fin), A. Flaherty (MD)
Immediate Holding Company: MERSEYSIDE SATELLITE CONSULTANTS LIMITED
Registration no: 01853657 **VAT No.:** GB 387 3867 90
Date established: 1984 **Turnover:** £500,000 - £1m
No.of Employees: 1 - 10 **Product Groups:** 37

Date of Accounts	Oct 11	Oct 10	Oct 09
Working Capital	22	1	5
Fixed Assets	598	600	602
Current Assets	114	91	160

Metaloffcuts
Arcadia Works Sefton Lane, Liverpool, L31 8BU
Tel: 0151-526 4777 **Fax:** 05601-157793
E-mail: sales@metaloffcuts.co.uk
Website: http://www.metaloffcuts.co.uk
Directors: J. Rutter (Prop)
Ultimate Holding Company: YAKIRA GROUP LIMITED
Immediate Holding Company: POLLARDS INTERNATIONAL LIMITED
Registration no: 06456147 **Date established:** 1996
Turnover: £10m - £20m **No.of Employees:** 1 - 10 **Product Groups:** 34

The Millennium Fire Company Ltd
Bridge Industrial Estate Speke Hall Road, Liverpool, L24 9HB
Tel: 0151-448 0111 **Fax:** 0151-448 0084
Directors: M. Bialeck (Fin)
Immediate Holding Company: THE MILLENNIUM FIRE COMPANY LIMITED
Registration no: 03698814 **Date established:** 1999
No.of Employees: 1 - 10 **Product Groups:** 38, 42

Date of Accounts	Mar 12	Mar 11	Mar 10
Working Capital	120	90	94
Current Assets	159	123	125

Millford Grain Ltd
Seafield House Crosby Road North, Liverpool, L22 0LG
Tel: 0151-949 0904 **Fax:** 0151-949 0485
Directors: A. Groves (MD)
Ultimate Holding Company: MILLGRAIN LIMITED
Immediate Holding Company: MILLFORD GRAIN LIMITED
Registration no: 00400052 **VAT No.:** GB 137 9376 33
Date established: 1945 **Turnover:** £50m - £75m **No.of Employees:** 1 - 10
Product Groups: 82

Date of Accounts	Dec 11	Dec 10	Dec 09
Sales Turnover	85m	69m	69m
Pre Tax Profit/Loss	105	153	-162
Working Capital	714	1m	2m
Current Assets	2m	3m	3m
Current Liabilities	612	433	276

Mobile Mini Ltd
Triumph Trading Park Triumph Way, Liverpool, L24 9GQ
Tel: 0151-448 1338 **Fax:** 0151-448 1929
E-mail: cthomas@mobilemini.co.uk
Website: http://www.mobilemini.co.uk
Managers: C. Thomas (District Mgr)
Registration no: 04283040 **Turnover:** £10m - £20m
No.of Employees: 11 - 20 **Product Groups:** 26, 35, 36

Morbridge International Ltd
Cunard Building Water Street, Liverpool, L3 1DS
Tel: 0151-236 9421 **Fax:** 0151-236 3313
E-mail: enquiry@morbridgeinternational.com
Website: http://www.morbridgeinternational.com
Managers: J. Bibby (Mgr)
Immediate Holding Company: MORBRIDGE INTERNATIONAL LIMITED
Registration no: 01770470 **Date established:** 1983
Turnover: £250,000 - £500,000 **No.of Employees:** 1 - 10
Product Groups: 35, 45, 72, 76, 83

Date of Accounts	Mar 11	Mar 10	Mar 07
Working Capital	1m	2m	2m
Fixed Assets	2m	959	43
Current Assets	2m	5m	1m

N P S Packaging Services Ltd
Edwards Lane Industrial Estate Edwards Lane, Liverpool, L24 9HX
Tel: 0151-486 5799 **Fax:** 0151-486 0990
Directors: R. Hannah (Fin), J. Forster (Dir)
Immediate Holding Company: NPS PACKAGING SERVICES LIMITED
Registration no: 03699167 **Date established:** 1999
No.of Employees: 1 - 10 **Product Groups:** 38, 42

Date of Accounts	Dec 07	Dec 06	Dec 05
Working Capital	-3	-5	-3
Fixed Assets	7	7	8
Current Assets	97	118	99
Current Liabilities	100	123	102

Newfab Services
Newstet Road Knowsley Industrial Park, Liverpool, L33 7TJ
Tel: 0151-549 1044 **Fax:** 0151-549 1044
E-mail: sales@newfab.co.uk
Directors: J. Roberts (Dir)
Immediate Holding Company: PG TRUCK SALES LTD
Registration no: 01879630 **Date established:** 2012
Turnover: £75m - £125m **No.of Employees:** 1 - 10 **Product Groups:** 35

Date of Accounts	Dec 10	Dec 09	Dec 08
Sales Turnover	57m	62m	120m
Pre Tax Profit/Loss	970	-2m	-2m
Working Capital	2m	2m	5m
Fixed Assets	8m	8m	9m
Current Assets	14m	12m	27m
Current Liabilities	2m	3m	5m

Newtons Engineers & Steel Fabricators Ltd
122 South Street, Liverpool, L8 3TN
Tel: 0151-727 5050 **Fax:** 0151-727 5370
Directors: J. Newton (Dir)
Ultimate Holding Company: NEWTONS INDUSTRIES (LIVERPOOL) LIMITED
Immediate Holding Company: NEWTONS INDUSTRIES (LIVERPOOL) LIMITED
Registration no: 00847025 **VAT No.:** GB 164 2487 56
Date established: 1965 **No.of Employees:** 1 - 10 **Product Groups:** 39

Date of Accounts	Dec 11	Dec 10	Dec 09
Working Capital	637	360	390
Fixed Assets	455	455	455
Current Assets	643	369	402

Nightfreight (GB) Ltd
2 Redfern Street, Liverpool, L20 8JB
Tel: 0151-933 8832 **Fax:** 0151-922 3138
E-mail: depot04@nightfreight.co.uk
Website: http://www.nightfreightgb.co.uk
Bank(s): HSBC Bank plc
Managers: P. Bosman (Chief Mgr)
Ultimate Holding Company: PENGLAIS INVESTMENTS LIMITED
Immediate Holding Company: NIGHTFREIGHT (GB) LIMITED
Registration no: 02402927 **Date established:** 1989
Turnover: £10m - £20m **No.of Employees:** 11 - 20 **Product Groups:** 72

Date of Accounts	Nov 11	Nov 10	Nov 09
Sales Turnover	121m	118m	122m
Pre Tax Profit/Loss	-4m	-2m	1m
Working Capital	16m	16m	5m
Fixed Assets	11m	15m	17m
Current Assets	47m	47m	52m
Current Liabilities	14m	12m	11m

North West Holdings 2005 Ltd
Brookfield Centre Aintree, Liverpool, L9 7AS
Tel: 0151-521 5215 **Fax:** 0151-521 5216
Directors: I. Randall (MD)
Immediate Holding Company: SOCIAL HOUSING BUILDING AND MAINTENANCE LIMITED
Date established: 2009 **No.of Employees:** 1 - 10 **Product Groups:** 35, 45

North West Tea Service Ltd
Units 70-72 Parliment Business Park Commerce Way, Liverpool, L8 7BA
Tel: 0151-703 0044 **Fax:** 0151-703 0055
E-mail: northwestteas@btinternet.com
Website: http://www.northwestteas.co.uk
Directors: T. Farricker (Sales), T. Torrible (Sales)
Managers: L. McInerney (Admin Off)
Immediate Holding Company: NORTH WEST TEA SERVICE LIMITED
Registration no: 04719044 **Date established:** 2003
No.of Employees: 1 - 10 **Product Groups:** 62

Date of Accounts	Mar 08	Mar 07	Mar 06
Working Capital	256	149	24
Fixed Assets	29	37	31
Current Assets	573	352	166
Current Liabilities	317	203	142

O S S Group Ltd
Stockpit Road Knowsley Industrial Park, Liverpool, L33 7TQ
Tel: 0151-549 1434 **Fax:** 0151-549 1444
E-mail: amcnair@ossgroupltd.com
Website: http://www.ossgroupltd.com
Directors: A. Mcnair (MD)
Ultimate Holding Company: OSS ENVIRONMENTAL HOLDINGS LIMITED
Immediate Holding Company: OSS GROUP LIMITED
Registration no: 03835964 **Date established:** 1999
Turnover: £20m - £50m **No.of Employees:** 101 - 250 **Product Groups:** 31

Date of Accounts	Dec 11	Dec 10	Dec 09
Sales Turnover	25m	25m	20m
Pre Tax Profit/Loss	1m	2m	-341
Working Capital	10m	10m	9m
Fixed Assets	5m	4m	4m
Current Assets	14m	14m	13m
Current Liabilities	2m	2m	2m

O'Neill Medicalia Ltd
10 Percy Street, Liverpool, L8 7LU
Tel: 0151-708 5268 **Fax:** 0151-707 1314
E-mail: vincent@medicalia.co.uk
Website: http://www.medicali.co.uk
Directors: V. O"neill (Grp Chief Exec)
Immediate Holding Company: MEDICALIA LTD
Registration no: 05400178 **Date established:** 2005
No.of Employees: 1 - 10 **Product Groups:** 38, 52, 85

Orion Paints Ltd
Unit 22 Manor Complex Kirkby Bank Road, Knowsley Industrial Park, Liverpool, L33 7SY
Tel: 0151-548 6756 **Fax:** 0151-549 2300
E-mail: info@orionpaints.co.uk
Website: http://www.orionpaints.co.uk
Directors: A. Cowell (MD)
Immediate Holding Company: ORION PAINTS LIMITED
Registration no: 02342512 **VAT No.:** GB 483 7090 26
Date established: 1989 **Turnover:** £1m - £2m **No.of Employees:** 1 - 10
Product Groups: 32

Date of Accounts	Sep 11	Sep 10	Sep 09
Working Capital	225	222	213
Fixed Assets	12	15	12
Current Assets	438	465	470

John O'Rourke
53a Allerton Road Mossley Hill, Liverpool, L18 2DA
Tel: 0151-281 2096 **Fax:** 0151-281 5955
E-mail: johnorourke@wwmail.co.uk
Directors: J. O'rourke (MD)
Immediate Holding Company: PARKER CAIN ASSOCIATES LIMITED
Date established: 2009 **No.of Employees:** 1 - 10 **Product Groups:** 35

Date of Accounts	Jun 10
Working Capital	-1
Fixed Assets	1

Otis Ltd
Unit 1e & H Wavertree Technology Park, Liverpool, L7 9PF
Tel: 0151-472 1500 **Fax:** 0151-472 1520
E-mail: john.okeefe@otis.com
Website: http://www.otis.com
Managers: J. O'keefe (Mgr)
Ultimate Holding Company: UNITED TECHNOLOGIES CORP INC (USA)
Immediate Holding Company: OTIS LIMITED
Registration no: 00147366 **VAT No.:** GB 114 0876 90
Date established: 2017 **Turnover:** £2m - £5m **No.of Employees:** 51 - 100
Product Groups: 45, 84

Date of Accounts	Nov 11	Nov 10	Nov 09
Sales Turnover	186m	200m	237m
Pre Tax Profit/Loss	35m	48m	37m
Working Capital	199m	179m	153m
Fixed Assets	233m	233m	208m
Current Assets	254m	241m	217m
Current Liabilities	39m	43m	49m

P E R Engineering
134 Buckingham Road Maghull, Liverpool, L31 7DR
Tel: 0151-520 1157
Directors: P. Rotherham (Prop)
Date established: 1994 **No.of Employees:** 1 - 10 **Product Groups:** 46

P & F Signs
129 Milton Avenue, Liverpool, L14 6TF
Tel: 0151-480 8840 **Fax:** 0151-480 8840
E-mail: sales@pfsigns.com
Website: http://www.pfsigns.com
Directors: C. Haggen (Prop)
Date established: 1975 **Turnover:** £250,000 - £500,000
No.of Employees: 1 - 10 **Product Groups:** 27, 28, 30, 35, 37, 39, 40, 45, 49

P K Marine Freight Services Ltd
1 Perimeter Road Knowsley Industrial Park, Liverpool, L33 3AY
Tel: 0151-547 3822 **Fax:** 0151-548 0884
E-mail: iankirkham@pkmarine.co.uk
Website: http://www.pkmarine.co.uk
Bank(s): National Westminster
Directors: I. Kirkham (MD)
Immediate Holding Company: P.K.MARINE FREIGHT SERVICES LIMITED
Registration no: 00980867 **VAT No.:** GB 673 6658 91
Date established: 1970 **Turnover:** £1m - £2m **No.of Employees:** 11 - 20
Product Groups: 25, 35, 76

Date of Accounts	May 11	May 10	May 09
Working Capital	544	591	667
Fixed Assets	1m	1m	1m
Current Assets	764	839	941

Pal Pak Corrugated Ltd
Unit C Bridge Industrial Estate Speke Hall Road, Liverpool, L24 9HB
Tel: 0151-486 5020 **Fax:** 0151-486 6400
E-mail: wford100@hotmail.com
Directors: P. Tobin (Fin), W. Ford (MD)
Immediate Holding Company: PAL PAK CORRUGATED LIMITED
Registration no: 03060021 **Date established:** 1995
Turnover: £500,000 - £1m **No.of Employees:** 1 - 10 **Product Groups:** 27, 45

Date of Accounts	Feb 08	Aug 11	Aug 10
Working Capital	72	-12	-16
Fixed Assets	27	95	105
Current Assets	330	314	340

Palace Chemicals Ltd
Unit 49 Spindus Road Speke Hall Industrial Estate, Liverpool, L24 1YA
Tel: 0151-486 6101 **Fax:** 0151-448 1982
E-mail: sales@palacechemicals.co.uk
Website: http://www.palacechemicals.co.uk
Bank(s): HSBC
Directors: C. Sweeney (Co Sec)
Immediate Holding Company: HOBSTAR LIMITED
Registration no: 02721142 **VAT No.:** GB 618 6195 20
Date established: 1992 **Turnover:** £10m - £20m
No.of Employees: 21 - 50 **Product Groups:** 32

Palatine Credit Information
PO Box 311, Liverpool, L69 2RH
Tel: 0151-243 1320 **Fax:** 0151-243 1321
E-mail: chris@palatine.co.uk
Website: http://www.palentine.co.uk
Directors: C. Booth (MD)
Registration no: 04366395 **VAT No.:** GB 487 8388 69
Date established: 2002 **Turnover:** £500,000 - £1m
No.of Employees: 1 - 10 **Product Groups:** 81, 82

Pearsons Glass Ltd
9-11 Maddrell Street, Liverpool, L3 7EH
Tel: 0151-207 2874 **Fax:** 0151-207 2110
E-mail: info@pearsonsglass.co.uk
Website: http://www.pearsonsglass.com
Directors: D. Vellins (Dir)
Immediate Holding Company: PEARSONS GLASS LIMITED
Registration no: 01312627 **VAT No.:** GB 303 5692 72
Date established: 1977 **Turnover:** £2m - £5m **No.of Employees:** 51 - 100
Product Groups: 33, 66

Date of Accounts	Feb 11	Feb 10	Feb 09
Working Capital	249	344	299
Fixed Assets	1m	1m	1m
Current Assets	2m	2m	2m

Penny Lane Electrical Wholesale Ltd
70 Rose Lane, Liverpool, L18 8AG
Tel: 0151-724 2200 **Fax:** 0151-729 0709
Website: http://www.aiew.co.uk
Directors: D. Smith (MD)
Immediate Holding Company: PENNY LANE ELECTRICAL WHOLESALE LTD
Registration no: 04491154 **Date established:** 2002
No.of Employees: 1 - 10 **Product Groups:** 36, 40

Date of Accounts	Aug 11	Aug 10	Aug 09
Sales Turnover	N/A	N/A	457
Pre Tax Profit/Loss	N/A	N/A	31
Working Capital	-5	-7	-9
Fixed Assets	5	7	10
Current Assets	55	54	63
Current Liabilities	N/A	N/A	15

Peter Cox Ltd
209 Century Building Summers Road, Brunswick Business Park, Liverpool, L3 4BL
Tel: 0800-030 4701 **Fax:** 0151-708 5304
Website: http://www.petercox.com
Managers: Y. O'brien (Mgr)
Ultimate Holding Company: GERALDTON SERVICES INC (USA)
Immediate Holding Company: PETER COX LIMITED
Registration no: 02438126 **Date established:** 1989
No.of Employees: 1 - 10 **Product Groups:** 07, 32, 52, 66

Date of Accounts	Dec 11	Dec 10	Dec 09
Sales Turnover	15m	15m	14m
Pre Tax Profit/Loss	645	282	-350
Working Capital	3m	3m	2m
Fixed Assets	459	542	643
Current Assets	6m	5m	4m
Current Liabilities	2m	2m	961

Pine Precision Engineering Ltd
45-51 Parliament Street, Liverpool, L8 5RN
Tel: 0151-709 4236 **Fax:** 0151-707 2212
E-mail: sutton@pine-engineering.co.uk
Website: http://www.pineprecisionengineering.co.uk
Directors: D. Sutton (MD)
Immediate Holding Company: PINE PRECISION ENGINEERING LIMITED
Registration no: 02669232 **Date established:** 1991
No.of Employees: 1 - 10 **Product Groups:** 35, 45

Date of Accounts	Jan 12	Jan 11	Jan 10
Working Capital	31	31	17
Fixed Assets	54	28	27
Current Assets	82	85	53

Plexus Cotton Ltd
Unity Building 20 Chapel Street, Liverpool, L3 9AG
Tel: 0151-650 8888 **Fax:** 0151-650 8889
E-mail: mail@plexus-cotton.com
Website: http://www.plexus-cotton.com
Directors: L. Kirby (Fin)
Managers: D. Cox (Tech Serv Mgr)
Immediate Holding Company: PLEXUS COTTON LIMITED
Registration no: 02548312 **Date established:** 1990
Turnover: £250m - £500m **No.of Employees:** 21 - 50 **Product Groups:** 66

Date of Accounts	Dec 08	Dec 07	Dec 06
Sales Turnover	454m	425m	447m
Pre Tax Profit/Loss	-13m	-4m	-3m
Working Capital	-4m	2m	3m
Fixed Assets	21m	25m	27m
Current Assets	63m	138m	112m
Current Liabilities	67m	136m	109m
Total Share Capital	360	360	360

Pollards International
83 Sefton Lane Maghull, Liverpool, L31 8BU
Tel: 0151-526 3456 **Fax:** 0151-526 6969
E-mail: info@pollardsinternational.com
Website: http://www.pollardsinternational.com
Bank(s): HSBC Bank plc
Directors: D. Thorn (Grp Chief Exec), G. Conway (MD), J. Hammond (Fin), M. Carberry (Dir)
Managers: M. Meehan (Sales Admin)
Immediate Holding Company: Yakira Group Ltd
Registration no: 02607129 **VAT No.:** GB 564 2360 48
Date established: 1946 **Turnover:** £2m - £5m **No.of Employees:** 21 - 50
Product Groups: 22, 27, 35, 38, 49

Date of Accounts	Jun 09	Jun 08	Jun 07
Sales Turnover	283	369	202
Pre Tax Profit/Loss	27	-49	20
Working Capital	5	-21	26
Fixed Assets	5	6	8
Current Assets	565	370	212
Current Liabilities	13	10	88

Popes Hightown Ltd
Moss Lane Hightown, Liverpool, L38 3RA
Tel: 0151-929 2514 **Fax:** 0151-929 2615
E-mail: popes@popeshightown.co.uk
Website: http://www.farming.co.uk
Directors: C. Pope (Dir)
Immediate Holding Company: POPES (HIGHTOWN) LIMITED
Registration no: 02054757 **Date established:** 1986
No.of Employees: 11 - 20 **Product Groups:** 30, 33, 51

Date of Accounts	Mar 12	Mar 11	Mar 10
Working Capital	-196	63	-147
Fixed Assets	451	266	467
Current Assets	157	419	282

Portia World Travel
6 North John Street, Liverpool, L2 4SD
Tel: 0151-227 3401 **Fax:** 0151- 2271176
E-mail: brian@portiaworldtravel.co.uk
Website: http://www.portiaworldtravel.co.uk
Directors: C. Marrison Gill (Co Sec)
Managers: B. Reilly (District Mgr)
Ultimate Holding Company: TOKENHOUSE LIMITED (ISLE OF MAN)
Immediate Holding Company: PORTIA WORLD TRAVEL LIMITED
Registration no: 01420160 **Date established:** 1979
Turnover: Up to £250,000 **No.of Employees:** 1 - 10 **Product Groups:** 69

Date of Accounts	Mar 11	Mar 10	Mar 09
Sales Turnover	163	190	202
Pre Tax Profit/Loss	12	33	38
Working Capital	444	432	400
Current Assets	639	621	665
Current Liabilities	18	45	57

Potter Group Ltd (Rail Freight Terminal)
Rail Freight Terminal Woodward Road, Knowsley Industrial Park, Liverpool, L33 7UY
Tel: 0151-290 0671 **Fax:** 0151-289 1310
E-mail: enquiries@pottergroup.co.uk
Website: http://www.pottergroup.co.uk
Managers: M. Crookall (Mgr)
Ultimate Holding Company: THE POTTER GROUP (HOLDINGS) PLC
Immediate Holding Company: THE POTTER GROUP LIMITED
Registration no: 01392251 **Date established:** 1978
Turnover: £500,000 - £1m **No.of Employees:** 21 - 50
Product Groups: 07, 39, 45, 72, 77, 80, 84

Date of Accounts	Apr 11	Apr 10	Apr 09
Sales Turnover	15m	15m	16m
Pre Tax Profit/Loss	447	355	28
Working Capital	7m	7m	6m
Fixed Assets	4m	3m	4m
Current Assets	11m	10m	11m
Current Liabilities	2m	1m	3m

Powder Systems Ltd
Unit 3 Estuary Business Park Speke, Liverpool, L24 8RG
Tel: 0151-448 7700 **Fax:** 0151-448 7702
E-mail: sales@powdersystems.com
Website: http://www.p-s-l.com
Directors: K. Pitcher (Fin)
Managers: E. Nagyova (Buyer), R. Benson, A. Pitcher (Sales & Mktg Mg)
Ultimate Holding Company: COBCO 892 LIMITED
Immediate Holding Company: POWDER SYSTEMS LIMITED
Registration no: 02233044 **Date established:** 1988 **Turnover:** £5m - £10m
No.of Employees: 21 - 50 **Product Groups:** 32, 38, 40, 42, 84

Date of Accounts	Mar 11	Mar 10	Mar 09
Sales Turnover	5m	5m	5m
Pre Tax Profit/Loss	-95	168	-273
Working Capital	899	911	760
Fixed Assets	79	60	94
Current Assets	3m	3m	3m
Current Liabilities	1m	1m	2m

Powertool Centre
49-51 London Road, Liverpool, L3 8HY
Tel: 0151-207 1400 **Fax:** 0151-298 1352
Website: http://www.powertoolcentre.co.uk
Managers: T. Mckeown (District Mgr)
Immediate Holding Company: POWER TOOL CENTRE LTD
Registration no: 04745386 **Date established:** 2003
Turnover: £500,000 - £1m **No.of Employees:** 1 - 10 **Product Groups:** 37

Date of Accounts	Apr 11	Apr 10	Apr 09
Working Capital	-3	-2	-3
Fixed Assets	4	4	5
Current Assets	209	177	150

Premier Forktrucks
10 Webber Road Knowsley Industrial Park, Liverpool, L33 7SW
Tel: 0151-548 2003 **Fax:** 0151-548 3779
Directors: P. Collier (Prop)
Date established: 1996 **No.of Employees:** 1 - 10 **Product Groups:** 35, 39, 45

Prestige Steel Fabrications
16 Cotton Street, Liverpool, L3 7DY
Tel: 0151-207 3207 **Fax:** 0151-207 5207
E-mail: dean.whalton@virgin.net
Website: http://www.prestigestainlesssteelsystems.co.uk
Directors: D. Walton (Dir)
Immediate Holding Company: PRESTIGE STEEL FABRICATION & SITE SERVICES LTD
Registration no: 06435070 **Date established:** 2007
No.of Employees: 11 - 20 **Product Groups:** 35

Date of Accounts	Feb 11	Feb 10	Feb 09
Working Capital	18	-25	N/A
Fixed Assets	27	18	N/A
Current Assets	130	63	N/A

Prism Chemicals Ltd
59-61 Sandhills Lane, Liverpool, L5 9XL
Tel: 0151-922 7871 **Fax:** 0151-944 1517
E-mail: info@bannerchemicals.com
Website: http://www.bannerchemicals.com
Managers: G. Mawdsley (Mgr)
Ultimate Holding Company: 2M GROUP LIMITED
Immediate Holding Company: PRISM CHEMICALS LIMITED
Registration no: 03659050 **Date established:** 1998
No.of Employees: 1 - 10 **Product Groups:** 32, 48

Date of Accounts	Apr 12	Apr 11	Apr 10
Sales Turnover	647	721	682
Pre Tax Profit/Loss	-246	-257	-246
Working Capital	-2m	-1m	-1m
Fixed Assets	876	923	981
Current Assets	569	586	500
Current Liabilities	97	90	42

Proweld Ltd
Unit 72 North Mersey Business Centre Woodward Road, Knowsley Industrial Park, Liverpool, L33 7UY
Tel: 0151-546 8271 **Fax:** 0151-546 8272
E-mail: proweldltd@btconnect.com
Website: http://www.proweld-ltd.co.uk
Directors: D. Blease (Prop)
Immediate Holding Company: PROWELD LIMITED
Registration no: 04178370 **Date established:** 2001
No.of Employees: 1 - 10 **Product Groups:** 46

Date of Accounts	Mar 12	Mar 11	Mar 10
Working Capital	-17	-21	-14
Fixed Assets	17	21	15
Current Assets	102	108	93

PureSil Technologies Ltd
Process House Acornfield Road Knowsley Industrial Estate, Knowsley Industrial Park, Liverpool, L33 7PA
Tel: 0151-548 4000 **Fax:** 0151-548 8000
E-mail: sales@puresil.com
Website: http://www.puresil.com
Directors: J. Scott (Fin), D. Scott (Sales)
Immediate Holding Company: PURESIL TECHNOLOGIES LIMITED
Registration no: 05202146 **Date established:** 2004
No.of Employees: 1 - 10 **Product Groups:** 30, 42

Date of Accounts	Jan 11	Jan 08	Jan 07
Working Capital	44	-4	1
Current Assets	84	13	16

R E A Metal Windows Ltd
126-136 Green Lane Stoneycroft, Liverpool, L13 7ED
Tel: 0151-228 6373 **Fax:** 0151-254 1828
E-mail: all@reametal.co.uk
Website: http://www.reametal.co.uk
Bank(s): HSBC
Directors: R. Smith (Co Sec), J. Chamberlain (Grp Chief Exec), B. McCabe (MD)
Managers: P. Richardson (Sales Prom Mgr)
Ultimate Holding Company: ETNA STREET INVESTMENTS LIMITED
Immediate Holding Company: REA METAL WINDOWS LIMITED
Registration no: 02678539 **VAT No.:** GB 164 5176 58
Date established: 1992 **Turnover:** £2m - £5m **No.of Employees:** 21 - 50
Product Groups: 35

Renshaw Napier Ltd
Crown Street, Liverpool, L8 7RF
Tel: 0151-706 8200 **Fax:** 0151-706 8201
E-mail: enquiries@renshawnapier.co.uk
Website: http://www.renshawnapier.co.uk
Bank(s): Barclays
Directors: M. McDonald (Fin), S. Gee (Dir), H. Billington (Pers)
Managers: D. Grive (Sales & Mktg Mg), M. Mcdonough (Fin Mgr), H. Billington (Personnel), R. Stead
Ultimate Holding Company: THE REAL GOOD FOOD COMPANY PLC
Immediate Holding Company: RENSHAWNAPIER LIMITED
Registration no: 01665672 **VAT No.:** GB 628 8571 01
Date established: 1982 **Turnover:** £125m - £250m
No.of Employees: 101 - 250 **Product Groups:** 20

Date of Accounts	Dec 10	Dec 09	Dec 08
Sales Turnover	179m	206m	201m
Pre Tax Profit/Loss	4m	3m	3m
Working Capital	6m	3m	-117
Fixed Assets	28m	28m	29m
Current Assets	37m	59m	47m
Current Liabilities	16m	17m	18m

Resman
22 Rose Lane, Liverpool, L18 5ED
Tel: 0151-729 0101 **Fax:** 0151-729 0202
E-mail: sales@sqlaccounts.com
Website: http://www.resman.co.uk

see next page

Resman - *Cont'd*
Directors: N. Willcox (Fin)
Immediate Holding Company: RESMAN LIMITED
Registration no: 02463322 **Date established:** 1990
Turnover: £500,000 - £1m **No.of Employees:** 11 - 20 **Product Groups:** 44

Date of Accounts	Feb 08	Feb 11	Feb 10
Working Capital	81	184	133
Fixed Assets	3	2	2
Current Assets	131	279	145
Current Liabilities	N/A	38	N/A

Rewinds & J Windsor & Sons Engineers Ltd
Regent Road Kirkdale, Liverpool, L5 9SY
Tel: 0151-207 2074 **Fax:** 0151-298 1442
E-mail: enquiries@rjweng.com
Website: http://www.rjweng.com
Bank(s): HSBC Bank plc
Directors: A. Windsor (Dir)
Immediate Holding Company: REWINDS AND J. WINDSOR & SONS (ENGINEERS) LIMITED
Registration no: 00603096 **VAT No.:** GB 150 2781 87
Date established: 1958 **Turnover:** £5m - £10m
No.of Employees: 51 - 100 **Product Groups:** 48

Date of Accounts	Apr 11	Apr 10	Apr 09
Sales Turnover	7m	6m	6m
Pre Tax Profit/Loss	20	33	-255
Working Capital	2m	2m	2m
Fixed Assets	1m	1m	2m
Current Assets	2m	2m	2m
Current Liabilities	227	213	162

Robinson & Neal Ltd
129 Sefton Street Toxteth, Liverpool, L8 5SN
Tel: 0151-709 9481 **Fax:** 0151-707 1377
Website: http://www.robinson-neal.com
Managers: E. Hannah (Mgr)
Immediate Holding Company: ROBINSON & NEAL LIMITED
Registration no: 00084087 **VAT No.:** 163 4722 68 **Date established:** 2005
Turnover: £1m - £2m **No.of Employees:** 1 - 10 **Product Groups:** 27, 30, 32

Date of Accounts	Dec 11	Dec 10	Dec 09
Working Capital	-79	-61	-38
Fixed Assets	465	477	492
Current Assets	306	336	251
Current Liabilities	N/A	13	N/A

Rodol Ltd
Richmond Row, Liverpool, L3 3BP
Tel: 0151-207 3161 **Fax:** 0151-207 3727
E-mail: accounts@rodol.co.uk
Website: http://www.rodol.co.uk
Bank(s): Lloyds TSB Bank plc
Directors: D. Robinson (Fin), G. Robinson (Dir)
Immediate Holding Company: RODOL LIMITED
Registration no: 00335087 **VAT No.:** GB 163 4088 66
Date established: 1937 **No.of Employees:** 21 - 50 **Product Groups:** 32

Date of Accounts	Jan 12	Jan 11	Jan 10
Working Capital	2m	2m	2m
Fixed Assets	6m	6m	5m
Current Assets	2m	2m	3m

Rotatools UK Ltd
2a Atherton Road, Liverpool, L9 7EL
Tel: 0151-525 8611 **Fax:** 0151-525 4868
E-mail: richard_dearn@hotmail.com
Directors: R. Dearn (MD)
Immediate Holding Company: ROTATOOLS (U.K.) LIMITED
Registration no: 00596045 **VAT No.:** GB 163 6792 37
Date established: 1957 **Turnover:** Up to £250,000
No.of Employees: 1 - 10 **Product Groups:** 35, 37, 40, 49

Date of Accounts	Dec 11	Dec 10	Dec 09
Working Capital	86	107	76
Fixed Assets	7	7	8
Current Assets	119	116	81

Rotunda Wrought Iron
12a Longmoor Lane, Liverpool, L9 0EF
Tel: 0151-521 5467
Directors: M. Gibbons (Prop)
Date established: 1992 **No.of Employees:** 1 - 10 **Product Groups:** 26, 35

Royal Institute Of British Architects (North West Region)
82 Wood Street, Liverpool, L1 4DQ
Tel: 0151-703 0107 **Fax:** 0151-703 0108
E-mail: berlinda.irlan-mowbrey@member.riba.org
Website: http://www.architcture.com
Bank(s): Natwest
Directors: B. Mowbray (Dir)
Immediate Holding Company: RIVER MEDIA LTD.
Registration no: FP012292 **VAT No.:** GB 232 3518 91
Date established: 1998 **No.of Employees:** 11 - 20 **Product Groups:** 80

Date of Accounts	Jul 10	Jul 09	Jul 08
Working Capital	-0	-8	17
Fixed Assets	32	39	43
Current Assets	129	156	219

Royal Liver Assurance
Royal Liver Building Pier Head, Liverpool, L3 1HT
Tel: 0151-236 1451 **Fax:** 0117-981 7449
E-mail: william.connelly@royalliver.com
Website: http://www.royalliver.co.uk
Bank(s): HSBC Bank plc
Directors: S. Burnet (Grp Chief Exec), W. Connelly (Grp Chief Exec), K. Dobson (Co Sec), D. Finney (Dir), C. Nugent (Dir), B. McCaul (Grp Chief Exec), G. Bowles (Non Exec)
Managers: D. Cross, P. Matthews, I. Hook (Mgr)
Ultimate Holding Company: ROYAL LIVER ASSURANCE LIMITED
Immediate Holding Company: ROYAL LIVER ASSET MANAGERS LIMITED
Registration no: 04130317 **Date established:** 2000 **Turnover:** £2m - £5m
No.of Employees: 101 - 250 **Product Groups:** 82

S & G Wrought Iron
2 Edwards Lane, Liverpool, L24 9HW
Tel: 0151-486 8651 **Fax:** 0151-486 0669

Directors: G. Speedf (Prop)
No.of Employees: 1 - 10 **Product Groups:** 26, 35

Sarah's Steels
1 Earp Street, Liverpool, L19 1RT
Tel: 0151-281 5305 **Fax:** 0151-281 5305
E-mail: sales@sarahssteels.co.uk
Website: http://www.sarahssteels.co.uk
Directors: I. Mcpoland (Prop)
Date established: 1997 **No.of Employees:** 1 - 10 **Product Groups:** 26, 35

Scientific Hospital Supplies International Ltd
100 Wavertree Boulevard Wavertree Technical Park, Liverpool, L7 9PT
Tel: 0151-228 8161 **Fax:** 0151-228 2650
Website: http://www.shs-nutrition.com
Bank(s): National Westminster
Directors: R. Crim (MD), S. Cassidy (Fin)
Managers: A. Nevin (Mktg Serv Mgr), G. Morrisey (District Mgr), J. Edwards (Admin Off)
Ultimate Holding Company: GROUPE DANONE SA (FRANCE)
Immediate Holding Company: SCIENTIFIC HOSPITAL SUPPLIES HOLDINGS LIMITED
Registration no: 02502240 **VAT No.:** GB 163 8936 29
Date established: 1990 **Turnover:** £75m - £125m
No.of Employees: 101 - 250 **Product Groups:** 20

Secure Bolts
Unit 19 Blenheim Way, Liverpool, L24 1YH
Tel: 0151-486 3154 **Fax:** 0151-486 3154
Directors: M. Ingham (Prop)
Immediate Holding Company: SECURE BOLTS LTD
Date established: 2011 **No.of Employees:** 1 - 10 **Product Groups:** 35

Sefton Fire Protection Ltd
4 Thornbeck Avenue Hightown, Liverpool, L38 0BE
Tel: 0151-285 9324 **Fax:** 0151-929 2406
Directors: D. Barker (MD)
Immediate Holding Company: SEFTON FIRE PROTECTION LTD
Registration no: 04885343 **Date established:** 2003
No.of Employees: 1 - 10 **Product Groups:** 38, 42

Date of Accounts	Mar 11	Mar 10	Mar 09
Working Capital	-0	N/A	18
Fixed Assets	1	1	1
Current Assets	14	12	18

Shand Higson & Co. Ltd
Lees Road Knowsley Industrial Park, Liverpool, L33 7SE
Tel: 0151-549 2210 **Fax:** 0151-549 1405
E-mail: info@shandhigson.co.uk
Website: http://www.shandhigson.co.uk
Bank(s): Barclays
Directors: S. Fisher (MD), S. Fisher (Dir)
Immediate Holding Company: SHAND HIGSON AND CO.LIMITED
Registration no: 00544915 **VAT No.:** GB 164 7499 24
Date established: 1955 **Turnover:** £2m - £5m **No.of Employees:** 21 - 50
Product Groups: 23, 27, 29, 30, 31, 32, 33, 42, 48, 49, 66, 68, 76

Date of Accounts	Mar 11	Mar 10	Mar 09
Working Capital	197	350	254
Fixed Assets	1m	1m	1m
Current Assets	951	831	647

J J Smith Technical Services Ltd
Moorgate Point Moorgate Road, Knowsley Industrial Park, Liverpool, L33 7DR
Tel: 0151-546 1308 **Fax:** 0151-546 1308
E-mail: pharrison@jjsmithtechserve.com
Website: http://www.jjsmithtechserv.com
Directors: P. Griffiths (Fin), P. Harrison (MD)
Immediate Holding Company: J.J. SMITH TECHNICAL SERVICES LTD
Registration no: 04221299 **VAT No.:** GB 618 8658 93
Date established: 2001 **Turnover:** £5m - £10m **No.of Employees:** 1 - 10
Product Groups: 48

Date of Accounts	Mar 11	Mar 10	Mar 09
Working Capital	7	6	9
Fixed Assets	1	1	2
Current Assets	45	47	58

Solaglas Ltd (part of the Saint-Gobain group)
Cheadle Avenue, Liverpool, L13 3AF
Tel: 0151-228 2696 **Fax:** 0151-259 2248
E-mail: solaglas.gpd@saint-gobain-glass.com
Website: http://www.solaglas.co.uk
Bank(s): National Westminster
Managers: R. Mackenzie (Mgr)
Ultimate Holding Company: COMPAGNIE DE SAINT GOBAIN (FRANCE)
Immediate Holding Company: GLASSOLUTIONS SAINT-GOBAIN LIMITED
Registration no: 02442570 **VAT No.:** GB 544 9390 18
Date established: 1989 **No.of Employees:** 21 - 50 **Product Groups:** 33, 66

Date of Accounts	Dec 11	Dec 10	Dec 09
Sales Turnover	116m	93m	97m
Pre Tax Profit/Loss	6m	-10m	-16m
Working Capital	-36m	-28m	-18m
Fixed Assets	23m	21m	15m
Current Assets	34m	33m	25m
Current Liabilities	64m	52m	15m

Sprague Equipment Ltd
2 Roberts Street, Liverpool, L3 7AS
Tel: 0151-236 0317 **Fax:** 0151-236 0260
Directors: P. Roberts (MD), L. Dobson (Co Sec), L. Dobson (Fin)
Immediate Holding Company: SPRAGUE BROS. LIMITED
Registration no: 00519850 **VAT No.:** GB 163 4158 71
Date established: 1953 **Turnover:** £500,000 - £1m
No.of Employees: 1 - 10 **Product Groups:** 48

Date of Accounts	Sep 09	Sep 08	Sep 07
Working Capital	118	106	77
Fixed Assets	3	5	N/A
Current Assets	149	129	98

Straight Talk In
45 Parton Street, Liverpool, L6 3AN
Tel: 0151-260 7345
E-mail: info@straighttalkin.com
Website: http://www.straighttalkin.co.uk
Directors: J. McNulty (Fin), R. Williams (Dir)
Immediate Holding Company: STRAIGHT TALK IN LIMITED
Registration no: 05744967 **Date established:** 2006
Turnover: Up to £250,000 **No.of Employees:** 11 - 20 **Product Groups:** 49

Date of Accounts	Mar 11	Mar 09	Mar 08
Working Capital	-17	-13	-11
Fixed Assets	1	1	2
Current Assets	9	9	9

Studley Engineering Ltd
17 Vulcan Street, Liverpool, L3 7BG
Tel: 0151-236 7825 **Fax:** 0151-255 0597
E-mail: frances.malone@studleyengineering.co.uk
Website: http://www.studleyengineering.co.uk
Directors: F. Malone (Fin)
Immediate Holding Company: STUDLEY ENGINEERING LIMITED
Registration no: 01754001 **Date established:** 1983 **Turnover:** £5m - £10m
No.of Employees: 51 - 100 **Product Groups:** 41

Date of Accounts	Oct 11	Oct 10	Oct 09
Sales Turnover	9m	8m	8m
Pre Tax Profit/Loss	426	178	214
Working Capital	444	218	466
Fixed Assets	21	14	19
Current Assets	2m	2m	2m
Current Liabilities	743	461	870

Supply Chain Solution Ltd
1-11 Mersey View Brighton-Le-Sands, Liverpool, L22 6QA
Tel: 0151-284 8867 **Fax:** 0151-213 3140
E-mail: sales@supplychainsolution.co.uk
Website: http://www.supplychainsolution.co.uk
Directors: L. Wright (Prop)
Immediate Holding Company: SUPPLY CHAIN SOLUTION LTD
Registration no: 06075296 **Date established:** 2007
Turnover: £250,000 - £500,000 **No.of Employees:** 1 - 10
Product Groups: 45, 67, 72, 74, 76

Date of Accounts	Jan 12	Jan 11	Jan 10
Sales Turnover	N/A	339	452
Pre Tax Profit/Loss	N/A	13	-8
Working Capital	12	-5	-13
Fixed Assets	5	6	7
Current Assets	58	48	100
Current Liabilities	6	47	5

Sureseal Windows Ltd
190-194 St Marys Road Garston, Liverpool, L19 2JJ
Tel: 0800-197 0217 **Fax:** 0151-280 5035
E-mail: info@surealwindows.co.uk
Website: http://www.surealwindows.co.uk
Directors: D. Melia (Dir), D. Melia (MD)
Immediate Holding Company: SURESEAL WINDOWS LTD
Registration no: 05990621 **No.of Employees:** 1 - 10 **Product Groups:** 35, 36, 52, 66

T J Engineering Supplies
51 Sandhills Lane, Liverpool, L5 9XJ
Tel: 0151-933 1599 **Fax:** 0151-922 5522
E-mail: tjengsupplies@btconnect.com
Website: http://www.tjengsupplies.co.uk
Directors: T. Bligh (MD), J. Bligh (Co Sec)
Immediate Holding Company: TJ ENGINEERING SUPPLIES LIMITED
Registration no: 04438005 **Date established:** 2002
Turnover: £250,000 - £500,000 **No.of Employees:** 1 - 10
Product Groups: 38, 42

Date of Accounts	May 11	May 10	May 09
Sales Turnover	N/A	N/A	314
Pre Tax Profit/Loss	N/A	N/A	31
Working Capital	-4	3	N/A
Fixed Assets	6	10	10
Current Assets	85	79	60
Current Liabilities	N/A	N/A	16

Techniflex Hygenic
Unit 1 Pride Point Ashcroft Road, Knowsley Industrial Park, Liverpool, L33 7TW
Tel: 0151-548 4000 **Fax:** 0151-548 8000
E-mail: sales@puresiltechniflex.co.uk
Website: http://www.puresiltechniflex.co.uk
Directors: D. Scott (Dir)
No.of Employees: 1 - 10 **Product Groups:** 29, 30, 36, 66, 84

Date of Accounts	Jan 08	Jan 07	Jan 06
Working Capital	-70	-46	16
Fixed Assets	164	177	171
Current Assets	71	68	135
Current Liabilities	141	114	119
Total Share Capital	1	1	1

Textile Fabrications
Unit C14 Commerce Way, Liverpool, L8 7BA
Tel: 0151-709 7969 **Fax:** 0151-709 6049
E-mail: flexibles@texfab.co.uk
Website: http://www.texfab.co.uk
Directors: P. Carmicheal (Prop)
No.of Employees: 1 - 10 **Product Groups:** 23, 40

Thurston (E A Clare & Son Ltd)
46-48 St Anne Street, Liverpool, L3 3DW
Tel: 0151-482 2700 **Fax:** 0151-298 1134
E-mail: thurston@eaclare.co.uk
Website: http://www.thurston.co.uk
Bank(s): Barclays
Directors: P. Clare (MD)
Ultimate Holding Company: E.A. CLARE & SON LIMITED
Immediate Holding Company: THURSTON & COMPANY,LIMITED
Registration no: 00046970 **VAT No.:** GB 166 0283 70
Date established: 1996 **Turnover:** £2m - £5m **No.of Employees:** 51 - 100
Product Groups: 49

Thurston Ash
21, Croxtheth Road sefton Park, Liverpool, L8 3SE
Tel: 0844-7407415
E-mail: info@thurston-ash.com
Website: http://www.thurston-ash.com
Date established: 2008 **No.of Employees:** 1 - 10 **Product Groups:** 80

TJ Hughes Ltd
Hughes House London Road, Liverpool, L3 8JA
Tel: 0151-207 2600 **Fax:** 0151-298 1373
Website: http://www.tjhughes.co.uk

Directors: P. Mcdonald (Fin), R. Dickie (MD), A. Juneja (Grp Chief Exec)
Ultimate Holding Company: T J HUGHES (HOLDINGS) COMPANY LIMITED
Immediate Holding Company: T J HUGHES LIMITED
Registration no: 00224422 **VAT No.:** GB 548 8214 19
Date established: 2027 **Turnover:** £75m - £125m
No.of Employees: 251 - 500 **Product Groups:** 61

Date of Accounts	Jan 09	Jan 10	Jan 07
Sales Turnover	261m	267m	239m
Pre Tax Profit/Loss	5m	7m	1m
Working Capital	27m	32m	14m
Fixed Assets	42m	42m	49m
Current Assets	74m	82m	62m
Current Liabilities	16m	18m	18m

Todd & Ledson

Martins Building 4 Water Street, Liverpool, L2 3SX
Tel: 0151-236 6864 **Fax:** 0151-236 1104
E-mail: liverpool@toddandledson.co.uk
Website: http://www.toddandledson.co.uk
Directors: S. Wands (Ptnr)
Immediate Holding Company: TODD & LEDSON LLP
Registration no: OC310715 **Date established:** 2004
No.of Employees: 11 - 20 **Product Groups:** 80, 84

Date of Accounts	Mar 11	Mar 10	Mar 09
Working Capital	350	224	349
Fixed Assets	116	123	130
Current Assets	669	529	636

TOPHtechnik Chiptuning

PO 75, Liverpool, L14 6WY
Tel: 0845-021 8674
E-mail: info@toph.co.uk
Website: http://www.toph.co.uk
Directors: C. jones (Prop)
Date established: 2004 **Turnover:** Up to £250,000
No.of Employees: 1 - 10 **Product Groups:** 39

Total Welding Supplies Ltd

Unit 12-13 Regal Works St Johns Road, Kirkdale, Liverpool, L20 8PR
Tel: 0151-933 7213 **Fax:** 0151-944 1177
E-mail: k.gill@totalweldingsupplies.com
Directors: K. Gill (MD)
Managers: T. Joyce (Chief Acct)
Immediate Holding Company: TOTAL WELDING SUPPLIES LIMITED
Registration no: 02038522 **Date established:** 1986
No.of Employees: 1 - 10 **Product Groups:** 46

Date of Accounts	Oct 11	Oct 10	Oct 09
Working Capital	75	37	25
Fixed Assets	17	6	6
Current Assets	223	149	113

Trade Mark Protection Society

Coopers Building Church Street, Liverpool, L1 3AB
Tel: 0151-709 3961 **Fax:** 0151-709 0162
E-mail: j-maddox@tmps.co.uk
Website: http://www.tmps.co.uk
Directors: J. Maddox (Dir)
Immediate Holding Company: PAPERACORN LIMITED
Registration no: 02293776 **Date established:** 1988
No.of Employees: 1 - 10 **Product Groups:** 80

Transcanada Turbines

Bechers Drive Aintree Racecourse Retail & Bus Pk, Liverpool, L9 5AY
Tel: 0151-525 5522 **Fax:** 0151-525 5185
Managers: S. Simonelli (Mgr)
Date established: 1999 **No.of Employees:** 1 - 10 **Product Groups:** 35, 36, 39

Transformers UK

14 Jordan Street, Liverpool, L1 0BP
Tel: 0151-709 0425 **Fax:** 0151-709 0405
E-mail: peter@transformers-uk.com
Website: http://www.sems-experts.co.uk
Directors: P. Marray (Co Sec)
Immediate Holding Company: TRANSFORMERS UK LIMITED
Registration no: 02548258 **Date established:** 1990
Turnover: £250,000 - £500,000 **No.of Employees:** 1 - 10
Product Groups: 30, 35, 36, 38, 39, 40, 41, 45, 46, 49, 62, 66

Date of Accounts	Apr 12	Apr 11	Apr 10
Working Capital	161	131	105
Fixed Assets	18	21	20
Current Assets	351	340	200

Trident Dental Lab Lancashire Ltd

90 Rose Lane Mossley Hill, Liverpool, L18 8AG
Tel: 0151-724 4656 **Fax:** 0151-724 6855
Directors: G. Roberts (MD)
Date established: 1980 **No.of Employees:** 21 - 50 **Product Groups:** 38, 67

Try & Lilly Ltd

95 Kempston Street, Liverpool, L3 8HE
Tel: 0151-207 2001 **Fax:** 0151-207 4878
E-mail: sales@tryandlilly.co.uk
Website: http://www.tryandlilly.co.uk
Bank(s): National Westminster Bank Plc
Directors: A. Jennions (MD)
Managers: A. Kirrane, S. Geron (Sales Prom Mgr)
Immediate Holding Company: TRY & LILLY LIMITED
Registration no: 00442264 **Date established:** 1947 **Turnover:** £1m - £2m
No.of Employees: 21 - 50 **Product Groups:** 24

Date of Accounts	Feb 12	Feb 11	Feb 10
Working Capital	630	601	580
Fixed Assets	49	54	56
Current Assets	816	856	794

Ultimate Dental Laboratory

40 Liverpool Road Formby, Liverpool, L37 6BZ
Tel: 08458-230230 **Fax:** 01704-832440
E-mail: sales@ultimatelab.co.uk
Website: http://www.ultimatelab.co.uk
Directors: N. Mansley (Dir)
Managers: M. Smith (Sales Admin)
No.of Employees: 21 - 50 **Product Groups:** 38, 67

W P Thompson & Co

Coopers Building Church Street, Liverpool, L1 3AB
Tel: 0151-709 3961 **Fax:** 01482-228366
E-mail: tlbrand@wpt.co.uk
Website: http://www.wpt.co.uk
Bank(s): Barclays
Directors: A. Walker (Ptnr)
Managers: C. Lawton (Chief Mgr)
Immediate Holding Company: PAPERACORN LIMITED
Registration no: 02293776 **Date established:** 1988
No.of Employees: 21 - 50 **Product Groups:** 80

Washbourn & Garrett Ltd

Ashcroft Road Knowsley Industrial Park, Liverpool, L33 7TW
Tel: 0151-546 2901 **Fax:** 0151-548 5562
E-mail: enquiries@washbourngarrett.co.uk
Website: http://www.washbourngarrett.co.uk
Managers: B. Jones (Mgr)
Immediate Holding Company: WASHBOURN & GARRETT LIMITED
Registration no: 00873793 **Date established:** 1966
Turnover: £500,000 - £1m **No.of Employees:** 1 - 10 **Product Groups:** 26, 36

Date of Accounts	Oct 07	Apr 11	Apr 10
Working Capital	18	65	71
Fixed Assets	140	8	N/A
Current Assets	288	99	105

John West Foods Ltd

1st Floor Lancaster House, Tithebarn Street, Liverpool, L2 2 GA
Tel: 0151-243 6200 **Fax:** 0151-236 5465
E-mail: paul.cottam@mwbrands.com
Website: http://www.john-west.co.uk
Managers: P. Cottam (Export Sales Mg)
Registration no: 00200767 **VAT No.:** GB 163 4599 41
No.of Employees: 51 **Product Groups:** 20

Date of Accounts	Dec 11	Dec 10	Mar 10
Sales Turnover	177m	112m	172m
Pre Tax Profit/Loss	3m	-1m	36m
Working Capital	36m	34m	69m
Fixed Assets	3m	4m	4m
Current Assets	74m	69m	86m
Current Liabilities	4m	6m	7m

World Trade Publishing Ltd

36 Crosby Road North, Liverpool, L22 4QQ
Tel: 0151-928 9288 **Fax:** 0151-928 4190
E-mail: wl@worldtrades.co.uk
Website: http://www.worldtrades.co.uk
Directors: S. Yarwood (MD), S. Cassidy (Fin)
Ultimate Holding Company: WORLD TRADES PUBLISHING LTD.
Immediate Holding Company: TEXTILE TRADES PUBLISHING LIMITED
Registration no: 03540804 **VAT No.:** GB 454 0583 53
Date established: 1998 **Turnover:** £500,000 - £1m
No.of Employees: 1 - 10 **Product Groups:** 81

Date of Accounts	Mar 11	Mar 10	Mar 09
Working Capital	34	51	36
Fixed Assets	17	19	32
Current Assets	751	1m	854

W R Wright & Sons Ltd

104-118 Cherry Lane, Liverpool, L4 8SF
Tel: 0151-270 2904 **Fax:** 0151-226 8833
E-mail: info@wrwright.co.uk
Website: http://www.wrwright.co.uk
Bank(s): Barclays
Directors: W. Wright (MD)
Immediate Holding Company: W. R. WRIGHT & SONS LIMITED
Registration no: 01297995 **VAT No.:** GB 166 6686 18
Date established: 1977 **Turnover:** £2m - £5m **No.of Employees:** 11 - 20
Product Groups: 20, 40, 67

Date of Accounts	Apr 11	Apr 10	Apr 09
Working Capital	2m	2m	2m
Fixed Assets	786	769	684
Current Assets	2m	2m	2m

Wrought Iron Shop

136 Prescot Road Fairfield, Liverpool, L7 0JB
Tel: 0151-252 0460 **Fax:** 0151-252 0460
Directors: F. Dutch (Prop)
Date established: 1990 **No.of Employees:** 1 - 10 **Product Groups:** 26, 35

www.mynetworkingpa.com

4th Floor 72 Church Street, Liverpool, L1 3AY
Tel: 08453-017406
E-mail: info@mynetworkingpa.com
Website: http://www.mynetworkingpa.com
Directors: H. Wood (Dir)
Immediate Holding Company: NETWORKING PA LIMITED
Registration no: 06501655 **Date established:** 2008
Turnover: £250,000 - £500,000 **No.of Employees:** 11 - 20
Product Groups: 44

Yeoward Shipping Ltd

The Logistics Office Port of Liverpool, Liverpool, L21 1JR
Tel: 0151-928 8173 **Fax:** 0151-928 8174
E-mail: yeowardshipping@btconnet.com
Directors: D. Bishop (MD), D. Bishop (Fin), K. Bishop (Dir)
Immediate Holding Company: YEOWARD SHIPPING LIMITED
Registration no: 03371237 **VAT No.:** GB 166 3627 49
Date established: 1997 **Turnover:** £500,000 - £1m
No.of Employees: 1 - 10 **Product Groups:** 74, 76

Date of Accounts	Jun 07	Jun 06
Sales Turnover	N/A	114
Pre Tax Profit/Loss	N/A	7
Working Capital	19	-2
Current Assets	75	95
Current Liabilities	56	97
Total Share Capital	1	1
ROCE% (Return on Capital Employed)		-368.2
ROT% (Return on Turnover)		5.8

Zim UK

Room 249 India Building Water Street, Liverpool, L2 0QD
Tel: 0151-258 1118 **Fax:** 0151-258 1117
E-mail: lbrauner@zim.uk.com
Website: http://www.zim.com
Bank(s): H S B C
Directors: G. Murray (Co Sec), I. Brauner (Dir)
Managers: G. Walters (Comm), E. Murphy (Personnel)
Immediate Holding Company: ZIM UK LIMITED
Registration no: 03556934 **Date established:** 1998 **Turnover:** £2m - £5m
No.of Employees: 51 - 100 **Product Groups:** 68, 74, 76

Date of Accounts	Dec 11	Dec 10	Dec 09
Sales Turnover	2m	2m	2m
Pre Tax Profit/Loss	44	120	48
Working Capital	432	375	257
Fixed Assets	81	104	142
Current Assets	586	558	463
Current Liabilities	101	182	206

Neston

Accutime Ltd

Casa Sarga Liverpool Road, Neston, CH64 7TW
Tel: 0151-353 0065 **Fax:** 0151-336 1964
E-mail: sales@accutime.co.uk
Website: http://www.accutime.co.uk
Directors: A. Lucas (Fin)
Immediate Holding Company: ACCUTIME LIMITED
Registration no: 06306209 **Date established:** 2007
No.of Employees: 1 - 10 **Product Groups:** 27, 38, 44, 48, 49, 65, 83

Date of Accounts	Jul 12	Jul 11	Jul 10
Working Capital	19	-57	-62
Fixed Assets	86	102	118
Current Assets	72	34	36

Borries

28 Coalbrookdale Road Clayhill Light Industrial Park, Neston, CH64 3UG
Tel: 0151-336 3101 **Fax:** 0151-336 3217
E-mail: rob.burslam@borries.com
Website: http://www.borries.com
Managers: L. Von Arnin, N. Ashton (Mgr), R. Burslam (Mgr)
Immediate Holding Company: BORRIES (UK) LIMITED
Registration no: 01848149 **VAT No.:** GB 422 9418 56
Date established: 1984 **Turnover:** Up to £250,000
No.of Employees: 1 - 10 **Product Groups:** 28, 42, 44, 46

Date of Accounts	Sep 10	Sep 09	Sep 08
Sales Turnover	90	92	135
Pre Tax Profit/Loss	3	4	9
Working Capital	-116	-44	-50
Fixed Assets	9	11	13
Current Assets	218	185	229
Current Liabilities	8	1	7

Channelwood Preservation Ltd

Unit 12-13 Coalbrookdale Road, Clayhill Light Industrial Park, Neston, CH64 3UG
Tel: 0151-342 3728 **Fax:** 0151-342 9472
E-mail: info@channelwood.co.uk
Website: http://www.channelwood.co.uk
Directors: C. Robertson (Dir), P. Robertson (Fin)
Immediate Holding Company: CHANNELWOOD PRESERVATIONS LIMITED
Registration no: 01662131 **VAT No.:** GB 406 2072 91
Date established: 1982 **Turnover:** Up to £250,000
No.of Employees: 1 - 10 **Product Groups:** 25, 32, 52, 66

Date of Accounts	Mar 11	Mar 10	Mar 09
Working Capital	137	223	220
Fixed Assets	4	6	7
Current Assets	265	314	341

Trade 1st Ltd

Field House Upper Raby Road, Neston, CH64 7TZ
Tel: 08448-004167
E-mail: enquiries@trade1st.co.uk
Website: http://www.trade1st.co.uk
Directors: T. Wild (MD)
Immediate Holding Company: TRADE 1ST LIMITED
Registration no: 06295221 **Date established:** 2007
Turnover: Up to £250,000 **No.of Employees:** 1 - 10 **Product Groups:** 49

Date of Accounts	Sep 11	Sep 10	Sep 09
Working Capital	1	-18	-20
Fixed Assets	43	38	29
Current Assets	56	44	40

Newton Le Willows

Brendon International Ltd

Sankey Valley Industrial Estate Junction Lane, Newton Le Willows, WA12 8DN
Tel: 01925-296000 **Fax:** 01925-296001
E-mail: info@brendon.uk.com
Website: http://www.brendon.uk.com
Directors: A. Hancox (Sales), H. James (MD)
Ultimate Holding Company: HMJ HOLDINGS LIMITED
Immediate Holding Company: BRENDON INTERNATIONAL LIMITED
Registration no: 01631731 **Date established:** 1982
No.of Employees: 21 - 50 **Product Groups:** 20, 25, 35, 48, 61, 72, 76, 80, 84

Date of Accounts	Dec 11	Dec 10	Dec 09
Working Capital	264	226	481
Fixed Assets	2m	3m	3m
Current Assets	2m	2m	1m

Busybee Clothing

PO Box 212, Newton Le Willows, WA12 8WL
Tel: 01925-227484 **Fax:** 01925-227484
E-mail: busybeeclothing@aol.com
Website: http://www.busybeeclothing.co.uk
Product Groups: 24, 29, 63

J M Dixon Associates Ltd

22 - 24 Willow Bank, Newton Le Willows, WA12 0DQ
Tel: 01925-222961 **Fax:** 01925-220410
E-mail: info@jmdixon.com
Website: http://www.jmdixon.com
Product Groups: 35, 37, 40, 41, 42, 44

see next page

J M Dixon Associates Ltd - Cont'd

Date of Accounts	May 11	May 10	May 09
Working Capital	196	206	183
Fixed Assets	69	44	32
Current Assets	227	246	212

New-Tonne Lifting Services Ltd
16 Junction Lane, Newton Le Willows, WA12 8DN
Tel: 01925-224471 **Fax:** 01925-223518
E-mail: sales@lifting-engineers.co.uk
Website: http://www.lifting-engineers.co.uk
Bank(s): Lloyds TSB Bank plc
Directors: G. Lindley (Dir)
Immediate Holding Company: NEW-TONNE LIFTING SERVICES LIMITED
Registration no: 02640968 **VAT No.:** GB 561 2908 44
Date established: 1991 **Turnover:** £500,000 - £1m
No.of Employees: 11 - 20 **Product Groups:** 39, 45, 84

Date of Accounts	Sep 11	Sep 10	Sep 09
Working Capital	-1	-67	32
Fixed Assets	67	90	107
Current Assets	505	502	511
Current Liabilities	73	60	55

Nichols plc
Laurel House 3 Woodlands Park Ashton Road, Newton Le Willows, WA12 0HH
Tel: 01925-222222 **Fax:** 01925-222233
E-mail: reception@nicholsplc.co.uk
Website: http://www.nicholsplc.co.uk
Bank(s): Royal Bank of Scotland, Manchester
Directors: T. Crosston (Fin)
Managers: L. Poole (Personnel), B. Hynes, A. Doyle (Tech Serv Mgr), N. Gibson
Immediate Holding Company: NICHOLS PLC
Registration no: 00238303 **VAT No.:** GB 519 9050 33
Date established: 2029 **Turnover:** £75m - £125m
No.of Employees: 21 - 50 **Product Groups:** 21

Date of Accounts	Dec 11	Dec 10	Dec 09
Sales Turnover	99m	84m	72m
Pre Tax Profit/Loss	18m	15m	12m
Working Capital	25m	19m	15m
Fixed Assets	18m	16m	14m
Current Assets	47m	35m	29m
Current Liabilities	16m	13m	10m

D J Sharpe
The Bungalow Vista Road, Newton Le Willows, WA12 0HD
Tel: 01925-224161 **Fax:** 01925-292201
Directors: D. Sharpe (Prop)
Date established: 1989 **No.of Employees:** 1 - 10 **Product Groups:** 41

Trafalgar Tools
116 Market Street, Newton Le Willows, WA12 9BU
Tel: 01925-298888 **Fax:** 01925-298888
E-mail: sales@trafalgar-tools.co.uk
Website: http://www.trafalgar-tools.co.uk
Directors: W. Morse (MD), W. Morse (Prop)
Date established: 2006 **No.of Employees:** 1 - 10 **Product Groups:** 22, 24, 25, 26, 30, 31, 32, 33, 34, 35, 36, 37, 38, 39, 40, 41, 42, 43, 44, 45, 46, 47, 48, 49, 51, 52, 54, 61, 62, 63, 66, 67, 68, 71, 79, 80, 83, 84, 85, 86, 87

Prenton

Deep Clean Cleaning Ltd
Unit 1 Badger Way, Prenton, CH43 3HQ
Tel: 0151-608 8860 **Fax:** 0151-647 0606
E-mail: deepcleancleaning@hotmail.com
Website: http://www.deepcleancleaning.co.uk
Directors: M. Mouse (Dir)
Immediate Holding Company: DEEP CLEAN CLEANING LIMITED
Registration no: 04790815 **Date established:** 2003
No.of Employees: 1 - 10 **Product Groups:** 33, 36

Date of Accounts	Jun 11	Jun 10	Jun 09
Working Capital	-12	-5	-3
Fixed Assets	5	7	8
Current Assets	25	11	11

J D Cleaning Solutions
Unit 7 Badger Way, Prenton, CH43 3HQ
Tel: 0845-3701238 **Fax:** 0845-3701239
E-mail: john@jdcleaningsolutions.com
Website: http://www.jdcleaningsolutions.com
Directors: J. Wallace (Prop)
No.of Employees: 1 - 10 **Product Groups:** 24, 32, 87

Pfaff-Silberblau Ltd
7 Durley Park Close North Cheshire Trading Estate, Prenton, CH43 3DZ
Tel: 01244-375375 **Fax:** 0151-609 0200
E-mail: anyone@pfaff-silberblau.co.uk
Website: http://www.pfaff-silberblau2.co.uk
Bank(s): National Westminster Bank Plc
Directors: J. Jones (Prop), P. Kelly (Dir), T. Dory (Dir)
Ultimate Holding Company: COLUMBUS MCKINNON CORP (USA)
Immediate Holding Company: PFAFF-SILBERBLAU LTD
Registration no: 01754473 **Date established:** 1983 **Turnover:** £2m - £5m
No.of Employees: 11 - 20 **Product Groups:** 45

Safeways Wirral Locksmiths Ltd
10 Grange Mount, Prenton, CH43 4XW
Tel: 0151-653 3414 **Fax:** 0151- 6533414
Website: http://www.safewaysltd.co.uk
Directors: G. Cassidy (MD)
Registration no: 00887416 **Date established:** 1966
No.of Employees: 1 - 10 **Product Groups:** 36, 52

Date of Accounts	Jun 06	Jun 05	Jun 04
Working Capital	-12	-15	1
Fixed Assets	4	4	6
Current Assets	19	22	21
Current Liabilities	31	37	20

The Shrewsbury Lodge
31 Shrewsbury Road, Prenton, CH43 2JB
Tel: 0151-652 4029
E-mail: info@shrewsbury-hotel.com
Website: http://www.shrewsbury-hotel.com
Directors: N. Champion (Ptnr)
Date established: 2004 **No.of Employees:** 1 - 10 **Product Groups:** 69

Sovex Ltd
Unit 2 Prenton Way Business Units Prenton Way, North Cheshire Trading Estate, Prenton, CH43 3EA
Tel: 0151-608 2323 **Fax:** 0151-608 2929
E-mail: info@sovexsystems.com
Website: http://www.sovexsystems.com
Directors: M. Dematteis (Comm), S. Nuttall (Sales), D. Lindfield (MD)
Managers: J. Bennett (Personnel)
Immediate Holding Company: SOVEX LIMITED
Registration no: 04598802 **Date established:** 2002 **Turnover:** £5m - £10m
No.of Employees: 51 - 100 **Product Groups:** 35, 39, 45

Date of Accounts	Dec 11	Dec 10	Dec 09
Sales Turnover	9m	N/A	N/A
Pre Tax Profit/Loss	283	N/A	N/A
Working Capital	-624	-795	-317
Fixed Assets	1m	989	740
Current Assets	3m	2m	3m
Current Liabilities	2m	N/A	1m

Prescot

Acorn Engineering Products
16 Bishopdale Drive Rainhill, Prescot, L35 4QH
Tel: 0151-426 7830 **Fax:** 0151-426 7830
Directors: B. Hendrick (Prop)
Date established: 1989 **No.of Employees:** 1 - 10 **Product Groups:** 26, 35

Bomac Electric Ltd
13a & 13b Randles Road Knowsley Business Park, Prescot, L34 9HX
Tel: 0151-546 4401 **Fax:** 0151-549 1661
E-mail: peter.bowen@bomac-elec.co.uk
Website: http://www.bomac-elec.co.uk
Directors: P. Bowen (MD)
Ultimate Holding Company: SPENCER COMMERCIAL PROPERTY LIMITED
Immediate Holding Company: BOMAC ELECTRIC LIMITED
Registration no: 01276494 **VAT No.:** GB 166 4950 37
Date established: 1976 **Turnover:** £5m - £10m **No.of Employees:** 1 - 10
Product Groups: 33, 37, 40

Date of Accounts	Dec 11	Dec 10	Dec 09
Working Capital	270	245	247
Fixed Assets	29	36	45
Current Assets	378	369	345

Bryken High Speed Turnings Ltd
Randles Road Knowsley Business Park, Prescot, L34 9HX
Tel: 0151-546 9314 **Fax:** 0151-549 1518
E-mail: admin@bryken.com
Website: http://www.bryken.com
Directors: B. Taylor (MD), K. Dovaston (Fin)
Ultimate Holding Company: BRYKEN (HOLDINGS) LIMITED
Immediate Holding Company: BRYKEN LIMITED
Registration no: 01672130 **Date established:** 1982
Turnover: £10m - £20m **No.of Employees:** 51 - 100 **Product Groups:** 46, 48

Date of Accounts	Nov 11	Nov 10	Nov 09
Sales Turnover	10m	N/A	6m
Pre Tax Profit/Loss	535	872	109
Working Capital	964	694	11
Fixed Assets	4m	2m	2m
Current Assets	4m	3m	2m
Current Liabilities	640	782	469

Burco
Stoney Lane Whiston, Prescot, L35 2XW
Tel: 08448-153744 **Fax:** 0844-815 3748
E-mail: sales@burco.co.uk
Website: http://www.burco.co.uk
Bank(s): National Westminster Bank Plc
Directors: S. Lopeman (Sales)
Ultimate Holding Company: GLEN DIMPLEX (ROI)
Immediate Holding Company: BURCO DEAN APPLIANCES LIMITED
Registration no: 01870098 **VAT No.:** GB 287 1315 50
Date established: 1984 **Turnover:** £5m - £10m **No.of Employees:** 21 - 50
Product Groups: 67

Date of Accounts	Mar 11	Mar 10	Mar 09
Sales Turnover	3m	3m	2m
Pre Tax Profit/Loss	664	-279	4
Working Capital	2m	2m	2m
Fixed Assets	98	125	179
Current Assets	3m	2m	2m
Current Liabilities	160	66	15

C P Kelco
Penrhyn Road Knowsley Business Park, Prescot, L34 9HY
Tel: 0151-632 8100 **Fax:** 0151-548 8032
Website: http://www.monsanto.com
Directors: J. Castagna (Dir)
Ultimate Holding Company: J M Huber Corp (USA)
Registration no: 03969110 **Date established:** 2000
Turnover: £20m - £50m **No.of Employees:** 51 - 100 **Product Groups:** 02, 32, 42

Central Electrical Armature Winding Company Ltd
Kitling Road Knowsley Industrial Park South, Knowsley Business Park, Prescot, L34 9JA
Tel: 0151-546 6000 **Fax:** 0151-549 1254
E-mail: sales@gocentral.co.uk
Website: http://www.centralelec.co.uk
Bank(s): Barclays
Directors: S. Sutton (Dir), T. Sutton (Dir)
Managers: D. Parry, I. Riley (Ops Mgr)
Ultimate Holding Company: ORANGEMEAD LIMITED
Immediate Holding Company: CENTRAL ELECTRICAL ARMATURE WINDING CO. LIMITED
Registration no: 01303644 **VAT No.:** GB 166 7650 34
Date established: 1977 **Turnover:** £5m - £10m **No.of Employees:** 21 - 50
Product Groups: 37, 38, 39, 48, 67

Date of Accounts	Dec 11	Dec 10	Dec 09
Sales Turnover	7m	6m	7m
Pre Tax Profit/Loss	224	331	116
Working Capital	522	698	429
Fixed Assets	818	822	837
Current Assets	2m	2m	2m
Current Liabilities	696	319	225

Chums Ltd
Unity Grove Knowsley Business Park, Prescot, L34 9AR
Tel: 08719-119999 **Fax:** 0151-548 6829
E-mail: sales@chums.co.uk
Website: http://www.chums.co.uk
Directors: G. Rubin (Dir)
Immediate Holding Company: CHUMS LIMITED
Registration no: 01561474 **VAT No.:** GB 325 1665 69
Date established: 1981 **Turnover:** £20m - £50m
No.of Employees: 101 - 250 **Product Groups:** 61

Date of Accounts	Dec 11	Dec 10	Dec 09
Sales Turnover	27m	28m	28m
Pre Tax Profit/Loss	710	2m	136
Working Capital	4m	3m	2m
Fixed Assets	1m	1m	1m
Current Assets	8m	8m	8m
Current Liabilities	2m	2m	3m

Contract Chemicals Ltd
Penrhyn Road Knowsley Business Park, Prescot, L34 9HY
Tel: 0151-548 8840 **Fax:** 0151-548 6548
E-mail: info@contract-chemicals.com
Website: http://www.contract-chemicals.com
Bank(s): The Royal Bank of Scotland
Managers: M. Howard (Personnel), E. Bonner (Comptroller), V. Ivkovic (Comm), J. Flatt, J. Bowers (Purch Mgr)
Ultimate Holding Company: CONTRACT CHEMICALS LIMITED
Immediate Holding Company: CONTRACT CHEMICALS LIMITED
Registration no: 02332554 **VAT No.:** GB 428 8340 36
Date established: 1989 **Turnover:** £10m - £20m
No.of Employees: 51 - 100 **Product Groups:** 66

Date of Accounts	Mar 11	Mar 10	Mar 09
Sales Turnover	19m	20m	25m
Pre Tax Profit/Loss	45	323	887
Working Capital	950	1m	570
Fixed Assets	10m	10m	11m
Current Assets	6m	6m	7m
Current Liabilities	4m	4m	4m

Counterline
12 Randles Road Knowsley Business Park, Prescot, L34 9HZ
Tel: 0151-548 2211 **Fax:** 0151-546 6666
E-mail: admin@counterline.co.uk
Website: http://www.counterline.co.uk
Directors: S. Dutton (Fin), T. Flood (Sales), T. Flood (Sales)
Managers: A. Ward (Fin Mgr), S. Simpson (Purch Mgr)
Ultimate Holding Company: COUNTERLINE HOLDINGS LIMITED
Immediate Holding Company: COUNTERLINE LIMITED
Registration no: 05471587 **Date established:** 2005 **Turnover:** £5m - £10m
No.of Employees: 101 - 250 **Product Groups:** 40, 48

Date of Accounts	Jun 11	Jun 10	Jun 09
Sales Turnover	10m	7m	7m
Pre Tax Profit/Loss	130	165	515
Working Capital	1m	1m	1m
Fixed Assets	1m	1m	1m
Current Assets	5m	4m	4m
Current Liabilities	2m	2m	2m

E G O UK Ltd
Unit 4 Caddick Road, Knowsley Business Park, Prescot, L34 9HP
Tel: 0151-549 1166 **Fax:** 0151-549 1124
E-mail: info.unitedkingdom@egoproducts.com
Website: http://www.egoproducts.com
Directors: S. Rowe (MD)
Immediate Holding Company: E.G.O. UNITED KINGDOM LIMITED
Registration no: 01708657 **Date established:** 1983
Turnover: £250,000 - £500,000 **No.of Employees:** 1 - 10
Product Groups: 37, 38, 40

Date of Accounts	Dec 11	Dec 10	Dec 09
Sales Turnover	401	399	N/A
Pre Tax Profit/Loss	51	27	N/A
Working Capital	452	410	392
Fixed Assets	6	11	18
Current Assets	488	453	417
Current Liabilities	29	34	N/A

E L M Construction
Blundells Lane Rainhill, Prescot, L35 6NB
Tel: 0151-426 3511 **Fax:** 0151-432 7000
E-mail: sales@elmsheds.co.uk
Website: http://www.elmconstruction.co.uk
Directors: P. Mawdsley (Snr Part)
Registration no: 00458339 **VAT No.:** GB 163 9569 25
Turnover: £250,000 - £500,000 **No.of Employees:** 1 - 10
Product Groups: 25, 33

Date of Accounts	Nov 11	Nov 10	Nov 09
Working Capital	29	37	53
Fixed Assets	55	59	80
Current Assets	112	145	147

Hartley Precision Engineering Company Ltd
Caddick Road Knowsley Business Park, Prescot, L34 9HP
Tel: 0151-548 0777 **Fax:** 0151-549 1191
E-mail: enquiries@hartleyprecision.co.uk
Website: http://www.hartleyprecision.co.uk
Bank(s): National Westminster Bank Plc
Directors: J. O'donnell (Chief Op Offcr), W. O'Donnell (Dir)
Managers: J. Short (Prod Mgr), R. Lamb (Tech Serv Mgr)
Ultimate Holding Company: STEWART HOLDINGS GROUP LIMITED
Immediate Holding Company: HARTLEY PRECISION ENGINEERING CO. LIMITED
Registration no: 01810334 **VAT No.:** GB 387 3509 19
Date established: 1984 **Turnover:** £500,000 - £1m
No.of Employees: 21 - 50 **Product Groups:** 48

Date of Accounts	Oct 11	Oct 10	Oct 09
Working Capital	879	642	656
Fixed Assets	385	452	388
Current Assets	2m	1m	1m

Hemsec Group
Stoney Lane Rainhill, Prescot, L35 9LL
Tel: 0151-426 7171 **Fax:** 0151-493 1331
E-mail: sales@hemsec.com
Website: http://www.hemsec.com

Bank(s): Midland, Liverpool
Directors: W. Hemmings (Ch)
Managers: K. Bowsher (Develop Mgr), M. Rotherham (Chief Acct)
Immediate Holding Company: HEMSEC DEVELOPMENTS LIMITED
Registration no: 01168503 **VAT No.:** GB 414 6208 77
Date established: 1974 **Turnover:** £2m - £5m **No.of Employees:** 21 - 50
Product Groups: 40, 48, 52

Date of Accounts	Jun 08	Jun 07	Dec 05
Working Capital	38	50	62
Fixed Assets	1	1	2
Current Assets	89	131	459
Current Liabilities	51	81	397

Henry Hollinghurst

Keepers Cottage School Lane, Knowsley, Prescot, L34 9EN
Tel: 0151-548 3238 **Fax:** 0151-548 3238
E-mail: havergil@globalnet.co.uk
Directors: H. Hollinghurst (Prop)
Immediate Holding Company: STUDIO ARGENT,LIMITED
Registration no: 00731254 **Date established:** 1962
No.of Employees: 1 - 10 **Product Groups:** 41

Date of Accounts	Jul 11	Jul 10	Jul 09
Working Capital	126	112	115
Fixed Assets	4	20	2
Current Assets	159	145	138

JHP group Limited (Part of J H P Group Ltd)

6 Tiger Court Kings Business Park, Knowsley, Prescot, L34 1BD
Tel: 0151-489 8259 **Fax:** 0151-227 2452
E-mail: manchester.business.centre@jhptraining.comv
Website: http://www.jhptraining.com
Directors: J. Pitman (MD)
Managers: D. Blake
Immediate Holding Company: J H P Group Ltd, Coventy
Registration no: 01729661 **No.of Employees:** 11 - 20 **Product Groups:** 86

L E K Sales

30 Cumber Lane Whiston, Prescot, L35 2XQ
Tel: 0151-430 7158 **Fax:** 0151-426 9116
E-mail: info@beka-max.co.uk
Website: http://www.beka-max.co.uk
Directors: A. Lay (Ptnr)
Immediate Holding Company: SPONSORSHIP INVESTMENT MANAGEMENT SERVICES LIMITED
Date established: 2010 **No.of Employees:** 1 - 10 **Product Groups:** 31, 36, 38, 39, 40, 42, 43, 45, 46, 48, 49, 66, 67, 68, 84

Lbk Packaging Limited

Overbrook Court Overbrook Lane, Knowsley Business Park, Prescot, L34 9FB
Tel: 0151-547 5380 **Fax:** 0151-549 0693
E-mail: sales@lbkpackaging.co.uk
Website: http://www.lbkpackaging.co.uk
Managers: S. Ainscough (Mgr)
Registration no: 04522213 **Turnover:** £5m - £10m
No.of Employees: 21 - 50 **Product Groups:** 24, 30

Manesty

Kitling Road Knowsley Business Park, Prescot, L34 9JS
Tel: 0151-547 8000 **Fax:** 0151-547 8001
E-mail: matthias.meyer@oystar.manesty.com
Website: http://www.oystar.manesty.com
Bank(s): HSBC
Directors: M. Meyer (MD), B. Jameson (MD)
Managers: A. Turrell (Purch Mgr), L. Cashmore (Sales & Mktg Mg)
Ultimate Holding Company: LIN VERMOGENSVERWALTUNG GMBH (GERMANY)
Immediate Holding Company: BWI PLC
Registration no: 04473562 **VAT No.:** GB 618 6029 37
Date established: 1951 **Turnover:** £2m - £5m
No.of Employees: 101 - 250 **Product Groups:** 41, 42

Minta Instrumentation Ltd

Unit 24a Caddick Road, Knowsley Business Park, Prescot, L34 9HP
Tel: 0151-548 6818 **Fax:** 0151-548 5578
E-mail: office@mintasensors.co.uk
Website: http://www.mintasensors.co.uk
Directors: M. Edwards (Dir)
Immediate Holding Company: MINTA INSTRUMENTATION LIMITED
Registration no: 01253132 **Date established:** 1976
Turnover: £250,000 - £500,000 **No.of Employees:** 11 - 20
Product Groups: 38, 40, 85

Date of Accounts	Mar 12	Mar 11	Mar 10
Working Capital	289	244	24
Fixed Assets	29	29	35
Current Assets	679	422	315

Rotofinish Rosler

1 Unity Grove Knowsley Business Park, Prescot, L34 9GT
Tel: 0151-547 3725 **Fax:** 0151-546 4759
E-mail: pmoorelandson@roesler-surfacefinish.com
Website: http://www.roesler-surfacefinish.com
Managers: P. Moorelandson (Mgr)
Date established: 1995 **No.of Employees:** 1 - 10 **Product Groups:** 46, 48

Staffords Ltd

Overbrook Court Overbrook Lane, Knowsley, Prescot, L34 9FB
Tel: 0151-907 0027 **Fax:** 0151-907 0028
E-mail: enquiries@staffords.ltd.uk
Website: http://www.staffords.ltd.uk
Bank(s): Barclays
Directors: M. Barnett (Fin), D. Latham (Dir), D. Lathan (Develop)
Immediate Holding Company: STAFFORDS LIMITED
Registration no: 01311369 **VAT No.:** GB 303 5474 82
Date established: 1977 **Turnover:** £2m - £5m **No.of Employees:** 51 - 100
Product Groups: 64, 67

Date of Accounts	Jun 11	Jun 10	Jun 09
Working Capital	289	237	33
Fixed Assets	789	1m	1m
Current Assets	805	949	806

Studio Argent Ltd

School Lane Knowsley, Prescot, L34 9EN
Tel: 0151-548 7722 **Fax:** 0151-549 1713
E-mail: images@studioargent.co.uk
Website: http://www.studioargent.co.uk
Directors: B. Jackson (MD)
Immediate Holding Company: STUDIO ARGENT,LIMITED
Registration no: 00731254 **VAT No.:** GB 164 7174 52
Date established: 1962 **Turnover:** £250,000 - £500,000
No.of Employees: 1 - 10 **Product Groups:** 81

Date of Accounts	Jul 11	Jul 10	Jul 09
Working Capital	126	112	115
Fixed Assets	4	20	2
Current Assets	159	145	138

South Wirral

Incon (Inspection Consultants) Ltd

Rosscliffe Road Ellesmere Port, South Wirral, CH65 3BS
Tel: 0151-356 5666 **Fax:** 0151-357 4181
E-mail: mail@incon.co.uk
Website: http://www.incon.co.uk
Directors: D. Whitfield (MD)
Managers: P. Prithchard (Quality Control), M. Gouldson (Accounts), R. Bailey (Sales Prom Mgr)
Registration no: 06219349 **Turnover:** £500,000 - £1m
No.of Employees: 11 - 20 **Product Groups:** 37, 38, 42, 48, 52, 54, 66, 67, 80, 84, 85, 86, 87

Southport

Abram Fencing

59 Old Park Lane, Southport, PR9 7BQ
Tel: 01704-224923 **Fax:** 01704-224923
E-mail: john@abramfencing.co.uk
Website: http://www.abramfencing.co.uk
Directors: J. Abram (Prop)
No.of Employees: 1 - 10 **Product Groups:** 25, 35, 36, 52

Alloi

Unit 4 The Mews 15a Liverpool Road, Southport, PR8 4AS
Tel: 01704-550451
E-mail: info@alloi.net
Website: http://www.alloi.net
Directors: A. Billingsley (Dir)
Immediate Holding Company: ALLOI UK LIMITED
Registration no: 07157852 **Date established:** 2010
No.of Employees: 1 - 10 **Product Groups:** 44

Date of Accounts	Feb 11
Working Capital	-2
Current Assets	4

Aqua Cure

Aqua Cure House Hall Street, Southport, PR9 0SE
Tel: 01704-501616 **Fax:** 01704-544916
E-mail: sales@aquacure.co.uk
Website: http://www.aquacure.co.uk
Bank(s): Barclays, Lord St, Southport
Directors: M. Brown (MD)
Managers: R. Stephenson (Tech Serv Mgr), T. McCullough (Purch Mgr)
Immediate Holding Company: AQUA CURE LIMITED
Registration no: 06330499 **VAT No.:** GB 477 4864 90
Date established: 2007 **Turnover:** £2m - £5m **No.of Employees:** 21 - 50
Product Groups: 40, 42

Date of Accounts	Dec 11	Dec 10	Dec 09
Sales Turnover	5m	10m	8m
Pre Tax Profit/Loss	1m	788	420
Working Capital	-443	-921	-1m
Fixed Assets	2m	4m	4m
Current Assets	2m	3m	2m
Current Liabilities	469	999	458

Arena Rooms Ltd

Five Pillars 50 Waterloo Road, Southport, PR8 2NB
Tel: 0845-6033139
E-mail: enquiries@arenarooms.com
Website: http://www.arenarooms.com
Directors: J. Pownall (Dir)
Immediate Holding Company: ARENA ROOMS LIMITED
Registration no: 05635825 **Date established:** 2005
No.of Employees: 1 - 10 **Product Groups:** 83

Date of Accounts	Dec 07	Dec 06
Working Capital	7	-14
Fixed Assets	6	5
Current Assets	40	10
Current Liabilities	32	24

Baumann Hinde & Co. Ltd

5 Church Street, Southport, PR9 0QS
Tel: 01704-543737 **Fax:** 01704-503601
E-mail: bh.trading@bahico.com
Website: http://www.bahico.com
Ultimate Holding Company: BARRICK INVESTMENT HOLDINGS LTD (BVI)
Immediate Holding Company: BAUMANN HINDE & CO.LIMITED
Registration no: 00553806 **Date established:** 1955 **Turnover:** £5m - £10m
No.of Employees: 1 - 10 **Product Groups:** 66

Bensons Waste Oils & Fats

55 Crowland Street, Southport, PR9 7RX
Tel: 01704-507757 **Fax:** 01704-507757
E-mail: info@bensonsuk.com
Website: http://www.bensonsuk.com
Directors: M. Holcroft (Prop), N. Holcroft (MD), J. Portnall (Co Sec)
Immediate Holding Company: MG WASTE TRANSPORT LIMITED
Registration no: 04796050 **Date established:** 2011
No.of Employees: 1 - 10 **Product Groups:** 20, 32, 41

Cartridge World Ltd

105 Manchester Road, Southport, PR9 9BB
Tel: 01704-500335
Website: http://www.southport.cartridgeworld.co.uk
Directors: C. Aitkin (Dir)
Immediate Holding Company: CARTRIDGE WORLD LIMITED
Registration no: 04124067 **Date established:** 2000 **Turnover:** £5m - £10m
No.of Employees: 1 - 10 **Product Groups:** 28, 30, 44, 64

Date of Accounts	Dec 11	Dec 10	Dec 09
Sales Turnover	6m	7m	8m
Pre Tax Profit/Loss	373	164	210
Working Capital	1m	967	878
Fixed Assets	403	455	524
Current Assets	7m	7m	6m
Current Liabilities	4m	1m	2m

Chrislec Lighting Manufactures

Gravel Lane Banks, Southport, PR9 8DE
Tel: 01704-507705 **Fax:** 01704-506970
Managers: D. Yardley (Mgr)
No.of Employees: 1 - 10 **Product Groups:** 37, 67

Churchtown Buildings Ltd

Lion Acre House Moss Lane, Banks, Southport, PR9 8EE
Tel: 01704-227826 **Fax:** 01704-220247
E-mail: sales@churchtown.co.uk
Website: http://www.churchtown.co.uk
Managers: W. Slater (Sales Prom Mgr)
Immediate Holding Company: CHURCHTOWN BUILDINGS LIMITED
Registration no: 01104508 **VAT No.:** GB 428 9248 19
Date established: 1973 **Turnover:** £250,000 - £500,000
No.of Employees: 1 - 10 **Product Groups:** 35

Date of Accounts	Jun 08	Jun 07	Jun 05
Working Capital	N/A	5	-20
Fixed Assets	81	115	175
Current Assets	56	34	42

Cooperheat UK Ltd

Unit 21-24 Slaidburn Industrial Estate Slaidburn Crescent, Southport, PR9 9YF
Tel: 01704-215600 **Fax:** 01695-713501
E-mail: nigel.bleackley@stork.com
Website: http://www.storktechnicalservices.com
Bank(s): Barclays
Directors: M. Eastwood (Co Sec)
Managers: S. Litherland, R. Davies (Tech Serv Mgr), R. Hardey (Personnel), N. Bleackley, A. Mitchell (Comptroller)
Ultimate Holding Company: STORK NV (NETHERLANDS)
Immediate Holding Company: STORK TECHNICAL SERVICES (STS) LTD
Registration no: 03809192 **VAT No.:** GB 732 3643 48
Date established: 1999 **Turnover:** £5m - £10m
No.of Employees: 101 - 250 **Product Groups:** 38, 40, 42, 46, 48, 51, 52, 83, 84, 85

Date of Accounts	Dec 11	Dec 10	Dec 09
Sales Turnover	8m	7m	8m
Pre Tax Profit/Loss	514	451	3m
Working Capital	3m	2m	2m
Fixed Assets	4m	4m	4m
Current Assets	5m	4m	4m
Current Liabilities	212	270	318

Doormen

Wennington Road, Southport, PR9 7TN
Tel: 01704-518000 **Fax:** 01704-518001
E-mail: jab@doormen.co.uk
Website: http://www.doormen.co.uk
Bank(s): Royal Bank of Scotland, Southport
Directors: M. Morse (Comm), M. Rimmer (Co Sec), C. Webb (Dir), A. Lack (Jt MD), A. Bache (Dir), G. Jackson (MD), J. Barlow (MD)
Managers: J. Barlow, G. Harrison, A. Farrington (Mats Contrlr)
Ultimate Holding Company: UNIPART GROUP OF COMPANIES LTD
Immediate Holding Company: HAZEFAMOUS LTD
Registration no: 00169770 **VAT No.:** GB 477 4659 91
Date established: 1994 **Turnover:** £5m - £10m **No.of Employees:** 11 - 20
Product Groups: 37, 39, 40

Date of Accounts	Dec 07
Working Capital	201
Current Assets	858
Current Liabilities	657
Total Share Capital	200

Edward Jackson

Suite 2 Victoria House 32 Hoghton Street, Southport, PR9 0PA
Tel: 01704-546686 **Fax:** 01704-501173
E-mail: ed.jack@mail.cybase.co.uk
Website: http://www.edwardjackson.co.uk
Directors: A. Sharman (Ptnr)
Date established: 1986 **No.of Employees:** 1 - 10 **Product Groups:** 35

Enterprise Fabrication Co

Virginia Street, Southport, PR8 6RZ
Tel: 01704-541544 **Fax:** 01704-544260
Website: http://www.eaststreetfurniture.com
Directors: S. Broomhead (MD)
Managers: D. Hunter (Mgr), D. Hunters (Mgr)
Immediate Holding Company: SOUTHPORT CAR WAREHOUSE LTD
VAT No.: GB 407 2681 60 **Date established:** 2011
Turnover: £500,000 - £1m **No.of Employees:** 1 - 10 **Product Groups:** 48

Garrick Fabrications Ltd

Crowland Street Industrial Estate Crowland Street, Southport, PR9 7RQ
Tel: 01704-534906 **Fax:** 01704-537952
E-mail: nina@gfab.co.uk
Website: http://www.gfab.co.uk
Bank(s): Barclays
Directors: N. Torpey (Sales)
Managers: N. Smith Crallan (Comptroller), N. Proud (Purch Mgr), N. Smith (Comptroller)
Immediate Holding Company: GARRICK ENGINEERING COMPANY LIMITED
Registration no: 00416335 **VAT No.:** GB 163 6376 51
Date established: 1946 **Turnover:** £2m - £5m **No.of Employees:** 11 - 20
Product Groups: 48

Date of Accounts	Sep 09	Sep 08	Sep 07
Sales Turnover	3m	N/A	N/A
Pre Tax Profit/Loss	108	N/A	N/A
Working Capital	-446	-516	-672
Fixed Assets	2m	2m	2m
Current Assets	854	2m	2m
Current Liabilities	599	N/A	N/A

Gate Place

140 Poulton Road, Southport, PR9 7DB
Tel: 01704-224365 **Fax:** 01704-507500
Website: http://www.gatemasteruk.com
Directors: G. Thierens (Prop)
Date established: 1979 **No.of Employees:** 1 - 10 **Product Groups:** 26, 35

Hunt & Edwards
Unit 22 Birkdale Trading Estate Liverpool Road, Southport, PR8 4PZ
Tel: 01704-550300 **Fax:** 01704-550700
E-mail: sales@huntandedwards.co.uk
Directors: P. Hunt (Fin)
Immediate Holding Company: HUNT & EDWARDS LIMITED
Registration no: 05470951 **Date established:** 2005
No.of Employees: 1 - 10 **Product Groups:** 46

Date of Accounts	Jun 11	Jun 10	Jun 09
Working Capital	5	4	5
Fixed Assets	1	1	1
Current Assets	15	20	39

Inciner8 Ltd
Inciner8 House Balmoral Business Centre Balmoral Drive, Southport, PR9 8PZ
Tel: 01704-506506 **Fax:** 01704-506666
E-mail: sales@inciner8.com
Website: http://www.inciner8.com
Directors: V. Ferguson (Fin)
Managers: P. Thorpe (Chief Mgr)
Immediate Holding Company: INCINER8 LIMITED
Registration no: 04866401 **Date established:** 2003
Turnover: £500,000 - £1m **No.of Employees:** 1 - 10 **Product Groups:** 40

Date of Accounts	Apr 11	Apr 10	Apr 09
Working Capital	2m	919	394
Fixed Assets	241	224	154
Current Assets	2m	1m	773

Insulation & Machining Services Ltd
Russell Road, Southport, PR9 7SB
Tel: 01704-226878 **Fax:** 01704-225857
E-mail: sales@ims-insulation.com
Website: http://www.ims-insulation.com
Bank(s): Barclays
Managers: D. Carington (Mgr)
Ultimate Holding Company: SIG PLC
Immediate Holding Company: INSULATION & MACHINING SERVICES LIMITED
Registration no: 02826466 **Date established:** 1993 **Turnover:** £2m - £5m
No.of Employees: 21 - 50 **Product Groups:** 30, 32, 33, 37, 42, 66

Date of Accounts	Dec 11	Dec 10	Dec 09
Working Capital	401	401	401
Current Assets	401	401	401

Inter-Group Communications Ltd
The Telecom Engineering Centre 113a Norwood Road, Southport, PR8 6EL
Tel: 01704-535977 **Fax:** 01704-535560
E-mail: enquiries@intergroup.co.uk
Website: http://www.intergroup.co.uk
Bank(s): The Royal Bank of Scotland
Directors: B. Barclay (Fin), C. Barclay (Dir)
Immediate Holding Company: INTER-GROUP COMMUNICATIONS LIMITED
Registration no: 01241499 **Date established:** 1976 **Turnover:** £1m - £2m
No.of Employees: 11 - 20 **Product Groups:** 37, 48, 84

Date of Accounts	Mar 12	Mar 11	Mar 10
Working Capital	375	104	-40
Fixed Assets	1m	1m	1m
Current Assets	946	1m	606

Isothermal Technology Ltd
42a St Lukes Road, Southport, PR9 9AP
Tel: 01704-543830 **Fax:** 01704-544799
E-mail: info@isotech.co.uk
Website: http://www.isotech.co.uk
Bank(s): Lloyds TSB Bank plc
Directors: J. Tavener (I.T. Dir)
Managers: L. Clark (Sales Admin), A. Holmes (Purch Mgr)
Immediate Holding Company: ISOTHERMAL TECHNOLOGY LIMITED
Registration no: 01530620 **VAT No.:** GB 32518979 **Date established:** 1980
Turnover: £2m - £5m **No.of Employees:** 21 - 50 **Product Groups:** 38, 67

Date of Accounts	Mar 12	Mar 11	Mar 10
Working Capital	1m	1m	1m
Fixed Assets	450	452	478
Current Assets	2m	2m	2m

Jewson Ltd
Meols Cop Bridge Bispham Road, Southport, PR9 7DD
Tel: 01704-229821 **Fax:** 01704-225557
Website: http://www.jewson.co.uk
Bank(s): Barclays
Managers: R. Berry (District Mgr)
Ultimate Holding Company: COMPAGNIE DE SAINT GOBAIN (FRANCE)
Immediate Holding Company: JEWSON LIMITED
Registration no: 00348407 **VAT No.:** GB 394 1212 63
Date established: 1939 **Turnover:** £2m - £5m **No.of Employees:** 11 - 20
Product Groups: 66

Date of Accounts	Dec 11	Dec 10	Dec 09
Sales Turnover	1606m	1547m	1485m
Pre Tax Profit/Loss	18m	100m	45m
Working Capital	-345m	-250m	-349m
Fixed Assets	496m	387m	461m
Current Assets	657m	1005m	1320m
Current Liabilities	66m	120m	64m

Kiddie Of Southport Ltd
91a Kensington Road, Southport, PR9 0SA
Tel: 01704-536464 **Fax:** 01704-543533
E-mail: sales@kiddie.co.uk
Website: http://www.kiddie.co.uk
Bank(s): Barclays
Directors: D. Sale (Dir), S. Holmes (Fin)
Managers: J. Edgerton (Sales Prom Mgr)
Immediate Holding Company: KIDDIE OF SOUTHPORT LIMITED
Registration no: 00446479 **VAT No.:** GB 163 8111 77
Date established: 1947 **Turnover:** £2m - £5m **No.of Employees:** 21 - 50
Product Groups: 26, 35

Date of Accounts	Nov 11	Nov 10	Nov 09
Working Capital	184	6	48
Fixed Assets	802	846	849
Current Assets	791	861	597

Lancashire Glass & Solar Ltd
Unit 1 George Business Park Cemetery Road, Southport, PR8 5EF
Tel: 01704-533888 **Fax:** 01704-501183
E-mail: admin@lancsglass.co.uk
Website: http://www.lancashire-glass.co.uk
Directors: G. Greenall (MD), L. Bonnar (Dir), J. Sutton (Ch), E. Pye (Co Sec)
Ultimate Holding Company: 01074315
Immediate Holding Company: LANCASHIRE GLASS & BUILDING LIMITED
Registration no: 01695510 **Date established:** 1983
Turnover: £500,000 - £1m **No.of Employees:** 1 - 10 **Product Groups:** 30, 36

Lattimer Ltd
79-83 Shakespeare Street, Southport, PR8 5AP
Tel: 01704-535040 **Fax:** 01704-541046
E-mail: mark.hailwood@lattimer.com
Website: http://www.lattimer.com
Bank(s): Barclays, Colmore Row
Directors: B. Hughes (Sales & Mktg), M. Hailwood (Dir)
Managers: J. Walsh (Purch Mgr), S. Cropper (Tech Serv Mgr), C. Stead
Ultimate Holding Company: LATTIMER HOLDINGS LIMITED
Immediate Holding Company: LATTIMER LIMITED
Registration no: 00370725 **VAT No.:** GB 582 3397 18
Date established: 1941 **Turnover:** £5m - £10m
No.of Employees: 51 - 100 **Product Groups:** 39, 48

Date of Accounts	Mar 12	Mar 11	Mar 10
Sales Turnover	6m	5m	5m
Pre Tax Profit/Loss	386	156	300
Working Capital	1m	2m	1m
Fixed Assets	1m	1m	1m
Current Assets	3m	2m	2m
Current Liabilities	350	340	210

Mentha & Halsall
95a Linaker Street, Southport, PR8 5BU
Tel: 01704-530800 **Fax:** 01704-500601
E-mail: sales@mentha-halsall.com
Website: http://www.mentha-halsall.com
Bank(s): National Westminster
Directors: P. Mentha (Dir)
Ultimate Holding Company: R M HOLDINGS
Immediate Holding Company: MENTHA & HALSALL (SHOPFITTERS) LIMITED
Registration no: 01256525 **VAT No.:** 325 0155 00 **Date established:** 1976
Turnover: £5m - £10m **No.of Employees:** 21 - 50 **Product Groups:** 26, 35, 37, 49, 52

Date of Accounts	Nov 11	Nov 10	Nov 09
Sales Turnover	N/A	N/A	5m
Pre Tax Profit/Loss	N/A	N/A	46
Working Capital	605	574	546
Fixed Assets	96	131	137
Current Assets	2m	2m	2m
Current Liabilities	N/A	N/A	432

Morgan Hope Industries Ltd
Unit 5-6 Blowick Business Park Crowland Street, Southport, PR9 7RU
Tel: 01704-512000 **Fax:** 01704-542632
E-mail: valerie.fisher@morganhope.com
Website: http://www.morganhope.com
Directors: V. Fisher (Dir)
Managers: S. Morris
Immediate Holding Company: MORGAN HOPE INDUSTRIES LIMITED
Registration no: 02708699 **Date established:** 1992
No.of Employees: 11 - 20 **Product Groups:** 37, 67

Date of Accounts	Jun 11	Jun 10	Jun 09
Working Capital	641	647	587
Fixed Assets	114	120	123
Current Assets	937	954	830

Greg Morris Photography
56 Forest Road, Southport, PR8 6HZ
Tel: 07802-392233
E-mail: greg@gregmorrisphoto.co.uk
Website: http://www.gregmorrisphoto.co.uk
Directors: G. Morris (Prop)
Date established: 1988 **Turnover:** £250,000 - £500,000
No.of Employees: 1 - 10 **Product Groups:** 81

Nvyro Ltd
100 Liverpool Road, Southport, PR8 4DA
Tel: 0161-408 4228
E-mail: paul@nvyro.com
Website: http://www.nvyro.com
Directors: P. Gregson (Prop)
Immediate Holding Company: NVYRO LIMITED
Registration no: 05272089 **Date established:** 2004
Turnover: £250,000 - £500,000 **No.of Employees:** 1 - 10
Product Groups: 30

Date of Accounts	Aug 11	Aug 10	Aug 09
Working Capital	-7	-5	-5
Current Assets	12	13	11

Newstrap
52 Promenade, Southport, PR9 0DY
Tel: 01704-532724 **Fax:** 01704-532724
Directors: M. Wakefield (Prop)
Date established: 2003 **No.of Employees:** 1 - 10 **Product Groups:** 38, 42

Nexus Emergency Lighting
Unit 8 Gravel Lane Banks, Southport, PR9 8DE
Tel: 01704-232783
Managers: D. Yardley (Mgr)
No.of Employees: 1 - 10 **Product Groups:** 37, 67

North West Packaging
34 Kempton Park Fold, Southport, PR8 5PL
Tel: 01704-544733
E-mail: sales@nwp-southport.co.uk
Website: http://www.nwp-southport.co.uk
Directors: P. Masters (Prop)
Date established: 1989 **No.of Employees:** 1 - 10 **Product Groups:** 38, 42

Optiquality Holdings Ltd
6a Larch Street, Southport, PR8 6DP
Tel: 01704-538921 **Fax:** 01704-544132
Directors: N. Huxtable (Fin), E. Huxtable (MD)
Immediate Holding Company: OPTIQUALITY (HOLDINGS) LIMITED
Registration no: 00377928 **Date established:** 1942
No.of Employees: 1 - 10 **Product Groups:** 45

Date of Accounts	Dec 11	Dec 10	Dec 09
Working Capital	129	160	188
Fixed Assets	350	350	350
Current Assets	200	232	256

R T D Products
Unit 10-11 A K Business Park Russell Road, Southport, PR9 7SA
Tel: 01704-507696 **Fax:** 01704-507055
E-mail: sales@rtd-products.co.uk
Website: http://www.rtd-products.co.uk
Bank(s): Barclays
Managers: B. Peach (Chief Mgr)
Immediate Holding Company: THERMOCOUPLE INSTRUMENTS LTD
VAT No.: GB 134 9494 45 **Turnover:** £5m - £10m
No.of Employees: 11 - 20 **Product Groups:** 36, 37, 38, 40, 67

Railex Filing Ltd
Crossens Way Marine Drive, Southport, PR9 9LY
Tel: 01704-222100 **Fax:** 01923-252211
E-mail: sales@railex.co.uk
Website: http://www.railexfiling.co.uk
Bank(s): Lloyds TSB Bank plc
Directors: P. McDade (Fin)
Managers: S. Burns
Ultimate Holding Company: RAILEX LIMITED
Immediate Holding Company: ELITE MANUFACTURING CO. LTD
Registration no: 00649469 **VAT No.:** GB 325 3630 78
Date established: 1960 **Turnover:** £2m - £5m **No.of Employees:** 21 - 50
Product Groups: 26, 49

Date of Accounts	Apr 08	Apr 07	Apr 06
Pre Tax Profit/Loss	N/A	-338	-2m
Working Capital	181	-68	336
Fixed Assets	382	519	866
Current Assets	1m	1m	2m
Current Liabilities	N/A	426	712

Royal Birkdale Golf Club
Waterloo Road, Southport, PR8 2LX
Tel: 01704-552020 **Fax:** 01704-552021
E-mail: secretary@royalbirkdale.com
Website: http://www.royalbirkdale.com
Managers: M. Gilyert (Mgr), M. Gilyeat (Sales Prom Mgr)
Immediate Holding Company: Royal Birkdale Golf Club Merchandising Company Limited(The)
Registration no: 01675820 **Date established:** 1982
No.of Employees: 21 - 50 **Product Groups:** 49, 65

Date of Accounts	Nov 05
Working Capital	1
Current Assets	1
Total Share Capital	1

S B Industrial Agencies
36a Kew Road, Southport, PR8 4HW
Tel: 01704-569940 **Fax:** 01704-569324
Directors: B. Done (Prop)
Date established: 1985 **No.of Employees:** 1 - 10 **Product Groups:** 38, 42

S F C Wholesale
Westminster Chambers Lord Street, Southport, PR8 1LF
Tel: 01704-548641 **Fax:** 01704-546412
E-mail: walter@sfcwholesale.co.uk
Website: http://www.sfcwholesale.co.uk
Managers: W. Horrocks (Chief Mgr)
Immediate Holding Company: RETAIL AND TRADE EVALUATION SERVICES UK LTD
Registration no: 01897546 **Date established:** 2011 **Turnover:** £2m - £5m
No.of Employees: 1 - 10 **Product Groups:** 20, 62

Date of Accounts	Mar 08	Mar 07	Mar 06
Working Capital	491	299	101
Fixed Assets	50	65	98
Current Assets	1467	648	469
Current Liabilities	975	349	368

Sally Hair & Beauty Supplies Ltd
321 Lord Street, Southport, PR8 1NH
Tel: 01704-538679
E-mail: admin@sallybeauty.co.uk
Website: http://www.sallybeauty.com
Managers: T. Wain Wright (Mgr)
Ultimate Holding Company: SALLY BEAUTY HOLDING INC (USA)
Immediate Holding Company: SALLY SALON SERVICES LIMITED
Registration no: 01060763 **Date established:** 1972
No.of Employees: 1 - 10 **Product Groups:** 30, 36, 40

Date of Accounts	Sep 11	Sep 10	Sep 09
Sales Turnover	128m	107m	82m
Pre Tax Profit/Loss	3m	2m	1m
Working Capital	10m	7m	6m
Fixed Assets	11m	12m	9m
Current Assets	63m	50m	45m
Current Liabilities	10m	7m	4m

Sensing Devices Ltd
97 Tithebarn Road, Southport, PR8 6AG
Tel: 01704-546161 **Fax:** 01704-564231
E-mail: sales@sensing-devices.co.uk
Website: http://www.sensing-devices.co.uk
Bank(s): Barclays,Lord Street, Southport
Directors: J. Halstead (MD)
Immediate Holding Company: SENSING DEVICES LIMITED
Registration no: 01018313 **VAT No.:** GB 163 6847 38
Date established: 1971 **Turnover:** £2m - £5m **No.of Employees:** 21 - 50
Product Groups: 37, 38, 85

Date of Accounts	Aug 12	Aug 11	Aug 10
Working Capital	560	457	423
Fixed Assets	269	253	241
Current Assets	881	736	798

Roger Stevenson Ltd
The Mews House 1b Bradley Street, Southport, PR9 9HW
Tel: 01704-534000 **Fax:** 01704-538094
Directors: R. Stevenson (MD)
Immediate Holding Company: ROGER STEVENSON LIMITED
Registration no: 00752292 **Date established:** 1963
Turnover: £500,000 - £1m **No.of Employees:** 1 - 10 **Product Groups:** 89

Date of Accounts	Jul 11	Jul 09	Jul 08
Working Capital	42	28	32
Fixed Assets	16	7	5
Current Assets	52	39	50

Travers Woodworking Machinery
86 Larkfield Lane, Southport, PR9 8NW
Tel: 01704-224674 **Fax:** 01704-222912
E-mail: awtravers@lineone.net

Directors: A. Travers (Prop)
Date established: 2000 **No.of Employees:** 1 - 10 **Product Groups:** 46

Unipart Rail Dorman

Wennington Road, Southport, PR9 7TN
Tel: 01704-518000 **Fax:** 01704-518001
E-mail: info@dorman.co.uk
Website: http://www.dorman.co.uk
Bank(s): Lloyds TSB
Directors: J. Barlow (MD)
Ultimate Holding Company: UNIPART GROUP OF COMPANIES LIMITED
Immediate Holding Company: UNIPART RAIL LIMITED
Registration no: 03038418 **VAT No.:** GB 568 3477 95
Date established: 1995 **Turnover:** Up to £250,000
No.of Employees: 51 - 100 **Product Groups:** 37, 39

Date of Accounts	Dec 10	Dec 09	Dec 08
Sales Turnover	165m	156m	201m
Pre Tax Profit/Loss	12m	6m	12m
Working Capital	57m	54m	60m
Fixed Assets	14m	15m	13m
Current Assets	91m	85m	91m
Current Liabilities	10m	7m	5m

United Automation Ltd

Southport Business Park Wight Moss Way, Southport, PR8 4HQ
Tel: 01704-516500 **Fax:** 01704-516501
E-mail: chloe@united-automation.com
Website: http://www.united-automation.com
Bank(s): Yorkshire Bank PLC
Directors: D. Fashoni (MD)
Immediate Holding Company: UNITED AUTOMATION LIMITED
Registration no: 02714552 **VAT No.:** GB 582 2416 45
Date established: 1992 **Turnover:** £1m - £2m **No.of Employees:** 21 - 50
Product Groups: 37, 38, 39, 40, 44, 45, 46, 67, 77, 84

Date of Accounts	Dec 11	Dec 10	Dec 09
Working Capital	531	420	394
Fixed Assets	392	405	420
Current Assets	700	560	522

Weber Sensors Ltd

66 Eastbourne Road, Southport, PR8 4DU
Tel: 01704-551684 **Fax:** 01704-533956
E-mail: sales@captor.co.uk
Website: http://www.captor.com
Directors: G. Livingstone (Dir)
Immediate Holding Company: WEBER SENSORS LIMITED
Registration no: 01839387 **VAT No.:** GB 402 0909 96
Date established: 1984 **Turnover:** £250,000 - £500,000
No.of Employees: 1 - 10 **Product Groups:** 38, 40

Date of Accounts	Dec 10	Dec 09	Dec 08
Working Capital	753	691	656
Fixed Assets	26	61	86
Current Assets	1m	1m	1m

Weldon Metal Fabrications

Unit 14 Birkdale Trading Estate 174 Liverpool Road, Southport, PR8 4PZ
Tel: 01704-562216 **Fax:** 01704-567440
Directors: A. Pierce (Prop)
Date established: 1955 **No.of Employees:** 1 - 10 **Product Groups:** 35

St Helens

A Line Mobility Ltd

58 Claughton Street, St Helens, WA10 1SN
Tel: 01744-602602 **Fax:** 01744-632610
Website: http://www.alinemobility.co.uk
Directors: C. Maddox (MD), H. Madox (MD)
Immediate Holding Company: ST. HELENS MOBILITY SHOP LIMITED
Registration no: 05038794 **Date established:** 2004
No.of Employees: 1 - 10 **Product Groups:** 35, 39, 45

Date of Accounts	Mar 11	Mar 10	Mar 09
Working Capital	10	6	-10
Fixed Assets	48	42	47
Current Assets	99	82	47

A & N Plant Ltd

Unit 9, Station Road Industrial Estate Sutton, St Helens, WA9 3JG
Tel: 0800-9171149 **Fax:** 01494-729240
E-mail: info@anplant.com
Website: http://www.anplant.com
Directors: A. Dibbo (MD)
Managers: B. Davies (Mgr), D. Mullinere (Sales Prom Mgr), D. Rainger (Develop Mgr)
Ultimate Holding Company: A & N Management Ltd
Immediate Holding Company: A & N Plant Ltd
Registration no: 06194683 **Date established:** 2007
Turnover: Up to £250,000 **No.of Employees:** 1 - 10 **Product Groups:** 46, 67, 83

Ace Controls International

404 Haydock Lane Haydock, St Helens, WA11 9TH
Tel: 01942-727440 **Fax:** 01942-717273
E-mail: info@ace-controls.co.uk
Website: http://www.acecontrols.co.uk
Bank(s): National Westminster, Leigh
Managers: E. Abbott (Chief Mgr)
Ultimate Holding Company: KAYDON
Immediate Holding Company: ACE CONTROLS INTERNATIONAL INC
Registration no: BR001473 **VAT No.:** GB 152 2202 20
Date established: 1984 **Turnover:** £1m - £2m **No.of Employees:** 11 - 20
Product Groups: 29, 35, 37, 39, 40, 45, 46, 66

Action Can Ltd (Formerly Plow Products Ltd)

Dixon Close Old Boston Trading Estate, Haydock, St Helens, WA11 9SF
Tel: 01942-713667 **Fax:** 01942-716235
E-mail: sales@actioncan.com
Website: http://www.actioncan.com
Bank(s): National Westminster Bank Plc
Directors: C. Garrity (Sales), M. Garrity (I.T. Dir), T. Garrity (MD)
Immediate Holding Company: ACTION CAN LIMITED
Registration no: 00550814 **VAT No.:** GB 344 1652 70
Date established: 1955 **Turnover:** £500,000 - £1m
No.of Employees: 11 - 20 **Product Groups:** 31, 40, 41

Date of Accounts	May 11	May 10	May 09
Working Capital	460	413	396
Fixed Assets	71	37	23
Current Assets	1m	954	776

Aimia Foods

Penny Lane Haydock, St Helens, WA11 0QZ
Tel: 01942-272900 **Fax:** 01942-272831
E-mail: customer.services@aimiafoods.com
Website: http://www.aimiafoods.com
Directors: G. Hodgson (Sales), A. Large (Co Sec)
Ultimate Holding Company: AIMIA FOODS HOLDINGS LIMITED
Immediate Holding Company: AIMIA FOODS LIMITED
Registration no: 01542173 **Date established:** 1981
Turnover: £50m - £75m **No.of Employees:** 251 - 500
Product Groups: 20, 62

Date of Accounts	Jun 12	Jun 11	Jun 10
Sales Turnover	59m	53m	51m
Pre Tax Profit/Loss	2m	1m	1m
Working Capital	16m	14m	13m
Fixed Assets	2m	2m	2m
Current Assets	30m	30m	29m
Current Liabilities	7m	7m	6m

Alumasc Exterior Building Products

White House Works Bold Road, St Helens, WA9 4JG
Tel: 01744-648400 **Fax:** 01744-648401
E-mail: littlewoodr@alumasc-exteriors.co.uk
Website: http://www.alumasc-exteriors.co.uk
Directors: A. Magson (Co Sec), G. Jackson (MD)
Managers: A. Horton (Mktg Serv Mgr), M. Walton (Purch Mgr), J. Doel (Systems Mgr), D. Woods
Ultimate Holding Company: THE ALUMASC GROUP PLC
Immediate Holding Company: ALUMASC EXTERIOR BUILDING PRODUCTS LIMITED
Registration no: 02992960 **Date established:** 1994
Turnover: £20m - £50m **No.of Employees:** 101 - 250
Product Groups: 14, 31

Date of Accounts	Jun 11	Jun 10	Jun 09
Sales Turnover	30m	26m	31m
Pre Tax Profit/Loss	456	763	864
Working Capital	11m	7m	6m
Fixed Assets	3m	3m	3m
Current Assets	17m	12m	12m
Current Liabilities	1m	1m	1m

ATG Access Ltd

CoBaCo House, North Florida Road Haydock Industrial Estate, Haydock, St Helens, WA11 9TP
Tel: 0845-6757574 **Fax:** 04856-759955
E-mail: sales@atgaccess.com
Website: http://www.atgaccess.com
Registration no: 02643622 **No.of Employees:** 21 - 50
Product Groups: 35, 37, 39, 68

Date of Accounts	Apr 08	Apr 07	Apr 06
Sales Turnover	N/A	5661	4923
Pre Tax Profit/Loss	390	331	263
Working Capital	2475	1063	754
Fixed Assets	183	238	210
Current Assets	4146	2325	1832
Current Liabilities	1672	1262	1078
Total Share Capital	3	3	3
ROCE% (Return on Capital Employed)	14.7	25.4	27.3
ROT% (Return on Turnover)		5.8	5.3

Bauer Group (Bauer Compressors)

Haydock Industrial Estate North Florida Road Haydock, St Helens, WA11 9TN
Tel: 01942-724248 **Fax:** 01942-270771
E-mail: general@bauer.uk.com
Website: http://www.bauergroup.co.uk
Bank(s): The Royal Bank of Scotland plc, Wigan
Directors: M. Illidge (MD)
Ultimate Holding Company: BAUER COMP HOLDING AG (GERMANY)
Immediate Holding Company: BAUER KOMPRESSOREN UK LIMITED
Registration no: 01325473 **VAT No.:** GB 294 9383 04
Date established: 1977 **Turnover:** £2m - £5m **No.of Employees:** 21 - 50
Product Groups: 31, 35, 36, 38, 39, 40, 42, 46, 67, 68

Date of Accounts	Dec 09	Dec 08	Dec 07
Sales Turnover	8m	8m	6m
Pre Tax Profit/Loss	-442	246	101
Working Capital	684	1m	906
Fixed Assets	358	401	318
Current Assets	4m	4m	3m
Current Liabilities	352	276	183

BIS ATG

Propect House Kilbuck Lane, Haydock, St Helens, WA11 9UX
Tel: 01942-868900 **Fax:** 01942-868901
E-mail: enquiries@bis-atg.co.uk
Website: http://www.bis-atg.co.uk
Directors: E. Higham (Pers), P. Atherton (Fin)
Managers: R. Woods (Mktg Serv Mgr), M. Warrilow (Tech Serv Mgr), V. Caswell (Personnel), L. Holmes (Purch Mgr)
Ultimate Holding Company: BILFINGER BERGER AG (GERMANY)
Immediate Holding Company: BIS ATG LIMITED
Registration no: 03864114 **Date established:** 1999
Turnover: £20m - £50m **No.of Employees:** 101 - 250
Product Groups: 30, 37, 38, 44, 81, 84, 85, 86

Date of Accounts	Dec 11	Sep 10	Sep 09
Sales Turnover	26m	20m	20m
Pre Tax Profit/Loss	989	2m	1m
Working Capital	960	6m	5m
Fixed Assets	537	601	671
Current Assets	6m	9m	9m
Current Liabilities	3m	2m	1m

Bold Recruitment

1st Floor Court Buildings Alexander Park Prescot Road, St Helens, WA10 3TP
Tel: 01744-758160 **Fax:** 01744-757588
E-mail: healthcare@boldac.co.uk
Website: http://www.boldrecruitment.co.uk
Directors: S. Haunch (MD)
Immediate Holding Company: BOLD RECRUITMENT SOLUTIONS LIMITED
Registration no: 05214012 **Date established:** 2009 **Turnover:** £1m - £2m
No.of Employees: 1 - 10 **Product Groups:** 79, 80

Date of Accounts	Aug 09	Aug 08	Aug 07
Sales Turnover	2m	1m	1m
Pre Tax Profit/Loss	82	64	73
Working Capital	24	23	27
Fixed Assets	4	N/A	1
Current Assets	414	312	320
Current Liabilities	191	121	181

C G I International Ltd

International House Millfield Lane, Haydock, St Helens, WA11 9GA
Tel: 01942-710720 **Fax:** 01942-710730
E-mail: info@cgii.co.uk
Website: http://www.cgii.co.uk
Bank(s): The Royal Bank of Scotland
Directors: D. Jolliffe (MD), S. Goodman (Sales)
Managers: D. Bowerbank (Fin Mgr)
Ultimate Holding Company: DUNEDIN ENTERPRISE INVESTMENT TRUST PLC
Immediate Holding Company: C.G.I. INTERNATIONAL LIMITED
Registration no: 03648124 **VAT No.:** GB 712 5291 57
Date established: 1998 **Turnover:** £10m - £20m
No.of Employees: 21 - 50 **Product Groups:** 33

Date of Accounts	Dec 11	Dec 10	Dec 09
Sales Turnover	12m	11m	12m
Pre Tax Profit/Loss	3m	3m	3m
Working Capital	12m	11m	11m
Fixed Assets	4m	4m	5m
Current Assets	13m	12m	12m
Current Liabilities	798	904	914

C & O Powder Coatings Ltd

1 Brindley Road Reginald Road Industrial Estate, St Helens, WA9 4HY
Tel: 01744-818776 **Fax:** 01744-819268
E-mail: sales@candocoatings.co.uk
Website: http://www.candocoatings.co.uk
Bank(s): Co-Operative
Directors: T. Holmes (Fin), T. Holmes (Dir)
Ultimate Holding Company: COBCO 811 LIMITED
Immediate Holding Company: C & O POWDER COATINGS LIMITED
Registration no: 01886104 **Date established:** 1985 **Turnover:** £1m - £2m
No.of Employees: 21 - 50 **Product Groups:** 48

Date of Accounts	May 11	May 10	May 09
Working Capital	324	275	249
Fixed Assets	145	192	252
Current Assets	1m	920	839

Caldo Oils Ltd

Worsley Brow, St Helens, WA9 3EZ
Tel: 01744-813535 **Fax:** 01744-816031
E-mail: info@caldo.co.uk
Website: http://www.caldo.co.uk
Directors: M. Scott (MD)
Immediate Holding Company: CALDO OILS LIMITED
Registration no: 00496486 **Date established:** 1951
Turnover: £10m - £20m **No.of Employees:** 21 - 50 **Product Groups:** 31, 48

Date of Accounts	Jun 11	Jun 10	Jun 09
Sales Turnover	15m	14m	15m
Pre Tax Profit/Loss	256	168	198
Working Capital	-18	-26	-45
Fixed Assets	969	1m	991
Current Assets	3m	3m	2m
Current Liabilities	321	2m	1m

Churchill Security Ltd

Rainford Hall Crank Road Crank, St Helens, WA11 7RP
Tel: 01744-25575 **Fax:** 0844-477 9992
E-mail: admin@churchill-security.co.uk
Website: http://www.churchill-security.co.uk
Managers: M. Cook (Mgr)
Immediate Holding Company: CHURCHILL SECURITY LIMITED
Registration no: 03156058 **Date established:** 1996
No.of Employees: 51 - 100 **Product Groups:** 38, 40, 44, 80, 81, 82

Date of Accounts	Jul 11	Jul 10	Jul 09
Working Capital	294	199	140
Fixed Assets	37	42	55
Current Assets	772	505	391

C J W T Solutions

Unit 20 Bold Business Centre Bold Lane, St Helens, WA9 4TX
Tel: 01925-220319 **Fax:** 08707-065878
E-mail: craig@cjwtsolutions.co.uk
Website: http://www.cjwtsolutions.co.uk
Directors: C. Tetlow (Prop)
Immediate Holding Company: CJWT SOLUTIONS LTD
Registration no: 07489834 **Date established:** 2011
Turnover: Up to £250,000 **No.of Employees:** 1 - 10 **Product Groups:** 44, 64

Company Cards (Plastic Card Solutions)

Worsley Brow, St Helens, WA9 3EZ
Tel: 01744-850872 **Fax:** 01744-604463
E-mail: info@companycards.co.uk
Website: http://www.companycards.co.uk
Directors: T. Scott (MD)
Managers: S. Sherman (Mktg Serv Mgr), S. Abbott (Tech Serv Mgr)
Immediate Holding Company: COMPANY CARDS LIMITED
Registration no: 05360059 **VAT No.:** GB 152 1950 83
Date established: 2005 **No.of Employees:** 21 - 50 **Product Groups:** 22, 23, 27, 28, 30, 35, 37, 38, 43, 44, 46, 48, 49, 64, 81

Date of Accounts	Jun 11	Jun 10	Jun 09
Working Capital	380	410	316
Fixed Assets	278	48	75
Current Assets	904	865	683

Compass Bearing & Engineering Supplies Ltd

Unit 5a Sandwash Close Rainford, St Helens, WA11 8LY
Tel: 01744-884888 **Fax:** 01744-886888
E-mail: sales@compassbearings.co.uk
Website: http://www.compassbearings.co.uk
Directors: C. Mccarthy (MD)
Immediate Holding Company: COMPASS BEARING AND ENGINEERING SUPPLIES LTD
Registration no: 04479142 **Date established:** 2002
No.of Employees: 1 - 10 **Product Groups:** 35, 61, 66

Date of Accounts	Jul 11	Jul 10	Jul 09
Working Capital	2	1	1
Fixed Assets	1	2	2
Current Assets	128	105	87

Cutlass Fasteners Ltd
Penny Lane Old Boston Trading Estate, Haydock, St Helens, WA11 9ST
Tel: 01942-712387 **Fax:** 01942-722306
E-mail: higton@cutlassfst.aol.com
Website: http://www.cutlass-studwelding.com
Bank(s): Barclays
Directors: D. Higton (MD), S. Sudworth (Fin)
Immediate Holding Company: CUTLASS FASTENERS LIMITED
Registration no: 01642509 **VAT No.:** GB 373 9034 41
Date established: 1982 **Turnover:** £1m - £2m **No.of Employees:** 11 - 20
Product Groups: 35, 46, 48

Date of Accounts	Dec 11	Dec 10	Dec 09
Working Capital	295	329	272
Fixed Assets	131	139	161
Current Assets	472	463	463

Delta Fluid Products Ltd
Delta Road, St Helens, WA9 2ED
Tel: 01744-611811 **Fax:** 01744-611818
E-mail: enquiry@deltafluidproducts.co.uk
Website: http://www.cranebsu.com
Bank(s): HSBC Bank plc
Directors: D. Pye (Dir), S. Cooper (Tech Serv), B. Travis (MD), S. Burr (Co Sec), D. Lewis (Dir)
Managers: S. Webster (Mgr)
Ultimate Holding Company: CRANE CO. (USA)
Immediate Holding Company: DELTA FLUID PRODUCTS LIMITED
Registration no: 04279520 **VAT No.:** GB 340 1992 70
Date established: 2001 **Turnover:** £10m - £20m
No.of Employees: 251 - 500 **Product Groups:** 36

Date of Accounts	Dec 10	Dec 09	Dec 08
Sales Turnover	N/A	N/A	21m
Pre Tax Profit/Loss	N/A	198	2m
Working Capital	3m	3m	5m
Fixed Assets	N/A	N/A	2m
Current Assets	3m	3m	9m
Current Liabilities	N/A	N/A	1m

Electrovision Group Ltd
Lancots Lane, St Helens, WA9 3EX
Tel: 01744-745000 **Fax:** 01744-745001
E-mail: richard@electrovision.co.uk
Website: http://www.electrovision.co.uk
Bank(s): Lloyds TSB Bank plc
Directors: R. Fox (MD)
Immediate Holding Company: ELECTROVISION LIMITED
Registration no: 01518942 **VAT No.:** GB 145 9185 51
Date established: 1980 **Turnover:** £20m - £50m
No.of Employees: 51 - 100 **Product Groups:** 37

Date of Accounts	Dec 11	Dec 10	Dec 09
Sales Turnover	25m	24m	23m
Pre Tax Profit/Loss	2m	2m	3m
Working Capital	12m	9m	8m
Fixed Assets	6m	7m	7m
Current Assets	17m	15m	13m
Current Liabilities	2m	3m	2m

Enspec Ltd
29 Shaw Street, St Helens, WA10 1DG
Tel: 01744-605613 **Fax:** 01744-634795
E-mail: sgjones@enspecpower.com
Website: http://www.enspecpower.com
Directors: S. Jones (Dir), S. Jones (Prop)
Immediate Holding Company: ENSPEC POWER LTD
Registration no: 04066153 **Date established:** 2000
No.of Employees: 11 - 20 **Product Groups:** 37, 38

Date of Accounts	Mar 10	Mar 09	Mar 08
Working Capital	-24	87	62
Fixed Assets	62	71	56
Current Assets	219	471	301

Equipe Enviromental Ltd
5 Norfolk Road, St Helens, WA10 3JN
Tel: 01744-731462 **Fax:** 01744-601736
E-mail: pamelaseymour@hotmail.co.uk
Website: http://www.equipeenvironmental.co.uk
Directors: E. Seymour (Co Sec)
Immediate Holding Company: EQUIPE ENVIRONMENTAL LIMITED
Registration no: 03774553 **Date established:** 1999
No.of Employees: 1 - 10 **Product Groups:** 23, 29, 30, 36, 38, 39

Date of Accounts	Mar 11	Mar 09	Mar 08
Working Capital	-4	3	1
Fixed Assets	5	9	9
Current Assets	37	51	77

European Metals Recycling Ltd
Reginald Road, St Helens, WA9 4JA
Tel: 01744-811105 **Fax:** 01744-813041
Website: http://www.emrltd.com
Managers: J. Bissett (Mgr)
Immediate Holding Company: EUROPEAN METAL RECYCLING LIMITED
Registration no: 02954623 **Date established:** 1994
Turnover: £10m - £20m **No.of Employees:** 1 - 10 **Product Groups:** 42, 66

Date of Accounts	Dec 11	Dec 10	Dec 09
Sales Turnover	3032m	2431m	1843m
Pre Tax Profit/Loss	116m	155m	91m
Working Capital	414m	371m	167m
Fixed Assets	518m	483m	480m
Current Assets	1027m	717m	557m
Current Liabilities	124m	118m	185m

Excel Garage Doors Ltd
Unit B Mosspark Warehousing Dairy Farm Road, Rainford, St Helens, WA11 7JR
Tel: 0800-652 2050 **Fax:** 01744-886224
Website: http://www.excelshutters.co.uk
Directors: P. Middlehurst (Ptnr), S. Middlehurst (MD)
Immediate Holding Company: MOSSPARK WAREHOUSING DAIRY FARM LIMITED
Registration no: 03186242 **Date established:** 1996
Turnover: £250,000 - £500,000 **No.of Employees:** 1 - 10
Product Groups: 35, 36

Ex Or Ltd
Haydock Lane Haydock Indl-Est, Haydock, St Helens, WA11 9UJ
Tel: 01942-719229 **Fax:** 01942-272767
E-mail: marketing@ex-or.com
Website: http://www.ex-or.com
Bank(s): HSBC Bank plc
Directors: A. Fowell (Ch), D. Murgatroyd (Fab), N. Jones (MD)
Managers: R. Townsend
Ultimate Holding Company: HONEYWELL INTERNATIONAL INC (USA)
Immediate Holding Company: EX-OR LIMITED
Registration no: 01780639 **VAT No.:** GB 732 5434 47
Date established: 1983 **Turnover:** £2m - £5m **No.of Employees:** 21 - 50
Product Groups: 37, 54, 67, 84

Date of Accounts	Dec 11	Dec 10	Dec 09
Working Capital	N/A	N/A	3m
Current Assets	N/A	N/A	3m

F D LPackaging Group LLP
Abbeyway South Vista Road, Haydock, St Helens, WA11 0RW
Tel: 01942-722299 **Fax:** 01942-271325
E-mail: sales@fdlgroup.co.uk
Website: http://www.fdlcontainers.co.uk
Directors: D. Scotting (Sales), F. Cunniffe (Dir), F. Cunnisse (Ch), R. Douse (Chief Op Offcr), S. Cunnisse (MD)
Managers: C. Atherton (Sales Admin), N. Jones (Mktg Serv Mgr), C. Dufficy (Sales Prom Mgr)
Immediate Holding Company: FDL Packaging Group LLP
Registration no: OC304583 **Date established:** 2003 **Turnover:** £2m - £5m
No.of Employees: 21 - 50 **Product Groups:** 27, 30, 35

F H Brundle
Unit 8 Haydock Lane Haydock, St Helens, WA11 9XE
Tel: 01942-868888 **Fax:** 01942-868899
E-mail: sales@brundle.com
Website: http://www.fhbrundle.co.uk
Managers: E. Heaton (District Mgr)
Immediate Holding Company: F H BRUNDLE
Registration no: 07168270 **Date established:** 2010
Turnover: £500,000 - £1m **No.of Employees:** 11 - 20
Product Groups: 30, 32, 34, 35, 36, 39, 46, 49, 66, 67

F W Fabrications
Unit 12 Mill Lane Rainford Industrial Estate, Rainford, St Helens, WA11 8LS
Tel: 01744-889866 **Fax:** 01744-889866
Directors: F. Woosey (Prop)
Immediate Holding Company: RAINFORD GROUP LIMITED
Registration no: 03372015 **Date established:** 1997 **Turnover:** £2m - £5m
No.of Employees: 1 - 10 **Product Groups:** 35

Fibre Drums Ltd
Abbeyway South Vista Road, Haydock, St Helens, WA11 0RW
Tel: 01942-722299 **Fax:** 01942-271325
E-mail: s.cunniffe@fdlgroup.co.uk
Website: http://www.fdlcontainers.co.uk
Bank(s): National Westminster Bank Plc
Directors: D. Scotting (Sales), R. Douse (Purch), S. Cunniffe (MD)
Managers: N. Jones (Mktg Serv Mgr), C. Atherton (I.T. Exec)
Immediate Holding Company: FIBRE DRUMS LIMITED
Registration no: 02519255 **Date established:** 1990 **Turnover:** £2m - £5m
No.of Employees: 21 - 50 **Product Groups:** 27, 30, 35

Date of Accounts	Mar 11	Mar 10	Mar 09
Working Capital	305	341	-540
Fixed Assets	2m	2m	2m
Current Assets	2m	1m	1m

Firemain Engineering Ltd
6 Harrier Court Eurolink Business Park, St Helens, WA9 4YR
Tel: 01744-850063 **Fax:** 01744-812014
E-mail: info@firemain.com
Website: http://www.firemain.com
Directors: P. Bayliss (MD)
Immediate Holding Company: FIREMAIN ENGINEERING LIMITED
Registration no: 02437760 **Date established:** 1989 **Turnover:** £1m - £2m
No.of Employees: 11 - 20 **Product Groups:** 40, 52, 67

Date of Accounts	Mar 11	Mar 10	Mar 09
Working Capital	347	345	198
Fixed Assets	159	142	151
Current Assets	770	716	669

First Stop Security Products
Unit 1 Hertford House Hertford Street, Parr Industrial Estate, St Helens, WA9 1BF
Tel: 01744-25038
Directors: S. Matthews (Prop)
Date established: 2003 **No.of Employees:** 1 - 10 **Product Groups:** 26, 35

Folglade Pipe & Fittings Ltd
Unit 9 Westside Industrial Estate, St Helens, WA9 3AT
Tel: 01744-24999 **Fax:** 01744-24447
E-mail: sales@folglade.co.uk
Website: http://www.folglade.co.uk
Bank(s): Barclays
Directors: E. Chisnall (Prop)
Immediate Holding Company: FOLGLADE (PIPES AND FITTINGS) LIMITED
Registration no: 01481388 **VAT No.:** GB 582 1223 61
Date established: 1980 **Turnover:** £2m - £5m **No.of Employees:** 11 - 20
Product Groups: 36, 66

Date of Accounts	Mar 11	Mar 10	Mar 09
Working Capital	64	-16	-21
Fixed Assets	351	360	360
Current Assets	423	501	212

Four Colour Digital Company Cards
Worsley Brow, St Helens, WA9 3EZ
Tel: 01744-850872 **Fax:** 01744-604463
E-mail: timscott@plastic-cards.co.uk
Website: http://www.companycards.co.uk
Directors: T. Scott (MD)
Immediate Holding Company: COMPANY CARDS LIMITED
Date established: 2005 **Turnover:** £2m - £5m **No.of Employees:** 21 - 50
Product Groups: 27, 28, 44, 64, 81

G D K Wrought Iron
9 The Portland Centre Sutton Road, St Helens, WA9 3DR
Tel: 01744-614043
Directors: G. Keely (Prop)
Date established: 1994 **No.of Employees:** 1 - 10 **Product Groups:** 26, 35

G P W Recruitment
Worsley House Windle Street, St Helens, WA10 2BL
Tel: 08453-301111 **Fax:** 0845-330 1112
E-mail: recruitment@gpw.uk.com
Website: http://www.gpw.uk.com
Bank(s): National Westminster Bank Plc
Directors: C. Worsley (Co Sec), G. Worsley (Dir), M. Parish (MD)
Immediate Holding Company: GPW DESIGN SERVICES LIMITED
Registration no: 05025730 **VAT No.:** GB 374 0528 55
Date established: 1976 **Turnover:** £2m - £5m **No.of Employees:** 21 - 50
Product Groups: 80

Date of Accounts	Apr 06	Apr 05	Apr 04
Working Capital	17	19	44
Fixed Assets	N/A	N/A	8
Current Assets	18	21	188

Glass Bond N W Ltd
Westside Industrial Estate Jackson Street, St Helens, WA9 3AT
Tel: 01744-730334 **Fax:** 01744-451661
E-mail: info@glassbond.co.uk
Website: http://www.glassbond.co.uk
Bank(s): Lloyds TSB Bank plc
Directors: P. Randell (Dir)
Managers: R. Randell, D. Birkitt (Sales & Mktg Mg)
Immediate Holding Company: GLASS BOND (N.W.) LIMITED
Registration no: 01378679 **VAT No.:** GB 295 0234 60
Date established: 1978 **Turnover:** £2m - £5m **No.of Employees:** 21 - 50
Product Groups: 31, 33, 66

Date of Accounts	Feb 11	Feb 10	Feb 09
Working Capital	1m	818	584
Fixed Assets	157	169	193
Current Assets	2m	1m	1m

Hi Tech Steel Services Ltd
Neills Road Bold Industrial Park, Bold, St Helens, WA9 4TU
Tel: 01744-818767 **Fax:** 01744-818706
E-mail: sales@hitechsteels.com
Website: http://www.hitechsteels.com
Directors: C. Gardner (Dir), I. Gorman (Dir), T. Young (Sales)
Managers: J. Flatt
Immediate Holding Company: HI-TECH STEEL SERVICES LIMITED
Registration no: 02702383 **Date established:** 1992
Turnover: £20m - £50m **No.of Employees:** 51 - 100 **Product Groups:** 66

Date of Accounts	Jun 10	Jun 09	Jun 08
Sales Turnover	34m	37m	39m
Pre Tax Profit/Loss	-524	-2m	861
Working Capital	-685	-342	1m
Fixed Assets	2m	2m	2m
Current Assets	15m	14m	18m
Current Liabilities	9m	8m	11m

Hoyles Fire & Safety Ltd
Sandwash Close Rainford Industrial Estate, Rainford, St Helens, WA11 8LY
Tel: 01744-885161 **Fax:** 01744-882410
E-mail: customer.service@hoyles.co.uk
Website: http://www.hoyles.co.uk
Bank(s): National Westminster Bank Plc
Directors: R. Pollard (Dir)
Ultimate Holding Company: EOI FIRE SARL (LUXEMBOURG)
Immediate Holding Company: HOYLES FIRE & SAFETY LIMITED
Registration no: 02575502 **VAT No.:** GB 535 0182 71
Date established: 1991 **Turnover:** £2m - £5m **No.of Employees:** 11 - 20
Product Groups: 27, 29, 30, 33, 35, 37, 38, 39, 40, 49, 52, 67, 84, 86

Date of Accounts	Dec 11	Dec 10	Dec 09
Sales Turnover	3m	2m	2m
Pre Tax Profit/Loss	22	45	62
Working Capital	-557	-531	1m
Fixed Assets	1m	1m	826
Current Assets	1m	908	2m
Current Liabilities	291	258	263

H Q C Ltd
North Florida Road Haydock Industrial Estate, Haydock, St Helens, WA11 9UB
Tel: 01942-722770 **Fax:** 01942-270235
E-mail: sbowden@hqc.co.uk
Website: http://www.cranehireuk.co.uk
Directors: P. O'Neale (MD), S. Bowden (Dir)
Managers: S. Bowden (Comptroller)
Ultimate Holding Company: HQC (LEIGH) LIMITED
Immediate Holding Company: HQC (HOLDINGS) LIMITED
Registration no: 05001448 **VAT No.:** GB 439 1193 45
Date established: 2003 **Turnover:** £2m - £5m **No.of Employees:** 21 - 50
Product Groups: 48

Date of Accounts	Aug 11	Aug 10	Aug 09
Working Capital	4	-82	-68
Fixed Assets	2m	2m	2m
Current Assets	4	2	5

Industrial Purification Systems
Unit 10 Lea Green Business Park Eurolink, St Helens, WA9 4TR
Tel: 01744-811652 **Fax:** 01744-24049
E-mail: sales@industrial-purification.co.uk
Website: http://www.industrial-purification.co.uk
Directors: S. Cupples (Dir)
Ultimate Holding Company: BRIGHT LIGHT HOLDINGS LIMITED
Immediate Holding Company: INDUSTRIAL PURIFICATION SYSTEMS LIMITED
Registration no: 01672816 **VAT No.:** GB 320 3887 71
Date established: 1982 **Turnover:** £1m - £2m **No.of Employees:** 1 - 10
Product Groups: 14, 33, 35, 37, 38, 39, 40, 41, 42, 52, 54, 67, 85

Date of Accounts	Jun 11	Jun 10	Jun 09
Working Capital	147	170	150
Fixed Assets	8	18	38
Current Assets	323	315	310

Johns Manville Limited
Unit 4 Roundwood Drive Sherdley Road Industrial Estate, St Helens, WA9 5JD
Tel: 01744-762500 **Fax:** 01744-451076
E-mail: jeff.nash@jm.com
Website: http://www.jm.com
Bank(s): Barclays
Directors: C. Tattam (Fin)
Managers: J. Nash (Sales Prom Mgr), P. Robinson (Plant), P. Saunders (Accounts)
Immediate Holding Company: Johns Manville Corp (USA)
Registration no: 00358002 **Date established:** 1997 **Turnover:** £2m - £5m
No.of Employees: 51 - 100 **Product Groups:** 30

Date of Accounts	Dec 07	Dec 06
Sales Turnover	3370	9961
Pre Tax Profit/Loss	-6	-6210

Working Capital	12563	11835
Fixed Assets	1810	2610
Current Assets	12777	12548
Current Liabilities	214	713
Total Share Capital	1	1
ROCE% (Return on Capital Employed)	-0.0	-43.0
ROT% (Return on Turnover)	-0.2	-62.3

K Hire Ltd

Unit 5 Sutton Oak Drive, St Helens, WA9 3PH
Tel: 01744-850888 **Fax:** 01744-850116
Directors: J. Spencer (Dir)
Immediate Holding Company: GAS SHOWROOM WAREHOUSE LIMITED
Registration no: 05778107 **Date established:** 2006
No.of Employees: 1 - 10 **Product Groups:** 46

Date of Accounts	Mar 10	Mar 09	Mar 08
Working Capital	11	-58	-76
Fixed Assets	75	80	85
Current Assets	52	78	61

Kingdom Security Ltd

Mill Brow Eccleston, St Helens, WA10 4QG
Tel: 08450-517700 **Fax:** 01744-616699
E-mail: terry@kingdomsecurity.co.uk
Website: http://www.kingdomsecurity.co.uk
Directors: T. Barton (MD)
Managers: M. Wallace (Sales Prom Mgr), P. Walsh, S. Bold
Immediate Holding Company: KINGDOM SECURITY LIMITED
Registration no: 02795197 **Date established:** 1993
Turnover: £20m - £50m **No.of Employees:** 21 - 50 **Product Groups:** 44, 80, 81

Date of Accounts	Mar 11	Mar 10	Mar 09
Sales Turnover	22m	14m	11m
Pre Tax Profit/Loss	2m	1m	1m
Working Capital	2m	2m	2m
Fixed Assets	2m	363	338
Current Assets	6m	5m	3m
Current Liabilities	4m	3m	2m

Kirkby Steel Tubes Ltd

Abbotsfield Road Reginald Road Industrial Estate, St Helens, WA9 4HU
Tel: 01744-830600 **Fax:** 01744-830609
E-mail: mail@kst.uk.com
Website: http://www.kst.uk.com
Bank(s): National Westminster Bank Plc
Directors: S. Ursell (Ch), C. Blakemore (Co Sec), P. Doyle (MD), P. McLean (Comm)
Ultimate Holding Company: WATTS CLIFT HOLDINGS LTD
Immediate Holding Company: KIRKBY STEEL TUBES LIMITED
Registration no: 00881802 **Date established:** 1966 **Turnover:** £1m - £2m
No.of Employees: 21 - 50 **Product Groups:** 36

Date of Accounts	Apr 11	Apr 10	Apr 09
Working Capital	658	592	620
Fixed Assets	2m	2m	2m
Current Assets	3m	2m	2m

Knauf Insulation Ltd

PO Box 10, St Helens, WA10 3NS
Tel: 01744-24022 **Fax:** 0870-400 5797
E-mail: sales@knaufinsulation.com
Website: http://www.knaufinsulation.co.uk
Bank(s): Barclays
Managers: L. Sharples (Mktg Serv Mgr)
Ultimate Holding Company: GEBRUEDER KNAUF VERWALTUNGS GESELLSCHAFT KG (GERMANY)
Immediate Holding Company: KNAUF INSULATION LIMITED
Registration no: 01926842 **Date established:** 1985
Turnover: £125m - £250m **No.of Employees:** 101 - 250
Product Groups: 33

Date of Accounts	Dec 11	Dec 10	Dec 09
Sales Turnover	195m	180m	180m
Pre Tax Profit/Loss	36m	40m	43m
Working Capital	224	-8m	-11m
Fixed Assets	105m	112m	119m
Current Assets	98m	82m	88m
Current Liabilities	18m	17m	15m

Label Line UK Ltd

94 Ravenhead Road, St Helens, WA10 3LR
Tel: 01744-754088 **Fax:** 01744-754088
E-mail: sales@labellineuk.co.uk
Website: http://www.labellineuk.co.uk
Managers: S. Jordan (Mgr)
Immediate Holding Company: LABEL LINE UK LTD
Registration no: 06583825 **Date established:** 2008
Turnover: £250,000 - £500,000 **No.of Employees:** 11 - 20
Product Groups: 42

Date of Accounts	Jun 11	Jun 10	Jun 09
Sales Turnover	N/A	298	167
Pre Tax Profit/Loss	N/A	48	9
Working Capital	13	9	-6
Fixed Assets	11	6	4
Current Assets	138	103	43
Current Liabilities	103	N/A	N/A

Linacre Plant & Sales Ltd

Boundary Road, St Helens, WA10 2PZ
Tel: 01744-751237 **Fax:** 01744-20318
E-mail: sales@linacrehire.co.uk
Website: http://www.linacrehire.co.uk
Directors: G. Ames (MD)
Immediate Holding Company: LINACRE PLANT HIRE AND SALES LIMITED
Registration no: 03588888 **Date established:** 1998
Turnover: £250,000 - £500,000 **No.of Employees:** 1 - 10
Product Groups: 24, 37, 41, 63, 83

Date of Accounts	Oct 11	Oct 10	Oct 09
Working Capital	-63	-74	-92
Fixed Assets	156	160	167
Current Assets	54	59	52

M & CT Ltd

Unit 12wharton St Sherdley Road Industrial Estate Sherdley Road Industrial Estate, St Helens, WA9 5AA
Tel: 01744-737274 **Fax:** 01744-739404
E-mail: admin@vitreous-enamel.com
Website: http://www.vitreous-enamel.com
Directors: C. Taylor (MD)
Immediate Holding Company: M.&C.T. LTD
Registration no: 04412725 **Date established:** 2002
Turnover: £250,000 - £500,000 **No.of Employees:** 1 - 10
Product Groups: 46, 48

Date of Accounts	Apr 11	Apr 10	Apr 09
Sales Turnover	N/A	414	249
Pre Tax Profit/Loss	N/A	59	-23
Working Capital	-28	-11	-60
Fixed Assets	155	172	171
Current Assets	115	93	86

E F G Matthews Office Furniture Ltd

Reginald Road, St Helens, WA9 4JE
Tel: 08456-084100 **Fax:** 01744-819431
E-mail: craig.howarth@efgoffice.co.uk
Website: http://www.efgoffice.co.uk
Directors: C. Howarth (MD)
Ultimate Holding Company: EFG HOLDING AB (SWEDEN)
Immediate Holding Company: EFG OFFICE FURNITURE LIMITED
Registration no: 00257489 **VAT No.:** GB 151 6840 71
Date established: 1931 **Turnover:** £75m - £125m
No.of Employees: 1 - 10 **Product Groups:** 26, 49

Date of Accounts	Dec 11	Dec 10	Dec 09
Sales Turnover	9m	8m	9m
Pre Tax Profit/Loss	-469	-280	-1m
Working Capital	2m	2m	3m
Fixed Assets	210	279	364
Current Assets	3m	4m	4m
Current Liabilities	324	381	333

Moore & Buckle Ltd

Unit 9 Sutton Fold, St Helens, WA9 3GL
Tel: 01744-733066 **Fax:** 01744-451000
E-mail: derek@mooreandbuckle.com
Website: http://www.mooreandbuckle.com
Directors: D. Hewitt (MD), J. Warwick (Co Sec)
Ultimate Holding Company: SECURITY RESEARCH GROUP PLC
Immediate Holding Company: MOORE & BUCKLE (FLEXIBLE PACKAGING) LIMITED
Registration no: 01559652 **Date established:** 1981 **Turnover:** £1m - £2m
No.of Employees: 1 - 10 **Product Groups:** 38, 42

Date of Accounts	Mar 12	Mar 11	Mar 10
Sales Turnover	1m	1m	1m
Pre Tax Profit/Loss	153	152	97
Working Capital	909	950	786
Fixed Assets	82	80	138
Current Assets	1m	2m	1m
Current Liabilities	115	114	90

Multi Mesh UK Ltd

Eurolink House Eurolink Way, St Helens, WA9 4QU
Tel: 01744-820666 **Fax:** 01744-821417
E-mail: steve@multimesh.co.uk
Website: http://www.multimesh.co.uk
Bank(s): National Westminster Bank Plc
Managers: S. Watson (Chief Mgr)
Ultimate Holding Company: Soar Group Limited
Immediate Holding Company: MULTIMESH (UK) LTD
Registration no: 07942009 **VAT No.:** GB 294 4848 11
Date established: 2012 **Turnover:** £2m - £5m **No.of Employees:** 21 - 50
Product Groups: 26, 28, 33, 34, 35, 45, 46

Date of Accounts	Feb 08	Feb 10	Feb 09
Working Capital	1m	-192	-158
Fixed Assets	579	43	53
Current Assets	3m	910	1m

N G F Europe Ltd

Lea Green Road, St Helens, WA9 4PR
Tel: 01744-853000 **Fax:** 01744-816147
E-mail: david.farmer@ngfeurope.com
Website: http://www.ngfeurope.com
Bank(s): National Westminster Bank Plc
Directors: D. Farmer (Fin), C. Hammond (Mkt Research)
Managers: J. Whittaker (Buyer)
Ultimate Holding Company: NIPPON SHEET GLASS CO LTD (JAPAN)
Immediate Holding Company: NGF EUROPE LIMITED
Registration no: 02586467 **VAT No.:** GB 535 0937 44
Date established: 1991 **Turnover:** £20m - £50m
No.of Employees: 101 - 250 **Product Groups:** 23, 29, 32, 33, 66

Date of Accounts	Dec 07	Mar 11	Mar 10
Sales Turnover	41m	49m	39m
Pre Tax Profit/Loss	4m	9m	818
Working Capital	13m	22m	17m
Fixed Assets	13m	9m	10m
Current Assets	20m	31m	26m
Current Liabilities	1m	2m	1m

Northern Connectors Ltd

Abbotsfield Road Reginald Road Industrial Estate, St Helens, WA9 4HU
Tel: 01744-815001 **Fax:** 01744-814040
E-mail: sales@northern-connectors.co.uk
Website: http://www.northern-connectors.co.uk
Bank(s): Lloyds TSB Bank plc
Directors: K. Hewitt (Dir), L. Hewitt (Dir)
Managers: S. Jones
Immediate Holding Company: NORTHERN CONNECTORS LIMITED
Registration no: 02425919 **Date established:** 1989 **Turnover:** £2m - £5m
No.of Employees: 21 - 50 **Product Groups:** 30, 33, 37, 39, 40

Date of Accounts	Jan 12	Jan 11	Jan 10
Working Capital	882	777	703
Fixed Assets	53	35	51
Current Assets	1m	1m	1m

Osram Ltd

Neills Road Bold, St Helens, WA9 4XG
Tel: 01744-812221
E-mail: thompsona@osram.co.uk
Website: http://www.osram.co.uk
Directors: M. Weber (Fin), T. Rice (Tech Serv)
Managers: A. Thompson (Sales Admin), S. Stark
Ultimate Holding Company: SIEMENS AG (GERMANY)
Immediate Holding Company: OSRAM LIMITED
Registration no: 01961715 **Date established:** 1985
Turnover: £50m - £75m **No.of Employees:** 21 - 50 **Product Groups:** 37, 67

Date of Accounts	Sep 11	Sep 10	Sep 09
Sales Turnover	58	56m	65m
Pre Tax Profit/Loss	5	4m	2m
Working Capital	9	9m	6m
Fixed Assets	1	1m	2m
Current Assets	16	14m	12m
Current Liabilities	6	4m	5m

P Owen

31 Haresfinch Road, St Helens, WA11 9NS
Tel: 01744-604605
E-mail: paul@powenwroughtiron.co.uk
Website: http://www.powenwroughtiron.co.uk
Directors: P. Owen (Prop)
Date established: 1981 **No.of Employees:** 1 - 10 **Product Groups:** 26, 35

Permadeck Systems Ltd

Unit 12 Westside Indl-Est Jackson Street, St Helens, WA9 3AT
Tel: 01744-751869 **Fax:** 01744-22551
E-mail: enquiries@nlwgroup.com
Website: http://www.nlwgroup.com
Directors: B. Williams (Dir), E. Williams (MD), B. Williams (MD), E. Williams (Fin)
Ultimate Holding Company: N.L. WILLIAMS GROUP LIMITED
Immediate Holding Company: PERMADECK SYSTEMS LIMITED
Registration no: 02824621 **VAT No.:** GB 152 9554 51
Date established: 1993 **Turnover:** £2m - £5m **No.of Employees:** 11 - 20
Product Groups: 29, 48, 52

Date of Accounts	May 11	May 10	May 04
Working Capital	-2	-2	-2
Current Liabilities	2	2	2

Pilkington Group Ltd

Prescot Road, St Helens, WA10 3TT
Tel: 01744-28882 **Fax:** 01744-692880
E-mail: ashtons@pilkington.com
Website: http://www.pilkington.com
Managers: S. Ashton (Mgr), C. Musyimi
Ultimate Holding Company: NIPPON SHEET GLASS CO LTD (JAPAN)
Immediate Holding Company: PILKINGTON GROUP LIMITED
Registration no: 00041495 **Date established:** 1994 **Turnover:** £1m - £2m
No.of Employees: 51 - 100 **Product Groups:** 33, 39

Date of Accounts	Mar 11	Mar 10	Mar 09
Sales Turnover	1m	16m	3m
Pre Tax Profit/Loss	685m	-26m	248m
Working Capital	13m	-92m	N/A
Fixed Assets	1097m	1096m	1100m
Current Assets	30m	31m	22m
Current Liabilities	8m	9m	18m

Pneumat Systems Ltd

Unit 22 Bold Business Centre Bold Lane, St Helens, WA9 4TX
Tel: 01925-290080 **Fax:** 01925-290085
E-mail: team@pneumat-europe.com
Website: http://www.pneumat-europe.com
Directors: S. Gallagher (MD)
Ultimate Holding Company: SGH ENGINEERING LIMITED
Immediate Holding Company: PNEUMAT SYSTEMS (EUROPE) LIMITED
Registration no: 03702090 **Date established:** 1999
No.of Employees: 1 - 10 **Product Groups:** 41

Date of Accounts	Dec 11	Dec 10	Dec 09
Working Capital	-12	40	57
Fixed Assets	44	42	25
Current Assets	36	87	89

Pro-Plan Projects Ltd

69a Corporation Street, St Helens, WA10 1SX
Tel: 01744-739700
E-mail: proplanprojects@btconnect.com
Website: http://www.proplanprojects.co.uk
Directors: D. Forsyth (MD)
Immediate Holding Company: PRO-PLAN PROJECTS LIMITED
Registration no: 01371414 **Date established:** 1978
No.of Employees: 1 - 10 **Product Groups:** 51, 84, 87

Date of Accounts	Mar 12	Mar 11	Mar 10
Working Capital	169	152	150
Fixed Assets	4	6	7
Current Assets	220	220	324

Rainford Fieldsports

21 Church Road Rainford, St Helens, WA11 8HE
Tel: 01744-885580 **Fax:** 01744-885580
E-mail: steve5580@googlemail.com
Website: http://www.rainfordfieldsports.com
Directors: S. Farrar (Prop)
Immediate Holding Company: Rainford Carpets Ltd
Registration no: 04522594 **Date established:** 2002
No.of Employees: 1 - 10 **Product Groups:** 36, 39, 40

Rainford Precision Machines

Pasture Lane Business Centre Pasture Lane, Rainford, St Helens, WA11 8PU
Tel: 01744-889726 **Fax:** 01744-885201
E-mail: sales@rainfordprecision.com
Website: http://www.rainfordprecision.com
Directors: A. Turner (MD)
Immediate Holding Company: RAINFORD PRECISION MACHINES LIMITED
Registration no: 03028893 **Date established:** 1995
Turnover: £250,000 - £500,000 **No.of Employees:** 1 - 10
Product Groups: 46, 47

Date of Accounts	Dec 11	Dec 10	Dec 09
Working Capital	-34	-29	-93
Fixed Assets	185	204	221
Current Assets	245	245	235

Royden Structures Ltd

Sandwash Building Sandwash Close Off Mill Lane, Rainford, St Helens, WA11 8LS
Tel: 01744-883636 **Fax:** 01744-885730
E-mail: ajones@royden.co.uk
Website: http://www.royden.co.uk
Bank(s): HSBC Bank plc
Directors: P. Bennett (MD), A. Jones (MD), S. Bennett (MD)
Managers: P. McDonald (Purch Mgr), K. Edwards (Sec), D. Doodson (Sales Admin), S. Noonan (Accounts), A. Poole (I.T. Exec), P. Murray (Est)
Immediate Holding Company: ROYDEN STRUCTURES LIMITED
Registration no: 07382781 **VAT No.:** GB 164 9722 37
Date established: 2010 **Turnover:** £5m - £10m
No.of Employees: 51 - 100 **Product Groups:** 26, 30, 34, 35, 36, 40, 45, 48, 51, 52

see next page

Royden Structures Ltd - *Cont'd*

Date of Accounts	Jul 07	Jul 06
Pre Tax Profit/Loss	334	137
Working Capital	699	391
Fixed Assets	2191	2305
Current Assets	5229	4838
Current Liabilities	4530	4447
ROCE% (Return on Capital Employed)	11.6	5.1

Saint Gobain Industrial Ceramics Ltd

Mill Lane Rainford, St Helens, WA11 8LP
Tel: 01744-882941 **Fax:** 01744-883514
E-mail: alun.oxenham@cduk.saint-gobain.com
Website: http://www.cduk.saint-gobain.com
Directors: A. Oxenham (Dir), R. Granger (MD)
Managers: A. Smith (Sales Prom Mgr), D. Anderton (Purch Mgr), N. Hales (Fin Mgr)
Ultimate Holding Company: COMPAGNIE DE SAINT GOBAIN (FRANCE)
Immediate Holding Company: SAINT-GOBAIN INDUSTRIAL CERAMICS LIMITED
Registration no: 00909697 **VAT No.:** GB 374 1376 47
Date established: 1967 **Turnover:** £5m - £10m **No.of Employees:** 1 - 10
Product Groups: 33

Date of Accounts	Dec 11	Dec 10	Dec 09
Sales Turnover	8m	6m	7m
Pre Tax Profit/Loss	541	167	212
Working Capital	7m	7m	8m
Fixed Assets	2m	3m	2m
Current Assets	9m	9m	9m
Current Liabilities	580	452	581

Screen Systems Wire Workers Ltd

Haydock Lane Industrial Estate Haydock Mersyside, St Helens, WA11 9UY
Tel: 01942-272895 **Fax:** 01942-274257
E-mail: david.greenall@screensystems.com
Website: http://www.screensystems.com
Bank(s): First Trust Bank
Managers: F. Garratt (Mktg Serv Mgr), P. Garratt (Import Mgr), D. Greenall (Mgr), D. Greeall (Purch Mgr), D. Greenall (Chief Mgr), D. Greenall (Prod Mgr), P. Garratt ()
Immediate Holding Company: SCREEN SYSTEMS (WIRE WORKERS) LIMITED
Registration no: 05423239 **VAT No.:** GB 860 5177 24
Date established: 2005 **Turnover:** £5m - £10m **No.of Employees:** 11 - 20
Product Groups: 33, 35, 42

Date of Accounts	Dec 10	Dec 09	Dec 08
Working Capital	232	193	N/A
Fixed Assets	5	7	N/A
Current Assets	467	483	N/A

Ena Shaw Ltd

Euro Link Lea Green, St Helens, WA9 4QF
Tel: 01744-851515 **Fax:** 01744-812412
E-mail: mark@richardbarrie.co.uk
Website: http://www.richardbarrie.co.uk
Directors: M. Gordon (Fin)
Managers: M. Potter (Sales & Mktg Mg), S. Murphy (Tech Serv Mgr)
Immediate Holding Company: ENA SHAW LIMITED
Registration no: 00590975 **Date established:** 1957
Turnover: £10m - £20m **No.of Employees:** 101 - 250
Product Groups: 24, 63

Date of Accounts	Jan 09	Jan 10	Jan 11
Sales Turnover	N/A	12m	12m
Pre Tax Profit/Loss	63	456	319
Working Capital	3m	3m	4m
Fixed Assets	1m	1m	889
Current Assets	5m	5m	5m
Current Liabilities	681	685	1m

Showers & Eyebaths Services Ltd

Safety House 23c Sandwash Close Rainford, St Helens, WA11 8LY
Tel: 01744-889677 **Fax:** 01744-885663
E-mail: janet@safety-showers.com
Website: http://www.safety-showers.com
Bank(s): The Royal Bank of Scotland
Directors: J. Dickinson (Fin)
Immediate Holding Company: SHOWERS & EYEBATHS SERVICES LIMITED
Registration no: 03447603 **VAT No.:** GB 703 9281 41
Date established: 1997 **Turnover:** £1m - £2m **No.of Employees:** 11 - 20
Product Groups: 29, 30, 31, 33, 36, 40, 44, 54, 67

Date of Accounts	Dec 11	Dec 10	Dec 09
Sales Turnover	1m	1m	N/A
Pre Tax Profit/Loss	191	139	N/A
Working Capital	499	324	317
Fixed Assets	410	401	207
Current Assets	1m	606	591
Current Liabilities	199	46	N/A

Signatime

5 Badbury Close Haydock, St Helens, WA11 0FF
E-mail: sales@signatime.co.uk
Website: http://www.signatime.co.uk
Directors: R. Cain (Dir)
Registration no: OC336208 **Date established:** 2008
Turnover: Up to £250,000 **No.of Employees:** 1 - 10 **Product Groups:** 49

Sinoway International Ltd

136 Chamberlain Street St Helens, St Helens, WA10 4NN
Tel: 01744-606018 **Fax:** 01744-730018
E-mail: sinoway@btinernet.com
Website: http://www.sinoway.com
Directors: M. Zhang (Fin), X. Zhou (MD)
Immediate Holding Company: SINOWAY INTERNATIONAL LIMITED
Registration no: 04514841 **Date established:** 2002
No.of Employees: 1 - 10 **Product Groups:** 27, 66

Date of Accounts	Aug 11	Aug 10	Aug 09
Working Capital	40	48	48
Current Assets	88	173	114

Sitelift Ltd

Unit F2a Sandwash Close Rainford, St Helens, WA11 8LY
Tel: 01744-883548
E-mail: chrissitelift@aol.com
Website: http://www.sitelift.co.uk
Directors: C. Pye (Co Sec)
Ultimate Holding Company: SITELIFT HOLDINGS LIMITED
Immediate Holding Company: SITELIFT LIMITED
Registration no: 03501550 **Date established:** 1998
No.of Employees: 1 - 10 **Product Groups:** 35, 39, 45

Date of Accounts	Apr 12	Apr 11	Apr 10
Working Capital	-23	-19	-856
Fixed Assets	2m	1m	1m
Current Assets	412	251	314

Speedy Hire Centres Northern Ltd

Lakeside Buildings, St Helens, WA10 3TT
Tel: 01744-697000 **Fax:** 01744-739975
Website: http://www.avoid.co.uk
Bank(s): Barclays
Directors: B. Halliwell (MD), N. O'brien (Dir), S. Corcoran (Dir), S. Richards (Fin), E. Arnold (Dir)
Immediate Holding Company: Speedy Hire plc
Registration no: 00245380 **VAT No.:** GB 151 9136 75
Date established: 1930 **Turnover:** Over £1,000m
No.of Employees: 501 - 1000 **Product Groups:** 83

Speedy Survey Ltd

Pye Close Haydock, St Helens, WA11 9SJ
Tel: 01942-723700 **Fax:** 01942-717200
Website: http://www.speedysurvey.co.uk
Bank(s): National Westminster Bank Plc
Directors: M. Burgess (MD), A. carter (MD), S. Page (Chief Op Offcr), M. Macara (Chief Op Offcr)
Ultimate Holding Company: 00927680
Immediate Holding Company: SPEEDY SURVEY LIMITED
Registration no: 03845497 **Date established:** 1999
No.of Employees: 21 - 50 **Product Groups:** 83

St Helens Mobility Shop

82 Unit 7 Barrow Arcades Claughton Street, St Helens, WA10 1RR
Tel: 01744-632611 **Fax:** 01744-632610
Managers: H. Maddox (Ops Mgr)
Immediate Holding Company: St Helens Mobility Shop Ltd
Registration no: 05038794 **Date established:** 2004
No.of Employees: 1 - 10 **Product Groups:** 45, 48, 67

Super Trucks Ltd

Beaufort Street, St Helens, WA9 3BQ
Tel: 01744-25348 **Fax:** 01744-27772
E-mail: supertrucks@btinternet.com
Website: http://www.supertrucks-uk.com
Bank(s): Nat West
Directors: L. Wright (Dir), R. Hitchen (MD), L. Wright (Co Sec)
Immediate Holding Company: SUPERTRUCKS LIMITED
Registration no: 03244516 **VAT No.:** GB 344 0948 54
Date established: 1996 **Turnover:** £1m - £2m **No.of Employees:** 11 - 20
Product Groups: 45

Date of Accounts	Jul 11	Jul 10	Jul 09
Working Capital	-86	-61	-105
Fixed Assets	145	172	224
Current Assets	257	278	296

Surefil Beauty Products

The Bedford Centre Bedford Street, Parr Industrial Estate, St Helens, WA9 1PN
Tel: 01744-758820 **Fax:** 01744-451859
E-mail: sales@surefil.co.uk
Website: http://www.surefil.co.uk
Bank(s): Lloyds TSB Bank plc
Directors: C. Critchley (Fin), P. Critchley (MD)
Managers: C. Jackson (Personnel), L. Hill (Purch Mgr)
Ultimate Holding Company: ELECTRICJUMP LIMITED
Immediate Holding Company: SUREFIL BEAUTY PRODUCTS LIMITED
Registration no: 01480297 **Date established:** 1980 **Turnover:** £5m - £10m
No.of Employees: 51 - 100 **Product Groups:** 32

Date of Accounts	Feb 08	Feb 11	Feb 10
Sales Turnover	N/A	6m	4m
Pre Tax Profit/Loss	220	278	-78
Working Capital	811	2m	2m
Fixed Assets	679	525	587
Current Assets	2m	3m	3m
Current Liabilities	185	782	728

Titan Distribution Ukltd

North Florida Road Haydock, St Helens, WA11 9UB
Tel: 01942-715333 **Fax:** 01942-715111
E-mail: enquiries@titandistributionuk.com
Website: http://www.titaneurope.com
Immediate Holding Company: TITAN DISTRIBUTION (UK) LIMITED
Registration no: 02352328 **Date established:** 1989 **Turnover:** £5m - £10m
No.of Employees: 1 - 10 **Product Groups:** 39

Date of Accounts	Dec 09	Dec 08	Dec 07
Sales Turnover	6m	11m	9m
Pre Tax Profit/Loss	311	2m	797
Working Capital	3m	3m	2m
Fixed Assets	3	5	7
Current Assets	5m	7m	5m
Current Liabilities	1m	3m	2m

T M Utley Offshore plc

Abbotsfield Road Reginald Road Industrial Estate, St Helens, WA9 4HU
Tel: 01744-850552 **Fax:** 01744-850510
E-mail: sales@utleyoffshore.co.uk
Website: http://www.utleyoffshore.co.uk
Directors: T. Utley (MD), M. Utley (Fin)
Immediate Holding Company: T M UTLEY (OFFSHORE) PLC
Registration no: 02100814 **VAT No.:** GB 439 2134 56
Date established: 1987 **Turnover:** £250,000 - £500,000
No.of Employees: 1 - 10 **Product Groups:** 25, 33, 35, 39

Date of Accounts	Apr 12	Apr 11	Apr 10
Sales Turnover	355	396	360
Pre Tax Profit/Loss	2	55	-68
Working Capital	242	301	307
Fixed Assets	11	12	10
Current Assets	393	477	422
Current Liabilities	45	50	39

V L C Stairlifts Ltd

366 Church Road Haydock, St Helens, WA11 0LG
Tel: 01942-719565 **Fax:** 0844-824 6428
E-mail: info@versatileliftcompany.co.uk
Website: http://www.versatileliftcompany.co.uk
Directors: J. Green (MD)
Immediate Holding Company: VLC (STAIRLIFTS) LIMITED
Registration no: 04657120 **Date established:** 2003
No.of Employees: 11 - 20 **Product Groups:** 35, 39, 45

Date of Accounts	Feb 12	Feb 11	Feb 10
Working Capital	48	15	-15
Fixed Assets	44	30	29
Current Assets	164	126	142

Valve Center

Unit 5 Bold Business Centre Bold Lane, St Helens, WA9 4TX
Tel: 01925-290660 **Fax:** 01925-227463
E-mail: sales@valvecenter.co.uk
Website: http://www.valvecenter.co.uk
Directors: D. Bowden (MD)
Managers: J. Glover (Mgr)
Ultimate Holding Company: THE CONCENTRIC GROUP OF COMPANIES
Registration no: 00671255 **Date established:** 1935 **Turnover:** £1m - £2m
No.of Employees: 1 - 10 **Product Groups:** 36

Vinyline Ltd

Unit 4b Delph Court Sullivans Way, St Helens, WA9 5GL
Tel: 01744-756644 **Fax:** 01744-454308
E-mail: keith@vinyline.co.uk
Website: http://www.vinyline.co.uk
Bank(s): Royal Bank of Scotland
Directors: S. Mitchell (Fin), K. Hughes (MD)
Immediate Holding Company: VINYLINE LIMITED
Registration no: 01813785 **Date established:** 1984
Turnover: £250,000 - £500,000 **No.of Employees:** 21 - 50
Product Groups: 28, 30

Date of Accounts	Aug 11	Aug 10	Aug 09
Working Capital	26	104	112
Fixed Assets	229	166	191
Current Assets	455	412	321

W Maass UK Ltd

Unit 2 Bedford Street Parr Industrial Estate, St Helens, WA9 1PN
Tel: 01744-453393 **Fax:** 01744-451707
E-mail: d.toone@w-maass.co.uk
Website: http://www.w-maass.co.uk
Bank(s): Barclays
Directors: D. Toone (Dir), D. Toone (MD)
Managers: G. McCann (), P. Clare (Projects), P. Greenwood (Product), J. Chadwick (Sales Prom Mgr), K. Toone (Accounts), F. Taylor
Ultimate Holding Company: FP004585
Immediate Holding Company: W MAASS (UK) LIMITED
Registration no: 01416453 **VAT No.:** GB 306 0920 92
Date established: 1979 **Turnover:** £2m - £5m **No.of Employees:** 21 - 50
Product Groups: 34, 36

Date of Accounts	Dec 10	Dec 09	Dec 08
Working Capital	1m	2m	2m
Fixed Assets	755	929	1m
Current Assets	2m	2m	4m

Wealdpark Ltd

Sutton Road, St Helens, WA9 3DJ
Tel: 01744-22567 **Fax:** 01744- 451339
E-mail: sales@wealdpark.co.uk
Website: http://www.wealdpark.co.uk
Bank(s): Royal Bank of Scotland
Directors: C. Smith (Dir)
Immediate Holding Company: WEALDPARK LIMITED
Registration no: 00846059 **VAT No.:** GB 152 1963 74
Date established: 1965 **Turnover:** £2m - £5m **No.of Employees:** 11 - 20
Product Groups: 30, 35

Date of Accounts	Jan 12	Jan 11	Jan 10
Working Capital	204	155	86
Fixed Assets	1m	1m	1m
Current Assets	890	753	539

Willochrome Ltd

Westside Jackson Street, St Helens, WA9 3AT
Tel: 01744-738488 **Fax:** 01744-23039
E-mail: graham.daniels@willochrome.co.uk
Website: http://www.willochrome.co.uk
Directors: G. Daniels (MD)
Immediate Holding Company: WILLOCHROME LIMITED
Registration no: 00611468 **Date established:** 1958
No.of Employees: 1 - 10 **Product Groups:** 46, 48

Date of Accounts	Aug 10	Aug 08	Aug 07
Working Capital	30	33	36
Fixed Assets	55	63	61
Current Assets	94	66	52

Woodwards S V S Ltd

Merton Street Merton Bank Road, St Helens, WA9 1HU
Tel: 01744-20266 **Fax:** 01744-752226
Website: http://www.woodwardssvsltd.co.uk
Directors: C. Newell (Prop)
Immediate Holding Company: WOODWARDS SVS LIMITED
Registration no: 02984370 **Date established:** 1994
Turnover: £500,000 - £1m **No.of Employees:** 1 - 10 **Product Groups:** 39, 45, 72

Date of Accounts	Mar 11	Mar 10	Mar 09
Sales Turnover	N/A	N/A	324
Pre Tax Profit/Loss	N/A	N/A	-89
Working Capital	-104	1	88
Fixed Assets	25	34	39
Current Assets	239	239	236
Current Liabilities	N/A	N/A	37

Wallasey

Action Seals Ltd

Westfield Road, Wallasey, CH44 7JA
Tel: 0151-652 6661 **Fax:** 0151-653 4994
E-mail: steve.quail@actionseals.co.uk
Website: http://www.actionseals.com
Directors: S. Quail (MD)
Ultimate Holding Company: BEACHBREEZE LIMITED
Immediate Holding Company: ACTION SEALS LTD
Registration no: 00750570 **VAT No.:** GB 163 3323 87
Date established: 1963 **Turnover:** £1m - £2m **No.of Employees:** 1 - 10
Product Groups: 22, 23, 25, 29, 30, 33, 36

Date of Accounts	Mar 12	Mar 11	Mar 10
Working Capital	560	553	570
Fixed Assets	3	1	2
Current Assets	658	629	623

Arrowe Brook Engineering Wallasey Ltd
2 The Grove, Wallasey, CH44 4BQ
Tel: 0151-638 8111 **Fax:** 0151-639 1776
E-mail: info@arrowebrookengineering.co.uk
Website: http://www.arrowebrookengineering.co.uk
Bank(s): HSBC Bank plc
Directors: P. Richards (MD)
Ultimate Holding Company: ARROWEBROOK HOLDINGS LIMITED
Immediate Holding Company: ARROWEBROOK ENGINEERING (WALLASEY) LIMITED (THE)
Registration no: 01096711 **VAT No.:** GB 165 3986 27
Date established: 1973 **Turnover:** £500,000 - £1m
No.of Employees: 11 - 20 **Product Groups:** 48

Date of Accounts	Jun 11	Jun 10	Jun 09
Working Capital	24	-7	55
Fixed Assets	N/A	25	29
Current Assets	201	90	160

Bailey & Birch Electrical Services Ltd
138 Seabank Road, Wallasey, CH45 1HG
Tel: 0151-639 3005 **Fax:** 0151-630 5027
E-mail: office@baileyandbirch.co.uk
Website: http://www.baileyandbirch.co.uk
Directors: R. Bailey (Dir)
Immediate Holding Company: BAILEY & BIRCH ELECTRICAL SERVICES LIMITED
Registration no: 07329081 **Date established:** 2010
Turnover: £500,000 - £1m **No.of Employees:** 11 - 20 **Product Groups:** 52

Date of Accounts	Oct 11
Working Capital	14
Fixed Assets	4
Current Assets	76

Builder Center Ltd
Cross Lane, Wallasey, CH45 8RQ
Tel: 0151-263 5544 **Fax:** 0151-263 1432
Website: http://www.sublimebydesign.co.uk
Directors: A. Barden (MD)
Managers: C. Latham (District Mgr), C. Lathan (Mgr)
Ultimate Holding Company: Wolseley plc
Immediate Holding Company: BUILD CENTER LIMITED
Registration no: 00462397 **Date established:** 1948 **Turnover:** £2m - £5m
No.of Employees: 21 - 50 **Product Groups:** 66, 83

C M L Treatments Ltd
Unit 5 Wheatland Business Park, Wallasey, CH44 7ER
Tel: 0151-631 5600 **Fax:** 0151-631 5601
E-mail: caroline.favager@cml-group.com
Website: http://www.cml.group.com
Bank(s): Intelek P.L.C.
Directors: G. Stewart (MD), D. Haydon (Fin), M. Allport (Dir), Allport (Dir)
Managers: H. Symonds, Z. Johnston (Admin Off), C. Favager (Admin Off), S. Crane (Mgr), P. Williams (Sales Prom Mgr), D. Hughes (Tech Serv Mgr), J. Allport (I.T. Exec)
Registration no: 01564040 **VAT No.:** GB 320 1086 18
Date established: 1992 **Turnover:** £1m - £2m **No.of Employees:** 21 - 50
Product Groups: 48, 54

J Smyth Welding
Unit D 33 Breck Road, Wallasey, CH44 3BB
Tel: 0151-639 8990 **Fax:** 0151-639 8990
E-mail: brian@solutionengineers.com
Directors: B. Bennett (Dir)
Date established: 1993 **No.of Employees:** 1 - 10 **Product Groups:** 35

Kohler Daryl Ltd
Alfred Road, Wallasey, CH44 7HY
Tel: 0151-606 5000 **Fax:** 0151-638 0303
E-mail: karger@daryl-showers.co.uk
Website: http://www.daryl-showers.co.uk
Bank(s): Lloyds
Directors: K. Kohler (Dir), N. Black (Co Sec)
Ultimate Holding Company: KOHLER CO (USA)
Immediate Holding Company: KOHLER DARYL LIMITED
Registration no: 00907700 **VAT No.:** 163 4694 47 **Date established:** 1967
Turnover: £5m - £10m **No.of Employees:** 51 - 100 **Product Groups:** 30, 36, 48

Date of Accounts	Dec 11	Dec 10	Dec 09
Sales Turnover	N/A	9m	9m
Pre Tax Profit/Loss	N/A	-3m	-3m
Working Capital	7m	7m	6m
Fixed Assets	N/A	N/A	4m
Current Assets	7m	7m	8m
Current Liabilities	N/A	N/A	590

Max Web Solutions Ltd
188 Liscard Road, Wallasey, CH44 5TN
Tel: 0151-691 4939 **Fax:** 01582
E-mail: info@maxwebsolutions.co.uk
Website: http://www.maxwebsolutions.co.uk
Directors: M. Ainsworth (Dir)
Immediate Holding Company: MAX WEB SOLUTIONS LIMITED
Registration no: 07544011 **Date established:** 2011
Turnover: £500,000 - £1m **No.of Employees:** 1 - 10 **Product Groups:** 83

Ross Care Cummunity Equipment Centre
2-3 Westfield Road, Wallasey, CH44 7HX
Tel: 0151-653 9988 **Fax:** 0151-653 8543
Bank(s): National Westminster
Directors: P. Smith (Fin)
Managers: D. Clay (Ops Mgr), S. Dean, A. Cavell (Mktg Serv Mgr)
Ultimate Holding Company: ROSS CARE HOLDINGS LTD
Registration no: 00469301 **Turnover:** £2m - £5m
No.of Employees: 11 - 20 **Product Groups:** 26, 39

Wirral Travel
259 Wallasey Village, Wallasey, CH45 3LR
Tel: 0151-638 7277 **Fax:** 0151- 6387077
E-mail: sales@cltvl.co.uk
Website: http://www.wirraltravelagency.com
Directors: K. Jones (Ptnr)
Immediate Holding Company: APH ACCOUNTANTS LTD
Registration no: 06856358 **Date established:** 2010
No.of Employees: 1 - 10 **Product Groups:** 69, 82, 84

Date of Accounts	Mar 12
Working Capital	5
Fixed Assets	9
Current Assets	15

Wirral

A N H Europe Refractories
Dock Road South, Wirral, CH62 4SP
Tel: 0151-641 5900 **Fax:** 0151-641 5910
E-mail: sales@anheurope.co.uk
Website: http://www.anheurope.co.uk
Bank(s): Barclays
Directors: P. Rooney (MD)
Managers: S. Kenny (Sales Admin), T. Williams (Eng Serv Mgr), A. Millard
Ultimate Holding Company: ANH REFRACTORIES CO (USA)
Immediate Holding Company: ANH REFRACTORIES EUROPE LIMITED
Registration no: 00175893 **Date established:** 2021 **Turnover:** £5m - £10m
No.of Employees: 21 - 50 **Product Groups:** 33

Date of Accounts	Dec 11	Dec 10	Dec 09
Working Capital	4m	3m	3m
Fixed Assets	479	457	495
Current Assets	5m	4m	4m

Alpine Vending Co. Ltd
2425 Carham Road Hoylake, Wirral, CH47 4FF
Tel: 08704-443989 **Fax:** 0151-632 1420
E-mail: sales@alpinevending.co.uk
Website: http://www.alpinevending.co.uk
Directors: J. Hazelhurst (MD)
Immediate Holding Company: ALPINE VENDING CO LIMITED
Registration no: 04654806 **Date established:** 2003
No.of Employees: 1 - 10 **Product Groups:** 48, 61

Date of Accounts	Oct 11	Oct 10	Oct 09
Working Capital	-72	-65	-63
Fixed Assets	114	112	126
Current Assets	283	279	249

B P Engineering Co. Ltd
5 Railway Buildings Carr Lane, Hoylake, Wirral, CH47 4AY
Tel: 0151-632 1364 **Fax:** 0151-632 3364
E-mail: bpeng@btconnect.com
Directors: A. Brierley (MD)
Immediate Holding Company: B. P. ENGINEERING CO. (WIRRAL) LIMITED
Registration no: 01031290 **VAT No.:** GB 163 7097 50
Date established: 1971 **Turnover:** £250,000 - £500,000
No.of Employees: 1 - 10 **Product Groups:** 36, 48

Date of Accounts	Mar 11	Mar 10	Mar 09
Working Capital	-52	16	4
Fixed Assets	10	13	18
Current Assets	39	85	94

B P I Films
40 Thursby Road Croft Business Park Bromborough, Wirral, CH62 3PZ
Tel: 0151-334 8091 **Fax:** 0151-334 0066
E-mail: davebeale@bpipoly.com
Website: http://www.bpifilms.com
Bank(s): The Royal Bank of Scotland
Directors: D. Beale (MD)
Immediate Holding Company: BRITISH POLYTHENE INDUSTRIES P.L.C.
Registration no: 00350729 **Date established:** 1982
Turnover: £20m - £50m **No.of Employees:** 51 - 100 **Product Groups:** 30

Beer & Co. Ltd
Harrisons Yard Bridle Road, Eastham, Wirral, CH62 8AS
Tel: 0151-327 6283 **Fax:** 0151-328 1067
E-mail: info@beersltd.co.uk
Website: http://www.beersltd.co.uk
Directors: M. Beer (Dir)
Date established: 1916 **No.of Employees:** 1 - 10 **Product Groups:** 25, 52, 66

Beers Timber & Building Supplies
Darlington Industrial Estate Chester Road, Heswall, Wirral, CH60 3SG
Tel: 0151-342 6222 **Fax:** 0151-342 9646
E-mail: info@beersltd.co.uk
Website: http://www.beersltd.co.uk
Managers: A. Davies (Mgr)
Immediate Holding Company: A&M TABIAT LIMITED
Date established: 2009 **No.of Employees:** 1 - 10 **Product Groups:** 25, 52, 66

Biffa Waste Services Ltd
Unit 16 Bandy Park Plantation Road, Bronborough, Wirral, CH62 3QS
Tel: 0151-343 3700 **Fax:** 0151-343 0893
E-mail: marketing@biffa.co.uk
Website: http://www.biffa.co.uk
Directors: M. Bettington (MD)
Managers: A. Coulton (District Mgr)
Immediate Holding Company: BIFFA WASTE SERVICES LIMITED
Registration no: 00946107 **Date established:** 1969
No.of Employees: 101 - 250 **Product Groups:** 32, 54

Date of Accounts	Mar 08	Mar 09	Apr 10
Sales Turnover	555m	574m	492m
Pre Tax Profit/Loss	23m	50m	30m
Working Capital	229m	271m	293m
Fixed Assets	371m	360m	378m
Current Assets	409m	534m	609m
Current Liabilities	50m	100m	115m

C C R Systems Northern Ltd
142 Bebington Road New Ferry, Wirral, CH62 5BJ
Tel: 0151-644 8296 **Fax:** 0151-645 8981
E-mail: epos@ccrsystems.co.uk
Website: http://www.ccrsystems.co.uk
Directors: R. Gunnery (Fin), G. Gunnery (Dir)
Immediate Holding Company: C.C.R.SYSTEMS (NORTHERN) LIMITED
Registration no: 02193147 **Date established:** 1987 **Turnover:** £1m - £2m
No.of Employees: 1 - 10 **Product Groups:** 44, 67

Date of Accounts	Dec 11	Dec 10	Dec 09
Working Capital	-69	-78	-71
Fixed Assets	28	29	31
Current Assets	52	61	50
Current Liabilities	N/A	100	N/A

C Q R Ltd
125 Pasture Road, Wirral, CH46 4TH
Tel: 0151-606 1000 **Fax:** 0151-606 1122
E-mail: info@cqr.co.uk
Website: http://www.cqr.co.uk
Directors: J. Roberts (Sales & Mktg), P. Benjamin (MD)
Immediate Holding Company: CHANNEL HOLDINGS P.L.C.
VAT No.: GB 319 8244 45 **Date established:** 1984
No.of Employees: 21 - 50 **Product Groups:** 36, 37, 40, 67

C S M UK Ltd
Stadium Road, Wirral, CH62 3NU
Tel: 0151-343 1600 **Fax:** 0151-346 1334
E-mail: orders@bakemark.co.uk
Website: http://www.arkady-craigmillar.co.uk
Bank(s): National Westminster Bank Plc
Directors: M. Bok (Fin), M. Ten Doesschate (Dir)
Ultimate Holding Company: CSM NV (NETHERLANDS)
Immediate Holding Company: ARKADY CRAIGMILLAR LIMITED
Registration no: 04927453 **VAT No.:** GB 595 9399 56
Date established: 2003 **No.of Employees:** 251 - 500 **Product Groups:** 20, 62

Chester Medical Solutions
Unit 3-4 Apex Court Bassendale Road, Bromborough, Wirral, CH62 3RE
Tel: 0151-343 1181 **Fax:** 0151-343 5380
E-mail: twilliams@ads-graphics.com
Website: http://www.chestermedical.com
Directors: J. Tindall (Dir), D. Pattison (MD), T. Williams (Sales)
Managers: T. Smith
Registration no: 04165479 **No.of Employees:** 21 - 50 **Product Groups:** 31

Cleaning and Catering Direct
Brooklet Brimstage, Wirral, CH63 6HE
Tel: 0151-342 5579 **Fax:** 0151-342 5310
E-mail: admin@cleaningandcatering.co.uk
Website: http://www.cleaningandcatering.co.uk
Managers: R. Tyson (Develop Mgr)
Date established: 2000 **No.of Employees:** 1 - 10 **Product Groups:** 32

Dantec Ltd
Tarran Way Tarran Industrial Estate, Wirral, CH46 4TL
Tel: 0151-678 2222 **Fax:** 0151-606 0188
E-mail: sales@dantec.com
Website: http://www.dantec.com
Bank(s): H S B C
Directors: J. Loach (Sales), H. Jones (Fin), J. Laidlaw (MD)
Managers: E. Lolley, R. Craig, K. Taylor (Purch Mgr)
Ultimate Holding Company: DANTEC HOSE LIMITED
Immediate Holding Company: DANTEC LIMITED
Registration no: 01057158 **Date established:** 1972 **Turnover:** £5m - £10m
No.of Employees: 21 - 50 **Product Groups:** 30

Date of Accounts	Apr 11	Apr 10	Apr 09
Sales Turnover	6m	5m	6m
Pre Tax Profit/Loss	466	496	614
Working Capital	3m	2m	2m
Fixed Assets	443	437	426
Current Assets	5m	4m	4m
Current Liabilities	328	344	442

Dee Sailing Club
Station Road Thurstaston, Wirral, CH61 0HN
Tel: 0151-648 2300
E-mail: wayfarers@dee-sc.co.uk
Website: http://www.dee-sc.co.uk
Managers: R. Clark
Date established: 2000 **No.of Employees:** 1 - 10 **Product Groups:** 37, 67, 68, 74

Easy 2 Move
19 Roslin Road, Wirral, CH61 3UH
Tel: 0151-648 3961
E-mail: info@easy2move.org
Website: http://www.easy2move.org/
Directors: M. Eymes (Prop)
Date established: 2000 **Turnover:** £20m - £50m **No.of Employees:** 1 - 10
Product Groups: 72

Elliott Properties
PO Box 46, Wirral, CH60 9LR
Tel: 0774-788 8181
Website: http://www.elliottproperties.co.uk
Directors: J. Elliott (Prop)
No.of Employees: 11 - 20 **Product Groups:** 80

J K Evans & Sons
1a Sandy Lane Heswall, Wirral, CH60 5SX
Tel: 0151-342 1801
E-mail: sales@jkevansandsons.co.uk
Website: http://www.jkevansandsons.co.uk
Directors: D. Evans (Ptnr)
Date established: 1957 **No.of Employees:** 1 - 10 **Product Groups:** 26, 40

F M C Chemicals Ltd
Lithium Division Commercial Road, Wirral, CH62 3NL
Tel: 0151-334 8085 **Fax:** 0151-334 8501
E-mail: stephen.lewis@fmc.com
Website: http://www.fmclithium.com
Directors: B. Curry (I.T. Dir), S. Price (Pers)
Ultimate Holding Company: FMC CORPORATION (USA)
Immediate Holding Company: FMC CHEMICALS LIMITED
Registration no: 04081622 **VAT No.:** GB 748 8534 82
Date established: 2000 **Turnover:** £20m - £50m
No.of Employees: 51 - 100 **Product Groups:** 31, 34

Date of Accounts	Dec 11	Dec 10	Dec 09
Sales Turnover	33m	34m	32m
Pre Tax Profit/Loss	5m	3m	-5m
Working Capital	6m	2m	-1m
Fixed Assets	13m	14m	15m
Current Assets	12m	10m	13m
Current Liabilities	1m	547	2m

Feedwater Ltd
Tarran Way West Tarran Industrial Estate, Wirral, CH46 4TU
Tel: 0151-606 0808 **Fax:** 0151-678 5459
E-mail: info@feedwater.co.uk
Website: http://www.feedwater.co.uk
Directors: S. Walker (Sales), T. Parkinson (MD)
Managers: C. Dodgson (Fin Mgr), C. Jowitt
Immediate Holding Company: FEEDWATER LIMITED
Registration no: 01274270 **Date established:** 1976 **Turnover:** £5m - £10m
No.of Employees: 51 - 100 **Product Groups:** 32, 38, 40, 42, 66

see next page

Feedwater Ltd - Cont'd

Date of Accounts	Jun 11	Jun 10	Jun 09
Working Capital	326	381	283
Fixed Assets	1m	905	793
Current Assets	1m	1m	1m

Fine Controls UK Ltd
Unit 15 Bassendale Road Croft Business Park, Bromborough, Wirral, CH62 3QL
Tel: 0151-343 9966 **Fax:** 0151-343 0062
E-mail: sales@fincon.co.uk
Website: http://finecontrols.com
Bank(s): National Westminster Bank Plc
Directors: M. Croft (Co Sec), G. Hall (Sales), J. Donaldson (I.T. Dir)
Immediate Holding Company: FINE CONTROLS (UK) LTD.
Registration no: 02916212 **VAT No.:** GB 618 8289 01
Date established: 1994 **Turnover:** £1m - £2m **No.of Employees:** 11 - 20
Product Groups: 37, 38

Date of Accounts	Mar 11	Mar 10	Mar 09
Working Capital	230	217	210
Fixed Assets	36	43	46
Current Assets	871	789	718

Givaudam UK Ltd
Dock Road South Bromborough Port, Wirral, CH62 4SU
Tel: 0151-645 2060 **Fax:** 0151-645 6975
E-mail: kevin.robinson@givaudan.com
Website: http://www.givaudam.com
Directors: P. Millington (Fin), K. Robinson (MD)
Managers: M. Lloyd (Personnel), M. Fishburne (Tech Serv Mgr), K. Peover (Purch Mgr)
VAT No.: GB 572 0185 55 **No.of Employees:** 101 - 250
Product Groups: 20

Heap & Partners Ltd
Britannia House 61-63 Newton Road, Hoylake, Wirral, CH47 3DG
Tel: 0151-632 3393 **Fax:** 0151-632 4453
E-mail: info@heaps.co.uk
Website: http://www.heaps.co.uk
Directors: D. Millar (MD)
Ultimate Holding Company: TEAL HOLDINGS LIMITED
Immediate Holding Company: HEAP & PARTNERS LIMITED
Registration no: 00196537 **Date established:** 2024 **Turnover:** £5m - £10m
No.of Employees: 21 - 50 **Product Groups:** 35, 66

Date of Accounts	Mar 12	Mar 11	Mar 10
Sales Turnover	7m	7m	7m
Pre Tax Profit/Loss	201	9	169
Working Capital	889	1m	1m
Fixed Assets	823	652	453
Current Assets	4m	4m	4m
Current Liabilities	1m	1m	1m

Hilsonic
Unit 9 Carrock Road Croft Business Park, Bromborough, Wirral, CH62 3RA
Tel: 0151-639 6020 **Fax:** 0151-334 7407
E-mail: sales@hilsonic.co.uk
Website: http://www.hilsonic.co.uk
Directors: J. Caza (Prop)
No.of Employees: 1 - 10 **Product Groups:** 37

Holt Springs Ltd
Carsgoe Road Carr Lane Industrial Estate, Hoylake, Wirral, CH47 4FE
Tel: 0151-632 5005 **Fax:** 0151-632 3856
E-mail: sales@holtsprings.co.uk
Website: http://www.holtsprings.co.uk
Directors: D. Nickson (Dir)
Immediate Holding Company: HOLT SPRINGS LIMITED
Registration no: 00527299 **Date established:** 1953
Turnover: £250,000 - £500,000 **No.of Employees:** 1 - 10
Product Groups: 34, 35, 36, 38, 39, 66

Date of Accounts	Dec 11	Dec 10	Dec 09
Working Capital	139	134	115
Fixed Assets	64	72	92
Current Assets	214	218	165

Innovation Engineering
PO Box 46, Wirral, CH60 9LR
Tel: 0151-348 4202
E-mail: info@innovation-engineering.co.uk
Website: http://www.innovation-engineering.co.uk
Directors: J. Elliott (Ptnr)
No.of Employees: 11 - 20 **Product Groups:** 45

International Translations Ltd
9 Queensway, Wirral, CH60 3SL
Tel: 0151-342 7044 **Fax:** 0151-342 9407
E-mail: admin@itltranslations.com
Website: http://www.itltranslations.com
Managers: C. Smith (Mgr)
Immediate Holding Company: INTERNATIONAL TRANSLATIONS LIMITED
Registration no: 01768839 **VAT No.:** GB 324 8585 38
Date established: 1983 **No.of Employees:** 1 - 10 **Product Groups:** 80

Date of Accounts	Apr 12	Apr 11	Apr 10
Working Capital	3	2	N/A
Fixed Assets	1	4	4
Current Assets	43	51	44

Italia Lighting Ltd
139 Telegraph Road Heswall, Wirral, CH60 7SE
Tel: 0151-342 6523
Website: http://www.taskersonline.com
Managers: P. Whitingham (Mgr)
Registration no: 02559953 **Date established:** 1990
No.of Employees: 1 - 10 **Product Groups:** 37, 67

J N Electrical Services
469 New Chester Road, Wirral, CH62 3LB
Tel: 0151-334 5660 **Fax:** 0151-334 8559
Website: http://www.electricianwirral.com
Directors: J. Nicholson (Prop)
No.of Employees: 1 - 10 **Product Groups:** 40, 52, 67, 84

J P M Associates
284 Irby Road, Wirral, CH61 2XQ
Tel: 0151-648 2035 **Fax:** 0151-648 2035
Website: http://www.constructionplus.net
Directors: J. Meacher (Prop)
Immediate Holding Company: JPM ASSOCIATES (NW) LTD
Registration no: 05907775 **Date established:** 2006
No.of Employees: 1 - 10 **Product Groups:** 35

Date of Accounts	Aug 10	Aug 08	Aug 07
Working Capital	-2	-2	6
Fixed Assets	1	2	2
Current Assets	2	16	16

Kimpton Building Services
Unit 5 Hawkshead Road, Bromborough, Wirral, CH62 3RJ
Tel: 0151-343 1963 **Fax:** 0151-343 5900
E-mail: enquiries@kimpton.ltd.uk
Website: http://www.kimpton.ltd.uk
Bank(s): HSBC, Birkenhead
Directors: D. Kimpton (Fin), R. Kimpton (MD)
Immediate Holding Company: KIMPTON LTD
Registration no: 00781553 **VAT No.:** GB 164 0596 61
Date established: 1963 **Turnover:** £5m - £10m
No.of Employees: 51 - 100 **Product Groups:** 52

Date of Accounts	Sep 11	Sep 10	Sep 09
Sales Turnover	9m	9m	10m
Pre Tax Profit/Loss	96	158	197
Working Capital	696	474	867
Fixed Assets	2m	2m	1m
Current Assets	3m	3m	4m
Current Liabilities	987	1m	1m

L S J Mortgages
21b Pensby Road Heswall, Wirral, CH60 7RA
Tel: 0151-342 3288 **Fax:** 0151-342 5246
Website: http://www.themortgagepartnership.com
Directors: M. Hutchinson (Dir)
Managers: H. Brown (Chief Mgr)
Registration no: 06721153 **Date established:** 2008
No.of Employees: 1 - 10 **Product Groups:** 80

Land & Marine Project Engineering
Dock Road North, Wirral, CH62 4LN
Tel: 0151-641 5600 **Fax:** 0151-644 9990
E-mail: info@landandmarine.com
Website: http://www.landandmarine.com
Managers: A. Ball, T. Ley (Sales & Mktg Mg)
Ultimate Holding Company: DANIEL CONTRACTORS
Date established: 1985 **Turnover:** £20m - £50m
No.of Employees: 101 - 250 **Product Groups:** 84

Date of Accounts	Sep 08
Sales Turnover	128800
Pre Tax Profit/Loss	2950
Working Capital	2730
Fixed Assets	6040
Current Assets	47610
Current Liabilities	44880
Total Share Capital	10
ROCE% (Return on Capital Employed)	33.6

Lomax Electrical
35 North Parade Hoylake, Wirral, CH47 3AJ
Tel: 0151-632 0032 **Fax:** 07006-036976
E-mail: enquiry@lomaxelectrical.co.uk
Website: http://www.lomaxelectrical.co.uk
Directors: S. Lomax (Prop)
No.of Employees: 1 - 10 **Product Groups:** 37, 38, 52, 84

Marldon Group Ltd
Unit 9 Carr Lane Industrial Estate Hoylake, Wirral, CH47 4AZ
Tel: 0151-632 3146 **Fax:** 0151-632 4517
E-mail: sales@marldon.com
Website: http://www.marldon.com
Bank(s): National Westminster Bank Plc
Directors: D. Ryder (MD), P. Hindle (MD)
Immediate Holding Company: MARLDON GROUP LIMITED
Registration no: 00883915 **VAT No.:** GB 157 5615 47
Date established: 1966 **No.of Employees:** 21 - 50 **Product Groups:** 46

Date of Accounts	Jun 11	Jun 10	Jun 09
Working Capital	72	82	128
Fixed Assets	10	12	15
Current Assets	111	105	143

Mercia Global Business Aviation
463 New Chester Road Bromborough, Wirral, CH62 3LB
Tel: 0151-343 0347 **Fax:** 0151-223 0171
E-mail: georgehlane@gmx.com
Website: http://www.merciaglobal.com
Directors: G. Lane (Prop)
Date established: 2007 **No.of Employees:** 1 - 10 **Product Groups:** 75

Metalkraft
China Place Farm Thurstaston, Wirral, CH61 0HH
Tel: 0151-677 1934
Directors: D. Rich (Prop)
Date established: 1985 **No.of Employees:** 1 - 10 **Product Groups:** 26, 35

Newhall Publications Ltd
Newhall Lane, Wirral, CH47 4BQ
Tel: 08445-458102 **Fax:** 08707-453003
E-mail: chris@candis.co.uk
Website: http://www.candis.co.uk
Directors: C. Blackford (Fin), C. Harman (Chief Op Offcr)
Managers: B. Douglas Dala
Ultimate Holding Company: NEWHALL GROUP LIMITED(THE)
Immediate Holding Company: NEWHALL PUBLICATIONS LIMITED
Registration no: 02099513 **Date established:** 1987 **Turnover:** £5m - £10m
No.of Employees: 21 - 50 **Product Groups:** 28

Date of Accounts	Mar 11	Mar 10	Mar 09
Sales Turnover	8m	8m	9m
Pre Tax Profit/Loss	339	517	422
Working Capital	422	1m	2m
Fixed Assets	230	266	378
Current Assets	3m	4m	4m
Current Liabilities	455	542	527

Osiris Projects
Unit 4 Brunel Road Croft Business Park, Bromborough, Wirral, CH62 3NY
Tel: 0151-328 1120 **Fax:** 0151-343 1057
E-mail: enquiries@osirisprojects.co.uk
Website: http://www.osirisprojects.co.uk
Directors: A. Mcleay (MD), G. Harris (Fin)
Managers: P. Burlington (Tech Serv Mgr), H. Blackford
Immediate Holding Company: OSIRIS HYDROGRAPHIC & GEOPHYSICAL PROJECTS LIMITED
Registration no: 03408060 **Date established:** 1997
No.of Employees: 21 - 50 **Product Groups:** 32, 38, 39, 51, 54, 84, 85, 87

Date of Accounts	Mar 12	Mar 11	Mar 10
Working Capital	116	-31	126
Fixed Assets	3m	3m	3m
Current Assets	3m	988	1m

Oxton & Hoylake Iron Works
Unit 5 Links Business Park Carr Lane Hoylake, Wirral, CH47 4AY
Tel: 0151-632 2110
Directors: N. Foster (Prop)
Immediate Holding Company: SKY HIGH ENGINEERING LTD
Date established: 2011 **No.of Employees:** 1 - 10 **Product Groups:** 26, 35

Peninsular Nameplates
Peninsular House Car Lane, Hoylake, Wirral, CH47 4AZ
Tel: 0151-632 5814 **Fax:** 0151-632 1090
E-mail: info@peninsular-nameplates.co.uk
Website: http://www.peninsular-nameplates.co.uk
Directors: T. Mccarthy (Prop)
Immediate Holding Company: PENINSULAR NAMEPLATES LTD
Registration no: 07426729 **Date established:** 2010
Turnover: Up to £250,000 **No.of Employees:** 1 - 10 **Product Groups:** 23, 27, 28, 30, 34, 35, 39, 40, 48, 49, 65, 84

Quickhire
Unit 8 Pemway Centre Carr Lane Industrial Estate, Hoylake, Wirral, CH47 4AZ
Tel: 0151-632 6945 **Fax:** 0151-632 6946
E-mail: quickhire@btinternet.com
Website: http://www.quickhire.co.uk
Directors: B. Culshaw (Prop)
Immediate Holding Company: RAWELL GROUP HOLDINGS LIMITED
Registration no: 03363719 **Date established:** 1993
No.of Employees: 1 - 10 **Product Groups:** 40, 67

Date of Accounts	Jun 11	Jun 10	Jun 09
Working Capital	45	45	50
Current Assets	45	45	50

R F Lifting & Access Ltd
Unit 18 Carrock Road Croft Business Park, Bromborough, Wirral, CH62 3RA
Tel: 0151-346 1365 **Fax:** 0151-346 1366
E-mail: sales@rflifting.co.uk
Website: http://www.rflifting.co.uk
Directors: R. Fleming (Dir)
Immediate Holding Company: R F LIFTING & ACCESS LIMITED
Registration no: 04779560 **Date established:** 2003
No.of Employees: 1 - 10 **Product Groups:** 23, 24, 25, 28, 30, 35, 37, 38, 39, 40, 41, 45, 48, 66, 67, 68, 80, 83, 84, 86

Date of Accounts	Mar 11	Mar 10	Mar 09
Working Capital	162	174	173
Fixed Assets	16	20	26
Current Assets	258	250	315

Rawell Environmental Ltd
Carr Lane Hoylake, Wirral, CH47 4AZ
Tel: 0151-632 5771 **Fax:** 0151-632 4363
E-mail: postmaster@rawell.com
Website: http://www.rawell.com
Bank(s): Lloyds TSB Bank plc
Directors: B. Flynn (Ch)
Ultimate Holding Company: RAWELL GROUP HOLDINGS LIMITED
Immediate Holding Company: RAWELL ENVIRONMENTAL LIMITED
Registration no: 02667720 **VAT No.:** GB 618 8657 95
Date established: 1991 **Turnover:** £1m - £2m **No.of Employees:** 11 - 20
Product Groups: 18

Date of Accounts	Jun 11	Jun 10	Jun 09
Working Capital	-523	-229	-297
Fixed Assets	414	446	481
Current Assets	396	594	401

Selo UK Ltd
3-4 Bankfield Court Commercial Road, Wirral, CH62 3NN
Tel: 08452-932910 **Fax:** 0151-645 2202
E-mail: uk@selo.com
Website: http://www.selo.com
Bank(s): Barclays City Office, Liverpool
Managers: C. Keenan (Mgr)
Immediate Holding Company: SELO UK LTD
Registration no: 00392399 **VAT No.:** GB 164 2439 67
Date established: 1945 **Turnover:** £5m - £10m **No.of Employees:** 21 - 50
Product Groups: 41, 42

Date of Accounts	Dec 11	Dec 10	Dec 09
Sales Turnover	6m	6m	N/A
Working Capital	905	1m	1m
Fixed Assets	125	144	163
Current Assets	2m	2m	2m

Spectacle Warehouse (Hoylake) Limited
Unit 3 Carr lane Industrial Estate Shepburn Units, Hoylake, Wirral, CH47 4AZ
Tel: 0151-632 4857 **Fax:** 0151-632 0505
E-mail: info@spectacle-warehouse.co.uk
Website: http://www.spectacle-warehouse.co.uk
Directors: N. Corke (MD)
Registration no: 04660175 **Date established:** 2003
Turnover: Up to £250,000 **No.of Employees:** 1 - 10 **Product Groups:** 38, 40, 49, 65, 67

Standard Industrial Systems Ltd
Stanton House Eastham Village Rd, Eastham, Wirral, CH62 0DE
Tel: 0845-2571985 **Fax:** 0845-2571986
E-mail: sales@standardindustrial.co.uk
Website: http://www.standardindustrial.co.uk
Directors: G. Greenlees (Dir)
Managers: A. Forbes (Admin Off)
Registration no: 02745677 **No.of Employees:** 11 - 20
Product Groups: 37, 46, 84

Date of Accounts	Mar 08	Mar 07	Mar 06
Working Capital	-21	-43	-30
Fixed Assets	30	37	N/A
Current Assets	122	7	64
Current Liabilities	142	49	94
Total Share Capital	1	1	1

Telegraph Contract Furniture

91 Telegraph Road Heswall, Wirral, CH60 0AE
Tel: 0151-342 7773 **Fax:** 0151-342 2262
E-mail: joe@tcfshowroom.com
Website: http://www.tcfshowroom.com
Directors: J. Pinnington (Prop)
Date established: 1994 **No.of Employees:** 1 - 10 **Product Groups:** 35, 36

Thermal Ceramics UK Ltd

Tebay Road, Wirral, CH62 3PH
Tel: 0151-334 4030 **Fax:** 0151-334 1684
E-mail: jsimons@thermalceramics.com
Website: http://www.thermalceramics.co.uk
Directors: J. Simons (MD)
Ultimate Holding Company: MORGAN CRUCIBLE COMPANY PLC(THE)
Immediate Holding Company: THERMAL CERAMICS UK LIMITED
Registration no: 00890443 **VAT No.:** GB 595 9507 79
Date established: 1966 **Turnover:** £10m - £20m
No.of Employees: 101 - 250 **Product Groups:** 33, 37

Date of Accounts	Jan 09	Jan 10	Jan 11
Sales Turnover	16m	12m	14m
Pre Tax Profit/Loss	948	17	2m
Working Capital	2m	5m	6m
Fixed Assets	6m	4m	4m
Current Assets	9m	8m	12m
Current Liabilities	1m	1m	3m

Thermaton Imaging Thermal Imaging Services

59 Queens Avenue Meols, Wirral, CH47 0LS
Tel: 0151-632 5192 **Fax:** 0151-632 5192
E-mail: thermalderek@hotmail.co.uk
Directors: D. Povall (Prop)
Turnover: £1m - £2m **No.of Employees:** 1 - 10 **Product Groups:** 38, 54, 67

Timber Coaters

187 Pensby Road Heswall, Wirral, CH61 6UB
Tel: 07778-461644 **Fax:** 0151-342 5205
E-mail: timbercoaters@aol.com
Website: http://www.timbercoaters.com
Directors: G. Thomas (Ptnr)
No.of Employees: 1 - 10 **Product Groups:** 31, 32, 48, 52

Toohey Maintenance

76 Beechwood Road, Wirral, CH62 7BJ
Tel: 0151-343 1555
E-mail: denroamin@ntlworld.com
Website: http://www.tooheymaint.co.uk
Directors: D. Toohey (Prop)
Date established: 1996 **No.of Employees:** 1 - 10 **Product Groups:** 20, 40, 41

Veolia

Dock Road South, Wirral, CH62 4SQ
Tel: 0151-644 4300 **Fax:** 0151-644 4301
E-mail: jenny.alexander@veolia.co.uk
Website: http://www.veolia.co.uk
Managers: J. Alexander (Mgr)
Registration no: 01774317 **Date established:** 1983
No.of Employees: 11 - 20 **Product Groups:** 34, 40, 42, 54

MIDDLESEX

Ashford

Activair UK Ltd
Unit 1 Action Court Ashford Road, Ashford, TW15 1XS
Tel: 01784-890005 **Fax:** 01784-890013
Website: http://www.activair.com
Directors: M. Evans (Dir), S. Mcwilliams (Dir)
Managers: P. Barret (Sales Prom Mgr), R. Windsor (Personnel)
Immediate Holding Company: ACTIVAIR (UK) LIMITED
Registration no: 01369940 **Date established:** 1978
Turnover: £20m - £50m **No.of Employees:** 51 - 100 **Product Groups:** 76

Date of Accounts	May 08	May 07	May 06
Sales Turnover	53823	46805	45761
Pre Tax Profit/Loss	4773	1709	1129
Working Capital	3500	3143	2051
Fixed Assets	1119	1021	961
Current Assets	9380	9329	8354
Current Liabilities	5879	6186	6303
Total Share Capital	50	50	50
ROCE% (Return on Capital Employed)	103.3	41.0	37.5
ROT% (Return on Turnover)	8.9	3.7	2.5

Chase Perrin Ltd
Unit 7 Littleton House Littleton Road, Ashford, TW15 1UU
Tel: 01784-250200 **Fax:** 01784-257283
E-mail: sidney@chaseperrin.co.uk
Directors: S. Chase (MD)
Immediate Holding Company: CHASE PERRIN LTD
Registration no: 04512208 **Date established:** 2002
Turnover: Up to £250,000 **No.of Employees:** 1 - 10 **Product Groups:** 80, 81

Date of Accounts	Sep 08	Sep 07	Sep 06
Working Capital	10	7	3
Fixed Assets	N/A	N/A	1
Current Assets	53	48	32
Current Liabilities	43	41	30

D J Lift Services Ltd
Unit 3 Challenge Road, Ashford, TW15 1AX
Tel: 01784-249133 **Fax:** 01784-243863
Directors: V. Speight (MD)
Immediate Holding Company: D. J. LIFT SERVICES LIMITED
Registration no: 01257637 **Date established:** 1976
No.of Employees: 1 - 10 **Product Groups:** 35, 39, 45

Date of Accounts	Jul 11	Jul 10	Jul 09
Working Capital	57	59	52
Fixed Assets	57	49	51
Current Assets	133	168	171

Alan Dale Pumps Ltd
75 Clockhouse Lane, Ashford, TW15 2HA
Tel: 01784-421114 **Fax:** 01784-421092
E-mail: info@alandalepumps.wanadoo.co.uk
Website: http://www.alandalepumps.co.uk
Directors: J. Dale (Fin)
Immediate Holding Company: ALAN DALE PUMPS LIMITED
Registration no: 02796529 **Date established:** 1993
Turnover: Up to £250,000 **No.of Employees:** 1 - 10 **Product Groups:** 39, 40, 45, 46

Date of Accounts	Mar 12	Mar 11	Mar 09
Working Capital	-4	-5	-6
Fixed Assets	1	N/A	N/A
Current Assets	5	21	11

E T R Tool Hire & Sales Centre Ltd
148 Woodthorpe Road, Ashford, TW15 3LH
Tel: 01784-254396 **Fax:** 01784-240254
E-mail: helpdesk@etrtools.co.uk
Website: http://www.etrtools.co.uk
Directors: D. Fennessy (MD)
No.of Employees: 1 - 10 **Product Groups:** 36

Freight Merchandising Services
19 Shield Road, Ashford, TW15 1AU
Tel: 01784-240840 **Fax:** 01784-248615
E-mail: info@fmslondon.co.uk
Website: http://www.fmslondon.co.uk
Directors: P. Delaloye (Prop)
Immediate Holding Company: FREIGHT MERCHANDISING SERVICES LIMITED
Registration no: 03041739 **VAT No.:** GB 797 4022 03
Date established: 1995 **Turnover:** £500,000 - £1m
No.of Employees: 1 - 10 **Product Groups:** 27, 28, 30, 40, 80

Date of Accounts	Aug 11	Aug 10	Aug 09
Sales Turnover	N/A	N/A	846
Pre Tax Profit/Loss	N/A	N/A	207
Working Capital	1m	849	738
Fixed Assets	4	4	N/A
Current Assets	1m	939	830
Current Liabilities	N/A	N/A	61

Freightserve Worldwide
32 Church Road, Ashford, TW15 2UY
Tel: 01784-421044 **Fax:** 05601-261644
E-mail: sales@freightserve.co.uk
Website: http://www.freightserve.co.uk
Directors: D. Montague (Prop)
Immediate Holding Company: TIMELESS COMPUTER SUPPORT SERVICES LIMITED
VAT No.: GB 584 4467 06 **Date established:** 2002
Turnover: £250,000 - £500,000 **No.of Employees:** 1 - 10
Product Groups: 76

Date of Accounts	Mar 12	Mar 11
Working Capital	31	8
Fixed Assets	3	2
Current Assets	65	27

H M W Computing
142 Feltham Hill Road, Ashford, TW15 1HN
Tel: 020-7112 5423 **Fax:** 07092-117740
E-mail: info@4xtra.com
Website: http://4xtra.com
Directors: C. Hogan (Dir)
Immediate Holding Company: MICHAEL REASON & PARTNERS LLP
Registration no: OC316587 **Date established:** 2006
Turnover: Up to £250,000 **No.of Employees:** 1 - 10 **Product Groups:** 80, 82

Date of Accounts	Sep 11	Sep 10	Sep 09
Working Capital	31	10	62
Fixed Assets	1	1	1
Current Assets	55	75	84

Isoquest
10 Fontmell Park, Ashford, TW15 2NW
Tel: 01784-252275
E-mail: info@isoquest.co.uk
Website: http://www.isoquest.co.uk
Directors: M. Beetham (MD)
No.of Employees: 1 - 10 **Product Groups:** 54, 80

M H V Products Ltd
33 Woodthorpe Road, Ashford, TW15 2RP
Tel: 01784-241628 **Fax:** 01784-255610
E-mail: sales@mhvproducts.co.uk
Website: http://www.mhvproducts.co.uk
Bank(s): National Westminster Bank Plc
Directors: S. Vincer (Dir)
Immediate Holding Company: M.H.V. PRODUCTS LIMITED
Registration no: 01207264 **VAT No.:** GB 209 3714 70
Date established: 1975 **Turnover:** £1m - £2m **No.of Employees:** 11 - 20
Product Groups: 48

Date of Accounts	Apr 12	Apr 11	Apr 10
Working Capital	13	-10	39
Fixed Assets	220	224	208
Current Assets	264	405	297

Moonbridge Air & Project Services Ltd
Unit 304 Bedfont Industrial Park Challenge Road, Ashford, TW15 1AX
Tel: 01784-259555 **Fax:** 01784-259599
E-mail: ryans@moonbridge.co.uk
Website: http://www.moonbridge.co.uk
Managers: R. Sargeant (Mgr)
Immediate Holding Company: MOONBRIDGE AIR AND PROJECT SERVICES LIMITED
Registration no: 02076946 **VAT No.:** GB 453 0928 51
Date established: 1986 **Turnover:** £5m - £10m **No.of Employees:** 1 - 10
Product Groups: 76

Date of Accounts	Mar 11	Mar 10	Mar 09
Working Capital	385	387	389
Fixed Assets	51	57	55
Current Assets	803	765	829

Phoenix Air Cargo
Unit 11 Ashford Industrial Estate Shield Road, Ashford, TW15 1AU
Tel: 01784-420114 **Fax:** 01425-673391
E-mail: mail@phoenix-cargo.com
Website: http://www.phoenix-cargo.com
Directors: A. York (Prop)
Registration no: 02564155 **Date established:** 1995 **Turnover:** £2m - £5m
No.of Employees: 1 - 10 **Product Groups:** 75, 76

Safety Flooring Supplies
132-134 Stanwell Road, Ashford, TW15 3QP
Tel: 01784-244577 **Fax:** 08704-020124
Directors: R. Smerdon (MD), R. Smerdon (Dir)
Turnover: £500,000 - £1m **No.of Employees:** 1 - 10 **Product Groups:** 29, 32, 40, 63

Sandrair
Unit 18 Ashford Industrial Estate Shield Road, Ashford, TW15 1AU
Tel: 01784-242081 **Fax:** 01784-420776
E-mail: peter.smith@heathrow.sandrair.com
Website: http://www.mistercargo.com
Directors: P. Smith (Grp Chief Exec)
Ultimate Holding Company: 03007622
Immediate Holding Company: SANDRAIR INTERNATIONAL LIMITED
Registration no: 01769361 **VAT No.:** 584 6652 01 **Date established:** 1983
Turnover: £5m - £10m **No.of Employees:** 1 - 10 **Product Groups:** 75, 76

Date of Accounts	Jan 08	Jan 07
Working Capital	141	173
Fixed Assets	47	69
Current Assets	2009	2084
Current Liabilities	1868	1911
Total Share Capital	40	40

Silicair Dryvent Ltd
Challenge Road, Ashford, TW15 1BF
Tel: 01784-424920 **Fax:** 01784-229676
E-mail: martin.wright@silicair.co.uk
Website: http://www.silicair.co.uk
Directors: M. Wright (Sales)
Immediate Holding Company: SILICAIR DRYVENT LIMITED
Registration no: 04563199 **VAT No.:** GB 222 9215 86
Date established: 2002 **Turnover:** £1m - £2m **No.of Employees:** 1 - 10
Product Groups: 31, 32, 37, 38, 39, 40, 42

Date of Accounts	Apr 11	Apr 10	Apr 09
Working Capital	-594	-594	-594
Fixed Assets	639	639	639

Uniglobe Gemini Travel Ltd
10 Woodthorpe Road, Ashford, TW15 2RY
Tel: 01784-254850 **Fax:** 01784-259640
E-mail: travel@uniglobegemini.co.uk
Website: http://www.uniglobegemini.co.uk
Directors: M. Hewett (MD)
Turnover: £500,000 - £1m **No.of Employees:** 11 - 20 **Product Groups:** 69

Brentford

Agfa Gevaert
Eleventh Floor Vantage West Great West Road, Brentford, TW8 9AX
Tel: 020-8231 4983 **Fax:** 020-8231 4951
E-mail: laurence.roberts@agfa.com
Website: http://www.agfa.com
Directors: J. Johnston (Co Sec), L. Roberts (Dir)
Ultimate Holding Company: AGFA GEVAERT NV (BELGIUM)
Immediate Holding Company: AGFA-GEVAERT LIMITED
Registration no: 00103198 **Date established:** 2009
Turnover: £10m - £20m **No.of Employees:** 101 - 250
Product Groups: 27, 28, 32, 38, 44

Date of Accounts	Dec 11	Dec 10	Dec 09
Sales Turnover	17m	18m	22m
Pre Tax Profit/Loss	-17m	-348	43
Working Capital	-8m	5m	5m
Fixed Assets	2m	2m	3m
Current Assets	7m	7m	7m
Current Liabilities	1m	2m	2m

Amcor Ltd
9 Ryan Drive, Brentford, TW8 9ER
Tel: 020-8560 4141 **Fax:** 020-8232 8814
E-mail: amcor@compuserve.com
Website: http://www.amcorgroup.com
Directors: Y. Poleg (MD), G. Macfadyen (Co Sec)
Managers: R. Adams (Sales Prom Mgr)
Ultimate Holding Company: Amcor Ltd (Israel)
Immediate Holding Company: Amcor Israel Ltd (Israel)
Registration no: 04595242 **Date established:** 1977 **Turnover:** £5m - £10m
No.of Employees: 11 - 20 **Product Groups:** 66

Date of Accounts	Dec 07	Dec 06	Dec 05
Sales Turnover	4614	3856	5191
Pre Tax Profit/Loss	-27	42	327
Working Capital	2472	2392	2263
Fixed Assets	2269	2412	2564
Current Assets	4109	3128	2647
Current Liabilities	1636	736	384
Total Share Capital	4521	4521	4521
ROCE% (Return on Capital Employed)	-0.6	0.9	6.8
ROT% (Return on Turnover)	-0.6	1.1	6.3

B S S Brentford

Transport Avenue, Brentford, TW8 9HF
Tel: 020-8232 2700 **Fax:** 020-8232 2730
E-mail: barry.hardy@bssgroup.com
Website: http://www.bssgroup.com
Bank(s): HSBC Bank plc
Managers: B. Hardy (District Mgr)
Immediate Holding Company: WEST SERVICES LIMITED
Registration no: 03106393 **Date established:** 1984 **Turnover:** £5m - £10m
No.of Employees: 21 - 50 **Product Groups:** 30, 36, 38, 39, 40, 42

Date of Accounts	Dec 10	Dec 09	Dec 08
Sales Turnover	N/A	N/A	138
Pre Tax Profit/Loss	N/A	N/A	-56
Working Capital	N/A	N/A	-96
Fixed Assets	44	44	46
Current Assets	N/A	N/A	124
Current Liabilities	N/A	N/A	12

Deckard Ltd

6 Brentford Business Centre Commerce Road, Brentford, TW8 8LG
Tel: 020-8995 5000 **Fax:** 020-8747 0190
E-mail: kim@deckard.co.uk
Website: http://www.deckard.co.uk
Directors: M. Redshaw (Dir)
Immediate Holding Company: DECKARD LTD
Registration no: 03209973 **Date established:** 1996
Turnover: £500,000 - £1m **No.of Employees:** 1 - 10 **Product Groups:** 35, 49, 64

Date of Accounts	Mar 11	Mar 10	Mar 09
Sales Turnover	888	N/A	N/A
Pre Tax Profit/Loss	62	N/A	N/A
Working Capital	137	179	149
Fixed Assets	2	3	4
Current Assets	263	391	398
Current Liabilities	87	N/A	N/A

Emcor UK plc

1 Thameside Centre Kew Bridge Road, Brentford, TW8 0HF
Tel: 020-8380 6700 **Fax:** 020-8380 6701
E-mail: ukinfo@emcoruk.com
Website: http://www.emcoruk.com
Bank(s): The Royal Bank of Scotland
Directors: G. Ingleton (Pers), M. Walker (Co Sec), S. Chatterton (Tech Serv)
Managers: K. Chanter, J. Hack (Mktg Serv Mgr)
Ultimate Holding Company: EMCOR GROUP INC (USA)
Immediate Holding Company: EMCOR (UK) LIMITED
Registration no: 02353544 **Date established:** 1989
Turnover: £250m - £500m **No.of Employees:** 21 - 50 **Product Groups:** 80

Date of Accounts	Dec 11	Dec 10	Dec 09
Sales Turnover	330m	298m	321m
Pre Tax Profit/Loss	7m	16m	11m
Working Capital	27m	22m	32m
Fixed Assets	6m	3m	2m
Current Assets	136m	116m	120m
Current Liabilities	56m	56m	59m

General Healthcare Group

4 Thameside Centre Kew Bridge Road, Brentford, TW8 0HF
Tel: 020-8232 5100 **Fax:** 020-8232 5101
E-mail: adrian.fawcett@generaldynamics.uk.com
Website: http://www.ghg.co.uk
Directors: E. Hayes (Fin), A. Fawcett (Grp Chief Exec)
Ultimate Holding Company: NETWORK HEALTHCARE HOLDINGS LIMITED (SOUTH AFRICA)
Immediate Holding Company: GENERAL HEALTHCARE MIXER PARTNERSHIP LLP
Registration no: OC319550 **Date established:** 2006
Turnover: £500m - £1,000m **No.of Employees:** 101 - 250
Product Groups: 88

Glaxosmithkline

G S K House 980 Great West Road, Brentford, TW8 9GS
Tel: 020-8047 5000 **Fax:** 020-8047 0525
Website: http://www.gsk.com
Directors: P. Blackburn (Dir)
Ultimate Holding Company: GLAXOSMITHKLINE PLC
Immediate Holding Company: SMITHKLINE BEECHAM (INVESTMENTS) LIMITED
Registration no: 00302065 **Date established:** 1935
Turnover: £20m - £50m **No.of Employees:** 1501 & over
Product Groups: 31

Date of Accounts	Dec 11	Dec 10	Dec 09
Sales Turnover	1529m	1946m	2035m
Pre Tax Profit/Loss	77m	98m	101m
Working Capital	374m	306m	244m
Fixed Assets	49m	57m	54m
Current Assets	865m	664m	800m
Current Liabilities	133m	148m	147m

Heidelberg Graphic Equipment Ltd

69-76 High Street, Brentford, TW8 0AA
Tel: 020-8490 3500 **Fax:** 020-8490 3589
E-mail: info@heidelberg.com
Website: http://www.heidelberg.com
Bank(s): Lloyds TSB Bank plc
Directors: R. Kirschenlohr (Fin), G. Heanue (MD)
Managers: V. Geeling, D. Davies (Personnel), M. Herbig (Tech Serv Mgr)
Ultimate Holding Company: HEIDELBERGER DRUCKMASCHINEN AG (GERMANY)
Immediate Holding Company: HEIDELBERG GRAPHIC EQUIPMENT LIMITED
Registration no: 01177224 **VAT No.:** GB 228 0793 55
Date established: 1974 **Turnover:** £75m - £125m
No.of Employees: 251 - 500 **Product Groups:** 44, 64

Date of Accounts	Mar 12	Mar 11	Mar 10
Sales Turnover	90m	117m	107m
Pre Tax Profit/Loss	651	-1m	-6m
Working Capital	7m	11m	8m
Fixed Assets	11m	9m	14m
Current Assets	36m	44m	44m
Current Liabilities	13m	16m	14m

Luvata Sales Oy (UK)

P.O. Box 640, Brentford, TW8 0AB
Tel: 01689-825677 **Fax:** 01926-459149
E-mail: enquiries@outokumpu.com
Website: http://www.luvata.com
Bank(s): HSBC Bank plc
Directors: P. Olin (MD)
Ultimate Holding Company: Outokumpu Copper Oyj (Finland)
Immediate Holding Company: Outokumpu Sales OY
Registration no: FC023261 **VAT No.:** GB 775 8185 78
Turnover: £2m - £5m **No.of Employees:** 11 - 20 **Product Groups:** 34, 35, 36

Mayer Enviromental Ltd

Transport Avenue, Brentford, TW8 9HA
Tel: 020-8847 3637 **Fax:** 020-8847 3638
E-mail: info@mayer-enviro.com
Website: http://www.mayer-enviro.com
Directors: N. Stinson (Co Sec), P. Davidson (Dir)
Ultimate Holding Company: EUROPEAN METAL RECYCLING LIMITED
Immediate Holding Company: MAYER ENVIRONMENTAL LTD.
Registration no: 03398932 **Date established:** 1997
Turnover: £500,000 - £1m **No.of Employees:** 1 - 10 **Product Groups:** 54

Date of Accounts	Dec 11	Dec 10	Dec 09
Sales Turnover	657	517	340
Pre Tax Profit/Loss	81	80	64
Working Capital	2m	2m	2m
Fixed Assets	10	2	N/A
Current Assets	5m	4m	4m
Current Liabilities	3m	907	898

N & J Tools Ltd

11 Shield Drive, Brentford, TW8 9EX
Tel: 020-8560 0885 **Fax:** 020-8390 4848
E-mail: nigel.stevens@njtools.co.uk
Website: http://www.njtools.co.uk
Directors: L. Fisher (Fin), N. Stevens (Dir)
Immediate Holding Company: N & J TOOLS LIMITED
Registration no: 04384643 **Date established:** 2002
Turnover: £500,000 - £1m **No.of Employees:** 1 - 10 **Product Groups:** 37

Date of Accounts	Mar 11	Mar 10	Mar 09
Working Capital	-165	-92	-34
Fixed Assets	1	1	1
Current Assets	172	160	203

New Box

29 New Road, Brentford, TW8 0NX
Tel: 020-8560 2442
E-mail: info@newbox.co.uk
Website: http://www.newbox.co.uk
Directors: T. Scott (Prop)
No.of Employees: 1 - 10 **Product Groups:** 37, 84

Penborn Technical Services

Garrett House 24 Windmill Road, Brentford, TW8 0QA
Tel: 020-8569 7979 **Fax:** 020-8568 1621
E-mail: enquiries@penborn.co.uk
Website: http://www.penborn.co.uk
Bank(s): National Westminster Bank Plc
Directors: A. Jameson (MD), A. Jamieson (MD), B. Britton (Dir), B. Burke (Dir)
Managers: H. Lee (Accounts)
Immediate Holding Company: Alectia Ltd
Registration no: 06363833 **VAT No.:** GB 228 3341 75
Date established: 2007 **Turnover:** £5m - £10m **No.of Employees:** 21 - 50
Product Groups: 20, 38, 41, 42, 48, 80, 84

Safety Kleen UK Ltd

Profile West 950 Great West Road, Brentford, TW8 9ES
Tel: 020-8490 9084 **Fax:** 020-8490 3859
E-mail: sbrain@sk-europe.com
Website: http://www.SK-europe.com
Directors: J. Ferguson (I.T. Dir)
Managers: S. Brain
Ultimate Holding Company: WP SAFETY-KLEEN (CAYMAN) LTD (CAYMAN ISLANDS)
Immediate Holding Company: SAFETY-KLEEN U.K. LIMITED
Registration no: 01190039 **Date established:** 1974
Turnover: £50m - £75m **No.of Employees:** 251 - 500
Product Groups: 32, 39, 41, 46, 48, 54

Date of Accounts	Dec 11	Dec 08	Jan 10
Sales Turnover	58m	59m	56m
Pre Tax Profit/Loss	13m	17m	14m
Working Capital	69m	36m	45m
Fixed Assets	15m	14m	14m
Current Assets	78m	51m	58m
Current Liabilities	7m	7m	6m

Samsung C & T UK Ltd

Samsung House 3 Riverbank Way, Brentford, TW8 9RE
Tel: 020-8232 3200 **Fax:** 020-8569 7165
Website: http://www.samsunguk.com
Directors: S. Kang (Fin), S. Lee (Co Sec)
Managers: A. Yoon, J. Lloyd (Personnel)
Ultimate Holding Company: SAMSUNG C & T CORPORATION
Immediate Holding Company: SAMSUNG C&T UK. LIMITED
Registration no: 01217165 **Date established:** 1975
Turnover: £10m - £20m **No.of Employees:** 21 - 50 **Product Groups:** 61

Date of Accounts	Dec 11	Dec 10	Dec 09
Sales Turnover	20m	29m	29m
Pre Tax Profit/Loss	-2m	-2m	-3m
Working Capital	18m	20m	22m
Fixed Assets	2m	489	476
Current Assets	20m	34m	28m
Current Liabilities	895	6m	830

Sega Europe Ltd

27 Great West Road, Brentford, TW8 9BW
Tel: 020-8995 3399 **Fax:** 020-8996 4499
E-mail: info@soe.sega.co.uk
Website: http://www.sega.com
Directors: M. Hayes (MD), N. Boxall (Co Sec)
Ultimate Holding Company: SEGA SAMMY HOLDINGS INC (JAPAN)
Immediate Holding Company: SEGA EUROPE LIMITED
Registration no: 01669057 **Date established:** 1982
Turnover: £75m - £125m **No.of Employees:** 101 - 250
Product Groups: 49

Date of Accounts	Mar 11	Mar 10	Mar 09
Sales Turnover	98m	193m	161m
Pre Tax Profit/Loss	2m	3m	10m
Working Capital	54m	52m	49m
Fixed Assets	3m	4m	4m
Current Assets	93m	118m	108m
Current Liabilities	5m	11m	13m

Teapigs

Unit 1 The Old Pumping Station Pump Alley, Brentford, TW8 0AP
Tel: 020-8568 1313
E-mail: help@teapigs.co.uk
Website: http://www.teapigs.co.uk
Ultimate Holding Company: TATA TEA LTD (INDIA)
Immediate Holding Company: TEAPIGS LIMITED
Registration no: 05426310 **Date established:** 2005 **Turnover:** £2m - £5m
No.of Employees: 1 - 10 **Product Groups:** 20, 62

Date of Accounts	Mar 11	Mar 10	Mar 09
Sales Turnover	3m	2m	822
Pre Tax Profit/Loss	163	132	-210
Working Capital	567	472	377
Fixed Assets	24	2	2
Current Assets	1m	909	533
Current Liabilities	179	64	37

Thames Valley Pressings Ltd (Transteel)

Unit 2-3 Leyton Road, Brentford, TW8 0QJ
Tel: 020-8847 3636 **Fax:** 020-8758 1236
E-mail: enquiries@tvpressings.co.uk
Directors: N. Ohayon (MD), M. Foreman (Fin)
Immediate Holding Company: THAMES VALLEY PRESSINGS LIMITED
Registration no: 02658815 **Date established:** 1991 **Turnover:** £1m - £2m
No.of Employees: 11 - 20 **Product Groups:** 37, 67

Date of Accounts	Dec 11	Dec 10	Dec 09
Working Capital	116	80	66
Fixed Assets	489	510	527
Current Assets	289	254	245
Current Liabilities	3	N/A	N/A

Thames Valley Supplies Ltd

Unit 7 Churchill House 114 Windmill Road, Brentford, TW8 9NA
Tel: 020-8560 3385 **Fax:** 020-8560 8553
E-mail: sales@tvsl.co.uk
Website: http://www.thamesvalleysupplies.co.uk
Directors: R. Haslett (MD)
Immediate Holding Company: THAMES VALLEY SUPPLIES LIMITED
Registration no: 02151101 **Date established:** 1987
Turnover: £500,000 - £1m **No.of Employees:** 1 - 10 **Product Groups:** 24, 29

Date of Accounts	Sep 11	Sep 10	Sep 09
Sales Turnover	565	637	557
Pre Tax Profit/Loss	-18	-10	-37
Working Capital	15	29	36
Fixed Assets	20	24	22
Current Assets	142	181	161
Current Liabilities	18	33	20

Tie Rack Ltd

Capital Interchange Way, Brentford, TW8 0EX
Tel: 020-8230 2300 **Fax:** 01208-230 2301
E-mail: reception@tie-rack.co.uk
Website: http://www.tie-rack.co.uk
Directors: J. Hunt (Fin), M. Marcheetta (Fin)
Managers: G. Pavanati, R. Caroli, M. Gujral (Personnel)
Ultimate Holding Company: TIE RACK RETAIL GROUP LIMITED
Immediate Holding Company: TIE RACK LIMITED
Registration no: 01524977 **VAT No.:** GB 443 9421 47
Date established: 1980 **Turnover:** £1m - £2m **No.of Employees:** 51 - 100
Product Groups: 24

Date of Accounts	Jan 12	Jan 11	Jan 10
Sales Turnover	1m	944	1m
Pre Tax Profit/Loss	787	-84	-1m
Working Capital	10m	8m	8m
Fixed Assets	8m	8m	8m
Current Assets	22m	22m	22m
Current Liabilities	215	493	669

UK Time Ltd

1000 Great West Road, Brentford, TW8 9DW
Tel: 020-8326 6900 **Fax:** 020-8326 6999
E-mail: sales@timex.com
Website: http://www.timex.com
Bank(s): National Westminster Bank Plc
Directors: K. Agnew (MD), M. Plancon (Dir), G. Crilly-Mckean (MD), F. Sherer (Co Sec)
Managers: B. Roberts (I.T. Exec), L. Dean, B. Roberts (Tech Serv Mgr)
Ultimate Holding Company: SWORD GROUP SA (FRANCE)
Immediate Holding Company: SWORD ACHIEVER LIMITED
Registration no: 02879513 **Date established:** 2012
Turnover: £500,000 - £1m **No.of Employees:** 21 - 50 **Product Groups:** 49

Date of Accounts	Dec 08	Dec 07	Dec 06
Sales Turnover	16473	14436	9380
Pre Tax Profit/Loss	-871	1058	476
Working Capital	3297	4689	3834
Fixed Assets	775	448	222
Current Assets	10336	8675	6004
Current Liabilities	7039	3986	2170
Total Share Capital	500	500	500
ROCE% (Return on Capital Employed)	-21.4	20.6	11.7
ROT% (Return on Turnover)	-5.3	7.3	5.1

W B S

5 Churchill House 114 Windmill Road, Brentford, TW8 9NB
Tel: 020-8847 2444 **Fax:** 020-8847 1444
E-mail: info@wbs-medical.co.uk
Website: http://www.wbs-medical.co.uk
Directors: B. Cunliffe (Prop)
Registration no: 05805012 **Date established:** 2006
No.of Employees: 1 - 10 **Product Groups:** 30, 35

Waterstone's Booksellers

Capital Court Capital Interchange Way, Brentford, TW8 0EX
Tel: 020-8742 3800 **Fax:** 020-8742 0215
E-mail: mike.giffin@waterstones.com
Website: http://www.waterstones.co.uk
Directors: M. Miles (Fin), M. Giffin (Dir), E. Marriner (Co Sec)
Managers: R. Hines (Mktg Serv Mgr), S. Monaghan (Tech Serv Mgr)
Ultimate Holding Company: HMV GROUP PLC
Immediate Holding Company: WATERSTONES BOOKSELLERS LIMITED
Registration no: 00610095 **Date established:** 1958
Turnover: £250m - £500m **No.of Employees:** 1501 & over
Product Groups: 64

Date of Accounts	Apr 11	Apr 08	Apr 09
Sales Turnover	477m	273m	521m
Pre Tax Profit/Loss	-21m	2m	4m
Working Capital	-39m	-157m	-92m
Fixed Assets	95m	231m	174m
Current Assets	138m	145m	129m
Current Liabilities	64m	65m	75m

Worley Parsond Ltd

Parkview Great West Road, Brentford, TW8 9AZ
Tel: 020-8326 5000 **Fax:** 020-8710 0220
Website: http://www.worleyparsond.com
Bank(s): Bank of America
Directors: M. Daly (Fin), P. Stoner (Pers), J. Thomson (Tech Serv), S. Brady (MD)
Immediate Holding Company: WORLEYPARSONS UK LIMITED
Registration no: 07441549 **Date established:** 2010
Turnover: £125m - £250m **No.of Employees:** 1501 & over
Product Groups: 85

Edgware

A B C Catering Equipment

196 Edgwarebury Lane, Edgware, HA8 8QW
Tel: 020-8958 1958 **Fax:** 020-8958 1958
E-mail: sales@abccatering.co.uk
Website: http://www.abccatering.co.uk
Directors: A. David (Prop)
Immediate Holding Company: ALLIED BUSINESS CONTRACTS LIMITED
Registration no: 03409426 **Date established:** 1997
Turnover: Up to £250,000 **No.of Employees:** 1 - 10 **Product Groups:** 24, 33, 36, 40, 41, 67, 83

Date of Accounts	Dec 11	Dec 10	Dec 09
Sales Turnover	62	66	43
Pre Tax Profit/Loss	-1	-3	5
Working Capital	10	10	14
Fixed Assets	2	2	1
Current Assets	24	32	25
Current Liabilities	N/A	N/A	6

Amber Safetywear Ltd

18 Howberry Close, Edgware, HA8 6TA
Tel: 020-8951 5868
E-mail: amber@btconnect.com
Website: http://www.ambersafetywear.co.uk
Managers: S. Lee (Comm)
Immediate Holding Company: AMBER SAFETYWEAR LTD
Registration no: 07335560 **Date established:** 2010 **Turnover:** £1m - £2m
No.of Employees: 1 - 10 **Product Groups:** 22

Crest Construction & Interiors Ltd

49 Highview Gardens, Edgware, HA8 9UD
Tel: 020-8958 4411
E-mail: info@crest-construction.co.uk
Website: http://www.crest-construction.co.uk
Directors: A. Payravi (Dir), J. Payravi (Fin)
Immediate Holding Company: CREST CONSTRUCTION & INTERIORS LIMITED
Registration no: 05995763 **Date established:** 2006
No.of Employees: 1 - 10 **Product Groups:** 25, 35, 52, 80

Date of Accounts	Mar 11	Mar 09	Mar 08
Working Capital	37	26	17
Fixed Assets	2	2	3
Current Assets	62	84	104

G K N Freight Services Ltd

Equity House 128-136 High Street, Edgware, HA8 7EL
Tel: 020-8905 6668 **Fax:** 020-8905 6951
E-mail: john.gillam@gknfreightservices.com
Website: http://www.gknauto.com
Directors: J. Gillam (MD)
Ultimate Holding Company: GKN PLC
Immediate Holding Company: GKN FREIGHT SERVICES LIMITED
Registration no: 00056211 **Date established:** 1998
Turnover: £20m - £50m **No.of Employees:** 21 - 50 **Product Groups:** 76

Date of Accounts	Dec 11	Dec 10	Dec 09
Sales Turnover	40m	36m	22m
Pre Tax Profit/Loss	2m	728	546
Working Capital	7m	5m	5m
Fixed Assets	402	594	751
Current Assets	15m	14m	11m
Current Liabilities	931	994	558

Head Promotions Ltd

16 Orchard Crescent, Edgware, HA8 9PW
Tel: 020-8959 7345
E-mail: headprom@aol.com
Website: http://www.headpromotions.com
Directors: S. Cooper (MD)
Immediate Holding Company: HEAD PROMOTIONS LIMITED
Registration no: 05065782 **Date established:** 2004
No.of Employees: 1 - 10 **Product Groups:** 32, 63

Date of Accounts	Mar 11	Mar 10	Mar 09
Working Capital	-0	1	1
Current Assets	8	7	6

Kimberley Trading Co Ltd

31 Burnt Oak Broadway, Edgware, HA8 5LD
Tel: 020-8200 1232 **Fax:** 020-8200 6101
E-mail: kimtrad@kimberleyhouse.co.uk
Website: http://www.kimberleyhouse.co.uk
Directors: C. Holding (Dir), K. Chandaria (Dir), B. Holding (MD)
Immediate Holding Company: Kimberley Trading Co. Limited(The)
Registration no: 01143984 **VAT No.:** GB 221 5780 81
Date established: 1973 **Turnover:** £1m - £2m **No.of Employees:** 1 - 10
Product Groups: 61

Date of Accounts	Jan 08	Jan 07	Jan 06
Working Capital	252	121	118
Fixed Assets	6	8	9
Current Assets	329	312	437
Current Liabilities	77	191	318
Total Share Capital	5	5	5

Madhouse

369-391 Burnt Oak Broadway, Edgware, HA8 5AW
Tel: 020-8905 7664 **Fax:** 020-8905 7654
Website: http://www.madhouse.co.uk
Directors: P. Samber (Prop)
Immediate Holding Company: ROY HOLT CONSTRUCTION DESIGN LIMITED
Registration no: 05234237 **VAT No.:** GB 226 8151 67
Date established: 2011 **No.of Employees:** 11 - 20 **Product Groups:** 61

Date of Accounts	Feb 11
Working Capital	-40
Fixed Assets	325
Current Assets	15

Pollard Weighing & Food Machinery

118a High Street, Edgware, HA8 7EL
Tel: 020-8952 0087 **Fax:** 020-8952 0087
Directors: C. Pollard (Prop)
Date established: 1994 **No.of Employees:** 1 - 10 **Product Groups:** 38, 42

Sagewood Ltd

48 Methuen Road, Edgware, HA8 6EX
Tel: 020-8951 0165 **Fax:** 020-8952 8466
E-mail: info@sagewood.com
Website: http://www.sagewood.com
Directors: M. Parekh (MD), N. Parekh (Fin)
Managers: N. Shah (Export Sales Mg)
Registration no: 02118488 **VAT No.:** GB 581 5512 40
Date established: 1987 **Turnover:** £500,000 - £1m
No.of Employees: 1 - 10 **Product Groups:** 41

Date of Accounts	Mar 08	Mar 07	Mar 06
Working Capital	233	167	160
Fixed Assets	16	16	17
Current Assets	716	294	398
Current Liabilities	482	128	238
Total Share Capital	11	11	2

Spectra International plc

Spectra House Spring Villa Road, Edgware, HA8 7EB
Tel: 020-8951 4323 **Fax:** 020-8951 4174
E-mail: neil@akura.com
Website: http://www.akura.com
Directors: N. Osgood (Fin)
Ultimate Holding Company: SAGEMOSS HOLDINGS LIMITED (JERSEY)
Immediate Holding Company: SPECTRA INTERNATIONAL LIMITED
Registration no: 01810853 **Date established:** 1984
Turnover: Up to £250,000 **No.of Employees:** 1 - 10 **Product Groups:** 49, 61

Date of Accounts	May 11	May 10	May 09
Sales Turnover	N/A	13	13
Pre Tax Profit/Loss	N/A	24	4
Working Capital	762	939	1m
Fixed Assets	666	460	460
Current Assets	774	1m	1m
Current Liabilities	N/A	7	10

Stage Control Ltd

20 Station Parade Whitchurch Lane, Edgware, HA8 6RW
Tel: 020-8952 8982 **Fax:** 020-8951 4178
E-mail: info@stagecontrol.com
Website: http://www.stagecontrol.com
Directors: D. Jenkins (Sales), I. New (Tech Serv)
Immediate Holding Company: STAGE CONTROL LIMITED
Registration no: 00896179 **VAT No.:** GB 229 4122 76
Date established: 1967 **Turnover:** £2m - £5m **No.of Employees:** 1 - 10
Product Groups: 37, 67

Date of Accounts	Jun 11	Jun 10	Jun 09
Working Capital	-76	-66	-63
Fixed Assets	50	52	54
Current Assets	25	29	51

Thurston

110 High Street, Edgware, HA8 7HF
Tel: 020-8952 2002 **Fax:** 020-8952 0222
E-mail: thurston@eaclare.co.uk
Website: http://www.thurstongames.co.uk
Directors: C. Felton (I.T. Dir), P. Clare (MD), P. Eggington (Fin), P. Crail (Dir)
Managers: A. Hillier (Mgr), A. Hillyer (Mgr), P. Crail (Mktg Serv Mgr)
Ultimate Holding Company: E.A. Clare & Son Group Ltd
Registration no: 06976220 **VAT No.:** GB 166 0283 70
Date established: 2009 **Turnover:** £2m - £5m **No.of Employees:** 1 - 10
Product Groups: 49

Enfield

AEG Power Solutions Ltd

Vision 25 Innova Park, Enfield, EN3 7XY
Tel: 01992-719 200 **Fax:** 01992-702 151
E-mail: uk.sales@aegps.com
Website: http://www.aegps.com
Directors: G. Marshall (Sales & Mktg), M. McLeavy (MD), M. Michaelides (Fin)
Ultimate Holding Company: ALCATEL-LUCENT SA (FRANCE)
Immediate Holding Company: AEG POWER SOLUTIONS LTD.
Registration no: 00407689 **Date established:** 1957
Turnover: £500m - £1,000m **No.of Employees:** 21 - 50
Product Groups: 37

Date of Accounts	Dec 07
Sales Turnover	8900
Pre Tax Profit/Loss	420
Working Capital	2400
Fixed Assets	70
Current Assets	6830
Current Liabilities	4430
Total Share Capital	30040
ROCE% (Return on Capital Employed)	17.0

Aimer Products Ltd

Unit 6 Plaza Business Centre, Enfield, EN3 7PH
Tel: 020-8804 8282 **Fax:** 020-8804 8821
E-mail: sales@aimer.co.uk
Website: http://www.aimer.co.uk
Directors: J. Leveridge (MD)
Immediate Holding Company: AIMER PRODUCTS LIMITED
Registration no: 00421867 **VAT No.:** GB 232 1756 85
Date established: 1946 **Turnover:** £250,000 - £500,000
No.of Employees: 11 - 20 **Product Groups:** 33, 63

Date of Accounts	Sep 11	Sep 10	Sep 09
Working Capital	-86	-95	-117
Fixed Assets	92	110	129
Current Assets	112	93	84

Ashby Plating Works

26 Alexandra Road, Enfield, EN3 7EH
Tel: 020-8804 1025 **Fax:** 020-8804 1025
Directors: D. Shipman (Prop)
Immediate Holding Company: BEST TREAT LTD
Registration no: 04650578 **Date established:** 2012
Turnover: Up to £250,000 **No.of Employees:** 1 - 10 **Product Groups:** 48

Date of Accounts	Jan 11	Jan 10	Jan 09
Sales Turnover	N/A	N/A	143
Pre Tax Profit/Loss	N/A	N/A	-1
Working Capital	24	20	25
Fixed Assets	1	1	1
Current Assets	33	31	32
Current Liabilities	7	8	3

Broadfell Ltd

Bullsmoor Lane, Enfield, EN1 4SF
Tel: 01992-762359 **Fax:** 01992-652992
E-mail: broadfell@btinternet.com
Directors: L. Josephs (MD)
Immediate Holding Company: BROADFELL LIMITED
Registration no: 01124668 **VAT No.:** GB 220 4606 11
Date established: 1973 **Turnover:** Up to £250,000
No.of Employees: 1 - 10 **Product Groups:** 30

Date of Accounts	Jul 11	Jul 10	Jul 07
Working Capital	6	4	-11
Fixed Assets	1	1	2
Current Assets	20	17	22

Business Link London Ltd

Link House 292-308 Southbury Road, Enfield, EN1 1TS
Tel: 08456-000787 **Fax:** 020-7215 5001
E-mail: irene.chung@bllondon.co.uk
Website: http://www.businesslink.gov.uk/london
Bank(s): National Westminster Bank Plc
Directors: I. Chung (Fin)
Managers: G. Clark (Mktg Serv Mgr), O. Burnett (Personnel)
Registration no: 03591108 **No.of Employees:** 101 - 250
Product Groups: 54, 65, 80, 81, 82, 84, 86, 87, 89

Charles Pugh Glass Ltd

Unit 1 69 Millmarsh Lane, Enfield, EN3 7QJ
Tel: 020-8805 5222 **Fax:** 020-8805 2251
E-mail: chalkd@pughs.co.uk
Website: http://www.pughs.co.uk
Bank(s): HSBC Bank plc
Managers: D. Chalk (District Mgr)
Ultimate Holding Company: CHARLES PUGH (HOLDINGS) LIMITED
Immediate Holding Company: CHARLES PUGH (GLASS) LIMITED
Registration no: 00301247 **VAT No.:** GB 580 9001 51
Date established: 1935 **Turnover:** £10m - £20m
No.of Employees: 11 - 20 **Product Groups:** 39

Date of Accounts	Jul 11	Aug 08	Aug 09
Sales Turnover	13m	13m	11m
Pre Tax Profit/Loss	821	-389	-309
Working Capital	5m	4m	4m
Fixed Assets	3m	3m	3m
Current Assets	7m	7m	6m
Current Liabilities	1m	419	337

Chela Ltd

68 Bilton Way, Enfield, EN3 7NH
Tel: 020-8805 2150 **Fax:** 020-8443 1868
E-mail: mail@chela.co.uk
Website: http://www.chela.co.uk
Directors: I. Fisher (MD), V. Darville (Co Sec)
Managers: R. Rushby (Sales Prom Mgr)
Ultimate Holding Company: FISHER DARVILLE HOLDINGS LIMITED
Immediate Holding Company: CHELA LTD
Registration no: 02768529 **Date established:** 1992
No.of Employees: 11 - 20 **Product Groups:** 31, 32, 39

Date of Accounts	Aug 11	Aug 10	Aug 09
Working Capital	162	162	158
Fixed Assets	24	35	38
Current Assets	242	288	268

Classic Signs Of London

11 Redburn Industrial Estate Woodall Road, Enfield, EN3 4LQ
Tel: 020-8805 4649 **Fax:** 020-8805 1847
E-mail: classicsigns@btconnect.com
Website: http://www.signsoflondon.co.uk
Directors: P. Hopkins (Prop)
Date established: 1993 **No.of Employees:** 1 - 10 **Product Groups:** 30, 39, 40

Comet Catering Equipment Co. Ltd

Comet Works Brimsdown Industrial Estate Lockfield Avenue, Brimsdown, Enfield, EN3 7XZ
Tel: 020-8804 4779 **Fax:** 020-8804 9470
E-mail: michael@cometcatering.com
Website: http://www.cometcatering.com
Directors: J. Webb (Fin), M. Webb (MD)
Ultimate Holding Company: CLEE & WEBB LIMITED
Immediate Holding Company: COMET CATERING EQUIPMENT CO. LIMITED
Registration no: 01415138 **VAT No.:** GB 330 6203 08
Date established: 1979 **Turnover:** Up to £250,000
No.of Employees: 1 - 10 **Product Groups:** 26, 67

Date of Accounts	Mar 11	Mar 10	Mar 09
Working Capital	366	211	270
Fixed Assets	353	379	420
Current Assets	731	484	530

D P S Software
Herewood House 288 Southbury Road, Enfield, EN1 1TR
Tel: 020-8804 1022 **Fax:** 020-8804 2875
E-mail: info@dpssoftware.co.uk
Website: http://www.dpssoftware.co.uk
Directors: O. Ismail (MD), S. Ridley (Tech Serv)
Managers: J. Voskou, F. Bongiorno (Sales Admin)
Ultimate Holding Company: PAGESTYLE LIMITED
Immediate Holding Company: D.P.S. SOFTWARE PLC
Registration no: 03755111 **Date established:** 1999 **Turnover:** £1m - £2m
No.of Employees: 21 - 50 **Product Groups:** 44

Date of Accounts	Mar 11	Mar 10	Mar 09
Working Capital	727	662	306
Fixed Assets	99	128	184
Current Assets	2m	2m	2m

Datasights Ltd
228-234 Alma Road, Enfield, EN3 7BB
Tel: 020-8805 4151 **Fax:** 020-8805 8084
E-mail: sales@datasights.com
Website: http://www.datasights.com
Directors: F. Sharpe (Dir)
Ultimate Holding Company: INSTRUMENT GLASSES,LIMITED
Immediate Holding Company: SDATASIGHTS LIMITED
Registration no: 01286165 **VAT No.:** GB 292 1386 50
Date established: 1976 **Turnover:** £500,000 - £1m
No.of Employees: 1 - 10 **Product Groups:** 33, 38

Date of Accounts	Mar 11	Mar 10	Mar 09
Working Capital	-35	-25	-9
Fixed Assets	3	3	5
Current Assets	64	70	98

Deco Floors Ltd
Unit 4 Leaside Industrial Estate, Enfield, EN3 7PH
Tel: 08456-580104 **Fax:** 08456-580105
E-mail: sales@decofloors.co.uk
Website: http://www.decofloors.co.uk
Directors: B. Mouradian (Comm), B. Baka (MD)
Immediate Holding Company: DECO FLOORS LIMITED
Registration no: 05131124 **Date established:** 2004
Turnover: £500,000 - £1m **No.of Employees:** 1 - 10 **Product Groups:** 23, 25, 29, 30, 31, 32, 33, 35, 49, 52, 66

Fairview New Homes Ltd
50 Lancaster Road, Enfield, EN2 0BY
Tel: 020-8366 1271 **Fax:** 020-8366 0189
E-mail: sales@fairview.co.uk
Website: http://www.fairviewnewhomes.co.uk
Directors: G. Malton (MD)
Ultimate Holding Company: FAIRVIEW HOLDINGS LIMITED
Immediate Holding Company: FAIRVIEW NEW HOMES LIMITED
Registration no: 04081723 **VAT No.:** GB 589 6820 73
Date established: 2000 **Turnover:** £75m - £125m
No.of Employees: 251 - 500 **Product Groups:** 80

Date of Accounts	Dec 11	Dec 10	Dec 09
Sales Turnover	4m	8m	6m
Pre Tax Profit/Loss	1m	-625	2m
Working Capital	23	-18m	-28m
Fixed Assets	38m	35m	42m
Current Assets	130m	118m	119m
Current Liabilities	1m	2m	967

G Farley & Sons Ltd
Unit 6 Plaza Business Centre Stockingswater Lane, Enfield, EN3 7PH
Tel: 020-8804 1367 **Fax:** 020-8804 8821
E-mail: sales@g-farleyandsons.co.uk
Website: http://www.g-farleyandsons.co.uk
Directors: D. Leveridge (MD)
Immediate Holding Company: G FARLEY & SONS LIMITED
Registration no: 01061822 **Date established:** 1972
Turnover: £500,000 - £1m **No.of Employees:** 1 - 10 **Product Groups:** 33, 63

Date of Accounts	Dec 10	Dec 08	Dec 07
Working Capital	4	11	21
Fixed Assets	3	6	3
Current Assets	21	36	43

Fischbein-Saxon
274 Alma Road, Enfield, EN3 7RS
Tel: 020-8805 6111 **Fax:** 020-8344 6625
E-mail: sales@fischbein-saxon.co.uk
Website: http://www.fischbein-saxon.co.uk
Bank(s): National Westminster Bank Plc
Managers: A. Bowie (Ops Mgr), H. Kilborn
Immediate Holding Company: THAMES SACK & BAG CO. LTD
Registration no: 00646917 **Turnover:** £2m - £5m
No.of Employees: 11 - 20 **Product Groups:** 42, 45, 85

Fisher Research Ltd
68 Bilton Way, Enfield, EN3 6EJ
Tel: 020-8804 1891 **Fax:** 020-8443 1868
E-mail: sales@fisherresearch.com
Website: http://www.fisherresearch.com
Bank(s): HSCB
Directors: I. Fisher (MD)
Managers: M. Fisher (Sales Admin)
Ultimate Holding Company: FISHER DARVILLE HOLDINGS LIMITED
Immediate Holding Company: FISHER RESEARCH LTD
Registration no: 02218702 **VAT No.:** GB 504 6506 68
Date established: 1988 **Turnover:** £500,000 - £1m
No.of Employees: 21 - 50 **Product Groups:** 32

Date of Accounts	Aug 11	Aug 10	Aug 09
Working Capital	121	197	248
Fixed Assets	2m	2m	2m
Current Assets	643	680	709

Gabriel Contractors Ltd
15 Edison Road Brimsdown Industrial Estate, Enfield, EN3 7BY
Tel: 020-8344 4300 **Fax:** 020-8344 4343
E-mail: volkerhighwayscallcentre@volkerhighways.co.uk
Website: http://www.volkerhighways.co.uk/bin/ibp.jsp?ibpPage=S3_HomePage
Bank(s): National Westminster Bank Plc
Directors: D. Grier (MD), P. Wain (Co Sec), R. Carter (Dir), H. Smith (Dir), N. Wilson (Dir), A. De Jong (Dir)
Managers: D. Pearson (I.T. Exec), O. Hermie (Accounts), J. Hutchinson (Purch Mgr)
Ultimate Holding Company: ROYAL VOLKER WESSELS STEVIN NV (NETHERLANDS)
Immediate Holding Company: Volkerhighways Crowley Ltd
Registration no: 00638559 **VAT No.:** GB 220 4300 35
Date established: 1943 **Turnover:** £5m - £10m **No.of Employees:** 21 - 50
Product Groups: 51

Date of Accounts	Dec 07	Dec 06	Dec 05
Sales Turnover	9338	15482	15043
Pre Tax Profit/Loss	324	506	1131
Working Capital	2308	1501	1368
Fixed Assets	766	1041	1123
Current Assets	4278	5585	5007
Current Liabilities	1970	4084	3639
Total Share Capital	463	463	463
ROCE% (Return on Capital Employed)	10.5	19.9	45.4
ROT% (Return on Turnover)	3.5	3.3	7.5

Hoults Group
Heritage house 345 Southbury Road, Enfield, EN1 1UP
Tel: 0800-515675 **Fax:** 0191-491 6009
E-mail: houltsremovals@hoults.co.uk
Website: http://www.hoults.co.uk
Directors: C. Kirk (Co Sec), G. Whitaker (MD)
Managers: A. Hardy (Personnel), G. Davies (Mgr), K. Barnes, M. Gaye (Purch Mgr)
Ultimate Holding Company: N F C P.L.C.
Immediate Holding Company: N.A.V.L.
Registration no: 04439154 **Date established:** 1989
Turnover: £500,000 - £1m **No.of Employees:** 1 - 10 **Product Groups:** 72

Date of Accounts	Dec 07
Working Capital	9
Current Assets	9
Total Share Capital	1

Hunter Vehicles Ltd
Crown Works Southbury Road, Enfield, EN1 1UD
Tel: 020-8344 3900 **Fax:** 020-8805 7292
E-mail: info@huntervehicles.co.uk
Website: http://www.huntervehicles.co.uk
Bank(s): Barclays
Directors: K. Mowbray (Dir), K. Elsley (Co Sec), P. Blackman (Dir)
Immediate Holding Company: HUNTER VEHICLES LIMITED
Registration no: 06070791 **VAT No.:** Gb 220 4164 17
Date established: 2007 **Turnover:** £250,000 - £500,000
No.of Employees: 21 - 50 **Product Groups:** 39, 72, 84

Date of Accounts	Apr 11	Apr 10	Apr 09
Working Capital	-4	-52	-124
Fixed Assets	746	612	663
Current Assets	674	526	675

Kebrell Nuts & Bolts Ltd
Imperial Works 93 Lockfield Avenue, Enfield, EN3 7PY
Tel: 020-8805 8510 **Fax:** 020-8805 1553
E-mail: alanweedon@kebrell.co.uk
Website: http://www.kebrell.co.uk
Managers: A. Weedon (Sales Admin)
Immediate Holding Company: KEBRELL NUTS AND BOLTS LIMITED
Registration no: 01475515 **Date established:** 1980 **Turnover:** £5m - £10m
No.of Employees: 1 - 10 **Product Groups:** 35, 66

Date of Accounts	Feb 11	Feb 10	Feb 09
Sales Turnover	N/A	3m	N/A
Pre Tax Profit/Loss	N/A	-9	150
Working Capital	1m	1m	1m
Fixed Assets	3m	3m	3m
Current Assets	4m	3m	3m
Current Liabilities	N/A	474	556

Mac Sash Weight
166 Lincoln Road, Enfield, EN1 1LN
Tel: 020-8367 4999 **Fax:** 020-8881 4100
E-mail: info@macsashweights.co.uk
Website: http://www.macsashweights.co.uk
Directors: R. Arbuckle (Prop)
Date established: 2004 **No.of Employees:** 1 - 10 **Product Groups:** 38, 42

Macfarlane Packaging UK Ltd
5 Delta Park Industrial Estate Millmarsh Lane, Enfield, EN3 7QJ
Tel: 08447-701409 **Fax:** 08708-500117
E-mail: enfield@macfarlanepackaging.com
Website: http://www.macfarlanegroup.net
Directors: G. Jarvis Brown (Dir)
Immediate Holding Company: MACFARLANE GROUP PLC
Registration no: 01630389 **No.of Employees:** 21 - 50
Product Groups: 27, 30, 48

MECG Ltd
Unit 28 Woodridge Close, Enfield, EN2 8HJ
Tel: 0845-474 4561 **Fax:** 0871-528 8032
E-mail: info@mecg.co.uk
Website: http://www.mecg.co.uk
Directors: T. Slessor (Comm)
Registration no: 06561816 **Date established:** 2008
Turnover: £250,000 - £500,000 **No.of Employees:** 11 - 20
Product Groups: 12, 34

Mercury Bearings Ltd
4 Redburn Industrial Estate Woodall Road, Enfield, EN3 4LE
Tel: 020-8805 1919 **Fax:** 020-8805 9599
E-mail: enfield@mercuryltd.co.uk
Website: http://www.mercuryltd.co.uk
Directors: C. Claydon (Dir)
Immediate Holding Company: MERCURY BEARINGS LIMITED
Registration no: 03598993 **VAT No.:** GB 718 7840 04
Date established: 1998 **Turnover:** £2m - £5m **No.of Employees:** 1 - 10
Product Groups: 22, 23, 29, 30, 32, 33, 34, 35, 39, 45, 48

Date of Accounts	Jul 08	Mar 11	Mar 10
Working Capital	573	-219	-120
Fixed Assets	33	1m	1m
Current Assets	1m	2m	1m

Metair Mechanical Services
Unit 21d Queensway, Enfield, EN3 4SZ
Tel: 020-8443 5777 **Fax:** 020-8443 3366
E-mail: metair@metair.co.uk
Website: http://www.metair.co.uk
Directors: W. Hughes (Dir)
Immediate Holding Company: METAIR MECHANICAL SERVICES LIMITED
Registration no: 05568243 **VAT No.:** GB 646 9214 18
Date established: 2005 **Turnover:** £500,000 - £1m
No.of Employees: 1 - 10 **Product Groups:** 52

Date of Accounts	Sep 11	Sep 10	Sep 09
Sales Turnover	N/A	554	492
Pre Tax Profit/Loss	N/A	-12	-47
Working Capital	116	162	173
Fixed Assets	1	1	N/A
Current Assets	213	334	269
Current Liabilities	N/A	68	28

Metal Teck Euro Ltd
Unit 15 Redburn Industrial Estate Woodall Road, Enfield, EN3 4LQ
Tel: 020-8443 2233
Directors: M. Michael (MD)
Immediate Holding Company: METAL TECK EURO LIMITED
Registration no: 07467708 **Date established:** 2010
No.of Employees: 1 - 10 **Product Groups:** 26, 35

Metalex Metalworks Ltd
15 & 15b Queensway, Enfield, EN3 4SA
Tel: 020-8443 4345 **Fax:** 020-8443 4168
E-mail: kerry.christou@btconnect.com
Website: http://www.metalexmetalworks.co.uk
Directors: K. Christou (Dir)
Immediate Holding Company: METALEX METALWORKS LTD
Registration no: 08006750 **Date established:** 2012
No.of Employees: 1 - 10 **Product Groups:** 35

Morelli Group Ltd
Unit 2 Baird Road, Enfield, EN1 1SJ
Tel: 020-8351 5171 **Fax:** 020-8351 5172
E-mail: enquiries@morelli.co.uk
Website: http://www.morelli.co.uk
Bank(s): National Westminster Bank Plc
Directors: A. Toms (Fin), J. Moring (MD)
Immediate Holding Company: MORELLI GROUP LIMITED
Registration no: 02711932 **Date established:** 1992
Turnover: £20m - £50m **No.of Employees:** 11 - 20 **Product Groups:** 32

Date of Accounts	May 11	May 10	May 09
Sales Turnover	32m	31m	30m
Pre Tax Profit/Loss	81	615	-991
Working Capital	5m	5m	5m
Fixed Assets	3m	3m	4m
Current Assets	11m	10m	10m
Current Liabilities	2m	2m	2m

N. J. Milroy Fibrous Plasterers
Drayton Nursery Cattlegate Road, Crews Hill, Enfield, EN2 9DJ
Tel: 020-8363 7586 **Fax:** 020-8445 9862
E-mail: enquiries@njmilroy.com
Website: http://www.njmilroy.com
Product Groups: 30, 66

National Office Of Animal Health Ltd
Crossfield Chambers Gladbeck Way, Enfield, EN2 7HF
Tel: 020-8367 3131 **Fax:** 020-8363 1155
E-mail: p.sketchley@noah.co.uk
Website: http://www.noah.co.uk
Directors: P. Sketchley (Co Sec)
Immediate Holding Company: NATIONAL OFFICE OF ANIMAL HEALTH LIMITED
Registration no: 02145809 **Date established:** 1987
Turnover: £500,000 - £1m **No.of Employees:** 1 - 10 **Product Groups:** 85

Date of Accounts	Dec 11	Dec 10	Dec 09
Sales Turnover	856	753	769
Pre Tax Profit/Loss	76	14	52
Working Capital	427	346	331
Fixed Assets	155	162	166
Current Assets	1m	1m	773
Current Liabilities	680	867	389

North London Chamber Of Commerce Ltd
Enfield Business Centre 201 Hertford Road, Enfield, EN3 5JH
Tel: 020-8443 4464 **Fax:** 020-8443 3822
E-mail: huw@nlcc.co.uk
Website: http://www.nlcc.co.uk
Managers: D. Wyatt (Chief Acct), H. Jones
Immediate Holding Company: NORTH LONDON CHAMBER OF COMMERCE
Registration no: 02923708 **Date established:** 1994
Turnover: £250,000 - £500,000 **No.of Employees:** 1 - 10
Product Groups: 87

Date of Accounts	Mar 11	Mar 10	Mar 09
Working Capital	6	59	71
Fixed Assets	N/A	1	2
Current Assets	49	110	115

O E M Group Ltd
Pavilion Business Centre 6 Kinetic Crescent, Enfield, EN3 7FJ
Tel: 020-8344 8777 **Fax:** 020-8344 8778
E-mail: cameron@secureseal.com
Website: http://www.secureseal.com
Directors: C. Grant (MD)
Ultimate Holding Company: O.E.M. MARKETING SERVICES LIMITED
Immediate Holding Company: OEM GROUP LIMITED
Registration no: 02004194 **VAT No.:** GB 439 9994 68
Date established: 1986 **Turnover:** £1m - £2m **No.of Employees:** 1 - 10
Product Groups: 39, 40, 66

Date of Accounts	May 11	May 10	May 09
Sales Turnover	1m	999	N/A
Pre Tax Profit/Loss	64	75	N/A
Working Capital	206	121	85
Fixed Assets	32	56	54
Current Assets	663	507	571
Current Liabilities	286	315	19

R Glover Ascroft Ltd
2a Catisfield Road, Enfield, EN3 6BD
Tel: 01992-717272 **Fax:** 01992-714040
E-mail: enquiries@r-glover-ascroft.com
Website: http://www.r-glover-ascroft.com
Managers: R. Cox (Chief Mgr)
Immediate Holding Company: R. GLOVER ASCROFT LIMITED
Registration no: 00482429 **Date established:** 1950
Turnover: £500,000 - £1m **No.of Employees:** 1 - 10 **Product Groups:** 22, 24, 29, 40, 63

see next page

R Glover Ascroft Ltd - Cont'd

Date of Accounts	Jun 12	Jun 11	Jun 10
Working Capital	84	52	49
Fixed Assets	14	20	23
Current Assets	204	172	150

Reed Accountancy Personnel Ltd

3 Cecil Court 49-55 London Road, Enfield, EN2 6DE
Tel: 020-8363 1344 **Fax:** 020-8363 6781
E-mail: rap.enfield@reed.co.uk
Website: http://www.reed.co.uk
Managers: R. Joshi (Comm)
Immediate Holding Company: REED PERSONNEL SERVICES LTD
Registration no: 00973629 **Turnover:** £125m - £250m
No.of Employees: 1 - 10 **Product Groups:** 80

Reed Employment Ltd

8 The Town, Enfield, EN2 6LE
Tel: 020-8370 3600 **Fax:** 020-8360 0223
E-mail: caroline.dyer@reed.co.uk
Website: http://www.reed.co.uk
Managers: M. Conroy (Mgr)
Ultimate Holding Company: REED GLOBAL LTD (MALTA)
Immediate Holding Company: REED EMPLOYMENT LIMITED
Registration no: 00669854 **Date established:** 1960
Turnover: £500m - £1,000m **No.of Employees:** 1 - 10
Product Groups: 80

Date of Accounts	Jun 11	Jun 10	Dec 07
Sales Turnover	618	450	287m
Pre Tax Profit/Loss	-2m	310	8m
Working Capital	23m	28m	28m
Fixed Assets	31	36	5m
Current Assets	28m	30m	74m
Current Liabilities	37	29	21m

Royfreight Ltd

2 Queen Annes Place, Enfield, EN1 2PX
Tel: 020-8360 3060 **Fax:** 020-8360 0440
E-mail: info@royfreight.co.uk
Website: http://www.royfreight.co.uk
Directors: S. Spenwyn (Fin), D. Spenwyn (MD)
Immediate Holding Company: ROYFREIGHT LIMITED
Registration no: 00935590 **Date established:** 1968
Turnover: £500,000 - £1m **No.of Employees:** 1 - 10 **Product Groups:** 76

Date of Accounts	Jul 11	Jul 10	Jul 09
Working Capital	100	140	159
Fixed Assets	184	186	188
Current Assets	215	243	242

Stealth Computer Services

119 Hertford Road, Enfield, EN3 5JF
Tel: 08704-460609 **Fax:** 020-8373 2519
E-mail: info@stealthuk.com
Website: http://www.stealthuk.com
Directors: E. Kaya (MD)
No.of Employees: 1 - 10 **Product Groups:** 44

Suncombe Ltd

Jade House Lockfield Avenue, Brimsdown, Enfield, EN3 7JY
Tel: 020-8443 3454 **Fax:** 020-8443 3969
E-mail: d.simpson@suncombe.com
Website: http://www.suncombe.com
Directors: D. Simpson (Fin), D. Overton (MD)
Immediate Holding Company: SUNCOMBE LIMITED
Registration no: 00745960 **Date established:** 1963
No.of Employees: 21 - 50 **Product Groups:** 38, 42

Date of Accounts	Jan 12	Jan 11	Jan 10
Working Capital	131	64	63
Fixed Assets	54	48	47
Current Assets	495	478	551

Texapin

85 Lockfield Avenue, Enfield, EN3 7PY
Tel: 020-8805 2275 **Fax:** 020-8443 3389
E-mail: andywells@texapin.co.uk
Website: http://www.texapin.co.uk
Managers: A. Wells (Chief Mgr)
Registration no: 01170801 **VAT No.:** 206 8128 76 **Date established:** 1974
Turnover: £1m - £2m **No.of Employees:** 1 - 10 **Product Groups:** 30

Two & A Half

9 Queens Road, Enfield, EN1 1NE
Tel: 020-8363 6709 **Fax:** 020-8363 6709
E-mail: enquiries@twoandahalf.co.uk
Website: http://www.twoandahalf.co.uk
Directors: C. Humphreys (Prop), C. Humphrys (Prop)
Turnover: Up to £250,000 **No.of Employees:** 1 - 10 **Product Groups:** 25, 33, 35, 41, 66

Tyrone Textiles Ltd

Unit 30-31 Riverwalk Business Park Riverwalk Road, Enfield, EN3 7QN
Tel: 020-8221 3300 **Fax:** 020-8221 3322
E-mail: enquiries@tyrone-group.com
Website: http://www.tyrone-group.com
Directors: M. Green (Dir)
Managers: L. Parsons (Personnel), T. Moyes (Chief Mgr)
Immediate Holding Company: TYRONE TEXTILES LIMITED
Registration no: 01406354 **Date established:** 1978 **Turnover:** £5m - £10m
No.of Employees: 21 - 50 **Product Groups:** 23

Date of Accounts	Jun 11	Jun 10	Jun 09
Sales Turnover	N/A	5m	5m
Pre Tax Profit/Loss	N/A	153	163
Working Capital	2m	3m	988
Fixed Assets	86	117	3m
Current Assets	4m	4m	2m
Current Liabilities	N/A	641	632

Wealden Computing Services Ltd

6 Sovereign Business Centre Stockingswater Lane, Enfield, EN3 7JX
Tel: 020-8364 7177 **Fax:** 020-8367 7181
E-mail: jane.broughton@wealden.net
Website: http://www.wealden.net
Bank(s): Barclays
Directors: G. Williams (Sales)
Managers: M. Haynes (Tech Serv Mgr), S. Rehal (Fin Mgr)
Ultimate Holding Company: RED RIVER 11 LIMITED
Immediate Holding Company: FALCONWOOD ASSOCIATES LIMITED
Registration no: 01693382 **Date established:** 1983 **Turnover:** £2m - £5m
No.of Employees: 11 - 20 **Product Groups:** 44

Date of Accounts	Mar 11	Mar 10	Mar 09
Working Capital	52	1	-1
Current Assets	52	61	66

Westmill Foods

26 Crown Road, Enfield, EN1 1DZ
Tel: 020-8345 8100 **Fax:** 01279-715280
E-mail: enquiries@westmill.co.uk
Website: http://www.westmill.co.uk
Bank(s): Lloyds TSB
Directors: R. Cook (Sales), A. Mealings (Pers), A. Nicholson (Mkt Research)
Managers: S. Hancke (Comptroller), J. Downes, B. Amon, J. Rutherford (Tech Serv Mgr)
Ultimate Holding Company: ASSOCIATED BRITISH FOODS P.L.C.
Immediate Holding Company: ALLIED GRAIN PRODUCTS LTD
Registration no: 00044394 **VAT No.:** 183 8080 48 **Date established:** 1895
Turnover: £50m - £75m **No.of Employees:** 101 - 250
Product Groups: 20, 41, 62, 67

WF Enfield

Unit 10 Trafalgar Trading Estate Jeffreys Road, Enfield, EN3 7TY
Tel: 020-8344 4170 **Fax:** 020-8804 9814
Website: http://www.wf-online.com
Bank(s): HSBC
Managers: C. Nicholson (Chief Mgr)
Immediate Holding Company: Hagemeyer
Registration no: 00434724 **No.of Employees:** 11 - 20 **Product Groups:** 67

Winther Browne & Company Ltd

75 Bilton Way, Enfield, EN3 7ER
Tel: 020-8344 9050 **Fax:** 020-8344 9051
E-mail: sales@wintherbrowne.co.uk
Website: http://www.wintherbrowne.co.uk
Bank(s): Bank of Scotland, 16 Piccadilly, London W1V 0AH
Directors: D. Smith (Tech Serv), S. Goldsmith (Fin)
Managers: M. Underwood, M. Evetts, M. Kurucoca
Immediate Holding Company: WINTHER,BROWNE & COMPANY LIMITED
Registration no: 00141940 **Date established:** 2015
Turnover: £10m - £20m **No.of Employees:** 101 - 250 **Product Groups:** 25

Date of Accounts	Dec 10	Dec 09	Dec 08
Sales Turnover	12m	13m	N/A
Pre Tax Profit/Loss	165	26	-2m
Working Capital	2m	1m	1m
Fixed Assets	217	359	607
Current Assets	5m	5m	6m
Current Liabilities	821	847	736

G R Wright & Sons Ltd

Ponders End Mills Wharf Road, Enfield, EN3 4TG
Tel: 020-8344 6900 **Fax:** 020-8804 0533
E-mail: sales@wrightsflour.co.uk
Website: http://www.wrightsflour.co.uk
Bank(s): Barclays
Directors: D. Wright (Dir), L. Morris (Dir)
Immediate Holding Company: G.R.WRIGHT & SONS LIMITED
Registration no: 00129755 **VAT No.:** GB 220 5876 74
Date established: 2013 **Turnover:** £20m - £50m
No.of Employees: 51 - 100 **Product Groups:** 20

Date of Accounts	Dec 11	Dec 10	Dec 09
Sales Turnover	35m	29m	28m
Pre Tax Profit/Loss	3m	3m	3m
Working Capital	11m	9m	7m
Fixed Assets	5m	5m	6m
Current Assets	14m	12m	9m
Current Liabilities	1m	2m	981

Feltham

Agility Logistics Ltd

Unit 6 Radius Park Faggs Road, Feltham, TW14 0NG
Tel: 020-8917 3000 **Fax:** 020-8917 3001
E-mail: info@agilitylogistics.com
Website: http://www.agilitylogistics.com
Directors: C. Hindley (Chief Op Offcr)
Managers: C. Price
Ultimate Holding Company: PUBLIC WAREHOUSING COMPANY K.S.C (KUWAIT)
Immediate Holding Company: AGILITY LOGISTICS LIMITED
Registration no: 00112456 **VAT No.:** GB 243 5125 87
Date established: 2010 **Turnover:** £20m - £50m
No.of Employees: 51 - 100 **Product Groups:** 76

Date of Accounts	Dec 11	Dec 10	Dec 09
Sales Turnover	7m	10m	41m
Pre Tax Profit/Loss	-7	66	2m
Working Capital	16m	16m	16m
Fixed Assets	30	58	60
Current Assets	18m	17m	18m
Current Liabilities	568	235	223

Air Duct Engineering Co.

Unit 16 By The Way Farm London Road, Feltham, TW14 8RW
Tel: 01784-257862 **Fax:** 01784-240249
Website: http://www.airduct.co.uk
Directors: M. Streeter (Ptnr)
Date established: 1986 **No.of Employees:** 1 - 10 **Product Groups:** 37, 40, 48

British International Freight Association

Redfern House Browells Lane, Feltham, TW13 7EP
Tel: 020-8844 2266 **Fax:** 020-8890 5546
E-mail: p.quantrill@bifa.org
Website: http://www.bifa.org
Managers: P. Quantrill
Immediate Holding Company: BRITISH INTERNATIONAL FREIGHT ASSOCIATION
Registration no: 00391973 **VAT No.:** GB 216 4763 63
Date established: 1944 **Turnover:** £1m - £2m **No.of Employees:** 11 - 20
Product Groups: 87

Date of Accounts	Dec 11	Dec 10	Dec 09
Sales Turnover	2m	2m	2m
Pre Tax Profit/Loss	51	35	53
Working Capital	540	487	444
Fixed Assets	241	256	274
Current Assets	1m	799	738
Current Liabilities	405	219	181

Buck & Hickman Ltd

Units 14-15 Vector Park Forest Road, Feltham, TW13 7EJ
Tel: 020-8587 9500 **Fax:** 020-8943 2826
E-mail: feltham@buckandhickman.com
Website: http://www.buckandhickman.com
Bank(s): Barclays
Managers: G. Miles (District Mgr)
Ultimate Holding Company: TRAVIS PERKINS PLC
Immediate Holding Company: BOSTON (2011) LIMITED
Registration no: 06028304 **Date established:** 2006
No.of Employees: 11 - 20 **Product Groups:** 24, 29, 33, 36, 37, 41, 46

Date of Accounts	Dec 10	Mar 10	Mar 09
Working Capital	6m	6m	6m
Current Assets	27m	27m	27m

Burgess Furniture Ltd

Hanworth Trading Estate Hampton Road West, Feltham, TW13 6EH
Tel: 020-8894 9231 **Fax:** 020-8894 2943
E-mail: sales@burgessfurniture.com
Website: http://www.burgessfurniture.com
Bank(s): National Westminster
Directors: C. Gillett (Fin), J. Burgess (MD), S. Richards (Sales)
Managers: D. Maidment (Purch Mgr), T. Gay (Tech Serv Mgr), S. Bateman (Mktg Serv Mgr)
Immediate Holding Company: BURGESS FURNITURE LTD
Registration no: 02222052 **Date established:** 1988
Turnover: £10m - £20m **No.of Employees:** 101 - 250
Product Groups: 26, 67

Date of Accounts	Dec 11	Dec 10	Dec 09
Sales Turnover	13m	12m	10m
Pre Tax Profit/Loss	-140	552	-265
Working Capital	2m	3m	2m
Fixed Assets	2m	2m	2m
Current Assets	4m	5m	4m
Current Liabilities	735	711	638

C M F

Falcon Way, Feltham, TW14 0XJ
Tel: 020-8844 0940 **Fax:** 020-8751 5793
E-mail: info@cmf.co.uk
Website: http://www.cmf.co.uk
Directors: S. Gregan (Fin), C. Roy (MD), N. Boyles (MD)
Managers: K. Deegan, T. Kennedy (Purch Mgr)
Ultimate Holding Company: CMF GROUP LIMITED
Immediate Holding Company: C.M.F. LIMITED
Registration no: 01688993 **VAT No.:** GB 226 3065 85
Date established: 1982 **Turnover:** £20m - £50m
No.of Employees: 51 - 100 **Product Groups:** 48

Date of Accounts	Jun 11	Jun 10	Jun 09
Sales Turnover	24m	21m	23m
Pre Tax Profit/Loss	-126	223	2m
Working Capital	2m	2m	1m
Fixed Assets	1m	2m	2m
Current Assets	4m	6m	6m
Current Liabilities	345	844	1m

Charles Kendall Packing Ltd

Spur Road, Feltham, TW14 0SL
Tel: 020-8893 2930 **Fax:** 020-8893 2476
E-mail: sales@charleskendall.com
Website: http://www.charleskendall.com
Directors: D. Harris (Chief Op Offcr), G. Mitchell (Fin)
Managers: S. Kadwell, L. Jenner (Mktg Serv Mgr)
Ultimate Holding Company: CHARLES KENDALL GROUP LIMITED
Immediate Holding Company: CHARLES KENDALL PACKING LIMITED
Registration no: 00661309 **VAT No.:** GB 238 4062 67
Date established: 1960 **Turnover:** £2m - £5m **No.of Employees:** 11 - 20
Product Groups: 76, 80, 84

Date of Accounts	Dec 11	Dec 10	Dec 09
Sales Turnover	2m	1m	2m
Pre Tax Profit/Loss	42	-86	-195
Working Capital	191	161	224
Current Assets	646	362	324
Current Liabilities	24	10	4

Citizen Systems Europe G M B H

643-651 Staines Road, Feltham, TW14 8PA
Tel: 020-8893 1900 **Fax:** 020-8893 0080
E-mail: sales@citizen.co.uk
Website: http://www.citizen-europe.com
Bank(s): HSBC
Managers: A. Pickett (District Mgr)
Ultimate Holding Company: CITIZEN WATCH CO LTD (JAPAN)
Immediate Holding Company: CITIZEN SYSTEMS EUROPE GMBH
Registration no: FC021780 **VAT No.:** GB 455 5711 39
Date established: 1999 **Turnover:** £20m - £50m
No.of Employees: 11 - 20 **Product Groups:** 38, 42, 44

Copiertec Ltd

3 Browells Lane, Feltham, TW13 7EQ
Tel: 020-8890 0900 **Fax:** 020-8890 0919
E-mail: sales@copiertec.co.uk
Website: http://www.copiertec.co.uk
Directors: R. Davis (Sales), S. Naidu (MD), W. Naidu (Co Sec)
Immediate Holding Company: COPIERTEC LIMITED
Registration no: 03502413 **Date established:** 1998 **Turnover:** £2m - £5m
No.of Employees: 1 - 10 **Product Groups:** 32, 44, 48, 67

Cosmotrans International Ltd

9 Felthambrook Way, Feltham, TW13 7DU
Tel: 020-8751 2109 **Fax:** 020-8751 2119
E-mail: ops@cosmotrans.co.uk
Website: http://www.cosmotrans.co.uk
Directors: I. Herdman Grant (Dir)
Managers: J. Branniff (Chief Acct)
Immediate Holding Company: COSMOTRANS INTERNATIONAL LTD
Registration no: 02663163 **Date established:** 1991
No.of Employees: 1 - 10 **Product Groups:** 39, 45, 74, 75, 76

Date of Accounts	Jun 12	Jun 11	Jun 10
Working Capital	101	92	75
Fixed Assets	4	4	N/A
Current Assets	406	423	308

Dnata

Unit 8 Radius Park Faggs Road, Feltham, TW14 0NG
Tel: 020-8890 6861 **Fax:** 020-8893 2543
E-mail: sales@planehandling.com
Website: http://www.dnata.co.uk
Directors: R. Williams (MD)
Ultimate Holding Company: DNATA WORLD TRAVEL (UNITED ARAB EMIRATES)

Immediate Holding Company: DNATA LIMITED
Registration no: 03091040 **Date established:** 1995
Turnover: £75m - £125m **No.of Employees:** 21 - 50 **Product Groups:** 76

Date of Accounts	Mar 11	Mar 10	Jun 08
Sales Turnover	85m	43m	58m
Pre Tax Profit/Loss	1m	2m	5m
Working Capital	6m	6m	-2m
Fixed Assets	7m	7m	12m
Current Assets	17m	19m	10m
Current Liabilities	7m	8m	5m

E C S Contract Services

68 Hereford Road, Feltham, TW13 5BS
Tel: 020-8893 1807 **Fax:** 020-8890 4947
E-mail: sales@ecscs.co.uk
Website: http://www.ecscs.co.uk
Bank(s): HSBC Bank plc
Directors: J. Baker (Snr Part)
Turnover: £500,000 - £1m **No.of Employees:** 21 - 50 **Product Groups:** 52

G B L

12 Mount Road, Feltham, TW13 6AR
Tel: 020-8867 2461 **Fax:** 020-8867 2475
E-mail: info@gblwheelchairs.com
Website: http://www.gblwheelchairs.com
Managers: G. Laker (Mgr)
Immediate Holding Company: GBL WHEELCHAIR SERVICES LIMITED
Registration no: 02810704 **Date established:** 1993
No.of Employees: 1 - 10 **Product Groups:** 24, 30, 38

Date of Accounts	Mar 11	Mar 10	Mar 09
Working Capital	17	-29	-18
Fixed Assets	76	92	94
Current Assets	353	398	382

G & H Fabrications

137 Bedfont Lane, Feltham, TW14 9NH
Tel: 020-8751 1748 **Fax:** 020-8844 9704
E-mail: ghfab@orange.net
Directors: G. Callaway (Prop)
No.of Employees: 1 - 10 **Product Groups:** 35

John Gardiner Airfreight Ltd

Unit 12 Maple Industrial Estate Maple Way, Feltham, TW13 7AW
Tel: 020-8894 3537 **Fax:** 020-8894 3542
E-mail: john@johngardinerfreight.com
Website: http://www.johngardiner.com
Directors: J. Gardiner (Dir)
Immediate Holding Company: JOHN GARDINER (AIR FREIGHT) LIMITED
Registration no: 00723291 **Date established:** 1962
Turnover: £500,000 - £1m **No.of Employees:** 1 - 10 **Product Groups:** 75, 76

Date of Accounts	Sep 11	Sep 10	Sep 09
Working Capital	-150	-135	-113
Fixed Assets	2	3	3
Current Assets	47	67	52

Mailflight Ltd

Unit 2 Central Way, Feltham, TW14 0RX
Tel: 020-8893 1477 **Fax:** 020- 88931459
E-mail: micko@mfcourier.com
Website: http://www.mfcourier.com
Bank(s): HSBC Bank plc
Directors: M. Odell (MD), M. O'Dell (MD)
Ultimate Holding Company: BTB MAILFLIGHT HOLDINGS LIMITED
Immediate Holding Company: MAILFLIGHT COURIER SERVICES LIMITED
Registration no: 01924311 **VAT No.:** GB 426 5985 17
Date established: 1985 **Turnover:** £5m - £10m **No.of Employees:** 21 - 50
Product Groups: 79, 81

Date of Accounts	Dec 10	Dec 09	Dec 08
Sales Turnover	8m	8m	10m
Pre Tax Profit/Loss	-89	-90	-127
Working Capital	14	74	132
Fixed Assets	N/A	9	15
Current Assets	2m	3m	2m
Current Liabilities	373	30	44

Merck Serono Ltd

Bedfont Cross Stanwell Road, Feltham, TW14 8NX
Tel: 020-8818 7200 **Fax:** 01895-420605
E-mail: serono_uk@serono.com
Website: http://www.merckserono.net
Directors: J. Vass (Fin)
Ultimate Holding Company: MERCK KGaA (GERMANY)
Immediate Holding Company: SERONO LIMITED
Registration no: 01192915 **Date established:** 1974
Turnover: £50m - £75m **No.of Employees:** 51 - 100 **Product Groups:** 31

Date of Accounts	Dec 09	Dec 08
Working Capital	4m	4m
Current Assets	4m	4m

Neate Brake Controls

Hanworth Trading Estate Hampton Road West, Feltham, TW13 6DN
Tel: 020-8898 6021 **Fax:** 020-8898 1246
E-mail: neatebrakecontrols@utdsl.com
Managers: C. Gates (Consultant)
Registration no: 00470537 **VAT No.:** GB 222 7667 61
Date established: 1949 **Turnover:** Up to £250,000
No.of Employees: 1 - 10 **Product Groups:** 35, 39

Date of Accounts	Mar 08	Mar 07	Mar 06
Sales Turnover	173	N/A	N/A
Pre Tax Profit/Loss	-19	N/A	N/A
Working Capital	45	64	79
Fixed Assets	103	103	103
Current Assets	83	91	116
Current Liabilities	38	27	36
Total Share Capital	8	8	8
ROCE% (Return on Capital Employed)	-12.7		
ROT% (Return on Turnover)	-10.8		

Norman Global Logistics Ltd

1 Griffin Centre Staines Road, Feltham, TW14 0HS
Tel: 020-8893 2999 **Fax:** 020-8893 1770
E-mail: pob@norman.co.uk
Website: http://www.norman.co.uk
Bank(s): The Royal Bank of Scotland
Directors: P. O'Brien (MD), G. Dean (Dir), N. Short (Co Sec)
Ultimate Holding Company: NG LOGISTICS LIMITED
Immediate Holding Company: NORMAN GLOBAL LOGISTICS LIMITED
Registration no: 00981771 **Date established:** 1970
Turnover: £20m - £50m **No.of Employees:** 21 - 50 **Product Groups:** 76, 84

Date of Accounts	Sep 11	Sep 10	Sep 09
Sales Turnover	20m	23m	18m
Pre Tax Profit/Loss	1m	1m	532
Working Capital	2m	2m	1m
Fixed Assets	300	280	230
Current Assets	6m	7m	6m
Current Liabilities	421	735	566

Panalpina World Transport Ltd

Great South West Road, Feltham, TW14 8NE
Tel: 020-8587 9000 **Fax:** 020-8587 9200
E-mail: info@panalpina.com
Website: http://www.panalpina.com
Bank(s): Lloyds
Directors: G. Barnes (MD)
Ultimate Holding Company: PANALPINA WORLD TRANSPORT (HOLDING) LTD (SWITZERLAND)
Immediate Holding Company: PANALPINA WORLD TRANSPORT LIMITED
Registration no: 00357697 **VAT No.:** GB 577 9009 00
Date established: 1939 **Turnover:** £125m - £250m
No.of Employees: 251 - 500 **Product Groups:** 72, 74, 75, 76

Date of Accounts	Dec 11	Dec 10	Dec 09
Sales Turnover	141m	153m	147m
Pre Tax Profit/Loss	-4m	-2m	-959
Working Capital	172	3m	3m
Fixed Assets	17m	18m	21m
Current Assets	31m	33m	32m
Current Liabilities	10m	7m	5m

Pisani plc

2a Plane Tree Crescent, Feltham, TW13 7AL
Tel: 020-8917 3350 **Fax:** 020-8847 3406
E-mail: sales@pisani.co.uk
Website: http://www.pisani.co.uk
Managers: C. Gray (Fin Mgr), D. Medlam (Ops Mgr)
Ultimate Holding Company: PISANI (HOLDINGS) LIMITED
Immediate Holding Company: PISANI PLC
Registration no: 00335887 **Date established:** 1938
Turnover: £10m - £20m **No.of Employees:** 21 - 50 **Product Groups:** 14, 33, 66

Date of Accounts	Dec 11	Dec 10	Dec 09
Sales Turnover	17m	22m	22m
Pre Tax Profit/Loss	-1m	225	168
Working Capital	9m	3m	3m
Fixed Assets	14m	13m	13m
Current Assets	14m	14m	16m
Current Liabilities	1m	1m	725

R A C

1 Forest Road, Feltham, TW13 7WB
Tel: 08457-414151 **Fax:** 020- 89172525
Website: http://www.rac.co.uk
Bank(s): National Westminster Bank Plc
Directors: P. Atkinson (MD), R. Pennycuik (Fin)
Managers: J. Hale (Mgr), N. Dunne (Mgr), J. Temblett (Mktg Serv Mgr), P. Trudgeon (Sec)
Ultimate Holding Company: AVIVA PLC
Immediate Holding Company: RAC PLC
Registration no: 01424399 **VAT No.:** GB 239 5058 47
Turnover: £20m - £50m **No.of Employees:** 251 - 500 **Product Groups:** 38

Ram Mount UK Ltd

5 Lion Centre Hanworth Trading Estate Hampton Road West, Feltham, TW13 6DS
Tel: 020-8755 2881 **Fax:** 020-8893 8439
E-mail: sales@ram-mount.co.uk
Website: http://www.ram-mount.co.uk
Managers: S. Dickenson
Immediate Holding Company: RAM MOUNT UK LIMITED
Registration no: 05219801 **Date established:** 2004
No.of Employees: 1 - 10 **Product Groups:** 39

Date of Accounts	Sep 11	Sep 10	Sep 09
Working Capital	114	83	48
Fixed Assets	1	N/A	N/A
Current Assets	433	164	130

Reed Employment Ltd

22 The Centre, Feltham, TW13 4AU
Tel: 020-8844608 **Fax:** 020- 87514608
E-mail: feltham@reed.co.uk
Website: http://www.reed.co.uk
Managers: J. Shorter (District Mgr)
Ultimate Holding Company: REED GLOBAL LTD (MALTA)
Immediate Holding Company: REED EMPLOYMENT LIMITED
Registration no: 00669854 **Date established:** 1960
Turnover: £75m - £125m **No.of Employees:** 1 - 10 **Product Groups:** 80

Date of Accounts	Jun 11	Jun 10	Dec 07
Sales Turnover	618	450	287m
Pre Tax Profit/Loss	-2m	310	8m
Working Capital	23m	28m	28m
Fixed Assets	31	36	5m
Current Assets	28m	30m	74m
Current Liabilities	37	29	21m

Renzacci UK plc

Unit 9 Marlin Park Central Way, Feltham, TW14 0AN
Tel: 020-8579 2661 **Fax:** 020-8579 2663
E-mail: mail@renzacci.co.uk
Website: http://www.renzacci.co.uk
Directors: J. Alexander (MD)
Ultimate Holding Company: RENZACCI (U.K.) PLC
Immediate Holding Company: RENZACCI (U.K.) PLC
Registration no: 01042547 **Date established:** 1972 **Turnover:** £1m - £2m
No.of Employees: 1 - 10 **Product Groups:** 43

Date of Accounts	Mar 12	Mar 11	Mar 10
Sales Turnover	2m	1m	1m
Pre Tax Profit/Loss	-14	2	-63
Working Capital	388	428	51
Fixed Assets	997	913	2m
Current Assets	796	780	399
Current Liabilities	116	95	82

Ricoh UK Ltd

1 Plane Tree Crescent, Feltham, TW13 7HG
Tel: 020-8261 4000 **Fax:** 020-8261 4004
E-mail: ukinfo@ricoh.co.uk
Website: http://www.ricoh.co.uk
Directors: R. Wallis (Pers), R. Hewitt (Fin), C. Moloney (Mkt Research), N. Downing (Co Sec)
Managers: P. Cheetham, D. O'Doherty, M. Greenhalgh
Ultimate Holding Company: RICOH COMPANY LIMITED (JAPAN)
Immediate Holding Company: NRG (RUK) LIMITED
Registration no: 01505381 **Date established:** 1980
No.of Employees: 251 - 500 **Product Groups:** 44

Date of Accounts	Mar 10	Mar 09	Mar 08
Sales Turnover	N/A	N/A	155m
Pre Tax Profit/Loss	31	527	5m
Working Capital	8m	19m	19m
Current Assets	8m	19m	19m
Current Liabilities	9	148	N/A

Russell Finex Ltd

Russell House Browells Lane, Feltham, TW13 7EW
Tel: 020-8818 2000 **Fax:** 020-8818 2060
E-mail: marketing@russellfinex.com
Website: http://www.russellfinex.com
Bank(s): HSBC Bank plc
Managers: R. Kay (Mktg Serv Mgr), R. Baker (Sales Prom Mgr), J. Cano (Export Sales Mg)
Immediate Holding Company: Russell-Hurst Trustees Ltd
Registration no: 00294532 **VAT No.:** GB 239 2642 53
Turnover: £10m - £20m **No.of Employees:** 101 - 250
Product Groups: 29, 32, 35, 41, 42, 44, 45, 47, 66, 67

Date of Accounts	Jan 12	Jan 11	Jan 10
Sales Turnover	22m	18m	15m
Pre Tax Profit/Loss	3m	1m	572
Working Capital	8m	8m	7m
Fixed Assets	6m	13m	10m
Current Assets	14m	12m	10m
Current Liabilities	4m	2m	2m

Schenkers Ltd

Schenker House Unitair Centre Great South West Road, Feltham, TW14 8NT
Tel: 020-8890 8899 **Fax:** 020-8751 0141
E-mail: per.holstnielsen@schenker.co.uk
Website: http://www.dbschenker.com
Bank(s): Barclays
Directors: D. Harrison (Comm), F. Sabbroni (Pers), R. Anderson (Tech Serv)
Managers: P. Hollst-Nielsen, P. Holst Nielsen
Ultimate Holding Company: DEUTSCHE BAHN AG (GERMANY)
Immediate Holding Company: SCHENKER LIMITED
Registration no: 00383914 **VAT No.:** GB 656 9213 13
Date established: 1943 **Turnover:** £250m - £500m
No.of Employees: 101 - 250 **Product Groups:** 72, 75, 76, 77, 84

Date of Accounts	Dec 11	Dec 10	Dec 09
Sales Turnover	307m	311m	232m
Pre Tax Profit/Loss	1m	341	-4m
Working Capital	21m	21m	22m
Fixed Assets	8m	8m	8m
Current Assets	74m	77m	71m
Current Liabilities	27m	26m	25m

Senior Hargreaves

622 Central Way, Feltham, TW14 0RX
Tel: 020-8890 4602 **Fax:** 020-8751 4376
E-mail: sales@hargreaves-ductwork.co.uk
Website: http://www.hargreaves-ductwork.co.uk
Managers: P. Heryet (Mgr)
Immediate Holding Company: SENIOR HARGREAVES LIMITED
Registration no: 00288899 **Date established:** 1934
Turnover: £75m - £125m **No.of Employees:** 1 - 10 **Product Groups:** 37, 40, 48

Stanmatic Precision UK Ltd T/A Axis Group (Axis Group)

Unit 5 Lion Centre Hanworth Trading Estate, Feltham, TW13 6DS
Tel: 020-8893 8339 **Fax:** 020-8893 8439
E-mail: sales@axis-gb.com
Website: http://www.axis-gb.com
Managers: R. Drake (Mgr)
Registration no: 03963323 **VAT No.:** GB 530 9440 60
Turnover: £500,000 - £1m **No.of Employees:** 1 - 10 **Product Groups:** 38

UK Accreditation Service

Accreditation House 21-47 High Street, Feltham, TW13 4UN
Tel: 020-8917 8400 **Fax:** 020-8917 8500
E-mail: sylvia.paice@ukas.com
Website: http://www.ukas.com
Bank(s): HSBC
Directors: A. Hill (Fin)
Managers: C. Forster (Tech Serv Mgr), S. Paice, D. Bartlett (Personnel)
Immediate Holding Company: UNITED KINGDOM ACCREDITATION SERVICE
Registration no: 03076190 **Date established:** 1995
Turnover: £10m - £20m **No.of Employees:** 101 - 250 **Product Groups:** 85

Date of Accounts	Mar 12	Mar 11	Mar 10
Sales Turnover	19m	19m	18m
Pre Tax Profit/Loss	884	1m	670
Working Capital	3m	3m	3m
Fixed Assets	1m	1m	750
Current Assets	6m	6m	5m
Current Liabilities	2m	2m	2m

U P S

U P S House Forest Road, Feltham, TW13 7DY
Tel: 08457-877877 **Fax:** 020-8844 2815
Website: http://www.aniteps.com
Directors: C. Cubias Jr (Fin), W. Flick (Pres)
Ultimate Holding Company: UNITED PARCEL SERVICE INC (USA)
Immediate Holding Company: UPS AIR COURIERS OF AMERICA LIMITED
Registration no: 00947724 **Date established:** 1969 **Turnover:** £5m - £10m
No.of Employees: 1 - 10 **Product Groups:** 79

Date of Accounts	Dec 11	Dec 10	Dec 09
Sales Turnover	10m	24m	21m
Pre Tax Profit/Loss	2m	821	1m
Working Capital	9m	8m	7m
Fixed Assets	462	478	448
Current Assets	11m	14m	13m
Current Liabilities	885	635	11

Unit Products Ltd
2 Mount Road, Feltham, TW13 6AR
Tel: 020-8755 4216 **Fax:** 020-8898 4711
E-mail: enquiries@unitproducts.co.uk
Website: http://www.unitproducts.co.uk
Directors: C. Hardy (Ptnr), L. Hardy (Co Sec)
Immediate Holding Company: UNIT PRODUCTS LIMITED
Registration no: 02091876 **Date established:** 1987
Turnover: £500,000 - £1m **No.of Employees:** 1 - 10 **Product Groups:** 52, 66

Date of Accounts	Apr 11	Apr 10	Apr 09
Working Capital	67	58	76
Fixed Assets	35	44	46
Current Assets	206	328	296

Universal Marking Systems Ltd
Unit 7 Mount Road, Feltham, TW13 6AR
Tel: 020-8984884 **Fax:** 020-8898 9891
E-mail: jeff@ums.co.uk
Website: http://www.ums.co.uk
Directors: J. Sawdy (MD), J. Sawdy (Dir), J. Sawdy (Co Sec), S. Sawdy (Mkt Research), S. Sawdy (Fin)
Managers: C. Sawdy (Sales Prom Mgr)
Immediate Holding Company: METALETCH LIMITED
Registration no: 01752977 **VAT No.:** GB 700 7695 42
Date established: 1983 **Turnover:** £1m - £2m **No.of Employees:** 1 - 10
Product Groups: 32, 42, 44, 46, 47

Date of Accounts	Feb 07	Feb 06
Working Capital	60	90
Fixed Assets	20	20
Current Assets	280	240
Current Liabilities	220	150

Valley Forge
By The Way Farm London Road, Feltham, TW14 8RW
Tel: 01784-244340
Website: http://www.valleyforgeltd.net
Directors: P. Johns (Ptnr)
Immediate Holding Company: VALLEY FORGE LIMITED
Registration no: 02572967 **Date established:** 1991
No.of Employees: 1 - 10 **Product Groups:** 34, 35

Warwick Engineering
3 River Gardens, Feltham, TW14 0RD
Tel: 020-8844 2268 **Fax:** 020-8751 0509
Directors: G. Yellop (Prop)
Ultimate Holding Company: PHOENIX TRANSPORT GROUP LIMITED
Immediate Holding Company: PHOENIX TRUCK & TRAILER MAINTENANCE LTD
Registration no: 04685196 **Date established:** 2002
Turnover: Up to £250,000 **No.of Employees:** 1 - 10 **Product Groups:** 48

Date of Accounts	Mar 12	Mar 11	Mar 10
Working Capital	-221	-216	-320
Fixed Assets	26	34	26
Current Assets	181	279	245

Greenford

A Wise Move Ltd
Wise Moves Vanguard Storage Services Ltd, Greenford, UB6 8AA
Tel: 07984-401264 **Fax:** 0845-3025440
E-mail: info@wisemovesltd.co.uk
Website: http://www.wisemovesltd.co.uk
Directors: T. Liebenberg (Dir)
Managers: J. Potgieter (Sales Prom), P. Liebenberg (Accounts)
Immediate Holding Company: A. WISE MOVE LIMITED
Registration no: 04368752 **Date established:** 2002
No.of Employees: 1 - 10 **Product Groups:** 72, 76

Date of Accounts	Mar 08	Mar 07
Sales Turnover	N/A	512
Pre Tax Profit/Loss	N/A	135
Working Capital	-22	34
Fixed Assets	25	22
Current Assets	152	156
Current Liabilities	174	122
ROCE% (Return on Capital Employed)		239.4
ROT% (Return on Turnover)		26.3

A40 Packaging
6 Fairway Drive, Greenford, UB6 8PW
Tel: 020-8575 1213 **Fax:** 020-8575 1213
E-mail: sales@a40packaging.co.uk
Website: http://www.a40packaging.co.uk
Directors: D. Smith (Dir)
Turnover: Up to £250,000 **No.of Employees:** 1 - 10 **Product Groups:** 27, 28, 48

Aerodyne Equipment
67 Bideford Avenue Perivale, Greenford, UB6 7PX
Tel: 020-8998 5042 **Fax:** 020-8991 4321
E-mail: sales@aerodyneuk.com
Website: http://www.aerodyneuk.com
Directors: A. Kingston (Snr Part)
Date established: 1980 **Turnover:** Up to £250,000
No.of Employees: 11 - 20 **Product Groups:** 39

Albe England Ltd
Newton Works 51 Bideford Avenue Perivale, Greenford, UB6 7PR
Tel: 020-8997 7282 **Fax:** 020-8998 2932
E-mail: terry.roff@albe.com
Website: http://www.albe.com
Bank(s): National Westminster Bank Plc
Directors: N. Roff (Sales), T. Roff (MD)
Ultimate Holding Company: ALBE (HOLDINGS) LIMITED
Immediate Holding Company: ALBE (ENGLAND) LIMITED
Registration no: 00853375 **Date established:** 1965 **Turnover:** £1m - £2m
No.of Employees: 11 - 20 **Product Groups:** 34, 36, 48

Date of Accounts	Jun 11	Jun 10	Jun 09
Working Capital	11	26	25
Fixed Assets	612	633	669
Current Assets	621	456	338
Current Liabilities	N/A	115	N/A

Assign Technology
Unit 1 Wadsworth Business Centre Wadsworth Road, Perivale, Greenford, UB6 7LQ
Tel: 020-8998 0806 **Fax:** 020-8998 1272
E-mail: info@assigntechnology.com
Website: http://www.assigntechnology.co.uk
Directors: D. Yori (Fin), D. Yori (Prop)
Immediate Holding Company: ASSIGN TECHNOLOGY LIMITED
Registration no: 03210316 **Date established:** 1996
Turnover: £500,000 - £1m **No.of Employees:** 1 - 10 **Product Groups:** 39, 40

Date of Accounts	Aug 10	Aug 09	Aug 08
Working Capital	13	8	6
Fixed Assets	4	5	9
Current Assets	99	114	105

Autoland Ltd
Prigee House 175 Bilton Road, Perivale, Greenford, UB6 7BD
Tel: 020-8998 8866 **Fax:** 020-8998 8869
E-mail: autoland@prigee.com
Website: http://www.prigee.com
Bank(s): National Westminster Bank Plc
Directors: M. Patel (MD), G. Patel (Co Sec)
Immediate Holding Company: Autoland Ltd
Registration no: 04654929 **VAT No.:** GB 424 1536 78
Date established: 1989 **Turnover:** £1m - £2m **No.of Employees:** 11 - 20
Product Groups: 39, 40, 45, 61, 68

B J S Biotechnologies Ltd
65 Bideford Avenue Perivale, Greenford, UB6 7PP
Tel: 020-8810 5779 **Fax:** 020-8810 5883
E-mail: info@bjsco.com
Website: http://www.bjsco.com
Bank(s): Lloyds TSB Bank plc
Directors: R. Lewis (MD)
Immediate Holding Company: BJS BIOTECHNOLOGIES LIMITED
Registration no: 02959160 **VAT No.:** GB 226 6109 76
Date established: 1994 **Turnover:** £1m - £2m **No.of Employees:** 11 - 20
Product Groups: 48

Bunzl Vending Services Ltd
19 Aintree Road Perivale, Greenford, UB6 7LG
Tel: 020-8998 2828 **Fax:** 020-8998 0704
E-mail: enquiries@bunzlvend.com
Website: http://www.bunzlvend.com
Bank(s): National Westminster Bank Plc
Directors: D. Abrahams (Fin), D. Wilmot (Sales), J. Sheehan (Tech Serv), S. Murray (MD), B. Shepherd (Pers)
Managers: S. Welcome (Buyer)
Ultimate Holding Company: BUNZL PUBLIC LIMITED COMPANY
Immediate Holding Company: AUTOBAR VENDING SERVICES LIMITED
Registration no: 02605313 **VAT No.:** GB 581 7059 24
Date established: 1991 **Turnover:** £75m - £125m
No.of Employees: 51 - 100 **Product Groups:** 20, 21, 27, 32, 40, 48, 49, 61, 83

Date of Accounts	Dec 10	Dec 09	Dec 08
Sales Turnover	68m	80m	110m
Pre Tax Profit/Loss	-6m	-6m	-2m
Working Capital	-36m	-33m	-32m
Fixed Assets	28m	29m	32m
Current Assets	43m	45m	49m
Current Liabilities	3m	4m	4m

Burlington Engineers Ltd
Unit 11 Perival Industrial Park Horsenden Lane South, Perivale, Greenford, UB6 7RL
Tel: 020-8810 7266 **Fax:** 020-8998 3517
E-mail: info@burlington-engineers.co.uk
Website: http://www.burlington-engineers.co.uk
Directors: J. Kluger (MD)
Immediate Holding Company: BURLINGTON ENGINEERS LIMITED
Registration no: 05875718 **Date established:** 2006 **Turnover:** £5m - £10m
No.of Employees: 1 - 10 **Product Groups:** 67

City Care Cleaning Ltd
Unit 5 Rockware Business Centre Rockware Avenue, Greenford, UB6 0AA
Tel: 07886-402065 **Fax:** 020-8578 1758
E-mail: info@citycarecleaning.co.uk
Website: http://www.citycarecleaning.co.uk
Directors: N. Perera (Dir)
Immediate Holding Company: CITY CARE CLEANING LIMITED
Registration no: 06020522 **Date established:** 2006
No.of Employees: 21 - 50 **Product Groups:** 52

Eri Refrigeration Ltd
Derby Road, Greenford, UB6 8UJ
Tel: 020-8575 9955 **Fax:** 020-8575 2984
E-mail: sales@erirefrigeration.co.uk
Website: http://www.erirefrigeration.co.uk
Directors: L. Granville (Dir), S. Granville (MD), A. Goss (I.T. Dir)
Immediate Holding Company: E.R.I. REFRIGERATION LIMITED
Registration no: 02330852 **Date established:** 1988
No.of Employees: 21 - 50 **Product Groups:** 40, 66

Date of Accounts	May 11	May 10	May 09
Working Capital	-76	-28	55
Fixed Assets	206	197	166
Current Assets	463	626	556

Euro Matic Ltd
Clausen House Perivale Industrial Park, Horsenden Lane South, Greenford, UB6 7QE
Tel: 020-8991 2211 **Fax:** 020-8997 5074
E-mail: adrian.wilkes@wppg.co.uk
Website: http://www.euro-matic.com
Directors: A. Wilkes (Dir)
Managers: F. Grage (Sales Prom), N. Childs (Accounts)
Registration no: 03851161 **VAT No.:** GB 222 5376 82
Turnover: £1m - £2m **No.of Employees:** 1 - 10 **Product Groups:** 30, 40, 49, 54

Date of Accounts	Dec 07	Dec 06	Dec 05
Sales Turnover	417	1841	2272
Pre Tax Profit/Loss	34	-96	-626
Working Capital	176	-141	-609
Fixed Assets	499	764	1743
Current Assets	289	168	1338
Current Liabilities	113	309	1947
Total Share Capital	50	50	50
ROCE% (Return on Capital Employed)	5.0	-15.4	-55.2
ROT% (Return on Turnover)	8.2	-5.2	-27.6

Forster & Hales Ltd
24 Wadsworth Road Perivale, Greenford, UB6 7JD
Tel: 020-8998 9057 **Fax:** 020-8998 2922
E-mail: sales@forsterandhales.com
Website: http://www.forsterandhales.com
Directors: C. Dunne (Dir)
Immediate Holding Company: FORSTER & HALES LIMITED
Registration no: 01765236 **Date established:** 1983 **Turnover:** £1m - £2m
No.of Employees: 11 - 20 **Product Groups:** 30, 35, 37, 42, 48

Date of Accounts	Mar 12	Mar 11	Mar 10
Working Capital	471	421	527
Fixed Assets	14	13	5
Current Assets	625	624	688

Geller Business Equipment Ltd
Unit 14-15 Fairway Drive, Greenford, UB6 8PW
Tel: 020-8839 1000 **Fax:** 020-8839 1030
E-mail: info@geller.co.uk
Website: http://www.geller.co.uk
Bank(s): Lloyds TSB Bank plc
Directors: S. Geller (Dir), N. Geller (MD)
Managers: I. Selby (Tech Serv Mgr), S. Lambert (Purch Mgr)
Ultimate Holding Company: CONSOLIS SYSTEMS LIMITED
Immediate Holding Company: GELLER BUSINESS EQUIPMENT LIMITED
Registration no: 00694719 **VAT No.:** GB 232 5209 94
Date established: 1961 **Turnover:** £2m - £5m **No.of Employees:** 21 - 50
Product Groups: 44

Date of Accounts	Jun 11	Jun 10	Jun 09
Working Capital	487	349	620
Fixed Assets	56	96	143
Current Assets	2m	2m	2m

Glove Club Ltd
Stewkley House 2 Wadsworth Road, Perivale, Greenford, UB6 7JD
Tel: 020-8991 4300 **Fax:** 020-8991 4301
E-mail: sales@gloveclub.co.uk
Website: http://www.gloveclub.co.uk
Managers: M. Parmar (Ops Mgr)
Immediate Holding Company: GLOVE CLUB LIMITED
Registration no: 02945157 **Date established:** 1994
No.of Employees: 1 - 10 **Product Groups:** 24, 27, 29

Date of Accounts	Dec 11	Dec 10	Jul 09
Working Capital	316	318	274
Fixed Assets	11	10	10
Current Assets	603	704	452

Graphics Arts Equipment Ltd
11 Aintree Road Perivale, Greenford, UB6 7LE
Tel: 020-8997 8053 **Fax:** 020-8997 7706
E-mail: brian.godwyn@gae.co.uk
Website: http://www.gae.co.uk
Bank(s): Barclays
Directors: B. Godwyn (Co Sec), B. Godwyn (MD), P. Hards (Pers), T. Hards (MD), A. Hards (MD)
Managers: V. Fletcher (Mktg Serv Mgr), C. Hammond (Tech Sales Mgr)
Immediate Holding Company: GRAPHIC ARTS EQUIPMENT LIMITED
Registration no: 02693151 **VAT No.:** GB 701 7808 49
Date established: 1992 **Turnover:** £5m - £10m **No.of Employees:** 21 - 50
Product Groups: 44

Lapp Group
Unit 3 Perivale Park Horsenden Lane South, Perivale, Greenford, UB6 7RL
Tel: 020-8758 7800 **Fax:** 020-8758 7880
E-mail: sales@lapplimited.com
Website: http://www.lapplimited.com
Bank(s): Barclays
Directors: C. McGovern (Fin), D. Clark (MD)
Managers: M. Ansell, C. Nice (Personnel)
Ultimate Holding Company: LAPP HOLDING AG (GERMANY)
Immediate Holding Company: LAPP LIMITED
Registration no: 01497180 **VAT No.:** GB 346 4076 53
Date established: 1980 **Turnover:** £10m - £20m
No.of Employees: 21 - 50 **Product Groups:** 37, 46, 67, 77

Date of Accounts	Sep 11	Sep 10	Sep 09
Sales Turnover	19m	13m	11m
Pre Tax Profit/Loss	2m	1m	-7
Working Capital	3m	2m	1m
Fixed Assets	266	130	164
Current Assets	7m	5m	4m
Current Liabilities	2m	1m	531

Mecalux UK Ltd
Unit 39 The Metropolitan Park Halifax Road, Greenford, UB6 8XU
Tel: 020-8575 1007 **Fax:** 020-8575 0705
E-mail: info@mecalux.com
Website: http://www.mecalux.com
Directors: D. Rabagliati (Fin), E. Bighin (MD)
Immediate Holding Company: MECALUX (U.K.) LIMITED
Registration no: 02053742 **Date established:** 1986 **Turnover:** £2m - £5m
No.of Employees: 11 - 20 **Product Groups:** 35, 42, 45

Date of Accounts	Dec 11	Dec 10	Dec 09
Sales Turnover	3m	2m	2m
Pre Tax Profit/Loss	-310	-405	-161
Working Capital	716	1m	1m
Fixed Assets	20	26	28
Current Assets	1m	1m	2m
Current Liabilities	279	157	115

Mercatron International Ltd
92a Empire Road Perivale, Greenford, UB6 7EG
Tel: 020-8998 4898 **Fax:** 020-8961 2106
E-mail: info@mercatron.co.uk
Website: http://www.mercatron.co.uk
Directors: I. Naqvi (MD), B. Mandora (Co Sec)
Immediate Holding Company: MERCATRON INTERNATIONAL LIMITED
Registration no: 01214129 **Date established:** 1975
No.of Employees: 1 - 10 **Product Groups:** 34, 35, 36

Date of Accounts	Jun 11	Jun 10	Jun 09
Working Capital	94	78	91
Fixed Assets	3	4	4
Current Assets	136	130	114

Mike Weaver Commmunications
I C G House Station Approach Oldfield Lane North, Greenford, UB6 0AL
Tel: 020-8575 1540 **Fax:** 024-7660 2609
Website: http://www.mwc.co.uk
Directors: M. Weaver (Prop)
Immediate Holding Company: RIGHT CHOICE EMPLOYMENT LIMITED
Date established: 2002 **No.of Employees:** 1 - 10 **Product Groups:** 37, 79

P R G Ltd

The Old Hoover Building Western Avenue, Perivale, Greenford, UB6 8DW
Tel: 08454-706400 **Fax:** 020-8575 0424
E-mail: info@prg.com
Website: http://www.prglighting.co.uk
Bank(s): Coutts
Directors: G. Boyd (Chief Op Offcr), B. Croft (MD)
Managers: D. March (Sales Prom Mgr), G. De-Winter (Mktg Serv Mgr), J. Douglas (Sales Prom Mgr), S. Blair (Comptroller)
Immediate Holding Company: PRODUCTION RESOURCE GROUP UK LTD
Registration no: 03014564 **VAT No.:** GB 629 8240 18
Turnover: £10m - £20m **No.of Employees:** 11 - 20 **Product Groups:** 37, 67

Date of Accounts	Sep 07	Sep 06	Sep 05
Sales Turnover	N/A	4408	3661
Pre Tax Profit/Loss	N/A	217	190
Working Capital	284	159	89
Fixed Assets	113	248	174
Current Assets	1255	1239	1106
Current Liabilities	972	1080	1017
Total Share Capital	1	1	1
ROCE% (Return on Capital Employed)		53.5	72.2
ROT% (Return on Turnover)		4.9	5.2

Panavision Grips Ltd

The Metropolitan Centre Bristol Road, Greenford, UB6 8GD
Tel: 020-8839 7333 **Fax:** 020-8839 7360
E-mail: enquiries@panavision.co.uk
Website: http://www.panavision.co.uk
Bank(s): National Westminster
Directors: J. Allen (MD)
Ultimate Holding Company: MAFCO IN USA
Immediate Holding Company: PANAVISION EUROPE LTD
Registration no: 02532311 **VAT No.:** GB 581 8551 15
Turnover: £2m - £5m **No.of Employees:** 51 - 100 **Product Groups:** 83

Perancea Ltd

Unit 36 Silicon Business Centre 28 Wadsworth Road, Perivale, Greenford, UB6 7JZ
Tel: 020-8365 2520 **Fax:** 020-8566 7217
E-mail: sales@perancea.com
Website: http://www.perancea.com
Bank(s): Barclays
Directors: P. Hendrick (Dir)
Immediate Holding Company: PERANCEA LIMITED
Registration no: 02061057 **VAT No.:** GB 455 2449 41
Date established: 1986 **Turnover:** £500,000 - £1m
No.of Employees: 11 - 20 **Product Groups:** 26, 29, 30, 35, 36, 37, 38, 39, 45, 48

Date of Accounts	May 12	May 11	May 10
Sales Turnover	816	777	833
Pre Tax Profit/Loss	110	72	74
Working Capital	187	135	105
Fixed Assets	37	47	42
Current Assets	288	241	214
Current Liabilities	54	45	45

Petroplastics & Chemicals Ltd

Unit 18 Silicon Business Centre Wadsworth Road, Perivale, Greenford, UB6 7JZ
Tel: 020-8997 2300 **Fax:** 020-8997 4964
E-mail: sales@petroplast.co.uk
Website: http://www.petroplast.co.uk
Directors: A. Chandaria (Fin)
Immediate Holding Company: PETROPLASTICS & CHEMICALS LIMITED
Registration no: 01145604 **VAT No.:** GB 241 3324 06
Date established: 1973 **Turnover:** £5m - £10m **No.of Employees:** 1 - 10
Product Groups: 61

Date of Accounts	Dec 11	Dec 10	Dec 09
Working Capital	679	801	888
Fixed Assets	537	487	481
Current Assets	795	1m	1m

Polybags Ltd

Lyon Way, Greenford, UB6 0AQ
Tel: 020-8575 8200 **Fax:** 020-8578 2247
E-mail: sales@polybags.co.uk
Website: http://www.polybags.co.uk
Bank(s): Barclays
Directors: G. Davies (Dir), J. Lomax (MD), S. Arbuthnott (Pers)
Managers: D. Perry (Chief Mgr)
Registration no: 00698834 **VAT No.:** GB 226 5049 73
Date established: 1961 **Turnover:** £5m - £10m
No.of Employees: 51 - 100 **Product Groups:** 30

Date of Accounts	Nov 09	Nov 08	Nov 07
Sales Turnover	8m	8m	7m
Pre Tax Profit/Loss	231	111	13
Working Capital	2m	2m	2m
Fixed Assets	1m	1m	1m
Current Assets	3m	3m	3m
Current Liabilities	524	653	490

Poselco Lighting Ltd

Unit 1 The Metropolitan Park Bristol Road, Greenford, UB6 8UW
Tel: 020-8813 0101 **Fax:** 020-8813 0099
E-mail: c.tribe@poselco.co.uk
Website: http://www.poselco.co.uk
Bank(s): HSBC
Directors: L. Eldridge (Fin), C. Tribe (MD)
Immediate Holding Company: POSELCO LIGHTING LIMITED
Registration no: 04021643 **VAT No.:** GB 629 0847 20
Date established: 2000 **No.of Employees:** 11 - 20 **Product Groups:** 37

Date of Accounts	Sep 11	Sep 10	Sep 09
Working Capital	9	7	23
Fixed Assets	19	24	30
Current Assets	197	302	272

Prestolite Electric

12-16 Bristol Road, Greenford, UB6 8UP
Tel: 020-8231 1000 **Fax:** 020-8575 9575
E-mail: bhounslow@prestolite.com
Website: http://www.prestoliteelectric.com
Bank(s): National Westminster Bank Plc
Directors: B. Hounslow (MD), B. Banford (Sales)
Managers: S. Biret (Mktg Serv Mgr), M. Fowler, J. Franks, L. Furby (Personnel)
Ultimate Holding Company: ATLANTIC EQUITY PARTNERS INTERNATIONAL II LP (USA)
Immediate Holding Company: PRESTOLITE ELECTRIC LIMITED
Registration no: 01189048 **Date established:** 1974
Turnover: £20m - £50m **No.of Employees:** 101 - 250
Product Groups: 37, 39

Date of Accounts	Dec 10	Dec 09	Dec 08
Sales Turnover	22m	19m	21m
Pre Tax Profit/Loss	-280	-1m	-853
Working Capital	2m	3m	355
Fixed Assets	13m	13m	14m
Current Assets	10m	9m	12m
Current Liabilities	2m	1m	2m

Signet Branded Tags & Seals

3 Aintree Road Perivale, Greenford, UB6 7LA
Tel: 08449-007300 **Fax:** 0844-900 7301
E-mail: sales@signetseals.com
Website: http://www.signetseals.com
Directors: I. Lyon (MD)
Turnover: Up to £250,000 **No.of Employees:** 1 - 10 **Product Groups:** 30, 36, 42, 49

Snopake Ltd

28 Perivale Park Horsenden Lane South, Perivale, Greenford, UB6 7RJ
Tel: 020-8991 1666 **Fax:** 020-8998 2000
E-mail: uksales@snopake.com
Website: http://www.snopake.com
Bank(s): Barclays
Directors: E. Popper (Co Sec), S. Fawke (Sales), T. Zaman (Fin)
Managers: A. McDermott
Ultimate Holding Company: THE SNOPAKE GROUP LIMITED
Immediate Holding Company: SNOPAKE LIMITED
Registration no: 02143057 **VAT No.:** GB 224 9911 54
Date established: 1987 **Turnover:** £5m - £10m **No.of Employees:** 21 - 50
Product Groups: 64

Date of Accounts	Dec 11	Dec 10	Dec 09
Sales Turnover	8m	9m	9m
Pre Tax Profit/Loss	1m	161	153
Working Capital	683	562	363
Fixed Assets	452	492	568
Current Assets	3m	5m	3m
Current Liabilities	2m	2m	2m

Tetley GB Ltd

325-327 Oldfield Lane North, Greenford, UB6 0AZ
Tel: 020-8338 4000 **Fax:** 020-8338 4532
E-mail: peter.unsworth@tetley.com
Website: http://www.tetley.co.uk
Directors: L. Allen (Dir), P. Unsworth (Dir), R. Price (Dir)
Ultimate Holding Company: Tata Tea (GB) Ltd
Immediate Holding Company: TATA GLOBAL BEVERAGES GB LIMITED
Registration no: 03019950 **Date established:** 1995
Turnover: £125m - £250m **No.of Employees:** 251 - 500
Product Groups: 20

Ultra Electronics Ltd

417 Bridport Road, Greenford, UB6 8UE
Tel: 020-8813 4567 **Fax:** 020-8813 4568
E-mail: information@ultra-electronics.com
Website: http://www.ultra-electronics.com
Bank(s): Royal Bank of Scotland
Directors: K. Thomson (Pers), P. Dean (Fin)
Managers: C. Trumper (Sales Admin)
Ultimate Holding Company: ULTRA ELECTRONICS HOLDINGS PLC
Immediate Holding Company: ULTRA ELECTRONICS LIMITED
Registration no: 02830644 **Date established:** 1993
Turnover: £250m - £500m **No.of Employees:** 11 - 20
Product Groups: 37, 39

Date of Accounts	Dec 11	Dec 10	Dec 09
Sales Turnover	379m	313m	286m
Pre Tax Profit/Loss	59m	19m	24m
Working Capital	37m	-27m	15m
Fixed Assets	70m	76m	73m
Current Assets	208m	135m	160m
Current Liabilities	79m	68m	58m

Varidex Overseas Ltd

14 Elton Avenue, Greenford, UB6 0PW
Tel: 020-8864 0701 **Fax:** 020-8426 8233
E-mail: varidex@greenford.demon.co.uk
Directors: K. Vibian (MD)
Immediate Holding Company: VARIDEX (OVERSEAS) LIMITED
Registration no: 02128923 **VAT No.:** GB 480 6133 57
Date established: 1987 **Turnover:** Up to £250,000
No.of Employees: 1 - 10 **Product Groups:** 61

Date of Accounts	Oct 11	Oct 09	Oct 08
Working Capital	32	27	26
Current Assets	54	48	40

Viking Precision Engineers Ltd

1 Wadsworth Road Perivale, Greenford, UB6 7JD
Tel: 020-8998 4353 **Fax:** 020-8997 0182
E-mail: sales@viking-precision.co.uk
Website: http://www.viking-precision.co.uk
Bank(s): National Westminster Bank Plc
Directors: S. Turner (Dir)
Immediate Holding Company: VIKING PRECISION ENGINEERS LIMITED
Registration no: 00848448 **Date established:** 1965 **Turnover:** £1m - £2m
No.of Employees: 11 - 20 **Product Groups:** 48

Date of Accounts	May 12	May 11	May 10
Working Capital	97	200	-54
Fixed Assets	1m	1m	1m
Current Assets	525	740	633

W G Wigginton

1-4 Rockware Avenue, Greenford, UB6 0AA
Tel: 020-8575 5942 **Fax:** 020-8575 5110
E-mail: info@wigginton.co.uk
Website: http://www.wigginton.co.uk
Directors: P. Keyland (MD)
Ultimate Holding Company: W.G. WIGGINTON GROUP LIMITED
Immediate Holding Company: W.G. WIGGINTON PROPERTIES LIMITED
Registration no: 04199748 **VAT No.:** 227 1324 91 **Date established:** 2001
Turnover: Up to £250,000 **No.of Employees:** 1 - 10 **Product Groups:** 52

Date of Accounts	Mar 11	Mar 10	Mar 09
Working Capital	100	356	60
Fixed Assets	718	730	741
Current Assets	129	423	90

Wiles Group

Walmgate Road Perivale, Greenford, UB6 7LN
Tel: 020-7587700 **Fax:** 020-8758 7722
E-mail: peter.duncan@wilesgreenworld.co.uk
Website: http://www.wiles.co.uk
Bank(s): HSBC Bank plc
Directors: I. Ezzard (Sales), J. Barber (Purch), P. Duncan (MD)
Managers: A. Gibson (I.T. Exec)
Immediate Holding Company: WILES GROUP LIMITED
Registration no: 00380423 **Date established:** 1943
No.of Employees: 21 - 50 **Product Groups:** 32, 44, 49, 64, 80

Date of Accounts	Jun 11	Jun 10	Jun 09
Working Capital	501	249	141
Fixed Assets	878	946	986
Current Assets	2m	1m	1m

Hampton

Atrium UK Ltd

Bourne House 10 Windmill Road, Hampton Hill, Hampton, TW12 1RH
Tel: 020-8979 8241 **Fax:** 020-8941 7595
E-mail: simon.davis@atriiumgroup.com
Website: http://www.atriiumgroup.com
Directors: S. Davis (MD)
Managers: K. Smith (Admin Off)
Immediate Holding Company: ATRIUM UK LIMITED
Registration no: 06907847 **Date established:** 2009
Turnover: £500,000 - £1m **No.of Employees:** 11 - 20 **Product Groups:** 44

Cartridge World Ltd

30 High Street Hampton Hill, Hampton, TW12 1PD
Tel: 020-8973 3919 **Fax:** 020-8973 3918
Website: http://www.cartridgeworld.org
Registration no: 04124067 **Date established:** 2000 **Turnover:** £5m - £10m
No.of Employees: 1 - 10 **Product Groups:** 28, 30, 44, 64

D & D Fine Limits Ltd

2 St Clare Business Park Holly Road, Hampton, TW12 1PZ
Tel: 020-8979 3545 **Fax:** 020-8979 3545
E-mail: info@sheetmetalproduction.com
Website: http://www.sheetmetalproduction.com
Directors: D. Costar (MD)
Immediate Holding Company: D AND D (FINE LIMITS S.M.W.) LIMITED
Registration no: 01170261 **Date established:** 1974
Turnover: £500,000 - £1m **No.of Employees:** 1 - 10 **Product Groups:** 48

Date of Accounts	May 11	May 10	May 09
Working Capital	-62	-54	57
Fixed Assets	221	238	67
Current Assets	191	134	271

Hallite Seals International Ltd

130 Oldfield Road, Hampton, TW12 2HT
Tel: 020-8941 2244 **Fax:** 020-8783 1669
E-mail: seals@hallite.com
Website: http://www.hallite.com
Bank(s): HSBC Bank plc
Directors: S. Davies (MD), V. Markanday (Fin)
Managers: L. Hutton (Personnel), J. Parker (Tech Serv Mgr), L. Gibbs (Cust Serv Mgr), N. Taylor (Mktg Serv Mgr), R. Shield (Purch Mgr)
Ultimate Holding Company: FENNER PLC
Immediate Holding Company: HALLITE SEALS INTERNATIONAL LIMITED
Registration no: 00310223 **Date established:** 1936 **Turnover:** £1m - £2m
No.of Employees: 101 - 250 **Product Groups:** 29, 30, 33, 36

Date of Accounts	Aug 11	Aug 10	Aug 09
Sales Turnover	22m	16m	14m
Pre Tax Profit/Loss	3m	2m	658
Working Capital	1m	1m	-454
Fixed Assets	6m	5m	6m
Current Assets	10m	8m	4m
Current Liabilities	5m	4m	3m

Hilton Banks Ltd

74 Oldfield Road, Hampton, TW12 2HR
Tel: 020-8979 8284 **Fax:** 020-8979 8294
E-mail: hiltonbanks@btinternet.com
Directors: R. Banks (MD)
Immediate Holding Company: HILTON BANKS LTD
Registration no: 01967612 **Date established:** 1985 **Turnover:** £2m - £5m
No.of Employees: 11 - 20 **Product Groups:** 66

Date of Accounts	Dec 11	Dec 10	Dec 09
Sales Turnover	3m	3m	2m
Pre Tax Profit/Loss	70	29	11
Working Capital	579	570	592
Fixed Assets	105	104	122
Current Assets	1m	1m	1m
Current Liabilities	175	162	166

I F M

Oldfield Road, Hampton, TW12 2HP
Tel: 020-8213 0000 **Fax:** 020-8213 0001
E-mail: enquiry_gb@ifm-electronic.com
Website: http://www.ifm.com
Directors: F. Kabir (MD), S. Evans (Sales), S. Kabir (Fin)
Managers: M. Langen, J. Allen (Ops Mgr), L. Venthan (Personnel)
Ultimate Holding Company: BAY GROUP LTD (BERMUDA)
Immediate Holding Company: BONDS MILL ESTATE LIMITED
Registration no: 01551804 **Date established:** 1985
Turnover: £10m - £20m **No.of Employees:** 51 - 100 **Product Groups:** 23, 28, 29, 30, 31, 35, 36, 37, 38, 39, 40, 41, 42, 43, 44, 45, 46, 52, 67, 68, 84, 85

Date of Accounts	Mar 11	Mar 10	Mar 09
Sales Turnover	N/A	N/A	753
Pre Tax Profit/Loss	N/A	N/A	-2m
Working Capital	2m	2m	2m
Fixed Assets	5m	4m	4m
Current Assets	3m	3m	3m
Current Liabilities	N/A	N/A	121

Orga

A1 Kingsway Business Park Oldfield Road, Hampton, TW12 2HD
Tel: 0870-6092452 **Fax:** 020-8941 6683
E-mail: t.howes@orga.nl
Website: http://www.orga.nl

see next page

Orga *- Cont'd*

Directors: R. Beest (Ch)
Managers: T. Howes (Sales Admin), C. Dieterich (Sales Prom), T. Howes (Mgr)
Ultimate Holding Company: Orga International BV (Netherlands)
Immediate Holding Company: Orga Holdings B.V.
Registration no: 01982586 **VAT No.:** GB 442 9216 54
Turnover: £2m - £5m **No.of Employees:** 1 - 10 **Product Groups:** 37, 40

Paint Research Association

14 Castle Mews High Street, Hampton, TW12 2NP
Tel: 020-8487 0800 **Fax:** 020-8487 0801
E-mail: coatings@pra.org.uk
Website: http://www.pra-world.com
Bank(s): National Westminster Bank Plc
Directors: J. Bourne (MD)
Managers: C. Webb (I.T. Exec)
Registration no: 00216387 **VAT No.:** GB 222 7875 54
Turnover: £2m - £5m **No.of Employees:** 21 - 50 **Product Groups:** 28, 81, 84, 85, 86

Petrolvalves GB Ltd

18-22 Church Street, Hampton, TW12 2EG
Tel: 020-8783 2350 **Fax:** 020-8783 2355
E-mail: sales@petrolvalves.co.uk
Website: http://www.petrolvalves.co.uk
Directors: G. Martines (MD)
Ultimate Holding Company: FIDUCIARIA BANKNORD SPA (ITALY)
Immediate Holding Company: PETROLVALVES (G.B.) LIMITED
Registration no: 01851035 **Date established:** 1984
Turnover: £75m - £125m **No.of Employees:** 11 - 20 **Product Groups:** 36, 37, 38

Date of Accounts	Dec 11	Dec 10	Dec 09
Sales Turnover	77m	98m	88m
Pre Tax Profit/Loss	5m	6m	2m
Working Capital	6m	8m	7m
Fixed Assets	1m	1m	123
Current Assets	74m	37m	64m
Current Liabilities	41m	14m	32m

Prospect Swetenhams

Field House 72 Oldfield Road, Hampton, TW12 2HQ
Tel: 020-8481 8730 **Fax:** 020-8783 1940
E-mail: sales@prospectshop.co.uk
Website: http://www.prospectswetenhams.com
Bank(s): Nordea
Directors: L. Williams (Co Sec), T. Daghed (Dir), A. Holmes (MD), A. Laidlaw (Dir)
Ultimate Holding Company: RATOS AB (SWEDEN)
Immediate Holding Company: CHECKIT (UK) LIMITED
Registration no: 02588823 **VAT No.:** GB 720 5355 62
Date established: 1994 **Turnover:** £2m - £5m **No.of Employees:** 21 - 50
Product Groups: 80, 81

Date of Accounts	Dec 08	Dec 07	Dec 06
Sales Turnover	3m	4m	7m
Pre Tax Profit/Loss	-363	36	-303
Working Capital	28	268	266
Fixed Assets	34	161	131
Current Assets	699	868	2m
Current Liabilities	671	599	1m

Rees Associates

9-11 High Street, Hampton, TW12 2SA
Tel: 020-8941 4225 **Fax:** 020-8979 4692
Website: http://www.reesfoodservice.com
Directors: A. Rees (Prop)
Immediate Holding Company: REED CONSTRUCTION LIMITED
Registration no: 06373359 **Date established:** 2007
No.of Employees: 1 - 10 **Product Groups:** 20, 40, 41

Sportsmans Choice

58 Park Road Hampton Hill, Hampton, TW12 1HP
Tel: 020-8941 8844 **Fax:** 020-8941 8900
E-mail: gpsportsman@aol.com
Directors: G. Posvey (MD)
Registration no: 1555599 **Date established:** 2007 **Turnover:** £2m - £5m
No.of Employees: 1 - 10 **Product Groups:** 89

World Transport Agency Ltd

Thameside House Kingsway Business Park Oldfield Road, Hampton, TW12 2HD
Tel: 020-8783 2100 **Fax:** 020-8783 2114
E-mail: kelvin.edmundson@wta.co.uk
Website: http://www.wta.co.uk
Bank(s): HSBC
Directors: K. Edmundson (Dir)
Managers: R. Wegner (Comptroller)
Ultimate Holding Company: SOMMER HOLDINGS LTD
Immediate Holding Company: WORLD TRANSPORT AGENCY LIMITED
Registration no: 00129014 **VAT No.:** 235 9766 24 **Date established:** 2013
Turnover: £50m - £75m **No.of Employees:** 21 - 50 **Product Groups:** 72, 76

Date of Accounts	Jun 11	Jun 10	Jun 09
Sales Turnover	58m	48m	48m
Pre Tax Profit/Loss	2m	1m	2m
Working Capital	3m	3m	3m
Fixed Assets	146	227	311
Current Assets	10m	10m	9m
Current Liabilities	872	477	754

Harrow

A & C Ltd

83 Headstone Road, Harrow, HA1 1PQ
Tel: 020-8427 5168 **Fax:** 020-8861 2469
E-mail: info@powerpod.co.uk
Website: http://www.powerpod.co.uk
Directors: F. Fletcher (MD)
Immediate Holding Company: ASA ACCOUNTANCY SERVICES LTD
Registration no: 06692643 **Date established:** 2008
Turnover: £250,000 - £500,000 **No.of Employees:** 1 - 10
Product Groups: 38, 46

Date of Accounts	Sep 11	Sep 10	Sep 09
Working Capital	-3	-3	-1
Fixed Assets	2	2	1
Current Assets	17	21	4

Alka International UK Ltd

756 Kenton Lane, Harrow, HA3 6AD
Tel: 020-8954 5447 **Fax:** 020-8420 6504
E-mail: sales@alkain.co.uk
Website: http://www.alkain.co.uk
Directors: P. Mehta (MD), J. Mehta (Fin)
Immediate Holding Company: ALKA INTERNATIONAL (U.K.) LIMITED
Registration no: 03169955 **Date established:** 1996
No.of Employees: 1 - 10 **Product Groups:** 33, 37

Date of Accounts	Oct 11	Oct 10	Oct 09
Working Capital	20	26	2
Fixed Assets	14	4	4
Current Assets	550	527	513

Allstar Services Ltd

25 Forward Drive, Harrow, HA3 8NT
Tel: 020-8861 6440 **Fax:** 020-8861 3134
E-mail: sales@allstar.co.uk
Website: http://www.allstar.co.uk
Bank(s): HSBC Bank plc
Directors: M. Warner (Fin)
Immediate Holding Company: ALLSTAR SERVICES LIMITED
Registration no: 01809515 **Date established:** 1984 **Turnover:** £1m - £2m
No.of Employees: 11 - 20 **Product Groups:** 28, 38, 44

Date of Accounts	Dec 11	Dec 10	Dec 09
Working Capital	193	215	182
Fixed Assets	208	233	211
Current Assets	340	400	448

Apt Controls Ltd

The Power House Chantry Place, Harrow, HA3 6NY
Tel: 020-8421 2411 **Fax:** 020-8421 3951
E-mail: sales@aptcontrols.co.uk
Website: http://www.aptcontrols-group.co.uk
Bank(s): Lloyds TSB Bank plc
Directors: N. Young (Sales), R. Adams (Dir)
Managers: S. Story (Tech Serv Mgr), A. Higgins (Mktg Serv Mgr)
Immediate Holding Company: APT CONTROLS LIMITED
Registration no: 02754698 **VAT No.:** GB 541 4255 67
Date established: 1992 **Turnover:** £20m - £50m
No.of Employees: 51 - 100 **Product Groups:** 35, 36, 39, 40, 49, 52, 83

Date of Accounts	Dec 11	Dec 10	Dec 09
Sales Turnover	25m	26m	27m
Pre Tax Profit/Loss	2m	3m	3m
Working Capital	6m	6m	5m
Fixed Assets	9m	9m	9m
Current Assets	14m	15m	15m
Current Liabilities	4m	4m	5m

Arcode UK Ltd

41 Ebrington Road Kenton, Harrow, HA3 0LS
Tel: 020-8907 1309 **Fax:** 020-8907 9132
E-mail: sales@arcode.co.uk
Website: http://www.arcode.co.uk
Directors: B. Hamilton Smith (Fin), M. Popa (MD), R. Popa (Sales)
Registration no: 03678047 **Date established:** 1998 **Turnover:** £5m - £10m
No.of Employees: 1 - 10 **Product Groups:** 29, 31, 41, 45, 49, 66, 67

Date of Accounts	Mar 10	Mar 09	Mar 08
Working Capital	1m	1m	921
Fixed Assets	21	12	17
Current Assets	2m	2m	2m

Bedhire.co.uk

213 Harrow View, Harrow, HA1 4SS
Tel: 020-8933 8888 **Fax:** 020-8427 6275
E-mail: sales@hotelbedhire.co.uk
Website: http://www.bedhire.co.uk
No.of Employees: 1 - 10 **Product Groups:** 26, 40

Russell Black Ltd

399a Kenton Lane, Harrow, HA3 8RZ
Tel: 020-8907 7757 **Fax:** 020-8909 1055
E-mail: sales@russellblack.co.uk
Website: http://www.russellblack.co.uk
Directors: A. Levy (MD)
Immediate Holding Company: RUSSELL BLACK LIMITED
Registration no: 00923135 **VAT No.:** 229 7184 39 **Date established:** 1967
Turnover: £1m - £2m **No.of Employees:** 1 - 10 **Product Groups:** 30, 38, 42, 52

Date of Accounts	Dec 11	Dec 10	Dec 09
Working Capital	446	442	430
Fixed Assets	193	215	224
Current Assets	584	711	701

Brandone Machine Tool Ltd

48 Station Road, Harrow, HA1 2SQ
Tel: 020-8863 7141 **Fax:** 020-8861 3658
E-mail: brandone@btconnect.com
Website: http://www.brandonemarking.co.uk
Directors: M. Blum (MD), R. Blum (Dir), M. Blum (Co Sec)
Immediate Holding Company: BRANDONE MACHINE TOOL LIMITED
Registration no: 00574777 **VAT No.:** GB 225 0904 90
Date established: 1956 **Turnover:** £500,000 - £1m
No.of Employees: 1 - 10 **Product Groups:** 36, 37, 46

Date of Accounts	Mar 11	Mar 10	Mar 09
Working Capital	-13	-39	45
Fixed Assets	2	3	4
Current Assets	40	21	45

Capital Hair & Beauty

Unit 5 Hawthorn Centre Elmgrove Road, Harrow, HA1 2RF
Tel: 020-8863 7371 **Fax:** 020-8861 2405
E-mail: harrow@capitalhb.co.uk
Website: http://www.capitalhairandbeauty.co.uk
Managers: D. Shattock (Develop Mgr)
Immediate Holding Company: CAPITAL (HAIR AND BEAUTY) LIMITED
Registration no: 00530201 **Date established:** 1954
No.of Employees: 1 - 10 **Product Groups:** 32, 40, 63, 67

Date of Accounts	Dec 11	Dec 10	Dec 09
Sales Turnover	32m	28m	24m
Pre Tax Profit/Loss	4m	749	2m
Working Capital	7m	4m	3m
Fixed Assets	3m	3m	2m
Current Assets	13m	8m	7m
Current Liabilities	4m	3m	3m

Chesham Chemicals Ltd

Cunningham House Westfield Lane, Harrow, HA3 9ED
Tel: 020-8907 7779 **Fax:** 020-8927 0686
E-mail: sales@cheshamchemicals.co.uk
Website: http://www.chesham-ingredients.com
Bank(s): Barclays
Directors: A. Eastwood (Sales), D. Mitchell (MD)
Managers: V. Halai (Quality Control)
Ultimate Holding Company: S & D GROUP LIMITED
Immediate Holding Company: CHESHAM CHEMICALS LIMITED
Registration no: 03036047 **Date established:** 1995 **Turnover:** £5m - £10m
No.of Employees: 11 - 20 **Product Groups:** 31, 32, 66

Date of Accounts	May 07	Nov 10	Nov 09
Working Capital	-812	-426	-874
Fixed Assets	3m	2m	2m
Current Assets	585	900	280

Computaform (t/a Computaform)

4 Merivale Road, Harrow, HA1 4BH
Tel: 020-8423 5005 **Fax:** 020-8422 7216
E-mail: mail@computaform.com
Website: http://www.abbeymg.net
Directors: P. Sineane (MD), P. Simeone (MD)
Managers: L. Merry (Sales Prom Mgr)
Immediate Holding Company: COMPUTER FAST FORMS LIMITED
Registration no: 01582079 **VAT No.:** GB 346 6421 52
Date established: 1981 **Turnover:** £2m - £5m **No.of Employees:** 1 - 10
Product Groups: 27, 44

Continental Ethicals Ltd

8 Churchill Court 58 Station Road, North Harrow, Harrow, HA2 7SA
Tel: 020-8424 2426 **Fax:** 020-8424 0469
E-mail: kansangra@tiscali.co.uk
Directors: S. Kansagra (Co Sec)
Immediate Holding Company: CONTINENTAL ETHICALS LIMITED
Registration no: 02257132 **Date established:** 1988
Turnover: £250,000 - £500,000 **No.of Employees:** 1 - 10
Product Groups: 61

Date of Accounts	Mar 12	Mar 11	Mar 10
Pre Tax Profit/Loss	-4	-22	-4
Working Capital	2	6	29
Current Assets	3	10	32
Current Liabilities	1	3	4

Cosmetochem UK Ltd

Cunningham House Westfield Lane, Harrow, HA3 9ED
Tel: 020-8907 7779 **Fax:** 020-8927 0686
E-mail: cosmetochem@cheshamchemicals.co.uk
Website: http://www.cheshamchemicals.co.uk
Directors: A. Eastwood (Dir)
Ultimate Holding Company: COSMETOCHEM INTERNATIONAL LTD (SWITZERLAND)
Immediate Holding Company: COSMETOCHEM (U.K.) LIMITED
Registration no: 01647880 **Date established:** 1982
Turnover: £500,000 - £1m **No.of Employees:** 1 - 10 **Product Groups:** 02, 32, 66

Date of Accounts	May 11	May 10	May 09
Sales Turnover	581	527	562
Pre Tax Profit/Loss	93	40	39
Working Capital	167	144	192
Current Assets	234	232	218
Current Liabilities	24	20	16

Crescent Hotel

58-62 Welldon Crescent, Harrow, HA1 1QR
Tel: 020-8863 5491 **Fax:** 020-8427 5965
E-mail: info@crescenthotels.co.uk
Website: http://www.crescenthotels.co.uk
Managers: S. Jivraj (Mgr)
Turnover: Up to £250,000 **No.of Employees:** 1 - 10 **Product Groups:** 69

Dawnlight Ltd

56 Lindsay Drive, Harrow, HA3 0TD
Tel: 020-8204 3828 **Fax:** 020-8204 3420
Website: http://www.btinternet.com
Directors: N. Shah (Fin)
Immediate Holding Company: DAWNLIGHT LIMITED
Registration no: 02101955 **Date established:** 1987
Turnover: £500,000 - £1m **No.of Employees:** 1 - 10 **Product Groups:** 30, 31

Date of Accounts	Apr 12	Apr 11	Apr 10
Working Capital	116	93	86
Fixed Assets	1	N/A	N/A
Current Assets	182	163	155

Deepak Sareen Associates Ltd

Ambassador House 2 Cavendish Avenue, Harrow, HA1 3RW
Tel: 020-8423 8855 **Fax:** 020-8423 8992
E-mail: sales@dsareen.com
Website: http://www.dsareen.com
Managers: T. Lawes (Mgr)
Immediate Holding Company: DEEPAK SAREEN ASSOCIATES LIMITED
Registration no: 01777098 **Date established:** 1983
Turnover: Up to £250,000 **No.of Employees:** 1 - 10 **Product Groups:** 44

Date of Accounts	Mar 11	Mar 10	Mar 09
Working Capital	-101	-101	-102
Fixed Assets	47	47	48
Current Assets	283	291	244

Disc Wizards Ltd

59a Palmerston Road, Harrow, HA3 7RR
Tel: 020-8861 5765 **Fax:** 020-8931 0001
E-mail: info@discwizards.com
Website: http://www.discwizards.com
Directors: V. Mehta (MD)
Immediate Holding Company: DISC WIZARDS LIMITED
Registration no: 06984224 **Date established:** 2009
Turnover: Up to £250,000 **No.of Employees:** 1 - 10 **Product Groups:** 37, 44, 89

Date of Accounts	Aug 11	Aug 10
Sales Turnover	181	72
Pre Tax Profit/Loss	N/A	49
Working Capital	120	2
Current Assets	196	87
Current Liabilities	56	17

Eternal Nursery
54 Somervell Road, Harrow, HA2 8TT
Tel: 07984-006616
E-mail: etnurseries@hotmail.co.uk
Website: http://www.eternalnursery.com
Directors: R. Bryan (Dir)
Date established: 2006 **Turnover:** Up to £250,000
No.of Employees: 1 - 10 **Product Groups:** 61

Europan
31-33 College Road, Harrow, HA1 1EJ
Tel: 020-8861 0242 **Fax:** 020-8861 6502
E-mail: sales@europanltd.com
Website: http://www.europanltd.com
Directors: J. Shah (Dir)
Immediate Holding Company: EUROPAN METAL CENTRE LIMITED
Registration no: 04457859 **Date established:** 2002
No.of Employees: 1 - 10 **Product Groups:** 34, 46, 66

Date of Accounts	Mar 11	Mar 10	Mar 09
Working Capital	31	28	29
Fixed Assets	2	2	1
Current Assets	153	215	172

G & T Resources Europe
Brent House 214 Kenton Road, Harrow, HA3 8BT
Tel: 020-8909 3099 **Fax:** 020-8909 2622
E-mail: europe.office@gtrw.com
Website: http://www.gtrw.com
Directors: S. Negandhi (Fin)
Immediate Holding Company: G & T RESOURCES (EUROPE) LIMITED
Registration no: 04203443 **Date established:** 2001 **Turnover:** £1m - £2m
No.of Employees: 1 - 10 **Product Groups:** 84

Date of Accounts	Mar 11	Mar 10	Mar 09
Working Capital	274	221	186
Fixed Assets	2	3	4
Current Assets	777	912	2m

Global Oil & Gas Procurement Services Gogps Ltd
63 Shaftesbury Avenue Kenton, Harrow, HA3 0RB
Tel: 020-8907 3554 **Fax:** 020-8907 3557
E-mail: info@gogps-ltd.co.uk
Website: http://www.gogps-ltd.co.uk
Directors: N. Kootiarab (Fin), M. Kootiarab (MD)
Immediate Holding Company: GLOBAL OIL & GAS PROCUREMENT SERVICES (GOGPS) LIMITED
Registration no: 05119927 **Date established:** 2004
No.of Employees: 1 - 10 **Product Groups:** 30, 33, 36, 37, 39, 45, 61, 67, 83

Date of Accounts	Oct 08	Oct 07	Apr 11
Working Capital	42	118	-66
Fixed Assets	6	1	N/A
Current Assets	107	189	3

Graydon UK Ltd
Hygeia Building 66-68 College Road, Harrow, HA1 1BE
Tel: 020-8515 1400 **Fax:** 020-8515 1499
E-mail: mail@graydon.co.uk
Website: http://www.graydon.co.uk
Bank(s): National Westminster Bank Plc
Directors: G. Skaljak (Mkt Research)
Managers: M. Samuel (Tech Serv Mgr)
Immediate Holding Company: GRAYDON UK LIMITED
Registration no: 00363849 **Date established:** 1940
Turnover: £10m - £20m **No.of Employees:** 51 - 100 **Product Groups:** 81, 82

Date of Accounts	Dec 11	Dec 10	Dec 09
Sales Turnover	10m	10m	9m
Pre Tax Profit/Loss	1m	637	572
Working Capital	861	1m	1m
Fixed Assets	1m	1m	1m
Current Assets	3m	3m	3m
Current Liabilities	1m	2m	1m

H B M UK Ltd
1 Churchill Court 58 Station Road, North Harrow, Harrow, HA2 7SA
Tel: 020-8515 6100 **Fax:** 020-8515 6149
E-mail: info@uk.hbm.com
Website: http://www.hbm.com
Directors: M. Johnson (MD)
Ultimate Holding Company: SPECTRIS PLC
Immediate Holding Company: HBM UNITED KINGDOM LIMITED
Registration no: 01589921 **Date established:** 1981
No.of Employees: 1 - 10 **Product Groups:** 26, 38, 44, 67, 85

Date of Accounts	Dec 11	Dec 10	Dec 09
Sales Turnover	8m	8m	8m
Pre Tax Profit/Loss	2m	1m	2m
Working Capital	2m	749	-2m
Fixed Assets	2m	2m	2m
Current Assets	4m	3m	4m
Current Liabilities	2m	2m	1m

J B Fashions
24 Railway App, Harrow, HA3 5AA
Tel: 020-8357 1170 **Fax:** 020-8861 1075
Website: http://www.jbfashions.co.uk
Directors: J. Lever (Dir)
No.of Employees: 11 - 20 **Product Groups:** 38, 65

John Strand M K Ltd
12-22 Herga Road, Harrow, HA3 5AS
Tel: 020-8930 6006 **Fax:** 020-8930 6008
E-mail: enquiry@johnstrand-mk.co.uk
Website: http://www.johnstrand-mk.co.uk
Directors: C. Reeves (MD)
Immediate Holding Company: JOHN STRAND MK LTD
Registration no: 03391732 **VAT No.:** GB 701 6037 79
Date established: 1997 **Turnover:** £500,000 - £1m
No.of Employees: 1 - 10 **Product Groups:** 63

Date of Accounts	Dec 07	Jun 11	Jun 10
Working Capital	178	197	165
Fixed Assets	2	1	2
Current Assets	536	416	345

Levolux Ltd
1 Forward Drive, Harrow, HA3 8NT
Tel: 020-8863 9111 **Fax:** 020-8863 8760
E-mail: info@leolux.com
Website: http://www.levolux.com
Directors: I. Rose (Co Sec), G. Simoni (MD), D. Gordon (Sales & Mktg)
Managers: C. Phippen (Tech Serv Mgr), N. Marriott (Personnel), R. Lumley (Chief Buyer), G. Gribbin (Admin Off)
Ultimate Holding Company: THE ALUMASC GROUP PLC
Immediate Holding Company: LEVOLUX LIMITED
Registration no: 01834176 **VAT No.:** GB 225 8418 59
Date established: 1984 **Turnover:** £10m - £20m
No.of Employees: 51 - 100 **Product Groups:** 35, 36

Date of Accounts	Jun 11	Jun 10	Jun 09
Sales Turnover	10m	8m	12m
Pre Tax Profit/Loss	835	1m	3m
Working Capital	5m	5m	5m
Fixed Assets	79	94	77
Current Assets	8m	6m	7m
Current Liabilities	706	636	747

Mba Developments
170 Woodcock Hill, Harrow, HA3 0NY
Tel: 020-8908 0595 **Fax:** 020-8537 2400
Website: http://www.go.to/taxigolftrolley
Directors: M. May (MD)
Immediate Holding Company: COINTREE LTD.
Registration no: 01831327 **Date established:** 1984
Turnover: Up to £250,000 **No.of Employees:** 1 - 10 **Product Groups:** 35, 49, 67

Middlesex Machines
4 B College Hill Road, Harrow, HA3 7HH
Tel: 020-8954 6664 **Fax:** 020-8933 6644
E-mail: middlesexmachines@hotmail.com
Directors: A. Di-Meo (Prop)
No.of Employees: 1 - 10 **Product Groups:** 37, 38, 46

Monarch
148 Greenford Road, Harrow, HA1 3QP
Tel: 020-8864 7446 **Fax:** 020-8864 6626
Directors: R. Patel (Prop)
Date established: 1985 **No.of Employees:** 1 - 10 **Product Groups:** 37, 38, 42

Parliament International Ltd
Servantes House 8 Headstone Road, Harrow, HA1 1PD
Tel: 020-8861 3505 **Fax:** 020-8861 2025
E-mail: sales@parliament-group.co.uk
Website: http://www.parliament-group.co.uk
Directors: R. Leaver (MD)
Ultimate Holding Company: THE PARLIAMENT GROUP LTD.
Immediate Holding Company: PARLIAMENT STEEL (TUBES) LIMITED
Registration no: 01917139 **Date established:** 1985 **Turnover:** £1m - £2m
No.of Employees: 1 - 10 **Product Groups:** 34, 35, 36, 84

Date of Accounts	Jul 11	Jul 10	Jul 09
Working Capital	-12	-27	-27
Current Assets	4	13	22

Philton Fire & Security Ltd
61 Lower Road, Harrow, HA2 0DE
Tel: 020-8864 7534 **Fax:** 020-8864 8631
E-mail: info@philton.com
Website: http://www.philton.com
Directors: M. Sloane (Dir)
Immediate Holding Company: PHILTON FIRE & SECURITY LIMITED
Registration no: 00882141 **Date established:** 1966
No.of Employees: 1 - 10 **Product Groups:** 38, 42

Date of Accounts	Apr 11	Apr 10	Apr 09
Working Capital	18	73	158
Fixed Assets	24	50	81
Current Assets	371	419	609

Pindoria Associates
213d Station Road, Harrow, HA1 2TP
Tel: 020-8863 8400 **Fax:** 020-8863 7018
E-mail: admin@pindoriaassociates.co.uk
Directors: K. Pindoria (Prop)
No.of Employees: 1 - 10 **Product Groups:** 35

Pinkerton Consulting & Investigations
Ferrari House 102 College Road, Harrow, HA1 1ES
Tel: 020-8424 8884 **Fax:** 020-8424 9744
E-mail: richard.rice@ci-pinkerton.com
Website: http://www.securitas.com/pinkerton
Directors: D. Ross Wood (Sales), J. Ross Wood (Fin), R. Rice (Dir)
Ultimate Holding Company: SECURITAS AB, SWEDEN
Immediate Holding Company: PINKERTON'S INC, USA
Registration no: 03308266 **VAT No.:** GB 749 1564 05
Date established: 1997 **Turnover:** £50m - £75m **No.of Employees:** 1 - 10
Product Groups: 54, 80, 81, 82, 84

Reed
310 Station Road, Harrow, HA1 2DX
Tel: 020-8427 0799 **Fax:** 020-8861 3117
E-mail: rapharrow@reed.co.uk
Website: http://www.reed.co.uk
Managers: R. Blood (Comm)
Immediate Holding Company: REED PERSONNEL SERVICES
Registration no: 00973629 **Turnover:** £125m - £250m
No.of Employees: 1 - 10 **Product Groups:** 80

Reed Employment Ltd
310 Station Road, Harrow, HA1 2DX
Tel: 020-8863 0244 **Fax:** 020-8861 2119
E-mail: pauline.chidgey@reed.co.uk
Website: http://www.reed.co.uk
Managers: P. Chidgey (District Mgr), J. Reed (District Mgr), R. Blood (Mgr), K. Nickleson (Mktg Serv Mgr)
Immediate Holding Company: REED EMPLOYMENT LIMITED
Registration no: 00669854 **Date established:** 1960
Turnover: £500m - £1,000m **No.of Employees:** 1 - 10
Product Groups: 80

S & D Chemicals Ltd
Cunningham House 19-21 Westfield Lane, Harrow, HA3 9ED
Tel: 020-8907 8822 **Fax:** 020-8927 0619
E-mail: peter.straus@sdcldn.com
Website: http://www.sd-chemicals.com
Bank(s): Barclays Bank
Directors: P. Straus (Dir)
Ultimate Holding Company: S & D GROUP LIMITED
Immediate Holding Company: S & D CHEMICALS LIMITED
Registration no: 03030758 **VAT No.:** GB 736 3456 23
Date established: 1995 **Turnover:** £20m - £50m
No.of Employees: 51 - 100 **Product Groups:** 66

Date of Accounts	Dec 11	May 10	May 09
Sales Turnover	27m	38m	38m
Pre Tax Profit/Loss	-295	120	73
Working Capital	-2m	4m	4m
Fixed Assets	55	111	82
Current Assets	17m	24m	21m
Current Liabilities	3m	813	974

Salix Mechanical Services
46 -48 Byron Road Wealdstone, Harrow, HA3 7SS
Tel: 020-8427 4088 **Fax:** 020-8427 4099
E-mail: enquiries@salixmechanical.com
Website: http://www.salixmechanical.com
Bank(s): Barclays
Directors: N. Purdon (Snr Part)
Immediate Holding Company: SALIX MECHANICAL SERVICES LLP
Registration no: OC363802 **Date established:** 2011
Turnover: £500,000 - £1m **No.of Employees:** 11 - 20 **Product Groups:** 52

Softwarebrands Ltd
35-37 Lowlands Road, Harrow, HA1 3AW
Tel: 020-8385 7443 **Fax:** 0871-5941236
E-mail: sales@softwarebrands.co.uk
Website: http://www.softwarebrands.co.uk/contact_us.php
Directors: A. Patel (MD)
Registration no: 05624662 **Date established:** 2005
Turnover: £250,000 - £500,000 **No.of Employees:** 1 - 10
Product Groups: 28, 44

Date of Accounts	Nov 09	Nov 08	Nov 07
Working Capital	-5	992	991
Current Assets	18	1m	1m

Gerald Summers Ltd
Chantry Works Chantry Road Headstone Lane, Harrow, HA3 6NU
Tel: 020-8428 6388 **Fax:** 020-8428 7119
E-mail: sales@gerald-summers.co.uk
Website: http://www.gerald-summers.co.uk
Directors: D. Summers (Dir), W. Summers (MD)
Managers: P. McDonald (Sales Prom Mgr)
Ultimate Holding Company: 05500626
Immediate Holding Company: GERALD SUMMERS LIMITED
Registration no: 00379562 **Date established:** 1943 **Turnover:** £1m - £2m
No.of Employees: 1 - 10 **Product Groups:** 30, 34, 35, 39

Date of Accounts	Mar 08	Mar 07	Mar 06
Sales Turnover	1120	1105	1333
Pre Tax Profit/Loss	-25	-14	-27
Working Capital	887	911	924
Fixed Assets	15	15	16
Current Assets	953	1007	1010
Current Liabilities	66	96	86
ROCE% (Return on Capital Employed)	-2.7	-1.5	-2.9
ROT% (Return on Turnover)	-2.2	-1.2	-2.0

Swiftpro Ltd
Congress House 14 Lyon Road, Harrow, HA1 2EN
Tel: 020-8861 6321 **Fax:** 08708-731271
E-mail: sales@swiftpro.com
Website: http://www.swiftpro.com
Managers: M. Ross (Develop Mgr)
Immediate Holding Company: SWIFTPRO LTD
Registration no: 03288010 **Date established:** 1996
Turnover: Up to £250,000 **No.of Employees:** 1 - 10 **Product Groups:** 44

Date of Accounts	Dec 11	Dec 10	Dec 09
Working Capital	-23	-25	-27
Fixed Assets	23	25	29
Current Assets	30	38	45

Trademark Consultants
54 Hillbury Avenue, Harrow, HA3 8EW
Tel: 020-8907 6066 **Fax:** 020-8421 4050
E-mail: info@trademarkco.co.uk
Website: http://www.trademarkco.co.uk
Directors: G. Myrants (MD)
Immediate Holding Company: TRADE MARK CONSULTANTS LIMITED
Registration no: 04665955 **VAT No.:** GB 224 5850 68
Date established: 2003 **No.of Employees:** 1 - 10 **Product Groups:** 80

Date of Accounts	Mar 11	Mar 10	Mar 09
Working Capital	-27	-2	34
Fixed Assets	4	7	14
Current Assets	102	112	167

Transcontinental Exports UK Ltd
Prestige House, Harrow, HA2 7HE
Tel: 020-8866 8880 **Fax:** 020-8429 4141
E-mail: shebs@tcexports.co.uk
Website: http://www.safari-surf.com
Directors: S. Merali (Dir)
Immediate Holding Company: TRANSCONTINENTAL EXPORTS (UK) LIMITED
Registration no: 02091839 **VAT No.:** GB 442 2399 55
Date established: 1987 **Turnover:** £1m - £2m **No.of Employees:** 1 - 10
Product Groups: 33, 37, 45, 61

Date of Accounts	Nov 11	Nov 10	Nov 09
Sales Turnover	N/A	1m	1m
Pre Tax Profit/Loss	N/A	21	24
Working Capital	57	48	46
Fixed Assets	1	1	2
Current Assets	399	473	351
Current Liabilities	N/A	282	120

Wahoo Enterprises Limited
9 Laburnum Court, Harrow, HA1 4YD
Tel: 0844-7403213
E-mail: info@wahooenterprises.biz
Website: http://www.wahooenterprises.biz
Directors: G. Wong (MD)
Registration no: 7229105 **Date established:** 2010 **Turnover:**
No.of Employees: 1 - 10 **Product Groups:** 26, 44, 61

Zanara Export & Import Agents
First Base Forward Drive, Harrow, HA3 8LT
Tel: 020-8909 3936 **Fax:** 020-8909 9917
E-mail: info@zanara.com
Website: http://www.zanara.com
Directors: S. Khan (MD)
Managers: A. Rai (Admin Off)
Date established: 2003 **No.of Employees:** 1 - 10 **Product Groups:** 37

Hayes

Ark Electrical Services Ltd
448 Uxbridge Road, Hayes, UB4 0SD
Tel: 020-8589 0777 **Fax:** 020-8589 0776
E-mail: micky@arkelectrical.co.uk
Directors: M. Koyce (MD)
Immediate Holding Company: ARK ELECTRICAL SERVICES LIMITED
Registration no: 05303633 **Date established:** 2004
No.of Employees: 1 - 10 **Product Groups:** 36, 40

Date of Accounts	Dec 11	Dec 10	Dec 09
Working Capital	368	319	242
Fixed Assets	851	867	871
Current Assets	743	652	581

Attewell Ltd
7ab Millington Road, Hayes, UB3 4AZ
Tel: 020-8571 0055 **Fax:** 020-8571 7139
E-mail: sales@attewell.co.uk
Website: http://www.attewell.co.uk
Bank(s): National Westminster Bank Plc
Directors: M. Dolan (Co Sec), J. Stowell (Fin)
Managers: N. Eary (Sales Prom Mgr), T. Crowter, M. Giggle (Chief Mgr), W. Chadwick (Tech Serv Mgr)
Ultimate Holding Company: HAMPSON INDUSTRIES P.L.C.
Immediate Holding Company: ATTEWELL LIMITED
Registration no: 00743760 **VAT No.:** GB 222 2396 91
Date established: 1962 **Turnover:** £10m - £20m
No.of Employees: 51 - 100 **Product Groups:** 30, 35, 48

Date of Accounts	Mar 11	Mar 10	Mar 09
Sales Turnover	15m	11m	13m
Pre Tax Profit/Loss	2m	2m	2m
Working Capital	5m	4m	3m
Fixed Assets	2m	2m	2m
Current Assets	9m	7m	5m
Current Liabilities	621	403	452

Avis Rent A Car Ltd
Trident House Station Road, Hayes, UB3 4DJ
Tel: 0844-5810147 **Fax:** 020-8569 1436
E-mail: info@avis.co.uk
Website: http://www.avis.co.uk
Directors: S. Gent (MD), P. Stallman (Sales & Mktg), J. Nicholson (Co Sec)
Ultimate Holding Company: SA D'LETEREN NV (BELGIUM)
Immediate Holding Company: Avis Europe Overseas Ltd
Registration no: 00802486 **VAT No.:** GB 222 6271 91
Date established: 1964 **Turnover:** £75m - £125m
No.of Employees: 501 - 1000 **Product Groups:** 72

Date of Accounts	Dec 07
Sales Turnover	124910
Pre Tax Profit/Loss	-3330
Working Capital	-79650
Fixed Assets	138850
Current Assets	72680
Current Liabilities	152330
Total Share Capital	18650
ROCE% (Return on Capital Employed)	-5.6

Convotherm Ltd Enodis UK Food Service
Unit 4 Brook Industrial Estate, Bullsbrook Road, Hayes, UB4 0JZ.
Tel: 020-8848 2980 **Fax:** 020-8756 1720
E-mail: info@convotherm.co.uk
Website: http://www.catercomm.net
Directors: S. Loughton (MD)
Managers: D. Jonston ()
Ultimate Holding Company: Enodis P.L.C.
Immediate Holding Company: Enodis P.L.C.
Registration no: 01172730 **No.of Employees:** 21 - 50
Product Groups: 40, 67, 69

Coolspan
23 Botwell Lane, Hayes, UB3 2AB
Tel: 020-8842 3344 **Fax:** 020-8842 3311
Website: http://www.coolspan.com
Directors: P. Harding (MD)
Immediate Holding Company: GALAXY TRAVEL SOLUTIONS LTD
Registration no: 07024161 **Date established:** 2010
Turnover: £250,000 - £500,000 **No.of Employees:** 1 - 10
Product Groups: 39, 40

D H L Global Fowarding
Unit 1 Dawley Park Kestrel Way, Hayes, UB3 1HJ
Tel: 020-8754 5000
E-mail: roger.olsson@dhl.com
Website: http://www.dhl.com
Managers: R. Olsson
Turnover: Up to £250,000 **No.of Employees:** 251 - 500
Product Groups: 75, 76

D T L Broadcast Ltd
5 Johnsons Industrial Estate Silverdale Road, Hayes, UB3 3BA
Tel: 020-8813 5200 **Fax:** 020-8813 5022
E-mail: sales@dtl-broadcast.com
Website: http://www.dtl-broadcast.com
Directors: A. Sultan (MD)
Immediate Holding Company: DTL BROADCAST LIMITED
Registration no: 02518517 **VAT No.:** GB 538 1813 39
Date established: 1990 **Turnover:** £250,000 - £500,000
No.of Employees: 1 - 10 **Product Groups:** 37

Date of Accounts	Dec 11	Dec 10	Dec 09
Sales Turnover	N/A	N/A	251
Pre Tax Profit/Loss	N/A	N/A	1
Working Capital	-10	-9	13
Fixed Assets	N/A	N/A	3
Current Assets	44	66	96
Current Liabilities	N/A	N/A	16

Floringo Ltd
Enterprise House 133 Blyth Road, Hayes, UB3 1DD
Tel: 020-8587 3400 **Fax:** 020-8569 1445
E-mail: des@floringouk.co.uk
Website: http://www.floringo.net
Directors: D. Johnson (MD), P. Hayes (Fin)
Immediate Holding Company: FLORINGO LIMITED
Registration no: 01714824 **Date established:** 1983 **Turnover:** £1m - £2m
No.of Employees: 1 - 10 **Product Groups:** 23, 24, 66, 67, 83

Date of Accounts	Jun 11	Jun 10	Jun 09
Sales Turnover	1m	1m	1m
Pre Tax Profit/Loss	-34	-65	-81
Working Capital	238	271	335
Fixed Assets	5	6	7
Current Assets	675	795	741
Current Liabilities	59	128	90

Fujitsu Europe Ltd
Hayes Park Central Building Hayes End Road, Hayes, UB4 8FE
Tel: 020-8573 4444 **Fax:** 020-8573 2643
E-mail: lesley.fry@fel.fujitsu.com
Website: http://www.fel.fujitsu.com
Bank(s): Barclays; Bank of Tokyo; Dai-Ichi Kangyo
Directors: H. Nishikori (Dir), J. Douglass (Fin), K. Uemura (Co Sec), A. Harris (MD), I. Hirose (Ch), S. Yamada (Dir), N. Torb (I.T. Dir)
Managers: L. Simpson (Purch Mgr), L. Fry (Mgr), T. Crowe (Sales Prom Mgr), A. Batty (Sales & Mktg Mg), H. Barker (Personnel)
Ultimate Holding Company: FP002448
Immediate Holding Company: PFU IMAGING SOLUTIONS EUROPE LIMITED
Registration no: 01578652 **Date established:** 1981
Turnover: £75m - £125m **No.of Employees:** 51 - 100
Product Groups: 37, 44

G 4 S Security Service G4S
Princess House Nobel Drive, Harlington, Hayes, UB3 5EY
Tel: 020-8564 3400 **Fax:** 020-8759 7345
E-mail: martin.aggar@uk.g4s.com
Website: http://www.uksystems.g4s.com
Directors: M. Aggar (MD)
Managers: D. Taylor (Comm)
Immediate Holding Company: G4S PLC
Registration no: 01412704 **Date established:** 1979 **Turnover:** £5m - £10m
No.of Employees: 51 - 100 **Product Groups:** 37, 40, 67

Gainsborough Electronic Controls
Unit 6 Warnford Industrial Estate, Hayes, UB3 1BQ
Tel: 020-8756 1411 **Fax:** 020-8569 2426
E-mail: kim@gainsborough-controls.co.uk
Website: http://www.-gainsborough.co.uk
Directors: K. Hemson (Fin)
Immediate Holding Company: GAINSBOROUGH ELECTRONIC CONTROLS LIMITED
Registration no: 01701041 **VAT No.:** GB 223 5175 86
Date established: 1983 **Turnover:** £500,000 - £1m
No.of Employees: 1 - 10 **Product Groups:** 45

Date of Accounts	Mar 12	Mar 11	Mar 10
Working Capital	214	127	67
Fixed Assets	5	3	4
Current Assets	285	399	135

Garrards Transport Ltd
Unit 3 Elder Farm Business Complex West End Lane, Harlington, Hayes, UB3 5LY
Tel: 020-8897 9979 **Fax:** 020-8759 8982
E-mail: office@garrardstransport.co.uk
Website: http://www.garrardstransport.co.uk
Directors: L. Garrard (Ptnr)
Immediate Holding Company: GARRARDS TRANSPORT LIMITED
Registration no: 05466107 **Date established:** 2005
Turnover: Up to £250,000 **No.of Employees:** 1 - 10 **Product Groups:** 72, 77

Date of Accounts	May 11	May 10	May 09
Working Capital	7	20	-7
Fixed Assets	17	N/A	N/A
Current Assets	76	56	36

H G Timber Ltd
Three Ways Wharf Rigby Lane, Hayes, UB3 1ET
Tel: 020-8561 3311 **Fax:** 020-8569 2122
E-mail: sales@hgtimber.co.uk
Website: http://www.hgtimber.co.uk
Bank(s): Barclays, Uxbridge
Directors: L. Pyle (Sales), V. Theo (MD), V. Theodoulou (MD)
Managers: L. Pyle (Sales Prom Mgr)
Immediate Holding Company: H.G.TIMBER LIMITED
Registration no: 00397092 **VAT No.:** GB 223 1221 28
Date established: 1945 **Turnover:** £2m - £5m **No.of Employees:** 21 - 50
Product Groups: 25, 26, 45

Date of Accounts	Feb 08	Feb 07	Feb 06
Working Capital	1369	2139	1782
Fixed Assets	2268	1242	1245
Current Assets	2450	3202	2919
Current Liabilities	1082	1063	1138
Total Share Capital	10	10	10

H J Heinz Co. Ltd
South Building Hayes Park, Hayes, UB4 8AL
Tel: 020-8573 7757 **Fax:** 020-8848 2325
E-mail: enquiries@heinz.co.uk
Website: http://www.heinz.co.uk
Bank(s): National Westminster Bank Plc
Directors: R. Biedzinski (Co Sec), J. Leiper (Co Sec)
Ultimate Holding Company: H J HEINZ COMPANY (USA)
Immediate Holding Company: H.J.HEINZ COMPANY LIMITED
Registration no: 00147624 **VAT No.:** GB 222 7497 60
Date established: 2017 **Turnover:** £500m - £1,000m
No.of Employees: 251 - 500 **Product Groups:** 20

Date of Accounts	Apr 08	Apr 09	Apr 10
Sales Turnover	676m	734m	766m
Pre Tax Profit/Loss	154m	146m	140m
Working Capital	-200	75m	17m
Fixed Assets	244m	179m	290m
Current Assets	257m	335m	301m
Current Liabilities	51m	59m	43m

Hi-Brite Polishing
160 Clayton Road, Hayes, UB3 1AN
Tel: 020-8561 5102 **Fax:** 020-8561 6949

Managers: G. Youlton (Mgr)
No.of Employees: 1 - 10 **Product Groups:** 48

Kezvale Ltd
5 Johnsons Industrial Estate Silverdale Road, Hayes, UB3 3BA
Tel: 020-8569 2731 **Fax:** 020-8569 2790
E-mail: info@kezvale.co.uk
Website: http://www.kezvale.co.uk
Directors: A. Sultan (MD)
Immediate Holding Company: KEZVALE LIMITED
Registration no: 01312171 **Date established:** 1977
Turnover: £250,000 - £500,000 **No.of Employees:** 1 - 10
Product Groups: 37, 38

Date of Accounts	May 11	May 10	May 09
Working Capital	89	71	53
Fixed Assets	6	8	29
Current Assets	158	179	170

Kings Road Tyres & Repairs Ltd
Pump Lane, Hayes, UB3 3NB
Tel: 020-8561 4747 **Fax:** 020-8561 4012
E-mail: accounts@kingsroadtyres.co.uk
Website: http://www.kingsroadtyres.co.uk
Bank(s): National Westminster Bank Plc
Directors: J. Lederhose (Fin)
Managers: T. Bader, A. Bader (Mgr), M. Stacey (Sales Prom Mgr), S. Jadhav (Tech Serv Mgr)
Ultimate Holding Company: THE KRT GROUP LIMITED
Immediate Holding Company: KINGS ROAD TYRES AND REPAIRS LIMITED
Registration no: 00627338 **VAT No.:** GB 228 7030 72
Date established: 1959 **Turnover:** £20m - £50m
No.of Employees: 101 - 250 **Product Groups:** 68

Date of Accounts	Dec 11	Dec 10	Dec 09
Sales Turnover	55m	50m	45m
Pre Tax Profit/Loss	336	60	-131
Working Capital	-928	83	137
Fixed Assets	1m	2m	2m
Current Assets	26m	22m	20m
Current Liabilities	1m	7m	6m

Leemark Engineering
Rigby Works Rigby Lane, Hayes, UB3 1ET
Tel: 020-8573 4229 **Fax:** 020-8573 3526
E-mail: mark@leemarkeng.freeserve.co.uk
Website: http://www.leemarkeng.co.uk
Bank(s): Lloyds
Directors: M. Stockwell (MD)
Immediate Holding Company: LEEMARK ENGINEERING (HAYES) LIMITED
Registration no: 00891734 **Date established:** 1966 **Turnover:** £1m - £2m
No.of Employees: 11 - 20 **Product Groups:** 48

Date of Accounts	Mar 11	Mar 10	Mar 09
Working Capital	97	-34	50
Fixed Assets	161	198	128
Current Assets	322	293	424

P J Mcgowan
Gethceln House Dawley Road, Hayes, UB3 1EH
Tel: 020-8573 1571 **Fax:** 020-8561 3750
Directors: T. Lawry (Ptnr), C. Lawry (Jt MD), J. Lawry (Jt MD), T. Lawry (Jt MD)
Registration no: 00911036 **VAT No.:** GB 422 4234 91
Date established: 1967 **Turnover:** Up to £250,000
No.of Employees: 1 - 10 **Product Groups:** 48

Murray Productions Ltd
Silverdale Road, Hayes, UB3 3BN
Tel: 020-8573 4354 **Fax:** 020-8573 0152
E-mail: sales@murray-productions.co.uk
Website: http://www.murray-productions.co.uk
Directors: W. Bell (MD)
Ultimate Holding Company: TRANSWORLD PACKAGING BV (NETHERLANDS)
Immediate Holding Company: MURRAY (PRODUCTIONS) LIMITED
Registration no: 01040266 **VAT No.:** GB 223 1696 78
Date established: 1972 **Turnover:** £500,000 - £1m
No.of Employees: 1 - 10 **Product Groups:** 37, 48, 85

Date of Accounts	Mar 11	Mar 10	Mar 09
Working Capital	-159	-145	-126
Fixed Assets	191	201	214
Current Assets	184	167	172

Netcargo International UK Ltd
1 Nestles Avenue, Hayes, UB3 4UZ
Tel: 020-8606 3602 **Fax:** 08452-308083
E-mail: sales@netcargouk.com
Website: http://www.netcargo-intl.co.uk
Directors: A. Onas (Dir)
Managers: J. Lardner (Chief Mgr), D. Onas (Export Sales Mg)
Immediate Holding Company: AOA RECRUIT LIMITED
Registration no: 07161862 **Date established:** 2011 **Turnover:** £1m - £2m
No.of Employees: 1 - 10 **Product Groups:** 76

Nitram Vacuum Heat Treatments Company Ltd
Pump Lane Industrial Estate Silverdale Road, Hayes, UB3 3BN
Tel: 020-8573 5111
Website: http://www.nitramvacuum.co.uk
Directors: D. King (Dir)
Immediate Holding Company: NITRAM VACUUM HEAT TREATMENTS COMPANY LIMITED
Registration no: 00356843 **Date established:** 1939
No.of Employees: 1 - 10 **Product Groups:** 46, 48

Date of Accounts	Sep 11	Sep 10	Sep 09
Working Capital	80	80	80
Fixed Assets	43	46	50
Current Assets	179	175	186

Original Addidtions
Ventura House Bullsbrook Road, Hayes, UB4 0UJ
Tel: 020-8573 9907 **Fax:** 020-8573 6824
E-mail: reception@originaladditions.co.uk
Website: http://www.originaladditions.co.uk
Directors: A. Newall (Co Sec), R. Steele (Dir), A. Toms (Fin), H. Makin (Co Sec), S. Zussman (MD)
Managers: K. Barnes (Mgr)
Ultimate Holding Company: AMALDIS (2008) LIMITED
Immediate Holding Company: ORIGINAL ADDITIONS (BEAUTY PRODUCTS) LIMITED

Registration no: 05094961 **Date established:** 2004
Turnover: £20m - £50m **No.of Employees:** 51 - 100 **Product Groups:** 63

Date of Accounts	Dec 07	Mar 09	Apr 10
Sales Turnover	18m	24m	24m
Pre Tax Profit/Loss	2m	2m	2m
Working Capital	3m	4m	5m
Fixed Assets	7m	6m	6m
Current Assets	6m	7m	9m
Current Liabilities	847	1m	1m

Owen Coyle Anodising Ltd

144 Blyth Road, Hayes, UB3 1DE
Tel: 020-8573 0184 **Fax:** 020-8848 1170
E-mail: sales@owencoyle-anodising.co.uk
Website: http://www.owencoyle-anodising.co.uk
Bank(s): HSBC
Directors: G. Longman (Sales)
Managers: F. Amelia-davis (Tech Serv Mgr)
Ultimate Holding Company: OWEN COYLE MANAGEMENTS LIMITED
Immediate Holding Company: OWEN COYLE (ANODISING) LIMITED
Registration no: 01503884 **VAT No.:** GB 225 6336 71
Date established: 1980 **Turnover:** £2m - £5m **No.of Employees:** 11 - 20
Product Groups: 48

Date of Accounts	Jun 11	Jun 10	Jun 09
Working Capital	421	281	229
Fixed Assets	306	342	375
Current Assets	551	399	484

Paramount Powders UK Ltd

4 Viveash Close, Hayes, UB3 4RY
Tel: 020-8561 5588 **Fax:** 020-8561 5599
E-mail: paramountpowders@hotmail.com
Website: http://www.paramountpowders.co.uk
Directors: D. Badyal (MD), V. Bij (Fin)
Managers: C. Brown (Sales Prom Mgr), E. Kansra
Immediate Holding Company: PARAMOUNT POWDERS (U.K.) LIMITED
Registration no: 02047691 **Date established:** 1986
No.of Employees: 11 - 20 **Product Groups:** 46, 48

Date of Accounts	Mar 11	Mar 10	Mar 09
Working Capital	426	329	351
Fixed Assets	3m	3m	4m
Current Assets	1m	2m	1m

Parmley Graham Ltd

Unit 6 Pasadena Close Trading Estate, Hayes, UB3 3NQ
Tel: 020-8848 9667 **Fax:** 020-8848 1968
E-mail: london@parmley-graham.co.uk
Website: http://www.parmley-graham.co.uk
Managers: S. Woodhall (District Mgr)
Immediate Holding Company: PARMLEY GRAHAM LIMITED
Registration no: 00172842 **Date established:** 2021
Turnover: £20m - £50m **No.of Employees:** 1 - 10 **Product Groups:** 67

Date of Accounts	Dec 11	Dec 10	Dec 09
Sales Turnover	34m	33m	26m
Pre Tax Profit/Loss	1m	910	353
Working Capital	4m	4m	3m
Fixed Assets	1m	1m	1m
Current Assets	10m	9m	7m
Current Liabilities	1m	900	415

Phoenix Lift Trucks Ltd

Unit 16 Warnford Industrial Estate Clayton Road, Hayes, UB3 1BQ
Tel: 020-8569 0313 **Fax:** 020-8569 0304
E-mail: barry@phoenixlifttrucks.co.uk
Website: http://www.phoenixlifttrucks.co.uk
Directors: B. Jenkins (MD)
Immediate Holding Company: PHOENIX LIFT TRUCKS LIMITED
Registration no: 05528448 **Date established:** 2005
No.of Employees: 1 - 10 **Product Groups:** 35, 39, 45

Date of Accounts	Mar 11	Mar 10	Mar 09
Working Capital	48	20	-7
Fixed Assets	310	244	261
Current Assets	123	98	95

Preheat Engineering Ltd

Unit 1 Adler Industrial Estate Betam Rd, Hayes, UB3 1ST
Tel: 020-8848 1912 **Fax:** 020-8848 1913
E-mail: sales@preheat.co.uk
Website: http://www.preheat.co.uk
Bank(s): Lloyds TSB Bank plc
Directors: M. Harrison (Co Sec)
Managers: B. Taylor (Sales Prom Mgr), A. Smith (Purch Mgr)
Registration no: 01796507 **VAT No.:** GB 409 7030 64
Date established: 1954 **Turnover:** £2m - £5m **No.of Employees:** 21 - 50
Product Groups: 37, 38, 40

Date of Accounts	Jul 08	Jul 07	Jul 06
Working Capital	154	138	154
Fixed Assets	70	72	61
Current Assets	181	154	171
Current Liabilities	27	16	17

Ridat Co

Unit 4 Benlow Works Silverdale Road, Hayes, UB3 3BW
Tel: 08450-505625 **Fax:** 0208-455 5056
E-mail: info@ridat.com
Website: http://www.ridat.com
Directors: D. Sen Gupta (MD), D. Sengupta (Dir)
Managers: D. Senguppa (Mgr)
Immediate Holding Company: TECHNOBEAM LTD
Registration no: 04010149 **Date established:** 1970 **Turnover:** £1m - £2m
No.of Employees: 1 - 10 **Product Groups:** 30, 42, 48

Sascal Displays Ltd

Unit 16 Hayes Metro Centre Springfield Road, Hayes, UB4 0LE
Tel: 020-8573 0303 **Fax:** 020-8569 1515
E-mail: sales@sascaldisplays.co.uk
Website: http://www.sascaldisplays.co.uk
Bank(s): Lloyds TSB Bank plc
Directors: S. Caldecourt (MD), L. Caldecourt (Fin)
Managers: R. Kashap (Purch Mgr)
Immediate Holding Company: SASCAL DISPLAYS LIMITED
Registration no: 02904141 **VAT No.:** GB 676 1019 35
Date established: 1994 **Turnover:** £2m - £5m **No.of Employees:** 21 - 50
Product Groups: 37, 44, 67

Date of Accounts	Mar 12	Mar 11	Mar 10
Working Capital	766	837	431
Fixed Assets	60	98	148
Current Assets	1m	2m	996

Steelcraft Jig & Tool Co.

Unit 1 Benlow Works Silverdale Road, Hayes, UB3 3BW
Tel: 020-8569 2442 **Fax:** 020-8569 2442
Directors: R. Maunder (Prop)
Registration no: 05702042 **Date established:** 2006 **Turnover:** £1m - £2m
No.of Employees: 1 - 10 **Product Groups:** 36

T M D Technologies Ltd

Unit 3 Swallowfield Way, Hayes, UB3 1DQ
Tel: 020-8573 5555 **Fax:** 020-8569 1839
E-mail: graham.brown@tmd.co.uk
Website: http://www.tmd.co.uk
Bank(s): The Royal Bank of Scotland
Directors: J. Hill (Fin), G. Brown (Sales)
Managers: J. Hill (Personnel), B. Gibney (Purch Mgr)
Ultimate Holding Company: TMD HOLDINGS LIMITED
Immediate Holding Company: TMD TECHNOLOGIES LIMITED
Registration no: 00952502 **VAT No.:** GB 662 9537 04
Date established: 1969 **Turnover:** £20m - £50m
No.of Employees: 101 - 250 **Product Groups:** 37

Date of Accounts	Mar 12	Mar 11	Mar 10
Sales Turnover	30m	28m	27m
Pre Tax Profit/Loss	7m	6m	4m
Working Capital	13m	10m	10m
Fixed Assets	2m	1m	1m
Current Assets	19m	16m	17m
Current Liabilities	3m	4m	5m

Trueform Engineering Ltd

Unit 12 Trading Estate Pasadena Close, Hayes, UB3 3NQ
Tel: 020-8561 4959 **Fax:** 020-8848 8761
E-mail: maxine.bailey@trueform.co.uk
Website: http://www.trueform.co.uk
Bank(s): HSBC Bank plc
Directors: M. Bailey (Fin), J. Morley (Sales & Mktg), K. Clarke (Tech Serv)
Managers: H. Russell (Personnel), S. Newton (Purch Mgr)
Immediate Holding Company: TRUEFORM ENGINEERING LIMITED
Registration no: 01324196 **Date established:** 1977
Turnover: £20m - £50m **No.of Employees:** 101 - 250
Product Groups: 30, 37, 40, 45, 48

Date of Accounts	Dec 10	Dec 09	Sep 08
Sales Turnover	23m	36m	N/A
Pre Tax Profit/Loss	3m	3m	1m
Working Capital	1m	2m	2m
Fixed Assets	1m	1m	1m
Current Assets	8m	12m	9m
Current Liabilities	4m	6m	3m

United Biscuits UK Ltd

Hayes Park Hayes End Road, Hayes, UB4 8EE
Tel: 020-8234 5000 **Fax:** 020-8734 5555
E-mail: mark.oldham@unitedbiscuits.com
Website: http://www.unitedbiscuits.com
Bank(s): The Royal Bank of Scotland
Directors: M. Oldham (Fin)
Ultimate Holding Company: UNITED BISCUITS (EQUITY) LTD (CAYMAN ISLANDS)
Immediate Holding Company: UNITED BISCUITS GROUP (INVESTMENTS) LIMITED
Registration no: 03877866 **Date established:** 1999
Turnover: £500m - £1,000m **No.of Employees:** 251 - 500
Product Groups: 20

Date of Accounts	Dec 11	Jan 09	Jan 10
Pre Tax Profit/Loss	N/A	-2m	N/A
Working Capital	-18m	-18m	-18m
Current Liabilities	18m	18m	18m

Windsor Wholesale Ltd

7 Nestles Avenue, Hayes, UB3 4SA
Tel: 020-8848 6169 **Fax:** 020-8848 6185
Directors: P. Hussey (Dir)
Ultimate Holding Company: BUNZL PUBLIC LIMITED COMPANY
Immediate Holding Company: WOW CATERING SUPPLIES LIMITED
Registration no: 01847116 **Date established:** 1984
Turnover: Up to £250,000 **No.of Employees:** 21 - 50 **Product Groups:** 20, 40, 41

Date of Accounts	Dec 10	Dec 09	Dec 08
Sales Turnover	N/A	76	142
Pre Tax Profit/Loss	-0	-47	-254
Working Capital	382	381	415
Current Assets	683	976	893

Hounslow

A B Pharos Marine Ltd

Steyning Way, Hounslow, TW4 6DL
Tel: 020-8538 1100 **Fax:** 020-8577 4170
E-mail: sales@pharosmarine.com
Website: http://www.pharosmarine.com
Bank(s): Svenska Handel Sbanken
Directors: E. Asplund (Dir), K. Solomons (Fin), O. James (MD)
Managers: N. Kearley (Comptroller)
Immediate Holding Company: PHAROS MARINE LIMITED
Registration no: 06757705 **VAT No.:** 222 6454 83 **Date established:** 2008
Turnover: £2m - £5m **No.of Employees:** 11 - 20 **Product Groups:** 37, 39, 40

Date of Accounts	Dec 11	Dec 10	Dec 09
Sales Turnover	4m	4m	3m
Pre Tax Profit/Loss	212	54	1m
Working Capital	1m	1m	994
Fixed Assets	15	22	2
Current Assets	2m	2m	2m
Current Liabilities	422	718	249

Airclaims Group Ltd

2nd Floor Building 947 Cardinal Point Heathrow Airport, Hounslow, TW6N 6EL
Tel: 020-8897 1066 **Fax:** 020-8859 6294
E-mail: info@airclaims.com
Website: http://www.airclaims.com
Directors: M. Hunter (Dir), T. Skelton (Fin)
Managers: D. Horne (Mktg Serv Mgr), J. Mitchell (Personnel), S. Davies
Ultimate Holding Company: AIRCLAIMS HOLDINGS LIMITED
Immediate Holding Company: AIRCLAIMS GROUP (OVERSEAS) LIMITED
Registration no: 01748797 **Date established:** 1983
Turnover: Up to £250,000 **No.of Employees:** 21 - 50 **Product Groups:** 82

Date of Accounts	Dec 10	Dec 09	Dec 08
Pre Tax Profit/Loss	782	298	306
Working Capital	1m	494	186
Fixed Assets	831	831	831
Current Assets	1m	502	270
Current Liabilities	N/A	N/A	55

Alldoor Systems Ltd

203a Enfield Road London Heathrow Airport, Hounslow, TW6 2RN
Tel: 020-8759 6633 **Fax:** 020-8759 6699
E-mail: rick@alldoorsystems.co.uk
Website: http://www.alldoorsystems.co.uk
Directors: R. Lomax (MD)
Immediate Holding Company: ALLDOOR SYSTEMS LTD
Registration no: 05652574 **Date established:** 2005
No.of Employees: 1 - 10 **Product Groups:** 25, 30, 35, 36

Date of Accounts	Mar 11	Mar 10	Mar 09
Working Capital	N/A	8	13
Fixed Assets	4	5	7
Current Assets	3	21	23

Am Safe Ltd

Tamian Way, Hounslow, TW4 6BL
Tel: 020-8572 0321 **Fax:** 020-8572 2096
E-mail: sales@amsafe.co.uk
Website: http://www.am-safe.co.uk
Bank(s): National Westminster Bank Plc
Directors: M. Brooks (Co Sec)
Immediate Holding Company: AM-SAFE LIMITED
Registration no: 01769054 **VAT No.:** GB 409 8917 15
Date established: 1983 **Turnover:** £1m - £2m **No.of Employees:** 21 - 50
Product Groups: 39

Areo Quality Sales Ltd

8 Air Links Industrial Estate Spitfire Way, Hounslow, TW5 9NR
Tel: 020-8561 4211 **Fax:** 020-8848 1568
E-mail: kgreene@aeroqualitysales.com
Website: http://www.aeroquality.com
Directors: M. Tannian (Sales & Mktg), M. Wilson (MD), J. Downey (Dep Pres)
Managers: K. Ramsden (Ops Mgr), K. Green (Chief Mgr), K. Greene (Mgr), G. Drake (Mktg Serv Mgr), D. Smith (Chief Acct), K. Greene (Ops Mgr)
Ultimate Holding Company: JLL PARTNERS (USA)
Immediate Holding Company: SATAIR UK LIMITED
Registration no: 03141268 **VAT No.:** GB 666 2394 11
Date established: 1995 **Turnover:** £5m - £10m **No.of Employees:** 1 - 10
Product Groups: 37, 39

Date of Accounts	Dec 11	Dec 10	Dec 09
Sales Turnover	5m	11m	9m
Pre Tax Profit/Loss	299	1m	1m
Working Capital	4m	3m	2m
Fixed Assets	6	4	10
Current Assets	6m	6m	3m
Current Liabilities	270	246	167

Avenance

Central House Balfour Road, Hounslow, TW3 1HY
Tel: 08450-300 100 **Fax:** 020-8569 4069
E-mail: info@elior.co.uk
Website: http://www.avenance.co.uk
Directors: M. Audis (Grp Chief Exec), M. Auids (MD)
Managers: B. McLaughlan (Develop Mgr), I. Stiles (Mktg Serv Mgr)
Ultimate Holding Company: PERNOD RICARD SA (FRANCE)
Immediate Holding Company: HOUSE OF CAMPBELL LIMITED
Registration no: 01106729 **Date established:** 1984
Turnover: £250m - £500m **No.of Employees:** 1001 - 1500
Product Groups: 69

Blue Star Infotech UK Ltd

50 Salisbury Road Vista Centre, Hounslow, TW4 6JH
Tel: 020-8863 6888 **Fax:** 020-8538 2709
E-mail: sales@bsil.com
Website: http://www.bsil.com
Directors: S. Advani (Dir)
Ultimate Holding Company: BLUE STAR INFOTECH LTD (INDIA)
Immediate Holding Company: BLUE STAR INFOTECH (UK) LIMITED
Registration no: 03624322 **Date established:** 1998 **Turnover:** £2m - £5m
No.of Employees: 11 - 20 **Product Groups:** 44

Date of Accounts	Mar 12	Mar 11	Mar 10
Sales Turnover	3m	3m	3m
Pre Tax Profit/Loss	18	127	33
Working Capital	490	475	377
Fixed Assets	2	3	4
Current Assets	1m	1m	1m
Current Liabilities	180	221	297

R D Campbell & Co. Ltd

Unit 14 Mill Farm Business Park Millfield Road, Hounslow, TW4 5PY
Tel: 020-8898 6611 **Fax:** 020-8898 6622
E-mail: info@rdcampbell.co.uk
Website: http://www.rdcampbell.co.uk
Directors: R. Campbell (MD)
Immediate Holding Company: R.D. CAMPBELL & COMPANY LIMITED
Registration no: 00519682 **Date established:** 1953
Turnover: Up to £250,000 **No.of Employees:** 1 - 10 **Product Groups:** 20, 31, 32, 66

Date of Accounts	Mar 11	Mar 10	Mar 09
Working Capital	7	7	7
Fixed Assets	11	11	11
Current Assets	44	44	44
Current Liabilities	2	2	2

Chawlas Fashion Centre

269 Bath Road, Hounslow, TW3 3DA
Tel: 020-8572 2902 **Fax:** 020-8572 2902
E-mail: rs@chawlas.com
Website: http://www.chawlas.com
Directors: R. Chawla (MD), R. Chawlas (Prop)
Immediate Holding Company: CHAWLA'S LIMITED
Registration no: 04475562 **Date established:** 2002
Turnover: £250,000 - £500,000 **No.of Employees:** 1 - 10
Product Groups: 63

Date of Accounts	Jul 09	Jul 08	Jul 07
Sales Turnover	302	161	118
Pre Tax Profit/Loss	195	121	111
Working Capital	-38	-119	-66
Fixed Assets	7m	7m	5m
Current Assets	114	54	62
Current Liabilities	131	164	126

Clorox Car Care Ltd

Kershaw House Great West Road, Hounslow, TW5 0BU
Tel: 020-8538 5400 **Fax:** 020-8569 5611
Website: http://www.clorox.com
Bank(s): National Westminster Bank Plc
Directors: K. Stokes (Dir), E. Sterry (Co Sec)
Managers: C. Stokes (Chief Mgr), S. Walsh (Cust Serv Mgr)
Registration no: 02362589 **VAT No.:** GB 528 9421 23
Turnover: £20m - £50m **No.of Employees:** 21 - 50 **Product Groups:** 32

Date of Accounts	Jun 08	Jun 07	Jun 06
Sales Turnover	36208	33945	29716
Pre Tax Profit/Loss	4208	4206	3331
Working Capital	16485	13392	10270
Fixed Assets	7326	7641	7988
Current Assets	24434	20660	15715
Current Liabilities	7949	7268	5445
Total Share Capital	10255	10255	10255
ROCE% (Return on Capital Employed)	17.7	20.0	18.2
ROT% (Return on Turnover)	11.6	12.4	11.2

Dewhurst plc

Inverness Road, Hounslow, TW3 3LT
Tel: 020-8607 7300 **Fax:** 020-8572 5986
E-mail: fixtures@dewhurst.co.uk
Website: http://www.dewhurst.co.uk
Bank(s): National Westminster
Directors: R. Dewhurst (Jt MD), D. Dewhurst (Jt MD), C. Johnson (MD), D. Dewhurst (Sales)
Managers: D. Dennis (I.T. Exec), N. Maxwell (Mktg Serv Mgr), A. Butcher (Personnel), M. Green (I.T. Exec), T. Peck (Comm), C. Olds (Purch Mgr), A. Crissle (Buyer)
Immediate Holding Company: DEWHURST PLC
Registration no: 00160314 **Date established:** 2019
Turnover: £20m - £50m **No.of Employees:** 51 - 100 **Product Groups:** 37, 38, 40, 45

Date of Accounts	Sep 11	Sep 10	Sep 09
Sales Turnover	41m	37m	36m
Pre Tax Profit/Loss	4m	5m	4m
Working Capital	12m	16m	14m
Fixed Assets	19m	13m	12m
Current Assets	18m	21m	19m
Current Liabilities	3m	2m	3m

ERIKS UK (Heathrow Electrical Mechanical)

Building 200c Elgin Crescent, London Heathrow Airport, Hounslow, TW6 2RX
Tel: 020-8897 2611 **Fax:** 020-8759 5696
E-mail: michael.fensome@wyko.co.uk
Website: http://www.eriks.co.uk
Managers: M. Fensome (Ops Mgr)
Immediate Holding Company: WYKO HOLDINGS LTD
Registration no: 00917112 **Turnover:** £250m - £500m
No.of Employees: 1 - 10 **Product Groups:** 35, 66

Euro Seals & Gaskets

Suite 13 Vista Office Centre 50 Salisbury Road, Hounslow, TW4 6JQ
Tel: 020-8538 0342 **Fax:** 020-8538 0343
Website: http://www.eurosealsandgaskets.co.uk
Directors: G. Timms (Dir)
Immediate Holding Company: EURO SEALS & GASKETS LIMITED
Registration no: 04980535 **Date established:** 2003
No.of Employees: 1 - 10 **Product Groups:** 38, 42

Date of Accounts	Dec 10	Dec 09	Dec 08
Working Capital	3	11	19
Fixed Assets	27	23	30
Current Assets	34	28	44

Gear Cutting Company Ltd

Kirby Works 122-124 Heston Road, Hounslow, TW5 0QU
Tel: 020-8570 5521 **Fax:** 020-8577 5158
E-mail: a.pendry@gearcutting.com
Website: http://www.gearcutting.com
Directors: A. Pendry (MD)
Immediate Holding Company: THE GEAR CUTTING CO. LIMITED
Registration no: 01249330 **Date established:** 1976
No.of Employees: 1 - 10 **Product Groups:** 35, 45

Date of Accounts	Sep 11	Sep 10	Sep 09
Working Capital	-73	-72	-107
Fixed Assets	174	190	120
Current Assets	76	149	111

Heldite Ltd

1a Bristow Road, Hounslow, TW3 1UP
Tel: 020-8577 9157 **Fax:** 020-8577 9057
E-mail: sales@heldite.com
Website: http://www.heldite.com
Managers: B. Naldrett (Mgr)
Immediate Holding Company: HELDITE LIMITED
Registration no: 00179847 **VAT No.:** GB 222 8044 92
Date established: 2022 **Turnover:** Up to £250,000
No.of Employees: 1 - 10 **Product Groups:** 18, 30, 32, 33, 35, 36, 37, 39, 40, 42, 45, 51, 52, 54, 66, 74

Date of Accounts	Mar 11	Mar 10	Mar 09
Working Capital	-3	-0	7
Fixed Assets	162	163	165
Current Assets	53	56	58

Jackson Plating Ltd

Unit 1 Fairfield Works Fairfields Road, Hounslow, TW3 1UZ
Tel: 020-8577 3452 **Fax:** 020-8570 4599
E-mail: martin.jackson7@btopenworld.com
Website: http://www.jacksonplating.co.uk
Directors: M. Jackson (Ptnr)
Immediate Holding Company: JACKSON PLATING LTD
Registration no: 04950242 **Date established:** 2003
Turnover: £500,000 - £1m **No.of Employees:** 11 - 20
Product Groups: 48, 84

Date of Accounts	Dec 11	Dec 10	Dec 09
Working Capital	429	356	335
Fixed Assets	114	122	135
Current Assets	504	411	404

Leon Jaeggi & Sons Ltd

2 National Works Bath Road, Hounslow, TW4 7EA
Tel: 020-8814 0268 **Fax:** 020- 88140268
Directors: R. Abrihim (Dir)
Immediate Holding Company: LEON JAEGGI & SONS LIMITED
Registration no: 00437389 **Date established:** 1947
No.of Employees: 1 - 10 **Product Groups:** 20, 40, 41

Date of Accounts	Mar 11	Mar 10	Mar 09
Sales Turnover	8m	8m	8m
Pre Tax Profit/Loss	354	360	179
Working Capital	357	240	81
Fixed Assets	86	111	126
Current Assets	3m	3m	3m
Current Liabilities	2m	1m	1m

Keyline Brands

Central House 3 Lampton Road, Hounslow, TW3 1HY
Tel: 020-8538 1250 **Fax:** 020-8814 0185
E-mail: info@keyline-brands.co.uk
Website: http://www.keyline-brands.com
Bank(s): Barclays
Managers: B. Hammersley (Comptroller), J. Melia (Tech Serv Mgr), J. Edwards (Mktg Serv Mgr), S. Selwood
Ultimate Holding Company: GODREJ CONSUMER PRODUCTS LTD (INDIA)
Immediate Holding Company: KEYLINE BRANDS LIMITED
Registration no: 02530797 **Date established:** 1990
Turnover: £20m - £50m **No.of Employees:** 21 - 50 **Product Groups:** 32, 63

Date of Accounts	Mar 12	Mar 11	Mar 10
Sales Turnover	27m	24m	29m
Pre Tax Profit/Loss	2m	2m	4m
Working Capital	1m	3m	3m
Fixed Assets	5m	5m	2m
Current Assets	10m	11m	12m
Current Liabilities	2m	2m	2m

Logic Office Group Ltd

155-157 Staines Road, Hounslow, TW3 3JB
Tel: 020-8572 7474 **Fax:** 020-8538 5998
E-mail: info@logic-office.co.uk
Website: http://www.logic-office.co.uk
Bank(s): The Royal Bank of Scotland
Directors: A. Edward (Grp Chief Exec), P. Edward (Dir), R. Waxman (Fin)
Managers: G. Sapra (Mktg Serv Mgr), E. Quinn (I.T. Exec)
Immediate Holding Company: Black Arrow Group P.L.C.
Registration no: 06863140 **VAT No.:** GB 199 0483 23
Date established: 1992 **Turnover:** £20m - £50m
No.of Employees: 21 - 50 **Product Groups:** 26, 49

Date of Accounts	Mar 08	Mar 07	Mar 06
Sales Turnover	8765	9002	10941
Pre Tax Profit/Loss	-4701	-1576	-943
Working Capital	-3413	417	1284
Fixed Assets	408	1048	1382
Current Assets	2837	2877	3394
Current Liabilities	6249	2460	2110
Total Share Capital	262	262	262
ROCE% (Return on Capital Employed)	156.5	-107.6	-35.4
ROT% (Return on Turnover)	-53.6	-17.5	-8.6

Nevill Long Interior Building Products

Centre House Victory Way, Hounslow, TW5 9NS
Tel: 020-8573 9898 **Fax:** 020-8813 5127
E-mail: a.nicholls@nevilllong.co.uk
Website: http://www.nevilllong.co.uk
Managers: A. Nicholls (Mgr)
Ultimate Holding Company: WOLSELEY GROUP HOLDINGS LTD
Immediate Holding Company: WOLSELEY UK LTD
Registration no: 00184628 **No.of Employees:** 11 - 20
Product Groups: 27, 33, 35, 37, 66, 67

Nippon Express UK Ltd

Unit A1-A2 Parkway West Cranford Lane, Hounslow, TW5 9NE
Tel: 020-8737 4000 **Fax:** 020-8737 4029
E-mail: mjacob@neuk.co.uk
Website: http://www.nipponexpress.net
Directors: M. Jacob (Fin)
Ultimate Holding Company: NIPPON EXPRESS COMPANY LIMITED (INCORPOR
Immediate Holding Company: NIPPON EXPRESS (U.K.) LIMITED
Registration no: 01534130 **VAT No.:** GB 340 4489 64
Date established: 1980 **Turnover:** £75m - £125m
No.of Employees: 251 - 500 **Product Groups:** 76

Date of Accounts	Dec 11	Dec 10	Dec 09
Sales Turnover	94m	94m	73m
Pre Tax Profit/Loss	3m	245	-1m
Working Capital	15m	8m	7m
Fixed Assets	2m	9m	10m
Current Assets	27m	19m	18m
Current Liabilities	1m	2m	2m

Parvend Coffee Services

Unit 23 Phoenix Way, Hounslow, TW5 9NB
Tel: 020-8990 9779 **Fax:** 020-8759 9152
E-mail: info@paravend.co.uk
Website: http://www.paravend.co.uk
Directors: G. Parry (Prop)
Ultimate Holding Company: GLOBAL SHIPPING MASTER UK LIMITED
Date established: 2003 **No.of Employees:** 1 - 10 **Product Groups:** 40, 69

Preheat Engineering Ltd

17 Dene Avenue, Hounslow, TW3 3AQ
Tel: 020-8570 7036
E-mail: info@preheat.co.uk
Website: http://www.preheat.co.uk
Directors: M. Harrison (Fin)
Registration no: 01796507 **Date established:** 1984
No.of Employees: 1 - 10 **Product Groups:** 37, 40

Q R Tools Ltd

251-253 Hanworth Road, Hounslow, TW3 3UF
Tel: 020-8570 5135 **Fax:** 020-8572 6833
Directors: S. Patel (Fin), J. Patel (MD)
Ultimate Holding Company: ROBERT SAMUELL & CO. LIMITED
Immediate Holding Company: Q.R. TOOLS LIMITED
Registration no: 00885906 **Date established:** 1966
No.of Employees: 1 - 10 **Product Groups:** 37

Date of Accounts	Sep 11	Sep 10	Sep 09
Working Capital	5	5	5
Current Assets	5	5	5

R S Components Ltd (West London Trade Counter)

Unit 8 Fairway Close, Hounslow, TW4 6BU
Tel: 020-8572 4225 **Fax:** 020-8572 2966
E-mail: rsint@rs-components.com
Website: http://www.rswww.com
Directors: B. Lawson (Ch), I. Mason (Grp Chief Exec)
Ultimate Holding Company: ELECTROCOMPONENTS PUBLIC LIMITED COMPANY
Immediate Holding Company: RS COMPONENTS LIMITED
Registration no: 01002091 **VAT No.:** GB 243 1640 91
Date established: 1971 **Turnover:** £500m - £1,000m
No.of Employees: 1 - 10 **Product Groups:** 67

Date of Accounts	Mar 11	Mar 10	Mar 09
Sales Turnover	579m	486m	494m
Pre Tax Profit/Loss	41m	26m	55m
Working Capital	19m	-6m	10m
Fixed Assets	89m	77m	83m
Current Assets	229m	177m	145m
Current Liabilities	33m	32m	30m

Rapat Freight Ltd

Rapat House Amberley Way, Hounslow, TW4 6BH
Tel: 020-8570 7777 **Fax:** 020-8577 3376
E-mail: info@rapat.co.uk
Website: http://www.rapat.co.uk
Bank(s): National Westminster
Directors: J. Suresh (Dir), P. Patel (Fin), H. Patel (MD)
Managers: K. Kotadia (Purch Mgr), A. Nanda (Accounts), J. Putra (Sales Admin)
Ultimate Holding Company: UNEEK FORWARDING LIMITED
Immediate Holding Company: UNEEK FREIGHT SERVICES LIMITED
Registration no: 04292114 **Date established:** 1978 **Turnover:** £5m - £10m
No.of Employees: 11 - 20 **Product Groups:** 71, 75, 76

Redberry Software (U.K.) Ltd

150 Cardington Square, Hounslow, TW4 6AL
Tel: 020-8893 7630 **Fax:** 020-8572 6119
E-mail: sales@redberry.com
Website: http://www.redberry.com
Managers: G. Stow (Gen Contact)
Registration no: 02337320 **Date established:** 1989
No.of Employees: 1 - 10 **Product Groups:** 44

Redsky House

Park Lane Cranford, Hounslow, TW5 9RW
Tel: 020-8897 3071 **Fax:** 020-8897 5325
E-mail: enquiry@redskyit.com
Website: http://www.redskyit.com
Directors: G. Mathews (Grp Chief Exec), P. Edwards (MD), S. Walder (Co Sec)
Managers: C. Knighton (Mktg Serv Mgr), C. Kniveston (Mgr), D. Waite (Sales Prom Mgr)
Registration no: 02698759 **Turnover:** £5m - £10m
No.of Employees: 51 - 100 **Product Groups:** 37, 44

Date of Accounts	Jun 08	Jun 07	May 06
Sales Turnover	N/A	5802	6306
Pre Tax Profit/Loss	N/A	-2081	508
Working Capital	-796	-954	2451
Fixed Assets	N/A	222	663
Current Assets	N/A	1489	3522
Current Liabilities	796	2442	1071
Total Share Capital	1511	1511	1511
ROCE% (Return on Capital Employed)		284.4	16.3
ROT% (Return on Turnover)		-35.9	8.0

Reed Accountancy Personnel Ltd

352 Bath Road, Hounslow, TW4 7HW
Tel: 020-8572 6990 **Fax:** 020-8572 9177
Website: http://www.reed.co.uk
Directors: J. Reed (Grp Chief Exec)
Managers: V. Basra (Consultant), T. Peters (Mgr)
Registration no: 00973629 **Date established:** 2001
Turnover: £250m - £500m **No.of Employees:** 1 - 10 **Product Groups:** 80

Rogers Chapman plc

Grantley House 9 Park Lane, Hounslow, TW5 9RW
Tel: 020-8759 4141 **Fax:** 020-8759 5367
E-mail: enquiries@rogerschapman.co.uk
Website: http://www.rogerschapman.co.uk
Bank(s): Barclays
Directors: J. Izett (MD), M. Kenney (Dir), R. Webster (Co Sec)
Managers: D. Dulai (I.T. Exec), D. Allen (Mktg Serv Mgr)
Immediate Holding Company: ROGERS CHAPMAN UK LIMITED
Registration no: 02094942 **VAT No.:** GB 636 1515 51
Date established: 1987 **Turnover:** £500,000 - £1m
No.of Employees: 51 - 100 **Product Groups:** 80

Date of Accounts	Dec 07
Pre Tax Profit/Loss	1278
Working Capital	12830
Current Assets	13385
Current Liabilities	556
Total Share Capital	339
ROCE% (Return on Capital Employed)	10.0

Solution Interiors

Mill Farm Business Park Millfield Road, Hounslow, TW4 5PY
Tel: 020-8898 0999 **Fax:** 020-8898 0997
E-mail: info@solutioninteriors.com
Website: http://www.solutioninteriors.com
Directors: A. Windsor (MD), D. Barker (MD), J. Munden (MD)
Registration no: 05820501 **VAT No.:** GB 226 1417 90
Date established: 2006 **Turnover:** £1m - £2m **No.of Employees:** 1 - 10
Product Groups: 22, 24, 40

Date of Accounts	Mar 08	Mar 07	Mar 06
Working Capital	72	58	71
Fixed Assets	423	439	106
Current Assets	125	134	129
Current Liabilities	53	76	58
Total Share Capital	80	80	80

Systat Software UK Ltd

50 Salisbury Road Vista Office Centre, Hounslow, TW4 6JQ
Tel: 020-8538 0128
E-mail: noorian@systat.com
Website: http://www.sigmaplot.com
Directors: N. Riaz (Dir)
Immediate Holding Company: IGP RECRUITMENT LIMITED
Registration no: 07201164 **Date established:** 2012
No.of Employees: 1 - 10 **Product Groups:** 28, 39, 44, 81, 85, 87

Thames Welding Supplies

Unit 22 Air Links Industrial Estate Spitfire Way, Hounslow, TW5 9NW
Tel: 020-8573 5773 **Fax:** 020-8813 0606
E-mail: thameswelding@btconnect.com
Website: http://www.thameswelding.co.uk

Directors: D. Harvey (MD), J. Harvey (Fin)
Immediate Holding Company: THAMES WELDING SUPPLIES LIMITED
Registration no: 03002322 **Date established:** 1994
Turnover: £500,000 - £1m **No.of Employees:** 1 - 10 **Product Groups:** 46

Date of Accounts	Apr 11	Apr 10	Apr 09
Sales Turnover	500	526	763
Pre Tax Profit/Loss	-43	30	44
Working Capital	11	64	53
Fixed Assets	71	77	82
Current Assets	208	220	284
Current Liabilities	81	99	122

Tics International Ltd
Unit 7 Derby Road Industrial Estate, Hounslow, TW3 3UH
Tel: 020-8572 5599 **Fax:** 08707-874920
E-mail: sales@tics.co.uk
Website: http://www.tics.co.uk
Directors: V. Deolia (Co Sec), R. Deolia (Dir)
Immediate Holding Company: T I C S INTERNATIONAL LIMITED
Registration no: 03936696 **VAT No.:** GB 584 5031 38
Date established: 2000 **No.of Employees:** 1 - 10 **Product Groups:** 37, 38, 44, 49, 67, 85

Date of Accounts	Mar 11	Mar 10	Mar 09
Working Capital	138	188	245
Fixed Assets	11	12	14
Current Assets	236	237	288

TNT Freight Management
Unit 5 & 6 Park Way Trading Estate Cranford Lane, Hounslow, TW5 9QA
Tel: 020-8814 7000 **Fax:** 020-8814 7078
E-mail: sales@tntfreight.com
Website: http://www.geodiswilson.com
Directors: J. Simpson (Dir), M. Carr (Fin), S. Finch (MD)
Managers: L. Tebble (Sales & Mktg Mg), M. Brown (I.T. Exec), T. Gregory (Personnel)
Immediate Holding Company: Wilson Logistics Holdings AB
Registration no: 01628530 **VAT No.:** GB 636 1573 37
No.of Employees: 1 - 10 **Product Groups:** 72, 74, 76, 77

Worldwide Logistic Service Ltd
34 Sutton Lane, Hounslow, TW3 3BD
Tel: 020-8569 4228 **Fax:** 020-8572 0184
E-mail: mail@worldwidelogisticsservice.com
Website: http://www.worldwidelogisticsservice.com
Directors: S. Rowe (Dir)
Immediate Holding Company: WORLDWIDE LOGISTICS SERVICE LIMITED
Registration no: 02068302 **Date established:** 1986
Turnover: Up to £250,000 **No.of Employees:** 1 - 10 **Product Groups:** 75, 76

Date of Accounts	Apr 08	Apr 07	Apr 06
Sales Turnover	N/A	N/A	24
Pre Tax Profit/Loss	N/A	N/A	4
Working Capital	9	2	-6
Current Assets	32	17	8
Current Liabilities	N/A	N/A	6

Yara Dry Ice
Unit 11-12 Central Park Estate Staines Road, Hounslow, TW4 5DJ
Tel: 020-8538 5350 **Fax:** 020-8384 5455
E-mail: richard.walker@yara.com
Website: http://www.yara.com
Directors: M. Bell (Prop)
Managers: R. Walker (Mgr)
No.of Employees: 21 - 50 **Product Groups:** 31, 40, 47

Isleworth

Braun Consumer
Great West Road, Isleworth, TW7 5NP
Tel: 0800-7837010 **Fax:** 020-8847 6165
Website: http://www.braun.com
Bank(s): National Westminster Bank Plc
Directors: S. Taylor (Mkt Research)
Managers: R. Murphy (Chief Mgr)
Immediate Holding Company: Gillette UK Ltd
Registration no: 00254912 **VAT No.:** GB 224 0729 88
No.of Employees: 501 - 1000 **Product Groups:** 36, 40, 63, 67

Business Systems UK Ltd
462 London Road, Isleworth, TW7 4ED
Tel: 020-8326 8200 **Fax:** 020-8326 8400
E-mail: sales@businesssystemsuk.com
Website: http://www.businesssystemsuk.co.uk
Directors: R. Mill (Dir)
Immediate Holding Company: BUSINESS SYSTEMS (U.K.) LIMITED
Registration no: 02199582 **Date established:** 1987 **Turnover:** £5m - £10m
No.of Employees: 51 - 100 **Product Groups:** 37, 79

Date of Accounts	Dec 11	Dec 10	Dec 09
Sales Turnover	11m	9m	12m
Pre Tax Profit/Loss	44	515	643
Working Capital	3m	3m	2m
Fixed Assets	802	766	796
Current Assets	7m	8m	7m
Current Liabilities	4m	4m	4m

C P Cases Ltd
Unit 11 Worton Hall Industrial Estate Worton Road, Isleworth, TW7 6ER
Tel: 020-8568 1881 **Fax:** 020-8568 1141
E-mail: info@cpcases.com
Website: http://www.cpcases.com
Bank(s): Barclays
Directors: C. Gers (Sales)
Managers: G. Kew (Purch Mgr), F. Haggerty (Admin Off)
Ultimate Holding Company: CP GLOBAL LIMITED
Immediate Holding Company: C P CASES LIMITED
Registration no: 01111889 **VAT No.:** GB 228 2844 54
Date established: 1973 **Turnover:** £2m - £5m **No.of Employees:** 21 - 50
Product Groups: 22, 24, 25, 26, 27, 29, 30, 34, 35, 36, 37, 38, 39, 40, 42, 43, 44, 49, 66, 76

Date of Accounts	Dec 07	Dec 06	Dec 05
Working Capital	607	569	594
Fixed Assets	37	36	31
Current Assets	1084	1089	1049
Current Liabilities	477	519	455
Total Share Capital	64	64	64

Caddie Products Ltd
Swan Court Swan Street, Isleworth, TW7 6RJ
Tel: 020-8847 4321 **Fax:** 020-8568 2100
E-mail: enquiries@caddieproducts.co.uk
Website: http://www.caddie.com
Managers: M. Amer
Immediate Holding Company: CADDIE PRODUCTS LIMITED
Registration no: 01014616 **Date established:** 1971 **Turnover:** £1m - £2m
No.of Employees: 1 - 10 **Product Groups:** 26, 40, 45, 67

Date of Accounts	Dec 10	Dec 09	Dec 08
Sales Turnover	2m	910	2m
Pre Tax Profit/Loss	-6	-68	-380
Working Capital	-845	-840	-773
Fixed Assets	2	3	4
Current Assets	348	425	1m
Current Liabilities	1m	1m	2m

Customs Clearance Ltd
1 The Metro Centre St Johns Road, Isleworth, TW7 6NJ
Tel: 020-8231 0900
E-mail: info@customsclearanceuk.com
Website: http://www.customsclearanceuk.com
Managers: A. Nawaz (Ops Mgr)
Immediate Holding Company: CUSTOMS CLEARANCE LIMITED
Registration no: 03719890 **Date established:** 1999
No.of Employees: 11 - 20 **Product Groups:** 61, 72, 74, 75, 76, 77, 79, 80, 82

Date of Accounts	Feb 08	Feb 11	Feb 10
Working Capital	-15	39	-50
Fixed Assets	274	226	245
Current Assets	243	540	236

Danfo UK Ltd
2 Victory Business Centre Fleming Way, Isleworth, TW7 6DB
Tel: 020-8380 7370 **Fax:** 020-8380 7371
E-mail: info@danfo.co.uk
Website: http://www.danfo.co.uk
Directors: R. Longbottom (MD)
Ultimate Holding Company: DANFO HOLDING AB (SWEDEN)
Immediate Holding Company: DANFO (UK) LIMITED
Registration no: 02682551 **Date established:** 1992
No.of Employees: 1 - 10 **Product Groups:** 36, 49

Date of Accounts	Dec 11	Dec 10	Dec 09
Sales Turnover	N/A	N/A	3m
Pre Tax Profit/Loss	N/A	N/A	455
Working Capital	1m	-99	-11
Fixed Assets	71	1m	1m
Current Assets	2m	1m	1m
Current Liabilities	N/A	N/A	573

F D B Electrical Ltd
Unit 20 Worton Hall Industrial Estate Worton Road, Isleworth, TW7 6ER
Tel: 020-8568 4621 **Fax:** 020-8569 7899
E-mail: brianjury@fdb.uk.com
Website: http://www.fdb.uk.com
Bank(s): National Westminster Bank Plc
Directors: K. Wheeler (MD)
Ultimate Holding Company: FINDLAY DURHAM & BRODIE LIMITED
Immediate Holding Company: FDB ELECTRICAL LIMITED
Registration no: 01036604 **Date established:** 1971 **Turnover:** £1m - £2m
No.of Employees: 11 - 20 **Product Groups:** 37

Date of Accounts	Sep 11	Sep 10	Sep 09
Sales Turnover	1m	1m	884
Pre Tax Profit/Loss	92	59	9
Working Capital	168	69	14
Fixed Assets	22	29	25
Current Assets	566	450	416
Current Liabilities	36	27	16

Failsafe Power Supplies Ltd
292 Worton Road, Isleworth, TW7 6EL
Tel: 020-8568 8090 **Fax:** 020-8568 6070
E-mail: carole.lundie@anix.co.uk
Website: http://www.failsafepower.com
Bank(s): Barclays
Directors: P. Cadogan Rawlinson (Fin), G. Gillespie (MD)
Managers: J. Hoyland (Sales Prom Mgr), A. Smith (Chief Mgr)
Immediate Holding Company: FAILSAFE POWER SUPPLIES LIMITED
Registration no: 01989655 **VAT No.:** GB 413 6503 81
Date established: 1986 **Turnover:** £500,000 - £1m
No.of Employees: 21 - 50 **Product Groups:** 37

Date of Accounts	Jul 05	Jul 04	Jul 03
Working Capital	78	89	62
Fixed Assets	4	5	5
Current Assets	182	194	162

Gillette UK Ltd
Great West Road, Isleworth, TW7 5NP
Tel: 020-8560 1234 **Fax:** 01784-431 080
E-mail: dick_cantwell@gillette.com
Website: http://www.gillette.com
Directors: J. Lingard (Fin), N. Allsey (Co Sec)
Ultimate Holding Company: Gillette Co. (USA)
Immediate Holding Company: Procter & Gamble Holdings UK Ltd
Registration no: 00254912 **Date established:** 1931
Turnover: £250m - £500m **No.of Employees:** 501 - 1000
Product Groups: 32, 36

Jain Europe Ltd
3rd Floor Grove House 551 London Road, Isleworth, TW7 4DS
Tel: 020-8326 5900
Website: http://www.jains.com
Managers: A. Gadi (Chief Mgr)
Ultimate Holding Company: JAIN IRRIGATION SYSTEMS LTD (INDIA)
Immediate Holding Company: JAIN (EUROPE) LIMITED
Registration no: 03215190 **Date established:** 1996
Turnover: £50m - £75m **No.of Employees:** 1 - 10 **Product Groups:** 30, 41

Date of Accounts	Mar 12	Mar 11	Mar 10
Sales Turnover	60m	36m	26m
Pre Tax Profit/Loss	-1m	-322	-736
Working Capital	-7m	-6m	-3m
Fixed Assets	6m	6m	2m
Current Assets	38m	30m	23m
Current Liabilities	706	1m	3m

Knapp Hicks & Partners
Prospect House 191 London Road, Isleworth, TW7 5XD
Tel: 020-8587 1000 **Fax:** 020-8587 1001
E-mail: info@knapphicks.co.uk
Website: http://www.knapphicks.co.uk
Bank(s): National Westminster Bank Plc
Directors: P. Nicholls (Dir), P. Armstrong (Fin)
Managers: P. Hicks (Sales & Mktg Mg)
Ultimate Holding Company: KHP SECURITIES LIMITED
Immediate Holding Company: KNAPP HICKS AND PARTNERS LIMITED
Registration no: 02886020 **VAT No.:** GB 676 4175 06
Date established: 1994 **Turnover:** £2m - £5m **No.of Employees:** 21 - 50
Product Groups: 84

Date of Accounts	Jan 11	Jan 10	Jan 09
Working Capital	889	826	755
Fixed Assets	14	18	31
Current Assets	1m	1m	1m

Linear Tools Ltd
1 Clock Tower Road, Isleworth, TW7 6DT
Tel: 020-8400 2020 **Fax:** 020-8400 2021
E-mail: sales@lineartools.co.uk
Website: http://www.lineartools.co.uk
Bank(s): Barclays
Directors: R. Brown (Sales)
Immediate Holding Company: LINEAR TOOLS LIMITED
Registration no: 01319862 **VAT No.:** 242 1020 30 **Date established:** 1977
Turnover: £2m - £5m **No.of Employees:** 11 - 20 **Product Groups:** 35, 38, 46

Date of Accounts	Jul 11	Jul 10	Jul 09
Working Capital	444	414	414
Fixed Assets	68	94	106
Current Assets	1m	1m	914

Nomadic Display
71 St Johns Road, Isleworth, TW7 6XQ
Tel: 020-8326 5555 **Fax:** 020-8326 5522
E-mail: info@nomadicdisplay.co.uk
Website: http://www.nomadicdisplay.co.uk
Bank(s): Lloyds TSB Bank plc
Managers: C. Stafford (Chief Mgr)
Ultimate Holding Company: NOMADIC STRUCTURES INC(USA)
Immediate Holding Company: NOMADIC STRUCTURES (UK) LIMITED
Registration no: 01994191 **Date established:** 1986
Turnover: £10m - £20m **No.of Employees:** 21 - 50 **Product Groups:** 26, 28, 49, 81

Date of Accounts	Dec 11	Dec 10	Dec 09
Working Capital	13	214	475
Fixed Assets	143	82	98
Current Assets	542	745	940

Ormiston Wire Ltd
1 Fleming Way, Isleworth, TW7 6EU
Tel: 020-8569 7287 **Fax:** 020-8569 8601
E-mail: info@ormiston-wire.co.uk
Website: http://www.ormiston-wire.co.uk
Bank(s): National Westminster Bank Plc
Directors: M. Ormiston (MD)
Immediate Holding Company: ORMISTON WIRE LIMITED
Registration no: 00189160 **VAT No.:** GB 226 7073 66
Date established: 2023 **Turnover:** £1m - £2m **No.of Employees:** 11 - 20
Product Groups: 29, 35, 37

Date of Accounts	Mar 12	Mar 11	Mar 10
Working Capital	1m	1m	746
Fixed Assets	501	521	876
Current Assets	1m	2m	1m

P & R Fabrications Ltd
The Arch St Johns Road, Isleworth, TW7 6NN
Tel: 020-8560 6655 **Fax:** 020-8847 2682
E-mail: pandroffice@gmail.com
Website: http://www.pandrfabrications.com
Managers: S. Henley (Mgr)
Immediate Holding Company: P & R FABRICATIONS LIMITED
Registration no: 03202323 **VAT No.:** GB 689 4441 76
Date established: 1996 **Turnover:** £250,000 - £500,000
No.of Employees: 1 - 10 **Product Groups:** 35, 48

Date of Accounts	May 11	May 10	May 09
Working Capital	-23	-13	-182
Fixed Assets	8	10	16
Current Assets	97	118	22

Pirtek
Isleworth Business Complex St Johns Road, Isleworth, TW7 6NL
Tel: 020-8847 5095 **Fax:** 020-8847 5092
E-mail: isleworth@pirtekcentre.co.uk
Website: http://www.pirtek.co.uk
Directors: A. Williams (Prop)
No.of Employees: 1 - 10 **Product Groups:** 29, 30

Robot Coupe UK Ltd
2 Fleming Way, Isleworth, TW7 6EU
Tel: 020-8232 1800 **Fax:** 020-8568 4966
E-mail: sales@robotcoupe.co.uk
Website: http://www.robotcoupe.co.uk
Directors: E. Cotterell (MD)
Ultimate Holding Company: HAMEUR SA (LUXEMBOURG)
Immediate Holding Company: ROBOT-COUPE (UK) LIMITED
Registration no: 01393429 **VAT No.:** GB 302 2253 22
Date established: 1978 **Turnover:** £2m - £5m **No.of Employees:** 11 - 20
Product Groups: 67

Date of Accounts	Dec 11	Dec 10	Dec 09
Working Capital	2m	3m	3m
Fixed Assets	207	213	234
Current Assets	3m	4m	4m

Telephone Recorders Direct
462 London Road, Isleworth, TW7 4ED
Tel: 0871-4242444 **Fax:** 020-8326 8400
E-mail: salesmanager@telephonerecordersdirect.com
Website: http://www.telephonerecordersdirect.com
Directors: R. Mill (MD)
Registration no: 04679145 **No.of Employees:** 51 - 100
Product Groups: 37

Valradio Electronic Ltd
1a Mandeville Road, Isleworth, TW7 6AD
Tel: 020-8560 3001 **Fax:** 020-8847 0783
E-mail: info@valradio.co.uk
Website: http://www.btinternet.com
Directors: B. Patal (Dir)
Immediate Holding Company: VALRADIO ELECTRONICS LIMITED
Registration no: 03120376 **VAT No.:** 745 0124 62 **Date established:** 1995
Turnover: Up to £250,000 **No.of Employees:** 1 - 10 **Product Groups:** 37, 39, 44

see next page

Valradio Electronic Ltd - Cont'd

Date of Accounts	Mar 11	Mar 10	Mar 09
Working Capital	-8	-4	-9
Fixed Assets	2	2	2
Current Assets	2	12	4

Vanco Group Ltd

John Busch House 277 London Road, Isleworth, TW7 5AX
Tel: 020-8380 1000 **Fax:** 020-8380 1001
E-mail: steve.dyde@vanco.co.uk
Website: http://www.vanco.co.uk
Directors: S. Dyde (Dir)
Ultimate Holding Company: RELIANCE COMMUNICATIONS LTD (INDIA)
Immediate Holding Company: RELIANCE VANCO GROUP LIMITED
Registration no: 02705350 **Date established:** 1992
No.of Employees: 1 - 10 **Product Groups:** 37, 44, 79, 80, 84, 85

Date of Accounts	Mar 12	Mar 11	Mar 10
Pre Tax Profit/Loss	-5m	5m	22m
Working Capital	113m	119m	97m
Fixed Assets	401	136	188
Current Assets	118m	124m	101m
Current Liabilities	361	21	119

Northolt

Arthur Removals Ltd

Unit 9 Magnolia Court 62 Aspen Lane, Northolt, UB5 6XE
Tel: 07725-020677
E-mail: service@kingarthurremovals.com
Website: http://www.kingarthurremovals.com
Directors: A. Swtag (MD)
Registration no: 06154880 **Date established:** 2007
Turnover: Up to £250,000 **No.of Employees:** 1 - 10 **Product Groups:** 72

Docuprint Ltd

Avad House Belvue Road, Northolt Industrial Estate, Northolt, UB5 5HY
Tel: 020-8537 7200 **Fax:** 020-8537 7219
E-mail: sales@docuprint.co.uk
Website: http://www.docuprint.co.uk
Directors: D. Patel (Dir)
Managers: S. Patel (Prod Mgr), I. Jones (Mgr)
No.of Employees: 11 - 20 **Product Groups:** 28

Date of Accounts	Dec 09	Dec 08	Dec 07
Working Capital	9	353	58
Fixed Assets	687	304	296
Current Assets	536	770	605

Premier CCTV Ltd

34 Union Road, Northolt, UB5 6UE
Tel: 020-8841 1196 **Fax:** 0870-111 8012
E-mail: info@premiercctv.co.uk
Website: http://www.premiercctv.co.uk
Directors: H. Mohamedali (Fin), S. Mohamedali (MD)
Immediate Holding Company: PREMIER CCTV LIMITED
Registration no: 04402483 **Date established:** 2002
Turnover: £250,000 - £500,000 **No.of Employees:** 1 - 10
Product Groups: 37, 38, 40, 67

Date of Accounts	Mar 11	Mar 10	Mar 09
Working Capital	7	11	4
Fixed Assets	2	2	2
Current Assets	73	58	51

Sabre Defence Industries Ltd

Sabre House Belvue Road, Northolt, UB5 5QJ
Tel: 020-8842 0603 **Fax:** 020-8845 4814
E-mail: sales@sabredefence.com
Website: http://www.sabredefence.com
Directors: G. Savage (Dir), A. Savage (Fin)
Immediate Holding Company: SABRE DEFENCE INDUSTRIES LIMITED
Registration no: 02989557 **Date established:** 1994
No.of Employees: 1 - 10 **Product Groups:** 36, 39, 40

Date of Accounts	Nov 09	Nov 08	Nov 07
Working Capital	900	-208	-100
Fixed Assets	399	676	721
Current Assets	2m	1m	772

Sterling

Hallmark House Rowdell Road, Northolt, UB5 6AG
Tel: 020-8841 7000 **Fax:** 020-8841 3500
E-mail: info@sterlingrelocation.com
Website: http://www.sterlingrelocation.com
Directors: R. Morley (Dir)
Managers: O. Shilling (Develop Mgr), E. Alcaraz (Personnel), M. Veck (Tech Serv Mgr), A. Sleth (Mktg Serv Mgr), N. Smith (Comptroller)
Ultimate Holding Company: HALCYON RELOCATION LIMITED
Immediate Holding Company: STERLING RELOCATION LIMITED
Registration no: 02670177 **Date established:** 1991
Turnover: £20m - £50m **No.of Employees:** 101 - 250 **Product Groups:** 80

Date of Accounts	Jun 11	Jun 10	Jun 09
Sales Turnover	37m	32m	37m
Pre Tax Profit/Loss	942	889	397
Working Capital	6m	5m	4m
Fixed Assets	682	707	841
Current Assets	18m	13m	19m
Current Liabilities	7m	5m	6m

Northwood

Bhardwaj Insolvency Practitioners

47-49 Green Lane, Northwood, HA6 3AE
Tel: 01923-820966 **Fax:** 01923-835311
E-mail: info@bhardwaj.co.uk
Website: http://www.bhardwaj.co.uk
Directors: A. Bhardwaj (Fin)
Immediate Holding Company: BHARDWAJ LIMITED
Registration no: 02599536 **Date established:** 1991
Turnover: Up to £250,000 **No.of Employees:** 1 - 10 **Product Groups:** 80, 81, 82

Date of Accounts	Dec 11	Dec 10	Dec 09
Sales Turnover	178	159	100
Pre Tax Profit/Loss	86	56	2
Working Capital	116	49	5
Fixed Assets	19	25	23
Current Assets	153	75	18
Current Liabilities	35	26	6

Roger F Jones Ltd

8 Northbrook Drive, Northwood, HA6 2YU
Tel: 01923-828995 **Fax:** 01923-820551
E-mail: rjones378@googlemail.com
Directors: R. Jones (MD), J. Jones (Fin)
Immediate Holding Company: ROGER F JONES LIMITED
Registration no: 04121354 **Date established:** 2000
Turnover: Up to £250,000 **No.of Employees:** 1 - 10 **Product Groups:** 80

Date of Accounts	Apr 11	Apr 10	Apr 08
Sales Turnover	N/A	9	46
Pre Tax Profit/Loss	-2	-2	1
Working Capital	N/A	-1	1
Fixed Assets	1	1	1
Current Assets	2	6	2
Current Liabilities	1	4	1

Pinner Tools Ltd

25 The Avenue, Northwood, HA6 2NJ
Tel: 01923-822893 **Fax:** 01923-835552
E-mail: jackie@pinnertools.net
Directors: J. Hart (MD)
Immediate Holding Company: PINNER TOOLS LIMITED
Registration no: 01170410 **Date established:** 1974
No.of Employees: 1 - 10 **Product Groups:** 46

Date of Accounts	Jun 11	Jun 09	Jun 08
Working Capital	1	4	6
Fixed Assets	1	N/A	1
Current Assets	10	12	23

Pinner

360vision.Co.Uk (T/A 360vision Co UK)

107 Marsh Road, Pinner, HA5 5PA
Tel: 020-8429 8285
E-mail: info@360travelguide.com
Website: http://www.360travelguide.com
Directors: P. Baderman (Dir)
Immediate Holding Company: 360 VISION LTD
Registration no: 03960108 **Date established:** 2000 **Turnover:** £1m - £2m
No.of Employees: 1 - 10 **Product Groups:** 89

Date of Accounts	Mar 10	Mar 09	Apr 11
Working Capital	-2	-3	1
Fixed Assets	2	3	2
Current Assets	53	52	24

Farrell Engineering Ltd

Westbury House 23-25 Bridge Street, Pinner, HA5 3HR
Tel: 020-3432 3291 **Fax:** 020-8965 7586
E-mail: info@farrellengineering.com
Website: http://www.farrellengineering.com
Directors: C. Chowdhry (MD), P. Chowdhry (Fin)
Ultimate Holding Company: VERACITY ASSOCIATES LIMITED
Immediate Holding Company: FARRELL ENGINEERING LIMITED
Registration no: 01723966 **VAT No.:** GB 371 0706 75
Date established: 1983 **Turnover:** £2m - £5m **No.of Employees:** 1 - 10
Product Groups: 34, 48, 67

Date of Accounts	Mar 12	Mar 11	Mar 10
Sales Turnover	3m	2m	1m
Pre Tax Profit/Loss	151	105	11
Working Capital	153	35	-57
Fixed Assets	2m	2m	514
Current Assets	802	767	180
Current Liabilities	35	27	6

Get Shot Ltd

Kingsbridge House 130 Marsh Road, Pinner, HA5 5LX
Tel: 020-3195 0092 **Fax:** 020-8429 5335
E-mail: studio@get-shot.co.uk
Website: http://www.get-shot.co.uk
Managers: J. Mason (Mgr)
Registration no: 07076343 **Product Groups:** 81

Inger Rose

5 Royston Park Road Hatch End, Pinner, HA5 4AA
Tel: 020-8421 1822 **Fax:** 020-8421 3187
E-mail: info@ingerrose.co.uk
Website: http://www.ingerrose.co.uk
Directors: J. Rose (Dir)
Registration no: 01717235 **Turnover:** Up to £250,000
No.of Employees: 1 - 10 **Product Groups:** 24

London Fire & Pump Co. Ltd

11 Bridle Road, Pinner, HA5 2SL
Tel: 020-8866 6342 **Fax:** 020-8429 1129
Directors: S. Willmore (MD)
Turnover: Up to £250,000 **No.of Employees:** 1 - 10 **Product Groups:** 38, 39, 40, 52

Mollisigns

546 Uxbridge Road, Pinner, HA5 3QA
Tel: 07973-662041 **Fax:** 01923-463354
E-mail: mollisigns@btinternet.com
Website: http://www.mollisigns.co.uk
Directors: S. Mollison (Prop)
No.of Employees: 1 - 10 **Product Groups:** 30, 39, 40

Ovenu Oven Valeting Service

49 West Towers, Pinner, HA5 1TZ
Tel: 020-8429 8279
Website: http://www.ovenu.co.uk
Directors: A. Hart (Prop)
Date established: 1999 **No.of Employees:** 1 - 10 **Product Groups:** 20, 40, 41

The Print Shop

4 Pinner Green, Pinner, HA5 2AA
Tel: 020-8429 0020 **Fax:** 020-8429 0020
E-mail: info@printshoppinner.co.uk
Website: http://www.printshoppinner.co.uk
Directors: L. Mcgregor (Prop), J. Bullock (Fin)
No.of Employees: 1 - 10 **Product Groups:** 28, 80, 81

Probus Electronics Ltd

Findon Southill Lane, Pinner, HA5 2EQ
Tel: 020-8866 7272 **Fax:** 020-8866 2999
E-mail: sales@probus.freeserve.co.uk
Website: http://www.probus.freeserve.co.uk
Directors: W. Rowe (Dir)
Immediate Holding Company: PROBUS ELECTRONICS LIMITED
Registration no: 02476829 **Date established:** 1990
Turnover: £250,000 - £500,000 **No.of Employees:** 1 - 10
Product Groups: 32, 37, 38

Date of Accounts	Mar 11	Mar 10	Mar 09
Working Capital	8	31	55
Fixed Assets	1	1	4
Current Assets	69	69	89

Ruislip

Admiral Microwaves Ltd

1 Kildare Close, Ruislip, HA4 9LG
Tel: 020-8869 9050 **Fax:** 020-8866 6513
E-mail: sales@admiral-microwaves.co.uk
Website: http://www.admiral-microwaves.co.uk
Directors: S. Cohen (MD)
Immediate Holding Company: ADMIRAL MICROWAVES LIMITED
Registration no: 02697531 **VAT No.:** GB 287 2335 15
Date established: 1992 **Turnover:** £500,000 - £1m
No.of Employees: 1 - 10 **Product Groups:** 37, 38

Date of Accounts	Jun 11	Jun 10	Jun 09
Working Capital	550	588	462
Fixed Assets	3	4	5
Current Assets	606	775	554

Always Under Pressure

4 Langley Avenue, Ruislip, HA4 9TT
Tel: 020-8868 6694 **Fax:** 020-8582 2773
E-mail: ryan@graffiti-removal.org.uk
Website: http://www.graffiti-removal.org.uk
Directors: R. Matthews (Prop)
No.of Employees: 1 - 10 **Product Groups:** 32, 52

Aspen Electronics Ltd

1-3 Kildare Close, Ruislip, HA4 9UR
Tel: 020-8868 1311 **Fax:** 020-8866 6596
E-mail: sales@aspen-electronics.com
Website: http://www.aspen-electronics.com
Bank(s): National Westminster Bank Plc
Directors: H. Venning (MD)
Immediate Holding Company: ASPEN ELECTRONICS LIMITED
Registration no: 01166826 **VAT No.:** GB 233 9576 48
Date established: 1974 **Turnover:** £500,000 - £1m
No.of Employees: 11 - 20 **Product Groups:** 37, 38

Date of Accounts	Jun 11	Jun 10	Jun 09
Working Capital	1m	973	847
Fixed Assets	678	677	645
Current Assets	2m	2m	2m

Bucon Ltd

Braintree House Braintree Road, Ruislip, HA4 0EJ
Tel: 020-8842 1440 **Fax:** 020-8842 3881
E-mail: info@bucon.co.uk
Website: http://www.bucon.co.uk
Registration no: 20909526 **No.of Employees:** 11 - 20
Product Groups: 26, 48, 67, 83

Date of Accounts	Dec 11	Dec 10	Dec 09
Working Capital	241	204	278
Fixed Assets	62	78	12
Current Assets	372	374	516

Fanuc Fa UK Ltd

Andrew Myhill Fanuc House, Ruislip, HA4 8LF
Tel: 01895-634182 **Fax:** 01895-676140
E-mail: info@fanuc.co.uk
Website: http://www.fanuc.eu
Directors: A. Myhill (MD)
Ultimate Holding Company: FANUC LIMITED (JAPAN)
Immediate Holding Company: FANUC CORPORATION
Registration no: FC011332 **Date established:** 1982
Turnover: Over £1,000m **No.of Employees:** 21 - 50 **Product Groups:** 44

Date of Accounts	Dec 09	Dec 08	Mar 12
Sales Turnover	3m	4m	9m
Pre Tax Profit/Loss	373	1m	2m
Working Capital	4m	10m	4m
Fixed Assets	22	34	2m
Current Assets	5m	11m	6m
Current Liabilities	520	627	1m

Hodge Engineering Ltd

5 Kildare Close, Ruislip, HA4 9LQ
Tel: 020-8868 5387 **Fax:** 020-8868 0078
E-mail: sales@hodge-eng.co.uk
Directors: S. Harding (MD)
Immediate Holding Company: HODGE ENGINEERING LIMITED
Registration no: 00707491 **Date established:** 1961
No.of Employees: 1 - 10 **Product Groups:** 44

Date of Accounts	Oct 11	Oct 10	Oct 09
Working Capital	75	91	100
Fixed Assets	7	9	13
Current Assets	94	116	132

Independent Power Systems

Canada House 272 Field End Road, Ruislip, HA4 9NA
Tel: 020-8866 4400 **Fax:** 020-8866 3725
Website: http://www.independent-power.co.uk
Directors: T. Hill (Fin)
Immediate Holding Company: INDEPENDENT POWER SYSTEMS LIMITED
Registration no: 02938816 **Date established:** 1994
Turnover: £250,000 - £500,000 **No.of Employees:** 1 - 10
Product Groups: 28

Date of Accounts	Sep 11	Sep 10	Sep 09
Sales Turnover	N/A	N/A	374
Pre Tax Profit/Loss	N/A	N/A	25

Working Capital	-16	50	88
Fixed Assets	16	21	28
Current Assets	30	79	147
Current Liabilities	N/A	N/A	24

J P Glass & Decor Ltd

Unit 1-6 Eastcote Industrial Estate Field End Road, Ruislip, HA4 9XG
Tel: 020-8429 2999 **Fax:** 020-8868 4314
E-mail: sales@jpglass.com
Website: http://www.jpglass.com
Directors: P. Spears (Dir)
Ultimate Holding Company: ALLMODELS ENGINEERING LIMITED
Immediate Holding Company: J.P. GLASS & DECOR LIMITED
Registration no: 01841932 **VAT No.:** GB 409 8645 22
Date established: 1984 **Turnover:** £500,000 - £1m
No.of Employees: 11 - 20 **Product Groups:** 33

Date of Accounts	Oct 11	Oct 10	Oct 09
Sales Turnover	N/A	N/A	712
Pre Tax Profit/Loss	N/A	N/A	-22
Working Capital	25	372	289
Fixed Assets	1m	1m	1m
Current Assets	182	576	550
Current Liabilities	N/A	N/A	108

Kall Kwik UK Ltd

Kall Kwik House 106 Pembroke Road, Ruislip, HA4 8NW
Tel: 0500-872060 **Fax:** 01895-872111
E-mail: roger.crudgington@adareodc.com
Website: http://www.adareodc.com
Directors: J. Blyth (Sales & Mktg), M. Hutter (MD), R. Crudgington (MD), K. Campbell (Pers)
Managers: A. Maddocks (I.T. Exec)
Immediate Holding Company: KALL KWIK UK LIMITED
Registration no: 01396406 **VAT No.:** GB 242 7193 66
Date established: 1978 **Turnover:** £2m - £5m **No.of Employees:** 1 - 10
Product Groups: 28

Noise & Pulsation Control Ltd

5 King Edwards Road, Ruislip, HA4 7AE
Tel: 01895-676215 **Fax:** 01895-676215
E-mail: noiseandpulsationuk@btinternet.com
Website: http://www.noiseandpulsation.co.uk
Directors: J. Sivarajah (Fin)
Immediate Holding Company: NOISE AND PULSATION CONTROL LIMITED
Registration no: 02142818 **VAT No.:** GB 460 8481 38
Date established: 1987 **Turnover:** £250,000 - £500,000
No.of Employees: 1 - 10 **Product Groups:** 37, 39, 40, 54

Date of Accounts	Mar 11	Mar 10	Mar 09
Working Capital	6	5	8
Fixed Assets	1	1	1
Current Assets	116	5	39

K Slingerland

1 Long Drive, Ruislip, HA4 0HG
Tel: 020-8845 8205
Directors: K. Slingerland (Prop)
Date established: 1990 **No.of Employees:** 1 - 10 **Product Groups:** 35

Starkstrom Ltd

256 Field End Road Eastcote, Ruislip, HA4 9UW
Tel: 020-8868 3732 **Fax:** 020-8868 3736
E-mail: info@starkstrom.com
Website: http://www.starkstrom.com
Bank(s): National Westminster
Directors: S. Tabibi (MD), A. King (Fin)
Ultimate Holding Company: STARKSTROM GROUP LIMITED
Immediate Holding Company: STARKSTROM LIMITED
Registration no: 01013256 **VAT No.:** GB 223 0111 40
Date established: 1971 **Turnover:** £5m - £10m **No.of Employees:** 21 - 50
Product Groups: 38

Date of Accounts	May 11	May 10	May 09
Sales Turnover	9m	N/A	N/A
Pre Tax Profit/Loss	945	N/A	N/A
Working Capital	3m	2m	2m
Fixed Assets	366	267	201
Current Assets	6m	6m	5m
Current Liabilities	2m	N/A	N/A

Technology Support Consultancy

6 Laburnum Grove, Ruislip, HA4 7XF
Tel: 01895-675347
E-mail: info@techsconsult.co.uk
Website: http://www.techsconsult.co.uk
Directors: D. Elliott (Prop)
Immediate Holding Company: TECHNOLOGY SUPPORT CONSULTANCY LIMITED
Registration no: 04821310 **Date established:** 2003
No.of Employees: 1 - 10 **Product Groups:** 44

Date of Accounts	Nov 11	Nov 10	Nov 09
Working Capital	19	16	13
Fixed Assets	1	N/A	N/A
Current Assets	23	20	19

Textiliana Ltd

Unit G Braintree Industrial Estate Braintree Road, Ruislip, HA4 0EJ
Tel: 020-8845 2323 **Fax:** 020-8845 1144
E-mail: info@textiliana.co.uk
Website: http://www.textiliana.co.uk
Directors: J. Swan (Dir), S. Bresley (MD)
Immediate Holding Company: TEXTILIANA LIMITED
Registration no: 00585251 **VAT No.:** GB 233 3260 01
Date established: 1957 **Turnover:** £1m - £2m **No.of Employees:** 1 - 10
Product Groups: 63

Date of Accounts	Dec 07	Dec 06	Dec 05
Working Capital	270	257	191
Fixed Assets	808	358	362
Current Assets	954	806	732
Current Liabilities	684	548	541
Total Share Capital	35	35	35

Wright Machinery Ltd (Head Office)

Stonefield Way, Ruislip, HA4 0JU
Tel: 020-8842 2244 **Fax:** 020-8842 1113
E-mail: sales@wright.co.uk
Website: http://www.wright.co.uk
Directors: V. Anderson (Co Sec), R. Treacher (Sales), M. Reed (Sales), J. Walsh (MD), A. Husbands (Tech Serv)
Managers: P. Morley (Purch Mgr), S. Dickson (Personnel), S. Tomlinson (Eng Serv Mgr), T. Hovell (Purch Mgr), M. Budd (Works Gen Mgr)
Immediate Holding Company: WRIGHT MACHINERY LIMITED
Registration no: 04361450 **VAT No.:** GB 222 9117 86
Date established: 2002 **Turnover:** £10m - £20m
No.of Employees: 51 - 100 **Product Groups:** 30, 38, 42, 45

Date of Accounts	Dec 08	Apr 08	Apr 07
Sales Turnover	14m	17m	21m
Pre Tax Profit/Loss	-2m	194	853
Working Capital	191	675	368
Fixed Assets	1m	2m	3m
Current Assets	10m	6m	7m
Current Liabilities	6m	3m	5m

Shepperton

Belimo Automation UK Ltd

Unit 10 Shepperton Business Park Govett Avenue, Shepperton, TW17 8BA
Tel: 01932-260460 **Fax:** 01932-269222
E-mail: andrew.bartlett@belimo.org
Website: http://www.belimo.org
Directors: A. Bartlett (MD)
Ultimate Holding Company: BELIMO HOLDING AG (SWITZERLAND)
Immediate Holding Company: BELIMO AUTOMATION UK LIMITED
Registration no: 01534607 **Date established:** 1980 **Turnover:** £2m - £5m
No.of Employees: 11 - 20 **Product Groups:** 38

Date of Accounts	Dec 11	Dec 10	Dec 09
Sales Turnover	9m	9m	8m
Pre Tax Profit/Loss	341	328	332
Working Capital	326	314	389
Fixed Assets	98	103	102
Current Assets	2m	2m	2m
Current Liabilities	295	883	821

Bridge Marine

Thames Meadow, Shepperton, TW17 8LT
Tel: 01932-245126 **Fax:** 01932-220331
Website: http://www.bridgemarine.co.uk
Managers: J. Beagle (Mgr)
Date established: 1985 **No.of Employees:** 1 - 10 **Product Groups:** 35, 36, 39

Chilly Pepper Hire

41 Broadlands Avenue, Shepperton, TW17 9DJ
Tel: 020-8844 1665 **Fax:** 020-8538 7797
E-mail: info@chillypepperhire.co.uk
Website: http://www.chillypepperhire.co.uk
Directors: J. Brassington (Prop)
Immediate Holding Company: CITYTOOLBOX FACILITIES MANAGEMENT LIMITED
Registration no: 03856187 **VAT No.:** GB 563 1847 31
Date established: 2009 **No.of Employees:** 1 - 10 **Product Groups:** 40, 52, 66, 81, 83, 84

Date of Accounts	Sep 06	Sep 05
Working Capital	-58	-94
Fixed Assets	81	65
Current Assets	184	97
Current Liabilities	241	191

Compass Forest Products Ltd

Clock House, Shepperton, TW17 8AN
Tel: 01932-256970 **Fax:** 01932-229974
E-mail: specialities@mbmfp.co.uk
Website: http://www.compassfp.co.uk
Bank(s): Barclays
Directors: J. Collins (Sales)
Ultimate Holding Company: CONSOLIDATED TIMBER HOLDINGS LIMITED
Immediate Holding Company: COMPASS FOREST PRODUCTS LIMITED
Registration no: 01893926 **VAT No.:** GB 429 6028 42
Date established: 1985 **Turnover:** £20m - £50m
No.of Employees: 21 - 50 **Product Groups:** 66

Date of Accounts	Dec 08	Dec 07	Mar 11
Sales Turnover	22m	24m	22m
Pre Tax Profit/Loss	354	681	606
Working Capital	3m	3m	3m
Fixed Assets	120	181	156
Current Assets	8m	9m	8m
Current Liabilities	3m	3m	3m

Consolidated Timber Holdings Ltd

Clock House Station App, Shepperton, TW17 8AN
Tel: 01932-256960 **Fax:** 01932-229974
E-mail: enquiries@cth.co.uk
Website: http://www.cth.co.uk
Bank(s): Barclays
Directors: S. Holdsworth (Fin), M. Meyer (Ch), M. Bacon (Dir), M. Laughlin (Dir)
Immediate Holding Company: CONSOLIDATED TIMBER HOLDINGS LIMITED
Registration no: 02295212 **Date established:** 1988
Turnover: £75m - £125m **No.of Employees:** 101 - 250
Product Groups: 61

Date of Accounts	Dec 08	Dec 07	Mar 11
Sales Turnover	86m	103m	91m
Pre Tax Profit/Loss	829	3m	2m
Working Capital	6m	6m	8m
Fixed Assets	4m	4m	5m
Current Assets	30m	36m	34m
Current Liabilities	13m	17m	13m

Falcon Panel Products Ltd

Clock House Station Approach, Shepperton, TW17 8AN
Tel: 01932-256580 **Fax:** 01932-230268
E-mail: sales@falconpp.co.uk
Website: http://www.falconpp.co.uk
Directors: A. Stead (Co Sec)
Managers: J. Hamblion
Ultimate Holding Company: CONSOLIDATED TIMBER HOLDINGS LIMITED
Immediate Holding Company: FALCON PANEL PRODUCTS LIMITED
Registration no: 02013545 **Date established:** 1986
Turnover: £10m - £20m **No.of Employees:** 21 - 50 **Product Groups:** 25, 66

Date of Accounts	Dec 08	Dec 07	Mar 11
Sales Turnover	20m	21m	18m
Pre Tax Profit/Loss	626	1m	564
Working Capital	2m	2m	2m
Fixed Assets	231	123	170
Current Assets	7m	9m	7m
Current Liabilities	3m	4m	2m

Ian Allan Group Ltd

Terminal House Station Approach, Shepperton, TW17 8AS
Tel: 01932-255500 **Fax:** 01932-252748
E-mail: ian.allan@ianallan.co.uk
Website: http://www.ianallangroup.com
Bank(s): Barclays
Managers: C. Oldfield (Mgr), D. Allan
Immediate Holding Company: IAN ALLAN GROUP LIMITED
Registration no: 00739567 **VAT No.:** GB 207 6524 72
Date established: 1962 **Turnover:** £50m - £75m
No.of Employees: 51 - 100 **Product Groups:** 28, 68, 69, 80

Date of Accounts	Nov 11	Nov 10	Nov 09
Sales Turnover	62m	59m	53m
Pre Tax Profit/Loss	-1m	-969	-892
Working Capital	3m	3m	4m
Fixed Assets	12m	13m	13m
Current Assets	10m	11m	10m
Current Liabilities	N/A	3m	2m

Middlesex Gates & Grilles

3 Bugle Nurseries Upper Halliford Road, Shepperton, TW17 8SN
Tel: 01932-770934 **Fax:** 01932-787818
Website: http://www.middlesexgateandgrille.com
Directors: M. Tomkins (Prop)
Date established: 2001 **No.of Employees:** 1 - 10 **Product Groups:** 26, 35

Nauticalia Ltd

Ferry Lane, Shepperton, TW17 9LQ
Tel: 01932-244396 **Fax:** 01753-850721
E-mail: sales@nauticalia.com
Website: http://www.nauticalia.com
Bank(s): National Westminster Bank Plc
Directors: C. Murdoch (MD), L. Lewis (Ch)
Managers: I. Thompson (Mktg Serv Mgr), M. Wilby (I.T. Exec)
Ultimate Holding Company: 01254803
Immediate Holding Company: NAUTICALIA LIMITED
Registration no: 02282064 **VAT No.:** GB 285 2641 44
Date established: 1988 **Turnover:** £5m - £10m **No.of Employees:** 21 - 50
Product Groups: 65

Date of Accounts	Sep 09	Sep 08	Sep 07
Sales Turnover	8m	8m	8m
Pre Tax Profit/Loss	21	N/A	-256
Working Capital	-66	-65	-143
Fixed Assets	3m	3m	2m
Current Assets	4m	4m	4m
Current Liabilities	638	738	593

Papersticks Ltd

Govett Avenue, Shepperton, TW17 8AB
Tel: 01932-228491 **Fax:** 01932-242828
E-mail: sales@papersticks.co.uk
Website: http://www.papersticks.co.uk
Bank(s): Barclays
Directors: P. Fisher (Co Sec)
Immediate Holding Company: PAPERSTICKS LIMITED
Registration no: 00870572 **Date established:** 1966 **Turnover:** £2m - £5m
No.of Employees: 11 - 20 **Product Groups:** 66

Date of Accounts	Sep 11	Sep 10	Sep 09
Working Capital	196	213	279
Fixed Assets	371	396	431
Current Assets	341	406	464

Pinewood Label Systems Ltd

Terminal House Station Approach, Shepperton, TW17 8AP
Tel: 01932-243724 **Fax:** 01932-246632
E-mail: sales@pinewoodlabels.com
Website: http://www.pinewoodlabels.com
Directors: A. Ridley (Dir)
Immediate Holding Company: PINEWOOD LABEL SYSTEMS LIMITED
Registration no: 01468976 **Date established:** 1979
No.of Employees: 1 - 10 **Product Groups:** 38, 42

Date of Accounts	Dec 11	Dec 10	Dec 09
Working Capital	50	51	33
Fixed Assets	2	3	3
Current Assets	104	109	92

Tarmac Southern Ltd

Littleton Lane, Shepperton, TW17 0NF
Tel: 01932-568561 **Fax:** 01932-569714
E-mail: info@tarmac-southern.co.uk
Website: http://www.tarmac.co.uk
Directors: M. Shipman (Dir), D. Cole (Comm)
Managers: P. Sullivan (Mgr)
Immediate Holding Company: TARMAC SOUTHERN LIMITED
Registration no: 00415260 **Date established:** 1946
Turnover: £20m - £50m **No.of Employees:** 11 - 20 **Product Groups:** 14, 31

Date of Accounts	Sep 10	Sep 09	Sep 08
Working Capital	45	46	47
Fixed Assets	2	5	7
Current Assets	112	113	126

Transmission TX

Sunit 1a Shepperton Studios Studios Road, Shepperton, TW17 0QD
Tel: 020-8783 1972 **Fax:** 01932-572571
E-mail: info@ttx.co.uk
Website: http://www.ttx.co.uk
Managers: S. Lloyd (Chief Mgr)
Immediate Holding Company: TRANSMISSION (TX) LIMITED
Registration no: 02331912 **Date established:** 1988
No.of Employees: 11 - 20 **Product Groups:** 37, 38, 79

Date of Accounts	Dec 11	Dec 10	Dec 09
Working Capital	-312	-637	-591
Fixed Assets	1m	1m	1m
Current Assets	571	420	292

Southall

Automatic Systems Equipment UK Ltd
Unit G4, Middlesex Business Centre Bridge Road, Southall, UB2 4AB
Tel: 020-8744 7669 **Fax:** 020-8744 7670
E-mail: sales@automaticsystems.co.uk
Website: http://www.automaticsystems.co.uk
Directors: C. Mcginn (MD), T. De Martin De Montmarin (Dir)
Immediate Holding Company: Automatic Systems Sa (Belgium)
Registration no: 02876526 **VAT No.:** GB 615 4270 60
Turnover: £1m - £2m **No.of Employees:** 1 - 10 **Product Groups:** 35, 39, 49

Date of Accounts	Dec 07	Dec 06
Sales Turnover	502	972
Pre Tax Profit/Loss	-335	-127
Working Capital	-220	107
Fixed Assets	5	14
Current Assets	282	419
Current Liabilities	502	312
Total Share Capital	54	54
ROCE% (Return on Capital Employed)	155.8	-104.9
ROT% (Return on Turnover)	-66.8	-13.1

Emanuel Malik
Unit 10 Endsleigh Industrial Estate Endsleigh Road, Southall, UB2 5QR
Tel: 020-8574 3299
Directors: E. Malik (Prop)
No.of Employees: 1 - 10 **Product Groups:** 37, 67

Golden Entertainment
Unit 1d 142 Johnson Street, Southall, UB2 5FD
Tel: 020-8577 7277 **Fax:** 020-8569 0093
E-mail: info@goldenentertainment.co.uk
Website: http://www.goldenentertainment.co.uk
Directors: K. Mahal (Prop)
Registration no: 06029684 **No.of Employees:** 1 - 10 **Product Groups:** 22, 24, 25, 26, 27, 30, 33, 34, 35, 36, 46, 48, 49, 52, 63, 65, 81, 82, 83, 84, 89

Date of Accounts	Dec 08	Dec 07	Mar 11
Working Capital	-130	-157	-9
Fixed Assets	536	543	376
Current Assets	99	111	118

Herting & Son plc
Frederick House 25 Armstrong Way, Southall, UB2 4SD
Tel: 020-8606 7000 **Fax:** 020-8606 7010
E-mail: sales@hertings.com
Website: http://www.hertings.com
Directors: J. Herting (Dir)
Managers: C. Francis (Chief Mgr)
Immediate Holding Company: F.P. HERTING & SON PLC
Registration no: 00709812 **VAT No.:** GB 226 7536 52
Date established: 1961 **Turnover:** £10m - £20m
No.of Employees: 101 - 250 **Product Groups:** 66

Date of Accounts	Dec 11	Dec 10	Dec 09
Sales Turnover	15m	14m	12m
Pre Tax Profit/Loss	1m	947	595
Working Capital	3m	1m	2m
Fixed Assets	3m	3m	3m
Current Assets	7m	6m	6m
Current Liabilities	3m	942	509

Interken Freighters Ltd
6 Grand Union Enterprise Park Grand Union Way, Southall, UB2 4EX
Tel: 020-8574 0313 **Fax:** 020-8574 0323
E-mail: info@interken-freighters.co.uk
Directors: R. Ghai (MD), S. Ghai (MD)
Managers: S. Bux (Mgr)
Immediate Holding Company: INTERKEN FREIGHTERS (U.K.) LIMITED
Registration no: 01871446 **VAT No.:** GB 409 8706 28
Date established: 1984 **Turnover:** £2m - £5m **No.of Employees:** 1 - 10
Product Groups: 45, 71, 74

Jas Musical Instruments
124 The Broadway, Southall, UB1 1QF
Tel: 020-8574 2686 **Fax:** 020-8571 7445
E-mail: info@jas-musicals.com
Website: http://www.jas-musicals.com
Directors: J. Shah (Fin)
Immediate Holding Company: JAS MUSICALS LIMITED
Registration no: 02595352 **Date established:** 1991
No.of Employees: 1 - 10 **Product Groups:** 49, 65

Date of Accounts	Mar 11	Mar 10	Mar 09
Working Capital	42	27	15
Fixed Assets	13	16	13
Current Assets	161	169	180

London Linen Supply Ltd
Unit 6-8 Jackson Way, Southall, UB2 4SF
Tel: 020-8574 5569 **Fax:** 020-8571 2487
E-mail: roger.oliver@londonlinen.co.uk
Website: http://www.londonlinen.co.uk
Directors: M. Bailey (Fin), R. Oliver (MD), C. Delacombe (Co Sec)
Managers: S. Sultan (Purch Mgr), R. Smith (Tech Serv Mgr)
Immediate Holding Company: LONDON LINEN SUPPLY LIMITED
Registration no: 00303039 **Date established:** 1935
Turnover: £20m - £50m **No.of Employees:** 251 - 500 **Product Groups:** 83

Date of Accounts	Oct 10	Oct 11	Oct 08
Sales Turnover	19m	22m	N/A
Pre Tax Profit/Loss	1m	2m	1m
Working Capital	5m	8m	7m
Fixed Assets	3m	3m	3m
Current Assets	10m	10m	10m
Current Liabilities	3m	1m	3m

M B S Kitchens & Bedrooms Ltd
220 Uxbridge Road, Southall, UB1 3DZ
Tel: 020-8571 0043 **Fax:** 020-843 0747
E-mail: mbsmanufacturing@btconnect.com
Directors: P. Mangat (MD)
Immediate Holding Company: EXECUTIVE WINDOWS LTD.
Registration no: 03498600 **Date established:** 2007
Turnover: £250,000 - £500,000 **No.of Employees:** 11 - 20
Product Groups: 26, 30

Date of Accounts	Aug 10	Aug 09
Working Capital	16	6
Current Assets	26	13

Current Liabilities	3	N/A

Maina Freight Forwarders plc
5 Featherstone Industrial Estate Dominion Road, Southall, UB2 5DP
Tel: 020-8843 1977 **Fax:** 020-8571 5628
E-mail: info@maina.com
Website: http://www.maina.com
Directors: M. Madlani (Fin), B. Madlani (MD)
Managers: N. Madlani (Sales Admin), K. Pattani (Transport), H. Rajkotwala (Personnel)
Immediate Holding Company: MAINA FREIGHT FORWARDERS PLC
Registration no: 01599041 **Date established:** 1981 **Turnover:** £2m - £5m
No.of Employees: 21 - 50 **Product Groups:** 76

Date of Accounts	Jun 11	Jun 10	Jun 09
Sales Turnover	5m	4m	5m
Pre Tax Profit/Loss	117	-53	128
Working Capital	-62	-151	195
Fixed Assets	243	239	211
Current Assets	630	715	1m
Current Liabilities	67	70	66

Noon Products Ltd
Windmill Lane, Southall, UB2 4NA
Tel: 020-8571 1866 **Fax:** 020-8571 2672
E-mail: bob.carnell@kerryfoods.co.uk
Website: http://www.noon.co.uk
Bank(s): National Westminster Bank Plc
Directors: B. Carnell (MD), W. Cadbury (Fin), D. Haywood (Sales)
Managers: J. Nel (Mats Contrlr), R. Patel (Personnel), H. Dogra (Tech Serv Mgr)
Ultimate Holding Company: KERRY GROUP PUBLIC LIMITED COMPANY
Immediate Holding Company: NOON PRODUCTS LIMITED
Registration no: 02166664 **Date established:** 1987
Turnover: £125m - £250m **No.of Employees:** 1001 - 1500
Product Groups: 20

Date of Accounts	Dec 11	Dec 10	Dec 09
Sales Turnover	184m	166m	149m
Pre Tax Profit/Loss	4m	1m	4m
Working Capital	14m	18m	17m
Fixed Assets	13m	14m	14m
Current Assets	51m	42m	44m
Current Liabilities	3m	2m	6m

Parkside Health Wheelchair Service
Unit G3 Middlesex Business Centre Bridge Road, Southall, UB2 4AB
Tel: 020-8813 9836 **Fax:** 020-8813 9842
Managers: R. Goodyear (Mgr)
No.of Employees: 1 - 10 **Product Groups:** 38

Pioneer Marquees
30 Villiers Rd, Southall, UB1 3BS
Tel: 020-8574 1742
E-mail: sales@pioneermarquees.com
Website: http://www.pioneermarquees.com
Managers: U. Ghafoor (Sales Prom Mgr)
Registration no: 06965134 **Date established:** 2004
Turnover: Up to £250,000 **No.of Employees:** 1 - 10 **Product Groups:** 24, 83

Quaker Oats Ltd
PO Box 24 Bridge Road, Southall, UB2 4AG
Tel: 020-8574 2388 **Fax:** 020-8574 6615
E-mail: marketing@quaker.co.uk
Website: http://www.quakeroats.com
Bank(s): National Westminster
Directors: G. Sewell (Pres), S. Fraser (Dir), C. Stone (Dir)
Managers: R. Potter (Purch Mgr)
Ultimate Holding Company: The Quaker Oats Co. Inc. (USA)
Immediate Holding Company: Quaker Holdings UK Ltd
Registration no: 00064262 **VAT No.:** GB 222 8136 87
Date established: 2007 **Turnover:** £50m - £75m
No.of Employees: 101 - 250 **Product Groups:** 20

Richard A Fores
Dagmar Road, Southall, UB2 5NX
Tel: 020-8574 5287 **Fax:** 020-8574 3105
E-mail: r.a.fores@btinternet.com
Website: http://www.btinternet.com
Directors: S. Fores (Fin)
Immediate Holding Company: RICHARD A. FORES LIMITED
Registration no: 00610990 **VAT No.:** GB 222 4430 10
Date established: 1958 **Turnover:** £250,000 - £500,000
No.of Employees: 1 - 10 **Product Groups:** 48

Date of Accounts	Mar 11	Mar 10	Mar 09
Working Capital	90	319	315
Fixed Assets	64	73	88
Current Assets	413	383	372

T R S Cash & Carry Ltd
3 Southbridge Way, Southall, UB2 4AX
Tel: 020-8843 5400 **Fax:** 020-8574 5254
E-mail: mail@trs.co.uk
Website: http://www.trs.co.uk
Bank(s): National Westminster Bank Plc
Directors: H. Suterwalla (MD)
Ultimate Holding Company: TRS CASH & CARRY (HOLDINGS) LIMITED
Immediate Holding Company: TRS CASH & CARRY LIMITED
Registration no: 00920682 **VAT No.:** GB 226 2890 59
Date established: 1967 **Turnover:** £20m - £50m
No.of Employees: 101 - 250 **Product Groups:** 61

Date of Accounts	Dec 10	Dec 09	Dec 08
Sales Turnover	48m	52m	49m
Pre Tax Profit/Loss	2m	2m	2m
Working Capital	18m	17m	16m
Fixed Assets	694	717	730
Current Assets	22m	25m	23m
Current Liabilities	960	4m	3m

Watts Industrial Tyres plc
9 Market Trading Estate Christopher Road, Southall, UB2 5YG
Tel: 020-8813 6660 **Fax:** 020-8813 7353
E-mail: southall@watts-tyres.co.uk
Website: http://www.watts-tyres.co.uk
Directors: J. Thurston (MD), J. Fullick (Div)
Managers: P. Fullick (Mgr), P. Fullick (District Mgr)
Ultimate Holding Company: TRELLEBORG AB (SWEDEN)
Immediate Holding Company: WATTS INDUSTRIAL TYRES LIMITED
Registration no: 01434811 **Date established:** 1979
No.of Employees: 1 - 10 **Product Groups:** 29, 68

Date of Accounts	Dec 10	Dec 09	Dec 08
Sales Turnover	10m	12m	14m
Pre Tax Profit/Loss	906	60	28
Working Capital	446	-398	-625
Fixed Assets	597	551	719
Current Assets	4m	5m	4m
Current Liabilities	541	565	610

Staines

Acton Bright Steel
Gordon Road The Causeway, Staines, TW18 3BG
Tel: 01784-455273 **Fax:** 01784-451748
E-mail: sales@actonbrightsteel.co.uk
Website: http://www.actonbrightsteel.co.uk
Bank(s): Barclays
Directors: A. Coghlan (Sales), N. Holland (Fin)
Immediate Holding Company: ACTON BRIGHT STEEL LIMITED
Registration no: 00755037 **VAT No.:** GB 207 5605 77
Date established: 1963 **Turnover:** £1m - £2m **No.of Employees:** 21 - 50
Product Groups: 34, 66

Date of Accounts	Apr 11	Apr 10	Apr 09
Working Capital	2m	2m	2m
Fixed Assets	355	384	422
Current Assets	3m	2m	2m

Alstec Ltd
Unit 3-5 The Camgate Centre Long Lane, Staines, TW19 7AX
Tel: 01784-420852 **Fax:** 01784-241740
Managers: J. Conway (Chief Mgr)
Ultimate Holding Company: Babcock International Group plc
Immediate Holding Company: ALSTEC LIMITED
Registration no: 03014476 **Date established:** 1995
No.of Employees: 51 - 100 **Product Groups:** 38, 42

Applebee Exports Ltd
2 Lord Knyvett Close Stanwell, Staines, TW19 7PF
Tel: 020-8150 6242 **Fax:** 020-8751 1337
E-mail: sales@abelparts.com
Website: http://www.abelparts.com
Directors: R. Gill (Dir), A. Gill (Dir)
Immediate Holding Company: APPLE BEE EXPORTS LTD
Registration no: 05180817 **Date established:** 2004
No.of Employees: 1 - 10 **Product Groups:** 67

Date of Accounts	Jul 07	Jul 06
Working Capital	6	7
Current Assets	22	13
Current Liabilities	16	6
Total Share Capital	1	1

Astellas Pharma Ltd (Associated Co. Yamanouchi)
Lovett House Causeway Corporate Centre Lovett Road, Staines, TW18 3AZ
Tel: 01784-419615 **Fax:** 01784-419401
Website: http://www.astellas-europe.co.uk
Bank(s): Midland, Hitchin
Directors: D. Ferguson (MD), R. Turnbull (Co Sec)
Ultimate Holding Company: ASTELLAS PHARMA INC (JAPAN)
Immediate Holding Company: ASTELLAS PHARMA EUROPE LTD.
Registration no: 02486792 **VAT No.:** GB 222 2295 00
Date established: 1990 **Turnover:** £500m - £1,000m
No.of Employees: 101 - 250 **Product Groups:** 31

Boden Sheet Metal Ltd
Drake House Drake Avenue, Staines, TW18 2AW
Tel: 01784-452683 **Fax:** 01784-465889
E-mail: info@bodensheetmetal.co.uk
Website: http://www.bodensheetmetal.co.uk
Directors: V. Borman (Dir)
Immediate Holding Company: BODEN SHEET METAL LIMITED
Registration no: 04454597 **VAT No.:** GB 290 3516 74
Date established: 2002 **Turnover:** £250,000 - £500,000
No.of Employees: 1 - 10 **Product Groups:** 48

Date of Accounts	Dec 11	Dec 10	Dec 09
Working Capital	-87	-109	-3
Fixed Assets	254	258	262
Current Assets	111	130	151
Current Liabilities	129	46	41

Capital Equipment & Machinery Ltd
Mill Mead, Staines, TW18 4UQ
Tel: 01784-456151 **Fax:** 01784-466481
E-mail: sales@capital-equipment.com
Website: http://www.capital-equipment.com
Directors: C. Hayes (I.T. Dir), N. Bongers (Ch), N. Bongers (Ch & MD)
Registration no: 00955816 **VAT No.:** GB 448 8101 40
Date established: 1981 **Turnover:** £500,000 - £1m
No.of Employees: 1 - 10 **Product Groups:** 44, 48, 66, 67

Date of Accounts	Jun 08	Jun 07	Jun 06
Working Capital	279	271	287
Fixed Assets	6	8	9
Current Assets	400	425	555
Current Liabilities	121	154	269
Total Share Capital	87	87	87

Celsur Plastics Ltd
3 Lovett Road The Causeway, Staines, TW18 3AZ
Tel: 01784-457175 **Fax:** 01784-454605
E-mail: info@celsurplastics.co.uk
Website: http://www.celsur.co.uk
Bank(s): Barclays, Slough
Directors: R. Freeman (MD), K. De Zoysa (Fin)
Ultimate Holding Company: CELSUR GROUP LIMITED
Immediate Holding Company: CELSUR PLASTICS LIMITED
Registration no: 00663439 **VAT No.:** GB 207 6564 60
Date established: 1960 **Turnover:** £5m - £10m
No.of Employees: 101 - 250 **Product Groups:** 48

Date of Accounts	Dec 11	Dec 10	Dec 09
Sales Turnover	6m	6m	6m
Pre Tax Profit/Loss	337	312	274
Working Capital	3m	2m	2m
Fixed Assets	228	248	165
Current Assets	4m	4m	4m
Current Liabilities	879	691	779

Courage Ltd
1 Bridge Street, Staines, TW18 4TP
Tel: 01784-466199 **Fax:** 01784-468131
E-mail: enquiries@f-n.com
Website: http://www.scottish-newcastle.com
Bank(s): National Westminster Bank Plc
Directors: B. Emms (Fin), D. O'flanagan (MD), J. Botie (Pers), J. Louden (I.T. Dir)
Managers: J. Mckenzie (Chief Acct), S. Brown (Nat Sales Mgr)
Ultimate Holding Company: SCOTTISH & NEWCASTLE LIMITED
Immediate Holding Company: Heineken UK Ltd
Registration no: 03043813 **Date established:** 1995
Turnover: Over £1,000m **No.of Employees:** 251 - 500
Product Groups: 21

D & N Carpentry
16 Florence Gardens, Staines, TW18 1HG
Tel: 07973-354003
E-mail: deanbriancox@hotmail.co.uk
Website: http://carpenter-and-joiner-surrey.co.uk/
Directors: D. Cox (Prop)
No.of Employees: 1 - 10 **Product Groups:** 30, 52

D S Freight Services Ltd
The Mill Horton Road, Staines, TW19 6BJ
Tel: 01753-682153 **Fax:** 01753-682154
E-mail: david.shawki@technicalwebservices.com
Website: http://www.dsfreight.co.uk
Directors: D. Shawki (MD)
Immediate Holding Company: D.S. FREIGHT SERVICES LIMITED
Registration no: 04257318 **Date established:** 2001
No.of Employees: 1 - 10 **Product Groups:** 76

Date of Accounts	Dec 11	Dec 10	Dec 09
Working Capital	-2	-7	-5
Fixed Assets	37	35	6
Current Assets	114	164	130

Dalkia plc
Elizabeth House 56-60 London Road, Staines, TW18 4BQ
Tel: 01784-496200 **Fax:** 01784-496222
E-mail: info@dalkia.co.uk
Website: http://www.dalkia.co.uk
Directors: P. Stevens (Fin), R. Bent (MD), S. Turnbull (Pers)
Ultimate Holding Company: VEOLIA ENVIRONNEMENT SA (FRANCE)
Immediate Holding Company: DALKIA PLC
Registration no: 00883131 **Date established:** 1966
Turnover: £125m - £250m **No.of Employees:** 251 - 500
Product Groups: 54, 84

Date of Accounts	Dec 11	Dec 10	Dec 09
Sales Turnover	151m	136m	134m
Pre Tax Profit/Loss	3m	8m	5m
Working Capital	-19m	29m	66m
Fixed Assets	97m	45m	73m
Current Assets	79m	99m	123m
Current Liabilities	26m	37m	30m

Design Incorporated UK Ltd
Centurion House London Road, Staines, TW18 4AX
Tel: 01784-410380 **Fax:** 01784-410310
E-mail: sales@designinc.co.uk
Website: http://www.designinc.co.uk
Directors: F. Norman (MD)
Immediate Holding Company: DESIGN INCORPORATED (UK) LIMITED
Registration no: 04618464 **Date established:** 2002
No.of Employees: 1 - 10 **Product Groups:** 81

Date of Accounts	Jan 12	Jan 11	Jan 10
Working Capital	49	41	84
Fixed Assets	20	17	20
Current Assets	211	253	228

Extem Tool Design
Mill Mead, Staines, TW18 4UQ
Tel: 01784-490630 **Fax:** 01784-490630
Directors: K. Fox (Dir)
Date established: 1997 **No.of Employees:** 1 - 10 **Product Groups:** 36

Fermod Ltd
Unit 2 Northumberland Close Stanwell, Staines, TW19 7LN
Tel: 01784-248376 **Fax:** 01784-257285
E-mail: sales@fermod.co.uk
Website: http://www.fermod.com
Directors: M. Strickland (Sales), R. Alger (MD), S. Alger (Co Sec)
Managers: B. Ashton (Sales Prom Mgr)
Immediate Holding Company: FERMOD LIMITED
Registration no: 00832943 **Date established:** 1964 **Turnover:** £2m - £5m
No.of Employees: 11 - 20 **Product Groups:** 40, 67

Date of Accounts	Apr 11	Apr 10	Apr 09
Working Capital	1m	1m	1m
Fixed Assets	5	9	28
Current Assets	2m	2m	2m

Intergrated Electronics Ltd
20 Ferry Lane Wraysbury, Staines, TW19 6HG
Tel: 01784-483633 **Fax:** 01784-483918
E-mail: contact@ielco.com
Website: http://www.ielco.com
Bank(s): HSBC Bank plc
Directors: R. Hall (MD), J. Wakefield (Fin)
Ultimate Holding Company: GARSTON DEVELOPMENTS LIMITED
Immediate Holding Company: INTEGRATED ELECTRONICS LIMITED
Registration no: 00695321 **VAT No.:** GB 207 7436 64
Date established: 1961 **Turnover:** £500,000 - £1m
No.of Employees: 11 - 20 **Product Groups:** 37

Date of Accounts	May 11	May 10	May 09
Working Capital	15	9	5
Fixed Assets	3	4	4
Current Assets	69	58	69

J P Kenny Ltd
Compass Point 79-87 Kingston Road, Staines, TW18 1DT
Tel: 01784-417200 **Fax:** 01784-417283
E-mail: dave.baker@jpkenny.com
Website: http://www.jpkenny.com
Bank(s): Lloyds TSB Bank plc
Directors: D. Baker (MD)
Ultimate Holding Company: JOHN WOOD GROUP P.L.C.
Immediate Holding Company: J P KENNY LIMITED
Registration no: 01398385 **Date established:** 1978
Turnover: £50m - £75m **No.of Employees:** 251 - 500 **Product Groups:** 84

Date of Accounts	Dec 11	Dec 10	Dec 09
Sales Turnover	56m	51m	55m
Pre Tax Profit/Loss	8m	6m	10m
Working Capital	5m	10m	7m
Fixed Assets	833	204	329
Current Assets	25m	28m	25m
Current Liabilities	14m	13m	14m

Jas Forwarding UK Ltd
Bedfont Road Stanwell, Staines, TW19 7NZ
Tel: 01784-229000 **Fax:** 01784-250643
E-mail: dholland@jasuk.com
Website: http://www.jasuk.com
Directors: N. Broadbent (Dir)
Managers: D. Holland (I.T. Exec)
Ultimate Holding Company: ATH AIR TRANSPORT HOLDINGS SA (SWITZERLAND)
Immediate Holding Company: JAS FORWARDING (UK) LIMITED
Registration no: 01824515 **Date established:** 1984
Turnover: £250m - £500m **No.of Employees:** 51 - 100
Product Groups: 76

Date of Accounts	Dec 11	Dec 10	Dec 09
Sales Turnover	32m	397m	303m
Pre Tax Profit/Loss	-3m	3m	925
Working Capital	5m	24m	28m
Fixed Assets	17m	3m	3m
Current Assets	11m	82m	80m
Current Liabilities	2m	13m	4m

Jewson Ltd
Moor Lane, Staines, TW18 4YN
Tel: 01784-457516 **Fax:** 01784-460106
Website: http://www.jewson.co.uk
Managers: M. Goymer (District Mgr)
Ultimate Holding Company: COMPAGNIE DE SAINT GOBAIN (FRANCE)
Immediate Holding Company: JEWSON LIMITED
Registration no: 00348407 **VAT No.:** GB 394 1212 63
Date established: 1939 **Turnover:** £500m - £1,000m
No.of Employees: 1 - 10 **Product Groups:** 66

Date of Accounts	Dec 11	Dec 10	Dec 09
Sales Turnover	1606m	1547m	1485m
Pre Tax Profit/Loss	18m	100m	45m
Working Capital	-345m	-250m	-349m
Fixed Assets	496m	387m	461m
Current Assets	657m	1005m	1320m
Current Liabilities	66m	120m	64m

K R Tools
173-175 Laleham Road, Staines, TW18 2NR
Tel: 01784-461225 **Fax:** 01784-455679
E-mail: keithrose@btinternet.com
Website: http://www.krtools.co.uk
Directors: K. Rose (Prop)
Turnover: £500,000 - £1m **No.of Employees:** 1 - 10 **Product Groups:** 36, 38, 40, 42, 46, 52, 67

Keep Able Hearing & Mobility
11-17 Kingston Road, Staines, TW18 4QX
Tel: 01784-440044
E-mail: staines@hearingandmobility.com
Website: http://www.hearingandmobility.co.uk
Managers: O. Nunn
No.of Employees: 1 - 10 **Product Groups:** 37, 38, 39

Kommerling International Ltd
6 The Courtyard 80 High Street, Staines, TW18 4DR
Tel: 01543-444900 **Fax:** 01784-455764
E-mail: enquiries@kommerling.co.uk
Website: http://www.kommerling.com
Bank(s): HSBC Bank plc
Directors: O. Schmid (Dir), P. Shmid-Kommerling (Dir), W. Posner (Dir)
Managers: C. Breeze (Chief Mgr)
Immediate Holding Company: Kommerling GmbH
Registration no: 01811296 **Date established:** 1984 **Turnover:** £5m - £10m
No.of Employees: 11 - 20 **Product Groups:** 52

Kuwait Petroleum GB Ltd
Burgan House The Causeway, Staines, TW18 3PA
Tel: 01784-467788 **Fax:** 01784-467600
E-mail: sales@kuwait.com
Website: http://www.q8.co.uk
Directors: B. Handley (Dir)
Managers: D. Hathaway (I.T. Exec), G. Timbers (Sales Prom Mgr), I. Rose (Mktg Serv Mgr), R. Exley (Sales Prom Mgr)
Ultimate Holding Company: MRH (GB) Ltd
Immediate Holding Company: Refined Holdings Ltd
Registration no: 02063581 **VAT No.:** GB 244 0317 00
Date established: 1963 **Turnover:** £500m - £1,000m
No.of Employees: 251 - 500 **Product Groups:** 13, 42

Premier Laboratory Services Ltd
142 Hithermoor Road, Staines, TW19 6BB
Tel: 01753-449415 **Fax:** 01753-449415
E-mail: info@premierlabserve.co.uk
Website: http://www.premierlabserve.co.uk
Directors: D. Buck (MD)
Immediate Holding Company: PREMIER LABORATORY SERVICES LIMITED
Registration no: 05478273 **VAT No.:** GB 225 7726 53
Date established: 2005 **Turnover:** Up to £250,000
No.of Employees: 1 - 10 **Product Groups:** 42

Date of Accounts	Jun 11	Jun 10	Jun 09
Sales Turnover	N/A	92	153
Pre Tax Profit/Loss	N/A	11	11
Working Capital	-9	-5	-8
Fixed Assets	10	7	9
Current Assets	37	8	14
Current Liabilities	N/A	10	18

Quantum Transportation Ltd
The Mill Horton Road, Staines, TW19 6BF
Tel: 01753-683399 **Fax:** 08704-324543
E-mail: info@quantumtransportation.co.uk
Website: http://www.quantumtransportation.co.uk
Directors: S. Francis (Fin), T. Francis (MD)
Immediate Holding Company: QUANTUM TRANSPORTATION LIMITED
Registration no: 03556788 **Date established:** 1998
No.of Employees: 1 - 10 **Product Groups:** 72, 74, 75

Date of Accounts	Dec 11	Dec 10	Dec 09
Working Capital	255	228	231
Fixed Assets	14	21	9
Current Assets	496	407	376

R & R Joinery
103 London Road, Staines, TW18 4HN
Tel: 01784-465308 **Fax:** 01784-450124
E-mail: sales@rrjoinery.co.uk
Website: http://www.rrjoinery.co.uk
Directors: R. Rough (MD)
Date established: 1984 **Turnover:** £2m - £5m **No.of Employees:** 11 - 20
Product Groups: 52

Rainbow Freight Services Ltd
Mill Mead, Staines, TW18 4UQ
Tel: 01784-455356 **Fax:** 01784-455350
E-mail: david@rainbowfreight.com
Website: http://www.rainbowfreight.com
Directors: D. Gicquel (MD)
Immediate Holding Company: RAINBOW FREIGHT SERVICES LIMITED
Registration no: 01044743 **Date established:** 1972 **Turnover:** £1m - £2m
No.of Employees: 1 - 10 **Product Groups:** 75

Date of Accounts	Mar 12	Mar 11	Mar 10
Working Capital	157	131	16
Fixed Assets	N/A	10	23
Current Assets	308	408	194

Reed Employment Ltd
91 High Street, Staines, TW18 4PQ
Tel: 01784-458526 **Fax:** 01784-466466
E-mail: staines@reed.co.uk
Website: http://www.reed.co.uk
Directors: P. Sharmer (MD)
Managers: C. Cantello (District Mgr), J. Brodie (District Mgr), N. Hardy (District Mgr)
Ultimate Holding Company: REED GLOBAL LTD (MALTA)
Immediate Holding Company: REED EMPLOYMENT LIMITED
Registration no: 00669854 **Date established:** 1960
Turnover: £500m - £1,000m **No.of Employees:** 1 - 10
Product Groups: 80

Date of Accounts	Jun 11	Jun 10	Dec 07
Sales Turnover	618	450	287m
Pre Tax Profit/Loss	-2m	310	8m
Working Capital	23m	28m	28m
Fixed Assets	31	36	5m
Current Assets	28m	30m	74m
Current Liabilities	37	29	21m

Remmington Consumer Products
Watermans Court Watermans Business Park Kingsbury CR, Staines, TW18 3BA
Tel: 01784-411411 **Fax:** 01784-411412
E-mail: sales@remmington-products.com
Website: http://www.remmington-products.com
Directors: D. Greenwood (Sales), G. Charles (Dir), K. Dawns (MD), G. Rowe (Co Sec)
Managers: C. Clark (I.T. Exec), I. Francis (Sales Admin), T. Sankey (Personnel)
Ultimate Holding Company: SPECTRUM BRANDS INC (USA)
Immediate Holding Company: REMINGTON CONSUMER PRODUCTS
Registration no: 01396316 **Date established:** 1978
Turnover: £50m - £75m **No.of Employees:** 21 - 50 **Product Groups:** 36, 40

Seriously Sorted Ltd t/a Microlimit
P.O. Box 542, Staines, TW18 9DG
Tel: 07768-461441 **Fax:** 020-8901 6511
E-mail: info@microlimit.co.uk
Website: http://www.microlimit.co.uk
Directors: N. Budgen (Prop), N. Budgen (Ptnr)
Registration no: 07130669 **Date established:** 1955
No.of Employees: 1 - 10 **Product Groups:** 35, 36

Date of Accounts	Mar 07
Sales Turnover	89
Pre Tax Profit/Loss	-1
Working Capital	8
Current Assets	53
Current Liabilities	45
ROCE% (Return on Capital Employed)	-15.4

Sesame Access Systems Ltd
Tims Boatyard Timsway, Staines, TW18 3JY
Tel: 01784-440088 **Fax:** 01784-440088
E-mail: info@wheelchairaccess.co.uk
Website: http://www.wheelchairaccess.co.uk
Managers: S. Lyons (Projects)
Immediate Holding Company: SESAME ACCESS SYSTEMS LIMITED
Registration no: 03259843 **Date established:** 1996
No.of Employees: 1 - 10 **Product Groups:** 39, 45, 67

Date of Accounts	Oct 11	Oct 10	Oct 09
Working Capital	103	38	37
Fixed Assets	17	20	14
Current Assets	305	92	58

Splicing & Allied Company Ltd
Eldorado Works Drake Avenue, Staines, TW18 2AP
Tel: 01784-455121 **Fax:** 01784-454788
E-mail: info@splicingallied.com
Website: http://www.splicingallied.com
Directors: D. Higgins (MD), S. Farmer (MD)
Immediate Holding Company: SPLICING AND ALLIED SERVICES COMPANY LIMITED
Registration no: 01103578 **Date established:** 1973
No.of Employees: 1 - 10 **Product Groups:** 35, 39, 45

Date of Accounts	Mar 12	Mar 11	Mar 10
Working Capital	372	409	433
Fixed Assets	2	2	3
Current Assets	431	459	514

Staines Steel Gate Company Ltd
18-24 Ruskin Road, Staines, TW18 2PX
Tel: 01784-454456 **Fax:** 01784-466668
Website: http://www.stainesgates.co.uk
Directors: C. Gingell (MD)
Immediate Holding Company: STAINES STEEL GATE COMPANY LIMITED
Registration no: 00479499 **Date established:** 1950
No.of Employees: 1 - 10 **Product Groups:** 26, 35

Date of Accounts	Dec 11	Dec 10	Dec 09
Working Capital	197	260	376
Fixed Assets	7	9	11
Current Assets	258	280	410

Tekni Kleen Computer Services Ltd
PO Box 200, Staines, TW18 4QE
Tel: 01784-469133 **Fax:** 01784-451277
E-mail: colin@teknikleen.co.uk
Website: http://www.teknikleen.co.uk
Directors: C. Buzzard (MD)
Managers: N. Sorrell (Develop Mgr)
Immediate Holding Company: TEKNI KLEEN COMPUTER SERVICES LTD
Registration no: 04849562 **VAT No.:** GB 529 9648 86
Date established: 2003 **Turnover:** Up to £250,000
No.of Employees: 21 - 50 **Product Groups:** 52

Date of Accounts	Aug 09	Aug 08	Sep 11
Working Capital	191	160	336
Fixed Assets	2	N/A	2
Current Assets	233	208	361

Thales Optronics Ltd
Heritage Court Thorpe Road, Staines, TW18 3HP
Tel: 0141-440 4000 **Fax:** 0141-440 4001
Website: http://www.thalesgroup.com
Directors: E. Mccrorie (Fin)
Ultimate Holding Company: Thales Holdings UK plc
Immediate Holding Company: Thales Optronics (Holdings) Ltd
Registration no: SC008495 **Turnover:** £125m - £250m
No.of Employees: 501 - 1000 **Product Groups:** 37, 38, 65

Stanmore

3E UK Ltd
14 Free Trade House Lowther Road, Queensbury, Stanmore, HA7 1EP
Tel: 0844-8849739
E-mail: solutions_3e@hotmail.com
Website: http://www.3esolutions.net
Directors: B. Dilawari (Sales)
Managers: A. Ward (Chief Acct)
Registration no: 06715061 **Date established:** 2005
Turnover: £250,000 - £500,000 **No.of Employees:** 11 - 20
Product Groups: 44

Date of Accounts	Oct 06
Sales Turnover	27
Pre Tax Profit/Loss	4
Working Capital	4
Current Assets	13
Current Liabilities	9

Automobile Trimmings Co.
Stonebridge Works Cumberland Road, Stanmore, HA7 1EL
Tel: 020-8204 8242 **Fax:** 020-8204 0255
E-mail: info@automobiletrim.com
Website: http://www.automobiletrim.com
Directors: J. David (Prop)
Immediate Holding Company: HOTEL PROMOTIONS SERVICES LIMITED
Registration no: 02593789 **VAT No.:** GB 226 5327 71
Date established: 1971 **No.of Employees:** 1 - 10 **Product Groups:** 36, 68

Date of Accounts	Dec 10	Dec 08	Dec 07
Working Capital	1	1	1
Fixed Assets	1	1	1
Current Assets	2	2	2

Chas A Blatchford & Sons Ltd
Royal National Orthopaedic Hospital Brockley Hill, Stanmore, HA7 4LP
Tel: 020-8954 5024 **Fax:** 020-8954 0182
Website: http://www.blatchford.co.uk
Managers: C. Wood
Immediate Holding Company: THE DISABILITY FOUNDATION LIMITED
Registration no: 02893346 **Date established:** 1999
Turnover: £250,000 - £500,000 **No.of Employees:** 21 - 50
Product Groups: 38, 67

Date of Accounts	Dec 11	Dec 10	Dec 09
Sales Turnover	193	239	260
Pre Tax Profit/Loss	-114	-80	45
Working Capital	593	707	787
Current Assets	715	905	859
Current Liabilities	121	198	72

Complex Ltd
1st Floor 19 Cumberland Road, Stanmore, HA7 1EL
Tel: 020-8206 2067 **Fax:** 020-8204 2294
E-mail: complex@jayaar.com
Website: http://www.jayaar.com
Directors: J. Haria (Fin), R. Haria (MD)
Immediate Holding Company: COMPLEX LIMITED
Registration no: 01604076 **VAT No.:** GB 379 6563 90
Date established: 1981 **Turnover:** £500,000 - £1m
No.of Employees: 1 - 10 **Product Groups:** 87

Date of Accounts	Mar 11	Mar 10	Mar 09
Working Capital	168	145	143
Fixed Assets	3	4	2
Current Assets	349	295	355

Data Sharp
Snaresbrook Drive, Stanmore, HA7 4QN
Tel: 020-8958 9602 **Fax:** 0870-050 5929
E-mail: info@dsvd.co.uk
Website: http://www.datasharp-vd.co.uk
Directors: J. Bardon (Prop)
Immediate Holding Company: DATASHARP VOICE & DATA LIMITED
Registration no: 04431058 **Date established:** 2002
No.of Employees: 1 - 10 **Product Groups:** 48

Date of Accounts	May 07	May 06
Working Capital	N/A	4
Fixed Assets	1	1
Current Assets	38	34
Current Liabilities	38	31

Glen Spectra Ltd
2 Dalston Gardens, Stanmore, HA7 1BQ
Tel: 020-8204 9517 **Fax:** 020-8204 5189
E-mail: info@glenspectra.co.uk
Website: http://www.glenspectra.co.uk
Directors: C. Kemp (MD), A. Benattar (MD), A. Benatter (MD)
Managers: S. Lewis (I.T. Exec), E. Gribbin ()
Ultimate Holding Company: HORIBA LTD
Immediate Holding Company: JOBIN YVON LTD
Registration no: 2242542 **VAT No.:** GB 468 2372 25
No.of Employees: 21 - 50 **Product Groups:** 33, 38

Date of Accounts	Dec 03	Dec 02	Dec 01
Working Capital	177	138	133
Fixed Assets	8	17	17
Current Assets	324	263	388
Current Liabilities	147	125	256

Honeypot Cosmetics & Perfumery Sales
Unit 4a Honeypot Business Centre Parr Road, Stanmore, HA7 1NL
Tel: 020-8951 3686
E-mail: info@honeypotcosmetics.com
Website: http://www.honeypotcosmetics.com
Directors: M. Lalji (Fin)
Immediate Holding Company: HONEYPOT COSMETICS (WHOLESALE) LIMITED
Registration no: 06276399 **Date established:** 2007
No.of Employees: 1 - 10 **Product Groups:** 32

Date of Accounts	Aug 11	Aug 10	Aug 09
Working Capital	111	146	139
Fixed Assets	6	13	21
Current Assets	381	330	325
Current Liabilities	130	39	N/A

Horiba Scientific
2 Dalston Gardens, Stanmore, HA7 1BQ
Tel: 020-8204 8142 **Fax:** 020-8204 6142
E-mail: jy@jyhoriba.co.uk
Website: http://www.horiba.com/uk/scientific
Directors: C. Kemp (MD)
Immediate Holding Company: HORIBA JOBIN YVON IBH LTD
Registration no: 01326526 **Date established:** 1977
No.of Employees: 21 - 50 **Product Groups:** 48

Date of Accounts	Dec 11	Dec 10	Dec 09
Working Capital	499	445	480
Fixed Assets	138	175	119
Current Assets	2m	2m	3m
Current Liabilities	N/A	N/A	1

Madison
Burnell House 8 Stanmore Hill, Stanmore, HA7 3BQ
Tel: 020-8385 3385 **Fax:** 020-8385 3444
E-mail: dominic.langan@madison.co.uk
Website: http://www.madison.co.uk
Bank(s): National Westminster
Directors: B. Baxter (Sales), D. Langan (MD), P. Barker (Comm), P. Clements (Fin)
Managers: G. Trent (Tech Serv Mgr), W. Fripp
Ultimate Holding Company: H. YOUNG HOLDINGS P.L.C.
Registration no: 00706712 **Turnover:** £20m - £50m
No.of Employees: 21 - 50 **Product Groups:** 39

M C C Group London Ltd
Buckingham House East Buckingham Parade The Broadway, Stanmore, HA7 4EB
Tel: 020-8954 5061 **Fax:** 020-8954 8628
E-mail: info@mccgrouplondon.com
Website: http://www.mccgrouplondon.com
Directors: T. Newman (Head)
Ultimate Holding Company: MEDICALS DIRECT HOLDINGS LIMITED
Immediate Holding Company: BRESLAUER LIMITED
Registration no: 04115597 **Date established:** 2006 **Turnover:** £1m - £2m
No.of Employees: 1 - 10 **Product Groups:** 66, 84

Date of Accounts	Mar 11	Mar 09	Mar 08
Working Capital	-61	-55	-13
Fixed Assets	N/A	10	14
Current Assets	76	70	71

Multi Installations
502 Honeypot Lane, Stanmore, HA7 1JR
Tel: 020-8731 1212 **Fax:** 020-8204 2888
E-mail: info@multi1.co.uk
Website: http://www.multi1.co.uk
Directors: M. Pindoria (Fin), N. Pindoria (Dir)
Immediate Holding Company: MULTI INSTALLATIONS LTD
Registration no: 03359115 **Date established:** 1997 **Turnover:** £5m - £10m
No.of Employees: 51 - 100 **Product Groups:** 25

Date of Accounts	Mar 11	Mar 10	Mar 09
Working Capital	166	120	117
Fixed Assets	142	170	231
Current Assets	1m	2m	2m

Si Property Consultants Ltd
39 Hermitage Way, Stanmore, HA7 2AX
Tel: 020-8930 1684 **Fax:** 020-8424 2557
E-mail: office@siproperty.co.uk
Website: http://www.siproperty.co.uk
Directors: K. Halai (Fin), R. Halai (MD)
Immediate Holding Company: SI PROPERTY CONSULTANTS LIMITED
Registration no: 05199565 **Date established:** 2004
No.of Employees: 1 - 10 **Product Groups:** 80

Date of Accounts	Aug 11	Aug 10	Aug 09
Working Capital	-2	-2	N/A
Fixed Assets	2	3	3
Current Assets	18	19	14

Tyco Electronics Ltd
Terminal House Merrion Avenue, Stanmore, HA7 4RS
Tel: 0870-6080208 **Fax:** 020-8954 6234
Website: http://www.tycoelectronics.com
Bank(s): The Royal Bank of Scotland
Directors: A. Clarke (MD), S. Allen (Pers), T. Gatt (MD), G. Quaegebeur (Fin)
Managers: S. Allen, M. Squire (I.T. Exec)
Immediate Holding Company: TYCO ELECTRONICS LIMITED
Registration no: 03871371 **Date established:** 1999 **Turnover:** £1m - £2m
No.of Employees: 251 - 500 **Product Groups:** 30, 35, 36, 37, 38, 39, 40, 41, 42, 44, 46, 47, 48, 63, 66, 67, 68, 85

Sunbury On Thames

ADT
Security House Summit Business Park Hanworth Road, Sunbury On Thames, TW16 5DB
Tel: 01932-743456 **Fax:** 01932-743222
E-mail: anton.alphonsus@adt.co.uk
Website: http://www.adt.co.uk
Bank(s): HSBC, Farnham
Directors: A. Alphonsus (Fin)
Ultimate Holding Company: TYCO INTERNATIONAL LIMITED (SWITZERLAND)
Immediate Holding Company: ADT (UK) LIMITED
Registration no: 01838517 **VAT No.:** GB 413 6330 86
Date established: 1984 **No.of Employees:** 51 - 100 **Product Groups:** 36, 37, 38, 40, 52, 81

Date of Accounts	Sep 11	Sep 10	Sep 09
Pre Tax Profit/Loss	2m	-1	-1m
Working Capital	-870m	-874m	-874m
Fixed Assets	299m	301m	301m
Current Assets	4m	2m	2m
Current Liabilities	5	4	N/A

AMETEK Airscrew Limited
111 Windmill Road, Sunbury On Thames, TW16 7EF
Tel: 01932-765822 **Fax:** 01932-761098
E-mail: mail.airscrew@ametek.co.uk
Website: http://www.airscrew.co.uk
Bank(s): HSBC Bank plc
Directors: J. Mockler (Pers), K. Sena (Co Sec)
Managers: G. Jones, P. Heapy, S. Rayner
Ultimate Holding Company: Ema Holdings UK Ltd
Immediate Holding Company: Airscrew Ltd
Registration no: 00499805 **VAT No.:** GB 384 4960 16
Date established: 2003 **Turnover:** £20m - £50m
No.of Employees: 101 - 250 **Product Groups:** 37, 38, 39, 40

Ardenta Ltd
Sunbury Business Centre Brooklands Close, Sunbury On Thames, TW16 7DX
Tel: 01932-724027 **Fax:** 08700-549829
E-mail: scott.hanson@ardenta.com
Website: http://www.ardenta.com
Directors: N. Truby (MD), S. Hanson (Tech Serv), S. Hanson (MD)
Managers: A. Calvert (Chief Acct), S. Morgan (Mktg Serv Mgr)
Immediate Holding Company: ARDENTA LIMITED
Registration no: 04181041 **Date established:** 2001 **Turnover:** £5m - £10m
No.of Employees: 21 - 50 **Product Groups:** 44

Date of Accounts	Oct 10	Oct 09	Oct 08
Working Capital	306	652	499
Fixed Assets	102	119	109
Current Assets	1m	2m	2m

Arrow Lift Engineers Ltd
Sunbury Business Centre Brooklands Close, Sunbury On Thames, TW16 7DX
Tel: 01932-724044 **Fax:** 01932-724344
Website: http://www.arrowlifts.co.uk
Directors: I. Phillips (MD), N. Phillips (Fin)
Immediate Holding Company: ARROW LIFT ENGINEERS LIMITED
Registration no: 03563387 **Date established:** 1998
No.of Employees: 1 - 10 **Product Groups:** 45, 48, 67

Date of Accounts	May 11	May 10	May 09
Working Capital	-37	-47	-52
Fixed Assets	41	60	77
Current Assets	272	256	237

Besam Ltd Assa Abloy Group
Washington House Brooklands Close, Sunbury On Thames, TW16 7EQ
Tel: 01932-765888 **Fax:** 01932-765864
E-mail: info@besam.co.uk
Website: http://www.besam.co.uk
Bank(s): National Westminster Bank Plc
Directors: A. Helps (Sales), A. Jaques (Co Sec), J. Jaques (Fin), U. Jonasson (Dir)
Managers: C. Espindula, J. Turpin (Personnel)
Ultimate Holding Company: ASSA ABLOY AB (PUBL) (SWEDEN)
Immediate Holding Company: BESAM LIMITED
Registration no: 00910858 **VAT No.:** GB 494 0601 49
Date established: 1967 **Turnover:** £10m - £20m
No.of Employees: 21 - 50 **Product Groups:** 37

Date of Accounts	Dec 11	Dec 10	Dec 09
Sales Turnover	18m	17m	18m
Pre Tax Profit/Loss	642	222	-6m
Working Capital	4m	5m	4m
Fixed Assets	223	139	87
Current Assets	10m	10m	10m
Current Liabilities	2m	2m	3m

Cameron Ltd
Cameron House 61-73 Staines Road West, Sunbury On Thames, TW16 7AH
Tel: 01932-732000 **Fax:** 01276-681107
E-mail: jane.turner@c-a-m.com
Website: http://www.c-a-m.com
Directors: J. Pellegrin (Pers)
Managers: N. Mendis (Tech Serv Mgr), R. Crook (Sales & Mktg Mg)
Ultimate Holding Company: CAMERON INTERNATIONAL CORP (USA)
Immediate Holding Company: CAMERON SYSTEMS LIMITED
Registration no: 04291991 **Date established:** 2001
Turnover: £20m - £50m **No.of Employees:** 101 - 250
Product Groups: 14, 32, 36, 40, 42, 45, 67

Date of Accounts	Dec 10	Dec 09	Dec 08
Sales Turnover	44m	30m	80m
Pre Tax Profit/Loss	12m	1m	14m
Working Capital	9m	4m	4m
Fixed Assets	16m	16m	16m
Current Assets	31m	24m	33m
Current Liabilities	9m	4m	5m

Cherry Active
99 Manor Lane, Sunbury On Thames, TW16 6JE
Tel: 0845-1705705
E-mail: enquiries@cherryactive.co.uk
Website: http://www.cherryactive.co.uk

Directors: P. Carey (Fin), J. Carey (Dir), J. Carey (MD)
Immediate Holding Company: CHERRY ACTIVE LIMITED
Registration no: 05585268 **Date established:** 2005
No.of Employees: 1 - 10 **Product Groups:** 21

Date of Accounts	Dec 09	Dec 08	Dec 07
Working Capital	315	202	107
Fixed Assets	5	8	8
Current Assets	413	290	161

Chubb Electronic Security Ltd

PO Box 233, Sunbury On Thames, TW16 7XY
Tel: 01932-738600 **Fax:** 01932-787989
E-mail: info@chubb.co.uk
Website: http://www.chubb.co.uk
Directors: C. Forbes (Dir), M. Moore (Co Sec)
Ultimate Holding Company: UNITED TECHNOLOGIES CORP INC (USA)
Immediate Holding Company: CHUBB FIRE & SECURITY LIMITED
Registration no: 00524469 **Date established:** 1953
Turnover: £125m - £250m **No.of Employees:** 501 - 1000
Product Groups: 38, 40, 52

Date of Accounts	Dec 11	Dec 10	Dec 09
Sales Turnover	215m	121m	133m
Pre Tax Profit/Loss	-40m	9m	6m
Working Capital	44m	35m	27m
Fixed Assets	337m	234m	249m
Current Assets	148m	94m	94m
Current Liabilities	56m	44m	52m

Chubb Fire & Security Ltd

Chubb House Staines Road West, Sunbury On Thames, TW16 7AR
Tel: 01932-785588 **Fax:** 01932-782654
E-mail: info@chubb.co.uk
Website: http://www.chubb.co.uk
Bank(s): Barclays
Directors: A. Birchall (Co Sec), C. Stevenson (Fin), J. Dennell (Pers)
Managers: S. Wetson
Ultimate Holding Company: UNITED TECHNOLOGIES CORP INC (USA)
Immediate Holding Company: CHUBB FIRE SECURITY (SA) LIMITED
Registration no: 02937745 **Date established:** 1994 **Turnover:** £2m - £5m
No.of Employees: 21 - 50 **Product Groups:** 39, 40, 52

Date of Accounts	Dec 11	Dec 10	Dec 09
Sales Turnover	215m	121m	133m
Pre Tax Profit/Loss	-40m	9m	6m
Working Capital	44m	35m	27m
Fixed Assets	337m	234m	249m
Current Assets	148m	94m	94m
Current Liabilities	56m	44m	52m

DPF Plastering

10 Mill Farm Avenue, Sunbury On Thames, TW16 7DG
Tel: 01932-770883 **Fax:** 07956-242392
E-mail: info@dpf-plastering.co.uk
Website: http://www.dpf-plastering.co.uk
Directors: D. Fisher (Prop)
No.of Employees: 1 - 10 **Product Groups:** 23, 32, 33, 52

Engineering Appliances Ltd

11 Brooklands Close, Sunbury On Thames, TW16 7DX
Tel: 01932-788888 **Fax:** 01932-761263
E-mail: marlon.foakes@engineering-appliances.com
Website: http://www.engineerings-appliances.com
Bank(s): National Westminster
Directors: M. Foakes (Chief Op Offcr)
Ultimate Holding Company: IMI PLC
Immediate Holding Company: ENGINEERING APPLIANCES LIMITED
Registration no: 02700518 **VAT No.:** 100 4295 24 **Date established:** 1992
Turnover: £500,000 - £1m **No.of Employees:** 11 - 20
Product Groups: 36, 42

Date of Accounts	Dec 11	Dec 10	Dec 09
Sales Turnover	520	3m	4m
Pre Tax Profit/Loss	377	184	-377
Working Capital	N/A	934	667
Fixed Assets	N/A	48	78
Current Assets	N/A	1m	1m
Current Liabilities	N/A	132	225

Gravity Internet Ltd

17 Fairlawns, Sunbury On Thames, TW16 6QR
Tel: 08707-651802 **Fax:** 08707-651803
E-mail: tema@gravityinternet.net
Website: http://www.gravityinternet.net
Directors: T. Hassan (Fin)
Immediate Holding Company: GRAVITY INTERNET LIMITED
Registration no: 05235905 **Date established:** 2004
Turnover: Up to £250,000 **No.of Employees:** 1 - 10 **Product Groups:** 37, 44

Date of Accounts	Dec 08	Dec 06	Dec 05
Sales Turnover	38	16	4
Pre Tax Profit/Loss	-18	-14	-18
Working Capital	8	12	4
Fixed Assets	9	12	15
Current Assets	19	10	8

Esmond Hellerman Ltd

Hellerman House Harris Way, Sunbury On Thames, TW16 7EW
Tel: 01932-781888 **Fax:** 01932-789573
E-mail: sales@hellermans.com
Website: http://www.hellermans.com
Directors: S. Fish (Fin), J. Fish (MD)
Immediate Holding Company: ESMOND HELLERMAN LIMITED
Registration no: 02978647 **VAT No.:** GB 652 8484 11
Date established: 1994 **Turnover:** £250,000 - £500,000
No.of Employees: 1 - 10 **Product Groups:** 26, 38, 64

Date of Accounts	Jan 12	Jan 11	Jan 10
Working Capital	31	30	34
Fixed Assets	3	4	4
Current Assets	62	83	89

I S Solutions

Windmill House 91-93 Windmill Road, Sunbury On Thames, TW16 7EF
Tel: 01932-893300 **Fax:** 01932-893433
E-mail: jim.dodkins@issolutions.co.uk
Website: http://www.issolutions.co.uk
Directors: J. Dodkins (Tech Serv), M. Tinling (Co Sec)
Immediate Holding Company: I S SOLUTIONS PLC
Registration no: 01892751 **Date established:** 1985 **Turnover:** £5m - £10m
No.of Employees: 51 - 100 **Product Groups:** 44

Date of Accounts	Dec 11	Dec 10	Dec 09
Sales Turnover	9m	11m	10m
Pre Tax Profit/Loss	830	684	594
Working Capital	1m	1m	1m
Fixed Assets	4m	4m	4m
Current Assets	3m	3m	4m
Current Liabilities	1m	1m	988

Ikegami Electronics

Unit E1 Cologne Court Brooklands Close, Sunbury On Thames, TW16 7EB
Tel: 01932-769700 **Fax:** 01932- 769710
E-mail: mark@ikegami.co.uk
Website: http://www.ikegami.co.uk
Managers: M. Capstick (Chief Mgr), J. Gibbs (Sales Admin)
Ultimate Holding Company: IKEGAMI TSUSHINKI CO. LTD
Immediate Holding Company: IKEGAMI ELECTRONICS (EUROPE) GMBH
VAT No.: GB 358 4102 59 **Turnover:** £2m - £5m **No.of Employees:** 1 - 10
Product Groups: 37

Impact

Europe House 170 Windmill Road West, Sunbury On Thames, TW16 7HB
Tel: 01932-733700 **Fax:** 01932-733711
E-mail: julian.phillips@impactmarcom.co.uk
Website: http://www.impact-europe.com
Directors: C. Steward (Co Sec), J. Phillips (Dir)
Ultimate Holding Company: IMPACT EUROPE GROUP AB (SWEDEN)
Immediate Holding Company: IMPACT MARCOM LTD
Registration no: 01166286 **Date established:** 1974
Turnover: £20m - £50m **No.of Employees:** 51 - 100 **Product Groups:** 37, 81

Date of Accounts	Dec 11	Dec 10	Dec 09
Sales Turnover	22m	20m	19m
Pre Tax Profit/Loss	410	54	771
Working Capital	3m	3m	3m
Fixed Assets	790	889	724
Current Assets	10m	10m	9m
Current Liabilities	4m	4m	3m

K P K Sheet Metal Ltd

Parkwood Works Brooklands Close, Sunbury On Thames, TW16 7DX
Tel: 01932-789866 **Fax:** 01932-789794
E-mail: sales@kpk-sheetmetal.co.uk
Website: http://www.kpk-sheetmetal.co.uk
Directors: A. Thorpe (Fin), S. Millwood (MD)
Managers: H. Russell (I.T. Exec)
Immediate Holding Company: BLYTH MANAGEMENT SERVICES LIMITED
Registration no: 01231895 **VAT No.:** GB 222 7028 95
Date established: 1975 **Turnover:** £1m - £2m **No.of Employees:** 11 - 20
Product Groups: 48

Date of Accounts	Oct 09	Oct 08	Oct 07
Working Capital	502	481	431
Fixed Assets	64	43	42
Current Assets	641	597	602

Lawton Precision Engineers Ltd

1 25a Hanworth Road, Sunbury On Thames, TW16 5DA
Tel: 01932-789001 **Fax:** 01932- 789003
Directors: M. Cox (Fin), C. Strudwick (Co Sec), S. Barnes (MD)
Ultimate Holding Company: PRECISION PARTNERS LIMITED
Immediate Holding Company: LAWTON PRECISION ENGINEERS LIMITED
Registration no: 00614553 **VAT No.:** GB 208 0179 87
Date established: 1958 **Turnover:** Up to £250,000
No.of Employees: 1 - 10 **Product Groups:** 48, 66, 85

Date of Accounts	Dec 11	Dec 10	Dec 09
Working Capital	34	142	69
Current Assets	50	168	83

Page Aerospace Ltd

Forge Lane, Sunbury On Thames, TW16 6EQ
Tel: 01932-787661 **Fax:** 01932-780349
E-mail: nmarks@pageaerospace.co.uk
Website: http://www.pageaerospace.co.uk
Directors: N. Marks (MD), S. Johnson (Dir)
Ultimate Holding Company: UNITED TECHNOLOGIES CORP INC (USA)
Immediate Holding Company: PAGE AEROSPACE LIMITED
Registration no: 00615793 **Date established:** 1958
Turnover: £10m - £20m **No.of Employees:** 101 - 250
Product Groups: 37, 39

Date of Accounts	Nov 10	Nov 09	Nov 08
Sales Turnover	17m	18m	18m
Pre Tax Profit/Loss	13m	4m	3m
Working Capital	21m	7m	5m
Fixed Assets	2m	1m	1m
Current Assets	49m	44m	47m
Current Liabilities	2m	3m	3m

Pepcon Ltd

PO Box 272, Sunbury On Thames, TW16 6WB
Tel: 01932-788545 **Fax:** 01932-788496
E-mail: sales@pepcon.org
Website: http://www.pepcon.org
Directors: A. Pepperell (Prop)
Immediate Holding Company: PEPCON LIMITED
Registration no: 01469490 **VAT No.:** GB 564 2099 33
Date established: 1979 **Turnover:** £250,000 - £500,000
No.of Employees: 1 - 10 **Product Groups:** 33, 35, 66

Date of Accounts	Mar 11	Mar 10	Mar 09
Working Capital	-117	-131	-123
Current Assets	107	95	49

Planer plc

110 Windmill Road, Sunbury On Thames, TW16 7HD
Tel: 01932-755000 **Fax:** 01932-781151
E-mail: sales@planer.com
Website: http://www.planer.com
Bank(s): Royal Bank of Scotland
Directors: A. Clements (Fin), P. Lakra (MD)
Managers: S. Delicata (Tech Serv Mgr), P. Morley (Buyer)
Ultimate Holding Company: PLANER PLC
Immediate Holding Company: PLANER PRODUCTS LIMITED
Registration no: 01116458 **VAT No.:** GB 208 1727 77
Date established: 1973 **Turnover:** £2m - £5m **No.of Employees:** 21 - 50
Product Groups: 38

Rayotec Ltd

Unit E2 Brooklands Close, Sunbury On Thames, TW16 7EB
Tel: 01932-784848 **Fax:** 01932-784849
E-mail: reza@rayotec.com
Website: http://www.rayotec.com
Directors: S. Sabba (Dir)
Immediate Holding Company: RAYOTEC LIMITED
Registration no: 02209397 **Date established:** 1987
No.of Employees: 21 - 50 **Product Groups:** 37, 40

Date of Accounts	Dec 11	Dec 10	Dec 09
Working Capital	2m	1m	1m
Fixed Assets	313	355	355
Current Assets	3m	2m	2m

Retell

53 Thames Street, Sunbury On Thames, TW16 5QH
Tel: 01932-779755 **Fax:** 01932-780383
E-mail: steve.cobley@retell.co.uk
Website: http://www.retellrecorders.co.uk
Directors: R. Herman (MD)
Registration no: 04871004 **VAT No.:** GB 442 4079 58
Turnover: £1m - £2m **No.of Employees:** 1 - 10 **Product Groups:** 37

Schindler

Benwell House Green Street, Sunbury On Thames, TW16 6QS
Tel: 01932-758100 **Fax:** 020-8818 7999
E-mail: simon.rose@gb.schindler.com
Website: http://www.schindler.com
Managers: S. Rose (Mgr)
Ultimate Holding Company: SCHINDLER HOLDING AG (SWITZERLAND)
Immediate Holding Company: SCHINDLER LTD.
Registration no: 00662746 **Date established:** 1960
Turnover: £75m - £125m **No.of Employees:** 1 - 10 **Product Groups:** 45, 48

Date of Accounts	Dec 11	Dec 10	Dec 09
Sales Turnover	80m	82m	88m
Pre Tax Profit/Loss	2m	-2m	-9m
Working Capital	10m	11m	18m
Fixed Assets	35m	2m	343
Current Assets	37m	37m	46m
Current Liabilities	21m	19m	16m

Storacall Engineering Ltd

Swan House 69-71 Windmill Road, Sunbury On Thames, TW16 7DT
Tel: 01932-710950 **Fax:** 01932-710811
E-mail: sales@storacall.co.uk
Website: http://www.storacall.co.uk
Directors: A. Kearsley (Fin), J. Leighton (Dir)
Ultimate Holding Company: STORACALL LIMITED
Immediate Holding Company: STORACALL ENGINEERING LIMITED
Registration no: 02102238 **Date established:** 1987 **Turnover:** £2m - £5m
No.of Employees: 1 - 10 **Product Groups:** 37

Date of Accounts	Mar 04	Mar 03	Mar 02
Sales Turnover	N/A	N/A	865
Pre Tax Profit/Loss	N/A	N/A	-114
Working Capital	N/A	44	-277
Current Assets	N/A	44	631
Current Liabilities	N/A	N/A	24

S B Weston Ltd

125 Harris Way, Sunbury On Thames, TW16 7EL
Tel: 01932-785544 **Fax:** 01932-761294
E-mail: sales@sbweston.com
Website: http://www.sbweston.com
Bank(s): Barclays
Directors: R. Weston (Dir)
Immediate Holding Company: S.B.WESTON LIMITED
Registration no: 00795590 **Date established:** 1964
Turnover: £500,000 - £1m **No.of Employees:** 11 - 20 **Product Groups:** 30

Date of Accounts	Mar 12	Mar 11	Mar 10
Working Capital	165	149	145
Fixed Assets	741	760	789
Current Assets	446	355	369

Worldwide Energy Logistics Ltd

Grosvenor House 4-7 Station Road, Sunbury On Thames, TW16 6SB
Tel: 020-8867 0330 **Fax:** 020-8867 0440
Website: http://www.well.uk.com
Managers: M. Burt (Mgr)
Immediate Holding Company: WORLDWIDE ENERGY LOGISTICS LIMITED
Registration no: 05036110 **Date established:** 2004 **Turnover:** £5m - £10m
No.of Employees: 11 - 20 **Product Groups:** 45, 68, 75

Date of Accounts	May 11	May 10	May 09
Sales Turnover	8m	8m	N/A
Pre Tax Profit/Loss	524	243	N/A
Working Capital	870	706	1m
Fixed Assets	31	22	38
Current Assets	5m	5m	4m
Current Liabilities	279	575	N/A

Teddington

Apropa Machinery Ltd

Coburg House 5 Gloucester Road, Teddington, TW11 0NS
Tel: 020-8902 1114 **Fax:** 020-8902 1115
E-mail: sales@apropa.co.uk
Website: http://www.apropa.co.uk
Directors: C. Borchard (Fin), H. Borchard (Mkt Research)
Immediate Holding Company: APROPA MACHINERY LIMITED
Registration no: 00641703 **VAT No.:** GB 240 8593 57
Date established: 1959 **Turnover:** £500,000 - £1m
No.of Employees: 1 - 10 **Product Groups:** 31, 38, 41, 42, 43, 67

Date of Accounts	Dec 11	Dec 10	Dec 09
Working Capital	-82	76	-110
Fixed Assets	172	176	184
Current Assets	192	442	161

Base 1 Limited

Harlequin House 7 High Street, Teddington, TW11 8EE
Tel: 020-8943 9999 **Fax:** 020-8943 8222
E-mail: hello@baseonegroup.co.uk
Website: http://www.base01.co.uk
Directors: J. Stanton (MD), R. Bush (Mkt Research)
Registration no: 02578715 **No.of Employees:** 21 - 50 **Product Groups:** 81

Butterworth Laboratories Ltd

54-56 Waldegrave Road, Teddington, TW11 8NY
Tel: 020-8977 0750 **Fax:** 020-8943 2624
E-mail: info@butterworth-labs.co.uk
Website: http://www.butterworth-labs.co.uk
Directors: J. Gearey (Fin), D. Butterworth (MD)
Managers: D. Hawkins (Tech Serv Mgr), J. Welch, J. Smith (Purch Mgr)
Immediate Holding Company: BUTTERWORTH LABORATORIES LIMITED
Registration no: 01185121 **Date established:** 1974 **Turnover:** £2m - £5m
No.of Employees: 21 - 50 **Product Groups:** 85

Date of Accounts	Sep 11	Sep 10	Sep 09
Working Capital	3m	2m	2m
Fixed Assets	711	706	675
Current Assets	3m	3m	3m

Chinese Channel

Teddington Studios Broom Road, Teddington, TW11 9NT
Tel: 020-8614 8300 **Fax:** 020-8943 0982
E-mail: lawrence@chinese-channel.co.uk
Website: http://www.chinese-channel.co.uk
Directors: L. Ma (Dir), W. Tam (Co Sec)
Ultimate Holding Company: TELEVISION BROADCASTS LIMITED (HONG KONG)
Immediate Holding Company: THE CHINESE CHANNEL LIMITED
Registration no: 02502925 **Date established:** 1990 **Turnover:** £2m - £5m
No.of Employees: 21 - 50 **Product Groups:** 89

Date of Accounts	Dec 11	Dec 10	Dec 09
Sales Turnover	3m	3m	3m
Pre Tax Profit/Loss	204	272	219
Working Capital	3m	3m	2m
Fixed Assets	42	32	74
Current Assets	3m	3m	3m
Current Liabilities	172	240	175

Euro Log Ltd

Orlando House 3 High Street, Teddington, TW11 8NP
Tel: 020-8977 4407 **Fax:** 020-8977 3714
E-mail: info@eurolog.co.uk
Website: http://www.eurolog.co.uk
Directors: L. Krantz (MD)
Immediate Holding Company: EURO LOG LIMITED
Registration no: 01872358 **VAT No.:** GB 410 8434 82
Date established: 1984 **Turnover:** £500,000 - £1m
No.of Employees: 1 - 10 **Product Groups:** 54, 80

Date of Accounts	Mar 11	Mar 10	Mar 09
Sales Turnover	941	875	951
Pre Tax Profit/Loss	11	-38	16
Working Capital	248	223	207
Fixed Assets	17	33	47
Current Assets	392	311	355
Current Liabilities	116	66	78

Gemini Electrical Supplies

186-188 Stanley Road, Teddington, TW11 8UE
Tel: 020-8977 5006 **Fax:** 020-8977 8999
Website: http://www.geminielectricalsupplies.co.uk
Managers: S. Croudace (Mgr)
Date established: 1984 **No.of Employees:** 1 - 10 **Product Groups:** 37, 40, 67

Haymarket Media Group

Teddington Studios Broom Road, Teddington, TW11 9BE
Tel: 020-8267 5000 **Fax:** 020-8267 5844
E-mail: ian.burrows@haymarket.com
Website: http://www.f1racing.co.uk
Managers: L. Candilio (Sales Prom Mgr)
Registration no: 00267189 **No.of Employees:** 11 - 20 **Product Groups:** 28

Jewson Hirepoint

Sandy Lane, Teddington, TW11 0DS
Tel: 020-8943 2890 **Fax:** 020-8943 2113
Website: http://www.hirepoint.co.uk
Directors: C. Kenward (Fin), P. Hindle (MD), T. Newman (Sales)
Managers: J. Griffin (District Mgr), N. Blackburn (District Mgr), S. Shorey (District Mgr)
Immediate Holding Company: JEWSON LIMITED
Registration no: 00348407 **Date established:** 1939
Turnover: £500m - £1,000m **No.of Employees:** 1 - 10
Product Groups: 66

KOTHEA

Fairfax Road, Teddington, TW11 9BX
Tel: 08702-854768
E-mail: info@kothea.com
Website: http://www.kothea.com
Directors: M. Gee (Dir)
Registration no: 3826388 **Date established:** 1997
Turnover: £500,000 - £1m **No.of Employees:** 1 - 10 **Product Groups:** 22, 23

Livingston UK

Livingston House 2 Queens Road, Teddington, TW11 0LB
Tel: 020-8943 5151 **Fax:** 020-8977 6431
E-mail: info@livingston.co.uk
Website: http://www.livingston.co.uk
Directors: P. Bagot (Dir), M. Porter (Grp Chief Exec)
Managers: J. Carroll, M. Porter
Ultimate Holding Company: LIVINGSTON GROUP LIMITED
Immediate Holding Company: LIVINGSTON GROUP LIMITED
Registration no: 04782833 **Date established:** 2003
Turnover: £10m - £20m **No.of Employees:** 21 - 50 **Product Groups:** 18, 28, 37, 38, 39, 44, 45, 46, 52, 61, 67, 68, 79, 80, 83, 84, 85

Date of Accounts	Dec 10	Dec 09	Dec 08
Sales Turnover	21m	42m	41m
Pre Tax Profit/Loss	-2m	-399	-2m
Working Capital	-13m	-2m	-1m
Fixed Assets	18m	28m	26m
Current Assets	9m	18m	19m
Current Liabilities	10m	12m	10m

National Physical Laboratory

Hampton Road, Teddington, TW11 0LW
Tel: 020-8977 3222 **Fax:** 020-8943 6458
E-mail: brian.bowsher@npl.co.uk
Website: http://www.npl.co.uk
Directors: S. Bennett (Fin), B. Bowsher (MD)
Managers: L. Fletcher, C. Hall (I.T. Exec), D. Hukins (Purch Mgr)
Immediate Holding Company: AIRTO LIMITED
Registration no: 02992144 **Date established:** 1975
Turnover: £20m - £50m **No.of Employees:** 501 - 1000
Product Groups: 54, 85

Date of Accounts	Jun 11	Jun 10	Jun 09
Sales Turnover	81	81	77
Pre Tax Profit/Loss	-16	-3	-2
Working Capital	61	77	81
Current Assets	74	101	96
Current Liabilities	12	22	15

Pine & Shine Wood Companions

77 High Street, Teddington, TW11 8HG
Tel: 020-8977 2888
Directors: V. Saroian (Prop)
Date established: 1997 **No.of Employees:** 1 - 10 **Product Groups:** 35, 36

Pinner Metal Window Services

102-104 Church Road, Teddington, TW11 8PY
Tel: 020-8943 2335 **Fax:** 020-8943 3151
Directors: R. Brown (Ptnr)
Ultimate Holding Company: URALITA SA (SPAIN)
Registration no: 03758068 **Date established:** 1999 **Turnover:** £5m - £10m
No.of Employees: 1 - 10 **Product Groups:** 35, 36

Rapier Precision Sheet Metal Ltd

1 Princes Works Princes Road, Teddington, TW11 0RW
Tel: 020-8943 4788 **Fax:** 020-8977 1686
E-mail: info@rapierprecision.co.uk
Website: http://www.rapierprecision.co.uk
Directors: D. Naylor (Fin)
Immediate Holding Company: RAPIER PRECISION SHEET METAL LIMITED
Registration no: 02221003 **VAT No.:** GB 493 4614 26
Date established: 1988 **Turnover:** £500,000 - £1m
No.of Employees: 1 - 10 **Product Groups:** 48

Date of Accounts	Mar 12	Mar 11	Mar 10
Working Capital	883	861	771
Fixed Assets	201	202	245
Current Assets	1m	957	823

Salco Self Adhesive Label Co. Ltd

2 Princes Works Princes Road, Teddington, TW11 0RW
Tel: 020-8943 0731 **Fax:** 020-8977 0142
Directors: K. Humphreys (Dir)
Immediate Holding Company: SALCO SELF-ADHESIVE LABEL CO. LIMITED
Registration no: 00958976 **Date established:** 1969
Turnover: £250,000 - £500,000 **No.of Employees:** 1 - 10
Product Groups: 38, 42

Date of Accounts	Mar 11	Mar 10	Mar 09
Working Capital	157	132	121
Fixed Assets	34	38	39
Current Assets	207	172	148

Sunny Aspects Ltd

36 Udney Park Road, Teddington, TW11 9BG
Tel: 020-8977 4149
E-mail: info@sunnyaspects.co.uk
Website: http://www.sunnyaspects.co.uk
Directors: I. Butcher (MD)
Turnover: Up to £250,000 **No.of Employees:** 1 - 10 **Product Groups:** 30, 42, 63

Date of Accounts	Oct 07	Oct 06	Oct 05
Working Capital	13	4	2
Fixed Assets	1	2	2
Current Assets	18	12	7

Teddington Studios

Broom Road, Teddington, TW11 9NT
Tel: 020-8977 3252 **Fax:** 020-8943 4050
E-mail: info@pinewoodgroup.com
Website: http://www.pinewoodgroup.com
Directors: P. Darbyshire (MD)
Immediate Holding Company: GROWTH IN COMMUNITY LIMITED
Registration no: 01959657 **VAT No.:** GB 689 7321 78
Date established: 1997 **Turnover:** £5m - £10m **No.of Employees:** 11 - 20
Product Groups: 89

Date of Accounts	Mar 11	Mar 10	Mar 09
Sales Turnover	N/A	22	13
Pre Tax Profit/Loss	N/A	8	-4
Working Capital	29	21	13
Current Assets	31	21	13

Twickenham

A To Z Computers

134 Heath Road, Twickenham, TW1 4BN
Tel: 020-8744 1029 **Fax:** 020-8744 1768
E-mail: sales@atoz-computers.co.uk
Website: http://www.atoz-computers.co.uk
Directors: S. Mok (Prop)
Turnover: £500m - £1,000m **No.of Employees:** 1 - 10
Product Groups: 26, 37, 67

Alsford Timber Ltd

63-69 Heath Road, Twickenham, TW1 4AT
Tel: 020-8892 2868 **Fax:** 020-8892 5474
E-mail: r.paget@alsfordtimber.com
Website: http://www.alsfordtimber.com
Managers: W. Lubbe (District Mgr)
Ultimate Holding Company: GEO. KINGSBURY HOLDINGS LIMITED
Immediate Holding Company: ALSFORD TIMBER LIMITED
Registration no: 02827724 **Date established:** 1993
Turnover: Up to £250,000 **No.of Employees:** 1 - 10 **Product Groups:** 66

Date of Accounts	Dec 11	Dec 10	Dec 09
Sales Turnover	28m	26m	25m
Pre Tax Profit/Loss	-577	-1m	-1m
Working Capital	4m	4m	5m
Fixed Assets	624	651	869
Current Assets	9m	8m	8m
Current Liabilities	532	479	535

Aquapure Water Treatment Equipment

9 Richmond Mansions Denton Road, Twickenham, TW1 2HH
Tel: 020-8892 9010 **Fax:** 020-8892 9010
E-mail: info@aquapure.co.uk
Website: http://www.aquapure.co.uk
Directors: B. Rogerson (Prop)
Immediate Holding Company: AQUAPURE LTD
Registration no: 05368731 **Date established:** 2005
Turnover: Up to £250,000 **No.of Employees:** 1 - 10 **Product Groups:** 31, 40, 42

Aston Manufacturing Co. Ltd

8-14 Staines Road, Twickenham, TW2 5AH
Tel: 020-8894 1971 **Fax:** 020-8755 1971
E-mail: astonmfg@aol.com
Website: http://www.astonmanufacturing.co.uk
Directors: S. Norgate (MD)
Immediate Holding Company: ASTON MANUFACTURING CO LIMITED
Registration no: 00291745 **VAT No.:** GB 222 2515 12
Date established: 1934 **Turnover:** £250,000 - £500,000
No.of Employees: 1 - 10 **Product Groups:** 27, 29, 35, 40

Date of Accounts	Sep 11	Sep 10	Sep 09
Working Capital	18	27	25
Fixed Assets	120	125	128
Current Assets	53	51	55

Autoscript Ltd

Unit 2 Heathlands Close, Twickenham, TW1 4BP
Tel: 020-8891 8900 **Fax:** 020-7515 9529
E-mail: hire@autoscript.tv
Website: http://www.autoscript.tv
Bank(s): Lloyds TSB Bank plc
Directors: J. Milton (Co Sec), B. Larter (Dir)
Managers: M. Washington (Tech Serv Mgr)
Ultimate Holding Company: THE VITEC GROUP PLC.
Immediate Holding Company: BROADCAST DEVELOPMENTS LIMITED
Registration no: 01833713 **VAT No.:** GB 410 2423 20
Date established: 1984 **Turnover:** £2m - £5m **No.of Employees:** 11 - 20
Product Groups: 81

Date of Accounts	Dec 11	Dec 10	Dec 09
Sales Turnover	2m	2m	1m
Pre Tax Profit/Loss	294	363	207
Working Capital	223	-126	51
Fixed Assets	618	636	182
Current Assets	563	1m	475
Current Liabilities	155	259	213

Barnett The Factory

61 Haliburton Road, Twickenham, TW1 1PD
Tel: 020-8891 0067 **Fax:** 020-8891 0067
E-mail: peter_barnett@hotmail.com
Website: http://www.barnettmanufacturing.co.uk
Directors: P. Barnett (Prop)
Turnover: £250,000 - £500,000 **No.of Employees:** 1 - 10
Product Groups: 24, 63

Raymond Clark Specialist Sprayer

27 Saville Road, Twickenham, TW1 4BQ
Tel: 020-8892 4326 **Fax:** 020-8892 4326
Directors: R. Clark (Prop)
Date established: 1982 **No.of Employees:** 1 - 10 **Product Groups:** 46, 48

Classic Miniatures Ltd

8 Heathlands Close, Twickenham, TW1 4BP
Tel: 020-8892 3686 **Fax:** 020-8744 1142
E-mail: sales@classicminiatures.co.uk
Website: http://www.classicminiatures.co.uk
Directors: F. Cross (Fin), F. Park (Chief Op Offcr)
Immediate Holding Company: CLASSIC MINIATURES LIMITED
Registration no: 01309832 **VAT No.:** GB 242 0902 01
Date established: 1977 **Turnover:** £500,000 - £1m
No.of Employees: 1 - 10 **Product Groups:** 49, 81

Date of Accounts	Dec 11	Dec 10	Dec 09
Working Capital	196	182	206
Fixed Assets	88	95	58
Current Assets	235	255	245

Connaught Facts Line Ltd

Maple House 11 Briar Road, Twickenham, TW2 6RB
Tel: 08708-333500 **Fax:** 0870-833 3501
E-mail: sales@connaught.co.uk
Website: http://www.connaught.co.uk
Directors: M. Bak (Dir), D. Bak (Fin)
Immediate Holding Company: CONNAUGHT FACTSLINE LIMITED
Registration no: 02845178 **Date established:** 1993
Turnover: £250,000 - £500,000 **No.of Employees:** 1 - 10
Product Groups: 79

Date of Accounts	Mar 12	Mar 11	Mar 10
Working Capital	316	247	175
Fixed Assets	43	48	57
Current Assets	486	427	321

Currie Motors Ltd

161 Chertsey Road, Twickenham, TW1 1ER
Tel: 020-8892 0041 **Fax:** 020-8891 3807
Website: http://www.curriemotors.co.uk
Bank(s): Barclays
Directors: N. Boutros (Co Sec)
Managers: J. Cheung (Mktg Serv Mgr)
Ultimate Holding Company: CURFIN (NA) NV (NETHERLANDS ANTILLES)
Immediate Holding Company: CURRIE MOTORS LIMITED
Registration no: 01437000 **VAT No.:** GB 225 2400 11
Date established: 1979 **Turnover:** £125m - £250m
No.of Employees: 101 - 250 **Product Groups:** 68

Date of Accounts	Apr 12	Apr 11	Apr 10
Sales Turnover	159m	153m	148m
Pre Tax Profit/Loss	6m	6m	3m
Working Capital	15m	13m	9m
Fixed Assets	81m	78m	79m
Current Assets	52m	44m	46m
Current Liabilities	14m	13m	17m

Langton Software Ltd

Holly Road, Twickenham, TW1 4EG
Tel: 08451-235714 **Fax:** 020-8831 7522
E-mail: colin.alcock@langton.com
Website: http://www.langton.com
Directors: C. Alcock (MD), C. Alcock (I.T. Dir), D. Elyan (Dir), K. Jackson (Dir)

Immediate Holding Company: LANGTON SOFTWARE LIMITED
Registration no: 02127442 **Date established:** 1987
Turnover: £500,000 - £1m **No.of Employees:** 1 - 10 **Product Groups:** 44

Date of Accounts	Mar 11	Mar 10	Mar 09
Working Capital	27	26	28
Fixed Assets	6	6	4
Current Assets	134	210	227
Current Liabilities	N/A	N/A	199

The London Seed Emporium

PO Box 301 The Royal Borough of Richmond-Upon-Thames, Twickenham, TW1 9AY
Tel: 05600-464323
E-mail: sales@londonseedemporium.co.uk
Website: http://www.flower-seed-gifts.co.uk
Product Groups: 24, 41, 62, 65

M H E Retail Ltd

Richmond Bridge House 419 Richmond Road, Twickenham, TW1 2EF
Tel: 020-3005 9860 **Fax:** 020-8891 5027
E-mail: info@mheretail.com
Website: http://www.mheretail.com
Directors: G. Wallace (Grp Chief Exec)
Ultimate Holding Company: LUVATA OY (FINLAND)
Immediate Holding Company: MHE RETAIL LIMITED
Registration no: 05051707 **Date established:** 2004 **Turnover:** £5m - £10m
No.of Employees: 1 - 10 **Product Groups:** 80, 81, 84

Matrix Security & Electrical Systems Ltd

Electroline House 15 Lion Road, Twickenham, TW1 4JH
Tel: 020-8744 2244 **Fax:** 0870-051 8310
E-mail: dan@matrixsecurity.demon.co.uk
Website: http://www.matrix-security.co.uk
Directors: D. Crowley (Dir)
Immediate Holding Company: MATRIX SECURITY AND ELECTRICAL SYSTEMS LTD
Registration no: 04391693 **Date established:** 2002
Turnover: Up to £250,000 **No.of Employees:** 1 - 10 **Product Groups:** 40, 52

Date of Accounts	Mar 12	Mar 11	Mar 10
Sales Turnover	N/A	71	N/A
Pre Tax Profit/Loss	N/A	11	N/A
Working Capital	10	-1	-8
Fixed Assets	1	1	1
Current Assets	27	8	10
Current Liabilities	N/A	4	N/A

Positive Metering Systems

88 Queens Road, Twickenham, TW1 4ET
Tel: 020-8892 7292 **Fax:** 020-8892 8090
Directors: P. Sims (Dir)
Date established: 1992 **No.of Employees:** 1 - 10 **Product Groups:** 38, 42

Rugby Football Union

Rugby Road, Twickenham, TW1 1DZ
Tel: 020-8892 2000 **Fax:** 020-8892 9816
E-mail: sales@fru.co.uk
Website: http://www.fru.co.uk
Directors: F. Baron (Grp Chief Exec), M. Thomas (Ch)
Managers: F. Baron (Sales Prom Mgr)
Registration no: 09000374 **Date established:** 2001
Turnover: Up to £250,000 **No.of Employees:** 501 - 1000
Product Groups: 89

S K S Business Services Ltd

148 Percy Road, Twickenham, TW2 6JF
Tel: 020-7096 0662 **Fax:** 020-8609 0313
E-mail: mail@sksbusinessservices.com
Website: http://www.sksbusinessservices.com
Directors: S. Swarup (Fin), S. Swarup (Dir)
Immediate Holding Company: SKS BUSINESS SERVICES LTD
Registration no: 06418541 **Date established:** 2007
No.of Employees: 1 - 10 **Product Groups:** 80

Date of Accounts	Nov 11	Nov 10	Nov 09
Working Capital	3	-69	-60
Fixed Assets	3	75	34
Current Assets	66	31	6
Current Liabilities	N/A	54	N/A

Sauflon Pharmaceuticals Ltd

49-53 York Street, Twickenham, TW1 3LP
Tel: 020-8322 4200 **Fax:** 020-8891 3001
E-mail: alanwells@sauflon.co.uk
Website: http://www.sauflon.com
Directors: J. Maynard (Fin), D. Gowing (Fin), A. Wells (MD), H. Griffiths (I.T. Dir)
Managers: B. Surenbranath (Tech Serv Mgr), S. Ings (Personnel)
Immediate Holding Company: SAUFLON PHARMACEUTICALS LIMITED
Registration no: 01071033 **Date established:** 1972
Turnover: £50m - £75m **No.of Employees:** 21 - 50 **Product Groups:** 38

Date of Accounts	Oct 11	Oct 10	Oct 09
Sales Turnover	68m	56m	47m
Pre Tax Profit/Loss	6m	4m	1m
Working Capital	9m	7m	6m
Fixed Assets	26m	21m	20m
Current Assets	35m	29m	23m
Current Liabilities	8m	4m	4m

TranScript

53 Fifth Cross Road, Twickenham, TW2 5LJ
Tel: 020-8893 4138
E-mail: bev.hetherington@btinternet.com
Website: http://www.transcript.uk.com
Directors: B. Hetherington (Prop)
Immediate Holding Company: TOM HETHERINGTON SERVICES LIMITED
Date established: 2010 **Turnover:** Up to £250,000
No.of Employees: 1 - 10 **Product Groups:** 80

Date of Accounts	Jun 11
Working Capital	23
Current Assets	38

Twiflex Ltd

9 Briar Road, Twickenham, TW2 6RB
Tel: 020-8894 1161 **Fax:** 020-8894 6056
E-mail: sales@twiflex.co.uk
Website: http://www.twiflex.com
Directors: J. Cooksley (Sales)
Ultimate Holding Company: ALTRA HOLDINGS INC (USA)
Immediate Holding Company: TWIFLEX LIMITED
Registration no: 00404531 **VAT No.:** GB 422 4813 75
Date established: 1946 **Turnover:** £10m - £20m **No.of Employees:** 1 - 10
Product Groups: 35, 43, 44, 45

Date of Accounts	Dec 11	Dec 10	Dec 09
Sales Turnover	14m	12m	7m
Pre Tax Profit/Loss	3m	905	723
Working Capital	8m	4m	4m
Fixed Assets	1m	1m	543
Current Assets	11m	11m	11m
Current Liabilities	705	336	710

Ventalution

Norcutt House Norcutt Road, Twickenham, TW2 6SR
Tel: 020-8898 5040 **Fax:** 020-8867 2859
E-mail: admin@ventaloo.co.uk
Website: http://www.ventalution.co.uk
Directors: J. Reynolds (MD)
Registration no: 04131307 **Date established:** 2000 **Turnover:** £1m - £2m
No.of Employees: 1 - 10 **Product Groups:** 30, 39, 40

Date of Accounts	Dec 11	Dec 10	Dec 09
Working Capital	564	588	544
Fixed Assets	124	125	128
Current Assets	905	803	632

Uxbridge

A G Refrigeration

Unit 1 Crows Nest Farm Breakspear Road South, Harefield, Uxbridge, UB9 6LT
Tel: 01895-636203 **Fax:** 01895-624620
Website: http://www.ag-refrigeration.co.uk
Directors: A. Glassbrook (Dir)
No.of Employees: 1 - 10 **Product Groups:** 40, 66

A & M Fencing Company Ltd

Harefield Oil Terminal Harvil Road, Harefield, Uxbridge, UB9 6JL
Tel: 08452-302205 **Fax:** 01895-270074
E-mail: enquiries@aandmfencing.co.uk
Website: http://www.aandmfencing.co.uk
Directors: B. Jordan (MD)
Immediate Holding Company: A & M FENCING COMPANY LIMITED
Registration no: 05138109 **Date established:** 2004
No.of Employees: 1 - 10 **Product Groups:** 52

Date of Accounts	Mar 11	Mar 09	Mar 08
Working Capital	242	97	58
Fixed Assets	65	102	104
Current Assets	373	180	127
Current Liabilities	N/A	53	N/A

Action Lighting Ltd

2 Pine Trees Drive, Uxbridge, UB10 8AE
Tel: 01895-256481
Registration no: 03258144 **Date established:** 1996
No.of Employees: 1 - 10 **Product Groups:** 37, 67

Adobe Systems UK Ltd

3 Roundwood Avenue Stockley Park, Uxbridge, UB11 1AY
Tel: 020-8606 1100 **Fax:** 020-8606 4004
E-mail: mhiggins@adobe.com
Website: http://www.adobe.co.uk
Directors: C. Tegal (MD), M. Higgins (MD)
Ultimate Holding Company: ADOBE SYSTEMS INC. (USA)
Registration no: SC101089 **No.of Employees:** 51 - 100
Product Groups: 44

Allied Irish Bank - GB

Bankcentre Belmont Road, Uxbridge, UB8 1SA
Tel: 01895-272222 **Fax:** 020-7606 4966
E-mail: info@aib.ie
Website: http://www.aibgb.co.uk
Managers: A. McKeon (Chief Mgr), A. Docherty (Mktg Serv Mgr)
Ultimate Holding Company: Allied Irish Banks PLC (Eire)
Immediate Holding Company: Allied Irish Banks P.L.C. (Eire)
Registration no: 00024173 **Date established:** 1988 **Turnover:** £1m - £2m
No.of Employees: 101 - 250 **Product Groups:** 82

Anchor Plastics Machinery

The Watermill Coppermill Lock, Harefield, Uxbridge, UB9 6SA
Tel: 01895-824301 **Fax:** 01895-825344
E-mail: sales@anchor-pm.co.uk
Website: http://www.anchor-pm.co.uk
Directors: R. Collins (Prop)
Immediate Holding Company: ANCHOR PLASTICS MACHINERY LIMITED
Registration no: 01085691 **Date established:** 1972
No.of Employees: 1 - 10 **Product Groups:** 42, 48, 66

Date of Accounts	Dec 11	Dec 10	Dec 09
Working Capital	214	410	499
Fixed Assets	52	42	55
Current Assets	606	734	796

Apple Computer UK Ltd

2 Furzeground Way Stockley Park, Uxbridge, UB11 1BB
Tel: 020-8218 1000 **Fax:** 020-8569 2957
E-mail: info@apple.com
Website: http://www.euro.apple.com/uk/
Directors: G. Wipfler (Dir), M. Rogers (MD)
Immediate Holding Company: APPLE (UK) LIMITED
Registration no: 01591116 **Date established:** 1981
Turnover: £50m - £75m **No.of Employees:** 101 - 250
Product Groups: 44, 67

Date of Accounts	Sep 07
Sales Turnover	27410
Pre Tax Profit/Loss	6870
Working Capital	15040
Fixed Assets	4400
Current Assets	19200
Current Liabilities	4160
Total Share Capital	1000
ROCE% (Return on Capital Employed)	35.3

Armstrong World Industries Ltd

Armstrong House 38 Market Square, Uxbridge, UB8 1NG
Tel: 01895-251122 **Fax:** 01895-274284
Website: http://www.gema-ceilings.com
Bank(s): Barclays, Uxbridge
Directors: M. Hewitson (Co Sec)
Managers: C. Dobson (Comptroller), M. Nicholl (Mktg Serv Mgr)
Ultimate Holding Company: ARMSTRONG WORLD INDUSTRIES INC (USA)
Immediate Holding Company: ARMSTRONG WORLD INDUSTRIES LIMITED
Registration no: 00207732 **VAT No.:** GB 226 1432 94
Date established: 2025 **Turnover:** £125m - £250m
No.of Employees: 11 - 20 **Product Groups:** 30, 33, 35, 37

Date of Accounts	Dec 10	Dec 09	Dec 08
Sales Turnover	103m	136m	154m
Pre Tax Profit/Loss	-1m	7m	8m
Working Capital	17m	21m	16m
Fixed Assets	13m	17m	18m
Current Assets	30m	38m	37m
Current Liabilities	2m	3m	2m

Arthur Sanderson Ltd

Chalfont House Oxford Road, Denham, Uxbridge, UB9 4DX
Tel: 08445-439500 **Fax:** 01895-830055
E-mail: enquiries@a-sanderson.co.uk
Website: http://www.sanderson-uk.com
Bank(s): Barclays
Directors: D. Walker (Sales), S. Whitfield (Chief Op Offcr), J. Redford (Fin), L. Stovell (Fin), V. Blair (Mkt Research)
Managers: D. Boughtflower, S. Shadbolt (Personnel)
Ultimate Holding Company: WALKER GREENBANK PLC.
Immediate Holding Company: ARTHUR SANDERSON & SONS LIMITED
Registration no: 01002898 **VAT No.:** GB 422 4413 91
Date established: 1971 **Turnover:** £10m - £20m
No.of Employees: 51 - 100 **Product Groups:** 24, 27

AVA packaging solutions Ltd

7 Union Buildings Wallingford Road, Uxbridge, UB8 2FR
Tel: 01895-590095 **Fax:** 01895-590096
E-mail: pack@ava-packaging.com
Website: http://www.AVA-packaging.com
Directors: A. Vincent (MD)
Registration no: 04385292 **Date established:** 2002
No.of Employees: 1 - 10 **Product Groups:** 20, 48, 84, 85, 86

Date of Accounts	Mar 08	Mar 07	Mar 06
Working Capital	25	3	-2
Fixed Assets	5	3	4
Current Assets	47	38	16
Current Liabilities	21	36	18
Total Share Capital	1	1	1

Berkley Precision Engineering Ltd

3b Eskdale Road, Uxbridge, UB8 2RT
Tel: 01895-258555 **Fax:** 01895-258255
E-mail: info@berkleyeng.co.uk
Website: http://www.berkleyeng.co.uk
Directors: C. Davis (Dir)
Ultimate Holding Company: ESTDALE-SCENEX LIMITED
Immediate Holding Company: BERKLEY PRECISION ENGINEERING LTD
Registration no: 05629159 **Date established:** 2005
No.of Employees: 1 - 10 **Product Groups:** 35, 39, 85

Date of Accounts	Oct 11	Oct 10	Oct 09
Working Capital	-6	-46	-75
Fixed Assets	60	43	76
Current Assets	156	130	98

Blue Dragon Dry Cleaners Ltd

Whiteleys Parade Uxbridge Road, Uxbridge, UB10 0NZ
Tel: 01895-236571 **Fax:** 01895-812950
Website: http://www.bluedragon.uk.com
Bank(s): HSBC, Marlborough Parade
Directors: J. Orford (Dir), W. Orford (MD), R. Orford (Ch), N. Kota (Fin), C. Hill (Dir), R. Orford (Prop)
Managers: W. Awford (Sales Prom Mgr)
Immediate Holding Company: BLUE DRAGON (HILLINGDON) LIMITED
Registration no: 00217817 **VAT No.:** GB 222 3364 02
Date established: 2026 **Turnover:** £2m - £5m **No.of Employees:** 51 - 100
Product Groups: 23

Date of Accounts	Mar 11	Mar 10	Mar 09
Sales Turnover	3m	2m	N/A
Pre Tax Profit/Loss	54	-32	59
Working Capital	272	254	358
Fixed Assets	4m	3m	3m
Current Assets	788	701	700
Current Liabilities	204	129	199

Robert Bosch Ltd

PO Box 93, Uxbridge, UB9 5HJ
Tel: 01895-834466 **Fax:** 01895-838388
E-mail: hermann.kaess@uk.bosch.com
Website: http://www.bosch.co.uk
Bank(s): Barclays
Directors: M. Firminger (Dir), P. Fouquet (Pres)
Ultimate Holding Company: ROBERT BOSCH GMBH (GERMANY)
Immediate Holding Company: ROBERT BOSCH FINANCE LIMITED
Registration no: 02998440 **Date established:** 1994
Turnover: £250m - £500m **No.of Employees:** 251 - 500
Product Groups: 35, 36, 37, 38, 39, 40, 41, 42, 45, 46, 47, 67, 68, 84

Date of Accounts	Dec 11	Dec 10	Dec 09
Sales Turnover	939	N/A	N/A
Pre Tax Profit/Loss	858	437	980
Working Capital	30m	30m	39m
Current Assets	95m	135m	39m
Current Liabilities	142	108	56

Bosch Security Systems

PO Box 750, Uxbridge, UB9 5ZJ
Tel: 01895-878088 **Fax:** 01895-878089
E-mail: paul.wong@uk.bosch.com
Website: http://www.boschsecurity.co.uk
Bank(s): National Westminster Bank Plc
Directors: P. Wong (MD)
Managers: D. Simons (Sales Prom Mgr), S. Horsfield (Comptroller), A. Breeze (Mktg Serv Mgr)
Ultimate Holding Company: ROBERT BOSCH GMBH (GERMANY)
Immediate Holding Company: BOSCH SECURITY SYSTEMS LIMITED
Registration no: 02865840 **Date established:** 1993
Turnover: £20m - £50m **No.of Employees:** 21 - 50 **Product Groups:** 37, 38, 40

see next page

Bosch Security Systems - *Cont'd*

Date of Accounts	Dec 11	Dec 10	Dec 09
Sales Turnover	24m	25m	31m
Pre Tax Profit/Loss	-24	-3m	-1m
Working Capital	-12m	-14m	-13m
Fixed Assets	13m	14m	16m
Current Assets	7m	6m	10m
Current Liabilities	2m	2m	2m

Bristol-Myers Squibb

Unit 2 Uxbridge Business Park Sanderson Road, Uxbridge, UB8 1DH
Tel: 01895-523000 **Fax:** 01895-523010
Website: http://www.bms.com
Bank(s): National Westminster Bank Plc
Directors: A. Hooper (MD)
Ultimate Holding Company: BRISTOL MYERS SQUIBB COMPANY (USA)
Immediate Holding Company: BRISTOL-MYERS SQUIBB TRUSTEES LIMITED
Registration no: 02546250 **VAT No.:** GB 163 5426 67
Date established: 1990 **Turnover:** £125m - £250m
No.of Employees: 251 - 500 **Product Groups:** 63

British Movietone News Ltd

North Orbital Road Denham, Uxbridge, UB9 5HQ
Tel: 01895-833071 **Fax:** 01895-834893
E-mail: barry@mtone.co.uk
Website: http://www.movietone.com
Directors: P. Higginson (Dir), B. Florin (MD)
Managers: C. Briers (Gen Contact)
Ultimate Holding Company: FP051591
Immediate Holding Company: BRITISH MOVIETONEWS LIMITED(THE)
Registration no: 00241313 **Date established:** 1929
Turnover: £250,000 - £500,000 **No.of Employees:** 1 - 10
Product Groups: 89

Budgens & Londis

Widewater Place Moorhall Road, Harefield, Uxbridge, UB9 6NS
Tel: 08700-500158 **Fax:** 0870-050 0159
E-mail: sales@musgrave.co.uk
Website: http://www.londis.co.uk
Directors: S. Fahy (Pers)
Managers: R. Mcfarnalane (Commun Mgr)
Ultimate Holding Company: MUSGRAVE GROUP PUBLIC LIMITED COMPANY
Immediate Holding Company: MUSGRAVE UK LIMITED
Registration no: 00221722 **Date established:** 2027
No.of Employees: 101 - 250 **Product Groups:** 61

Date of Accounts	Dec 11	Dec 10	Dec 09
Working Capital	67m	67m	67m
Fixed Assets	23m	23m	23m
Current Assets	67m	67m	67m

Burkard Scientific Sales Ltd

Eskdale Road, Uxbridge, UB8 2RT
Tel: 01895-230056 **Fax:** 01895-230058
E-mail: sales@burkardscientific.co.uk
Website: http://www.burkardscientific.co.uk
Directors: B. Wili (MD), I. Wili (Fin)
Ultimate Holding Company: BURKARD SCIENTIFIC (SALES) LIMITED
Registration no: 00868514 **Date established:** 1966 **Turnover:** £2m - £5m
No.of Employees: 1 - 10 **Product Groups:** 38, 40, 42, 85

Date of Accounts	Mar 11	Mar 10	Mar 09
Working Capital	213	203	193
Fixed Assets	2	1	1
Current Assets	266	267	258

Clancy Docwra Ltd

Clare House Coppermill Lane, Harefield, Uxbridge, UB9 6HZ
Tel: 01895-823711 **Fax:** 01895-825263
E-mail: marian.webb@theclancygroup.co.uk
Website: http://www.theclancygroup.co.uk
Bank(s): AIB Group
Directors: D. Pegg (Co Sec)
Managers: N. Childs, M. Webb, M. Sirrell, P. Kerry, T. Euvraid (Personnel)
Ultimate Holding Company: THE CLANCY GROUP PLC
Immediate Holding Company: CLANCY DEVELOPMENTS LIMITED
Registration no: 00763197 **VAT No.:** GB 226 5552 64
Date established: 1963 **Turnover:** £1m - £2m
No.of Employees: 101 - 250 **Product Groups:** 51

Date of Accounts	Mar 12	Mar 11	Mar 10
Sales Turnover	483	1m	2m
Pre Tax Profit/Loss	-217	-373	286
Working Capital	35	158	428
Current Assets	19m	11m	7m
Current Liabilities	2m	2m	430

Classic Powder Coating Ltd

Bridge Works Iver Lane, Uxbridge, UB8 2JG
Tel: 01895-270616 **Fax:** 020-8892 4048
Directors: T. Chase (Dir)
Immediate Holding Company: CLASSIC POWDER COATING LIMITED
Registration no: 02249818 **Date established:** 1988
Turnover: Up to £250,000 **No.of Employees:** 1 - 10 **Product Groups:** 48

Date of Accounts	Mar 11	Mar 10	Mar 06
Working Capital	30	24	28
Fixed Assets	2	3	4
Current Assets	44	29	34

Coats

1 The Square Stockley Park, Uxbridge, UB11 1TD
Tel: 020-8210 5000 **Fax:** 020-8210 5069
E-mail: gary.weiss@coats.com
Website: http://www.coats.com
Managers: P. Foreman, R. Norman (Personnel), R. Bevan (Comptroller), G. Weiss
Ultimate Holding Company: GUINESS PEAT GROUP PLC
Immediate Holding Company: COATS PLC
Registration no: 04620973 **Date established:** 2002
Turnover: Over £1,000m **No.of Employees:** 21 - 50 **Product Groups:** 23, 24, 63

Date of Accounts	Dec 07
Pre Tax Profit/Loss	508000
Working Capital	1064m
Fixed Assets	959000
Current Assets	1065m
Current Liabilities	1000
Total Share Capital	280000
ROCE% (Return on Capital Employed)	25.1

Compass Group PLC

Parkview 82 Oxford Road, Uxbridge, UB8 1UX
Tel: 01895-554554 **Fax:** 01895-554555
Website: http://www.compass-group.co.uk
Directors: L. Potter (Dir)
Immediate Holding Company: COMPASS GROUP PLC
Registration no: 04083914 **Date established:** 2000 **Turnover:** £5m - £10m
No.of Employees: 251 - 500 **Product Groups:** 69

Date of Accounts	Sep 11	Sep 10	Sep 09
Sales Turnover	15833m	14468m	13444m
Pre Tax Profit/Loss	958m	913m	773m
Working Capital	-515m	-487m	-549m
Fixed Assets	5935m	5502m	5091m
Current Assets	3475m	2752m	2550m
Current Liabilities	2615m	1979m	2036m

Complete Crown & Bridge Dental Laboratory

1 Station Approach Denham, Uxbridge, UB9 5EL
Tel: 01895-834311 **Fax:** 01895-832428
Directors: S. Jordon (Prop)
No.of Employees: 1 - 10 **Product Groups:** 38, 67

Convatec Ltd

Harrington House Milton Road, Uxbridge, UB10 8PU
Tel: 01895-628300 **Fax:** 01895-628456
Website: http://www.convatec.com
Directors: P. Forsyth (Mkt Research)
Ultimate Holding Company: CIDRON HEALTHCARE LTD (JERSEY)
Immediate Holding Company: CONVATEC LIMITED
Registration no: 01309639 **Date established:** 1977 **Turnover:** £2m - £5m
No.of Employees: 101 - 250 **Product Groups:** 61

Date of Accounts	Dec 11	Dec 10	Dec 09
Sales Turnover	161m	201m	238m
Pre Tax Profit/Loss	28m	58m	41m
Working Capital	132m	93m	43m
Fixed Assets	100m	101m	117m
Current Assets	156m	137m	136m
Current Liabilities	7m	12m	7m

Copp Wilson Pettitt Moore

7 Brook Business Centre Cowley Mill Road, Cowley, Uxbridge, UB8 2FX
Tel: 01895-231000 **Fax:** 01895-230044
E-mail: cwpmconsultants@btconnect.com
Website: http://www.cwpmconsultants.co.uk
Directors: S. Hopkins (Ptnr)
No.of Employees: 1 - 10 **Product Groups:** 35

Danfoss Ltd

Capswood Business Centre Oxford Road, Denham, Uxbridge, UB9 4LH
Tel: 0870-6080008 **Fax:** 0870-6080009
E-mail: henrik.hansen@danfoss.com
Website: http://www.danfoss.co.uk
Bank(s): HSBC Bank plc
Directors: G. Strauss (MD), H. Hansen (Co Sec)
Managers: P. Scarratt (Sales Prom Mgr)
Ultimate Holding Company: FP000599
Immediate Holding Company: DANFOSS LIMITED
Registration no: 00624322 **VAT No.:** GB 222 2169 05
Date established: 1959 **Turnover:** £20m - £50m
No.of Employees: 101 - 250 **Product Groups:** 35, 36, 37, 38, 40

Date of Accounts	Dec 09	Dec 08	Dec 07
Sales Turnover	37m	39m	37m
Pre Tax Profit/Loss	64	17m	1m
Working Capital	3m	3m	3m
Fixed Assets	12	60	206
Current Assets	12m	11m	9m
Current Liabilities	1m	1m	2m

Deluxe London

North Orbital Road Denham, Uxbridge, UB9 5HQ
Tel: 01895-832323 **Fax:** 01895-833617
E-mail: k.biggins@bydeluxe.com
Website: http://www.bydeluxe.com
Bank(s): National Westminster Bank Plc
Directors: C. Catterall (Co Sec), K. Biggins (MD), M. Doughty (Dir)
Managers: S. Morrison (Tech Serv Mgr), G. Lowrey (Personnel), I. Robinson (Sales & Mktg Mg)
Ultimate Holding Company: MACANDREWS & FORBES HOLDINGS INC (USA)
Immediate Holding Company: DELUXE LABORATORIES LIMITED
Registration no: 00309123 **VAT No.:** GB 422 4546 72
Date established: 1936 **Turnover:** £50m - £75m
No.of Employees: 101 - 250 **Product Groups:** 81

Date of Accounts	Dec 11	Dec 10	Dec 09
Sales Turnover	45m	50m	70m
Pre Tax Profit/Loss	-1m	672	1m
Working Capital	2m	5m	15m
Fixed Assets	21m	21m	22m
Current Assets	14m	21m	28m
Current Liabilities	5m	5m	5m

Diesel Services Ltd

Unit 19 Sarum Complex Salisbury Road, Uxbridge, UB8 2RZ
Tel: 01895-270693 **Fax:** 01895-234336
Website: http://www.dieselservicesltd.com
Directors: S. Kassam (Dir)
Immediate Holding Company: DIESEL SERVICES LIMITED
Registration no: 03206342 **Date established:** 1996
No.of Employees: 1 - 10 **Product Groups:** 39, 40, 48

Date of Accounts	May 11	May 10	May 09
Working Capital	-92	-108	-120
Fixed Assets	321	338	358
Current Assets	187	165	175

E T Enterprises Ltd

Riverside Way Cowley, Uxbridge, UB8 2YF
Tel: 01895-200880 **Fax:** 01895-270873
E-mail: sales@et-enterprises.com
Website: http://www.et-enterprises.com
Directors: G. Chambers (Fin), R. Mcalpine (MD), R. Stubbersfield (Sales & Mktg)
Managers: A. Cormack (Tech Serv Mgr), M. Petrafek (Purch Mgr)
Immediate Holding Company: ET ENTERPRISES LIMITED
Registration no: 06081468 **VAT No.:** GB 629 0520 52
Date established: 2007 **Turnover:** £5m - £10m
No.of Employees: 51 - 100 **Product Groups:** 37

Date of Accounts	Dec 11	Dec 10	Dec 09
Sales Turnover	7m	7m	6m
Pre Tax Profit/Loss	268	750	185
Working Capital	2m	3m	2m
Fixed Assets	3m	1m	1m
Current Assets	4m	4m	3m
Current Liabilities	511	558	355

Equipline

Ashley House Ashley Road, Uxbridge, UB8 2GA
Tel: 01895-272236 **Fax:** 01895-256360
E-mail: walker@equipline.co.uk
Website: http://www.equipline.co.uk
Directors: J. Walker (Ch)
Registration no: 02969227 **No.of Employees:** 21 - 50
Product Groups: 35, 40, 41, 48, 49, 63, 67, 83

Date of Accounts	Jan 08
Working Capital	452
Fixed Assets	197
Current Assets	1292
Current Liabilities	840
Total Share Capital	3

Esselte UK Ltd

Waterside House 4 Cowley Business Park, Cowley, Uxbridge, UB8 2HP
Tel: 01895-878700 **Fax:** 01895-878874
E-mail: marketinguk@esselte.com
Website: http://www.esselte.com
Bank(s): Barclays
Directors: R. Startin (Fin)
Managers: M. Adams (Tech Serv Mgr), N. Hall, V. Thompson (Sales Admin)
Ultimate Holding Company: ESSELTE GROUP HOLDINGS (LUXEMBOURG)SA LUXEMBOURG
Immediate Holding Company: ESSELTE LIMITED
Registration no: 01451078 **VAT No.:** GB 503 2915 77
Date established: 1979 **Turnover:** £5m - £10m **No.of Employees:** 21 - 50
Product Groups: 22, 27, 28, 29, 32

Date of Accounts	Dec 11	Dec 10	Dec 09
Sales Turnover	6m	6m	5m
Pre Tax Profit/Loss	-966	-1m	-2m
Working Capital	-33m	-30m	-28m
Fixed Assets	238	235	231
Current Assets	18m	18m	17m
Current Liabilities	1m	1m	662

F S L Aerospace Ltd

33 Riverside Way Cowley, Uxbridge, UB8 2YF
Tel: 01895-817600 **Fax:** 01895-817601
E-mail: sales@fslaerospace.co.uk
Website: http://www.fslaerospace.co.uk
Directors: T. Halliday (MD)
Managers: R. Woodward (Sales Prom Mgr), H. Stoke (Tech Serv Mgr)
Immediate Holding Company: FSL AEROSPACE LIMITED
Registration no: 01889558 **VAT No.:** GB 417 4169 53
Date established: 1985 **Turnover:** £1m - £2m **No.of Employees:** 11 - 20
Product Groups: 22, 23, 30, 35, 38, 39, 42, 46, 49, 63

Date of Accounts	Jun 11	Jun 10	Jun 09
Working Capital	696	544	632
Fixed Assets	112	67	86
Current Assets	2m	2m	2m

Fiserv Europe Ltd

7 Roundwood Avenue Stockley Park, Uxbridge, UB11 1AX
Tel: 020-8833 3000 **Fax:** 020-8833 3033
E-mail: bower@cbs.fiserv.com
Website: http://www.fiserv.com
Bank(s): Citibank International plc
Directors: D. Dyamond (Fin), J. Bower (Dir)
Ultimate Holding Company: FISERV INC (USA)
Immediate Holding Company: FISERV (EUROPE) LIMITED
Registration no: 02467435 **VAT No.:** GB 577 0295 18
Date established: 1990 **Turnover:** £20m - £50m
No.of Employees: 101 - 250 **Product Groups:** 44

Date of Accounts	Dec 11	Dec 10	Dec 09
Sales Turnover	28m	36m	27m
Pre Tax Profit/Loss	907	7m	5m
Working Capital	14m	16m	11m
Fixed Assets	2m	756	681
Current Assets	20m	25m	19m
Current Liabilities	5m	9m	7m

Galliford Try plc (Head Office)

Cowley Business Park No2 Cowley, Uxbridge, UB8 2AL
Tel: 01895-855000 **Fax:** 01895-855298
E-mail: info@gallifordtry.co.uk
Website: http://www.gallifordtry.co.uk
Bank(s): National Westminster Bank Plc
Directors: F. Nelson (Fin), P. Cooper (MD)
Managers: H. Walker, R. Gorbert (Purch Mgr)
Ultimate Holding Company: GALLIFORD TRY PLC
Immediate Holding Company: TRY GROUP LIMITED
Registration no: 01989257 **Date established:** 1986
Turnover: £10m - £20m **No.of Employees:** 101 - 250
Product Groups: 52, 80, 84

Date of Accounts	Jun 10	Jun 09	Jun 08
Working Capital	10m	10m	10m
Current Assets	10m	10m	10m

General Mills UK Ltd

Harman House 1 George Street, Uxbridge, UB8 1QQ
Tel: 01895-201100 **Fax:** 01895-201101
E-mail: info@genmills.com
Website: http://www.genmills.com
Bank(s): Barclays, Ruislip
Directors: J. Coward (Dir)
Ultimate Holding Company: GENERAL MILLS INC (USA)
Immediate Holding Company: GENERAL MILLS UK LIMITED
Registration no: 04633664 **Date established:** 2003
Turnover: £250m - £500m **No.of Employees:** 101 - 250
Product Groups: 20, 62

Date of Accounts	Apr 11	Apr 10	Apr 09
Sales Turnover	251m	239m	234m
Pre Tax Profit/Loss	2m	3m	4m
Working Capital	35m	34m	32m
Fixed Assets	5m	4m	6m
Current Assets	103m	99m	81m
Current Liabilities	20m	15m	14m

H & S Enamelling UK Ltd

Unit 7 Cowley Mill Trading Estate Longbridge Way, Cowley, Uxbridge, UB8 2YG
Tel: 01895-233251 **Fax:** 01895-810800
E-mail: sales@hsenamelling.co.uk
Website: http://www.hsenamelling.co.uk

Directors: K. Saggar (Prop)
Immediate Holding Company: H.& S.ENAMELLING LIMITED
Registration no: 00896066 **VAT No.:** GB 223 6522 86
Date established: 1967 **Turnover:** £20m - £50m **No.of Employees:** 1 - 10
Product Groups: 48

Date of Accounts	Jul 11	Jul 10	Jul 09
Working Capital	-35	-30	-12
Fixed Assets	2	11	6
Current Assets	68	78	108

Haes Systems Ltd

Columbia House Packet Boat Lane, Uxbridge, UB8 2JP
Tel: 01895-422066 **Fax:** 01895-420603
E-mail: enquiries@haes-systems.co.uk
Website: http://www.haes-systems.co.uk
Bank(s): Barclays
Directors: J. Ivey (MD), L. Ivey (Co Sec)
Ultimate Holding Company: BFS (HOLDINGS) LTD
Immediate Holding Company: HAES SYSTEMS (MANUFACTURING) LIMITED
Registration no: 01427223 **VAT No.:** GB 223 8255 73
Date established: 1979 **Turnover:** £500,000 - £1m
No.of Employees: 21 - 50 **Product Groups:** 38, 40

Date of Accounts	Dec 11	Dec 10	Dec 09
Sales Turnover	N/A	N/A	941
Pre Tax Profit/Loss	N/A	N/A	-174
Working Capital	15	15	15
Current Assets	38	38	38
Current Liabilities	22	22	22

Hale Hamilton Ltd

Cowley Road, Uxbridge, UB8 2AF
Tel: 01895-236525 **Fax:** 01895-231407
E-mail: agoodbrand@halehamilton.com
Website: http://www.halehamilton.com
Bank(s): HSBC Bank plc
Directors: P. Hunter (Fin), A. Goodbrand (Grp Chief Exec)
Managers: I. Ibrahim (Tech Serv Mgr), I. Davies, B. Dormer, L. Smart (Personnel), C. Day (Purch Mgr)
Ultimate Holding Company: CIRCOR INTERNATIONAL INC (USA)
Immediate Holding Company: CAMBRIDGE FLUID SYSTEMS LIMITED
Registration no: 03246262 **Date established:** 1987
Turnover: £10m - £20m **No.of Employees:** 101 - 250
Product Groups: 36, 40

Date of Accounts	Dec 11	Dec 10	Dec 09
Sales Turnover	23m	28m	12m
Pre Tax Profit/Loss	4m	5m	1m
Working Capital	6m	5m	3m
Fixed Assets	252	240	218
Current Assets	9m	11m	5m
Current Liabilities	2m	2m	470

Hasbro UK Ltd

2 Roundwood Avenue Stockley Park, Uxbridge, UB11 1AZ
Tel: 020-8569 1234 **Fax:** 020-8569 1133
E-mail: john.harper@hasbro.co.uk
Website: http://www.hasbro.co.uk
Directors: A. Emrich (Co Sec), J. Harper (MD)
Ultimate Holding Company: HASBRO INC (USA)
Immediate Holding Company: HASBRO U.K. LIMITED
Registration no: 01981543 **Date established:** 1986
Turnover: £20m - £50m **No.of Employees:** 251 - 500 **Product Groups:** 49

Date of Accounts	Dec 08	Dec 09	Dec 10
Sales Turnover	136m	133m	132m
Pre Tax Profit/Loss	10m	6m	6m
Working Capital	30m	34m	37m
Fixed Assets	4m	4m	3m
Current Assets	92m	97m	96m
Current Liabilities	10m	11m	12m

Ickenham Travel Group plc

6th Floor Armstrong House 38 Market Square, Uxbridge, UB8 1NG
Tel: 01895-450700 **Fax:** 01895-621658
E-mail: bbeesley@businesstraveldirect.co.uk
Website: http://www.businesstraveldirect.co.uk
Directors: P. Reglar (MD), H. Sawyer (Comm), J. Oliver (Dir)
Managers: V. Beesley (), V. Beesley
Immediate Holding Company: ICKENHAM TRAVEL GROUP PLC
Registration no: 00986305 **Date established:** 1970
Turnover: £20m - £50m **No.of Employees:** 21 - 50 **Product Groups:** 72, 74

Date of Accounts	Sep 11	Sep 10	Sep 09
Sales Turnover	48m	48m	44m
Pre Tax Profit/Loss	66	145	449
Working Capital	662	493	615
Fixed Assets	776	708	670
Current Assets	3m	4m	4m
Current Liabilities	222	388	455

Industria Bearings & Transmissions

76 Cowley Mill Road, Uxbridge, UB8 2QE
Tel: 01895-237971 **Fax:** 01895-272191
E-mail: sales@industria.co.uk
Website: http://www.industria.co.uk
Directors: G. Williams (MD)
Registration no: 06006121 **Turnover:** £1m - £2m
No.of Employees: 1 - 10 **Product Groups:** 35

Interserve Project Services Ltd

Dolphin Bridge House Rockingham Road, Uxbridge, UB8 2XL
Tel: 01895-238111 **Fax:** 01895-238237
E-mail: uxbridge.civils@interserveprojects.com
Website: http://www.interserveprojects.com
Directors: J. O'neil (MD)
Managers: D. Baker (Buyer)
Ultimate Holding Company: INTERSERVE PLC
Immediate Holding Company: INTERSERVE PROJECT SERVICES LIMITED
Registration no: 03299588 **Date established:** 1997
Turnover: £500m - £1,000m **No.of Employees:** 51 - 100
Product Groups: 51, 52

Gilbert Laurence Ltd

1 Union Buildings Wallingford Road, Uxbridge, UB8 2FR
Tel: 01895-455980 **Fax:** 01895-455999
E-mail: sales@gilbertlaurence.co.uk
Website: http://www.gilbertlaurence.co.uk
Bank(s): Barclays.
Directors: T. Warren (MD)
Immediate Holding Company: GILBERT LAURENCE LIMITED
Registration no: 01215180 **VAT No.:** GB 224 2433 02
Date established: 1975 **Turnover:** £1m - £2m **No.of Employees:** 11 - 20
Product Groups: 35

Date of Accounts	Apr 11	Apr 10	Apr 09
Working Capital	17	35	69
Fixed Assets	514	275	235
Current Assets	353	357	340

L D J

Bridge Works Iver Lane, Uxbridge, UB8 2JG
Tel: 01895-231880 **Fax:** 01895-271825
E-mail: sales@ldjmetal.co.uk
Website: http://www.ldjmetal.co.uk
Directors: D. Sawyer (Ptnr)
Registration no: 00240284 **VAT No.:** GB 224 8541 66
Date established: 1929 **Turnover:** £250,000 - £500,000
No.of Employees: 1 - 10 **Product Groups:** 48

M & A Locksmiths

31 Nelson Road, Uxbridge, UB10 0PU
Tel: 0800-695 4195
E-mail: john@a-jlocksmiths.com
Website: http://www.a-jlocksmiths.com
Directors: J. Ritter (Prop)
No.of Employees: 1 - 10 **Product Groups:** 36, 52

M E B Equipment Ltd

Broadwater Lane Harefield, Uxbridge, UB9 6AH
Tel: 01895-821002 **Fax:** 01895-824845
E-mail: sales@mebequipment.co.uk
Website: http://www.mebequipment.co.uk
Directors: E. Bolger (MD)
Immediate Holding Company: MEB EQUIPMENT LIMITED
Registration no: 03645415 **Date established:** 1998
No.of Employees: 1 - 10 **Product Groups:** 35, 39, 45

Date of Accounts	Nov 11	Nov 10	Nov 09
Working Capital	69	44	-30
Fixed Assets	9	11	14
Current Assets	190	182	100

M S D Animal Health

Breakspear Road South Harefield, Uxbridge, UB9 6LS
Tel: 0370-060 3380 **Fax:** 01895-672429
E-mail: spahuk@spcorp.com
Website: http://www.intervet.co.uk
Directors: D. Brown (Prop)
Immediate Holding Company: SDR REFRIDGERATION LIMITED
Registration no: 06793031 **Date established:** 2005
No.of Employees: 21 - 50 **Product Groups:** 63

Date of Accounts	Mar 11	Mar 10	Mar 09
Working Capital	-17	-24	-31
Fixed Assets	23	29	34
Current Assets	21	14	N/A

Manpower UK Ltd

Capital Court 30 Windsor Street, Uxbridge, UB8 1AB
Tel: 01895-205200 **Fax:** 01895-205201
E-mail: mark.cahill@manpower.co.uk
Website: http://www.manpower.co.uk
Bank(s): National Westminster Bank Plc
Directors: F. Broadfield (Fin), M. Cahill (Dir), T. Howard (MD)
Ultimate Holding Company: FP007619
Immediate Holding Company: MANPOWER UK LIMITED
Registration no: 03841918 **Date established:** 1999 **Turnover:** £2m - £5m
No.of Employees: 101 - 250 **Product Groups:** 80

Date of Accounts	Dec 09	Dec 08	Dec 07
Sales Turnover	523m	577m	588m
Pre Tax Profit/Loss	-2m	7m	2m
Working Capital	22m	24m	17m
Fixed Assets	1m	2m	2m
Current Assets	127m	140m	125m
Current Liabilities	43m	42m	50m

Maplin Electronics Ltd

148-154 Bakers Road, Uxbridge, UB8 1RG
Tel: 01895-270949 **Fax:** 01895-270918
Website: http://www.maplin.co.uk
Managers: E. Parchman (Mgr)
Ultimate Holding Company: MONTAGU PRIVATE EQUITY LLP
Immediate Holding Company: MAPLIN ELECTRONICS LIMITED
Registration no: 01264385 **Date established:** 1976
Turnover: £125m - £250m **No.of Employees:** 1 - 10 **Product Groups:** 37, 61

Date of Accounts	Dec 07	Dec 08	Dec 09
Sales Turnover	180m	204m	204m
Pre Tax Profit/Loss	24m	32m	35m
Working Capital	28m	49m	75m
Fixed Assets	26m	28m	28m
Current Assets	78m	108m	142m
Current Liabilities	44m	51m	59m

Marine Engine Services Ltd

Unit 3 549 Eskdale Road, Uxbridge, UB8 2RT
Tel: 01895-236246 **Fax:** 01895-813322
E-mail: pr-thompson@marineengine.co.uk
Website: http://www.marineengine.co.uk
Directors: P. Thompson (MD)
Immediate Holding Company: MARINE ENGINE SERVICES LIMITED
Registration no: 02438393 **Date established:** 1989
Turnover: £250,000 - £500,000 **No.of Employees:** 1 - 10
Product Groups: 35, 36, 39

Date of Accounts	Mar 12	Mar 11	Mar 10
Working Capital	-83	-99	-95
Fixed Assets	115	116	117
Current Assets	69	57	117

Metro Plating

3 Chartridge Development Eskdale Road, Uxbridge, UB8 2RT
Tel: 01895-238641 **Fax:** 01895-270278
E-mail: enquiries@metroplating.co.uk
Website: http://www.metroplating.co.uk
Directors: S. Etheridge (Dir)
Immediate Holding Company: METRO ENGINEERING AND PLATING WORKS LIMITED
Registration no: 00422946 **VAT No.:** GB 222 9625 67
Date established: 1946 **Turnover:** £1m - £2m **No.of Employees:** 1 - 10
Product Groups: 48

Date of Accounts	Nov 11	Nov 10	Nov 09
Working Capital	125	108	88
Fixed Assets	661	659	677
Current Assets	891	604	526

Microlimit

Iver Lane, Uxbridge, UB8 2JG
Tel: 01895-235252 **Fax:** 01895-813800
E-mail: neil@microlimit.co.uk
Website: http://www.microlimit.co.uk
Directors: N. Budgen (MD)
Immediate Holding Company: VMG UXBRIDGE LTD
Registration no: 00240284 **VAT No.:** GB 413 5896 41
Date established: 2010 **Turnover:** Up to £250,000
No.of Employees: 1 - 10 **Product Groups:** 37

MJF Corporate Guarding Ltd

River House Riverside Way, Uxbridge, UB8 2YF
Tel: 0808-1280001 **Fax:** 01895-909060
E-mail: info@mjf.co.uk
Website: http://www.mjf.co.uk
Managers: A. Young (Develop Mgr)
Registration no: 02961309 **Date established:** 1987 **Turnover:** £2m - £5m
No.of Employees: 101 - 250 **Product Groups:** 81, 86

Date of Accounts	Dec 07	Dec 06	Feb 06
Sales Turnover	6161	3487	N/A
Pre Tax Profit/Loss	134	-84	N/A
Working Capital	178	127	216
Fixed Assets	89	12	6
Current Assets	1731	1086	972
Current Liabilities	1553	959	756
ROCE% (Return on Capital Employed)	50.3	-60.4	
ROT% (Return on Turnover)	2.2	-2.4	

Norgine International Ltd (Head Office)

Chaplin House Widewater Place Moorhall Road, Harefield, Uxbridge, UB9 6NS
Tel: 01895-826600 **Fax:** 01895-825865
E-mail: enquiries@norgine.com
Website: http://www.norgine.com
Bank(s): Barclays
Directors: D. Todd (Co Sec), K. Scrimgeour (Dir)
Ultimate Holding Company: NORGINE (EUROPE) BV (NETHERLANDS)
Immediate Holding Company: NORGINE PHARMACEUTICALS LIMITED
Registration no: 03527131 **VAT No.:** GB 235 0839 68
Date established: 1998 **Turnover:** £20m - £50m
No.of Employees: 21 - 50 **Product Groups:** 63

Date of Accounts	Dec 11	Dec 10	Dec 09
Sales Turnover	39m	47m	46m
Pre Tax Profit/Loss	504	2m	2m
Working Capital	6m	5m	4m
Fixed Assets	66	104	2
Current Assets	12m	14m	15m
Current Liabilities	2m	2m	2m

Premiair Aircraft Services

Tilehouse Lane Denham, Uxbridge, UB9 5DF
Tel: 01895-830900 **Fax:** 01895-830950
E-mail: charter@premiair-aviation.com
Website: http://www.premiair-aviation.com
Directors: M. Harding (Fin)
Managers: R. Kinder (Tech Serv Mgr), C. Forrest, S. Coles (Personnel)
Ultimate Holding Company: VON ESSEN AVIATION LTD
Immediate Holding Company: PREMIAIR AVIATION GROUP LTD
Registration no: 02263711 **Turnover:** £10m - £20m
No.of Employees: 1 - 10 **Product Groups:** 31, 39, 75

Date of Accounts	Dec 07	Oct 06	Oct 05
Sales Turnover	10692	8187	8275
Pre Tax Profit/Loss	288	133	93
Working Capital	-8	932	-211
Fixed Assets	827	894	1993
Current Assets	2963	3482	2692
Current Liabilities	2971	2550	2903
Total Share Capital	10	10	10
ROCE% (Return on Capital Employed)	35.2	7.3	5.2
ROT% (Return on Turnover)	2.7	1.6	1.1

Protech Land & Marine Project Engineering Ltd

The Grand Union Office Park Packet Boat Lane, Uxbridge, UB8 2GH
Tel: 01895-434744 **Fax:** 01895-458010
E-mail: adrian.wilson@landandmarine.com
Website: http://www.protechengineering-uk.com
Bank(s): Barclays
Directors: F. Fricker (MD)
Managers: P. Harnden, A. Wilson (Chief Mgr), A. Wilson (Projects), W. Carr
Ultimate Holding Company: STORK NV
Registration no: 07132100 **VAT No.:** GB 531 3021 07
Date established: 1910 **Turnover:** £2m - £5m **No.of Employees:** 11 - 20
Product Groups: 37, 42, 44, 51, 61, 80, 84

Radiall Ltd

Ground Floor 6 The Ground Union Office Park, Uxbridge, UB8 2GH
Tel: 01895-425000 **Fax:** 01895-425010
E-mail: infouk@radiall.com
Website: http://www.radiall.com
Managers: P. Mcdavitt (Sales Prom Mgr)
Ultimate Holding Company: RADIALL SA (FRANCE)
Immediate Holding Company: RADIALL LTD
Registration no: 00377015 **VAT No.:** GB 226 7600 69
Date established: 1942 **Turnover:** £5m - £10m **No.of Employees:** 1 - 10
Product Groups: 37, 38

Date of Accounts	Dec 11	Dec 10	Dec 09
Sales Turnover	7m	5m	6m
Pre Tax Profit/Loss	180	147	254
Working Capital	144	69	2m
Fixed Assets	218	299	339
Current Assets	2m	1m	3m
Current Liabilities	365	287	299

Reed Accountancy Personnel Ltd

20 High Street, Uxbridge, UB8 1JN
Tel: 01895-274297 **Fax:** 01895-259885
E-mail: uxbridge.employment@reed.co.uk
Website: http://www.reed.co.uk
Directors: J. Reed (MD)
Managers: S. Cave (Personnel), D. Parminter (Mgr), E. Whickham (District Mgr)

see next page

***Reed Accountancy Personnel Ltd** - Cont'd*

Immediate Holding Company: Reed Personnel Services Ltd
Registration no: 00973629 **VAT No.:** GB 216 3577 65
Turnover: £125m - £250m **No.of Employees:** 1 - 10 **Product Groups:** 80

Reed Specialist Recruitment

20 High Street, Uxbridge, UB8 1JN
Tel: 01895-251665 **Fax:** 01895-810977
E-mail: dianne.parminter@reedglobal.com
Website: http://www.reed.co.uk
Managers: D. Parminter (Mgr)
Ultimate Holding Company: REED GLOBAL LTD (MALTA)
Immediate Holding Company: REED EMPLOYMENT LIMITED
Registration no: 00669854 **Date established:** 1960
Turnover: £500m - £1,000m **No.of Employees:** 1 - 10
Product Groups: 80

Date of Accounts	Jun 11	Jun 10	Dec 07
Sales Turnover	618	450	287m
Pre Tax Profit/Loss	-2m	310	8m
Working Capital	23m	28m	28m
Fixed Assets	31	36	5m
Current Assets	28m	30m	74m
Current Liabilities	37	29	21m

Reliance Security Group Ltd

Boundary House Cricketfield Road, Uxbridge, UB8 1QG
Tel: 01895-205000 **Fax:** 01895-205100
E-mail: brian.kingham@reliancegroup.co.uk
Website: http://www.reliancefm.com
Directors: B. Kingham (Ch)
Managers: O. Cassidy (Personnel)
Ultimate Holding Company: RELIANCE TRUST LIMITED
Immediate Holding Company: RELIANCE PROPERTY HOLDINGS LIMITED
Registration no: 01033997 **Date established:** 1971
Turnover: Up to £250,000 **No.of Employees:** 1 - 10 **Product Groups:** 40, 80, 81

Date of Accounts	Mar 12	Apr 11	Apr 10
Sales Turnover	39	58	117
Pre Tax Profit/Loss	27	1m	1m
Working Capital	2m	2m	961
Fixed Assets	617	628	1m
Current Assets	3m	3m	2m
Current Liabilities	16	200	55

The Right Address

Second Floor Salamander Quay West, Harefield, Uxbridge, UB9 6NZ
Tel: 01895-827800 **Fax:** 01895-827801
E-mail: info@therightaddress.co.uk
Website: http://www.therightaddress.co.uk
Directors: J. French (Dir)
Immediate Holding Company: MEINE EUROPE LIMITED
Date established: 2002 **Turnover:** £1m - £2m **No.of Employees:** 1 - 10
Product Groups: 87

Rio Tinto plc

Hunton House Unit 1 Highbridge Industrial Estate Oxford Road, Uxbridge, UB8 1HU
Tel: 01895-213200 **Fax:** 01895-213299
Website: http://www.riotintoalcan.com
Bank(s): National Westminster Bank Plc
Directors: T. Kilbryne (Fin), K. Anthony Wilkinson (Co Sec)
Managers: C. Hockley (I.T. Exec), J. Gardner
Immediate Holding Company: Alcan Aluminium Ltd (Canada)
Registration no: 00719885 **Date established:** 1944
Turnover: Over £1,000m **No.of Employees:** 21 - 50 **Product Groups:** 34, 35

Date of Accounts	Dec 07	Dec 06
Pre Tax Profit/Loss	-4000	-1000
Working Capital	-1000	2000
Fixed Assets	259000	259000
Current Assets	9000	16000
Current Liabilities	10000	14000
Total Share Capital	46000	46000
ROCE% (Return on Capital Employed)	-1.6	-0.4

S & G Machinery Ltd

106 Denecroft Crescent, Uxbridge, UB10 9HZ
Tel: 01895-270362 **Fax:** 01895-271926
E-mail: sandgmachinery@btconnect.com
Website: http://www.sandgmachinery.co.uk
Directors: G. Hughes (MD), S. Hughes (Fin)
Immediate Holding Company: S & G MACHINERY LTD
Registration no: 05541357 **Date established:** 2005
Turnover: Up to £250,000 **No.of Employees:** 1 - 10 **Product Groups:** 46

Date of Accounts	Aug 11	Aug 10	Aug 09
Sales Turnover	N/A	N/A	136
Pre Tax Profit/Loss	N/A	N/A	30
Working Capital	20	11	13
Fixed Assets	598	617	628
Current Assets	58	40	40
Current Liabilities	N/A	N/A	8

S P C International

Unit 5 The Grand Union Office Park Packet Boat Lane, Uxbridge, UB8 2GH
Tel: 01895-430900 **Fax:** 01963-435927
E-mail: sales@spcint.com
Website: http://www.spcint.com
Bank(s): National Westminster
Directors: D. Clarke (Sales)
Managers: T. Spall (Tech Serv Mgr), B. Orr
Ultimate Holding Company: SPC INTERNATIONAL LIMITED
Immediate Holding Company: SPC INTERNATIONAL LIMITED
Registration no: 04722278 **VAT No.:** GB710 5916 5500
Date established: 2003 **Turnover:** £10m - £20m
No.of Employees: 101 - 250 **Product Groups:** 26, 44, 48, 67

Date of Accounts	Sep 11	Sep 10	Sep 09
Sales Turnover	16m	15m	13m
Pre Tax Profit/Loss	393	419	-366
Working Capital	873	601	-363
Fixed Assets	5m	5m	5m
Current Assets	4m	4m	4m
Current Liabilities	1m	1m	1m

Sitexorbis plc

Beaufort House Cricket Field Road, Uxbridge, UB8 1QG
Tel: 01895-465500 **Fax:** 01895-465499
E-mail: info@sitexorbis.com
Website: http://www.sitexorbis.com
Directors: S. Crabb (Co Sec), O. Cunningham (Fin)
Managers: P. Tonks (Purch Mgr), C. Simmons (Personnel), M. Cosh (Sales & Mktg Mg), A. Debanfu, P. Docherty (Tech Serv Mgr)
Ultimate Holding Company: SITEXORBIS HOLDINGS LIMITED
Immediate Holding Company: SITEXORBIS LIMITED
Registration no: 02476859 **Date established:** 1990
Turnover: £20m - £50m **No.of Employees:** 21 - 50 **Product Groups:** 33

Date of Accounts	Mar 11	Mar 10	Mar 09
Sales Turnover	30m	30m	41m
Pre Tax Profit/Loss	-10m	-546	131
Working Capital	13m	12m	9m
Fixed Assets	15m	26m	27m
Current Assets	19m	18m	16m
Current Liabilities	4m	4m	4m

Small Order Springs & Pressings Ltd

Unit 2 Packet Boat Lane, Uxbridge, UB8 2JP
Tel: 01895-420149 **Fax:** 01895-421910
E-mail: keeley@sosltd.co.uk
Website: http://www.sosltd.co.uk
Bank(s): National Westminster Bank Plc
Directors: K. Swadling (Dir)
Immediate Holding Company: SMALL ORDER SPRINGS & PRESSINGS LIMITED
Registration no: 02072870 **VAT No.:** GB 453 0962 51
Date established: 1986 **Turnover:** £1m - £2m **No.of Employees:** 11 - 20
Product Groups: 35, 37, 48

Date of Accounts	Jan 12	Jan 11	Jan 10
Working Capital	593	241	246
Fixed Assets	248	312	335
Current Assets	946	584	462

Smiths Welding Services

Old Mill Lane, Uxbridge, UB8 2JH
Tel: 01895-251145 **Fax:** 01895-251145
Directors: C. Smith (Prop)
Immediate Holding Company: FINE WOODEN FURNITURE LIMITED
Registration no: 02962921 **Date established:** 2006
No.of Employees: 1 - 10 **Product Groups:** 46

Date of Accounts	Mar 11	Mar 10	Mar 06
Working Capital	-12	-2	31
Fixed Assets	176	183	173
Current Assets	22	6	35

Stork Food & Dairy Systems

Unit 9 Brook Business Centre Cowley Mill Road, Cowley, Uxbridge, UB8 2FX
Tel: 01895-251621
E-mail: dlambie@stork-uk.co.uk
Website: http://www.storkgroup.com
Managers: L. Axel-Berg (Chief Mgr)
Immediate Holding Company: DRUMFISH COMMUNICATIONS LIMITED
Registration no: 01104963 **Date established:** 2003 **Turnover:** £2m - £5m
No.of Employees: 1 - 10 **Product Groups:** 38, 42

Date of Accounts	Sep 11	Sep 10	Sep 09
Working Capital	454	380	446
Fixed Assets	21	23	70
Current Assets	913	773	958

Surespeed Couriers Systems Ltd

Unit 4a Tomo Industrial Estate Packet Boat Lane, Uxbridge, UB8 2JP
Tel: 01895-444622 **Fax:** 0871-123 1715
E-mail: sales@surespeed-couriers.com
Website: http://www.surespeed-couriers.com
Directors: C. Ryan (Ptnr)
Immediate Holding Company: SURESPEED COURIER SYSTEMS LIMITED
Registration no: 05549036 **Date established:** 2005
No.of Employees: 1 - 10 **Product Groups:** 39, 72, 77

Date of Accounts	Jul 11	Jul 10	Jul 09
Working Capital	3	-9	-35
Fixed Assets	12	12	15
Current Assets	6	N/A	5

Sykes Enterprises, Incorporated

Beaufort House Cricket Field Road, Uxbridge, UB8 1QD
Tel: 01895-274900 **Fax:** 01895-274880
E-mail: sykesausfinancialservices@sykes.com
Website: http://www.ictgroup.com
Directors: M. Simms (Develop), M. Puttock (MD)
Managers: R. Akinlawon (Comptroller)
No.of Employees: 251 - 500 **Product Groups:** 44

Date of Accounts	Dec 04
Sales Turnover	325530
Pre Tax Profit/Loss	-4330
Working Capital	48740
Fixed Assets	62570
Current Assets	98010
Current Liabilities	49270
Total Share Capital	51880
ROCE% (Return on Capital Employed)	-3.9

T C Ltd

Unit 6 Packet Boat Lane, Uxbridge, UB8 2GH
Tel: 01895-252222 **Fax:** 01895-273540
E-mail: info@tc.co.uk
Website: http://www.tc.co.uk
Bank(s): Midland
Directors: M. Ross (MD), R. Taylor (MD), R. Taylor (Dir), E. Ross (Dir)
Immediate Holding Company: T C LIMITED
Registration no: 01125377 **VAT No.:** GB 223 7880 55
Date established: 1973 **Turnover:** £10m - £20m
No.of Employees: 11 - 20 **Product Groups:** 37, 38

Date of Accounts	Oct 11	Oct 10	Oct 09
Sales Turnover	14m	11m	11m
Pre Tax Profit/Loss	913	64	149
Working Capital	2m	1m	1m
Fixed Assets	744	726	697
Current Assets	5m	5m	4m
Current Liabilities	2m	2m	2m

Tactiq Ltd

8 The Square Stockley Park, Uxbridge, UB11 1FW
Tel: 0845-8058925 **Fax:** 0845-8058928
E-mail: enquiries@tactiq.co.uk
Website: http://www.tactiq.co.uk
Managers: V. Ellis (Mktg Serv Mgr)
Registration no: 5837744 **Date established:** 1996
Turnover: £500,000 - £1m **No.of Employees:** 11 - 20
Product Groups: 44, 84

Date of Accounts	Dec 09	Dec 08	Dec 07
Working Capital	149	127	-68
Fixed Assets	7	9	2
Current Assets	340	273	159

Tamo Ltd

Unit 22 Sarum Complex Salisbury Road, Uxbridge, UB8 2RZ
Tel: 01895-200015 **Fax:** 01895-859888
E-mail: info@tamo.co.uk
Website: http://www.tamo.co.uk
Directors: D. Grant (MD)
Managers: R. Moses (Tech Sales Mgr)
Ultimate Holding Company: H & G HOLDINGS LIMITED
Immediate Holding Company: TAMO LIMITED
Registration no: 00596266 **Date established:** 1958 **Turnover:** £1m - £2m
No.of Employees: 1 - 10 **Product Groups:** 36, 38

Date of Accounts	Dec 11	Dec 10	Dec 09
Working Capital	363	267	221
Fixed Assets	34	44	32
Current Assets	518	416	363

Tec Line

Ashley House Ashley Road, Uxbridge, UB8 2GA
Tel: 01895-251666 **Fax:** 01895-256360
E-mail: post@equipline.co.uk
Website: http://www.equipline.co.uk
Directors: J. Krebs (Tech Serv)
Registration no: 02548525 **No.of Employees:** 11 - 20
Product Groups: 20, 40, 41

Date of Accounts	Jan 08	Jan 07	Jan 06
Working Capital	815	751	647
Fixed Assets	134	123	126
Current Assets	1232	1115	905
Current Liabilities	417	363	258
Total Share Capital	95	95	95

Total Butler

Harefield Oil Terminal Harvil Road, Harefield, Uxbridge, UB9 6JL
Tel: 01895-233440 **Fax:** 01442-841901
Website: http://www.hemal.co.uk
Directors: S. Palmer (MD)
Immediate Holding Company: LTC (SOUTHERN) LIMITED
Registration no: 01162536 **VAT No.:** GB 579 3674 80
Date established: 2002 **Turnover:** £50m - £75m **No.of Employees:** 1 - 10
Product Groups: 31

Date of Accounts	Feb 11	Feb 10	Feb 09
Working Capital	96	-201	-197
Fixed Assets	404	430	427
Current Assets	617	489	111

Tracker Network Ltd

Otter House 5 Cowley Business Park High Street, Cowley, Uxbridge, UB8 2AD
Tel: 01895-234567 **Fax:** 01895-234117
E-mail: enquiries@tracker.co.uk
Website: http://www.tracker.co.uk
Managers: A. Stephans, G. Hinds (Fin Mgr), J. Breeds (Tech Serv Mgr), M. Williams (Sales Prom Mgr), P. Patel (Mktg Serv Mgr), S. Mahoney, A. Stephens
Ultimate Holding Company: THE ROYAL BANK OF SCOTLAND GROUP PUBLIC LIMITED COMPANY
Immediate Holding Company: TRACKER NETWORK (UK) LIMITED
Registration no: 02632771 **Date established:** 1991
Turnover: £10m - £20m **No.of Employees:** 101 - 250 **Product Groups:** 72

Date of Accounts	Dec 11	Dec 10	Dec 09
Sales Turnover	19m	21m	23m
Pre Tax Profit/Loss	27	887	1m
Working Capital	14m	13m	12m
Fixed Assets	1m	1m	1m
Current Assets	23m	24m	24m
Current Liabilities	7m	9m	11m

Try Construction Ltd

Cowley Business Park Cowley, Uxbridge, UB8 2AL
Tel: 01895-855000 **Fax:** 01895-855099
E-mail: david.hinton@gallifordtry.co.uk
Website: http://www.gallifordtry.co.uk
Bank(s): National Westminster
Directors: D. Calverley (Grp Chief Exec), D. Hinton (Dir), F. Nelson (Fin), H. Try (Ch), R. Barraclough (Co Sec)
Ultimate Holding Company: Galliford Try plc
Immediate Holding Company: TRY CONSTRUCTION LIMITED
Registration no: 01983966 **VAT No.:** GB 223 4135 06
Date established: 1986 **Turnover:** £250,000 - £500,000
No.of Employees: 251 - 500 **Product Groups:** 52

Date of Accounts	Jun 10	Jun 09	Jun 08
Sales Turnover	N/A	395	441
Pre Tax Profit/Loss	281	18	-116
Working Capital	135	-54	-67
Fixed Assets	171	171	171
Current Assets	1m	2m	2m
Current Liabilities	998	2m	2m

Varta Automotive Batteries Ltd

Broadwater Park North Orbital Road Denham, Uxbridge, UB9 5HR
Tel: 01895-838999 **Fax:** 01895-838981
E-mail: info-uk@varta-automotive.com
Website: http://www.varta-automotive.com
Directors: P. Matarewicz (MD), M. Mehring (Co Sec), M. Mehring (Fin)
Managers: P. Thornton (Cust Serv Mgr), R. Bosch (I.T. Exec), A. Mavar (Sales & Mktg Mg), A. Sutton (Mktg Serv Mgr)
Ultimate Holding Company: INTERCONTINENTAL HOTELS GROUP PLC
Immediate Holding Company: SIX CONTINENTS LIMITED
Registration no: 02651473 **Date established:** 1967
Turnover: £10m - £20m **No.of Employees:** 1 - 10 **Product Groups:** 37

Date of Accounts	Dec 10	Dec 09	Dec 08
Pre Tax Profit/Loss	-886	-822	6m
Working Capital	155m	162m	78m
Fixed Assets	372m	373m	459m
Current Assets	174m	182m	187m
Current Liabilities	N/A	640	2m

W M F UK Ltd

31 Riverside Way Cowley, Uxbridge, UB8 2YF
Tel: 01895-816100 **Fax:** 01895-816105
E-mail: sales@wmf.uk.com
Website: http://www.wmf.uk.com

Directors: F. Lehmann (MD)
Managers: J. Seehawer (Mktg Serv Mgr)
Immediate Holding Company: WMF UNITED KINGDOM LIMITED
Registration no: 03690400 **Date established:** 1998
No.of Employees: 21 - 50 **Product Groups:** 22, 24, 26, 27, 30, 32, 33, 34, 35, 36, 37, 38, 39, 40, 41, 42, 45, 48, 49, 63, 64, 66, 67, 69, 83

Date of Accounts	Dec 11	Dec 10	Dec 09
Sales Turnover	12m	11m	10m
Pre Tax Profit/Loss	2m	1m	700
Working Capital	7m	5m	4m
Fixed Assets	96	201	222
Current Assets	9m	8m	6m
Current Liabilities	2m	2m	1m

Zoffany

Chalfont House Oxford Road, Denham, Uxbridge, UB9 4DX
Tel: 08445-434600 **Fax:** 0844-543 4602
E-mail: enquiries@zoffany.uk.com
Website: http://www.zoffany.uk.com
Directors: L. Stovell (Fin)
Managers: S. Carbutt, S. Whitfield (Comm), S. Shabolt (Personnel), V. Blair (Mktg Serv Mgr)
Ultimate Holding Company: WALKER GREENBANK PLC.
Immediate Holding Company: ZOFFANY LIMITED
Registration no: 01735081 **Date established:** 1983
No.of Employees: 21 - 50 **Product Groups:** 27, 66

Wembley

Arc Fabrications

3 Tower Lane East Lane Business Park, Wembley, HA9 7NB
Tel: 020-8908 5675 **Fax:** 020-8908 5676
E-mail: sales@arcfabrications.com
Website: http://www.arcfabrications.com
Directors: S. Gibb (Dir)
Registration no: 02813087 **No.of Employees:** 1 - 10 **Product Groups:** 35, 36, 48, 49, 51, 52, 66, 84

Argent Litho Ltd

259 Water Road, Wembley, HA0 1HX
Tel: 020-8998 0284 **Fax:** 020-8566 7107
E-mail: print@argentlitho.co.uk
Website: http://www.argentlitho.co.uk
Directors: B. Harwood (MD)
Immediate Holding Company: ARGENT LITHO LIMITED
Registration no: 01591344 **Date established:** 1981
No.of Employees: 11 - 20 **Product Groups:** 27, 28, 44, 80, 81

Date of Accounts	Mar 12	Mar 11	Mar 10
Working Capital	45	52	42
Fixed Assets	145	159	196
Current Assets	637	618	501

BugBusters UK Ltd

79 Wembley Park Drive, Wembley, HA9 8HE
Tel: 0800-916 9898 **Fax:** 020-8795 2664
E-mail: tobias@bugbustersuk.net
Website: http://www.bugbustersuk.net
Directors: T. Batkim (MD)
Immediate Holding Company: BUGBUSTERS UK LTD
Registration no: 05387391 **Date established:** 2005
No.of Employees: 1 - 10 **Product Groups:** 23, 32, 44, 52

Date of Accounts	Dec 11	Dec 10	Dec 09
Working Capital	-6	-6	-5
Fixed Assets	3	3	5

Carey Group P.L.C.

Carey House Great Central Way, Wembley, HA9 0HR
Tel: 020-8900 0221 **Fax:** 020-8795 9987
E-mail: enquiries@careysplc.ie
Website: http://www.carey-plc.co.uk
Directors: J. Carey (MD), J. Stephenson (Dir), T. Carey (Dir)
Managers: M. Bonna (Mktg Serv Mgr), P. Francis (Purch Mgr)
Registration no: 02644192 **Turnover:** £20m - £50m
No.of Employees: 251 - 500 **Product Groups:** 51

Date of Accounts	Mar 08
Sales Turnover	213220
Pre Tax Profit/Loss	9130
Working Capital	72950
Fixed Assets	14770
Current Assets	140860
Current Liabilities	67910
Total Share Capital	250
ROCE% (Return on Capital Employed)	10.4

Cartridge World Ltd

8 Main Drive East Lane Business Park, Wembley, HA9 7NA
Tel: 020-8904 1551
Website: http://www.wembley.cartridgeworld.co.uk
Managers: A. Windle (Mgr)
Immediate Holding Company: CARTRIDGE WORLD LIMITED
Registration no: 04124067 **Date established:** 2000 **Turnover:** £5m - £10m
No.of Employees: 1 - 10 **Product Groups:** 28, 30, 44

Date of Accounts	Dec 11	Dec 10	Dec 09
Sales Turnover	6m	7m	8m
Pre Tax Profit/Loss	373	164	210
Working Capital	1m	967	878
Fixed Assets	403	455	524
Current Assets	7m	7m	6m
Current Liabilities	4m	1m	2m

Cofit T Shirts Deals

6 Wharfeside Rosemont Road, Wembley, HA0 4PE
Tel: 020-8795 5700 **Fax:** 020-8902 2566
E-mail: h.chakardjian@sky.com
Website: http://www.tshirtdeals.co.uk
Directors: H. Chakardjian (MD)
No.of Employees: 1 - 10 **Product Groups:** 63

Dhamecha Foods Ltd

First Way, Wembley, HA9 0TU
Tel: 020-8903 8181 **Fax:** 020-8902 4420
E-mail: info@dhamecha.com
Website: http://www.dhamecha.com
Directors: B. Dhamecha (MD), R. Cowley (Fin)
Managers: R. Shah (Mktg Serv Mgr), G. Jarvis (Tech Serv Mgr), M. Vithlani, J. Shah (Personnel)
Ultimate Holding Company: DHAMECHA HOLDINGS LIMITED
Immediate Holding Company: DHAMECHA FOODS LIMITED
Registration no: 01163739 **VAT No.:** GB 228 2248 70
Date established: 1974 **Turnover:** £500m - £1,000m
No.of Employees: 51 - 100 **Product Groups:** 61

Date of Accounts	Mar 12	Mar 11	Mar 10
Sales Turnover	565m	527m	428m
Pre Tax Profit/Loss	12m	10m	9m
Working Capital	42m	37m	33m
Fixed Assets	2m	2m	2m
Current Assets	110m	110m	100m
Current Liabilities	5m	5m	4m

E M R Sliverthorn Ltd

4 Abercorn Commercial Centre Manor Farm Road, Wembley, HA0 1AN
Tel: 020-8903 1390 **Fax:** 020-8903 9092
E-mail: sales@emrsilverthorn.co.uk
Website: http://www.emrsilverthorn.co.uk
Directors: C. Fletcher (MD)
Registration no: 01395770 **Date established:** 1978 **Turnover:** £1m - £2m
No.of Employees: 1 - 10 **Product Groups:** 23, 30, 31, 33, 34, 35, 36, 37, 38, 40, 48, 66, 67, 83

Fantasy Island

Watford Road, Wembley, HA0 3HG
Tel: 020-8904 9044 **Fax:** 020-8904 9046
Website: http://www.wherekidsplay.co.uk
Directors: C. Lousada (MD), P. Sharp (MD), T. Brook (Co Sec)
Immediate Holding Company: THE LEARNING HUB LIMITED
Registration no: 02585537 **Date established:** 2005
Turnover: Up to £250,000 **No.of Employees:** 21 - 50 **Product Groups:** 89

Date of Accounts	Mar 11	Mar 10	Mar 09
Working Capital	3	2	2
Fixed Assets	1	1	2
Current Assets	66	62	53

Formula Sound Ltd

Unit 23 Stadium Business Centre North End Road, Wembley, HA9 0AT
Tel: 020-8900 0947 **Fax:** 020-8903 8657
E-mail: info@formula-sound.com
Website: http://www.formula-sound.com
Directors: B. Penaligon (Sales), D. Gami (Dir)
Immediate Holding Company: Naina International Ltd
Registration no: 01134234 **VAT No.:** GB 298 6353 04
Date established: 1996 **Turnover:** £500,000 - £1m
No.of Employees: 1 - 10 **Product Groups:** 37

Date of Accounts	Dec 07	Dec 06	Dec 05
Working Capital	149	174	208
Fixed Assets	17	20	24
Current Assets	229	261	288
Current Liabilities	80	87	80

Friarnoll Ltd

Unit 41 Hallmark Industrial Estate Fourthway, Wembley, HA9 0LB
Tel: 020-8902 7722 **Fax:** 020-8795 4187
E-mail: sales@colonnademetal.com
Website: http://www.colonnademetal.com
Directors: J. Dormer (MD)
Ultimate Holding Company: CONTEMPORARY METALWARE LIMITED
Immediate Holding Company: FRIARNOLL LIMITED
Registration no: 01351314 **Date established:** 1978
No.of Employees: 11 - 20 **Product Groups:** 46, 48

Date of Accounts	Apr 11	Apr 10	Apr 09
Working Capital	140	130	112
Fixed Assets	36	45	58
Current Assets	220	201	230

G W Wiring Products Ltd

Unit 2 Wharfeside Rosemont Road, Wembley, HA0 4PE
Tel: 020-8795 0652 **Fax:** 020-8795 0797
E-mail: gwcabletie@aol.com
Website: http://www.gwcabletie.com
Managers: J. Chow (Mgr)
Immediate Holding Company: GW WIRING PRODUCTS LIMITED
Registration no: 04333217 **Date established:** 2001
Turnover: £500,000 - £1m **No.of Employees:** 1 - 10 **Product Groups:** 30

Date of Accounts	Jan 12	Jan 11	Jan 10
Working Capital	989	826	444
Fixed Assets	25	29	32
Current Assets	1m	1m	607

gabicci

York House Empire Way, Wembley, HA9 0PA
Tel: 020-8903 9037 **Fax:** 020-8903 2493
E-mail: info@gabicci.com
Website: http://www.gabicci.com
Directors: J. Keogh (MD), J. Keoth (MD), S. Hamed (Ch)
Managers: K. Patel (Sales Prom Mgr)
Immediate Holding Company: Gabicci International Ltd
Registration no: 06958543 **Date established:** 2003
Turnover: Up to £250,000 **No.of Employees:** 1 - 10 **Product Groups:** 24

Date of Accounts	Jun 07	Jun 06
Working Capital	-6863	-7138
Fixed Assets	13097	13569
Current Assets	151	80
Current Liabilities	7014	7218
Total Share Capital	5	5

G K P Partnership

109-110 Biglen House Elperton Lane, Wembley, HA0 1HD
Tel: 020-8998 3456 **Fax:** 020-8998 1612
E-mail: info@gkpp.com
Website: http://www.gkpp.com
Directors: A. Sharma (MD)
Immediate Holding Company: GKP PARTNERSHIP LIMITED
Registration no: 04931787 **Date established:** 2003
No.of Employees: 11 - 20 **Product Groups:** 80

Gobina London Ltd

Unit 8-10 Hallmark Trading Estate Fourth Way, Wembley, HA9 0LB
Tel: 020-8900 2707 **Fax:** 020-8903 9171
Website: http://www.gobina.co.uk
Bank(s): Natwest
Directors: H. Bharwani (Dir), B. Bharwani (Fin)
Immediate Holding Company: GOBINA (LONDON) LIMITED
Registration no: 01405927 **VAT No.:** GB 228 8865 16
Date established: 1978 **Turnover:** £2m - £5m **No.of Employees:** 11 - 20
Product Groups: 23, 24

Date of Accounts	Sep 11	Sep 10	Jun 09
Sales Turnover	N/A	N/A	2m
Pre Tax Profit/Loss	N/A	N/A	-646
Working Capital	257	4	-903
Fixed Assets	2m	2m	2m
Current Assets	2m	2m	2m
Current Liabilities	N/A	N/A	163

Ice Cream Container Co. Ltd

6 Beresford Avenue, Wembley, HA0 1SA
Tel: 020-8903 9021 **Fax:** 020-8900 2472
E-mail: sales@icecream-cont.co.uk
Website: http://www.icecream-alfred.co.uk
Directors: B. Marsh (MD), G. Wilcock (Fin), R. Wadge (Sales)
Immediate Holding Company: ICE CREAM CONTAINER COMPANY LIMITED(THE)
Registration no: 01483665 **VAT No.:** GB 346 4328 52
Date established: 1980 **Turnover:** £2m - £5m **No.of Employees:** 1 - 10
Product Groups: 30

Date of Accounts	Apr 11	Apr 10	Apr 09
Working Capital	182	102	35
Fixed Assets	5	6	12
Current Assets	574	543	626

Jewson Ltd

33 Manor Farm Road, Wembley, HA0 1AB
Tel: 020-8902 8671 **Fax:** 020-8900 0291
E-mail: sam.williamson@jewson.co.uk
Website: http://www.jewson.co.uk
Managers: S. Williamson (Mgr)
Ultimate Holding Company: COMPAGNIE DE SAINT GOBAIN (FRANCE)
Immediate Holding Company: JEWSON LIMITED
Registration no: 00348407 **VAT No.:** GB 394 1212 63
Date established: 1939 **Turnover:** £2m - £5m **No.of Employees:** 1 - 10
Product Groups: 66

Date of Accounts	Dec 11	Dec 10	Dec 09
Sales Turnover	1606m	1547m	1485m
Pre Tax Profit/Loss	18m	100m	45m
Working Capital	-345m	-250m	-349m
Fixed Assets	496m	387m	461m
Current Assets	657m	1005m	1320m
Current Liabilities	66m	120m	64m

Loot Ltd

Wembley Point 1 Harrow Road, Wembley, HA9 6DA
Tel: 0871-2225000 **Fax:** 020-8900 4505
E-mail: marketing@loot.com
Website: http://www.loot.com
Directors: A. Perry (Fin), S. Winfield (MD)
Immediate Holding Company: LOOT LIMITED
Registration no: 07310736 **Date established:** 2010
Turnover: £20m - £50m **No.of Employees:** 251 - 500
Product Groups: 80, 81

Date of Accounts	Sep 07	Sep 06	Sep 05
Sales Turnover	N/A	N/A	19719
Pre Tax Profit/Loss	-5006	14419	5988
Working Capital	56696	54301	52450
Fixed Assets	10762	19030	38762
Current Assets	58376	55135	53449
Current Liabilities	1680	834	999
Total Share Capital	500	500	500
ROCE% (Return on Capital Employed)	-7.4	19.7	6.6
ROT% (Return on Turnover)			30.4

Mcgee Group Ltd

340-342 Athlon Road, Wembley, HA0 1BX
Tel: 020-8998 1101 **Fax:** 020-8997 7689
E-mail: mail@mcgee.co.uk
Website: http://www.mcgee.co.uk
Bank(s): The Royal Bank of Scotland
Directors: B. Mcgee (MD), G. Payne (Fin)
Managers: K. Brown
Ultimate Holding Company: DEALPRIDE LIMITED
Immediate Holding Company: MCGEE GROUP (HOLDINGS) LIMITED
Registration no: 00933689 **Date established:** 1968
Turnover: £75m - £125m **No.of Employees:** 251 - 500
Product Groups: 51

Date of Accounts	May 09	May 08	Nov 11
Sales Turnover	65m	75m	92m
Pre Tax Profit/Loss	-1m	2m	3m
Working Capital	-2m	2m	1m
Fixed Assets	15m	14m	12m
Current Assets	15m	17m	22m
Current Liabilities	3m	4m	5m

Mitex Ltd

4 Towers Business Park Carey Way, Wembley, HA9 0LQ
Tel: 020-8900 0440 **Fax:** 020-8900 1908
Directors: M. Earl (Jt MD), E. Earl (Jt MD)
Managers: S. Hooper (Sales Admin)
Immediate Holding Company: MITEX LIMITED
Registration no: 01708531 **Date established:** 1983
Turnover: Up to £250,000 **No.of Employees:** 1 - 10 **Product Groups:** 22, 24

Date of Accounts	Jun 08
Pre Tax Profit/Loss	38
Working Capital	376
Fixed Assets	891
Current Assets	404
Current Liabilities	28
ROCE% (Return on Capital Employed)	3.0

N S Welding & Metal Works

455 Sunleigh Road, Wembley, HA0 4LY
Tel: 020-8795 1855 **Fax:** 020-8795 1855
Directors: N. Sidbura (Prop)
No.of Employees: 1 - 10 **Product Groups:** 35, 36, 52

Oakland Financial Advisors

Unit 2 Popi Business Centre South Way, Wembley, HA9 0HB
Tel: 020-8903 4054 **Fax:** 020-8903 8045
Website: http://www.orkin.co.uk
Directors: M. Patel (MD), M. Patel (Prop)
Immediate Holding Company: OAKLAND FINANCIAL CONSULTANTS LLP
Registration no: OC332761 **Date established:** 2007
Turnover: Up to £250,000 **No.of Employees:** 1 - 10 **Product Groups:** 32, 66

Omega Import Export Ltd
6 Beresford Avenue, Wembley, HA0 1SA
Tel: 020-8902 6222 **Fax:** 020-8903 5011
E-mail: enquiry@elftone.com
Website: http://www.elftone.com
Directors: S. Vaswani (Dir)
Immediate Holding Company: OMEGA IMPORT EXPORT LIMITED
Registration no: 00989599 **VAT No.:** GB 244 9890 22
Date established: 1970 **Turnover:** £1m - £2m **No.of Employees:** 11 - 20
Product Groups: 37, 40, 44, 67

Date of Accounts	Mar 12	Mar 11	Mar 10
Sales Turnover	N/A	1m	N/A
Pre Tax Profit/Loss	N/A	49	N/A
Working Capital	220	185	169
Fixed Assets	2m	2m	2m
Current Assets	943	1m	982
Current Liabilities	N/A	419	N/A

The Quintessa Art Collection
8 Watkin Road, Wembley, HA9 0NL
Tel: 020-8795 3620 **Fax:** 020-8795 3634
E-mail: robert@quintessa-art.com
Website: http://www.quintessa-art.com
Directors: R. Lunzer (Prop)
Registration no: 04215204 **Turnover:** £500,000 - £1m
No.of Employees: 1 - 10 **Product Groups:** 81

Synel Industries UK Ltd
Transputec House Heather Park Drive, Wembley, HA0 1SS
Tel: 020-8900 9991 **Fax:** 020-8902 3595
E-mail: sales@synel.co.uk
Website: http://www.synel.co.uk
Directors: D. Furber (MD)
Ultimate Holding Company: SYNEL INDUSTRIES LTD (ISRAEL)
Immediate Holding Company: SYNEL INDUSTRIES (UK) LIMITED
Registration no: 02499677 **Date established:** 1990
No.of Employees: 11 - 20 **Product Groups:** 40

Date of Accounts	Dec 11	Dec 10	Dec 09
Working Capital	-70	-71	-14
Fixed Assets	163	164	126
Current Assets	969	1m	998

T R A UK
Unit 7 Liberty Centre Mount Pleasant, Wembley, HA0 1TX
Tel: 020-8537 0000 **Fax:** 020-8537 5601
Website: http://www.trauk.com
Managers: A. Rehman (Mgr)
Immediate Holding Company: TRA (UK) LIMITED
Registration no: 04222478 **Date established:** 2001
No.of Employees: 1 - 10 **Product Groups:** 37, 67, 84

Date of Accounts	May 11	May 10	May 09
Working Capital	-300	-194	69
Fixed Assets	30	35	35
Current Assets	468	473	246

2d 3d Ltd
263 Abbeydale Road, Wembley, HA0 1TW
Tel: 020-8998 3199 **Fax:** 020-8998 7767
E-mail: rob@2d3d.co.uk
Website: http://www.2d3d.co.uk
Directors: R. Edkins (MD), S. Bramall (Fin)
Immediate Holding Company: 2D: 3D LIMITED
Registration no: 03003985 **Date established:** 1994
No.of Employees: 1 - 10 **Product Groups:** 30, 49

Date of Accounts	Dec 11	Dec 10	Dec 09
Working Capital	23	-64	-84
Fixed Assets	93	74	82
Current Assets	529	312	191

Unitrust Protection Services Ltd
Unitrust House Heather Park Drive, Wembley, HA0 1SS
Tel: 020-8903 8303 **Fax:** 020-8903 5526
E-mail: info@unitrust.co.uk
Website: http://www.unitrust.co.uk
Bank(s): National Westminster
Directors: P. Griffin (MD)
Ultimate Holding Company: UNITRUST PROTECTION SERVICES HOLDINGS LIMITED
Immediate Holding Company: UNITRUST PROTECTION SERVICES (U.K.) LIMITED
Registration no: 01335720 **VAT No.:** GB 296 1960 20
Date established: 1977 **Turnover:** £5m - £10m
No.of Employees: 101 - 250 **Product Groups:** 81

Date of Accounts	Mar 12	Mar 11	Mar 10
Sales Turnover	5m	5m	7m
Pre Tax Profit/Loss	137	118	93
Working Capital	722	841	968
Fixed Assets	68	279	315
Current Assets	2m	2m	2m
Current Liabilities	648	642	942

Variety Silk House Ltd
150-152 Ealing Road, Wembley, HA0 4PY
Tel: 020-8903 6302 **Fax:** 020-8900 2497
E-mail: variety@mailbox.co.uk
Website: http://www.varietysilkhouse.com
Directors: C. Shah (Dir)
Immediate Holding Company: VARIETY SILK
Registration no: 01801332 **VAT No.:** GB 228 1772 58
Date established: 1984 **Turnover:** £1m - £2m **No.of Employees:** 1 - 10
Product Groups: 24

Date of Accounts	Jun 11	Jun 10	Jun 09
Working Capital	283	191	174
Fixed Assets	327	359	411
Current Assets	815	863	788

Vendo plc
215 East Lane, Wembley, HA0 3NG
Tel: 020-8908 1234 **Fax:** 020-8904 2698
E-mail: enquiries@pvcvendo.com
Website: http://www.pvcvendo.com
Directors: I. Calhoun (MD)
Immediate Holding Company: VENDO PLC
Registration no: 01571834 **Date established:** 1981
Turnover: £500,000 - £1m **No.of Employees:** 11 - 20 **Product Groups:** 39

Date of Accounts	Sep 11	Sep 10	Sep 09
Sales Turnover	524	548	644
Pre Tax Profit/Loss	114	149	223
Working Capital	211	194	192
Fixed Assets	5	7	9
Current Assets	538	544	552
Current Liabilities	64	71	88

W S M U Ltd
15 Monks Park, Wembley, HA9 6JF
Tel: 0791-742 0009 **Fax:** 020-8900 8404
E-mail: info@wsmunited.com
Website: http://www.wsmunited.com
Directors: Y. Pavelchuk (Dir)
Immediate Holding Company: WSMU LIMITED
Registration no: 06819535 **Date established:** 2009
No.of Employees: 1 - 10 **Product Groups:** 25, 35

Date of Accounts	Feb 12	Feb 11	Feb 10
Working Capital	-6	-6	-10
Fixed Assets	6	7	10
Current Assets	5	5	23

Westlake Wembley Ltd
440 High Road, Wembley, HA9 6AH
Tel: 020-8902 2392 **Fax:** 020-8902 1780
E-mail: enquiries@westlakes.uk.com
Website: http://www.westlakes.uk.com
Directors: P. Patel (MD)
Immediate Holding Company: WESTLAKE(WEMBLEY) LIMITED
Registration no: 00752545 **Date established:** 1963 **Turnover:** £1m - £2m
No.of Employees: 1 - 10 **Product Groups:** 22, 23, 25, 26, 27, 28, 29, 30, 32, 35, 36, 38, 39, 43, 44, 48, 49, 61, 64, 67

Date of Accounts	Dec 11	Dec 10	Dec 09
Working Capital	942	908	926
Fixed Assets	5	7	10
Current Assets	1m	1m	1m

West Drayton

All Metal Services Ltd
6 Horton Industrial Park Horton Road, West Drayton, UB7 8JD
Tel: 01895-444066 **Fax:** 01895-420963
E-mail: sales@allmetal.co.uk
Website: http://www.allmetal.co.uk
Bank(s): HSBC Bank plc
Directors: D. Potts (MD)
Ultimate Holding Company: ALUMINIUM SERVICES (UK) LIMITED
Immediate Holding Company: ALL METAL SERVICES LIMITED
Registration no: 01159685 **VAT No.:** GB 223 8977 35
Date established: 1974 **Turnover:** £75m - £125m
No.of Employees: 21 - 50 **Product Groups:** 34

Date of Accounts	Dec 11	Dec 10	Dec 09
Sales Turnover	130m	96m	102m
Pre Tax Profit/Loss	5m	3m	9m
Working Capital	48m	45m	53m
Fixed Assets	6m	5m	5m
Current Assets	109m	81m	91m
Current Liabilities	37m	3m	24m

British Airways plc
Waterside P O Box 365, Harmondsworth, West Drayton, UB7 0GB
Tel: 01805-266522 **Fax:** 020-8738 9990
E-mail: contactbade@email.ba.com
Website: http://www.peacocktravelsandtours.com
Bank(s): Barclays
Directors: M. Read (Grp Chief Exec), C. Marshall (Ch)
Registration no: 01777777 **Date established:** 1983
Turnover: Up to £250,000 **No.of Employees:** 1001 - 1500
Product Groups: 75

Date of Accounts	Mar 08	Mar 07	Mar 06
Sales Turnover	8753m	8492m	8213m
Pre Tax Profit/Loss	883000	611000	616000
Working Capital	-96000	-194000	234000
Fixed Assets	7975m	7953m	8508m
Current Assets	3148m	3431m	3666m
Current Liabilities	3244m	3625m	3432m
Total Share Capital	288000	288000	283000
ROCE% (Return on Capital Employed)	11.2	7.9	7.0
ROT% (Return on Turnover)	10.1	7.2	7.5

Comag
Tavistock Road, West Drayton, UB7 7QE
Tel: 01895-433600 **Fax:** 01895-433602
Website: http://www.comag.co.uk
Bank(s): Lloyds TSB Bank plc
Directors: M. Mirams (MD), S. Pounder (Tech Serv)
Managers: S. Smith (Sales Admin)
Ultimate Holding Company: THE HEARST CORPORATION
Immediate Holding Company: NATIONAL MAGAZINE COMPANY & CONDE NAST PUBLICATION
Registration no: 01319853 **VAT No.:** GB 579 1003 40
Turnover: £125m - £250m **No.of Employees:** 101 - 250
Product Groups: 64

Continental Tyre Group Ltd
Continental House 191 High Street, Yiewsley, West Drayton, UB7 7XW
Tel: 01895-425900 **Fax:** 01895-425982
E-mail: info@conti.de
Website: http://www.conti-online.com
Directors: D. Smith (MD), G. Frobisher (Mkt Research), N. Pritchard (Fin)
Managers: A. Gregg
Ultimate Holding Company: CONTINENTAL AG (GERMANY)
Immediate Holding Company: CONTINENTAL TYRE GROUP LTD.
Registration no: 00296602 **Date established:** 1935
Turnover: £250m - £500m **No.of Employees:** 101 - 250
Product Groups: 29

Date of Accounts	Dec 11	Dec 10	Dec 09
Sales Turnover	382m	305m	257m
Pre Tax Profit/Loss	8m	7m	4m
Working Capital	22m	16m	10m
Fixed Assets	5m	5m	4m
Current Assets	153m	111m	93m
Current Liabilities	124m	89m	79m

H D S Freight Services Ltd
Unit 5 Saxon Way Trading Centre Saxon Way, Harmondsworth, West Drayton, UB7 0LW
Tel: 020-8564 9955 **Fax:** 020-8564 7060
E-mail: transport@electronichandling.co.uk
Website: http://www.hdsfreight.co.uk
Directors: D. Keen (Dir)
Immediate Holding Company: H. D. S. FREIGHT SERVICES LIMITED
Registration no: 01621588 **VAT No.:** GB 226 0155 02
Date established: 1982 **No.of Employees:** 11 - 20 **Product Groups:** 75, 76

Date of Accounts	Aug 11	Aug 10	Aug 09
Sales Turnover	1m	1m	1m
Pre Tax Profit/Loss	6	24	-61
Working Capital	101	94	65
Fixed Assets	3	4	5
Current Assets	318	369	271
Current Liabilities	132	57	60

John Guest
Horton Road, West Drayton, UB7 8JL
Tel: 01895-449233 **Fax:** 01895-420321
E-mail: info@johnguest.co.uk
Website: http://www.johnguest.co.uk
Directors: J. Guest (Dir)
Managers: C. Gray (Mktg Serv Mgr)
Ultimate Holding Company: JOHN GUEST HOLDINGS LIMITED
Immediate Holding Company: JOHN GUEST INTERNATIONAL LIMITED
Registration no: 03880612 **VAT No.:** GB 649 7726 80
Date established: 1999 **Turnover:** £75m - £125m
No.of Employees: 501 - 1000 **Product Groups:** 36

Date of Accounts	Dec 11	Dec 10	Dec 09
Sales Turnover	109m	104m	88m
Pre Tax Profit/Loss	16m	13m	5m
Working Capital	39m	33m	24m
Fixed Assets	43m	43m	45m
Current Assets	54m	48m	38m
Current Liabilities	6m	7m	4m

K Controls Ltd
2 Crown Way Crown Business Centre, West Drayton, UB7 8HZ
Tel: 01895-449601 **Fax:** 01895-448586
E-mail: sales@k-controls.co.uk
Website: http://www.k-controls.co.uk
Bank(s): Lloyds TSB Bank plc
Directors: D. Yates (Ptnr)
Immediate Holding Company: K CONTROLS LIMITED
Registration no: 00953427 **Date established:** 1969 **Turnover:** £1m - £2m
No.of Employees: 11 - 20 **Product Groups:** 36, 37, 38, 68

Date of Accounts	Dec 11	Dec 10	Dec 09
Working Capital	1m	1m	979
Fixed Assets	103	101	116
Current Assets	1m	1m	1m

New Pro Foundries Ltd
Unit C Horton Close, West Drayton, UB7 8EB
Tel: 01895-443194 **Fax:** 01895-442968
E-mail: info@newpro.co.uk
Website: http://www.newpro.co.uk
Bank(s): National Westminster
Directors: D. Taylor (Fin)
Immediate Holding Company: NEW PRO FOUNDRIES LIMITED
Registration no: 00606481 **VAT No.:** 222 8363 76 **Date established:** 1958
Turnover: £500,000 - £1m **No.of Employees:** 11 - 20 **Product Groups:** 34

Date of Accounts	Jun 11	Jun 10	Jun 09
Working Capital	96	137	170
Fixed Assets	27	32	38
Current Assets	178	194	244

Parker Merchanting Ltd
4 Horton Industrial Park Horton Road, West Drayton, UB7 8JD
Tel: 01895-444040 **Fax:** 01895-420036
E-mail: pparker.nationalsales@parkermerchanting.co.uk
Website: http://www.parker-merchanting.com
Managers: E. Finingham (Mgr)
Ultimate Holding Company: RAY INVESTMENT SARL (LUXEMBOURG)
Immediate Holding Company: PARKER MERCHANTING LIMITED
Registration no: 00224779 **VAT No.:** GB 614 2136 80
Date established: 2027 **Turnover:** £75m - £125m
No.of Employees: 21 - 50 **Product Groups:** 22, 23, 24, 29, 30, 32, 33, 37, 39, 40, 45, 63, 66, 68

Date of Accounts	Dec 10	Dec 09	Dec 08
Working Capital	51	51	51
Current Assets	51	51	51

Pourshins plc
The Lodge Harmondsworth Lane, Harmondsworth, West Drayton, UB7 0AB
Tel: 020-8917 5777 **Fax:** 020-8917 5791
E-mail: sales@pourshins.com
Website: http://www.pourshins.com
Bank(s): Natwest
Directors: R. Powell (Co Sec), M. Diviney (Dir)
Ultimate Holding Company: GATEGROUP HOLDING AG (SWITZERLAND)
Immediate Holding Company: POURSHINS LIMITED
Registration no: 01576522 **VAT No.:** GB 584 5403 27
Date established: 1981 **Turnover:** £50m - £75m
No.of Employees: 21 - 50 **Product Groups:** 61, 62

Date of Accounts	Dec 11	Dec 10	Dec 09
Sales Turnover	79m	72m	59m
Pre Tax Profit/Loss	2m	886	274
Working Capital	3m	1m	81
Fixed Assets	6	9	160
Current Assets	12m	11m	11m
Current Liabilities	1m	1m	2m

System Sound & Light Ltd
1 Liddall Way, West Drayton, UB7 8PG
Tel: 01895-432995 **Fax:** 01895-432976
E-mail: simon@systemsound.com
Website: http://www.systemsoundandlight.co.uk
Directors: S. Biddulph (MD)
Immediate Holding Company: SYSTEM SOUND & LIGHT LIMITED
Registration no: 02022374 **Date established:** 1986
No.of Employees: 1 - 10 **Product Groups:** 81

Date of Accounts	Jan 12	Jan 11	Jan 10
Working Capital	5	-9	9
Fixed Assets	183	138	164
Current Assets	302	273	299

Teledyne Ltd
Aviation House The Lodge Harmondsworth Lane, Harmondsworth, West Drayton, UB7 0LQ
Tel: 020-8759 3455 **Fax:** 020-8990 5900
E-mail: reception@flightdata.co.uk
Website: http://www.teledyne-controls.com

Directors: P. Clapp (Dir)
Ultimate Holding Company: TELEDYNE TECHNOLOGIES INC (USA)
Immediate Holding Company: TELEDYNE LIMITED
Registration no: 03863642 **VAT No.:** GB 226 0944 72
Date established: 1999 **Turnover:** £20m - £50m
No.of Employees: 11 - 20 **Product Groups:** 39, 44, 84

Date of Accounts	Dec 11	Dec 10	Dec 09
Sales Turnover	31m	20m	21m
Pre Tax Profit/Loss	7m	9m	4m
Working Capital	8m	15m	7m
Fixed Assets	58m	58m	58m
Current Assets	23m	24m	10m
Current Liabilities	4m	2m	2m

Viasat Broadcasting Group Ltd

7 Horton Industrial Park Horton Road, West Drayton, UB7 8JD
Tel: 01895-433433 **Fax:** 01895-446606
E-mail: info@viasat.se
Website: http://www.viasat.se
Directors: M. Zagar (Co Sec), J. Lundqvist (Mkt Research)
Ultimate Holding Company: MODERN TIMES GROUP AB (SWEDEN)
Immediate Holding Company: VIASAT BROADCASTING UK LIMITED
Registration no: 02228654 **Date established:** 1988
Turnover: Over £1,000m **No.of Employees:** 101 - 250
Product Groups: 89

VOA Services

West Drayton, West Drayton, UB7 7QA
Tel: 07773-033675
E-mail: contact@voaservices.co.uk
Website: http://www.voaservices.co.uk
Directors: S. Cousins (Prop)
Date established: 2006 **Turnover:** Up to £250,000
No.of Employees: 1 - 10 **Product Groups:** 44

Wessex Guild

26-36 Horton Road, West Drayton, UB7 8JE
Tel: 01895-449595 **Fax:** 01895-431665
E-mail: cmf@lineonewest.co.uk
Website: http://www.cmf.co.uk
Directors: R. Pocock (MD), S. Punj (MD), J. Smith (Ch), N. Boyles (Dir)
Managers: K. Deegan (Est), A. Punj (Mgr)
Ultimate Holding Company: WELDWORK INTERNATIONAL
Immediate Holding Company: FOCUSCRETE LTD
Registration no: 02451447 **Turnover:** £1m - £2m
No.of Employees: 1 - 10 **Product Groups:** 35, 36, 49

Date of Accounts	Jun 11	Jun 10	Jun 09
Sales Turnover	24m	21m	23m
Pre Tax Profit/Loss	-126	223	2m
Working Capital	2m	2m	1m
Fixed Assets	1m	2m	2m
Current Assets	4m	6m	6m
Current Liabilities	345	844	1m

WEST MIDLANDS

Bilston

Joseph Ash
Unit C Springvale Industrial Park, Bilston, WV14 0QL
Tel: 01902-353935 **Fax:** 01902-405115
E-mail: bilston@josephash.co.uk
Website: http://www.josephash.co.uk
Directors: S. Hopkins (MD)
Managers: J. Wright
Date established: 1997 **No.of Employees:** 51 - 100 **Product Groups:** 46, 48

Douglas Baker Plastics Ltd
Doubak Works Barton Industrial Estate Mount Pleasant, Bilston, WV14 7LH
Tel: 01902-353800 **Fax:** 01902-353855
E-mail: sales@dbplastics.co.uk
Website: http://www.dbplastics.com
Directors: B. Lloyd (MD)
Ultimate Holding Company: C L HOLDINGS LTD
Immediate Holding Company: DOUGLAS BAKER PLASTICS LIMITED
Registration no: 01172715 **VAT No.:** GB 101 3516 33
Date established: 1974 **Turnover:** £2m - £5m **No.of Employees:** 11 - 20
Product Groups: 32

Date of Accounts	Jun 11	Jun 10	Jun 09
Working Capital	797	771	819
Fixed Assets	42	54	47
Current Assets	2m	1m	1m

Barton Storage Systems Ltd
Mount Pleasant, Bilston, WV14 7NG
Tel: 01902-499500 **Fax:** 01902-353098
E-mail: enquiries@bartonstorage.com
Website: http://www.barton-storage-systems.co.uk
Bank(s): Barclays
Directors: D. Rodbourne (Sales), K. Bibb (MD)
Immediate Holding Company: KDI PARTNERSHIP LIMITED
Registration no: 00804331 **Date established:** 1964 **Turnover:** £2m - £5m
No.of Employees: 11 - 20 **Product Groups:** 26, 30, 35, 36, 45, 49, 84

Berry Systems
Springvale Industrial Park, Bilston, WV14 0QL
Tel: 01902-491100 **Fax:** 01902-494080
E-mail: sales@berrysystems.co.uk
Website: http://www.optimumbarriers.co.uk
Directors: I. Smith (Purch), I. Darlington (MD), R. Ravone (Fin), S. Bradbury (Sales)
Managers: T. Hedges (Tech Serv Mgr), A. Griffin (Personnel)
Ultimate Holding Company: HILL & SMITH HOLDINGS PLC
Immediate Holding Company: BERRY SAFETY SYSTEMS LIMITED.
Registration no: 03134071 **Date established:** 1999
Turnover: £50m - £75m **No.of Employees:** 11 - 20 **Product Groups:** 35, 45, 48, 49, 67, 68

C P L Petroleum
Trinity Road, Bilston, WV14 7EF
Tel: 01902-409438 **Fax:** 01902-490789
E-mail: bilston@cplpetroleum.co.uk
Website: http://www.cplpetroleum.co.uk
Managers: D. Ashabury (Mgr), D. Astvury (Depot Mgr)
Ultimate Holding Company: CPL INDUSTRIES HOLDINGS LTD
Immediate Holding Company: CPL PETROLEUM LIMITED
Registration no: 03003860 **Date established:** 1994
No.of Employees: 1 - 10 **Product Groups:** 66, 71

Camtool Engineering Ltd
6b Purdy Road, Bilston, WV14 8UB
Tel: 01902-403562 **Fax:** 01902-403562
E-mail: camtool.eng@btconnect.com
Website: http://www.camtoolengineering.co.uk
Directors: C. Lloyd (MD)
Immediate Holding Company: CAMTOOL ENGINEERING LIMITED
Registration no: 05455935 **Date established:** 2005
Turnover: Up to £250,000 **No.of Employees:** 1 - 10 **Product Groups:** 46, 48

Date of Accounts	May 11	May 10	May 09
Working Capital	-12	-31	-21
Fixed Assets	19	23	29
Current Assets	46	39	68

Chase Equipment Ltd
Wellington House Wellington Industrial Estate, Bilston, WV14 9EE
Tel: 01902-675835 **Fax:** 01902-674998
E-mail: sales@chaseequipment.com
Website: http://www.chaseequipment.com
Bank(s): The Bank of Nova Scotia
Directors: D. Sweeney (MD), A. Luckett (Fin)
Immediate Holding Company: CHASE EQUIPMENT LIMITED
Registration no: 01963631 **VAT No.:** GB 413 5796 45
Date established: 1985 **Turnover:** £1m - £2m **No.of Employees:** 21 - 50
Product Groups: 30, 39, 45, 77

Date of Accounts	Dec 11	Dec 10	Dec 09
Working Capital	385	324	320
Fixed Assets	49	49	51
Current Assets	925	953	948

Chemsearch (a division of N C H (UK) Ltd)
Nch House Springvale Avenue, Bilston, WV14 0QL
Tel: 01902-510334 **Fax:** 01902-510341
E-mail: patrick.toye1@btinternet.com
Website: http://www.chemsearch.com
Bank(s): Barclays
Directors: R. Price (Dir)
Managers: M. Reynolds (Sales Admin)
Ultimate Holding Company: NCH Corporation (USA)
Immediate Holding Company: N C H (UK) Ltd
Registration no: 00816221 **VAT No.:** GB 276 8590 06
Date established: 1996 **Turnover:** £1m - £2m
No.of Employees: 101 - 250 **Product Groups:** 32

Delta Plastics Ltd
Unit 2 Bilston Industrial Estate Oxford St, Bilston, WV14 7EG
Tel: 01902-409627 **Fax:** 01902-409673
E-mail: sales@deltaplastics.co.uk
Website: http://www.deltaplastics.co.uk
Date established: 1994 **Product Groups:** 29, 30, 36, 48

Date of Accounts	Dec 11	Dec 10	Dec 09
Working Capital	25	-55	-169
Fixed Assets	179	87	99
Current Assets	427	312	233

Dudley Tubes Ltd
Meadow Lane, Bilston, WV14 9NQ
Tel: 01902-671747 **Fax:** 01902-354049
E-mail: dudleytubes@btconnect.com
Website: http://www.dudleytubes.com
Bank(s): Lloyds TSB Bank plc
Directors: N. Peters (Dir)
Managers: B. Peters (Mgr), P. Hunt (Sales Prom Mgr)
Registration no: 01100531 **VAT No.:** GB 277 0159 50
Date established: 1973 **Turnover:** £1m - £2m **No.of Employees:** 11 - 20
Product Groups: 66

Date of Accounts	Sep 08	Aug 07	Aug 06
Pre Tax Profit/Loss	182	120	N/A
Working Capital	-195	-243	-262
Fixed Assets	1751	1695	1679
Current Assets	6611	5382	3149
Current Liabilities	6806	5625	3411
Total Share Capital	1	1	1
ROCE% (Return on Capital Employed)	11.7	8.2	

E D M
E D M House Village Way, Bilston, WV14 0UJ
Tel: 01902-406200 **Fax:** 01902-406296
E-mail: enquiries@edmgroup.co.uk
Website: http://www.edmgroup.co.uk
Bank(s): Barclays
Managers: A. James
Ultimate Holding Company: EDM GROUP (HOLDINGS) LIMITED
Immediate Holding Company: EDM GROUP LIMITED
Registration no: 01193648 **Date established:** 1974
Turnover: £10m - £20m **No.of Employees:** 251 - 500
Product Groups: 27, 38, 81

Date of Accounts	Mar 11	Mar 10	Mar 09
Sales Turnover	16m	14m	14m
Pre Tax Profit/Loss	2m	607	358
Working Capital	4m	3m	3m
Fixed Assets	4m	3m	3m
Current Assets	14m	11m	11m
Current Liabilities	5m	4m	4m

Ellison Coatings Systems Ltd
Unit 15 Cannon Business Park Gough Road, Bilston, WV14 8XR
Tel: 01902-408005 **Fax:** 01902-490941
Website: http://www.ellisoncoatingsystems.co.uk
Bank(s): National Westminster Bank plc
Directors: D. Till (MD), J. Heathcote (Co Sec)
Managers: D. Smith (Admin Off), J. Hunter (Asst Gen Mgr)
Immediate Holding Company: CANNON STEELSTOCK LTD
Registration no: 04165617 **Date established:** 2000 **Turnover:** £1m - £2m
No.of Employees: 21 - 50 **Product Groups:** 35, 48, 66

Date of Accounts	Jul 11	Jul 10	Jul 09
Working Capital	-0	-0	-0

Enzone Plastics 1990 Ltd
Cross Street, Bilston, WV14 8TP
Tel: 01902-353972 **Fax:** 01902-353178
E-mail: mark@enzone-plastics.co.uk
Website: http://www.enzone-plastics.co.uk
Directors: G. Coggins (MD), M. Richards (Fin)
Managers: L. Rodgers (Sales Admin)
Ultimate Holding Company: ENZONE HOLDINGS LIMITED
Immediate Holding Company: ENZONE HOLDINGS LIMITED
Registration no: 06116824 **Date established:** 2007 **Turnover:** £2m - £5m
No.of Employees: 21 - 50 **Product Groups:** 26, 30, 48, 66

Date of Accounts	Mar 11	Mar 10	Mar 09
Working Capital	-1m	-881	-795
Fixed Assets	2m	2m	2m
Current Assets	165	59	37

Feenix Fabs Ltd
Unit 51 Wellington Industrial Estate, Bilston, WV14 9EE
Tel: 01902-676780 **Fax:** 01902- 663397
Directors: Y. Foley (Fin)
Immediate Holding Company: CHASE EQUIPMENT LIMITED
Registration no: 03860843 **Date established:** 1985
No.of Employees: 11 - 20 **Product Groups:** 35, 48

Date of Accounts	Oct 11	Oct 10	Oct 09
Working Capital	72	68	68
Fixed Assets	8	11	14
Current Assets	118	104	99

M F Hawkins & Sons Ltd
Murdoch Road, Bilston, WV14 7HG
Tel: 01902-492329 **Fax:** 01902-354397
Directors: L. Hawkins (Fin), M. Hawkins (MD)
Immediate Holding Company: M.F.HAWKINS & SONS(ELECTRO-PLATERS)LIMITED
Registration no: 01039231 **Date established:** 1972
No.of Employees: 11 - 20 **Product Groups:** 46, 48

Hill & Smith Ltd
Springvale Industrial Park, Bilston, WV14 0QL
Tel: 01902-499400 **Fax:** 01902-499419
E-mail: mark@hill-smith.co.uk
Website: http://www.hill-smith.co.uk
Bank(s): Midland
Directors: A. Dean (Chief Op Offcr), M. Tonks (MD), R. Rabone (Fin)
Managers: T. Hedges (Tech Serv Mgr), A. Griffin (Personnel)
Ultimate Holding Company: HILL & SMITH HOLDINGS PLC
Immediate Holding Company: HILL & SMITH LIMITED
Registration no: 01270322 **VAT No.:** GB 369 6846 85
Date established: 1976 **Turnover:** £50m - £75m
No.of Employees: 51 - 100 **Product Groups:** 35, 46, 48

Date of Accounts	Dec 11	Dec 10	Dec 09
Sales Turnover	57m	76m	76m
Pre Tax Profit/Loss	7m	9m	6m
Working Capital	16m	17m	11m
Fixed Assets	14m	17m	20m
Current Assets	33m	32m	34m
Current Liabilities	6m	5m	8m

E C Hopkins Ltd
Unit 1-3 Barton Industrial Estate Mount Pleasant, Bilston, WV14 7LH
Tel: 01902-401755 **Fax:** 01902-495097
E-mail: enquiries@echopkins.co.uk
Website: http://www.echopkins.co.uk
Bank(s): Lloyds TSB
Directors: S. Worrall (Pers), M. Light (Fin), B. Hopkins (Ptnr)
Immediate Holding Company: E.C.HOPKINS,LIMITED
Registration no: 00340631 **VAT No.:** GB 101 3917 15
Date established: 1938 **Turnover:** £5m - £10m
No.of Employees: 51 - 100 **Product Groups:** 35

Date of Accounts	Sep 11	Sep 10	Sep 09
Sales Turnover	7m	6m	5m
Pre Tax Profit/Loss	285	208	-78
Working Capital	1m	854	763
Fixed Assets	2m	2m	1m
Current Assets	2m	2m	2m
Current Liabilities	572	467	327

Hub Le Bas (a division of Caparo Precision Tubes Ltd)

Rose Street, Bilston, WV14 8TS
Tel: 01902-493506 **Fax:** 01902-353687
E-mail: m.benbow@hublebas.co.uk
Website: http://www.hublebas.co.uk
Bank(s): HSBC Bank plc
Directors: M. Benbow (Dir), T. Moris (Fin)
Managers: T. Mansfield (Purch Mgr)
Ultimate Holding Company: TYCO INTERNATIONAL LTD
Immediate Holding Company: TYCO EUROPEAN TUBING LTD
Registration no: 05172071 **VAT No.:** GB 670 3254 51
Turnover: £2m - £5m **No.of Employees:** 21 - 50 **Product Groups:** 36

Hudley Trading Co. Ltd

22 Hickman Road, Bilston, WV14 0QW
Tel: 01902-492991 **Fax:** 01902-405078
E-mail: sales@hudleytrading.com
Directors: R. Hudson (MD), J. Hudson (Dir)
Registration no: 00827915 **Date established:** 1964
Turnover: £500,000 - £1m **No.of Employees:** 1 - 10 **Product Groups:** 39, 40, 42, 68, 84

Impacta Ltd

Field Street, Bilston, WV14 8RW
Tel: 01902-496307 **Fax:** 01902-493937
E-mail: sales@impacta.co.uk
Website: http://www.impacta.co.uk
Directors: L. Morgan (Fin), W. Morgan (MD)
Immediate Holding Company: IMPACTA LIMITED
Registration no: 04018411 **Date established:** 2000 **Turnover:** £1m - £2m
No.of Employees: 21 - 50 **Product Groups:** 22, 23, 24, 29, 30, 37, 39, 40, 42, 45, 46, 47, 48, 67, 68, 76, 84

Date of Accounts	Jun 11	Jun 10	Jun 09
Working Capital	97	207	302
Fixed Assets	426	84	92
Current Assets	456	421	684

The Invincible Spring Co. Ltd

Batmans Hill Industrial Estate Purdy Road, Bilston, WV14 8UB
Tel: 01902-497068 **Fax:** 01902-496652
E-mail: enquiries@invinciblespring.co.uk
Website: http://www.invinciblespring.co.uk
Directors: A. Smith (MD), A. Smith (Prop), W. Smith (MD), M. Smith (Dir), M. Smith (MD)
Managers: N. Smith (Mktg Serv Mgr), T. Bradley (Sales Admin)
Immediate Holding Company: INVINCIBLE SPRING CO. LIMITED(THE)
Registration no: 01480137 **VAT No.:** GB 346 8406 38
Date established: 1980 **Turnover:** £250,000 - £500,000
No.of Employees: 1 - 10 **Product Groups:** 35

Date of Accounts	Apr 08	Apr 07	Apr 06
Working Capital	41	60	64
Fixed Assets	57	5	5
Current Assets	187	177	137
Current Liabilities	146	117	73
Total Share Capital	1	1	1

Leemoore Ltd

Unit 52b Wellington Industrial Estate, Bilston, WV14 9EE
Tel: 01902-496511 **Fax:** 01902-672118
E-mail: leemoore@btconnect.com
Website: http://www.leemoore.co.uk
Directors: T. Moore (Fin)
Managers: S. Harrison
Immediate Holding Company: LEEMOORE LIMITED
Registration no: 03242937 **Date established:** 1996
No.of Employees: 1 - 10 **Product Groups:** 35, 39, 45

Date of Accounts	Sep 11	Sep 10	Sep 09
Working Capital	59	55	101
Fixed Assets	5	5	6
Current Assets	177	168	250
Current Liabilities	45	N/A	N/A

Merridale Polishing & Plating Co. Ltd

Oxford Street, Bilston, WV14 7EA
Tel: 01902-404191 **Fax:** 01902-405872
Bank(s): Lloyds TSB
Directors: H. Nijjar (Dir)
Immediate Holding Company: MERRIDALE POLISHING AND PLATING COMPANY LIMITED
Registration no: 01167251 **VAT No.:** GB 101 3368 22
Date established: 1974 **Turnover:** £1m - £2m **No.of Employees:** 11 - 20
Product Groups: 33

Date of Accounts	Mar 11	Mar 10	Mar 09
Working Capital	-156	-197	-198
Fixed Assets	133	138	169
Current Assets	759	666	670

Millstock Stainless Ltd

Alloys House Dale Street, Bilston, WV14 7JY
Tel: 01902-409409 **Fax:** 01902-409411
E-mail: info@millstockstainless.com
Website: http://www.millstockstainless.com
Directors: D. Smith (Dir), G. Lloyd (Dir)
Immediate Holding Company: MILLSTOCK STAINLESS LIMITED
Registration no: 03260745 **Date established:** 1996
No.of Employees: 1 - 10 **Product Groups:** 34, 35, 36

Date of Accounts	Mar 12	Mar 11	Mar 10
Working Capital	354	373	417
Fixed Assets	342	49	56
Current Assets	2m	1m	2m

Mueller Europe Ltd

Oxford Street, Bilston, WV14 7DS
Tel: 01902-499700 **Fax:** 01902-405838
E-mail: sales@muellereurope.com
Website: http://www.muellereurope.com
Directors: N. York (Tech Serv), P. Marsh (MD)
Managers: E. O'Hagan (Buyer), A. Gutteridge (Personnel)
Ultimate Holding Company: MUELLER INDUSTRIES INC (USA)
Immediate Holding Company: MUELLER EUROPE LIMITED
Registration no: 03316088 **Date established:** 1997
Turnover: £75m - £125m **No.of Employees:** 101 - 250
Product Groups: 34, 36

Date of Accounts	Dec 11	Dec 08	Dec 09
Sales Turnover	131m	102m	72m
Pre Tax Profit/Loss	301	-6m	2m
Working Capital	42m	29m	30m
Fixed Assets	29m	33m	31m
Current Assets	52m	58m	43m
Current Liabilities	1m	3m	7m

N & W Global Vending Ltd

Dudley Street, Bilston, WV14 0LA
Tel: 01902-355000 **Fax:** 01902-402272
E-mail: david.ward@nwglobalvending.co.uk
Website: http://www.nwglobalvending.co.uk
Bank(s): Barclays
Directors: D. Ward (MD)
Managers: M. Butler, M. Goodwin (Tech Serv Mgr), R. Cox (Comptroller)
Ultimate Holding Company: VENDING HOLDINGS SARL (LUXEMBOURG)
Immediate Holding Company: N & W GLOBAL VENDING LIMITED
Registration no: 03806034 **Date established:** 1999 **Turnover:** £5m - £10m
No.of Employees: 51 - 100 **Product Groups:** 49, 61, 82

Date of Accounts	Dec 11	Dec 10	Dec 09
Sales Turnover	5m	6m	5m
Pre Tax Profit/Loss	1m	2m	932
Working Capital	3m	2m	623
Fixed Assets	2m	2m	2m
Current Assets	5m	4m	2m
Current Liabilities	726	976	619

Optimum Barriers

Springvale Industrial Park, Bilston, WV14 0QL
Tel: 01902-403197 **Fax:** 01902- 494080
E-mail: sales@berrysystems.co.uk
Website: http://www.optimumbarriers.co.uk
Bank(s): The Royal Bank of Scotland
Directors: I. Darlinton (MD), I. Darlington (MD), M. Fellows (MD)
Managers: D. Wright (District Mgr), M. Simspon (Mgr), L. Cole (Admin Off)
Ultimate Holding Company: DUNDEC HOLDINGS LTD
Immediate Holding Company: DUNDEC CONTRACTS LTD
Registration no: 01270322 **VAT No.:** GB 726 8995 72
Date established: 2000 **Turnover:** £2m - £5m **No.of Employees:** 51 - 100
Product Groups: 35, 39

Parker Precision Ltd

Vulcan Road, Bilston, WV14 7HW
Tel: 01902-353453 **Fax:** 01902-493108
E-mail: sales@parkerprecision.co.uk
Website: http://www.parkerprecision.co.uk
Bank(s): Lloyds
Directors: M. Parker (MD), P. Parker (Works)
Immediate Holding Company: PARKER PRECISION LIMITED
Registration no: 00638576 **VAT No.:** GB 100 3334 45
Date established: 1959 **Turnover:** £250,000 - £500,000
No.of Employees: 21 - 50 **Product Groups:** 48

Date of Accounts	Dec 11	Dec 10	Dec 09
Working Capital	2m	1m	1m
Fixed Assets	1m	1m	1m
Current Assets	2m	2m	1m

Quest 4 Alloys Ltd

Alloys House Dale Street, Bilston, WV14 7JY
Tel: 01902-409316 **Fax:** 01902-409304
E-mail: info@quest4alloys.co.uk
Website: http://www.quest4alloys.com
Bank(s): National Westminster Bank Plc
Directors: A. Jones (Fin)
Immediate Holding Company: QUEST 4 ALLOYS LIMITED
Registration no: 02857040 **VAT No.:** GB 661 0054 75
Date established: 1993 **Turnover:** £2m - £5m **No.of Employees:** 11 - 20
Product Groups: 34, 36, 48, 66

Date of Accounts	Mar 12	Mar 11	Mar 10
Working Capital	463	362	321
Fixed Assets	423	135	139
Current Assets	1m	1m	888

R S S Edge Shoes Ltd

184 Wellington Road, Bilston, WV14 6BE
Tel: 01902-353007 **Fax:** 01902-353823
E-mail: sales@edgeshoes.com
Website: http://www.edgeshoes.com
Directors: R. Singh (MD)
Immediate Holding Company: EDGE SHOES LIMITED
Registration no: 07144441 **VAT No.:** 488 3983 74 **Date established:** 2010
No.of Employees: 1 - 10 **Product Groups:** 22

Date of Accounts	Mar 11
Working Capital	10
Current Assets	10

Ramsay Rubber & Plastics

Vulcan Road, Bilston, WV14 7HT
Tel: 01902-407150 **Fax:** 01902-407160
E-mail: sales@ramsayrubber.com
Website: http://www.ramsayrubber.com
Bank(s): Barclays, West Bromwich
Directors: M. Dell (MD)
Managers: L. Botfield (Fin Mgr), G. Perrins (Purch Mgr), D. Bewitt (Tech Serv Mgr)
Ultimate Holding Company: RAM CELLULAR PRODUCTS LIMITED
Immediate Holding Company: R A S REALISATIONS LIMITED
Registration no: 05602431 **Date established:** 2005 **Turnover:** £5m - £10m
No.of Employees: 11 - 20 **Product Groups:** 29, 33, 63

Date of Accounts	Dec 09	Dec 08	Dec 07
Sales Turnover	N/A	5m	N/A
Pre Tax Profit/Loss	N/A	21	64
Working Capital	-459	-210	-278
Fixed Assets	858	1m	1m
Current Assets	2m	1m	2m
Current Liabilities	N/A	684	893

Rapid Grinding Services Ltd

3 Bilston Key Industrial Estate Oxford Street, Bilston, WV14 7DW
Tel: 01902-354040 **Fax:** 01902-354055
E-mail: rapidgrinding@hotmail.com
Website: http://www.rapidgrinding.co.uk
Directors: R. Jeavons (MD)
Immediate Holding Company: RAPID GRINDING SERVICES LIMITED
Registration no: 01012938 **Date established:** 1971
No.of Employees: 11 - 20 **Product Groups:** 46

Date of Accounts	May 11	May 10	May 09
Working Capital	-13	-6	-17
Fixed Assets	70	61	78
Current Assets	77	87	69

Scientific & Chemical Supplies Ltd

Carlton House Livingstone Road, Bilston, WV14 0QZ
Tel: 01902-402402 **Fax:** 01902-402343
E-mail: info@scichem.co.uk
Website: http://www.scichem.co.uk
Bank(s): Barclays
Directors: E. Parkin (Purch), P. Poulter (Tech Serv), P. Jordan (Fin), J. Turton (Grp Chief Exec), G. Owen (Fin), S. D'arcy (Sales)
Managers: S. Vinter (Mktg Serv Mgr), R. Bailey (Mktg Serv Mgr), G. Smith (Sales Prom Mgr)
Ultimate Holding Company: SCICHEM UK LIMITED
Immediate Holding Company: SCIENTIFIC AND CHEMICAL SUPPLIES LIMITED
Registration no: 00588778 **VAT No.:** GB 277 0531 56
Date established: 1957 **Turnover:** £10m - £20m
No.of Employees: 101 - 250 **Product Groups:** 28, 32, 33, 36, 37, 38, 40, 42, 47, 49, 65, 67

Date of Accounts	Dec 11	Dec 10	Dec 09
Sales Turnover	17m	17m	14m
Pre Tax Profit/Loss	302	-527	49
Working Capital	-273	-477	-94
Fixed Assets	2m	2m	2m
Current Assets	5m	5m	4m
Current Liabilities	2m	3m	2m

Scott Packaging

Biddings Lane, Bilston, WV14 9NW
Tel: 01902-403631 **Fax:** 01902-492308
E-mail: enquiries@scottgroupltd.com
Website: http://www.scottgroupltd.com
Bank(s): Barclays
Directors: T. Trotter (Fin), J. Kench (MD)
Managers: S. Smith (Site Co-ord)
Ultimate Holding Company: SCOTT GROUP INVESTMENTS LIMITED
Immediate Holding Company: GEORGE HILL LIMITED
Registration no: 00435919 **Date established:** 1947 **Turnover:** £2m - £5m
No.of Employees: 21 - 50 **Product Groups:** 25, 27, 45

Date of Accounts	Dec 11	Dec 10	Dec 09
Working Capital	336	1m	1m
Fixed Assets	N/A	612	664
Current Assets	336	3m	2m

Secure Fasteners Midlands Ltd

Webb Street, Bilston, WV14 8XL
Tel: 01902-405258 **Fax:** 01902-401763
E-mail: sales@secure-fasteners.co.uk
Website: http://www.secure-fasteners.co.uk
Directors: L. Smith (Fin), J. Smith (MD)
Immediate Holding Company: SECURE FASTENERS (MIDLANDS) LIMITED
Registration no: 01831461 **Date established:** 1984
Turnover: £250,000 - £500,000 **No.of Employees:** 1 - 10
Product Groups: 30, 32, 35, 36, 37, 40, 66

Date of Accounts	Jul 11	Jul 10	Jul 09
Working Capital	-29	-33	-37
Fixed Assets	7	8	9
Current Assets	86	86	87

Simply Foam Products Ltd Simply Foam Products Ltd

Unit 20 Barton Industrial Estate Mount Pleasant, Bilston, WV14 7LH
Tel: 01902-405100 **Fax:** 01902-405300
E-mail: info@efoam.co.uk
Website: http://www.efoam.co.uk
Immediate Holding Company: SIMPLY FOAM PRODUCTS LIMITED
Registration no: 03988665 **Date established:** 2000 **Turnover:** £1m - £2m
No.of Employees: 1 - 10 **Product Groups:** 26, 29, 30, 39, 40

Date of Accounts	May 11	May 10	May 09
Sales Turnover	N/A	768	653
Pre Tax Profit/Loss	N/A	109	60
Working Capital	75	84	30
Fixed Assets	564	578	581
Current Assets	257	219	152
Current Liabilities	N/A	115	73

Sterling Filtration Ltd

Unit 2-4 Meadwood Industrial Estate Bath Street, Bilston, WV14 0ST
Tel: 01902-491118 **Fax:** 01902-491119
E-mail: sales@sterlingfiltration.co.uk
Website: http://www.sterlingfiltration.co.uk
Managers: T. Ward (Sales Admin)
Immediate Holding Company: STERLING FILTRATION LIMITED
Registration no: 03226779 **Date established:** 1996
No.of Employees: 1 - 10 **Product Groups:** 38, 42

Date of Accounts	Mar 12	Mar 11	Mar 10
Working Capital	193	165	173
Fixed Assets	38	51	33
Current Assets	430	404	383

T P S Fronius

108 Highfields Road, Bilston, WV14 0LD
Tel: 01902-495686 **Fax:** 01902-496461
E-mail: info@tps-fronius.co.uk
Website: http://www.tps-fronius.co.uk
Managers: K. Palmer (Mgr)
Immediate Holding Company: TPS-FRONIUS LTD
Registration no: SC053928 **Date established:** 1973
No.of Employees: 1 - 10 **Product Groups:** 35, 36, 37, 42, 45, 46, 48, 67, 83, 84

Date of Accounts	Dec 08	Dec 07	Dec 06
Sales Turnover	8100	N/A	N/A
Pre Tax Profit/Loss	581	371	N/A
Working Capital	669	617	559
Fixed Assets	1617	1459	1392
Current Assets	3203	2725	2297
Current Liabilities	2534	2108	1738
Total Share Capital	150	150	150
ROCE% (Return on Capital Employed)	25.4	17.9	
ROT% (Return on Turnover)	7.2		

Triple S

14 Loxdale Industrial Estate Northcott Road, Bilston, WV14 0TP
Tel: 01902-495536 **Fax:** 01902- 497314
E-mail: garyrsefton@aol.com
Directors: G. Sefton (Prop)
Immediate Holding Company: SPARKY MARKY ELECTRICAL SERVICES LIMITED
Registration no: 05151827 **Date established:** 2012
No.of Employees: 1 - 10 **Product Groups:** 46, 48

see next page

Triple S - Cont'd

Date of Accounts	Mar 11	Mar 10	Mar 09
Pre Tax Profit/Loss	N/A	N/A	222
Working Capital	733	390	433
Fixed Assets	1m	1m	2m
Current Assets	2m	2m	2m
Current Liabilities	N/A	N/A	348

Triplefast International Ltd

Unit C Oxford Street Industrial Park Vulcan Road, Bilston, WV14 7LF
Tel: 01902-357600 **Fax:** 01902-609880
E-mail: jayneb@triplefast.co.uk
Website: http://www.triplefast-ltd.com
Bank(s): Royal Bank of Scotland
Directors: B. Williams (MD), S. Lawrence (Sales), G. Latham (Fin)
Managers: J. Bradley, D. Riley
Ultimate Holding Company: LSP HOLDING SARL (LUXEMBOURG)
Immediate Holding Company: TRIPLEFAST INTERNATIONAL LIMITED
Registration no: 02460987 **VAT No.:** GB 489 7836 61
Date established: 1990 **Turnover:** £5m - £10m
No.of Employees: 51 - 100 **Product Groups:** 30, 35, 36, 66

Date of Accounts	Dec 11	Dec 10	Dec 09
Sales Turnover	8m	6m	8m
Pre Tax Profit/Loss	588	672	676
Working Capital	2m	3m	3m
Fixed Assets	275	220	285
Current Assets	4m	5m	4m
Current Liabilities	677	469	635

Truck Wise

Unit 12 Perry Street Industrial Estate, Bilston, WV14 8RP
Tel: 01902-496596
E-mail: info@truckwiseuk.com
Website: http://www.truckwiseuk.com
Directors: G. Burton (Prop)
Immediate Holding Company: TRUCKWISE (UK) LIMITED
Registration no: 05021139 **Date established:** 2004
No.of Employees: 1 - 10 **Product Groups:** 33, 39, 40

Date of Accounts	Jan 12	Jan 11	Jan 10
Working Capital	-23	-17	-14
Fixed Assets	64	75	22
Current Assets	288	281	195

Unit Metal Construction Co. Ltd

Dale Street, Bilston, WV14 7JY
Tel: 01902-491436 **Fax:** 01902-491665
E-mail: unitmetal@btconnect.com
Website: http://www.unitmetal.net
Directors: G. Cartwright (MD), K. Cartwright (Co Sec), K. Cartwright (Fin)
Immediate Holding Company: UNIT METAL CONSTRUCTIONS CO. LIMITED
Registration no: 00417278 **VAT No.:** GB 100 0206 69
Date established: 1946 **Turnover:** Up to £250,000
No.of Employees: 1 - 10 **Product Groups:** 48

Date of Accounts	Mar 11	Mar 10	Mar 09
Working Capital	-16	22	52
Fixed Assets	21	26	21
Current Assets	45	62	89

D S Willetts Stainless Ltd

Murdoch Road, Bilston, WV14 7HG
Tel: 01902-404221 **Fax:** 01902-405705
E-mail: sales@dswilletts.co.uk
Website: http://www.dswilletts.co.uk
Bank(s): Barclays
Directors: I. Willetts (Co Sec), D. Willetts (MD)
Immediate Holding Company: D.S. WILLETTS (STAINLESS) LIMITED
Registration no: 01845419 **VAT No.:** GB 431 4377 68
Date established: 1984 **Turnover:** £1m - £2m **No.of Employees:** 21 - 50
Product Groups: 48

Date of Accounts	Mar 12	Mar 11	Mar 10
Working Capital	1m	1m	1m
Fixed Assets	91	107	106
Current Assets	2m	2m	2m

Yeoman Pressings Ltd

Unit 10 Cannon Business Park Gough Road, Bilston, WV14 8XR
Tel: 01902-385260 **Fax:** 01902-385332
E-mail: sales@yeomanpressings.com
Website: http://www.yeomanpressings.com
Directors: G. Yeoman (Dir), G. Yeomans (Dir), S. Butler (Dir)
Managers: B. Checketts (Buyer)
Ultimate Holding Company: APTON PARTITIONING LIMITED
Immediate Holding Company: YEOMAN PRESSINGS LIMITED
Registration no: 00764180 **Date established:** 2009 **Turnover:** £2m - £5m
No.of Employees: 21 - 50 **Product Groups:** 48

Date of Accounts	Sep 11	Sep 10
Working Capital	-28	-39
Fixed Assets	103	122
Current Assets	721	765
Current Liabilities	423	501

Birmingham

3rd Eye Broadcast

2 Warstone Parade East, Birmingham, B18 6NR
Tel: 0121-693 9977 **Fax:** 0121-693 9976
E-mail: info@3rdeyebroadcast.com
Website: http://www.3rdeyecamerahire.co.uk
Directors: M. Bradley (Dir)
Immediate Holding Company: 3RD EYE BROADCAST LIMITED
Registration no: 04423821 **Date established:** 2002
Turnover: Up to £250,000 **No.of Employees:** 11 - 20 **Product Groups:** 37, 44

Date of Accounts	Jan 07	Jan 06	Jan 05
Sales Turnover	81	N/A	N/A
Pre Tax Profit/Loss	23	N/A	N/A
Working Capital	8	-12	1
Fixed Assets	23	21	27
Current Assets	31	9	13
Current Liabilities	11	N/A	N/A

A B D I Machine Tool

67 Camden Street, Birmingham, B1 3DD
Tel: 0121-236 1517 **Fax:** 0121-236 9342
E-mail: dereckcornock@abditools.fsnet.co.uk
Website: http://www.abditools.fsnet.co.uk
Directors: D. Cornock (Prop)
Registration no: 01614646 **VAT No.:** GB 110 9831 91
Turnover: Up to £250,000 **No.of Employees:** 1 - 10 **Product Groups:** 48

A B L Aluminium Components Ltd

Premier House Garretts Green Trading Estate Valepits Road, Birmingham, B33 0TD
Tel: 0121-789 8686 **Fax:** 0121-789 8778
E-mail: stephen.richardson@ablcomponents.co.uk
Website: http://www.ablcomponents.co.uk
Bank(s): The Royal Bank of Scotland
Directors: A. McLoughin (Sales & Mktg), S. Richardson (MD)
Managers: J. Venables (Chief Acct), S. Quinn (Buyer)
Ultimate Holding Company: ABL HOLDINGS LIMITED
Immediate Holding Company: ABL (ALUMINIUM COMPONENTS) LIMITED
Registration no: 03603229 **VAT No.:** GB 614 4825 47
Date established: 1998 **Turnover:** £5m - £10m **No.of Employees:** 21 - 50
Product Groups: 34, 35, 36, 37, 46, 48

Date of Accounts	Mar 11	Mar 10	Mar 09
Working Capital	-183	-159	-140
Fixed Assets	2m	2m	2m
Current Assets	1m	1m	1m

A C Jigs

10 Porters Way, Birmingham, B9 5RR
Tel: 0121-753 0304 **Fax:** 0121-753 0304
Directors: R. Pegg (Dir)
VAT No.: GB **Turnover:** Up to £250,000 **No.of Employees:** 1 - 10
Product Groups: 46

A D & C Group Ltd

80 Wrentham Street, Birmingham, B5 6QL
Tel: 0121-666 6070 **Fax:** 0121-666 7585
E-mail: sales@ad-c.co.uk
Website: http://www.ad-c.net
Directors: D. Austin (Co Sec), D. Smith (Dir)
Immediate Holding Company: A D & C GROUP LIMITED
Registration no: 02688274 **Date established:** 1992 **Turnover:** £1m - £2m
No.of Employees: 21 - 50 **Product Groups:** 34, 48

Date of Accounts	Apr 11	Apr 10	Apr 09
Working Capital	310	303	304
Fixed Assets	79	92	106
Current Assets	445	390	389

A E S Birmingham Ltd

Unit 39 Rovex Business Park Hay Hall Road, Birmingham, B11 2AG
Tel: 0121-706 8251 **Fax:** 0121-706 5080
E-mail: sales@aesbirmingham.com
Directors: B. Douglas (Dir)
Immediate Holding Company: A.E.S. (BIRMINGHAM) LIMITED
Registration no: 02012176 **VAT No.:** GB 377 5164 24
Date established: 1986 **Turnover:** £500,000 - £1m
No.of Employees: 1 - 10 **Product Groups:** 67

Date of Accounts	May 12	May 11	May 10
Working Capital	120	108	60
Fixed Assets	23	34	44
Current Assets	240	260	204

A E Southgate Ltd

Station Road Coleshill, Birmingham, B46 1HT
Tel: 01675-463096 **Fax:** 01675-467455
E-mail: rita@brushexpert.com
Website: http://www.brushexpert.com
Directors: R. Southgate (MD)
Immediate Holding Company: A.E.SOUTHGATE LIMITED
Registration no: 00218628 **Date established:** 2027 **Turnover:** £1m - £2m
No.of Employees: 1 - 10 **Product Groups:** 49

Date of Accounts	Dec 11	Dec 10	Dec 09
Working Capital	190	184	189
Fixed Assets	28	39	45
Current Assets	359	353	316

A Edmonds & Co. Ltd (Head Office)

89 Constitution Hill, Birmingham, B19 3JY
Tel: 0121-236 8351 **Fax:** 0121-236 4793
E-mail: info@edmonds.uk.com
Website: http://www.edmonds.uk.com
Directors: D. Edmonds (Dir), C. Kettel (Fin)
Managers: I. Parker (Mktg Serv Mgr), G. Dytor
Immediate Holding Company: A.EDMONDS & CO.LIMITED
Registration no: 00134794 **Date established:** 2014 **Turnover:** £2m - £5m
No.of Employees: 1 - 10 **Product Groups:** 25, 26, 35, 36, 48, 52

Date of Accounts	Sep 08	Sep 09	Sep 10
Sales Turnover	7m	5m	4m
Pre Tax Profit/Loss	782	276	355
Working Capital	5m	5m	5m
Fixed Assets	765	795	682
Current Assets	7m	7m	7m
Current Liabilities	1m	628	353

A F S Services Ltd

41 Great Lister Street, Birmingham, B7 4LW
Tel: 0121-359 5048 **Fax:** 0121-359 4562
Directors: L. Marshall (MD)
Immediate Holding Company: A.F.S. SERVICES LIMITED
Registration no: 04427073 **Date established:** 2002
Turnover: £500,000 - £1m **No.of Employees:** 1 - 10 **Product Groups:** 35, 40, 46, 48

Date of Accounts	May 11	May 10	May 09
Working Capital	-155	2m	2m
Fixed Assets	2m	48	63
Current Assets	216	2m	2m

A G Hydraulics Ltd

Unit 40 Plume Street Industrial Estate Plume Street, Birmingham, B6 7RT
Tel: 0121-326 6395 **Fax:** 0121-328 2923
E-mail: sales@aghydraulics.com
Website: http://www.aghydraulics.co.uk
Directors: S. Pugh (Fin)
Immediate Holding Company: A.G. HYDRAULICS LIMITED
Registration no: 01952624 **Date established:** 1985
Turnover: £500,000 - £1m **No.of Employees:** 1 - 10 **Product Groups:** 40, 67

Date of Accounts	Jan 12	Jan 11	Jan 10
Working Capital	72	16	-6
Fixed Assets	9	10	13
Current Assets	203	167	143

A G I Media Packaging Birmingham

98-138 Barford Street, Birmingham, B5 6AP
Tel: 0121-607 7300 **Fax:** 0121-607 7400
E-mail: john.hargreaves@agimedia.com
Website: http://www.agimedia.com
Directors: C. Lammie (Co Sec), C. Lammie (Fin), J. Hargreaves (Dir)
Ultimate Holding Company: MEADWESTVACO CORP (USA)
Immediate Holding Company: MWV DORMANT LIMITED
Registration no: 01117887 **Date established:** 1973 **Turnover:** £5m - £10m
No.of Employees: 21 - 50 **Product Groups:** 37, 44

Date of Accounts	Dec 09	Dec 08	Dec 07
Sales Turnover	N/A	N/A	6m
Pre Tax Profit/Loss	N/A	N/A	-2m
Working Capital	N/A	4m	4m
Current Assets	N/A	4m	5m
Current Liabilities	N/A	N/A	662

A J H

Unit 15 West Wood Road, Birmingham, B6 7DU
Tel: 0121-326 9624 **Fax:** 0121-784 1139
E-mail: john@ajhpumpsupply.co.uk
Website: http://www.ajhpumpsupply.co.uk
Directors: A. Howells (Prop)
Date established: 2001 **No.of Employees:** 1 - 10 **Product Groups:** 46, 48

A J Paveley & Co.

416 Golden Hillock Road Sparkbrook, Birmingham, B11 2QH
Tel: 0121-772 1739 **Fax:** 0121-771 1386
E-mail: peterpavely@aol.com
Website: http://www.ajpaveley.co.uk
Directors: P. Hancox (Ptnr)
VAT No.: GB 443 6122 72 **Turnover:** £1m - £2m **No.of Employees:** 1 - 10
Product Groups: 66

A L N Circuits Ltd

Units 11-15 Bickford Road, Birmingham, B6 7EE
Tel: 0121-326 7409 **Fax:** 0121-322 2176
E-mail: alm@btconnect.com
Website: http://www.alnpcb.co.uk
Bank(s): T.S.B.
Managers: F. Taylor (Sales Admin)
Immediate Holding Company: ALN CIRCUITS LTD
Registration no: 02683998 **VAT No.:** GB 580 3687 21
Date established: 1992 **Turnover:** £500,000 - £1m
No.of Employees: 11 - 20 **Product Groups:** 37, 48

Date of Accounts	Mar 11	Mar 10	Mar 09
Working Capital	17	17	82
Fixed Assets	64	68	77
Current Assets	176	214	243

A P S Metal Pressings Ltd

8 Great King Street, Birmingham, B19 3AR
Tel: 0121-523 0011 **Fax:** 0121-554 7244
E-mail: info@apsmith.co.uk
Website: http://www.apsmith.co.uk
Bank(s): Lloyds TSB Bank plc
Directors: A. Parr (MD), B. Andrews (Fin), P. Smith (Purch)
Managers: M. Iliffe (Personnel), R. Arnold (Tech Serv Mgr), T. Plum (Mktg Serv Mgr)
Immediate Holding Company: APS METAL PRESSINGS LIMITED
Registration no: 01529017 **Date established:** 1980 **Turnover:** £5m - £10m
No.of Employees: 51 - 100 **Product Groups:** 48

Date of Accounts	Dec 11	Dec 10	Dec 09
Sales Turnover	10m	7m	6m
Pre Tax Profit/Loss	701	123	300
Working Capital	2m	2m	1m
Fixed Assets	1m	1m	1m
Current Assets	4m	3m	2m
Current Liabilities	278	188	220

A Wardle & Co.

51 Albion Street, Birmingham, B1 3EA
Tel: 0121-236 2733 **Fax:** 0121-200 3056
E-mail: info@wardle.co.uk
Website: http://www.awardle.co.uk
Directors: N. Wardle (MD)
Immediate Holding Company: A.WARDLE & COMPANY(CASTERS)LIMITED
Registration no: 00789001 **Date established:** 1964
Turnover: £250,000 - £500,000 **No.of Employees:** 1 - 10
Product Groups: 34, 48, 49

Date of Accounts	May 11	May 10	May 09
Working Capital	5	-5	25
Fixed Assets	20	21	14
Current Assets	71	52	52

A Webbs Power Tools Ltd

1346-1352 Pershore Road Stirchley, Birmingham, B30 2XS
Tel: 0121-213 5000 **Fax:** 0121-213 5001
E-mail: info@webbs-site.co.uk
Website: http://www.webbs-site.co.uk
Managers: S. Taylor (Mgr)
Immediate Holding Company: WEBBS PROPERTY SERVICES LTD
Registration no: 00523599 **No.of Employees:** 1 - 10 **Product Groups:** 37

Date of Accounts	Sep 07	Sep 06	Sep 05
Working Capital	75	65	55
Fixed Assets	439	439	439
Current Assets	134	120	113
Current Liabilities	60	54	57
Total Share Capital	3	3	3

A C Fluid Technology

2 Batemans Lane Wythall, Birmingham, B47 6NG
Tel: 01564-825145 **Fax:** 01564-825100
E-mail: enquiries@ac-fluid.co.uk
Website: http://www.ac-fluid.co.uk
Managers: M. Thomas (Mgr)
Immediate Holding Company: AC FLUID TECHNOLOGY LIMITED
Registration no: 04001959 **Date established:** 2000
No.of Employees: 1 - 10 **Product Groups:** 29, 36, 38, 40, 42, 67

Ace Grind

Wainwright Street, Birmingham, B6 5TG
Tel: 0121-326 9122 **Fax:** 0121-327 4492

Directors: J. Fabo (Dir)
Date established: 1983 **No.of Employees:** 1 - 10 **Product Groups:** 36

Adaptaflex Ltd
C M G House Station Road Industrial Estate Station Road, Coleshill, Birmingham, B46 1HT
Tel: 01675-468222 **Fax:** 01675-462090
E-mail: duncan.mckinlay@adaptaflex.co.uk
Website: http://www.adaptaflex.co.uk
Bank(s): Lloyds TSB Bank plc
Directors: M. Vitty (Fin), D. Mckinlay (Dir)
Ultimate Holding Company: DUNDAS GROUP HOLDINGS LIMITED
Immediate Holding Company: ADAPTAFLEX LIMITED
Registration no: 01085977 **Date established:** 1972
Turnover: £10m - £20m **No.of Employees:** 101 - 250
Product Groups: 30, 36, 37, 39

Date of Accounts	Jul 10	Jul 09	Jul 08
Working Capital	250m	250m	250
Fixed Assets	101	101	N/A
Current Assets	250m	250m	250

Advanced Colour Coatings Ltd
Bannerley Road Garretts Green, Birmingham, B33 0SL
Tel: 0121-789 6991 **Fax:** 0121-789 6992
E-mail: kevin.mann@accoatings.co.uk
Website: http://www.accoatings.co.uk
Directors: K. Mann (Dir), K. Phipps (Co Sec)
Ultimate Holding Company: KAM HOLDINGS LIMITED
Immediate Holding Company: ADVANCED COLOUR COATINGS LIMITED
Registration no: 05112665 **Date established:** 2004 **Turnover:** £1m - £2m
No.of Employees: 21 - 50 **Product Groups:** 30, 48

Date of Accounts	May 11	May 10	May 09
Working Capital	62	104	168
Fixed Assets	15	22	28
Current Assets	465	298	270

Airtec Great Britain
45 Shenstone Road Maypole, Birmingham, B14 4TH
Tel: 0121-474 3337 **Fax:** 07917-666159
E-mail: airtec@airtec.co.uk
Website: http://www.airtecsolutions.co.uk
Product Groups: 40, 42, 46

Ajax Tocco International Ltd (a division of AjaxTOCCO Magnethermic Corporation)
2 Dorset Road Saltley Business Park, Saltley, Birmingham, B8 1BG
Tel: 0121-322 8000 **Fax:** 0121-322 8080
E-mail: phyland@ajaxtocco.com
Website: http://www.ajaxtocco.co.uk
Bank(s): Fortis
Directors: M. Smith (Tech Serv)
Managers: P. Hyland, C. Kenward, S. Pearson, P. Berry, S. Cockfield, B. Hockey (Tech Sales Eng), T. Lee, M. Guest, S. Barber, L. Townsend (Prod Mgr), G. Ball, S. Dennis, C. Rudge
Registration no: 02676033 **Date established:** 1933
Turnover: £50m - £75m **No.of Employees:** 21 - 50 **Product Groups:** 37, 46, 48, 67, 83, 84

Date of Accounts	Dec 07
Sales Turnover	5014
Pre Tax Profit/Loss	15
Working Capital	2389
Fixed Assets	1349
Current Assets	2947
Current Liabilities	558
ROCE% (Return on Capital Employed)	0.4

Akzo Nobel Packaging Coatings Ltd
Bordesley Green Road Bordesley Green, Birmingham, B9 4TQ
Tel: 0121-766 6600 **Fax:** 0121-766 6601
E-mail: enquiries@ici.com
Website: http://www.akzonobel.com/packaging
Bank(s): Lloyds TSB Bank plc
Managers: S. Johnson
Ultimate Holding Company: AKZO NOBEL NV (NETHERLANDS)
Immediate Holding Company: AKZO NOBEL PACKAGING COATINGS LIMITED
Registration no: 00059837 **Date established:** 1998
Turnover: £50m - £75m **No.of Employees:** 101 - 250 **Product Groups:** 32

Date of Accounts	Dec 11	Dec 10	Dec 09
Sales Turnover	103m	77m	68m
Pre Tax Profit/Loss	11m	21m	15m
Working Capital	25m	21m	18m
Fixed Assets	18m	14m	11m
Current Assets	51m	51m	48m
Current Liabilities	10m	13m	10m

Alabaster & Wilson Ltd
9-11 Legge Lane, Birmingham, B1 3LD
Tel: 0121-236 2356 **Fax:** 0121-233 0774
E-mail: info@alabasterandwilson.com
Website: http://www.alabasterandwilson.com
Directors: W. Alabaster (MD)
Immediate Holding Company: ALABASTER AND WILSON LIMITED
Registration no: 00442583 **VAT No.:** GB 109 3043 02
Date established: 1947 **Turnover:** £500,000 - £1m
No.of Employees: 11 - 20 **Product Groups:** 49

Date of Accounts	Dec 11	Dec 10	Dec 09
Working Capital	83	73	41
Fixed Assets	85	85	86
Current Assets	305	292	279

Alcoa Europe Flat Rolled Products Ltd
PO Box 383, Birmingham, B33 9QR
Tel: 0121-252 8000 **Fax:** 0121-252 8001
E-mail: info@alcoa.com
Website: http://www.alcoa.com
Bank(s): The Royal Bank of Scotland
Directors: I. Sayce (Fin), J. Wallace (Dir)
Managers: V. Massey (Mktg Serv Mgr), C. Davis, I. Watson (Tech Serv Mgr), A. Scott (Personnel), A. Wyrobek (Purch Mgr)
Ultimate Holding Company: ALCOA INC
Immediate Holding Company: LUXFER GROUP
VAT No.: GB 762 3259 28 **Date established:** 1938
Turnover: £125m - £250m **No.of Employees:** 251 - 500
Product Groups: 34, 36, 39, 68, 84

Alecto Optical Solutions Ltd
Hastingwood Industrial Park Wood Lane, Erdington, Birmingham, B24 9QR
Tel: 0121-356 1112 **Fax:** 0121-356 8743
Directors: N. Tredell (Dir)
Immediate Holding Company: ALECTO OPTICAL SOLUTIONS LIMITED
Registration no: 07191586 **Date established:** 2010
Turnover: £500,000 - £1m **No.of Employees:** 1 - 10 **Product Groups:** 38, 47, 67

Date of Accounts	Mar 12	Mar 11
Working Capital	12	13
Fixed Assets	9	5
Current Assets	79	98

Frank Allart & Co. Ltd
15-35 Great Tindal Street, Birmingham, B16 8DR
Tel: 0121-410 6000 **Fax:** 0121-456 2234
E-mail: sales@allart.co.uk
Website: http://www.allart.co.uk
Bank(s): HSBC Bank plc
Directors: N. Mcgrail (MD), S. Broom (Chief Op Offcr)
Managers: N. Smith (Sales Prom Mgr), R. Davies, H. McLaughlin (Chief Acct)
Ultimate Holding Company: ARMAC BRASSFOUNDERS GROUP LIMITED
Immediate Holding Company: FRANK ALLART & COMPANY LIMITED
Registration no: 00398726 **VAT No.:** GB 109 4112 04
Date established: 1945 **Turnover:** £2m - £5m **No.of Employees:** 51 - 100
Product Groups: 35, 36, 81

Date of Accounts	Dec 11	Dec 10	Dec 09
Sales Turnover	4m	4m	5m
Pre Tax Profit/Loss	-222	116	-274
Working Capital	-134	148	69
Fixed Assets	1m	1m	2m
Current Assets	2m	2m	2m
Current Liabilities	1m	1m	1m

Allegheny Technologies Ltd (ATI)
Granby Avenue, Birmingham, B33 0SP
Tel: 0121-789 8030 **Fax:** 0121-789 8027
E-mail: graeme.parkinson@atimetals.com
Website: http://www.atimetals.com
Directors: P. Broeker (MD), P. Broeker (MD), T. Dudill (Fin)
Managers: G. Parkinson (Sales Prom Mgr)
Ultimate Holding Company: ALLEGHENY TECHNOLOGIES INC (USA)
Immediate Holding Company: ALLEGHENY TECHNOLOGIES LIMITED
Registration no: 00960067 **VAT No.:** GB 580 3516 48
Date established: 1969 **Turnover:** £5m - £10m **No.of Employees:** 11 - 20
Product Groups: 34, 35, 36, 39, 46, 66, 80

Date of Accounts	Dec 11	Dec 10	Dec 09
Sales Turnover	9m	8m	8m
Pre Tax Profit/Loss	1m	847	-1m
Working Capital	10m	9m	8m
Fixed Assets	11m	11m	11m
Current Assets	13m	11m	11m
Current Liabilities	1m	199	2m

Allgood
63-83 Brearley Street Hockley, Birmingham, B19 3NT
Tel: 0121-359 4415 **Fax:** 0121-359 5832
E-mail: info@allgood.co.uk
Website: http://www.allgood.co.uk
Directors: A. Foxwell (Fin)
No.of Employees: 51 - 100 **Product Groups:** 26, 35

Allround Door Services Allround Door Services
27 Lundy View, Birmingham, B36 0LY
Tel: 07922-368367
E-mail: davenfish@hotmail.com
Directors: D. Northall (Prop)
No.of Employees: 1 - 10 **Product Groups:** 25, 30, 35, 66

Alstain Metal Services Ltd
Sapcote Trading Centre Small Heath Highway, Birmingham, B10 0HR
Tel: 0121-773 5655 **Fax:** 0121-773 5220
E-mail: sales@alstain.co.uk
Website: http://www.alstain.co.uk
Bank(s): Barclays
Managers: R. Grant (Mgr)
Immediate Holding Company: ALSTAIN METAL SERVICES LIMITED
Registration no: 02538732 **VAT No.:** GB 547 4989 01
Date established: 1990 **Turnover:** £2m - £5m **No.of Employees:** 11 - 20
Product Groups: 66

Date of Accounts	Dec 11	Dec 10	Dec 09
Working Capital	117	85	-29
Fixed Assets	198	230	263
Current Assets	985	1m	782

Alwayse Engineering Ltd
6 Miller Street Aston, Birmingham, B6 4NF
Tel: 0121-380 4700 **Fax:** 0121-380 4701
E-mail: sales@alwayse.co.uk
Website: http://www.alwayse.com
Bank(s): H S B C
Directors: Z. Lawton (Co Sec), L. Pinnick (Ch), G. Golby (MD)
Managers: S. O'Neil (Accounts), C. Branch (Eng Serv Mgr), M. Haddon (Prod Mgr), P. Hogg (Sales Prom Mgr)
Registration no: 00362715 **VAT No.:** GB 559 0679 02
Turnover: £2m - £5m **No.of Employees:** 21 - 50 **Product Groups:** 35, 36, 38, 39, 41, 42, 45, 46, 67

Date of Accounts	Mar 10	Mar 09	Mar 08
Pre Tax Profit/Loss	N/A	537	618
Working Capital	1m	1m	1m
Fixed Assets	406	460	3m
Current Assets	2m	2m	2m
Current Liabilities	N/A	484	350

American Express Europe (Business Travel Centre)
Mclaren Building 35 Dale End, Birmingham, B4 7WN
Tel: 08706-000548 **Fax:** 0121-710 5512
Managers: M. Allen (Mgr)
Immediate Holding Company: AMERICAN EXPRESS EUROPE LIMITED
Registration no: FC011790 **Date established:** 1983
No.of Employees: 21 - 50 **Product Groups:** 69

American Express Travel (Branch Office, Travel Division)
34 Union Street, Birmingham, B2 4SR
Tel: 0121-644 5500 **Fax:** 0121-644 5512
E-mail: birmingham@amexfranchise.co.uk
Website: http://www.americanexpress.co.uk
Managers: S. Penn (Mgr)
Immediate Holding Company: AMERICAN EXPRESS EUROPE LIMITED
Registration no: FC011790 **VAT No.:** GB 190 1985 48
Date established: 1983 **Turnover:** £2m - £5m **No.of Employees:** 11 - 20
Product Groups: 69

AMG Forwarding Ltd
Unit S25 Hastingwood Industrial Park Wood Lane, Erdington, Birmingham, B24 9QR
Tel: 0121-386 6780 **Fax:** 0121-386 6785
E-mail: andrew@amglogistics.co.uk
Website: http://www.amglogistics.co.uk
Directors: A. Griffiths (Dir)
Immediate Holding Company: AMG FORWARDING LIMITED
Registration no: 04851641 **Date established:** 2003
No.of Employees: 1 - 10 **Product Groups:** 61, 72, 74, 75, 76, 77, 79, 80, 84

Date of Accounts	Mar 11	Mar 10	Mar 09
Working Capital	91	86	68
Fixed Assets	2	2	2
Current Assets	172	159	125

Amico Birmingham Ltd
119-121 Barr Street, Birmingham, B19 3DE
Tel: 0121-551 2786 **Fax:** 0121-551 4786
Website: http://www.amico.uk.com
Directors: I. Suleman (MD)
Registration no: 06775348 **Date established:** 2008
No.of Employees: 1 - 10 **Product Groups:** 38, 42

Amyco Industrial Doors Ltd
Unit 23 Century Park Garrison Lane, Birmingham, B9 4NZ
Tel: 0121-771 0395 **Fax:** 0121-773 3766
E-mail: info@amycodoors.co.uk
Website: http://www.amycodoors.co.uk
Directors: A. Grady (Fin)
Immediate Holding Company: AMYCO INDUSTRIAL DOORS LTD.
Registration no: 01741841 **VAT No.:** GB 377 6381 11
Date established: 1983 **Turnover:** £1m - £2m **No.of Employees:** 11 - 20
Product Groups: 35, 36

Date of Accounts	Mar 12	Mar 11	Mar 10
Working Capital	289	291	435
Fixed Assets	20	36	45
Current Assets	446	452	604

Andrews Water Heaters
Wood Lane Erdington, Birmingham, B24 9QP
Tel: 08450-701055 **Fax:** 0121-506 7434
E-mail: rebecca.johnson@baxigroup.com
Website: http://www.andrewswaterheaters.co.uk
Managers: R. Johnson
Immediate Holding Company: NEWMOND GROUP
Registration no: 03879156 **VAT No.:** GB 562 3227 57
Turnover: £5m - £10m **No.of Employees:** 51 - 100 **Product Groups:** 40

Anopol Ltd
70 Bordesley Street, Birmingham, B5 5QA
Tel: 0121-632 6888 **Fax:** 0121-631 2274
E-mail: info@anopol.co.uk
Website: http://www.anopol.co.uk
Bank(s): TSB P.L.C., Birmingham
Directors: A. Dallaway (Fin), J. Swain (MD)
Managers: J. Bradley (Personnel), T. Duell (Tech Serv Mgr)
Ultimate Holding Company: ANOPOL LIMITED
Immediate Holding Company: ANOPOL LIMITED
Registration no: 00925237 **VAT No.:** GB 443 6521 58
Date established: 1967 **Turnover:** £5m - £10m **No.of Employees:** 21 - 50
Product Groups: 46, 48

Date of Accounts	Dec 11	Dec 10	Dec 09
Working Capital	650	609	540
Fixed Assets	752	724	723
Current Assets	940	1m	1m

Anthony Collins Solicitors
134 Edmund Street, Birmingham, B3 2ES
Tel: 0121-200 3242 **Fax:** 0121-200 2408
E-mail: peter.baldwin@anthonycollinssolicitors.com
Website: http://www.anthonycollins.com
Directors: A. Harper (Fin), A. Collins (Fin), R. Thompson (Snr Part)
Managers: A. Skuse (Tech Serv Mgr), C. Sobolewska (Personnel), C. Ingram
Immediate Holding Company: ANTHONY COLLINS SOLICITORS LLP
Registration no: OC313432 **Date established:** 2005
Turnover: £10m - £20m **No.of Employees:** 101 - 250 **Product Groups:** 80

Date of Accounts	Apr 12	Apr 11	Apr 10
Sales Turnover	14m	13m	13m
Pre Tax Profit/Loss	4m	2m	2m
Working Capital	4m	2m	3m
Fixed Assets	2m	2m	2m
Current Assets	7m	6m	6m
Current Liabilities	2m	1m	1m

Apex Agencies International Ltd
155 Tame Road, Birmingham, B6 7DG
Tel: 0121-328 9190 **Fax:** 0121-328 4175
E-mail: info@apex.world.com
Directors: D. Nathwani (Dir)
Immediate Holding Company: APEX AGENCIES INTERNATIONAL LIMITED
Registration no: 01719065 **VAT No.:** GB 346 2717 51
Date established: 1983 **Turnover:** £1m - £2m **No.of Employees:** 1 - 10
Product Groups: 22, 24, 25, 26, 27, 29, 30, 32, 33, 35, 36, 37, 38, 39, 40, 44, 45, 46, 49, 52, 61, 62, 63, 65, 66, 67, 80

Date of Accounts	Apr 11	Apr 10	Apr 09
Working Capital	90	85	64
Fixed Assets	3	2	3
Current Assets	241	260	117

Apex Plastics Ltd
Unit 4 Mount St Business Centre Mount Street, Nechells, Birmingham, B7 5RD
Tel: 0121-326 6800 **Fax:** 0121-326 6390
E-mail: jeffcox@apexplasticsuk.com
Website: http://www.apexplasticsuk.com
Directors: J. Cox (Dir)
Immediate Holding Company: APEX PLASTICS MIDLANDS LIMITED
Registration no: 07647645 **Date established:** 2011
No.of Employees: 1 - 10 **Product Groups:** 26, 30, 49

A-Plant Ltd
67 Davey Road, Birmingham, B20 3DR
Tel: 0121-356 9672 **Fax:** 0121-356 9672
Website: http://www.toolhireshops.com
Directors: D. Plant (Snr Part)
Immediate Holding Company: A.PLANT LIMITED
Registration no: 05407712 **Date established:** 2005
No.of Employees: 1 - 10 **Product Groups:** 35, 39, 45

Date of Accounts	Mar 07	Mar 06
Working Capital	12	-3
Fixed Assets	9	12
Current Assets	35	8

Applied Window Films Ltd
Halesfield House 909 Aldridge Road, Great Barr, Birmingham, B44 8NS
Tel: 0121-693 2412 **Fax:** 0121-693 2415
E-mail: claire@appliedwindowfilms.co.uk
Website: http://www.appliedwindowfilms.co.uk
Directors: T. Raynor (MD)
Immediate Holding Company: APPLIED WINDOW FILMS LIMITED
Registration no: 02512909 **Date established:** 1990
No.of Employees: 1 - 10 **Product Groups:** 30, 32, 33, 35, 39, 68

Date of Accounts	Nov 11	Nov 10	Nov 09
Working Capital	22	65	36
Fixed Assets	6	7	15
Current Assets	173	128	141

Argus Services
H R S House H R S Industrial Estate Garretts Green Lane, Birmingham, B33 0UE
Tel: 0121-683 1168 **Fax:** 0121- 6831167
E-mail: jerry.matthews@argus-services.co.uk
Website: http://www.argus-services.co.uk
Directors: J. Matthews (Co Sec)
Immediate Holding Company: ARGUS SERVICES LTD
Registration no: 03793798 **Date established:** 1999
Turnover: Up to £250,000 **No.of Employees:** 11 - 20 **Product Groups:** 36, 37, 40, 67

Date of Accounts	Jun 12	Jun 11	Jun 10
Working Capital	136	277	137
Fixed Assets	84	66	64
Current Assets	565	620	466
Current Liabilities	260	254	170

Armac Brassworks
160 Dollman Street, Birmingham, B7 4RS
Tel: 0121-359 4821 **Fax:** 0121-359 4698
E-mail: sales@martin.co.uk
Website: http://www.martin.co.uk
Bank(s): HSBC, Birmingham
Directors: B. Morby (Mkt Research), M. Mcgrail (MD)
Managers: M. Savage (Sales Admin)
Ultimate Holding Company: ARMAC BRASSFOUNDERS GROUP LIMITED
Immediate Holding Company: ARMAC BRASSFOUNDERS GROUP LIMITED
Registration no: 00523440 **VAT No.:** GB 294 5922 20
Date established: 1953 **Turnover:** £5m - £10m **No.of Employees:** 21 - 50
Product Groups: 34, 35, 36

Date of Accounts	Dec 11	Dec 10	Dec 09
Sales Turnover	8m	8m	8m
Pre Tax Profit/Loss	-266	428	-266
Working Capital	2m	2m	2m
Fixed Assets	4m	4m	5m
Current Assets	4m	4m	4m
Current Liabilities	396	530	399

Artistic Trims Ltd
Aston House 77 Upper Trinity Street, Birmingham, B9 4EG
Tel: 0121-766 6167 **Fax:** 0121-766 6360
E-mail: sales@artistictrims.co.uk
Website: http://www.artistictrims.co.uk
Directors: R. Bagga (MD)
Immediate Holding Company: ARTISTIC TRIMS LIMITED
Registration no: 02641953 **Date established:** 1991
Turnover: £500,000 - £1m **No.of Employees:** 1 - 10 **Product Groups:** 23

Date of Accounts	Aug 11	Aug 10	Aug 09
Working Capital	464	489	502
Fixed Assets	326	341	316
Current Assets	576	611	643

Ashbourne Products
Newton Industrial Estate 84-96 Bordesley Green, Birmingham, B9 4TS
Tel: 0121-766 6019 **Fax:** 0121-766 6019
Directors: A. Ashbourne (Prop)
Registration no: 01748518 **Date established:** 1983
No.of Employees: 1 - 10 **Product Groups:** 35

Ashtenne Ltd
35 Spring Road Tyseley, Birmingham, B11 3EA
Tel: 0121-778 2233 **Fax:** 0121-702 1760
E-mail: mcloughlin.c@ashtenne.co.uk
Website: http://www.ashtenne-online.co.uk
Managers: V. Mathews (Admin Off), J. Havery (District Mgr), C. Mcloughlin (Reg Mgr), R. Mccrewmen (Fin Mgr)
Immediate Holding Company: CORE LEGAL SERVICES LIMITED
Registration no: 04293795 **Date established:** 2005
No.of Employees: 1 - 10 **Product Groups:** 80

Date of Accounts	Nov 11	Nov 10	Nov 09
Working Capital	2	-6	-15
Fixed Assets	N/A	1	1
Current Assets	14	15	14

Ashton & Moore Ltd
12 Smith Street Hockley, Birmingham, B19 3EX
Tel: 0121-554 4415 **Fax:** 0845-618 8197
E-mail: contact@ashton-moore.co.uk
Website: http://www.ashtonandmoore.co.uk
Bank(s): Lloyds TSB Bank plc
Directors: K. Tucker (MD), M. Hudson (Works)
Managers: T. Brownsword (Chief Acct), S. Agnew (Purch Mgr)
Ultimate Holding Company: ASHTON & MOORE HOLDINGS LIMITED
Immediate Holding Company: ASHTON & MOORE LIMITED
Registration no: 00195160 **Date established:** 2024 **Turnover:** £2m - £5m
No.of Employees: 51 - 100 **Product Groups:** 28, 48, 85

Date of Accounts	Mar 12	Mar 11	Mar 10
Working Capital	723	637	497
Fixed Assets	6	7	340
Current Assets	1m	1m	796

Aston Fittings
2 Springcroft Road, Birmingham, B11 3EL
Tel: 0121-778 6001 **Fax:** 0121-778 6001
E-mail: sales@astonfittings.com
Website: http://www.astonfittings.com
Bank(s): Barclays
Directors: R. Brown (Dir)
Immediate Holding Company: ASTON FITTINGS MANUFACTURING LIMITED
Registration no: 02913370 **VAT No.:** GB 614 3760 54
Date established: 1994 **Turnover:** £1m - £2m **No.of Employees:** 11 - 20
Product Groups: 36

Date of Accounts	Mar 11	Mar 10	Mar 09
Working Capital	460	354	251
Fixed Assets	55	45	62
Current Assets	1m	813	704

Aston University
The Aston Triangle, Birmingham, B4 7ET
Tel: 0121-204 3000 **Fax:** 0121-333 6350
E-mail: admissions@aston.ac.uk
Website: http://www.aston.ac.uk
Bank(s): Lloyds TSB Bank plc
Directors: J. Saunders (Head)
Managers: M. Lyne (Mgr)
Immediate Holding Company: ASTON UNIVERSITY ENGINEERING ACADEMY BIRMINGHAM
Registration no: 07166427 **Date established:** 2010 **Turnover:** £2m - £5m
No.of Employees: 11 - 20 **Product Groups:** 86

Date of Accounts	Feb 11
Sales Turnover	35
Current Assets	20
Current Liabilities	20

Astra Engineering Products Ltd
Queens Road Aston, Birmingham, B6 7NH
Tel: 0121-327 3571 **Fax:** 0121-327 6381
E-mail: hallj@astrapressings.co.uk
Website: http://www.astrapressings.co.uk
Bank(s): The Royal Bank of Scotland
Directors: J. Hall (Dir), J. Findley (Fin)
Managers: P. Stafford (Buyer)
Immediate Holding Company: ASTRA ENGINEERING PRODUCTS LIMITED
Registration no: 02542704 **VAT No.:** GB 555 0647 39
Date established: 1990 **Turnover:** £2m - £5m **No.of Employees:** 21 - 50
Product Groups: 37, 48

Date of Accounts	Sep 11	Sep 10	Sep 09
Working Capital	-169	-125	-48
Fixed Assets	450	312	433
Current Assets	947	997	529

Athlone Extrusions (UK) Ltd
Equipoint Coventry Road, Birmingham, B25 8AD
Tel: 0121-764 4848 **Fax:** 0121-764 4443
E-mail: sales@athloneuk.com
Website: http://www.athloneextrusions.ie
Managers: J. McGee, E. Cunningham, J. Browne, J. Ferreira, J. Palmer (Sales Admin), C. Wright, A. Dickson (Mgr), A. Lee (Mgr)
Immediate Holding Company: Athlone Extrusions Ltd
Registration no: 01831340 **Turnover:** £20m - £50m
No.of Employees: 1 - 10 **Product Groups:** 30, 31, 42

Date of Accounts	Sep 11	Sep 10	Sep 09
Sales Turnover	162	N/A	185
Pre Tax Profit/Loss	25	23	27
Working Capital	527	507	489
Current Assets	698	665	656
Current Liabilities	17	5	5

Atkins
The Axis 10 Holliday Street, Birmingham, B1 1TF
Tel: 0121-483 5000 **Fax:** 0121-483 5252
E-mail: emma.frost@fgould.com
Website: http://www.atkinsglobal.com
Bank(s): National Westminster Bank Plc
Directors: R. Barrett (MD)
Ultimate Holding Company: W.S. ATKINS
Immediate Holding Company: W S ATKINS
No.of Employees: 501 - 1000 **Product Groups:** 44, 80, 84

Atlantic Plastics
Eddison Road Hams Hall Distribution Park Coleshill, Birmingham, B46 1AB
Tel: 01675-437900 **Fax:** 01675-437909
E-mail: sdrain@tyco-valves.com
Website: http://www.tmproducts.com
Bank(s): Royal Bank of Scotland
Directors: D. Murr (Sales), S. Godfrey (MD)
Ultimate Holding Company: TARPAN LUXCO SARL (LUXEMBOURG)
Immediate Holding Company: ATLANTIC PLASTICS LIMITED
Registration no: 01154347 **Date established:** 1974
Turnover: £20m - £50m **No.of Employees:** 21 - 50 **Product Groups:** 36

Date of Accounts	Sep 11	Sep 10	Sep 08
Sales Turnover	24m	21m	29m
Pre Tax Profit/Loss	352	-1m	2m
Working Capital	7m	7m	29m
Fixed Assets	10m	10m	11m
Current Assets	11m	10m	36m
Current Liabilities	1m	1m	1m

Atlantis Forwarding Ltd
1607 Pershore Road Stirchley, Birmingham, B30 2JF
Tel: 0121-451 1588 **Fax:** 0121-433 4034
E-mail: stuart.law@stirchley4.freeserve.co.uk
Website: http://www.atlantisltd.co.uk
Directors: S. Law (Dir)
Ultimate Holding Company: ATLANTIS FORWARDING HOLDINGS LIMITED
Immediate Holding Company: ATLANTIS FORWARDING LIMITED
Registration no: 01298851 **VAT No.:** GB 301 4438 06
Date established: 1977 **Turnover:** £1m - £2m **No.of Employees:** 1 - 10
Product Groups: 72

Date of Accounts	Oct 09	Oct 08	Feb 12
Working Capital	-363	-373	-384
Fixed Assets	713	749	666
Current Assets	191	87	227

A T M S plc
Unit 1 Holt Court South Jennens Road, Birmingham, B7 4EJ
Tel: 0121-628 9000 **Fax:** 0121-359 4200
E-mail: atms@atms.co.uk
Website: http://www.atmsglobal.com
Bank(s): Natwest
Directors: S. Cross (MD), D. Hughes (Sales), S. Warburton (Fin)
Managers: D. Stevens
Immediate Holding Company: A.T.M.S. PLC
Registration no: 01825688 **VAT No.:** GB 405 2978 49
Date established: 1984 **Turnover:** £1m - £2m **No.of Employees:** 11 - 20
Product Groups: 47

Date of Accounts	Apr 11	Apr 10	Apr 09
Sales Turnover	1m	2m	2m
Pre Tax Profit/Loss	44	60	32
Working Capital	-129	-47	44
Fixed Assets	262	220	109
Current Assets	581	562	768
Current Liabilities	396	389	376

Auto Windscreens
112-116 Electric Avenue, Birmingham, B6 7EB
Tel: 0121-322 2455 **Fax:** 0121-322 2108
Website: http://www.racautowindscreens.co.uk
Directors: B. Duffy (MD), D. Watkins (MD)
Managers: A. Grey (Transport), C. Turner (), D. Watkin (), L. King (I.T. Exec), M. Gale (Tech Serv Mgr)
Ultimate Holding Company: Aviva plc
Immediate Holding Company: Rac plc
Registration no: 01424399 **Date established:** 1996 **Turnover:** £5m - £10m
No.of Employees: 101 - 250 **Product Groups:** 39

Autospin (Oil Seals) Ltd
Birkdale Avenue Selly Oak, Birmingham, B29 6UB
Tel: 0121-472 1243 **Fax:** 0121-471 3348
E-mail: sales@autospin.co.uk
Website: http://www.autospin.co.uk
Bank(s): Lloyds TSB Bank plc
Directors: A. Hill (MD)
Immediate Holding Company: Autospin(Oil Seals)Limited
Registration no: 01206807 **VAT No.:** GB 112 7644 88
Date established: 1973 **Turnover:** £500,000 - £1m
No.of Employees: 11 - 20 **Product Groups:** 23, 29, 30, 36, 63

Date of Accounts	Sep 09	Sep 08	Sep 07
Working Capital	201	196	121
Fixed Assets	7	13	19
Current Assets	309	478	382

B H S F
Gamgee House 2 Darnley Road, Birmingham, B16 8TE
Tel: 0121-454 3601 **Fax:** 0121-454 7725
E-mail: enquiries@bhsf.co.uk
Website: http://www.bhsf.co.uk
Bank(s): Lloyds TSB Bank plc
Directors: P. Ashbourne (MD), P. Maskell (Grp Chief Exec), C. Taylor (Co Sec), B. Hall (Sales & Mktg)
Managers: S. Mendy, M. Sims (Tech Serv Mgr), J. White (Personnel), N. Wright
Ultimate Holding Company: BHSF GROUP LIMITED
Immediate Holding Company: BHSF LIMITED
Registration no: 00035500 **Date established:** 1991
Turnover: Up to £250,000 **No.of Employees:** 51 - 100
Product Groups: 82

Date of Accounts	Dec 11	Dec 10	Dec 09
Pre Tax Profit/Loss	1m	3m	3m
Fixed Assets	24m	24m	23m
Current Assets	5m	5m	4m
Current Liabilities	1m	2m	1m

B J Tool & Cutters Grinding
172 Stockfield Road Acocks Green, Birmingham, B27 6AU
Tel: 0121-706 9893 **Fax:** 0121-706 9893
E-mail: bjgrinding@live.co.uk
Directors: B. James (Prop)
No.of Employees: 1 - 10 **Product Groups:** 36

B S A Guns UK Ltd
Armoury Road, Birmingham, B11 2PP
Tel: 0121-772 8543 **Fax:** 0121-773 0845
E-mail: sales@bsaguns.com
Website: http://www.bsaguns.com
Bank(s): Lloyds TSB Bank plc
Managers: M. Suleman (Comptroller), P. Knight (Mgr), P. Martineau (Sales & Mktg Mg)
Immediate Holding Company: BSA GUNS (UK) LIMITED
Registration no: 02003295 **VAT No.:** GB 444 5894 18
Date established: 1986 **Turnover:** £2m - £5m **No.of Employees:** 21 - 50
Product Groups: 36

Date of Accounts	Dec 11	Dec 10	Dec 09
Working Capital	812	1m	1m
Fixed Assets	155	177	152
Current Assets	2m	2m	2m

B S A Machine Tools
Mackadown Lane, Birmingham, B33 0LE
Tel: 0121-783 4071 **Fax:** 0121-789 9509
E-mail: sales@bsamachinetools.co.uk
Website: http://www.bsamachinetools.co.uk
Bank(s): Barclays
Directors: T. Mawbey (Fin), A. Aucott (MD), S. Brittan (MD)
Managers: R. Lakin (Purch Mgr)
Ultimate Holding Company: AUTOMATION INVESTMENTS LIMITED
Immediate Holding Company: BSA MACHINE TOOLS LIMITED
Registration no: 03031017 **VAT No.:** GB 486 8755 74
Date established: 1995 **Turnover:** £10m - £20m
No.of Employees: 21 - 50 **Product Groups:** 38, 46, 47, 86, 87

Date of Accounts	Mar 12	Mar 11	Mar 10
Working Capital	-119	-378	-594
Fixed Assets	56	11	25
Current Assets	3m	3m	2m

B S Executive Travel Ltd
Albany House Hurst Street, Birmingham, B5 4BD
Tel: 0121-666 6336 **Fax:** 0121-666 7620
E-mail: mike.barnard@bstravel.co.uk
Website: http://www.bsexec.co.uk
Directors: M. Barnard (MD), J. Harrison Jones (Fin)
Ultimate Holding Company: PHAEDRE LIMITED
Immediate Holding Company: B.S. EXECUTIVE TRAVEL LIMITED
Registration no: 00452614 **VAT No.:** GB 661 5374 32
Date established: 1948 **Turnover:** £2m - £5m **No.of Employees:** 1 - 10
Product Groups: 69

Date of Accounts	Sep 11	Sep 10	Sep 09
Working Capital	48	36	43
Fixed Assets	8	11	14
Current Assets	674	497	443

B Sky Cars
A 147 Soho Road, Birmingham, B21 9ST
Tel: 0121-554 5555
E-mail: info@skyradiocars.co.uk
Website: http://www.skyradiocars.co.uk
Directors: M. Akram (Prop)
Managers: A. hussain (Chief Mgr)
Registration no: 06801875 **Date established:** 2009
No.of Employees: 11 - 20 **Product Groups:** 39

Badger Anodising Birmingham Ltd
42-50 Bissell Street, Birmingham, B5 7HP
Tel: 0121-622 1850 **Fax:** 0121-622 1218
E-mail: sales@badgeranodising.co.uk
Website: http://www.badgeranodising.co.uk
Directors: A. Law (MD)
Immediate Holding Company: BADGER ANODISING (BIRMINGHAM) LIMITED
Registration no: 01945626 **VAT No.:** GB 443 6563 42
Date established: 1985 **Turnover:** £1m - £2m **No.of Employees:** 11 - 20
Product Groups: 48

Date of Accounts	Mar 12	Mar 11	Mar 10
Working Capital	181	181	132
Fixed Assets	198	194	209
Current Assets	382	342	249

Badgerblue Solutions Ltd
Somerset House 40-49 Price Street, Birmingham, B4 6LZ
Tel: 0845-8332475 **Fax:** 0845-2265908
E-mail: info@badgerblue.com
Website: http://www.badgerblue.com
Managers: D. Bucklow (Chief Acct)
Registration no: 06076867 **Date established:** 2007
Turnover: Up to £250,000 **No.of Employees:** 1 - 10 **Product Groups:** 44, 67

Date of Accounts	Mar 08
Working Capital	5
Fixed Assets	1
Current Assets	8
Current Liabilities	3

Bailey & Mackey Ltd
Baltimore Road, Birmingham, B42 1DE
Tel: 0121-357 5351 **Fax:** 0121-357 8319
E-mail: enquiries@baileymackey.com
Website: http://www.baileymackey.com
Bank(s): HSBC, West Bromwich
Directors: F. Caddy (Fin), E. Sparks (MD)
Managers: D. Blunt (Sales Admin)
Immediate Holding Company: BAILEY & MACKEY LIMITED
Registration no: 02140400 **VAT No.:** GB 462 0986 36
Date established: 1987 **Turnover:** £2m - £5m **No.of Employees:** 51 - 100
Product Groups: 37, 38, 40

Date of Accounts	Oct 11	Oct 10	Oct 09
Working Capital	1m	911	793
Fixed Assets	1m	1m	1m
Current Assets	2m	1m	1m

Baker & Finnemore Ltd
199 Newhall Street, Birmingham, B3 1SN
Tel: 0121-236 2347 **Fax:** 0121-236 7224
E-mail: sales@bakfin.com
Website: http://www.bakfin.com
Bank(s): HSBC
Directors: I. Packer (Fin), P. Yates (Sales & Mktg)
Managers: D. Wilkinson (Works Gen Mgr), P. Watkins Burk (Purch Mgr)
Ultimate Holding Company: BAKFIN LIMITED
Immediate Holding Company: BAKER & FINNEMORE LIMITED
Registration no: 00116591 **Date established:** 2011 **Turnover:** £2m - £5m
No.of Employees: 51 - 100 **Product Groups:** 35, 48

Date of Accounts	Dec 11	Dec 10	Dec 09
Sales Turnover	5m	5m	3m
Pre Tax Profit/Loss	840	839	167
Working Capital	4m	4m	3m
Fixed Assets	887	920	872
Current Assets	5m	5m	4m
Current Liabilities	327	370	108

Balfour Beatty Construction Ltd (Midlands Region)
Neville House 42-46 Hagley Road, Birmingham, B16 8PE
Tel: 0121-224 6600 **Fax:** 0121-224 6601
E-mail: peter.hollins@bbcc.co.uk
Website: http://www.balfourbeattyconstruction.co.uk
Bank(s): Royal Bank of Scotland, Edinburgh
Directors: D. Ronon (Dir), L. Wild (Mkt Research)
Managers: D. Ronan (Ops Mgr), T. Rogers (Buyer)
Ultimate Holding Company: Balfour Beatty plc
Immediate Holding Company: BALFOUR BEATTY CONSTRUCTION LIMITED
Registration no: SC106247 **Date established:** 1987
Turnover: £20m - £50m **No.of Employees:** 11 - 20 **Product Groups:** 52, 80, 84

Bambi Air Compressors Ltd
152 Thimble Mill Lane, Birmingham, B7 5HT
Tel: 0121-322 2299 **Fax:** 0121-322 2297
E-mail: sales@bambi-air.co.uk
Website: http://www.bambi-air.co.uk
Bank(s): HSBC Bank plc
Directors: L. Clutterbuck (Dir)
Immediate Holding Company: BAMBI AIR COMPRESSORS LIMITED
Registration no: 01318759 **Date established:** 1977
Turnover: £500,000 - £1m **No.of Employees:** 21 - 50 **Product Groups:** 40

Date of Accounts	Sep 11	Sep 10	Sep 09
Working Capital	1m	1m	753
Fixed Assets	86	111	552
Current Assets	2m	2m	1m

Barker Brettell LLP
100 Hagley Road Edgbaston, Birmingham, B16 8QQ
Tel: 0121-456 0000 **Fax:** 0121-456 1368
E-mail: info@barkerbrettell.co.uk
Website: http://www.barkerbrettell.co.uk
Managers: R. Beswick (Sales Admin), J. Williams (Personnel)
Immediate Holding Company: BARKER BRETTELL SERVICES LIMITED
Registration no: 07995323 **Date established:** 2012
Turnover: £10m - £20m **No.of Employees:** 51 - 100 **Product Groups:** 80, 87

Date of Accounts	Mar 11	Mar 10	Mar 09
Sales Turnover	18m	16m	16m
Pre Tax Profit/Loss	4m	3m	2m
Working Capital	4m	4m	2m
Fixed Assets	849	720	164
Current Assets	7m	6m	5m
Current Liabilities	1m	606	619

Barkley Plastics Ltd
120 Highgate Street, Birmingham, B12 0XR
Tel: 0121-440 1303 **Fax:** 0121-440 4902
E-mail: jgrassby@barkley.co.uk
Website: http://www.barkley.co.uk
Bank(s): Barclays
Directors: M. Harwood (MD), M. Cassidy (Comm)
Managers: M. Powell (Sales Prom Mgr), K. Goodwin (Purch Mgr), J. Grassby (Fin Mgr), P. Tedd (Mgr)
Ultimate Holding Company: BARKLEY HOLDINGS LIMITED
Immediate Holding Company: BARKLEY PLASTICS LIMITED
Registration no: 00838669 **VAT No.:** GB 109 6603 72
Date established: 1965 **Turnover:** £5m - £10m
No.of Employees: 51 - 100 **Product Groups:** 30, 48

Date of Accounts	Feb 12	Feb 11	Feb 10
Sales Turnover	5m	5m	5m
Pre Tax Profit/Loss	176	327	231
Working Capital	419	377	168
Fixed Assets	2m	2m	2m
Current Assets	2m	2m	2m
Current Liabilities	811	873	1m

C H Barnett Ltd
18 Tyseley Industrial Estate Seeleys Road, Birmingham, B11 2LQ
Tel: 0121-773 5222 **Fax:** 0121-773 7800
E-mail: sales@chbarnett.co.uk
Website: http://www.chbarnett.co.uk
Directors: S. Pickering (MD)
Managers: M. Dodson (Purch Mgr), C. Raybone (Tech Serv Mgr)
Ultimate Holding Company: C H BARNETT (HOLDINGS) LIMITED
Immediate Holding Company: C.H. BARNETT LTD.
Registration no: 02581045 **Date established:** 1991 **Turnover:** £1m - £2m
No.of Employees: 51 - 100 **Product Groups:** 35, 48

Date of Accounts	Dec 11	Dec 10	Dec 09
Working Capital	175	134	124
Fixed Assets	800	831	888
Current Assets	1m	1m	1m

Bassra Ltd
99 Spring Road Tyseley, Birmingham, B11 3DJ
Tel: 0121-707 4343 **Fax:** 0121-707 3535
E-mail: sales@bassra.com
Website: http://www.bassra.com
Directors: B. Bassra (MD)
Immediate Holding Company: BASSRA MACHINE TOOLS LIMITED
Registration no: 03403339 **Date established:** 1997
Turnover: £250,000 - £500,000 **No.of Employees:** 11 - 20
Product Groups: 32, 45

Date of Accounts	Dec 11	Dec 10	Dec 09
Working Capital	93	-134	-97
Fixed Assets	400	415	424
Current Assets	419	400	208

Bean2Bed Ltd
Lonsdale House 52 Blucher Street, Birmingham, B1 1QU
Tel: 0121-616 5178
E-mail: sales@bean2bed.com
Website: http://www.bean2bed.com
Directors: M. Roberts (Dir)
Immediate Holding Company: BEAN2BED LIMITED
Registration no: 05489359 **Date established:** 2005
No.of Employees: 1 - 10 **Product Groups:** 26

Date of Accounts	Jun 11	Jun 10	Jun 09
Working Capital	-11	-11	-10
Fixed Assets	4	4	5
Current Assets	7	9	17

Bearwood Engineering Supplies (Inc. Bearwood Intl Ltd)
11 Vernon Road, Birmingham, B16 9SQ
Tel: 0121-454 7227 **Fax:** 0121-454 5991
E-mail: jon.laxton@btconnect.com
Website: http://www.bearwoodinternational.co.uk
Directors: J. Laxton (Dir)
Immediate Holding Company: BEARWOOD ENGINEERING SUPPLIES LIMITED
Registration no: 02686492 **VAT No.:** GB 428 7423 37
Date established: 1992 **Turnover:** £1m - £2m **No.of Employees:** 1 - 10
Product Groups: 22, 23, 24, 29, 30, 32, 34, 35, 36, 37, 38, 39, 40, 41, 42, 44, 45, 46, 61, 63, 66, 67, 68, 80, 83

Date of Accounts	Apr 11	Apr 10	Apr 09
Working Capital	13	51	80
Fixed Assets	1	1	2
Current Assets	70	94	139

Beauvale Floorcoverings
Coleshill Distribution Centre Gorsey Lane, Coleshill, Birmingham, B46 1JU
Tel: 01675-433034 **Fax:** 01675-433534
E-mail: headlamgroup@headlam.com
Website: http://www.headlammidlands.co.uk
Directors: D. Price (MD)
Managers: R. Paisley (Mgr)
Ultimate Holding Company: SERTEC GROUP LIMITED
Immediate Holding Company: CCT (HINCKLEY) LIMITED
Registration no: 00460129 **Date established:** 2000
Turnover: £500m - £1,000m **No.of Employees:** 51 - 100
Product Groups: 25, 30, 66

Date of Accounts	Mar 12	Mar 11	Mar 10
Working Capital	-1m	-961	-552
Fixed Assets	N/A	110	114
Current Assets	211	195	415
Current Liabilities	2	N/A	N/A

J W Beddows & Son
1-11 New Summer Street, Birmingham, B19 3QN
Tel: 0121-359 3747 **Fax:** 0121-359 8550
Directors: M. Beddows (Dir), D. Beddows (Dir)
Immediate Holding Company: J.W. BEDDOWS & SON (HOLDINGS) LIMITED
Registration no: 01013701 **Date established:** 1971
No.of Employees: 21 - 50 **Product Groups:** 46, 48

Date of Accounts	Feb 08	Feb 11	Feb 10
Working Capital	669	240	549
Fixed Assets	208	192	198
Current Assets	671	250	584

Bedestone Ltd
41 Icknield Street Hockley, Birmingham, B18 5AY
Tel: 0121-554 3283 **Fax:** 0121-507 0140
E-mail: enquiries@bedestone.co.uk
Website: http://www.bedestone.co.uk
Directors: R. Tromans (Dir)
Managers: E. Lowry (Sales Admin)
Immediate Holding Company: BEDESTONE LIMITED
Registration no: 01344839 **VAT No.:** GB 113 5882 76
Date established: 1977 **Turnover:** £1m - £2m **No.of Employees:** 21 - 50
Product Groups: 30, 37, 42, 46, 48, 85

Date of Accounts	Jul 11	Jul 10	Jul 09
Working Capital	74	55	64
Fixed Assets	225	260	334
Current Assets	409	326	325

Beeches 24 Hour Rescue & Recovery Service Ltd
Paper Mill End Industrial Estate, Birmingham, B44 8NH
Tel: 0121-344 4644 **Fax:** 0121-344 4786
E-mail: info@beechesrecovery.co.uk
Website: http://www.beechesrecovery.co.uk
Immediate Holding Company: DESIGNER APPAREL LIMITED
Date established: 2009 **No.of Employees:** 21 - 50 **Product Groups:** 39, 72

Date of Accounts	Oct 11	Oct 10
Working Capital	N/A	1
Current Assets	N/A	1

Beeline Promotional Products Ltd
Sapphire Heights 32 Tenby Street, Birmingham, B1 3ES
Tel: 0121-212 1220 **Fax:** 0121-212 1230
E-mail: sales@beeline-promo.co.uk
Website: http://www.beeline-promo.co.uk
Directors: P. Welch (Dir), S. Yeomans (Co Sec)
Immediate Holding Company: BEELINE PROMOTIONAL PRODUCTS PROPERTIES LIMITED
Registration no: 04826577 **Date established:** 2003 **Turnover:** £1m - £2m
No.of Employees: 1 - 10 **Product Groups:** 24, 27, 28, 29, 30

Date of Accounts	Jul 11	Jul 10	Jul 09
Working Capital	41	39	28
Fixed Assets	210	210	210
Current Assets	74	67	58

Bemco (t/a Bemco)
11-12 Carver Street, Birmingham, B1 3AS
Tel: 0121-236 5868 **Fax:** 0121-236 8211
E-mail: info@bemco.com
Website: http://www.bemco.uk.com
Bank(s): HSBC Bank plc
Directors: D. Rafferty (MD), R. Larcomb (MD)
Immediate Holding Company: GLOBEMARKET LIMITED
Registration no: 03424074 **VAT No.:** GB 486 8735 80
Date established: 1997 **Turnover:** £1m - £2m **No.of Employees:** 11 - 20
Product Groups: 30, 35, 36, 40, 46

Date of Accounts	Jul 11	Jul 10	Jul 09
Working Capital	-5	-35	-34
Fixed Assets	73	66	83
Current Assets	356	294	217
Current Liabilities	N/A	N/A	98

Betterware Ltd
Stanley House Park Lane Castle Vale, Birmingham, B35 6LJ
Tel: 08451-294500 **Fax:** 08451-294654
E-mail: r.way@betterware.co.uk
Website: http://www.betterware.co.uk
Bank(s): Barclays, Birmingham
Directors: R. Way (MD)
Managers: J. Embray (Tech Serv Mgr), G. Peel, R. Smith (Mktg Serv Mgr)
Ultimate Holding Company: BWI REALISATIONS 2012 LIMITED
Immediate Holding Company: BW REALISATIONS 2012 LIMITED
Registration no: 01715427 **VAT No.:** GB 580 7060 45
Date established: 1983 **Turnover:** £20m - £50m
No.of Employees: 251 - 500 **Product Groups:** 24, 30, 49, 66

Date of Accounts	Dec 07	Dec 08	Jan 10
Sales Turnover	26m	29m	34m
Pre Tax Profit/Loss	-189	572	1m
Working Capital	10m	11m	11m
Fixed Assets	770	525	935
Current Assets	18m	19m	19m
Current Liabilities	3m	3m	3m

The Binding Site Ltd
PO Box 11712, Birmingham, B14 4ST
Tel: 0121-436 1000 **Fax:** 0121-430 7061
E-mail: info@bindingsite.co.uk
Website: http://www.bindingsite.co.uk
Bank(s): Natwest, City Office, PO Box 87, Colmore Centre, 103 Colmore Row, Birmingham, B3 3NS
Directors: S. Calderbank (Co Sec), T. Sykes (Co Sec), A. Rowland (Dir), W. Hetzog (Sales)
Managers: P. Duncan (Mktg Serv Mgr), D. Wall (Mktg Serv Mgr)
Immediate Holding Company: THE BINDING SITE LIMITED
Registration no: 01644144 **VAT No.:** GB 614 2438 64
Date established: 1982 **Turnover:** £20m - £50m
No.of Employees: 251 - 500 **Product Groups:** 31

Binney & Son Ltd
Unit H Spring Hill Industrial Park Steward Street, Birmingham, B18 7AF
Tel: 0121-454 4545 **Fax:** 0121-454 1145
E-mail: binney.eng@btconnect.com

see next page

Binney & Son Ltd - Cont'd

Directors: D. Yoxall (Fin), F. Yoxall (Dir)
Immediate Holding Company: BINNEY AND SON LIMITED
Registration no: 04018440 **VAT No.:** GB 754 3048 36
Date established: 2000 **Turnover:** £500,000 - £1m
No.of Employees: 1 - 10 **Product Groups:** 31, 48, 66, 67

Date of Accounts	Mar 09	Mar 08	Mar 07
Working Capital	-0	1	1
Fixed Assets	1	1	1
Current Assets	145	170	157

W Birch & Sons Ltd

42 Bissell Street, Birmingham, B5 7HP
Tel: 0121-666 6164 **Fax:** 0121-622 1218
E-mail: sales@badgeranodising.co.uk
Website: http://www.badgeranodising.co.uk
Directors: A. Law (Jt MD), M. Law (Jt MD), T. Law (MD)
Immediate Holding Company: W.BIRCH & SONS(POLISHERS)LIMITED
Registration no: 00418677 **Date established:** 1946
Turnover: Up to £250,000 **No.of Employees:** 11 - 20 **Product Groups:** 48

Date of Accounts	Mar 11	Mar 10	Mar 09
Working Capital	294	347	352
Fixed Assets	10	11	13
Current Assets	434	468	379

Birmingham Airport

Diamond House Birmingham International Airport, Birmingham, B26 3QJ
Tel: 08445-766000 **Fax:** 0121-782 8802
Website: http://www.birminghamairport.co.uk
Bank(s): National Westminster Bank Plc
Directors: L. Gregory (Dir), W. Smith (Tech Serv), M. Kelly (Co Sec), S. Richards (Fin)
Managers: T. Dunning (Purch Mgr)
Ultimate Holding Company: BIRMINGHAM AIRPORT HOLDINGS LIMITED
Immediate Holding Company: BIRMINGHAM AIRPORT LIMITED
Registration no: 02078273 **VAT No.:** GB 687 9037 77
Date established: 1986 **Turnover:** £75m - £125m
No.of Employees: 251 - 500 **Product Groups:** 71

Date of Accounts	Mar 11	Mar 10	Mar 09
Sales Turnover	103m	104m	108m
Pre Tax Profit/Loss	9m	3m	14m
Working Capital	-7m	-11m	-20m
Fixed Assets	446m	437m	429m
Current Assets	24m	20m	18m
Current Liabilities	29m	29m	35m

Birmingham Business School

Edgbaston, Birmingham, B15 2TT
Tel: 0121-414 6225 **Fax:** 0121-414 7380
E-mail: j@business.bham.ac.uk
Website: http://www.business.bham.ac.uk
Managers: J. Michie
Immediate Holding Company: BIRMINGHAM BUSINESS SUPPLIES LIMITED
Registration no: 01148399 **Date established:** 1973
No.of Employees: 21 - 50 **Product Groups:** 86

Date of Accounts	Jul 11	Jul 10	Jul 09
Working Capital	-31	-29	-23
Fixed Assets	205	208	211
Current Assets	49	60	116

Birmingham Business Supplies Ltd

25 Adams Street, Birmingham, B7 4LT
Tel: 0121-354 7881 **Fax:** 0121-355 7288
Directors: D. Cookson (Fin), J. Cookson (MD)
Immediate Holding Company: BIRMINGHAM BUSINESS SUPPLIES LIMITED
Registration no: 01148399 **Date established:** 1973
Turnover: £500,000 - £1m **No.of Employees:** 1 - 10 **Product Groups:** 22, 26, 28, 33, 36, 44, 49, 52, 63, 64, 65, 66, 67, 80, 83, 84

Date of Accounts	Jul 11	Jul 10	Jul 09
Working Capital	-31	-29	-23
Fixed Assets	205	208	211
Current Assets	49	60	116

Birmingham Chambers Of Commerce & Industry

75 Harborne Road, Birmingham, B15 3DH
Tel: 0121-454 6171 **Fax:** 0121-455 8670
E-mail: enquiries@birminghamchamber.org.uk
Website: http://www.birmingham-chamber.com
Bank(s): National Westminster Bank Plc
Directors: M. Hibbert (Fin), M. Hibbert (Fin), M. Hubbert (Fin), J. Blackett (Grp Chief Exec), J. Smith (Sales)
Managers: K. Johnson (Sales & Mktg Mg), G. Fiddler (Personnel), A. Duncan (Tech Serv Mgr), D. Bradford (Sales Admin), A. Duncan (I.T. Exec), R. Deans
Immediate Holding Company: BIRMINGHAM CHAMBER OF COMMERCE AND INDUSTRY
Registration no: 00078731 **Date established:** 2003
Turnover: £10m - £20m **No.of Employees:** 251 - 500
Product Groups: 69, 80, 81, 83, 86, 87

Date of Accounts	Mar 12	Mar 11	Mar 10
Sales Turnover	8m	11m	10m
Pre Tax Profit/Loss	89	-130	171
Working Capital	205	789	724
Fixed Assets	3m	3m	3m
Current Assets	1m	2m	3m
Current Liabilities	529	892	2m

Birmingham City Laboratories

Valepits Road, Birmingham, B33 0TD
Tel: 0121-303 9300 **Fax:** 0121-303 9301
E-mail: bcl@birmingham.gov.uk
Website: http://www.birmingham.gov.uk/bcl
Managers: T. Box
Ultimate Holding Company: BIRMINGHAM CITY COUNCIL, BIRMINGHAM
Immediate Holding Company: BIRMINGHAM CITY COUNCIL, ENVIRONMENTAL SERVICES
Turnover: £1m - £2m **No.of Employees:** 21 - 50 **Product Groups:** 84, 85

Birmingham Coldform & Special Fasteners Ltd

Unit 11 120 Sydenham Road New Shires Industrial Estate, Birmingham, B11 1DQ
Tel: 0121-772 0562 **Fax:** 0121-771 2419
E-mail: kev-bcsfltd@btconnect.com
Website: http://www.kellysearch.com/partners/birminghamcoldformspec.asp
Managers: K. Jordan (Chief Mgr), K. Jordon (Chief Mgr)
Ultimate Holding Company: HYDROBOLT GROUP HOLDINGS LIMITED
Immediate Holding Company: BIRMINGHAM COLDFORM & SPECIAL FASTENERS LIMITED
Registration no: 02227339 **VAT No.:** GB 487 0507 30
Date established: 1988 **Turnover:** £500,000 - £1m
No.of Employees: 1 - 10 **Product Groups:** 35, 66

Date of Accounts	Mar 12	Mar 11	Mar 10
Working Capital	887	411	297
Fixed Assets	86	162	178
Current Assets	1m	646	457

Birmingham Glass Fibre Mouldings

5 Weston Works Weston Lane, Birmingham, B11 3RP
Tel: 0121-708 1400 **Fax:** 0121-707 5312
E-mail: info@birminghamglassfibre.co.uk
Website: http://www.birminghamglassfibre.co.uk
Directors: S. Pearson (Prop)
Date established: 1986 **No.of Employees:** 1 - 10 **Product Groups:** 30, 33

Birmingham Heat Exchangers Ltd

17 Tile Cross Trading Estate Tile Cross Road, Birmingham, B33 0NW
Tel: 0121-788 2450 **Fax:** 0121-788 2587
E-mail: sales@bheat.co.uk
Website: http://www.aandgheatexchangers.com
Directors: G. Griffiths (Fin)
Immediate Holding Company: A & G HEAT EXCHANGERS LIMITED
Registration no: 06226628 **Date established:** 2007
Turnover: Up to £250,000 **No.of Employees:** 1 - 10 **Product Groups:** 37, 40, 48

Date of Accounts	Jul 09	Jul 08
Sales Turnover	240	N/A
Pre Tax Profit/Loss	39	N/A
Working Capital	3	1
Current Assets	65	1
Current Liabilities	22	N/A

Birmingham LDV

Aston Cross Business Park 50 Rocky Lane, Aston, Birmingham, B6 5RQ
Tel: 0121-624 9000 **Fax:** 0121-624 9001
E-mail: chris.morse@pendragon.uk.com
Website: http://www.birmingham.ldv.com
Directors: T. Finn (Ch)
Managers: C. Morse (Sales Prom), J. May (Mgr)
Ultimate Holding Company: DE RIGO SPA (ITALY)
Immediate Holding Company: DOLLOND & AITCHISON SAVINGS PLAN LIMITED
Registration no: 03379725 **Date established:** 1997
No.of Employees: 1 - 10 **Product Groups:** 68

Birmingham Mailing Cases Ltd

Machin Road, Birmingham, B23 6DR
Tel: 0121-373 0401 **Fax:** 0121-377 7671
E-mail: sales@birminghammailingcases.com
Website: http://www.birminghammailingcases.com
Directors: W. Davies (Sales)
Immediate Holding Company: BIRMINGHAM MAILING CASES LIMITED
Registration no: 00191153 **Date established:** 2023
Turnover: £500,000 - £1m **No.of Employees:** 1 - 10 **Product Groups:** 27

Date of Accounts	Aug 11	Aug 10	Aug 09
Working Capital	254	234	189
Fixed Assets	73	74	88
Current Assets	512	428	389

Birmingham Partitioning Supplies Ltd

Unit 54 Rovex Business Park Hay Hall Road, Birmingham, B11 2AQ
Tel: 0121-706 0666 **Fax:** 0121-708 1355
E-mail: sales@bhampartitions.co.uk
Directors: S. Shaw (MD)
Immediate Holding Company: BIRMINGHAM PARTITIONING SUPPLIES LIMITED
Registration no: 01947975 **Date established:** 1985 **Turnover:** £1m - £2m
No.of Employees: 1 - 10 **Product Groups:** 24, 25, 33, 35

Date of Accounts	Sep 11	Sep 10	Sep 09
Working Capital	377	349	327
Fixed Assets	20	33	46
Current Assets	575	545	537

Birmingham Powder Coatings (a division of Tomburn Ltd)

Clonmel Road Stirchley, Birmingham, B30 2BU
Tel: 0121-459 4341 **Fax:** 0121-451 1735
E-mail: sales@tomburn.co.uk
Website: http://www.tomburn.co.uk
Bank(s): Bank of Scotland
Managers: M. Hyde (Comptroller)
Immediate Holding Company: TOMBURN LIMITED
Registration no: 03134975 **VAT No.:** GB 673 8846 80
Turnover: £20m - £50m **No.of Employees:** 21 - 50 **Product Groups:** 34, 48

Date of Accounts	Dec 08	Dec 07	Dec 06
Working Capital	780	780	780
Current Assets	780	780	780
Total Share Capital	6080	6080	6080

Birmingham Pump Supplies

7 Network Park Industrial Estate Duddeston Mill Road, Saltley, Birmingham, B8 1AU
Tel: 0121-503 3000 **Fax:** 0121-503 3002
E-mail: sales@birminghampumps.co.uk
Website: http://www.birminghampumps.co.uk
Directors: K. Pearson (MD)
Immediate Holding Company: BIRMINGHAM PUMP SUPPLIES LIMITED
Registration no: 03360865 **VAT No.:** GB 591 9659 80
Date established: 1997 **Turnover:** £2m - £5m **No.of Employees:** 1 - 10
Product Groups: 39, 40, 42, 45, 46, 48

Date of Accounts	Dec 11	Dec 10	Dec 09
Working Capital	-14	2	104
Fixed Assets	311	354	33
Current Assets	354	363	308
Current Liabilities	N/A	142	N/A

Birmingham Science Park Aston

Faraday Wharf Holt Street, Birmingham, B7 4BB
Tel: 0121-260 6000 **Fax:** 0121-260 6003
E-mail: info@bsp-a.com
Website: http://www.bsp-a.com
Bank(s): Lloyds TSB Bank plc
Directors: D. Hardman (MD)
Managers: B. Hughes (Tech Serv Mgr), I. Good (Mktg Serv Mgr), J. Tinley (Personnel), R. Kumar (Fin Mgr)
Ultimate Holding Company: BIRMINGHAM TECHNOLOGY LIMITED
Immediate Holding Company: BIRMINGHAM SCIENCE PARK ASTON LIMITED
Registration no: 01720256 **VAT No.:** 486 7807 86 **Date established:** 1983
Turnover: £1m - £2m **No.of Employees:** 21 - 50 **Product Groups:** 80

Date of Accounts	Mar 11	Mar 10	Mar 09
Sales Turnover	2m	2m	1m
Pre Tax Profit/Loss	107	16	24
Working Capital	-36	-150	-77
Fixed Assets	475	231	93
Current Assets	12m	10m	10m
Current Liabilities	1m	965	921

Birmingham Specialities Ltd

Moor Lane, Birmingham, B6 7HE
Tel: 0121-356 5026 **Fax:** 0121-356 9198
E-mail: sales@bhamspec.co.uk
Website: http://www.bhamspec.co.uk
Bank(s): National Westminster Bank Plc
Directors: K. Stonehill (MD), W. Hickson (Co Sec)
Immediate Holding Company: BIRMINGHAM SPECIALITIES LIMITED
Registration no: 00230677 **VAT No.:** GB 295 8924 92
Date established: 2028 **Turnover:** £5m - £10m
No.of Employees: 51 - 100 **Product Groups:** 35, 36, 37, 39, 48

Date of Accounts	Mar 11	Mar 10	Mar 09
Sales Turnover	6m	5m	N/A
Pre Tax Profit/Loss	710	402	440
Working Capital	2m	2m	2m
Fixed Assets	425	433	451
Current Assets	3m	3m	3m
Current Liabilities	982	774	760

Birmingham Stopper Ltd Incorporating Hickton Pressings Ltd

235 Icknield Street Hockley, Birmingham, B18 6QU
Tel: 0121-551 7781 **Fax:** 0121-554 4567
E-mail: info@birminghamstopper.co.uk
Website: http://www.birminghamstopper.co.uk
Bank(s): Barclays, Colmore Row
Directors: R. Paton (Dir)
Immediate Holding Company: BIRMINGHAM STOPPER LIMITED
Registration no: 03401000 **VAT No.:** GB 109 6035 83
Date established: 1997 **Turnover:** £5m - £10m
No.of Employees: 51 - 100 **Product Groups:** 34, 35, 48

Date of Accounts	Dec 11	Dec 10	Dec 09
Sales Turnover	6m	5m	4m
Pre Tax Profit/Loss	546	238	-261
Working Capital	1m	1m	1m
Fixed Assets	3m	2m	2m
Current Assets	3m	2m	2m
Current Liabilities	872	302	181

Birmingham Welding Supplies Ltd

Unit 1 62-64 Northwood Street, Birmingham, B3 1TT
Tel: 0121-236 3888 **Fax:** 0121-236 3888
E-mail: bws1@btinternet.com
Directors: C. Jones (MD)
Immediate Holding Company: BIRMINGHAM WELDING SUPPLIES LIMITED
Registration no: 04203646 **Date established:** 2001
No.of Employees: 1 - 10 **Product Groups:** 46

Date of Accounts	Mar 11	Mar 10	Mar 09
Working Capital	17	14	11
Fixed Assets	3	4	6
Current Assets	37	39	34

Blackacre Ltd

Austin Way Hampstead Industrial Estate, Birmingham, B42 1DU
Tel: 0121-358 5066 **Fax:** 0121-358 1721
E-mail: sales@blackacre.co.uk
Website: http://www.blackacre.co.uk
Bank(s): National Westminster Bank Plc
Directors: C. Gratwick (MD)
Immediate Holding Company: BLAKEACRE LIMITED
Registration no: 02019304 **VAT No.:** GB 444 6128 54
Date established: 1986 **Turnover:** £500,000 - £1m
No.of Employees: 11 - 20 **Product Groups:** 35

Date of Accounts	Jan 12	Jan 11	Jan 10
Working Capital	681	653	596
Fixed Assets	179	206	243
Current Assets	1m	1m	968

A F Blakemore & Son Ltd

Arden Industrial Estate Arden Road, Saltley, Birmingham, B8 1DL
Tel: 0121-328 2111 **Fax:** 0121-327 7366
Website: http://www.afblakemore.com
Managers: D. Pugh (Sales Prom Mgr), C. Sturman (Chief Mgr)
Immediate Holding Company: A.F.BLAKEMORE AND SON LIMITED
Registration no: 00391135 **Date established:** 1944
No.of Employees: 21 - 50 **Product Groups:** 61

Date of Accounts	Apr 11	Apr 10	Apr 09
Sales Turnover	912m	816m	779m
Pre Tax Profit/Loss	10m	9m	9m
Working Capital	14m	33m	19m
Fixed Assets	119m	68m	65m
Current Assets	162m	132m	130m
Current Liabilities	42m	27m	22m

Blaze Neon Ltd

Units 3-4 Arden Road Rednal, Birmingham, B45 0JA
Tel: 0121-457 7715 **Fax:** 0121-453 9356
E-mail: rduncan@blazeneon.com
Website: http://www.blazeneon.com
Bank(s): HSBC Bank plc
Managers: K. Mulkerrins (Chief Mgr), R. Duncan
Ultimate Holding Company: BLAZE SIGNS HOLDINGS LIMITED
Immediate Holding Company: BLAZE NEON LIMITED
Registration no: 01524697 **VAT No.:** GB 472 6768 09
Date established: 1980 **Turnover:** £10m - £20m
No.of Employees: 21 - 50 **Product Groups:** 37, 39, 49

Date of Accounts	Mar 12	Mar 11	Mar 10
Sales Turnover	15m	15m	11m
Pre Tax Profit/Loss	1m	1m	85
Working Capital	3m	3m	3m
Fixed Assets	3m	2m	2m
Current Assets	6m	7m	5m
Current Liabilities	708	952	537

Blue Seal Ltd
Unit 67 Gravelly Industrial Park, Birmingham, B24 8TQ
Tel: 0121-327 5575 **Fax:** 0121-327 9711
E-mail: goconnell@blue-seal.co.uk
Website: http://www.blue-seal.co.uk
Directors: G. O'Connell (MD), M. Allen (Co Sec)
Ultimate Holding Company: ALI SPA (ITALY)
Immediate Holding Company: BLUE SEAL LIMITED
Registration no: 03437267 **Date established:** 1997 **Turnover:** £5m - £10m
No.of Employees: 11 - 20 **Product Groups:** 20, 22, 24, 27, 30, 32, 33, 35, 36, 37, 38, 40, 41, 42, 44, 45, 48, 49, 62, 63, 64, 66, 67, 69, 83

Date of Accounts	Aug 11	Aug 10	Aug 09
Sales Turnover	9m	9m	8m
Pre Tax Profit/Loss	476	317	-110
Working Capital	2m	2m	1m
Fixed Assets	154	134	143
Current Assets	4m	4m	3m
Current Liabilities	234	237	189

Bournville Engineering
Unit 1a Lifford Trading Estate Lifford Lane, Birmingham, B30 3DY
Tel: 0121-459 9339 **Fax:** 0121-459 9242
E-mail: jack.r.eaton@googlemail.com
Website: http://www.bournvilleengineering.co.uk
Directors: J. Eaton (Prop)
Date established: 1988 **Turnover:** Up to £250,000
No.of Employees: 1 - 10 **Product Groups:** 30, 34, 36, 42, 46, 48

The Box Warehouse
10 Arden Oak Road, Birmingham, B26 3LX
Tel: 0121-693 9090
E-mail: sales@theboxwarehouse.co.uk
Website: http://www.theboxwarehouse.co.uk
Directors: P. Hopkins (MD)
Immediate Holding Company: THE BOX WAREHOUSE LIMITED
Registration no: 05683544 **Date established:** 2006
No.of Employees: 1 - 10 **Product Groups:** 35, 42, 85

Date of Accounts	Jan 11	Jan 10	Jan 09
Working Capital	-21	2	-12
Fixed Assets	21	4	3
Current Assets	33	33	16

Boxes And Packaging Limited
Lifford Hall, Lifford Lane, Kings Norton, Birmingham, B30 3JN
Tel: 0121-328 8900 **Fax:** 01472-350315
E-mail: birmingham@boxesandpackaging.co.uk,
E-mail: birmingham@boxesandpackaging.co.ukbrimingham@boxesandpackaging.co.uk
Website: http://www.boxesandpackaging.co.uk
Directors: P. Corby (MD), S. Welsh (MD)
Registration no: 05291434 **Date established:** 1960
No.of Employees: 21 - 50 **Product Groups:** 27, 28, 49, 85

Bracebridge Engineering Ltd
75-97 Walsall Road Perry Barr, Birmingham, B42 1TX
Tel: 0121-331 1503 **Fax:** 0121-331 1506
E-mail: sales@bracebridgeengineering.co.uk
Website: http://www.bracebridgeengineering.co.uk
Bank(s): Royal Bankof Scotland
Directors: K. Street (Sales), J. Reynolds (Fin), J. Reynolds (MD)
Managers: K. Street (Mktg Serv Mgr), J. Reynolds (Chief Acct), G. Cordelle (Sales Admin), C. Casby (Buyer), W. O'Flaherty (Ops Mgr), S. Dunbar (Comm)
Immediate Holding Company: BRACEBRIDGE ENGINEERING LIMITED
Registration no: 01299727 **VAT No.:** GB 295 5897 477
Date established: 1977 **Turnover:** £1m - £2m **No.of Employees:** 21 - 50
Product Groups: 34, 48

Date of Accounts	Oct 11	Oct 10	Oct 09
Working Capital	364	275	175
Fixed Assets	80	44	41
Current Assets	694	499	338

Brandauer Precision Pressings
235 Bridge Street West, Birmingham, B19 2YU
Tel: 0121-359 2822 **Fax:** 0121-359 2836
E-mail: aedwards@brandauer.co.uk
Website: http://www.brandauer.co.uk
Bank(s): Barclays, Erdington
Directors: R. Crozier (Sales & Mktg), T. Williams (Fin)
Managers: A. Edwards (Ops Mgr), T. Whelan
Ultimate Holding Company: BRANDAUER HOLDINGS LIMITED
Immediate Holding Company: C.BRANDAUER & CO. LIMITED
Registration no: 00071835 **VAT No.:** GB 109 3914 70
Date established: 2001 **Turnover:** £5m - £10m
No.of Employees: 51 - 100 **Product Groups:** 35, 37, 48

Date of Accounts	Mar 11	Mar 10	Mar 09
Sales Turnover	10m	8m	7m
Pre Tax Profit/Loss	547	448	-292
Working Capital	2m	1m	854
Fixed Assets	1m	1m	2m
Current Assets	4m	3m	2m
Current Liabilities	421	209	172

Braythorn Ltd
Phillips Street, Birmingham, B6 4PT
Tel: 0121-359 8800 **Fax:** 0121-359 8412
E-mail: m@braythorn.co.uk
Website: http://www.braythorn.co.uk
Bank(s): Lloyds TSB Bank plc
Directors: M. Kirkham (Fin), M. Crossley (MD)
Managers: A. Cromwell (Chief Mgr)
Ultimate Holding Company: K & C HOLDINGS LIMITED
Immediate Holding Company: BRAYTHORN LIMITED
Registration no: 02993638 **Date established:** 1994 **Turnover:** £2m - £5m
No.of Employees: 21 - 50 **Product Groups:** 27, 30, 49

Date of Accounts	Dec 10	Dec 09	Dec 08
Working Capital	873	765	680
Fixed Assets	N/A	4	9
Current Assets	1m	1m	1m

Breckenridge Intersearch
5 George Road Edgbaston, Birmingham, B15 1NP
Tel: 0121-455 9568 **Fax:** 0870-4299843
E-mail: paul@intersearchuk.com
Website: http://www.intersearchuk.com
Directors: P. Holmes (MD), K. Tracy (Dir)
Managers: K. Werrett (Mktg Serv Mgr)
Immediate Holding Company: MAINTENANCE MANAGER (SOFTWARE) LIMITED

Date established: 1998 **No.of Employees:** 1 - 10 **Product Groups:** 80

Alan Bridgens Associates
65 Presthope Road, Birmingham, B29 4NL
Tel: 0121-475 6818 **Fax:** 0121-475 6818
Directors: A. Bridgens (Prop)
Date established: 1988 **No.of Employees:** 1 - 10 **Product Groups:** 35

H T Brigham & Co. Ltd
Station Road Coleshill, Birmingham, B46 1JQ
Tel: 01675-463882 **Fax:** 01675-467441
E-mail: enquiries@htbrigham.co.uk
Website: http://www.htbrigham.co.uk
Bank(s): Lloyds TSB Bank plc
Directors: B. Smith (MD)
Managers: P. Tanner (Sales & Mktg Mg)
Ultimate Holding Company: H.T. BRIGHAM & COMPANY (HOLDINGS) LIMITED
Immediate Holding Company: H.T. BRIGHAM & COMPANY LIMITED
Registration no: 00598418 **Date established:** 1947 **Turnover:** £2m - £5m
No.of Employees: 21 - 50 **Product Groups:** 48

Date of Accounts	Apr 12	Apr 11	Apr 10
Working Capital	98	92	278
Fixed Assets	453	518	742
Current Assets	1m	895	873
Current Liabilities	187	N/A	N/A

Brilec Power Tools Ltd
109 Grove Lane Handsworth, Birmingham, B21 9HF
Tel: 0121-554 4989 **Fax:** 0121-554 5488
E-mail: brilecsales@btconnect.com
Directors: G. Stait (Fin), M. Stait (MD)
Immediate Holding Company: BRILEC POWER TOOLS LIMITED
Registration no: 01329572 **VAT No.:** GB 295 9828 83
Date established: 1977 **Turnover:** £500,000 - £1m
No.of Employees: 1 - 10 **Product Groups:** 83

Date of Accounts	Sep 11	Sep 10	Sep 09
Working Capital	14	17	20
Fixed Assets	27	28	30
Current Assets	56	66	66

Bristol Street Birmingham
156-182 Bristol Street, Birmingham, B5 7AZ
Tel: 0121-666 6000 **Fax:** 0121-666 6340
E-mail: martin.leach@bristolstreet.co.uk
Website: http://www.bristolstreetmotors.co.uk
Directors: M. Walsh (Sales)
Managers: M. Croson (Fin Mgr), M. Leach (Chief Mgr), P. Rumbles (Sales Prom Mgr)
Ultimate Holding Company: TED JOHNSON (HOLDINGS) LTD.
Immediate Holding Company: TED JOHNSON VEHICLE MANAGEMENT LIMITED
Registration no: 04214746 **Date established:** 2001
Turnover: £10m - £20m **No.of Employees:** 101 - 250
Product Groups: 39, 68

Date of Accounts	Dec 09	Dec 08	Dec 07
Working Capital	3	3	3
Current Assets	3	3	3

Bristol Street Motors
40 Granby Avenue, Birmingham, B33 0TJ
Tel: 0121-785 3400 **Fax:** 0121-785 3421
E-mail: rob.graver@bristolstreet.co.uk
Website: http://www.bristolstreet.co.uk
Managers: N. Parnelle (Tech Serv Mgr), S. O'Donnell, K. Taylor (Chief Mgr), Z. Wallis
Ultimate Holding Company: TED JOHNSON (HOLDINGS) LTD.
Immediate Holding Company: TED JOHNSON VEHICLE MANAGEMENT LIMITED
Registration no: 04214746 **Date established:** 2001
No.of Employees: 51 - 100 **Product Groups:** 68

Date of Accounts	Oct 11	Oct 10
Working Capital	2	33
Fixed Assets	25	31
Current Assets	2	33

Broadway Brass Ltd
1 Brunswick Industrial Estate Hertford Street, Birmingham, B12 8NJ
Tel: 0121-440 3173 **Fax:** 0121-440 2661
E-mail: sales@broadwaybrass.co.uk
Website: http://www.broadwaybrass.co.uk
Directors: A. Shah (Dir)
Immediate Holding Company: BROADWAY BRASS LIMITED
Registration no: 03142120 **Date established:** 1995
No.of Employees: 11 - 20 **Product Groups:** 32, 46, 48

Date of Accounts	Dec 11	Dec 10	Dec 09
Working Capital	21	16	5
Fixed Assets	18	23	23
Current Assets	156	135	118

Bromwich Insurance Brokers
311a Kingstanding Road, Birmingham, B44 9TH
Tel: 0121-384 8499 **Fax:** 0121-384 2114
E-mail: mikenuttal@btconnect.com
Website: http://www.big4insurance.co.uk
Directors: K. Nuttall (MD)
Managers: E. Simpson (Mgr)
No.of Employees: 1 - 10 **Product Groups:** 82

Brookes & Adams Ltd
Shady Lane, Birmingham, B44 9DX
Tel: 0121-360 1588 **Fax:** 0121-360 1580
E-mail: brookadam@aol.com
Website: http://www.banda.co.uk
Directors: A. Brookes (Fin), J. Brookes (MD)
Immediate Holding Company: BROOKES & ADAMS,LIMITED
Registration no: 00162914 **VAT No.:** GB 109 3145 91
Date established: 2020 **Turnover:** £500,000 - £1m
No.of Employees: 21 - 50 **Product Groups:** 34, 46, 48

Date of Accounts	Dec 11	Dec 10	Dec 09
Working Capital	729	738	719
Fixed Assets	73	71	87
Current Assets	787	806	769

Buck & Hickman Ltd
Unit 9 Spitfire Park Spitfire Road, Birmingham, B24 9PR
Tel: 0121-386 8000 **Fax:** 0121-386 8011
E-mail: birmingham@buckandhickman.com
Website: http://www.buckandhickman.com
Managers: R. Whitehouse (Mgr)
Ultimate Holding Company: TRAVIS PERKINS PLC
Immediate Holding Company: BOSTON (2011) LIMITED
Registration no: 06028304 **Date established:** 2006
No.of Employees: 11 - 20 **Product Groups:** 24, 33, 36, 37, 45, 46, 66

Date of Accounts	Dec 10	Mar 10	Mar 09
Working Capital	6m	6m	6m
Current Assets	27m	27m	27m

Bullet Lift Services
166 Highfield Road Hall Green, Birmingham, B28 0HT
Tel: 0121-258 2214 **Fax:** 0121-258 2214
E-mail: blsbirmingham@msn.com
Website: http://www.bulletliftservices.co.uk
Directors: P. Larkin (MD), R. Larkin (Fin)
Immediate Holding Company: BULLET LIFT SERVICES LIMITED
Registration no: 04689288 **Date established:** 2003
No.of Employees: 1 - 10 **Product Groups:** 35, 39, 45

Date of Accounts	Mar 11	Mar 10	Mar 09
Working Capital	59	65	56
Fixed Assets	11	13	15
Current Assets	126	141	93

Burcas Ltd
Park Lane Handsworth, Birmingham, B21 8LT
Tel: 0121-553 2777 **Fax:** 0121-553 1284
E-mail: info@burcas.co.uk
Website: http://www.burcas.co.uk
Bank(s): Bank of Ireland
Directors: M. Burrows (Fin)
Managers: C. Hayword (Tech Serv Mgr), S. Bounds (Ops Mgr), R. Vicary
Immediate Holding Company: BURCAS LIMITED
Registration no: 00437989 **VAT No.:** GB 110 0020 76
Date established: 1947 **Turnover:** £2m - £5m **No.of Employees:** 51 - 100
Product Groups: 34, 35, 44, 46, 48, 80

Date of Accounts	Mar 11	Mar 10	Mar 09
Sales Turnover	4m	4m	N/A
Pre Tax Profit/Loss	139	-131	140
Working Capital	1m	1m	1m
Fixed Assets	2m	3m	3m
Current Assets	4m	3m	3m
Current Liabilities	326	625	1m

W & M Burden
15-17 Regent Place, Birmingham, B1 3NL
Tel: 0121-236 6686 **Fax:** 0121-236 3252
E-mail: mabuck46@gmail.com
Directors: M. Burden (Ptnr)
Date established: 1988 **No.of Employees:** 1 - 10 **Product Groups:** 46, 48

John Burn & Co Birmingham Ltd
74 Albert Road Stechford, Birmingham, B33 9AJ
Tel: 0121-508 4144 **Fax:** 0121-508 4145
E-mail: info@johnburn.co.uk
Website: http://www.johnburn.co.uk
Bank(s): HSBC, Washwood Heath
Directors: B. Land (MD), F. Hawley (Dir)
Ultimate Holding Company: HALIFAX INDUSTRIAL LIMITED
Immediate Holding Company: JOHN BURN & COMPANY (BIRMINGHAM) LIMITED
Registration no: 00151048 **VAT No.:** GB 109 5317 78
Date established: 2018 **Turnover:** £2m - £5m **No.of Employees:** 11 - 20
Product Groups: 31, 32, 33, 35, 36, 38, 46, 48

Date of Accounts	Mar 08	Sep 11	Sep 10
Working Capital	661	1m	1m
Fixed Assets	677	526	562
Current Assets	1m	2m	2m

Business Post Ltd
Wolseley Drive Heartlands, Birmingham, B8 2SQ
Tel: 0121-335 1000 **Fax:** 0121-335 1003
E-mail: marketing@businesspost.biz
Website: http://www.ukmail.biz
Bank(s): The Royal Bank of Scotland
Directors: A. Ross (Chief Op Offcr), D. Baxter (I.T. Dir), G. Buswell (Comm), P. Kane (Ch)
Managers: C. Spencer, N. Procter (Sales Prom Mgr), S. Glew, D. Ball
Immediate Holding Company: UK Mail Group plc
Registration no: 02283789 **Turnover:** £250m - £500m
No.of Employees: 251 - 500 **Product Groups:** 79

Butler Valves & Fittings Limited
Unit D2
OYO Business Park
187 ParkLane
CastleVale, Birmingham, B35 6AN
Tel: 0121-730 2333 **Fax:** 0121-730 2332
E-mail: sales@butlervalves.co.uk
Website: http://www.butlervalves.co.uk
Directors: R. Butler (MD)
Managers: L. Harris (Sales Admin), G. Worviell (Accounts), D. Butler (Sales Prom Mgr)
Registration no: 00290234 **No.of Employees:** 1 - 10 **Product Groups:** 35, 36, 39, 40, 61, 66, 67

Date of Accounts	Apr 12	Apr 11	Apr 10
Working Capital	166	144	142
Fixed Assets	9	16	18
Current Assets	382	277	301

BUYAPRESS.CO.UK GLOBALINDUSTRIALSERVICES.CO.UK
Unit 7 Paper Mill End Industrial Estate, Birmingham, B44 8NH
Tel: 0121-356 7437 **Fax:** 0121-705 6500
E-mail: martinhodson3@hotmail.com
Website: http://www.buyapress.co.uk
Managers: M. Hodson (Chief Eng)
Immediate Holding Company: DESIGNER APPAREL LIMITED
Date established: 2009 **No.of Employees:** 1 - 10 **Product Groups:** 35, 46, 68

Date of Accounts	Oct 11	Oct 10
Working Capital	N/A	1
Current Assets	N/A	1

C A P Group Of Companies
Head Office The Crescent Hockley, Birmingham, B18 5NL
Tel: 0121-554 9811 **Fax:** 0121-554 3791
E-mail: veronica@capproductions.co.uk
Website: http://www.capproductions.co.uk
Bank(s): HSBC Bank plc

see next page

C A P Group Of Companies - *Cont'd*
Managers: V. Colley
Ultimate Holding Company: J. & G. SMART (HOLDINGS) LIMITED
Immediate Holding Company: C.A.P. PRODUCTIONS LIMITED
Registration no: 00430637 **Date established:** 1947 **Turnover:** £5m - £10m
No.of Employees: 21 - 50 **Product Groups:** 35, 48

Date of Accounts	Mar 11	Mar 10	Mar 09
Working Capital	610	616	661
Fixed Assets	182	188	209
Current Assets	2m	2m	2m

C B Cable Clips
235 Bridge Street West, Birmingham, B19 2YU
Tel: 0121-359 2822 **Fax:** 0121-359 2836
E-mail: info@cbcableclips.com
Website: http://www.cbcableclips.com
Directors: M. McCalister (Prop)
Ultimate Holding Company: Brandauer & Co Ltd
Registration no: 04547640 **Turnover:** £250,000 - £500,000
No.of Employees: 1 - 10 **Product Groups:** 37

C B Frost & Co. Ltd
Green Street, Birmingham, B12 0NE
Tel: 0121-773 8494
E-mail: info@cbfrost-rubber.com
Website: http://www.cbfrost-rubber.com
Bank(s): Barclays, Birmingham South Group
Directors: D. Dunn (Purch), P. Beadle (Comm), P. Kennedy (Tech Serv)
Managers: A. Ross
Ultimate Holding Company: C B FROST HOLDINGS LIMITED
Immediate Holding Company: C.B.FROST & CO LIMITED
Registration no: 00458421 **VAT No.:** GB 110 3284 27
Date established: 1948 **Turnover:** £2m - £5m **No.of Employees:** 21 - 50
Product Groups: 23, 27, 29, 30, 31, 32, 37, 40, 48, 49, 63, 66

Date of Accounts	Jul 11	Jul 10	Jul 09
Working Capital	327	401	395
Fixed Assets	141	109	103
Current Assets	848	998	776

C B Richard Ellis Ltd
Cornwall Court 19 Cornwall Street, Birmingham, B3 2DT
Tel: 0121-609 7666 **Fax:** 0121-233 3986
E-mail: martin.guest@cbre.com
Website: http://www.cbre.com
Directors: M. Guest (MD)
Managers: D. Smith, J. Clifton (Sales Admin)
Ultimate Holding Company: CB RICHARD ELLIS GROUP INC (USA)
Immediate Holding Company: CB RICHARD ELLIS LIMITED
Registration no: 02704074 **Date established:** 1992
No.of Employees: 21 - 50 **Product Groups:** 80

Date of Accounts	Dec 11	Dec 10	Dec 09
Sales Turnover	207m	202m	174m
Pre Tax Profit/Loss	52m	14m	8m
Working Capital	237m	40m	18m
Fixed Assets	120m	117m	124m
Current Assets	394m	187m	144m
Current Liabilities	103m	70m	53m

C D Finishing Ltd
9 Bissell Street, Birmingham, B5 7HP
Tel: 0121-622 3386 **Fax:** 0121-622 3386
E-mail: cdfinishingltd@unicombox.co.uk
Directors: C. Dixon (Jt MD), M. Chapman (Dir), C. Dixon (Ptnr)
Immediate Holding Company: C D FINISHING LIMITED
Registration no: 04497756 **VAT No.:** GB 307 8242 64
Date established: 2002 **Turnover:** Up to £250,000
No.of Employees: 1 - 10 **Product Groups:** 48

Date of Accounts	Mar 10	Mar 09	Mar 08
Working Capital	30	29	12
Fixed Assets	7	10	13
Current Assets	95	88	59

C P B Innovative Technology Ltd
Cameron Price Ltd Charlotte Road, Stirchley, Birmingham, B30 2BT
Tel: 0121-459 2121 **Fax:** 0121-451 2303
Directors: S. Bailey (Fin)
Immediate Holding Company: CPB INNOVATIVE TECHNOLOGY LIMITED
Registration no: 02863644 **Date established:** 1993
Turnover: £250,000 - £500,000 **No.of Employees:** 1 - 10
Product Groups: 29, 30, 31

C 3 Consulting
2 The Hawthorns Woodbridge Road, Birmingham, B13 9DY
Tel: 0121-449 8717 **Fax:** 0121-442 4082
E-mail: contact@c3consulting.co.uk
Website: http://www.c3consulting.co.uk
Directors: L. Jones (Grp Chief Exec)
Immediate Holding Company: C3 CONSULTING LIMITED
Registration no: 02264865 **VAT No.:** GB 487 0973 01
Date established: 1988 **Turnover:** Up to £250,000
No.of Employees: 1 - 10 **Product Groups:** 80, 81

Date of Accounts	Dec 11	Dec 10	Dec 09
Sales Turnover	N/A	N/A	21
Pre Tax Profit/Loss	N/A	N/A	-12
Working Capital	-119	-107	-99
Fixed Assets	9	11	14
Current Assets	6	14	16
Current Liabilities	N/A	N/A	1

C2C Services Ltd
2308 Coventry Road Sheldon, Birmingham, B26 3JZ
Tel: 0121-722 6181
E-mail: post@c2cgroup.co.uk
Website: http://www.c2cservices.co.uk
Managers: D. Godfrey (Chief Mgr)
Ultimate Holding Company: SEVERN TRENT PLC
Immediate Holding Company: SEVERN TRENT COSTAIN SERVICES LIMITED
Registration no: 04052522 **Date established:** 2000
Turnover: £10m - £20m **No.of Employees:** 51 - 100 **Product Groups:** 18

Cameron Price Ltd
1a Charlotte Road Stirchley, Birmingham, B30 2BT
Tel: 0121-459 2121 **Fax:** 0121-451 2303
E-mail: info@cameron-price.co.uk
Website: http://www.cameron-price.co.uk
Bank(s): HSBC Bank plc
Directors: B. Moor (MD), S. Bailey (Fin)
Managers: C. Bennett
Ultimate Holding Company: FORAY 902 LIMITED
Immediate Holding Company: CPB INNOVATIVE TECHNOLOGY LIMITED
Registration no: 02863644 **VAT No.:** GB 670 3124 64
Date established: 1993 **Turnover:** Up to £250,000
No.of Employees: 21 - 50 **Product Groups:** 30, 38, 39, 42, 48

Date of Accounts	Apr 11	Apr 10	Apr 09
Sales Turnover	150	250	154
Pre Tax Profit/Loss	12	118	61
Working Capital	226	216	126
Current Assets	340	323	190
Current Liabilities	2	29	14

Cameron Robb Ltd
48-52 Lombard Street, Birmingham, B12 0QN
Tel: 0121-772 8311 **Fax:** 0121-771 3562
E-mail: cathy@cameron-robb.co.uk
Website: http://www.cameron-robb.co.uk
Bank(s): Barclays
Directors: C. Barnes (Comm)
Immediate Holding Company: CAMERON ROBB LIMITED
Registration no: 00509951 **VAT No.:** GB 109 5083 77
Date established: 1952 **No.of Employees:** 21 - 50 **Product Groups:** 35, 66

Date of Accounts	Dec 11	Dec 10	Dec 09
Sales Turnover	2m	3m	2m
Pre Tax Profit/Loss	98	157	37
Working Capital	560	509	522
Fixed Assets	758	829	634
Current Assets	953	971	1m
Current Liabilities	162	128	103

Camp Steels Ltd
29 Grafton Road Sparkbrook, Birmingham, B11 1JP
Tel: 0121-772 7821 **Fax:** 0121-771 0435
E-mail: dave-campsteel@btconnect.com
Website: http://www.campsteel.co.uk
Bank(s): National Westminster Bank Plc
Directors: J. Ratledge (MD)
Immediate Holding Company: MARSTON FABRICATIONS LTD
Registration no: 11170471 **VAT No.:** GB 111 7047 15
Date established: 2011 **Turnover:** £1m - £2m **No.of Employees:** 11 - 20
Product Groups: 48, 66

Date of Accounts	Jun 12
Working Capital	3
Fixed Assets	4
Current Assets	32

Camsierra Ltd
6 Rear of 34 Heath Green Road, Birmingham, B18 4EZ
Tel: 0798-990 5288
E-mail: zjalloh@aol.com
Directors: T. Ayukonchong (Fin), Z. Jalloh (Dir)
Immediate Holding Company: CAMSIERRA LIMITED
Registration no: 06426568 **Date established:** 2007
No.of Employees: 1 - 10 **Product Groups:** 02, 20

Cannon.Co.Uk
214-224 Barr Street, Birmingham, B19 3AG
Tel: 0121-551 4131 **Fax:** 0121-554 9292
E-mail: peter.cannon@cannon.co.uk
Website: http://www.cannon.co.uk
Directors: P. Cannon (Prop)
Immediate Holding Company: A.T. Cannon Ltd
VAT No.: GB 580 3226 57 **Date established:** 1972
No.of Employees: 1 - 10 **Product Groups:** 33, 49

Cap Gemini
1 Avenue Road Aston, Birmingham, B6 4DU
Tel: 0121-333 3536 **Fax:** 0121-333 3308
E-mail: info@capgemini.co.uk
Website: http://www.capgemini.com
Directors: C. Williams (Grp Chief Exec)
Immediate Holding Company: CGS HOLDINGS LTD
Registration no: 00943935 **Turnover:** £125m - £250m
No.of Employees: 1 - 10 **Product Groups:** 44, 84, 86

Capture Services
397 Barrows Lane Sheldon, Birmingham, B26 1QQ
Tel: 0121-288 4110
E-mail: info@capture-services.co.uk
Website: http://www.clocking-machine.com
Directors: A. Meaking (Prop)
Date established: 2003 **No.of Employees:** 1 - 10 **Product Groups:** 67

Carbide Dies B'Ham
5 Port Hope Road, Birmingham, B11 1JS
Tel: 0121-772 0817 **Fax:** 0121-773 9342
E-mail: sales@ctr-uk.com
Website: http://www.ctr-uk.com
Managers: G. Tyler (Mgr)
Ultimate Holding Company: HERON GREEN LIMITED
Immediate Holding Company: CARBIDE DIES (BIRMINGHAM) LIMITED
Registration no: 01599587 **VAT No.:** GB 705 3305 71
Date established: 1981 **Turnover:** £2m - £5m **No.of Employees:** 21 - 50
Product Groups: 31, 34, 36, 42, 44, 46

Date of Accounts	Dec 11	Dec 10	Dec 09
Working Capital	557	546	917
Fixed Assets	312	159	176
Current Assets	1m	1m	2m

Carlzeiss Vision
Unit 9 Holford Way, Holford, Birmingham, B6 7AX
Tel: 08453-007788 **Fax:** 0121-356 7678
E-mail: marketing@vision.zeiss.com
Website: http://www.vision.zeiss.com
Bank(s): Natwest
Directors: P. Green (Fin), A. Leonson (MD), P. Robertson (Mkt Research)
Managers: J. Nock, V. Lancaster, T. Delaney (Personnel)
Ultimate Holding Company: CARL ZEISS AG (GERMANY)
Immediate Holding Company: CARL ZEISS VISION UK LIMITED
Registration no: 02838963 **Date established:** 1993
Turnover: £20m - £50m **No.of Employees:** 51 - 100 **Product Groups:** 33

Date of Accounts	Sep 11	Sep 10	Sep 09
Sales Turnover	35m	37m	32m
Pre Tax Profit/Loss	2m	16m	5m
Working Capital	23m	22m	-3m
Fixed Assets	374	422	9m
Current Assets	58m	57m	37m
Current Liabilities	3m	4m	2m

Carrtech Engineering Products (Raffle Court Ltd)
Crossfield Road, Birmingham, B33 9HP
Tel: 0121-683 2600 **Fax:** 0121-683 2601
E-mail: sales@carrtech.com
Website: http://www.carrtech.com
Bank(s): National Westminster Bank Plc
Directors: S. Carr (MD), A. Carr (Fin)
Managers: R. Angle
Immediate Holding Company: CARRTECH LIMITED
Registration no: SC119826 **Date established:** 1989 **Turnover:** £1m - £2m
No.of Employees: 21 - 50 **Product Groups:** 46, 48

Date of Accounts	Sep 11	Sep 10	Sep 09
Working Capital	-4	N/A	-2
Fixed Assets	9	12	16
Current Assets	17	16	16

Cartel Communications Ltd
Radio House 15 Sutton Street, Birmingham, B1 1PG
Tel: 0121-622 5555 **Fax:** 0121-622 3328
E-mail: sales@cartel.co.uk
Website: http://www.cartel.co.uk
Directors: I. Sharratt (MD)
Immediate Holding Company: CARTEL COMMUNICATIONS LIMITED
Registration no: 05087055 **Date established:** 2004
No.of Employees: 11 - 20 **Product Groups:** 37, 44, 79

Carter Ceramics
627 Kingsbury Road Erdington Erdington, Birmingham, B24 9PP
Tel: 0121-350 8086 **Fax:** 0121-350 8175
E-mail: estimating@carterceramics.co.uk
Website: http://www.carterceramics.co.uk
Managers: R. Suckling
Immediate Holding Company: CARTER CERAMICS NORTHERN LIMITED
Registration no: 07518415 **Date established:** 2011 **Turnover:**
No.of Employees: 51 - 100 **Product Groups:** 33, 52

Carter Retail Equipment Ltd
90 Lea Ford Road, Birmingham, B33 9TX
Tel: 0121-250 1111 **Fax:** 0121-250 1122
E-mail: info@cre-ltd.co.uk
Website: http://www.cre-ltd.co.uk
Bank(s): Barclays
Directors: N. Gardener (MD), N. Gardiner (MD), A. Santer (Fin)
Managers: K. Northall (Personnel), J. Downes (Purch Mgr), G. McInerney (Tech Serv Mgr)
Ultimate Holding Company: LONGDON ESTATES LIMITED
Immediate Holding Company: CARTER RETAIL EQUIPMENT LIMITED
Registration no: 00618898 **VAT No.:** GB 109 7690 43
Date established: 1959 **Turnover:** £20m - £50m
No.of Employees: 251 - 500 **Product Groups:** 26, 40, 41, 44, 48, 49, 66, 67

Date of Accounts	Dec 11	Dec 10	Dec 09
Sales Turnover	39m	34m	26m
Pre Tax Profit/Loss	2m	1m	-452
Working Capital	3m	2m	925
Fixed Assets	2m	2m	2m
Current Assets	10m	11m	8m
Current Liabilities	2m	2m	1m

Carter Thermal Industries Ltd
Redhill Road Hay Mills, Yardley, Birmingham, B25 8EY
Tel: 0121-250 1000 **Fax:** 0121-250 1005
E-mail: reception@cti-ltd.co.uk
Website: http://www.cartersynergy.co.uk
Bank(s): Barclays, Colmore Row
Directors: A. Bews (Pers), J. Scott (Dir)
Managers: J. Askew (Tech Serv Mgr)
Ultimate Holding Company: LONGDON ESTATES LIMITED
Immediate Holding Company: LONGDON ESTATES LIMITED
Registration no: 00502673 **VAT No.:** GB 109 7690 46
Date established: 1951 **Turnover:** £75m - £125m
No.of Employees: 501 - 1000 **Product Groups:** 40, 42, 48, 54, 84, 85

Date of Accounts	Dec 11	Dec 10	Dec 09
Sales Turnover	110m	104m	93m
Pre Tax Profit/Loss	3m	3m	1m
Working Capital	17m	16m	16m
Fixed Assets	12m	13m	12m
Current Assets	36m	39m	32m
Current Liabilities	7m	6m	4m

Castors & Wheel Direct Ltd
Unit C 98-104 Lombard Street, Birmingham, B12 0QR
Tel: 0121-622 4007 **Fax:** 0121-622 4006
E-mail: castors2@btinternet.com
Website: http://www.cwdl.co.uk
Directors: Z. Hussein (Prop)
Immediate Holding Company: CASTORS AND WHEELS DIRECT LIMITED
Registration no: 03601326 **Date established:** 1998
Turnover: £250,000 - £500,000 **No.of Employees:** 1 - 10
Product Groups: 30, 35, 39, 66

Date of Accounts	Jul 11	Jul 10	Jul 09
Working Capital	-186	-209	-212
Fixed Assets	317	321	315
Current Assets	262	220	217

Catering Suppliers
PO Box 12976, Birmingham, B6 7AP
Tel: 0121-331 4200 **Fax:** 0121-331 4200
E-mail: sales@chefset.co.uk
Website: http://www.catering-suppliers.com
Directors: V. Korotane (MD)
Immediate Holding Company: B M S COOKWARE LTD
Registration no: 02561944 **VAT No.:** GB 555 2946 19
Turnover: £2m - £5m **No.of Employees:** 1 - 10 **Product Groups:** 36

Catton Control Cables Ltd
33-35 Kings Road Yardley, Birmingham, B25 8JB
Tel: 0121-772 4297 **Fax:** 0121-766 6075
E-mail: rich@catton.co.uk
Website: http://www.catton.co.uk
Bank(s): HSBC Bank plc
Directors: R. Catton (Dir)
Ultimate Holding Company: CATTON HOLDINGS LIMITED
Immediate Holding Company: CATTON CONTROL CABLES LIMITED
Registration no: 00597288 **VAT No.:** GB 109 4089 70
Date established: 1958 **Turnover:** £2m - £5m **No.of Employees:** 21 - 50
Product Groups: 35, 39, 41

Date of Accounts	Jul 11	Jul 10	Jul 09
Working Capital	123	114	117
Fixed Assets	20	28	20
Current Assets	2m	1m	930

CCR UK Ltd A division of CCR SAS France

129 Sydenham Road, Birmingham, B11 1DG
Tel: 0121-766 8401 **Fax:** 0121-766 8407
E-mail: atran@ccrcontainers.com
Website: http://www.ccr-sa.fr
Registration no: 03877621 **No.of Employees:** 1 - 10 **Product Groups:** 35, 42, 76

Central Autotech

29 Freeth Street, Birmingham, B16 0QN
Tel: 0121-455 8392 **Fax:** 0121-455 8392
Directors: H. Shemar (Prop)
No.of Employees: 1 - 10 **Product Groups:** 39

Central Diesel

Unit 18 Erdington Industrial Park Chester Road, Birmingham, B24 0RD
Tel: 0121-386 1700 **Fax:** 0121-386 1744
E-mail: chris.key@central-diesel.co.uk
Website: http://www.central-diesel.co.uk
Directors: G. Knox (MD)
Managers: C. Key (District Mgr), C. Key (Mgr)
Ultimate Holding Company: Turner Group of Companies
Immediate Holding Company: Mitchell Diesel Ltd
Registration no: 01179564 **VAT No.:** GB 118 2891 60
Turnover: £5m - £10m **No.of Employees:** 21 - 50 **Product Groups:** 40

Centresoft Ltd

6 Pavilion Drive Holford, Birmingham, B6 7BB
Tel: 0121-625 3388 **Fax:** 0121-625 3236
E-mail: sales@centresoft.co.uk
Website: http://www.centresoft.co.uk
Bank(s): Bank of Scotland
Managers: L. Harston (Sales Prom Mgr)
Ultimate Holding Company: VIVENDI SA (FRANCE)
Immediate Holding Company: CENTRESOFT LIMITED
Registration no: 01673860 **VAT No.:** GB 580 7155 34
Date established: 1982 **Turnover:** £250m - £500m
No.of Employees: 101 - 250 **Product Groups:** 44, 49

Date of Accounts	Dec 11	Dec 10	Dec 09
Sales Turnover	276m	254m	279m
Pre Tax Profit/Loss	8m	9m	18m
Working Capital	32m	27m	24m
Fixed Assets	1m	987	808
Current Assets	113m	92m	89m
Current Liabilities	4m	7m	8m

Certus UK Ltd

Unit 45 Gravelly Industrial Park, Birmingham, B24 8TG
Tel: 0121-327 5362 **Fax:** 0121-328 2934
E-mail: info@certuss.demon.co.uk
Website: http://www.certus.co.uk
Directors: D. Ward (MD)
Managers: R. Timmins (Sales Prom Mgr)
Ultimate Holding Company: CERTUSS GROUP HOLDINGS LIMITED
Immediate Holding Company: CERTUSS (UK) LIMITED
Registration no: 02405483 **Date established:** 1989
Turnover: £500,000 - £1m **No.of Employees:** 1 - 10 **Product Groups:** 40, 83

Date of Accounts	Dec 09	Dec 08	Apr 11
Working Capital	66	83	2
Fixed Assets	55	43	72
Current Assets	626	990	623

Chambers & Cook Frieght Ltd

Perrywell Road Witton, Birmingham, B6 7AT
Tel: 0121-356 1441 **Fax:** 0121-356 7880
E-mail: julie-anne@ccfreight.com
Website: http://www.ccfreight.com
Bank(s): Barclays
Directors: P. Blackburn (MD)
Ultimate Holding Company: CHAMBERS AND COOK (EUROPEAN SERVICES) LIMITED
Immediate Holding Company: CHAMBERS AND COOK (EUROPEAN SERVICES) LIMITED
Registration no: 00938984 **VAT No.:** GB 109 5450 76
Date established: 1968 **Turnover:** £10m - £20m
No.of Employees: 51 - 100 **Product Groups:** 72, 76

Date of Accounts	Sep 11	Sep 10	Sep 09
Sales Turnover	19m	15m	11m
Pre Tax Profit/Loss	676	333	126
Working Capital	855	1m	886
Fixed Assets	5m	3m	4m
Current Assets	5m	4m	3m
Current Liabilities	1m	713	586

Channelglaze Ltd

21a Rushey Lane, Birmingham, B11 2BL
Tel: 0121-706 5777 **Fax:** 0121-706 7177
E-mail: enquiry@channelglaze.com
Website: http://www.channelglaze.com
Directors: D. Pearson (Dir), J. Pearson (Co Sec)
Immediate Holding Company: CHANNELGLAZE LIMITED
Registration no: 05211090 **Date established:** 2004
No.of Employees: 1 - 10 **Product Groups:** 26, 35

Date of Accounts	Aug 11	Aug 10	Aug 09
Working Capital	-12	-23	-25
Fixed Assets	24	25	29
Current Assets	67	35	57

Charles Neal Birmingham Ltd

Boulton Industrial Centre Icknield Street, Hockley, Birmingham, B18 5AU
Tel: 0121-554 4344 **Fax:** 0121-554 0888
E-mail: sales@charlesneal.co.uk
Website: http://www.charlesneal.co.uk
Directors: S. Turley (Dir)
Immediate Holding Company: CHARLES NEAL BIRMINGHAM LIMITED
Registration no: 07508690 **VAT No.:** GB 229 2341 74
Date established: 2011 **Turnover:** £500,000 - £1m
No.of Employees: 1 - 10 **Product Groups:** 30, 35, 48, 49

Chidlow & Cheshire Ltd

Steward Street, Birmingham, B18 7AE
Tel: 0121-454 1003 **Fax:** 0121-456 3935
E-mail: chidlow@btconnect.com
Directors: G. Chidlow (MD), R. Chidlow (Dir)
Immediate Holding Company: CHIDLOW & CHESHIRE LIMITED
Registration no: 00264229 **Date established:** 1932
Turnover: £500,000 - £1m **No.of Employees:** 1 - 10 **Product Groups:** 37, 48

Date of Accounts	Mar 11	Mar 10	Mar 09
Working Capital	163	169	150
Fixed Assets	103	159	163
Current Assets	216	213	221

Citroen Birmingham

100 Small Heath Highway, Birmingham, B10 0BT
Tel: 0121-766 7060 **Fax:** 0121-766 7042
E-mail: sisav@supanet.com
Website: http://www.citroen-birmingham.co.uk
Managers: J. Bishop, R. Laidler (Chief Mgr)
No.of Employees: 1 - 10 **Product Groups:** 39, 45, 68, 72

Clifton Steel Ltd

122 Fazeley Industrial Estate Fazeley Street, Birmingham, B5 5RS
Tel: 0121-603 4000 **Fax:** 0121-603 4001
E-mail: sales@cliftonsteel.co.uk
Website: http://www.cliftonsteel.co.uk
Bank(s): T.S.B.
Directors: R. Shafi (Dir), R. Shafi (Dir), S. Holland (Co Sec), Z. Holland (Co Sec)
Immediate Holding Company: CLIFTON STEEL LIMITED
Registration no: 01179413 **Date established:** 1974 **Turnover:** £5m - £10m
No.of Employees: 11 - 20 **Product Groups:** 34, 77

Date of Accounts	Dec 09	Sep 11	Sep 10
Sales Turnover	9m	N/A	N/A
Pre Tax Profit/Loss	-129	N/A	N/A
Working Capital	553	416	700
Fixed Assets	507	397	473
Current Assets	1m	2m	2m
Current Liabilities	88	N/A	N/A

Climatize Upvc Windows

Shady Lane, Birmingham, B44 9ER
Tel: 0121-325 1792 **Fax:** 0121-325 1799
Website: http://www.climatizewindows.co.uk
Directors: N. Bartlam (Prop)
Immediate Holding Company: FLITZ HAIR & BEAUTY LIMITED
Registration no: 06027289 **Date established:** 2008
Turnover: £250,000 - £500,000 **No.of Employees:** 1 - 10
Product Groups: 25, 30, 35, 39

Date of Accounts	Jul 11	Jul 10	Jul 09
Working Capital	-25	-29	-22
Fixed Assets	7	10	13
Current Assets	13	10	10

Coleman & Co.

Shady Lane, Birmingham, B44 9ER
Tel: 0121-325 2424 **Fax:** 0121-325 2425
E-mail: contracts@coleman-co.com
Website: http://www.coleman-co.com
Managers: J. Harrod (Mgr), M. Reid (Personnel), J. Kirwan
Ultimate Holding Company: CNC GROUP HOLDINGS LIMITED
Immediate Holding Company: COLEMAN & COMPANY LIMITED
Registration no: 00737922 **Date established:** 1962
Turnover: £10m - £20m **No.of Employees:** 51 - 100 **Product Groups:** 14, 32, 36, 45, 51, 54, 66, 72, 84, 86

Date of Accounts	Apr 12	Apr 11	Apr 10
Sales Turnover	15m	17m	11m
Pre Tax Profit/Loss	564	514	-889
Working Capital	2m	2m	1m
Fixed Assets	5m	5m	5m
Current Assets	5m	6m	4m
Current Liabilities	1m	981	513

Coleshill Aluminium Ltd

Gorsey Lane Coleshill, Birmingham, B46 1JU
Tel: 01675-463170 **Fax:** 01675-463748
E-mail: office@coleshill-aluminium.com
Website: http://www.yearsley.co.uk
Bank(s): Barclays, Coleshill
Directors: A. Evans (Sales), A. Evans (Dir), D. Evans (MD), R. Evans (Dir)
Managers: A. Evans (Fin Mgr)
Immediate Holding Company: COLESHILL ALUMINIUM LIMITED
Registration no: 00585158 **VAT No.:** GB 584 9575 75
Date established: 1957 **Turnover:** £10m - £20m
No.of Employees: 21 - 50 **Product Groups:** 34

Date of Accounts	Aug 11	Aug 10	Aug 09
Sales Turnover	14m	12m	7m
Pre Tax Profit/Loss	254	275	34
Working Capital	3m	2m	2m
Fixed Assets	203	185	185
Current Assets	6m	5m	5m
Current Liabilities	2m	2m	2m

Coleshill Freight Services Ltd

Coleshill Freight Terminal Station Road, Coleshill, Birmingham, B46 1JJ
Tel: 01675-463869 **Fax:** 01675-465727
E-mail: andrewwilliams@dangerousgoodspacking.com
Website: http://www.coleshillfreight.com
Directors: A. Williams (Dir)
Immediate Holding Company: COLESHILL FREIGHT SERVICES LIMITED
Registration no: 02197260 **VAT No.:** GB 487 4022 34
Date established: 1987 **Turnover:** £2m - £5m **No.of Employees:** 11 - 20
Product Groups: 76

Date of Accounts	Mar 11	Mar 10	Mar 09
Working Capital	70	51	38
Fixed Assets	9	12	20
Current Assets	291	195	205

Computronic Controls Ltd

41-46 Railway Terrace Nechells, Birmingham, B7 5NG
Tel: 0121-327 8500 **Fax:** 0121-327 8501
E-mail: sales@computroniccontrols.com
Website: http://www.computroniccontrols.com
Directors: P. Gay (MD)
Managers: T. Kimber (Personnel), C. Rattlidge (Buyer), N. Rattlidge (Design Mgr)
Ultimate Holding Company: MURPHY INDUSTRIES INC (USA)
Immediate Holding Company: COMPUTRONIC CONTROLS LIMITED
Registration no: 01779131 **VAT No.:** GB 371 6128 59
Date established: 1983 **Turnover:** £1m - £2m **No.of Employees:** 21 - 50
Product Groups: 37, 38

Concrete Developments Great Barr Ltd

Baltimore Road, Birmingham, B42 1DD
Tel: 0121-356 5575 **Fax:** 0121-344 3285
E-mail: sales@concretedevelopments.com
Website: http://www.concretedevelopments.com
Directors: I. Thorneywork (MD)
Immediate Holding Company: CONCRETE DEVELOPMENTS (GREAT BARR) LIMITED
Registration no: 00488576 **VAT No.:** GB 109 4843 62
Date established: 1950 **Turnover:** £1m - £2m **No.of Employees:** 1 - 10
Product Groups: 33, 66

Date of Accounts	Oct 11	Oct 10	Oct 09
Working Capital	48	39	42
Fixed Assets	1m	1m	1m
Current Assets	275	302	350

Connaught Resourcing

111 Hagley Road, Birmingham, B16 8LB
Tel: 0121-452 5117 **Fax:** 0121-452 5118
E-mail: enquiries@connaughteducation.com
Website: http://www.connaught-resourcing.com
Directors: A. O'Neill (Dir), S. Aston (Dir)
Managers: L. Tulloch, R. Condon, S. Jackson (Tech Serv Mgr)
Immediate Holding Company: CONNAUGHT PARTNERS LIMITED
Registration no: 04054587 **Date established:** 2000 **Turnover:** £1m - £2m
No.of Employees: 21 - 50 **Product Groups:** 80

Date of Accounts	Dec 11	Dec 10	Dec 09
Working Capital	1	37	31
Fixed Assets	N/A	2	7
Current Assets	5	135	100

Connect Distibution

Medco House Connect Business Park Bordesley Green Road, Birmingham, B9 4UA
Tel: 08704-423700 **Fax:** 0121-766 7138
E-mail: sales@connect-distribution.co.uk
Website: http://www.connect-distribution.co.uk
Directors: M. Depper (Prop)
Immediate Holding Company: ELECTRUEPART LTD
Registration no: 03004798 **VAT No.:** GB 655 1290 41
Date established: 1994 **Turnover:** £50m - £75m
No.of Employees: 501 - 1000 **Product Groups:** 30, 33, 35, 37, 40, 45, 67, 85

Contacto Ltd

Unit 3 Key Business Park Kingsbury Road, Erdington, Birmingham, B24 9PT
Tel: 0121-605 5522 **Fax:** 0121-605 5523
E-mail: info@contacto.co.uk
Website: http://www.contacto.co.uk
Directors: S. Goodliff (Fin)
Ultimate Holding Company: CONTACTO BANDER GMBH (GERMANY)
Immediate Holding Company: CONTACTO LIMITED
Registration no: 02728674 **Date established:** 1992
Turnover: £500,000 - £1m **No.of Employees:** 1 - 10 **Product Groups:** 67

Date of Accounts	Dec 11	Dec 10	Dec 09
Working Capital	480	401	343
Fixed Assets	5	7	8
Current Assets	607	504	443

The Control Shop

19 Stockmans Close Bilton Indus Trial Estate, Birmingham, B38 9TS
Tel: 0121-451 1030 **Fax:** 0121-459 1511
E-mail: sales@controlshop.co.uk
Website: http://www.controlshop.co.uk
Bank(s): Barclays
Directors: J. Hare (Fin), N. Fonyodi (Prop)
Immediate Holding Company: THE CONTROL SHOP LIMITED
Registration no: 03132753 **VAT No.:** GB 669 5760 76
Date established: 1995 **Turnover:** £250,000 - £500,000
No.of Employees: 11 - 20 **Product Groups:** 38

Date of Accounts	Dec 11	Dec 10	Dec 09
Working Capital	131	93	85
Fixed Assets	12	17	23
Current Assets	253	210	209

Conway Precision Engineering Ltd

106 Tame Road, Birmingham, B6 7EZ
Tel: 0121-327 2301 **Fax:** 0121-328 4885
E-mail: cliff@gauges.co.uk
Website: http://www.gauges.co.uk
Bank(s): HSBC Bank plc
Directors: C. Connick (MD)
Immediate Holding Company: CONWAY PRECISION ENGINEERING GROUP LIMITED
Registration no: 00715589 **VAT No.:** GB 109 4305 90
Date established: 1962 **Turnover:** £250,000 - £500,000
No.of Employees: 11 - 20 **Product Groups:** 38, 46, 48

Date of Accounts	Apr 12	Apr 11	Apr 10
Working Capital	104	34	-1
Fixed Assets	99	72	40
Current Assets	326	244	251

Cookson Precious Metals Ltd

59-83 Vittoria Street, Birmingham, B1 3NZ
Tel: 0121-200 3232 **Fax:** 0121-200 3222
E-mail: richard.powers@cooksongold.com
Website: http://www.cooksongold.com
Bank(s): Lloyds TSB Bank plc
Directors: R. Powers (Dir)
Ultimate Holding Company: COOKSON GROUP PLC
Immediate Holding Company: COOKSON PRECIOUS METALS LIMITED
Registration no: 02775187 **VAT No.:** GB 614 1113 00
Date established: 1993 **Turnover:** £50m - £75m
No.of Employees: 101 - 250 **Product Groups:** 31

Date of Accounts	Dec 11	Dec 10	Dec 09
Sales Turnover	55m	57m	59m
Pre Tax Profit/Loss	2m	2m	2m
Working Capital	14m	9m	6m
Fixed Assets	3m	6m	6m
Current Assets	20m	19m	15m
Current Liabilities	3m	3m	2m

Coopers

69 Sydenham Road, Birmingham, B11 1DG
Tel: 0121-693 1405 **Fax:** 0121- 6931406
Directors: G. Cooper (Dir)
Date established: 1999 **No.of Employees:** 1 - 10 **Product Groups:** 46

Coopers Needleworks Ltd
261-265 Aston Lane Handsworth, Birmingham, B20 3HS
Tel: 0121-356 4719 **Fax:** 0121-356 3050
E-mail: sales@coopersnw.com
Website: http://www.finestainlesstube.com
Bank(s): Barclays, Birmingham
Directors: L. Saunders (Co Sec), K. Saunders (Dir)
Ultimate Holding Company: SAUNROW LIMITED
Immediate Holding Company: COOPERS NEEDLE WORKS LIMITED
Registration no: 00315430 **Date established:** 1936
Turnover: £500,000 - £1m **No.of Employees:** 11 - 20 **Product Groups:** 38

Date of Accounts	Feb 08	Feb 11	Feb 10
Working Capital	370	426	347
Fixed Assets	47	67	60
Current Assets	444	539	446

Corporate Media Supplies Ltd
Centre Court 1301 Stratford Road, Hall Green, Birmingham, B28 9HH
Tel: 0121-702 1445 **Fax:** 0121-608 1445
E-mail: sales@corporate-media.co.uk
Website: http://www.corporate-media.co.uk
Directors: G. Tanner (Fin)
Immediate Holding Company: CORPORATE MEDIA SUPPLIES LIMITED
Registration no: 02739656 **Date established:** 1992
Turnover: £250,000 - £500,000 **No.of Employees:** 1 - 10
Product Groups: 44, 49

Date of Accounts	Dec 11	Dec 10	Dec 09
Working Capital	344	313	281
Fixed Assets	4	7	9
Current Assets	713	662	667

Craig Anthony Productions
15 Haunch Close, Birmingham, B13 0PZ
Tel: 07730-577404
E-mail: info@craiganthonyproductions.co.uk
Website: http://www.craiganthonyproductions.co.uk
Directors: C. Anthony (Prop)
Registration no: 06540925 **Date established:** 2008
No.of Employees: 1 - 10 **Product Groups:** 38, 81, 89

Crane Care Ltd
50 Avenue Road Aston, Birmingham, B6 4DY
Tel: 0121-333 3995 **Fax:** 0121-333 3996
E-mail: sales@cranecare.ltd.uk
Website: http://www.cranecare.ltd.uk
Directors: S. Evans (Dir), G. Handy (Dir)
Immediate Holding Company: CRANE CARE LIMITED
Registration no: 03450411 **Date established:** 1997 **Turnover:** £2m - £5m
No.of Employees: 21 - 50 **Product Groups:** 45, 67, 85

Date of Accounts	Dec 11	Dec 10	Dec 09
Working Capital	624	522	457
Fixed Assets	232	276	294
Current Assets	1m	1m	1m

Cranlea & Co.
Sandpit Acacia Road, Birmingham, B30 2AH
Tel: 0121-472 0361 **Fax:** 0121-472 6262
E-mail: info@cranlea.co.uk
Website: http://www.cranlea.co.uk
Directors: S. Skett (Ptnr)
Immediate Holding Company: CRANLEA HUMAN PERFORMANCE LIMITED
Registration no: 07869243 **Date established:** 2011
No.of Employees: 1 - 10 **Product Groups:** 38, 67

Paul Craythorne Associates
50 Boswell Road Kingstanding, Birmingham, B44 8EH
Tel: 07779-516462 **Fax:** 0121-270 1212
E-mail: paulc@pcraythorne.co.uk
Website: http://www.pcraythorne.co.uk
Directors: P. Craythorne (Ptnr), K. Craythorne (Ptnr)
Turnover: Up to £250,000 **No.of Employees:** 1 - 10 **Product Groups:** 54, 84

Croft & Assinder Ltd
95 Lombard Street, Birmingham, B12 0QU
Tel: 0121-622 1074 **Fax:** 0121-622 5718
E-mail: general@crofts.co.uk
Website: http://www.crofts.co.uk
Bank(s): HSBC Bank plc
Directors: T. Bird (Sales & Mktg)
Managers: L. Hazelton (Fin Mgr), A. Croft, M. Shaunasey (Purch Mgr), L. Hazelton (Fin Mgr)
Ultimate Holding Company: CROFTS & ASSINDER HOLDINGS LIMITED
Immediate Holding Company: CROFTS & ASSINDER LIMITED
Registration no: 01237954 **VAT No.:** GB 487 2043 36
Date established: 1975 **No.of Employees:** 11 - 20 **Product Groups:** 36

Date of Accounts	Mar 11	Mar 10	Mar 09
Working Capital	673	656	607
Fixed Assets	41	39	31
Current Assets	1m	1m	1m

Cross Channel Time Critical
Impex House Garretts Green Trading Estate Valepits Road, Birmingham, B33 0TD
Tel: 0121-683 1100 **Fax:** 0121-683 1176
E-mail: xchannelfrt@ukonline.co.uk
Website: http://www.cross-channel.com
Directors: G. Tamana (Dir), L. Thomas (MD)
Managers: L. Powell (Ops Mgr)
Ultimate Holding Company: THOMAS PLANT (BIRMINGHAM) LIMITED
Immediate Holding Company: RGF LOGISTICS BIRMINGHAM LIMITED
Registration no: 00219394 **Date established:** 2001
Turnover: £250,000 - £500,000 **No.of Employees:** 1 - 10
Product Groups: 74, 76

Date of Accounts	Mar 11	Mar 09	Mar 08
Working Capital	168	65	102
Current Assets	484	119	434

Cross Huller UK Ltd
Fourth Floor Fort Dunlop Fort Parkway, Birmingham, B24 9FD
Tel: 0121-306 5600
Registration no: 05567165 **Date established:** 2005
No.of Employees: 51 - 100 **Product Groups:** 45, 46, 67

Cross & Morse
Shady Lane Great Barr, Birmingham, B44 9EU
Tel: 0121-360 0155 **Fax:** 0121-325 1079
E-mail: sales@crossmorse.com
Website: http://www.crossmorse.com
Bank(s): Barclays Bank PLC
Directors: D. Shadbolt (MD), M. Scudamore (Comm)
Managers: D. Wordley (Export Sales Mg), P. Pearson (Buyer), C. Till (Prod Mgr), D. Keatley (Sales Prom Mgr), A. Bone (Tech Serv Mgr), P. Wheeler (Sales Prom Mgr)
Ultimate Holding Company: Cross Holdings Ltd
Registration no: 01631813 **VAT No.:** GB 377 3361 32
Date established: 1982 **Turnover:** £2m - £5m **No.of Employees:** 51 - 100
Product Groups: 35, 38, 41, 43, 45, 46

Date of Accounts	Dec 11	Dec 10	Dec 09
Working Capital	783	511	310
Fixed Assets	1m	1m	2m
Current Assets	2m	2m	2m

T D Cross Ltd
Shady Lane Great Barr, Birmingham, B44 9EU
Tel: 0121-360 0155 **Fax:** 0121-325 1079
E-mail: accounts@cross-morse.co.uk
Website: http://www.crossmorse.com
Bank(s): HSBC
Directors: D. Shadbolt (Fin), D. Shadbolt (MD), M. Harris (MD)
Managers: A. Bone (Export Sales Mg), M. Scudamore (I.T. Exec), P. Rowan (Mgr)
Ultimate Holding Company: CROSS HOLDINGS LIMITED
Immediate Holding Company: T.D. CROSS LIMITED
Registration no: 01631813 **Date established:** 1982 **Turnover:** £2m - £5m
No.of Employees: 51 - 100 **Product Groups:** 35

Date of Accounts	Dec 10	Dec 09	Dec 08
Pre Tax Profit/Loss	N/A	N/A	303
Working Capital	511	310	279
Fixed Assets	1m	2m	2m
Current Assets	2m	2m	2m
Current Liabilities	N/A	N/A	316

Crowncom Ltd
109 Clifton Road Sparkbrook, Birmingham, B12 8SR
Tel: 0121-449 7111 **Fax:** 0121-449 7222
E-mail: shop@crowncom.ltd.uk
Website: http://www.crowncom.ltd.uk
Managers: I. Simjee (Sales Prom Mgr), S. Simjee (Export Sales Mg)
Registration no: 02768533 **Turnover:** £2m - £5m
No.of Employees: 11 - 20 **Product Groups:** 36, 63

Date of Accounts	Mar 10	Mar 09	Mar 08
Working Capital	64	59	62
Fixed Assets	78	79	78
Current Assets	151	145	159

Croy Glass Fibre Products
3 Lower Dartmouth Street, Birmingham, B9 4LG
Tel: 0121-773 8714 **Fax:** 0121-773 8714
Directors: P. Fox (Ptnr)
Turnover: Up to £250,000 **No.of Employees:** 1 - 10 **Product Groups:** 30

G M Cruxton
55 Price Street, Birmingham, B4 6JZ
Tel: 0121-359 6806 **Fax:** 0121-359 6806
Directors: G. Cruxton (Prop)
Date established: 1971 **No.of Employees:** 1 - 10 **Product Groups:** 36, 39, 40

Crystal Occasions
32 Silver Birch Drive Hollywood, Birmingham, B47 5RB
Tel: 0121-474 2143 **Fax:** 0121-474 2143
E-mail: sales@crystaloccasions.co.uk
Website: http://www.crystaloccasions.co.uk
Directors: K. Smith (Prop)
Date established: 1989 **No.of Employees:** 1 - 10 **Product Groups:** 36, 37, 67

Cunningham Cashless Systems
Headley Technology Park Middle Lane, Kings Norton, Birmingham, B38 0DS
Tel: 01564-829999 **Fax:** 01564-826999
E-mail: services@cunninghams.co.uk
Website: http://www.cunninghams.co.uk
Directors: C. Quinn (MD)
Immediate Holding Company: CUNNINGHAMS EPOS SOLUTIONS LTD
Registration no: 01596629 **Date established:** 1981 **Turnover:** £2m - £5m
No.of Employees: 51 - 100 **Product Groups:** 30, 37, 44

Date of Accounts	Jul 07
Working Capital	1
Current Assets	1

D C Grinding Ltd
Unit 6 Tyseley Industrial Estate Seeleys Road Tysley, Birmingham, B11 2LF
Tel: 0121-766 6620 **Fax:** 0121-766 6620
Directors: K. Powell (Fin), D. Clinton (MD)
Ultimate Holding Company: EASYFIT HARDWARE LIMITED
Immediate Holding Company: MIDLAND PUMP HOLDINGS LIMITED
Registration no: 05287853 **Date established:** 2005
No.of Employees: 1 - 10 **Product Groups:** 46

Date of Accounts	Apr 11	Apr 10	Apr 09
Working Capital	603	481	483
Fixed Assets	606	557	626
Current Assets	966	759	667

D H L Freight
Starley Way, Birmingham, B37 7HB
Tel: 0121-767 6000 **Fax:** 0121-767 6005
E-mail: penny.darnbrook@dhl.com
Website: http://www.dhl.com
Managers: R. Alridge (District Mgr)
Ultimate Holding Company: PALLETLINE PLC
Immediate Holding Company: PALLETLINE PLC
Registration no: 01439507 **Date established:** 1988
No.of Employees: 51 - 100 **Product Groups:** 72, 74, 75, 76

Date of Accounts	Mar 12	Mar 11	Mar 10
Working Capital	37	60	48
Current Assets	58	107	100

D M F
6 Grafton Road Sparkbrook, Birmingham, B11 1JP
Tel: 0121-773 3335 **Fax:** 0121-773 3141
E-mail: adriandmf@aol.com
Website: http://dmfdirect.co.uk
Directors: A. Rainey (Fin)
No.of Employees: 51 - 100 **Product Groups:** 46, 48

D R B Engineering Ltd
71-75 New Summer Street, Birmingham, B19 3TE
Tel: 0121-359 3777 **Fax:** 0121-359 5410
E-mail: reg@drbengineering.com
Website: http://www.drbengineering.com
Bank(s): Yorkshire
Directors: R. Jones (MD), R. Aldworth (Sales), B. Devlin (Fin), R. Jones (Grp Chief Exec)
Managers: B. Devlin (Accounts), R. Aldworth (Quality Control), R. Hill (Chief Mgr), M. Clarke (Buyer)
Immediate Holding Company: D.R.B. ENGINEERING LIMITED
Registration no: 02337609 **VAT No.:** GB 486 8722 89
Date established: 1989 **Turnover:** £2m - £5m **No.of Employees:** 51 - 100
Product Groups: 46, 48

Date of Accounts	Mar 08	Mar 09	Apr 10
Sales Turnover	5m	5m	4m
Pre Tax Profit/Loss	-76	76	12
Working Capital	1m	1m	1m
Fixed Assets	2m	2m	2m
Current Assets	3m	3m	2m
Current Liabilities	205	728	470

D & R Racking Ltd
Unit 1-3 Kings Road Industrial Estate Tyseley, Birmingham, B11 2AX
Tel: 0121-773 2121 **Fax:** 0121-773 3121
E-mail: sales@dnr.uk.com
Website: http://www.dandrracking.co.uk
Directors: D. Rogers (MD), E. Whitehall (Fin)
Immediate Holding Company: D & R RACKING LIMITED
Registration no: 03113241 **Date established:** 1995
Turnover: £500,000 - £1m **No.of Employees:** 11 - 20
Product Groups: 26, 35, 67

Date of Accounts	Dec 11	Dec 10	Dec 09
Working Capital	84	76	75
Fixed Assets	8	12	15
Current Assets	220	174	179

D R Warehouse Ltd
60-64 Great Hampton Street, Birmingham, B18 6EL
Tel: 0121-551 4920 **Fax:** 0121-551 6504
Website: http://www.drwarehouse.co.uk
Directors: K. Kaur (Dir), R. Lal (Dir)
Immediate Holding Company: D.R. WAREHOUSE LIMITED
Registration no: 02304469 **Date established:** 1988
No.of Employees: 1 - 10 **Product Groups:** 25, 35, 77

Date of Accounts	Mar 12	Mar 11	Mar 10
Working Capital	346	159	135
Fixed Assets	21	23	25
Current Assets	824	842	388

D S Technology UK Ltd
43-45 Avenue Close, Birmingham, B7 4NU
Tel: 0121-359 3637 **Fax:** 0121-359 1868
E-mail: info@dstechnology.co.uk
Website: http://www.dstechnology.co.uk
Directors: J. Fallon (Co Sec), J. Macdonald (Dir)
Managers: P. Connor (Tech Serv Mgr)
Ultimate Holding Company: STARRAGHECKERT HOLDING AG (SWITZERLAND)
Immediate Holding Company: DS TECHNOLOGY (UK) LIMITED
Registration no: 03326219 **Date established:** 1997 **Turnover:** £2m - £5m
No.of Employees: 21 - 50 **Product Groups:** 46, 48, 67, 85

Date of Accounts	Dec 11	Dec 10	Dec 09
Sales Turnover	N/A	4m	4m
Pre Tax Profit/Loss	N/A	105	129
Working Capital	755	893	810
Fixed Assets	N/A	211	227
Current Assets	755	1m	1m
Current Liabilities	N/A	153	205

D V R Fabrications
Unit 10 Winster Grove Industrial Estate Winster Grove, Birmingham, B44 9EG
Tel: 0121-325 0087 **Fax:** 0121-325 0087
E-mail: sales@phoenixfab.co.uk
Website: http://www.phoenixfab.co.uk
Directors: D. Reynolds (Prop)
VAT No.: GB 486 6167 04 **Turnover:** £250,000 - £500,000
No.of Employees: 1 - 10 **Product Groups:** 48

Dalen Ltd
Garretts Green Trading Estate Valepits Road, Birmingham, B33 0TD
Tel: 0121-784 9399 **Fax:** 0121-784 6348
E-mail: clive.beardmore@top-tec.co.uk
Website: http://www.top-tec.co.uk
Bank(s): HSBC Bank plc
Directors: C. Beardmore (Dir), C. Beardmore (MD), A. Broadbridge (MD), C. Beardmore (Fin)
Immediate Holding Company: DALEN LIMITED
Registration no: 01542645 **VAT No.:** GB 352 3438 67
Date established: 1981 **Turnover:** £2m - £5m **No.of Employees:** 21 - 50
Product Groups: 26, 30, 35, 36, 40, 48

Date of Accounts	Jun 09	Jun 08	Jun 07
Working Capital	72	-14	-77
Fixed Assets	459	464	487
Current Assets	2m	2m	820

W H Darby Ltd
16 Well Street, Birmingham, B19 3BJ
Tel: 0121-554 9817 **Fax:** 0121-523 3585
E-mail: info@whdarby.co.uk
Website: http://www.whdarby.co.uk
Bank(s): HSBC
Directors: S. Hobbis (MD)
Immediate Holding Company: W H DARBY LIMITED
Registration no: 05337453 **VAT No.:** GB 377 6465 05
Date established: 2005 **Turnover:** £500,000 - £1m
No.of Employees: 21 - 50 **Product Groups:** 49

Date of Accounts	Dec 11	Dec 10	Dec 09
Working Capital	-126	-62	-26
Fixed Assets	503	529	491
Current Assets	277	222	267

Dare Pro-Audio
10 Carver Street, Birmingham, B1 3AS
Tel: 0121-693 9292
Website: http://www.dareproaudio.com

Directors: S. Dehavilland (MD)
No.of Employees: 1 - 10 **Product Groups:** 37

Dataproof Ltd

46 Lower Tower Street, Birmingham, B19 3NH
Tel: 0121-753 7930 **Fax:** 0121-753 7939
E-mail: office@dataproof.biz
Website: http://www.dataproof.biz
Directors: P. Knight (Grp Chief Exec)
Immediate Holding Company: DATAPROOF LIMITED
Registration no: 01452327 **VAT No.:** GB 349 2056 51
Date established: 1979 **Turnover:** £1m - £2m **No.of Employees:** 1 - 10
Product Groups: 28

Date of Accounts	Dec 11	Dec 10	Dec 09
Working Capital	7	N/A	-12
Fixed Assets	5	6	6
Current Assets	102	79	101

Davies Turner & Co. Ltd Surface Freight

Station Road Coleshill, Birmingham, B46 1DT
Tel: 01675-462171 **Fax:** 01675-466804
E-mail: express@daviesturner.co.uk
Website: http://www.daviesturner.co.uk
Bank(s): National Westminster Bank Plc
Directors: M. Dean (MD), M. Gransbury (Fin)
Managers: G. McBride (Personnel), S. Butler, K. Scott (Mktg Serv Mgr), S. Lyncook (Tech Serv Mgr)
Ultimate Holding Company: DAVIES TURNER HOLDINGS PLC
Immediate Holding Company: DAVIES TURNER HOLDINGS PLC
Registration no: 04402085 **VAT No.:** GB 235 6746 45
Date established: 2002 **Turnover:** £125m - £250m
No.of Employees: 51 - 100 **Product Groups:** 44, 45, 61, 72, 74, 76, 77, 80, 82, 84

Date of Accounts	Mar 12	Mar 11	Mar 10
Sales Turnover	147m	149m	132m
Pre Tax Profit/Loss	5m	3m	3m
Working Capital	11m	7m	5m
Fixed Assets	24m	24m	25m
Current Assets	38m	37m	34m
Current Liabilities	8m	8m	7m

Davies Turner Air Cargo Ltd

Unit 3-4 The Gateway Estate West Midlands Freeport Airport Cargo, Birmingham International Airport, Birmingham, B26 3QD
Tel: 0121-782 8060 **Fax:** 0121-782 0516
Website: http://www.davisturner.co.uk
Managers: C. Mills (Mgr)
Ultimate Holding Company: DAVIES TURNER HOLDINGS PLC
Immediate Holding Company: DAVIES TURNER AIR CARGO LIMITED
Registration no: 02513979 **Date established:** 1990
No.of Employees: 1 - 10 **Product Groups:** 75, 76

Date of Accounts	Mar 12	Mar 11	Mar 10
Sales Turnover	50m	48m	41m
Pre Tax Profit/Loss	2m	1m	952
Working Capital	6m	5m	5m
Fixed Assets	365	433	436
Current Assets	16m	15m	13m
Current Liabilities	4m	4m	3m

Davis Decade Ltd

30 Spring Lane, Birmingham, B24 9BX
Tel: 0121-377 6292 **Fax:** 0121-377 6645
E-mail: enquiries@decade.co.uk
Website: http://www.decade.co.uk
Directors: I. Kimberley (MD), I. Kimberley (Dir), L. Kimberley (Co Sec)
Immediate Holding Company: DAVIS (DECADE) LIMITED
Registration no: 01887394 **Date established:** 1985
Turnover: £500,000 - £1m **No.of Employees:** 11 - 20
Product Groups: 38, 44, 45, 46

Date of Accounts	Apr 09	Apr 08	Apr 07
Working Capital	434	339	290
Fixed Assets	65	85	114
Current Assets	655	544	437
Current Liabilities	N/A	N/A	31

Davis & Hill

50-60 Pritchett Street Aston, Birmingham, B6 4EY
Tel: 0121-359 4091 **Fax:** 0121-333 3163
E-mail: sales@davisandhill.co.uk
Website: http://www.davisandhill.co.uk
Bank(s): HSBC Bank plc
Directors: N. Hill (MD), J. Hill (Jt MD), K. Hill (Jt MD), K. Hills (Dir)
Managers: B. Parton (Foundry Mgr), L. Spencer (Accounts)
Immediate Holding Company: Jesse Hill Ltd
Registration no: 07213554 **VAT No.:** GB 377 5756 96
Turnover: £500,000 - £1m **No.of Employees:** 21 - 50
Product Groups: 34, 66

Davran Jewellery Ltd

38-40 Hylton Street, Birmingham, B18 6HN
Tel: 0121-523 5575 **Fax:** 0121-523 7737
E-mail: info@davran-jewellery.com
Website: http://www.britishjewelleryworkshops.com
Directors: A. Grose (MD)
Immediate Holding Company: DAVRAN JEWELLERY LIMITED
Registration no: 01831144 **VAT No.:** GB 295 8525 09
Date established: 1984 **No.of Employees:** 1 - 10 **Product Groups:** 24, 25, 27, 33, 35, 47, 48, 49, 61, 65, 81

Date of Accounts	May 11	May 10	May 09
Working Capital	16	36	61
Fixed Assets	42	43	48
Current Assets	148	165	187

Davroy Contracts Ltd

510 Queslett Road, Birmingham, B43 7EJ
Tel: 0121-325 0936 **Fax:** 0121-360 6840
E-mail: neil.reynolds@davroy.co.uk
Website: http://www.davroy.co.uk
Directors: N. Reynolds (MD)
Ultimate Holding Company: DAVROY CONTRACTS (HOLDINGS) LIMITED
Immediate Holding Company: DAVROY CONTRACTS LIMITED
Registration no: 02545782 **VAT No.:** GB 580 4497 21
Date established: 1990 **Turnover:** £2m - £5m **No.of Employees:** 1 - 10
Product Groups: 24, 25, 26, 27, 30, 33, 35, 40, 41, 45, 52, 66

Date of Accounts	Mar 12	Mar 11	Mar 10
Working Capital	220	243	211
Fixed Assets	82	60	74
Current Assets	1m	1m	748

Dawes

35 Tameside Drive Castle Vale, Birmingham, B35 7AG
Tel: 0121-748 8050 **Fax:** 0121-748 8060
E-mail: julie.hayward@dawescycles.com
Website: http://www.dawescycles.com
Bank(s): Barclays
Directors: J. Hayward (Sales)
Ultimate Holding Company: TANDEM GROUP PLC
Immediate Holding Company: DAWES CYCLES LIMITED
Registration no: 04207519 **Date established:** 2001 **Turnover:** £5m - £10m
No.of Employees: 11 - 20 **Product Groups:** 39

Date of Accounts	Jan 10	Jan 09
Sales Turnover	6m	6m
Pre Tax Profit/Loss	197	167
Working Capital	-200	-442
Fixed Assets	514	559
Current Assets	2m	3m
Current Liabilities	176	147

Daytona

Units 2 & 3 Eckersall Road Kings Norton, Birmingham, B38 8SS
Tel: 0121-433 3174 **Fax:** 0121-433 3175
E-mail: partsforyou2@aol.com
Directors: T. Green (Prop)
Date established: 1982 **Turnover:** £500,000 - £1m
No.of Employees: 1 - 10 **Product Groups:** 68

Deakin & Francis Ltd

15-17 Regent Place, Birmingham, B1 3NL
Tel: 0121-236 7751 **Fax:** 0121-233 2588
E-mail: james@deakinanadfrancis.com
Website: http://www.deakinandfrancis.co.uk
Bank(s): Lloyds TSB Bank plc
Directors: J. Deakin (MD)
Immediate Holding Company: DEAKIN AND FRANCIS LIMITED
Registration no: 00162115 **VAT No.:** GB 109 3323 93
Date established: 2019 **Turnover:** £2m - £5m **No.of Employees:** 11 - 20
Product Groups: 49

Date of Accounts	Mar 11	Mar 10	Mar 09
Working Capital	811	795	927
Fixed Assets	33	41	53
Current Assets	1m	1m	1m

Declare Gate Mnfrs

Hylton Street, Birmingham, B18 6HJ
Tel: 0121-523 3700
Directors: J. Wilson (Prop)
Date established: 1999 **No.of Employees:** 1 - 10 **Product Groups:** 26, 35

Deepak Fasteners

12-14 Tower Street, Birmingham, B19 3RR
Tel: 0121-333 4610 **Fax:** 0121-333 4525
E-mail: andesh.gupter@deepakfastners.com
Website: http://www.deepakfastners.com
Managers: A. Gupter (Chief Mgr)
Immediate Holding Company: DEEPAK FASTENERS (UK) LIMITED
Registration no: 05888065 **Date established:** 2006
No.of Employees: 1 - 10 **Product Groups:** 35

Date of Accounts	Mar 11	Mar 10	Mar 09
Working Capital	155	4	-59
Fixed Assets	579	596	610
Current Assets	3m	2m	2m

Delcam plc

Talbot Way, Birmingham, B10 0HJ
Tel: 0121-766 5544 **Fax:** 0121-766 5511
E-mail: marketing@delcam.com
Website: http://www.delcam.com
Directors: K. Singh (Fin), E. Lambourne (Tech Serv), C. Martell (MD)
Managers: M. Corrigan (Sales Prom Mgr), P. Dickin (Mktg Serv Mgr), D. Sheffield (Comptroller)
Immediate Holding Company: DELCAM PLC
Registration no: 02311487 **Date established:** 1988
Turnover: £20m - £50m **No.of Employees:** 101 - 250
Product Groups: 35, 38, 44, 46, 48, 80, 81, 84, 85

Date of Accounts	Dec 11	Dec 10	Dec 09
Sales Turnover	42m	37m	32m
Pre Tax Profit/Loss	4m	2m	1m
Working Capital	7m	7m	6m
Fixed Assets	12m	12m	13m
Current Assets	19m	20m	15m
Current Liabilities	11m	12m	8m

Deloitte LLP

4 Brindley Place, Birmingham, B1 2HZ
Tel: 020-7936 3000 **Fax:** 0121-695 5678
E-mail: cloughran@deloitte.co.uk
Website: http://www.deloitte.co.uk
Directors: R. Edwards (Snr Part), C. Loughran (Ptnr)
Immediate Holding Company: DELOITTE LLP
Registration no: OC303675 **Date established:** 2003
Turnover: Up to £250,000 **No.of Employees:** 501 - 1000
Product Groups: 44, 80, 81, 82, 86

Date of Accounts	May 11	May 10	May 09
Sales Turnover	2098m	1953m	1969m
Pre Tax Profit/Loss	510m	543m	564m
Working Capital	263m	365m	435m
Fixed Assets	242m	251m	235m
Current Assets	623m	623m	659m
Current Liabilities	300m	239m	206m

Deva Dog Ware Ltd

320 Witton Road, Birmingham, B6 6PA
Tel: 0121-327 1108 **Fax:** 0121-328 2699
E-mail: info@devadogware.com
Website: http://www.devadogware.com
Directors: M. Swingler (Dir)
Immediate Holding Company: DEVA DOG WARE LIMITED
Registration no: 02455941 **VAT No.:** GB 554 9332 25
Date established: 1989 **Turnover:** Up to £250,000
No.of Employees: 1 - 10 **Product Groups:** 35, 49

Date of Accounts	Mar 08	Mar 07	Mar 06
Working Capital	-15	-20	-14
Fixed Assets	N/A	N/A	1
Current Assets	4	N/A	N/A
Current Liabilities	19	20	14

Diepress Refresherator Ltd

27-31 Cato Street North, Birmingham, B7 5AP
Tel: 0121-333 3139 **Fax:** 0121-359 1729
Website: http://www.diepress.co.uk
Directors: C. Papachristophorou (Dir)
Immediate Holding Company: DIEPRESS (REFRESHERATOR) LIMITED
Registration no: 00903305 **Date established:** 1967
Turnover: £250,000 - £500,000 **No.of Employees:** 1 - 10
Product Groups: 34, 35

Date of Accounts	Apr 11	Apr 10	Apr 09
Working Capital	-46	-24	-21
Fixed Assets	29	33	36
Current Assets	90	78	81

Dinkum Products Ltd

St Clements House St Clements Road, Birmingham, B7 5AF
Tel: 0121-245 1945 **Fax:** 0121-328 1966
E-mail: admin@dinkum.net
Website: http://www.dinkum.net
Directors: A. Christley (Dir), K. Richards (Fin)
Immediate Holding Company: DINKUM PRODUCTS LIMITED
Registration no: 04098234 **Date established:** 2000
No.of Employees: 1 - 10 **Product Groups:** 62

Date of Accounts	May 11	May 10	May 09
Working Capital	448	276	207
Fixed Assets	245	239	266
Current Assets	483	328	252

Direct Mail Publicity Birmingham Ltd

PO Box 581, Birmingham, B6 7ER
Tel: 0121-327 1172 **Fax:** 0121-326 6139
E-mail: info@dmpb.co.uk
Website: http://www.dmpb.co.uk
Directors: P. Allan-Smith (Dir), S. Allan-Smith (MD), E. Allan Smith (Co Sec)
Immediate Holding Company: DIRECT MAIL PUBLICITY(BIRMINGHAM)LIMITED
Registration no: 00831827 **Date established:** 1964
Turnover: £500,000 - £1m **No.of Employees:** 1 - 10 **Product Groups:** 81

Date of Accounts	Jul 11	Jul 10	Jul 09
Working Capital	40	55	90
Fixed Assets	12	11	13
Current Assets	88	105	130

Direct Roofing Supplies

The Roofing Centre Wharf Road, Tyseley, Birmingham, B11 2DX
Tel: 0121-708 1515 **Fax:** 0121-708 1511
E-mail: petergoodson@sigroofing.co.uk
Website: http://sigplc.co.uk
Managers: P. Goodson (District Mgr)
Ultimate Holding Company: SIG PLC
Immediate Holding Company: DIRECT ROOFING SUPPLIES LIMITED
Registration no: 02459661 **VAT No.:** GB 558 8569 72
Date established: 1990 **Turnover:** £2m - £5m **No.of Employees:** 11 - 20
Product Groups: 63, 66

Doaba Balloons

247-249 Rookery Road Handsworth, Birmingham, B21 9PU
Tel: 0121-551 6006 **Fax:** 0121-551 0808
E-mail: info@doaba.net
Website: http://www.doaba.net
Directors: K. Bharaj (Prop)
No.of Employees: 1 - 10 **Product Groups:** 24, 49, 65, 83

Dolland & Aitchison Ltd

Aston Cross Business Park 50 Rocky Lane, Aston, Birmingham, B6 5RQ
Tel: 0115-950 6111 **Fax:** 0121-697 2700
E-mail: contactus@danda.co.uk
Website: http://www.danda.co.uk
Directors: A. Bailey (Comm), A. Ferguson (Grp Chief Exec), P. Willows (I.T. Dir)
Managers: N. Durman (Mgr)
Ultimate Holding Company: DE RIGO SPA (ITALY)
Immediate Holding Company: EUROPEAN VISION LIMITED
Registration no: 00575754 **VAT No.:** GB 111 7544 01
Date established: 1956 **Turnover:** £2m - £5m **No.of Employees:** 1 - 10
Product Groups: 38

Doorfit Products Ltd

Icknield House 90 Heaton Street, Birmingham, B18 5BA
Tel: 0121-523 4171 **Fax:** 0121-554 3859
E-mail: enquiries@doorfit.co.uk
Website: http://www.doorfit.co.uk
Bank(s): National Westminster Bank Plc
Directors: J. Neil (MD)
Managers: R. Chew, M. Smith (Buyer)
Ultimate Holding Company: DOORFIT PRODUCTS LIMITED
Immediate Holding Company: DOORFIT LIMITED
Registration no: 03463329 **VAT No.:** GB 110 0893 17
Date established: 1997 **Turnover:** £2m - £5m **No.of Employees:** 51 - 100
Product Groups: 35, 36

Dowding & Mills Ltd

193 Camp Hill Bordesley, Birmingham, B12 0JJ
Tel: 0121-766 6161 **Fax:** 0121-766 6098
E-mail: simon.balem@dowdingandmills.com
Website: http://www.salzer.co.uk
Directors: R. Huser (Fin), S. Balem (Fin)
Ultimate Holding Company: SULZER AG (SWITZERLAND)
Immediate Holding Company: DOWDING & MILLS (OVERSEAS) LIMITED
Registration no: 01396382 **Date established:** 1978
No.of Employees: 251 - 500 **Product Groups:** 37, 44, 45, 48, 84, 85

Date of Accounts	Dec 11	Dec 10	Jun 10
Pre Tax Profit/Loss	21	28	55
Working Capital	-702	148	168
Fixed Assets	915	44	44
Current Assets	N/A	346	878
Current Liabilities	N/A	20	N/A

Dowding & Mills Engineering Services Ltd

Unit 14 Maple Business Park Walter Street, Birmingham, B7 5ET
Tel: 0121-326 6306 **Fax:** 0121-326 9379
E-mail: electronics.birmingham@dowdingandmills.com
Website: http://www.dowdingandmills.com
Managers: A. Porter (District Mgr), B. Scott (Chief Mgr), D. Wright (I.T. Exec)
Ultimate Holding Company: Castle Support Services plc
Immediate Holding Company: Dowding & Mills plc
Registration no: SC028056 **No.of Employees:** 21 - 50
Product Groups: 37

Down & Francis Industrial Products Ltd (Part of MRX Engineering Services)
Ardath Road Kings Norton, Birmingham, B38 9PN
Tel: 0121-433 3300 **Fax:** 0121- 4333325
E-mail: reception@downandfrancis.co.uk
Website: http://www.downandfrancis.co.uk
Bank(s): Barclays
Directors: G. Chatwin (MD), M. Stock (Fin), D. McKenzie (Grp Chief Exec), T. Sidwell (Dir), M. Jones (MD)
Managers: J. Bibb (Buyer), P. Meakin (Purch Mgr)
Ultimate Holding Company: METALRAX GROUP PLC
Immediate Holding Company: DOWN & FRANCIS INDUSTRIAL PRODUCTS LIMITED
Registration no: 00706828 **Date established:** 1961
Turnover: Up to £250,000 **No.of Employees:** 21 - 50 **Product Groups:** 35, 36, 45, 48

Date of Accounts	Dec 10	Dec 09	Dec 08
Pre Tax Profit/Loss	-2	-3	-3
Working Capital	-2	-2	-2
Fixed Assets	178	180	216
Current Assets	8	8	8
Current Liabilities	N/A	N/A	4

Drum Systems Ltd (Fenner Engineering Ltd)
2 Forge Mills Park Station Road, Coleshill, Birmingham, B46 1JH
Tel: 01675-467636 **Fax:** 01675-467582
E-mail: info@drumsystems.com
Website: http://www.drumsystems.com
Registration no: 06975732 **No.of Employees:** 21 - 50
Product Groups: 35, 41

Dual Metallising Ltd (Vacuum Metallising, Injection Moulding & Paint Spraying)
12-14 The Business Centre James Road, Tyseley, Birmingham, B11 2BA
Tel: 0121-708 2748 **Fax:** 0121-708 2256
E-mail: sales@dual-metallising.co.uk
Website: http://www.dual-metallising.co.uk
Directors: O. Franks (Fin), P. Franks (MD)
Immediate Holding Company: DUAL METALLISING LIMITED
Registration no: 01775336 **Date established:** 1983
Turnover: £250,000 - £500,000 **No.of Employees:** 11 - 20
Product Groups: 30, 31, 32, 33, 35, 37, 39, 48, 49, 66

Date of Accounts	Aug 11	Aug 10	Aug 09
Working Capital	160	150	144
Fixed Assets	125	109	108
Current Assets	331	277	288

Durose Ltd
33-35 Adams Street, Birmingham, B7 4LT
Tel: 0121-333 3096 **Fax:** 0121-359 6408
E-mail: enquiries@durose.co.uk
Website: http://www.durose.co.uk
Directors: C. Durose (Fin)
Immediate Holding Company: DUROSE LIMITED
Registration no: 02996589 **VAT No.:** GB 389 1689 86
Date established: 1994 **Turnover:** £250,000 - £500,000
No.of Employees: 1 - 10 **Product Groups:** 25, 35, 36, 48

Date of Accounts	Dec 11	Dec 10	Dec 09
Working Capital	121	152	194
Fixed Assets	15	17	20
Current Assets	177	219	298

E & B Engineering
Unit 5 Empire Works, Sydenham Road, Birmingham, B11 1DG
Tel: 0121-773 9137 **Fax:** 0121-773946
Directors: G. Roberts (Prop)
No.of Employees: 1 - 10 **Product Groups:** 35

E J Bowman Birmingham Ltd
Aston Brook Street East, Birmingham, B6 4AP
Tel: 0121-359 5401 **Fax:** 0121-359 7495
E-mail: info@ejbowman.co.uk
Website: http://www.ejbowman.co.uk
Directors: R. Bowman (MD), M. Patel (I.T. Dir), D. Moseley (Pers)
Managers: W. Moseley (Maint), M. Cook (Buyer), J. Moore, G. Pierce (Tech Serv Mgr)
VAT No.: GB 444 5241 63 **Date established:** 1919
No.of Employees: 21 - 50 **Product Groups:** 36, 37, 40, 41, 42, 45, 46

E M R Midland Shredders Ltd
Landor Street, Birmingham, B8 1AE
Tel: 0121-322 2399 **Fax:** 0121-327 4160
E-mail: phil.thompson@emrltd.com
Website: http://www.emrltd.com
Directors: N. Stinson (Co Sec), P. Thompson (Dir)
Ultimate Holding Company: EUROPEAN METAL RECYCLING LIMITED
Immediate Holding Company: EMR MIDLAND SHREDDERS LIMITED
Registration no: 01018817 **Date established:** 1971
Turnover: £75m - £125m **No.of Employees:** 21 - 50 **Product Groups:** 42, 66

Date of Accounts	Dec 10	Dec 09	Dec 08
Sales Turnover	N/A	N/A	79m
Pre Tax Profit/Loss	N/A	N/A	6m
Working Capital	103	103	14m
Current Assets	140	140	14m
Current Liabilities	37	37	37

Ease-E-Load Trolleys Ltd
Saunders House Moor Lane, Birmingham, B6 7HH
Tel: 0121-356 2228 **Fax:** 0121-356 2220
E-mail: info@ease-e-load.co.uk
Website: http://www.ease-e-load.co.uk
Bank(s): Barclays
Directors: S. Dallow (Dir)
Ultimate Holding Company: ARDEN MANUFACTURING LIMITED
Immediate Holding Company: EASE-E-LOAD TROLLEYS LIMITED
Registration no: 00994500 **VAT No.:** GB 100 9120 34
Date established: 1970 **Turnover:** Up to £250,000
No.of Employees: 11 - 20 **Product Groups:** 26, 35, 67

Date of Accounts	Dec 11	Dec 10	Dec 09
Sales Turnover	133	129	89
Pre Tax Profit/Loss	4	-11	-2
Working Capital	201	197	208
Current Assets	236	246	241
Current Liabilities	3	4	8

East End Foods Midlands Ltd
P S W Buildings 58-66 Darwin Street, Birmingham, B12 0TY
Tel: 0121-772 5201 **Fax:** 0121-772 4079
E-mail: jasonwourhra@eastendfoods.co.uk
Website: http://www.eastendfoods.co.uk
Bank(s): HSBC, Birmingham
Directors: J. Wouhra (Dir)
Managers: N. Mahmood (Purch Mgr)
Registration no: 01159183 **VAT No.:** GB 101 3292 29
Turnover: £50m - £75m **No.of Employees:** 21 - 50 **Product Groups:** 62

Easy Air Conditioning
262 Baldwins Lane, Birmingham, B28 0XB
Tel: 0121-746 3500 **Fax:** 0121-746 3505
E-mail: info@easyairconditioning.com
Website: http://www.easyairconditioning.com
Directors: A. Terrett (Dir)
Ultimate Holding Company: EASYAIRCONDITIONING GROUP LIMITED
Immediate Holding Company: EASYAIRCONDITIONING LIMITED
Registration no: 04356699 **Date established:** 2002
No.of Employees: 1 - 10 **Product Groups:** 40, 66

Eaton Electric Ltd
Reddings Lane Tyseley, Birmingham, B11 3EZ
Tel: 0121-685 2100 **Fax:** 08700-507525
E-mail: s.parker@mem250.com
Website: http://www.mem250.com
Directors: G. Sutton (Comm), S. Smith (Comm), J. Owens (MD), P. Hoare (MD)
Managers: M. Storey (Mktg Serv Mgr), J. McFarland (), A. Tipper (Personnel), A. Higgins (Purch Mgr), S. Parker (District Mgr), R. Box (Accounts), L. Hayes (Mgr), K. Smith (Sales & Mktg Mg)
Ultimate Holding Company: EATON CORPORATION (USA)
Immediate Holding Company: EATON ELECTRIC LIMITED
Registration no: 04617032 **Date established:** 2002
Turnover: £10m - £20m **No.of Employees:** 21 - 50 **Product Groups:** 37

Date of Accounts	Dec 08	Dec 07	Dec 06
Sales Turnover	81890	78950	77880
Pre Tax Profit/Loss	-9510	-12170	-17740
Working Capital	18640	-39730	-29060
Fixed Assets	22350	24170	25650
Current Assets	32580	33080	33250
Current Liabilities	13940	72810	62310
ROCE% (Return on Capital Employed)	-23.2	78.2	520.2
ROT% (Return on Turnover)	-11.6	-15.4	-22.8

W G Eaton Ltd
61-63 Lower Essex Street, Birmingham, B5 6SN
Tel: 0121-622 2611 **Fax:** 0121-666 6367
E-mail: sales@wgeaton.co.uk
Website: http://www.wgeaton.co.uk
Bank(s): Lloyds TSB Bank plc
Directors: M. Wheeler (MD)
Immediate Holding Company: TAILS LIMITED
Registration no: 01507693 **VAT No.:** GB 112 5166 11
Date established: 1980 **Turnover:** £500,000 - £1m
No.of Employees: 11 - 20 **Product Groups:** 23, 24, 30, 40

Date of Accounts	Mar 12	Mar 11	Mar 10
Working Capital	28	39	-85
Fixed Assets	257	218	57
Current Assets	53	78	61

Ecland Engraving
A10 Seedbed Centre Avenue Road, Nechells, Birmingham, B7 4NT
Tel: 0121-333 6880 **Fax:** 0121-333 6897
Directors: J. Eccleston (Prop)
Turnover: Up to £250,000 **No.of Employees:** 1 - 10 **Product Groups:** 28, 35, 42, 48

Ecorys UK
Albert House 92-93 Edward Street, Birmingham, B1 2RA
Tel: 0121-212 8800 **Fax:** 0121-616 3699
E-mail: chris.ralph@uk.ecorys.com
Website: http://www.uk.ecorys.com
Bank(s): National Westminster Bank Plc
Directors: C. Ralph (MD), M. Higham (Fin)
Immediate Holding Company: ECORYS UK LIMITED
Registration no: 01650169 **VAT No.:** GB 558 9423 95
Date established: 1982 **Turnover:** £10m - £20m
No.of Employees: 51 - 100 **Product Groups:** 54, 87

Date of Accounts	Dec 11	Dec 10	Dec 09
Sales Turnover	19m	20m	19m
Pre Tax Profit/Loss	114	166	-81
Working Capital	52	121	-54
Fixed Assets	1m	1m	1m
Current Assets	7m	7m	6m
Current Liabilities	2m	3m	3m

Eef Ltd
St James House Frederick Road, Edgbaston, Birmingham, B15 1JJ
Tel: 0121-456 2222 **Fax:** 0121-454 6745
E-mail: mail@eef.org.uk
Website: http://www.eef.org.uk
Managers: R. Halstead (Reg Mgr)
Immediate Holding Company: EEF (WM) ONE LIMITED
Registration no: 04898142 **Date established:** 2003
No.of Employees: 21 - 50 **Product Groups:** 87

Patrick Eggle
63 Water Street, Birmingham, B3 1HN
Tel: 0121-212 1989 **Fax:** 0121-212 1990
E-mail: gordon@patrickeggleguitars.com
Website: http://www.patrickeggleguitars.com
Directors: G. Tilly (MD)
Managers: L. Tilley (Sales Prom Mgr)
Ultimate Holding Company: Musical Exchangers
Registration no: 02089978 **VAT No.:** GB 111 4652 13
Date established: 1997 **No.of Employees:** 1 - 10 **Product Groups:** 65

Ehrhardt G V & Hereward Ltd
The Crescent Hockley, Birmingham, B18 5NL
Tel: 0121-554 1573 **Fax:** 0121-554 3791
Directors: J. Murray (Fin), D. Swene (Sales), M. Turley (MD), J. Smart (Ch)
Immediate Holding Company: G.V.EHRHARDT & HEREWARD LIMITED
Registration no: 00107511 **Date established:** 2010 **Turnover:** £1m - £2m
No.of Employees: 1 - 10 **Product Groups:** 35, 48

Elba Designs
151 Warstone Lane, Birmingham, B18 6NZ
Tel: 0121-236 8491
Website: http://www.elbadesigns.co.uk
Directors: C. Hayes (Prop)
No.of Employees: 1 - 10 **Product Groups:** 25, 26, 36

Eldis Electrical Distributors
239-242 Great Lister Street, Birmingham, B7 4BS
Tel: 0121-359 4521 **Fax:** 0121-333 1432
E-mail: david.small@eldis.co.uk
Website: http://www.eldis.co.uk
Directors: D. Hendry (MD), D. Henry (Ch)
Managers: D. Small (Chief Mgr), A. Clarke, A. Murphy (Chief Mgr)
Immediate Holding Company: MEDISAFE DISPENSING SYSTEMS LIMITED
Registration no: 04242974 **Date established:** 2011 **Turnover:** £5m - £10m
No.of Employees: 1 - 10 **Product Groups:** 67

Electronic Business Systems Ltd
852 Tyburn Road, Birmingham, B24 9NT
Tel: 0121-384 2513 **Fax:** 0121-377 6014
E-mail: info@e-b-s.co.uk
Website: http://www.e-b-s.co.uk
Directors: J. Tullah (Fin), R. Torr (Dir)
Managers: D. Price, A. Tullah, N. Phillips, R. Agar (Comptroller)
Immediate Holding Company: ELECTRONIC BUSINESS SYSTEMS LIMITED
Registration no: 01457911 **VAT No.:** GB 346 0020 03
Date established: 1979 **Turnover:** £500,000 - £1m
No.of Employees: 11 - 20 **Product Groups:** 44

Date of Accounts	Dec 11	Dec 10	Dec 09
Working Capital	89	183	180
Fixed Assets	103	73	37
Current Assets	608	742	674

Elite Metal Finishing
Unit 43 Birch Road East Industrial Estate Birch Road East, Birmingham, B6 7DA
Tel: 0121-326 9263 **Fax:** 0121-326 9263
Directors: B. Roberts (Prop)
Date established: 1992 **No.of Employees:** 1 - 10 **Product Groups:** 46, 48

Emhart Teknologies (Tucker Fasteners Ltd)
177 Walsall Rd Perry Barr, Birmingham, B42 1BP
Tel: 0121-356 4811 **Fax:** 0121-356 1598
E-mail: uk.marketing@bdk.com
Website: http://www.emhart.com
Bank(s): Bank of America N.A., 5 Canada Sq, London E14 5AQ
Directors: I. Bovis (Fab)
Managers: G. Weeks (Eng Serv Mgr), A. Horne (Prod Mgr), C. Lubascher, D. Madden, J. Beckett (Purch Mgr), J. Kennell, S. Smith (Fin Mgr), C. Mason
Ultimate Holding Company: Black & Decker Corp (U.S.A.)
Registration no: 00077952 **VAT No.:** GB 554 9932 01
Date established: 1903 **Turnover:** £20m - £50m
No.of Employees: 251 - 500 **Product Groups:** 30, 35, 36, 37, 39, 40, 46, 66

Emi Turn Engineering Ltd
129-133 Weston Lane, Birmingham, B11 3RR
Tel: 0121-706 4110 **Fax:** 0121-706 4830
E-mail: sales@emiturn.co.uk
Website: http://www.emiturn.co.uk
Directors: C. Tailor (Dir)
Immediate Holding Company: EMI-TURN ENGINEERING LIMITED
Registration no: 02415185 **VAT No.:** GB 377 4983 90
Date established: 1989 **Turnover:** Up to £250,000
No.of Employees: 1 - 10 **Product Groups:** 35

English Antique Glass
Bordesley Hall The Holloway, Alvechurch, Birmingham, B48 7QB
Tel: 01527-61100 **Fax:** 01527-61110
E-mail: info@englishantiqueglass.co.uk
Website: http://www.englishantiqueglass.co.uk
Managers: M. Tuffey (Chief Mgr)
Immediate Holding Company: DATATECH UK LTD
Registration no: 03986495 **Date established:** 2006 **Turnover:** £1m - £2m
No.of Employees: 1 - 10 **Product Groups:** 63

Date of Accounts	Feb 12	Feb 11	Feb 10
Working Capital	-0	-1	-1
Current Assets	1	N/A	N/A
Current Liabilities	N/A	1	N/A

Ensinger Ltd
Mainstream Industrial Park Mainstream Way, Birmingham, B7 4SN
Tel: 0121-333 4188 **Fax:** 0121-333 4189
E-mail: sales@ensinger.co.uk
Website: http://www.ensinger.ltd.uk
Managers: L. Gwilliams
Ultimate Holding Company: ENSINGER HOLDING GMBG & CO KG (GERMANY)
Immediate Holding Company: ENSINGER LIMITED
Registration no: 02190301 **VAT No.:** GB 570 2402 75
Date established: 1987 **Turnover:** £20m - £50m **No.of Employees:** 1 - 10
Product Groups: 30, 31, 48

Date of Accounts	Mar 12	Mar 11	Mar 10
Sales Turnover	18m	18m	14m
Pre Tax Profit/Loss	2m	2m	2m
Working Capital	874	886	1m
Fixed Assets	93	79	80
Current Assets	7m	7m	6m
Current Liabilities	962	1m	676

Environmental Landscape Contractors
Coopers Hill Alvechurch, Birmingham, B48 7BX
Tel: 0121-447 7313 **Fax:** 0121-447 7799
E-mail: admin@elccontractors.co.uk
Website: http://www.elccontractors.co.uk
Directors: A. Bytom (Prop)
Immediate Holding Company: TOTAL PROJECT RESOURCING LIMITED
Registration no: 04162235 **Date established:** 2001
No.of Employees: 1 - 10 **Product Groups:** 25, 35, 49

Epicor Software Ltd
Unit 2630 Kings Court The Crescent, Birmingham Business Park, Birmingham, B37 7YE
Tel: 0121-779 1000 **Fax:** 0121-779 1111
E-mail: euromarketing@epicor.com
Website: http://www.epicor.com

Directors: N. Beckett (Grp Chief Exec), D. Kershaw (Dir), S. Scott (Grp Chief Exec)
Ultimate Holding Company: TRANSTEC PLC
Immediate Holding Company: N.S.B. Retail Systems P.L.C.
Registration no: 00015997 **Date established:** 1981 **Turnover:** £5m - £10m
No.of Employees: 1 - 10 **Product Groups:** 44

Erhard Valves Ltd

Edison Road Hams Hall Distribution Park, Coleshill, Birmingham, B46 1AB
Tel: 01675-437940 **Fax:** 01675-437949
E-mail: erharduksales@talis-group.com
Website: http://www.erhard.de
Directors: D. Melrose (MD)
Registration no: 02474413 **Turnover:** £2m - £5m
No.of Employees: 1 - 10 **Product Groups:** 36, 38, 39, 40, 48

Date of Accounts	Sep 08	Sep 07	Sep 06
Sales Turnover	5379	5942	3684
Pre Tax Profit/Loss	89	594	428
Working Capital	2589	2472	1891
Fixed Assets	2	7	9
Current Assets	3617	3618	3616
Current Liabilities	1027	1146	1725
ROCE% (Return on Capital Employed)	3.4	24.0	22.5
ROT% (Return on Turnover)	1.7	10.0	11.6

Eriks Industrial Services (Digbeth Electro Mechanical)

70 Lower Essex Street, Birmingham, B5 6SU
Tel: 0121-692 1473 **Fax:** 0121-666 6018
E-mail: digbeth.repair@eriks.co.uk
Website: http://www.eriks.co.uk
Bank(s): Bank of Scotland
Managers: M. Allen (Ops Mgr)
Registration no: 03142338 **Turnover:** £2m - £5m
No.of Employees: 21 - 50 **Product Groups:** 37, 48, 84

Eriks UK

Great Lister Street Nechells Green, Birmingham, B7 4DA
Tel: 0121-359 1591 **Fax:** 0121-359 4546
E-mail: birmingham@eriks.co.uk
Website: http://www.eriks.co.uk
Managers: N. Moore (Mgr)
Immediate Holding Company: CIVIL PRIVATE INVESTIGATIONS LTD
Registration no: 03142339 **Date established:** 2012
Turnover: £250m - £500m **No.of Employees:** 1 - 10 **Product Groups:** 35

Ernst & Young Ltd

1 Colmore Square, Birmingham, B4 6HQ
Tel: 0121-535 2000 **Fax:** 0121-535 2001
E-mail: rbowker@uk.ey.com
Website: http://www.ey.com
Directors: R. Bowker (Snr Part)
Ultimate Holding Company: ERNST & YOUNG EUROPE LLP
Immediate Holding Company: ERNST & YOUNG LIMITED
Registration no: 05458987 **VAT No.:** GB 524 1472 70
Date established: 2005 **Turnover:** £10m - £20m
No.of Employees: 251 - 500 **Product Groups:** 80

Date of Accounts	Jun 08	Jul 09	Jul 10
Sales Turnover	217	2m	4m
Pre Tax Profit/Loss	N/A	529	649
Working Capital	N/A	155	303
Fixed Assets	N/A	N/A	21
Current Assets	500	2m	2m
Current Liabilities	500	902	679

Euro Export UK Ltd

240 Grove Lane Handsworth, Birmingham, B20 2EY
Tel: 0121-686 5116
E-mail: sonir@blueyonder.co.uk
Website: http://www.euroexportuk.com
Directors: R. Lal (MD), A. Mehra (Fin)
Immediate Holding Company: EURO EXPORT (UK) LIMITED
Registration no: 03967473 **VAT No.:** GB 775 4158 04
Date established: 2000 **Turnover:** £500,000 - £1m
No.of Employees: 1 - 10 **Product Groups:** 23, 29, 30, 40, 41, 54, 61, 63, 66, 68

Date of Accounts	Apr 11	Apr 10	Apr 09
Working Capital	2	5	1
Current Assets	28	28	15

Euro Gate Logictics Ltd

Garret Green Freight Depot Bannerley Road, Birmingham, B33 0SL
Tel: 0121-785 0270 **Fax:** 0121-785 0271
E-mail: birmingham@eurogate.co.uk
Website: http://www.eurogate.co.uk
Directors: G. Nagy (MD)
Managers: G. Larder (District Mgr), R. Possee (Chief Mgr), V. Evans (Sales Admin)
Immediate Holding Company: STEVE BENTON TRANSPORT LIMITED
Registration no: 01113069 **Date established:** 1999
Turnover: £20m - £50m **No.of Employees:** 1 - 10 **Product Groups:** 76

Date of Accounts	Dec 07	Dec 06	Dec 05
Sales Turnover	13083	12395	14320
Pre Tax Profit/Loss	58	151	218
Working Capital	994	982	809
Fixed Assets	138	127	126
Current Assets	3494	3514	3708
Current Liabilities	2500	2532	2900
Total Share Capital	500	500	500
ROCE% (Return on Capital Employed)	5.2	13.6	23.3
ROT% (Return on Turnover)	0.4	1.2	1.5

Euro Packaging Ltd

20 Brickfield Road, Birmingham, B25 8HE
Tel: 0121-706 6181 **Fax:** 01708-524621
E-mail: info@europackaging.co.uk
Website: http://www.europackaging.co.uk
Directors: A. Majid (MD), D. Taylor (Comm), S. Bostock (Fin), L. Connop (Pers)
Managers: G. Weaver (Purch Mgr), P. Timmins (Tech Serv Mgr), P. Brindley (Cr Control)
Ultimate Holding Company: EPL ACQUISITIONS (SUB) NV
Immediate Holding Company: EURO PACKAGING LIMITED
Registration no: 01328600 **Date established:** 1977
Turnover: £20m - £50m **No.of Employees:** 101 - 250
Product Groups: 27, 31

Date of Accounts	Dec 11	Dec 10	Dec 09
Sales Turnover	2m	2m	2m
Pre Tax Profit/Loss	344	464	696

Working Capital	761	-10m	205
Fixed Assets	15m	15m	19m
Current Assets	973	726	602
Current Liabilities	212	10m	396

Euro Precision

Unit 29 Rovex Business Park Hay Hall Road, Birmingham, B11 2AG
Tel: 0121-248 8844 **Fax:** 0121-248 8807
E-mail: europrecision@compuserve.com
Directors: N. Quiney (MD)
Immediate Holding Company: PARTQUEST ELECTRICAL SYSTEMS LIMITED
Registration no: 03039982 **VAT No.:** GB 660 7335 38
Date established: 1988 **Turnover:** Up to £250,000
No.of Employees: 1 - 10 **Product Groups:** 48

Evac+Chair International Ltd

Paraid House Weston Lane, Birmingham, B11 3RS
Tel: 0845-230 2253 **Fax:** 0121-706 6746
E-mail: info@evacchair.co.uk
Website: http://www.evacchair.co.uk
Bank(s): Lloyds TSB Bank plc
Directors: M. Wallace (MD), B. Scholes (Fin)
Managers: G. Hubbleday (Sales Prom Mgr), P. Colder ()
Registration no: 03593826 **VAT No.:** GB 443 6586 30
Date established: 1995 **Turnover:** £5m - £10m
No.of Employees: 51 - 100 **Product Groups:** 40, 67

Date of Accounts	Dec 11	Dec 10	Dec 09
Sales Turnover	5m	5m	6m
Pre Tax Profit/Loss	123	175	673
Working Capital	2m	2m	2m
Fixed Assets	408	435	416
Current Assets	5m	3m	4m
Current Liabilities	645	413	703

J W Evans & Sons Ltd

52-57 Albion Street, Birmingham, B1 3EA
Tel: 0121-236 1775 **Fax:** 0121-236 7966
Directors: A. Kenyon (Co Sec), J. Evans (Fab), P. Evans (Dir), A. Evans (MD)
Registration no: 00161980 **VAT No.:** GB 109 8496 37
Date established: 1919 **Turnover:** £250,000 - £500,000
No.of Employees: 1 - 10 **Product Groups:** 48, 49, 65

Date of Accounts	Dec 06	Dec 05
Working Capital	67	66
Fixed Assets	1	2
Current Assets	72	94
Current Liabilities	4	28
Total Share Capital	12	12

Eversheds Solicitors Bridge Trustees Ltd

115 Colmore Row, Birmingham, B3 3AL
Tel: 0121-232 1000 **Fax:** 0121-232 1900
E-mail: ronaldgraham@eversheds.com
Website: http://www.eversheds.com
Directors: R. Graham (Dir)
Managers: K. Flemming (Fin Mgr)
Ultimate Holding Company: EVERSHEDS LLP
Immediate Holding Company: BRIDGE TRUSTEES LIMITED
Registration no: 02600168 **Date established:** 1991 **Turnover:** £2m - £5m
No.of Employees: 251 - 500 **Product Groups:** 80

Date of Accounts	Apr 11	Apr 10	Apr 09
Sales Turnover	3m	2m	2m
Current Assets	2m	1m	1m
Current Liabilities	8	57	35

Exact Copy

270 Moseley Road Highgate, Birmingham, B12 0BS
Tel: 0121-248 8151 **Fax:** 0121-248 8153
E-mail: exactcopysales@aol.com
Website: http://www.exactcopy.co.uk
Directors: I. Atkin (Prop), I. Atkins (Prop)
Date established: 1973 **Turnover:** £500,000 - £1m
No.of Employees: 1 - 10 **Product Groups:** 27, 28, 81

Executive Network Ltd

Network House 119 Hagley Road, Birmingham, B16 8LB
Tel: 0121-450 5000 **Fax:** 0121-450 5010
E-mail: admin@ensales.co.uk
Website: http://www.ensales.co.uk
Directors: A. Ratcliffe (Pers), N. Dudley (Co Sec)
Registration no: 06701205 **Turnover:** Up to £250,000
No.of Employees: 21 - 50 **Product Groups:** 80

Express Moulds Ltd

Jubilee Works 40 Alma Crescent, Birmingham, B7 4RH
Tel: 0121-359 6378 **Fax:** 0121-359 3792
E-mail: paul.yeomans@expressmoulds.co.uk
Website: http://www.expressmoulds.co.uk
Bank(s): Barclays
Directors: P. Yeomans (MD)
Immediate Holding Company: EXPRESS MOULDS LIMITED
Registration no: 04573908 **VAT No.:** GB 313 7213 93
Date established: 2002 **Turnover:** £500,000 - £1m
No.of Employees: 21 - 50 **Product Groups:** 28, 30, 36, 42, 48, 49, 81

Date of Accounts	Nov 11	Nov 10	Nov 09
Working Capital	329	215	110
Fixed Assets	93	67	105
Current Assets	674	592	509

Express Packaging Ltd

79-107 Barford Street, Birmingham, B5 6AH
Tel: 0121-622 5414 **Fax:** 0121-622 2848
E-mail: sales@expresspkg.fsnet.co.uk
Website: http://www.expresspkg.co.uk
Directors: C. Jones (MD), J. Jones (Fin), B. Cope (Sales)
Immediate Holding Company: EXPRESS PACKAGING LIMITED
Registration no: 01642630 **Date established:** 1982
Turnover: Up to £250,000 **No.of Employees:** 1 - 10 **Product Groups:** 27, 28, 30

Date of Accounts	Jun 11	Jun 10	Jun 09
Working Capital	23	15	16
Fixed Assets	2	2	3
Current Assets	90	104	68

F G F Insulators Ltd

Shadwell House Shadwell Street, Birmingham, B4 6LJ
Tel: 0121-214 2459 **Fax:** 0121-333 5755
E-mail: jimwhite@fgfinsulaters.co.uk
Website: http://www.fgfltd.co.uk
Managers: J. White (Chief Mgr)
Ultimate Holding Company: F.G.F. LIMITED
Immediate Holding Company: FGF INSULATERS LIMITED
Registration no: 02561986 **VAT No.:** GB 559 0806 21
Date established: 1990 **Turnover:** £20m - £50m **No.of Employees:** 1 - 10
Product Groups: 23, 25, 30, 33, 36

Date of Accounts	Apr 11	Apr 10	Apr 09
Working Capital	411	372	419
Fixed Assets	N/A	39	45
Current Assets	411	525	472

F G H Products Ltd

68 Hunters Vale, Birmingham, B19 2XH
Tel: 0121-554 4329 **Fax:** 0121-554 1857
E-mail: fghsilver@btconnect.com
Directors: J. Hibbs (Fin), D. Higgs (MD), D. Higgs (Dir), J. Higgs (Fin)
Managers: J. Higgs (I.T. Exec)
Immediate Holding Company: F.G.H.PRODUCTS LIMITED
Registration no: 00787921 **VAT No.:** GB 109 5979 32
Date established: 1964 **Turnover:** £250,000 - £500,000
No.of Employees: 1 - 10 **Product Groups:** 36

Date of Accounts	Dec 10	Dec 09	Dec 08
Working Capital	N/A	-8	10
Fixed Assets	18	13	12
Current Assets	71	92	83

F & G Smart Shopfittings Ltd

Unit 16 Tyseley Industrial Estate Seeleys Road, Birmingham, B11 2LA
Tel: 0121-772 5634 **Fax:** 0121-766 8995
E-mail: sales@smartshopfittings.co.uk
Website: http://www.smartshopfittings.co.uk
Directors: N. Smart (Dir)
Immediate Holding Company: SMART SHOPFITTINGS LIMITED
Registration no: 01762490 **VAT No.:** GB 110 0336 49
Date established: 1983 **Turnover:** £250,000 - £500,000
No.of Employees: 1 - 10 **Product Groups:** 26, 49

Date of Accounts	Jun 95	Jun 11	Jun 10
Working Capital	1	1	1
Current Assets	1	1	1

F H Brundle

Saltley Business Park Dorset Road, Saltley, Birmingham, B8 1BG
Tel: 0121-327 8999 **Fax:** 0121-327 8555
E-mail: sales@brundle.com
Website: http://www.fhbrundle.com
Managers: C. Westwood (Mgr)
Immediate Holding Company: F H BRUNDLE
Registration no: 07168270 **Date established:** 2010
No.of Employees: 11 - 20 **Product Groups:** 30, 32, 34, 35, 36, 39, 46, 49, 66, 67

F I S Loveday Ltd

16-18 Princip Street, Birmingham, B4 6LE
Tel: 0121-359 3176 **Fax:** 0121-359 1098
E-mail: andrew.forrest@fisloveday.com
Website: http://www.fisloveday.com
Bank(s): National Westminster Bank Plc
Directors: A. Forrest (MD), K. Stait (Fin)
Immediate Holding Company: F.I.S. LOVEDAY LIMITED
Registration no: 01163199 **VAT No.:** GB 112 2572 15
Date established: 1974 **Turnover:** £1m - £2m **No.of Employees:** 11 - 20
Product Groups: 48

Date of Accounts	Mar 11	Mar 10	Mar 09
Working Capital	388	394	413
Fixed Assets	95	110	106
Current Assets	576	586	917

Fakir Halal Doners

Unit 2 19-23 Green Lane, Small Heath, Birmingham, B9 5BU
Tel: 0121-753 2226 **Fax:** 0121-753 2228
Directors: K. Minhas (Prop)
Date established: 1993 **Turnover:** £250,000 - £500,000
No.of Employees: 1 - 10 **Product Groups:** 20, 62

Fancy Metal Goods Ltd

71 Lifford Lane, Birmingham, B30 3DY
Tel: 0121-459 9777 **Fax:** 0121-459 9595
E-mail: fancy.metalgoods@btinternet.com
Website: http://www.fancymetalgoods.co.uk
Directors: P. Woodyatt (Sales), D. Woodyatt (Dir)
Immediate Holding Company: FANCY METAL GOODS LIMITED
Registration no: 00360471 **Date established:** 1940 **Turnover:** £1m - £2m
No.of Employees: 1 - 10 **Product Groups:** 65

Date of Accounts	Mar 12	Mar 11	Mar 10
Sales Turnover	N/A	N/A	1m
Pre Tax Profit/Loss	N/A	N/A	176
Working Capital	546	544	527
Fixed Assets	526	543	552
Current Assets	667	641	644
Current Liabilities	N/A	N/A	80

Fans & Spares

72 Cheston Road Nechells, Birmingham, B7 5EJ
Tel: 0121-328 1011 **Fax:** 0121-322 0201
E-mail: mudassar.ali@fansandspares.co.uk
Website: http://www.fansandspares.co.uk
Bank(s): Barclays
Directors: M. Ali (Co Sec)
Ultimate Holding Company: SYSTEMAIR AB (SWEDEN)
Immediate Holding Company: SYSTEMAIR FANS & SPARES LTD
Registration no: 04997065 **Date established:** 2003
Turnover: £10m - £20m **No.of Employees:** 21 - 50 **Product Groups:** 40

Date of Accounts	Apr 12	Apr 11	Apr 10
Sales Turnover	16m	14m	9m
Pre Tax Profit/Loss	763	-2m	-41
Working Capital	2m	1m	845
Fixed Assets	893	970	921
Current Assets	6m	6m	3m
Current Liabilities	619	665	273

Farmfoods Ltd

1507 Coventry Road Yardley, Birmingham, B25 8LW
Tel: 0121-707 5775
E-mail: cusomerservices@farmfoods.co.uk
Website: http://www.farmfoods.co.uk
Directors: W. McCreadie (Dir), E. Herd (MD), A. Henderson (Mkt Research), S. Crombie (Co Sec)

see next page

Farmfoods Ltd - Cont'd

Immediate Holding Company: FARMFOODS LIMITED
Registration no: SC030186 **VAT No.:** GB 265 5846 25
Date established: 1954 **Turnover:** £250m - £500m
No.of Employees: 11 - 20 **Product Groups:** 20, 62

Date of Accounts	Dec 11	Dec 10	Dec 09
Sales Turnover	578m	558m	469m
Pre Tax Profit/Loss	24m	17m	13m
Working Capital	-3m	-8m	-8m
Fixed Assets	88m	85m	81m
Current Assets	51m	45m	45m
Current Liabilities	12m	10m	11m

Thomas Fattorini (Insignia, Medals, Trophies, Swords)

Regent Street Works, Birmingham, B1 3HQ
Tel: 0121-236 1307 Freephone 0800 018 0369 **Fax:** 0121-200 1568
E-mail: sales@fattorini.co.uk
Website: http://www.fattorini.co.uk/Insignia_Makers.aspx
Bank(s): Barclays Bank
Directors: G. Fattorini (MD), T. Fattorini (Sales)
Ultimate Holding Company: Thomas Fattorini
Registration no: 00153351 **VAT No.:** GB 343 4128 78
Date established: 1827 **Turnover:** £2m - £5m
No.of Employees: 101 - 250 **Product Groups:** 23, 24, 25, 32, 33, 35, 36, 41, 46, 49, 63, 65

Date of Accounts	Dec 11	Dec 10	Dec 09
Sales Turnover	10m	N/A	N/A
Pre Tax Profit/Loss	1m	N/A	N/A
Working Capital	3m	3m	2m
Fixed Assets	734	429	386
Current Assets	5m	5m	3m
Current Liabilities	795	N/A	N/A

First Call

23 Bincomb Avenue, Birmingham, B26 2UY
Tel: 0121-722 2525
Directors: M. Quinton (Prop)
Immediate Holding Company: FIRST CALL LIMITED
Registration no: 06290670 **Date established:** 2007
No.of Employees: 1 - 10 **Product Groups:** 36, 40

Date of Accounts	Jun 11	Jun 10	Jun 09
Working Capital	16	14	2
Fixed Assets	11	2	3
Current Assets	23	24	12

1st 4 Home Improvements

4a Cranes Park Road, Birmingham, B26 3SG
Tel: 0121-743 8520 **Fax:** 0121-743 8522
Directors: R. Allatt (Prop)
Date established: 2003 **No.of Employees:** 1 - 10 **Product Groups:** 35, 36

flaskstore.com

23 - 24 Warstone Lane Hockley, Birmingham, B18 6JQ
Tel: 0121-233 4757
E-mail: sales@flaskstore.com
Website: http://www.flaskstore.com
No.of Employees: 1 - 10 **Product Groups:** 30, 36, 49, 65

Flexicon Ltd

Roman Way Coleshill, Birmingham, B46 1HG
Tel: 01675-466900 **Fax:** 01675-466901
E-mail: sales@flexicon.uk.com
Website: http://www.flexicon.uk.com
Bank(s): Lloyds TSB Bank plc
Directors: A. Poulton (MD), I. Gibson (I.T. Dir), J. Parkinson (Sales), S. Dale (Fin)
Managers: E. Robbins
Immediate Holding Company: FLEXICON LIMITED
Registration no: 03824181 **VAT No.:** GB 753 7316 23
Date established: 1999 **Turnover:** £10m - £20m
No.of Employees: 51 - 100 **Product Groups:** 30, 36, 37, 39

Date of Accounts	Dec 11	Dec 10	Dec 09
Sales Turnover	17m	14m	11m
Pre Tax Profit/Loss	657	502	172
Working Capital	4m	4m	4m
Fixed Assets	3m	3m	3m
Current Assets	8m	7m	6m
Current Liabilities	3m	2m	2m

Frederick Follows Ltd

129 Phillips Street, Birmingham, B6 4PT
Tel: 0121-359 5026 **Fax:** 0121-359 1822
E-mail: sales@frederickfollows.co.uk
Website: http://www.frederickfollows.co.uk
Bank(s): Lloyds TSB Bank plc
Directors: C. Rhodes (MD)
Immediate Holding Company: FREDERICK FOLLOWS LIMITED
Registration no: 00443336 **Date established:** 1947
Turnover: £250,000 - £500,000 **No.of Employees:** 11 - 20
Product Groups: 28, 36, 43, 44, 46, 47, 48, 49, 81

Date of Accounts	Sep 11	Sep 10	Sep 09
Working Capital	96	84	57
Fixed Assets	336	341	339
Current Assets	211	193	113

Fordwater Pumping Supplies Ltd

49-51 Stratford Road Sparkhill, Birmingham, B11 1RQ
Tel: 0121-772 8336 **Fax:** 0121-771 0530
E-mail: info@pumpsuk.com
Website: http://www.fordwaterpumps.co.uk
Bank(s): HSBC Bank plc
Directors: B. Powell (MD)
Immediate Holding Company: FORDWATER PUMPING SUPPLIES LIMITED
Registration no: 01311286 **VAT No.:** GB 113 4398 86
Date established: 1977 **Turnover:** £1m - £2m **No.of Employees:** 11 - 20
Product Groups: 39, 40, 41, 42, 45, 46, 48, 49, 67, 83

Date of Accounts	Jun 12	Jun 11	Jun 10
Working Capital	42	51	65
Fixed Assets	345	351	358
Current Assets	284	263	244

Fork Truck Centre Ltd

43 Steward Street, Birmingham, B18 7AE
Tel: 0121-454 7514 **Fax:** 0121-456 1792
E-mail: rwilliams@wilmat-handling.co.uk
Website: http://www.wilmat-handling.co.uk
Directors: R. Williams (Ch), T. Hands (MD)
Managers: K. Mackenzie (Accounts), A. Wye (Sales Prom)
Registration no: 02527881 **VAT No.:** GB 558 9542 87
Turnover: £500,000 - £1m **No.of Employees:** 1 - 10 **Product Groups:** 83

Date of Accounts	Jun 10	Jun 09	Jun 08
Working Capital	N/A	168	164
Fixed Assets	N/A	N/A	5
Current Assets	N/A	168	226

Forresters

Chamberlain House Paradise Place, Birmingham, B3 3HP
Tel: 0121-236 0484 **Fax:** 0121-233 1064
E-mail: dwardley@forresters.co.uk
Website: http://www.forresters.co.uk
Directors: G. Harrison (Ptnr), G. Harrison (Snr Part), J. Leach (Ptnr), A. Louckey (Ptnr), D. Lucking (Snr Part), M. Shaw (Ptnr), M. Shore (Ptnr), D. Wardley (Ptnr), D. Wardley (Snr Part)
Managers: D. Lucking (Mgr), W. Tolley (Asst Gen Mgr)
Immediate Holding Company: FORRESTER & BOEHMERT LIMITED
Registration no: 05135883 **Date established:** 2004
No.of Employees: 21 - 50 **Product Groups:** 80

Forward Induction

6 Burbidge Road, Birmingham, B9 4US
Tel: 0121-773 2425 **Fax:** 0121- 7732417
E-mail: frank@forward-induction.co.uk
Website: http://www.forward-induction.co.uk
Directors: F. Hallworth (Prop)
Date established: 2000 **No.of Employees:** 1 - 10 **Product Groups:** 46, 48

Forward Industrial Products Group Ltd

Unit 2-4 Tyseley Park Wharfdale Road, Birmingham, B11 2DF
Tel: 0121-708 2555 **Fax:** 0121-708 3081
E-mail: martyncleaver@forwardindustrial.com
Website: http://www.forwardindustrial.com
Directors: M. Cleaver (MD)
Managers: J. Lonie (Purch Mgr), A. Bailley (Sales Prom Mgr)
Immediate Holding Company: FORWARD INDUSTRIAL PRODUCTS GROUP LIMITED
Registration no: 03341583 **Date established:** 1997
Turnover: £10m - £20m **No.of Employees:** 51 - 100 **Product Groups:** 22, 23, 24, 25, 27, 29, 30, 31, 32, 33, 34, 35, 36, 37, 38, 39, 40, 41, 42, 43, 44, 45, 46, 47, 48, 49, 61, 63, 66, 67, 83, 84

Date of Accounts	Aug 07	Aug 06
Sales Turnover	7508	N/A
Pre Tax Profit/Loss	421	N/A
Working Capital	153	133
Fixed Assets	77	100
Current Assets	2981	2258
Current Liabilities	2828	2125
Total Share Capital	1	1
ROCE% (Return on Capital Employed)	183.3	
ROT% (Return on Turnover)	5.6	

B J & G J Fox

Erskine Street, Birmingham, B7 4RU
Tel: 0121-359 6396 **Fax:** 0121-359 6396
E-mail: garyfox58@hotmail.com
Directors: G. Fox (Ptnr)
Date established: 1967 **No.of Employees:** 1 - 10 **Product Groups:** 35

Frame Tec

8 Greenfield Road Harborne, Birmingham, B17 0EE
Tel: 0121-428 1038
E-mail: pfrith@btconnect.com
Website: http://www.frametec.co.uk
Directors: P. Frith (Prop)
Immediate Holding Company: FRAMETEC LIMITED
Registration no: 07546321 **Date established:** 2011
Turnover: Up to £250,000 **No.of Employees:** 1 - 10 **Product Groups:** 25, 30, 36, 47

Francis Graves Partnership LLP

54 Hagley Road, Birmingham, B16 8PE
Tel: 0121-603 9000 **Fax:** 0121-643 9190
E-mail: mark.bevan@francisgraves.co.uk
Website: http://www.francisgraves.co.uk
Directors: M. Bevan (Ptnr), S. Ansell (Co Sec), S. Brailsford (Mkt Research)
Ultimate Holding Company: HENRY RILEY LLP
Immediate Holding Company: FRANCIS GRAVES PARTNERSHIP LLP
Registration no: OC349907 **VAT No.:** GB 294 6147 31
Date established: 2009 **Turnover:** £2m - £5m **No.of Employees:** 1 - 10
Product Groups: 80

Date of Accounts	Mar 11	Mar 10
Working Capital	-157	-112
Fixed Assets	29	39
Current Assets	132	150

Friary Metal Products Ltd

106-110 Bishop Street, Birmingham, B5 6JP
Tel: 0121-622 7291 **Fax:** 0121-666 7277
E-mail: info@thefriarygroup.co.uk
Website: http://www.thefriarygroup.co.uk
Bank(s): Lloyds TSB Bank plc
Directors: B. Smith (Sales)
Immediate Holding Company: FRIARY METAL PRODUCTS LIMITED
Registration no: 01067260 **VAT No.:** GB 110 0605 48
Date established: 1972 **Turnover:** £1m - £2m **No.of Employees:** 11 - 20
Product Groups: 48

Date of Accounts	Mar 11	Mar 10	Mar 09
Working Capital	171	182	192
Fixed Assets	84	106	114
Current Assets	382	356	401

Frost Electroplating Ltd

19-21 Great Hampton Street, Birmingham, B18 6AX
Tel: 0121-236 4135 **Fax:** 0121-236 5823
E-mail: wsouthall@frost-electroplating.co.uk
Website: http://www.frost-electroplating.co.uk
Bank(s): Lloyds TSB Bank plc
Directors: W. Southall (MD), M. Griffith (Fin)
Managers: H. Fairbotham (Transport), D. Tannahill (Purch Mgr), D. Tannehill (Buyer), M. Jaggard (Fin Mgr)
Immediate Holding Company: FROST ELECTROPLATING LIMITED
Registration no: 03916194 **VAT No.:** GB 109 3297 68
Date established: 2000 **Turnover:** £5m - £10m **No.of Employees:** 21 - 50
Product Groups: 48

Date of Accounts	Dec 11	Dec 10	Dec 09
Working Capital	2m	2m	2m
Fixed Assets	481	586	675
Current Assets	3m	3m	2m

Fujitsu Telecommunications Europe Ltd

Unit 6000 Solihull Parkway Birmingham Business Park, Birmingham, B37 7YU
Tel: 0121-717 6000 **Fax:** 0121-717 6014
E-mail: a.stevenson@ftel.co.uk
Website: http://www.uk.fujitsu.com
Directors: A. Stevenson (Dir)
Ultimate Holding Company: FUJITSU LIMITED (JAPAN)
Immediate Holding Company: FUJITSU TELECOMMUNICATIONS EUROPE LIMITED
Registration no: 02548187 **Date established:** 1990
Turnover: £125m - £250m **No.of Employees:** 501 - 1000
Product Groups: 37, 38, 43, 44, 48, 52, 80, 84

Date of Accounts	Mar 12	Mar 11	Mar 10
Sales Turnover	170m	121m	138m
Pre Tax Profit/Loss	7m	10m	-13m
Working Capital	8m	11m	17m
Fixed Assets	22m	16m	19m
Current Assets	66m	61m	60m
Current Liabilities	47m	37m	32m

Fulda Tyres

88-98 Wingfoot Way Erdington, Birmingham, B24 9HY
Tel: 01902-327000 **Fax:** 01902-327494
E-mail: fuldainfo-uk@fulda.com
Website: http://www.fulda.com
Product Groups: 29

Future Access Ltd

Unit E2 Salford Trading Estate, Birmingham, B6 7SH
Tel: 0121-328 0554 **Fax:** 0121-326 0274
E-mail: vccutters@btconnect.com
Website: http://www.vccutters.co.uk
Managers: T. Coughlin (Mgr)
Immediate Holding Company: FUTURE ACCESS LIMITED
Registration no: 03081918 **Date established:** 1995
No.of Employees: 1 - 10 **Product Groups:** 27, 44

Date of Accounts	Jul 11	Jul 10	Jul 09
Working Capital	56	60	54
Fixed Assets	75	85	95
Current Assets	157	110	103

G K N Aerospace Transparancy Systems Ltd

Eckersall Road, Birmingham, B38 8SR
Tel: 0121-606 4100 **Fax:** 0121-458 6880
Website: http://www.gknplc.com
Directors: A. Dutton (Co Sec)
Managers: A. Wilson, M. Payne (Fin Mgr), S. Tenant (Personnel)
Ultimate Holding Company: GKN PLC
Immediate Holding Company: GKN AEROSPACE TRANSPARENCY SYSTEMS (KINGS NORTON) LIMITED
Registration no: 01999018 **VAT No.:** GB 151 6225 91
Date established: 1986 **Turnover:** £20m - £50m
No.of Employees: 251 - 500 **Product Groups:** 33, 39

Date of Accounts	Dec 11	Dec 10	Dec 09
Pre Tax Profit/Loss	-67	127	1m
Working Capital	8m	7m	7m
Fixed Assets	3m	3m	3m
Current Assets	8m	7m	7m
Current Liabilities	N/A	27	131

G M S

175 Booth Street, Birmingham, B21 0NU
Tel: 0121-551 5440 **Fax:** 0121-554 5344
E-mail: enquiries@gmspolymer.co.uk
Website: http://www.gmspolymer.co.uk
Directors: J. Toons (MD), T. Clives (Fin)
Registration no: 01585798 **VAT No.:** 294 6678 00 **Date established:** 2004
Turnover: £500,000 - £1m **No.of Employees:** 1 - 10 **Product Groups:** 29

G P M Engineering Systems Ltd

1575 Bristol Road South Rednal, Birmingham, B45 9UA
Tel: 0121-457 7132 **Fax:** 0121-457 9035
E-mail: scrow@gpmengineering.com
Website: http://www.gpmengineering.com
Directors: S. Crow (Dir)
Immediate Holding Company: GPM ENGINEERING SYSTEMS LIMITED
Registration no: 02998191 **VAT No.:** GB 377 1062 52
Date established: 1994 **Turnover:** £5m - £10m **No.of Employees:** 1 - 10
Product Groups: 45

Date of Accounts	Mar 11	Mar 10	Mar 09
Working Capital	-38	-110	-85
Current Assets	122	28	52

G & S Brough Ltd

28-40 Leopold Street, Birmingham, B12 0UR
Tel: 0121-440 4406 **Fax:** 0121-440 4409
E-mail: sales@gandsbrough.co.uk
Website: http://www.gandsbrough.co.uk
Bank(s): Barclays
Managers: G. Scriven (Chief Acct), M. Dunbar (Nat Sales Mgr), I. Healey (Personnel), J. Russell (Buyer)
Immediate Holding Company: G.& S.BROUGH LIMITED
Registration no: 00306579 **VAT No.:** GB 389 4487 63
Date established: 1935 **Turnover:** £1m - £2m **No.of Employees:** 51 - 100
Product Groups: 22, 23, 25, 27, 29, 30, 31, 33, 35, 36, 40

Date of Accounts	Mar 11	Mar 10	Mar 09
Working Capital	166	59	73
Fixed Assets	729	762	774
Current Assets	375	399	304

G S Fire Protection

46 Gotham Road, Birmingham, B26 1LB
Tel: 0121-244 4747 **Fax:** 0121-693 3883
E-mail: info@gsfireprotection.co.uk
Website: http://www.gsfireprotection.co.uk
Directors: G. Green (Prop)
Date established: 1996 **Turnover:** Up to £250,000
No.of Employees: 1 - 10 **Product Groups:** 39, 40, 52

Gabriel & Co. Ltd

10 Hay Hall Road, Birmingham, B11 2AU
Tel: 0121-248 3333 **Fax:** 0121-248 3330
E-mail: sales@gabrielco.com
Website: http://www.gabrielco.com

Directors: A. Gabriel (Ch), J. Gabriel (MD), A. Gabriel (MD), J. Gabriel (Ch), P. Turner (Chief Op Offcr)
Managers: J. Stephens (Buyer), L. Cooper (Quality Control), R. Southall (Accounts), B. Baker (Buyer), C. Rowen (Sales Prom Mgr), J. Price (Sales Prom Mgr), D. Holland (Accounts)
Immediate Holding Company: GABRIEL & CO,LIMITED
Registration no: 00235891 **VAT No.:** GB 109 8605 58
Date established: 1928 **Turnover:** £2m - £5m **No.of Employees:** 1 - 10
Product Groups: 34, 39

Galvanised Sheet & Coil Ltd

Doris Road Bordesley Green, Birmingham, B9 4SJ
Tel: 0121-773 8341 **Fax:** 0121-771 0024
E-mail: davidreeves@galvsheet.co.uk
Bank(s): National Westminster Bank Plc
Directors: D. Reeves (Comm)
Immediate Holding Company: GALVANISED SHEETS & COIL LIMITED
Registration no: 01035162 **VAT No.:** GB 109 4572 67
Date established: 1971 **Turnover:** £5m - £10m **No.of Employees:** 11 - 20
Product Groups: 34

Date of Accounts	Dec 11	Dec 10	Dec 09
Sales Turnover	9m	7m	6m
Pre Tax Profit/Loss	291	555	200
Working Capital	5m	5m	5m
Fixed Assets	199	274	292
Current Assets	7m	7m	6m
Current Liabilities	309	407	210

Gauge Master

93 Leopold Street, Birmingham, B12 0UD
Tel: 0121-773 6331 **Fax:** 0121-772 4046
E-mail: mick.sheasby@gaugemaster.net
Website: http://www.gaugemaster.net
Bank(s): Lloyds TSB Bank plc
Directors: M. Sheasby (MD)
Ultimate Holding Company: GAUGEMASTER HOLDINGS LIMITED
Immediate Holding Company: GAUGEMASTER COMPANY LIMITED
Registration no: 00660348 **VAT No.:** GB 109 9052 68
Date established: 1960 **No.of Employees:** 21 - 50 **Product Groups:** 48

Date of Accounts	May 11	May 10	May 09
Working Capital	991	754	542
Fixed Assets	191	185	182
Current Assets	1m	1m	1m

Gazbags Packaging Supplies

246 Frankley Beeches Road, Birmingham, B31 5LZ
Tel: 0121-476 1702 **Fax:** 0121-476 1702
E-mail: sales@gazbags.co.uk
Website: http://www.gazbags.co.uk
Directors: G. Blake (Prop)
Date established: 1987 **No.of Employees:** 1 - 10 **Product Groups:** 38, 42

GB Precision Engineering Co.

1 Port Hope Road, Birmingham, B11 1JS
Tel: 0121-766 7008 **Fax:** 0121-773 2824
E-mail: info@gbprecision.co.uk
Website: http://www.gbprecision.co.uk
Directors: G. Turner (MD), P. Turner (Fin)
Registration no: 01188381 **VAT No.:** GB 112 4755 94
Turnover: £250,000 - £500,000 **No.of Employees:** 1 - 10
Product Groups: 42, 48

GB Quality Assurance Ltd

Unit 9 Chancel Way Moor Lane Industrial Estate, Birmingham, B6 7AU
Tel: 0121-356 7430 **Fax:** 0121-344 3837
E-mail: sales@gbqualityassurance.co.uk
Website: http://www.gbquality.com
Directors: T. Stacey (MD)
Immediate Holding Company: G.B. QUALITY ASSURANCE (CONSULTANTS) & N.D.T. LIMITED
Registration no: 01331317 **Date established:** 1977
Turnover: Up to £250,000 **No.of Employees:** 1 - 10 **Product Groups:** 85

Date of Accounts	Oct 11	Oct 10	Oct 09
Working Capital	9	13	-11
Fixed Assets	60	53	16
Current Assets	69	62	21

General Fabrications Ltd

26 Orphanage Road, Birmingham, B24 9HT
Tel: 0121-377 6070 **Fax:** 0121-377 7175
E-mail: info@genfab.co.uk
Website: http://www.genfab.co.uk
Directors: J. Hession (Dir), A. Ross (Sales)
Immediate Holding Company: GENERAL FABRICATIONS LIMITED
Registration no: 00453031 **Date established:** 1948 **Turnover:** £1m - £2m
No.of Employees: 11 - 20 **Product Groups:** 23, 27, 28, 29, 30, 31, 32, 33, 35, 37, 38, 40, 42, 48, 49, 64, 65, 66, 67, 68, 80

Date of Accounts	Apr 11	Apr 10	Apr 09
Working Capital	-63	-137	-184
Fixed Assets	386	487	514
Current Assets	619	442	455

Geti Ltd

44 Hockley Street, Birmingham, B18 6BH
Tel: 0121-507 0994 **Fax:** 0121-523 6849
E-mail: getiuk@aol.com
Website: http://www.gegi.cc
Directors: A. Hadley (Dir)
Immediate Holding Company: GETI LTD
Registration no: 04892067 **Date established:** 2003
No.of Employees: 1 - 10 **Product Groups:** 45

Date of Accounts	Aug 11	Aug 10	Aug 09
Working Capital	40	23	15
Fixed Assets	71	99	77
Current Assets	129	112	82

GGB UK

Wellington House Starley Way, Birmingham International Park, Birmingham, B37 7HB
Tel: 0121-767 9100 **Fax:** 0121-781 7313
E-mail: greatbritain@ggbearings.com
Website: http://www.ggbearings.com
Managers: J. Dunn (Sales Prom Mgr)
Product Groups: 35

James Gibbons Format Ltd

Unit 214-216 Telsen Industrial Centre 55 Thomas Street, Birmingham, B6 4TN
Tel: 0121-333 5201 **Fax:** 0121-359 9068
E-mail: info@jgf.co.uk
Website: http://www.jgf.co.uk
Directors: R. Blakey (MD)
Immediate Holding Company: JAMES GIBBONS FORMAT LIMITED
Registration no: 04240188 **VAT No.:** GB 346 9500 41
Date established: 2001 **Turnover:** £5m - £10m **No.of Employees:** 1 - 10
Product Groups: 36

Date of Accounts	Dec 11
Working Capital	89
Fixed Assets	238
Current Assets	1m

Gifts Of Distinction

23-24 Warstone Lane, Birmingham, B18 6JQ
Tel: 0121-233 4757
E-mail: david.hendley@gifts-of-distinction.co.uk
Website: http://www.gifts-of-distinction.co.uk
Directors: D. Hendley (Prop)
No.of Employees: 1 - 10 **Product Groups:** 30, 35, 36, 49

A J Gilbert Birmingham Ltd

66-77 Buckingham Street, Birmingham, B19 3HU
Tel: 0121-236 7774 **Fax:** 0121-236 6024
E-mail: lucycooperajg@aol.com
Website: http://www.ajgilbert.co.uk
Bank(s): Lloyds, Hockley
Directors: R. Cooper (Dir)
Ultimate Holding Company: A.J.GILBERT(BIRMINGHAM)LIMITED
Immediate Holding Company: EXECUTIVE KEY RECOVERY LIMITED
Registration no: 02206381 **VAT No.:** GB 109 7653 52
Date established: 1987 **Turnover:** £1m - £2m **No.of Employees:** 21 - 50
Product Groups: 35, 48, 49

Date of Accounts	Dec 10	Dec 09	Dec 06
Working Capital	1	1	3
Current Assets	1	1	4

Gilbert & Mellish Ltd

3 Lightning Way, Birmingham, B31 3PH
Tel: 0121-475 1101 **Fax:** 0121-478 0163
E-mail: sales@gilbert-mellish.co.uk
Website: http://www.gilbert-mellish.co.uk
Bank(s): Bank of Scotland
Managers: S. Morris (Mgr)
Immediate Holding Company: GILBERT & MELLISH LIMITED
Registration no: 04354646 **VAT No.:** GB 695 4715 89
Date established: 2002 **Turnover:** £2m - £5m **No.of Employees:** 11 - 20
Product Groups: 38

Date of Accounts	Mar 11	Mar 10	Mar 09
Working Capital	709	181	-188
Fixed Assets	4m	4m	5m
Current Assets	3m	2m	2m

P S Gill & Sons

261-277 Rookery Road Handsworth, Birmingham, B21 9PT
Tel: 0121-554 7521 **Fax:** 0121-554 9033
E-mail: sales@psgill.com
Website: http://www.psg.com
Directors: S. Gill (Prop)
Immediate Holding Company: P S GILL LIMITED
Registration no: 04430606 **VAT No.:** GB 112 6012 33
Date established: 2002 **Turnover:** £2m - £5m **No.of Employees:** 1 - 10
Product Groups: 24

Date of Accounts	May 11	May 10	May 08
Working Capital	2	-0	-1
Fixed Assets	2	2	2
Current Assets	39	38	27

E Gilligan & Sons Ltd

25 Allcock Street, Birmingham, B9 4DY
Tel: 0121-766 7666 **Fax:** 0121-766 7601
E-mail: gilligan@btconnect.com
Website: http://www.agilligan.co.uk
Bank(s): HSBC Bank plc
Directors: A. Gilligan (MD), A. Gilligan (MD), J. Oliver (Co Sec), J. Oliver (Fin)
Managers: J. Silvers (Chief Mgr)
Immediate Holding Company: E.GILLIGAN & SONS LIMITED
Registration no: 00754300 **VAT No.:** GB 109 7038 72
Date established: 1963 **Turnover:** £500,000 - £1m
No.of Employees: 11 - 20 **Product Groups:** 48

Date of Accounts	Apr 08	Apr 07	Apr 06
Working Capital	248	248	150
Fixed Assets	348	348	432
Current Assets	253	270	298
Current Liabilities	5	23	148
Total Share Capital	54	54	54

Gillman Group Ltd

Chipstead Road Erdington, Birmingham, B23 5HD
Tel: 0121-244 4141 **Fax:** 0121-244 4142
E-mail: david@gillmangroup.com
Website: http://www.gillmangroup.com
Bank(s): Barclays
Directors: D. Millman (MD)
Managers: J. Gill (Mktg Serv Mgr)
Immediate Holding Company: GILLMAN GROUP LIMITED
Registration no: 03209438 **Date established:** 1996
Turnover: £250,000 - £500,000 **No.of Employees:** 11 - 20
Product Groups: 52, 84

Date of Accounts	Jun 09	Jun 08	Jun 07
Sales Turnover	278	366	320
Pre Tax Profit/Loss	4	16	33
Working Capital	10	4	10
Fixed Assets	8	10	14
Current Assets	265	197	197
Current Liabilities	197	192	173

Giro Food Ltd

Welcome House Glover Street, Birmingham, B9 4EP
Tel: 0121-773 5811 **Fax:** 0121-202 1555
E-mail: javedsarwar@girofood.com
Website: http://www.girofood.com
Directors: T. Akram (Purch), I. Sarwar (Mkt Research), J. Sarwar (MD), M. Sarwar (Sales)
Managers: K. Arthur (Tech Serv Mgr)
Immediate Holding Company: GIRO FOOD LIMITED
Registration no: 00947901 **Date established:** 1969
Turnover: £20m - £50m **No.of Employees:** 51 - 100 **Product Groups:** 61

Date of Accounts	Mar 11	Mar 10	Mar 09
Sales Turnover	25m	25m	N/A
Pre Tax Profit/Loss	69	262	308
Working Capital	2m	2m	2m
Fixed Assets	3m	3m	3m
Current Assets	7m	6m	5m
Current Liabilities	424	196	316

Gladman & Norman Ltd

51-53 Tenby Street North, Birmingham, B1 3EG
Tel: 0121-236 5752 **Fax:** 0121-233 4539
E-mail: information@gladman-norman.co.uk
Website: http://www.gladman-norman.co.uk
Bank(s): National Westminster
Directors: P. McDermott (MD), K. McDermott (Co Sec)
Managers: J. Holdsworth (Chief Mgr)
Registration no: 00320491 **VAT No.:** GB 109 5189 61
Date established: 1910 **Turnover:** £500,000 - £1m
No.of Employees: 21 - 50 **Product Groups:** 32, 35, 48, 49, 65

Date of Accounts	May 08	May 07	May 06
Sales Turnover	N/A	640	478
Pre Tax Profit/Loss	N/A	53	39
Working Capital	167	150	133
Fixed Assets	107	90	77
Current Assets	402	361	257
Current Liabilities	235	211	124
Total Share Capital	20	20	20
ROCE% (Return on Capital Employed)		22.0	18.4
ROT% (Return on Turnover)		8.3	8.1

Global

90 Stratford Road Sparkhill, Birmingham, B11 1AN
Tel: 0121-773 4440 **Fax:** 0121-773 4441
E-mail: glopbal786@aol.com
Website: http://www.glabolcateringequiptment.com
Directors: A. Shaikh (Prop)
No.of Employees: 1 - 10 **Product Groups:** 20, 40, 41

Global Industrial Services

91 Blakeland Road, Birmingham, B44 8AT
Tel: 0121-356 7437 **Fax:** 0121-705 6500
E-mail: martinhodson3@hotmail.com
Website: http://www.globalindustrialservices.co.uk
Directors: R. Billington (Prop)
Immediate Holding Company: BAYLINK LTD
Registration no: 02490185 **Date established:** 2009
No.of Employees: 1 - 10 **Product Groups:** 48

Global Metal Trading UK Ltd

Unit 5 Chelmsley Wood Industrial Estate Waterloo Avenue, Kingshurst, Birmingham, B37 6QQ
Tel: 0121-788 8065 **Fax:** 0121-788 3362
E-mail: salesuk@gmttitanium.com
Website: http://www.gmttitanium.com
Directors: A. Litchfield (Co Sec), F. Perrins (Sales)
Managers: B. Singh (Buyer), D. Gould (Quality Control)
Registration no: 04028834 **VAT No.:** GB 754 3303 46
Date established: 2003 **Turnover:** £2m - £5m **No.of Employees:** 1 - 10
Product Groups: 34, 35, 36, 46

Date of Accounts	Dec 07	Dec 06	Dec 05
Sales Turnover	2810	1714	N/A
Pre Tax Profit/Loss	68	125	N/A
Working Capital	356	311	253
Fixed Assets	75	60	N/A
Current Assets	1408	1477	461
Current Liabilities	1052	1165	208
Total Share Capital	60	60	60
ROCE% (Return on Capital Employed)	15.7	33.8	
ROT% (Return on Turnover)	2.4	7.3	

Glopac Ltd

Eddison Road Hams Hall Distribution Park, Coleshill, Birmingham, B46 1AB
Tel: 01675-431000 **Fax:** 01675-431066
E-mail: neil.morrish@glopac.co.uk
Website: http://www.glopac.co.uk
Bank(s): HSBC Bank plc
Directors: N. Morrish (Dir)
Ultimate Holding Company: RETAIL SUPPLY GROUP LIMITED
Immediate Holding Company: GLOPAC LIMITED
Registration no: 01243706 **Date established:** 1976
Turnover: £10m - £20m **No.of Employees:** 21 - 50 **Product Groups:** 30

Date of Accounts	Dec 11	Dec 10	Dec 09
Sales Turnover	20m	18m	20m
Pre Tax Profit/Loss	119	893	-1m
Working Capital	2m	2m	1m
Fixed Assets	4m	4m	4m
Current Assets	11m	11m	12m
Current Liabilities	534	466	528

Goliath International Ltd

Unit 2 Aston Express Way Industrial Estate 64 Pritchett Street, Birmingham, B6 4EX
Tel: 0121-359 6621 **Fax:** 0121-359 6882
E-mail: info@goliathinternational.com
Website: http://www.goliathinternational.com
Bank(s): HSBC Bank plc
Directors: N. Moore (MD), P. Wozniak (Dir), M. Brooke (Fin)
Managers: V. Brook, S. Middlesbrook (Chief Buyer)
Ultimate Holding Company: GOLIATH INTERNATIONAL (TOOLS) LIMITED
Immediate Holding Company: GOLIATH THREADING TOOLS LIMITED
Registration no: 00730026 **Date established:** 1962 **Turnover:** £1m - £2m
No.of Employees: 21 - 50 **Product Groups:** 36, 46

Golley Slater Group

Unit 205 Fort Dunlop Fort Parkway, Birmingham, B24 9FD
Tel: 0121-384 9700 **Fax:** 0121-384 9790
E-mail: enquiries@golleyslater.co.uk
Website: http://www.golleyslater.co.uk
Directors: A. Walton (MD)
Immediate Holding Company: NAUTIC STEELS (HOLDINGS) LIMITED
Registration no: 02302004 **Date established:** 1988 **Turnover:** £5m - £10m
No.of Employees: 21 - 50 **Product Groups:** 81

Goodyear Dunlop UK Ltd
Tyrefort 88-98 Wingfoot Way, Erdington, Birmingham, B24 9HY
Tel: 0121-306 6000
E-mail: info@dunloptyres.co.uk
Website: http://www.dunlop-tires.com
Directors: G. Rietvergen (MD), J. Robinson (Fin), G. Rietbergen (MD), N. Burrows (Mkt Research), M. Brickhill (MD)
Managers: J. Beddow, S. Page (I.T. Exec), S. Durston-Smith (Mktg Serv Mgr), N. Burrows (Sales & Mktg Mg), M. Gabel (I.T. Exec), A. Davis (Purch Mgr), J. Cowell (Fin Mgr)
Immediate Holding Company: GOODYEAR DUNLOP TYRES UK (PENSION TRUSTEES) LTD.
Registration no: 01792066 **Date established:** 1984
Turnover: £250m - £500m **No.of Employees:** 101 - 250
Product Groups: 29

Grahams Heating Spares
Unit 2 Bromford Central Bromford Industrial Estate Bromford Lane, Washwood Heath, Birmingham, B8 2SE
Tel: 0121-325 8372 **Fax:** 0121-325 8351
Website: http://www.graham-group.com
Bank(s): HSBC Bank plc
Managers: A. Ogle (District Mgr), J. Darnell (District Mgr)
Immediate Holding Company: SAINT GOBAIN (FRANCE)
Registration no: LP003081 **VAT No.:** GB 394 1212 63
Turnover: £500m - £1,000m **No.of Employees:** 21 - 50
Product Groups: 66

Grant Allen Designer Homes
11 Gracemere Crescent Hall Green, Birmingham, B28 OUA
Tel: 0121-744 7849 **Fax:** 07908-513 923
E-mail: info@grantallendesignerhomes.co.uk
Website: http://www.gadh.co.uk
Bank(s): Barclays
Directors: D. Littlehales (Dir), T. Hursthouse (Ch)
Managers: J. Covey (I.T. Exec)
Immediate Holding Company: Imtech UK Ltd
Registration no: 00443522 **VAT No.:** GB 116 6043 95
Turnover: £20m - £50m **No.of Employees:** 51 - 100 **Product Groups:** 52

Date of Accounts	Dec 08	Dec 07	Dec 06
Sales Turnover	35461	31228	26387
Pre Tax Profit/Loss	1956	2149	1682
Working Capital	5382	4680	3880
Fixed Assets	1303	1531	1633
Current Assets	14039	12522	8566
Current Liabilities	8657	7842	4687
Total Share Capital	5	5	5
ROCE% (Return on Capital Employed)	29.3	34.6	30.5
ROT% (Return on Turnover)	5.5	6.9	6.4

Grayson Thermal Systems
257 Wharfdale Road, Birmingham, B11 2DP
Tel: 0121-708 1830 **Fax:** 0121-706 1886
E-mail: sales@graysonts.com
Website: http://www.graysonts.com
Bank(s): Lloyds TSB Bank plc
Directors: B. Szypulski (Fin)
Managers: A. Minister, H. Mohammed (Tech Serv Mgr), I. Butler (Purch Mgr), O. Morris (Personnel)
Immediate Holding Company: GRAYSON AUTOMOTIVE SERVICES LIMITED
Registration no: 01223712 **VAT No.:** GB 112 9207 03
Date established: 1975 **Turnover:** £10m - £20m
No.of Employees: 101 - 250 **Product Groups:** 29, 32, 35, 36, 39, 40, 48, 66, 67, 68

Date of Accounts	Mar 11	Mar 10	Mar 09
Sales Turnover	16m	15m	N/A
Pre Tax Profit/Loss	244	157	341
Working Capital	814	568	773
Fixed Assets	2m	2m	2m
Current Assets	8m	7m	7m
Current Liabilities	1m	1m	907

Greenwoods Coleshill Ltd
Jeynes House 3 Highway Point Gorsey Lane, Coleshill, Birmingham, B46 1JU
Tel: 01675-464280 **Fax:** 01675-464738
E-mail: sales@greenwoodscomms.com
Website: http://www.greenwoodscomms.com
Bank(s): Lloyds
Directors: T. Lane (Fin), D. Akrell (Fin)
Managers: A. Swain (Sales Admin), E. Lander (Personnel), J. Holcroft (Tech Serv Mgr)
Ultimate Holding Company: GREENWOODS GROUP LIMITED
Immediate Holding Company: GREENWOODS COLESHILL LIMITED
Registration no: 03444792 **VAT No.:** GB 600 6855 59
Date established: 1997 **Turnover:** £1m - £2m **No.of Employees:** 11 - 20
Product Groups: 37

Date of Accounts	Dec 11	Dec 10	Dec 09
Sales Turnover	N/A	N/A	4m
Pre Tax Profit/Loss	N/A	N/A	-111
Working Capital	995	603	452
Fixed Assets	43	53	49
Current Assets	3m	2m	3m
Current Liabilities	N/A	N/A	157

Griflex
Roman Way Coleshill, Birmingham, B46 1HG
Tel: 01675-464803 **Fax:** 01675-465924
E-mail: sales@griflex.uk.com
Website: http://www.griflex.uk.com
Directors: S. Dale (Co Sec)
Managers: I. Marshall (Mgr)
Ultimate Holding Company: FLEXICON LIMITED
Immediate Holding Company: TEKFLEX LIMITED
Registration no: 06395496 **Date established:** 2007
No.of Employees: 21 - 50 **Product Groups:** 30

Groundwork UK
Lockside 5 Scotland Street, Birmingham, B1 2RR
Tel: 0121-236 8565 **Fax:** 0121-236 7356
E-mail: info@groundwork.org.uk
Website: http://www.groundwork.org.uk
Directors: R. Sharland (Dir), S. Bennett (Fin)
Managers: A. Hawkhead (Sales Admin), S. Grundy (Mktg Serv Mgr), D. Stevens (Purch Mgr)
Registration no: 07422194 **Date established:** 1989
No.of Employees: 51 - 100 **Product Groups:** 80

Grundfos Pumps Ltd
39 Gravelly Industrial Park, Birmingham, B24 8TG
Tel: 0121-328 3336 **Fax:** 0121-328 4332
E-mail: hberger@grundfos.com
Website: http://www.grundfos.com
Directors: B. Jensen (Fin), H. Berger (Sales)
Ultimate Holding Company: POUL DUE JENSENS FOUNDATION (DENMARK)
Immediate Holding Company: GRUNDFOS PUMPS LIMITED
Registration no: 00805960 **Date established:** 1964 **Turnover:** £1m - £2m
No.of Employees: 1 - 10 **Product Groups:** 67

Date of Accounts	Dec 11	Dec 10	Dec 09
Sales Turnover	97m	92m	86m
Pre Tax Profit/Loss	12m	14m	10m
Working Capital	8m	8m	6m
Fixed Assets	6m	8m	9m
Current Assets	26m	28m	25m
Current Liabilities	12m	13m	12m

Guhring Ltd
Castle Bromwich Business Park Tameside Drive, Castle Vale, Birmingham, B35 7AG
Tel: 0121-749 5544 **Fax:** 0121-776 7224
E-mail: info@guhring.co.uk
Website: http://www.guhring.co.uk
Bank(s): Lloyds TSB
Directors: M. Dinsdale (Dir)
Managers: D. Hudson (Sales Prom Mgr), Y. Clune (Tech Serv Mgr)
Ultimate Holding Company: GUEHRING OHG (GERMANY)
Immediate Holding Company: GUHRING LIMITED
Registration no: 01114577 **VAT No.:** GB 195 4424 43
Date established: 1973 **Turnover:** £10m - £20m
No.of Employees: 51 - 100 **Product Groups:** 36, 46

Date of Accounts	Dec 11	Dec 10	Dec 09
Sales Turnover	14m	11m	9m
Pre Tax Profit/Loss	1m	405	502
Working Capital	7m	6m	6m
Fixed Assets	563	598	566
Current Assets	10m	8m	8m
Current Liabilities	1m	1m	382

A & J Gummers Ltd
Unit H Redfern Park Way, Birmingham, B11 2DN
Tel: 0121-706 2241 **Fax:** 0121-706 2960
E-mail: sales@gummers.co.uk
Website: http://www.sirrusshowers.co.uk
Directors: G. Balls (Fin)
Managers: J. Shade (Mgr)
Ultimate Holding Company: MASCO CORP INC (USA)
Immediate Holding Company: A & J GUMMERS LIMITED
Registration no: 02756137 **VAT No.:** GB 417 0222 95
Date established: 1992 **Turnover:** £10m - £20m **No.of Employees:** 1 - 10
Product Groups: 36, 38, 39

H A S T A M
10 Sovereign Court 8 Graham Street, Birmingham, B1 3JR
Tel: 08445-610434 **Fax:** 01621-851756
E-mail: info@hastam.co.uk
Website: http://www.hastam.co.uk
Directors: M. Vyvyan (Grp Chief Exec)
Ultimate Holding Company: CONTINENTAL HOLDINGS LIMITED (HONG KONG)
Immediate Holding Company: HASTAM LIMITED
Registration no: 02343863 **VAT No.:** GB 393 1015 71
Date established: 1989 **Turnover:** £500,000 - £1m
No.of Employees: 1 - 10 **Product Groups:** 84

H K L Gas Power Ltd
260 Windsor Street, Birmingham, B7 4DX
Tel: 0121-359 6131 **Fax:** 0121-359 8580
E-mail: info@hkl-gaspower.co.uk
Website: http://www.hkl-gaspower.co.uk
Directors: K. Knight (MD), S. Woodward (Co Sec)
Immediate Holding Company: H. K. L. GAS POWER LIMITED
Registration no: 01222527 **Date established:** 1975
Turnover: Up to £250,000 **No.of Employees:** 1 - 10 **Product Groups:** 30, 31, 35, 36, 37, 38, 39, 40, 42, 45, 63, 68, 72, 77

Date of Accounts	Mar 07	Sep 10	Sep 09
Working Capital	574	-302	-30
Fixed Assets	563	836	958
Current Assets	2m	399	719
Current Liabilities	373	33	12

H P P UK Ltd
82 Cliveland Street, Birmingham, B19 3SN
Tel: 0121-359 6465 **Fax:** 0121-359 0746
E-mail: hppukltd@aol.com
Website: http://www.hppuk.com
Directors: M. Barford (Fin), J. Roberts (MD)
Immediate Holding Company: H.P.P. (U.K.) LIMITED
Registration no: 01632190 **VAT No.:** GB 377 3111 55
Date established: 1982 **Turnover:** £500,000 - £1m
No.of Employees: 1 - 10 **Product Groups:** 40, 49

Date of Accounts	Mar 11	Mar 10	Mar 09
Working Capital	82	117	59
Fixed Assets	2	2	3
Current Assets	464	449	440

H V R
Unit 2 Tudor Industrial Estate Wharfdale Road, Birmingham, B11 2DG
Tel: 0121-707 7922 **Fax:** 0121-706 6176
E-mail: info@pentagonelectric.co.uk
Website: http://www.pentagonelectric.co.uk
Bank(s): Lloyds TSB Bank plc
Directors: J. Ketchin (Co Sec)
Ultimate Holding Company: HVR LIMITED
Immediate Holding Company: HVR PENTAGON LIMITED
Registration no: 01125953 **VAT No.:** GB 112 2297 11
Date established: 1973 **Turnover:** £500,000 - £1m
No.of Employees: 11 - 20 **Product Groups:** 37, 38

Date of Accounts	May 11	May 10	May 09
Working Capital	256	234	262
Fixed Assets	36	25	28
Current Assets	350	369	385

Hall & Kay Fire Engineering Ltd (a division of Staveley Fire Services Ltd)
Sterling Park Clapgate Lane, Birmingham, B32 3BU
Tel: 0121-421 3311 **Fax:** 0121-422 7312
E-mail: birmingham@hkfire.co.uk
Website: http://www.hkfire.co.uk
Bank(s): National Westminster Bank Plc
Directors: T. Pierson (Fin)
Managers: M. Nock (Ops Mgr), P. Apperley (Personnel)
Ultimate Holding Company: UNITED TECHNOLOGIES CORP INC (USA)
Immediate Holding Company: HALL & KAY FIRE ENGINEERING LTD
Registration no: 05515962 **VAT No.:** GB 239 3550 53
Date established: 2005 **Turnover:** £50m - £75m
No.of Employees: 21 - 50 **Product Groups:** 40

Hallam Catering Equipment Ltd
Unit F9-F10 Aston Seedbed Centreavenue Road Nechells, Birmingham, B7 4NT
Tel: 0121-359 4411 **Fax:** 0121-359 4425
E-mail: hallamcatequip@btconnect.com
Website: http://www.hallamcatering.co.uk
Directors: C. Hallam (Prop)
Immediate Holding Company: HALLAM CATERING EQUIPMENT LTD
Registration no: 05538065 **Date established:** 2005
No.of Employees: 1 - 10 **Product Groups:** 20, 40, 41

G S Halligan
175 Knightlow Road, Birmingham, B17 8PY
Tel: 0121-420 2227 **Fax:** 0121-434 3967
Directors: G. Halligan (Prop)
Date established: 1986 **No.of Employees:** 1 - 10 **Product Groups:** 38, 67

Hammond Lubricants & Chemicals Ltd
Unit 2-4 Porters Way, Birmingham, B9 5RR
Tel: 0121-772 1375 **Fax:** 0121-772 3530
E-mail: sales@hammondlubricants.co.uk
Website: http://www.hammondlubricants.co.uk
Directors: M. Hammond (Dir)
Immediate Holding Company: HAMMOND LUBRICANTS AND CHEMICALS LIMITED
Registration no: 04602531 **Date established:** 2002
Turnover: £500,000 - £1m **No.of Employees:** 1 - 10 **Product Groups:** 31, 32, 33, 36, 38, 40, 45, 48, 54, 63, 66, 67, 68

Date of Accounts	Apr 11	Apr 10	Apr 09
Working Capital	-247	-351	-315
Fixed Assets	1m	1m	1m
Current Assets	288	238	146

The Hampton Works Ltd
Twyning Road Stirchley, Birmingham, B30 2XZ
Tel: 0121-458 2901 **Fax:** 0121-433 3819
E-mail: sales@hamptonworks.co.uk
Website: http://www.hamptonworks.co.uk
Bank(s): National Westminster Bank Plc
Directors: R. Cull (Dir), S. Cull (Dir)
Ultimate Holding Company: CLEVERLYN LIMITED
Immediate Holding Company: HAMPTON WORKS(STAMPINGS),LIMITED(THE)
Registration no: 00299640 **VAT No.:** GB 109 7302 81
Date established: 1935 **Turnover:** £1m - £2m **No.of Employees:** 11 - 20
Product Groups: 24, 49, 61, 65

Date of Accounts	Mar 11	Mar 10	Mar 09
Working Capital	117	98	91
Fixed Assets	101	113	131
Current Assets	327	317	297

Hans Motors
Unit 22 Fort Industrial Park, Castle Vale, Birmingham, B35 7AR
Tel: 0121-749 8820 **Fax:** 0121-749 8821
E-mail: sales@gsfcarparts.com
Website: http://www.hansmotors.co.uk
Managers: L. Parchment (Sales Prom Mgr)
Registration no: 02095672 **No.of Employees:** 11 - 20
Product Groups: 31, 39

Happich Vehicle & Industrial Components Ltd
Unit 30 Fort Industrial Park Chester Road, Castle Vale, Birmingham, B35 7AR
Tel: 0121-747 4400 **Fax:** 0121-747 4977
Website: http://www.happich.com
Directors: R. Grice (Fin)
Ultimate Holding Company: Aksia Group Spa (Italy)
Registration no: 02590020 **Date established:** 1991 **Turnover:** £2m - £5m
No.of Employees: 1 - 10 **Product Groups:** 29, 36, 49

Harness Flex Ltd
Station Road Industrial Estate Station Road, Coleshill, Birmingham, B46 1HT
Tel: 01675-468222 **Fax:** 01675-464930
E-mail: sales@harnessflex.co.uk
Website: http://www.harnessflex.co.uk
Directors: D. Mckinlay (MD)
Managers: E. Robins (Buyer), M. Turner (Mktg Serv Mgr), S. Bradley (Nat Sales Mgr)
Ultimate Holding Company: DUNDAS GROUP HOLDINGS LIMITED
Immediate Holding Company: HARNESSFLEX LIMITED
Registration no: 02130654 **VAT No.:** GB 486 9127 07
Date established: 1987 **Turnover:** £10m - £20m **No.of Employees:** 1 - 10
Product Groups: 30, 37, 39

Date of Accounts	Jul 08	Jul 07	Jul 06
Working Capital	50	50	755
Current Assets	50	50	755

Hawker Electronics Ltd
57 The Avenue Rubery, Rednal, Birmingham, B45 9AL
Tel: 0121-453 8911 **Fax:** 0121-453 3777
E-mail: info@hawker-electronics.co.uk
Website: http://www.hawker-electronics.co.uk
Bank(s): Lloyds TSB Bank plc
Directors: J. Slevin (MD), M. Armstrong (Tech Serv)
Managers: B. Ashfield (Sales Eng)
Immediate Holding Company: HAWKER ELECTRONICS LIMITED
Registration no: 00758105 **VAT No.:** GB 109 9898 12
Date established: 1963 **No.of Employees:** 21 - 50 **Product Groups:** 38

Date of Accounts	Aug 11	Aug 10	Aug 09
Working Capital	1m	1m	1m
Fixed Assets	243	258	274
Current Assets	2m	2m	2m

William Hawkes Holdings Ltd
183-184 High Street Deritend, Birmingham, B12 0LH
Tel: 0121-772 2694 **Fax:** 0121-772 2694
Directors: R. Hawkes (Fin)
Immediate Holding Company: WILLIAM HAWKES (HOLDINGS) LIMITED
Registration no: 03888999 **Date established:** 1999
Turnover: Up to £250,000 **No.of Employees:** 1 - 10 **Product Groups:** 48, 51

Date of Accounts	Apr 11	Apr 10	Apr 07
Working Capital	578	549	747
Fixed Assets	194	194	1
Current Assets	582	750	763

Hay Group Ltd
6120 Knights Court Solihull Parkway, Birmingham Business Park, Birmingham, B37 7WY
Tel: 0121-717 4600 **Fax:** 0121-717 4601
Website: http://www.haygroup.com
Directors: L. Wilkins (MD)
Ultimate Holding Company: TRANSTEC PLC
Immediate Holding Company: THE HAY GROUP HOLDINGS LTD
Registration no: 00015997 **VAT No.:** GB 497 6415 95
Date established: 1998 **Turnover:** £5m - £10m **No.of Employees:** 1 - 10
Product Groups: 80

Hazard Warning Systems Ltd
52-57 Bristol Road, Birmingham, B5 7TU
Tel: 0121-446 4433 **Fax:** 0121-446 4230
E-mail: sales@hazard.co.uk
Website: http://www.hazard.co.uk
Managers: B. Ward (Develop Mgr)
Immediate Holding Company: HAZARD WARNING SYSTEMS LTD
Registration no: 04596567 **Date established:** 2002 **Turnover:** £2m - £5m
No.of Employees: 11 - 20 **Product Groups:** 23, 39, 40

Date of Accounts	Nov 11	Nov 10	Nov 09
Working Capital	107	98	N/A
Current Assets	549	100	13

Heart Of England Ltd
The Hampton Works,Twyning Road,Twyning Road Stirchley, Birmingham, B30 2XZ
Tel: 0121-458 2470 **Fax:** 0121-433 5799
E-mail: sales@heartofenglandltd.co.uk
Website: http://www.heartofenglandltd.co.uk
Directors: A. Jones (Dir), D. Jones (MD)
Managers: R. Thompson (Comm), D. Edwards (Accounts)
Registration no: 06041255 **VAT No.:** GB 109 4203 01
Turnover: Up to £250,000 **No.of Employees:** 1 - 10 **Product Groups:** 35, 36, 48

Heartland Catering Spares
1187 Bristol Road South Northfield, Birmingham, B31 2SL
Tel: 0121-243 3336 **Fax:** 0121-243 2236
E-mail: sharptez@aol.com
Directors: T. Sharps (Prop), T. Sharpe (Prop)
Immediate Holding Company: WHITEHOT LIMITED
Registration no: 06677364 **Date established:** 2000
No.of Employees: 1 - 10 **Product Groups:** 20, 40, 41

Samuel Heath & Sons plc
Cobden Works Leopold Street, Birmingham, B12 0UJ
Tel: 0121-772 2303 **Fax:** 0121-772 3334
E-mail: info@samuel-heath.com
Website: http://www.samuel-heath.com
Bank(s): Barclays
Directors: P. Turner (Fin), D. Pick (MD), A. Cogzell (Pers)
Managers: S. Richardson (Purch Mgr), G. Hand (Sales Prom Mgr), V. Allan (Mktg Serv Mgr), N. Titley (Tech Serv Mgr)
Ultimate Holding Company: SAMUEL HEATH AND SONS PUBLIC LIMITED COMPANY
Immediate Holding Company: PERKINS & POWELL LIMITED
Registration no: 00238382 **VAT No.:** GB 109 5249 69
Date established: 2029 **Turnover:** £10m - £20m
No.of Employees: 101 - 250 **Product Groups:** 36

Helm-X Ltd
27-29 Speedwell Road Yardley, Birmingham, B25 8HT
Tel: 0121-766 6755 **Fax:** 0121-766 6752
E-mail: brentandcarole@yahoo.co.uk
Website: http://www.helmx.co.uk
Bank(s): AIB Group
Directors: B. Brown (MD)
Immediate Holding Company: HELM-X LIMITED
Registration no: 04981690 **VAT No.:** GB 559 0747 11
Date established: 2003 **Turnover:** £2m - £5m **No.of Employees:** 11 - 20
Product Groups: 35, 81

Date of Accounts	Dec 11	Dec 10	Dec 09
Working Capital	20	-99	24
Fixed Assets	13	12	15
Current Assets	305	193	304

Help Organisation Ltd
Lawford House Lawford Close, Birmingham, B7 4HJ
Tel: 0121-202 0200 **Fax:** 0121-359 3712
E-mail: mn@moenawaz.com
Website: http://www.ukadvice.com
Directors: P. Jordan (Dir)
Immediate Holding Company: HELP ORGANISATION LIMITED
Registration no: 06009381 **Date established:** 2006
No.of Employees: 11 - 20 **Product Groups:** 80

Date of Accounts	Nov 11	Nov 10	Nov 09
Working Capital	510	510	497
Fixed Assets	1	2	2
Current Assets	524	518	520

Henley Research International Ltd
Concorde House Trinity Park Solihul, Birmingham, B37 7UQ
Tel: 0121-635 5177 **Fax:** 0121-635 5001
E-mail: helen@henleyresearch.com
Website: http://www.henleyresearch.com
Managers: H. Davies
Immediate Holding Company: HENLEY RESEARCH INTERNATIONAL LIMITED
Registration no: 02991221 **VAT No.:** GB 655 2212 56
Date established: 1994 **Turnover:** £500,000 - £1m
No.of Employees: 1 - 10 **Product Groups:** 80

Date of Accounts	Mar 11	Mar 10	Mar 09
Working Capital	59	59	64
Fixed Assets	6	5	7

Current Assets	108	83	110
Current Liabilities	N/A	N/A	33

Henshaw Manufacturing Co Birmingham Ltd
Diamond Place Stratford Street North, Birmingham, B11 1BF
Tel: 0121-771 3633 **Fax:** 0121-771 1788
E-mail: weekshenshaw@aol.com
Bank(s): HSBC Bank plc
Directors: R. Weeks (MD)
Immediate Holding Company: HENSHAW MANUFACTURING CO. (BIRMINGHAM) LIMITED
Registration no: 01017382 **VAT No.:** GB 109 8329 56
Date established: 1971 **No.of Employees:** 11 - 20 **Product Groups:** 35, 45, 48

Date of Accounts	Jul 11	Jul 10	Jul 09
Working Capital	-48	-36	-93
Fixed Assets	343	346	346
Current Assets	224	217	209

Hewden Hire Centres Ltd
39-40 New Summer Street, Birmingham, B19 3QN
Tel: 0121-359 4282 **Fax:** 0121-333 6866
Website: http://www.hewden.co.uk
Directors: B. Sherlock (Grp MD)
Managers: P. Clarke (Mgr), J. Schofield (Grp Mktg Mgr), P. Clark (Mgr)
Immediate Holding Company: HEWDEN HIRE CENTRES LIMITED
Registration no: SC046005 **Date established:** 1968
No.of Employees: 11 - 20 **Product Groups:** 83

Hexa Sports Ltd
Unit D 70 Albert Road, Stechford, Birmingham, B33 9AH
Tel: 0121-783 0312 **Fax:** 0121-786 2472
E-mail: sales@hexasports.co.uk
Website: http://www.hexasports.co.uk
Directors: C. Styles (Dir), E. Styles (MD)
Registration no: 01135282 **Date established:** 1993
Turnover: £250,000 - £500,000 **No.of Employees:** 1 - 10
Product Groups: 49

Date of Accounts	Oct 09	Oct 08	Oct 07
Sales Turnover	290	304	305
Pre Tax Profit/Loss	-1	-12	2
Working Capital	57	58	66
Fixed Assets	6	6	9
Current Assets	117	140	145
Current Liabilities	11	21	22

Hi Tech Selection Ltd
123-131 Bradford Street, Birmingham, B12 0NS
Tel: 0121-766 6626 **Fax:** 0121-772 2016
E-mail: recruit@hts.co.uk
Website: http://www.hdf.co.uk
Directors: M. Hannon (MD), M. Hannon (Dir)
Immediate Holding Company: CLOCKWORK FACILITIES LIMITED
Registration no: 06659091 **Date established:** 2008
Turnover: £250,000 - £500,000 **No.of Employees:** 1 - 10
Product Groups: 80

Highwood Engineering Ltd
Parkfield Road, Birmingham, B8 3AZ
Tel: 0121-327 9212 **Fax:** 0121-327 4329
Directors: J. Smith (MD), P. Truran (Fin), Y. Yakub (Dir)
Immediate Holding Company: P S BODY HIRE LIMITED
Registration no: 02951872 **VAT No.:** GB 614 4531 64
Date established: 2009 **Turnover:** Up to £250,000
No.of Employees: 1 - 10 **Product Groups:** 40, 48

Date of Accounts	Mar 11	Mar 10
Working Capital	-17	-41
Fixed Assets	14	45
Current Assets	5	6

Hills Numberplate Holdings Ltd
Unit 6 Electric Avenue, Birmingham, B6 7JJ
Tel: 0121-623 8050 **Fax:** 0121-623 8011
E-mail: orders@hillsnumberplates.com
Website: http://www.hillsnumberplates.com
Bank(s): Barclays
Directors: R. Taffinder (Dir), K. Jenkins (Fin)
Managers: D. Floyd (Tech Serv Mgr), J. Cane, A. Berry
Immediate Holding Company: HILLS NUMBERPLATE HOLDINGS LIMITED
Registration no: 04227068 **Date established:** 2001
Turnover: £10m - £20m **No.of Employees:** 51 - 100 **Product Groups:** 39

Date of Accounts	Dec 11	Dec 10	Dec 09
Sales Turnover	10m	8m	8m
Pre Tax Profit/Loss	368	-148	-306
Working Capital	-1m	-1m	-2m
Fixed Assets	3m	3m	4m
Current Assets	3m	2m	2m
Current Liabilities	563	215	315

Hilti GT Britain Ltd
Priory Road Aston, Birmingham, B6 7LG
Tel: 0800-886100 **Fax:** 0800-886200
Website: http://www.hilti.co.uk
Directors: J. Rood (MD), A. Murphy (Sales), F. Dannheim (Fin)
Ultimate Holding Company: HILTI AG (LIECHTENSTEIN)
Immediate Holding Company: HILTI (GT.BRITAIN) LIMITED
Registration no: 00479786 **Date established:** 1950
No.of Employees: 1 - 10 **Product Groups:** 30, 35, 36, 37, 40

Date of Accounts	Dec 10	Dec 09	Dec 08
Sales Turnover	65m	66m	79m
Pre Tax Profit/Loss	766	-379	-48
Working Capital	12m	15m	12m
Fixed Assets	5m	5m	6m
Current Assets	33m	25m	23m
Current Liabilities	6m	4m	5m

H Hipkiss & Co. Ltd
Park House Clapgate Lane, Birmingham, B32 3BL
Tel: 0121-421 5777 **Fax:** 0121-421 5333
E-mail: info@hipkiss.co.uk
Website: http://www.hipkiss.co.uk
Bank(s): Lloyds TSB Bank plc
Directors: S. Rogers (Sales), P. Farrington (Fin), M. Evans (Dir)
Ultimate Holding Company: HIPKISS HOLDINGS LIMITED
Immediate Holding Company: H.HIPKISS AND COMPANY,LIMITED
Registration no: 00071382 **Date established:** 2001 **Turnover:** £2m - £5m
No.of Employees: 21 - 50 **Product Groups:** 35, 36, 48, 66

Date of Accounts	Oct 11	Oct 10	Oct 09
Working Capital	1m	1m	1m
Fixed Assets	101	72	83
Current Assets	2m	2m	2m

J Hipwell & Son Ltd
427 Warwick Road Greet, Tyseley, Birmingham, B11 2JU
Tel: 0121-706 5471 **Fax:** 0121-706 0502
Directors: P. Hipwell (Dir)
Immediate Holding Company: J.HIPWELL & SON LIMITED
Registration no: 00701085 **VAT No.:** GB 111 0082 48
Date established: 1961 **Turnover:** Up to £250,000
No.of Employees: 1 - 10 **Product Groups:** 48

Date of Accounts	Mar 11	Mar 10	Mar 09
Working Capital	-57	-53	-44
Fixed Assets	16	18	20
Current Assets	127	122	123

Hire Association Europe Ltd
Unit 2450 Regent Court The Crescent, Birmingham Business Park, Birmingham, B37 7YE
Tel: 0121-380 4600 **Fax:** 0121-333 4109
E-mail: melanie.kilkenny@hae.org.uk
Website: http://www.hae.org.uk
Directors: G. Arundell (MD)
Immediate Holding Company: HIRE ASSOCIATION EUROPE LIMITED
Registration no: 01183652 **VAT No.:** GB 247 7099 28
Date established: 1974 **Turnover:** £500,000 - £1m
No.of Employees: 1 - 10 **Product Groups:** 80, 82

Date of Accounts	Sep 11	Sep 10	Sep 09
Sales Turnover	975	969	957
Pre Tax Profit/Loss	57	-9	-165
Working Capital	127	53	135
Fixed Assets	133	141	70
Current Assets	462	443	515
Current Liabilities	268	255	273

Hoare Lea & Partners
Auchinleck House Broad Street, Birmingham, B15 1DP
Tel: 0121-643 6331 **Fax:** 0121-643 2419
E-mail: birmingham@hoarelea.com
Website: http://www.hoarelea.com
Directors: G. Andrew (Ptnr), G. Tucker (Snr Part), M. West (Ptnr)
Immediate Holding Company: Hoare Lea & Partners Ltd
Registration no: 01854244 **Turnover:** £10m - £20m
No.of Employees: 21 - 50 **Product Groups:** 84

Hoerbiger UK
1649 Pershore Road Stirchley, Kings Norton, Birmingham, B30 3DR
Tel: 0121-433 3636 **Fax:** 0121-459 7794
E-mail: timothy.haviland@hoerbiger.co.uk
Website: http://www.hoerbiger.com
Bank(s): ABN AMRO Bank NV
Directors: M. Tomlinson (Co Sec), S. Harvey (MD), T. Haviland (Dir)
Ultimate Holding Company: HOERBIGER HOLDING AG (SWITZERLAND)
Immediate Holding Company: HOERBIGER UK LIMITED
Registration no: 02072970 **Date established:** 1986 **Turnover:** £5m - £10m
No.of Employees: 101 - 250 **Product Groups:** 36, 40, 48

Date of Accounts	Dec 10	Dec 09	Dec 08
Sales Turnover	8m	9m	10m
Pre Tax Profit/Loss	-814	-18	-2m
Working Capital	1m	2m	263
Fixed Assets	3m	3m	3m
Current Assets	3m	3m	3m
Current Liabilities	557	332	1m

Holdens Supaseal Ltd
505 Garretts Green Lane, Birmingham, B33 0SG
Tel: 0121-789 7766 **Fax:** 0121-789 7237
E-mail: info@holdens-supaseal.co.uk
Website: http://www.holdens-supaseal.co.uk
Bank(s): Barclays
Directors: M. Holden (MD), C. Pearse (Fin)
Managers: T. Whitehall
Immediate Holding Company: HOLDENS SUPASEAL LIMITED
Registration no: 01296553 **Date established:** 1977 **Turnover:** £1m - £2m
No.of Employees: 21 - 50 **Product Groups:** 33

Date of Accounts	Dec 11	Dec 10	Dec 09
Working Capital	10	21	70
Fixed Assets	566	605	621
Current Assets	604	625	637

Holec Electrical Goods
Reddings Lane Tyseley, Birmingham, B11 3EZ
Tel: 0121-685 1326 **Fax:** 0121-685 2072
E-mail: barryholt@eaton.com
Website: http://www.eaton.com
Managers: B. Holt (Mgr)
Date established: 1999 **No.of Employees:** 1 - 10 **Product Groups:** 36, 40

Holloway Tools
71-75 New Summer Street, Birmingham, B19 3TE
Tel: 0121-359 3777 **Fax:** 0121-359 5410
E-mail: reg@drbengineering.com
Website: http://www.drbengineering.com
Bank(s): Barclays
Directors: B. Devlin (Fin), R. Hill (Fab), R. Jones (Grp Chief Exec), R. Jones (MD)
Managers: M. Brookes (Prod Mgr), N. Clansey (Purch Mgr)
Ultimate Holding Company: DRB Engineering Ltd
Immediate Holding Company: D.R.B. ENGINEERING LIMITED
Registration no: 02337609 **Date established:** 1989 **Turnover:** £5m - £10m
No.of Employees: 51 - 100 **Product Groups:** 37, 46, 48

Date of Accounts	Mar 08	Mar 09	Apr 10
Sales Turnover	5m	5m	4m
Pre Tax Profit/Loss	-76	76	12
Working Capital	1m	1m	1m
Fixed Assets	2m	2m	2m
Current Assets	3m	3m	2m
Current Liabilities	205	728	470

Holmes UK Ltd
Unit 6 Monarch Industrial Park 198 Kings Road, Tyseley, Birmingham, B11 2AP
Tel: 0121-706 6936 **Fax:** 0121-707 9913
E-mail: tim@holmesmachines.co.uk
Website: http://www.holmesmachines.co.uk

see next page

***Holmes UK Ltd** - Cont'd*

Directors: A. Hopton (Dir)
Immediate Holding Company: HOLMES UK LIMITED
Registration no: 02708391 **VAT No.:** GB 614 0077 80
Date established: 1992 **Turnover:** £500,000 - £1m
No.of Employees: 1 - 10 **Product Groups:** 46

Date of Accounts	Dec 11	Dec 10	Dec 09
Working Capital	361	291	286
Fixed Assets	187	152	189
Current Assets	462	415	384

Honeywell Control Systems Ltd

2480 Regents Court The Crescent, Birmingham Business Park, Birmingham, B37 7YE
Tel: 0121-480 5200
Website: http://www.honeywell.com
Ultimate Holding Company: Honeywell International Inc (USA)
Immediate Holding Company: HONEYWELL CONTROL SYSTEMS LIMITED
Registration no: 00217803 **Date established:** 1926
Turnover: £250m - £500m **No.of Employees:** 1 - 10 **Product Groups:** 38, 39, 68

Hopkins Blind & Shutter Fittings

Prospect House Jameson Road, Birmingham, B6 7SJ
Tel: 08454-563018 **Fax:** 08454- 563019
E-mail: brian@hopkinsfittings.co.uk
Website: http://www.hopkinsfittings.co.uk
Directors: R. Hopkins (MD), A. Hopkins (MD)
Ultimate Holding Company: HOPKINS HOLDINGS LIMITED
Immediate Holding Company: HOPKINS HOLDINGS LIMITED
Registration no: 03725091 **Date established:** 1999 **Turnover:** £1m - £2m
No.of Employees: 1 - 10 **Product Groups:** 24, 25

Date of Accounts	Oct 09	Oct 08	Oct 07
Working Capital	-56	-63	-61
Fixed Assets	219	226	234
Current Assets	64	3	N/A
Current Liabilities	N/A	49	47

E C Hopkins Ltd

82 Kettles Wood Drive, Birmingham, B32 3DB
Tel: 0121-506 6090 **Fax:** 0121-421 8286
E-mail: steve@echopkins-bham.co.uk
Website: http://www.echopkins.co.uk
Managers: S. Seedhouse (Mgr)
Immediate Holding Company: E.C.HOPKINS,LIMITED
Registration no: 00340631 **VAT No.:** GB 101 3917 15
Date established: 1938 **Turnover:** £5m - £10m **No.of Employees:** 1 - 10
Product Groups: 37, 40, 45

Date of Accounts	Sep 11	Sep 10	Sep 09
Sales Turnover	7m	6m	5m
Pre Tax Profit/Loss	285	208	-78
Working Capital	1m	854	763
Fixed Assets	2m	2m	1m
Current Assets	2m	2m	2m
Current Liabilities	572	467	327

Hoskins Medical Equipment Ltd

Admail 1001, Birmingham, B1 1HJ
Tel: 0121-707 6600 **Fax:** 0121-607 5555
E-mail: sales@hoskinsme.co.uk
Website: http://www.hoskinsme.co.uk
Bank(s): Barclays, St. Albans
Directors: G. Cox (MD), M. Simpson (Dir)
Managers: G. Gladwin (Sales Prom Mgr), C. Jones (Sec)
Immediate Holding Company: Huntleigh Technology Ltd
Registration no: 03255575 **VAT No.:** GB 580 3495 30
Turnover: £5m - £10m **No.of Employees:** 251 - 500 **Product Groups:** 26, 38

House Of Flags Ltd

1048 Coventry Road Yardley, Birmingham, B25 8DP
Tel: 0121-773 6789 **Fax:** 0121-773 6757
E-mail: solutions@flags.co.uk
Website: http://www.flags.co.uk
Managers: M. Percy (District Mgr)
Ultimate Holding Company: KORAMIC INDUSTRIES SA (BELGIUM)
Immediate Holding Company: HOUSE OF FLAGS LIMITED
Registration no: 02213723 **VAT No.:** GB 491 0233 70
Date established: 1988 **Turnover:** £2m - £5m **No.of Employees:** 1 - 10
Product Groups: 49

Date of Accounts	Mar 12	Mar 11	Mar 10
Sales Turnover	4m	3m	N/A
Pre Tax Profit/Loss	330	214	N/A
Working Capital	1m	973	779
Fixed Assets	79	70	99
Current Assets	2m	1m	1m
Current Liabilities	689	219	N/A

Howard Bros Engravers Ltd

89-91 Barr Street, Birmingham, B19 3DE
Tel: 0121-554 6318 **Fax:** 0121-507 0601
E-mail: info@howardbros.co.uk
Website: http://www.howardbros.co.uk
Directors: J. Howard (MD)
Immediate Holding Company: HOWARD BROS.(ENGRAVERS)LIMITED
Registration no: 00490805 **VAT No.:** GB 109 6192 67
Date established: 1951 **Turnover:** £250,000 - £500,000
No.of Employees: 1 - 10 **Product Groups:** 48, 49

Date of Accounts	Dec 11	Dec 10	Dec 09
Working Capital	138	163	153
Fixed Assets	281	245	282
Current Assets	225	296	257

Hudson

Victoria Square House Victoria Square, Birmingham, B2 4AJ
Tel: 0121-633 0010 **Fax:** 0121-633 0862
E-mail: eleanor.patterson@hudson.com
Website: http://www.hudson.com
Directors: C. Haynes (Fin)
Managers: E. Patterson (Ops Mgr)
Immediate Holding Company: HUDSON GLOBAL RESOURCES LIMITED
Registration no: 03206355 **Date established:** 1996
Turnover: £500,000 - £1m **No.of Employees:** 1 - 10 **Product Groups:** 80

Date of Accounts	Dec 07	Dec 06	Dec 05
Sales Turnover	161800	182660	205550
Pre Tax Profit/Loss	5240	11690	3800
Working Capital	53440	64350	51410
Fixed Assets	2730	2510	2530
Current Assets	94240	103430	83040
Current Liabilities	40800	39080	31630
Total Share Capital	270	270	270
ROCE% (Return on Capital Employed)	9.3	17.5	7.0
ROT% (Return on Turnover)	3.2	6.4	1.8

Hyder Consulting Ltd

Aston Cross Business Village 50 Rocky Lane, Aston, Birmingham, B6 5RQ
Tel: 0121-345 9000 **Fax:** 0121-333 4275
E-mail: chris.evans@hyderconsulting.com
Website: http://www.hyderconsulting.com
Directors: J. Matthews (Mkt Research), G. Reid (Dir), C. Evans (Div)
Ultimate Holding Company: DE RIGO SPA (ITALY)
Immediate Holding Company: DOLLOND & AITCHISON SAVINGS PLAN LIMITED
Registration no: 03379725 **Date established:** 1997
Turnover: £20m - £50m **No.of Employees:** 51 - 100 **Product Groups:** 54, 84

Hydrajaws Ltd

Unit 1 The Courtyard Roman Way, Coleshill, Birmingham, B46 1HQ
Tel: 01675-430370 **Fax:** 01675-465950
E-mail: adrian@hydrajaws.co.uk
Website: http://www.hydrajaws.co.uk
Directors: A. Morgan (MD)
Immediate Holding Company: HYDRAJAWS LIMITED
Registration no: 02230733 **Date established:** 1988
Turnover: £500,000 - £1m **No.of Employees:** 1 - 10 **Product Groups:** 38

Date of Accounts	Jul 11	Jul 10	Jul 09
Working Capital	188	340	350
Fixed Assets	342	333	339
Current Assets	364	484	448

Hydrapower Dynamics Ltd

St Marks Street, Birmingham, B1 2UN
Tel: 0121-456 5656 **Fax:** 0121-456 5668
E-mail: pbrowne@hdl.uk.net
Website: http://www.hydrapower-dynamics.com
Directors: P. Browne (Co Sec)
Managers: D. Smith (Purch Mgr), S. Allsop (Sales & Mktg Mg), A. Whitfield, A. Sogi (Personnel), P. Brown (Tech Serv Mgr)
Immediate Holding Company: HYDRAPOWER DYNAMICS LIMITED
Registration no: 01737504 **Date established:** 1983 **Turnover:** £5m - £10m
No.of Employees: 51 - 100 **Product Groups:** 29, 30, 35, 36

Date of Accounts	Dec 11	Dec 10	Dec 09
Sales Turnover	8m	6m	4m
Pre Tax Profit/Loss	306	-191	150
Working Capital	442	176	463
Fixed Assets	2m	2m	2m
Current Assets	3m	3m	2m
Current Liabilities	1m	391	126

Hydraulic Cylinders

4 Birmingham New Enterprise Workshops All Saints Road, Birmingham, B18 7RL
Tel: 0121-523 8400 **Fax:** 0121-523 8400
E-mail: roy@hydraulic-pneumatic-cylinders.co.uk
Website: http://www.hydraulic-pneumatic-cylinders.co.uk
Directors: R. Targonski (Dir)
Immediate Holding Company: CASTLEBEST LIMITED
Registration no: 04528850 **Date established:** 2003
Turnover: Up to £250,000 **No.of Employees:** 1 - 10 **Product Groups:** 38, 40, 48, 76, 83, 84

I C S

Birmingham Science Park Aston Faraday Wharf Holt Street, Birmingham, B7 4BB
Tel: 0121-326 7771 **Fax:** 0121-327 4114
E-mail: info@icstemp.com
Website: http://www.icstemp.com
Managers: I. Morgan (District Mgr)
Immediate Holding Company: GLOBETRACK TECHNOLOGIES LIMITED
Registration no: 02432069 **VAT No.:** GB 541 7905 39
Date established: 2007 **Turnover:** £10m - £20m **No.of Employees:** 1 - 10
Product Groups: 40, 42, 52

Date of Accounts	Mar 11	Mar 10	Mar 07
Working Capital	-4	-19	19
Fixed Assets	5	7	N/A
Current Assets	23	12	20
Current Liabilities	N/A	N/A	1

I & M Controls Ltd

75 Villa Street, Birmingham, B19 2XL
Tel: 0121-551 7877 **Fax:** 0121-554 3846
E-mail: sales@iandmcontrols.co.uk
Website: http://www.iandmcontrols.co.uk
Bank(s): Barclays
Directors: P. Mcclenaghan (Dir)
Immediate Holding Company: I AND M CONTROLS LIMITED
Registration no: 00986962 **VAT No.:** GB 110 1239 42
Date established: 1970 **Turnover:** £500,000 - £1m
No.of Employees: 21 - 50 **Product Groups:** 30, 37

Date of Accounts	Nov 11	Nov 10	Nov 09
Working Capital	678	610	662
Fixed Assets	142	170	160
Current Assets	1m	2m	2m

I M I Components Ltd

Nobel Way, Birmingham, B6 7ES
Tel: 0121-344 5800 **Fax:** 0121-344 3056
E-mail: p.evans@imicomponents.com
Website: http://www.imicomponents.com
Directors: M. Evans (Co Sec), P. Evans (MD)
Managers: A. Floyd (Tech Serv Mgr), A. Guise (Personnel)
Ultimate Holding Company: IMI PLC
Immediate Holding Company: IMI COMPONENTS LIMITED
Registration no: 01640862 **VAT No.:** GB 405 2661 78
Date established: 1982 **Turnover:** £20m - £50m
No.of Employees: 101 - 250 **Product Groups:** 34, 52, 63, 67

Date of Accounts	Dec 11	Dec 10	Dec 09
Sales Turnover	47m	1m	1m
Pre Tax Profit/Loss	975	538	1m
Working Capital	3m	3m	2m
Current Assets	67m	61m	53m
Current Liabilities	259	160	358

I M S International Marketing Services Ltd

Boulton Works 54 College Road, Perry Barr, Birmingham, B44 8BS
Tel: 0121-344 5500 **Fax:** 0121-344 5505/0121 344 5524
E-mail: djbiggs@ims-ltd.co.uk
Website: http://www.ims-ltd.co.uk
Bank(s): The Royal Bank of Scotland
Directors: D. Biggs (MD), M. Biggs (Fin)
Managers: B. White (Sales Prom Mgr)
Immediate Holding Company: I M S INTERNATIONAL MARKETING SERVICES LIMITED
Registration no: 01418504 **VAT No.:** GB 313 9030 91
Date established: 1979 **Turnover:** £2m - £5m **No.of Employees:** 21 - 50
Product Groups: 24, 35, 39

Date of Accounts	May 11	May 10	May 09
Working Capital	2m	2m	2m
Fixed Assets	285	250	259
Current Assets	3m	3m	3m

I T Fusions Ltd

51 Netherhall Avenue Great Barr, Birmingham, B43 7EU
Tel: 08456-435198 **Fax:** 08456-435199
E-mail: farb@mynetwork.co.uk
Website: http://www.fixmynetwork.co.uk
Directors: F. Randhawa (MD)
Immediate Holding Company: IT FUSIONS LTD
Registration no: 06648874 **Date established:** 2008
Turnover: Up to £250,000 **No.of Employees:** 1 - 10 **Product Groups:** 44, 80

Date of Accounts	Mar 12	Mar 11	Mar 10
Sales Turnover	18	30	47
Working Capital	2	5	4
Fixed Assets	1	1	2
Current Assets	11	9	12

Illston & Robson Ltd

Herbert Road Small Heath, Birmingham, B10 0QQ
Tel: 0121-772 5674 **Fax:** 0121-766 6452
E-mail: info@illstonandrobson.com
Website: http://www.illstonandrobson.com
Directors: C. Reid (MD), S. Holder (Fin), M. Reid (Dir)
Managers: N. Williams (Sales Prom Mgr)
Immediate Holding Company: ILLSTON & ROBSON LIMITED
Registration no: 04729590 **VAT No.:** GB 110 7592 93
Date established: 2003 **Turnover:** £500,000 - £1m
No.of Employees: 21 - 50 **Product Groups:** 39

Date of Accounts	May 12	May 11	May 10
Working Capital	212	276	119
Fixed Assets	379	222	197
Current Assets	551	557	379

Imirp Rapid Prototyping Ltd

Aston Cross Industrial Estate 51 Lichfield Road, Birmingham, B6 5RW
Tel: 0121-327 3525 **Fax:** 0121-328 5982
E-mail: paul@imirp.co.uk
Website: http://www.imirp.co.uk
Directors: D. Potter (Sales), P. Bingham (Comm), R. Ray (I.T. Dir)
Immediate Holding Company: IMIRP RAPID PROTOTYPING LTD
Registration no: 03930210 **Date established:** 2000 **Turnover:** £1m - £2m
No.of Employees: 1 - 10 **Product Groups:** 28, 30, 34, 42, 44, 46, 47, 48, 49, 66, 84

Date of Accounts	Jun 11	Jun 10	Jun 09
Working Capital	110	83	75
Fixed Assets	22	12	19
Current Assets	254	184	188

Industrial Hose & Pipe Fittings Ltd

Bannerley Road, Birmingham, B33 0SR
Tel: 0121-783 8118 **Fax:** 0121-784 4844
E-mail: sales@ihp.co.uk
Website: http://www.ihp.co.uk
Bank(s): HSBC Bank plc
Directors: A. Caldecott (MD), C. Elwell (MD)
Immediate Holding Company: INDUSTRIAL HOSE & PIPE FITTINGS LIMITED
Registration no: 00596613 **VAT No.:** GB 109 7947 35
Date established: 1958 **Turnover:** £1m - £2m **No.of Employees:** 11 - 20
Product Groups: 22, 30, 36

Date of Accounts	Jul 12	Jul 11	Jul 10
Working Capital	671	585	564
Fixed Assets	41	38	21
Current Assets	900	772	750

I W M Ltd

Facet Road, Birmingham, B38 9PT
Tel: 0121-451 2788 **Fax:** 0121-459 9001
E-mail: carl@indwash.co.uk
Website: http://www.indwash.co.uk
Bank(s): Barclays Bank
Directors: C. Hollier (MD)
Managers: S. Wakeman (Buyer), M. Round (Tech Serv Mgr)
Immediate Holding Company: INDUSTRIAL WASHING MACHINES LIMITED
Registration no: 04636452 **VAT No.:** GB 614 0017 01
Date established: 2003 **Turnover:** £2m - £5m **No.of Employees:** 21 - 50
Product Groups: 24, 40, 41

Date of Accounts	Dec 11	Dec 10	Dec 09
Working Capital	354	326	202
Fixed Assets	658	652	662
Current Assets	1m	858	716

Infometal (t/a Barnies)

Moseley Street, Birmingham, B12 0RT
Tel: 0121-693 3800 **Fax:** 0121-693 3803
E-mail: info@barnies.co.uk
Directors: D. O'Grady (Jt MD)
Registration no: 01673545 **Date established:** 1982
Turnover: Up to £250,000 **No.of Employees:** 1 - 10 **Product Groups:** 35

Date of Accounts	Mar 08	Mar 07	Mar 06
Working Capital	356	356	218
Fixed Assets	499	535	486
Current Assets	3492	3676	2195
Current Liabilities	3136	3319	1977

Initial Electronic Security Systems Ltd

Woodgate Business Centre 6 Kettles Wood Drive, Birmingham, B32 3DB
Tel: 0121-421 1111 **Fax:** 0121-421 5533
Website: http://www.ies.uk.com

Managers: M. Perks (Mgr), R. Goodger (Mgr)
Immediate Holding Company: Mitie Group plc
Registration no: 00715168 **Turnover:** £20m - £50m
No.of Employees: 1 - 10 **Product Groups:** 40

Instrumentation Concept Ltd

754 Alum Rock Road, Birmingham, B8 3PP
Tel: 0121-328 3261 **Fax:** 0845-463 1984
E-mail: info@instconcept.co.uk
Website: http://www.instconcept.co.uk
Managers: S. Ishaque (Mgr)
Immediate Holding Company: INSTRUMENTATION CONCEPT LIMITED
Registration no: 06472683 **Date established:** 2008
Turnover: Up to £250,000 **No.of Employees:** 1 - 10 **Product Groups:** 38

Date of Accounts	Jan 11	Jan 10	Jan 09
Sales Turnover	75	38	N/A
Working Capital	3	-9	-6
Fixed Assets	1	1	1
Current Assets	20	7	6
Current Liabilities	N/A	6	N/A

Integrated Designs & Associates Ltd

38 Old Walsall Road, Birmingham, B42 1NP
Tel: 0121-358 2233 **Fax:** 0121-357 7492
E-mail: contact@integratedesigns.co.uk
Website: http://www.integratedesigns.co.uk
Directors: P. Sehdeva (MD)
Immediate Holding Company: INTEGRATED DESIGNS & ASSOCIATES LIMITED
Registration no: 06712665 **Date established:** 2008
No.of Employees: 1 - 10 **Product Groups:** 84

Date of Accounts	Mar 12	Mar 11	Mar 10
Working Capital	82	19	-7
Fixed Assets	5	6	7
Current Assets	252	165	167

Intercity Telecom Ltd

101-114 Holloway Head, Birmingham, B1 1QP
Tel: 0121-643 7373 **Fax:** 0121-643 6160
E-mail: sales@intercity-uk.com
Website: http://www.intercity-uk.com
Directors: A. Jackson (Fin), A. Jackson (MD)
Ultimate Holding Company: GIFTSIGN LIMITED
Immediate Holding Company: INTERCITY TELECOM LIMITED
Registration no: 01938625 **Date established:** 1985
Turnover: £20m - £50m **No.of Employees:** 101 - 250 **Product Groups:** 37

Date of Accounts	Dec 11	Dec 10	Dec 09
Sales Turnover	22m	22m	21m
Pre Tax Profit/Loss	2m	3m	2m
Working Capital	41m	40m	38m
Fixed Assets	1m	1m	1m
Current Assets	56m	54m	53m
Current Liabilities	743	843	820

Interdream Web Development

604 ROTUNDA NEW STREET, Birmingham, B2 4PA
Tel: 07722-836302
E-mail: contact@interdream-web-development.com
Website: http://www.interdream.co.uk
Directors: J. Allardice (Pres)
Date established: 2006 **No.of Employees:** 1 - 10 **Product Groups:** 44

International Convention Centre

Broad Street, Birmingham, B1 2EA
Tel: 0121-200 2000
Website: http://www.theicc.co.uk
Directors: A. Jowett (Dir)
Managers: A. McManus, K. Davidson
Ultimate Holding Company: PERFORMANCES BIRMINGHAM LIMITED
Immediate Holding Company: PERFORMANCES BIRMINGHAM LIMITED
Registration no: 03169600 **Date established:** 1996
Turnover: £10m - £20m **No.of Employees:** 51 - 100 **Product Groups:** 69

Date of Accounts	Mar 11	Mar 10	Mar 09
Sales Turnover	1m	1m	539
Working Capital	-25	-33	N/A
Fixed Assets	25	33	N/A
Current Assets	141	132	87

International Training Service Ltd (ITS)

37 Parkfield Road Coleshill, Birmingham, B46 3LD
Tel: 01675-466466 **Fax:** 01675-466404
E-mail: johnh@itsconsult.com
Website: http://www.itsconsult.com
Directors: A. Conway (Dir), D. Harvey (Dir), J. Hillier (Grp Chief Exec), J. Doyle (Dir), P. Kenrick (MD), M. Forster (Co Sec)
Managers: A. Young
Ultimate Holding Company: ITS CONSULTANTS LIMITED
Immediate Holding Company: INTERNATIONAL TRAINING SERVICE LIMITED
Registration no: 00638133 **VAT No.:** GB 238 8401 51
Date established: 1959 **Turnover:** £2m - £5m **No.of Employees:** 1 - 10
Product Groups: 54, 80, 86

Date of Accounts	Mar 08	Mar 07	Mar 06
Sales Turnover	2969	N/A	2452
Pre Tax Profit/Loss	40	N/A	18
Working Capital	647	634	608
Fixed Assets	21	15	8
Current Assets	1117	1104	935
Current Liabilities	470	470	327
ROCE% (Return on Capital Employed)	5.9		2.9
ROT% (Return on Turnover)	1.3		0.7

Iscar Tools

Woodgate Business Park Bartley Green, Birmingham, B32 3DE
Tel: 0121-422 8585 **Fax:** 0121-421 8255
E-mail: sales@iscar.co.uk
Website: http://www.iscar.co.uk
Bank(s): National Westminster Bank Plc
Managers: M. Jones (Mktg Serv Mgr), A. Warr (Tech Serv Mgr), B. Williams (Personnel), P. King (Fin Mgr), I. Pearce (Sales Prom Mgr), D. Beale (Purch Mgr), G. Taylor (Chief Mgr)
Ultimate Holding Company: BERKSHIRE HATHAWAY INC (USA)
Immediate Holding Company: ISCAR TOOLS LIMITED
Registration no: 01194326 **VAT No.:** GB 281 4434 63
Date established: 1974 **Turnover:** £20m - £50m
No.of Employees: 21 - 50 **Product Groups:** 36, 46

Date of Accounts	Dec 11	Dec 10	Dec 09
Sales Turnover	28m	24m	24m
Pre Tax Profit/Loss	413	-392	-2m
Working Capital	1m	643	983
Fixed Assets	981	1m	1m
Current Assets	10m	8m	8m
Current Liabilities	2m	1m	576

Isher Hangers

51-53 Steward Street, Birmingham, B18 7AE
Tel: 0121-456 1833 **Fax:** 0121-456 1833
E-mail: rs-chatha@isherhangers.co.uk
Website: http://www.isherhangers.co.uk
Managers: R. Chatha (Chief Mgr)
No.of Employees: 21 - 50 **Product Groups:** 25, 30, 35, 40, 48, 67

I T T Ltd

61 Charlotte Street, Birmingham, B3 1PX
Tel: 0121-248 1632 **Fax:** 0121-248 1633
E-mail: richard.ashton@i-t-t.com
Website: http://www.i-t-t.com
Directors: R. Ashton (Grp Chief Exec)
Immediate Holding Company: ITT.COM LIMITED
Registration no: 04222607 **Date established:** 2001 **Turnover:** £1m - £2m
No.of Employees: 1 - 10 **Product Groups:** 80

J E S Manufacturing Company Ltd

53 Wharf Road Tyseley, Birmingham, B11 2DX
Tel: 0121-706 1425 **Fax:** 0121-707 3988
E-mail: sales@jesmanufacturing.co.uk
Website: http://www.jesmanufacturing.co.uk
Directors: N. Storey (MD)
Immediate Holding Company: J.E.S. MANUFACTURING COMPANY LIMITED
Registration no: 02894218 **VAT No.:** GB 110 6260 26
Date established: 1994 **Turnover:** £500,000 - £1m
No.of Employees: 1 - 10 **Product Groups:** 26, 34, 35, 36, 49, 67

Date of Accounts	Dec 11	Dec 10	Dec 09
Working Capital	61	79	63
Fixed Assets	6	8	10
Current Assets	129	150	134

J H P Training Ltd

Norfolk House Smallbrook Queensway, Birmingham, B5 4LJ
Tel: 0121-643 4200 **Fax:** 0121-633 4681
E-mail: bda.birmingham@jhp-group.com
Website: http://www.jhptraining.com
Bank(s): National Westminster Bank Plc
Directors: C. Fisher (Reg), J. Pitman (Ch)
Managers: J. Candlish (Mktg Serv Mgr), P. Allard (Mgr), R. Patel (I.T. Exec), S. Cooper (Sales Prom Mgr), J. Bray (Personnel)
Immediate Holding Company: JHP TRAINING LIMITED
Registration no: 03247918 **Date established:** 1996
No.of Employees: 21 - 50 **Product Groups:** 86

J H Richards & Co.

112 Saltley Road, Birmingham, B7 4TD
Tel: 0121-359 2257 **Fax:** 0121-359 7340
E-mail: info@jhrichards.co.uk
Website: http://www.jhrichards.co.uk
Bank(s): Lloyds TSB Bank plc
Directors: A. Jeeves (Fin), K. Greenhall (MD)
Immediate Holding Company: J.H.RICHARDS AND CO.LIMITED
Registration no: 00141346 **VAT No.:** GB 110 2906 24
Date established: 2015 **Turnover:** £1m - £2m **No.of Employees:** 21 - 50
Product Groups: 34, 35, 36, 39, 40, 48

Date of Accounts	Dec 11	Dec 10	Dec 09
Working Capital	539	596	642
Fixed Assets	530	573	425
Current Assets	876	932	1m

J Hudson & Co Whistles Ltd

244 Barr Street, Birmingham, B19 3AH
Tel: 0121-554 2124 **Fax:** 0121-551 9293
E-mail: info@acmewhistles.co.uk
Website: http://www.acmewhistles.co.uk
Bank(s): Barclays
Directors: S. Topman (MD)
Managers: D. Topman (Personnel), B. McFarlane (Purch Mgr)
Immediate Holding Company: J. HUDSON AND CO. (WHISTLES) LIMITED
Registration no: 00473291 **VAT No.:** GB 109 9022 77
Date established: 1949 **Turnover:** £2m - £5m **No.of Employees:** 21 - 50
Product Groups: 39, 49

Date of Accounts	Dec 11	Dec 10	Dec 09
Working Capital	650	644	543
Fixed Assets	136	123	109
Current Assets	800	843	683

J J Engineering

Granby Avenue, Birmingham, B33 0TJ
Tel: 0121-784 9990 **Fax:** 0121-784 8588
E-mail: jonathand@jjeng.co.uk
Website: http://www.jjeng.co.uk
Bank(s): Lloyds TSB Bank plc
Directors: J. Davis (Prop)
Managers: K. Swallow (Personnel)
Immediate Holding Company: J J ENGINEERING (HOLDINGS) LTD
Registration no: 01089418 **VAT No.:** GB 111 5335 20
Turnover: £2m - £5m **No.of Employees:** 21 - 50 **Product Groups:** 48

Date of Accounts	Dec 07	Dec 06	Dec 05
Working Capital	-254	-35	112
Fixed Assets	1283	1257	1161
Current Assets	985	1105	934
Current Liabilities	1239	1140	822
Total Share Capital	10	10	50

J Lacey Steeplejack Contractors Ltd

50 Bickford Road, Birmingham, B6 7EE
Tel: 0121-327 6376 **Fax:** 0121-328 4692
E-mail: info@jlacey.com
Website: http://www.jlacey.com
Directors: J. Lacey (MD)
Immediate Holding Company: J. LACEY INDUSTRIAL SERVICES LIMITED
Registration no: 01788368 **Date established:** 1984
No.of Employees: 1 - 10 **Product Groups:** 07, 23, 30, 37, 40, 52, 67

Date of Accounts	Dec 11	Dec 10	Dec 09
Working Capital	25	23	33
Fixed Assets	3	3	4
Current Assets	38	63	39

Jaffabox Ltd

Starley Way, Birmingham, B37 7HB
Tel: 0121-250 2000 **Fax:** 0121-250 2001
E-mail: sales@jaffabox.com
Website: http://www.jaffabox.com
Bank(s): Barclays
Directors: J. Amyes (Dir)
Immediate Holding Company: JAFFABOX LIMITED
Registration no: 01259298 **Date established:** 1976 **Turnover:** £5m - £10m
No.of Employees: 21 - 50 **Product Groups:** 27

Date of Accounts	Jul 11	Jul 10	Jul 09
Sales Turnover	8m	7m	5m
Pre Tax Profit/Loss	514	314	308
Working Capital	220	-106	-60
Fixed Assets	4m	5m	5m
Current Assets	2m	1m	1m
Current Liabilities	638	465	335

James Lister & Sons Ltd

2 Dartmouth Industrial Estate Miller Street, Birmingham, B6 4NF
Tel: 0121-359 3774 **Fax:** 01827-52291
E-mail: birmingham@lister.co.uk
Website: http://www.lister.co.uk
Directors: T. Cotterell (MD)
Ultimate Holding Company: JAMES LISTER HOLDINGS LIMITED
Immediate Holding Company: JAMES LISTER & SONS LIMITED
Registration no: 00591148 **Date established:** 1957
Turnover: £10m - £20m **No.of Employees:** 1 - 10 **Product Groups:** 34, 37, 63, 66, 67

Date of Accounts	Sep 11	Sep 10	Sep 09
Sales Turnover	15m	14m	16m
Pre Tax Profit/Loss	334	103	84
Working Capital	4m	5m	5m
Fixed Assets	578	1m	1m
Current Assets	8m	9m	8m
Current Liabilities	517	635	395

Jewson Ltd

Stechford Station Wharf Station Road, Stechford, Birmingham, B33 9AF
Tel: 0121-783 2287 **Fax:** 0121-789 7179
E-mail: clive.richardson@jewson.co.uk
Website: http://www.jewson.co.uk
Managers: C. Richardson (District Mgr)
Ultimate Holding Company: COMPAGNIE DE SAINT GOBAIN (FRANCE)
Immediate Holding Company: JEWSON LIMITED
Registration no: 00348407 **Date established:** 1939
Turnover: £500m - £1,000m **No.of Employees:** 11 - 20
Product Groups: 66

Date of Accounts	Dec 11	Dec 10	Dec 09
Sales Turnover	1606m	1547m	1485m
Pre Tax Profit/Loss	18m	100m	45m
Working Capital	-345m	-250m	-349m
Fixed Assets	496m	387m	461m
Current Assets	657m	1005m	1320m
Current Liabilities	66m	120m	64m

Jewson Ltd

Unit 7 Sandy Lane Aston, Birmingham, B6 5TP
Tel: 0121-327 1451 **Fax:** 0121-328 7713
Website: http://www.jewson.co.uk
Managers: N. Falukner (Mgr)
Ultimate Holding Company: COMPAGNIE DE SAINT GOBAIN (FRANCE)
Immediate Holding Company: JEWSON LIMITED
Registration no: 00348407 **VAT No.:** GB 394 1212 63
Date established: 1939 **Turnover:** £500m - £1,000m
No.of Employees: 1 - 10 **Product Groups:** 25, 66

Date of Accounts	Dec 11	Dec 10	Dec 09
Sales Turnover	1606m	1547m	1485m
Pre Tax Profit/Loss	18m	100m	45m
Working Capital	-345m	-250m	-349m
Fixed Assets	496m	387m	461m
Current Assets	657m	1005m	1320m
Current Liabilities	66m	120m	64m

Jigs R Us Ltd

16 New Bartholomew Street, Birmingham, B5 5QS
Tel: 0121-643 0727 **Fax:** 0121-633 3392
Website: http://www.premierplatingjigs.com
Directors: A. Bott (Dir), K. Trueman (Fin)
Immediate Holding Company: JIGS R US LIMITED
Registration no: 07060807 **Date established:** 2009
Turnover: £250,000 - £500,000 **No.of Employees:** 1 - 10
Product Groups: 46

Date of Accounts	Oct 11	Oct 10
Working Capital	17	10
Fixed Assets	8	11
Current Assets	75	91

Johnson Apparel Master Ltd

Aldridge Road Perry Barr, Birmingham, B42 2EU
Tel: 0121-356 4512 **Fax:** 0121-344 3520
E-mail: davidray@johnsonplc.com
Website: http://www.apparelmaster.co.uk
Bank(s): National Westminster Bank Plc
Managers: D. Ray (Chief Mgr), H. Baggott (Sales Admin), I. Stevenson
Ultimate Holding Company: JOHNSONS APPARELMASTER
Immediate Holding Company: JOHNSON SERVICE GROUP P.L.C.
Registration no: 02970406 **VAT No.:** 71 5152 71 **Turnover:** £10m - £20m
No.of Employees: 101 - 250 **Product Groups:** 83

J E Jones S & D Ltd

Moor Lane, Birmingham, B6 7HH
Tel: 0121-356 9169 **Fax:** 0121-356 0595
E-mail: jejdrums@globalnet.co.uk
Website: http://www.jejdrums.co.uk
Bank(s): Lloyds TSB Bank plc
Directors: M. Jones (Dir)
Immediate Holding Company: J.E. JONES (SALES AND DISTRIBUTION) LIMITED
Registration no: 01888433 **VAT No.:** GB 425 3482 59
Date established: 1985 **Turnover:** £1m - £2m **No.of Employees:** 11 - 20
Product Groups: 35, 48, 66

Date of Accounts	Mar 12	Mar 11	Mar 10
Working Capital	240	274	204
Fixed Assets	268	293	274
Current Assets	536	581	483

Jones Lang Lasalle
45 Church Street, Birmingham, B3 2RT
Tel: 0121-643 6440 **Fax:** 0121-643 3121
E-mail: ian.cornock@eu.jll.com
Website: http://www.joneslanglasalle.co.uk
Directors: I. Cornock (Dir)
Immediate Holding Company: MOVESTARTER LTD
Registration no: 01081258 **Date established:** 2008
No.of Employees: 51 - 100 **Product Groups:** 80

Date of Accounts	Dec 11	Dec 10
Working Capital	-72	-137
Fixed Assets	205	232
Current Assets	62	76

Jones & Palmer Ltd
95 Carver Street, Birmingham, B1 3AR
Tel: 0121-236 9007 **Fax:** 0121-236 5513
E-mail: james.houston@jonesandpalmer.co.uk
Website: http://www.jonesandpalmer.co.uk
Bank(s): National Westminster Bank Plc
Directors: M. Judd (Co Sec), J. Houston (Dir)
Managers: M. Hill (Tech Serv Mgr)
Ultimate Holding Company: JONES AND PALMER HOLDINGS LIMITED
Immediate Holding Company: JONES AND PALMER LIMITED
Registration no: 00239324 **VAT No.:** GB 444 5678 24
Date established: 2029 **Turnover:** £2m - £5m **No.of Employees:** 21 - 50
Product Groups: 28

Date of Accounts	Mar 08	Sep 11	Sep 10
Working Capital	193	785	596
Fixed Assets	334	487	541
Current Assets	770	2m	1m

Jones & Webb Ltd
431 Tyburn Road, Birmingham, B24 8HJ
Tel: 0121-328 6199 **Fax:** 0121- 3280471
E-mail: sales@jonesandwebb.co.uk
Website: http://www.jonesandwebb.co.uk
Directors: L. Webb (MD)
Immediate Holding Company: JONES AND WEBB LIMITED
Registration no: 04346808 **Date established:** 2002
Turnover: £500,000 - £1m **No.of Employees:** 11 - 20 **Product Groups:** 34

Date of Accounts	Mar 11	Mar 10	Mar 09
Working Capital	37	98	228
Fixed Assets	1	2	2
Current Assets	112	190	321

Juice Master
22 Moseley Gate, Birmingham, B13 8JJ
Tel: 08451-302829 **Fax:** 0121-449 5392
E-mail: info@juicemaster.com
Website: http://www.juicemaster.com
Directors: J. Bow (MD)
Immediate Holding Company: THE JUICE MASTER LTD
Registration no: 04632887 **Date established:** 2003
No.of Employees: 1 - 10 **Product Groups:** 31, 32

Junction Media
Waterside House 46 Gas Street, Birmingham, B1 2JT
Tel: 0121-248 4466 **Fax:** 0121-634 4701
E-mail: paul@junctionmedia.co.uk
Website: http://www.junctionmedia.co.uk
Directors: P. Davies (MD)
Immediate Holding Company: TELEVISION JUNCTION HOLDINGS LIMITED
Registration no: 03269213 **Date established:** 1996
Turnover: £250m - £500m **No.of Employees:** 1 - 10 **Product Groups:** 79, 89

Date of Accounts	Dec 11	Dec 10	Dec 09
Working Capital	83	185	209
Fixed Assets	19	24	25
Current Assets	108	324	430

K B Extruders
Westwood Road, Birmingham, B6 7DU
Tel: 0121-328 4442 **Fax:** 0121-326 7767
E-mail: sales@kbextruders.co.uk
Website: http://www.kbextruders.co.uk
Directors: A. Ahmed (MD)
Immediate Holding Company: K.B. EXTRUDERS LTD
Registration no: 07533755 **Date established:** 2011
No.of Employees: 11 - 20 **Product Groups:** 38, 42

K N Manufacturing
17 Ebury Road, Birmingham, B30 3JJ
Tel: 0121-451 2200 **Fax:** 0121-451 2200
Directors: D. Brown (Prop)
Date established: 1991 **No.of Employees:** 1 - 10 **Product Groups:** 46, 48

K P D Midlands Ltd
Unit 1 St Andrews Street, Birmingham, B9 4JT
Tel: 0121-766 8226
E-mail: kpdmidlands@hotmail.com
Directors: K. Jackson (MD), J. Holder (Fin)
Immediate Holding Company: K P D (MIDLANDS) LIMITED
Registration no: 03586893 **Date established:** 1998
Turnover: Up to £250,000 **No.of Employees:** 1 - 10 **Product Groups:** 46, 48

Date of Accounts	Mar 11	Mar 10	Mar 08
Sales Turnover	171	164	171
Pre Tax Profit/Loss	3	2	8
Working Capital	-16	-15	3
Fixed Assets	17	16	20
Current Assets	91	95	81
Current Liabilities	13	24	7

Kalamazoo - Reynolds Ltd
1200 Bristol Road South Northfield, Birmingham, B31 2RW
Tel: 0121-483 2000 **Fax:** 0121-475 7566
E-mail: marketing@kalamazoo.co.uk
Website: http://www.kalamazoo.co.uk
Bank(s): Lloyds
Directors: P. Daniels (MD), A. Boulter (Fin)
Managers: A. Franks (Sales Prom Mgr), M. Snowdon, H. Barnett (Mktg Serv Mgr), J. Wilson (Personnel)
Ultimate Holding Company: UNIVERSAL COMPUTER SYSTEMS HOLDINGS INC (USA)
Immediate Holding Company: KALAMAZOO - REYNOLDS LIMITED
Registration no: 04286244 **Date established:** 2001
Turnover: £10m - £20m **No.of Employees:** 101 - 250
Product Groups: 44, 86

Date of Accounts	Dec 11	Dec 10	Dec 09
Sales Turnover	15m	17m	18m
Pre Tax Profit/Loss	1m	2m	-349
Working Capital	12m	10m	22m
Fixed Assets	9m	10m	11m
Current Assets	25m	23m	32m
Current Liabilities	2m	2m	2m

Kaleidoscope Imaging Ltd
Unit 1 Auckland Road, Birmingham, B11 1RH
Tel: 0121-771 1171 **Fax:** 0121-771 2075
E-mail: sales@tkpnet.com
Website: http://www.kal.uk.com
Directors: S. Eade (Dir)
Immediate Holding Company: KALEIDOSCOPE IMAGING LIMITED
Registration no: 04968663 **Date established:** 2003
Turnover: £500,000 - £1m **No.of Employees:** 1 - 10 **Product Groups:** 28, 81

Date of Accounts	Mar 11	Mar 10	Mar 09
Working Capital	-162	-153	-171
Fixed Assets	175	186	208
Current Assets	102	125	127

Kappa Paper Recycling
Mount Street, Birmingham, B7 5RE
Tel: 0121-327 1381 **Fax:** 0121-322 6300
E-mail: sales@sskpaper.co.uk
Website: http://www.smurfitkappa.com
Bank(s): HSBC Bank plc
Directors: K. Clish (Co Sec), P. Mcneill (Dir)
Ultimate Holding Company: SMURFIT KAPPA GROUP PUBLIC LIMITED COMPANY
Immediate Holding Company: SMURFIT KAPPA SSK LIMITED
Registration no: 00040681 **Date established:** 1994
Turnover: £50m - £75m **No.of Employees:** 101 - 250 **Product Groups:** 27

Date of Accounts	Dec 08
Working Capital	27m
Current Assets	27m

Kaug Refinery Services Ltd
31 Green Street, Birmingham, B12 0NB
Tel: 0121-772 4029
E-mail: info@kaugrefinery.co.uk
Website: http://www.kaugrefinery.co.uk
Directors: A. Coldicutt (Dir)
Immediate Holding Company: KAUG REFINERY SERVICES LIMITED
Registration no: 04685454 **Date established:** 2003
No.of Employees: 11 - 20 **Product Groups:** 37, 47, 48, 66

Date of Accounts	Mar 11	Mar 10	Mar 09
Working Capital	-174	-167	6
Fixed Assets	275	268	283
Current Assets	797	656	388

Keiper UK Ltd
Woodgate Business Park Clapgate Lane, Birmingham, B32 3BZ
Tel: 0121-423 2828 **Fax:** 0121-423 2561
E-mail: info@keiper.com
Website: http://www.keiper.com
Directors: B. Mandall (Co Sec)
Immediate Holding Company: KEIPER UK LIMITED
Registration no: 01662465 **Date established:** 1982
Turnover: £20m - £50m **No.of Employees:** 101 - 250 **Product Groups:** 39

Date of Accounts	Dec 11	Dec 10	Dec 09
Sales Turnover	35m	31m	17m
Pre Tax Profit/Loss	2m	888	892
Working Capital	4m	3m	2m
Fixed Assets	3m	3m	3m
Current Assets	9m	8m	6m
Current Liabilities	2m	2m	1m

J H Kemp Ltd
409 Tyburn Road, Birmingham, B24 8HJ
Tel: 0121-327 3154 **Fax:** 0121-326 7542
E-mail: info@jhkemp.co.uk
Website: http://www.jhkemp.co.uk
Directors: J. Kemp (MD), J. Robson (Fin)
Immediate Holding Company: J H KEMP LIMITED
Registration no: 03924219 **Date established:** 2000
No.of Employees: 11 - 20 **Product Groups:** 72, 84

Date of Accounts	Jun 11	Jun 10	Jun 09
Working Capital	169	101	-47
Fixed Assets	116	168	166
Current Assets	553	640	421

Kemps Publishing Ltd
11 Swan Courtyard Charles Edward Road, Birmingham, B26 1BU
Tel: 0121-765 4144 **Fax:** 0121-706 6210
E-mail: info@kempspublishing.co.uk
Website: http://www.kempspublishing.co.uk
Directors: M. Jennings (Dir)
Ultimate Holding Company: KEMPS HOLDINGS LIMITED
Immediate Holding Company: KEMPS PUBLISHING LIMITED
Registration no: 02685392 **Date established:** 1992 **Turnover:** £5m - £10m
No.of Employees: 21 - 50 **Product Groups:** 28, 87

Date of Accounts	Mar 12	Mar 11	Mar 10
Working Capital	1m	947	1m
Fixed Assets	31	68	104
Current Assets	2m	2m	2m

Kemwell Thermal Ltd
Roma Road, Birmingham, B11 2JH
Tel: 0121-708 1188 **Fax:** 0121-706 3390
E-mail: enquiries@kemwellthermal.com
Website: http://www.kemwellthermal.co.uk
Bank(s): Lloyds TSB Bank plc
Directors: G. Buckley (Fin)
Managers: T. Buckley (Chief Mgr)
Immediate Holding Company: KEMWELL THERMAL LIMITED
Registration no: 02829049 **VAT No.:** GB 614 1735 63
Date established: 1993 **Turnover:** £1m - £2m **No.of Employees:** 21 - 50
Product Groups: 33, 37, 40, 46, 48

Date of Accounts	Dec 11	Dec 10	Dec 09
Working Capital	500	502	403
Fixed Assets	79	87	106
Current Assets	880	684	542

Charles Kendall Freight Ltd
2241 Coventry Road Sheldon, Birmingham, B26 3NW
Tel: 0121-722 3088 **Fax:** 0121-722 3035
E-mail: lmartin@charleskendallfreight.com
Website: http://www.charleskendall.com
Managers: L. Martin (District Mgr)
Ultimate Holding Company: CHARLES KENDALL GROUP LIMITED
Immediate Holding Company: CHARLES KENDALL FREIGHT LIMITED
Registration no: 00540121 **Date established:** 1954
No.of Employees: 1 - 10 **Product Groups:** 76

Date of Accounts	Dec 11	Dec 10	Dec 09
Sales Turnover	19m	21m	20m
Pre Tax Profit/Loss	445	248	107
Working Capital	3m	2m	2m
Current Assets	13m	9m	7m
Current Liabilities	167	150	95

Kentex Jeans & Casuals (Labmen Ltd, A Division of SLK Kentex Fashions Ltd)
33 Hampton Street, Birmingham, B19 3LS
Tel: 0121-233 0203
E-mail: kentex@btinternet.com
Website: http://www.kentex.co.uk
Directors: P. Kenth (Dir), P. Kenth (Prop)
Managers: H. Jheeta (Sales Prom Mgr)
Immediate Holding Company: KENTEX FASHIONS (UK) LIMITED
Registration no: 01503528 **VAT No.:** GB 487 1583 09
Date established: 1980 **Turnover:** £1m - £2m **No.of Employees:** 1 - 10
Product Groups: 23, 24, 63

Keter UK Ltd
12-14 Kettles Wood Drive, Birmingham, B32 3DB
Tel: 0121-422 6633 **Fax:** 0121-422 0808
E-mail: sales@outstanding-keter.com
Website: http://www.keter.com
Managers: I. Morely (Mgr)
Ultimate Holding Company: KETER PLASTIC LIMITED (ISRAEL)
Immediate Holding Company: KETER (UK) LIMITED
Registration no: 02186562 **VAT No.:** GB 494 6809 92
Date established: 1987 **Turnover:** £500,000 - £1m
No.of Employees: 21 - 50 **Product Groups:** 30

Date of Accounts	Dec 11	Dec 10	Dec 09
Sales Turnover	28m	29m	35m
Pre Tax Profit/Loss	66	71	-89
Working Capital	2m	2m	2m
Fixed Assets	18	24	38
Current Assets	3m	3m	5m
Current Liabilities	187	379	353

Key Lighting Ltd
37 Dulverton Road, Birmingham, B6 7EQ
Tel: 0121-322 2300 **Fax:** 0121-328 5050
Managers: M. Palmer (Mgr)
Immediate Holding Company: KEYLIGHTING LIMITED
Registration no: 01810394 **Date established:** 1984
Turnover: Up to £250,000 **No.of Employees:** 1 - 10 **Product Groups:** 37

Date of Accounts	Jan 11	Jan 10	Jan 09
Working Capital	811	762	673
Fixed Assets	489	499	545
Current Assets	2m	2m	1m

Keystone Castor Co.
Unit 1, St Andrews Trading Estate
111 Gt Barr Street
Digbeth, Birmingham, B9 4 BB
Tel: 0121-772 1010 **Fax:** 0121-773 1103
E-mail: info@keystonecastors.com
Website: http://www.keystonecastors.co.uk
Bank(s): National Westminster Bank Plc
Directors: J. Wood (MD), L. Montali (MD)
Managers: A. Partridge (Mgr)
Ultimate Holding Company: Keystone Wood Ltd
Immediate Holding Company: KEYSTONE WOOD LIMITED
Registration no: 00541197 **Date established:** 1954 **Turnover:** £2m - £5m
No.of Employees: 21 - 50 **Product Groups:** 35, 39, 66

Date of Accounts	Dec 11	Dec 10	Dec 09
Working Capital	2m	2m	2m
Fixed Assets	104	81	39
Current Assets	3m	3m	2m

Kilby Packaging
192 Alcester Road Hollywood, Birmingham, B47 5HH
Tel: 01564-823176 **Fax:** 01564-334594
E-mail: info@kilby.co.uk
Website: http://www.kilby.co.uk
Bank(s): Barclays
Directors: J. Kilby (MD), K. Williams (Fin)
Managers: A. Sutton (Tech Serv Mgr), J. Blackburn
Immediate Holding Company: JOHN KILBY & SON LIMITED
Registration no: 00557587 **VAT No.:** GB 109 6330 81
Date established: 1955 **Turnover:** £2m - £5m **No.of Employees:** 21 - 50
Product Groups: 25, 27

Date of Accounts	Mar 12	Mar 11	Mar 10
Working Capital	1m	1m	1m
Fixed Assets	630	647	641
Current Assets	2m	2m	2m

King Dick Tools
Unit 11 Roman Way, Coleshill, Birmingham, B46 1HG
Tel: 01675-467776 **Fax:** 01675-464277
E-mail: info@kingdicktools.co.uk
Website: http://www.kingdicktools.co.uk
Bank(s): The Royal Bank of Scotland
Directors: G. Roberts (MD)
Immediate Holding Company: A.E.T. LTD
Registration no: 03461518 **VAT No.:** GB 688 1948 70
Date established: 1997 **Turnover:** £2m - £5m **No.of Employees:** 11 - 20
Product Groups: 35, 36

Date of Accounts	Mar 11	Mar 10	Sep 08
Working Capital	-41	-25	N/A
Fixed Assets	315	76	38
Current Assets	27	60	30

Kingsbury Engineering Birmingham Ltd
842 Kingsbury Road Erdington, Birmingham, B24 9PS
Tel: 0121-377 6383 **Fax:** 0121-377 6694
E-mail: cad@kingsbury-eng.com
Website: http://www.kingsbury.eng.com
Bank(s): Lloyds TSB Bank plc

Directors: R. Left (MD), C. Wilkins (Ch)
Managers: P. Cox (Mgr), S. Burke (Accounts)
Ultimate Holding Company: KINGSBURY JIG & TOOL GROUP LIMITED
Immediate Holding Company: KINGSBURY ENGINEERING (BIRMINGHAM) LIMITED
Registration no: 00810495 **VAT No.:** GB 346 1751 56
Date established: 1964 **Turnover:** £2m - £5m **No.of Employees:** 11 - 20
Product Groups: 46, 67

Date of Accounts	Sep 11	Sep 10	Sep 09
Working Capital	-14	-58	107
Fixed Assets	22	37	30
Current Assets	309	209	607

Kirmell Ltd

Eyre Street, Birmingham, B18 7AA
Tel: 0121-456 3141 **Fax:** 0121-456 3151
E-mail: sales@kirmell.co.uk
Website: http://www.kirmell.co.uk
Bank(s): Barclays
Directors: A. Riaz (Fin), D. Keene (MD)
Immediate Holding Company: KIRMELL LIMITED
Registration no: 01936908 **VAT No.:** GB 109 5416 76
Date established: 1985 **Turnover:** £2m - £5m **No.of Employees:** 51 - 100
Product Groups: 46, 48

Date of Accounts	Mar 11	Mar 10	Mar 09
Working Capital	351	253	326
Fixed Assets	466	457	482
Current Assets	1m	1m	1m

Kitsons Environmental Europe Ltd

179b Gravelly Lane, Birmingham, B23 6LT
Tel: 0121-377 6675 **Fax:** 0121-377 6175
E-mail: info@kitsons.co.uk
Website: http://www.kitsons.co.uk
Directors: P. Dolan (MD), R. Hardy (Dir)
Managers: R. Hardy (District Mgr)
Ultimate Holding Company: SILVERDELL PLC
Immediate Holding Company: KITSONS ENVIRONMENTAL EUROPE LIMITED
Registration no: 02749577 **VAT No.:** 628 8843 91 **Date established:** 1992
No.of Employees: 1 - 10 **Product Groups:** 54

Date of Accounts	Sep 11	Sep 10	Sep 09
Sales Turnover	26m	26m	28m
Pre Tax Profit/Loss	2m	2m	2m
Working Capital	8m	7m	5m
Fixed Assets	338	370	436
Current Assets	14m	11m	11m
Current Liabilities	2m	3m	4m

Knight Strip Metals Ltd

Saltley Business Park Cumbria Way, Saltley, Birmingham, B8 1BH
Tel: 0121-322 8400 **Fax:** 0121-322 8401
E-mail: alan.woodhouse@knight-group.co.uk
Website: http://www.knight-group.co.uk
Directors: A. Woodhouse (Dir)
Immediate Holding Company: KNIGHT STRIP METALS LIMITED
Registration no: 00382978 **VAT No.:** GB 780 3621 35
Date established: 1943 **Turnover:** £10m - £20m
No.of Employees: 21 - 50 **Product Groups:** 34, 48

Date of Accounts	May 11	May 10	May 09
Sales Turnover	20m	15m	13m
Pre Tax Profit/Loss	944	534	19
Working Capital	8m	7m	7m
Fixed Assets	977	918	704
Current Assets	12m	10m	8m
Current Liabilities	1m	731	305

L V H Coatings Ltd

Station Road Coleshill, Birmingham, B46 1HT
Tel: 01675-466888 **Fax:** 01675-466260
E-mail: ron@lvh-coatings.co.uk
Website: http://www.lvh-coatings.co.uk
Bank(s): National Westminster Bank Plc
Directors: R. Vanes (Dir), E. Vanes (Co Sec)
Immediate Holding Company: L.V.H. COATINGS LIMITED
Registration no: 02536276 **VAT No.:** GB 545 1587 33
Date established: 1990 **Turnover:** £1m - £2m **No.of Employees:** 11 - 20
Product Groups: 32, 48, 66

Date of Accounts	Dec 11	Dec 10	Dec 09
Working Capital	409	424	389
Fixed Assets	219	200	153
Current Assets	753	723	659

Landor Cartons Ltd

45 Devon Street, Birmingham, B7 4SL
Tel: 0121-359 8511 **Fax:** 0121-359 6392
E-mail: phil@landorcartons.co.uk
Website: http://www.landorcartons.co.uk
Bank(s): Barclays
Directors: P. Morley (MD), R. McHardy (Fin)
Ultimate Holding Company: LANDOR CARTONS HOLDINGS LIMITED
Immediate Holding Company: LANDOR CARTONS LIMITED
Registration no: 03193683 **Date established:** 1996 **Turnover:** £5m - £10m
No.of Employees: 21 - 50 **Product Groups:** 27, 28, 42

Date of Accounts	Mar 12	Mar 11	Mar 10
Working Capital	1m	2m	2m
Fixed Assets	937	712	753
Current Assets	2m	3m	2m

George Lane & Sons Ltd

Bannerley Road, Birmingham, B33 0SL
Tel: 0121-784 5525 **Fax:** 0121-783 6988
E-mail: info@georgelane.co.uk
Website: http://www.georgelane.co.uk
Bank(s): National Westminster Bank Plc
Directors: M. Morris (Dir)
Immediate Holding Company: GEORGE LANE & SONS LTD
Registration no: 00103539 **VAT No.:** GB 110 3114 52
Date established: 2009 **Turnover:** £1m - £2m **No.of Employees:** 11 - 20
Product Groups: 35, 41, 42, 45

Date of Accounts	Dec 11	Dec 10	Dec 09
Working Capital	57	91	93
Fixed Assets	571	623	619
Current Assets	372	462	443

Lap Tab Ltd

205 Tyburn Road, Birmingham, B24 8NB
Tel: 0121-328 1697 **Fax:** 0121-328 9787
E-mail: neill.m@thewheelspecialist.co.uk
Website: http://www.thewheelspecialist.co.uk
Directors: N. Murphy (MD), L. Murphy (Fin)
Immediate Holding Company: LAP-TAB LIMITED
Registration no: 00911974 **VAT No.:** GB 110 0278 37
Date established: 1967 **Turnover:** Up to £250,000
No.of Employees: 1 - 10 **Product Groups:** 48

Date of Accounts	Jan 12	Jan 11	Jan 10
Working Capital	175	118	70
Fixed Assets	414	417	410
Current Assets	208	144	84

Latch & Batchelor

Hay Mills, Birmingham, B25 8DW
Tel: 0121-772 1386 **Fax:** 0121-772 0762
E-mail: sales@latchandbatchelor.co.uk
Website: http://www.latchandbatchelor.co.uk
Bank(s): National Westminster Bank Plc
Directors: R. Horsfall (Mkt Research), H. Dueli (Fin), G. Coshan (MD), G. Horsfall (MD), C. Horsfall (Dir)
Managers: M. Sherwood (Personnel), A. Parkinson (Buyer), B. Field (Personnel), E. O'Neil (Sales Prom Mgr)
Ultimate Holding Company: LATCH & BATCHELOR (HOLDINGS) LIMITED
Immediate Holding Company: LATCH & BATCHELOR LIMITED
Registration no: 00541289 **VAT No.:** GB 111 6299 90
Date established: 1954 **Turnover:** £2m - £5m **No.of Employees:** 51 - 100
Product Groups: 23, 35, 36

Date of Accounts	Dec 10	Dec 07	Dec 08
Working Capital	524	521	394
Fixed Assets	17	90	234
Current Assets	2m	2m	2m

B H Leake & Sons Ltd

Dogpool Lane, Birmingham, B30 2XH
Tel: 0121-472 0657 **Fax:** 0121-414 1135
E-mail: sales@bhleakerubber.co.uk
Website: http://www.bhleakerubber.co.uk
Directors: L. Leake (MD)
Managers: G. Adams (Chief Mgr), D. Rollinson (Sales Admin), K. Kendal
Immediate Holding Company: B.H.LEAKE & SONS LIMITED
Registration no: 01061853 **VAT No.:** 111 2009 48 **Date established:** 1972
Turnover: £500,000 - £1m **No.of Employees:** 21 - 50 **Product Groups:** 29

Date of Accounts	Aug 11	Aug 10	Aug 09
Working Capital	251	137	138
Fixed Assets	231	190	200
Current Assets	611	336	361

The Learning Path

Bordesley Hall The Holloway, Alvechurch, Birmingham, B48 7QA
Tel: 01527-585310
E-mail: ellen@thelearningpath.co.uk
Website: http://www.thelearningpath.co.uk
Directors: E. Boswick (Dir)
Immediate Holding Company: JOHN ATKINS CONSULTING LIMITED
Registration no: 06484457 **Date established:** 2005
Turnover: Up to £250,000 **No.of Employees:** 1 - 10 **Product Groups:** 86

Date of Accounts	Feb 12	Feb 11	Feb 10
Working Capital	-0	-1	-1
Current Assets	1	N/A	N/A
Current Liabilities	N/A	1	N/A

Lecol Engineering

125 Barr Street, Birmingham, B19 3DE
Tel: 0121-523 0404 **Fax:** 0121-523 2372
Directors: B. Holmes (Fin)
Immediate Holding Company: LECOL ENGINEERING (BIRMINGHAM) LTD
Registration no: 03200630 **Date established:** 1996
Turnover: £250,000 - £500,000 **No.of Employees:** 1 - 10
Product Groups: 48

Legrand

20 Great King Street North, Birmingham, B19 2LF
Tel: 0121-515 0515 **Fax:** 0121-515 0516
E-mail: philip.middlemast@legrand.co.uk
Website: http://www.legrand.com
Directors: P. Beddall (Pers), P. Middlemast (Fin)
Managers: D. Brindley (Purch Mgr), D. Evans (Tech Serv Mgr), M. Graham (Sales Prom Mgr), M. Evans (Mktg Serv Mgr)
Ultimate Holding Company: LEGRAND SA (FRANCE)
Immediate Holding Company: LEGRAND ELECTRIC LIMITED
Registration no: 00115834 **VAT No.:** GB 634 3341 60
Date established: 2011 **Turnover:** £50m - £75m
No.of Employees: 51 - 100 **Product Groups:** 30, 37, 38, 40, 44, 49, 67

Date of Accounts	Dec 11	Dec 10	Dec 09
Sales Turnover	58m	54m	58m
Pre Tax Profit/Loss	-2m	607	-3m
Working Capital	-5m	-3m	-4m
Fixed Assets	28m	29m	31m
Current Assets	22m	22m	24m
Current Liabilities	10m	10m	9m

Lifting Equipment Supplies Ltd

18 James Road Tyseley, Birmingham, B11 2BA
Tel: 0121-694 0094
E-mail: liambullough@hotmail.com
Website: http://www.liftingequipmentsupplies.co.uk
Directors: B. Taylor (Dir), L. Bullough (MD), S. Dorme (MD)
Immediate Holding Company: LIFTING EQUIPMENT SUPPLIES LIMITED
Registration no: 04053382 **Date established:** 2000
Turnover: £250,000 - £500,000 **No.of Employees:** 11 - 20
Product Groups: 45

Date of Accounts	Mar 05
Working Capital	-68
Fixed Assets	41
Current Assets	172
Current Liabilities	239

Light & Boston Ltd

32 New John Street West, Birmingham, B19 3NB
Tel: 0121-359 1500 **Fax:** 0121-359 1300
E-mail: sales@lightboston.co.uk
Website: http://www.lightboston.co.uk
Directors: D. Boston (MD)
Immediate Holding Company: LIGHT AND BOSTON LIMITED
Registration no: 01935412 **Date established:** 1985
Turnover: £500,000 - £1m **No.of Employees:** 1 - 10 **Product Groups:** 28, 30, 49, 65

Date of Accounts	Dec 09	Dec 08	Dec 07
Working Capital	-24	-28	-13
Fixed Assets	31	29	36
Current Assets	200	221	192

Linpac Allibert Ltd

17 Ridgeway Quinton Business Park, Quinton, Birmingham, B32 1AF
Tel: 0121-506 0100 **Fax:** 0121-422 1771
E-mail: linpacallibert-uk@linpac.com
Website: http://www.linpacallibert.com
Directors: S. Knights (Sales), R. Taylor (Pers), J. Blackiston (Fin), B. Faulkner (MD)
Managers: S. Wrighton, S. Mendes (Mktg Serv Mgr), D. Bishop (Tech Serv Mgr), S. Knight (Sales Prom Mgr)
Ultimate Holding Company: LINPAC SENIOR HOLDINGS LIMITED
Immediate Holding Company: LINPAC ALLIBERT LIMITED
Registration no: 07632708 **Date established:** 2011 **Turnover:** £2m - £5m
No.of Employees: 51 - 100 **Product Groups:** 21, 25, 26, 27, 29, 30, 32, 33, 35, 36, 37, 38, 39, 40, 41, 42, 44, 45, 66, 67

Linpac Group

Unit 3180 Park Square Solihull Parkway, Birmingham Business Park, Birmingham, B37 7YN
Tel: 0121-607 6700 **Fax:** 0121-607 6600
Website: http://www.linpac.com
Managers: J. Hayes
Ultimate Holding Company: LINPAC SENIOR HOLDINGS LIMITED
Immediate Holding Company: LINPAC GROUP LIMITED
Registration no: 04792926 **Date established:** 2003
Turnover: Over £1,000m **No.of Employees:** 11 - 20 **Product Groups:** 30, 31

Date of Accounts	Dec 11	Dec 10	Dec 09
Sales Turnover	N/A	N/A	1092m
Pre Tax Profit/Loss	-22m	-51m	526m
Working Capital	-429m	-412m	213m
Fixed Assets	20m	20m	499m
Current Assets	4m	14m	478m
Current Liabilities	410	410	139m

Linton Metalware

Linton Works Studley Street, Birmingham, B12 8JD
Tel: 0121-772 4491 **Fax:** 0121-766 7218
E-mail: action@linton.co.uk
Website: http://www.littersolutions.co.uk
Bank(s): Barclays
Directors: A. Phabet (MD)
Ultimate Holding Company: REELTIME TECHNOLOGIES LIMITED
Immediate Holding Company: LINTON METALWARE LIMITED
Registration no: 00198898 **VAT No.:** GB 109 3310 05
Date established: 2024 **Turnover:** £1m - £2m **No.of Employees:** 11 - 20
Product Groups: 26, 30, 35, 36, 49

Date of Accounts	Jun 11	Jun 10	Jun 09
Working Capital	400	316	259
Fixed Assets	702	711	365
Current Assets	1m	1m	1m

Llewellyn Ryland Ltd

Haden Street, Birmingham, B12 9DB
Tel: 0121-440 2284 **Fax:** 0121-440 0281
E-mail: sales@llewellyn-ryland.co.uk
Website: http://www.llewellyn-ryland.co.uk
Bank(s): HSBC
Directors: C. Kier (MD), H. Law (Dir), K. Adams (Works)
Managers: R. Reynolds (Sales Admin), A. Breen (Sales & Mktg Mg)
Immediate Holding Company: LLEWELLYN RYLAND LIMITED
Registration no: 00058528 **VAT No.:** GB 110 6341 26
Date established: 1998 **Turnover:** £2m - £5m **No.of Employees:** 21 - 50
Product Groups: 32

Date of Accounts	Dec 11	Dec 10	Dec 09
Sales Turnover	5m	5m	N/A
Pre Tax Profit/Loss	120	144	74
Working Capital	2m	2m	2m
Fixed Assets	2m	2m	2m
Current Assets	3m	3m	2m
Current Liabilities	152	156	130

Lodge Cottrell Ltd

George Street, Birmingham, B3 1QQ
Tel: 0121-214 1300 **Fax:** 0121-200 2555
E-mail: irf@lodgecottrell.com
Website: http://www.lodgecottrell.com
Directors: K. Park (MD)
Managers: I. Fantom (Mktg Serv Mgr)
Immediate Holding Company: LODGE COTTRELL LTD.
Registration no: 02937032 **VAT No.:** GB 792 4120 33
Date established: 1994 **Turnover:** £10m - £20m **No.of Employees:** 1 - 10
Product Groups: 38, 39, 40, 41, 42, 44, 45, 46, 48, 52, 54, 67, 81, 82, 84, 85, 86, 87

Lodge Tyre

25-29 Lord Street, Birmingham, B7 4DE
Tel: 0121-380 3207 **Fax:** 0121-359 0046
E-mail: martin@lodgetyre.com
Website: http://www.lodgetyre.com
Directors: A. Christmas (MD), M. Lodge (Fin)
Ultimate Holding Company: LODGE HOLDINGS (UK) LIMITED
Immediate Holding Company: LODGE TYRE COMPANY LIMITED(THE)
Registration no: 00531793 **Date established:** 1954
Turnover: £10m - £20m **No.of Employees:** 11 - 20 **Product Groups:** 68

Date of Accounts	Mar 12	Mar 11	Mar 10
Sales Turnover	15m	14m	12m
Pre Tax Profit/Loss	322	706	325
Working Capital	1m	1m	777
Fixed Assets	473	340	676
Current Assets	4m	4m	4m
Current Liabilities	627	739	418

Edwin Lowe Ltd

Perry Bridge Works Aldridge Road, Perry Barr, Birmingham, B42 2HB
Tel: 0121-356 5255 **Fax:** 0121-344 3172
E-mail: info@edwinlowe.com
Website: http://www.edwinlowe.com
Directors: A. Cook (MD)
Immediate Holding Company: EDWIN LOWE,LIMITED
Registration no: 00142543 **VAT No.:** GB 109 7873 38
Date established: 2015 **Turnover:** £1m - £2m **No.of Employees:** 1 - 10
Product Groups: 45

Date of Accounts	Jun 11	Jun 10	Jun 09
Working Capital	43	39	-37
Fixed Assets	827	925	754
Current Assets	307	337	321

Luminaire UK Ltd
9-15 Henley Street, Birmingham, B11 1JD
Tel: 0121-766 1490 **Fax:** 0121-766 1491
E-mail: info@luminaireuk.com
Website: http://www.luminaireuk.com
Bank(s): Barclays, Erdington
Directors: I. Bury (Dir)
Managers: D. Hughes, W. Boyde (Buyer)
Immediate Holding Company: LUMINAIRE (UK) LIMITED
Registration no: 01948852 **VAT No.:** GB 338 0859 36
Date established: 1985 **Turnover:** £2m - £5m **No.of Employees:** 21 - 50
Product Groups: 37

Date of Accounts	Nov 11	Nov 10	Nov 09
Working Capital	264	122	-80
Fixed Assets	356	341	369
Current Assets	940	843	632

Lunt's Castings Ltd
Hawthorns Industrial Estate Middlemore Road, Handsworth, Birmingham, B21 0BJ
Tel: 0121-551 4301 **Fax:** 0121-523 7954
E-mail: info@luntscastings.co.uk
Website: http://www.luntscastings.co.uk
Bank(s): National Westminster, Milton Keynes
Directors: A. Limb (Dir)
Managers: D. McKay (Mgr)
Immediate Holding Company: LUNTS CASTINGS LIMITED
Registration no: 03121448 **VAT No.:** 669 6031 09 **Date established:** 1995
Turnover: £1m - £2m **No.of Employees:** 21 - 50 **Product Groups:** 48, 49

Date of Accounts	Dec 11	Dec 10	Dec 09
Working Capital	198	201	203
Fixed Assets	106	106	110
Current Assets	349	350	324

Lustre Powder Coating Ltd
4 Carisbrooke Road Edgbaston, Birmingham, B17 8NW
Tel: 0121-429 3307
Directors: G. Wharrad (MD)
Registration no: 04977889 **No.of Employees:** 1 - 10 **Product Groups:** 32, 48

Lutz (UK) Ltd
Gateway Estate West Midlands Freeport, Birmingham, B26 3QD
Tel: 0121-782 2662 **Fax:** 0121-782 2680
E-mail: lutzpump@aol.com
Website: http://www.lutz-pumps.co.uk
Directors: R. Gooch (MD), J. Gooch (Fin)
Managers: J. Philips (Sales Prom), J. McGurk (Purch Mgr)
Immediate Holding Company: Lutz (U.K.) Ltd
Registration no: 02236496 **VAT No.:** GB 487 1536 18
Date established: 1988 **Turnover:** £1m - £2m **No.of Employees:** 1 - 10
Product Groups: 40

Date of Accounts	Dec 09	Dec 08	Dec 07
Working Capital	48	67	34
Fixed Assets	2	1	24
Current Assets	164	220	191

Lux Lighting Ltd
100 Icknield Street Hockley, Birmingham, B18 6RU
Tel: 0121-236 7595 **Fax:** 0121-236 6548
E-mail: steve@luxlighting.co.uk
Website: http://www.luxlighting.co.uk
Directors: J. Townsend (Co Sec), S. Townsend (MD)
Immediate Holding Company: LUX LIGHTING LIMITED
Registration no: 01610701 **VAT No.:** GB 361 9433 46
Date established: 1982 **Turnover:** £500,000 - £1m
No.of Employees: 1 - 10 **Product Groups:** 35, 36, 37

Date of Accounts	Feb 12	Feb 11	Feb 10
Working Capital	-3	7	-12
Fixed Assets	18	24	31
Current Assets	323	231	157

M A Lloyd & Son Ltd
47 Princip Street, Birmingham, B4 6LW
Tel: 0121-359 6434 **Fax:** 0121-333 5333
E-mail: info@malloyd.com
Website: http://www.malloyd.com
Bank(s): Lloyds TSB Bank plc
Directors: J. Key (MD)
Managers: R. Johnson (Mktg Serv Mgr)
Immediate Holding Company: M.A.LLOYD & SON LTD
Registration no: 01036738 **Date established:** 1971 **Turnover:** £1m - £2m
No.of Employees: 21 - 50 **Product Groups:** 28, 30, 33, 35, 36, 38, 39, 40, 48, 49, 68, 84

Date of Accounts	May 11	May 10	May 09
Working Capital	394	-168	404
Fixed Assets	101	627	52
Current Assets	958	388	915

M C A Aston Ltd
40 Victoria Road Aston, Birmingham, B6 5HF
Tel: 0121-554 6644 **Fax:** 0121-554 7854
E-mail: colin@mca-aston.co.uk
Website: http://www.mca-aston.com
Directors: D. Brown (Dir)
Ultimate Holding Company: POSITIVE ENGINEERING LIMITED
Immediate Holding Company: M.C.A.(ASTON)LIMITED
Registration no: 00530321 **VAT No.:** GB 110 6737 01
Date established: 1954 **Turnover:** £1m - £2m **No.of Employees:** 1 - 10
Product Groups: 30

Date of Accounts	Dec 11	Dec 10	Dec 09
Working Capital	760	724	680
Fixed Assets	48	51	46
Current Assets	876	863	794

M J W Engineering Ltd
199 Warstone Lane, Birmingham, B18 6JR
Tel: 0121-236 7776 **Fax:** 0121-236 0461
E-mail: sales@mjwengineering.com
Website: http://www.mjwengineering.com
Bank(s): HSBC
Directors: J. Marshall (Fin), J. Rochester (Ch)
Managers: I. Furlong (Sales Prom Mgr), M. Walker (Admin Off)
Immediate Holding Company: M.J.W. (Engineering) Ltd
Registration no: 01918740 **Date established:** 1985 **Turnover:** £5m - £10m
No.of Employees: 11 - 20 **Product Groups:** 33, 36, 37, 39, 40, 42, 43, 45, 46, 47, 48, 67

Date of Accounts	Dec 09	Dec 08	Dec 07
Working Capital	18	28	55
Fixed Assets	199	150	156
Current Assets	515	771	535

M K L Automations Ltd
Unit 16 Industrial Estate Tame Road, Birmingham, B6 7HS
Tel: 0121-327 6637 **Fax:** 0121-328 8178
Directors: J. Hughes (Prop)
Immediate Holding Company: JOSEPH ALEX ASSOCIATES LIMITED
Registration no: 03603891 **Date established:** 2007
Turnover: Up to £250,000 **No.of Employees:** 1 - 10 **Product Groups:** 38, 45, 46

Date of Accounts	Jul 07	Jul 06
Working Capital	-7	-8
Fixed Assets	8	9
Current Assets	55	77
Current Liabilities	62	85

M N B Mould Services Ltd
Unit 2b Tamebridge Industrial Estate Aldridge Road, Perry Barr, Birmingham, B42 2TX
Tel: 0121-331 4006 **Fax:** 0121-356 3098
E-mail: info@mnbmoulds.com
Website: http://www.mnbmoulds.com
Bank(s): HSBC Bank plc
Directors: C. Ryan (Fin), F. Ryan (MD)
Immediate Holding Company: MNB MOULD SERVICES LIMITED
Registration no: 04023113 **VAT No.:** GB 754 2010 66
Date established: 2000 **Turnover:** £1m - £2m **No.of Employees:** 21 - 50
Product Groups: 30, 42, 45, 46, 48

Date of Accounts	Aug 11	Aug 10	Aug 09
Working Capital	8	-51	-52
Fixed Assets	244	305	210
Current Assets	393	369	209

M P M Presstools
1 Chancel Way Industrial Estate Chancel Way, Birmingham, B6 7AU
Tel: 0121-356 7600 **Fax:** 0121-356 9766
E-mail: mpm.presstools@btconnect.com
Website: http://www.mpmpresstools.co.uk
Directors: A. Pugh (Prop)
Date established: 1975 **Turnover:** Up to £250,000
No.of Employees: 1 - 10 **Product Groups:** 46

M R J Furnaces Ltd
Bordesley Hall Alvechurch, Birmingham, B48 7QA
Tel: 01527-61100 **Fax:** 01527-61110
E-mail: help@mrjfurnaces.co.uk
Website: http://www.mrjfurnaces.co.uk
Directors: M. Tuffey (MD)
Immediate Holding Company: M.R.J. Furnaces Ltd
Registration no: 03012431 **VAT No.:** GB 646 9878 65
Date established: 2008 **Turnover:** £500,000 - £1m
No.of Employees: 1 - 10 **Product Groups:** 40

M S J Asian Directories Ltd
42 Cherry Orchard Road Handsworth Wood, Birmingham, B20 2LD
Tel: 0121-551 5568
E-mail: info@msjdirect.co.uk
Website: http://www.msjdirect.co.uk
Managers: G. Johal (Mgr)
Immediate Holding Company: MSJ ASIAN DIRECTORIES LTD
Registration no: 05654565 **Date established:** 2005
No.of Employees: 1 - 10 **Product Groups:** 24, 61, 81

Date of Accounts	Mar 11	Mar 10	Mar 08
Working Capital	6	5	13
Fixed Assets	1	2	1
Current Assets	36	32	44

M V Sport & Leisure Ltd
35 Tameside Drive Castle Vale, Birmingham, B35 7AG
Tel: 0121-748 8000 **Fax:** 0121-748 8010
E-mail: john.bellamy@mvsports.com
Website: http://www.mvsports.com
Directors: J. Bellamy (Chief Op Offcr), P. Ratcliffe (Sales & Mktg), G. Kaur (Fin)
Managers: S. Cannon (Tech Serv Mgr)
Ultimate Holding Company: TANDEM GROUP PLC
Immediate Holding Company: MV SPORTS & LEISURE LIMITED
Registration no: 01700202 **Date established:** 1983 **Turnover:** £2m - £5m
No.of Employees: 21 - 50 **Product Groups:** 49

Date of Accounts	Dec 11	Jan 11	Jan 10
Sales Turnover	4m	3m	4m
Pre Tax Profit/Loss	-29	-3m	-78
Working Capital	-3m	-3m	-2m
Fixed Assets	530	591	603
Current Assets	2m	2m	6m
Current Liabilities	1m	1m	1m

Mcgeoch Technology Ltd
86 Lower Tower Street, Birmingham, B19 3PA
Tel: 0121-687 5850 **Fax:** 0121-333 3089
E-mail: info@mcgeoch.co.uk
Website: http://www.mcgeoch.co.uk
Directors: G. Randle (Sales), J. Dambrogio (MD), S. Swallow (MD)
Managers: R. Ahmed (Tech Serv Mgr)
Immediate Holding Company: MCGEOCH TECHNOLOGY LIMITED
Registration no: 03253370 **Date established:** 1996 **Turnover:** £5m - £10m
No.of Employees: 51 - 100 **Product Groups:** 37

Date of Accounts	Dec 11	Dec 10	Dec 09
Sales Turnover	8m	7m	6m
Pre Tax Profit/Loss	37	5	39
Working Capital	626	587	613
Fixed Assets	2m	1m	1m
Current Assets	3m	3m	3m
Current Liabilities	834	496	515

Alistair Mackintosh Ltd
Bannerley Road Garretts Green Industrial Estate, Birmingham, B33 0SL
Tel: 0121-784 6800 **Fax:** 0121-789 7068
E-mail: info@alistairmackintosh.co.uk
Website: http://www.alistairmackintosh.co.uk
Directors: A. Mackintosh (Dir)
Immediate Holding Company: ALISTAIR MACKINTOSH LIMITED
Registration no: 01113069 **Date established:** 1973 **Turnover:** £1m - £2m
No.of Employees: 1 - 10 **Product Groups:** 14, 66

Date of Accounts	Dec 11	Dec 10	Dec 09
Working Capital	421	429	606
Fixed Assets	1m	1m	1m
Current Assets	567	682	904

Rudd Macnamara Ltd
Holyhead Road, Birmingham, B21 0BS
Tel: 0121-523 8437 **Fax:** 0121-551 7032
E-mail: enquiries@ruddmacnamara.com
Website: http://www.ruddmacnamara.com
Bank(s): Lloyds TSB
Directors: L. Caunce (Fin), G. Caunce (MD)
Immediate Holding Company: RUDD MACNAMARA LIMITED
Registration no: 01136271 **VAT No.:** GB 705 3302 77
Date established: 1973 **Turnover:** £2m - £5m **No.of Employees:** 21 - 50
Product Groups: 28, 30, 35

Date of Accounts	Mar 11	Mar 10	Mar 09
Working Capital	905	744	829
Fixed Assets	277	301	365
Current Assets	1m	1m	1m

Magbility
25 Watford Road, Birmingham, B30 1JB
Tel: 01527-837076 **Fax:** 0121-459 5560
Directors: M. Grant (Prop), P. Grant (Prop)
No.of Employees: 11 - 20 **Product Groups:** 38

Magic World Toys Limited
105 Coventry Street, Birmingham, B5 5NY
Tel: 0121-665 6842 **Fax:** 0121-632 6404
E-mail: info@magicworldtoys.com
Website: http://www.magicworldtoys.com
Managers: T. Tu (Cust Serv Mgr)
Immediate Holding Company: Magic World Toys Ltd
Registration no: 05757387 **Date established:** 2006
Turnover: £500,000 - £1m **No.of Employees:** 1 - 10 **Product Groups:** 49, 65

Date of Accounts	Mar 09	Mar 08	Mar 07
Sales Turnover	1m	853	35
Pre Tax Profit/Loss	18	18	-10
Working Capital	-10	79	65
Fixed Assets	11	14	3
Current Assets	66	209	66
Current Liabilities	77	129	1

Main Event Products Ltd
Unit 25 Coleshill Industrial Estate Station Road, Coleshill, Birmingham, B46 1JP
Tel: 01675-464224 **Fax:** 01675-466082
E-mail: sales@mainevent.co.uk
Website: http://www.mainevent.co.uk
Directors: O. Cowen (Fin), R. Cowen (Dir)
Immediate Holding Company: MAIN EVENT PRODUCTS LIMITED
Registration no: 04002104 **Date established:** 2000
No.of Employees: 1 - 10 **Product Groups:** 26, 30, 35, 49, 67, 83

Date of Accounts	May 09	May 08	Nov 11
Working Capital	125	135	90
Fixed Assets	141	177	86
Current Assets	236	292	241

Mainstream
1020 Yardley Wood Road, Birmingham, B14 4BW
Tel: 0121-430 9150 **Fax:** 0121-430 9155
E-mail: richard@mainstream-windows.co.uk
Website: http://www.windowsbirmingham.co.uk
Directors: S. Lake (Dir), B. Dhillon (Dir)
Managers: R. Elson (Mgr)
Immediate Holding Company: MAINSTREAM DESIGN AND BUILD LIMITED
Registration no: 07995526 **Date established:** 2012
No.of Employees: 11 - 20 **Product Groups:** 46

Date of Accounts	Apr 11	Apr 10
Working Capital	-201	-146
Fixed Assets	121	126
Current Assets	25	139

Manor Enterprises
3 Beacon Court Birmingham Road, Great Barr, Birmingham, B43 6NN
Tel: 0121-358 7771 **Fax:** 0121-358 1105
E-mail: mandy@scoutbadges.org.uk
Website: http://www.scoutbadges.org.uk
Directors: M. Mould (Dir)
Immediate Holding Company: MANOR LIMITED
Registration no: 01342107 **Date established:** 1977
No.of Employees: 1 - 10 **Product Groups:** 22, 23, 24, 49

Date of Accounts	Mar 11	Mar 10	Mar 09
Working Capital	-4	9	8
Fixed Assets	6	N/A	N/A
Current Assets	2	14	13

Marflow Engineering Ltd
Britannia House Austin Way, Hampstead Industrial Estate, Birmingham, B42 1DU
Tel: 0121-358 1555 **Fax:** 0121-358 1444
E-mail: sales@marflow.co.uk
Website: http://www.marflow.co.uk
Bank(s): Midland, West Bromwich
Directors: P. Davies (Fin), C. Forbes (Chief Op Offcr), P. Cheshire (Dir), P. Dawes (Sales), P. Fennell (Ch)
Managers: P. Lowe (Sales Off Mgr)
Ultimate Holding Company: MARFLOW PROPERTIES HOLDINGS LIMITED
Immediate Holding Company: MARFLOW ENGINEERING LIMITED
Registration no: 00928322 **VAT No.:** GB 277 2141 59
Date established: 1968 **Turnover:** £2m - £5m **No.of Employees:** 21 - 50
Product Groups: 66

Date of Accounts	Feb 12	Feb 11	Feb 10
Working Capital	182	244	230
Fixed Assets	113	112	108
Current Assets	1m	1m	1m

Mark's & Clerk LLP
Alpha Tower Suffolk Street Queensway, Birmingham, B1 1TT
Tel: 0121-643 5881 **Fax:** 0116-233 0192
E-mail: birmingham@marks-clerk.com
Website: http://www.marks-clerk.com
Managers: A. Williams, I. Hull (Sales Admin), S. Hackett (Mgr), Z. Obden
Immediate Holding Company: MARKS & CLERK LLP
Registration no: OC343273 **Date established:** 2009
No.of Employees: 21 - 50 **Product Groups:** 80

Date of Accounts	Jul 11	Jul 10	Jul 09
Sales Turnover	68m	61m	64m
Pre Tax Profit/Loss	16m	11m	11m

Working Capital	18m	15m	11m
Fixed Assets	10m	7m	9m
Current Assets	29m	25m	22m
Current Liabilities	4m	4m	4m

Marque Models Ltd

Station Road Stechford, Birmingham, B33 9AQ
Tel: 0121-784 3955 **Fax:** 01885-410266
E-mail: marquemodels@aol.com
Website: http://www.marquemodels.com
Directors: T. Power (Prop), M. Power (Dir), T. Power (Dir)
Immediate Holding Company: MARQUE MODELS LIMITED
Registration no: 01197092 **Date established:** 1975
Turnover: £250,000 - £500,000 **No.of Employees:** 1 - 10
Product Groups: 49

Date of Accounts	Mar 11	Mar 10	Mar 09
Working Capital	-28	-60	-81
Fixed Assets	2	2	3
Current Assets	35	43	40

Martin Co. Ltd (Armac)

160 Dollman Street Duddeston, Birmingham, B7 4RS
Tel: 0121-359 2111 **Fax:** 0121-359 4698
E-mail: sales@martin.co.uk
Website: http://www.martin.co.uk
Bank(s): Lloyds TSB
Directors: B. Morby (MD), P. Mcgrail (MD)
Managers: G. Barnes (Sales Prom Mgr), I. Harvey (Export Sales Mg)
Registration no: 00124649 **VAT No.:** GB 444 5240 65
Date established: 1945 **Turnover:** £2m - £5m **No.of Employees:** 51 - 100
Product Groups: 48

Martineau Johnson Solicitors

1 Colmore Square, Birmingham, B4 6AA
Tel: 0121-233 0318 **Fax:** 0870-763 2001
E-mail: lawyers@martineau-uk.com
Website: http://www.martineau-johnson.co.uk
Directors: D. Allison (Dir), W. Barker (MD), D. Gwyther (Snr Part)
Managers: D. Price (Personnel), L. Collins (Cust Serv Mgr), K. Agnew (I.T. Exec), J. Preston (Mktg Serv Mgr), D. Draser (Accounts), B. Lunnen (I.T. Exec)
Immediate Holding Company: MARTINEAU JOHNSON LIMITED
Registration no: 02279908 **Date established:** 1988
Turnover: £10m - £20m **No.of Employees:** 1 - 10 **Product Groups:** 80, 86

B Mason & Sons Ltd

Wharf Street Aston, Birmingham, B6 5SA
Tel: 0121-327 0181 **Fax:** 0121-322 8341
E-mail: sales@bmason.co.uk
Website: http://www.bmason.co.uk
Directors: D. Westbrook (Fin), R. Herold (MD)
Managers: T. Laird (Sales Prom Mgr), H. Meeson (Personnel)
Ultimate Holding Company: WIELAND-WERKE AG (GERMANY)
Immediate Holding Company: B.MASON & SONS LIMITED
Registration no: 00139599 **Date established:** 2015
Turnover: £75m - £125m **No.of Employees:** 101 - 250
Product Groups: 34

Date of Accounts	Sep 11	Sep 10	Sep 09
Sales Turnover	85m	71m	35m
Pre Tax Profit/Loss	3m	2m	-665
Working Capital	6m	4m	2m
Fixed Assets	12m	13m	14m
Current Assets	27m	28m	20m
Current Liabilities	4m	3m	2m

Harry Mason Ltd

217 Thimble Mill Lane, Birmingham, B7 5HS
Tel: 0121-328 5900 **Fax:** 0121-327 7257
E-mail: info@harrymason.co.uk
Website: http://www.harrymason.co.uk
Directors: G. Townsend (MD)
Immediate Holding Company: HARRY MASON LIMITED
Registration no: 00838508 **VAT No.:** GB 109 7475 50
Date established: 1965 **Turnover:** £2m - £5m **No.of Employees:** 21 - 50
Product Groups: 40, 49

Date of Accounts	Feb 12	Feb 11	Feb 10
Working Capital	244	285	272
Fixed Assets	484	476	512
Current Assets	364	439	368

Masteel UK Ltd

The Cedars Coton Road, Coleshill, Birmingham, B46 2HH
Tel: 01675-437733 **Fax:** 01675-437734
E-mail: enquiries@masteel.co.uk
Website: http://www.masteel.co.uk
Directors: M. Connell (MD)
Immediate Holding Company: MASTEEL (UK) LIMITED
Registration no: 04500564 **Date established:** 2002
Turnover: £20m - £50m **No.of Employees:** 21 - 50 **Product Groups:** 33, 34, 36, 40, 48, 66

Date of Accounts	Aug 11	Aug 10	Aug 09
Sales Turnover	23m	16m	24m
Pre Tax Profit/Loss	1m	663	1m
Working Capital	3m	3m	2m
Fixed Assets	91	84	113
Current Assets	9m	8m	4m
Current Liabilities	852	451	597

E F G Matthews Office Furniture Ltd

100 Hagley Road, Birmingham, B16 8NJ
Tel: 0121-454 8121 **Fax:** 0121-454 2430
E-mail: sales@efgoffice.co.uk
Website: http://www.efgmatthews.co.uk
Directors: C. Howarth (Dir), M. Matthews (MD)
Managers: G. Thorp (Mgr)
Ultimate Holding Company: E.F.G Sweden
Immediate Holding Company: E.F.G. Matthews (UK) Ltd
Registration no: 00257489 **VAT No.:** GB 151 6840 71
Date established: 2008 **Turnover:** £10m - £20m **No.of Employees:** 1 - 10
Product Groups: 26

Matts & Jenkins Ltd

Garland Street, Birmingham, B9 4DE
Tel: 0121-772 4718 **Fax:** 0121-773 0023
E-mail: sales@mattsandjenkins.co.uk
Website: http://www.mattsandjenkins.co.uk
Directors: M. Bolton (Fin)
Immediate Holding Company: MATTS AND JENKINS LTD.
Registration no: 00800801 **Date established:** 1964
No.of Employees: 11 - 20 **Product Groups:** 46, 48

Date of Accounts	Mar 11	Mar 10	Mar 09
Working Capital	66	42	41
Fixed Assets	29	32	45
Current Assets	161	130	90

Max Power Sports Co.

126 Edward Road Balsall Heath, Birmingham, B12 9LS
Tel: 0121-440 1841 **Fax:** 0121-440 6279
E-mail: rkumar@maxpowersports.co.uk
Website: http://www.maxpowersports.co.uk
Directors: R. Kumar (Prop)
VAT No.: GB 109 3121 08 **Date established:** 1973
Turnover: Up to £250,000 **No.of Employees:** 1 - 10 **Product Groups:** 23, 24

Mayflex UK Ltd

Junction 6 Industrial Park 66 Electric Avenue, Birmingham, B6 7JJ
Tel: 0121-326 7557 **Fax:** 0121-327 5886
E-mail: sales@mayflex.com
Website: http://www.mayflex.com
Bank(s): The Royal Bank of Scotland
Directors: M. Simmons (Sales), R. Mayall (MD), M. Butterfield (Fin)
Managers: J. Beech (Tech Serv Mgr), T. Hillifer (Personnel), A. Philips, T. Calcutt (Mktg Serv Mgr)
Ultimate Holding Company: MAYFLEX HOLDINGS LIMITED
Immediate Holding Company: MAYALL & CO LIMITED
Registration no: 00146594 **VAT No.:** GB 110 2109 50
Date established: 2017 **Turnover:** £20m - £50m
No.of Employees: 101 - 250 **Product Groups:** 30, 35, 37, 38

Date of Accounts	Mar 11	Mar 10	Mar 09
Sales Turnover	N/A	N/A	45m
Pre Tax Profit/Loss	33	-3m	6m
Working Capital	502	461	479
Fixed Assets	17	17	18
Current Assets	502	464	3m
Current Liabilities	N/A	3	169

Maypole Ltd

162 Clapgate Lane, Birmingham, B32 3DE
Tel: 0121-270 4301 **Fax:** 0121-423 3020
E-mail: sales@maypole.ltd.uk
Website: http://www.maypole.ltd.uk
Bank(s): Lloyds
Directors: B. Harrison (Sales), C. Howe (Co Sec), K. Hambleton (Dir), R. Dunn (Fin)
Managers: J. Hendry (Purch Mgr), P. Hambleton
Ultimate Holding Company: MAYPOLE HOLDINGS LIMITED
Immediate Holding Company: MAYPOLE LIMITED
Registration no: 01502304 **VAT No.:** GB 352 2140 00
Date established: 1980 **Turnover:** £5m - £10m **No.of Employees:** 21 - 50
Product Groups: 32, 35, 37, 39, 40, 46

Date of Accounts	Oct 11	Oct 10	Oct 09
Sales Turnover	9m	9m	8m
Pre Tax Profit/Loss	458	230	355
Working Capital	3m	3m	2m
Fixed Assets	131	180	207
Current Assets	5m	4m	4m
Current Liabilities	648	639	577

Mechanical Cleansing Services Ltd

Unit G Salford Trading Estate Salford Street, Birmingham, B6 7SH
Tel: 0121-327 3103 **Fax:** 0121-327 3105
E-mail: droemcsltd@aol.com
Website: http://www.mechanicalcleansing.co.uk
Directors: D. Roe (Dir), M. Roe (Fin)
Immediate Holding Company: MECHANICAL CLEANSING SERVICES LIMITED
Registration no: 03351981 **Date established:** 1997
Turnover: £500,000 - £1m **No.of Employees:** 11 - 20
Product Groups: 30, 32, 39, 40, 42, 52, 54

Date of Accounts	Jul 11	Jul 10	Jul 09
Working Capital	-28	16	101
Fixed Assets	283	319	210
Current Assets	162	207	240

Meditelle

Meditelle Product Division Beautelle Manufacturing Centre, Birmingham, B6 7HH
Tel: 0121-332 1850 **Fax:** 0121-332 1851
E-mail: enquiry@meditelle.co.uk
Website: http://www.meditelle.co.uk
Directors: S. Howells (Sales)
Immediate Holding Company: MEDITELLE LTD
Registration no: 06735158 **Date established:** 2008
Turnover: £500,000 - £1m **No.of Employees:** 1 - 10 **Product Groups:** 26, 38, 67

Date of Accounts	Oct 09	Mar 11
Working Capital	N/A	-3
Fixed Assets	N/A	11
Current Assets	N/A	86

Merchandising & Promotional Products

Millenium Place 7 Coventry Road, Coleshill, Birmingham, B46 3BB
Tel: 01675-466907 **Fax:** 01675-466908
Website: http://www.mappltd.com
Directors: G. Marston (MD)
Immediate Holding Company: Merchandising & Promotional Products Ltd
Registration no: 03949133 **Date established:** 2000
No.of Employees: 1 - 10 **Product Groups:** 30, 44, 65

Merlin Metal Products

23-24 Warstone Lane, Birmingham, B18 6JQ
Tel: 0121-236 5146
Website: http://www.merlinmetalproducts.co.uk
Directors: J. Evans (Prop)
Date established: 1968 **No.of Employees:** 1 - 10 **Product Groups:** 35

Metal Fusions Welding Supplies Ltd

73 Metchley Lane, Birmingham, B17 0HT
Tel: 0121-426 3020 **Fax:** 0121-426 2333
E-mail: p-devaney@blueyonder.co.uk
Directors: P. Delaney (MD)
No.of Employees: 1 - 10 **Product Groups:** 46

Metalor Technologies UK Ltd

74 Warstone Lane, Birmingham, B18 6NG
Tel: 0121-236 3241 **Fax:** 0121-236 3568
E-mail: info@metalor.com
Website: http://www.metalor.com
Bank(s): Barclays
Managers: M. Wild (Site Co-ord), S. Burling, E. Greenaway (Fin Mgr)
Ultimate Holding Company: METALOR TECHNOLOGIES INTERNATIONAL SA (SWITZERLAND)
Immediate Holding Company: METALOR TECHNOLOGIES (UK) LTD
Registration no: 01510877 **Date established:** 1980
Turnover: £250m - £500m **No.of Employees:** 21 - 50
Product Groups: 31, 32, 34, 35, 36, 37, 38, 47, 48, 49, 65, 66

Date of Accounts	Dec 11	Dec 10	Dec 09
Sales Turnover	265m	169m	76m
Pre Tax Profit/Loss	2m	880	665
Working Capital	3m	2m	770
Fixed Assets	243	279	293
Current Assets	9m	10m	9m
Current Liabilities	610	477	422

Metalweb

Unit 1 Stargate Business Park Cuckoo Road, Nechells, Birmingham, B7 5SE
Tel: 0121-328 7700 **Fax:** 0121-328 8381
E-mail: info@metalweb.co.uk
Website: http://www.metalweb.co.uk
Directors: D. Webb (MD)
Registration no: 04130945 **Date established:** 2000
Turnover: £20m - £50m **No.of Employees:** 21 - 50 **Product Groups:** 34, 36, 48, 66

Date of Accounts	Dec 07	May 07	May 06
Sales Turnover	15135	26219	22156
Pre Tax Profit/Loss	319	895	859
Working Capital	1469	728	1283
Fixed Assets	3008	3101	1265
Current Assets	12412	12451	11001
Current Liabilities	10943	11723	9719
Total Share Capital	551	551	405
ROCE% (Return on Capital Employed)	7.1	23.4	33.7
ROT% (Return on Turnover)	2.1	3.4	3.9

Meyer Timber Ltd

Bromford Gate Bromford Lane, Erdington, Birmingham, B24 8DW
Tel: 0121-326 3200 **Fax:** 0121-326 3230
E-mail: timber@meyertimber.com
Website: http://www.meyertimber.co.uk
Directors: J. Hunter (Fin), D. Barnett (Fin), R. Lazenby (MD)
Managers: S. McErlean (Sales Prom Mgr), S. Cope (Mktg Serv Mgr), P. Glover, L. Johnsone (Tech Serv Mgr)
Ultimate Holding Company: MONTAGUE MEYER TIMBER LTD
Immediate Holding Company: MEYER TIMBER GROUP LIMITED
Registration no: 03524920 **Date established:** 1998
Turnover: £20m - £50m **No.of Employees:** 21 - 50 **Product Groups:** 25

Date of Accounts	Dec 11	Dec 10	Mar 10
Sales Turnover	N/A	N/A	132m
Pre Tax Profit/Loss	17	-936	599
Working Capital	15	3m	8m
Fixed Assets	11	11m	22m
Current Assets	21	36m	41m
Current Liabilities	N/A	363	15m

Micron Metrology 2000 Ltd

Unit 10 Garretts Green Trading Estate Valepits Road, Birmingham, B33 0TD
Tel: 0121-784 7498 **Fax:** 0121-783 6031
E-mail: sales@micron-metrology.co.uk
Website: http://www.micron-metrology.co.uk
Managers: A. Smith (Grp Mgr)
Immediate Holding Company: MICRON METROLOGY 2000 LIMITED
Registration no: 04070905 **Date established:** 2000 **Turnover:** £1m - £2m
No.of Employees: 21 - 50 **Product Groups:** 38, 44, 67, 85, 86

Date of Accounts	Oct 10	Oct 09	Oct 08
Sales Turnover	N/A	N/A	967
Pre Tax Profit/Loss	N/A	N/A	94
Working Capital	233	147	51
Fixed Assets	26	12	23
Current Assets	383	335	259
Current Liabilities	N/A	N/A	107

Microstat

Kings Norton Business Centre Crown Road, Birmingham, B30 3HY
Tel: 0121-486 2020 **Fax:** 0121-486 2424
E-mail: stephencave@microstat.co.uk
Website: http://www.microstat.co.uk
Bank(s): Barclays
Directors: T. Myatt (MD), S. Cave (MD)
Immediate Holding Company: MICROSTAT
Date established: 1982 **Turnover:** £250,000 - £500,000
No.of Employees: 21 - 50 **Product Groups:** 44

Date of Accounts	Mar 11	Mar 10	Mar 09
Working Capital	294	206	176
Fixed Assets	5	7	9
Current Assets	376	296	214
Current Liabilities	N/A	N/A	34

Midland Brass Fittings Ltd

Wynford Industrial Trading Estate Wynford Road, Birmingham, B27 6JT
Tel: 0121-707 6666 **Fax:** 0121-708 1270
E-mail: sales@midbras.co.uk
Bank(s): Lloyds
Directors: T. Mcintosh (MD)
Ultimate Holding Company: MIDBRAS GROUP HOLDINGS LIMITED
Immediate Holding Company: MIDLAND BRASS FITTINGS CO.LIMITED
Registration no: 01058858 **VAT No.:** GB 110 2534 35
Date established: 1972 **Turnover:** £5m - £10m **No.of Employees:** 11 - 20
Product Groups: 34, 35, 36, 39

Date of Accounts	Mar 11	Mar 10	Mar 09
Working Capital	36	201	342
Fixed Assets	19	26	20
Current Assets	3m	3m	3m

Midland Decorative Surfaces Ltd

St Andrews House 76 St. Andrews Road, Bordesley, Birmingham, B9 4LN
Tel: 0121-766 8705 **Fax:** 0121-753 1979
E-mail: matt@fbservices.co.uk
Website: http://www.decorativesurfaces.co.uk
Directors: P. Weldon (MD)
Registration no: 04275528 **Turnover:** Up to £250,000
No.of Employees: 11 - 20 **Product Groups:** 51, 52

Date of Accounts	Mar 08	Mar 07	Mar 06
Working Capital	30	6	17
Fixed Assets	31	39	17
Current Assets	163	81	75
Current Liabilities	132	75	58

Midland Linen Services Ltd
Unit 3 Klaxon Tysley Industrial Estate 747-751 Warwick Road, Tyseley, Birmingham, B11 2HA
Tel: 0121-707 4355 **Fax:** 0121-707 4686
E-mail: info@midlandlinen.co.uk
Website: http://www.midland-linen.co.uk
Directors: J. Yap (MD)
Immediate Holding Company: MIDLAND LINEN SERVICES LIMITED
Registration no: 01901138 **Date established:** 1985
No.of Employees: 21 - 50 **Product Groups:** 23, 83

Date of Accounts	Mar 12	Mar 11	Mar 10
Working Capital	-33	-25	-4
Fixed Assets	353	399	223
Current Assets	190	174	177

Midland Marble Ltd
Masonry Works 80 Dollman Street, Birmingham, B7 4RP
Tel: 0121-359 3699 **Fax:** 0121-333 3052
E-mail: enquiries@midlandmarbleltd.co.uk
Website: http://www.midlandmarbleltd.co.uk
Directors: J. McKeon (MD), D. McKeon (Fin)
Ultimate Holding Company: MIDLAND MARBLE HOLDINGS LIMITED
Immediate Holding Company: MIDLAND MARBLE LIMITED
Registration no: 01091195 **VAT No.:** GB 478 2975 85
Date established: 1973 **Turnover:** £1m - £2m **No.of Employees:** 21 - 50
Product Groups: 14, 33

Date of Accounts	Aug 11	Aug 10	Aug 09
Working Capital	293	217	193
Fixed Assets	33	30	52
Current Assets	1m	847	963

Midland Paint & Powder Coaters Ltd
44-45 Prince Albert Street, Birmingham, B9 5AZ
Tel: 0121-766 8267 **Fax:** 0121-753 3195
E-mail: enquiries@mppcltd.co.uk
Website: http://www.mppcltd.co.uk
Directors: G. Carless (Co Sec), S. Carless (MD)
Ultimate Holding Company: MIDLAND PAINT & POWDER COATERS (HOLDINGS) LIMITED
Immediate Holding Company: MIDLAND PAINT AND POWDER COATERS LIMITED
Registration no: 02473357 **Date established:** 1990
No.of Employees: 1 - 10 **Product Groups:** 46, 48

Date of Accounts	Dec 11	Dec 10	Dec 09
Working Capital	72	77	62
Fixed Assets	13	12	38
Current Assets	153	197	235

Midland Precision Diamond Tools
44 Hockley Street, Birmingham, B18 6BH
Tel: 0121-554 3434 **Fax:** 0121-554 9674
Website: http://www.panachediamond.com
Directors: A. Heinz (MD), I. Heinz (Fin)
Immediate Holding Company: JULIE PATRICIA BERRY LIMITED
Registration no: 03490496 **Date established:** 1987
Turnover: Up to £250,000 **No.of Employees:** 1 - 10 **Product Groups:** 36, 47, 66

Date of Accounts	Mar 11	Mar 10	Mar 09
Working Capital	164	216	264
Fixed Assets	3	4	3
Current Assets	266	285	350

Midland Pump Manufacturing Co. Ltd
Unit 19a Tyseley Industrial Estate Seeleys Road, Birmingham, B11 2LF
Tel: 0121-773 8862 **Fax:** 0121-771 4363
E-mail: alan@midlandpump.co.uk
Website: http://www.midlandpump.co.uk
Directors: A. Parker (MD), M. Parker (Co Sec)
Ultimate Holding Company: EASYFIT HARDWARE LIMITED
Immediate Holding Company: MIDLAND PUMP MANUFACTURING COMPANY LIMITED
Registration no: 01103911 **VAT No.:** GB 111 9082 03
Date established: 1973 **Turnover:** £500,000 - £1m
No.of Employees: 1 - 10 **Product Groups:** 40, 42, 45, 46

Date of Accounts	Sep 11	Sep 10	Sep 09
Working Capital	350	265	155
Fixed Assets	22	14	14
Current Assets	427	322	361

Midland Systems Ltd
Charnwood House 21 Fairyfield Ave, Birmingham, B43 6AG
Tel: 0121-233 4242 **Fax:** 0121-357 0350
E-mail: info@knightkit.co.uk
Website: http://www.knightkit.co.uk
Managers: P. Waldron (District Mgr)
Registration no: 04677140 **Date established:** 2003
Turnover: Up to £250,000 **No.of Employees:** 1 - 10 **Product Groups:** 37, 39

Midland Tank & Ironplate Co. Ltd
241-243 Heneage Street, Birmingham, B7 4LY
Tel: 0121-359 4377 **Fax:** 0121-333 3035
E-mail: info@mti.uk.com
Website: http://www.mti.uk.com
Bank(s): HSBC Bank plc
Managers: D. Cox (Chief Mgr), D. Cox (Mgr)
Immediate Holding Company: MIDLAND TANK AND IRON PLATE COMPANY LIMITED(THE)
Registration no: 00581107 **VAT No.:** GB 110 3064 41
Date established: 1957 **Turnover:** £1m - £2m **No.of Employees:** 11 - 20
Product Groups: 35, 36, 46, 48

Date of Accounts	Mar 12	Mar 11	Mar 10
Working Capital	474	448	338
Fixed Assets	1m	926	989
Current Assets	1m	929	677

Midlands Reclamation
3 Yarwood Works Ledsam Street, Birmingham, B16 8DW
Tel: 0121-454 6159 **Fax:** 0121- 4546159
Directors: C. Peterkin (Prop)
Date established: 1994 **No.of Employees:** 1 - 10 **Product Groups:** 36

Miller Plating Co.
Unit 15 All Saints Industrial Estate All Saints Street, Birmingham, B18 7RJ
Tel: 0121-523 3348 **Fax:** 0121-515 3187
Directors: L. Miller (Prop)
Turnover: Up to £250,000 **No.of Employees:** 1 - 10 **Product Groups:** 48

Miniature Pressure Gauge Co.
52-54 Hylton Street, Birmingham, B18 6HN
Tel: 0121-551 9910 **Fax:** 0121-551 3860
E-mail: info@miniaturepressuregauge.com
Website: http://www.miniaturepressuregauge.com
Directors: M. Scott (MD)
Immediate Holding Company: MINIATURE PRESSURE GAUGE LIMITED
Registration no: 04444053 **Date established:** 2002
Turnover: £500,000 - £1m **No.of Employees:** 1 - 10 **Product Groups:** 38, 39, 49, 67

Date of Accounts	May 11	May 10	May 09
Working Capital	35	21	11
Fixed Assets	14	16	19
Current Assets	87	63	54

Mini-Batch Plating Co. Ltd
31 Hatchett Street Hockley, Birmingham, B19 3NX
Tel: 0121-359 8234 **Fax:** 0121-359 4934
E-mail: sales@mini-batch.co.uk
Website: http://www.mini-batch.co.uk
Directors: I. Downing (MD)
Immediate Holding Company: MINI BATCH PLATING LIMITED
Registration no: 04707005 **Date established:** 2003
No.of Employees: 1 - 10 **Product Groups:** 46, 48

Date of Accounts	Mar 11	Mar 10	Mar 09
Working Capital	-15	-15	-13
Fixed Assets	15	16	19
Current Assets	28	32	27

Minuteman Press
3 & 5 Highfield Road Hall Green, Birmingham, B28 0EL
Tel: 0121-777 0018 **Fax:** 0121-777 5810
E-mail: karl.mccabe@hallgreen.minutemanpress.com
Website: http://www.hallgreen.minutemanpress.com
Managers: K. McCabe (Mgr)
Turnover: £500,000 - £1m **No.of Employees:** 1 - 10 **Product Groups:** 28

Mitsubishi Electric Europe
Mylen House Wagon Lane, Birmingham, B26 3DU
Tel: 0121-741 2800 **Fax:** 0121-741 2801
Ultimate Holding Company: MITSUBISHI ELECTRIC CORP (JAPAN)
Immediate Holding Company: MITSUBISHI ELECTRIC EUROPE B.V.
Registration no: FC019156 **Date established:** 1996
Turnover: Over £1,000m **No.of Employees:** 11 - 20 **Product Groups:** 40, 66

M & M Steel Stockholders & Fabricators Ltd
Riverside Works Trevor Street Industrial Estate Trevor Street, Birmingham, B7 5RG
Tel: 0121-327 1695 **Fax:** 0121-327 1708
E-mail: info@mmsteelstock.co.uk
Website: http://www.mmsteelstock.co.uk
Directors: M. Halbert (Fin), C. Mcguire (MD)
Immediate Holding Company: M & M STEEL STOCK LIMITED
Registration no: 05747661 **VAT No.:** GB 555 1664 34
Date established: 2006 **Turnover:** £500,000 - £1m
No.of Employees: 11 - 20 **Product Groups:** 66

Date of Accounts	Mar 11	Mar 10	Mar 09
Working Capital	-26	-90	-70
Fixed Assets	225	270	304
Current Assets	179	60	117
Current Liabilities	N/A	100	68

Moflash Signalling Ltd
Unit 18 Klaxon Industrial Estate Warwick Road, Tyseley, Birmingham, B11 2HA
Tel: 0121-707 6681 **Fax:** 0121-707 8305
E-mail: uksales@moflash.co.uk
Website: http://www.moflash.co.uk
Bank(s): National Westminster
Directors: M. Bailey (Comm)
Immediate Holding Company: MOFLASH SIGNALLING LIMITED
Registration no: 03430666 **VAT No.:** 695 7711 82 **Date established:** 1997
Turnover: £1m - £2m **No.of Employees:** 11 - 20 **Product Groups:** 30, 37, 39, 40, 45, 67, 68

Date of Accounts	Dec 11	Dec 10	Dec 09
Working Capital	248	79	68
Fixed Assets	214	236	265
Current Assets	737	515	492

Monk Metal Windows Ltd
Hansons Bridge Road, Birmingham, B24 0QP
Tel: 0121-351 4411 **Fax:** 0121-351 3673
E-mail: neil.holding@monkmetal.co.uk
Website: http://www.monkmetalwindows.co.uk
Bank(s): Midland
Directors: N. Holding (Dir), R. Smith (Co Sec)
Ultimate Holding Company: ETNA STREET HOLDINGS LIMITED
Immediate Holding Company: MONK METAL WINDOWS LIMITED
Registration no: 02279468 **VAT No.:** GB 486 7800 03
Date established: 1988 **Turnover:** £1m - £2m **No.of Employees:** 21 - 50
Product Groups: 35, 36

Morelli Birmingham
1 Stratford Street North, Birmingham, B11 1BY
Tel: 0121-772 7100 **Fax:** 0121-772 7713
Bank(s): Barclays
Directors: B. Morris (Dir)
Immediate Holding Company: MORELLI GROUP LIMITED
Registration no: 02711932 **Date established:** 1992
Turnover: £10m - £20m **No.of Employees:** 21 - 50 **Product Groups:** 32

Morflin Precision Castings Ltd
21 Northampton Street, Birmingham, B18 6DU
Tel: 0121-233 9361 **Fax:** 0121-233 0713
E-mail: sales@morflin.com
Website: http://www.morflin.co.uk
Directors: P. Griffiths (MD), N. Griffiths (Fin)
Immediate Holding Company: MORFLIN PRECISION CASTINGS LIMITED
Registration no: 00514976 **Date established:** 1953
No.of Employees: 1 - 10 **Product Groups:** 46

Date of Accounts	Apr 11	Apr 10	Apr 09
Working Capital	54	59	57
Fixed Assets	43	30	33
Current Assets	86	80	86

Mortimer Spinks
Unit 4302 Waterside Centre Solihull Parkway, Birmingham Business Park, Birmingham, B37 7YN
Tel: 0121-329 1400 **Fax:** 0121-329 1414
E-mail: info@mortimerspinks.com
Website: http://www.mortimerspinks.com
Managers: D. Owen (Sales Admin)
Date established: 1989 **Turnover:** £2m - £5m **No.of Employees:** 1 - 10
Product Groups: 80

Moss Lighting Ltd
Unit 2a Bordesley Street, Birmingham, B5 5PG
Tel: 0121-643 0529 **Fax:** 0121-633 4576
E-mail: enquiries@mosslighting.co.uk
Directors: V. Zavoli (Fin)
Immediate Holding Company: MOSS LIGHTING LIMITED
Registration no: 01345974 **VAT No.:** GB 113 4757 82
Date established: 1977 **No.of Employees:** 1 - 10 **Product Groups:** 37

Date of Accounts	Dec 11	Dec 10	Dec 08
Working Capital	20	19	17
Fixed Assets	2	2	4
Current Assets	32	33	30

Mott Macdonald Ltd
85 New Hall Street, Birmingham, B3 1LZ
Tel: 0121-237 4000 **Fax:** 0121-237 4001
E-mail: birmingham@mottmacdonald.com
Website: http://www.mottmac.com
Managers: A. Taylor, D. Mangam
Ultimate Holding Company: MOTT MACDONALD GROUP LIMITED
Immediate Holding Company: MOTT MACDONALD LIMITED
Registration no: 01243967 **Date established:** 1976
No.of Employees: 51 - 100 **Product Groups:** 42, 54, 80, 84

Date of Accounts	Dec 11	Dec 10	Dec 09
Sales Turnover	531m	573m	610m
Pre Tax Profit/Loss	13m	25m	21m
Working Capital	288m	302m	299m
Fixed Assets	19m	19m	19m
Current Assets	498m	505m	502m
Current Liabilities	124m	120m	131m

Multibrasive Ltd
133 New John Street, Birmingham, B6 4LD
Tel: 0121-333 4760 **Fax:** 0121-333 4761
E-mail: jeffcater@multibrasive.co.uk
Website: http://www.multibrasive.co.uk
Directors: J. Cater (Ptnr)
Immediate Holding Company: MULTIBRASIVE LIMITED
Registration no: 06581277 **Date established:** 2008
Turnover: Up to £250,000 **No.of Employees:** 1 - 10 **Product Groups:** 42, 48

M Y Living Space
PO Box 13459, Birmingham, B11 9BX
Tel: 0121-622 1772
E-mail: general@mylivingspace.co.uk
Website: http://www.mylivingspace.co.uk
Managers: A. Croft
Turnover: Up to £250,000 **No.of Employees:** 1 - 10 **Product Groups:** 26, 30, 33, 36

myM-link Limited
4 Greenfield Crescent Edgbaston, Birmingham, B15 3BE
Tel: 0121-452 5636 **Fax:** 0121-452 5361
E-mail: sue@mym-link.co.uk
Website: http://www.mym-link.co.uk
Registration no: 06575316 **Date established:** 2008
Turnover: £250,000 - £500,000 **No.of Employees:** 1 - 10
Product Groups: 81

Nairda Ltd
1 St Johns Wood Rednal, Birmingham, B45 8DL
Tel: 0121-457 9571 **Fax:** 0121-457 9571
E-mail: info@nairda.co.uk
Website: http://www.nairda.co.uk
Directors: A. O'Donnell (MD)
Immediate Holding Company: NAIRDA LIMITED
Registration no: 04841346 **VAT No.:** GB 818 1091 41
Date established: 2003 **No.of Employees:** 1 - 10 **Product Groups:** 37, 38

Date of Accounts	Jul 10	Jul 09	Jul 08
Working Capital	10	15	29
Fixed Assets	5	6	7
Current Assets	18	20	36

Naturalvent Ltd
510 Queslett Road Great Barr, Birmingham, B43 7EJ
Tel: 08704-431923 **Fax:** 0121-3605140
E-mail: sales.office@naturalvent.com
Website: http://www.naturalvent.com
Directors: L. Levy (Dir), N. Levy (Dir), R. Levy (Dir)
Immediate Holding Company: NATURALVENT LIMITED
Registration no: 06797237 **Date established:** 2009
No.of Employees: 1 - 10 **Product Groups:** 40

Nec Group
National Exhibition Centre, Birmingham, B40 1NT
Tel: 0121-780 4141 **Fax:** 0121-767 3815
E-mail: feedback@necgroup.co.uk
Website: http://www.necgroup.co.uk
Directors: C. Stretton (Co Sec)
Managers: P. Thandi
Ultimate Holding Company: NATIONAL EXHIBITION CENTRE LIMITED (THE)
Immediate Holding Company: NEC FINANCE PLC
Registration no: 02652843 **Date established:** 1991
Turnover: £75m - £125m **No.of Employees:** 1 - 10 **Product Groups:** 69, 81

Date of Accounts	Mar 11	Mar 10	Mar 09
Pre Tax Profit/Loss	N/A	N/A	1
Working Capital	38	38	38
Fixed Assets	200m	200m	200m
Current Assets	46	46	46
Current Liabilities	8	8	8

Needham & James Limited
Shakespeare Putsman LLP Somerset House, Temple Street, Birmingham, B2 5DJ
Tel: 0121-237 3000 **Fax:** 0121-237 3011
E-mail: sales@needhamandjames.com
Website: http://www.needhamandjames.com
Directors: D. Whiting (Ptnr), J. Hughes (Snr Part), K. James (Ptnr), R. Mason (Ptnr), J. Webster (Dir)
Managers: C. Buckley (Sales Admin)
Immediate Holding Company: College Barns Management Ltd
Registration no: 02263603 **Date established:** 2004
Turnover: £500,000 - £1m **No.of Employees:** 21 - 50 **Product Groups:** 80

Netlink Trading Ltd
108 Harvington Road, Birmingham, B29 5ER
Tel: 08707-202742 **Fax:** 07050-801628
E-mail: richard@netlinktrading.co.uk
Website: http://www.netlinktrading.co.uk
Directors: R. Tubb (MD)
Immediate Holding Company: NETLINK TRADING LIMITED
Registration no: 03718735 **Date established:** 1999
Turnover: Up to £250,000 **No.of Employees:** 1 - 10 **Product Groups:** 44

Date of Accounts	Apr 11	Apr 10	Apr 09
Working Capital	-12	-15	-17
Fixed Assets	N/A	N/A	3
Current Assets	2	1	6

Network HR Recruitment
Network House 119 Hagley Road, Birmingham, B16 8LB
Tel: 0121-450 5030 **Fax:** 0121-450 5031
E-mail: sales@networkhr.co.uk
Website: http://www.networkhr.co.uk
Directors: C. Watson (Dir), M. Ellis (MD)
Registration no: 04331963 **No.of Employees:** 1 - 10 **Product Groups:** 80

New Edge Cutting Tools
21b Vyse Street Hockley, Birmingham, B18 6LE
Tel: 0121-523 9086 **Fax:** 0121- 5239086
Directors: M. Davis (Prop)
Date established: 1980 **No.of Employees:** 1 - 10 **Product Groups:** 36

Newey & Eyre
Yardley Court 11-13 Frederick Rd, Edgbaston, Birmingham, B15 1JD
Tel: 0800-783 6909 **Fax:** 0121-455 1413
E-mail: customer.info@hagemeyer.co.uk
Website: http://www.neweysonline.co.uk
Bank(s): Barclays
Directors: A. Fraser (Grp Chief Exec), L. Pattinson (Sales), T. Hammerschmid (Fin), D. O'Byrne (Comm), C. Gibson (Sales), J. Hogan (Grp Chief Exec), L. Henderson (Fin)
Managers: J. Harris (Mktg Serv Mgr), A. Holland (Chief Mgr), L. Biddle (Mktg Serv Mgr), A. McDamez
Ultimate Holding Company: Hagemeyer NV
Immediate Holding Company: Hagemeyer (UK) Ltd
Registration no: 00216596 **VAT No.:** GB 614 2136 80
Turnover: £250m - £500m **No.of Employees:** 101 - 250
Product Groups: 30, 37, 39, 40, 63, 66, 67

J Nicklin & Sons Ltd
36 Erskine Street, Birmingham, B7 4LL
Tel: 0121-359 8101 **Fax:** 0121-359 6673
E-mail: enquiries@nicklin.com
Website: http://www.nicklin.com
Bank(s): HSBC Bank plc
Directors: D. Nicklin (Dir)
Ultimate Holding Company: NICKLIN TRANSIT PACKAGING LIMITED
Immediate Holding Company: J. NICKLIN & SONS LIMITED
Registration no: 00410867 **Date established:** 1946 **Turnover:** £5m - £10m
No.of Employees: 21 - 50 **Product Groups:** 25, 27, 45

Date of Accounts	May 11	May 10	May 09
Sales Turnover	5m	4m	5m
Pre Tax Profit/Loss	149	121	220
Working Capital	646	842	886
Fixed Assets	2m	2m	2m
Current Assets	3m	3m	2m
Current Liabilities	1m	868	802

Nitrotec Services Ltd
5-8 Bickford Road, Birmingham, B6 7EE
Tel: 0121-322 2280 **Fax:** 0121-322 2236
E-mail: mikefielden@ttigroup.co.uk
Website: http://www.ttigroup.co.uk
Managers: A. Locke (Sales Prom Mgr), M. Fielden (Mgr)
No.of Employees: 21 - 50 **Product Groups:** 46, 48

Nobisco Ltd
68 Wyrley Road, Birmingham, B6 7BN
Tel: 0121-328 3889 **Fax:** 0121-328 2375
E-mail: info@nobisco.co.uk
Website: http://www.nobisco.co.uk
Directors: D. Marshall (MD)
Immediate Holding Company: NOBISCO LIMITED
Registration no: 01945617 **Date established:** 1985
No.of Employees: 11 - 20 **Product Groups:** 24, 27, 30, 40, 67

Date of Accounts	Mar 12	Mar 11	Mar 10
Working Capital	1m	1m	936
Fixed Assets	172	172	126
Current Assets	2m	2m	1m

Non Standard Socket Screws Ltd
358-364 Farm Street, Birmingham, B19 2TZ
Tel: 0121-515 0100 **Fax:** 0121-523 4440
E-mail: sales@nssocketscrews.com
Website: http://www.nssocketscrews.com
Bank(s): HSBC
Managers: M. Talbot (Purch Mgr), M. Wolsey, P. Glover (Fin Mgr), R. Trezise
Immediate Holding Company: NON STANDARD SOCKET SCREW LIMITED
Registration no: 01008405 **VAT No.:** GB 112 7880 76
Date established: 1971 **Turnover:** £5m - £10m
No.of Employees: 51 - 100 **Product Groups:** 35, 66

Date of Accounts	Apr 12	Apr 11	Apr 10
Sales Turnover	7m	6m	5m
Pre Tax Profit/Loss	724	538	77
Working Capital	3m	2m	2m
Fixed Assets	1m	1m	1m
Current Assets	4m	3m	3m
Current Liabilities	514	441	267

Nouveau Ceramics
223 Longbridge Lane, Birmingham, B31 4RE
Tel: 0121-477 2038 **Fax:** 0121-475 4004
Directors: G. Payne (Ptnr)
Date established: 1995 **No.of Employees:** 1 - 10 **Product Groups:** 38, 67, 88

O S R International Ltd
361-365 Moseley Road, Birmingham, B12 9DE
Tel: 0121-440 3655 **Fax:** 0121-446 4183
E-mail: info@osrinternational.com
Website: http://www.osrinternational.com
Directors: M. Verma (MD)
Immediate Holding Company: O.S.R. INTERNATIONAL LIMITED
Registration no: 01696298 **VAT No.:** GB 378 2287 17
Date established: 1983 **Turnover:** £2m - £5m **No.of Employees:** 1 - 10
Product Groups: 24, 63

Date of Accounts	Mar 11	Mar 10	Mar 09
Working Capital	134	162	188
Fixed Assets	13	13	19
Current Assets	355	545	414

Oakley Steel Limited
Lonsdale House 52 Blucher Street, Birmingham, B1 1QU
Tel: 0121-288 0371 **Fax:** 0121-345 0775
E-mail: sales@oakleysteel.co.uk
Website: http://www.oakleysteel.co.uk
Directors: S. Oakley (Export)
Registration no: 06118170 **Date established:** 2007
Turnover: £500,000 - £1m **No.of Employees:** 1 - 10 **Product Groups:** 61

Ocean Video & Multi Media Productions
Benson House 98-104 Lombard Street Digbeth, Birmingham, B12 0QR
Tel: 07000-191920 **Fax:** 07000-191921
E-mail: solutions@oceanmultimedia.com
Website: http://www.oceanmultimedia.com
Managers: R. Pallett (Sales Prom Mgr)
Immediate Holding Company: BLACK TIGER LIMITED
Registration no: 04715959 **VAT No.:** GB 444 6997 04
Date established: 2003 **No.of Employees:** 11 - 20 **Product Groups:** 44, 89

Date of Accounts	Dec 11	Dec 10	Dec 09
Working Capital	6	6	7
Current Assets	7	7	8

Old Iron Fabrications
Unit 10 Mount Street Business Centre Mount Street, Nechells, Birmingham, B7 5RD
Tel: 0121-327 1946 **Fax:** 0121-327 1946
Directors: T. Mullins (Prop)
No.of Employees: 1 - 10 **Product Groups:** 35, 49

Orbit International
Dugdale Street, Birmingham, B18 4JA
Tel: 0121-558 8444 **Fax:** 0121-565 0385
E-mail: sales@orbit-int.co.uk
Website: http://www.orbit-int.co.uk
Bank(s): HSBC
Managers: J. Thomas (Ops Mgr), E. Yi (Purch Mgr), K. Sohal
Immediate Holding Company: ORBIT INTERNATIONAL PLC
Registration no: 01866035 **VAT No.:** GB 388 6650 94
Date established: 1984 **Turnover:** £10m - £20m
No.of Employees: 21 - 50 **Product Groups:** 24

Date of Accounts	Sep 11	Sep 10	Sep 09
Sales Turnover	12m	8m	8m
Pre Tax Profit/Loss	2m	693	555
Working Capital	8m	6m	6m
Fixed Assets	280	221	213
Current Assets	11m	8m	8m
Current Liabilities	566	398	432

P J M Microwaves
Unit 12-13 Deykin Park Industrial Estate Deykin Avenue, Birmingham, B6 7HN
Tel: 07721-586208
E-mail: pjmmicrowaves@hotmail.co.uk
Website: http://www.pjmmicrowaves.co.uk
Directors: P. Melsopp (Prop)
Registration no: 05441376 **Date established:** 2005
Turnover: Up to £250,000 **No.of Employees:** 1 - 10 **Product Groups:** 36, 40

P & P Seating Ltd
429 The Meadway, Birmingham, B33 0DZ
Tel: 0121-784 4001 **Fax:** 0121-789 7061
E-mail: info@viperint.co.uk
Website: http://www.ppseat.co.uk
Directors: J. Brain (Prop)
Ultimate Holding Company: ESTEEMSPRINT LIMITED
Immediate Holding Company: P & P SEATING LIMITED
Registration no: 01420822 **VAT No.:** GB 313 9118 77
Date established: 1979 **Turnover:** £1m - £2m **No.of Employees:** 11 - 20
Product Groups: 22, 26, 39, 63

Date of Accounts	Jul 11	Jul 10	Jul 09
Working Capital	131	139	121
Fixed Assets	23	25	28
Current Assets	203	196	194

P.D.Q
Unit 6 Pavilion Drive, Holford, Birmingham, B6 7BB
Tel: 0121-625 3377 **Fax:** 0121-356 1652
Website: http://www.centresoft.co.uk
Managers: A. Waterhouse (Mgr)
Ultimate Holding Company: VIVENDI SA (FRANCE)
Immediate Holding Company: P.D.Q. DISTRIBUTION LIMITED
Registration no: 02105582 **Date established:** 1987 **Turnover:** £5m - £10m
No.of Employees: 101 - 250 **Product Groups:** 44

Date of Accounts	Dec 11	Dec 10	Dec 09
Sales Turnover	7m	8m	12m
Pre Tax Profit/Loss	244	287	440
Working Capital	6m	6m	7m
Fixed Assets	163	166	247
Current Assets	16m	19m	13m
Current Liabilities	2m	2m	4m

Pacific Solutions International Ltd
Bordesley Hall The Holloway, Alvechurch, Birmingham, B48 7QA
Tel: 08450-589686 **Fax:** 01252-846333
E-mail: support@pacsol.co.uk
Website: http://www.pacsol.co.uk
Directors: M. Coulthard (Dir)
Immediate Holding Company: PACIFIC SOLUTIONS INTERNATIONAL LIMITED
Registration no: 03113771 **Date established:** 1995 **Turnover:** £1m - £2m
No.of Employees: 1 - 10 **Product Groups:** 44, 80

Date of Accounts	Sep 11	Sep 10	Sep 09
Working Capital	164	151	100
Fixed Assets	45	51	52
Current Assets	581	603	414

R T Palmer Ltd
100 Unett Street, Birmingham, B19 3BZ
Tel: 0121-523 4363 **Fax:** 0121-523 5923
E-mail: sales@ae-uk.net
Website: http://www.rtnet.co.uk
Bank(s): Barclays
Directors: N. Carter (Fin), T. Pedley (MD)
Managers: B. Hall (Sales Prom Mgr)
Ultimate Holding Company: R T PALMER LIMITED
Immediate Holding Company: ADVANCED ENGINEERING (UK) LIMITED
Registration no: 01388943 **Date established:** 1978 **Turnover:** £1m - £2m
No.of Employees: 21 - 50 **Product Groups:** 35, 46, 48, 67, 84

Date of Accounts	Oct 11	Oct 10	Oct 09
Working Capital	222	-29	13
Fixed Assets	2m	1m	1m
Current Assets	1m	764	586

Paperchasers Ltd
Logistics House, Birmingham, B28 9HL
Tel: 08456-344170 **Fax:** 08456-344170
E-mail: sales@paperchasers.biz
Website: http://www.paperchasers.biz
Directors: L. Langdon (MD)
Immediate Holding Company: PAPERCHASERS LIMITED
Registration no: 05982749 **Date established:** 2006
No.of Employees: 1 - 10 **Product Groups:** 27

Date of Accounts	Mar 11	Mar 10	Mar 09
Working Capital	-1	-0	-1
Fixed Assets	14	3	4
Current Assets	21	16	13

Paraid Medical
Paraid House Weston Lane, Birmingham, B11 3RS
Tel: 0121-700 7455 **Fax:** 0121-700 7454
E-mail: info@paraid.co.uk
Website: http://www.paraid.co.uk
Directors: M. Wallace (MD), B. Scholes (Fin), D. Smith (Sales), A. Whitmore (Fab)
Managers: P. Colder ()
Product Groups: 26, 38, 40, 45, 63, 86

Pareto Golf Ltd
Unit 25 Aston Cross Business Centre 19 Wainwright Street, Birmingham, B6 5TH
Tel: 0121-325 9100 **Fax:** 0121-325 9220
Website: http://www.paretogolf.co.uk
Directors: C. Treharne (MD), T. Treharne (Ch)
Managers: P. Ruck (I.T. Exec)
Immediate Holding Company: PARETO GOLF LIMITED
Registration no: 06742796 **VAT No.:** GB 528 4177 33
Date established: 2008 **Turnover:** £1m - £2m **No.of Employees:** 1 - 10
Product Groups: 49

Parker Merchanting Ltd
Chester Street Aston, Birmingham, B6 4AE
Tel: 0121-503 4500 **Fax:** 0121-503 4501
E-mail: info.parker@hagemeyer.co.uk
Website: http://www.parker-merchanting.com
Directors: L. Pattison (MD)
Managers: F. Galvin (District Mgr)
Ultimate Holding Company: RAY INVESTMENT SARL (LUXEMBOURG)
Immediate Holding Company: PARKER MERCHANTING LIMITED
Registration no: 00224779 **VAT No.:** GB 614 2136 80
Date established: 2027 **No.of Employees:** 1 - 10 **Product Groups:** 22, 23, 24, 30, 39, 40, 45, 63, 66, 68

Parklines Buildings Ltd
Gala House 3 Raglan Road, Birmingham, B5 7RA
Tel: 0121-446 6030 **Fax:** 0121-446 5991
E-mail: sales@parklines.co.uk
Website: http://www.parklines.co.uk
Directors: J. Wernick (Dir)
Immediate Holding Company: PARK LINES (BUILDINGS) LIMITED
Registration no: 01129239 **Date established:** 1973
Turnover: Up to £250,000 **No.of Employees:** 1 - 10 **Product Groups:** 25, 35

Date of Accounts	Dec 11	Dec 10	Dec 09
Working Capital	-5	-0	-6
Fixed Assets	15	17	11
Current Assets	64	102	67

Parsons Brinckerhoff
Quadrant Court 45 Calthorpe Road, Edgbaston, Birmingham, B15 1TH
Tel: 0121-452 7400 **Fax:** 0121-452 1799
Website: http://www.pbworld.com
Managers: R. Hughes (Mgr)
Ultimate Holding Company: BALFOUR BEATTY PLC
Immediate Holding Company: PARSONS BRINCKERHOFF LTD
Registration no: 02554514 **Date established:** 1990
Turnover: £50m - £75m **No.of Employees:** 21 - 50 **Product Groups:** 84

Partex Marking Systems UK Ltd
Unit 61-64 0 Station Road Coleshill, Birmingham, B46 1JT
Tel: 01675-463670 **Fax:** 01675-463520
E-mail: sales@partex.co.uk
Website: http://www.partex.co.uk
Bank(s): Scandinavian, Cannon Street, London EC4M 6XX
Directors: P. Symonds (MD)
Managers: S. Hooper (Tech Serv Mgr)
Ultimate Holding Company: PARTEX HOLDING AB (SWEDEN)
Immediate Holding Company: PARTEX MARKING SYSTEMS (UK) LIMITED
Registration no: 00850894 **Date established:** 1965 **Turnover:** £2m - £5m
No.of Employees: 21 - 50 **Product Groups:** 30, 37

Date of Accounts	Dec 11	Dec 10	Dec 09
Working Capital	2m	2m	1m
Fixed Assets	294	317	184
Current Assets	3m	3m	2m

Pascal & Co. Ltd
112 Cherrywood Road, Birmingham, B9 4JJ
Tel: 0121-753 7720 **Fax:** 0121-771 1179
E-mail: sales@lloydpascal.co.uk
Website: http://www.lloydpascal.co.uk
Bank(s): Barclays, Birmingham
Directors: K. Bates (Dir), M. Bates (Ch), H. Hamilton (Fin)
Managers: S. Bates (Sales Prom Mgr), M. Oxland (Mgr)
Ultimate Holding Company: SLEMCKA (DMS) LIMITED
Immediate Holding Company: LLOYD PASCAL & CO.LIMITED
Registration no: 00369093 **VAT No.:** GB 110 3500 47
Date established: 1941 **Turnover:** £5m - £10m **No.of Employees:** 21 - 50
Product Groups: 22, 26, 35, 36

Date of Accounts	Dec 11	Dec 10	Dec 09
Sales Turnover	12m	11m	7m
Pre Tax Profit/Loss	576	671	338
Working Capital	6m	5m	4m
Fixed Assets	4m	4m	5m
Current Assets	7m	6m	5m
Current Liabilities	544	349	977

Patrol Alarm Systems Ltd
505 Reddings Lane Tyseley, Birmingham, B11 3DF
Tel: 0121-777 4075 **Fax:** 0121-702 2307
E-mail: info@patrolalarmsystems.co.uk
Website: http://www.patrolalarmsystems.co.uk
Directors: P. Stevens (MD)
Immediate Holding Company: PATROL ALARM SYSTEMS LIMITED
Registration no: 00971786 **Date established:** 1970
Turnover: £500,000 - £1m **No.of Employees:** 1 - 10 **Product Groups:** 37, 38, 40, 46, 47

Date of Accounts	Mar 12	Mar 11	Mar 10
Working Capital	136	146	237
Fixed Assets	1m	1m	852
Current Assets	395	385	447

Pennant Automotive & Industrial Supplies
University Farm Wasthill Lane, Kings Norton, Birmingham, B38 9EP
Tel: 0121-459 4276 **Fax:** 0121-451 2488
Directors: G. Jones (Prop)
Registration no: 04588185 **Date established:** 2002 **Turnover:** £2m - £5m
No.of Employees: 1 - 10 **Product Groups:** 68

Permat Machines Ltd
Station Road Coleshill, Birmingham, B46 1JG
Tel: 01675-463351 **Fax:** 01675-465816
E-mail: sales@permat.com
Website: http://www.permat.com
Directors: W. Koch (MD), I. Bott (Fin)
Ultimate Holding Company: NAGEL MASCHINEN UND WERKZUNGFABRIK GMBH (GERMANY)
Immediate Holding Company: PERMAT MACHINES LIMITED
Registration no: 00980466 **Date established:** 1970 **Turnover:** £2m - £5m
No.of Employees: 1 - 10 **Product Groups:** 36, 37, 46, 48, 47

Date of Accounts	Dec 11	Dec 10	Dec 09
Working Capital	990	1m	1m
Fixed Assets	2m	755	761
Current Assets	1m	1m	1m

Petrel Ltd
Fortnum Close, Birmingham, B33 0LB
Tel: 0121-783 7161 **Fax:** 0121-783 5717
E-mail: sales@petrel-ex.co.uk
Website: http://www.petrel-ex.co.uk
Bank(s): HSBC, Walsall
Directors: C. Holmes (Sales & Mktg), J. Tipper (Fin)
Managers: J. Myatt (Buyer)
Ultimate Holding Company: CHAMBERLIN PLC
Immediate Holding Company: PETREL LIMITED
Registration no: 01539429 **VAT No.:** GB 377 3648 12
Date established: 1981 **Turnover:** £2m - £5m **No.of Employees:** 21 - 50
Product Groups: 37

Date of Accounts	Mar 12	Mar 11	Mar 10
Sales Turnover	3m	3m	3m
Pre Tax Profit/Loss	175	307	203
Working Capital	1m	903	887
Fixed Assets	195	170	182
Current Assets	2m	2m	2m
Current Liabilities	167	175	218

Philip Cornes & Company Ltd
Unit 4 The Cofton Centre, Birmingham, B31 4PT
Tel: 01527-555000 **Fax:** 01527-547000
E-mail: ian.cruxton@twmetals.co.uk
Website: http://www.philipcornes.com
Bank(s): Lloyds TSB, The Rotunda, Birmingham
Directors: L. Brown (Co Sec)
Managers: T. Neale (Mgr), I. Cruxton (Sales Prom Mgr)
Ultimate Holding Company: O'NEAL STEEL INC (USA)
Immediate Holding Company: PHILIP CORNES & COMPANY LIMITED
Registration no: 00599724 **Date established:** 1958
Turnover: £10m - £20m **No.of Employees:** 11 - 20 **Product Groups:** 34, 66

Date of Accounts	Dec 11	Dec 10	Dec 09
Sales Turnover	18m	13m	14m
Pre Tax Profit/Loss	2m	1m	1m
Working Capital	6m	13m	12m
Fixed Assets	26	29	27
Current Assets	11m	17m	15m
Current Liabilities	559	415	206

Phillips Hybrid
40 Bickford Road, Birmingham, B6 7EE
Tel: 0121-327 0428 **Fax:** 0121-328 9050
E-mail: lhp@p-hybrid.demon.co.uk
Directors: L. Phillips (Prop)
No.of Employees: 1 - 10 **Product Groups:** 33, 48, 84

Pike Signals Ltd
7-11 Phoenix Business Park Avenue Close, Birmingham, B7 4NU
Tel: 0121-359 4034 **Fax:** 0121-333 3167
E-mail: enquiries@pikesignals.com
Website: http://www.pikesignals.com
Bank(s): Barclays, Erdington
Directors: C. Pearson (MD)
Ultimate Holding Company: THE TRAFFIC GROUP LIMITED
Immediate Holding Company: PIKE SIGNALS LIMITED
Registration no: 01586729 **VAT No.:** GB 307 7047 67
Date established: 1981 **Turnover:** £2m - £5m **No.of Employees:** 11 - 20
Product Groups: 39

Date of Accounts	Sep 11	Sep 10	Sep 09
Working Capital	861	602	948
Fixed Assets	297	281	2m
Current Assets	2m	2m	2m

Pilkington Automotives
Triplex House Eckersall Road, Birmingham, B38 8SR
Tel: 0121-254 3000 **Fax:** 0121-254 3188
E-mail: tim.bayliss@pilkington.com
Website: http://www.pilkington.com
Bank(s): National Westminster, St Helens
Directors: T. Bowlas (Fin)
Managers: D. Sword (Plant), R. Batchelor (Mktg Serv Mgr), S. Ash, A. Manley (Personnel), S. McKenna, M. Nuttall (Buyer)
Ultimate Holding Company: NIPPON SHEET GLASS CO LTD (JAPAN)
Immediate Holding Company: PILKINGTON AUTOMOTIVE LIMITED
Registration no: 02803344 **VAT No.:** 151622591006
Date established: 1993 **Turnover:** £500m - £1,000m
No.of Employees: 101 - 250 **Product Groups:** 33, 39

Pinstripe Print Ltd
60 Hampton Street, Birmingham, B19 3LU
Tel: 0121-236 0101 **Fax:** 0121-236 3059
E-mail: nigel.lyon@pinstripegroup.co.uk
Website: http://www.acornprintuk.com
Directors: N. Lyon (MD)
Ultimate Holding Company: PINSTRIPE HOLDINGS LIMITED
Immediate Holding Company: PINSTRIPE PRINT LIMITED
Registration no: 03556407 **Date established:** 1998
No.of Employees: 21 - 50 **Product Groups:** 80, 81

Date of Accounts	Nov 11	Nov 10	Nov 09
Working Capital	423	371	264
Fixed Assets	126	148	232
Current Assets	751	827	874

Pipe Center (Head Office)
PO Box 41, Birmingham, B5 6LU
Tel: 0121-666 6343 **Fax:** 0121-666 6574
Managers: B. Chance (Mgr)
Immediate Holding Company: PROFIT FOCUS (UK) LIMITED
Registration no: 03244411 **VAT No.:** GB 109 6076 69
Date established: 1996 **Turnover:** £20m - £50m **No.of Employees:** 1 - 10
Product Groups: 66

Date of Accounts	Jun 11	Jun 10	Jun 09
Sales Turnover	87m	96m	96m
Pre Tax Profit/Loss	-2m	5m	5m
Working Capital	-2m	1m	4m
Fixed Assets	36m	34m	26m
Current Assets	34m	33m	45m
Current Liabilities	9m	7m	9m

Pipe Center
PO Box 297, Birmingham, B21 0AH
Tel: 0121-553 6666 **Fax:** 0121-553 6102
E-mail: john.hancock@wolseley.co.uk
Website: http://www.wolseley.co.uk
Directors: W. Woodward (Co Sec), M. Storey (Dir), J. Smith (Dir), C. Wadsworth (Dir), C. Buckett (Fin), A. Barden (MD), B. Stanton (Grp Chief Exec)
Managers: J. Hancock (Mgr), S. Brightwell (Mgr), P. Mountford, J. Hancox (Mgr), C. Green (District Mgr)
Immediate Holding Company: WOLSELEY CENTRES LTD
Registration no: 03244411 **Turnover:** £75m - £125m
No.of Employees: 21 - 50 **Product Groups:** 30, 34, 35, 36, 38, 40

The Plastic Fan Co. Ltd
Unit Z Hamstead Industrial Estate, Austin Way, Great Barr, Birmingham, B42 1DU
Tel: 0121-358 6949 **Fax:** 0121-357 4159
E-mail: pfan1@btconnect.com
Website: http://www.fabricationsinplastic.co.uk
Registration no: 00564679 **Turnover:** £250,000 - £500,000
No.of Employees: 1 - 10 **Product Groups:** 29, 30, 34, 35, 37, 38, 40, 41, 42, 46, 48, 49, 52, 54, 84

Date of Accounts	Mar 08	Mar 07	Mar 06
Working Capital	177	99	88
Fixed Assets	7	6	8
Current Assets	344	184	164
Current Liabilities	167	85	76
Total Share Capital	2	2	2

Plastics Centre
Unit 13 Boulton Industrial Centre Icknield Street, Hockley, Birmingham, B18 5AU
Tel: 0121-554 5225 **Fax:** 0121-515 4664
Website: http://www.countyplastics.co.uk
Managers: T. Hubbard (District Mgr)
No.of Employees: 1 - 10 **Product Groups:** 30

Pobs Precision Tools
44 Bickford Road, Birmingham, B6 7EE
Tel: 0121-327 5736 **Fax:** 0121-328 5261
E-mail: pobs.tools@btconnect.com
Website: http://www.pobs.co.uk
Directors: E. Lane (Prop)
Turnover: Up to £250,000 **No.of Employees:** 1 - 10 **Product Groups:** 48

Polishcraft Ltd
68g Sapcote Trading Centre Wyrley Road, Birmingham, B6 7BN
Tel: 0121-322 2344 **Fax:** 0121-322 2344
E-mail: glovers123@tiscali.co.uk
Website: http://www.polishcraft.net
Directors: S. Glover (MD)
Immediate Holding Company: POLISHCRAFT LIMITED
Registration no: 04428119 **VAT No.:** GB 456 8040 39
Date established: 2002 **Turnover:** Up to £250,000
No.of Employees: 1 - 10 **Product Groups:** 48

Date of Accounts	Mar 11	Mar 10	Mar 09
Working Capital	-2	-2	23
Fixed Assets	15	18	15
Current Assets	81	74	99

Polyfashions Ltd
27 Whitmore Road Small Heath, Birmingham, B10 0NR
Tel: 0121-772 7754 **Fax:** 0121-766 6744
E-mail: info@polyfashion.co.uk
Website: http://www.polyfashion.co.uk
Directors: A. Rauf (Dir), A. Rauf (MD)
Managers: N. Qasim (Sales Prom Mgr), M. Farooq (Accounts)
Immediate Holding Company: POLYFASHION LIMITED
Registration no: 01154474 **VAT No.:** GB 112 1926 11
Date established: 1974 **No.of Employees:** 1 - 10 **Product Groups:** 24

Date of Accounts	Dec 06	Dec 05	Dec 04
Working Capital	-78	-80	-10
Fixed Assets	4	11	18
Current Assets	47	18	73

Polyfibre Ltd
18 Wainwright Street Aston, Birmingham, B6 5TJ
Tel: 0121-327 2360 **Fax:** 0121-327 3089
E-mail: info@polyfibre.co.uk
Website: http://www.polyfibre.co.uk
Directors: K. Greenaway (MD)
Immediate Holding Company: POLYFIBRE (UK) LIMITED
Registration no: 04647208 **Date established:** 2003 **Turnover:** £1m - £2m
No.of Employees: 1 - 10 **Product Groups:** 30

Date of Accounts	Mar 11	Mar 10	Mar 09
Working Capital	1m	1m	871
Fixed Assets	13	N/A	3
Current Assets	1m	1m	1m

Poole & Son Scoops Ltd
Unit 15 Delta House Adderley Street, Birmingham, B9 4ED
Tel: 0121-753 0912 **Fax:** 0121-753 0912
E-mail: janeannheath@hotmail.com
Website: http://www.scoopsforscales.com
Directors: M. Heath (MD)
Immediate Holding Company: POOLE & SON (SCOOPS) LIMITED
Registration no: 00554723 **Date established:** 1955
Turnover: Up to £250,000 **No.of Employees:** 1 - 10 **Product Groups:** 38, 42

Date of Accounts	Mar 12	Mar 11	Mar 10
Working Capital	-2	3	5
Fixed Assets	1	1	1
Current Assets	12	23	15

T Pope Ltd (Nameplates & Labels)
47 Ward Street, Birmingham, B19 3TA
Tel: 0121-359 4618 **Fax:** 0121-359 1027
E-mail: tpopeltd@btconnect.com
Website: http://www.t-popeltd.co.uk
Directors: P. Booker (MD)
Immediate Holding Company: T. POPE LIMITED
Registration no: 04597357 **Date established:** 2002
Turnover: £500,000 - £1m **No.of Employees:** 1 - 10 **Product Groups:** 28, 30, 35, 36, 46, 48, 49, 65

Date of Accounts	Dec 11	Dec 10	Dec 09
Working Capital	80	66	10
Fixed Assets	4	7	6
Current Assets	220	218	140

Porter Precision Grinding Ltd
188-192 Barr Street, Birmingham, B19 3AE
Tel: 0121-554 6959 **Fax:** 0121-554 9129
E-mail: surfacegrinders@aol.com
Directors: S. Nagar (MD)
Immediate Holding Company: KHAYLAN ENTERPRISES LTD
Registration no: 00481857 **Date established:** 2010
No.of Employees: 1 - 10 **Product Groups:** 46

Portman Travel Ltd
15th Floor Edgbaston House 3 Duchess Place, Birmingham, B16 8NH
Tel: 0121-452 8800 **Fax:** 0121-452 8810
E-mail: mhumphries@portmantravel.co.uk
Website: http://www.portmantravel.com
Bank(s): HSBC
Managers: M. Wells (Chief Mgr)
Ultimate Holding Company: SUPER SELECTOR SARL
Immediate Holding Company: PORTMAN TRAVEL LIMITED
Registration no: 00620104 **VAT No.:** 680 4034 53 **Date established:** 1959
Turnover: £75m - £125m **No.of Employees:** 11 - 20 **Product Groups:** 69

Date of Accounts	Dec 11	Dec 10	Dec 09
Sales Turnover	260m	257m	239m
Pre Tax Profit/Loss	4m	4m	2m
Working Capital	14m	13m	15m
Fixed Assets	6m	5m	4m
Current Assets	27m	30m	29m
Current Liabilities	2m	3m	2m

Powder Coatings Ltd
215 Tyburn Road, Birmingham, B24 8NB
Tel: 0121-250 2145 **Fax:** 0121-250 2154
E-mail: sales@powder-coatings.ltd.uk
Website: http://www.powder-coatings.ltd.uk
Bank(s): National Westminster Bank Plc
Directors: E. Murphy (Fin), R. Murphy (MD)
Immediate Holding Company: POWDER COATINGS LIMITED
Registration no: 02680452 **VAT No.:** GB 580 3690 32
Date established: 1992 **Turnover:** £500,000 - £1m
No.of Employees: 11 - 20 **Product Groups:** 48

Date of Accounts	Jun 11	Jun 10	Jun 09
Working Capital	246	304	265
Fixed Assets	66	19	30
Current Assets	501	437	355

Power Capacitors Ltd
30 Redfern Road Tyseley, Birmingham, B11 2BH
Tel: 0121-708 4511 **Fax:** 0121-765 4054
E-mail: sales@powercapacitors.co.uk
Website: http://www.powercapacitors.co.uk
Bank(s): National Westminster, Solihull
Directors: P. Moss (MD)
Managers: T. Brown (Tech Serv Mgr)
Immediate Holding Company: POWER CAPACITORS LIMITED
Registration no: 01701108 **VAT No.:** 378 2589 01 **Date established:** 1983
Turnover: £1m - £2m **No.of Employees:** 11 - 20 **Product Groups:** 37, 38

Date of Accounts	Dec 11	Mar 11	Mar 10
Working Capital	5	94	19
Fixed Assets	87	34	31
Current Assets	850	841	604

Practical Car & Van Rental
Practical House 21-23 Little Broom Street, Camp Hill, Birmingham, B12 0EU
Tel: 0121-772 8599 **Fax:** 0121-766 6229
E-mail: info@practicalburton.co.uk
Website: http://www.practical.co.uk

Directors: B. Agnew (Dir)
Ultimate Holding Company: PRACTICAL HOLDINGS LIMITED
Immediate Holding Company: PRACTICAL CAR AND VAN RENTAL LIMITED
Registration no: 01675341 **Date established:** 1982 **Turnover:** £2m - £5m
No.of Employees: 21 - 50 **Product Groups:** 72, 82

Date of Accounts	Sep 11	Sep 10	Sep 09
Sales Turnover	N/A	N/A	4m
Pre Tax Profit/Loss	N/A	N/A	119
Working Capital	-2m	-1m	-2m
Fixed Assets	4m	3m	4m
Current Assets	2m	2m	1m
Current Liabilities	N/A	N/A	254

Precise Saw & Tool Co. Ltd

Unit 3 Deykin Avenue, Birmingham, B6 7HN
Tel: 0121-327 7733 **Fax:** 0121-558 7506
E-mail: enquiries@cuttingtoolsolutions.co.uk
Website: http://www.cuttingtoolsolutions.co.uk
Directors: D. Easterlow (MD)
Immediate Holding Company: PRECISE SAW AND TOOL CO LTD.
Registration no: 04058462 **Date established:** 2000
No.of Employees: 1 - 10 **Product Groups:** 34, 36, 41, 46, 47, 48, 67

Date of Accounts	Aug 11	Aug 10	Aug 09
Working Capital	-33	-21	-25
Fixed Assets	68	41	52
Current Assets	97	71	82

Precision Ceramics (a division of McGeoch - Technology Ltd)

86 Lower Tower Street, Birmingham, B19 3PA
Tel: 0121-687 5858 **Fax:** 0121-687 5857
E-mail: info@precision-ceramics.co.uk
Website: http://www.precision-ceramics.co.uk
Directors: S. Swallow (MD), T. Hudson (Fin)
Managers: R. Ahmed (Tech Serv Mgr)
Ultimate Holding Company: EASTACRE INTERNATIONAL LTD (BRITISH VIRGIN ISLANDS)
Immediate Holding Company: PRECISION CERAMICS LIMITED
Registration no: 02748497 **VAT No.:** GB 580 5066 43
Date established: 1992 **Turnover:** £2m - £5m **No.of Employees:** 51 - 100
Product Groups: 33, 35, 37, 48, 84

Precision Micro

Vantage Way Erdington, Birmingham, B24 9GZ
Tel: 0121-380 0100 **Fax:** 0121-359 3313
E-mail: info@precisionmicro.com
Website: http://www.precisionmicro.com
Directors: I. Whateley (Sales)
Registration no: 01745834 **VAT No.:** GB 687 8971 46
Date established: 1960 **Turnover:** £5m - £10m
No.of Employees: 101 - 250 **Product Groups:** 34, 35, 37, 38, 39, 42, 44, 48

Date of Accounts	Mar 11	Mar 10	Mar 09
Sales Turnover	9m	7m	N/A
Pre Tax Profit/Loss	930	671	456
Working Capital	4m	3m	2m
Fixed Assets	890	816	947
Current Assets	6m	5m	4m
Current Liabilities	637	310	399

Premier Metal Finishers

16 Warstone Parade East Hockley, Birmingham, B19 6NR
Tel: 0121-212 4787 **Fax:** 0121-212 4787
E-mail: enquires@premier-polishing.co.uk
Website: http://www.premier-polishing.co.uk
Directors: C. Cairnes (Prop)
Date established: 1996 **No.of Employees:** 1 - 10 **Product Groups:** 46, 48

Presslite Ltd

Essex Works Holborn Hill, Birmingham, B6 7QT
Tel: 0121-327 1428 **Fax:** 0121-327 9241
Website: http://www.sertec.co.uk
Bank(s): Lloyds TSB
Directors: G. Adams (MD), M. Hughes (Fin)
Managers: T. Willet (Personnel), D. Steggles (Mktg Serv Mgr), D. Cox (Tech Serv Mgr), J. Chahill (Purch Mgr), J. Harris (Sales Prom Mgr)
Ultimate Holding Company: SERTEC GROUP LIMITED
Immediate Holding Company: PRESSLITE LIMITED
Registration no: 02944354 **VAT No.:** GB 661 5464 31
Date established: 1994 **Turnover:** £10m - £20m
No.of Employees: 51 - 100 **Product Groups:** 48

Date of Accounts	Mar 12	Mar 11	Mar 10
Sales Turnover	15m	13m	10m
Pre Tax Profit/Loss	1m	1m	531
Working Capital	3m	2m	2m
Fixed Assets	2m	2m	2m
Current Assets	7m	5m	4m
Current Liabilities	497	450	304

Prestision Metal Work

St Andrews Industrial Estate Sydney Road, Birmingham, B9 4QB
Tel: 0121-772 4414 **Fax:** 0121-771 0472
E-mail: geoff@prestision.co.uk
Website: http://www.prestision.co.uk
Directors: G. Quinney (Ptnr)
VAT No.: GB 346 0227 78 **Turnover:** Up to £250,000
No.of Employees: 1 - 10 **Product Groups:** 48, 66

Primaflow Ltd

Unit 2 Stargate Business Park Cuckoo Road, Birmingham, B7 5SE
Tel: 0121-327 4000 **Fax:** 01543-571851
E-mail: sales@muellerprimaflow.com
Website: http://www.muellerprimaflow.com
Directors: M. Millerchip (MD)
Managers: E. O'Hagan (Buyer)
Ultimate Holding Company: MUELLER INDUSTRIES INC (USA)
Immediate Holding Company: INSTOX LIMITED
Registration no: 02831837 **Date established:** 1993
Turnover: £20m - £50m **No.of Employees:** 21 - 50 **Product Groups:** 30, 36

Date of Accounts	Dec 10	Dec 09	Dec 08
Working Capital	2m	2m	2m
Current Assets	2m	2m	2m

The Priory Castor & Engineering Co. Ltd

160 Aston Hall Road, Birmingham, B6 7LA
Tel: 0121-327 0832 **Fax:** 0121-322 2123
E-mail: enquiries@priorycastor.co.uk
Website: http://www.priorycastor.co.uk
Bank(s): Lloyds TSB Bank plc
Directors: N. Cooper (MD), N. Cooper (MD)
Immediate Holding Company: THE PRIORY CASTOR & ENGINEERING COMPANY LIMITED
Registration no: 00336626 **VAT No.:** GB 110 0994 11
Date established: 1938 **Turnover:** £500,000 - £1m
No.of Employees: 11 - 20 **Product Groups:** 26, 30, 35, 39

Date of Accounts	Dec 11	Dec 10	Dec 09
Working Capital	160	208	191
Fixed Assets	421	427	436
Current Assets	210	264	238

Pro Chill Ltd

89 Chester Road Castle Bromwich, Birmingham, B36 9DS
Tel: 0121-730 1526 **Fax:** 0121-730 1536
E-mail: info@prochill.co.uk
Website: http://www.prochill.co.uk
Directors: R. Lampton (MD), M. Lampton (Fin)
Immediate Holding Company: PRO CHILL LIMITED
Registration no: 03622336 **VAT No.:** GB 715 2598 49
Date established: 1998 **Turnover:** Up to £250,000
No.of Employees: 1 - 10 **Product Groups:** 40, 66

Date of Accounts	Aug 11	Aug 10	Aug 09
Working Capital	3	1	4
Fixed Assets	3	1	1
Current Assets	15	11	14

Pro Moto

Unit 48 Imex Business Park Kings Road, Tyseley, Birmingham, B11 2AL
Tel: 0121-706 2250 **Fax:** 0121-706 2250
Website: http://www.promoto.co.uk
Directors: A. Conway (Prop)
VAT No.: GB 687 6017 01 **Turnover:** Up to £250,000
No.of Employees: 1 - 10 **Product Groups:** 39

Probrand Ltd

37-55 Camden Street, Birmingham, B1 3BP
Tel: 0121-605 1000 **Fax:** 0121-605 6600
E-mail: gensalles@program.co.uk
Website: http://www.probrand.co.uk
Bank(s): The Royal Bank of Scotland
Directors: C. Griesbach (Fin), P. Robbins (Dir)
Managers: A. Garvey (Personnel), J. Dawson (Sales Prom Mgr), I. Nethercot
Immediate Holding Company: PROBRAND LIMITED
Registration no: 02653446 **Date established:** 1991
Turnover: £20m - £50m **No.of Employees:** 51 - 100 **Product Groups:** 26, 32, 37, 44, 67

Date of Accounts	Dec 11	Dec 10	Dec 09
Sales Turnover	37m	51m	58m
Pre Tax Profit/Loss	329	783	647
Working Capital	-112	-396	-36
Fixed Assets	2m	2m	2m
Current Assets	6m	5m	9m
Current Liabilities	291	465	555

Produsit Ltd

340 Summer Lane, Birmingham, B19 3QL
Tel: 0121-359 5571 **Fax:** 0121-359 5572
E-mail: produsit@msn.com
Website: http://www.produsit.co.uk
Directors: R. Hicks (MD)
Immediate Holding Company: PRODUSIT PRECISION LIMITED
Registration no: 00446778 **VAT No.:** GB 109 7256 62
Date established: 1947 **Turnover:** £250,000 - £500,000
No.of Employees: 1 - 10 **Product Groups:** 46, 48, 84

Date of Accounts	Jul 11	Jul 10	Jul 09
Working Capital	4	23	42
Fixed Assets	253	253	253
Current Assets	4	23	42

Propbrook Engineering Ltd

32 Cato Street, Birmingham, B7 4TS
Tel: 0121-359 7097
E-mail: sales@propbrook-eng.co.uk
Website: http://www.propbrook-eng.co.uk
Directors: H. Middleton (Dir)
Immediate Holding Company: PROPBROOK ENGINEERING LIMITED
Registration no: 04211112 **Date established:** 2001
No.of Employees: 11 - 20 **Product Groups:** 35, 48, 49, 85

Date of Accounts	Dec 11	Dec 10	Dec 09
Working Capital	1m	937	849
Fixed Assets	191	117	140
Current Assets	1m	1m	992

Protective Textured Coatings UK Ltd

Unit 16 Haywards Industrial Park Orton Way, Birmingham, B35 7BT
Tel: 0121-749 5088 **Fax:** 0121-693 7688
Website: http://www.ptcoatings.co.uk
Directors: I. Evans (Fin), D. Gibbons (MD)
Immediate Holding Company: PROTECTIVE TEXTURED COATINGS (U.K.) LIMITED
Registration no: 01539735 **Date established:** 1981
No.of Employees: 1 - 10 **Product Groups:** 46, 48

Date of Accounts	May 11	May 10	May 09
Working Capital	181	332	319
Fixed Assets	213	51	62
Current Assets	296	417	371

Pure Bathrooms

Reflections Studio, Grove House 473 Dudley Road, Smethwick, Birmingham, B18 4HE
Tel: 0121-565 3445 **Fax:** 0121-555 7039
E-mail: esales@purebathrooms.net
Website: http://www.purekbb.com
Directors: K. Virdi (Dir)
Registration no: 05216256 **Date established:** 1970
Turnover: £250,000 - £500,000 **No.of Employees:** 51 - 100
Product Groups: 66

Quadgate Ltd

73-75 Pershore Street, Birmingham, B5 4RW
Tel: 0121-622 2826 **Fax:** 0121-622 2985
Website: http://www.quadgate.co.uk
Directors: L. Tin (Co Sec)
Immediate Holding Company: QUADGATE LIMITED
Registration no: 02277832 **Date established:** 1988
No.of Employees: 1 - 10 **Product Groups:** 20, 40, 41

Date of Accounts	Mar 11	Mar 10	Mar 08
Working Capital	191	193	208
Fixed Assets	13	20	12
Current Assets	201	206	227

Qualplast 1991 Ltd

Old Walsall Road Great Barr, Hampstead Industrial Estate, Birmingham, B42 1EA
Tel: 0121-357 5858 **Fax:** 0121-357 5855
E-mail: enquiries@qualplast.com
Website: http://www.qualplast.com
Bank(s): Barclays, Soho Road
Directors: D. Caro (MD)
Managers: J. Curtain (Quality Control)
Immediate Holding Company: QUALPLAST (1991) LIMITED
Registration no: 05650232 **VAT No.:** GB 295 9313 19
Date established: 1977 **Turnover:** £2m - £5m **No.of Employees:** 21 - 50
Product Groups: 27, 28, 30, 48, 63

Date of Accounts	Mar 12	Mar 11	Mar 10
Working Capital	115	1	-11
Current Assets	549	243	229

Qualtec Systems Ltd

Qualtec House The Courtyard Roman Way, Coleshill, Birmingham, B46 1HQ
Tel: 01675-465332 **Fax:** 01675-466106
E-mail: info@qualtec.co.uk
Website: http://www.qualtec.co.uk
Directors: P. Griffiths (MD)
Immediate Holding Company: QUALTEC SYSTEMS LIMITED
Registration no: 02444962 **Date established:** 1989
Turnover: £250,000 - £500,000 **No.of Employees:** 1 - 10
Product Groups: 44

Date of Accounts	Dec 11	Dec 10	Dec 09
Sales Turnover	320	311	283
Pre Tax Profit/Loss	68	53	30
Working Capital	94	109	119
Fixed Assets	38	31	10
Current Assets	229	220	209
Current Liabilities	84	78	75

Quicksilver Automotive

11-15 Stoney Lane Balsall Heath, Birmingham, B12 8DL
Tel: 0121-773 7000 **Fax:** 0121-773 9420
E-mail: mail@satnavshop.com
Website: http://www.bettercarlighting.co.uk
Directors: G. Franks (Chief Op Offcr), M. Keane (Co Sec), G. Keane (Fin), G. Keane (Ch)
Managers: G. Franks (Mktg Serv Mgr)
Immediate Holding Company: TOTALCONTROL LTD
Registration no: 03367607 **Date established:** 1997
Turnover: Up to £250,000 **No.of Employees:** 1 - 10 **Product Groups:** 37

Quinton Dental Air Services

P.O.Box 6686, Birmingham, B63 3LJ
Tel: 0845-4722013
E-mail: quintonair@btinternet.com
Website: http://www.quintondentalairservices.co.uk
Managers: S. francis (Sales Admin)
Date established: 1985 **No.of Employees:** 1 - 10 **Product Groups:** 38

R & E Presswork Ltd

72-77 Lower Tower Street, Birmingham, B19 3NF
Tel: 0121-359 3023 **Fax:** 0121-359 3644
E-mail: contact@represswork.co.uk
Website: http://www.represswork.co.uk
Bank(s): HSBC Bank plc
Directors: A. Yates (MD)
Immediate Holding Company: R. & E. PRESSWORK LIMITED
Registration no: 01707067 **Date established:** 1983
Turnover: £500,000 - £1m **No.of Employees:** 21 - 50
Product Groups: 34, 35, 36, 37, 46, 48, 66

Date of Accounts	Jun 12	Jun 11	Jun 10
Working Capital	283	256	264
Fixed Assets	510	540	460
Current Assets	760	699	605

R G T Fire Protection Ltd

95 Beaumont Road, Birmingham, B30 2EB
Tel: 0121-433 5175 **Fax:** 0121-486 1847
E-mail: reg@rgtfire.com
Website: http://www.rgtfire.com
Directors: R. Tilston (Dir)
Immediate Holding Company: RGT FIRE PROTECTION LIMITED
Registration no: 04595572 **Date established:** 2002
No.of Employees: 1 - 10 **Product Groups:** 38, 42

Date of Accounts	Mar 11	Mar 10	Mar 09
Working Capital	13	-32	-29
Fixed Assets	39	35	49
Current Assets	149	77	52
Current Liabilities	20	7	N/A

R H Nuttall Ltd

Great Brook Street, Birmingham, B7 4EN
Tel: 0121-359 2484 **Fax:** 0121-359 4439
E-mail: sales@rhnuttall.co.uk
Website: http://www.rhnuttall.co.uk
Bank(s): Barclays
Directors: I. Nutall (MD), S. Nuttall (Dir)
Immediate Holding Company: R.H.NUTTALL LIMITED
Registration no: 00900093 **VAT No.:** GB 110 1329 41
Date established: 1967 **Turnover:** £500,000 - £1m
No.of Employees: 21 - 50 **Product Groups:** 22, 23, 29, 30, 36

Date of Accounts	Mar 12	Mar 11	Mar 10
Working Capital	253	200	318
Fixed Assets	348	333	174
Current Assets	739	709	644

R N A Automation Ltd

Hayward Industrial Park Tameside Drive, Castle Vale, Birmingham, B35 7AG
Tel: 0121-749 2566 **Fax:** 0121-749 6217
E-mail: rparnham@rna-uk.com
Website: http://www.rna-uk.com
Directors: B. Borggreve (Fin), S. Brettell (Fin)
Managers: Y. Zhang, J. Appleby
Immediate Holding Company: RNA AUTOMATION LIMITED
Registration no: 02037916 **Date established:** 1986
No.of Employees: 21 - 50 **Product Groups:** 35, 39, 45

Date of Accounts	Dec 11	Dec 10	Dec 09
Working Capital	2m	2m	1m
Fixed Assets	123	63	83
Current Assets	3m	2m	2m

Radshape Sheet Metal Ltd
Shefford Road, Birmingham, B6 4PL
Tel: 0121-242 3323 **Fax:** 0121-242 3385
E-mail: k.chadwick@radshape.co.uk
Website: http://www.radshape.co.uk
Bank(s): HSBC, Kings Heath, Birmingham
Directors: J. Morrall (Fin), K. Chadwick (MD), K. Brown (Sales)
Managers: M. Ward (Eng)
Immediate Holding Company: RADSHAPE SHEET METAL LIMITED
Registration no: 01248311 **VAT No.:** GB 113 0255 31
Date established: 1976 **Turnover:** £2m - £5m **No.of Employees:** 51 - 100
Product Groups: 35, 36, 44, 48, 49, 87

Date of Accounts	Mar 12	Mar 11	Mar 10
Working Capital	644	684	549
Fixed Assets	838	900	973
Current Assets	1m	1m	876

Railtech UK Ltd
5 Catesby Park Kings Norton, Birmingham, B38 8SE
Tel: 0121-486 4444
E-mail: enquiries@railtech-uk.com
Website: http://www.railtech-uk.com
Directors: B. Destailleurs (MD)
Ultimate Holding Company: DELACHAUX SA (FRANCE)
Immediate Holding Company: RAILTECH (UK) LIMITED
Registration no: 02767803 **Date established:** 1992 **Turnover:** £1m - £2m
No.of Employees: 1 - 10 **Product Groups:** 39, 45, 48

Date of Accounts	Dec 11	Dec 10	Dec 09
Sales Turnover	2m	2m	3m
Pre Tax Profit/Loss	67	14	327
Working Capital	112	97	112
Fixed Assets	966	987	1m
Current Assets	559	595	646
Current Liabilities	351	106	222

Rainsford & Lynes Ltd
Diaden Works Kings Road, Tyseley, Birmingham, B11 2AJ
Tel: 0121-706 6301 **Fax:** 0121-707 0995
E-mail: sales@rainsford-lynes.co.uk
Website: http://www.rainsford-lynes.co.uk
Directors: A. Williams (MD)
Immediate Holding Company: RAINSFORD & LYNES,LIMITED
Registration no: 00049364 **VAT No.:** GB 110 5961 01
Date established: 1996 **Turnover:** £1m - £2m **No.of Employees:** 1 - 10
Product Groups: 34, 48

Date of Accounts	Jun 11	Jun 10	Jun 09
Working Capital	807	786	797
Fixed Assets	209	217	250
Current Assets	992	983	974

Raja Frozen Foods Ltd
Unit A4 Amyco Works Doris Road, Bordesley Green, Birmingham, B9 4SJ
Tel: 0121-771 0039 **Fax:** 0121-771 0030
E-mail: rajafrozenfoods@btconnect.com
Website: http://www.rajafrozenfoods.co.uk
Directors: A. Hussain (MD)
Immediate Holding Company: RAJA FROZEN FOODS LTD
Registration no: 08086880 **Date established:** 2012
Turnover: £250,000 - £500,000 **No.of Employees:** 1 - 10
Product Groups: 20

Date of Accounts	Dec 10	Dec 09	Dec 08
Sales Turnover	7m	6m	N/A
Pre Tax Profit/Loss	555	200	525
Working Capital	5m	5m	5m
Fixed Assets	274	292	341
Current Assets	7m	6m	6m
Current Liabilities	407	210	338

Range Steel Stockholders
Unit 8 Duddeston Mill Trading Estate, Saltley, Birmingham, B8 1AP
Tel: 0121-359 7666 **Fax:** 0121-359 7599
E-mail: nobarnes@rangesteel.co.uk
Website: http://www.rangesteel.co.uk
Directors: N. Barnes (Dir), D. Hughes (Co Sec)
Immediate Holding Company: RANGE STEEL STOCKHOLDERS LTD
Registration no: 01302744 **Date established:** 1977
Turnover: £500,000 - £1m **No.of Employees:** 1 - 10 **Product Groups:** 66

Date of Accounts	Aug 12	Aug 11	Aug 10
Sales Turnover	N/A	N/A	722
Pre Tax Profit/Loss	N/A	N/A	20
Working Capital	193	179	154
Fixed Assets	30	20	27
Current Assets	361	372	330
Current Liabilities	37	33	24

Raves Clothing Ltd
101-113 Branston Street, Birmingham, B18 6BA
Tel: 0121-554 4142 **Fax:** 0121-554 4452
E-mail: info@ravesuk.com
Directors: J. Khalgure (Dir)
Immediate Holding Company: RAVES CLOTHING LIMITED
Registration no: 01801010 **Date established:** 1984
No.of Employees: 1 - 10 **Product Groups:** 24

Date of Accounts	Apr 11	Apr 10	Apr 09
Working Capital	1m	2m	1m
Fixed Assets	55	23	31
Current Assets	2m	2m	2m

Recon Catering Equipment Suppliers
141 Fazeley Street, Birmingham, B5 5RX
Tel: 0121-633 3080 **Fax:** 0121-633 3081
Directors: M. Qureshi (Prop)
Date established: 2005 **No.of Employees:** 1 - 10 **Product Groups:** 20, 40, 41

Redfern Stevens Ltd
40 Brickfield Road, Birmingham, B25 8HE
Tel: 0121-766 6464 **Fax:** 0121-766 6651
E-mail: info@redfernstevens.co.uk
Website: http://www.redfernstevens.co.uk
Bank(s): Lloyds TSB Bank plc
Directors: C. Murley (Fin), A. Murley (MD)
Immediate Holding Company: REDFERN STEVENS LIMITED
Registration no: 06763736 **Date established:** 2008 **Turnover:** £1m - £2m
No.of Employees: 11 - 20 **Product Groups:** 35, 36, 46, 48

Date of Accounts	Mar 11	Mar 10
Working Capital	-50	-67
Fixed Assets	83	94
Current Assets	286	304

Reed Accountancy Personnel Ltd
Interchange Place 151-165 Edmund Street, Birmingham, B3 2TA
Tel: 0121-237 8800 **Fax:** 0121-237 8801
E-mail: ranjit.singh@reed.co.uk
Website: http://www.reed.co.uk
Managers: R. Singh (Mgr)
Registration no: 00973629 **Date established:** 1987 **Turnover:** £1m - £2m
No.of Employees: 21 - 50 **Product Groups:** 80

Ren Tools Ltd
247 Great Lister Street, Birmingham, B7 4BS
Tel: 0121-359 7231 **Fax:** 0121-359 7502
E-mail: sales@rentools.co.uk
Website: http://www.rentools.co.uk
Bank(s): Lloyds TSB
Directors: S. Jennings (MD)
Immediate Holding Company: SYDENHAM TOOL CO. LTD
Registration no: 01178175 **VAT No.:** GB 110 7648 92
Date established: 1974 **Turnover:** £1m - £2m **No.of Employees:** 11 - 20
Product Groups: 46

Renatex Ltd
Nam House 22-26 Spencer Street, Birmingham, B18 6DS
Tel: 0121-233 9999 **Fax:** 0121-236 9295
E-mail: sales@renatex.com
Website: http://www.renatex.com
Directors: B. Minhas (Dir)
Immediate Holding Company: RENATEX LIMITED
Registration no: 02918450 **Date established:** 1994
No.of Employees: 1 - 10 **Product Groups:** 37

Date of Accounts	Dec 11	Dec 10	Dec 09
Working Capital	879	610	487
Fixed Assets	116	138	147
Current Assets	1m	968	750

Response Generation
199 Tyburn Road, Birmingham, B24 8NB
Tel: 0870-4421862 **Fax:** 0870-0664267
E-mail: enquiries@responsegeneration.co.uk
Website: http://www.responsegeneration.co.uk
Directors: J. Dyson (MD), J. Linney (Co Sec)
Immediate Holding Company: RESPONSE GENERATION LIMITED
Registration no: 05371959 **Date established:** 2005
No.of Employees: 1 - 10 **Product Groups:** 81

Righton Ltd
Righton House Elliott Way, Nexus Point, Holford, Birmingham, B6 7AP
Tel: 0121-356 1141 **Fax:** 0121-332 3829
E-mail: marketing@righton.co.uk
Website: http://www.righton.co.uk
Directors: T. Whalley (Sales), G. Wright (MD), C. Hussey (Comm)
Managers: R. Mann (Comptroller), J. Gardani (Mktg Serv Mgr), P. Hoskison (Export Sales Mg), L. Chandler (Export Sales Mg)
Immediate Holding Company: Amari Metals
Registration no: 00143411 **Date established:** 1891
Turnover: £50m - £75m **No.of Employees:** 51 - 100 **Product Groups:** 30, 31, 34, 36

Date of Accounts	Dec 11	Dec 10	Dec 09
Sales Turnover	71m	74m	50m
Pre Tax Profit/Loss	943	1m	-632
Working Capital	11m	7m	6m
Fixed Assets	1m	2m	2m
Current Assets	31m	30m	27m
Current Liabilities	2m	4m	2m

Righton Fasteners Ltd
Unit H2 Elliott Way Nexus Point, Holford, Birmingham, B6 7AP
Tel: 0121-356 8181 **Fax:** 0121-344 4028
E-mail: sales@rightonfasteners.com
Website: http://www.righton.co.uk
Managers: L. Wem (Sales Prom)
Registration no: 03460135 **Date established:** 1990
Turnover: £500,000 - £1m **No.of Employees:** 1 - 10 **Product Groups:** 35

Robert Horne Sign & Display
Huntsman House 40 Tameside Drive, Birmingham, B35 7BD
Tel: 0121-776 5555 **Fax:** 0121-327 2818
E-mail: rh.birmingham@roberthorne.co.uk
Website: http://www.roberthorne.co.uk
Directors: A. Gough (Chief Op Offcr), M. Stears (Purch), P. Shipley (Sales), R. Latham (Mkt Research), T. Marchant (MD)
Managers: A. Dennis (District Mgr), C. Green, P. Lewis (Mgr)
Registration no: 00584756 **Turnover:** £20m - £50m
No.of Employees: 11 - 20 **Product Groups:** 66

Frank Roberts
Anvic House 84 Vyse Street, Hockley, Birmingham, B18 6HA
Tel: 0121-554 2754 **Fax:** 0121-554 2754
E-mail: frobertsenamelers@aol.com
Directors: F. Roberts (Ptnr)
Date established: 1989 **No.of Employees:** 1 - 10 **Product Groups:** 46, 48

Robins & Day Peugeot Birmingham East (t/a Clock Garage)
Coleshill Road, Birmingham, B36 8BQ
Tel: 0121-747 4712 **Fax:** 0121-749 4243
E-mail: clock@peugeotmail.co.uk
Website: http://www.robinsanddaybirminghameast.co.uk
Bank(s): HSBC Bank plc
Managers: L. Lapworth (Nat Sales Mgr), P. Cole
Immediate Holding Company: CITY MOTORS LTD.
Registration no: 01917962 **Date established:** 1985
No.of Employees: 51 - 100 **Product Groups:** 68

Rodway & Taylor
85 Buckingham Street, Birmingham, B19 3HU
Tel: 0121-236 4027 **Fax:** 0121-233 2972
E-mail: paul.rodway@virgin.net
Bank(s): Midland
Directors: G. Hale (Prop)
Immediate Holding Company: CGH FABRICATIONS LIMITED
Registration no: 06392914 **VAT No.:** GB 110 3019 46
Date established: 2007 **Turnover:** £500,000 - £1m
No.of Employees: 11 - 20 **Product Groups:** 42

Date of Accounts	Mar 12	Mar 11	Mar 10
Working Capital	-34	-87	-87
Fixed Assets	430	458	486
Current Assets	164	76	77

Roemheld UK Ltd
Rubery House The Avenue Rednal, Birmingham, B45 9AL
Tel: 0121-453 1414 **Fax:** 0121-460 1798
E-mail: sales@roemheld.co.uk
Website: http://www.roemheld.co.uk
Directors: B. Neal (MD)
Ultimate Holding Company: A ROMHELD GMBH & CO KG (GERMANY)
Immediate Holding Company: ROEMHELD UK LTD
Registration no: 01941520 **Date established:** 1985 **Turnover:** £1m - £2m
No.of Employees: 1 - 10 **Product Groups:** 35, 38, 40, 45, 46, 47, 67

Date of Accounts	Dec 11	Dec 10	Dec 09
Working Capital	120	-138	-116
Fixed Assets	11	5	2
Current Assets	831	758	495

Roman Originals plc
Unit 1 Vantage Point 5 Wingfoot Close Erdington, Birmingham, B24 9JH
Tel: 0121-380 1900 **Fax:** 0121-380 1912
E-mail: enquiries@romanoriginals.co.uk
Website: http://www.romanoriginals.co.uk
Bank(s): Barclays
Directors: R. Christo (MD)
Immediate Holding Company: ROMAN ORIGINALS PLC
Registration no: 00980843 **VAT No.:** GB 111 3607 23
Date established: 1970 **Turnover:** £20m - £50m
No.of Employees: 251 - 500 **Product Groups:** 63

Date of Accounts	Dec 11	Dec 10	Dec 09
Sales Turnover	23m	21m	23m
Pre Tax Profit/Loss	-396	293	528
Working Capital	3m	3m	4m
Fixed Assets	5m	5m	6m
Current Assets	6m	6m	6m
Current Liabilities	654	798	1m

Rotadex Systems Ltd
Systems House Central Business Park, Birmingham, B33 0JL
Tel: 0121-783 7411 **Fax:** 0121-783 1876
E-mail: sales@rotadex.co.uk
Website: http://www.rotadex.co.uk
Bank(s): Barclays, Marston Green
Directors: W. White (MD)
Ultimate Holding Company: REDACELL LIMITED
Immediate Holding Company: REDACELL LIMITED
Registration no: 01863986 **Date established:** 1984 **Turnover:** £2m - £5m
No.of Employees: 51 - 100 **Product Groups:** 26, 27, 28, 30, 49

Date of Accounts	Dec 11	Dec 10	Dec 09
Working Capital	-112	-112	-112
Fixed Assets	1m	1m	1m
Current Assets	3	3	3

Rowan Precision Ltd
2-4 Poplar Drive Witton, Birmingham, B6 7AD
Tel: 0121-356 9981 **Fax:** 0121-356 9982
E-mail: martin.barker@rowanprecision.co.uk
Website: http://www.rowanprecision.co.uk
Bank(s): National Westminster Bank plc
Directors: C. Kent (Fin), M. Barker (Ptnr)
Ultimate Holding Company: STANDTRADE
Immediate Holding Company: ROWAN PRECISION LIMITED
Registration no: 01817185 **VAT No.:** GB 389 3471 06
Date established: 1984 **Turnover:** £2m - £5m **No.of Employees:** 11 - 20
Product Groups: 30, 35, 37, 39, 45, 48, 67, 68, 84

Date of Accounts	Apr 11	Apr 10	Apr 09
Working Capital	211	111	67
Current Assets	945	610	457

Charles Rowley & Co. Ltd
22 Athole Street, Birmingham, B12 0DA
Tel: 0121-440 7711 **Fax:** 0121-440 4837
E-mail: sales@charlesrowley.co.uk
Website: http://www.charlesrowley.co.uk
Directors: B. Wilson (Dir), W. Davis (Fin)
Immediate Holding Company: CHARLES ROWLEY & CO. LIMITED
Registration no: 05383397 **VAT No.:** GB 327 6262 54
Date established: 2005 **Turnover:** £500,000 - £1m
No.of Employees: 1 - 10 **Product Groups:** 30, 35, 36

Date of Accounts	Dec 11	Dec 10	Dec 09
Sales Turnover	N/A	509	477
Pre Tax Profit/Loss	N/A	-32	-44
Working Capital	103	132	160
Fixed Assets	10	8	13
Current Assets	197	242	235
Current Liabilities	4	34	20

Royal Institute Of British Architects
The Birmingham & Midland Institute Margaret Street, Birmingham, B3 3SP
Tel: 0121-233 2321 **Fax:** 0121-233 4946
E-mail: matthew.dobson@inst.riba.org
Website: http://www.architecture.com
Directors: M. Dobson (Reg)
Registration no: FP012292 **VAT No.:** GB 232 3518 91
No.of Employees: 1 - 10 **Product Groups:** 87

Royal Society For The Prevention Of Accidents Ltd
353 Bristol Road Edgbaston, Birmingham, B5 7ST
Tel: 0121-248 2000 **Fax:** 0121-248 2001
E-mail: help@rospa.com
Website: http://www.mohsg.org.uk
Bank(s): National Westminster Bank Plc
Directors: D. Fenemore (Develop), E. Wiles (Fin), J. Le M. Howard (Safety), P. Moss (Fin), A. Edwards (Grp Chief Exec)
Managers: D. Rogers, F. Mulla (Mgr), J. Cave, M. Ellis, M. Gomberg, R. Bibbings
Immediate Holding Company: ROYAL SOCIETY FOR THE PREVENTION OF ACCIDENTS(THE)
Registration no: 00231435 **VAT No.:** GB 655 1316 49
Date established: 1928 **Turnover:** £10m - £20m
No.of Employees: 51 - 100 **Product Groups:** 40, 54, 84, 86, 89

Date of Accounts	Mar 08	Mar 07	Mar 06
Sales Turnover	8482	7816	7959
Pre Tax Profit/Loss	212	-84	157
Working Capital	1155	924	811
Fixed Assets	529	184	202
Current Assets	4468	3783	3141
Current Liabilities	3313	2859	2330
ROCE% (Return on Capital Employed)	12.6	-7.6	15.5
ROT% (Return on Turnover)	2.5	-1.1	2.0

Royce Thompson
Unit 13-15 Ace Business Park Mackadown Lane, Birmingham, B33 0LD
Tel: 0121-785 4700 **Fax:** 0121-785 4717
E-mail: jeremy.farrow@tnb.com
Website: http://www.roycethompson.com
Directors: G. Farrow (MD), J. Farrow (MD)
Managers: N. James (Personnel), T. Finney (Sales Prom Mgr)
No.of Employees: 21 - 50 **Product Groups:** 37, 38

S Lilley & Son Ltd
80 Alcester Street, Birmingham, B12 0QE
Tel: 0121-622 2385 **Fax:** 0121-666 6148
E-mail: sales@s-lilley.co.uk
Website: http://www.s-lilley.co.uk
Directors: S. Lilley (Co Sec), J. Lilley (MD)
Ultimate Holding Company: S. LILLEY & SON HOLDINGS LTD
Immediate Holding Company: S.LILLEY & SON LIMITED
Registration no: 00218678 **Date established:** 2027 **Turnover:** £2m - £5m
No.of Employees: 21 - 50 **Product Groups:** 34, 35, 36, 37, 48, 67

Date of Accounts	Dec 11	Dec 10	Dec 09
Working Capital	586	550	524
Fixed Assets	53	79	51
Current Assets	842	776	716

S N D Electrical Wholesalers
23 Constitution Hill, Birmingham, B19 3LG
Tel: 0121-236 5012 **Fax:** 0121-233 3654
E-mail: sales@sndelectrical.co.uk
Website: http://www.sndelectrical.co.uk
Directors: J. Banborough (Dir)
Ultimate Holding Company: SND ELECTRICAL GROUP
Immediate Holding Company: SND ELECTRICAL
Turnover: £5m - £10m **No.of Employees:** 11 - 20 **Product Groups:** 52

S P Engineering
M Hawthorns Industrial Estate Middlemore Road, Handsworth, Birmingham, B21 0BH
Tel: 0121-554 1404 **Fax:** 0121-523 5834
Managers: B. Collins (Mgr)
Turnover: Up to £250,000 **No.of Employees:** 1 - 10 **Product Groups:** 46, 48

S P Group
58 Lower Tower Street, Birmingham, B19 3NE
Tel: 0121-248 3151 **Fax:** 0121-248 3130
E-mail: steve.fisher@spgroup.co.uk
Website: http://www.spgroup.co.uk
Managers: S. Fisher (Chief Mgr)
Ultimate Holding Company: St Ives plc
Immediate Holding Company: Retail Communications Ltd
Registration no: 01240968 **Turnover:** £5m - £10m
No.of Employees: 101 - 250 **Product Groups:** 28, 64, 81

S T B Polishing
Unit 13 Green Lane Industrial Estate, Bordesley Green, Birmingham, B9 5QP
Tel: 0121-772 1044 **Fax:** 0121-772 1267
E-mail: darrenjnorris@hotmail.com
Website: http://www.wmccm.co.uk
Directors: D. Norris (Prop)
No.of Employees: 1 - 10 **Product Groups:** 46, 48

Sabre Jetting Services Ltd
Unit 26-27 The Business Centre 20 James Road, Tyseley, Birmingham, B11 2BA
Tel: 0121-706 9801 **Fax:** 0121-706 9894
E-mail: enq@sabrejetting.co.uk
Website: http://www.sabrejetting.co.uk
Bank(s): Barclays
Directors: D. Malin (MD), T. Malin (Fin)
Immediate Holding Company: SABRE JETTING SERVICES LIMITED
Registration no: 01827657 **Date established:** 1984
No.of Employees: 21 - 50 **Product Groups:** 51, 52

Date of Accounts	Mar 12	Mar 11	Mar 10
Working Capital	272	267	236
Fixed Assets	282	292	321
Current Assets	465	483	490

Sally Hair & Beauty Supplies Ltd
Unit 57 Grosvenor Centre Bristol Road, Northfield, Birmingham, B31 2JU
Tel: 0121-476 5110
E-mail: admin@sallybeauty.co.uk
Website: http://www.sallybeauty.com
Managers: K. Morten (Mgr)
Ultimate Holding Company: SALLY BEAUTY HOLDING INC (USA)
Immediate Holding Company: SALLY SALON SERVICES LIMITED
Registration no: 01060763 **Date established:** 1972
No.of Employees: 1 - 10 **Product Groups:** 30, 36, 40

Date of Accounts	Sep 11	Sep 10	Sep 09
Sales Turnover	128m	107m	82m
Pre Tax Profit/Loss	3m	2m	1m
Working Capital	10m	7m	6m
Fixed Assets	11m	12m	9m
Current Assets	63m	50m	45m
Current Liabilities	10m	7m	4m

Salt & Sadler Ltd
71 Rea Street, Birmingham, B5 6BB
Tel: 0121-622 3887 **Fax:** 0121-666 6530
E-mail: info@saltandsadler.co.uk
Website: http://www.saltandsadler.co.uk
Directors: M. Sadler (Co Sec)
Immediate Holding Company: SALT & SADLER LIMITED
Registration no: 02127396 **Date established:** 1987
No.of Employees: 11 - 20 **Product Groups:** 48

Date of Accounts	Mar 11	Mar 10	Mar 09
Working Capital	102	87	105
Fixed Assets	36	45	28
Current Assets	234	229	188

Salts Healthcare
Unit 1 Richard Street, Birmingham, B7 4AA
Tel: 0121-333 2000 **Fax:** 0121-359 0830
E-mail: philipsalt@salts.co.uk
Website: http://www.salts.co.uk
Bank(s): Lloyds
Directors: P. Salt (Dir), I. Taylor (Fin)
Managers: G. Rossiter (Tech Serv Mgr), W. Kerley (Personnel), C. Cowin (Mktg Serv Mgr), N. Bromley (Purch Mgr)
Immediate Holding Company: SALTS HEALTHCARE LIMITED
Registration no: 00074096 **VAT No.:** GB 110 3990 04
Date established: 2002 **Turnover:** £20m - £50m
No.of Employees: 101 - 250 **Product Groups:** 30

Date of Accounts	Dec 11	Dec 10	Dec 09
Sales Turnover	53m	48m	43m
Pre Tax Profit/Loss	4m	4m	3m
Working Capital	5m	4m	4m
Fixed Assets	13m	10m	7m
Current Assets	16m	13m	13m
Current Liabilities	2m	2m	2m

Sampling Services Ltd
2 Forge Mills Park Station Road, Coleshill, Birmingham, B46 1JH
Tel: 01675-466992 **Fax:** 01675-466994
E-mail: info@sampling.co.uk
Website: http://www.sampling.co.uk
Directors: J. Fenner (MD)
Immediate Holding Company: SAMPLING SYSTEMS LIMITED
Registration no: 01731816 **Date established:** 1983
No.of Employees: 1 - 10 **Product Groups:** 38, 40, 41, 42

Date of Accounts	Mar 11	Mar 10	Mar 09
Working Capital	392	283	205
Fixed Assets	124	99	73
Current Assets	830	637	484

Sapphire Products Ltd
Unit 4-6 Dunton Trading Estate Mount Street, Birmingham, B7 5QL
Tel: 0121-326 6000 **Fax:** 0121-328 5518
E-mail: sapphireproducts@cw.com.net
Website: http://www.sapphireproducts.co.uk
Directors: D. Wood (Fin), J. Wood (MD)
Immediate Holding Company: SAPPHIRE PRODUCTS LIMITED
Registration no: 02761807 **VAT No.:** GB 580 5120 63
Date established: 1992 **Turnover:** £500,000 - £1m
No.of Employees: 1 - 10 **Product Groups:** 35

Date of Accounts	Nov 11	Nov 10	Nov 09
Working Capital	620	721	716
Fixed Assets	11	12	9
Current Assets	670	824	806

Savada Metal Finishing
255 Tame Road, Birmingham, B6 7HL
Tel: 0121-327 1655 **Fax:** 0121-326 6522
Directors: R. Wheeler (Prop)
Immediate Holding Company: SAVADA METAL FINISHING LIMITED
Registration no: 01088817 **Date established:** 1972
No.of Employees: 1 - 10 **Product Groups:** 46, 48

Scala Agenturen UK
Unit 6 Roman Way, Coleshill, Birmingham, B46 1HG
Tel: 01675-430300 **Fax:** 01675-430444
E-mail: scalab46@yahoo.co.uk
Website: http://www.scala-nl.com
Directors: C. Gore (Sales), F. Bergman (MD)
Managers: C. Gore (Mgr)
Immediate Holding Company: SCALA AGENTUREN (UK) LIMITED
Registration no: 03503072 **VAT No.:** GB 112 3400 39
Date established: 1998 **Turnover:** £2m - £5m **No.of Employees:** 1 - 10
Product Groups: 29

Date of Accounts	Dec 10	Dec 09	Dec 08
Working Capital	424	2m	2m
Fixed Assets	33	33	23
Current Assets	696	2m	2m

Howard Scale Co. Ltd
14 Oughton Road, Birmingham, B12 0DF
Tel: 0121-446 5190 **Fax:** 0121-446 5191
E-mail: david@howardscales.co.uk
Website: http://www.howardscales.co.uk
Directors: D. Dear (MD)
Immediate Holding Company: HOWARD SCALE CO. LIMITED(THE)
Registration no: 00608264 **Date established:** 1958
No.of Employees: 1 - 10 **Product Groups:** 38, 42

Date of Accounts	May 11	May 10	May 09
Working Capital	31	20	22
Fixed Assets	64	57	60
Current Assets	113	71	95

Scale Warehouse
14 Oughton Road, Birmingham, B12 0DF
Tel: 0121-440 8978 **Fax:** 0121-440 8978
E-mail: sales@scalewarehouse.co.uk
Website: http://www.scalewarehouse.co.uk
Directors: A. Brown (Dir)
Immediate Holding Company: SCALE WAREHOUSE LIMITED
Registration no: 06876352 **Date established:** 2009
No.of Employees: 1 - 10 **Product Groups:** 38, 42

Date of Accounts	Apr 11	Apr 10
Current Assets	3	N/A

Sea Products International Ltd
Ocean House Wholesale Markets Pershore Street, Birmingham, B5 6UU
Tel: 0121-622 5111 **Fax:** 0121-622 6123
E-mail: paul.pearce@fisherfoods.com
Website: http://www.seaproductsint.com
Directors: P. Pearce (Fin), T. Hansen (Dir)
Ultimate Holding Company: WESTINDIA AB (SWEDEN)
Immediate Holding Company: SEA PRODUCTS INTERNATIONAL LIMITED
Registration no: 04449016 **VAT No.:** GB 111 9111 22
Date established: 2002 **Turnover:** £20m - £50m
No.of Employees: 21 - 50 **Product Groups:** 20

Date of Accounts	Dec 11	Dec 10	Dec 09
Sales Turnover	27m	23m	19m
Pre Tax Profit/Loss	450	524	656
Working Capital	3m	2m	2m
Fixed Assets	68	72	64
Current Assets	11m	9m	8m
Current Liabilities	325	311	378

Seca Ltd
40 Barn Street, Birmingham, B5 5QB
Tel: 0121-643 9349 **Fax:** 0121-633 3403
E-mail: sales@seca.co.uk
Website: http://www.seca.com
Bank(s): Barclays
Directors: G. Christie (MD)
Ultimate Holding Company: SECA GMBH (GERMANY)
Immediate Holding Company: SECA LIMITED
Registration no: 01430864 **VAT No.:** GB 338 0211 88
Date established: 1979 **Turnover:** £2m - £5m **No.of Employees:** 11 - 20
Product Groups: 31, 37, 38

Date of Accounts	Dec 11	Dec 10	Dec 09
Working Capital	2m	2m	2m
Fixed Assets	204	200	172
Current Assets	2m	3m	2m

Securitas UK Ltd
Ts2 Pinewood Business Park Coleshill Road, Birmingham, B37 7HG
Tel: 0121-779 8198 **Fax:** 01622-710478
Website: http://www.securitas.co.uk
Directors: N. Shotten (MD)
Managers: M. Driver (Admin Off), C. Aram (Mgr)
Registration no: 06006615 **No.of Employees:** 51 - 100
Product Groups: 81

Date of Accounts	Dec 07	Dec 06	Dec 05
Sales Turnover	112510	105900	100340
Pre Tax Profit/Loss	-680	3630	3380
Working Capital	2920	5930	5130
Fixed Assets	35580	37250	37310
Current Assets	27080	21190	21370
Current Liabilities	24160	15260	16240
Total Share Capital	20440	20440	20440
ROCE% (Return on Capital Employed)	-1.8	8.4	8.0
ROT% (Return on Turnover)	-0.6	3.4	3.4

Selco Builders Warehouse
1 Charlotte Road Stirchley, Birmingham, B30 2BT
Tel: 0121-433 3355 **Fax:** 0121-458 5996
Website: http://www.selcobw.com
Bank(s): Lloyds Bank Plc
Directors: V. Patel (MD)
Managers: J. Hodgson (Sales Prom Mgr)
Ultimate Holding Company: GRAFTON GROUP P.L.C.
Registration no: 02182671 **VAT No.:** GB 110 4121 50
No.of Employees: 21 - 50 **Product Groups:** 66

Selection Partnership
17 High Street Harborne, Birmingham, B17 9NT
Tel: 0121-427 4255 **Fax:** 0121-427 2077
E-mail: info@martindady.co.uk
Website: http://www.t-s-p.com
Directors: K. Payne (Fin), R. Furlow (MD)
Immediate Holding Company: THE SELECTION PARTNERSHIP LTD
Registration no: 04679041 **Date established:** 2003
No.of Employees: 1 - 10 **Product Groups:** 80

Date of Accounts	Mar 08	Sep 11	Sep 10
Working Capital	-90	-36	-70
Fixed Assets	93	40	56
Current Assets	18	19	7

Selwood Pump Company Ltd
188 Robin Hood Lane, Birmingham, B28 0LG
Tel: 0121-777 5631 **Fax:** 0121-702 2195
E-mail: graham.gallen@selwood-pumps.co.uk
Website: http://www.selwood-pumps.com
Bank(s): Lloyds TSB Bank plc
Directors: M. Morris (Co Sec), G. Gallen (MD)
Managers: S. Allan (I.T. Exec), A. Moore (Personnel), S. Allan (Tech Serv Mgr), A. Moore (Personnel)
Immediate Holding Company: SELWOOD PUMP COMPANY LIMITED
Registration no: 02835747 **VAT No.:** GB 614 3989 22
Date established: 1993 **Turnover:** £2m - £5m **No.of Employees:** 21 - 50
Product Groups: 39, 40, 45, 46

Date of Accounts	Jul 11	Jul 10	Jul 09
Working Capital	609	594	535
Fixed Assets	106	79	91
Current Assets	1m	1m	1m

Serck Heat Exchange
Unit 34-38 Mucklow Industrial Estate Station Road, Coleshill, Birmingham, B46 1JP
Tel: 01675-466396 **Fax:** 01675-466397
E-mail: jimkerr@uees.co.uk
Website: http://www.serckservices.co.uk
Managers: J. Kerr (Ops Mgr)
Date established: 1998 **No.of Employees:** 21 - 50 **Product Groups:** 37, 40, 48

Serina Glass & Miror Processing
Sherbourne Road Balsall Heath, Birmingham, B12 9DJ
Tel: 0121-440 3820 **Fax:** 0121-440 1091
E-mail: ramzan26@hotmail.com
Website: http://www.serinaglassprocessing.com
Directors: M. Ramzan (Dir)
Date established: 2000 **No.of Employees:** 1 - 10 **Product Groups:** 26, 35

Sertec Birmingham Ltd
Gorsey Lane Coleshill, Birmingham, B46 1JU
Tel: 01675-463361 **Fax:** 01675-465539
E-mail: graham.mosedale@sertec.co.uk
Website: http://www.sertec.co.uk
Bank(s): Lloyds TSB
Directors: D. Steggles (Comm), G. Mosedale (MD), M. Hughes (Fin), R. Jessop (Pers)
Managers: D. Cox, J. Cahill (Buyer)
Ultimate Holding Company: SERTEC GROUP LIMITED
Immediate Holding Company: SERTEC(BIRMINGHAM)LIMITED
Registration no: 00719490 **VAT No.:** GB 661 5464 31
Date established: 1962 **Turnover:** £50m - £75m
No.of Employees: 251 - 500 **Product Groups:** 46, 48

Date of Accounts	Mar 12	Mar 11	Mar 10
Sales Turnover	61m	43m	34m
Pre Tax Profit/Loss	4m	3m	895
Working Capital	6m	4m	4m
Fixed Assets	8m	7m	7m
Current Assets	19m	15m	12m
Current Liabilities	3m	2m	1m

SGT Electrical Contractors
Stuart House 97 Station Road, Erdington, Birmingham, B23 6UG
Tel: 0121-377 2980 **Fax:** 0121-384 1178
E-mail: info@sgtelectrical.co.uk
Website: http://www.sgtelectrical.co.uk/
Product Groups: 37, 52, 84

Shakespeares
Somerset House 37 Temple Street, Birmingham, B2 5DJ
Tel: 0121-632 4199 **Fax:** 0121-237 3011
E-mail: paul.wilson@sp-legal.co.uk
Website: http://www.shakespeares.co.uk
Directors: C. Laird (Ptnr), M. Beesley (Ptnr), P. Willson (Ptnr), P. Wilson (Grp Chief Exec)
Managers: L. Watts (Mktg Serv Mgr)
Immediate Holding Company: SHAKESPEARES LEGAL LLP
Registration no: OC319029 **Date established:** 2006
Turnover: £10m - £20m **No.of Employees:** 101 - 250 **Product Groups:** 80

Date of Accounts	Apr 11	Apr 10	Apr 09
Sales Turnover	24m	17m	18m
Pre Tax Profit/Loss	6m	5m	6m
Working Capital	7m	6m	5m
Fixed Assets	1m	454	618
Current Assets	11m	8m	9m
Current Liabilities	2m	800	4m

Henry Shaw & Sons Ltd
Crown Road Bordesley Green, Birmingham, B9 4TY
Tel: 0121-772 5561 **Fax:** 0121-766 6047
E-mail: sales@henryshaw.co.uk
Website: http://www.henryshaw.co.uk
Bank(s): Barclays
Directors: M. Lambert (Dir)
Ultimate Holding Company: LAMBERT HOLDINGS LIMITED
Immediate Holding Company: HENRY SHAW & SONS LIMITED
Registration no: 01573615 **VAT No.:** GB 109 5797 38
Date established: 1981 **Turnover:** £2m - £5m **No.of Employees:** 21 - 50
Product Groups: 35, 66

Date of Accounts	Dec 11	Dec 10	Dec 09
Sales Turnover	N/A	N/A	3m
Working Capital	739	728	723
Fixed Assets	35	60	63
Current Assets	1m	1m	1m
Current Liabilities	N/A	N/A	161

Shaw Munster Ltd
Winster Grove, Birmingham, B44 9EG
Tel: 0121-360 4279 **Fax:** 0121-360 4265
E-mail: office@shawmunstergroup.co.uk
Website: http://www.shawmunstergroup.co.uk
Bank(s): Lloyds TSB
Directors: W. Tyler (Fin), M. Tyler (MD)
Managers: A. Eaten (Tech Serv Mgr)
Immediate Holding Company: SHAW MUNSTER LIMITED
Registration no: 00956969 **VAT No.:** 110 4335 31 **Date established:** 1969
Turnover: £1m - £2m **No.of Employees:** 11 - 20 **Product Groups:** 34, 49

Date of Accounts	May 11	May 10	May 09
Working Capital	89	72	57
Fixed Assets	47	57	55
Current Assets	828	800	793
Current Liabilities	38	30	N/A

Shaw & Underwood Advertising Services Ltd
Monaco House Bristol Street, Birmingham, B5 7AW
Tel: 0121-622 6868 **Fax:** 0121-666 6551
E-mail: admin@shawandunderwood.co.uk
Website: http://www.shawandunderwood.co.uk
Directors: C. Twigger (Fin), S. Trott (MD)
Immediate Holding Company: SHAW AND UNDERWOOD (ADVERTISING SERVICES) LIMITED
Registration no: 00468291 **VAT No.:** GB 110 9547 88
Date established: 1949 **Turnover:** £1m - £2m **No.of Employees:** 1 - 10
Product Groups: 81

Date of Accounts	Mar 12	Mar 11	Mar 10
Working Capital	205	220	201
Fixed Assets	4	4	18
Current Assets	376	352	367

Shelforce
Unit 21-23 Erdington Industrial Park Chester Road, Birmingham, B24 0RD
Tel: 0121-603 5262 **Fax:** 0121-603 2771
E-mail: andrew_fellows@birmingham.gov.uk
Website: http://www.shelforce.co.uk
Directors: K. Geddes (Fin)
Managers: A. Fellows (Mgr), B. Pearson (Purch Mgr), T. Griffiths (Tech Serv Mgr)
VAT No.: GB 112 0821 30 **Date established:** 1981 **Turnover:** £2m - £5m
No.of Employees: 51 - 100 **Product Groups:** 30, 66

Sign & Screen Print Supplies Ltd
55 Great Tindal Street, Birmingham, B16 8DR
Tel: 0121-454 9070 **Fax:** 0121-456 2385
E-mail: sales@signtrays.net
Website: http://www.signtrays.net
Directors: W. Devonshire (MD)
Immediate Holding Company: SIGN AND SCREEN PRINT SUPPLIES LTD
Registration no: 04406001 **Date established:** 2002
No.of Employees: 1 - 10 **Product Groups:** 46, 48

Date of Accounts	Mar 11	Mar 10	Mar 09
Working Capital	-73	-33	11
Fixed Assets	147	143	101
Current Assets	293	244	247

Signarama Ltd
1819-1821 Pershore Road Kings Norton, Birmingham, B30 3DN
Tel: 0121-433 3307 **Fax:** 0121-433 3334
E-mail: preston@sign-a-rama.co.uk
Website: http://www.signarama.co.uk
Directors: S. Walton (MD)
Immediate Holding Company: SIGNARAMA (BIRMINGHAM WEST) LTD
Registration no: 07106075 **Date established:** 2009
No.of Employees: 1 - 10 **Product Groups:** 30, 37, 39, 40, 49

Date of Accounts	Dec 11	Dec 10
Working Capital	-10	N/A

Sil-Mid Ltd
Unit 2 Roman Park Off Roman Way Coleshill, Birmingham, B46 1HG
Tel: 01675-432850 **Fax:** 01675-432870
E-mail: info@silmid.com
Website: http://www.silmid.com
Bank(s): Barclays
Managers: S. Flint (Sales Prom Mgr)
Ultimate Holding Company: CILDARN LIMITED
Immediate Holding Company: SIL-MID LIMITED
Registration no: 01460851 **Date established:** 1979 **Turnover:** £5m - £10m
No.of Employees: 21 - 50 **Product Groups:** 31, 32, 66

Date of Accounts	Dec 11	Dec 10	Dec 09
Sales Turnover	9m	N/A	N/A
Pre Tax Profit/Loss	847	N/A	N/A
Working Capital	2m	2m	1m
Fixed Assets	91	90	96
Current Assets	4m	3m	3m
Current Liabilities	482	N/A	N/A

Skerritt Electrical Ltd
1087 Kingsbury Road Castle Vale, Birmingham, B35 6AJ
Tel: 0121-776 5710 **Fax:** 0121-322 2216
E-mail: admin@skerrittelectrical.co.uk
Website: http://www.skerrittelectrical.co.uk
Directors: S. Gaunt (Fin), S. Hulse (MD)
Immediate Holding Company: SKERRITT ELECTRICAL LTD.
Registration no: 01980263 **VAT No.:** GB 455 7024 48
Date established: 1986 **Turnover:** £1m - £2m **No.of Employees:** 1 - 10
Product Groups: 52

Date of Accounts	Oct 11	Oct 10	Oct 09
Working Capital	86	102	74
Fixed Assets	66	85	106
Current Assets	581	723	588

Skygates International Ltd
18 Sugden Grove, Birmingham, B5 7DH
Tel: 0121-622 1011
E-mail: itviskas@hotmail.com
Website: http://www.skygates.co.uk
Directors: R. Rezgys (MD)
Immediate Holding Company: SCALA INVESTMENTS LIMITED
Registration no: 05044561 **Date established:** 2008
No.of Employees: 1 - 10 **Product Groups:** 63

Slib Design
156 Bordesley Middleway Camp Hill, Birmingham, B11 1BN
Tel: 0121-288 9047 **Fax:** 0870-8381196
E-mail: studio@slibdesign.com
Website: http://www.slibdesign.com
Directors: B. Llewellyn (Comm), B. Llewellyn (Prop)
Immediate Holding Company: HEATER BANDS LTD.
Date established: 2008 **Turnover:** Up to £250,000
No.of Employees: 1 - 10 **Product Groups:** 44

C H Smith & Sons
Unit G F1 63 Price Street, Birmingham, B4 6JZ
Tel: 0121-359 1680 **Fax:** 0121-359 1680
Directors: M. Smith (Ptnr)
Date established: 1840 **No.of Employees:** 1 - 10 **Product Groups:** 36, 39, 40

Smith Francis Tools Ltd
Priory Works 66 Moseley Street, Birmingham, B12 0RT
Tel: 0121-622 3311 **Fax:** 0121-666 7201
E-mail: sales@smithfrancistools.co.uk
Website: http://www.smithfrancistools.co.uk
Bank(s): HSBC
Directors: A. Smith (MD)
Immediate Holding Company: SMITH FRANCIS TOOLS LIMITED
Registration no: 00966302 **VAT No.:** GB 110 9434 04
Date established: 1969 **Turnover:** £1m - £2m **No.of Employees:** 11 - 20
Product Groups: 35, 36

Date of Accounts	Oct 11	Oct 10	Oct 09
Working Capital	746	652	586
Fixed Assets	134	156	178
Current Assets	978	956	880

Socket & Allied Screws Ltd
Austin Way Hamstead, Birmingham, B42 1DU
Tel: 0121-386 7200 **Fax:** 0121-386 7210
E-mail: sales@socket-allied.com
Website: http://www.socket-allied.com
Directors: K. Bradley (MD), S. Matthews (Dir)
Registration no: 02000030 **VAT No.:** GB 444 5562 43
Turnover: £500,000 - £1m **No.of Employees:** 11 - 20
Product Groups: 35, 36, 37

Date of Accounts	Apr 08	Apr 07	Apr 06
Sales Turnover	697	748	715
Pre Tax Profit/Loss	78	152	138
Working Capital	337	772	731
Fixed Assets	544	47	33
Current Assets	491	956	878
Current Liabilities	153	184	147
ROCE% (Return on Capital Employed)	8.8	18.5	18.0
ROT% (Return on Turnover)	11.1	20.3	19.3

Soda Blast Systems
Morgan Works River Lee Road, Birmingham, B11 2JG
Tel: 0121-706 7772 **Fax:** 0121-706 9174
E-mail: info@soda-blast.co.uk
Website: http://www.soda-blast.co.uk
Directors: J. Grantham (Co Sec), R. Grantham (MD), R. Grantham (Dir)
Managers: M. Steiner (Research & Deve)
Immediate Holding Company: SODA-BLAST-SYSTEMS (UK) LIMITED
Registration no: 05422921 **Date established:** 2005
Turnover: Up to £250,000 **No.of Employees:** 21 - 50 **Product Groups:** 39, 40, 45, 46, 47, 48, 52, 83

Date of Accounts	May 11	Apr 10	Apr 09
Sales Turnover	N/A	235	178
Pre Tax Profit/Loss	N/A	53	30
Working Capital	49	16	2
Fixed Assets	10	9	20
Current Assets	86	62	24

Solo Fabrications Ltd
Landor Street, Birmingham, B8 1AE
Tel: 0121-327 3378 **Fax:** 0121-327 3757
E-mail: info@solofabs.com
Website: http://www.solofabs.com
Directors: D. Hunt (MD)
Ultimate Holding Company: SOLO FABS LIMITED
Immediate Holding Company: SOLO FABRICATIONS LIMITED
Registration no: 04797394 **Date established:** 2003
No.of Employees: 21 - 50 **Product Groups:** 26, 35

Date of Accounts	Jun 11	Jun 10	Jun 09
Sales Turnover	N/A	N/A	4m
Pre Tax Profit/Loss	N/A	N/A	341
Working Capital	555	464	445
Current Assets	1m	1m	964
Current Liabilities	N/A	N/A	294

Sonic Communications International Ltd
Starley Way, Birmingham, B37 7HB
Tel: 0121-781 4400 **Fax:** 0121-781 4404
E-mail: sales@sonic-comms.com
Website: http://www.sonic-comms.com
Bank(s): Barclays
Directors: A. Wright (I.T. Dir), M. Beale (Fin), N. Barker (MD), R. Bowmer (Co Sec), S. Jones (Mkt Research)
Managers: D. Sutton (Purch Mgr), J. Burden (Tech Serv Mgr), M. Briant (Personnel)
Ultimate Holding Company: BOWMER AND KIRKLAND LIMITED
Immediate Holding Company: SONIC COMMUNICATIONS (INTERNATIONAL) LIMITED
Registration no: 01248257 **VAT No.:** GB 113 2427 18
Date established: 1976 **Turnover:** £10m - £20m
No.of Employees: 101 - 250 **Product Groups:** 37

Date of Accounts	Aug 11	Aug 10	Aug 09
Sales Turnover	13m	15m	11m
Pre Tax Profit/Loss	4	1m	1m
Working Capital	8m	8m	7m
Fixed Assets	2m	3m	3m
Current Assets	10m	10m	9m
Current Liabilities	1m	2m	741

C A Sothers Ltd
156 Hockley Hill, Birmingham, B18 5AN
Tel: 0121-554 2054 **Fax:** 0121-554 4090
E-mail: robert.hinton@sothers.com
Website: http://www.hastiegroup.com.au/rotarygroup
Directors: R. Hinton (MD), S. Craddock (Fin)
Managers: P. Barnett
Ultimate Holding Company: HASTIE GROUP LIMITED (AUSTRALIA)
Immediate Holding Company: C.A. SOTHERS LIMITED
Registration no: 02325172 **VAT No.:** GB 110 5086 21
Date established: 1988 **Turnover:** £20m - £50m
No.of Employees: 51 - 100 **Product Groups:** 48, 52, 84

Date of Accounts	Mar 10	Mar 09	Mar 08
Sales Turnover	25m	N/A	N/A
Pre Tax Profit/Loss	117	187	245
Working Capital	1m	1m	1m
Fixed Assets	234	332	260
Current Assets	6m	7m	6m
Current Liabilities	571	1m	771

Spysure
109a Digbeth, Birmingham, B5 6DT
Tel: 08702-004200
E-mail: info@spysure.com
Website: http://www.spysure.com
Directors: Z. Majid (Dir)
Managers: Z. Majid (Chief Acct)
Date established: 2005 **No.of Employees:** 1 - 10 **Product Groups:** 44

Squirrel Enterprises Ltd
77 Camden Street Birmngham, Birmingham, B1 3DD
Tel: 01886-853625 **Fax:** 01886-853625
E-mail: jhjosephh@aol.com
Directors: J. Hemingway (Dir)
Immediate Holding Company: SQUIRREL ENTERPRISES LIMITED
Registration no: 08192354 **Date established:** 2012 **Turnover:** £1m - £2m
No.of Employees: 1 - 10 **Product Groups:** 30

Date of Accounts	Sep 06	Jun 05	Jun 04
Working Capital	3	1	1
Fixed Assets	N/A	1	1
Current Assets	4	3	2
Current Liabilities	1	1	1

Stacatruc
Unit 12 Stechford Trading Estate Stechford, Birmingham, B33 8BU
Tel: 0121-244 4700 **Fax:** 0121-244 4900
E-mail: service@stacatruc.co.uk
Website: http://www.stacatruc.co.uk
Directors: N. Stanton (Dir)
Immediate Holding Company: STACATRUC LIMITED
Registration no: 07096530 **Date established:** 2009 **Turnover:** £5m - £10m
No.of Employees: 11 - 20 **Product Groups:** 45, 48, 67, 71, 83

Date of Accounts	Jan 12	Jan 11
Working Capital	-213	32
Fixed Assets	465	184
Current Assets	572	700

Stanco Electrical Systems
Unit 13 Indl-Est National Exhibition Centre, Birmingham, B40 1PJ
Tel: 0121-782 3388 **Fax:** 0121- 7823443
E-mail: electrics@stanco.co.uk
Website: http://www.stanco.co.uk
Directors: R. Melon (Chief Op Offcr), N. Jackson (Dep Ch), P. O'Neill (Prop), P. Slaney (MD), J. Standerline (Dir & Co Sec), D. O'Beirne (Sales), P. Johnson (Admin), E. Grant (Fin), D. O'Berne (Ch)
Managers: J. Sanderline (I.T. Exec), E. Jayne (Purch Mgr)
Immediate Holding Company: OPEX EXHIBITION SERVICES LTD
Registration no: 07625633 **Turnover:** Up to £250,000
No.of Employees: 1 - 10 **Product Groups:** 81

Date of Accounts	Dec 07	Oct 06	Oct 05
Sales Turnover	16807	13935	13539
Pre Tax Profit/Loss	61	212	512
Working Capital	27	419	143
Fixed Assets	1904	1492	1721
Current Assets	4251	2708	2706
Current Liabilities	4225	2289	2563
Total Share Capital	331	331	331
ROCE% (Return on Capital Employed)	3.2	11.1	27.5
ROT% (Return on Turnover)	0.4	1.5	3.8

Stanmor Floors Ltd
Holly Park Industrial Estate Unit 6 Spitfire Road, Birmingham, B24 9PB
Tel: 0121-384 8868 **Fax:** 0121-384 6424
E-mail: info@stanmorfloors.co.uk
Website: http://www.stanmorfloors.co.uk
Directors: H. Curtis (MD)
Immediate Holding Company: STANMOR FLOORS LIMITED
Registration no: 01334017 **Date established:** 1977
Turnover: £250,000 - £500,000 **No.of Employees:** 1 - 10
Product Groups: 52

Date of Accounts	Dec 11	Dec 10	Dec 09
Working Capital	209	262	294
Fixed Assets	153	154	154
Current Assets	240	289	344

Star Industrial Tools Ltd
42 Westfield Road Kings Heath, Birmingham, B14 7ST
Tel: 0121-444 4354 **Fax:** 0121-441 1838
E-mail: admin@starindustrialtools.co.uk
Bank(s): Barclays, Horsefair
Directors: C. Chandler (MD), J. Chandler (Co Sec)
Immediate Holding Company: STAR INDUSTRIAL TOOLS LIMITED
Registration no: 00711361 **VAT No.:** GB 109 7597 36
Date established: 1961 **Turnover:** £500,000 - £1m
No.of Employees: 21 - 50 **Product Groups:** 33, 36, 49

Date of Accounts	Dec 11	Dec 10	Dec 09
Working Capital	30	37	66
Fixed Assets	44	46	49
Current Assets	112	116	132

Staystrip Group Ltd
11-16 Eyre Street, Birmingham, B18 7AA
Tel: 0121-455 0111 **Fax:** 0121-454 5524
E-mail: sales@staystrip.co.uk
Website: http://www.staystrip.co.uk
Bank(s): Barclays
Directors: D. Myers (Grp Chief Exec), J. Haynes (Fin), P. Leadbeater (MD)
Managers: L. Myers (Tech Serv Mgr)
Immediate Holding Company: STAYSTRIP GROUP LIMITED
Registration no: 01481306 **VAT No.:** GB 559 1939 94
Date established: 1980 **Turnover:** £5m - £10m
No.of Employees: 51 - 100 **Product Groups:** 34, 48

Date of Accounts	Dec 11	Dec 10	Dec 09
Sales Turnover	6m	6m	5m
Pre Tax Profit/Loss	-90	107	-93
Working Capital	2m	2m	2m
Fixed Assets	247	286	248
Current Assets	3m	3m	3m
Current Liabilities	281	348	287

Stephens Birmingham Ltd
1 Stephens Industrial Estate 635 Warwick Road, Tyseley, Birmingham, B11 2EZ
Tel: 0121-693 2522 **Fax:** 0121- 6932521
E-mail: tonyjabest@aol.com
Website: http://www.jspv.com
Directors: V. Burling (Fin)
Immediate Holding Company: STEPHENS (BIRMINGHAM) LTD
Registration no: 00515754 **VAT No.:** GB 110 0244 54
Date established: 1953 **Turnover:** £1m - £2m **No.of Employees:** 1 - 10
Product Groups: 80

Date of Accounts	Jul 08	Jul 07	Jul 06
Pre Tax Profit/Loss	12	12	10
Working Capital	363	352	339
Current Assets	365	352	339
Current Liabilities	1	N/A	N/A
Total Share Capital	4	4	4
ROCE% (Return on Capital Employed)	3.4		

Sterex Electrolysis International Ltd
174 Kings Road Tyseley, Birmingham, B11 2AP
Tel: 0121-708 2404 **Fax:** 0121-707 0028
E-mail: sales@sterex.com
Website: http://www.sterex.com
Bank(s): HSBC
Directors: L. Cartmell (Dir)
Ultimate Holding Company: CARTMELL HOLDINGS LIMITED
Immediate Holding Company: STEREX ELECTROLYSIS INTERNATIONAL LIMITED
Registration no: 01666827 **Date established:** 1982
No.of Employees: 21 - 50 **Product Groups:** 38

Date of Accounts	Jul 11	Jul 10	Jul 09
Working Capital	298	314	362
Fixed Assets	667	667	686
Current Assets	559	531	566

Strip Tinning Ltd
Arden Business Park Arden Road, Rednal, Birmingham, B45 0JA
Tel: 0121-457 7675
E-mail: sales@striptinning.com
Website: http://www.striptinning.com
Directors: R. Barton (MD), S. Oconner (Dir)
Immediate Holding Company: STRIP TINNING LIMITED
Registration no: 00594845 **Date established:** 1957
No.of Employees: 21 - 50 **Product Groups:** 33, 35, 39, 48

Date of Accounts	Dec 11	Dec 10	Dec 09
Working Capital	806	562	372
Fixed Assets	1m	1m	745
Current Assets	2m	2m	1m

Subaru (UK) Ltd
I M House South Drive, Coleshill, Birmingham, B46 1DF
Tel: 0844-6626612 **Fax:** 0121-730 8269
E-mail: info@subaru.co.uk
Website: http://www.subaru.co.uk
Bank(s): Bank of America; National Westminster; TSB;
Directors: R. Edmiston (Grp Chief Exec), E. Swatman (MD)
Ultimate Holding Company: I.M. Group Ltd
Immediate Holding Company: International Motors Ltd
Registration no: 01295214 **VAT No.:** GB 351 5643 62
Turnover: £50m - £75m **No.of Employees:** 101 - 250 **Product Groups:** 39

Date of Accounts	Dec 09	Dec 08	Dec 07
Sales Turnover	71m	74m	95m
Pre Tax Profit/Loss	571	-5m	-5m
Working Capital	893	-3m	2m
Fixed Assets	108	3m	3m
Current Assets	39m	60m	54m
Current Liabilities	2m	1m	2m

Sumari Business Systems Ltd
Suite 2 364 - 366 High Street, Harborne, Birmingham, B17 9PY
Tel: 0121-244 8111 **Fax:** 0121-244 8811
E-mail: info@sumari.co.uk
Website: http://www.sumari.net
Directors: S. Randle (Dir), S. Chadda (MD)
Managers: L. Baldock (Accounts), R. Randle (Purch Mgr)
Registration no: 03034096 **VAT No.:** GB 660 9069 23
Date established: 1995 **Turnover:** £500,000 - £1m
No.of Employees: 1 - 10 **Product Groups:** 44, 67

Date of Accounts	May 08	May 07	May 06
Working Capital	-4	-6	-7
Fixed Assets	7	7	8
Current Assets	101	84	160
Current Liabilities	104	90	167

Summit Instruments Ltd
16 James Road Tyseley, Birmingham, B11 2BA
Tel: 0121-706 5751 **Fax:** 0121-706 4011
E-mail: stephen.savage@summitinstruments.co.uk
Website: http://www.summitinstruments.co.uk
Directors: S. Savage (MD)
Immediate Holding Company: SUMMIT INSTRUMENTS LIMITED
Registration no: 01293737 **VAT No.:** GB 113 4124 26
Date established: 1977 **Turnover:** £250,000 - £500,000
No.of Employees: 1 - 10 **Product Groups:** 38

Date of Accounts	Mar 11	Mar 10	Mar 09
Sales Turnover	N/A	317	321
Pre Tax Profit/Loss	N/A	76	65
Working Capital	-0	-1	-1
Fixed Assets	1	1	1
Current Assets	107	81	61
Current Liabilities	N/A	25	21

Sunny Digital Prints
Unit 15 272 Montgomery Street, Birmingham, B11 1DS
Tel: 07732-297261
E-mail: xsunnychana@hotmail.com
Website: http://www.sunnydigitalprints.com
Directors: S. Chana (Prop)
Date established: 2008 **Turnover:** Up to £250,000
No.of Employees: 1 - 10 **Product Groups:** 23, 32, 44, 81

Surface Technology Products Ltd
244 Heneage Street, Birmingham, B7 4LY
Tel: 0121-359 4322 **Fax:** 0121-359 1817
E-mail: sales@surtech.co.uk
Website: http://www.surtech.co.uk
Directors: A. Lehnen (MD)
Ultimate Holding Company: MIDPEX LIMITED
Immediate Holding Company: SURFACE TECHNOLOGY PRODUCTS LIMITED
Registration no: 01009612 **Date established:** 1971
No.of Employees: 1 - 10 **Product Groups:** 33, 40, 46

Date of Accounts	Mar 11	Mar 10	Mar 09
Working Capital	377	362	358
Fixed Assets	15	15	15
Current Assets	517	477	511

Survirn Engineering Ltd
1581 Bristol Road South Rednal, Birmingham, B45 9UA
Tel: 0121-453 7718 **Fax:** 0121-453 6915
E-mail: sales@survirn.co.uk
Website: http://www.survirn.co.uk
Bank(s): Barclays
Directors: N. Kench (Dir), P. Kench (Co Sec)
Managers: N. Foster (Tech Serv Mgr)
Immediate Holding Company: SURVIRN ENGINEERING LIMITED
Registration no: 02019965 **VAT No.:** GB 443 6577 31
Date established: 1986 **No.of Employees:** 21 - 50 **Product Groups:** 46, 48

Date of Accounts	Sep 11	Sep 10	Sep 09
Working Capital	191	98	147
Fixed Assets	320	353	411
Current Assets	795	858	368

System Air Fans & Spares Ltd
72 Cheston Road, Birmingham, B7 5EJ
Tel: 0121-322 0200 **Fax:** 0121-322 0859
E-mail: neil.rapley@fansandspares.co.uk
Website: http://www.fansandspares.co.uk
Bank(s): Svenskhandelsbankan
Directors: N. Rapley (MD)
Ultimate Holding Company: SYSTEMAIR AB (SWEDEN)
Immediate Holding Company: SYSTEMAIR FANS & SPARES LTD
Registration no: 04997065 **VAT No.:** GB 662 0088 52
Date established: 2003 **Turnover:** £10m - £20m
No.of Employees: 21 - 50 **Product Groups:** 30, 40

Date of Accounts	Apr 12	Apr 11	Apr 10
Sales Turnover	16m	14m	9m
Pre Tax Profit/Loss	763	-2m	-41
Working Capital	2m	1m	845
Fixed Assets	893	970	921
Current Assets	6m	6m	3m
Current Liabilities	619	665	273

T & J Installations Ltd
2 Central Business Park Mackadown Lane, Birmingham, B33 0JL
Tel: 0121-783 8925 **Fax:** 0121-789 6011
E-mail: info@tjinstall.co.uk
Website: http://www.tjinstall.co.uk
Directors: P. Jones (Fin), W. Chandler (Pers), I. Jones (Dir)
Immediate Holding Company: T & J INSTALLATIONS LTD
Registration no: 03307179 **Date established:** 1997 **Turnover:** £5m - £10m
No.of Employees: 51 - 100 **Product Groups:** 20, 40, 41

Date of Accounts	Mar 11	Mar 10	Mar 09
Sales Turnover	7m	5m	7m
Pre Tax Profit/Loss	-624	-822	-697
Working Capital	2m	2m	3m
Fixed Assets	402	414	625
Current Assets	3m	3m	4m
Current Liabilities	229	231	221

T L Fire
59 Hawthorn Road, Birmingham, B44 8QT
Tel: 0783-674 1528 **Fax:** 0121-384 1557
E-mail: atlong@blueyonder.co.uk
Directors: A. Long (Prop)
Date established: 1983 **No.of Employees:** 1 - 10 **Product Groups:** 38, 42

T M A Engineering Ltd
95-111 Tyburn Road, Birmingham, B24 8NQ
Tel: 0121-328 1908 **Fax:** 0121-322 2017
E-mail: sales@tmaeng.co.uk
Website: http://www.tmaeng.co.uk
Bank(s): Barclays
Directors: M. Albutt (MD), B. Rogers (Fin)
Immediate Holding Company: T.M.A. ENGINEERING LIMITED
Registration no: 01126971 **Date established:** 1973 **Turnover:** £2m - £5m
No.of Employees: 21 - 50 **Product Groups:** 48

Date of Accounts	Feb 12	Feb 11	Feb 10
Working Capital	61	151	35
Fixed Assets	980	960	991
Current Assets	360	514	298

T M L Housewares
Unit 1 85 Eyre Street, Birmingham, B18 7AD
Tel: 0121-454 9945 **Fax:** 0121-454 9883
Website: http://www.tmlhw.co.uk
Directors: J. Johal (Fin)
Managers: J. Singh
Immediate Holding Company: TML HOUSEWARES LIMITED
Registration no: 05124366 **Date established:** 2004
No.of Employees: 21 - 50 **Product Groups:** 30

Date of Accounts	May 11	May 10	May 09
Working Capital	299	290	-45
Fixed Assets	236	194	211
Current Assets	748	679	540

T N A Europe Ltd
166 Clapgate Lane, Birmingham, B32 3DE
Tel: 0121-628 8900 **Fax:** 0121-628 8700
E-mail: alf.taylor@tnasolutions.com
Website: http://www.tnasolutions.com
Directors: A. Taylor (Dir), J. Boulton (Co Sec)
Ultimate Holding Company: T N A AUSTRALIA PTY LIMITED (AUSTRALIA)
Immediate Holding Company: T.N.A. EUROPE LIMITED
Registration no: 02668491 **Date established:** 1991 **Turnover:** £5m - £10m
No.of Employees: 1 - 10 **Product Groups:** 38, 42

Date of Accounts	Jun 11	Jun 10	Jun 09
Sales Turnover	7m	8m	13m
Pre Tax Profit/Loss	-336	224	104
Working Capital	1m	2m	2m
Fixed Assets	2m	3m	3m
Current Assets	7m	5m	5m
Current Liabilities	3m	504	809

T P S Tools
1 Lea End Cottages Lea End Lane Hopwood, Alvechurch, Birmingham, B48 7AY
Tel: 0121-445 6297 **Fax:** 0121-445 6297
E-mail: bob@tpstools.com
Website: http://www.tpstools.com
Directors: B. Sedgwick (MD)
No.of Employees: 1 - 10 **Product Groups:** 36

T R W Automotive Electronics
College Road Perry Barr, Birmingham, B44 8DU
Tel: 0121-623 4299 **Fax:** 0121-344 3396
E-mail: norman.taylor@trw.com
Website: http://www.trw.com
Managers: N. Taylor (Personnel), M. Nash (Personnel), B. Elms (Fin Mgr), C. Jackson (I.T. Exec)
No.of Employees: 251 - 500 **Product Groups:** 38, 39

T & T Maintenance Services Ltd
PO Box 383, Birmingham, B33 9QR
Tel: 0121-252 8243 **Fax:** 0121-789 7645
E-mail: t.dunn@totalise.co.uk
Directors: T. Dunn (MD)
Immediate Holding Company: T & T MAINTENANCE SERVICES LIMITED
Registration no: 04097773 **Date established:** 2000
Turnover: £500,000 - £1m **No.of Employees:** 1 - 10 **Product Groups:** 35, 39, 45

Date of Accounts	Oct 11	Oct 10	Oct 09
Sales Turnover	N/A	N/A	664
Pre Tax Profit/Loss	N/A	N/A	235
Working Capital	420	334	308
Fixed Assets	50	63	79
Current Assets	690	492	356

T W Stamping Ltd
112-117 Charles Henry Street, Birmingham, B12 0SJ
Tel: 0121-622 2600 **Fax:** 0121-622 2700
E-mail: vic.ensor@tgstamping.co.uk
Website: http://www.thomaswalker.co.uk
Directors: J. Norton (Sales & Mktg), V. Ensor (Dir), A. McKelly (Fin)
Ultimate Holding Company: THOMAS WALKER P.L.C.
Immediate Holding Company: T W STAMPING LTD
Registration no: 02719675 **VAT No.:** GB 559 2906 07
Date established: 1992 **Turnover:** £5m - £10m
No.of Employees: 51 - 100 **Product Groups:** 48

Date of Accounts	Jun 07	Jun 06	Jun 05
Sales Turnover	6m	4m	2m
Pre Tax Profit/Loss	437	264	142
Working Capital	-201	10	856
Fixed Assets	2m	1m	396
Current Assets	2m	2m	1m
Current Liabilities	886	435	125

Tacho-Fit
Unit 17 Haywards Industrial Park, Birmingham, B35 7BT
Tel: 0121-747 7220 **Fax:** 0121-747 7138
E-mail: sales@tacho-fit.co.uk
Website: http://www.tacho-fit.co.uk
Directors: D. Mccarthy (Dir)
Immediate Holding Company: TACHO-SERVE LTD
Registration no: 03416282 **No.of Employees:** 1 - 10 **Product Groups:** 38, 39

Date of Accounts	Mar 08	Mar 07	Mar 06
Working Capital	-8	-79	-32
Fixed Assets	N/A	38	42
Current Assets	9	104	65
Current Liabilities	17	183	97

Talbots Birmingham Ltd
56-60 Princip Street, Birmingham, B4 6LN
Tel: 0121-333 3544 **Fax:** 0121-333 3520
E-mail: sales@talbotsbirm.co.uk
Website: http://www.talbotsbirm.co.uk
Bank(s): Barclays
Directors: R. Randall (Fin), J. Fowler Drake (MD)
Immediate Holding Company: TALBOTS (BIRMINGHAM) LIMITED
Registration no: 00366112 **VAT No.:** GB 111 5452 16
Date established: 1941 **Turnover:** £5m - £10m **No.of Employees:** 21 - 50
Product Groups: 22, 27

Date of Accounts	Mar 11	Mar 10	Mar 09
Sales Turnover	6m	7m	N/A
Pre Tax Profit/Loss	-356	-32	-285
Working Capital	2m	4m	2m
Fixed Assets	1m	1m	1m
Current Assets	3m	6m	5m
Current Liabilities	160	324	170

Tastees UK
Aspect Court 4 Temple Row, Birmingham, B2 5HG
Tel: 0121-222 2327
E-mail: hello@tastees.info
Website: http://www.templarfoods.co.uk
Directors: J. Roblings (Dir)
Registration no: 05997965 **Date established:** 2006
Turnover: Up to £250,000 **No.of Employees:** 1 - 10 **Product Groups:** 20

Tate Circuit Industries Ltd
190 High Street Aston, Birmingham, B6 4XA
Tel: 0121-359 3102 **Fax:** 0121-359 4108
E-mail: neil@tatecircuits.com
Website: http://www.tatecircuits.com
Bank(s): Nat West
Directors: N. Stevenson (MD), S. Stevenson (MD), S. Stevenson (Dir), A. Knight-Adams (Dir)
Immediate Holding Company: TATE CIRCUIT INDUSTRIES LIMITED
Registration no: 01183623 **VAT No.:** 112 4459 01 **Date established:** 1974
Turnover: £250,000 - £500,000 **No.of Employees:** 11 - 20
Product Groups: 37

Date of Accounts	Mar 10	Mar 09	Mar 08
Working Capital	249	171	209
Fixed Assets	79	140	190
Current Assets	423	505	603
Current Liabilities	26	N/A	N/A

Taylor Engineering
Unit D St Clements Road, Birmingham, B7 5AF
Tel: 0121-326 9035
E-mail: tony@taylorengineer.co.uk
Website: http://www.taylorengineer.co.uk
Managers: T. Taylor (Mgr)
Immediate Holding Company: TAYLOR ENGINEERING & FABRICATIONS LIMITED
Registration no: 04989359 **Date established:** 2003
No.of Employees: 1 - 10 **Product Groups:** 40, 48

Date of Accounts	Nov 11	Nov 10	Nov 09
Working Capital	142	28	5
Fixed Assets	49	22	27
Current Assets	313	184	144

Taylor Plate
60-62 Branston Street, Birmingham, B18 6BP
Tel: 0121-236 3046 **Fax:** 0121-200 1430
E-mail: taylor@plate.freeserve.co.uk
Website: http://www.plate.freeserv.co.uk
Directors: A. Taylor (Prop)
Registration no: 02521748 **Date established:** 1990
No.of Employees: 1 - 10 **Product Groups:** 46, 48

Taylor Precision Components Ltd
18 Porters Way, Birmingham, B9 5RR
Tel: 0121-766 8065 **Fax:** 0121-766 7551
E-mail: taylorprecision@btconnect.com
Website: http://www.tpclimited.co.uk
Directors: J. Taylor (MD)
Immediate Holding Company: TAYLOR PRECISION COMPONENTS LIMITED
Registration no: 02657733 **Date established:** 1991
No.of Employees: 11 - 20 **Product Groups:** 36, 37, 38

Date of Accounts	Oct 11	Oct 10	Oct 09
Working Capital	88	54	59
Fixed Assets	8	5	7
Current Assets	130	85	93

Technispray Coating Ltd
Linton House Catherine Street, Birmingham, B6 5RS
Tel: 0121-326 8020 **Fax:** 0121-326 8020
E-mail: info@kolorbond.co.uk
Website: http://www.kolorbond.co.uk
Directors: J. White (Fin), D. Kershaw (MD)
Ultimate Holding Company: TECHNISPRAY LIMITED
Immediate Holding Company: TECHNISPRAY COATINGS LIMITED
Registration no: 03821155 **Date established:** 1999
No.of Employees: 1 - 10 **Product Groups:** 46, 48

Date of Accounts	Mar 12	Mar 11	Mar 10
Working Capital	119	71	20
Fixed Assets	13	15	21
Current Assets	148	108	52

Tek Ltd
Unit 14 Seeleys Road, Birmingham, B11 2LQ
Tel: 0121-766 5005 **Fax:** 0121-766 5010
E-mail: sales@tekltd.uk
Website: http://www.tekltd.com
Bank(s): National Westminster
Directors: M. Callard (MD), P. Virgo (Fin)
Ultimate Holding Company: TEK UK LIMITED
Immediate Holding Company: TEK LIMITED
Registration no: 02787537 **VAT No.:** GB 614 1193 73
Date established: 1993 **Turnover:** £2m - £5m **No.of Employees:** 21 - 50
Product Groups: 35, 40, 42, 52, 54, 66

Date of Accounts	Mar 12	Mar 11	Mar 10
Working Capital	160	34	29
Fixed Assets	126	N/A	N/A
Current Assets	1m	936	1m

Terraspan Pipe Fittings
Unit 4 135 Manor Farm Road, Birmingham, B11 2HT
Tel: 0121-707 9921 **Fax:** 0121-708 1752
E-mail: markp@terraspan.co.uk
Website: http://www.terraspan.co.uk
Directors: M. Phillips (Dir)
Immediate Holding Company: TERRASPAN PIPE FITTINGS LIMITED
Registration no: 00706106 **VAT No.:** GB 111 5227 23
Date established: 1961 **Turnover:** £500,000 - £1m
No.of Employees: 1 - 10 **Product Groups:** 36

Date of Accounts	Dec 11	Dec 10	Dec 09
Working Capital	394	263	276
Fixed Assets	104	95	104
Current Assets	552	456	512

The Little Trucker
Wholesale Markets Precinct Pershore Street, Birmingham, B5 6UB
Tel: 0121-666 7123 **Fax:** 0121-608 5097
Directors: R. Humpage (Prop)
Immediate Holding Company: J. VICKERSTAFF HOLDINGS LIMITED
Registration no: 04168172 **Date established:** 2001
No.of Employees: 1 - 10 **Product Groups:** 35, 39, 45

The Office Furniture Warehouse
Unit 3-5 Speedwell Trading Estate 108 Kings Road, Tyseley, Birmingham, B11 2AT
Tel: 0121-771 4944 **Fax:** 01384-231215
E-mail: sales@officefurn.co.uk
Website: http://www.officefurn.co.uk
Directors: J. Burrell (Prop)
Registration no: 02882641 **Turnover:** £2m - £5m
No.of Employees: 11 - 20 **Product Groups:** 26, 28, 49, 61, 67, 80

The Pewter Sheet Company Ltd
River Lee Road, Birmingham, B11 2JG
Tel: 0121-706 2649 **Fax:** 0121-707 7682
E-mail: chris@pewtersheet.co.uk
Website: http://www.pewtersheet.co.uk
Directors: C. Griffiths (MD)
Immediate Holding Company: PEWTER SHEET COMPANY LIMITED
Registration no: 05734027 **Date established:** 2006
Turnover: Up to £250,000 **No.of Employees:** 1 - 10 **Product Groups:** 34, 66

Date of Accounts	Jun 11	Jun 10	Jun 09
Working Capital	27	-2	-8
Fixed Assets	1	3	19
Current Assets	151	137	80

The Running Fox Ltd
Langley Drive Castle Bromwich, Birmingham, B35 7AD
Tel: 0121-747 2806 **Fax:** 0121-748 7541
Directors: P. Smythe (MD), W. Smythe (Jt MD), W. Smythe (Co Sec), P. Smythe (Jt MD)
Immediate Holding Company: SALAMANDER WALKING LIMITED
Registration no: 01429263 **Date established:** 1977
No.of Employees: 1 - 10 **Product Groups:** 28

Date of Accounts	Dec 06	Dec 05
Working Capital	-46	-69
Fixed Assets	77	106
Current Assets	152	170
Current Liabilities	197	239

The Tool Box
630 Bristol Road South Northfield, Birmingham, B31 2JR
Tel: 0121-477 5222 **Fax:** 0121-477 5222
E-mail: sales@thetoolbox.uk.com
Website: http://www.thetoolbox.uk.com
Directors: K. Clarke (Prop)
Date established: 1982 **No.of Employees:** 1 - 10 **Product Groups:** 46

Thermofrost Cryo plc
Robert Fawkes House Rea Street South, Birmingham, B5 6LB
Tel: 0121-622 6325 **Fax:** 0121-622 7268
E-mail: sales@thermofrostcryo.co.uk
Website: http://www.thermofrostcryo.co.uk
Bank(s): National Westminster Bank Plc
Directors: P. Sloper (MD)
Ultimate Holding Company: LANSING SECURITIES LTD (BRITISH VIRGIN ISLANDS)
Immediate Holding Company: THERMOFROST CRYO PLC
Registration no: 01036288 **VAT No.:** GB 193 1918 45
Date established: 1971 **Turnover:** £10m - £20m
No.of Employees: 21 - 50 **Product Groups:** 29, 32, 35, 36, 37, 38, 39, 40, 42, 66

Date of Accounts	Mar 12	Mar 11	Mar 10
Sales Turnover	10m	11m	10m
Pre Tax Profit/Loss	92	334	82
Working Capital	1m	1m	2m
Fixed Assets	268	217	207
Current Assets	4m	4m	4m
Current Liabilities	2m	640	479

Thomas Plant Birmingham
Plumb Bob House Valepits Road, Birmingham, B33 0TD
Tel: 0121-604 6000 **Fax:** 0121-604 2222
E-mail: info@kitchencraft.co.uk
Website: http://www.kitchencraft.co.uk
Directors: A. Plant (Dir), A. Perry (Co Sec)
Managers: C. Budgen (Sales & Mktg Mg), L. Comrie (Tech Serv Mgr)
Ultimate Holding Company: THOMAS PLANT (BIRMINGHAM) LIMITED
Immediate Holding Company: THOMAS PLANT (BIRMINGHAM 1927) LIMITED
Registration no: 00219394 **Date established:** 2027
Turnover: £20m - £50m **No.of Employees:** 51 - 100 **Product Groups:** 63

Date of Accounts	Dec 10	Dec 09	Dec 08
Working Capital	615	615	615
Current Assets	615	615	615

Thyssenkrupp Aerospace UK Ltd
Apollo House Redfern Road, Birmingham, B11 2BH
Tel: 0121-335 5000 **Fax:** 0121-335 5070
E-mail: allan.walters@thyssenkrupp.com
Website: http://www.thyssenkruppaerospace.com
Managers: A. Walters
Ultimate Holding Company: THYSSEN KRUPP AG (GERMANY)
Immediate Holding Company: THYSSENKRUPP AEROSPACE UK LTD
Registration no: 01914559 **Date established:** 1985
Turnover: £75m - £125m **No.of Employees:** 51 - 100
Product Groups: 34, 36

Date of Accounts	Sep 11	Sep 10	Sep 09
Sales Turnover	101m	95m	101m
Pre Tax Profit/Loss	5m	3m	7m
Working Capital	27m	26m	27m
Fixed Assets	3m	4m	4m
Current Assets	64m	59m	68m
Current Liabilities	7m	8m	10m

Timet UK Ltd
PO Box 704, Birmingham, B6 7UR
Tel: 0121-356 1155 **Fax:** 0121-356 5413
E-mail: eurosales@timet.com
Website: http://www.timet.com
Bank(s): Lloyds
Directors: D. Roberts (Dir), M. Goodwin (Co Sec)
Ultimate Holding Company: TITANIUM METALS CORPORATION (USA)
Immediate Holding Company: TIMET UK LIMITED
Registration no: 00530589 **VAT No.:** GB 405 2661 78
Date established: 1954 **Turnover:** £125m - £250m
No.of Employees: 251 - 500 **Product Groups:** 34, 35, 39

Date of Accounts	Dec 11	Dec 10	Dec 09
Sales Turnover	186m	155m	110m
Pre Tax Profit/Loss	32m	18m	2m
Working Capital	108m	98m	80m
Fixed Assets	46m	46m	49m
Current Assets	144m	131m	103m
Current Liabilities	15m	7m	6m

Derek Timms Seals Ltd
90 Evelyn Road, Birmingham, B11 3JJ
Tel: 0121-773 7666 **Fax:** 0121-766 5590
E-mail: derek_timms_seals@yahoo.co.uk
Directors: D. Timms (MD)
Immediate Holding Company: DT SEALS (UK) LTD
Registration no: 03188829 **VAT No.:** 670 2505 57 **Date established:** 1996
Turnover: £250,000 - £500,000 **No.of Employees:** 1 - 10
Product Groups: 29, 36

Date of Accounts	Dec 11	Dec 10	Dec 09
Working Capital	54	45	36
Fixed Assets	3	2	4
Current Assets	350	263	220

Titanium Engineering Ltd
Unit 42 Great Western Industrial Estate Great Western Close, Birmingham, B18 4QF
Tel: 0121-523 6932 **Fax:** 0121-523 5991
E-mail: titanium.engineering@hotmail.com
Directors: M. Singh (Dir)
Immediate Holding Company: TITANIUM ENGINEERING LIMITED
Registration no: 07835674 **Date established:** 2011
Turnover: £250,000 - £500,000 **No.of Employees:** 1 - 10
Product Groups: 48

Titanium Industries UK Ltd
Unit 38 Elmdon Trading Estate Bickenhill Lane, Birmingham, B37 7HE
Tel: 08707-507557 **Fax:** 0121-782 9705
E-mail: uksales@titanium.com
Website: http://www.titanium.com
Directors: C. Simpson (Prop)
Immediate Holding Company: TITANIUM INDUSTRIES U.K LIMITED
Registration no: 05113123 **Date established:** 2004 **Turnover:** £2m - £5m
No.of Employees: 21 - 50 **Product Groups:** 34, 36

Date of Accounts	Dec 11	Dec 10	Dec 09
Working Capital	2m	2m	1m
Fixed Assets	169	190	58
Current Assets	3m	2m	2m

Tobbletag Ltd
30 Somery Road, Birmingham, B29 5RY
Tel: 0121-342 0791
E-mail: info@tobbletag.com
Website: http://www.tobbletag.co.uk
Directors: D. Harvey (MD), D. Harvey (Prop)
Immediate Holding Company: TOBBLETAG LTD
Registration no: 06386418 **Date established:** 2007
No.of Employees: 1 - 10 **Product Groups:** 22

Toptec
Garretts Green Trading Estate Valepits Road, Birmingham, B33 0TD
Tel: 0121-783 3838 **Fax:** 0121-784 6348
E-mail: claire.beardmore@top-tec.co.uk
Website: http://www.top-tec.co.uk
Directors: C. Beardmore (Co Sec)
Immediate Holding Company: AMINGTON LIMITED
Registration no: 01516435 **Date established:** 1980
No.of Employees: 21 - 50 **Product Groups:** 26, 36, 45

Tornado International Ltd
Unit 28 Green Lane Industrial Estate Bordesley Green, Birmingham, B9 5QP
Tel: 0121-773 1827 **Fax:** 0121-772 6056
E-mail: sales@tornado-uk.com
Website: http://www.tornado-uk.com
Bank(s): HSBC Bank plc
Directors: S. Roberts (Fin), S. Bland (MD)
Ultimate Holding Company: TORNADO INTERNATIONAL LEISURE LIMITED
Immediate Holding Company: TORNADO INTERNATIONAL LIMITED
Registration no: 01099092 **Date established:** 1973
Turnover: Up to £250,000 **No.of Employees:** 11 - 20 **Product Groups:** 49

Date of Accounts	Nov 11	Nov 10	Nov 09
Working Capital	336	378	326
Fixed Assets	51	31	39
Current Assets	588	643	673

Total Finishing Solutions
67-70 Mott Street, Birmingham, B19 3HE
Tel: 0121-233 3505 **Fax:** 0121-233 9207
E-mail: wesley.jenkinson@totalfinishingsolutions.co.uk
Bank(s): HSBC Bank plc
Directors: K. Jekinson (MD), W. Jenkinson (Prop)
Immediate Holding Company: METTAFIN 2010 LIMITED
Registration no: 06675528 **VAT No.:** GB 313 9123 84
Date established: 2010 **Turnover:** £250,000 - £500,000
No.of Employees: 11 - 20 **Product Groups:** 48

Toye Kenning Spencer Stadden
77 Warstone Lane, Birmingham, B18 6NL
Tel: 0121-236 3253 **Fax:** 0121-236 7217
E-mail: bryan.toye@toye.com
Website: http://www.toye.co.uk
Bank(s): Lloyds TSB Bank plc
Directors: B. Toye (Prop)
Immediate Holding Company: TOYE & CO. P.L.C.
Registration no: 00692479 **VAT No.:** GB 232 5841 74
Turnover: £1m - £2m **No.of Employees:** 51 - 100 **Product Groups:** 23, 24, 35, 49

The Translation People
Concorde House Trinity Park Bickenhill Lane, Birmingham, B37 7UQ
Tel: 08456-430726 **Fax:** 0121-635 5061
E-mail: birmingham@thetranslationpeople.com
Website: http://www.thetranslationpeople.com
Managers: J. Schneider (District Mgr)
Ultimate Holding Company: ACTIVE HUMAN CAPITAL GROUP LIMITED
Immediate Holding Company: BUSINESS PATHWAYS LTD
Registration no: 04241666 **Date established:** 2010 **Turnover:** £2m - £5m
No.of Employees: 1 - 10 **Product Groups:** 28, 80, 86

Date of Accounts	Jul 11	Jul 10	Jul 09
Working Capital	-5	1	12
Current Assets	6	5	19

Travel West Midlands Ltd
51 Bordesley Green, Birmingham, B9 4BZ
Tel: 0121-254 7272 **Fax:** 0121-254 7277
Website: http://www.nationalexpresswestmidlands.co.uk
Directors: P. Snape (Dir), J. Giles (Dir), J. Casson (Co Sec), T. Fletcher (Dir), P. White (Dir), G. Wellings (Dir), D. Leeder (Dir), C. Child (Dir), A. Kelsey (Dir), P. Cox (Dir)
Ultimate Holding Company: NATIONAL EXPRESS GROUP PLC
Immediate Holding Company: TRAVEL WEST MIDLANDS LIMITED
Registration no: 00775806 **Date established:** 1963
Turnover: £125m - £250m **No.of Employees:** 1501 & over
Product Groups: 72

Date of Accounts	Dec 11	Dec 10	Dec 09
Working Capital	3	3	3
Current Assets	3	3	3

Travis Perkins plc
1 South Road Hockley, Birmingham, B18 5LT
Tel: 0121-554 3396 **Fax:** 0121-554 6811
Website: http://www.travisperkins.co.uk
Directors: A. Pike (Co Sec)
Immediate Holding Company: TRAVIS PERKINS PLC
Registration no: 00824821 **Date established:** 1964
Turnover: £75m - £125m **No.of Employees:** 11 - 20 **Product Groups:** 66

Date of Accounts	Dec 11	Dec 10	Dec 09
Sales Turnover	4779m	3153m	2931m
Pre Tax Profit/Loss	270m	197m	213m
Working Capital	133m	159m	248m
Fixed Assets	2771m	2749m	2108m
Current Assets	1421m	1329m	1035m
Current Liabilities	473m	412m	109m

Trewhella Brothers Ltd
Bowyer Street, Birmingham, B10 0SA
Tel: 0121-766 7525 **Fax:** 0121-766 8841
E-mail: sales@trewhella.co.uk
Website: http://www.trewhella.co.uk
Directors: S. Cullen (MD)
Immediate Holding Company: TREWHELLA BROTHERS LTD
Registration no: 02518361 **VAT No.:** GB 687 5365 84
Date established: 1990 **Turnover:** £500,000 - £1m
No.of Employees: 1 - 10 **Product Groups:** 35, 36, 39, 41, 45

Date of Accounts	May 11	May 10	May 08
Working Capital	57	63	86
Current Assets	105	126	148

Tri World Ltd
Unit 16 Tame Road, Birmingham, B6 7HS
Tel: 0121-327 8323 **Fax:** 0121-327 8324
Directors: G. Taylor (Dir)
No.of Employees: 1 - 10 **Product Groups:** 46

Trojan Special Fasteners Ltd
18 Fortnum Close, Birmingham, B33 0LG
Tel: 0121-789 8586 **Fax:** 0121-789 8006
E-mail: sales@trojanspecialfastenersltd.co.uk
Website: http://www.trojanspecialfastenersltd.co.uk
Directors: A. Mohammed (MD), M. Bashir (Sales)
Immediate Holding Company: TROJAN SPECIAL FASTENERS LIMITED
Registration no: 02668394 **Date established:** 1991
Turnover: £500,000 - £1m **No.of Employees:** 11 - 20
Product Groups: 35, 66

Date of Accounts	Jan 12	Jan 11	Jan 10
Working Capital	90	122	117
Fixed Assets	176	158	153
Current Assets	189	217	178

Trolquote Ltd
Unit 23 Birch Road East Wyrley Trading Estate Witton, Birmingham, B6 7DA
Tel: 0121-326 6735 **Fax:** 0121-327 2437
Website: http://www.trolquote.co.uk
Directors: N. Batchelor (MD)
Immediate Holding Company: TROLQUOTE LIMITED
Registration no: 01705075 **VAT No.:** GB 377 5261 26
Date established: 1983 **Turnover:** £250,000 - £500,000
No.of Employees: 1 - 10 **Product Groups:** 26, 40, 48

Date of Accounts	Mar 12	Mar 11	Mar 10
Working Capital	-16	-28	-32
Fixed Assets	59	58	61
Current Assets	83	79	79

Truflo Gas Turbines Ltd (A fluid controls business of IMI plc)
Westwood Road, Birmingham, B6 7JF
Tel: 0121-327 4789 **Fax:** 0121-327 4132
E-mail: robert.bowser@truflo-marine.com
Website: http://www.fcx-truflow-marine.com
Bank(s): Barclays
Directors: A. Staten (Co Sec), P. Adams (Sales), R. Bowser (Dir), R. Watson (Eng Serv), R. Bowser (MD), S. Chapman (Fab)
Managers: D. Bowen (Sales Prom Mgr), R. Beathe (Chief Buyer)
Immediate Holding Company: TRUFLO MARINE LIMITED
Registration no: 00993167 **Date established:** 1970
Turnover: £10m - £20m **No.of Employees:** 51 - 100 **Product Groups:** 36, 39, 40, 48

Date of Accounts	Dec 09	Dec 08	Dec 07
Sales Turnover	13m	10m	15m
Pre Tax Profit/Loss	2m	1m	3m
Working Capital	8m	7m	6m
Fixed Assets	673	430	504
Current Assets	12m	11m	9m
Current Liabilities	3m	2m	1m

Trulaw Fabs Ltd
338 Summer Lane, Birmingham, B19 3QL
Tel: 0121-359 1191 **Fax:** 0121-359 4855
E-mail: trb2218@aol.com
Directors: T. Brown (MD)
Immediate Holding Company: TRULAW ENGINEERING LTD
Registration no: 06741077 **Date established:** 2008 **Turnover:** £1m - £2m
No.of Employees: 1 - 10 **Product Groups:** 35, 48

T-Tech Tooling Ltd
70 Prince of Wales Lane, Birmingham, B14 4JZ
Tel: 0121-474 2255 **Fax:** 0121-474 2066
E-mail: sales@t-tech.co.uk
Website: http://www.t-tech.co.uk
Bank(s): HSBC
Directors: R. Gray (Sales)
Ultimate Holding Company: P.T.T. HOLDINGS LIMITED
Immediate Holding Company: T-TECH TOOLING LIMITED
Registration no: 03833067 **VAT No.:** GB 747 4017 31
Date established: 1999 **Turnover:** £500,000 - £1m
No.of Employees: 11 - 20 **Product Groups:** 36, 46

Date of Accounts	Dec 11	Dec 10	Dec 09
Working Capital	102	70	50
Fixed Assets	43	38	35
Current Assets	205	159	136

Tube Heat Ltd
Unit 15 Tile Cross Trading Estate Tile Cross Road, Birmingham, B33 0NW
Tel: 0121-779 5253 **Fax:** 0121-779 2867
E-mail: info@tubeheat.co.uk
Website: http://www.tubeheat.co.uk
Directors: T. Handley (MD)
Managers: K. Burrows (Chief Mgr)
Registration no: 00409828 **VAT No.:** GB 109 9315 62
Date established: 1946 **Turnover:** Up to £250,000
No.of Employees: 1 - 10 **Product Groups:** 40

Date of Accounts	Sep 07	Sep 06	Sep 05
Working Capital	48	39	30
Fixed Assets	9	11	12
Current Assets	64	61	47
Current Liabilities	16	22	17
Total Share Capital	4	4	4

Tuckey Print Ltd
79 Moseley Road, Birmingham, B12 0HL
Tel: 0121-773 7411 **Fax:** 0121-766 7339
E-mail: nicola.holland@tuckeyprint.co.uk
Website: http://www.tuckeyprint.co.uk
Directors: N. Holland (Fin)
Immediate Holding Company: TUCKEY PRINT LIMITED
Registration no: 02401464 **Date established:** 1989
No.of Employees: 1 - 10 **Product Groups:** 28, 81

Date of Accounts	Sep 11	Sep 10	Sep 09
Working Capital	45	41	53
Fixed Assets	143	166	191
Current Assets	171	185	202

Tyresonline.NET
Units 8&9 Sandpits Ind Est Summerhill Street, Birmingham, B1 2PD
Tel: 0845-260 1600 **Fax:** 0845-260 1603
E-mail: sales@tyresonline.net
Website: http://www.tyresonline.net
Turnover: £500,000 - £1m **No.of Employees:** 1 - 10 **Product Groups:** 29, 68

United Optical Industries Ltd
583 Moseley Road, Birmingham, B12 9BL
Tel: 0121-442 2222 **Fax:** 0121-449 9993
E-mail: sales@bog.co.uk
Website: http://www.bog.co.uk
Bank(s): Bank of Scotland
Directors: C. Tyler (Sales), J. Cooper (Jt MD), S. Jones (MD)
Managers: T. Tyler (I.T. Exec), Z. Haywood (Mktg Serv Mgr)
Ultimate Holding Company: SECKLOE 302 LIMITED
Immediate Holding Company: UNITED OPTICAL INDUSTRIES LIMITED
Registration no: 03052147 **Date established:** 1995
Turnover: £10m - £20m **No.of Employees:** 51 - 100 **Product Groups:** 67

Date of Accounts	Oct 10	Oct 09	Oct 08
Working Capital	-4m	-4m	-4m
Current Assets	6m	6m	6m
Current Liabilities	25	25	25

University of Birmingham (The Business School)
Edgbaston, Birmingham, B15 2TT
Tel: 0121-414 3344 **Fax:** 0121-414 7453
E-mail: m.e.a.mackenzie@bham.ac.uk
Website: http://www.is.bham.ac.uk/cm/bindery
Directors: G. Ball (Fin)
Managers: B. Higgins, M. Mackenzie, P. Collier, H. Taver (Personnel), S. Duffy (Tech Serv Mgr)
Immediate Holding Company: THE UNIVERSITY OF BIRMINGHAM SCHOOL AND SIXTH FORM
Registration no: 07960887 **Date established:** 2012 **Turnover:** £2m - £5m
No.of Employees: 1 - 10 **Product Groups:** 86

Utensa Ltd
Kings Road Tyseley, Birmingham, B11 2AS
Tel: 0121-706 0271 **Fax:** 0121-706 6169
E-mail: sales@utensa.co.uk
Website: http://www.utensa.co.uk
Bank(s): HSBC Bank plc
Directors: G. Dunnett (MD), G. Cressey (Co Sec), G. Dunnett (Ch), G. Cressey (Dir)
Managers: S. Edwards ()
Immediate Holding Company: UTENSA LIMITED
Registration no: 06425317 **VAT No.:** GB 109 7450 66
Date established: 2007 **Turnover:** £1m - £2m **No.of Employees:** 21 - 50
Product Groups: 36, 41

Date of Accounts	Jan 11	Jan 10	Jan 09
Working Capital	56	169	-14
Fixed Assets	81	84	49
Current Assets	740	692	441

V S N Steels Ltd
395 Lichfield Road, Birmingham, B6 7SS
Tel: 0121-327 1783 **Fax:** 0121-327 6897
E-mail: info@vsn-steels.co.uk
Website: http://www.vsn-steels.co.uk
Bank(s): HSBC Bank plc
Directors: R. Stockton (MD), R. Stockton (MD)
Immediate Holding Company: V.S.N.(STEELS)LIMITED
Registration no: 00706440 **VAT No.:** GB 110 7391 06
Date established: 1961 **Turnover:** £2m - £5m **No.of Employees:** 21 - 50
Product Groups: 48

Date of Accounts	Mar 12	Mar 11	Mar 10
Sales Turnover	N/A	N/A	4m
Pre Tax Profit/Loss	N/A	N/A	205
Working Capital	2m	1m	1m
Fixed Assets	1m	646	660
Current Assets	3m	3m	3m
Current Liabilities	N/A	N/A	217

V T G Rail UK Ltd
Sir Stanley Clarke House Ridgeway Quinton Business Park, Quinton, Birmingham, B32 1AF
Tel: 0121-421 9180 **Fax:** 0121-421 9192
E-mail: joanne.cobley@vtg.com
Website: http://www.vtg.com
Managers: J. Cobley
Ultimate Holding Company: VTG AG (GERMANY)
Immediate Holding Company: VTG RAIL UK LTD
Registration no: 04474641 **Date established:** 2002
Turnover: £10m - £20m **No.of Employees:** 11 - 20 **Product Groups:** 72

Date of Accounts	Dec 11	Dec 10	Dec 09
Sales Turnover	14m	13m	12m
Pre Tax Profit/Loss	3m	2m	1m
Working Capital	10m	15m	14m
Fixed Assets	51m	49m	48m
Current Assets	15m	18m	18m
Current Liabilities	3m	2m	1m

Valor Heating
Wood Lane Erdington, Birmingham, B24 9QP
Tel: 0121-373 8111 **Fax:** 0121- 3738181
E-mail: darren.mcmahon@baxigroup.com
Website: http://www.valor.co.uk
Directors: D. Mcmahon (Dir), N. Friend (Dir), S. Gay (Co Sec)
Managers: I. Brookes (Buyer)
No.of Employees: 251 - 500 **Product Groups:** 40

Valspar Powder Coatings Ltd (Global Coatings Division)
95 Aston Church Road Nechells, Birmingham, B7 5RQ
Tel: 0121-322 6900 **Fax:** 0121-322 6901
E-mail: infoeurope@powderstore.com
Website: http://www.valsparglobal.com
Bank(s): Lloyds TSB Bank plc
Managers: D. Mathias (Sales & Mktg Mgr), L. Gabb (Fin Mgr), T. Mccarthy
Ultimate Holding Company: VALSPAR CORPORATION INC (USA)
Immediate Holding Company: VALSPAR POWDER COATINGS LIMITED
Registration no: 02849106 **VAT No.:** GB 580 6887 95
Date established: 1993 **Turnover:** £10m - £20m
No.of Employees: 51 - 100 **Product Groups:** 30, 32

Date of Accounts	Sep 11	Sep 10	Dec 09
Sales Turnover	11m	6m	8m
Pre Tax Profit/Loss	-535	-1m	-1m
Working Capital	3m	3m	4m
Fixed Assets	2m	2m	2m
Current Assets	6m	7m	7m
Current Liabilities	554	517	560

Vanstead Ltd
Unit 6 Manor Farm Road, Birmingham, B11 2HT
Tel: 0121-707 4929 **Fax:** 0121-707 2155
E-mail: office@vanstead.com
Website: http://www.vanstead.com
Directors: B. Mcgovern (MD)
Immediate Holding Company: VANSTEAD LIMITED
Registration no: 01242089 **VAT No.:** GB 112 9919 65
Date established: 1976 **Turnover:** £250,000 - £500,000
No.of Employees: 1 - 10 **Product Groups:** 76

Date of Accounts	Mar 11	Mar 10	Mar 09
Working Capital	131	104	85
Fixed Assets	13	17	21
Current Assets	196	158	138

Varley & Gulliver Ltd
Alfred Street Sparkbrook, Birmingham, B12 8JR
Tel: 0121-773 2441 **Fax:** 0121-766 6875
E-mail: reception@v-and-g.co.uk
Website: http://www.v-and-g.co.uk
Bank(s): Barclays
Directors: D. Copeland (Tech Serv), T. Abrey (Fin)
Ultimate Holding Company: HILL & SMITH HOLDINGS PLC
Immediate Holding Company: VARLEY & GULLIVER LIMITED
Registration no: 00330433 **VAT No.:** GB 110 9719 85
Date established: 1937 **Turnover:** £5m - £10m **No.of Employees:** 21 - 50
Product Groups: 26, 35, 39, 48

Date of Accounts	Dec 11	Dec 10	Dec 09
Sales Turnover	7m	13m	16m
Pre Tax Profit/Loss	-425	2m	3m
Working Capital	2m	4m	3m
Fixed Assets	1m	2m	2m
Current Assets	4m	7m	6m
Current Liabilities	548	1m	1m

H Varley Ltd
Unit 173 Argyle Street, Birmingham, B7 5TE
Tel: 0121-328 8396 **Fax:** 0121-328 3476
E-mail: midsales@varley.co.uk
Website: http://www.varley.co.uk
Managers: L. Callan (Mgr)
Immediate Holding Company: H.VARLEY LIMITED
Registration no: 00344712 **Date established:** 1938
No.of Employees: 1 - 10 **Product Groups:** 29, 39

Veolia Environmental Services plc
Waste Services Centre 201 Armoury Road, Birmingham, B11 2RH
Tel: 0121-773 8353 **Fax:** 0121-773 1194
Website: http://www.cleanaway.com
Managers: N. Phillips (Mgr)
Ultimate Holding Company: VIVENDI GROUP
Registration no: 02215767 **No.of Employees:** 51 - 100
Product Groups: 34, 54

Vertik Al
Yardley Brook Industrial Park Lea Ford Road Shard End, Birmingham, B33 9TX
Tel: 0121-608 7171 **Fax:** 0121-693 7787
E-mail: info@vertik-al.com
Website: http://www.vertik-al.com
Directors: M. Lock (Sales), R. Gibbs (Fab), W. Lock (Dir), M. Lock (Fin)
Immediate Holding Company: VERTIK-AL LIMITED
Registration no: 02634525 **Date established:** 1991 **Turnover:** £2m - £5m
No.of Employees: 51 - 100 **Product Groups:** 48

Date of Accounts	Mar 11	Mar 10	Mar 09
Working Capital	301	234	242
Current Assets	1m	1m	1m

Vincent Timber Ltd
8 Montgomery Street, Birmingham, B11 1DU
Tel: 0121-772 5511 **Fax:** 0121-766 6002
E-mail: allen@vincenttimber.co.uk
Website: http://www.vincenttimber.co.uk
Bank(s): HSBC, Birmingham
Directors: A. Allen (Sales), A. Allen (MD), N. Crespi (Fin)
Ultimate Holding Company: W.J.VINCENT GROUP LIMITED
Immediate Holding Company: VINCENT TIMBER LIMITED
Registration no: 00107182 **VAT No.:** GB 109 5821 67
Date established: 2010 **Turnover:** £10m - £20m
No.of Employees: 51 - 100 **Product Groups:** 66

Date of Accounts	Mar 11	Mar 10	Mar 09
Sales Turnover	11m	10m	11m
Pre Tax Profit/Loss	56	89	77
Working Capital	2m	2m	2m
Fixed Assets	391	458	508
Current Assets	5m	5m	5m
Current Liabilities	662	485	840

Vision Tech International Ltd
44 Harford Street Hockley, Birmingham, B19 3EB
Tel: 0121-554 8282 **Fax:** 0121-554 2121
E-mail: sales@visiontech.co.uk
Website: http://www.visiontech.co.uk
Directors: S. Nawaz (MD), R. Nawaz (Fin)
Immediate Holding Company: VISION TECH INTERNATIONAL LIMITED
Registration no: 04616517 **Date established:** 2002
No.of Employees: 1 - 10 **Product Groups:** 36, 40

Date of Accounts	Dec 08	Dec 07	Dec 06
Working Capital	669	400	222
Fixed Assets	62	68	55
Current Assets	1m	751	468

Vitis PR
32-35 Hall Street Jewellery Quarter, Birmingham, B18 6BS
Tel: 0121-242 8048
E-mail: jas@vitispr.com
Website: http://www.vitispr.com
Directors: J. Sahota (Dir)
Immediate Holding Company: VITIS BUSINESS CONSULTING LIMITED
Registration no: 06501637 **Date established:** 2008
No.of Employees: 1 - 10 **Product Groups:** 81

W J Sutton Ltd
St Helens House 23-31 Vittoria Street, Birmingham, B1 3ND
Tel: 0121-604 5446 **Fax:** 0121-236 9866
E-mail: kenneth.sutton@wjsutton.co.uk
Website: http://www.wjsutton.co.uk
Directors: K. Sutton (MD)
Immediate Holding Company: W.J.SUTTON LIMITED
Registration no: 00303132 **Date established:** 1935
Turnover: £250,000 - £500,000 **No.of Employees:** 1 - 10
Product Groups: 35, 65

Date of Accounts	Jun 11	Jun 10	Jun 09
Working Capital	1m	1m	953
Fixed Assets	264	280	294
Current Assets	1m	1m	1m

W M T P
228 Kings Road Kingstanding, Birmingham, B44 0SA
Tel: 0121-354 2094 **Fax:** 0121-354 2094
E-mail: timberanddamp@wmtp.co.uk
Website: http://www.wmtp.co.uk
Directors: E. Murphy (Prop)
No.of Employees: 1 - 10 **Product Groups:** 25, 31, 52, 66

Wallwork Heat Treatment Birmingham Ltd
Sydenham Road New Shires Industrial Estate, Birmingham, B11 1DQ
Tel: 0121-628 2552 **Fax:** 0121-628 1555
E-mail: enquiries@wallworkht.com
Website: http://www.wallworkht.com
Bank(s): National Westminster
Directors: R. Carpenter (Dir)
Managers: B. Harradence (Purch Mgr), C. Chettoe (Fin Mgr), C. Richards (Personnel)
Immediate Holding Company: WALLWORK HEAT TREATMENT (BIRMINGHAM) LIMITED
Registration no: 02293573 **VAT No.:** GB 519 0343 63
Date established: 1988 **Turnover:** £2m - £5m **No.of Employees:** 51 - 100
Product Groups: 46, 48

Date of Accounts	Mar 11	Mar 10	Mar 09
Sales Turnover	4m	4m	4m
Pre Tax Profit/Loss	474	207	41
Working Capital	441	626	2m
Fixed Assets	569	550	643
Current Assets	1m	1m	3m
Current Liabilities	383	237	200

F H Warden Steel Ltd
Landor Street, Birmingham, B8 1AE
Tel: 0121-327 7575 **Fax:** 0121-327 7212
E-mail: sales@fhwarden.co.uk
Website: http://www.fhwarden.co.uk
Bank(s): Barclays, Birmingham
Directors: D. Hughes (MD)
Immediate Holding Company: F. H. WARDEN (STEEL) LIMITED
Registration no: 03037789 **VAT No.:** GB 661 1838 36
Date established: 1995 **Turnover:** £1m - £2m **No.of Employees:** 11 - 20
Product Groups: 34, 66

Date of Accounts	Mar 11	Mar 10	Mar 09
Working Capital	280	239	180
Fixed Assets	363	384	410
Current Assets	860	766	726

Warman C N C Ltd
214 Moseley Street, Birmingham, B5 6LE
Tel: 0121-622 4045 **Fax:** 0121-666 6539
E-mail: warmancnc@aol.com
Bank(s): Midland
Directors: A. Khaliq (MD)
Managers: M. Stevenson (Comptroller)
Immediate Holding Company: WARMAN C.N.C. (BIRMINGHAM) LIMITED
Registration no: 00952067 **Date established:** 1969
Turnover: £500,000 - £1m **No.of Employees:** 21 - 50 **Product Groups:** 48

Date of Accounts	Mar 11	Mar 10	Mar 09
Working Capital	353	258	295
Fixed Assets	123	103	93
Current Assets	534	397	437

W P Warren Engineering Ltd
177-179 Alma Street, Birmingham, B19 2RL
Tel: 0121-359 2808 **Fax:** 0121-359 0027
Directors: M. Warren (MD), S. Docker (Fin)
Immediate Holding Company: W.P.WARREN ENGINEERING COMPANY LIMITED
Registration no: 00628283 **Date established:** 1959
Turnover: Up to £250,000 **No.of Employees:** 1 - 10 **Product Groups:** 48

Date of Accounts	Jul 12	Jul 11	Jul 10
Working Capital	622	626	627
Fixed Assets	160	164	171
Current Assets	642	648	663

Washcraft Appliances UK Ltd
St Clements Road, Birmingham, B7 5AF
Tel: 0121-328 4445 **Fax:** 01384-411415
E-mail: sales@washcraft.co.uk
Website: http://www.kingdomappliances.co.uk
Managers: M. Ibrar (District Mgr)
Immediate Holding Company: WASHCRAFT APPLIANCES (UK) LIMITED
Registration no: 04915397 **Date established:** 2003
No.of Employees: 11 - 20 **Product Groups:** 36, 40

Date of Accounts	Dec 11	Dec 10	Dec 09
Working Capital	507	321	162
Fixed Assets	1m	1m	994
Current Assets	645	578	951

Waterbury Bathroom Accessories Ltd
60 Adams Street, Birmingham, B7 4LT
Tel: 0121-333 6062 **Fax:** 0121-333 6459
E-mail: sales@waterbury.co.uk
Website: http://www.waterbury.co.uk
Bank(s): Barclays, Coventry Road
Managers: W. Smith (Sales Admin)
Immediate Holding Company: WATERBURY BATHROOM ACCESSORIES LTD.
Registration no: 01669010 **Date established:** 1982
No.of Employees: 11 - 20 **Product Groups:** 36

Date of Accounts	Sep 11	Sep 10	Sep 09
Working Capital	641	722	657
Fixed Assets	192	201	211
Current Assets	904	1m	966

Watson Engineering
12 Upper Gough Street, Birmingham, B1 1JG
Tel: 0121-643 1922 **Fax:** 0121-633 4019
Website: http://www.titanium-fasteners.com
Directors: G. Watson (Prop)
Immediate Holding Company: WATSON ENGINEERING (BHAM) LIMITED
Registration no: 03061963 **VAT No.:** GB 110 8873 80
Date established: 1995 **Turnover:** £1m - £2m **No.of Employees:** 1 - 10
Product Groups: 35, 48

Web Spiders Ltd
IBIC Holt Court South Jennens Road, Birmingham Science Park - Asto, Birmingham, B7 4EJ
Tel: 0845-1232592 **Fax:** 0870-7515124
E-mail: products@webspiders.com
Website: http://www.webspiders.com
Directors: S. Agarwalla (Dir)
Registration no: 04268772 **Turnover:** Up to £250,000
No.of Employees: 1 - 10 **Product Groups:** 37

Date of Accounts	Mar 10	Mar 09	Mar 08
Working Capital	30	21	19
Fixed Assets	5	4	5
Current Assets	185	196	132

G W Webb Plastics Ltd
Brookside Works Tyseley Industrial Estate Seeleys Road, Birmingham, B11 2LA
Tel: 0121-772 5968 **Fax:** 0121-773 7653
E-mail: sales@webbplastics.co.uk
Website: http://www.webbplastics.com
Bank(s): Lloyds TSB Bank plc
Directors: G. Osborne (MD), A. Osborne (Fin)
Managers: Y. Sullivan
Ultimate Holding Company: G A OSBORNE LIMITED
Immediate Holding Company: G.W.WEBB(PLASTICS)LIMITED
Registration no: 00682331 **VAT No.:** GB 111 5287 05
Date established: 1961 **Turnover:** £500,000 - £1m
No.of Employees: 21 - 50 **Product Groups:** 30, 31, 66

Date of Accounts	Jan 12	Jan 11	Jan 10
Working Capital	857	773	661
Fixed Assets	55	66	40
Current Assets	1m	1m	1m

Webster & Horsfall Ltd
Fordrough, Birmingham, B25 8DW
Tel: 0121-772 2555 **Fax:** 0121-772 0762
E-mail: sales@websterandhorsfall.co.uk
Website: http://www.websterandhorsfall.co.uk
Bank(s): National Westminster Bank Plc
Directors: E. O'Neill (Sales), H. Dulai (Fin), C. Horsfall (Ch)
Managers: M. Sherwood (Personnel), A. Parkinson (Purch Mgr)
Immediate Holding Company: WEBSTER & HORSFALL LIMITED
Registration no: 00035630 **VAT No.:** GB 110 1654 30
Date established: 1992 **Turnover:** £5m - £10m
No.of Employees: 101 - 250 **Product Groups:** 35

Date of Accounts	Dec 10	Dec 07	Dec 08
Sales Turnover	7m	N/A	N/A
Pre Tax Profit/Loss	554	762	437
Working Capital	3m	3m	3m
Fixed Assets	838	292	421
Current Assets	4m	4m	4m
Current Liabilities	573	424	651

Wells Fabrications & Developments Ltd
Unit 39a Wyrley Trading Estate Wyrley Road, Birmingham, B6 7DB
Tel: 0121-327 3354 **Fax:** 0121-327 3418
E-mail: ian.1.godwin@btconnect.com
Directors: E. Godwin (Fin), I. Godwin (MD)
Immediate Holding Company: WELLS FABRICATIONS & DEVELOPMENTS LIMITED
Registration no: 01014106 **VAT No.:** GB 110 7662 01
Date established: 1971 **Turnover:** £250,000 - £500,000
No.of Employees: 1 - 10 **Product Groups:** 84

Date of Accounts	Jun 11	Jun 10	Jun 09
Working Capital	-5	2	22
Fixed Assets	84	84	85

Current Assets	60	96	83

West Midlands Enterprise Ltd
Wellington House 31-34 Waterloo Street, Birmingham, B2 5TJ
Tel: 0121-236 8855 **Fax:** 0121-233 3942
E-mail: martynb@wm-enterprise.co.uk
Website: http://www.wm-enterprise.co.uk
Directors: M. Booth (Grp Chief Exec)
Ultimate Holding Company: WME GROUP LIMITED
Immediate Holding Company: SOUTH EAST GROWTH FUND MANAGERS LIMITED
Registration no: 03963896 **VAT No.:** GB 377 5212 39
Date established: 2000 **Turnover:** Up to £250,000
No.of Employees: 1 - 10 **Product Groups:** 80, 82

Date of Accounts	Mar 11	Mar 10	Mar 09
Sales Turnover	1	1	1
Pre Tax Profit/Loss	1	1	1
Working Capital	9	8	7
Current Assets	11	10	9
Current Liabilities	N/A	3	3

West Midlands Salvage
Aston Church Road Saltley, Birmingham, B8 1QF
Tel: 0121-328 1111 **Fax:** 0121-327 4140
E-mail: spares@taroni.co.uk
Directors: R. Taroni (MD)
Immediate Holding Company: WEST MIDLANDS LEISURE LIMITED
Registration no: 04530587 **Date established:** 2002
Turnover: £500,000 - £1m **No.of Employees:** 21 - 50 **Product Groups:** 66

Date of Accounts	Dec 11	Dec 10	Dec 09
Working Capital	-64	-110	-94
Fixed Assets	183	237	278
Current Assets	41	30	61
Current Liabilities	1	3	19

West Midlands Thermocouples
Unit 203 Telsen Industrial Centre Thomas Street, Birmingham, B6 4TN
Tel: 0121-359 0535 **Fax:** 0121-359 4005
E-mail: thermocouplesrus@aol.com
Website: http://www.westmidlandsthermocouples.com
Directors: M. Davies (Ptnr)
Immediate Holding Company: WEST MIDLAND THERMOCOUPLES LTD.
Registration no: 03349232 **Date established:** 1997
No.of Employees: 1 - 10 **Product Groups:** 38

Date of Accounts	Jun 11	Jun 10	Jun 09
Working Capital	71	64	63
Current Assets	161	125	119

Westley Engineering Ltd
120 Pritchett Street, Birmingham, B6 4EH
Tel: 0121-333 1925 **Fax:** 0121-333 1926
E-mail: engineering@westleyrichards.co.uk
Website: http://www.westleyengineering.co.uk
Directors: G. Dunne (MD)
Ultimate Holding Company: WESTLEY RICHARDS (HOLDINGS) LIMITED
Immediate Holding Company: WESTLEY ENGINEERING LIMITED
Registration no: 03612940 **Date established:** 1998 **Turnover:** £2m - £5m
No.of Employees: 11 - 20 **Product Groups:** 36, 39, 40

Date of Accounts	Sep 11	Sep 10	Sep 09
Working Capital	-112	-169	-222
Fixed Assets	461	534	648
Current Assets	812	831	630

Weston Beamor Ltd
3-8 Vyse Street Hockley, Birmingham, B18 6LT
Tel: 0121-236 3688 **Fax:** 0121-236 8100
E-mail: info@domino-wb.co.uk
Website: http://www.domino-wb.co.uk
Directors: M. Senior (MD), P. Fuller (Jt MD), V. Fuller (Dir)
Ultimate Holding Company: WESTON BEAMOR HOLDINGS LIMITED
Immediate Holding Company: WB THE CREATIVE JEWELLERY GROUP LIMITED
Registration no: 00465213 **VAT No.:** GB 109 7079 58
Date established: 1949 **Turnover:** £20m - £50m
No.of Employees: 51 - 100 **Product Groups:** 33

Date of Accounts	Dec 10	Dec 09	Dec 08
Sales Turnover	24m	21m	20m
Pre Tax Profit/Loss	2m	1m	892
Working Capital	5m	4m	4m
Fixed Assets	2m	1m	1m
Current Assets	8m	7m	7m
Current Liabilities	2m	2m	2m

Wheatsheaf Jewellers Tools
35 Spencer Street Hockley, Birmingham, B18 6DE
Tel: 0844-477 8193
E-mail: sales@wheatsheafproducts.com
Website: http://www.wheatsheafonline.co.uk
Directors: P. Parker (Admin)
Date established: 1920 **No.of Employees:** 11 - 20 **Product Groups:** 47

Wheeler Fabrications Ltd
Orchard House Sherbourne Road East, Balsall Heath, Birmingham, B12 9DJ
Tel: 0121-440 2345 **Fax:** 0121-440 4008
E-mail: wheelerfabs@btconnect.com
Website: http://www.wheelerfabrications.com
Directors: E. Onions (Fin), B. Wheeler (MD)
Immediate Holding Company: WHEELER FABRICATIONS LIMITED
Registration no: 04189377 **Date established:** 2001
No.of Employees: 1 - 10 **Product Groups:** 48

Date of Accounts	Jun 12	Jun 11	Jun 10
Working Capital	3	-5	-4
Fixed Assets	44	47	79
Current Assets	70	75	55

Widney Manufacturing Ltd
PO Box 133, Birmingham, B6 7SA
Tel: 0121-327 5500 **Fax:** 0121-328 2466
E-mail: info@widney.co.uk
Website: http://www.widney.co.uk
Bank(s): Barclays
Directors: M. Devers (Fin), S. Roberts (Dir)
Ultimate Holding Company: WIDNEY PLC
Immediate Holding Company: WIDNEY UK LIMITED
Registration no: 00950388 **VAT No.:** GB 971 5338 05
Date established: 1969 **Turnover:** £10m - £20m
No.of Employees: 101 - 250 **Product Groups:** 24, 33, 35, 36, 39, 68

Date of Accounts	Sep 07	Sep 06	Sep 05
Sales Turnover	16m	15m	14m
Pre Tax Profit/Loss	446	669	796

Working Capital	-495	215	-362
Fixed Assets	1m	1m	942
Current Assets	6m	5m	5m
Current Liabilities	636	342	609

John Wilde & Co Metals Ltd
66-72 Devon Street, Birmingham, B7 4SL
Tel: 0121-380 0300 **Fax:** 0121-359 5438
E-mail: enquiries@johnwilde.co.uk
Website: http://www.johnwilde.co.uk
Directors: R. Wilde (MD)
Ultimate Holding Company: J.M.B.R. HOLDINGS LIMITED
Immediate Holding Company: JOHN WILDE & CO.(METALS)LIMITED
Registration no: 00664767 **Date established:** 1960 **Turnover:** £2m - £5m
No.of Employees: 51 - 100 **Product Groups:** 23, 49

Date of Accounts	Dec 11	Dec 10	Dec 09
Working Capital	766	654	701
Fixed Assets	371	504	476
Current Assets	2m	2m	2m

A E Williams
6 Well Lane, Birmingham, B5 5TE
Tel: 0121-643 4756 **Fax:** 0121-643 2977
E-mail: info@pewtergiftware.com
Website: http://www.pewtergiftware.com
Directors: D. Williams (Ptnr)
Turnover: £1m - £2m **No.of Employees:** 11 - 20 **Product Groups:** 48, 49

E C Williams Ltd
17-25 Spencer Street, Birmingham, B18 6DN
Tel: 0121-236 2524 **Fax:** 0121-233 4931
E-mail: plating@ecwilliams.co.uk
Website: http://www.ecwilliams.co.uk
Bank(s): Barclays
Directors: H. Skouby (MD)
Immediate Holding Company: E.C.WILLIAMS LIMITED
Registration no: 00542108 **VAT No.:** GB 110 0503 56
Date established: 1954 **Turnover:** £1m - £2m **No.of Employees:** 21 - 50
Product Groups: 48

Date of Accounts	Dec 11	Dec 10	Dec 09
Working Capital	745	725	744
Fixed Assets	781	804	777
Current Assets	882	888	861

Willpower Breathing Air Ltd
6 Granby Business Park Granby Avenue, Birmingham, B33 0TJ
Tel: 0121-605 2600 **Fax:** 0121-605 2800
E-mail: info@willpower-ltd.co.uk
Website: http://willpower-ltd.co.uk
Directors: M. Williams (MD)
Immediate Holding Company: WILLPOWER BREATHING AIR LIMITED
Registration no: 01122356 **VAT No.:** GB 139 5670 41
Date established: 1973 **Turnover:** Up to £250,000
No.of Employees: 1 - 10 **Product Groups:** 38, 40, 42

Date of Accounts	Aug 11	Aug 10	Aug 09
Working Capital	97	96	107
Fixed Assets	20	26	24
Current Assets	122	133	130

Wilmat Ltd
Wilmat House 43 Steward Street, Birmingham, B18 7AE
Tel: 0121-454 7514 **Fax:** 0121-456 1792
E-mail: sales@wilmat-handling.co.uk
Website: http://www.wilmat-handling.co.uk
Bank(s): HSBC, Darlaston
Directors: T. Hands (MD)
Immediate Holding Company: WILMAT LIMITED
Registration no: 06498876 **VAT No.:** GB 110 1559 24
Date established: 2008 **Turnover:** £2m - £5m **No.of Employees:** 21 - 50
Product Groups: 45

Date of Accounts	Jun 12	Jun 11	Jun 10
Sales Turnover	N/A	N/A	2m
Pre Tax Profit/Loss	N/A	N/A	494
Working Capital	730	977	727
Fixed Assets	1m	853	862
Current Assets	1m	2m	1m
Current Liabilities	N/A	N/A	329

Wilts Wholesale Electrical
Units 1 & 2 Lichfield Road, Birmingham, B6 5SN
Tel: 0121-328 7070 **Fax:** 0121-328 0234
E-mail: lee.mills@wilts.co.uk
Website: http://www.wilts.co.uk
Managers: L. Mills (District Mgr)
Immediate Holding Company: WILTS WHOLESALE ELECTRICAL COMPANY,LIMITED
Registration no: 00679117 **Date established:** 1960 **Turnover:** £2m - £5m
No.of Employees: 21 - 50 **Product Groups:** 77

Wizard Pro-Gear Ltd
Unit 6 The 3b Business Village Alexandra Road, Handsworth, Birmingham, B21 0PD
Tel: 0121-507 1311 **Fax:** 0121-507 1311
E-mail: steven@wizardpro-gear.co.uk
Website: http://www.wizardpro-gear.co.uk
Directors: N. Kumar (Ptnr), S. Kumar (Ptnr)
Immediate Holding Company: WIZARD PRO GEAR LIMITED
Registration no: 05028816 **Date established:** 2004
Turnover: Up to £250,000 **No.of Employees:** 1 - 10 **Product Groups:** 24, 30, 49, 63

E V Wood Anodising Ltd
421 Tyburn Road, Birmingham, B24 8HJ
Tel: 0121-328 7646 **Fax:** 0121-327 1854
E-mail: carolyn@ebwood.co.uk
Website: http://www.anodised.co.uk
Directors: E. Wood (MD)
Immediate Holding Company: E.V. WOOD (ANODISING) LIMITED
Registration no: 01280765 **VAT No.:** GB 313 8831 62
Date established: 1976 **No.of Employees:** 11 - 20 **Product Groups:** 48

Date of Accounts	Jan 12	Jan 11	Jan 10
Working Capital	56	57	45
Fixed Assets	14	15	17
Current Assets	127	131	96

Workdirections Recruitment Agency
Town Hall Chambers 88-91 New Street, Birmingham, B2 4BA
Tel: 0121-329 7300 **Fax:** 0121-329 7301
E-mail: birgham@windsor-recruit.co.uk
Website: http://www.workdirections.co.uk
Managers: S. Opuni (District Mgr), S. Hughes, C. Davis (Mkt Research), S. Hoskins (Ops Mgr)
Date established: 2004 **No.of Employees:** 11 - 20 **Product Groups:** 86, 87

World Of Picture Frames
353 Upper Balsall Heath Road, Birmingham, B12 9DR
Tel: 0121-440 3340 **Fax:** 0121-440 2270
E-mail: mr_iqbal@hotmail.com
Website: http://www.worldofpictureframes.co.uk
Directors: M. Iqbal (Dir)
VAT No.: GB 109 3836 64 **Turnover:** Up to £250,000
No.of Employees: 1 - 10 **Product Groups:** 26, 36, 65

Wragge & Co LLP
55 Colmore Row, Birmingham, B3 2AS
Tel: 08709-031000 **Fax:** 08709-041099
E-mail: john_crabtree@wragge.com
Website: http://www.wragge.com
Bank(s): Lloyds, Birmingham
Directors: N. Blackwood (Tech Serv), P. Phayer (Fin), Q. Poole (Snr Part), L. Bellis (Pers), K. Crossley (Pers)
Immediate Holding Company: WRAGGE & CO LIMITED
Registration no: 02253188 **VAT No.:** GB 110 3363 31
Date established: 1988 **Turnover:** £75m - £125m
No.of Employees: 501 - 1000 **Product Groups:** 80

Wyko Industrial Distribution Ltd
Industrial Distribution Service Centre Great Lister Street, Nechells Green, Birmingham, B7 4DA
Tel: 0121-359 1591 **Fax:** 0121-359 4546
E-mail: birmingham@eriks.co.uk
Website: http://www.eriks.co.uk
Managers: R. Ellingson (District Mgr)
Immediate Holding Company: Wyko Holdings Ltd
Registration no: 03142338 **Turnover:** £250m - £500m
No.of Employees: 1 - 10 **Product Groups:** 66

Zero Clips Ltd
100 Charles Henry Street, Birmingham, B12 0SJ
Tel: 0121-622 3211 **Fax:** 0121-622 2813
E-mail: sales@zeroclips.com
Website: http://www.zeroclips.com
Directors: J. Lymer (Dir), B. Bates (Co Sec)
Immediate Holding Company: ZERO CLIPS LIMITED
Registration no: 01361665 **VAT No.:** GB 113 6321 14
Date established: 1978 **Turnover:** £500,000 - £1m
No.of Employees: 1 - 10 **Product Groups:** 30, 36

Date of Accounts	May 11	May 10	May 09
Working Capital	271	199	116
Fixed Assets	5	6	7
Current Assets	382	359	258

Zodiac Screw Gauge Ltd
15-17 Fortnum Close, Birmingham, B33 0LG
Tel: 0121-784 0474 **Fax:** 0121-789 7210
Managers: D. Lockley (Works Gen Mgr)
Immediate Holding Company: ZODIAC SCREW GAUGE LIMITED
Registration no: 01889248 **VAT No.:** GB 425 3504 75
Date established: 1985 **Turnover:** £500,000 - £1m
No.of Employees: 11 - 20 **Product Groups:** 35

Date of Accounts	Mar 08	Mar 07	Mar 06
Working Capital	58	110	93
Fixed Assets	71	70	79
Current Assets	315	327	298

Zodiac Stainless Products Co. Ltd
Selly Oak Industrial Estate Elliott Road, Birmingham, B29 6LR
Tel: 0121-472 7206 **Fax:** 0121-471 5109
E-mail: sales@zodiacspco.co.uk
Website: http://www.zodiacspco.co.uk
Directors: J. Burman (Sales), W. Lee (MD)
Managers: K. Evans (Tech Serv Mgr), J. Harvey (Personnel), B. Murray
Immediate Holding Company: ASTROLUXE LTD
Registration no: 11277497 **Turnover:** £5m - £10m
No.of Employees: 21 - 50 **Product Groups:** 49

Zoki UK Ltd
44 Alcester Street, Birmingham, B12 0PH
Tel: 0121-766 7888 **Fax:** 0121-766 7962
E-mail: zokiuk@btconnect.com
Website: http://www.zokiuk.co.uk
Directors: T. Overington (Dir)
Managers: T. Overington (Admin Off)
Immediate Holding Company: ZOKI U.K. LIMITED
Registration no: 03188109 **Date established:** 1996
Turnover: Up to £250,000 **No.of Employees:** 11 - 20 **Product Groups:** 40

Date of Accounts	Apr 09	Apr 08	Apr 07
Working Capital	-95	-94	-104
Fixed Assets	99	102	104
Current Assets	149	181	145

Brierley Hill

3d Engineering Midland Ltd
Unit 15 The Wallows Industrial Estate Fens Pool Avenue, Brierley Hill, DY5 1QA
Tel: 01384-480604 **Fax:** 01384-480604
E-mail: 3dengineering@btconnect.com
Directors: D. Butler (MD)
Immediate Holding Company: 3D ENGINEERING (MIDLANDS) LIMITED
Registration no: 04457418 **Date established:** 2002
Turnover: £250,000 - £500,000 **No.of Employees:** 1 - 10
Product Groups: 46

Date of Accounts	Aug 11	Aug 10	Aug 09
Working Capital	-10	-15	-21
Fixed Assets	29	25	30
Current Assets	40	46	47

A J T Equipment Ltd
Premier Partnership Estate Leys Road, Brierley Hill, DY5 3UP
Tel: 01384-482848 **Fax:** 01384-482849
E-mail: admin@ajtequipment.co.uk
Website: http://www.ajtequipment.co.uk
Directors: P. Gordon (MD)
Ultimate Holding Company: GORDON HOLDINGS LIMITED
Immediate Holding Company: A.J.T. EQUIPMENT LIMITED
Registration no: 00496932 **Date established:** 1951 **Turnover:** £1m - £2m
No.of Employees: 1 - 10 **Product Groups:** 38, 44, 67, 85

Date of Accounts	Sep 11	Sep 10	Sep 09
Sales Turnover	N/A	2m	544
Pre Tax Profit/Loss	N/A	265	-85
Working Capital	166	230	44
Fixed Assets	117	62	37
Current Assets	842	791	230
Current Liabilities	N/A	160	66

Acclaim Fasteners & Turned Parts
Unit 17 Premier Partnership Estate Leys Road, Brierley Hill, DY5 3UP
Tel: 01384-76263 **Fax:** 01384-76268
Website: http://www.acclaimfasteners.co.uk
Directors: G. Valentine (Prop)
Turnover: £250,000 - £500,000 **No.of Employees:** 1 - 10
Product Groups: 35

Airbloc
AmbiRad Ltd (Airbloc Division) Fens Pool Avenue, Brierley Hill, DY5 1QA
Tel: 01384-489700 **Fax:** 01384-489707
E-mail: marketing@airbloc.co.uk
Website: http://www.airbloc.co.uk
Bank(s): Barclays Bank Plc, High Street, Worcester
Directors: M. Brookes (MD), P. O'Donohue (Fin), C. Yates (Fab), F. Staniland (Sales), J. Fletcher (Ch)
Managers: S. Hartles
Registration no: 01390934 **Turnover:** £1m - £2m **Product Groups:** 40

Alloy Wire International Ltd
Unit 5a Narrowboat Way Hurst Business Park, Brierley Hill, DY5 1UF
Tel: 01384-566775 **Fax:** 01384-410074
E-mail: sales@alloywire.com
Website: http://www.alloywire.com
Directors: M. Cobb (Fin), M. Venables (MD)
Immediate Holding Company: ALLOY WIRE INTERNATIONAL LIMITED
Registration no: 03722788 **Date established:** 1999
No.of Employees: 11 - 20 **Product Groups:** 35, 37

Date of Accounts	Mar 11	Mar 10	Mar 09
Working Capital	1m	840	342
Fixed Assets	727	520	559
Current Assets	3m	2m	2m

Arcwell Mobile Welding
64 Tansey Green Road, Brierley Hill, DY5 4TE
Tel: 07860-419626 **Fax:** 01384-78009
Directors: J. Hopton (Prop), J. Hopton (MD)
No.of Employees: 1 - 10 **Product Groups:** 35, 48, 84

Arvon Die & Tool Company
Oak Street Quarry Bank, Brierley Hill, DY5 2JH
Tel: 01384-567970 **Fax:** 01384-567970
E-mail: enquires@arvon.co.uk
Directors: R. Cartright (Prop)
Turnover: Up to £250,000 **No.of Employees:** 1 - 10 **Product Groups:** 30, 35, 36, 42, 46, 48, 67

Ashworth Europe Ltd
Unit E5 The Wallows Industrial Estate Fens Pool Avenue, Brierley Hill, DY5 1QA
Tel: 01384-355000 **Fax:** 01384-355001
E-mail: vdavies@ashwortheurope.co.uk
Website: http://www.ashworth.com
Directors: P. Copeland (Co Sec)
Managers: V. Davies (Sales Admin)
Ultimate Holding Company: ASHWORTH BROS INC (USA)
Immediate Holding Company: ASHWORTH EUROPE LIMITED
Registration no: 02918177 **VAT No.:** GB 648 5178 04
Date established: 1994 **Turnover:** £5m - £10m **No.of Employees:** 1 - 10
Product Groups: 30, 35, 39, 41, 45, 48

Date of Accounts	Dec 11	Dec 10	Dec 09
Working Capital	641	728	283
Fixed Assets	240	243	211
Current Assets	2m	2m	2m

B S Burner Services Ltd
Unit E1 The Wallows Industrial Estate Fens Pool Avenue, Brierley Hill, DY5 1QA
Tel: 01384-571162 **Fax:** 01384-442998
E-mail: davidgorst@burnerservices.co.uk
Website: http://www.burnerservices.co.uk
Directors: D. Gorst (MD)
Immediate Holding Company: B.S. BURNER SERVICES LIMITED
Registration no: 02293993 **Date established:** 1988
No.of Employees: 1 - 10 **Product Groups:** 35, 36, 39

Date of Accounts	Sep 11	Sep 10	Sep 09
Working Capital	69	79	63
Fixed Assets	83	29	9
Current Assets	293	189	142

J Barnsley Cranes Ltd
Unit 1 The Wallows Indl-Est Wallows Road, Brierley Hill, DY5 1QB
Tel: 01384-484811 **Fax:** 01384- 484333
E-mail: sales@jbarnsleycranes.com
Website: http://www.jbarnsleycranes.com
Bank(s): Barclays
Directors: D. Barnsley (Sales), J. Satchwell (Dir), J. Slim (Works), J. Satchwell (MD), M. Banner (Dir)
Immediate Holding Company: J. BARNSLEY CRANES LIMITED
Registration no: 02369982 **VAT No.:** GB 610 9545 52
Date established: 1989 **Turnover:** £10m - £20m
No.of Employees: 21 - 50 **Product Groups:** 35, 38, 39, 45, 67

Date of Accounts	Mar 11	Mar 10	Mar 09
Sales Turnover	10m	6m	7m
Pre Tax Profit/Loss	2m	607	497
Working Capital	3m	2m	1m
Fixed Assets	607	491	549
Current Assets	4m	4m	3m
Current Liabilities	588	674	301

Baxcrest Ltd
Unit 5 Canal View Industrial Estate Brettell Lane, Brierley Hill, DY5 3LQ
Tel: 01384-261412 **Fax:** 01384-70167
E-mail: sales@baxcrest.co.uk
Website: http://www.baxcrest.co.uk

see next page

***Baxcrest Ltd** - Cont'd*

Directors: S. Benson (Fin)
Managers: C. Hughes, N. Aston (Chief Mgr)
Immediate Holding Company: BAXCREST LIMITED
Registration no: 02068927 **VAT No.:** GB 441 8541 54
Date established: 1986 **Turnover:** £1m - £2m **No.of Employees:** 21 - 50
Product Groups: 35, 36

Date of Accounts	Dec 11	Dec 10	Dec 09
Working Capital	155	124	137
Fixed Assets	138	148	104
Current Assets	609	630	468

M Billingham & Co. Ltd

Little Cottage Street, Brierley Hill, DY5 1RG
Tel: 01384-482828 **Fax:** 01384-482399
E-mail: martin@billingham.co.uk
Website: http://www.billingham.co.uk
Bank(s): Lloyds TSB
Directors: R. Billingham (Dir), M. Billingham (MD), M. Billingham (Ch & MD)
Managers: H. Billingham (Purch Mgr)
Immediate Holding Company: M. BILLINGHAM & CO. LIMITED
Registration no: 01714494 **VAT No.:** 281 2026 88 **Date established:** 1983
Turnover: Up to £250,000 **No.of Employees:** 21 - 50 **Product Groups:** 22

Date of Accounts	Dec 07	Dec 06	Dec 05
Working Capital	244	183	125
Fixed Assets	54	66	63
Current Assets	444	368	331
Current Liabilities	200	185	206
Total Share Capital	5	5	5

Black Country Stoves

36 High Street, Brierley Hill, DY5 3AE
Tel: 01384-262060
Directors: D. Wellings (Prop)
Immediate Holding Company: BLACK COUNTRY SWEEPERS LIMITED
Date established: 2012 **No.of Employees:** 1 - 10 **Product Groups:** 40

Date of Accounts	Mar 11	Mar 10	Mar 09
Working Capital	-135	-147	-145
Fixed Assets	286	290	300
Current Assets	31	14	18
Current Liabilities	N/A	12	116

Noah Bloomer & Sons Ltd

Oak Street Quarry Bank, Brierley Hill, DY5 2JH
Tel: 01384-566021 **Fax:** 01384-410793
E-mail: rjbloomer@noahbloomer.co.uk
Website: http://www.noahbloomer.co.uk
Directors: R. Bloomer (MD), N. Bloomer (Fin)
Immediate Holding Company: NOAH BLOOMER LIMITED
Registration no: 00104308 **Date established:** 2009
No.of Employees: 1 - 10 **Product Groups:** 35, 45

Date of Accounts	Jun 11	Jun 10	Jun 09
Working Capital	85	40	-20
Fixed Assets	958	982	908
Current Assets	105	77	46
Current Liabilities	N/A	2	N/A

Bord Na Mona Ltd

4 Harbour Buildings Waterfront West Dudley Road, Brierley Hill, DY5 1LN
Tel: 01384-486978 **Fax:** 01384-486979
E-mail: enquiriesuk@bnm.ie
Website: http://www.bnm.ie
Directors: B. Malony (MD), J. Ryan (Co Sec)
Managers: F. Pietrzak (Sales Prom Mgr), I. Jackson (I.T. Exec)
Ultimate Holding Company: BORD NA MONA PUBLIC LIMITED COMPANY
Immediate Holding Company: BORD NA MONA ENVIRONMENTAL PRODUCTS UK LIMITED
Registration no: 02788583 **Date established:** 1993
Turnover: £500,000 - £1m **No.of Employees:** 1 - 10 **Product Groups:** 40, 42, 52, 54

Brandenburg UK Ltd (a division of Astec Europe Ltd)

29 Navigation Drive Hurst Business Park, Brierley Hill, DY5 1UT
Tel: 01384-472900 **Fax:** 01384-472911
E-mail: sales@b-one.com
Website: http://www.b-one.com
Directors: M. Kaye (Dir)
Managers: L. Collins, T. Ragg (Chief Buyer), S. Underwood, N. Roberts (Mktg Serv Mgr), M. Szczepanik (Tech Serv Mgr), M. Cubbin (Mgr)
Ultimate Holding Company: BRANDENBURG HOLDINGS LIMITED
Immediate Holding Company: BRANDENBURG (UK) LIMITED
Registration no: 03604238 **Date established:** 1998 **Turnover:** £5m - £10m
No.of Employees: 51 - 100 **Product Groups:** 37, 38

Date of Accounts	Jan 11	Jan 10	Feb 09
Sales Turnover	8m	6m	N/A
Pre Tax Profit/Loss	1m	616	311
Working Capital	2m	1m	725
Fixed Assets	374	309	474
Current Assets	4m	3m	2m
Current Liabilities	778	783	401

British Crystal Ltd (Brierley Hill Crystal)

Pedmore Road, Brierley Hill, DY5 1TJ
Tel: 01384-77701 **Fax:** 01384-482580
E-mail: sales@britishcrystal.co.uk
Website: http://www.brierleyhillcrystal.co.uk
Product Groups: 33, 48, 49, 65

Brockmoor Foundry Co. Ltd

The Leys, Brierley Hill, DY5 3UJ
Tel: 01384-480026 **Fax:** 01384-480032
E-mail: reception@brockmoor.co.uk
Website: http://www.brockmoor.co.uk
Bank(s): Barclays
Directors: J. Leppington (MD)
Immediate Holding Company: BROCKMOOR FOUNDRY COMPANY LIMITED(THE)
Registration no: 00317267 **VAT No.:** GB 276 8038 28
Date established: 1936 **Turnover:** £10m - £20m
No.of Employees: 101 - 250 **Product Groups:** 34

Date of Accounts	Mar 12	Mar 11	Mar 10
Sales Turnover	15m	12m	7m
Pre Tax Profit/Loss	907	476	-138
Working Capital	3m	2m	2m
Fixed Assets	3m	2m	2m
Current Assets	5m	5m	4m
Current Liabilities	399	452	307

Bronx Engineering Ltd

Unit 48 Enterprise Trading Estate Pedmore Road, Brierley Hill, DY5 1TX
Tel: 01384-486648 **Fax:** 01384-486440
E-mail: operations@bronx.co.uk
Website: http://www.bronx.co.uk
Directors: B. Lunn (MD)
Immediate Holding Company: BRONX ENGINEERING LIMITED
Registration no: 04253229 **Date established:** 2001 **Turnover:** £2m - £5m
No.of Employees: 11 - 20 **Product Groups:** 46

Date of Accounts	Oct 11	Oct 10	Oct 09
Sales Turnover	3m	3m	2m
Pre Tax Profit/Loss	15	223	156
Working Capital	170	135	90
Fixed Assets	46	21	31
Current Assets	669	1m	996
Current Liabilities	234	682	719

C P L Petroleum Ltd

The Leys Leys Road, Brockmoor, Brierley Hill, DY5 3UQ
Tel: 01384-76211 **Fax:** 01384-572664
E-mail: sales@cplpetroleum.co.uk
Website: http://www.cplpetroleum.co.uk
Managers: D. Astbury (Depot Mgr)
Ultimate Holding Company: DCC Ltd
Immediate Holding Company: Energy Acquisitions UK Ltd
Registration no: 03003860 **VAT No.:** GB 275 0972 38
Turnover: £250m - £500m **No.of Employees:** 1 - 10 **Product Groups:** 66

Camis Ltd (Incorporating Advance Power)

Unit A-B Station Drive, Brierley Hill, DY5 3JZ
Tel: 01384-471360 **Fax:** 01384-471361
E-mail: sales@camis-group.com
Website: http://www.camis.com
Directors: B. Hockley (MD), J. Russell (Sales)
Managers: L. Brookes (Fin Mgr), R. Calderbank
Ultimate Holding Company: CHILTERN GROUP LIMITED
Immediate Holding Company: CAMIS LIMITED
Registration no: 02038599 **Date established:** 1986
Turnover: £500,000 - £1m **No.of Employees:** 11 - 20
Product Groups: 35, 37, 38, 39, 40, 67

Date of Accounts	Mar 12	Mar 11	Mar 10
Working Capital	583	524	545
Fixed Assets	101	122	139
Current Assets	1m	1m	1m

Carbern Pipes & Fittings

Unit 3 Bevan Industrial Estate, Brierley Hill, DY5 3TF
Tel: 01384-76111 **Fax:** 01384- 262309
E-mail: sales@carbern.co.uk
Website: http://www.carbern.co.uk
Bank(s): Yorkshire Bank PLC
Directors: J. Rankine (Fin), M. Carey (MD)
Immediate Holding Company: CAREY HOLDINGS LTD
Registration no: 03042157 **Date established:** 1981 **Turnover:** £1m - £2m
No.of Employees: 11 - 20 **Product Groups:** 34, 35, 36, 48

Chapel Windows Ltd

Bevan Industrial Estate, Brierley Hill, DY5 3TF
Tel: 01384-571315 **Fax:** 01384-480403
Bank(s): Barclays
Directors: C. Carroll (MD), W. Carroll (Co Sec)
Ultimate Holding Company: CHAPEL HOLDINGS LIMITED
Immediate Holding Company: CHAPEL WINDOWS LIMITED
Registration no: 01782706 **VAT No.:** GB 409 3392 50
Date established: 1984 **No.of Employees:** 21 - 50 **Product Groups:** 25, 35

Date of Accounts	Feb 08	Feb 11	Feb 10
Working Capital	460	450	424
Fixed Assets	N/A	43	N/A
Current Assets	860	818	749

Citizen Machinery UK Ltd

9a Navigation Drive Hurst Business Park, Brierley Hill, DY5 1UT
Tel: 01384-489500 **Fax:** 01384-489501
E-mail: sales@citizen-miyano.co.uk
Website: http://www.citizenmachinery.co.uk
Managers: G. Bryant (Mgr)
Immediate Holding Company: MIYANO MACHINERY UK LIMITED
Registration no: 01744265 **VAT No.:** GB 388 6617 92
Date established: 1983 **Turnover:** £2m - £5m **No.of Employees:** 1 - 10
Product Groups: 46

Date of Accounts	Dec 11	Dec 10	Dec 09
Sales Turnover	N/A	6m	N/A
Pre Tax Profit/Loss	-811	158	N/A
Working Capital	N/A	495	652
Fixed Assets	N/A	316	86
Current Assets	N/A	3m	1m
Current Liabilities	N/A	416	N/A

Cooper & Jackson Ltd

Evans Works Pedmore Road Industrial Estate, Brierley Hill, DY5 1TJ
Tel: 01384-486600 **Fax:** 01384-480444
E-mail: chris.cooper@cooperandjackson.co.uk
Website: http://www.cooperandjackson.co.uk
Directors: C. Cooper (MD)
Immediate Holding Company: COOPER & JACKSON (SHEARING) LIMITED
Registration no: 06432773 **Date established:** 2007 **Turnover:** £2m - £5m
No.of Employees: 11 - 20 **Product Groups:** 48, 66, 84

Cotmor Tool & Presswork Co. Ltd

Unit 1A Albion Works Moor Street, Brierley Hill, DY5 3SZ
Tel: 01384-482993 **Fax:** 01384-482995
E-mail: david.cotterill@cotmor.co.uk
Website: http://www.cotmor.co.uk
Bank(s): Lloyds, Dudley
Directors: D. Cotterill (MD)
Immediate Holding Company: COTMOR TOOL & PRESSWORK CO. LIMITED
Registration no: 00517804 **Date established:** 1953 **Turnover:** £1m - £2m
No.of Employees: 11 - 20 **Product Groups:** 48

Date of Accounts	Nov 11	Nov 10	Nov 09
Working Capital	276	433	428
Fixed Assets	6	120	193
Current Assets	678	582	641

Cromwell Plastics Ltd

53-54 New Street Quarry Bank, Brierley Hill, DY5 2AZ
Tel: 01384-564146 **Fax:** 01384-561645
E-mail: sales@cromwell-plastics.co.uk
Website: http://www.cromwellplastics.co.uk
Directors: R. McLaughlin (Dir)
Immediate Holding Company: CROMWELL PLASTICS LIMITED
Registration no: 01082373 **VAT No.:** GB 227 835 020
Date established: 1972 **Turnover:** £500,000 - £1m
No.of Employees: 1 - 10 **Product Groups:** 30

Date of Accounts	Jan 11	Jan 10	Jan 09
Working Capital	105	53	57
Fixed Assets	2	2	3
Current Assets	333	205	290
Current Liabilities	N/A	N/A	38

Davicon Mezzazine Floors Ltd

The Wallows Industrial Estate Fens Pool Avenue, Brierley Hill, DY5 1QA
Tel: 01384-572851 **Fax:** 01384-265098
E-mail: sales@davicon.com
Website: http://www.davicon.com
Directors: D. Kettleborough (Comm), P. Watson (Dir)
Ultimate Holding Company: GROVE INDUSTRIES LIMITED
Immediate Holding Company: DAVICON MEZZANINE FLOORS LIMITED
Registration no: 07014080 **Date established:** 2009 **Turnover:** £5m - £10m
No.of Employees: 21 - 50 **Product Groups:** 29, 30, 35, 67

Date of Accounts	Mar 12	Mar 11	Mar 10
Working Capital	397	137	-25
Fixed Assets	364	264	176
Current Assets	2m	1m	854

Definitive Computing Ltd

Haldon House 385 Brettell Lane, Brierley Hill, DY5 3LQ
Tel: 01384-261727 **Fax:** 01384-261727
E-mail: info@dclsoftware.co.uk
Website: http://www.dclsoftware.co.uk
Directors: A. Aaaa (MD)
Immediate Holding Company: DEFINITIVE COMPUTING LIMITED
Registration no: 01590372 **VAT No.:** GB 428 6638 21
Date established: 1981 **Turnover:** Up to £250,000
No.of Employees: 1 - 10 **Product Groups:** 84

Date of Accounts	Sep 11	Sep 10	Sep 09
Working Capital	-34	-2	-2
Fixed Assets	1	2	2
Current Assets	5	30	38

Drakeset Ltd

Unit 3 Tansey Green Road, Brierley Hill, DY5 4TL
Tel: 01384-79487 **Fax:** 01384-70143
E-mail: tony.pope@btconnect.com
Website: http://www.drakeset.com
Bank(s): Lloyds TSB Bank plc
Directors: A. Pope (MD), T. Pope (Dir), L. Moore (Fin)
Immediate Holding Company: DRAKESET LIMITED
Registration no: 01770337 **VAT No.:** GB 388 6674 80
Date established: 1983 **Turnover:** £500,000 - £1m
No.of Employees: 11 - 20 **Product Groups:** 52

Date of Accounts	Jan 12	Jan 11	Jan 10
Working Capital	45	12	25
Fixed Assets	45	52	66
Current Assets	401	323	340

Dustair Ltd

Unit 13 Pedmore Industrial Estate Pedmore Rd, Brierley Hill, DY5 1TJ
Tel: 01384-76662 **Fax:** 01384-77227
E-mail: sales@dustair.co.uk
Website: http://www.dustair.co.uk
Directors: I. Marshall (Dir)
Registration no: 00925805 **Turnover:** £500,000 - £1m
No.of Employees: 11 - 20 **Product Groups:** 30, 40, 41, 42, 52, 54

Date of Accounts	Jan 12	Jan 11	Jan 10
Working Capital	217	153	158
Fixed Assets	143	133	137
Current Assets	395	387	239

Dyson Products Ltd

Moor Street Unit G Brockmoore Park Industrial Estate, Brierley Hill, DY5 3TG
Tel: 01384-77833 **Fax:** 01384- 263724
Website: http://www.dysonproductsltd.com
Directors: L. Evans (Dir)
Ultimate Holding Company: EASIFLO INVESTMENTS LIMITED
Immediate Holding Company: DYSON PRODUCTS LIMITED
Registration no: 00416853 **VAT No.:** GB 277 2190 46
Date established: 1946 **Turnover:** £1m - £2m **No.of Employees:** 1 - 10
Product Groups: 40, 48, 61, 63, 84

Date of Accounts	Jul 11	Jul 10	Jul 09
Working Capital	450	459	459
Fixed Assets	16	28	29
Current Assets	624	590	680

Easiflo Investments Ltd

Unit 1 Moor Street Industrial Estate Moor Street, Brierley Hill, DY5 3TS
Tel: 01384-77833 **Fax:** 01384-263724
E-mail: sales@dyson.com
Website: http://www.dysonproducts.com
Bank(s): HSBC Bank plc
Directors: H. Evans (Dir), S. Evans (Co Sec), L. Evans (Dir), E. Newman (Dir)
Immediate Holding Company: Easiflo Investments Ltd
Registration no: 00737906 **VAT No.:** GB 277 2190 46
Turnover: £250,000 - £500,000 **No.of Employees:** 11 - 20
Product Groups: 48

Electro Arc Co. Ltd

The Wallows Industrial Estate Fens Pool Avenue, Brierley Hill, DY5 1QA
Tel: 01384-263426 **Fax:** 01384-79017
E-mail: sales@electroarc.co.uk
Website: http://www.electroarc.com
Directors: B. Harvey (Fin), H. Stark (MD)
Immediate Holding Company: ELECTRO ARC COMPANY LIMITED
Registration no: 01141402 **VAT No.:** GB 112 1131 50
Date established: 1973 **Turnover:** £500,000 - £1m
No.of Employees: 1 - 10 **Product Groups:** 36, 38

Date of Accounts	Apr 11	Apr 10	Apr 09
Working Capital	-100	-30	70
Fixed Assets	201	209	223
Current Assets	178	145	129

Express Valve Services Ltd

Dudley Road, Brierley Hill, DY5 1HR
Tel: 01384-263872 **Fax:** 01384-480148
E-mail: marketing@expressvalves.co.uk
Website: http://www.expressvalves.co.uk
Bank(s): HSBC Bank plc

Directors: V. Crompton (Dir)
Immediate Holding Company: EXPRESS VALVE SERVICES LIMITED
Registration no: 01935013 **VAT No.:** GB 428 6818 19
Date established: 1985 **Turnover:** £1m - £2m **No.of Employees:** 11 - 20
Product Groups: 36, 66

Date of Accounts	Aug 11	Aug 10	Aug 09
Working Capital	232	219	227
Fixed Assets	4	7	11
Current Assets	501	411	395

Falcon Shipping Ltd
Two Locks Hurst Business Park, Brierley Hill, DY5 1UU
Tel: 01384-471600 **Fax:** 01384-471610
E-mail: sales@falconshipping.co.uk
Website: http://www.falconshipping.co.uk
Directors: J. Silvey (MD)
Managers: J. Rudge
Ultimate Holding Company: TRANS GLOBAL PLC
Immediate Holding Company: FALCON SHIPPING LIMITED
Registration no: 01312379 **VAT No.:** GB 113 4497 84
Date established: 1977 **Turnover:** £2m - £5m **No.of Employees:** 1 - 10
Product Groups: 76

Date of Accounts	Dec 11	Jun 10	Jun 09
Working Capital	27	82	54
Fixed Assets	51	313	337
Current Assets	605	1m	911

Fibercill
The Moorings Hurst Business Park, Brierley Hill, DY5 1UF
Tel: 01384-482221 **Fax:** 01384-482212
E-mail: mail@fibercill.com
Website: http://www.fibercill.co.uk
Directors: J. Stoker (Legal), M. Burlton (MD)
Managers: I. Cameron (Sales Prom Mgr), P. Price (Mgr), D. Bradley (Sales Admin)
Immediate Holding Company: Hickman Industries Ltd
Registration no: 00437587 **Turnover:** £10m - £20m
No.of Employees: 1 - 10 **Product Groups:** 25

Formula One Pipelines Ltd
Unit 20 Delph Road, Brierley Hill, DY5 2TW
Tel: 01384-482211 **Fax:** 01384-482223
E-mail: mike@mikeformula1.org.uk
Website: http://www.yescomputers.co.uk
Directors: M. Leadbeater (MD)
Immediate Holding Company: FORMULA ONE PIPELINES LIMITED
Registration no: 02953171 **Date established:** 1994
Turnover: Up to £250,000 **No.of Employees:** 1 - 10 **Product Groups:** 36

Date of Accounts	Oct 11	Oct 10	Oct 09
Working Capital	461	442	379
Fixed Assets	10	11	12
Current Assets	625	782	621

Freecom Internet Services Ltd
E4 Hagley Court North The Waterfront Level Street, Brierley Hill, DY5 1XF
Tel: 01384-487800 **Fax:** 08444-720 033
E-mail: enquiries@freecom.net
Website: http://www.freecom.net
Managers: M. Geer (Chief Mgr)
Immediate Holding Company: FREECOM INTERNET SERVICES LIMITED
Registration no: 06657464 **Date established:** 2008 **Turnover:** £2m - £5m
No.of Employees: 11 - 20 **Product Groups:** 79

Date of Accounts	Dec 09	Apr 11	Apr 10
Working Capital	128	33	-62
Fixed Assets	21	10	19
Current Assets	152	150	88

G C G Electrical Wholesalers
58-64 Albion Street, Brierley Hill, DY5 3EE
Tel: 01384-74681 **Fax:** 01384-78246
Website: http://www.edmundson-electrical.co.uk/
Managers: T. Follows (District Mgr)
Immediate Holding Company: MARLOWE HOLDINGS LTD
Registration no: 01297669 **VAT No.:** GB 287 6691 94
Turnover: £2m - £5m **No.of Employees:** 1 - 10 **Product Groups:** 77

G N J Equipment Ltd
Meeting Lane, Brierley Hill, DY5 3LB
Tel: 01384-480818 **Fax:** 01384-78176
E-mail: info@gnjengineering.co.uk
Website: http://www.gnjengineering.co.uk
Directors: A. James (MD)
Immediate Holding Company: G.N.J. (EQUIPMENT) LIMITED
Registration no: 01446409 **VAT No.:** GB 300 2623 27
Date established: 1979 **Turnover:** £1m - £2m **No.of Employees:** 1 - 10
Product Groups: 48

Date of Accounts	Mar 12	Mar 11	Mar 10
Working Capital	2	2	2
Current Assets	2	2	3

Global Fasteners Ltd
Unit 19 Delph Industrial Estate Delph Road, Brierley Hill, DY5 2UA
Tel: 01384-480793 **Fax:** 01384-482522
E-mail: sales@global-fasteners.co.uk
Website: http://www.global-fasteners.co.uk
Directors: A. Hickman (MD)
Immediate Holding Company: GLOBAL FASTENERS LIMITED
Registration no: 05258240 **Date established:** 2004
No.of Employees: 1 - 10 **Product Groups:** 22, 24, 30, 35, 36, 37, 40, 45, 46, 49, 66

Date of Accounts	Oct 11	Oct 10	Oct 09
Working Capital	6	5	4
Fixed Assets	2	2	3
Current Assets	67	68	67

Grant Handling Ltd
23-24 Delph Road, Brierley Hill, DY5 2TW
Tel: 01384-77881 **Fax:** 01384- 480779
E-mail: johncooper@forktrucks.co.uk
Website: http://www.forktrucks.co.uk
Managers: J. Cooper (Depot Mgr)
Ultimate Holding Company: GHL HOLDINGS LIMITED
Immediate Holding Company: GRANT HANDLING LIMITED
Registration no: 01109065 **Date established:** 1973
No.of Employees: 11 - 20 **Product Groups:** 35, 39, 45

Harco Engineering Ltd
Canal Street, Brierley Hill, DY5 1JJ
Tel: 01384-480280 **Fax:** 01384-480399
E-mail: martyn@harcoeng.co.uk
Website: http://www.harcoengineering.co.uk
Directors: M. Hughes (MD), K. Hughes (MD)
Immediate Holding Company: HARCO ENGINEERING LIMITED
Registration no: 03621534 **Date established:** 1998
Turnover: £250,000 - £500,000 **No.of Employees:** 21 - 50
Product Groups: 48

Date of Accounts	Feb 12	Feb 11	Feb 10
Working Capital	-177	-155	-158
Fixed Assets	799	664	675
Current Assets	334	243	164
Current Liabilities	511	N/A	N/A

Harris Walton Lifting Gear Ltd
Two Woods Lane, Brierley Hill, DY5 1TR
Tel: 01384-74071 **Fax:** 01384-74070
E-mail: sales@harriswaltonliftinggear.co.uk
Website: http://www.harriswaltonliftinggear.co.uk
Directors: C. Hemmings (MD)
Immediate Holding Company: HARRIS-WALTON LIFTING GEAR LIMITED
Registration no: 00636077 **Date established:** 1959
Turnover: £500,000 - £1m **No.of Employees:** 11 - 20
Product Groups: 23, 35, 48

Date of Accounts	Aug 11	Aug 10	Aug 09
Working Capital	550	495	535
Fixed Assets	180	234	246
Current Assets	699	664	795

Heath Lambert
Admiral House Waterfront East Level Street, Brierley Hill, DY5 1XG
Tel: 01384-822222 **Fax:** 01782-618851
E-mail: bduffin@heathlambert.com
Website: http://www.heathlambert.com
Directors: B. Duffin (Dir), B. Duffin (Chief Op Offcr), D. Ghiglieri (Dir), M. Bruce (MD)
Ultimate Holding Company: HLG HOLDINGS LTD
Immediate Holding Company: FRIARY INTERMEDIATE LTD
Registration no: 01199129 **Turnover:** £125m - £250m
No.of Employees: 21 - 50 **Product Groups:** 80, 82

Hinton Perry Davenhill
Dreadnought Works, Brierley Hill, DY5 4TH
Tel: 01384-77405 **Fax:** 01384-74553
E-mail: office@drednort.tiles.co.uk
Website: http://www.dreadnought-tiles.co.uk
Bank(s): HSBC Bank plc
Directors: C. Davenhill (Fin)
Managers: D. Francis (Sales Admin), D. Patrick-smith (Mktg Serv Mgr)
Immediate Holding Company: HINTON PERRY & DAVENHILL LIMITED
Registration no: 00610931 **VAT No.:** GB 276 9589 83
Date established: 1958 **Turnover:** £2m - £5m **No.of Employees:** 21 - 50
Product Groups: 33

Date of Accounts	Mar 12	Mar 11	Mar 10
Sales Turnover	4m	4m	4m
Pre Tax Profit/Loss	90	5	297
Working Capital	5m	5m	5m
Fixed Assets	3m	3m	3m
Current Assets	6m	6m	5m
Current Liabilities	405	378	386

Hudsons Of Dudley Ltd
Canal Street, Brierley Hill, DY5 1JJ
Tel: 01384-262126 **Fax:** 01384-481170
E-mail: hudsonsofdudley@aol.com
Directors: M. Hudson (Dir)
Immediate Holding Company: HUDSONS OF DUDLEY LIMITED
Registration no: 00824137 **VAT No.:** GB 278 1002 72
Date established: 1964 **Turnover:** £1m - £2m **No.of Employees:** 1 - 10
Product Groups: 66, 72

Date of Accounts	Oct 11	Oct 10	Oct 09
Sales Turnover	1m	2m	1m
Pre Tax Profit/Loss	158	755	155
Working Capital	778	961	630
Fixed Assets	720	713	799
Current Assets	866	1m	718
Current Liabilities	49	268	66

Imperial Metal Polishing Ltd
Unit 48c Premier Partnership Estate Leys Road, Brierley Hill, DY5 3UP
Tel: 01384-77099 **Fax:** 01384-483892
E-mail: imperialpol@aol.com
Directors: A. Rudge (Fin), R. Clewes (MD)
Immediate Holding Company: IMPERIAL METAL POLISHING LIMITED
Registration no: 07017624 **Date established:** 2009
Turnover: Up to £250,000 **No.of Employees:** 1 - 10 **Product Groups:** 46, 48

Date of Accounts	Sep 11	Sep 10
Working Capital	3	-1
Fixed Assets	12	14
Current Assets	44	33

Improvement Systems Ltd
Waterfront Business Park, Brierley Hill, DY5 3ZU
Tel: 07791-256808 **Fax:** 01384-74936
E-mail: info@improvement-systems.co.uk
Website: http://www.improvement-systems.co.uk
Managers: P. Smith
Immediate Holding Company: IMPROVEMENT SYSTEMS LIMITED
Registration no: 05831051 **Date established:** 2006
No.of Employees: 1 - 10 **Product Groups:** 80

Date of Accounts	May 09	Nov 11	Nov 10
Working Capital	N/A	1	1
Current Assets	N/A	4	6

Justkarndean
85 Blewitt Street, Brierley Hill, DY5 4AL
Tel: 07981-878863
E-mail: jason@justkarndean.co.uk
Website: http://www.justkarndean.co.uk
Directors: J. Hall (Prop)
No.of Employees: 1 - 10 **Product Groups:** 30, 52, 63, 66

K D S Engineering
Unit 7 Moor Street Industrial Estate, Brierley Hill, DY5 3ST
Tel: 01384-265826
Directors: D. Rew (Prop)
No.of Employees: 1 - 10 **Product Groups:** 34, 35, 48

Lifting Gear Direct
Unit 17 The Wallows Industrial Estate Fens Pool Avenue, Brierley Hill, DY5 1QA
Tel: 01384-76961 **Fax:** 01384-75181
E-mail: liftinggeardirect@hotmail.com
Website: http://www.liftinggeardirect.co.uk
Directors: D. Shaw (Fin), S. Shaw (Dir)
Ultimate Holding Company: LGD HOLDINGS LIMITED
Immediate Holding Company: LIFTING GEAR DIRECT LIMITED
Registration no: 04958113 **Date established:** 2003
Turnover: £500,000 - £1m **No.of Employees:** 11 - 20
Product Groups: 35, 39, 45

Date of Accounts	Apr 12	Apr 11	Apr 10
Working Capital	878	830	759
Fixed Assets	15	16	19
Current Assets	1m	986	900

Magnetic Industries
Unit 28 Premier Partnership Estate Leys Road, Brierley Hill, DY5 3UP
Tel: 01384-77644 **Fax:** 01384-77505
E-mail: mail@magnetic-industries.co.uk
Website: http://www.magnetic-industries.co.uk
Directors: N. Robinson (Fin)
Immediate Holding Company: MAGNETIC INDUSTRIES LIMITED
Registration no: 04278050 **Date established:** 2001
No.of Employees: 1 - 10 **Product Groups:** 34

Date of Accounts	Aug 11	Aug 10	Aug 09
Working Capital	497	490	490
Fixed Assets	N/A	12	12
Current Assets	506	552	552

Mantech UK Ltd
7 Acres Road, Brierley Hill, DY5 2XS
Tel: 01384-824051 **Fax:** 01384-359131
E-mail: mantechmachinery@gmail.com
Website: http://www.mantechmachinery.co.uk
Directors: B. Van Cleven (Fin), N. Cartwright (MD)
Immediate Holding Company: MANTECH (U.K.) LIMITED
Registration no: 04147199 **Date established:** 2001 **Turnover:** £1m - £2m
No.of Employees: 1 - 10 **Product Groups:** 67

Date of Accounts	Mar 11	Mar 10	Mar 09
Sales Turnover	N/A	N/A	1m
Pre Tax Profit/Loss	N/A	N/A	110
Working Capital	447	449	351
Fixed Assets	62	63	64
Current Assets	502	521	426
Current Liabilities	N/A	N/A	63

Maplin Electronics Ltd
Unit 2 Pedmore Road Merry Hill, Brierley Hill, DY5 1SY
Tel: 08432-277376 **Fax:** 01384-70185
E-mail: customercare@maplin.co.uk
Website: http://www.maplin.co.uk
Ultimate Holding Company: MONTAGU PRIVATE EQUITY LLP
Immediate Holding Company: MAPLIN ELECTRONICS LIMITED
Registration no: 01264385 **Date established:** 1976
Turnover: £125m - £250m **No.of Employees:** 1 - 10 **Product Groups:** 37, 61

Date of Accounts	Dec 11	Dec 08	Dec 09
Sales Turnover	205m	204m	204m
Pre Tax Profit/Loss	25m	32m	35m
Working Capital	118m	49m	75m
Fixed Assets	27m	28m	28m
Current Assets	207m	108m	142m
Current Liabilities	78m	51m	59m

Merek Engineering Ltd
25-26 Premier Partnership Estate Leys Road, Brierley Hill, DY5 3UP
Tel: 01384-262138 **Fax:** 01384-265183
E-mail: sales@merek.co.uk
Website: http://www.merek.co.uk
Directors: E. Hackett (MD)
Immediate Holding Company: MEREK ENGINEERING LIMITED
Registration no: 01712894 **Date established:** 1983
Turnover: £500,000 - £1m **No.of Employees:** 11 - 20
Product Groups: 29, 30, 33, 35, 36, 40, 45, 46, 48, 61, 66

Date of Accounts	Jun 11	Jun 10	Jun 09
Working Capital	221	247	276
Fixed Assets	15	25	40
Current Assets	528	555	653
Current Liabilities	N/A	N/A	282

Moor Storage Ltd
Waterside Business Park Brettell Lane, Brierley Hill, DY5 3LH
Tel: 01384-480011 **Fax:** 01384-480051
E-mail: robert@moorstorage.co.uk
Website: http://www.moorstorage.co.uk
Managers: R. Plant (Ops Mgr)
Immediate Holding Company: MOOR STORAGE LIMITED
Registration no: 02402975 **Date established:** 1989
No.of Employees: 1 - 10 **Product Groups:** 26, 35

Date of Accounts	Aug 11	Aug 10	Aug 09
Working Capital	60	33	67
Fixed Assets	18	47	39
Current Assets	345	261	275

Dr D Mueller UK Ltd
15 Dunsford Close, Brierley Hill, DY5 3PR
Tel: 01384-482806 **Fax:** 01384-482808
E-mail: info.uk@mueller-ahlhorn.com
Website: http://www.mueller-ahlhorn.com
Directors: J. Nock (MD), M. Nock (Fin)
Immediate Holding Company: DR. D. MUELLER (UK) LTD
Registration no: 05349390 **Date established:** 2005
Turnover: Up to £250,000 **No.of Employees:** 1 - 10 **Product Groups:** 32, 37

Date of Accounts	Mar 11	Mar 10	Mar 08
Working Capital	-2	20	22
Fixed Assets	60	17	5
Current Assets	97	66	122

News Fittings Flanges & Fasteners Ltd
Unit 3 Bevan Industrial Estate, Brierley Hill, DY5 3TS
Tel: 01384-761111
E-mail: sales@carbern.co.uk

see next page

News Fittings Flanges & Fasteners Ltd - Cont'd

Directors: M. Carey (MD)
Ultimate Holding Company: CAREY HOLDINGS LIMITED
Immediate Holding Company: NEWS (FITTINGS, FLANGES AND FASTENERS) LTD
Registration no: 05423544 **Date established:** 2005
No.of Employees: 11 - 20 **Product Groups:** 36, 46

Date of Accounts	Jul 11	Jul 10	Jul 09
Working Capital	22	122	314
Fixed Assets	2	2	1
Current Assets	425	363	620

Plastic Supplies Dudley Ltd

Unit 4-5 Breener Industrial Estate Station Drive, Brierley Hill, DY5 3JZ
Tel: 01384-77569 **Fax:** 01384-486660
E-mail: info@plasticsuppliesdudley.co.uk
Website: http://www.plasticsuppliesdudley.co.uk
Bank(s): HSBC
Directors: T. Loverock (MD)
Immediate Holding Company: PLASTIC SUPPLIES DUDLEY LIMITED
Registration no: 04858657 **VAT No.:** GB 488 4998 56
Date established: 2003 **Turnover:** £500,000 - £1m
No.of Employees: 11 - 20 **Product Groups:** 30

Date of Accounts	Sep 11	Sep 10	Sep 09
Working Capital	-207	-210	-205
Fixed Assets	389	341	304
Current Assets	263	253	210

Pratt Triumph 94 Ltd

Unit 18 Premier Partnership Estate Leys Road, Brierley Hill, DY5 3UP
Tel: 01384-265255 **Fax:** 01384-265255
Directors: N. Hodgkins (Fin)
Immediate Holding Company: PRATT TRIUMPH 94 LIMITED
Registration no: 02979295 **Date established:** 1994
Turnover: Up to £250,000 **No.of Employees:** 1 - 10 **Product Groups:** 46

Date of Accounts	Oct 11	Oct 10	Oct 09
Working Capital	83	70	77
Fixed Assets	3	5	6
Current Assets	109	80	93

Q A D Europe Ltd

Waterfront Business Park Dudley Road, Brierley Hill, DY5 1LX
Tel: 01384-487700 **Fax:** 01384-487501
E-mail: peg@qad.com
Website: http://www.qad.com
Bank(s): Lloyds TSB Bank plc
Directors: P. Geddes (Dir), P. Geddes (Fin), G. Munn (Co Sec)
Managers: J. Smith (I.T. Exec), M. Brewer (Mktg Serv Mgr)
Ultimate Holding Company: QAD INC (USA)
Immediate Holding Company: QAD EUROPE LIMITED
Registration no: 03653092 **Date established:** 1998 **Turnover:** £5m - £10m
No.of Employees: 51 - 100 **Product Groups:** 44, 81

Date of Accounts	Jan 11	Jan 10	Jan 09
Sales Turnover	9m	9m	10m
Pre Tax Profit/Loss	520	181	-2m
Working Capital	9m	6m	9m
Fixed Assets	2m	2m	3m
Current Assets	11m	11m	13m
Current Liabilities	397	482	521

Quality Kernels Ltd

Unit 23 Enterprise Trading Estate, Brierley Hill, DY5 1TX
Tel: 01384-74477 **Fax:** 01384-76382
E-mail: rob.whitehead@zubrance.co.uk
Website: http://www.qualitykernels.co.uk
Directors: D. Woodwards (Fin)
Managers: T. Hoy (Buyer), A. Quinn (Comm)
Ultimate Holding Company: ZUBRANCE LIMITED
Immediate Holding Company: QUALITY KERNELS LIMITED
Registration no: 03771493 **Date established:** 1999 **Turnover:** £5m - £10m
No.of Employees: 11 - 20 **Product Groups:** 20, 40, 41

Date of Accounts	Jun 08	Jun 09	Jun 10
Sales Turnover	5m	5m	6m
Pre Tax Profit/Loss	369	187	149
Working Capital	411	509	604
Fixed Assets	163	229	245
Current Assets	2m	2m	3m
Current Liabilities	169	74	116

R & J Mesh Ltd

2 The Wallows Industrial Estate Fens Pool Avenue, Brierley Hill, DY5 1QA
Tel: 01384-70488 **Fax:** 01384- 265663
E-mail: sales@rjmesh.co.uk
Website: http://www.rjmesh.co.uk
Directors: M. Harris (MD)
Immediate Holding Company: R AND J MESH LIMITED
Registration no: 01314597 **Date established:** 1977
No.of Employees: 1 - 10 **Product Groups:** 26, 35

Date of Accounts	Jun 12	Jun 11	Jun 10
Working Capital	298	302	201
Fixed Assets	520	527	540
Current Assets	556	514	510

R J T Conveyors

Unit 16 Bevan Indl-Est, Brierley Hill, DY5 3TF
Tel: 01384-864458 **Fax:** 01384-827777
E-mail: sales@rjtconveyors.com
Website: http://www.rjtconveyors.com
Directors: J. Brettelle (Dir), T. Brettell (Dir)
Immediate Holding Company: R. J. T. CONVEYORS (INTERNATIONAL) LIMITED
Registration no: 02947359 **Date established:** 1994 **Turnover:** £1m - £2m
No.of Employees: 1 - 10 **Product Groups:** 35, 41, 43, 44, 45

Date of Accounts	Apr 11	Apr 10	Apr 09
Working Capital	161	148	142
Fixed Assets	65	35	47
Current Assets	440	324	361

R S Paskin & Co. Ltd

Mount Pleasant, Brierley Hill, DY5 2YR
Tel: 01384-78081 **Fax:** 01384-76480
E-mail: sales@rspaskin.co.uk
Website: http://www.rspaskin.co.uk
Bank(s): Lloyds Merryhill
Directors: R. Paskin (MD), S. Paskin (MD)
Immediate Holding Company: R.S. Paskin Group Ltd
Registration no: 00647868 **VAT No.:** GB 277 1380 46
Date established: 1960 **Turnover:** £2m - £5m **No.of Employees:** 11 - 20
Product Groups: 30, 36

Race Industrial Products Ltd

Unit A1 The Wallows Industrial Estate Fens Pool Avenue, Brierley Hill, DY5 1QA
Tel: 01384-263614 **Fax:** 01384-261154
E-mail: sales@raceindustrial.com
Website: http://www.raceindustrial.com
Directors: A. Harris (Dir), C. Fell (Dir)
Managers: A. Harris
Immediate Holding Company: RACE INDUSTRIAL (PRODUCTS) LIMITED
Registration no: 01882376 **Date established:** 1985 **Turnover:** £1m - £2m
No.of Employees: 21 - 50 **Product Groups:** 22, 29, 30, 31, 32, 33, 34, 35, 36, 37, 39, 40, 45, 46, 48, 51, 52, 65, 66, 67, 68, 84

Date of Accounts	Apr 12	Apr 11	Apr 10
Working Capital	147	89	12
Fixed Assets	130	190	218
Current Assets	2m	2m	1m

Robec Gears Ltd

Unit 10 Pedmore Industrial Estate, Brierley Hill, DY5 1TJ
Tel: 01384-76461 **Fax:** 01384-76461
Directors: E. Dudley (Fin), C. Dudley (MD)
Immediate Holding Company: ROBEC GEARS LIMITED
Registration no: 00978258 **Date established:** 1970
No.of Employees: 1 - 10 **Product Groups:** 35, 45

Date of Accounts	Apr 11	Apr 10	Apr 09
Working Capital	12	1	9
Fixed Assets	6	7	8
Current Assets	44	50	35

S S A B Swedish Steel Ltd

Unit 17 Narrowboat Way Hurst Business Park, Brierley Hill, DY5 1UF
Tel: 01384-74660 **Fax:** 01384-77575
E-mail: paul.cartwright@ssab.com
Website: http://www.dobel.co.uk
Bank(s): HSBC Bank plc
Directors: P. Cartwright (MD), P. Carle (Mkt Research)
Managers: S. Bristow (Sales Admin)
Ultimate Holding Company: SSAB SVENSKT STAL AB (SWEDEN)
Immediate Holding Company: SSAB SWEDISH STEEL LIMITED
Registration no: 00710624 **Date established:** 1961
Turnover: £10m - £20m **No.of Employees:** 21 - 50 **Product Groups:** 34, 48, 66

Date of Accounts	Dec 11	Dec 10	Dec 09
Sales Turnover	14m	16m	19m
Pre Tax Profit/Loss	743	611	189
Working Capital	5m	5m	4m
Fixed Assets	2m	2m	2m
Current Assets	7m	7m	9m
Current Liabilities	715	414	232

Sebden Colours

Thorns Road, Brierley Hill, DY5 2PJ
Tel: 01384-422242 **Fax:** 01384-893641
E-mail: colours@sebden.com
Website: http://www.sebden.com
Managers: S. Hill
No.of Employees: 21 - 50 **Product Groups:** 34, 61, 66

Solor Plastics

Meeting Lane, Brierley Hill, DY5 3LB
Tel: 01384-78078 **Fax:** 01384-77373
E-mail: solorplastics@fastmail.fm
Website: http://www.solor-plastics.co.uk
Directors: J. Gibbons (MD), J. Gibbins (MD)
Managers: R. Gibbons (Tech Serv Mgr), R. Harper (Sales & Mktg Mg)
Registration no: 01504159 **VAT No.:** GB 351 4256 74
Turnover: £500,000 - £1m **No.of Employees:** 1 - 10 **Product Groups:** 23, 30, 31, 32

Specsafe Eyewear

Mill Street, Brierley Hill, DY5 2RG
Tel: 01543-492449 **Fax:** 01543-492328
E-mail: cf@specsafe.co.uk
Website: http://www.specsafe.co.uk
Directors: C. Flanagan (Sales)
Immediate Holding Company: WRIGHT SIGNS LIMITED
Registration no: 04712952 **Date established:** 2003
No.of Employees: 1 - 10 **Product Groups:** 24, 33, 38, 40

Date of Accounts	Apr 11	Apr 10	Apr 09
Working Capital	3	1	-1
Fixed Assets	4	5	6
Current Assets	10	8	13

Staffordshire Crystal Ltd

Unit 14 Pedmore Road Industrial Estate Pedmore Road, Brierley Hill, DY5 1TJ
Tel: 01384-77701 **Fax:** 01384- 482580
E-mail: sales@staffordshirecrystal.net
Website: http://www.shirecrystal.com
Managers: N. Marsh (Admin Off)
Immediate Holding Company: BRITISH CRYSTAL LTD
Registration no: 05407951 **Date established:** 2005
Turnover: £250,000 - £500,000 **No.of Employees:** 11 - 20
Product Groups: 33

Date of Accounts	Aug 11	Aug 10	Aug 09
Working Capital	45	47	70
Fixed Assets	17	18	19
Current Assets	114	120	132
Current Liabilities	N/A	30	N/A

Summerhill Steels Ltd

Chiltern House Leys Road, Brierley Hill, DY5 3UP
Tel: 01384-482048 **Fax:** 01384-482022
E-mail: pmale@aol.com
Directors: M. Male (MD), S. Male (Co Sec)
Immediate Holding Company: SUMMERHILL STEELS LIMITED
Registration no: 02524167 **VAT No.:** GB 547 4468 14
Date established: 1990 **Turnover:** £1m - £2m **No.of Employees:** 1 - 10
Product Groups: 66

Date of Accounts	Aug 09	Aug 08	Jun 11
Working Capital	162	172	32
Fixed Assets	180	173	164
Current Assets	460	795	336

Sunrise Medical Ltd

High Street, Brierley Hill, DY5 4PS
Tel: 01384-446688 **Fax:** 01384-446699
E-mail: peter.riley@sunmed.co.uk
Website: http://www.sunrisemedical.co.uk
Bank(s): HSBC
Directors: M. Passant (Fin)
Managers: A. Handley, P. Riley, S. Johnson (Tech Serv Mgr), H. Hackett (Personnel), J. Elsworth (Mktg Serv Mgr)
Ultimate Holding Company: SUNRISE MEDICAL HOLDINGS INC (USA)
Immediate Holding Company: SUNRISE MEDICAL LIMITED
Registration no: 03570204 **VAT No.:** GB 388 6068 02
Date established: 1998 **Turnover:** £20m - £50m
No.of Employees: 101 - 250 **Product Groups:** 67

Date of Accounts	Jul 09	Jul 08	Jul 10
Sales Turnover	36m	38m	34m
Pre Tax Profit/Loss	1m	3m	3m
Working Capital	21m	19m	25m
Fixed Assets	7m	8m	5m
Current Assets	31m	31m	37m
Current Liabilities	5m	6m	5m

Tower Analysis & Design

21b Bell Street, Brierley Hill, DY5 3EU
Tel: 01384-263920 **Fax:** 01384-263922
E-mail: tower.ad@btinternet.com
Directors: B. Hamblin (Prop)
Date established: 2001 **No.of Employees:** 1 - 10 **Product Groups:** 35

Trimat Ltd

Narrowboat Way Hurst Business Pk, Brierley Hill, DY5 1UF
Tel: 01384-473400 **Fax:** 01384-261010
E-mail: sales@trimat.co.uk
Website: http://www.trimat.co.uk
Bank(s): National Westminster Bank Plc
Directors: S. Magee (Tech Serv), D. Taylor (MD)
Managers: D. James (Sales Prom Mgr)
Ultimate Holding Company: Donoco Ltd
Registration no: 02557968 **VAT No.:** GB 547 5659 02
Turnover: £2m - £5m **No.of Employees:** 21 - 50 **Product Groups:** 30, 33, 34, 35

Date of Accounts	Aug 11	Aug 10	Aug 09
Working Capital	-84	-98	-144
Fixed Assets	234	234	280
Current Assets	1m	1m	2m

Van Leeuwen Wheeler Ltd

Nine Lock Works Mill Street, Brierley Hill, DY5 2SX
Tel: 01384-487600 **Fax:** 01384-487619
E-mail: sales@vlwheeler.co.uk
Website: http://www.vanleeuwen.co.uk
Managers: G. Fellows, K. Bowling (Sales Prom Mgr), M. Davies (Fin Mgr), T. Desmond (Comm), J. Spicer (Personnel)
Ultimate Holding Company: VAN LEEUWEN PIPE & TUBE GROUP BV (NETHER
Immediate Holding Company: VAN LEEUWEN LIMITED
Registration no: 01991207 **Date established:** 1986
Turnover: £20m - £50m **No.of Employees:** 51 - 100 **Product Groups:** 66

Date of Accounts	Dec 11	Dec 10	Dec 09
Sales Turnover	41m	32m	28m
Pre Tax Profit/Loss	1m	1m	-130
Working Capital	10m	9m	7m
Fixed Assets	1m	1m	1m
Current Assets	19m	16m	13m
Current Liabilities	2m	1m	324

Volkobind Engineering Company Ltd

Unit 1 Tansey Green Road, Brierley Hill, DY5 4TL
Tel: 01384-79746 **Fax:** 01384-75737
E-mail: sales@volkobind.co.uk
Website: http://www.volkobind.co.uk
Directors: P. Standish (Dir)
Immediate Holding Company: VOLKOBIND ENGINEERING CO. LIMITED
Registration no: 00836273 **VAT No.:** GB 277 0709 41
Date established: 1965 **Turnover:** £250,000 - £500,000
No.of Employees: 1 - 10 **Product Groups:** 46

Date of Accounts	Jul 11	Jul 10	Jul 09
Working Capital	159	181	172
Fixed Assets	281	218	247
Current Assets	304	282	281

Welin Lambie

Britannia House Old Bush Street, Brierley Hill, DY5 1UB
Tel: 01384-78294 **Fax:** 01384- 265100
E-mail: admin@welin-lambie.co.uk
Website: http://www.welin-lambie.co.uk
Directors: N. Rose (MD), S. Rose (Fin)
Immediate Holding Company: WELIN LAMBIE LIMITED
Registration no: 02367406 **VAT No.:** GB 488 5634 89
Date established: 1989 **Turnover:** £2m - £5m **No.of Employees:** 21 - 50
Product Groups: 29, 39

Date of Accounts	Dec 11	Dec 10	Dec 09
Working Capital	3m	3m	2m
Fixed Assets	736	830	676
Current Assets	3m	3m	3m

Bromwich

Seagull Balustrades

90 Roebuck Lane, Bromwich, B70 6QX
Tel: 0121-5250020 **Fax:** 0121-5251116
E-mail: sales@seagullfittings.co.uk
Website: http://www.seagullbalustrades.com
Product Groups: 35, 36, 39

Date of Accounts	Oct 11	Oct 10	Oct 09
Working Capital	256	237	236
Fixed Assets	106	87	100
Current Assets	489	413	383

Coventry

A A H Pharmaceuticals

Sapphire Court Paradise Way, Coventry Walsgrave Triangle, Coventry, CV2 2TX
Tel: 024-7643 2000 **Fax:** 024-7643 2001
E-mail: it@aah.co.uk
Website: http://www.aah.co.uk

Directors: T. Beer (Fin), M. James (MD), D. Rollinson (Sales)
Managers: J. Attenborough (Personnel)
Ultimate Holding Company: FRANZ HANIEL & CIE GMBH (GERMANY)
Immediate Holding Company: AAH PHARMACEUTICALS LIMITED
Registration no: 00123458 **Date established:** 2012
Turnover: Over £1,000m **No.of Employees:** 1 - 10 **Product Groups:** 63

Date of Accounts	Dec 11	Dec 10	Dec 09
Sales Turnover	2892m	2996m	3118m
Pre Tax Profit/Loss	100m	106m	112m
Working Capital	606m	601m	579m
Fixed Assets	35m	28m	29m
Current Assets	1073m	1100m	1199m
Current Liabilities	93m	82m	44m

A Blundell Jewel Bearing Ltd

203 Torrington Avenue, Coventry, CV4 9UT
Tel: 024-7647 3625 **Fax:** 024-7646 6399
Directors: D. Blundell (MD)
Immediate Holding Company: A.BLUNDELL (JEWEL BEARINGS) LIMITED
Registration no: 00525728 **Date established:** 1953
Turnover: Up to £250,000 **No.of Employees:** 1 - 10 **Product Groups:** 49

Date of Accounts	Dec 11	Dec 10	Dec 09
Working Capital	37	31	61
Fixed Assets	504	505	507
Current Assets	61	57	84

A G Gears Of Coventry

Phoenix House Holbrook Lane, Coventry, CV6 4AD
Tel: 024-7658 1854 **Fax:** 024-7668 0446
Directors: P. Russell (Dir)
Registration no: 01377101 **Date established:** 1978 **Turnover:** £5m - £10m
No.of Employees: 1 - 10 **Product Groups:** 35, 45

A M P C O Metal Ltd

17 Binns Close, Coventry, CV4 9TB
Tel: 024-7646 7011 **Fax:** 024-7646 1455
E-mail: info@ampcometal.com
Website: http://www.ampcometal.com
Directors: J. Bovey (Fin)
Managers: C. Fahy (Sales Prom Mgr)
Ultimate Holding Company: AMPCO METAL SA (SWITZERLAND)
Immediate Holding Company: AMPCO METAL LIMITED
Registration no: 00972795 **VAT No.:** GB 272 3640 66
Date established: 1970 **Turnover:** £1m - £2m **No.of Employees:** 1 - 10
Product Groups: 34, 35, 36, 48

Date of Accounts	Dec 11	Dec 10	Dec 09
Working Capital	-87	-131	-73
Fixed Assets	N/A	N/A	4
Current Assets	208	240	173

Ace Signs Group Ltd

Oak Tree Road Binley, Coventry, CV3 2UL
Tel: 024-7660 8200 **Fax:** 024-7660 8201
E-mail: info@asg.co.uk
Website: http://www.asg.co.uk
Directors: S. Lloyd (MD)
Managers: K. Mulkerrins (Ops Mgr), M. Nichols (Buyer), R. Eldridge (Fin Mgr)
Immediate Holding Company: ACE SIGNS GROUP LIMITED
Registration no: 04427113 **Date established:** 2002 **Turnover:** £2m - £5m
No.of Employees: 21 - 50 **Product Groups:** 26, 37, 39, 49, 52, 81

Activ-Step

Faraday House Electric Wharf, Coventry, CV1 4JF
Tel: 0845-226 3213
E-mail: info@activstep.com
Website: http://www.activstep.co.uk
Directors: M. Carver (Dir), P. Fedoroff (Dir)
Immediate Holding Company: Activ-Step Ltd
Registration no: 05014939 **Date established:** 2008
No.of Employees: 1 - 10 **Product Groups:** 81

Acton Finishing

213 Torrington Avenue, Coventry, CV4 9HN
Tel: 024-7646 6914 **Fax:** 024-7646 7551
E-mail: enquiries@acton-finishing.co.uk
Website: http://www.acton-finishing.co.uk
Bank(s): NAT WEST
Directors: S. Gulati (Dir)
Immediate Holding Company: ACTON FINISHING LIMITED
Registration no: 04566548 **VAT No.:** GB 807 8017 31
Date established: 2002 **Turnover:** £1m - £2m **No.of Employees:** 21 - 50
Product Groups: 33, 40, 41, 42, 46, 47, 48

Date of Accounts	Mar 12	Mar 11	Mar 10
Working Capital	299	644	537
Fixed Assets	828	803	228
Current Assets	888	1m	936

Adams Lubetech Ltd

Unit 6 Binns Close, Coventry, CV4 9TB
Tel: 024-7646 7941 **Fax:** 024-7669 4002
E-mail: info@adamslube.com
Website: http://www.adamslube.com
Bank(s): The Royal Bank of Scotland
Directors: T. Tostles (MD)
Immediate Holding Company: ADAMS LUBETECH LIMITED
Registration no: 03720077 **VAT No.:** GB 729 6804 00
Date established: 1999 **No.of Employees:** 11 - 20 **Product Groups:** 36

Date of Accounts	May 11	May 10	May 09
Working Capital	303	291	276
Fixed Assets	167	147	177
Current Assets	462	421	426

Adecs Ltd

69 Albany Road, Coventry, CV5 6JR
Tel: 024-7667 1220 **Fax:** 08453-109600
E-mail: services@adecs.co.uk
Website: http://www.adecs.co.uk
Directors: M. Chaplin (Co Sec), A. Bhabra (MD)
Managers: J. Howells (Tech Serv Mgr)
Immediate Holding Company: ADECS LIMITED
Registration no: 02741308 **Date established:** 1992
No.of Employees: 11 - 20 **Product Groups:** 80, 86

Date of Accounts	Aug 11	Aug 09	Aug 08
Working Capital	-5	-38	-27
Fixed Assets	33	54	59
Current Assets	137	147	175

Advanced Surface Treatments Ltd

Unit 11 Alpha Business Park, Coventry, CV2 1EQ
Tel: 024-7660 3232 **Fax:** 024-7661 1776
E-mail: desmond_willis@astec-uk.com
Website: http://www.surfacetechnology.co.uk
Bank(s): Yorkshire Bank PLC
Directors: A. Courtney (Sales)
Managers: M. Gimmock, R. Hurrell (Prod Mgr), P. Darlaston
Immediate Holding Company: SUPERDREAM LIMITED
Registration no: 02522017 **VAT No.:** GB 545 0857 35
Date established: 1990 **Turnover:** £1m - £2m **No.of Employees:** 21 - 50
Product Groups: 48

Date of Accounts	Aug 11	Aug 10	Aug 09
Working Capital	-96	-88	-76
Fixed Assets	132	132	132
Current Assets	898	898	911

Aereco Ventilation Ltd

The Technocentre Coventry University Technology Park Puma Way, Coventry, CV1 2TT
Tel: 024-7623 6066 **Fax:** 024-7623 6077
Website: http://www.aereco.com
Directors: D. Glass (Co Sec), M. Jardinier (Dir)
Ultimate Holding Company: Aereco Sa (France)
Immediate Holding Company: AERECO VENTILATION LIMITED
Registration no: 02171632 **Date established:** 1987
Turnover: £250,000 - £500,000 **No.of Employees:** 1 - 10
Product Groups: 40, 66

Agie Charmilles Ltd

North View Coventry Walsgrave Triangle, Coventry, CV2 2SJ
Tel: 024-7653 8666 **Fax:** 024-7653 0023
E-mail: info@uk.gfac.com
Website: http://www.gfac.com
Bank(s): HSBC, Coventry
Directors: M. Spencer (MD)
Managers: D. Outhwaite (Comptroller), O. Pennington (Buyer), N. Baines (Personnel)
Ultimate Holding Company: GEORG FISCHER AG (SWITZERLAND)
Immediate Holding Company: AGIE CHARMILLES LIMITED
Registration no: 03240378 **Date established:** 1996
Turnover: £20m - £50m **No.of Employees:** 21 - 50 **Product Groups:** 33, 35, 42

Date of Accounts	Dec 11	Dec 10	Dec 09
Sales Turnover	22m	17m	13m
Pre Tax Profit/Loss	609	190	-186
Working Capital	2m	2m	1m
Fixed Assets	551	588	638
Current Assets	7m	6m	4m
Current Liabilities	2m	2m	1m

AIC

8 Holbrook Lane, Coventry, CV6 4AD
Tel: 024-7666 2423
Website: http://www.artistic-iron.co.uk
Directors: N. Kelly (Ptnr)
Immediate Holding Company: DESAI CONSULTANCY LIMITED
Registration no: 07461700 **Date established:** 2010
No.of Employees: 1 - 10 **Product Groups:** 26, 35

Alpaca Select

82 Frobisher Road, Coventry, CV3 6NA
Tel: 024-7641 1776 **Fax:** 024-7641 1776
E-mail: sales@alpaca-select.co.uk
Website: http://www.alpaca-select.co.uk
Directors: I. Langdon (Prop)
Date established: 1992 **Turnover:** **No.of Employees:** 1 - 10
Product Groups: 23, 24

Aluminium Surface Engineering Ltd

Bodmin Road, Coventry, CV2 5DX
Tel: 024-7661 1921 **Fax:** 024-7660 2196
E-mail: admin@ase4anodising.co.uk
Website: http://www.ase4anodising.co.uk
Directors: J. Alksnitis (Prop), J. Alksnitis (Prop)
Ultimate Holding Company: BRITA FINISH 2002 LIMITED
Immediate Holding Company: BRITA FINISH LIMITED
Registration no: 04479237 **VAT No.:** GB 272 3533 67
Date established: 2002 **Turnover:** £2m - £5m **No.of Employees:** 21 - 50
Product Groups: 34, 46, 48

Date of Accounts	Oct 11	Oct 10	Oct 09
Working Capital	489	335	271
Fixed Assets	1m	1m	1m
Current Assets	760	554	497

The Amtico Co. Ltd

Kingfield Road, Coventry, CV6 5AA
Tel: 024-7686 1400 **Fax:** 024-7686 1552
E-mail: info@amtico.com
Website: http://www.amtico.co.uk
Bank(s): Royal Bank of Scotland
Directors: S. Mills (Dir), T. Morrow (Co Sec), O. Kluge (Dir)
Managers: S. Smith (Tech Serv Mgr), J. Shelley (Personnel)
Ultimate Holding Company: ABN AMRO CAPITAL UK BUY OUT FUND
Immediate Holding Company: THE AMTICO COMPANY LIMITED
Registration no: 02303730 **Date established:** 1988
Turnover: £50m - £75m **No.of Employees:** 251 - 500
Product Groups: 25, 30, 32, 33, 35, 66

Date of Accounts	Mar 11	Mar 10	Mar 09
Sales Turnover	64m	55m	55m
Pre Tax Profit/Loss	4m	97	8m
Working Capital	36m	31m	33m
Fixed Assets	7m	5m	6m
Current Assets	56m	47m	47m
Current Liabilities	5m	3m	4m

Anca UK Ltd

2 Eastwood Business Village Harry Weston Road, Coventry, CV3 2UB
Tel: 024-7644 7000 **Fax:** 024-7644 7333
E-mail: ukinfo@anca.com
Website: http://www.anca.com
Managers: N. Kendrick (Tech Serv Mgr), P. Moore (Chief Mgr), V. Harms (Fin Mgr)
Ultimate Holding Company: ANCA PTY LTD (AUSTRALIA)
Immediate Holding Company: ANCA (U.K.) LIMITED
Registration no: 01975150 **VAT No.:** GB 423 6153 75
Date established: 1986 **Turnover:** £2m - £5m **No.of Employees:** 1 - 10
Product Groups: 46, 47

Date of Accounts	Jun 11	Jun 10	Jun 09
Sales Turnover	N/A	4m	11m
Pre Tax Profit/Loss	N/A	65	29

Working Capital	483	601	570
Fixed Assets	550	703	733
Current Assets	4m	5m	5m
Current Liabilities	N/A	398	279

Anchor Inserts

11 Bayton Road Industrial Estate Bayton Road, Exhall, Coventry, CV7 9EL
Tel: 024-7636 3979 **Fax:** 024-7636 6303
E-mail: info@anchorinserts.co.uk
Website: http://www.anchorinserts.co.uk
Directors: A. Wade (MD)
Immediate Holding Company: ANCHOR INSERTS LIMITED
Registration no: 05448586 **VAT No.:** GB 273 7380 40
Date established: 2005 **Turnover:** £500,000 - £1m
No.of Employees: 11 - 20 **Product Groups:** 30, 35, 36, 37, 48

Date of Accounts	May 11	May 09	May 07
Working Capital	333	160	-25
Fixed Assets	19	30	43
Current Assets	388	299	309

Andantex Ltd

Rowley Drive Baginton, Coventry, CV3 4LS
Tel: 0161-330 5331 **Fax:** 0161-344 0210
E-mail: sales@andantex.co.uk
Website: http://www.andantex-kinematic.com
Directors: H. Travis (Co Sec)
Managers: A. Stuart (Prod Mgr), W. Linsdell (Sales Prom Mgr), L. Bent (Sales Prom Mgr), G. Edwards (Estimating), H. Cividino
Immediate Holding Company: ANDANTEX LIMITED
Registration no: 00359637 **VAT No.:** GB 145 0554 85
Date established: 1940 **Turnover:** £1m - £2m **No.of Employees:** 1 - 10
Product Groups: 35, 46

Date of Accounts	Dec 11	Dec 10	Dec 09
Working Capital	299	231	223
Fixed Assets	714	710	715
Current Assets	737	575	553

Anglo Building Products & Rustoleum UK Ltd

Unit 6 Spitfire Close Coventry Business Park, Coventry, CV5 6UR
Tel: 01483-427777 **Fax:** 01483-428888
E-mail: sales@anglobuild.co.uk
Website: http://www.ro-m.com
Directors: A. Stevens (Sales & Mktg), R. Rice (Dir)
Managers: M. Hadden (Sales Prom Mgr), S. Chanter (Sales Prom Mgr), M. Johnstone (Personnel)
Immediate Holding Company: ANGLO BUILDING PRODUCTS LIMITED
Registration no: 01860623 **Date established:** 1984
Turnover: Up to £250,000 **No.of Employees:** 1 - 10 **Product Groups:** 49, 52

Date of Accounts	May 08	May 07	Dec 05
Sales Turnover	851	972	N/A
Pre Tax Profit/Loss	96	80	N/A
Working Capital	225	158	102
Current Assets	379	250	201
Current Liabilities	154	93	99
Total Share Capital	1	1	1
ROCE% (Return on Capital Employed)	42.6	50.8	
ROT% (Return on Turnover)	11.3	8.3	

Apprise Consulting Ltd

Oddicombe Croft, Coventry, CV3 5PB
Tel: 024-7641 3149
E-mail: info@appriseconsulting.co.uk
Website: http://www.appriseconsulting.co.uk
Directors: G. Richards (MD)
Immediate Holding Company: APPRISE CONSULTING LTD
Registration no: 04987218 **Date established:** 2003
Turnover: Up to £250,000 **No.of Employees:** 1 - 10 **Product Groups:** 44, 80, 84, 86

Date of Accounts	Dec 11	Dec 10	Dec 09
Working Capital	15	14	8
Current Assets	41	38	25

Arbil Ltd

Brandon Road Binley, Coventry, CV3 2AG
Tel: 024-7645 6667 **Fax:** 024-7663 5113
E-mail: coventry@arbil.co.uk
Website: http://www.arbil.co.uk
Managers: C. Maughan (Mgr)
Ultimate Holding Company: BILLS GROUP LIMITED
Immediate Holding Company: ARBIL LIMITED
Registration no: 01406906 **Date established:** 1978 **Turnover:** £2m - £5m
No.of Employees: 1 - 10 **Product Groups:** 45, 48, 84

Date of Accounts	Dec 11	Dec 10	Dec 09
Sales Turnover	8m	7m	7m
Pre Tax Profit/Loss	373	118	1
Working Capital	1m	1m	1m
Fixed Assets	251	200	184
Current Assets	3m	2m	3m
Current Liabilities	345	205	163

Architectural Panels Ltd

66 Bayton Road Exhall, Coventry, CV7 9EJ
Tel: 024-7636 6266
E-mail: architect.panels@btconnect.com
Website: http://www.architecturalpanels.co.uk
Directors: T. Morrissey (Co Sec)
Immediate Holding Company: ARCHITECTURAL PANELS LIMITED
Registration no: 02138398 **Date established:** 1987
No.of Employees: 1 - 10 **Product Groups:** 26, 35

Date of Accounts	Jun 11	Jun 10	Jun 09
Working Capital	109	96	87
Fixed Assets	65	66	50
Current Assets	296	295	186

Ashtead Plant Hire Ltd

7-9 Broad St Jetty Broad Street, Coventry, CV6 5BE
Tel: 024-7668 5556 **Fax:** 024-7663 8199
E-mail: coventry@aplant.com
Website: http://www.aplant.com
Directors: A. Latief (Mkt Research), G. Thompson (Sales), P. Fereday (MD)
Managers: W. Walker (Chief Mgr), T. Reynolds (Sales & Mktg Mg), R. Corbett (Sales Prom Mgr), J. Brookes (Mgr)
Immediate Holding Company: Ashtead Plant Hire Co. Ltd
No.of Employees: 11 - 20 **Product Groups:** 83

Association Of Plumbing & Heating Contractors

Unit 14 Ensign Business Centre Westwood Way, Westwood Business Park, Coventry, CV4 8JA
Tel: 0121-711 5030 **Fax:** 024-7647 0942
E-mail: enquiries@aphc.co.uk
Website: http://www.aphc.co.uk
Bank(s): HSBC Bank plc
Directors: R. Newhouse (Dir)
Immediate Holding Company: ASSOCIATION OF PLUMBING AND HEATING CONTRACTORS LIMITED
Registration no: 05302003 **Date established:** 2004
Turnover: Up to £250,000 **No.of Employees:** 11 - 20 **Product Groups:** 52

Date of Accounts	Dec 11	Dec 10	Dec 09
Working Capital	979	1m	489
Fixed Assets	588	130	157
Current Assets	1m	2m	676

Atritor Ltd

PO Box 101, Coventry, CV6 5RE
Tel: 024-7666 2266 **Fax:** 024-7666 5751
E-mail: sales@atritor.com
Website: http://www.atritor.com
Bank(s): HSBC
Directors: D. Wilkinson (MD), D. Wilkinson (MD)
Managers: G. Lynch (Buyer), M. Hulme (Sales & Mktg Mg), B. Percival
Ultimate Holding Company: HELDOMO AG (SWITZERLAND)
Immediate Holding Company: ATRITOR LIMITED
Registration no: 01481073 **VAT No.:** GB 307 3444 77
Date established: 1980 **Turnover:** £2m - £5m **No.of Employees:** 21 - 50
Product Groups: 34, 41, 48

Date of Accounts	Aug 11	Aug 10	Aug 09
Working Capital	2m	2m	2m
Fixed Assets	230	249	322
Current Assets	3m	3m	2m

Auric Metal Finishers Ltd

14 Herald Way Binley Industrial Estate, Coventry, CV3 2RP
Tel: 024-7644 7431 **Fax:** 024-7663 5719
E-mail: info@auric.co.uk
Website: http://www.auric.co.uk
Directors: J. Ross (MD), M. Ross (Fin), T. Mitchell (Dir)
Immediate Holding Company: AURIC METAL FINISHERS LIMITED
Registration no: 01476891 **VAT No.:** GB 346 1016 86
Date established: 1980 **Turnover:** £2m - £5m **No.of Employees:** 21 - 50
Product Groups: 48

Date of Accounts	Mar 12	Mar 11	Mar 10
Working Capital	2m	1m	981
Fixed Assets	483	472	461
Current Assets	3m	3m	2m

Austin Research

74 Whoberley Avenue, Coventry, CV5 8EQ
Tel: 024-7671 4545
E-mail: enquiries@austinresearch.co.uk
Website: http://www.austinresearch.co.uk
Directors: G. Austin (Prop)
Immediate Holding Company: AUSTIN RESEARCH LIMITED
Registration no: 06741180 **Date established:** 2008
Turnover: Up to £250,000 **No.of Employees:** 1 - 10 **Product Groups:** 81

Date of Accounts	Nov 11	Nov 10	Nov 09
Working Capital	14	31	9
Fixed Assets	1	1	1
Current Assets	32	49	17

Auto Sport Engineering Ltd (t/a Hadden & Abbots)

Brandon Road Binley, Coventry, CV3 2AH
Tel: 024-7643 7100 **Fax:** 024-7645 9757
E-mail: aclarke@autosporteng.com
Bank(s): Lloyds TSB Bank plc
Directors: A. Clarke (Fin)
Immediate Holding Company: BINLEY PROPERTIES LIMITED
Registration no: 03678166 **Date established:** 1998 **Turnover:** £1m - £2m
No.of Employees: 21 - 50 **Product Groups:** 39, 48

Date of Accounts	Aug 11	Aug 10	Aug 09
Working Capital	N/A	N/A	-14
Fixed Assets	2m	2m	3m
Current Assets	19	N/A	566

Avon Coatings Ltd

Unit 8a Spring Hill Industrial Estate Colliers Way, Arley, Coventry, CV7 8HN
Tel: 01676-542203 **Fax:** 01676-540849
E-mail: richard.moreby@gmail.com
Directors: R. Moreby (MD)
Immediate Holding Company: AVON COATINGS LIMITED
Registration no: 06943591 **Date established:** 2009
Turnover: Up to £250,000 **No.of Employees:** 1 - 10 **Product Groups:** 46, 48

Date of Accounts	Jun 11	Jun 10
Working Capital	-5	14
Fixed Assets	12	15
Current Assets	49	37

B K International Freight Ltd

Unit 13-14 Maguire Industrial Estate 219 Torrington Avenue, Coventry, CV4 9HN
Tel: 024-7646 4983 **Fax:** 024-7669 4184
E-mail: admin@bkfreight.co.uk
Website: http://www.bkfreight.co.uk
Directors: J. Cave (Fin)
Managers: P. Cullen
Immediate Holding Company: BK INTERNATIONAL FREIGHT LIMITED
Registration no: 01660258 **VAT No.:** GB 307 6001 96
Date established: 1982 **Turnover:** £500,000 - £1m
No.of Employees: 1 - 10 **Product Groups:** 76

Date of Accounts	Oct 11	Oct 10	Oct 09
Working Capital	151	233	197
Fixed Assets	128	14	20
Current Assets	278	353	305

B M S Engineering Ltd

Unit 3 403 Broad Lane, Coventry, CV5 7AX
Tel: 024-7646 6442
E-mail: info@bmsengineering.co.uk
Website: http://www.bmsengineering.co.uk
Directors: P. Boffin (MD)
Immediate Holding Company: BMS ENGINEERING LIMITED
Registration no: 05952135 **Date established:** 2006
No.of Employees: 1 - 10 **Product Groups:** 35, 48, 68

Date of Accounts	Oct 11	Oct 10	Oct 09
Working Capital	-18	2	-17
Fixed Assets	138	92	90
Current Assets	88	69	21

B S S

Unit 17 Torrington Avenue, Coventry, CV4 9HN
Tel: 024-7669 4744 **Fax:** 024-7647 0574
Website: http://www.bssgroup.com
Managers: S. Wells (Mgr)
No.of Employees: 11 - 20 **Product Groups:** 33, 37, 40

B T P Craftscreen Ltd

Harefield Road, Coventry, CV2 4BT
Tel: 024-7665 4000 **Fax:** 024-7665 4001
E-mail: reception@btpc.co.uk
Website: http://www.btpc.co.uk
Bank(s): National Westminster Bank Plc
Directors: M. Charlton (MD), M. Charlton (MD)
Immediate Holding Company: BTP CRAFTSCREEN LIMITED
Registration no: 02191784 **Date established:** 1987
Turnover: £500,000 - £1m **No.of Employees:** 21 - 50
Product Groups: 23, 28

Date of Accounts	Dec 11	Dec 10	Dec 09
Working Capital	361	233	62
Fixed Assets	1m	1m	1m
Current Assets	866	677	476

B U P A

Dale Buildings Cook Street, Coventry, CV1 1JH
Tel: 024-7681 1700 **Fax:** 024-7622 7363
E-mail: barrya@bupa.com
Website: http://www.bupa.co.uk/cashplan
Managers: A. Barry (Mgr)
Ultimate Holding Company: BRITISH UNITED PROVIDENT ASSOCIATION LIMITED(THE)
Immediate Holding Company: COVENTRY & WARWICKSHIRE HOSPITAL SATURDAY FUND (THE)
Registration no: 02991773 **Date established:** 1956
No.of Employees: 21 - 50 **Product Groups:** 80, 82

Baileigh Industrial

Unit 1 Fullwood Close Aldermans Green Industrial Estate, Coventry, CV2 2SS
Tel: 024-7661 9267 **Fax:** 024-7661 9276
E-mail: sales@bifabuk.co.uk
Website: http://www.bifabuk.co.uk
Directors: C. Staeth (MD)
Ultimate Holding Company: BAILEIGH INDUSTRIAL INC (UNITED STATES)
Immediate Holding Company: BAILEIGH INDUSTRIAL LIMITED
Registration no: 05672861 **Date established:** 2006
No.of Employees: 1 - 10 **Product Groups:** 34, 36, 37, 42, 43, 46, 47, 48, 67, 83

Date of Accounts	Dec 11	Dec 10	Dec 09
Working Capital	237	-66	-99
Fixed Assets	58	50	23
Current Assets	2m	1m	1m

BBI Business Interiors Ltd

Unit A Quinn Close, Coventry, CV3 4LH
Tel: 024-7630 3000 **Fax:** 024-7630 3099
E-mail: david@bbiltd.co.uk
Website: http://www.bbi.uk.com
Bank(s): Barclays
Directors: J. Bee (Dir)
Immediate Holding Company: BBI BUSINESS INTERIORS LIMITED
Registration no: 02590455 **VAT No.:** GB 584 9241 07
Date established: 1991 **Turnover:** £2m - £5m **No.of Employees:** 11 - 20
Product Groups: 26, 52

Date of Accounts	Oct 07	Oct 06	Jan 10
Working Capital	32	42	17
Fixed Assets	72	62	51
Current Assets	595	572	489
Current Liabilities	22	N/A	N/A

Bicycle Association Of GB Ltd

3 The Quadrant, Coventry, CV1 2DY
Tel: 024-7655 3838 **Fax:** 024-7622 8366
E-mail: office@ba-gb.com
Website: http://www.bicycleassociation.org.uk
Managers: P. Morris (Mgr)
Immediate Holding Company: BICYCLE ASSOCIATION OF GREAT BRITAIN LIMITED(THE)
Registration no: 01111307 **Date established:** 1973
Turnover: £250,000 - £500,000 **No.of Employees:** 1 - 10
Product Groups: 87

Date of Accounts	Dec 11	Dec 10	Dec 09
Sales Turnover	N/A	N/A	448
Working Capital	1m	1m	1m
Fixed Assets	N/A	N/A	1
Current Assets	1m	1m	1m

Bilz Tool

304 Bedworth Road, Coventry, CV6 6LA
Tel: 024-7636 9700 **Fax:** 024-7636 9701
E-mail: dennis.butler@morristooling.com
Website: http://www.morristooling.com
Directors: D. Butler (MD), T. Braun (Fin)
Ultimate Holding Company: ITS INTERNATIONAL TOOL SYSTEMS GMBH & CO KG (GERMANY)
Immediate Holding Company: BILZ TOOL LIMITED
Registration no: 01558030 **VAT No.:** GB 307 5393 58
Date established: 1981 **Turnover:** £2m - £5m **No.of Employees:** 1 - 10
Product Groups: 46

Date of Accounts	Dec 11	Dec 10	Dec 09
Working Capital	982	977	1m
Fixed Assets	4	5	7
Current Assets	1m	1m	1m

Blundell Production Equipment

Unit C-D Seven Stars Industrial Estate Quinn Close, Coventry, CV3 4LH
Tel: 024-7621 0270 **Fax:** 024-7669 4155
E-mail: sales@blundell.co.uk
Website: http://www.blundell.co.uk
Bank(s): Bank of Scotland
Directors: N. Blundell (Fin)
Immediate Holding Company: BLUNDELL PRODUCTION EQUIPMENT LIMITED
Registration no: 00929625 **Date established:** 1968 **Turnover:** £2m - £5m
No.of Employees: 11 - 20 **Product Groups:** 37, 38

Date of Accounts	Dec 11	Dec 10	Dec 09
Working Capital	2m	1m	1m
Fixed Assets	316	242	263
Current Assets	2m	2m	2m

Bodycote Ltd

Thermal House Colliery Lane, Exhall, Coventry, CV7 9NW
Tel: 024-7636 7786 **Fax:** 024-7636 8158
E-mail: adrian.campbell@bodycote.com
Website: http://www.bodycote.com
Bank(s): HSBC, Manchester
Managers: A. Campbell (Site Co-ord), J. Jervis, J. Starsmore
Immediate Holding Company: PINNACLE MACHINE TOOLS LIMITED
Registration no: 00849216 **Date established:** 1998
Turnover: £50m - £75m **No.of Employees:** 21 - 50 **Product Groups:** 48

Bosch Rexroth Ltd

38 Herald Way Binley Industrial Estate, Coventry, CV3 2RQ
Tel: 024-7663 5711 **Fax:** 024-7663 5041
E-mail: sales@boschrexroth.co.uk
Website: http://www.boschrexroth.co.uk
Directors: S. Storci (Mkt Research), G. Rowell (Co Sec)
Managers: R. Benton (Mktg Serv Mgr)
Ultimate Holding Company: ROBERT BOSCH GMBH (GERMANY)
Immediate Holding Company: BOSCH REXROTH LIMITED
Registration no: 00768471 **VAT No.:** GB 401 0540 27
Date established: 1963 **Turnover:** £5m - £10m **No.of Employees:** 1 - 10
Product Groups: 36, 40, 67

Date of Accounts	Dec 11	Dec 10	Dec 09
Sales Turnover	168m	117m	77m
Pre Tax Profit/Loss	13m	4m	-6m
Working Capital	21m	17m	13m
Fixed Assets	15m	13m	14m
Current Assets	53m	40m	28m
Current Liabilities	7m	6m	3m

Bowater Building Products Ltd

Bowater Doors Courtaulds House, Courtaulds Way,, Coventry, CV6 5NH
Tel: 024-7683 5300 **Fax:** 024-7683 5255
Website: http://www.bowaterwindows.com
Directors: C. Watson (Dir), E. Patterson (Dir), K. Franklin (Fin), P. Duguid (Dir)
Registration no: 05088708 **Turnover:** £50m - £75m
No.of Employees: 1 - 10 **Product Groups:** 66

Breeze Building Services

Unit 4 Brindley Road Bayton Road Industrial Estate, Coventry, CV7 9EP
Tel: 024-7636 6100 **Fax:** 024-7636 6123
No.of Employees: 1 - 10 **Product Groups:** 40, 66

Brett Martin Daylight Systems

Sanford Close Aldermans Green Industrial Estate, Coventry, CV2 2QU
Tel: 024-7660 2022 **Fax:** 01363-775842
E-mail: davidbiggs@brettmartin.co.uk
Website: http://www.brettmartin.co.uk
Directors: D. Biggs (Sales)
Ultimate Holding Company: BRETT MARTIN HOLDINGS LTD
Immediate Holding Company: BRETT MARTIN DAYLIGHT SYSTEMS LIMITED
Registration no: 01225853 **Date established:** 1975
Turnover: £10m - £20m **No.of Employees:** 101 - 250
Product Groups: 26, 35

Date of Accounts	Dec 11	Dec 10	Dec 09
Sales Turnover	17m	16m	14m
Pre Tax Profit/Loss	840	751	727
Working Capital	8m	7m	6m
Fixed Assets	883	1m	1m
Current Assets	13m	12m	9m
Current Liabilities	3m	3m	3m

Brical Finishers Ltd

Bay 5 Unit 38 Bayton Road, Exhall, Coventry, CV7 9EJ
Tel: 024-7636 2032 **Fax:** 024-7636 2032
Directors: B. Hammersley (MD)
Immediate Holding Company: BRICAL FINISHERS LIMITED
Registration no: 03129929 **Date established:** 1995
No.of Employees: 11 - 20 **Product Groups:** 46, 48

Date of Accounts	Mar 12	Mar 11	Mar 10
Working Capital	175	183	190
Fixed Assets	86	96	98
Current Assets	346	360	389

Brindley Twist Tafft & James LLP

Lowick Gate Siskin Drive, Middlemarch Business Park, Coventry, CV3 4FJ
Tel: 024-7653 1532 **Fax:** 024-7630 1300
E-mail: enquiries@bttj.com
Website: http://www.bttj.com
Directors: J. Ruddick (Fin)
Managers: M. Acton (Tech Serv Mgr), P. Kershaw (Chief Acct), V. Sinar (Admin Off), J. Sinar (Sales Admin)
Immediate Holding Company: BRINDLEY TWIST TAFFT & JAMES LLP
Registration no: OC361443 **Date established:** 2011
Turnover: £75m - £125m **No.of Employees:** 51 - 100
Product Groups: 80, 82

Briton Shutters & Grilles

20 Carter Road, Coventry, CV3 1BX
Tel: 0800-035 2515 **Fax:** 024-7645 6966
E-mail: sales@bsgnation.com
Website: http://www.fastrackcad.co.uk
Directors: W. Holmes (Snr Part), W. Holmes (Ptnr)
VAT No.: GB 307 2569 62 **Turnover:** £1m - £2m **No.of Employees:** 1 - 10
Product Groups: 25, 26, 30, 34, 35, 36, 37, 39, 40, 48, 52, 66, 81

Broker Ltd

Banner Lane, Coventry, CV4 9GH
Tel: 024-7685 5200 **Fax:** 024-7646 5317
E-mail: reception@broker.co.uk
Website: http://www.broker.co.uk
Bank(s): Barclays

Directors: R. Ladbury (MD)
Ultimate Holding Company: BRUKER CORPORATION (USA)
Immediate Holding Company: BRUKER UK LIMITED
Registration no: 00923986 **Date established:** 1967
Turnover: £20m - £50m **No.of Employees:** 21 - 50 **Product Groups:** 37, 38

Date of Accounts	Dec 10	Dec 09	Dec 08
Sales Turnover	21m	19m	16m
Pre Tax Profit/Loss	392	1m	270
Working Capital	2m	2m	4m
Fixed Assets	2m	2m	2m
Current Assets	19m	13m	12m
Current Liabilities	11m	8m	7m

Bromark Ltd
22 Stoneton Crescent Balsall Common, Coventry, CV7 7QG
Tel: 01676-532562 **Fax:** 01676-532562
E-mail: bromark@aol.com
Website: http://www.geocities.com/bromarkltd/bromark.html
Directors: C. Brookes (MD)
Immediate Holding Company: BROMARK LIMITED
Registration no: 03224930 **Date established:** 1996
No.of Employees: 1 - 10 **Product Groups:** 80

Date of Accounts	Nov 11	Nov 10	Nov 09
Working Capital	27	10	-5
Fixed Assets	1	35	35
Current Assets	44	49	39

Brose
Colliery Lane Exhall, Coventry, CV7 9NW
Tel: 024-7664 6410 **Fax:** 024-7664 6400
E-mail: coventry@brose.com
Website: http://www.brose.com
Bank(s): National Westminster Bank Plc
Directors: S. Park (Fin)
Managers: D. Richite (Personnel), S. Sabir (Purch Mgr), A. Ali (Tech Serv Mgr), T. Kohlbauer (Plant)
Ultimate Holding Company: BROSE INTERNATIONAL GMBH (GERMANY)
Immediate Holding Company: BROSE LIMITED
Registration no: 00849216 **Date established:** 1965
Turnover: £50m - £75m **No.of Employees:** 101 - 250
Product Groups: 39, 61

Date of Accounts	Dec 11	Dec 10	Dec 09
Sales Turnover	64m	50m	42m
Pre Tax Profit/Loss	3m	8m	2m
Working Capital	25m	30m	27m
Fixed Assets	11m	9m	8m
Current Assets	36m	36m	32m
Current Liabilities	4m	3m	2m

Buck & Hickman
Siskin Parkway East Middlemarch Business Park, Coventry, CV3 4PE
Tel: 024-7630 6444 **Fax:** 024-7651 4214
E-mail: enquiries@buckandhickman.com
Website: http://www.buckandhickman.co.uk
Bank(s): Barclays
Directors: N. Harrison (MD), F. Guard (Dir)
Managers: G. Preist (District Mgr), J. Sheringham (Sales Prom Mgr), A. Payne (Export Sales Mg)
Immediate Holding Company: BUCK & HICKMAN LIMITED
Registration no: 06028304 **VAT No.:** GB 169 6803 22
Date established: 2006 **Turnover:** £50m - £75m
No.of Employees: 101 - 250 **Product Groups:** 36, 66

Burbidge & Son Ltd
Burnsall Road, Coventry, CV5 6BS
Tel: 024-7667 1600 **Fax:** 024-7669 1010
E-mail: sales@burbidge.co.uk
Website: http://www.burbidge.co.uk
Bank(s): National Westminster Bank Plc
Directors: B. Burbidge (Ch), G. Heaven (Fin)
Managers: J. Sheehan (Sales & Mktg Mg), S. Matthews (Tech Serv Mgr), P. Fennel (Buyer)
Ultimate Holding Company: BURBIDGE HOLDINGS LIMITED
Immediate Holding Company: BURBIDGE & SON LIMITED
Registration no: 00376700 **Date established:** 1942 **Turnover:** £5m - £10m
No.of Employees: 51 - 100 **Product Groups:** 25, 26

Date of Accounts	Sep 11	Sep 10	Sep 09
Sales Turnover	10m	9m	9m
Pre Tax Profit/Loss	1m	1m	794
Working Capital	3m	3m	7m
Fixed Assets	2m	2m	3m
Current Assets	5m	5m	8m
Current Liabilities	1m	788	605

Burnsall Engineering Co. Ltd
Brandon Road Binley, Coventry, CV3 2AN
Tel: 024-7644 0444 **Fax:** 024-7665 2696
E-mail: info@burnsallengineering.com
Website: http://www.burnsallengineering.com
Directors: R. Pladdys (MD)
Ultimate Holding Company: RON & JILL PLADDYS LTD
Immediate Holding Company: BURNSALL ENGINEERING CO. LIMITED
Registration no: 03480496 **VAT No.:** GB 705 3180 65
Date established: 1997 **Turnover:** Up to £250,000
No.of Employees: 21 - 50 **Product Groups:** 37

Date of Accounts	Dec 11	Dec 10	Dec 09
Working Capital	234	170	129
Fixed Assets	523	391	457
Current Assets	822	719	623

Bystronic UK Ltd
6 Wayside Business Park Wilsons Lane, Coventry, CV6 6NY
Tel: 024-7658 5100 **Fax:** 0844-848 5851
E-mail: sales.uk@bystronic.com
Website: http://www.bystronic.co.uk
Bank(s): Lloyds TSB Bank plc
Managers: D. Griffith (Comm), D. Griffith (Comm)
Ultimate Holding Company: TEGULA AG (SWITZERLAND)
Immediate Holding Company: BYSTRONIC UK LIMITED
Registration no: 02276120 **VAT No.:** GB 185 3259 44
Date established: 1988 **Turnover:** £20m - £50m
No.of Employees: 51 - 100 **Product Groups:** 36, 46, 48

Date of Accounts	Dec 11	Dec 10	Dec 09
Sales Turnover	22m	22m	20m
Pre Tax Profit/Loss	761	867	147
Working Capital	4m	5m	5m
Fixed Assets	258	431	281
Current Assets	9m	9m	9m
Current Liabilities	4m	4m	3m

C C S Technology Ltd
Old School School Street Wolston, Coventry, CV8 3HG
Tel: 024-7654 5711 **Fax:** 024-7654 5722
E-mail: sales@ccstech.co.uk
Website: http://www.ccstech.co.uk
Bank(s): HSBC Bank plc
Directors: M. Fursland (MD)
Immediate Holding Company: C C S TECHNOLOGY LIMITED
Registration no: 02356050 **Date established:** 1989
Turnover: £500,000 - £1m **No.of Employees:** 21 - 50 **Product Groups:** 46

Date of Accounts	Aug 11	Aug 10	Aug 09
Working Capital	233	223	155
Fixed Assets	66	87	47
Current Assets	908	719	546
Current Liabilities	N/A	N/A	391

C L A Tools Ltd
10 Binns Close, Coventry, CV4 9TB
Tel: 024-7646 5535 **Fax:** 024-7669 4543
E-mail: info@clatools.co.uk
Website: http://www.clatools.co.uk
Bank(s): HSBC, Coventry
Directors: J. Flinn (Fin), M. Flinn (MD)
Ultimate Holding Company: C.L.A. TOOLS LIMITED
Immediate Holding Company: C. L. A. MANUFACTURING LIMITED
Registration no: 00935543 **VAT No.:** GB 273 5569 30
Date established: 1968 **Turnover:** £2m - £5m **No.of Employees:** 11 - 20
Product Groups: 46

Date of Accounts	Jul 11	Jul 10	Jul 09
Working Capital	129	129	129
Current Assets	129	129	129

Caldwell Hardware Ltd
Herald Way Binley Industrial Estate, Coventry, CV3 2RQ
Tel: 024-7643 7900 **Fax:** 024-7643 7969
E-mail: amacaulay@caldwell.co.uk
Website: http://www.caldwell.co.uk
Bank(s): Lloyds TSB
Directors: A. Macaulay (Dir), R. Procinski (Fin)
Managers: B. Humphries (Sales & Mktg Mg), K. Garnett (Tech Serv Mgr), P. Fellingham (Mats Contrlr), W. Hodgkinson (Personnel)
Ultimate Holding Company: CALDWELL MANUFACTURING CO (USA)
Immediate Holding Company: CALDWELL HARDWARE (UK) LIMITED
Registration no: 00517067 **Date established:** 1953 **Turnover:** £5m - £10m
No.of Employees: 51 - 100 **Product Groups:** 36

Date of Accounts	Dec 11	Dec 10	Dec 09
Sales Turnover	10m	9m	8m
Pre Tax Profit/Loss	1m	1m	878
Working Capital	12m	11m	10m
Fixed Assets	2m	2m	2m
Current Assets	13m	12m	11m
Current Liabilities	654	611	439

Cam Tech Engineering
Unit 4 Bodmin Road, Coventry, CV2 5DB
Tel: 024-7662 2567 **Fax:** 024-7662 2494
E-mail: info@cam-tech-engineering.co.uk
Website: http://www.cam-tech-engineering.co.uk
Directors: J. Bolger (MD)
Immediate Holding Company: CAM-TECH ENGINEERING (COVENTRY) LIMITED
Registration no: 03616014 **Date established:** 1998
No.of Employees: 11 - 20 **Product Groups:** 35

Date of Accounts	Aug 11	Aug 10	Aug 09
Working Capital	-63	-75	-31
Fixed Assets	520	407	260
Current Assets	351	239	155

Cameron Roofing
Hollyhurst Farm Coventry Road, Aldermans Green, Coventry, CV2 1NU
Tel: 024-7631 1497
E-mail: stuart@cameronroofing.co.uk
Website: http://www.cameroroofing.co.uk
Directors: A. Cameron (Prop)
Registration no: 05009992 **Date established:** 1989
Turnover: £250,000 - £500,000 **No.of Employees:** 1 - 10
Product Groups: 52

Camping & Caravanning Club Ltd
Greenfields House Westwood Way, Westwood Business Park, Coventry, CV4 8JH
Tel: 08451-307631 **Fax:** 024-7669 4886
Website: http://www.campingandcaravanningclub.co.uk
Directors: D. Welsford (Dir & Gen Mgr), E. Simpson (Fin)
Managers: M. Jewel (Mktg Serv Mgr), L. Johnson (I.T. Exec)
Ultimate Holding Company: CAMPING AND CARAVANNING CLUB LIMITED(THE)
Immediate Holding Company: CAMPING AND CARAVANNING CLUB LIMITED(THE)
Registration no: 00445520 **Date established:** 1947
Turnover: £50m - £75m **No.of Employees:** 1 - 10 **Product Groups:** 84, 87, 89

Date of Accounts	Feb 08	Feb 11	Feb 10
Sales Turnover	44m	65m	57m
Pre Tax Profit/Loss	211	3m	3m
Working Capital	667	-20m	-10m
Fixed Assets	62m	74m	67m
Current Assets	6m	11m	15m
Current Liabilities	3m	19m	18m

Capital Kiosk Co. Ltd
Unit 10 Maguire Industrial Estate 219 Torrington Avenue, Coventry, CV4 9HN
Tel: 024-7647 1666 **Fax:** 024-7647 1666
E-mail: sales@capitalkiosk.co.uk
Website: http://www.capitalkiosk.co.uk
Directors: S. Hartopp (Dir)
Immediate Holding Company: CAPITAL KIOSK CO LTD
Registration no: 05988766 **Date established:** 2006
Turnover: Up to £250,000 **No.of Employees:** 1 - 10 **Product Groups:** 30, 33, 37, 68

Date of Accounts	Mar 12	Mar 11	Mar 10
Working Capital	-38	-55	-45
Fixed Assets	102	122	143
Current Assets	63	9	18

Paul Carr Fabrications
Unit 7-8 Bodmin Road, Coventry, CV2 5DB
Tel: 024-7662 2121 **Fax:** 024-7660 3784
E-mail: pcfabrication@btinternet.com
Website: http://www.paulcarrfabrications.co.uk
Directors: P. Carr (Prop)
No.of Employees: 1 - 10 **Product Groups:** 35

Cash Register Services
176 Albany Road, Coventry, CV5 6NG
Tel: 024-7644 3728 **Fax:** 024-7644 3728
E-mail: simon@crs-coventry.co.uk
Website: http://www.cashregisterservices.co.uk
Directors: S. Rickard (Prop)
Turnover: £250,000 - £500,000 **No.of Employees:** 1 - 10
Product Groups: 27, 28, 36, 40, 44, 48, 66, 67

Champ Telephones Ltd
11-15 Station Street East, Coventry, CV6 5FL
Tel: 024-7666 7757 **Fax:** 024-7668 2290
E-mail: lynn-aleca.chambers@champtel.co.uk
Website: http://www.champtelephones.co.uk
Directors: G. Chambers (Prop), G. Chambers (MD), R. Lee (Sales), L. Chambers (Fin)
Managers: M. Robinson (Sales Prom Mgr)
Immediate Holding Company: CHAMP TELEPHONES HOLDINGS LIMITED
Registration no: 02761723 **Date established:** 1992
No.of Employees: 1 - 10 **Product Groups:** 37

Date of Accounts	Mar 10	Mar 09	Mar 08
Working Capital	58	73	73
Current Assets	100	108	102

Chromalock Ltd
Beechwood House Falkland Close, Charter Avenue Industrial Estate, Coventry, CV4 8HQ
Tel: 024-7646 6277 **Fax:** 024-7646 5298
E-mail: sales@chromalock.com
Website: http://www.chromalock.com
Directors: G. Devall (Fin), M. Arji (MD)
Ultimate Holding Company: ELECTROSTORE GROUP LIMITED
Immediate Holding Company: CHROMALOCK LIMITED
Registration no: 01332017 **VAT No.:** GB 307 1287 77
Date established: 1977 **Turnover:** £1m - £2m **No.of Employees:** 11 - 20
Product Groups: 38

Date of Accounts	Jun 11	Jun 10	Jun 09
Working Capital	426	508	428
Fixed Assets	6	8	7
Current Assets	570	670	568

Chromatica
Alvis Works Bubbenhall Road, Baginton, Coventry, CV8 3BB
Tel: 024-7630 7744 **Fax:** 024-7630 7799
E-mail: kevinc@chromatica-led.com
Website: http://www.chromatica-led.com
Directors: K. Clark (Dir)
Immediate Holding Company: CHROMATICA LTD
Registration no: 05113256 **Date established:** 2004
No.of Employees: 1 - 10 **Product Groups:** 37, 67

Date of Accounts	Mar 11	Mar 10	Mar 09
Working Capital	41	38	20
Fixed Assets	56	60	41
Current Assets	187	328	165

Class Building Services
226 Lythalls Lane, Coventry, CV6 6GF
Tel: 024-7670 5498 **Fax:** ERROR
E-mail: classbuilding@btconnect.com
Website: http://www.classconstruction.co.uk
Directors: D. Dunne (Prop)
Registration no: 6757367 **Date established:** 2005
Turnover: Up to £250,000 **No.of Employees:** 1 - 10 **Product Groups:** 52

Cleanright Steel Fabrications
14 Lythalls Lane Industrial Estate, Coventry, CV6 6FJ
Tel: 024-7666 6870
Website: http://www.sb-steel.co.uk
Directors: J. Wright (Prop)
Date established: 1993 **No.of Employees:** 1 - 10 **Product Groups:** 35

S J Clifford & Co. Ltd
Unit B 19 Bayton Road Industrial Estate Bayton Road, Exhall, Coventry, CV7 9EL
Tel: 024-7636 3961 **Fax:** 024-7664 4097
E-mail: info@sjclifford.co.uk
Website: http://www.sjclifford.co.uk
Bank(s): Barclays
Directors: D. Prescott (MD)
Immediate Holding Company: S.J. CLIFFORD & COMPANY LIMITED
Registration no: 02217663 **VAT No.:** GB 272 3676 45
Date established: 1988 **Turnover:** £500,000 - £1m
No.of Employees: 21 - 50 **Product Groups:** 48

Date of Accounts	Jul 11	Jul 10	Jul 09
Working Capital	-101	-103	-158
Fixed Assets	58	71	84
Current Assets	263	235	243

Coleshill Plastics Ltd
Bodmin Road, Coventry, CV2 5DB
Tel: 024-7672 4900 **Fax:** 024-7672 4901
E-mail: martinpilley@coleshillplastics.co.uk
Website: http://www.coleshillplastics.co.uk
Bank(s): Bank of Scotland plc
Directors: M. Pilley (MD)
Ultimate Holding Company: COLESHILL PLASTICS GROUP LIMITED
Immediate Holding Company: COLESHILL PLASTICS LIMITED
Registration no: 02597705 **VAT No.:** GB 273 5727 38
Date established: 1991 **Turnover:** £2m - £5m **No.of Employees:** 21 - 50
Product Groups: 30, 33, 36, 38, 39, 40, 48, 49, 63, 65, 66, 67, 68

Date of Accounts	Jan 12	Jan 11	Jan 10
Working Capital	99	111	100
Fixed Assets	127	153	184
Current Assets	838	868	613
Current Liabilities	78	N/A	116

Cov Rad Heat Transfer
Canley Works Sir Henry Parkes Road, Coventry, CV5 6BN
Tel: 024-7671 3316 **Fax:** 024-7671 3316
E-mail: bernard.ronchetti@covrad.co.uk
Website: http://www.covrad.co.uk
Bank(s): Lloyds
Managers: M. Hackleton (I.T. Exec), R. Cooper (Sales Prom Mgr), B. Ronchetti (Mgr)

see next page

Cov Rad Heat Transfer - Cont'd

Ultimate Holding Company: THERMASYS GROUP HOLDING COMPANY INC (USA)
Immediate Holding Company: COVRAD HEAT TRANSFER LIMITED
Registration no: 00714170 **VAT No.:** GB 705 3358 50
Date established: 1962 **Turnover:** £20m - £50m
No.of Employees: 101 - 250 **Product Groups:** 39, 40, 68

Date of Accounts	Dec 11	Dec 10	Dec 09
Sales Turnover	35m	28m	22846m
Pre Tax Profit/Loss	3m	844	658m
Working Capital	4m	2m	1354m
Fixed Assets	2m	2m	2548m
Current Assets	10m	9m	7945m
Current Liabilities	1m	2m	3239m

Coventry Chemicals

Woodhams Road Siskin Drive, Coventry, CV3 4FX
Tel: 024-7663 9739 **Fax:** 024-7663 9717
E-mail: info@coventrychemicals.com
Website: http://www.coventrychemicals.com
Directors: K. Blogg (Fin), M. Ward (Purch), P. Staniland (Comm), S. Quinlan (MD)
Ultimate Holding Company: THE COVENTRY GROUP LIMITED
Immediate Holding Company: COVENTRY CHEMICALS LIMITED
Registration no: 01205963 **Date established:** 1975
Turnover: £10m - £20m **No.of Employees:** 51 - 100 **Product Groups:** 66

Date of Accounts	Dec 10	Dec 09	Jun 08
Sales Turnover	13m	15m	9m
Pre Tax Profit/Loss	417	-23	43
Working Capital	686	433	771
Fixed Assets	2m	2m	1m
Current Assets	6m	4m	4m
Current Liabilities	3m	2m	2m

Coventry Evening Telegraph

PO Box 34, Coventry, CV1 1FP
Tel: 024-7663 3633 **Fax:** 024-7655 0868
E-mail: editorial@go2coventry.co.uk
Website: http://www.go2coventry.co.uk
Bank(s): National Westminster Bank Plc
Directors: D. Faulkner (MD), N. Sheen (Fin)
Managers: G. Deaves (Tech Serv Mgr), I. Randle (Purch Mgr), E. Cook (Personnel), M. Brain (Sales & Mktg Mg)
Immediate Holding Company: TRINITY MIRROR PLC
Registration no: 01917810 **VAT No.:** GB 440 3567 67
Turnover: £10m - £20m **No.of Employees:** 251 - 500 **Product Groups:** 28

Coventry Fabrication Services Ltd

34 H Bayton Road Exhall, Coventry, CV7 9EJ
Tel: 024-7636 1414 **Fax:** 024-7636 1414
Directors: D. Hughes (MD)
Immediate Holding Company: COVENTRY FABRICATION SERVICES LIMITED
Registration no: 04450664 **Date established:** 2002
No.of Employees: 1 - 10 **Product Groups:** 35

Date of Accounts	May 12	May 11	May 09
Working Capital	33	59	148
Fixed Assets	18	20	27
Current Assets	78	98	172

Coventry Manufavturingn Ltd

Unit 1 Telford Road, Exhall, Coventry, CV7 9ES
Tel: 024-7636 5490 **Fax:** 024-7636 5465
E-mail: asaptooling@btconnect.com
Directors: L. Hartlett (Dir)
Immediate Holding Company: COVENTRY MANUFACTURING LIMITED
Registration no: 07040678 **VAT No.:** GB 273 1621 74
Date established: 2009 **Turnover:** £250,000 - £500,000
No.of Employees: 1 - 10 **Product Groups:** 46

Date of Accounts	Oct 11	Oct 10
Working Capital	42	3
Fixed Assets	9	N/A
Current Assets	77	3

Coventry Powder Coating Ltd

Unit 5-7 Bilton Industrial Estate Humber Avenue, Coventry, CV3 1JL
Tel: 024-7645 4694 **Fax:** 024- 76454476
E-mail: info@covpow.co.uk
Website: http://www.covpow.co.uk
Directors: S. Hillyard (MD)
Ultimate Holding Company: PAB GROUP LIMITED
Immediate Holding Company: COVENTRY POWDER COATING LIMITED
Registration no: 01932456 **VAT No.:** GB 418 6513 48
Date established: 1985 **Turnover:** £500,000 - £1m
No.of Employees: 1 - 10 **Product Groups:** 46, 48

Date of Accounts	May 11	May 10	May 09
Working Capital	-189	-88	-304
Fixed Assets	67	66	66
Current Assets	159	108	76
Current Liabilities	N/A	48	238

Coventry Silvercraft Co. Ltd

6 Lamb Street, Coventry, CV1 4AD
Tel: 024-7622 3374 **Fax:** 024-7622 7166
E-mail: sales@coventry-silvercraft.co.uk
Website: http://www.coventry-silvercraft.com
Directors: A. Oakley (Dir)
Immediate Holding Company: COVENTRY SILVERCRAFT COMPANY LIMITED (THE)
Registration no: 00967390 **Date established:** 1969
Turnover: £250,000 - £500,000 **No.of Employees:** 1 - 10
Product Groups: 28, 48, 49

Date of Accounts	Dec 11	Dec 10	Dec 09
Working Capital	37	45	45
Fixed Assets	10	11	12
Current Assets	77	85	76

Coventry Toolholders Ltd

Unit 7 9 & 11 Paragon Way, Bayton Road Industrial Estate, Coventry, CV7 9QS
Tel: 024-7664 5999 **Fax:** 024-7664 4081
E-mail: rgordon@coveng.co.uk
Website: http://www.coveng.co.uk
Bank(s): Lloyds
Directors: R. Gordon (Fin)
Ultimate Holding Company: CEL 2003 LTD
Immediate Holding Company: CTL REALISATIONS LIMITED
Registration no: 03668462 **VAT No.:** GB 705 3515 60
Date established: 1998 **Turnover:** £2m - £5m **No.of Employees:** 21 - 50
Product Groups: 46

D B S Midlands Ltd

Bourne Brook Station Road, Arley, Coventry, CV7 8FG
Tel: 01676-540453 **Fax:** 01676-542844
Directors: H. Fellows (Co Sec)
Immediate Holding Company: DBS MIDLANDS LIMITED
Registration no: 02450386 **Date established:** 1989
No.of Employees: 1 - 10 **Product Groups:** 38, 42

Date of Accounts	Mar 12	Mar 11	Mar 10
Working Capital	-6	50	91
Fixed Assets	8	4	5
Current Assets	150	222	203

D C Machine Tool Services Ltd

30 Alderminster Road Mount Nod, Coventry, CV5 7JQ
Tel: 024-7647 0733
E-mail: supportdm@activewebs.co.uk
Website: http://www.dandmmachinetools.co.uk
Directors: M. Coulson (Fin), D. Coulson (MD)
Immediate Holding Company: D.C. MACHINE TOOL SERVICES LIMITED
Registration no: 04688893 **Date established:** 2003
Turnover: Up to £250,000 **No.of Employees:** 1 - 10 **Product Groups:** 46

Date of Accounts	Mar 11	Mar 10	Mar 09
Sales Turnover	N/A	N/A	18
Pre Tax Profit/Loss	N/A	N/A	-6
Working Capital	53	58	41
Fixed Assets	1	1	1
Current Assets	92	87	44
Current Liabilities	N/A	N/A	2

D Drill Master Drillers Ltd

Unit D Shilton Industrial Estate Bulkington Road, Coventry, CV7 9QL
Tel: 024-7661 8602 **Fax:** 024-7660 4409
E-mail: admin@d-drill.co.uk
Website: http://www.d-drill.co.uk
Directors: J. White (Dir)
Ultimate Holding Company: D-DRILL LIMITED
Immediate Holding Company: WHITE DIAMOND PRODUCTS LIMITED
Registration no: 01220625 **Date established:** 1975
No.of Employees: 1 - 10 **Product Groups:** 51

D J S Power Ltd

Aldermans Green Aldermans Green Industrial Estate, Coventry, CV2 2LE
Tel: 024-7661 6115
E-mail: sales@djspower.co.uk
Website: http://www.djspower.co.uk
Directors: F. Pulley (Dir)
Immediate Holding Company: DJS POWER LIMITED
Registration no: 04192865 **Date established:** 2001
No.of Employees: 1 - 10 **Product Groups:** 35, 38, 40

Dampco UK Ltd

21 Lythalls Lane, Coventry, CV6 6FN
Tel: 024-7668 7683 **Fax:** 01536-410944
E-mail: info@dampco.org
Website: http://www.dampco.org
Directors: I. Middleton (MD), B. Middleton (MD), B. Middleton (Dir)
Immediate Holding Company: DAMPCO (U.K.) LIMITED
Registration no: 00940156 **Date established:** 1968
No.of Employees: 11 - 20 **Product Groups:** 32, 52

Date of Accounts	Oct 09	Oct 08	Oct 07
Working Capital	44	70	127
Fixed Assets	212	228	245
Current Assets	272	250	348

Davidson Products & Services

Truggist Lane Berkswell, Coventry, CV7 7BX
Tel: 01676-532606
Directors: T. Taylor (Ptnr)
Date established: 1989 **No.of Employees:** 1 - 10 **Product Groups:** 35

Depilex Ltd

C/O Ellisons 43 Bayton Road, Exhall, Coventry, CV7 9EF
Tel: 024-7636 9768 **Fax:** 01282-602541
E-mail: sales@depilex.co.uk
Website: http://www.depilex.co.uk
Directors: B. Peers (Dir), C. Blakey (Co Sec), C. Braithwaite (Ch), J. Houghton (MD), D. Burkhill (Comm)
Managers: J. Hargreaves (Purch Mgr)
Ultimate Holding Company: Braithwaite Holdings Ltd
Immediate Holding Company: Netspark Ltd
Registration no: 03383722 **Date established:** 1997 **Turnover:** £2m - £5m
No.of Employees: 1 - 10 **Product Groups:** 26, 31, 32, 38

Date of Accounts	Sep 09	Sep 08	Sep 07
Working Capital	-124	6	9
Fixed Assets	13	18	24
Current Assets	226	320	330
Current Liabilities	N/A	108	N/A

Doncasters Sterling Ltd

Colliery Lane Exhall, Coventry, CV7 9NW
Tel: 024-7664 5252 **Fax:** 024-7664 5312
E-mail: info@doncasters.com
Website: http://www.doncasters.com
Bank(s): National Westminster, Birmingham & Barclays, Wolverhampton
Directors: C. Thomas (MD)
Managers: A. Smith, C. Bradshaw (Admin Off), J. McIlvenny, K. Blocksidge (Comptroller), T. Hagen (Personnel)
Immediate Holding Company: PINNACLE MACHINE TOOLS LIMITED
Registration no: 00849216 **Date established:** 1998
Turnover: £50m - £75m **No.of Employees:** 101 - 250
Product Groups: 34, 40

Dongor Ltd

Unit 44 Hotchkiss Way Binley Industrial Estate, Coventry, CV3 2RL
Tel: 024-7644 9298 **Fax:** 024-7644 8642
E-mail: sales@dongor.com
Website: http://www.dongor.com
Directors: T. Hope (Fin), N. Hope (MD)
Immediate Holding Company: DONGOR LIMITED
Registration no: 03977833 **Date established:** 2000
No.of Employees: 1 - 10 **Product Groups:** 26, 35

Date of Accounts	Apr 11	Apr 10	Apr 09
Working Capital	49	48	69
Fixed Assets	28	30	42
Current Assets	148	76	140

Driair International Ltd

9 Maguire Industrial Estate Torrington Avenue, Coventry, CV4 9HN
Tel: 024-7646 6061 **Fax:** 024-7669 4516
E-mail: paulclark@driair.co.uk
Website: http://www.driair.co.uk
Directors: P. Clark (MD)
Immediate Holding Company: DRIAIR INTERNATIONAL LIMITED
Registration no: 02326288 **Date established:** 1988
Turnover: £500,000 - £1m **No.of Employees:** 1 - 10 **Product Groups:** 40

Date of Accounts	Jan 12	Jan 11	Jan 10
Working Capital	61	106	69
Fixed Assets	13	16	24
Current Assets	115	292	271

Ducati Coventry

204 Keresley Road, Coventry, CV6 2JJ
Tel: 024-7633 5300 **Fax:** 024-7633 5307
E-mail: parts@ducaticoventry.com
Website: http://www.ducaticoventry.com
Directors: J. Hackett (Prop)
Immediate Holding Company: JH PERFORMANCE RACING LIMITED
Date established: 2004 **No.of Employees:** 11 - 20 **Product Groups:** 24, 39, 40

Date of Accounts	Mar 11	Mar 10	Mar 09
Working Capital	-65	-54	-33
Fixed Assets	193	230	236
Current Assets	756	730	729

Eagle Ottawa UK Ltd

Unit 2 Coventry Innovation Village, Coventry, CV1 2TL
Tel: 024-7623 4160 **Fax:** 024-7630 8756
Website: http://www.eagleottawa.com
Directors: A. Ross (Sales & Mktg), J. Sumpter (Dir)
Ultimate Holding Company: EVERETT SMITH GROUP LTD (USA)
Immediate Holding Company: EAGLE OTTAWA UK LTD
Registration no: 02645641 **Date established:** 1991
Turnover: £250,000 - £500,000 **No.of Employees:** 1 - 10
Product Groups: 39

Date of Accounts	Nov 11	Nov 08	Nov 09
Sales Turnover	803	19m	442
Pre Tax Profit/Loss	2m	-2m	-335
Working Capital	20m	18m	18m
Fixed Assets	5	271	N/A
Current Assets	20m	19m	18m
Current Liabilities	302	535	92

Eckold Ltd

15 Lifford Way Binley Industrial Estate, Coventry, CV3 2RN
Tel: 024-7645 5580 **Fax:** 024-7630 2777
E-mail: sales@eckold.co.uk
Website: http://www.eckold.co.uk
Directors: L. Green (MD)
Immediate Holding Company: ECKOLD LIMITED
Registration no: 01517315 **Date established:** 1980
Turnover: £500,000 - £1m **No.of Employees:** 1 - 10 **Product Groups:** 30, 35, 36, 39, 40, 46, 66, 67, 72

Date of Accounts	Dec 11	Dec 10	Dec 09
Working Capital	326	322	362
Fixed Assets	172	181	190
Current Assets	476	417	475

Edm Plus UK Ltd

192 Fletchamstead Highway Industrial Estate Fletchamstead Highway, Coventry, CV4 7BB
Tel: 024-7667 8888 **Fax:** 024-7671 2059
E-mail: info@edmplus.co.uk
Website: http://www.edmplus.co.uk
Directors: T. Mercer (Dir)
Immediate Holding Company: EDM PLUS INDUSTRIES LIMITED
Registration no: 07877844 **Date established:** 2011
Turnover: £250,000 - £500,000 **No.of Employees:** 1 - 10
Product Groups: 32, 34, 37, 45, 46

e-loans4you

Office 1 Little Heath Industrial Estate, Old church Road, Coventry, CV6 7NB
Tel: 024-76663250
E-mail: admin@e-loans4you.co.uk
Website: http://www.e-loans4you.co.uk
Managers: A. Reed (Admin Off)
Date established: 2003 **Turnover:** Up to £250,000
No.of Employees: 1 - 10 **Product Groups:** 82

Engine Power

7 Bryant Road Bayton Road Industrial Estate, Coventry, CV7 9EN
Tel: 024-7664 4660 **Fax:** 024-7664 4634
E-mail: enginepower@tiscali.co.uk
Directors: N. Wilkinson (Dir)
Date established: 1995 **Turnover:** £250,000 - £500,000
No.of Employees: 1 - 10 **Product Groups:** 39, 40, 48

Engineering Diamonds Ltd

Bodmin Road Wyken, Coventry, CV2 5DL
Tel: 024-7661 8676
E-mail: sales@endia.co.uk
Website: http://www.endia.co.uk
Directors: R. Laing (MD)
Immediate Holding Company: ENGINEERING DIAMONDS LIMITED
Registration no: 04104009 **Date established:** 2000
No.of Employees: 21 - 50 **Product Groups:** 36, 46

Date of Accounts	Dec 11	Dec 10	Dec 09
Working Capital	-244	-118	-113
Fixed Assets	788	540	605
Current Assets	411	350	299

Eriks (Coventry Service Centre)

Unit 2 Hotchkiss Way Binley Industrial Estate, Coventry, CV3 2RL
Tel: 024-7623 3745 **Fax:** 024-7623 3701
E-mail: coventry@eriks.co.uk
Website: http://www.eriks.co.uk
Managers: M. Powell (District Mgr)
Immediate Holding Company: JIGSAW BEDROOMS LIMITED
Registration no: 03142338 **Date established:** 2004
Turnover: £250m - £500m **No.of Employees:** 1 - 10 **Product Groups:** 22, 66

Ets Gap Electrical Wholesalers (Head Office)
Energy House Falkland Close, Charter Avenue Industrial Estate, Coventry, CV4 8AU
Tel: 024-7646 8259 **Fax:** 024-7669 4090
E-mail: carl.tranter@uk-electric.net
Website: http://www.ukelectric.com
Managers: C. Tranter (Mgr)
Ultimate Holding Company: MNB PRECISION LIMITED
Immediate Holding Company: J.K. LYNCH LIMITED
Registration no: 02769483 **VAT No.:** GB 338 2468 41
Date established: 1972 **Turnover:** £1m - £2m **No.of Employees:** 1 - 10
Product Groups: 67

Date of Accounts	Jun 11	Jun 10	Jun 09
Working Capital	-95	-137	-62
Fixed Assets	370	379	368
Current Assets	213	88	156

Euro Fabrications Coventry Ltd
Unit 5 Brindley Road, Bayton Road Industrial Estate, Coventry, CV7 9EP
Tel: 024-7636 7721 **Fax:** 024-7636 1172
E-mail: david.shorthose@woodcraft-coventry.co.uk
Website: http://www.eurofab.com
Directors: D. Shorthose (Dir), D. Blackford (Fin)
Immediate Holding Company: EURO FABRICATIONS (COVENTRY) LIMITED
Registration no: 03734377 **VAT No.:** GB 545 1854 36
Date established: 1999 **Turnover:** Up to £250,000
No.of Employees: 1 - 10 **Product Groups:** 48

Date of Accounts	Mar 11	Mar 10	Mar 09
Working Capital	-3	-29	-102
Fixed Assets	21	22	26
Current Assets	148	119	98

Evobus UK Ltd
Ashcroft Way Cross Point Business Park, Coventry, CV2 2TU
Tel: 024-7662 6000 **Fax:** 024-7662 6010
Website: http://www.evobus.com
Bank(s): National Westminster Bank Plc
Directors: H. Mader (MD), K. Dodd (Mkt Research), C. Laws (Co Sec)
Managers: M. Beagrie, P. Homles (Tech Serv Mgr), M. Granger (Personnel)
Ultimate Holding Company: DAIMLER AKTIENGESELLSCHAFT (GERMANY)
Immediate Holding Company: EVOBUS (UK) LIMITED
Registration no: 02882442 **Date established:** 1993
Turnover: £20m - £50m **No.of Employees:** 101 - 250 **Product Groups:** 68

Date of Accounts	Dec 11	Dec 10	Dec 09
Sales Turnover	36m	47m	57m
Pre Tax Profit/Loss	-124	2m	-2m
Working Capital	-1m	-2m	-5m
Fixed Assets	16m	10m	6m
Current Assets	14m	13m	13m
Current Liabilities	6m	6m	5m

Evolution Automotive Components Ltd
17 Lythalls Lane, Coventry, CV6 6FN
Tel: 024-7663 7337 **Fax:** 024-7663 7351
E-mail: sales@eacparts.com
Website: http://www.eacparts.com
Directors: S. Hall (MD), J. Hall (Fin)
Immediate Holding Company: EVOLUTION AUTOMOTIVE COMPONENTS LIMITED
Registration no: 02090721 **VAT No.:** GB 478 4413 20
Date established: 1987 **Turnover:** £2m - £5m **No.of Employees:** 1 - 10
Product Groups: 22, 29, 30, 35, 36, 39, 40, 61, 68

Date of Accounts	Dec 11	Dec 10	Dec 09
Working Capital	141	166	198
Fixed Assets	101	96	49
Current Assets	907	997	936

Excel Machine Tools Ltd
Colliery Lane Exhall, Coventry, CV7 9NW
Tel: 024-7664 5038 **Fax:** 024-7636 6666
E-mail: sales@excelmachinetools.co.uk
Website: http://www.excel-machine-tools.co.uk
Directors: F. Sokhi (MD)
Immediate Holding Company: EXCEL MACHINE TOOLS LIMITED
Registration no: 01596813 **VAT No.:** GB 585 1581 17
Date established: 1981 **Turnover:** £5m - £10m **No.of Employees:** 1 - 10
Product Groups: 46, 48, 67

Date of Accounts	Dec 11	Dec 10	Dec 09
Working Capital	894	855	809
Fixed Assets	1m	1m	1m
Current Assets	2m	2m	2m

Expert Tooling & Automation
1 Banner Park Wickmans Drive, Coventry, CV4 9XA
Tel: 024-7642 8520 **Fax:** 024-7642 8501
E-mail: sales@exta.co.uk
Website: http://www.experttooling.co.uk
Bank(s): Barclays
Directors: A. Luciano (MD)
Immediate Holding Company: EXPERT TOOLING & AUTOMATION LIMITED
Registration no: 03489117 **VAT No.:** GB 580 3151 62
Date established: 1998 **Turnover:** £5m - £10m
No.of Employees: 51 - 100 **Product Groups:** 37, 40, 42, 45, 46, 47, 84

Date of Accounts	Jun 11	Jun 10	Jun 09
Working Capital	229	43	-132
Fixed Assets	657	253	466
Current Assets	7m	3m	2m

FANUC Robotics
Seven Stars Industrial Estate Quinn Close, Coventry, CV3 4LB
Tel: 024-7663 9669 **Fax:** 024-7630 4305
E-mail: sales@fanucrobotics.co.uk
Website: http://www.fanucrobotics.co.uk
Bank(s): National Westminster Bank Plc
Directors: C. Sumner (MD)
Managers: M. Hanley (Sales Prom), M. Arbon (Eng Serv Mgr)
Ultimate Holding Company: FANUC Ltd (Japan)
Immediate Holding Company: FANUC Robotics Europe GmbH (Luxemburg)
Registration no: 00153227 **VAT No.:** GB 386 7888 68
Date established: 1983 **Turnover:** £10m - £20m
No.of Employees: 21 - 50 **Product Groups:** 37, 45, 48, 84

Date of Accounts	Dec 09	Dec 08	Mar 12
Sales Turnover	10m	14m	16m
Pre Tax Profit/Loss	303	1m	838
Working Capital	3m	3m	3m
Fixed Assets	102	130	63
Current Assets	5m	5m	8m
Current Liabilities	2m	2m	3m

Federal Express Europe Incorporated
Sutherland House Matlock Road, Coventry, CV1 4JQ
Tel: 08456-070809 **Fax:** 024-7666 2127
Website: http://www.fedex.com
Managers: R. Whitehouse, S. Parrott (Comptroller), L. Mason
Immediate Holding Company: FEDERAL EXPRESS AVIATION SERVICES INTERNATIONAL LIMITED
Registration no: FC014330 **Date established:** 1987
Turnover: £500,000 - £1m **No.of Employees:** 251 - 500
Product Groups: 79

Fire Angel Ltd
vanguard Centre Sir William Lyons Road, Coventry, CV4 7EZ
Tel: 024-7632 3232 **Fax:** 024-7669 3610
E-mail: info@fireangel.co.uk
Website: http://www.fireangel.co.uk
Directors: G. Whitworth (Ch), W. Payne (Fin)
Immediate Holding Company: Sprue Aegis plc
Registration no: 03641019 **Date established:** 2005 **Turnover:** £5m - £10m
No.of Employees: 1 - 10 **Product Groups:** 38, 42

Date of Accounts	Dec 07	Dec 06
Sales Turnover	7263	3269
Pre Tax Profit/Loss	313	707
Working Capital	1682	1423
Fixed Assets	43	16
Current Assets	3190	2176
Current Liabilities	1508	753
ROCE% (Return on Capital Employed)	18.1	49.1
ROT% (Return on Turnover)	4.3	21.6

George Fischer Sales Ltd
Paradise Way, Coventry, CV2 2ST
Tel: 024-7653 5535 **Fax:** 024-7653 0450
E-mail: uk.ps@georgfischer.com
Website: http://www.georgefischer.co.uk
Bank(s): National Westminster Bank Plc
Directors: R. Alsem (Sales & Mktg), R. Trevaskis (MD), E. Ward (Fin)
Managers: M. Lane, I. Ross, S. Alder
Ultimate Holding Company: Georg Fischer AG (Switzerland)
Immediate Holding Company: George Fischer (Holding) Ltd
Registration no: 00273569 **VAT No.:** GB 927 2609 14
Date established: 1930 **Turnover:** £20m - £50m
No.of Employees: 101 - 250 **Product Groups:** 30, 36, 38, 40

Date of Accounts	Dec 11	Dec 10	Dec 09
Sales Turnover	28m	24m	23m
Pre Tax Profit/Loss	479	91	-83
Working Capital	5m	4m	4m
Fixed Assets	5m	5m	5m
Current Assets	8m	7m	7m
Current Liabilities	2m	2m	2m

Flawless Floors
92c Vinecote Road Longford, Coventry, CV6 6EA
Tel: 024-7636 5909
E-mail: lee@flawless-floors.com
Website: http://www.flawless-floors.com
Directors: L. Corrigan (Prop)
Date established: 2004 **No.of Employees:** 1 - 10 **Product Groups:** 25

Foleshill Metal Finishing Ltd
13 Bayton Road Exhall, Coventry, CV7 9EJ
Tel: 024-7664 4225 **Fax:** 024-7636 5876
E-mail: queries@foleshill.co.uk
Website: http://www.foleshill.co.uk
Bank(s): Lloyds TSB Bank plc
Directors: H. Minhas (MD), J. Minhas (Dir)
Ultimate Holding Company: K.S.M. HOLDINGS LIMITED
Immediate Holding Company: FOLESHILL METAL FINISHING LIMITED
Registration no: 03227623 **VAT No.:** GB 418 5751 37
Date established: 1996 **Turnover:** £1m - £2m **No.of Employees:** 11 - 20
Product Groups: 30, 32, 46, 48

Date of Accounts	Mar 11	Mar 10	Mar 09
Working Capital	-236	-284	-305
Fixed Assets	236	281	325
Current Assets	297	186	189

Foleshill Plating Co. Ltd
32 Bayton Rd Exhall, Coventry, CV7 9EJ
Tel: 024-7636 1101 /363505 **Fax:** 024-7636 7783
E-mail: enquiries@foleshillplating.co.uk
Website: http://www.foleshillplating.co.uk
Bank(s): National Westminster Bank Plc
Directors: K. Aojula (MD), M. Singh (Ch)
Registration no: 01656795 **VAT No.:** GB 307 0716 85
Turnover: £1m - £2m **No.of Employees:** 51 - 100 **Product Groups:** 32, 48

Date of Accounts	Aug 11	Aug 10	Aug 09
Working Capital	N/A	N/A	-280
Fixed Assets	N/A	N/A	329
Current Assets	446	585	406

Foremost Filters Ltd
896 Charter Avenue Canley, Coventry, CV4 8AT
Tel: 024-7646 7821 **Fax:** 024-7646 8419
E-mail: foremostfilters@btconnect.com
Website: http://www.foremostfilters.co.uk
Directors: A. Kavanagh (MD), C. Kavanagh (Fin)
Immediate Holding Company: FOREMOST FILTERS LIMITED
Registration no: 04422324 **Date established:** 2002
No.of Employees: 1 - 10 **Product Groups:** 38, 42

Date of Accounts	Oct 11	Oct 10	Oct 09
Working Capital	130	255	112
Fixed Assets	156	17	28
Current Assets	786	588	447

Fraikin Ltd
Fraikin House Torwood Close, Westwood Business Park, Coventry, CV4 8HX
Tel: 024-7669 4494 **Fax:** 024-7647 0419
E-mail: enquiries@vilresins.co.uk
Website: http://www.fraikin.co.uk
Bank(s): National Westminster Bank Plc
Directors: M. Jowett (Co Sec)
Managers: A. Wood (Purch Mgr), N. Finch
Ultimate Holding Company: BABCOCK INTERNATIONAL GROUP PLC
Immediate Holding Company: BABCOCK CRITICAL SERVICES LIMITED
Registration no: SC046710 **VAT No.:** GB 243 2890 53
Date established: 1969 **Turnover:** £50m - £75m
No.of Employees: 51 - 100 **Product Groups:** 72

Date of Accounts	Mar 12	Mar 11	Mar 10
Sales Turnover	65m	60m	60m
Pre Tax Profit/Loss	5m	3m	1m
Working Capital	20m	18m	12m
Fixed Assets	11m	11m	12m
Current Assets	36m	39m	36m
Current Liabilities	13m	18m	18m

G H Pearman Engineers Ltd
Musson Hall Green End Road, Fillongley, Coventry, CV7 8DT
Tel: 01676-540238 **Fax:** 01676-542204
Website: http://www.pearman-agri.co.uk
Directors: M. Northall (Ptnr)
No.of Employees: 1 - 10 **Product Groups:** 41

G & N Tool Ltd
Unit 8 Napier Street, Coventry, CV1 5PR
Tel: 024-7623 1500 **Fax:** 024-7623 1500
E-mail: gandn4tools@btconnect.com
Website: http://www.gandntools.co.uk
Directors: N. Eaves (Dir), G. Judge (Dir)
Date established: 1994 **No.of Employees:** 1 - 10 **Product Groups:** 36

G S N Machine Tools
22/23 Albion Industrial Estate Endermere Road, Holbrooks, Coventry, CV6 5PY
Tel: 024-766 65654 **Fax:** 024-766 65648
E-mail: paul@kwi.uk.com
Website: http://www.gsnmachinetools.net
Turnover: £250,000 - £500,000 **No.of Employees:** 11 - 20
Product Groups: 35, 39, 40, 45, 46, 47, 48, 67, 84

G & T Plastics
Unit 37 Lythalls Lane Industrial Estate Lythalls Lane, Coventry, CV6 6FL
Tel: 024-7663 7983 **Fax:** 024-7663 7983
E-mail: georgegoldie@gtplastics.co.uk
Directors: G. Goldie (Prop)
Immediate Holding Company: ASPIRE FABRICATIONS LIMITED
Date established: 2009 **Turnover:** Up to £250,000
No.of Employees: 1 - 10 **Product Groups:** 30

Gaia Active Ltd
The Techno Centre Coventry University Technology Park, Puma Way, Coventry, CV1 2TT
Tel: 0800-4334040 **Fax:** 024-7623 6024
E-mail: enquiry@savegaia.net
Website: http://www.gaiaactive.com
Directors: H. Young (MD)
Managers: S. Thompson (Mktg Serv Mgr)
Registration no: 06081530 **Date established:** 2007
No.of Employees: 1 - 10 **Product Groups:** 44

Date of Accounts	Mar 08
Working Capital	-14
Fixed Assets	8
Current Assets	7
Current Liabilities	21
Total Share Capital	1

George's Wrought Iron
Unit D5 Little Heath Industrial Estate Old Church Road, Coventry, CV6 7ND
Tel: 024-7666 6660 **Fax:** 024-7666 6662
Website: http://www.georgesiron.com
Directors: L. Carson (Co Sec)
Date established: 1995 **No.of Employees:** 1 - 10 **Product Groups:** 26, 35

Gilbert Curry Industrial Plastics
16 Bayton Road Exhall, Coventry, CV7 9EJ
Tel: 024-7658 8388 **Fax:** 024-7658 8389
E-mail: plastics@gcip.co.uk
Website: http://www.gcip.co.uk
Directors: A. Cole (MD)
Immediate Holding Company: GILBERT CURRY INDUSTRIAL PLASTICS COMPANY LIMITED
Registration no: 01644094 **Date established:** 1982 **Turnover:** £2m - £5m
No.of Employees: 1 - 10 **Product Groups:** 29, 30, 63

Date of Accounts	Jun 11	Jun 10	Jun 09
Working Capital	109	80	78
Fixed Assets	333	291	363
Current Assets	1m	938	734

Goodrem Nicholson
Export House Rowley Road, Coventry, CV3 4FR
Tel: 024-7630 5601 **Fax:** 024-7630 4663
E-mail: clarke@goodrem.co.uk
Website: http://www.goodrem.co.uk
Directors: S. Clarke (MD)
Managers: A. Furbank, C. Baillie (Ops Mgr), L. Poulton (Sales Prom Mgr)
Immediate Holding Company: COVENTRY(CIVIL)AVIATION,LIMITED
Registration no: 02941794 **VAT No.:** GB 418 7092 41
Date established: 1932 **No.of Employees:** 21 - 50 **Product Groups:** 76

Date of Accounts	Dec 11	Dec 10	Dec 09
Working Capital	177	166	151
Current Assets	286	246	217

Gudel Lineartec (UK) Ltd
Unit 5 Wickmans Drive, Coventry, CV4 9XA
Tel: 024-7669 5444 **Fax:** 024-7669 5666
E-mail: info@uk.gudel.com
Website: http://www.gudel.com
Directors: G. Ottley (Jt MD), J. Niven (Jt MD)
Managers: R. Kerry (Eng Serv Mgr)
Ultimate Holding Company: GUDEL GROUP AG (SWITZERLAND)
Immediate Holding Company: GUDEL LINEARTEC (U.K.) LIMITED
Registration no: 02710424 **Date established:** 1992 **Turnover:** £2m - £5m
No.of Employees: 1 - 10 **Product Groups:** 35, 37, 45

Date of Accounts	Dec 11	Dec 10	Dec 09
Sales Turnover	2m	2m	3m
Pre Tax Profit/Loss	37	62	49
Working Capital	-226	-259	33
Fixed Assets	412	421	445
Current Assets	2m	2m	2m
Current Liabilities	1m	244	424

H B Graphics
5 Maguire Industrial Estate Torrington Avenue, Coventry, CV4 9HN
Tel: 024-7646 6447 **Fax:** 024-7646 6445
Directors: S. Hiron (Ptnr)
No.of Employees: 1 - 10 **Product Groups:** 30, 37

Habasitrossi Rossi Gear Motors Ltd
Unit 7-8 Phoenix Park, Bayton Road Industrial Estate, Coventry, CV7 9QN
Tel: 024-7664 4646 **Fax:** 024-7664 4535
E-mail: info.uk@habasitrossi.com
Website: http://www.habasitrossi.com
Bank(s): HSBC Bank plc
Directors: R. Smith (Co Sec)
Managers: C. Bower (Chief Mgr)
Immediate Holding Company: ROSSI GEARMOTORS LIMITED
Registration no: 02127971 **Date established:** 1987 **Turnover:** £1m - £2m
No.of Employees: 11 - 20 **Product Groups:** 35, 37, 39

Date of Accounts	Dec 09	Dec 07
Working Capital	971	971
Current Assets	971	971

Helical Components Coventry Ltd
Telford Road Exhall, Coventry, CV7 9ES
Tel: 024-7636 1058 **Fax:** 024-7636 7270
Directors: K. Norbury (Co Sec)
Immediate Holding Company: HELICAL COMPONENTS (COVENTRY) LIMITED
Registration no: 02957078 **VAT No.:** GB 646 8617 01
Date established: 1994 **Turnover:** Up to £250,000
No.of Employees: 1 - 10 **Product Groups:** 46, 48

Date of Accounts	Aug 11	Aug 10	Aug 09
Working Capital	59	46	52
Fixed Assets	2	2	2
Current Assets	106	71	61

Hennig UK Ltd
Unit 5 Challenge Business Park Challenge Close, Coventry, CV1 5JG
Tel: 024-7655 5690 **Fax:** 024-7625 6591
E-mail: sales@henniguk.com
Website: http://www.henniguk.com
Directors: J. Manning (MD)
Immediate Holding Company: HENNIG (U.K.) LIMITED
Registration no: 01628757 **VAT No.:** GB 307 6724 56
Date established: 1982 **Turnover:** £500,000 - £1m
No.of Employees: 1 - 10 **Product Groups:** 29, 30, 35, 37, 40, 46, 67

Date of Accounts	May 11	May 10	May 09
Working Capital	220	199	183
Fixed Assets	6	9	14
Current Assets	343	288	257

Herbert Tooling Ltd
Rosne Sandy Lane, Fillongley, Coventry, CV7 8DD
Tel: 01676-540040 **Fax:** 01676-542093
E-mail: info@herberttooling.com
Website: http://www.herberttooling.com
Directors: G. Todd (MD), L. Todd (Fin)
Immediate Holding Company: HERBERT TOOLING LIMITED
Registration no: 03243522 **Date established:** 1996
Turnover: Up to £250,000 **No.of Employees:** 1 - 10 **Product Groups:** 46, 48

Date of Accounts	Mar 12	Mar 11	Mar 10
Working Capital	1	5	8
Fixed Assets	7	9	1
Current Assets	22	24	27

Hey Machine Tools Ltd
Lythalls Lane, Coventry, CV6 6FX
Tel: 024-7668 8641 **Fax:** 024-7663 7162
E-mail: heytool@mindspring.com
Website: http://www.mindspring.com
Directors: P. Gilbert (MD), S. Daniels (Fin)
Immediate Holding Company: HAY MACHINE TOOLS LIMITED
Registration no: 01165610 **Date established:** 1974
No.of Employees: 1 - 10 **Product Groups:** 46, 67

Date of Accounts	Jun 11	Jun 10	Jun 09
Working Capital	-282	-282	-220
Fixed Assets	735	735	673
Current Assets	2	2	2

Hitex UK Ltd
Millburn Hill Road, Coventry, CV4 7HS
Tel: 024-7669 2066 **Fax:** 024-7669 2131
E-mail: info@hitex.co.uk
Website: http://www.hitex.co.uk
Bank(s): HSBC Bank plc
Managers: L. Taylor (Sales Admin)
Ultimate Holding Company: INFINEON TECHNOLOGIES AG (GERMANY)
Immediate Holding Company: HITEX (UK) LIMITED
Registration no: 02282162 **VAT No.:** GB 487 6422 08
Date established: 1988 **Turnover:** £2m - £5m **No.of Employees:** 11 - 20
Product Groups: 37, 44, 67, 84, 86, 87

Date of Accounts	Sep 11	Sep 10	Sep 09
Working Capital	955	701	452
Fixed Assets	31	26	18
Current Assets	2m	1m	816

I S O S Engineering Ltd
21 Queens Road, Coventry, CV1 3EG
Tel: 024-7622 3226 **Fax:** 024-7622 8221
E-mail: symon@isos.co.uk
Website: http://www.isos.co.uk
Directors: S. Whitehouse (MD), H. Whitehouse (Fin)
Immediate Holding Company: ISOS ENGINEERING LIMITED
Registration no: 03792888 **Date established:** 1999
Turnover: Up to £250,000 **No.of Employees:** 1 - 10 **Product Groups:** 36, 40, 67

Date of Accounts	Jun 11	Jun 10	Jun 09
Sales Turnover	N/A	71	71
Working Capital	13	8	9
Fixed Assets	2	2	3
Current Assets	48	37	40
Current Liabilities	N/A	3	N/A

Image Plus Ltd
Unit 1 The Depot, Coventry, CV1 4JP
Tel: 024-7683 4780 **Fax:** 024-7683 4781
E-mail: info@image-plus.co.uk
Website: http://www.image-plus.co.uk
Directors: A. Hartin (Dir), S. Whitworth (Prop), A. Hartin (Prop)
Managers: J. Day (Accounts), A. Gill (Sales & Mktg Mg), J. Day (Sales Prom Mgr)
Immediate Holding Company: IMAGE + LIMITED
Registration no: 03009044 **Date established:** 1995
Turnover: Up to £250,000 **No.of Employees:** 1 - 10 **Product Groups:** 44, 89

Inta Audio
PO BOX 4558, Coventry, CV1 9DL
Tel: 024-7636 9898 **Fax:** 0870-1992277
E-mail: sales@inta-audio.com
Website: http://www.inta-audio.com
Managers: I. Lucas (Chief Mgr)
Date established: 2001 **No.of Employees:** 1 - 10 **Product Groups:** 28, 37

J D Neuhaus Ltd
Unit 8 Herald Business Park Golden Acres Lane, Coventry, CV3 2SY
Tel: 024-7665 2500 **Fax:** 024-7665 2555
E-mail: info@jdneuhaus.co.uk
Website: http://www.jdneuhaus.co.uk
Directors: A. Hedley (MD)
Ultimate Holding Company: J D NEUHAUS HEBEZEUGE GMBH & CO (GERMANY)
Immediate Holding Company: J.D. NEUHAUS LIMITED
Registration no: 03642088 **Date established:** 1998 **Turnover:** £2m - £5m
No.of Employees: 1 - 10 **Product Groups:** 39, 41, 45, 46, 67, 83

Date of Accounts	Dec 11	Dec 10	Dec 08
Sales Turnover	2m	463	N/A
Pre Tax Profit/Loss	367	-24	N/A
Working Capital	129	-269	234
Fixed Assets	724	467	199
Current Assets	1m	689	864
Current Liabilities	210	59	N/A

J S Marketing
7 Wheler Road Seven Stars Industrial Estate, Coventry, CV3 4LJ
Tel: 024-7651 1155 **Fax:** 024-7651 8877
Website: http://www.jsmarketing.com
Directors: S. Jandu (Prop)
Immediate Holding Company: JANDU DEVELOPMENTS LTD
VAT No.: GB 585 0137 4 **Date established:** 2002 **Turnover:** £5m - £10m
No.of Employees: 1 - 10 **Product Groups:** 24

Date of Accounts	Dec 07	Dec 06
Working Capital	-22	77
Fixed Assets	145	12
Current Assets	N/A	861
Current Liabilities	22	784

Jade Engineering (Coventry) Ltd
70 Bayton Road Industrial Estate Exhall, Coventry, CV7 9EJ
Tel: 024-7636 5336 **Fax:** 024-7664 4308
E-mail: sales@jade-eng.co.uk
Website: http://www.jade-eng.co.uk
Bank(s): HSBC Bank plc
Directors: D. Thomas (Jt MD), J. Wiberley (Jt MD)
Managers: G. Price (Sales Prom Mgr), J. Rowse (Chief Mgr), M. Price (I.T. Exec), S. Simms (Buyer), T. Ottley (Chief Mgr)
Registration no: 02064486 **VAT No.:** GB 307 0114 16
Date established: 1986 **Turnover:** £250,000 - £500,000
No.of Employees: 21 - 50 **Product Groups:** 67

Date of Accounts	Dec 09	Dec 08	Dec 07
Working Capital	384	525	575
Fixed Assets	326	392	478
Current Assets	482	747	895

Jewson Ltd (t/a Grahams)
Merchant House Binley Business Park Harry Weston Road, Coventry, CV3 2TT
Tel: 024-7643 8400 **Fax:** 024-7643 8401
E-mail: peter.hindle@jewson.co.uk
Website: http://www.jewson.co.uk
Bank(s): HSBC Bank plc
Directors: C. Kenward (Fin), P. Hindle (MD), P. Hindle (Grp Chief Exec)
Managers: J. Yates (District Mgr)
Ultimate Holding Company: COMPAGNIE DE SAINT GOBAIN (FRANCE)
Immediate Holding Company: JEWSON LIMITED
Registration no: 00348407 **VAT No.:** GB 394 1212 63
Date established: 1939 **Turnover:** Over £1,000m
No.of Employees: 1501 & over **Product Groups:** 52

Date of Accounts	Dec 10	Dec 09	Dec 08
Sales Turnover	1547m	1485m	1795m
Pre Tax Profit/Loss	100m	45m	47m
Working Capital	-250m	-349m	-332m
Fixed Assets	387m	461m	549m
Current Assets	1005m	1320m	1146m
Current Liabilities	120m	64m	57m

Jobs@Pertemps
Meriden Hall Main Road, Meriden, Coventry, CV7 7PT
Tel: 01676-525000 **Fax:** 01676-525259
E-mail: press.office@pertemps.co.uk
Website: http://www.pertemps.co.uk
Directors: J. Smith (I.T. Dir), M. Owen (Dir), R. Engelfield (Dir), T. Watts (Ch), J. Jackson (Dir)
Managers: T. Jones (Mgr), A. Hull (Sales Prom Mgr)
Ultimate Holding Company: Network Group Holdings plc
Immediate Holding Company: Pertemps People Development Group Ltd
Registration no: 06515679 **VAT No.:** GB 585 1800 31
Date established: 2008 **Turnover:** £125m - £250m
No.of Employees: 1 - 10 **Product Groups:** 80

John Astley & Son Ltd
Renown Avenue Coventry Business Park, Coventry, CV5 6UF
Tel: 024-7685 4545 **Fax:** 01926-407270
E-mail: sales@astleys.co.uk
Website: http://www.astleys.co.uk
Bank(s): Lloyds TSB Bank plc
Directors: D. Astley (Fin)
Ultimate Holding Company: ASTLEY GROUP LTD
Immediate Holding Company: JOHN ASTLEY & SONS LIMITED
Registration no: 00035885 **VAT No.:** GB 272 3323 78
Date established: 1992 **Turnover:** £5m - £10m **No.of Employees:** 21 - 50
Product Groups: 22, 24, 30

Date of Accounts	Sep 11	Sep 10	Sep 09
Working Capital	557	494	444
Fixed Assets	154	181	192
Current Assets	1m	1m	1m

Johnsons Sectionals
91a Jubilee Crescent, Coventry, CV6 3EX
Tel: 024-7659 6813 **Fax:** 024-7659 4645
E-mail: sales@compton-buildings.co.uk
Website: http://www.comptonbuildings.co.uk
Directors: A. Johnson (Ptnr)
Turnover: Up to £250,000 **No.of Employees:** 1 - 10 **Product Groups:** 25, 33, 35, 66

Keller Foundations Ltd
Oxford Road Ryton on Dunsmore, Coventry, CV8 3EG
Tel: 024-7651 1266 **Fax:** 024-7630 5230
E-mail: info@colcrete-eurodrill.co.uk
Website: http://www.keller.co.uk
Directors: J. Dewaele (Dir), J. Atkinson (Fin), L. Moffit (Pers), D. Taylor (Sales)
Managers: C. Riley (Tech Serv Mgr)
Ultimate Holding Company: KELLER GROUP PLC
Immediate Holding Company: KELLER LIMITED
Registration no: 00485692 **VAT No.:** GB 544 9250 34
Date established: 1950 **Turnover:** £50m - £75m
No.of Employees: 251 - 500 **Product Groups:** 51

Date of Accounts	Dec 11	Dec 10	Dec 09
Sales Turnover	54m	50m	36m
Pre Tax Profit/Loss	-5m	-3m	275
Working Capital	-3m	-448	-2m
Fixed Assets	10m	9m	11m
Current Assets	21m	18m	17m
Current Liabilities	3m	3m	3m

Kite Packaging
186 Torrington Avenue, Coventry, CV4 9AJ
Tel: 024-7642 0088 **Fax:** 024-7642 0062
E-mail: enquiries@kitepackaging.co.uk
Website: http://www.kitepackaging.co.uk
Directors: G. Ashe (Snr Part)
Managers: S. Buckton (Tech Serv Mgr), K. Beale (Fin Mgr), M. Ash (Comptroller)
Ultimate Holding Company: KPG HOLDINGS LIMITED
Immediate Holding Company: KITE PACKAGING LIMITED
Registration no: 04680835 **Date established:** 2003
Turnover: £20m - £50m **No.of Employees:** 51 - 100 **Product Groups:** 27

Date of Accounts	Dec 11	Dec 10	Dec 09
Sales Turnover	25m	21m	17m
Pre Tax Profit/Loss	2m	2m	906
Working Capital	76	-300	-882
Fixed Assets	3m	3m	3m
Current Assets	8m	7m	4m
Current Liabilities	3m	2m	2m

Kramark Gauge & Tool Ltd
27-31 Westwood Road, Coventry, CV5 6GF
Tel: 024-7671 2591 **Fax:** 024-7671 5708
Directors: B. McGuire (Fin), M. Mcguire (MD)
Immediate Holding Company: KRAMARK GAUGE & TOOL LIMITED
Registration no: 02705005 **Date established:** 1992
No.of Employees: 1 - 10 **Product Groups:** 46

Date of Accounts	Feb 08	Feb 11	Feb 10
Working Capital	754	739	694
Fixed Assets	22	9	12
Current Assets	813	848	736

L S Court Ltd
Red Hill Coventry Road, Fillongley, Coventry, CV7 8DA
Tel: 01676-540282 **Fax:** 01676-541110
Website: http://www.ic24.net
Directors: J. Purchase (Co Sec)
Immediate Holding Company: L.S. COURT LIMITED
Registration no: 00458934 **Date established:** 1948
No.of Employees: 1 - 10 **Product Groups:** 37, 39, 72, 79

Date of Accounts	Sep 11	Sep 10	Sep 09
Working Capital	29	-7	33
Fixed Assets	165	87	56
Current Assets	64	87	118

The Landscape Group Ltd
3 Rye Hill Office Park Birmingham Road, Allesley, Coventry, CV5 9AB
Tel: 024-7640 5660 **Fax:** 01635-202050
E-mail: coventry@thelandscapegroup.co.uk
Website: http://www.thelandscapegroup.co.uk
Bank(s): Bank of Scotland
Managers: H. Cole (Sales Admin), J. Francis (Mktg Serv Mgr)
Ultimate Holding Company: HARE NEWCO LIMITED
Immediate Holding Company: THE LANDSCAPE GROUP LIMITED
Registration no: 03542918 **VAT No.:** GB 190 1736 69
Date established: 1998 **Turnover:** £20m - £50m
No.of Employees: 21 - 50 **Product Groups:** 02, 07

Date of Accounts	Mar 11	Mar 10	Sep 08
Sales Turnover	25m	32m	21m
Pre Tax Profit/Loss	2m	1m	483
Working Capital	4m	3m	1m
Fixed Assets	2m	2m	2m
Current Assets	10m	6m	5m
Current Liabilities	3m	2m	2m

Langford Electronics UK Ltd
Unit B19 Little Heath Industrial Estate Old Church Road, Coventry, CV6 7NB
Tel: 024-7670 0320 **Fax:** 024-7670 0321
E-mail: sales@langfordelectronics.co.uk
Website: http://www.langfordelectronics.co.uk
Directors: A. James (Prop)
Immediate Holding Company: LANGFORD ELECTRONICS UK LIMITED
Registration no: 05297964 **Date established:** 2004
Turnover: £250,000 - £500,000 **No.of Employees:** 1 - 10
Product Groups: 32, 37, 38, 46, 47, 48

Date of Accounts	Dec 10	Dec 09	Dec 08
Working Capital	-44	-41	-34
Fixed Assets	10	8	9
Current Assets	122	102	99
Current Liabilities	N/A	N/A	4

Langston Jones & Co. Ltd
Station St West Business Park, Coventry, CV6 5BP
Tel: 024-7666 8592 **Fax:** 024-7666 8593
E-mail: rakeshd@langston-jones.co.uk
Website: http://www.langston-jones.co.uk
Managers: R. Dhameja (Sales Prom Mgr)
Immediate Holding Company: R. LANGSTON JONES & COMPANY LIMITED

Registration no: 02686030 **VAT No.:** GB 608 9177 14
Date established: 1992 **Turnover:** £500,000 - £1m
No.of Employees: 1 - 10 **Product Groups:** 52, 85

Date of Accounts	Mar 12	Mar 11	Mar 10
Working Capital	529	613	578
Fixed Assets	22	27	26
Current Assets	782	741	738

Laroc Coventry Ltd

Curriers Close Charter Avenue Industrial Estate, Coventry, CV4 8AW
Tel: 024-7646 6085 **Fax:** 024-7646 6085
Directors: R. Callen (Dir)
Immediate Holding Company: LAROC (COVENTRY) LIMITED
Registration no: 00414206 **Date established:** 1946
Turnover: Up to £250,000 **No.of Employees:** 1 - 10 **Product Groups:** 48

Date of Accounts	Mar 11	Mar 10	Mar 09
Working Capital	14	3	-4
Fixed Assets	17	18	19
Current Assets	138	114	103

Lawton Tube Co. Ltd

Torrington Avenue, Coventry, CV4 9AB
Tel: 024-7646 6203 **Fax:** 024-7669 4183
E-mail: simon@lawtontubes.co.uk
Website: http://www.lawtontubes.co.uk
Bank(s): Barclays
Directors: O. Lawton (MD), S. Waldron (Fin)
Immediate Holding Company: LAWTON TUBE COMPANY LIMITED(THE)
Registration no: 00165130 **Date established:** 2020
Turnover: £75m - £125m **No.of Employees:** 51 - 100 **Product Groups:** 36

Date of Accounts	Sep 11	Sep 10	Sep 09
Sales Turnover	104m	87m	52m
Pre Tax Profit/Loss	2m	2m	2m
Working Capital	12m	10m	9m
Fixed Assets	3m	3m	3m
Current Assets	27m	23m	19m
Current Liabilities	4m	3m	2m

Lee Beesley Ltd

Quinn Close, Coventry, CV3 4LH
Tel: 024-7651 6060 **Fax:** 024-7630 6474
E-mail: aharvey@leebeesley.co.uk
Website: http://www.leebeesley.co.uk
Managers: N. Bampton (District Mgr)
Ultimate Holding Company: VINCI SA (FRANCE)
Immediate Holding Company: LEE BEESLEY HOLDINGS LIMITED
Registration no: 01234891 **VAT No.:** GB 545 1884 27
Date established: 1975 **Turnover:** £20m - £50m **No.of Employees:** 1 - 10
Product Groups: 37, 48, 52, 84, 85

Date of Accounts	Dec 10	Dec 09	Dec 08
Working Capital	N/A	1m	1m
Fixed Assets	N/A	300	300
Current Assets	N/A	1m	1m

Lifeline Fire & Safety Systems Ltd

Burnsall Road Industrial Estate Burnsall Road, Coventry, CV5 6BU
Tel: 024-7671 2999 **Fax:** 024-7671 2998
E-mail: sales@lifeline-fire.co.uk
Website: http://www.lifeline-fire.co.uk
Bank(s): National Westminster Bank Plc
Directors: J. Morris (MD)
Immediate Holding Company: LIFELINE FIRE AND SAFETY SYSTEMS LIMITED
Registration no: 02898515 **VAT No.:** GB 585 3848 90
Date established: 1994 **No.of Employees:** 11 - 20 **Product Groups:** 40

Date of Accounts	Mar 12	Mar 11	Mar 10
Working Capital	1m	795	525
Fixed Assets	158	169	173
Current Assets	1m	1m	874

Lifting Gear Centre

Brandon Road Binley, Coventry, CV3 2JD
Tel: 024-7645 6666 **Fax:** 024-7663 5113
E-mail: info@arbil.co.uk
Website: http://www.arbil.co.uk
Managers: C. Maughan
Date established: 1960 **No.of Employees:** 1 - 10 **Product Groups:** 35, 39, 45

Lightning Aerospace Ltd

Falkland Close Charter Avenue Industrial Estate, Coventry, CV4 8AU
Tel: 024-7642 2038 **Fax:** 024-7646 4745
E-mail: info@lightningaerospace.co.uk
Website: http://www.lightningaerospace.co.uk
Bank(s): HSBC
Directors: S. Kirkham (MD)
Managers: J. Ramsey (Chief Acct), A. Redfearn, A. Redfern (Mktg Serv Mgr), D. Levay (Project Eng)
Ultimate Holding Company: PLAYFELS LIMITED
Immediate Holding Company: LIGHTNING AEROSPACE LIMITED
Registration no: 02769483 **VAT No.:** GB 585 1545 21
Date established: 1992 **Turnover:** £1m - £2m **No.of Employees:** 11 - 20
Product Groups: 46, 48

Date of Accounts	Mar 11	Mar 10	Mar 09
Working Capital	409	420	400
Fixed Assets	350	358	160
Current Assets	1m	2m	1m
Current Liabilities	N/A	N/A	756

Linear Projects

7 Browett Road Coundon, Coventry, CV6 1BA
Tel: 024-7659 5813
Managers: G. Brown (Mgr)
Immediate Holding Company: LINEAR PROJECTS UK LTD
Registration no: 05858907 **Date established:** 2006
No.of Employees: 1 - 10 **Product Groups:** 46

Lionbridge UK Ltd

Enterprise Centre Coventry University Technology Park Puma Way, Coventry, CV1 2TT
Tel: 024-7682 6500 **Fax:** 024-7663 2925
E-mail: info.cov@lionbridge.com
Website: http://www.lionbridge.com
Directors: I. Middlemiss (Fin), R. Cowan (Grp Chief Exec)
Managers: A. Doggett (Tech Serv Mgr), C. Voisey
Ultimate Holding Company: LIONBRIDGE TECHNOLOGIES INC (USA)
Immediate Holding Company: LIONBRIDGE (UK) LIMITED
Registration no: 01295207 **Date established:** 1977 **Turnover:** £5m - £10m
No.of Employees: 21 - 50 **Product Groups:** 80

Date of Accounts	Dec 11	Dec 10	Dec 09
Sales Turnover	10m	9m	8m
Pre Tax Profit/Loss	75	14	-127
Working Capital	2m	2m	2m
Fixed Assets	179	124	179
Current Assets	10m	6m	6m
Current Liabilities	995	782	758

The London Taxi Company

Holyhead Road, Coventry, CV5 8JJ
Tel: 024-7657 2040 **Fax:** 024-7657 2001
E-mail: jloakes@london-taxis.co.uk
Website: http://www.london-taxis.co.uk
Directors: J. Russell (Dir), P. Shellcock (MD), P. Shilcock (MD), M. Devin (Co Sec), M. Cheyne (Sales & Mktg), J. Shillcock (MD), G. Jones (Pers), A. Pearman (Fin)
Managers: J. Loakes (Chief Mgr), E. Osmond
Ultimate Holding Company: MANGANESE BRONZE HOLDINGS PLC
Immediate Holding Company: THE LONDON TAXI COMPANY LIMITED
Registration no: 03422115 **Date established:** 1997
Turnover: £75m - £125m **No.of Employees:** 1 - 10 **Product Groups:** 39

Lyntech Systems Ltd

Maguire Industrial Estate Torrington Avenue, Coventry, CV4 9HN
Tel: 024-7646 8710 **Fax:** 024-7646 6111
E-mail: sales@lyntech-systems.ltd.uk
Website: http://www.lyntechsystems.co.uk
Directors: P. Ellis (Dir)
Immediate Holding Company: LYNTECH SYSTEMS LIMITED
Registration no: 02279358 **VAT No.:** GB 487 6671 84
Date established: 1988 **Turnover:** £2m - £5m **No.of Employees:** 1 - 10
Product Groups: 26, 35, 36, 52

Date of Accounts	Jun 11	Jun 10	Jun 09
Working Capital	342	334	338
Fixed Assets	7	8	10
Current Assets	410	455	468

M B K Motor Rewinds Ltd

10a Lythalls Lane, Coventry, CV6 6FG
Tel: 024-7668 9510 **Fax:** 024-7666 2944
E-mail: sales@mbk-rewinds.co.uk
Website: http://www.mbk-rewinds.co.uk
Bank(s): HSBC Bank plc
Directors: T. Evans (Dir)
Ultimate Holding Company: MONTSPUR PLC
Immediate Holding Company: MBK MOTOR REWINDS LIMITED
Registration no: 02429411 **VAT No.:** GB 584 9378 77
Date established: 1989 **No.of Employees:** 11 - 20 **Product Groups:** 35, 36, 37, 40

Date of Accounts	Jun 11	Jun 10	Jun 09
Working Capital	38	44	28
Fixed Assets	46	24	25
Current Assets	308	252	271

M C S Control Systems Ltd

Unit 4 Phoenix Park Bayton Road Industrial Estate, Coventry, CV7 9QN
Tel: 024-7636 0211 **Fax:** 024-7636 8219
E-mail: sales@mcscontrolsystems.co.uk
Website: http://www.mcscontrolsystems.co.uk
Directors: S. Foster (Sales), K. Parsons (Fin)
Managers: P. Jones (Transport), N. Sallabank, A. Powell (Mktg Serv Mgr)
Ultimate Holding Company: W.J. HOLDINGS LIMITED
Immediate Holding Company: MCS CONTROL SYSTEMS LIMITED
Registration no: 01279131 **VAT No.:** GB 293 9643 10
Date established: 1976 **Turnover:** £5m - £10m **No.of Employees:** 1 - 10
Product Groups: 37

Date of Accounts	Nov 11	Nov 10	Nov 09
Sales Turnover	9m	7m	8m
Pre Tax Profit/Loss	306	-158	144
Working Capital	690	503	703
Fixed Assets	62	71	83
Current Assets	3m	2m	2m
Current Liabilities	1m	462	821

M E L Secure Systems Ltd

2020 House Siskin Drive, Middlemarch Business Park, Coventry, CV3 4FJ
Tel: 024-7630 6606 **Fax:** 024-7630 6100
E-mail: sales@melsecuresystems.com
Website: http://www.melsecuresystems.com
Directors: P. Druzyc (Dir)
Immediate Holding Company: MEL SECURE SYSTEMS LIMITED
Registration no: 04440452 **Date established:** 2002
No.of Employees: 11 - 20 **Product Groups:** 36, 37, 38, 40, 44, 67, 81, 83

M H C Fabrications Ltd

654 Kenilworth Road Balsall Common, Coventry, CV7 7DY
Tel: 01676-530308
Directors: J. Catley (Dir)
Immediate Holding Company: DOVEDALE FENCING SUPPLY AND MANUFACTURE LIMITED
Registration no: 06948348 **Date established:** 2009
No.of Employees: 1 - 10 **Product Groups:** 26, 35

M P L Fabrications

Dutton Road Aldermans Green Industrial Estate, Coventry, CV2 2LE
Tel: 024-7661 0778 **Fax:** 024-7661 9499
E-mail: ian.gurney@mplfabrications.com
Website: http://www.mplfabrications.com
Directors: I. Gurney (Ptnr)
Immediate Holding Company: DJS POWER LIMITED
Registration no: 04192865 **VAT No.:** GB 376 0168 47
Date established: 2001 **Turnover:** £250,000 - £500,000
No.of Employees: 11 - 20 **Product Groups:** 48

Macfarlane Group UK Ltd

Siskin Parkway East Middlemarch Business Park, Coventry, CV3 4PE
Tel: 024-7621 7000 **Fax:** 024-7651 1302
E-mail: enquiries@macfarlanepackaging.com
Website: http://www.macfarlanegroup.net
Directors: G. Young (Co Sec), G. Young (Dir)
Ultimate Holding Company: MACFARLANE GROUP PLC
Immediate Holding Company: MACFARLANE GROUP UK LIMITED
Registration no: 01630389 **Date established:** 1982
Turnover: £75m - £125m **No.of Employees:** 501 - 1000
Product Groups: 27, 30, 48

Date of Accounts	Dec 10	Dec 09	Dec 08
Sales Turnover	117m	97m	104m
Pre Tax Profit/Loss	4m	1m	4m
Working Capital	5m	5m	11m
Fixed Assets	15m	11m	12m
Current Assets	41m	34m	33m
Current Liabilities	5m	8m	4m

Marque Restore Chrome Plating Ltd

4 Shilton Industrial Estate Bulkington Road, Coventry, CV7 9JY
Tel: 024-7662 2225 **Fax:** 024-7662 2677
E-mail: alan.olner@marquerestore.co.uk
Website: http://www.marquerestore.co.uk
Directors: E. Davies (Fin), A. Olner (MD)
Immediate Holding Company: MARQUE RESTORE CHROME PLATING LIMITED
Registration no: 04089702 **Date established:** 2000
No.of Employees: 1 - 10 **Product Groups:** 46, 48

Date of Accounts	Oct 11	Oct 10	Oct 09
Working Capital	36	21	-5
Fixed Assets	21	22	24
Current Assets	100	48	37

Marrill Engineering Co. Ltd

Waterman Road, Coventry, CV6 5TP
Tel: 024-7668 9221 **Fax:** 024-7666 8114
E-mail: sales@marrill.co.uk
Website: http://www.marrill.co.uk
Bank(s): Barclays
Directors: J. Phillips (MD)
Managers: D. Redding (Ops Mgr), K. Brooks (Buyer), M. Baker (Comptroller)
Ultimate Holding Company: MARRILL GROUP LTD
Immediate Holding Company: MARRILL ENGINEERING COMPANY LIMITED
Registration no: 00819905 **VAT No.:** GB 114 4493 86
Date established: 1964 **Turnover:** £10m - £20m
No.of Employees: 21 - 50 **Product Groups:** 39, 46

Date of Accounts	Aug 10	Aug 09	Aug 08
Sales Turnover	13m	12m	15m
Pre Tax Profit/Loss	-475	102	380
Working Capital	1m	2m	2m
Fixed Assets	1m	2m	1m
Current Assets	6m	6m	6m
Current Liabilities	1m	961	584

Masonic Collection

PO Box 4726, Coventry, CV6 9ES
Tel: 024-7668 8357
E-mail: sales@masoniccollection.co.uk
Website: http://www.masoniccollection.com
Turnover: Up to £250,000 **No.of Employees:** 1 - 10 **Product Groups:** 35, 49

Matrix Machine Tool Coventry Ltd

Unit 2 Earl Place Business Park Fletchamstead Highway, Coventry, CV4 9XL
Tel: 024-7671 8886 **Fax:** 024-7667 8899
E-mail: hackletondean@matrixgrinding.co.uk
Website: http://www.matrix-machine.com
Directors: D. Hackleton (Dir)
Managers: N. Chiow, B. Hilton, M. Lester (Sales Prom Mgr)
Ultimate Holding Company: COVENTRY MATRIX TECHNOLOGIES LIMITED
Immediate Holding Company: MATRIX MACHINE TOOL (COVENTRY) LIMITED
Registration no: 04939500 **Date established:** 2003
No.of Employees: 11 - 20 **Product Groups:** 46

Date of Accounts	Dec 11	Dec 10	Dec 09
Sales Turnover	3m	3m	989
Pre Tax Profit/Loss	320	-512	-1m
Working Capital	-42	-397	-1m
Fixed Assets	447	530	711
Current Assets	3m	3m	2m
Current Liabilities	384	518	2m

Max Buch Cables

19 Far Gosford Street, Coventry, CV1 5DT
Tel: 024-7622 8285
Directors: M. Buch (Prop)
Date established: 1971 **No.of Employees:** 1 - 10 **Product Groups:** 36, 40

Mccarthy & Associates Ltd

Broad Lane, Coventry, CV5 7AX
Tel: 024-7646 8866 **Fax:** 024-7669 4486
E-mail: enquiries@mccarthyinteriors.co.uk
Website: http://www.mccarthygroup.co.uk
Directors: B. Mc Carthy (Co Sec), S. Mccarthy (MD)
Ultimate Holding Company: MCCARTHY GROUP LIMITED
Immediate Holding Company: MCCARTHY & ASSOCIATES LIMITED
Registration no: 01692577 **Date established:** 1983 **Turnover:** £2m - £5m
No.of Employees: 11 - 20 **Product Groups:** 26, 38, 49, 52, 84

Date of Accounts	Jul 12	Jul 09	Jan 12
Sales Turnover	2m	2m	2m
Pre Tax Profit/Loss	147	-89	-34
Working Capital	182	108	35
Fixed Assets	4	59	4
Current Assets	755	734	765
Current Liabilities	37	150	200

Metprep Ltd

Unit 10 Curriers Close Charter Avenue Industrial Estate, Coventry, CV4 8AW
Tel: 024-7642 1222 **Fax:** 024-7642 1192
E-mail: sales@metprep.co.uk
Website: http://www.metprep.co.uk
Directors: J. Ashby (MD)
Immediate Holding Company: METPREP LIMITED
Registration no: 02639800 **VAT No.:** GB 581 2168 44
Date established: 1991 **Turnover:** £2m - £5m **No.of Employees:** 1 - 10
Product Groups: 38, 42

Date of Accounts	Dec 11	Dec 10	Dec 09
Working Capital	1m	1m	871
Fixed Assets	43	53	34
Current Assets	2m	1m	1m

Midland Mobility Ltd

194 Torrington Avenue, Coventry, CV4 9BL
Tel: 024-7646 2424 **Fax:** 024-7646 5288
E-mail: sales@midlandmobility.co.uk
Website: http://www.midlandmobility.co.uk

see next page

Midland Mobility Ltd - Cont'd

Directors: I. Tippett (Co Sec)
Immediate Holding Company: MIDLAND MOBILITY LIMITED
Registration no: 02012080 **VAT No.:** GB 669 5318 73
Date established: 1986 **Turnover:** £250,000 - £500,000
No.of Employees: 1 - 10 **Product Groups:** 26, 39

Date of Accounts	Mar 12	Mar 11	Mar 10
Working Capital	43	43	62
Fixed Assets	12	12	23
Current Assets	80	74	116

Mills Forgings Ltd

Charterhouse Road, Coventry, CV1 2BJ
Tel: 024-7622 4985 **Fax:** 024-7652 5453
E-mail: sales@millsforgings.co.uk
Website: http://www.millsforgings.co.uk
Bank(s): Barclays
Directors: L. Joyce (Ch), J. O'Brien (Co Sec)
Immediate Holding Company: MILLS FORGINGS LIMITED
Registration no: 00424123 **Date established:** 1946 **Turnover:** £2m - £5m
No.of Employees: 21 - 50 **Product Groups:** 46, 48

Date of Accounts	Feb 08	Feb 11	Feb 10
Working Capital	-62	-35	-60
Fixed Assets	515	415	434
Current Assets	654	497	495

Mil-Ver Metal Company Ltd

Coronel Avenue Rowleys Green Industrial Estate, Longford, Coventry, CV6 6AP
Tel: 024-7666 6292 **Fax:** 024-7666 2299
E-mail: hamish.brown@milver.co.uk
Website: http://www.milvermetal.com
Bank(s): Barclay
Directors: S. Miles (MD), J. Gazey (Pers), M. Ibberson (Sales), H. Brown (Fin), H. Ibberson (Sales), G. Miles (Dir), H. Ibberson (Sales)
Managers: P. Wright (Comptroller), P. White (Comptroller), B. Morton (Buyer)
Ultimate Holding Company: AMCO INVESTMENTS LIMITED
Immediate Holding Company: MIL-VER METAL COMPANY LIMITED
Registration no: 01634739 **VAT No.:** GB 307 5678 36
Date established: 1982 **Turnover:** £20m - £50m
No.of Employees: 51 - 100 **Product Groups:** 34

Date of Accounts	Dec 11	Dec 10	Dec 09
Sales Turnover	50m	44m	25m
Pre Tax Profit/Loss	372	518	104
Working Capital	5m	4m	697
Fixed Assets	3m	4m	4m
Current Assets	13m	12m	8m
Current Liabilities	619	556	320

Modulamb Ltd

Peter Hall Farm Peter Hall Lane, Walsgrave On Sowe, Coventry, CV2 2DR
Tel: 024-7661 1647 **Fax:** 024-7661 3866
E-mail: info@modulamb.com
Website: http://www.modulamb.com
Directors: R. Meakin (MD)
Immediate Holding Company: MODULAMB LIMITED
Registration no: 01443779 **Date established:** 1979
Turnover: £250,000 - £500,000 **No.of Employees:** 1 - 10
Product Groups: 41

Date of Accounts	Feb 08	Feb 11	Feb 10
Sales Turnover	328	384	400
Pre Tax Profit/Loss	2	3	13
Working Capital	29	48	37
Fixed Assets	10	20	15
Current Assets	102	112	108
Current Liabilities	3	1	3

Motaquip Ltd

PO Box 126 Torrington Avenue, Tile Hill, Coventry, CV4 0UX
Tel: 024-7688 3002 **Fax:** 024-7647 3235
E-mail: info@motamail.net
Website: http://www.motaquip.co.uk
Bank(s): HSBC Bank plc
Directors: D. Higgins (MD), R. Dyson (Dir)
Ultimate Holding Company: P S A Peugeot Citroen
Immediate Holding Company: Peugeot Motor Co. P.L.C.
Registration no: 04418860 **Date established:** 1981
Turnover: £20m - £50m **No.of Employees:** 501 - 1000
Product Groups: 29, 35, 37, 38, 39, 40, 42, 68

Date of Accounts	Dec 03	Dec 02	Dec 01
Working Capital	180	180	180
Current Assets	180	180	180
Total Share Capital	180	180	180

Murray Uniforms

Bodmin Road Bodmin Road Industrial Estate, Coventry, CV2 5DZ
Tel: 024-7658 7980 **Fax:** 024-7658 7981
E-mail: sales@murray-uniforms.co.uk
Website: http://www.murray-uniforms.co.uk
Bank(s): Lloyds TSB
Directors: M. Vas (MD)
Ultimate Holding Company: ELMDENE GROUP LIMITED
Immediate Holding Company: MURRAY UNIFORMS LTD
Registration no: 06840659 **VAT No.:** 273 7062 54 **Date established:** 2009
Turnover: £250,000 - £500,000 **No.of Employees:** 11 - 20
Product Groups: 22, 24

Date of Accounts	Dec 10	Dec 09
Sales Turnover	N/A	356
Pre Tax Profit/Loss	N/A	27
Working Capital	625	729
Fixed Assets	152	128
Current Assets	836	980
Current Liabilities	N/A	54

Mustard Presentations

Herald Business Park Golden Acres Lane, Coventry, CV3 2SY
Tel: 024-7644 2422 **Fax:** 024-7644 2416
E-mail: solutions@mustard.uk.net
Website: http://www.mustard.uk.net
Directors: K. Hunt (Chief Op Offcr), C. Macleod (MD)
Managers: A. Bayliss (Chief Acct)
Immediate Holding Company: THE PRESENTATION SOLUTIONS GROUP LIMITED
Registration no: 03942824 **Date established:** 2000 **Turnover:** £1m - £2m
No.of Employees: 11 - 20 **Product Groups:** 37, 38, 67

Date of Accounts	Jun 11	Jun 10	Jun 09
Working Capital	-117	-83	-68
Fixed Assets	249	367	200
Current Assets	238	356	234

N P Aerospace Ltd

473 Foleshill Road, Coventry, CV6 5AQ
Tel: 024-7670 2802 **Fax:** 024-7668 7313
E-mail: info@np-aerospace.co.uk
Website: http://www.np-aerospace.com
Bank(s): HSBC
Directors: B. Singh Shergill (Fin), D. Eldridge (MD)
Managers: D. Wadge, A. Tiwana (Tech Serv Mgr), M. Larwood (Purch Mgr)
Ultimate Holding Company: MORGAN CRUCIBLE COMPANY PLC(THE)
Immediate Holding Company: NP AEROSPACE LIMITED
Registration no: 03472480 **VAT No.:** GB 704 7087 41
Date established: 1997 **Turnover:** £75m - £125m
No.of Employees: 101 - 250 **Product Groups:** 25, 30

Date of Accounts	Dec 08	Jan 10	Jan 11
Sales Turnover	70m	185m	122m
Pre Tax Profit/Loss	10m	27m	16m
Working Capital	27m	50m	63m
Fixed Assets	2m	4m	4m
Current Assets	54m	98m	101m
Current Liabilities	6m	15m	7m

N U M UK Ltd

Unit 5 Fairfield Court Seven Stars Industrial Estate Wheler Road, Coventry, CV3 4LJ
Tel: 024-7630 1259 **Fax:** 08717-504021
E-mail: sales.uk@num.com
Website: http://www.num.com
Managers: S. Moore (Mgr)
Ultimate Holding Company: VERDOSO INVESTMENTS SA (LUXEMBOURG)
Immediate Holding Company: NUM (UK) LIMITED
Registration no: 02198020 **Date established:** 1987
Turnover: £500,000 - £1m **No.of Employees:** 1 - 10 **Product Groups:** 35, 37, 38, 39, 44, 46, 67

Date of Accounts	Dec 11	Dec 10	Dec 09
Sales Turnover	833	670	689
Pre Tax Profit/Loss	93	-103	-37
Working Capital	348	275	334
Fixed Assets	3	20	30
Current Assets	551	496	1m
Current Liabilities	74	37	637

Nationwide Access Ltd

Old Church Road, Coventry, CV6 7BZ
Tel: 024-7668 8855 **Fax:** 024-7668 2119
E-mail: mail@nationwideaccess.co.uk
Website: http://www.nationwideaccess.co.uk
Directors: H. Walters (Mkt Research)
Managers: A. Briggs (District Mgr)
Ultimate Holding Company: Lavendon Group plc
Immediate Holding Company: NATIONWIDE ACCESS LIMITED
Registration no: 04405299 **Date established:** 2002
No.of Employees: 1 - 10 **Product Groups:** 45, 83

Newco Catering Equipment Ltd

Unit 1-2 Broad Lane, Tile Hill, Coventry, CV5 7AX
Tel: 024-7642 6000 **Fax:** 024-7646 2090
E-mail: info@newcocatering.com
Website: http://www.newcocatering.com
Directors: J. Waters (Dir)
Registration no: 04763034 **No.of Employees:** 1 - 10 **Product Groups:** 20, 40, 41

Newcomer UK Ltd

Deeming Taylor Estate Blackhorse Road, Exhall, Coventry, CV7 9FW
Tel: 024-7636 3535 **Fax:** 024-7636 1777
E-mail: gary-wyatt@btconnect.com
Website: http://www.newcomer.co.uk
Directors: G. Wyatt (MD)
Immediate Holding Company: NEWCOMER UK LIMITED
Registration no: 02666403 **Date established:** 1991
Turnover: £250,000 - £500,000 **No.of Employees:** 1 - 10
Product Groups: 46, 47

Date of Accounts	Feb 08	Feb 11	Feb 10
Sales Turnover	698	N/A	421
Pre Tax Profit/Loss	7	N/A	1
Working Capital	88	121	88
Fixed Assets	11	5	7
Current Assets	253	244	176
Current Liabilities	36	18	15

Nixon Industrial Diamonds Ltd

Albion Industrial Estate Endermere Road, Coventry, CV6 5RR
Tel: 024-7668 6069 **Fax:** 024-7663 7213
E-mail: office@nixondiamonds.co.uk
Website: http://www.nixondiamonds.co.uk
Bank(s): National Westminster Bank Plc
Directors: T. Nichols (Fin)
Immediate Holding Company: NIXON INDUSTRIAL DIAMONDS LIMITED
Registration no: 00940303 **VAT No.:** GB 272 7345 48
Date established: 1968 **Turnover:** £1m - £2m **No.of Employees:** 11 - 20
Product Groups: 36, 46, 48, 66

Date of Accounts	Oct 11	Oct 10	Oct 09
Working Capital	56	50	81
Fixed Assets	25	21	31
Current Assets	209	171	182
Current Liabilities	N/A	39	N/A

Norman Hay plc

Godiva Place, Coventry, CV1 5PN
Tel: 024-7622 9373 **Fax:** 024-7622 4420
E-mail: info@normanhay.com
Website: http://www.normanhay.com
Bank(s): Bank of Scotland
Directors: B. Cattle (Co Sec)
Managers: N. Ogden, V. Bellanti
Ultimate Holding Company: NORMAN HAY PLC
Immediate Holding Company: NORMAN HAY PLC
Registration no: 00405025 **VAT No.:** GB 222 5248 91
Date established: 1946 **Turnover:** £20m - £50m
No.of Employees: 101 - 250 **Product Groups:** 42

Date of Accounts	Dec 11	Dec 10	Dec 09
Sales Turnover	30m	25m	26m
Pre Tax Profit/Loss	3m	2m	865
Working Capital	7m	6m	4m
Fixed Assets	8m	8m	10m
Current Assets	20m	12m	12m
Current Liabilities	7m	3m	5m

Notedome Ltd

34 Herald Way Binley Industrial Estate, Coventry, CV3 2RQ
Tel: 024-7663 5192 **Fax:** 024-7663 5509
E-mail: sales@notedome.co.uk
Website: http://www.notedome.co.uk
Directors: H. Tunnicliffe (I.T. Dir), B. Lear (MD)
Immediate Holding Company: NOTEDOME LIMITED
Registration no: 01326364 **Date established:** 1977 **Turnover:** £2m - £5m
No.of Employees: 11 - 20 **Product Groups:** 30, 31

Date of Accounts	Dec 11	Dec 10	Dec 09
Working Capital	787	1m	857
Fixed Assets	1m	281	285
Current Assets	3m	3m	2m

Notice Board Company

Po Box 2986, Coventry, CV3 6YP
Tel: 024-7601 0076 **Fax:** 024-7601 2862
E-mail: sales@noticeboardcompany.com
Website: http://www.noticeboardcompany.com
Product Groups: 26, 28, 30, 35, 49, 64, 66, 67

Nullifire Ltd A Division of Tremco Illbruck Coatings Ltd

Torrington Avenue, Coventry, CV4 9TJ
Tel: 024-7685 5000 **Fax:** 024-7646 9547
E-mail: protect@nullifire.com
Website: http://www.nullifire.com
Bank(s): Lloyds TSB
Directors: D. Hughes (Comm)
Managers: S. Quinn (I.T. Exec), J. Gordon (Chief Mgr)
Ultimate Holding Company: Dore Holdings
Immediate Holding Company: R P M Inc
Registration no: 01238924 **Turnover:** £10m - £20m
No.of Employees: 21 - 50 **Product Groups:** 32, 36, 40, 51, 52

Date of Accounts	May 11	May 10	May 09
Sales Turnover	N/A	7m	14m
Pre Tax Profit/Loss	-9	69	1m
Working Capital	4m	4m	4m
Fixed Assets	N/A	N/A	645
Current Assets	4m	4m	5m
Current Liabilities	32	61	1m

OCS Worldwide Ltd

Unit 1B Siskin Parkway East, 4020 Middlemarch Business Park, Coventry, CV3 4SU
Tel: 0845-6789800 **Fax:** 020-7640 3909
E-mail: coventry@ocsworldwide.co.uk
Website: http://www.ocsworldwide.co.uk
Managers: M. Davis (Warehouse Mgr), N. Blunt (District Mgr)
Immediate Holding Company: Overseas Courier Service (London) Ltd
Registration no: 06746489 **Turnover:** £20m - £50m
No.of Employees: 11 - 20 **Product Groups:** 72, 76, 79

Odin

Unit 4 Fullwood Close, Aldermans Green Industrial Estate, Coventry, CV2 2SS
Tel: 024-7660 2622 **Fax:** 024-7660 2649
Website: http://www.odinengineering.co.uk
Directors: J. Barker (Dir), A. Barker (MD)
Immediate Holding Company: ODIN ENGINEERING LIMITED
Registration no: 02390367 **Date established:** 1989
Turnover: £500,000 - £1m **No.of Employees:** 1 - 10 **Product Groups:** 46

Date of Accounts	Jul 08	Jul 07	Jul 06
Working Capital	70	97	39
Fixed Assets	22	18	26
Current Assets	202	208	152

Oleo International Ltd

Grovelands Estate Longford Road, Exhall, Coventry, CV7 9ND
Tel: 024-7664 5555 **Fax:** 024-7664 5777
E-mail: roy@oleo.co.uk
Website: http://www.oleo.co.uk
Bank(s): Barclays
Directors: J. Jowett (Dir), C. Brown (Dir), C. Brown (MD)
Managers: C. Sarson (Accounts), D. Priest (Prod Mgr), I. Dawkins (I.T. Exec), M. Leckie, R. Curvy (Purch Mgr), R. Hunt (Sales & Mktg Mg)
Ultimate Holding Company: Wagon Industrial Holdings P.L.C.
Immediate Holding Company: OLEO INTERNATIONAL LIMITED
Registration no: 06843192 **Date established:** 2009
Turnover: £10m - £20m **No.of Employees:** 101 - 250
Product Groups: 35, 39, 40, 45

One Vision Imaging

Herald Way Binley Industrial Estate, Coventry, CV3 2NY
Tel: 024-7644 0404 **Fax:** 024-7644 4219
E-mail: info@onevisionimaging.com
Website: http://www.onevisionimaging.com
Directors: D. Poulston (MD)
Immediate Holding Company: PHILIP JAMES PRECISION ENGINEERS LTD
Registration no: 01832011 **Date established:** 2000 **Turnover:** £5m - £10m
No.of Employees: 21 - 50 **Product Groups:** 28, 38, 80, 81

Date of Accounts	Apr 12	Apr 11	Apr 10
Working Capital	1m	944	822
Fixed Assets	1m	830	952
Current Assets	2m	1m	1m

Oz Box UK Ltd

Herald Way Binley Industrial Estate, Coventry, CV3 2RQ
Tel: 024-7656 1561 **Fax:** 024-7656 1555
E-mail: sales@ozbox.co.uk
Website: http://www.ozbox.co.uk
Bank(s): Royal Bank of Scotland, Leicester
Directors: D. Corbett (MD), D. Corbett (MD)
Managers: S. O'Grady, C. Hawker, S. Wragg (Comm)
Ultimate Holding Company: CALDWELL MANUFACTURING CO (USA)
Immediate Holding Company: OZBOX (UK) LIMITED
Registration no: 04892281 **VAT No.:** GB 398 3152 21
Date established: 2003 **Turnover:** £5m - £10m **No.of Employees:** 21 - 50
Product Groups: 27

Date of Accounts	Sep 11	Sep 10	Sep 09
Working Capital	-33	-92	-136
Fixed Assets	224	246	227
Current Assets	676	720	552

P B K Micron Ltd
Unit 6 Kingfield Industrial Estate, Coventry, CV1 4DW
Tel: 024-7622 0376 **Fax:** 024-7660 7819
E-mail: sales@pbk-micron.co.uk
Website: http://www.pbk-micron.co.uk
Bank(s): Bank of Scotland
Directors: C. Cummiskey (MD)
Ultimate Holding Company: UMBERTO GREEN LIMITED
Immediate Holding Company: P.B.K. MICRON LIMITED
Registration no: 03708886 **VAT No.:** GB 823 8050 43
Date established: 1999 **Turnover:** £1m - £2m **No.of Employees:** 21 - 50
Product Groups: 48

Date of Accounts	Jun 11	Jun 10	Jun 09
Working Capital	709	644	688
Fixed Assets	462	481	381
Current Assets	2m	2m	1m

P C G Hydraulics Ltd
Dutton Road Aldermans Green Industrial Estate, Coventry, CV2 2LE
Tel: 024-7661 8533 **Fax:** 024-7661 5944
E-mail: sales@pcg-hydraulics.co.uk
Website: http://www.pcg-hydraulics.co.uk
Bank(s): National Westminster Bank Plc
Directors: H. Pulley (Fin), F. Pulley (MD)
Immediate Holding Company: P C G HYDRAULICS LIMITED
Registration no: 01538814 **VAT No.:** GB 307 4840 64
Date established: 1981 **Turnover:** £1m - £2m **No.of Employees:** 11 - 20
Product Groups: 39, 40

Date of Accounts	Jan 12	Jan 11	Jan 10
Working Capital	148	159	114
Fixed Assets	311	317	324
Current Assets	278	396	269

P C Removal
20 Mary Slessor Street, Coventry, CV3 3BY
Tel: 024-7663 9154
Website: http://www.pcremoval.co.uk
Directors: M. Wilkins (Prop)
Turnover: £250,000 - £500,000 **No.of Employees:** 1 - 10
Product Groups: 30

P G & Ar Engineering
12 Bayton Road Exhall, Coventry, CV7 9EJ
Tel: 024-7664 5710 **Fax:** 024-7664 5710
E-mail: info@pgareng.co.uk
Website: http://www.pgareng.co.uk
Directors: C. Spadafora (Prop)
Immediate Holding Company: PG & AR ENGINEERING (MIDLANDS) LTD
Registration no: 06773387 **Date established:** 2008
No.of Employees: 1 - 10 **Product Groups:** 20, 40, 41

Date of Accounts	Dec 11	Dec 10	Dec 09
Working Capital	16	22	22
Fixed Assets	1	2	2
Current Assets	102	101	93

P J C Welding
46 Hotchkiss Way Binley Industrial Estate, Coventry, CV3 2RL
Tel: 024-7645 7111
Directors: P. Cooper (Prop)
Immediate Holding Company: P J C WELDING LTD
Registration no: 05735695 **Date established:** 2006
No.of Employees: 1 - 10 **Product Groups:** 35, 84

Date of Accounts	Mar 11	Mar 10	Mar 08
Working Capital	-2	-9	-4
Fixed Assets	43	52	69
Current Assets	32	31	29

P M D UK Ltd
Broad Lane, Coventry, CV5 7AY
Tel: 024-7646 6691 **Fax:** 024-7647 3034
E-mail: sales@pmdgroup.co.uk
Website: http://www.pmdgroup.co.uk
Bank(s): National Westminster Bank Plc
Directors: A. Naylor (MD), B. Fisher (Fin), S. Fisher (Fin)
Immediate Holding Company: PMD LIMITED
Registration no: 02429669 **VAT No.:** GB 272 7238 49
Date established: 1989 **Turnover:** £2m - £5m **No.of Employees:** 51 - 100
Product Groups: 32, 46

Pab Coventry Ltd
Falkland Close Charter Avenue Industrial Estate, Coventry, CV4 8AU
Tel: 024-7669 4419 **Fax:** 024-7646 7799
E-mail: info@pabcoventry.co.uk
Website: http://www.pabgroup.co.uk
Directors: M. Braizer (MD), M. Brazier (MD), V. Braizer (Fin)
Managers: D. Wheldon (Personnel), L. Allan (Buyer), R. Lewis (Sales Prom Mgr)
Immediate Holding Company: PAB COVENTRY LIMITED
Registration no: 03646267 **Date established:** 1998
No.of Employees: 21 - 50 **Product Groups:** 34, 66

Date of Accounts	May 11	May 10	May 09
Working Capital	-191	-280	-330
Fixed Assets	588	652	747
Current Assets	1m	1m	799
Current Liabilities	N/A	632	N/A

Pailton Engineering Ltd
Phoenix House Holbrook Lane, Coventry, CV6 4AD
Tel: 024-7668 0445 **Fax:** 024-7668 0446
E-mail: mailbox@pailton.com
Website: http://www.pailton.com
Directors: H. Ward (Fin), J. Nollett (MD)
Managers: A. Lancashire (Personnel), J. Murton (Tech Serv Mgr), M. Kynaston, L. Shropshire (Purch Mgr)
Immediate Holding Company: PAILTON ENGINEERING LIMITED
Registration no: 01377101 **VAT No.:** GB 307 1134 05
Date established: 1978 **Turnover:** £10m - £20m
No.of Employees: 101 - 250 **Product Groups:** 35, 36, 39, 68

Date of Accounts	Dec 11	Dec 10	Dec 09
Sales Turnover	14m	14m	13m
Pre Tax Profit/Loss	268	2m	2m
Working Capital	5m	5m	4m
Fixed Assets	4m	3m	4m
Current Assets	9m	9m	7m
Current Liabilities	3m	3m	3m

Parkes Machine Tools Ltd
PO Box 2709, Coventry, CV7 7WF
Tel: 01676-530053 **Fax:** 01676-530030
E-mail: info@parkesmachinetools.co.uk
Website: http://www.parkesmachinetools.co.uk
Directors: R. Parkes (MD)
Immediate Holding Company: PARKES (MACHINE TOOLS) LIMITED
Registration no: 00390860 **VAT No.:** GB 110 1457 32
Date established: 1944 **Turnover:** £1m - £2m **No.of Employees:** 1 - 10
Product Groups: 46

Date of Accounts	Dec 11	Dec 10	Dec 09
Working Capital	431	314	196
Fixed Assets	136	132	135
Current Assets	867	657	472

Parkside Packaging Ltd
Willenhall Lane Binley, Coventry, CV3 2AS
Tel: 024-7645 5455 **Fax:** 024-7645 6056
E-mail: sales@parkside-pkg.co.uk
Website: http://www.parkside-pkg.co.uk
Bank(s): National Westminster Bank Plc
Directors: G. Whitehead (Sales), K. Hobbs (MD), C. Wragg (Comm), C. Wragg (Fin)
Managers: A. Brushett (Purch Mgr), A. Anderson (Sales Off Mgr)
Ultimate Holding Company: PAPERLINX LIMITED (AUSTRALIA)
Immediate Holding Company: PARKSIDE PACKAGING LIMITED
Registration no: 03243805 **VAT No.:** GB 670 7326 32
Date established: 1996 **Turnover:** £5m - £10m **No.of Employees:** 21 - 50
Product Groups: 27

Date of Accounts	Jun 11	Jun 10	Jun 09
Sales Turnover	8m	6m	6m
Pre Tax Profit/Loss	487	310	269
Working Capital	3m	3m	2m
Fixed Assets	3m	3m	3m
Current Assets	5m	4m	4m
Current Liabilities	260	224	415

Peugeot Motor Company plc
Pinley House 2 Sunbeam Way, Coventry, CV3 1ND
Tel: 024-7688 4000 **Fax:** 024-7688 4001
E-mail: info@robinsandday.co.uk
Website: http://www.peugeot.co.uk
Bank(s): HSBC
Directors: J. Goodman (MD), R. Lewis (Co Sec)
Ultimate Holding Company: PEUGEOT SA (FRANCE)
Immediate Holding Company: PEUGEOT MOTOR COMPANY PLC
Registration no: 00148545 **VAT No.:** GB 272 3691 49
Date established: 2017 **Turnover:** Over £1,000m
No.of Employees: 251 - 500 **Product Groups:** 39

Date of Accounts	Dec 11	Dec 10	Dec 09
Sales Turnover	1291m	1358m	1210m
Pre Tax Profit/Loss	-1m	-3m	-28m
Working Capital	53m	64m	78m
Fixed Assets	49m	51m	52m
Current Assets	500m	664m	559m
Current Liabilities	202m	192m	180m

Pharos Engineering Ltd
228 Lythalls Lane Foleshill, Coventry, CV6 6GF
Tel: 024-7668 7235 **Fax:** 024-7666 6355
E-mail: mwinstone@pharosengineering.co.uk
Website: http://www.pharosgroupuk.com
Bank(s): HSBC Studley
Directors: R. Apted (Ch)
Managers: C. Jones (Comptroller), G. Lawrence (Chief Mgr), M. Dearden (Prod Mgr)
Immediate Holding Company: PHAROS BUILDING SERVICES LIMITED
Registration no: 04392694 **VAT No.:** GB 378 2256 28
Date established: 2002 **Turnover:** £1m - £2m **No.of Employees:** 21 - 50
Product Groups: 31, 34, 36, 38, 40, 43, 45, 46, 48, 67

Date of Accounts	Sep 11	Sep 10	Sep 09
Working Capital	-7	-2	-7
Current Assets	101	56	41

Pinpoint Presentation
Green Zone 3b 54 Bayton Road Industrial Estate Bayton Road, Exhall, Coventry, CV7 9TH
Tel: 024-7664 6103 **Fax:** 0121-275 6183
E-mail: sales@pinpointpresentation.co.uk
Website: http://www.pinpointpresentation.co.uk
Directors: B. Johnson (MD)
Date established: 2006 **Turnover:** £250,000 - £500,000
No.of Employees: 1 - 10 **Product Groups:** 28

Planet Granite
Devitts Green Farm Devitts Green Lane, Arley, Coventry, CV7 8GF
Tel: 01926-855005 **Fax:** 024-7667 8818
E-mail: sales@planetgranite.co.uk
Website: http://www.planetgranite.co.uk
Directors: S. Mitchell (Prop)
Registration no: 04659707 **No.of Employees:** 1 - 10 **Product Groups:** 14, 33, 66

Plant Installations Coventry Ltd
Crondal Road Exhall, Coventry, CV7 9NH
Tel: 024-7636 0421 **Fax:** 024-7664 4303
E-mail: info@plantinstallations.co.uk
Website: http://www.plantinstallations.co.uk
Bank(s): Barclays
Directors: M. Cullinane (Co Sec), S. Cullinane (MD)
Managers: K. Barlow (Transport)
Immediate Holding Company: PLANT INSTALLATIONS (COVENTRY) LIMITED
Registration no: 00966319 **VAT No.:** GB 272 8013 68
Date established: 1969 **Turnover:** £2m - £5m **No.of Employees:** 51 - 100
Product Groups: 51, 72

Date of Accounts	Nov 11	Nov 10	Nov 09
Working Capital	1m	1m	1m
Fixed Assets	289	275	300
Current Assets	1m	1m	1m

Plastech Whetherseals
Blackhorse Road Longford, Coventry, CV6 6DG
Tel: 024-7664 4565 **Fax:** 024-7664 4599
E-mail: sales@plastechweatherseals.co.uk
Directors: R. Whelan (Fin)
Immediate Holding Company: PLASTECH WEATHERSEALS LIMITED
Registration no: 06702200 **Date established:** 2008 **Turnover:** £1m - £2m
No.of Employees: 1 - 10 **Product Groups:** 29, 30, 36

Date of Accounts	Oct 11	Oct 10	Oct 09
Working Capital	19	-5	-17
Fixed Assets	161	166	160
Current Assets	277	265	197

Power Torque Engineering
Herald Way Binley Industrial Estate, Coventry, CV3 2RQ
Tel: 024-7663 5757 **Fax:** 024-7663 5878
E-mail: j.townley@powertorque.co.uk
Website: http://www.powertorque.co.uk
Bank(s): National Westminster Bank Plc
Directors: J. Plumb (Fin), J. Townley (Sales), J. Townley (Sales)
Immediate Holding Company: POWER TORQUE ENGINEERING LIMITED
Registration no: 00217422 **VAT No.:** GB 272 5173 61
Date established: 2026 **Turnover:** £10m - £20m
No.of Employees: 21 - 50 **Product Groups:** 29, 30, 35, 36, 37, 38, 39, 40, 48, 68

Date of Accounts	Apr 11	Apr 10	Apr 09
Sales Turnover	13m	10m	10m
Pre Tax Profit/Loss	140	17	74
Working Capital	2m	2m	2m
Fixed Assets	3m	3m	3m
Current Assets	5m	5m	4m
Current Liabilities	664	503	277

Process Management International Ltd
Unit 6 Villiers Court Meriden Business Park Copse Drive, Coventry, CV5 9RN
Tel: 01676-522766 **Fax:** 024-7641 9480
E-mail: richard.seddon@pmi.co.uk
Website: http://www.pmi.co.uk
Managers: P. Mathis
Ultimate Holding Company: THE PMI & EG GROUP LIMITED
Immediate Holding Company: PROCESS MANAGEMENT INTERNATIONAL LIMITED
Registration no: 02541912 **Date established:** 1990
No.of Employees: 1 - 10 **Product Groups:** 44

Date of Accounts	Jun 11	Jun 10	Jun 09
Working Capital	441	452	706
Fixed Assets	31	14	35
Current Assets	1m	1m	1m

Profab Coventry Ltd
Unit 1 Brindley Road, Bayton Road Industrial Estate, Coventry, CV7 9EP
Tel: 024-7636 1762 **Fax:** 024-7636 2319
E-mail: profabcoventry@tiscali.co.uk
Website: http://www.profabcoventry.com
Managers: L. Greves (Mgr)
Immediate Holding Company: PROFAB (COVENTRY) LIMITED
Registration no: 02397039 **VAT No.:** GB 487 7337 91
Date established: 1989 **Turnover:** Up to £250,000
No.of Employees: 1 - 10 **Product Groups:** 48

Date of Accounts	Jun 12	Jun 11	Jun 10
Working Capital	141	137	122
Fixed Assets	106	117	125
Current Assets	219	222	183

Protopipe Ltd
Unit 15 Windmill Industrial Estate Birmingham Road, Allesley, Coventry, CV5 9QE
Tel: 024-7640 3111 **Fax:** 024-7640 5444
E-mail: paul.ashmore@protopipe.co.uk
Website: http://www.protopipe.co.uk
Directors: P. Ashmore (Dir)
Immediate Holding Company: PROTOPIPE LIMITED
Registration no: 04075467 **Date established:** 2000
No.of Employees: 1 - 10 **Product Groups:** 35, 36, 46, 48

Date of Accounts	Oct 11	Oct 10	Oct 09
Working Capital	207	123	31
Fixed Assets	65	63	70
Current Assets	322	255	103

Quest Trade Services
Back Lane Meriden, Coventry, CV7 7LD
Tel: 01676-522997 **Fax:** 01676-523622
E-mail: qts@btinternet.com
Directors: M. Burns (Ptnr)
Turnover: £2m - £5m **No.of Employees:** 1 - 10 **Product Groups:** 87

R D Taylor
Unit 14 Napier Street, Coventry, CV1 5PR
Tel: 024-7663 2296 **Fax:** 024-7663 2506
E-mail: covsale@rdtaylor.demon.co.uk
Website: http://www.rdtaylor.co.uk
Managers: A. Wilks (Mgr)
No.of Employees: 1 - 10 **Product Groups:** 27, 32, 66

R F R Coventry Precision Engineering Ltd
16 Midland Oak Industrial Estate Lythalls Lane, Coventry, CV6 6FJ
Tel: 024-7668 9427 **Fax:** 024-7668 9427
Directors: W. Robinson (Fin), P. Robertson (Dir), P. Robinson (Dir), R. Robinson (MD)
Immediate Holding Company: R.F.R. (COVENTRY) PRECISION ENGINEERING LIMITED
Registration no: 01003461 **VAT No.:** GB 272 6959 18
Date established: 1971 **Turnover:** Up to £250,000
No.of Employees: 1 - 10 **Product Groups:** 48

Date of Accounts	Jan 12	Jan 11	Jan 10
Working Capital	13	12	9
Fixed Assets	4	4	4
Current Assets	33	20	12

R G Engineering Coventry Ltd
3 Stoney Court Hotchkiss Way, Binley Industrial Estate, Coventry, CV3 2RL
Tel: 024-7644 0508 **Fax:** 024-7663 6680
E-mail: r.g.eng@dial.pipex.com
Directors: J. Colley (MD)
Immediate Holding Company: R G ENGINEERING (COVENTRY) LTD
Registration no: 04899508 **VAT No.:** 307 0995 55 **Date established:** 2003
Turnover: £250,000 - £500,000 **No.of Employees:** 1 - 10
Product Groups: 46, 48

Date of Accounts	Mar 11	Mar 10	Mar 09
Working Capital	30	9	22
Fixed Assets	6	4	5
Current Assets	68	31	58

R S M Industries Ltd
School Lane Exhall, Coventry, CV7 9NN
Tel: 024-7636 2082 **Fax:** 024-7655 3715
E-mail: admin@rsmindustries.co.uk
Website: http://www.rsmindustries.co.uk
Bank(s): Royal Bank of Scotland
Directors: M. Williams (MD), A. Corbett (Fin), J. Cooper (Dir)
Managers: D. Crawley (Mats Contrlr)
Immediate Holding Company: RSM INDUSTRIES LIMITED
Registration no: 01908874 **VAT No.:** GB 441 6713 61
Date established: 1985 **Turnover:** £10m - £20m
No.of Employees: 101 - 250 **Product Groups:** 48

Date of Accounts	May 12	May 11	May 10
Sales Turnover	N/A	17m	13m
Pre Tax Profit/Loss	-213	2m	1m
Working Capital	3m	4m	2m
Fixed Assets	1m	2m	2m
Current Assets	6m	7m	5m
Current Liabilities	1m	1m	814

Racar Technologies Ltd
Oakwood Court Spring Hill, Coventry, CV7 8FF
Tel: 0845-226 7731 **Fax:** 0845-2267732
E-mail: info@racartechnologies.com
Website: http://www.racartechnologies.com
Directors: N. Mistry (Dir), Y. Carpenter (Dir)
Registration no: 04170436 **Date established:** 2001
No.of Employees: 1 - 10 **Product Groups:** 80

Date of Accounts	Mar 07	Mar 06	Mar 05
Working Capital	-0	-4	12
Fixed Assets	1	1	1
Current Assets	10	9	20
Current Liabilities	10	13	8

Radford Leather Fashions
270 Radford Road, Coventry, CV6 3BU
Tel: 024-7659 7260
E-mail: info@radfordleathers.co.uk
Website: http://www.radfordleather.co.uk
No.of Employees: 1 - 10 **Product Groups:** 22, 24, 63

Red House Industrial Services Ltd
Cromwell Street, Coventry, CV6 5EZ
Tel: 024-7663 7700 **Fax:** 024-7666 7777
E-mail: sales@redhouseuk.com
Website: http://www.redhouseuk.com
Directors: R. Morris-Jones (MD), J. Morris Jones (Co Sec)
Immediate Holding Company: REDHOUSE INDUSTRIAL SERVICES LIMITED
Registration no: 01190855 **Date established:** 1974
Turnover: £250,000 - £500,000 **No.of Employees:** 1 - 10
Product Groups: 37, 39, 40, 42, 45, 46, 47, 48, 61, 66, 67, 72, 77, 83, 84, 87

Date of Accounts	Oct 11	Oct 10	Oct 09
Working Capital	76	75	95
Fixed Assets	713	717	347
Current Assets	131	126	108

Reed Employment Ltd
13-15 Cross Cheaping, Coventry, CV1 1HF
Tel: 024-7625 6097 **Fax:** 024-7625 6068
Website: http://www.reed.co.uk
Managers: T. Shirley (Mgr)
Ultimate Holding Company: REED GLOBAL LTD (MALTA)
Immediate Holding Company: REED EMPLOYMENT LIMITED
Registration no: 00669854 **Date established:** 1960
Turnover: £75m - £125m **No.of Employees:** 1 - 10 **Product Groups:** 80

Date of Accounts	Jun 11	Jun 10	Dec 07
Sales Turnover	618	450	287m
Pre Tax Profit/Loss	-2m	310	8m
Working Capital	23m	28m	28m
Fixed Assets	31	36	5m
Current Assets	28m	30m	74m
Current Liabilities	37	29	21m

Remotec UK Ltd
Unit 5 Quinn Close, Coventry, CV3 4LH
Tel: 024-7651 6000 **Fax:** 024-7651 6041
E-mail: sales@remotec.co.uk
Website: http://www.northropgrummaninternational.com
Directors: P. Hunter (Fin)
Ultimate Holding Company: NORTHROP GRUMMAN CORPORATION (USA)
Immediate Holding Company: REMOTEC UK LIMITED
Registration no: 03958799 **Date established:** 2000
Turnover: £10m - £20m **No.of Employees:** 51 - 100 **Product Groups:** 36, 37, 40, 42, 45

Date of Accounts	Dec 11	Dec 10	Dec 09
Sales Turnover	24m	17m	10m
Pre Tax Profit/Loss	-343	-1m	-3m
Working Capital	-10m	-7m	-6m
Fixed Assets	760	799	938
Current Assets	16m	12m	14m
Current Liabilities	3m	2m	1m

Rentaclamp Coventry Ltd
Unit 1 31-41 Cross Road, Coventry, CV6 5GR
Tel: 024-7668 8879 **Fax:** 024-7668 5758
Website: http://www.rentaclamp-coventry.co.uk
Directors: M. Fletcher (MD)
Immediate Holding Company: Rentaclamp (Coventry) Ltd
Registration no: 01261297 **Date established:** 1976
No.of Employees: 1 - 10 **Product Groups:** 35, 39, 45

Date of Accounts	Jun 10	Jun 09	Jun 08
Working Capital	197	169	169
Fixed Assets	16	26	41
Current Assets	297	250	347

Repanco Bartlett Ltd
24 Albion Industrial Estate Endermere Road, Coventry, CV6 5NT
Tel: 024-7666 5666 **Fax:** 024-7666 2820
E-mail: repanco@btconnect.com
Website: http://www.repancobartlett.co.uk
Directors: H. Jagatia (MD), S. Jagatia (Co Sec)
Immediate Holding Company: REPANCO BARTLETT LIMITED
Registration no: 02017843 **VAT No.:** GB 418 8202 55
Date established: 1986 **Turnover:** £500,000 - £1m
No.of Employees: 1 - 10 **Product Groups:** 37

Date of Accounts	May 12	May 11	May 10
Working Capital	27	39	32
Fixed Assets	10	12	14
Current Assets	75	102	76

Resource Development International Ltd
Midland Management Centre 1a Brandon Lane, Coventry, CV3 3RD
Tel: 024-7651 5700 **Fax:** 024-7651 5701
E-mail: reception@rdi.co.uk
Website: http://www.rdi.co.uk
Managers: C. Rice (Mktg Serv Mgr), C. Gordon
Immediate Holding Company: RESOURCE DEVELOPMENT INTERNATIONAL LIMITED
Registration no: 02450180 **VAT No.:** GB 705 3350 66
Date established: 1989 **Turnover:** £5m - £10m
No.of Employees: 51 - 100 **Product Groups:** 86

Date of Accounts	Oct 11	Jul 10	Jul 09
Sales Turnover	9m	9m	8m
Pre Tax Profit/Loss	-2m	70	236
Working Capital	-2m	-761	-230
Fixed Assets	916	923	623
Current Assets	3m	4m	4m
Current Liabilities	2m	3m	3m

Revolving Stage Company Ltd
Unit F5 Little Heath Industrial Estate Old Church Road, Coventry, CV6 7ND
Tel: 024-7668 7055 **Fax:** 024-7668 9355
E-mail: enquiries@therevolvingstagecompany.co.uk
Website: http://www.therevolvingstagecompany.com
Directors: P. Hulston (MD)
Immediate Holding Company: THE REVOLVING STAGE COMPANY LIMITED
Registration no: 04146506 **Date established:** 2001
No.of Employees: 1 - 10 **Product Groups:** 26

Date of Accounts	Mar 11	Mar 10	Mar 09
Working Capital	195	154	128
Fixed Assets	8	6	4
Current Assets	268	201	184

Robins & Day
Kenpas Highway, Coventry, CV3 6PE
Tel: 024-7641 1515 **Fax:** 024-7669 2044
E-mail: mark.warrilow@peugeotmail.co.uk
Managers: M. Warrilow (Chief Mgr)
Immediate Holding Company: CITY MOTORS LTD.
Registration no: 01917962 **Date established:** 1985
Turnover: £250m - £500m **No.of Employees:** 21 - 50 **Product Groups:** 68

Rockwell Sheet Sales Ltd
Rockwell House Birmingham Road, Millisons Wood, Coventry, CV5 9AZ
Tel: 01676-522224 **Fax:** 01676-523630
E-mail: ann@rockwellsheet.com
Website: http://www.rockwellsheet.com
Directors: J. Flin (Jt MD), A. Quinn (MD), J. Flynn (Dir), G. McErlean (Comm)
Immediate Holding Company: ROCKWELL SHEET SALES (HOLDINGS) LIMITED
Registration no: 06371790 **VAT No.:** GB 418 6774 20
Date established: 2007 **Turnover:** Up to £250,000
No.of Employees: 1 - 10 **Product Groups:** 30

Date of Accounts	Sep 10	Sep 09	Sep 08
Sales Turnover	63	50	35
Pre Tax Profit/Loss	62	50	29
Working Capital	-242	-223	-205
Fixed Assets	1m	1m	1m
Current Liabilities	242	76	58

Rotatech Ltd
20 Cavans Way Binley Industrial Estate, Coventry, CV3 2SF
Tel: 024-7645 2600 **Fax:** 024-7645 2645
E-mail: sales@rotatech.com
Website: http://www.rotatech.com
Directors: A. Williams (Dir)
Immediate Holding Company: ROTATECH LIMITED
Registration no: 04073662 **Date established:** 2000
No.of Employees: 1 - 10 **Product Groups:** 46

Date of Accounts	Dec 11	Dec 10	Dec 09
Working Capital	159	92	158
Fixed Assets	44	62	51
Current Assets	521	381	373

R T C Electronics Ltd
Systems House Willenhall Lane, Binley, Coventry, CV3 2AS
Tel: 024-7644 4000 **Fax:** 024-7644 9801
E-mail: sales@rtcelectronics.co.uk
Website: http://www.rtcelectronics.co.uk
Bank(s): Investec Bank (UK) Ltd
Directors: N. French (MD)
Immediate Holding Company: RTC ELECTRONICS LTD
Registration no: 05242429 **VAT No.:** GB 487 5153 14
Date established: 2004 **Turnover:** £500,000 - £1m
No.of Employees: 21 - 50 **Product Groups:** 37, 38

Date of Accounts	Jun 11	Jun 10	Jun 09
Working Capital	592	425	464
Fixed Assets	18	18	9
Current Assets	696	574	588
Current Liabilities	52	31	66

S A Schrader Ltd
Unit 2 Castle Place Adelaide Street, Coventry, CV1 5TS
Tel: 024-7655 0880 **Fax:** 024-7655 1118
Website: http://www.schraderspd.com
Directors: A. Beard (Co Sec)
Managers: G. Leonard (Chief Mgr), R. Eaden (Sales Prom Mgr)
Immediate Holding Company: SCHRADER SA
Registration no: FC013219 **Date established:** 1984
Turnover: £250m - £500m **No.of Employees:** 1 - 10 **Product Groups:** 36, 37, 38

Saint-Gobain Limited
Saint-Gobain House Binley Business Park, Coventry, CV3 2TT
Tel: 024-7656 0700 **Fax:** 024-7656 0705
E-mail: info@saint-gobain.co.uk
Website: http://www.saint-gobain.co.uk
Bank(s): Natwest, Andover
Directors: G. De Landhseer (MD)
Managers: L. Loaiza (Sales Prom Mgr), B. Pendsay (Fin Mgr)
Immediate Holding Company: Brunswick Technologies Inc
Registration no: 03291592 **VAT No.:** GB 711 8432 56
Turnover: £10m - £20m **No.of Employees:** 21 - 50 **Product Groups:** 61

Sally Hair & Beauty Supplies Ltd
13 Sherbourne Arcade Off Lower Precinct, Coventry, CV1 1DN
Tel: 024-7622 7077
E-mail: admin@sallybeauty.co.uk
Website: http://www.sallybeauty.com
Managers: B. Shivshanker (Mgr)
Ultimate Holding Company: SALLY BEAUTY HOLDING INC (USA)
Immediate Holding Company: SALLY SALON SERVICES LIMITED
Registration no: 01060763 **Date established:** 1972
No.of Employees: 1 - 10 **Product Groups:** 30, 36, 40

Date of Accounts	Sep 11	Sep 10	Sep 09
Sales Turnover	128m	107m	82m
Pre Tax Profit/Loss	3m	2m	1m
Working Capital	10m	7m	6m
Fixed Assets	11m	12m	9m
Current Assets	63m	50m	45m
Current Liabilities	10m	7m	4m

Sanderson Group plc
Sanderson House Manor Road, Coventry, CV1 2GF
Tel: 03331-231400 **Fax:** 024-7625 6705
E-mail: christopher.winn@sanderson.com
Website: http://www.sanderson.com
Bank(s): The Royal Bank of Scotland
Directors: A. Frost (Co Sec), C. Winn (Ch)
Managers: K. Simpson (Sales & Mktg Mg), M. Whitham (Tech Serv Mgr)
Ultimate Holding Company: SANDERSON GROUP PLC
Immediate Holding Company: SANDERSON LIMITED
Registration no: 03743507 **VAT No.:** GB 391 1710 65
Date established: 1999 **Turnover:** £5m - £10m **No.of Employees:** 21 - 50
Product Groups: 44, 79, 80, 84, 86

Date of Accounts	Sep 11	Sep 10	Sep 09
Sales Turnover	6m	6m	6m
Pre Tax Profit/Loss	-39	148	-3m
Working Capital	8m	9m	6m
Fixed Assets	4m	4m	5m
Current Assets	11m	13m	10m
Current Liabilities	3m	3m	3m

Sandvik Hard Materials Ltd
PO Box 89, Coventry, CV4 9XG
Tel: 024-7647 6000 **Fax:** 024-7647 6010
E-mail: terry.alison@sandvik.com
Website: http://www.sandvik.com
Bank(s): Barclays, Sheffield
Directors: T. Alison (Dir)
Ultimate Holding Company: SANDVIK AKTIEBOLAG (SWEDEN)
Immediate Holding Company: SANDVIK LTD
Registration no: 00136547 **VAT No.:** GB 281 4525 600 003
No.of Employees: 251 - 500 **Product Groups:** 34, 36, 41, 45, 46, 48

Sarginsons Industries Sarginsons Precision Components & Advance Tooling
Torrington Avenue, Coventry, CV4 9AG
Tel: 024-7646 6291 **Fax:** 024-7646 8135
E-mail: reception@sarginsons.co.uk
Website: http://www.sarginsons.co.uk
Bank(s): Allied Irish Bank (GB)
Directors: R. Simms (MD), R. Sims (MD), J. Lazenby (Fin)
Managers: P. Shelley (Mgr), P. Harrison (Purch Mgr)
Ultimate Holding Company: COVENTRY DIECASTING LIMITED
Immediate Holding Company: SIL INDUSTRIES LIMITED
Registration no: 03355694 **VAT No.:** GB 687 8956 42
Date established: 1997 **Turnover:** £5m - £10m
No.of Employees: 51 - 100 **Product Groups:** 34

Date of Accounts	Apr 10	Apr 09	Apr 08
Sales Turnover	7m	9m	10m
Pre Tax Profit/Loss	-859	-159	183
Working Capital	-4	286	480
Fixed Assets	238	274	196
Current Assets	2m	2m	3m
Current Liabilities	187	188	392

Scaleaway Tools & Equipment Ltd
Station Street West Business Park, Coventry, CV6 5BP
Tel: 024-7666 1326 **Fax:** 024-7668 8603
E-mail: sales@scaleaway-tools.co.uk
Website: http://www.scaleaway-tools.co.uk
Directors: R. Hobbs (Dir)
Ultimate Holding Company: CHERRINGTON ENGINEERING LIMITED
Immediate Holding Company: SCALEAWAY TOOLS AND EQUIPMENT LIMITED
Registration no: 01234948 **VAT No.:** GB 273 7548 28
Date established: 1975 **Turnover:** £500,000 - £1m
No.of Employees: 1 - 10 **Product Groups:** 35, 36, 37, 40, 42, 43, 46, 49, 66, 67

Date of Accounts	Dec 11	Dec 10	Dec 09
Working Capital	99	88	93
Fixed Assets	6	7	8
Current Assets	178	183	201

Schmitt Europe Ltd
Unit 4 Sir William Lyons Road University of Warwick Science Park, Coventry, CV4 7EZ
Tel: 024-7669 7192 **Fax:** 024-7641 2697
E-mail: jon@schmitt.co.uk
Website: http://www.schmitteurope.com
Directors: J. Atkinson (Fin), J. Atkinson (Co Sec), D. White (MD), W. Case (Pres)
Managers: B. Craddock (Sales & Mktg Mg)
Immediate Holding Company: SCHMITT EUROPE LIMITED
Registration no: 03202316 **VAT No.:** GB 670 0267 57
Date established: 1996 **Turnover:** £500,000 - £1m
No.of Employees: 1 - 10 **Product Groups:** 29, 35, 37, 38, 39, 46, 47, 48, 85

Date of Accounts	May 10	May 09	May 08
Sales Turnover	732	879	930
Pre Tax Profit/Loss	-33	64	198
Working Capital	-49	-23	-72
Current Assets	285	360	254
Current Liabilities	28	53	28

Select Sourcing
The Technocentre, Coventry Technology Park Puma Way, Coventry, CV1 2TT
Tel: 024-7623 6818 **Fax:** 024-7623 6024
E-mail: enquiry@selectsourcing.com
Website: http://www.selectsourcing.com

Directors: L. Brian (Dir)
Managers: P. Sangha (Mgr)
Registration no: 05206649 **No.of Employees:** 11 - 20 **Product Groups:** 61

Serck Controls Ltd

Stonebridge Trading Estate Rowley Drive, Coventry, CV3 4FH
Tel: 024-7651 1069 **Fax:** 024-7630 2437
E-mail: sales@serck-controls.co.uk
Website: http://www.serck-controls.co.uk
Directors: M. Stansfield (MD), N. Howland (Fin)
Ultimate Holding Company: SCADA GROUP PTY LTD
Immediate Holding Company: SERCK CONTROLS LIMITED
Registration no: 04353634 **Date established:** 2002
Turnover: £10m - £20m **No.of Employees:** 101 - 250
Product Groups: 37, 44

Date of Accounts	Dec 11	Dec 10	Jun 09
Sales Turnover	16m	20m	12m
Pre Tax Profit/Loss	5m	5m	2m
Working Capital	5m	4m	3m
Fixed Assets	2m	2m	2m
Current Assets	11m	8m	6m
Current Liabilities	4m	3m	3m

Serigraphia Digital Ltd

Stonebridge Trading Estate Sibree Road, Coventry, CV3 4FD
Tel: 024-7663 7744 **Fax:** 024-7651 1582
E-mail: bryan@serigraphia.co.uk
Website: http://www.serigraphiadigita.co.uk
Directors: B. Fisher (MD)
Immediate Holding Company: SERIGRAPHIA DIGITAL LIMITED
Registration no: 06049489 **Date established:** 2007 **Turnover:** £1m - £2m
No.of Employees: 1 - 10 **Product Groups:** 28, 44

Date of Accounts	Sep 11	Sep 10	Sep 09
Working Capital	109	56	24
Fixed Assets	56	78	80
Current Assets	205	183	201

Severn Trent Water

Customer Relations Po Box 5310, Coventry, CV3 9FJ
Tel: 0800-7834444 **Fax:** 0121-722 4800
E-mail: customer.relations@severntrent.co.uk
Website: http://www.stwater.co.uk
Bank(s): Lloyds
Directors: A. Wray (Dir), M. McKeon (Fin), R. Mcpheely (Dir), T. Wray (MD), F. Smith (Co Sec), K. Porritt (Co Sec)
Immediate Holding Company: SEVERN TRENT PLC
Registration no: 02366686 **VAT No.:** GB 486 9855 65
Date established: 1989 **Turnover:** Over £1,000m
No.of Employees: 1501 & over **Product Groups:** 18, 42, 84

Date of Accounts	Mar 09	Mar 08	Mar 07
Sales Turnover	1325m	1265m	1207m
Pre Tax Profit/Loss	282m	240m	300m
Working Capital	-144m	-133m	-908m
Fixed Assets	5685m	5418m	5220m
Current Assets	449m	756m	282m
Current Liabilities	593m	889m	1190m
Total Share Capital	1000m	1000m	1000m

Seymour Paper & Packaging

70-86 Lower Ford Street, Coventry, CV1 5PW
Tel: 024-7622 3021 **Fax:** 024-7652 0779
E-mail: sales@seymourpackaging.co.uk
Website: http://www.seymourpackaging.co.uk
Directors: Q. Seymour-Smith (Prop)
Registration no: 01698149 **VAT No.:** GB 272 9221 56
Date established: 1983 **Turnover:** £500,000 - £1m
No.of Employees: 1 - 10 **Product Groups:** 27, 64

Shilton Cast Iron & Welding Ltd

Shilton Industrial Estate Bulkington Road, Coventry, CV7 9QL
Tel: 024-7660 4899 **Fax:** 024-7660 4899
E-mail: sales@shiltoncastironandwelding.co.uk
Website: http://www.shiltoncastironandwelding.co.uk
Directors: N. Shilton (MD)
Immediate Holding Company: SHILTON CAST IRON & WELDING LIMITED
Registration no: 05486928 **Date established:** 2005
No.of Employees: 1 - 10 **Product Groups:** 34, 35, 48

Date of Accounts	Jun 11	Jun 10	Jun 09
Working Capital	132	113	83
Fixed Assets	20	23	25
Current Assets	177	153	133

Showerlux UK Ltd

Stonebridge Trading Estate Sibree Road, Coventry, CV3 4FD
Tel: 024-7663 9400 **Fax:** 024-7630 5457
E-mail: reception@showerlux.co.uk
Website: http://www.showerlux.co.uk
Directors: R. Bowler (MD)
Ultimate Holding Company: DUSCHOLUX SCHIEDAM HOLDING BV (THE NETHERLANDS)
Immediate Holding Company: SHOWERLUX U.K. LIMITED
Registration no: 01102862 **Date established:** 1973 **Turnover:** £5m - £10m
No.of Employees: 11 - 20 **Product Groups:** 30, 35, 36

Date of Accounts	Dec 10	Dec 09	Dec 08
Sales Turnover	N/A	6m	9m
Pre Tax Profit/Loss	N/A	-852	-3m
Working Capital	170	313	952
Fixed Assets	35	63	128
Current Assets	2m	3m	4m
Current Liabilities	N/A	516	281

Sita UK Ltd

Packington House Packington Lane, Meriden, Coventry, CV7 7HN
Tel: 01675-434700 **Fax:** 01675-465740
E-mail: geraint.rees@sita.co.uk
Website: http://www.sita.co.uk
Bank(s): National Westminster
Managers: G. Rees (Chief Mgr)
Ultimate Holding Company: GDF SUEZ SA (FRANCE)
Immediate Holding Company: SITA UK LIMITED
Registration no: 02291198 **VAT No.:** GB 444 0858 47
Date established: 1988 **Turnover:** £10m - £20m
No.of Employees: 21 - 50 **Product Groups:** 54

Date of Accounts	Dec 11	Dec 10	Dec 09
Sales Turnover	279m	282m	270m
Pre Tax Profit/Loss	6m	6m	90m
Working Capital	77m	73m	142m
Fixed Assets	90m	89m	95m
Current Assets	120m	111m	188m
Current Liabilities	43m	38m	43m

Spa Plastics Ltd

4 Herald Business Park Golden Acres Lane, Coventry, CV3 2SY
Tel: 024-7665 0670 **Fax:** 024-7665 0680
E-mail: sales@spaplastics.com
Website: http://www.spaplastics.com
Directors: D. Turrell (Fin)
Immediate Holding Company: SPA PLASTICS LIMITED
Registration no: 02688174 **Date established:** 1992 **Turnover:** £1m - £2m
No.of Employees: 1 - 10 **Product Groups:** 30, 52

Date of Accounts	Dec 11	Dec 10	Dec 09
Working Capital	174	146	126
Fixed Assets	83	58	68
Current Assets	567	487	460

Spectron Gas Control Systems Ltd

Unit 4 Advanced Technology Unit 1 University of Warwick Science Park, Coventry, CV4 7EZ
Tel: 024-7641 6234 **Fax:** 024-7641 1987
E-mail: sales@spectron-gcs.com
Website: http://www.spectron-gcs.com
Managers: M. Arber (Fin Mgr)
Immediate Holding Company: SPECTRON GAS CONTROL SYSTEMS LIMITED
Registration no: 05976951 **Date established:** 2006
No.of Employees: 1 - 10 **Product Groups:** 38, 42

Date of Accounts	Dec 11	Dec 10	Dec 09
Working Capital	292	139	68
Fixed Assets	26	15	24
Current Assets	556	532	563

Sphinx Industrial Supplies Ltd

26 Brindley Road Bayton Road Industrial Estate, Coventry, CV7 9EP
Tel: 024-7636 4411 **Fax:** 024-7636 4411
E-mail: sales@sphinxindustrial.co.uk
Website: http://www.sphinxindustrial.co.uk
Directors: J. Fletcher (Dir), W. Fletcher (Fin)
Immediate Holding Company: SPHINX INDUSTRIAL SUPPLIES LIMITED
Registration no: 05414127 **Date established:** 2005
No.of Employees: 1 - 10 **Product Groups:** 46

Date of Accounts	Apr 11	Apr 10	Apr 09
Working Capital	107	53	48
Fixed Assets	8	5	7
Current Assets	312	210	159

Spindle Services

Unit 9-10 Central City Industrial Estate Red Lane, Coventry, CV6 5RY
Tel: 024-7663 7771 **Fax:** 024-7663 7772
E-mail: sales@spindleservices.co.uk
Website: http://www.spindleservices.co.uk
Bank(s): HSBC Bank plc
Directors: S. Emms (MD)
Immediate Holding Company: SPINDLE SERVICES LIMITED
Registration no: 02442279 **VAT No.:** GB 544 9009 39
Date established: 1989 **Turnover:** £500,000 - £1m
No.of Employees: 11 - 20 **Product Groups:** 46, 48, 67

Date of Accounts	Mar 11	Mar 10	Mar 09
Working Capital	290	266	309
Fixed Assets	45	53	64
Current Assets	493	441	450

Stable Forge

Rectory Cottage Packington Lane, Meriden, Coventry, CV7 7HN
Tel: 01675-443756
Website: http://www.stableforge.com
Directors: B. Wright (Prop)
Date established: 1987 **No.of Employees:** 1 - 10 **Product Groups:** 41

Stainless steel cleaner ltd

17 Treforest Road, Coventry, CV3 IFN
Tel: 024-7665 0012 **Fax:** 024-7665 0012
E-mail: sales@stainlesssteelcleaner.co.uk
Website: http://www.stainlesssteelcleaner.co.uk
Directors: D. green (Dir), C. park (Dir)
Registration no: 05522568 **Date established:** 2006
Turnover: Up to £250,000 **No.of Employees:** 1 - 10 **Product Groups:** 26, 32, 34, 35

Date of Accounts	Dec 10	Dec 09	Dec 08
Working Capital	6	1	1
Fixed Assets	1	N/A	1
Current Assets	10	7	3

Sun Hydraulics Ltd

Wheler Road, Coventry, CV3 4LA
Tel: 024-7621 7400 **Fax:** 024-7621 7488
E-mail: sales@sunuk.com
Website: http://www.sunhydraulics.co.uk
Bank(s): Lloyds TSB Bank plc
Directors: R. Glasspole (Fin)
Managers: S. Hancox (Chief Mgr)
Ultimate Holding Company: SUN HYDRAULICS CORPORATION (USA)
Immediate Holding Company: SUN HYDRAULICS LIMITED
Registration no: 01914045 **VAT No.:** GB 307 5830 62
Date established: 1985 **Turnover:** £10m - £20m
No.of Employees: 51 - 100 **Product Groups:** 40

Date of Accounts	Dec 11	Dec 08	Jan 10
Sales Turnover	16m	13m	9m
Pre Tax Profit/Loss	3m	2m	333
Working Capital	9m	5m	6m
Fixed Assets	3m	4m	4m
Current Assets	11m	6m	7m
Current Liabilities	702	839	226

Superior Systems

39 Deerhurst Road Whitmore Park, Coventry, CV6 4EJ
Tel: 024-7666 3321 **Fax:** 024-7666 3321
E-mail: sales@superior-systems.co.uk
Website: http://www.superior-systems.co.uk
Directors: J. Ferris (Prop)
No.of Employees: 1 - 10 **Product Groups:** 37

Sure Names Internet Solutions Ltd

3 The Quadrant, Coventry, CV1 2DY
Tel: 024-7667 5112 **Fax:** 024-7667 5161
Website: http://www.surenames.co.uk
Directors: K. Khan (MD)
Managers: K. Khan (Sales Prom Mgr)
Immediate Holding Company: SURENAMES INTERNET SOLUTIONS LIMITED
Registration no: 04099403 **Date established:** 2000
Turnover: Up to £250,000 **No.of Employees:** 1 - 10 **Product Groups:** 44

Date of Accounts	Oct 09	Oct 07	Oct 06
Working Capital	-8	-4	-1
Fixed Assets	1	1	1
Current Assets	1	N/A	N/A
Current Liabilities	9	4	1

System 3 R UK

Paradise Way Coventry Walsgrave Triangle, Coventry, CV2 2ST
Tel: 024-7653 8653 **Fax:** 01844-348800
E-mail: info.uk@system-3r.com
Website: http://www.system3r.com
Managers: P. Lampitt
Ultimate Holding Company: GEORG FISCHER AG (SWITZERLAND)
Immediate Holding Company: GEORGE FISCHER CASTINGS LIMITED
Registration no: 01489834 **VAT No.:** GB 348 2293 43
Date established: 1959 **Turnover:** £1m - £2m **No.of Employees:** 1 - 10
Product Groups: 46

Date of Accounts	Dec 04	Dec 03	Dec 02
Sales Turnover	1m	5m	5m
Pre Tax Profit/Loss	2m	-3m	-130
Working Capital	N/A	1m	826
Fixed Assets	N/A	1m	2m
Current Assets	N/A	2m	1m
Current Liabilities	N/A	78	103

T V H UK Ltd

Unit 17 Paragon Way Bayton Road Industrial Estate, Coventry, CV7 9QS
Tel: 024-7658 5000 **Fax:** 024-7658 5001
E-mail: sales@tvh.com
Website: http://www.tvh.com
Bank(s): Fortis, London
Managers: D. Mcallister (Mgr)
Ultimate Holding Company: TVH FORKLIFT PARTS NV (BELGIUM)
Immediate Holding Company: TVH U.K. LIMITED
Registration no: 03859070 **Date established:** 1999 **Turnover:** £2m - £5m
No.of Employees: 11 - 20 **Product Groups:** 45

Date of Accounts	Dec 09	Dec 08	Sep 11
Working Capital	1m	3m	2m
Fixed Assets	341	363	458
Current Assets	2m	4m	3m

Tallon International Ltd

Unit4 Cyan Park, Coventry, CV2 4QP
Tel: 024-7643 7000 **Fax:** 024-7645 2946
E-mail: ericquantrill@tallon.co.uk
Website: http://www.tallon.co.uk
Bank(s): HSBC
Managers: E. Quantrill, L. Debnath, B. Heath (Design Mgr)
Ultimate Holding Company: ZINTELLO MERCHANTS LIMITED
Immediate Holding Company: TALLON INTERNATIONAL LIMITED
Registration no: 01153586 **VAT No.:** GB 307 0797 59
Date established: 1973 **Turnover:** £10m - £20m
No.of Employees: 21 - 50 **Product Groups:** 27, 28, 49

Date of Accounts	Mar 12	Mar 11	Mar 10
Sales Turnover	13m	11m	10m
Pre Tax Profit/Loss	607	424	220
Working Capital	2m	2m	2m
Fixed Assets	250	309	320
Current Assets	3m	3m	2m
Current Liabilities	623	861	415

Tangi-Flow Products Limited

Automatic House Discovery WayLeofric Business Park, Binley, Coventry, CV3 2TD
Tel: 024-7642 1200 **Fax:** 024-7642 1459
E-mail: enquiries@tangi-flow.com
Website: http://www.tangi-flow.com
Bank(s): Lloyds TSB Bank plc
Directors: M. Tilson (Dir), P. Setchell (Dir), E. Setchell (MD)
Managers: J. Pargetor (Mgr)
Immediate Holding Company: MNB PRECISION (HOLDINGS) LIMITED
Registration no: 07033652 **VAT No.:** GB 646 8537 96
Date established: 1950 **Turnover:** £5m - £10m **No.of Employees:** 21 - 50
Product Groups: 36, 46, 48

Tarmac Concrete Meriden

Cornets End Lane Meriden, Coventry, CV7 7LG
Tel: 01675-442922 **Fax:** 0121-504 4696
Managers: S. Parkes (Mgr)
Ultimate Holding Company: ANGLO AMERICAN PLC
Immediate Holding Company: TARMAC CENTRAL LIMITED
Registration no: 03140503 **Date established:** 1995
No.of Employees: 1 - 10 **Product Groups:** 52

Teliteci

27 Bantock Road, Coventry, CV4 9LZ
Tel: 08450-060822
E-mail: robert@teliteci.co.uk
Website: http://www.teliteci.co.uk
Directors: R. Edward (Prop)
No.of Employees: 1 - 10 **Product Groups:** 37, 44, 67

Terex UK Ltd

PO Box 26, Coventry, CV6 4BX
Tel: 024-7633 9400 **Fax:** 024-7633 9500
E-mail: sales@terexce.com
Website: http://www.terexce.com
Bank(s): National Westminster Bank Plc
Managers: M. Lingard (Purch Mgr), P. Barfield (Mktg Serv Mgr)
Ultimate Holding Company: TEREX CORP (USA)
Immediate Holding Company: TEREX UNITED KINGDOM LIMITED
Registration no: 00494347 **VAT No.:** GB 272 3280 70
Date established: 1951 **No.of Employees:** 251 - 500 **Product Groups:** 35, 45, 49

Date of Accounts	Dec 10	Dec 09	Dec 08
Sales Turnover	89m	56m	121m
Pre Tax Profit/Loss	-12m	-21m	-17m
Working Capital	-29m	-19m	5m
Fixed Assets	8m	8m	7m
Current Assets	67m	80m	104m
Current Liabilities	2m	3m	4m

TGT Consulting
Archery Ground Cottage Birmingham Road, Meriden, Coventry, CV7 7JS
Tel: 01676-544259 **Fax:** 01676-523177
E-mail: sales@tgtconsult.com
Website: http://www.tgtconsult.com
Directors: B. Fisher (Grp Chief Exec)
Date established: 2007 **Turnover:** Up to £250,000
No.of Employees: 1 - 10 **Product Groups:** 68

Tooling & Equipment Engineers Ltd
114a Earlsdon Avenue South, Coventry, CV5 6DN
Tel: 024-7669 1522 **Fax:** 024-7669 1544
E-mail: info@tandee.co.uk
Website: http://www.tandee.co.uk
Bank(s): Lloyds
Directors: S. Lawrence (Dir)
Immediate Holding Company: TOOLING AND EQUIPMENT ENGINEERS LIMITED
Registration no: 04624181 **VAT No.:** 545 2144 62 **Date established:** 2002
Turnover: £500,000 - £1m **No.of Employees:** 11 - 20
Product Groups: 38, 46

Date of Accounts	Mar 11	Mar 10	Mar 09
Working Capital	280	214	269
Fixed Assets	376	402	470
Current Assets	496	336	372

Toughnuts Fasteners & Fixing Devices
46 Bayton Road Bayton Road Industrial Estate, Exhall, Coventry, CV7 9EL
Tel: 024-7636 4440
Directors: P. Neale (Prop)
Immediate Holding Company: BOLYER ENGINEERING COMPANY LIMITED
Registration no: 00624688 **Date established:** 1959
No.of Employees: 1 - 10 **Product Groups:** 35

Transtherm Cooling Industries Ltd
Unit 12 Wickmans Drive, Coventry, CV4 9XA
Tel: 024-7647 1120 **Fax:** 024-7647 1125
E-mail: sales@transtherm.ltd.uk
Website: http://www.transtherm.ltd.uk
Bank(s): Lloyds TSB Bank plc
Directors: L. Bound (Co Sec)
Managers: N. Bound (Comm)
Immediate Holding Company: TRANSTHERM LIMITED
Registration no: 04922881 **VAT No.:** GB 795 0503 19
Date established: 2003 **Turnover:** £1m - £2m **No.of Employees:** 11 - 20
Product Groups: 29, 30, 37, 38, 40, 42, 45, 52, 66, 84

Trelleborg Automotive UK Ltd
Holbrook Lane, Coventry, CV6 4QX
Tel: 024-7629 3300 **Fax:** 024-7629 3390
E-mail: diane.whitworth@trelleborg.com
Website: http://www.trelleborg.com
Bank(s): Lloyds TSB Bank plc
Managers: P. Brown (Sales & Mktg Mg), V. Saville (), P. Copie (Sales Prom Mgr), S. Basra (Buyer), W. Laur (Sales Prom Mgr), J. Badrinas, D. Briscoe (Comptroller), C. Davis (Mgr), M. Castiel
Immediate Holding Company: TRELLEBORG HOLDINGS UK LTD
Registration no: 03847966 **VAT No.:** GB 742 2052 69
Turnover: £500m - £1,000m **No.of Employees:** 251 - 500
Product Groups: 29, 30, 35, 39, 40

Date of Accounts	Dec 10	Dec 09	Dec 08
Sales Turnover	10m	9m	N/A
Pre Tax Profit/Loss	403	385	2m
Working Capital	1m	1m	1m
Fixed Assets	727	741	498
Current Assets	4m	4m	4m
Current Liabilities	720	1m	1m

Trinity Expert Systems
1 The Oaks Westwood Way, Westwood Business Park, Coventry, CV4 8JB
Tel: 024-7642 0100 **Fax:** 024-7642 0111
E-mail: info@tesl.com
Website: http://www.tesl.com
Bank(s): Barclays Bank PLC
Managers: R. Thorburn (Consultant)
Ultimate Holding Company: TES GROUP LIMITED
Immediate Holding Company: TRINITY EXPERT SYSTEMS LIMITED
Registration no: 02830123 **Date established:** 1993
Turnover: £20m - £50m **No.of Employees:** 101 - 250
Product Groups: 44, 67, 79, 80, 84

Date of Accounts	Oct 10	Oct 09	Oct 08
Sales Turnover	22m	26m	26m
Pre Tax Profit/Loss	907	3m	4m
Working Capital	5m	5m	6m
Fixed Assets	610	730	695
Current Assets	6m	6m	8m
Current Liabilities	1m	743	1m

Unipart Eberspcher Exhaust Systems Ltd
Durbar Avenue, Coventry, CV6 5LZ
Tel: 024-7663 8663 **Fax:** 024-7666 1084
E-mail: enquiries@unipart.co.uk
Website: http://www.uees.co.uk
Directors: N. Squires (Fin), A. Davis (MD)
Managers: D. Lloyd (Purch Mgr), D. Jokes (Tech Serv Mgr), I. Garrett (Personnel), A. Perry Ogden
Immediate Holding Company: UNIPART EBERSPACHER EXHAUST SYSTEMS LIMITED
Registration no: 03496115 **Date established:** 1998
Turnover: £50m - £75m **No.of Employees:** 251 - 500 **Product Groups:** 40

Date of Accounts	Dec 11	Dec 10	Dec 09
Sales Turnover	69m	51m	37m
Pre Tax Profit/Loss	2m	1m	489
Working Capital	5m	5m	3m
Fixed Assets	2m	2m	3m
Current Assets	20m	17m	14m
Current Liabilities	4m	4m	2m

Unitemps
Gibbet Hill Road, Coventry, CV4 7AL
Tel: 024-7652 8118 **Fax:** 024-7657 3126
E-mail: admin@unitemps.co.uk
Website: http://www.unitemps.co.uk
Managers: K. Martin (Mgr)
Immediate Holding Company: MEMBERSHIP SOLUTIONS LIMITED
Registration no: 01659656 **Date established:** 2005 **Turnover:** £5m - £10m
No.of Employees: 1 - 10 **Product Groups:** 80

Date of Accounts	Jul 11
Sales Turnover	7m
Pre Tax Profit/Loss	265
Working Capital	194
Fixed Assets	134
Current Assets	1m
Current Liabilities	844

Veasey & Smith Ltd
Hawthorn Tree Works Broad Lane, Coventry, CV5 7AX
Tel: 024-7647 4090 **Fax:** 024-7647 3553
E-mail: veasey-smith@tiscali.co.uk
Website: http://www.veaseyandsmithsheds.co.uk
Directors: J. Veasey (Dir)
Immediate Holding Company: VEASEY & SMITH LIMITED
Registration no: 02329741 **VAT No.:** GB 487 6653 86
Date established: 1988 **Turnover:** Up to £250,000
No.of Employees: 1 - 10 **Product Groups:** 46, 48, 67

Date of Accounts	Feb 08	Feb 11	Feb 10
Working Capital	11	34	27
Fixed Assets	3	2	2
Current Assets	40	56	49

Volumatic Ltd
1a Taurus House Endemere Road, Coventry, CV6 5PY
Tel: 024-7668 4217 **Fax:** 024-7663 8155
E-mail: info@volumatic.com
Website: http://www.volumatic.com
Bank(s): HSBC
Directors: J. Summerfield (Fin), D. Johnson (Dir), J. Harris (Dir)
Managers: P. Coombes (Tech Serv Mgr)
Ultimate Holding Company: HALMA PUBLIC LIMITED COMPANY
Immediate Holding Company: VOLUMATIC LIMITED
Registration no: 01069143 **VAT No.:** 272 7575 31 **Date established:** 1972
Turnover: £5m - £10m **No.of Employees:** 21 - 50 **Product Groups:** 40

Date of Accounts	Mar 08	Mar 09	Apr 10
Sales Turnover	6m	4m	3m
Pre Tax Profit/Loss	796	-177	23
Working Capital	751	764	992
Fixed Assets	1m	788	488
Current Assets	2m	2m	2m
Current Liabilities	600	258	330

R L Walsh & Sons Ltd
17 Lythalls Lane, Coventry, CV6 6FN
Tel: 024-7668 7241 **Fax:** 024-7666 2870
E-mail: office@rlwalsh.co.uk
Website: http://www.rlwalsh.co.uk
Directors: D. Walsh (MD)
Registration no: 01139514 **VAT No.:** GB 273 5423 58
Turnover: £2m - £5m **No.of Employees:** 21 - 50 **Product Groups:** 48

Warwickshire Fire Protection
17 Sanders Road, Coventry, CV6 6DH
Tel: 024-7636 4729 **Fax:** 024-7636 4729
Directors: C. Turbitt (Ptnr)
Date established: 1989 **No.of Employees:** 1 - 10 **Product Groups:** 38, 42

Wheelabrator Group Ltd (t/a U S F Impact Finishers Ltd)
Unit 5 Sandy Lane Business Park Sandy Lane, Coventry, CV1 4DQ
Tel: 024-7625 8811 **Fax:** 024-7625 8822
Website: http://www.noricangroup.com
Managers: C. Tyroll (Site Co-ord)
Ultimate Holding Company: NORICAN HOLDINGS LTD (DENMARK)
Immediate Holding Company: WHEELABRATOR GROUP LIMITED
Registration no: 00033672 **Date established:** 1991
No.of Employees: 1 - 10 **Product Groups:** 48

Date of Accounts	Dec 11	Dec 10	Dec 09
Sales Turnover	32m	33m	30m
Pre Tax Profit/Loss	-684	1m	378
Working Capital	24m	25m	24m
Fixed Assets	4m	4m	5m
Current Assets	37m	38m	37m
Current Liabilities	5m	4m	2m

George Wilson Industries Ltd
Barlow Road, Coventry, CV2 2TD
Tel: 024-7660 3336 **Fax:** 024-7660 3128
E-mail: gwi@bi-group.com
Bank(s): Lloyds TSB Bank plc
Directors: D. Pemblington (Dir)
Managers: R. Barnes (Personnel), P. Phipps (Comptroller), M. Grimes (Grp Purch Mgr), G. Morris (Tech Serv Mgr), M. Worthington (Sales Prom Mgr)
Ultimate Holding Company: NATIONAL INDUSTRIES GROUP (HOLDING) SAK (KUWAIT)
Immediate Holding Company: GEORGE WILSON INDUSTRIES LIMITED
Registration no: 02873275 **Date established:** 1993 **Turnover:** £5m - £10m
No.of Employees: 51 - 100 **Product Groups:** 38

Date of Accounts	Nov 11	Nov 10	Nov 09
Sales Turnover	5m	7m	12m
Pre Tax Profit/Loss	-881	-3m	-4m
Working Capital	1m	-2m	-3m
Fixed Assets	1m	2m	3m
Current Assets	2m	3m	5m
Current Liabilities	344	847	813

Windmill Products Ltd
Walsh Lane Meriden, Coventry, CV7 7JY
Tel: 01676-523838 **Fax:** 01676-522532
Website: http://www.windmillmachines.co.uk
Directors: J. Weaver (MD)
Immediate Holding Company: WINDMILL PRODUCTS LIMITED
Registration no: 05925290 **Date established:** 2006
Turnover: Up to £250,000 **No.of Employees:** 1 - 10 **Product Groups:** 46

Wright Safety Solutions
Shuna Croft, Coventry, CV2 2RY
Tel: 024-7661 8235
E-mail: safety@jabw.demon.co.uk
Website: http://www.wrightsafety.co.uk
Directors: J. Wright (Prop)
Date established: 2006 **No.of Employees:** 1 - 10 **Product Groups:** 54, 84

Wyken Tools Ltd
Unit 3 Bodmin Road, Coventry, CV2 5DB
Tel: 024-7662 1525 **Fax:** 024-7662 1472
E-mail: s.oxnard@talk21.com
Directors: S. Oxnard (Fin)
Immediate Holding Company: BODMIN ROAD LIMITED
Registration no: 04257802 **Date established:** 2001 **Turnover:** £1m - £2m
No.of Employees: 1 - 10 **Product Groups:** 46, 48

Date of Accounts	Dec 10	Dec 09	Dec 08
Working Capital	277	79	-124
Fixed Assets	154	153	201
Current Assets	904	494	509

Wyko Torrintool Engineering
Unit 2 Hotchkiss Way Binley Industrial Estate, Coventry, CV3 2RL
Tel: 024-7644 8644 **Fax:** 024-7663 5085
Website: http://www.wyko.co.uk
Directors: I. McQueem (Sales)
Immediate Holding Company: JIGSAW BEDROOMS LIMITED
Registration no: 05085767 **Date established:** 2004
No.of Employees: 1 - 10 **Product Groups:** 35, 45

Date of Accounts	Mar 11	Mar 10	Mar 09
Working Capital	-34	-26	-47
Fixed Assets	13	16	19
Current Assets	86	104	69

X K Engineering Ltd
Shilton Industrial Estate Bulkington Road, Coventry, CV7 9JY
Tel: 024-7662 2288 **Fax:** 024-7661 9323
E-mail: info@xkengineering.com
Website: http://www.xkengineering.com
Directors: D. Woods (Dir)
Ultimate Holding Company: XKE HOLDINGS LTD
Immediate Holding Company: XK ENGINEERING LIMITED
Registration no: 01870587 **VAT No.:** GB 372 2942 47
Date established: 1984 **Turnover:** £2m - £5m **No.of Employees:** 21 - 50
Product Groups: 39, 84

Date of Accounts	Jul 11	Jul 10	Jul 09
Working Capital	2m	2m	1m
Fixed Assets	50	59	400
Current Assets	2m	2m	2m

Cradley Heath

A Perry Hinges
Doulton Road, Cradley Heath, B64 5QW
Tel: 01384-414000 **Fax:** 01384-411100
E-mail: ian@hinges.co.uk
Website: http://www.hinges.co.uk
Directors: A. Dunnaker (MD), I. Dunnaker (Dir)
Managers: J. Hodgkinson (Purch Mgr), P. Wright (Tech Serv Mgr)
Immediate Holding Company: A.PERRY & CO.(HINGES)LIMITED
Registration no: 00363827 **Date established:** 1940 **Turnover:** £5m - £10m
No.of Employees: 51 - 100 **Product Groups:** 35, 36

Date of Accounts	Dec 11	Dec 10	Dec 09
Sales Turnover	9m	8m	3m
Pre Tax Profit/Loss	27	36	30
Working Capital	1m	1m	1m
Fixed Assets	265	215	227
Current Assets	3m	3m	3m
Current Liabilities	930	533	566

Aremco Products
Foxoak Street, Cradley Heath, B64 5DQ
Tel: 01384-568566 **Fax:** 01384-634601
E-mail: sales@aremco-products.co.uk
Website: http://www.aremco-products.co.uk
Directors: C. Blair (MD)
Managers: J. Coley (Chief Acct), S. Hackett (Buyer), J. Coley (Sales Prom Mgr)
Immediate Holding Company: H. CASE & SON (CRADLEY HEATH) LTD
Registration no: 00430324 **VAT No.:** GB 276 8367 09
Date established: 1947 **Turnover:** £500,000 - £1m
No.of Employees: 1 - 10 **Product Groups:** 35, 39

B D Profiles Ltd
PO Box 65, Cradley Heath, B64 5PP
Tel: 0121-559 5136 **Fax:** 0121-561 4265
E-mail: info@bdprofiles.co.uk
Website: http://www.bdprofiles.co.uk
Bank(s): Lloyds TSB Bank plc
Directors: S. Young (MD), A. Bowater (Fin)
Managers: D. Cartwright (Product), P. Hipkiss (Works Gen Mgr)
Ultimate Holding Company: UNISANT (HOLDINGS) LIMITED
Immediate Holding Company: BD PROFILES LIMITED
Registration no: 02120435 **VAT No.:** GB 488 3307 17
Date established: 1987 **Turnover:** £2m - £5m **No.of Employees:** 21 - 50
Product Groups: 30, 36, 37, 40, 43

Date of Accounts	Jul 11	Jul 10	Jul 09
Working Capital	3m	4m	4m
Fixed Assets	190	189	220
Current Assets	4m	4m	5m

B & W Billiards Ltd
Unit 3 Sapcote Trading Centre Powke Lane, Cradley Heath, B64 5QR
Tel: 01384-638191 **Fax:** 01384-638195
E-mail: sales@bandwbilliards.co.uk
Website: http://www.bandwbilliards.co.uk
Directors: Y. Westwood (Dir)
Immediate Holding Company: B & W BILLIARDS AND SNOOKER SERVICES LIMITED
Registration no: 04829057 **Date established:** 2003
Turnover: Up to £250,000 **No.of Employees:** 1 - 10 **Product Groups:** 49

Birmingham Saw Blades Ltd
117 Station Road, Cradley Heath, B64 6PL
Tel: 0121-559 5931 **Fax:** 0121-561 5121
E-mail: sales@dynashape.co.uk
Website: http://www.dynashape.co.uk
Directors: G. Mason (Dir)
Ultimate Holding Company: SOLUTIONS WORK LIMITED
Immediate Holding Company: BIRMINGHAM SAW BLADES LIMITED
Registration no: 01079240 **Date established:** 1972 **Turnover:** £2m - £5m
No.of Employees: 21 - 50 **Product Groups:** 36, 46, 47

Date of Accounts	Dec 11	Dec 10	Dec 09
Working Capital	-201	-219	-160
Fixed Assets	68	104	122
Current Assets	239	212	210

Brighton-Best Socket Screw Manufacturing Ltd
Unit D1 Cradley Business Park Overend Road, Cradley Heath, B64 7DW
Tel: 01384-568144 **Fax:** 01384-413719
E-mail: sales@brightonbest.org
Website: http://www.brightonbest.co.uk
Bank(s): Barclays, Bank of New Jersey
Managers: A. Dodd (Sales Prom Mgr), S. Gooding (Sales Prom Mgr)
Immediate Holding Company: BRIGHTON-BEST INTERNATIONAL, (UK) LIMITED
Registration no: 05908636 **VAT No.:** GB 390 6684 51
Date established: 2006 **Turnover:** £5m - £10m **No.of Employees:** 11 - 20
Product Groups: 35, 36

Date of Accounts	Dec 11	Dec 10	Dec 09
Sales Turnover	5m	2m	2m
Pre Tax Profit/Loss	449	-438	-188
Working Capital	1m	758	1m
Fixed Assets	337	379	154
Current Assets	7m	4m	2m
Current Liabilities	104	3m	18

British Standard Gratings
Unit B1 Cradley Business Park Overend Road, Cradley Heath, B64 7DW
Tel: 01384-563434 **Fax:** 01952-277778
E-mail: sales@bsgratings.com
Website: http://www.bsgratings.com
Bank(s): National Westminster Bank Plc
Directors: B. Trubshaw (MD)
Managers: B. Pilon (Tech Serv Mgr)
Immediate Holding Company: ACCESS TECHNOLOGIES LTD
Registration no: 04885681 **VAT No.:** GB 655 2396 20
Date established: 2003 **Turnover:** £2m - £5m **No.of Employees:** 21 - 50
Product Groups: 35

Brook Crompton
Unit 11 Waterfall Lane Trading Estate, Cradley Heath, B64 6PU
Tel: 0121-698 3100 **Fax:** 0121-698 3160
E-mail: steve.hurley@brookcrompton.com
Website: http://www.brookcrompton.com
Directors: S. Hurley (Chief Op Offcr)
Immediate Holding Company: WESTERN ELECTRICS
Registration no: 00476716 **Turnover:** £5m - £10m
No.of Employees: 21 - 50 **Product Groups:** 37

Brooks Forgings Ltd
Doulton Road, Cradley Heath, B64 5QJ
Tel: 01384-566434 **Fax:** 01384-637380
E-mail: sales@brooksforgings.co.uk
Website: http://www.brooksforgings.co.uk
Bank(s): HSBC Bank plc
Directors: S. Brooks (MD), A. Brooks (Dir)
Managers: S. Mills (Sales Prom Mgr)
Immediate Holding Company: BROOKS FORGINGS LIMITED
Registration no: 01289695 **Date established:** 1976
No.of Employees: 21 - 50 **Product Groups:** 30, 35, 48, 49

Date of Accounts	Mar 11	Mar 10	Mar 09
Working Capital	1m	1m	2m
Fixed Assets	664	587	518
Current Assets	2m	2m	2m

C & J International Windows Ltd
Unit 10 Peacocks Estate Providence Street, Cradley Heath, B64 5DG
Tel: 01384-411884 **Fax:** 01384-411884
E-mail: clive.cockram@liftinggear.co.uk
Website: http://www.candjinternationalwindows.co.uk
Directors: C. Cockram (Dir)
Immediate Holding Company: C & J INTERNATIONAL WINDOWS LIMITED
Registration no: 02865021 **Date established:** 1993
Turnover: Up to £250,000 **No.of Employees:** 1 - 10 **Product Groups:** 35, 39

Date of Accounts	Dec 11	Dec 10	Dec 09
Working Capital	6	3	1
Fixed Assets	1	1	1
Current Assets	25	24	24

C M T Steel Services Ltd
6 Overend Road Corngreaves Trading Estate, Cradley Heath, B64 7DD
Tel: 01384-632111 **Fax:** 01384-633586
E-mail: sales@shop4steel.com
Website: http://www.cmt-steel.co.uk
Directors: A. Warcup (MD), M. Dobbs (MD)
Managers: C. Smith (Mgr)
Immediate Holding Company: CMT STEEL SERVICES LIMITED
Registration no: 03704539 **Date established:** 1999
No.of Employees: 21 - 50 **Product Groups:** 34, 66

C M T Tube Fittings Ltd (Division of CMT Engineering)
PO Box 36, Cradley Heath, B64 7DQ
Tel: 01384-563200 **Fax:** 01384-563225
E-mail: sales@cmt-engineering.co.uk
Website: http://www.cmt-engineering.co.uk
Bank(s): Barclays, Birmingham
Directors: I. Whale (MD)
Managers: S. Humphries (Fin Mgr)
Immediate Holding Company: TUBE FITTINGS LIMITED
Registration no: 00532930 **VAT No.:** GB 245 2598 47
Date established: 1954 **Turnover:** £5m - £10m
No.of Employees: 51 - 100 **Product Groups:** 35, 36

Caparo Insulation (a division of C M T Engineering)
PO Box 36, Cradley Heath, B64 7DQ
Tel: 01384-563210 **Fax:** 01384-563225
E-mail: ian.whale@cmt-engineering.co.uk
Website: http://www.cmt-engineering.co.uk
Bank(s): Barclays, Colmore Row, Birmingham
Directors: I. Whale (Dir), S. Humphries (Fin)
Ultimate Holding Company: CAPARO GROUP LTD
Immediate Holding Company: CAPARO ENGINEERING LTD
Registration no: 00212644 **VAT No.:** GB 245 2598 47
Turnover: £1m - £2m **No.of Employees:** 51 - 100 **Product Groups:** 30, 33, 66

Claron Hydraulic Seals Ltd
Station Road, Cradley Heath, B64 6PN
Tel: 0121-559 9711 **Fax:** 02155-91036
E-mail: seals@claron.co.uk
Website: http://www.claron.co.uk
Bank(s): Barclays Bank PLC
Directors: C. Stanley (MD)
Managers: A. Lockhead (Fin Mgr), R. Walker (Tech Serv Mgr), J. Brimmell (Buyer)
Immediate Holding Company: CLARON HYDRAULIC SEALS LIMITED
Registration no: 01229690 **VAT No.:** GB 281 5636 46
Date established: 1975 **Turnover:** £1m - £2m **No.of Employees:** 21 - 50
Product Groups: 29, 30, 36, 39, 40, 66, 67

Date of Accounts	Mar 11	Mar 10	Mar 09
Working Capital	271	333	333
Fixed Assets	245	248	252
Current Assets	573	579	624

Clubsafe Case Manufacturers
Unit 1 Oldfield Trading Estate Oldfields Corngreaves Road, Cradley Heath, B64 6BS
Tel: 01384-411311 **Fax:** 01384-411311
E-mail: enquiries@cslclubsafe.co.uk
Website: http://www.cslclubsafe.co.uk
Directors: L. Beards (Prop)
Date established: 2002 **No.of Employees:** 1 - 10 **Product Groups:** 49

CMT Engineering Ltd (Division of CMT Engineering)
Po Box 36Corngreaves Road, Cradley Heath, B64 7DQ
Tel: 01384-563220 **Fax:** 01384-563225
E-mail: sales@caparo-dynamics.com
Website: http://www.cmt-dynamics.co.uk
Bank(s): Barclays, Birmingham
Directors: P. Taylor (MD), S. Gooding (Chief Op Offcr)
Managers: M. Raybould (Comm)
Ultimate Holding Company: Caparo Group Ltd
Immediate Holding Company: Caparo Engineering Ltd
Registration no: 00212644 **VAT No.:** GB 245 2598 47
Turnover: Up to £250,000 **No.of Employees:** 11 - 20 **Product Groups:** 29, 35, 39, 46

Cradley Doors & Shutters Ltd
Peacocks Estate Providence Street, Cradley Heath, B64 5DG
Tel: 01384-411366 **Fax:** 01384-573155
E-mail: info@cradleydoors.co.uk
Website: http://www.cradleydoors.co.uk
Directors: J. Bayliss (MD), J. Bayliss (Prop)
Date established: 1989 **No.of Employees:** 1 - 10 **Product Groups:** 30, 35, 36

Cradley Plating Co. Ltd
Woods Lane, Cradley Heath, B64 7AA
Tel: 01384-634111 **Fax:** 01384-413110
E-mail: cradleyplate@btinternet.com
Directors: D. Jones (Dir)
Immediate Holding Company: CRADLEY PLATING CO. LIMITED
Registration no: 00631527 **Date established:** 1959
Turnover: Up to £250,000 **No.of Employees:** 1 - 10 **Product Groups:** 36, 48

Date of Accounts	Jun 11	Jun 10	Jun 09
Working Capital	99	89	90
Fixed Assets	59	49	51
Current Assets	122	97	101

Dart Products Ltd
Garratts Lane, Cradley Heath, B64 5RE
Tel: 0121-559 1414 **Fax:** 0121-559 8675
E-mail: sales@dart.biz
Website: http://www.dart.biz
Managers: L. Deville (Personnel), A. Spicer
Immediate Holding Company: DART PRODUCTS LIMITED
Registration no: 02067427 **Date established:** 1986
No.of Employees: 51 - 100 **Product Groups:** 24, 27, 29, 30, 49, 67

Date of Accounts	Dec 11	Dec 10	Dec 09
Sales Turnover	13m	13m	12m
Pre Tax Profit/Loss	322	537	458
Working Capital	9m	8m	12m
Fixed Assets	4m	4m	5m
Current Assets	10m	9m	13m
Current Liabilities	160	506	276

Davies Woven Wire Ltd
Unit 38 Cradley Heath Factory Centre Woods Lane, Cradley Heath, B64 7AQ
Tel: 01384-411991 **Fax:** 01384-410999
E-mail: peter@davieswilliams.co.uk
Website: http://www.davieswovenwire.co.uk
Directors: P. Davies (MD)
Managers: C. Capewell (Sales Prom Mgr)
Immediate Holding Company: DAVIES WOVEN WIRE LIMITED
Registration no: 03472100 **Date established:** 1997
No.of Employees: 21 - 50 **Product Groups:** 35, 45

Date of Accounts	Dec 11	Dec 10	Dec 09
Working Capital	393	337	296
Fixed Assets	59	53	53
Current Assets	1m	1m	854

Deacon Products Ltd
Unit 5 Penn Industrial Estate Providence Street, Cradley Heath, B64 5DJ
Tel: 01384-416931 **Fax:** 01384-635172
E-mail: info@wire-rope.co.uk
Website: http://www.chain-fittings.co.uk
Directors: B. Connop (Dir)
Immediate Holding Company: DEACON PRODUCTS LIMITED
Registration no: 02440650 **Date established:** 1989
Turnover: £500,000 - £1m **No.of Employees:** 21 - 50
Product Groups: 35, 36, 37, 39, 45, 66

Date of Accounts	Jul 11	Jul 10	Jul 09
Working Capital	2m	2m	1m
Fixed Assets	299	280	510
Current Assets	2m	2m	1m

Dynashape Ltd
117 Station Rd Old Hill, Cradley Heath, B64 6PL
Tel: 0121-559 5931 **Fax:** 0121-559 2008
E-mail: sales@dynashape.co.uk
Website: http://www.dynashape.co.uk
Bank(s): Barclays, Birmingham
Directors: G. Mason (MD)
Registration no: 01451585 **VAT No.:** GB 333 1439 83
Turnover: £2m - £5m **No.of Employees:** 21 - 50 **Product Groups:** 36, 41, 66

Date of Accounts	Dec 09	Dec 08	Dec 07
Working Capital	9	6	10
Current Assets	335	311	395

Easygates Ltd
Unit 4 Broadcott Industrial Estate, Cradley Heath, B64 6NT
Tel: 08707-606536 **Fax:** 0121-561 3395
E-mail: info@easygates.co.uk
Website: http://www.easygates.co.uk
Directors: D. Gooding (MD)
Immediate Holding Company: EASYGATES LIMITED
Registration no: 03051720 **Date established:** 1995
No.of Employees: 11 - 20 **Product Groups:** 25, 30, 35, 36, 37, 39, 40, 49, 52, 66, 67, 68, 81, 83

Date of Accounts	Mar 11	Mar 10	Mar 09
Working Capital	319	266	203
Fixed Assets	31	15	20
Current Assets	728	516	378

Electra Engineering Services Midlands Ltd
Unit 19 Charlton Drive Corngreaves Trading Estate, Cradley Heath, B64 7BJ
Tel: 01384-561000 **Fax:** 01384-411142
E-mail: sales@electraengineering.com
Website: http://www.electraengineering.com
Bank(s): National Westminster Bank Plc
Directors: P. Marsh (MD)
Managers: L. Woodall (Sales Admin)
Ultimate Holding Company: ELECTRA ENGINEERING SERVICES HOLDINGS LIMITED
Immediate Holding Company: ELECTRA ENGINEERING SERVICES (MIDLANDS) LIMITED
Registration no: 01299251 **Date established:** 1977 **Turnover:** £2m - £5m
No.of Employees: 21 - 50 **Product Groups:** 30, 35, 66

Date of Accounts	Apr 11	Apr 10	Apr 09
Working Capital	597	657	637
Fixed Assets	3	10	16
Current Assets	2m	2m	1m

FastClamp
Cradley Business Park Overend Road, Cradley Heath, B64 7DW
Tel: 01952-632387 **Fax:** 01952-632384
E-mail: info@fastclamp.com
Website: http://www.fastclamp.com
Product Groups: 36

W H Foster & Sons Ltd
Stourdale Road, Cradley Heath, B64 7BG
Tel: 08453-313491 **Fax:** 01384-415185
E-mail: sales@whfoster.co.uk
Website: http://www.whfoster.co.uk
Bank(s): Lloyds TSB
Directors: A. Lowe (MD), D. Payne (Co Sec), J. Hardwick (Dir), R. Foster (Dir)
Managers: G. Turner (Sales Prom Mgr)
Ultimate Holding Company: APOLLO GROUP LIMITED
Immediate Holding Company: W H FOSTER & SONS LIMITED
Registration no: 05138028 **VAT No.:** 276 9432 19 **Date established:** 2004
Turnover: £2m - £5m **No.of Employees:** 21 - 50 **Product Groups:** 48

Date of Accounts	Dec 10	Dec 09	Dec 08
Working Capital	-141	-132	-176
Fixed Assets	322	275	316
Current Assets	1m	1m	1m

H Reis T R Ltd
Powke Lane, Cradley Heath, B64 5QF
Tel: 01384-567727 **Fax:** 01384-410317
E-mail: terry.reis@chromebar.co.uk
Website: http://www.chromebar.co.uk
Directors: T. Reis (MD), T. Reis (Dir)
Immediate Holding Company: H REIS (TR) LIMITED
Registration no: 05227541 **VAT No.:** GB 277 9683 85
Date established: 2004 **Turnover:** £1m - £2m **No.of Employees:** 21 - 50
Product Groups: 32, 48

Date of Accounts	Oct 11	Oct 10	Oct 09
Working Capital	230	226	211
Fixed Assets	66	68	70
Current Assets	404	559	405

Holtite Ltd
Jubilee Works Woods Lane, Cradley Heath, B64 7BA
Tel: 01384-560611 **Fax:** 01384-410214
E-mail: holtite@aol.com
Bank(s): HSBC Bank plc
Directors: D. Bills (Dir)
Immediate Holding Company: HOLTITE LIMITED
Registration no: 00565481 **VAT No.:** GB 277 0575 36
Date established: 1956 **Turnover:** £1m - £2m **No.of Employees:** 11 - 20
Product Groups: 35, 39

Date of Accounts	Apr 11	Apr 10	Apr 09
Working Capital	124	138	138
Fixed Assets	115	134	120
Current Assets	434	485	697

Industrial Combustion Engineers Ltd
Bannister Street, Cradley Heath, B64 5EQ
Tel: 01384-564160 **Fax:** 01384-635628
Website: http://www.indcom.co.uk
Directors: D. Neade (MD)
Immediate Holding Company: INDUSTRIAL COMBUSTION ENGINEERS LIMITED
Registration no: 01835648 **Date established:** 1984
No.of Employees: 1 - 10 **Product Groups:** 35, 36, 39

Date of Accounts	Dec 11	Dec 10	Dec 09
Working Capital	29	28	20
Fixed Assets	4	4	5
Current Assets	85	116	99

J C D Cranes & Lifting Gear Ltd
Unit 12-13 Peacocks Estate Providence Street, Cradley Heath, B64 5DG
Tel: 01384-568444 **Fax:** 01384-568777
E-mail: info@jcdcranes.co.uk
Website: http://www.jcdcranes.co.uk
Directors: B. Walker (Dir)
Immediate Holding Company: J C D CRANE AND LIFTING GEAR COMPANY LIMITED

see next page

J C D Cranes & Lifting Gear Ltd - Cont'd

Registration no: 02582520 **Date established:** 1991
Turnover: Up to £250,000 **No.of Employees:** 1 - 10 **Product Groups:** 23, 35, 39, 45, 83, 85

Date of Accounts	Dec 10	Dec 09	Dec 08
Working Capital	33	44	55
Fixed Assets	6	7	8
Current Assets	157	120	125

Katoll Metals & Industrial Products Ltd
Unit 4 Corngreaves Industrial Estate Central Avenue, Cradley Heath, B64 7BY
Tel: 01384-634001 **Fax:** 01384-410776
E-mail: sales@katollmetals.co.uk
Website: http://www.katollmetals.co.uk
Directors: K. Williams (Co Sec)
Immediate Holding Company: KATOLL METALS AND INDUSTRIAL PRODUCTS LIMITED
Registration no: 01664462 **VAT No.:** GB 388 5182 09
Date established: 1982 **Turnover:** £2m - £5m **No.of Employees:** 1 - 10
Product Groups: 34, 48, 67

Date of Accounts	Jan 12	Jan 11	Jan 10
Working Capital	424	407	407
Fixed Assets	57	64	64
Current Assets	735	672	672

Kendrick Sheet Metal Ltd
Unit 3 Peacocks Estate Providence Street, Cradley Heath, B64 5DG
Tel: 01384-638363 **Fax:** 01384-637881
Website: http://www.kendricksheetmetal.co.uk
Directors: M. Kendrick (Dir)
Immediate Holding Company: KENDRICK SHEET METAL LIMITED
Registration no: 01309284 **VAT No.:** GB 300 0394 26
Date established: 1977 **Turnover:** Up to £250,000
No.of Employees: 1 - 10 **Product Groups:** 48

Date of Accounts	Aug 11	Aug 10	Aug 09
Working Capital	88	70	22
Fixed Assets	N/A	1	1
Current Assets	195	123	65

Samuel Lewis Ltd
PO Box 65, Cradley Heath, B64 5PP
Tel: 0121-561 2157 **Fax:** 0121-561 5273
Bank(s): Lloyds
Directors: A. Bowater (Co Sec)
Ultimate Holding Company: UNISANT (HOLDINGS) LIMITED
Immediate Holding Company: SAMUEL LEWIS LIMITED
Registration no: 00334669 **VAT No.:** GB 188 3307 17
Date established: 1937 **Turnover:** £2m - £5m **No.of Employees:** 11 - 20
Product Groups: 67

Date of Accounts	Jul 11	Jul 10	Jul 09
Working Capital	1m	2m	2m
Fixed Assets	25	29	35
Current Assets	2m	2m	3m

Lift & Engineering Services Ltd
16 Portersfield Road, Cradley Heath, B64 7BE
Tel: 01384-633115 **Fax:** 01384-633119
E-mail: mailbox@lift-engineering.co.uk
Website: http://www.lift-engineering.co.uk
Bank(s): Lloyds TSB Bank plc
Directors: D. Haywood (MD)
Immediate Holding Company: LIFT AND ENGINEERING SERVICES LIMITED
Registration no: 01913516 **VAT No.:** GB 377 3555 19
Date established: 1985 **Turnover:** £5m - £10m **No.of Employees:** 21 - 50
Product Groups: 45

Date of Accounts	Mar 11	Mar 10	Mar 09
Sales Turnover	8m	7m	N/A
Pre Tax Profit/Loss	1m	1m	449
Working Capital	700	644	452
Fixed Assets	659	585	565
Current Assets	2m	2m	2m
Current Liabilities	712	528	329

Lifting Tackles Suppliers Ltd
Silverthorne Lane, Cradley Heath, B64 5AP
Tel: 01384-569910 **Fax:** 01384-569972
E-mail: sales@liftingtackle.com
Website: http://www.liftingtackle.com
Bank(s): Bank of Scotland
Directors: B. Robinson (Fin), P. Jackson (Ch), P. Jackson (MD)
Managers: J. Harris (Sales Prom Mgr)
Immediate Holding Company: RADICAL FINANCIAL SERVICES LIMITED
Registration no: 03210565 **VAT No.:** GB 360 6702 66
Date established: 2002 **Turnover:** £1m - £2m **No.of Employees:** 11 - 20
Product Groups: 35, 45, 48, 84

Date of Accounts	May 11	May 10	May 09
Working Capital	170	155	115
Fixed Assets	230	230	279
Current Assets	402	410	284

M I F Filter Systems
Waterfall Lane Trading Estate, Cradley Heath, B64 6PU
Tel: 0121-561 3580 **Fax:** 0121- 5593711
E-mail: mikeg@mif-filters.com
Website: http://www.mif-filters.com
Directors: M. Grainger (Fin)
Ultimate Holding Company: NECTON LIMITED
Immediate Holding Company: MIF FILTER SYSTEMS LIMITED
Registration no: 01456776 **Date established:** 1979
No.of Employees: 11 - 20 **Product Groups:** 23, 24, 33, 34, 35, 38, 39, 40, 41, 42, 45, 68

Date of Accounts	Sep 11	Sep 10	Sep 09
Working Capital	518	252	127
Fixed Assets	204	416	545
Current Assets	1m	1m	1m
Current Liabilities	106	N/A	452

Main Man Supplies Ltd
12-17 Charlton Drive Corngreaves Trading Estate, Cradley Heath, B64 7BJ
Tel: 01384-411101 **Fax:** 01384-411718
E-mail: sales@mmsgroup.co.uk
Website: http://www.mmsgroup.co.uk
Bank(s): Midland P.L.C., Dudley
Directors: A. Cook (Sales), M. Brooker (MD), E. Williams (Co Sec)
Managers: A. Elwell, L. Norwood (Purch Mgr)
Immediate Holding Company: MAIN MAN SUPPLIES LIMITED
Registration no: 02422319 **VAT No.:** GB 462 3720 59
Date established: 1989 **Turnover:** £10m - £20m
No.of Employees: 101 - 250 **Product Groups:** 24

Date of Accounts	Dec 10	Dec 09	Dec 08
Sales Turnover	17m	16m	N/A
Pre Tax Profit/Loss	282	2	739
Working Capital	4m	4m	4m
Fixed Assets	244	301	488
Current Assets	7m	7m	8m
Current Liabilities	2m	260	536

Metal & Waste Recycling
Powke Lane, Cradley Heath, B64 5PT
Tel: 0121-559 1156 **Fax:** 0121-561 5371
E-mail: john.wright@metalandwaste.com
Website: http://www.metalandwaste.com
Bank(s): Barclays
Directors: J. Rice (Co Sec), J. Wright (MD)
Ultimate Holding Company: BROOMCO (3958) LIMITED
Immediate Holding Company: N.BROOKES & BROTHERS LIMITED
Registration no: 00346720 **VAT No.:** GB 276 9842 00
Date established: 1938 **Turnover:** £10m - £20m
No.of Employees: 21 - 50 **Product Groups:** 66

Date of Accounts	Oct 10	Oct 09	Oct 08
Working Capital	3m	3m	3m
Fixed Assets	190	190	190
Current Assets	3m	3m	4m
Current Liabilities	11	11	10

Midland Tube & Fabrications
4 Corngreaves Works Corngreaves Road, Cradley Heath, B64 7DA
Tel: 01384-566364 **Fax:** 01384-566365
E-mail: keithcadman@btconnect.com
Website: http://www.midlandtubeandfabrications.co.uk
Directors: K. Cadman (Prop)
VAT No.: GB 333 1155 00 **Turnover:** Up to £250,000
No.of Employees: 1 - 10 **Product Groups:** 35, 36, 48

M S R
Unit 6 Bay 4 Stourdale Road, Cradley Heath, B64 7BG
Tel: 01384-636683 **Fax:** 01384-634245
E-mail: info@msrfab.co.uk
Website: http://www.msrfab.co.uk
Directors: R. Gower (Prop)
Ultimate Holding Company: APOLLO GROUP LIMITED
Immediate Holding Company: APOLLO AEROSPACE COMPONENTS LIMITED
Registration no: 02023463 **Date established:** 1986
No.of Employees: 1 - 10 **Product Groups:** 35

Date of Accounts	Mar 12	Mar 11	Mar 10
Working Capital	966	918	1m
Fixed Assets	92	91	66
Current Assets	2m	2m	2m

N E Fasteners
2 Waterfall Lane Trading Estate, Cradley Heath, B64 6PU
Tel: 0121-559 8866 **Fax:** 0121-559 8862
E-mail: m.elliot@nefasteners.co.uk
Website: http://www.nefasteners.co.uk
Managers: M. Elliot (Mgr)
Registration no: 01941690 **Turnover:** £500,000 - £1m
No.of Employees: 1 - 10 **Product Groups:** 30, 35, 66

Date of Accounts	Jun 08	Jun 07	Jun 06
Working Capital	78	60	41
Fixed Assets	23	20	26
Current Assets	216	225	213
Current Liabilities	138	165	172

Old Park Engineering Services
36b Woods Lane, Cradley Heath, B64 7AN
Tel: 01384-412550 **Fax:** 01384-410784
E-mail: info@oldparklpg.co.uk
Website: http://www.oldparklpg.co.uk
Directors: G. Cornforth (Dir), C. Cornforth (Co Sec)
Immediate Holding Company: OLD PARK ENGINEERING SERVICES LIMITED
Registration no: 03636597 **Date established:** 1998 **Turnover:** £1m - £2m
No.of Employees: 1 - 10 **Product Groups:** 77

Date of Accounts	Dec 11	Dec 10	Dec 09
Working Capital	-6	-6	-31
Fixed Assets	188	183	176
Current Assets	495	385	301

Orbit Bearings & Transmission Ltd
7 Hillcrest Industrial Estate Corngreaves Road, Cradley Heath, B64 7BT
Tel: 01384-410700 **Fax:** 01384-410900
E-mail: info@orbitbearings.co.uk
Website: http://www.orbitbearings.co.uk
Directors: A. Burton (Fin)
Immediate Holding Company: ORBIT BEARINGS AND TRANSMISSION LIMITED
Registration no: 02529511 **Date established:** 1990
No.of Employees: 1 - 10 **Product Groups:** 22, 23, 25, 29, 30, 31, 33, 34, 35, 36, 37, 38, 39, 40, 43, 45, 46, 47, 48, 49, 66, 67, 68, 84

Date of Accounts	Dec 11	Dec 10	Dec 09
Working Capital	67	56	39
Fixed Assets	59	61	62
Current Assets	178	146	122

Palmer Timber Ltd
104 Station Road, Cradley Heath, B64 6PW
Tel: 0121-559 5511 **Fax:** 0121-561 4562
E-mail: sales@palmertimber.com
Website: http://www.palmertimber.com
Directors: P. Kerr (Fin), R. Palmer (Sales)
Managers: K. Edmunds (Tech Serv Mgr), P. Waddington (Sales & Mktg Mg)
Immediate Holding Company: PALMER TIMBER LIMITED
Registration no: 00365289 **Date established:** 1941
Turnover: £20m - £50m **No.of Employees:** 51 - 100 **Product Groups:** 08, 66

Date of Accounts	Sep 11	Sep 10	Sep 09
Sales Turnover	30m	27m	24m
Pre Tax Profit/Loss	943	621	-218
Working Capital	3m	3m	2m
Fixed Assets	3m	3m	3m
Current Assets	14m	12m	10m
Current Liabilities	2m	2m	2m

Parasene
Unit 20 Waterfall Lane Trading Estate, Cradley Heath, B64 6PU
Tel: 0121-508 6570 **Fax:** 0121-508 6590
E-mail: sales@tarasen.com
Website: http://www.parasene.com
Directors: R. Tye (Purch)
Immediate Holding Company: PARASENE LIMITED
Registration no: 05871436 **Date established:** 2006
No.of Employees: 101 - 250 **Product Groups:** 40

Professional Cycle Marketing
Forge Lane, Cradley Heath, B64 5AL
Tel: 01384-568521 **Fax:** 01384-634494
E-mail: enquires@pcmgroup.co.uk
Website: http://www.pcmgroup.co.uk
Bank(s): Barclays
Directors: D. Overton (Co Sec)
Registration no: 02943544 **No.of Employees:** 11 - 20 **Product Groups:** 39

Rainbow Upholstery
51 Compton Road, Cradley Heath, B64 5BB
Tel: 01384-634059 **Fax:** 01384-411733
E-mail: paul@rainbowupholstery.co.uk
Website: http://www.rainbowupholstery.co.uk
Directors: P. Round (MD), M. Bate (Dir), T. Jenkins (Sales & Mktg)
Immediate Holding Company: RAINBOW UPHOLSTERY LIMITED
Registration no: 01763459 **Date established:** 1983
No.of Employees: 21 - 50 **Product Groups:** 23, 26

Date of Accounts	Dec 11	Dec 10	Dec 09
Working Capital	129	121	217
Fixed Assets	459	431	292
Current Assets	434	511	449

Rapid Industrial Fasteners Ltd
9 Gun Barrel Industrial Centre Hayseech, Cradley Heath, B64 7JZ
Tel: 0121-501 3903 **Fax:** 0121-585 5163
E-mail: sales@rapidfast.co.uk
Website: http://www.rapidfast.co.uk
Directors: R. White (Dir)
Immediate Holding Company: RAPID INDUSTRIAL FASTENERS LIMITED
Registration no: 01812731 **Date established:** 1984 **Turnover:** £2m - £5m
No.of Employees: 11 - 20 **Product Groups:** 35, 66

Date of Accounts	Apr 11	Apr 10	Apr 09
Working Capital	383	376	406
Fixed Assets	33	40	36
Current Assets	749	628	675

William Rowland Ltd
Powke Lane, Cradley Heath, B64 5PS
Tel: 0121-559 3031 **Fax:** 0121-561 5474
E-mail: info@william-rowland.co.uk
Website: http://www.william-rowland.co.uk
Directors: D. Cooper (Dir)
Ultimate Holding Company: AMCO INVESTMENTS LIMITED
Immediate Holding Company: WILLIAM ROWLAND LIMITED
Registration no: 00853661 **Date established:** 1965
Turnover: £20m - £50m **No.of Employees:** 11 - 20 **Product Groups:** 34

Date of Accounts	Dec 11	Dec 10	Dec 09
Sales Turnover	74m	63m	28m
Pre Tax Profit/Loss	2m	1m	599
Working Capital	11m	11m	6m
Fixed Assets	998	978	961
Current Assets	19m	19m	10m
Current Liabilities	623	425	1m

Security Fasteners & Fixings (UK) ltd
Unit 19 Charlton Drive, Corngreaves Trading Estate, Cradley Heath, B64 7BJ
Tel: 01384-561000 **Fax:** 01384-411142
E-mail: info@securityfastenersandfixings.com
Website: http://www.securityfastenersandfixings.com
Directors: Shelton (MD)
Registration no: 02373522 **No.of Employees:** 1 - 10 **Product Groups:** 35, 66

Service Business Forms
Cokeland Place, Cradley Heath, B64 6AN
Tel: 01384-569934 **Fax:** 01384-569937
E-mail: guy@service1.co.uk
Website: http://www.service1.co.uk
Directors: J. O'neil (Co Sec), S. Trow (MD), R. Trow (MD), G. Thornbery (MD), G. Thornbury (MD)
Managers: M. Kirkham (Purch Mgr), J. O'Neill (Comptroller), K. Wilson (Develop Mgr)
Ultimate Holding Company: DURMAST GROUP LIMITED
Immediate Holding Company: SERVICE BUSINESS FORMS LIMITED
Registration no: 01674441 **Date established:** 1982
Turnover: £500,000 - £1m **No.of Employees:** 21 - 50 **Product Groups:** 28

Date of Accounts	Dec 10	Dec 09	Dec 08
Working Capital	359	239	81
Fixed Assets	120	189	217
Current Assets	1m	845	740

Solid Stampings Ltd
Porters Field Road, Cradley Heath, B64 7BL
Tel: 01384-636421 **Fax:** 01384-639163
E-mail: aledw@solidswivel.co.uk
Website: http://www.solidswivel.co.uk
Directors: A. Williams (Fin)
Immediate Holding Company: SOLID STAMPINGS LIMITED
Registration no: 01035249 **VAT No.:** 277 2220 63 **Date established:** 1971
No.of Employees: 1 - 10 **Product Groups:** 48

Date of Accounts	Mar 12	Mar 11	Mar 10
Working Capital	169	247	239
Fixed Assets	N/A	N/A	5
Current Assets	355	370	351

T T C Lifting Gear Ltd
Newlyn Road, Cradley Heath, B64 6BE
Tel: 01384-564059 **Fax:** 01384-410587
E-mail: info@ttclifting.co.uk
Website: http://www.ttclifting.co.uk
Directors: D. Billington (Dir)
Immediate Holding Company: T T C (LIFTING GEAR) LIMITED
Registration no: 01283805 **Date established:** 1976
No.of Employees: 11 - 20 **Product Groups:** 35, 39, 45

Date of Accounts	Oct 11	Oct 10	Oct 09
Working Capital	190	187	107
Fixed Assets	74	80	31
Current Assets	525	413	239

Truck-Lite Co. Ltd
Waterfall Lane, Cradley Heath, B64 6QB
Tel: 0121-561 7000 **Fax:** 0121-561 1415
E-mail: jhamilton@uk.truck-lite.com
Website: http://www.truck-lite.eu.com
Bank(s): Royal Bank of Scotland, 35 Princes St, Wolverhampton
Directors: K. Jones (Fin)
Managers: M. Elsworth, S. Wearing (Tech Serv Mgr), S. Walker (Personnel), A. Lloyd (Plant)
Ultimate Holding Company: PENSKE CORP INC (USA)
Immediate Holding Company: TRUCK-LITE CO. LIMITED
Registration no: 00460489 **VAT No.:** GB 276 8483 07
Date established: 1948 **Turnover:** £50m - £75m
No.of Employees: 101 - 250 **Product Groups:** 37, 39, 68

Date of Accounts	Dec 11	Dec 10	Dec 09
Sales Turnover	61m	52m	38m
Pre Tax Profit/Loss	-2m	-2m	195
Working Capital	11m	11m	9m
Fixed Assets	18m	19m	20m
Current Assets	20m	20m	14m
Current Liabilities	2m	2m	1m

Westley Group Ltd
PO Box 1, Cradley Heath, B64 5QS
Tel: 01384-410111 **Fax:** 08701-290865
E-mail: james.salisbury@westley.co.uk
Website: http://www.westleygroup.co.uk
Bank(s): Barclays
Directors: J. Salisbury (MD), M. Richard (Fin), I. McWhirter (Sales & Mktg)
Managers: D. Wheeler (Personnel)
Ultimate Holding Company: MUSGRAVE HOLDINGS LIMITED
Immediate Holding Company: WESTLEY GROUP LIMITED
Registration no: 01150600 **VAT No.:** GB 281 3470 64
Date established: 1973 **Turnover:** £20m - £50m
No.of Employees: 101 - 250 **Product Groups:** 30, 34, 35, 36, 39, 40, 45, 46, 48, 66, 67

Date of Accounts	Aug 11	Aug 10	Aug 09
Sales Turnover	42m	39m	37m
Pre Tax Profit/Loss	-1m	238	2m
Working Capital	4m	3m	3m
Fixed Assets	6m	10m	9m
Current Assets	15m	18m	13m
Current Liabilities	1m	3m	3m

Westley Plastics Ltd
PO Box 1, Cradley Heath, B64 5QY
Tel: 01384-414840 **Fax:** 01384-414849
E-mail: sales@plasticsuk.com
Website: http://www.plasticsuk.com
Bank(s): Lloyds TSB Bank plc
Directors: T. Chandler (Dir), T. Westley (Ch)
Registration no: 00807351 **Date established:** 1964 **Turnover:** £2m - £5m
No.of Employees: 21 - 50 **Product Groups:** 30, 31, 33, 35, 39, 48, 66

Date of Accounts	Aug 09	Aug 08	Aug 07
Sales Turnover	3m	2m	3m
Pre Tax Profit/Loss	198	66	22
Working Capital	-177	-189	-121
Fixed Assets	3m	3m	2m
Current Assets	1m	1m	999
Current Liabilities	197	241	275

Darlaston

George Dyke Ltd
Imperial Works Heath Road, Darlaston, WS10 8LP
Tel: 0121-526 7138 **Fax:** 0121-568 8956
E-mail: gsmith@george-dyke.co.uk
Website: http://www.george-dyke.co.uk
Bank(s): Lloyds TSB Bank plc
Managers: G. Smith (Sales Prom Mgr), G. Smith (Export Sales Mg), D. McTighe (Chief Mgr), G. Smith (Mktg Serv Mgr), M. Bissell (Works Gen Mgr), N. Scribner (Purch Mgr), N. Turner (Tech Serv Mgr), D. Lovatt (Tech Serv Mgr), D. Lovatt (Mgr)
Registration no: 01523799 **Date established:** 1830 **Turnover:** £5m - £10m
No.of Employees: 51 - 100 **Product Groups:** 46, 48, 66

Date of Accounts	Nov 11	Nov 09	Nov 08
Sales Turnover	5m	4m	N/A
Pre Tax Profit/Loss	82	-135	49
Working Capital	1m	1m	1m
Fixed Assets	1m	1m	1m
Current Assets	3m	2m	2m
Current Liabilities	246	380	343

Dudley

A C Ford Dudley Ltd
1 Churchfield Street, Dudley, DY2 8QU
Tel: 01384-253701 **Fax:** 01384-457542
Website: http://www.acforddudley.co.uk
Directors: J. Wilde (MD)
Immediate Holding Company: A.C. FORD (DUDLEY) LIMITED
Registration no: 01245699 **Date established:** 1976
No.of Employees: 1 - 10 **Product Groups:** 37, 67

Date of Accounts	Jun 11	Jun 10	Jun 09
Working Capital	14	24	38
Fixed Assets	35	38	35
Current Assets	39	49	73

All Seasons Blinds & Shutters
27 Woodland Avenue, Dudley, DY1 4AX
Tel: 01384-231425 **Fax:** 01384-231425
Directors: J. Pearson (Snr Part)
Date established: 1991 **No.of Employees:** 1 - 10 **Product Groups:** 26, 35

Alomgate Ltd
Unit 1 Shaw Road, Dudley, DY2 8TS
Tel: 01384-238786 **Fax:** 01384-455261
E-mail: john@alomgate.com
Website: http://www.midtherm.com
Bank(s): Lloyds TSB Bank plc
Directors: M. Andrews (MD)
Immediate Holding Company: ALOMGATE LIMITED
Registration no: 01426828 **VAT No.:** GB 409 4277 45
Date established: 1979 **Turnover:** £1m - £2m **No.of Employees:** 21 - 50
Product Groups: 36, 40

Date of Accounts	Mar 10	Mar 09	Jun 11
Working Capital	-31	-13	-43
Fixed Assets	563	585	537
Current Assets	316	337	243

Alpha Bearings
Kingsley Street, Dudley, DY2 0PZ
Tel: 01384-255151 **Fax:** 01384-457509
E-mail: info@alpha-bearings.com
Website: http://www.alpha-bearings.com
Bank(s): Lloyds TSB
Directors: C. Williams (Prop), A. Fitzgerald (Co Sec)
Immediate Holding Company: ALPHA BEARINGS LIMITED
Registration no: 00524495 **VAT No.:** GB 276 8266 15
Date established: 1953 **Turnover:** £250,000 - £500,000
No.of Employees: 11 - 20 **Product Groups:** 39, 40

Date of Accounts	Dec 08	Dec 07	Dec 06
Working Capital	21	52	95
Fixed Assets	38	47	51
Current Assets	234	210	230

Anastel Ltd
67 Gospel End Street, Dudley, DY3 3LR
Tel: 01902-679494 **Fax:** 01902-664080
E-mail: sales@anstel.co.uk
Website: http://www.anastel.co.uk
Directors: J. Roberts (Fin), R. Wimhurst (MD)
Immediate Holding Company: ANASTEL LIMITED
Registration no: 04356074 **Date established:** 2002
Turnover: £10m - £20m **No.of Employees:** 1 - 10 **Product Groups:** 34

Date of Accounts	Dec 07	Dec 06	Dec 05
Sales Turnover	6586	7370	7033
Pre Tax Profit/Loss	-121	72	65
Working Capital	851	961	951
Fixed Assets	54	59	44
Current Assets	6275	7111	4907
Current Liabilities	5423	6150	3955
Total Share Capital	400	400	400
ROCE% (Return on Capital Employed)	-13.3	7.0	6.5
ROT% (Return on Turnover)	-1.8	1.0	0.9

B F Entron Ltd
Castle Mill Works Birmingham New Road, Dudley, DY1 4DA
Tel: 01384-455401 **Fax:** 01384-455551
E-mail: sales@bfentron.co.uk
Website: http://www.bfentron.co.uk
Bank(s): Lloyds TSB Bank plc
Directors: J. Stanway (MD)
Immediate Holding Company: BF ENTRON LIMITED
Registration no: 05434301 **VAT No.:** GB 758 1697 82
Date established: 2005 **Turnover:** £1m - £2m **No.of Employees:** 11 - 20
Product Groups: 34, 35, 36, 37, 38, 45, 46, 47, 48, 84, 85

Date of Accounts	Dec 11	Dec 10	Dec 09
Working Capital	377	308	283
Fixed Assets	7	8	11
Current Assets	739	646	472

C Beech & Sons Netherton Ltd
Primrose Hill Cradley Road, Dudley, DY2 9RG
Tel: 01384-456654 **Fax:** 01384-238656
E-mail: sales@cbeech-steel.co.uk
Website: http://www.cbeech-steel.co.uk
Bank(s): HSBC Bank plc
Directors: M. Beech (MD)
Immediate Holding Company: C.BEECH & SONS (NETHERTON) LIMITED
Registration no: 00795354 **VAT No.:** GB 276 8425 21
Date established: 1964 **Turnover:** £2m - £5m **No.of Employees:** 11 - 20
Product Groups: 66

Date of Accounts	Apr 11	Apr 10	Apr 09
Working Capital	974	921	955
Fixed Assets	2m	2m	2m
Current Assets	2m	2m	2m

Birchfield Engineering Ltd
Northfield Road Netherton, Dudley, DY2 9JQ
Tel: 01384-237171 **Fax:** 01384-237273
E-mail: peter@birchfieldengineering.co.uk
Website: http://www.birchfieldengineering.co.uk
Registration no: 3263682 **Turnover:** £500,000 - £1m
No.of Employees: 1 - 10 **Product Groups:** 35, 38, 46, 48

Date of Accounts	Mar 12	Mar 11	Mar 10
Working Capital	926	802	699
Fixed Assets	332	387	263
Current Assets	1m	1m	834

Bodycote plc
Blackbrook Business Park Narrowboat Way, Dudley, DY2 0XQ
Tel: 01384-455880 **Fax:** 01384-457250
E-mail: info@bodycote.com
Website: http://www.bodycote.com
Directors: D. Shipley (Develop), C. Fowler (Dir), P. Dent (MD)
Ultimate Holding Company: Bodycote International PLC
Registration no: 00519057 **VAT No.:** GB 553 5266 38
Turnover: £500,000 - £1m **No.of Employees:** 51 - 100
Product Groups: 39, 51, 54, 84, 85

Bradney Chain & Engineering Co. Ltd
Quarry Road, Dudley, DY2 0EB
Tel: 01384-636233 **Fax:** 01384-634289
E-mail: sales@bradneychain.co.uk
Website: http://www.bradneychain.com
Directors: C. Wiggins (Fin)
Ultimate Holding Company: BRADNEY HOLDINGS LIMITED
Immediate Holding Company: BRADNEY CHAIN AND ENGINEERING COMPANY LIMITED
Registration no: 04618203 **VAT No.:** GB 276 8633 14
Date established: 2002 **Turnover:** £1m - £2m **No.of Employees:** 1 - 10
Product Groups: 35, 45, 48, 84

Date of Accounts	Sep 11	Sep 10	Sep 09
Working Capital	194	101	43
Fixed Assets	3	3	10
Current Assets	675	584	536

Bruck UK Ltd
28-30 Wolverhampton Street, Dudley, DY1 1DB
Tel: 01905-796999 **Fax:** 01905-796898
E-mail: klaus.scheid@bruck-uk.com
Website: http://www.bruck-uk.com
Directors: K. Scheid (MD)
Immediate Holding Company: BRUCK UK LIMITED
Registration no: 02628719 **VAT No.:** GB 589 5419 79
Date established: 1991 **Turnover:** £2m - £5m **No.of Employees:** 1 - 10
Product Groups: 36, 48

Date of Accounts	Dec 11	Dec 10	Dec 09
Working Capital	2m	2m	2m
Fixed Assets	21	19	24
Current Assets	2m	3m	2m

John Buckley Dudley Ltd
Alma Place, Dudley, DY2 8QH
Tel: 01384-252554 **Fax:** 01384-456172
E-mail: sales@buckleybrass.co.uk
Website: http://www.jbuckley.co.uk
Directors: T. Rowe (Dir)
Immediate Holding Company: JOHN BUCKLEY(DUDLEY)LIMITED
Registration no: 00105158 **Date established:** 2009 **Turnover:** £1m - £2m
No.of Employees: 1 - 10 **Product Groups:** 48

Date of Accounts	Mar 12	Mar 11	Mar 10
Working Capital	863	859	800
Fixed Assets	230	238	248
Current Assets	1m	1m	913

Caparo Forging Dudley
Marriott Road, Dudley, DY2 0LA
Tel: 01384-252587 **Fax:** 01384-231005
E-mail: jane.f@clydesdale-forge.co.uk
Website: http://www.caparoforging.co.uk
Bank(s): Barclays, Birmingham
Directors: J. Beck (Fin), K. Newton (Sales)
Managers: D. Pearson (Personnel), S. Harris, M. Haythorne (Tech Serv Mgr), K. Llewellyn (Mktg Serv Mgr)
Ultimate Holding Company: CAPARO INDUSTRIES P.L.C.
Immediate Holding Company: CARPARO ENGINEERING LTD
Registration no: 03450375 **VAT No.:** GB 245 2598 47
Turnover: £20m - £50m **No.of Employees:** 101 - 250 **Product Groups:** 48

Castle Engineering Resources Ltd
4 Central Works Peartree Lane, Dudley, DY2 0QU
Tel: 01384-230233 **Fax:** 01384-230757
E-mail: sales@castletanks.co.uk
Directors: M. Castle (MD)
Immediate Holding Company: CASTLE ENGINEERING RESOURCES LIMITED
Registration no: 02017400 **VAT No.:** GB 409 3494 42
Date established: 1986 **Turnover:** £500,000 - £1m
No.of Employees: 1 - 10 **Product Groups:** 26, 29, 30, 35, 36, 40, 42, 45, 48, 84

Date of Accounts	May 11	May 10	May 06
Working Capital	12	14	18
Fixed Assets	3	4	2
Current Assets	30	42	56

Chinal Management Services Ltd (Head Office)
King Charles House 2 Castle Hill, Dudley, DY1 4PS
Tel: 01384-234234 **Fax:** 01384-456183
E-mail: info@chinal.co.uk
Website: http://www.chinal.co.uk
Directors: S. Chinal (Fin), E. Chinal (MD)
Immediate Holding Company: CHINAL MANAGEMENT SERVICES LIMITED
Registration no: 01212391 **Date established:** 1975 **Turnover:** £2m - £5m
No.of Employees: 1 - 10 **Product Groups:** 80

Date of Accounts	May 12	May 11	May 10
Working Capital	402	343	329
Fixed Assets	8	13	6
Current Assets	474	412	457

Civica UK Ltd
Castlegate House Castlegate Drive, Dudley, DY1 4TD
Tel: 01384-453400 **Fax:** 01384-453600
E-mail: enquiries@civica.co.uk
Website: http://www.civica.co.uk
Bank(s): HSBC Bank plc
Directors: D. Roots (MD)
Managers: F. Russel (Sales Prom Mgr)
Ultimate Holding Company: CORNWALL TOPCO LIMITED
Immediate Holding Company: CIVICA CONNECT LIMITED
Registration no: 03413938 **Date established:** 1997 **Turnover:** £2m - £5m
No.of Employees: 51 - 100 **Product Groups:** 44

Date of Accounts	Sep 11	Sep 10	Sep 07
Sales Turnover	N/A	N/A	2m
Pre Tax Profit/Loss	N/A	N/A	325
Working Capital	2m	2m	2m
Current Assets	2m	2m	2m

Compact Fork Trucks Ltd
Unit 8B Blackbrook Business Park Narrowboat Way, Dudley, DY2 0XQ
Tel: 01384-238000 **Fax:** 01384-240300
E-mail: info@thecompactgroup.com
Website: http://www.thecompactgroup.com
Directors: B. Tilt (Prop)
Ultimate Holding Company: STURGE INDUSTRIES LIMITED
Immediate Holding Company: COMPACT FORK TRUCKS LIMITED
Registration no: 04593061 **Date established:** 2002
No.of Employees: 11 - 20 **Product Groups:** 45, 48, 67, 71, 83, 86

Date of Accounts	Mar 12	Mar 11	Mar 10
Sales Turnover	N/A	N/A	2m
Pre Tax Profit/Loss	N/A	N/A	70
Working Capital	77	64	140
Fixed Assets	104	139	52
Current Assets	688	546	581
Current Liabilities	N/A	N/A	169

Computeach International Ltd
PO Box 51, Dudley, DY3 2AH
Tel: 01384-458515 **Fax:** 01384-455650
E-mail: customercare@computeach.co.uk
Website: http://www.computeach.co.uk
Bank(s): HSBC Bank plc

see next page

Computeach International Ltd - *Cont'd*

Directors: T. Morroll (Co Sec), A. Coleyshaw (Dir)
Managers: R. Boichat (Tech Serv Mgr), D. Edwards (Personnel)
Immediate Holding Company: COMPUTEACH INTERNATIONAL LIMITED
Registration no: 01242854 **Date established:** 1976 **Turnover:** £5m - £10m
No.of Employees: 51 - 100 **Product Groups:** 86

Date of Accounts	Dec 08	Dec 09	Jan 11
Sales Turnover	13m	9m	7m
Pre Tax Profit/Loss	3m	6m	1m
Working Capital	-2m	-682	813
Fixed Assets	2m	2m	2m
Current Assets	9m	4m	3m
Current Liabilities	10m	4m	2m

Container Products

Unit 7 Castle Mill Works Birmingham New Road, Dudley, DY1 4DA
Tel: 01384-251391 **Fax:** 01384-251390
E-mail: info@containerproducts.co.uk
Website: http://www.containerproducts.co.uk
Directors: S. Fletcher (Dir), J. Fletcher (Fin)
Immediate Holding Company: CONTAINER PRODUCTS LIMITED
Registration no: 03271086 **Date established:** 1996
No.of Employees: 1 - 10 **Product Groups:** 25, 27

Date of Accounts	Oct 11	Oct 10	Oct 09
Working Capital	-6	-9	-12
Fixed Assets	3	3	4
Current Assets	94	94	65

Control Equipment Ltd

Cinder Bank, Dudley, DY2 9AP
Tel: 01384-458651 **Fax:** 01384-458972
E-mail: kwalters@tycoint.com
Website: http://www.controlequipment.com
Directors: D. Neale (Co Sec), K. Walters (MD)
Managers: M. Adams (Personnel), D. Whitefoot (Mktg Serv Mgr), S. Alhaklami (Tech Serv Mgr)
Ultimate Holding Company: TYCO INTERNATIONAL LIMITED (SWITZERLAND)
Immediate Holding Company: CONTROL EQUIPMENT LIMITED
Registration no: 01769524 **Date established:** 1983
Turnover: £10m - £20m **No.of Employees:** 101 - 250
Product Groups: 37, 40, 67

Date of Accounts	Sep 11	Sep 08	Sep 09
Sales Turnover	13m	7m	8m
Pre Tax Profit/Loss	66	595	164
Working Capital	3m	3m	3m
Fixed Assets	395	55	580
Current Assets	6m	5m	6m
Current Liabilities	390	309	381

Cottage Blinds Of Sedgley Ltd

Old Nail Works Brick Street, Dudley, DY3 1NT
Tel: 01902-661267 **Fax:** 01902-884312
E-mail: sales@cottageblinds.co.uk
Website: http://www.cottageblinds.co.uk
Directors: P. Thompson (MD)
Immediate Holding Company: COTTAGE BLINDS OF SEDGLEY LIMITED
Registration no: 02369008 **Date established:** 1989
Turnover: £500,000 - £1m **No.of Employees:** 11 - 20
Product Groups: 24, 25, 30, 35, 37, 38, 39, 48, 49, 63, 66

Date of Accounts	May 11	May 10	May 09
Working Capital	-101	-59	-25
Fixed Assets	16	13	24
Current Assets	310	335	385

D R Harvey & Co.

7 North Street, Dudley, DY2 7DT
Tel: 01384-253200 **Fax:** 01384-253200
E-mail: gateshouse2@tiscali.co.uk
Website: http://www.drharvey.co.uk
Directors: S. Harvey (Dir)
Immediate Holding Company: D R HARVEY & CO LIMITED
Registration no: 06198009 **Date established:** 2007
Turnover: Up to £250,000 **No.of Employees:** 1 - 10 **Product Groups:** 34, 35, 37, 46, 49, 66

Deepdale Engineering Co. Ltd

Pedmore Road, Dudley, DY2 0RD
Tel: 01384-480022 **Fax:** 01384-480489
E-mail: sales@deepdale-eng.co.uk
Website: http://www.deepdale-eng.co.uk
Bank(s): Barclays, High St
Directors: J. Marsh (Co Sec)
Managers: A. Hodgekins, P. Cutler, M. Wood (Personnel), S. Phipson (Tech Serv Mgr)
Immediate Holding Company: DEEPDALE ENGINEERING CO. LIMITED
Registration no: 00473086 **VAT No.:** GB 277 1599 17
Date established: 1949 **Turnover:** £2m - £5m **No.of Employees:** 21 - 50
Product Groups: 34, 35, 36, 48

Date of Accounts	Jul 11	Jul 10	Jul 09
Working Capital	983	986	924
Fixed Assets	339	354	370
Current Assets	2m	2m	2m

Dudley College

The Broadway, Dudley, DY1 4AS
Tel: 01384-363363 **Fax:** 01384-363311
E-mail: sarah.cooper@dudleycol.ac.uk
Website: http://www.dudleycol.ac.uk
Directors: G. Turton (Fin)
Managers: N. Marsh (Tech Serv Mgr), J. Turner, S. Cooper (Mktg Serv Mgr)
Immediate Holding Company: DUDLEY COLLEGE ENTERPRISES LIMITED
Registration no: 02786849 **Date established:** 1993
Turnover: Up to £250,000 **No.of Employees:** 501 - 1000
Product Groups: 80, 86

Date of Accounts	Jul 11	Jul 10	Jul 09
Sales Turnover	N/A	N/A	181
Pre Tax Profit/Loss	-6	-7	2
Working Capital	-516	-517	-514
Fixed Assets	504	510	517
Current Assets	13	212	224
Current Liabilities	4	107	116

Dudley Electro Plating

Dudley Central Trading Estate Shaw Road, Dudley, DY2 8QX
Tel: 01384-237427 **Fax:** 01384-255741
No.of Employees: 1 - 10 **Product Groups:** 32, 48

Thomas Dudley Ltd

295 Birmingham New Road, Dudley, DY1 4SJ
Tel: 0121-557 5411 **Fax:** 0121-557 5345
E-mail: info@thomasdudley.co.uk
Website: http://www.thomasdudley.co.uk
Bank(s): Barclays, West Bromwich
Directors: M. Dudley (MD)
Ultimate Holding Company: THOMAS DUDLEY GROUP LIMITED
Immediate Holding Company: THOMAS DUDLEY GROUP LIMITED
Registration no: 00732459 **VAT No.:** GB 488 5315 08
Date established: 1962 **Turnover:** £20m - £50m
No.of Employees: 251 - 500 **Product Groups:** 30, 34, 36, 49

Date of Accounts	Jul 11	Jul 10	Jul 09
Sales Turnover	27m	25m	26m
Pre Tax Profit/Loss	5m	4m	3m
Working Capital	20m	18m	17m
Fixed Assets	16m	15m	13m
Current Assets	25m	23m	21m
Current Liabilities	2m	2m	1m

Dyform Jenkins Dunn

Dudley Central Trading Estate Shaw Road, Dudley, DY2 8QX
Tel: 01384-232844 **Fax:** 01384-455628
Website: http://www.jenkinsdunn.co.uk
Bank(s): HSBC Bank plc
Managers: R. O'neill (Sales Prom Mgr)
Immediate Holding Company: MT SKIPS LIMITED
Registration no: 03261694 **VAT No.:** GB 300 2241 41
Date established: 2010 **Turnover:** £1m - £2m **No.of Employees:** 11 - 20
Product Groups: 48

Date of Accounts	Aug 11	Aug 10	Aug 09
Working Capital	75	75	83
Fixed Assets	44	25	19
Current Assets	360	336	214

Ehrco UK Ltd

Unit H Peartree Industrial Park Crackley Way Peartree Lane, Dudley, DY2 0UW
Tel: 01384-245000 **Fax:** 01384-245001
E-mail: bob@ehrco.ltd.uk
Website: http://www.ehrco.ltd.uk
Bank(s): Lloyds TSB Bank plc
Directors: A. Russell (Co Sec), B. Couzens (MD)
Ultimate Holding Company: SPRINGSTAR SRL (ITALY)
Immediate Holding Company: EHRCO LIMITED
Registration no: 02671603 **VAT No.:** GB 610 8140 83
Date established: 1991 **Turnover:** £2m - £5m **No.of Employees:** 11 - 20
Product Groups: 29, 30, 36, 66, 67

Date of Accounts	Dec 11	Dec 10	Dec 09
Working Capital	1m	1m	1m
Fixed Assets	882	878	868
Current Assets	2m	2m	2m

Emerson Network Power Embedded Power

Astec House Waterfront Business Park, Merry Hill, Dudley, DY5 1LX
Tel: 0800-032 1546 **Fax:** 01384-843355
E-mail: sales@emerson.com
Website: http://www.powerconversion.com
Bank(s): Barclays
Directors: P. Lamb (MD)
Managers: A. Muircroft
Ultimate Holding Company: Emerson Electric Co
Immediate Holding Company: AIL Holdings Ltd
Registration no: 00644867 **VAT No.:** GB 441 7337 58
Turnover: £500,000 - £1m **Product Groups:** 37, 38, 44

Estil Ltd

Charlotte Street, Dudley, DY1 1TD
Tel: 01384-243643 **Fax:** 01384-243644
E-mail: sales@estil.co.uk
Website: http://www.estil.co.uk
Bank(s): HSBC Bank plc
Directors: A. Newbould (Dir), R. Hobson (Fin)
Managers: R. Woolley (Buyer)
Immediate Holding Company: ESTIL LIMITED
Registration no: 01758295 **Date established:** 1983 **Turnover:** £2m - £5m
No.of Employees: 51 - 100 **Product Groups:** 52

Date of Accounts	Oct 11	Oct 10	Oct 09
Working Capital	557	488	465
Fixed Assets	542	557	576
Current Assets	2m	1m	1m

Eurocraft Trustees Ltd

Cinderbank Netherton, Dudley, DY2 9AE
Tel: 01384-230101 **Fax:** 01384-256883
E-mail: sales@eurocraft.co.uk
Website: http://www.eurocraft.co.uk
Bank(s): Royal bank of Scotland
Directors: K. O'Toole (Dir), M. Bate (I.T. Dir), M. Hamblett (Pers)
Managers: L. Loveys (Prod Mgr)
Immediate Holding Company: Eurocraft Group Ltd
Registration no: 02445667 **Date established:** 1989 **Turnover:** £5m - £10m
No.of Employees: 51 - 100 **Product Groups:** 26, 48

Fellows Stringer Ltd

Unit 7 Bagley Industrial Park Railwharf Sidings, Dudley, DY2 9DY
Tel: 01384-459978 **Fax:** 01384-458963
E-mail: tim@fellows-stringer.co.uk
Website: http://www.fellows-stringer.co.uk
Directors: S. Jackson (Fin), T. Jackson (MD)
Immediate Holding Company: FELLOWS STRINGER CRANES & HOISTS LIMITED
Registration no: 02610287 **Date established:** 1991
No.of Employees: 1 - 10 **Product Groups:** 45, 67

Date of Accounts	Mar 09	Mar 08	Mar 07
Working Capital	-167	-52	-49
Fixed Assets	12	22	19
Current Assets	220	387	424
Current Liabilities	N/A	194	222

Glasscoat International Ltd

Chapel Street, Dudley, DY2 9PN
Tel: 01384-400789 **Fax:** 01384-400787
E-mail: info@glasscoat.co.uk
Website: http://www.glasscoat.co.uk
Directors: A. Cripps (Fin)
Managers: C. Hands
Ultimate Holding Company: TYPEWRITER & EQUIPMENT COMPANY LIMITED
Immediate Holding Company: GLASSCOAT INTERNATIONAL LIMITED
Registration no: 05333100 **Date established:** 2005 **Turnover:** £2m - £5m
No.of Employees: 1 - 10 **Product Groups:** 33

Date of Accounts	Mar 11	Mar 10	Mar 09
Working Capital	201	207	174
Fixed Assets	10	12	N/A
Current Assets	424	352	356

Griff Chains Ltd

Quarry Road Dudley Wood, Dudley, DY2 0ED
Tel: 01384-569512 **Fax:** 01384-410580
E-mail: sales@griffchains.co.uk
Website: http://www.griffchains.co.uk
Bank(s): National Westminster Bank Plc
Directors: T. Wood (MD)
Immediate Holding Company: JOSEPH WOODHOUSE (CHAINS) LIMITED
Registration no: 03756730 **VAT No.:** GB 715 7410 47
Date established: 1999 **Turnover:** £1m - £2m **No.of Employees:** 21 - 50
Product Groups: 34, 35, 39, 41, 45, 48, 84

Griffin Bros Dudley Ltd

10 Wellington Road, Dudley, DY1 1RB
Tel: 01384-252063 **Fax:** 01384-237820
E-mail: sue@griffenbros.co.uk
Website: http://www.griffinbros.co.uk
Bank(s): HSBC Bank plc
Directors: A. Griffin (Dir), C. Coxson (Jt MD), J. Saunders (Dir), M. Griffin (Co Sec)
Immediate Holding Company: GRIFFIN BROS (DUDLEY)LIMITED
Registration no: 00625177 **Date established:** 1959
Turnover: £500,000 - £1m **No.of Employees:** 11 - 20 **Product Groups:** 35

Date of Accounts	Dec 07	Dec 06	Dec 05
Working Capital	-310	-280	-250
Fixed Assets	216	213	209
Current Assets	209	181	183
Current Liabilities	519	461	434
Total Share Capital	23	23	23

Holemoor Engineering Ltd

Shaw Road, Dudley, DY2 8TP
Tel: 01384-237574 **Fax:** 01384-230013
Directors: E. Nightingale (Fin), M. Nightingale (MD)
Immediate Holding Company: HOLEMOOR ENGINEERING LIMITED
Registration no: 01569543 **Date established:** 1981
Turnover: £250,000 - £500,000 **No.of Employees:** 1 - 10
Product Groups: 48

Date of Accounts	Oct 11	Oct 10	Oct 09
Working Capital	80	63	79
Fixed Assets	3	4	5
Current Assets	113	101	104

I V M

11 Ley Rise, Dudley, DY3 3EU
Tel: 01902-650094
E-mail: kevin@i-v-m.co.uk
Website: http://www.knotweed-uk.com
Managers: K. Alderwick (Mgr)
Immediate Holding Company: INVASIVE VEGETATION MANAGEMENT AND TREATMENT LIMITED
Registration no: 06381111 **Date established:** 2007
No.of Employees: 1 - 10 **Product Groups:** 07

Date of Accounts	Mar 12	Mar 11	Mar 10
Working Capital	62	46	38
Fixed Assets	2	1	2
Current Assets	105	113	71
Current Liabilities	N/A	N/A	21

Indtherm Ltd

120 Wellington Road, Dudley, DY1 1UB
Tel: 01384-456666 **Fax:** 01384-456666
E-mail: alan.faulkner@indtherm.co.uk
Website: http://www.indtherm.co.uk
Directors: C. Walker (Ch), T. Moore (MD), P. Stokes (Co Sec), M. France (MD), A. Faulkner (Dir)
Managers: L. Watson (Sales & Mktg Mg), S. Walker (Mktg Serv Mgr), S. Robinson (I.T. Exec), M. Whitehouse (Sales Prom Mgr)
Ultimate Holding Company: GG133 LIMITED
Immediate Holding Company: INDTHERM LIMITED
Registration no: 01054496 **Date established:** 1972 **Turnover:** £5m - £10m
No.of Employees: 51 - 100 **Product Groups:** 52

Date of Accounts	Sep 11	Sep 10	Sep 09
Sales Turnover	10m	8m	9m
Pre Tax Profit/Loss	123	-451	-576
Working Capital	-90	-128	-346
Fixed Assets	392	236	926
Current Assets	3m	3m	3m
Current Liabilities	896	970	318

Industrial Machine Guards

2 Dormston Trading Estate Burton Road, Dudley, DY1 2UF
Tel: 01902-676485 **Fax:** 01902-880987
Directors: B. Evans (Ptnr), B. Evans (Head)
Managers: S. Raybold (Mgr)
Ultimate Holding Company: ROBERT LICKLEY HOLDINGS LIMITED
Immediate Holding Company: ROBERT LICKLEY REFRACTORIES LIMITED
Registration no: 00620638 **VAT No.:** GB 278 2964 09
Date established: 1977 **Turnover:** Up to £250,000
No.of Employees: 1 - 10 **Product Groups:** 35, 40

Date of Accounts	Jul 10	Jul 09	Jul 08
Working Capital	-4	-6	-8
Fixed Assets	2	3	3
Current Assets	11	37	34

Industrial Valves Ltd

Units 1 & 2 Washington Street, Dudley, DY2 9PH
Tel: 01384-458411 **Fax:** 01384-246952
E-mail: sales@industrialvalve.co.uk
Website: http://www.industrialvalve.co.uk
Managers: A. Williams, R. Collins, A. Morgan (Sales Prom Mgr)
Ultimate Holding Company: F.J.HOLDINGS LIMITED
Immediate Holding Company: INDUSTRIAL VALVES LIMITED
Registration no: 04270582 **Date established:** 2001 **Turnover:** £2m - £5m
No.of Employees: 11 - 20 **Product Groups:** 29, 30, 31, 32, 33, 34, 35, 36, 37, 38, 39, 40, 41, 45, 46, 48, 49, 66, 67, 68

Date of Accounts	Dec 11	Dec 10	Dec 09
Sales Turnover	6m	5m	N/A
Pre Tax Profit/Loss	33	28	N/A

Working Capital	315	295	300
Fixed Assets	220	254	219
Current Assets	2m	2m	2m
Current Liabilities	396	621	N/A

Ingram Foods Ltd

4 Blackbrook Valley Industrial Estate Narrowboat Way, Dudley, DY2 0XQ
Tel: 01384-237551 **Fax:** 01384-240017
E-mail: ingramfoodslimited@btinternet.com
Website: http://www.ingramfoods.com
Bank(s): HSBC Bank plc
Directors: G. Strain (MD), K. Pinfield (Co Sec)
Ultimate Holding Company: STURGE INDUSTRIES LIMITED
Immediate Holding Company: NDC POLYTHENES LIMITED
Registration no: 01160038 **VAT No.:** GB 300 2393 18
Date established: 1999 **Turnover:** £5m - £10m **No.of Employees:** 21 - 50
Product Groups: 20

Date of Accounts	Aug 08	Aug 07	Aug 06
Working Capital	-161	-95	-98
Fixed Assets	512	499	127
Current Assets	942	794	503
Current Liabilities	1104	889	602
Total Share Capital	5	5	5

Initial Facilities Services Ltd

Castlegate House Castlegate Way, Dudley, DY1 4RR
Tel: 01384-455055 **Fax:** 01384-246085
E-mail: dpofficer@rentokil-initial.com
Website: http://www.initial.co.uk
Directors: M. Brown (MD)
Ultimate Holding Company: RENTOKIL INITIAL PLC
Immediate Holding Company: RENTOKIL INITIAL FACILITIES SERVICES (UK) LIMITED
Registration no: 02329448 **Date established:** 1988
Turnover: £125m - £250m **No.of Employees:** 101 - 250
Product Groups: 52

Date of Accounts	Dec 11	Dec 10	Dec 09
Sales Turnover	206m	199m	191m
Pre Tax Profit/Loss	5m	2m	648
Working Capital	-23m	-22m	-14m
Fixed Assets	63m	54m	37m
Current Assets	122m	47m	59m
Current Liabilities	33m	28m	20m

International Power Presses (Hulbert Engineering Limited)

Peartree Lodge Grazebrook Industrial Park Peartree Lane, Dudley, DY2 0XW
Tel: 01384-457595 **Fax:** 01384-457280
E-mail: enq@hulbert-group.co.uk
Website: http://www.int-power-presses.co.uk
Directors: G. Knowles (MD), L. Willetts (Co Sec)
Ultimate Holding Company: HULBERT ENGINEERING LIMITED
Immediate Holding Company: INTERNATIONAL POWER PRESSES LIMITED
Registration no: 03901974 **VAT No.:** GB 748 0924 12
Date established: 2000 **Turnover:** £5m - £10m **No.of Employees:** 1 - 10
Product Groups: 42, 46, 67

J & M Steels

Unit 14 Deepdale Lane, Dudley, DY3 2AF
Tel: 01384-253223 **Fax:** 01384-253299
Directors: M. Jones (MD)
Immediate Holding Company: J. & M. STEELS (MIDLANDS) LIMITED
Registration no: 01714132 **VAT No.:** GB 371 5131 75
Date established: 1983 **No.of Employees:** 1 - 10 **Product Groups:** 66

Date of Accounts	Dec 11	Dec 10	Dec 09
Working Capital	6	2	6
Fixed Assets	6	8	2
Current Assets	238	281	181

J Powell Electrical Ltd

53 Churchfield Street, Dudley, DY2 8QN
Tel: 01384-259911 **Fax:** 01384-211446
E-mail: john@powellelectrical.co.uk
Website: http://www.powellelectrical.co.uk
Directors: J. Powell (MD)
Immediate Holding Company: POWELL ELECTRICAL LIMITED
Registration no: 04231465 **VAT No.:** GB 669 5936 65
Date established: 2001 **Turnover:** £1m - £2m **No.of Employees:** 1 - 10
Product Groups: 52

Date of Accounts	Jun 08	Jun 07	Jun 06
Working Capital	24	16	66
Fixed Assets	80	61	68
Current Assets	370	300	301

James Walker Rotabolt Ltd

Unit F Peartree Industrial Park Crackley Way Peartree Lane, Dudley, DY2 0UW
Tel: 01384-214442 **Fax:** 01384-455186
E-mail: sales@rotabolt.co.uk
Website: http://www.rotabolt.co.uk
Bank(s): HSBC, Wednesbury
Directors: D. Galloway (Fin), R. Corbett (MD)
Ultimate Holding Company: JAMES WALKER GROUP LIMITED
Immediate Holding Company: JAMES WALKER ROTABOLT LIMITED
Registration no: 01545486 **VAT No.:** GB 351 5728 54
Date established: 1981 **Turnover:** £1m - £2m **No.of Employees:** 11 - 20
Product Groups: 35, 48

Date of Accounts	Mar 12	Mar 11	Mar 10
Working Capital	2m	1m	2m
Fixed Assets	491	545	495
Current Assets	3m	2m	2m

Jewson Ltd

Woodside Works Pedmore Road, Dudley, DY2 0RH
Tel: 01384-480886 **Fax:** 01384-480880
Website: http://www.jewson.co.uk
Bank(s): Barclays
Directors: P. Hindle (MD)
Managers: S. Goodacre (District Mgr)
Ultimate Holding Company: COMPAGNIE DE SAINT GOBAIN (FRANCE)
Immediate Holding Company: JEWSON LIMITED
Registration no: 00348407 **VAT No.:** GB 394 1212 63
Date established: 1939 **No.of Employees:** 11 - 20 **Product Groups:** 66

Date of Accounts	Dec 11	Dec 10	Dec 09
Sales Turnover	1606m	1547m	1485m
Pre Tax Profit/Loss	18m	100m	45m

Working Capital	-345m	-250m	-349m
Fixed Assets	496m	387m	461m
Current Assets	657m	1005m	1320m
Current Liabilities	66m	120m	64m

Robert Lickley Refractries Ltd

PO Box 24, Dudley, DY1 2RL
Tel: 01902-880123 **Fax:** 01902-880019
E-mail: admin@robertlickley.co.uk
Website: http://www.robertlickley.co.uk
Bank(s): HSBC
Directors: B. Bridgen (Ch), A. Winwood (MD), K. Winchurch (Sales)
Managers: T. Oliver, M. Hartill (Purch Mgr)
Ultimate Holding Company: ROBERT LICKLEY HOLDINGS LIMITED
Immediate Holding Company: ROBERT LICKLEY HOLDINGS LIMITED
Registration no: 01303146 **VAT No.:** GB 300 0060 55
Date established: 1977 **Turnover:** £5m - £10m **No.of Employees:** 21 - 50
Product Groups: 33

Date of Accounts	Aug 11	Aug 10	Aug 09
Sales Turnover	10m	9m	7m
Pre Tax Profit/Loss	191	129	142
Working Capital	2m	1m	1m
Fixed Assets	1m	1m	1m
Current Assets	4m	3m	3m
Current Liabilities	671	541	331

M & G Sheds & Fencing

Unit J9 Dudley Trading Estate Shaw Road, Dudley, DY2 8QX
Tel: 01384-240956 **Fax:** 01384-255741
Directors: M. Enright (Prop)
No.of Employees: 1 - 10 **Product Groups:** 08, 25, 35, 52

M G Stainless Ltd

Unit 1-2 Shaw Road, Dudley, DY2 8TS
Tel: 01384-232175 **Fax:** 01384-232177
E-mail: mail@mgstainless.co.uk
Website: http://www.mgstainless.co.uk
Directors: M. Gillett (Dir)
Immediate Holding Company: M G STAINLESS LIMITED
Registration no: 03185706 **Date established:** 1996
Turnover: £250,000 - £500,000 **No.of Employees:** 1 - 10
Product Groups: 26, 35, 36, 66

Date of Accounts	Sep 11	Sep 10	Sep 09
Working Capital	1	6	-3
Fixed Assets	10	13	17
Current Assets	81	75	96

Malroy Products Dudley Ltd

Shaw Road, Dudley, DY2 8TR
Tel: 01384-254178 **Fax:** 01384- 230126
E-mail: mhadley@malroyco.freeserve.co.uk
Website: http://www.malroy.co.uk
Bank(s): Lloyds TSB
Directors: M. Hadley (MD)
Immediate Holding Company: MALROY PRODUCTS(DUDLEY)LIMITED
Registration no: 00864619 **VAT No.:** GB 277 7389 95
Date established: 1965 **Turnover:** £1m - £2m **No.of Employees:** 11 - 20
Product Groups: 25, 26, 35, 36, 45

Date of Accounts	Jan 12	Jan 11	Jan 10
Working Capital	527	533	-3
Fixed Assets	116	148	311
Current Assets	530	561	178

Marcegaglia UK Ltd

New Road, Dudley, DY2 8TA
Tel: 01384-242812 **Fax:** 01384-242813
E-mail: uk@marcegaglia.com
Website: http://www.gruppo-marcegaglia.com
Directors: N. Grinsell (Co Sec), S. Marcegaglia (Dir)
Managers: J. Ingram (Sales Prom Mgr), I. Cotterell, G. Tristan (Tech Serv Mgr)
Ultimate Holding Company: MARCEGAGLIA SPA (ITALY)
Immediate Holding Company: MARCEGAGLIA (UK) LIMITED
Registration no: 02677001 **VAT No.:** GB 589 3586 70
Date established: 1992 **Turnover:** £20m - £50m
No.of Employees: 51 - 100 **Product Groups:** 34, 36

Date of Accounts	Dec 11	Dec 10	Dec 09
Sales Turnover	48m	41m	30m
Pre Tax Profit/Loss	4m	4m	2m
Working Capital	20m	17m	13m
Fixed Assets	5m	5m	6m
Current Assets	27m	24m	19m
Current Liabilities	2m	1m	559

Meridian Metal Trading Ltd

Meridian House Grazebrook Industrial Park Peartree Lane, Dudley, DY2 0XW
Tel: 01384-250665 **Fax:** 01384-250289
E-mail: info@meridianmetals.com
Website: http://www.meridianmetals.com
Directors: D. Myatt (Ch), S. Roadway (Fin), S. Crowe (Trans)
Managers: P. Broxholme, S. Corbett
Immediate Holding Company: MERIDIAN METAL TRADING LIMITED
Registration no: 02052884 **Date established:** 1986
Turnover: £75m - £125m **No.of Employees:** 101 - 250
Product Groups: 48, 66

Date of Accounts	May 11	May 10	May 09
Sales Turnover	76m	64m	53m
Pre Tax Profit/Loss	2m	2m	700
Working Capital	-5m	-4m	-2m
Fixed Assets	17m	15m	12m
Current Assets	40m	39m	26m
Current Liabilities	2m	2m	2m

Metallisation Ltd

Peartree Lane, Dudley, DY2 0XH
Tel: 01384-252464 **Fax:** 01384-237196
E-mail: sales@metallisation.com
Website: http://www.metallisation.com
Bank(s): Lloyds TSB Bank plc
Directors: R. Hill (Fin), S. Barker (Chief Op Offcr)
Managers: T. Lester, C. Arrow, J. Moore (Purch Mgr), S. Milton (Sales & Mktg Mg)
Registration no: 00270156 **VAT No.:** GB 109 3635 74
Date established: 1922 **Turnover:** £5m - £10m
No.of Employees: 51 - 100 **Product Groups:** 31, 32, 33, 34, 35, 36, 39, 40, 44, 46, 48, 51, 66, 84

Date of Accounts	Dec 09	Dec 08	Dec 07
Sales Turnover	7m	7m	9m
Pre Tax Profit/Loss	127	217	187

Working Capital	960	584	522
Fixed Assets	128	840	928
Current Assets	2m	2m	2m
Current Liabilities	216	402	267

Midtherm Engineering Ltd

Staffordshire House New Road, Dudley, DY2 8TA
Tel: 01384-455811 **Fax:** 01384-241252
E-mail: sales@mideng.net
Website: http://www.naturallydriven.co.uk
Bank(s): Lloyds
Directors: J. Walsh (MD), M. Andrews (Fin)
Managers: C. Boroughs (Sales Prom), D. Walker (Contracts Eng)
Immediate Holding Company: MIDTHERM ENGINEERING LIMITED
Registration no: 01690818 **VAT No.:** GB 388 5113 28
Date established: 1983 **Turnover:** £1m - £2m **No.of Employees:** 11 - 20
Product Groups: 52

Date of Accounts	Dec 09	Dec 08	Dec 07
Working Capital	176	147	277
Fixed Assets	405	417	115
Current Assets	1m	922	1m

Mitchell Oil Co. Ltd

Unit 4 Thornleigh Trading Estate, Dudley, DY2 8UB
Tel: 01384-233803 **Fax:** 01384-456279
E-mail: mitchelloilltd@tiscali.co.uk
Directors: S. Ward (MD)
Immediate Holding Company: MITCHELL OIL COMPANY LIMITED
Registration no: 02218837 **VAT No.:** GB 488 4982 71
Date established: 1988 **Turnover:** Up to £250,000
No.of Employees: 1 - 10 **Product Groups:** 31, 32, 66

Date of Accounts	Mar 12	Mar 11	Mar 10
Working Capital	19	19	14
Fixed Assets	5	3	6
Current Assets	89	95	78

Mitek

Mitek House Grazebrook Industrial Park, Dudley, DY2 0XW
Tel: 01384-451400 **Fax:** 01384-451411
E-mail: sgriffiths@mitek.co.uk
Website: http://www.mitek.co.uk
Bank(s): National Westminster, Birmingham
Directors: S. Griffiths (MD)
Managers: L. Fox (Tech Serv Mgr), R. Troman (Sales & Mktg Mg), J. Tudor (Comptroller)
Ultimate Holding Company: BERKSHIRE HATHAWAY INC (USA)
Immediate Holding Company: MITEK INDUSTRIES LIMITED
Registration no: 00944342 **VAT No.:** GB 281 3557 52
Date established: 1968 **Turnover:** £20m - £50m
No.of Employees: 101 - 250 **Product Groups:** 25, 35

Date of Accounts	Dec 11	Dec 10	Dec 09
Sales Turnover	25m	23m	19m
Pre Tax Profit/Loss	1m	1m	1m
Working Capital	4m	3m	4m
Fixed Assets	2m	1m	1m
Current Assets	8m	7m	8m
Current Liabilities	2m	2m	2m

Northwood Castings Ltd

Dormston Trading Estate Burton Road, Dudley, DY1 2UF
Tel: 01902-884411 **Fax:** 01902-884412
E-mail: northwood@hotmail.co.uk
Website: http://www.kprincegroup.co.uk
Bank(s): Lloyds TSB
Directors: K. Stanton (Dir)
Immediate Holding Company: NORTHWOOD CASTINGS LIMITED
Registration no: 06821580 **VAT No.:** GB 278 0059 48
Date established: 2009 **Turnover:** Up to £250,000
No.of Employees: 11 - 20 **Product Groups:** 34, 48

Date of Accounts	Feb 11	Feb 10
Sales Turnover	N/A	120
Pre Tax Profit/Loss	N/A	10
Working Capital	-2	-2
Fixed Assets	2	2
Current Assets	51	43
Current Liabilities	N/A	2

Alan Nuttall Ltd

Hall Street, Dudley, DY2 7DQ
Tel: 01384-245100 **Fax:** 01384-245102
E-mail: nino.calandra@nuttalls.co.uk
Website: http://www.nuttalls.co.uk
Bank(s): Barclays, Nuneaton
Directors: G. Smith (Fin), I. Bishop (Sales), N. Westwick (Tech Serv), N. Calandra (Dir)
Managers: M. Priest (Purch Mgr), S. Judge (Personnel)
Ultimate Holding Company: THE NUTTALL GROUP LIMITED
Immediate Holding Company: ALAN NUTTALL LIMITED
Registration no: 01191211 **Date established:** 1974
Turnover: £20m - £50m **No.of Employees:** 251 - 500 **Product Groups:** 26

Date of Accounts	May 11	May 10	May 09
Sales Turnover	48m	35m	49m
Pre Tax Profit/Loss	950	-2m	677
Working Capital	6m	6m	7m
Fixed Assets	4m	4m	4m
Current Assets	19m	15m	14m
Current Liabilities	2m	900	2m

Offspring International

Unit 8 Castle Court 2 Castlegate Way, Dudley, DY1 4RH
Tel: 01384-415540 **Fax:** 01384-415544
E-mail: david.rowley@offspringinternational.com
Website: http://www.offspringinternational.com
Directors: D. Rowley (Dir), A. Grainger (Dir)
Managers: J. Smart (Sales Admin)
Immediate Holding Company: N T (UK) LTD
Registration no: 06343137 **VAT No.:** GB 589 1057 10
Date established: 2007 **No.of Employees:** 1 - 10 **Product Groups:** 23, 35, 39, 41, 45

Date of Accounts	Apr 06
Working Capital	93
Fixed Assets	8
Current Assets	2842
Current Liabilities	2749
Total Share Capital	40

Ovako Ltd
Unit 2 Yorks Park Blowers Green Road, Dudley, DY2 8UL
Tel: 01384-213940
E-mail: graham.butler@ovako.com
Website: http://www.ovaka.com
Managers: J. Bartley (Ops Mgr)
Immediate Holding Company: OVAKO LIMITED
Registration no: 03879876 **VAT No.:** GB 456 7229 24
Date established: 1999 **Turnover:** £2m - £5m **No.of Employees:** 1 - 10
Product Groups: 34, 36, 48

Date of Accounts	Dec 11	Dec 10	Dec 09
Sales Turnover	4m	4m	3m
Pre Tax Profit/Loss	133	-2m	-7
Working Capital	1m	1m	1m
Fixed Assets	33	40	59
Current Assets	2m	2m	2m
Current Liabilities	183	172	183

Parmley Graham Ltd
Peartree Lane, Dudley, DY2 0QX
Tel: 01384-573231 **Fax:** 01384-265418
E-mail: birmingham@parmley-graham.co.uk
Website: http://www.parmley-graham.co.uk
Directors: N. Wilson (MD), M. Eggitt (Admin)
Managers: A. Gunnell (District Mgr), A. Gunnell (Mgr), B. Jewkes (Sales Prom)
Immediate Holding Company: PARMLEY GRAHAM LIMITED
Registration no: 00172842 **VAT No.:** GB 176 7006 54
Date established: 1921 **Turnover:** £10m - £20m **No.of Employees:** 1 - 10
Product Groups: 52

People Seating Ltd
9 Washington Street Industrial Estate Halesowen Road, Dudley, DY2 9RE
Tel: 01384-257124 **Fax:** 01384-242106
E-mail: david@peopleseating.com
Website: http://www.peopleseating.co.uk
Directors: D. Poston (Fin), D. Poston (MD), T. Poston (Co Sec)
Immediate Holding Company: PEOPLE SEATING LIMITED
Registration no: 02636490 **Date established:** 1991
No.of Employees: 11 - 20 **Product Groups:** 39

Date of Accounts	Mar 11	Mar 10	Mar 09
Working Capital	12	57	75
Current Assets	143	153	207

Petrofast Global Supplies Ltd
Unit B Grazebrook Industrial Park, Dudley, DY2 0XW
Tel: 01384-217617 **Fax:** 01384-217618
E-mail: paul.bailey@petrofast.com
Website: http://www.petrofast.com
Directors: P. Bailey (Dir)
Immediate Holding Company: Fastener Network Holdings Ltd
Registration no: 06674588 **No.of Employees:** 11 - 20 **Product Groups:** 36

Polystyrene Packaging Supplies Ltd (t/a Vertapak)
Unit J6 Dudley Central Trading Estate Shaw Road, Dudley, DY2 8QX
Tel: 01384-457730 **Fax:** 01384-237360
E-mail: admin@vertapak.co.uk
Website: http://www.vertapak.co.uk
Directors: M. Thomas (Dir), N. Stallard (Dir), B. Adams (Dir)
Managers: T. Thomas (Sales Prom Mgr)
Immediate Holding Company: P P S Ltd
Registration no: 02629030 **VAT No.:** GB 547 6149 20
Date established: 1965 **Turnover:** £500,000 - £1m
No.of Employees: 1 - 10 **Product Groups:** 30, 31

Date of Accounts	Aug 07	Aug 06
Working Capital	106	105
Current Assets	218	213
Current Liabilities	112	109

Precision Chains Ltd
Clee Road, Dudley, DY2 0YG
Tel: 01384-455455 **Fax:** 01384-230751
E-mail: julia.gorton@precision-chains.com
Website: http://www.precision-chains.com
Bank(s): Barclays, Dudley
Directors: N. Dayman (Fin), J. Gorton (MD)
Managers: D. Landon (Tech Serv Mgr), I. Thomas (Purch Mgr), M. Kyte (Sales Prom Mgr)
Immediate Holding Company: PRECISION CHAINS LIMITED
Registration no: 00709436 **VAT No.:** GB 277 8005 37
Date established: 1961 **Turnover:** £2m - £5m **No.of Employees:** 21 - 50
Product Groups: 35, 41, 45

Date of Accounts	Feb 11	Feb 10	Feb 09
Working Capital	792	665	683
Fixed Assets	645	750	734
Current Assets	2m	1m	1m

Profab Holdings Ltd
Westminster Industrial Estate Cradley Road, Dudley, DY2 9SW
Tel: 01384-560291 **Fax:** 01384-636608
E-mail: profab@msn.com
Website: http://www.profab.co.uk
Bank(s): Barclays
Directors: P. Simkins (Co Sec), B. Simkins (MD)
Managers: J. Lowe (Purch Mgr), H. Cartwright (Chief Acct)
Immediate Holding Company: PROFAB HOLDINGS LIMITED
Registration no: 01569415 **VAT No.:** GB 351 5995 31
Date established: 1981 **Turnover:** £1m - £2m **No.of Employees:** 21 - 50
Product Groups: 34, 35, 46, 48

Date of Accounts	Oct 11	Oct 10	Oct 09
Sales Turnover	1m	1m	1m
Pre Tax Profit/Loss	73	76	87
Working Capital	212	194	167
Fixed Assets	875	929	988
Current Assets	535	503	399
Current Liabilities	117	102	66

Quatroserve Ltd
Bay 11 Central Works Peartree Lane, Dudley, DY2 0QU
Tel: 01384-480326 **Fax:** 01384-74119
E-mail: s.anderson@quatroserve.co.uk
Website: http://www.quatroserve.co.uk
Bank(s): Barclays
Directors: S. Anderson (Fin), S. Anderson (Dir)
Immediate Holding Company: QUATROSERVE LIMITED
Registration no: 03285583 **VAT No.:** GB 632 1474 63
Date established: 1996 **Turnover:** £500,000 - £1m
No.of Employees: 21 - 50 **Product Groups:** 42, 45, 48, 84

Date of Accounts	Jun 11	Jun 10	Jun 09
Working Capital	22	64	80
Fixed Assets	148	159	134
Current Assets	389	341	358

R T Clocks
103 Knowle Hill Road, Dudley, DY2 0HW
Tel: 01384-212544 **Fax:** 01384-212544
E-mail: roger@rhmiddleton.fsnet.co.uk
Website: http://www.rhmiddleton.fsnet.co.uk
Directors: R. Middleton (Ptnr)
Date established: 1990 **Turnover:** Up to £250,000
No.of Employees: 1 - 10 **Product Groups:** 49

Ramsay Rubber & Plastics Ltd
84 Birmingham Road, Dudley, DY1 4RJ
Tel: 01384-453160 **Fax:** 0121-535 7108
E-mail: sales@ramsayrubber.com
Website: http://www.ramsayrubber.com
Bank(s): Lloyds
Directors: P. Johnson (Dir), P. Woolridge (I.T. Dir)
Immediate Holding Company: Ram Cellular Products Ltd
Registration no: 01716027 **VAT No.:** GB 388 5739 83
Turnover: £1m - £2m **No.of Employees:** 21 - 50 **Product Groups:** 49, 63

Refractory & Industrial Services Ltd
118 Longfellow Road, Dudley, DY3 3EH
Tel: 01902-672995 **Fax:** 01902-672995
Website: http://www.ris.homestead.com
Directors: T. Green (Dir)
Immediate Holding Company: REFRACTORY & INDUSTRIAL SERVICES LIMITED
Registration no: 02079241 **Date established:** 1986
No.of Employees: 1 - 10 **Product Groups:** 40, 42, 46

Date of Accounts	Nov 10	Nov 09	Nov 08
Working Capital	-26	-33	-16
Fixed Assets	12	7	9
Current Assets	35	20	29

Repair & Maintenance Services Ltd
Woodside House Pedmore Road, Dudley, DY2 0RL
Tel: 01384-350136 **Fax:** 01384-350269
Directors: W. Sambrook (Fin), J. Sambrook (MD)
Immediate Holding Company: REPAIR AND MAINTENANCE SERVICES LIMITED
Registration no: 01865256 **Date established:** 1984
Turnover: Up to £250,000 **No.of Employees:** 1 - 10 **Product Groups:** 40, 41, 45, 67

Date of Accounts	Oct 11	Oct 10	Oct 09
Working Capital	34	32	28
Fixed Assets	5	5	7
Current Assets	109	84	85
Current Liabilities	17	N/A	6

Revolvo Ltd
Unit 4 Yorks Park Blowers Green Road, Dudley, DY2 8UL
Tel: 01384-245370 **Fax:** 01384-458345
E-mail: nick.dent@revolvo.com
Website: http://www.revolvo.com
Directors: A. Menzies (Sales), N. Dent (MD)
Managers: D. Osborne (Tech Serv Mgr), M. Blythe (Buyer), P. Salter (Fin Mgr)
Ultimate Holding Company: SHV HOLDINGS NV (NETHERLANDS)
Immediate Holding Company: REVOLVO LIMITED
Registration no: 03582649 **Date established:** 1998
Turnover: £10m - £20m **No.of Employees:** 51 - 100 **Product Groups:** 35, 45

Date of Accounts	Dec 11	Dec 10	Dec 09
Sales Turnover	5m	5m	5m
Pre Tax Profit/Loss	128	-68	-214
Working Capital	105	-242	-263
Fixed Assets	1m	2m	2m
Current Assets	4m	3m	4m
Current Liabilities	322	271	269

Bob Richardson Tools & Fasteners Ltd
Pedmore Road, Dudley, DY2 0RL
Tel: 01384-482789 **Fax:** 01384-481888
E-mail: sales@toolstoday.co.uk
Website: http://www.toolstoday.co.uk
Directors: R. Richardson (MD), S. Richardson (MD)
Immediate Holding Company: BOB RICHARDSON TOOLS & FASTENERS LIMITED
Registration no: 01741080 **VAT No.:** GB 388 6053 15
Date established: 1983 **Turnover:** £500,000 - £1m
No.of Employees: 21 - 50 **Product Groups:** 66

Date of Accounts	Sep 11	Sep 10	Sep 09
Working Capital	353	343	238
Fixed Assets	366	373	380
Current Assets	927	920	684

H. Rollet Waveguide & Components Ltd
Castle Mill Works Birmingham New Road, Dudley, DY1 4DA
Tel: 01384-255300 **Fax:** 01384-255400
E-mail: admin@hrollet.co.uk
Website: http://www.hrollet.co.uk
Product Groups: 34, 37

Roof Units Ltd (t/a Vent-Axia Incorp Roof Units)
Blackbrook Road Narrowboat Way, Dudley, DY2 0NB
Tel: 01384-418800 **Fax:** 01384-418831
E-mail: ru@roofunitsltd.co.uk
Website: http://www.vent-axia.com
Bank(s): Barclays
Directors: K. Sargeant (MD), R. Geroge (MD)
Managers: C. Farrer, D. Clark, N. Sproston (District Mgr)
Ultimate Holding Company: Volution Group Ltd
Immediate Holding Company: ROOF UNITS LIMITED
Registration no: 01000703 **VAT No.:** GB 300 0687 11
Date established: 1971 **Turnover:** £10m - £20m
No.of Employees: 21 - 50 **Product Groups:** 35, 38, 40

Date of Accounts	Jul 07	Jul 06
Working Capital	1	1
Fixed Assets	61	61
Current Assets	1	1
Total Share Capital	62	62

Royal Brierley Crystal Ltd
Tipton Road, Dudley, DY1 4SH
Tel: 0121-530 5607 **Fax:** 01384-457302
E-mail: rhixon@dartington.co.uk
Website: http://www.royalbrierley.com
Directors: N. Hughes (MD)
Managers: R. Hixon (Mgr), R. Hixon
Ultimate Holding Company: THE BLACK COUNTRY LIVING MUSEUM TRUST
Immediate Holding Company: BLACK COUNTRY LIVING MUSEUM ENTERPRISES LIMITED
Registration no: 01226321 **VAT No.:** GB 276 8154 26
Date established: 1995 **Turnover:** £5m - £10m **No.of Employees:** 1 - 10
Product Groups: 33

Date of Accounts	Mar 11	Mar 10	Mar 09
Sales Turnover	2m	N/A	1m
Pre Tax Profit/Loss	N/A	N/A	303
Working Capital	-18	-4	-4
Fixed Assets	20	6	6
Current Assets	150	585	387
Current Liabilities	90	N/A	314

S G Dieplas Ltd
Unit J8 Dudley Central Trading Estate Shaw Road, Dudley, DY2 8QX
Tel: 01384-258494 **Fax:** 01384-258494
E-mail: patricia.ward@court.co.uk
Website: http://www.court.co.uk
Directors: P. Ward (Fin)
Immediate Holding Company: S.G. DIEPLAS LIMITED
Registration no: 01605476 **Date established:** 1981
Turnover: Up to £250,000 **No.of Employees:** 1 - 10 **Product Groups:** 30, 42

Date of Accounts	Mar 11	Mar 10	Mar 09
Working Capital	9	13	51
Fixed Assets	73	75	78
Current Assets	58	51	98

S L H Metal Finishes
Waterside Estate Cradley Road, Dudley, DY2 9RG
Tel: 01384-235333 **Fax:** 01384-243333
E-mail: slhmetalfinishes@btconnect.com
Directors: S. Hardwick (Prop)
Date established: 2002 **No.of Employees:** 1 - 10 **Product Groups:** 46, 48

S T Lifting Ltd
Unit 2-3 Washington Street Halesowen Road, Dudley, DY2 9RE
Tel: 01384-233122 **Fax:** 01384-230433
E-mail: steve.turton@btconnect.com
Website: http://www.st-lifting.co.uk
Directors: S. Turton (MD)
Immediate Holding Company: S T LIFTING HOLDINGS LIMITED
Registration no: 05131475 **Date established:** 2004
Turnover: £500,000 - £1m **No.of Employees:** 11 - 20
Product Groups: 35, 39, 45

Date of Accounts	Nov 11	Nov 10	Nov 09
Working Capital	665	652	660
Fixed Assets	81	40	40
Current Assets	776	785	738

Speedy Hire Centre
Unit 2 Crescent Industrial Park Peartree Lane, Dudley, DY2 0QQ
Tel: 01384-239966 **Fax:** 01384-455782
E-mail: rob.langford@speedyhire.com
Website: http://www.speedyhire.co.uk
Managers: R. Langford (Mgr)
Immediate Holding Company: SPEEDY LIFTING LIMITED
Registration no: 04529136 **Date established:** 2002
Turnover: £20m - £50m **No.of Employees:** 11 - 20 **Product Groups:** 35, 37, 38, 39, 45, 48, 83

Stainless Fittings Ltd glenwood pipe systems
Tipton Road, Dudley, DY1 4SQ
Tel: 0121-557 1188
E-mail: sales@dpluk.co.uk
Website: http://www.dpluk.co.uk
Directors: D. Atter (Fin), S. Sharps (MD)
Managers: L. Lawrence (Personnel), T. Wilson, P. Mackintosh (Tech Serv Mgr)
Ultimate Holding Company: STAINLESS TECHNOLOGIES LIMITED
Immediate Holding Company: STAINLESS FITTINGS LIMITED
Registration no: 06377506 **Date established:** 2007 **Turnover:** £5m - £10m
No.of Employees: 21 - 50 **Product Groups:** 36, 37, 38

Date of Accounts	Feb 11	Feb 10	Feb 09
Working Capital	166	255	105
Fixed Assets	N/A	N/A	32
Current Assets	516	518	713
Current Liabilities	N/A	N/A	162

Steelco UK Ltd
12 Blackbrook Business Park Narrowboat Way, Dudley, DY2 0XQ
Tel: 01384-455535 **Fax:** 01384-456860
E-mail: sales@steelcouk.com
Website: http://www.steelcouk.com
Bank(s): National Westminster
Directors: A. Fowle (Fin)
Managers: P. Warren, K. Brazil (Mgr)
Immediate Holding Company: STEELCO (UK) LIMITED
Registration no: 02319502 **VAT No.:** GB 488 4499 74
Date established: 1988 **Turnover:** £10m - £20m
No.of Employees: 21 - 50 **Product Groups:** 34, 66

Date of Accounts	Mar 11	Mar 10	Mar 09
Sales Turnover	19m	14m	27m
Pre Tax Profit/Loss	783	353	339
Working Capital	-420	-559	-669
Fixed Assets	1m	1m	2m
Current Assets	3m	2m	2m
Current Liabilities	3m	3m	3m

Strong Recycling Balers Ltd
26 Edenbridge View, Dudley, DY1 2JJ
Tel: 01384-567773 **Fax:** 01384-567773
E-mail: jrwebster2000@yahoo.co.uk
Website: http://www.strongrecyclingbalers.co.uk
Directors: J. Webster (MD)
Immediate Holding Company: STRONG RECYCLING BALERS LIMITED
Registration no: 07077408 **Date established:** 2009
Turnover: £250,000 - £500,000 **No.of Employees:** 1 - 10
Product Groups: 42

Date of Accounts	Nov 11	Nov 10
Working Capital	2	-5
Fixed Assets	1	2
Current Assets	53	72

Surfacetechnik Oldhill Ltd
Sovereign Works Deepdale Lane, Dudley, DY3 2AF
Tel: 01384-457610 **Fax:** 01384-238563
E-mail: info@surfacetechnik.co.uk
Website: http://www.surfacetechnik.co.uk
Managers: P. Zambra (Chief Mgr)
Immediate Holding Company: SURFACE TECHNIK (OLD HILL) LIMITED
Registration no: 01996845 **Date established:** 1986
Turnover: £500,000 - £1m **No.of Employees:** 21 - 50 **Product Groups:** 48

Date of Accounts	Dec 11	Dec 10	Dec 09
Working Capital	276	222	163
Fixed Assets	105	101	110
Current Assets	543	448	366

Teepee Materials Handling Ltd
8 Bagley Industrial Park Railwharf Sidings, Dudley, DY2 9DY
Tel: 01384-256969 **Fax:** 01384-240405
E-mail: sales@teepee.co.uk
Website: http://www.teepee.co.uk
Directors: S. Toop (MD), E. Hazeldine (Co Sec)
Immediate Holding Company: TEEPEE MATERIALS HANDLING LIMITED
Registration no: 02073740 **Date established:** 1986 **Turnover:** £1m - £2m
No.of Employees: 11 - 20 **Product Groups:** 35, 39, 45

Date of Accounts	Mar 12	Mar 11	Mar 10
Working Capital	562	499	578
Fixed Assets	137	161	178
Current Assets	1m	2m	2m

Telford Tanks Ltd
Unit 3c Central Works Peartree Lane, Dudley, DY2 0QU
Tel: 01384-212167 **Fax:** 01384-457757
E-mail: enquiries@telfordtanks.co.uk
Website: http://www.telfordtanks.co.uk
Directors: J. Moore (MD)
Ultimate Holding Company: TELFORD TANKS LIMITED
Immediate Holding Company: WINGATE TRADING LIMITED
Registration no: 01650186 **Date established:** 1982
No.of Employees: 1 - 10 **Product Groups:** 35, 42, 45

Date of Accounts	Mar 09
Working Capital	18
Fixed Assets	18
Current Assets	98

Thorn Polishing Ltd
Quarry Road, Dudley, DY2 0ED
Tel: 01384-566161 **Fax:** 01384-410580
E-mail: sales@thornpolishing.co.uk
Directors: T. Wood (MD), P. Wood (Fin)
Immediate Holding Company: THORN POLISHING LIMITED
Registration no: 04280725 **Date established:** 2001
No.of Employees: 1 - 10 **Product Groups:** 46, 48

Date of Accounts	Dec 11	Dec 10	Dec 09
Working Capital	23	14	18
Fixed Assets	12	14	17
Current Assets	100	83	89

Towerglens Ltd
Turner Street, Dudley, DY1 1TX
Tel: 01384-455025 **Fax:** 01384-451300
E-mail: info@towerglens.com
Website: http://www.towerglens.com
Bank(s): Lloyds TSB Bank plc
Directors: R. Davies (MD), N. Davies (Fin)
Immediate Holding Company: TOWERGLENS TECHNOLOGY LIMITED
Registration no: 04610327 **VAT No.:** GB 287 5983 86
Date established: 2002 **Turnover:** £1m - £2m **No.of Employees:** 11 - 20
Product Groups: 35, 37

Date of Accounts	Sep 11	Sep 10	Sep 08
Working Capital	45	35	14
Fixed Assets	8	10	27
Current Assets	88	60	61

Ultima Designer Furniture
70 Northfield Road, Dudley, DY2 9JQ
Tel: 01384-242500 **Fax:** 01384-242500
Directors: I. Ralley (Ptnr)
Date established: 1988 **No.of Employees:** 1 - 10 **Product Groups:** 35, 36

Waterfit
PO Box 28, Dudley, DY1 4SJ
Tel: 0121-520 7987 **Fax:** 0121-557 0357
E-mail: enquiries@waterfit.co.uk
Website: http://www.waterfit.co.uk
Managers: S. Hickman (Mgr)
Ultimate Holding Company: THOMAS DUDLEY GROUP LIMITED
Immediate Holding Company: WATERFIT LIMITED
Registration no: 05420758 **VAT No.:** 189 6472 05 **Date established:** 2005
Turnover: £500,000 - £1m **No.of Employees:** 11 - 20
Product Groups: 31, 44

Date of Accounts	Jul 11	Jul 10	Jul 09
Working Capital	109	86	23
Fixed Assets	91	83	118
Current Assets	1m	1m	1m

Woodall Steels Ltd
Town Works Washington Street, Dudley, DY2 9PH
Tel: 01384-456888 **Fax:** 01384-457755
E-mail: sales@woodallsteels.co.uk
Website: http://www.woodallsteels.co.uk
Directors: R. Roe (Dir), J. Roe (MD), J. Clarke (Dir)
Immediate Holding Company: WOODALL STEELS LIMITED
Registration no: 00941751 **VAT No.:** GB 278 1645 30
Date established: 1968 **Turnover:** £1m - £2m **No.of Employees:** 1 - 10
Product Groups: 34, 66

Date of Accounts	Mar 12	Mar 11	Mar 10
Working Capital	182	132	130
Fixed Assets	47	44	45
Current Assets	470	435	438

Worcester Doors
Unit A2 Windmill Industrial Park Peartree Lane, Dudley, DY2 0UY
Tel: 01384-237999 **Fax:** 01384-233302
E-mail: enquiries@worcesterdoors.co.uk
Website: http://www.worcesterdoors.co.uk
Directors: P. Rogers (Fin)
Immediate Holding Company: WORCESTER DOORS LIMITED
Registration no: 04891407 **Date established:** 2003
No.of Employees: 1 - 10 **Product Groups:** 26, 35

Date of Accounts	Dec 11	Dec 10	Dec 09
Working Capital	36	66	52
Fixed Assets	20	11	25
Current Assets	99	156	122

Halesowen

Acco UK Ltd
Hereward Rise, Halesowen, B62 8AN
Tel: 0121-550 8883 **Fax:** 0121-550 7755
E-mail: richard.burgess@acco.com
Website: http://www.acco.com
Managers: R. Burgess (Dist Mgr)
Ultimate Holding Company: ACCO BRANDS CORP (USA)
Immediate Holding Company: ACCO UK LIMITED
Registration no: 00197754 **Date established:** 2024
No.of Employees: 51 - 100 **Product Groups:** 37

Date of Accounts	Dec 11	Dec 10	Dec 09
Sales Turnover	80m	80m	73m
Pre Tax Profit/Loss	-2m	5m	4m
Working Capital	2m	-6m	-8m
Fixed Assets	53m	51m	52m
Current Assets	60m	59m	52m
Current Liabilities	7m	8m	7m

Alderdale Fixing Systems
New John Street, Halesowen, B62 8HT
Tel: 0121-561 5500 **Fax:** 0121-561 3535
E-mail: sales@alderdale.com
Website: http://www.alderdale.com
Directors: C. Powell (MD)
Ultimate Holding Company: CWP HOLDINGS LIMITED
Immediate Holding Company: ALDERDALE FIXING SYSTEMS LIMITED
Registration no: 01807429 **Date established:** 1984
No.of Employees: 21 - 50 **Product Groups:** 34, 35, 36, 45, 66

Date of Accounts	Sep 11	Sep 10	Sep 09
Working Capital	576	539	561
Fixed Assets	37	45	66
Current Assets	876	1m	864

Alphamation Ltd
9 Bassett Road, Halesowen, B63 2RE
Tel: 01384-412255 **Fax:** 01384-413191
E-mail: info@alphamation.co.uk
Website: http://www.alphamation.co.uk
Directors: P. Smith (MD)
Managers: D. Bailey (Tech Serv Mgr)
Immediate Holding Company: ALPHAMATION LIMITED
Registration no: 01610382 **Date established:** 1982
Turnover: £500,000 - £1m **No.of Employees:** 11 - 20 **Product Groups:** 45

Date of Accounts	Mar 12	Mar 11	Mar 10
Working Capital	497	480	436
Fixed Assets	66	19	28
Current Assets	641	619	520

Anca Industrial Supplies
Unit D4b Coombswood Way, Halesowen, B62 8BH
Tel: 0121-508 6500 **Fax:** 0121-585 5483
E-mail: enquiry@anca.co.uk
Website: http://www.anca.co.uk
Bank(s): HSBC Bank plc
Directors: P. Dainty (MD), R. Downing (Mkt Research)
Immediate Holding Company: ANCA INDUSTRIAL SUPPLIES LIMITED
Registration no: 01801236 **VAT No.:** GB 409 3579 34
Date established: 1984 **Turnover:** £1m - £2m **No.of Employees:** 11 - 20
Product Groups: 23, 27

Date of Accounts	Jun 11	Jun 10	Jun 09
Working Capital	66	61	65
Fixed Assets	55	43	35
Current Assets	666	607	491

Arnold & Fleet Ltd
39 Hambleton Road, Halesowen, B63 1HH
Tel: 07885-255138 **Fax:** 0121-585 9315
Directors: G. Fleet (Fin), A. Fleet (MD)
Immediate Holding Company: ARNOLD & FLEET LIMITED
Registration no: 04801859 **Date established:** 2003
No.of Employees: 1 - 10 **Product Groups:** 38, 42

Date of Accounts	Mar 11	Mar 10	Mar 09
Working Capital	16	15	12
Fixed Assets	N/A	N/A	3
Current Assets	24	26	27

B & S Chains Ltd
29 Toys Lane, Halesowen, B63 2JX
Tel: 01384-413088 **Fax:** 01384-413066
E-mail: sales@bandschains.co.uk
Website: http://www.bandschains.co.uk
Directors: A. Steele (MD)
Immediate Holding Company: B & S CHAINS (MIDLANDS) LIMITED
Registration no: 03014683 **VAT No.:** 547 3302 53 **Date established:** 1995
Turnover: £250,000 - £500,000 **No.of Employees:** 1 - 10
Product Groups: 35, 49

Date of Accounts	Jan 12	Jan 11	Jan 10
Working Capital	74	105	88
Fixed Assets	31	36	16
Current Assets	146	164	162

Bahco Tools Ltd
Manor Way, Halesowen, B62 8QZ
Tel: 01709-731600 **Fax:** 0121-504 5252
E-mail: info@bahco.com
Website: http://www.bahco.com
Directors: J. Lovatt (Sales), W. Johnson (Fin), T. O'Brien (MD)
Managers: W. Johnson (Accounts), S. Allen (Chief Mgr), K. Lowe (Sales & Mktg Mg), M. Lee (Sales & Mktg Mg)
Ultimate Holding Company: SANDVIK AB (SWEDEN)
Immediate Holding Company: SANDVIK HOLDINGS LIMITED
Registration no: 03689641 **Date established:** 1993 **Turnover:** £2m - £5m
No.of Employees: 21 - 50 **Product Groups:** 36, 37, 47

Date of Accounts	Dec 10	Dec 09	Dec 08
Pre Tax Profit/Loss	-6m	9m	938
Working Capital	156m	161m	188m
Fixed Assets	194m	192m	193m
Current Assets	174m	176m	196m
Current Liabilities	1m	1m	2m

Barratt West Midlands
60 White Hall Road, Halesowen, B63 3JS
Tel: 0121-585 5303 **Fax:** 0121-585 5304
E-mail: adrian.farr@barratthomes.co.uk
Website: http://www.barratthomes.co.uk
Directors: A. Farr (MD), G. Worthing (Sales), R. Whittaker (Co Sec)
Managers: G. Devane (Personnel), M. Beckett (Buyer), S. Webb
Ultimate Holding Company: BARRATT DEVELOPMENTS P L C
Immediate Holding Company: BARRATT WEST MIDLANDS LIMITED
Registration no: 00595244 **VAT No.:** GB 428 6040 58
Date established: 1957 **No.of Employees:** 21 - 50 **Product Groups:** 52

Date of Accounts	Jun 09
Working Capital	18m
Fixed Assets	879
Current Assets	18m

Chemix Autocentres
Maypole Fields, Halesowen, B63 2QB
Tel: 01384-411819 **Fax:** 01384-638098
E-mail: sales@chemix-autocentres.co.uk
Website: http://www.chemix-autocentres.co.uk
Directors: R. Fellows (Dir), R. Fellows (Fin), M. McCarron (MD)
Managers: K. Clay (Chief Acct)
Immediate Holding Company: INDUSVENT ENGINEERING LIMITED
Registration no: 01566479 **VAT No.:** GB 277 1813 41
Date established: 1967 **Turnover:** £2m - £5m **No.of Employees:** 1 - 10
Product Groups: 37, 68

Corus
PO Box 6329, Halesowen, B63 2RN
Tel: 01384-897377 **Fax:** 01384-898018
Website: http://www.corusgroup.com
Managers: D. Green (Sales Prom Mgr), S. Tromans (Chief Mgr), S. Tromans (Mgr)
Ultimate Holding Company: Corus Group P.L.C.
Immediate Holding Company: CORUS GROUP LIMITED
Registration no: 03811373 **Date established:** 1999
Turnover: £250,000 - £500,000 **No.of Employees:** 51 - 100
Product Groups: 34, 46, 66

Crosland Cutters Ltd
Nimmings Road, Halesowen, B62 9JE
Tel: 0121-559 7915 **Fax:** 0121-561 3064
E-mail: sales@croslandcuttersltd.co.uk
Website: http://www.croslandcuttersltd.co.uk
Bank(s): HSBC Bank plc
Directors: E. Gilley (Fin), J. Rose (MD)
Managers: M. Smith, M. Dodd (Comm), P. Male (Admin Off)
Immediate Holding Company: CROSLAND CUTTERS LIMITED
Registration no: 01049175 **VAT No.:** GB 276 8665 01
Date established: 1972 **Turnover:** £500,000 - £1m
No.of Employees: 11 - 20 **Product Groups:** 48

Date of Accounts	Mar 12	Mar 11	Mar 10
Working Capital	425	370	368
Fixed Assets	163	184	162
Current Assets	598	513	500

D C B Automation Ltd
Unit 10 Belfont Trading Estate Mucklow Hill, Halesowen, B62 8DR
Tel: 0121-585 9229 **Fax:** 0121-585 9339
E-mail: info@dcbautomation.com
Website: http://www.dcbautomation.com
Directors: S. Bowen (MD)
Immediate Holding Company: DCB AUTOMATION LIMITED
Registration no: 04426020 **Date established:** 2002
Turnover: Up to £250,000 **No.of Employees:** 1 - 10 **Product Groups:** 38

Date of Accounts	Jun 11	Jun 10	Jun 09
Working Capital	50	50	56
Fixed Assets	1	1	2
Current Assets	50	76	97

Delta GB N Ltd
115 Lodgefield Road, Halesowen, B62 8AX
Tel: 0121-602 1221 **Fax:** 0121-602 3222
E-mail: rogerw@deltagbn.co.uk
Website: http://www.deltagbn.co.uk
Bank(s): The Royal Bank of Scotland
Directors: J. Ramsay (Co Sec), M. Snape (Dir), R. Birmingham (MD)
Ultimate Holding Company: GALVANISED BOLTS AND NUTS LIMITED
Immediate Holding Company: DELTA G.B.N. LIMITED
Registration no: 01842767 **VAT No.:** GB 541 3245 75
Date established: 1984 **Turnover:** £2m - £5m **No.of Employees:** 11 - 20
Product Groups: 32, 48

Date of Accounts	Sep 11	Sep 10	Sep 09
Working Capital	-130	-106	-153
Fixed Assets	258	168	191
Current Assets	2m	1m	1m

Dolphin Stairlifts Central Ltd
Cradley Enterprise Centre Maypole Fields, Halesowen, B63 2QB
Tel: 01384-898933 **Fax:** 01384-891189
E-mail: dolphin@dolphincentral.co.uk
Website: http://www.dolphincentral.co.uk
Directors: J. Broome (MD)
Immediate Holding Company: DOLPHIN STAIRLIFTS (CENTRAL) LIMITED
Registration no: 04867489 **Date established:** 2003
No.of Employees: 1 - 10 **Product Groups:** 35, 39, 45

Date of Accounts	Dec 11	Dec 10	Dec 09
Working Capital	-3	-6	5
Fixed Assets	30	33	35
Current Assets	35	35	53

Drivall Ltd
Narrow Lane, Halesowen, B62 9PA
Tel: 0121-423 1212 **Fax:** 0121-422 9498
E-mail: ray.hill@drivall.com
Website: http://www.drivall.co.uk
Bank(s): Lloyds TSB Bank plc
Directors: R. Hill (Co Sec), A. Eaton (MD), F. Wall (Sales)
Managers: P. Beck
Immediate Holding Company: DRIVALL LIMITED
Registration no: 00474060 **VAT No.:** GB 661 5523 41
Date established: 1949 **Turnover:** £500,000 - £1m
No.of Employees: 11 - 20 **Product Groups:** 37

see next page

Drivall Ltd - Cont'd

Date of Accounts	Dec 11	Dec 10	Dec 09
Working Capital	13	3	-3
Fixed Assets	59	62	63
Current Assets	2m	2m	1m

Drywite Ltd

The House of Lee Park Lane, Halesowen, B63 2RA
Tel: 01384-569556 **Fax:** 01384-410583
E-mail: enquiries@drywite.co.uk
Website: http://www.drywite.co.uk
Bank(s): Barclays, Upper High Street, Cradley Heath, Warley
Directors: K. Lee (MD), L. Law (Co Sec)
Immediate Holding Company: DRYWITE LIMITED
Registration no: 00278011 **VAT No.:** GB 276 8586 94
Date established: 1933 **Turnover:** £1m - £2m **No.of Employees:** 21 - 50
Product Groups: 17, 20, 32, 35

Date of Accounts	Mar 12	Mar 11	Mar 10
Working Capital	1m	1m	1m
Fixed Assets	177	206	243
Current Assets	2m	2m	2m

Ductbusters Ltd

1 Victoria Road, Halesowen, B62 8HY
Tel: 0121-559 1555 **Fax:** 0121-559 8555
E-mail: enquiries@ductbusters.co.uk
Website: http://www.ductbusters.co.uk
Directors: D. Quinn (MD), I. Wall (Dir), G. Quinn (Dir), S. Quinn (Fin)
Immediate Holding Company: DUCTBUSTERS LIMITED
Registration no: 03255812 **Date established:** 1996
No.of Employees: 21 - 50 **Product Groups:** 40, 52, 84

Date of Accounts	Mar 12	Mar 11	Mar 10
Working Capital	316	303	390
Fixed Assets	178	192	81
Current Assets	741	840	620

E T M A Engineering Ltd

Victoria Road, Halesowen, B62 8HY
Tel: 0121-559 5333 **Fax:** 0121-559 2236
E-mail: quality@etma.co.uk
Website: http://www.etma.co.uk
Bank(s): National Westminster
Directors: P. Coley (Co Sec)
Managers: M. Taylor (Mgr)
Ultimate Holding Company: GLOBAL STRATEGIC ALLIANCE GROUP LIMITED
Immediate Holding Company: ETMA (ENGINEERING) LIMITED
Registration no: 00687372 **VAT No.:** GB 276 9809 95
Date established: 1961 **Turnover:** £2m - £5m **No.of Employees:** 11 - 20
Product Groups: 34

Date of Accounts	Mar 12	Mar 11	Mar 10
Working Capital	555	536	441
Fixed Assets	324	349	358
Current Assets	1m	1m	1m

Eagle Supplies Ltd

Lyde Green, Halesowen, B63 2PF
Tel: 01384-633933 **Fax:** 01384-413440
E-mail: adrianjball@btinternet.co.uk
Directors: A. Ball (MD), C. Ball (Fin)
Immediate Holding Company: EAGLE SUPPLIES LIMITED
Registration no: 01851694 **VAT No.:** GB 369 6194 05
Date established: 1984 **Turnover:** Up to £250,000
No.of Employees: 1 - 10 **Product Groups:** 66

Date of Accounts	Oct 11	Jul 10	Jul 09
Working Capital	10	48	52
Current Assets	125	153	142

Ellwood Steel Ltd

Unit 2 Park Lane, Halesowen, B63 2NT
Tel: 01384-564935 **Fax:** 01384-410577
Directors: D. Attwood (MD)
Immediate Holding Company: ELLWOOD STEELS LIMITED
Registration no: 01606535 **VAT No.:** GB 369 5352 18
Date established: 1982 **Turnover:** £500,000 - £1m
No.of Employees: 1 - 10 **Product Groups:** 34

Date of Accounts	Jan 11	Jan 10	Jan 09
Working Capital	-1	-7	-7
Fixed Assets	8	9	10
Current Assets	56	56	55

Entec International Ltd

Unit C3 Coombswood Way, Halesowen, B62 8BH
Tel: 08708-507101 **Fax:** 0121-585 8899
E-mail: enquiries@entec-int.com
Website: http://www.entec-int.com
Directors: C. Syner (Prop), P. Carter (Fin), C. Brearley (Co Sec)
Managers: H. Hughes (Personnel), J. Evans (Tech Serv Mgr)
Immediate Holding Company: ENTEC INTERNATIONAL LIMITED
Registration no: 02370079 **Date established:** 1989
Turnover: £10m - £20m **No.of Employees:** 11 - 20 **Product Groups:** 84

Date of Accounts	Jan 11	Jan 10	Jan 09
Sales Turnover	14m	13m	N/A
Pre Tax Profit/Loss	447	427	N/A
Working Capital	488	333	109
Fixed Assets	735	697	780
Current Assets	5m	5m	4m
Current Liabilities	683	792	N/A

Erik's UK

Amberway, Halesowen, B62 8WG
Tel: 0121-508 6000 **Fax:** 0121-508 6009
E-mail: enquiries@eriks.co.uk
Website: http://www.eriks.co.uk
Directors: D. Wood (Pers), D. White (Fin)
Managers: R. Ludlam (Mktg Serv Mgr), D. Murtagh (Tech Serv Mgr)
Ultimate Holding Company: WYKO HOLDINGS LIMITED
Immediate Holding Company: WYKO INDUSTRIAL SERVICES LIMITED
Registration no: 00917112 **Date established:** 1967
Turnover: £250m - £500m **No.of Employees:** 101 - 250
Product Groups: 66

Extavator Buckets

Victoria Road, Halesowen, B62 8HY
Tel: 0121-559 1479
E-mail: sales@ebmidlands.co.uk
Website: http://www.ebmidlands.co.uk
Directors: D. Roberts (Prop)
Immediate Holding Company: GLOBAL STRATEGIC ALLIANCE GROUP LIMITED
Registration no: 05570003 **Date established:** 2010
No.of Employees: 1 - 10 **Product Groups:** 35

Date of Accounts	Mar 11
Working Capital	-694
Fixed Assets	696
Current Assets	20

Falcontec Ltd

Falcon House Mucklow Hill, Halesowen, B62 8DT
Tel: 0121-550 1076 **Fax:** 0121-585 5126
E-mail: info@falcontec.co.uk
Website: http://www.falcontec.co.uk
Bank(s): National Westminster Bank Plc
Directors: D. Evans (Co Sec)
Ultimate Holding Company: AMAGERBANKEN AKTIESELSKAB (DENMARK)
Immediate Holding Company: FALCONTEC LIMITED
Registration no: 02695535 **VAT No.:** GB 610 9041 80
Date established: 1992 **Turnover:** £1m - £2m **No.of Employees:** 21 - 50
Product Groups: 44

Date of Accounts	Dec 11	Dec 10	Dec 09
Sales Turnover	1m	1m	1m
Pre Tax Profit/Loss	137	-361	9
Working Capital	375	210	386
Fixed Assets	58	77	256
Current Assets	703	498	670
Current Liabilities	219	189	174

Feridax 1957 Ltd

Park Lane, Halesowen, B63 2NT
Tel: 01384-413841 **Fax:** 01384-638287
E-mail: robin.harris@feridax.com
Website: http://www.feridax.com
Bank(s): National Westminster Bank Plc
Directors: A. White (Co Sec), R. Harris (MD)
Managers: M. Ingleby (Mktg Serv Mgr)
Ultimate Holding Company: FERIDAX GROUP LIMITED
Immediate Holding Company: FERIDAX (1957) LIMITED
Registration no: 02904875 **Date established:** 1994
Turnover: £10m - £20m **No.of Employees:** 21 - 50 **Product Groups:** 22, 24, 68

Date of Accounts	Dec 11	Dec 10	Dec 09
Sales Turnover	12m	12m	13m
Pre Tax Profit/Loss	552	602	994
Working Capital	9m	8m	8m
Fixed Assets	571	643	721
Current Assets	10m	9m	9m
Current Liabilities	196	237	352

Forge Lifting Gear Ltd

29 Toys Lane, Halesowen, B63 2JX
Tel: 01384-567722 **Fax:** 01384-569977
E-mail: sales@forgeliftinggear.com
Website: http://www.forgeliftinggear.com
Directors: A. Steele (MD), I. Silvera (Fin)
Immediate Holding Company: FORGE LIFTING GEAR LIMITED
Registration no: 01970097 **Date established:** 1985
No.of Employees: 1 - 10 **Product Groups:** 35, 39, 45

Date of Accounts	Jul 11	Jul 10	Jul 09
Working Capital	136	181	98
Fixed Assets	44	45	49
Current Assets	276	350	300

Galvanised Bolts & Nuts Ltd

115 Lodgefield Road, Halesowen, B62 8AX
Tel: 0121-602 3333 **Fax:** 0121-602 4040
E-mail: galvanised.boltsandnuts@btconnect.com
Directors: A. Ramsey (Dir)
Immediate Holding Company: GALVANISED BOLTS AND NUTS LIMITED
Registration no: 00818110 **VAT No.:** GB 541 3245 75
Date established: 1964 **Turnover:** £2m - £5m **No.of Employees:** 1 - 10
Product Groups: 35

Date of Accounts	Sep 11	Sep 10	Sep 09
Working Capital	595	538	548
Fixed Assets	215	226	238
Current Assets	2m	2m	2m

Glass Works Hounsell Ltd

Park Lane, Halesowen, B63 2QS
Tel: 01384-560666 **Fax:** 01384-561363
E-mail: b.hicks@glassworkshounsell.co.uk
Website: http://www.glassworkshounsell.co.uk
Bank(s): Barclays
Directors: G. Patel (Co Sec), B. Hicks (MD), W. Brinkman (Sales)
Ultimate Holding Company: GLASSWORKS EQUIPMENT LIMITED
Immediate Holding Company: GLASSWORKS HOUNSELL LIMITED
Registration no: 00371181 **VAT No.:** GB 276 9382 08
Date established: 1941 **Turnover:** £2m - £5m **No.of Employees:** 11 - 20
Product Groups: 40, 45, 48

Date of Accounts	Mar 11	Mar 10	Mar 09
Working Capital	1m	941	899
Fixed Assets	264	294	220
Current Assets	2m	2m	2m

Graphite Trading Company

72 Carters Lane, Halesowen, B62 0BS
Tel: 0783-110 9201 **Fax:** 0121-421 2215
E-mail: enquiries@graphitetrading.co.uk
Website: http://www.graphitetrading.co.uk
Directors: S. Bullock (Prop)
Turnover: Up to £250,000 **No.of Employees:** 1 - 10 **Product Groups:** 20, 33

James Grove & Sons Properties Ltd

Bloomfield Works 136 Stourbridge Road, Halesowen, B63 3UW
Tel: 0121-550 4015 **Fax:** 0121-501 3905
E-mail: john.brougham@jamesgroveandsons.co.uk
Website: http://www.jamesgroveandsons.co.uk
Directors: J. Brougham (Ch), J. Brougham (Dir), N. Grove (MD)
Managers: D. Potter (Publicity), N. Grove (Export Sales Mg), C. Hill (Accounts), C. Turner (Shipping Mgr)
Immediate Holding Company: JAMES GROVE & SONS (PROPERTIES) LIMITED
Registration no: 05010716 **VAT No.:** GB 276 9536 07
Date established: 2004 **Turnover:** £1m - £2m **No.of Employees:** 1 - 10
Product Groups: 24, 25, 30, 33, 35, 48

Halesowen Business Services Ltd

61 Broadway Avenue, Halesowen, B63 3DF
Tel: 0121-550 0185 **Fax:** 0121-550 2572
E-mail: paul@halesowen.net
Website: http://www.halesowen.net
Directors: L. Hill (Fin), P. Hill (MD)
Immediate Holding Company: HALESOWEN BUSINESS SERVICES LIMITED
Registration no: 04617169 **Date established:** 2002
No.of Employees: 1 - 10 **Product Groups:** 46

Date of Accounts	Dec 11	Dec 10	Dec 08
Working Capital	9	8	-43
Fixed Assets	1	2	3
Current Assets	34	66	33

Harris Steels Ltd

PO Box 29, Halesowen, B62 8AF
Tel: 0121-561 2221 **Fax:** 0121-561 1283
E-mail: info@harrissteels.co.uk
Website: http://www.harrissteels.co.uk
Bank(s): Lloyds TSB Bank plc
Directors: R. Price (Dir), J. Price (Sales), S. Price (MD)
Managers: B. Roden (Accounts), D. Price
Immediate Holding Company: HARRIS (STEELS) LIMITED
Registration no: 00674976 **VAT No.:** GB 277 7567 00
Date established: 1960 **Turnover:** £5m - £10m **No.of Employees:** 11 - 20
Product Groups: 34

Date of Accounts	Jun 11	Jun 10	Jun 09
Working Capital	1m	945	800
Fixed Assets	291	219	193
Current Assets	2m	2m	2m

Hawking Electrotechnology Ltd

19 Hereward Rise, Halesowen, B62 8AN
Tel: 0121-585 6263 **Fax:** 0121-585 6178
E-mail: sales@hawking.co.uk
Website: http://www.hawking.co.uk
Directors: J. Metaxas (MD), R. Hayward (Fin)
Immediate Holding Company: HAWKING ELECTROTECHNOLOGY LIMITED
Registration no: 06773622 **Date established:** 2008
No.of Employees: 1 - 10 **Product Groups:** 46, 48

Date of Accounts	Dec 11	Dec 10	Dec 09
Working Capital	329	221	22
Fixed Assets	8	10	6
Current Assets	371	301	88

Headstock Distribution

Unit G1 Steelpark Road, Halesowen, B62 8HD
Tel: 0121-508 6666 **Fax:** 0121-508 6677
E-mail: sales@headstockdistribution.com
Website: http://www.headstockdistribution.com
Directors: D. Hirons (Tech Serv), J. Laney (Sales & Mktg), J. Waldron (Fin)
Managers: S. McKenzie (Tech Serv Mgr)
Immediate Holding Company: HEADSTOCK DISTRIBUTION LIMITED
Registration no: 01486774 **VAT No.:** GB 441 8875 25
Date established: 1980 **Turnover:** £10m - £20m
No.of Employees: 51 - 100 **Product Groups:** 37

Date of Accounts	Jun 11	Jun 10	Jun 09
Sales Turnover	12m	12m	12m
Pre Tax Profit/Loss	251	379	383
Working Capital	5m	5m	4m
Fixed Assets	527	579	1m
Current Assets	6m	6m	5m
Current Liabilities	510	504	481

Hockley Pattern & Tool Company Ltd

Lodgefield Road, Halesowen, B62 8AR
Tel: 0121-561 4665 **Fax:** 0121-525 0595
E-mail: sales@hockleypattern.co.uk
Website: http://www.hockleypattern.co.uk
Directors: G. Williams (Dir), N. Williams (Dir)
Immediate Holding Company: HOCKLEY PATTERN & TOOL CO LIMITED
Registration no: 01708663 **Date established:** 1983 **Turnover:** £2m - £5m
No.of Employees: 21 - 50 **Product Groups:** 31, 34, 39, 42, 46, 47, 48, 84

Date of Accounts	Mar 11	Mar 10	Mar 09
Working Capital	-299	-154	-445
Fixed Assets	1m	2m	2m
Current Assets	1m	795	1m
Current Liabilities	N/A	N/A	1m

Indespension Ltd

38a Nimmings Road, Halesowen, B62 9JE
Tel: 0121-561 5467 **Fax:** 0121-561 2180
E-mail: westmids@indespention.com
Website: http://www.indespension.com
Managers: S. Taylor (Mgr)
Ultimate Holding Company: D.R.A. LTD
Immediate Holding Company: INDESPENSION LTD
Registration no: 02125263 **Date established:** 1987
Turnover: Up to £250,000 **No.of Employees:** 1 - 10 **Product Groups:** 39

Date of Accounts	Jun 11	Jun 10	Jun 09
Sales Turnover	17m	15m	19m
Pre Tax Profit/Loss	550	192	137
Working Capital	2m	1m	2m
Fixed Assets	4m	5m	6m
Current Assets	8m	8m	8m
Current Liabilities	3m	527	783

Industrial Brushware Ltd

Ibex House Malt Mill Lane, Halesowen, B62 8JJ
Tel: 0121-559 3862 **Fax:** 0121-559 9404
E-mail: andrew.biggs@industrialbrushware.co.uk
Website: http://www.industrialbrushware.co.uk
Bank(s): Natwest
Directors: J. Palmer (MD), H. Palmer (Tech Serv), N. Palmer (Dir)
Registration no: 00392424 **VAT No.:** GB 277 2415 48
Turnover: £500,000 - £1m **No.of Employees:** 11 - 20
Product Groups: 33, 38, 42, 49

Date of Accounts	Apr 11	Apr 10	Apr 09
Working Capital	97	110	224
Fixed Assets	488	497	460
Current Assets	306	276	417

K D Electrical Co. Ltd

Lyde Green, Halesowen, B63 2PG
Tel: 01384-560333 **Fax:** 01384-560423

Directors: K. Dimmock (MD)
Immediate Holding Company: K.D. ELECTRICAL CO. LIMITED
Registration no: 00856508 **VAT No.:** GB 278 0034 64
Date established: 1965 **Turnover:** £500,000 - £1m
No.of Employees: 11 - 20 **Product Groups:** 52

Date of Accounts	Aug 11	Aug 10	Aug 09
Working Capital	69	80	54
Fixed Assets	6	9	8
Current Assets	142	150	165

Kay Safe Engineering Ltd
2 Pound Lane Industrial Estate Maypole Fields, Halesowen, B63 2QB
Tel: 01384-566991 **Fax:** 01384-566884
Directors: P. Russell (MD), P. Russell (Dir)
Immediate Holding Company: KAYSAFE ENGINEERING LIMITED
Registration no: 02768247 **Date established:** 1992
No.of Employees: 1 - 10 **Product Groups:** 38, 42

Date of Accounts	Mar 11	Mar 10	Mar 09
Working Capital	379	430	294
Fixed Assets	2	3	1
Current Assets	489	665	822

Mayweld Engineering Co.
Banners Lane, Halesowen, B63 2SD
Tel: 01384-560285 **Fax:** 01384-411456
E-mail: sales@mayweld.co.uk
Website: http://www.mayweld.co.uk
Directors: M. May (Fin)
Managers: B. Cope (Chief Mgr)
Immediate Holding Company: BANNERS LANE ENGINEERING COMPANY LTD
Registration no: 00898462 **Date established:** 1967
No.of Employees: 11 - 20 **Product Groups:** 35, 42, 45

Midland Oil Refinery Ltd
Shelah Road, Halesowen, B63 3PN
Tel: 0121-585 6006 **Fax:** 0121-585 5405
E-mail: admin@midlandoil.co.uk
Website: http://www.midlandoil.co.uk
Bank(s): Barclays Bank plc
Directors: C. Dutton (MD), R. Walliker (Co Sec)
Managers: M. Hayes (Mgr), M. Elliker, M. Bradley (Sales Prom Mgr)
Immediate Holding Company: MIDLAND OIL REFINERY LIMITED
Registration no: 04832747 **VAT No.:** GB 519 5743 72
Date established: 2003 **Turnover:** £10m - £20m
No.of Employees: 21 - 50 **Product Groups:** 31, 32, 54

Date of Accounts	Jul 11	Jul 10	Jul 09
Sales Turnover	10m	8m	6m
Pre Tax Profit/Loss	420	223	237
Working Capital	161	285	66
Fixed Assets	2m	2m	2m
Current Assets	3m	3m	1m
Current Liabilities	2m	841	644

Midlands Technical Mouldings Ltd
Park Lane, Halesowen, B63 2QP
Tel: 01384-414403 **Fax:** 01384-415429
Bank(s): Barclays
Directors: T. Cox (MD)
Managers: K. Crawford (Mktg Serv Mgr)
Immediate Holding Company: BRADLEY STEELS LIMITED
Registration no: 05618732 **VAT No.:** GB 705 3145 67
Date established: 2008 **Turnover:** £2m - £5m **No.of Employees:** 51 - 100
Product Groups: 30

Date of Accounts	Dec 06
Pre Tax Profit/Loss	-267
Working Capital	-671
Fixed Assets	1317
Current Assets	2381
Current Liabilities	3052
ROCE% (Return on Capital Employed)	-41.3

N T S Aluminium Systems Ltd
Gainsford Drive, Halesowen, B62 8BQ
Tel: 0121-501 3814 **Fax:** 0121-585 5492
E-mail: colin@ntsltd.freeserve.co.uk
Website: http://www.ntsaluminium.co.uk
Directors: C. Taylor (Fin), G. Savastio (Dir)
Immediate Holding Company: N.T.S. Aluminium Systems Ltd
Registration no: 02116901 **Date established:** 1987
No.of Employees: 1 - 10 **Product Groups:** 26, 35

John Neale Ltd
25 Fairfield Road, Halesowen, B63 4PT
Tel: 0121-585 8793 **Fax:** 0121-585 8793
E-mail: info@johnnealeltd.co.uk
Website: http://www.johnnealeltd.co.uk
Directors: J. Neale (Dir)
Immediate Holding Company: JOHN NEALE LTD
Registration no: 04476463 **Date established:** 2002
No.of Employees: 1 - 10 **Product Groups:** 31

Date of Accounts	Jun 12	Jun 11	Jun 10
Working Capital	162	108	54
Current Assets	233	210	109
Current Liabilities	N/A	21	N/A

Network Catering Engineers Ltd
Unit 4 Building A7 Coombswood Business Estate, Halesowen, B62 8BH
Tel: 08700-628772 **Fax:** 0121-585 8029
Website: http://www.network-ltd.com
Directors: T. Church (Prop)
Immediate Holding Company: Network (Catering Engineers) Ltd
Registration no: 04081826 **Date established:** 2000
No.of Employees: 21 - 50 **Product Groups:** 40, 48, 69

Optimax Ltd
36 Douglas Road, Halesowen, B62 9HX
Tel: 0121-561 1122 **Fax:** 0121-559 0541
Managers: C. Wood (Mgr)
Immediate Holding Company: OPTIMAX LIMITED
Registration no: 01199897 **Date established:** 1975
No.of Employees: 21 - 50 **Product Groups:** 37, 38, 65

Date of Accounts	Apr 11	Apr 10	Apr 09
Working Capital	223	177	189
Fixed Assets	73	92	120
Current Assets	312	321	316

Parker Hannison Ltd
Belfont Industrial Estate Mucklow Hill, Halesowen, B62 8DR
Tel: 0121-504 3400 **Fax:** 0121-550 4274
Website: http://www.parker.com
Directors: L. Challoner (Dir)
Managers: A. Wordley
Ultimate Holding Company: STERLING POWER GROUP HOLDINGS LIMITED
Immediate Holding Company: STERLING CARBON MANAGEMENT LIMITED
Registration no: 05433768 **Date established:** 2005
No.of Employees: 21 - 50 **Product Groups:** 42, 45

Date of Accounts	Mar 10	Mar 09	Mar 08
Working Capital	-78	-46	N/A
Current Assets	75	101	N/A

Pioneer Weston
Amber Way, Halesowen, B62 8WG
Tel: 01925-853000 **Fax:** 01925-853030
E-mail: sales@pioneer.weston.co.uk
Website: http://www.pwi-ltd.com
Bank(s): Bank of Scotland, Birmingham
Directors: P. Greenway (Fin)
Managers: S. Bullen (I.T. Exec), M. Newton (Export Sales Mg)
Registration no: 03142338 **VAT No.:** GB 277 2632 40
Turnover: £2m - £5m **No.of Employees:** 21 - 50 **Product Groups:** 22, 29, 33

H S Pitt & Co. Ltd
Park Lane, Halesowen, B63 2QP
Tel: 01384-564949 **Fax:** 01384-411102
E-mail: andrew.haden@hspitt.co.uk
Bank(s): HSBC Bank plc
Directors: A. Haden (MD)
Ultimate Holding Company: BOSWELL & CO. (STEELS) LIMITED
Immediate Holding Company: H.S. PITT & CO. LIMITED
Registration no: 00211899 **Date established:** 2026
Turnover: Up to £250,000 **No.of Employees:** 11 - 20 **Product Groups:** 48

Date of Accounts	Mar 11	Mar 10	Mar 09
Working Capital	17	78	104
Fixed Assets	905	907	909
Current Assets	519	597	530

G. John Power Ltd
Hayseech Road, Halesowen, B63 3PF
Tel: 0121-550 3112 **Fax:** 0121-585 5147
E-mail: sales@gjohnpower.co.uk
Website: http://www.gjohnpower.co.uk
Bank(s): Barclays, Dudley
Directors: N. Shott (Fin), W. Stothert (MD), M. Jarvis (Fin)
Immediate Holding Company: G. John Power Ltd
Registration no: 00436185 **VAT No.:** GB 277 7037 29
Date established: 1947 **No.of Employees:** 11 - 20 **Product Groups:** 34, 35

Date of Accounts	Apr 08	Apr 07	Apr 06
Working Capital	1171	989	922
Fixed Assets	470	516	528
Current Assets	2066	1554	1655
Current Liabilities	895	566	733
Total Share Capital	10	10	10

Powlift Handling Systems Ltd
3a Blackberry Lane, Halesowen, B63 4NX
Tel: 0121-550 4750 **Fax:** 0121-585 5226
E-mail: sales@powlift.co.uk
Website: http://www.powlift.co.uk
Directors: A. Woodhall (MD)
Immediate Holding Company: POWLIFT HANDLING SYSTEMS LIMITED
Registration no: 00952289 **Date established:** 1969 **Turnover:** £1m - £2m
No.of Employees: 1 - 10 **Product Groups:** 67

Date of Accounts	Sep 11	Sep 10	Sep 09
Working Capital	-20	-4	13
Fixed Assets	22	16	30
Current Assets	63	64	69

Premier Filters Ltd
9 Radcliffe Drive, Halesowen, B62 8PL
Tel: 0121-423 4610 **Fax:** 0121-423 4611
E-mail: sales@premierfilters.co.uk
Website: http://www.premierfilters.co.uk
Directors: A. Williams (Fin), G. Williams (MD)
Immediate Holding Company: PREMIER FILTERS LIMITED
Registration no: 04765252 **Date established:** 2003
No.of Employees: 1 - 10 **Product Groups:** 38, 42

Date of Accounts	May 12	May 11	May 10
Working Capital	23	17	5
Current Assets	64	118	35

Quality Optical Services
4 Birmingham Street, Halesowen, B63 3HN
Tel: 0121-550 3345 **Fax:** 0121-503 0218
E-mail: info@qualityopticalservices.co.uk
Website: http://www.youseemeeyestyles.co.uk
Managers: S. Harbutt (Mgr)
Immediate Holding Company: PHASE TRUST
Registration no: 04927820 **Date established:** 2003
Turnover: Up to £250,000 **No.of Employees:** 1 - 10 **Product Groups:** 37, 38, 65

Richley Dental Studio
1 Nimmings Road, Halesowen, B62 9JQ
Tel: 0121-561 4444 **Fax:** 0121-561 4563
E-mail: sales@richleydental.co.uk
Website: http://www.richleydental.co.uk
Directors: S. Macconnachie (Prop)
Registration no: 06238883 **Date established:** 2007
No.of Employees: 11 - 20 **Product Groups:** 38, 67

Roberts Precision Tools Ltd
Victoria Road, Halesowen, B62 8HY
Tel: 0121-559 1477
E-mail: sales@robertstools.net
Website: http://www.robertstools.net
Directors: D. Roberts (Prop)
Immediate Holding Company: ROBERTS PRECISION TOOLS LIMITED
Registration no: 03030510 **Date established:** 1995
No.of Employees: 1 - 10 **Product Groups:** 35, 48, 49, 85

Date of Accounts	May 11	May 10	May 09
Working Capital	30	39	28
Fixed Assets	109	121	100

Current Assets	135	141	116

Angela Russell Technical Services Ltd
39 Instone Road, Halesowen, B63 4SA
Tel: 0121-602 5303
E-mail: angrusuk@yahoo.com
Directors: R. Franklin (MD), A. Hammond Franklin (Co Sec)
Immediate Holding Company: ANGELA RUSSELL TECHNICAL SERVICES LTD
Registration no: 04321825 **Date established:** 2001
No.of Employees: 1 - 10 **Product Groups:** 84

Date of Accounts	Mar 11	Mar 10	Mar 09
Working Capital	2	-4	N/A
Fixed Assets	N/A	N/A	1
Current Assets	13	5	7

St Turier
Unit 7 Block 5 Shenstone Trading Estate Bromsgrove Road, Halesowen, B63 3XB
Tel: 0121-501 6880 **Fax:** 0121-501 6881
E-mail: sales@turierscales.co.uk
Website: http://www.turierscales.co.uk
Managers: C. Rogers (Mgr)
Registration no: 00782286 **VAT No.:** GB 275 0057 70
Date established: 2006 **Turnover:** £2m - £5m **No.of Employees:** 1 - 10
Product Groups: 38

Sandvik Process Systems UK
Manor Way, Halesowen, B62 8QZ
Tel: 0121-504 5750 **Fax:** 0121-504 5151
E-mail: smc@sandvik.com
Website: http://www.processsystems.sandvik.com
Managers: N. Flivell (Mgr)
Ultimate Holding Company: SANDVIK AB (SWEDEN)
Immediate Holding Company: SANDVIK LIMITED
Registration no: 00136547 **Date established:** 2014
Turnover: £75m - £125m **No.of Employees:** 1 - 10 **Product Groups:** 34, 36, 66

Date of Accounts	Dec 11	Dec 10	Dec 09
Sales Turnover	162m	120m	84m
Pre Tax Profit/Loss	10m	4m	-5m
Working Capital	17m	6m	790
Fixed Assets	30m	33m	34m
Current Assets	46m	35m	25m
Current Liabilities	5m	8m	4m

Sealco International Ltd
Unit 1 Saltbrook Estate Saltbrook Trading Road, Cradley Heath, Halesowen, B63 2QU
Tel: 01384-413058 **Fax:** 01384-568729
E-mail: sales@sealco.co.uk
Website: http://www.sealco.co.uk
Directors: R. Fowkes (MD), C. Bradbury (MD)
Managers: S. McCairn (Sales Prom Mgr), P. Haywood (Mgr)
Immediate Holding Company: SEALCO INTERNATIONAL LIMITED
Registration no: 02585264 **Date established:** 1991
Turnover: £500,000 - £1m **No.of Employees:** 1 - 10 **Product Groups:** 29, 30, 36, 48

Date of Accounts	Dec 11	Dec 10	Dec 09
Working Capital	159	44	29
Fixed Assets	66	104	75
Current Assets	797	578	446

Securiclear Aluminum Systems Ltd
Forge Lane, Halesowen, B62 8EJ
Tel: 0121-585 0822 **Fax:** 0121-585 0801
E-mail: alan.walker@cbcgrp.co.uk
Website: http://www.cbcgrp.co.uk
Directors: A. Walker (MD)
Ultimate Holding Company: GOGLASS LIMITED
Immediate Holding Company: SECURICLEAR ALUMINIUM SYSTEMS LIMITED
Registration no: 02511342 **Date established:** 1990
No.of Employees: 11 - 20 **Product Groups:** 26, 35

Date of Accounts	Oct 11	Oct 10	Oct 09
Working Capital	2m	825	857
Fixed Assets	943	2m	2m
Current Assets	2m	1m	1m

SKF Economos UK Ltd NDC/Wyko
Hereward Rise, Halesowen, B62 8AN
Tel: 0121-5016701 **Fax:** 0121-5016745
E-mail: halesowen@economos.com
Website: http://www.economos.co.uk
Directors: P. Chambers (MD), R. Kumra (MD)
Product Groups: 29, 30, 33, 36, 40, 42, 45, 46, 48

Skilled
Victoria Road, Halesowen, B62 8HY
Tel: 0121-561 3251 **Fax:** 0121-559 0801
Directors: S. Green (Fin)
Immediate Holding Company: GLOBAL STRATEGIC ALLIANCE GROUP LIMITED
Registration no: 02567448 **Date established:** 2010 **Turnover:** £1m - £2m
No.of Employees: 1 - 10 **Product Groups:** 35, 49

Date of Accounts	Dec 06
Working Capital	640
Fixed Assets	71
Current Assets	1035
Current Liabilities	395

Solid Auto UK Ltd
Coombswood Way, Halesowen, B62 8BH
Tel: 0121-561 6444 **Fax:** 0121-561 6464
E-mail: uksales@solidautouk.co.uk
Website: http://www.solidautouk.co.uk
Directors: M. Price (MD)
Immediate Holding Company: SOLID AUTO (U.K.) LIMITED
Registration no: 02446727 **Date established:** 1989 **Turnover:** £2m - £5m
No.of Employees: 11 - 20 **Product Groups:** 39

Date of Accounts	Dec 11	Dec 10	Dec 09
Working Capital	835	810	816
Fixed Assets	108	117	127
Current Assets	2m	2m	2m

Somers Forge Ltd

Haywood Forge Prospect Road, Halesowen, B62 8DZ
Tel: 0121-585 5959 **Fax:** 0121-585 7154
E-mail: sales@somersforge.com
Website: http://www.somersforge.com
Directors: J. Warr (Sales), T. Ingles (Fin), P. Mitchell (MD)
Managers: M. Addison (Export Sales Mg), G. Abbott, M. White, J. Wood
Ultimate Holding Company: Folkes Holdings
Immediate Holding Company: Folkes Forgings Ltd
Registration no: 02532900 **Date established:** 1866
Turnover: £10m - £20m **Product Groups:** 34, 46, 48, 66

Somers Totalkare Ltd

Unit 15 Forge Trading Estate Mucklow Hill, Halesowen, B62 8TP
Tel: 0121-585 2700 **Fax:** 0121-501 1458
E-mail: sales@somerstotalkare.co.uk
Website: http://www.stkare.co.uk
Directors: J. Radford (Sales), T. Jackson (MD)
Managers: D. Hems (Fin Mgr), A. Chumber (Mktg Serv Mgr)
Immediate Holding Company: SOMERS TOTALKARE LIMITED
Registration no: 05256574 **VAT No.:** GB 705 3507 59
Date established: 2004 **Turnover:** £5m - £10m **No.of Employees:** 1 - 10
Product Groups: 39, 45

Date of Accounts	Dec 11	Dec 10	Dec 09
Working Capital	105	7	669
Fixed Assets	250	111	57
Current Assets	2m	1m	1m

Sponmech Safety Systems Ltd

Hayseech Road, Halesowen, B63 3PD
Tel: 0121-585 8730 **Fax:** 0121-585 5128
E-mail: sales@sponmech.co.uk
Website: http://www.sponmech.co.uk
Directors: D. Sheppard (Fin)
Immediate Holding Company: SPONMECH SAFETY SYSTEMS LIMITED
Registration no: 02621238 **Date established:** 1991
No.of Employees: 11 - 20 **Product Groups:** 26, 30, 35, 40, 51

Date of Accounts	Mar 12	Mar 11	Mar 10
Working Capital	210	147	92
Fixed Assets	61	72	85
Current Assets	407	352	218

Stannah Lift Services Ltd

Unit A6 Coombswood Way, Halesowen, B62 8BH
Tel: 0121-559 2260 **Fax:** 0121-559 8171
E-mail: enquiries@stannah.co.uk
Website: http://www.stannah.co.uk
Managers: J. Pearshouse (Mgr)
Ultimate Holding Company: STANNAH LIFTS HOLDINGS LIMITED
Immediate Holding Company: STANNAH LIFT SERVICES LIMITED
Registration no: 01189799 **Date established:** 1974
No.of Employees: 21 - 50 **Product Groups:** 35, 39, 45

Date of Accounts	Dec 11	Dec 10	Dec 09
Sales Turnover	84m	82m	87m
Pre Tax Profit/Loss	191	2m	2m
Working Capital	12m	14m	15m
Fixed Assets	4m	4m	3m
Current Assets	21m	24m	24m
Current Liabilities	6m	6m	7m

Steel Doors By Design Ltd

Units 8-10 Western Business Park Coombs Road, Halesowen, B62 8AE
Tel: 0121-561 1912 **Fax:** 0121-561 5232
E-mail: susan@walltowalluk.com
Website: http://www.walltowalluk.com
Directors: S. Wall (Dir)
Immediate Holding Company: STEEL DOORS BY DESIGN LTD
Registration no: 07335782 **Date established:** 2010
No.of Employees: 1 - 10 **Product Groups:** 26, 35

Date of Accounts	Jul 11
Working Capital	-8
Fixed Assets	10
Current Assets	171

Swindale Parks

Trinity Point New Road, Halesowen, B63 3HY
Tel: 0121-585 6079 **Fax:** 0121-585 7625
E-mail: enquiries@swindaleparks.co.uk
Website: http://www.swindaleparks.co.uk
Directors: P. Cash (Dir)
Immediate Holding Company: SWINDALE PARKS LTD
Registration no: 07122659 **Date established:** 2010
Turnover: £250,000 - £500,000 **No.of Employees:** 1 - 10
Product Groups: 80

Date of Accounts	Dec 11	Oct 10
Working Capital	-7	N/A
Fixed Assets	12	N/A
Current Assets	59	N/A

Thompson Friction Welding

Hereward Rise, Halesowen, B62 8AN
Tel: 0121-585 0800 **Fax:** 0121-585 0810
E-mail: sales@thompson.co
Website: http://www.thompson.co
Directors: P. Lovegrove (MD)
Managers: N. Edge (Sales Prom Mgr), N. Edge (Sales Prom Mgr)
Immediate Holding Company: THOMPSON FRICTION WELDING LIMITED
Registration no: 01154477 **VAT No.:** GB 614 8091 46
Date established: 1974 **Turnover:** £10m - £20m
No.of Employees: 21 - 50 **Product Groups:** 46, 48, 85

Date of Accounts	Dec 11	Dec 10	Dec 09
Sales Turnover	20m	17m	15m
Pre Tax Profit/Loss	-526	919	-64
Working Capital	2m	2m	169
Fixed Assets	4m	4m	5m
Current Assets	13m	11m	12m
Current Liabilities	3m	3m	2m

Top Tower Ltd

Access House Bromsgrove Road, Halesowen, B63 3HJ
Tel: 0121-585 5858 **Fax:** 0121-585 7989
E-mail: sales@toptower.co.uk
Website: http://www.toptower.co.uk
Directors: M. Smith (Dir)
Immediate Holding Company: TOPTOWER LIMITED
Registration no: 02685951 **Date established:** 1992
Turnover: £500,000 - £1m **No.of Employees:** 1 - 10 **Product Groups:** 35

Date of Accounts	Dec 11	Dec 10	Dec 09
Working Capital	17	49	44
Fixed Assets	28	18	25

Current Assets	179	205	217

Trac Ltd

Shelah Road, Halesowen, B63 3PG
Tel: 0121-585 1080 **Fax:** 0121-585 1090
E-mail: enquiries@trac-aircon.co.uk
Website: http://www.trac-aircon.co.uk
Bank(s): HSBC
Directors: I. Lowe (MD), N. Guest (Dir), P. Stephens (Dir)
Immediate Holding Company: TRAC LIMITED
Registration no: 01200842 **VAT No.:** GB 281 5268 49
Date established: 1975 **Turnover:** £500,000 - £1m
No.of Employees: 21 - 50 **Product Groups:** 52

Date of Accounts	Jul 11	Jul 10	Jul 09
Working Capital	193	242	195
Fixed Assets	191	109	134
Current Assets	695	898	1m

Ultravalve Ltd

Diamond Works, Maple Tree Lane Colley Gate, Halesowen, B63 2BN
Tel: 01384-411888 **Fax:** 01384-411114
E-mail: sales@ultravalve.co.uk
Website: http://www.ultravalve.co.uk
Product Groups: 36, 40

Date of Accounts	Apr 12	Apr 11	Apr 10
Working Capital	173	163	157
Fixed Assets	179	187	200
Current Assets	373	372	394

Vacuum Furnace Engineering

Hayes Trading Estate Hingley Road, Halesowen, B63 2RR
Tel: 01384-426170 **Fax:** 01384-426180
E-mail: sales@vfe.co.uk
Website: http://www.vfe.co.uk
Bank(s): HSBC Bank plc
Managers: M. Bridgewater
Immediate Holding Company: VACUUM FURNACE ENGINEERING LIMITED
Registration no: 01920664 **VAT No.:** GB 428 6905 24
Date established: 1985 **Turnover:** £10m - £20m
No.of Employees: 21 - 50 **Product Groups:** 34, 40, 42, 46, 48, 84

Date of Accounts	Dec 11	Dec 10	Dec 09
Sales Turnover	11m	8m	11m
Pre Tax Profit/Loss	1m	571	408
Working Capital	3m	2m	2m
Fixed Assets	60	71	89
Current Assets	5m	5m	6m
Current Liabilities	780	446	386

Warley Polishing Ltd

Unit 4-5 James Scott Road, Halesowen, B63 2QT
Tel: 01384-634036 **Fax:** 01384-411025
E-mail: sales@warleypolishing.co.uk
Website: http://www.warleypolishing.co.uk
Bank(s): HSBC, Dudley
Directors: J. Gutteridge (Sales)
Immediate Holding Company: WARLEY POLISHING COMPANY LIMITED
Registration no: 01476525 **VAT No.:** GB 351 4637 62
Date established: 1980 **Turnover:** £500,000 - £1m
No.of Employees: 11 - 20 **Product Groups:** 48

Date of Accounts	Dec 11	Dec 10	Dec 09
Working Capital	196	168	199
Fixed Assets	350	350	378
Current Assets	325	227	257

Westmid Fans

Zephyr House Mucklow Hill, Halesowen, B62 8DN
Tel: 0121-550 0315 **Fax:** 0121-585 5185
E-mail: info@westmidfans.co.uk
Website: http://www.westmidfans.co.uk
Directors: A. Jones (Dir)
Immediate Holding Company: WESTMIDVENT LIMITED
Registration no: 01375073 **Date established:** 1978 **Turnover:** £1m - £2m
No.of Employees: 1 - 10 **Product Groups:** 40

Date of Accounts	Jul 11	Jul 10	Jul 09
Working Capital	5	-13	-16
Fixed Assets	123	128	120
Current Assets	390	353	354

T H Withers

Unit 2 1 Blackberry Lane, Halesowen, B63 4NX
Tel: 0121-550 1517 **Fax:** 0121-550 1517
Directors: J. Withers (Prop)
Date established: 1982 **No.of Employees:** 1 - 10 **Product Groups:** 26, 35

Henley In Arden

Bourne Taylor Neville Ltd

Neville House 66 High Street, Henley In Arden, B95 5BX
Tel: 01564-793232 **Fax:** 01564-794784
E-mail: advice@btneville.co.uk
Website: http://www.btneville.co.uk
Directors: R. Swithenby (Fin)
Immediate Holding Company: BOURNE TAYLOR NEVILLE LIMITED
Registration no: 02190964 **Date established:** 1987
Turnover: £500,000 - £1m **No.of Employees:** 1 - 10 **Product Groups:** 80, 82

Date of Accounts	Mar 11	Mar 10	Mar 09
Working Capital	12	14	7
Fixed Assets	15	23	26
Current Assets	54	66	57
Current Liabilities	N/A	42	N/A

Goldsmith & Co. Ltd

221 High Street, Henley In Arden, B95 5BG
Tel: 01564-794616 **Fax:** 01564-794451
E-mail: enquiries@fgoldsmith.co.uk
Website: http://www.fgoldsmith.co.uk
Directors: K. Clifford (Dir)
Immediate Holding Company: F. GOLDSMITH & CO. LIMITED
Registration no: 00699067 **VAT No.:** GB 559 0626 23
Date established: 1961 **Turnover:** £1m - £2m **No.of Employees:** 1 - 10
Product Groups: 49

Date of Accounts	Jul 11	Jul 10	Jul 09
Working Capital	4m	4m	4m
Fixed Assets	158	176	138
Current Assets	4m	4m	4m

Haigh Thornley Design Ltd

6 Ardent Court William James Way, Henley In Arden, B95 5GF
Tel: 01564-797420 **Fax:** 0844-567 0410
E-mail: post@htdl.co.uk
Website: http://www.htdl.co.uk
Managers: A. Thornley
Immediate Holding Company: HTDL LTD
Registration no: 03147945 **VAT No.:** GB 487 0368 18
Date established: 1996 **Turnover:** £500m - £1,000m
No.of Employees: 1 - 10 **Product Groups:** 27, 28, 37, 44, 49, 64, 80, 81, 84, 87

Date of Accounts	Apr 12	Apr 11	Apr 10
Working Capital	-2	-7	-48
Fixed Assets	33	43	50
Current Assets	256	281	264

Lambournes B'Ham Ltd

Unit 1 Shallowford Court, Henley In Arden, B95 5BY
Tel: 01564-794971 **Fax:** 01564-793075
Directors: K. Lambourne (Ch)
Immediate Holding Company: LAMBOURNES(B HAM)LIMITED
Registration no: 00262071 **Date established:** 1932
No.of Employees: 11 - 20 **Product Groups:** 37

Date of Accounts	Jun 11	Jun 10	Jun 09
Working Capital	575	908	1m
Fixed Assets	504	167	167
Current Assets	594	912	1m

Kingswinford

Accurate Section Benders Ltd

Dawley Brook Road, Kingswinford, DY6 7AU
Tel: 01384-402402 **Fax:** 01384-402462
E-mail: sales@accuratesectionbenders.co.uk
Website: http://www.fullers-group.com
Bank(s): Barclays, Lymington
Directors: T. Mocroft (MD)
Managers: K. Edwards (Buyer), J. Heagh (Tech Serv Mgr), T. Ralph (Sales Prom Mgr)
Immediate Holding Company: ACCURATE SECTION BENDERS LIMITED
Registration no: 02463108 **VAT No.:** GB 547 3671 22
Date established: 1990 **Turnover:** £1m - £2m **No.of Employees:** 21 - 50
Product Groups: 34, 35, 45, 48

Date of Accounts	Mar 11	Mar 10	Mar 09
Working Capital	854	764	734
Fixed Assets	785	832	887
Current Assets	2m	1m	1m

Arpel Ltd

Building 70 Third Avenue, Pensnett Trading Estate, Kingswinford, DY6 7FE
Tel: 01384-296660 **Fax:** 01384-280320
E-mail: sales@arpelchilterns.com
Website: http://www.arpelchilterns.com
Directors: P. Wallis (Dir)
Immediate Holding Company: ARPEL LIMITED
Registration no: 02335833 **VAT No.:** GB 007 9818 80
Date established: 1989 **Turnover:** £500,000 - £1m
No.of Employees: 1 - 10 **Product Groups:** 35, 36, 37, 39, 40, 46, 66

Date of Accounts	May 11	May 10	May 09
Working Capital	56	45	42
Fixed Assets	8	10	11
Current Assets	309	320	230

Blackburns Metals Ltd

Building 43 Third Avenue Pensnett Trading Estate, Kingswinford, DY6 7UU
Tel: 01384-282360 **Fax:** 01902-431899
E-mail: info@blackburnsmetals.co.uk
Website: http://www.blackburnsmetals.co.uk
Bank(s): The Royal Bank of Scotland
Managers: M. Ray (Comm), A. Palmer (Chief Mgr)
Ultimate Holding Company: HENLEY MANAGEMENT COMPANY (USA)
Immediate Holding Company: BLACKBURNS METALS LIMITED
Registration no: 04632083 **Date established:** 2003
Turnover: £50m - £75m **No.of Employees:** 21 - 50 **Product Groups:** 34

Date of Accounts	Dec 11	Dec 10	Dec 09
Sales Turnover	68m	58m	48m
Pre Tax Profit/Loss	599	616	-328
Working Capital	4m	3m	3m
Fixed Assets	1m	1m	1m
Current Assets	26m	26m	18m
Current Liabilities	2m	2m	1m

C M L Alloys

Building 8 8 First Avenue Pensnett Trading Estate, Kingswinford, DY6 7TG
Tel: 01384-282400 **Fax:** 01384-270800
E-mail: sales@cmlalloys.com
Website: http://www.cmlalloys.com
Directors: D. Megson (Sales)
Managers: J. Davies, M. Parkes, P. Moriarty (Mgr), T. Karalios (Sales Prom Mgr)
Immediate Holding Company: A.M. CASTLE CO. LTD
Registration no: 05726897 **VAT No.:** GB 686 0037 31
Date established: 2006 **No.of Employees:** 21 - 50 **Product Groups:** 34, 61

V B S Centurion Blinds

Oakdale Trading Estate Ham Lane, Kingswinford, DY6 7JH
Tel: 01384-276240 **Fax:** 01384-292354
E-mail: sales@vbscenturion.co.uk
Bank(s): National Westminster
Managers: I. Marsh (Mgr)
Immediate Holding Company: BAGGERIDGE JOINERY LIMITED
Registration no: 03565208 **Date established:** 2004 **Turnover:** £1m - £2m
No.of Employees: 11 - 20 **Product Groups:** 24, 25, 35

Date of Accounts	Mar 12	Mar 11	Mar 10
Working Capital	171	173	204
Fixed Assets	16	21	17
Current Assets	231	235	276

Charles Advertising Ltd (Charles Advertising Ltd)

Hampshire House High Street, Kingswinford, DY6 8AW
Tel: 01384-400114 **Fax:** 01384-277833
E-mail: info@charlesadvertising.co.uk
Website: http://www.charlesdesign.co.uk

Directors: C. Hanmer (MD), J. Hanmer (Fin)
Immediate Holding Company: CHARLES ADVERTISING LIMITED
Registration no: 01621330 **Date established:** 1982
Turnover: £500,000 - £1m **No.of Employees:** 11 - 20 **Product Groups:** 81

Date of Accounts	Mar 11	Mar 10	Mar 09
Working Capital	236	223	239
Fixed Assets	14	16	24
Current Assets	405	513	453

Clamason Industries Ltd

Unit 9 Gibbons Industrial Park Dudley Road, Kingswinford, DY6 8XG
Tel: 01384-400000 **Fax:** 01384-400588
E-mail: dennisw@clamason.co.uk
Website: http://www.clamason.com
Bank(s): Lloyds TSB Bank plc
Directors: D. Whitmore (Co Sec)
Immediate Holding Company: CLAMASON INDUSTRIES LIMITED
Registration no: 00420452 **VAT No.:** GB 276 9035 29
Date established: 1946 **Turnover:** £10m - £20m
No.of Employees: 101 - 250 **Product Groups:** 35, 37, 48

Date of Accounts	Dec 11	Dec 10	Dec 09
Sales Turnover	14m	13m	11m
Pre Tax Profit/Loss	77	107	96
Working Capital	270	202	237
Fixed Assets	3m	3m	3m
Current Assets	5m	5m	4m
Current Liabilities	101	154	167

C M W Stainless Steel & Alloy Products

Stallings Lane, Kingswinford, DY6 7HP
Tel: 01384-400232 **Fax:** 01384-402001
Directors: D. Mackenzie (Dir), D. Mackenzine (Co Sec), I. Whittaker (Dir), N. Cartwright (MD)
Immediate Holding Company: C.M.W. STAINLESS STEEL AND ALLOY PRODUCTS LIMITED
Registration no: 02371582 **Date established:** 1989
Turnover: Up to £250,000 **No.of Employees:** 1 - 10 **Product Groups:** 40, 67

Date of Accounts	Sep 08	Sep 07	Sep 06
Working Capital	8	16	23
Fixed Assets	7	8	9
Current Assets	32	34	44
Current Liabilities	24	18	22

Alexander Comley Ltd

Pensnett Trading Estate, Kingswinford, DY6 7ND
Tel: 01384-401080 **Fax:** 01384-273935
E-mail: sales@alexandercomley.co.uk
Website: http://www.alexandercomley.co.uk
Bank(s): Lloyds TSB Bank plc
Directors: A. Jones (Sales), A. Roper (Dir)
Immediate Holding Company: ALEXANDER COMLEY LIMITED
Registration no: 00170369 **VAT No.:** GB 670 3088 42
Date established: 2020 **Turnover:** £2m - £5m **No.of Employees:** 21 - 50
Product Groups: 36

Date of Accounts	Dec 11	Dec 10	Dec 09
Working Capital	1m	1m	1m
Fixed Assets	63	71	20
Current Assets	3m	2m	2m

Dudley Designs & Technical Services Ltd

LCP House Building 36 First Avenue, Pensnett Trading Estate, Kingswinford, DY6 7NA
Tel: 01384-291139 **Fax:** 01384-400944
E-mail: email@dudley-designs.co.uk
Website: http://www.dudley-designs.co.uk
Directors: M. Arnold (MD), L. Fithern (Fin)
Immediate Holding Company: DUDLEY DESIGNS & TECHNICAL SERVICES LIMITED
Registration no: 04865669 **VAT No.:** GB 488 2704 12
Date established: 2003 **Turnover:** £500,000 - £1m
No.of Employees: 1 - 10 **Product Groups:** 44, 81, 84

Date of Accounts	Aug 11	Aug 10	Aug 09
Working Capital	25	1	-15
Fixed Assets	10	14	16
Current Assets	135	147	134

Easiflo Fabrications

4 Building 64 Third Avenue, Pensnett Trading Estate, Kingswinford, DY6 7XX
Tel: 01384-279245 **Fax:** 01384-400030
Website: http://www.easiflofabs.co.uk
Bank(s): HSBC Bank plc
Directors: A. Malek (Co Sec)
Ultimate Holding Company: EASIFLO INVESTMENTS LIMITED
Immediate Holding Company: EASIFLO FABRICATIONS LIMITED
Registration no: 00842618 **VAT No.:** GB 277 2190 46
Date established: 1965 **Turnover:** £500,000 - £1m
No.of Employees: 11 - 20 **Product Groups:** 35, 36, 45, 48

Date of Accounts	Jul 11	Jul 10	Jul 09
Working Capital	155	124	129
Fixed Assets	24	36	45
Current Assets	362	257	274

Electroflock Ltd

Unit 7-8 Building 33 Second Avenue, Pensnett Trading Estate, Kingswinford, DY6 7UG
Tel: 01384-402660 **Fax:** 01384-402662
E-mail: electroflock@btinternet.com
Website: http://www.electroflock.co.uk
Directors: A. Kirszniok (Fin), A. Butler (Dir)
Immediate Holding Company: ELECTROFLOCK LIMITED
Registration no: 03028619 **VAT No.:** GB 655 1949 10
Date established: 1995 **Turnover:** £250,000 - £500,000
No.of Employees: 1 - 10 **Product Groups:** 23, 48

Date of Accounts	Mar 11	Mar 10	Mar 09
Working Capital	-27	-37	26
Fixed Assets	2	2	3
Current Assets	119	86	85

Elta Group Ltd

Building 46 Third Avenue, Pensnett Trading Estate, Kingswinford, DY6 7US
Tel: 01384-275760 **Fax:** 01384-275770
E-mail: info@eltagroup.co.uk
Website: http://www.eltagroup.com
Managers: S. Hunt
Registration no: 03008449 **VAT No.:** GB 670 3097 41
Turnover: £20m - £50m **No.of Employees:** 1 - 10 **Product Groups:** 40

Date of Accounts	Mar 10	Mar 09	Mar 08
Sales Turnover	70m	63m	52m
Pre Tax Profit/Loss	6m	5m	5m
Working Capital	19m	17m	13m
Fixed Assets	8m	7m	7m
Current Assets	37m	29m	24m
Current Liabilities	9m	4m	3m

Essexcare Trenching Ltd

Unit 1-3 Oak Lane, Kingswinford, DY6 7JS
Tel: 01384-402376 **Fax:** 01384-296974
E-mail: essexcare@aol.com
Website: http://www.essexcaretrenching.co.uk
Product Groups: 41, 45, 84

Date of Accounts	Oct 09	Oct 08	Oct 07
Working Capital	-142	-163	-256
Fixed Assets	914	1m	977
Current Assets	667	633	516

Fullex Locks Ltd

Building 84 First Avenue, Pensnett Trading Estate, Kingswinford, DY6 7FN
Tel: 01384-401312 **Fax:** 01384-400420
E-mail: iansouthall@fullex-locks.com
Website: http://www.fullex-locks.com
Directors: J. Mason (Dir), S. Plant (Co Sec), I. Southall (MD)
Immediate Holding Company: FULLEX LOCKS LIMITED
Registration no: 04549025 **Date established:** 2002 **Turnover:** £1m - £2m
No.of Employees: 11 - 20 **Product Groups:** 36

Date of Accounts	Dec 11	Dec 10	Dec 09
Working Capital	298	223	55
Fixed Assets	253	274	289
Current Assets	2m	2m	1m

General Kinematics Ltd

Dawley House Dawley Brook Road, Kingswinford, DY6 7BB
Tel: 01384-273303 **Fax:** 01384-273404
E-mail: mail@generalkinematics.com
Website: http://www.generalkinematics.com
Directors: N. Clegg (Co Sec)
Ultimate Holding Company: GENERAL KINEMATICS CORP (USA)
Immediate Holding Company: GENERAL KINEMATICS LIMITED
Registration no: 01784852 **VAT No.:** GB 409 3124 75
Date established: 1984 **Turnover:** £2m - £5m **No.of Employees:** 1 - 10
Product Groups: 45, 46

Date of Accounts	Dec 11	Dec 10	Dec 09
Sales Turnover	N/A	N/A	4m
Pre Tax Profit/Loss	N/A	N/A	-1m
Working Capital	341	2m	2m
Fixed Assets	79	84	142
Current Assets	2m	3m	3m
Current Liabilities	N/A	N/A	190

Glendenning Plastics Ltd

Building 27 First Avenue Pensnett Trading Estate, Kingswinford, DY6 7TZ
Tel: 01384-278256 **Fax:** 01384-400091
E-mail: sales@glendenningplastics.co.uk
Website: http://www.garlandproducts.com
Bank(s): Lloyds TSB Bank plc
Directors: S. Glendenning (MD)
Managers: M. Glendenning (Mktg Serv Mgr), P. King Scott (Purch Mgr)
Ultimate Holding Company: GARLAND PRODUCTS LIMITED
Immediate Holding Company: GLENDENNING PLASTICS LIMITED
Registration no: 00853676 **VAT No.:** GB 276 9502 24
Date established: 1965 **No.of Employees:** 51 - 100 **Product Groups:** 30, 66

Date of Accounts	Dec 11	Dec 10	Dec 09
Working Capital	538	616	520
Fixed Assets	1m	1m	947
Current Assets	1m	1m	1m

Handicare

Building 82 First Avenue, Pensnett Trading Estate, Kingswinford, DY6 7FJ
Tel: 01384-408700
E-mail: sales@handicare.co.uk
Website: http://www.handicare.co.uk
Directors: I. Burrows (Chief Op Offcr), D. Temple (Fin)
Managers: F. Worrall (Personnel), S. Cutler (Mktg Serv Mgr), M. Hatton (Tech Serv Mgr), L. Jones
Ultimate Holding Company: HANDICARE AS (NORWAY)
Immediate Holding Company: HANDICARE HOLDING LIMITED
Registration no: 07111460 **Date established:** 2009
Turnover: £20m - £50m **No.of Employees:** 251 - 500
Product Groups: 35, 39, 45

Date of Accounts	Dec 11	Dec 10	Dec 09
Sales Turnover	44m	42m	40m
Pre Tax Profit/Loss	-1m	2m	2m
Working Capital	5m	7m	6m
Fixed Assets	3m	2m	2m
Current Assets	31m	25m	23m
Current Liabilities	3m	2m	2m

Howden UK Ltd

6 & 7 Baird House Dudley Innovation Centre, Pensnett Trading Estate, Kingswinford, DY6 7FX
Tel: 01384-401021 **Fax:** 01384-401039
Website: http://www.howden.com
Managers: N. Frances (Chief Mgr), N. Francis (Chief Mgr)
Ultimate Holding Company: CHARTER INTERNATIONAL PLC (JERSEY)
Immediate Holding Company: HOWDEN UK LIMITED
Registration no: R0000173 **Date established:** 1998
No.of Employees: 11 - 20 **Product Groups:** 36, 40

Date of Accounts	Dec 11	Dec 10	Dec 09
Sales Turnover	54m	50m	74m
Pre Tax Profit/Loss	10m	7m	6m
Working Capital	79m	70m	65m
Fixed Assets	4m	5m	5m
Current Assets	101m	97m	90m
Current Liabilities	11m	18m	14m

J & S Handling Ltd

Building 53 1 Third Avenue, Pensnett Trading Estate, Kingswinford, DY6 7XQ
Tel: 01384-401342 **Fax:** 01384-401342
E-mail: enquiries@jandshandling.co.uk
Website: http://www.jandshandling.co.uk
Directors: S. Elkes (Fin), A. Elkes (MD)
Immediate Holding Company: J & S HANDLING LIMITED
Registration no: 04749745 **Date established:** 2003
No.of Employees: 1 - 10 **Product Groups:** 35, 39, 45

Date of Accounts	Apr 11	Apr 10	Apr 09
Working Capital	4	-20	-33
Fixed Assets	33	35	42
Current Assets	139	57	41

Jackson Products Ltd

Unit 10 Gibbons Industrial Park Dudley Road, Kingswinford, DY6 8XF
Tel: 01384-286190 **Fax:** 01384-286197
E-mail: sales@jacksonproducts.co.uk
Website: http://www.jacksonproducts.co.uk
Ultimate Holding Company: JACKSON PRODUCTS INC (USA)
Registration no: 03472233 **Date established:** 1997
No.of Employees: 11 - 20 **Product Groups:** 46

Date of Accounts	Dec 07	Dec 06	Dec 05
Working Capital	689	956	1045
Fixed Assets	177	103	79
Current Assets	2245	1621	1462
Current Liabilities	1556	665	418
Total Share Capital	1600	1600	1600

Kennametal UK Ltd

PO Box 29, Kingswinford, DY6 7NP
Tel: 01384-401000 **Fax:** 01384-408015
E-mail: andy.godwin@kennametal.com
Website: http://www.kennametal.co.uk
Bank(s): National Westminster Bank Plc
Directors: A. Godwin (Fin)
Managers: S. Cooper (Tech Serv Mgr), P. Gutteridge (Buyer), J. Evans (Personnel)
Ultimate Holding Company: KENNAMETAL INC (USA)
Immediate Holding Company: KENNAMETAL UK LIMITED
Registration no: 03425094 **VAT No.:** GB 488 4769 71
Date established: 1997 **Turnover:** £20m - £50m
No.of Employees: 101 - 250 **Product Groups:** 33, 34, 35, 36, 46

Date of Accounts	Jun 11	Jun 10	Jun 09
Sales Turnover	36m	32m	31m
Pre Tax Profit/Loss	957	-893	1m
Working Capital	18m	8m	6m
Fixed Assets	7m	7m	628
Current Assets	24m	12m	11m
Current Liabilities	1m	1m	2m

Keymas Ltd

4 Darwin House Dudley Innovation Centre Second Avenue, Pensnett Trading Estate, Kingswinford, DY6 7YB
Tel: 01384-401162 **Fax:** 01384- 400942
E-mail: info@keymas.co.uk
Website: http://www.keymas.co.uk
Directors: J. Barton (MD), H. Barton (Co Sec)
Managers: M. Waldron (Systems Mgr)
Immediate Holding Company: KEYMAS LIMITED
Registration no: 02029255 **Date established:** 1986
No.of Employees: 1 - 10 **Product Groups:** 44, 45

Date of Accounts	Jan 12	Jan 11	Jan 10
Working Capital	490	517	486
Fixed Assets	5	5	1
Current Assets	626	684	1m

Kingswinford Fire Protection Ltd

9 Redruth Close, Kingswinford, DY6 7RL
Tel: 01384-279149 **Fax:** 01384-359643
Website: http://www.kingswinfordfireprotection.co.uk
Directors: L. Matton (Fin), S. Matton (MD)
Immediate Holding Company: KINGSWINFORD FIRE PROTECTION LIMITED
Registration no: 04591763 **Date established:** 2002
No.of Employees: 1 - 10 **Product Groups:** 38, 42

Date of Accounts	Dec 11	Dec 10	Dec 09
Working Capital	6	-1	-7
Fixed Assets	7	8	10
Current Assets	39	38	32

Laidler Steels Ltd

Stallings Lane, Kingswinford, DY6 7LE
Tel: 01384-400442 **Fax:** 01384-294295
E-mail: sales@laidlersteels.co.uk
Bank(s): Lloyds TSB Bank plc
Directors: R. Waring (Sales), A. Laidler (MD)
Immediate Holding Company: LAIDLER STEELS LIMITED
Registration no: 01292879 **Date established:** 1976
Turnover: £10m - £20m **No.of Employees:** 21 - 50 **Product Groups:** 48

Date of Accounts	Sep 11	Sep 10	Sep 09
Sales Turnover	10m	8m	7m
Pre Tax Profit/Loss	516	442	242
Working Capital	3m	2m	2m
Fixed Assets	337	415	348
Current Assets	4m	4m	4m
Current Liabilities	344	257	181

Midland Bearings Ltd

Building 33 Second Avenue, Pensnett Trading Estate, Kingswinford, DY6 7UG
Tel: 01384-841400 **Fax:** 01384-841450
E-mail: sales@midlandbearings.com
Website: http://www.midlandbearings.com
Directors: P. Chesworth (Dir)
Immediate Holding Company: MIDLAND BEARINGS LIMITED
Registration no: 02839330 **Date established:** 1993 **Turnover:** £5m - £10m
No.of Employees: 21 - 50 **Product Groups:** 29, 30, 33, 35, 36, 37, 38, 39, 40, 43, 45, 48, 49, 61, 66, 68

Date of Accounts	Jul 11	Jul 10	Jul 09
Working Capital	2m	2m	2m
Fixed Assets	141	135	130
Current Assets	4m	3m	3m

Midland Pallet Trucks

Unit 33 Second Avenue, Pensnett Trading Estate, Kingswinford, DY6 7UG
Tel: 01384-841440 **Fax:** 01384-841450
E-mail: sales@midlandpallettrucks.com
Website: http://www.midlandpallettrucks.com
Managers: P. Chesworth ()
Product Groups: 45

Midland Presswood & Plastics

109 Ridge Road, Kingswinford, DY6 9RG
Tel: 01384-258010
Website: http://www.m-pp.co.uk
Directors: P. Wood (Prop)
No.of Employees: 1 - 10 **Product Groups:** 30, 48, 49

Midland Scales

Unit 33 Second Avenue, Pennsett Trading Estate, Kingswinford, DY6 7UG
Tel: 01384-841430 **Fax:** 01384-841450
E-mail: sales@midlandscales.com
Website: http://www.midlandscales.com
Managers: T. Lellow (Sales Prom)
Registration no: 02839330 **Date established:** 1984 **Turnover:** £1m - £2m
No.of Employees: 11 - 20 **Product Groups:** 38, 49, 67

Midsteel Flanges & Fittings Ltd

Building 51 Third Avenue, Pensnett Trading Estate, Kingswinford, DY6 7XE
Tel: 01384-400290 **Fax:** 01384-400461
E-mail: sales@midsteel.com
Website: http://www.midsteelflangesandfittings.com
Bank(s): Barclays
Directors: M. Reding (MD), P. Jones (Fin)
Managers: J. Street (Purch Mgr)
Ultimate Holding Company: WOMBOURNE HOLDINGS LIMITED
Immediate Holding Company: WOMBOURNE HOLDINGS LIMITED
Registration no: 02508457 **Date established:** 1990
Turnover: £10m - £20m **No.of Employees:** 21 - 50 **Product Groups:** 35

Date of Accounts	Jun 11	Jun 10	Jun 09
Sales Turnover	14m	10m	20m
Pre Tax Profit/Loss	905	2m	769
Working Capital	4m	3m	3m
Fixed Assets	159	159	800
Current Assets	7m	6m	6m
Current Liabilities	448	491	995

Plastic Coatings Ltd

Ham Lane, Kingswinford, DY6 7JY
Tel: 01384-400066 **Fax:** 01384-298740
E-mail: sales@plastic-coatings.com
Website: http://www.plasticcoatings.co.uk
Bank(s): Bank of Scotland
Directors: K. Bilham (Fin)
Managers: G. Astley, S. Brehler, M. Edwards (Site Co-ord), N. Skidmore (Comptroller)
Ultimate Holding Company: INTERNATIONAL PROCESS TECHNOLOGIES LIMITED
Immediate Holding Company: PLASTIC COATINGS LIMITED
Registration no: 04452705 **VAT No.:** GB 211 3232 32
Date established: 2002 **Turnover:** £5m - £10m
No.of Employees: 101 - 250 **Product Groups:** 30, 32, 48

Date of Accounts	Dec 11	Dec 10	Dec 09
Sales Turnover	6m	5m	5m
Pre Tax Profit/Loss	685	536	344
Working Capital	1m	515	2m
Fixed Assets	2m	2m	2m
Current Assets	3m	3m	3m
Current Liabilities	714	524	469

PLCS Ltd

Wartell Bank, Kingswinford, DY6 7QQ
Tel: 01384-298000 **Fax:** 01384-400845
E-mail: sales@pressleakage.com
Website: http://www.pressleakage.com
Bank(s): National Westminster Bank Plc
Directors: M. Bailey (MD), E. Mathews (Fin)
Immediate Holding Company: PRESS LEAKAGE CONTROL SERVICES LIMITED
Registration no: 02413567 **Date established:** 1989 **Turnover:** £1m - £2m
No.of Employees: 11 - 20 **Product Groups:** 62, 84

Date of Accounts	Mar 12	Mar 11	Mar 10
Working Capital	308	22	-9
Fixed Assets	62	74	71
Current Assets	1m	1m	1m

Quasartronics Ltd

3 Watt House Dudley Innovation Centre Second Avenue, Pensnett Trading Estate, Kingswinford, DY6 7YD
Tel: 01384-401132 **Fax:** 01384-400754
E-mail: karencapewell@quasartronics.com
Website: http://www.quasartronics.com
Bank(s): Barclays
Directors: R. Webb (Co Sec), K. Webb (MD)
Immediate Holding Company: QUASARTRONICS LIMITED
Registration no: 02456654 **Date established:** 1990
Turnover: £500,000 - £1m **No.of Employees:** 11 - 20
Product Groups: 38, 85

Date of Accounts	Mar 12	Mar 11	Mar 10
Working Capital	1m	941	751
Fixed Assets	71	65	54
Current Assets	1m	1m	1m

R G R Fabrications & Welding Services Ltd

Unit 23 Pensnett Trading Estate Second Avenue, Pensnett Trading Estate, Kingswinford, DY6 7PP
Tel: 01384-401055 **Fax:** 01384-400068
E-mail: david.yellowley@btconnect.com
Website: http://www.rgrltd.com
Directors: G. Ness (MD)
Immediate Holding Company: RGR FABRICATING AND WELDING SERVICES LIMITED
Registration no: 03995543 **VAT No.:** GB 346 9388 09
Date established: 2000 **Turnover:** £500,000 - £1m
No.of Employees: 1 - 10 **Product Groups:** 35, 36, 40, 48

Date of Accounts	Nov 11	Nov 10	Nov 08
Working Capital	6	17	32
Fixed Assets	18	24	29
Current Assets	128	92	72

S J G Site Services Ltd

35 Lynwood Avenue Wallheath, Kingswinford, DY6 9AL
Tel: 01384-830827 **Fax:** 01384-830827
Directors: K. Silwood (Fin), S. Gellatly (MD)
No.of Employees: 1 - 10 **Product Groups:** 26, 35

Smithpack Ltd (Smithpack)

Building 55 Second Avenue, Pensnett Trading Estate, Kingswinford, DY6 7XL
Tel: 01384-402424 **Fax:** 01384-402090
E-mail: midlands@smithpack.co.uk
Website: http://www.smithpack.co.uk
Managers: K. Alwood (Mgr)
Ultimate Holding Company: WSPH LIMITED
Immediate Holding Company: SMITHPACK LIMITED
Registration no: 01850712 **Date established:** 1984 **Turnover:** £5m - £10m
No.of Employees: 11 - 20 **Product Groups:** 27, 49, 66

Date of Accounts	Apr 11	Apr 10	Apr 09
Sales Turnover	7m	7m	7m
Pre Tax Profit/Loss	105	73	-400
Working Capital	226	66	-187
Fixed Assets	431	528	752
Current Assets	2m	2m	2m
Current Liabilities	872	1m	1m

Sound Image

14 High Street Pensnett, Kingswinford, DY6 8XD
Tel: 08709-224110 **Fax:** 01384-295419
E-mail: david@sound-i.co.uk
Website: http://www.sound-i.co.uk
Directors: D. Jenkins (Sales), D. Jenkins (Ptnr)
Managers: J. Psaras
No.of Employees: 1 - 10 **Product Groups:** 84

Stillages.com Ltd

Unit 10 Gibbons Industrial Park, Dudley Road, Kingswinford, DY6 8XF
Tel: 01384-408 951 **Fax:** 01384-408968
E-mail: ops@stillages.com
Website: http://www.stillages.com
Directors: K. Halladay (MD), J. Farndon (Fin)
Registration no: 04027026 **No.of Employees:** 1 - 10 **Product Groups:** 29, 45, 67

Supply Technologies

Unit 6 Gibbons Industrial Park Dudley Road, Kingswinford, DY6 8XF
Tel: 01384-402200 **Fax:** 01384-402201
E-mail: garry.attwood@supplytechnologies.com
Website: http://www.supplytechnologies.com
Directors: M. Filipowicz (Co Sec)
Managers: G. Attwood
Ultimate Holding Company: HARLAN LABORATORIES INCORPORATED (UNITED STATES)
Immediate Holding Company: ILS LIMITED
Registration no: 03009343 **Date established:** 1995 **Turnover:** £5m - £10m
No.of Employees: 1 - 10 **Product Groups:** 27, 28, 29, 30, 31, 32, 34, 35, 36, 39, 49, 66

Date of Accounts	Dec 11	Dec 10	Dec 09
Sales Turnover	7m	6m	6m
Pre Tax Profit/Loss	1m	1m	934
Working Capital	1m	1m	984
Fixed Assets	187	93	142
Current Assets	2m	2m	2m
Current Liabilities	325	243	130

Syscom plc

Hampshire House High Street, Kingswinford, DY6 8AW
Tel: 01384-400600 **Fax:** 01384-400601
E-mail: chris.brentnall@syscom.plc.uk
Website: http://www.syscom.plc.uk
Bank(s): Barclays, Wolverhampton
Directors: C. Brentnall (Fin)
Managers: D. Armitage (Tech Serv Mgr), D. Wesley (Mktg Serv Mgr), R. Gibbs
Ultimate Holding Company: SYSCOM GROUP LIMITED
Immediate Holding Company: SYSCOM GROUP LIMITED
Registration no: 02513529 **Date established:** 1990 **Turnover:** £1m - £2m
No.of Employees: 21 - 50 **Product Groups:** 44

Date of Accounts	Mar 11	Mar 10	Mar 09
Sales Turnover	2m	2m	2m
Pre Tax Profit/Loss	-103	53	-159
Working Capital	212	284	192
Fixed Assets	403	457	559
Current Assets	1m	1m	1m
Current Liabilities	855	610	644

Troax Lee Ltd

Building 52 Third Avenue, Pensnett Trading Estate, Kingswinford, DY6 7XF
Tel: 01384-277441 **Fax:** 01384-273627
E-mail: david.teulon@troax.co.uk
Website: http://www.troax.com
Directors: D. Teulon (MD), S. Hodgkiss (Tech Sales), K. Cooper (Fin)
Managers: D. Chapman (Purch Mgr)
Ultimate Holding Company: GUNNEBO AB (SWEDEN)
Immediate Holding Company: LEE MANUFACTURING LIMITED
Registration no: 02565032 **Date established:** 1990 **Turnover:** £2m - £5m
No.of Employees: 21 - 50 **Product Groups:** 35, 40

Date of Accounts	Dec 11	Dec 10	Dec 09
Sales Turnover	5m	5m	4m
Pre Tax Profit/Loss	661	293	-27
Working Capital	674	526	540
Fixed Assets	147	110	136
Current Assets	1m	2m	1m
Current Liabilities	361	388	222

Ultra Furniture

Building 66 Third Avenue, Pensnett Trading Estate, Kingswinford, DY6 7GA
Tel: 01384-400240 **Fax:** 01384-405048
E-mail: glyn.aston@ultra-furniture.co.uk
Website: http://www.ultra-furniture.co.uk
Directors: P. Whitelocks (Dir), G. Aston (Fin)
Managers: N. Dudley (Prod Mgr), K. Billingham (Personnel), P. Wildman (Tech Serv Mgr)
Ultimate Holding Company: RAVEN HOLDINGS LIMITED
Immediate Holding Company: ULTRA FURNITURE LIMITED
Registration no: 02052358 **Date established:** 1986
Turnover: £10m - £20m **No.of Employees:** 101 - 250 **Product Groups:** 26

Date of Accounts	Dec 11	Dec 10	Dec 09
Sales Turnover	22m	19m	17m
Pre Tax Profit/Loss	382	315	152
Working Capital	594	517	369
Fixed Assets	525	519	651
Current Assets	6m	4m	4m
Current Liabilities	922	839	515

United Steels

Gibbons Industrial Park Dudley Road, Kingswinford, DY6 8XF
Tel: 01384-401166 **Fax:** 01384-401167
E-mail: admin@unitedsteels.com
Website: http://www.unitedsteels.com
Directors: K. Sawyer (MD)
Managers: R. Bairsley (Tech Serv Mgr)
Immediate Holding Company: UNITED STEELS LIMITED
Registration no: 02517863 **VAT No.:** GB 610 9859 29
Date established: 1990 **Turnover:** £20m - £50m
No.of Employees: 51 - 100 **Product Groups:** 66

Date of Accounts	Dec 11	Dec 10	Dec 09
Sales Turnover	30m	38m	28m
Pre Tax Profit/Loss	3m	662	172
Working Capital	8m	-284	196
Fixed Assets	11m	11m	10m
Current Assets	21m	16m	15m
Current Liabilities	1m	1m	1m

Oldbury

A Mir & Co. Ltd

Taylors Lane, Oldbury, B69 2BN
Tel: 0121-544 1999 **Fax:** 0121-544 4951
E-mail: office@a-mir.co.uk
Website: http://www.a-mir.co.uk
Bank(s): Barclays
Directors: A. Mir (MD), F. Mir (Fin)
Immediate Holding Company: A. MIR & CO. LIMITED
Registration no: 02470744 **VAT No.:** GB 554 9022 40
Date established: 1990 **Turnover:** £5m - £10m **No.of Employees:** 11 - 20
Product Groups: 35, 36

Date of Accounts	Nov 11	Nov 10	Nov 09
Sales Turnover	9m	8m	6m
Pre Tax Profit/Loss	487	211	69
Working Capital	3m	3m	2m
Fixed Assets	6m	6m	6m
Current Assets	4m	3m	4m
Current Liabilities	99	92	178

Accurus Ltd

Giles Road, Oldbury, B68 8JG
Tel: 0121-544 5335 **Fax:** 0121-544 5339
E-mail: johndavies7263@hotmail.com
Bank(s): Yorkshire Bank PLC
Directors: J. Davies (Dir)
Immediate Holding Company: ACCURUS LIMITED
Registration no: 01846893 **VAT No.:** GB 409 4317 59
Date established: 1984 **Turnover:** £250,000 - £500,000
No.of Employees: 11 - 20 **Product Groups:** 46

Date of Accounts	Oct 11	Oct 10	Oct 09
Working Capital	-42	-16	-29
Fixed Assets	162	150	142
Current Assets	70	76	59
Current Liabilities	54	N/A	N/A

Acme Spinning Co

36-38 Fisher Road, Oldbury, B69 4EL
Tel: 0121-552 1813 **Fax:** 0121-511 1089
E-mail: sales@acmespinningbedale.co.uk
Directors: P. Davis (MD), P. Davis (Prop)
Managers: A. Johnson
Immediate Holding Company: ACME METAL SPINNING & BEDALE LIMITED
Registration no: 05602773 **Date established:** 2005
Turnover: Up to £250,000 **No.of Employees:** 1 - 10 **Product Groups:** 48

All Alloy Slitting Services Ltd

Anchor Bridge House Blakeley Hall Road, Oldbury, B69 4ES
Tel: 0121-544 9889 **Fax:** 0121-544 4555
E-mail: kerry.allalloy@btconnect.com
Website: http://www.allalloyslittingservicesltd.co.uk
Managers: K. Attwell (Admin Off)
Immediate Holding Company: ALL ALLOY SLITTING SERVICES LIMITED
Registration no: 03859499 **Date established:** 1999
No.of Employees: 11 - 20 **Product Groups:** 27, 34, 48, 77

Date of Accounts	Nov 11	Nov 10	Nov 09
Working Capital	82	144	104
Fixed Assets	529	510	551
Current Assets	368	382	260

A-Plant Ltd

Unit A 100 Dudley Road East, Oldbury, B69 3EB
Tel: 0121-544 1333 **Fax:** 0121-544 2822
E-mail: enquiries@aplant.com
Website: http://www.aplant.com
Managers: S. Elkington (Mgr)
Immediate Holding Company: A.PLANT LIMITED
Registration no: 05407712 **Date established:** 2005
Turnover: £500,000 - £1m **No.of Employees:** 11 - 20 **Product Groups:** 83

Date of Accounts	Mar 07	Mar 06
Working Capital	12	-3
Fixed Assets	9	12
Current Assets	35	8

B F S Ltd

2 Hainge Road Tividale, Oldbury, B69 2NH
Tel: 0121-557 1935 **Fax:** 0121-557 4245
E-mail: sales@bfsltd.co.uk
Website: http://www.bfsltd.co.uk
Directors: I. Baker (Dir)
Immediate Holding Company: BAKERS FORKLIFT SERVICES LIMITED
Registration no: 03142014 **Date established:** 1995
No.of Employees: 1 - 10 **Product Groups:** 35, 45, 67

Date of Accounts	Dec 11	Dec 10	Dec 09
Working Capital	49	31	28
Fixed Assets	16	26	32
Current Assets	371	439	293

B C Barton & Son Ltd

1 Hainge Road Tividale, Oldbury, B69 2NR
Tel: 0121-557 2272 **Fax:** 0121-557 2276
E-mail: website@bcbarton.co.uk
Website: http://www.bcbarton.co.uk
Bank(s): Barclays, Birmingham
Directors: B. Keys (Sales), I. Hunter (MD), J. Arrowsmith (Co Sec)
Managers: B. Ketts (Sales Prom Mgr)
Immediate Holding Company: B.C. Barton & Son Ltd
Registration no: 00270354 **VAT No.:** GB 276 8129 25
Date established: 2005 **Turnover:** £5m - £10m **No.of Employees:** 21 - 50
Product Groups: 30, 35, 39, 48

Date of Accounts	Jul 08	Jul 07	Jul 06
Pre Tax Profit/Loss	448	-53	-17
Working Capital	1174	888	922
Fixed Assets	875	877	914
Current Assets	2320	1958	1689
Current Liabilities	1146	1070	767
Total Share Capital	234	234	234
ROCE% (Return on Capital Employed)	21.9	-3.0	-0.9

Berry Polishing
Unit 79 Percy Business Park Rounds Green Road, Oldbury, B69 2RE
Tel: 0121-544 5192 **Fax:** 0121-558 0086
Directors: J. Pearce (Prop)
Date established: 1998 **No.of Employees:** 1 - 10 **Product Groups:** 46, 48

Beta Heat Treatment Ltd
Summerton Road, Oldbury, B69 2EL
Tel: 0121-511 1190 **Fax:** 0121-511 1192
E-mail: dl@claytonholdings.com
Website: http://www.claytonholdings.com
Bank(s): Barclays
Directors: D. Lord (MD), D. Lord (MD)
Managers: P. Cox (Mktg Serv Mgr)
Ultimate Holding Company: CLAYTON HOLDINGS LIMITED
Immediate Holding Company: BETA HEAT TREATMENT LIMITED
Registration no: 02195866 **VAT No.:** GB 661 5410 54
Date established: 1987 **Turnover:** £500,000 - £1m
No.of Employees: 11 - 20 **Product Groups:** 48

Date of Accounts	Dec 11	Dec 10	Dec 09
Working Capital	294	268	401
Fixed Assets	783	833	748
Current Assets	742	711	573

Betco Stapling & Nailing
12 Gregston Industrial Estate Birmingham Road, Oldbury, B69 4EX
Tel: 0121-552 8400 **Fax:** 0121-511 1324
E-mail: sales@betcofasteners.co.uk
Website: http://www.betcofasteners.co.uk
Directors: R. Simson (Ptnr)
Date established: 1975 **Turnover:** £250,000 - £500,000
No.of Employees: 1 - 10 **Product Groups:** 35, 66

Bohler Welding Group Ltd
European Business Park Taylors Lane, Oldbury, B69 2BN
Tel: 0121-569 7700 **Fax:** 0121-544 2876
E-mail: sales@bwguk.co.uk
Website: http://www.bwguk.co.uk
Bank(s): Barclays West Bromwich
Directors: D. Webster (MD), S. Lebedez (Fin)
Managers: P. Jones (Develop Mgr), P. De Prez (Tech Serv Mgr)
Ultimate Holding Company: VOEST-ALPINE AG (AUSTRIA)
Immediate Holding Company: BOHLER WELDING GROUP UK LIMITED
Registration no: 01760660 **VAT No.:** GB 695 8217 85
Date established: 1983 **Turnover:** £5m - £10m **No.of Employees:** 11 - 20
Product Groups: 35

Date of Accounts	Mar 12	Mar 11	Mar 10
Sales Turnover	10m	8m	7m
Pre Tax Profit/Loss	913	725	601
Working Capital	1m	968	1m
Fixed Assets	355	356	552
Current Assets	5m	4m	3m
Current Liabilities	1m	740	698

C M K Treatments Ltd
Unit 12 Granada Industrial Estate, Oldbury, B69 4LH
Tel: 0121-552 3131 **Fax:** 0121-552 1791
E-mail: admin@cmkgroup.co.uk
Website: http://www.cmkgroup.co.uk
Directors: B. Gardiner (Comm), J. Gardiner (Fab)
Immediate Holding Company: CMK (TREATMENTS) LIMITED
Registration no: 02187713 **VAT No.:** GB 547 2015 61
Date established: 1987 **No.of Employees:** 21 - 50 **Product Groups:** 32, 46

Date of Accounts	Jul 11	Jul 10	Jul 09
Working Capital	388	403	-50
Current Assets	913	760	991

Caparo Precision Tubes (Walsall Division)
PO Box 13, Oldbury, B69 4PF
Tel: 0121-543 5700 **Fax:** 0121-543 5750
E-mail: sales@caparoprecisiontubes.co.uk
Website: http://www.caparosteelproducts.com
Bank(s): HSBC Bank plc
Directors: D. Farrell (MD), R. Sockalingam (Fin)
Managers: A. Manlove (Buyer), B. Sharrett (Tech Serv Mgr)
Ultimate Holding Company: CAPARO INDUSTRIES P.L.C.
Immediate Holding Company: CAPARO STEEL PRODUCTS LTD
Registration no: 00318635 **Turnover:** £10m - £20m
No.of Employees: 101 - 250 **Product Groups:** 36

Cemex UK Ltd
Wolverhampton Road, Oldbury, B69 4RJ
Tel: 0121-552 6699 **Fax:** 0121-544 7447
Website: http://www.cemex.co.uk
Directors: S. Keighley (Prop)
Managers: P. Blackwell (Sales & Mktg Mg), S. Richards (Chief Mgr)
Ultimate Holding Company: CEMEX S A B DE CV (MEXICO)
Immediate Holding Company: CEMEX UK
Registration no: 05196131 **Date established:** 2004
Turnover: Over £1,000m **No.of Employees:** 1 - 10 **Product Groups:** 14

Date of Accounts	Dec 10	Dec 09	Dec 08
Pre Tax Profit/Loss	-64m	612m	-101m
Working Capital	-2m	-3m	-452m
Fixed Assets	2432m	2432m	1721m
Current Assets	N/A	218	11m
Current Liabilities	2m	3m	10m

Cenpart Ltd
Twydale Works Dudley Road West, Tividale, Oldbury, B69 2PF
Tel: 0121-520 9400 **Fax:** 0121-520 9211
E-mail: office@cenpart.co.uk
Website: http://www.cenpart.co.uk
Registration no: 03987619 **Date established:** 2000
Turnover: £250,000 - £500,000 **No.of Employees:** 1 - 10
Product Groups: 33, 35, 39, 40, 45, 51, 66, 68

Date of Accounts	Sep 11	Sep 10	Sep 09
Sales Turnover	N/A	N/A	1m
Pre Tax Profit/Loss	N/A	N/A	22
Working Capital	254	264	227
Fixed Assets	2	4	4
Current Assets	642	642	484

Clayton Thermal Processes Ltd
2 Summerton Road, Oldbury, B69 2EL
Tel: 0121-511 1203 **Fax:** 0121-511 1192
E-mail: dw@claytonholdings.com
Website: http://www.claytonholdings.com
Bank(s): Barclays
Directors: D. Pugh (Fin), D. Walker (MD)
Ultimate Holding Company: CLAYTON HOLDINGS LIMITED
Immediate Holding Company: CLAYTON THERMAL PROCESSES LIMITED
Registration no: 02240210 **VAT No.:** GB 661 5410 54
Date established: 1988 **No.of Employees:** 21 - 50 **Product Groups:** 40, 42, 46, 48

Date of Accounts	Dec 11	Dec 10	Dec 09
Working Capital	57	270	161
Fixed Assets	3	3	2
Current Assets	491	305	215

Concept Stainless Ltd
Hainge Park Hainge Road, Oldbury, B69 2NU
Tel: 0121-521 5850 **Fax:** 0121-521 5851
E-mail: sales@concept-stainless.co.uk
Website: http://www.concept-stainless.co.uk
Directors: S. Jones (Fin), R. Jones (MD)
Managers: A. Goode (Ops Mgr), N. Stevens (Sales Prom Mgr)
Registration no: 02552389 **Date established:** 1990 **Turnover:** £2m - £5m
No.of Employees: 1 - 10 **Product Groups:** 36, 38

Date of Accounts	Sep 07	Sep 06	Sep 05
Working Capital	715	631	533
Fixed Assets	126	71	82
Current Assets	1460	1345	1104
Current Liabilities	745	714	571

Cottam & Preedy Ltd
68 Lower City Road Tividale, Oldbury, B69 2HF
Tel: 0121-552 5281 **Fax:** 0121-552 6895
E-mail: enquiries@cottamandpreedy.co.uk
Website: http://www.cottamandpreedy.co.uk
Directors: S. Cottam (Dir)
Immediate Holding Company: COTTAM & PREEDY.LIMITED
Registration no: 00562817 **VAT No.:** GB 276 8706 13
Date established: 1956 **Turnover:** £2m - £5m **No.of Employees:** 1 - 10
Product Groups: 36, 39, 40

Date of Accounts	Jul 12	Jul 11	Jul 10
Working Capital	1m	1m	500
Fixed Assets	74	61	490
Current Assets	2m	1m	1m

Crawford Amber
4 Raby Close Tividale, Oldbury, B69 1US
Tel: 01384-253900
E-mail: keith.haywood@crawfordsolutions.com
Website: http://www.crawfordamber.co.uk
Directors: D. Butwell (Prop)
Immediate Holding Company: CRAWFORD DOOR LTD
Registration no: 00937594 **Date established:** 1983
No.of Employees: 1 - 10 **Product Groups:** 26, 35

Currall Lewis & Martin Construction Ltd
89-93 Broadwell Road, Oldbury, B69 4BL
Tel: 0121-552 9292 **Fax:** 0121-544 9899
E-mail: office@clmconstruction.com
Website: http://www.clmconstruction.com
Bank(s): Barclays, London
Directors: E. Pinfield (MD), E. Lewis (Co Sec)
Ultimate Holding Company: CP HOLDINGS LIMITED
Immediate Holding Company: CURRALLS LIMITED
Registration no: 00833456 **VAT No.:** GB 322 5064 93
Date established: 1965 **Turnover:** Up to £250,000
No.of Employees: 21 - 50 **Product Groups:** 51, 52, 84

Date of Accounts	Dec 11	Dec 10	Dec 09
Sales Turnover	N/A	7	16
Pre Tax Profit/Loss	-60	-11	N/A
Working Capital	-86	-56	-44
Current Assets	4	23	35
Current Liabilities	27	20	2

Cuxson Gerrard & Company Ltd
125 Broadwell Road, Oldbury, B69 4BF
Tel: 0121-544 7117 **Fax:** 0121-544 8616
E-mail: info@cuxsongerrard.com
Website: http://www.cuxsongerrard.com
Bank(s): HSBC Bank plc
Directors: C. Mullen (Fin), D. Wain (MD)
Managers: A. Whitehouse (Chief Acct), D. Smith (Purch Mgr)
Immediate Holding Company: CUXSON GERRARD & COMPANY LIMITED
Registration no: 00080715 **VAT No.:** GB 276 8469 01
Date established: 2004 **Turnover:** £5m - £10m
No.of Employees: 51 - 100 **Product Groups:** 24, 27

Date of Accounts	Mar 11	Mar 10	Mar 09
Sales Turnover	7m	7m	7m
Pre Tax Profit/Loss	2m	1m	2m
Working Capital	10m	9m	9m
Fixed Assets	1m	2m	2m
Current Assets	11m	10m	10m
Current Liabilities	834	756	642

D J R Electrical Services
6 Suffolk Close, Oldbury, B68 8RP
Tel: 0121-541 1658
E-mail: info@djrelectrical.org
Website: http://www.djrelectrical.pwp.blueyonder.co.uk
Directors: D. Rowlands (Prop)
Registration no: 06513465 **Date established:** 2003
Turnover: Up to £250,000 **No.of Employees:** 1 - 10 **Product Groups:** 37, 38, 52, 67

Dudley Iron & Steel Co. Ltd
Unit 8 Tividale, Oldbury, B69 3HU
Tel: 0121-601 5000 **Fax:** 0121-601 5001
E-mail: sales@tubes-uk-steel.co.uk
Website: http://www.tubes-uk-steel.co.uk
Bank(s): HSBC Bank plc
Directors: S. Berry (Sales), R. Robinson (MD)
Managers: G. Wright, A. Leigh (Sales Prom Mgr), G. Wright
Ultimate Holding Company: BARRETT STEEL LIMITED
Immediate Holding Company: DUDLEY IRON & STEEL CO. LIMITED
Registration no: 02788759 **Date established:** 1993 **Turnover:** £5m - £10m
No.of Employees: 51 - 100 **Product Groups:** 34, 35, 36, 46

Date of Accounts	Sep 08
Working Capital	1
Current Assets	1

D G Evitts & Son Ltd
Gate 2 Caparo Precision Tubes Popes Lane, Oldbury, B69 4PF
Tel: 0121-202 4430 **Fax:** 0121-543 5744
E-mail: tonyfegan_evitts@btconnect.com
Directors: K. Round (Dir), R. Evitt (MD)
Immediate Holding Company: D G EVITTS & SON LIMITED
Registration no: 06496011 **Date established:** 2008
No.of Employees: 11 - 20 **Product Groups:** 72

Date of Accounts	May 11	May 10	May 09
Sales Turnover	937	1m	N/A
Working Capital	-44	-40	-56
Fixed Assets	199	263	144
Current Assets	119	124	104

John A Gaunt Electrical Contractors Ltd
Computer House Rood End Road, Oldbury, B68 8SF
Tel: 0121-511 2101 **Fax:** 0121-544 8292
Website: http://www.johnagaunt.co.uk
Directors: P. Gaunt (Dir)
Immediate Holding Company: GAUNT PROPERTY MANAGEMENT LIMITED
Registration no: 02201009 **Date established:** 1987 **Turnover:** £1m - £2m
No.of Employees: 11 - 20 **Product Groups:** 52

Date of Accounts	Mar 11	Mar 10	Mar 09
Working Capital	338	479	750
Fixed Assets	106	106	108
Current Assets	487	617	871

Gilca Ltd
Wolverhampton Road, Oldbury, B69 2RU
Tel: 0121-544 1929 **Fax:** 0121-544 6301
E-mail: info@gilca.biz
Website: http://www.foam-warehouse.com
Bank(s): HSBC Bank plc
Directors: K. Smith (MD), B. Ayas (Fin)
Immediate Holding Company: GILCA LIMITED
Registration no: 02108757 **VAT No.:** GB 462 3002 89
Date established: 1987 **Turnover:** £1m - £2m **No.of Employees:** 11 - 20
Product Groups: 29, 44, 49

Date of Accounts	Dec 11	Dec 10	Dec 09
Working Capital	-5	-34	-53
Fixed Assets	54	61	70
Current Assets	191	177	167

Goodwill Trophy Company Ltd
Unit 7 Junction 2 Indust Estate Demuth Way, Oldbury, B69 4LT
Tel: 0121-544 3444 **Fax:** 0121-544 1947
E-mail: sales@goodwill-trophy.co.uk
Website: http://www.goodwilltrophy.co.uk
Bank(s): HSBC Bank plc
Directors: J. Goodwin (Dir), G. Broodryk (Dir)
Managers: T. Trinder (Sales Admin)
Immediate Holding Company: GOODWILL TROPHY COMPANY LIMITED
Registration no: 03755262 **VAT No.:** GB 729 9417 89
Date established: 1999 **Turnover:** £2m - £5m **No.of Employees:** 21 - 50
Product Groups: 49

Date of Accounts	Dec 11	Dec 10	Dec 09
Working Capital	833	788	663
Fixed Assets	41	59	86
Current Assets	1m	1m	925

Granada Cranes & Handling
Parsonage Street, Oldbury, B69 4PH
Tel: 0121-552 4503 **Fax:** 0121-511 1152
E-mail: info@granada-cranes.co.uk
Website: http://www.granada-cranes.co.uk
Directors: B. Mcloughlin (Dir)
Immediate Holding Company: WHITON TOOLS LIMITED
Registration no: 06719767 **Date established:** 1973
No.of Employees: 11 - 20 **Product Groups:** 35, 39, 45

Date of Accounts	Jul 11	Jul 10	Jul 09
Working Capital	-29	-21	-23
Fixed Assets	105	110	120
Current Assets	47	49	38

H K B Steels Services Ltd
Autobase Industrial Estate Tipton Road, Tividale, Oldbury, B69 3HU
Tel: 0121-557 8361 **Fax:** 0121-520 8810
E-mail: sales@hkb-steel.co.uk
Website: http://www.hkb-steel.co.uk
Directors: R. Robinson (MD)
Immediate Holding Company: BARRETT STEELS
Registration no: 00713342 **Turnover:** £10m - £20m
No.of Employees: 101 - 250 **Product Groups:** 34, 35, 38, 66

Hooper Engineering Products Ltd
Nelson Street, Oldbury, B69 4NY
Tel: 0121-552 2835 **Fax:** 0121-552 3821
E-mail: hooper.sheetmetal@virgin.net
Directors: M. Pedley (Fin), R. Hooper (MD), S. Fletcher (Sales & Mktg), W. Hooper (MD)
Managers: M. Pedley (Accounts)
Immediate Holding Company: HOOPER ENGINEERING PRODUCTS LIMITED
Registration no: 00490845 **VAT No.:** GB 428 7526 27
Date established: 1951 **Turnover:** £2m - £5m **No.of Employees:** 1 - 10
Product Groups: 30, 48

Date of Accounts	Mar 10	Mar 09	Mar 08
Working Capital	-141	-117	-52
Fixed Assets	480	508	371
Current Assets	46	15	103

Independent Slitters Ltd
Park Street, Oldbury, B69 4LE
Tel: 0121-552 9628 **Fax:** 0121-552 9631
E-mail: sales@independentslitters.co.uk
Website: http://www.independentslitters.co.uk
Directors: D. Warren (Dir)
Immediate Holding Company: INDEPENDENT SLITTERS LIMITED
Registration no: 02495434 **Date established:** 1990
No.of Employees: 1 - 10 **Product Groups:** 77

Date of Accounts	Mar 12	Mar 11	Mar 10
Working Capital	-88	-150	-127
Fixed Assets	20	N/A	593
Current Assets	296	249	196

Industrial Power Units Ltd
Churchbridge, Oldbury, B69 2AS
Tel: 0121-511 0400 **Fax:** 0121-511 0401
E-mail: robert.beebee@ipu.co.uk
Website: http://www.ipu.co.uk
Bank(s): Lloyds TSB Bank plc
Directors: I. Cleary (Dir), R. Beebee (MD)
Immediate Holding Company: INDUSTRIAL POWER UNITS LIMITED
Registration no: 00641876 **VAT No.:** GB 100 0123 73
Date established: 1959 **Turnover:** £10m - £20m
No.of Employees: 51 - 100 **Product Groups:** 40

Date of Accounts	Oct 11	Oct 10	Oct 09
Sales Turnover	13m	10m	10m
Pre Tax Profit/Loss	558	-68	113
Working Capital	1m	903	456
Fixed Assets	2m	2m	2m
Current Assets	5m	4m	4m
Current Liabilities	2m	1m	1m

M G Steels Ltd
Phoenix House Dudley Road West, Tividale, Oldbury, B69 2PJ
Tel: 0121-522 4520 **Fax:** 0121-520 0191
E-mail: mgsteels@madasafish.com
Directors: J. Gwinnell (Ptnr)
Immediate Holding Company: MG STEELS LIMITED
Registration no: 02465924 **VAT No.:** GB 547 3640 33
Date established: 1990 **Turnover:** £250,000 - £500,000
No.of Employees: 1 - 10 **Product Groups:** 34

Date of Accounts	Mar 11	Mar 10	Mar 09
Working Capital	49	46	40
Current Assets	173	152	140

Marwel Conveyors
Dudley Road East, Oldbury, B69 3EB
Tel: 0121-552 4418 **Fax:** 0121-552 4018
E-mail: sales@marwel.com
Website: http://www.marwel.uk.com
Bank(s): Barclays
Directors: A. Reavenall (Fin), I. Marshall (MD)
Immediate Holding Company: MARWEL CONVEYORS LIMITED
Registration no: 02714790 **VAT No.:** GB 610 9180 66
Date established: 1992 **No.of Employees:** 11 - 20 **Product Groups:** 35, 45, 46, 84

Date of Accounts	Feb 08	Feb 11	Feb 10
Working Capital	13	109	107
Current Assets	467	546	1m

Mercian Industrial Doors
Pearsall Drive Industrial Estate, Oldbury, B69 2RA
Tel: 0121-544 6124 **Fax:** 0121-552 6793
E-mail: info@merciandoors.co.uk
Website: http://www.merciandoors.co.uk
Directors: R. Gear (Fin)
Managers: A. Langston (Fin Mgr)
Ultimate Holding Company: STONESHARE LIMITED
Immediate Holding Company: MERCIAN INDUSTRIAL DOORS (SOUTH WALES) LIMITED
Registration no: 04726250 **VAT No.:** 632 1310 93 **Date established:** 2003
Turnover: £1m - £2m **No.of Employees:** 21 - 50 **Product Groups:** 35

Date of Accounts	Mar 10	Mar 09	Mar 07
Working Capital	1	1	-76
Fixed Assets	N/A	N/A	6
Current Assets	1	19	50
Current Liabilities	N/A	18	N/A

Metsec plc
Broadwell Road, Oldbury, B69 4HF
Tel: 0121-601 6000 **Fax:** 0121-601 6136
E-mail: wolfgang.spreitzer@metsec.com
Website: http://www.metsec.com
Directors: T. Baumgartner (Fin), J. Andrew (MD)
Managers: T. Whale, H. Punz (Comptroller), N. Woodward (Tech Serv Mgr)
Ultimate Holding Company: VOEST-ALPINE AG (AUSTRIA)
Immediate Holding Company: METSEC PLC
Registration no: 01551970 **Date established:** 1981
Turnover: £75m - £125m **No.of Employees:** 251 - 500
Product Groups: 34

Date of Accounts	Mar 12	Mar 11	Mar 10
Sales Turnover	81m	74m	62m
Pre Tax Profit/Loss	15m	9m	3m
Working Capital	2m	-5m	-13m
Fixed Assets	22m	24m	26m
Current Assets	27m	17m	10m
Current Liabilities	7m	5m	3m

Midland Food Equipment
513 Wolverhampton Road, Oldbury, B68 8DD
Tel: 0121-552 2110
Directors: D. Thomas (Prop)
No.of Employees: 1 - 10 **Product Groups:** 38, 42

N J Bradford Ltd
Ashes Road, Oldbury, B69 4RA
Tel: 0121-559 5555 **Fax:** 0121-559 3826
E-mail: ian.bradford@nj-bradford.co.uk
Website: http://www.nj-bradford.co.uk
Bank(s): Barclays, West Bromwich
Directors: P. Badger (Fin), T. Bradford (MD)
Managers: C. Good (Sales Prom Mgr)
Immediate Holding Company: N.J.BRADFORD LIMITED
Registration no: 00489777 **VAT No.:** GB 276 8042 37
Date established: 1950 **Turnover:** £2m - £5m **No.of Employees:** 21 - 50
Product Groups: 26, 30, 33, 34, 40, 45, 48

Date of Accounts	Oct 10	Oct 11	Nov 08
Working Capital	85	137	60
Fixed Assets	995	941	1m
Current Assets	434	445	409

The Natural Rug Store Style International Limited
Unit 1 Gregston Trading Estate Birmingham Road, Oldbury, B69 4EX
Tel: 08450-760086
E-mail: info@naturalrugstore.co.uk
Website: http://www.naturalrugstore.co.uk
Directors: J. Hughes (Prop)
Turnover: £250,000 - £500,000 **No.of Employees:** 1 - 10
Product Groups: 23, 24, 39

Nero Pipeline Connections Ltd
31 Hainge Road Tividale, Oldbury, B69 2NY
Tel: 0121-557 9000 **Fax:** 0121-544 5601
E-mail: info@nero.co.uk
Website: http://www.nero.co.uk
Bank(s): Lloyds TSB Bank plc
Directors: R. Mooney (MD)
Immediate Holding Company: NERO PIPELINE CONNECTIONS LIMITED
Registration no: 02740604 **Date established:** 1992 **Turnover:** £1m - £2m
No.of Employees: 11 - 20 **Product Groups:** 34, 36, 40, 66

Date of Accounts	Aug 11	Aug 10	Aug 09
Working Capital	171	90	75
Fixed Assets	379	381	370
Current Assets	754	600	537

Passenger Lift Services Ltd
Pearsall Drive, Oldbury, B69 2RA
Tel: 0121-552 0660 **Fax:** 0121-552 0200
E-mail: enquiries@pls-access.co.uk
Website: http://www.pls-access.co.uk
Directors: C. Thomas (Comm)
Managers: M. Pitt
Ultimate Holding Company: PASSENGER LIFT (HOLDINGS) LIMITED
Immediate Holding Company: PASSENGER LIFT SERVICES LIMITED
Registration no: 02544902 **Date established:** 1990
Turnover: £500,000 - £1m **No.of Employees:** 21 - 50
Product Groups: 35, 39, 45

Date of Accounts	Mar 11	Mar 10	Mar 09
Working Capital	2m	2m	2m
Fixed Assets	273	294	331
Current Assets	4m	4m	3m
Current Liabilities	645	N/A	386

Pegrex Ltd
Unit 1e Pearsall Drive, Oldbury, B69 2RA
Tel: 0121-511 1475 **Fax:** 0121-511 1474
E-mail: info@pegrex.co.uk
Website: http://www.pegrex.co.uk
Directors: N. Trueman (MD)
Immediate Holding Company: PEGREX LIMITED
Registration no: 03951034 **VAT No.:** GB 748 2668 91
Date established: 2000 **Turnover:** £500,000 - £1m
No.of Employees: 1 - 10 **Product Groups:** 46

Date of Accounts	Dec 11	Dec 10	Dec 09
Working Capital	105	59	38
Fixed Assets	36	41	13
Current Assets	213	165	134

Petrofit Ltd
Unit 9 Credenda Road, Oldbury, B70 7JE
Tel: 0121-544 9938 **Fax:** 0121-544 9132
E-mail: info@petrofit.com
Website: http://www.petrofit.com
Registration no: 03533800 **VAT No.:** GB 714 8607 29
Date established: 1998 **No.of Employees:** 1 - 10 **Product Groups:** 23, 29, 30, 33, 34, 35, 36, 40, 66, 67

Date of Accounts	Mar 08	Mar 07	Mar 06
Working Capital	-10	3	-4
Fixed Assets	11	13	18
Current Assets	249	112	127
Current Liabilities	259	109	130

Premier M & D Windows
34 Strawberry Close Tividale, Oldbury, B69 1NU
Tel: 01384-565787 **Fax:** 01384- 410951
E-mail: sales@premierglass.co.uk
Website: http://www.premierglass.co.uk
Directors: T. Chattin (Prop), C. Trickett (Dir)
Ultimate Holding Company: DP PARTNERSHIP LIMITED
Immediate Holding Company: MTM LIMITED
Registration no: 03921934 **Date established:** 1998 **Turnover:** £2m - £5m
No.of Employees: 1 - 10 **Product Groups:** 51

Pressure Gauges Ltd
Park Street, Oldbury, B69 4LE
Tel: 0121-544 4408 **Fax:** 0121-544 7332
E-mail: enquiries@pressure-gauges-ltd.com
Website: http://www.pressure-gauges-ltd.com
Directors: L. Cutler (Fin)
Immediate Holding Company: PRESSURE GAUGES LIMITED
Registration no: 01834648 **VAT No.:** GB 409 4159 51
Date established: 1984 **Turnover:** £250,000 - £500,000
No.of Employees: 1 - 10 **Product Groups:** 38, 68

Date of Accounts	Mar 11	Mar 10	Mar 09
Working Capital	243	252	216
Fixed Assets	9	13	15
Current Assets	263	279	247

Reliance Security Group Limited
3rd Floor East Wing Trigate, 210-222 Hagley Road West, Oldbury, B68 ONP
Tel: 0870-6068999 **Fax:** 0121-429 6733
E-mail: info@reliancesecurity.co.uk
Website: http://www.reliancesecurity.co.uk
Managers: C. Burnell (Chief Mgr)
Registration no: 01473721 **Turnover:** Over £1,000m
No.of Employees: 51 - 100 **Product Groups:** 81

J E Roberts & Son
47 Moat Road, Oldbury, B68 8EB
Tel: 0121-552 3189
E-mail: house.doctor@btinternet.com
Website: http://www.aatishoo.co.uk
Directors: K. Roberts (Prop)
Turnover: £250,000 - £500,000 **No.of Employees:** 1 - 10
Product Groups: 52

Ronis-Dom Ltd
Unit 1 Junction Two Industrial Estate Demuth Way, Oldbury, B69 4LT
Tel: 0800-988 4348 **Fax:** 0800-988 4349
E-mail: sales@ronis-dom.co.uk
Website: http://www.ronis-dom.co.uk
Bank(s): H S B C, Harlow
Directors: J. Denis (MD)
Ultimate Holding Company: SECURIDEV (FRANCE)
Immediate Holding Company: RONIS-DOM LIMITED
Registration no: 02324698 **Date established:** 1988 **Turnover:** £2m - £5m
No.of Employees: 11 - 20 **Product Groups:** 36, 40

Date of Accounts	Dec 11	Dec 10	Dec 09
Sales Turnover	3m	3m	3m
Pre Tax Profit/Loss	100	150	-46
Working Capital	590	567	485
Fixed Assets	162	152	177
Current Assets	2m	2m	1m
Current Liabilities	176	179	128

S G S UK Ltd
1 Johns Lane Tividale, Oldbury, B69 3HX
Tel: 0121-520 6454 **Fax:** 0121-522 4116
E-mail: admin@sgsuk.com
Website: http://www.sgs.com
Managers: J. Byrne
Ultimate Holding Company: SGS SA (SWITZERLAND)
Immediate Holding Company: SGS UNITED KINGDOM LIMITED
Registration no: 01193985 **Date established:** 1974 **Turnover:** £5m - £10m
No.of Employees: 21 - 50 **Product Groups:** 44, 54, 84, 85

Date of Accounts	Dec 11	Dec 10	Dec 09
Sales Turnover	101m	90m	97m
Pre Tax Profit/Loss	19m	7m	10m
Working Capital	8m	8m	12m
Fixed Assets	32m	27m	22m
Current Assets	34m	29m	35m
Current Liabilities	20m	18m	14m

Samuel Groves
Station Road Western Road, Oldbury, B69 4LY
Tel: 0121-569 7900 **Fax:** 0121-523 2924
E-mail: sales@samuelgroves.co.uk
Website: http://www.samuelgroves.co.uk
Bank(s): Lloyds TSB Bank plc
Directors: M. Cahill (Fin)
Managers: T. Wilkinson (Personnel), P. Boardman (Sales & Mktg Mg), J. Brain (Purch Mgr)
Immediate Holding Company: MIDLAND WALLBOARDS LIMITED
Registration no: 00149246 **VAT No.:** GB 109 3383 75
Date established: 1999 **Turnover:** £5m - £10m **No.of Employees:** 21 - 50
Product Groups: 30, 36, 40, 48, 63

Date of Accounts	Jun 11	Jun 10	Jun 09
Working Capital	20	20	20
Current Assets	20	20	20

Sca Packaging Oldbury Heavy Duty Division (Industrial Division)
Unit A Rood End Road, Oldbury, B69 4HT
Tel: 0121-552 0696 **Fax:** 0121-552 0623
E-mail: david.sanders@sca.com
Website: http://www.sca.com
Managers: D. Sanders (Mgr)
Registration no: 00053913 **No.of Employees:** 11 - 20
Product Groups: 27, 28, 30, 49

Schoeller-Bleckmann UK
European Business Pk Taylors La, Oldbury, B69 2BN
Tel: 0121-552 1535 **Fax:** 0121-627 9282
E-mail: sales@schoeller-bleckmann.co.uk
Website: http://www.schoeller-bleckmann.co.uk
Bank(s): Barclays
Directors: R. Morgan (MD)
Managers: K. Taylor (Mgr), R. Coates (Mgr)
Ultimate Holding Company: Voest Alpine
Immediate Holding Company: Bohler Uddeholm UK Ltd
Registration no: 02819214 **VAT No.:** GB 610 9847 36 003
Date established: 1993 **Turnover:** £10m - £20m
No.of Employees: 21 - 50 **Product Groups:** 36

Date of Accounts	Mar 10	Mar 09	Mar 08
Sales Turnover	13m	18m	21m
Pre Tax Profit/Loss	1m	930	2m
Working Capital	3m	4m	3m
Fixed Assets	N/A	167	192
Current Assets	3m	9m	10m
Current Liabilities	N/A	792	1m

Sheetmetal Machinery Service & Sales Ltd
92 Bristnall Hall Lane, Oldbury, B68 9PB
Tel: 0121-544 1444 **Fax:** 0121-544 1244
Directors: M. Evans (Fin)
Immediate Holding Company: SHEETMETAL MACHINERY SERVICE & SALES LIMITED
Registration no: 02736910 **Date established:** 1992
No.of Employees: 1 - 10 **Product Groups:** 46

Date of Accounts	Aug 11	Aug 10	Aug 09
Working Capital	4	13	20
Fixed Assets	1	1	1
Current Assets	35	42	50

Signature Ltd
51 Hainge Road Tividale, Oldbury, B69 2NF
Tel: 0121-557 0234 **Fax:** 0121-557 0995
E-mail: sales@signatureltd.com
Website: http://www.signatureltd.com
Directors: R. Land (Dir)
Managers: V. O'Brien (Comptroller), E. Gumbley (Sales Prom Mgr), R. Benson, D. Spiteri (Purch Mgr)
Ultimate Holding Company: PLASTIC OMNIUM SA (FRANCE)
Immediate Holding Company: SIGNATURE LIMITED
Registration no: 01645551 **VAT No.:** GB 369 7775 77
Date established: 1982 **Turnover:** £5m - £10m
No.of Employees: 51 - 100 **Product Groups:** 30, 39

Date of Accounts	Dec 11	Dec 10	Dec 09
Sales Turnover	11m	10m	10m
Pre Tax Profit/Loss	1m	1m	1m
Working Capital	1m	607	2m
Fixed Assets	8m	8m	5m
Current Assets	5m	5m	7m
Current Liabilities	1m	2m	1m

A Smith Sandwell Ltd
Unit 2c Union Road, Oldbury, B69 3EU
Tel: 0121-544 6575 **Fax:** 0121-552 1537
E-mail: asmithsandwell@yahoo.co.uk
Website: http://www.sandwellsteels.ffnet.co.uk
Directors: M. Jones (MD)
Immediate Holding Company: A. SMITH (SANDWELL) LIMITED
Registration no: 01422336 **VAT No.:** GB 333 0819 78
Date established: 1979 **Turnover:** £500,000 - £1m
No.of Employees: 1 - 10 **Product Groups:** 66

Date of Accounts	Sep 11	Sep 10	Sep 09
Working Capital	-37	-43	-65
Fixed Assets	15	23	26
Current Assets	62	72	144

N Smith Ltd

Hainge Road Tividale, Oldbury, B69 2NZ
Tel: 0121-557 1891 **Fax:** 0121-521 5700
E-mail: sales@nsmithbox.co.uk
Website: http://www.nsmithbox.co.uk
Bank(s): National Westminster Bank Plc
Directors: A. Loynes (Fin), M. Loynes (MD)
Ultimate Holding Company: GOLDENCRESS ASSOCIATES LIMITED
Immediate Holding Company: N.SMITH & COMPANY LIMITED
Registration no: 00190120 **VAT No.:** GB 276 8190 22
Date established: 2023 **Turnover:** £2m - £5m **No.of Employees:** 21 - 50
Product Groups: 27

Date of Accounts	Mar 12	Mar 11	Mar 10
Working Capital	12	-78	-102
Fixed Assets	764	779	865
Current Assets	1m	990	904

Stephens Gaskets Ltd (Incorporating S J Feasey Ltd)

Unit 1-4 Portway Road Industrial Estate Alston Road, Oldbury, B69 2PP
Tel: 0121-544 5808 **Fax:** 0121-544 4188
E-mail: sales@stephensgaskets.co.uk
Website: http://www.stephensgaskets.co.uk
Bank(s): HSBC Bank plc
Directors: R. Baynton (Dir)
Managers: P. Baynton (Sales Prom Mgr)
Immediate Holding Company: STEPHENS GASKETS LIMITED
Registration no: 00433304 **Date established:** 1947 **Turnover:** £1m - £2m
No.of Employees: 21 - 50 **Product Groups:** 22, 23, 24, 25, 27, 29, 30, 33, 34, 35, 36, 37, 40, 45, 46, 47, 48, 84

Date of Accounts	Mar 12	Mar 11	Mar 10
Working Capital	659	543	352
Fixed Assets	109	123	91
Current Assets	1m	797	583

Style International Ltd

Unit 1 Gregston Industrial Estate Birmingham Road, Oldbury, B69 4EX
Tel: 0121-665 3870 **Fax:** 0845-076 0079
E-mail: info@naturalrugstore.co.uk
Website: http://www.naturalrugstore.co.uk
Directors: L. Darlington (Prop)
Immediate Holding Company: STYLE INTERNATIONAL LIMITED
Registration no: 05728357 **Date established:** 2006
Turnover: Up to £250,000 **No.of Employees:** 1 - 10 **Product Groups:** 23

Date of Accounts	Mar 11	Mar 10	Mar 09
Working Capital	2	10	10
Current Assets	64	101	77

T C L Scaffolding

31 Oakdale Road, Oldbury, B68 8AZ
Tel: 0121-533 0439
Website: http://www.tclscaffolding.co.uk
Directors: T. Peacock (Ptnr)
No.of Employees: 1 - 10 **Product Groups:** 35, 52, 66, 83

Taylor Special Steels Ltd

Unit 1-2 Pearsall Drive, Oldbury, B69 2RA
Tel: 0121-552 2741 **Fax:** 0121-511 1240
E-mail: accounts@taylorspecialsteels.co.uk
Website: http://www.taylorspecialsteels.co.uk
Bank(s): HSBC Bank plc
Managers: A. Brentnall (Sales Prom Mgr), D. Hastings (Chief Acct)
Immediate Holding Company: TAYLOR SPECIAL STEELS LIMITED
Registration no: 02542464 **VAT No.:** GB 547 5319 26
Date established: 1990 **Turnover:** £5m - £10m **No.of Employees:** 11 - 20
Product Groups: 34

Date of Accounts	Dec 11	Dec 10	Dec 09
Working Capital	388	152	73
Fixed Assets	456	362	346
Current Assets	3m	3m	2m
Current Liabilities	1m	1m	756

Truscanian Foundries Ltd

St Martins Industrial Estate Engine Street, Oldbury, B69 4NL
Tel: 0121-552 3011 **Fax:** 0121-552 4672
E-mail: graham@truscanian.co.uk
Website: http://www.truscanian.co.uk
Bank(s): Lloyds
Directors: G. Shore (MD)
Ultimate Holding Company: TRUSCANIAN LIMITED
Immediate Holding Company: TRUSCANIAN LIMITED
Registration no: 04872978 **VAT No.:** GB 369 5914 02
Date established: 2003 **Turnover:** £1m - £2m **No.of Employees:** 11 - 20
Product Groups: 34, 48

Date of Accounts	Sep 11	Sep 10	Sep 09
Working Capital	-58	120	120
Fixed Assets	254	254	254
Current Assets	N/A	120	120

Uddeholm Steel Stockholders

European Business Park Taylors Lane, Oldbury, B69 2BN
Tel: 0121-552 5530 **Fax:** 0121-544 3036
E-mail: sales@uddeholm.co.uk
Website: http://www.uddeholm.com
Bank(s): Barclays
Directors: T. Gowan (MD)
Managers: P. Nash (Tech Serv Mgr), B. Smith (Personnel)
Ultimate Holding Company: VOEST-ALPINE AG (AUSTRIA)
Immediate Holding Company: BOHLER-UDDEHOLM (UK) LIMITED
Registration no: 00229550 **VAT No.:** GB 610 9847 36
Date established: 2028 **Turnover:** £20m - £50m
No.of Employees: 51 - 100 **Product Groups:** 34, 35, 44

Date of Accounts	Mar 12	Mar 11	Mar 10
Sales Turnover	71m	52m	27m
Pre Tax Profit/Loss	4m	4m	2m
Working Capital	10m	11m	5m
Fixed Assets	4m	4m	5m
Current Assets	40m	31m	24m
Current Liabilities	5m	3m	2m

Universal Boltforgers Ltd

Unit 28 Dudley Road West Tividale, Oldbury, B69 2PJ
Tel: 0121-522 5950 **Fax:** 0121-520 5333
E-mail: paul@universal-boltforgers.co.uk
Website: http://www.universal-boltforgers.co.uk
Bank(s): Barclays
Directors: P. Watkins (MD), S. Bailey (Fin)
Immediate Holding Company: UNIVERSAL BOLTFORGERS LIMITED
Registration no: 01525523 **VAT No.:** GB 351 5120 94
Date established: 1980 **Turnover:** £1m - £2m **No.of Employees:** 21 - 50
Product Groups: 35

Date of Accounts	Dec 11	Dec 10	Dec 09
Working Capital	-18	-18	15
Fixed Assets	75	63	79
Current Assets	426	432	510

Wellman Thermal Services Ltd (a Wellman Thermal Products Company)

Newfield Road, Oldbury, B69 3ET
Tel: 0121-543 0000 **Fax:** 0121-543 0199
E-mail: info@wellman-thermal.com
Website: http://www.wellman-thermal.com
Bank(s): National Westminster
Directors: G. Shannon (Fin), G. Shannon (Fin)
Managers: A. Baillie (Tech Serv Mgr), M. Elleston (Personnel), S. Watson, J. Hawkins (Sales & Mktg Mg), J. Beagley
Ultimate Holding Company: INMED VENTURES LIMITED (GIBRALTAR)
Immediate Holding Company: WELLMAN THERMAL PRODUCTS LIMITED
Registration no: 04594328 **VAT No.:** GB 276 4737 22
Date established: 2002 **Turnover:** £10m - £20m
No.of Employees: 101 - 250 **Product Groups:** 36, 40, 42

Date of Accounts	Dec 10	Dec 09	Dec 08
Sales Turnover	18m	24m	32m
Pre Tax Profit/Loss	-900	-589	51
Working Capital	2m	5m	4m
Fixed Assets	463	833	3m
Current Assets	8m	13m	12m
Current Liabilities	4m	6m	4m

West Mercia Fork Truck Services Ltd

23 Hainge Road Tividale, Oldbury, B69 2NR
Tel: 0121-522 2211 **Fax:** 0121-557 2665
E-mail: sales@westmercia.co.uk
Website: http://www.westmercia.co.uk
Directors: D. Pugh (MD), K. Pugh (Sales)
Immediate Holding Company: WEST MERCIA FORK TRUCK SERVICE LTD
Registration no: SC051867 **Date established:** 1971 **Turnover:** £2m - £5m
No.of Employees: 21 - 50 **Product Groups:** 45, 48, 67, 83

Rowley Regis

Air & Liquid Filtration Ltd

Long Meadow Rowley Village, Rowley Regis, B65 9EN
Tel: 0121-559 1638 **Fax:** 0121-559 7204
E-mail: enquiries@filters-uk.com
Website: http://www.filters-uk.com
Directors: K. Gibbins (MD), R. Danks (Fin)
Immediate Holding Company: AIR & LIQUID FILTRATION LIMITED
Registration no: 00563608 **Date established:** 1956
Turnover: £250,000 - £500,000 **No.of Employees:** 1 - 10
Product Groups: 42

Date of Accounts	Apr 12	Apr 11	Apr 10
Working Capital	79	105	64
Fixed Assets	2	3	2
Current Assets	109	136	85

Aprilia Birmingham

78 Oldbury Road, Rowley Regis, B65 0JS
Tel: 0121-559 6023 **Fax:** 0121-559 4256
Website: http://www.speedaway.co.uk
Directors: S. Bastable (MD)
Immediate Holding Company: MOTO SPEEDAWAY LLP
Date established: 2010 **No.of Employees:** 11 - 20 **Product Groups:** 39, 40

Birmingham Garage & Industrial Doors Ltd

Griffin Industrial Estate, Rowley Regis, B65 0SN
Tel: 0121-559 8666 **Fax:** 0121-561 5373
E-mail: sales@bgid.co.uk
Website: http://www.bgid.co.uk
Bank(s): National Westminster Bank Plc
Directors: J. Foulds (Dir), P. Fitzpatrick (Fin)
Managers: B. Righton (Sales & Mktg Mg), P. Doswell
Immediate Holding Company: BIRMINGHAM GARAGE & INDUSTRIAL DOORS LIMITED
Registration no: 01404492 **VAT No.:** GB 600 2674 10
Date established: 1978 **Turnover:** £1m - £2m **No.of Employees:** 21 - 50
Product Groups: 35, 36

Date of Accounts	Dec 11	Dec 10	Dec 09
Working Capital	305	209	108
Fixed Assets	504	510	546
Current Assets	848	652	544

Cube Precision Engineering Ltd

Cakemore Road, Rowley Regis, B65 0QW
Tel: 0121-559 3096 **Fax:** 0121-561 5661
E-mail: enquiries@cubeprecision.co.uk
Website: http://www.cubeprecision.co.uk
Bank(s): HSBC Bank plc
Directors: D. Workman (Fin), N. Clifton (MD)
Ultimate Holding Company: WEST MIDLAND FORM TOOLS LIMITED
Immediate Holding Company: CLIFTON PRECISION TOOLS LIMITED
Registration no: 02375947 **VAT No.:** GB 729 8574 78
Date established: 1989 **Turnover:** £2m - £5m **No.of Employees:** 21 - 50
Product Groups: 46, 48

Date of Accounts	May 07	May 06	May 05
Working Capital	8	-341	21
Fixed Assets	137	199	299
Current Assets	673	882	923

D T M

Unit 9 Griffin Industrial Estate Penncricket Lane, Rowley Regis, B65 0SN
Tel: 0121-559 8431 **Fax:** 0121-559 7551
E-mail: info@dtmfab.co.uk
Directors: J. Hoskins (Prop)
Immediate Holding Company: D.T.M FABRICATIONS LIMITED
Registration no: 05079329 **Date established:** 2004
No.of Employees: 1 - 10 **Product Groups:** 35

Date of Accounts	Mar 11	Mar 10	Mar 09
Working Capital	N/A	-1	-4
Fixed Assets	N/A	1	3
Current Assets	42	38	52

Decma Ltd

9 J A S Industrial Park Titford Lane, Rowley Regis, B65 0PY
Tel: 0121-561 4906 **Fax:** 0121-561 3249
E-mail: decma_ltd@hotmail.com
Website: http://www.worleyholdings.com
Directors: S. Gould (MD)
Ultimate Holding Company: WARLEY HOLDINGS LIMITED
Immediate Holding Company: DECMA LIMITED
Registration no: 01740679 **Date established:** 1983 **Turnover:** £1m - £2m
No.of Employees: 51 - 100 **Product Groups:** 48

Date of Accounts	Apr 12	Apr 11	Apr 10
Working Capital	245	230	250
Fixed Assets	79	79	54
Current Assets	372	397	381

Doulton Doors Ltd

Doulton Trading Estate, Rowley Regis, B65 8JQ
Tel: 01384-413331 **Fax:** 01384-569484
E-mail: tony@doultondoors.co.uk
Website: http://www.doultondoors.co.uk
Directors: T. Binner (MD)
Immediate Holding Company: DOULTON DOORS LIMITED
Registration no: 06200999 **Date established:** 2007 **Turnover:** £2m - £5m
No.of Employees: 1 - 10 **Product Groups:** 26, 35

Date of Accounts	Mar 12	Mar 11	Mar 09
Working Capital	-10	-8	-8
Fixed Assets	31	34	43
Current Assets	49	26	13

Emi-Mec Ltd

Unit E2 Doulton Trading Estate Doulton Road, Rowley Regis, B65 8JQ
Tel: 01384-633968 **Fax:** 01384-633946
E-mail: sales@emi-mec.eu
Website: http://www.emi-mec.eu
Directors: J. Oliver (MD)
Immediate Holding Company: EMI-MEC LIMITED
Registration no: 06247936 **Date established:** 2007
Turnover: £250,000 - £500,000 **No.of Employees:** 1 - 10
Product Groups: 46, 48

Excelsior Lifts

334-336 Oldbury Road, Rowley Regis, B65 0QJ
Tel: 0121-559 4831 **Fax:** 0121-559 6384
Website: http://www.excelsior-lifts.co.uk
Directors: J. Goodey (Dir)
Date established: 1992 **No.of Employees:** 1 - 10 **Product Groups:** 35, 39, 45

G B Springs Ltd

Hawes Lane, Rowley Regis, B65 9AL
Tel: 07768-551326 **Fax:** 0121-559 5637
Directors: P. Stone (Fin)
Registration no: 03702966 **Date established:** 1999
No.of Employees: 1 - 10 **Product Groups:** 35, 66

Grasam Samson Ltd

Unit E1 Doulton Trading Estate Doulton Road, Rowley Regis, B65 8JQ
Tel: 01384-634162 **Fax:** 01384-568051
E-mail: sales@grasamsamson.co.uk
Directors: G. Phillips (MD)
Immediate Holding Company: GRASAM SAMSON LIMITED
Registration no: 01015901 **VAT No.:** GB 278 1850 29
Date established: 1971 **Turnover:** £250,000 - £500,000
No.of Employees: 1 - 10 **Product Groups:** 66, 67

Date of Accounts	Apr 11	Apr 10	Apr 09
Working Capital	642	598	573
Fixed Assets	76	75	78
Current Assets	711	656	638

H & H Alloy Sales Ltd

J A S Industrial Park Titford Lane, Rowley Regis, B65 0PY
Tel: 0121-559 6466 **Fax:** 0121-559 8723
E-mail: mark.hilsdon@warleyholdings.co.uk
Website: http://www.warleyholdings.co.uk
Directors: A. Hilsdon (MD), M. Hilsdon (Dir)
Ultimate Holding Company: WARLEY HOLDINGS LIMITED
Immediate Holding Company: H. & H. ALLOY SALES LIMITED
Registration no: 01418949 **Date established:** 1979 **Turnover:** £5m - £10m
No.of Employees: 21 - 50 **Product Groups:** 35, 39, 66

Date of Accounts	Apr 12	Apr 11	Apr 10
Working Capital	151	-58	112
Fixed Assets	244	177	207
Current Assets	912	682	828
Current Liabilities	46	102	55

Impact Metal Services Ltd

Unit 3 Phoenix Park Industrial Estate Station Road, Rowley Regis, B65 0JY
Tel: 0121-561 2030 **Fax:** 0121-561 1158
E-mail: chris@impactmetal.co.uk
Website: http://www.impactmetal.co.uk
Managers: C. Potter (Mgr)
Immediate Holding Company: IMPACT METAL SERVICES LIMITED
Registration no: 01838879 **VAT No.:** GB 428 7567 13
Date established: 1984 **Turnover:** £1m - £2m **No.of Employees:** 1 - 10
Product Groups: 34, 35, 36

Date of Accounts	Jan 12	Jan 11	Jan 10
Working Capital	84	87	95
Fixed Assets	36	21	23
Current Assets	636	496	474

Keytracker Ltd

Station Road Industrial Estate Station Road, Rowley Regis, B65 0JY
Tel: 0121-559 9000 **Fax:** 0121-559 9000
E-mail: sales@keytracker.com
Website: http://www.keytracker.com
Managers: A. Smith (Chief Mgr)
Immediate Holding Company: KEYTRACKER LIMITED
Registration no: 03271557 **Date established:** 1996
No.of Employees: 1 - 10 **Product Groups:** 30, 35, 36, 40, 81

Date of Accounts	Apr 11	Apr 10	Apr 09
Working Capital	-42	-61	-61
Fixed Assets	278	240	238
Current Assets	339	305	161

M T M Ltd

Unit 1-9 Waterside Industrial Estate Doulton Road, Rowley Regis, B65 8JG
Tel: 01384-633321 **Fax:** 01384-565782
E-mail: sales@mtm.ltd.uk
Website: http://www.mtm.ltd.uk
Bank(s): National Westminster Bank Plc
Directors: D. Clarke Brereton (Dir)
Managers: G. Gutteridge (Mgr)
Ultimate Holding Company: DP PARTNERSHIP LIMITED
Immediate Holding Company: MAWSON TRITON MOULDINGS LIMITED
Registration no: 04451433 **VAT No.:** GB 747 8896 54
Date established: 2002 **Turnover:** £5m - £10m
No.of Employees: 51 - 100 **Product Groups:** 30, 48, 66

Midland Brakes Ltd

4 Station Road Industrial Estate Station Road, Rowley Regis, B65 0JY
Tel: 0121-561 2212 **Fax:** 0121-561 2285
E-mail: office@midlandbrakes.com
Website: http://www.midlandbrakes.com
Directors: V. Burgess (MD)
Immediate Holding Company: MIDLAND BRAKES (PROPERTIES) LIMITED
Registration no: 01169363 **Date established:** 1974
No.of Employees: 1 - 10 **Product Groups:** 35, 45

Date of Accounts	Apr 11	Apr 10	Apr 09
Working Capital	64	87	-32
Fixed Assets	162	162	220
Current Assets	82	101	393

B A Overton

8 Saxon Drive, Rowley Regis, B65 9RD
Tel: 0121-559 6459
Directors: B. Overton (Prop), A. Overton (Prop)
Immediate Holding Company: KINGDOMCREST LIMITED
Registration no: 03039261 **Date established:** 1995
No.of Employees: 1 - 10 **Product Groups:** 37, 40, 48

Date of Accounts	Mar 11	Mar 10	Mar 09
Working Capital	18	43	73
Fixed Assets	1	1	1
Current Assets	114	146	148

Simark Engineering Co.

Griffin Industrial Estate, Rowley Regis, B65 0SN
Tel: 0121-559 1351 **Fax:** 0121-559 3205
E-mail: sales@simarkengineering.co.uk
Website: http://www.simarkengineering.co.uk
Directors: P. Mccann (Dir), K. McCann (Co Sec)
Immediate Holding Company: SIMARK ENGINEERING COMPANY LIMITED
Registration no: 06248104 **Date established:** 2007
No.of Employees: 11 - 20 **Product Groups:** 35, 39, 45

Thomas Howse Ltd

Cakemore Road, Rowley Regis, B65 0RD
Tel: 0121-559 1451 **Fax:** 0121-559 2722
E-mail: sales@howsepaints.co.uk
Website: http://www.howsepaints.co.uk
Bank(s): Barclays, West Bromwich
Directors: A. Greenfield (Fin), E. Greenfield (Ch)
Immediate Holding Company: THOMAS HOWSE,LIMITED
Registration no: 00109575 **VAT No.:** GB 276 9066 18
Date established: 2010 **Turnover:** £2m - £5m **No.of Employees:** 21 - 50
Product Groups: 32

Date of Accounts	Dec 11	Dec 10	Dec 09
Working Capital	1m	1m	1m
Fixed Assets	623	633	541
Current Assets	2m	2m	2m

Three Pears Ltd

Unit 6 Station Road Industrial Estate Station Road, Rowley Regis, B65 0JY
Tel: 0121-559 5351 **Fax:** 0121-559 5353
E-mail: edunn@btconnect.com
Website: http://www.threepears.co.uk
Bank(s): Lloyds TSB Bank plc
Directors: K. Tonks (Co Sec), E. Dunn (MD)
Ultimate Holding Company: THREE PEARS HOLDINGS LIMITED
Immediate Holding Company: THREE PEARS LIMITED
Registration no: 01107147 **Date established:** 1973
Turnover: £10m - £20m **No.of Employees:** 11 - 20 **Product Groups:** 63

Date of Accounts	Feb 12	Feb 11	Feb 10
Sales Turnover	11m	11m	12m
Pre Tax Profit/Loss	79	86	104
Working Capital	2m	1m	1m
Fixed Assets	907	1m	1m
Current Assets	3m	3m	2m
Current Liabilities	40	27	82

Truck & Trailer Equipment Ltd

Dial House 37-39 Hawes Lane, Rowley Regis, B65 9AL
Tel: 0121-559 7711 **Fax:** 0121-559 5637
E-mail: sales@trucktrailerequip.co.uk
Website: http://www.trucktrailerequip.co.uk
Managers: J. Keeling (Mgr)
Ultimate Holding Company: E.M.S. (TRUCK AND TRAILER PARTS) LIMITED
Immediate Holding Company: TRUCK & TRAILER EQUIPMENT LIMITED
Registration no: 05649281 **VAT No.:** GB 281 3235 74
Date established: 2005 **No.of Employees:** 1 - 10 **Product Groups:** 39, 68

Date of Accounts	Jul 11	Jul 10	Jul 09
Working Capital	214	152	124
Fixed Assets	100	28	32
Current Assets	626	568	455

Smethwick

2 Sisters Food Group

Unit 3 Bevan Way, Smethwick, B66 1AW
Tel: 08704-589700 **Fax:** 0870-4589911
Website: http://www.2sfg.co.uk
Directors: M. Glanfield (Fin), R. Coomar (MD), R. Gitsingh (MD)
Immediate Holding Company: LLOYD MAUNDER LIMITED
Registration no: 00234992 **Date established:** 1928
No.of Employees: 101 - 250 **Product Groups:** 01, 20, 84

Albion Hose Ltd

Albion Works Alma Street, Smethwick, B66 2RL
Tel: 0121-565 4103 **Fax:** 0121-558 7220
E-mail: sales@albionhose.co.uk
Website: http://www.albionhose.co.uk
Bank(s): Barclays, High Street, West Bromwich
Directors: D. West (MD), P. Feasey (Co Sec)
Immediate Holding Company: ALBION HOSE LIMITED
Registration no: 01733698 **Date established:** 1983 **Turnover:** £1m - £2m
No.of Employees: 11 - 20 **Product Groups:** 29, 30

Date of Accounts	Dec 11	Dec 10	Dec 09
Working Capital	13	-471	-141
Fixed Assets	615	831	468
Current Assets	955	720	654

W & S Allely Ltd (Head Office)

Alma Street, Smethwick, B66 2RL
Tel: 0121-558 3301 **Fax:** 0121-555 5194
E-mail: sales@allely.co.uk
Website: http://www.allely.co.uk
Bank(s): Lloyds TSB Bank plc
Directors: M. Whitmore (Dir), J. Hollies (Fin)
Ultimate Holding Company: ALLELY EDEN HOLDINGS LIMITED
Immediate Holding Company: W. & S. ALLELY LIMITED
Registration no: 00292572 **VAT No.:** GB 547 6741 12
Date established: 1934 **Turnover:** £10m - £20m
No.of Employees: 11 - 20 **Product Groups:** 34, 37, 49, 66

Date of Accounts	Dec 11	Dec 10	Dec 09
Working Capital	465	401	371
Fixed Assets	22	25	43
Current Assets	3m	2m	2m
Current Liabilities	N/A	N/A	166

Allied Rubber Products P J Donnelly Rubber Ltd

15 Cornwall Road Industrial Park, Smethwick, B66 2JT
Tel: 0121-565 0961 **Fax:** 0121-565 0976
Bank(s): National Westminster Bank Plc
Directors: A. Donnelly (MD)
Immediate Holding Company: ALLIED RUBBER PRODUCTS & ENGINEERING COMPANY LIMITED
Registration no: 03309811 **Date established:** 1997
No.of Employees: 11 - 20 **Product Groups:** 29

Ansul Fabrication

Downing Street, Smethwick, B66 2JL
Tel: 0121-565 3108 **Fax:** 0121-558 1339
E-mail: ansulfabricationsuk@tyco-valves.com
Website: http://www.tyco-bspd.com
Directors: P. Clarke (MD)
Managers: P. Clarke (Mgr)
Registration no: 02857339 **Date established:** 1993
Turnover: £250,000 - £500,000 **No.of Employees:** 21 - 50
Product Groups: 48

Ash & Lacy Perforators Ltd

PO Box 58, Smethwick, B66 2RP
Tel: 0121-565 8000 **Fax:** 0121-565 1354
E-mail: dnock@ashlacyperf.co.uk
Website: http://www.ashlacyperf.co.uk
Bank(s): Lloyds TSB Bank plc
Directors: M. Baker (Chief Op Offcr), J. Keating (MD), D. Nock (Dir), D. Nock (Sales & Mktg)
Managers: D. Collinson (Purch Mgr)
Immediate Holding Company: ASH & LACY PERFORATORS LIMITED
Registration no: 00529602 **Date established:** 1954 **Turnover:** £5m - £10m
No.of Employees: 51 - 100 **Product Groups:** 30, 33, 34, 35, 45, 48

Date of Accounts	Dec 10	Dec 09	Dec 08
Sales Turnover	6m	7m	10m
Pre Tax Profit/Loss	59	-575	-228
Working Capital	3m	3m	2m
Fixed Assets	745	1m	3m
Current Assets	5m	5m	5m
Current Liabilities	569	650	300

Atlas Metals Ltd

Cranford Street, Smethwick, B66 2RX
Tel: 0121-555 5000 **Fax:** 0121-558 8600
E-mail: atlasmetalsltd@msn.com
Directors: J. Cartmill (MD), S. McCann (Fin)
Immediate Holding Company: ATLAS METALS LIMITED
Registration no: 01326250 **Date established:** 1977
No.of Employees: 1 - 10 **Product Groups:** 66

Date of Accounts	Jun 11	Jun 10	Jun 09
Working Capital	365	454	507
Fixed Assets	878	820	868
Current Assets	754	825	799

Aurubis UK Ltd

Unit 6 Rabone Park, Smethwick, B66 2NN
Tel: 0121-555 1199 **Fax:** 0121-555 1188
E-mail: b.middleton@aurubis.co.uk
Website: http://www.aurubis.co.uk
Directors: P. Tromans (Fin), B. Middleton (MD)
Immediate Holding Company: AURUBIS UK LTD
Registration no: 05169749 **Date established:** 2004
Turnover: £20m - £50m **No.of Employees:** 21 - 50 **Product Groups:** 34, 35, 66

Date of Accounts	Sep 11	Sep 10	Sep 09
Sales Turnover	29m	25m	15m
Pre Tax Profit/Loss	271	349	-236
Working Capital	859	486	58
Fixed Assets	739	943	1m
Current Assets	10m	11m	6m
Current Liabilities	4m	5m	325

Avery Berkel Ab Ltd

Foundry Lane, Smethwick, B66 2LP
Tel: 08709-034343 **Fax:** 0121-555 6062
Website: http://www.averyweigh-tronix.com
Directors: E. Ufland (Dir), J. Ghuman (Fin)
Managers: C. Taylor (Tech Serv Mgr)
Ultimate Holding Company: ILLINOIS TOOL WORKS INC (USA)
Immediate Holding Company: AVERY WEIGH-TRONIX LIMITED
Registration no: 00595129 **Date established:** 1957
Turnover: £20m - £50m **No.of Employees:** 501 - 1000
Product Groups: 38, 42

Date of Accounts	Dec 11	Nov 10	Nov 09
Sales Turnover	48m	45m	48m
Pre Tax Profit/Loss	-2m	3m	3m
Working Capital	15m	14m	11m
Fixed Assets	4m	5m	6m
Current Assets	76m	75m	84m
Current Liabilities	9m	8m	9m

Avery Weigh-Tronix Ltd

Soho Foundry Foundry Lane, Smethwick, B66 2LP
Tel: 08459-002244 **Fax:** 0870-900 0366
E-mail: info@awtxglobal.com
Website: http://www.averyweigh-tronix.com
Bank(s): Midland, West Bromwich
Directors: P. Branston (MD)
Ultimate Holding Company: ILLINOIS TOOL WORKS INC (USA)
Immediate Holding Company: AVERY WEIGH-TRONIX LIMITED
Registration no: 00595129 **VAT No.:** GB 239 3550 53
Date established: 1957 **Turnover:** £20m - £50m
No.of Employees: 251 - 500 **Product Groups:** 38

Date of Accounts	Dec 11	Nov 10	Nov 09
Sales Turnover	48m	45m	48m
Pre Tax Profit/Loss	-2m	3m	3m
Working Capital	15m	14m	11m
Fixed Assets	4m	5m	6m
Current Assets	76m	75m	84m
Current Liabilities	9m	8m	9m

Ayrshire Metal Products plc

41 Anne Road, Smethwick, B66 2NZ
Tel: 0121-558 7739 **Fax:** 0121-558 7772
E-mail: martin.brown@ayrshire.co.uk
Website: http://www.ayrshire.co.uk
Bank(s): The Royal Bank of Scotland
Directors: M. Brown (MD)
Immediate Holding Company: AYRSHIRE METAL PRODUCTS PUBLIC LIMITED COMPANY
Registration no: SC006517 **Date established:** 2007
No.of Employees: 11 - 20 **Product Groups:** 34

Date of Accounts	Dec 11	Dec 10	Dec 09
Sales Turnover	23m	23m	19m
Pre Tax Profit/Loss	1m	448	534
Working Capital	5m	5m	5m
Fixed Assets	2m	2m	2m
Current Assets	9m	10m	8m
Current Liabilities	3m	2m	1m

Bearwood Builders Supply Co Smethwick Ltd

Three Shires Oak Road, Smethwick, B67 5BS
Tel: 0121-429 2011 **Fax:** 0121-429 2226
Directors: J. Reece (Dir)
Immediate Holding Company: BEARWOOD BUILDERS SUPPLY CO. (SMETHWICK) LIMITED
Registration no: 00509932 **Date established:** 1952
Turnover: £500,000 - £1m **No.of Employees:** 1 - 10 **Product Groups:** 25, 66

Date of Accounts	Dec 11	Dec 10	Dec 09
Working Capital	-90	17	105
Fixed Assets	1m	1m	950
Current Assets	389	500	613

Benteler Distribution Ltd

Unit 6b Heath Street Industrial Estate, Smethwick, B66 2QZ
Tel: 0121-555 6161 **Fax:** 0121-555 6176
E-mail: info@perchcourt.co.uk
Website: http://www.benteler-distribution.co.uk
Directors: C. Cook (MD), C. Cooke (Dir), J. Busby (Dir), K. Mann (Dir)
Managers: R. Thomas (Eng Serv Mgr)
Immediate Holding Company: Perch Realisations Ltd
Registration no: 00456349 **VAT No.:** GB 378 1119 43
Date established: 1980 **Turnover:** £2m - £5m **No.of Employees:** 1 - 10
Product Groups: 66

Date of Accounts	Jul 08	Jul 07	Jul 06
Working Capital	413	321	380
Fixed Assets	449	439	435
Current Assets	1830	2133	1893
Current Liabilities	1417	1811	1513

Birmingham Plastic Recycling (Hartchain Limited)

Bridge Street North, Smethwick, B66 2BJ
Tel: 0121-565 4188 **Fax:** 0121-565 3900
E-mail: johnandritagerry@hotmail.com
Directors: J. Gerry (Dir)
Immediate Holding Company: BIRMINGHAM PLATING COMPANY LTD.
Registration no: 02701529 **Date established:** 1992 **Turnover:** £2m - £5m
No.of Employees: 11 - 20 **Product Groups:** 30, 42, 61, 66

Date of Accounts	Sep 11	Sep 10	Sep 09
Working Capital	1m	765	2m
Fixed Assets	841	859	900
Current Assets	2m	2m	2m

Birmingham Plating Co. Ltd

142 Lewisham Road, Smethwick, B66 2ER
Tel: 0121-558 2341 **Fax:** 0121-558 3923
E-mail: sales@birmingham-plating.co.uk
Website: http://www.birmingham-plating.co.uk
Directors: A. Gakhal (Dir), T. Kelly (Fin)
Managers: G. Edwards (Tech Serv Mgr)
Immediate Holding Company: BIRMINGHAM PLATING COMPANY LTD.
Registration no: 02701529 **Date established:** 1992 **Turnover:** £1m - £2m
No.of Employees: 21 - 50 **Product Groups:** 48

Date of Accounts	Sep 11	Sep 10	Sep 09
Working Capital	1m	765	2m
Fixed Assets	841	859	900
Current Assets	2m	2m	2m

Bonnell Industries

Solar Works Cornwall Road, Smethwick, B66 2JR
Tel: 0121-558 0520 **Fax:** 0121-555 6157
E-mail: info@bonnellonline.co.uk
Website: http://www.bonnellonline.co.uk
Directors: T. Bonnell (Prop)
Immediate Holding Company: BONNELL LIMITED
Registration no: 07463313 **VAT No.:** GB 478 6311 18
Date established: 2010 **Turnover:** £500,000 - £1m
No.of Employees: 11 - 20 **Product Groups:** 38, 48, 67

Date of Accounts	Mar 12
Working Capital	-3
Current Assets	37

D K Rewinds Ltd
23 Cranford Street, Smethwick, B66 2RT
Tel: 0121-555 5532 **Fax:** 0121-558 6251
E-mail: sales@dkrewinds.co.uk
Website: http://www.dkrewinds.co.uk
Directors: K. Bhogal (Co Sec), B. Bhogal (MD), P. Bhogal (Sales)
Immediate Holding Company: D.K. REWINDS LIMITED
Registration no: 01265800 **Date established:** 1976 **Turnover:** £1m - £2m
No.of Employees: 1 - 10 **Product Groups:** 37

Date of Accounts	Jun 11	Jun 10	Jun 09
Working Capital	671	863	476
Fixed Assets	541	567	576
Current Assets	896	1m	801

Direct Manufacturing Supply Co
19 Anne Road, Smethwick, B66 2PJ
Tel: 0121-558 4591 **Fax:** 0121-565 7513
E-mail: kevinh@slemcka.co.uk
Website: http://www.directo.co.uk
Directors: K. Bate (Dir), K. Bates (MD)
Managers: R. Leeson (Purch Mgr)
Immediate Holding Company: METRIC MARKETING LIMITED
Registration no: 00303240 **VAT No.:** GB 300 1984 00
Date established: 1993 **Turnover:** £1m - £2m **No.of Employees:** 1 - 10
Product Groups: 65

Eclipse Sprayers Ltd
120 Beakes Road, Smethwick, B67 5AB
Tel: 0121-420 2494 **Fax:** 0121-429 1668
E-mail: davepennock@btconnect.com
Website: http://www.eclipsesprayers.com
Bank(s): Barclays, Wolverhampton
Directors: D. Pennock (MD), D. Pennock (MD)
Ultimate Holding Company: LONGITUDE ENGINEERING LIMITED
Immediate Holding Company: ECLIPSE SPRAYERS LIMITED
Registration no: 00227588 **VAT No.:** GB 547 4638 15
Date established: 2028 **Turnover:** £500,000 - £1m
No.of Employees: 21 - 50 **Product Groups:** 45

Date of Accounts	Dec 11	Dec 10	Dec 09
Working Capital	346	344	308
Fixed Assets	452	463	479
Current Assets	1m	1m	1m

Gaylee Ltd (t/a Brooks Fork Lift Service)
Pope Street, Smethwick, B66 2JP
Tel: 0121-558 2027 **Fax:** 0121-558 2029
Directors: I. Jones (Fin), R. Jones (Grp Chief Exec), R. Jones (MD)
Immediate Holding Company: GAYLEE LIMITED
Registration no: 00407500 **VAT No.:** GB 276 9339 09
Date established: 1946 **No.of Employees:** 1 - 10 **Product Groups:** 45, 83

Date of Accounts	May 10	May 09	May 08
Working Capital	-40	40	90
Fixed Assets	1	2	3
Current Assets	73	82	140

Goodwin & Price Ltd
Unit 16 Willow Court Crystal Drive, Smethwick, B66 1RD
Tel: 0121-552 3920 **Fax:** 0121-511 1162
E-mail: enquiries@goodwinandprice.co.uk
Website: http://www.goodwinandprice.co.uk
Directors: D. Price (Dir), G. Goodwin (Dir)
Immediate Holding Company: GOODWIN & PRICE LIMITED
Registration no: 01942008 **VAT No.:** GB 488 5182 01
Date established: 1985 **Turnover:** £2m - £5m **No.of Employees:** 21 - 50
Product Groups: 52

Date of Accounts	Mar 12	Mar 11	Mar 10
Working Capital	312	312	284
Fixed Assets	69	64	91
Current Assets	920	1m	1m

Hadley Sections Ltd
PO Box 92, Smethwick, B66 2PA
Tel: 0121-555 1330 **Fax:** 0121-555 1331
E-mail: enquiries@hadleygroup.co.uk
Website: http://www.hadleygroup.co.uk
Bank(s): HSBC, Wolverhampton
Directors: R. Neale (Fin), S. Towe (MD), J. Flynn (Sales), G. Deeley (I.T. Dir)
Managers: D. Linthwaite (Tech Serv Mgr), B. Dunthorne (Sales & Mktg Mg), I. Woolley (Personnel)
Ultimate Holding Company: HADLEY INDUSTRIES PLC
Immediate Holding Company: HADLEY INDUSTRIES HOLDINGS LIMITED
Registration no: 00831538 **VAT No.:** GB 409 4460 54
Date established: 1964 **Turnover:** £50m - £75m
No.of Employees: 251 - 500 **Product Groups:** 48

Date of Accounts	Apr 12	Apr 11	Apr 10
Sales Turnover	80m	75m	61m
Pre Tax Profit/Loss	5m	4m	3m
Working Capital	15m	11m	10m
Fixed Assets	30m	30m	29m
Current Assets	40m	37m	41m
Current Liabilities	4m	4m	4m

Haws Watering Cans
120 Beakes Road, Smethwick, B67 5AB
Tel: 0121-420 2494 **Fax:** 0121-429 1668
E-mail: davepennock@btconnect.com
Website: http://www.haws.co.uk
Bank(s): Barclays P.L.C.
Directors: D. Pennock (Prop), D. Pennock (MD), G. Blocksidge (Co Sec)
Managers: S. Riley (Sales Prom Mgr)
Ultimate Holding Company: LONGITUDE ENGINEERING LIMITED
Immediate Holding Company: ECLIPSE SPRAYERS LIMITED
Registration no: 01639207 **VAT No.:** GB 547 4638 15
Date established: 2028 **Turnover:** £2m - £5m **No.of Employees:** 21 - 50
Product Groups: 30, 36, 41

Date of Accounts	Dec 10	Dec 09	Dec 08
Working Capital	344	308	269
Fixed Assets	463	479	525
Current Assets	1m	1m	821

Heartlands Manufacturing
Alma Street, Smethwick, B66 2RL
Tel: 0121-555 8528 **Fax:** 0121-555 8643
Directors: A. Grant (MD)
Immediate Holding Company: A K TRAVEL LIMITED
Registration no: 04436455 **Date established:** 2004
No.of Employees: 1 - 10 **Product Groups:** 20, 40, 41

Date of Accounts	Dec 07	Dec 06	Dec 05
Working Capital	25	-22	18
Fixed Assets	559	344	171
Current Assets	321	195	165

K C Hickson Ltd
89-91 Rolfe Street, Smethwick, B66 2AY
Tel: 0121-558 1884 **Fax:** 0121-558 0017
E-mail: kchickson@george-jones-engineering.co.uk
Website: http://www.kchickson.com
Directors: A. Guest (MD), S. Hunt (Co Sec)
Ultimate Holding Company: SMETHWICK MAINTENANCE COMPANY LIMITED
Immediate Holding Company: K.C.HICKSON LIMITED
Registration no: 00739627 **VAT No.:** GB 300 2118 40
Date established: 1962 **No.of Employees:** 1 - 10 **Product Groups:** 35, 37, 39, 40, 52

Date of Accounts	Nov 11	Nov 10	Nov 09
Working Capital	-374	-270	-139
Fixed Assets	10	13	18
Current Assets	350	353	275

Incanite Foundries Ltd
Cornwall Road, Smethwick, B66 2JR
Tel: 0121-565 2882 **Fax:** 0121-555 5190
E-mail: sales@incanite.co.uk
Website: http://www.incanite.co.uk
Bank(s): Barclays
Directors: E. Richards (MD), J. Howell (Fin)
Ultimate Holding Company: M & SB LIMITED
Immediate Holding Company: INCANITE FOUNDRIES LIMITED
Registration no: 00167997 **VAT No.:** GB 277 8404 23
Date established: 2020 **Turnover:** £2m - £5m **No.of Employees:** 51 - 100
Product Groups: 34, 36

Date of Accounts	Aug 11	Aug 10	Aug 09
Working Capital	513	425	663
Fixed Assets	30	36	37
Current Assets	1m	803	950

Interlink Express Parcels Ltd
Roebuck Lane, Smethwick, B66 1BY
Tel: 0121-500 2500
E-mail: marketing@geopostuk.com
Website: http://www.interlinkexpress.com
Directors: T. Jones (Mkt Research), S. Mills (Tech Serv), D. Poole (Pers), E. Kerr (Sales)
Managers: D. Adams, M. Hamilton
Ultimate Holding Company: LA POSTE (FRANCE)
Immediate Holding Company: INTERLINK EXPRESS PARCELS LIMITED
Registration no: 01421773 **Date established:** 1979
Turnover: £125m - £250m **No.of Employees:** 1501 & over
Product Groups: 79

Date of Accounts	Dec 08	Jan 10	Jan 11
Sales Turnover	129m	128m	135m
Pre Tax Profit/Loss	15m	15m	15m
Working Capital	17m	20m	21m
Current Assets	27m	29m	31m
Current Liabilities	9m	8m	9m

Isuzu (UK) Ltd
Halfords Lane, Smethwick, B66 1EL
Tel: 0121-500 1720 **Fax:** 0121-500 1721
Website: http://www.isuzu.co.uk
Bank(s): Bank of America NA & Barclays Bank PLC
Directors: A. Edmanston (MD), D. Napier (Co Sec), E. Swatman (Grp Chief Exec), J. Nealon (Mkt Research), P. Kinnaird (MD), P. Williams (I.T. Dir), R. Edmiston (Ch), S. Burton (Sales), J. Tytler (Co Sec)
Managers: M. Forgeham (Buyer)
Ultimate Holding Company: I M Group Ltd
Immediate Holding Company: International Motors Ltd
Registration no: 02064489 **VAT No.:** GB 351 5643 62
Turnover: £20m - £50m **No.of Employees:** 21 - 50 **Product Groups:** 39

J W Rudge & Co. Ltd
Anne Road, Smethwick, B66 2NZ
Tel: 0121-558 5519 **Fax:** 0121-558 0053
E-mail: millssteve@btconnect.com
Bank(s): National Westminster Bank Plc
Directors: S. Mills (MD)
Immediate Holding Company: J.W.RUDGE & CO.LIMITED
Registration no: 00607184 **VAT No.:** GB 110 1455 36
Date established: 1958 **Turnover:** £500,000 - £1m
No.of Employees: 11 - 20 **Product Groups:** 48

Date of Accounts	Mar 11	Mar 10	Mar 08
Working Capital	263	247	232
Fixed Assets	33	41	43
Current Assets	486	464	453
Current Liabilities	N/A	N/A	18

George Jones Engineering Services Ltd
Lionel Works 89-91 Rolfe Street, Smethwick, B66 2AY
Tel: 0121-558 1884 **Fax:** 0121-558 0017
E-mail: sales.georgejonesengservices@zyworld.com
Website: http://www.george-jones-engineering.co.uk
Bank(s): Barclays, High Street
Directors: D. Cooper (Dir), R. Dovey (MD), S. Hunt (Co Sec)
Managers: K. Harvey (Design Eng)
Immediate Holding Company: Smethwick Maintenance Company Ltd
Registration no: 01913091 **VAT No.:** GB 300 2118 40
Date established: 1985 **Turnover:** £500,000 - £1m
No.of Employees: 11 - 20 **Product Groups:** 40, 46, 48, 84

K & K Engineering
Unit 54 The Bridge Trading Estate Bridge Street North, Smethwick, B66 2BZ
Tel: 0121-555 8144 **Fax:** 0121-555 8144
Directors: K. Howen (MD)
Date established: 1990 **No.of Employees:** 1 - 10 **Product Groups:** 35

Komfort Workspace Ltd
Globe House 1 Middlemore Road, Smethwick, B66 2DR
Tel: 0121-555 0333 **Fax:** 0121-555 0301
E-mail: phil.pritchard@komfort.net
Website: http://www.komfort.com
Managers: P. Pritchard (Chief Mgr)
Immediate Holding Company: YULE CATTO & CO. P.L.C.
Registration no: 01111722 **No.of Employees:** 21 - 50 **Product Groups:** 26

L J Grinding Services
3 Smethwick Enterprise Centre Rolfe Street, Smethwick, B66 2AR
Tel: 0121-558 0777 **Fax:** 0121-558 0777
Directors: L. Williams (Prop)
Date established: 1997 **No.of Employees:** 1 - 10 **Product Groups:** 46

La Metals Ltd
Roebuck Lane, Smethwick, B66 1BY
Tel: 0121-553 6846 **Fax:** 0121-553 3270
E-mail: sales@lametals.co.uk
Website: http://www.lametals.co.uk
Bank(s): National Westminster Bank Plc
Directors: M. Withers (Fin)
Managers: J. Mullally (Sales Prom Mgr)
Immediate Holding Company: L.A. METALS LIMITED
Registration no: 02131280 **VAT No.:** GB 462 3406 65
Date established: 1987 **Turnover:** £2m - £5m **No.of Employees:** 11 - 20
Product Groups: 34

Date of Accounts	Jun 11	Jun 10	Jun 09
Working Capital	713	700	679
Fixed Assets	30	35	41
Current Assets	2m	1m	1m

Lancing Linde Creighton Ltd
Radial Point Dartmouth Road, Smethwick, B66 1BG
Tel: 0121-524 3300 **Fax:** 0121-524 3399
E-mail: enquiries@linde-creighton.co.uk
Website: http://www.linde-creighton.co.uk
Directors: R. Hinton (MD), T. Bauld (Sales), D. Woodward (Fin)
Managers: C. Fellows (Sales Admin), J. Roberts (Personnel)
Immediate Holding Company: J.B. LANGFORD & CO. LIMITED
Registration no: 02794355 **Date established:** 1973
Turnover: £10m - £20m **No.of Employees:** 251 - 500
Product Groups: 45, 67

Date of Accounts	Dec 11	Dec 10	Dec 09
Sales Turnover	42m	34m	34m
Pre Tax Profit/Loss	3m	2m	1m
Working Capital	5m	5m	3m
Fixed Assets	6m	6m	8m
Current Assets	19m	19m	15m
Current Liabilities	12m	11m	7m

Linak UK
Actuation House Crystal Drive Sandwell Business Park, Smethwick, B66 1RJ
Tel: 0121-544 2211 **Fax:** 0121-544 2552
E-mail: louisee@linak.co.uk
Website: http://www.linak.co.uk
Bank(s): Nordea Bank Ltd, London
Directors: G. Fellows (Co Sec), M. Palmer (MD)
Managers: J. Turner (Ops Mgr), L. Aris, M. Blake, A. Stock, G. Fellows (Comptroller)
Ultimate Holding Company: FP031284
Immediate Holding Company: LINAK-UK LIMITED
Registration no: 02483800 **VAT No.:** GB 558 8776 67
Date established: 1990 **Turnover:** £10m - £20m
No.of Employees: 21 - 50 **Product Groups:** 26, 35, 37, 38, 40, 41, 42, 45

Date of Accounts	Jun 11	Jun 10	Jun 09
Sales Turnover	10m	11m	12m
Pre Tax Profit/Loss	347	351	384
Working Capital	2m	2m	2m
Fixed Assets	1m	1m	1m
Current Assets	4m	5m	5m
Current Liabilities	715	746	433

Made Of Music
Punjabi Roots Music Centre 7 Tollgate Shopping Centre, High Street, Smethwick, B66 3AP
Tel: 0121-558 1767 **Fax:** 0121-525 0021
E-mail: info@madeofmusic.com
Website: http://www.madeofmusic.com
Directors: T. Seetra (Dir), T. Sehra (Prop)
Turnover: Up to £250,000 **No.of Employees:** 1 - 10 **Product Groups:** 49

Midland Door Services Ltd
Booth Street, Smethwick, B66 2PF
Tel: 0121-565 0022 **Fax:** 0121-565 0055
E-mail: info@mdsind.co.uk
Website: http://www.mdsind.co.uk
Directors: M. Davis (Fin), R. Simmons (I.T. Dir)
Immediate Holding Company: KENRICK DOOR SYSTEMS LIMITED
Registration no: 03420999 **Date established:** 1997
No.of Employees: 21 - 50 **Product Groups:** 35

Date of Accounts	Apr 07	Apr 06	Apr 05
Working Capital	15	-45	-48
Fixed Assets	241	152	138
Current Assets	2m	1m	1m

Midland Industrial Glass
51 Downing Street, Smethwick, B66 2PP
Tel: 0121-565 6500 **Fax:** 0121-565 6501
E-mail: enquire@miglass.com
Website: http://www.miglass.com
Bank(s): HSBC Bank plc
Directors: A. Gardner (Dir), P. Johnson (Co Sec)
Managers: L. Cooper (Comptroller), M. Whitwel (Sales Prom Mgr)
Ultimate Holding Company: MI GLASS MIDCO LIMITED
Immediate Holding Company: MI GLASS LIMITED
Registration no: 00551629 **Date established:** 1955
Turnover: Up to £250,000 **No.of Employees:** 21 - 50 **Product Groups:** 33, 39, 48

Date of Accounts	Aug 11	Aug 10	Aug 09
Working Capital	720	412	236
Fixed Assets	1m	977	870
Current Assets	2m	1m	842

Neway Doors Ltd
Lionel Works 8991 Rolfe Street, Smethwick, B66 2AY
Tel: 0121-558 6406 **Fax:** 0121-555 7140
E-mail: sales@priory-group.co.uk
Website: http://www.priory-group.co.uk
Directors: G. Cooper (MD)
Ultimate Holding Company: SMETHWICK MAINTENANCE COMPANY LIMITED
Immediate Holding Company: NEWAY DOORS LIMITED
Registration no: 01044958 **Date established:** 1972
No.of Employees: 1 - 10 **Product Groups:** 30

Date of Accounts	Nov 11	Nov 10	Nov 09
Working Capital	222	160	115
Fixed Assets	10	13	18
Current Assets	818	888	838

Orapi Ltd

15 Spring Road, Smethwick, B66 1PT
Tel: 0121-525 4000 **Fax:** 01274-822002
E-mail: info@orapiapplied.com
Website: http://www.orapi.com
Bank(s): The Royal Bank of Scotland
Directors: X. De Bourleuf (Co Sec), M. Duncan (MD)
Ultimate Holding Company: ORAPI SA (FRANCE)
Immediate Holding Company: ORAPI PACIFIQUE LIMITED
Registration no: 03375422 **VAT No.:** GB 765337508001
Date established: 1997 **Turnover:** £2m - £5m **No.of Employees:** 11 - 20
Product Groups: 23, 24, 30, 32, 66

Date of Accounts	Dec 10	Dec 09	Dec 08
Sales Turnover	7m	7m	N/A
Pre Tax Profit/Loss	428	188	-939
Working Capital	-653	-1m	-2m
Fixed Assets	1m	2m	2m
Current Assets	4m	3m	3m
Current Liabilities	887	666	601

Parceline Ltd

Roebuck Lane, Smethwick, B66 1BY
Tel: 08459-505505 **Fax:** 0121-500 2646
E-mail: info@geopostuk.com
Website: http://www.parceline.com
Bank(s): Barclays, Nottingham
Directors: K. Philips (Grp Chief Exec), C. Millbanks (Grp Chief Exec)
Managers: M. Dolin, M. Hamilton (Mktg Serv Mgr), S. Mills (I.T. Exec), J. Bench (Accounts), J. Akton (Mktg Serv Mgr), J. Acton (Mktg Serv Mgr), D. Macdonald (Sales Prom Mgr)
Ultimate Holding Company: LA POSTE (FRANCE)
Immediate Holding Company: PARCELINE LIMITED
Registration no: 04130503 **VAT No.:** GB 385 1017 56
Date established: 2000 **Turnover:** £75m - £125m
No.of Employees: 501 - 1000 **Product Groups:** 72, 79

Polypack Polythene Co.

4 Heath St Industrial Estate Abberley Street, Smethwick, B66 2QZ
Tel: 0121-558 9977 **Fax:** 0121-555 6077
E-mail: info@polypackuk.com
Website: http://www.polypackuk.com
Directors: S. Ghattaura (Fin), M. Ghattaura (MD)
Managers: S. Wilson
Immediate Holding Company: POLYPACK POLYTHENE LIMITED
Registration no: 04075029 **Date established:** 2000
Turnover: £500,000 - £1m **No.of Employees:** 11 - 20
Product Groups: 30, 31

Date of Accounts	Sep 11	Sep 10	Sep 09
Working Capital	86	-13	-36
Fixed Assets	69	94	111
Current Assets	855	900	773

Premier World Trading Ltd

Raintex House, Smethwick, B66 2AA
Tel: 0121-555 6479 **Fax:** 0121-555 6532
E-mail: sales@pwtltd.co.uk
Website: http://www.jackorton.com
Bank(s): Midland, High St, West Bromwich
Directors: K. Sahota (Dir), P. Raindi (Fin)
Immediate Holding Company: Raindi Group
Registration no: 03357844 **Date established:** 1992 **Turnover:** £1m - £2m
No.of Employees: 21 - 50 **Product Groups:** 24, 61

Date of Accounts	Sep 07	Sep 06
Sales Turnover	N/A	1609
Pre Tax Profit/Loss	N/A	44
Working Capital	21	40
Fixed Assets	40	46
Current Assets	421	323
Current Liabilities	399	283
ROCE% (Return on Capital Employed)		51.4
ROT% (Return on Turnover)		2.8

Presscraft Components Ltd

3 Woodburn Road, Smethwick, B66 2PU
Tel: 0121-558 1888 **Fax:** 0121-555 5498
E-mail: info@presscraft-limited.co.uk
Website: http://www.presscraft-limited.co.uk
Directors: J. Smith (MD)
Immediate Holding Company: PRESSCRAFT (COMPONENTS) LIMITED
Registration no: 02013033 **VAT No.:** GB 110 4844 10
Date established: 1986 **Turnover:** £500,000 - £1m
No.of Employees: 1 - 10 **Product Groups:** 39

Date of Accounts	Jun 12	Jun 11	Jun 10
Working Capital	128	127	110
Fixed Assets	27	13	10
Current Assets	225	188	174

Professional Polishing Services Ltd

Unit 18b Parkrose Industrial Estate Middlemore Road, Smethwick, B66 2DZ
Tel: 0121-555 6569 **Fax:** 0121-555 6613
E-mail: admin@professionalpolishing.co.uk
Website: http://www.professionalpolishing.co.uk
Managers: S. Wright
Immediate Holding Company: PROFESSIONAL POLISHING SERVICES LIMITED
Registration no: 01162175 **Date established:** 1974
No.of Employees: 11 - 20 **Product Groups:** 46, 48

Date of Accounts	Jun 11	Jun 10	Jun 09
Working Capital	-120	-200	-159
Fixed Assets	772	812	861
Current Assets	259	210	234

Reeve Metal Finishing Co. Ltd

40 Anne Road, Smethwick, B66 2NZ
Tel: 0121-558 0692 **Fax:** 0121-558 4708
E-mail: sales@reevemetalfinishing.co.uk
Website: http://www.reevemetalfinishing.co.uk
Bank(s): Barclays
Managers: D. Lippitt (Fin Mgr)
Immediate Holding Company: REEVE METAL FINISHING CO. LIMITED(THE)
Registration no: 00637814 **VAT No.:** GB 277 4116 48
Date established: 1959 **Turnover:** £1m - £2m **No.of Employees:** 11 - 20
Product Groups: 48

Date of Accounts	Mar 11	Mar 10	Mar 09
Working Capital	214	204	232
Fixed Assets	372	371	375
Current Assets	336	283	271

Reid Electonics Ltd

Unit 20 Smethwick Enterprise Centre Rolfe Street, Smethwick, B66 2AR
Tel: 0121-555 7003 **Fax:** 0121-555 7003
Website: http://www.reidelectronics.co.uk
Directors: A. Reid (Prop)
No.of Employees: 1 - 10 **Product Groups:** 37, 48, 84

The Rical Ltd

Tramway Oldbury Road, Smethwick, B66 1NY
Tel: 0121-558 2694 **Fax:** 0121-558 4239
E-mail: info@ricalltd.com
Website: http://www.ricalltd.com
Directors: B. Head (Ch), F. Moody (MD), P. Marsh (Fin)
Managers: P. Bytherway (Sales Prom Mgr), R. McHugo (Chief Mgr)
Immediate Holding Company: RICAL LIMITED
Registration no: 00088330 **Date established:** 2006
Turnover: £20m - £50m **No.of Employees:** 51 - 100 **Product Groups:** 39, 48

Date of Accounts	Aug 11	Aug 10	Aug 09
Sales Turnover	24m	21m	20m
Pre Tax Profit/Loss	1m	654	430
Working Capital	5m	4m	4m
Fixed Assets	6m	6m	6m
Current Assets	10m	9m	8m
Current Liabilities	1m	1m	2m

Rollform Sections Ltd

PO Box 92, Smethwick, B66 2PA
Tel: 0121-555 1310 **Fax:** 0121-555 1311
E-mail: belinda.fleming@hadleygroup.co.uk
Website: http://www.hadleygroup.co.uk
Bank(s): HSBC, Wolverhampton
Directors: G. Deeley (Tech Serv), S. Towe (MD), R. French (Dir), G. Mayo (Dir), J. Flynn (Sales)
Managers: R. Dunphorne (Mktg Serv Mgr), I. Woolley (Personnel)
Immediate Holding Company: ROLLFORM SECTIONS LIMITED
Registration no: 01844012 **VAT No.:** GB 409 4460 54
Date established: 1984 **Turnover:** £2m - £5m **No.of Employees:** 51 - 100
Product Groups: 34, 36

Sections & Profiles

Gaitskell Way, Smethwick, B66 1BF
Tel: 0121-555 1430 **Fax:** 0121-555 1431
E-mail: admin@hadleygroup.co.uk
Website: http://www.hadleygroup.co.uk
Bank(s): HSBC, Wolverhampton
Directors: N. Plant (Dir), J. Flynn (Sales), G. Deeley (I.T. Dir)
Immediate Holding Company: SECTIONS & PROFILES LIMITED
Registration no: 01302201 **VAT No.:** GB 409 4460 54
Date established: 1977 **Turnover:** £2m - £5m **No.of Employees:** 21 - 50
Product Groups: 34

Date of Accounts	Apr 09	Apr 08
Working Capital	10	10
Current Assets	10	10

Shoreheat Ltd

Unit 9 Oak Court Crystal Drive, Smethwick, B66 1QG
Tel: 0121-544 8008 **Fax:** 0121-544 8785
Managers: M. Clarke (District Mgr)
Ultimate Holding Company: PROGRESS GROUP LIMITED
Immediate Holding Company: SHOREHEAT LIMITED
Registration no: 01566154 **VAT No.:** GB 484 6058 12
Date established: 1981 **Turnover:** £5m - £10m **No.of Employees:** 1 - 10
Product Groups: 36, 38, 40

Date of Accounts	Dec 10	Dec 09	Dec 08
Sales Turnover	17m	13m	14m
Pre Tax Profit/Loss	540	327	393
Working Capital	2m	2m	2m
Fixed Assets	461	505	481
Current Assets	6m	6m	5m
Current Liabilities	480	388	504

Skeldings Ltd

126 Oldbury Road, Smethwick, B66 1JE
Tel: 0121-558 0622 **Fax:** 0121-558 6115
Bank(s): National Westminster
Directors: D. Skelding (Dir), M. Whitby (MD), G. Whitby (Co Sec)
Managers: C. New (Purch Mgr), K. New (Personnel)
Immediate Holding Company: SKELDINGS LIMITED
Registration no: 00187063 **Date established:** 2023 **Turnover:** £1m - £2m
No.of Employees: 21 - 50 **Product Groups:** 35, 48

Date of Accounts	Dec 11	Dec 10	Dec 09
Working Capital	-82	-51	3
Fixed Assets	583	592	602
Current Assets	196	209	212

Steel Fence Supplies (a division of Hadley Industries Ltd

Gaitskell Way, Smethwick, B66 1BF
Tel: 0121-555 1430 **Fax:** 0121-555 1431
E-mail: neil.plant@hadleygroup.co.uk
Website: http://www.hadleygroup.co.uk
Bank(s): HSBC, Wolverhampton
Directors: N. Plant (Dir)
Immediate Holding Company: STEEL FENCE SUPPLIES LIMITED
Registration no: 01843612 **VAT No.:** GB 409 4460 54
Date established: 1984 **Turnover:** Up to £250,000
No.of Employees: 51 - 100 **Product Groups:** 34, 35

Date of Accounts	Apr 06
Working Capital	1m
Current Assets	1m

Sunrise Bakery Ltd

Woodlands Street, Smethwick, B66 3TF
Tel: 0121-565 1647 **Fax:** 0121-558 7409
E-mail: info@sunrisebakery.co.uk
Website: http://www.sunrisebakery.co.uk
Directors: E. Drummond (Dir)
Immediate Holding Company: SUNRISE BAKERY LIMITED
Registration no: 04603872 **Date established:** 2002
Turnover: £250,000 - £500,000 **No.of Employees:** 21 - 50
Product Groups: 20, 30, 41

T W M Die Tools Ltd

1 Spring Court Cranford Street, Smethwick, B66 2RT
Tel: 0121-565 5208 **Fax:** 0121-565 3098
E-mail: mark@twmdietools.co.uk
Website: http://www.twmdietools.co.uk
Directors: M. Tanner (MD)
Immediate Holding Company: TWM DIE TOOLS LIMITED
Registration no: 07195401 **Date established:** 2010
Turnover: Up to £250,000 **No.of Employees:** 1 - 10 **Product Groups:** 33, 35, 46, 48

Date of Accounts	Mar 11
Working Capital	-5
Fixed Assets	8
Current Assets	35

Workrest Blades Ltd

3 Wattville Road Industrial Estate Wattville Road, Smethwick, B66 2NT
Tel: 0121-558 4339 **Fax:** 0121-558 3666
E-mail: neal@workrestblades.co.uk
Website: http://www.workrestblades.co.uk
Directors: N. Lanchbury (MD)
Immediate Holding Company: WORKREST BLADES LIMITED
Registration no: 06129623 **Date established:** 2007
No.of Employees: 1 - 10 **Product Groups:** 46

Date of Accounts	Feb 08	Feb 11	Feb 10
Sales Turnover	N/A	158	N/A
Working Capital	7	2	-16
Fixed Assets	4	13	17
Current Assets	29	58	23

Worson Die Cushions Ltd

89-91 Rolfe Street, Smethwick, B66 2AY
Tel: 0121-558 0939 **Fax:** 0121-558 0017
Directors: K. Harvey (Dir), A. Sorrell (MD), R. Dovey (Dir), S. Hunt (Fin)
Immediate Holding Company: WORSON DIE CUSHIONS LIMITED
Registration no: 02570059 **Date established:** 1990
Turnover: Up to £250,000 **No.of Employees:** 1 - 10 **Product Groups:** 46

Date of Accounts	Nov 08	Nov 06	Nov 05
Working Capital	3	3	3
Current Assets	4	4	4
Current Liabilities	1	1	N/A

Solihull

Advertising Matters Ltd

3 Cranford Grove, Solihull, B91 3GP
Tel: 0121-711 3423 **Fax:** 01299-823225
E-mail: info@advertisingmatters.com
Website: http://www.advertisingmatters.com
Directors: M. Pittaway (MD)
Immediate Holding Company: ADVERTISING MATTERS LIMITED
Registration no: 02073875 **Date established:** 1986
Turnover: £250,000 - £500,000 **No.of Employees:** 1 - 10
Product Groups: 28, 44, 81

Date of Accounts	Sep 11	Sep 10	Sep 09
Working Capital	-7	-7	-9
Fixed Assets	9	10	12
Current Assets	9	7	13

Aim Software Ltd

21b Station Road Knowle, Solihull, B93 0HL
Tel: 01564-770400 **Fax:** 01564-771066
E-mail: tcp@aimsoftware.co.uk
Website: http://www.aimsoftware.co.uk
Directors: T. Platt (MD)
Immediate Holding Company: AIM SOFTWARE LIMITED
Registration no: 02321807 **Date established:** 1988
Turnover: £250,000 - £500,000 **No.of Employees:** 1 - 10
Product Groups: 44

Date of Accounts	Apr 11	Apr 10	Apr 09
Working Capital	1	31	50
Fixed Assets	11	3	4
Current Assets	109	115	192

Allbatteries UK Ltd (Powerpacks Division)

Unit 20 Monkspath Business Park Highlands Road Shirley, Solihull, B90 4NZ
Tel: 0121-506 8600 **Fax:** 0121-711 3604
E-mail: sales@allbatteries.com
Website: http://www.allbatteries.com
Bank(s): Barclays
Directors: D. Buffelard (MD)
Managers: T. Willis (Sales Prom Mgr)
Ultimate Holding Company: VDI SAS (FRANCE)
Immediate Holding Company: ALLBATTERIES U.K. LIMITED
Registration no: 02045875 **Date established:** 1986 **Turnover:** £2m - £5m
No.of Employees: 51 - 100 **Product Groups:** 37, 48

Date of Accounts	Dec 11	Dec 10	Dec 09
Working Capital	1m	476	387
Fixed Assets	62	86	115
Current Assets	3m	3m	2m

Andrews Metals & Alloys Ltd

42 Stratford Road Shirley, Solihull, B90 3LS
Tel: 0121-745 1138 **Fax:** 0121-733 1700
E-mail: stevemike@btopenworld.com
Website: http://www.andrewsmetals.co.uk
Directors: S. Andrews (Dir)
Immediate Holding Company: ANDREWS METALS & ALLOYS LIMITED
Registration no: 00727892 **Date established:** 1962 **Turnover:** £1m - £2m
No.of Employees: 1 - 10 **Product Groups:** 66

Date of Accounts	Mar 12	Mar 11	Mar 10
Working Capital	224	110	98
Fixed Assets	20	24	17
Current Assets	320	255	305

Arden Precision Ltd

5 Maidwell Drive Shirley, Solihull, B90 4QN
Tel: 0121-683 5200 **Fax:** 0121-683 5210
E-mail: don.ryan@ardenprecision.com
Website: http://www.ardenprecision.com
Bank(s): Barclays
Directors: D. Ryan (MD), D. Ryan (MD), T. Mansell (Chief Op Offcr)
Managers: A. Sidwell (Ops Mgr), I. Gleed (Eng Serv Mgr), T. Davies (Fin Mgr)
Immediate Holding Company: ARDEN PRECISION LIMITED
Registration no: 01852372 **Date established:** 1984 **Turnover:** £1m - £2m
No.of Employees: 21 - 50 **Product Groups:** 48

Date of Accounts	Jun 11	Jun 10	Jun 09
Working Capital	-560	-531	-165
Fixed Assets	1m	1m	1m
Current Assets	1m	947	1m

Arup
Blythe Valley Park Shirley, Solihull, B90 8AE
Tel: 0121-213 3000 **Fax:** 0121-213 3001
E-mail: solihull@arup.com
Website: http://www.arup.com
Directors: R. Shields (Dir)
Immediate Holding Company: ARUP GROUP LTD
Registration no: SC062237 **No.of Employees:** 501 - 1000
Product Groups: 44

Atomic Engineering Co.
9 Radway Industrial Estate Radway Road, Shirley, Solihull, B90 4NR
Tel: 0121-709 1127 **Fax:** 0121-709 1128
E-mail: sales@atomicengineering.co.uk
Website: http://www.atomicengineering.co.uk
Directors: S. Thompson (Fin)
Immediate Holding Company: ATOMIC ENGINEERING LIMITED
Registration no: 02886193 **VAT No.:** GB 614 2868 39
Date established: 1994 **Turnover:** Up to £250,000
No.of Employees: 1 - 10 **Product Groups:** 30, 35, 37

Date of Accounts	Apr 11	Apr 10	Apr 09
Working Capital	173	130	102
Fixed Assets	11	13	15
Current Assets	247	228	199

Bernwell C N C Ltd
Valley Road Earlswood, Solihull, B94 6AA
Tel: 01564-702717 **Fax:** 01564-702717
Website: http://www.bernwells.fsnet.co.uk
Directors: B. Wells (Dir)
Immediate Holding Company: BERNWELL CNC LIMITED
Registration no: 04990959 **Date established:** 2003
No.of Employees: 1 - 10 **Product Groups:** 46

Date of Accounts	Mar 12	Mar 11	Mar 10
Working Capital	1	-1	-1
Fixed Assets	2	2	3
Current Assets	27	14	28

Biotest UK Ltd
Unit 28 Monkspath Business Park Highlands Road, Shirley, Solihull, B90 4NZ
Tel: 0121-733 3393 **Fax:** 0121-733 3066
E-mail: chris_hyde@biotestuk.com
Website: http://www.biotestuk.com
Directors: H. Allen (Fin)
Managers: C. Hyde (Chief Mgr)
Ultimate Holding Company: BIOTEST AG (GERMANY)
Immediate Holding Company: BIOTEST (U.K.) LIMITED
Registration no: 01126745 **VAT No.:** GB 112 0314 47
Date established: 1973 **Turnover:** £10m - £20m **No.of Employees:** 1 - 10
Product Groups: 31, 38, 41, 42, 67

Date of Accounts	Dec 11	Dec 10	Dec 09
Sales Turnover	14m	17m	14m
Pre Tax Profit/Loss	513	861	202
Working Capital	1m	1m	1m
Fixed Assets	42	42	56
Current Assets	3m	4m	4m
Current Liabilities	211	256	219

Chain Products Ltd
Stirling Road Shirley, Solihull, B90 4NE
Tel: 0121-359 0697 **Fax:** 0121-359 3672
E-mail: r.cartwright@chainproducts.co.uk
Website: http://www.chainproducts.co.uk
Bank(s): Barclays, SmallHeath
Directors: E. Cartwright (Dir)
Managers: J. Cartwright (Mgr)
Immediate Holding Company: CHAIN PRODUCTS LIMITED
Registration no: 01714125 **VAT No.:** GB 109 6531 71
Date established: 1983 **Turnover:** £2m - £5m **No.of Employees:** 11 - 20
Product Groups: 35

Date of Accounts	Dec 11	Jul 10	Jul 09
Working Capital	185	672	427
Fixed Assets	2m	391	581
Current Assets	880	975	951

C H L Equipment Ltd (Formerly Verstegen Grabs & Cunnington Handling)
24 Solihull Road Shirley, Solihull, B90 3HD
Tel: 0121-733 8100 **Fax:** 0121-733 2796
E-mail: sales@chlequipment.com
Website: http://www.chlequipment.com
Managers: J. Hinder (Chief Mgr)
Immediate Holding Company: CHL EQUIPMENT LIMITED
Registration no: 02631564 **Date established:** 1991
No.of Employees: 1 - 10 **Product Groups:** 45

Date of Accounts	Jul 11	Jul 10	Jul 09
Working Capital	54	39	44
Fixed Assets	1	1	4
Current Assets	177	55	110

City Air Weapons & Firearms
247 Lyndon Road, Solihull, B92 7QP
Tel: 0121-742 1329 **Fax:** 0121-742 1329
E-mail: enquiries@cityairweapons.com
Website: http://www.cityairweapons.com
Directors: S. Parrack (Prop)
Date established: 1978 **No.of Employees:** 1 - 10 **Product Groups:** 36, 39, 40

Cleaner Systems Ltd
50 Richmond Road, Solihull, B92 7RP
Tel: 0800-756 1331 **Fax:** 0800-756 9821
E-mail: info@cleaner-systems.co.uk
Website: http://www.cleaner-systems.co.uk
Directors: D. Budden (MD)
Immediate Holding Company: CLEANER SYSTEMS LTD
Registration no: 05163873 **Date established:** 2004
Turnover: Up to £250,000 **No.of Employees:** 1 - 10 **Product Groups:** 44

Date of Accounts	Mar 12	Mar 11	Mar 10
Working Capital	1	3	4
Fixed Assets	3	7	11
Current Assets	22	19	15

Climaveneta UK Ltd
Highlands Road Shirley, Solihull, B90 4NL
Tel: 0871-663 0664 **Fax:** 0871-6631664
E-mail: tony.holmes@waltermeirer.com
Website: http://www.climaveneta.com
Bank(s): HSBC, Birmingham
Directors: S. Shepherd (MD), A. Manotia (Fin)
Managers: A. Davis (I.T. Exec), N. Speakman (Mktg Serv Mgr)
Immediate Holding Company: Climaventa SPA
Registration no: 00788610 **Date established:** 1964 **Turnover:** £5m - £10m
No.of Employees: 21 - 50 **Product Groups:** 37, 38, 40, 52, 66

G A Docker
Rushbrook Farm Rushbrook Lane, Tanworth-in-Arden, Solihull, B94 5HW
Tel: 01564-742606
Directors: G. Docker (Prop)
Immediate Holding Company: ANCHORDOWN LIMITED
Registration no: 03027319 **Date established:** 1995
No.of Employees: 1 - 10 **Product Groups:** 26, 35

Drive2arrive Light Haulage Services Ltd
18 Quinton Close, Solihull, B92 9BL
Tel: 0121-684 0107
E-mail: sales@drive2arrive.org.uk
Website: http://www.drive2arrive.org.uk
Directors: D. Morris (Dir), P. Morris (Fin)
Registration no: 06495589 **Date established:** 2004
Turnover: Up to £250,000 **No.of Employees:** 1 - 10 **Product Groups:** 72, 76

E H Smith
357-363 Haslucks Green Road Shirley, Solihull, B90 2NG
Tel: 0121-713 7100 **Fax:** 0121-713 7101
E-mail: john.parker@ehsmith.co.uk
Website: http://www.ehsmith.co.uk
Bank(s): Barclays, Acocks Green
Managers: A. Webb (Prod Mgr)
Ultimate Holding Company: E H SMITH HOLDINGS LTD
Immediate Holding Company: E H SMITH (BUILDERS MERCHANTS) LIMITED
Registration no: 00800907 **Date established:** 1964
Turnover: £75m - £125m **No.of Employees:** 21 - 50 **Product Groups:** 27, 30, 32, 33, 67

Date of Accounts	Jun 11	Jun 10	Jun 09
Sales Turnover	95m	80m	82m
Pre Tax Profit/Loss	218	-795	-2m
Working Capital	10m	9m	10m
Fixed Assets	9m	10m	10m
Current Assets	26m	21m	20m
Current Liabilities	1m	977	1m

Easy-Vend Limited
29 Thornton Road Shirley, Solihull, B90 4TL
Tel: 0121-684 1117 **Fax:** 0121-733 1091
E-mail: sales@easyvend.com
Website: http://www.easy-vend.co.uk
Directors: M. Slater (Dir)
Registration no: 05132095 **No.of Employees:** 11 - 20 **Product Groups:** 48

European Squash Federation
The Firs Barston Lane, Barston, Solihull, B92 0JP
Tel: 01675-443922 **Fax:** 01675-443440
E-mail: info@europeansquash.com
Website: http://www.europeansquash.com
Directors: E. Warburton (MD), J. Khan (Pres), P. Derrick (Co Sec)
Managers: C. Leighton (Mgr)
Immediate Holding Company: European Squash Federation
Registration no: 04628339 **Turnover:** £250,000 - £500,000
No.of Employees: 1 - 10 **Product Groups:** 89

Fleet Hire
Station Court Old Station Road, Hampton-In-Arden, Solihull, B92 0HA
Tel: 01675-445100 **Fax:** 01675-445101
E-mail: info@fleethire.co.uk
Website: http://www.fleethire.co.uk
Directors: K. Sharpe (Fin), A. Obrien (Co Sec), N. Poole (Sales)
Managers: D. Page (Buyer), J. Bourne (Tech Serv Mgr)
Ultimate Holding Company: FLEET HIRE HOLDINGS LIMITED
Immediate Holding Company: FLEET HIRE LIMITED
Registration no: 04110984 **Date established:** 2000
Turnover: £20m - £50m **No.of Employees:** 21 - 50 **Product Groups:** 82

Date of Accounts	Mar 12	Mar 11	Mar 10
Sales Turnover	31m	32m	24m
Pre Tax Profit/Loss	805	724	602
Working Capital	8m	7m	10m
Fixed Assets	6m	7m	3m
Current Assets	20m	22m	24m
Current Liabilities	7m	9m	10m

Folex Ltd
Suite 10 Cranmore Place Cranmore Drive, Shirley, Solihull, B90 4RZ
Tel: 0121-733 3833 **Fax:** 0121-733 3222
E-mail: sales@folex.co.uk
Website: http://www.folex.co.uk
Directors: J. Pocock (MD)
Managers: S. Warren (Sales & Mktg Mg), H. Sawers
Ultimate Holding Company: CELFA AG (SWITZERLAND)
Immediate Holding Company: FOLEX LIMITED
Registration no: 01919578 **Date established:** 1985 **Turnover:** £1m - £2m
No.of Employees: 1 - 10 **Product Groups:** 27, 28, 30, 31, 38, 44, 47

Date of Accounts	Dec 11	Dec 10	Dec 09
Working Capital	631	689	675
Fixed Assets	20	32	30
Current Assets	1m	1m	1m

Goodrich Control Systems
Stratford Road Shirley, Solihull, B90 4LA
Tel: 0121-451 5975 **Fax:** 0121-451 6111
E-mail: martin.butler@goodrich.com
Website: http://www.goodrich.com
Managers: M. Butler (Commun Mgr)
Ultimate Holding Company: GOODRICH CORP (USA)
Immediate Holding Company: GOODRICH CONTROL SYSTEMS
Registration no: 04482312 **Date established:** 2002
Turnover: £125m - £250m **No.of Employees:** 51 - 100
Product Groups: 33, 36, 37, 38, 39, 68

Date of Accounts	Dec 11	Dec 10	Dec 09
Sales Turnover	253m	238m	232m
Pre Tax Profit/Loss	42m	41m	33m
Working Capital	274m	236m	186m
Fixed Assets	70m	74m	74m
Current Assets	456m	402m	311m
Current Liabilities	32m	29m	9m

H M V & Waterstones
Royal House Princes Gate Buildings Homer Road, Solihull, B91 3QQ
Tel: 0121-703 8000 **Fax:** 0121-711 7478
Website: http://www.waterstones.co.uk
Managers: I. Wagg (Tech Serv Mgr), J. Parker (Fin Mgr), J. Gleeson (I.T. Exec), P. Willis (Purch Mgr), S. Potter Price
Ultimate Holding Company: S & U PLC
Immediate Holding Company: COMMUNITAS FINANCE LIMITED
Registration no: 00610095 **Date established:** 2005
Turnover: Up to £250,000 **No.of Employees:** 101 - 250
Product Groups: 64

Date of Accounts	Jun 11	Jun 10	Jun 09
Working Capital	-1m	-1m	-1m

High Tech Living
112 Prospect Lane, Solihull, B91 1HT
Tel: 08450-090237 **Fax:** 08712-364804
E-mail: sales@high-tech-living.com
Website: http://www.high-tech-living.com
Directors: N. De Faria (Dir)
Immediate Holding Company: C & J RECYCLING LIMITED
Date established: 2010 **No.of Employees:** 1 - 10 **Product Groups:** 37, 63, 66

Date of Accounts	Mar 12
Working Capital	257
Fixed Assets	3
Current Assets	429

Brian Hyde Ltd
Stirling Road Shirley, Solihull, B90 4LZ
Tel: 0121-705 7987 **Fax:** 0121-711 2465
E-mail: richard@brianhyde.co.uk
Website: http://www.brianhyde.co.uk
Bank(s): HSBC
Directors: R. Hyde (MD)
Managers: A. Musty (Purch Mgr), C. Kelly (Personnel), P. Lovell (Tech Serv Mgr), J. Dabb (Mktg Serv Mgr)
Immediate Holding Company: BRIAN HYDE LIMITED
Registration no: 00549267 **VAT No.:** GB 109 3336 84
Date established: 1955 **Turnover:** £2m - £5m **No.of Employees:** 21 - 50
Product Groups: 35

Date of Accounts	May 12	May 11	May 10
Working Capital	2m	2m	2m
Fixed Assets	327	219	239
Current Assets	2m	2m	2m

Impress Your Boss Ltd
68 Berkeley Road Shirley, Solihull, B90 2HT
Tel: 07813-796792
E-mail: iybinfo@yahoo.co.uk
Website: http://www.enhanceconsulting.com
Directors: A. Heys (Dir), D. Heys (Fin)
Immediate Holding Company: ENHANCE MANAGEMENT CONSULTING LIMITED
Registration no: 04522435 **Date established:** 2002
No.of Employees: 1 - 10 **Product Groups:** 80

Date of Accounts	Aug 11	Aug 10	Aug 09
Working Capital	35	8	2
Current Assets	69	61	29

Industrial Power Cooling Ltd
Orchard Cottage Barston Lane Barston, Solihull, B92 0JP
Tel: 08458-739916 **Fax:** 0845-873 9924
E-mail: nick.hart@ipcuk.com
Website: http://www.ipcuk.com
Directors: N. Hart (MD)
Immediate Holding Company: (IPC) INDUSTRIAL POWER COOLING LIMITED
Registration no: 03792602 **Date established:** 1999
No.of Employees: 1 - 10 **Product Groups:** 40, 66, 67

Date of Accounts	Dec 11	Jun 11	Jun 10
Working Capital	71	79	98
Fixed Assets	7	2	3
Current Assets	147	128	132

J B Forklifts
30 Woodfield Road, Solihull, B91 2DN
Tel: 0121-704 2939 **Fax:** 0121-704 2939
Directors: J. Box (Fin), S. Box (Dir)
Immediate Holding Company: JB FORKLIFTS LIMITED
Registration no: 06300387 **Date established:** 2007
No.of Employees: 1 - 10 **Product Groups:** 35, 39, 45

Date of Accounts	Mar 12	Mar 11	Mar 10
Working Capital	-71	-57	-54
Fixed Assets	81	64	57
Current Assets	70	49	43

Jewels & Finery
488 Lode Lane, Solihull, B92 8NU
Tel: 0121-684 2013
E-mail: sales@jewelsandfinery.co.uk
Website: http://www.jewelsandfinery.co.uk
Directors: M. Weaver (MD)
Turnover: Up to £250,000 **No.of Employees:** 1 - 10 **Product Groups:** 25, 30, 35, 49, 63, 65

J P S
7 Radway Industrial Estate Radway Road, Shirley, Solihull, B90 4NR
Tel: 0121-711 2115 **Fax:** 0121-711 2584
E-mail: jps12345@btconnect.com
Website: http://www.jps-engineering.com
Directors: M. Soltau (Prop)
Registration no: 01145607 **VAT No.:** GB 112 2975 90
Turnover: Up to £250,000 **No.of Employees:** 1 - 10 **Product Groups:** 38

Laranca Engineering Ltd
Earlswood Trading Estate Poolhead Lane, Earlswood, Solihull, B94 5EW
Tel: 01564-702651 **Fax:** 01564-702341
E-mail: laranca@btinternet.com
Website: http://www.laranca.com
Directors: R. Shaw (MD), R. Shaw (Fin)
Immediate Holding Company: LARANCA ENGINEERING LIMITED
Registration no: 00902059 **VAT No.:** GB 110 6836 96
Date established: 1967 **No.of Employees:** 11 - 20 **Product Groups:** 84

Date of Accounts	Mar 11	Mar 10	Mar 09
Working Capital	99	15	-14
Fixed Assets	459	311	390
Current Assets	569	481	532

Larchwood Machine Tools Ltd
24 Browns Lane Knowle, Solihull, B93 8BA
Tel: 01564-776234 **Fax:** 01564-779270
E-mail: sales@larchwoodltd.co.uk
Website: http://www.larchwoodltd.co.uk
Directors: R. Pollard (MD)
Immediate Holding Company: LARCHWOOD MACHINE TOOLS LIMITED
Registration no: 01096903 **VAT No.:** GB 111 6358 03
Date established: 1973 **Turnover:** £1m - £2m **No.of Employees:** 1 - 10
Product Groups: 46, 67

Date of Accounts	Mar 12	Mar 11	Mar 10
Working Capital	99	113	122
Fixed Assets	3	3	2
Current Assets	212	240	264

Lil-lets UK Ltd
PO Box 14568, Solihull, B91 9LN
Tel: 08456-020061 **Fax:** 0121-327 6172
E-mail: corporate@lil-lets.com
Website: http://www.lil-lets.co.uk
Bank(s): Lloyds
Directors: C. Ward (Mkt Research)
Ultimate Holding Company: LIL-LETS GROUP LTD.
Immediate Holding Company: LIL-LETS UK LTD
Registration no: 00548990 **VAT No.:** GB 109 3539 70
Date established: 1955 **Turnover:** £10m - £20m
No.of Employees: 51 - 100 **Product Groups:** 23, 24

Date of Accounts	Dec 11	Dec 10	Dec 09
Sales Turnover	18m	16m	19m
Pre Tax Profit/Loss	287	2m	5m
Working Capital	56m	52m	48m
Fixed Assets	24m	28m	33m
Current Assets	59m	55m	51m
Current Liabilities	2m	2m	2m

Lush Ltd
12 Mill Lane, Solihull, B91 3AX
Tel: 0121-713 2199 **Fax:** 0121-713 2199
Website: http://www.lush.co.uk
Managers: K. Baxter
Ultimate Holding Company: LUSH COSMETICS LIMITED
Immediate Holding Company: LUSH LTD.
Registration no: 02940032 **Date established:** 1994
No.of Employees: 1 - 10 **Product Groups:** 32, 63

Date of Accounts	Jun 11	Jun 10	Jun 09
Sales Turnover	25m	21m	22m
Pre Tax Profit/Loss	3m	7m	6m
Working Capital	6m	13m	11m
Fixed Assets	14m	12m	10m
Current Assets	17m	22m	20m
Current Liabilities	3m	3m	4m

M C P Consulting & Training
Blythe Valley Innovation Centre Central Boulevard Shirley, Solihull, B90 8AJ
Tel: 0121-506 9034 **Fax:** 0121-506 9033
E-mail: info@mcpeurope.com
Website: http://www.mcpeurope.com
Directors: P. Gagg (MD)
Managers: C. Cionnagh (Ops Mgr)
Immediate Holding Company: I-WAVE LIMITED
Registration no: 04285925 **Date established:** 2003
No.of Employees: 11 - 20 **Product Groups:** 86

Date of Accounts	Feb 12	Feb 11	Feb 10
Working Capital	26	24	3
Fixed Assets	7	4	7
Current Assets	63	47	15

Maplin Electronics Ltd
Unit 1 1519 High Street, Solihull, B91 3SJ
Tel: 08432-277369 **Fax:** 0121-704 0380
E-mail: customercare@maplin.co.uk
Website: http://www.maplin.co.uk
Managers: T. Teesdale (Mgr)
Ultimate Holding Company: MONTAGU PRIVATE EQUITY LLP
Immediate Holding Company: MAPLIN ELECTRONICS LIMITED
Registration no: 01264385 **Date established:** 1976
Turnover: £125m - £250m **No.of Employees:** 21 - 50
Product Groups: 37, 61

Date of Accounts	Dec 11	Dec 08	Dec 09
Sales Turnover	205m	204m	204m
Pre Tax Profit/Loss	25m	32m	35m
Working Capital	118m	49m	75m
Fixed Assets	27m	28m	28m
Current Assets	207m	108m	142m
Current Liabilities	78m	51m	59m

Meteor Group plc
Unit 1 Enterprise House Meadow Drive, Hampton-in-Arden, Solihull, B92 0BD
Tel: 01675-445890 **Fax:** 0870-088 0044
Directors: K. Thorpe (Grp MD), S. Miles (Fin)
Ultimate Holding Company: WARWICK HOLDINGS LIMITED
Immediate Holding Company: METEOR GROUP PLC
Registration no: 00525582 **VAT No.:** GB 338 0841 55
Date established: 1953 **Turnover:** £125m - £250m
No.of Employees: 1 - 10 **Product Groups:** 80

Date of Accounts	Dec 11	Dec 10	Dec 09
Sales Turnover	151m	151m	137m
Pre Tax Profit/Loss	-199	2m	2m
Working Capital	6m	7m	6m
Fixed Assets	905	1m	1m
Current Assets	31m	25m	23m
Current Liabilities	2m	2m	N/A

Miracon Conveyors Ltd
Drayton Road Shirley, Solihull, B90 4NG
Tel: 0121-705 8468 **Fax:** 0121-711 2074
E-mail: sales@miracon.com
Website: http://www.miracon.com
Managers: P. Lungley (Projects)
Immediate Holding Company: MIRACON CONVEYORS LIMITED
Registration no: 05987542 **VAT No.:** GB 111 6255 13
Date established: 2006 **Turnover:** £500,000 - £1m
No.of Employees: 1 - 10 **Product Groups:** 45

Date of Accounts	Dec 08	Dec 07
Working Capital	3	N/A
Fixed Assets	23	20
Current Assets	162	148

Niglon Ltd
Highlands Road Shirley, Solihull, B90 4NP
Tel: 0121-711 1990 **Fax:** 0121-711 1344
E-mail: s.hinley@niglon.co.uk
Website: http://www.niglon.co.uk
Directors: S. Hinley (Dir), J. Wilson (Fin)
Managers: N. Clive (Tech Serv Mgr)
Immediate Holding Company: NIGLON LIMITED
Registration no: 00891753 **VAT No.:** GB 110 3670 22
Date established: 1966 **Turnover:** £5m - £10m **No.of Employees:** 21 - 50
Product Groups: 67

Date of Accounts	Apr 11	Apr 10	Apr 09
Sales Turnover	8m	8m	8m
Pre Tax Profit/Loss	771	795	653
Working Capital	5m	5m	4m
Fixed Assets	2m	2m	2m
Current Assets	7m	6m	6m
Current Liabilities	1m	1m	1m

Nokell Fabrications Ltd
18 Radway Industrial Estate Radway Road, Shirley, Solihull, B90 4NR
Tel: 0121-705 4771 **Fax:** 0121-711 3681
E-mail: karl@nokell.co.uk
Directors: K. Nokes (Dir)
Immediate Holding Company: NOKELL FABRICATIONS LIMITED
Registration no: 04541563 **VAT No.:** GB 487 3700 21
Date established: 2002 **Turnover:** Up to £250,000
No.of Employees: 1 - 10 **Product Groups:** 48

Date of Accounts	Dec 10	Dec 08	Dec 07
Working Capital	30	31	43
Fixed Assets	7	5	6
Current Assets	131	100	110

Paragon Group Of Companies plc
St Catherines Court Herbert Road, Solihull, B91 3QE
Tel: 0121-712 2345 **Fax:** 0121-711 1330
E-mail: info@paragon-group.co.uk
Website: http://www.paragon-group.co.uk
Bank(s): National Westminster
Directors: J. Herron (MD), N. Keen (Dir), N. Keen (Fin), J. Perry (Ch), J. Gemmell (Co Sec), N. Terrington (Grp Chief Exec)
Managers: J. Fedefski (Mktg Serv Mgr)
Ultimate Holding Company: THE PARAGON GROUP OF COMPANIES PLC
Immediate Holding Company: PARAGON HOLDINGS GROUP LIMITED
Registration no: 03303807 **VAT No.:** GB 487 3605 16
Date established: 1997 **No.of Employees:** 501 - 1000 **Product Groups:** 82

The Piper Group
132 Widney Lane, Solihull, B91 3LH
Tel: 0121-704 1217
E-mail: rjp@pipergroup.co.uk
Website: http://www.pipergroup.co.uk
Directors: R. Parkin (MD)
Ultimate Holding Company: PIPER SECURITIES HOLDINGS LIMITED
Immediate Holding Company: PIPER CONSTRUCTION MIDLANDS LIMITED
Registration no: 00993275 **VAT No.:** GB 487 2608 14
Date established: 1970 **Turnover:** £5m - £10m **No.of Employees:** 1 - 10
Product Groups: 52

Date of Accounts	Mar 07	Mar 06	Mar 05
Pre Tax Profit/Loss	-198	-259	39
Working Capital	424	114	331
Fixed Assets	45	66	95
Current Assets	4m	2m	3m
Current Liabilities	325	70	152

Primary Fasteners Ltd
PO Box 10571 Shirley, Solihull, B90 4WP
Tel: 0121-247 5191 **Fax:** 0121-535 7094
E-mail: mailroom@prifast.co.uk
Website: http://www.prifast.co.uk
Directors: M. Davis (Dir), N. Coulson (Export), J. Lewise (Dir)
Registration no: 03356321 **Date established:** 1985 **Turnover:** £2m - £5m
No.of Employees: 11 - 20 **Product Groups:** 35, 66

Date of Accounts	Mar 08	Mar 07	Mar 06
Sales Turnover	233	265	219
Pre Tax Profit/Loss	1	2	11
Working Capital	47	46	44
Current Assets	80	96	73
Current Liabilities	33	50	29

Roskel Contracts Ltd
Old Bank House 50 St Johns Close, Knowle, Solihull, B93 0NN
Tel: 01564-732292 **Fax:** 01564-732296
E-mail: ian.horton@roskel.co.uk
Website: http://www.roskel.co.uk
Managers: I. Horton (Chief Mgr)
Ultimate Holding Company: ROSKEL HOLDINGS LIMITED
Immediate Holding Company: ROSKEL CONTRACTS LIMITED
Registration no: 00925981 **Date established:** 1968 **Turnover:** £5m - £10m
No.of Employees: 1 - 10 **Product Groups:** 33, 35, 52

Date of Accounts	Dec 11	Dec 10	Dec 09
Sales Turnover	9m	11m	10m
Pre Tax Profit/Loss	205	308	105
Working Capital	402	444	429
Current Assets	2m	2m	4m
Current Liabilities	630	784	2m

Sasol UK Ltd
1 Hockley Court 2401 Stratford Road, Hockley Heath, Solihull, B94 6NW
Tel: 01564-783060 **Fax:** 01564-784088
E-mail: info@sasol.com
Website: http://www.sasol.com
Bank(s): Barclays Bank P.L.C.
Directors: J. Ward (MD), K. Bernstone (MD)
Ultimate Holding Company: SASOL LIMITED (SOUTH AFRICA)
Immediate Holding Company: SASOL UK LTD
Registration no: 02858889 **VAT No.:** GB 644 1471 50
Date established: 1993 **Turnover:** £500,000 - £1m
No.of Employees: 11 - 20 **Product Groups:** 32

Date of Accounts	Jun 12	Jun 11	Jun 10
Sales Turnover	532	538	552
Pre Tax Profit/Loss	262	247	223
Working Capital	427	424	397
Fixed Assets	24	11	19
Current Assets	530	544	473
Current Liabilities	65	82	45

Scuber & Outdoor Pursuits Centre
380 Stratford Road Shirley, Solihull, B90 4AQ
Tel: 0121-733 8228 **Fax:** 0121-733 8448
Website: http://www.scubapursuits.com
Directors: M. Turner (MD)
Immediate Holding Company: QUADLANCE LIMITED
Date established: 1985 **No.of Employees:** 1 - 10 **Product Groups:** 40, 68, 89

Seamless Aluminium International Ltd
Unit 6b Solihull Building Trade Centre Richmond Road, Solihull, B92 7RN
Tel: 0121-765 4355 **Fax:** 0121-764 5603
E-mail: sales@seaukltd.co.uk
Website: http://www.seamlessaluminium.ie
Managers: S. Colvin (District Mgr)
Immediate Holding Company: SEAMLESS ALUMINIUM INTERNATIONAL LIMITED
Registration no: 02219191 **Date established:** 1988
Turnover: £500,000 - £1m **No.of Employees:** 1 - 10 **Product Groups:** 35, 36, 37, 39, 40

Date of Accounts	Dec 11	Dec 10	Dec 09
Working Capital	-842	-785	-295
Fixed Assets	16	25	31
Current Assets	483	465	436

H V Skan Ltd
425-433 Stratford Road Shirley, Solihull, B90 4AE
Tel: 0121-733 3003 **Fax:** 0121-733 1030
E-mail: info@skan.co.uk
Website: http://www.skan.co.uk
Bank(s): Barclays, Birmingham South Group
Directors: D. Oates (Fin), R. Skan (MD)
Managers: J. Drew (Mgr)
Ultimate Holding Company: SKAN GROUP HOLDINGS LIMITED
Immediate Holding Company: H.V. SKAN LIMITED
Registration no: 00996954 **VAT No.:** GB 614 2166 71
Date established: 1970 **Turnover:** £2m - £5m **No.of Employees:** 11 - 20
Product Groups: 32, 33, 38, 48, 49

Date of Accounts	Sep 11	Sep 10	Sep 09
Sales Turnover	5m	5m	5m
Pre Tax Profit/Loss	-80	96	-289
Working Capital	186	252	170
Fixed Assets	182	175	181
Current Assets	2m	2m	2m
Current Liabilities	244	255	195

Skytrader Ltd
Unit 12 Four Ashes Road Bentley Heath, Solihull, B93 8LX
Tel: 08704-422979 **Fax:** 0870-442 2978
E-mail: info@skytraderuk.com
Website: http://www.skytraderuk.com
Directors: A. Webb (Dir), R. Harrison (Dir)
Immediate Holding Company: SKYTRADER LIMITED
Registration no: 03330309 **Date established:** 1997
No.of Employees: 1 - 10 **Product Groups:** 75

Date of Accounts	Mar 07	Mar 06	Mar 05
Working Capital	-1	-2	2
Fixed Assets	3	3	4
Current Assets	26	38	35
Current Liabilities	5	15	11

Store 21
Tureck House Drayton Road Shirley, Solihull, B90 4NG
Tel: 0121-705 8286 **Fax:** 01273-874433
E-mail: recruitment@storetwentyone.co.uk
Website: http://www.gsgroup.co.uk
Directors: A. Jhunjhunwala (Grp Chief Exec), P. Bacon (Dir), S. Khela (Dir), N. Wanstall (Grp Chief Exec)
Immediate Holding Company: HIGHFIELD INVESTMENTS LIMITED
Registration no: 01682473 **Date established:** 1955 **Turnover:** £1m - £2m
No.of Employees: 101 - 250 **Product Groups:** 63

T R W Ltd
Technical Centre Stratford Road, Shirley, Solihull, B90 4GW
Tel: 0121-627 4141 **Fax:** 0121-627 4243
E-mail: conekt.enquiries@trw.com
Website: http://www.trw.com
Directors: D. Chew (Grp Chief Exec), M. Furber (Pers)
Managers: M. Southwell (Chief Mgr), M. Pym, S. Baddeley, A. Buchanan, A. Mitcham, C. Tarling, D. Richard
Immediate Holding Company: LUCAS AUTOMOTIVE LIMITED
Registration no: 00870649 **Date established:** 1966
No.of Employees: 501 - 1000 **Product Groups:** 35, 37, 38, 39, 44, 45, 54, 67, 68, 81, 84, 85

T R W Ltd
Stratford Road Shirley, Solihull, B90 4AX
Tel: 0121-506 5000 **Fax:** 0121-506 5001
E-mail: enquiries@lucasestateagents.co.uk
Website: http://www.trw.com
Directors: G. Plumley (Pers), A. Neogy (Co Sec), J. Pegg (Co Sec)
Managers: K. Holland (Personnel), N. Lloyd (Mktg Serv Mgr), K. Foster (Buyer), A. Joseph
Ultimate Holding Company: TRW AUTOMOTIVE HOLDINGS CORP (USA)
Immediate Holding Company: LUCAS LIMITED
Registration no: 00872804 **Date established:** 1966
Turnover: £250m - £500m **No.of Employees:** 251 - 500
Product Groups: 38, 39, 68, 84

Thor Hammer Company Ltd
Highlands Road Shirley, Solihull, B90 4NJ
Tel: 0121-705 4695 **Fax:** 0121-705 4727
E-mail: info@thorhammer.com
Website: http://www.thorhammer.com
Bank(s): HSBC Bank plc
Directors: H. Stephens (Co Sec), J. O'Connell (Dir)
Immediate Holding Company: THOR HAMMER COMPANY LIMITED
Registration no: 00189360 **VAT No.:** GB 110 6305 30
Date established: 2023 **Turnover:** £2m - £5m **No.of Employees:** 21 - 50
Product Groups: 29, 36, 43, 47

Date of Accounts	Dec 11	Dec 10	Dec 09
Working Capital	2m	2m	2m
Fixed Assets	809	756	689
Current Assets	2m	2m	2m

Titanium Products Ltd
96 Widney Lane, Solihull, B91 3LL
Tel: 0121-705 1483 **Fax:** 0121-705 1483
E-mail: sales@titaniumproducts.co.uk
Website: http://www.titaniumproducts.co.uk

Directors: J. Turner (MD)
Immediate Holding Company: TITANIUM PRODUCTS LIMITED
Registration no: 02549470 **Date established:** 1990
Turnover: Up to £250,000 **No.of Employees:** 1 - 10 **Product Groups:** 34, 35, 36

Date of Accounts	Jan 12	Jan 11	Jan 10
Working Capital	20	29	17
Current Assets	80	80	57

Total Process Cooling Ltd
94 Heaton Road, Solihull, B91 2DZ
Tel: 0121-711 4014 **Fax:** 0121- 7054012
E-mail: sales@totalprocesscooling.co.uk
Website: http://www.totalprocesscooling.co.uk
Directors: M. Gallagher (MD), M. Gallagher (Fin), R. Smith (Sales)
Managers: R. Smith (Sales Prom Mgr)
Immediate Holding Company: TOTAL PROCESS COOLING LIMITED
Registration no: 02598183 **Date established:** 1991 **Turnover:** £1m - £2m
No.of Employees: 1 - 10 **Product Groups:** 40, 48, 49, 52, 84, 85

Date of Accounts	Apr 11	Apr 10	Apr 09
Sales Turnover	N/A	N/A	1m
Pre Tax Profit/Loss	N/A	N/A	134
Working Capital	235	221	249
Fixed Assets	2	5	8
Current Assets	848	356	611
Current Liabilities	N/A	N/A	126

Trelleborg Ceiling Solutions Ltd
Pegasus House Cranbrook Way, Shirley, Solihull, B90 4GT
Tel: 0121-733 2442 **Fax:** 0121-733 2442
E-mail: d.brown@trelleborg.com
Website: http://www.trelleborg.com
Bank(s): HSBC Bank plc
Directors: P. Taylor (Sales), O. Cooksey (Fin)
Managers: D. Brown (Chief Mgr), B. Clough (Mktg Serv Mgr)
Ultimate Holding Company: SMITHS INDUSTRIES
VAT No.: GB 610 3886 56 **Date established:** 1975
Turnover: Up to £250,000 **No.of Employees:** 21 - 50 **Product Groups:** 29, 30, 36, 37, 40

Van Der Lande Industries
59 Marsh Lane Hampton-in-Arden, Solihull, B92 0AJ
Tel: 01675-443743 **Fax:** 01675-443169
E-mail: grahame.bacon@vanderlande.com
Website: http://www.vanderlande.com
Bank(s): National Westminster Bank Plc
Directors: G. Bacon (Co Sec)
Managers: R. Peart (Mktg Serv Mgr)
Ultimate Holding Company: VANDERLANDE INDUSTRIES BV-THE NETHERLAND
Immediate Holding Company: VANDERLANDE INDUSTRIES UNITED KINGDOM LIMITED
Registration no: 03298374 **VAT No.:** GB 687 9920 58
Date established: 1997 **Turnover:** £75m - £125m
No.of Employees: 21 - 50 **Product Groups:** 37, 38, 39, 43, 45, 67, 84

Date of Accounts	Mar 11	Mar 10	Mar 09
Sales Turnover	76m	55m	46m
Pre Tax Profit/Loss	11m	6m	1m
Working Capital	9m	3m	1m
Fixed Assets	252	355	457
Current Assets	30m	26m	17m
Current Liabilities	16m	18m	10m

Watson Group Ltd
Netherwood Heath Farmhouse Netherwood Lane, Solihull, B93 0BB
Tel: 01724-898252 **Fax:** 0121-711 1086
E-mail: enquiries@watson-group.co.uk
Website: http://www.watson-group.co.uk
Bank(s): Barclays, Solihull
Directors: G. Hughes (MD), D. Thorton (Co Sec), J. Wood (Dir & Co Sec)
Managers: S. Cooper (Chief Mgr), Hardman (Admin Off), J. Hardman (Sales Admin), L. Hobday (Export Sales Mg), S. Hardman (Admin Off)
Ultimate Holding Company: The Watson Group Ltd
Registration no: 07007421 **VAT No.:** GB 416 9773 19
Turnover: £5m - £10m **No.of Employees:** 21 - 50 **Product Groups:** 49, 65

Whale Tankers Ltd
Ravenshaw, Solihull, B91 2SU
Tel: 0121-704 5700 **Fax:** 0121-704 5701
E-mail: r.turner@whale.co.uk
Website: http://www.whale.co.uk
Bank(s): HSBC Bank plc
Directors: C. Anderson (Sales), C. Williams (Co Sec), K. Van Hagen (Sales), R. Turner (Dir)
Managers: L. Terry (Personnel), T. Pile (Tech Serv Mgr)
Immediate Holding Company: WHALE TANKERS LIMITED
Registration no: 04251423 **VAT No.:** GB 112 2243 34
Date established: 2001 **Turnover:** £20m - £50m
No.of Employees: 101 - 250 **Product Groups:** 39, 45, 72

Date of Accounts	Dec 11	Dec 10	Dec 09
Sales Turnover	20m	17m	22m
Pre Tax Profit/Loss	80	-165	482
Working Capital	2m	2m	2m
Fixed Assets	8m	8m	9m
Current Assets	7m	6m	6m
Current Liabilities	1m	918	2m

W M Web Design
50 Chelveston Crescent, Solihull, B91 3YH
Tel: 0121-705 6502
E-mail: info@wmwebdesign.co.uk
Website: http://www.wmwebdesign.co.uk
Directors: H. Davis (Mkt Research)
Date established: 2008 **Turnover:** Up to £250,000
No.of Employees: 1 - 10 **Product Groups:** 44

Wyckham Blackwell Ltd
Old Station Road Hampton-in-Arden, Solihull, B92 0HB
Tel: 01675-442233 **Fax:** 01675-442227
E-mail: info@wyckham-blackwell.co.uk
Website: http://www.wyckham-blackwell.co.uk
Directors: C. Golby (Pers), J. Taylor (Grp Chief Exec), H. Taylor (Fin)
Managers: D. Himmons
Ultimate Holding Company: WYCKHAM BLACKWELL GROUP LIMITED
Immediate Holding Company: WYCKHAM BLACKWELL GROUP LIMITED
Registration no: 00256080 **VAT No.:** GB 110 7052 28
Date established: 1931 **Turnover:** Up to £250,000
No.of Employees: 21 - 50 **Product Groups:** 25

Date of Accounts	Mar 11	Mar 10	Mar 09
Sales Turnover	81	30	166
Pre Tax Profit/Loss	1	-72	119
Working Capital	512	564	699
Fixed Assets	1m	1m	1m
Current Assets	630	689	846
Current Liabilities	24	31	53

Stourbridge

Acme Jewellery Ltd
2 Hartle Lane Belbroughton, Stourbridge, DY9 9TG
Tel: 01562-730172 **Fax:** 01562-730450
E-mail: carolem@acmejewellery.co.uk
Website: http://www.acmejewellery.co.uk
Directors: P. Mason (MD), C. Mason (Sales & Mktg), C. Mason (Sales)
Immediate Holding Company: ACME JEWELLERY LIMITED
Registration no: 01364535 **Date established:** 1978 **Turnover:** £5m - £10m
No.of Employees: 51 - 100 **Product Groups:** 49

Date of Accounts	Jul 10	Jul 09	Jul 08
Working Capital	394	382	432
Fixed Assets	410	470	432
Current Assets	2m	2m	2m

Addison Saws Ltd
Attwood Street, Stourbridge, DY9 8RU
Tel: 01384-264950 **Fax:** 01384-456331
E-mail: sales@addisonsaws.co.uk
Website: http://www.addisonsaws.co.uk
Bank(s): National Westminster Bank Plc
Directors: A. Jones (Co Sec), M. Knight (Sales)
Managers: J. Haddy (Mktg Serv Mgr)
Ultimate Holding Company: SAW MART LIMITED
Immediate Holding Company: ADDISON SAWS LIMITED
Registration no: 04109103 **VAT No.:** GB 765 1373 22
Date established: 2000 **Turnover:** £2m - £5m **No.of Employees:** 21 - 50
Product Groups: 33, 36, 37, 46, 67

Date of Accounts	Mar 11	Mar 10	Mar 09
Working Capital	545	526	629
Fixed Assets	57	64	72
Current Assets	2m	2m	2m

Arrowsmith Marketing Ltd
Sunningdale Wollaston Road, Stourbridge, DY7 6RX
Tel: 01384-376299
E-mail: info@arrowsmithmarketing.co.uk
Website: http://www.arrowsmithmarketing.co.uk
Directors: G. Edwards (MD)
Immediate Holding Company: ARROWSMITH MARKETING LIMITED
Registration no: 05914041 **Date established:** 2006
Turnover: Up to £250,000 **No.of Employees:** 1 - 10 **Product Groups:** 81

Date of Accounts	Aug 11	Aug 10	Aug 09
Working Capital	7	9	5
Fixed Assets	2	2	2
Current Assets	19	17	22

Avanti Fitted Kitchens Ltd
Avanti House Hayes Lane, Stourbridge, DY9 8RD
Tel: 01384-893929 **Fax:** 01384-896734
E-mail: info@avantikb.co.uk
Website: http://www.avantikb.co.uk
Directors: B. Hopkins (Sales), L. Hopkins (Sales), K. Dearn (Fin)
Managers: T. Bills (Purch Mgr), J. Pearce (Mktg Serv Mgr)
Ultimate Holding Company: AVANTI FITTED KITCHENS (HOLDINGS) LIMITED
Immediate Holding Company: AVANTI FITTED KITCHENS LIMITED
Registration no: 01527338 **VAT No.:** GB 361 9292 38
Date established: 1980 **Turnover:** £5m - £10m **No.of Employees:** 21 - 50
Product Groups: 26

Date of Accounts	Dec 11	Dec 10	Dec 09
Sales Turnover	9m	10m	9m
Pre Tax Profit/Loss	330	687	519
Working Capital	3m	3m	3m
Fixed Assets	1m	1m	1m
Current Assets	5m	5m	4m
Current Liabilities	425	538	447

B G Bullas Ltd
Fletcher Street, Stourbridge, DY9 8TH
Tel: 01384-424400 **Fax:** 01384-893359
E-mail: sales@bgbullas.com
Website: http://www.bgbullas.com
Directors: N. Bullas (MD)
Immediate Holding Company: B.G.BULLAS LIMITED
Registration no: 00757234 **Date established:** 1963
Turnover: £500,000 - £1m **No.of Employees:** 1 - 10 **Product Groups:** 30, 40, 42

Date of Accounts	Oct 11	Oct 10	Oct 09
Working Capital	683	510	484
Fixed Assets	184	201	222
Current Assets	819	607	609

Bache Pallets Ltd
Bromley Street, Stourbridge, DY9 8HU
Tel: 01384-897799 **Fax:** 01384-891351
E-mail: sales@bache-pallets.co.uk
Website: http://www.bache-pallets.co.uk
Bank(s): Barclays Dudley
Directors: G. Bentley (Sales), R. Bache (MD)
Immediate Holding Company: BACHE PALLETS LIMITED
Registration no: 01351410 **VAT No.:** GB 333 8726 45
Date established: 1978 **Turnover:** £2m - £5m **No.of Employees:** 21 - 50
Product Groups: 45, 67

Date of Accounts	Sep 11	Sep 10	Jun 09
Working Capital	234	195	157
Fixed Assets	56	95	82
Current Assets	1m	784	606

Boro Foundry Ltd
Stourvale Road, Stourbridge, DY9 8PR
Tel: 01384-422277 **Fax:** 01384-424836
E-mail: info@borofoundry.co.uk
Website: http://www.borofoundery.co.uk
Managers: N. Norton (Ops Mgr)
Immediate Holding Company: BORO FOUNDRY LIMITED(THE)
Registration no: 00447495 **Date established:** 1948 **Turnover:** £2m - £5m
No.of Employees: 1 - 10 **Product Groups:** 34, 48

Date of Accounts	Jan 12	Jan 11	Jan 10
Sales Turnover	2m	2m	2m
Pre Tax Profit/Loss	191	73	-187
Working Capital	457	358	-19
Fixed Assets	520	509	1m
Current Assets	836	721	690
Current Liabilities	113	80	73

Brassart Ltd
76 Attwood St, Stourbridge, DY9 8RY
Tel: 01384-894814 **Fax:** 01384-423824
E-mail: davidgregory@brassards.co.uk
Website: http://www.brassard.com
Bank(s): Barclays
Directors: D. Corbett (MD)
Managers: T. Prat (Sales Prom Mgr), D. Dawson (Mktg Serv Mgr), D. Gregory (Ops Mgr), T. Esser
Registration no: 03528097 **VAT No.:** GB 110 6214 33
Turnover: £1m - £2m **No.of Employees:** 21 - 50 **Product Groups:** 36

Brierley Lifting Tackle Ltd
Timmis Road, Stourbridge, DY9 7BQ
Tel: 01384-893000 **Fax:** 01384-898000
E-mail: brilift@aol.com
Website: http://www.brierleyliftingtackle.com
Directors: C. Austin (MD), S. Austin (Fin)
Immediate Holding Company: BRIERLEY LIFTING TACKLE COMPANY LIMITED
Registration no: 01927426 **VAT No.:** GB 547 2911 33
Date established: 1985 **Turnover:** £2m - £5m **No.of Employees:** 1 - 10
Product Groups: 45, 83

Date of Accounts	Jun 11	Jun 10	Jun 09
Working Capital	2m	1m	2m
Fixed Assets	913	933	991
Current Assets	3m	3m	3m

C Y Electrical & Cranes Co. Ltd
Hayes Lane, Stourbridge, DY9 8QT
Tel: 01384-895570 **Fax:** 01384-892877
E-mail: info@cyequip.co.uk
Website: http://www.cyequip.co.uk
Directors: J. Clarke (Dir), P. Cook (Dir)
Immediate Holding Company: C.Y. ELECTRICAL AND CRANES COMPANY LIMITED
Registration no: 01199536 **Date established:** 1975
No.of Employees: 21 - 50 **Product Groups:** 48

Date of Accounts	Mar 12	Mar 11	Mar 10
Working Capital	65	73	71
Fixed Assets	114	87	82
Current Assets	440	397	385

The Camera Co UK Ltd
Unit 4-6 Rufford Road, Stourbridge, DY9 7NE
Tel: 01384-877006 **Fax:** 01384-877009
E-mail: sales@thecamera.co.uk
Website: http://www.thecamera.co.uk
Directors: C. Reid (Dir)
Immediate Holding Company: THE CAMERA COMPANY (U.K.) LIMITED
Registration no: 05053558 **Date established:** 2004
No.of Employees: 1 - 10 **Product Groups:** 38, 49, 65

The Chair Clinic Ltd
High Street Wordsley, Stourbridge, DY8 5SD
Tel: 01384-480030 **Fax:** 01384-480031
E-mail: sales@chairclinic.co.uk
Website: http://www.chairclinic.co.uk
Directors: A. Staples (Dir)
Immediate Holding Company: THE CHAIR CLINIC LIMITED
Registration no: 04323942 **Date established:** 2001
Turnover: £250,000 - £500,000 **No.of Employees:** 1 - 10
Product Groups: 26

Date of Accounts	Nov 11	Nov 10	Nov 09
Sales Turnover	367	452	316
Working Capital	8	9	-3
Fixed Assets	10	13	8
Current Assets	103	116	67

Chapel Windows Ltd
118 High Street Wordsley, Stourbridge, DY8 5QR
Tel: 01384-288722 **Fax:** 01384-294357
Directors: C. Carroll (MD)
Ultimate Holding Company: CHAPEL HOLDINGS LIMITED
Immediate Holding Company: CHAPEL WINDOWS LIMITED
Registration no: 01782706 **VAT No.:** GB 409 3392 50
Date established: 1984 **No.of Employees:** 1 - 10 **Product Groups:** 30, 33

Date of Accounts	Feb 08	Feb 11	Feb 10
Working Capital	460	450	424
Fixed Assets	N/A	43	N/A
Current Assets	860	818	749

Coote Engineering
Sheraton Grange, Stourbridge, DY8 2BE
Tel: 01384-443572
Website: http://www.coote.co.uk
Directors: R. Coote (Prop)
Date established: 2005 **No.of Employees:** 1 - 10 **Product Groups:** 45

Crane Services Ltd
Platts Road, Stourbridge, DY8 4YR
Tel: 01384-370318 **Fax:** 01384-440203
E-mail: admin@craneservices.co.uk
Website: http://www.craneservices.co.uk
Directors: R. Lewis (MD)
Immediate Holding Company: CRANE SERVICES LIMITED
Registration no: 00590896 **VAT No.:** GB 274 1669 40
Date established: 1957 **Turnover:** £500,000 - £1m
No.of Employees: 11 - 20 **Product Groups:** 35, 45, 48

Date of Accounts	Sep 11	Sep 10	Sep 09
Working Capital	287	217	199
Fixed Assets	74	77	59
Current Assets	535	429	297

Croxgrove Powder Coaters 1987 Ltd
Unit 10-11 The Hayes Trading Estate Folkes Road, Stourbridge, DY9 8RN
Tel: 01384-422000 **Fax:** 01384-423941
E-mail: info@croxgrovepowdercoaters.co.uk
Website: http://www.croxgrovepowdercoaters.co.uk
Directors: K. Jones (Co Sec)
Immediate Holding Company: CROXGROVE POWDER COATERS (1987) LIMITED

see next page

Croxgrove Powder Coaters 1987 Ltd - Cont'd

Registration no: 02136548 **VAT No.:** GB 478 6185 94
Date established: 1987 **Turnover:** £500,000 - £1m
No.of Employees: 1 - 10 **Product Groups:** 48

Date of Accounts	Mar 11	Mar 10	Mar 09
Working Capital	73	90	121
Fixed Assets	17	16	12
Current Assets	303	286	274

Defensive Driver Training Ltd

2 Worcester Street, Stourbridge, DY8 1AN
Tel: 01384-442233 **Fax:** 01384-440010
E-mail: sales@ddtgroup.com
Website: http://www.ddtgroup.com
Directors: P. Beresford (Dir)
Immediate Holding Company: DEFENSIVE DRIVER TRAINING LIMITED
Registration no: 02402475 **Date established:** 1989
No.of Employees: 1 - 10 **Product Groups:** 51, 86

Date of Accounts	Dec 11	Dec 10	Dec 09
Working Capital	-58	-27	-12
Fixed Assets	327	328	332
Current Assets	78	72	106

Ducatt Heating Co. Ltd

Platts Road, Stourbridge, DY8 4YT
Tel: 01384-394641 **Fax:** 01384-440455
E-mail: info@ducatt.co.uk
Website: http://www.ducatt.co.uk
Bank(s): Bank of Scotland, Dudley
Directors: P. Dainty (MD), S. Singleton (Fin)
Managers: M. Stinton (Tech Serv Mgr), S. Williams
Immediate Holding Company: DUCATT HEATING COMPANY LIMITED(THE)
Registration no: 00157925 **VAT No.:** GB 277 1345 48
Date established: 2019 **Turnover:** £2m - £5m **No.of Employees:** 21 - 50
Product Groups: 48, 52

Date of Accounts	Dec 11	Dec 10	Dec 09
Working Capital	470	566	625
Fixed Assets	331	340	347
Current Assets	892	1m	1m

Dudley Tool Presswork & Engineering Ltd

Mill Street Wordsley, Stourbridge, DY8 5SX
Tel: 01384-571181 **Fax:** 01384-265435
E-mail: andrew.millard@dudley-tool.co.uk
Website: http://www.dudley-tool.co.uk
Directors: A. Millard (Fin), J. Millard (Dir), P. Millard (Dir)
Ultimate Holding Company: DUDLEY TOOL & ENGINEERING CO. LIMITED
Immediate Holding Company: DUDLEY TOOL & ENGINEERING CO. LIMITED
Registration no: 00834804 **VAT No.:** GB 276 9251 23
Date established: 1965 **Turnover:** £1m - £2m **No.of Employees:** 21 - 50
Product Groups: 48

Date of Accounts	Feb 08	Feb 11	Feb 10
Working Capital	78	264	61
Fixed Assets	467	260	463
Current Assets	149	269	66

Folkes Holdings

Forge House, Stourbridge, DY9 8EL
Tel: 01384-424242 **Fax:** 01384-424425
E-mail: info@folkesholdings.com
Website: http://www.folkesholdings.com
Bank(s): HSBC Bank plc
Directors: P. Turner (Fin), C. Folkes (Dir), M. Harris (Property), J. Thompson (Fin), A. Parker (Property)
Managers: P. Tomilinson
Ultimate Holding Company: FOLKES HOLDINGS LIMITED
Immediate Holding Company: FOLKES GROUP LIMITED
Registration no: 00353957 **Date established:** 1939
Turnover: £20m - £50m **No.of Employees:** 11 - 20 **Product Groups:** 77, 80

Date of Accounts	Dec 11	Dec 10	Dec 09
Pre Tax Profit/Loss	-49	2	-22
Working Capital	34m	34m	34m
Fixed Assets	2m	2m	2m
Current Assets	36m	36m	36m
Current Liabilities	12	17	2

The Garden Gate Co UK Ltd

Pepperhill Works Hungary Hill, Stourbridge, DY9 7NH
Tel: 01384-392300 **Fax:** 01384-372948
E-mail: enquiries@thegardengate.biz
Website: http://www.thegardengate.biz
Directors: A. Brettell (Dir)
Immediate Holding Company: THE GARDEN GATE CO (UK) LTD
Registration no: 05376991 **Date established:** 2005
Turnover: £250,000 - £500,000 **No.of Employees:** 1 - 10
Product Groups: 49

Date of Accounts	Jun 11	Jun 10	Jun 09
Working Capital	31	28	22
Fixed Assets	N/A	1	2
Current Assets	82	72	55

Gardener Shaw (South East)

50a Cemetery Road, Stourbridge, DY9 7EF
Tel: 01384-869888 **Fax:** 01384-863777
Bank(s): HSBC Bank plc
Directors: A. Dusanj (Dir), S. Kaur (Fin), S. Dusanj (MD)
Registration no: 02688845 **VAT No.:** GB 660 9212 44
Date established: 1998 **No.of Employees:** 11 - 20 **Product Groups:** 21

Genwork Ltd

Bromley Street, Stourbridge, DY9 8HU
Tel: 01384-636588 **Fax:** 01384-410306
E-mail: robert@bache-pallets.co.uk
Website: http://www.firstmesh.co.uk
Bank(s): Barclays
Directors: R. Bache (MD)
Immediate Holding Company: GENWORK LIMITED
Registration no: 01538251 **VAT No.:** GB 349 3981 11
Date established: 1981 **Turnover:** £500,000 - £1m
No.of Employees: 11 - 20 **Product Groups:** 35, 45, 46

Date of Accounts	Mar 12	Mar 11	Mar 10
Working Capital	48	16	14
Fixed Assets	30	23	25
Current Assets	697	350	331

H C M Engineering Ltd

Pedmore Road, Stourbridge, DY9 7DZ
Tel: 01384-422643 **Fax:** 01384-899210
E-mail: mikeh@hcmeng.co.uk
Website: http://www.hcmeng.co.uk
Bank(s): National Westminster Bank Plc
Directors: M. Hanson (MD), S. Hanson (MD)
Managers: S. Pearson (Tech Serv Mgr), M. Hussain (Fin Mgr)
Immediate Holding Company: H.C.M. ENGINEERING LIMITED
Registration no: 01195702 **VAT No.:** GB 287 5366 13
Date established: 1975 **Turnover:** £500,000 - £1m
No.of Employees: 21 - 50 **Product Groups:** 48

Date of Accounts	Apr 11	Apr 10	Apr 09
Working Capital	-49	-122	-121
Fixed Assets	282	330	368
Current Assets	600	392	295

Helix Trading Ltd

PO Box 15, Stourbridge, DY9 7AJ
Tel: 01384-424441 **Fax:** 01384-892617
E-mail: info@helixhq.com
Website: http://www.helix.co.uk
Bank(s): Barclays
Managers: M. Pell (Chief Mgr)
Ultimate Holding Company: HELIX GROUP PLC
Immediate Holding Company: HELIX GROUP PLC
Registration no: 00155151 **VAT No.:** GB 478 6818 81
Date established: 2019 **Turnover:** £10m - £20m
No.of Employees: 21 - 50 **Product Groups:** 27, 30, 32, 35, 36, 38, 49

Date of Accounts	Dec 09	Dec 08	Dec 07
Sales Turnover	13m	14m	13m
Pre Tax Profit/Loss	97	-804	113
Working Capital	824	731	2m
Fixed Assets	365	479	480
Current Assets	5m	7m	7m
Current Liabilities	656	583	499

Higgins & Hewins Ltd

Titan Works High Street, Amblecote, Stourbridge, DY8 4LR
Tel: 01384-397700 **Fax:** 01384-397701
E-mail: sales@handhltd.co.uk
Website: http://handhltd.co.uk
Directors: M. Higgins (MD)
Immediate Holding Company: HIGGINS & HEWINS LIMITED
Registration no: 05399234 **VAT No.:** GB 388 5918 83
Date established: 2005 **Turnover:** £500,000 - £1m
No.of Employees: 1 - 10 **Product Groups:** 46

Date of Accounts	Mar 12	Mar 11	Mar 10
Working Capital	736	702	606
Fixed Assets	107	4	7
Current Assets	941	1m	925

Highley Steel Ltd

Stourbridge Industrial Estate Mill Race Lane, Stourbridge, DY8 1JN
Tel: 01384-396660 **Fax:** 01384-396662
E-mail: david.goodsir@highleysteel.co.uk
Website: http://www.highleysteel.com
Directors: E. Pierdziwol (Fin)
Managers: D. Goodsir (Mgr)
Ultimate Holding Company: FRIEDR. GUSTAV THEIS GMBH (GERMANY)
Immediate Holding Company: HIGHLEY STEEL LIMITED
Registration no: 06880960 **Date established:** 2009 **Turnover:** £2m - £5m
No.of Employees: 1 - 10 **Product Groups:** 34

Date of Accounts	Aug 11	Aug 10	Sep 09
Working Capital	286	217	N/A
Fixed Assets	77	40	N/A
Current Assets	1m	1m	N/A

Indentec Hardness Testing Machines Ltd

Unit 9-10 Lye Valley Industrial Estate, Stourbridge, DY9 8HX
Tel: 01384-896949 **Fax:** 01384-424470
E-mail: john.piller@indentec.com
Website: http://www.indentec.com
Bank(s): Lloyds TSB Bank plc
Directors: J. Piller (MD)
Ultimate Holding Company: ZWICK ROELL AG (GERMANY)
Immediate Holding Company: INDENTEC HARDNESS TESTING MACHINES LIMITED
Registration no: 01252140 **VAT No.:** GB 287 5311 38
Date established: 1976 **Turnover:** £1m - £2m **No.of Employees:** 11 - 20
Product Groups: 38

Date of Accounts	Dec 11	Dec 10	Dec 09
Working Capital	799	773	554
Fixed Assets	100	49	56
Current Assets	1m	1m	842

Insight Training & Development Ltd

PO Box 1234, Stourbridge, DY8 2GE
Tel: 01384-371432 **Fax:** 01384-371432
E-mail: jeffsmith@askinsight.com
Website: http://www.askinsight.com
Directors: J. Smith (MD)
Immediate Holding Company: INSIGHT TRAINING & DEVELOPMENT LIMITED
Registration no: 07584152 **Date established:** 2011
Turnover: £250,000 - £500,000 **No.of Employees:** 1 - 10
Product Groups: 28

Date of Accounts	Nov 11
Working Capital	18
Current Assets	80

J W & C J Phillips 1969 Ltd

Unit 3 Stambermill Industrial Estate Lye, Stourbridge, DY9 7BJ
Tel: 01384-897324 **Fax:** 01384-895435
E-mail: sales@bradleeboilers.com
Website: http://www.bradleeboilers.com/phillips
Managers: C. Longbottom (Chief Mgr)
Immediate Holding Company: J.W. & C.J. PHILLIPS (1969) LIMITED
Registration no: 03025912 **Date established:** 1995
Turnover: Up to £250,000 **No.of Employees:** 1 - 10 **Product Groups:** 30, 32

Date of Accounts	Dec 10	Dec 08	Dec 07
Working Capital	N/A	N/A	2
Current Assets	26	26	23

Jasun Technology Ltd

1b Timmis Road, Stourbridge, DY9 7BQ
Tel: 01384-422420 **Fax:** 01384-422464
E-mail: info@jasunengineering.com
Website: http://www.jasunengineering.com
Directors: M. Nixon (Dir), V. Nixon (Co Sec)
Managers: C. Nixon (Prod Mgr)
Immediate Holding Company: JASUN TECHNOLOGY LIMITED
Registration no: 02807537 **VAT No.:** GB 551 4275 54
Date established: 1993 **Turnover:** Up to £250,000
No.of Employees: 1 - 10 **Product Groups:** 35, 37, 46

Date of Accounts	May 05	May 04	May 03
Working Capital	39	32	8
Fixed Assets	13	15	17
Current Assets	97	86	47
Current Liabilities	58	53	39
Total Share Capital	1	24	24

Keymesh Ltd

Unit 5 Premier Business Centre Attwood Street, Stourbridge, DY9 8RU
Tel: 01384-898899 **Fax:** 01384-898775
E-mail: sales@keymesh.co.uk
Website: http://www.keymesh.co.uk
Directors: S. Hawkeswood (Dir)
Immediate Holding Company: KEYMESH LIMITED
Registration no: 02842036 **VAT No.:** GB 431 4085 81
Date established: 1993 **Turnover:** £500,000 - £1m
No.of Employees: 1 - 10 **Product Groups:** 23, 27, 30

Date of Accounts	Jan 12	Jan 11	Jan 10
Working Capital	180	155	143
Fixed Assets	24	14	10
Current Assets	336	311	327
Current Liabilities	1	3	3

Laidler Products

35 Fairfield Rise, Stourbridge, DY8 3PQ
Tel: 01384-442815 **Fax:** 01384-441065
E-mail: mail@laidlerproducts.co.uk
Directors: K. Laidler (Fin)
Immediate Holding Company: INCRO LIMITED
Registration no: 04580499 **Date established:** 1993
Turnover: Up to £250,000 **No.of Employees:** 1 - 10 **Product Groups:** 30

Date of Accounts	Oct 11	Oct 10	Oct 09
Working Capital	14	6	7
Fixed Assets	1	2	2
Current Assets	63	59	56

Light Ideas Inc Hunza Europe

Suite 3 Faraday House King William Street, Stourbridge, DY8 4HD
Tel: 01384-377378 **Fax:** 01384-377387
E-mail: orders@lightideas.co.uk
Website: http://www.lightideas.co.uk
Directors: R. Heath (MD)
Immediate Holding Company: LIGHT IDEAS INTERNATIONAL LIMITED
Registration no: 03945883 **Date established:** 2000
No.of Employees: 1 - 10 **Product Groups:** 37, 67

Date of Accounts	Dec 11	Dec 10	Dec 09
Working Capital	242	566	601
Fixed Assets	7	13	28
Current Assets	703	963	1m

Lovato UK Ltd

Lovato House Providence Drive Lye, Stourbridge, DY9 8HQ
Tel: 0845-8110023 **Fax:** 0845-8110024
E-mail: sales@lovato.co.uk
Website: http://www.lovato.co.uk
Bank(s): Barclays
Directors: D. Cross (MD), G. Forcella (Co Sec)
Managers: M. Phipps (Admin Off)
Registration no: 02616851 **VAT No.:** GB 547 6763 02
Date established: 1991 **Turnover:** £2m - £5m **No.of Employees:** 11 - 20
Product Groups: 37

Date of Accounts	Dec 07	Dec 06	Dec 05
Sales Turnover	2840	N/A	N/A
Pre Tax Profit/Loss	76	36	N/A
Working Capital	1147	1074	1064
Fixed Assets	53	77	67
Current Assets	1820	1779	1771
Current Liabilities	673	705	707
ROCE% (Return on Capital Employed)	6.3	3.1	
ROT% (Return on Turnover)	2.7		

Micron Alloy Castings Ltd

Platts Road, Stourbridge, DY8 4YR
Tel: 01384-393247 **Fax:** 01384-444860
E-mail: sales@micronalloys.co.uk
Website: http://www.micronalloys.co.uk
Bank(s): Barclays
Directors: R. Bills (Fin), S. Mcmurray (MD)
Immediate Holding Company: MICRON ALLOY CASTINGS LIMITED
Registration no: 02358271 **Date established:** 1989 **Turnover:** £1m - £2m
No.of Employees: 11 - 20 **Product Groups:** 34, 48

Date of Accounts	Jul 11	Jul 10	Jul 09
Working Capital	251	247	240
Fixed Assets	24	28	35
Current Assets	468	429	438

Microplus Engineering Ltd

Unit 12 Gainsborough Trading Estate Rufford Road, Stourbridge, DY9 7ND
Tel: 01384-442991 **Fax:** 01384-441164
Directors: A. Marshall (MD)
Immediate Holding Company: MICROPLUS ENGINEERING LIMITED
Registration no: 01514509 **Date established:** 1980
No.of Employees: 1 - 10 **Product Groups:** 46

Date of Accounts	Dec 11	Dec 10	Dec 09
Working Capital	-79	-66	-71
Fixed Assets	144	156	181
Current Assets	101	100	77

Mid-Ven Doors Ltd

The Hayes Trading Estate Folkes Road, Stourbridge, DY9 8RG
Tel: 01384-424924 **Fax:** 01384-424929
E-mail: dav@mid-ven.co.uk
Website: http://www.mid-ven.co.uk
Bank(s): HSBC Wolverhampton
Directors: D. Vickery (MD), D. Vickery (Fin), C. Chatterton (Sales & Mktg), J. Goode (MD)
Managers: J. Howard (Buyer)
Immediate Holding Company: MID-VEN DOORS LIMITED
Registration no: 04408811 **VAT No.:** GB 670 7855 05
Date established: 2002 **Turnover:** £2m - £5m **No.of Employees:** 21 - 50
Product Groups: 25, 26

Date of Accounts	Aug 10	Aug 09	Aug 08
Working Capital	23	-67	-79
Fixed Assets	6	2	3

Current Assets	573	238	554

Norton Fire Protection
Unit 12 Lye Business Centre Enterprise Drive, Stourbridge, DY9 8QH
Tel: 01384-441267 **Fax:** 01384-891255
E-mail: enquiries@nortonfire.co.uk
Website: http://www.nortonfire.co.uk
Directors: M. Hancock (Prop)
Date established: 1992 **No.of Employees:** 1 - 10 **Product Groups:** 38, 42

P V S Ltd
Britch Farm Compton, Kinver, Stourbridge, DY7 5NW
Tel: 01384-872747 **Fax:** 01384-872238
E-mail: sales@pvsgroup.co.uk
Website: http://www.pvsl.uk.com
Directors: D. Hughes (Chief Op Offcr)
Immediate Holding Company: PROCESS & VESSEL SYSTEMS LIMITED
Registration no: 02028330 **Date established:** 1986 **Turnover:** £1m - £2m
No.of Employees: 1 - 10 **Product Groups:** 20, 40, 41

Date of Accounts	Oct 08	Oct 07	Mar 11
Working Capital	177	168	182
Fixed Assets	13	27	32
Current Assets	722	774	468

Palace Furniture Ltd
Stour House High Street, Wollaston, Stourbridge, DY8 4PF
Tel: 01384-377771 **Fax:** 01384-377772
E-mail: nina.thornton@palace-furniture.co.uk
Website: http://www.palace-furniture.co.uk
Directors: A. Cooper (Fin), N. Collins (Sales), T. Thornton (Sales), N. Thornton (Co Sec)
Managers: N. Shilvock (Tech Serv Mgr)
Immediate Holding Company: PALACE FURNITURE LIMITED
Registration no: 02767140 **VAT No.:** GB 610 9858 31
Date established: 1992 **Turnover:** £1m - £2m **No.of Employees:** 21 - 50
Product Groups: 26

Date of Accounts	Apr 11	Apr 10	Apr 09
Working Capital	1m	1m	1m
Fixed Assets	469	482	474
Current Assets	2m	2m	1m

Parasene
Allfor House Hayes Lane, Stourbridge, DY9 8QT
Tel: 01384-898911 **Fax:** 01384-899100
E-mail: jpc@bretshaweltex.com
Website: http://www.parasene.com
Bank(s): Barclays, Stourbridge
Directors: C. Steele (Dir), D. Cope (Sales), J. Cartwright (MD), J. Scott (Dir), E. Cartwright (Co Sec)
Managers: R. Horne (Sales Prom Mgr), R. Hill (Sales Admin)
Immediate Holding Company: BRETTELL & SHAW,LIMITED
Registration no: 00126111 **VAT No.:** GB 300 0907 23
Date established: 2012 **Turnover:** £5m - £10m
No.of Employees: 101 - 250 **Product Groups:** 30, 35, 36, 40, 41, 42, 49

Date of Accounts	Dec 07	Dec 06	Dec 05
Working Capital	791	285	681
Current Assets	1777	1496	1633
Current Liabilities	985	1211	952
Total Share Capital	5	5	5

Plowden & Thompson Ltd
Dial Glass Work Stewkins, Stourbridge, DY8 4YN
Tel: 01384-393398 **Fax:** 01384-376638
E-mail: sales@plowden-thompson.com
Website: http://www.plowden-thompson.com
Bank(s): Midland, Stourbridge
Directors: B. Beadman (Dir)
Immediate Holding Company: BEADMAN PT LIMITED
Registration no: 00977294 **VAT No.:** GB 277 1999 01
Date established: 1970 **Turnover:** £500,000 - £1m
No.of Employees: 11 - 20 **Product Groups:** 33, 66

Date of Accounts	Aug 11	Aug 10	Aug 09
Working Capital	8	113	197
Fixed Assets	226	235	244
Current Assets	191	235	261

Polymac Services Ltd
Timmis Road, Stourbridge, DY9 7BQ
Tel: 01384-892441 **Fax:** 01384-893303
E-mail: info@polymacservices.co.uk
Website: http://www.polymacservices.co.uk
Bank(s): National Westminster
Managers: L. Curtis (Mgr)
Immediate Holding Company: POLYMAC SERVICES LIMITED
Registration no: 03727174 **VAT No.:** GB 729 6132 23
Date established: 1999 **Turnover:** £500,000 - £1m
No.of Employees: 11 - 20 **Product Groups:** 30

Date of Accounts	Mar 11	Mar 10	Mar 09
Working Capital	56	50	56
Fixed Assets	34	37	51
Current Assets	263	183	143

Portway Tool & Gauge Ltd
27 Dudley Road Lye, Stourbridge, DY9 8EX
Tel: 01384-892458 **Fax:** 01384-424371
E-mail: info@portwaytool.co.uk
Website: http://www.portwaytool.co.uk
Bank(s): Barclays
Directors: H. Dunn (Fin), M. Dunn (MD)
Managers: A. Treece (Design Eng), L. Hook (Sales Prom Mgr)
Registration no: 02326800 **VAT No.:** GB 488 5512 06
Date established: 1988 **Turnover:** £1m - £2m **No.of Employees:** 21 - 50
Product Groups: 46, 48

Date of Accounts	Mar 07	Mar 06
Working Capital	324	177
Fixed Assets	702	791
Current Assets	509	721
Current Liabilities	186	544
Total Share Capital	55	55

Martyn Price Ltd
PO Box 48, Stourbridge, DY9 8QF
Tel: 01384-424767 **Fax:** 01384-424833
E-mail: sales@martynprice.co.uk
Website: http://www.martynprice.co.uk
Bank(s): HSBC
Directors: L. Dowd (Dir), J. Murphy (Co Sec)
Ultimate Holding Company: MARTYN PRICE HOLDINGS LIMITED
Immediate Holding Company: MARTYN PRICE HOLDINGS LIMITED
Registration no: 01507613 **VAT No.:** GB 488 4132 21
Date established: 1980 **Turnover:** £2m - £5m **No.of Employees:** 11 - 20
Product Groups: 35

Date of Accounts	Jun 11	Jun 10	Jun 09
Pre Tax Profit/Loss	N/A	N/A	-774
Working Capital	-3	-3	-3
Fixed Assets	9	9	9
Current Liabilities	3	N/A	3

Probox UK Ltd
PO Box 4222, Stourbridge, DY7 6WW
Tel: 01384-878794 **Fax:** 01384-878795
E-mail: a.beddow@probox-uk.com
Website: http://www.probox-uk.com
Directors: A. Beddow (Sales), A. Beddow (Dir)
Managers: S. Mason (Sales Admin)
Immediate Holding Company: PROBOX UK LTD
Registration no: 07190536 **Date established:** 2010 **Turnover:** £1m - £2m
No.of Employees: 1 - 10 **Product Groups:** 25, 27, 46, 49, 85

Date of Accounts	Mar 11
Working Capital	3
Current Assets	56

Q M P
Timmis Road, Stourbridge, DY9 7BQ
Tel: 01384-899800 **Fax:** 01384-899801
E-mail: sales@qmp.uk.com
Website: http://www.qmp.uk.com
Bank(s): Lloyds TSB Bank plc
Directors: M. Wright (Fin), N. Higgitt (MD)
Managers: C. Jones, M. Lowe (Mktg Serv Mgr), P. Waite (Tech Serv Mgr)
Immediate Holding Company: STOURBRIDGE MP LIMITED
Registration no: 06800530 **VAT No.:** GB 443 6828 32
Date established: 2009 **Turnover:** £2m - £5m **No.of Employees:** 51 - 100
Product Groups: 36

Date of Accounts	Apr 11	Apr 10
Sales Turnover	5m	4m
Pre Tax Profit/Loss	-1m	-741
Working Capital	1m	1m
Fixed Assets	314	378
Current Assets	2m	2m
Current Liabilities	127	122

R & M Metal Finishing Ltd
Unit 8 Old Forge Trading Estate Dudley Road, Stourbridge, DY9 8EL
Tel: 01384-266022 **Fax:** 01384-898766
E-mail: enquiries@rmmetalfinishing.co.uk
Website: http://www.rmmetalfinishing.co.uk
Directors: M. Rogers (Prop)
Managers: R. Hunt (Eng Serv Mgr)
Immediate Holding Company: R & M METAL FINISHING LTD
Registration no: 05218098 **Date established:** 2004
No.of Employees: 11 - 20 **Product Groups:** 32, 48

Date of Accounts	Sep 11	Sep 10	Sep 09
Working Capital	80	18	4
Current Assets	307	156	182

S Y R Ltd
Lye Bypass Lye, Stourbridge, DY9 8HG
Tel: 01384-892021 **Fax:** 01384-422675
E-mail: info@syrclean.com
Website: http://www.syrclean.com
Bank(s): National Westminster Bank Plc
Directors: S. Young (Ch), D. Deo (Fin), C. Adams (Dep Ch)
Managers: T. Jones (Prod Mgr), J. Jasper (Sales Prom Mgr)
Ultimate Holding Company: SCOT YOUNG LIMITED (CANADA)
Immediate Holding Company: SCOT YOUNG RESEARCH LIMITED
Registration no: 00481830 **VAT No.:** GB 277 2297 28
Date established: 1950 **Turnover:** £10m - £20m
No.of Employees: 21 - 50 **Product Groups:** 37

Date of Accounts	Aug 10	Aug 09	Aug 08
Sales Turnover	17m	16m	N/A
Pre Tax Profit/Loss	795	766	-517
Working Capital	3m	3m	2m
Fixed Assets	4m	2m	2m
Current Assets	7m	7m	7m
Current Liabilities	1m	2m	1m

Bob Sanderson Video Production
82 Chapel Street Wordsley, Stourbridge, DY8 5QP
Tel: 01384-271073 **Fax:** 01384-271073
E-mail: info@voxvisionvideoproductions.co.uk
Website: http://www.voxvisionvideoproductions.co.uk
Directors: B. Sanderson (MD)
Registration no: 05937662 **Date established:** 2006
No.of Employees: 1 - 10 **Product Groups:** 81, 89

Date of Accounts	Sep 09	Sep 08	Sep 07
Working Capital	26	17	5
Fixed Assets	4	5	5
Current Assets	33	23	8

The Screw Shop
Unit 3 Monarch Works Hill Street, Lye, Stourbridge, DY9 8TW
Tel: 01384-350100 **Fax:** 01384-825077
Website: http://www.screwshop.co.uk
Directors: T. Kirton (Fin), J. Elliott (MD)
Managers: R. Pritchard (Tech Serv Mgr)
No.of Employees: 21 - 50 **Product Groups:** 35

Shelectric Control Panel Mnfrs
1 Stone Lane Kinver, Stourbridge, DY7 6EQ
Tel: 01384-878855 **Fax:** 01384-878866
E-mail: frank.shelectric@hotmail.co.uk
Managers: F. Probert (Chief Eng)
Immediate Holding Company: SHELECTRIC LIMITED
Registration no: 06955711 **Date established:** 2009
Turnover: Up to £250,000 **No.of Employees:** 1 - 10 **Product Groups:** 37

Date of Accounts	Jul 10
Working Capital	6
Fixed Assets	1
Current Assets	17

Static Safe Ltd
6 Timmis Road, Stourbridge, DY9 7BQ
Tel: 01384-898599 **Fax:** 01384-898577
E-mail: sse@static-safe.demon.co.uk
Website: http://www.static-safe.co.uk
Directors: P. Dickens (MD)
Ultimate Holding Company: KITE CONNEXION HOLDINGS LIMITED
Immediate Holding Company: STATIC SAFE ENVIRONMENTS LIMITED
Registration no: 01358881 **VAT No.:** GB 443 6828 32
Date established: 1978 **Turnover:** £1m - £2m **No.of Employees:** 1 - 10
Product Groups: 23, 36, 45

Date of Accounts	Jan 12	Jan 11	Jan 10
Working Capital	475	421	286
Fixed Assets	10	14	13
Current Assets	700	623	383

Stourbridge Lion Ltd
Parkbrook House Talbot Street, Lye, Stourbridge, DY9 8UH
Tel: 01384-891297 **Fax:** 01384-423940
E-mail: general@brockway-conveyors.com
Website: http://www.stourbridge.co.uk
Bank(s): Lloyds TSB Bank plc
Directors: J. Noble (Prop)
Registration no: 04807167 **Date established:** 2007 **Turnover:** £1m - £2m
No.of Employees: 11 - 20 **Product Groups:** 45

Date of Accounts	Jun 08	Jun 07	Jun 06
Working Capital	-16	-94	-54
Fixed Assets	109	117	85
Current Assets	428	424	426
Current Liabilities	444	518	480
Total Share Capital	1	1	1

Stourbridge Turning & Grinding Ltd
Rufford Road, Stourbridge, DY9 7NE
Tel: 01384-443050 **Fax:** 01384-443051
E-mail: enquiries@stag-eng.co.uk
Website: http://www.stag-eng.co.uk
Bank(s): Yorkshire
Directors: G. Pargeter (MD)
Ultimate Holding Company: STOURBRIDGE TURNING & GRINDING (HOLDINGS) LIMITED
Immediate Holding Company: STOURBRIDGE TURNING & GRINDING LIMITED
Registration no: 03002690 **VAT No.:** GB 277 2373 38
Date established: 1994 **Turnover:** £1m - £2m **No.of Employees:** 11 - 20
Product Groups: 35, 48

Date of Accounts	Mar 12	Mar 11	Mar 10
Working Capital	6	-2	-42
Fixed Assets	837	718	780
Current Assets	621	651	375

T W Blaymires Ltd
Orchard Lane, Stourbridge, DY9 8JD
Tel: 01384-895151 **Fax:** 01384-895725
E-mail: sales@twblaymires.com
Website: http://www.twblaymires.com
Bank(s): Lloyds TSB
Directors: A. Hughes (Ch), M. Hughes (MD), P. Rowse (MD)
Managers: M. Luckman (I.T. Exec)
Ultimate Holding Company: A.K.HUGHES LIMITED
Immediate Holding Company: T.W. BLAYMIRES LIMITED
Registration no: 00333983 **VAT No.:** GB 276 8125 33
Date established: 1937 **Turnover:** £1m - £2m **No.of Employees:** 11 - 20
Product Groups: 48

Date of Accounts	Mar 11	Mar 10	Mar 09
Working Capital	10	-49	291
Fixed Assets	N/A	60	20
Current Assets	19	638	428

Travis Perkins plc
45 Stourbridge Road, Stourbridge, DY9 7DG
Tel: 01384-422314 **Fax:** 01384-422860
E-mail: stourbridge@travisperkins.co.uk
Website: http://www.travisperkins.co.uk
Directors: T. Travis (Ch)
Managers: N. Ashton (District Mgr)
Immediate Holding Company: TRAVIS PERKINS PLC
Registration no: 00824821 **Date established:** 1964
No.of Employees: 1 - 10 **Product Groups:** 66

Date of Accounts	Dec 11	Dec 10	Dec 09
Sales Turnover	4779m	3153m	2931m
Pre Tax Profit/Loss	270m	197m	213m
Working Capital	133m	159m	248m
Fixed Assets	2771m	2749m	2108m
Current Assets	1421m	1329m	1035m
Current Liabilities	473m	412m	109m

Vanguard Foundry
Bott Lane, Stourbridge, DY9 7AW
Tel: 01384-422557 **Fax:** 01384-423338
E-mail: bhiggins@vanguardfoundry.co.uk
Website: http://www.vanguardfoundry.co.uk
Bank(s): Barclays
Directors: C. Mintern (MD)
Immediate Holding Company: VANGUARD FOUNDRY LIMITED
Registration no: 01743426 **VAT No.:** GB 388 6103 26
Date established: 1983 **Turnover:** £5m - £10m
No.of Employees: 101 - 250 **Product Groups:** 34

Date of Accounts	Sep 11	Sep 10	Sep 09
Sales Turnover	10m	7m	5m
Pre Tax Profit/Loss	233	368	-630
Working Capital	1m	938	523
Fixed Assets	1m	830	950
Current Assets	2m	2m	1m
Current Liabilities	235	297	98

Vaughans Hope Works Ltd
Baker House The Hayes, Stourbridge, DY9 8RS
Tel: 01384-424232 **Fax:** 01384-893171
E-mail: sales@anvils.co.uk
Website: http://www.anvils.co.uk
Directors: D. Butterworth (Dir), G. Cattell (Sales), M. Bourne (Dir), T. Bourne (Co Sec)
Managers: A. Thompson (Sales Prom Mgr), J. Whitehouse (Accounts)
Immediate Holding Company: VAUGHANS (HOPE WORKS) LIMITED
Registration no: 03355759 **VAT No.:** GB 799 6048 60
Date established: 1997 **Turnover:** £500,000 - £1m
No.of Employees: 1 - 10 **Product Groups:** 14, 24, 25, 34, 35, 36, 38, 40, 41, 42, 45, 46, 47, 48, 49, 66, 67

Vee Bee Filtration UK Ltd
Old Wharf Road, Stourbridge, DY8 4LS
Tel: 01384-378884 **Fax:** 01384-374179
E-mail: bradleyr@veebee.co.uk
Website: http://www.veebee.co.uk

see next page

Vee Bee Filtration UK Ltd - Cont'd

Directors: R. Bradley (Dir)
Ultimate Holding Company: VEE BEE LIMITED
Immediate Holding Company: VEE BEE FILTRATION UK LIMITED
Registration no: 02713463 **VAT No.:** 786 7092 77 **Date established:** 1992
Turnover: £2m - £5m **No.of Employees:** 51 - 100 **Product Groups:** 42

Date of Accounts	Sep 11	Jun 10	Jun 09
Sales Turnover	8m	7m	7m
Pre Tax Profit/Loss	281	817	494
Working Capital	2m	1m	752
Fixed Assets	100	107	75
Current Assets	4m	4m	3m
Current Liabilities	384	472	818

W H Hill & Sons Holloware Ltd
Attwood Street, Stourbridge, DY9 8RU
Tel: 01384-422661 **Fax:** 01384-423163
E-mail: info@whhill.co.uk
Website: http://www.whhill.co.uk
Directors: J. Hill (MD), J. Collins (Fin)
Ultimate Holding Company: W.H. HILL & SON (HOLLOWARE) LIMITED
Immediate Holding Company: MAIN LINE PRODUCTS (RICHARDS)
Registration no: 00490006 **Date established:** 1950
Turnover: Up to £250,000 **No.of Employees:** 1 - 10 **Product Groups:** 34

Date of Accounts	Mar 11	Mar 10	Mar 08
Working Capital	152	161	153
Fixed Assets	14	3	6
Current Assets	160	166	159

Webgear Design Solutions
87 Barnett Lane, Stourbridge, DY8 5PS
Tel: 01384-352153
E-mail: info@webgear.co.uk
Website: http://www.webgear.co.uk
Directors: A. Harper (Prop)
Registration no: 07190171 **Date established:** 2006
No.of Employees: 1 - 10 **Product Groups:** 44

Worcester Presses (a division of Jones & Attwood Ltd)
Titan Works Old Wharf Road, Amblecote, Stourbridge, DY8 4LR
Tel: 01384-392266 **Fax:** 01384-374261
E-mail: sales@worcesterpresses.co.uk
Website: http://www.worcesterpresses.co.uk
Directors: C. Higgins (Dir)
Immediate Holding Company: WORCESTER PRESSES LIMITED
Registration no: 05399230 **Date established:** 2005 **Turnover:** £5m - £10m
No.of Employees: 1 - 10 **Product Groups:** 40, 42, 46, 47, 48

Date of Accounts	Mar 12	Mar 11	Mar 10
Working Capital	334	280	221
Fixed Assets	14	38	41
Current Assets	808	829	547

Sutton Coldfield

A.S.A.P. Tyres & Exhausts Limited
Beechoak House 38 Knighton Road, Sutton Coldfield, B74 4NX
Tel: 0121-270 6555 **Fax:** 0870-7625202
E-mail: admin@asaptyres.com
Website: http://www.asaptyres.com
Directors: T. Hunt (Dir)
Managers: K. Hunt (Sales Admin)
Registration no: 02759259 **Date established:** 1992
Turnover: £250,000 - £500,000 **No.of Employees:** 1 - 10
Product Groups: 29

Date of Accounts	Nov 07	Nov 06	Nov 05
Working Capital	-34	4	4
Fixed Assets	2	2	3
Current Assets	72	87	80
Current Liabilities	105	82	76

Accles & Shelvoke Ltd
Selco Way Off First Avenue Minworth Industrial Estate, Minworth, Sutton Coldfield, B76 1BA
Tel: 0121-313 4567 **Fax:** 0121-313 4569
E-mail: stewartmorris@eley.co.uk
Website: http://www.acclesandshelvoke.co.uk
Bank(s): Lloyds TSB Bank plc
Managers: S. Morris (Mgr)
Ultimate Holding Company: IMI PLC
Immediate Holding Company: ACCLES & SHELVOKE LIMITED
Registration no: 00220533 **VAT No.:** GB 405 2661 78
Date established: 2027 **Turnover:** £2m - £5m **No.of Employees:** 51 - 100
Product Groups: 36, 41

Date of Accounts	Dec 11	Dec 10	Dec 09
Sales Turnover	5m	4m	4m
Pre Tax Profit/Loss	2m	2m	1m
Working Capital	2m	2m	5m
Fixed Assets	287	311	14
Current Assets	6m	6m	6m
Current Liabilities	585	538	439

Allied Garage Doors
Langley Gorse Fox Hollies Road, Sutton Coldfield, B76 2RU
Tel: 0121-626 0055 **Fax:** 0870-633891
E-mail: alliedgaragedoors@talktalk.net
Website: http://www.alliedgaragedoors.co.uk
Directors: P. Morris (Prop)
Date established: 1993 **No.of Employees:** 1 - 10 **Product Groups:** 30, 35, 36

Aluminium Powder Co. Ltd
Forge Lane Minworth Industrial Park, Minworth, Sutton Coldfield, B76 1AH
Tel: 0121-351 6119 **Fax:** 0121-351 7604
E-mail: sales@alpoco.co.uk
Website: http://www.alpoco.co.uk
Bank(s): Barclays, Sheffield
Directors: D. Beare (Co Sec), J. Hamer (Co Sec)
Ultimate Holding Company: AMG ADVANCED METALLURGICAL GROUP (NETHERLANDS)
Immediate Holding Company: ALUMINIUM POWDER COMPANY LIMITED (THE)
Registration no: 00961050 **VAT No.:** GB 798 6326 65
Date established: 1969 **Turnover:** £20m - £50m
No.of Employees: 51 - 100 **Product Groups:** 34

Date of Accounts	Dec 07	Dec 06	Dec 05
Sales Turnover	62438	50339	43277
Pre Tax Profit/Loss	20	87	1382
Working Capital	10175	9543	8739
Fixed Assets	4606	5416	6249
Current Assets	16798	15245	13798
Current Liabilities	6623	5702	5059
Total Share Capital	837	837	837
ROCE% (Return on Capital Employed)	0.1	0.6	9.2
ROT% (Return on Turnover)	0.0	0.2	3.2

B1 Marketing
12 Squires Croft, Sutton Coldfield, B76 2RY
Tel: 07852-552008
E-mail: info@marketinghype.co.uk
Website: http://www.marketinghype.co.uk
Managers: M. Cotton (Sales Prom Mgr)
Date established: 2008 **No.of Employees:** 1 - 10 **Product Groups:** 81

Batt Cables
1st Floor 11 Emmanuel Court 12 Reddicroft, Sutton Coldfield, B73 6AZ
Tel: 0121-321 1745 **Fax:** 0121-313 2891
E-mail: battindustrial.sales@batt.co.uk
Website: http://www.batt.co.uk
Managers: M. Evans (Sales Admin)
Immediate Holding Company: JAMES HOFTON & CO. (BIRMINGHAM) LIMITED
Registration no: 01353688 **Date established:** 1984
No.of Employees: 1 - 10 **Product Groups:** 30, 35, 36, 37, 38, 44, 66, 67

Bead Technologies Ltd
2 Union House Union Drive, Sutton Coldfield, B73 5TN
Tel: 0121-354 3854 **Fax:** 0845-017 6269
E-mail: admin@beadtech.co.uk
Website: http://www.beadtech.co.uk
Directors: S. Rathod (MD)
Immediate Holding Company: BEAD TECHNOLOGIES LTD
Registration no: 04607253 **Date established:** 2002
Turnover: £250,000 - £500,000 **No.of Employees:** 1 - 10
Product Groups: 29, 45, 61

Date of Accounts	Mar 12	Mar 11	Mar 10
Working Capital	57	79	31
Fixed Assets	4	6	N/A
Current Assets	110	243	114

Brookvale Manufacturing Co. Ltd
15 Reddicap Trading Estate, Sutton Coldfield, B75 7DQ
Tel: 0121-378 0833 **Fax:** 0121-311 1794
E-mail: jtidball@brookvale-manufacturing.co.uk
Website: http://www.brookvale-manufacturing.co.uk
Bank(s): Royal Bank of Scotland, Birmingham
Directors: G. Chadwick (Co Sec), J. Tidball (MD)
Immediate Holding Company: BROOKVALE MANUFACTURING CO. LIMITED(THE)
Registration no: 00465373 **VAT No.:** GB 109 3102 12
Date established: 1949 **Turnover:** £1m - £2m **No.of Employees:** 21 - 50
Product Groups: 35, 39, 46, 48

Date of Accounts	Mar 12	Mar 11	Mar 10
Working Capital	698	675	682
Fixed Assets	120	114	120
Current Assets	809	788	770

Burroughes & Watts
Carroway Head Farm Carroway Head, Canwell, Sutton Coldfield, B75 5RY
Tel: 0121-323 2043 **Fax:** 0121-323 2043
E-mail: sales@burroughesandwatts.com
Website: http://www.burroughesandwatts.com
Directors: M. Jones (Prop)
Immediate Holding Company: BURROUGHES & WATTS LIMITED
Registration no: 04463729 **Date established:** 2002
No.of Employees: 1 - 10 **Product Groups:** 23, 26, 49, 65

Cembre Ltd
Estate Office Dunton Park Kingsbury Road, Curdworth, Sutton Coldfield, B76 9EB
Tel: 01675-470440 **Fax:** 01675-470220
E-mail: sales@cembre.co.uk
Website: http://www.cembre.com
Bank(s): Lloyds TSB
Directors: B. Davies (MD), B. Davies (MD), S. Laraway (Comm)
Managers: I. Wood (Tech Serv Mgr), D. Davies (Fin Mgr)
Ultimate Holding Company: LYSNE SPA (ITALY)
Immediate Holding Company: CEMBRE LTD.
Registration no: 02072165 **VAT No.:** GB 455 7372 25
Date established: 1986 **Turnover:** £10m - £20m
No.of Employees: 51 - 100 **Product Groups:** 36, 37, 39, 40, 45

Date of Accounts	Dec 11	Dec 10	Dec 09
Sales Turnover	14m	12m	11m
Pre Tax Profit/Loss	1m	1m	1m
Working Capital	4m	3m	3m
Fixed Assets	4m	4m	4m
Current Assets	7m	6m	5m
Current Liabilities	964	709	595

Centre Tank Services
41 Forge Lane Minworth Industrial Park, Minworth, Sutton Coldfield, B76 1AH
Tel: 0121-351 4445 **Fax:** 0121-351 4442
E-mail: sales@centretank.com
Website: http://www.centretank.com
Bank(s): Lloyds TSB Bank plc
Directors: M. Terry (MD)
Managers: D. Dogan, J. Ferrar (Mktg Serv Mgr), R. Terry (Tech Serv Mgr)
Ultimate Holding Company: FLOWMAX HOLDINGS LIMITED (BVI)
Immediate Holding Company: CENTRE TANK SERVICES LIMITED
Registration no: 02136427 **VAT No.:** GB 478 2038 30
Date established: 1987 **Turnover:** £2m - £5m **No.of Employees:** 11 - 20
Product Groups: 23, 29, 36, 38, 39, 40, 42, 68

Date of Accounts	Apr 12	Apr 11	Apr 10
Working Capital	955	162	503
Fixed Assets	52	793	52
Current Assets	3m	2m	2m
Current Liabilities	574	492	313

Chambers Ford
Coleshill Road, Sutton Coldfield, B75 7BS
Tel: 0121-311 1133 **Fax:** 0121-311 1118
E-mail: nhowes@chambers.ford.co.uk
Website: http://www.chambers-ford.co.uk
Directors: A. Howes (Fin), N. Howes (MD)
Managers: J. Smith (Buyer), M. Yates (Tech Serv Mgr), J. Westwood (Personnel), D. Howes
Immediate Holding Company: CHAMBERS OF SUTTON LIMITED
Registration no: 00315732 **Date established:** 1936
Turnover: £20m - £50m **No.of Employees:** 101 - 250 **Product Groups:** 68

Date of Accounts	Dec 11	Dec 10	Dec 09
Sales Turnover	23m	26m	25m
Pre Tax Profit/Loss	-158	220	405
Working Capital	-972	-641	-538
Fixed Assets	4m	4m	4m
Current Assets	5m	6m	7m
Current Liabilities	590	402	327

Cleaning Associates
18 All Saints Drive, Sutton Coldfield, B74 4AG
Tel: 0121-323 3232 **Fax:** 0121-323 3232
E-mail: admin@cleaningassociates.co.uk
Website: http://www.cleaningassociates.co.uk
Directors: K. Nicolson (Prop)
Immediate Holding Company: CHEMSPEC DIRECT LIMITED
Registration no: 06069177 **Date established:** 2007
No.of Employees: 1 - 10 **Product Groups:** 23

Clevedon Fasteners Ltd
Unit 11 Reddicap Trading Estate, Sutton Coldfield, B75 7BU
Tel: 0121-378 0619 **Fax:** 0121-378 3186
E-mail: sales@clevedon-fasteners.co.uk
Website: http://www.clevedon-fasteners.co.uk
Bank(s): Lloyds TSB Bank plc
Directors: S. Hardeman (MD), S. Hardieman (MD), C. Hopkins (Fin), C. Langam (Ch)
Managers: S. Morris (Sales Off Mgr)
Ultimate Holding Company: LANGHAM INDUSTRIES LIMITED
Immediate Holding Company: CLEVEDON FASTENERS LIMITED
Registration no: 03859239 **VAT No.:** GB 747 7844 78
Date established: 1999 **Turnover:** £2m - £5m **No.of Employees:** 21 - 50
Product Groups: 35

Date of Accounts	Dec 10	Dec 09	Dec 08
Sales Turnover	3m	3m	3m
Pre Tax Profit/Loss	193	6	-212
Working Capital	1m	1m	1m
Fixed Assets	480	567	580
Current Assets	2m	1m	2m
Current Liabilities	117	57	82

Coltman Precast Concrete Ltd
London Road Canwell, Sutton Coldfield, B75 5SX
Tel: 01543-480482 **Fax:** 01543-481587
E-mail: martin.smethurst@coltman.co.uk
Website: http://www.coltman.co.uk
Bank(s): Barclays
Directors: M. Smethurst (Co Sec)
Managers: L. Gilbert (Personnel), R. Stephenson (Sales & Mktg Mg), C. Bayton (Purch Mgr), R. Hackett (Tech Serv Mgr)
Ultimate Holding Company: VALERIE COLTMAN HOLDINGS LIMITED
Immediate Holding Company: COLTMAN PRECAST CONCRETE LIMITED
Registration no: 01032721 **VAT No.:** GB 109 5802 71
Date established: 1971 **Turnover:** £5m - £10m
No.of Employees: 101 - 250 **Product Groups:** 33

Date of Accounts	Mar 11	Mar 10	Mar 09
Sales Turnover	9m	9m	N/A
Pre Tax Profit/Loss	-630	-323	173
Working Capital	2m	2m	2m
Fixed Assets	867	1m	2m
Current Assets	5m	5m	5m
Current Liabilities	243	318	421

Compass Window Systems Ltd
Unit 19 Reddicap Trading Estate, Sutton Coldfield, B75 7BU
Tel: 0121-311 0128 **Fax:** 0121-311 0129
Website: http://www.compasswindows.com
Directors: D. Hunt (MD), L. Bird (Fin)
Immediate Holding Company: COMPASS WINDOW SYSTEMS LIMITED
Registration no: 04094523 **Date established:** 2000
No.of Employees: 1 - 10 **Product Groups:** 33, 35

Date of Accounts	Nov 11	Nov 10	Nov 09
Working Capital	15	8	-7
Fixed Assets	12	15	20
Current Assets	91	70	58

Creative Media Company
Coppice View Studio Mountford Drive, Sutton Coldfield, B75 6TA
Tel: 08453-130970
E-mail: studio@creative-media.biz
Website: http://www.creative-media.biz
Directors: S. Bridges (MD)
Immediate Holding Company: THE CREATIVE MEDIA COMPANY (UK) LIMITED
Registration no: 04850507 **Date established:** 2003
Turnover: Up to £250,000 **No.of Employees:** 1 - 10 **Product Groups:** 27, 28, 44, 80, 81, 84, 86, 89

Date of Accounts	Mar 12	Mar 11	Mar 10
Working Capital	-2	-4	17
Fixed Assets	3	5	5
Current Assets	37	32	45

Cunningham & Co
Europa House 384 Boldmere Road, Sutton Coldfield, B73 5EZ
Tel: 0121-244 2929 **Fax:** 0121-244 6040
E-mail: mail@cunninghamandco.co.uk
Website: http://www.housesurveyors.org
Directors: A. Cunningham (MD), E. Cunningham (Fin)
Immediate Holding Company: CUNNINGHAM & CO LIMITED
Registration no: 05156065 **Date established:** 2004
No.of Employees: 1 - 10 **Product Groups:** 35

Date of Accounts	Mar 10	Mar 09	Mar 08
Working Capital	-30	-11	-17
Fixed Assets	3	4	145
Current Assets	10	46	68

Cyril Charlesworth & Co. Ltd
Wishaw Lane Curdworth, Sutton Coldfield, B76 9EL
Tel: 01675-470382 **Fax:** 01675-470467
E-mail: sales@charlesworthmouldings.co.uk
Website: http://www.charlesworthmouldings.co.uk
Directors: J. Cummings (MD), S. Cummings (Fin)
Immediate Holding Company: CYRIL CHARLESWORTH & CO. LIMITED
Registration no: 01178804 **VAT No.:** 109 5940 59 **Date established:** 1974
Turnover: Up to £250,000 **No.of Employees:** 1 - 10 **Product Groups:** 30, 48

Date of Accounts	Dec 11	Dec 10	Dec 07
Working Capital	-40	-40	-40
Fixed Assets	80	80	80

Current Liabilities	N/A	N/A	40

Doors & Hardware Ltd
Taskmaster Works Maybrook Road, Minworth, Sutton Coldfield, B76 1AL
Tel: 0121-351 5276 **Fax:** 0121-313 1228
E-mail: sales@taskmaster.co
Website: http://www.doors-and-hardware.com
Directors: A. Fitzpatrick (Prop), R. Warmington (MD), G. Drury (Co Sec), A. Fitzpatrick (MD), D. Warmington (MD)
Managers: R. Warmington (Sales Prom Mgr)
Immediate Holding Company: DOORS & HARDWARE LIMITED
Registration no: 01447886 **Date established:** 1979 **Turnover:** £2m - £5m
No.of Employees: 21 - 50 **Product Groups:** 35, 36, 39, 40, 66

Date of Accounts	Dec 09	Dec 08	Dec 07
Sales Turnover	N/A	4m	3m
Pre Tax Profit/Loss	N/A	151	-116
Working Capital	-126	215	73
Fixed Assets	69	83	77
Current Assets	1m	2m	1m
Current Liabilities	842	775	632

Encoders UK
Unit 5a The Courtyard Reddicap Trading Estate, Sutton Coldfield, B75 7BU
Tel: 0121-378 5577 **Fax:** 0121-378 5599
E-mail: info@encoders-uk.com
Website: http://www.encoders-uk.com
Directors: M. Perkins (MD)
Immediate Holding Company: ENCODERS UK LIMITED
Registration no: 02900854 **Date established:** 1994
Turnover: £500,000 - £1m **No.of Employees:** 1 - 10 **Product Groups:** 37, 38, 44, 46

Date of Accounts	Feb 08	Feb 11	Feb 10
Working Capital	17	-15	1
Fixed Assets	31	23	17
Current Assets	188	170	155

Enviro Call Ltd
Gate Lane, Sutton Coldfield, B73 5TT
Tel: 0121-355 5500 **Fax:** 0121-355 5514
E-mail: mick@envirocall.co.uk
Website: http://www.envirocall.co.uk
Directors: M. Tynan (MD), L. Tynan (Co Sec)
Ultimate Holding Company: KEELEX 273 LIMITED
Immediate Holding Company: ENVIROCALL LIMITED
Registration no: 02290784 **Date established:** 1988
No.of Employees: 21 - 50 **Product Groups:** 54, 84, 85

Date of Accounts	Feb 08	Feb 11	Feb 10
Working Capital	511	464	415
Fixed Assets	67	103	117
Current Assets	962	719	715

Eventsi Ltd
8 Silvermead Road, Sutton Coldfield, B73 5SR
Tel: 0121-240 1470
E-mail: enquiries@eventsimarquees.co.uk
Website: http://www.eventsimarquees.co.uk
Directors: Broad (MD), S. Smith (Prop)
Registration no: 03812899 **No.of Employees:** 1 - 10 **Product Groups:** 24, 34, 48, 83, 84

GB Inspection Systems
Unit 8c2 Maybrook Business Park Minworth, Sutton Coldfield, B76 1AL
Tel: 0121-351 5025 **Fax:** 0121-351 1178
E-mail: sales@gbinspection.com
Directors: R. Gauge (MD)
Immediate Holding Company: GB INSPECTION SYSTEMS LIMITED
Registration no: 03021497 **VAT No.:** GB 405 2514 91
Date established: 1995 **No.of Employees:** 1 - 10 **Product Groups:** 31, 32, 37, 38, 48, 85

Date of Accounts	Apr 12	Apr 11	Apr 10
Working Capital	369	223	152
Fixed Assets	144	172	205
Current Assets	494	364	395

G K N Driveline Services Ltd
5 Kingsbury Business Park Kingsbury Road, Minworth, Sutton Coldfield, B76 9DL
Tel: 0121-313 1661 **Fax:** 0121-313 2074
E-mail: sales@gkn.com
Website: http://www.gkndriveline.co.uk
Directors: A. Henstock (Co Sec)
Managers: D. Rogers (Personnel), S. Taylor (Chief Mgr)
Ultimate Holding Company: GKN PLC
Immediate Holding Company: GKN DRIVELINE SERVICE LIMITED
Registration no: 00649576 **Date established:** 1960
Turnover: £10m - £20m **No.of Employees:** 21 - 50 **Product Groups:** 39, 68

Date of Accounts	Dec 11	Dec 10	Dec 09
Sales Turnover	11m	11m	10m
Pre Tax Profit/Loss	623	-2m	554
Working Capital	9m	3m	5m
Fixed Assets	707	748	570
Current Assets	10m	4m	6m
Current Liabilities	471	296	329

H R P Sales Ltd
Unit 16 Fulford Drive Minworth Industrial Park, Minworth, Sutton Coldfield, B76 1DR
Tel: 0121-313 6720 **Fax:** 0121-313 2801
E-mail: birmingham@hrpltd.co.uk
Website: http://www.hrponline.co.uk
Managers: D. Mutton (Mgr)
Immediate Holding Company: HRP LIMITED
Registration no: 00832237 **Date established:** 1964
Turnover: £50m - £75m **No.of Employees:** 1 - 10 **Product Groups:** 40, 66

Haslimann Taylor Ltd
1 Wrens Court 53 Lower Queen Street, Sutton Coldfield, B72 1RT
Tel: 0121-355 3446 **Fax:** 0121-355 3393
E-mail: reception@htpr.com
Website: http://www.haslimanntaylor.com
Bank(s): Co-operative Bank
Directors: J. Lees (Co Sec), B. Eames (Dir)
Managers: B. Mathias
Ultimate Holding Company: HUNTSWORTH PLC
Immediate Holding Company: HASLIMANN TAYLOR LIMITED
Registration no: 02167675 **VAT No.:** GB 478 2493 06
Date established: 1987 **Turnover:** £500,000 - £1m
No.of Employees: 11 - 20 **Product Groups:** 44, 52, 81, 84

Date of Accounts	Dec 10	Dec 09
Current Assets	101	101

Heartlands Business Gifts Ltd
Unit 8e-F Maybrook Road Maybrook Business Park, Minworth, Sutton Coldfield, B76 1AL
Tel: 0121-313 0944 **Fax:** 0121-313 0945
E-mail: sales@heartlandsbusinessgifts.co.uk
Website: http://www.heartlandsbusinessgifts.co.uk
Directors: E. Sampson (Sales)
Immediate Holding Company: HEARTLANDS BUSINESS GIFTS LIMITED
Registration no: 04436384 **Date established:** 2002
No.of Employees: 1 - 10 **Product Groups:** 22, 23, 24, 25, 28, 29, 30, 33, 40, 49, 63, 64, 65, 67, 77, 80, 81, 87, 89

Date of Accounts	May 12	May 11	May 10
Working Capital	74	76	61
Fixed Assets	13	11	13
Current Assets	211	259	328
Current Liabilities	N/A	52	N/A

Hi Roller
34 Thornhill Park, Sutton Coldfield, B74 2LG
Tel: 0121-580 8410 **Fax:** 0121- 5808410
Directors: N. Crutchley (Prop)
Date established: 2004 **No.of Employees:** 1 - 10 **Product Groups:** 26, 35

Hozelock Ltd
Midpoint Park Kingsbury Road, Minworth, Sutton Coldfield, B76 1AB
Tel: 0121-313 1122 **Fax:** 0121-313 4243
E-mail: lorraine.thompson@hozelock.com
Website: http://www.hozelock.com
Directors: A. Cooper (Pers), P. Rush (MD)
Managers: D. Tuner (Comptroller), G. Coonbs (I.T. Exec), S. Reynolds (Purch Mgr)
Ultimate Holding Company: RASINDECK LIMITED
Immediate Holding Company: HOZELOCK LIMITED
Registration no: 00645367 **Date established:** 1959
Turnover: £20m - £50m **No.of Employees:** 1 - 10 **Product Groups:** 30

Date of Accounts	Sep 08	Sep 09	Oct 10
Sales Turnover	42m	43m	54m
Pre Tax Profit/Loss	-4m	2m	4m
Working Capital	2m	6m	10m
Fixed Assets	9m	7m	8m
Current Assets	28m	15m	18m
Current Liabilities	6m	6m	2m

Hydrop Enviromental Consultancy Services
Wrens Court 55 Lower Queen Street, Sutton Coldfield, B72 1RT
Tel: 0121-354 2030 **Fax:** 0121-354 8030
E-mail: info@hydrop.com
Website: http://www.hydrop.com
Directors: M. Koumi (Ptnr)
Turnover: Up to £250,000 **No.of Employees:** 1 - 10 **Product Groups:** 52, 54, 84, 86

Imek Precision Ltd
Unit 5a The Courtyard Reddicap Trading Estate, Sutton Coldfield, B75 7BU
Tel: 0121-378 5577 **Fax:** 0121-378 5599
E-mail: info@encoders-uk.com
Website: http://www.imek-precision.com
Directors: M. Perkins (MD), M. Perkins (Prop)
Immediate Holding Company: RARE ESTATE LIMITED
Registration no: 04245910 **Date established:** 2011
Turnover: £500,000 - £1m **No.of Employees:** 1 - 10 **Product Groups:** 38

J B Furnace Engineering Ltd
Unit 2a 21-2 Forge Lane Minworth Industrial Park, Minworth, Sutton Coldfield, B76 1AH
Tel: 0121-351 3496 **Fax:** 0121-313 1432
E-mail: sales@jbfurnace.com
Website: http://www.jbfurnace.com
Directors: A. Hillier (Comm)
Immediate Holding Company: J. B. FURNACE ENGINEERING LIMITED
Registration no: 01036890 **Date established:** 1972
Turnover: £500,000 - £1m **No.of Employees:** 1 - 10 **Product Groups:** 33, 40, 42, 46, 48, 51, 67, 84

Date of Accounts	Oct 11	Oct 10	Oct 09
Working Capital	103	104	104
Fixed Assets	32	4	7
Current Assets	283	150	217

J M G Engineering Co UK Ltd
PO Box 4451, Sutton Coldfield, B75 7QG
Tel: 07973-672149
E-mail: jim@jmgengineering.co.uk
Website: http://www.jmgengineering.co.uk
Directors: J. Gwilliam (MD), A. Gwilliam (Fin)
Immediate Holding Company: JMG ENGINEERING COMPANY (UK) LTD
Registration no: 04866673 **Date established:** 2003
No.of Employees: 1 - 10 **Product Groups:** 38, 40, 48

Date of Accounts	Mar 11	Mar 10	Mar 09
Working Capital	-113	-94	-90
Fixed Assets	7	9	13
Current Assets	27	24	16

Johnsons Veterinary Products Ltd
5 Reddicap Trading Estate, Sutton Coldfield, B75 7DF
Tel: 0121-378 1684 **Fax:** 0121-311 1758
E-mail: info@johnsons-vet.com
Website: http://www.johnsons-vet.com
Bank(s): Barclays
Directors: N. Franks (Chief Op Offcr), P. Gwynn (MD)
Managers: C. Ray (Purch Mgr), J. Robson (Personnel)
Immediate Holding Company: JOHNSONS VETERINARY PRODUCTS LIMITED
Registration no: 00489549 **VAT No.:** GB 109 6106 86
Date established: 1950 **Turnover:** £5m - £10m **No.of Employees:** 21 - 50
Product Groups: 62

Date of Accounts	Dec 11	Dec 10	Dec 09
Sales Turnover	8m	7m	8m
Pre Tax Profit/Loss	884	850	878
Working Capital	2m	2m	2m
Fixed Assets	643	395	400
Current Assets	3m	3m	3m
Current Liabilities	600	590	517

Kuehne & Nagel UK Ltd
Midpoint Park Kingsbury Road, Minworth, Sutton Coldfield, B76 1BL
Tel: 0121-625 2468 **Fax:** 0121-625 2426
Website: http://www.kuehne-nagel.com
Managers: C. Toot
Ultimate Holding Company: KUEHNE & NAGEL INTERNATIONAL AG (SWITZERLAND)
Immediate Holding Company: KUEHNE + NAGEL (UK) LIMITED
Registration no: 01463105 **VAT No.:** GB 584 6403 22
Date established: 1979 **No.of Employees:** 251 - 500 **Product Groups:** 76

Kween B Ltd
29 Dalkeith Road, Sutton Coldfield, B73 6PW
Tel: 0121-355 2662 **Fax:** 0121-355 8566
E-mail: duncan@kweenb.co.uk
Website: http://www.kweenb.co.uk
Directors: E. Bamforth (MD), S. Taylor (Fin)
Immediate Holding Company: Kween B. Ltd
Registration no: 01901857 **VAT No.:** GB 425 3602 75
Date established: 1985 **Turnover:** £1m - £2m **No.of Employees:** 1 - 10
Product Groups: 35, 37, 39, 42, 43, 44, 45, 84

Date of Accounts	Jul 08	Jul 07	Jul 06
Working Capital	121	120	113
Fixed Assets	1	1	3
Current Assets	219	197	175
Current Liabilities	98	77	63

Lampitt Fire Escapes
Lymore Ltd Keepers Road, Sutton Coldfield, B74 3AX
Tel: 0121-353 1522 **Fax:** 0121-353 1917
E-mail: richard@lymore.com
Website: http://www.lymore.com
Directors: R. Brosche (MD), R. Brosch (Dir), J. Lowe (Co Sec), J. Lowe (Fin)
Managers: R. Brosch (Sales Prom Mgr)
Immediate Holding Company: LYMORE LTD
Registration no: 02064282 **VAT No.:** GB 461 9844 17
Date established: 1986 **Turnover:** Up to £250,000
No.of Employees: 1 - 10 **Product Groups:** 35, 40, 52

Date of Accounts	Jan 11	Jan 09	Jan 08
Working Capital	-5	9	29
Fixed Assets	13	26	29
Current Assets	23	26	38

LBW Machines
7 Millbrook House 24 South Parade, Sutton Coldfield, B72 1QY
Tel: 0121-448 9660
E-mail: kieran@lineboringandwelding.com
Website: http://www.lineboringandwelding.com
Directors: K. Courtney (MD)
Registration no: 07641074 **Date established:** 2010 **Turnover:**
No.of Employees: 1 - 10 **Product Groups:** 46

Lifting Gear Hire plc
630 Chester Road, Sutton Coldfield, B73 5JR
Tel: 0121-350 5325 **Fax:** 01384- 455782
Website: http://www.lgh.co.uk
Directors: D. Rogers (Prop)
Ultimate Holding Company: SPEEDY HIRE PLC
Immediate Holding Company: SPEEDY LIFTING LIMITED
Registration no: 04529136 **Date established:** 2002
No.of Employees: 1 - 10 **Product Groups:** 35, 39, 45

Logico Control Systems
154 Station Road Wylde Green, Sutton Coldfield, B73 5LD
Tel: 0121-354 2587 **Fax:** 0121-354 2587
E-mail: info@logicosystems.co.uk
Website: http://www.logicosystems.co.uk
Directors: M. Stamoulis (MD)
No.of Employees: 1 - 10 **Product Groups:** 37, 84

Luhrfilter Ltd
58a Thornhill Road, Sutton Coldfield, B74 3EN
Tel: 0121-353 0176 **Fax:** 0121-353 4066
E-mail: sales@luhrgb.demon.co.uk
Website: http://www.luhrfiltergb.com
Managers: R. Jones (Chief Mgr)
Immediate Holding Company: LUHRFILTER LIMITED
Registration no: 01172350 **VAT No.:** GB 124 3706 93
Date established: 1974 **Turnover:** £1m - £2m **No.of Employees:** 1 - 10
Product Groups: 40, 42, 52, 54

Date of Accounts	Dec 11	Dec 10	Dec 09
Working Capital	613	794	1m
Fixed Assets	80	78	74
Current Assets	718	934	2m

M B E Computer Systems
14 Shooters Hill, Sutton Coldfield, B72 1HX
Tel: 0121-240 5989 **Fax:** 0121-240 5708
E-mail: tellmemore@m-b-e.co.uk
Website: http://www.m-b-e.co.uk
Directors: J. Roberts (Ptnr)
Immediate Holding Company: ANGLIAN WATER (AWG PLC)
Registration no: 02591424 **Date established:** 1991
Turnover: £250m - £500m **No.of Employees:** 1 - 10 **Product Groups:** 35, 52, 80

Mats4U
17 Maybrook Road Minworth, Sutton Coldfield, B76 1AL
Tel: 0800-1804024 **Fax:** 0121-351 1991
E-mail: sales@mats4u.co.uk
Website: http://www.mats4u.co.uk
Directors: S. Rawlins (MD)
Date established: 1969 **Turnover:** £500,000 - £1m
No.of Employees: 11 - 20 **Product Groups:** 23, 29, 30

Mayday Commercial Catering Services
21 Walmley Ash Road, Sutton Coldfield, B76 1HY
Tel: 0121-313 0301
Directors: D. Allman (Prop)
No.of Employees: 1 - 10 **Product Groups:** 20, 40, 41

Melting Solutions Ltd
Unit E Dunton Park Kingsbury Road, Curdworth, Sutton Coldfield, B76 9EB
Tel: 01675-470551 **Fax:** 01675-470645
E-mail: info@meltingsolutions.co.uk
Website: http://www.meltingsolutions.co.uk
Bank(s): Lloyds TSB Bank plc

see next page

Melting Solutions Ltd - Cont'd

Directors: D. Rankin (MD)
Ultimate Holding Company: MELTING SOLUTIONS (MIDLANDS) LIMITED
Immediate Holding Company: MELTING SOLUTIONS LIMITED
Registration no: 02724156 **VAT No.:** GB 444 5945 27
Date established: 1992 **Turnover:** £2m - £5m **No.of Employees:** 11 - 20
Product Groups: 40, 46, 48

Date of Accounts	Dec 11	Dec 10	Dec 09
Working Capital	468	425	585
Fixed Assets	77	110	170
Current Assets	769	951	1m

Mercian Science Ltd

Unit 8d2 Maybrook Road, Minworth, Sutton Coldfield, B76 1AL
Tel: 0121-352 3711 **Fax:** 0121-352 3722
E-mail: info@mercianscience.co.uk
Website: http://www.mercianscience.co.uk
Directors: J. Lewis (MD)
Managers: J. Usher (Lab Mgr), J. Usher (Mgr)
Immediate Holding Company: MERCIAN SCIENCE LIMITED
Registration no: 03626148 **Date established:** 1998
Turnover: £500,000 - £1m **No.of Employees:** 1 - 10 **Product Groups:** 54, 84

Date of Accounts	Sep 09	Sep 08	Sep 07
Working Capital	-6	11	14
Fixed Assets	32	30	40
Current Assets	167	104	98
Current Liabilities	N/A	N/A	11

Midland Security & Surveillance

14 Clarry Drive, Sutton Coldfield, B74 2RA
Tel: 0121-323 2126 **Fax:** 0121-323 2165
E-mail: enquiries@mss-security.co.uk
Website: http://www.mss-security.co.uk
Directors: D. Rooker (Prop)
Date established: 2002 **No.of Employees:** 1 - 10 **Product Groups:** 37, 40, 67

Newey & Eyre Ltd

Unit 34 Forge Lane Minworth Industrial Park, Minworth, Sutton Coldfield, B76 1AH
Tel: 0121-313 1001 **Fax:** 0121-351 4851
Website: http://www.neweyandeyre.co.uk
Directors: M. Smith (Dir & Gen Mgr)
Managers: C. White (Mgr)
Immediate Holding Company: NEWEY & EYRE LIMITED
Registration no: 00216596 **Date established:** 1926
Turnover: Up to £250,000 **No.of Employees:** 21 - 50 **Product Groups:** 37, 67

Nippon Distribution

8c Reddicap Trading Estate, Sutton Coldfield, B75 7BU
Tel: 0121-311 0313 **Fax:** 0121-311 0338
E-mail: nippondis@hotmail.com
Website: http://www.nippon-dis.co.uk
Directors: B. Gough (Dir)
Immediate Holding Company: NIPPON DISTRIBUTION LIMITED
Registration no: 02450424 **VAT No.:** GB 111 3961 05
Date established: 1989 **Turnover:** £500,000 - £1m
No.of Employees: 1 - 10 **Product Groups:** 39

C J Penn Sales Ltd

49 Hardwick Road, Sutton Coldfield, B74 3DN
Tel: 0121-580 9099 **Fax:** 0121-580 9088
Directors: M. Golland (Fin), B. Stokes (MD)
Immediate Holding Company: C. J. PENN (SALES) LIMITED
Registration no: 00473901 **VAT No.:** GB 101 7176 11
Date established: 1949 **Turnover:** Up to £250,000
No.of Employees: 1 - 10 **Product Groups:** 34, 37, 68, 87

Date of Accounts	Aug 11	Aug 10	Aug 09
Working Capital	16	17	12
Current Assets	44	19	15

Premier Paper Group

Midpoint Park Kingsbury Road, Minworth, Sutton Coldfield, B76 1AF
Tel: 0121-313 1115 **Fax:** 0121-313 2390
E-mail: graham.griffiths@paper.co.uk
Website: http://www.paper.co.uk
Directors: C. Candler (Fin), D. Jones (Mkt Research), G. Griffiths (MD), R. Jackson (Pers)
Managers: A. Day (Tech Serv Mgr), J. Hinds, N. Maritu (Personnel)
Ultimate Holding Company: G. C. PAPER LIMITED
Immediate Holding Company: PREMIER PAPER GROUP LIMITED
Registration no: 03672117 **Date established:** 1998
Turnover: £125m - £250m **No.of Employees:** 51 - 100
Product Groups: 66

Date of Accounts	Dec 11	Dec 10	Dec 09
Sales Turnover	155m	151m	141m
Pre Tax Profit/Loss	6m	6m	1m
Working Capital	18m	16m	7m
Fixed Assets	3m	3m	15m
Current Assets	62m	63m	53m
Current Liabilities	5m	4m	4m

Denis Rawlins Ltd

Unit 17 Castle Vale Industrial Estate Maybrook Road, Minworth, Sutton Coldfield, B76 1AL
Tel: 0121-351 4444 **Fax:** 0121-351 1991
E-mail: stephen.rawlins@rawlins.co.uk
Website: http://www.rawlins.co.uk
Directors: S. Rawlins (MD)
Immediate Holding Company: DENIS RAWLINS LIMITED
Registration no: 01546492 **Date established:** 1981 **Turnover:** £1m - £2m
No.of Employees: 11 - 20 **Product Groups:** 23, 27, 29, 30, 40, 42, 49, 68

Date of Accounts	Jun 12	Jun 11	Jun 10
Working Capital	495	658	609
Fixed Assets	662	683	679
Current Assets	762	905	945

Selco

First Avenue Minworth, Sutton Coldfield, B76 1BA
Tel: 0121-313 2020 **Fax:** 0121-313 0523
E-mail: mark.bramwell@selcobw.com
Website: http://www.selcobw.com
Bank(s): Lloyds
Directors: M. Aldridge (MD)
Managers: B. Deadman (Buyer), M. Greenslade (Mgr), M. Bramwell (Mgr), M. Branwell (Mgr), N. Fern (District Mgr)
Immediate Holding Company: 1ST AVENUE PROPERTIES LIMITED
Date established: 2007 **Turnover:** £2m - £5m **No.of Employees:** 21 - 50
Product Groups: 66

Severn Trent Water Ltd (t/a Severn Trent Services)

Park Lane Minworth, Sutton Coldfield, B76 9BL
Tel: 0121-722 4000 **Fax:** 0121-313 1938
E-mail: tony.ray@severntrent.co.uk
Website: http://www.severntrent.co.uk
Directors: M. Ashley (MD), R. Picken (Fin), T. Ray (Grp Chief Exec), S. Tilley (Prop), B. Hastings (Sales), A. Lloyd (Chief Op Offcr)
Managers: T. Duffy, R. Mayberry, N. Bradley, M. Sears (Sales Prom Mgr), L. Filoni, G. Perazzo, D. Shepherd, B. Hanson (Projects), A. Scudieri (Purch Mgr), A. Beech, R. Lewis
Ultimate Holding Company: 02366619
Immediate Holding Company: SEVERN TRENT WATER LIMITED
Registration no: 02366686 **VAT No.:** GB 486 9855 65
Date established: 1989 **Turnover:** £2m - £5m **No.of Employees:** 1 - 10
Product Groups: 31, 32, 35, 36, 38, 39, 41, 42, 43, 52, 54, 67, 85

W H Smith & Sons Tools Ltd

Water Orton Lane Minworth, Sutton Coldfield, B76 9BG
Tel: 0121-748 7777 **Fax:** 0121-749 6213
E-mail: peterr@whstools.co.uk
Website: http://www.whstools.co.uk
Bank(s): HSBC, Birmingham
Directors: P. Rushton (Fin), A. Kendrick (Sales)
Managers: M. Tetley (Tech Serv Mgr), A. Sharrocks (Buyer), D. Ticer (Personnel)
Ultimate Holding Company: W.H. SMITH & SONS HOLDINGS LIMITED
Immediate Holding Company: W.H.SMITH & SONS(TOOLS)LIMITED
Registration no: 00689319 **VAT No.:** GB 670 3127 58
Date established: 1961 **Turnover:** £10m - £20m
No.of Employees: 101 - 250 **Product Groups:** 30

Date of Accounts	Apr 10	Apr 11	May 08
Sales Turnover	12m	12m	17m
Pre Tax Profit/Loss	68	158	254
Working Capital	3m	3m	4m
Fixed Assets	1m	1m	2m
Current Assets	5m	6m	9m
Current Liabilities	796	728	1m

Spray Direct Ltd

75 Inglewood Grove, Sutton Coldfield, B74 3LW
Tel: 0121-353 7175 **Fax:** 0121-353 7041
E-mail: spraydirect@supanet.com
Website: http://www.spray-direct.com
Directors: K. Sealey (MD)
Immediate Holding Company: SPRAY DIRECT LIMITED
Registration no: 04446614 **Date established:** 2002
No.of Employees: 1 - 10 **Product Groups:** 38, 42

Date of Accounts	May 11	May 10	May 09
Working Capital	33	32	31
Current Assets	124	116	118

R Stahl Ltd (Switchgear Division)

Unit 11 Maybrook Road Maybrook Business Park, Minworth, Sutton Coldfield, B76 1AL
Tel: 0121-767 6400 **Fax:** 0121-767 6480
E-mail: info@rstahl.co.uk
Website: http://www.rstahl.co.uk
Bank(s): Barclays
Directors: T. Boden (Fin), C. Payne (Sales), P. Baker (MD)
Managers: C. Payne, M. Webb (Purch Mgr)
Ultimate Holding Company: R STAHL AG (GERMANY)
Immediate Holding Company: R. STAHL LIMITED
Registration no: 01046854 **Date established:** 1972
Turnover: £10m - £20m **No.of Employees:** 21 - 50 **Product Groups:** 35, 37, 40

Date of Accounts	Dec 11	Dec 10	Dec 09
Sales Turnover	11m	19m	9m
Pre Tax Profit/Loss	43	1m	507
Working Capital	-618	-215	1m
Fixed Assets	2m	2m	141
Current Assets	4m	6m	4m
Current Liabilities	662	1m	642

Sutton Coldfield Dairies

47 Ashfurlong Crescent, Sutton Coldfield, B75 6EN
Tel: 0121-448 0269 **Fax:** 0121-311 1893
E-mail: sales@scdairies.co.uk
Website: http://www.scdairies.co.uk
Directors: P. Mitchell (Prop)
Date established: 2004 **No.of Employees:** 1 - 10 **Product Groups:** 23, 24

Ti Tek

Bulls Lane Wishaw, Sutton Coldfield, B76 9QN
Tel: 0121-313 3355 **Fax:** 0121-313 3366
E-mail: info@titek.co.uk
Website: http://www.titek.co.uk
Directors: J. Price (MD)
Immediate Holding Company: SIGMA PUBLICITY & SHOPFITTING SERVICES LIMITED
Date established: 2007 **No.of Employees:** 1 - 10 **Product Groups:** 34, 35, 36, 37, 38, 39, 40, 42, 46, 48, 49, 66

Date of Accounts	Aug 11	Feb 08	Feb 10
Working Capital	N/A	31	N/A
Fixed Assets	10	30	10
Current Assets	N/A	31	N/A

Trasfor Electric Ltd

Belwell House 1a Belwell Lane Four Oaks, Sutton Coldfield, B74 4SA
Tel: 0121-323 3339 **Fax:** 0121-323 3301
E-mail: sales@firstinservice.co.uk
Website: http://www.trasfor.com
Directors: C. Zehnder (Fin)
Managers: A. Jackson (Sales & Mktg Mg)
Ultimate Holding Company: ABB LTD (SWITZERLAND)
Immediate Holding Company: TRASFOR ELECTRIC LIMITED
Registration no: 02666236 **VAT No.:** GB 559 2293 14
Date established: 1991 **Turnover:** £2m - £5m **No.of Employees:** 1 - 10
Product Groups: 37

Date of Accounts	Dec 11	Dec 10	Dec 09
Working Capital	80	141	284
Fixed Assets	17	14	1
Current Assets	152	220	359

W H S Halo

Midpoint Park Kingsbury Road Minworth, Sutton Coldfield, B76 1AF
Tel: 0121-749 3000 **Fax:** 0121-749 2511
E-mail: gemma.handley@bowaterbuildingproducts.com
Website: http://www.bowaterbuildingproducts.com
Bank(s): HSBC
Directors: R. Pearce (I.T. Dir), C. Baranowski (Fin), M. Stevenson (Sales & Mktg)
Managers: J. Holland, A. Winn (Personnel)
Ultimate Holding Company: G. C. PAPER LIMITED
Immediate Holding Company: WHS HALO LIMITED
Registration no: 05717265 **VAT No.:** GB 238 5870 31
Date established: 2006 **Turnover:** £50m - £75m
No.of Employees: 101 - 250 **Product Groups:** 30

Wave Tec

29 Planetree Road, Sutton Coldfield, B74 3SP
Tel: 0121-353 2474 **Fax:** 0121-353 2474
Directors: S. Taylor (Prop)
Date established: 1995 **No.of Employees:** 1 - 10 **Product Groups:** 36, 40

Webasto Roof Systems

Unit 7 Kingsbury Business Park Kingsbury Road, Minworth, Sutton Coldfield, B76 9DL
Tel: 0121-313 5600 **Fax:** 0121-351 4905
Website: http://www.webasto.com
Directors: K. Green (Fin), R. Strahanner (MD)
Managers: G. Twigg (Purch Mgr), A. Lowe (Personnel)
Ultimate Holding Company: WEBASTO AG FAHRZEUGTECHNIK (GERMANY)
Immediate Holding Company: WEBASTO ROOF SYSTEMS LTD.
Registration no: 02630029 **VAT No.:** GB 486 6727 89
Date established: 1991 **Turnover:** £20m - £50m
No.of Employees: 251 - 500 **Product Groups:** 39

Date of Accounts	Dec 11	Dec 10	Dec 09
Sales Turnover	55m	47m	25m
Pre Tax Profit/Loss	-3m	313	-2m
Working Capital	3m	7m	7m
Fixed Assets	2m	2m	3m
Current Assets	23m	19m	17m
Current Liabilities	5m	3m	2m

Tipton

A Q Central Ltd

Factory Road, Tipton, DY4 9AU
Tel: 0121-557 7131 **Fax:** 0121-520 2663
E-mail: a.q.central@btopenworld.com
Website: http://www.a.q.central.co.uk
Directors: L. Rodenhurst (Fin)
Managers: M. Ward (Chief Mgr)
Immediate Holding Company: A. Q. (CENTRAL) LIMITED
Registration no: 03353634 **Date established:** 1997
Turnover: £500,000 - £1m **No.of Employees:** 1 - 10 **Product Groups:** 40, 84

Date of Accounts	Dec 11	Dec 10	Dec 09
Working Capital	-27	-66	-30
Fixed Assets	240	244	198
Current Assets	178	207	213

Acorn Industrial Services Ltd Midlands

Units 17-21 Bloomfield Park Bloomfield Road, Tipton, DY4 9AH
Tel: 0121-521 5999 **Fax:** 0121-521 5888
E-mail: astokes@acorn-ind.co.uk
Website: http://www.acorn-ind.co.uk
Directors: D. Spilling (MD)
Managers: A. Stokes (Mgr), R. Hewitt (Mktg Serv Mgr)
Ultimate Holding Company: ACORN INDUSTRIAL SERVICES GROUP LTD
Immediate Holding Company: ACORN INDUSTRIAL SERVICES LIMITED
Registration no: 01733820 **Date established:** 1983
No.of Employees: 1 - 10 **Product Groups:** 30, 35, 38

Aeroplas UK Ltd

Great Western Way, Tipton, DY4 7AB
Tel: 0121-522 3000 **Fax:** 0121-522 3333
E-mail: mail@aeroplas.net
Website: http://www.aeroplas.net
Bank(s): Barclays
Directors: A. Gakhal (Dir)
Ultimate Holding Company: AEROPLAS HOLDINGS LTD.
Immediate Holding Company: AEROPLAS (U.K.) LIMITED
Registration no: 01376171 **Date established:** 1978
Turnover: £10m - £20m **No.of Employees:** 51 - 100 **Product Groups:** 30

Date of Accounts	Dec 11	Dec 10	Dec 09
Sales Turnover	11m	11m	N/A
Pre Tax Profit/Loss	186	232	244
Working Capital	1m	1m	591
Fixed Assets	4m	4m	4m
Current Assets	5m	5m	4m
Current Liabilities	171	183	450

Aire Body Care

Coneygre Road, Tipton, DY4 8XQ
Tel: 08454-301133 **Fax:** 0121-520 3001
Website: http://www.aire-trucks.com
Managers: A. Hawkyard (Chief Mgr)
Immediate Holding Company: CARRS TOOL STEELS LIMITED
Date established: 1991 **No.of Employees:** 1 - 10 **Product Groups:** 35, 39, 44

Date of Accounts	Mar 12	Mar 11	Mar 10
Sales Turnover	5m	N/A	N/A
Pre Tax Profit/Loss	507	N/A	N/A
Working Capital	636	408	375
Fixed Assets	2m	2m	2m
Current Assets	2m	2m	2m
Current Liabilities	908	N/A	N/A

Anglo Metals Ltd

Unit 1-2 Brymill Industrial Estate Brown Lion Street, Tipton, DY4 9EG
Tel: 0121-522 3350 **Fax:** 0121-522 3860
E-mail: anglometal@btconnect.com
Website: http://www.anglometals.co.uk

Directors: J. Sutton (MD)
Immediate Holding Company: ANGLO METALS LIMITED
Registration no: 04339091 **Date established:** 2001
Turnover: Up to £250,000 **No.of Employees:** 1 - 10 **Product Groups:** 34, 66

Date of Accounts	Dec 11	Dec 10	Dec 09
Working Capital	-8	-5	-6
Fixed Assets	9	10	13
Current Assets	98	77	47

Arte Engineering Co.
Unit 8 Great Bridge Industrial Estate, Tipton, DY4 0HR
Tel: 0121-520 8953 **Fax:** 0121- 5208953
Directors: R. Bhogal (Prop)
Registration no: 02764254 **Turnover:** Up to £250,000
No.of Employees: 1 - 10 **Product Groups:** 38, 48

Date of Accounts	Jul 11	Jul 10	Jul 09
Working Capital	292	285	335
Fixed Assets	374	386	406
Current Assets	943	662	764

B H J UK Protein Foods Ltd
Ramsey Road, Tipton, DY4 9DU
Tel: 0121-521 4300 **Fax:** 0121-521 4301
E-mail: info@bhj.co.uk
Website: http://www.bhj.co.uk
Directors: R. Parnell (Sales), L. Clark (Fin)
Ultimate Holding Company: LAURIDSEN GROUP INC (USA)
Immediate Holding Company: BHJ UK PROTEIN FOODS LIMITED
Registration no: 00946600 **Date established:** 1969
Turnover: £10m - £20m **No.of Employees:** 51 - 100 **Product Groups:** 20

Date of Accounts	Dec 08	Dec 09	Jan 11
Sales Turnover	9m	10m	11m
Pre Tax Profit/Loss	387	92	1m
Working Capital	1m	1m	2m
Fixed Assets	2m	2m	2m
Current Assets	3m	3m	4m
Current Liabilities	336	325	471

Beesley Fuel Services Ltd
Whitehall Road Great Bridge, Tipton, DY4 7JT
Tel: 0121-553 5413 **Fax:** 0121-520 4536
Directors: W. Beesley (Dir)
Managers: A. Beesley (Sec)
Immediate Holding Company: BEESLEY FUEL SERVICES LIMITED
Registration no: 01024928 **VAT No.:** GB 276 9208 24
Date established: 1971 **Turnover:** £10m - £20m **No.of Employees:** 1 - 10
Product Groups: 31

Date of Accounts	Sep 09	Sep 08	Sep 07
Working Capital	451	360	296
Fixed Assets	64	69	90
Current Assets	1m	2m	1m

Bloomfield Packaging Ltd
Unit 33 Bloomfield Park Bloomfield Road, Tipton, DY4 9AH
Tel: 0121-520 5480 **Fax:** 01432-272727
E-mail: sales@bloomfieldpackaging.co.uk
Website: http://www.bloomfieldpackaging.co.uk
Bank(s): Barclays
Directors: S. Jones (Sales)
Immediate Holding Company: BLOOMFIELD PACKAGING LIMITED
Registration no: 03901914 **VAT No.:** GB 747 9006 11
Date established: 2000 **Turnover:** £1m - £2m **No.of Employees:** 11 - 20
Product Groups: 30

Date of Accounts	Mar 12	Mar 11	Mar 10
Working Capital	216	276	271
Fixed Assets	231	118	110
Current Assets	925	982	987

Bodill Parker Group Ltd
Barnfield Industrial Estate Speed Road, Tipton, DY4 9DY
Tel: 0121-557 4164 **Fax:** 0121-557 4177
E-mail: sales@bodill-parker.co.uk
Website: http://www.bodill-parker.co.uk
Bank(s): Barclays
Directors: D. Gittins (Dir)
Immediate Holding Company: BODILL PARKER LIMITED
Registration no: 00415079 **VAT No.:** GB 278 0907 31
Date established: 1946 **Turnover:** £500,000 - £1m
No.of Employees: 11 - 20 **Product Groups:** 22, 27, 34, 35, 36, 46, 47, 48, 66

Date of Accounts	Mar 12	Mar 11	Mar 10
Working Capital	254	288	279
Fixed Assets	366	443	454
Current Assets	371	435	398

Bolt & Nut Services Ltd
Dolton Way, Tipton, DY4 9AW
Tel: 0121-520 4003 **Fax:** 0121-557 6665
E-mail: nutbolt@btconnect.com
Directors: M. Walker (MD)
Immediate Holding Company: BOLT & NUT SERVICES LTD
Registration no: 05466881 **Date established:** 2005 **Turnover:** £2m - £5m
No.of Employees: 1 - 10 **Product Groups:** 30, 34, 35

Date of Accounts	Aug 11	Aug 10	Aug 09
Working Capital	17	21	21
Fixed Assets	2	3	4
Current Assets	37	55	54

Broen Valves Ltd
Unit 7 Cleton Street Business Park, Tipton, DY4 7TR
Tel: 0121-522 4515 **Fax:** 0121-522 4535
E-mail: as@broen.com
Website: http://www.broen.co.uk
Managers: A. Spence (Sales Admin)
Ultimate Holding Company: AALBERTS INDUSTRIES NV (NETHERLANDS)
Immediate Holding Company: BROEN VALVES LIMITED
Registration no: 01179101 **VAT No.:** GB 191 8296 30
Date established: 1974 **Turnover:** £2m - £5m **No.of Employees:** 1 - 10
Product Groups: 30, 36

Date of Accounts	Dec 11	Dec 10	Dec 09
Sales Turnover	2m	2m	3m
Pre Tax Profit/Loss	124	49	100
Working Capital	1m	1m	1m
Fixed Assets	46	72	64
Current Assets	1m	1m	2m
Current Liabilities	127	120	97

C B C International Ltd
Coneygre Industrial Estate, Tipton, DY4 8XP
Tel: 0121-557 3154 **Fax:** 0121-557 9570
E-mail: mjbull@cbcint.com
Website: http://www.cbcint.com
Directors: C. Lowe (MD)
Ultimate Holding Company: CBC HOLDINGS LIMITED
Immediate Holding Company: CBC INTERNATIONAL LIMITED
Registration no: 02418705 **VAT No.:** GB 729 8562 85
Date established: 1989 **Turnover:** £500,000 - £1m
No.of Employees: 11 - 20 **Product Groups:** 66

Date of Accounts	Dec 11	Dec 10
Working Capital	1	1
Current Assets	1	1

C & M Access Scaffolding
Unit A Tinsley Street, Tipton, DY4 7LH
Tel: 0121-520 1007 **Fax:** 0121-520 2007
E-mail: chrishughes42@btconnect.com
Directors: T. Silvester (Co Sec), J. Francis (Dir)
No.of Employees: 1 - 10 **Product Groups:** 35, 48, 52, 66, 83

Celltex Fabrications Ltd
Unit 9a Barnfield Trading Estate Ramsey Road, Tipton, DY4 9DU
Tel: 0121-520 3443 **Fax:** 0121-520 1772
E-mail: sales@celltex.co.uk
Website: http://www.celltex.co.uk
Managers: S. Evans (Chief Mgr)
Immediate Holding Company: CELLTEX FABRICATIONS LIMITED
Registration no: 02645090 **VAT No.:** GB 589 1902 96
Date established: 1991 **Turnover:** £1m - £2m **No.of Employees:** 1 - 10
Product Groups: 30, 42

Date of Accounts	Sep 11	Sep 10	Sep 09
Working Capital	317	257	229
Fixed Assets	86	92	105
Current Assets	554	519	431

Coating & Converting Solutions Ltd
Bloomfield Park Bloomfield Road, Tipton, DY4 9AP
Tel: 0121-557 1155 **Fax:** 0121-557 9997
Bank(s): National Westminster Bank Plc
Directors: T. Webb (Prop)
Ultimate Holding Company: JOH WINKLHOFER BETEILIGUNGS GMBH & CO KG (GERMANY)
Immediate Holding Company: IWIS DRIVE SYSTEMS LIMITED
Registration no: 03784066 **Date established:** 1994 **Turnover:** £1m - £2m
No.of Employees: 11 - 20 **Product Groups:** 23, 27, 30, 31, 66, 68

Date of Accounts	Dec 11	Dec 10	Dec 09
Working Capital	477	551	618
Fixed Assets	24	23	48
Current Assets	958	955	985

Dale
1 Eagle Industrial Estate Bagnall Street, Great Bridge, Tipton, DY4 7BS
Tel: 0121-520 8499 **Fax:** 0121- 5208699
E-mail: info@daleuk.co.uk
Website: http://www.dalestructuralengineers.co.uk
Directors: G. Dale (Prop)
Immediate Holding Company: DALE (UK) LIMITED
Registration no: 04560366 **Date established:** 2002
No.of Employees: 1 - 10 **Product Groups:** 35

Date of Accounts	Sep 11	Sep 10	Sep 09
Working Capital	387	120	58
Fixed Assets	702	655	696
Current Assets	1m	952	749

Emi Mec
23 Avern Close, Tipton, DY4 7ND
Tel: 0121-522 4823 **Fax:** 0121-522 4823
E-mail: sales@emi-mec.co.uk
Website: http://www.emi-mec.co.uk
Directors: M. Evans (Prop), M. Evens (MD)
Date established: 1994 **No.of Employees:** 1 - 10 **Product Groups:** 40, 46, 47, 67

Eriks (Tipton Service Centre)
Groveland Road, Tipton, DY4 7UD
Tel: 0121-520 2151 **Fax:** 0121-557 4813
E-mail: tipton@eriks.co.uk
Website: http://www.fptgroup.uk.com
Directors: D. Batty (Jt MD)
Managers: R. Beech (Mgr), R. Beach (District Mgr)
Immediate Holding Company: CONWAY PACKAGING SERVICES HOLDINGS LIMITED
Date established: 2003 **Turnover:** £250m - £500m
No.of Employees: 11 - 20 **Product Groups:** 66

Ervin Amasteel Ltd
George Henry Road, Tipton, DY4 7BZ
Tel: 0121-522 2777 **Fax:** 0121-522 2927
E-mail: sales@ervinindustries.com
Website: http://www.ervinindustries.com
Bank(s): Barclays
Managers: S. Mills (Comptroller)
Ultimate Holding Company: ERVIN INDUSTRIES INC (USA)
Immediate Holding Company: ERVIN AMASTEEL
Registration no: 02830693 **VAT No.:** GB 632 0665 61
Date established: 1993 **Turnover:** £20m - £50m
No.of Employees: 51 - 100 **Product Groups:** 33, 34

Date of Accounts	Dec 11	Dec 10	Dec 09
Sales Turnover	29m	21m	14m
Pre Tax Profit/Loss	2m	-823	-3m
Working Capital	2m	-466	-2m
Fixed Assets	2m	2m	2m
Current Assets	12m	10m	7m
Current Liabilities	496	433	328

Eurodoors Systems
16 High Street Princes End, Tipton, DY4 9JF
Tel: 0500-608610
Directors: N. Mayo (MD)
No.of Employees: 1 - 10 **Product Groups:** 26, 35

Foil Specialist Company Ltd
Unit 17 Sedgley Road West, Tipton, DY4 8AH
Tel: 0121-313 3858 **Fax:** 0121-313 3868
E-mail: keith@foil-specialists.co.uk
Website: http://www.foil-specialists.co.uk
Directors: E. Hinton-Platt (Dir), K. Thompson (Dir)
Immediate Holding Company: THE FOIL SPECIALIST COMPANY LIMITED
Registration no: 04129678 **Date established:** 2000
Turnover: £500,000 - £1m **No.of Employees:** 1 - 10 **Product Groups:** 34

Frederick Spring Co.
Unit 4a Princes End Industrial Park Nicholls Road, Tipton, DY4 9LG
Tel: 0121-557 4080 **Fax:** 0121-557 6959
E-mail: sales@reliablespring.co.uk
Website: http://www.reliablespring.co.uk
Bank(s): Lloyds TSB Bank plc
Directors: R. Jenkins (Prop)
Immediate Holding Company: MODLIT HOLDINGS LIMITED
Registration no: 01743427 **VAT No.:** GB 277 8610 17
Date established: 1997 **Turnover:** Up to £250,000
No.of Employees: 11 - 20 **Product Groups:** 35

Date of Accounts	Mar 11	Mar 10	Mar 09
Sales Turnover	N/A	N/A	140
Pre Tax Profit/Loss	N/A	N/A	-29
Working Capital	18	16	16
Fixed Assets	10	11	13
Current Assets	53	70	77
Current Liabilities	N/A	N/A	14

Gustair Materials Handling Equipment Ltd
Unit 1 Denbigh Road, Tipton, DY4 7QF
Tel: 0121-520 0555 **Fax:** 0121-520 0777
E-mail: i.hollingworth@gustair.co.uk
Website: http://www.gustair.co.uk
Directors: I. Hollingworth (Dir)
Immediate Holding Company: GUSTAIR (INCORP ARO UK) LIMITED
Registration no: 01611320 **Date established:** 1982
Turnover: Up to £250,000 **No.of Employees:** 1 - 10 **Product Groups:** 40, 45, 67, 83

Date of Accounts	Apr 10	Apr 09	Apr 08
Working Capital	99	93	97
Fixed Assets	9	12	15
Current Assets	136	141	194

H & R Chempharm UK Ltd
Tiptone Works Dudley Road, Tipton, DY4 8EH
Tel: 0121-522 0100 **Fax:** 0121-522 0115
E-mail: neil.herman@hur-esp.com
Website: http://www.hur.com
Directors: N. Herman (Fin)
Managers: S. Davies (Mktg Serv Mgr), P. Waterfield (Tech Serv Mgr), N. Bassi (Personnel)
Immediate Holding Company: H&R CHEMPHARM (UK) LIMITED
Registration no: 05641816 **Date established:** 2005
Turnover: £20m - £50m **No.of Employees:** 21 - 50 **Product Groups:** 31, 66

Date of Accounts	Dec 11	Dec 10	Dec 09
Sales Turnover	45m	42m	29m
Pre Tax Profit/Loss	2m	2m	2m
Working Capital	6m	4m	4m
Fixed Assets	2m	2m	2m
Current Assets	12m	12m	12m
Current Liabilities	1m	2m	2m

H U F - UK Ltd
Black Country New Road, Tipton, DY4 0PT
Tel: 0121-521 1300 **Fax:** 0121-521 1326
E-mail: info@hufuk.com
Website: http://www.hufuk.com
Bank(s): HSBC, Willenhall
Directors: J. Dawes (MD)
Ultimate Holding Company: HULSBECK AND FURST GMBH & CO. KG (GERMAN
Immediate Holding Company: HUF U.K. LIMITED
Registration no: 02121160 **VAT No.:** GB 456 8071 28
Date established: 1987 **Turnover:** £20m - £50m
No.of Employees: 101 - 250 **Product Groups:** 36, 39

Date of Accounts	Dec 11	Dec 10	Dec 09
Sales Turnover	26m	28m	28m
Pre Tax Profit/Loss	-159	3m	2m
Working Capital	1m	-518	-1m
Fixed Assets	4m	6m	7m
Current Assets	8m	6m	5m
Current Liabilities	484	817	431

Harris Extrusion Tools
Unit 18 Bloomfield Park Bloomfield Road, Tipton, DY4 9AH
Tel: 0121-520 8697 **Fax:** 0121-520 8610
Directors: S. Harris (Prop)
Date established: 1987 **No.of Employees:** 1 - 10 **Product Groups:** 46

Hickman Sheet Metal
8b Sedgley Road West, Tipton, DY4 8AH
Tel: 0121-520 2022 **Fax:** 0121-520 2021
Directors: P. Hickman (Prop)
Immediate Holding Company: CENTRAL WELDING (SALES) LIMITED
Registration no: 05913637 **Date established:** 2004
No.of Employees: 1 - 10 **Product Groups:** 37, 40, 48

Huttenes-Albertus UK Ltd
Vision Point Sedgley Road East, Tipton, DY4 7UJ
Tel: 0121-270 0834 **Fax:** 0121-270 0839
E-mail: info@huttenes-albertus.co.uk
Website: http://www.huttenes-albertus.co.uk
Managers: R. Bentley (Chief Mgr)
Ultimate Holding Company: HUTTENES ALBERTUS CHEMISCHE WERKE GMBH (GERMANY)
Immediate Holding Company: HUTTENES-ALBERTUS U.K. LIMITED
Registration no: 01359479 **VAT No.:** GB 278 0739 26
Date established: 1978 **Turnover:** Up to £250,000
No.of Employees: 1 - 10 **Product Groups:** 32, 46, 84

Date of Accounts	Dec 11	Dec 10	Dec 09
Working Capital	588	501	591
Fixed Assets	558	549	588
Current Assets	1m	949	1m

Ibp Conex Ltd
Whitehall Road, Tipton, DY4 7JU
Tel: 0121-557 2831 **Fax:** 0121-520 8778
E-mail: jayne.round@ibpgroup.com
Website: http://www.ibpconex.co.uk

see next page

Ibp Conex Ltd - Cont'd
Managers: J. Round (Admin Off), A. Mason (Comptroller)
Ultimate Holding Company: SUN CAPITAL PARTNERS LIMITED
Immediate Holding Company: ICB REALISATIONS LIMITED
Registration no: 04294361 **Date established:** 2001
Turnover: £75m - £125m **No.of Employees:** 101 - 250
Product Groups: 35, 36

Date of Accounts	Dec 09	Dec 08	Dec 07
Sales Turnover	87m	82m	103m
Pre Tax Profit/Loss	-14m	-14m	-6m
Working Capital	-34m	5m	37m
Fixed Assets	1m	977	3m
Current Assets	38m	49m	48m
Current Liabilities	5m	2m	2m

Image Wheels International Ltd
Unit 3 Fountain Lane, Tipton, DY4 9HA
Tel: 0121-522 2442 **Fax:** 0121-520 9311
E-mail: jane@imagewheels.co.uk
Website: http://www.imagewheels.co.uk
Directors: J. Nicklin (Co Sec)
Immediate Holding Company: IMAGE WHEELS INTERNATIONAL LIMITED
Registration no: 02296565 **VAT No.:** GB 488 2739 90
Date established: 1988 **Turnover:** £500,000 - £1m
No.of Employees: 1 - 10 **Product Groups:** 39

Date of Accounts	Nov 11	Nov 09	Nov 08
Working Capital	157	192	236
Fixed Assets	166	169	146
Current Assets	313	334	407

Iwis Drive Systems
Unit 8c Bloomfield Park Bloomfield Road, Tipton, DY4 9AP
Tel: 0121-521 3600 **Fax:** 0121-520 0822
E-mail: salesuk@iwis.com
Website: http://www.iwis.com
Directors: A. Fletcher (MD)
Ultimate Holding Company: JOH WINKLHOFER BETEILIGUNGS GMBH & CO KG (GERMANY)
Immediate Holding Company: IWIS DRIVE SYSTEMS LIMITED
Registration no: 02969829 **Date established:** 1994
No.of Employees: 1 - 10 **Product Groups:** 35, 45, 67, 68, 84

Date of Accounts	Dec 11	Dec 10	Dec 09
Working Capital	477	551	618
Fixed Assets	24	23	48
Current Assets	958	955	985

J P Polymer Sheetings Ltd
Unit 24 Coneygre Industrial Estate, Tipton, DY4 8XP
Tel: 0121-520 5020 **Fax:** 0121-522 4610
E-mail: sales@jppolymer.co.uk
Website: http://www.jppolymer.co.uk
Directors: P. Fenton (MD)
Immediate Holding Company: J.P. POLYMER SHEETINGS LIMITED
Registration no: 02461800 **VAT No.:** GB 559 3151 29
Date established: 1990 **Turnover:** £1m - £2m **No.of Employees:** 11 - 20
Product Groups: 29

Date of Accounts	Mar 11	Mar 10	Mar 09
Working Capital	81	64	128
Fixed Assets	119	130	73
Current Assets	1m	1m	1m

Jabez Barker
Coneygre Industrial Estate, Tipton, DY4 8XP
Tel: 0121-520 7058 **Fax:** 0121-522 3229
Directors: C. Pritchard (Prop)
VAT No.: GB 377 7913 96 **Date established:** 1995
Turnover: £500,000 - £1m **No.of Employees:** 1 - 10 **Product Groups:** 39

Kingsland Engineering
Unit 9 Eagle Industrial Estate Bagnall Street, Great Bridge, Tipton, DY4 7BS
Tel: 0121-522 4929 **Fax:** 0121-522 3174
E-mail: steve@kingsland.com
Website: http://www.kingsland.com
Managers: S. Basrai (Sales Prom Mgr)
Registration no: 06396427 **Date established:** 2007
No.of Employees: 1 - 10 **Product Groups:** 46

Date of Accounts	Sep 11	Sep 10	Sep 09
Working Capital	387	120	58
Fixed Assets	702	655	696
Current Assets	1m	952	749

M & S Sewing Machines
Coppice Street, Tipton, DY4 9BE
Tel: 07721-584653 **Fax:** 0121-520 4726
E-mail: mandssewingmachines@hotmail.co.uk
Directors: T. Clarke (Prop)
Date established: 1989 **No.of Employees:** 1 - 10 **Product Groups:** 43

Mainwaring Metals Ltd
The Field House Johns Lane, Tipton, DY4 7PT
Tel: 0121-557 1809
E-mail: mainwaring@britishproductsdirectory.co.uk
Website: http://www.britishproductsdirectory.co.uk
Directors: S. Partridge (Fin)
Immediate Holding Company: MAINWARING METALS LIMITED
Registration no: 02288954 **VAT No.:** GB 488 4057 09
Date established: 1988 **Turnover:** Up to £250,000
No.of Employees: 1 - 10 **Product Groups:** 34

Date of Accounts	Dec 08	Dec 07	Dec 06
Working Capital	-18	N/A	-12
Fixed Assets	39	38	43
Current Assets	174	197	174
Current Liabilities	192	196	186

Melba Ornamental Designs
1 Lee Trading Estate Factory Road, Tipton, DY4 9AU
Tel: 0121-557 9697
Directors: B. Mellor (Prop)
Registration no: 03868308 **Date established:** 1999
No.of Employees: 1 - 10 **Product Groups:** 26, 35

Metrology Calibration Services Limited
Metropolitan Borough Council Coneygre Industrial Estate Coneygre Road, Tipton, DY4 8XR
Tel: 0121-569 6733 **Fax:** 0121-569 6647
E-mail: calibration@metrologygroup.co.nz
Website: http://www.metrologygroup.co.nz
Managers: A. Taylor (Mgr)
No.of Employees: 1 - 10 **Product Groups:** 38, 42

Midland Power Press Services Ltd
Unit 2 High Street Princes End, Tipton, DY4 9JA
Tel: 0121-520 4320 **Fax:** 0121-557 7395
E-mail: admin@mpps.co.uk
Website: http://www.mpps.co.uk
Bank(s): LloydsTSB Dudley
Directors: R. Crow (Dir)
Immediate Holding Company: MIDLAND POWER PRESS SERVICES LIMITED
Registration no: 02407284 **VAT No.:** GB 369 7979 61
Date established: 1989 **Turnover:** £500,000 - £1m
No.of Employees: 21 - 50 **Product Groups:** 46, 83

Date of Accounts	Aug 11	Aug 10	Aug 09
Working Capital	3	41	-45
Fixed Assets	65	50	103
Current Assets	713	587	320

Midland Tool & Design Ltd
Units 19-20 Barnfield Road, Tipton, DY4 9DF
Tel: 0121-520 1171 **Fax:** 0121-557 3410
E-mail: sales@mtdltd.co.uk
Website: http://www.mtdltd.co.uk
Bank(s): Nat West, Letchworth
Directors: D. Booton (Dir), L. Barrows (Fin)
Managers: N. Brittle (Sales Prom Mgr)
Ultimate Holding Company: DALION ENGINEERING LIMITED
Immediate Holding Company: MIDLAND TOOL AND DESIGN LIMITED
Registration no: 00962501 **VAT No.:** GB 277 0400 71
Date established: 1969 **Turnover:** £500,000 - £1m
No.of Employees: 21 - 50 **Product Groups:** 46

Date of Accounts	Dec 11	Dec 10	Dec 09
Working Capital	695	507	265
Fixed Assets	239	165	180
Current Assets	2m	2m	811

Moseley Brothers Ltd
Vaughan Trading Estate Vaughan Trading Sedgley Road East, Tipton, DY4 7UJ
Tel: 0121-520 6703 **Fax:** 0121-520 4118
E-mail: admin@moseleybrothers.co.uk
Website: http://www.moseleybrothers.co.uk
Directors: P. Aust (Co Sec), A. Taylor (Chief Op Offcr), J. Hickman (MD)
Managers: L. Butler (Admin Off)
Immediate Holding Company: MOSELEY BROTHERS TOOLS LIMITED
Registration no: 00259312 **VAT No.:** GB 109 5625 67
Date established: 1931 **Turnover:** £2m - £5m **No.of Employees:** 21 - 50
Product Groups: 46, 48

Date of Accounts	Oct 04	Mar 08	Mar 07
Working Capital	411	716	707
Fixed Assets	1m	1m	1m
Current Assets	1m	2m	2m

Narrow Aisle Ltd
Great Western Way Great Bridge, Tipton, DY4 7AU
Tel: 0121-557 6242 **Fax:** 0121-520 8585
E-mail: info@flexi.co.uk
Website: http://www.flexi.co.uk
Bank(s): Lloyds TSB Bank plc
Directors: C. Randle (Fin), P. Wooldridge (MD), J. Maguire (Sales & Mktg)
Ultimate Holding Company: V.N.A. TRUCKS LIMITED
Immediate Holding Company: NARROW AISLE MANAGEMENT LTD
Registration no: 01250894 **VAT No.:** GB 101 9551 01
Date established: 1975 **Turnover:** £10m - £20m
No.of Employees: 51 - 100 **Product Groups:** 45, 67, 83

Date of Accounts	Dec 11	Dec 10	Dec 09
Sales Turnover	N/A	282	389
Pre Tax Profit/Loss	N/A	353	82
Working Capital	726	642	790
Fixed Assets	48	48	48
Current Assets	2m	1m	1m
Current Liabilities	N/A	16	33

Naylor Specialists Plastics
Unit 47 Coneygree Industrial Estate, Tipton, DY4 8XP
Tel: 0121-522 0290 **Fax:** 0121-522 0299
E-mail: specialistplastics@naylor.co.uk
Website: http://www.naylor.co.uk
Directors: J. Grice (MD)
Registration no: 01810207 **Turnover:** £1m - £2m
No.of Employees: 11 - 20 **Product Groups:** 30, 36, 40, 42, 46, 48, 66, 84

Olympus Distribution Ltd
Olympus Drive Great Bridge, Tipton, DY4 7HY
Tel: 0121-522 5600 **Fax:** 0121-522 5601
E-mail: sales@olympusglobal.co.uk
Website: http://www.olympusglobal.co.uk
Bank(s): National Westminster Bank Plc
Directors: K. Rice (Dir), D. Watson (Fin)
Managers: I. Playford (Purch Mgr)
Immediate Holding Company: OLYMPUS DISTRIBUTION LIMITED
Registration no: 01702340 **VAT No.:** GB 369 8592 80
Date established: 1983 **Turnover:** £5m - £10m **No.of Employees:** 21 - 50
Product Groups: 30, 35, 36, 48

Date of Accounts	Mar 12	Mar 11	Mar 10
Sales Turnover	12m	9m	7m
Pre Tax Profit/Loss	904	863	233
Working Capital	3m	3m	2m
Fixed Assets	478	350	201
Current Assets	6m	6m	4m
Current Liabilities	2m	426	167

P & O Aerosols
2 Hale Indl-Est Lower Church Lane, Tipton, DY4 7PQ
Tel: 0121-520 8883 **Fax:** 0121-520 8080
E-mail: info@pxoaerosols.co.uk
Website: http://www.pxoaerosols.co.uk
Directors: A. Lewis (Fin), M. Lewis (Co Sec), M. Lewis (Fin)
Immediate Holding Company: THE HARE AND FIVE HOUNDS LIMITED
Date established: 2010 **No.of Employees:** 1 - 10 **Product Groups:** 35, 45

Date of Accounts	Dec 10
Working Capital	-243
Fixed Assets	252
Current Assets	93

P R Fastening
Waterside Park Golds Hill Way, Tipton, DY4 0WP
Tel: 01299-252500 **Fax:** 01299-251566
E-mail: marketing@trfastenings.co.uk
Website: http://www.trfastening.com
Directors: S. Auld (MD)
Immediate Holding Company: Trifast PLC
VAT No.: GB 486 8001 28 **Date established:** 1935 **Turnover:** £20m - £50m
No.of Employees: 51 - 100 **Product Groups:** 30, 35, 36, 37, 66

P S U Designs Ltd
7 Bloomfield Park Bloomfield Road, Tipton, DY4 9AP
Tel: 0121-557 6499 **Fax:** 0121-557 6498
E-mail: sales@psudesigns.co.uk
Website: http://www.psudesigns.co.uk
Directors: N. Arkell (MD), T. Shillingford (Fin)
Managers: G. Potter (Purch Mgr)
Immediate Holding Company: PSU DESIGNS LIMITED
Registration no: 02600288 **Date established:** 1991 **Turnover:** £2m - £5m
No.of Employees: 51 - 100 **Product Groups:** 37, 44

Date of Accounts	Aug 11	Aug 10	Aug 09
Working Capital	77	214	387
Fixed Assets	149	154	118
Current Assets	2m	2m	1m

Pointer
22 Bloomfield Park Bloomfield Road, Tipton, DY4 9AH
Tel: 0121-520 7186 **Fax:** 0121-520 7756
E-mail: andrew.wiedeman@pointerfire.com
Website: http://www.pointer.co.uk
Managers: A. Wiedeman (District Mgr)
No.of Employees: 11 - 20 **Product Groups:** 40, 80

R C F Bolt & Nut Co Tipton Ltd
Park Lane East, Tipton, DY4 8RF
Tel: 0121-522 2353 **Fax:** 0121-522 2304
E-mail: ray.cooper@dial.pipex.com
Website: http://www.rcfboltnut.co.uk
Directors: C. Cooper (Fin), R. Cooper (MD)
Immediate Holding Company: RCF BOLT & NUT CO (TIPTON) LIMITED
Registration no: 01266907 **Date established:** 1976 **Turnover:** £2m - £5m
No.of Employees: 21 - 50 **Product Groups:** 35

Date of Accounts	Dec 11	Dec 10	Dec 09
Sales Turnover	N/A	N/A	2m
Working Capital	114	72	91
Fixed Assets	487	505	520
Current Assets	1m	1m	1m

Ramsden Steel Drums Ltd
Unit 1 Harrold Street, Tipton, DY4 0JF
Tel: 0121-522 2344 **Fax:** 0121-522 3144
Website: http://www.ramsdenandwhale.co.uk
Directors: S. Ramsden (MD), D. Richardson (Co Sec)
Ultimate Holding Company: RAMSDEN AND WHALE LIMITED
Immediate Holding Company: RAMSDEN STEEL DRUMS LIMITED
Registration no: 03304771 **Date established:** 1997
No.of Employees: 21 - 50 **Product Groups:** 35, 36, 45

Date of Accounts	Mar 11	Mar 10	Mar 08
Working Capital	761	510	543
Current Assets	2m	1m	2m

Ramsden & Whale Ltd
Unit 1 Harrold Street, Tipton, DY4 0JF
Tel: 0121-557 3656 **Fax:** 0121-522 3144
E-mail: sales@ramsdenandwhale.co.uk
Website: http://www.ramsdenandwhale.co.uk
Directors: S. Ramsden (MD), D. Richardson (Fin)
Managers: J. Haffner (Sales Admin)
Ultimate Holding Company: RAMSDEN AND WHALE LIMITED
Immediate Holding Company: RAMSDEN STEEL DRUMS LIMITED
Registration no: 03304771 **Date established:** 1997
No.of Employees: 21 - 50 **Product Groups:** 35, 36, 45

Date of Accounts	Mar 11	Mar 10	Mar 08
Working Capital	761	510	543
Current Assets	2m	1m	2m

Rhino Coat Ltd
Nicholls Road, Tipton, DY4 9LG
Tel: 0121-522 4394 **Fax:** 0121-522 4394
E-mail: info@rhinocoat.co.uk
Website: http://www.rhinocoat.co.uk
Directors: D. Phillips (Dir)
Immediate Holding Company: RHINO COAT LIMITED
Registration no: 04505706 **Date established:** 2002
No.of Employees: 1 - 10 **Product Groups:** 46, 48

Date of Accounts	Dec 11	Dec 10	Dec 09
Working Capital	1	11	9
Fixed Assets	N/A	N/A	2
Current Assets	69	154	95

S P C Bearings Ltd
Unit 39 Coneygre Industrial Estate, Tipton, DY4 8XP
Tel: 0121-557 1371 **Fax:** 0121-557 3793
Website: http://www.cbcint.com
Directors: C. Lowe (MD)
Ultimate Holding Company: CBC HOLDINGS LIMITED
Immediate Holding Company: SPC BEARINGS LIMITED
Registration no: 02369785 **Date established:** 1989
No.of Employees: 11 - 20 **Product Groups:** 35, 45

Sant Castings Ltd
Unit 45 Coneygre Industrial Estate, Tipton, DY4 8XP
Tel: 0121-522 2434 **Fax:** 0121-557 2007
E-mail: sans@santgroup.com
Website: http://www.santgroup.com
Directors: S. Suman (MD)
Immediate Holding Company: SANT CASTINGS LIMITED
Registration no: 02338522 **Date established:** 1989
No.of Employees: 11 - 20 **Product Groups:** 46

Date of Accounts	Sep 11	Sep 10	Sep 09
Working Capital	3	-11	-27
Fixed Assets	176	196	214
Current Assets	343	324	385
Current Liabilities	N/A	178	243

Sant Products Ltd
Unit 42 Coneygre Industrial Estate, Tipton, DY4 8XP
Tel: 0121-557 7066 **Fax:** 0121-557 2007
E-mail: sales@santgroup.com

Managers: S. Suman (Mgr)
Immediate Holding Company: SANT PRODUCTS LIMITED
Registration no: 03852026 **Date established:** 1999
No.of Employees: 1 - 10 **Product Groups:** 46, 48

Date of Accounts	Sep 11	Sep 10	Sep 09
Working Capital	-198	63	12
Fixed Assets	242	158	178
Current Assets	662	679	728
Current Liabilities	N/A	293	312

Servacrane Investments Ltd
Bagnall Street Industrial Estate George Henry Road, Tipton, DY4 7BZ
Tel: 0121-557 4401 **Fax:** 0121-557 3788
Website: http://www.servacrane.com
Directors: G. Taylor (Fin), K. Taylor (MD)
Immediate Holding Company: SERVACRANE INVESTMENTS LIMITED
Registration no: 01197102 **Date established:** 1975
Turnover: Up to £250,000 **No.of Employees:** 11 - 20 **Product Groups:** 35, 39, 45

Date of Accounts	Jul 11	Jul 10	Jul 09
Sales Turnover	21	21	N/A
Pre Tax Profit/Loss	19	19	N/A
Working Capital	-98	-61	-40
Fixed Assets	300	300	300
Current Assets	94	82	56
Current Liabilities	5	5	N/A

Simonswerk UK Ltd
Burcot Works Spring Street, Tipton, DY4 8TF
Tel: 0121-522 2848 **Fax:** 0121-557 7042
E-mail: sales@simonswerk.co.uk
Website: http://www.simonswerk.co.uk
Directors: R. Guy (MD)
Managers: D. Boon (Mktg Serv Mgr), S. Slater (Sales Admin)
Ultimate Holding Company: FAMILIE JULIUS THYSSEN VERWALTUNGSGESELLSCHAFT MBH(GER)
Immediate Holding Company: SIMONSWERK UK LIMITED
Registration no: 01318326 **Date established:** 1977
No.of Employees: 21 - 50 **Product Groups:** 35, 36, 40, 66

Date of Accounts	Dec 11	Dec 10	Dec 09
Working Capital	1m	952	857
Fixed Assets	363	339	311
Current Assets	1m	1m	1m

Smith Bros Quinton Ltd The Wooden Packaging Company
Smith Bros Quinton Castle Street, Tipton, DY4 8HP
Tel: 0121-557 0077 **Fax:** 0121-557 0177
E-mail: harveysmith@smith-bros.co.uk
Website: http://www.enviro-materials.co.uk
Directors: H. Smith (MD), B. Smith (Sales), H. Smith (Prop)
Immediate Holding Company: SMITH BROS. (QUINTON) LIMITED
Registration no: 00610393 **Date established:** 1958
Turnover: Up to £250,000 **No.of Employees:** 1 - 10 **Product Groups:** 25, 45, 66, 67

Date of Accounts	Dec 07	Dec 06
Pre Tax Profit/Loss	98210	88020
Working Capital	-291760	-65230
Fixed Assets	564180	218810
Current Assets	390	5890
Current Liabilities	292150	71120
Total Share Capital	22550	21010
ROCE% (Return on Capital Employed)	36.1	57.3

Staffordshire Builders Supplies Ltd
27 Bagnall Street Ocker Hill, Tipton, DY4 0EQ
Tel: 0121-556 0496 **Fax:** 0121-505 3409
E-mail: r.spooner@staffordshirebuilders.co.uk
Website: http://www.staffordshirebuilders.co.uk
Directors: R. Spooner (MD)
Immediate Holding Company: STAFFORDSHIRE BUILDERS SUPPLIES LIMITED
Registration no: 00214111 **Date established:** 2026
No.of Employees: 1 - 10 **Product Groups:** 66, 67

Date of Accounts	Mar 11	Mar 10	Mar 09
Working Capital	101	100	140
Fixed Assets	189	198	221
Current Assets	199	206	250

Swift Abrasive Wheels Ltd (t/a Swift & Whitmore Limited)
Toll End Road, Tipton, DY4 0HF
Tel: 0121-557 8337 **Fax:** 0121-520 4770
E-mail: sales@swiftabrasives.com
Website: http://www.swiftabrasivewheels.com
Bank(s): HSBC Bank plc
Directors: R. Whitmore (Dir), J. Tierney (Co Sec)
Managers: L. Horton (Sales Prom Mgr), K. Brooks (Comptroller)
Ultimate Holding Company: PHOENIX ABRASIVE WHEEL CO.LIMITED(THE)
Immediate Holding Company: SWIFT ABRASIVES LIMITED
Registration no: 01312358 **VAT No.:** 300 2227 35 **Date established:** 1977
Turnover: £2m - £5m **No.of Employees:** 21 - 50 **Product Groups:** 33

Date of Accounts	Mar 11	Mar 10	Feb 09
Working Capital	268	118	96
Fixed Assets	83	95	114
Current Assets	490	504	451

T Masters & Sons Ltd
Salem Street, Tipton, DY4 7JH
Tel: 0121-520 1422 **Fax:** 0121-520 1431
E-mail: steve@tmasters.co.uk
Website: http://www.tmasters.co.uk
Directors: S. White (MD)
Immediate Holding Company: T. MASTERS & SONS LIMITED
Registration no: 00380170 **VAT No.:** GB 277 6931 10
Date established: 1943 **Turnover:** £1m - £2m **No.of Employees:** 1 - 10
Product Groups: 46

Date of Accounts	Mar 11	Mar 10	Mar 09
Working Capital	584	614	633
Fixed Assets	279	281	292
Current Assets	771	763	808

T Norton Ltd
Tinsley Street, Tipton, DY4 7LQ
Tel: 0121-557 6413 **Fax:** 0121-557 5124
E-mail: sales@jameswshenton.co.uk
Website: http://www.jameswshenton.co.uk
Bank(s): Barclays
Directors: M. Daniels (MD), M. Shenton (Dir)
Managers: J. Carey (Chief Acct)
Ultimate Holding Company: EDISON HOLDINGS LTD
Immediate Holding Company: T. NORTON LIMITED
Registration no: 01730000 **Date established:** 1983
Turnover: Up to £250,000 **No.of Employees:** 21 - 50 **Product Groups:** 46

T & T Dudley Tools & Engineering Ltd
Unit 4-7 Factory Road, Tipton, DY4 9AU
Tel: 0121-557 8922
E-mail: sales@ttbearinghousings.co.uk
Website: http://www.ttbearinghousings.co.uk
Directors: D. Jones (Dir)
Immediate Holding Company: T.& T.(DUDLEY)TOOLS AND ENGINEERING LIMITED
Registration no: 00750399 **Date established:** 1963
No.of Employees: 1 - 10 **Product Groups:** 35, 37, 45

Date of Accounts	Mar 11	Mar 09	Mar 08
Working Capital	6	-1	16
Fixed Assets	13	22	12
Current Assets	32	27	66

The Anglering Company
Bloomfield Road, Tipton, DY4 9EH
Tel: 0121-557 7241 **Fax:** 0121-522 4555
E-mail: sales@anglering.com
Website: http://www.anglering.com
Bank(s): HSBC Bank plc
Directors: D. Springthorpe (Prop)
Ultimate Holding Company: ANGLE RING HOLDINGS LIMITED
Immediate Holding Company: THE RINGLEADERS (SECTION BENDERS) LIMITED
Registration no: 06080905 **VAT No.:** GB 276 8533 18
Date established: 2007 **Turnover:** £5m - £10m
No.of Employees: 101 - 250 **Product Groups:** 34, 35, 36, 45, 48

Thermal Spray Material Services Ltd
Brook Street Business Centre Brook Street, Tipton, DY4 9DD
Tel: 0121-520 0720 **Fax:** 0121-520 3002
E-mail: thermalsprayuk@aol.com
Website: http://www.thermalspray.co.uk
Directors: M. Proctor (MD)
Immediate Holding Company: THERMAL-SPRAY MATERIALS & SERVICES LIMITED
Registration no: 02339969 **Date established:** 1989
Turnover: Up to £250,000 **No.of Employees:** 1 - 10 **Product Groups:** 31, 32, 33, 34, 35, 36, 37, 40, 46, 48, 66, 67

Date of Accounts	Mar 12	Mar 11	Mar 10
Working Capital	73	69	64
Fixed Assets	N/A	N/A	1
Current Assets	110	99	87

Tipton & Coseley Building Society
70 Owen Street, Tipton, DY4 8HG
Tel: 0121-557 2551 **Fax:** 0121-557 8570
E-mail: mail@thetipton.co.uk
Website: http://www.thetipton.co.uk
Bank(s): Barclays
Directors: C. Martin (Grp Chief Exec)
Managers: L. Judson (Mktg Serv Mgr), R. Newton (Fin Mgr), R. Savage (Tech Serv Mgr)
Immediate Holding Company: TIPTON & COSELEY BUILDING SOCIETY CHARITABLE FOUNDATION
Registration no: 03869002 **Date established:** 1999
Turnover: Up to £250,000 **No.of Employees:** 21 - 50 **Product Groups:** 82

Date of Accounts	May 11	May 10	May 09
Sales Turnover	11	10	11
Pre Tax Profit/Loss	3	-2	2
Working Capital	4	1	3
Current Assets	10	10	9
Current Liabilities	6	9	6

Tipton & Mill Steels Ltd
Hobart Road, Tipton, DY4 9LQ
Tel: 0121-557 7251 **Fax:** 0121-557 7258
E-mail: sales@tiptonandmillsteels.com
Website: http://www.tiptonandmillsteels.com
Bank(s): Barclays
Managers: R. Pitt (Chief Mgr)
Ultimate Holding Company: MURRAY INTERNATIONAL HOLDINGS LIMITED
Immediate Holding Company: TIPTON & MILL STEELS LIMITED
Registration no: 00513077 **VAT No.:** GB 277 2320 59
Date established: 1952 **Turnover:** £20m - £50m
No.of Employees: 21 - 50 **Product Groups:** 34

Date of Accounts	Jan 08	Jun 11	Jun 10
Sales Turnover	15m	N/A	11m
Pre Tax Profit/Loss	667	N/A	-188
Working Capital	2m	3m	3m
Fixed Assets	155	N/A	N/A
Current Assets	9m	3m	3m
Current Liabilities	156	N/A	N/A

Transformotor Ltd
Unit 43 Coneygre Industrial Estate, Tipton, DY4 8XU
Tel: 0121-557 4491 **Fax:** 0121-557 3175
E-mail: enquiries@transformotor.co.uk
Website: http://www.transformotor.co.uk
Directors: A. Snaddon (Sales)
Immediate Holding Company: TRANSFORMOTOR LIMITED
Registration no: 01508067 **VAT No.:** GB 277 4165 35
Date established: 1980 **Turnover:** £250,000 - £500,000
No.of Employees: 1 - 10 **Product Groups:** 48

Date of Accounts	Dec 11	Dec 10	Dec 09
Working Capital	143	130	138
Fixed Assets	19	25	32
Current Assets	222	211	266

Truflo Air Movement
Station Street, Tipton, DY4 8UG
Tel: 0121-557 4101 **Fax:** 0121-557 4108
E-mail: wolpelenski@truflo-airmovement.com
Website: http://www.truflo-airmovement.com
Bank(s): Barclays
Directors: W. Pelenski (Co Sec), S. Bourne (Pers)
Managers: A. Marwaha (Sales Prom Mgr), R. Tipler (Purch Mgr), R. Mehmet-harding (Mktg Serv Mgr)
Ultimate Holding Company: PHILTEM HOLDINGS INC (UNITED STATES OF AMERICA)
Immediate Holding Company: TRUFLO AIR MOVEMENT LIMITED
Registration no: 05500950 **VAT No.:** 559 6043 17 **Date established:** 2005
Turnover: £10m - £20m **No.of Employees:** 101 - 250 **Product Groups:** 39

Date of Accounts	Sep 11	Sep 10	Sep 09
Sales Turnover	11m	8m	6m
Pre Tax Profit/Loss	432	-2m	-4m
Working Capital	801	-2m	-256
Fixed Assets	4m	5m	7m
Current Assets	4m	3m	2m
Current Liabilities	388	370	222

W R T L Exterior Lighting Ltd
Waterside Park Golds Hill Way, Tipton, DY4 0PU
Tel: 0121-521 1234 **Fax:** 0121-521 1250
E-mail: r.schmit@wrtl.co.uk
Website: http://www.wrtle.co.uk
Bank(s): National Westminster, Manchester
Directors: G. Walker (Fin), R. Curtiss (MD)
Managers: E. Lloyd
Ultimate Holding Company: INDUSTRIAS DERIVADAS DEL ALUMNIO SL (SPAIN)
Immediate Holding Company: W R T L EXTERIOR LIGHTING LIMITED
Registration no: 03896819 **VAT No.:** GB 146 6958 25
Date established: 1999 **Turnover:** £20m - £50m
No.of Employees: 21 - 50 **Product Groups:** 37, 67, 84

Date of Accounts	Dec 11	Dec 10	Dec 09
Sales Turnover	29m	24m	19m
Pre Tax Profit/Loss	1m	957	646
Working Capital	5m	4m	3m
Fixed Assets	206	259	229
Current Assets	7m	7m	5m
Current Liabilities	2m	1m	1m

Wade Building Services Ltd
Groveland Road, Tipton, DY4 7TN
Tel: 0121-520 8121 **Fax:** 0121-557 7061
E-mail: sales@wade-bs.co.uk
Website: http://www.wade-bs.co.uk
Bank(s): HSBC, West Bromwich
Directors: A. Clowes (Dir), W. Pierce (MD)
Immediate Holding Company: WADE BUILDING SERVICES LIMITED
Registration no: 02615062 **VAT No.:** GB 559 5391 96
Date established: 1991 **Turnover:** £2m - £5m **No.of Employees:** 21 - 50
Product Groups: 35, 52

Date of Accounts	Aug 11	Aug 10	Aug 09
Working Capital	375	396	321
Fixed Assets	477	440	558
Current Assets	1m	1m	836

West Mercia Sections Ltd
Nicholls Road, Tipton, DY4 9LG
Tel: 0121-557 9927 **Fax:** 0121-520 3133
E-mail: sales@westmerciasections.co.uk
Website: http://www.westmerciasections.co.uk
Bank(s): Lloyds TSB Bank plc
Directors: J. Tuckey (MD)
Immediate Holding Company: WEST MERCIA SECTIONS LIMITED
Registration no: 01743427 **VAT No.:** GB 388 6604 04
Date established: 1983 **No.of Employees:** 11 - 20 **Product Groups:** 34

Date of Accounts	Dec 11	Dec 10	Dec 09
Working Capital	391	366	415
Fixed Assets	161	179	184
Current Assets	871	863	781

Walsall

A J Plastics Ltd
Unit 2 Leamore Lane, Walsall, WS2 7DE
Tel: 01922-406779 **Fax:** 01922-402470
E-mail: sales@ajplastics.co.uk
Website: http://www.ajplastics.co.uk
Directors: T. Cotton (Fin), R. Woolaston (Grp Chief Exec), G. Cooper (MD)
Managers: M. Proffitt, M. Proffitt (), R. Wollaston (Mgr)
Ultimate Holding Company: ALBERT JAGGER HOLDINGS LIMITED
Immediate Holding Company: A. J. PLASTICS LIMITED
Registration no: 01295005 **VAT No.:** GB 101 8305 21
Date established: 1977 **Turnover:** £250,000 - £500,000
No.of Employees: 1 - 10 **Product Groups:** 32

Date of Accounts	Jul 08
Working Capital	513
Fixed Assets	42
Current Assets	927
Current Liabilities	414

Abbey Mechanical Services Ltd
James House Northgate, Aldridge, Walsall, WS9 8TH
Tel: 01922-457778 **Fax:** 01922-743332
Website: http://www.abbey-mechanical.co.uk
Directors: J. Lakin (Fin), B. Lakin (Fin)
Immediate Holding Company: ABBEY MECHANICAL SERVICES LIMITED
Registration no: 02818205 **Date established:** 1993
No.of Employees: 1 - 10 **Product Groups:** 35, 39, 45

Date of Accounts	Jun 11	Jun 10	Jun 09
Working Capital	-12	-29	-19
Fixed Assets	77	91	97
Current Assets	166	139	135

Acorn Services
Unit 3 Willenhall Lane Industrial Estate Willenhall Lane, Bloxwich, Walsall, WS3 2XN
Tel: 01922-491676 **Fax:** 01922-710305
E-mail: business@acornpowdercoating.com
Website: http://www.acornpowdercoating.com
Directors: S. Welch (Fin), J. Swingle (MD)
Immediate Holding Company: ACORN SERVICES LIMITED
Registration no: 01559361 **Date established:** 1981
Turnover: £250,000 - £500,000 **No.of Employees:** 1 - 10
Product Groups: 32, 37, 48, 67

Date of Accounts	Jul 11	Jul 10	Jul 09
Working Capital	19	-7	-37
Fixed Assets	41	50	63
Current Assets	146	128	103

Airguard Filters Ltd
Unit 9 Gill & Russell Business Park Pleck Road, Walsall, WS2 9ES
Tel: 01922-628782 **Fax:** 01922-645441
E-mail: m.garrigan@airguard.co.uk
Website: http://www.airguardfilters.co.uk
Directors: M. Garrigan (MD)
Immediate Holding Company: AIRGUARD FILTERS LIMITED
Registration no: 01955674 **VAT No.:** GB 100 9383 02
Date established: 1985 **Turnover:** Up to £250,000
No.of Employees: 1 - 10 **Product Groups:** 23, 24, 34, 35, 37, 38, 39, 40, 42, 67

Date of Accounts	Jun 12	Jun 11	Jun 10
Working Capital	58	44	34
Fixed Assets	45	32	32
Current Assets	170	149	106

Aldridge Ironcraft
Rear of 196 Walsall Wood Road, Walsall, WS9 8HB
Tel: 01922-440001 **Fax:** 01922-865784
E-mail: d.j.peace@hotmail.co.uk
Website: http://www.aldridgeironcraft.com
Directors: D. Peace (Prop)
Immediate Holding Company: JENKINS & NEWELL LIMITED
Date established: 1977 **No.of Employees:** 1 - 10 **Product Groups:** 26, 35

Date of Accounts	Jun 11	Jun 10	Jun 09
Working Capital	15	29	39
Fixed Assets	44	47	49
Current Assets	54	68	72
Current Liabilities	N/A	13	N/A

Robert Allan Associates
6 Oakenhayes Drive, Walsall, WS8 7QB
Tel: 01543-452795 **Fax:** 01543-453693
E-mail: theteam@robertallan.co.uk
Website: http://www.robertallan.co.uk
Directors: A. Page (Prop), R. Page (Dir)
Managers: M. Page (Accounts)
VAT No.: GB 101 7727 00 **Date established:** 1993
Turnover: Up to £250,000 **No.of Employees:** 1 - 10 **Product Groups:** 81

Ancol Pet Products Ltd
Ancol House 113 Leamore Lane, Walsall, WS2 7DA
Tel: 01922-402428 **Fax:** 01922-404983
E-mail: sales@ancol.co.uk
Website: http://www.ancol.co.uk
Bank(s): HSBC Bank plc
Directors: J. Lane (Dir), S. Lane (Mkt Research), S. Lane (Sales)
Managers: R. Whithouse (Buyer)
Immediate Holding Company: ANCOL PET PRODUCTS LIMITED
Registration no: 01019480 **VAT No.:** GB 100 0116 70
Date established: 1971 **Turnover:** £2m - £5m **No.of Employees:** 51 - 100
Product Groups: 22, 49

Date of Accounts	Dec 11	Dec 10	Dec 09
Sales Turnover	9m	N/A	N/A
Pre Tax Profit/Loss	878	933	1m
Working Capital	3m	2m	2m
Fixed Assets	1m	1m	1m
Current Assets	4m	4m	3m
Current Liabilities	2m	2m	1m

Anochrome Ltd
Reservoir Place, Walsall, WS2 9RZ
Tel: 01922-627404 **Fax:** 01922-722572
E-mail: enquiries@anochrome-group.co.uk
Website: http://www.anochrome-group.co.uk
Directors: M. Oliver (Fin)
Managers: J. Oliver
Ultimate Holding Company: ANOCHROME GROUP LIMITED
Immediate Holding Company: ANOCHROME LIMITED
Registration no: 00405120 **Date established:** 1946
No.of Employees: 51 - 100 **Product Groups:** 46, 48

Date of Accounts	Mar 11	Mar 10	Mar 09
Working Capital	406	410	292
Fixed Assets	917	1m	2m
Current Assets	2m	2m	2m

Apollo Flow Measurement Ltd
Charles Street, Walsall, WS2 9LZ
Tel: 01922-645647 **Fax:** 01922-640326
E-mail: sales@apolloflow.co.uk
Website: http://www.apolloflow.co.uk
Directors: I. Maclaren (Fin)
Immediate Holding Company: APOLLO FLOW MEASUREMENT LIMITED
Registration no: 02781691 **Date established:** 1993
No.of Employees: 1 - 10 **Product Groups:** 38, 85

Date of Accounts	Mar 11	Mar 10	Mar 09
Working Capital	509	405	432
Fixed Assets	541	479	443
Current Assets	739	583	632

Approved Design Ltd
Coppice Side Industrial Estate Brownhills, Walsall, WS8 7EX
Tel: 01543-377033 **Fax:** 01543-377422
E-mail: sales@adl1.demon.co.uk
Website: http://www.adl.net
Directors: J. Page (Ptnr)
Immediate Holding Company: APPROVED DESIGN LIMITED
Registration no: 03781799 **Date established:** 1999
No.of Employees: 11 - 20 **Product Groups:** 20, 35, 38, 41, 45, 67, 84

Date of Accounts	Dec 11	Dec 10	Dec 09
Working Capital	687	597	655
Fixed Assets	242	243	258
Current Assets	897	855	891

Aqua Chill Ltd
Unit 28 Manor Industrial Estate Pleck Road, Walsall, WS2 9XX
Tel: 01922-709090 **Fax:** 08712-420497
Directors: R. Waite (Prop)
Immediate Holding Company: TEXTILES WEST MIDS LIMITED
Date established: 2011 **No.of Employees:** 1 - 10 **Product Groups:** 40, 66

Date of Accounts	Jun 11	Jun 10
Current Assets	1	1

Arjay Automation
Unit 2a Gatehouse Trading Estate Lichfield Road, Brownhills, Walsall, WS8 6JZ
Tel: 01543-375670 **Fax:** 01543-375670
Directors: A. Jarvis (Prop)
Date established: 1984 **No.of Employees:** 1 - 10 **Product Groups:** 46

Joseph Ash Walsall
Briteon Street Off Pleck Road, Walsall, WS2 9HW
Tel: 01922-628141 **Fax:** 01922-623451
E-mail: davidh@josephash.co.uk
Website: http://www.josephash.co.uk
Bank(s): National Westminster Bank Plc
Managers: D. Hanson (Mgr), J. Harney (Buyer), J. Beckford (Sales Prom Mgr)
Ultimate Holding Company: ASH & LACY P.L.C.
Immediate Holding Company: JOSEPH ASH & SON LTD
Registration no: 00154773 **Date established:** 1992 **Turnover:** £2m - £5m
No.of Employees: 21 - 50 **Product Groups:** 48

Ashley Competition Exhausts Ltd
1 New Street, Walsall, WS1 3DF
Tel: 01922-720767 **Fax:** 01922-721354
E-mail: brian@ashleycompetitionexhausts.com
Website: http://www.ashleycompetitionexhausts.com
Directors: B. Ashley (MD)
Registration no: 03485826 **Date established:** 1997
Turnover: Up to £250,000 **No.of Employees:** 1 - 10 **Product Groups:** 39, 68

Atlas Ball & Bearing Co. Ltd
Leamore Lane, Walsall, WS2 7DE
Tel: 01922-710515 **Fax:** 01922-710575
E-mail: sales@atlasball.co.uk
Website: http://www.atlasball.co.uk
Directors: A. Chandler (MD)
Ultimate Holding Company: ATLAS BEARINGS LIMITED
Immediate Holding Company: ATLAS BALL AND BEARING CO. LIMITED
Registration no: 01339603 **VAT No.:** GB 313 6157 82
Date established: 1977 **Turnover:** £2m - £5m **No.of Employees:** 11 - 20
Product Groups: 35

Date of Accounts	Dec 11	Dec 10	Dec 09
Working Capital	698	666	644
Fixed Assets	56	63	54
Current Assets	1m	928	1m

Aulton & Butler Ltd
Ashtree Works Bentley Lane Industrial Park Bentley Lane, Walsall, WS2 8TL
Tel: 01922-623297 **Fax:** 01922-613586
E-mail: aulton-butler@tiscali.co.uk
Directors: J. Unitt (Fin), K. Aulton (MD)
Immediate Holding Company: AULTON & BUTLER LIMITED
Registration no: 00555212 **VAT No.:** GB 101 2160 51
Date established: 1955 **Turnover:** Up to £250,000
No.of Employees: 1 - 10 **Product Groups:** 25

Date of Accounts	Oct 11	Oct 10	Oct 09
Working Capital	-5	-12	2
Fixed Assets	2	3	4
Current Assets	55	45	46

B C Plastic Mouldings
Unit B Leamore Enterprise Park Commercial Road, Walsall, WS2 7NQ
Tel: 01922-497888 **Fax:** 01922-478600
E-mail: cjms@btconnect.com
Directors: A. Jansen (MD), A. Jansen (Fin)
Immediate Holding Company: OPAL TRANSPORT EQUIPMENT LIMITED
Registration no: 05649894 **VAT No.:** GB 648 6625 00
Date established: 1976 **Turnover:** £2m - £5m **No.of Employees:** 1 - 10
Product Groups: 30, 66

A J Baker Grinding Ltd
Middlemore Lane West Aldridge, Walsall, WS9 8BG
Tel: 01922-745075 **Fax:** 0121-378 3291
E-mail: enquiries@ajbaker.com
Website: http://www.ajbaker.com
Directors: A. Baker (MD)
Immediate Holding Company: A.J. BAKER (GRINDING) LIMITED
Registration no: 01268617 **Date established:** 1976 **Turnover:** £1m - £2m
No.of Employees: 1 - 10 **Product Groups:** 46

Date of Accounts	Aug 11	Aug 10	Aug 09
Working Capital	72	22	61
Fixed Assets	2m	2m	2m
Current Assets	269	185	222

Battery Distribution Group
Unit 2 Fellows Court Lockside Anchor Brook Industrial Park, Aldridge, Walsall, WS9 8BZ
Tel: 01922-741710 **Fax:** 01922-741719
E-mail: sales@batterydistribution.com
Website: http://www.batterydistribution.com
Directors: W. Daniels (Prop)
Immediate Holding Company: BATTERY DISTRIBUTION GROUP LIMITED
Registration no: 03567783 **Date established:** 1998
No.of Employees: 11 - 20 **Product Groups:** 37, 67

Date of Accounts	Mar 12	Mar 11	Mar 10
Working Capital	154	196	133
Fixed Assets	242	117	111
Current Assets	3m	3m	2m

Bernstein Ltd
Unit 1 Westgate Park Industrial Estate, Aldridge, Walsall, WS9 8ER
Tel: 01922-744999 **Fax:** 01922-457555
E-mail: sales@bernstein-ltd.co.uk
Website: http://www.bernstein-ltd.co.uk
Bank(s): Barclays
Directors: R. Norden (Co Sec), R. Emms (Dir)
Ultimate Holding Company: BERNSTEIN AG (GERMANY)
Immediate Holding Company: BERNSTEIN LTD
Registration no: 02051250 **VAT No.:** GB 449 6230 33
Date established: 1986 **Turnover:** £1m - £2m **No.of Employees:** 11 - 20
Product Groups: 30, 37

Date of Accounts	Dec 11	Dec 10	Dec 09
Sales Turnover	3m	2m	2m
Pre Tax Profit/Loss	131	134	-46
Working Capital	355	254	159
Fixed Assets	366	368	362
Current Assets	597	618	604
Current Liabilities	13	133	67

Birmingham Burner Ltd
Unit 6 Field Gate, Walsall, WS1 3DJ
Tel: 01922-635831 **Fax:** 01922-724332
E-mail: info@birminghamburner.co.uk
Website: http://www.birminghamburner.co.uk
Directors: C. Mcglone (MD)
Immediate Holding Company: BIRMINGHAM BURNER (WALSALL) LIMITED
Registration no: 01392185 **VAT No.:** GB 316 5280 70
Date established: 1978 **Turnover:** Up to £250,000
No.of Employees: 1 - 10 **Product Groups:** 40

Date of Accounts	Jun 11	Jun 10	Jun 09
Working Capital	-22	-31	-25
Fixed Assets	37	41	47
Current Assets	79	73	117

Birmingham Seals Company Ltd
Unit 31 Regal Drive Walsall Enterprise Park, Walsall, WS2 9HQ
Tel: 08454-501585 **Fax:** 0845-450 1584
E-mail: d.mace@birminghamseals.co.uk
Website: http://www.birminghamseals.co.uk
Directors: D. Mace (Dir)
Immediate Holding Company: BIRMINGHAM SEALS COMPANY LIMITED
Registration no: 03615681 **VAT No.:** GB 714 9713 25
Date established: 1998 **Turnover:** £1m - £2m **No.of Employees:** 1 - 10
Product Groups: 29, 30, 31, 33, 34, 35, 36, 40

Date of Accounts	Jan 12	Jan 11	Jan 10
Working Capital	788	621	480
Fixed Assets	23	27	53
Current Assets	1m	1m	712

Black Country Metal Polishers
Unit 12 Short Acre Street, Walsall, WS2 8HW
Tel: 01922-616837 **Fax:** 01922-616837
E-mail: enquiries@metalpolish.co.uk
Website: http://www.metalpolish.co.uk
Directors: P. Grant (Ptnr)
Immediate Holding Company: BLACK COUNTRY SNACKS LTD
Registration no: 05606508 **Date established:** 2005
No.of Employees: 1 - 10 **Product Groups:** 36, 48

J W Bonser Ltd Dalby Holdings of Leicester
Albert Street, Walsall, WS2 8EX
Tel: 01922-621448 **Fax:** 01922-720263
E-mail: sales@jwbonser.co.uk
Website: http://www.jwbonser.co.uk
Directors: H. Dalby (MD), H. Darly (MD), R. Bonser (Co Sec)
Managers: A. Burton (Sales & Mktg Mg), R. Dalvy (Chief Mgr), R. Darly (Chief Mgr), J. Henworth (Mgr), L. Horton (Purch Mgr)
Registration no: 02477843 **Turnover:** £500,000 - £1m
No.of Employees: 21 - 50 **Product Groups:** 34, 66

Brineton Engineering Co. Ltd
Alma Street, Walsall, WS2 8JQ
Tel: 01922-620070 **Fax:** 01922-722875
E-mail: michael.hope@brineton-eng.co.uk
Website: http://www.brineton-eng.co.uk
Directors: M. Hope (Dir)
Immediate Holding Company: BRINETON ENGINEERING COMPANY LIMITED
Registration no: 00897961 **VAT No.:** GB 100 0947 27
Date established: 1967 **Turnover:** £1m - £2m **No.of Employees:** 1 - 10
Product Groups: 67

Date of Accounts	Dec 11	Dec 10	Dec 09
Working Capital	-392	-328	-282
Fixed Assets	773	804	854
Current Assets	103	110	122

Bullock Construction Ltd
Northgate Aldridge, Walsall, WS9 8TU
Tel: 01922-458311 **Fax:** 01922-459589
E-mail: daniels@bullock.co.uk
Website: http://www.bullock.co.uk
Bank(s): Barclays, Chiltern Hse, Station Approach
Directors: K. Maxwell (Co Sec)
Managers: M. Vitty, S. Daniels (Mgr)
Ultimate Holding Company: SFH 123 LIMITED
Immediate Holding Company: BULLOCK CONSTRUCTION LIMITED
Registration no: 00545646 **Date established:** 1955
Turnover: £125m - £250m **No.of Employees:** 51 - 100
Product Groups: 51, 52

Date of Accounts	Sep 10	Sep 09	Sep 08
Sales Turnover	159m	191m	181m
Pre Tax Profit/Loss	4m	7m	7m
Working Capital	38m	37m	35m
Fixed Assets	280	216	247
Current Assets	85m	86m	77m
Current Liabilities	38m	39m	31m

Burrafirm Ltd
Croxstalls Road, Walsall, WS3 2XY
Tel: 01922-476836 **Fax:** 01922-479442
E-mail: terryfryer@burrafirm.co.uk
Website: http://www.albert-jagger.co.uk
Directors: T. Fryer (MD)
Ultimate Holding Company: ALBERT JAGGER HOLDINGS LIMITED
Immediate Holding Company: BURRAFIRM LIMITED
Registration no: 00462061 **Date established:** 1948 **Turnover:** £1m - £2m
No.of Employees: 21 - 50 **Product Groups:** 48

Date of Accounts	Jul 11	Jul 10	Jul 09
Working Capital	946	1m	1m
Fixed Assets	16	25	37
Current Assets	1m	1m	1m

Howard Butler Ltd (t/a Hobut)
Crown Works Lincoln Rd, Walsall, WS1 2EB
Tel: 01922-640003 **Fax:** 01922-723626
E-mail: sales@hobut.co.uk
Website: http://www.hobut.co.uk
Bank(s): Lloyds TSB Bank plc
Managers: P. Collins (Export Sales Mg), T. Spink
Registration no: 00255259 **VAT No.:** GB 100 1746 32
Turnover: £2m - £5m **No.of Employees:** 101 - 250 **Product Groups:** 30, 37, 38, 67

Date of Accounts	Mar 12	Mar 11	Mar 10
Working Capital	2m	1m	1m
Fixed Assets	148	188	136
Current Assets	3m	2m	2m

C H Jones Walsall Ltd
Queen Street Premier Business Park, Walsall, WS2 9PB
Tel: 01922-704400 **Fax:** 01922-704440
E-mail: info@keyfuels.co.uk
Website: http://www.chjones.co.uk

Directors: J. Bennett (I.T. Dir), S. Pisciotta (Fin), M. Hoffmann (Tech Serv), G. Anslow (MD), C. Welsh (MD)
Managers: V. Hyde (Admin Off), M. Barnett (Serv Mgr), S. Clifford (Sales Prom)
Immediate Holding Company: C H JONES LIMITED
Registration no: 00305804 **Date established:** 1935
Turnover: £50m - £75m **No.of Employees:** 51 - 100 **Product Groups:** 38, 44, 80

Date of Accounts	Dec 10	Dec 09	Dec 08
Sales Turnover	89m	60m	34m
Pre Tax Profit/Loss	6m	4m	6m
Working Capital	22m	15m	12m
Fixed Assets	9m	10m	384
Current Assets	57m	37m	33m
Current Liabilities	3m	2m	277

C N C Speedwell Ltd
260 Lichfield Road Brownhills, Walsall, WS8 6LH
Tel: 01543-363880 **Fax:** 01543-444512
E-mail: mail@cncspeedwell.co.uk
Website: http://www.cncspeedwell.co.uk
Directors: J. Roby (Fin), M. Lewis (MD)
Managers: N. Spiers (Tech Serv Mgr), N. Spiers (I.T. Exec), C. Allport (Personnel)
Ultimate Holding Company: CASTINGS PUBLIC LIMITED COMPANY
Immediate Holding Company: C N C SPEEDWELL LIMITED
Registration no: 03124721 **Date established:** 1995
Turnover: £10m - £20m **No.of Employees:** 51 - 100 **Product Groups:** 46, 48

Date of Accounts	Mar 11	Mar 10	Mar 09
Sales Turnover	20m	8m	11m
Pre Tax Profit/Loss	4m	-652	798
Working Capital	-5m	-4m	-4m
Fixed Assets	17m	13m	14m
Current Assets	4m	4m	2m
Current Liabilities	3m	2m	1m

Tom Carrington & Co. Ltd
Willenhall Lane Bloxwich, Walsall, WS3 2XN
Tel: 01922-406611 **Fax:** 01922-493493
E-mail: info@tomcarrington.co.uk
Website: http://www.tomcarrington.co.uk
Bank(s): HSBC, Willenhall
Directors: T. Carrington (MD)
Immediate Holding Company: TOM CARRINGTON & CO.LIMITED
Registration no: 00785929 **VAT No.:** GB 276 8225 29
Date established: 1963 **No.of Employees:** 11 - 20 **Product Groups:** 33, 36, 46

Date of Accounts	Mar 11	Mar 10	Mar 09
Working Capital	994	813	841
Fixed Assets	365	365	391
Current Assets	2m	2m	2m

Cashmores
Upper Brook Street, Walsall, WS2 9PD
Tel: 01922-720930 **Fax:** 01922-648304
E-mail: csparrow@cashmores.co.uk
Website: http://www.cashmores.co.uk
Bank(s): National Westminster Bank Plc
Managers: D. Townsend (District Mgr)
Ultimate Holding Company: HENLEY MANAGEMENT LTD
Immediate Holding Company: AMARI METALS LTD
Registration no: 03308899 **Turnover:** £20m - £50m
No.of Employees: 21 - 50 **Product Groups:** 34, 66

Date of Accounts	Dec 07
Sales Turnover	22320
Pre Tax Profit/Loss	-270
Working Capital	-900
Fixed Assets	420
Current Assets	9470
Current Liabilities	10370
Total Share Capital	1950
ROCE% (Return on Capital Employed)	56.3

Castings plc
Lichfield Road Brownhills, Walsall, WS8 6JZ
Tel: 01543-374341 **Fax:** 01543-377483
E-mail: brian.cooke@castings.plc.uk
Website: http://www.castings.plc.uk
Bank(s): HSBC Bank plc
Directors: S. Mant (Fin), M. Everton (Sales), B. Cooke (Ch), J. Roby (Fin)
Immediate Holding Company: CASTINGS PUBLIC LIMITED COMPANY
Registration no: 00091580 **VAT No.:** GB 100 0216 66
Date established: 2007 **Turnover:** £75m - £125m
No.of Employees: 251 - 500 **Product Groups:** 34, 36, 48

Date of Accounts	Mar 12	Mar 11	Mar 10
Sales Turnover	126m	105m	61m
Pre Tax Profit/Loss	23m	16m	10m
Working Capital	35m	29m	26m
Fixed Assets	63m	56m	52m
Current Assets	57m	56m	42m
Current Liabilities	10m	11m	7m

Castle Packaging
2 Selborne Street, Walsall, WS1 2JN
Tel: 01922-625451 **Fax:** 01922-722202
E-mail: sales@castlepackaging.co.uk
Website: http://www.castlepackaging.co.uk
Bank(s): HSBC
Directors: S. Parkes (Fin)
Managers: D. Lord (Chief Mgr)
Immediate Holding Company: CASTLE PACKAGING LIMITED
Registration no: 01639241 **VAT No.:** GB 369 7403 17
Date established: 1982 **Turnover:** £2m - £5m **No.of Employees:** 11 - 20
Product Groups: 23, 27, 28, 30, 64, 66

Date of Accounts	Jan 12	Jan 11	Jan 10
Working Capital	N/A	N/A	140
Current Assets	N/A	N/A	140

Circuit Coatings Ltd
Marlow Street, Walsall, WS2 8AQ
Tel: 01922-635589 **Fax:** 01922-638444
E-mail: sales@circuit-coating.co.uk
Website: http://www.circuit-coating.co.uk
Directors: D. Shalts (Sales), C. Jones (I.T. Dir)
Immediate Holding Company: CIRCUIT COATINGS LIMITED
Registration no: 01418978 **Date established:** 1979 **Turnover:** £2m - £5m
No.of Employees: 51 - 100 **Product Groups:** 48

Date of Accounts	Mar 11	Mar 10	Mar 09
Working Capital	209	44	217
Fixed Assets	52	60	100
Current Assets	747	696	782

Classic Continuous Ltd
1st Floor 315 Chester Road Aldridge, Walsall, WS9 0PH
Tel: 0121-353 0113 **Fax:** 0121-353 5995
E-mail: sales@classic-continuous.co.uk
Website: http://www.classic-continuous.co.uk
Directors: R. Hibbs (Dir)
Immediate Holding Company: CLASSIC CONTINUOUS LIMITED
Registration no: 02123129 **Date established:** 1987
Turnover: Up to £250,000 **No.of Employees:** 1 - 10 **Product Groups:** 27, 28, 44

Date of Accounts	Aug 11	Aug 10	Aug 09
Working Capital	83	73	70
Fixed Assets	17	15	20
Current Assets	176	175	141

Coinadrink Ltd
Unit 11 Maple Leaf Industrial Estate, Walsall, WS2 8TF
Tel: 01922-640777 **Fax:** 01922-635270
E-mail: roger@coinadrink.co.uk
Website: http://www.coinadrink.co.uk
Bank(s): Lloyds TSB Bank plc
Directors: R. Williams (MD)
Immediate Holding Company: COIN-A-DRINK LIMITED
Registration no: 00870282 **VAT No.:** GB 100 4624 31
Date established: 1966 **Turnover:** £2m - £5m **No.of Employees:** 51 - 100
Product Groups: 48, 61, 83

Date of Accounts	Jul 11	Jul 10	Jul 09
Working Capital	1m	1m	478
Fixed Assets	753	658	619
Current Assets	1m	2m	964

Comlec Units
Northgate Way Northgate, Aldridge, Walsall, WS9 8TH
Tel: 01922-456237 **Fax:** 01922-455251
E-mail: sales@comlec.co.uk
Website: http://www.comlec.demon.co.uk
Directors: R. Blackwell (Co Sec)
Managers: L. Wilson (Accounts), N. Blackwell (Sales Prom Mgr)
Immediate Holding Company: Comlec Units Ltd
Registration no: 02365269 **VAT No.:** GB 489 6717 74
Date established: 1985 **Turnover:** £500,000 - £1m
No.of Employees: 1 - 10 **Product Groups:** 37, 40, 48

Date of Accounts	Sep 07	Sep 06	Sep 05
Working Capital	7	-4	-19
Fixed Assets	21	32	20
Current Assets	171	65	169
Current Liabilities	164	69	188

Cooke Brothers Ltd
Northgate Aldridge, Walsall, WS9 8TL
Tel: 01922-740001 **Fax:** 01922-456227
E-mail: customerservices@cookebrothers.co.uk
Website: http://www.cookebrothers.co.uk
Bank(s): National Westminster Bank Plc
Directors: P. Dicken (Sales), P. Cooke (MD), T. Cooke (Comm)
Managers: N. Winall (Chief Acct)
Immediate Holding Company: COOKE BROTHERS LIMITED
Registration no: 00521209 **VAT No.:** GB 100 0253 60
Date established: 1953 **Turnover:** £2m - £5m **No.of Employees:** 21 - 50
Product Groups: 35, 36, 46, 48

Date of Accounts	Jun 11	Jun 10	Jun 09
Working Capital	622	788	730
Fixed Assets	47	51	61
Current Assets	2m	1m	1m

Copper & Automotive Washer Co. Ltd
Northgate Aldridge, Walsall, WS9 8TW
Tel: 01922-743951 **Fax:** 01922-743830
E-mail: sales@copwash.co.uk
Website: http://www.copwash.co.uk
Bank(s): Lloyds TSB, New St, Birmingham
Directors: S. Yates (Sales), D. Yates (MD), M. Yates (Works)
Managers: J. Collins (Purch Mgr)
Immediate Holding Company: COPPER & AUTOMOTIVE WASHER COMPANY LIMITED
Registration no: 00263608 **Date established:** 1932 **Turnover:** £2m - £5m
No.of Employees: 21 - 50 **Product Groups:** 23, 24, 27, 29, 30, 31, 32, 33, 34, 35, 36, 37, 38, 39, 40, 41, 43, 44, 46, 47, 49, 66, 68

Date of Accounts	Jul 11	Jul 10	Jul 09
Working Capital	2m	2m	1m
Fixed Assets	252	254	328
Current Assets	2m	2m	2m

Craig & Derricott Ltd
Hall Lane Walsall Wood, Walsall, WS9 9DP
Tel: 01543-375541 **Fax:** 01543-452610
E-mail: kmorris@craigandderricott.com
Website: http://www.craigandderricott.com
Bank(s): National Westminster
Directors: K. Morris (Co Sec), P. Cranshaw (Sales)
Managers: A. Tucker (Tech Serv Mgr), C. Burgess (Purch Mgr), P. Mehmi (Mktg Serv Mgr)
Ultimate Holding Company: VICTORY TRANSFORMERS AND SWITCHGEAR LTD (INDIA)
Immediate Holding Company: CRAIG & DERRICOTT LIMITED
Registration no: 00388918 **VAT No.:** GB 100 0002 85
Date established: 1944 **Turnover:** £5m - £10m
No.of Employees: 51 - 100 **Product Groups:** 37, 38

Date of Accounts	Dec 11	Dec 10	Dec 09
Working Capital	413	496	523
Fixed Assets	474	365	318
Current Assets	2m	2m	2m

Crystal Mortgages Ltd
66 Lysways Street, Walsall, WS1 3AA
Tel: 01922-722007 **Fax:** 01922-722008
E-mail: info@crystalmortgages.co.uk
Website: http://www.loanbank.co.uk
Directors: A. Dewsbery (Fin), P. Cosnett (Dir), A. Dewsbury (MD)
Registration no: 04407643 **Date established:** 2002 **Turnover:** £2m - £5m
No.of Employees: 1 - 10 **Product Groups:** 80, 82

Date of Accounts	Sep 09	Sep 08	Sep 07
Working Capital	-197	-275	230
Fixed Assets	469	603	13
Current Assets	24	4	499

D J & C Macinnes & Sons Ltd
4 Dawes Lane, Walsall, WS8 7QJ
Tel: 01543-361519 **Fax:** 01543-361519
E-mail: donald.macinnes@sky.com
Directors: D. Macinnes (Dir)
Immediate Holding Company: D.J. & C. MACINNES LLP
Registration no: OC306937 **Date established:** 2004
No.of Employees: 1 - 10 **Product Groups:** 38, 42

Datasave Ltd
Landywood Holly Lane, Great Wyrley, Walsall, WS6 6BD
Tel: 01922-418564 **Fax:** 01922-415060
E-mail: sales@datasave.ltd.uk
Website: http://www.datasave.ltd.uk
Managers: G. Eade (Mgr)
Immediate Holding Company: DATASAVE LIMITED
Registration no: 03007864 **Date established:** 1995
No.of Employees: 1 - 10 **Product Groups:** 44, 80

Date of Accounts	Jan 11	Jan 10	Jan 09
Working Capital	276	248	186
Fixed Assets	31	38	46
Current Assets	346	334	314

Diegrave Co. Ltd
Everest Works Mount Street, Walsall, WS1 3PF
Tel: 01922-641420 **Fax:** 01922-725263
Directors: F. Forrest (Fin), D. Forrest (MD)
Ultimate Holding Company: DIEGRAVE HOLDINGS LIMITED
Immediate Holding Company: DIEGRAVE HOLDINGS LIMITED
Registration no: 01024325 **Date established:** 1971
No.of Employees: 1 - 10 **Product Groups:** 46, 48

Date of Accounts	Sep 11	Sep 10	Sep 06
Working Capital	-7	-7	24
Fixed Assets	33	36	57
Current Assets	10	4	35

Joseph Dixon Tool Co. Ltd
Unit 2 Charles Street, Walsall, WS2 9LZ
Tel: 01922-622051 **Fax:** 01922-721168
E-mail: sales@josephdixon.co.uk
Website: http://www.josephdixon.co.uk
Bank(s): Lloyds TSB Bank plc
Directors: C. Williamson (Dir)
Immediate Holding Company: JOSEPH DIXON TOOL COMPANY LIMITED(THE)
Registration no: 00447777 **VAT No.:** GB 100 1687 22
Date established: 1948 **Turnover:** £1m - £2m **No.of Employees:** 11 - 20
Product Groups: 35, 36, 42, 43, 44, 46

Date of Accounts	Apr 11	Apr 10	Apr 09
Working Capital	-144	-114	-110
Fixed Assets	308	324	343
Current Assets	150	155	110

Driver Southall Ltd
Unit 18 Maybrook Industrial Estate Maybrook Road, Walsall, WS8 7DG
Tel: 01543-375566 **Fax:** 01543-375979
E-mail: robert.allison@driversouthall.co.uk
Website: http://www.driversouthall.co.uk
Directors: R. Allison (MD), R. Allison (Dir), D. York (Comm)
Immediate Holding Company: DRIVER SOUTHALL LIMITED
Registration no: 02546899 **Date established:** 1990
Turnover: £500,000 - £1m **No.of Employees:** 1 - 10 **Product Groups:** 38, 45

Date of Accounts	Nov 09	Nov 08	Nov 07
Working Capital	3	6	20
Fixed Assets	12	14	20
Current Assets	130	286	189

E Jeffries & Sons Ltd
Unit 32 New Firms Centre Fairground Way, Walsall, WS1 4NU
Tel: 01922-642222 **Fax:** 01922-615043
E-mail: d.kent@ejeffries.co.uk
Website: http://www.ejeffries.co.uk
Bank(s): HSBC Bank plc
Directors: B. Evans (Sales & Mktg), S. Longdon (Fin)
Managers: D. Richards (Fin Mgr), D. Plant
Ultimate Holding Company: E. JEFFRIES HOLDINGS LIMITED
Immediate Holding Company: E.JEFFRIES & SONS LIMITED
Registration no: 00710564 **VAT No.:** GB 333 9613 53
Date established: 1961 **Turnover:** £2m - £5m **No.of Employees:** 51 - 100
Product Groups: 22, 23, 24, 49, 66

Date of Accounts	Dec 11	Dec 10	Dec 09
Sales Turnover	N/A	N/A	3m
Pre Tax Profit/Loss	N/A	N/A	-77
Working Capital	434	441	949
Fixed Assets	80	89	14
Current Assets	1m	1m	1m
Current Liabilities	N/A	N/A	324

Electrolytic Plating Co. Ltd
Crown Works Wednesbury Road, Walsall, WS1 4JJ
Tel: 01922-627466 **Fax:** 01922-723844
E-mail: info@electrolytic.co.uk
Website: http://www.electrolytic.co.uk
Bank(s): HSBC Bank plc
Directors: N. Toon (Co Sec), A. Toon (MD)
Managers: A. Dawson (Works Gen Mgr)
Immediate Holding Company: ELECTROLYTIC PLATING COMPANY LIMITED(THE)
Registration no: 00306348 **VAT No.:** GB 100 1656 33
Date established: 1935 **Turnover:** £2m - £5m **No.of Employees:** 21 - 50
Product Groups: 48

Date of Accounts	Dec 11	Dec 10	Dec 09
Working Capital	-864	-540	-355
Fixed Assets	2m	2m	2m
Current Assets	911	872	794

Equestrian Manufacturing & Supply
52 Mount Street, Walsall, WS1 3PL
Tel: 01922-613988 **Fax:** 01922-613988
Directors: A. Fox (Prop)
VAT No.: GB 101 7128 22 **Date established:** 1976
Turnover: £500,000 - £1m **No.of Employees:** 1 - 10 **Product Groups:** 22, 63

Foundry Machinery & Spares

Unit H Fryers Close, Walsall, WS3 2XQ
Tel: 01922-493603 **Fax:** 01922-713729
E-mail: info@fmslimited.co.uk
Website: http://www.fmslimited.co.uk
Directors: C. Perkins (Dir)
Immediate Holding Company: FOUNDRY MACHINERY & SPARES LIMITED
Registration no: 06610843 **Date established:** 2008
No.of Employees: 1 - 10 **Product Groups:** 45

Date of Accounts	Dec 11	Dec 10	Dec 09
Working Capital	197	178	59
Current Assets	505	589	180

Fuelvend Ltd

Queen Street Premier Business Park, Walsall, WS2 9PB
Tel: 01922-704407 **Fax:** 01922-704403
Website: http://www.keyfuels.co.uk
Managers: P. Mcarthy (Mgr)
Ultimate Holding Company: FLEETCOR TECHNOLOGIES INC (USA)
Immediate Holding Company: FUELVEND LIMITED
Registration no: 01914742 **Date established:** 1985
Turnover: £500,000 - £1m **No.of Employees:** 51 - 100
Product Groups: 38, 39, 54, 68

Date of Accounts	Dec 11	Dec 10	Dec 09
Working Capital	270	270	270
Current Assets	270	270	270

G E I Electronic Industries Ltd

Linley Lodge Works Westgate, Aldridge, Walsall, WS9 8EX
Tel: 01922-458020 **Fax:** 01922-452608
E-mail: adrian@gei-elec.com
Website: http://www.gei-elec.com
Directors: A. Beech (MD)
Immediate Holding Company: G.E.I.ELECTRONIC INDUSTRIES LIMITED
Registration no: 00367906 **VAT No.:** GB 486 8116 11
Date established: 1941 **Turnover:** £500,000 - £1m
No.of Employees: 1 - 10 **Product Groups:** 26, 35, 36, 38, 45, 48, 84

Date of Accounts	Jul 11	Jul 10	Jul 09
Working Capital	86	95	92
Fixed Assets	23	27	33
Current Assets	335	328	353
Current Liabilities	63	66	49

G K N Driveline Walsall

2, Walsall, WS9 8DT
Tel: 01922-453371 **Fax:** 01922-451716
E-mail: ryan.callaghan@gkndriveline.com
Website: http://www.gknplc.com
Bank(s): Barclays, Birmingham
Directors: R. Callaghan (Fin)
Managers: M. Habgood (Personnel)
Ultimate Holding Company: GKN plc
Immediate Holding Company: GKN DRIVELINE WALSALL LIMITED
Registration no: 00361671 **Date established:** 1940
Turnover: £20m - £50m **No.of Employees:** 51 - 100 **Product Groups:** 35, 39

Date of Accounts	Dec 09	Dec 08	Dec 07
Sales Turnover	38m	49m	54m
Pre Tax Profit/Loss	-4m	797	-290
Working Capital	6m	6m	4m
Fixed Assets	10m	12m	17m
Current Assets	11m	11m	11m
Current Liabilities	750	1m	1m

Gainsborough Bathrooms Ltd

Brickyard Road Aldridge, Walsall, WS9 8SR
Tel: 01922-743314 **Fax:** 01922-743207
Ultimate Holding Company: GEORGE TAYLOR & CO. LIFTING GEAR (EUROPE) LIMITED
Immediate Holding Company: ROADWAY INTERNATIONAL HAULIERS LIMITED
Date established: 1999 **No.of Employees:** 51 - 100 **Product Groups:** 26, 36

Date of Accounts	Dec 11	Dec 10	Dec 09
Sales Turnover	N/A	N/A	5m
Pre Tax Profit/Loss	N/A	N/A	82
Working Capital	777	582	465
Current Assets	4m	3m	3m
Current Liabilities	N/A	N/A	601

Genex UK Ltd

Fryers Road, Walsall, WS2 7NA
Tel: 01922-710050 **Fax:** 01922-495813
E-mail: info@genexuk.co.uk
Website: http://www.genexuk.co.uk
Directors: D. Moss (MD)
Immediate Holding Company: GENEX UK LIMITED
Registration no: 04157489 **VAT No.:** GB 427 4704 50
Date established: 2001 **No.of Employees:** 11 - 20 **Product Groups:** 26, 34, 35, 36, 37, 39, 40, 48, 66, 68

Date of Accounts	Feb 12	Feb 11	Feb 10
Working Capital	74	26	-2
Fixed Assets	30	27	33
Current Assets	403	341	311

Grammer Seating Systems Ltd

Willenhall Lane Industrial Estate Willenhall Lane, Bloxwich, Walsall, WS3 2XN
Tel: 01922-407035 **Fax:** 01922-710552
E-mail: info@grammer.com
Website: http://grammer.com
Directors: D. Bignell (MD)
Ultimate Holding Company: GRAMMER AG (GERMANY)
Immediate Holding Company: GRAMMER SEATING SYSTEMS LIMITED
Registration no: 00906728 **Date established:** 1967
Turnover: Up to £250,000 **No.of Employees:** 1 - 10 **Product Groups:** 26, 39, 41, 45, 67, 68

Date of Accounts	Dec 11	Dec 10	Dec 09
Sales Turnover	112	N/A	1m
Pre Tax Profit/Loss	-50	N/A	164
Working Capital	2m	2m	2m
Fixed Assets	141	147	154
Current Assets	2m	2m	2m
Current Liabilities	55	N/A	113

Greenaway Pipeline Products

Hayward Industrial Park Vigo Place, Walsall, WS9 8UG
Tel: 01922-743322 **Fax:** 01922-743163
E-mail: chris.greenaway@mjsections.co.uk
Website: http://www.greenaways.co.uk
Directors: C. Greenaway (MD)
Immediate Holding Company: M. GREENAWAY & SON LIMITED
Registration no: 01267147 **VAT No.:** GB 101 7466 02
Date established: 1976 **No.of Employees:** 1 - 10 **Product Groups:** 36

Date of Accounts	Mar 12	Mar 11	Mar 10
Working Capital	2m	2m	2m
Fixed Assets	673	642	627
Current Assets	2m	2m	2m

H C L Safety Ltd Latchways Group Plc

Unit 1 Ball Street, Walsall, WS1 2HG
Tel: 01922-619470 **Fax:** 01922-619471
E-mail: birmingham@hclsafety.com
Website: http://www.hclsafety.com
Managers: P. Davies (Reg Mgr)
Ultimate Holding Company: LATCHWAYS PLC
Immediate Holding Company: HCL-SAFETY LIMITED
Registration no: 02691137 **Date established:** 1992
No.of Employees: 11 - 20 **Product Groups:** 37, 40, 67, 86

Date of Accounts	Mar 11	Mar 10	Mar 09
Sales Turnover	9m	8m	10m
Pre Tax Profit/Loss	971	1m	1m
Working Capital	2m	2m	1m
Fixed Assets	251	311	360
Current Assets	3m	3m	3m
Current Liabilities	1m	783	640

H & D Developments

Westgate House Westgate, Aldridge, Walsall, WS9 8EX
Tel: 01922-457310 **Fax:** 01922-745692
Website: http://www.handddevelopments.co.uk
Directors: A. Higgs (Prop)
Immediate Holding Company: TJM HOLDINGS LIMITED
Registration no: 01132731 **Date established:** 1987
No.of Employees: 1 - 10 **Product Groups:** 35, 37

Date of Accounts	Aug 11	Aug 10	Aug 09
Working Capital	-1m	-1m	-1m
Fixed Assets	5m	4m	4m
Current Assets	489	458	391
Current Liabilities	N/A	150	N/A

H H Plastics Ltd

12 Navigation Street, Walsall, WS2 9NE
Tel: 01922-638454 **Fax:** 01922-720947
E-mail: sales@hhplastics.com
Website: http://www.hhplastics.com
Managers: P. Machin (Chief Mgr)
Immediate Holding Company: H. H. PLASTICS LIMITED
Registration no: 01449340 **Date established:** 1979 **Turnover:** £2m - £5m
No.of Employees: 21 - 50 **Product Groups:** 30

Date of Accounts	Mar 12	Mar 11	Mar 10
Working Capital	-112	-95	-109
Fixed Assets	169	127	122
Current Assets	917	876	855

Hartshorne Motor Services Ltd

Bentley Mill Close, Walsall, WS2 0BN
Tel: 01922-704600 **Fax:** 01922-704601
E-mail: info@hartshornegroup.co.uk
Website: http://www.hartshornegroup.co.uk
Directors: M. Cronin (MD), I. Mason (Co Sec)
Immediate Holding Company: HARTSHORNE MOTOR SERVICES LIMITED
Registration no: 00940949 **VAT No.:** GB 100 2107 61
Date established: 1968 **Turnover:** £50m - £75m
No.of Employees: 101 - 250 **Product Groups:** 68

Date of Accounts	Dec 11	Dec 10	Dec 09
Sales Turnover	52m	33m	61m
Pre Tax Profit/Loss	2m	-6m	-980
Working Capital	678	-837	2m
Fixed Assets	3m	4m	5m
Current Assets	19m	14m	12m
Current Liabilities	3m	3m	3m

Heathyards Engineering Co. Ltd

30 - 31 Industrial House Maybrook Road, Walsall, WS8 7DG
Tel: 01543-376754 **Fax:** 01543-452645
E-mail: sales@heathyards.com
Website: http://www.heathyards.com
Bank(s): Lloyds
Directors: D. Nash (Dir), L. Nash (Fin)
Ultimate Holding Company: EUROPEAN INDUSTRIAL GROUP LIMITED
Immediate Holding Company: HEATHYARDS ENGINEERING CO. LIMITED
Registration no: 01164808 **VAT No.:** GB 101 4380 27
Date established: 1974 **Turnover:** £2m - £5m **No.of Employees:** 21 - 50
Product Groups: 48

Date of Accounts	Mar 11	Mar 10	Mar 09
Working Capital	1m	1m	925
Fixed Assets	78	85	93
Current Assets	2m	2m	2m
Current Liabilities	530	86	196

Hollaender Rainer

Leamore Close Leamore Enterprise Park, Walsall, WS2 7PL
Tel: 01922-711474 **Fax:** 01922-497943
E-mail: rainer@hollaenderrainer.com
Website: http://www.hollaenderrainer.com
Bank(s): Yorkshire Bank PLC
Directors: R. Clover (Dir), A. Clover (Fin), G. May (MD), A. Clover (Dir), R. Clover (Prop)
Ultimate Holding Company: FOX HOLLIES PROPERTIES LIMITED
Immediate Holding Company: FOX HOLLIES PROPERTIES LIMITED
Registration no: 02373542 **VAT No.:** GB 559 6058 04
Date established: 1989 **Turnover:** £2m - £5m **No.of Employees:** 21 - 50
Product Groups: 35, 36

Date of Accounts	Mar 11	Mar 10	Mar 09
Working Capital	-0	-0	-0
Current Assets	1	1	1

Holloway Plastics Ltd

Willenhall Lane Industrial Estate Willenhall Lane, Bloxwich, Walsall, WS3 2XN
Tel: 01922-492777 **Fax:** 01922-495820
E-mail: sales@holloway-plastics.co.uk
Website: http://www.holloway-plastics.co.uk
Bank(s): Lloyds TSB Bank plc
Directors: N. Holloway (MD)
Managers: L. Street (Sales Admin)
Immediate Holding Company: HOLLOWAY PLASTICS LIMITED
Registration no: 02108830 **VAT No.:** GB 100 3192 39
Date established: 1987 **Turnover:** £500,000 - £1m
No.of Employees: 21 - 50 **Product Groups:** 30, 48

Date of Accounts	May 12	May 11	May 10
Working Capital	29	42	84
Fixed Assets	227	266	249
Current Assets	488	533	447

Stanley Horne & Sons Ltd

Bentley Mill Way, Walsall, WS2 0BN
Tel: 01922-611451 **Fax:** 01922-726070
E-mail: sales@stanleyhorne.co.uk
Website: http://www.stanleyhorne.co.uk
Bank(s): National Westminster Bank Plc
Directors: M. Horne (MD)
Immediate Holding Company: STANLEY HORNE & SONS LIMITED
Registration no: 00385438 **Date established:** 1944 **Turnover:** £1m - £2m
No.of Employees: 11 - 20 **Product Groups:** 48

Date of Accounts	Mar 12	Mar 11	Mar 10
Working Capital	792	541	471
Fixed Assets	224	251	272
Current Assets	1m	806	643

A C F Howell

Croft Street, Walsall, WS2 8JR
Tel: 01922-649992 **Fax:** 01922-624405
E-mail: adam@acfhowell.com
Website: http://www.acfhowell.com
Directors: A. Howell (Prop)
Registration no: 05917890 **Date established:** 2006
No.of Employees: 11 - 20 **Product Groups:** 46, 48

Howell Tomkins Ltd

Stockton Close, Walsall, WS2 8LH
Tel: 01922-633151 **Fax:** 01922-648593
E-mail: mail@howelltomkins.com
Website: http://www.howelltomkins.com
Bank(s): Barclays & HSBC
Directors: A. Howell (MD)
Managers: L. Price (Sales Admin), G. Cavanagh
Ultimate Holding Company: A C F HOWELL HOLDINGS LIMITED
Immediate Holding Company: HOWELL TOMKINS LIMITED
Registration no: 00517653 **Date established:** 1953
No.of Employees: 21 - 50 **Product Groups:** 48

Date of Accounts	Dec 09	Dec 08	Dec 07
Working Capital	55	96	72
Fixed Assets	41	30	51
Current Assets	401	361	376

E Hulme & Son Ltd

13 Cecil Street, Walsall, WS4 2BD
Tel: 01922-622082 **Fax:** 01922-722442
E-mail: robert@ehulme.co.uk
Website: http://www.ehulme.co.uk
Directors: R. Hulme (Prop)
Immediate Holding Company: E. HULME & SON LIMITED
Registration no: 04810048 **VAT No.:** GB 346 9051 44
Date established: 2003 **Turnover:** £500,000 - £1m
No.of Employees: 1 - 10 **Product Groups:** 22, 35, 49, 65

Date of Accounts	Mar 12	Mar 11	Mar 10
Working Capital	588	575	505
Fixed Assets	110	108	108
Current Assets	647	642	627

Ibstock Building Products Ltd

Brickyard Road Aldridge, Walsall, WS9 8TB
Tel: 01922-741400 **Fax:** 01922-743086
E-mail: r.hall@ibstock.co.uk
Website: http://www.ibstock.co.uk
Bank(s): HSBC Bank plc
Directors: S. Hardy (Co Sec)
Managers: R. Hall (Factory Mgr)
Ultimate Holding Company: CRH PUBLIC LIMITED COMPANY
Immediate Holding Company: IBSTOCK BUILDING PRODUCTS LIMITED
Registration no: 00784339 **VAT No.:** GB 101 8383 01
Date established: 1963 **Turnover:** £5m - £10m **No.of Employees:** 21 - 50
Product Groups: 33

Date of Accounts	Dec 11	Dec 10	Dec 09
Sales Turnover	3m	3m	2m
Pre Tax Profit/Loss	2m	7m	2m
Working Capital	22m	20m	16m
Fixed Assets	191m	191m	192m
Current Assets	22m	20m	16m

Impalloy

Willenhall Lane Industrial Estate Willenhall Lane, Bloxwich, Walsall, WS3 2XN
Tel: 01922-714400 **Fax:** 01922-714411
E-mail: sales@impalloy.com
Website: http://www.impalloy.com
Bank(s): Barclays
Managers: A. Wood (Sales & Mktg Mg), N. Moseley (Chief Mgr)
Ultimate Holding Company: IMPALLOY HOLDINGS APS LIMITED (DENMARK)
Immediate Holding Company: IMPALLOY LIMITED
Registration no: 05482132 **VAT No.:** GB 864 8742 77
Date established: 2005 **Turnover:** £5m - £10m **No.of Employees:** 21 - 50
Product Groups: 35, 37, 39, 51, 52, 54, 67, 68, 84

Date of Accounts	Dec 11	Jun 10	Jun 09
Sales Turnover	9m	6m	7m
Pre Tax Profit/Loss	-654	-95	641
Working Capital	152	635	777
Fixed Assets	277	448	374
Current Assets	2m	3m	2m
Current Liabilities	275	1m	1m

The Imperial Bathroom Company Ltd

Empire Industrial Park Brickyard Road, Aldridge, Walsall, WS9 8XT
Tel: 01922-743074 **Fax:** 01922-743180
E-mail: sales@imperial-bathrooms.co.uk
Website: http://www.imperial-bathrooms.co.uk

Directors: D. Wooldridge (Co Sec), N. Gore (MD), K. Johnson (Fab), J. Stevenson (Comm)
Ultimate Holding Company: KINDBURLY LIMITED
Immediate Holding Company: THE IMPERIAL BATHROOM COMPANY LIMITED
Registration no: 02196824 **Date established:** 1987 **Turnover:** £5m - £10m
No.of Employees: 21 - 50 **Product Groups:** 25, 33, 36

Date of Accounts	Mar 11	Mar 10	Mar 09
Sales Turnover	7m	6m	N/A
Pre Tax Profit/Loss	62	-262	138
Working Capital	1m	1m	1m
Fixed Assets	796	860	1m
Current Assets	3m	3m	3m
Current Liabilities	539	591	313

In-Comm Business Services Ltd

Unit 12 Hayward Industrial Park Vigo Place, Walsall, WS9 8UG
Tel: 01922-457686 **Fax:** 01922-453211
E-mail: info@in-comm.co.uk
Website: http://www.in-comm.co.uk
Bank(s): HSBC Bank plc
Directors: C. Mills (Fin)
Managers: G. Jones, M. Busby, J. Collins (Admin Off)
Immediate Holding Company: IN-COMM BUSINESS SERVICES LIMITED
Registration no: 02882089 **VAT No.:** GB 361 9729 25
Date established: 1993 **Turnover:** £1m - £2m **No.of Employees:** 21 - 50
Product Groups: 86

Date of Accounts	Mar 11	Mar 10	Mar 09
Working Capital	279	233	192
Fixed Assets	31	18	22
Current Assets	366	323	297

Incotech Ltd (Spraymation Ltd)

9 Lion Industrial Park Northgate Way, Walsall, WS9 8RL
Tel: 01922-455299 **Fax:** 01922-452288
E-mail: colin@incotech.co.uk
Website: http://www.incotech.co.uk
Directors: C. Robinson (Dir)
Immediate Holding Company: INCOTECH LIMITED
Registration no: 02821339 **Date established:** 1993
Turnover: £500,000 - £1m **No.of Employees:** 1 - 10 **Product Groups:** 48

Date of Accounts	Mar 12	Mar 11	Mar 10
Working Capital	250	167	135
Fixed Assets	5	4	5
Current Assets	389	331	291

Ingersoll Rand Security Technologies

Bescot Crescent, Walsall, WS1 4DL
Tel: 01922-707400 **Fax:** 01922-646303
E-mail: info@ingersollrand.co.uk
Website: http://www.ingersollrand.co.uk
Directors: C. Crampton (Fin)
Managers: J. Stanley (Mgr), C. Howett (Personnel), J. Shields (Mktg Serv Mgr)
Ultimate Holding Company: INGERSOLL-RAND COMPANY LIMITED
Immediate Holding Company: INGERSOLL RAND SECURITY TECHNOLOGIES LIMITED
Registration no: 00029131 **Date established:** 1989
Turnover: £50m - £75m **No.of Employees:** 51 - 100 **Product Groups:** 35, 36, 49, 66

Date of Accounts	Dec 11	Dec 10	Dec 09
Sales Turnover	50m	51m	50m
Pre Tax Profit/Loss	400	-37m	-1m
Working Capital	87m	87m	53m
Fixed Assets	11m	19m	18m
Current Assets	197m	197m	158m
Current Liabilities	4m	4m	4m

Intensiv Filter UK

Bath House Bath Street, Walsall, WS1 3DB
Tel: 01922-628893 **Fax:** 01922-613875
E-mail: jim.macmillan@intensiv-filter.co.uk
Website: http://www.intensiv-filter.com
Directors: J. Macmillan (MD)
Ultimate Holding Company: INTENSIV FILTER GMBH & CO KG (GERMANY)
Immediate Holding Company: INTENSIV FILTER (UK) LTD.
Registration no: 03699110 **VAT No.:** GB 669 8810 72
Date established: 1999 **Turnover:** £20m - £50m **No.of Employees:** 1 - 10
Product Groups: 23, 35, 40, 41, 42, 45, 52, 66, 83

Date of Accounts	Dec 11	Dec 10	Dec 09
Working Capital	3	-14	-42
Fixed Assets	20	26	21
Current Assets	187	703	223

International Yacht Sales

23 Old Oak Close, Walsall, WS9 8SE
Tel: 01922-459072 **Fax:** 01922- 453420
E-mail: alfagius@intyachtsales.com
Website: http://www.intyachtsales.com
Directors: A. Agius (Prop)
VAT No.: GB 661 2086 52 **Turnover:** Up to £250,000
No.of Employees: 1 - 10 **Product Groups:** 39, 61

J B Electrical Ltd

5-6 Lion Industrial Park Northgate Way, Walsall, WS9 8RL
Tel: 01922-459351 **Fax:** 01922- 743506
E-mail: jeff.bird@fsmail.net
Website: http://www.jbelectrical.co.uk
Directors: J. Bird (MD), J. Bird (Co Sec)
Managers: R. Nichols (Sales Prom Mgr)
Immediate Holding Company: J.B. ELECTRICAL LIMITED
Registration no: 02323925 **VAT No.:** GB 489 7820 76
Date established: 1988 **Turnover:** £250,000 - £500,000
No.of Employees: 1 - 10 **Product Groups:** 37

Date of Accounts	Dec 10	Dec 09	Dec 08
Working Capital	-91	-74	13
Fixed Assets	N/A	1	1
Current Assets	61	24	116

J & E Sedgwick & Co. Ltd

Reservoir Place, Walsall, WS2 9RX
Tel: 01922-622797 **Fax:** 01922-724344
E-mail: sales@je-sedgwick.co.uk
Website: http://www.je-sedgwick.co.uk
Bank(s): Barclays
Directors: M. Lawson (Co Sec), M. Nazaruk (Dir), R. Farrow (MD)
Ultimate Holding Company: J&E SEDGWICK HOLDINGS LIMITED
Immediate Holding Company: J & E SEDGWICK & COMPANY LIMITED
Registration no: 02393038 **VAT No.:** GB 643 0374 59
Date established: 1989 **Turnover:** £2m - £5m **No.of Employees:** 21 - 50
Product Groups: 22, 40, 63, 66

Date of Accounts	Sep 11	Sep 10	Sep 09
Working Capital	1m	1m	1m
Fixed Assets	334	371	411
Current Assets	2m	2m	2m

J & J Engineering Walsall Ltd

Leamore Enterprise Park Fryers Road, Walsall, WS3 2XJ
Tel: 01922-710204 **Fax:** 01922-710191
E-mail: j.woodall@btconnect.com
Website: http://www.j-jengwalsall-ltd.co.uk
Bank(s): Barclays
Directors: J. Woodall (MD)
Immediate Holding Company: J & J ENGINEERING (WALSALL) LIMITED
Registration no: 01669967 **VAT No.:** GB 316 4890 48
Date established: 1982 **Turnover:** £1m - £2m **No.of Employees:** 11 - 20
Product Groups: 30, 34, 35, 46, 47, 48

Date of Accounts	Oct 11	Oct 10	Oct 09
Working Capital	199	133	211
Fixed Assets	201	201	211
Current Assets	446	262	316

J K L Industrial Engineering Ltd

Canalside Close, Walsall, WS3 1NZ
Tel: 01922-409949 **Fax:** 01922-710457
E-mail: sales@jklengineering.fsnet.co.uk
Directors: K. Woolley (MD)
Immediate Holding Company: JKL INDUSTRIAL SERVICES LTD
Registration no: 04550005 **VAT No.:** GB 346 8958 96
Date established: 2002 **Turnover:** £500,000 - £1m
No.of Employees: 1 - 10 **Product Groups:** 48

Date of Accounts	Feb 07	Feb 06
Working Capital	-84	93
Fixed Assets	481	494
Current Assets	422	503
Current Liabilities	506	410
Total Share Capital	7	7

J P Metal Treatments Ltd

Crescent Works Pleck Road, Walsall, WS2 9ES
Tel: 01922-613295 **Fax:** 01922-724611
E-mail: jpmt@btconnect.com
Website: http://www.jpmetaltreatments.com
Bank(s): Yorkshire Bank PLC
Directors: L. Cottrell (MD)
Immediate Holding Company: J.P. METAL TREATMENTS LIMITED
Registration no: 01036007 **VAT No.:** GB 110 0474 37
Date established: 1971 **Turnover:** £250,000 - £500,000
No.of Employees: 11 - 20 **Product Groups:** 48

Date of Accounts	Dec 11	Dec 10	Dec 09
Sales Turnover	400	402	350
Pre Tax Profit/Loss	-42	-63	-105
Working Capital	326	359	412
Fixed Assets	37	46	56
Current Assets	384	402	447
Current Liabilities	16	16	12

J S F Stainless Ltd

Chase Road Brownhills, Walsall, WS8 6JT
Tel: 01543-374688 **Fax:** 01543-454030
E-mail: info@jsfstainless.co.uk
Website: http://www.jsfstainless.com
Directors: M. Ottewell (MD), R. Lancaster (Dir), M. Ottewell (MD)
Immediate Holding Company: JSF STAINLESS LIMITED
Registration no: 04618535 **Date established:** 2002
Turnover: £500,000 - £1m **No.of Employees:** 11 - 20
Product Groups: 35, 36, 48, 67

Date of Accounts	Dec 11	Dec 09	Dec 08
Working Capital	-63	19	N/A
Fixed Assets	155	41	47
Current Assets	589	406	483

Jabez Cliff Company Ltd

Aldridge Road, Walsall, WS4 2JP
Tel: 01922-621676 **Fax:** 01922-722575
E-mail: jennifer@barnsby.com
Website: http://www.barnsby.com
Bank(s): Lloyds TSB Bank plc
Directors: K. Kirby (MD), T. Sharland (Co Sec), T. Sharland (Fin), J. Hickton (Ch)
Managers: C. Kirby (Mktg Serv Mgr)
Immediate Holding Company: JABEZ CLIFF & COMPANY LIMITED
Registration no: 00159339 **VAT No.:** GB 100 0155 60
Date established: 2019 **No.of Employees:** 21 - 50 **Product Groups:** 22, 49

Date of Accounts	Dec 10	Dec 09	Dec 08
Working Capital	193	-1m	-1m
Fixed Assets	682	2m	2m
Current Assets	484	491	483
Current Liabilities	77	102	N/A

Albert Jagger Ltd

Centaur Works Green Lane, Walsall, WS2 8HG
Tel: 01922-471000 **Fax:** 01922-648021
E-mail: export@albert-jagger.co.uk
Website: http://www.albert-jagger.co.uk
Bank(s): Lloyds TSB Bank plc
Directors: G. Cooper (MD), A. Cotton (Fin), J. Wollaston (Sales)
Managers: D. Cocker (Purch Mgr), D. Blackham (Export Sales Mg)
Registration no: 00325249 **VAT No.:** GB 806 6470 27
Date established: 1887 **Turnover:** £10m - £20m
No.of Employees: 51 - 100 **Product Groups:** 30, 35, 36, 37, 39, 40, 41, 42, 43, 44, 45, 46, 61, 66, 67, 68, 87

Date of Accounts	Jul 11	Jul 10	Jul 09
Sales Turnover	10m	8m	8m
Pre Tax Profit/Loss	308	2	-129
Working Capital	9m	9m	9m
Fixed Assets	142	116	183
Current Assets	12m	11m	12m
Current Liabilities	416	220	246

Jetter UK Ltd

43 Leighswood Road Aldridge, Walsall, WS9 8AH
Tel: 01922-745200 **Fax:** 01922-745045
E-mail: jetteruk@btinternet.com
Website: http://www.jetter.de
Directors: M. Matchet (Sales), N. Barnett (Tech Sales)
Immediate Holding Company: Jetter A.G.
Registration no: 02681945 **VAT No.:** GB 589 2839 72
Turnover: £1m - £2m **No.of Employees:** 1 - 10 **Product Groups:** 35, 37, 38, 44

R D Jukes & Co. Ltd

Walsingham Works 1 Walsingham Street, Walsall, WS1 2JZ
Tel: 01922-624222 **Fax:** 01922-630587
E-mail: enquiries@rdjukes.co.uk
Website: http://www.rdjukes.co.uk
Bank(s): HSBC Bank plc
Directors: J. Jukes (Dir)
Managers: A. Jukes (Personnel), S. Snoddy
Immediate Holding Company: R.D. JUKES & CO. LIMITED
Registration no: 01159706 **Date established:** 1974 **Turnover:** £1m - £2m
No.of Employees: 21 - 50 **Product Groups:** 52

Date of Accounts	Apr 12	Apr 11	Apr 10
Working Capital	503	390	445
Fixed Assets	53	73	102
Current Assets	1m	881	901

Kirkpatrick Ltd

PO Box 17, Walsall, WS2 9NF
Tel: 01922-620026 **Fax:** 01922-722525
E-mail: enquiries@kirkpatrick.co.uk
Website: http://www.kirkpatrick.co.uk
Bank(s): Lloyds TSB Bank plc
Directors: J. Anderson (MD), S. Preston (MD)
Managers: D. Jones (Fin Mgr)
Immediate Holding Company: KIRKPATRICK LIMITED
Registration no: 00071325 **VAT No.:** GB 100 1726 38
Date established: 2001 **Turnover:** £2m - £5m
No.of Employees: 101 - 250 **Product Groups:** 34, 35, 36

Date of Accounts	Dec 11	Dec 10	Dec 09
Sales Turnover	2m	3m	3m
Pre Tax Profit/Loss	-11	26	-37
Working Capital	2m	2m	2m
Fixed Assets	293	227	250
Current Assets	2m	2m	2m
Current Liabilities	227	221	179

L & R Saddles Ltd

Clifford House 10-14 Butts Road, Walsall, WS4 2AR
Tel: 01922-630740 **Fax:** 01922-721149
E-mail: landrsaddles@btconnect.com
Website: http://www.landrsaddles.com
Directors: S. Lovatt (Dir)
Immediate Holding Company: L & R SADDLES LTD.
Registration no: 02756473 **VAT No.:** GB 559 7531 96
Date established: 1992 **Turnover:** £250,000 - £500,000
No.of Employees: 1 - 10 **Product Groups:** 22

Date of Accounts	Aug 12	Aug 11	Aug 10
Working Capital	33	20	34
Fixed Assets	16	14	16
Current Assets	79	74	94

L & S Engineers Ltd

Unit 5 West Coppice Road, Walsall, WS8 7HB
Tel: 01543-378189 **Fax:** 01543-370006
Website: http://www.lsengineers.co.uk
Directors: B. Lees (Dir)
Managers: D. Vernon (Mgr)
Immediate Holding Company: L & S ENGINEERS LIMITED
Registration no: 04224976 **VAT No.:** GB 100 5565 12
Date established: 2001 **Turnover:** Up to £250,000
No.of Employees: 11 - 20 **Product Groups:** 67, 87

Date of Accounts	Nov 11	Nov 10	Nov 09
Working Capital	7m	6m	6m
Fixed Assets	37	13	17
Current Assets	8m	7m	7m

Lee Beesley Ltd

Frederick Street, Walsall, WS2 9NJ
Tel: 01922-615616 **Fax:** 01922-615696
Website: http://www.leebeesley.co.uk
Bank(s): Barclays, Queens Square, Wolverhampton
Directors: D. Fisher (Mkt Research), P. Rooney (Ch & MD)
Managers: K. Blogg (Fin Mgr), P. Pearson (Chief Mgr)
Ultimate Holding Company: VINCI SA (FRANCE)
Immediate Holding Company: LEE BEESLEY HOLDINGS LIMITED
Registration no: 01234891 **VAT No.:** GB 545 1884 27
Date established: 1975 **Turnover:** £20m - £50m
No.of Employees: 21 - 50 **Product Groups:** 48, 52, 85

Date of Accounts	Dec 10	Dec 09	Dec 08
Working Capital	N/A	1m	1m
Fixed Assets	N/A	300	300
Current Assets	N/A	1m	1m

Letchford Swifts Ltd

Leamore Lane, Walsall, WS2 7BU
Tel: 01922-402460 **Fax:** 01922-402460
Directors: A. Wall (Fin), S. Wall (MD)
Immediate Holding Company: LETCHFORD SWIFTS LIMITED
Registration no: 01678642 **Date established:** 1982
Turnover: Up to £250,000 **No.of Employees:** 1 - 10 **Product Groups:** 48

Date of Accounts	Mar 11	Mar 10	Mar 09
Working Capital	22	21	24
Current Assets	31	28	32
Current Liabilities	5	5	5

Lichtgitter UK Ltd

Fryers Road Bloxwich, Walsall, WS2 7LZ
Tel: 01922-711611 **Fax:** 01922-711612
E-mail: sales@lichtgitter.co.uk
Website: http://www.lichtgitter.co.uk
Bank(s): Bank of Scotland
Directors: A. Grice (Sales), M. Grice (Fin)
Managers: R. Murray (Buyer)
Ultimate Holding Company: LICHTGITTER GMBH (GERMANY)
Immediate Holding Company: LICHTGITTER (U.K.) LIMITED
Registration no: 02469611 **Date established:** 1990 **Turnover:** £2m - £5m
No.of Employees: 21 - 50 **Product Groups:** 35

Date of Accounts	Dec 11	Dec 10	Dec 09
Working Capital	756	577	564
Fixed Assets	633	647	650
Current Assets	2m	2m	1m

Lones UK Ltd (t/a Workplace Products)
7 Middlemore Lane West Aldridge, Walsall, WS9 8BG
Tel: 01922-743833 **Fax:** 01922-743760
E-mail: sales@workplace-products.co.uk
Website: http://www.workplace-products.co.uk
Bank(s): HSBC Bank plc
Directors: J. Lones (Fin)
Immediate Holding Company: LONES (UK) LIMITED
Registration no: 05175628 **VAT No.:** GB 101 6767 90
Date established: 2004 **No.of Employees:** 11 - 20 **Product Groups:** 26, 37, 45, 49, 67, 84

Date of Accounts	Oct 10	Oct 09	Oct 08
Working Capital	318	90	123
Fixed Assets	229	16	23
Current Assets	1m	829	790

Lowe & Fletcher Metal Finishing Ltd
Leamore Industrial Estate Fryers Road, Walsall, WS2 7LZ
Tel: 01922-475555 **Fax:** 01922-408711
E-mail: sales@metal-finishing.co.uk
Website: http://www.metal-finishing.co.uk
Bank(s): Lloyds TSB
Directors: G. Birt (Co Sec), G. Tonks (MD)
Ultimate Holding Company: LOWE AND FLETCHER LIMITED
Immediate Holding Company: LOWE AND FLETCHER METAL FINISHING LIMITED
Registration no: 01176463 **VAT No.:** GB 101 5929 95
Date established: 1974 **Turnover:** £1m - £2m **No.of Employees:** 21 - 50
Product Groups: 48

Date of Accounts	Dec 11	Dec 10	Dec 09
Sales Turnover	1m	1m	1m
Pre Tax Profit/Loss	-210	-255	80
Working Capital	229	330	406
Fixed Assets	1m	1m	1m
Current Assets	523	543	607
Current Liabilities	85	69	61

M J P Gates
5 Crossings Indl-Est Fryers Road, Walsall, WS3 2XJ
Tel: 01922-409773
Website: http://www.mjpgates.co.uk
Directors: M. Stathan (Ptnr)
No.of Employees: 1 - 10 **Product Groups:** 26, 35

M K G Food Products Ltd
Westgate Aldridge, Walsall, WS9 8DE
Tel: 01922-453131 **Fax:** 01922-743077
E-mail: sales@mkgfoods.co.uk
Website: http://www.mkgfoods.co.uk
Bank(s): National Westminster
Directors: J. Soulsby (Co Sec), A. Jefferson (Dir), B. Mayling (Sales), J. Mayling (Jt MD), P. Mayling (Dir), R. Mayling (MD)
Managers: S. Mayling (Sales & Mktg Mg)
Ultimate Holding Company: M.K.G. HOLDINGS LIMITED
Immediate Holding Company: M.K.G.(FOOD PRODUCTS)LIMITED
Registration no: 00478772 **VAT No.:** GB 559 6595 75
Date established: 1950 **Turnover:** £10m - £20m
No.of Employees: 51 - 100 **Product Groups:** 20, 62

Date of Accounts	Mar 11	Mar 10	Mar 09
Sales Turnover	11m	14m	N/A
Pre Tax Profit/Loss	100	246	449
Working Capital	2m	2m	2m
Fixed Assets	902	864	907
Current Assets	3m	3m	4m
Current Liabilities	327	496	1m

M W Equipment
Unit 5 Maybrook Industrial Estate Maybrook Road, Walsall, WS8 7DG
Tel: 01543-378805 **Fax:** 0161-429 0296
Bank(s): Royal Bank of Scotland
Directors: T. Whelan (Prop), T. Willis (Dir)
Date established: 1929 **No.of Employees:** 11 - 20 **Product Groups:** 46

Date of Accounts	Apr 11	Apr 10	Apr 09
Working Capital	124	113	93
Fixed Assets	72	49	64
Current Assets	307	312	259

Mackwell Electronics Ltd
Vigo Place Aldridge, Walsall, WS9 8UG
Tel: 01922-458255 **Fax:** 01922-451263
E-mail: nick.brangwin@mackwell.com
Website: http://www.mackwell.com
Bank(s): Lloyds TSB Bank plc
Directors: N. Brangwin (MD), P. Dupont (Purch), T. Ballard (Fin)
Managers: G. Cupitt (Sales Prom Mgr), G. Mack (Tech Serv Mgr), K. McCann (Mktg Serv Mgr), S. Dunmill (Personnel)
Ultimate Holding Company: F.W. THORPE PUBLIC LIMITED COMPANY
Immediate Holding Company: MACKWELL ELECTRONICS LIMITED
Registration no: 01414873 **Date established:** 1979
Turnover: £10m - £20m **No.of Employees:** 101 - 250 **Product Groups:** 37

Date of Accounts	Jun 11	Jun 10	Jun 09
Sales Turnover	13m	11m	12m
Pre Tax Profit/Loss	1m	705	1m
Working Capital	5m	4m	4m
Fixed Assets	551	507	502
Current Assets	7m	7m	6m
Current Liabilities	894	553	661

Majestic Aluminium Anodising Ltd
Queen Street Premier Business Park, Walsall, WS2 9NU
Tel: 01922-628596 **Fax:** 01922-724290
E-mail: amirkhan@majestics.org.uk
Website: http://www.majestics.org.uk
Directors: A. Khan (MD), B. Hems (Co Sec)
Immediate Holding Company: MAJESTIC ALUMINIUM ANODISING LIMITED
Registration no: 05611292 **Date established:** 2005
No.of Employees: 1 - 10 **Product Groups:** 46, 48

Date of Accounts	Mar 11	Mar 10	Mar 09
Working Capital	-2	-22	-16
Fixed Assets	61	72	81
Current Assets	293	198	142

Maple Leaf Bakery
38 Raleigh Street, Walsall, WS2 8RB
Tel: 01922-444546 **Fax:** 01922-444550
E-mail: info@mapleleaf.ca
Website: http://www.mapleleaf.ca
Managers: M. Hempstock (Chief Mgr)
Turnover: £50m - £75m **No.of Employees:** 101 - 250 **Product Groups:** 20

F Martin & Son Ltd
Bridgeman Street, Walsall, WS2 9NR
Tel: 01922-624666 **Fax:** 01922-724198
E-mail: info@fmartinandson.co.uk
Website: http://www.fmartinandson.co.uk
Directors: P. Taylor (MD)
Ultimate Holding Company: MARTIN HOLDINGS (WALSALL) LIMITED
Immediate Holding Company: F. MARTIN AND SON LIMITED
Registration no: 01345609 **VAT No.:** GB 100 2318 48
Date established: 1977 **Turnover:** £500,000 - £1m
No.of Employees: 1 - 10 **Product Groups:** 35

Date of Accounts	Mar 12	Mar 11	Mar 10
Working Capital	852	801	735
Fixed Assets	52	55	58
Current Assets	900	839	776

Mckechnie Brass
Middlemore Lane, Walsall, WS9 8DN
Tel: 01922-742400 **Fax:** 01922-451566
E-mail: sales@mckbrass.com
Website: http://www.mckbrass.com
Bank(s): Scandinaviska Enskilda Banken
Directors: R. Crilly (Comm)
Immediate Holding Company: MBL REALISATIONS LIMITED
Registration no: 02489169 **VAT No.:** GB 559 3370 17
Date established: 1990 **Turnover:** £20m - £50m
No.of Employees: 51 - 100 **Product Groups:** 34, 35

Date of Accounts	Jul 10	Jul 09	Apr 09
Sales Turnover	N/A	N/A	33m
Pre Tax Profit/Loss	N/A	N/A	-6m
Working Capital	250	2m	2m
Fixed Assets	1m	4m	5m
Current Assets	4m	17m	17m
Current Liabilities	N/A	N/A	2m

Metafin Group Holdings Ltd
Green Lane Birchills, Walsall, WS2 8JG
Tel: 01922-626073 **Fax:** 01922-720673
E-mail: info@metafin.co.uk
Website: http://www.metafin.co.uk
Bank(s): Barclays
Directors: M. Flannery (MD), G. Davis (Fin), P. Bundy (Dir)
Managers: G. Povey (Sales Prom Mgr)
Immediate Holding Company: METAFIN GROUP HOLDINGS LIMITED
Registration no: 01513707 **VAT No.:** GB 559 5492 90
Date established: 1980 **Turnover:** £2m - £5m
No.of Employees: 101 - 250 **Product Groups:** 48

Date of Accounts	Feb 12	Feb 11	Feb 10
Working Capital	224	617	486
Fixed Assets	2m	577	677
Current Assets	1m	1m	1m

Metal Finishing Ltd
16-18 Station Street, Walsall, WS2 9JZ
Tel: 01922-720720 **Fax:** 01922-723400
E-mail: paul.walford@lbparkes.net
Website: http://www.lbparkes.net
Bank(s): Barclays
Directors: P. Walford (MD)
Immediate Holding Company: METAL FINISHING LIMITED
Registration no: 05400499 **VAT No.:** GB 101 9167 02
Date established: 2005 **Turnover:** £1m - £2m **No.of Employees:** 21 - 50
Product Groups: 30, 48

Date of Accounts	Aug 11	Aug 10	Aug 09
Working Capital	-48	-107	-123
Fixed Assets	33	29	12
Current Assets	213	194	169

Metelec Ltd
Vulcan Industrial Estate, Walsall, WS2 7BZ
Tel: 01922-712665 **Fax:** 01922-710919
E-mail: sales@metelec.co.uk
Website: http://www.metelec.co.uk
Directors: D. Bird (Fin), P. Bird (MD)
Immediate Holding Company: METELEC LIMITED
Registration no: 04416364 **Date established:** 2002
Turnover: £20m - £50m **No.of Employees:** 11 - 20 **Product Groups:** 34, 35, 37

Date of Accounts	Dec 11	Dec 10	Dec 09
Sales Turnover	32m	26m	19m
Pre Tax Profit/Loss	2m	2m	2m
Working Capital	5m	4m	3m
Fixed Assets	371	233	196
Current Assets	11m	11m	7m
Current Liabilities	3m	4m	871

Midland Safe Load Indicators
Watling Street Works Watling Street, Brownhills, Walsall, WS8 7JT
Tel: 01543-453166 **Fax:** 01543-453167
E-mail: midlandsafeload@aol.com
Directors: H. Degville (Fin)
Managers: C. Degville (Sales Admin)
Immediate Holding Company: MIDLAND SAFE LOAD INDICATORS LIMITED
Registration no: 01259382 **VAT No.:** GB 101 7148 16
Date established: 1976 **Turnover:** £500,000 - £1m
No.of Employees: 1 - 10 **Product Groups:** 45, 48

Date of Accounts	Apr 11	Apr 10	Apr 09
Working Capital	-6	13	50
Fixed Assets	19	24	23
Current Assets	79	94	99

MITIE Tilley Roofing Ltd
Middlemore Lane, Walsall, WS9 8AN
Tel: 01922-457911 **Fax:** 01922-459829
E-mail: karly.hodgkiss@mitie.com
Website: http://www.mitie.com
Managers: I. Village (Mgr)
Ultimate Holding Company: MITIE GROUP PLC
Immediate Holding Company: MITIE TILLEY ROOFING LIMITED
Registration no: 00937663 **Date established:** 1968
Turnover: £20m - £50m **No.of Employees:** 1 - 10 **Product Groups:** 52

Date of Accounts	Mar 11	Mar 10	Mar 07
Working Capital	-3	-3	-37
Fixed Assets	5	10	40
Current Assets	77	87	76

T Morgan & Sons Ltd
136 Wolverhampton Road, Walsall, WS2 8PP
Tel: 01922-637022 **Fax:** 01922-631811
E-mail: sales@tmorgan.co.uk
Website: http://www.tmorgan.co.uk
Bank(s): Lloyds TSB P.L.C.
Directors: D. Morton (Dir)
Immediate Holding Company: T.MORGAN & SONS(LOCK MANUFACTURERS)LIMITED
Registration no: 00875548 **Date established:** 1966
Turnover: £500,000 - £1m **No.of Employees:** 11 - 20
Product Groups: 30, 36, 66

Date of Accounts	Mar 12	Mar 11	Mar 10
Working Capital	73	47	48
Fixed Assets	133	133	135
Current Assets	167	140	132

Myatt & Degville Fabrications Ltd
Selborne Street, Walsall, WS1 2JN
Tel: 01922-648222 **Fax:** 01922-613565
E-mail: myattanddegville@btconnect.com
Directors: D. Robinson (Dir)
Immediate Holding Company: MYATT & DEGVILLE FABRICATIONS LIMITED
Registration no: 01519856 **Date established:** 1980
No.of Employees: 1 - 10 **Product Groups:** 26, 35

Date of Accounts	Sep 10	Sep 09	Sep 08
Working Capital	-121	-82	-2
Fixed Assets	15	17	17
Current Assets	94	100	285
Current Liabilities	42	28	N/A

Nameplate UK Ltd
Unit 11 Westgate Trading Estate Westgate, Aldridge, Walsall, WS9 8EX
Tel: 01922-745735 **Fax:** 01922-745755
E-mail: info@nameplateuk.com
Website: http://www.nameplateuk.com
Directors: J. Redmond (Dir), M. Collins (Co Sec), M. Collins (Dir)
Immediate Holding Company: NAMEPLATE UK LIMITED
Registration no: 03602387 **Date established:** 1998 **Turnover:** £1m - £2m
No.of Employees: 1 - 10 **Product Groups:** 49

Date of Accounts	Dec 11	Dec 10	Dec 09
Working Capital	125	98	81
Fixed Assets	34	39	43
Current Assets	227	203	166

Netzsch-Instruments
Hayward Industrial Park Vigo Place, Walsall, WS9 8UG
Tel: 01922-459006 **Fax:** 01922-453320
E-mail: sales@netzsch-therma1.co.uk
Website: http://www.netzsch-thermal.co.uk
Directors: P. Davies (Chief Op Offcr)
Registration no: 01267147 **Date established:** 1976
No.of Employees: 1 - 10 **Product Groups:** 38, 42, 85

New Tech Finishing
Commercial Road, Walsall, WS2 7NQ
Tel: 01922-404604 **Fax:** 01922-711083
E-mail: enquiries@ntfltd.co.uk
Website: http://www.anoltd.co.uk
Bank(s): HSBC Bank plc
Directors: J. Oliver (I.T. Dir), M. Oliver (Co Sec)
Immediate Holding Company: OPAL TRANSPORT EQUIPMENT LIMITED
Registration no: 02072352 **Date established:** 1976
Turnover: £250,000 - £500,000 **No.of Employees:** 21 - 50
Product Groups: 46, 48

Noirit Ltd Newman & Field Ltd
21 Portland Street, Walsall, WS2 8AB
Tel: 01922-625471 **Fax:** 01922-722339
E-mail: sales@noirit.com
Website: http://www.noirit.com
Directors: J. Conquest (MD)
Ultimate Holding Company: NEWMAN & FIELD LIMITED
Immediate Holding Company: NEWMAN & FIELD LIMITED
Registration no: 00627251 **VAT No.:** GB 100 2178 38
Date established: 1959 **No.of Employees:** 1 - 10 **Product Groups:** 24, 34, 36, 37, 39, 74

Date of Accounts	Mar 11	Mar 10	Mar 09
Working Capital	N/A	-3	-3
Fixed Assets	302	460	337
Current Assets	N/A	N/A	1

One Stop Stores Ltd
Apex Road Brownhills, Walsall, WS8 7TS
Tel: 01543-363000 **Fax:** 01543-361073
E-mail: david.turner@onestop.co.uk
Website: http://www.onestop.co.uk
Directors: D. Turner (Grp Chief Exec)
Managers: B. Shingler-Day (Commun Mgr)
Ultimate Holding Company: TESCO PLC
Immediate Holding Company: T&S STORES LIMITED
Registration no: 01228935 **Date established:** 1975
Turnover: £500m - £1,000m **No.of Employees:** 251 - 500
Product Groups: 61

Date of Accounts	Feb 09	Feb 10	Feb 11
Sales Turnover	499m	530m	551m
Pre Tax Profit/Loss	16m	25m	21m
Working Capital	-52m	-20m	10m
Fixed Assets	200m	187m	178m
Current Assets	207m	205m	246m
Current Liabilities	20m	21m	23m

Onsite Resources Ltd
Green Lane, Walsall, WS2 7PD
Tel: 01922-638282 **Fax:** 01922-723631
E-mail: sales@onsite.co.uk
Website: http://www.onsite.co.uk
Directors: B. Whitty (Fin), R. Harley (Dir)
Ultimate Holding Company: Hydriades V Ltd
Immediate Holding Company: ONSITE SOUTH LIMITED
Registration no: 03152213 **Date established:** 1996
Turnover: £20m - £50m **No.of Employees:** 11 - 20 **Product Groups:** 54, 84

Date of Accounts	Mar 08	Mar 07	Mar 06
Pre Tax Profit/Loss	-175	-387	-165
Working Capital	-4759	-4637	-4315

Fixed Assets	110	108	108
Current Assets	23	N/A	86
Current Liabilities	4782	4637	4401
Total Share Capital	50	50	50
ROCE% (Return on Capital Employed)	3.8	8.5	3.9

Orbik Electronics Ltd

Orbik House Northgate Way, Aldridge, Walsall, WS9 8TX
Tel: 01922-743515 **Fax:** 01922-743173
E-mail: pauldawson@orbik.co.uk
Website: http://www.orbik.co.uk
Bank(s): Barclays
Directors: C. Goldspink (Sales), P. Dawson (Fin)
Managers: R. Williams (Tech Serv Mgr), D. Wilkes (Purch Mgr), K. Woolley (Personnel)
Immediate Holding Company: ORBIK ELECTRONICS LIMITED
Registration no: 01693311 **Date established:** 1983
Turnover: £10m - £20m **No.of Employees:** 101 - 250 **Product Groups:** 37

Date of Accounts	Mar 11	Mar 10	Mar 09
Sales Turnover	10m	9m	9m
Pre Tax Profit/Loss	101	73	74
Working Capital	2m	2m	1m
Fixed Assets	1m	1m	1m
Current Assets	4m	4m	4m
Current Liabilities	406	318	502

Owens Conveyor

Westgate House Westgate, Aldridge, Walsall, WS9 8EX
Tel: 01922-452333 **Fax:** 01922-458777
E-mail: sales@ocon.co.uk
Website: http://www.ocon.co.uk
Directors: A. Owen (Fin), K. Owen (Ptnr)
Immediate Holding Company: OWENS
Registration no: 03485517 **Date established:** 1997
No.of Employees: 11 - 20 **Product Groups:** 35, 39, 45

Paddock Fabrications Ltd

Fryers Road, Walsall, WS2 7LZ
Tel: 01922-711722 **Fax:** 01922-476021
E-mail: sales@paddockfabrications.co.uk
Website: http://www.paddockfabrications.co.uk
Bank(s): Midland
Directors: A. King (Co Sec), N. Hutchinson (MD), P. Atkinson (Sales)
Managers: J. Walker (Mktg Serv Mgr)
Ultimate Holding Company: ASSA ABLOY AB (PUBL) (SWEDEN)
Immediate Holding Company: PADDOCK FABRICATIONS LIMITED
Registration no: 03697765 **VAT No.:** 729 5783 84 **Date established:** 1999
Turnover: £10m - £20m **No.of Employees:** 101 - 250
Product Groups: 30, 35, 36

Date of Accounts	Dec 11	Dec 10	Dec 09
Sales Turnover	16m	28m	26m
Pre Tax Profit/Loss	41m	2m	1m
Working Capital	99	-1m	2m
Fixed Assets	757	4m	4m
Current Assets	166	12m	12m
Current Liabilities	67	2m	4m

Parmelee Ltd

PO Box 9 Middlemore Lane West, Walsall, WS9 8DZ
Tel: 01922-457421 **Fax:** 01922-473275
E-mail: gary@parmelee-safety.com
Website: http://www.parmelee-safety.com
Bank(s): Barclays
Directors: B. Howlett (Sales), G. Dawson (MD), A. Hinton (Co Sec)
Managers: B. Howlett (Mgr), C. Dawson (Mktg Serv Mgr), I. Lloyd (Stores Contrlr), R. Ferreday (Mgr), A. Hinton (Sales Admin), J. Brown (Accounts), M. Harvey
Ultimate Holding Company: PARMELEE INDUSTRIES INC (USA)
Immediate Holding Company: PARMELEE LIMITED
Registration no: 00517490 **VAT No.:** GB 208 0854 75
Date established: 1953 **Turnover:** £1m - £2m **No.of Employees:** 21 - 50
Product Groups: 38, 40

Date of Accounts	Dec 07
Working Capital	1171
Fixed Assets	180
Current Assets	1373
Current Liabilities	202
Total Share Capital	2

Piquant Ltd

Piquant House Willenhall Lane Industrial Estate Willenhall Lane, Bloxwich, Walsall, WS3 2XN
Tel: 01922-711116 **Fax:** 01922-473240
E-mail: salesinfo@piquant.co.uk
Website: http://www.piquant.co.uk
Directors: S. Nagendram (Fin), S. Khera (MD)
Managers: M. Hooker (Sales Prom Mgr)
Immediate Holding Company: PIQUANT LIMITED
Registration no: 01990129 **Date established:** 1986
No.of Employees: 21 - 50 **Product Groups:** 20

Date of Accounts	Jun 11	Jun 10	Jun 09
Working Capital	-172	-213	-156
Fixed Assets	1m	1m	1m
Current Assets	906	622	607

Plas Com

Unit 10 Merchants Way Aldridge, Walsall, WS9 8SW
Tel: 01922-743839 **Fax:** 01922-743491
E-mail: jenny@plascom.co.uk
Website: http://www.plascom.co.uk
Directors: R. Jones (Dir)
Date established: 2005 **No.of Employees:** 1 - 10 **Product Groups:** 46, 48

Date of Accounts	Nov 08	Nov 07
Pre Tax Profit/Loss	52	43
Working Capital	-69	-32
Fixed Assets	10	7
Current Assets	137	110
Current Liabilities	206	142
ROCE% (Return on Capital Employed)	-89.6	-169.7

Power Utilities Ltd

Queen Street Premier Business Park, Walsall, WS2 9QE
Tel: 01922-720561 **Fax:** 01922-720461
E-mail: info@power-utilities.com
Website: http://www.power-utilities.com
Bank(s): Lloyds
Directors: J. Cannavan (Co Sec), J. Gardner (Dir)
Ultimate Holding Company: POWER UTILITIES (HOLDINGS) LIMITED
Immediate Holding Company: POWER UTILITIES LIMITED
Registration no: 00293210 **Date established:** 1934
No.of Employees: 21 - 50 **Product Groups:** 40, 42, 67

Date of Accounts	Dec 11	Dec 10	Dec 09
Working Capital	2m	2m	2m
Fixed Assets	283	324	268
Current Assets	3m	3m	3m

Presco Components

Selborne Street, Walsall, WS1 2JN
Tel: 01922-620202 **Fax:** 01922-632695
E-mail: cparkes@presco.co.uk
Website: http://www.presco.co.uk
Bank(s): Midland
Directors: C. Parkes (Prop), D. Quinn (Fin)
Managers: J. Morgan (Prod Mgr), L. Argyle (Personnel)
Registration no: 05405613 **Turnover:** £5m - £10m
No.of Employees: 51 - 100 **Product Groups:** 35

Date of Accounts	Jan 08	Jan 07	Jan 06
Pre Tax Profit/Loss	674	299	282
Working Capital	779	324	137
Fixed Assets	691	685	679
Current Assets	5451	3397	2802
Current Liabilities	4672	3073	2665
ROCE% (Return on Capital Employed)	45.9	29.7	34.6

Prestwood Engineering Co. Ltd

Marlow Street, Walsall, WS2 8AQ
Tel: 01922-633476 **Fax:** 01922-724988
E-mail: john.higginbottom@prestwoodengineering.com
Website: http://www.prestwoodengineering.co.uk
Directors: J. Higginbottom (Dir)
Immediate Holding Company: PRESTWOOD ENGINEERING COMPANY LIMITED
Registration no: 01007338 **Date established:** 1971
No.of Employees: 11 - 20 **Product Groups:** 46

Date of Accounts	Feb 08	Feb 11	Feb 10
Working Capital	223	186	136
Fixed Assets	54	19	34
Current Assets	496	454	356

Q A Electrical Products Ltd

Queen Street Premier Business Park, Walsall, WS2 9NT
Tel: 01922-621329 **Fax:** 01922-626902
E-mail: sales@qaelectricalproducts.co.uk
Website: http://www.qaelectricalproducts.co.uk
Bank(s): National Westminster Bank Plc
Directors: A. Patel (MD)
Immediate Holding Company: Q.A.ELECTRICAL PRODUCTS LIMITED
Registration no: 01013948 **VAT No.:** GB 101 0581 37
Date established: 1971 **Turnover:** £250,000 - £500,000
No.of Employees: 11 - 20 **Product Groups:** 37

Date of Accounts	Mar 12	Mar 11	Mar 10
Working Capital	104	96	58
Fixed Assets	282	222	197
Current Assets	209	265	157

Rabtherm International Ltd

Shelco House Northgate, Aldridge, Walsall, WS9 8TH
Tel: 01922-743273 **Fax:** 01922-743119
E-mail: bgas@rabtherm.co.uk
Website: http://www.rabtherm.co.uk
Directors: S. Bennett (MD)
Immediate Holding Company: RABTHERM INTERNATIONAL LIMITED
Registration no: 00748561 **VAT No.:** GB 369 8684 75
Date established: 1963 **Turnover:** £1m - £2m **No.of Employees:** 1 - 10
Product Groups: 29, 32, 40

Date of Accounts	Apr 11	Apr 10	Apr 09
Working Capital	-39	-31	-21
Fixed Assets	1	2	2
Current Assets	13	13	20

Ramsell Naber Ltd

Vigo Place Aldridge, Walsall, WS9 8YB
Tel: 01922-455521 **Fax:** 01922-455277
E-mail: info@ramsell-naber.co.uk
Website: http://www.ramsell-naber.co.uk
Directors: C. Jackson (MD), J. Ramsell (Co Sec)
Ultimate Holding Company: RAMSELL THERMAL EQUIPMENT LIMITED
Immediate Holding Company: RAMSELL-NABER LIMITED
Registration no: 01911389 **VAT No.:** GB 489 4113 19
Date established: 1985 **Turnover:** £2m - £5m **No.of Employees:** 1 - 10
Product Groups: 33, 37, 40, 46

Date of Accounts	Sep 11	Sep 10	Sep 09
Working Capital	249	218	204
Current Assets	545	557	426

W Raybould & Sons Ltd

Croxstalls Close, Walsall, WS3 2XT
Tel: 01922-479196 **Fax:** 01922-494616
E-mail: info@raybould.co.uk
Website: http://www.raybould.co.uk
Directors: A. Raybould (Co Sec), J. Raybould (Dir)
Immediate Holding Company: W. RAYBOULD & SONS LIMITED
Registration no: 01185931 **VAT No.:** GB 101 4100 59
Date established: 1974 **Turnover:** £500,000 - £1m
No.of Employees: 1 - 10 **Product Groups:** 34

Date of Accounts	Oct 11	Oct 10	Oct 09
Working Capital	112	160	219
Fixed Assets	114	119	124
Current Assets	137	188	249

Rayburn Plastics Ltd

Whitehouse Street, Walsall, WS2 8HR
Tel: 01922-625572 **Fax:** 01922-723333
E-mail: nigel.evans@rayburn.co.uk
Website: http://www.rayburn.co.uk
Bank(s): Barclays, Aldridge
Managers: N. Evans (Chief Mgr), P. Moseley (Purch Mgr), B. Devey (Fin Mgr)
Ultimate Holding Company: RAYBURN HOLDINGS LIMITED
Immediate Holding Company: RAYBURN PLASTICS LIMITED
Registration no: 00628866 **Date established:** 1959 **Turnover:** £2m - £5m
No.of Employees: 21 - 50 **Product Groups:** 30, 31, 35, 48, 49

Date of Accounts	May 11	May 10	May 09
Working Capital	983	799	804
Fixed Assets	371	411	472
Current Assets	2m	1m	1m

Relko Restoration & Masonry Ltd

Cadnam House Long Street, Premier Business Park, Walsall, WS2 9DY
Tel: 08451-211955 **Fax:** 01922-623223
E-mail: enquiries@relkogroup.co.uk
Website: http://www.relkogroup.co.uk
Directors: M. Newland (Dir), P. Newland (MD)
Immediate Holding Company: RELKO RESTORATION & MASONRY LIMITED
Registration no: 03172114 **Date established:** 1996
No.of Employees: 21 - 50 **Product Groups:** 32, 52

Date of Accounts	Mar 11	Mar 10	Mar 09
Working Capital	266	615	667
Fixed Assets	102	121	107
Current Assets	474	850	1m

R & G Satalite Services

7 Spinney Close, Walsall, WS3 4LB
Tel: 07976-622001
E-mail: garyrapson@msn.com
Website: http://www.randgsataliteservices.com
Directors: G. Rapson (Prop)
No.of Employees: 1 - 10 **Product Groups:** 37

RMD Kwikform Limited

Brickyard Rd Aldridge, Walsall, WS9 8BW
Tel: 01922-743743 **Fax:** 01922-743400
E-mail: info@rmdkwikform.com
Website: http://www.rmdkwikform.com
Directors: M. Pickard (Fin), R. Bafico (Dir), G. Jacks (Dir), M. Follett (Dir), T. Ainscough (Dir)
Managers: M. Jones, P. Davis, S. Dance
Ultimate Holding Company: Interserve PLC
Registration no: 00301199 **VAT No.:** GB 248 4590 35
Turnover: £50m - £75m **No.of Employees:** 501 - 1000
Product Groups: 18, 33, 35, 37, 40, 45, 51, 52, 66, 83

Date of Accounts	Dec 11	Dec 10	Dec 09
Sales Turnover	19m	20m	20m
Pre Tax Profit/Loss	1m	1m	27m
Working Capital	50m	40m	46m
Fixed Assets	12m	13m	15m
Current Assets	54m	48m	94m
Current Liabilities	3m	2m	8m

Rotometrics International Ltd

Walsall Business Park Walsall Road, Aldridge, Walsall, WS9 0SW
Tel: 01922-610000 **Fax:** 01922-610100
E-mail: eddie.salter@rotometrics.com
Website: http://www.rotometrics.com
Directors: N. Lilley (Sales), A. Speed (Fin)
Managers: S. Howard, V. Ball (Personnel)
Ultimate Holding Company: ROTO HOLDINGS INC (UNITED STATES)
Immediate Holding Company: ROTOMETRICS INTERNATIONAL LIMITED
Registration no: 02368722 **Date established:** 1989
Turnover: £10m - £20m **No.of Employees:** 101 - 250 **Product Groups:** 44

Date of Accounts	Sep 11	Sep 10	Sep 09
Sales Turnover	16m	10m	9m
Pre Tax Profit/Loss	985	552	-706
Working Capital	3m	2m	2m
Fixed Assets	5m	4m	4m
Current Assets	6m	3m	3m
Current Liabilities	719	378	248

Rubbernek Fittings Ltd

Lichfield Road Brownhills, Walsall, WS8 6LH
Tel: 01543-453533 **Fax:** 01543-453531
E-mail: mcreighton@rubbernek.co.uk
Website: http://www.rubbernek.co.uk
Bank(s): National Westminster Bank Plc
Directors: M. Creighton (MD), L. Guest (Fin)
Managers: M. Jones (Tech Sales Mgr), J. Murphy (Chief Mgr)
Immediate Holding Company: RUBBERNEK FITTINGS LIMITED
Registration no: 00851444 **VAT No.:** GB 110 6778 84
Date established: 1965 **Turnover:** £2m - £5m **No.of Employees:** 21 - 50
Product Groups: 35, 36

Date of Accounts	Apr 11	Apr 10	Apr 09
Working Capital	1m	1m	1m
Fixed Assets	587	555	596
Current Assets	3m	2m	2m

Satchrome Ltd

Birchills House Industrial Estate Green Lane, Walsall, WS2 8LF
Tel: 01922-622721 **Fax:** 01922-625353
E-mail: satchrome@yahoo.co.uk
Website: http://www.satchrome.co.uk
Directors: S. Dawkins (MD), J. Dawkins (Dir)
Immediate Holding Company: SATCHROME LIMITED
Registration no: 00859974 **Date established:** 1965
Turnover: £500,000 - £1m **No.of Employees:** 11 - 20
Product Groups: 32, 46, 48, 67

Date of Accounts	Oct 11	Oct 10	Oct 09
Working Capital	192	562	606
Fixed Assets	152	55	62
Current Assets	401	725	759

Select Windows Home Improvements Ltd

Barons Court Trading Estate Walsall Road, Walsall Wood, Walsall, WS9 9AQ
Tel: 01543-370666 **Fax:** 01543-370270
E-mail: sales@selectwindows.co.uk
Website: http://www.selectwindows.co.uk
Bank(s): Lloyds
Directors: J. Wood (Dir)
Ultimate Holding Company: SELECT GROUP HOLDINGS LIMITED
Immediate Holding Company: SELECT WINDOWS (HOME IMPROVEMENTS) LIMITED
Registration no: 02616087 **Date established:** 1991
No.of Employees: 51 - 100 **Product Groups:** 33

Date of Accounts	Nov 11	Nov 10	Nov 09
Working Capital	38	-7	-70
Fixed Assets	136	159	172
Current Assets	1m	2m	2m

Sertronics Ltd

45 Regal Drive Walsall Enterprise Park, Walsall, WS2 9HQ
Tel: 01922-624412 **Fax:** 01922-608008
E-mail: admin@sertronics.org
Website: http://www.sertronics.com

see next page

Sertronics Ltd - Cont'd
Directors: A. Anderson (Chief Op Offcr)
Immediate Holding Company: SERTRONICS LIMITED
Registration no: 06984556 **Date established:** 2009
Turnover: £250,000 - £500,000 **No.of Employees:** 1 - 10
Product Groups: 63

Date of Accounts	Aug 11	Aug 10
Working Capital	-36	4
Fixed Assets	1	N/A
Current Assets	67	67

Smiths Of Walsall Ltd
Anchor House 4 Bridgeman Street, Walsall, WS2 9NW
Tel: 01922-627644 **Fax:** 01922-616522
E-mail: smithsofwalsall@hotmail.com
Website: http://www.smithsofwalsall.co.uk
Directors: D. Smith (MD), D. Chappelle (Fin)
Immediate Holding Company: SMITHS OF WALSALL LTD
Registration no: 04834639 **VAT No.:** GB 101 5331 35
Date established: 2003 **Turnover:** Up to £250,000
No.of Employees: 1 - 10 **Product Groups:** 24

Date of Accounts	Mar 11	Mar 10	Mar 09
Working Capital	10	1	6
Fixed Assets	N/A	1	1
Current Assets	26	38	43

Special Formwork Ltd
Stubbers Green Road, Walsall, WS9 8BN
Tel: 01922-451909 **Fax:** 01922-454520
E-mail: sales@formwork.co.uk
Website: http://www.formwork.co.uk
Bank(s): HSBC Bank plc
Directors: S. Williams (Dir), S. Williams (Sales)
Immediate Holding Company: SPECIAL FORMWORK LIMITED
Registration no: 06621406 **Date established:** 2008 **Turnover:** £1m - £2m
No.of Employees: 21 - 50 **Product Groups:** 35, 45, 52, 66

Spraymation Ltd
9 Lion Industrial Park Northgate Way, Walsall, WS9 8RL
Tel: 01922-455299 **Fax:** 01922-452288
E-mail: sales@spraymation.co.uk
Website: http://www.spraymation.co.uk
Directors: C. Robinson (Dir), R. Sim (Dir)
Immediate Holding Company: SPRAYMATION LIMITED
Registration no: 03794176 **Date established:** 1999
No.of Employees: 1 - 10 **Product Groups:** 38, 42

Date of Accounts	Mar 12	Mar 11	Mar 10
Working Capital	61	66	66
Fixed Assets	3	N/A	N/A
Current Assets	86	90	97

G H Stafford & Son Ltd
1 Regal Drive Walsall Enterprise Park, Walsall, WS2 9HQ
Tel: 01922-623993 **Fax:** 01922-723403
E-mail: info@ghstafford.com
Website: http://www.ghstafford.com
Bank(s): Lloyds TSB Bank plc
Directors: C. Stafford (Sales), P. Stafford (Fin)
Managers: H. Stafford
Immediate Holding Company: G.H.STAFFORD & SON LIMITED
Registration no: 00750659 **VAT No.:** GB 100 6611 30
Date established: 1963 **Turnover:** £2m - £5m **No.of Employees:** 11 - 20
Product Groups: 22, 49

Date of Accounts	Dec 11	Dec 10	Dec 09
Working Capital	1m	1m	1m
Fixed Assets	3m	3m	3m
Current Assets	3m	2m	2m

Stainless Steel World Ltd
27 Holmbridge Grove Shelfield, Walsall, WS4 1RA
Tel: 01922-693053 **Fax:** 01922-694250
E-mail: sales@ssworld.co.uk
Website: http://www.ssworld.co.uk
Directors: W. Ashwell Fisher (MD)
Immediate Holding Company: STAINLESS STEEL WORLD LIMITED
Registration no: 04577742 **Date established:** 2002
No.of Employees: 1 - 10 **Product Groups:** 20, 40, 41

Date of Accounts	Dec 11	Dec 10	Dec 09
Working Capital	-33	-32	-23
Fixed Assets	110	112	114
Current Assets	61	61	58

Stainless Steel World Ltd
14b Croxstalls Close, Walsall, WS3 2XT
Tel: 01922-403049
Website: http://www.ssworld.co.uk
Directors: A. Fisher (MD)
Registration no: 04577742 **Date established:** 2002
No.of Employees: 1 - 10 **Product Groups:** 38, 41, 45, 67

Stepco
12 Sunnybank Close Aldridge, Walsall, WS9 0YR
Tel: 0121-352 0952
Website: http://www.stepco.co.uk
Directors: R. Tye (Prop)
No.of Employees: 1 - 10 **Product Groups:** 35, 36

Strapex a division of ITW Limited
50 Empire Industrial Park
Empire Close
Aldridge, Walsall, WS9 8UQ
Tel: 01922-742500 **Fax:** 01922-742501
E-mail: sales@strapex.co.uk
Website: http://www.strapex.co.uk
Bank(s): Lloyds TSB, Erdington
Managers: P. Evans (Mgr)
Ultimate Holding Company: STRAPEX HOLDING AG (SWITZERLAND)
Immediate Holding Company: STRAPEX AG (SWITZERLAND)
Registration no: 01991245 **Date established:** 2005 **Turnover:** £5m - £10m
No.of Employees: 11 - 20 **Product Groups:** 29, 30, 35, 42

Strimech Engineering Ltd
Longmore Avenue, Walsall, WS2 0BW
Tel: 01922-649700 **Fax:** 01922-649802
E-mail: info@strimech.com
Website: http://www.strimech.co.uk
Directors: S. Henderson (MD)
Managers: L. Collins (Sales Prom Mgr), R. Porter (Chief Mgr)
Immediate Holding Company: STRIMECH ENGINEERING LIMITED
Registration no: 01247524 **Date established:** 1976 **Turnover:** £2m - £5m
No.of Employees: 21 - 50 **Product Groups:** 41, 45

Date of Accounts	Mar 11	Mar 10	Mar 09
Working Capital	381	274	181
Fixed Assets	76	57	75
Current Assets	2m	1m	871

Sullivan Holdings Ltd
West Coppice Road, Walsall, WS8 7HB
Tel: 01543-453779 **Fax:** 01543-373079
E-mail: vicraft@lineone.net
Website: http://www.sullivanholdings.co.uk
Directors: J. O'sullivan (Prop), A. O'Sullivan (Co Sec)
Immediate Holding Company: SULLIVAN HOLDINGS LIMITED
Registration no: 00861568 **Date established:** 1965 **Turnover:** £2m - £5m
No.of Employees: 1 - 10 **Product Groups:** 35, 39, 67, 72

Date of Accounts	Dec 11	Dec 10	Dec 09
Working Capital	-115	-69	-63
Fixed Assets	819	821	822
Current Assets	78	77	94

Superite Tools Ltd
Unit 3 Hayward Industrial Park Vigo Place, Walsall, WS9 8UG
Tel: 01922-451151 **Fax:** 01922-743176
E-mail: enquiries@superite.co.uk
Website: http://www.superite.co.uk
Bank(s): National Westminster
Directors: M. Collins (Dir)
Ultimate Holding Company: COLLINS GROUP INTERNATIONAL LIMITED
Immediate Holding Company: SUPERITE TOOLS LIMITED
Registration no: 00616970 **VAT No.:** GB 100 0350 62
Date established: 1958 **Turnover:** £2m - £5m **No.of Employees:** 11 - 20
Product Groups: 48

Date of Accounts	Apr 11	Apr 10	Apr 09
Working Capital	112	81	74
Fixed Assets	3	3	269
Current Assets	564	467	430

Swift Business Solutions Ltd
Northgate Aldridge, Walsall, WS9 8TH
Tel: 01922-743454 **Fax:** 01922-743134
E-mail: sales@thinkswift.co.uk
Website: http://www.thinkswift.co.uk
Bank(s): HSBC, Aldridge
Directors: S. Grice (MD), N. Brittle (MD), N. Brittle (MD)
Ultimate Holding Company: BULLDOG SUPPLIES LIMITED
Immediate Holding Company: SWIFT BUSINESS SOLUTIONS LIMITED
Registration no: 00936069 **VAT No.:** GB 100 4547 23
Date established: 1968 **Turnover:** £1m - £2m **No.of Employees:** 21 - 50
Product Groups: 26

Date of Accounts	Dec 11	Dec 10	Dec 09
Working Capital	365	307	312
Fixed Assets	707	718	739
Current Assets	635	544	615

T Spinks Fabrications
Maybrook Industrial Estate Maybrook Road, Walsall, WS8 7DG
Tel: 01543-379015 **Fax:** 01543-452856
E-mail: t-spinks@btconnect.com
Directors: C. Spinks (Prop)
VAT No.: GB 100 8614 14 **Turnover:** Up to £250,000
No.of Employees: 1 - 10 **Product Groups:** 48

Tardis Environmental UK Ltd
Leighmore Enterprise Park Fryers Road, Walsall, WS2 7LZ
Tel: 01922-402410 **Fax:** 01922-402085
E-mail: info@tardishire.co.uk
Website: http://www.tardishire.co.uk
Directors: C. Boydon (MD), D. Furlong (Sales), R. Boydon (Chief Op Offcr)
Managers: M. Westerley (Transport)
Ultimate Holding Company: TARDIS ENVIRONMENTAL UK (HOLDINGS) LIMITED
Immediate Holding Company: TARDIS ENVIRONMENTAL UK LIMITED
Registration no: 02581818 **Date established:** 1991 **Turnover:** £5m - £10m
No.of Employees: 21 - 50 **Product Groups:** 35, 39, 40, 52, 54, 83

Date of Accounts	Feb 12	Feb 11	Feb 10
Sales Turnover	7m	N/A	N/A
Pre Tax Profit/Loss	2m	N/A	N/A
Working Capital	3m	2m	1m
Fixed Assets	2m	2m	2m
Current Assets	4m	2m	2m
Current Liabilities	728	N/A	N/A

Taurus Supplies
Unit 34 Landywood Enterprise Park Holly Lane, Great Wyrley, Walsall, WS6 6BD
Tel: 01922-701111 **Fax:** 01922-701107
E-mail: sales@taurussupplies.co.uk
Website: http://www.taurussupplies.co.uk
Directors: G. Bednall (Ptnr)
Immediate Holding Company: HOLLIS ELECTRICAL & MECHANICAL SERVICES LIMITED
Date established: 2007 **Turnover:** £250,000 - £500,000
No.of Employees: 1 - 10 **Product Groups:** 22, 40, 63

Date of Accounts	Dec 09	Dec 08	Dec 07
Working Capital	-5	-11	-11
Fixed Assets	6	7	6
Current Assets	42	29	47

Taylor Fabrications
Unit 24 New Firms Centre Fairground Way, Walsall, WS1 4NU
Tel: 01922-639981 **Fax:** 01922-639981
Directors: G. Taylor (Prop)
Date established: 1999 **No.of Employees:** 1 - 10 **Product Groups:** 35

The Trilite Zone
8 Fryers road, Walsall, WS2 7LZ
Tel: 01922-713 713 **Fax:** 01922-713 717
E-mail: lew.james@nec-g.com
Website: http://trilite-zone.co.uk
Directors: L. James (MD)
Managers: J. Brett (Product)
Registration no: 07436403 **Date established:** 1990
No.of Employees: 1 - 10 **Product Groups:** 26, 49

The Wright K-9 Academy
49 Stanley Road, Walsall, WS4 1EJ
Tel: 07527-652706 **Fax:** 7527-652706
E-mail: thewrightk-9academy@live.co.uk
Website: http://www.thewrightk-9academy.webs.com
Directors: J. Wright (Prop)
Date established: 2004 **Turnover:** **No.of Employees:** 1 - 10
Product Groups: 01, 07, 09, 20, 22, 31, 49

F H Tomkins Buckle Company Ltd
Brockhurst Crescent, Walsall, WS5 4QG
Tel: 01922-723003 **Fax:** 01922-723149
E-mail: sales@fhtomkins.com
Website: http://www.fhtomkins.com
Bank(s): Barclays
Directors: R. Parkes (MD), R. Parks (Prop)
Managers: G. Benson (Mgr), G. Benton (Works Gen Mgr), G. Benson (Works Gen Mgr), J. Hinton (Sales Prom Mgr), S. Turner (I.T. Exec)
Immediate Holding Company: F.H. TOMKINS BUCKLE PENSION TRUSTEES LIMITED
Registration no: 03745302 **VAT No.:** GB 643 0552 61
Date established: 1999 **Turnover:** £2m - £5m **No.of Employees:** 21 - 50
Product Groups: 22, 24, 35, 36, 49, 63

Tomlin Engineering
76 Station Road Great Wyrley, Walsall, WS6 6LJ
Tel: 01922-415755 **Fax:** 01922-415830
Directors: T. Hunter (Ptnr)
Date established: 1990 **No.of Employees:** 1 - 10 **Product Groups:** 35

Transaxle Ltd
Bescot House Walstead Road West, Walsall, WS5 4NY
Tel: 01922-471300 **Fax:** 01922-725072
E-mail: meddings@transaxle-ltd.co.uk
Website: http://www.transaxle-ltd.co.uk
Directors: R. Meddings (Dir)
Immediate Holding Company: TRANSAXLE LIMITED
Registration no: 02964225 **Date established:** 1994
Turnover: Up to £250,000 **No.of Employees:** 11 - 20 **Product Groups:** 68

Date of Accounts	Sep 11	Sep 10	Sep 09
Working Capital	56	64	86
Fixed Assets	11	9	10
Current Assets	241	246	296

Travis Perkins plc
Queen Street Sawmills Queen Street, Walsall, WS2 9PE
Tel: 01922-631254 **Fax:** 01922-721516
E-mail: sanjeev.kalsay@travisperkins.co.uk
Website: http://www.travisperkins.co.uk
Managers: S. Kalsay (District Mgr)
Immediate Holding Company: TRAVIS PERKINS PLC
Registration no: 00824821 **Date established:** 1964
Turnover: £500,000 - £1m **No.of Employees:** 1 - 10 **Product Groups:** 66

Date of Accounts	Dec 11	Dec 10	Dec 09
Sales Turnover	4779m	3153m	2931m
Pre Tax Profit/Loss	270m	197m	213m
Working Capital	133m	159m	248m
Fixed Assets	2771m	2749m	2108m
Current Assets	1421m	1329m	1035m
Current Liabilities	473m	412m	109m

Trophy Distributors UK Ltd
Unit 4 Westgate Park Industrial Estate, Aldridge, Walsall, WS9 8ER
Tel: 01922-455545 **Fax:** 01922-459966
E-mail: info@trophydistributors.co.uk
Website: http://www.trophydistributors.co.uk
Directors: A. Gremson (Dir), R. Gremson (Dir)
Managers: M. Sajjad (Tech Serv Mgr), T. Webster
Immediate Holding Company: TROPHY DISTRIBUTORS UK LIMITED
Registration no: 01506129 **Date established:** 1980 **Turnover:** £1m - £2m
No.of Employees: 11 - 20 **Product Groups:** 33, 49

Date of Accounts	Dec 11	Dec 10	Dec 09
Working Capital	837	814	777
Fixed Assets	1m	1m	1m
Current Assets	960	1m	1m

Turnock Ltd
Reaymer Close, Walsall, WS2 7QZ
Tel: 01922-710422 **Fax:** 01922-710428
E-mail: sales@turnock.co.uk
Website: http://www.turnock.co.uk
Bank(s): Barclays
Directors: T. Stone (MD)
Ultimate Holding Company: A.E.E. LTD.
Immediate Holding Company: TURNOCK LIMITED
Registration no: 00320293 **VAT No.:** GB 100 1463 44
Date established: 1936 **Turnover:** £2m - £5m **No.of Employees:** 21 - 50
Product Groups: 30, 37, 48, 66

Date of Accounts	Jun 11	Jun 10	Jun 09
Working Capital	54	35	N/A
Fixed Assets	788	809	835
Current Assets	451	446	457

UK Strategic Study Centre
The Coach House 38h Stafford, Walsall, WS3 3NL
Tel: 01922-711100
E-mail: doughoward@btconnect.com
Website: http://www.ukstrategicstudycentre.co.uk
Directors: D. Howard (Dir), L. Harding (Fin)
Immediate Holding Company: UK STRATEGIC STUDY CENTRE LIMITED
Registration no: 06077395 **Date established:** 2007
Turnover: Up to £250,000 **No.of Employees:** 1 - 10 **Product Groups:** 80, 81

Date of Accounts	Jan 10	Jan 09	Jan 08
Sales Turnover	N/A	90	N/A
Working Capital	-6	9	-4
Current Assets	5	9	2

U S S Manufacturing Ltd
Unit 1 Fryers Road, Walsall, WS2 7NA
Tel: 01922-476973 **Fax:** 01922-408828
E-mail: sales@ussmfg.co.uk
Website: http://www.frfsystems.co.uk
Directors: D. Mcelroy (Sales)
Immediate Holding Company: U.S.S. MANUFACTURING LIMITED
Registration no: 04024335 **Date established:** 2000
No.of Employees: 1 - 10 **Product Groups:** 22, 23, 24, 25, 26, 27, 28, 29, 30, 32, 33, 35, 36, 37, 38, 39, 40, 41, 42, 43, 44, 45, 46, 48, 49, 51, 52, 54, 61, 63, 66, 67, 68, 74, 77, 80, 81, 83, 84, 85, 86, 87

Date of Accounts	Sep 11	Sep 10	Sep 09
Working Capital	-8	-22	-9
Fixed Assets	26	26	18
Current Assets	287	-22	304

Vale Brothers

Long Street, Walsall, WS2 9QG
Tel: 01922-624363 **Fax:** 01922-720994
E-mail: sales@valebrothers.co.uk
Website: http://www.valebrothers.co.uk
Directors: P. Wilkes (Dir), J. Wilkes (Co Sec)
Managers: S. Coates (Sales & Mktg Mg)
Immediate Holding Company: VALE BROTHERS LIMITED
Registration no: 03819106 **VAT No.:** GB 112 7777 69
Date established: 1999 **Turnover:** £500,000 - £1m
No.of Employees: 51 - 100 **Product Groups:** 29

Date of Accounts	Dec 11	Dec 10	Dec 09
Working Capital	466	422	234
Fixed Assets	504	633	729
Current Assets	2m	1m	2m

Venture Building Plastics Ltd

Brickyard Road Aldridge, Walsall, WS9 8SR
Tel: 01922-458882
Managers: J. Hunt (Chief Mgr)
Ultimate Holding Company: GEORGE TAYLOR & CO. LIFTING GEAR (EUROPE) LIMITED
Immediate Holding Company: VENTURE BUILDING PLASTICS LIMITED
Registration no: 04456068 **Date established:** 2002
No.of Employees: 1 - 10 **Product Groups:** 30

Date of Accounts	Dec 11	Jul 10	Jul 09
Sales Turnover	4m	N/A	N/A
Pre Tax Profit/Loss	88	N/A	N/A
Working Capital	445	388	115
Fixed Assets	45	72	63
Current Assets	647	825	753
Current Liabilities	66	N/A	N/A

Veolia plc

Lindon Road Brownhills, Walsall, WS8 7BB
Tel: 01543-452121 **Fax:** 01543-378196
E-mail: richard.berry@veolia.co.uk
Website: http://www.veolia.co.uk
Bank(s): Barclays
Directors: R. Berry (Dir)
Managers: M. Perry, L. Haynes (Sales & Mktg Mg), A. Wragg (Comptroller), C. Thorpe (Personnel)
Ultimate Holding Company: VEOLIA ENVIRONNEMENT SA (FRANCE)
Immediate Holding Company: SARP UK LIMITED
Registration no: 03467664 **Date established:** 1997
Turnover: Over £1,000m **No.of Employees:** 101 - 250
Product Groups: 32, 34, 40, 42, 54, 84, 85

Date of Accounts	Dec 10	Dec 09	Dec 08
Working Capital	-43m	-43m	-43m
Current Assets	23	23	23

Vicraft Housewares

West Coppice Road, Walsall, WS8 7HB
Tel: 01543-377280 **Fax:** 01543-373079
Website: http://www.sullivanholdings.co.uk
Directors: D. Sullivan (MD)
Immediate Holding Company: L & S ENGINEERS LIMITED
Registration no: 04224976 **Date established:** 2001
No.of Employees: 11 - 20 **Product Groups:** 30, 36, 40

Date of Accounts	Nov 11	Nov 10	Nov 09
Working Capital	7m	6m	6m
Fixed Assets	37	13	17
Current Assets	8m	7m	7m

Walsall Box Company

22 Bank Street, Walsall, WS1 2ER
Tel: 01922-628118 **Fax:** 01922-723395
E-mail: mail@thewalsallbox.co.uk
Website: http://www.thewalsallbox.co.uk
Bank(s): National Westminster Bank Plc
Directors: H. Mitchell (Ch), H. Mitchell Jr (Fin)
Immediate Holding Company: WALSALL BOX COMPANY LIMITED(THE)
Registration no: 00287916 **Date established:** 1934 **Turnover:** £1m - £2m
No.of Employees: 21 - 50 **Product Groups:** 27

Date of Accounts	Mar 11	Mar 10	Mar 09
Working Capital	-75	-145	-182
Fixed Assets	516	534	456
Current Assets	155	119	135

Walsall Locks Ltd

Leamore Close Leamore Enterprise Park, Walsall, WS2 7NL
Tel: 01922-494101 **Fax:** 01922-403772
E-mail: sales@walsall-locks.co.uk
Website: http://www.walsall-locks.co.uk
Bank(s): HSBC Bank plc
Directors: P. Preece (MD)
Immediate Holding Company: WALSALL LOCKS LIMITED
Registration no: 01990247 **VAT No.:** GB 431 3885 54
Date established: 1986 **Turnover:** £1m - £2m **No.of Employees:** 11 - 20
Product Groups: 36

Date of Accounts	Dec 11	Dec 10	Dec 09
Working Capital	384	368	349
Fixed Assets	20	14	18
Current Assets	582	546	496

Walsall Pressings Co. Ltd

Wednesbury Road, Walsall, WS1 4JW
Tel: 01922-721152 **Fax:** 01922-721106
E-mail: info@walpres.co.uk
Website: http://www.walpres.co.uk
Directors: P. Woolley (MD), E. Woolley (Ch)
Managers: G. Boyd (Sales & Mktg Mg), P. Chandler (I.T. Exec)
Immediate Holding Company: WALSALL PRESSINGS COMPANY LIMITED
Registration no: 00888236 **Date established:** 1966
Turnover: £20m - £50m **No.of Employees:** 101 - 250 **Product Groups:** 48

Date of Accounts	Jun 11	Jun 10	Jun 09
Sales Turnover	23m	16m	14m
Pre Tax Profit/Loss	-152	-707	883
Working Capital	5m	6m	6m
Fixed Assets	1m	1m	1m
Current Assets	12m	10m	9m
Current Liabilities	1m	1m	1m

Weatherite Air Conditioning Ltd

Weatherite House Westgate Park, Aldridge, Walsall, WS9 8EX
Tel: 01922-741641 **Fax:** 01922-741642
Website: http://www.weatheritegroup.co.uk
Managers: K. Friar (Sales Admin)
Immediate Holding Company: WEATHERITE AIR CONDITIONING LIMITED
Registration no: 04738814 **Date established:** 2003
No.of Employees: 51 - 100 **Product Groups:** 30, 39, 40

Whitehouse Cox & Co. Ltd

Unit F1 Fellows Court, Aldridge, Walsall, WS9 8BZ
Tel: 01922-458881 **Fax:** 01922-458889
E-mail: customerservice@whitehouse-cox.co.uk
Website: http://www.leathergoodsonline.com
Directors: S. Cox (Dir), T. Beard (Fin)
Managers: A. Standley (Purch Mgr)
Immediate Holding Company: WHITEHOUSE COX & CO. LIMITED
Registration no: 02934682 **VAT No.:** 648 5018 26 **Date established:** 1994
Turnover: £1m - £2m **No.of Employees:** 21 - 50 **Product Groups:** 22, 49

Date of Accounts	Mar 11	Mar 10	Mar 09
Working Capital	1m	1m	1m
Fixed Assets	75	64	57
Current Assets	1m	1m	1m

Willenhall Tube & Forging

Bloxwich Lane Industrial Estate Bloxwich Lane, Walsall, WS2 8TF
Tel: 01922-725505 **Fax:** 01922-720131
E-mail: graham.barrows@willenhalltube.co.uk
Website: http://www.willenhalltube.co.uk
Bank(s): Barclays
Directors: G. Barrows (MD)
Immediate Holding Company: WILLENHALL TUBE AND FORGING CO. LIMITED
Registration no: 00443049 **Date established:** 1947 **Turnover:** £2m - £5m
No.of Employees: 21 - 50 **Product Groups:** 48

Date of Accounts	Sep 08	Sep 07	Sep 06
Working Capital	298	2m	866
Fixed Assets	532	310	637
Current Assets	792	3m	1m

Win Metal Polishing

140c Wednesbury Road, Walsall, WS1 4JJ
Tel: 01922-647600 **Fax:** 01922-647600
Directors: H. Singh (Prop), H. Singh (Dir)
Immediate Holding Company: H & R KITCHEN FABRICATIONS (WALSALL) LIMITED
Registration no: 05250756 **Date established:** 2010
Turnover: Up to £250,000 **No.of Employees:** 1 - 10 **Product Groups:** 46, 48

Date of Accounts	Oct 09	Oct 08	Oct 07
Working Capital	47	31	12
Fixed Assets	12	14	14
Current Assets	118	121	72
Current Liabilities	N/A	48	38

Yansport Safetywear Ltd

91 Frederick Street, Walsall, WS2 9NE
Tel: 01922-721721 **Fax:** 01922-723710
E-mail: ian@yansport.co.uk
Website: http://www.yansport.co.uk
Bank(s): Barclays
Directors: I. Cousins (MD)
Ultimate Holding Company: YANSPORT (HOLDINGS) LIMITED
Immediate Holding Company: YANSPORT SAFETYWEAR LIMITED
Registration no: 04208237 **Date established:** 2001 **Turnover:** £1m - £2m
No.of Employees: 21 - 50 **Product Groups:** 24

Date of Accounts	Jun 11	Jun 10	Jun 09
Working Capital	97	17	-33
Fixed Assets	8	10	13
Current Assets	640	284	187
Current Liabilities	222	N/A	N/A

Peter Yates Leathergoods Ltd

Unit 31 Empire Industrial Park, Aldridge, Walsall, WS9 8UY
Tel: 08452-411412 **Fax:** 01922-453808
E-mail: paul.yates@peteryatesleathergoods.com
Website: http://www.peteryatesleathergoods.co.uk
Bank(s): HSBC Bank plc
Directors: P. Yates (MD), C. Yates (Fin)
Managers: C. Yates
Immediate Holding Company: PETER YATES LEATHERGOODS LIMITED
Registration no: 00539508 **VAT No.:** GB 100 2323 55
Date established: 1954 **Turnover:** £500,000 - £1m
No.of Employees: 11 - 20 **Product Groups:** 22, 49, 66

Date of Accounts	Dec 10	Dec 09	Dec 08
Working Capital	-4	-39	-35
Fixed Assets	3	3	17
Current Assets	218	276	245
Current Liabilities	N/A	N/A	21

D Young

120 Leighswood Avenue, Walsall, WS9 8BB
Tel: 01922-745710
E-mail: young@blueyonder.co.uk
Directors: D. Young (Prop)
Date established: 2000 **No.of Employees:** 1 - 10 **Product Groups:** 36

Zinco Midlands Ltd

Midland House 52 Lower Forster Street, Walsall, WS1 1XB
Tel: 01922-723672 **Fax:** 0800-028 6370
E-mail: enquiries@zincomids.co.uk
Website: http://www.zincomids.co.uk
Directors: P. Holloway (MD)
Managers: K. Swindell (Sales Prom Mgr)
Immediate Holding Company: ZINCO (MIDLANDS) LIMITED
Registration no: 01980848 **VAT No.:** GB 417 0850 66
Date established: 1986 **Turnover:** £500,000 - £1m
No.of Employees: 1 - 10 **Product Groups:** 30, 35, 36

Date of Accounts	Feb 12	Feb 11	Feb 10
Working Capital	105	100	95
Fixed Assets	5	7	11
Current Assets	445	383	310

Wednesbury

Allied Tank & Fabrications Ltd

Phoenix Works Industrial Estate Richards Street, Wednesbury, WS10 8BZ
Tel: 0121-568 8166 **Fax:** 0121-568 8177
E-mail: sales@alliedtanks.co.uk
Website: http://www.alliedtanks.co.uk
Bank(s): Lloyds TSB Bank plc
Directors: T. Cornaby (Co Sec), C. Powers (Dir), G. Mosgrove (Dir)
Managers: S. Abbott (Sales Admin)
Ultimate Holding Company: ALLIED TANKS GROUP LIMITED
Immediate Holding Company: ALLIED TANKS & FABRICATIONS LTD
Registration no: 01805063 **Date established:** 1984 **Turnover:** £2m - £5m
No.of Employees: 21 - 50 **Product Groups:** 26

Date of Accounts	Mar 11	Mar 10	Mar 09
Working Capital	596	530	295
Fixed Assets	171	26	30
Current Assets	2m	1m	1m

Aqualux Products Holdings Ltd

Universal Point Steelmans Road, Wednesbury, WS10 9UZ
Tel: 0121-526 7600 **Fax:** 0121-526 7601
E-mail: enquiries@aqualux.co.uk
Website: http://www.aqualux.co.uk
Directors: A. Murray (Fin)
Immediate Holding Company: AQUALUX PRODUCTS HOLDINGS LIMITED
Registration no: 05171320 **Date established:** 2004
Turnover: £10m - £20m **No.of Employees:** 101 - 250 **Product Groups:** 36

Date of Accounts	Dec 11	Dec 10	Dec 09
Sales Turnover	19m	25m	25m
Pre Tax Profit/Loss	-5m	-6m	-4m
Working Capital	5m	4m	6m
Fixed Assets	1m	3m	6m
Current Assets	13m	14m	15m
Current Liabilities	4m	8m	9m

B S J Fixings

Unit 1-2 A Old Park Industrial Estate, Wednesbury, WS10 9LR
Tel: 0121-556 2006 **Fax:** 0121-556 9922
E-mail: info@bsjfixings.com
Website: http://www.bsjfixings.com
Directors: T. Sagoo (Prop)
Registration no: 4504514 **Date established:** 1999
Turnover: Over £1,000m **No.of Employees:** 1 - 10 **Product Groups:** 30, 35

Barnfather Wire Ltd

Willenhall Road, Wednesbury, WS10 8JG
Tel: 0121-526 2880 **Fax:** 0121-526 3130
E-mail: sales@barnfatherwire.co.uk
Website: http://www.barnfatherwire.co.uk
Bank(s): HSBC
Directors: M. Fenney (Dir), R. Barnfather (MD), T. Dalley (Dir)
Managers: S. Pamter (Admin Off)
Ultimate Holding Company: BARNFATHER HOLDINGS LIMITED
Immediate Holding Company: AGS DORMANT 1 LIMITED
Registration no: 00417146 **VAT No.:** GB 521 5838 52
Date established: 1946 **Turnover:** £2m - £5m **No.of Employees:** 21 - 50
Product Groups: 34, 35, 48

Date of Accounts	Dec 11	Dec 10	Dec 09
Working Capital	8	8	8
Current Assets	39	39	39

Biffa Waste Services Ltd

Wednesbury Treatment Centre Potters Lane, Wednesbury, WS10 7NR
Tel: 0121-502 5500 **Fax:** 0121-505 2120
E-mail: wednesbury@biffa.co.uk
Website: http://www.biffa.co.uk
Managers: S. Milnes, T. Owen (Sales Prom Mgr)
Immediate Holding Company: BIFFA WASTE SERVICES LIMITED
Registration no: 00946107 **Date established:** 1969
Turnover: £20m - £50m **No.of Employees:** 21 - 50 **Product Groups:** 32, 54

Date of Accounts	Mar 08	Mar 09	Apr 10
Sales Turnover	555m	574m	492m
Pre Tax Profit/Loss	23m	50m	30m
Working Capital	229m	271m	293m
Fixed Assets	371m	360m	378m
Current Assets	409m	534m	609m
Current Liabilities	50m	100m	115m

Bradken UK Ltd

Box 4 Heath Road, Wednesbury, WS10 8LZ
Tel: 0121-526 4111 **Fax:** 0121-526 4174
Bank(s): Barclays
Managers: C. Sadler (Site Co-ord)
Ultimate Holding Company: BRADKEN LTD (AUSTRALIA)
Immediate Holding Company: BRADKEN UK LIMITED
Registration no: 01144329 **Date established:** 1973 **Turnover:** £5m - £10m
No.of Employees: 51 - 100 **Product Groups:** 34

Date of Accounts	Jun 11	Jun 10	Jun 09
Sales Turnover	16m	17m	23m
Pre Tax Profit/Loss	-2m	-3m	-2m
Working Capital	5m	7m	8m
Fixed Assets	7m	7m	9m
Current Assets	11m	11m	11m
Current Liabilities	379	393	344

Bridge Aluminium Ltd

84 Bridge Street, Wednesbury, WS10 0AN
Tel: 0121-556 0995 **Fax:** 0121-556 9971
E-mail: info@bridgealuminium.com
Website: http://www.bridgealuminium.com
Directors: J. Pay (Co Sec), M. Melvin (Fin), W. Priest (MD)
Managers: C. Allen (Purch Mgr), D. Pearson (Personnel)
Ultimate Holding Company: CAPARO GROUP LIMITED
Immediate Holding Company: BRIDGE ALUMINIUM LIMITED
Registration no: 04687227 **VAT No.:** GB 307 6632 61
Date established: 2003 **Turnover:** £20m - £50m
No.of Employees: 101 - 250 **Product Groups:** 34, 48

Date of Accounts	Dec 11	Dec 10	Dec 09
Sales Turnover	21m	19m	10m
Pre Tax Profit/Loss	693	323	-1m

see next page

Bridge Aluminium Ltd - Cont'd

Working Capital	1m	295	364
Fixed Assets	314	406	496
Current Assets	6m	6m	3m
Current Liabilities	1m	1m	769

Caparo Atlas Fastenings Ltd

Heath Road Darlaston, Wednesbury, WS10 8XL
Tel: 0121-224 2000 **Fax:** 0121-224 2001
E-mail: andy.harland@atlasfastenings.com
Website: http://www.atlasfastenings.com
Bank(s): Barclays
Directors: L. Marshall (Co Sec), A. Nuttall (Sales & Mktg), I. Monzur (Fin)
Managers: D. Franklin (Purch Mgr), J. Bate (Tech Serv Mgr), A. Jarvis
Ultimate Holding Company: CAPARO GROUP LIMITED
Immediate Holding Company: CAPARO ATLAS FASTENINGS LIMITED
Registration no: 05817189 **VAT No.:** GB 245 2598 470 088
Date established: 2006 **Turnover:** £50m - £75m
No.of Employees: 101 - 250 **Product Groups:** 35

Date of Accounts	Dec 11	Dec 10	Dec 09
Sales Turnover	22m	16m	10m
Pre Tax Profit/Loss	817	-5m	-3m
Working Capital	-444	-4m	-3m
Fixed Assets	4m	4m	5m
Current Assets	8m	5m	7m
Current Liabilities	2m	1m	1m

Central Fencing Ltd

5 Potters Lane, Wednesbury, WS10 0AS
Tel: 0121-556 6390 **Fax:** 0121-556 6070
No.of Employees: 1 - 10 **Product Groups:** 25, 35, 36, 49, 66

Central Plate Services Ltd

Phoenix Works Industrial Estate Richards Street, Wednesbury, WS10 8BZ
Tel: 0121-526 3770 **Fax:** 0121-526 4770
E-mail: info@centralplateservices.com
Website: http://www.centralplateservices.com
Directors: C. Horton (Dir)
Immediate Holding Company: CENTRAL PLATE SERVICES LIMITED
Registration no: 01746004 **VAT No.:** GB 409 3249 55
Date established: 1983 **Turnover:** £2m - £5m **No.of Employees:** 11 - 20
Product Groups: 34

Date of Accounts	Feb 12	Feb 11	Feb 10
Working Capital	827	870	863
Fixed Assets	155	132	127
Current Assets	3m	3m	2m
Current Liabilities	N/A	N/A	881

Charles Cantrill Ltd

Block 2 Unit 3 Wednesbury Trading Estate, Wednesbury, WS10 7JN
Tel: 0121-567 3140 **Fax:** 0121-567 3149
E-mail: sales@charlescantrill.com
Website: http://www.charlescantrill.com
Directors: J. Billington (Dir)
Immediate Holding Company: CHARLES CANTRILL LIMITED
Registration no: 00715748 **VAT No.:** GB 109 4358 69
Date established: 1962 **Turnover:** £1m - £2m **No.of Employees:** 1 - 10
Product Groups: 22, 25, 27, 29, 30, 39, 49, 66, 68

Date of Accounts	Aug 11	Aug 10	Aug 09
Working Capital	93	74	44
Fixed Assets	29	36	47
Current Assets	208	218	152

Chas B Pugh Walsall Ltd

C B Pugh Ltd Heath Road, Wednesbury, WS10 8LU
Tel: 0121-568 7568 **Fax:** 0121-568 8666
E-mail: manightingale@cbpugh.co.uk
Website: http://www.chaspughscrapmetal.co.uk
Bank(s): HSBC Bank plc
Directors: M. Nightingale (MD)
Immediate Holding Company: CHAS.B.PUGH(WALSALL),LIMITED
Registration no: 00300289 **VAT No.:** GB 100 0881 31
Date established: 1935 **Turnover:** £2m - £5m **No.of Employees:** 11 - 20
Product Groups: 51, 66

Date of Accounts	Mar 11	Mar 10	Mar 09
Pre Tax Profit/Loss	N/A	N/A	294
Working Capital	256	300	387
Fixed Assets	1m	1m	1m
Current Assets	2m	1m	1m
Current Liabilities	N/A	N/A	361

Cox Building Products Ltd

Unit 1 Bilport Lane, Wednesbury, WS10 0NT
Tel: 0121-530 4230 **Fax:** 01902-371810
E-mail: sales@coxdome.co.uk
Website: http://www.coxbp.com
Managers: S. Cowley (Chief Mgr)
Ultimate Holding Company: CRH PUBLIC LIMITED COMPANY
Immediate Holding Company: COX BUILDING PRODUCTS LIMITED
Registration no: 00229110 **Date established:** 2028 **Turnover:** £2m - £5m
No.of Employees: 1 - 10 **Product Groups:** 35, 66

Date of Accounts	Dec 10	Dec 09	Dec 08
Sales Turnover	2m	2m	2m
Pre Tax Profit/Loss	-236	-227	-804
Working Capital	-2m	-2m	-1m
Fixed Assets	67	15	32
Current Assets	7m	7m	7m
Current Liabilities	142	190	332

Deanson Wilkes Forms & Systems Ltd

1 Cramp Hill, Wednesbury, WS10 8ES
Tel: 0121-568 7123 **Fax:** 0121-568 7122
E-mail: sales@deansonwilkes.co.uk
Website: http://www.deansonwilkes.co.uk
Directors: S. Cornwell (Fin), G. Cornwell (Sales & Mktg), J. Cornwell (MD)
Managers: S. Swindell (Sales Admin), S. Broadhead (Accounts)
Immediate Holding Company: DEANSON WILKES (FORMS AND SYSTEMS) LIMITED
Registration no: 02776372 **Date established:** 1992 **Turnover:** £1m - £2m
No.of Employees: 11 - 20 **Product Groups:** 27, 28

Date of Accounts	Sep 10	Sep 09	Sep 08
Working Capital	21	175	175
Fixed Assets	18	2	N/A
Current Assets	256	254	272

Diamond Rubber Co. Ltd

Unit E Alma Industrial Estate, Stafford Road, Wednesbury, WS10 8SX
Tel: 0121-526 6626 **Fax:** 0121-526 2900
Directors: P. Tinsley (MD)
Immediate Holding Company: DIAMOND RUBBER COMPANY LTD
Registration no: 03927358 **Date established:** 2000
Turnover: £250,000 - £500,000 **No.of Employees:** 1 - 10
Product Groups: 29, 66

Ellison Switchgear

Mounts Road, Wednesbury, WS10 0DU
Tel: 0121-505 2000 **Fax:** 0121-556 1981
E-mail: enquiries@ellison.co.uk
Website: http://www.ellison.co.uk
Bank(s): National Westminster Bank Plc
Directors: K. Connors (MD)
Ultimate Holding Company: TIMIK LIMITED
Immediate Holding Company: PURITY SOFT DRINKS LIMITED
Registration no: 00358349 **VAT No.:** GB 554 8478 02
Date established: 1939 **Turnover:** £250,000 - £500,000
No.of Employees: 11 - 20 **Product Groups:** 30, 35, 37

Date of Accounts	Mar 12	Mar 11	Mar 10
Sales Turnover	16m	15m	14m
Pre Tax Profit/Loss	944	1m	1m
Working Capital	2m	358	52
Fixed Assets	2m	3m	3m
Current Assets	5m	4m	3m
Current Liabilities	1m	2m	1m

Enerpac UK

Unit 601 Axcess 10 Business Park Bentley Road South, Wednesbury, WS10 8LQ
Tel: 0121-505 0787 **Fax:** 01527-585500
E-mail: james.mitchell@enerpac.com
Website: http://www.enerpac.com
Directors: S. Brittain (Co Sec)
Managers: J. Mitchell (Comm)
Ultimate Holding Company: ACTUANT CORP (USA)
Immediate Holding Company: ENERPAC LIMITED
Registration no: 00833720 **Date established:** 1965
Turnover: £10m - £20m **No.of Employees:** 1 - 10 **Product Groups:** 36, 38, 39, 40, 42, 45, 46

Date of Accounts	Aug 11	Aug 10	Aug 09
Sales Turnover	12m	8m	5m
Pre Tax Profit/Loss	1m	966	558
Working Capital	3m	555	316
Fixed Assets	7m	8m	7m
Current Assets	5m	2m	2m
Current Liabilities	474	446	485

European Metal Recycling Ltd

Heath Road Darlaston, Wednesbury, WS10 8XL
Tel: 0121-568 6266 **Fax:** 0121-568 7900
Website: http://www.elrltd.com
Managers: M. Turner (Mgr)
Immediate Holding Company: EUROPEAN METAL RECYCLING LIMITED
Registration no: 02954623 **Date established:** 1994
No.of Employees: 1 - 10 **Product Groups:** 42, 66

Date of Accounts	Dec 11	Dec 10	Dec 09
Sales Turnover	3032m	2431m	1843m
Pre Tax Profit/Loss	116m	155m	91m
Working Capital	414m	371m	167m
Fixed Assets	518m	483m	480m
Current Assets	1027m	717m	557m
Current Liabilities	124m	118m	185m

Fabory UK Ltd

Unit 9 Block D Bescot Industrial Estate Woden Road West, Wednesbury, WS10 7SG
Tel: 0121-556 3474 **Fax:** 0121-556 7337
E-mail: john.rollins@fabory.com
Website: http://www.fabory.com
Directors: J. Rollins (MD)
Ultimate Holding Company: BMF HOLDINGS BV (HOLLAND)
Immediate Holding Company: FABORY UK LIMITED
Registration no: 02225266 **VAT No.:** GB 488 3158 08
Date established: 1988 **Turnover:** £1m - £2m **No.of Employees:** 11 - 20
Product Groups: 35

Date of Accounts	Dec 11	Dec 10	Dec 09
Working Capital	1m	1m	1m
Fixed Assets	60	35	48
Current Assets	1m	1m	1m

First Choice Uniforms (School & Workwear)

26 Union Street, Wednesbury, WS10 7HD
Tel: 0121-505 7100
E-mail: sales.firstchoice@gmail.com
Website: http://www.firstchoiceuniforms.co.uk
Directors: M. Malhi (MD)
No.of Employees: 1 - 10 **Product Groups:** 24, 63

G & P Batteries Ltd

Crescent Works Industrial Park Willenhall Road, Wednesbury, WS10 8JR
Tel: 0121-568 3200 **Fax:** 0121-568 3201
E-mail: enquiries@g-pbatt.co.uk
Website: http://www.g-pbatt.co.uk
Bank(s): Lloyds TSB Bank plc
Directors: G. Cummings (Co Sec), G. Clementson (Sales), M. Green (MD)
Managers: J. Kerr, S. Poole
Ultimate Holding Company: EB HOLDINGS II INC (NEVADA)
Immediate Holding Company: G. & P. BATTERIES LIMITED
Registration no: 01420451 **VAT No.:** GB 687 8896 34
Date established: 1979 **Turnover:** £10m - £20m
No.of Employees: 51 - 100 **Product Groups:** 42, 54, 66

Date of Accounts	Dec 11	Dec 10	Dec 09
Sales Turnover	15m	13m	10m
Pre Tax Profit/Loss	475	976	2m
Working Capital	-2m	-1m	944
Fixed Assets	7m	6m	3m
Current Assets	1m	1m	3m
Current Liabilities	292	447	114

G T A Welding Ltd

324-326 Crankhall Lane, Wednesbury, WS10 0DX
Tel: 0121-502 3251 **Fax:** 0121-556 5200
Website: http://www.weldalloy.fsnet.co.uk
Directors: G. Durrell (MD), T. Duffy (MD)
Immediate Holding Company: A.OAKESWELL LIMITED
Registration no: 01325672 **Date established:** 2010
No.of Employees: 1 - 10 **Product Groups:** 46

Date of Accounts	Aug 08	Aug 07	Aug 06
Working Capital	1	-3	3
Fixed Assets	3	3	5
Current Assets	153	110	122
Current Liabilities	152	113	119
Total Share Capital	3	3	3

Gisco

18 Wolverhampton Street, Wednesbury, WS10 8UQ
Tel: 0121-568 6868 **Fax:** 01922-611384
E-mail: info@giscouk.com
Website: http://www.giscouk.com
Directors: S. Gibbs (Prop)
Date established: 2000 **Turnover:** £250,000 - £500,000
No.of Employees: 1 - 10 **Product Groups:** 37, 39, 67

W W Grew & Co. Ltd

Stafford Street, Wednesbury, WS10 7JX
Tel: 0121-556 3337 **Fax:** 0121-556 8171
E-mail: info@wwgrew.com
Website: http://www.wwgrew.com
Bank(s): HSBC Bank plc
Directors: R. Grew (Co Sec)
Immediate Holding Company: W.W.GREW & COMPANY LIMITED
Registration no: 00603840 **VAT No.:** GB 277 0719 38
Date established: 1958 **Turnover:** £1m - £2m **No.of Employees:** 11 - 20
Product Groups: 35

Date of Accounts	Apr 12	Apr 11	Apr 10
Working Capital	25	5	3
Fixed Assets	51	50	45
Current Assets	167	153	158

Grove Packaging

Unit 2c Old Park Industrial Estate Old Park Road, Wednesbury, WS10 9LR
Tel: 0121-556 4735 **Fax:** 0121-556 4579
Directors: D. Norgrove (MD)
VAT No.: GB 441 7435 58 **Turnover:** £500,000 - £1m
No.of Employees: 1 - 10 **Product Groups:** 27, 66

Hallen Engineering Ltd

PO Box 27, Wednesbury, WS10 7SZ
Tel: 0121-556 3324 **Fax:** 0121-502 0194
E-mail: charles@hallen.co.uk
Website: http://www.hallen.co.uk
Bank(s): Barclays
Directors: K. Collins (Sales), C. Carver (MD)
Immediate Holding Company: HALLEN ENGINEERING LIMITED
Registration no: 00530535 **Date established:** 1954 **Turnover:** £1m - £2m
No.of Employees: 11 - 20 **Product Groups:** 30, 35, 36

Date of Accounts	Mar 12	Mar 11	Mar 10
Working Capital	800	749	799
Fixed Assets	106	120	111
Current Assets	981	935	845

Haropa Products

Unit 35 Darlaston Central Trading Estate, Wednesbury, WS10 8XB
Tel: 0121-526 2228
Managers: C. Rushdon (Mgr)
Registration no: 03294372 **Date established:** 1996
No.of Employees: 1 - 10 **Product Groups:** 36

Hydraulic Supplies Ltd

Unit 5-6 Block 2 Wednesbury Trading Estate, Wednesbury, WS10 7JN
Tel: 0121-505 3663 **Fax:** 0121-505 3375
E-mail: sales@hydraulicsupplies.co.uk
Website: http://www.hydraulicsupplies.co.uk
Directors: G. Cadd (MD)
Ultimate Holding Company: TU.LE. TUBI LEVIGATI SA (ITALY)
Immediate Holding Company: HYDRAULIC SUPPLIES LIMITED
Registration no: 02651256 **VAT No.:** GB 547 6733 11
Date established: 1991 **Turnover:** £1m - £2m **No.of Employees:** 1 - 10
Product Groups: 48

Date of Accounts	Mar 11	Mar 10	Mar 09
Working Capital	572	432	410
Fixed Assets	5	11	11
Current Assets	1m	797	1m

Imperial Heat Treatments

Imperial Works Heath Road, Wednesbury, WS10 8LP
Tel: 0121-526 7138 **Fax:** 0121-568 6104
E-mail: info@george-dyke.co.uk
Managers: C. Neale (Mgr)
Ultimate Holding Company: CROFTACRE HOLDINGS LTD
Immediate Holding Company: HHT LIMITED
Registration no: 00661185 **Date established:** 1960 **Turnover:** £2m - £5m
No.of Employees: 1 - 10 **Product Groups:** 46, 48

Irpen UK Ltd

Unit 1 Block A Bescot Industrial Estate Woden Road West, Wednesbury, WS10 7SG
Tel: 0121-556 5534 **Fax:** 0121-556 1744
E-mail: sales@irpen.co.uk
Website: http://www.irpen.co.uk
Managers: J. Clarke (Mgr)
Ultimate Holding Company: Irpen SA (Spain)
Immediate Holding Company: IRPEN (UK) LIMITED
Registration no: 02118430 **Date established:** 1987 **Turnover:** £1m - £2m
No.of Employees: 11 - 20 **Product Groups:** 30

Date of Accounts	Dec 11	Dec 10	Dec 09
Sales Turnover	2m	2m	2m
Pre Tax Profit/Loss	1	N/A	-72
Working Capital	103	101	99
Fixed Assets	2	2	4
Current Assets	873	1m	1m
Current Liabilities	82	92	69

J & M Pattern & Dye Co.

Unit 9 Holloway Bank Trading Estate Globe Street, Wednesbury, WS10 0NN
Tel: 0121-556 9461 **Fax:** 0121-556 9461
E-mail: john.jmpatterns@btconnect.com
Directors: J. Potts (Dir)
Turnover: £250,000 - £500,000 **No.of Employees:** 1 - 10
Product Groups: 34, 44, 48

Keep-it Security Products

Imperial Works Heath Road, Darlaston, Wednesbury, WS10 8LP
Tel: 0870-444 2820 **Fax:** 0870-444 2826
E-mail: sales@keep-it.co.uk
Website: http://www.keep-it.co.uk

Directors: R. Ward (MD)
Product Groups: 36, 39, 66, 68

Kepston Ltd

Unit 13-15 Western Way, Wednesbury, WS10 7BW
Tel: 0121-502 2972 **Fax:** 0121-556 5300
E-mail: sales@kepston.co.uk
Website: http://www.kepston.co.uk
Bank(s): Barclays
Directors: B. Millage (Ch), A. Pitt (Co Sec)
Managers: T. Smith (Mgr), A. McCracken (Sales Prom Mgr), M. Goldsmith (I.T. Exec)
Ultimate Holding Company: KEPSTON HOLDINGS LIMITED
Immediate Holding Company: KEPSTON LIMITED
Registration no: 00191194 **Date established:** 1923 **Turnover:** £2m - £5m
No.of Employees: 21 - 50 **Product Groups:** 46, 48, 84

Date of Accounts	Jun 11	Jun 10	Jun 09
Sales Turnover	N/A	N/A	3m
Pre Tax Profit/Loss	N/A	N/A	-637
Working Capital	473	262	132
Fixed Assets	2m	2m	2m
Current Assets	2m	1m	866
Current Liabilities	N/A	N/A	232

Kingfisher Enamelling

Unit 2-3 Moxley Industrial Centre Western Way, Wednesbury, WS10 7BG
Tel: 0121-556 5494 **Fax:** 0121-556 5852
E-mail: fg.hill@blueyonder.co.uk
Website: http://www.kingfisherenamelling.com
Directors: F. Hill (MD), M. Nutting (Fin)
Immediate Holding Company: KINGFISHER ENAMELLING COMPANY LIMITED
Registration no: 03167285 **Date established:** 1996
No.of Employees: 11 - 20 **Product Groups:** 46, 48

Date of Accounts	Jul 10	Jul 09	Jul 08
Working Capital	74	216	345
Fixed Assets	200	222	244
Current Assets	202	313	426

M W A International Ltd

Bridge Street, Wednesbury, WS10 0AW
Tel: 0121-556 6366 **Fax:** 0121-556 5566
E-mail: sales@mwa-international.com
Website: http://www.mwa-international.com
Bank(s): National Westminster Bank Plc
Directors: N. Collett (MD)
Immediate Holding Company: MWA INTERNATIONAL LIMITED
Registration no: 00960787 **Date established:** 1969
Turnover: £500,000 - £1m **No.of Employees:** 11 - 20
Product Groups: 24, 30, 32, 33, 34, 35, 36, 38

Date of Accounts	Dec 11	Dec 10	Dec 09
Working Capital	282	276	280
Fixed Assets	363	367	370
Current Assets	425	412	356
Current Liabilities	14	20	N/A

Malcolm Enamellers Acp Ltd

Automotive Components Park Hallens Drive, Wednesbury, WS10 7DD
Tel: 0121-505 7474 **Fax:** 0121-505 0519
E-mail: ghall@malcolm.co.uk
Website: http://www.malcolms.co.uk
Directors: G. Hall (Comm), L. Stanaway (MD), M. Beddows (Tech Serv)
Managers: D. Smith (Chief Acct), M. Ivery
Immediate Holding Company: MALCOLM ENAMELLERS ACP LIMITED
Registration no: 03296389 **Date established:** 1996
No.of Employees: 51 - 100 **Product Groups:** 46, 48

Date of Accounts	Mar 11	Mar 10	Mar 09
Working Capital	3	-179	-221
Fixed Assets	236	273	333
Current Assets	27m	700	668
Current Liabilities	N/A	N/A	506

Monks & Crane Industrial Group Ltd

Unit 2 Atlantic Way, Wednesbury, WS10 7WW
Tel: 0121-506 4000 **Fax:** 01952-684064
E-mail: twd@mcrane.co.uk
Website: http://www.monks-crane.com/branch
Bank(s): HSBC Plc
Directors: R. Veitch (Sales), P. Watts (Dir), G. Thompson (MD), F. Piazza (Fin), R. Baxter (Chief Op Offcr)
Managers: P. McDermott (Mgr), T. Drury (District Mgr), S. Hill (Mgr), R. Veitch (Mgr), P. Barber (Mgr), A. McDonald (Mgr)
Ultimate Holding Company: ADOLF WURTH GMBH & CO KG (GERMANY)
Immediate Holding Company: MONKS & CRANE INDUSTRIAL GROUP LIMITED
Registration no: 00342072 **VAT No.:** GB000368184325
Date established: 1938 **Turnover:** £50m - £75m
No.of Employees: 251 - 500 **Product Groups:** 22, 23, 24, 25, 26, 27, 29, 30, 31, 32, 33, 36, 46

Date of Accounts	Dec 10	Dec 09	Dec 08
Sales Turnover	43m	48m	70m
Pre Tax Profit/Loss	-1m	-2m	-694
Working Capital	3m	3m	-278
Fixed Assets	701	556	786
Current Assets	15m	17m	22m
Current Liabilities	1m	2m	4m

Muller England Ltd

1 Block A Bescot Industrial Estate Woden Road West, Wednesbury, WS10 7SG
Tel: 0121-502 6676 **Fax:** 0121-502 6656
E-mail: sales@muller-england.co.uk
Website: http://www.muller-england.co.uk
Directors: C. Walker (Fin), J. Clifford (Sales), P. Bethell (MD)
Managers: E. Jackson (Tech Serv Mgr), B. McConkey (Purch Mgr)
Ultimate Holding Company: MULLER HOLDINGS LIMITED
Immediate Holding Company: MULLER ENGLAND LIMITED
Registration no: 01687555 **Date established:** 1982
Turnover: £10m - £20m **No.of Employees:** 21 - 50 **Product Groups:** 48

Date of Accounts	Dec 11	Dec 10	Dec 09
Sales Turnover	13m	10m	7m
Pre Tax Profit/Loss	288	-648	454
Working Capital	2m	1m	2m
Fixed Assets	4m	4m	2m
Current Assets	5m	5m	4m
Current Liabilities	460	315	724

Nationwide Access Ltd

Willenhall Road, Wednesbury, WS10 8JG
Tel: 0121-568 8444 **Fax:** 0121-568 6862
E-mail: davidprice@nationwideplatforms.co.uk
Website: http://www.nationwideplatforms.co.uk
Directors: A. Merrell (Fin), D. Price (Ch)
Ultimate Holding Company: LAVENDON GROUP PLC
Immediate Holding Company: NATIONWIDE ACCESS LIMITED
Registration no: 04405299 **Date established:** 2002
Turnover: £20m - £50m **No.of Employees:** 21 - 50 **Product Groups:** 45, 83

Date of Accounts	Dec 11	Dec 10	Dec 09
Working Capital	-91	-87	-61
Fixed Assets	913	939	925
Current Assets	1m	2m	997

Nationwide Platforms

Willenhall Road, Wednesbury, WS10 8JR
Tel: 0845-7450000 **Fax:** 0121-544 9837
E-mail: birmingham@nationwideplatforms.co.uk
Website: https://www.nationwideplatforms.co.uk
Directors: H. Walters (Mkt Research)
Managers: A. Parker (Mgr)
Ultimate Holding Company: Lavendon Group plc
Immediate Holding Company: Zooom Holdings UK Ltd
Registration no: 02268921 **Date established:** 1996
Turnover: £20m - £50m **No.of Employees:** 11 - 20 **Product Groups:** 45, 83

Newby Holdings Ltd

Smith Road, Wednesbury, WS10 0PB
Tel: 0121-556 4451 **Fax:** 0121-502 5480
E-mail: sales@newbyfoundries.co.uk
Website: http://www.newbyfoundries.co.uk
Bank(s): HSBC, West Bromwich
Directors: P. Baggott (Fin), P. Grubb (MD)
Immediate Holding Company: NEWBY HOLDINGS LIMITED
Registration no: 00344599 **VAT No.:** GB 277 2261 49
Date established: 1938 **Turnover:** £10m - £20m
No.of Employees: 101 - 250 **Product Groups:** 34

Date of Accounts	Dec 11	Dec 10	Dec 09
Sales Turnover	15m	10m	6m
Pre Tax Profit/Loss	1m	639	62
Working Capital	3m	3m	3m
Fixed Assets	9m	7m	7m
Current Assets	6m	6m	4m
Current Liabilities	1m	1m	520

Oxi-Black & Phosphate Ltd

Darlaston Centre Trading Estate, Wednesbury, WS10 8XB
Tel: 0121-526 7381 **Fax:** 0121-568 6721
E-mail: oxi-black@btconnect.com
Website: http://www.oxi-black.co.uk
Directors: N. Smith (MD), V. Smith (Fin)
Immediate Holding Company: OXI-BLACK AND PHOSPHATE LIMITED
Registration no: 01723789 **Date established:** 1983
Turnover: Up to £250,000 **No.of Employees:** 1 - 10 **Product Groups:** 48

Date of Accounts	Jun 11	Jun 10	Jun 09
Working Capital	65	69	51
Fixed Assets	78	81	85
Current Assets	140	129	133

P A L Group Operations (incorporating Rustin Allen)

Darlaston Road Industrial Estate, Wednesbury, WS10 7TN
Tel: 0121-526 4048 **Fax:** 0121-526 4658
E-mail: peter.lowe@palgroup.co.uk
Website: http://www.palglazing.co.uk
Bank(s): Barclays
Directors: N. Walton (Fin)
Managers: B. Humphries (Buyer), R. Herbert, P. Lowe (Mgr)
Immediate Holding Company: PAL EXTRUSIONS LIMITED
Registration no: 02933043 **VAT No.:** GB 361 8235 55
Date established: 1994 **Turnover:** £10m - £20m
No.of Employees: 101 - 250 **Product Groups:** 30, 35

Date of Accounts	Mar 11	Mar 10	Mar 09
Sales Turnover	11m	10m	10m
Pre Tax Profit/Loss	343	268	21
Working Capital	-35	-60	185
Fixed Assets	3m	3m	2m
Current Assets	4m	4m	3m
Current Liabilities	2m	2m	2m

Powell Gee & Co. Ltd

Rigby Street, Wednesbury, WS10 0NP
Tel: 0121-556 1495 **Fax:** 0121-556 6729
E-mail: sales@powellgee.co.uk
Website: http://www.selfdrillingscrew.co.uk
Bank(s): Barclays
Directors: B. Powell (MD)
Immediate Holding Company: POWELL, GEE & COMPANY LIMITED
Registration no: 00689940 **VAT No.:** GB 277 2597 16
Date established: 1961 **Turnover:** £2m - £5m **No.of Employees:** 11 - 20
Product Groups: 14, 30, 32, 33, 35

Date of Accounts	Aug 11	Aug 10	Aug 09
Working Capital	584	510	512
Fixed Assets	161	130	144
Current Assets	1m	999	960

Pritchard Gears Ltd

5 Brunswick Park Tarding Estate Brunswick Park Road, Wednesbury, WS10 9QR
Tel: 0121-556 0275 **Fax:** 0121-505 1278
E-mail: nigel@pritchardgearsltd.co.uk
Website: http://www.pritchardgears.co.uk
Directors: P. Pritchard (Fin), N. Pritchard (MD)
Immediate Holding Company: PRITCHARD GEARS LIMITED
Registration no: 01471031 **Date established:** 1980
Turnover: Up to £250,000 **No.of Employees:** 1 - 10 **Product Groups:** 35, 45

Date of Accounts	Jan 12	Jan 11	Jan 10
Working Capital	94	73	52
Fixed Assets	86	78	49
Current Assets	157	120	103

Queen Anne Tableware Ltd

Classic Works Holyhead Road, Wednesbury, WS10 7PD
Tel: 0121-556 1471 **Fax:** 0121-556 4966
E-mail: info@queenanneuk.com
Website: http://www.queenanneuk.com
Bank(s): National Westminster
Directors: N. Lockley (Fin), P. Lawrence (MD)
Managers: G. Sadler (Comm)
Immediate Holding Company: QUEEN ANNE TABLEWARE LIMITED
Registration no: 04050469 **VAT No.:** 004 0504 69 **Date established:** 2000
Turnover: £1m - £2m **No.of Employees:** 21 - 50 **Product Groups:** 36, 49

Date of Accounts	Aug 11	Aug 10	Aug 09
Working Capital	412	460	369
Fixed Assets	582	391	419
Current Assets	771	780	836

R D Techniques

3 Mounts Road, Wednesbury, WS10 0BU
Tel: 0121-502 0570 **Fax:** 0121-505 3238
E-mail: rd.techniques@cableinet.co.uk
Directors: R. Dunkley (Ptnr)
Immediate Holding Company: R D TECHNIQUES LIMITED
Registration no: 06030595 **VAT No.:** GB 547 4204 48
Date established: 2006 **Turnover:** Up to £250,000
No.of Employees: 1 - 10 **Product Groups:** 48

Date of Accounts	Mar 11	Mar 10
Working Capital	212	147
Fixed Assets	31	52
Current Assets	509	437

R J T Furnaces Ltd

Unit 10 Holland Park Bentley Road South, Wednesbury, WS10 8LN
Tel: 0121-568 6474 **Fax:** 0121-568 6269
Directors: J. Thompson (Fin)
Immediate Holding Company: R.J.T. FURNACES LIMITED
Registration no: 03032474 **Date established:** 1995
No.of Employees: 1 - 10 **Product Groups:** 40, 42, 46

Date of Accounts	Sep 11	Sep 10	Sep 09
Working Capital	84	119	131
Fixed Assets	1	1	1
Current Assets	150	236	222

Rapid Steel Profiling

Unit 2 William Burton Works St James Street, Wednesbury, WS10 7DY
Tel: 0121-505 2808 **Fax:** 0121-505 2744
Website: http://www.keitonengineering.co.uk
Managers: B. Gould (Sales Prom Mgr)
No.of Employees: 11 - 20 **Product Groups:** 34, 66

Regent Engineering Company

Darlaston Central Trading Estate Salisbury Street, Wednesbury, WS10 8BQ
Tel: 0121-568 6063 **Fax:** 0121-526 4789
E-mail: alan@regenteng.com
Website: http://www.regenteng.com
Managers: J. Shaw (Eng Serv Mgr), A. Shaw (Export Sales Mg), J. Shaw (Accounts)
Immediate Holding Company: REGENT ENGINEERING CO (WALSALL) LIMITED(THE)
Registration no: 00551421 **VAT No.:** GB 100 6375 16
Date established: 1955 **Turnover:** £2m - £5m **No.of Employees:** 1 - 10
Product Groups: 34, 48

Date of Accounts	Mar 12	Mar 11	Mar 10
Working Capital	55	63	132
Fixed Assets	518	541	536
Current Assets	2m	1m	1m

Robert Gordon Europe Ltd

Kings Hill Business Park Darlaston Road, Wednesbury, WS10 7SH
Tel: 0121-506 7700 **Fax:** 0121-506 7701
E-mail: uksales@rg-inc.com
Website: http://www.rg-inc.com
Bank(s): National Westminster, Wolverhampton
Directors: R. Harris (MD), G. Stainke (Fin)
Managers: G. Whitehouse, N. Blythin (Tech Serv Mgr)
Ultimate Holding Company: ROBERTS GORDON LLC (USA)
Immediate Holding Company: ROBERTS-GORDON EUROPE LIMITED
Registration no: 02955148 **Date established:** 1994 **Turnover:** £5m - £10m
No.of Employees: 11 - 20 **Product Groups:** 40

Date of Accounts	Dec 11	Dec 10	Dec 09
Sales Turnover	N/A	6m	5m
Pre Tax Profit/Loss	N/A	-1m	-1m
Working Capital	-3m	-2m	-1m
Fixed Assets	42	72	169
Current Assets	5m	4m	6m
Current Liabilities	N/A	243	274

Rotech Laboratories Ltd (Rubery Owen Group)

Unit 6 Moxley Industrial Centre Western Way, Wednesbury, WS10 7BG
Tel: 0121-505 4050 **Fax:** 0121-505 1115
E-mail: info@rotechlabs.co.uk
Website: http://www.rotechlabs.co.uk
Directors: R. Smith (MD), E. Eaton (Fin)
Ultimate Holding Company: RUBERY,OWEN HOLDINGS LIMITED
Immediate Holding Company: ROTECH LABORATORIES LIMITED
Registration no: 00562845 **Date established:** 1956
Turnover: £500,000 - £1m **No.of Employees:** 21 - 50
Product Groups: 33, 34, 38, 40, 42, 48, 85

Date of Accounts	Sep 10	Sep 09	Sep 08
Sales Turnover	1m	1m	1m
Pre Tax Profit/Loss	23	2	57
Working Capital	31	12	15
Fixed Assets	152	148	171
Current Assets	290	299	317
Current Liabilities	61	66	81

Rushall Tool & Engineering

Darlaston Central Trading Estate, Wednesbury, WS10 8XB
Tel: 0121-526 3617 **Fax:** 0121-568 6015
Bank(s): HSBC
Directors: E. Morris (Dir), E. Morris (Fin), S. Morris (Fab), R. Morris (MD), D. Leverett (Dir), P. Carr (Co Sec)
Ultimate Holding Company: CHESHIRE TOOL AND PRESSING COMPANY LIMITED
Immediate Holding Company: RUSHALL TOOL & ENGINEERING LIMITED
Registration no: 00998526 **VAT No.:** GB 100 1860 34
Date established: 1970 **No.of Employees:** 21 - 50 **Product Groups:** 46, 48

Date of Accounts	Sep 07	Jun 10	Jun 09
Working Capital	1m	211	232
Fixed Assets	53	158	177
Current Assets	1m	672	697

SKF Economos U.K. Ltd Wednesbury Branch

Unit 17, Block D Wednesbury Trading Estate Darlaston Rd, Wednesbury, WS10 7JN
Tel: 0121-505 2112 **Fax:** 0121-505 2045
E-mail: wednesbury@economos.com
Website: http://www.economos.co.uk
Directors: R. Kumra (MD), P. Chambers (MD)
Ultimate Holding Company: Economos AG (Austria)
Immediate Holding Company: Economos Ltd
Registration no: 02414449 **VAT No.:** 532 1465 72 **Turnover:** £2m - £5m
No.of Employees: 1 - 10 **Product Groups:** 29, 30, 33, 40, 42, 48

Swift Maintenance Services

Unit 2 Albert Street, Wednesbury, WS10 7EW
Tel: 0121-505 4001 **Fax:** 0121-502 2065
E-mail: mail@swiftmain.co.uk
Directors: C. Birch (Ptnr)
Immediate Holding Company: SWIFT MAINTENANCE SERVICES (1973) LIMITED
Registration no: 07649586 **Date established:** 2011
No.of Employees: 11 - 20 **Product Groups:** 20, 40, 41

Top Tubes Ltd

2 Smith Road, Wednesbury, WS10 0PD
Tel: 0121-506 1080 **Fax:** 01902-674110
E-mail: enquiries@toptubes.co.uk
Website: http://www.toptubes.co.uk
Directors: M. Bradley (Fin), A. Bradley (MD)
Managers: S. Taylor
Immediate Holding Company: TOP TUBES LIMITED
Registration no: 03000662 **Date established:** 1994
Turnover: £20m - £50m **No.of Employees:** 51 - 100 **Product Groups:** 36, 37

Date of Accounts	Mar 11	Mar 10	Mar 09
Sales Turnover	27m	23m	N/A
Pre Tax Profit/Loss	882	385	1m
Working Capital	744	600	379
Fixed Assets	3m	2m	2m
Current Assets	12m	9m	7m
Current Liabilities	6m	5m	2m

Tower Input

Phoenix Works Industrial Estate Richards Street, Wednesbury, WS10 8BZ
Tel: 0121-568 7003 **Fax:** 0121-568 7371
Website: http://www.towerinput.com
Managers: S. Wesley (Mgr), S. Westwood (Mgr)
Immediate Holding Company: 4 G STEEL STOCKHOLDER LTD
Registration no: 04458439 **Date established:** 2010
No.of Employees: 1 - 10 **Product Groups:** 46

Date of Accounts	May 11
Working Capital	33
Current Assets	98

Tuke & Bell Ltd

Patent Drive, Wednesbury, WS10 7XD
Tel: 0121-506 7330 **Fax:** 0121-506 7333
E-mail: sales@tukeandbell.co.uk
Website: http://www.tukeandbell.co.uk
Bank(s): HSBC Bank plc
Directors: R. Lewis (MD)
Managers: P. Daniel (Comm)
Immediate Holding Company: TUKE AND BELL LIMITED
Registration no: 00125585 **Date established:** 2012 **Turnover:** £5m - £10m
No.of Employees: 21 - 50 **Product Groups:** 38, 42, 54

Date of Accounts	Dec 11	Dec 10	Dec 09
Sales Turnover	3m	N/A	N/A
Pre Tax Profit/Loss	15	N/A	N/A
Working Capital	274	423	528
Fixed Assets	2m	2m	2m
Current Assets	2m	2m	2m
Current Liabilities	264	N/A	N/A

Turton Safety Ltd

1 Britannia Park Trident Drive, Wednesbury, WS10 7XB
Tel: 08709-007560 **Fax:** 0121-567 4141
E-mail: sales@turtonsafety.co.uk
Website: http://www.turton.co.uk
Directors: M. Parsons (MD), R. Monro (Co Sec)
Managers: S. Davies
Ultimate Holding Company: SIG PLC
Immediate Holding Company: SIG DORMANT COMPANY NUMBER THREE LIMITED
Registration no: 02098236 **VAT No.:** GB 428 7071 42
Date established: 1987 **Turnover:** £10m - £20m **No.of Employees:** 1 - 10
Product Groups: 22, 24, 29, 40

Date of Accounts	Dec 11	Dec 10	Dec 09
Working Capital	173	173	173
Current Assets	173	173	173

W P A Furnaces & Engineering Projects Ltd

Mounts Road, Wednesbury, WS10 0DU
Tel: 01902-631155 **Fax:** 01902-602615
E-mail: wkdave@yahoo.co.uk
Directors: D. Page (MD), C. Page (Fin)
Ultimate Holding Company: TIMIK LIMITED
Immediate Holding Company: W.P.A. FURNACES & ENGINEERING PROJECTS LIMITED
Registration no: 01105418 **Date established:** 1973
No.of Employees: 1 - 10 **Product Groups:** 40, 42, 46

Date of Accounts	May 11	May 10	May 09
Working Capital	738	712	701
Fixed Assets	1	1	1
Current Assets	800	755	758

West Midlands Gates & Trailers

3 Jubilee Buildings Tamebridge Service Station Holloway, Wednesbury, WS10 0NF
Tel: 0121-505 1150 **Fax:** 0121-505 1150
Directors: S. Richards (Prop)
Date established: 1994 **No.of Employees:** 1 - 10 **Product Groups:** 26, 35

Z F Lenforder UK Ltd

PO Box 35, Wednesbury, WS10 8BH
Tel: 0121-526 4441 **Fax:** 0121-526 3579
E-mail: roger.homer@zf.com
Website: http://www.zf.com
Bank(s): Lloyds TSB Bank plc
Directors: T. Summerfield (MD)
Managers: C. Newman (Comptroller), R. Homer (Sales Prom Mgr)
Ultimate Holding Company: ZF FRIEDRICHSHAFEN AG (GERMANY)
Immediate Holding Company: ZF LEMFORDER UK LIMITED
Registration no: 02370396 **VAT No.:** GB 547 6665 02
Date established: 1989 **Turnover:** £125m - £250m
No.of Employees: 251 - 500 **Product Groups:** 39, 84

Date of Accounts	Dec 11	Dec 10	Dec 09
Sales Turnover	148m	125m	82m
Pre Tax Profit/Loss	2m	1m	-3m
Working Capital	358	4m	2m
Fixed Assets	11m	5m	3m
Current Assets	42m	37m	28m
Current Liabilities	4m	3m	2m

West Bromwich

A B R Specialists Welding Ltd

2 Haines Street, West Bromwich, B70 7DS
Tel: 0121-525 1319 **Fax:** 0121-525 1311
E-mail: enquiries@abrspecialistwelding.co.uk
Website: http://www.abrspecialistwelding.co.uk
Directors: W. Hewitson (MD), J. Hewitson (Fin)
Immediate Holding Company: A.B.R. (SPECIALIST WELDING) LIMITED
Registration no: 01795984 **Date established:** 1984
Turnover: £500,000 - £1m **No.of Employees:** 1 - 10 **Product Groups:** 30, 48

Date of Accounts	Apr 11	Apr 10	Apr 09
Working Capital	1m	1m	930
Fixed Assets	33	51	83
Current Assets	1m	1m	1m

A D I Treatments Ltd

Unit D Doranda Way Industrial Park Doranda Way, West Bromwich, B71 4LE
Tel: 0121-525 0303 **Fax:** 0121-525 0404
E-mail: sales@chta.co.uk
Website: http://www.aditreatments.com
Bank(s): Lloyds TSB Bank plc
Directors: A. Rimmer (Dir), S. Day (Fin)
Immediate Holding Company: ADI TREATMENTS LIMITED
Registration no: 03840660 **VAT No.:** GB 729 8504 02
Date established: 1999 **Turnover:** £2m - £5m **No.of Employees:** 21 - 50
Product Groups: 46, 48

Date of Accounts	Dec 11	Dec 10	Dec 09
Sales Turnover	4m	3m	N/A
Pre Tax Profit/Loss	751	351	N/A
Working Capital	-280	-209	113
Fixed Assets	1m	2m	2m
Current Assets	1m	1m	949
Current Liabilities	1m	768	N/A

J T Adams Springs Ltd

Matlock Works Union Street, West Bromwich, B70 6BZ
Tel: 0121-525 9758 **Fax:** 0121-553 6113
E-mail: sales@jt-adams.co.uk
Website: http://www.jt-adams-springs.co.uk
Directors: S. Hodson (Dir)
Immediate Holding Company: J. T. ADAMS (SPRINGS) LIMITED
Registration no: 01663368 **VAT No.:** GB 369 6967 73
Date established: 1982 **Turnover:** £250,000 - £500,000
No.of Employees: 1 - 10 **Product Groups:** 35, 48

Date of Accounts	Dec 11	Dec 10	Dec 09
Working Capital	13	-14	-1
Fixed Assets	45	40	50
Current Assets	137	89	79

Adwin Spring Co. Ltd

Elwell Street, West Bromwich, B70 0DW
Tel: 0121-557 1473
E-mail: sales@adwinspring.co.uk
Website: http://www.adwin.co.uk
Bank(s): Barclays
Directors: J. Harris (Grp Chief Exec), P. Cottrill (MD)
Managers: S. Garbett (Sales Prom Mgr), M. Angell (Sales Prom Mgr), V. Payton (Sales Prom Mgr)
Immediate Holding Company: MORRIS SPRINGS LIMITED
Registration no: 03706332 **VAT No.:** GB 276 8871 95
Date established: 1999 **Turnover:** £2m - £5m **No.of Employees:** 51 - 100
Product Groups: 35, 36, 41, 48, 66

Date of Accounts	Aug 11	Aug 10	Aug 09
Working Capital	371	376	369
Fixed Assets	307	322	348
Current Assets	694	630	582

Air Liquide Ltd

Johnsons Bridge Road Church Lane, West Bromwich, B71 1AR
Tel: 0121-500 1000 **Fax:** 0121-500 1111
E-mail: info@uk.linde-gas.com
Website: http://www.linde-gas.co.uk
Bank(s): Barclays
Directors: A. Reynolds (Fin), O. Petit (Dir), P. Humber (Fin), T. Longley (Sales), W. Ingerson (MD)
Managers: R. Sharma (Mktg Serv Mgr), S. Mole (Systems Mgr)
Ultimate Holding Company: Linde AG
Immediate Holding Company: Air Liquide UK Ltd
Registration no: 02103630 **VAT No.:** GB 537 6738 08
Date established: 1987 **Turnover:** £20m - £50m
No.of Employees: 251 - 500 **Product Groups:** 31

Albion Section Ltd

2 Albion Road, West Bromwich, B70 8BD
Tel: 0121-553 1877 **Fax:** 0121-553 5507
E-mail: sales@albionsections.co.uk
Website: http://www.albionsections.co.uk
Bank(s): Lloyds TSB Bank plc
Directors: E. King (Sales), P. Chilton (Co Sec)
Ultimate Holding Company: THE SEBDEN GROUP LIMITED
Immediate Holding Company: ALBION SECTIONS LIMITED
Registration no: 02744609 **VAT No.:** GB 611 0055 11
Date established: 1992 **Turnover:** £5m - £10m **No.of Employees:** 21 - 50
Product Groups: 34, 35

Date of Accounts	Apr 11	Apr 10	Apr 09
Sales Turnover	N/A	N/A	6m
Pre Tax Profit/Loss	N/A	N/A	575
Working Capital	136	80	315
Fixed Assets	2m	2m	2m
Current Assets	2m	2m	2m
Current Liabilities	N/A	N/A	667

Aluminium Products Ltd

Alpro Foundry Haines Street, West Bromwich, B70 7DA
Tel: 0121-553 1911 **Fax:** 0121-500 5796
E-mail: mike@alpro.co.uk
Website: http://www.aluminiumproductsltd.co.uk
Bank(s): Lloyds TSB Bank plc
Directors: M. Laker (MD), G. Steventon (Co Sec)
Immediate Holding Company: ALUMINIUM PRODUCTS LIMITED
Registration no: 00331072 **VAT No.:** GB 276 8159 16
Date established: 1937 **Turnover:** £1m - £2m **No.of Employees:** 21 - 50
Product Groups: 34

Date of Accounts	Dec 11	Dec 10	Dec 09
Working Capital	153	88	101
Fixed Assets	82	95	107
Current Assets	527	399	369

Anchorfast Ltd

Doranda Way, West Bromwich, B71 4LU
Tel: 0121-525 0525 **Fax:** 0121-580 3555
E-mail: d.dobson@reca-uk.com
Website: http://www.reca-uk.com
Bank(s): HSBC Bank plc
Directors: D. Dobson (MD)
Managers: S. Herlihy (Purch Mgr), W. Westall (Sales Prom Mgr)
Ultimate Holding Company: REINHOLD WURTH HOLDING GMBH (GERMANY)
Immediate Holding Company: RECA-UK LTD
Registration no: 02738056 **VAT No.:** GB 368 1843 25
Date established: 1992 **Turnover:** £5m - £10m **No.of Employees:** 21 - 50
Product Groups: 30, 32, 33, 35, 36, 49, 66

Aquaid Birmingham & Midlands Central

Unit 35 Kelvin Way Trading Estate Kelvin Way, West Bromwich, B70 7TP
Tel: 0121-525 4533 **Fax:** 0121-525 3502
Website: http://www.aquaidwatercoolers.co.uk
Managers: S. Barnbrook (Mgr)
No.of Employees: 1 - 10 **Product Groups:** 40, 66

ARCO West Bromwich

PO Box 2210, West Bromwich, B71 1DQ
Tel: 0121-500 4444 **Fax:** 0121-553 7554
E-mail: steve.westerby@arco.co.uk
Website: http://www.arco.co.uk
Managers: S. Westerby (District Mgr)
Immediate Holding Company: ARCO LTD
Registration no: 02017269 **Date established:** 1986
Turnover: £125m - £250m **No.of Employees:** 21 - 50
Product Groups: 24, 29, 30, 84

Asco Fixings Ltd

Colliery Road, West Bromwich, B71 4JT
Tel: 0121-553 1177 **Fax:** 0121-553 1199
E-mail: info@ascofixings.co.uk
Website: http://www.ascofixings.co.uk
Directors: K. Anand (MD)
Managers: A. Chandan, A. Chandan, A. Singh (Mgr)
Immediate Holding Company: ASCO FIXINGS LIMITED
Registration no: 03494733 **VAT No.:** GB 710 0101 28
Date established: 1998 **Turnover:** £1m - £2m **No.of Employees:** 1 - 10
Product Groups: 23, 26, 33, 34, 35, 36, 39, 46, 48, 66, 67, 84

Date of Accounts	Mar 08	Mar 07	Mar 06
Working Capital	123	55	13
Fixed Assets	204	217	272
Current Assets	1403	1152	976
Current Liabilities	1280	1097	963
Total Share Capital	270	270	270

Ash & Lacy Building Systems Ltd

Bromford Lane, West Bromwich, B70 7JJ
Tel: 0121-525 1444 **Fax:** 0121-525 3444
E-mail: sales@ashandlacy.com
Website: http://www.ashandlacy.com
Bank(s): Barclays, Dudley
Directors: A. Waterhouse (Fin), D. Wright (MD), D. Hoey (Chief Op Offcr)
Ultimate Holding Company: HILL & SMITH HOLDINGS PLC
Immediate Holding Company: ASH & LACY BUILDING SYSTEMS LIMITED
Registration no: 00149058 **VAT No.:** GB 277 0118 64
Date established: 2017 **Turnover:** £20m - £50m
No.of Employees: 51 - 100 **Product Groups:** 35

Date of Accounts	Dec 11	Dec 10	Dec 09
Sales Turnover	25m	22m	20m
Pre Tax Profit/Loss	-339	-450	-1m
Working Capital	2m	2m	2m
Fixed Assets	879	1m	1m
Current Assets	12m	8m	8m
Current Liabilities	1m	817	1m

Baron UK

Unit 32 Phoenix International Industrial Estate Charles Street, West Bromwich, B70 0AY
Tel: 0121-520 2200 **Fax:** 0121-520 3200
E-mail: enquiries@baronukltd.com
Website: http://www.baron-mixer.com
No.of Employees: 1 - 10 **Product Groups:** 36, 40, 41

Beeswift Ltd

West Wing Delta House Delta Point Greets Green Road, West Bromwich, B70 9PL
Tel: 0121-524 2323 **Fax:** 0121-524 2325
E-mail: sales@beeswift.com
Website: http://www.beeswift.com
Directors: T. Haigh (Purch), D. Griffin (Fin), A. Stonehill (Sales)
Managers: J. Chambers (Tech Serv Mgr), J. Fellows (Mktg Serv Mgr)
Ultimate Holding Company: GERBER GLOBAL CAPITAL LLC (USA)
Immediate Holding Company: BEESWIFT LIMITED
Registration no: 01569085 **VAT No.:** GB 351 7367 50
Date established: 1981 **Turnover:** £20m - £50m
No.of Employees: 51 - 100 **Product Groups:** 22, 24, 29, 30, 36, 40, 41, 63

Date of Accounts	Sep 11	Sep 10	Sep 09
Sales Turnover	30m	28m	24m
Pre Tax Profit/Loss	1m	506	6

Working Capital	7m	6m	6m
Fixed Assets	154	124	164
Current Assets	15m	13m	11m
Current Liabilities	1m	789	508

Berck Ltd

Titan Works Pleasant Street, Lyng Industrial Estate, West Bromwich, B70 7DP
Tel: 0121-553 2726 **Fax:** 0121-553 1087
E-mail: sales@bercklimited.co.uk
Website: http://www.bercklimited.co.uk
Bank(s): Barclays
Directors: A. Jackson (Jt MD), D. Yates (Jt MD), B. Yates (Ch), R. Jones (Comm)
Managers: D. Pring (I.T. Exec)
Registration no: 00440136 **VAT No.:** GB 276 8200 45
Turnover: £5m - £10m **No.of Employees:** 101 - 250 **Product Groups:** 34, 35, 36, 37, 48, 68, 84

Date of Accounts	Jul 11	Jul 10	Jul 09
Sales Turnover	5m	5m	4m
Pre Tax Profit/Loss	47	184	-624
Working Capital	1m	1m	882
Fixed Assets	30	58	153
Current Assets	3m	3m	3m
Current Liabilities	150	268	1m

Black Country Rag & Wiper Co.

4a-4b Greets Green Industrial Estate Greets Green Road, West Bromwich, B70 9EW
Tel: 0121-520 7586 **Fax:** 0121-522 3340
E-mail: mail@bcrglobaltextiles.co.uk
Website: http://www.bcrglobaltextiles.co.uk
Directors: M. Sault (Dir)
Immediate Holding Company: BLACK COUNTRY RAG & WIPER CO. LIMITED
Registration no: 06071381 **Date established:** 2007 **Turnover:** £1m - £2m
No.of Employees: 1 - 10 **Product Groups:** 63

Boc Ltd

305-307 Bromford Lane, West Bromwich, B70 7JA
Tel: 0121-544 1513 **Fax:** 0121-544 1514
E-mail: paulcooper@boc.com
Website: http://www.boc.com
Managers: P. Cooper (Mgr)
Ultimate Holding Company: LINDE AG (GERMANY)
Immediate Holding Company: BOC LIMITED
Registration no: 00337663 **Date established:** 1938
No.of Employees: 1 - 10 **Product Groups:** 46

Date of Accounts	Dec 11	Dec 10	Dec 08
Sales Turnover	726m	691m	721m
Pre Tax Profit/Loss	122m	125m	67m
Working Capital	409m	278m	-219m
Fixed Assets	480m	492m	538m
Current Assets	724m	578m	371m
Current Liabilities	64m	68m	73m

Bridge Steel Sections Ltd

Ridgeacre Road, West Bromwich, B71 1BB
Tel: 0121-555 1460 **Fax:** 0121-555 1461
E-mail: bss@hadleygroup.co.uk
Website: http://www.hadleygroup.co.uk
Directors: G. Deeley (I.T. Dir), J. Flynn (Sales & Mktg), P. Hadley (MD), S. Towe (Fin)
Managers: I. Woolley (Personnel), M. Collier (I.T. Exec)
Immediate Holding Company: Hadley Industries plc
Registration no: 01601346 **VAT No.:** GB 409 4460 54
Turnover: £2m - £5m **No.of Employees:** 1 - 10 **Product Groups:** 34

British Castors Ltd

Golds Green Works Bagnall Street Hill Top West Bromwich, West Bromwich, B70 0TZ
Tel: 0121-556 7221 **Fax:** 0121-502 2658
E-mail: info@colson-castors.co.uk
Website: http://www.colson-castors.co.uk
Directors: B. Lilly (MD), D. Towell (Fin)
Managers: R. Hudson (Tech Serv Mgr), J. Simmons (Buyer)
Ultimate Holding Company: COLSON GROUP INC (USA)
Immediate Holding Company: BRITISH CASTORS LIMITED
Registration no: 00153369 **Date established:** 2019 **Turnover:** £1m - £2m
No.of Employees: 51 - 100 **Product Groups:** 25, 30, 36, 39, 66

Brockhouse Group Ltd

Hill Top Howard Street, West Bromwich, B70 0SN
Tel: 0121-556 1241 **Fax:** 0121-502 3076
E-mail: sales@brockhouse.co.uk
Website: http://www.brockhouse.co.uk
Directors: S. Chilvers (Sales & Mktg), S. Walters (Fin), J. Pickering (MD), C. Hutton-Penman (Ch)
Managers: S. Millward (I.T. Exec), T. Roberts (Sales Prom Mgr), S. Shahzad (Cust Serv Mgr)
Registration no: 03737163 **Turnover:** £10m - £20m
No.of Employees: 101 - 250 **Product Groups:** 48, 66

Date of Accounts	Mar 12	Mar 09	Mar 10
Sales Turnover	12m	11m	8m
Pre Tax Profit/Loss	434	87	-206
Working Capital	605	256	246
Fixed Assets	2m	2m	2m
Current Assets	3m	3m	2m
Current Liabilities	538	641	482

Bromford Iron & Steel Co. Ltd

Bromford Lane, West Bromwich, B70 7JJ
Tel: 0121-553 6121 **Fax:** 0121-525 0913
E-mail: martyn@bisteel.co.uk
Website: http://www.bromfordsteels.co.uk
Bank(s): Lloyds TSB Bank plc
Directors: M. Coles (Fin)
Managers: A. Williams (Maint Eng), A. Smith
Ultimate Holding Company: HILL & SMITH HOLDINGS PLC
Immediate Holding Company: BROMFORD IRON AND STEEL COMPANY LIMITED
Registration no: 00447036 **Date established:** 1947
Turnover: £10m - £20m **No.of Employees:** 21 - 50 **Product Groups:** 35, 46, 48

Date of Accounts	Dec 11	Dec 10	Dec 09
Sales Turnover	14m	13m	13m
Pre Tax Profit/Loss	73	469	373

Working Capital	1m	1m	950
Fixed Assets	2m	2m	2m
Current Assets	8m	6m	6m
Current Liabilities	133	2m	3m

Carlyle Parts Ltd

Carlyle Business Park Great Bridge Street, Swan Village, West Bromwich, B70 0XA
Tel: 0121-524 1200 **Fax:** 0121-524 1201
E-mail: neilbottrill@carlyle.com
Website: http://www.carlyleplc.co.uk
Directors: J. Turton (Fin), M. Fortt (Sales), N. Bottrill (Dir)
Managers: S. Dunn (Sales & Mktg Mg)
Ultimate Holding Company: CARLYLE PLC
Immediate Holding Company: CARLYLE PARTS & SERVICE LIMITED
Registration no: 03666290 **Date established:** 1998
Turnover: £10m - £20m **No.of Employees:** 21 - 50 **Product Groups:** 39

Ceva Container Logistics

Unit A Doranda Way Industrial Park Doranda Way, West Bromwich, B71 4LE
Tel: 0121-525 6060 **Fax:** 0121-525 2442
E-mail: martin.thornhill@cevalogistics.com
Website: http://www.cevalogistics.com
Bank(s): Barclays, Manchester
Directors: M. Thornhill (MD)
Managers: J. Bland (Sales Prom Mgr), D. Marchant-smith (Purch Mgr), A. Durnall, G. Upton, M. Gledhill
Ultimate Holding Company: TPG (THE POSTGROUP)
Immediate Holding Company: TNT LOGISTICS
Registration no: 01628530 **VAT No.:** GB 354 7150 57
Turnover: £10m - £20m **No.of Employees:** 51 - 100 **Product Groups:** 27, 30, 36, 45

Chase Castings Ltd

Albion Industrial Estate Oldbury Road, West Bromwich, B70 9BP
Tel: 0121-500 5437 **Fax:** 0121-525 0587
E-mail: sales@chasecastings.co.uk
Website: http://www.chasecastings.co.uk
Directors: D. Hurford (Fin)
Immediate Holding Company: CHASE CASTINGS LIMITED
Registration no: 02037220 **Date established:** 1986
Turnover: £500,000 - £1m **No.of Employees:** 1 - 10 **Product Groups:** 34

Date of Accounts	Jan 12	Jan 11	Jan 10
Working Capital	35	41	26
Fixed Assets	23	28	35
Current Assets	164	170	168

China Clothing Co. (Contract Manufacturer & General Agencyship for Large Customers)

Unit 29 Phoenix International Industrial Estate Charles Street, West Bromwich, B70 0AY
Tel: 0121-601 8026 **Fax:** 0121-601 8039
E-mail: info@chinaclothing.co.uk
Website: http://www.chinaclothing.co.uk
Directors: J. Jin (MD)
Immediate Holding Company: THE CHINA CLOTHING CO. LTD.
Registration no: 07917130 **VAT No.:** GB 559 7175 92
Date established: 2012 **Turnover:** £2m - £5m **No.of Employees:** 1 - 10
Product Groups: 22, 23, 24, 25, 29, 40, 49, 61, 63, 77

China Industrial Materials Ltd

Unit 29 Phoenix International Industrial Estate Charles Street, West Bromwich, B70 0AY
Tel: 0121-601 8007 **Fax:** 0121-601 8039
E-mail: jyjin@cimukltd.com
Website: http://www.cimukltd.com
Directors: J. Jin (MD)
Immediate Holding Company: CHINA INDUSTRIAL MATERIALS LIMITED
Registration no: 03098384 **VAT No.:** GB 559 7175 92
Date established: 1995 **Turnover:** £5m - £10m **No.of Employees:** 1 - 10
Product Groups: 12, 17, 20, 31, 32, 34, 66

Date of Accounts	Mar 11	Mar 10	Mar 09
Working Capital	900	1m	953
Fixed Assets	1	2	2
Current Assets	973	1m	2m

Cleaning 2000 Ltd

7 Ridgeacre Enterprise Park Ridgeacre Road, West Bromwich, B71 1BW
Tel: 0121-525 7726 **Fax:** 0121-525 9594
E-mail: enquiries@cleaning2000.co.uk
Website: http://www.cleaning2000.co.uk
Directors: J. Hollinshead (Co Sec)
Immediate Holding Company: CLEANING 2000 LIMITED
Registration no: 03085830 **Date established:** 1995
No.of Employees: 1 - 10 **Product Groups:** 36, 49

Date of Accounts	Sep 11	Sep 10	Sep 09
Working Capital	35	34	46
Current Assets	87	99	114

Colson Castors Ltd

Bagnall Street Golds Hill, West Bromwich, B70 0TS
Tel: 0121-556 7221 **Fax:** 0121-502 6258
E-mail: info@colson-castors.co.uk
Website: http://www.colson-castors.co.uk
Bank(s): National Westminster Bank Plc
Directors: R. Lilly (Dir), D. Towell (Fin)
Ultimate Holding Company: COLSON GROUP INC (USA)
Immediate Holding Company: COLSON CASTORS LIMITED
Registration no: 00411142 **Date established:** 1946
Turnover: £10m - £20m **No.of Employees:** 51 - 100 **Product Groups:** 29, 39

Date of Accounts	Dec 11	Dec 10	Dec 09
Sales Turnover	19m	17m	13m
Pre Tax Profit/Loss	1m	-13	-2m
Working Capital	5m	4m	3m
Fixed Assets	4m	4m	4m
Current Assets	40m	32m	34m
Current Liabilities	846	764	641

Kate Crown Ltd

Trinity Way, West Bromwich, B70 6NU
Tel: 0121-500 6348 **Fax:** 0121-580 0749
E-mail: katecrown@fsmail.net
Directors: H. Kang (Co Sec)
Immediate Holding Company: KATECROWN LIMITED
Registration no: 02408709 **Date established:** 1989
Turnover: £500,000 - £1m **No.of Employees:** 1 - 10 **Product Groups:** 48

Date of Accounts	Jun 11	Jun 10	Jun 09
Working Capital	159	196	255
Fixed Assets	36	40	53
Current Assets	225	245	308

Cubra Casting Co. Ltd

Pikehelve Street, West Bromwich, B70 0TU
Tel: 0121-557 2321 **Fax:** 0121-520 8462
E-mail: admin@cubracastings.co.uk
Website: http://www.cubracastings.co.uk
Directors: A. Banks (MD), J. Bowater (Dir)
Managers: K. Bourne (Admin Off), S. Fellowes (Mgr)
Immediate Holding Company: THE CUBRA CASTING COMPANY LIMITED
Registration no: 04103234 **VAT No.:** GB 276 8370 20
Date established: 2000 **Turnover:** £1m - £2m **No.of Employees:** 21 - 50
Product Groups: 34

Date of Accounts	Dec 11	Dec 10	Dec 09
Working Capital	302	252	190
Fixed Assets	412	460	344
Current Assets	552	524	402
Current Liabilities	N/A	N/A	42

Davico Industrial Ltd

Charles Street, West Bromwich, B70 0AZ
Tel: 0121-520 7101 **Fax:** 0121-520 7775
E-mail: sales@davico.co.uk
Website: http://www.davico.co.uk
Bank(s): Barclays, Dudley
Directors: B. Davies (MD), D. Washbrook (Fin), N. Hodson (Sales)
Managers: M. Evans (Buyer)
Immediate Holding Company: DAVICO INDUSTRIAL LIMITED
Registration no: 00900196 **VAT No.:** GB 101 2500 53
Date established: 1967 **Turnover:** £10m - £20m
No.of Employees: 21 - 50 **Product Groups:** 30, 36, 37, 39

Date of Accounts	Dec 11	Dec 10	Dec 09
Working Capital	-44	-65	-255
Fixed Assets	689	671	770
Current Assets	2m	2m	2m

Dudley Factory Doors Ltd

G6 Grice Street, West Bromwich, B70 7EZ
Tel: 0121-555 8989 **Fax:** 0121-558 4616
Website: http://www.priory-group.com
Directors: D. Cooper (Ch), G. Cooper (Dir)
Immediate Holding Company: DUDLEY FACTORY DOORS LIMITED
Registration no: 03682062 **Date established:** 1998
Turnover: £250,000 - £500,000 **No.of Employees:** 1 - 10
Product Groups: 25, 30, 33, 35, 40

Date of Accounts	Nov 07	Nov 06	Nov 05
Working Capital	106	106	69
Fixed Assets	N/A	3	5
Current Assets	113	130	186

Eagle Power Ltd

Johnsons Bridge Road, West Bromwich, B71 1DG
Tel: 0121-580 3222 **Fax:** 0121-525 4796
Website: http://www.kw1.com
Directors: N. Nijim (MD)
Managers: N. Nijim (Purch Mgr), R. Davis (Sales Prom Mgr), N. Nijim (Sales Prom Mgr)
Ultimate Holding Company: EAGLE MACHINERY HOLDINGS LIMITED
Immediate Holding Company: EAGLE POWER LIMITED
Registration no: 05040774 **VAT No.:** GB 369 3912 16
Date established: 2004 **Turnover:** £2m - £5m **No.of Employees:** 1 - 10
Product Groups: 37, 40, 52, 67, 83

Date of Accounts	Jul 10	Jul 09	Jul 08
Working Capital	4	93	73
Fixed Assets	494	461	31
Current Assets	891	2m	1m

East End Foods plc

Eastend House Kenrick Way, West Bromwich, B71 4EA
Tel: 0121-553 1999 **Fax:** 0121-525 6565
E-mail: info@eastendfoods.co.uk
Website: http://www.eastendfoods.co.uk
Directors: T. Deep (MD), J. Wuhra (Sales)
Managers: H. Kumar (I.T. Exec), L. Vallely, K. Khambe (Mktg Serv Mgr), C. Wilson (Personnel)
Immediate Holding Company: EAST END FOODS PLC
Registration no: 01159183 **Date established:** 1974
Turnover: £125m - £250m **No.of Employees:** 251 - 500
Product Groups: 61, 72, 76, 77, 85

Date of Accounts	Apr 11	Apr 10	Apr 09
Sales Turnover	126m	122m	115m
Pre Tax Profit/Loss	5m	6m	392
Working Capital	7m	4m	61
Fixed Assets	10m	9m	9m
Current Assets	25m	21m	21m
Current Liabilities	4m	4m	10m

Eurofix Ltd

Doranda Way, West Bromwich, B71 4LU
Tel: 0121-553 5151 **Fax:** 0121-500 5001
E-mail: sales@reca-uk.com
Website: http://www.eurofix.co.uk
Bank(s): HSBC Bank plc
Directors: D. Dobson (MD)
Managers: J. Cavener (Fin Mgr), S. Herlihy (Purch Mgr)
Ultimate Holding Company: REINHOLD WURTH HOLDING GMBH (GERMANY)
Immediate Holding Company: EURO FIX LTD
Registration no: 07630254 **VAT No.:** GB 368 1843 25
Date established: 2011 **Turnover:** £5m - £10m **No.of Employees:** 21 - 50
Product Groups: 35, 37, 46, 66

Fiamma Ltd

Siddon Factory Estate Howard Street, Hill Top, West Bromwich, B70 0TE
Tel: 0121-505 3371 **Fax:** 0121-556 2132
E-mail: melaniepoole@talktalkbusiness.net
Website: http://www.trpoole.co.uk
Directors: R. Poole (MD)
Managers: J. O'Donnell (Spares Mgr)
Registration no: 03885605 **VAT No.:** GB 281 3232 80
No.of Employees: 1 - 10 **Product Groups:** 40

Filtex Filters Ltd
Unit 4-7 Union Park Navigation Way, West Bromwich, B70 9DF
Tel: 0121-553 1283 **Fax:** 0121-500 5284
E-mail: sales@ioi.co.uk
Website: http://www.filtex.co.uk
Bank(s): Lloyds TSB Bank plc
Directors: J. Volante (Fin), T. Rose (MD)
Immediate Holding Company: FILTEX FILTERS LIMITED
Registration no: 01011929 **VAT No.:** GB 277 0236 58
Date established: 1971 **Turnover:** £500,000 - £1m
No.of Employees: 11 - 20 **Product Groups:** 40, 54

Date of Accounts	Jun 12	Jun 11	Jun 10
Working Capital	94	92	167
Fixed Assets	52	44	47
Current Assets	387	313	333

Flexello Ltd
Bagnall Street Hill Top, Golds Hill, West Bromwich, B70 0TS
Tel: 0121-506 1770 **Fax:** 0121-502 2658
E-mail: info@flexello.co.uk
Website: http://www.flexello.co.uk
Bank(s): Barclays
Directors: D. Towell (Fin)
Managers: R. Hudson (Tech Serv Mgr), L. Jordan (Mktg Serv Mgr)
Immediate Holding Company: FLEXELLO LIMITED
Registration no: 04198442 **Date established:** 2001 **Turnover:** £2m - £5m
No.of Employees: 21 - 50 **Product Groups:** 39

Date of Accounts	Dec 11	Dec 10	Dec 09
Sales Turnover	4m	4m	3m
Pre Tax Profit/Loss	385	384	-298
Working Capital	5m	5m	4m
Fixed Assets	55	101	149
Current Assets	13m	10m	20m
Current Liabilities	7	7	6

Formbend Ltd
Unit 4-5 Charles Street, West Bromwich, B70 0AZ
Tel: 0121-557 0555 **Fax:** 0121-557 0888
E-mail: email@formbend.com
Website: http://www.formbend.com
Directors: J. Hateley (Fin), M. Hateley (MD)
Immediate Holding Company: FORMBEND LIMITED
Registration no: 00884148 **VAT No.:** GB 277 1650 43
Date established: 1966 **Turnover:** £2m - £5m **No.of Employees:** 21 - 50
Product Groups: 26, 34, 35, 36, 40, 45, 46, 48

Date of Accounts	Oct 11	Oct 10	Oct 09
Working Capital	308	244	195
Fixed Assets	238	135	140
Current Assets	936	971	674

G & B Repair Services
Unit 47 Phoenix International Industrial Estate Charles Street, West Bromwich, B70 0AY
Tel: 0121-557 5746 **Fax:** 0121-520 1313
Directors: B. Stern (Prop)
Date established: 1984 **No.of Employees:** 1 - 10 **Product Groups:** 37

G & C Scaffolding
52 Turner Street, West Bromwich, B70 9HY
Tel: 07878-273276
E-mail: leephillipgardner@hotmail.co.uk
Directors: W. Crowley (Ptnr)
No.of Employees: 1 - 10 **Product Groups:** 35, 52, 66

G P X Group plc
Brandon Way, West Bromwich, B70 8JH
Tel: 0121-580 3080 **Fax:** 0121-580 3081
E-mail: enquiries@gpxgroup.com
Website: http://www.gpxgroup.com
Directors: A. Glazer (MD), J. Baggett (Co Sec)
Managers: S. Priestly (Sales Prom Mgr)
Immediate Holding Company: GPX Holdings Ltd
Registration no: 03977756 **VAT No.:** GB 226 6785 51
Date established: 1901 **Turnover:** £2m - £5m **No.of Employees:** 51 - 100
Product Groups: 30

G T Certification Ltd
204 Great Bridge Street, West Bromwich, B70 0DE
Tel: 0121-522 3957 **Fax:** 0121-522 4958
E-mail: sales@gtcertification.com
Website: http://www.gtcertification.com
Directors: G. Thompson (MD)
Immediate Holding Company: G.T. CERTIFICATION LIMITED
Registration no: 04295617 **VAT No.:** GB 785 5711 91
Date established: 2001 **Turnover:** £500,000 - £1m
No.of Employees: 1 - 10 **Product Groups:** 36, 38, 85

Date of Accounts	Jan 12	Jan 11	Jan 10
Sales Turnover	N/A	N/A	492
Pre Tax Profit/Loss	N/A	N/A	-13
Working Capital	-5	-18	-32
Fixed Assets	6	8	11
Current Assets	92	89	69
Current Liabilities	N/A	N/A	82

Guest Motors Ltd
Kenrick Way, West Bromwich, B70 6BY
Tel: 0121-553 2737 **Fax:** 0121-500 5932
E-mail: info@guests.co.uk
Website: http://www.guests.co.uk
Directors: R. Spittle (MD)
Ultimate Holding Company: IAN GUEST HOLDINGS LIMITED
Immediate Holding Company: GUEST MOTORS LIMITED
Registration no: 00585041 **VAT No.:** GB 729 8547 81
Date established: 1957 **Turnover:** £50m - £75m
No.of Employees: 51 - 100 **Product Groups:** 68

Date of Accounts	Dec 11	Dec 10	Dec 09
Sales Turnover	75m	66m	45m
Pre Tax Profit/Loss	302	109	-652
Working Capital	2m	3m	3m
Fixed Assets	2m	2m	1m
Current Assets	19m	15m	11m
Current Liabilities	1m	941	634

Heat Treatment 2000
Bull Lane Works Brandon Way, West Bromwich, B70 9PQ
Tel: 0121-526 2000 **Fax:** 0121-500 5837
E-mail: paul.handley@heattreat2000.co.uk
Website: http://www.heattreat2000.co.uk
Directors: P. Handley (Fin)
Immediate Holding Company: HEAT TREATMENT 2000 LIMITED
Registration no: 02714973 **Date established:** 1992
No.of Employees: 21 - 50 **Product Groups:** 46, 48

Date of Accounts	Mar 11	Mar 10	Mar 09
Working Capital	910	521	501
Fixed Assets	699	723	738
Current Assets	1m	1m	807

Robert Hopkins Environmental Services Ltd
Bullock Street, West Bromwich, B70 7HE
Tel: 0121-553 0403 **Fax:** 0121-525 6448
E-mail: info@roberthopkins.co.uk
Website: http://www.roberthopkins.co.uk
Directors: P. Hopkins (MD), D. Hopkins (Fin)
Ultimate Holding Company: ROBERT HOPKINS AND SON LIMITED
Immediate Holding Company: ROBERT HOPKINS AND SON LIMITED
Registration no: 00278885 **Date established:** 1933 **Turnover:** £2m - £5m
No.of Employees: 21 - 50 **Product Groups:** 35, 36, 42, 45

Date of Accounts	Oct 11	Oct 10	Oct 09
Working Capital	-190	-178	-199
Fixed Assets	607	610	612
Current Assets	62	85	111

Industrial Door Systems Midlands Ltd
Unit 43 Trading Estate Kelvin Way, West Bromwich, B70 7TP
Tel: 0121-525 0220 **Fax:** 0121-525 3035
Website: http://www.indoorsystems.co.uk
Directors: J. Barnett (Fin)
Ultimate Holding Company: INDUSTRIAL DOOR SYSTEMS LIMITED
Immediate Holding Company: INDUSTRIAL DOOR SYSTEMS (MIDLANDS) LIMITED
Registration no: 03262249 **Date established:** 1996
No.of Employees: 1 - 10 **Product Groups:** 26, 35

J B R Recovery Ltd
Izons Industrial Estate Oldbury Road, West Bromwich, B70 9BS
Tel: 0121-525 1691 **Fax:** 0121-553 3107
E-mail: punt@jbr.co.uk
Website: http://www.jbr.co.uk
Bank(s): Barclays Bank plc
Directors: B. Meddings (Grp Chief Exec), C. Phipps (Ch), J. Rutherford (Fin), R. Punt (Chief Op Offcr)
Ultimate Holding Company: PHIPPS & COMPANY LIMITED
Immediate Holding Company: JBR RECOVERY LIMITED
Registration no: 02623872 **VAT No.:** GB 547 6446 14
Date established: 1991 **Turnover:** £20m - £50m
No.of Employees: 21 - 50 **Product Groups:** 32, 34, 46

Date of Accounts	Mar 12	Mar 11	Mar 10
Sales Turnover	81m	27m	22m
Pre Tax Profit/Loss	2m	2m	432
Working Capital	3m	2m	963
Fixed Assets	823	596	676
Current Assets	13m	9m	6m
Current Liabilities	1m	505	385

J H Lavender Holdings Ltd
Hall Green Works Crankhall Lane, West Bromwich, B71 3JZ
Tel: 0121-588 2273 **Fax:** 0121-588 7936
E-mail: itimings@lavender-diecast.com
Website: http://www.lavender-diecast.com
Directors: A. Taylor (Fin), I. Timings (MD), A. Rose (Ch), A. Taylor (Co Sec), J. Warner (Dir)
Managers: A. Magher
Immediate Holding Company: J. H. LAVENDER (HOLDINGS) LIMITED
Registration no: 00202442 **VAT No.:** GB 655 1348 36
Date established: 1924 **Turnover:** £5m - £10m **No.of Employees:** 1 - 10
Product Groups: 34

Date of Accounts	Oct 10	Oct 09	Oct 08
Sales Turnover	6m	4m	N/A
Pre Tax Profit/Loss	-93	-558	134
Working Capital	601	514	1m
Fixed Assets	2m	2m	627
Current Assets	3m	1m	1m
Current Liabilities	119	118	30

J & J Coil Slitting Ltd
217 Sams Lane, West Bromwich, B70 7EX
Tel: 0121-553 1131 **Fax:** 0121-525 2411
E-mail: sales@jjcoil.co.uk
Website: http://www.jjcoil.co.uk
Directors: T. Barker (MD)
Immediate Holding Company: J & J COIL SLITTING LIMITED
Registration no: 04287641 **VAT No.:** GB 281 5850 44
Date established: 2001 **Turnover:** Up to £250,000
No.of Employees: 1 - 10 **Product Groups:** 48

Date of Accounts	Sep 04
Working Capital	-53
Fixed Assets	120
Current Liabilities	53

Jbi Technology Ltd
Unit 2-3 Bond Street, West Bromwich, B70 7DQ
Tel: 0121-553 0500 **Fax:** 0121-553 5333
E-mail: info@jbitechnology.co.uk
Website: http://www.jbitechnology.co.uk
Directors: B. Johal (MD), H. Johal (Tech Serv), K. Johal (Mkt Research)
Immediate Holding Company: JBI TECHNOLOGY LIMITED
Registration no: 03900197 **VAT No.:** GB 281 3495 48
Date established: 1999 **Turnover:** £500,000 - £1m
No.of Employees: 1 - 10 **Product Groups:** 41, 42, 45, 46, 48

Date of Accounts	Jan 10	Jan 09	Jan 08
Working Capital	-171	-89	-67
Fixed Assets	102	105	76
Current Assets	231	231	245

Jones & Wilson Ltd
Unit 5 Brandon Way Industrial Estate Brandon Way, West Bromwich, B70 9PW
Tel: 0121-525 4973 **Fax:** 0121-553 4013
E-mail: jonesr383@aol.com
Website: http://www.jonesandwilsonltd.com
Directors: R. Jones (Dir)
Registration no: 02395497 **VAT No.:** GB 488 5962 72
Turnover: £250,000 - £500,000 **No.of Employees:** 1 - 10
Product Groups: 35, 40

Date of Accounts	Jul 07	Jul 06
Working Capital	-5	5
Fixed Assets	3	3
Current Assets	27	30
Current Liabilities	32	25

Joseph & Jesse Siddons Ltd
Howard Street Hill Top, West Bromwich, B70 0TB
Tel: 0121-556 0218 **Fax:** 0121-556 3843
E-mail: ian.parker@jjsiddons.co.uk
Website: http://www.jjsiddons.co.uk
Bank(s): Barclays
Directors: I. Parker (MD), T. Fox (Co Sec)
Immediate Holding Company: JOSEPH AND JESSE SIDDONS LIMITED
Registration no: 00015793 **Date established:** 1981 **Turnover:** £5m - £10m
No.of Employees: 51 - 100 **Product Groups:** 34, 48

Date of Accounts	Jun 11	Jun 10	Jun 09
Sales Turnover	8m	5m	6m
Pre Tax Profit/Loss	1m	813	889
Working Capital	3m	2m	2m
Fixed Assets	6m	6m	5m
Current Assets	4m	3m	3m
Current Liabilities	932	620	613

Keltruck Ltd
Kenrick Way, West Bromwich, B71 4JW
Tel: 0121-525 7000 **Fax:** 0121-524 1855
E-mail: info@keltruck.com
Website: http://www.keltruck.com
Bank(s): HSBC Bank plc
Directors: A. Jamieson (MD)
Managers: A. Bentley (Mktg Serv Mgr), P. Radford (Personnel), T. Joynes (Fin Mgr), M. Kelly (Sales Prom Mgr), C. Glover (Tech Serv Mgr)
Immediate Holding Company: KELTRUCK LIMITED
Registration no: 02880543 **VAT No.:** GB 547 6934 01
Date established: 1993 **Turnover:** £75m - £125m
No.of Employees: 51 - 100 **Product Groups:** 39, 45, 72

Date of Accounts	Dec 11	Dec 10	Dec 09
Sales Turnover	94m	71m	84m
Pre Tax Profit/Loss	3m	3m	1m
Working Capital	6m	6m	5m
Fixed Assets	11m	9m	9m
Current Assets	36m	22m	23m
Current Liabilities	8m	9m	9m

Archibald Kenrick & Sons
Union Street, West Bromwich, B70 6DB
Tel: 0121-553 2741 **Fax:** 0121-500 6332
E-mail: sales@kenricks.co.uk
Website: http://www.kenricks.co.uk
Bank(s): Barclays
Directors: S. Williams (Sales), M. Freebury (Fin), S. Jones (MD)
Managers: S. Hewitt (Comm), J. Turner (Personnel)
Immediate Holding Company: ARCHIBALD KENRICK & SONS LIMITED
Registration no: 00018712 **VAT No.:** 489 7826 64 **Date established:** 1983
Turnover: £5m - £10m **No.of Employees:** 21 - 50 **Product Groups:** 30, 34, 35, 36, 39

Date of Accounts	Mar 05
Working Capital	170
Fixed Assets	157
Current Assets	170

William King Ltd
Atlas Centre Union Road, West Bromwich, B70 9DR
Tel: 0121-500 4100 **Fax:** 0121-500 0400
E-mail: sales@williamking.co.uk
Website: http://www.williamking.co.uk
Bank(s): Barclays, Birmingham
Directors: M. Worley (MD), R. Graville (Fin), J. Moore (Sales), D. Patel (Co Sec)
Managers: K. Fletcher (Tech Serv Mgr)
Immediate Holding Company: WILLIAM KING LIMITED
Registration no: 00498601 **VAT No.:** GB 277 7247 18
Date established: 1951 **Turnover:** £75m - £125m
No.of Employees: 101 - 250 **Product Groups:** 34, 66

Date of Accounts	Jun 11	Jun 10	Jun 09
Sales Turnover	91m	67m	67m
Pre Tax Profit/Loss	3m	3m	120
Working Capital	20m	18m	18m
Fixed Assets	12m	11m	10m
Current Assets	37m	36m	25m
Current Liabilities	4m	3m	1m

J B & S Lees
Trident Steel Works Albion Road, West Bromwich, B70 8BH
Tel: 0121-553 3031 **Fax:** 0121-553 7680
E-mail: eugene.harkins@jbslees.co.uk
Website: http://www.caparo.com
Bank(s): HSBC Midland
Directors: E. Harkins (MD), R. Lane (Fin), J. Watts (Fin), M. Adnitt (Sales)
Managers: S. Moore (Ops Mgr), M. Banks (Sales Prom Mgr), C. Jones (Tech Serv Mgr), C. Jones (I.T. Exec), A. Smith (Buyer)
Ultimate Holding Company: TYCO INTERNATIONAL LTD
Immediate Holding Company: TYCO EUROPEAN STEEL STRIP LTD
Registration no: 05234781 **Turnover:** £20m - £50m
No.of Employees: 101 - 250 **Product Groups:** 34, 66

Longwear Products Ltd
Pleasant Street Lyng, West Bromwich, B70 7DP
Tel: 0121-553 4974 **Fax:** 0121-500 5388
E-mail: sales@longwear.co.uk
Website: http://www.longwear.co.uk
Directors: A. Whittle (Comm), W. Daniels (MD), S. Cottrell (Fin), S. Jones (Sales & Mktg), W. Daniel (MD)
Managers: C. Hunt (Tech Sales Mgr)
Registration no: 00604454 **VAT No.:** GB 340 6320 94
Date established: 1958 **Turnover:** £5m - £10m **No.of Employees:** 21 - 50
Product Groups: 34

Date of Accounts	Oct 09	Oct 08	Oct 07
Working Capital	921	813	722
Fixed Assets	197	205	219
Current Assets	2m	3m	3m

Longwear Surface Treatments Ltd
Pleasant Street Lyng, West Bromwich, B70 7DP
Tel: 0121-580 1120 **Fax:** 0121-500 5388
E-mail: longwear_nitriding@hotmail.com
Website: http://www.longwear-nitriding.co.uk
Directors: I. Macdonald (MD)
Immediate Holding Company: LONGWEAR SURFACE TREATMENTS LIMITED
Registration no: 02621971 **Date established:** 1991
Turnover: Up to £250,000 **No.of Employees:** 1 - 10 **Product Groups:** 48, 84

Date of Accounts	Oct 11	Oct 10	Oct 09
Working Capital	93	53	77
Fixed Assets	28	21	24
Current Assets	160	117	128

M D L

Unit 42 Queens Court Trading Estate Greets Green Road, West Bromwich, B70 9EG
Tel: 0121-520 3291 **Fax:** 0121-520 2020
E-mail: sales@mdl-uk.com
Website: http://www.mdl-uk.com
Directors: M. Leighton (Prop)
Registration no: 06638833 **Date established:** 2008
No.of Employees: 1 - 10 **Product Groups:** 38, 42

M D S Architectural Fabrications Ltd

Unit 3a Brandon Way, West Bromwich, B70 8JB
Tel: 0121-525 3338 **Fax:** 0121- 5253348
E-mail: john.pardoe@mdsarchitectural.com
Website: http://www.mdsarchitectural.com
Directors: J. Pardoe (Dir)
Immediate Holding Company: MDS ARCHITECTURAL FABRICATIONS LIMITED
Registration no: 02137858 **Date established:** 1987 **Turnover:** £1m - £2m
No.of Employees: 11 - 20 **Product Groups:** 26, 35

Date of Accounts	Jun 11	Jun 10	Jun 09
Sales Turnover	1m	866	2m
Pre Tax Profit/Loss	26	-155	126
Working Capital	-111	-139	47
Fixed Assets	66	93	121
Current Assets	401	224	399
Current Liabilities	212	198	231

Midland Funeral Supplies Ltd

Unit 1-2 Richmond Street South, West Bromwich, B70 0DG
Tel: 0121-520 1815 **Fax:** 0121-520 1817
E-mail: stewart.jukes@midlandfuneralsupplies.co.uk
Website: http://www.midlandfuneralsupplies.co.uk
Bank(s): Barclays
Directors: S. Jukes (Prop)
Ultimate Holding Company: JUKES HOLDINGS LIMITED
Immediate Holding Company: MIDLAND FUNERAL SUPPLIES LIMITED
Registration no: 01342411 **VAT No.:** GB 054 3000 99
Date established: 1977 **Turnover:** £500,000 - £1m
No.of Employees: 11 - 20 **Product Groups:** 49

Date of Accounts	Dec 11	Dec 10	Dec 09
Working Capital	283	238	211
Fixed Assets	63	80	87
Current Assets	739	689	674

Midland Industrial Metals Ltd

Sams Lane, West Bromwich, B70 7ED
Tel: 0121-553 4321 **Fax:** 0121-500 6092
E-mail: info@mimltd.co.uk
Website: http://www.mimltd.co.uk
Managers: J. Foster (Mgr)
Immediate Holding Company: MIDLAND INDUSTRIAL METALS LIMITED
Registration no: 01325405 **Date established:** 1977
Turnover: £10m - £20m **No.of Employees:** 21 - 50 **Product Groups:** 34, 35, 54, 66

Date of Accounts	Nov 11	Nov 10	Nov 09
Sales Turnover	21m	20m	11m
Pre Tax Profit/Loss	216	967	436
Working Capital	2m	2m	1m
Fixed Assets	217	232	190
Current Assets	6m	7m	4m
Current Liabilities	113	605	334

Oak Mobility Ltd

14 Bustleholme Lane, West Bromwich, B71 3AP
Tel: 0845-111 0313
E-mail: customerservice@oakmobility.co.uk
Website: http://www.oakmobility.co.uk
Directors: S. Oakley (Fin)
Immediate Holding Company: OAK MOBILITY LIMITED
Registration no: 05511560 **Date established:** 2005
No.of Employees: 1 - 10 **Product Groups:** 67

Date of Accounts	Dec 07	Dec 06
Working Capital	5	1
Fixed Assets	1	N/A
Current Assets	14	10

Oaktree Packaging Ltd

Units 5 & 6 Church Lane, West Bromwich, B71 1AR
Tel: 0121-553 2754 **Fax:** 0121-500 5460
E-mail: info@mcarthur-group.com
Website: http://www.mcarthur-group.com
Bank(s): HSBC Bank plc
Directors: M. Osbourne (MD), D. McArthur (Ch), J. McArthur (Dir)
Managers: C. McVee
Ultimate Holding Company: Hall & Rice Ltd
Immediate Holding Company: MacArthur Group
Registration no: 00633330 **Date established:** 1959 **Turnover:** £1m - £2m
No.of Employees: 21 - 50 **Product Groups:** 35

Phoenix Scales Ltd

34 Oldbury Road, West Bromwich, B70 9ED
Tel: 08456-017464 **Fax:** 08456-024205
E-mail: sales@phoenixscales.co.uk
Website: http://www.phoenixscales.co.uk
Directors: J. Darroch (MD)
Ultimate Holding Company: PHOENIX SCALES HOLDINGS LIMITED
Immediate Holding Company: PHOENIX SCALES LIMITED
Registration no: 03918379 **Date established:** 2000
No.of Employees: 1 - 10 **Product Groups:** 38, 42

Date of Accounts	Feb 12	Feb 11	Feb 10
Working Capital	-85	-140	-102
Fixed Assets	459	481	395
Current Assets	218	149	107

Polmeric Mouldings Ltd (Polmeric Mouldings Ltd)

Unit 1 Spon Lane Trading Estate Varney Avenue, West Bromwich, B70 6AE
Tel: 0121-525 7887 **Fax:** 0121-500 6495
E-mail: fred.green@polmeric.co.uk
Website: http://www.pollmeric.co.uk
Bank(s): Bank of Ireland
Managers: F. Green (Chief Mgr)
Immediate Holding Company: POLMERIC MOULDINGS LIMITED
Registration no: FC012637 **VAT No.:** GB 409 4154 61
Date established: 1984 **Turnover:** £500,000 - £1m
No.of Employees: 11 - 20 **Product Groups:** 30, 39, 66

Date of Accounts	Jul 95	Jul 94	Jul 93
Sales Turnover	885	653	N/A
Pre Tax Profit/Loss	229	103	N/A
Working Capital	218	61	N/A
Fixed Assets	14	17	N/A
Current Assets	480	290	171
Current Liabilities	142	59	N/A

Power Plant Gears

1 Eagle Works Greets Green Road, West Bromwich, B70 9EJ
Tel: 0121-557 6334 **Fax:** 0121-520 0951
E-mail: uk@davidbrown.com
Website: http://www.davidbrown.com
Managers: I. Sumner (Works Gen Mgr)
Ultimate Holding Company: DAVID BROWN SPECIAL PRODUCTS LTD
Registration no: 02303060 **Date established:** 1992
No.of Employees: 1 - 10 **Product Groups:** 35, 39, 44

Date of Accounts	Dec 02
Fixed Assets	23
Total Share Capital	23

Premax Engineering Ltd

Unit 8 Swan Lane Industrial Estate Swan Lane, West Bromwich, B70 0NU
Tel: 0121-525 9716 **Fax:** 0121-525 4979
E-mail: matt@premax.co.uk
Website: http://www.premax.co.uk
Directors: M. Snaddon (MD)
Managers: M. Snaddon (Quality Control), G. Moore (Chief Mgr), I. Rochell (Works Gen Mgr), C. Hatfield (Tech Serv Mgr)
Immediate Holding Company: PREMAX ENGINEERING LIMITED
Registration no: 01647761 **VAT No.:** GB 377 4484 11
Date established: 1982 **Turnover:** £1m - £2m **No.of Employees:** 11 - 20
Product Groups: 38, 46, 48

Date of Accounts	Dec 11	Dec 10	Dec 09
Working Capital	418	346	344
Fixed Assets	239	241	245
Current Assets	633	472	472

Rhombus Castors Ltd

Gold Green Works Bagnall Street Golds Hill, West Bromwich, B70 0TS
Tel: 01455-633371 **Fax:** 01455-251204
E-mail: sales@rhombusuk.co.uk
Website: http://www.colson-castors.co.uk
Bank(s): Barclays, Bradford
Directors: F. Newey (MD), N. Bamford (MD), R. Lilly (Dir), S. Newey (MD), S. Peckham (Dir)
Managers: D. Hemsley (Comptroller), L. Turner (Sales Admin)
Immediate Holding Company: RHOMBUS CASTORS LIMITED
Registration no: 01562038 **VAT No.:** GB 184 4733 43
Date established: 1981 **Turnover:** £500,000 - £1m
No.of Employees: 51 - 100 **Product Groups:** 66

Date of Accounts	Mar 08	Mar 07	Mar 06
Sales Turnover	1139	1056	1178
Pre Tax Profit/Loss	-25	-31	56
Working Capital	917	938	941
Fixed Assets	6	10	17
Current Assets	1288	1228	1154
Current Liabilities	371	290	213
Total Share Capital	1	1	1
ROCE% (Return on Capital Employed)	-2.7	-3.3	5.8
ROT% (Return on Turnover)	-2.2	-2.9	4.8

Robinson Brothers Ltd

Phoenix Street, West Bromwich, B70 0AH
Tel: 0121-553 2451 **Fax:** 0121-500 5183
E-mail: enquiries@robinsonbrothers.co.uk
Website: http://www.rbltd.co.uk
Bank(s): Barclays
Directors: A. Hanrahan (MD), G. Parker (Fin)
Managers: J. Owens (Personnel), N. Smith (Tech Serv Mgr), P. Middleton (Purch Mgr)
Ultimate Holding Company: ROBINSON BROTHERS (RYDERS GREEN) LIMITED
Immediate Holding Company: ROBINSON BROTHERS LIMITED
Registration no: 00201053 **VAT No.:** GB 300 0247 39
Date established: 2024 **Turnover:** £20m - £50m
No.of Employees: 101 - 250 **Product Groups:** 31, 32

Date of Accounts	Dec 11	Dec 10	Dec 09
Sales Turnover	27m	23m	23m
Pre Tax Profit/Loss	865	-254	-492
Working Capital	7m	6m	5m
Fixed Assets	6m	7m	8m
Current Assets	11m	9m	9m
Current Liabilities	941	451	687

S & D Nonferrous Ltd

130 Roebuck Street, West Bromwich, B70 6RB
Tel: 0121-525 5500 **Fax:** 0121-525 3803
E-mail: sales@copperandbrass.co.uk
Website: http://www.sanddnonferrous.co.uk
Directors: A. Silvers (MD)
Immediate Holding Company: S & D (STORAGE AND DISTRIBUTION) LIMITED
Registration no: 02796261 **VAT No.:** GB 112 5420 23
Date established: 1993 **Turnover:** £2m - £5m **No.of Employees:** 1 - 10
Product Groups: 32

Sandwell Field Sports

13 Queens Court Trading Estate Greets Green Road, West Bromwich, B70 9EG
Tel: 0121-520 2000 **Fax:** 0121-520 9999
E-mail: sandwellfs@yahoo.co.uk
Website: http://www.sandwellfieldsports.co.uk
Directors: R. Stanton (Ptnr)
Date established: 1997 **No.of Employees:** 1 - 10 **Product Groups:** 36, 39, 40

Seagull Fittings Ltd

90 Roebuck Lane, West Bromwich, B70 6QX
Tel: 0121-525 0020 **Fax:** 0121-525 1116
E-mail: sales@seagullfittings.co.uk
Website: http://www.seagullfittings.co.uk
Directors: D. Worley (Ch), D. Worley (Fin), T. Warley (MD)
Managers: E. Cribbin (Purch Mgr), M. Fenton (Sales Admin)
Immediate Holding Company: SEAGULL FITTINGS LIMITED
Registration no: 02866634 **Date established:** 1993 **Turnover:** £1m - £2m
No.of Employees: 11 - 20 **Product Groups:** 30, 36

Date of Accounts	Oct 09	Oct 08	Oct 07
Working Capital	236	359	295
Fixed Assets	100	67	82
Current Assets	383	544	533

Simcron Food Machinery

Unit 20 Spartan Industrial Centre Brickhouse Lane, West Bromwich, B70 0DH
Tel: 0121-522 4061 **Fax:** 0121-522 4392
E-mail: info@simcron.co.uk
Website: http://www.simcron.co.uk
Directors: T. Cronin (Fin), S. Cronin (MD)
Immediate Holding Company: SIMCRON FOOD MACHINERY LIMITED
Registration no: 04286684 **Date established:** 2001
No.of Employees: 1 - 10 **Product Groups:** 20, 40, 41

Date of Accounts	Oct 11	Oct 10	Oct 09
Working Capital	4	42	18
Fixed Assets	11	14	18
Current Assets	189	225	130

Smethwick Maintenance Co. Ltd

336 Spon Lane South, West Bromwich, B70 6AZ
Tel: 0121-553 3941 **Fax:** 0121-553 5371
E-mail: enquiries@sis-group.co.uk
Website: http://www.sis-group.co.uk
Bank(s): Barclays, Smethwick
Directors: M. Cooper (Ch), S. Cox (Co Sec)
Ultimate Holding Company: SMETHWICK MAINTENANCE COMPANY LIMITED
Immediate Holding Company: SMETHWICK INDUSTRIAL SERVICES LIMITED
Registration no: 01081607 **Date established:** 1972 **Turnover:** £2m - £5m
No.of Employees: 11 - 20 **Product Groups:** 35, 48, 52

Date of Accounts	Nov 11	Nov 10	Nov 09
Working Capital	590	1m	2m
Fixed Assets	57	74	61
Current Assets	1m	2m	3m

Spire Group Ltd

Union Street, West Bromwich, B70 6DB
Tel: 0121-553 4446
Website: http://www.probusmayfair.co.uk
Directors: S. Jones (MD), S. Jones (Dir)
Immediate Holding Company: SPIRE GROUP LIMITED
Registration no: 03522780 **Date established:** 1998 **Turnover:** £5m - £10m
No.of Employees: 21 - 50 **Product Groups:** 23, 24, 48

Stainless & Alloy Products Ltd

Unit 8 Greets Green Road Industrial Estate Greets Green Road, West Bromwich, B70 9EW
Tel: 0121-557 0033 **Fax:** 0121-557 7775
E-mail: info@stainless-alloy.co.uk
Website: http://www.stainless-alloy.co.uk
Directors: C. Mcgoldrick (Dir)
Immediate Holding Company: STAINLESS & ALLOY PRODUCTS LIMITED
Registration no: 02181664 **VAT No.:** GB 478 6548 84
Date established: 1987 **Turnover:** £250,000 - £500,000
No.of Employees: 1 - 10 **Product Groups:** 48

Date of Accounts	Nov 11	Nov 10	Nov 09
Working Capital	121	112	126
Fixed Assets	17	25	33
Current Assets	206	171	215

Steel & Alloy Processing Ltd

Trafalgar Works Union Street, West Bromwich, B70 6BZ
Tel: 0121-553 5292 **Fax:** 0121-553 3864
E-mail: info@steelalloy.co.uk
Website: http://www.steelalloy.co.uk
Bank(s): Barclays
Directors: P. Whitehouse (Fin)
Managers: S. Watkins, S. Dean (Sales Prom Mgr), G. Jewkes (Tech Serv Mgr), M. Fleetwood (Personnel)
Ultimate Holding Company: STEEL & ALLOY HOLDINGS LIMITED
Immediate Holding Company: STEEL & ALLOY HOLDINGS LIMITED
Registration no: 03326521 **Date established:** 1997
Turnover: £125m - £250m **No.of Employees:** 101 - 250
Product Groups: 66

Date of Accounts	Mar 11	Mar 10	Mar 09
Sales Turnover	142m	106m	123m
Pre Tax Profit/Loss	2m	77	33
Working Capital	18m	16m	30m
Fixed Assets	8m	9m	10m
Current Assets	48m	36m	40m
Current Liabilities	5m	4m	2m

Steel Sections Warley Ltd

2 Howard Street, West Bromwich, B70 0ST
Tel: 0121-556 9111 **Fax:** 0121-502 5611
E-mail: sales@steelsections.co.uk
Website: http://www.steelsections.co.uk
Bank(s): Barclays, Birmingham
Directors: F. Evans (MD), T. Smith (Sales)
Managers: N. Jackson (Chief Acct)
Immediate Holding Company: STEEL SECTIONS (WARLEY) LIMITED
Registration no: 01301924 **VAT No.:** GB 300 1828 14
Date established: 1977 **Turnover:** £10m - £20m
No.of Employees: 21 - 50 **Product Groups:** 34, 35

Date of Accounts	Sep 11	Sep 10	Sep 09
Sales Turnover	13m	10m	9m
Pre Tax Profit/Loss	1m	642	278
Working Capital	5m	4m	4m
Fixed Assets	732	796	823
Current Assets	7m	6m	6m
Current Liabilities	521	447	260

Stephens Midlands Ltd

Unit 6 Greets Green Industrial Estate Greets Green Road, West Bromwich, B70 9EW
Tel: 0121-522 2221 **Fax:** 0116-286 4957
E-mail: info@stephenslube.co.uk
Website: http://www.stephenslube.co.uk

see next page

Stephens Midlands Ltd - Cont'd

Managers: P. Cherry (Chief Mgr)
Immediate Holding Company: SM (2012) REALISATIONS LIMITED
Registration no: 02687911 **VAT No.:** GB 610 8482 55
Date established: 1992 **Turnover:** £500,000 - £1m
No.of Employees: 1 - 10 **Product Groups:** 35, 36, 39, 40, 46

Date of Accounts	Sep 10	Sep 09	Sep 08
Working Capital	88	90	139
Fixed Assets	N/A	N/A	2
Current Assets	275	232	293

Styrotech Ltd

Unit 33 Phoenix International Industrial Estate Charles Street, West Bromwich, B70 0AY
Tel: 0121-520 6343 **Fax:** 0121-520 4851
E-mail: info@styrotech.uk.com
Website: http://www.styrotech.uk.com
Directors: B. Holton (MD), S. Hayes (Co Sec)
Immediate Holding Company: STYRO-TECH LIMITED
Registration no: 03664969 **Date established:** 1998
No.of Employees: 11 - 20 **Product Groups:** 30, 31, 49, 65

Date of Accounts	Dec 11	Dec 10	Dec 09
Working Capital	293	319	254
Fixed Assets	100	36	80
Current Assets	476	473	342

Surface Coatings

Unit 12c Izons Industrial Estate Oldbury Road, West Bromwich, B70 9BS
Tel: 0121-525 8788 **Fax:** 0121-525 8857
E-mail: p.stokes@blueyonder.co.uk
Website: http://www.surface-coatings.co.uk
Directors: P. Stokes (Prop)
Immediate Holding Company: SURFACE COATINGS (WEST BROMWICH) LIMITED
Registration no: 04780855 **Date established:** 2003
No.of Employees: 1 - 10 **Product Groups:** 46, 48

Date of Accounts	Aug 11	Aug 10	Aug 09
Working Capital	277	235	177
Fixed Assets	41	58	75
Current Assets	372	321	249

T R C Midlands Ltd

Mount Pleasant Street, West Bromwich, B70 7DL
Tel: 0121-500 6181 **Fax:** 0121-500 5075
E-mail: info@totalroofcontrol.co.uk
Website: http://www.totalroofcontrol.co.uk
Bank(s): Royal Bank of Scotland
Directors: S. Brown (Dir), S. Brown (Dir)
Immediate Holding Company: T.R.C. (MIDLANDS) LIMITED
Registration no: 01314915 **VAT No.:** GB 559 5115 23
Date established: 1977 **Turnover:** £1m - £2m **No.of Employees:** 11 - 20
Product Groups: 52

Date of Accounts	Apr 11	Apr 10	Apr 09
Working Capital	169	123	126
Fixed Assets	44	69	72
Current Assets	359	337	233

Technical Glass Ltd

Kelvin Way, West Bromwich, B70 7LB
Tel: 0121-553 3334 **Fax:** 0121-553 3336
E-mail: technicalglass@btclick.com
Website: http://www.technicalglass.net
Directors: S. Cutler (MD), S. Farmer (Ch), S. Farmer (Fin)
Managers: M. Williams (Sales Prom Mgr), C. Farmer (Personnel), L. Redshaw (Accounts)
Immediate Holding Company: TECHNICAL GLASS LIMITED
Registration no: 01333138 **VAT No.:** GB 313 9962 42
Date established: 1977 **Turnover:** £1m - £2m **No.of Employees:** 21 - 50
Product Groups: 33

Date of Accounts	Dec 09	Dec 08	Dec 07
Working Capital	-99	99	129
Fixed Assets	601	711	822
Current Assets	462	745	765

Tentec Ltd

Plymouth House Guns Lane, West Bromwich, B70 9HS
Tel: 0121-524 1990 **Fax:** 0121-525 1999
E-mail: sales@tentec.net
Website: http://www.tentec.net
Bank(s): National Westminster Bank Plc
Directors: M. Gethings (MD), R. Sheldon (Sales)
Managers: S. Chambers
Immediate Holding Company: TENTEC LIMITED
Registration no: 02269292 **VAT No.:** GB 487 1201 49
Date established: 1988 **Turnover:** £2m - £5m **No.of Employees:** 21 - 50
Product Groups: 35, 36, 37, 40, 45, 47, 48

Date of Accounts	Dec 11	Dec 10	Dec 09
Sales Turnover	8m	N/A	N/A
Pre Tax Profit/Loss	368	N/A	N/A
Working Capital	1m	639	218
Fixed Assets	2m	1m	1m
Current Assets	3m	2m	2m
Current Liabilities	395	N/A	N/A

3 Dimensional

244 Bromford Lane, West Bromwich, B70 7HX
Tel: 0121-525 5599 **Fax:** 0121-525 3644
E-mail: sales@3dimensional.co.uk
Website: http://www.3dimensional.co.uk
Directors: J. Callaghan (MD)
Immediate Holding Company: 3 DIMENSIONAL LIMITED
Registration no: 04301086 **Date established:** 2001
No.of Employees: 11 - 20 **Product Groups:** 34, 39, 46, 48

Date of Accounts	Jan 12	Jan 11	Jan 10
Working Capital	-146	-153	-160
Fixed Assets	478	352	387
Current Assets	408	251	192

Titanium Metals UK Ltd

206 Great Bridge Street Great Bridge, West Bromwich, B70 0DE
Tel: 0121-557 7557 **Fax:** 0121-557 7556
E-mail: bal@titaniummetals.co.uk
Website: http://www.titaniummetals.co.uk
Directors: B. Singh (MD)
Immediate Holding Company: TITANIUM METALS UK LIMITED
Registration no: 04776512 **Date established:** 2003
No.of Employees: 1 - 10 **Product Groups:** 34, 35, 36

Date of Accounts	Dec 11	Dec 10	Dec 09
Working Capital	356	243	213
Fixed Assets	60	64	60
Current Assets	569	450	325

E W Turner & Co. Ltd

Shaw Street, West Bromwich, B70 0TX
Tel: 0121-556 1141 **Fax:** 0121-556 3911
E-mail: sales@ewturner.co.uk
Website: http://www.ewturner.co.uk
Bank(s): Lloyds TSB Bank plc
Directors: N. Clarke (MD)
Immediate Holding Company: E W TURNER AND COMPANY LIMITED
Registration no: 03497066 **Date established:** 1998
Turnover: £250,000 - £500,000 **No.of Employees:** 11 - 20
Product Groups: 25, 45

Date of Accounts	Mar 11	Mar 10	Mar 09
Working Capital	74	90	102
Fixed Assets	130	98	103
Current Assets	540	510	399
Current Liabilities	N/A	65	N/A

Valbruna UK Ltd (Head Office)

Oldbury Road, West Bromwich, B70 9BT
Tel: 0121-553 5384 **Fax:** 0121-500 5095
E-mail: philip.wood@valbruna-uk.com
Website: http://www.valbruna-uk.com
Bank(s): Barclays
Directors: V. Viero (Co Sec), P. Wood (MD)
Managers: C. Hunter (Tech Serv Mgr), M. Dean (Personnel)
Ultimate Holding Company: AMENDUNI ACCIAIO SPA (ITALY)
Immediate Holding Company: VALBRUNA UK LIMITED
Registration no: 02015096 **VAT No.:** GB 441 7292 54
Date established: 1986 **Turnover:** £20m - £50m
No.of Employees: 21 - 50 **Product Groups:** 34, 35

Date of Accounts	Dec 11	Dec 10	Dec 09
Sales Turnover	31m	24m	20m
Pre Tax Profit/Loss	1m	632	35
Working Capital	10m	7m	4m
Fixed Assets	4m	4m	4m
Current Assets	24m	20m	18m
Current Liabilities	1m	904	311

W S S Couriers

6 Vale Street, West Bromwich, B71 4DN
Tel: 0121-553 7718 **Fax:** 0121-553 6041
E-mail: steve@stevejukes9.wanadoo.co.uk
Directors: S. Jukes (Prop), S. Jukes (Dir)
Date established: 1994 **No.of Employees:** 1 - 10 **Product Groups:** 79

West Bromwich Building Society

374 High Street, West Bromwich, B70 8LR
Tel: 08453-300611 **Fax:** 0161-237 5448
E-mail: mark.brayford@westbrom.co.uk
Website: http://www.westbrom.co.uk
Directors: J. Westhoff (Grp Chief Exec), R. Hopwood (Div)
Managers: M. Brayford (Sales Admin), P. Collinbridge (Tech Serv Mgr), J. Randle (Personnel), S. Hemmings (Mktg Serv Mgr)
Ultimate Holding Company: WEST BROMWICH BUILDING SOCIETY
Immediate Holding Company: WEST BROMWICH FINANCIAL SERVICES LIMITED
Registration no: 09000246 **Date established:** 2001 **Turnover:** £2m - £5m
No.of Employees: 1 - 10 **Product Groups:** 82

Date of Accounts	Mar 11	Mar 10	Mar 09
Sales Turnover	5m	5m	6m
Pre Tax Profit/Loss	-2m	204	-13m
Working Capital	-2m	2m	3m
Fixed Assets	114m	116m	114m
Current Assets	2m	2m	3m
Current Liabilities	3m	212	309

West Bromwich Sheet Metal Ltd

Unit 37 Siddons Factory Estate Howard Street, West Bromwich, B70 0SU
Tel: 0121-556 9120 **Fax:** 0121-556 9120
Directors: R. Woodley (MD), H. Woodley (Fin)
Immediate Holding Company: WEST BROMWICH SHEET METAL LIMITED
Registration no: 01762075 **VAT No.:** GB 388 6570 92
Date established: 1983 **Turnover:** Up to £250,000
No.of Employees: 1 - 10 **Product Groups:** 48

Date of Accounts	Oct 11	Oct 10	Oct 09
Working Capital	-2	3	19
Fixed Assets	5	7	9
Current Assets	32	98	107

West Midlands Foundry Co. Ltd

Blakemore Road, West Bromwich, B70 8JF
Tel: 0121-553 1515 **Fax:** 0121-500 5839
Bank(s): HSBC
Directors: M. Backhouse (MD)
Immediate Holding Company: WEST MIDLANDS FOUNDRY CO. LIMITED
Registration no: 00734214 **VAT No.:** GB 277 1753 33
Date established: 1962 **Turnover:** £1m - £2m **No.of Employees:** 11 - 20
Product Groups: 34

Date of Accounts	Sep 11	Sep 10	Sep 09
Working Capital	554	598	600
Fixed Assets	575	577	602
Current Assets	807	809	863

Woods & Hughes Bolts & Screws Ltd (Incorperating Taylor Embex Fasteners)

Unit 9 Hill Top Industrial Estate, West Bromwich, B70 0TX
Tel: 0121-505 7551 **Fax:** 0121-505 7652
E-mail: sales@socketscrews.co.uk
Website: http://www.socketscrews.co.uk
Bank(s): HSBC
Managers: G. Hardeman (Comm)
Registration no: 02263316 **VAT No.:** GB 488 2866 83
Date established: 1988 **Turnover:** £1m - £2m **No.of Employees:** 11 - 20
Product Groups: 35

Date of Accounts	Apr 08	Apr 07	Apr 06
Working Capital	-38	-41	-21
Fixed Assets	74	94	117
Current Assets	645	568	601
Current Liabilities	683	610	622
Total Share Capital	1	1	2

Wrights Plastics

Brandon Way, West Bromwich, B70 8JH
Tel: 0121-580 3080 **Fax:** 0121-580 3081
E-mail: sales@wrightsplastics.co.uk
Website: http://www.wrightsplastics.co.uk
Bank(s): HSBC
Directors: J. Wright (Dir), M. Wright (MD)
Managers: B. Jones, A. Watkins (Comm), P. Duke (Sales Prom Mgr)
Immediate Holding Company: WRIGHTS PLASTICS LIMITED
Registration no: 02108847 **VAT No.:** GB 100 6764 05
Date established: 1987 **Turnover:** £2m - £5m **No.of Employees:** 21 - 50
Product Groups: 30

Date of Accounts	Apr 11	Apr 10	Apr 09
Sales Turnover	4m	3m	3m
Pre Tax Profit/Loss	-3	48	288
Working Capital	2m	3m	3m
Fixed Assets	1m	903	902
Current Assets	3m	3m	3m
Current Liabilities	201	99	210

Willenhall

A J M Metal Polishing Co

A J M Buildings Villiers Street, Willenhall, WV13 1DF
Tel: 01902-630511 **Fax:** 01902- 630511
Directors: G. Marsh (Snr Part)
Date established: 1987 **No.of Employees:** 1 - 10 **Product Groups:** 46, 48

Adams Rite Europe Ltd

School Street, Willenhall, WV13 3PW
Tel: 0845-873 4837 **Fax:** 0845-8734839
E-mail: info@adamsrite.co.uk
Website: http://www.adamsrite.co.uk
Bank(s): Barclays
Directors: A. Swan (MD), I. Mackay (Ch), K. Gallon (Co Sec), L. Kitson-Harris (Fin)
Managers: T. Ainsworth (Mktg Serv Mgr)
Ultimate Holding Company: ASSA ABLOY AB (PUBL) (SWEDEN)
Registration no: 01217948 **VAT No.:** GB 207 0718 89
Date established: 1975 **Turnover:** £5m - £10m **No.of Employees:** 21 - 50
Product Groups: 36

Date of Accounts	Dec 07	Dec 06	Sep 05
Sales Turnover	7765	8147	6314
Pre Tax Profit/Loss	685	595	718
Working Capital	4601	4058	3656
Fixed Assets	185	254	250
Current Assets	5756	4842	4525
Current Liabilities	1155	784	869
Total Share Capital	50	50	50
ROCE% (Return on Capital Employed)	14.3	13.8	18.4
ROT% (Return on Turnover)	8.8	7.3	11.4

Assaabloy Group

Portebello Works School Street, Willenhall, WV13 3PW
Tel: 01902-366911 **Fax:** 01902-368535
E-mail: john.middleton@assaabloyuk.com
Website: http://www.assaabloyuk.com
Bank(s): National Westminster
Directors: S. Merry (Tech Serv), C. Bailey (Fin)
Managers: A. Cooper (Personnel), J. Middleton, R. Roberts (Buyer)
Ultimate Holding Company: ASSA ABLOY AB (PUBL) (SWEDEN)
Immediate Holding Company: ASSA ABLOY (UK) PENSION TRUSTEES LIMITED
Registration no: 04007863 **VAT No.:** GB 439 4758 08
Date established: 2000 **Turnover:** £75m - £125m
No.of Employees: 251 - 500 **Product Groups:** 36

Aural Plastics Ltd

134 Victoria Street, Willenhall, WV13 1DW
Tel: 01902-607412 **Fax:** 01902-606938
Website: http://www.ukf.net
Directors: R. Dixon (Dir), R. Dixon (Jt MD), C. Bateson (MD), C. Bateson (Fin)
Immediate Holding Company: AURAL PLASTICS LIMITED
Registration no: 01677974 **VAT No.:** GB 559 4429 05
Date established: 1982 **Turnover:** Up to £250,000
No.of Employees: 1 - 10 **Product Groups:** 32

Date of Accounts	Sep 09	Sep 08	Sep 07
Working Capital	12	17	28
Fixed Assets	73	74	75
Current Assets	48	53	54

B & G Lock & Tool Company Ltd

Chapel Green, Willenhall, WV13 1RD
Tel: 01902-605946 **Fax:** 01902-633794
E-mail: sales@bgpadlocks.co.uk
Website: http://www.bgpadlocks.co.uk
Directors: D. Bate (Fab)
Immediate Holding Company: B.& G.LOCK & TOOL CO.LIMITED
Registration no: 00505123 **Date established:** 1952
No.of Employees: 21 - 50 **Product Groups:** 36

Date of Accounts	Mar 12	Mar 11	Mar 10
Working Capital	916	728	635
Fixed Assets	42	8	2
Current Assets	1m	993	921

Barpoint Ltd

Willenhall Trading Estate Midacre, Willenhall, WV13 2JW
Tel: 01902-608021 **Fax:** 01902-601652
E-mail: sales@barpointltd.com
Website: http://www.barpointltd.com
Bank(s): Lloyds TSB
Directors: P. Hall (MD), C. Barker (Dir)
Managers: J. Colbourn (Sales Prom Mgr)
Ultimate Holding Company: CHROMELABEL LIMITED
Immediate Holding Company: BARPOINT LIMITED
Registration no: 01342503 **VAT No.:** GB 313 6854 60
Date established: 1977 **Turnover:** £1m - £2m **No.of Employees:** 11 - 20
Product Groups: 34

Date of Accounts	Jan 12	Jan 11	Jan 10
Working Capital	721	758	840
Fixed Assets	19	30	26
Current Assets	1m	2m	2m
Current Liabilities	393	454	405

A F Blakemore & Son Ltd

Longacre Industrial Estate, Willenhall, WV13 2JP
Tel: 01902-366066 **Fax:** 01902-602361
E-mail: ghallam@afblakemore.com
Website: http://www.afblakemore.com

Directors: G. Hallam (MD), S. Munroe-morris (Fin)
Managers: M. Walton (Purch Mgr)
Immediate Holding Company: A.F.BLAKEMORE AND SON LIMITED
Registration no: 00391135 **Date established:** 1944
Turnover: £500m - £1,000m **No.of Employees:** 1501 & over
Product Groups: 61

Date of Accounts	Apr 11	Apr 10	Apr 09
Sales Turnover	912m	816m	779m
Pre Tax Profit/Loss	10m	9m	9m
Working Capital	14m	33m	19m
Fixed Assets	119m	68m	65m
Current Assets	162m	132m	130m
Current Liabilities	42m	27m	22m

Bollhoss Fastenings Ltd

Midacre Willenhall Trading Estate Midacre, Willenhall, WV13 2JW
Tel: 01902-637161 **Fax:** 01902-609495
E-mail: enquiries@bollhoff.co.uk
Website: http://www.bollhoss.com
Bank(s): Lloyds TSB Bank plc
Managers: W. Webb (I.T. Exec)
Ultimate Holding Company: WILHELM BOLLHOFF GMBH & CO KG (GERMANY)
Immediate Holding Company: BOLLHOFF FASTENINGS LIMITED
Registration no: 01856255 **Date established:** 1984 **Turnover:** £5m - £10m
No.of Employees: 11 - 20 **Product Groups:** 30, 35, 36, 37, 39, 46, 66

Date of Accounts	Dec 11	Dec 10	Dec 09
Working Capital	1000	902	727
Fixed Assets	27	36	33
Current Assets	2m	2m	1m

Brookside Metal Co. Ltd

28 Bilston Lane, Willenhall, WV13 2QE
Tel: 01902-365500 **Fax:** 01902-636671
E-mail: ian.kirk@brooksidemetal.com
Website: http://www.brooksidemetal.com
Bank(s): Barclays
Directors: R. Payne (Sales & Mktg)
Managers: I. Kirk (Ops Mgr)
Ultimate Holding Company: AMCO INVESTMENTS LIMITED
Immediate Holding Company: BROOKSIDE METAL COMPANY LIMITED
Registration no: 03059787 **VAT No.:** GB 366 9963 84
Date established: 1995 **Turnover:** £50m - £75m
No.of Employees: 51 - 100 **Product Groups:** 31, 34

Date of Accounts	Dec 11	Dec 10	Dec 09
Sales Turnover	67m	47m	32m
Pre Tax Profit/Loss	174	-977	9
Working Capital	3m	3m	3m
Fixed Assets	3m	3m	3m
Current Assets	18m	19m	12m
Current Liabilities	266	1m	175

Central Pattern Making Ltd

Stringes Lane, Willenhall, WV13 1LU
Tel: 01902-605205 **Fax:** 01902-366009
E-mail: mjs@centralpatternmaking.co.uk
Website: http://www.centralpatternmaking.co.uk
Directors: M. Sawbridge (MD)
Immediate Holding Company: CENTRAL PATTERNMAKING LIMITED
Registration no: 01245144 **Date established:** 1976
No.of Employees: 21 - 50 **Product Groups:** 48

Date of Accounts	Nov 11	Nov 10	Nov 09
Working Capital	698	582	433
Fixed Assets	1m	1m	799
Current Assets	1m	1m	1m
Current Liabilities	7	7	6

Clarydon Electronics Services Ltd

Unit 2-2a Strawberry Lane, Willenhall, WV13 3RS
Tel: 01902-606000 **Fax:** 01902-606868
E-mail: sales@clarydon.com
Website: http://www.clarydon.com
Directors: S. Stockley (MD)
Ultimate Holding Company: RALPH MARTINDALE AND COMPANY LIMITED
Immediate Holding Company: M. A. C. (WILLENHALL) LIMITED
Registration no: 03005967 **Date established:** 2003
No.of Employees: 11 - 20 **Product Groups:** 37, 84

Date of Accounts	Jul 11	Jul 10	Jul 09
Sales Turnover	N/A	63	104
Pre Tax Profit/Loss	N/A	1	14
Working Capital	N/A	14	13
Fixed Assets	1	2	2
Current Assets	11	19	25

Clesse UK Ltd

8 Planetary Industrial Estate Planetary Road, Willenhall, WV13 3XQ
Tel: 01902-383233 **Fax:** 01902-383234
E-mail: sales@clesse.co.uk
Website: http://www.clesse.co.uk
Directors: K. Dzialarski (MD), N. Ormord (Sales), B. Hadacek (Sales)
Managers: N. Ormrod (Sales & Mktg Mg), K. Dziamarski (Sales & Mktg Mg)
Immediate Holding Company: CLESSE (UK) LIMITED
Registration no: 04535858 **Date established:** 2002 **Turnover:** £2m - £5m
No.of Employees: 1 - 10 **Product Groups:** 36

Clydesdale Jones Ltd

Neachells Lane, Willenhall, WV13 3SJ
Tel: 01902-308000 **Fax:** 01902-308047
E-mail: sales@clydesdale-jones.com
Website: http://www.clydesdale-jones.com
Bank(s): Barclays
Directors: T. Collins (Dir), P. Pearson (Fin)
Managers: I. Underhill (Buyer), D. Keats (Tech Serv Mgr)
Immediate Holding Company: ASKEY PRECISION ENGINEERING LIMITED
Registration no: 03295047 **VAT No.:** GB 245 2598 47
Date established: 1996 **Turnover:** £2m - £5m **No.of Employees:** 51 - 100
Product Groups: 39

Date of Accounts	Mar 12	Mar 11	Mar 10
Working Capital	213	195	236
Fixed Assets	460	364	294
Current Assets	744	547	566

Cold Rolled Strip Stock

Charles Street, Willenhall, WV13 1HG
Tel: 01902-365434 **Fax:** 01902-365435
E-mail: uksales@dscm.co.uk
Website: http://www.dscm.co.uk
Directors: K. Taylor (Dir)
Registration no: 5234781 **Date established:** 1995 **Turnover:** £1m - £2m
No.of Employees: 1 - 10 **Product Groups:** 34

Colter Steels Ltd

Unit 10 Owen Road Industrial Estate, Willenhall, WV13 2PY
Tel: 0121-526 6066 **Fax:** 0121-526 3044
E-mail: sales@coltersteels.co.uk
Website: http://www.coltersteels.co.uk
Directors: S. Smallman (Dir)
Ultimate Holding Company: COLTER STEELS HOLDINGS LIMITED
Immediate Holding Company: COLTER STEELS LIMITED
Registration no: 01585791 **Date established:** 1981
No.of Employees: 1 - 10 **Product Groups:** 34, 66, 77

Date of Accounts	Nov 11	Nov 10	Nov 09
Working Capital	434	525	399
Fixed Assets	47	50	57
Current Assets	1m	1m	843

Comar Engineering Services Ltd

D Key Industrial Park Fernside Road, Willenhall, WV13 3YA
Tel: 01902-383000 **Fax:** 01902-739430
E-mail: graham@comarfluidpower.com
Website: http://www.comarfluidpower.com
Bank(s): National Westminster Bank Plc
Directors: G. Martin (MD), S. Martin (Fin)
Immediate Holding Company: COMAR ENGINEERING SERVICES LIMITED
Registration no: 01406705 **Date established:** 1978 **Turnover:** £1m - £2m
No.of Employees: 11 - 20 **Product Groups:** 38

Date of Accounts	Jun 11	Jun 10	Jun 09
Working Capital	96	208	31
Fixed Assets	321	58	45
Current Assets	2m	978	578

Davenport Burgess

47 Wednesfield Road, Willenhall, WV13 1AL
Tel: 01902-366448 **Fax:** 01902-602472
E-mail: jenny@davenport-burgess.com
Website: http://www.davenport-burgess.com
Bank(s): Lloyds TSB Bank plc
Directors: J. Davenport (MD), S. Davenport (Sales), J. Davenport (Dir)
Ultimate Holding Company: 01026710
Immediate Holding Company: DAVENPORT BURGESS LIMITED
Registration no: 00195145 **VAT No.:** GB 100 2825 31
Date established: 1924 **Turnover:** £2m - £5m **No.of Employees:** 21 - 50
Product Groups: 36

Date of Accounts	Dec 09	Dec 08	Dec 07
Working Capital	22	22	22
Current Assets	22	22	22

Diode Electrics Ltd

King Street, Willenhall, WV13 1QT
Tel: 01902-608125 **Fax:** 01902-633694
E-mail: stuart@diodeelectrics.co.uk
Website: http://www.diodeelectricsltd.co.uk
Directors: S. Clews (MD)
Immediate Holding Company: DIODE ELECTRICS LIMITED
Registration no: 04659974 **Date established:** 2003
No.of Employees: 1 - 10 **Product Groups:** 35, 39, 45

Date of Accounts	Sep 11	Sep 10	Sep 09
Working Capital	308	274	322
Fixed Assets	30	38	49
Current Assets	362	340	390

Ductile Stourbridge Cold Mills Ltd

Charles Street, Willenhall, WV13 1HG
Tel: 01902-365400 **Fax:** 01902-365444
E-mail: uksales@dscm.co.uk
Website: http://www.dscm.co.uk
Bank(s): Midland, Birmingham
Directors: K. Taylor (Dir), R. Lane (Fin)
Managers: S. Moore (Personnel), M. Banks (Sales Prom Mgr), C. Jones (Tech Serv Mgr)
Immediate Holding Company: TYCO INTERNATIONAL LTD
Registration no: 00533160 **VAT No.:** GB 388 6658 78
Date established: 1987 **Turnover:** £5m - £10m **No.of Employees:** 21 - 50
Product Groups: 34

Ecotex Coatings Ltd

Orion House Harper Street, Willenhall, WV13 1SW
Tel: 01902-366196 **Fax:** 01902-366197
Website: http://www.ecotexcoating.co.uk
Directors: C. Wright (Fin)
Immediate Holding Company: ECOTEX COATINGS LIMITED
Registration no: 02997527 **Date established:** 1994
No.of Employees: 1 - 10 **Product Groups:** 46, 48

Date of Accounts	Dec 09	Dec 08	Dec 07
Working Capital	-52	-18	-14
Fixed Assets	9	11	12
Current Assets	46	81	126

Era Products Ltd

Straight Road, Willenhall, WV12 5RA
Tel: 01922-490049 **Fax:** 01922-494420
E-mail: davidh@era-security.com
Website: http://www.era-security.com
Bank(s): HSBC Bank plc
Directors: D. Hill (Sales), L. Coleman (Pers)
Managers: S. Lloyd, S. Smith (Fin Mgr), B. Williams (Purch Mgr)
Ultimate Holding Company: LUPUS CAPITAL PLC
Immediate Holding Company: ERA PRODUCTS LIMITED
Registration no: 00342771 **Date established:** 1938
Turnover: £10m - £20m **No.of Employees:** 51 - 100 **Product Groups:** 36

Date of Accounts	Dec 11	Dec 10	Dec 08
Pre Tax Profit/Loss	N/A	266	N/A
Working Capital	2m	2m	2m
Fixed Assets	N/A	N/A	952
Current Assets	2m	2m	2m

Ercon Group Ltd

Midacre Block C, Willenhall, WV13 2JW
Tel: 01902-601312 **Fax:** 01902-605081
E-mail: mail@ercongroup.com
Website: http://www.ercongroup.com
Bank(s): Barclays
Directors: C. Waterhouse (Sales), M. Green (Chief Op Offcr)
Ultimate Holding Company: ERCON FINISHING SYSTEMS LIMITED
Immediate Holding Company: ERCON METAL FINISHING SYSTEMS LIMITED
Registration no: 01385618 **VAT No.:** GB 489 5560 86
Date established: 1978 **Turnover:** £1m - £2m **No.of Employees:** 21 - 50
Product Groups: 38, 45

Date of Accounts	Mar 11	Mar 10	Mar 09
Working Capital	3	3	3
Current Assets	3	3	3

Essential Equipment Ltd

Unit 24 Planetary Industrial Estate Planetary Road, Willenhall, WV13 3XA
Tel: 01902-725055 **Fax:** 01902-862684
E-mail: info@essentialequipment.co.uk
Website: http://www.essentialequipment.co.uk
Directors: B. Davis (MD)
Immediate Holding Company: ESSENTIAL EQUIPMENT LIMITED
Registration no: 02755222 **Date established:** 1992 **Turnover:** £1m - £2m
No.of Employees: 1 - 10 **Product Groups:** 29

Date of Accounts	May 11	May 10	May 09
Working Capital	322	282	285
Fixed Assets	64	75	85
Current Assets	680	721	643

Eurofast Petrochemical Supplies Ltd

Unit 30 Planetary Industrial Estate Planetary Road, Willenhall, WV13 3XA
Tel: 01902-307788 **Fax:** 01902-307744
E-mail: brianw@eurofast.co.uk
Website: http://www.eurofast.co.uk
Bank(s): Bank of Wales PLC
Directors: P. Lawton (Co Sec), B. Williams (MD)
Managers: K. Godbold (Sales Prom Mgr), L. Wynn (Buyer)
Ultimate Holding Company: LSP HOLDING SARL (LUXEMBOURG)
Immediate Holding Company: EUROFAST PETROCHEMICAL SUPPLIES LIMITED
Registration no: 01952397 **VAT No.:** GB 489 7836 61
Date established: 1985 **Turnover:** £10m - £20m
No.of Employees: 101 - 250 **Product Groups:** 30, 35, 36, 66

Date of Accounts	Dec 11	Dec 10	Dec 09
Sales Turnover	12m	10m	9m
Pre Tax Profit/Loss	2m	1m	856
Working Capital	7m	6m	5m
Fixed Assets	726	637	580
Current Assets	8m	7m	7m
Current Liabilities	461	668	547

F T L Foundry Equipment Ltd

6-11 Riley Street, Willenhall, WV13 1RH
Tel: 01902-630222 **Fax:** 01902-636593
E-mail: sales@ftl-foundry.co.uk
Website: http://www.ftl-foundry.co.uk
Bank(s): The Royal Bank of Scotland
Directors: B. Griffiths (Comm)
Managers: M. Horton (Buyer)
Immediate Holding Company: F T L FOUNDRY EQUIPMENT LIMITED
Registration no: 02035882 **Date established:** 1986 **Turnover:** £2m - £5m
No.of Employees: 21 - 50 **Product Groups:** 40, 42, 46

Date of Accounts	Dec 10	Dec 09	Dec 08
Working Capital	373	419	371
Fixed Assets	79	92	107
Current Assets	1m	1m	2m

Falcon Grinding Co. Ltd

Ann Street, Willenhall, WV13 1EN
Tel: 01902-601478 **Fax:** 01902-606055
E-mail: antony.johnson@wrr-pedley.com
Website: http://www.falcongrinding.co.uk
Directors: A. Johnson (Dir)
Immediate Holding Company: FALCON GRINDING CO. LIMITED
Registration no: 01373316 **VAT No.:** GB 101 9946 75
Date established: 1978 **No.of Employees:** 1 - 10 **Product Groups:** 48

Date of Accounts	Sep 11	Sep 10	Sep 09
Working Capital	21	29	51
Fixed Assets	9	11	12
Current Assets	113	111	110

Flexo Trade Print

Unit 6 Owen Road Industrial Estate, Willenhall, WV13 2PY
Tel: 0121-526 4779 **Fax:** 0121-568 7870
E-mail: info@flexotradeprint.co.uk
Website: http://www.flexotradeprint.co.uk
Managers: A. Wilcox (Mgr)
Turnover: Up to £250,000 **No.of Employees:** 1 - 10 **Product Groups:** 28, 44

G E A Industrial Services Ltd

John Harper Street, Willenhall, WV13 1RE
Tel: 01902-604111 **Fax:** 01902-607356
E-mail: smith.pat@gea-industrialservices.com
Website: http://www.gea-industrialservices.com
Bank(s): National Westminster
Directors: M. Smith (Fin), J. Gattley (Co Sec), P. Smith (Dir), P. Smith (MD), M. Smith (Co Sec)
Ultimate Holding Company: GEA GROUP AG (GERMANY)
Immediate Holding Company: GEA INDUSTRIAL SERVICES LIMITED
Registration no: 03182511 **Date established:** 1996 **Turnover:** £2m - £5m
No.of Employees: 21 - 50 **Product Groups:** 30, 40

Date of Accounts	Dec 09	Dec 08	Mar 08
Sales Turnover	3m	2m	N/A
Pre Tax Profit/Loss	-204	-154	N/A
Working Capital	-90	49	162
Fixed Assets	42	58	69
Current Assets	943	720	794
Current Liabilities	210	228	N/A

Accura Geometric Ltd

Stringes Close, Willenhall, WV13 1NS
Tel: 01902-606206 **Fax:** 01902-609517
E-mail: mike@geometric.co.uk
Website: http://www.geometric.co.uk
Bank(s): Lloyds TSB Bank plc
Directors: M. Richards (MD)
Managers: M. Harper (Develop Mgr), M. Barnett (Comptroller), J. Ellis (Works Gen Mgr)
Ultimate Holding Company: ACCURA GROUP LIMITED
Immediate Holding Company: ACCURA GEOMETRIC LIMITED
Registration no: 01442283 **Date established:** 1979 **Turnover:** £2m - £5m
No.of Employees: 51 - 100 **Product Groups:** 46, 47, 48, 84

Date of Accounts	Mar 11	Mar 10	Mar 09
Working Capital	1m	1m	954
Fixed Assets	358	353	440
Current Assets	3m	2m	2m

Grenadier Guard Security
Planetary Road, Willenhall, WV13 3SW
Tel: 01902-866499 **Fax:** 01902-866455
Website: http://www.grenadiersecurity.co.uk
Directors: S. Taylor (Dir)
Ultimate Holding Company: THE W S B GROUP LIMITED
Immediate Holding Company: UNIVERSAL COATINGS (WSB) LIMITED
Registration no: 04943657 **Date established:** 2005
No.of Employees: 1 - 10 **Product Groups:** 35, 81

Hewden Hire Centres Ltd
Ashmore Lake Way Ashmore Lake Industrial Estate, Willenhall, WV12 4LF
Tel: 01902-608666 **Fax:** 01902-606555
E-mail: jon.hatton@hewden.co.uk
Website: http://www.hewden.co.uk
Managers: J. Hatton, G. Buchan
Ultimate Holding Company: FP053669
Immediate Holding Company: DESIGNED CONSTRUCTION LIMITED
Registration no: SC046005 **Date established:** 2009
Turnover: £20m - £50m **No.of Employees:** 51 - 100 **Product Groups:** 83

Date of Accounts	Sep 11	Sep 10	Sep 09
Working Capital	306	257	233
Fixed Assets	79	46	49
Current Assets	633	533	390

Holland Engineering Midlands Ltd
Ashmore Lake Road, Willenhall, WV12 4LB
Tel: 01902-632424 **Fax:** 01902-604526
E-mail: contactholland@aol.com
Website: http://www.hollandengineeringmidlands.com
Bank(s): Barclays
Directors: D. Hoskins (Chief Op Offcr), D. Hyde (Dir)
Immediate Holding Company: HOLLAND ENGINEERING (MIDLANDS) LIMITED
Registration no: 06867912 **Date established:** 2009
Turnover: £500,000 - £1m **No.of Employees:** 21 - 50 **Product Groups:** 46

Date of Accounts	Apr 11	Apr 10
Working Capital	-72	-43
Fixed Assets	35	31
Current Assets	78	100

Hopton Engineering Ltd
Unit 8-9 Tractor Spares Industrial Estate Strawberry Lane, Willenhall, WV13 3RN
Tel: 01902-606336 **Fax:** 01902-607339
E-mail: hopton.eng@virgin.net
Directors: D. Marriott (Tech Serv)
Immediate Holding Company: HOPTON ENGINEERING LIMITED
Registration no: 02775088 **Date established:** 1992
Turnover: £250,000 - £500,000 **No.of Employees:** 1 - 10
Product Groups: 26, 28, 38, 67

Date of Accounts	Dec 11	Dec 10	Dec 09
Working Capital	152	84	55
Fixed Assets	76	74	82
Current Assets	260	196	200

Edward Howell Galvanizers Ltd (Wedge Group Galvanizing)
Watery Lane, Willenhall, WV13 3SU
Tel: 01902-637463 **Fax:** 01902-630923
E-mail: edward.howell@wedge-galv.co.uk
Website: http://www.wedge-galv.co.uk
Bank(s): HSBC Bank plc
Directors: D. Lynam (Fin), T. Beech (Sales)
Ultimate Holding Company: B.E. WEDGE HOLDINGS LIMITED
Immediate Holding Company: EDWARD HOWELL GALVANIZERS LIMITED
Registration no: 00296766 **Date established:** 1935
No.of Employees: 51 - 100 **Product Groups:** 46, 48

Date of Accounts	Mar 11	Mar 10	Mar 09
Pre Tax Profit/Loss	12	12	12
Working Capital	20	20	20
Current Assets	23	23	22
Current Liabilities	3	3	2

Hydravalve Ltd
Unit 4 Noose Lane, Willenhall, WV13 3BX
Tel: 01902-637263 **Fax:** 01902-637264
E-mail: andy@hydravalve.co.uk
Website: http://www.hydravalve.co.uk
Directors: M. Shaw (Fin), A. Newham (MD)
Immediate Holding Company: HYDRAVALVE (UK) LIMITED
Registration no: 02213870 **Date established:** 1988 **Turnover:** £1m - £2m
No.of Employees: 11 - 20 **Product Groups:** 36, 38, 39, 40

Date of Accounts	Jun 11	Jun 10	Jun 09
Working Capital	578	450	376
Fixed Assets	45	16	18
Current Assets	1m	985	817

I B Construction
Construction House Spring Lane, Willenhall, WV12 4HW
Tel: 01902-364455 **Fax:** 01902-364456
E-mail: info@ibconstruction.co.uk
Website: http://www.ibconstruction.co.uk
Bank(s): Lloyds, Wolverhampton
Directors: P. Lewis (MD)
Immediate Holding Company: I.B. CONSTRUCTION LIMITED
Registration no: 00642276 **VAT No.:** GB 100 2961 23
Date established: 1959 **Turnover:** £2m - £5m **No.of Employees:** 21 - 50
Product Groups: 52

Date of Accounts	Sep 11	Sep 10	Sep 09
Sales Turnover	8m	7m	6m
Pre Tax Profit/Loss	152	46	24
Working Capital	2m	2m	2m
Fixed Assets	478	419	430
Current Assets	3m	3m	3m
Current Liabilities	142	114	145

J T B Pressings Ltd
Unit 29-31 & 34 Owen Road Industrial Estate, Willenhall, WV13 2PY
Tel: 0121-526 4020 **Fax:** 0121-526 4023
E-mail: jtbarker.ltd@virgin.net
Website: http://www.jtb-pressings.co.uk
Directors: I. Evans (Prop)
Immediate Holding Company: J T B PRESSINGS LIMITED
Registration no: 02503879 **Date established:** 1990
Turnover: £500,000 - £1m **No.of Employees:** 11 - 20 **Product Groups:** 48

Date of Accounts	Jun 12	Jun 11	Jun 10
Working Capital	324	289	221
Fixed Assets	307	323	356
Current Assets	470	454	338

Jackdaw Tools Ltd
Leveson Street, Willenhall, WV13 1DB
Tel: 01902-366551 **Fax:** 01902-366552
E-mail: sales@jackdaw.co.uk
Website: http://www.jackdaw.co.uk
Bank(s): HSBC Bank PLC
Directors: D. Webb (Tech Serv), S. Pearson (MD)
Managers: L. Rogers (Comptroller)
Immediate Holding Company: JACKDAW TOOLS LIMITED
Registration no: 02902720 **Date established:** 1994 **Turnover:** £5m - £10m
No.of Employees: 21 - 50 **Product Groups:** 48

Date of Accounts	Jul 11	Jul 10	Jul 09
Working Capital	278	279	265
Fixed Assets	178	139	146
Current Assets	2m	2m	2m

Laidlaw Solutions Ltd
Strawberry Lane Industrial Estate Strawberry Lane, Willenhall, WV13 3RS
Tel: 01902-600400 **Fax:** 01902-600490
E-mail: info@laidlaw.net
Website: http://www.laidlaw.net
Directors: S. Peckmore (Tech Serv), S. Sharif (Sales & Mktg), D. Beech (Fin)
Managers: B. Fox (Mgr), B. Rogers, A. Scott
Ultimate Holding Company: LAIDLAW INTERIORS GROUP LIMITED
Immediate Holding Company: LAIDLAW SOLUTIONS LIMITED
Registration no: 04552005 **VAT No.:** GB 110 6214 33
Date established: 2002 **Turnover:** £20m - £50m
No.of Employees: 21 - 50 **Product Groups:** 66

Date of Accounts	Sep 11	Sep 10	Sep 09
Sales Turnover	26m	26m	25m
Pre Tax Profit/Loss	154	137	564
Working Capital	-194	-301	-211
Fixed Assets	3m	3m	3m
Current Assets	8m	10m	8m
Current Liabilities	3m	6m	4m

A Lewis & Sons Willenhall Ltd
47 Church Street, Willenhall, WV13 1QW
Tel: 01902-605428 **Fax:** 01902-601181
E-mail: lewislocksltd@aol.com
Website: http://www.lewislocksltd.co.uk
Directors: J. Lewis (MD)
Immediate Holding Company: A. LEWIS AND SONS (WILLENHALL) LIMITED
Registration no: 00446028 **VAT No.:** GB 100 5154 37
Date established: 1947 **Turnover:** £250,000 - £500,000
No.of Employees: 1 - 10 **Product Groups:** 35, 36

Date of Accounts	Jun 11	Jun 10	Jun 09
Working Capital	67	52	53
Fixed Assets	34	30	26
Current Assets	171	150	128

Manor Forklift Services
18 Harvesters Road, Willenhall, WV12 4AG
Tel: 01902-633390 **Fax:** 01902-633390
Directors: P. Vass (Prop)
Immediate Holding Company: MANOR FORKLIFT SERVICES LIMITED
Registration no: 06911712 **Date established:** 2009
No.of Employees: 1 - 10 **Product Groups:** 35, 39, 45

Date of Accounts	Jun 11
Working Capital	-56
Fixed Assets	57
Current Assets	62

Mercia Lifting Gear Ltd
Mercia House Chapel Green, Willenhall, WV13 1QY
Tel: 01902-608259 **Fax:** 01902-608972
E-mail: info@mercialiftinggear.com
Website: http://www.mercialiftinggear.com
Directors: R. Clarke (MD)
Immediate Holding Company: MERCIA LIFTING GEAR LIMITED
Registration no: 01611229 **Date established:** 1982
Turnover: £500,000 - £1m **No.of Employees:** 21 - 50 **Product Groups:** 45

Date of Accounts	Feb 08	Feb 11	Feb 10
Working Capital	17	71	61
Fixed Assets	55	38	56
Current Assets	1m	854	628
Current Liabilities	151	303	226

Middleton Catering Equipment Ltd
Somerford Place, Willenhall, WV13 3DT
Tel: 01902-608852 **Fax:** 01902-630828
E-mail: middletoncat@btconnect.com
Website: http://www.middletoncatering.co.uk
Immediate Holding Company: MIDDLETON CATERING EQUIPMENT LIMITED
Registration no: 01378634 **Date established:** 1978
Turnover: £500,000 - £1m **No.of Employees:** 1 - 10 **Product Groups:** 20, 40, 41

Date of Accounts	Oct 09	Oct 08	Oct 07
Working Capital	-26	-30	-32
Fixed Assets	10	11	13
Current Assets	117	151	171

L & S Middleton Ltd
665 Willenhall Road, Willenhall, WV13 3LH
Tel: 01902-608122 **Fax:** 01902-609550
E-mail: middletonpaper@compuserve.com
Website: http://www.middleton-paper.com
Bank(s): Barclays Walsall
Directors: G. Middleton (Dir)
Immediate Holding Company: L. & S. MIDDLETON LIMITED
Registration no: 01331325 **VAT No.:** GB 101 6634 12
Date established: 1977 **Turnover:** £10m - £20m
No.of Employees: 21 - 50 **Product Groups:** 27, 64, 66

Date of Accounts	Oct 11	Oct 10	Oct 09
Sales Turnover	13m	12m	12m
Pre Tax Profit/Loss	336	184	250
Working Capital	2m	2m	2m
Fixed Assets	226	271	302
Current Assets	4m	4m	3m
Current Liabilities	345	542	401

Morelock Signs Ltd
Morelock House Strawberry Lane, Willenhall, WV13 3RS
Tel: 01902-637575 **Fax:** 01902-637576
E-mail: mail@morelock.co.uk
Website: http://www.morelock.co.uk
Bank(s): National Westminster
Directors: E. Guilmartin (Fin), K. Chester (MD)
Managers: J. Flavell (Personnel), S. Garrett, M. Bradford
Immediate Holding Company: MORELOCK SIGNS LIMITED
Registration no: 03193048 **VAT No.:** Gb 670 8170 32
Date established: 1996 **Turnover:** £5m - £10m
No.of Employees: 51 - 100 **Product Groups:** 28, 30, 35, 37, 39

Date of Accounts	Dec 11	Dec 10	Dec 09
Sales Turnover	7m	9m	9m
Pre Tax Profit/Loss	-632	69	271
Working Capital	482	1m	1m
Fixed Assets	1m	1m	1m
Current Assets	2m	2m	3m
Current Liabilities	648	174	282

Niagara Lasalle
Planetary Road, Willenhall, WV13 3SW
Tel: 01902-308600 **Fax:** 0121-522 3737
E-mail: tsingh@niag.com
Website: http://www.niag.com
Directors: C. Ross (MD), T. Singh (MD), T. Sing (MD), C. Ross (Sales & Mktg), C. Singh (MD)
Immediate Holding Company: JJ & N ASSOCIATES LIMITED
Registration no: 03725308 **Date established:** 2007
Turnover: £50m - £75m **No.of Employees:** 51 - 100 **Product Groups:** 34, 66

Date of Accounts	Dec 11
Sales Turnover	93m
Pre Tax Profit/Loss	13m
Working Capital	12m
Fixed Assets	11m
Current Assets	35m
Current Liabilities	3m

P R D Fasteners Ltd
Unit 10-15 Monmer Close, Willenhall, WV13 1JR
Tel: 01902-636246 **Fax:** 01902-605759
E-mail: sales@prdfasteners.co.uk
Website: http://www.prdfasteners.co.uk
Directors: S. Roden (Sales), D. May (Tech Serv), N. Sutcliffe (Sales), S. Howarth (Fin)
Managers: C. Farrell (Purch Mgr)
Ultimate Holding Company: LSP HOLDING SARL (LUXEMBOURG)
Immediate Holding Company: P.R.D. FASTENERS LIMITED
Registration no: 01754121 **Date established:** 1983
Turnover: £10m - £20m **No.of Employees:** 101 - 250 **Product Groups:** 35

Date of Accounts	Dec 11	Dec 10	Dec 09
Sales Turnover	15m	12m	12m
Pre Tax Profit/Loss	2m	2m	1m
Working Capital	6m	9m	6m
Fixed Assets	886	685	776
Current Assets	9m	11m	9m
Current Liabilities	591	661	796

Pendeford Metal Spinnings Ltd
Neachells Lane, Willenhall, WV13 3SF
Tel: 01902-733145 **Fax:** 01902-721136
E-mail: info@pendeford.co.uk
Website: http://www.pendeford.co.uk
Bank(s): Lloyds
Directors: R. Humphries (MD)
Immediate Holding Company: PENDEFORD METAL SPINNINGS LIMITED
Registration no: 01013760 **VAT No.:** GB 100 4788 01
Date established: 1971 **No.of Employees:** 11 - 20 **Product Groups:** 36, 63

Date of Accounts	Jul 11	Jul 10	Jul 09
Working Capital	273	251	156
Fixed Assets	160	56	62
Current Assets	880	914	606

Pommier Furgocar Ltd
Unit L Key Industrial Park Fernside Road, Willenhall, WV13 3YA
Tel: 01902-731106 **Fax:** 01902-738630
E-mail: sales@furgocaruk.co.uk
Directors: M. Owen (MD)
Ultimate Holding Company: FIMAPO SA (FRANCE)
Immediate Holding Company: POMMIER FURGOCAR UK LIMITED
Registration no: 04058903 **Date established:** 2000
No.of Employees: 1 - 10 **Product Groups:** 35, 39

Date of Accounts	Dec 11	Dec 10	Dec 09
Working Capital	253	197	92
Fixed Assets	40	43	53
Current Assets	886	860	681

Poundland Ltd
Wellmans Road, Willenhall, WV13 2QT
Tel: 0121-568 7000 **Fax:** 0121-568 7003
E-mail: jim.mccarthy@poundland.co.uk
Website: http://www.poundland.co.uk
Bank(s): Barclays
Directors: J. Mccarthy (Grp Chief Exec)
Managers: D. Coxon, M. Gray (Tech Serv Mgr), N. Hateley (Fin Mgr), S. Sharples (Personnel)
Ultimate Holding Company: WARBURG PINCUS PRIVATE EQUITY X LP (USA)
Immediate Holding Company: POUNDLAND LIMITED
Registration no: 02495645 **VAT No.:** GB 547 5122 45
Date established: 1990 **Turnover:** £500m - £1,000m
No.of Employees: 251 - 500 **Product Groups:** 61

Date of Accounts	Mar 10	Mar 11	Apr 12
Sales Turnover	510m	642m	780m
Pre Tax Profit/Loss	23m	21m	32m
Working Capital	31m	42m	60m
Fixed Assets	27m	33m	41m
Current Assets	85m	117m	157m
Current Liabilities	32m	47m	62m

R J Ornamental Steel Work
Victoria Building New Railway Street, Willenhall, WV13 1LJ
Tel: 01902-606979 **Fax:** 01902-606979
Directors: R. Jinks (Prop)
Date established: 1998 **No.of Employees:** 1 - 10 **Product Groups:** 26, 35

Raybloc Ltd
32 Bilston Lane, Willenhall, WV13 2QD
Tel: 01902-633383 **Fax:** 01902-609453
E-mail: info@raybloc.net
Website: http://www.raybloc.net
Directors: S. Haydon (MD)
Immediate Holding Company: RAYBLOC (X-RAY PROTECTION) LIMITED
Registration no: 04098881 **Date established:** 2000
No.of Employees: 11 - 20 **Product Groups:** 33, 35

Date of Accounts	Jan 12	Jan 11	Jan 10
Working Capital	-108	-43	-79
Fixed Assets	323	412	403
Current Assets	185	229	489

Reiter UK LTD
Marina Building 94 Newhall Street, Willenhall, WV13 1LQ
Tel: 01902-415000 **Fax:** 01902-418992
E-mail: info@reiter.co.uk
Website: http://www.reiter.co.uk
No.of Employees: 1 - 10 **Product Groups:** 30, 32, 33, 35, 36, 37, 39, 40, 42, 44, 46, 47, 67, 83

Date of Accounts	Nov 07	Nov 06	Nov 05
Working Capital	324	257	229
Fixed Assets	43	51	27
Current Assets	423	364	302
Current Liabilities	99	106	72

Roadlink International Ltd
Strawberry Lane, Willenhall, WV13 3RL
Tel: 01902-606210 **Fax:** 01902-631515
E-mail: sales@roadlink-international.co.uk
Website: http://www.roadlink-international.co.uk
Directors: H. Arthur (Ptnr), E. Sedgley (Fin), D. Sedgley (Ch)
Managers: R. Reynolds (Sales & Mktg Mg), N. Harvey (Purch Mgr)
Ultimate Holding Company: ROADLINK INTERNATIONAL LIMITED
Immediate Holding Company: ROADLINK EUROPE LIMITED
Registration no: 02483958 **Date established:** 1990 **Turnover:** £5m - £10m
No.of Employees: 21 - 50 **Product Groups:** 30, 33, 35, 36, 39, 40, 46, 67, 68, 84

Date of Accounts	Mar 96	Mar 95	Mar 11
Working Capital	78	55	78
Fixed Assets	N/A	15	N/A
Current Assets	99	413	78

Peter Rushton Ltd
Albion Street, Willenhall, WV13 1NN
Tel: 01902-368444 **Fax:** 01902-601757
E-mail: sales@peterrushton.co.uk
Website: http://www.peterrushton.co.uk
Directors: I. Rushton (Dir)
Immediate Holding Company: PETER RUSHTON LIMITED
Registration no: 01213260 **Date established:** 1975
Turnover: £500,000 - £1m **No.of Employees:** 1 - 10 **Product Groups:** 36, 37, 41, 46, 47, 48, 66, 67

Date of Accounts	Mar 12	Mar 11	Mar 10
Working Capital	300	286	295
Fixed Assets	4	4	5
Current Assets	313	307	310

W & J Smith Metal Stockists Ltd
Ashmore Lake Way, Willenhall, WV12 4LF
Tel: 01902-607336 **Fax:** 01902-634905
Website: http://www.rsjcentre.com
Directors: A. Smith (Dir)
Immediate Holding Company: W. & J. SMITH (METAL STOCKISTS) LIMITED
Registration no: 00789605 **VAT No.:** GB 100 5157 31
Date established: 1964 **Turnover:** £250,000 - £500,000
No.of Employees: 1 - 10 **Product Groups:** 66

Date of Accounts	May 11	May 10	May 09
Working Capital	37	45	109
Fixed Assets	58	66	64
Current Assets	236	226	193

Starchem Ltd
Strawberry Lane, Willenhall, WV13 3RS
Tel: 01902-838880 **Fax:** 01902-838881
E-mail: sales@starchem.co.uk
Website: http://www.starchem.co.uk
Bank(s): HSBC
Directors: A. Scott (Fin), R. Mills (MD)
Immediate Holding Company: STARCHEM LIMITED
Registration no: 01016000 **VAT No.:** GB 100 6369 11
Date established: 1971 **Turnover:** £5m - £10m **No.of Employees:** 21 - 50
Product Groups: 23, 24, 27

Date of Accounts	Dec 11	Dec 10	Dec 09
Sales Turnover	7m	7m	7m
Pre Tax Profit/Loss	1m	1m	1m
Working Capital	5m	4m	3m
Fixed Assets	637	650	659
Current Assets	6m	5m	5m
Current Liabilities	1m	410	1m

Uniclad Systems Ltd
Planetary Road, Willenhall, WV13 3SW
Tel: 01902-866411 **Fax:** 01902-866465
E-mail: sales@uncladsystems.co.uk
Website: http://www.unicladsystems.co.uk
Managers: P. Millard (Mgr)
Ultimate Holding Company: MOORHEN HOLDINGS LIMITED
Immediate Holding Company: UNICLAD SYSTEMS LIMITED
Registration no: 02729822 **Date established:** 1992 **Turnover:** £2m - £5m
No.of Employees: 1 - 10 **Product Groups:** 35

Date of Accounts	Jun 11	Jun 10	Jun 09
Working Capital	2m	1m	3m
Current Assets	2m	2m	4m

W H Tildesley Ltd
Clifford Works Bow Street, Willenhall, WV13 2AN
Tel: 01902-366440 **Fax:** 01902-366216
E-mail: sales@whtildesley.com
Website: http://www.whtildesley.com
Bank(s): HSBC Bank plc
Directors: J. Tildesley (MD), T. Tildesley (Fin)
Managers: J. Coles (Mktg Serv Mgr), S. Thompson, B. Burden (Tech Serv Mgr)
Immediate Holding Company: W.H. TILDESLEY LIMITED
Registration no: 00188101 **VAT No.:** GB 431 4762 65
Date established: 2023 **Turnover:** £2m - £5m **No.of Employees:** 21 - 50
Product Groups: 35, 41, 48

Date of Accounts	Jun 11	Jun 10	Jun 09
Sales Turnover	N/A	2m	3m
Pre Tax Profit/Loss	N/A	32	126
Working Capital	2m	2m	3m
Fixed Assets	3m	3m	2m
Current Assets	3m	3m	3m
Current Liabilities	N/A	188	196

Wedge Galvanizing Group Ltd
Stafford Street, Willenhall, WV13 1RZ
Tel: 01902-630311 **Fax:** 01902-366353
E-mail: sales@wedge-galv.co.uk
Website: http://www.wedge-galv.co.uk
Bank(s): HSBC Bank plc
Directors: J. Woolridge (MD), J. Parsons (Fin)
Managers: T. Messer
Ultimate Holding Company: B.E. WEDGE HOLDINGS LIMITED
Immediate Holding Company: WEDGE GROUP GALVANIZING LIMITED
Registration no: 00515891 **Date established:** 1953
Turnover: £50m - £75m **No.of Employees:** 51 - 100 **Product Groups:** 48

Date of Accounts	Mar 11	Mar 10	Mar 09
Sales Turnover	56m	54m	64m
Pre Tax Profit/Loss	2m	3m	5m
Working Capital	21m	20m	18m
Fixed Assets	9m	10m	10m
Current Assets	30m	31m	26m
Current Liabilities	3m	2m	3m

Weishaupt UK Ltd
Neachells Lane, Willenhall, WV13 3RG
Tel: 01902-609841 **Fax:** 01902-633343
E-mail: info@weishaupt.co.uk
Website: http://www.weishaupt.co.uk
Directors: B. Fox (MD)
Immediate Holding Company: WEISHAUPT (U.K.) LIMITED
Registration no: 01030670 **Date established:** 1971
No.of Employees: 1 - 10 **Product Groups:** 40, 42, 46

Date of Accounts	Dec 11	Dec 10	Dec 09
Working Capital	799	690	367
Fixed Assets	67	78	83
Current Assets	1m	1m	836

Whittingham Design & Manufacturing Co. Ltd
Chapel Works Chapel Green, Willenhall, WV13 1QY
Tel: 01902-607272 **Fax:** 01902-637884
E-mail: david.whittingham@live.co.uk
Directors: D. Whittingham (Dir)
Immediate Holding Company: WHITTINGHAM DESIGN & MANUFACTURING LIMITED
Registration no: 01128234 **Date established:** 1973
No.of Employees: 1 - 10 **Product Groups:** 46

Date of Accounts	Mar 11	Mar 10	Mar 09
Working Capital	55	102	48
Fixed Assets	69	82	98
Current Assets	144	182	142

Willenhall Fasteners Ltd
Frederick William Street, Willenhall, WV13 1NE
Tel: 01902-630760 **Fax:** 01902-636447
E-mail: sales@willenfast.co.uk
Website: http://www.willenfast.co.uk
Bank(s): HSBC
Directors: V. Fitzmaurice (Fin), N. Parr (Dir), J. Parr (Dir)
Ultimate Holding Company: WILLENHALL FASTENERS (HOLDINGS) LIMITED
Immediate Holding Company: WILLENHALL FASTENERS (HOLDINGS) LIMITED
Registration no: 02969849 **VAT No.:** GB 650 3742 52
Date established: 1994 **Turnover:** £500,000 - £1m
No.of Employees: 21 - 50 **Product Groups:** 35, 66

Date of Accounts	Mar 12	Mar 11	Mar 10
Fixed Assets	333	333	333

Wilson UK Ltd
Forge Road, Willenhall, WV12 4HD
Tel: 01922-725800 **Fax:** 01922-649888
E-mail: uksales@wilsononline.com
Website: http://www.wilsononline.com
Bank(s): National Westminster Bank Plc
Directors: G. Chantrey (Co Sec), M. Kochalski (MD), D. Hopkinson (Sales), R. Carter (Co Sec), G. Chantrey (Co Sec)
Managers: D. Morgan (Buyer), J. Mark (), J. Cuthbert (Sales Prom Mgr), J. Sand (Ops Mgr), R. Bowlcott (Chief Mgr)
Ultimate Holding Company: Smith International (USA)
Immediate Holding Company: Wilson Industries Inc (U.S.A.)
Registration no: 00885990 **Turnover:** £10m - £20m
No.of Employees: 51 - 100 **Product Groups:** 35, 36, 45, 46, 47, 67, 83

Wolverhampton Handling Ltd
Unit 10 Planetary Indl-Est Planetary Road, Willenhall, WV13 3XQ
Tel: 01902-726481 **Fax:** 01902-864744
E-mail: sales@roller.co.uk
Website: http://www.roller.co.uk
Directors: B. Stokes (MD)
Managers: B. Hancox (Sales Prom Mgr), J. Wall (Sales Prom Mgr)
Immediate Holding Company: WOLVERHAMPTON HANDLING LIMITED
Registration no: 00889624 **Date established:** 1966 **Turnover:** £1m - £2m
No.of Employees: 11 - 20 **Product Groups:** 35, 45

Date of Accounts	Jan 12	Jan 11	Jan 10
Working Capital	137	107	129
Fixed Assets	44	37	39
Current Assets	389	311	343

Wolverson X-Ray Ltd
Walsall Street, Willenhall, WV13 2DY
Tel: 01902-637333 **Fax:** 01902-637333
E-mail: deyoung@wolversonx-ray.co.uk
Website: http://www.wolverson.uk.com
Bank(s): National Westminster
Directors: D. Young (Fin)
Immediate Holding Company: WOLVERSON X-RAY LIMITED
Registration no: 03997914 **VAT No.:** GB 100 5418 29
Date established: 2000 **Turnover:** £2m - £5m **No.of Employees:** 21 - 50
Product Groups: 37

Date of Accounts	Mar 12	Mar 11	Mar 10
Working Capital	179	137	240
Fixed Assets	319	412	291
Current Assets	1m	1m	1m

Worrall Locks Ltd
Unit A2 Erebus Works Albion Road, Willenhall, WV13 1NH
Tel: 01902-605038 **Fax:** 01902-633558
E-mail: dcooper@worrall-locks.co.uk
Website: http://www.worrall-locks.co.uk
Directors: D. Cooper (Dir)
Immediate Holding Company: WORRALL LOCKS LIMITED
Registration no: 02221799 **Date established:** 1988
No.of Employees: 1 - 10 **Product Groups:** 36

Date of Accounts	Mar 11	Mar 10	Mar 09
Working Capital	-50	-56	-58
Fixed Assets	1	1	N/A
Current Assets	22	22	23

Zincast Foundry Ltd
Strawberry Lane, Willenhall, WV13 3NG
Tel: 01902-606226 **Fax:** 01902-634607
E-mail: pheath@zincast.co.uk
Website: http://www.zincast.co.uk
Bank(s): Barclays
Directors: P. Heath (MD), S. Heath (Fin)
Managers: P. Horton (Projects)
Ultimate Holding Company: ZINCAST (HOLDINGS) LIMITED
Immediate Holding Company: ZINCAST FOUNDRY LIMITED
Registration no: 02692531 **VAT No.:** GB 559 6833 85
Date established: 1992 **Turnover:** £2m - £5m **No.of Employees:** 51 - 100
Product Groups: 34

Date of Accounts	Aug 11	Aug 10	May 09
Working Capital	52	58	51
Fixed Assets	270	202	226
Current Assets	1m	828	562
Current Liabilities	408	267	N/A

Wolverhampton

A C Cleaning Services Ltd
Unit A1 Guy Motors Industrial Park Park Lane, Wolverhampton, WV10 9QF
Tel: 01902-307070 **Fax:** 01902-398598
E-mail: sales@thecleaningwarehouse.co.uk
Website: http://www.accleaningservicesltd.co.uk
Directors: A. Cartwright (MD)
Immediate Holding Company: A. C. CLEANING SERVICES (WOLVERHAMPTON) LIMITED
Registration no: 04539477 **Date established:** 2002
No.of Employees: 1 - 10 **Product Groups:** 24, 32, 66

Date of Accounts	Nov 11	Nov 10	Nov 09
Working Capital	104	111	58
Fixed Assets	10	13	15
Current Assets	142	170	119

A J Controls
Derry Street, Wolverhampton, WV2 1EY
Tel: 01902-454111 **Fax:** 01902-454111
E-mail: rupygill@hotmail.com
Website: http://www.ajcontrols.co.uk
Directors: R. Gill (Prop)
Immediate Holding Company: NATIONWIDE SIGNS LIMITED
Registration no: 06390830 **Date established:** 1994
No.of Employees: 1 - 10 **Product Groups:** 20, 40, 41

Date of Accounts	Jul 11
Working Capital	-37
Fixed Assets	99
Current Assets	728

A1 Marquees
25 Castlecroft Road, Wolverhampton, WV3 8BS
Tel: 01902-765353 **Fax:** 01902-765353
E-mail: hire@a1marquees.co.uk
Website: http://www.a1marquees.co.uk
Directors: O. Kainth (Prop)
Turnover: Up to £250,000 **No.of Employees:** 1 - 10 **Product Groups:** 24, 26, 36, 83

Aba Cranes
52 Sneyd Lane Essington, Wolverhampton, WV11 2DU
Tel: 01922-478543 **Fax:** 01922-711210
E-mail: info@abacranehire.co.uk
Website: http://www.abacranehire.co.uk
Managers: D. England
Registration no: 00002210 **Turnover:** Up to £250,000
No.of Employees: 1 - 10 **Product Groups:** 83

Acumen Waste Services
Lincoln Street, Wolverhampton, WV10 0DX
Tel: 01902-352100
E-mail: sales@acumenwaste.co.uk
Website: http://www.acumenwaste.co.uk
Managers: A. Wray (Sales Admin), A. Carr (Personnel)
Immediate Holding Company: SIGNCAST LIMITED
Date established: 2009 **Turnover:** £10m - £20m
No.of Employees: 51 - 100 **Product Groups:** 32, 39, 40, 41, 42, 44, 54, 72, 74

Date of Accounts	Mar 11	Mar 10	Mar 09
Working Capital	2	-17	-14
Fixed Assets	117	123	45
Current Assets	74	90	112

Adverc B M Ltd
245 Trysull Road, Wolverhampton, WV3 7LG
Tel: 01902-380494 **Fax:** 01902-380435
E-mail: techsales@adverc.co.uk
Website: http://www.adverc.co.uk
Directors: A. Mapperson (MD)
Immediate Holding Company: ADVERC B.M. LIMITED
Registration no: 01932971 **VAT No.:** GB 431 3431 93
Date established: 1985 **Turnover:** £500,000 - £1m
No.of Employees: 1 - 10 **Product Groups:** 37, 39, 45

Date of Accounts	Mar 12	Mar 11	Mar 10
Working Capital	115	78	122
Fixed Assets	1	12	14
Current Assets	145	146	189

Aesthetic Dental Laboratory
19 Bilbrook Road Codsall, Wolverhampton, WV8 1EU
Tel: 01902-844825 **Fax:** 01902-845471

see next page

***Aesthetic Dental Laboratory** - Cont'd*
Directors: M. Mcglynn (Prop)
No.of Employees: 11 - 20 **Product Groups:** 38, 67

Aldridge
Castle House Drayton Street, Wolverhampton, WV2 4EF
Tel: 01902-710805 **Fax:** 01902-427474
E-mail: mail@aldridge.co.uk
Website: http://www.aldridge.co.uk
Bank(s): Lloyds TSB Bank plc
Directors: S. Aldridge (Prop)
Managers: J. Austin (Mgr)
Registration no: 36980431 **VAT No.:** GB 369 8043 16
Turnover: £500,000 - £1m **No.of Employees:** 21 - 50
Product Groups: 39, 48

Alphagraphics
68 Darlington Street, Wolverhampton, WV1 4ND
Tel: 01902-711151 **Fax:** 01902-710174
E-mail: info@alphagraphics-wolves.co.uk
Website: http://www.alphagraphics.co.uk/uk016
Directors: M. Taylor (MD)
Managers: D. Elliot (Mgr)
Registration no: 02913558 **VAT No.:** GB 489 7839 55
Date established: 1989 **Turnover:** £1m - £2m **No.of Employees:** 1 - 10
Product Groups: 28

Andrews Coatings Ltd
Carver Building Littles Lane, Wolverhampton, WV1 1JY
Tel: 01902-429190 **Fax:** 01902-426574
E-mail: info@andrewscoatings.co.uk
Website: http://www.rustoleumaerosols.co.uk
Directors: C. Bullock (Fin), M. Bullock (MD)
Managers: L. Bills (Sales Prom Mgr)
Ultimate Holding Company: CARVER (WOLVERHAMPTON) LIMITED
Immediate Holding Company: ANDREWS COATINGS LIMITED
Registration no: 04327568 **Date established:** 2001
Turnover: £250,000 - £500,000 **No.of Employees:** 1 - 10
Product Groups: 66

Date of Accounts	Dec 11	Dec 10	Dec 09
Working Capital	3	8	21
Fixed Assets	12	15	5
Current Assets	85	68	107

Andrews Sykes Hire Ltd
Premier House Darlington Street, Wolverhampton, WV1 4JJ
Tel: 01902-328700 **Fax:** 01902-422466
E-mail: info@andrews-sykes.com
Website: http://www.andrews-sykes.com
Directors: K. Ford (Fin), M. Calderbank (Co Sec), N. Gill (Purch), S. Reeve (Sales)
Managers: N. Burson (Personnel)
Immediate Holding Company: ANDREWS SYKES HIRE LIMITED
Registration no: 02985657 **Date established:** 1994
Turnover: £20m - £50m **No.of Employees:** 251 - 500 **Product Groups:** 83

Date of Accounts	Dec 11	Dec 10	Dec 09
Sales Turnover	35m	36m	34m
Pre Tax Profit/Loss	10m	10m	8m
Working Capital	8m	6m	2m
Fixed Assets	7m	7m	9m
Current Assets	33m	35m	35m
Current Liabilities	7m	7m	5m

Anglo European Workforce Ltd
Wulfrun House 51 Waterloo Road, Wolverhampton, WV1 4QJ
Tel: 01902-422224 **Fax:** 01902-421895
E-mail: jacqueline.c@angloew.com
Website: http://www.angloew.com
Directors: J. Cope (Dir)
Managers: P. Rowley (Contracts Mgr)
Ultimate Holding Company: ROMAN ROADS LIMITED
Immediate Holding Company: ANGLO EUROPEAN WORKFORCE LIMITED
Registration no: 02924774 **VAT No.:** GB 101 7945 87
Date established: 1994 **Turnover:** £2m - £5m **No.of Employees:** 1 - 10
Product Groups: 48

Date of Accounts	Dec 06	Dec 05	Dec 04
Sales Turnover	N/A	N/A	3m
Pre Tax Profit/Loss	N/A	N/A	-47
Working Capital	87	-73	-8
Fixed Assets	10	16	28
Current Assets	463	810	703
Current Liabilities	N/A	N/A	673

Anochrome Technologies Ltd
Wood Lane, Wolverhampton, WV10 8HN
Tel: 01902-567567 **Fax:** 01902-567777
E-mail: enquiries@anochrome-group.co.uk
Website: http://www.anochrome.co.uk
Directors: J. Oliver (I.T. Dir), M. Oliver (Fin), S. Rolls (Sales & Mktg)
Managers: V. Sherwood (Chief Mgr)
Immediate Holding Company: ANOCHROME TECHNOLOGIES LIMITED
Registration no: 03507309 **Date established:** 1998
No.of Employees: 21 - 50 **Product Groups:** 46, 48

Date of Accounts	Mar 11	Mar 10	Mar 09
Working Capital	389	-866	-956
Fixed Assets	1m	2m	2m
Current Assets	699	432	470

Aptus Interiors Ltd
31 Lawn Lane Coven, Wolverhampton, WV9 5AX
Tel: 01902-791293 **Fax:** 01902-790792
E-mail: info@aptusinteriors.co.uk
Website: http://www.aptusinteriors.co.uk
Directors: P. Roberts (Fin)
Immediate Holding Company: APTUS INTERIORS LIMITED
Registration no: 05857422 **Date established:** 2006
Turnover: Up to £250,000 **No.of Employees:** 1 - 10 **Product Groups:** 26

Date of Accounts	Dec 11	Dec 10	Dec 09
Working Capital	-8	-19	12
Fixed Assets	1	1	1
Current Assets	12	11	68

Arcgen (t/a Hilta Pumps)
Station Road Four Ashes Industrial Estate, Four Ashes, Wolverhampton, WV10 7DB
Tel: 01902-790824 **Fax:** 01902-790355
E-mail: info@arcgenhilta.com
Website: http://www.arcgenhilta.com
Managers: D. McCormack, J. Brogan (Ops Mgr), M. Collins (Purch Mgr), J. Simkiss, R. Homer (Mktg Serv Mgr)
Ultimate Holding Company: ENERGYST BV (NETHERLANDS)
Immediate Holding Company: ENERGYST UK LIMITED
Registration no: 01063091 **Date established:** 2002 **Turnover:** £5m - £10m
No.of Employees: 21 - 50 **Product Groups:** 40

Date of Accounts	Dec 11	Dec 10	Dec 09
Working Capital	90	80	70
Current Assets	90	80	70

Armoloy UK Ltd
Mammoth Drive Wolverhampton Science Park, Wolverhampton, WV10 9TF
Tel: 01902-310375 **Fax:** 01902-310075
E-mail: steve.c@armoloy.co.uk
Website: http://www.armoloy.co.uk
Directors: B. Cooper (Dir), S. Cooper (MD), K. Foster (Dir)
Immediate Holding Company: ARMOLOY (U.K.) LIMITED
Registration no: 02360196 **Date established:** 1989 **Turnover:** £1m - £2m
No.of Employees: 21 - 50 **Product Groups:** 32, 48

Date of Accounts	May 11	May 10	May 09
Working Capital	-7	-6	42
Fixed Assets	717	711	721
Current Assets	222	211	228

Ashworth
Neachells Lane, Wolverhampton, WV11 3QF
Tel: 01902-867400 **Fax:** 01902-867499
E-mail: carl.green@ashworth.eu.com
Website: http://www.ashworth.eu.com
Bank(s): Lloyds TSB
Directors: A. Oxenham (Co Sec), C. Green (Dir)
Ultimate Holding Company: SAINT GOBAIN GROUP P.L.C.
Immediate Holding Company: SANT-GOBIAN PIPE SYSTEMS
Turnover: £2m - £5m **No.of Employees:** 21 - 50 **Product Groups:** 33, 34, 35, 40, 66

Assystem UK Ltd
St. Johns House Church Street, Wolverhampton, WV2 4LS
Tel: 01902-427463 **Fax:** 01902-714239
E-mail: careers@assystemuk.com
Website: http://www.assystem.com
Bank(s): Lloyds TSB Bank plc
Directors: C. Pearce (Dir)
Managers: D. Lowe (I.T. Exec), P. Delilloye (Reg Mgr)
Immediate Holding Company: Assystem Group UK Ltd
Registration no: 01147167 **Turnover:** £2m - £5m
No.of Employees: 21 - 50 **Product Groups:** 39, 44, 80, 81, 84, 85

A-Stat
20 Henwood Court Henwood Road, Wolverhampton, WV6 8PG
Tel: 01902-725222 **Fax:** 01902-342333
E-mail: admin@astat.co.uk
Website: http://www.astat.co.uk
Directors: D. Westwood (MD)
Immediate Holding Company: A-STAT OFFICE TECHNOLOGY LIMITED
Registration no: 02434307 **Date established:** 1989
No.of Employees: 11 - 20 **Product Groups:** 32, 44

Date of Accounts	Oct 11	Oct 10	Oct 09
Working Capital	97	57	241
Fixed Assets	996	900	63
Current Assets	498	383	433

Atec Security Ltd
1 Element Court Featherstone, Wolverhampton, WV10 7QZ
Tel: 08452-426000 **Fax:** 01922-743186
E-mail: info@atec-security.co.uk
Website: http://www.atec-security.co.uk
Bank(s): National Westminster Bank Plc
Directors: S. Adcock (MD), C. Adcock (Fin)
Immediate Holding Company: ATEC SECURITY LIMITED
Registration no: 01936399 **VAT No.:** GB 431 3211 10
Date established: 1985 **Turnover:** £500,000 - £1m
No.of Employees: 21 - 50 **Product Groups:** 35, 36, 40

Date of Accounts	Apr 11	Apr 10	Apr 09
Working Capital	260	131	246
Fixed Assets	42	59	92
Current Assets	2m	1m	1m

Axyz Automation UK Ltd
Albrighton Business Park Newport Road, Albrighton, Wolverhampton, WV7 3ET
Tel: 01902-375600 **Fax:** 01902-375662
E-mail: sales@axyz.co.uk
Website: http://www.axyz.co.uk
Bank(s): National Westminster Bank Plc
Managers: T. Scarth (Mgr)
Ultimate Holding Company: AXYZ INTERNATIONAL INC (CANADA)
Immediate Holding Company: AXYZ AUTOMATION (U.K.) LIMITED
Registration no: 03263276 **VAT No.:** GB 416 2435 74
Date established: 1996 **No.of Employees:** 11 - 20 **Product Groups:** 47

Date of Accounts	Sep 11	Sep 10	Sep 09
Working Capital	486	220	120
Fixed Assets	155	189	235
Current Assets	1m	1m	1m
Current Liabilities	N/A	41	N/A

B S Engineering UK Ltd
Unit D18 Hilton Trading Estate Hilton Road, Lanesfield, Wolverhampton, WV4 6DW
Tel: 01902-408335 **Fax:** 01902-492470
E-mail: sales@bs-engineering.co.uk
Website: http://www.bs-engineering.co.uk
Directors: B. Bunger (MD)
Immediate Holding Company: B. S. ENGINEERING UK LTD
Registration no: 04467267 **Date established:** 2002
No.of Employees: 1 - 10 **Product Groups:** 46, 48

Date of Accounts	Mar 12	Mar 11	Mar 10
Working Capital	24	23	-14
Fixed Assets	138	149	173
Current Assets	125	114	91

Barr & Grosvenor Ltd
Jenner Street, Wolverhampton, WV2 2AE
Tel: 01902-352390 **Fax:** 01902-871342
E-mail: sales@bargrosvenorwannado.co.uk
Website: http://www.barrandgrosvenor.wanadoo.co.uk
Directors: L. Grosvenor (Co Sec)
Immediate Holding Company: BARR & GROSVENOR LIMITED
Registration no: 03981134 **VAT No.:** GB 456 7020 50
Date established: 2000 **Turnover:** £1m - £2m **No.of Employees:** 11 - 20
Product Groups: 34, 38, 48, 83

Date of Accounts	Jun 11	Jun 10	Jun 09
Working Capital	-70	-83	-79
Fixed Assets	74	78	87
Current Assets	269	238	244

Baynell Ltd
85-86 Darlington Street, Wolverhampton, WV1 4EX
Tel: 01902-425616 **Fax:** 01902-311242
Directors: B. Bayliss (Jt MD), L. Roper (Co Sec), J. Bayliss (Dir)
Ultimate Holding Company: 00432505
Immediate Holding Company: BAYNELL LIMITED
Registration no: 00348880 **VAT No.:** GB 100 0405 63
Date established: 1939 **Turnover:** Up to £250,000
No.of Employees: 1 - 10 **Product Groups:** 24, 26, 30

Date of Accounts	Jan 08	Jan 07	Jan 06
Working Capital	9	9	13
Fixed Assets	189	192	195
Current Assets	15	16	18
Current Liabilities	6	8	5
Total Share Capital	1	1	1

Bearing Man Ltd
Unit 1 Ashford Industrial Estate, Wolverhampton, WV2 2BX
Tel: 01902-454151 **Fax:** 01902-459382
E-mail: timcoley@bmltd.co.uk
Website: http://www.bmltd.co.uk
Managers: T. Coley (Mgr)
Ultimate Holding Company: HAYLEY GROUP PUBLIC LIMITED COMPANY
Immediate Holding Company: BEARING MAN LIMITED
Registration no: 02399424 **VAT No.:** GB 434 0683 63
Date established: 1989 **Turnover:** £5m - £10m **No.of Employees:** 1 - 10
Product Groups: 35, 48

Date of Accounts	May 11	May 10	May 09
Sales Turnover	9m	7m	7m
Pre Tax Profit/Loss	777	159	142
Working Capital	1m	1m	1m
Fixed Assets	77	94	111
Current Assets	3m	3m	3m
Current Liabilities	605	319	247

Belpac Ltd
Heath Mill Road Wombourne, Wolverhampton, WV5 8AP
Tel: 01902-897343 **Fax:** 01902-893708
E-mail: info@belpac.co.uk
Website: http://www.belpac.co.uk
Bank(s): Barclays
Directors: C. Deeley (Fin), I. Blunt (Dir), I. Nicholls (Sales & Mktg)
Managers: A. Rogers (Site Co-ord)
Immediate Holding Company: BELPAC LIMITED
Registration no: 01273309 **VAT No.:** GB 287 6191 17
Date established: 1976 **Turnover:** £2m - £5m **No.of Employees:** 21 - 50
Product Groups: 20, 30

Date of Accounts	Aug 10	Aug 09	Mar 08
Sales Turnover	N/A	4m	4m
Pre Tax Profit/Loss	N/A	-3	356
Working Capital	117	995	873
Fixed Assets	558	576	695
Current Assets	738	2m	2m
Current Liabilities	N/A	189	327

Bendfast UK Ltd
Unit F3 Primrose Avenue, Wolverhampton, WV10 8AW
Tel: 01902-397337 **Fax:** 01902-780359
E-mail: sales@bendfast.co.uk
Website: http://www.bendfast.co.uk
Directors: A. Bentley (Fin), H. Smith (MD)
Immediate Holding Company: BENDFAST UK LIMITED
Registration no: 06382830 **Date established:** 2007
No.of Employees: 1 - 10 **Product Groups:** 35, 66

Date of Accounts	Oct 11	Oct 10	Oct 09
Working Capital	329	236	165
Fixed Assets	40	39	28
Current Assets	489	381	396

Birmingham Midshires Financial Services Ltd
PO Box 81, Wolverhampton, WV9 5HZ
Tel: 08456-022828 **Fax:** 01902-302811
E-mail: info@birminghammidshires.co.uk
Website: http://www.bmsavings.co.uk
Directors: P. Beddows (Fin)
Managers: M. Reynold, S. Clarke, S. Kearsley, N. Ball (I.T. Exec)
Ultimate Holding Company: LLOYDS BANKING GROUP PLC
Immediate Holding Company: BIRMINGHAM MIDSHIRES FINANCIAL SERVICES LIMITED
Registration no: 02319628 **Date established:** 1988
No.of Employees: 1001 - 1500 **Product Groups:** 82

Date of Accounts	Dec 11	Dec 10	Dec 09
Working Capital	6m	6m	6m
Current Assets	6m	6m	6m

Bodycote Metallurgical Coatings Ltd
Shakespeare Street, Wolverhampton, WV1 3LR
Tel: 01902-452915 **Fax:** 01902-352917
E-mail: sales.bmc@bodycote.co.uk
Website: http://www.bodycote.co.uk
Bank(s): HSBC Bank plc
Directors: R. Blakemore (Sales)
Managers: S. Henley (Admin Off), B. Davenport (Tech Sales Mgr), I. Davies
Ultimate Holding Company: BODYCOTE PLC
Immediate Holding Company: BODYCOTE METALLURGICAL COATINGS LIMITED
Registration no: 00187961 **Date established:** 2023
Turnover: £10m - £20m **No.of Employees:** 101 - 250 **Product Groups:** 48

Date of Accounts	Dec 11	Dec 10	Dec 09
Sales Turnover	18m	16m	14m
Pre Tax Profit/Loss	2m	2m	532
Working Capital	6m	5m	-7m
Fixed Assets	17m	18m	18m
Current Assets	12m	10m	6m
Current Liabilities	3m	3m	3m

Brammer Ltd (Export Division)
National Distribution Centre Headway Road, Wolverhampton, WV10 6PZ
Tel: 01902-395959 **Fax:** 01902-395988
E-mail: export@brammer.biz
Website: http://www.brammer.co.uk/

Directors: G. Holride (Dir)
Ultimate Holding Company: LUPUS CAPITAL PLC
Immediate Holding Company: EWS (MANUFACTURING) LTD.
Registration no: 00569290 **Date established:** 1984
Turnover: £75m - £125m **No.of Employees:** 51 - 100
Product Groups: 29, 35

Date of Accounts	Dec 11	Dec 10	Dec 09
Sales Turnover	N/A	11m	20m
Pre Tax Profit/Loss	N/A	903	717
Working Capital	1m	1m	2m
Fixed Assets	N/A	N/A	2m
Current Assets	1m	1m	7m
Current Liabilities	N/A	N/A	1m

British Mensa Ltd
St Johns House St Johns Square, Wolverhampton, WV2 4AH
Tel: 01902-772771 **Fax:** 01902-392500
E-mail: enquiries@mensa.org.uk
Website: http://www.mensa.org.uk
Managers: C. Skitt
Immediate Holding Company: BRITISH MENSA LIMITED
Registration no: 00971663 **Date established:** 1970
Turnover: £500,000 - £1m **No.of Employees:** 11 - 20 **Product Groups:** 87

Date of Accounts	Dec 11	Dec 10	Dec 09
Sales Turnover	825	865	898
Pre Tax Profit/Loss	3	5	-8
Working Capital	172	163	150
Fixed Assets	3	9	17
Current Assets	263	251	229
Current Liabilities	49	46	36

N D Brown Ltd
Old Stafford Road Slade Heath, Wolverhampton, WV10 7PD
Tel: 01902-791991 **Fax:** 01902-790910
E-mail: jon@ndbrown.co.uk
Website: http://www.ndbrown.co.uk
Directors: N. Brown (Prop)
Immediate Holding Company: N.D. BROWN LIMITED
Registration no: 01471913 **Date established:** 1980
No.of Employees: 21 - 50 **Product Groups:** 39, 40, 45, 68, 72

Date of Accounts	Mar 12	Mar 11	Mar 10
Pre Tax Profit/Loss	713	718	650
Working Capital	-2m	-3m	-3m
Fixed Assets	9m	7m	8m
Current Assets	1m	1m	1m
Current Liabilities	404	653	653

Broyce Control Ltd
Pool Street, Wolverhampton, WV2 4HN
Tel: 01902-773746 **Fax:** 01902-420639
E-mail: sales@broycecontrol.com
Website: http://www.broycecontrol.com
Bank(s): Barclays, Queen St
Directors: M. Gough (MD)
Immediate Holding Company: BROYCE CONTROL LIMITED
Registration no: 00868370 **Date established:** 1966 **Turnover:** £2m - £5m
No.of Employees: 21 - 50 **Product Groups:** 37, 38, 40, 49

Date of Accounts	Dec 11	Dec 10	Dec 09
Working Capital	749	603	574
Fixed Assets	87	108	94
Current Assets	1m	935	1m

Bushbury Landrover Parts Services
Bushbury Lane, Wolverhampton, WV10 9TT
Tel: 01902-393200 **Fax:** 01902-393211
E-mail: steve.moore@stratstone.com
Website: http://www.stratstone.com
Managers: S. Moore
No.of Employees: 11 - 20 **Product Groups:** 68

Carillion
Construction House 24 Birch Street, Wolverhampton, WV1 4HY
Tel: 01902-422431 **Fax:** 0113-264 4702
Website: http://www.carillionplc.com
Bank(s): National Westminster Bank Plc & Barclays Bank PLC
Managers: J. Dennings
Ultimate Holding Company: CARILLION PLC
Immediate Holding Company: CARILLION HOLDINGS LIMITED
Registration no: 03783019 **VAT No.:** GB 100 6366 17
Date established: 1999 **No.of Employees:** 251 - 500 **Product Groups:** 84

Date of Accounts	Dec 11	Dec 10	Dec 09
Pre Tax Profit/Loss	5m	7m	3m
Working Capital	20m	15m	8m
Fixed Assets	3m	3m	3m
Current Assets	20m	15m	8m
Current Liabilities	23	40	29

Carvers Wolverhampton Ltd
Littles Lane, Wolverhampton, WV1 1JY
Tel: 01902-577000 **Fax:** 01902-712145
E-mail: sales@carvers.co.uk
Website: http://www.carvers.co.uk
Bank(s): Lloyds TSB Bank plc
Directors: R. Kendrick (Co Sec), R. Bolt (Dir), D. Carver (Asst MD), B. Turslow (Chief Op Offcr), A. Dinham (Sales), S. Moore (Pers)
Managers: R. Groom (Mktg Serv Mgr)
Ultimate Holding Company: CARVER (WOLVERHAMPTON) LIMITED
Immediate Holding Company: CARVER GASES LIMITED
Registration no: 01272289 **VAT No.:** GB 100 0333 62
Date established: 1976 **Turnover:** £20m - £50m
No.of Employees: 101 - 250 **Product Groups:** 66

Ceandess Wolverhampton Ltd
Ashford Indl-Est Dixon Street, Wolverhampton, WV2 2BX
Tel: 01902-872000 **Fax:** 01902-872019
E-mail: peter.killey@ceandess.co.uk
Website: http://www.ceandess.co.uk
Bank(s): HSBC Bank plc
Directors: S. Killey (Fin), M. Davies (Dir), P. Killey (Dir)
Managers: C. Smallman (Eng Serv Mgr), M. Chadha (Sales Admin)
Immediate Holding Company: CEANDESS (WOLVERHAMPTON) LIMITED
Registration no: 06896909 **VAT No.:** GB 738 8432 00
Date established: 2009 **Turnover:** £1m - £2m **No.of Employees:** 11 - 20
Product Groups: 35, 48

Date of Accounts	May 11	May 10
Sales Turnover	1m	948
Pre Tax Profit/Loss	37	29
Working Capital	13	50
Fixed Assets	107	100
Current Assets	394	358
Current Liabilities	239	220

Challenge Power Transmission Ltd
Unit 1-2 Merryhills Enterprise Park Park Lane, Wolverhampton, WV10 9TJ
Tel: 01902-866116 **Fax:** 01902-866117
E-mail: uk@challengept.com
Website: http://www.challengept.com
Directors: M. Pope (Fin)
Managers: G. Hopkins (Tech Serv Mgr)
Immediate Holding Company: CHALLENGE POWER TRANSMISSION LIMITED
Registration no: 03196154 **Date established:** 1996 **Turnover:** £5m - £10m
No.of Employees: 11 - 20 **Product Groups:** 29, 35, 45, 46, 66, 67

Date of Accounts	Dec 11	Dec 10	Dec 09
Sales Turnover	6m	6m	5m
Pre Tax Profit/Loss	657	373	353
Working Capital	2m	2m	2m
Fixed Assets	225	234	278
Current Assets	4m	3m	3m
Current Liabilities	787	779	802

Chambers Electrical Wolverhampton Ltd
74 Aldersley Road, Wolverhampton, WV6 9LZ
Tel: 01902-752094 **Fax:** 01902-752891
E-mail: chambers.electrical@btinternet.com
Website: http://www.chambers-electrical.co.uk
Directors: L. Chambers (MD)
Immediate Holding Company: CHAMBERS ELECTRICAL (WOLVERHAMPTON)LIMITED
Registration no: 01047567 **Date established:** 1972 **Turnover:** £1m - £2m
No.of Employees: 1 - 10 **Product Groups:** 52

Date of Accounts	Apr 11	Apr 10	Apr 09
Working Capital	178	144	148
Fixed Assets	72	81	87
Current Assets	275	283	296

Chromebar
Neachells Lane, Wolverhampton, WV11 3PY
Tel: 01902-725011 **Fax:** 01902- 305068
E-mail: sales@chromebaruk.com
Directors: M. Jones (Fin)
Immediate Holding Company: CHROMEBAR UK LTD
Registration no: 01620333 **VAT No.:** GB 489 5801 90
Date established: 1982 **Turnover:** £2m - £5m **No.of Employees:** 11 - 20
Product Groups: 34, 48

Date of Accounts	Aug 10	Aug 09	Aug 08
Working Capital	-145	-122	-17
Fixed Assets	11	16	35
Current Assets	195	217	197
Current Liabilities	N/A	N/A	94

Clipperlight Ltd
PO Box 3950, Wolverhampton, WV7 3BT
Tel: 01902-373217 **Fax:** 01902-375317
E-mail: clipperlight@aol.com
Website: http://www.clipperlight.com
Directors: M. Pate (MD)
Immediate Holding Company: CLIPPERLIGHT LIMITED
Registration no: 05378329 **Date established:** 2005
Turnover: Up to £250,000 **No.of Employees:** 1 - 10 **Product Groups:** 33, 38

College Engineering Supply
2 Sandy Lane Codsall, Wolverhampton, WV8 1EJ
Tel: 01902-842284 **Fax:** 01902-842284
E-mail: howard@collegeengineering.co.uk
Website: http://www.collegeengineering.co.uk
Directors: H. Proffitt (Snr Part)
Registration no: 03918566 **Date established:** 2000
Turnover: Up to £250,000 **No.of Employees:** 1 - 10 **Product Groups:** 34, 36, 45, 46, 64, 66

Components Automotive 73 Ltd
Unit 4-6 Wulfrun Trading Estate Stafford Road, Wolverhampton, WV10 6HG
Tel: 01902-311499 **Fax:** 01902-715213
E-mail: sales@comp.co.uk
Website: http://www.comp.co.uk
Bank(s): HSBC Bank plc
Directors: B. Dixon (MD)
Immediate Holding Company: COMPONENTS AUTOMOTIVES 73 LIMITED
Registration no: 01144938 **VAT No.:** GB 333 9173 55
Date established: 1973 **Turnover:** £2m - £5m **No.of Employees:** 21 - 50
Product Groups: 39

Date of Accounts	Dec 11	Dec 10	Dec 09
Working Capital	90	129	138
Fixed Assets	667	746	794
Current Assets	654	613	668

Concept Mouldings
63 Major Street, Wolverhampton, WV2 2HX
Tel: 01902-450902 **Fax:** 01902-870410
E-mail: ian.finney@conceptmouldings.co.uk
Website: http://www.conceptmouldings.co.uk
Directors: I. Finney (MD)
Immediate Holding Company: CONCEPT MOULDINGS LIMITED
Registration no: 02343052 **Date established:** 1989
Turnover: Up to £250,000 **No.of Employees:** 11 - 20 **Product Groups:** 22, 23, 25, 26, 29, 30, 31, 32, 39, 40, 42, 48, 49, 66, 67, 68, 84, 85

Date of Accounts	May 08
Working Capital	-513
Fixed Assets	658
Current Assets	750
Current Liabilities	1263
Total Share Capital	1

Concept Steel Ltd
Unit 5 Parkside Indl-Est Hickman Avenue, Wolverhampton, WV1 2EN
Tel: 01902-450444 **Fax:** 01902-455365
E-mail: ian.austin@concept-steels.co.uk
Website: http://www.conceptsteels.co.uk
Directors: G. Richards (Sales), I. Austin (MD)
Managers: P. Gomes (Export Sales Mg), G. Boyle (Sec)
Ultimate Holding Company: ACCURA GROUP LIMITED
Immediate Holding Company: CONCEPT STEELS LIMITED
Registration no: 01136933 **Date established:** 1973 **Turnover:** £1m - £2m
No.of Employees: 11 - 20 **Product Groups:** 36, 45, 66

Date of Accounts	Mar 11	Mar 10	Mar 09
Working Capital	1m	1m	1m
Fixed Assets	26	40	59
Current Assets	3m	2m	3m

Corus Ltd
PO Box 4 Bridgnorth Road, Wombourne, Wolverhampton, WV5 8AT
Tel: 01902-324444 **Fax:** 01902-324204
E-mail: enquiries@corus.com
Website: http://www.corusgroup.com
Managers: D. Guild (Purch Mgr), J. Day (Mgr), M. Salt (Sales Prom Mgr), T. Day (Chief Mgr)
Ultimate Holding Company: Corus Group P.L.C.
Immediate Holding Company: Corus
Registration no: 03811373 **Turnover:** £500m - £1,000m
No.of Employees: 51 - 100 **Product Groups:** 34

Cosgriff Whitehouse Electrical Ltd
Brickheath Road, Wolverhampton, WV1 2SR
Tel: 01902-451961 **Fax:** 01902-870971
E-mail: orders@coswhielec.co.uk
Website: http://www.coswhielec.co.uk
Bank(s): National Westminster
Directors: P. Whitehouse (Dir)
Managers: J. Whitehouse (Mktg Serv Mgr), A. Timmins
Immediate Holding Company: COSGRIFF WHITEHOUSE ELECTRICAL LIMITED
Registration no: 00420511 **Date established:** 1946 **Turnover:** £1m - £2m
No.of Employees: 21 - 50 **Product Groups:** 52

Date of Accounts	Sep 11	Sep 10	Sep 09
Working Capital	310	343	417
Fixed Assets	88	109	117
Current Assets	533	582	609

Cozens & Cole Ltd
Spring Road Ettingshall, Wolverhampton, WV4 6JT
Tel: 01902-405971 **Fax:** 01902-497021
E-mail: sales@cozensandcole.co.uk
Website: http://www.cozensandcole.co.uk
Directors: J. Zambra (Co Sec)
Ultimate Holding Company: H.A.C. (HOLDINGS) LIMITED
Immediate Holding Company: COZENS & COLE LIMITED
Registration no: 00682754 **VAT No.:** GB 100 0314 66
Date established: 1961 **Turnover:** £500,000 - £1m
No.of Employees: 1 - 10 **Product Groups:** 22, 23, 29, 30, 35, 45

Date of Accounts	Mar 11	Mar 10	Mar 09
Working Capital	259	228	204
Fixed Assets	36	32	38
Current Assets	696	629	628

D G S Abrasive Ltd
92 Dovedale Road, Wolverhampton, WV4 6RA
Tel: 01902-661111 **Fax:** 01902-880311
E-mail: sales@dgsabrasives.co.uk
Website: http://www.dgsabrasives.co.uk
Directors: D. Stevens (Fin), A. Stevens (Dir)
Immediate Holding Company: D.G.S. (GRINDING WHEELS & MACHINES) LIMITED
Registration no: 00896862 **Date established:** 1967 **Turnover:** £1m - £2m
No.of Employees: 1 - 10 **Product Groups:** 33

Date of Accounts	Dec 11	Dec 10	Dec 09
Working Capital	-193	-187	-196
Fixed Assets	304	309	301
Current Assets	621	952	994

D J D Components Wolverhampton Ltd
Unit 12b Showell Road, Wolverhampton, WV10 9LU
Tel: 01902-426228 **Fax:** 01902-424706
E-mail: office@djd.co.uk
Website: http://www.djd.co.uk
Directors: S. Castle (MD)
Immediate Holding Company: B.J.PLASTICS(WOLVERHAMPTON)LIMITED
Registration no: 01011816 **VAT No.:** GB 100 3138 458
Date established: 1971 **Turnover:** £250,000 - £500,000
No.of Employees: 1 - 10 **Product Groups:** 35

Date of Accounts	May 08	May 07	May 06
Working Capital	-42	-46	-57
Fixed Assets	11	10	11
Current Assets	27	35	51
Current Liabilities	69	80	107

D & J Steels Ltd
Colliery Road, Wolverhampton, WV1 2RD
Tel: 01902-453680 **Fax:** 01902-455431
E-mail: info@dandjsteels.com
Website: http://www.dandjsteels.com
Directors: S. Huggins (MD), D. Grove (Fin), C. Hutton-Penman (Ch)
Ultimate Holding Company: OFFSHORE SOURCING LIMITED
Immediate Holding Company: J D REALISATIONS LIMITED
Registration no: 00993624 **Date established:** 1970
No.of Employees: 11 - 20 **Product Groups:** 34

Date of Accounts	Mar 11	Mar 10	Mar 09
Sales Turnover	5m	N/A	N/A
Pre Tax Profit/Loss	55	N/A	N/A
Working Capital	643	889	675
Fixed Assets	745	480	497
Current Assets	4m	3m	2m
Current Liabilities	147	N/A	N/A

D S Metals Ltd
Trigstone House Nurton Hill Road, Pattingham, Wolverhampton, WV6 7HG
Tel: 01902-701539 **Fax:** 01902-701557
E-mail: dsmetals@btconnect.com
Website: http://www.dsmetals.com
Directors: P. Wraight (Dir), D. Sandford (MD), D. Bickley (Co Sec), P. Wraight (Co Sec)
Managers: J. Bickley (Accounts)
Registration no: 04077252 **VAT No.:** GB 754 3873 05
No.of Employees: 1 - 10 **Product Groups:** 31, 34, 35, 66

Date of Accounts	Dec 11	Dec 10	Dec 09
Working Capital	1m	1m	807
Fixed Assets	1	1	1
Current Assets	2m	1m	2m

Dalvie Storage Systems Ltd
Hilton Lane Essington, Wolverhampton, WV11 2BQ
Tel: 08450-178866 **Fax:** 0845-017 8877
E-mail: info@dalviestorage.co.uk
Website: http://www.dalviestorage.co.uk
Directors: T. Mckelvie (MD)
Immediate Holding Company: DALVIE STORAGE SYSTEMS LIMITED
Registration no: 04096375 **Date established:** 2000
No.of Employees: 1 - 10 **Product Groups:** 35, 42, 45

Date of Accounts	Mar 12	Mar 11	Mar 10
Working Capital	36	35	45
Fixed Assets	13	17	19
Current Assets	197	211	123

Deansfield Metal Finishing Co. Ltd
Colliery Road, Wolverhampton, WV1 2RD
Tel: 01902-351811 **Fax:** 01902-458165
E-mail: admin@deansfield.fsbusiness.co.uk
Directors: G. Clifford (Dir), G. Clifford (MD)
Managers: I. Jarvis (Works Gen Mgr), Y. Smith (Sales Admin)
Immediate Holding Company: DEANSFIELD METAL FINISHING COMPANY LIMITED
Registration no: 00707198 **VAT No.:** GB 100 3194 35
Date established: 1961 **Turnover:** £500,000 - £1m
No.of Employees: 1 - 10 **Product Groups:** 48

Date of Accounts	Dec 10	Dec 09	Dec 08
Working Capital	334	327	475
Fixed Assets	55	57	60
Current Assets	397	770	768

Debut Design Ltd
Technology Centre Glaisher Drive, Wolverhampton Science Park, Wolverhampton, WV10 9RU
Tel: 01902-837424
E-mail: studio@debutcreate.com
Website: http://www.debutcreate.com
Directors: S. Campbell (Prop), S. Campbell (MD)
Immediate Holding Company: DEBUT DESIGN LTD
Registration no: 05475024 **Date established:** 2005
Turnover: Up to £250,000 **No.of Employees:** 1 - 10 **Product Groups:** 28, 44, 49

Dependable Springs & Pressings Ltd (Head Office & Factory)
Stewart Street, Wolverhampton, WV2 4JZ
Tel: 01902-420934 **Fax:** 01902-423453
E-mail: mail@dependablesprings.co.uk
Website: http://www.dependablesprings.co.uk
Bank(s): Barclays
Directors: A. Turner (Dir), G. Turner (MD)
Managers: A. Turner, A. Turner
Immediate Holding Company: DEPENDABLE SPRINGS & PRESSINGS LIMITED
Registration no: 00332847 **Date established:** 1937
No.of Employees: 11 - 20 **Product Groups:** 34, 35, 36, 37, 39, 40, 48

Deritend
PO Box 36, Wolverhampton, WV2 4PB
Tel: 01902-426390 **Fax:** 01922-723128
E-mail: induction@deritend.co.uk
Website: http://www.deritend.co.uk
Managers: L. Miller (Personnel)
Immediate Holding Company: DERITEND INDUSTRIES LIMITED
Registration no: 05394932 **Date established:** 2005
Turnover: £20m - £50m **No.of Employees:** 1 - 10 **Product Groups:** 35, 37, 40, 46, 48, 52, 66, 85

Date of Accounts	Dec 11	Dec 10	Dec 09
Sales Turnover	20m	19m	21m
Pre Tax Profit/Loss	27	-412	-459
Working Capital	1m	1m	-390
Fixed Assets	4m	5m	6m
Current Assets	8m	6m	6m
Current Liabilities	1m	902	1m

DE-STA-CO U.K
Unit 7, Calibre Industrial Park Laches Close, Four Ashes, Wolverhampton, WV10 7DZ
Tel: 01902-797980 **Fax:** 01902-797981
E-mail: uk@destaco.com
Website: http://www.destaco.com
Managers: J. Smith (Chief Mgr)
Ultimate Holding Company: Dover Corporation (USA)
Immediate Holding Company: De Sta CO Metallerzeugnisse GmbH (Germany)
Registration no: 02581562 **No.of Employees:** 1 - 10 **Product Groups:** 28, 35

E F D Induction Ltd
Unit 1-2 Well Lane, Wolverhampton, WV11 1XP
Tel: 01902-308800 **Fax:** 01902-739222
E-mail: pjg@efdinduction.co.uk
Website: http://www.efd-induction.com
Directors: P. Greaves (Co Sec), W. Marsh (Fin)
Immediate Holding Company: EFD INDUCTION LIMITED
Registration no: 01193252 **Date established:** 1974 **Turnover:** £2m - £5m
No.of Employees: 11 - 20 **Product Groups:** 37, 40

Date of Accounts	Dec 11	Dec 10	Dec 09
Working Capital	609	395	247
Fixed Assets	129	45	80
Current Assets	1m	962	757

E T N A Assist UK
Unit 30 Calibre Industrial Park Laches Close, Four Ashes, Wolverhampton, WV10 7DZ
Tel: 01902-798606 **Fax:** 01902-798686
E-mail: info@etna-ct.com
Website: http://www.etna-ct.com
Directors: S. Matharu (Prop)
Immediate Holding Company: ETNA ASSIST UK LIMITED
Registration no: 04665111 **Date established:** 2003
No.of Employees: 1 - 10 **Product Groups:** 62

Date of Accounts	Feb 11	Feb 10	Feb 09
Working Capital	-64	-38	55
Fixed Assets	1	2	N/A
Current Assets	15	54	314

E W S Manufacturing Ltd
Headway Road, Wolverhampton, WV10 6PZ
Tel: 01902-623333 **Fax:** 01902-623300
E-mail: info@ewsproducts.com
Website: http://www.ews-ltd.com
Directors: A. McKeown (Chief Op Offcr), M. Russell (Sales)
Managers: D. Waters, S. Jones (Tech Serv Mgr), L. Stait (Comptroller)
Ultimate Holding Company: LUPUS CAPITAL PLC
Immediate Holding Company: EWS (MANUFACTURING) LTD.
Registration no: 01874264 **Date established:** 1984
Turnover: £10m - £20m **No.of Employees:** 51 - 100 **Product Groups:** 34

Date of Accounts	Dec 11	Dec 10	Dec 09
Sales Turnover	N/A	11m	20m
Pre Tax Profit/Loss	N/A	903	717
Working Capital	1m	1m	2m
Fixed Assets	N/A	N/A	2m
Current Assets	1m	1m	7m
Current Liabilities	N/A	N/A	1m

Ecolec Ltd
Sharrocks Street, Wolverhampton, WV1 3RP
Tel: 01902-457575 **Fax:** 01902-457797
E-mail: info@ecolec.co.uk
Website: http://www.ecolec.co.uk
Directors: C. Ray (MD)
Immediate Holding Company: MIDDLEMORE LIMITED
Registration no: 00121986 **VAT No.:** GB 417 8474 28
Date established: 2012 **No.of Employees:** 1 - 10 **Product Groups:** 38, 40, 66

Date of Accounts	Dec 10	Dec 09	Dec 08
Sales Turnover	N/A	N/A	285
Pre Tax Profit/Loss	N/A	-61	16
Working Capital	685	685	746
Current Assets	685	685	762
Current Liabilities	N/A	N/A	2

Edbros Fixings
Unit B2 Blakenhall Business Park Moorfield Road, Wolverhampton, WV2 4QT
Tel: 01902-715500 **Fax:** 01902-715501
Website: http://www.edbrosfixings.co.uk
Directors: S. Coleman (Dir)
Registration no: 06332172 **Date established:** 2007
No.of Employees: 1 - 10 **Product Groups:** 35

B S Ellis
Unit 5 Chillington Fields, Wolverhampton, WV1 2BY
Tel: 01902-459111 **Fax:** 01902-459111
Directors: B. Ellis (Prop)
Immediate Holding Company: B S ELLIS JIG & TOOL CO LTD
Registration no: 04659520 **VAT No.:** GB 101 1770 29
Date established: 2003 **Turnover:** Up to £250,000
No.of Employees: 1 - 10 **Product Groups:** 46, 48

Date of Accounts	Mar 11	Mar 10	Mar 07
Working Capital	-1	-4	-3
Current Assets	14	5	7
Current Liabilities	13	N/A	10

Emag UK Ltd
Chestnut House Kingswood Business Park, Albrighton, Wolverhampton, WV7 3AU
Tel: 01902-373121 **Fax:** 01902-376091
E-mail: sales@emag-vsc.co.uk
Website: http://www.emag-vsc.co.uk
Directors: E. York (MD)
Ultimate Holding Company: EMAG MASCHINENFABRIK GMBH (GERMANY)
Immediate Holding Company: EMAG (U.K.) LIMITED
Registration no: 01774955 **VAT No.:** GB 396 8160 09
Date established: 1983 **No.of Employees:** 1 - 10 **Product Groups:** 46

Date of Accounts	Dec 11	Dec 10	Dec 09
Working Capital	42	52	107
Fixed Assets	7	12	8
Current Assets	315	323	483

Enviroflo Engineering Ltd
Unit 10a Newton Court Westrand Pendeford Business Park, Wolverhampton, WV9 5HB
Tel: 01902-784848 **Fax:** 01902-784242
E-mail: sales@envirofloeng.com
Website: http://www.envirofloeng.com
Managers: S. Parkes (Mgr)
Ultimate Holding Company: NALCO COMPANY (USA)
Immediate Holding Company: ENVIROFLO ENGINEERING LIMITED
Registration no: 01463262 **Date established:** 1979
No.of Employees: 1 - 10 **Product Groups:** 40, 45

Date of Accounts	Dec 11	Dec 10	Dec 09
Sales Turnover	461	372	243
Pre Tax Profit/Loss	-962	-90	53
Working Capital	5m	5m	5m
Fixed Assets	257	1m	1m
Current Assets	5m	5m	5m
Current Liabilities	117	19	8

European Mezzanine Systems Ltd
Berrington Lodge 93 Tettenhall Road, Wolverhampton, WV3 9PE
Tel: 0845-2609601 **Fax:** 0845-2609602
E-mail: info@mezzstore.com
Website: http://www.mezzstore.com
Registration no: 04407634 **Product Groups:** 25, 26, 29, 30, 35, 36, 40, 52, 66, 67

European Mezzanine Systems
303 Tettenhall Road, Wolverhampton, WV6 0LB
Tel: 08452-609601 **Fax:** 08452-609602
E-mail: sales@mezzstore.com
Managers: D. Elliot (Mgr)
No.of Employees: 1 - 10 **Product Groups:** 35, 40, 52

Eurovan Express
Fibbersley, Wolverhampton, WV11 3SU
Tel: 07841-030335 **Fax:** 01902-410095
E-mail: info@eurovanexpress.com
Website: http://www.eurovanexpress.com
Directors: I. Shaw (Prop)
Registration no: 04473512 **Date established:** 2002
Turnover: Up to £250,000 **No.of Employees:** 1 - 10 **Product Groups:** 72

Gordon Evans Welding Supplies
Lower Horseley Field, Wolverhampton, WV1 3DZ
Tel: 01902-450200 **Fax:** 01902-351257
E-mail: sales@gordonevanswelding.co.uk
Directors: G. Evans (Prop)
Immediate Holding Company: ASWM LTD.
Registration no: 05929648 **Date established:** 2006
No.of Employees: 1 - 10 **Product Groups:** 46

Evans Halshaw Motors Ltd
67-71 Bilston Road, Wolverhampton, WV2 2QH
Tel: 01902-352352 **Fax:** 01902-458728
E-mail: paul.cooper@evanshalshaw.com
Website: http://www.evanshalshaw.com
Managers: P. Cooper (Mgr)
Ultimate Holding Company: PENDRAGON PLC
Immediate Holding Company: EVANS HALSHAW MOTORS LIMITED
Registration no: 01359849 **VAT No.:** GB 655 1306 52
Date established: 1978 **No.of Employees:** 21 - 50 **Product Groups:** 68

Date of Accounts	Dec 11	Dec 10	Dec 09
Working Capital	11m	11m	11m
Fixed Assets	9m	9m	9m
Current Assets	14m	14m	14m
Current Liabilities	3m	4m	4m

Expocet
113 Millfields Road, Wolverhampton, WV4 6JQ
Tel: 01902-836653
E-mail: martin@expocet.com
Website: http://www.expocet.com
Directors: M. Thomas (MD), M. Thomas (Sales), B. Dills (Sales), F. Ciampo (Sales), M. Thomas (Export), B. Dills (Export), F. Ciampo (Export), M. Thomas (Fin)
Managers: M. Thomas ()
Date established: 1996 **Product Groups:** 34, 80

Express & Star
Queen Street, Wolverhampton, WV1 1ES
Tel: 01902-313131 **Fax:** 01902-319721
E-mail: business@expressandstar.co.uk
Website: http://www.expressandstar.co.uk
Bank(s): Barclays, Wolverhampton
Directors: M. Graham (Ch), K. Parker (MD), G. Evers (Dir), E. Graham (Dir), D. Hughes (Dir), R. Green (Fab)
Managers: L. Young (Grp Mktg Mgr), V. Birch (Publicity)
Ultimate Holding Company: CLAVERLEY COMPANY
Immediate Holding Company: EXPRESS & STAR GROUP PENSION SCHEME LIMITED
Registration no: 01166216 **VAT No.:** GB 661 5365 33
Date established: 1974 **Turnover:** £20m - £50m
No.of Employees: 251 - 500 **Product Groups:** 28

Fablink UK Ltd
Stafford Road Fordhouses, Wolverhampton, WV10 7EJ
Tel: 01902-397766 **Fax:** 01902-788912
E-mail: m.singleton@fablink.co.uk
Website: http://www.fablink.co.uk
Bank(s): National Westminster Bank Plc
Directors: M. Singleton (MD)
Managers: E. Hesson (Personnel), D. Stephens (Fin Mgr), J. Baylay
Ultimate Holding Company: FABLINK LIMITED
Immediate Holding Company: FABLINK UK LIMITED
Registration no: 05745399 **VAT No.:** GB 100 4941 19
Date established: 2006 **Turnover:** £10m - £20m
No.of Employees: 101 - 250 **Product Groups:** 48

Date of Accounts	Mar 11	Mar 10	Mar 09
Sales Turnover	15m	8m	13m
Pre Tax Profit/Loss	255	-571	89
Working Capital	111	-99	467
Fixed Assets	2m	1m	1m
Current Assets	8m	4m	3m
Current Liabilities	4m	742	1m

Fellows (Pressings & Presswork Products Division)
Graiseley Row, Wolverhampton, WV2 4HL
Tel: 01902-576400 **Fax:** 01902- 576404
E-mail: sue.shinton@fellowstld.co.uk
Website: http://www.ricalltd.com
Directors: B. Head (Ch), M. Pemberton (Fin)
Managers: R. Worsey (Chief Mgr), S. Shinton (Purch Mgr), R. Worsey (Works Gen Mgr), M. Poole (I.T. Exec), M. Pool (I.T. Exec), I. Bubb (Sales & Mktg Mg)
Ultimate Holding Company: RICAL LTD
Immediate Holding Company: RICAL GROUP
Registration no: 00043995 **Date established:** 1895 **Turnover:** £2m - £5m
No.of Employees: 21 - 50 **Product Groups:** 48, 67

Fern Plastic Products Ltd
Macrome Road, Wolverhampton, WV6 9HD
Tel: 01902-758282 **Fax:** 01902-757500
E-mail: igraham@fern-plastics.co.uk
Website: http://www.fern-plastics.co.uk
Bank(s): HSBC Bank plc
Directors: I. Graham (Co Sec), G. Harper (Dir)
Ultimate Holding Company: FERN MANUFACTURING GROUP LIMITED
Immediate Holding Company: FERN PLASTIC PRODUCTS LIMITED
Registration no: 00624855 **VAT No.:** GB 100 0540 57
Date established: 1959 **Turnover:** £5m - £10m
No.of Employees: 101 - 250 **Product Groups:** 29, 30, 31, 38, 48, 66

Date of Accounts	Mar 12	Mar 11	Mar 10
Sales Turnover	7m	7m	7m
Pre Tax Profit/Loss	46	74	120
Working Capital	2m	2m	2m
Fixed Assets	838	916	1000
Current Assets	5m	4m	4m
Current Liabilities	1m	1m	1m

Freshway Chilled Foods Ltd
Stafford Court Boundary Industrial Estate Stafford Road, Wolverhampton, WV10 7EL
Tel: 01902-783666 **Fax:** 01902-781141
E-mail: brendag@freshway-foods.co.uk
Website: http://www.freshlay.co.uk
Directors: T. Britton (MD)
Managers: B. Gibbons (Personnel), T. Gilbride (Chief Acct)
Ultimate Holding Company: RECORDLINE LIMITED
Immediate Holding Company: FRESHWAY CHILLED FOODS LIMITED
Registration no: 06790279 **Date established:** 2009 **Turnover:** £5m - £10m
No.of Employees: 101 - 250 **Product Groups:** 20

Date of Accounts	Jan 10	Jan 11
Sales Turnover	21m	29m
Pre Tax Profit/Loss	-245	7
Working Capital	-89	-381
Fixed Assets	785	1m
Current Assets	4m	5m
Current Liabilities	418	249

Gardner Technical Services

Unit 4-5 New Cross Industrial Estate Brickheath Road, Wolverhampton, WV1 2RZ
Tel: 01902-870736 **Fax:** 01902-832749
E-mail: colin@gardnertechnicalservices.co.uk
Website: http://www.forklifttrucksuk.com
Directors: C. Gardner (MD)
Registration no: 01912911 **Date established:** 1985
No.of Employees: 1 - 10 **Product Groups:** 35, 39, 45

Glaze Autoparts

Dixon Street, Wolverhampton, WV2 2BP
Tel: 01902-455434 **Fax:** 01902-456210
E-mail: glazeautoparts@hotmail.com
Directors: M. Leason (Dir), R. Williams (Dir)
Immediate Holding Company: GLAZE AUTO PARTS LIMITED
Registration no: 04101271 **Date established:** 2000 **Turnover:** £1m - £2m
No.of Employees: 1 - 10 **Product Groups:** 68

Date of Accounts	Nov 11	Nov 10	Nov 09
Working Capital	307	305	300
Fixed Assets	22	13	16
Current Assets	644	601	545

Global Fabrications

7 Tower Works Industrial Estate Pelham Street, Wolverhampton, WV3 0BW
Tel: 01902-711174 **Fax:** 01902- 711174
Directors: B. Hollis (Prop)
Date established: 1995 **No.of Employees:** 1 - 10 **Product Groups:** 35

W Groves

3 Cullwick Street, Wolverhampton, WV1 2UL
Tel: 01902-404300 **Fax:** 01902-353112
E-mail: sales@wgroves.co.uk
Website: http://www.wgroves.co.uk
Bank(s): Barclays
Managers: E. Phelan (Chief Mgr)
VAT No.: GB 109 6183 68 **Turnover:** £250,000 - £500,000
No.of Employees: 11 - 20 **Product Groups:** 37

Guardrail Engineering Ltd

Pountney Street, Wolverhampton, WV2 4HX
Tel: 01902-871208 **Fax:** 01902-453330
E-mail: enquiries@guardrailgroup.com
Website: http://www.guardrailgroup.com
Directors: K. Burns (Dir)
Ultimate Holding Company: PF MANAGEMENT HOLDING A/S (DENMARK)
Immediate Holding Company: GUARDRAIL ENGINEERING LIMITED
Registration no: 03020408 **Date established:** 1995
Turnover: £500,000 - £1m **No.of Employees:** 11 - 20 **Product Groups:** 35

Date of Accounts	Dec 11	Dec 10	Dec 09
Working Capital	355	319	285
Fixed Assets	93	148	175
Current Assets	682	635	505

Gunnebo UK Ltd

Woden Road, Wolverhampton, WV10 0BY
Tel: 01902-455111 **Fax:** 01902-351961
E-mail: marketing@gunnebo.com
Website: http://www.gunnebo.com
Bank(s): Scandinaviska Enskilda Banken
Directors: T. Rochford (Dir)
Ultimate Holding Company: GUNNEBO AB (SWEDEN)
Immediate Holding Company: GUNNEBO UK LIMITED
Registration no: 00495726 **Date established:** 1951
Turnover: £20m - £50m **No.of Employees:** 11 - 20 **Product Groups:** 25, 26, 33, 35, 36, 39, 44, 48, 84

Date of Accounts	Dec 11	Dec 10	Dec 09
Sales Turnover	43m	39m	30m
Pre Tax Profit/Loss	3m	3m	779
Working Capital	8m	8m	6m
Fixed Assets	4m	5m	5m
Current Assets	18m	17m	10m
Current Liabilities	5m	5m	1m

H C Two Ltd

3 Brunel Court Enterprise Drive, Four Ashes, Wolverhampton, WV10 7DF
Tel: 01902-790805
Directors: R. Johnson (MD), D. Johnson (Fin)
Immediate Holding Company: H.C. TWO LIMITED
Registration no: 01741601 **Date established:** 1983
No.of Employees: 1 - 10 **Product Groups:** 25, 30, 49

Date of Accounts	Mar 11	Mar 10	Mar 09
Working Capital	25	19	18
Fixed Assets	63	75	84
Current Assets	40	30	29

H R O D C

122a Bhylls Lane, Wolverhampton, WV3 8DZ
Tel: 01902-763607 **Fax:** 01902-569133
E-mail: sales@hrodc.com
Website: http://www.hrod-consultancy.com
Directors: R. Crawford (Grp Chief Exec)
Managers: Crawford
Immediate Holding Company: HUMAN RESOURCE AND ORGANISATIONAL DEVELOPMENT CONSULTANCY (HRODC) LIMI
Registration no: 06088763 **Date established:** 2007
Turnover: Up to £250,000 **No.of Employees:** 1 - 10 **Product Groups:** 44, 45

Date of Accounts	Feb 08	Feb 11	Feb 10
Working Capital	-9	-22	4
Fixed Assets	5	7	4
Current Assets	N/A	12	30

H Y Ten Welded Mesh Co.

Dunstall Hill Industrial Estate Gorsebrook Road, Wolverhampton, WV6 0PJ
Tel: 01902-712200 **Fax:** 01902-714096
E-mail: sales@hy-ten.co.uk
Website: http://www.hy-ten.co.uk
Managers: P. Nichols (District Mgr)
No.of Employees: 11 - 20 **Product Groups:** 35, 66

G Hadley & Sons Sheet Metal Ltd

Sedgley Street, Wolverhampton, WV2 3AJ
Tel: 01902-458990 **Fax:** 01902-454926
E-mail: davidhadley8@aol.com
Directors: G. Hadley (MD)
Immediate Holding Company: G.HADLEY & SONS(SHEET METAL)LIMITED
Registration no: 01031441 **VAT No.:** 100 6231 40 **Date established:** 1971
No.of Employees: 1 - 10 **Product Groups:** 52

Date of Accounts	Nov 11	Nov 10	Nov 09
Working Capital	144	132	106
Fixed Assets	24	28	24
Current Assets	260	240	162

Hallett Oils Ltd

19 Tyninghame Avenue, Wolverhampton, WV6 9PP
Tel: 01902-745800 **Fax:** 07958-344202
E-mail: richard@hallettoil.co.uk
Website: http://www.hallettoil.co.uk
Directors: R. Hallett (MD), R. Hallett (Prop)
Immediate Holding Company: HALLETT OILS LIMITED
Registration no: 04637858 **Date established:** 2003
No.of Employees: 1 - 10 **Product Groups:** 31, 32

Hart Materials Ltd

Carrier House Carriers Fold Church Road, Wombourne, Wolverhampton, WV5 9DH
Tel: 01902-895446 **Fax:** 01902-897469
E-mail: info@hartmaterials.com
Website: http://www.hartmaterials.com
Directors: A. Hart (MD)
Immediate Holding Company: HART MATERIALS LIMITED
Registration no: 06504658 **VAT No.:** GB 351 5265 68
Date established: 2008 **Turnover:** Up to £250,000
No.of Employees: 1 - 10 **Product Groups:** 31, 32, 35, 37, 46, 48

Date of Accounts	Mar 11	Mar 10	Mar 09
Working Capital	17	-47	-50
Fixed Assets	172	182	191
Current Assets	274	332	205

Henry Squire & Sons Ltd

Unit 2 Hilton Cross Business Park Featherstone, Wolverhampton, WV10 7QZ
Tel: 01902-308050 **Fax:** 01902-308051
E-mail: info@henry-squire.co.uk
Website: http://www.squirelocks.co.uk
Directors: J. Squire (MD)
Ultimate Holding Company: HENRY SQUIRE & SONS HOLDINGS LIMITED
Immediate Holding Company: HENRY SQUIRE & SONS LIMITED
Registration no: 00088907 **VAT No.:** GB 100 1214 65
Date established: 2006 **No.of Employees:** 21 - 50 **Product Groups:** 36

Date of Accounts	Dec 11	Dec 10	Dec 09
Working Capital	288	364	55
Fixed Assets	325	307	325
Current Assets	3m	3m	3m

High Performance Alloys Ltd a division of Non Ferrous Stockholders Ltd

The Nfs Group, Dock Meadow Lanesfield Drive, Wolverhampton, WV4 6LE
Tel: 01902-353747 **Fax:** 01902-491030
E-mail: sales@non-ferrous.co.uk
Website: http://www.high-performance-alloys.com
Directors: B. Burt (MD)
Registration no: 04022117 **Date established:** 1983 **Turnover:** £5m - £10m
No.of Employees: 11 - 20 **Product Groups:** 34

Home Furnishings

16 Station Road Albrighton, Wolverhampton, WV7 3QG
Tel: 01902-373647 **Fax:** 01902-373647
E-mail: info@homefurnishingsshop.net
Website: http://www.homefurnishingsshop.net
Directors: R. Ganner (Prop)
No.of Employees: 1 - 10 **Product Groups:** 23, 24, 26

Hotchkiss Air Supply

Heath Mill Road Wombourne, Wolverhampton, WV5 8AP
Tel: 01902-895161 **Fax:** 01902-892045
E-mail: glattimer@hotchkissairsupply.co.uk
Website: http://www.hotchkissairsupply.co.uk
Bank(s): The Royal Bank of Scotland, Eastbourne
Directors: G. Latimer (Dir)
Managers: J. Black (Comptroller), P. Slater (Comm), B. Cook (Prod Mgr)
Ultimate Holding Company: SOLIOS THERMAL LIMITED
Immediate Holding Company: FATSPANNER LIMITED
Registration no: 00900611 **Date established:** 2002
Turnover: £10m - £20m **No.of Employees:** 51 - 100 **Product Groups:** 23, 30, 35, 36, 39, 40, 46, 52, 66

Date of Accounts	Mar 12	Mar 11	Mar 10
Sales Turnover	1m	2m	2m
Pre Tax Profit/Loss	143	1	-189
Working Capital	372	186	112
Fixed Assets	36	160	242
Current Assets	807	896	690
Current Liabilities	100	52	92

Arthur Hough & Sons Ltd

Hilton Cross Business Park Cannock Road, Featherstone, Wolverhampton, WV10 7QZ
Tel: 01902-867717 **Fax:** 01902-867719
E-mail: sales@ahough.com
Website: http://www.ahough.com
Bank(s): HSBC, Bloxwich
Directors: B. Appleby (Tech Serv), R. Evans (MD)
Immediate Holding Company: ARTHUR HOUGH & SONS LIMITED
Registration no: 00927416 **Date established:** 1968 **Turnover:** £2m - £5m
No.of Employees: 21 - 50 **Product Groups:** 35, 36, 37, 48, 66

Date of Accounts	Feb 12	Feb 11	Feb 10
Working Capital	514	445	131
Fixed Assets	3m	3m	3m
Current Assets	1m	1m	1m

Howard Shipping Services Ltd

Showell Road, Wolverhampton, WV10 9JY
Tel: 01902-738838 **Fax:** 01902-862962
E-mail: stuarthoward@hoship.com
Website: http://www.hoship.com
Directors: S. Howard (Dir)
Immediate Holding Company: HOWARD SHIPPING SERVICES LIMITED
Registration no: 00568207 **Date established:** 1956 **Turnover:** £1m - £2m
No.of Employees: 21 - 50 **Product Groups:** 72, 76

Date of Accounts	Jun 11	Jun 10	Jun 09
Working Capital	396	365	363
Fixed Assets	24	24	25
Current Assets	1m	757	798

Industrial Brakes Ltd

Unit 14-15 Webnor Industrial Estate Ettingshall Road, Wolverhampton, WV2 2LD
Tel: 01902-492337 **Fax:** 01902-404420
E-mail: sales@industrialbrakes.co.uk
Website: http://www.industrialbrakes.co.uk
Directors: B. Holmes (Dir)
Immediate Holding Company: INDUSTRIAL BRAKES LIMITED
Registration no: 01831530 **Date established:** 1984 **Turnover:** £1m - £2m
No.of Employees: 11 - 20 **Product Groups:** 33, 34, 35, 39, 45, 46, 48, 66

Date of Accounts	Sep 11	Sep 10	Sep 09
Working Capital	593	531	493
Fixed Assets	112	93	122
Current Assets	737	639	601

Industrial Cleaning Machines

Icm House Showell Road, Wolverhampton, WV10 9LN
Tel: 01902-306039 **Fax:** 01902-304774
E-mail: bob@industrialcleaningmachines.co.uk
Website: http://www.industrialcleaningmachines.co.uk
Directors: R. Evans (Dir)
Immediate Holding Company: TODCO THREE LIMITED
Registration no: 02352928 **Date established:** 1989 **Turnover:** £1m - £2m
No.of Employees: 11 - 20 **Product Groups:** 36, 40

Date of Accounts	Oct 11	Oct 10	Oct 09
Working Capital	-44	109	107
Fixed Assets	356	308	389
Current Assets	468	435	412

J A Seals Ltd

Unit 23 Essington Industrial Estate, Bognop Road, Essington, Wolverhampton, WV11 2BJ
Tel: 01922-710888 **Fax:** 01922-710999
E-mail: sales@jaseals.co.uk
Website: http://www.jaseals.co.uk
Directors: W. Thorpe (Dir), R. Thorpe (Dir)
Registration no: 05541133 **Date established:** 1997
No.of Employees: 1 - 10 **Product Groups:** 29, 30, 32, 33, 35, 36, 39, 41, 45, 49, 66

Date of Accounts	Dec 11	Dec 10	Dec 08
Working Capital	-17	N/A	-2
Fixed Assets	81	81	131
Current Assets	191	179	125

J & M Tubes Ltd

Unit 31 Central Industrial Estate Cable Street, Wolverhampton, WV2 2RL
Tel: 01902-450163 **Fax:** 01902-450169
E-mail: j.m.tubes.ltd@btconnect.com
Website: http://www.jandmtubesltd.co.uk
Directors: M. Gower (Fin), P. Gower (MD)
Immediate Holding Company: J & M TUBES LIMITED
Registration no: 04275005 **Date established:** 2001
Turnover: Up to £250,000 **No.of Employees:** 1 - 10 **Product Groups:** 34, 36, 37, 45, 46, 48, 66

Date of Accounts	Nov 11	Nov 10	Nov 09
Working Capital	83	66	63
Fixed Assets	2	16	31
Current Assets	178	175	110

Jenks & Cattell Engineering Ltd

Neachells Lane, Wolverhampton, WV11 3PU
Tel: 01902-305530 **Fax:** 01902-305529
E-mail: sales@jcel.co.uk
Website: http://www.jcel.co.uk
Bank(s): National Westminster Bank Plc
Directors: A. Harrison (Co Sec)
Managers: D. Dawson (Ops Mgr), N. George (Sales Prom Mgr), G. Palmer
Ultimate Holding Company: NEWSHIP PRODUCTS GROUP LIMITED
Immediate Holding Company: JENKS & CATTELL ENGINEERING LIMITED
Registration no: 02064801 **Date established:** 1986 **Turnover:** £2m - £5m
No.of Employees: 51 - 100 **Product Groups:** 48

Date of Accounts	Sep 11	Sep 10	Sep 09
Sales Turnover	4m	3m	4m
Pre Tax Profit/Loss	-64	-765	-921
Working Capital	1m	567	786
Fixed Assets	511	596	712
Current Assets	2m	1m	2m
Current Liabilities	142	126	257

John Handley Bearings Ltd

Unit 2 Heath Mill Business Centre Wombourne, Wolverhampton, WV5 8AP
Tel: 01902-898560 **Fax:** 01902-898561
E-mail: sales@johnhandleybearings.com
Website: http://www.hhttp://www.johnhandleybearings.com
Directors: W. Ellis (MD)
Immediate Holding Company: JOHN HANDLEY (BEARINGS) LIMITED
Registration no: 00787398 **Date established:** 1964 **Turnover:** £1m - £2m
No.of Employees: 1 - 10 **Product Groups:** 35

Date of Accounts	Dec 11	Dec 10	Dec 09
Working Capital	578	576	580
Fixed Assets	4	5	8
Current Assets	979	928	889

K & K Fashions Ltd

Kainth House 54 Stewart Street, Wolverhampton, WV2 4JW
Tel: 01902-714855 **Fax:** 01902-689972
E-mail: sales@kkfashionsltd.co.uk
Website: http://www.kkfashionsltd.co.uk
Directors: R. Rattenbury (Sales)
Immediate Holding Company: K & K FASHIONS LIMITED
Registration no: 03564089 **Date established:** 1998
Turnover: Up to £250,000 **No.of Employees:** 11 - 20 **Product Groups:** 24

Date of Accounts	May 12	May 11	May 10
Working Capital	-10	-5	6
Fixed Assets	15	18	21
Current Assets	63	49	49

Kenworth H & V Products Ltd
27 St Andrews Drive Perton, Wolverhampton, WV6 7YL
Tel: 01902-741259 **Fax:** 01902-750900
E-mail: info@kenworthgrilles.co.uk
Website: http://www.kenworthgrilles.co.uk
Directors: A. Rickuss (Fin)
Immediate Holding Company: KENWORTH H & V PRODUCTS LIMITED
Registration no: 01790065 **Date established:** 1984
No.of Employees: 1 - 10 **Product Groups:** 40, 66

Date of Accounts	Apr 11	Apr 10	Apr 09
Working Capital	-4	-3	-1
Fixed Assets	N/A	1	1
Current Assets	24	22	30

L P Hangers
Unit 5-9 Sunbeam Street, Wolverhampton, WV2 4PF
Tel: 01902-420653 **Fax:** 01902-714716
E-mail: info@lphangers.co.uk
Website: http://www.lphangers.co.uk
Directors: R. Birdi (Ptnr)
VAT No.: GB 369 8221 18 **Turnover:** £250,000 - £500,000
No.of Employees: 1 - 10 **Product Groups:** 30

Langley Tube Machines
Unit F2 Primrose Avenue, Wolverhampton, WV10 8AW
Tel: 01902-783956 **Fax:** 01902-787464
Directors: R. Ball (Prop)
Immediate Holding Company: TERMOROS (UK) LIMITED
Registration no: 05610200 **Date established:** 2005
Turnover: Up to £250,000 **No.of Employees:** 1 - 10 **Product Groups:** 46

Laystall Engineering Company Ltd
Dixon Street, Wolverhampton, WV2 2BU
Tel: 01902-451789 **Fax:** 01902-451539
E-mail: martin.bowers@laystall.co.uk
Website: http://www.laystall.co.uk
Bank(s): Barclays, 63 Colmore Row, B'ham B3
Directors: D. Richards (Fin), M. Bowers (MD)
Managers: J. Miller (Sales Prom), L. Haden (Purch Mgr)
Ultimate Holding Company: LAYSTALL (HOLDINGS) LIMITED
Immediate Holding Company: LAYSTALL ENGINEERING COMPANY LIMITED
Registration no: 02178374 **Date established:** 1987 **Turnover:** £5m - £10m
No.of Employees: 51 - 100 **Product Groups:** 40, 48, 67, 68

Date of Accounts	Mar 08	Mar 09	Apr 10
Sales Turnover	10m	5m	410
Pre Tax Profit/Loss	137	-708	-487
Working Capital	887	125	-243
Fixed Assets	4m	2m	2m
Current Assets	3m	1m	1m
Current Liabilities	250	207	214

Legg Brothers Ltd
Spring Road Ettingshall, Wolverhampton, WV4 6JT
Tel: 01902-408188 **Fax:** 01902-408228
E-mail: mail@leggbrothers.co.uk
Website: http://www.leggbrothers.co.uk
Bank(s): Barclays
Managers: C. Bailey (Fin Mgr), J. Legg (Mgr), M. Guest (Works Gen Mgr), M. Key (Purch Mgr)
Ultimate Holding Company: FORELLON LIMITED
Immediate Holding Company: LEGG BROTHERS HOLDINGS LIMITED
Registration no: 01608414 **VAT No.:** GB 308 7454 48
Date established: 1982 **Turnover:** £2m - £5m **No.of Employees:** 21 - 50
Product Groups: 34

Date of Accounts	Apr 12	Apr 11	Apr 10
Working Capital	58	64	17
Fixed Assets	1m	1m	2m
Current Assets	103	110	99

Lichfield Fire & Safety Equipment Co. Ltd
Saturn Centre 2nd Floor Suite 4 Spring Road, Ettingshall, Wolverhampton, WV4 6JX
Tel: 0870-066 4401 **Fax:** 0870-0664402
E-mail: info@lifeco-uk.com
Website: http://www.lifeco-uk.com
Managers: A. Abdalla (Mktg Serv Mgr), M. Hussein (Chief Mgr)
Immediate Holding Company: Lichfield Fire & Safety Equipment Co Ltd
Registration no: 03718790 **Date established:** 1999
Turnover: £500,000 - £1m **No.of Employees:** 1 - 10 **Product Groups:** 23, 33, 37, 40

Date of Accounts	Dec 07	Dec 06	Dec 05
Working Capital	110	93	112
Fixed Assets	2	3	4
Current Assets	304	318	254
Current Liabilities	194	225	143
Total Share Capital	10	10	10

Linear Motion Ltd
Park Street South, Wolverhampton, WV2 3JH
Tel: 01902-425588 **Fax:** 01902-425504
E-mail: linear.motion@yahoo.co.uk
Directors: P. Cooper (Dir)
Immediate Holding Company: LINEAR MOTION LIMITED
Registration no: 04870931 **VAT No.:** GB 488 3171 16
Date established: 2003 **Turnover:** £250,000 - £500,000
No.of Employees: 1 - 10 **Product Groups:** 48

Date of Accounts	Aug 11	Aug 10	Aug 09
Working Capital	59	44	46
Fixed Assets	54	55	59
Current Assets	182	168	121

Linvic Engineering Ltd
Hickman Avenue, Wolverhampton, WV1 2DW
Tel: 01902-456333 **Fax:** 01902-455856
E-mail: sales@linvic.co.uk
Website: http://www.linvic.co.uk
Bank(s): HSBC Bank PLC
Directors: A. Wilcox (Comm), D. Ralph (Dir), P. Westwood (MD), S. Duffen (Sales)
Ultimate Holding Company: ACCURA GROUP LIMITED
Immediate Holding Company: LINVIC ENGINEERING LIMITED
Registration no: 01036047 **VAT No.:** 705 3445 55 **Date established:** 1971
Turnover: £2m - £5m **No.of Employees:** 51 - 100 **Product Groups:** 36

Date of Accounts	Mar 11	Mar 10	Mar 09
Sales Turnover	N/A	5m	N/A
Pre Tax Profit/Loss	N/A	222	2m

Working Capital	2m	2m	2m
Fixed Assets	286	349	446
Current Assets	4m	4m	4m
Current Liabilities	N/A	401	685

Luxury Leather Goods
6 Watson Road, Wolverhampton, WV10 6SB
Tel: 01902-579423
E-mail: bpd01@blueyonder.co.uk
Website: http://www.luxury-leather-goods.co.uk
Directors: H. Bartram (Prop)
No.of Employees: 1 - 10 **Product Groups:** 24

M I S Fuel Monitoring Ltd
Lower Walsall Street, Wolverhampton, WV1 2EU
Tel: 01902-870037 **Fax:** 01902-871661
E-mail: info@merridale.co.uk
Website: http://www.merridale.co.uk
Directors: J. Russell (Dir)
Immediate Holding Company: M.I.S. FUEL MONITORING LIMITED
Registration no: 02990709 **Date established:** 1994
Turnover: £500,000 - £1m **No.of Employees:** 11 - 20
Product Groups: 38, 39, 47, 48, 49

Date of Accounts	Nov 11	Nov 10	Nov 09
Working Capital	463	265	224
Fixed Assets	80	110	155
Current Assets	765	660	437

Mccain Foods GB Ltd
Heath Mill Road Wombourne, Wolverhampton, WV5 8AE
Tel: 01902-894022 **Fax:** 01902-897998
E-mail: richard.hopkins@mccain.co.uk
Website: http://www.mccain.co.uk
Bank(s): Lloyds
Managers: A. Waver (I.T. Exec), S. O'leary (Plant), L. Penn (Personnel), S. Atter (Personnel)
Ultimate Holding Company: MCCAIN FOODS GROUP INC (CANADA)
Immediate Holding Company: McCAIN FOODS (G.B.) LIMITED
Registration no: 00733218 **Date established:** 1962
Turnover: £250m - £500m **No.of Employees:** 101 - 250
Product Groups: 20

Date of Accounts	Jun 11	Jun 10	Jun 09
Sales Turnover	372m	358m	351m
Pre Tax Profit/Loss	40m	46m	39m
Working Capital	42m	35m	39m
Fixed Assets	122m	106m	98m
Current Assets	90m	84m	87m
Current Liabilities	29m	25m	27m

Maclellan Rubber Ltd
Plasmar Ltd Neachells Lane, Wolverhampton, WV11 3QG
Tel: 01902-307711 **Fax:** 01902-305201
E-mail: sales@maclellanrubber.com
Website: http://www.maclellanrubber.com
Bank(s): HSBC
Directors: A. Onions (Dir), S. Winfield (Dir)
Managers: I. Littleton (Sales Prom Mgr), M. Mclaren (Sales Prom Mgr)
Ultimate Holding Company: ASC BROOKLANDS LIMITED
Immediate Holding Company: MACLELLAN RUBBER LIMITED
Registration no: 05173370 **VAT No.:** GB 972 1880 00
Date established: 2010 **Turnover:** £2m - £5m **No.of Employees:** 11 - 20
Product Groups: 23, 29

J H Marshall Pressings Ltd
Stadium Works Sedgley Street, Wolverhampton, WV2 3AJ
Tel: 01902-459764 **Fax:** 01902-351597
E-mail: jhmarshallpressings@btconnect.com
Website: http://www.jhmarshallpressings.co.uk
Directors: R. Marshall (MD)
Ultimate Holding Company: J H MARSHALL (HOLDINGS) LIMITED
Immediate Holding Company: J H MARSHALL (HOLDINGS) LIMITED
Registration no: 01103701 **VAT No.:** GB 101 0193 46
Date established: 1973 **Turnover:** Up to £250,000
No.of Employees: 1 - 10 **Product Groups:** 34

Date of Accounts	Mar 12	Mar 11	Mar 10
Working Capital	536	441	434
Fixed Assets	423	423	423
Current Assets	579	478	438

Marstons plc
Marstons House Brewery Road, Wolverhampton, WV1 4JT
Tel: 01902-711811 **Fax:** 01902-429136
E-mail: ralph.findlay@wdbbrands.co.uk
Website: http://www.marstonsplc.co.uk
Bank(s): Lloyds TSB Bank plc
Directors: R. Findlay (Grp Chief Exec), R. Findley (Grp Chief Exec)
Ultimate Holding Company: MARSTON'S PLC
Immediate Holding Company: MARSTON'S TRADING LIMITED
Registration no: 00040590 **VAT No.:** GB 185 3454 46
Date established: 1994 **Turnover:** £125m - £250m
No.of Employees: 501 - 1000 **Product Groups:** 20, 21, 62

Date of Accounts	Oct 08	Oct 09	Oct 10
Sales Turnover	666m	645m	651m
Pre Tax Profit/Loss	76m	21m	53m
Working Capital	-18m	36m	-37m
Fixed Assets	2296m	2224m	2264m
Current Assets	170m	207m	142m
Current Liabilities	116m	112m	135m

Allen Martin Conservation Ltd
504 Dudley Road, Wolverhampton, WV2 3AA
Tel: 01902-560065 **Fax:** 01902-560066
E-mail: support@allen-martin.co.uk
Website: http://www.allen-martin.co.uk
Directors: L. Checketts (Fin), P. Davies (MD)
Immediate Holding Company: ALLEN-MARTIN CONSERVATION LIMITED
Registration no: 01800086 **Date established:** 1984 **Turnover:** £2m - £5m
No.of Employees: 21 - 50 **Product Groups:** 44

Date of Accounts	Sep 11	Sep 10	Sep 09
Working Capital	127	265	339
Fixed Assets	127	125	37
Current Assets	376	513	581

Mcgean Rohco UK Ltd (CEE BEE Products Division)
Qualcast Road, Wolverhampton, WV1 2QP
Tel: 01902-451312 **Fax:** 01902-457443
E-mail: sales@mcgean-rohco.co.uk
Website: http://www.mcgean.com
Bank(s): Barclays
Directors: D. Whitney Junior (Dir)
Ultimate Holding Company: MCGEAN-ROHCO INC (USA)
Immediate Holding Company: MCGEAN-ROHCO (U.K.) LIMITED
Registration no: 01177941 **Date established:** 1974 **Turnover:** £2m - £5m
No.of Employees: 11 - 20 **Product Groups:** 32

Date of Accounts	Sep 11	Sep 10	Sep 09
Working Capital	1m	1m	1m
Fixed Assets	892	924	907
Current Assets	3m	2m	2m

Meltech Ltd
185 Cannock Road Westcroft, Wolverhampton, WV10 8QL
Tel: 01902-722588 **Fax:** 01902-730142
E-mail: steve@induction-furnaces.co.uk
Website: http://www.induction-furnaces.co.uk
Directors: S. Macey (Dir)
Immediate Holding Company: MELTECH LIMITED
Registration no: 03780047 **Date established:** 1999
No.of Employees: 1 - 10 **Product Groups:** 40, 42, 46

Date of Accounts	Mar 12	Mar 11	Mar 10
Working Capital	238	113	126
Fixed Assets	15	30	17
Current Assets	404	282	261

Midland Combustion Ltd
Station Works Four Ashes, Wolverhampton, WV10 7BX
Tel: 01902-790541 **Fax:** 01902-791526
E-mail: paul.smith@mid-com.co.uk
Website: http://www.mid-com.co.uk
Bank(s): Lloyds TSB
Directors: P. Smith (MD), M. Morris (Co Sec)
Managers: J. McQuillan, T. Pearce
Immediate Holding Company: MIDLAND COMBUSTION LIMITED
Registration no: 02835741 **VAT No.:** GB 648 5364 07
Date established: 1993 **Turnover:** £2m - £5m **No.of Employees:** 21 - 50
Product Groups: 40, 42, 48

Date of Accounts	Jul 11	Jul 10	Jul 09
Working Capital	291	291	291
Current Assets	995	986	1m

Midland Cryogenics Ltd (Midland Cryogenics)
Brock Building Aspley Close, Four Ashes, Wolverhampton, WV10 7DE
Tel: 01902-791999 **Fax:** 01902-791909
E-mail: david@midlandcryogenics.com
Website: http://www.midlandcryogenics.com
Directors: D. Brocklesby (MD)
Immediate Holding Company: MCL (OFFSHORE) LIMITED
Registration no: 01983021 **Date established:** 1986
Turnover: £250,000 - £500,000 **No.of Employees:** 1 - 10
Product Groups: 14, 33, 48

Date of Accounts	Mar 10	Mar 09	Mar 11
Working Capital	587	580	586
Fixed Assets	84	131	50
Current Assets	948	2m	910

Midland Heat Treatments Ltd
PO Box 45, Wolverhampton, WV1 2BU
Tel: 01902-450757 **Fax:** 01902-459093
E-mail: treatment@midlant-heat.co.uk
Website: http://www.midland-heat.co.uk
Bank(s): The Bank of Scotland, Colmore Row, Birmingham
Directors: M. Czyzyk (Dir), H. Cowie (Co Sec), A. Cowie (MD)
Managers: D. Williams (Purch Mgr), A. Cowie (Sales Admin), S. Berry (Quality Control)
Immediate Holding Company: MIDLAND HEAT TREATMENTS LIMITED
Registration no: 01744756 **VAT No.:** GB 369 7710 08
Date established: 1983 **Turnover:** £250,000 - £500,000
No.of Employees: 11 - 20 **Product Groups:** 48

Date of Accounts	Dec 06	Jun 10	Jun 09
Working Capital	-76	-130	-74
Fixed Assets	389	376	386
Current Assets	103	78	128

Midland Polishing & Plating Ltd
Unit 1 Marston Road Industrial Estate Marston Road, Wolverhampton, WV2 4LX
Tel: 01902-421174 **Fax:** 01902-713613
E-mail: info@midlandpolishing.co.uk
Website: http://www.midlandpolishing.co.uk
Directors: J. Dudrah (MD)
Immediate Holding Company: LEFROY BROOKS MIDLAND LIMITED
Registration no: 02233630 **Date established:** 1993
No.of Employees: 51 - 100 **Product Groups:** 46, 48

Date of Accounts	Feb 08	Feb 11	Feb 10
Working Capital	2m	2m	2m
Fixed Assets	86	92	110
Current Assets	2m	3m	2m

Moog Aircraft Group
Wobaston Road, Wolverhampton, WV9 5EW
Tel: 01902-397700 **Fax:** 01902-394394
Website: http://www.geaviation.com
Bank(s): HSBC Bank plc
Directors: T. Patterson (MD), P. Richards (Fin), D. Sharples (Fin)
Managers: C. Coombes (Purch Mgr), S. Chester (Tech Serv Mgr), L. Hamilton (Personnel), G. Reader (Personnel)
Ultimate Holding Company: DOWTY GROUP P.L.C.
Immediate Holding Company: SMITHS
Registration no: 00293428 **VAT No.:** GB 100 2487 25
Date established: 1989 **No.of Employees:** 251 - 500 **Product Groups:** 39

N L Cullis & Sons Crane Hire
9 Willow Road, Wolverhampton, WV3 8AF
Tel: 01902-339825 **Fax:** 01902-339825
Directors: N. Cullis (Dir)
Date established: 1981 **Turnover:** Up to £250,000
No.of Employees: 1 - 10 **Product Groups:** 83

Nathan Holdings Ltd
5 Neachells Lane Industrial Estate Neachells Lane, Wolverhampton, WV11 3RG
Tel: 01902-722255 **Fax:** 01902-739042
E-mail: nathanholdings@hotmail.com
Directors: A. Hughes (MD)
Immediate Holding Company: NATHAN HOLDINGS LIMITED
Registration no: 01982313 **VAT No.:** GB 775 9311 94
Date established: 1986 **No.of Employees:** 1 - 10 **Product Groups:** 48

Date of Accounts	Dec 11	Dec 10	Dec 09
Working Capital	31	1	77
Fixed Assets	580	647	662
Current Assets	55	51	219

Nationwide Signs Ltd
Derry Street, Wolverhampton, WV2 1EY
Tel: 01902-871116 **Fax:** 01902-351195
E-mail: roadframes@aol.com
Directors: D. Brookes (Dir), H. Ross (Fin)
Immediate Holding Company: NATIONWIDE SIGNS LIMITED
Registration no: 02970238 **Date established:** 1994
Turnover: Up to £250,000 **No.of Employees:** 11 - 20 **Product Groups:** 30, 35, 36, 37, 39, 48, 49, 67, 68, 81, 84

Date of Accounts	Sep 11	Sep 10	Sep 09
Working Capital	266	240	224
Fixed Assets	6	20	28
Current Assets	593	548	521

Non Ferrous Stockholders Ltd Subsidary of the CLAL Group, France
Dock Meadow Drive, Wolverhampton, WV4 6LE
Tel: 01902-353747 **Fax:** 01902-491030
E-mail: sales@non-ferrous.co.uk
Website: http://www.non-ferrous.co.uk
Bank(s): National Westminster Bank Plc
Directors: R. Burt (MD), C. Farkas (Dir)
Immediate Holding Company: NON-FERROUS STOCKHOLDERS LIMITED
Registration no: 01650805 **VAT No.:** GB 369 8669 71
Date established: 1982 **Turnover:** £20m - £50m
No.of Employees: 21 - 50 **Product Groups:** 34

Date of Accounts	Dec 11	Dec 10	Dec 09
Working Capital	768	717	627
Fixed Assets	192	155	155
Current Assets	2m	2m	2m

O S F Ltd
Unit 6 Station Road Four Ashes Industrial Estate, Four Ashes, Wolverhampton, WV10 7DB
Tel: 01902-798080 **Fax:** 01902-794750
E-mail: sales@osfltd.com
Website: http://www.jjplasticfabricationsltd.co.uk
Bank(s): National Westminster Bank Plc
Directors: D. Howell (Dir)
Immediate Holding Company: O.S.F. LIMITED
Registration no: 02287905 **VAT No.:** GB 489 5260 01
Date established: 1988 **Turnover:** £500,000 - £1m
No.of Employees: 11 - 20 **Product Groups:** 48

Date of Accounts	Mar 12	Mar 11	Mar 10
Working Capital	543	397	356
Fixed Assets	49	13	19
Current Assets	793	566	575

Off The Wall Graffiti Solutions
Carver Buildings Littles Lane, Wolverhampton, WV1 1JY
Tel: 01902-426479 **Fax:** 01902-426574
E-mail: sales@antigraffiti.co.uk
Website: http://www.antigraffiti.co.uk
Directors: M. Bollock (MD)
Managers: L. Bills (Sales & Mktg Mg), P. Kay (I.T. Exec)
Product Groups: 32, 52

Orchard Environmental Systems
Marston Road Industrial Estate Marston Road, Wolverhampton, WV2 4LX
Tel: 01902-429933 **Fax:** 01902-711175
E-mail: oesgroup@aol.com
Website: http://www.orchardenvironmentalsystems.co.uk
Directors: R. Smith (Prop)
Immediate Holding Company: ORCHARD ENVIRONMENTAL SYSTEMS LTD
Registration no: 07912332 **Date established:** 2012
No.of Employees: 1 - 10 **Product Groups:** 30, 35, 37, 40

Ovivo UK Ltd
Kennicott House Well Lane, Wolverhampton, WV11 1XR
Tel: 01902-721212 **Fax:** 01902-721333
E-mail: info.uk@ovivowater.com
Website: http://www.ovivowater.com
Bank(s): National Westminster Bank Plc
Directors: I. Richards (Fin), H. Joshua (Pers), B. Hook (MD), J. Fryer (Co Sec)
Managers: D. Lee (Personnel), R. Smith (Tech Serv Mgr), K. Holland (I.T. Exec), J. McLoughlin, C. Burleigh (Sales Prom Mgr), C. Burley (Sales & Mktg Mg), G. Cann (Purch Mgr)
Ultimate Holding Company: GLV INC (CANADA)
Immediate Holding Company: OVIVO UK LIMITED
Registration no: 00104655 **Date established:** 2009 **Turnover:** £5m - £10m
No.of Employees: 21 - 50 **Product Groups:** 18, 32, 36, 40, 42, 48, 51, 52, 54, 67

Date of Accounts	Mar 12	Mar 11	Mar 10
Sales Turnover	40m	26m	25m
Pre Tax Profit/Loss	-3m	-5m	-2m
Working Capital	23m	-398	3m
Fixed Assets	7m	12m	14m
Current Assets	50m	21m	14m
Current Liabilities	N/A	10m	4m

P D I C
The Stables Patshull Park, Burnhill Green, Wolverhampton, WV6 7HY
Tel: 01902-374451
Directors: C. Yates (Prop)
Date established: 1989 **No.of Employees:** 1 - 10 **Product Groups:** 26, 35

P J Polishing Services
Unit 3 The Vulcan Centre Dixon Street, Wolverhampton, WV2 2BS
Tel: 01902-871311 **Fax:** 01902-871311
Website: http://www.pjpolishing.com
Directors: P. Singer (Prop)
Date established: 2001 **No.of Employees:** 1 - 10 **Product Groups:** 46, 48

P O D Stainless Steel Products Ltd
25 Waterside Industrial Estate Ettingshall Road, Wolverhampton, WV2 2RQ
Tel: 01902-494036 **Fax:** 01902-494822
E-mail: phil@podstainless.co.uk
Website: http://www.podstainless.co.uk
Directors: P. Smith (Sales)
Immediate Holding Company: P.O.D. STAINLESS STEEL PRODUCTS LIMITED

Registration no: 04304317 **Date established:** 2001
No.of Employees: 1 - 10 **Product Groups:** 20, 40, 41

Date of Accounts	Oct 11	Oct 10	Oct 09
Working Capital	51	60	59
Fixed Assets	7	8	9
Current Assets	133	228	180

Parkrow Alloys Ltd
Millfields Road, Wolverhampton, WV4 6JQ
Tel: 01902-402727 **Fax:** 01902-403737
E-mail: sales@parkrow-alloys.co.uk
Website: http://www.parkrow-alloys.co.uk
Directors: S. Baker (Fin), M. Baker (Ptnr)
Ultimate Holding Company: BAKER ALLOYS LIMITED
Immediate Holding Company: PARKROW ALLOYS LIMITED
Registration no: 03831886 **Date established:** 1999
Turnover: £500,000 - £1m **No.of Employees:** 1 - 10 **Product Groups:** 34, 35

Date of Accounts	Sep 11	Sep 10	Sep 09
Working Capital	100	90	75
Fixed Assets	512	514	529
Current Assets	1m	2m	1m

Paybare
Paycare House George Street, Wolverhampton, WV2 4DX
Tel: 01902-371000 **Fax:** 01902-371030
E-mail: enquiries@paycare.org
Website: http://www.paycare.org
Directors: K. Rogers (Chief Op Offcr), G. Maltdy (Grp Chief Exec)
Immediate Holding Company: PAYCARE
Registration no: 00820791 **Date established:** 1964 **Turnover:** £2m - £5m
No.of Employees: 21 - 50 **Product Groups:** 82

Date of Accounts	Dec 09	Dec 08	Dec 07
Pre Tax Profit/Loss	590	-338	320
Fixed Assets	4m	4m	5m
Current Assets	2m	1m	1m
Current Liabilities	447	387	422

Perry Castings
Bank Street, Wolverhampton, WV10 9DU
Tel: 01902-732910 **Fax:** 01902-721046
E-mail: ericperry@live.co.uk
Website: http://www.perrycastings.co.uk
Directors: E. Perry (Prop)
Immediate Holding Company: NIMAG PRECISION ENGINEERING LIMITED
Registration no: 01707583 **VAT No.:** GB 316 4209 81
Date established: 1983 **Turnover:** £500,000 - £1m
No.of Employees: 1 - 10 **Product Groups:** 34

Date of Accounts	Mar 12	Mar 11	Mar 10
Working Capital	633	696	638
Fixed Assets	139	136	137
Current Assets	679	782	702

Plant & Lift Truck Training
Unit 30 Fallings Park Industrial Estate Park Lane, Wolverhampton, WV10 9QB
Tel: 01902-862777
E-mail: info@plttraining.co.uk
Website: http://www.plttraining.co.uk
Directors: N. Bennett (Prop)
Registration no: 05918541 **No.of Employees:** 1 - 10 **Product Groups:** 35, 39, 45

Date of Accounts	Aug 11	Aug 09	Aug 08
Working Capital	-15	-4	-5
Fixed Assets	21	25	11
Current Assets	39	26	17

Polymer Recruitment Services
4 Almar Cour Catisfield Crescent, Pendeford, Wolverhampton, WV8 1YT
Tel: 01902-746933 **Fax:** 01902-344631
E-mail: admin@polymerrecserv.co.uk
Website: http://www.polymerrecserv.co.uk
Directors: M. Bunce (Dir), R. Bradley (Fin)
Immediate Holding Company: Polymer Recruitment Services Ltd
Registration no: 03743557 **Date established:** 1999
No.of Employees: 1 - 10 **Product Groups:** 80

Power Assemblies Ltd
Cooper Street, Wolverhampton, WV2 2JL
Tel: 01902-456767 **Fax:** 01902-456761
Website: http://www.pump.net
Directors: G. Butterfield (MD)
Immediate Holding Company: POWER ASSEMBLIES LIMITED
Registration no: 03707186 **VAT No.:** GB 729 5456 02
Date established: 1999 **Turnover:** Up to £250,000
No.of Employees: 1 - 10 **Product Groups:** 40

Date of Accounts	Apr 11	Apr 10	Apr 09
Working Capital	195	147	203
Fixed Assets	21	9	12
Current Assets	598	432	627

Powerwave Technologies, Inc
Enterprise Drive Station Road, Four Ashes, Wolverhampton, WV10 7DF
Tel: 01902-798204 **Fax:** 01902-798205
Website: http://www.powerwave.com
Directors: J. Fletcher (MD)
Managers: D. Cannell (Site Co-ord)
Immediate Holding Company: Filtronic P.L.C.
Registration no: 03406063 **No.of Employees:** 1 - 10 **Product Groups:** 37

Premier Washers
3 Merryhills Enterprise Park Park Lane, Wolverhampton, WV10 9TJ
Tel: 01902-307121 **Fax:** 01902-307122
E-mail: sales@premierwashers.co.uk
Website: http://www.premierwashers.co.uk
Directors: D. Armstrong (MD)
Immediate Holding Company: PREMIER WASHERS LIMITED
Registration no: 04759535 **VAT No.:** GB 559 4943 88
Date established: 2003 **Turnover:** £1m - £2m **No.of Employees:** 11 - 20
Product Groups: 35, 48

Date of Accounts	May 11	May 10	May 09
Working Capital	169	81	74
Fixed Assets	36	37	39
Current Assets	506	366	331

Press Computer Systems Ltd
Castle Street, Wolverhampton, WV1 3AD
Tel: 01902-374757 **Fax:** 01902-373622
E-mail: info@presscomputers.com
Website: http://www.presscomputers.com
Bank(s): Barclays
Directors: P. Walker (MD), R. Cross (Co Sec), L. Hollaway (Fin)
Managers: L. Hill (Mktg Serv Mgr), S. Welch (Tech Serv Mgr), K. Jones (Buyer)
Ultimate Holding Company: CLAVERLEY COMPANY
Immediate Holding Company: PRESS COMPUTER SYSTEMS LIMITED
Registration no: 01148045 **VAT No.:** GB 101 2765 17
Date established: 1973 **Turnover:** £1m - £2m **No.of Employees:** 51 - 100
Product Groups: 44

Date of Accounts	Dec 11	Dec 08	Jan 10
Sales Turnover	2m	2m	2m
Pre Tax Profit/Loss	-810	440	-322
Working Capital	-89	-263	289
Fixed Assets	2m	1m	1m
Current Assets	709	1m	1m
Current Liabilities	618	378	297

Priory Steels Ltd
Unit 27-29 Central Indl-Est Cable Street, Wolverhampton, WV2 2RL
Tel: 01902-351001 **Fax:** 01902-871345
E-mail: sales@priorysteel.co.uk
Website: http://www.priorysteel.fsnet.co.uk
Bank(s): Lloyds
Directors: B. Davies (Jt MD), B. Davies (Dir), I. Cross (Dir)
Managers: J. Cross (Sales Prom Mgr), P. James (Buyer), M. Hudson (Buyer), J. Foulkes (Buyer)
Ultimate Holding Company: PRIORY STEEL HOLDINGS LIMITED
Immediate Holding Company: PRIORY STEEL GROUP LIMITED
Registration no: 02940278 **Date established:** 1994 **Turnover:** £5m - £10m
No.of Employees: 21 - 50 **Product Groups:** 34, 66

Date of Accounts	Dec 11	Dec 10	Dec 09
Sales Turnover	7m	6m	5m
Pre Tax Profit/Loss	268	239	124
Working Capital	1m	862	784
Fixed Assets	433	471	500
Current Assets	3m	3m	2m
Current Liabilities	522	679	532

Pro Metal Polishing
15 Salisbury Place Industrial Estate Roseberry Street, Wolverhampton, WV3 0BD
Tel: 01902-426161 **Fax:** 01902-426161
Directors: B. Sighn (Prop)
Date established: 1993 **No.of Employees:** 1 - 10 **Product Groups:** 46, 48

Process & Plant Equipment Ltd
Unit 4 Dock Meadow Industrial Estate Lanesfield Drive, Wolverhampton, WV4 6UD
Tel: 01902-495913 **Fax:** 01902-498945
E-mail: sales@pps-awb.co.uk
Website: http://www.processandplant.com
Directors: P. Jones (MD), A. Baxter (MD)
Immediate Holding Company: PROCESS & PLANT EQUIPMENT LIMITED
Registration no: 03466456 **Date established:** 1997
Turnover: £250,000 - £500,000 **No.of Employees:** 11 - 20
Product Groups: 45

Date of Accounts	Mar 11	Mar 10	Mar 04
Working Capital	2	2	-0
Current Assets	2	2	2

Purpose Electrical Controls Ltd
Unit 7 Salisbury Place Industrial Estate Rosebery Street, Wolverhampton, WV3 0BD
Tel: 01902-712909 **Fax:** 01902-712909
E-mail: brian@bridot.wanadoo.co.uk
Directors: B. Williams (MD), D. Williams (Fin)
Immediate Holding Company: PURPOSE ELECTRICAL CONTROLS LIMITED
Registration no: 00962938 **VAT No.:** GB 100 5518 25
Date established: 1969 **Turnover:** Up to £250,000
No.of Employees: 1 - 10 **Product Groups:** 38, 40

Date of Accounts	Jun 08	Jun 07	Jun 06
Working Capital	3	10	14
Fixed Assets	N/A	N/A	1
Current Assets	36	41	38
Current Liabilities	33	32	24
Total Share Capital	1	1	1

Quality Manufacturing Services Ltd
Coteleasowe Heath House Lane Codsall, Wolverhampton, WV8 2HW
Tel: 01902-842022 **Fax:** 01902-842022
E-mail: andy@qmsgb.co.uk
Website: http://www.qmsgb.co.uk
Directors: S. Holden (Fin)
Immediate Holding Company: QUALITY MANUFACTURING SERVICES LIMITED
Registration no: 05241236 **Date established:** 2004
No.of Employees: 1 - 10 **Product Groups:** 37, 46, 48, 84

Date of Accounts	Aug 11	Aug 10	Aug 09
Working Capital	5	6	6
Fixed Assets	2	2	3
Current Assets	8	9	10

R N J Engineering Ltd T/A Jackson Lifting
Unit 4a-4b Aspley Close Four Ashes, Wolverhampton, WV10 7DE
Tel: 01902-703588 **Fax:** 01902-703589
E-mail: rich.jacksonbus@tiscali.co.uk
Website: http://www.jackson-lifting.com
Directors: R. Jackson (Prop)
Immediate Holding Company: R N J ENGINEERING LTD
Registration no: 07575876 **Date established:** 2011
Turnover: £500,000 - £1m **No.of Employees:** 1 - 10 **Product Groups:** 35, 48, 67, 84

R W M Wolverhampton Ltd
34 Commercial Road, Wolverhampton, WV1 3RD
Tel: 01902-871272
E-mail: sales@rwmltd.co.uk
Website: http://www.rwmltd.co.uk
Directors: G. White (MD), G. White (Fin)
Immediate Holding Company: R.W.M. (WOLVERHAMPTON) LIMITED
Registration no: 01763944 **Date established:** 1983
No.of Employees: 1 - 10 **Product Groups:** 46

see next page

R W M Wolverhampton Ltd - Cont'd

Date of Accounts	Oct 11	Oct 10	Oct 09
Working Capital	41	39	36
Fixed Assets	75	77	79
Current Assets	110	99	53

Radleigh Metal Coatings Ltd

Unit 30 Cable Street, Wolverhampton, WV2 2HX
Tel: 01902-870606 **Fax:** 01902-351130
E-mail: sales@radleigh.co.uk
Website: http://www.radleighmetalcoatings.co.uk
Bank(s): National Westminster
Directors: C. Tyler (Sales), J. Law (Fin), J. Shingler (Dir)
Immediate Holding Company: RADLEIGH METAL COATINGS LIMITED
Registration no: 01965518 **VAT No.:** GB 431 3950 69
Date established: 1985 **Turnover:** £1m - £2m **No.of Employees:** 11 - 20
Product Groups: 29, 31, 32

Date of Accounts	Mar 11	Mar 10	Mar 09
Working Capital	36	29	24
Fixed Assets	85	99	113
Current Assets	258	230	248

Rainbow Signs & Graphics Ltd

Unit A-B Landport Road, Wolverhampton, WV2 2QJ
Tel: 01902-456949 **Fax:** 01902-450350
E-mail: sales@rainbowsafety.co.uk
Website: http://www.rainbowsafety.co.uk
Directors: D. Taylor (MD), N. Taylor (Fin)
Immediate Holding Company: RAINBOW SIGNS AND GRAPHICS LIMITED
Registration no: 03331021 **Date established:** 1997
Turnover: £250,000 - £500,000 **No.of Employees:** 11 - 20
Product Groups: 27, 28, 30, 35, 39, 40, 45, 49, 68

Date of Accounts	Sep 11	Sep 10	Sep 09
Working Capital	34	45	32
Fixed Assets	61	18	19
Current Assets	234	285	201

Recycled Plastic UK Ltd

Freeman Street Heath Town, Wolverhampton, WV10 0ES
Tel: 01902-458111 **Fax:** 01902-458 444
E-mail: info@recycledplasticsuk.com
Website: http://www.recycledplasticuk.com
Directors: F. Mukhtar (Dir)
Immediate Holding Company: RECYCLED PLASTICS (UK) LIMITED
Registration no: 06645314 **Date established:** 2008
Turnover: £500,000 - £1m **No.of Employees:** 1 - 10 **Product Groups:** 30, 42, 66

Date of Accounts	Jul 11	Jul 10	Jul 09
Working Capital	302	519	188
Fixed Assets	948	195	223
Current Assets	813	910	322
Current Liabilities	61	45	N/A

Robertson Collection Ltd

Unit 45 Wombourne Enterprise Park Bridgnorth Road, Wombourne, Wolverhampton, WV5 0AL
Tel: 01902-324243 **Fax:** 01902-324825
E-mail: sales@robertsoncollection.co.uk
Website: http://www.robertsoncollection.co.uk
Directors: E. Pritchard (MD), E. Robertson (Fin)
Immediate Holding Company: ROBERTSON COLLECTION LIMITED
Registration no: 02489839 **VAT No.:** GB 559 4449 96
Date established: 1990 **No.of Employees:** 1 - 10 **Product Groups:** 27

Date of Accounts	Dec 10	Dec 09	Dec 08
Working Capital	601	615	614
Fixed Assets	8	8	10
Current Assets	652	615	660

Rolevet Ltd

Ashland Street, Wolverhampton, WV3 0BN
Tel: 01902-421252 **Fax:** 01902-715585
E-mail: sales@rolevet.com
Website: http://www.rolevet.com
Bank(s): Barclays
Directors: A. Lawless (Sales), D. Sudlow (MD), D. Ward (Dir), T. Jones (Co Sec)
Immediate Holding Company: ROLEVET LIMITED
Registration no: 02435435 **VAT No.:** GB 489 7521 86
Date established: 1989 **No.of Employees:** 21 - 50 **Product Groups:** 35

Date of Accounts	Jan 12	Jan 11	Jan 10
Working Capital	-52	-44	55
Fixed Assets	527	504	533
Current Assets	1m	1m	724
Current Liabilities	N/A	1m	N/A

Rosch Engineering

Unit 1-2 Laches Close, Four Ashes, Wolverhampton, WV10 7DZ
Tel: 01902-798100 **Fax:** 01902-798844
E-mail: info@rosch.co.uk
Website: http://www.rosch.co.uk
Directors: B. Smith (MD), S. Smith (Fin)
Immediate Holding Company: ROSCH ENGINEERING LIMITED
Registration no: 02972007 **Date established:** 1994 **Turnover:** £1m - £2m
No.of Employees: 1 - 10 **Product Groups:** 30, 32, 35, 66

Rothley Ltd Dept. K.E

Macrome Road, Wolverhampton, WV6 9HG
Tel: 01902-756461 **Fax:** 01902-745554
E-mail: alan.bowell@rothley.co.uk
Website: http://www.rothley.co.uk
Managers: A. Bowell (Mktg Serv Mgr)
Immediate Holding Company: ROTHLEY LIMITED
Registration no: 05791651 **Date established:** 2006
Turnover: £10m - £20m **No.of Employees:** 21 - 50 **Product Groups:** 35, 36

Date of Accounts	Jun 12	Jun 11	Jun 10
Working Capital	439	141	161
Fixed Assets	85	119	152
Current Assets	3m	2m	3m

Rudge & Co UK

Unit E2 Hilton Trading Estate Hilton Road, Lanesfield, Wolverhampton, WV4 6DW
Tel: 01902-402225 **Fax:** 01902-404477
E-mail: sales@rudgeandco.com
Website: http://www.rudgeandco.com
Directors: J. Dhaliwal (MD)
Immediate Holding Company: RUDGE & CO (UK) LIMITED
Registration no: 04917951 **VAT No.:** GB 687 8906 57
Date established: 2003 **Turnover:** £1m - £2m **No.of Employees:** 1 - 10
Product Groups: 36, 66

Date of Accounts	Mar 11	Mar 10	Mar 09
Working Capital	-9	15	-75
Fixed Assets	42	45	53
Current Assets	176	85	131

Russell Hobbs Ltd

Bridgnorth Road Wombourne, Wolverhampton, WV5 8AQ
Tel: 0161-947 3000 **Fax:** 0161-682 1708
E-mail: service@russellhobbs.com
Website: http://www.saltoneurope.com
Bank(s): National Westminster
Directors: H. Sharples (Tech Serv), K. Stillwell (Purch), B. Martin (Mkt Research), M. Burns (Grp Chief Exec), A. Streets (Co Sec), A. Derry (Pers), A. Breen (Pers), M. Burnes (Grp Chief Exec)
Managers: J. Smethurst (Sales Prom Mgr), D. Kenyon (Public Relation), B. O'Shea (I.T. Exec)
Ultimate Holding Company: SPECTRUM BRANDS INC (USA)
Immediate Holding Company: RUSSELL HOBBS LIMITED
Registration no: 00073700 **Date established:** 2002
Turnover: Over £1,000m **No.of Employees:** 51 - 100 **Product Groups:** 36, 37, 40

Date of Accounts	Dec 09	Sep 10	Jun 08
Sales Turnover	110m	57m	69m
Pre Tax Profit/Loss	11m	14m	4m
Working Capital	28m	33m	22m
Fixed Assets	5m	4m	5m
Current Assets	65m	74m	62m
Current Liabilities	7m	6m	3m

S B S Trailers

Macrome Road, Wolverhampton, WV6 9HD
Tel: 08452-305670 **Fax:** 01902-755363
E-mail: sales@sbstrailers.co.uk
Website: http://www.sbstrailers.co.uk
Directors: A. Wyer (MD), A. Wyer (MD)
Managers: L. Bowyer, R. Walker (Prod Mgr)
Ultimate Holding Company: FERN MANUFACTURING GROUP LIMITED
Immediate Holding Company: FERN MANUFACTURING GROUP LIMITED
Registration no: 00750034 **Date established:** 2008
No.of Employees: 21 - 50 **Product Groups:** 39, 45, 68

Date of Accounts	Mar 12	Mar 11	Mar 10
Sales Turnover	7m	7m	7m
Pre Tax Profit/Loss	149	176	192
Working Capital	21	9	9
Fixed Assets	3m	3m	3m
Current Assets	3m	3m	2m
Current Liabilities	1m	1m	1m

S C F Group

35 Eagle Street, Wolverhampton, WV2 2AQ
Tel: 01902-351900
Website: http://www.mixandmatch.co.uk
Directors: S. Ferrier (Prop)
Registration no: 03251977 **Date established:** 1996
No.of Employees: 11 - 20 **Product Groups:** 26, 30, 33

S G G Engineering

Unit 10 Sprint Industrial Estate Station Road, Four Ashes, Wolverhampton, WV10 7DA
Tel: 01902-798055
Directors: D. Firkins (Prop)
Immediate Holding Company: TCK CASTINGS LIMITED
Date established: 2010 **No.of Employees:** 1 - 10 **Product Groups:** 26, 35

S P S

Owen Road, Wolverhampton, WV3 0AL
Tel: 01902-772679 **Fax:** 01902-711141
E-mail: info@spsbrassware.co.uk
Website: http://www.spsbrassware.co.uk
Bank(s): Barclays
Directors: S. Randhawa (Dir)
Managers: S. Randhawa (Sales Admin)
Ultimate Holding Company: MTDS LIMITED
Immediate Holding Company: SPS BRASSWARE LIMITED
Registration no: 04329971 **VAT No.:** GB 333 8928 33
Date established: 2001 **Turnover:** £1m - £2m **No.of Employees:** 11 - 20
Product Groups: 36, 37, 48, 67

Date of Accounts	Aug 11	Aug 10	Aug 09
Working Capital	220	216	212
Fixed Assets	47	55	61
Current Assets	457	428	386

Sage Aluminium Products Ltd

Heathmill Road Industrial Estate Wombourne, Wolverhampton, WV5 8AJ
Tel: 01902-892611 **Fax:** 01902-897685
E-mail: hstuart@btconnect.com
Website: http://www.sagealuminium.com
Bank(s): Barclays, George St, Luton, Bedfordshire
Directors: C. Taylor (MD), S. Hamilton (Fin)
Immediate Holding Company: SAGE ALUMINIUM PRODUCTS LIMITED
Registration no: 01910459 **Date established:** 1985 **Turnover:** £2m - £5m
No.of Employees: 21 - 50 **Product Groups:** 34

Date of Accounts	Dec 11	Dec 10	Dec 09
Working Capital	339	334	418
Fixed Assets	1m	522	571
Current Assets	706	660	579

Samrex Textiles

24 Church Lane, Wolverhampton, WV2 4BU
Tel: 01902-427733 **Fax:** 01902-427765
E-mail: sam@samrex.com
Website: http://www.samrex.com
Directors: K. Samra (MD), P. Samra (Dir)
Immediate Holding Company: SAMREX TEXTILES LIMITED
Registration no: 02144822 **Date established:** 1987
Turnover: £250,000 - £500,000 **No.of Employees:** 21 - 50
Product Groups: 24

Date of Accounts	Apr 11	Apr 10	Apr 09
Working Capital	927	946	951
Fixed Assets	303	355	414
Current Assets	2m	2m	2m

Saredon Steel Buildings Ltd

Saredon Works Malthouse Lane, Great Saredon, Wolverhampton, WV10 7LN
Tel: 01922-415425 **Fax:** 01922-414246
E-mail: info@saredonsteelbuildings.co.uk
Website: http://www.saredonsteelbuildings.co.uk
Bank(s): HSBC Bank plc
Directors: L. Roberts (Fin)
Ultimate Holding Company: KITPAC (HOLDINGS) 2004 LIMITED
Immediate Holding Company: KITPAC HOLDINGS LTD.
Registration no: 02745898 **VAT No.:** GB 632 0418 78
Date established: 1992 **Turnover:** £2m - £5m **No.of Employees:** 11 - 20
Product Groups: 35, 52

Date of Accounts	Jan 10	Jan 09	Jan 08
Working Capital	133	135	116
Fixed Assets	15	27	25
Current Assets	500	649	693

Sauter Automation Ltd (Sales Office)

Bath Avenue, Wolverhampton, WV1 4EG
Tel: 01902-796920 **Fax:** 01902-796928
Website: http://www.sauterautomation.co.uk
Managers: A. Costello (Purch Mgr)
Ultimate Holding Company: FR SAUTER AG BASLE (SWITZERLAND)
Immediate Holding Company: SAUTER AUTOMATION LIMITED
Registration no: 01292827 **Date established:** 1976 **Turnover:** £5m - £10m
No.of Employees: 51 - 100 **Product Groups:** 37, 49

Date of Accounts	Dec 11	Dec 10	Dec 09
Sales Turnover	9m	10m	10m
Pre Tax Profit/Loss	629	1m	695
Working Capital	3m	3m	2m
Fixed Assets	925	969	1m
Current Assets	5m	5m	5m
Current Liabilities	943	2m	2m

Security Guards UK Ltd

445 Dudley Road, Wolverhampton, WV2 3AQ
Tel: 01902-459501 **Fax:** 01902-450703
E-mail: info@securityguardsuk.com
Website: http://www.securityguardsuk.com
Directors: A. Belal (Dir)
Immediate Holding Company: SECURITY GUARDS UK LIMITED
Registration no: 06084898 **Date established:** 2007
Turnover: Up to £250,000 **No.of Employees:** 11 - 20 **Product Groups:** 35, 81

Date of Accounts	Mar 10	Mar 09	Mar 08
Working Capital	-3	-3	-5
Fixed Assets	3	4	5
Current Assets	130	33	8

Shelley Transmission Services Ltd

Eagle Street Off Bilston Road, Wolverhampton, WV2 2AQ
Tel: 01902-351178 **Fax:** 01902-352545
E-mail: sales@shelleytransmission.co.uk
Website: http://www.shelleytransmission.co.uk
Directors: A. Shelley Gray (Fin), A. Shelley-gray (Fin)
Immediate Holding Company: SHELLEY TRANSMISSION SERVICES LIMITED
Registration no: 05855391 **Date established:** 2006
No.of Employees: 21 - 50 **Product Groups:** 35, 45

Date of Accounts	Jul 11	Jul 10	Jul 09
Working Capital	4	-44	-72
Fixed Assets	83	89	96
Current Assets	142	121	97

Shinehill Ltd

127 Ettingshall Road, Wolverhampton, WV2 2JP
Tel: 01902-451322 **Fax:** 01902-870621
E-mail: shinehillexports@hotmail.com
Directors: R. Edgley (Dir)
Ultimate Holding Company: SHINEHILL (ASSETS) LIMITED
Immediate Holding Company: SHINEHILL LIMITED
Registration no: 04181814 **VAT No.:** 765 3318 20 **Date established:** 2001
Turnover: £250,000 - £500,000 **No.of Employees:** 1 - 10
Product Groups: 61

Date of Accounts	Mar 11	Mar 10	Mar 09
Working Capital	106	51	35
Current Assets	316	280	227

SIA TRAINING UK LTD

Sunbeam Studios Sunbeam Street, Wolverhampton, WV2 4PF
Tel: 01902-399688 **Fax:** 01902-399688
E-mail: enquiries@siatraininguktd.com
Website: http://www.siatraininguk.org
Immediate Holding Company: SIA TRAINING UK LTD
Registration no: 06386096 **Date established:** 2007
Turnover: Up to £250,000 **No.of Employees:** 1 - 10 **Product Groups:** 80, 86

Date of Accounts	Sep 09	Sep 08
Sales Turnover	N/A	97
Pre Tax Profit/Loss	N/A	65
Working Capital	1	-1
Fixed Assets	2	3
Current Assets	32	19
Current Liabilities	N/A	15

Simplex Metal Finishers Ltd

12 Stewart Street, Wolverhampton, WV2 4JW
Tel: 01902-717164 **Fax:** 01902-717169
Website: http://www.simplexltd.com
Directors: D. Raj (MD), J. Singh (Dir)
Immediate Holding Company: SIMPLEX METAL FINISHERS LIMITED
Registration no: 03816027 **Date established:** 1999
No.of Employees: 11 - 20 **Product Groups:** 46, 48

Date of Accounts	Oct 11	Oct 10	Oct 09
Working Capital	76	14	-0
Fixed Assets	36	34	37
Current Assets	283	184	158

Skiffy

Unit 5 Wombourne Enterprise Park Bridgnorth Road, Wombourne, Wolverhampton, WV5 0AL
Tel: 01902-894658 **Fax:** 01902-894661
E-mail: skiffyuk@btconnect.com
Website: http://www.skiffy.com

Directors: J. Green (Co Sec)
Managers: M. Green (Sales Prom Mgr), P. Herreaman (Sales Prom Mgr)
Ultimate Holding Company: FILTRONA PLC
Immediate Holding Company: SKIFFY LIMITED
Registration no: 02383222 **Date established:** 1989
Turnover: £500,000 - £1m **No.of Employees:** 1 - 10 **Product Groups:** 29, 30, 35

Date of Accounts	Dec 10	Dec 09	Dec 08
Sales Turnover	1m	852	943
Pre Tax Profit/Loss	64	45	57
Working Capital	314	264	236
Fixed Assets	7	12	10
Current Assets	573	572	708
Current Liabilities	103	49	89

Mike Smith Designs Ltd

Unit 10 Fordhouse Road Industrial Estate Steel Drive, Wolverhampton, WV10 9XE
Tel: 01902-784400 **Fax:** 01902-785980
E-mail: sales@mikesmithdesigns.com
Website: http://www.mikesmithdesigns.com
Bank(s): Barclays
Directors: R. Rayner (Fin)
Immediate Holding Company: MIKE SMITH DESIGNS LIMITED
Registration no: 03847683 **Date established:** 1999
Turnover: £10m - £20m **No.of Employees:** 11 - 20 **Product Groups:** 33, 37

Date of Accounts	Oct 11	Oct 10	Oct 09
Working Capital	69	59	55
Fixed Assets	40	47	51
Current Assets	193	208	172

Smith Welding Factors Ltd

Unit 38 Wombourne Enterprise Park Bridgnorth Road, Wombourne, Wolverhampton, WV5 0AL
Tel: 01902-896083 **Fax:** 01902-892613
E-mail: swf@chessmail.co.uk
Directors: J. Bromley (Co Sec)
Immediate Holding Company: SMITH WELDING FACTORS LIMITED
Registration no: 02559031 **Date established:** 1990
No.of Employees: 1 - 10 **Product Groups:** 46

Date of Accounts	Nov 11	Nov 10	Nov 09
Working Capital	64	74	78
Fixed Assets	5	6	3
Current Assets	106	133	133

Solois Thermal Ltd

Heathbrook House Heath Mill Road, Wombourne, Wolverhampton, WV5 8AP
Tel: 01902-324000
E-mail: stephen.augustine@fivesgroup.com
Website: http://www.fivesgroup.com
Directors: S. Augustine (MD)
Managers: C. Mialet (Fin Mgr)
Ultimate Holding Company: FL INVESTCO (FRANCE)
Immediate Holding Company: SOLIOS THERMAL LIMITED
Registration no: 00144198 **VAT No.:** GB 101 0575 32
Date established: 2016 **Turnover:** £2m - £5m **No.of Employees:** 21 - 50
Product Groups: 40, 46, 48, 84

Date of Accounts	Dec 11	Dec 10	Dec 09
Sales Turnover	7m	3m	12m
Pre Tax Profit/Loss	-406	-223	-2m
Working Capital	156	1m	608
Fixed Assets	1m	1m	1m
Current Assets	4m	3m	4m
Current Liabilities	2m	655	2m

Spa Conservatories Ltd

Hollybush Garden Centre Warstones Road, Shareshill, Wolverhampton, WV10 7LX
Tel: 01922-701121 **Fax:** 01922-701163
E-mail: spacon@theinternetpages.co.uk
Website: http://www.comptonbuildings.co.uk
Directors: C. Guest (Fin), R. Guest (MD)
Ultimate Holding Company: JACK MOODY HOLDINGS PLC
Immediate Holding Company: SPA CONSERVATORIES LTD
Registration no: 07056285 **Date established:** 2009
Turnover: £10m - £20m **No.of Employees:** 11 - 20 **Product Groups:** 25, 33, 35, 66

Specialist Contractors Supplies Ltd

Unit 29 Fallings Park Industrial Estate Park Lane, Wolverhampton, WV10 9QB
Tel: 01902-728381 **Fax:** 01902-728401
E-mail: mail@scslimited.co.uk
Website: http://www.s-c-s.co.uk
Directors: G. Holmes (Dir)
Immediate Holding Company: SPECIALIST CONTRACTORS SUPPLIES LIMITED
Registration no: 02565527 **Date established:** 1990
Turnover: £500,000 - £1m **No.of Employees:** 1 - 10 **Product Groups:** 33, 36, 66

Date of Accounts	Dec 11	Dec 10	Dec 09
Working Capital	24	70	87
Fixed Assets	8	22	29
Current Assets	305	402	390

Spillard Safety Systems Ltd

Solutions House Deepmore Close, Four Ashes, Wolverhampton, WV10 7DB
Tel: 01902-797930 **Fax:** 01902-797931
E-mail: sales@spillard.com
Website: http://www.spillard.com
Directors: P. Spillard (MD)
Immediate Holding Company: SPILLARD SAFETY SYSTEMS LIMITED
Registration no: 02972484 **Date established:** 1994
No.of Employees: 11 - 20 **Product Groups:** 33, 37, 38, 40, 45, 67

Date of Accounts	Sep 11	Sep 10	Sep 09
Working Capital	-123	-91	176
Fixed Assets	799	775	749
Current Assets	866	907	1m
Current Liabilities	375	327	N/A

Stabilised Transformers Ltd

Unit 3 Cullwick Street, Wolverhampton, WV1 2UL
Tel: 01902-404070 **Fax:** 01902-353112
E-mail: sales@stabtran.co.uk
Website: http://www.birford.co.uk
Directors: C. Wase (Sales), T. Wase (MD)
Immediate Holding Company: STABILISED TRANSFORMERS LIMITED
Registration no: 01317567 **Date established:** 1977
No.of Employees: 21 - 50 **Product Groups:** 37

Date of Accounts	Dec 11	Dec 10	Dec 09
Working Capital	586	446	365
Fixed Assets	97	110	88
Current Assets	817	653	488

Steelway

Queensgate Works Bilston Rd, Wolverhampton, WV2 2NJ
Tel: 01902-451733 **Fax:** 01902-452256
E-mail: sales@steelway.co.uk
Website: http://www.steelway.co.uk
Bank(s): National Westminster Bank Plc
Directors: C. Ager (Sales), S. Sahota (Ch), D. Houghton (MD), J. Hankey (Sales)
Managers: I. Whiting, M. Brandon
Registration no: 03872973 **VAT No.:** GB 753 9463 00
Date established: 1928 **Turnover:** £5m - £10m
No.of Employees: 101 - 250 **Product Groups:** 30, 35, 48, 66

Date of Accounts	Jun 11	Jun 10	Jun 09
Sales Turnover	12m	10m	12m
Pre Tax Profit/Loss	222	-486	392
Working Capital	77	-77	648
Fixed Assets	483	551	2m
Current Assets	3m	3m	4m
Current Liabilities	935	695	2m

Sterling Metal Services Ltd

Unit A Smestow Bridge Industrial Estate Bridgnorth Road, Wombourne, Wolverhampton, WV5 8AY
Tel: 01902-326202 **Fax:** 01902-897673
E-mail: am@sterlingmetalservices.co.uk
Website: http://www.sterlingmetalservices.co.uk
Directors: A. Morris (Sales)
Immediate Holding Company: STERLING METAL SERVICES LIMITED
Registration no: 02964603 **Date established:** 1994 **Turnover:** £1m - £2m
No.of Employees: 1 - 10 **Product Groups:** 36

Date of Accounts	Sep 11	Sep 10	Sep 09
Working Capital	33	32	23
Fixed Assets	90	105	128
Current Assets	598	535	349

D A Stuart Ltd

Lincoln Street, Wolverhampton, WV10 0DZ
Tel: 01902-456111 **Fax:** 01902-453764
E-mail: dastuart@dastuart.co.uk
Website: http://www.dastuart.co.uk
Bank(s): Natwest, Queen Square, Wolverhampton
Directors: C. Dutton (Sales), D. Jukes (Fin), P. Ladleif (Dir)
Managers: P. Jones (Sales Prom), M. Dain (Comptroller), P. Lloyd (Ops Mgr), S. Egan-Smith (I.T. Exec), T. Padget (Buyer)
Ultimate Holding Company: WILH WERHAHN KG(GERMANY)
Immediate Holding Company: Houghton Holdings Ltd
Registration no: 00700337 **VAT No.:** GB 100 6060 41
Date established: 1961 **Turnover:** £10m - £20m
No.of Employees: 101 - 250 **Product Groups:** 31, 32, 33, 66

Date of Accounts	Dec 07
Sales Turnover	19495
Pre Tax Profit/Loss	629
Working Capital	3197
Fixed Assets	5226
Current Assets	7361
Current Liabilities	4164
Total Share Capital	3130
ROCE% (Return on Capital Employed)	7.5

Surface Heating Systems UK Ltd

Unit 1 Heath Mill Business Park Road Wombourne, Wolverhampton, WV5 8AP
Tel: 01902-326062 **Fax:** 01902-892866
E-mail: surfheat@aol.com
Directors: H. Cummings (Fin), D. Robins (MD)
Immediate Holding Company: SURFACE HEATING SYSTEMS LIMITED
Registration no: SC178376 **Date established:** 1997
Turnover: £250,000 - £500,000 **No.of Employees:** 1 - 10
Product Groups: 37

Date of Accounts	Sep 11	Sep 10	Sep 09
Sales Turnover	N/A	N/A	353
Working Capital	218	55	116
Fixed Assets	27	13	8
Current Assets	359	66	156

Tarmac Ltd

Millfields Road Ettingshall, Wolverhampton, WV4 6JP
Tel: 01902-353522 **Fax:** 01423-864049
E-mail: enquiries@tarmac.co.uk
Website: http://www.tarmac.co.uk
Managers: T. Last, S. Maynard (Mktg Serv Mgr)
Ultimate Holding Company: ANGLO AMERICAN PLC
Immediate Holding Company: TARMAC LIMITED
Registration no: 00453791 **Date established:** 1948
Turnover: £20m - £50m **No.of Employees:** 251 - 500 **Product Groups:** 31

Date of Accounts	Dec 08
Working Capital	433
Current Assets	433

Tarmac Topblock Ltd (Western)

Hilton Main Industrial Estate Cannock Road, Featherstone, Wolverhampton, WV10 7HP
Tel: 01902-305060 **Fax:** 01902-384543
E-mail: enquiries@tarmac.co.uk
Website: http://www.topblock.co.uk
Directors: D. Billson (Fin), P. Robinson (MD)
Managers: N. Iddenhen (Mgr)
Ultimate Holding Company: Anglo American plc
Immediate Holding Company: Tarmac Ltd
Registration no: 03224202 **No.of Employees:** 51 - 100
Product Groups: 33

Timken UK Ltd

PO Box 667, Wolverhampton, WV2 4UH
Tel: 01902-719300 **Fax:** 01902-719301
E-mail: scott.scherff@timken.com
Website: http://www.timken.com
Directors: S. Scherff (Fin)
Managers: M. Jones (Mgr), M. Williams (Comptroller), S. Ford (Tech Serv Mgr), S. Hartshorne
Ultimate Holding Company: TIMKEN COMPANY (USA)
Immediate Holding Company: TIMKEN UK LIMITED
Registration no: 03392504 **Date established:** 1997
Turnover: £20m - £50m **No.of Employees:** 51 - 100 **Product Groups:** 35, 49

Date of Accounts	Dec 10	Dec 09	Dec 08
Sales Turnover	22m	24m	23m
Pre Tax Profit/Loss	-307	1m	2m
Working Capital	6m	16m	14m
Fixed Assets	1m	2m	2m
Current Assets	24m	19m	18m
Current Liabilities	2m	442	1m

TopDeck Parking

Springvale Business & Industrial Park Bilston, Wolverhampton, WV14 0QL
Tel: 01902-499400 **Fax:** 01902-494080
E-mail: info@topdeckparking.co.uk
Website: http://www.topdeckparking.co.uk
Directors: P. Smythe (Comm)
Registration no: 1270322 **Date established:** 2007
No.of Employees: 1 - 10 **Product Groups:** 35, 83

Turner Gear & Engineering Co.

Unit 3 Fort Works 0 Pelham Street, Wolverhampton, WV3 0BW
Tel: 01902-427617 **Fax:** 01902-681911
E-mail: turner@turnergear.co.uk
Website: http://www.turnergear.co.uk
Directors: C. Turner (Snr Part)
Date established: 1995 **No.of Employees:** 1 - 10 **Product Groups:** 35, 45

UK Security & Fire Services Ltd

Security House 31 Broad Lane, Wolverhampton, WV3 9BN
Tel: 08451-259637
E-mail: asddan@aol.com
Website: http://www.uksecurityandfire.co.uk
Directors: A. Davis (Dir)
Immediate Holding Company: UK SECURITY AND FIRE SERVICES LTD.
Registration no: 04708076 **Date established:** 2003
No.of Employees: 1 - 10 **Product Groups:** 40, 86

Date of Accounts	Mar 11	Mar 10	Mar 09
Working Capital	-1	-3	-5
Fixed Assets	3	4	5
Current Assets	27	29	22

Ultra Blinds

Enterprise Drive Four Ashes, Wolverhampton, WV10 7DF
Tel: 01902-798063 **Fax:** 01902-798065
E-mail: sales@ultrablinds.com
Website: http://www.ultrablinds.com
Managers: S. Doble (Mgr)
Immediate Holding Company: ULTRA BLINDS LIMITED
Registration no: 03007895 **Date established:** 1995
Turnover: £500,000 - £1m **No.of Employees:** 11 - 20
Product Groups: 23, 24, 33, 63, 66

Date of Accounts	Mar 11	Mar 10	Mar 09
Sales Turnover	626	N/A	N/A
Pre Tax Profit/Loss	-24	N/A	N/A
Working Capital	-23	8	94
Fixed Assets	46	58	37
Current Assets	139	212	302
Current Liabilities	71	N/A	N/A

United Bright Bar Co. Ltd

Station Road Four Ashes, Wolverhampton, WV10 7DG
Tel: 01902-791010 **Fax:** 01902-790044
E-mail: kfrench@unitedbrightbar.co.uk
Website: http://www.unitedbrightbar.co.uk
Directors: K. French (Fin)
Immediate Holding Company: UNITED BRIGHT BAR CO. LIMITED
Registration no: 01376360 **VAT No.:** GB 361 9724 35
Date established: 1978 **Turnover:** £5m - £10m **No.of Employees:** 11 - 20
Product Groups: 34

Date of Accounts	Mar 12	Mar 11	Mar 10
Sales Turnover	7m	6m	4m
Pre Tax Profit/Loss	57	-28	-439
Working Capital	1m	1m	1m
Fixed Assets	1m	1m	1m
Current Assets	3m	3m	2m
Current Liabilities	394	428	243

VW Company ltd

Phoenix Works, Satellite Industrial Estate Neachells Lane, Wednesfield, Wolverhampton, WV11 3PU
Tel: 0870-1654545 **Fax:** 0870-1654646
E-mail: info@vwcompany.co.uk
Website: http://www.vwcompany.com
Directors: R. Derby (Dir)
Registration no: 01952280 **Date established:** 2005
No.of Employees: 1 - 10 **Product Groups:** 38

Date of Accounts	Sep 08
Pre Tax Profit/Loss	158
Working Capital	23
Fixed Assets	534
Current Assets	23
Total Share Capital	50

Victorian Baking Ovens Ltd

Unit 40 Central Trading Estate Cable Street, Wolverhampton, WV2 2RL
Tel: 01902-351477 **Fax:** 01902-351437
E-mail: sales@victorianovens.co.uk
Website: http://www.victorianovens.co.uk
Directors: J. Hickman (MD)
Immediate Holding Company: VICTORIAN BAKING OVENS LIMITED
Registration no: 01639413 **Date established:** 1982
Turnover: £500,000 - £1m **No.of Employees:** 11 - 20
Product Groups: 40, 41

Date of Accounts	May 11	May 10	May 09
Working Capital	81	360	290
Fixed Assets	64	76	88
Current Assets	374	476	449

The Vintage Paint Company

Unit 6 Four Ashes Enterprise Centre, Wolverhampton, WV10 7BY
Tel: 01902-798292
E-mail: mail@vintagepaint.com
Website: http://www.vintagepaint.com
Directors: M. Pursglove (Ch)
Date established: 2000 **Turnover:** £500,000 - £1m
No.of Employees: 1 - 10 **Product Groups:** 32, 39

Walker Grinding
Unit 41 Fordhouse Road Industrial Estate Steel Drive, Wolverhampton, WV10 9XF
Tel: 01902-785804 **Fax:** 01902-789228
E-mail: enquiries@paragon-eng-log.com
Website: http://www.paragon-eng-log.com
Directors: J. Harper (Dir)
Immediate Holding Company: WALKER GRINDING COMPANY LIMITED
Registration no: 03981664 **Date established:** 2000
No.of Employees: 1 - 10 **Product Groups:** 46

Date of Accounts	Mar 12	Mar 11	Mar 10
Working Capital	21	8	4
Current Assets	26	11	7

Wear Belting
Little Poutney Street, Wolverhampton, WV2 4JH
Tel: 01925-259058 **Fax:** 01902-427442
E-mail: sales@wearbelting.co.uk
Website: http://www.wearbelting.com
Managers: S. Brennan (Sales Admin), S. Brennan (Admin Off)
No.of Employees: 1 - 10 **Product Groups:** 35, 45

Webgibb Welding & Fabrications
Unit 11 Bluebird Industrial Estate Park Lane, Wolverhampton, WV10 9QQ
Tel: 01902-722040 **Fax:** 01902-722040
E-mail: shane@webgibb.u-net.com
Website: http://www.webgibb.u-net.com
Directors: S. Gibbons (MD)
Immediate Holding Company: WEBGIBB WELDING AND FABRICATIONS LIMITED
Registration no: 02237513 **VAT No.:** GB 410 0371 23
Date established: 1988 **Turnover:** Up to £250,000
No.of Employees: 1 - 10 **Product Groups:** 48

Date of Accounts	Mar 11	Mar 10	Mar 09
Working Capital	4	3	6
Fixed Assets	11	13	15
Current Assets	28	25	26

Wescol
PO Box 41, Wolverhampton, WV1 2RZ
Tel: 01902-351283 **Fax:** 01902-351475
E-mail: sales@wescol.com
Website: http://www.wescol.com
Directors: S. Taylor (Fin)
Immediate Holding Company: GENWELD SUPPLIES LIMITED
Registration no: 01393521 **VAT No.:** GB 100 2935 24
Date established: 1978 **Turnover:** £1m - £2m **No.of Employees:** 1 - 10
Product Groups: 29, 34, 37, 38, 40, 46

Date of Accounts	Dec 03	Dec 02	Mar 04
Working Capital	44	31	45
Fixed Assets	2	2	1
Current Assets	190	184	146
Current Liabilities	46	34	N/A

Wheelabrator Allevard
Creative Industries Centre Wolverhampton Science Park, Glaisher Drive, Wolverhampton, WV10 9TG
Tel: 01902-792610 **Fax:** 01902-712058
E-mail: sales@metabrasive.com
Website: http://www.wabrasives.com
Bank(s): H S B C
Directors: A. Carmichael (MD), N. Moseley (Fin), M. Speak (Sales)
Managers: C. Ward (Mktg Serv Mgr), L. Pryke (Tech Serv Mgr)
Ultimate Holding Company: Vivendi SA
Immediate Holding Company: US Filter
Registration no: 00033672 **VAT No.:** GB 561 0079 67
Turnover: £2m - £5m **No.of Employees:** 251 - 500 **Product Groups:** 40, 42, 46

Willis European Ltd
Unit 7 Four Ashes Enterprise Centre Latherford Close, Four Ashes, Wolverhampton, WV10 7BY
Tel: 01902-798880 **Fax:** 01902-490896
E-mail: info@williseuropean.com
Website: http://www.williseuropean.com
Directors: T. Willis (MD)
Immediate Holding Company: WILLIS EUROPEAN LIMITED
Registration no: 05238851 **VAT No.:** GB 100 9701 14
Date established: 2004 **Turnover:** £1m - £2m **No.of Employees:** 1 - 10
Product Groups: 42

Date of Accounts	Sep 11	Sep 10	Sep 09
Working Capital	6	4	-31
Fixed Assets	62	26	35
Current Assets	163	250	188

Wirs (Wolverhampton) Limited
Church Lane, Wolverhampton, WV2 4AL
Tel: 01902-712525 **Fax:** 01902-429016
E-mail: enquiry@wirs.co.uk
Website: http://www.wirs.co.uk
Bank(s): National Westminster Bank Plc
Directors: J. Brian (MD), P. Marsh (Comm), W. Hayward (Dir)
Managers: J. Smith (Accounts), M. Ansell (Sales Prom Mgr)
Immediate Holding Company: Pces Ltd
Registration no: 02088761 **VAT No.:** GB 456 7461 20
Date established: 1987 **Turnover:** £2m - £5m **No.of Employees:** 21 - 50
Product Groups: 46

Date of Accounts	Sep 09	Sep 08	Sep 07
Working Capital	2m	2m	2m
Fixed Assets	862	873	751
Current Assets	2m	2m	2m

Wolverhampton Electro Plating Ltd
Wood Lane, Wolverhampton, WV10 8HN
Tel: 01902-397333 **Fax:** 01902-785372
E-mail: info@anochrome-group.co.uk
Website: http://www.anochrome-group.co.uk
Directors: J. Oliver (Tech Serv), M. Oliver (Fin), V. Warr (Co Sec)
Managers: A. Warner (Tech Serv Mgr), I. Smith (Sales Prom Mgr), P. James
Ultimate Holding Company: W.E.P. GROUP LIMITED
Immediate Holding Company: WOLVERHAMPTON ELECTRO PLATING LIMITED
Registration no: 01583889 **Date established:** 1981 **Turnover:** £1m - £2m
No.of Employees: 51 - 100 **Product Groups:** 48

Date of Accounts	Mar 11	Mar 10	Mar 09
Pre Tax Profit/Loss	N/A	N/A	-569
Working Capital	991	617	60
Fixed Assets	1m	1m	2m
Current Assets	3m	2m	2m
Current Liabilities	N/A	N/A	1m

Wolverhampton Pressings Co. Ltd
Fordhouse Road, Wolverhampton, WV10 9EX
Tel: 01902-307799 **Fax:** 01902-721026
E-mail: ptanner@wpc.ralphmartindale.com
Website: http://www.ralphmartindale.com
Directors: L. Smith (Fin), M. Smith (MD), N. Betteridge (Sales), S. Fox (Co Sec)
Managers: R. Bood (Buyer), G. Jurance (Sales & Mktg Mg), L. Weaver (Personnel)
Ultimate Holding Company: RALPH MARTINDALE AND COMPANY LIMITED
Immediate Holding Company: WOLVERHAMPTON PRESSINGS COMPANY LIMITED
Registration no: 01145374 **VAT No.:** GB 346 3189 45
Date established: 1973 **Turnover:** £2m - £5m **No.of Employees:** 51 - 100
Product Groups: 41, 48

Date of Accounts	Dec 10	Dec 09	Dec 08
Sales Turnover	2m	3m	3m
Pre Tax Profit/Loss	-184	-447	-294
Working Capital	-373	-450	93
Fixed Assets	396	443	492
Current Assets	1m	1m	2m
Current Liabilities	45	57	54

WyseGroup
Unit 1 Clear Water Industrial Estate, Wolverhampton, WV2 2JP
Tel: 01902-872600 **Fax:** 01920-453152
E-mail: bristol@wysepower.com
Website: http://www.wysepower.com
Directors: K. Linnane (MD), M. Curran (MD)
Managers: D. Garner (Purch Mgr), N. James (Mktg Serv Mgr)
Ultimate Holding Company: P & O Group & Carillion
Registration no: 05379085 **VAT No.:** GB 196 2687 15
Turnover: £10m - £20m **No.of Employees:** 11 - 20 **Product Groups:** 45, 48, 84

Date of Accounts	Dec 07	Dec 06	Dec 05
Sales Turnover	532	4972	1537
Pre Tax Profit/Loss	158	4216	-742
Working Capital	-637	30037	27862
Fixed Assets	30	157	2002
Current Assets	1609	34340	28430
Current Liabilities	2246	4303	568
Total Share Capital	N/A	40000	40000
ROCE% (Return on Capital Employed)	-26.0	14.0	-2.5
ROT% (Return on Turnover)	29.7	84.8	-48.3

Zaun Ltd
Steel Drive, Wolverhampton, WV10 9ED
Tel: 01902-796699 **Fax:** 01902-796698
E-mail: ian.wright@zaun.co.uk
Website: http://www.zaun.co.uk
Managers: I. Wright (Comm)
Immediate Holding Company: ZAUN LIMITED
Registration no: 03275214 **Date established:** 1996 **Turnover:** £5m - £10m
No.of Employees: 21 - 50 **Product Groups:** 35, 49, 66

Date of Accounts	Dec 11	Dec 10	Dec 09
Sales Turnover	11m	8m	11m
Pre Tax Profit/Loss	1m	622	1m
Working Capital	2m	1m	2m
Fixed Assets	4m	4m	3m
Current Assets	5m	3m	4m
Current Liabilities	826	343	814

NORFOLK

Attleborough

Advanced Research Associates Ltd

65 Mill Lane, Attleborough, NR17 2NW
Tel: 01953-450921 **Fax:** 01953-452751
E-mail: stevejones27@aol.com
Directors: A. Jones (Fin), S. Jones (MD), S. Jones (Dir)
Immediate Holding Company: ADVANCED RESEARCH ASSOCIATES LIMITED
Registration no: 04918723 **Date established:** 2003
No.of Employees: 1 - 10 **Product Groups:** 80

Date of Accounts	Oct 08	Oct 07	Oct 06
Pre Tax Profit/Loss	-0	-1	-1
Working Capital	N/A	N/A	3
Fixed Assets	N/A	N/A	1
Current Assets	N/A	N/A	3

Attleborough Diesel Services

Bunns Bank Old Buckenham, Attleborough, NR17 1QD
Tel: 01953-455431 **Fax:** 01953-455431
Directors: P. Howlett (Prop)
Immediate Holding Company: LEE & PLUMPTON LIMITED
Registration no: 01201175 **Date established:** 1975
No.of Employees: 1 - 10 **Product Groups:** 40

Date of Accounts	Feb 08	Feb 11	Feb 10
Sales Turnover	N/A	6m	6m
Pre Tax Profit/Loss	686	-240	-516
Working Capital	6m	6m	6m
Fixed Assets	6m	5m	5m
Current Assets	7m	6m	6m
Current Liabilities	393	109	33

Hamilton Acorn Ltd

Halford Road, Attleborough, NR17 2HZ
Tel: 01953-453201 **Fax:** 01953-454943
E-mail: info@hamilton-acorn.co.uk
Website: http://www.hamilton-acorn.co.uk
Bank(s): Bank of Scotland
Directors: S. Edwards (MD), A. Carpenter (Fin), T. Wortley (Mkt Research), T. Weir (Sales)
Managers: D. Woodrow (Tech Serv Mgr)
Ultimate Holding Company: JORDAN A/S (NORWAY)
Immediate Holding Company: HAMILTON ACORN LIMITED.
Registration no: 03149785 **VAT No.:** 558 4073 24 **Date established:** 1996
Turnover: £5m - £10m **No.of Employees:** 21 - 50 **Product Groups:** 36, 49

Date of Accounts	Dec 11	Dec 10	Dec 09
Sales Turnover	9m	9m	9m
Pre Tax Profit/Loss	301	-452	-1m
Working Capital	3m	3m	3m
Fixed Assets	1m	1m	1m
Current Assets	7m	7m	8m
Current Liabilities	885	972	1m

Protech Engineering

Unit 5 Ash Farm Hill Common, Attleborough, NR17 1AF
Tel: 01953-453666
Directors: J. Barker (Prop)
No.of Employees: 1 - 10 **Product Groups:** 37, 47

Reel Furniture

Unit 11a Bunns Bank, Old Buckenham, Attleborough, NR17 1QD
Tel: 01953-457247
E-mail: gainstay@hotmail.com
Website: http://www.davidmeddingsdesign.co.uk
Directors: D. Meddings (Prop)
No.of Employees: 1 - 10 **Product Groups:** 26

Reinforcements Norwich

Stalland Common Off Hingham Road, Great Ellingham, Attleborough, NR17 1JF
Tel: 01953-456999 **Fax:** 01953-456044
Managers: M. Pallet (Mgr)
No.of Employees: 1 - 10 **Product Groups:** 34, 66

Rendells Precision Engineering

12 Maurice Gaymer Road, Attleborough, NR17 2QZ
Tel: 01953-455801
E-mail: rendells@tiscali.co.uk
Directors: D. Rendells (Ptnr)
Immediate Holding Company: RENDELLS PRECISION ENGINEERING LTD
Date established: 2011 **No.of Employees:** 1 - 10 **Product Groups:** 36

Ultimet Films Ltd

Unit 16 Maurice Gaymer Road, Attleborough, NR17 2QZ
Tel: 01953-457220 **Fax:** 01953-457227
E-mail: sales@ultimetfilms.com
Website: http://www.ultimetfilms.com
Directors: M. Stott (MD)
Managers: M. Stott
Immediate Holding Company: ULTIMET FILMS LIMITED
Registration no: 03083304 **Date established:** 1995
No.of Employees: 11 - 20 **Product Groups:** 38, 42

Date of Accounts	Dec 11	Dec 10	Dec 09
Working Capital	2m	2m	1m
Fixed Assets	1m	2m	2m
Current Assets	2m	2m	2m

Cromer

Bournlea Instruments Ltd

The Old Rectory 34 Pauls Lane, Overstrand, Cromer, NR27 0PF
Tel: 01263-578186 **Fax:** 01263-579186
E-mail: harry@bournlea.com
Website: http://www.bournlea.com
Directors: H. Kitchin (Dir)
Immediate Holding Company: BOURNLEA INSTRUMENTS LIMITED
Registration no: 01840648 **Date established:** 1984
No.of Employees: 1 - 10 **Product Groups:** 38

Date of Accounts	Oct 11	Oct 10	Oct 09
Working Capital	-148	-136	-128
Fixed Assets	3	2	2
Current Assets	21	16	16

Cromer Crab Company

33 Holt Road, Cromer, NR27 9EB
Tel: 01263-519800 **Fax:** 01263- 514496
Website: http://www.theseafoodcompany.co.uk
Directors: P. Marshall (Fin), M. Grey (Dir), M. Gray (MD), G. Steggall (Pers), T. Muldoon (Dir), M. Bray (MD)
Managers: G. Steggall, N. Plant (Buyer), I. Rowland (Sales Prom Mgr)
Immediate Holding Company: THE SEAFOOD COMPANY LTD
Registration no: 02140583 **VAT No.:** GB 673 7410 25
No.of Employees: 101 - 250 **Product Groups:** 62

Date of Accounts	Sep 07	Dec 06	Dec 05
Sales Turnover	20259	27429	12648
Pre Tax Profit/Loss	103	1535	705
Working Capital	291	-87	-1244
Fixed Assets	4119	4310	4275
Current Assets	4700	6926	4098
Current Liabilities	4409	7014	5342
ROCE% (Return on Capital Employed)	2.3	36.3	23.3
ROT% (Return on Turnover)	0.5	5.6	5.6

Dereham

A & E Systems Ltd

3 Charles Wood Road, Dereham, NR19 1SX
Tel: 01362-694915 **Fax:** 01362-695350
E-mail: uk@ae-sys.com
Website: http://www.ae-sys.com
Managers: C. Frost (Sales Admin)
Immediate Holding Company: A&E SYSTEMS LIMITED
Registration no: 06271390 **Date established:** 2007
No.of Employees: 1 - 10 **Product Groups:** 32, 51, 52

Date of Accounts	Dec 11	Dec 10	Dec 09
Working Capital	141	-27	41
Fixed Assets	261	253	51
Current Assets	373	281	377

Anglia Epos

Hall Lodges Gateley, Dereham, NR20 5EF
Tel: 01328-829607 **Fax:** 01328-829607
E-mail: j.cowan@tills.net
Website: http://www.tills.net
Directors: J. Cowan (Ptnr)
Date established: 1999 **No.of Employees:** 1 - 10 **Product Groups:** 37, 40, 44, 67

Anglia Protective Coatings

28 De Havilland Road, Dereham, NR19 2XN
Tel: 01362-697463 **Fax:** 01362-697463
E-mail: chris@angliaprotectivecoatings.fsnet.co.uk
Directors: C. Maher (Prop)
Date established: 1993 **No.of Employees:** 1 - 10 **Product Groups:** 46, 48

Batoyle Freedom Group

1 Charles Wood Road, Dereham, NR19 1SX
Tel: 01362-698728 **Fax:** 01362-690254
Website: http://www.batoyle.co.uk
Managers: H. Franklin (Mgr)
Registration no: 00935764 **Turnover:** £5m - £10m
No.of Employees: 1 - 10 **Product Groups:** 31, 32, 66

Battley Marine Ltd

East End House Billingford, Dereham, NR20 4RD
Tel: 01362-668641 **Fax:** 01362-668930
E-mail: batmar@croftfk.fsnet.co.uk
Website: http://www.battleymarine.com
Directors: K. Croft (Dir)
Immediate Holding Company: BATTLEY MARINE LTD.
Registration no: 01395430 **VAT No.:** GB 324 3275 78
Date established: 1978 **Turnover:** £250,000 - £500,000
No.of Employees: 1 - 10 **Product Groups:** 84

Date of Accounts	Mar 11	Mar 10	Mar 09
Working Capital	-35	-42	-45
Fixed Assets	132	135	138
Current Assets	12	12	12

Churchills Of Dereham

24 Norwich Street, Dereham, NR19 1BX
Tel: 01362-696926 **Fax:** 01362-696926
E-mail: c.bennington@churchillsofdereham.co.uk
Website: http://www.churchillsofdereham.co.uk
Directors: C. Bennington (Prop), S. Bennington (Prop)
Date established: 1993 **No.of Employees:** 1 - 10 **Product Groups:** 36, 39, 40

Date of Accounts	Mar 07	Mar 06
Working Capital	-8	-25
Fixed Assets	63	62
Current Assets	135	120
Current Liabilities	143	145

Engineering Tech Recruitment

1 Keith Road Swanton Morley, Dereham, NR20 4NQ
Tel: 01362-637744 **Fax:** 0845-257716
E-mail: barry@engtechjobs.co.uk
Website: http://www.engtechjobs.co.uk
Directors: B. Gough (Dir)
Immediate Holding Company: ENG TECH RECRUITMENT LIMITED
Registration no: 06585443 **Date established:** 2008 **Turnover:** £2m - £5m
No.of Employees: 1 - 10 **Product Groups:** 80

Date of Accounts	May 11	May 10	May 09
Working Capital	-76	-66	-53
Fixed Assets	1	2	4
Current Assets	5	2	1

First Line Services

37 Colin Mclean Road, Dereham, NR19 2RY
Tel: 01362-699456 **Fax:** 01362-699456
E-mail: drivetrain9@hotmail.com
Directors: B. Thacker (Prop)
Date established: 2002 **No.of Employees:** 1 - 10 **Product Groups:** 35, 39, 45

Jark plc

Beechurst Commercial Road, Dereham, NR19 1AE
Tel: 01362-697888 **Fax:** 01362-694888
Website: http://www.jark.co.uk
Directors: D. Jaffrey (Co Sec), P. Mizen (MD), D. Parr (Tech Serv)
Ultimate Holding Company: JARK HOLDINGS LIMITED
Immediate Holding Company: JARK PLC
Registration no: 03224862 **Date established:** 1996
No.of Employees: 21 - 50 **Product Groups:** 80

Date of Accounts	Mar 12	Mar 11	Mar 10
Sales Turnover	57m	65m	66m
Pre Tax Profit/Loss	139	1m	-2m
Working Capital	-983	-2m	-2m
Fixed Assets	6m	5m	6m
Current Assets	11m	10m	12m
Current Liabilities	12m	11m	12m

Milne Partnership Ltd
Mill Works Harkers Lane, Swanton Morley, Dereham, NR20 4PA
Tel: 01362-637404 **Fax:** 01362-637692
E-mail: contact@themilnepartnership.co.uk
Website: http://www.themilnepartnership.co.uk
Directors: N. Blackledge (Dir), F. Milne (Fin)
Immediate Holding Company: THE MILNE PARTNERSHIP LLP
Registration no: OC302662 **Date established:** 2002
No.of Employees: 1 - 10 **Product Groups:** 35

Norfine Nets
The Broadway Fen Road, Scarning, Dereham, NR19 2LH
Tel: 01362-690900 **Fax:** 01362-695912
E-mail: info@norfinenets.co.uk
Website: http://www.norfinenets.co.uk
Directors: D. Shreeve (Prop)
Immediate Holding Company: NORFINE NETS LIMITED
Registration no: 06038283 **VAT No.:** GB 451 2669 51
Date established: 2006 **Turnover:** Up to £250,000
No.of Employees: 1 - 10 **Product Groups:** 23

Date of Accounts	Jan 12	Jan 11	Jan 10
Working Capital	7	17	10
Fixed Assets	33	33	34
Current Assets	20	22	17

Premier Pallet Systems Ltd
The Green Gressenhall, Dereham, NR20 4DT
Tel: 01362-861066 **Fax:** 01362-861160
E-mail: sales@premierpal.co.uk
Website: http://www.premierpal.co.uk
Directors: P. Davis (Dir)
Immediate Holding Company: PREMIER PALLET SYSTEMS LIMITED
Registration no: 02789457 **VAT No.:** GB 595 4282 05
Date established: 1993 **Turnover:** £2m - £5m **No.of Employees:** 1 - 10
Product Groups: 45

Date of Accounts	Dec 11	Dec 10	Dec 09
Working Capital	1m	1m	781
Fixed Assets	212	224	187
Current Assets	2m	1m	1m

Rima UK Ltd
Unit 2 Rashs Green, Dereham, NR19 1JG
Tel: 01362-697772 **Fax:** 01362-696444
E-mail: info@rima-uk.com
Website: http://www.rima-uk.com
Directors: C. Salvi (MD), N. Alcock (Co Sec)
Immediate Holding Company: RIMA UK LIMITED
Registration no: 04713781 **Date established:** 2003
No.of Employees: 1 - 10 **Product Groups:** 35, 40, 45

Date of Accounts	Dec 10	Dec 09	Dec 08
Working Capital	-50	-127	-86
Fixed Assets	5	7	8
Current Assets	532	258	259

Russell Scientific Instruments Ltd
Rashs Green Industrial Estate, Dereham, NR19 1JG
Tel: 01362-693481 **Fax:** 01362-698548
E-mail: sales@russell-scientific.co.uk
Website: http://www.russell-scientific.co.uk
Bank(s): Barclays
Directors: E. Allen (MD)
Ultimate Holding Company: WEST ALLEN HOLDINGS LIMITED
Immediate Holding Company: RUSSELL SCIENTIFIC INSTRUMENTS LIMITED
Registration no: 01188173 **VAT No.:** GB 451 2199 62
Date established: 1974 **Turnover:** £500,000 - £1m
No.of Employees: 11 - 20 **Product Groups:** 37, 38, 40, 48, 49, 85

Date of Accounts	Apr 12	Apr 11	Apr 10
Sales Turnover	471	583	522
Pre Tax Profit/Loss	-10	75	-38
Working Capital	164	169	110
Fixed Assets	18	23	24
Current Assets	248	273	238
Current Liabilities	17	34	55

Diss

Anglia Aircraft Services
The Patch Norwich Road, Dickleburgh, Diss, IP21 4NR
Tel: 07860-545812 **Fax:** 01379-741188
E-mail: stu@angliasailplanes.co.uk
Website: http://www.angliasailplanes.co.uk
Directors: S. Hoy (Prop)
Date established: 2002 **No.of Employees:** 1 - 10 **Product Groups:** 39, 40

Barric Ltd
Vinces Road, Diss, IP22 4WY
Tel: 01379-644202 **Fax:** 01379-652361
E-mail: sales@barric.co.uk
Website: http://www.barric.co.uk
Bank(s): Barclays
Directors: M. Bayley (MD), P. Kibble (Fin)
Managers: P. Jay (Mats Contrlr)
Ultimate Holding Company: BARRIC LIMITED
Immediate Holding Company: BARRIC LIMITED
Registration no: 04239530 **VAT No.:** GB 496 7366 83
Date established: 2001 **Turnover:** £5m - £10m **No.of Employees:** 21 - 50
Product Groups: 37

Date of Accounts	Sep 11	Sep 10	Sep 09
Working Capital	219	152	41
Fixed Assets	482	530	573
Current Assets	1m	887	883

Cadlow Enclosures
Bridge House The Green, Redgrave, Diss, IP22 1RR
Tel: 01379-898810 **Fax:** 01379-898812
E-mail: info@cadlow.co.uk
Website: http://www.cadlow.co.uk
Directors: D. Wright (Prop), S. Medhurst (Fin)
VAT No.: GB 571 4426 45 **Turnover:** Up to £250,000
No.of Employees: 1 - 10 **Product Groups:** 30

Cyprium Motor Sport Systems
Unit 3a Redgrave Business Centre Gallows Hill, Redgrave, Diss, IP22 1RZ
Tel: 01379-897262
E-mail: deswenn@cyprium.co.uk
Website: http://www.cyprium.co.uk
Directors: D. Wenn (MD), J. Wenn (Fin)
Immediate Holding Company: CYPRIUM LTD
Registration no: 04417742 **Date established:** 2002
No.of Employees: 11 - 20 **Product Groups:** 36, 40

Date of Accounts	Oct 11	Oct 10	Oct 08
Working Capital	291	221	152
Fixed Assets	43	45	55
Current Assets	370	284	293

Diss Ironworks Ltd
7 St Nicholas Street, Diss, IP22 4LB
Tel: 01379-643978 **Fax:** 01379-641026
E-mail: info@dissironworks.co.uk
Managers: M. Hyde (Mgr)
Immediate Holding Company: DISS IRONWORKS LIMITED
Registration no: 04875898 **Date established:** 2003
No.of Employees: 1 - 10 **Product Groups:** 40

Date of Accounts	Mar 11	Mar 10	Mar 09
Working Capital	149	121	100
Fixed Assets	39	45	55
Current Assets	266	248	253

Eras Ltd
Providence Court 104-106 Denmark Street, Diss, IP22 4WN
Tel: 01379-652171 **Fax:** 01379-644225
E-mail: expertise@eras.co.uk
Website: http://www.eras.co.uk
Directors: A. Pearce (MD)
Immediate Holding Company: ERAS LIMITED
Registration no: 01832022 **Date established:** 1984 **Turnover:** £1m - £2m
No.of Employees: 11 - 20 **Product Groups:** 80

Date of Accounts	Mar 12	Mar 11	Mar 10
Working Capital	123	108	103
Fixed Assets	10	13	10
Current Assets	272	342	193

Fairgreen Fish Bar
37 Denmark Street, Diss, IP22 4BE
Tel: 01379-642412 **Fax:** 01379-643857
E-mail: merdanadiguzel@hotmail.co.uk
Website: http://www.fairgreenco.com
Directors: M. Adiguzel (Prop)
Turnover: Up to £250,000 **No.of Employees:** 1 - 10 **Product Groups:** 26, 33, 48, 63, 67

Gas Arc Group Ltd
Vinces Road, Diss, IP22 4WW
Tel: 01379-652263 **Fax:** 01379-644235
E-mail: sales@gas-arc.co.uk
Website: http://www.gas-arc.co.uk
Bank(s): Bank of Scotland
Directors: D. Whiting (Sales), S. Bacon (Fin), C. Matthews (Comm)
Managers: M. Turner (Tech Serv Mgr), P. Fountain (Purch Mgr)
Immediate Holding Company: GAS ARC GROUP LIMITED
Registration no: 01569200 **VAT No.:** GB 363 5450 54
Date established: 1981 **Turnover:** £5m - £10m
No.of Employees: 51 - 100 **Product Groups:** 38, 46

Date of Accounts	Apr 11	Apr 10	Apr 09
Sales Turnover	7m	6m	6m
Pre Tax Profit/Loss	3m	3m	3m
Working Capital	4m	4m	5m
Fixed Assets	1m	1m	1m
Current Assets	6m	5m	6m
Current Liabilities	766	654	608

Jackaman's
Park House Mere Street, Diss, IP22 4JY
Tel: 01379-643555 **Fax:** 01379-652221
E-mail: james.laband@jackamans.co.uk
Website: http://www.jackamans.co.uk
Directors: J. Laband (Ptnr)
Immediate Holding Company: BUILDING CLEANING SERVICES LTD.
Registration no: 02676579 **Date established:** 1983 **Turnover:** £1m - £2m
No.of Employees: 1 - 10 **Product Groups:** 80

K & C Mouldings England Ltd
Spa House Church Road, Shelfanger, Diss, IP22 2DF
Tel: 01379-642660 **Fax:** 01379-650304
E-mail: sales@kcmouldings.co.uk
Website: http://www.kcmouldings.co.uk
Directors: W. Clendening (MD)
Immediate Holding Company: K. & C. MOULDINGS (ENGLAND) LIMITED
Registration no: 00616579 **VAT No.:** GB 104 9842 69
Date established: 1958 **Turnover:** £1m - £2m **No.of Employees:** 1 - 10
Product Groups: 30, 42

Date of Accounts	Feb 08	Feb 11	Feb 10
Working Capital	302	164	242
Fixed Assets	26	26	26
Current Assets	544	385	501

Linton & Co Engineering Ltd
Unit 11 Forge Business Centre, Diss, IP22 1AP
Tel: 01379-651344 **Fax:** 01379-650970
E-mail: mail@lintoninst.co.uk
Website: http://www.lintoninst.co.uk
Directors: P. Gunning (MD), J. Gunning (Co Sec)
Managers: R. Jones (Sales Prom Mgr)
Immediate Holding Company: Linton & Co. (Engineering) Ltd
Registration no: 01362774 **VAT No.:** GB 215 3230 12
Date established: 1978 **Turnover:** £1m - £2m **No.of Employees:** 1 - 10
Product Groups: 37, 38, 42, 44, 63

Date of Accounts	Oct 07	Oct 06	Oct 05
Working Capital	139	185	234
Fixed Assets	61	69	74
Current Assets	345	493	651
Current Liabilities	205	308	416
Total Share Capital	100	100	100

Midwich Security Ltd
Vinces Road, Diss, IP22 4YT
Tel: 01379-647529 **Fax:** 01379-652448
E-mail: anands@ubiqz.com
Website: http://www.ubiqz.com
Directors: A. Subbiah (Dir)
Ultimate Holding Company: M&R 320 LIMITED
Immediate Holding Company: MIDWICH LIMITED
Registration no: 01436289 **VAT No.:** GB 765 3317 22
Date established: 1979 **Turnover:** £125m - £250m
No.of Employees: 1 - 10 **Product Groups:** 37, 38, 44

Date of Accounts	Dec 11	Dec 10	Dec 09
Sales Turnover	182m	184m	174m
Pre Tax Profit/Loss	9m	7m	6m
Working Capital	12m	14m	10m
Fixed Assets	4m	3m	2m
Current Assets	53m	60m	50m
Current Liabilities	6m	4m	5m

Mondi Packaging Limited
Pulham St. Mary, Diss, IP21 4QH
Tel: 01379-676531 **Fax:** 01379-676275
E-mail: sales.bux@mondipackaging.com
Website: http://www.mondigroup.com
Directors: C. White (Sales), M. Mabbutt (MD)
Registration no: 01846191 **Turnover:** £500,000 - £1m
No.of Employees: 101 - 250 **Product Groups:** 27, 28, 49, 85

Norfolk Feather Co. Ltd
Park Road, Diss, IP22 4AS
Tel: 01379-643187 **Fax:** 01379-650413
E-mail: sales@norfolkfeathercompany.co.uk
Website: http://www.norfolkfeathercompany.co.uk
Bank(s): National Westminster Bank Plc
Directors: M. Flitcroft (MD), M. Edwards (Dir), J. Cummin (Fin)
Immediate Holding Company: WYCOMBE FEATHER GROUP LTD
Registration no: 02824984 **VAT No.:** GB 637 7610 21
Date established: 1993 **Turnover:** £2m - £5m **No.of Employees:** 21 - 50
Product Groups: 24, 26, 43

Date of Accounts	Dec 07	Dec 06	Dec 05
Working Capital	293	228	229
Fixed Assets	210	191	210
Current Assets	1295	988	937
Current Liabilities	1002	760	708
Total Share Capital	100	100	100

Open Field (a division of S C A T S Grain Ltd)
Low Road Bressingham, Diss, IP22 2DB
Tel: 01379-688111 **Fax:** 01379-688246
E-mail: info@openfield.co.uk
Website: http://www.grainfarmers.co.uk
Bank(s): National Westminster Bank Plc
Managers: S. Howlett (Chief Mgr)
Ultimate Holding Company: SOUTHERN COUNTIES AGRICULTURAL TRADING LIMITED
Immediate Holding Company: OPENFIELD ARABLE LIMITED
Registration no: 03613532 **Date established:** 1998
Turnover: £250m - £500m **No.of Employees:** 11 - 20
Product Groups: 02, 20

Date of Accounts	Jul 08	Jun 09
Sales Turnover	55m	46m
Pre Tax Profit/Loss	1m	2m
Working Capital	905	N/A
Fixed Assets	95	N/A
Current Assets	15m	N/A
Current Liabilities	5m	N/A

Pace Racing Developments Ltd
V19 Vinces Road, Diss, IP22 4HQ
Tel: 01379-652550 **Fax:** 01379-652200
E-mail: sales@paceracing.co.uk
Website: http://www.paceracing.fsnet.co.uk
Directors: Z. Watson (Fin), M. Watson (MD)
Immediate Holding Company: PACE RACING DEVELOPMENTS LIMITED
Registration no: 01841444 **VAT No.:** GB 394 4728 13
Date established: 1984 **Turnover:** £500,000 - £1m
No.of Employees: 1 - 10 **Product Groups:** 48

Date of Accounts	Nov 11	Nov 10	Nov 09
Working Capital	-40	-38	-35
Fixed Assets	89	92	97
Current Assets	68	79	65

Regal Gate Systems Ltd
The Gatehouse Hall Lane, Dickleburgh, Diss, IP21 4PT
Tel: 0800-169 4969 **Fax:** 01379-741153
E-mail: tkillick@regalgates.com
Website: http://www.regalgates.com
Directors: T. Killick (MD), T. Killick (Fin)
Immediate Holding Company: REGAL GATE SYSTEMS LIMITED
Registration no: 03436958 **Date established:** 1997
No.of Employees: 1 - 10 **Product Groups:** 26, 35

Date of Accounts	Sep 11	Sep 10	Sep 06
Working Capital	7	8	-3
Fixed Assets	5	6	13
Current Assets	29	29	35

Stadium Power Ltd
23-29 Owen Road, Diss, IP22 4YU
Tel: 01379-644233 **Fax:** 01379-650118
E-mail: sales@stadiumpower.co.uk
Website: http://www.stadiumpower.co.uk
Bank(s): NatWest
Directors: S. Applegate (MD)
Managers: F. Harding (Sales & Mktg Mg), K. Lansdale (Purch Mgr), S. Harding
Ultimate Holding Company: STADIUM GROUP PLC
Immediate Holding Company: STADIUM POWER LIMITED
Registration no: 02844194 **VAT No.:** 637 8174 10 **Date established:** 1993
Turnover: £2m - £5m **No.of Employees:** 21 - 50 **Product Groups:** 37

Date of Accounts	Dec 11	Dec 10	Dec 09
Sales Turnover	5m	4m	3m
Pre Tax Profit/Loss	794	461	60
Working Capital	1m	2m	1m
Fixed Assets	198	105	163
Current Assets	3m	3m	2m
Current Liabilities	209	239	236

Suffolk Communication
15a Mere Street, Diss, IP22 4AD
Tel: 01603-789898
Website: http://www.bt.com/btlocalbusiness/suffolk
Directors: M. Jones (Dir)
No.of Employees: 1 - 10 **Product Groups:** 37, 67, 79

Henry Watson Potteries Ltd
Pottery Hill Wattisfield, Diss, IP22 1NH
Tel: 01359-251239 **Fax:** 01359-250984
E-mail: sales@henrywatson.com
Website: http://www.henrywatson.com
Directors: J. Watson (Dir)
Immediate Holding Company: HENRY WATSON'S POTTERIES LIMITED
Registration no: 00378071 **VAT No.:** GB 102 0801 43
Date established: 1942 **Turnover:** £1m - £2m **No.of Employees:** 1 - 10
Product Groups: 33, 63

Date of Accounts	Dec 11	Dec 10	Dec 09
Working Capital	151	198	240
Fixed Assets	477	476	508
Current Assets	217	264	304

Wyatt Engineering
Darrow Wood Farm Shelfanger Road, Diss, IP22 4XY
Tel: 01379-640200 **Fax:** 01379-640200
E-mail: wyattengineering@aol.com
Website: http://wyattengineering.co.uk
Directors: J. Wyatt (Ptnr)
Immediate Holding Company: WYATT ENGINEERING LTD
Registration no: 05773145 **Date established:** 2006
No.of Employees: 1 - 10 **Product Groups:** 39, 40

Date of Accounts	Aug 11	Aug 10	Aug 09
Working Capital	-0	4	1
Fixed Assets	16	14	17
Current Assets	42	42	36

Downham Market

Fuel Pump Installations FPI PTT Ltd
Whitegate Farm Salters Lode, Downham Market, PE38 0AY
Tel: 01366-388056 **Fax:** 01366-388056
E-mail: jotagg@live.com
Directors: M. Longmuir (Prop)
Date established: 1988 **No.of Employees:** 1 - 10 **Product Groups:** 40

Masson Seeley & Co. Ltd
Rouses Lane, Downham Market, PE38 9AN
Tel: 01366-388000 **Fax:** 01366-385222
E-mail: admin@masson-seeley.co.uk
Website: http://www.masson-seeley.co.uk
Directors: C. Coussell (Fin), C. Mason (Comm), M. Potten (Dir)
Immediate Holding Company: MASSON SEELEY AND COMPANY,LIMITED
Registration no: 00162382 **VAT No.:** GB 104 6567 80
Date established: 2020 **Turnover:** £1m - £2m **No.of Employees:** 1 - 10
Product Groups: 40, 49

Date of Accounts	Apr 12	Apr 11	Apr 10
Working Capital	1m	1m	995
Fixed Assets	370	377	425
Current Assets	2m	1m	1m

Nicholson Machinery Ltd
33 Common Lane Southery, Downham Market, PE38 0PB
Tel: 01366-377444 **Fax:** 01366-377331
E-mail: sales@nicholson-machinery.co.uk
Website: http://www.nicholson-machinery.co.uk
Directors: D. Nicholson (Dir)
Managers: P. Nunn (Chief Acct)
Immediate Holding Company: NICHOLSON MACHINERY LIMITED
Registration no: 01618021 **Date established:** 1982 **Turnover:** £2m - £5m
No.of Employees: 21 - 50 **Product Groups:** 41

Date of Accounts	Sep 11	Sep 10	Sep 09
Working Capital	477	417	383
Fixed Assets	110	121	135
Current Assets	995	963	1m

Saturn Seeds
78 Howdale Road, Downham Market, PE38 9AH
Tel: 01366-385249 **Fax:** 01366-385158
E-mail: saturnseeds@btopenworld.com
Website: http://www.saturnseeds.com
Directors: C. Linford (Fin), M. Linford (MD)
Immediate Holding Company: SATURN SEEDS LIMITED
Registration no: 04505885 **VAT No.:** GB 784 4884 71
Date established: 2002 **No.of Employees:** 1 - 10 **Product Groups:** 07

Date of Accounts	Jul 11	Jul 10	Jul 07
Working Capital	95	75	23
Fixed Assets	130	131	126
Current Assets	125	99	44

Wood-Crafts Pet & Poultry
12 London Road, Downham Market, PE38 9AW
Tel: 01366-500878
E-mail: amanda@wood-crafts.co.uk
Website: http://www.wood-crafts.co.uk
Directors: A. woodcraft (Ptnr)
Date established: 2005 **No.of Employees:** 1 - 10 **Product Groups:** 41

X L Scales Ltd
Units 7-8 Trafalgar Industrial Estate Sovereign Way, Downham Market, PE38 9SW
Tel: 01366-384554 **Fax:** 01366-385300
E-mail: contact@xlscales.com
Website: http://www.xlscales.com
Directors: H. Duncan (Co Sec), D. Duncan (Sales)
Immediate Holding Company: XL SCALES LIMITED
Registration no: 03037185 **Date established:** 1995
No.of Employees: 1 - 10 **Product Groups:** 38, 42

Date of Accounts	Apr 12	Apr 11	Apr 10
Working Capital	65	70	82
Fixed Assets	24	32	38
Current Assets	136	132	147

Fakenham

A 1 Electronics
Warren Avenue Koloma, Fakenham, NR21 8NP
Tel: 01328-856226 **Fax:** 0845-166 5227
E-mail: repairs@a1electronics.co.uk
Website: http://www.a1electronics.co.uk
Directors: A. Warnes (Prop)
Date established: 1987 **No.of Employees:** 1 - 10 **Product Groups:** 48

Barber & Lyles Tractors
Tadorna Raynham Road, Helhoughton, Fakenham, NR21 7BH
Tel: 01485-528601 **Fax:** 01485-528544
Directors: P. Woodhouse (Dir)
Date established: 1980 **No.of Employees:** 1 - 10 **Product Groups:** 41

Delta Dampacure Fakenham Ltd
Heath Barn Norwich Road, Fakenham, NR21 8LZ
Tel: 01328-863451 **Fax:** 01328-855050
E-mail: elderton@deltadampacure.com
Website: http://www.deltadampacure.com
Directors: R. Elderton (MD), H. Broughton (MD), A. Broughton (Fin)
Immediate Holding Company: DELTA DAMPACURE (FAKENHAM) LIMITED
Registration no: 02997808 **VAT No.:** GB 651 1438 59
Date established: 1994 **Turnover:** Up to £250,000
No.of Employees: 1 - 10 **Product Groups:** 52

Date of Accounts	Mar 11	Mar 10	Mar 09
Working Capital	-46	-12	-5
Fixed Assets	41	89	91
Current Assets	30	31	28

N E S Electrical
Rear of 11 Bridge Street, Fakenham, NR21 9AG
Tel: 01328-853322 **Fax:** 01328-853311
Directors: N. Sturman (Prop)
Date established: 2000 **No.of Employees:** 1 - 10 **Product Groups:** 36, 40

P4 Ltd
1 Wymans Way, Fakenham, NR21 8NT
Tel: 01328-850555 **Fax:** 01462-851123
E-mail: info@p4fastel.co.uk
Website: http://www.p4fastel.co.uk
Bank(s): Abby National
Managers: P. Warner
Immediate Holding Company: P4 LIMITED
Registration no: 02339872 **VAT No.:** GB 490 5739 19
Date established: 1989 **Turnover:** £1m - £2m **No.of Employees:** 11 - 20
Product Groups: 37

Date of Accounts	Dec 11	Dec 10	Dec 09
Working Capital	-70	-95	-135
Fixed Assets	373	361	348
Current Assets	1m	924	703
Current Liabilities	505	N/A	N/A

Tapmatic Engineers' Merchants
7d Millers Close, Fakenham, NR21 8NW
Tel: 01328-863676 **Fax:** 01328-856118
E-mail: info@tapmatic.co.uk
Website: http://www.tapmatic.co.uk
Directors: D. Robotham (Fin), K. Robotham (MD)
Immediate Holding Company: TAPMATIC (U.K.) LIMITED
Registration no: 01982893 **Date established:** 1986
Turnover: £250,000 - £500,000 **No.of Employees:** 1 - 10
Product Groups: 25, 29, 33, 35, 36, 38, 39, 40, 46, 47, 48, 61, 66, 67

Date of Accounts	Jan 12	Jan 11	Jan 10
Working Capital	123	116	127
Fixed Assets	11	16	14
Current Assets	145	139	148

Great Yarmouth

A T I Tank Hire Ltd
Thamesfield Way Off Pasteur Road, Great Yarmouth, NR31 0DW
Tel: 01493-441747 **Fax:** 01493-442717
E-mail: info@atitanks.co.uk
Website: http://www.atitanks.co.uk
Bank(s): Clydesdale Bank
Directors: J. Bool (Fin)
Managers: D. Bullard (Chief Mgr)
Immediate Holding Company: ATI TANK HIRE LIMITED
Registration no: 01766265 **VAT No.:** GB 394 1622 44
Date established: 1983 **Turnover:** £1m - £2m **No.of Employees:** 11 - 20
Product Groups: 25, 30, 32, 33, 35, 41, 45, 66, 72, 76, 83

Date of Accounts	Jul 12	Jul 11	Jul 10
Sales Turnover	2m	1m	1m
Pre Tax Profit/Loss	541	492	435
Working Capital	-207	-648	-814
Fixed Assets	2m	2m	2m
Current Assets	417	397	348
Current Liabilities	300	323	284

Ace Tubular Services Ltd
14 Carrel Road Gorleston, Great Yarmouth, NR31 7RF
Tel: 01493-667392
E-mail: ace.tubular@tesco.net
Directors: J. Leggett (Fin), J. Leggett (MD)
Immediate Holding Company: ACE TUBULAR SERVICES LIMITED
Registration no: 04487549 **Date established:** 2002
No.of Employees: 1 - 10 **Product Groups:** 85

Date of Accounts	Jul 11	Jul 10	Jul 08
Working Capital	64	52	35
Fixed Assets	2	1	3
Current Assets	74	60	41

Alma Ironcraft
Charles Street, Great Yarmouth, NR30 3LA
Tel: 01493-857709 **Fax:** 01493-857709
E-mail: almaironcraft1982@tiscali.co.uk
Website: http://www.almaironcraft.co.uk
Directors: S. Thompson (Tech Serv)
Ultimate Holding Company: BENDART LIMITED
Immediate Holding Company: ADVANTAGE MEDIA DESIGN & PRINT LIMITED
Registration no: 03463558 **Date established:** 1997
No.of Employees: 1 - 10 **Product Groups:** 26, 35

Date of Accounts	Dec 11	Dec 10	Dec 09
Working Capital	-62	-62	-62
Current Liabilities	N/A	N/A	62

Anglia Catering Equipment East Ltd
1 Hobland Hall Cottages Hobland Road, Bradwell, Great Yarmouth, NR31 9AR
Tel: 01493-653111 **Fax:** 01493-656606
Directors: A. Gilham (Dir)
Immediate Holding Company: ANGLIA CATERING EQUIPMENT (EAST) LIMITED
Registration no: 02318088 **Date established:** 1988
No.of Employees: 1 - 10 **Product Groups:** 20, 40, 41

Date of Accounts	Dec 11	Dec 10	Dec 09
Working Capital	-20	-12	-14
Fixed Assets	2	2	2
Current Assets	33	44	53

Antech Engineering Ltd
Gapton Hall Industrial Estate Hewett Road, Great Yarmouth, NR31 0NN
Tel: 01493-440600 **Fax:** 01493-440606
E-mail: sales@antech.org.uk
Website: http://www.antech.org.uk
Directors: D. Gunn (Fin)
Managers: A. Stevens (Tech Serv Mgr), T. Allum
Immediate Holding Company: ANTECH ENGINEERING LIMITED
Registration no: 02225636 **Date established:** 1988 **Turnover:** £1m - £2m
No.of Employees: 21 - 50 **Product Groups:** 85

Date of Accounts	Mar 11	Mar 10	Mar 09
Working Capital	932	757	650
Fixed Assets	172	251	349
Current Assets	1m	990	998

Applied Acoustic Engineering Ltd
Unit 4 Marine Park Gapton Hall Road, Great Yarmouth, NR31 0NB
Tel: 01493-440355 **Fax:** 01493-440720
E-mail: adamdarling@appliedacoustics.com
Website: http://www.appliedacoustic.com
Directors: A. Darling (MD), T. Darling (Fin)
Managers: G. Willoughby (Sales Prom Mgr), J. Bush (Purch Mgr), S. Wiggins (Design Eng), N. Pearce, S. Meeken
Immediate Holding Company: APPLIED ACOUSTIC ENGINEERING LIMITED
Registration no: 02357352 **Date established:** 1989
Turnover: £500,000 - £1m **No.of Employees:** 21 - 50 **Product Groups:** 67

Date of Accounts	Feb 08	Feb 11	Feb 10
Working Capital	1m	2m	2m
Fixed Assets	953	1m	1m
Current Assets	2m	2m	2m

Aquablast Ltd
South Denes Road, Great Yarmouth, NR30 3PR
Tel: 01493-330139 **Fax:** 01493- 330139
E-mail: donaldblair@aquablast.co.uk
Website: http://www.aquablast.com
Directors: D. Blair (MD)
Immediate Holding Company: AQUABLAST LIMITED
Registration no: 02210129 **Date established:** 1988 **Turnover:** £1m - £2m
No.of Employees: 11 - 20 **Product Groups:** 40, 46, 67

Date of Accounts	Dec 11	Dec 10	Dec 09
Working Capital	-595	-433	-190
Fixed Assets	221	123	96
Current Assets	761	899	1m

Argo Electronic Components Ltd
Leyden Works Station Road, Great Yarmouth, NR31 0HB
Tel: 01493-652752 **Fax:** 01493-655433
E-mail: sales@norfolk-capacitors.com
Website: http://www.norfolk-capacitors.com
Bank(s): HSBC Bank plc
Directors: J. Murfitt (MD), J. Murfitt (MD)
Managers: A. Mitchell (Sales & Mktg Mg)
Immediate Holding Company: Norfolk Capacitors Ltd
Registration no: 02237532 **Date established:** 1988
Turnover: £500,000 - £1m **No.of Employees:** 21 - 50
Product Groups: 35, 36, 37

Atlas Industrial & Marine Supply Ltd
26-28 Southgates Road, Great Yarmouth, NR30 3LL
Tel: 01493-855464 **Fax:** 01493-842784
E-mail: sales@atlasindustrial.co.uk
Website: http://www.atlasindustrial.co.uk
Directors: B. Knappett (MD)
Registration no: 03835386 **Date established:** 1999
No.of Employees: 11 - 20 **Product Groups:** 36, 67, 74

Augesco International Ltd
Albatross Quay Beccles Road, St Olaves, Great Yarmouth, NR31 9HG
Tel: 01493-488444 **Fax:** 01493-488233
E-mail: sales@augesco.co.uk
Website: http://www.augesco.co.uk
Directors: V. Kilford (Fin)
Immediate Holding Company: AUGESCO INTERNATIONAL LIMITED
Registration no: 01584352 **Date established:** 1981
No.of Employees: 1 - 10 **Product Groups:** 29, 39

Date of Accounts	Mar 11	Mar 10	Mar 09
Working Capital	75	81	78
Fixed Assets	4	6	3
Current Assets	95	132	112

B J Services Co UK Ltd
Marine Base Southtown Road, Great Yarmouth, NR31 0JJ
Tel: 01493-680680 **Fax:** 01493-680780
E-mail: enquiries@bjservices.co.uk
Website: http://www.bjservices.co.uk
Directors: J. Taylor (Dir), E. Stephen (Dir)
Managers: L. Ridge (Personnel)
Ultimate Holding Company: GARDLINE SHIPPING LIMITED
Immediate Holding Company: RICHARDS DRY DOCK AND ENGINEERING LIMITED
Registration no: 04621093 **Date established:** 1994
Turnover: £50m - £75m **No.of Employees:** 21 - 50 **Product Groups:** 84

see next page

***B J Services Co UK Ltd** - Cont'd*

Date of Accounts	Apr 11	Apr 10	Apr 09
Working Capital	827	720	211
Fixed Assets	107	109	712
Current Assets	1m	1m	1m

Birds Baskets

Old School House Butt Lane, Burgh Castle, Great Yarmouth, NR31 9QE
Tel: 01493-780524 **Fax:** 01493-331813
E-mail: basketsatbirds@aol.com
Directors: A. Bird (Dir)
Date established: 2000 **Turnover:** £250,000 - £500,000
No.of Employees: 1 - 10 **Product Groups:** 25

British Metal Treatment Ltd (Galvanising Division)

40 Battery Road, Great Yarmouth, NR30 3NN
Tel: 01493-844153 **Fax:** 01493-330303
E-mail: sales@bmtgalv.co.uk
Website: http://www.bmtgalv.co.uk
Bank(s): Barclays Bank PLC
Directors: D. Cowley (MD)
Ultimate Holding Company: LINTON PARK P.L.C.
Immediate Holding Company: BRITISH METAL TREATMENTS LTD
Registration no: 00616411 **VAT No.:** GB 595 2018 32
Date established: 1958 **Turnover:** £1m - £2m **No.of Employees:** 11 - 20
Product Groups: 25, 30, 32, 33, 34, 40, 46, 48

C A P Fabrications Ltd

James Court Faraday Road Harfreys Industrial Estate, Great Yarmouth, NR31 0NF
Tel: 01493-650686 **Fax:** 01493-445678
E-mail: capfabrications@aol.com
Bank(s): HSBC Bank plc
Directors: R. Perry (Dir)
Immediate Holding Company: C.A.P. FABRICATIONS LIMITED
Registration no: 04284796 **VAT No.:** GB 442 9444 41
Date established: 2001 **Turnover:** £500,000 - £1m
No.of Employees: 21 - 50 **Product Groups:** 48

Date of Accounts	Oct 11	Oct 10	Oct 09
Working Capital	74	-39	-12
Fixed Assets	85	102	109
Current Assets	618	400	430

Certex UK Ltd

Britannia House Admiralty Road, Great Yarmouth, NR30 3PQ
Tel: 01493-857705 **Fax:** 01493-843607
E-mail: dbutler@certex.co.uk
Website: http://www.certex.co.uk
Managers: D. Butler (District Mgr)
Ultimate Holding Company: AXEL JOHNSON INTERNATIONAL AB (SWEDEN)
Immediate Holding Company: CERTEX (UK) LIMITED
Registration no: 00928803 **Date established:** 1968
No.of Employees: 21 - 50 **Product Groups:** 23, 30, 35

Cmac Micro Circuits Ltd (C-MAC MicroTechnology)

Fenner Road, Great Yarmouth, NR30 3PX
Tel: 01493-743100 **Fax:** 01493-858536
E-mail: info@api.com
Website: http://www.cmac.com
Directors: M. Bracher (MD), K. Henderson (Sales), B. Antell (Dir)
Managers: S. Clifton, I. Hall
Ultimate Holding Company: C-MAC UK HOLDING LIMITED
Immediate Holding Company: RF2M MICROELECTRONICS LTD
Registration no: 02721281 **VAT No.:** GB 595 3229 14
Date established: 1992 **Turnover:** £10m - £20m
No.of Employees: 101 - 250 **Product Groups:** 37, 44

Date of Accounts	Aug 07	Aug 08	Aug 09
Sales Turnover	21m	19m	20m
Pre Tax Profit/Loss	860	1m	1m
Working Capital	7m	8m	7m
Fixed Assets	3m	3m	2m
Current Assets	10m	14m	12m
Current Liabilities	621	1m	875

Compass Process Management Ltd

James Watt Close, Great Yarmouth, NR31 0NX
Tel: 01493-667037 **Fax:** 01493-653603
E-mail: intray@compass-hq.com
Website: http://www.compass-hq.com
Bank(s): HSBC Bank plc
Directors: J. Jennings (Dir), S. Jennings (MD)
Immediate Holding Company: COMPASS PROCESS MANAGEMENT LIMITED
Registration no: 01968563 **VAT No.:** GB 410 5801 96
Date established: 1985 **Turnover:** £5m - £10m **No.of Employees:** 21 - 50
Product Groups: 36, 38, 40, 42, 45, 61, 67, 80, 84

Date of Accounts	Sep 09	Sep 08	Sep 07
Working Capital	331	223	99
Fixed Assets	99	94	118
Current Assets	860	1m	717

Controlled Repair Instruments Ltd

1-5 Dock Tavern Lane Gorleston, Great Yarmouth, NR31 6PY
Tel: 01493-602060 **Fax:** 01493-441782
E-mail: sales@controlvalverepairs.co.uk
Website: http://www.controlvalverepairs.co.uk
Directors: J. Taylor (Fin)
Immediate Holding Company: CONTROLLED REPAIR (INSTRUMENTS) LIMITED
Registration no: 01573970 **Date established:** 1981
Turnover: £500,000 - £1m **No.of Employees:** 1 - 10 **Product Groups:** 48

Date of Accounts	Feb 08	Feb 11	Feb 10
Working Capital	29	48	14
Fixed Assets	68	68	76
Current Assets	395	559	520

Day Lewis plc Medical Supplies

54 Springfield Road Gorleston, Great Yarmouth, NR31 6AD
Tel: 01493-602673 **Fax:** 01493-651106
E-mail: david.eastwood@daylewisplc.co.uk
Website: http://www.daylewisplc.com
Managers: D. Eastwood (Mgr)
Ultimate Holding Company: DAY LEWIS LTD
VAT No.: GB 284 7312 44 **Date established:** 1985
No.of Employees: 1 - 10 **Product Groups:** 24, 38

Derrick Services UK Ltd

Falcongate House Gapton Hall Industrial Estate, Great Yarmouth, NR31 0NF
Tel: 01493-669141 **Fax:** 01493-668409
E-mail: enquiries@derricksl.com
Website: http://www.derricksl.com
Directors: J. Knight (Fin), M. Smith (MD), K. Smith (Fin)
Managers: M. Smith (Mktg Serv Mgr), A. Lambard (Personnel), A. Fewkes, R. Hill (Tech Serv Mgr)
Immediate Holding Company: DERADMIN LIMITED
Registration no: 04976859 **Date established:** 2003
Turnover: £10m - £20m **No.of Employees:** 21 - 50 **Product Groups:** 84

Date of Accounts	Nov 06	Nov 05	Nov 04
Sales Turnover	17m	6m	2m
Pre Tax Profit/Loss	-113	324	-79
Working Capital	-650	277	96
Fixed Assets	740	349	197
Current Assets	9m	3m	862
Current Liabilities	4m	1m	274

Edeco Petroleum Services Ltd

Bessemer Way, Great Yarmouth, NR31 0LX
Tel: 01493-653555 **Fax:** 01493-657428
E-mail: enquiries@edeco.co.uk
Website: http://www.edeco.co.uk
Bank(s): Lloyds TSB Bank plc
Managers: D. Heskins (Sales Prom Mgr), G. Lincoln (Div Mgr)
Ultimate Holding Company: SIMMONS GROUP INC (CANADA)
Immediate Holding Company: SIMMONS EDECO EUROPE LIMITED
Registration no: 02977551 **VAT No.:** GB 667 3717 02
Date established: 1994 **Turnover:** £20m - £50m
No.of Employees: 21 - 50 **Product Groups:** 48

Date of Accounts	Dec 11	Dec 10	Dec 09
Sales Turnover	13m	9m	9m
Pre Tax Profit/Loss	506	-47	190
Working Capital	2m	1m	986
Fixed Assets	2m	2m	2m
Current Assets	4m	2m	2m
Current Liabilities	1m	562	529

Equipment Supply Co Gy Ltd

Main Cross Road, Great Yarmouth, NR30 3NZ
Tel: 01493-857857 **Fax:** 01493-850255
E-mail: sales@kirkgroup.co.uk
Website: http://www.kirkgroup.com
Directors: J. Lambert (Co Sec), T. Boyes (MD)
Ultimate Holding Company: KIRKLANDS LIMITED
Immediate Holding Company: EQUIPMENT SUPPLY COMPANY (G.Y.) LIMITED
Registration no: 02185092 **Date established:** 1987 **Turnover:** £2m - £5m
No.of Employees: 1 - 10 **Product Groups:** 30, 36, 66

Date of Accounts	Feb 12	Feb 11	Feb 10
Sales Turnover	N/A	2m	2m
Pre Tax Profit/Loss	N/A	-13	31
Working Capital	248	236	237
Fixed Assets	65	68	74
Current Assets	865	907	673
Current Liabilities	N/A	74	61

Erik's Industrial Services (Yarmouth Service Centre)

7 James Court Faraday Road, Great Yarmouth, NR31 0NF
Tel: 01493-655505 **Fax:** 01493-653640
E-mail: yarmouth@eriks.co.uk
Website: http://www.eriks.co.uk
Managers: I. Merridale (District Mgr)
Immediate Holding Company: WYKO HOLDINGS LTD
Registration no: 00917112 **Turnover:** £250m - £500m
No.of Employees: 1 - 10 **Product Groups:** 66

Date of Accounts	Dec 11	Dec 10	Dec 09
Sales Turnover	231m	216m	210m
Pre Tax Profit/Loss	16m	10m	4m
Working Capital	35m	31m	22m
Fixed Assets	9m	10m	11m
Current Assets	101m	93m	80m
Current Liabilities	16m	13m	8m

E-Tech Group Ltd

The E-Tech Centre Boundary Road, Great Yarmouth, NR31 0LY
Tel: 01493-419800 **Fax:** 01493-650012
E-mail: gary.williams@etechcentre.com
Website: http://www.etech-group.co.uk
Bank(s): National Westminster
Directors: G. Williams (Grp), J. Brown (I.T. Dir)
Ultimate Holding Company: E-TECH GROUP LIMITED
Registration no: 04080287 **VAT No.:** GB 638 1788 04
Date established: 2000 **Turnover:** £1m - £2m **No.of Employees:** 21 - 50
Product Groups: 37, 38

Date of Accounts	Mar 11	Mar 10	Mar 09
Sales Turnover	21m	27m	N/A
Pre Tax Profit/Loss	68	2m	418
Working Capital	907	1m	124
Fixed Assets	645	669	671
Current Assets	9m	7m	8m
Current Liabilities	757	763	971

G W L Security

Shop 10 Row 48 North Quay, Great Yarmouth, NR30 1HU
Tel: 01493-857434 **Fax:** 01493-857434
Directors: M. Smith (Prop), P. Bonham (Prop)
Ultimate Holding Company: ABBEY WASTE CONTROL LIMITED
Immediate Holding Company: GWL SECURITY LIMITED
Registration no: 05191435 **Date established:** 2004
Turnover: Up to £250,000 **No.of Employees:** 1 - 10 **Product Groups:** 52

Date of Accounts	Apr 11	Apr 10	Apr 09
Working Capital	-4	-7	-14
Fixed Assets	6	6	6
Current Assets	20	20	19

Gall Thomson Environmental Ltd

Pommers Lane, Great Yarmouth, NR30 3PE
Tel: 01493-857936 **Fax:** 01493-850888
E-mail: mail@gall-thomson.co.uk
Website: http://www.gall-thomson.co.uk
Bank(s): Bank of Scotland
Directors: A. Virgin (MD), M. Virgin (MD), M. Smith (Co Sec)
Managers: T. Howe (Purch Mgr), C. Wilks (Fin Mgr), D. Stephenson (Sales Prom Mgr)
Ultimate Holding Company: LUPUS CAPITAL PLC
Immediate Holding Company: GALL THOMSON ENVIRONMENTAL LIMITED
Registration no: 02852924 **VAT No.:** GB 640 3810 68
Date established: 1993 **Turnover:** £10m - £20m
No.of Employees: 21 - 50 **Product Groups:** 36, 39, 40

Date of Accounts	Dec 11	Dec 10	Dec 09
Sales Turnover	19m	14m	13m
Pre Tax Profit/Loss	10m	6m	6m
Working Capital	6m	875	5m
Fixed Assets	567	446	438
Current Assets	9m	6m	9m
Current Liabilities	3m	3m	4m

Grapevine International

28 Clay Road Caister-on-Sea, Great Yarmouth, NR30 5HB
Tel: 01622-734619
E-mail: office@grapevine-int.co.uk
Website: http://www.grapevine-int.co.uk
Directors: R. Burnay (MD)
Registration no: 02362286 **No.of Employees:** 1 - 10 **Product Groups:** 80, 86

Date of Accounts	Apr 06
Sales Turnover	44
Pre Tax Profit/Loss	20
Working Capital	5
Fixed Assets	1
Current Assets	25
Current Liabilities	20
Total Share Capital	5
ROCE% (Return on Capital Employed)	344.4

Great Yarmouth Port Company Ltd

Eastport UK House South Beach Parade, Great Yarmouth, NR30 3GY
Tel: 01493-335500 **Fax:** 01493-852480
E-mail: rlewin@eastportuk.co.uk
Website: http://www.eastportuk.co.uk
Bank(s): Barclays
Managers: R. Lewin (Sales Prom Mgr)
Ultimate Holding Company: GLOBAL INFRASTRUCTURE IPH ACQUISITION PARTNERS LP
Immediate Holding Company: GREAT YARMOUTH PORT COMPANY LTD
Registration no: 05971330 **VAT No.:** GB 105 0899 79
Date established: 2006 **Turnover:** £10m - £20m
No.of Employees: 11 - 20 **Product Groups:** 71, 72, 74, 76, 77, 84

Date of Accounts	Dec 11	Dec 10	Dec 09
Sales Turnover	14m	10m	6m
Pre Tax Profit/Loss	6m	3m	1m
Working Capital	7m	-2m	2m
Fixed Assets	95m	91m	84m
Current Assets	12m	7m	4m
Current Liabilities	4m	8m	2m

Herbert Woods

Broads Haven Bridge Road, Potter Heigham, Great Yarmouth, NR29 5JD
Tel: 01692-670711 **Fax:** 01692-670734
E-mail: info@herbertwoods.co.uk
Website: http://www.herbertwoods.co.uk
Managers: J. Butler (Mgr), J. Gingell (Chief Acct), M. Whittaker (Mgr), E. Butler (Personnel)
Immediate Holding Company: HERBERT WOODS LLP
Registration no: OC352044 **VAT No.:** GB 532 8406 53
Date established: 2010 **Turnover:** £500,000 - £1m
No.of Employees: 21 - 50 **Product Groups:** 68, 74, 84

Date of Accounts	Mar 12	Mar 11
Working Capital	-797	-1m
Fixed Assets	7m	7m
Current Assets	738	684

J & M Edwards Ltd

Lefevre Way, Great Yarmouth, NR31 0NW
Tel: 01493-604312 **Fax:** 01493-655719
E-mail: sales@jmedwards.co.uk
Website: http://www.jmedwards.co.uk
Bank(s): National Westminster Bank Plc
Directors: G. Edwards (Dir)
Immediate Holding Company: J. & M. EDWARDS PRECISION ENGINEERS LIMITED
Registration no: 02427924 **VAT No.:** GB 283 4449 38
Date established: 1989 **Turnover:** £500,000 - £1m
No.of Employees: 11 - 20 **Product Groups:** 48

Date of Accounts	Oct 11	Oct 10	Oct 09
Working Capital	332	290	269
Fixed Assets	331	321	330
Current Assets	500	416	352

Jenex Ltd

5 Shuttleworth Close, Great Yarmouth, NR31 0NQ
Tel: 01493-602211 **Fax:** 01493-602221
E-mail: val@jenex.co.uk
Website: http://www.jenexltd.co.uk
Directors: V. Fishburne (MD), K. Fishburne (Fin)
Ultimate Holding Company: KONGSBERG GRUPPEN ASA (NORWAY)
Immediate Holding Company: JENEX LIMITED
Registration no: 03209885 **Date established:** 1996
Turnover: £250,000 - £500,000 **No.of Employees:** 1 - 10
Product Groups: 36, 38, 40, 41, 42, 46, 51, 66, 67, 80, 81

Date of Accounts	Mar 12	Mar 11	Mar 10
Working Capital	269	251	279
Fixed Assets	10	15	11
Current Assets	432	348	367

Lindchem Ltd

245 Southtown Road, Great Yarmouth, NR31 0JJ
Tel: 01493-850303 **Fax:** 01493-332292
E-mail: paul@abbeychemicals.co.uk
Website: http://www.abbey-chemicals.co.uk
Directors: P. Bonham (Dir), T. Bonham (MD)
Managers: J. Jones (Sales Prom Mgr), T. Tailford (I.T. Exec)
Ultimate Holding Company: ABBEY WASTE CONTROL LIMITED
Immediate Holding Company: LINDCHEM LIMITED
Registration no: 02243621 **Date established:** 1988
Turnover: £500,000 - £1m **No.of Employees:** 1 - 10 **Product Groups:** 17, 31, 32

Date of Accounts	Apr 11	Apr 10	Apr 09
Working Capital	105	50	43
Fixed Assets	9	6	2
Current Assets	298	222	88

Midstream Coatings Ltd

Boundary Road, Great Yarmouth, NR31 0LW
Tel: 01493-440478 **Fax:** 01493-440478
E-mail: tom-midstream@btconnect.com

Managers: T. Blackett (Mgr)
Immediate Holding Company: MIDSTREAM COATINGS LIMITED
Registration no: 04808941 **Date established:** 2003
No.of Employees: 1 - 10 **Product Groups:** 46, 48

Date of Accounts	Oct 11	Oct 10	Oct 09
Working Capital	33	7	-13
Fixed Assets	40	43	50
Current Assets	115	126	121

Moores Message Boards

Ludham Road Catfield, Wateringpiece Estate, Great Yarmouth, NR29 5PY
Tel: 01692-670011 **Fax:** 01692-670108
E-mail: sales@moores-mb.co.uk
Website: http://www.moores-trays.com
Directors: G. Woodhouse (Ch & MD), M. Nicholson (Co Sec), S. West (Dir)
Immediate Holding Company: Moores Message Boards Ltd
Registration no: 06306129 **VAT No.:** GB 304 7134 90
Date established: 2007 **Turnover:** £2m - £5m **No.of Employees:** 1 - 10
Product Groups: 49

Date of Accounts	Jun 10	Jun 09	Jun 08
Working Capital	16	50	43
Fixed Assets	28	34	50
Current Assets	80	97	80

Oilfield Testing Services

Qualtest House Viking Road, Great Yarmouth, NR31 0NU
Tel: 01493-440555 **Fax:** 01493-440737
E-mail: ots@dial.pipex.com
Website: http://www.oilfieldtesting.co.uk
Bank(s): National Westminster Bank Plc
Directors: P. Furlong (MD)
Managers: S. Calvert (Chief Acct)
Immediate Holding Company: OILFIELD TESTING SERVICES LIMITED
Registration no: 04210596 **VAT No.:** GB 426 2131 87
Date established: 2001 **Turnover:** £1m - £2m **No.of Employees:** 11 - 20
Product Groups: 48, 51, 85

Date of Accounts	May 08	Mar 11	Mar 10
Working Capital	236	231	133
Fixed Assets	44	67	54
Current Assets	493	521	378

Omni-Pac UK Ltd

South Denes Road, Great Yarmouth, NR30 3QD
Tel: 08456-013040 **Fax:** 01493-855563
E-mail: scooke@pactiv.com
Website: http://www.omni-pac.de
Managers: S. Cooke (Chief Mgr)
Ultimate Holding Company: PACKAGING HOLDINGS LTD (NEW ZEALAND)
Immediate Holding Company: OMNI-PAC U.K. LIMITED
Registration no: 00502216 **VAT No.:** GB 283 3345 55
Date established: 1951 **Turnover:** £5m - £10m **No.of Employees:** 1 - 10
Product Groups: 27, 84

Date of Accounts	Dec 11	Dec 10	Dec 09
Sales Turnover	3m	5m	5m
Pre Tax Profit/Loss	1m	499	-37
Working Capital	299	336	-336
Fixed Assets	N/A	272	269
Current Assets	1m	2m	2m
Current Liabilities	267	465	451

Paramode Ltd

Unit 1 Bessemer Way, Great Yarmouth, NR31 0LX
Tel: 01493-412940 **Fax:** 01502-501503
E-mail: info@paramode.co.uk
Website: http://www.paramode.co.uk
Bank(s): Barclays
Directors: D. Mosing (Fin), P. Sibille (Dir)
Immediate Holding Company: PARAMODE LIMITED
Registration no: 02053297 **VAT No.:** GB 443 0844 64
Date established: 1986 **Turnover:** £1m - £2m **No.of Employees:** 11 - 20
Product Groups: 80

Date of Accounts	Dec 11	Dec 10	Dec 09
Working Capital	961	939	910
Fixed Assets	22	38	61
Current Assets	2m	1m	1m

Pasta Foods Ltd

Pasteur Road, Great Yarmouth, NR31 0DW
Tel: 01493-416200 **Fax:** 01493-653346
E-mail: enquiries@pastafoods.com
Website: http://www.pastafoods.com
Bank(s): Lloyds TSB Bank plc
Directors: T. Woolner (Fin), P. Foster (Sales), K. Jermyn (Dir)
Managers: K. Johnson (Personnel), S. Pleasance (Tech Serv Mgr), J. Bagley (Purch Mgr)
Ultimate Holding Company: PRETTY 210 LIMITED
Immediate Holding Company: PASTA FOODS LIMITED
Registration no: 00566338 **VAT No.:** GB 197 0214 62
Date established: 1956 **Turnover:** £20m - £50m
No.of Employees: 101 - 250 **Product Groups:** 20, 41, 62

Date of Accounts	Apr 11	May 08	May 09
Sales Turnover	22m	17m	22m
Pre Tax Profit/Loss	1m	-601	99
Working Capital	11m	8m	9m
Fixed Assets	1m	3m	3m
Current Assets	17m	13m	12m
Current Liabilities	3m	2m	924

Perfect Engineering

Harfreys Road, Great Yarmouth, NR31 0JL
Tel: 01493-657131 **Fax:** 01493-441526
E-mail: della@lgperfects.co.uk
Bank(s): HSBC Bank plc
Directors: P. Green (Prop)
Managers: R. Pygall
Immediate Holding Company: NORTHOLD LIMITED
Registration no: 00458601 **VAT No.:** GB 443 0077 81
Date established: 2006 **Turnover:** £500,000 - £1m
No.of Employees: 11 - 20 **Product Groups:** 39, 72

Pertwee & Back Ltd

Gapton Hall Road Gapton Hall Industrial Estate, Great Yarmouth, NR31 0NJ
Tel: 01493-664151 **Fax:** 01493-658160
E-mail: rcoller@pertwee-and-back.co.uk
Website: http://www.pertwee-and-back.co.uk
Bank(s): Barclays
Directors: R. Coller (MD)
Managers: D. Langham (Tech Serv Mgr), D. Webb (Sales Prom Mgr), S. Hatton
Immediate Holding Company: PERTWEE & BACK,LIMITED
Registration no: 00237370 **VAT No.:** GB 105 1018 35
Date established: 2029 **Turnover:** £20m - £50m
No.of Employees: 51 - 100 **Product Groups:** 68

Date of Accounts	Oct 11	Oct 10	Oct 09
Sales Turnover	27m	33m	23m
Pre Tax Profit/Loss	-76	135	312
Working Capital	1m	1m	1m
Fixed Assets	1m	1m	1m
Current Assets	4m	5m	3m
Current Liabilities	678	259	299

Prior Diesel Ltd

Gapton Hall Road, Great Yarmouth, NR31 0NL
Tel: 01493-441383 **Fax:** 01493-441796
E-mail: info@priordiesel.com
Website: http://www.priordiesel.com
Bank(s): Barclays
Directors: A. Maclean (Dir), C. Conroy (Fin), G. Maclean (Sales & Mktg)
Ultimate Holding Company: GAPTON PARTNERS LIMITED
Immediate Holding Company: PRIOR DIESEL LIMITED
Registration no: 01499503 **VAT No.:** 353 2424 77 **Date established:** 1980
Turnover: £10m - £20m **No.of Employees:** 51 - 100 **Product Groups:** 37, 40, 45, 48

Date of Accounts	Mar 12	Mar 11	Mar 10
Sales Turnover	11m	10m	11m
Pre Tax Profit/Loss	81	73	160
Working Capital	2m	2m	2m
Fixed Assets	1m	1m	1m
Current Assets	5m	4m	4m
Current Liabilities	1m	652	501

Probe Oil Tools Ltd

Edison Way Gapton Hall Industrial Estate, Great Yarmouth, NR31 0NG
Tel: 01493-655471 **Fax:** 01493-652746
E-mail: sales@probe-oil-tools.co.uk
Website: http://www.probe-oil-tools.co.uk
Directors: J. Mobbs (Dir), K. Ford (Dir)
Registration no: 01168238 **Turnover:** £10m - £20m
No.of Employees: 21 - 50 **Product Groups:** 42, 45

Date of Accounts	May 08	May 07	May 06
Sales Turnover	11673	10357	N/A
Pre Tax Profit/Loss	1504	1606	N/A
Working Capital	2145	1060	185
Fixed Assets	1800	1832	1551
Current Assets	7818	5794	4294
Current Liabilities	5672	4734	4109
Total Share Capital	1	1	1
ROCE% (Return on Capital Employed)	38.1	55.5	
ROT% (Return on Turnover)	12.9	15.5	

Repro Arts Ltd

Monument Road, Great Yarmouth, NR30 3PS
Tel: 01493-855515 **Fax:** 01493-851557
E-mail: marissa@reproart.co.uk
Website: http://www.reproart.co.uk
Managers: M. Phillips
Immediate Holding Company: REPRO ARTS LIMITED
Registration no: 00774703 **VAT No.:** GB 105 2912 06
Date established: 1963 **Turnover:** £2m - £5m **No.of Employees:** 1 - 10
Product Groups: 23, 27, 28

Date of Accounts	Oct 11	Oct 10	Oct 09
Working Capital	-59	-33	-39
Fixed Assets	325	382	442
Current Assets	111	117	102

Rotating Electrics

2 Estcourt House Estcourt Road, Great Yarmouth, NR30 4JQ
Tel: 01493-330404 **Fax:** 01493-330404
E-mail: rotatingelectrics@jhis.net
Website: http://www.rotatingelectrics.members.easyspace.com
Directors: P. Waters (Prop)
No.of Employees: 1 - 10 **Product Groups:** 37, 39, 84

S S C S Lifting

Unit A Harfreys Road, Great Yarmouth, NR31 0LS
Tel: 01493-443380 **Fax:** 01493-443390
E-mail: info@sscsystems.com
Website: http://www.sscslifting.co.uk
Bank(s): Bank of Scotland
Managers: P. Chynoweth (Div Mgr), P. Teasdel
Immediate Holding Company: M.D.F. (GT YARMOUTH) LTD.
Registration no: 02459166 **VAT No.:** GB 521 4233 91
Date established: 1995 **Turnover:** £1m - £2m **No.of Employees:** 11 - 20
Product Groups: 23, 33, 35, 39, 45, 48, 63, 66, 83, 84, 85

S T M Rewinds Ltd

Abc Wharf Southgates Road, Great Yarmouth, NR30 3LQ
Tel: 01493-843510 **Fax:** 01493-845780
E-mail: paul@stmrewinds.co.uk
Website: http://www.stmrewinds.co.uk
Bank(s): Lloyds TSB Bank plc
Directors: P. Gowland (Eng Serv)
Ultimate Holding Company: STM ENGINEERING LIMITED
Immediate Holding Company: STM REWINDS LIMITED
Registration no: 05367691 **VAT No.:** GB 442 9749 19
Date established: 2005 **Turnover:** £10m - £20m
No.of Employees: 11 - 20 **Product Groups:** 35, 37, 38, 40, 47, 48, 52, 67, 83

Date of Accounts	Jul 11	Jul 10	Jul 09
Working Capital	17	17	17
Current Assets	17	17	17

Seacon Europe

Seacon House Hewett Road Gapton Hall Industrial Estate, Great Yarmouth, NR31 0RB
Tel: 01493-652733 **Fax:** 01493-652840
E-mail: sales@seaconeurope.com
Website: http://www.seaconeurope.com
Directors: N. Foreman (Fin), D. Parker (MD), K. Hall (Sales)
Ultimate Holding Company: BRANTNER & ASSOCIATES INC (USA)
Immediate Holding Company: SEA CONNECTIONS SYSTEMS LIMITED
Registration no: 03615404 **Date established:** 1998 **Turnover:** £5m - £10m
No.of Employees: 51 - 100 **Product Groups:** 37

Soft Start UK

Unit 14 Brinell Way, Great Yarmouth, NR31 0LU
Tel: 01493-660510 **Fax:** 01493-669647
E-mail: sales@silverteam.co.uk
Website: http://www.silverteam.co.uk
Directors: B. Neech (Fin)
Immediate Holding Company: SILVERTEAM LIMITED
Registration no: 04935734 **Date established:** 2003
Turnover: £500,000 - £1m **No.of Employees:** 1 - 10 **Product Groups:** 37

Date of Accounts	Sep 11	Sep 10	Sep 09
Working Capital	10	10	63
Fixed Assets	N/A	N/A	9
Current Assets	10	10	211

Sprunt Engineering Services Ltd

Unit 11 Suffolk Road, Great Yarmouth, NR31 0LN
Tel: 01493-650883 **Fax:** 01493-650530
E-mail: sales@ses-engineering.co.uk
Website: http://www.ses-engineering.co.uk
Directors: M. Mancini (Dir)
Immediate Holding Company: SPRUNT ENGINEERING SERVICES LIMITED
Registration no: 04684624 **VAT No.:** GB 571 1449 48
Date established: 2003 **Turnover:** £1m - £2m **No.of Employees:** 11 - 20
Product Groups: 48

Date of Accounts	Apr 11	Apr 10	Apr 09
Working Capital	-28	-27	N/A
Fixed Assets	42	40	44
Current Assets	172	253	265

Ssaf Window Films Ltd

Workshop 21 Hemsby Road, Martham, Great Yarmouth, NR29 4QG
Tel: 01493-749174 **Fax:** 01493-749175
E-mail: sales@ssafwindowfilms.com
Website: http://www.ssafwindowfilms.com
Directors: S. Ashton (Dir), D. Ashton (Co Sec)
Immediate Holding Company: SSAF WINDOW FILMS LIMITED
Registration no: 04436905 **Date established:** 2002
No.of Employees: 1 - 10 **Product Groups:** 30, 33, 35, 49, 66

Date of Accounts	May 11	May 10	May 09
Working Capital	-28	-51	95
Fixed Assets	220	239	75
Current Assets	144	144	125

Tech Safe Systems Ltd

Shuttleworth Close, Great Yarmouth, NR31 0NQ
Tel: 01493-444454 **Fax:** 01493-603944
E-mail: info@techsafe.co.uk
Website: http://www.techsafe.co.uk
Directors: R. Evans (Fin), P. Evans (MD)
Managers: D. Blood (Design Eng)
Ultimate Holding Company: STM ENGINEERING LIMITED
Immediate Holding Company: TECH SAFE SYSTEMS LIMITED
Registration no: 03172985 **Date established:** 1996
No.of Employees: 11 - 20 **Product Groups:** 35, 42, 45

Date of Accounts	Mar 11	Mar 10	Mar 09
Working Capital	842	876	715
Fixed Assets	158	181	212
Current Assets	1m	1m	1m

Traymaster Ltd

New Road Catfield, Great Yarmouth, NR29 5BQ
Tel: 01692-582100 **Fax:** 01692-582211
E-mail: sales@traymaster.co.uk
Website: http://www.traymaster.co.uk
Directors: R. Woodcock (MD)
Immediate Holding Company: TRAYMASTER LIMITED
Registration no: 00956298 **Date established:** 1969
No.of Employees: 11 - 20 **Product Groups:** 41

Date of Accounts	Dec 11	Dec 10	Dec 09
Working Capital	-137	-121	-155
Fixed Assets	280	293	302
Current Assets	175	576	236

Trevross Hotel

57 Apsley Road, Great Yarmouth, NR30 2HG
Tel: 01493-842030 **Fax:** 01493-858053
E-mail: info@trevross.co.uk
Website: http://www.trevross.co.uk
Directors: T. Fellas (Prop)
Date established: 1963 **Turnover:** Up to £250,000
No.of Employees: 1 - 10 **Product Groups:** 80

Vetco Gray UK Ltd

Gapton Hall Road, Great Yarmouth, NR31 0NL
Tel: 01493-444777 **Fax:** 01493-414221
E-mail: shaun.bradley@vetco.com
Website: http://www.vetco.com
Directors: S. Bradley (MD)
Managers: I. Smith (Mgr), S. Bradbey (Ops Mgr)
Immediate Holding Company: VETCO GRAY U.K. LIMITED
Registration no: 01521132 **Date established:** 1980 **Turnover:** £2m - £5m
No.of Employees: 11 - 20 **Product Groups:** 36

Date of Accounts	Dec 10	Dec 09	Dec 08
Sales Turnover	275m	259m	398m
Pre Tax Profit/Loss	-5m	16m	41m
Working Capital	81m	81m	67m
Fixed Assets	75m	74m	44m
Current Assets	360m	365m	248m
Current Liabilities	129m	132m	103m

Viking Life Saving Equipment

Ferry House South Denes Road, Great Yarmouth, NR30 3PJ
Tel: 01493-850250 **Fax:** 01493-851222
E-mail: vikingldn@viking-life.com
Website: http://www.viking-life.com
Directors: M. Harriman (MD)
Immediate Holding Company: VIKING LIFE-SAVING EQUIPMENT LIMITED
Registration no: 01350590 **VAT No.:** GB 249 8435 21
Date established: 1978 **No.of Employees:** 1 - 10 **Product Groups:** 23, 24, 26, 29, 32, 36, 37, 38, 39, 40, 42, 45, 67, 74

Date of Accounts	Dec 11	Dec 10	Dec 09
Sales Turnover	N/A	N/A	5m
Pre Tax Profit/Loss	N/A	N/A	557
Working Capital	1m	585	971
Fixed Assets	991	900	626
Current Assets	2m	2m	1m
Current Liabilities	N/A	N/A	171

Weatherford UK Ltd

Harfreys Road, Great Yarmouth, NR31 0LS
Tel: 01493-657516 **Fax:** 01493-653925
Website: http://www.weatherford.com

see next page

Weatherford UK Ltd - Cont'd

Managers: A. Crane (Mgr)
Ultimate Holding Company: WEATHERFORD INTERNATIONAL LIMITED (BERMUDA)
Immediate Holding Company: WEATHERFORD U.K. LIMITED
Registration no: 00862925 **VAT No.:** GB 735 2277 34
Date established: 1965 **Turnover:** £20m - £50m
No.of Employees: 21 - 50 **Product Groups:** 45, 67

Date of Accounts	Dec 10	Dec 09	Dec 08
Sales Turnover	185m	155m	190m
Pre Tax Profit/Loss	34m	5m	33m
Working Capital	122m	94m	82m
Fixed Assets	198m	203m	205m
Current Assets	377m	342m	343m
Current Liabilities	15m	14m	15m

Yarmouth Steel

Edison Way, Great Yarmouth, NR31 0NG
Tel: 01493-602241 **Fax:** 01493-417204
E-mail: sales@yarmouth-steel.co.uk
Website: http://www.yarmouth-steel.co.uk
Bank(s): HSBC Bank plc
Directors: M. Mcbean (MD)
Managers: M. Seaman (Sales Prom Mgr)
Immediate Holding Company: BARRETT STEEL LTD
Registration no: 02761850 **VAT No.:** GB 651 0327 73
Turnover: £5m - £10m **No.of Employees:** 11 - 20 **Product Groups:** 34, 66

Yarmouth Stores Ltd

117 South Quay, Great Yarmouth, NR30 3LD
Tel: 01493-842289 **Fax:** 01493-853416
E-mail: sales@ybeauty-uniforms.co.uk
Website: http://www.yarmo.co.uk
Directors: C. Knight (MD)
Immediate Holding Company: YARMOUTH STORES,LIMITED(THE)
Registration no: 00055930 **VAT No.:** GB 105 5680 83
Date established: 1998 **Turnover:** £1m - £2m **No.of Employees:** 1 - 10
Product Groups: 24, 74

Date of Accounts	Jan 12	Jan 11	Jan 10
Working Capital	605	636	638
Fixed Assets	434	449	458
Current Assets	936	905	898

Youngmans Sporting Guns

19-20 Market Row, Great Yarmouth, NR30 1PB
Tel: 01493-859814 **Fax:** 01493-331022
E-mail: sales@youngmans.com
Website: http://www.youngmans.com
Directors: C. Youngman (Ptnr)
Date established: 1985 **No.of Employees:** 1 - 10 **Product Groups:** 36, 39, 40

Harleston

Brian Fisher & Sons Ltd

40 Fuller Road, Harleston, IP20 9EA
Tel: 01379-853052 **Fax:** 01379-854713
E-mail: sales@brianfisher.co.uk
Website: http://www.brianfisher.co.uk
Directors: B. Fisher (Ptnr), P. Fisher (Dir), P. Fisher (MD), S. Fisher (Dir)
Immediate Holding Company: BRIAN FISHER & SONS LIMITED
Registration no: 04452337 **Date established:** 2002
Turnover: Up to £250,000 **No.of Employees:** 21 - 50 **Product Groups:** 24, 52, 63

Date of Accounts	Oct 10	May 09	May 08
Working Capital	-130	-62	-50
Fixed Assets	98	82	98
Current Assets	201	112	137

Coatings Direct

42 Fuller Road, Harleston, IP20 9EA
Tel: 01379-852121 **Fax:** 01379-853592
E-mail: msharma@coatingsdirect.co.uk
Directors: M. Sharma (Dir)
No.of Employees: 21 - 50 **Product Groups:** 27, 32

Jenelec Ltd

Fuller Road Industrial Estate, Harleston, IP20 9EA
Tel: 01379-853666 **Fax:** 01379-854414
E-mail: sales@jenelec.co.uk
Website: http://www.jenelec.com
Directors: J. Hall (Sales), M. Seaman (Dir)
Immediate Holding Company: PRECISION REFRIGERATION LIMITED
Registration no: 04069159 **Date established:** 2000 **Turnover:** £1m - £2m
No.of Employees: 1 - 10 **Product Groups:** 37

Date of Accounts	Jan 12	Jan 11	Jan 10
Sales Turnover	N/A	N/A	2m
Pre Tax Profit/Loss	N/A	N/A	-254
Working Capital	841	550	127
Fixed Assets	284	359	224
Current Assets	1m	1m	1m
Current Liabilities	N/A	N/A	23

Lings Motorcycles

Mendham Lane, Harleston, IP20 9DW
Tel: 01379-853764 **Fax:** 01379-854373
Website: http://www.lings.com
No.of Employees: 11 - 20 **Product Groups:** 37, 39, 40, 61

N L Roper & Sons Ltd

Fuller Road, Harleston, IP20 9EA
Tel: 01379-852739 **Fax:** 01379-853738
E-mail: info@nlrflatlapping.co.uk
Website: http://www.nlrflatlapping.co.uk
Directors: K. Roper (MD)
Immediate Holding Company: N.L.ROPER & SONS LIMITED
Registration no: 01080719 **VAT No.:** GB 105 7575 70
Date established: 1972 **Turnover:** £250,000 - £500,000
No.of Employees: 1 - 10 **Product Groups:** 33, 42, 46, 48, 49

Date of Accounts	Jan 12	Jan 11	Jan 10
Working Capital	77	71	139
Fixed Assets	191	200	210
Current Assets	106	89	179

Holt

Allison Heating Plumbing Ltd

Old Station Way, Holt, NR25 6DH
Tel: 01263-713260 **Fax:** 01263-713174
E-mail: info@allisongroup.co.uk
Website: http://www.allisongroup.co.uk
Directors: S. Rogers (Fin)
Immediate Holding Company: ALLISON HEATING AND PLUMBING LIMITED
Registration no: 03869959 **Date established:** 1999
No.of Employees: 1 - 10 **Product Groups:** 37, 38, 52

Date of Accounts	Dec 11	Dec 10	Dec 09
Working Capital	-53	-63	-73
Fixed Assets	10	14	18
Current Assets	61	110	103

Arterial Engineering Works Ltd

Morston Road Blakeney, Holt, NR25 7BE
Tel: 01263-740444 **Fax:** 01263- 740444
Website: http://www.pottersequipment.co.uk
Directors: R. Smith (Dir)
Immediate Holding Company: ARTERIAL ENGINEERING WORKS LTD
Registration no: 00722664 **Date established:** 1962
Turnover: £250,000 - £500,000 **No.of Employees:** 1 - 10
Product Groups: 42, 45, 49

Date of Accounts	Apr 07	Apr 06	Apr 05
Working Capital	6	2	1
Fixed Assets	37	41	42
Current Assets	41	54	49
Current Liabilities	35	52	48
Total Share Capital	1	1	1

Bakers & Larners Of Holt t/a Bakers of Holt

10 Market Place, Holt, NR25 6BW
Tel: 01263-712323 **Fax:** 01263-712720
E-mail: sales@bakersandlarners.com
Website: http://www.bakersandlarners.com
Directors: M. Baker (MD)
Registration no: 00067886 **Date established:** 2003
No.of Employees: 1 - 10 **Product Groups:** 26, 32, 41, 49, 63, 66

Crestbury Engineering

Hempstead Road Industrial Estate, Holt, NR25 6DL
Tel: 01263-711648 **Fax:** 01263-713066
E-mail: mallison@crestbury.co.uk
Website: http://www.crestbury.co.uk
Managers: M. Allison (Mgr)
No.of Employees: 1 - 10 **Product Groups:** 33, 34, 36

Kongskilde UK Ltd (Industrial Division)

The Kongskilde Building Hempstead Road, Holt, NR25 6EE
Tel: 01263-713291 **Fax:** 01263-712922
E-mail: mail@kongskilde.com
Website: http://www.kongskilde.com
Bank(s): HSBC Bank plc
Managers: J. Garrod, S. Smith
Ultimate Holding Company: KONGSKILDE MASKINGABRIK A/S (DENMARK)
Immediate Holding Company: KONGSKILDE U.K. LIMITED
Registration no: 01119305 **VAT No.:** GB 105 6657 73
Date established: 1973 **Turnover:** £5m - £10m **No.of Employees:** 21 - 50
Product Groups: 36, 40, 42, 45, 52

Date of Accounts	Dec 11	Dec 10	Dec 09
Sales Turnover	7m	5m	6m
Pre Tax Profit/Loss	32	-322	214
Working Capital	348	420	791
Fixed Assets	506	403	391
Current Assets	4m	3m	3m
Current Liabilities	749	239	285

Hunstanton

Swains International plc

Eastland House Westgate, Hunstanton, PE36 5EW
Tel: 01485-536200 **Fax:** 01485-536211
E-mail: sales@swains.co.uk
Website: http://www.swains.co.uk
Bank(s): National Westminster
Directors: D. Williams (Dir), R. Sealey (Dir)
Managers: S. Agate (Personnel)
Ultimate Holding Company: CWS HOLDINGS LIMITED
Immediate Holding Company: SWAINS INTERNATIONAL PLC
Registration no: 00522068 **VAT No.:** GB 106 3674 82
Date established: 1953 **Turnover:** £10m - £20m
No.of Employees: 21 - 50 **Product Groups:** 65

Date of Accounts	Mar 12	Mar 11	Mar 10
Sales Turnover	12m	14m	18m
Pre Tax Profit/Loss	116	97	300
Working Capital	2m	2m	2m
Fixed Assets	2m	2m	2m
Current Assets	4m	4m	5m
Current Liabilities	294	551	741

Kings Lynn

A S D

Hamlin Way, Kings Lynn, PE30 4LQ
Tel: 01553-761431 **Fax:** 01553-692394
E-mail: enquiries@asdmetalservices.co.uk
Website: http://www.asdplc.co.uk
Bank(s): National Westminster Bank Plc
Managers: D. Eggleton (Sales Prom Mgr), S. Bishop (Reg Mgr)
Immediate Holding Company: A R MITCHELL PLASTERERS LIMITED
Registration no: 02361372 **Date established:** 1994
Turnover: £500,000 - £1m **No.of Employees:** 11 - 20
Product Groups: 48, 66, 77

Academy Driving School

318 Wootton Road, Kings Lynn, PE30 3EB
Tel: 01553-675777
E-mail: bookings@academy.me.uk
Website: http://www.academy.me.uk
Directors: P. Brason (Prop)
Date established: 1988 **No.of Employees:** 1 - 10 **Product Groups:** 86

Accuramatic Laboratory Equipment

42 Windsor Road, Kings Lynn, PE30 5PL
Tel: 01553-777253 **Fax:** 01553-777253
E-mail: info@accuramatic.co.uk
Website: http://www.accuramatic.co.uk
Directors: D. Cooper (Ptnr)
VAT No.: GB 104 8006 13 **Turnover:** Up to £250,000
No.of Employees: 1 - 10 **Product Groups:** 40, 42

Aquarius Saw & Tool

Unit 3 Enterprise Way, Kings Lynn, PE30 4LJ
Tel: 01553-769370 **Fax:** 01553-765164
E-mail: sales@aquariuseng.co.uk
Directors: K. Cartwright (Ptnr)
No.of Employees: 1 - 10 **Product Groups:** 46, 48

Arc Training UK

3 Garage Lane Setchey, Kings Lynn, PE33 0BE
Tel: 01553-811800
E-mail: sales@arc-training.com
Website: http://www.arc-training.com
Directors: M. Wells (MD)
Immediate Holding Company: ARC TRAINING (UK) LIMITED
Registration no: 04477034 **Date established:** 2002
No.of Employees: 1 - 10 **Product Groups:** 35, 39, 45

Archives Express

3 Acer Road Saddlebow, Kings Lynn, PE34 3HN
Tel: 01553-660308 **Fax:** 01553- 660269
E-mail: jez@a10corporation.co.uk
Website: http://www.a10corporation.co.uk
Directors: J. Splude (MD), J. Splude (Dir)
Date established: 2001 **Turnover:** Up to £250,000
No.of Employees: 1 - 10 **Product Groups:** 67, 72

Berthoud Sprayers

Waterford Industrial Estate Mill Lane, Great Massingham, Kings Lynn, PE32 2HT
Tel: 01485-520626
E-mail: sales@berthoud.co.uk
Website: http://www.berthoud.co.uk
Directors: P. Ballu (Dir), P. Denizet (Co Sec)
Immediate Holding Company: BERTHOUD SPRAYERS LIMITED
Registration no: 01999544 **Date established:** 1986
No.of Employees: 1 - 10 **Product Groups:** 40, 41, 46

Date of Accounts	Aug 11	Aug 10	Aug 09
Working Capital	640	488	679
Fixed Assets	29	16	25
Current Assets	845	673	1m

Broste Ltd

Unit 8 North Lynn Business Village, North Lynn Indl-Est, Kings Lynn, PE30 2JG
Tel: 01323-640485 **Fax:** 01553- 767319
E-mail: uk@azelis.co.uk
Website: http://www.broste.com
Directors: A. Johnson (MD), A. Johnson (Dir), J. Schroder (Dir)
Ultimate Holding Company: AZELIS SA (LUXEMBOURG)
Immediate Holding Company: AZELIS UK INDUSTRIAL CHEMICALS LIMITED
Registration no: 02068721 **Date established:** 1986 **Turnover:** £5m - £10m
No.of Employees: 1 - 10 **Product Groups:** 17, 20, 41, 62, 63

Date of Accounts	Dec 09	Dec 08	Dec 07
Sales Turnover	12m	8m	7m
Pre Tax Profit/Loss	1m	-128	211
Working Capital	2m	564	579
Fixed Assets	153	218	289
Current Assets	5m	3m	2m
Current Liabilities	564	220	187

Ben Burgess Beeston

Dereham Road Beeston, Kings Lynn, PE32 2LE
Tel: 01328-701347 **Fax:** 01328-700111
E-mail: raymondsumner@benburgess.co.uk
Website: http://www.benburgess.co.uk
Directors: J. Rupp (Dir), A. Piercy (Co Sec)
Ultimate Holding Company: BEN BURGESS HOLDINGS LIMITED
Immediate Holding Company: BEN BURGESS (BEESTON)
Registration no: 00664883 **Date established:** 1960 **Turnover:** £2m - £5m
No.of Employees: 21 - 50 **Product Groups:** 07, 41, 48, 67

C P C Packaging

Oldmedow Road King's Lynn, Kings Lynn, PE30 4LL
Tel: 01553-761481 **Fax:** 01553-766203
E-mail: max.eaton@cpcpackaging.co.uk
Website: http://www.interglas-technologies.com
Directors: M. Holyland (MD), J. Dalby (I.T. Dir)
Managers: C. Nussey (Chief Mgr), D. Clark (Chief Mgr), J. Dalby (I.T. Exec), M. Eaton, M. Eaton (Sales Prom Mgr), R. Watson (Buyer), J. Cox, J. Cox, J. Shadford, J. Shadford (Personnel)
Ultimate Holding Company: COMPAGNIE POUR LA COMMUNICATION SA (FRANCE)
Immediate Holding Company: BERKSHIRE PRINTING COMPANY LIMITED
Registration no: 00067404 **Date established:** 2011
Turnover: £250,000 - £500,000 **No.of Employees:** 1 - 10
Product Groups: 27, 84

C W Engineering Ltd

Hamlin Way Hardwick Narrows Industrial Estate, Kings Lynn, PE30 4NG
Tel: 01553-775565 **Fax:** 01553-692080
E-mail: tony.jolley@cw-engineering.co.uk
Website: http://www.cw-engineering.co.uk
Bank(s): Lloyds TSB Bank plc
Directors: A. Jolley (Dir)
Immediate Holding Company: CW ENGINEERING LIMITED
Registration no: 04239690 **VAT No.:** GB 304 7578 54
Date established: 2001 **Turnover:** £1m - £2m **No.of Employees:** 11 - 20
Product Groups: 48

Date of Accounts	Sep 11	Sep 10	Sep 09
Working Capital	126	89	75
Fixed Assets	59	41	48

Current Assets	494	283	293

Charger Bay Solutions
7 Fitton Road St Germans, Kings Lynn, PE34 3AU
Tel: 07723-391485 **Fax:** 01553-617619
E-mail: sales@chargerbaysolutions.co.uk
Website: http://www.chargerbaysolutions.co.uk
Directors: P. Wiseman (Prop)
Date established: 2005 **Turnover:** £250,000 - £500,000
No.of Employees: 1 - 10 **Product Groups:** 26, 37

Circulating Pumps Ltd
56 Oldmedow Road, Kings Lynn, PE30 4PP
Tel: 01553-764821 **Fax:** 01553-760965
E-mail: sales@circulatingpumps.co.uk
Website: http://www.circulatingpumps.net
Bank(s): Barclays
Directors: S. Blake (Pers), I. Weaver Pope (Works)
Managers: I. Hayes (Purch Mgr), I. Henry (Comptroller), P. Farrow (Tech Serv Mgr)
Immediate Holding Company: CIRCULATING PUMPS LIMITED
Registration no: 04216373 **Date established:** 2001 **Turnover:** £5m - £10m
No.of Employees: 21 - 50 **Product Groups:** 40

Date of Accounts	Dec 11	Dec 10	Dec 09
Sales Turnover	7m	7m	N/A
Pre Tax Profit/Loss	909	518	-831
Working Capital	997	485	-208
Fixed Assets	487	623	783
Current Assets	3m	3m	2m
Current Liabilities	587	562	338

Concept Catering Equipment
79 Lynn Road, Kings Lynn, PE30 4PR
Tel: 01553-771400 **Fax:** 01553-771400
Directors: K. Wood (Prop)
No.of Employees: 1 - 10 **Product Groups:** 20, 33, 40

Cooper Roller Bearings Co. Ltd
Wisbech Road, Kings Lynn, PE30 5JX
Tel: 01553-763447 **Fax:** 01553-761113
E-mail: jruskin@raydon.com
Website: http://www.cooperbearings.com
Bank(s): Barclays
Directors: P. Smith (Dir), S. Gates (MD), P. Leggett (Pers), G. Scott (Co Sec), C. Ross (Fin)
Managers: D. Burns (Mktg Serv Mgr), A. Hattigan (Tech Serv Mgr), R. Ludlow (Purch Mgr)
Ultimate Holding Company: KAYDON CORPORATION (USA)
Immediate Holding Company: COOPER ROLLER BEARINGS COMPANY LIMITED
Registration no: 01643976 **VAT No.:** GB 426 4320 74
Date established: 1982 **Turnover:** £20m - £50m
No.of Employees: 101 - 250 **Product Groups:** 35, 45

Date of Accounts	Dec 11	Nov 09	Nov 10
Sales Turnover	24m	19m	19m
Pre Tax Profit/Loss	5m	2m	4m
Working Capital	7m	7m	10m
Fixed Assets	5m	5m	4m
Current Assets	13m	14m	17m
Current Liabilities	1m	2m	2m

Dancing Anvils Forge
Wallington Runcton Holme, Kings Lynn, PE33 0EP
Tel: 01553-813732
Directors: R. Hurcomb (Prop)
Date established: 2004 **No.of Employees:** 1 - 10 **Product Groups:** 26, 35

Decorative Sleeves Holdings Ltd
Rollesby Road Hardwick Industrial Estate, Kings Lynn, PE30 4LS
Tel: 01553-769319 **Fax:** 01553-767097
E-mail: dhambilton@decorativesleeves.co.uk
Website: http://www.decorativesleeves.co.uk
Bank(s): Bank of Scotland
Directors: D. Hambilton (Dir), J. Cowan (Sales & Mktg)
Managers: T. Smith (Comptroller), D. Rissmann (Buyer), A. Whitney
Ultimate Holding Company: HAVEN BOOKS LIMITED
Immediate Holding Company: OLIVER MICHAEL BOOKS LTD
Registration no: 06448235 **VAT No.:** GB 660 0414 41
Date established: 2007 **Turnover:** £10m - £20m
No.of Employees: 101 - 250 **Product Groups:** 30

Disco Drive Kings Lynn Ltd
Oldmedow Road, Kings Lynn, PE30 4LE
Tel: 01553-761331 **Fax:** 01553-692137
E-mail: sales@discodrives.co.uk
Website: http://www.discodrives.com
Bank(s): Barclays
Directors: R. Massingham (Fin)
Immediate Holding Company: DISCO DRIVES (KING'S LYNN) LIMITED
Registration no: 02993740 **VAT No.:** GB 636 9967 73
Date established: 1994 **Turnover:** £500,000 - £1m
No.of Employees: 11 - 20 **Product Groups:** 35, 48

Date of Accounts	Mar 12	Mar 11	Mar 10
Working Capital	225	328	319
Fixed Assets	34	36	43
Current Assets	406	448	468

Downham Components
Church Lane Whittington, Kings Lynn, PE33 9TG
Tel: 01366-500737 **Fax:** 01366-501156
Directors: S. Hawkins (Prop), J. Hawkins (Prop)
Managers: J. Hawkins (Sales Prom Mgr)
VAT No.: GB 105 9026 93 **Date established:** 1968
Turnover: Up to £250,000 **No.of Employees:** 1 - 10 **Product Groups:** 67

Enterprise Works
Bergen Way North Lynn Industrial Estate, Kings Lynn, PE30 2JG
Tel: 01553-760431
E-mail: emmascrafts@tiscali.co.uk
Website: http://www.qualitopsuk.co.uk
Managers: M. Henry (Serv Mgr)
Ultimate Holding Company: BEJAY HOLDINGS LIMITED
Immediate Holding Company: ENTERPRISE WORKS
Registration no: 06470615 **Date established:** 2008 **Turnover:** £5m - £10m
No.of Employees: 1 - 10 **Product Groups:** 23, 24

Date of Accounts	Dec 11	Dec 10	Dec 09
Sales Turnover	124	172	121
Pre Tax Profit/Loss	-15	42	-9
Working Capital	67	83	40
Current Assets	77	99	64
Current Liabilities	8	10	14

Evergreen Tractors Ltd
Lynn Road, Kings Lynn, PE34 3ES
Tel: 01553-617666 **Fax:** 01553-617673
E-mail: mail@evergreentractors.co.uk
Website: http://www.evergreentractors.co.uk
Directors: J. Rose (Fin), G. Collishaw (Sales), J. Doubleday (MD)
Managers: R. Pickett (Serv Mgr), Z. Doubleday (Personnel)
Ultimate Holding Company: J W D HOLDINGS LIMITED
Immediate Holding Company: EVERGREEN TRACTORS LIMITED
Registration no: 03723672 **Date established:** 1999
Turnover: £10m - £20m **No.of Employees:** 11 - 20 **Product Groups:** 48

Date of Accounts	Apr 11	Apr 10	Apr 09
Sales Turnover	13m	9m	10m
Pre Tax Profit/Loss	1m	473	948
Working Capital	733	502	72
Fixed Assets	3m	3m	2m
Current Assets	4m	4m	3m
Current Liabilities	744	415	743

Exaclair Ltd
Oldmedow Road, Kings Lynn, PE30 4LW
Tel: 01553-696600 **Fax:** 01553-767235
E-mail: enquiries@exaclair.co.uk
Website: http://www.exaclair.co.uk
Bank(s): National Westminster
Directors: M. Daisley (MD), C. Nusse (Dir)
Managers: N. Parry
Immediate Holding Company: EXACLAIR LIMITED
Registration no: 00118112 **Date established:** 2011 **Turnover:** £5m - £10m
No.of Employees: 51 - 100 **Product Groups:** 27, 28, 49, 64

Date of Accounts	Dec 11	Dec 10	Dec 09
Sales Turnover	10m	9m	9m
Pre Tax Profit/Loss	-72	-388	-457
Working Capital	4m	3m	3m
Fixed Assets	3m	3m	3m
Current Assets	7m	6m	6m
Current Liabilities	767	813	700

Flowpack Ltd
64 Ferry Road Clenchwarton, Kings Lynn, PE34 4BT
Tel: 01553-775577 **Fax:** 01553-763333
E-mail: andrew.gathercole@flowpack.co.uk
Website: http://www.flowpack.co.uk
Directors: R. Gathercole (Fin), A. Gathercole (MD)
Immediate Holding Company: FLOWPACK LIMITED
Registration no: 04081864 **Date established:** 2000
No.of Employees: 1 - 10 **Product Groups:** 35, 39, 45

Date of Accounts	Oct 11	Oct 10	Oct 09
Working Capital	12	13	13
Fixed Assets	26	11	7
Current Assets	77	46	25

Foodcare Systems Ltd
Unit 1 North Lynn Business Village Bergen Way, North Lynn Industrial Estate, Kings Lynn, PE30 2JG
Tel: 01553-770148 **Fax:** 01553-770146
E-mail: sales@foodcaresystems.com
Website: http://www.foodcaredirect.com
Directors: B. Wells (MD)
Ultimate Holding Company: BEJAY HOLDINGS LIMITED
Immediate Holding Company: FOODCARE SYSTEMS LTD
Registration no: 03575941 **Date established:** 1998 **Turnover:** £1m - £2m
No.of Employees: 11 - 20 **Product Groups:** 25, 30, 33, 36, 63

Date of Accounts	Mar 11	Mar 10	Mar 09
Sales Turnover	1m	778	760
Pre Tax Profit/Loss	23	12	9
Working Capital	57	44	42
Fixed Assets	48	50	8
Current Assets	364	265	193
Current Liabilities	109	45	32

Foster Refrigerator UK Ltd
Oldmeadow Road Hardwick Industrial Estate, Kings Lynn, PE30 4JU
Tel: 01553-691122 **Fax:** 01553-691447
E-mail: sales@foster-uk.com
Website: http://www.fosterrefrigerator.co.uk
Bank(s): Barclays
Directors: A. Sword (Sales), M. Cousins (Fin), P. Veried (MD)
Managers: N. Denham (Tech Serv Mgr), S. Ennis, L. Kirk (Mktg Serv Mgr)
Ultimate Holding Company: ILLINOIS TOOL WORKS INC (USA)
Immediate Holding Company: FOSTER REFRIGERATOR (U.K.)
Registration no: 00924235 **Date established:** 1967
Turnover: £20m - £50m **No.of Employees:** 101 - 250
Product Groups: 38, 40, 41

Germains Seed Technology
Hansa Road, Kings Lynn, PE30 4LG
Tel: 01553-774012 **Fax:** 01553-773145
E-mail: info@germains.com
Website: http://www.germains.com
Directors: R. Mendelsohn (Co Sec), P. Mullan (MD), V. Hayes (Mkt Research)
Managers: S. Power (Tech Serv Mgr), T. Drew (Personnel), T. Lecore (Comptroller)
Ultimate Holding Company: ASSOCIATED BRITISH FOODS P.L.C.
Immediate Holding Company: BRITISH SUGAR P.L.C.
Registration no: 00371996 **Turnover:** £10m - £20m
No.of Employees: 51 - 100 **Product Groups:** 20

Golfsim - Mobile Golf Simulator Hire
30 Elvington Kings Lynn, Kings Lynn, PE30 4TA
Tel: 07956-090436
E-mail: sales@golfsimulation.co.uk
Website: http://www.golfsimulation.co.uk
Directors: J. Greenfeld (Prop)
Turnover: Up to £250,000 **No.of Employees:** 1 - 10 **Product Groups:** 49

Harpley Engineering Ltd
Cross Street Harpley, Kings Lynn, PE31 6TJ
Tel: 01485-520355 **Fax:** 01485-520062
E-mail: sales@ctmharpley.co.uk
Website: http://www.ctmharpley.co.uk
Directors: N. Mountain (Dir)
Immediate Holding Company: HARPLEY ENGINEERING LIMITED
Registration no: 01326091 **Date established:** 1977
Turnover: £500,000 - £1m **No.of Employees:** 11 - 20
Product Groups: 41, 42, 67

Date of Accounts	Apr 11	Apr 10	Apr 09
Working Capital	1m	1m	941
Fixed Assets	264	369	324
Current Assets	2m	2m	1m

Hodgsons Forge
The Forge Wesley Road, Terrington St Clement, Kings Lynn, PE34 4NG
Tel: 01553-828637 **Fax:** 01553-828637
Directors: J. Hodgson (Ptnr)
Date established: 1983 **No.of Employees:** 1 - 10 **Product Groups:** 26, 35

Impactbond Ltd (t/a H & S Engineering)
Enterprise Way Harwick Narrows Industrial Estate, Kings Lynn, PE30 4LJ
Tel: 01553-767467 **Fax:** 01553-769151
E-mail: enquiries@hs-engineering.co.uk
Website: http://www.hs-engineering.co.uk
Directors: S. Bond (Fin)
Managers: J. Stitchman (Mgr), M. Belson
Immediate Holding Company: IMPACTBOND LIMITED
Registration no: 01701688 **Date established:** 1983
Turnover: £500,000 - £1m **No.of Employees:** 11 - 20 **Product Groups:** 48

Date of Accounts	Mar 11	Jan 10	Jan 09
Working Capital	71	188	140
Fixed Assets	81	103	90
Current Assets	345	363	404

Jay Craft Food Machinery Ltd
Downham Road Fincham, Kings Lynn, PE33 9HF
Tel: 01366-347971 **Fax:** 01366-347971
Directors: J. Murphy (Fin)
Immediate Holding Company: JAY-CRAFT FOOD MACHINERY LIMITED
Registration no: 04754510 **Date established:** 2003
No.of Employees: 1 - 10 **Product Groups:** 20, 40, 41

Date of Accounts	May 11	May 10	May 09
Working Capital	146	158	151
Fixed Assets	46	38	23
Current Assets	245	253	290

K M P Crusader Manufacturing Co. Ltd
Oldmedow Road, Kings Lynn, PE30 4LD
Tel: 01553-817200 **Fax:** 01553-691909
E-mail: sales@kmp-uk.co.uk
Website: http://www.kmp-europe.com
Bank(s): Barclays
Directors: J. Davies (MD)
Managers: J. Smith (Comptroller), C. De Waal (Sales Admin)
Ultimate Holding Company: KMP PRINTTECHNIK GMBH (GERMANY)
Immediate Holding Company: KMP CRUSADER MANUFACTURING LIMITED
Registration no: 00355221 **VAT No.:** GB 104 7285 85
Date established: 1997 **No.of Employees:** 21 - 50 **Product Groups:** 23, 44

Date of Accounts	Dec 10	Dec 09	Dec 08
Working Capital	326	428	346
Fixed Assets	195	227	249
Current Assets	1m	957	1m

Kings Lynn Conservancy Board
Common Staithe Quay, Kings Lynn, PE30 1LL
Tel: 01553-773411 **Fax:** 01553-763431
E-mail: sales@portauthoritykingslynn.fsnet.co.uk
Website: http://www.portauthoritykingslynn.fsnet.co.uk
Managers: J. Lorking
Date established: 1903 **Turnover:** £500,000 - £1m
No.of Employees: 1 - 10 **Product Groups:** 71, 74

Kingsway Print
Unit 18 Narborough Industrial Esate, Kings Lynn, PE32 1TE
Tel: 01760-339178
E-mail: info@kingswayprint.com
Website: http://www.kingswayprint.com
Directors: S. Jackson (Ptnr)
Managers: J. Jackson (Develop Mgr)
Date established: 1975 **Turnover:** Up to £250,000
No.of Employees: 1 - 10 **Product Groups:** 28

Lawtronic Ltd
Unit 3 Hamlin Way, Kings Lynn, PE30 4NG
Tel: 01553-765247 **Fax:** 01553-692147
E-mail: sales@lawtronic.co.uk
Website: http://www.lawtronic.co.uk
Directors: R. Mills (Fin), D. Tester (MD), D. Tester (MD)
Managers: A. Lloyd (Admin Off)
Ultimate Holding Company: LAWTRONIC HOLDINGS LIMITED
Immediate Holding Company: LAWTRONIC LIMITED
Registration no: 05184820 **VAT No.:** GB 451 3239 71
Date established: 2004 **Turnover:** £500,000 - £1m
No.of Employees: 51 - 100 **Product Groups:** 37

Date of Accounts	Mar 11	Mar 10	Mar 09
Working Capital	542	463	358
Fixed Assets	79	88	80
Current Assets	2m	1m	1m

M P G Biddles Ltd
24 Rollesby Road, Kings Lynn, PE30 4LS
Tel: 01553-764728 **Fax:** 01553-764633
E-mail: enquiries@biddles.co.uk
Website: http://www.biddles.co.uk
Bank(s): Lloyds TSB Bank plc
Managers: S. White (Buyer), G. Mackney, N. Prentis (Mktg Serv Mgr), R. Willett (Mgr)
Ultimate Holding Company: MPG BOOKS GROUP LIMITED
Immediate Holding Company: MPG BIDDLES LIMITED
Registration no: 06731115 **Date established:** 2008 **Turnover:** £5m - £10m
No.of Employees: 51 - 100 **Product Groups:** 28

Date of Accounts	Dec 11	Dec 10	Dec 09
Sales Turnover	6m	6m	8m
Pre Tax Profit/Loss	22	523	261
Working Capital	-594	-119	-404
Fixed Assets	3m	608	751
Current Assets	1m	2m	1m
Current Liabilities	125	316	290

Manley Engineering
Manor Farm Fakenham Road, Weasenham, Kings Lynn, PE32 2TF
Tel: 0800-027 7469 **Fax:** 01328-838772
Website: http://www.manleyengineering.co.uk
Directors: N. Manley (Prop), R. Manley (Prop)
No.of Employees: 1 - 10 **Product Groups:** 35

R J Marriott Engineering Ltd
The Street Marham, Kings Lynn, PE33 9JP
Tel: 01760-337332 **Fax:** 01760-338602
Directors: M. Marriott (Fin), R. Marriott (MD)
Immediate Holding Company: R. J. MARRIOTT (ENGINEERING) LIMITED
Registration no: 04131733 **Date established:** 2000
No.of Employees: 1 - 10 **Product Groups:** 20, 40, 41

Date of Accounts	Mar 12	Mar 11	Mar 10
Working Capital	57	57	72
Fixed Assets	24	18	22
Current Assets	144	92	133

Maxview Ltd
Common Lane Setchey, Kings Lynn, PE33 0AT
Tel: 01553-813300 **Fax:** 01553-813301
E-mail: info@maxview.ltd.uk
Website: http://www.maxview.ltd.uk
Bank(s): HSBC
Directors: S. Clark (Co Sec), A. Clark (MD)
Managers: M. Bush, S. Panks (Chief Acct)
Immediate Holding Company: MAXVIEW LIMITED
Registration no: 00791435 **VAT No.:** GB 283 2337 59
Date established: 1964 **Turnover:** £2m - £5m **No.of Employees:** 21 - 50
Product Groups: 37

Date of Accounts	Jun 11	Jun 10	Jun 09
Sales Turnover	N/A	N/A	5m
Pre Tax Profit/Loss	N/A	N/A	-60
Working Capital	453	373	269
Fixed Assets	2m	2m	2m
Current Assets	3m	3m	3m
Current Liabilities	N/A	N/A	875

Mr Signs Ltd
9 Austin Fields, Kings Lynn, PE30 1PH
Tel: 01553-761100 **Fax:** 01553-773535
E-mail: sales@mrsigns.ltd.uk
Directors: D. Pratt (Dir)
Immediate Holding Company: MR. SIGNS LIMITED
Registration no: 04131455 **Date established:** 2000
Turnover: Up to £250,000 **No.of Employees:** 1 - 10 **Product Groups:** 30

Date of Accounts	Dec 10	Dec 09	Dec 07
Working Capital	-11	-11	-4
Fixed Assets	73	76	71
Current Assets	12	13	19

Multitone Electronics plc
Hansa Road, Kings Lynn, PE30 4HX
Tel: 01553-760061 **Fax:** 01553-765945
E-mail: info@multitone.com
Website: http://www.multitone.com
Bank(s): National Westminster
Managers: D. Heighton (Ops Mgr)
Ultimate Holding Company: CHAMPION TECHNOLOGY HOLDINGS LTD (CAYMAN ISLANDS)
Immediate Holding Company: MULTITONE ELECTRONICS P L C
Registration no: 00256314 **Date established:** 1931
No.of Employees: 51 - 100 **Product Groups:** 37, 84

Date of Accounts	Jun 11	Jun 10	Jun 09
Sales Turnover	13m	15m	15m
Pre Tax Profit/Loss	-269	614	917
Working Capital	3m	4m	5m
Fixed Assets	4m	4m	3m
Current Assets	9m	11m	12m
Current Liabilities	4m	4m	4m

Night Shift Graphics
113 Hay Green Road South Terrington St Clement, Kings Lynn, PE34 4PU
Tel: 01553-829911 **Fax:** 01553-601329
E-mail: john@nightshiftgraphics.co.uk
Website: http://www.nsg-ltd.com
Directors: J. Osborne (Prop)
Immediate Holding Company: NIGHT SHIFT GRAPHICS LTD
Registration no: 07061705 **Date established:** 2009
No.of Employees: 1 - 10 **Product Groups:** 81

Date of Accounts	Dec 11	Dec 10
Working Capital	-49	-53
Fixed Assets	50	51
Current Assets	14	5

Norfolk Lavender Trading Ltd
Caley Mill Lynn Road, Heacham, Kings Lynn, PE31 7JE
Tel: 01485-570384 **Fax:** 01485-571176
E-mail: info@norfolk-lavender.co.uk
Website: http://www.norfolk-lavender.co.uk
Bank(s): Barclays
Managers: J. Winter
Immediate Holding Company: NORFOLK LAVENDER TRADING LIMITED
Registration no: 06800063 **Date established:** 2009 **Turnover:** £2m - £5m
No.of Employees: 21 - 50 **Product Groups:** 31, 32

Date of Accounts	Dec 11	Dec 10	Dec 09
Working Capital	-196	-237	-18
Fixed Assets	290	271	80
Current Assets	199	257	207

Omex Environmental Ltd
Riverside Industrial Estate, Kings Lynn, PE30 2HH
Tel: 01553-770092 **Fax:** 01553-776547
E-mail: alistarr@omex.com
Website: http://www.omex.co.uk
Directors: A. Rubie (Co Sec)
Ultimate Holding Company: OMEX INTERNATIONAL LIMITED (BERMUDA)
Immediate Holding Company: OMEX ENVIRONMENTAL LIMITED
Registration no: 02387507 **Date established:** 1989 **Turnover:** £2m - £5m
No.of Employees: 1 - 10 **Product Groups:** 31, 32, 42, 54, 66

Date of Accounts	Dec 11	Dec 10	Dec 09
Working Capital	1m	1m	1m
Fixed Assets	208	197	133
Current Assets	2m	5m	3m

Outback Autos
Walcups Lane Great Massingham, Kings Lynn, PE32 2HR
Tel: 01485-520394 **Fax:** 01485-520394
E-mail: outbackautos2000@yahoo.co.uk
Website: http://www.outbackautos.co.uk
Directors: S. Drewery (Prop)
Date established: 1989 **No.of Employees:** 1 - 10 **Product Groups:** 46, 48

Paramount Fire Armour
50 Marsh Lane, Kings Lynn, PE30 3AE
Tel: 01553-679001
E-mail: paramount@firearmour.fsnet.co.uk
Website: http://www.firearmour.fsnet.co.uk
Directors: R. Palmer (Ptnr)
No.of Employees: 1 - 10 **Product Groups:** 38, 42

Payne Pallet Inverters Ltd
Dereham Road Beeston, Kings Lynn, PE32 2NQ
Tel: 01328-700138 **Fax:** 01328-701879
E-mail: david@paynepalletinverters.co.uk
Website: http://www.paynepalletinverters.co.uk
Bank(s): Barclays
Directors: D. Payne (Dir), C. Payne (Fin)
Immediate Holding Company: PAYNE PALLET INVERTERS LIMITED
Registration no: 02899910 **VAT No.:** GB 636 8516 14
Date established: 1994 **Turnover:** £500,000 - £1m
No.of Employees: 11 - 20 **Product Groups:** 45, 84

Date of Accounts	Jul 12	Jul 11	Jul 10
Working Capital	1m	941	817
Fixed Assets	358	468	527
Current Assets	1m	1m	938

Petroleum Equipment Maintenance Service
9 Long Road Terrington St Clement, Kings Lynn, PE34 4JL
Tel: 01553-828873 **Fax:** 01553-828873
E-mail: a.barber515@btinternet.com
Directors: A. Barber (Prop)
Date established: 1995 **No.of Employees:** 1 - 10 **Product Groups:** 40

Porvair plc
7 Regis Place Bergen Way, North Lynn Industrial Estate, Kings Lynn, PE30 2JN
Tel: 01553-765500 **Fax:** 01553-765599
E-mail: sales@porvair-sciences.com
Website: http://www.porvair-sciences.com
Directors: B. Stocks (Grp Chief Exec), C. Tyler (Fin)
Immediate Holding Company: PORVAIR PLC
Registration no: 01661935 **Date established:** 1982
Turnover: £50m - £75m **No.of Employees:** 1 - 10 **Product Groups:** 30, 31, 33, 34, 35, 36, 37, 39, 40, 41, 42

Date of Accounts	Nov 11	Nov 10	Nov 09
Sales Turnover	68m	64m	55m
Pre Tax Profit/Loss	5m	3m	1m
Working Capital	12m	11m	11m
Fixed Assets	47m	48m	51m
Current Assets	26m	25m	21m
Current Liabilities	7m	6m	4m

R P D Precision Drawings
Unit 7 North Lynn Industrial Estate Bryggen Road, Kings Lynn, PE30 2HZ
Tel: 01553-774765 **Fax:** 01553-764816
E-mail: rpd@mywebpage.net
Website: http://www.mywebpage.net/rpd
Directors: J. Phipps (Fin), R. Phipps (MD)
Immediate Holding Company: B. & B. ENGINEERING LIMITED
Registration no: 01239383 **Date established:** 1985
Turnover: Up to £250,000 **No.of Employees:** 1 - 10 **Product Groups:** 38, 65

Date of Accounts	Apr 12	Apr 11	Apr 10
Working Capital	671	553	537
Fixed Assets	67	95	109
Current Assets	866	729	678

Guy Raymond Engineering Company Ltd
Rollesby Road, Kings Lynn, PE30 4LX
Tel: 01553-761401 **Fax:** 01553-767459
E-mail: cedricdaniels@guy-raymond.co.uk
Website: http://www.guy-raymond.co.uk
Bank(s): National Westminster Bank Plc
Directors: C. Daniels (MD)
Managers: S. Bown
Immediate Holding Company: GUY-RAYMOND ENGINEERING COMPANY LIMITED
Registration no: 00877932 **Date established:** 1966 **Turnover:** £2m - £5m
No.of Employees: 51 - 100 **Product Groups:** 26, 29, 30, 35, 36, 39, 66

Date of Accounts	Sep 11	Sep 10	Sep 09
Sales Turnover	4m	4m	N/A
Pre Tax Profit/Loss	140	184	228
Working Capital	2m	2m	3m
Fixed Assets	1m	1m	1m
Current Assets	2m	2m	3m
Current Liabilities	96	117	134

Dick Ropa
Carrstone Lodge Pullover Road, Tilney All Saints, Kings Lynn, PE34 4SG
Tel: 01553-692035
E-mail: support@dickropa.com
Website: http://www.dickropa.com
Directors: D. Ropa (Prop)
Turnover: Up to £250,000 **No.of Employees:** 1 - 10 **Product Groups:** 26, 49, 83

Sandringham Ironcraft
Unit 4 Cheney Crescent Heacham, Kings Lynn, PE31 7BT
Tel: 01485-571129 **Fax:** 01485-571129
Directors: N. Winter (Prop)
Date established: 1996 **No.of Employees:** 1 - 10 **Product Groups:** 26, 35

Sensient
Oldmedow Road, Kings Lynn, PE30 4LA
Tel: 01553-669444 **Fax:** 01553-776409
E-mail: mark.connolly@eu.sensient-tech.com
Website: http://www.sensient-tech.com
Bank(s): HSBC
Directors: M. Demeyer (MD), R. Creighton (Fin)
Managers: N. Bussey (Tech Serv Mgr), N. Laroiya, S. Mandham (Personnel)
Ultimate Holding Company: SENSIENT TECHNOLOGIES CORP (USA)
Immediate Holding Company: SENSIENT COLORS UK LTD
Registration no: 00741008 **VAT No.:** GB 342 5578 48
Date established: 1962 **Turnover:** £20m - £50m
No.of Employees: 101 - 250 **Product Groups:** 31, 32

Date of Accounts	Dec 11	Dec 10	Dec 09
Sales Turnover	29m	28m	24m
Pre Tax Profit/Loss	3m	3m	2m
Working Capital	8m	6m	12m
Fixed Assets	4m	4m	4m
Current Assets	16m	15m	19m
Current Liabilities	3m	1m	865

Sensitised Coatings Ltd
Bergen Way North Lynn Industrial Estate, Kings Lynn, PE30 2JL
Tel: 01553-764836 **Fax:** 01553-760377
E-mail: sales@senco.co.uk
Website: http://www.senco.co.uk
Bank(s): Barclays, Tuesday Market Place, Kings Lynn
Directors: D. Eatwell (MD)
Immediate Holding Company: SENSITISED COATINGS LIMITED
Registration no: 00583651 **VAT No.:** GB 394 2861 21
Date established: 1957 **Turnover:** £2m - £5m **No.of Employees:** 11 - 20
Product Groups: 27, 64

Date of Accounts	Jun 11	Jun 10	Jun 09
Working Capital	253	249	227
Fixed Assets	34	43	55
Current Assets	333	379	334

Smartlift Bulk Packaging
364 Wootton Road Kings Lynn, Kings Lynn, PE30 3EB
Tel: 01553-675688 **Fax:** 01553-675546
E-mail: sales@smartliftbulkpackaging.co.uk
Website: http://www.smartliftbulkpackaging.co.uk
Directors: T. Bland (Fin)
Immediate Holding Company: SMARTLIFT BULK PACKAGING LTD.
Registration no: 06370540 **Date established:** 2007
No.of Employees: 1 - 10 **Product Groups:** 22, 24, 27, 30, 66

Date of Accounts	Dec 11	Dec 10	Dec 09
Working Capital	216	168	116
Fixed Assets	19	13	19
Current Assets	556	457	365

Snap On
12-17 Denney Road, Kings Lynn, PE30 4HG
Tel: 01553-692422 **Fax:** 01553-691844
E-mail: uksales@snapon.com
Website: http://www.snapon.co.uk
Bank(s): Barclays
Managers: C. Farra (Site Co-ord)
Immediate Holding Company: SNAP-ON TOOLS CORPORATION (USA)
Registration no: 00667618 **VAT No.:** GB 105 7758 62
Turnover: £20m - £50m **No.of Employees:** 51 - 100 **Product Groups:** 38, 39

Thompson Forktrucks
Bergen Way Business Park North Lynn Industrial Estate, Kings Lynn, PE30 2DD
Tel: 01553-769310 **Fax:** 01553-760734
E-mail: thompson1957@aol.com
Website: http://www.thompsonforktrucks.com
Directors: T. Thompson (Prop)
Immediate Holding Company: SOLAR SCAFFOLDING LIMITED
Registration no: 03927841 **Date established:** 2000
No.of Employees: 1 - 10 **Product Groups:** 35, 39, 45

V S A Products Ltd
Rollesby Road, Kings Lynn, PE30 4JS
Tel: 01553-761521 **Fax:** 01553-691464
E-mail: vsa-enquiries@btconnect.com
Bank(s): Lloyds TSB Bank plc
Directors: R. Smith (MD)
Managers: J. Hall (Comm)
Immediate Holding Company: VSA PRODUCTS LIMITED
Registration no: 00745498 **VAT No.:** GB 105 9996 36
Date established: 1962 **Turnover:** £1m - £2m **No.of Employees:** 11 - 20
Product Groups: 30, 48

Date of Accounts	Mar 11	Mar 10	Mar 09
Working Capital	-29	-30	-328
Fixed Assets	644	656	691
Current Assets	347	319	315

Stuart D Warren
43 Stow Road Magdalen, Kings Lynn, PE34 3BX
Tel: 01553-810260 **Fax:** 01553-811136
E-mail: warrenstuartd@aol.co.uk
Directors: S. Warren (Prop)
Date established: 1924 **No.of Employees:** 1 - 10 **Product Groups:** 41

Williams Refrigeration
Bryggen Road, Kings Lynn, PE30 2HZ
Tel: 01553-817000 **Fax:** 01553-817111
E-mail: info@williams-refrigeration.co.uk
Website: http://www.williams-refrigeration.com
Bank(s): Lloyds TSB Bank plc
Directors: M. Harlin (Sales), S. Hallam (Fin), T. Smith (MD)
Managers: N. Franklin (Mktg Serv Mgr), D. Tyers (Fin Mgr), M. Rippon (Tech Serv Mgr), M. Laws (Mktg Serv Mgr), R. Smith (Purch Mgr), J. Wilks (Personnel)
Ultimate Holding Company: ALI SPA (ITALY)
Immediate Holding Company: WILLIAMS REFRIGERATION LIMITED
Registration no: 01504974 **VAT No.:** GB 100 5835 13
Date established: 1980 **Turnover:** £20m - £50m
No.of Employees: 251 - 500 **Product Groups:** 36, 38, 39, 40, 45, 48, 52

Date of Accounts	Aug 11	Aug 10	Aug 09
Pre Tax Profit/Loss	N/A	1m	368
Fixed Assets	282	282	347

Melton Constable

Derrick Barham
24 Mill Lane Briston, Melton Constable, NR24 2JG
Tel: 01263-860711 **Fax:** 01263-860711
Directors: D. Barham (Prop)
Date established: 1977 **No.of Employees:** 1 - 10 **Product Groups:** 41

Structure Flex
Peacock Way, Melton Constable, NR24 2AZ
Tel: 01263-863100 **Fax:** 01263-863115
E-mail: enquiries@structure-flex.co.uk
Website: http://www.structure-flex.co.uk
Managers: S. Davis (Fin Mgr), A. Willey, M. Doughty (Sales & Mktg Mg), J. Dawber (Tech Serv Mgr), K. Doughty (Personnel)

Ultimate Holding Company: RESOLUTE CORPORATE HOLDINGS LIMITED
Immediate Holding Company: STRUCTURE-FLEX LIMITED
Registration no: 00981555 **VAT No.:** GB 595 3542 10
Date established: 1970 **Turnover:** £5m - £10m
No.of Employees: 51 - 100 **Product Groups:** 23, 24, 27, 29, 30, 31, 35, 39, 45, 66, 68, 83

Date of Accounts	Aug 11	Aug 10	Aug 09
Sales Turnover	8m	5m	4m
Pre Tax Profit/Loss	2m	293	-351
Working Capital	2m	1m	1m
Fixed Assets	1m	968	940
Current Assets	5m	2m	2m
Current Liabilities	986	292	299

North Walsham

Ashford Commercial Ltd
7 Folgate Road, North Walsham, NR28 0AJ
Tel: 01692-500432 **Fax:** 01692-500483
E-mail: enquiries@ashfordcommercial.co.uk
Website: http://www.ashfordcommercial.co.uk
Bank(s): Barclays
Directors: B. Quinney (Fin), K. Lawrence (MD), M. Neale (Fin)
Managers: B. Manley (Comm), S. Mack (Tech Serv Mgr)
Immediate Holding Company: ASHFORD COMMERCIAL LIMITED
Registration no: 01973153 **VAT No.:** GB 426 3582 49
Date established: 1985 **No.of Employees:** 21 - 50 **Product Groups:** 30

Date of Accounts	Mar 11	Mar 10	Mar 09
Working Capital	2m	1m	419
Fixed Assets	325	387	537
Current Assets	4m	3m	2m

Broadland Transport Engineering Ltd
Stanford Tuck Road, North Walsham, NR28 0TY
Tel: 01692-500004 **Fax:** 01692-500091
E-mail: emptymytank@live.co.uk
Website: http://www.broadlandtankering.viviti.com/
Directors: K. Wharton (Dir), M. Wharton (Fin)
Immediate Holding Company: BROADLAND TRANSPORT ENGINEERING LTD
Registration no: 04929753 **Date established:** 2003 **Turnover:** £5m - £10m
No.of Employees: 1 - 10 **Product Groups:** 30, 39, 52

Date of Accounts	Oct 11	Oct 10	Oct 09
Working Capital	4	-3	-14
Fixed Assets	27	37	25
Current Assets	77	82	41

Coda Plastics Ltd
Folgate Road, North Walsham, NR28 0AJ
Tel: 01692-501020 **Fax:** 01692-501030
E-mail: nicktate@coda-plastics.co.uk
Website: http://www.coda-plastics.co.uk
Bank(s): Barclays
Directors: J. Campbell (Dir), N. Tate (Dir), J. Campbell (Fin)
Managers: A. Banks (Accounts), P. Middleton (Sales Prom Mgr), S. Alden (I.T. Exec)
Immediate Holding Company: CODA PLASTICS LIMITED
Registration no: 01116956 **VAT No.:** GB 107 1895 70
Date established: 1973 **No.of Employees:** 21 - 50 **Product Groups:** 30, 33

Date of Accounts	May 10	May 09	May 08
Working Capital	2m	2m	1m
Fixed Assets	1m	1m	1m
Current Assets	3m	2m	2m

Girovac Ltd
2 Douglas Bader Close, North Walsham, NR28 0TZ
Tel: 01692-403008 **Fax:** 01692-404611
E-mail: enquiries@girovac.com
Website: http://www.girovac.com
Directors: R. Lee (MD)
Immediate Holding Company: GIROVAC LIMITED
Registration no: 01758137 **VAT No.:** GB 403 9392 56
Date established: 1983 **Turnover:** £500,000 - £1m
No.of Employees: 1 - 10 **Product Groups:** 28, 36, 40, 42, 45, 46, 67

Date of Accounts	Dec 11	Dec 10	Dec 09
Working Capital	55	42	49
Fixed Assets	N/A	N/A	1
Current Assets	90	108	110

Group Precision Engineering Services
1c Cornish Way, North Walsham, NR28 0AW
Tel: 01692-402131 **Fax:** 01692-404317
E-mail: info@gpes.co.uk
Website: http://www.gpes.co.uk
Directors: P. Hart (Ptnr)
Immediate Holding Company: ASHFORD WINDOWS LIMITED
Registration no: 05210166 **Date established:** 2006
No.of Employees: 1 - 10 **Product Groups:** 29, 30, 48

GTH Photography
3 Birds Road, North Walsham, NR28 0WE
Tel: 01692-402501
E-mail: sales@gthphotography.co.uk
Website: http://www.gthphotography.co.uk
Directors: G. Hathaway (Prop)
Date established: 2006 **Turnover:** Up to £250,000
No.of Employees: 1 - 10 **Product Groups:** 81

Hardy Marine Ltd
Gaymers Way, North Walsham, NR28 0AN
Tel: 01692-408700 **Fax:** 01692-406483
E-mail: sales@hardymarine.co.uk
Website: http://www.hardymarine.co.uk
Bank(s): Barclays, Norwich
Directors: M. Funnell (MD)
Immediate Holding Company: HARDY MARINE LIMITED
Registration no: 03355341 **VAT No.:** GB 532 8406 53
Date established: 1997 **Turnover:** £2m - £5m **No.of Employees:** 21 - 50
Product Groups: 39

Date of Accounts	Mar 12	Mar 11	Mar 10
Working Capital	1m	1m	854
Fixed Assets	563	495	503
Current Assets	1m	1m	1m

Lake & Nicholls Engineering
4 Cornish Way, North Walsham, NR28 0AW
Tel: 01692-404602 **Fax:** 01692-406723
E-mail: info@lakeandnicholls.co.uk
Directors: S. Lake (Ptnr)
VAT No.: GB 324 4118 89 **Turnover:** Up to £250,000
No.of Employees: 1 - 10 **Product Groups:** 48

Mustang Tools Ltd
7 Cornish Way, North Walsham, NR28 0AW
Tel: 01692-404005 **Fax:** 01692-409943
E-mail: sales@mustangtools.co.uk
Website: http://www.mustangtools.co.uk
Directors: E. Baines (Fin), C. Utting (Dir)
Immediate Holding Company: MUSTANG TOOLS LIMITED
Registration no: 00903340 **VAT No.:** GB 105 8072 91
Date established: 1967 **Turnover:** Up to £250,000
No.of Employees: 1 - 10 **Product Groups:** 36, 45, 66

North Walsham Fire Protection
131 Mundesley Road, North Walsham, NR28 0DD
Tel: 01692-406604 **Fax:** 01692-400928
E-mail: nwfireprotection@tiscali.co.uk
Directors: L. Barnard (Prop)
Date established: 1998 **No.of Employees:** 1 - 10 **Product Groups:** 38, 42

P G Products Ltd
1 Folgate Road, North Walsham, NR28 0AJ
Tel: 01692-500390 **Fax:** 01692-402863
E-mail: info@pgproducts.com
Website: http://www.pgproducts.com
Bank(s): Royal Bank of Scotland
Directors: D. Simpson (MD)
Immediate Holding Company: P G PRODUCTS LTD.
Registration no: 00946981 **VAT No.:** GB 256 5067 50
Date established: 1969 **Turnover:** £500,000 - £1m
No.of Employees: 11 - 20 **Product Groups:** 24, 40

Date of Accounts	Mar 11	Mar 10	Mar 09
Working Capital	268	244	227
Fixed Assets	341	17	18
Current Assets	637	513	555

P S S
Lyngate Industrial Estate Folgate Road, North Walsham, NR28 0AJ
Tel: 01692-406017 **Fax:** 01692-406957
E-mail: sales@pss.co.uk
Website: http://www.pss.co.uk
Directors: A. Brammer (Comm), L. Pratt (Pers)
Managers: M. Pollard (Comptroller), M. Swann (Buyer), G. Bayles (Sales Prom Mgr)
Immediate Holding Company: FASTCOURT LIMITED
Registration no: 03345358 **VAT No.:** GB 629 8801 04
Date established: 1993 **Turnover:** £2m - £5m **No.of Employees:** 51 - 100
Product Groups: 40, 48

Date of Accounts	Dec 10	Dec 09	Dec 08
Working Capital	88	65	133
Fixed Assets	1m	1m	1m
Current Assets	104	80	149

Pumptronics Europe Ltd
Folgate Road, North Walsham, NR28 0AJ
Tel: 01692-500640 **Fax:** 01692-406710
E-mail: sales@pumptronics.co.uk
Website: http://www.pumptronics.co.uk
Directors: K. Owen (Fin)
Managers: A. Olive (Chief Mgr)
Ultimate Holding Company: THE PREMIER PUMP AND TANK COMPANY LIMITED
Immediate Holding Company: PUMPTRONICS EUROPE LIMITED
Registration no: 03404236 **Date established:** 1997 **Turnover:** £1m - £2m
No.of Employees: 11 - 20 **Product Groups:** 29, 33, 40, 48

Date of Accounts	Sep 11	Sep 10	Sep 09
Sales Turnover	1m	2m	2m
Pre Tax Profit/Loss	28	114	135
Working Capital	370	340	251
Fixed Assets	28	37	40
Current Assets	617	639	484
Current Liabilities	64	55	29

Rowlands Woodhouse Equipment Ltd
Laundry Loke Industrial Estate, North Walsham, NR28 0AJ
Tel: 01692-405129 **Fax:** 01692-406569
E-mail: info@rowood.co.uk
Website: http://www.rowlandswoodhouse.co.uk
Directors: M. Howlett (Fin), C. Rowlands (MD)
Immediate Holding Company: ROWLANDS-WOODHOUSE EQUIPMENT LIMITED
Registration no: 01300467 **Date established:** 1977
No.of Employees: 21 - 50 **Product Groups:** 35, 42, 45

Date of Accounts	May 11	May 10	May 09
Working Capital	46	-35	143
Fixed Assets	808	852	899
Current Assets	656	620	807

Tekpro
Laundry Loke, North Walsham, NR28 0BD
Tel: 01692-403403 **Fax:** 01692-404955
E-mail: info@tekpro.com
Website: http://www.tekpro.com
Directors: J. Catchpole (MD)
Immediate Holding Company: TEKPRO LIMITED
Registration no: 03894578 **Date established:** 1999 **Turnover:** £1m - £2m
No.of Employees: 11 - 20 **Product Groups:** 41

Date of Accounts	Apr 12	Apr 11	Apr 10
Working Capital	597	351	546
Fixed Assets	37	18	19
Current Assets	959	609	843

Wall Engineering Co. Ltd
Cromer Road, North Walsham, NR28 0NB
Tel: 01692-403701 **Fax:** 01692-406610
E-mail: info@wallengineering.co.uk
Website: http://www.wallengineering.co.uk
Bank(s): Bank of Scotland
Directors: P. Hemstock (MD), S. Tully (Chief Op Offcr)
Immediate Holding Company: WALL ENGINEERING COMPANY LIMITED(THE)
Registration no: 00471090 **VAT No.:** GB 105 8536 75
Date established: 1949 **Turnover:** £5m - £10m
No.of Employees: 51 - 100 **Product Groups:** 30, 35, 45, 48

Date of Accounts	Mar 12	Mar 11	Mar 10
Sales Turnover	8m	7m	6m
Pre Tax Profit/Loss	136	56	360
Working Capital	3m	3m	3m
Fixed Assets	318	380	388
Current Assets	5m	4m	5m
Current Liabilities	501	482	437

Norwich

Aa Sheet Metal Ltd
Unit 1 Fletcher Way Weston Road, Norwich, NR3 3ST
Tel: 01603-417030 **Fax:** 01603-417128
E-mail: alanlappin@aasheetmetal.info
Directors: A. Lappin (MD)
Immediate Holding Company: AA SHEET METAL LIMITED
Registration no: 04589987 **Date established:** 2002
Turnover: £250,000 - £500,000 **No.of Employees:** 11 - 20
Product Groups: 48

Date of Accounts	Dec 11	Dec 10	Dec 09
Working Capital	89	86	59
Fixed Assets	133	178	217
Current Assets	254	219	168

A T B Laurence Scott Ltd
PO Box 25, Norwich, NR1 1JD
Tel: 01603-628333 **Fax:** 01603-610604
E-mail: admin@laurence-scott.com
Website: http://www.laurence-scott.com
Bank(s): Barclays, Bradford, Yorks
Directors: I. Walker (Fin), I. Atkins (MD)
Managers: R. Nicholls (Buyer), A. Fox (Personnel), B. Scales (Sales & Mktg Mg), C. Holmes (Tech Serv Mgr)
Ultimate Holding Company: A-TEC INDUSTRIES GMBH (AUSTRIA)
Immediate Holding Company: ATB LAURENCE SCOTT LIMITED
Registration no: 06241009 **VAT No.:** GB 184 4733 43
Date established: 2007 **Turnover:** £20m - £50m
No.of Employees: 101 - 250 **Product Groups:** 35, 37, 39, 48

Date of Accounts	Dec 11	Dec 10	Dec 09
Sales Turnover	19m	24m	22m
Pre Tax Profit/Loss	2m	6m	5m
Working Capital	3m	5m	3m
Fixed Assets	10m	9m	8m
Current Assets	10m	9m	8m
Current Liabilities	3m	1m	2m

Aalco
Roundtree Way, Norwich, NR7 8SR
Tel: 01603-787878 **Fax:** 01603-789999
E-mail: callen@aalco.co.uk
Website: http://www.aalco.co.uk
Bank(s): National Westminster
Managers: C. Allen (Mgr)
Ultimate Holding Company: UK STEELSTOCK LTD
Immediate Holding Company: AMARI METALS LTD
Registration no: 03551533 **Date established:** 1969
Turnover: £125m - £250m **No.of Employees:** 21 - 50
Product Groups: 34, 35, 36, 66

Abfab Ltd
The Forge Blacksmith Lane, Happisburgh, Norwich, NR12 0QT
Tel: 01692-651291 **Fax:** 01692-651291
Website: http://www.abfabltd.com
Directors: J. Grimmer (MD)
Immediate Holding Company: ABFAB LIMITED
Registration no: 04251513 **Date established:** 2001
No.of Employees: 1 - 10 **Product Groups:** 26, 35

Date of Accounts	Oct 11	Oct 10	Oct 09
Working Capital	-30	-29	-31
Fixed Assets	2	3	3
Current Assets	1	2	1

Acorn Planting Products Ltd
Little Money Road Loddon, Norwich, NR14 6JD
Tel: 01621-874200 **Fax:** 01508-528775
E-mail: sales@acorn-p-p.co.uk
Website: http://www.acorn-p-p.co.uk
Directors: S. Towler (MD), R. Chamings (Co Sec)
Immediate Holding Company: ACORN PLANTING PRODUCTS LIMITED
Registration no: 01996376 **VAT No.:** GB 363 5946 25
Date established: 1986 **Turnover:** £250,000 - £500,000
No.of Employees: 21 - 50 **Product Groups:** 30

Date of Accounts	Apr 08	Apr 07	Apr 06
Working Capital	454	387	312
Fixed Assets	182	205	245
Current Assets	676	557	488
Current Liabilities	222	170	176

Adams & Howling Ltd
Granary Offices Manor Farm The Green, Little Plumstead, Norwich, NR13 5EL
Tel: 01603-722372 **Fax:** 01603-722472
E-mail: enquiries@adamsandhowling.co.uk
Website: http://www.adamsandhowling.co.uk
Directors: P. Adams (Snr Part)
Immediate Holding Company: ADAMS & HOWLING LIMITED
Registration no: 01076707 **Date established:** 1972
No.of Employees: 11 - 20 **Product Groups:** 61, 62

Date of Accounts	Mar 12	Mar 11	Mar 10
Working Capital	1m	894	889
Fixed Assets	43	60	59
Current Assets	2m	2m	2m

Aladdins Lighting
Unit 7 Wellesley Road Tharston, Norwich, NR15 2PD
Tel: 01508-532528 **Fax:** 01508-532538
E-mail: simon@aladdins-lighting.co.uk
Directors: S. Hifcox (Prop)
Immediate Holding Company: INTERNET TRADING LTD
Date established: 2010 **No.of Employees:** 1 - 10 **Product Groups:** 37, 67

Date of Accounts	Jul 11
Working Capital	4
Fixed Assets	27
Current Assets	12

Aldous Electrical Ltd
116 Hellesdon Park Road Drayton High Road, Norwich, NR6 5DR
Tel: 01603-425075 **Fax:** 01603-788453
E-mail: accounts@aldouselectrical.co.uk
Website: http://www.aldouselectricalnorwich.co.uk
Bank(s): National Westminster Bank Plc
Directors: D. Alderson (Dir)
Immediate Holding Company: ALDOUS ELECTRICAL LIMITED
Registration no: 02488309 **VAT No.:** GB 324 2932 73
Date established: 1990 **Turnover:** £500,000 - £1m
No.of Employees: 11 - 20 **Product Groups:** 52

Date of Accounts	Apr 11	Apr 10	Apr 09
Working Capital	5	39	48
Fixed Assets	30	47	155
Current Assets	556	436	582

Althon Ltd
Vulcan Road South, Norwich, NR6 6AF
Tel: 01603-488700 **Fax:** 01603-488598
E-mail: sales@althon.co.uk
Website: http://www.althon.co.uk
Directors: T. Gates (Dir), K. Price (Sales)
Ultimate Holding Company: MAG GROUP LIMITED
Immediate Holding Company: ALTHON LIMITED
Registration no: 01579423 **Date established:** 1981
No.of Employees: 1 - 10 **Product Groups:** 30, 35, 36, 38, 42, 45, 51, 54, 67, 83

Date of Accounts	Nov 11	Nov 10	Nov 09
Working Capital	541	415	393
Fixed Assets	36	50	77
Current Assets	953	816	849

Andrewpougher.co.uk
43 Caernarvon Road, Norwich, NR2 3HZ
Tel: 01603-46085
E-mail: info@andrewpougher.co.uk
Website: http://www.andrewpougher.co.uk
Directors: A. Pougher (Dir)
Turnover: Up to £250,000 **No.of Employees:** 1 - 10 **Product Groups:** 44, 81

Anglia Television Ltd
Anglia House Agricultural Hall Plain, Norwich, NR1 3JG
Tel: 08448-816920 **Fax:** 01603-631032
E-mail: neil.thompson@itv.com
Website: http://www.itv.com
Bank(s): Lloyds TSB Bank plc & National Westminster Bank Plc
Directors: N. Thompson (MD)
Managers: M. Beasley (Fin Mgr), C. McGowan
Ultimate Holding Company: ITV PLC
Immediate Holding Company: ANGLIA TELEVISION LIMITED
Registration no: 05959958 **Date established:** 2006
Turnover: £75m - £125m **No.of Employees:** 101 - 250
Product Groups: 89

Anglia Pipework Ltd
94 Hellesdon Park Road, Norwich, NR6 5DS
Tel: 01603-400012
Website: http://www.angliapipeworkltd.co.uk
Directors: J. Yallop (Fin)
Registration no: 03186295 **Date established:** 1996
No.of Employees: 1 - 10 **Product Groups:** 40, 48, 54, 84

Anglia Springs
Little Money Road Loddon, Norwich, NR14 6JD
Tel: 01508-528396 **Fax:** 01508-528396
E-mail: info@angliasprings.com
Website: http://www.angliasprings.com
Directors: K. Cuskeran (Dir)
Immediate Holding Company: ANGLIA SPRINGS LIMITED
Registration no: 05926334 **Date established:** 2006
Turnover: Up to £250,000 **No.of Employees:** 1 - 10 **Product Groups:** 35, 66

Date of Accounts	Sep 11	Sep 10	Sep 09
Working Capital	5	-3	5
Fixed Assets	3	4	4
Current Assets	46	47	52

Anglian Developments Ltd
The Granary School Road, Neatishead, Norwich, NR12 8BU
Tel: 01692-630808 **Fax:** 01692-631591
E-mail: angdev@btconnect.com
Website: http://www.angdev
Bank(s): National Westminster, Norwich
Directors: J. Mason (Fin), L. Pryse (MD)
Immediate Holding Company: ANGLIAN DEVELOPMENTS LIMITED
Registration no: 01574628 **VAT No.:** GB 394 1567 26
Date established: 1981 **Turnover:** £2m - £5m **No.of Employees:** 11 - 20
Product Groups: 30

Date of Accounts	Mar 11	Mar 10	Mar 08
Working Capital	2m	1m	929
Fixed Assets	1m	1m	1m
Current Assets	2m	2m	1m

Apex Print & Promotion Ltd
Apex House Sapphire Way Diamond Road Rhombus Business Park, Norwich, NR6 6NN
Tel: 01603-410035 **Fax:** 01634-10049
E-mail: apex@promotion.co.uk
Website: http://www.appuk.com
Bank(s): Barclays
Directors: N. Chudasama (MD), J. Webster (Co Sec)
Immediate Holding Company: APEX PRINT & PROMOTION LIMITED
Registration no: 04020746 **VAT No.:** GB 751 0247 63
Date established: 2000 **Turnover:** £250,000 - £500,000
No.of Employees: 11 - 20 **Product Groups:** 23, 28, 49

Date of Accounts	Jun 11	Jun 10	Jun 09
Working Capital	-42	-80	-84
Fixed Assets	250	244	220
Current Assets	98	78	101

Archant Community Media Ltd
Prospect House Rouen Road, Norwich, NR1 1RE
Tel: 01603-772772 **Fax:** 01603-612930
E-mail: john.ellison@archant.co.uk
Website: http://www.archant.co.uk
Bank(s): Barclays, Norwich
Directors: J. Ellison (Co Sec), D. Willmott (Pers)
Managers: J. Parsons (Tech Serv Mgr), N. Jones, G. Parton, B. McCarthy
Ultimate Holding Company: ARCHANT LIMITED
Immediate Holding Company: ARCHANT COMMUNITY MEDIA LIMITED
Registration no: 00019300 **Date established:** 1984
Turnover: £75m - £125m **No.of Employees:** 251 - 500
Product Groups: 28

Date of Accounts	Dec 11	Dec 10	Dec 09
Sales Turnover	95m	92m	97m
Pre Tax Profit/Loss	70m	-260	-18m
Working Capital	7m	-2m	-2m
Fixed Assets	156m	229m	235m
Current Assets	30m	15m	15m
Current Liabilities	18m	13m	12m

Arthur Brett
17 Concorde Road, Norwich, NR6 6BJ
Tel: 01603-480720 **Fax:** 01603-788984
E-mail: enquiries@arthur-brett.com
Website: http://www.arthurbrett.com
Bank(s): HSBC
Directors: D. Salmon (Prop)
Managers: B. Collins (Comptroller)
Immediate Holding Company: ABS REALISATIONS LTD
Registration no: 06520665 **Date established:** 1870
No.of Employees: 11 - 20 **Product Groups:** 26

Date of Accounts	Dec 05
Sales Turnover	2914
Pre Tax Profit/Loss	-1208
Working Capital	-1612
Fixed Assets	2024
Current Assets	1811
Current Liabilities	3423
Total Share Capital	13
ROCE% (Return on Capital Employed)	-293.1

Aspect Roofing Gang-Nail Systems Ltd
The Old Mill Harling Road, Norwich, NR16 2QW
Tel: 01953-717777 **Fax:** 01953-717164
E-mail: enquiries@aspectroofing.co.uk
Website: http://www.aspectroofing.co.uk
Directors: A. Howard (Dir)
Immediate Holding Company: ASPECT EAST ANGLIA LIMITED
Registration no: 02529333 **Date established:** 1990 **Turnover:** £5m - £10m
No.of Employees: 21 - 50 **Product Groups:** 35, 52, 66

Date of Accounts	Jun 11	Jun 10	Jun 09
Working Capital	750	657	648
Fixed Assets	445	453	464
Current Assets	1m	1m	1m

B F Engineering
Woodgate Farm Woodgate, Aylsham, Norwich, NR11 6UJ
Tel: 01263-733656
E-mail: barry521@btinternet.com
Directors: B. Fairclough (Prop), B. Faircloth (Prop)
Date established: 1988 **No.of Employees:** 1 - 10 **Product Groups:** 35

Badger Associates Ltd
Willows Cottage Pottergate Street, Aslacton, Norwich, NR15 2JU
Tel: 01508-536013 **Fax:** 0871-750 1925
E-mail: info@badgerassociates.co.uk
Website: http://www.badgerassociates.co.uk
Directors: M. Bolger (MD)
Immediate Holding Company: BADGER ASSOCIATES LIMITED
Registration no: 04286713 **Date established:** 2001
Turnover: £250,000 - £500,000 **No.of Employees:** 1 - 10
Product Groups: 44, 80, 84

Date of Accounts	Sep 11	Sep 10	Sep 09
Working Capital	126	148	158
Fixed Assets	2	2	3
Current Assets	174	195	198

Bath Remedies
6 Catton Grove Road, Norwich, NR3 3NH
Tel: 01603-404295 **Fax:** 01603-404295
Directors: D. Johnson (Prop)
Date established: 1983 **No.of Employees:** 1 - 10 **Product Groups:** 46, 48

Beardshaw
Stalham Road Industrial Estate Hoveton, Norwich, NR12 8DZ
Tel: 01603-783811 **Fax:** 01603-783859
E-mail: sales@beardshaw.co.uk
Website: http://www.beardshaw.co.uk
Directors: J. Beardshaw (Fin), C. Beardshaw (MD)
Immediate Holding Company: BEARDSHAW BROS LIMITED
Registration no: 01623710 **VAT No.:** GB 287 7753 93
Date established: 1982 **Turnover:** £500,000 - £1m
No.of Employees: 1 - 10 **Product Groups:** 35, 66

Date of Accounts	Mar 11	Mar 10	Mar 09
Working Capital	-23	-48	-38
Fixed Assets	15	26	31
Current Assets	231	198	188

bjsedgwick.com (B J Sedgwick)
23 Meadowbrook Close, Norwich, NR1 2HJ
Tel: 01603-618514
E-mail: barry@supasedg.freeserve.co.uk
Website: http://www.bjsedgwick.com
Directors: B. Sedgwick (Prop)
No.of Employees: 1 - 10 **Product Groups:** 26, 37, 40, 66

Black Sheep Ltd
9 Penfold Street Aylsham, Norwich, NR11 6ET
Tel: 01263-733142 **Fax:** 01263-735074
E-mail: email@blacksheep.ltd.uk
Website: http://www.blacksheep.ltd.uk
Directors: R. Hoare (MD)
Immediate Holding Company: BLACK SHEEP LIMITED
Registration no: 01679915 **Date established:** 1982
Turnover: £250,000 - £500,000 **No.of Employees:** 1 - 10
Product Groups: 23, 24

Date of Accounts	Jan 12	Jan 11	Jan 10
Working Capital	7	1	-3
Current Assets	118	104	105

Broadland Radiators & Heat Exchangers Ltd
Burton Road, Norwich, NR6 6AU
Tel: 01603-413050 **Fax:** 01603-413066
E-mail: sales@broadlandradiators.co.uk
Website: http://www.broadlandradiators.co.uk
Bank(s): The Royal Bank of Scotland
Directors: B. Craig (Dir)
Immediate Holding Company: BROADLAND RADIATORS AND HEAT EXCHANGERS LIMITED
Registration no: 02541299 **VAT No.:** GB 571 1483 48
Date established: 1990 **Turnover:** £1m - £2m **No.of Employees:** 11 - 20
Product Groups: 39, 40, 48

Date of Accounts	Dec 11	Oct 10	Oct 09
Sales Turnover	3m	N/A	N/A
Pre Tax Profit/Loss	644	N/A	N/A
Working Capital	1m	645	542
Fixed Assets	74	40	50
Current Assets	1m	940	851
Current Liabilities	161	N/A	N/A

Broadland Welding Supplies
Hillcroft 11 Tungate Way, Horstead, Norwich, NR12 7EN
Tel: 01603-737968 **Fax:** 01603-736355
Directors: S. Stone (Prop)
Date established: 1989 **No.of Employees:** 1 - 10 **Product Groups:** 46

Bush Property Management
1 Bridge Court Fishergate, Norwich, NR3 1UF
Tel: 01603-614004 **Fax:** 01603-761276
E-mail: info@bushmanagement.co.uk
Website: http://www.bushmanagement.co.uk
Directors: D. Bush (MD)
Immediate Holding Company: BUSH PROPERTY MANAGEMENT LIMITED
Registration no: 02990063 **Date established:** 1994
Turnover: £250,000 - £500,000 **No.of Employees:** 21 - 50
Product Groups: 80

Date of Accounts	Dec 11	Dec 10	Dec 09
Working Capital	253	262	191
Fixed Assets	56	68	84
Current Assets	336	345	237

C & H Quickmix Ltd (a division of Tarmac Southern Ltd)
Woodlands Dereham Road, New Costessey, Norwich, NR5 0TL
Tel: 01603-740333 **Fax:** 01603-741336
E-mail: enquiries@tarmac-southern.co.uk
Website: http://www.tarmac.co.uk
Directors: G. Drake (Co Sec)
Immediate Holding Company: C. & H. QUICK-MIX LIMITED
Registration no: 00839216 **Date established:** 1965
No.of Employees: 11 - 20 **Product Groups:** 33

Date of Accounts	Dec 11	Dec 10	Dec 09
Working Capital	756	1m	1m
Fixed Assets	990	967	1m
Current Assets	2m	2m	2m

C N C Machine Tools Ltd
Unit 8s Chalk Lane Snetterton, Norwich, NR16 2JZ
Tel: 08701-662529 **Fax:** 08701-662527
E-mail: sales@cncmachinetools.co.uk
Website: http://www.cncmachinetools.co.uk
Directors: P. Lee (MD)
Immediate Holding Company: CNC MACHINE TOOLS LIMITED
Registration no: 04088102 **Date established:** 2000 **Turnover:** £1m - £2m
No.of Employees: 1 - 10 **Product Groups:** 46

Date of Accounts	Dec 09	Dec 08	Mar 12
Working Capital	106	54	258
Fixed Assets	263	212	286
Current Assets	603	419	2m

C P L Petroleum
Drayton Road, Norwich, NR3 2AJ
Tel: 01603-779005 **Fax:** 01553-776439
E-mail: sales@cplpetroleum.co.uk
Website: http://www.cplpetroleum.co.uk
Managers: C. Robinson (Mktg Serv Mgr)
Ultimate Holding Company: CPL INDUSTRIES HOLDINGS LIMITED
Immediate Holding Company: CPL PETROLEUM LIMITED
Registration no: 03003860 **Date established:** 1994
Turnover: £500m - £1,000m **No.of Employees:** 1 - 10
Product Groups: 66

Date of Accounts	Mar 12	Mar 11	Mar 10
Pre Tax Profit/Loss	N/A	878	904
Working Capital	31	30m	30m
Fixed Assets	26	26m	26m
Current Assets	57	56m	56m
Current Liabilities	26	246	253

Cameron Creative Ltd
33 School Lane Sprowston, Norwich, NR7 8TG
Tel: 01603-495487 **Fax:** 01603-495487
E-mail: info@cameroncreative.co.uk
Website: http://www.cameroncreative.co.uk
Directors: E. Cameron (MD)
Immediate Holding Company: CAMERON CREATIVE LTD
Registration no: 05042939 **Date established:** 2004
Turnover: Up to £250,000 **No.of Employees:** 1 - 10 **Product Groups:** 81

Date of Accounts	Mar 11	Mar 10	Mar 09
Working Capital	-4	-5	4
Fixed Assets	4	5	7
Current Assets	7	4	7

Capital Hair & Beauty
3 Burton Road, Norwich, NR6 6AX
Tel: 01603-788778 **Fax:** 01603-788856
E-mail: norwich@capitalhb.co.uk
Website: http://www.capitalhairandbeauty.co.uk
Managers: A. Seamons (Develop Mgr)
Immediate Holding Company: CAPITAL (HAIR AND BEAUTY) LIMITED
Registration no: 00530201 **Date established:** 1954
No.of Employees: 1 - 10 **Product Groups:** 32, 40, 67

Date of Accounts	Dec 11	Dec 10	Dec 09
Sales Turnover	32m	28m	24m
Pre Tax Profit/Loss	4m	749	2m

Working Capital	7m	4m	3m
Fixed Assets	3m	3m	2m
Current Assets	13m	8m	7m
Current Liabilities	4m	3m	3m

Catershop Catering Equipment Ltd

3 Robberds Way Bowthorpe Employment Area, Norwich, NR5 9JF
Tel: 01603-741133 **Fax:** 01603-744255
E-mail: sales@catershop.co.uk
Website: http://www.catershop.co.uk
Directors: D. Holborow (Sales)
Immediate Holding Company: CATERSHOP LIMITED
Registration no: 03273558 **VAT No.:** GB 688 3072 02
Date established: 1996 **Turnover:** £1m - £2m **No.of Employees:** 1 - 10
Product Groups: 40

Date of Accounts	Dec 11	Dec 10	Dec 09
Working Capital	244	224	120
Fixed Assets	14	9	13
Current Assets	1m	818	616

Chapelfield Veterinary Surgeons

Wellesley Road Tharston, Norwich, NR15 2PD
Tel: 01508-530686 **Fax:** 01508-532411
E-mail: cvp.stratton@virgin.net
Directors: D. Stockton (Ptnr)
No.of Employees: 21 - 50 **Product Groups:**

Chatsworth

31 Norwich Road Strumpshaw, Norwich, NR13 4AG
Tel: 01603-716815 **Fax:** 01603-715440
E-mail: sales@chatsworth-dec.co.uk
Website: http://www.chatsworth-dec.co.uk
Directors: W. Hubbard (Dir)
Ultimate Holding Company: MISTROOM LIMITED
Immediate Holding Company: MISTROOM LIMITED
Registration no: 00964739 **Date established:** 1985 **Turnover:** £2m - £5m
No.of Employees: 1 - 10 **Product Groups:** 24, 27, 30, 32, 49

Date of Accounts	Jul 11	Jul 10	Jul 09
Working Capital	N/A	31	31
Fixed Assets	220	220	220
Current Assets	N/A	31	31

Childwise

Queens House Queens Road, Norwich, NR1 3PL
Tel: 01603-630054 **Fax:** 01603-664083
E-mail: research@childwise.co.uk
Website: http://www.childwise.co.uk
Directors: J. Davies (MD)
Immediate Holding Company: CHILDWISE RESEARCH LTD
Registration no: 04285610 **Date established:** 2001
Turnover: £250,000 - £500,000 **No.of Employees:** 1 - 10
Product Groups: 81

Date of Accounts	Jul 11	Jul 10	Jul 09
Sales Turnover	N/A	N/A	307
Pre Tax Profit/Loss	N/A	N/A	-31
Working Capital	-293	-325	-280
Fixed Assets	106	114	122
Current Assets	91	20	64
Current Liabilities	N/A	N/A	11

John Clayden & Partners Lubysil Ltd

9 Frensham Road Sweet Briar Road Industrial Estate, Norwich, NR3 2BT
Tel: 01603-789924 **Fax:** 01603-417335
E-mail: sales@clayden-lubricants.co.uk
Website: http://www.clayden-lubricants.co.uk
Directors: M. Clayden (MD)
Immediate Holding Company: JOHN CLAYDEN & PARTNERS (LUBYSIL) LIMITED
Registration no: 00780157 **VAT No.:** GB 106 0847 92
Date established: 1963 **No.of Employees:** 1 - 10 **Product Groups:** 31, 32, 66

Date of Accounts	Mar 12	Mar 11	Mar 10
Working Capital	85	70	84
Fixed Assets	273	282	231
Current Assets	355	316	260

Colins Mobile Services

The Bungalow Bure Valley Lane, Aylsham, Norwich, NR11 6UA
Tel: 01263-734317 **Fax:** 01263-734317
Directors: C. Chamberlain (Prop)
Date established: 1996 **No.of Employees:** 1 - 10 **Product Groups:** 41

Colour Composites Ltd

Ashtree Works Mill Road, Barnham Broom, Norwich, NR9 4DE
Tel: 01603-759711 **Fax:** 01603-758150
Website: http://www.abcoatings.com
Directors: A. Birchell (MD), C. Sexton (MD), S. Birchall (Co Sec)
Ultimate Holding Company: C A SEXTON (HOLDINGS) LIMITED
Immediate Holding Company: COLOUR COMPOSITES LTD
Registration no: 02770792 **Date established:** 1992
No.of Employees: 11 - 20 **Product Groups:** 46, 48

Date of Accounts	Dec 09	Dec 08	Dec 07
Working Capital	-66	-14	-49
Fixed Assets	162	183	201
Current Assets	116	273	93

Continental Product Engineering Ltd

Loddon Industrial Park Loddon, Norwich, NR14 6JD
Tel: 01508-528060 **Fax:** 01508-528061
E-mail: enquiries@continental-uk.com
Website: http://www.continentalproduct.co.uk
Directors: L. Price (Sales), P. Taylor (Fin)
Managers: N. Hollyoak (Buyer), C. Burton, B. Skinner (Sales Admin), F. Murren (Personnel)
Ultimate Holding Company: FRAMINGHAM HOUSE INVESTMENTS LIMITED
Immediate Holding Company: CONTINENTAL PRODUCT ENGINEERING LIMITED
Registration no: 02700257 **Date established:** 1992 **Turnover:** £5m - £10m
No.of Employees: 21 - 50 **Product Groups:** 13, 33, 36

Date of Accounts	Mar 11	Mar 10	Mar 09
Sales Turnover	N/A	7m	7m
Pre Tax Profit/Loss	N/A	251	140
Working Capital	565	211	54
Fixed Assets	197	157	104
Current Assets	3m	3m	3m
Current Liabilities	N/A	225	213

Cooks Brushes

52 The Street Costessey, Norwich, NR8 5DD
Tel: 01603-748339 **Fax:** 01603-271896
E-mail: sales@cooks-brushes.co.uk
Website: http://www.cooks-brushes.co.uk
Directors: P. Cook (Prop)
Registration no: 01720294 **VAT No.:** GB 426 4753 43
Date established: 1814 **Turnover:** £250,000 - £500,000
No.of Employees: 1 - 10 **Product Groups:** 23, 24, 25, 26, 27, 29, 30, 32, 33, 34, 35, 36, 40, 41, 43, 49, 63, 66

Coombe Video Productions

89 Beloe Avenue, Norwich, NR5 9BL
Tel: 01603-747990
E-mail: sales@coombevideo.com
Website: http://www.coombevideo.com
Directors: J. Wilson (Prop)
No.of Employees: 1 - 10 **Product Groups:** 37, 89

W A Cordaroy

Old Farm Forge East Ruston, Norwich, NR12 9JE
Tel: 01692-650724 **Fax:** 01692-650724
Directors: B. Cordaroy (Prop)
Date established: 1977 **No.of Employees:** 1 - 10 **Product Groups:** 26, 35

Cruz Yardy Engineering

Roundwell Works Dereham Road, New Costessey, Norwich, NR5 0SQ
Tel: 01603-746774 **Fax:** 01603-746774
Directors: T. Gay (Ptnr)
Date established: 1994 **Turnover:** Up to £250,000
No.of Employees: 1 - 10 **Product Groups:** 48

D T Systems Ltd

Lodge Farm Barns New Road, Bawburgh, Norwich, NR9 3LZ
Tel: 01603-731900 **Fax:** 01603-740764
E-mail: info@dtsystems.co.uk
Website: http://www.dtsystems.co.uk
Directors: P. May (Dir)
Immediate Holding Company: D.T. SYSTEMS LIMITED
Registration no: 01667405 **Date established:** 1982
Turnover: £500,000 - £1m **No.of Employees:** 1 - 10 **Product Groups:** 44

Date of Accounts	Dec 11	Dec 10	Dec 09
Working Capital	47	35	49
Fixed Assets	4	2	7
Current Assets	75	87	119

Danwood Group

Seymour House Little Money Road, Loddon, Norwich, NR14 6JD
Tel: 01508-521300 **Fax:** 01508-521319
E-mail: sales@danwood.co.uk
Website: http://www.danwood.co.uk
Managers: R. Wells (Mgr)
Immediate Holding Company: DANWOOD GROUP HOLDINGS LIMITED
Registration no: 06548014 **Date established:** 2008
Turnover: £125m - £250m **No.of Employees:** 11 - 20 **Product Groups:** 44

Date of Accounts	Sep 10	Sep 09	Sep 08
Sales Turnover	220m	194m	86
Pre Tax Profit/Loss	4m	2m	-1
Working Capital	39m	24m	17
Fixed Assets	106m	92m	90
Current Assets	98m	62m	58
Current Liabilities	29m	16m	17

Diatron Assembly Systems Ltd

40 Hurricane Way, Norwich, NR6 6JB
Tel: 01603-484747 **Fax:** 01603-485025
E-mail: sales@diatron.co.uk
Website: http://www.diatron.co.uk
Directors: S. Keeler (Fin), E. Fisher (Dir)
Immediate Holding Company: DIATRON ASSEMBLY SYSTEMS LIMITED
Registration no: 02568000 **Date established:** 1990
No.of Employees: 11 - 20 **Product Groups:** 37

Date of Accounts	Apr 12	Apr 11	Apr 10
Working Capital	250	209	218
Fixed Assets	82	96	113
Current Assets	325	289	272

Dodd Group Eastern Ltd

Delta Close, Norwich, NR6 6BG
Tel: 01603-482288 **Fax:** 01603-487300
E-mail: norwich@doddgroup.com
Website: http://www.doddgroup.com
Bank(s): National Westminster Bank Plc
Directors: T. Dodd (MD)
Managers: G. Arundell (Buyer)
Ultimate Holding Company: DODD GROUP HOLDINGS LIMITED
Immediate Holding Company: DODD GROUP (EASTERN) LIMITED
Registration no: 02842232 **Date established:** 1993
Turnover: £20m - £50m **No.of Employees:** 101 - 250 **Product Groups:** 52

Date of Accounts	Mar 11	Mar 10	Mar 09
Sales Turnover	27m	28m	30m
Pre Tax Profit/Loss	383	159	1m
Working Capital	4m	4m	4m
Fixed Assets	82	132	98
Current Assets	13m	13m	12m
Current Liabilities	2m	1000	1m

Drain Centre a division of Wolseley UK

Green Lane West Rackheath, Norwich, NR13 6LF
Tel: 01603-720611 **Fax:** 01603-721355
E-mail: p18.norwich@wolseley.co.uk
Website: http://www.capperplastics.com
Managers: P. Mureley (District Mgr)
VAT No.: GB 595 4941 88 **No.of Employees:** 1 - 10 **Product Groups:** 30, 31, 35, 36, 39, 40, 42, 48, 66

Drayton Tyre & Battery

16 Drayton Industrial Estate Taverham Road, Drayton, Norwich, NR8 6RL
Tel: 01603-260777 **Fax:** 01603-860879
E-mail: draytontyreandbattery@o2.co.uk
Website: http://www.draytontyres.co.uk
Directors: K. Howard (Dir)
Immediate Holding Company: DRAYTON TYRE & BATTERY LIMITED
Registration no: 05393099 **Date established:** 2005
Turnover: £500,000 - £1m **No.of Employees:** 1 - 10 **Product Groups:** 29, 68

Date of Accounts	Apr 11	Apr 10	Apr 09
Working Capital	-6	-6	-20
Fixed Assets	57	63	68
Current Assets	230	175	160

W L Duffield & Sons Ltd

Ipswich Road Saxlingham Thorpe, Norwich, NR15 1TY
Tel: 01508-470661 **Fax:** 01508-471364
E-mail: alistor.duffield@duffields.co.uk
Website: http://www.duffields.co.uk
Bank(s): National Westminster
Directors: A. Duffield (MD), P. Chase (Co Sec), D. Hills (Fin)
Managers: S. Green (Personnel), R. Wunderle (Buyer), L. Anison (Mktg Serv Mgr)
Ultimate Holding Company: DUFFIELDS MILLS LIMITED
Immediate Holding Company: W.L. DUFFIELD & SONS LIMITED
Registration no: 00320320 **Date established:** 1936
Turnover: £20m - £50m **No.of Employees:** 51 - 100 **Product Groups:** 20

Date of Accounts	Sep 08	Sep 09	Sep 10
Sales Turnover	23m	23m	32m
Pre Tax Profit/Loss	939	522	1m
Working Capital	2m	2m	2m
Fixed Assets	4m	5m	5m
Current Assets	5m	6m	7m
Current Liabilities	426	302	488

Dunhams Of Norwich

Hellesdon Park Road Drayton High Road, Norwich, NR6 5DR
Tel: 01603-424855 **Fax:** 01603-413336
Directors: M. Dunham (Ptnr)
VAT No.: GB 105 2240 29 **Date established:** 1966
No.of Employees: 11 - 20 **Product Groups:** 30

E C Landamore & Co. Ltd

Tunstead Road Hoveton, Norwich, NR12 8QN
Tel: 01603-782212 **Fax:** 01603-784166
E-mail: mail@landamores.co.uk
Website: http://www.landamores.co.uk
Bank(s): HSBC
Directors: A. Landamore (Dir), K. Webster (Pers)
Immediate Holding Company: E.C.LANDAMORE & CO.LIMITED
Registration no: 00548560 **VAT No.:** 105 3351 15 **Date established:** 1955
Turnover: £5m - £10m **No.of Employees:** 51 - 100 **Product Groups:** 39

Date of Accounts	Jun 11	Jun 10	Jun 09
Sales Turnover	6m	5m	6m
Pre Tax Profit/Loss	314	466	395
Working Capital	4m	4m	4m
Fixed Assets	351	379	392
Current Assets	5m	5m	4m
Current Liabilities	645	647	637

E S E Direct

150 Northumberland Street, Norwich, NR2 4EE
Tel: 01603-629956
E-mail: lee@ese.co.uk
Website: http://www.ese.co.uk
Directors: S. Francis (Dir)
Managers: L. Newell (Sales Admin)
Immediate Holding Company: ESE PROJECTS LIMITED
Registration no: 05443891 **Date established:** 2005 **Turnover:**
No.of Employees: 1 - 10 **Product Groups:** 26, 29, 30, 35, 41, 45

Earth and Fire Beads

103 Woodland Road Hellesdon, Norwich, NR6 5RJ
Tel: 01603-424355
E-mail: mail@earthandfirebeads.co.uk
Website: http://earthandfirebeads.blogspot.com
Directors: R. Dawes (Prop)
Date established: 2004 **No.of Employees:** 1 - 10 **Product Groups:** 33

Eastern Cash Registers Ltd

123 Oak Street, Norwich, NR3 3BP
Tel: 01603-610559 **Fax:** 01603-610002
E-mail: tina@ecr-tech.co.uk
Website: http://www.ecr-retail.co.uk
Managers: T. Smith (Sales Admin)
Immediate Holding Company: EASTERN CASH REGISTERS (NORWICH) LIMITED
Registration no: 01215144 **Date established:** 1975
Turnover: £500,000 - £1m **No.of Employees:** 1 - 10 **Product Groups:** 44

Date of Accounts	Oct 11	Oct 10	Oct 09
Working Capital	-4	-54	-145
Fixed Assets	2	8	14
Current Assets	138	150	124

Eastern Storage Equipment Ltd

150 Northumberland Street, Norwich, NR2 4EE
Tel: 01603-629956 **Fax:** 01603-630113
E-mail: simon@ese.co.uk
Website: http://www.esedirect.co.uk
Bank(s): Barclays
Directors: S. Francis (MD), C. Francis (Fin)
Immediate Holding Company: EASTERN STORAGE EQUIPMENT LIMITED
Registration no: 01279230 **VAT No.:** GB 283 2550 59
Date established: 1976 **Turnover:** £1m - £2m **No.of Employees:** 11 - 20
Product Groups: 49, 61, 67

Date of Accounts	Dec 11	Dec 10	Dec 09
Working Capital	210	293	263
Fixed Assets	77	72	25
Current Assets	635	695	522

Eastern Water Treatment Ltd

241 Heigham Street, Norwich, NR2 4LN
Tel: 01603-877222 **Fax:** 01603-877223
E-mail: keith@dolphinspas.co.uk
Website: http://www.easternwatertreatment.com
Directors: K. Parker (MD)
Immediate Holding Company: EASTERN WATER TREATMENT LIMITED
Registration no: 03831728 **Date established:** 1999
No.of Employees: 1 - 10 **Product Groups:** 30, 36, 40

Date of Accounts	Dec 10	Dec 09	Dec 08
Working Capital	-56	-47	-36
Fixed Assets	24	18	16
Current Assets	38	35	36

Easy Lighting (Aladdins Lighting)

Unit 7 Wellesley Road Tharston, Norwich, NR15 2PD
Tel: 01508-532528
E-mail: info@easylighting.co.uk
Website: http://www.easylighting.co.uk

see next page

Easy Lighting (Aladdins Lighting) *- Cont'd*

Directors: S. Hiscox (Prop)
Immediate Holding Company: INTERNET TRADING LTD
Date established: 2010 **No.of Employees:** 1 - 10 **Product Groups:** 37, 67, 84

Date of Accounts	Jul 11
Working Capital	4
Fixed Assets	27
Current Assets	12

Elephant I T

42 Wolfe Road, Norwich, NR1 4HT
Tel: 01603-498999
E-mail: sales@elephant-it.co.uk
Website: http://www.elephant-it.co.uk
Directors: T. Wiseman (Prop)
Immediate Holding Company: NORWICH I.T. LTD
Registration no: 06151427 **Date established:** 2007
Turnover: Up to £250,000 **No.of Employees:** 1 - 10 **Product Groups:** 44

Date of Accounts	Mar 11	Mar 10
Working Capital	-12	N/A
Fixed Assets	17	1
Current Assets	15	N/A

Elite Gift Boxes

Arena Building Vulcan Road North, Norwich, NR6 6AQ
Tel: 01603-418153 **Fax:** 01603-417333
E-mail: info@elitegiftboxes.co.uk
Website: http://www.elitegiftboxes.co.uk
Directors: A. Bovington (MD)
Registration no: 02053063 **Date established:** 1986
Turnover: Up to £250,000 **No.of Employees:** 1 - 10 **Product Groups:** 22, 30, 35

Eriks Electrical Mechanical Services Ltd (Norwich Service Centre)

Lansdowne Road Fifers Lane Industrial Estate, Norwich, NR6 6NF
Tel: 01603-416621 **Fax:** 01603-418213
E-mail: david.burroughs@eriks.co.uk
Website: http://www.eriks.co.uk
Bank(s): The Royal bank Of Scotland
Managers: D. Burroughs (Mgr)
Registration no: 03142338 **VAT No.:** GB 277 2632 40
Date established: 1960 **Turnover:** £50m - £75m
No.of Employees: 11 - 20 **Product Groups:** 48, 85

Euro Frame Ltd

20 Murrayfield Road, Norwich, NR6 6NQ
Tel: 01603-418880 **Fax:** 01603-418881
Directors: J. Rix (Dir), C. Watts (Co Sec)
Immediate Holding Company: EUROFRAME LIMITED
Registration no: 04663557 **Date established:** 2003
No.of Employees: 1 - 10 **Product Groups:** 46

Date of Accounts	Mar 12	Mar 11	Mar 10
Working Capital	119	89	58
Fixed Assets	90	89	72
Current Assets	299	236	145

F D A Packaging Machinery

11 Mahoney Green Green Lane West, Rackheath, Norwich, NR13 6JY
Tel: 01603-721804 **Fax:** 01603-721814
E-mail: sales@fda-packaging.com
Website: http://www.fda-packaging.com
Directors: P. Hodgkinson (Dir)
Date established: 1991 **No.of Employees:** 1 - 10 **Product Groups:** 38, 42

F6 Ltd

Unit 30 Witchcraft Way Rackheath, Norwich, NR13 6GA
Tel: 01603-722997 **Fax:** 01603-722998
E-mail: info@fsix.co.uk
Website: http://fsix.co.uk
Directors: M. Ottolangui (MD)
Immediate Holding Company: F6 LIMITED
Registration no: 04146290 **Date established:** 2001
Turnover: £250,000 - £500,000 **No.of Employees:** 1 - 10
Product Groups: 36, 40, 41, 67

Date of Accounts	Apr 11	Apr 10	Apr 09
Working Capital	13	19	7
Fixed Assets	1	1	2
Current Assets	34	33	43

Fabcon Projects Ltd

Delta Close, Norwich, NR6 6BG
Tel: 01603-482338 **Fax:** 01603-484064
E-mail: sales@fabcon.co.uk
Website: http://www.fabcon.co.uk
Directors: A. Peek (MD)
Immediate Holding Company: FABCON PROJECTS LIMITED
Registration no: 02663523 **Date established:** 1991
No.of Employees: 21 - 50 **Product Groups:** 35

Date of Accounts	Mar 11	Mar 10	Mar 09
Working Capital	-217	-239	-144
Fixed Assets	141	160	176
Current Assets	472	202	345
Current Liabilities	N/A	N/A	15

Feilden & Mawson LLP

1 Ferry Road, Norwich, NR1 1SU
Tel: 01603-629571 **Fax:** 01603-633569
E-mail: roberttodd@feildenandmawson.com
Website: http://www.feildenandmawson.com
Bank(s): Barclays
Directors: R. Todd (Snr Part), H. Feilden (Ptnr)
Immediate Holding Company: FEILDEN + MAWSON LLP
Registration no: OC300486 **VAT No.:** GB 105 1174 21
Date established: 2001 **Turnover:** £2m - £5m **No.of Employees:** 21 - 50
Product Groups: 80, 84

Date of Accounts	Mar 12	Mar 11	Mar 10
Working Capital	1m	1m	1m
Fixed Assets	290	282	298
Current Assets	2m	2m	1m

Fendercare

Enterprise House Harveys Lane, Seething, Norwich, NR15 1EN
Tel: 01508-482691 **Fax:** 01508-482710
E-mail: sales@fendercare.com
Website: http://www.fendercare.com
Managers: J. Rogers (Mgr)
Registration no: 03075910 **Turnover:** £1m - £2m
No.of Employees: 51 - 100 **Product Groups:** 39

Fereday Lewin Associates

1 Cathedral Street, Norwich, NR1 1LU
Tel: 01603-633832 **Fax:** 01603-633832
Directors: M. Lewin (Ptnr)
Immediate Holding Company: STAIRLIFTS AND SCOOTERS LIMITED
Registration no: 04974509 **Date established:** 2009
No.of Employees: 1 - 10 **Product Groups:** 35

Find A Part Ltd

The Royal Business Centre 25 Bank Plain, Norwich, NR2 4SF
Tel: 01603-283555
E-mail: matt@find-a-part.com
Website: http://www.find-a-part.com
Managers: J. Dobson (I.T. Exec), M. Campbell (Mgr)
Immediate Holding Company: FIND-A-PART LIMITED
Registration no: 02853712 **Date established:** 1993
Turnover: Up to £250,000 **No.of Employees:** 1 - 10 **Product Groups:** 34, 68

Date of Accounts	Dec 10	Dec 09	Dec 08
Sales Turnover	219m	157m	208m
Pre Tax Profit/Loss	3m	2m	3m
Working Capital	4m	5m	3m
Fixed Assets	362	295	369
Current Assets	31m	28m	33m
Current Liabilities	8m	11m	11m

Finlex International Ltd

1 Bunkell Road Rackheath Industrial Estate, Rackheath, Norwich, NR13 6PU
Tel: 08452-410487 **Fax:** 0845-241 2241
E-mail: kay.partner@finlexuk.com
Website: http://www.finlexuk.co.uk
Managers: K. Partner
Ultimate Holding Company: VANCEBUILD LIMITED
Immediate Holding Company: FINLEX INTERNATIONAL LIMITED
Registration no: 05756419 **Date established:** 2006
No.of Employees: 1 - 10 **Product Groups:** 35

Date of Accounts	Dec 11	Dec 10	Dec 09
Working Capital	423	188	39
Fixed Assets	9	6	9
Current Assets	753	756	621

Fitzmaurice Carriers Ltd

Avian Way Salhouse Road, Norwich, NR7 9AJ
Tel: 01603-788444 **Fax:** 01603-788562
E-mail: admin@fitzmaurice.co.uk
Website: http://www.fitzmaurice.co.uk
Bank(s): Lloyds TSB Bank plc
Directors: D. Fitzmaurice (Dir)
Immediate Holding Company: FITZMAURICE CARRIERS LIMITED
Registration no: 00841538 **Date established:** 1965 **Turnover:** £2m - £5m
No.of Employees: 21 - 50 **Product Groups:** 72, 77

Date of Accounts	Nov 11	Nov 10	Nov 09
Working Capital	1m	1m	981
Fixed Assets	499	510	492
Current Assets	2m	1m	1m

The Florida Group

Dibden Road, Norwich, NR3 4RR
Tel: 01603-426341 **Fax:** 01603-424354
E-mail: mailroom@floridagroup.co.uk
Website: http://www.floridagroup.co.uk
Bank(s): Barclays
Directors: S. Goodman (Ch), P. Clarke (Fin)
Managers: A. Stone (Purch Mgr), G. Hadley, J. Larke (Mktg Serv Mgr), J. McAvoy (Tech Serv Mgr)
Immediate Holding Company: EASTLEA LIMITED
Registration no: 01990262 **Date established:** 1986 **Turnover:** £5m - £10m
No.of Employees: 51 - 100 **Product Groups:** 22

Date of Accounts	Dec 11	Dec 10	Dec 09
Working Capital	974	947	689
Fixed Assets	645	645	820
Current Assets	989	969	714

Flowrite Industrial Dampers Ltd

The Glass House Kings Lane, Norwich, NR1 3PS
Tel: 01603-633163 **Fax:** 01603-633763
E-mail: sales@industrialdampers.com
Website: http://www.industrialdampers.com
Directors: P. Stevens (Co Sec)
Immediate Holding Company: FLOWRITE INDUSTRIAL DAMPERS LIMITED
Registration no: 02889661 **Date established:** 1994
Turnover: £500,000 - £1m **No.of Employees:** 1 - 10 **Product Groups:** 38

Date of Accounts	Mar 11	Mar 10	Mar 09
Working Capital	101	105	124
Fixed Assets	8	6	7
Current Assets	227	189	275

Franchise Development Services Ltd

Franchise House 56 Surrey Street, Norwich, NR1 3FD
Tel: 01603-620301 **Fax:** 01603-630174
E-mail: roy@fdsltd.com
Website: http://www.fdsfranchise.com
Bank(s): Barclays
Directors: R. Seaman (MD)
Immediate Holding Company: FRANCHISE DEVELOPMENT SERVICES LIMITED
Registration no: 01592312 **Date established:** 1981
No.of Employees: 11 - 20 **Product Groups:** 28, 80, 81

Date of Accounts	Mar 11	Mar 10	Mar 09
Working Capital	-18	-45	-94
Fixed Assets	79	92	106
Current Assets	269	193	195

Freightforce Distribution Ltd

1a Guardian Road Industrial Estate Guardian Road, Norwich, NR5 8PF
Tel: 01603-630011 **Fax:** 01603-630012
E-mail: sales@freightforce.co.uk
Website: http://www.freightforce.co.uk
Directors: N. Jolley (Chief Op Offcr)
Turnover: £2m - £5m **No.of Employees:** 11 - 20 **Product Groups:** 77

Date of Accounts	Dec 07	Dec 06	Dec 05
Working Capital	266	-85	-176
Fixed Assets	754	934	699
Current Assets	1196	712	1088
Current Liabilities	930	797	1263
Total Share Capital	6	6	7

French Marine Motors Ltd

Unit 19 Rackheath Industrial Estate Rackheath, Norwich, NR13 6LR
Tel: 01603-722079 **Fax:** 01603-721311
E-mail: norfolk@frenchmarine.com
Website: http://www.frenchmarine.com
Managers: S. Partridge (Mgr)
Immediate Holding Company: FRENCH MARINE MOTORS LIMITED
Registration no: 01455234 **Date established:** 1979
No.of Employees: 1 - 10 **Product Groups:** 35, 36, 39

Date of Accounts	Oct 11	Oct 10	Oct 09
Working Capital	19	57	125
Fixed Assets	143	122	139
Current Assets	666	677	794

G H P Solicitors Greenland Houchen Pomeroy

36 - 40 Prince of Wales Road, Norwich, NR1 1HZ
Tel: 01603-660744 **Fax:** 01603-610700
E-mail: james-knight@ghlaw.co.uk
Website: http://www.greenlandhp-solicitors.co.uk
Managers: J. Knight
Immediate Holding Company: GREENLAND HOUCHEN POMEROY LIMITED
Registration no: 02697947 **Date established:** 1992
No.of Employees: 21 - 50 **Product Groups:** 80

Genesis Lifts Ltd

Drayton Old Lodge 146 Drayton High Road, Drayton, Norwich, NR8 6AN
Tel: 01603-861631 **Fax:** 0700-585 0036
E-mail: enquiries@genesislifts.co.uk
Website: http://www.genesislifts.co.uk
Directors: T. Sherwood (MD)
Immediate Holding Company: GENESIS LIFTS LIMITED
Registration no: 04064590 **Date established:** 2000
No.of Employees: 1 - 10 **Product Groups:** 34, 37, 38, 45, 48, 67, 83, 84

Date of Accounts	Sep 11	Sep 10	Sep 09
Working Capital	491	370	261
Fixed Assets	9	11	5
Current Assets	886	742	588

Grain Handling Services

96 School Road Drayton, Norwich, NR8 6EN
Tel: 01603-867468 **Fax:** 01603-867468
E-mail: peter@ghsnorwich.plus.com
Directors: P. Reeve (Prop)
Date established: 2002 **No.of Employees:** 1 - 10 **Product Groups:** 41

Griffin Marine

10 Griffin Lane, Norwich, NR7 0SL
Tel: 01603-433253
Website: http://www.griffinmarine.org.uk
Directors: L. Culyer (Ptnr)
Immediate Holding Company: GRIFFIN MARINA LIMITED
Registration no: 08136539 **Date established:** 2012
No.of Employees: 1 - 10 **Product Groups:** 35, 36, 39

Date of Accounts	Apr 11	Apr 09	Apr 08
Working Capital	10	31	43
Fixed Assets	1	1	1
Current Assets	20	43	53

H R P Ltd

4-6 Murrayfield Road, Norwich, NR6 6NQ
Tel: 01603-409616 **Fax:** 01603-400464
E-mail: norwich@hrponline.co.uk
Website: http://www.hrponline.co.uk
Managers: A. Reynolds (District Mgr)
Ultimate Holding Company: HRP HOLDINGS LIMITED
Immediate Holding Company: HRP LIMITED
Registration no: 00832237 **Date established:** 1964
Turnover: £50m - £75m **No.of Employees:** 1 - 10 **Product Groups:** 40, 66

Date of Accounts	Dec 11	Dec 10	Dec 09
Sales Turnover	55m	52m	46m
Pre Tax Profit/Loss	1m	1m	651
Working Capital	8m	7m	6m
Fixed Assets	2m	2m	3m
Current Assets	22m	22m	17m
Current Liabilities	3m	4m	3m

Hamlin Electronics Europe Ltd

Broadland Business Park, Norwich, NR7 0WG.
Tel: 01603-257700 **Fax:** 01379-649702
E-mail: sales.uk@hamlin.com
Website: http://www.hamlin.com
Bank(s): National Westminster Bank Plc
Directors: A. Howell (Pres), M. Scharff (Dir), S. Boyd (MD), L. Guptill (Fin)
Managers: J. Bird (Intern Sales En), M. Beal (Sales Prom)
Ultimate Holding Company: KEY SAFETY SYSTEMS INC (USA)
Registration no: 00691700 **VAT No.:** GB 363 5992 18
Date established: 1961 **Turnover:** £10m - £20m
No.of Employees: 101 - 250 **Product Groups:** 37, 39

Date of Accounts	Dec 07	Dec 06	Dec 05
Sales Turnover	18433	18233	17376
Pre Tax Profit/Loss	2011	1944	1418
Working Capital	6545	4696	3117
Fixed Assets	2201	2602	2932
Current Assets	8925	6752	4690
Current Liabilities	2380	2056	1573
Total Share Capital	5004	5004	5004
ROCE% (Return on Capital Employed)	23.0	26.6	23.4
ROT% (Return on Turnover)	10.9	10.7	8.2

Harford Attachments Ltd

The Coach Works Burton Road, Norwich, NR6 6AX
Tel: 01603-403099 **Fax:** 01603-402399
E-mail: info@harfordattachments.co.uk
Website: http://www.harfordattachments.co.uk
Directors: A. Kidd (Fin), S. Kidd (Dir)
Managers: A. Lake (Tech Serv Mgr)
Immediate Holding Company: HARFORD MANUFACTURING LIMITED
Registration no: 02732002 **Date established:** 1992 **Turnover:** £2m - £5m
No.of Employees: 21 - 50 **Product Groups:** 67

Date of Accounts	Jul 07	Jul 06	Jul 05
Pre Tax Profit/Loss	233	217	N/A
Working Capital	511	356	170

Fixed Assets	683	717	798
Current Assets	2m	2m	2m
Current Liabilities	785	469	N/A

Harrison Group Enviromental Ltd
12 Kimberley Street, Norwich, NR2 2RJ
Tel: 01603-613111 **Fax:** 01603-618120
E-mail: info@harrisongroupuk.com
Website: http://www.harrisongroupuk.com
Directors: A. Stewart (Fin), S. Williams (MD), L. Harrison (Fin)
Managers: A. Cottam (Tech Serv Mgr), H. Chapman (Buyer)
Immediate Holding Company: HARRISON GROUP ENVIRONMENTAL LIMITED
Registration no: 01306165 **Date established:** 1977
No.of Employees: 21 - 50 **Product Groups:** 54, 85

Date of Accounts	Mar 11	Mar 10	Mar 09
Working Capital	70	110	34
Fixed Assets	104	112	145
Current Assets	625	531	516

Hartwell Norwich South
591 Hall Road, Norwich, NR4 6AJ
Tel: 08443-247410 **Fax:** 01603-203007
E-mail: jason.watts@hartwell.co.uk
Website: http://www.hartwell.co.uk
Bank(s): Barclays
Directors: J. Watts (MD)
Managers: J. Watts (Chief Mgr), M. Hanford (Sales Prom Mgr), J. Watt (Chief Mgr), S. Olley (Chief Acct)
Immediate Holding Company: HARTWELL HOLDINGS LTD
Registration no: 00155302 **VAT No.:** GB 194 3655 35
Turnover: £250,000 - £500,000 **No.of Employees:** 21 - 50
Product Groups: 39, 68, 82

Heath Lambert Group
Grosvenor House 112-114 Prince of Wales Road, Norwich, NR1 1NS
Tel: 01603-828200 **Fax:** 01603-760852
E-mail: marketing@heathlambert.com
Website: http://www.heathlambert.com
Managers: G. Threadgill
Ultimate Holding Company: HLG HOLDINGS LIMITED
Immediate Holding Company: HEATH LAMBERT GROUP LIMITED
Registration no: 05347036 **Date established:** 2005
Turnover: £125m - £250m **No.of Employees:** 21 - 50
Product Groups: 80, 82

Date of Accounts	Dec 10	Dec 09	Dec 07
Sales Turnover	N/A	N/A	114m
Pre Tax Profit/Loss	N/A	N/A	24m
Working Capital	N/A	N/A	68m
Fixed Assets	N/A	N/A	14m
Current Assets	N/A	N/A	376m
Current Liabilities	N/A	N/A	308m

Heatrae Sadia
1 Hurricane Way, Norwich, NR6 6EA
Tel: 01603-420100 **Fax:** 01603-420219
E-mail: paul.rivett@baxigroup.com
Website: http://www.heatraesadia.com
Bank(s): Lloyds TSB Bank plc
Directors: P. Rivett (MD)
Managers: K. Fisher (Comptroller), M. Leam (Tech Serv Mgr), P. Hundleby (Purch Mgr), J. King (Personnel), J. Cockburn (Sales & Mktg Mg)
Immediate Holding Company: HEATRAE SADIA HEATING LIMITED
Registration no: 00313551 **VAT No.:** GB 439 4758 08
Date established: 1936 **Turnover:** £50m - £75m
No.of Employees: 101 - 250 **Product Groups:** 35, 37, 40

Helionova Ltd
19 Frensham Road, Norwich, NR3 2BT
Tel: 01603-789010 **Fax:** 01603-789453
E-mail: sales@helionova.co.uk
Website: http://www.helionova.co.uk
Bank(s): Barclays
Directors: R. Warden (MD), J. Fabels (Fin)
Managers: M. Ivany (Tech Serv Mgr)
Immediate Holding Company: HELIONOVA LIMITED
Registration no: 01735738 **VAT No.:** GB 394 1706 38
Date established: 1983 **Turnover:** £2m - £5m **No.of Employees:** 21 - 50
Product Groups: 37, 40, 61, 83

Date of Accounts	Dec 11	Dec 10	Dec 09
Working Capital	-762	-860	-950
Fixed Assets	93	197	290
Current Assets	899	886	976

Howarth R A Engineering Ltd
Unit 28 Earl Road Rackheath, Norwich, NR13 6NT
Tel: 01603-721155 **Fax:** 01603-721648
E-mail: sales@howarthengineering.com
Website: http://www.howarthengineering.com
Bank(s): Barclays
Directors: C. Randall (Co Sec), A. Randall (MD)
Immediate Holding Company: R.A. HOWARTH (ENGINEERING) LIMITED
Registration no: 01660166 **VAT No.:** GB 107 0799 71
Date established: 1982 **Turnover:** £1m - £2m **No.of Employees:** 11 - 20
Product Groups: 46, 48

Date of Accounts	Sep 11	Sep 10	Sep 09
Working Capital	32	49	155
Fixed Assets	240	276	311
Current Assets	233	213	341

Hubbard Architectural Metal Work Ltd
3 Hurricane Way, Norwich, NR6 6HS
Tel: 01603-424817 **Fax:** 01603-487158
E-mail: email@hubbardsmetalwork.co.uk
Website: http://www.hubbardsmetalwork.co.uk
Bank(s): National Westminster Bank Plc
Directors: A. Hubbard (Sales), D. Spashett (Co Sec), D. O'Conner (Fin), M. Hubbard (Dir), T. Hubbard (MD)
Managers: C. Coulthard (Personnel), M. Didwell (Buyer), M. Watson (Tech Serv Mgr)
Immediate Holding Company: HUBBARD ARCHITECTURAL METALWORK LIMITED
Registration no: 00702744 **VAT No.:** GB 105 5363 95
Date established: 1961 **Turnover:** £5m - £10m
No.of Employees: 51 - 100 **Product Groups:** 35, 39

Date of Accounts	Sep 11	Sep 10	Sep 09
Sales Turnover	6m	5m	6m
Pre Tax Profit/Loss	-127	-203	306
Working Capital	835	767	983
Fixed Assets	1m	1m	1m
Current Assets	2m	3m	2m
Current Liabilities	255	380	446

Ibonhart
20 Barnard Road Bowthorpe Employment Area, Norwich, NR5 9JB
Tel: 01603-747456 **Fax:** 01603-749757
E-mail: sales@ibonhart.co.uk
Website: http://www.ibonhart.co.uk
Bank(s): Barclays
Directors: C. Barfe (Sales)
Ultimate Holding Company: BARFE HOLDINGS LIMITED
Immediate Holding Company: IBONHART (NORWICH) LIMITED
Registration no: 01503766 **Date established:** 1980 **Turnover:** £1m - £2m
No.of Employees: 11 - 20 **Product Groups:** 41, 42, 84

Date of Accounts	Sep 11	Sep 10	Sep 09
Working Capital	189	135	187
Fixed Assets	13	12	12
Current Assets	617	347	431

I C T C Ltd
3 Caley Close Sweet Briar Road Industrial Estate, Norwich, NR3 2BU
Tel: 01603-488019 **Fax:** 01603-488020
E-mail: sales@ictc.co.uk
Website: http://www.ictc.co.uk
Bank(s): National Westminster Bank Plc
Directors: B. Crane (MD), W. Poyton (Fin)
Managers: F. Elliott (Sales Admin)
Ultimate Holding Company: ICTC
Immediate Holding Company: HETHEL PROPERTIES LTD
Registration no: 04329008 **VAT No.:** GB 625 6400 56
Turnover: £2m - £5m **No.of Employees:** 21 - 50 **Product Groups:** 33

Inchcape East Anglia Ltd
Cromer Road, Norwich, NR6 6NA
Tel: 01603-788887 **Fax:** 01473-462117
Website: http://www.inchcape.co.uk/vovlo/norwich
Managers: M. Lawrence
Ultimate Holding Company: INCHCAPE PLC
Immediate Holding Company: INCHCAPE EAST (ACRE) LIMITED
Registration no: 02948466 **Date established:** 1994
Turnover: £250,000 - £500,000 **No.of Employees:** 51 - 100
Product Groups: 68

Date of Accounts	Dec 11	Dec 10	Dec 09
Sales Turnover	N/A	N/A	490
Pre Tax Profit/Loss	-487	-617	44
Working Capital	N/A	-13	623
Fixed Assets	N/A	500	500
Current Assets	N/A	N/A	2m
Current Liabilities	N/A	N/A	14

Incotes Ltd
The Street Lamas, Norwich, NR10 5AF
Tel: 01603-279995 **Fax:** 01603-279928
E-mail: incotes@btinternet.com
Directors: H. Gregory (Dir)
Immediate Holding Company: INCOTES LIMITED
Registration no: 00831444 **VAT No.:** GB 234 6431 76
Date established: 1964 **Turnover:** £1m - £2m **No.of Employees:** 1 - 10
Product Groups: 45

Date of Accounts	Dec 11	Dec 10	Dec 09
Working Capital	150	141	237
Fixed Assets	12	5	8
Current Assets	472	473	750
Current Liabilities	30	34	25

Initial Cleaning Services
1 Naylor Road Sweet Briar Road Industrial Estate, Norwich, NR3 2BZ
Tel: 01603-787101 **Fax:** 01603-406431
E-mail: ian.pickett@rentokil-initial.com
Website: http://www.initial.co.uk
Managers: J. Stathan (Sales Admin), I. Pickett (Mgr), S. Fiske (Mgr)
Ultimate Holding Company: RENTOKIL INITIAL PLC
Immediate Holding Company: BET UK LTD
Registration no: 02329448 **VAT No.:** GB 625 9496 02
Turnover: £75m - £125m **No.of Employees:** 1 - 10 **Product Groups:** 52

Inviron Ltd
40 Curtis Road, Norwich, NR6 6RB
Tel: 01603-258500 **Fax:** 01603-301398
Website: http://www.inviron.co.uk
Bank(s): HSBC Bank plc
Managers: A. Woodrow
Ultimate Holding Company: IMTECH NV (NETHERLANDS)
Immediate Holding Company: INVIRON LIMITED
Registration no: 04956673 **VAT No.:** GB 229 9038 40
Date established: 2003 **Turnover:** £75m - £125m
No.of Employees: 51 - 100 **Product Groups:** 52

Date of Accounts	Dec 11	Dec 10	Dec 09
Sales Turnover	137m	130m	137m
Pre Tax Profit/Loss	3m	1m	2m
Working Capital	12m	11m	11m
Fixed Assets	1m	774	844
Current Assets	42m	39m	38m
Current Liabilities	9m	7m	9m

Jeckells & Son Ltd
Riverside Road Hoveton, Norwich, NR12 8UQ
Tel: 01603-784488 **Fax:** 01603-783234
E-mail: jeckellstrimmers@ukgateway.net
Website: http://www.jeckells.net
Bank(s): National Westminster Bank Plc
Directors: P. Jeckells (Dir)
Immediate Holding Company: JECKELLS & SON LIMITED
Registration no: 00226663 **VAT No.:** GB 105 3396 90
Date established: 2027 **Turnover:** £500,000 - £1m
No.of Employees: 11 - 20 **Product Groups:** 23, 24, 26, 74

Date of Accounts	Oct 11	Oct 10	Oct 09
Working Capital	133	101	140
Fixed Assets	43	55	32
Current Assets	393	450	377

Jeckells Of Wroxham Ltd
Station Road Hoveton, Norwich, NR12 8UT
Tel: 01603-782223 **Fax:** 01603-784023
E-mail: sales@jeckells.co.uk
Website: http://www.jeckells.co.uk
Bank(s): Natwest
Directors: C. Jeckells (MD)
Immediate Holding Company: JECKELLS OF WROXHAM LIMITED
Registration no: 03574531 **VAT No.:** GB 711 6897 22
Date established: 1998 **Turnover:** £500,000 - £1m
No.of Employees: 11 - 20 **Product Groups:** 23, 24, 35

Date of Accounts	Oct 11	Oct 10	Oct 09
Working Capital	134	138	135
Fixed Assets	60	62	66
Current Assets	338	339	318

Jewson Ltd
8 Fletcher Way Weston Road, Norwich, NR3 3ST
Tel: 01603-402201 **Fax:** 01603-403811
E-mail: talk2dave@frazer.eu.com
Website: http://www.frazer.eu.com
Directors: S. Warrick (MD)
Managers: D. Potter (District Mgr)
Registration no: 00348407 **VAT No.:** GB 451 2528 69
Turnover: £2m - £5m **No.of Employees:** 1 - 10 **Product Groups:** 30, 36, 39, 40, 66

Joining Techologies Eastern Ltd
9 Furze Road, Norwich, NR7 0AS
Tel: 01603-437036 **Fax:** 01603-431106
Website: http://www.paston.co.uk
Directors: B. Gayton (Prop)
Immediate Holding Company: JOINING TECHNOLOGIES (EASTERN) LIMITED
Registration no: 04622968 **Date established:** 2002
No.of Employees: 1 - 10 **Product Groups:** 46

Date of Accounts	Dec 11	Dec 10	Dec 09
Working Capital	11	18	6
Fixed Assets	N/A	N/A	1
Current Assets	111	82	70

Jones & Cane
Unit 3-4 Oaktree Business Park Basey Road Rackheath, Norwich, NR13 6PZ
Tel: 01603-722264 **Fax:** 01603-722269
E-mail: enquiries@jonesandcane.co.uk
Website: http://www.jonesandcane.co.uk
Directors: B. Jones (Ptnr)
Date established: 1999 **No.of Employees:** 1 - 10 **Product Groups:** 38, 42

B W Keenan
83 Barker Street, Norwich, NR2 4TN
Tel: 01603-617553
Directors: B. Keenan (Prop)
Date established: 1988 **No.of Employees:** 1 - 10 **Product Groups:** 35

Keep I.T. Clean
258 Dereham Road New Costessey, Norwich, NR5 0SN
Tel: 01603-813170
E-mail: info@keep-it-clean.co.uk
Website: http://www.keep-it-clean.co.uk
Directors: C. Burke (Prop)
Registration no: 06506971 **Date established:** 1997
No.of Employees: 1 - 10 **Product Groups:** 44, 52

Kelcrow
Unit 7 Damgate Lane Acle, Norwich, NR13 3DJ
Tel: 01493-750780
E-mail: kelcrow@ymail.com
Website: http://www.acle.fsbusiness.co.uk
Directors: K. Crowson (Prop)
Date established: 1990 **No.of Employees:** 1 - 10 **Product Groups:** 35

Kenninghall Engineering
Fersfield Road Kenninghall, Norwich, NR16 2DP
Tel: 01379-688286 **Fax:** 01379-688041
Website: http://www.kegroup.co.uk
Directors: S. Condick (Co Sec)
Immediate Holding Company: KENNINGHALL ENGINEERING LIMITED
Registration no: 06119025 **Date established:** 2007
Turnover: £500,000 - £1m **No.of Employees:** 21 - 50
Product Groups: 35, 39, 45

Date of Accounts	Aug 11	Aug 10	Aug 09
Sales Turnover	540	511	530
Pre Tax Profit/Loss	N/A	4	19
Working Capital	-48	3	3
Fixed Assets	148	79	47
Current Assets	301	258	219
Current Liabilities	N/A	170	50

Kirton Health Care Group Ltd
The Street Hempnall, Norwich, NR15 2AD
Tel: 01508-498413 **Fax:** 01508-498491
No.of Employees: 11 - 20 **Product Groups:** 26, 36, 40

D Knowles
Cromer Road Lower Gresham, Norwich, NR11 8RF
Tel: 01263-577371 **Fax:** 01263-577371
E-mail: davidknowles@tesco.com
Directors: D. Knowles (Prop)
Date established: 1986 **No.of Employees:** 1 - 10 **Product Groups:** 40

Linacre Locksmiths
41 Linacre Avenue Sprowston, Norwich, NR7 8JZ
Tel: 07977-576655
E-mail: linacrelocks@aol.com
Website: http://www.linacrelocksmiths.com
Directors: W. Lever (Prop)
Turnover: Up to £250,000 **No.of Employees:** 1 - 10 **Product Groups:** 52

Litho Supplies
3 Hellesdon Park Road Drayton High Road, Norwich, NR6 5DR
Tel: 01603-416783 **Fax:** 01603-485735
E-mail: enquiries@litho.co.uk
Website: http://www.litho.co.uk
Directors: M. Hammond (Grp Chief Exec), J. Byford (Ch)
Managers: A. Jones (Buyer), B. Mayler (Sales Prom Mgr), B. Naylor (Mgr)
Ultimate Holding Company: HILCO TRADING LLC (UNITED STATES OF AMERICA)
Immediate Holding Company: LITHO SUPPLIES (UK) LIMITED
Registration no: 07088832 **Date established:** 2009
Turnover: £50m - £75m **No.of Employees:** 1 - 10 **Product Groups:** 28, 38, 44, 67

see next page

***Litho Supplies** - Cont'd*

Date of Accounts	Dec 10
Sales Turnover	14m
Pre Tax Profit/Loss	-408
Working Capital	-491
Fixed Assets	83
Current Assets	4m
Current Liabilities	3m

Loddon Engineering Ltd
Little Money Road Loddon, Norwich, NR14 6JJ
Tel: 01508-520744 **Fax:** 01508-528055
E-mail: sales@loddon.co.uk
Website: http://www.loddon.co.uk
Directors: R. Buck (MD)
Ultimate Holding Company: PPJ LTD (IOM)
Immediate Holding Company: ROOFLITE LIMITED
Registration no: 02293123 **VAT No.:** GB 532 8801 47
Date established: 1988 **Turnover:** £1m - £2m **No.of Employees:** 11 - 20
Product Groups: 25

Date of Accounts	Mar 07	Dec 10	Dec 09
Working Capital	504	226	437
Fixed Assets	728	N/A	N/A
Current Assets	1m	258	476

Lomax Technical Services Ltd
Unit 4 Snetterton Business Park Chalk Lane, Snetterton, Norwich, NR16 2JZ
Tel: 01953-888967 **Fax:** 01953-887807
E-mail: gen@lomaxtech.com
Website: http://www.lomaxtech.com
Managers: S. Humphrey (Sales Admin)
Immediate Holding Company: LOMAX TECHNICAL SERVICES LIMITED
Registration no: 03458788 **Date established:** 1997
No.of Employees: 1 - 10 **Product Groups:** 40, 41

Date of Accounts	Oct 11	Oct 10	Oct 09
Working Capital	1m	946	804
Fixed Assets	195	136	121
Current Assets	2m	2m	1m

Maplin Electronics Ltd
Castle Meadow, Norwich, NR1 3DH
Tel: 01603-630044 **Fax:** 01603-661823
Website: http://www.maplin.co.uk
Managers: J. Norman (Mgr)
Ultimate Holding Company: MONTAGU PRIVATE EQUITY LLP
Immediate Holding Company: MAPLIN ELECTRONICS LIMITED
Registration no: 01264385 **Date established:** 1976
Turnover: £125m - £250m **No.of Employees:** 11 - 20
Product Groups: 37, 61

Date of Accounts	Dec 07	Dec 08	Dec 09
Sales Turnover	180m	204m	204m
Pre Tax Profit/Loss	24m	32m	35m
Working Capital	28m	49m	75m
Fixed Assets	26m	28m	28m
Current Assets	78m	108m	142m
Current Liabilities	44m	51m	59m

Marel Ltd
Gresham House Pinetrees Road, Norwich, NR7 9BB
Tel: 01603-700755 **Fax:** 01603-700844
E-mail: norwich@marel.com
Website: http://www.marel.co.uk
Directors: A. Hay (Co Sec)
Managers: K. Debacker (Factory Mgr)
Ultimate Holding Company: MAREL HF (ICELAND)
Immediate Holding Company: MAREL LTD
Registration no: 05772856 **Date established:** 2006
Turnover: £20m - £50m **No.of Employees:** 51 - 100 **Product Groups:** 20, 40, 41

Date of Accounts	Dec 11	Dec 10	Dec 09
Sales Turnover	27m	21m	19m
Pre Tax Profit/Loss	1m	-819	-2m
Working Capital	-1m	-2m	-1m
Fixed Assets	6m	6m	6m
Current Assets	11m	9m	9m
Current Liabilities	915	2m	1m

Marinepower Engineering
Riverside Estate Brundall, Norwich, NR13 5PS
Tel: 01603-717525 **Fax:** 01603-717273
E-mail: gary@marinepower.freeserve.co.uk
Website: http://www.marinepower.freeserve.co.uk
Directors: G. McLagan (Dir), C. McLagan (Fin)
Immediate Holding Company: FENCRAFT LIMITED
Registration no: 03743798 **Date established:** 2002
No.of Employees: 1 - 10 **Product Groups:** 35, 36, 39

Date of Accounts	Dec 11	Dec 10	Dec 09
Working Capital	-141	-166	-190
Fixed Assets	306	316	315
Current Assets	162	142	64
Current Liabilities	N/A	42	N/A

Markwell Ltd
Unit 25 Littlewood Lane, Hoveton, Norwich, NR12 8DZ
Tel: 01603-783053 **Fax:** 01603-783053
Directors: K. Guy (Prop)
Immediate Holding Company: MARKWELL LIMITED
Registration no: 01521827 **Date established:** 1980
No.of Employees: 1 - 10 **Product Groups:** 35, 36, 39

Date of Accounts	Oct 11	Oct 10	Oct 09
Working Capital	-12	-26	-31
Fixed Assets	2	2	3
Current Assets	16	10	10

Bernard Matthews Farms Ltd
Great Witchingham Hall Great Witchingham, Norwich, NR9 5QD
Tel: 01603-872611 **Fax:** 01603-871118
E-mail: noel.bartram@bernardmatthews.com
Website: http://www.bernardmatthews.com
Bank(s): Barclays
Managers: N. Bartram
Ultimate Holding Company: BERNARD MATTHEWS HOLDINGS LIMITED
Immediate Holding Company: BERNARD MATTHEWS KITCHENS LIMITED
Registration no: 00701293 **Date established:** 1961
Turnover: £250m - £500m **No.of Employees:** 1501 & over
Product Groups: 20

Mcarthur Tring Architects
14a The Close, Norwich, NR1 4DZ
Tel: 01603-766750 **Fax:** 01603-633740
E-mail: mail@mcarthurtring.co.uk
Website: http://www.mcarthurtring.co.uk
Directors: G. Mcarthur (Ptnr)
Immediate Holding Company: MCARTHUR TRING ARCHITECTS LLP
Registration no: OC303838 **Date established:** 2003
Turnover: Up to £250,000 **No.of Employees:** 1 - 10 **Product Groups:** 52, 84

Date of Accounts	Mar 11	Mar 10	Mar 09
Sales Turnover	N/A	56	N/A
Pre Tax Profit/Loss	N/A	23	N/A
Working Capital	49	14	20
Fixed Assets	9	9	11
Current Assets	89	53	54
Current Liabilities	N/A	38	N/A

Meadows Bridal Shoes Ltd
Cordova Building Starling Road, Norwich, NR3 3ED
Tel: 01603-219174 **Fax:** 01603-762690
E-mail: sales@meadowsbridal.co.uk
Website: http://www.meadowsbridal.co.uk
Directors: J. Barrett (MD)
Immediate Holding Company: MEADOWS BRIDAL SHOES LIMITED
Registration no: 03123234 **Date established:** 1995
No.of Employees: 1 - 10 **Product Groups:** 22

Date of Accounts	Sep 11	Sep 10	Sep 09
Working Capital	50	70	72
Fixed Assets	4	6	8
Current Assets	156	123	108

Meltemi Co Clothing Ltd
Barnard Road, Norwich, NR5 9JB
Tel: 01603-731330 **Fax:** 08707-871759
E-mail: sales@meltemi.co.uk
Website: http://www.meltemi.co.uk
Directors: J. Mehew (Dir), S. Brothers (MD), C. Mehew (Fin), S. Brothers (MD)
Immediate Holding Company: MELTEMI COMPANY CLOTHING LIMITED
Registration no: 00980612 **Date established:** 1970 **Turnover:** £2m - £5m
No.of Employees: 51 - 100 **Product Groups:** 24, 63

Date of Accounts	Sep 11	Sep 10	Sep 09
Sales Turnover	4m	N/A	N/A
Pre Tax Profit/Loss	375	N/A	N/A
Working Capital	945	826	815
Fixed Assets	540	573	600
Current Assets	2m	1m	1m
Current Liabilities	318	N/A	318

Miganglia Ltd
Thorpe Road Southrepps, Norwich, NR11 8NQ
Tel: 01263-834941 **Fax:** 01263-834950
E-mail: sales@miganglia.co.uk
Website: http://www.miganglia.co.uk
Directors: B. Chapman (Dir)
Immediate Holding Company: MIG ANGLIA LIMITED
Registration no: 02156816 **Date established:** 1987
No.of Employees: 1 - 10 **Product Groups:** 46

Date of Accounts	Jul 11	Jul 10	Jul 09
Working Capital	193	213	193
Fixed Assets	113	109	111
Current Assets	312	356	296

Modbay
235 Holt Road Horsford, Norwich, NR10 3EB
Tel: 01603-890051
Website: http://www.modbayltd.co.uk
Directors: C. Bond (Dir)
Immediate Holding Company: MODBAY LIMITED
Registration no: 02339888 **Date established:** 1989
No.of Employees: 1 - 10 **Product Groups:** 29, 35, 52

Date of Accounts	Jul 11	Jul 10	Jul 09
Working Capital	45	31	27
Fixed Assets	3	4	5
Current Assets	104	79	74

Models Direct-National Model Register Men/Women Children Centre
King Street, Norwich, NR1 1QH
Tel: 08705-010101 **Fax:** 01603-767858
E-mail: email@modelsdirect.co.uk
Website: http://www.modelsdirect.com
Directors: D. O'Connnor (MD)
No.of Employees: 1 - 10 **Product Groups:** 89

Money Centre (t/a Money Centre)
Iceni Court Delft Way, Norwich, NR6 6BB
Tel: 01603-428500 **Fax:** 01603-428545
E-mail: info@themoneycentre.net
Website: http://www.themoneycentre.co.uk
Directors: M. Alexander (MD)
Immediate Holding Company: I/O U.K., LTD.
Registration no: 04218362 **Date established:** 2001
Turnover: £250,000 - £500,000 **No.of Employees:** 11 - 20
Product Groups: 80

Date of Accounts	Dec 10	Dec 09	Dec 08
Sales Turnover	N/A	297	5m
Pre Tax Profit/Loss	-2m	-773	2m
Working Capital	3	2m	3m
Fixed Assets	N/A	9	58
Current Assets	3	14m	16m
Current Liabilities	N/A	379	1m

Moneyfacts Group plc
66-70 Thorpe Road, Norwich, NR1 1BJ
Tel: 01603-476476 **Fax:** 01603-476477
E-mail: enquiries@moneyfacts.co.uk
Website: http://www.moneyfactsgroup.co.uk
Managers: D. Dillon (Personnel)
Ultimate Holding Company: MONEYFACTS GROUP HOLDINGS LIMITED
Immediate Holding Company: MONEYFACTS LIMITED
Registration no: 02256244 **VAT No.:** GB 525 3307 69
Date established: 1988 **Turnover:** £5m - £10m
No.of Employees: 51 - 100 **Product Groups:** 28

Date of Accounts	Jul 10	Jul 09
Working Capital	1	1
Current Assets	1	1

Mouldline Ltd (formerly ADOP Ltd)
The Old Granary Station Road, Eccles, Norwich, NR16 2JG
Tel: 01953-887544 **Fax:** 01953-887072
E-mail: sales@mouldline.com
Website: http://www.mouldline.com
Directors: R. Cole (MD)
Immediate Holding Company: MOULDLINE LIMITED
Registration no: 05059964 **VAT No.:** GB 640 4565 50
Date established: 2004 **Turnover:** £1m - £2m **No.of Employees:** 1 - 10
Product Groups: 30, 42, 48

Date of Accounts	Dec 11	Dec 10	Dec 09
Working Capital	-54	23	-13
Fixed Assets	105	109	117
Current Assets	114	164	142

N P N Mower Service
7 Zobel Close Sweet Briar Industrial Estate, Sweet Briar Road Industrial Estate, Norwich, NR3 2BY
Tel: 01603-425156 **Fax:** 01603-425156
E-mail: n.cushion@npnmowerservice.co.uk
Website: http://www.npnmowerservice.co.uk
Directors: N. Cushion (Prop)
No.of Employees: 1 - 10 **Product Groups:** 30, 35, 37, 40, 41, 42

Norfolk Industry
Oak Street, Norwich, NR3 3BP
Tel: 01603-667957 **Fax:** 01603-624265
E-mail: s.tooke@norfolk-industries.co.uk
Website: http://www.norfolk-industries.co.uk
Managers: S. Tooke (Chief Mgr), J. Ames (Admin Off)
Date established: 1978 **No.of Employees:** 21 - 50 **Product Groups:** 35

Norfolk Stoves
1 Norwich Road Lenwade, Norwich, NR9 5SH
Tel: 01603-879065 **Fax:** 01603-879783
E-mail: norfolkstoves@hotmail.co.uk
Website: http://www.norfolkstoves.co.uk
Directors: P. Grint (Prop)
No.of Employees: 1 - 10 **Product Groups:** 40

Norfolk Zinc Plating Co.
Little Money Road Loddon, Norwich, NR14 6JD
Tel: 01508-528307 **Fax:** 01508-521284
Directors: T. Jones (MD)
Immediate Holding Company: NORFOLK ZINC PLATING COMPANY LIMITED
Registration no: 07077437 **Date established:** 2009
No.of Employees: 1 - 10 **Product Groups:** 46, 48

Date of Accounts	Nov 11	Nov 10
Working Capital	8	2
Fixed Assets	120	155
Current Assets	49	120

Norwich City Football Club
Carrow Road, Norwich, NR1 1JE
Tel: 01603-760760 **Fax:** 01603-628373
E-mail: edward.jones@ncfc-canaries.co.uk
Website: http://www.canaries.co.uk
Directors: S. Gordon (Co Sec), S. Gordon (Fin), E. Wynn Jones (Dir)
Managers: W. Hoy (Sales & Mktg Mg), S. Sheen (Tech Serv Mgr), K. Coverdale (Purch Mgr)
Immediate Holding Company: NORWICH CITY FOOTBALL CLUB PLC
Registration no: 00154044 **VAT No.:** GB 105 4810 04
Date established: 2019 **Turnover:** £20m - £50m
No.of Employees: 101 - 250 **Product Groups:** 89

Date of Accounts	May 11	May 10	May 09
Sales Turnover	23m	17m	18m
Pre Tax Profit/Loss	-7m	-6m	-6m
Working Capital	-19m	-27m	-6m
Fixed Assets	36m	36m	37m
Current Assets	15m	9m	8m
Current Liabilities	29m	30m	11m

Norwich Engine Centre Ltd
Vulcan Road South Mile Cross Lane, Norwich, NR6 6AF
Tel: 01603-425701 **Fax:** 01603-484046
E-mail: info@norwichenginecentre.co.uk
Website: http://www.norwichenginecentre.co.uk
Directors: R. Quantrell (Dir)
Ultimate Holding Company: MAG GROUP LIMITED
Immediate Holding Company: STEVENSONS PLASTERWORK LIMITED
Registration no: 01655235 **Date established:** 2004
No.of Employees: 1 - 10 **Product Groups:** 35, 36, 39

Date of Accounts	Nov 11	Nov 10	Nov 09
Working Capital	304	325	405
Fixed Assets	76	115	92
Current Assets	1m	867	998

Norwich Plating Ltd
Unit 66 Hellesdon Park Road Drayton High Road, Norwich, NR6 5DR
Tel: 01603-403185 **Fax:** 01603-748622
Website: http://www.hayley-group.co.uk
Directors: I. Bowler (Dir)
Immediate Holding Company: NORWICH PLATING LIMITED
Registration no: 01968837 **Date established:** 1985
No.of Employees: 1 - 10 **Product Groups:** 46, 48

Date of Accounts	Oct 11	Oct 10	Oct 09
Working Capital	23	165	161
Fixed Assets	151	4	5
Current Assets	195	200	204

Odsock Ltd
2-4 Wellington Road Tharston, Norwich, NR15 2PE
Tel: 01508-532545 **Fax:** 01508-532516
E-mail: info@odsock.co.uk
Website: http://www.odsock.co.uk
Directors: T. Remfry (MD)
No.of Employees: 1 - 10 **Product Groups:** 37, 67

1-2-1 Consultancy Services
48 Prince Andrews Road, Norwich, NR6 6XG
Tel: 01603-789673
E-mail: 121consultancy@tiscali.co.uk
Directors: J. Woods (Ptnr)
Turnover: Up to £250,000 **No.of Employees:** 1 - 10 **Product Groups:** 37, 84, 87

One Way Circuit Ltd
Station Road Lenwade, Norwich, NR9 5LY
Tel: 01603-875100 **Fax:** 0870-751 7518
E-mail: sales@owcg.co.uk
Website: http://www.onewaypcb.com
Bank(s): National Westminster Bank Plc
Directors: R. Lyons (MD)
Managers: R. Urry (Tech Serv Mgr)
Immediate Holding Company: ONE WAY CIRCUITS LIMITED
Registration no: 02438188 **VAT No.:** GB 552 7229 40
Date established: 1989 **Turnover:** £1m - £2m **No.of Employees:** 21 - 50
Product Groups: 37, 48, 81, 84

Date of Accounts	Dec 10	Dec 09	Dec 08
Working Capital	32	39	-541
Fixed Assets	103	128	757
Current Assets	450	654	893

Onetwotree.Co.Uk
7 Frensham Road, Norwich, NR3 2BT
Tel: 01603-406972 **Fax:** 01603-406915
E-mail: info@onetwotree.co.uk
Website: http://www.onetwotree.co.uk
Directors: M. Wilson (Prop)
Immediate Holding Company: A.G.M. WHOLESALE LIMITED
Date established: 2002 **No.of Employees:** 1 - 10 **Product Groups:** 07, 30, 62

Date of Accounts	Dec 11	Dec 10	Dec 09
Working Capital	-48	-55	-52
Fixed Assets	65	67	72
Current Assets	459	447	380

P & D Tank Services
Intwood Lane East Carleton, Norwich, NR14 8LD
Tel: 01508-570629 **Fax:** 01508-570629
Directors: P. Dell (Prop)
Date established: 1984 **No.of Employees:** 1 - 10 **Product Groups:** 35, 42, 45

Page Bros Norwich Ltd
Mile Cross Lane, Norwich, NR6 6SA
Tel: 01603-778800 **Fax:** 01603-778801
E-mail: sales@pagebros.co.uk
Website: http://www.pagebros.co.uk
Bank(s): Royal Bank of Scotland
Directors: A. Spelman (Sales & Mktg), C. Eastaugh (Fin), D. Longfoot (Tech Serv), I. Johnston (Fin), S. Commons (Sales), T. Attwood (MD)
Managers: S. Bryanton, J. Forkes
Ultimate Holding Company: MILEX LIMITED
Immediate Holding Company: PAGE BROS. (NORWICH) LIMITED
Registration no: 00170008 **VAT No.:** GB 595 3185 08
Date established: 2020 **Turnover:** £5m - £10m
No.of Employees: 51 - 100 **Product Groups:** 28

Date of Accounts	Sep 11	Sep 10	Sep 09
Sales Turnover	8m	8m	8m
Pre Tax Profit/Loss	-315	-86	70
Working Capital	-31	76	76
Fixed Assets	3m	3m	3m
Current Assets	2m	2m	2m
Current Liabilities	317	264	323

Panema Trailer Engineering Ltd
Chalk Lane Snetterton, Norwich, NR16 2JZ
Tel: 01953-887622 **Fax:** 01953-888515
E-mail: info@panematrailers.co.uk
Website: http://www.panematrailers.co.uk
Bank(s): Barclays
Directors: A. Anema (Dir)
Immediate Holding Company: PANEMA TRAILER ENGINEERING LIMITED
Registration no: 01255752 **VAT No.:** GB 283 4461 48
Date established: 1976 **Turnover:** £500,000 - £1m
No.of Employees: 11 - 20 **Product Groups:** 39, 72

Date of Accounts	Mar 12	Mar 11	Mar 10
Working Capital	192	150	133
Fixed Assets	145	155	157
Current Assets	291	260	265

Parker Hydraulic & Pneumatics Ltd
Unit 5 Ashbourne Industrial Estate, Norwich, NR6 6LY
Tel: 01603-403190 **Fax:** 01603-485337
E-mail: david@parkerhydraulics.co.uk
Website: http://www.parkerhydraulics.co.uk
Directors: D. Willimott (MD), T. Betts (Fin)
Ultimate Holding Company: ASHBOURNE GROUP HOLDINGS LIMITED
Immediate Holding Company: PARKER HYDRAULICS AND PNEUMATICS LIMITED
Registration no: 01273399 **Date established:** 1976 **Turnover:** £1m - £2m
No.of Employees: 11 - 20 **Product Groups:** 40, 48, 52, 66, 84

Date of Accounts	Mar 12	Mar 11	Mar 10
Working Capital	193	249	94
Fixed Assets	780	784	809
Current Assets	1m	1m	1m

Pearl Water Softners East Anglia
Oshawa Highland Road, Taverham, Norwich, NR8 6QP
Tel: 01603-860368 **Fax:** 01603-260928
E-mail: pearl@get-the-web.com
Website: http://www.pearlwatersofteners.co.uk
Directors: B. Dye (Prop)
Immediate Holding Company: PEARL WATER SOFTENERS (EAST ANGLIA) LIMITED
Registration no: 01620151 **Date established:** 1982
No.of Employees: 1 - 10 **Product Groups:** 38, 42

Date of Accounts	Sep 11	Sep 10	Sep 09
Working Capital	1	2	-8
Fixed Assets	5	7	9
Current Assets	24	30	21

Pioner Fristads
Unit 7 Low Road Hellesdon, Norwich, NR6 5AT
Tel: 01282-858304 **Fax:** 01603-414540
E-mail: sales@fristads-co.com
Website: http://www.pionerfristads.co.uk
Directors: P. Moore (MD)
Ultimate Holding Company: KWINTET A/S (DENMARK)
Immediate Holding Company: PIONER FRISTADS (UK) LIMITED
Registration no: 03131122 **VAT No.:** GB 665 6657 88
Date established: 1995 **Turnover:** £5m - £10m **No.of Employees:** 1 - 10
Product Groups: 22, 23, 24, 63

Date of Accounts	Dec 11	Dec 10	Dec 09
Sales Turnover	6m	5m	6m
Pre Tax Profit/Loss	444	144	-191
Working Capital	1m	1m	906
Fixed Assets	N/A	3	5
Current Assets	2m	2m	1m
Current Liabilities	354	288	237

Place UK Ltd
Church Farm Church Road, Tunstead, Norwich, NR12 8RQ
Tel: 01692-536225 **Fax:** 01692-536928
E-mail: info@placeuk.com
Website: http://www.placeuk.com
Bank(s): Barclays
Directors: J. Starling (Fin), J. Walker (Sales), T. Place (MD)
Managers: J. Chambers (Personnel), D. Smith (Purch Mgr)
Ultimate Holding Company: R.& J.M.PLACE LIMITED
Immediate Holding Company: PLACE UK LIMITED
Registration no: 04155171 **Date established:** 2001
Turnover: £10m - £20m **No.of Employees:** 51 - 100 **Product Groups:** 62

Date of Accounts	Jan 12	Jan 11	Jan 10
Sales Turnover	13m	11m	9m
Pre Tax Profit/Loss	2m	1m	439
Working Capital	2m	2m	1m
Fixed Assets	665	590	654
Current Assets	3m	4m	3m
Current Liabilities	904	783	565

Premier Inn
Prince of Wales Road, Norwich, NR1 1DX
Tel: 08715-278842 **Fax:** 0870-850 6347
E-mail: reservations.norwichnelson@whitbread.com
Website: http://www.premierinn.com
Bank(s): Barclays
Managers: E. Cluett (Chief Mgr)
Ultimate Holding Company: WHITBREAD PLC
Immediate Holding Company: P I HOTELS LTD
Registration no: 05137608 **Turnover:** £2m - £5m
No.of Employees: 21 - 50 **Product Groups:** 69

Proton Cars UK Ltd
Potash Lane Hethel, Norwich, NR14 8EZ
Tel: 01953-713939 **Fax:** 01953-713949
E-mail: sales@proton.co.uk
Website: http://www.proton.co.uk
Directors: S. Green (Co Sec), B. Collier (MD), S. Green (Fin)
Managers: S. Park (Chief Mgr)
Ultimate Holding Company: GROUP LOTUS PLC
Immediate Holding Company: PROTON CARS (UK) LIMITED
Registration no: 01857505 **Date established:** 1984 **Turnover:** £5m - £10m
No.of Employees: 51 - 100 **Product Groups:** 68

Date of Accounts	Mar 11	Mar 10	Mar 09
Sales Turnover	6m	8m	10m
Pre Tax Profit/Loss	-818	-161	-1m
Working Capital	-595	-5m	-4m
Fixed Assets	6m	6m	6m
Current Assets	2m	4m	6m
Current Liabilities	825	647	683

Pyramid Windows East Anglia Ltd
13-14 Guardian Road Industrial Estate Guardian Road, Norwich, NR5 8PF
Tel: 01603-615674 **Fax:** 01603-623552
E-mail: paul.joyce@pyramidwindows.co.uk
Website: http://www.pyramidwindows.co.uk
Directors: P. Joyce (Dir)
Managers: J. Symonds (Fin Mgr)
Immediate Holding Company: PPA DEPOSITS 108 LIMITED
Registration no: 04147050 **Date established:** 2001
No.of Employees: 21 - 50 **Product Groups:** 46

Date of Accounts	Mar 10	Mar 09	Mar 08
Working Capital	-128	-91	-127
Fixed Assets	177	178	216
Current Assets	665	514	414
Current Liabilities	342	73	63

J C Quantrell & Sons Ltd
Vulcan Road South, Norwich, NR6 6AF
Tel: 01603-425701
E-mail: r.quantrell@eurodiesel.co.uk
Directors: R. Quantrell (MD)
Immediate Holding Company: J.C. QUANTRELL AND SONS LIMITED
Registration no: 01455130 **Date established:** 1979
No.of Employees: 1 - 10 **Product Groups:** 35, 36, 39

Date of Accounts	Dec 06	Dec 05
Working Capital	-4	4
Fixed Assets	161	169
Current Assets	115	163
Current Liabilities	120	160

Quantum Industries Ltd
Diamond Road, Norwich, NR6 6AN
Tel: 01603-789000 **Fax:** 01603-405476
E-mail: enquiries@quantum-ind.co.uk
Website: http://www.quantum-ind.co.uk
Bank(s): National Westminster
Directors: T. Manning (MD), D. Cole (Fin)
Managers: R. Murray (Tech Serv Mgr)
Ultimate Holding Company: QUANTUM HOLDINGS NORFOLK LIMITED
Immediate Holding Company: QUANTUM INDUSTRIES LIMITED
Registration no: 04871807 **Date established:** 2003 **Turnover:** £2m - £5m
No.of Employees: 21 - 50 **Product Groups:** 26, 52

Date of Accounts	Sep 11	Sep 10	Sep 09
Working Capital	398	291	248
Fixed Assets	181	163	162
Current Assets	2m	1m	1m

Quentor Ltd (T/A Quentor Cases)
10 Fitzmaurice Court Rackheath, Norwich, NR13 6PY
Tel: 01603-721604 **Fax:** 01603-721992
E-mail: info@quentor.com
Website: http://www.quentor.com
Directors: C. Asbury (Co Sec)
Managers: D. Perry
Ultimate Holding Company: Q HOLDINGS NORWICH LIMITED
Immediate Holding Company: QUENTOR LIMITED
Registration no: 02144668 **VAT No.:** GB 282 1462 67
Date established: 1987 **Turnover:** £2m - £5m **No.of Employees:** 11 - 20
Product Groups: 22, 25, 49

Date of Accounts	Jun 11	Jun 10	Jun 09
Working Capital	2m	1m	1m
Fixed Assets	58	80	102
Current Assets	2m	2m	1m

R G Carter Ltd
9-11 Drayton High Road Drayton, Norwich, NR8 6AH
Tel: 01603-867355 **Fax:** 01603-260151
E-mail: mail@rgcarter-drayton.co.uk
Website: http://www.rgcarter-construction.co.uk
Directors: G. Keys (MD)
Managers: H. Rochford (Purch Mgr), D. Coventry (Fin Mgr)
Ultimate Holding Company: RG CARTER GROUP LIMITED
Immediate Holding Company: BULLEN DEVELOPMENTS LIMITED
Registration no: 01005917 **VAT No.:** GB 104 6247 01
Date established: 1971 **Turnover:** £10m - £20m
No.of Employees: 51 - 100 **Product Groups:** 52

Date of Accounts	Dec 11	Dec 10	Dec 09
Working Capital	16m	13m	7m
Fixed Assets	365	37	23
Current Assets	16m	13m	7m

R P I Engineering Ltd
Wayside Garage 312 Holt Road, Horsford, Norwich, NR10 3EE
Tel: 01603-891209 **Fax:** 01603-890330
E-mail: info@v8engines.com
Website: http://www.v8engines.com
Directors: C. Crane (MD), L. Hislop (Fin)
No.of Employees: 1 - 10 **Product Groups:** 40, 61

Redpack Packaging Machinery
Bunkell Road Rackheath Industrial Estate, Rackheath, Norwich, NR13 6PU
Tel: 01603-722280 **Fax:** 01603-720906
E-mail: stuart@redpack.co.uk
Website: http://www.redpack.co.uk
Directors: S. Briston (Ptnr)
Immediate Holding Company: VANCEBUILD LIMITED
Registration no: 01360588 **Date established:** 1978
No.of Employees: 21 - 50 **Product Groups:** 38, 42

Date of Accounts	Dec 11	Dec 10	Dec 09
Working Capital	863	425	392
Fixed Assets	1m	820	896
Current Assets	2m	1m	1m

Regional Freight Services Ltd
Airport Cargo Terminal Liberator Road, Norwich Airport Industrial Estate, Norwich, NR6 6EU
Tel: 01603-414125 **Fax:** 01603-402542
E-mail: cbr@regfrt.co.uk
Website: http://www.regionalfreight.co.uk
Directors: C. Bryant (Grp Chief Exec), P. Hearn (MD), T. Roberts (Co Sec)
Managers: G. Peck (Systems Mgr), A. Chew (Mgr)
Registration no: 01589269 **VAT No.:** GB 363 6063 56
Date established: 2007 **Turnover:** £5m - £10m **No.of Employees:** 21 - 50
Product Groups: 75, 76

Date of Accounts	Dec 07
Working Capital	13
Fixed Assets	48
Current Assets	1196
Current Liabilities	1184
Total Share Capital	8

Richardsons Stalham Ltd
The Staithe Stalham, Norwich, NR12 9BX
Tel: 01692-581081 **Fax:** 01692-581522
E-mail: info@richardsonsgroup.net
Website: http://www.richardsonsboatingholidays.co.uk
Directors: M. Wilkinson (Pers), R. Cox (Tech Serv)
Managers: G. Mundford (Grp Gen Mgr), E. Day
Immediate Holding Company: RICHARDSONS (STALHAM) LIMITED
Registration no: 02192460 **Date established:** 1987 **Turnover:** £2m - £5m
No.of Employees: 101 - 250 **Product Groups:** 74

Date of Accounts	Mar 08	Mar 09	Mar 10
Sales Turnover	N/A	N/A	4m
Pre Tax Profit/Loss	95	-47	375
Working Capital	954	242	517
Fixed Assets	2m	2m	2m
Current Assets	2m	3m	4m
Current Liabilities	1m	713	4m

Ripblast & Co. Ltd
Oakwood Yard Harling Road, Snetterton, Norwich, NR16 2JU
Tel: 01953-888200 **Fax:** 01953-887453
E-mail: enquiries@ripblast.co.uk
Website: http://www.ripblast.co.uk
Directors: J. Ripley (MD), L. Ripley (Fin)
Immediate Holding Company: RIPBLAST & CO LIMITED
Registration no: 03425822 **Date established:** 1997
No.of Employees: 1 - 10 **Product Groups:** 46, 48

Date of Accounts	Dec 11	Dec 10	Dec 09
Working Capital	-155	-182	-118
Fixed Assets	2m	2m	2m
Current Assets	84	99	89

Robinsons Soft Drinks Ltd
Carrow Works Bracondale, Norwich, NR1 2DD
Tel: 01603-632633 **Fax:** 01603- 724106
Website: http://www.britvic.co.uk
Bank(s): Nat West
Directors: P. Moody (Sales), J. Gibney (Fin), J. Howard (Dir)
Managers: G. Howard (Chief Mgr)
Ultimate Holding Company: BRITVIC PLC
Immediate Holding Company: ROBINSONS SOFT DRINKS LIMITED
Registration no: 02987077 **VAT No.:** GB 232 1538 95
Date established: 1994 **Turnover:** £50m - £75m
No.of Employees: 251 - 500 **Product Groups:** 21, 62

Date of Accounts	Sep 08	Sep 09	Oct 10
Pre Tax Profit/Loss	27m	26m	26m
Working Capital	8m	-45m	-39m
Fixed Assets	395m	404m	395m
Current Assets	38m	N/A	1m
Current Liabilities	30m	30m	30m

Rocolec Ltd
Unit 10 Shepherds Business Park Norwich Road, Lenwade, Norwich, NR9 5SG
Tel: 01603-879000
E-mail: info@rocolec.com
Website: http://www.rocolec.com

see next page

***Rocolec Ltd** - Cont'd*

Directors: A. Barrett (MD)
Immediate Holding Company: ROCOLEC LIMITED
Registration no: 04549378 **Date established:** 2002
No.of Employees: 1 - 10 **Product Groups:** 84

Date of Accounts	Mar 12	Mar 11	Mar 10
Working Capital	7	9	5
Fixed Assets	8	3	4
Current Assets	81	81	80

St Andrews Fire Equipment

3 St Williams Way, Norwich, NR7 0AH
Tel: 07796-172233 **Fax:** 01603-448640
E-mail: standrewsfire@ntlworld.com
Website: http://www.standrewsfireequipment.co.uk
Directors: B. Nobes (MD)
Immediate Holding Company: ST.ANDREWS FIRE EQUIPMENT LIMITED
Registration no: 03550220 **Date established:** 1998
No.of Employees: 1 - 10 **Product Groups:** 38, 42

Date of Accounts	Jun 12	Jun 11	Jun 10
Working Capital	7	13	11
Fixed Assets	11	10	6
Current Assets	34	33	24

Sam's Fabrications

Unit 17 Morgan Way Bowthorpe Employment Area, Norwich, NR5 9JJ
Tel: 01603-743252 **Fax:** 01603-746927
E-mail: sales@samsfabrications.co.uk
Website: http://www.samsfabrications.co.uk
Directors: G. Waterhouse (Dir)
Turnover: Up to £250,000 **No.of Employees:** 1 - 10 **Product Groups:** 48

Sapphire Investigations Bureau Ltd

Sapphire House Ipswich Road, Long Stratton, Norwich, NR15 2TH
Tel: 01508-530324 **Fax:** 01508-531682
E-mail: peachman@sib-ltd.co.uk
Website: http://www.sib-ltd.co.uk
Directors: M. Peachman (MD)
Immediate Holding Company: SAPPHIRE INVESTIGATIONS BUREAU LIMITED
Registration no: 00777693 **VAT No.:** GB 105 0681 09
Date established: 1963 **Turnover:** Up to £250,000
No.of Employees: 1 - 10 **Product Groups:** 80, 81, 82

Date of Accounts	Oct 11	Oct 10	Oct 09
Sales Turnover	110	123	126
Pre Tax Profit/Loss	-5	1	-4
Working Capital	16	35	39
Fixed Assets	168	167	161
Current Assets	31	44	49
Current Liabilities	14	7	7

SATCO Tapes (t/a SATCO)

34 Europa Way Martineau Lane, Norwich, NR1 2EN
Tel: 01603-613434 **Fax:** 01603-699987
E-mail: sales@satco.co.uk
Website: http://www.satco.co.uk
Directors: P. James (MD)
Managers: A. Pearman (Sales Prom Mgr), R. James (Prod Mgr)
Registration no: 00264573 **VAT No.:** GB 196 9140 26
Turnover: £500,000 - £1m **No.of Employees:** 1 - 10 **Product Groups:** 23, 27, 42

Scanfit International Ltd

11-14 Burton Close, Norwich, NR6 6AZ
Tel: 01603-480400 **Fax:** 01603-424547
E-mail: bernard.garner@scanfit.co.uk
Website: http://www.scanfit.co.uk
Bank(s): Barclays
Managers: A. Warnes (Chief Mgr), A. Warnes (Mgr)
Immediate Holding Company: MRC SPF SCANFIT LIMITED
Registration no: 02299105 **VAT No.:** GB 525 2564 54
Date established: 1988 **Turnover:** £2m - £5m **No.of Employees:** 11 - 20
Product Groups: 36

Date of Accounts	Dec 11	Nov 09	Nov 08
Sales Turnover	8m	6m	N/A
Pre Tax Profit/Loss	944	423	773
Working Capital	4m	3m	3m
Fixed Assets	58	672	736
Current Assets	5m	4m	4m
Current Liabilities	158	138	241

Shelters R Us

17-18 Morgan Way Bowthorpe Employment Area, Norwich, NR5 9JJ
Tel: 01603-743252 **Fax:** 01603-746927
E-mail: sales@samsfabrications.co.uk
Website: http://www.shelters-r-us.co.uk
Managers: G. Waterhouse (Chief Mgr)
Date established: 1988 **No.of Employees:** 1 - 10 **Product Groups:** 40, 49

Shelters-R-Us

17-18 Morgan Way Bowthorpe Employment Area, Norwich, NR5 9JJ
Tel: 01603-743252 **Fax:** 01603-746927
E-mail: sales@shelters-r-us.co.uk
Website: http://www.shelters-r-us.co.uk
Managers: G. Waterhouse (Mgr)
Date established: 1988 **No.of Employees:** 1 - 10 **Product Groups:** 25, 35

Shoreheat Ltd

16 Morgan Way Bowthorpe Employment Area, Norwich, NR5 9JJ
Tel: 01603-744468 **Fax:** 01603-741188
Managers: W. Bunker (District Mgr)
Ultimate Holding Company: PROGRESS GROUP LIMITED
Immediate Holding Company: SHOREHEAT LIMITED
Registration no: 01566154 **Date established:** 1981
No.of Employees: 1 - 10 **Product Groups:** 36, 38, 40

Date of Accounts	Dec 11	Dec 10	Dec 09
Sales Turnover	14m	17m	13m
Pre Tax Profit/Loss	28	540	327
Working Capital	2m	2m	2m
Fixed Assets	560	461	505
Current Assets	6m	6m	6m
Current Liabilities	247	480	388

Shrinkit Ltd

148 Manor Road Newton St Faith, Norwich, NR10 3LG
Tel: 01603-897566 **Fax:** 01603-893550
E-mail: enquiries@shrinkit.co.uk
Website: http://www.shrinkit.co.uk
Directors: M. Greengrass (Dir)
Immediate Holding Company: SHRINKIT LIMITED
Registration no: 02926555 **Date established:** 1994
No.of Employees: 1 - 10 **Product Groups:** 38, 42

Date of Accounts	Jul 11	Jul 10	Jul 09
Working Capital	50	35	47
Fixed Assets	33	35	38
Current Assets	231	194	176

Signs Express Ltd National Headquarters

Franchise Headquarters 1-2 The Old Church St Matthews Road, Norwich, NR1 1SP
Tel: 01603-625925 **Fax:** 01603-613136
E-mail: sales@signsexpress.co.uk
Website: http://www.signsexpress.co.uk
Bank(s): Barclays
Managers: R. Dack (Mktg Serv Mgr), J. Bean (Fin Mgr)
Immediate Holding Company: SIGNS EXPRESS LIMITED
Registration no: 02375913 **Date established:** 1989
Turnover: £10m - £20m **No.of Employees:** 11 - 20 **Product Groups:** 26, 27, 28, 30, 33, 35, 37, 39, 40, 45, 49, 52, 67, 68, 81

Date of Accounts	May 11	May 10	May 09
Working Capital	2m	1m	988
Fixed Assets	112	87	105
Current Assets	2m	2m	1m

Siskin Dental Centre

Bowthorpe Road, Norwich, NR2 3TU
Tel: 01603-776834 **Fax:** 01603-776854
E-mail: aideen.mcquistin@nchc.nhs.uk
Managers: A. Mcquistin
No.of Employees: 21 - 50 **Product Groups:** 38, 67

Slater & Frith Ltd

Lurista House Stalham Road, Hoveton, Norwich, NR12 8DZ
Tel: 01603-783061 **Fax:** 01603-783991
E-mail: slater@frithltd.freeserve.co.uk
Website: http://www.frithltd.freeserve.co.uk
Directors: A. Slater (Dir)
Immediate Holding Company: SLATER & FRITH LIMITED
Registration no: 01961917 **VAT No.:** GB 426 2821 62
Date established: 1985 **Turnover:** £1m - £2m **No.of Employees:** 1 - 10
Product Groups: 02, 20, 31, 32

Date of Accounts	Dec 11	Dec 10	Dec 09
Working Capital	192	113	150
Fixed Assets	60	84	97
Current Assets	488	545	649
Current Liabilities	N/A	N/A	49

Smurfit Kappa Sheetfeeding

Fishergate, Norwich, NR3 1SJ
Tel: 01603-679888 **Fax:** 01603-679889
E-mail: alex.kelly@smurfitkappa.co.uk
Website: http://www.smurfitsheetfeeding.co.uk
Bank(s): National Westminster
Directors: A. Kelly (MD), M. Betts (Fin), M. Richards (Sales & Mktg), M. Wasden (Fin)
Managers: C. Pope (Sales Prom Mgr), S. Hailes (Transport), T. Chettleburgh (I.T. Exec)
Immediate Holding Company: Norcor Holdings Ltd
Registration no: 01021052 **VAT No.:** 806 6276 23 **Date established:** 1974
Turnover: £20m - £50m **No.of Employees:** 101 - 250 **Product Groups:** 27

Stannah Lift Services Ltd

27-28 Morgan Way Bowthorpe Employment Area, Norwich, NR5 9JJ
Tel: 01603-748021 **Fax:** 01603-743097
E-mail: keith_peters@stannah.co.uk
Website: http://www.stannah.co.uk
Managers: K. Peters (Mgr)
Ultimate Holding Company: STANNAH LIFTS HOLDINGS LIMITED
Immediate Holding Company: STANNAH LIFT SERVICES LIMITED
Registration no: 01189799 **Date established:** 1974
No.of Employees: 11 - 20 **Product Groups:** 35, 39, 45

Date of Accounts	Dec 11	Dec 10	Dec 09
Sales Turnover	84m	82m	87m
Pre Tax Profit/Loss	191	2m	2m
Working Capital	12m	14m	15m
Fixed Assets	4m	4m	3m
Current Assets	21m	24m	24m
Current Liabilities	6m	6m	7m

Steel Masters

5 Wendover Road Rackheath Industrial Estate, Rackheath, Norwich, NR13 6LH
Tel: 01603-720542 **Fax:** 01603-722226
Directors: C. Tyrrell (Ptnr)
Immediate Holding Company: STEEL MASTERS (NORWICH) LTD
Registration no: 04656742 **Date established:** 2003
No.of Employees: 1 - 10 **Product Groups:** 35

Date of Accounts	Apr 11	Apr 10	Apr 09
Working Capital	50	107	61
Fixed Assets	25	12	13
Current Assets	130	250	158

Stratstan Ltd

Wendover Road Rackheath Industrial Estate, Rackheath, Norwich, NR13 6LH
Tel: 01603-721797 **Fax:** 01603-721812
E-mail: sales@stratstan.co.uk
Website: http://www.stratstan.co.uk
Directors: S. Tuffen (MD)
Immediate Holding Company: STRATSTAN LIMITED
Registration no: 01086328 **VAT No.:** GB 209 0782 68
Date established: 1972 **Turnover:** £2m - £5m **No.of Employees:** 1 - 10
Product Groups: 36, 66

Date of Accounts	Mar 11	Mar 10	Mar 09
Working Capital	860	983	740
Fixed Assets	595	426	423
Current Assets	1m	2m	2m

Strongbar Ltd

Unit 1b Aylsham Industrial Estate, Aylsham, Norwich, NR11 6SS
Tel: 01263-734034 **Fax:** 01263-734790
E-mail: sales@strongbar.co.uk
Website: http://www.strongbar.co.uk
Managers: A. Jordan (Chief Mgr)
Ultimate Holding Company: 1211004 ONTARIO LIMITED (CANADA)
Immediate Holding Company: STRONGBAR LIMITED
Registration no: 01773256 **Date established:** 1983
Turnover: £500,000 - £1m **No.of Employees:** 11 - 20 **Product Groups:** 35

Date of Accounts	Feb 12	Feb 11	Feb 10
Working Capital	379	354	219
Fixed Assets	56	68	30
Current Assets	593	575	354

Sun-Blinds

C/O Quotatis Ltd, Suite 1, Joseph King House Abbey Farm Industrial Estate, Horsham St Faith, Norwich, NR10 3JU
Tel: 08448-044344 **Fax:** 01603-899919
Website: http://www.sunblinds.net
Registration no: NI066795 **Product Groups:** 25, 30, 35, 36, 63

Sycamore Services

Frost Industrial Estate Bidewell Close, Drayton, Norwich, NR8 6AP
Tel: 01603-260340 **Fax:** 01603-262695
E-mail: keith@sycamoreservices.co.uk
Website: http://www.sycamoreservices.co.uk
Directors: K. Canham (Ptnr)
Date established: 1983 **No.of Employees:** 1 - 10 **Product Groups:** 35, 39, 45

Syfer Technology Ltd

Old Stoke Road Arminghall, Norwich, NR14 8SQ
Tel: 01603-723300 **Fax:** 01603-665001
E-mail: hingleson@syfer.co.uk
Website: http://www.syfer.co.uk
Bank(s): National Westminster Bank Plc
Directors: H. Ingleson (MD), D. Cook (Fin)
Managers: J. Howard (Tech Serv Mgr), C. Noad (Mktg Serv Mgr), M. Evans (Personnel)
Ultimate Holding Company: DOVER CORPORATION (U.S.A.)
Immediate Holding Company: SYFER TECHNOLOGY LIMITED
Registration no: 02092166 **VAT No.:** GB 595 3387 93
Date established: 1987 **Turnover:** £20m - £50m
No.of Employees: 251 - 500 **Product Groups:** 37

Date of Accounts	Dec 11	Dec 10	Dec 09
Sales Turnover	22m	22m	16m
Pre Tax Profit/Loss	6m	7m	3m
Working Capital	17m	13m	8m
Fixed Assets	3m	3m	3m
Current Assets	20m	17m	10m
Current Liabilities	2m	3m	1m

T M L Precision Engineering Ltd

Brunel House Potash Lane, Hethel, Norwich, NR14 8EY
Tel: 01953-601700 **Fax:** 01953-603505
E-mail: info@tmlcnc.com
Website: http://www.tmlcnc.com
Directors: N. Dyer (MD)
Immediate Holding Company: TML PRECISION ENGINEERING LIMITED
Registration no: 06229823 **Date established:** 2007
No.of Employees: 1 - 10 **Product Groups:** 48

Date of Accounts	Apr 11	Apr 10	Apr 09
Working Capital	133	105	-23
Fixed Assets	321	289	285
Current Assets	369	368	154

T S Industrial Ltd

Dunkirk Aylsham, Norwich, NR11 6SU
Tel: 01263-731411 **Fax:** 01263-731413
Managers: S. Wright (Mgr)
Immediate Holding Company: AYLSHAM FARM MACHINERY LIMITED
Registration no: 03884266 **Date established:** 1990
No.of Employees: 1 - 10 **Product Groups:** 35

Date of Accounts	Mar 11	Mar 10	Mar 09
Working Capital	116	56	10
Fixed Assets	333	402	519
Current Assets	364	326	363

The Stationery Office

St Crispins Duke Street, Norwich, NR3 1PD
Tel: 08706-005522 **Fax:** 01603-696784
E-mail: customer.services@tso.co.uk
Website: http://www.tso.co.uk
Bank(s): Bank of Scotland
Directors: W. Duncan (Co Sec), R. Dell (Grp Chief Exec), R. Coward (Fin)
Managers: S. Rodwell (Personnel), L. Hallett (Mktg Serv Mgr), A. Damier (Sales Prom Mgr), K. Williams (Tech Serv Mgr)
Ultimate Holding Company: DEUTSCHE POST AG (GERMANY)
Immediate Holding Company: THE STATIONERY OFFICE LIMITED
Registration no: 03049649 **Date established:** 1995
Turnover: £50m - £75m **No.of Employees:** 51 - 100 **Product Groups:** 28

Date of Accounts	Dec 11	Dec 10	Dec 09
Sales Turnover	60m	63m	69m
Pre Tax Profit/Loss	21m	15m	18m
Working Capital	146m	130m	136m
Fixed Assets	5m	6m	7m
Current Assets	177m	160m	165m
Current Liabilities	20m	16m	19m

Tapley Instrumentation (a division of D. Evans Electrical Ltd)

Diamond Road,, Norwich, NR6 6AW
Tel: 01603-485153 **Fax:** 01603-418150
E-mail: info@bowmonk.com
Website: http://www.tapley.org.uk
Managers: R. Broughn (Mgr)
Registration no: 06451315 **VAT No.:** GB 686 5636 81
Date established: 2007 **No.of Employees:** 1 - 10 **Product Groups:** 38, 39, 67, 85

Teknomek Industries Ltd

1 Brunel Way Sweet Briar Road Industrial Estate, Norwich, NR3 2BD
Tel: 01603-788833 **Fax:** 01603-418380
E-mail: sales@teknomek.co.uk
Website: http://www.teknomek.co.uk
Directors: H. Mclellan (MD)
Ultimate Holding Company: A H WORTH AND COMPANY LIMITED
Immediate Holding Company: TEKNOMEK LIMITED
Registration no: 02054645 **Date established:** 1986 **Turnover:** £2m - £5m
No.of Employees: 21 - 50 **Product Groups:** 20, 40, 41

Date of Accounts	May 11	May 10	May 09
Sales Turnover	5m	N/A	N/A
Pre Tax Profit/Loss	651	N/A	N/A
Working Capital	2m	2m	1m
Fixed Assets	310	417	470
Current Assets	5m	5m	4m
Current Liabilities	370	N/A	N/A

Teleologic Ltd

Lion House Muspole Street, Norwich, NR3 1DJ
Tel: 01603-765737
E-mail: info@teleologic.co.uk
Website: http://www.teleologic.co.uk
Directors: R. Jackson (Fin)
Immediate Holding Company: TELEOLOGIC LIMITED
Registration no: 02623511 **Date established:** 1991
Turnover: £250,000 - £500,000 **No.of Employees:** 1 - 10
Product Groups: 44

Date of Accounts	Mar 12	Mar 11	Mar 10
Working Capital	78	35	94
Fixed Assets	39	59	4
Current Assets	260	117	197
Current Liabilities	53	N/A	N/A

Thanehall Ltd (Thanehall Ltd)

2 Riverside Road, Norwich, NR1 1SQ
Tel: 01603-760595 **Fax:** 01603-761486
E-mail: mike.boyd@thanehall.co.uk
Website: http://www.thanehall.ltd.uk
Directors: D. Blanks (Fin), M. Boyd (MD)
Immediate Holding Company: THANEHALL LIMITED
Registration no: 01937948 **Date established:** 1985
Turnover: Up to £250,000 **No.of Employees:** 1 - 10 **Product Groups:** 37, 44, 80

Date of Accounts	Mar 11	Mar 10	Mar 09
Working Capital	-61	-62	-14
Fixed Assets	4	5	7
Current Assets	47	27	81

Thomas Wilch & High

38 Europa Way Martineau Lane, Norwich, NR1 2EN
Tel: 01603-620644 **Fax:** 01603-762194
E-mail: benturner@benburgess.co.uk
Directors: B. Turner (MD)
Immediate Holding Company: NELSON MUSEUM
Registration no: 03938079 **VAT No.:** GB 106 3809 85
Date established: 2001 **No.of Employees:** 1 - 10 **Product Groups:** 48

Thomson & Joseph Ltd

119 Plumstead Road, Norwich, NR1 4JT
Tel: 01603-439511 **Fax:** 01603-700243
E-mail: enquiries@tandj.co.uk
Website: http://www.tandj.co.uk
Directors: G. Hill (Co Sec)
Immediate Holding Company: THOMSON & JOSEPH LIMITED
Registration no: 02121298 **VAT No.:** GB 105 8503 90
Date established: 1987 **Turnover:** £2m - £5m **No.of Employees:** 1 - 10
Product Groups: 02, 20, 31, 32, 66

Date of Accounts	Jun 11	Jun 10	Jun 09
Working Capital	416	406	453
Fixed Assets	114	125	100
Current Assets	692	683	741

Thurton Foundries Ltd

Loddon Road Thurton, Norwich, NR14 6AN
Tel: 01508-480301 **Fax:** 01508-480303
E-mail: ian@thurtonfoundries.co.uk
Website: http://www.thurtonfoundries.co.uk
Bank(s): National Westminster Bank Plc
Directors: I. Capps (MD), E. Capps (Fin)
Immediate Holding Company: THURTON FOUNDRIES LIMITED
Registration no: 00764438 **VAT No.:** GB 106 2785 78
Date established: 1963 **Turnover:** £250,000 - £500,000
No.of Employees: 11 - 20 **Product Groups:** 26, 33, 34, 35, 36, 38, 39, 45, 49

Date of Accounts	Dec 11	Dec 10	Dec 09
Working Capital	-44	-5	1
Fixed Assets	597	481	450
Current Assets	270	270	277

D C Townend

15 Devon Way Trowse, Norwich, NR14 8GE
Tel: 01603-766787
E-mail: dctownend@talktalk.net
Directors: D. Townend (Head)
Immediate Holding Company: DAVID TOWNEND & COMPANY LIMITED
Registration no: 05319307 **Date established:** 1994
Turnover: Up to £250,000 **No.of Employees:** 1 - 10 **Product Groups:** 35

Date of Accounts	Feb 11	Feb 10	Feb 09
Working Capital	-18	-17	-4
Fixed Assets	N/A	N/A	1

Trade Handles Provide Online Ltd

Unit 11 Shepherds Business Park Norwich Road, Lenwade, Norwich, NR9 5SH
Tel: 01603-871055
E-mail: support@provide.co.uk
Website: http://www.tradehandles.co.uk
Immediate Holding Company: PROVIDE ONLINE LIMITED
Registration no: 03699751 **Date established:** 1999 **Turnover:** £2m - £5m
No.of Employees: 1 - 10 **Product Groups:** 25, 30, 33, 36, 66

Date of Accounts	Dec 11	Dec 10	Dec 09
Working Capital	-44	1	-9
Fixed Assets	94	71	11
Current Assets	21	51	38

Truck Masters Handling

Norwich Livestock Hall Road, Norwich, NR4 6EQ
Tel: 01603-458817 **Fax:** 01603-452789
E-mail: mail@truckmasters.co.uk
Website: http://www.truckmasters.co.uk
Directors: G. Alsom (MD)
Registration no: 02555001 **VAT No.:** GB 598 6488 54
Turnover: £2m - £5m **No.of Employees:** 11 - 20 **Product Groups:** 45

Tyco Fire & Integrated Solutions Ltd (a division of Wormald Ansul UK)

Jarrold Way Bowthorpe Employment Area, Norwich, NR5 9JD
Tel: 01603-201201 **Fax:** 01603-201333
E-mail: amansbridge@tycoint.com
Website: http://www.tycoint.com
Bank(s): National Westminster
Managers: B. Heywood (Chief Mgr), C. Haylock (I.T. Exec), A. Mansbridge (Sales Prom Mgr), J. Crooke (Comm)
Immediate Holding Company: TYCO ELECTRONICS UK HOLDINGS LTD
Registration no: 00550926 **VAT No.:** GB 519 4313 52
Turnover: £20m - £50m **No.of Employees:** 101 - 250
Product Groups: 37, 38

Tyrrell Engineering

14a Middletons Lane, Norwich, NR6 5NG
Tel: 01603-425001 **Fax:** 01603-425001
E-mail: danieltyrrell@live.co.uk
Directors: D. Tyrrell (Prop)
Date established: 1990 **No.of Employees:** 1 - 10 **Product Groups:** 38, 42

Ultipac Packaging Supplies

Oulton, Norwich, NR11 6NX
Tel: 01263-587272 **Fax:** 01263-587743
E-mail: admin@ultipac.co.uk
Website: http://www.ultipac.co.uk
Directors: R. Coxall (Prop)
Date established: 1996 **No.of Employees:** 1 - 10 **Product Groups:** 38, 42

Date of Accounts	Aug 11	Aug 10
Working Capital	1	1
Current Assets	9	7

Vincents Norwich Ltd

Priory Works Newton Street Newton St Faith, Norwich, NR10 3AD
Tel: 01603-891050 **Fax:** 01603-890689
E-mail: post@vincents.co.uk
Website: http://www.vincents.co.uk
Bank(s): Lloyds
Directors: A. Vincent (Ch)
Managers: S. Wigney (Chief Acct)
Immediate Holding Company: VINCENTS (NORWICH) LIMITED
Registration no: 04967326 **VAT No.:** GB 105 7199 72
Date established: 2003 **Turnover:** £10m - £20m
No.of Employees: 21 - 50 **Product Groups:** 52

Date of Accounts	Dec 10	Dec 09	Dec 08
Pre Tax Profit/Loss	N/A	N/A	55
Working Capital	122	123	124
Fixed Assets	245	249	252
Current Assets	123	124	126
Current Liabilities	N/A	N/A	1

W.G. Photo

Sweetbriar Cottage The Street, Oulton, Norwich, NR11 6AF
Tel: 0844-8002990 **Fax:** 01903-200528
E-mail: mike@wgphoto.co.uk
Website: http://www.wgphoto.co.uk
Directors: M. Hemsley (Snr Part), C. Hemsley (Ptnr)
VAT No.: GB 194 1137 67 **Date established:** 1900
Turnover: Up to £250,000 **No.of Employees:** 1 - 10 **Product Groups:** 81

F C Walker

The Archway Bracondale, Norwich, NR1 2EE
Tel: 01603-626903 **Fax:** 01603-762194
E-mail: benturner@benburgess.co.uk
Website: http://www.benburgess.co.uk
Directors: B. Turner (MD)
Ultimate Holding Company: BEN BURGESS & CO. LTD
Registration no: 00790443 **VAT No.:** GB 104 6681 82
Turnover: Up to £250,000 **No.of Employees:** 1 - 10 **Product Groups:** 48

Walker Rubber & Plastics Ltd

Last House 21-23 Burnet Road, Sweet Briar Road Industrial Estate, Norwich, NR3 2BS
Tel: 01603-415045 **Fax:** 01603-406502
E-mail: info@walker-rubber.co.uk
Website: http://www.walker-rubber.co.uk
Bank(s): National Westminster Bank Plc
Directors: L. Walker (MD)
Immediate Holding Company: WALKER RUBBER & PLASTICS LIMITED
Registration no: 00505040 **VAT No.:** GB 105 8408 84
Date established: 1952 **Turnover:** £1m - £2m **No.of Employees:** 11 - 20
Product Groups: 29

Date of Accounts	Feb 12	Feb 11	Feb 10
Working Capital	1m	1m	1m
Fixed Assets	731	667	671
Current Assets	2m	1m	1m

Watersavers

Earl Road Rackheath Industrial Estate, Rackheath, Norwich, NR13 6NT
Tel: 01603-720999 **Fax:** 01603-721499
E-mail: sales@watersavers.co.uk
Website: http://www.watersavers.co.uk
Directors: S. Richards (Dir)
Immediate Holding Company: WATERSAVERS LIMITED
Registration no: 07006899 **Date established:** 2009
No.of Employees: 1 - 10 **Product Groups:** 36, 38

Waveform Electroforming Ltd

26 Meteor Close, Norwich, NR6 6HR
Tel: 01603-418691 **Fax:** 01603-418691
E-mail: info@electroform.co.uk
Website: http://www.electroform.com
Directors: J. Dye (MD)
Immediate Holding Company: WAVEFORM (ELECTROFORMING) LIMITED
Registration no: 02306526 **Date established:** 1988
Turnover: Up to £250,000 **No.of Employees:** 1 - 10 **Product Groups:** 35, 37, 46, 48

Date of Accounts	Jul 11	Jul 10	Jul 09
Working Capital	40	34	38
Fixed Assets	34	37	41
Current Assets	75	51	51

Wilki Engineering

Willow Barn Arminghall Lane, Arminghall, Norwich, NR14 8SD
Tel: 01508-493205 **Fax:** 01508-494637
E-mail: info@wilkiengineering.co.uk
Website: http://www.wilkiengineering.co.uk
Directors: B. Willcock (MD)
Date established: 1977 **Turnover:** £250,000 - £500,000
No.of Employees: 1 - 10 **Product Groups:** 42, 44

Williams Fasteners Anglia

3 Burton Close, Norwich, NR6 6AZ
Tel: 01603-483447 **Fax:** 01603-482145
E-mail: darren.ray@williamsfasteners.com
Website: http://www.williamsfasteners.com
Managers: P. Reetz (Mgr)
Immediate Holding Company: WILLIAMS FASTENERS SHEFFIELD
Registration no: 01588974 **VAT No.:** GB 363 6368 34
Turnover: £500,000 - £1m **No.of Employees:** 1 - 10 **Product Groups:** 35, 66

Windmill Buying Services Ltd

4 Derby Street, Norwich, NR2 4PU
Tel: 01603-632008 **Fax:** 01603-612236
E-mail: wwindmill@compuserve.com
Website: http://www.windmill-buying.co.uk
Directors: S. Drew (Fin), K. Drew (MD)
Immediate Holding Company: WINDMILL BUYING SERVICES LIMITED
Registration no: 01571627 **VAT No.:** GB 451 3973 43
Date established: 1981 **Turnover:** £250,000 - £500,000
No.of Employees: 1 - 10 **Product Groups:** 61, 64

Date of Accounts	Mar 11	Mar 10	Mar 09
Sales Turnover	N/A	306	187
Pre Tax Profit/Loss	N/A	20	10
Working Capital	114	78	57
Fixed Assets	1	2	1
Current Assets	276	203	189
Current Liabilities	N/A	4	5

Window Medic Ltd

Unit 58 Hellesdon Park Road Drayton High Road, Norwich, NR6 5DR
Tel: 01603-882244 **Fax:** 01603-747977
E-mail: email@window-medic.co.uk
Website: http://www.window-medic.co.uk
Directors: E. Powell (MD)
Immediate Holding Company: WINDOW MEDIC LIMITED
Registration no: 04140156 **Date established:** 2001
No.of Employees: 1 - 10 **Product Groups:** 25, 30, 35

Date of Accounts	Jan 11	Jan 10	Jan 09
Working Capital	-3	-11	14
Fixed Assets	2	3	4
Current Assets	28	21	35

Woodforde's Norfolk Ales (t/a Woodforde's Norfolk Ales)

Broadland Brewery Woodbastwick, Norwich, NR13 6SW
Tel: 01603-720353 **Fax:** 01603-721806
E-mail: dennis@woodfordes.co.uk
Website: http://www.woodfordes.co.uk
Directors: D. Nudd (Prop), M. Betts (Fin)
Managers: S. Chatten
Ultimate Holding Company: WOODFORDE'S LIMITED
Immediate Holding Company: WOODFORDE'S NORFOLK ALES LIMITED
Registration no: 01718342 **VAT No.:** GB 353 3154 75
Date established: 1983 **Turnover:** £2m - £5m **No.of Employees:** 21 - 50
Product Groups: 62

Woodland Stoves

Whitehouse Mill Road, Ashby St Mary, Norwich, NR14 7BN
Tel: 01508-480351 **Fax:** 01508-480355
Website: http://www.woodlandstoves.co.uk
Directors: A. Chapman (Ptnr)
Date established: 1980 **No.of Employees:** 1 - 10 **Product Groups:** 40

Young's Doors

City Road Works, Norwich, NR1 3AN
Tel: 01603-629889 **Fax:** 01603-764650
E-mail: mail@youngs-doors.co.uk
Website: http://www.youngs-doors.co.uk
Bank(s): HSBC Bank plc
Directors: G. Daniels (Fin)
Managers: C. Whitehead (Ops Mgr)
Ultimate Holding Company: R.G. CARTER HOLDINGS LTD
Immediate Holding Company: DRAYTON BUILDING SERVICES LTD
Registration no: 01944848 **VAT No.:** GB 426 2932 53
Date established: 1977 **Turnover:** £2m - £5m **No.of Employees:** 11 - 20
Product Groups: 25, 30, 40, 66

Date of Accounts	Dec 07	Dec 06	Dec 05
Sales Turnover	N/A	N/A	2522
Pre Tax Profit/Loss	N/A	N/A	17
Working Capital	161	187	156
Fixed Assets	209	195	245
Current Assets	984	721	620
Current Liabilities	823	534	463
ROCE% (Return on Capital Employed)			4.2
ROT% (Return on Turnover)			0.7

Zenith Staybrite Ltd Weatherseal Holdings

Joseph King House Horsham St Faith, Norwich, NR10 3JU
Tel: 01603-892100 **Fax:** 01708-737460
E-mail: customer.services@zsltd.co.uk
Website: http://www.zenithwindows.co.uk
Managers: S. Adamson, S. Coleson (Mgr)
Ultimate Holding Company: EBUILDERS LIMITED
Immediate Holding Company: ZENITH STAYBRITE LIMITED
Registration no: 06516827 **Date established:** 2008
No.of Employees: 21 - 50 **Product Groups:** 30

Date of Accounts	Oct 11	Oct 10	Oct 09
Sales Turnover	30m	30m	35m
Pre Tax Profit/Loss	585	633	710
Working Capital	4m	3m	338
Fixed Assets	207	288	341
Current Assets	8m	8m	8m
Current Liabilities	3m	3m	6m

Sheringham

Kingsland Engineering Company Ltd

Weybourne Road, Sheringham, NR26 8HE
Tel: 01263-822153 **Fax:** 01263-825667
E-mail: peter@kingsland.com
Website: http://www.kingsland.com
Bank(s): Barclays
Directors: B. De Muynck (MD), P. Lowagie (MD)
Managers: C. Gascoigne (Chief Acct), D. Hill (Purch Mgr), L. Gotts (Mktg Serv Mgr), J. Palmer
Ultimate Holding Company: HACO NV (BELGIUM)
Immediate Holding Company: KINGSLAND ENGINEERING COMPANY LIMITED(THE)

see next page

Kingsland Engineering Company Ltd - *Cont'd*
Registration no: 01772496 **VAT No.:** GB 394 3911 27
Date established: 1983 **Turnover:** £2m - £5m **No.of Employees:** 21 - 50
Product Groups: 37, 46

Date of Accounts	Mar 12	Mar 11	Mar 10
Sales Turnover	4m	4m	4m
Pre Tax Profit/Loss	75	5	111
Working Capital	4m	4m	4m
Fixed Assets	2m	2m	2m
Current Assets	5m	5m	5m
Current Liabilities	461	862	835

Swaffham

I R S Ltd
59 Turbine Way, Swaffham, PE37 7XD
Tel: 01760-721399 **Fax:** 01760-723726
E-mail: l.forster@irs.uk.com
Website: http://www.irs.uk.com
Bank(s): Barclays
Directors: L. Forster (MD)
Immediate Holding Company: IRS ESTATES LIMITED
Registration no: 00259372 **VAT No.:** GB 104 6241 13
Date established: 1931 **Turnover:** £1m - £2m **No.of Employees:** 11 - 20
Product Groups: 30, 39, 40

Date of Accounts	Dec 11	Dec 10	Dec 09
Working Capital	-16	12	35
Fixed Assets	170	169	170
Current Assets	25	30	40

Kitfix Swallow Group Ltd
Castle Acre Road, Swaffham, PE37 7HU
Tel: 01760-721390 **Fax:** 01760-723717
E-mail: sales@ksg.co.uk
Website: http://www.sequinart.com
Directors: P. Marcus (MD)
Immediate Holding Company: KITFIX SWALLOW GROUP LIMITED
Registration no: 00736596 **Date established:** 1962 **Turnover:** £1m - £2m
No.of Employees: 11 - 20 **Product Groups:** 49, 61

Date of Accounts	May 11	May 10	May 09
Working Capital	1m	799	728
Fixed Assets	5m	5m	4m
Current Assets	2m	1m	1m

Mansell Construction Services Ltd
Roman House Turbine Way, Swaffham, PE37 7XD
Tel: 01760-721388 **Fax:** 01760-724693
E-mail: swaffham@mansell.plc.uk
Website: http://www.mansell.plc.uk
Bank(s): Barclays, Croydon
Directors: W. Courtman (Fin), D. Lusher (Reg), D. Lusher (MD), B. Jones (MD)
Managers: A. Fake (Mktg Serv Mgr), J. Peagram (Buyer), Soamer (Sales Prom), A. Soamer (Sales Prom), M. Bailey (Mgr)
Ultimate Holding Company: BALFOUR BEATTY PLC
Immediate Holding Company: MANSELL CONSTRUCTION SERVICES LIMITED
Registration no: 01197246 **VAT No.:** 737 8509 94 **Date established:** 1975
Turnover: £10m - £20m **No.of Employees:** 101 - 250 **Product Groups:** 52

Date of Accounts	Dec 11	Dec 10	Dec 09
Sales Turnover	868m	772m	859m
Pre Tax Profit/Loss	14m	15m	20m
Working Capital	86m	85m	102m
Fixed Assets	37m	38m	32m
Current Assets	379m	383m	366m
Current Liabilities	232m	258m	248m

Read Scientific Ltd
32 Brancaster Way, Swaffham, PE37 7RY
Tel: 01760-724546 **Fax:** 01760-724546
E-mail: bill.read1@virgin.net
Directors: W. Read (Prop)
Immediate Holding Company: READ SCIENTIFIC LIMITED
Registration no: 04663148 **VAT No.:** GB 485 9664 78
Date established: 2003 **Turnover:** Up to £250,000
No.of Employees: 1 - 10 **Product Groups:** 27, 38, 44, 48

Date of Accounts	Mar 11	Mar 10	Mar 09
Working Capital	-5	-14	-23
Fixed Assets	21	22	24
Current Assets	18	9	3

Woods Of Swaffham
7-11 Mangate Street, Swaffham, PE37 7QN
Tel: 01760-722609 **Fax:** 01760-725384
E-mail: woodsofswaffham@hotmail.com
Directors: W. Woods (Prop)
Date established: 1987 **No.of Employees:** 1 - 10 **Product Groups:** 36, 39, 40

Thetford

A G A Group
Merton Hall Ponds Merton, Thetford, IP25 6QH
Tel: 01953-886824 **Fax:** 01953-889644
E-mail: ash@agagroup.org.uk
Website: http://www.agagroup.co.uk
Directors: A. Gurdler (Prop)
Immediate Holding Company: MUSIC TECHNOLOGY BOOKS LIMITED
Registration no: 05353798 **VAT No.:** GB 474 1245 54
Date established: 1999 **Turnover:** £2m - £5m **No.of Employees:** 1 - 10
Product Groups: 84

Date of Accounts	Dec 10	Dec 09	Dec 08
Working Capital	10	11	14
Fixed Assets	3	3	4
Current Assets	24	22	36

Allen & Page Ltd
Norfolk Mill Shipdham, Thetford, IP25 7SD
Tel: 01362-822900 **Fax:** 01362-822910
E-mail: helpline@allenandpage.co.uk
Website: http://www.allenandpage.com
Bank(s): Barclays
Directors: B. Page (MD), T. Page (Sales)
Managers: J. Saunders, M. Donaldson (Chief Acct), C. Baillie-lane, E. Mendes (Personnel)
Immediate Holding Company: ALLEN & PAGE,LIMITED
Registration no: 00318101 **VAT No.:** GB 104 7339 88
Date established: 1936 **No.of Employees:** 21 - 50 **Product Groups:** 20, 62

Date of Accounts	Aug 08	Aug 09	Aug 10
Working Capital	423	569	807
Fixed Assets	1m	922	859
Current Assets	1m	1m	2m

Anglian Tool Agency
Unit 9 Lodge Way, Thetford, IP24 1HE
Tel: 01842-765751 **Fax:** 01842-752997
E-mail: ata.thetford@btconnect.com
Directors: H. Woods (Prop)
No.of Employees: 1 - 10 **Product Groups:** 36, 66

Anoca Ltd
24 Roman Way, Thetford, IP24 1XB
Tel: 01842-766131 **Fax:** 01842-762929
E-mail: michael.abbott@anoca.co.uk
Website: http://www.anoca.co.uk
Directors: M. Abbott (Dir)
Immediate Holding Company: ANOCA LIMITED
Registration no: 02058224 **VAT No.:** 460 3077 70 **Date established:** 1986
Turnover: £500,000 - £1m **No.of Employees:** 1 - 10 **Product Groups:** 76

Date of Accounts	Mar 09	Mar 08	Mar 07
Sales Turnover	N/A	N/A	811
Pre Tax Profit/Loss	N/A	N/A	29
Working Capital	-33	-13	27
Fixed Assets	4	4	11
Current Assets	100	70	101
Current Liabilities	N/A	N/A	18

Aquadec Decorative Coatings Ltd
16-20 Howlett Way, Thetford, IP24 1HZ
Tel: 01842-762800 **Fax:** 01842-820151
E-mail: sales@aquadec.co.uk
Website: http://www.aquadec.co.uk
Directors: J. Daines (Sales & Mktg), J. Grint (MD)
Managers: H. Humhpries (Sales Admin)
Registration no: 04434796 **Turnover:** £500,000 - £1m
No.of Employees: 11 - 20 **Product Groups:** 27, 32, 66

Arcbase Valve Services
8 Faraday Place, Thetford, IP24 3RG
Tel: 01842-763580 **Fax:** 01842-762166
E-mail: arcbase@btconnect.com
Website: http://www.arcbase.co.uk
Directors: N. Russell (Prop)
Date established: 1997 **No.of Employees:** 1 - 10 **Product Groups:** 36, 37, 38

Atkin Automation Ltd
11 Howlett Way, Thetford, IP24 1HZ
Tel: 01842-753521 **Fax:** 01842-763614
E-mail: sales@atkinautomation.com
Website: http://www.atkinautomation.com
Directors: C. Ward (Fin)
Immediate Holding Company: ATKIN AUTOMATION LIMITED
Registration no: 05047146 **VAT No.:** GB 833 6158 26
Date established: 2004 **Turnover:** £2m - £5m **No.of Employees:** 1 - 10
Product Groups: 37, 46, 48, 67

Date of Accounts	Dec 11	Dec 10	Dec 09
Working Capital	178	277	109
Fixed Assets	32	12	16
Current Assets	836	616	242

B P C Anglia Ltd
Unit 1 Brunel Business Court Brunel Way, Thetford, IP24 1HP
Tel: 01842-762670 **Fax:** 01842-762633
E-mail: mail@bpc-anglia.co.uk
Website: http://www.bpc-anglia.co.uk
Directors: I. Rolph (Dir)
Immediate Holding Company: BPC (ANGLIA) LIMITED
Registration no: 04486201 **Date established:** 2002
Turnover: Up to £250,000 **No.of Employees:** 1 - 10 **Product Groups:** 40, 52

Date of Accounts	Aug 11	Aug 10	Aug 09
Working Capital	98	79	70
Fixed Assets	61	69	76
Current Assets	128	108	97

Baxter Health Care Ltd
Caxton Way, Thetford, IP24 3SE
Tel: 01842-767000 **Fax:** 01842-767099
E-mail: csob@baxter.co.uk
Website: http://www.baxter.com
Directors: G. Braham (Dir)
Ultimate Holding Company: BAXTER INTERNATIONAL INC (USA)
Immediate Holding Company: BAXTER HEALTHCARE LIMITED
Registration no: 00461365 **Date established:** 1948
Turnover: £125m - £250m **No.of Employees:** 251 - 500
Product Groups: 38

Date of Accounts	Dec 11	Dec 10	Dec 09
Sales Turnover	154m	138m	127m
Pre Tax Profit/Loss	13m	15m	8m
Working Capital	-33m	-34m	-51m
Fixed Assets	94m	92m	90m
Current Assets	93m	86m	103m
Current Liabilities	12m	13m	16m

Blake & Boughton Ltd
Unit 2 Roman Way, Thetford, IP24 1XB
Tel: 01842-751555 **Fax:** 01842-755577
E-mail: sales@blakeandboughton.co.uk
Website: http://www.scalesandbalances.co.uk
Directors: J. Boughton (Sales), P. Blake (Dir)
Immediate Holding Company: BLAKE AND BOUGHTON LIMITED
Registration no: 04297770 **Date established:** 2001
Turnover: £500,000 - £1m **No.of Employees:** 1 - 10 **Product Groups:** 38, 48

Date of Accounts	Oct 11	Oct 10	Oct 09
Working Capital	107	127	109
Fixed Assets	24	17	15
Current Assets	330	322	253

Breckland Finishing Ltd
12-14 Napier Place, Thetford, IP24 3RL
Tel: 01842-763740
E-mail: brecklandfinishing@btconnect.com
Website: http://www.brecklandfinishing.co.uk
Directors: C. Wilson (MD)
Immediate Holding Company: BRECKLAND FINISHING LIMITED
Registration no: 07636449 **Date established:** 2011
No.of Employees: 1 - 10 **Product Groups:** 46, 48

Caligraving
Brunel Way, Thetford, IP24 1HP
Tel: 01842-752116 **Fax:** 01842-755512
E-mail: info@caligraving.co.uk
Website: http://www.caligraving.co.uk
Bank(s): Barclays
Directors: C. Makings (Co Sec), O. Makings (Dir)
Ultimate Holding Company: PRINT AND PRESS SERVICES LIMITED
Immediate Holding Company: CALIGRAVING LIMITED
Registration no: 00570619 **Date established:** 1956
No.of Employees: 21 - 50 **Product Groups:** 28, 44

Date of Accounts	Aug 11	Aug 10	Aug 09
Working Capital	224	570	593
Fixed Assets	2m	2m	1m
Current Assets	810	1m	1m

Camvac Ltd
Burrell Way, Thetford, IP24 3QY
Tel: 01842-755021 **Fax:** 01842-762424
E-mail: info@camvaclimited.com
Website: http://www.camvaclimited.com
Bank(s): Barclays
Directors: S. Jackson (MD)
Immediate Holding Company: CAMVAC LIMITED
Registration no: 06582196 **VAT No.:** GB 238 5870 30
Date established: 2008 **Turnover:** £20m - £50m
No.of Employees: 101 - 250 **Product Groups:** 30

Date of Accounts	Jun 11	Jun 10	Jun 09
Sales Turnover	29m	22m	16m
Pre Tax Profit/Loss	1m	-72	181
Working Capital	-524	1m	1m
Fixed Assets	3m	3m	3m
Current Assets	9m	7m	7m
Current Liabilities	4m	2m	2m

Centurion Safety Products Ltd
21 Howlett Way, Thetford, IP24 1HZ
Tel: 01842-754266 **Fax:** 01842-765590
E-mail: sales@centurionsafety.co.uk
Website: http://www.centurionsafety.co.uk
Directors: D. Adler (Fin), D. Holdham (Grp Chief Exec), T. Epps (Fin)
Managers: M. Locke (Mktg Serv Mgr), S. Tuck (Purch Mgr)
Immediate Holding Company: CENTURION SAFETY PRODUCTS LTD
Registration no: 00013067 **VAT No.:** GB 102 0808 29
Date established: 1979 **Turnover:** £10m - £20m
No.of Employees: 101 - 250 **Product Groups:** 30, 40

Date of Accounts	Dec 11	Dec 10	Dec 09
Sales Turnover	12m	12m	11m
Pre Tax Profit/Loss	2m	3m	2m
Working Capital	7m	7m	6m
Fixed Assets	2m	2m	2m
Current Assets	9m	9m	7m
Current Liabilities	1m	1m	1m

Component Solutions For Industry Ltd
Unit 12-14 Brunel Way, Thetford, IP24 1HP
Tel: 01842-752775
E-mail: info@csi-solutions.co.uk
Website: http://www.csi-solutions.co.uk
Directors: G. Werrell (Dir)
Managers: G. Werrell (Mgr)
Immediate Holding Company: COMPONENT SOLUTIONS FOR INDUSTRY LIMITED
Registration no: 03730849 **Date established:** 1999
No.of Employees: 21 - 50 **Product Groups:** 33, 36, 46, 52

Date of Accounts	Dec 11	Dec 10	Dec 09
Working Capital	664	475	630
Fixed Assets	1m	1m	1m
Current Assets	2m	2m	2m

Comtek Ltd
41 St Helens Way, Thetford, IP24 1HG
Tel: 01842-753907 **Fax:** 01842-762924
E-mail: enquiries@comtek-ltd.com
Website: http://www.comtek-ltd.com
Directors: D. Dixon (Co Sec), M. Grossman (Dir)
Ultimate Holding Company: GARMET HOLDINGS LIMITED
Immediate Holding Company: COMTEK LTD
Registration no: 04300468 **Date established:** 2001
No.of Employees: 11 - 20 **Product Groups:** 38, 42

Date of Accounts	Jul 11	Jul 10	Jul 09
Working Capital	141	124	97
Fixed Assets	28	15	31
Current Assets	346	294	223

Marshall Cooke Ltd
Burrell Way, Thetford, IP24 3RW
Tel: 01842-764312 **Fax:** 01842-761033
E-mail: sales@marshallcooke.com
Website: http://www.marshallcooke.com
Directors: D. Marshall (MD), C. Marshall (Fin)
Managers: A. Marshall (Tech Serv Mgr), J. Weibel (Personnel)
Immediate Holding Company: MARSHALL COOKE LIMITED
Registration no: 01578678 **VAT No.:** GB 363 6284 40
Date established: 1981 **Turnover:** £1m - £2m **No.of Employees:** 1 - 10
Product Groups: 42, 45

Eastwood Catering Equipment & Consulting Ltd
51 Vicarage Walk Watton, Thetford, IP25 6PH
Tel: 01953-885192 **Fax:** 01953-885192
E-mail: enquiries@equipment4catering.co.uk
Website: http://www.equipment4catering.co.uk
Directors: A. Eastwood (Prop)
Immediate Holding Company: EASTWOOD CATERING EQUIPMENT & CONSULTING LTD
Registration no: 05231519 **Date established:** 2004
No.of Employees: 1 - 10 **Product Groups:** 20, 40, 41

Date of Accounts	Sep 11	Sep 10	Sep 09
Working Capital	-7	-6	6
Fixed Assets	2	6	9
Current Assets	17	15	26

EXHEAT Ltd

Threxton Road Industrial Estate Watton, Thetford, IP25 6NG
Tel: 01953-886200 **Fax:** 01953-886222
E-mail: sales@exheat.com
Website: http://www.exheat.com
Directors: P. Smithers (Grp Ch), S. Lyon (Tech Serv), S. Hudson (Purch), J. Cawcutt (MD), D. Webster (Fab)
Managers: R. Whadcoat (Quality Control), K. Parrot, K. Modha, J. Fahim, D. Lim, J. van der Meulen (Mktg Serv Mgr), L. Adams
Immediate Holding Company: EXHEAT LIMITED
Registration no: 02624818 **VAT No.:** GB 595 1441 26
Date established: 1991 **Turnover:** £5m - £10m **No.of Employees:** 1 - 10
Product Groups: 33, 35, 36, 37, 38, 39, 40, 41, 42, 44, 45, 46, 54, 63, 66, 67, 83

Date of Accounts	Aug 09	Aug 08	Aug 10
Sales Turnover	18m	N/A	13m
Pre Tax Profit/Loss	4m	3m	2m
Working Capital	5m	5m	4m
Fixed Assets	331	165	487
Current Assets	9m	10m	10m
Current Liabilities	2m	4m	4m

Guardline Technology Ltd

5 Brunel Way, Thetford, IP24 1HP
Tel: 01842-822150 **Fax:** 01842-820300
E-mail: sales@guardline.co.uk
Website: http://www.guardline.co.uk
Directors: A. Broughton (Sales), K. Wheeler (Fin), R. Wheeler (MD), K. Green (Cust Serv)
Managers: M. Dolman (Personnel), D. Everitt
Immediate Holding Company: GUARDLINE TECHNOLOGY LIMITED
Registration no: 01556397 **Date established:** 1981 **Turnover:** £2m - £5m
No.of Employees: 51 - 100 **Product Groups:** 24, 30, 67

Date of Accounts	Apr 11	Apr 10	Apr 09
Working Capital	410	290	200
Fixed Assets	336	428	423
Current Assets	2m	1m	1m

Industrial Controls Ltd

Unit 1 Audley Court Lodge Way, Thetford, IP24 1HT
Tel: 01842-750800 **Fax:** 01842-765900
E-mail: sales@industrialcontrols.co.uk
Website: http://www.industrialcontrols.co.uk
Directors: M. Clutton (MD)
Registration no: 01968589 **Turnover:** £500,000 - £1m
No.of Employees: 1 - 10 **Product Groups:** 37, 38, 40, 45, 84

Industrial Plastic Coatings

St Helens Way, Thetford, IP24 1HG
Tel: 01842-753529 **Fax:** 01842-754060
E-mail: sales@industrialplasticcoatings.co.uk
Website: http://www.industrialplasticcoatings.co.uk
Directors: D. Cunningham (MD)
Ultimate Holding Company: CREATIVE DISPLAYS (U.K.) LTD.
Immediate Holding Company: INDUSTRIAL PLASTIC COATING LIMITED
Registration no: 00813336 **VAT No.:** GB 103 6513 12
Date established: 1964 **Turnover:** £250,000 - £500,000
No.of Employees: 51 - 100 **Product Groups:** 48

Date of Accounts	May 09	May 08
Working Capital	1	1
Current Assets	1	1

J M Ayres Sons

Mayes Farm Severalls Road, Methwold Hythe, Thetford, IP26 4QU
Tel: 01366-728769
Directors: N. Ayres (Ptnr)
Date established: 1978 **No.of Employees:** 1 - 10 **Product Groups:** 41

Jeyes

Brunel Way, Thetford, IP24 1HF
Tel: 01842-757575 **Fax:** 01842-757824
E-mail: bernard.daymon@jeyes.co.uk
Website: http://www.jeyes.co.uk
Managers: M. Tyldesley
Ultimate Holding Company: JEYES HOLDINGS LIMITED
Immediate Holding Company: JEYES GROUP LIMITED
Registration no: 04440301 **VAT No.:** GB 428 0668 42
Date established: 2002 **Turnover:** £2m - £5m
No.of Employees: 251 - 500 **Product Groups:** 32

Date of Accounts	Dec 11	Aug 10	Aug 09
Sales Turnover	4m	3m	5m
Pre Tax Profit/Loss	-17m	-23m	-6m
Working Capital	5m	14m	21m
Fixed Assets	27m	50m	58m
Current Assets	6m	15m	36m
Current Liabilities	832	668	6

John Mayes Engineers

13 Roman Way, Thetford, IP24 1XB
Tel: 01842-753400 **Fax:** 01842-754285
E-mail: sales@pipe-fittings.co.uk
Website: http://www.pipe-fittings.co.uk
Directors: J. Mayes (Prop)
Immediate Holding Company: JOHN MAYES ENGINEERS LIMITED
Registration no: 04571975 **Date established:** 2002
Turnover: £250,000 - £500,000 **No.of Employees:** 11 - 20
Product Groups: 36, 66

Date of Accounts	Mar 11	Mar 10	Mar 09
Working Capital	1m	860	705
Fixed Assets	181	222	172
Current Assets	2m	1m	1m

R K & J Jones

Southery Road Seltwell, Feltwell, Thetford, IP26 4EH
Tel: 01842-828101
E-mail: r.jones@birdbrand.co.uk
Website: http://www.birdbrand.co.uk
Directors: R. Jones (Sales)
Managers: K. Jones (Mgr)
Immediate Holding Company: R K & J JONES LIMITED
Registration no: 03738345 **Date established:** 1999
No.of Employees: 1 - 10 **Product Groups:** 25, 31, 32

Machined Precision Components Ltd

4f Threxton Road Industrial Estate Watton, Thetford, IP25 6NG
Tel: 01953-889944 **Fax:** 01953-889955
E-mail: sales@mpcltd.net
Website: http://www.mpcltd.net
Directors: L. Hunton (Fin)
Immediate Holding Company: MACHINED PRECISION COMPONENTS LIMITED
Registration no: 05093377 **Date established:** 2004
No.of Employees: 1 - 10 **Product Groups:** 48, 84

Date of Accounts	Apr 11	Apr 10	Apr 09
Working Capital	40	19	36
Fixed Assets	80	90	100
Current Assets	108	65	70

Nets2go

Unit 1 Breckland House Norwich Road, Watton, Thetford, IP25 6JT
Tel: 01953-889215
E-mail: ashley.woodyate@nets2go.co.uk
Website: http://www.nets2go.co.uk
Directors: A. Woodyate (Prop), A. Woodyet (MD)
Turnover: Up to £250,000 **No.of Employees:** 1 - 10 **Product Groups:** 23

Peerless Plastics & Coatings

16-20 Howlett Way, Thetford, IP24 1HZ
Tel: 01842-750333 **Fax:** 01842-750770
E-mail: sales@peerless-coatings.co.uk
Website: http://www.peerless-coatings.co.uk
Bank(s): Lloyds TSB Bank plc
Directors: J. Grint (MD), H. Humphries (Fin)
Immediate Holding Company: PEERLESS PLASTICS AND COATINGS LIMITED
Registration no: 07079469 **Date established:** 2009 **Turnover:** £2m - £5m
No.of Employees: 11 - 20 **Product Groups:** 30, 31, 32, 33, 37, 44, 48, 49, 84

Date of Accounts	Apr 11
Working Capital	27
Fixed Assets	58
Current Assets	351

Pemco International

3 Rutherford Way, Thetford, IP24 1HA
Tel: 01842-855700 **Fax:** 01842-763500
E-mail: info@pemco.kpl.net
Website: http://www.kpl.net
Managers: S. Robertson (Chief Mgr)
Date established: 1986 **No.of Employees:** 1 - 10 **Product Groups:** 38, 42

Premier Plastics Ltd

Unit 43 St Helens Court St Helens Way, Thetford, IP24 1HG
Tel: 01842-750461 **Fax:** 01842-754743
E-mail: enquiries@premierplastics.org.uk
Website: http://www.premierplastics.org.uk
Directors: B. Green (Dir)
Immediate Holding Company: PREMIER PLASTICS THETFORD LTD.
Registration no: 04378508 **Date established:** 2002 **Turnover:** £1m - £2m
No.of Employees: 11 - 20 **Product Groups:** 30, 35, 42, 46, 48, 84

Date of Accounts	Nov 11	Nov 10	Nov 09
Working Capital	79	45	-82
Fixed Assets	108	117	141
Current Assets	219	253	184

R P D Mouldings

1c Market Street Shipdham, Thetford, IP25 7LY
Tel: 01362-821211 **Fax:** 01362-821211
E-mail: relement@aol.com
Directors: R. Element (Prop)
Turnover: £250,000 - £500,000 **No.of Employees:** 1 - 10
Product Groups: 30, 33

Rowlinson Packaging

1-5 Caxton Way, Thetford, IP24 3RY
Tel: 01842-753262 **Fax:** 01842-752026
E-mail: packaging@rowlinson.co.uk
Website: http://www.rowlinson.co.uk
Managers: A. King (Mgr), J. King (Develop Mgr), S. Drew (Personnel), S. Bickell (Sales Admin)
Immediate Holding Company: ROWLINSON PACKAGING LTD
Registration no: 02429702 **VAT No.:** GB 521 4166 80
No.of Employees: 21 - 50 **Product Groups:** 25, 48, 76

Sabrefix UK Ltd

Threxton Road Indl-Est Watton, Thetford, IP25 6NG
Tel: 01953-883919 **Fax:** 01953-884229
E-mail: g.tweed@sabrefix.com
Website: http://www.sabrefix.com
Directors: G. Tweed (MD)
Immediate Holding Company: D.E. PANELS LIMITED
Registration no: 02693077 **Date established:** 1992
No.of Employees: 21 - 50 **Product Groups:** 26, 35

Date of Accounts	Mar 11	Mar 10	Mar 09
Working Capital	-53	-71	-59
Fixed Assets	282	269	271
Current Assets	94	86	104

Solar Essence

Energy House Fisons Way Industrial Estate 45 St Helens Court, Thetford, IP24 1HG
Tel: 01842-845845
E-mail: info@solaressence.co.uk
Website: http://www.solaressence.co.uk
Directors: B. Wittam (MD)
Ultimate Holding Company: CREATIVE DISPLAYS (U.K.) LTD.
Immediate Holding Company: WALTON DESIGNS LIMITED
Registration no: 03459019 **Date established:** 1997 **Turnover:** £5m - £10m
No.of Employees: 11 - 20 **Product Groups:** 37

Date of Accounts	Dec 10	Dec 09	Dec 08
Working Capital	-0	-0	-0

Specialised Belting Supplies Ltd

26 Brunel Way, Thetford, IP24 1HP
Tel: 01842-754392 **Fax:** 01842-765264
E-mail: geoff.toft@sbsbelting.com
Website: http://www.sbsbelting.com
Bank(s): Lloyds TSB Bank plc
Directors: G. Toft (MD), P. Lord (Co Sec), P. Webster (Jt MD), P. Lord (MD)
Managers: L. Kitchen (Mgr)
Immediate Holding Company: SPECIALISED BELTING SUPPLIES LIMITED
Registration no: 02393041 **VAT No.:** GB 571 0994 28
Date established: 1989 **Turnover:** £10m - £20m
No.of Employees: 21 - 50 **Product Groups:** 30, 35, 45

Date of Accounts	Dec 10	Dec 09	Dec 08
Working Capital	1m	898	948
Fixed Assets	2m	2m	2m
Current Assets	3m	2m	3m

Specialised Polishing Services

Unit 3 Hill Fort Close, Thetford, IP24 1HS
Tel: 01842-762700 **Fax:** 01842-762700
Website: http://www.specialisedpolishingservices.co.uk
Directors: N. Thynne (Prop)
Date established: 1994 **No.of Employees:** 1 - 10 **Product Groups:** 46, 48

Sultans Ltd

Stephenson Way, Thetford, IP24 3RH
Tel: 01842-751515 **Fax:** 01842-764269
E-mail: info@sultans.co.uk
Website: http://www.sultans.co.uk
Bank(s): HSBC
Directors: N. Darbaz (MD), K. Darbaz (Co Sec)
Immediate Holding Company: SULTANS LIMITED
Registration no: 01452181 **VAT No.:** GB 342 5904 61
Date established: 1979 **Turnover:** £2m - £5m **No.of Employees:** 11 - 20
Product Groups: 20

Date of Accounts	Mar 11	Mar 10	Mar 09
Sales Turnover	4m	4m	N/A
Pre Tax Profit/Loss	-214	320	215
Working Capital	4m	4m	3m
Fixed Assets	5m	6m	4m
Current Assets	5m	4m	4m
Current Liabilities	968	187	424

The Fireplace & Plaster Centre

Station Lane, Thetford, IP24 1ND
Tel: 01842-766999 **Fax:** 01842-761122
E-mail: admin@astrellita.co.uk
Website: http://www.astrellita.co.uk
Directors: N. Cardwell (Prop)
Immediate Holding Company: CUNNINGHAM MOTORS LIMITED
Registration no: 04575653 **Date established:** 2002
No.of Employees: 1 - 10 **Product Groups:** 35, 49

Date of Accounts	Mar 11	Mar 10	Mar 09
Working Capital	42	43	37
Fixed Assets	21	21	23
Current Assets	81	85	77

Thetford Door Services

21 Edith Cavell Close, Thetford, IP24 1TJ
Tel: 01842-764730 **Fax:** 01842-764643
E-mail: jhutt@thetforddoorservicesltd.co.uk
Website: http://www.thetforddoorservicesltd.co.uk
Directors: J. Hutt (Prop)
Date established: 2003 **No.of Employees:** 1 - 10 **Product Groups:** 26, 35

Thetford International

Rymer Point Bury Road, Barnham, Thetford, IP24 2PN
Tel: 01842-890500 **Fax:** 01842-890077
E-mail: sales-serv@thetford-int.co.uk
Website: http://www.thetford-int.co.uk
Directors: K. Ellis (Ch)
Immediate Holding Company: THETFORD INTERNATIONAL COMPACTORS LIMITED
Registration no: 00968063 **Date established:** 1969 **Turnover:** £2m - £5m
No.of Employees: 21 - 50 **Product Groups:** 42, 44, 45, 47, 52, 54, 67

Date of Accounts	Dec 11	Dec 10	Dec 09
Working Capital	375	184	134
Fixed Assets	552	575	584
Current Assets	2m	2m	2m

The Traditional Rope Company

40 Oak Street Feltwell, Thetford, IP26 4DD
Tel: 0781-383 2693
E-mail: neil@traditionalropecompany.co.uk
Website: http://www.traditionalropecompany.co.uk
Directors: N. Gladwell (Prop)
Immediate Holding Company: KINGSBURY PARTNERSHIP LIMITED
Date established: 2005 **No.of Employees:** 1 - 10 **Product Groups:** 23, 35, 63

TS Associates Storage Equipment Ltd

New Green Business Park Norwich Road, Watton, Thetford, IP25 6JX
Tel: 0845-370 3750 **Fax:** 0845-2602361
E-mail: sales@storage-equipment-uk.co.uk
Website: http://www.tsequipment.co.uk
Directors: S. Etheridge (Fin), S. Swallow (MD)
Immediate Holding Company: TS Associates (Storage Equipment) Ltd
Registration no: 04225561 **Date established:** 1901
No.of Employees: 1 - 10 **Product Groups:** 35, 42, 45

Date of Accounts	Jun 08	Jun 07	Jun 06
Working Capital	-3	10	5
Fixed Assets	46	28	20
Current Assets	121	110	185
Current Liabilities	123	100	180
Total Share Capital	1	1	1

Weco Engineering Ltd

Griston Road Watton, Thetford, IP25 6DL
Tel: 01953-881142 **Fax:** 01953-882795
Website: http://www.weco.fsnet.co.uk
Directors: L. McCarthy (Fin), J. McCarthy (MD)
Immediate Holding Company: WECO (HOLDINGS) LIMITED
Registration no: 01570478 **VAT No.:** GB 106 7521 87
Date established: 1981 **Turnover:** £500,000 - £1m
No.of Employees: 11 - 20 **Product Groups:** 48

Date of Accounts	Jun 11	Jun 10	Jun 07
Working Capital	-3	-10	-18
Fixed Assets	426	445	344
Current Assets	27	25	18

Willis Builders Merchants

Wyatts Way, Thetford, IP24 1HB
Tel: 01842-821200 **Fax:** 01359-253881
E-mail: tim.warner@civilsandlintels.co.uk
Website: http://www.civilsandlintels.co.uk
Managers: T. Warner (Mgr)
No.of Employees: 11 - 20 **Product Groups:** 30, 33

G L Woods & Sons

Carbrooke Road Ovington, Thetford, IP25 6SD
Tel: 01953-881223
Directors: C. Woods (Ptnr)
Date established: 1943 **No.of Employees:** 1 - 10 **Product Groups:** 36, 39, 40

Wymondham

B B C Fire Protection Ltd

St Florian House Ayton Road, Wymondham, NR18 0QH
Tel: 01953-857700 **Fax:** 01953-857750
E-mail: sales@bbcfire.co.uk
Website: http://www.bbcfire.co.uk
Bank(s): Barclays
Directors: N. Copeman (Dir)
Managers: E. Copeman, S. Cavill (Sales Prom Mgr), D. Adams (Sales Admin), M. Church (Tech Serv Mgr)
Immediate Holding Company: B.B.C. FIRE PROTECTION LIMITED
Registration no: 01454397 **Date established:** 1979 **Turnover:** £5m - £10m
No.of Employees: 51 - 100 **Product Groups:** 40, 52

Date of Accounts	Dec 11	Dec 10	Dec 09
Sales Turnover	8m	8m	8m
Pre Tax Profit/Loss	453	372	397
Working Capital	3m	3m	3m
Fixed Assets	814	789	820
Current Assets	6m	5m	5m
Current Liabilities	2m	2m	2m

Barley Chalu Ltd

Ayton Road, Wymondham, NR18 0QH
Tel: 01953-602771 **Fax:** 01953-606631
E-mail: sales@barleychalu.co.uk
Website: http://www.barleychalu.co.uk
Bank(s): National Westminster
Directors: D. Carman (Dir), J. Chalu (MD), R. Chalu (Fin)
Managers: D. Palmer, J. Evans (Mktg Serv Mgr), P. Gardiner (Tech Serv Mgr)
Ultimate Holding Company: FUTURE METAL HOLDINGS LIMITED
Immediate Holding Company: BARLEY CHALU LIMITED
Registration no: 00923921 **VAT No.:** 104 6598 69 **Date established:** 1967
Turnover: £5m - £10m **No.of Employees:** 51 - 100 **Product Groups:** 34, 48

Date of Accounts	Dec 11	Dec 10	Dec 09
Sales Turnover	6m	6m	5m
Pre Tax Profit/Loss	312	199	-87
Working Capital	1m	980	767
Fixed Assets	993	1m	1m
Current Assets	3m	3m	2m
Current Liabilities	1m	1m	977

Curtains Curtains Curtains

19 Penfold Drive, Wymondham, NR18 0WZ
Tel: 01953-603529
E-mail: andy@attentiongrabbers.co.uk
Website: http://www.curtainscurtainscurtains.co.uk
Directors: D. Cooper (Prop)
Immediate Holding Company: CURTAINS CURTAINS CURTAINS LTD
Registration no: 06978175 **Date established:** 2009
No.of Employees: 1 - 10 **Product Groups:** 23, 24, 63

Date of Accounts	Mar 11	Mar 10
Working Capital	-263	-293
Fixed Assets	305	341
Current Assets	68	64

Norfolk Sporting Guns

18a Market Street, Wymondham, NR18 0BB
Tel: 01953-605517 **Fax:** 01953-600060
E-mail: christanner1957@tiscali.co.uk
Website: http://www.norfolk-sporting-guns.co.uk
Directors: C. Tanner (Prop)
Date established: 1991 **No.of Employees:** 1 - 10 **Product Groups:** 36, 39, 40

Pruce Newman Pipework Ltd

Ayton Road, Wymondham, NR18 0QJ
Tel: 01953-605123 **Fax:** 01953-601115
E-mail: mail@prucenewman.co.uk
Website: http://www.prucenewman.co.uk
Bank(s): National Westminster Bank Plc
Directors: S. Pruce (Co Sec), B. Edwards (MD)
Managers: J. Tanner (Transport), A. Gare (Chief Acct)
Immediate Holding Company: PRUCE NEWMAN PIPEWORK LIMITED
Registration no: 01111151 **VAT No.:** GB 247 3879 22
Date established: 1973 **Turnover:** £5m - £10m
No.of Employees: 101 - 250 **Product Groups:** 35, 36, 38, 48, 51, 52, 80

Date of Accounts	May 12	May 11	May 10
Sales Turnover	8m	8m	8m
Pre Tax Profit/Loss	78	89	491
Working Capital	847	899	1m
Fixed Assets	867	834	852
Current Assets	3m	2m	2m
Current Liabilities	680	600	702

Quick-Strip Ltd

Unit 2 Bridge Industrial Estate, Silfield Road, Wymondham, NR18 9AU
Tel: 01953-604399 **Fax:** 01953-602556
E-mail: sales@quickstrips.co.uk
Website: http://www.quickstrips.co.uk
Directors: D. Chapman (MD)
Managers: J. Edwards (Sales Admin), K. Mortlock (Mgr)
VAT No.: GB 525 3067 63 **Date established:** 1983
Turnover: £250,000 - £500,000 **No.of Employees:** 11 - 20
Product Groups: 54

Sherpa Packaging Supplies

Unit 9 Oak Tree Business Park Philip Ford Way, Silfield, Wymondham, NR18 9AQ
Tel: 01953-605700 **Fax:** 01953-606535
E-mail: bernard.allan@raepak.co.uk
Website: http://www.sherpa-packaging.com
Directors: P. Randle (MD), B. Allen (MD), A. Paterson (MD)
Managers: P. Edwards (Sales Prom Mgr)
Immediate Holding Company: GREEN FROG CAB COMPANY LIMITED
Registration no: 04365799 **Date established:** 2011
No.of Employees: 1 - 10 **Product Groups:** 38, 42

Date of Accounts	Apr 11	Apr 10	Apr 09
Working Capital	831	617	715
Fixed Assets	21	30	11
Current Assets	1m	778	817

Stauff Anglia Ltd

Unit 405 Copper Smith Way, Wymondham, NR18 0WY
Tel: 01953-857158 **Fax:** 01953-857159
E-mail: sales@stauffanglia.co.uk
Website: http://www.stauffanglia.co.uk
Directors: K. Rodgers (Prop)
Immediate Holding Company: STAUFF ANGLIA LIMITED
Registration no: 05673586 **Date established:** 2006 **Turnover:** £1m - £2m
No.of Employees: 1 - 10 **Product Groups:** 29, 30, 36

Date of Accounts	Jan 12	Jan 11	Jan 10
Working Capital	35	17	9
Fixed Assets	15	22	25
Current Assets	418	356	361

NORTHAMPTONSHIRE

Brackley

A C S Window Treatments
73 Manor Road, Brackley, NN13 6ED
Tel: 01327-855550 **Fax:** 01327-855550
Directors: F. Smith (Snr Part)
No.of Employees: 1 - 10 **Product Groups:** 24, 30

B P Y Plastics
J Lincoln Park Borough Road, Buckingham Road Industrial Estate, Brackley, NN13 7BE
Tel: 01280-706335 **Fax:** 01280-705675
E-mail: tony@bpy-plastics.com
Website: http://www.bpy-plastics.com
Directors: S. Boyd (Fin), A. Boyd (MD)
Immediate Holding Company: B.P.Y. PLASTICS LIMITED
Registration no: 04226013 **VAT No.:** GB 581 3149 43
Date established: 2001 **No.of Employees:** 1 - 10 **Product Groups:** 30

Date of Accounts	Jul 11	Jul 10	Jul 09
Working Capital	-32	-46	-74
Fixed Assets	62	77	87
Current Assets	33	35	26

H Bronnley & Co. Ltd
Bronnley Works Radstone Road, Brackley, NN13 5AU
Tel: 01280-702291 **Fax:** 01280-703912
E-mail: declan.salter@bronnley.co.uk
Website: http://www.bronnley.co.uk
Bank(s): Midland, Banbury
Directors: N. Towers (Fin), G. Revis (MD)
Managers: J. Capel (Personnel), B. Tite (Purch Mgr), A. Glenton (Mktg Serv Mgr), J. Vallis (Sales Prom Mgr), T. Millington (Tech Serv Mgr)
Ultimate Holding Company: KAYE ENTERPRISES LIMITED
Immediate Holding Company: HBCL REALISATIONS LIMITED
Registration no: 00046883 **VAT No.:** GB 443 8711 43
Date established: 1996 **Turnover:** £5m - £10m
No.of Employees: 101 - 250 **Product Groups:** 32

Date of Accounts	Dec 10	Dec 09	Dec 08
Sales Turnover	7m	7m	6m
Pre Tax Profit/Loss	-533	-1m	-2m
Working Capital	-2m	-943	187
Fixed Assets	3m	3m	4m
Current Assets	3m	4m	4m
Current Liabilities	2m	2m	2m

Cantor & Nissel Ltd
Market Place, Brackley, NN13 7NN
Tel: 01280-702002 **Fax:** 01280-703003
E-mail: info@cantor-nissel.co.uk
Website: http://www.cantor-nissel.co.uk
Directors: D. Cantor (Dir)
Immediate Holding Company: CANTOR & NISSEL LIMITED
Registration no: 01215483 **VAT No.:** GB 293 9703 18
Date established: 1975 **Turnover:** Up to £250,000
No.of Employees: 21 - 50 **Product Groups:** 38

Date of Accounts	Jul 11	Jul 10	Jul 09
Working Capital	123	150	201
Fixed Assets	1m	1m	1m
Current Assets	499	505	553

Caterparts Catering Equipment
The Engine Shed Top Station Road Industrial Estate Top Station Road, Brackley, NN13 7UG
Tel: 01280-845344 **Fax:** 01280-845345
E-mail: sales@caterparts.com
Website: http://www.caterparts.com
Directors: R. Keith (MD)
Ultimate Holding Company: CRYSTAL HOUSE HOLDINGS LIMITED
Immediate Holding Company: CATERPARTS LIMITED
Registration no: 06745472 **Date established:** 2008 **Turnover:** £2m - £5m
No.of Employees: 21 - 50 **Product Groups:** 20, 40, 41

Date of Accounts	Dec 11	Dec 10	Dec 09
Sales Turnover	N/A	3m	N/A
Pre Tax Profit/Loss	N/A	128	N/A
Working Capital	187	180	86
Fixed Assets	49	8	7
Current Assets	1m	1m	1m
Current Liabilities	105	309	271

Celef Audio Ltd
1 Riding Court Riding Road, Buckingham Road Industrial Estate, Brackley, NN13 7BH
Tel: 01280-700147 **Fax:** 01280-700148
E-mail: stewart@proac-loudspeakers.com
Website: http://www.proac-loudspeakers.com
Directors: S. Tyler (MD)
Immediate Holding Company: CELEF AUDIO INTERNATIONAL LIMITED
Registration no: 01225917 **Date established:** 1975
Turnover: £250,000 - £500,000 **No.of Employees:** 1 - 10
Product Groups: 37

Date of Accounts	Nov 11	Nov 10	Nov 09
Working Capital	201	221	282
Fixed Assets	70	65	63
Current Assets	581	580	714

Coppell Oak Ltd
Burwell Hill Farm Turweston Road, Brackley, NN13 7DD
Tel: 01280-700090
E-mail: coppell.oak_ltd@btinternet.com
Website: http://www.oakgardenfurniture.co.uk
Directors: D. Coppell (MD)
Immediate Holding Company: COPPELL OAK LIMITED
Registration no: 05856743 **Date established:** 2006
Turnover: Up to £250,000 **No.of Employees:** 1 - 10 **Product Groups:** 26

Date of Accounts	Jun 08	Jun 07
Working Capital	-14	-10
Fixed Assets	6	2
Current Assets	13	12
Current Liabilities	27	22
Total Share Capital	1	1

Dynoptic Systems Ltd
Furlong House Crowfield, Brackley, NN13 5TW
Tel: 01280-850521 **Fax:** 01280-850568
E-mail: sales@dynoptic.com
Website: http://www.dynoptic.com
Directors: J. Jones (Dir)
Immediate Holding Company: DYNOPTIC SYSTEMS LIMITED
Registration no: 01950437 **Date established:** 1985
Turnover: £500,000 - £1m **No.of Employees:** 1 - 10 **Product Groups:** 29, 38, 40, 45

Date of Accounts	Sep 11	Sep 10	Sep 09
Working Capital	353	196	161
Fixed Assets	48	57	71
Current Assets	484	405	232

F P International UK Ltd
Boundary Road Buckingham Road Industrial Estate, Brackley, NN13 7ES
Tel: 01280-703161 **Fax:** 01280-701915
E-mail: james.blood@fpintl.com
Website: http://www.flo-pak.co.uk
Directors: I. Drummond-smilie (Sales), I. Drummond-Smiley (Sales)
Managers: S. Theckley (Comptroller), S. Higgins, L. Stanley, A. Coleman (Mktg Serv Mgr)
Ultimate Holding Company: FREEFLOW PACKAGING INC (USA)
Immediate Holding Company: FP INTERNATIONAL (UK) LIMITED
Registration no: 01200088 **Date established:** 1975 **Turnover:** £2m - £5m
No.of Employees: 21 - 50 **Product Groups:** 30, 31

Date of Accounts	Sep 11	Sep 10	Sep 09
Sales Turnover	4m	4m	4m
Pre Tax Profit/Loss	-664	-526	-1m
Working Capital	-771	-1m	-916
Fixed Assets	1m	2m	3m
Current Assets	2m	2m	2m
Current Liabilities	285	439	467

Faccenda Group Ltd
Willow Road, Brackley, NN13 7EX
Tel: 01280-703641 **Fax:** 01280-705335
E-mail: mail@faccenda.co.uk
Website: http://www.faccenda.co.uk
Directors: S. Faccenda (Fin), R. Faccenda (Ch)
Managers: L. Dexter
Ultimate Holding Company: HILLESDEN INVESTMENTS LIMITED
Immediate Holding Company: FACCENDA FARMS LIMITED
Registration no: 01611081 **Date established:** 1982 **Turnover:** £1m - £2m
No.of Employees: 51 - 100 **Product Groups:** 62

Date of Accounts	Sep 11	Sep 10	Apr 09
Sales Turnover	N/A	N/A	1m
Pre Tax Profit/Loss	N/A	N/A	991
Working Capital	6m	5m	4m
Fixed Assets	7m	7m	7m
Current Assets	7m	5m	5m
Current Liabilities	N/A	N/A	136

J Green
5 Halse Road, Brackley, NN13 6EH
Tel: 01280-703838 **Fax:** 01280-703838
Directors: J. Green (Prop)
Date established: 1986 **No.of Employees:** 1 - 10 **Product Groups:** 35

Greenbarnes Ltd
7 Barrington Court Ward Road, Buckingham Road Industrial Estate, Brackley, NN13 7LE
Tel: 01280-701093 **Fax:** 01280-702843
E-mail: mike@greenbarnes.co.uk
Website: http://www.greenbarnes.co.uk
Directors: M. Barnes (Fin)
Immediate Holding Company: GREENBARNES LIMITED
Registration no: 02158191 **Date established:** 1987
No.of Employees: 1 - 10 **Product Groups:** 25, 26, 30, 39, 49

Date of Accounts	Mar 11	Mar 10	Mar 09
Working Capital	242	230	236
Fixed Assets	3	3	5
Current Assets	382	355	353

Knight Design Lighting
PO Box 15, Brackley, NN13 5YN
Tel: 01280-851092 **Fax:** 01280-851093
E-mail: mail@knightdesignlighting.co.uk
Website: http://www.knightdesignlighting.co.uk
Directors: M. Knight (Prop)
No.of Employees: 1 - 10 **Product Groups:** 37, 67

Liftability Ltd
Unit 2Avonbury Court Country Road, Buckingham Road Industrial Estate, Brackley, NN13 7AX
Tel: 01280-841661 **Fax:** 01280-841971
E-mail: sales@liftabilityltd.com
Website: http://www.liftabilityltd.com
Directors: A. Fenwick (Sales), D. Kennard (Dir)
Registration no: 03782380 **No.of Employees:** 1 - 10 **Product Groups:** 35, 39, 45

Date of Accounts	Jun 08	Jun 07	Jun 06
Working Capital	261	203	394
Fixed Assets	87	111	67
Current Assets	680	597	713
Current Liabilities	420	394	318

Maidaid Halcyon
The Engine Shed Top Station Road Industrial Estate Top Station Road, Brackley, NN13 7UG
Tel: 01280-845344 **Fax:** 01280-845340
E-mail: sales@maidaid-halcyon.co.uk
Website: http://www.maidaid.co.uk
Directors: A. Palmer (Dir), M. Gregory (Co Sec)
Immediate Holding Company: BUTTRESS GROUP
Registration no: 06745594 **Date established:** 2008
No.of Employees: 11 - 20 **Product Groups:** 40

Oliver Overhead Doors Ltd
Berkeley House Syresham, Brackley, NN13 5YF
Tel: 01280-850206 **Fax:** 01280-850077
E-mail: r.oliver@oohd.co.uk
Website: http://www.oliveroverhead.co.uk
Directors: R. Oliver (MD), T. Oliver (Sales)
Immediate Holding Company: OLIVER OVERHEAD DOOR COMPANY LIMITED
Registration no: 02811522 **Date established:** 1993 **Turnover:** £1m - £2m
No.of Employees: 1 - 10 **Product Groups:** 26, 35

Date of Accounts	Dec 11	Dec 10	Dec 09
Working Capital	153	155	87
Fixed Assets	6	1	3
Current Assets	394	552	252

Plasmotec
Ward Road Lincoln Park, Buckingham Road Industrial Estate, Brackley, NN13 7LE
Tel: 01280-701335 **Fax:** 01280-701341
E-mail: sales@plasmotec.co.uk
Website: http://www.plasmotec.co.uk
Bank(s): National Westminster
Directors: A. O Neill (Dir), L. Hibble (Dir)
Immediate Holding Company: PLASMOTEC LIMITED
Registration no: 02281896 **VAT No.:** GB 486 1280 33
Date established: 1988 **Turnover:** £2m - £5m **No.of Employees:** 21 - 50
Product Groups: 30, 48

Date of Accounts	Dec 11	Dec 10	Dec 09
Working Capital	218	429	333
Fixed Assets	587	298	413

see next page

***Plasmotec** - Cont'd*

Current Assets	743	884	726

Priory Publications Ltd
The Priory 36 Wappenham Road, Syresham, Brackley, NN13 5HH
Tel: 01280-850603 **Fax:** 01280-850576
E-mail: info@signpost.co.uk
Website: http://www.signpost.co.uk
Directors: M. Orr-Ewing (MD), C. Orr Ewing (Fin)
Immediate Holding Company: PRIORY PUBLICATIONS LIMITED
Registration no: 02235273 **VAT No.:** GB 486 0171 43
Date established: 1988 **Turnover:** £250,000 - £500,000
No.of Employees: 1 - 10 **Product Groups:** 28

Date of Accounts	Mar 12	Mar 11	Mar 10
Working Capital	-15	-14	-7
Fixed Assets	11	1	1
Current Assets	62	90	71

Rational Labelling & Marking Systems
Unit B 13 Borough Road Backingham Road Insdustrial Esta, Buckingham Road Industrial Estate, Brackley, NN13 7BE
Tel: 01280-840988 **Fax:** 01280-705874
E-mail: admin@rational-labelling.com
Website: http://www.rational-labelling.com
Directors: L. Malkoutzis (Fin), I. Malkoutzis (Dir)
Immediate Holding Company: RATIONAL LABELLING & MARKING SYSTEMS LIMITED (THE)
Registration no: 01203423 **Date established:** 1975 **Turnover:** £1m - £2m
No.of Employees: 1 - 10 **Product Groups:** 20, 21, 27, 28, 30, 32, 37, 41, 42, 44, 46, 47, 48, 49, 64, 67

Date of Accounts	Feb 11	Feb 10	Feb 09
Working Capital	345	326	360
Fixed Assets	87	122	124
Current Assets	517	545	496
Current Liabilities	26	28	20

Stannah Lift Services Ltd
4 Boundary Road Buckingham Road Industrial Estate, Brackley, NN13 7ES
Tel: 01280-704600 **Fax:** 01280-701187
Managers: G. Knight (Mgr)
Ultimate Holding Company: STANNAH LIFTS HOLDINGS LIMITED
Immediate Holding Company: STANNAH LIFT SERVICES LIMITED
Registration no: 01189799 **Date established:** 1974
No.of Employees: 21 - 50 **Product Groups:** 35, 39, 45

Date of Accounts	Dec 11	Dec 10	Dec 09
Sales Turnover	84m	82m	87m
Pre Tax Profit/Loss	191	2m	2m
Working Capital	12m	14m	15m
Fixed Assets	4m	4m	3m
Current Assets	21m	24m	24m
Current Liabilities	6m	6m	7m

Ubbink UK Ltd
Borough Road Buckingham Road Industrial Estate, Brackley, NN13 7TB
Tel: 01280-700211 **Fax:** 01280-705331
E-mail: sales@ubbink.co.uk
Website: http://www.ubbink.co.uk
Managers: K. Shaw (Mktg Serv Mgr), J. Donovan (Mgr), L. Chang, G. Player-jones (Sales Prom Mgr), J. Stevens (Purch Mgr), I. Davies (Tech Serv Mgr)
Ultimate Holding Company: CENTROTEC SUSTAINABLE AG (GERMANY)
Immediate Holding Company: UBBINK (U.K.) LIMITED
Registration no: 01168143 **VAT No.:** GB 195 9827 93
Date established: 1974 **Turnover:** £5m - £10m **No.of Employees:** 1 - 10
Product Groups: 30, 40

Date of Accounts	Dec 10	Dec 09	Dec 08
Sales Turnover	6m	5m	8m
Pre Tax Profit/Loss	-796	-540	15
Working Capital	2m	820	1m
Fixed Assets	35	30	48
Current Assets	4m	2m	3m
Current Liabilities	399	416	696

Unique Business Strategies
1 Highfield Mews Highfield Court, Brackley, NN13 7HE
Tel: 01280-844966 **Fax:** 01208-801137
Website: http://www.real-results.org
Directors: A. Pearson (Dir)
No.of Employees: 1 - 10 **Product Groups:** 80

Corby

A M C UK Fasteners
4 Darwin Road Willowbrook East Industrial Estate, Corby, NN17 5XZ
Tel: 01536-271920 **Fax:** 01536-271929
E-mail: david.vines@amcukfasteners.co.uk
Website: http://www.amcukfasteners.co.uk
Directors: D. Vines (Dir)
Immediate Holding Company: A. M. C. (U.K.) FASTENERS LIMITED
Registration no: 01333549 **VAT No.:** GB 313 0243 22
Date established: 1977 **Turnover:** £1m - £2m **No.of Employees:** 1 - 10
Product Groups: 35, 66

Date of Accounts	Dec 11	Dec 10	Dec 09
Working Capital	102	78	92
Fixed Assets	493	515	524
Current Assets	633	583	455

Aluminium Shapes Ltd
Princewood Road Earlstrees, Earlstrees Industrial Estate, Corby, NN17 4AP
Tel: 01536-262437 **Fax:** 01536-204216
E-mail: sales@alishapes.co.uk
Website: http://www.alishapes.co.uk
Directors: C. Bellamy (Fin), M. Patterson (MD), J. Williams (MD)
Managers: N. James, J. Seddon, D. Cook (I.T. Exec), B. Morgan (Prod Mgr)
Ultimate Holding Company: DOMES OF SILENCE HOLDINGS LIMITED
Immediate Holding Company: ALUMINIUM SHAPES LIMITED
Registration no: 03921671 **Date established:** 2000 **Turnover:** £5m - £10m
No.of Employees: 21 - 50 **Product Groups:** 34

Date of Accounts	Jun 11	Jun 10	Jun 09
Sales Turnover	9m	7m	10m
Pre Tax Profit/Loss	-415	30	138
Working Capital	3m	4m	3m
Fixed Assets	3m	3m	3m
Current Assets	6m	7m	6m
Current Liabilities	2m	2m	2m

Ashbury Chocolates
Darwin Road Willowbrook East Industrial Estate, Corby, NN17 5XZ
Tel: 01536-401229 **Fax:** 01536-401176
E-mail: reception@ashbury.co.uk
Website: http://www.ashbury.co.uk
Bank(s): Lloyds
Directors: M. Singh (Fin)
Managers: T. Cutting (Buyer), D. Knight (Sales & Mktg Mg), M. Mahmood (Tech Serv Mgr)
Immediate Holding Company: ASHBURY CHOCOLATES LIMITED
Registration no: 06454894 **VAT No.:** GB 167 0154 75
Date established: 2007 **Turnover:** £20m - £50m
No.of Employees: 101 - 250 **Product Groups:** 20

Date of Accounts	Dec 11	Dec 10	Dec 09
Sales Turnover	29m	32m	22m
Pre Tax Profit/Loss	-396	623	-720
Working Capital	-956	-86	-657
Fixed Assets	3m	3m	2m
Current Assets	8m	8m	7m
Current Liabilities	4m	4m	2m

AVK UK Ltd
Sondes Road Willowbrook East Industrial Estate, Corby, NN17 5XL
Tel: 01536-446920
Website: http://www.avkuk.co.uk
Managers: S. Brody (Mgr)
Ultimate Holding Company: ASX 14,145 APS (DENMARK)
Immediate Holding Company: AVK UK LIMITED
Registration no: 01838290 **Date established:** 1984
No.of Employees: 1 - 10 **Product Groups:** 36, 37, 38

Date of Accounts	Sep 11	Sep 10	Sep 09
Sales Turnover	26m	27m	29m
Pre Tax Profit/Loss	518	537	735
Working Capital	3m	3m	3m
Fixed Assets	546	575	462
Current Assets	9m	9m	10m
Current Liabilities	2m	2m	2m

B B Motors
St James Road St James Industrial Estate, Corby, NN18 8AL
Tel: 01536-202207 **Fax:** 01536-202207
E-mail: bbmotors@fsmail.net
Website: http://www.bbmotors.co.uk
Directors: K. Norris (Prop)
No.of Employees: 1 - 10 **Product Groups:** 38, 39

B D Technical Polymer Ltd
Unit 202b Cooks Road Weldon North Industrial Estate, Corby, NN17 5JT
Tel: 01536-200913 **Fax:** 01536-400836
E-mail: sales@bdtechnicalpolymer.co.uk
Website: http://www.bdtechnicalpolymer.co.uk
Directors: D. Shah (MD)
Immediate Holding Company: BD TECHNICAL POLYMER LIMITED
Registration no: 01681062 **VAT No.:** GB 395 7296 92
Date established: 1982 **Turnover:** £500,000 - £1m
No.of Employees: 1 - 10 **Product Groups:** 23, 29, 49, 63

Date of Accounts	Sep 11	Sep 10	Sep 09
Working Capital	177	159	136
Fixed Assets	49	46	41
Current Assets	336	283	200

Ball & Young Division Of Vitafoan Ltd (a division of Vitafoam Ltd)
53 Causeway Road Earlstrees Industrial Estate, Corby, NN17 4DU
Tel: 01536-200502 **Fax:** 01536-269554
E-mail: sales@underlay.com
Website: http://www.underlay.com
Bank(s): National Westminster Bank Plc
Directors: M. Stirzaker (Fin), D. McLaughlin (Dir)
Ultimate Holding Company: BRITISH VITA P.L.C.
Immediate Holding Company: VITAFOAM LTD
Registration no: 00901282 **VAT No.:** GB 606 3421 71
Date established: 1983 **Turnover:** £10m - £20m
No.of Employees: 101 - 250 **Product Groups:** 25, 29

Bedatec Ltd
Unit 10 Enterprise Park Hunters Road, Weldon North Industrial Estate, Corby, NN17 5JE
Tel: 01536-205488 **Fax:** 01536-205494
E-mail: sales@bedatec.co.uk
Website: http://www.bedatec.co.uk
Directors: J. Heggs (MD)
Registration no: 05719142 **Date established:** 2006
Turnover: Up to £250,000 **No.of Employees:** 1 - 10 **Product Groups:** 46, 48

Briggs Irrigation
Boyle Road Willowbrook East Industrial Estate, Corby, NN17 5XU
Tel: 01536-260338 **Fax:** 01536-263972
E-mail: warrenbriggs@briggsirrigation.co.uk
Website: http://www.briggsirrigation.co.uk
Directors: A. Colwill (Sales), W. Briggs (MD)
Immediate Holding Company: BRIGGS (U.K.) LIMITED
Registration no: 01800222 **Date established:** 1984 **Turnover:** £1m - £2m
No.of Employees: 21 - 50 **Product Groups:** 40, 67

Date of Accounts	Jan 12	Jan 11	Jan 10
Working Capital	2m	1m	2m
Fixed Assets	1m	1m	1m
Current Assets	3m	3m	3m

C R Services
5 Rutherford Court Earlstrees Industrial Estate, Corby, NN17 4SJ
Tel: 01536-261621
Directors: C. Robertson (Prop)
Date established: 1996 **No.of Employees:** 1 - 10 **Product Groups:** 35

Cellular Mouldings Ltd
18 Cronin Courtyard Weldon South Industrial Estate, Corby, NN18 8AG
Tel: 01536-275000 **Fax:** 01536-203653
E-mail: enquiries@cellularmouldings.co.uk
Website: http://www.cellularmouldings.co.uk
Bank(s): Barclays, Kettering
Directors: D. Matthews (MD), J. Matthews (Fin)
Managers: I. Minard (Factory Mgr), B. Bloomfield (Maint), J. Taylor
Registration no: 02956286 **VAT No.:** GB 359 9157 03
Date established: 1994 **Turnover:** £1m - £2m **No.of Employees:** 11 - 20
Product Groups: 30

Date of Accounts	Sep 08	Sep 07	Sep 06
Working Capital	83	94	99
Fixed Assets	157	182	206
Current Assets	509	436	419
Current Liabilities	426	342	321

Chemence Ltd
13 Princewood Road Earlstrees Industrial Estate, Corby, NN17 4XD
Tel: 01536-402600 **Fax:** 01536-400266
E-mail: hugh@chemence.com
Website: http://www.chemence.com
Bank(s): Barclays, King Street, London W6
Managers: B. Niasseri (Tech Serv Mgr), M. Russell (Chief Mgr), N. Cooper (Fin Mgr), R. Adams (Purch Mgr)
Immediate Holding Company: CHEMENCE LIMITED
Registration no: 01746313 **VAT No.:** GB 238 0180 81
Date established: 1983 **Turnover:** £10m - £20m
No.of Employees: 51 - 100 **Product Groups:** 28, 31, 32, 44

Date of Accounts	Dec 11	Dec 08	Aug 10
Sales Turnover	13m	12m	11m
Pre Tax Profit/Loss	-163	-3m	-52
Working Capital	419	481	784
Fixed Assets	2m	3m	3m
Current Assets	4m	7m	6m
Current Liabilities	2m	2m	1m

Commtel
56 Causeway Road Earlstrees Industrial Estate, Corby, NN17 4DU
Tel: 01536-403943 **Fax:** 01536-408482
E-mail: john.cook@commteluk.com
Website: http://www.commteluk.com
Directors: J. Cook (Dir), R. Drewnicki (MD), Y. Drewnicki (Dir)
Managers: B. Bennett (Sales Prom Mgr)
Immediate Holding Company: COMMTEL CHINA LIMITED
Registration no: 07013261 **Date established:** 2009 **Turnover:** £5m - £10m
No.of Employees: 21 - 50 **Product Groups:** 37

Cooper Ostlund
37 Bramblewood Road Weldon, Corby, NN17 3ED
Tel: 01536-205532 **Fax:** 01536-205532
Website: http://www.cooperostlund.com
Directors: S. Cooper (MD)
No.of Employees: 1 - 10 **Product Groups:** 37, 39, 80

Coopers Carpets & Lighting Centre
109-111 Rockingham Road, Corby, NN17 1JW
Tel: 01536-266364 **Fax:** 01536-400395
E-mail: eve@cooperscarpets.co.uk
Directors: R. Cooper (Prop)
No.of Employees: 1 - 10 **Product Groups:** 23, 33, 37, 67

Corby Radio Services Ltd
Dale Street, Corby, NN17 2BQ
Tel: 01536-401600
E-mail: sales@corbyradioservices.com
Website: http://www.corbyradioservices.com
Directors: C. Strachan (Fin), J. Strachan (MD)
Immediate Holding Company: CORBY RADIO SERVICES LIMITED
Registration no: 03800506 **Date established:** 1999
No.of Employees: 1 - 10 **Product Groups:** 37, 38, 52, 67, 83

Date of Accounts	Aug 10	Aug 09	Aug 08
Working Capital	57	61	65
Fixed Assets	7	11	15
Current Assets	109	98	138

Corby Steel Supplies Ltd
Sondes Road Willowbrook East Industrial Estate, Corby, NN17 5XL
Tel: 01536-261164 **Fax:** 01536-402971
E-mail: graham@corbysteel.co.uk
Website: http://www.corbysteel.co.uk
Directors: G. Wadsworth (MD)
Immediate Holding Company: CORBY STEEL SUPPLIES LIMITED
Registration no: 01841093 **VAT No.:** GB 395 9572 84
Date established: 1984 **Turnover:** £500,000 - £1m
No.of Employees: 1 - 10 **Product Groups:** 66

Date of Accounts	Aug 11	Aug 10	Aug 09
Working Capital	-105	-41	-14
Fixed Assets	391	394	403
Current Assets	179	237	169

C R P Print & Packaging Ltd
Cooks Road Weldon North Industrial Estate, Corby, NN17 5JT
Tel: 01536-200333 **Fax:** 01536-403329
E-mail: sales@crpprint.co.uk
Website: http://www.crpprint.com
Bank(s): Barclays
Directors: D. Brahmachari (Sales & Mktg), P. Sangster (Ch), C. Buckenham (Fin)
Managers: A. Prattis (Personnel), A. Gillard, Z. Hill (Sales Prom Mgr)
Ultimate Holding Company: CRP PRINT & PACKAGING HOLDINGS LIMITED
Immediate Holding Company: CRP PRINT & PACKAGING LIMITED
Registration no: 02866696 **VAT No.:** GB 638 2959 95
Date established: 1993 **Turnover:** £20m - £50m
No.of Employees: 101 - 250 **Product Groups:** 27, 28, 49

Date of Accounts	Dec 11	Dec 10	Dec 09
Sales Turnover	25m	21m	16m
Pre Tax Profit/Loss	2m	1m	879
Working Capital	4m	4m	4m
Fixed Assets	5m	5m	2m
Current Assets	11m	11m	9m
Current Liabilities	2m	3m	2m

Damixa Ltd
Edison Courtyard Brunel Road, Earlstrees Industrial Estate, Corby, NN17 4LS
Tel: 01536-409222 **Fax:** 01536-400144
E-mail: uksales@damixa.com
Website: http://www.damixa.com
Directors: S. Gannon (Ch), S. Mepsted (MD), D. Peterson (Chief Op Offcr)
Managers: B. Shaefer, B. Andersen, A. Gannon, J. Colmer (Nat Sales Mgr), J. Langfor, L. Hansen, M. Hepplestone, A. James (Quality Control), S. Southam, A. Boardman (Grp Mktg Mgr)

Ultimate Holding Company: EURAMAX INTERNATIONAL INC (USA)
Immediate Holding Company: Bristan Group Ltd
Registration no: 01861206 **VAT No.:** GB 638 6624 25
Date established: 1996 **Turnover:** £20m - £50m **No.of Employees:** 1 - 10
Product Groups: 29, 30, 36, 40, 66

Dubois Ltd t/a AGI Amaray

Arkwright Road Willowbrook North Industrial Estate, Corby, NN17 5AE
Tel: 01536-274800 **Fax:** 01536-274902
E-mail: ian.poore@uk.agimedia.com
Website: http://www.amaray.com
Bank(s): National Westminster Bank Plc
Directors: I. Poore (Dir)
Managers: A. Middleton
Ultimate Holding Company: MEADWESTVACO CORP (USA)
Immediate Holding Company: DUBOIS LIMITED
Registration no: 00070808 **Date established:** 2001
Turnover: £50m - £75m **No.of Employees:** 101 - 250
Product Groups: 30, 38

Date of Accounts	Dec 11	Dec 10	Dec 09
Sales Turnover	58m	54m	50m
Pre Tax Profit/Loss	4m	2m	4m
Working Capital	13m	8m	11m
Fixed Assets	12m	14m	18m
Current Assets	22m	20m	21m
Current Liabilities	3m	2m	3m

Eggbox Graphics

Crawley House Shelton Road, Willowbrook East Industrial Estate, Corby, NN17 5XH
Tel: 01536-260038 **Fax:** 01536-407927
E-mail: emailus@eggboxgraphics.co.uk
Website: http://www.eggboxgraphics.co.uk
Directors: C. Turner (Ptnr)
Ultimate Holding Company: NAKAGAWA SANGYO CO LTD (JAPAN)
Immediate Holding Company: NSUK LIMITED
Registration no: OC321089 **Date established:** 1997
No.of Employees: 1 - 10 **Product Groups:** 28, 44, 81

Date of Accounts	Mar 12	Mar 11	Mar 10
Working Capital	286	324	365
Fixed Assets	772	798	824
Current Assets	546	527	641
Current Liabilities	67	155	56

ERIKS UK (Corby Service Centre)

Unit 5 Perth House Corby Gate Business Park Priors Haw Road, Corby, NN17 5JG
Tel: 01536-204444 **Fax:** 01536-400803
E-mail: corby@eriks.co.uk
Website: http://www.eriks.co.uk
Managers: R. Bester (District Mgr)
Immediate Holding Company: WYKO HOLDINGS LTD
Registration no: 00917112 **Turnover:** £250m - £500m
No.of Employees: 1 - 10 **Product Groups:** 66

Fastrax Conveyor Rollers Ltd

Unit 1 Baird Road Willowbrook North Industrial Estate, Corby, NN17 5ZA
Tel: 01536-403662 **Fax:** 01536-747990
E-mail: sales@rollersfast.com
Website: http://www.rollersfast.com
Directors: S. Millar (MD)
Immediate Holding Company: FASTRAX CONVEYOR ROLLERS LIMITED
Registration no: 05520208 **Date established:** 2005 **Turnover:** £1m - £2m
No.of Employees: 11 - 20 **Product Groups:** 29, 30, 35, 41, 45

Date of Accounts	Dec 11	Dec 10	Dec 09
Working Capital	64	97	107
Fixed Assets	186	190	197
Current Assets	405	382	339

Filter House Ltd

Edison Courtyard Earlstree Industrial Estate, Earlstrees Industrial Estate, Corby, NN17 4LS
Tel: 01536-206120 **Fax:** 01536-407818
Directors: C. Carter (Fin), I. Carter (MD)
Immediate Holding Company: FILTER HOUSE LIMITED
Registration no: 04419977 **Date established:** 2002
No.of Employees: 1 - 10 **Product Groups:** 38, 42

Date of Accounts	Mar 11	Mar 10	Mar 08
Working Capital	23	16	8
Fixed Assets	11	11	11
Current Assets	49	37	41
Current Liabilities	1	2	23

Fourways Fabrications Ltd

14 Rutherford Court Earlstrees Industrial Estate, Corby, NN17 4SJ
Tel: 01536-266067 **Fax:** 01536-401693
Directors: I. Goody (Fin), I. Goody (MD)
Managers: J. Goody ()
Immediate Holding Company: FOURWAYS FABRICATIONS LIMITED
Registration no: 03477403 **Date established:** 1997
No.of Employees: 1 - 10 **Product Groups:** 48

Date of Accounts	Dec 07	Mar 11	Mar 10
Working Capital	-2	14	23
Fixed Assets	10	10	15
Current Assets	154	140	158

Global Technologies Europe Ltd

Unit I Tyson Courtyard, Weldon South Industrial Estate, Corby, NN18 8AZ
Tel: 01536-407740 **Fax:** 01536-268043
E-mail: vainsworth@globaltec.uk.com
Website: http://www.globaltec.uk.com
Directors: V. Ainsworth (Dir)
Immediate Holding Company: GLOBAL TECHNOLOGIES EUROPE LIMITED
Registration no: 03313611 **Date established:** 1997
Turnover: £250,000 - £500,000 **No.of Employees:** 1 - 10
Product Groups: 67

Date of Accounts	Dec 11	Dec 10	Dec 09
Sales Turnover	N/A	N/A	318
Pre Tax Profit/Loss	N/A	N/A	56
Working Capital	53	76	87
Fixed Assets	3	4	8
Current Assets	113	111	126
Current Liabilities	N/A	N/A	29

T J Grimley

65 Occupation Road, Corby, NN17 1EE
Tel: 01536-260719 **Fax:** 01536-408764
Directors: T. Grimley (Prop)
Date established: 1979 **No.of Employees:** 1 - 10 **Product Groups:** 36, 39, 40

Hi Bond Tapes Ltd

1 Crucible Road, Corby, NN17 5TS
Tel: 01536-260022 **Fax:** 01536-260044
E-mail: sales@hi-bondtapes.co.uk
Website: http://www.hi-bondtapes.com
Directors: H. Waser (Mkt Research), L. Fairbairn (Fin), M. Fairbairn (MD), M. Fairbairn (Sales)
Managers: G. Pearce (Tech Serv Mgr), D. Ashby (Sales Admin)
Immediate Holding Company: HI-BOND TAPES LIMITED
Registration no: 03985595 **Date established:** 2000
No.of Employees: 11 - 20 **Product Groups:** 27

Date of Accounts	Oct 11	Oct 10	Oct 09
Working Capital	940	765	628
Fixed Assets	128	138	152
Current Assets	1m	1m	861

Hingerose Ltd (UK Distributor for Dosatron International)

5 Ryder Court, Corby, NN18 9NX
Tel: 01536-461441 **Fax:** 01536-461600
E-mail: info@hingerose.co.uk
Website: http://www.hingerose.co.uk
Directors: R. Buttery (Fin), T. Jessiman (Co Sec)
Immediate Holding Company: HINGEROSE LTD
Registration no: 01455884 **Date established:** 1979 **Turnover:** £1m - £2m
No.of Employees: 1 - 10 **Product Groups:** 40, 46

Date of Accounts	Dec 11	Dec 10	Dec 09
Working Capital	290	340	163
Fixed Assets	10	13	23
Current Assets	491	518	426

Interroll Ltd

Brunel Road Earlstrees Industrial Estate, Corby, NN17 4UX
Tel: 01536-200322 **Fax:** 01536-748505
E-mail: c.middleton@interroll.com
Website: http://www.interroll.com
Directors: C. Middleton (MD), S. Cortese (Fin)
Managers: L. Preston (Sales & Mktg Mg)
Ultimate Holding Company: INTERROLL HOLDING AG (SWITZERLAND)
Immediate Holding Company: INTERROLL LIMITED
Registration no: 01577408 **VAT No.:** GB 196 5424 32
Date established: 1981 **Turnover:** £5m - £10m **No.of Employees:** 21 - 50
Product Groups: 45

Date of Accounts	Dec 11	Dec 10	Dec 09
Sales Turnover	11m	7m	6m
Pre Tax Profit/Loss	159	170	-31
Working Capital	982	878	826
Fixed Assets	146	115	179
Current Assets	3m	2m	2m
Current Liabilities	421	488	241

J M E Civils

1 Adelaide House Corby Gate Business Park Priors Haw Road, Corby, NN17 5JG
Tel: 01536-206688 **Fax:** 01536-206544
E-mail: iain@jme3d.co.uk
Website: http://www.jmecivils.co.uk
Directors: J. Moore (MD), A. Moore (Fin)
Immediate Holding Company: NORTHAMPTONSHIRE INDUSTRIAL TRAINING ASSOCIATION LIMITED
Date established: 1977 **Turnover:** **No.of Employees:** 1 - 10
Product Groups: 37, 80, 81, 84, 85

Keen Cut Ltd

Baird Road Willowbrook North Industrial Estate, Corby, NN17 5ZA
Tel: 01536-263158 **Fax:** 01536-204227
E-mail: info@keencut.co.uk
Website: http://www.keencut.co.uk
Directors: L. Lockwood (Co Sec)
Immediate Holding Company: KEENCUT LIMITED
Registration no: 01631036 **Date established:** 1982
No.of Employees: 11 - 20 **Product Groups:** 46

Date of Accounts	May 11	May 10	May 09
Working Capital	914	755	1m
Fixed Assets	549	588	576
Current Assets	1m	1m	1m

Key Packaging Machinery Ltd

Unit F Trevithick Road, Willowbrook East Industrial Estate, Corby, NN17 5XY
Tel: 01536-264844 **Fax:** 01536-264755
E-mail: sales@keypackaging.co.uk
Website: http://www.keypackaging.co.uk
Directors: G. Ingram (Dir)
Immediate Holding Company: KEY PACKAGING MACHINERY LIMITED
Registration no: 03737877 **Date established:** 1999
No.of Employees: 1 - 10 **Product Groups:** 38, 42

Date of Accounts	Oct 11	Oct 10	Oct 09
Working Capital	77	79	58
Fixed Assets	165	178	193
Current Assets	159	199	119

Living Space Ltd

12a Earlstrees Road Earlstrees Industrial Estate, Corby, NN17 4AZ
Tel: 01536-446980 **Fax:** 01536-446981
E-mail: sales@livingspaceltd.co.uk
Website: http://www.livingspaceltd.co.uk
Directors: A. Lucas (MD)
Immediate Holding Company: LIVING SPACE (UK) LIMITED
Registration no: 02627932 **Date established:** 1991 **Turnover:** £2m - £5m
No.of Employees: 11 - 20 **Product Groups:** 24, 30, 35

Date of Accounts	Dec 11	Dec 10	Dec 09
Sales Turnover	2m	2m	2m
Pre Tax Profit/Loss	38	100	204
Working Capital	107	122	100
Fixed Assets	852	813	766
Current Assets	821	786	670
Current Liabilities	351	319	313

Lurejumbo Ltd

Unit 2 Darwin Road, Willowbrook East Industrial Estate, Corby, NN17 5XZ
Tel: 01536-401971 **Fax:** 01536-401972
E-mail: p.walshaw@metalico.org.uk
Website: http://www.metalico.org.uk
Directors: C. Kettle (Co Sec), G. Carter (MD), P. Walshaw (MD)
Managers: P. Jeffries (Mgr), P. Walshaw (Purch Mgr)
Ultimate Holding Company: WH 345 LIMITED
Immediate Holding Company: METALICO LIMITED
Registration no: 02160801 **Date established:** 1987
Turnover: £500,000 - £1m **No.of Employees:** 11 - 20
Product Groups: 26, 49

Date of Accounts	May 11	May 10	May 09
Working Capital	32	4	-5
Fixed Assets	232	258	266
Current Assets	42	17	20

L V P Conveyors Ltd

Garston Road, Corby, NN18 8NH
Tel: 01536-747740
Website: http://www.conyerors.ie
Directors: J. Farquhar (Sales)
No.of Employees: 1 - 10 **Product Groups:** 38, 45, 46, 84

M Ormond Fabrications

13 Rutherford Court Earlstrees Industrial Estate, Corby, NN17 4SJ
Tel: 01536-402005 **Fax:** 01536-264908
E-mail: mormondfabs@btinternet.com
Directors: M. Ormond (Prop)
No.of Employees: 1 - 10 **Product Groups:** 35

Mace Industries

1-3 Macadam Road Earlstrees Industrial Estate, Corby, NN17 4JN
Tel: 01536-206600 **Fax:** 01536-206173
E-mail: sales@maceindustries.co.uk
Website: http://www.maceindustries.co.uk
Bank(s): National Westminster
Directors: J. Pollock (Fin), K. Mace (Fin)
Managers: T. Richards (Sales Prom Mgr), L. Mace (Sales Prom Mgr)
Immediate Holding Company: MACE INDUSTRIES LIMITED
Registration no: 02591930 **VAT No.:** GB 745 5247 21
Date established: 1991 **Turnover:** £250,000 - £500,000
No.of Employees: 21 - 50 **Product Groups:** 84

Date of Accounts	Apr 11	Apr 10	Apr 09
Working Capital	373	343	279
Fixed Assets	78	94	110
Current Assets	568	627	458

Mail Solutions Ltd

Cronin Courtyard Weldon South Industrial Estate, Corby, NN18 8AG
Tel: 01536-400558 **Fax:** 01536-400889
E-mail: print@mailsolutions.com
Website: http://www.mailsolutions.com
Directors: C. Reid (Fin), T. Banks (MD), P. Reid (Fin)
Managers: M. Souster (Sales & Mktg Mg), M. Souster (Sales & Mktg Mgr)
Ultimate Holding Company: MAIL SOLUTIONS GROUP LIMITED
Immediate Holding Company: MAIL SOLUTIONS LIMITED
Registration no: 02413935 **Date established:** 1989 **Turnover:** £5m - £10m
No.of Employees: 21 - 50 **Product Groups:** 27

Date of Accounts	Mar 11	Mar 10	Mar 09
Sales Turnover	6m	7m	10m
Pre Tax Profit/Loss	665	1m	4m
Working Capital	12m	12m	11m
Fixed Assets	675	793	976
Current Assets	14m	14m	14m
Current Liabilities	472	899	1m

Marlec Engineering Co. Ltd

Rutland House Trevithick Road, Willowbrook East Industrial Estate, Corby, NN17 5XY
Tel: 01536-201588 **Fax:** 01536-400211
E-mail: sales@marlec.co.uk
Website: http://www.marlec.co.uk
Bank(s): Barclays
Directors: T. Auciello (Sales), I. Fawkes (MD), N. Pucacco (Fin)
Managers: M. Seager (Purch Mgr)
Immediate Holding Company: MARLEC ENGINEERING COMPANY LIMITED
Registration no: 01388473 **VAT No.:** GB 330 2016 27
Date established: 1978 **Turnover:** £10m - £20m
No.of Employees: 21 - 50 **Product Groups:** 37, 40

Date of Accounts	Dec 11	Dec 10	Dec 09
Sales Turnover	12m	N/A	N/A
Pre Tax Profit/Loss	823	N/A	N/A
Working Capital	3m	2m	1m
Fixed Assets	187	147	132
Current Assets	5m	3m	2m
Current Liabilities	1m	N/A	N/A

Orchard House Foods Ltd

Bell House 3 Fleming Road, Earlstrees Industrial Estate, Corby, NN17 4SW
Tel: 01536-261599 **Fax:** 01536-274016
E-mail: info@ohf.co.uk
Website: http://www.ohf.co.uk
Directors: M. Lane (Fin), T. Varinder (MD), P. O'connor (Grp Chief Exec), J. Hather (Co Sec)
Managers: D. Jackson (Personnel), R. Dickson (Tech Serv Mgr)
Ultimate Holding Company: LYDIAN CAPITAL PARTNERSHIP LP (JERSEY)
Immediate Holding Company: ORCHARD HOUSE FOODS LIMITED
Registration no: 01897751 **Date established:** 1985
Turnover: £75m - £125m **No.of Employees:** 501 - 1000
Product Groups: 20, 21

Date of Accounts	Dec 11	Dec 10	Dec 09
Sales Turnover	97m	93m	93m
Pre Tax Profit/Loss	3m	-2m	415
Working Capital	311	-2m	-6m
Fixed Assets	12m	13m	19m
Current Assets	16m	13m	11m
Current Liabilities	2m	3m	4m

Ortomotion Ltd

2 Cockerell Road, Corby, NN17 5DU
Tel: 01536-407000 **Fax:** 01536-407999
E-mail: info@ortomotion.com
Website: http://www.ortomotion.com
Directors: C. Fenton (MD), C. Hishin (I.T. Dir)
Immediate Holding Company: ORTOMOTION LIMITED
Registration no: 04178769 **Date established:** 2001
No.of Employees: 1 - 10 **Product Groups:** 26, 38, 39

Date of Accounts	Apr 11	Apr 10	Apr 09
Working Capital	-33	-24	-0
Fixed Assets	6	8	7
Current Assets	80	102	106
Current Liabilities	N/A	13	17

P F M Counting Solutions

2 Perth House Corby Gate Business Park, Corby, NN17 5JG
Tel: 01536-511010 **Fax:** 01536-513653
E-mail: info@pfm-counts.com
Website: http://www.pfm-counts.com
Directors: D. Sturdy (MD)
Managers: P. Dixon (Tech Serv Mgr), L. Warwick (Chief Acct)
Immediate Holding Company: COUNTING SOLUTIONS LIMITED
Registration no: 04289312 **Date established:** 2001
Turnover: £500,000 - £1m **No.of Employees:** 11 - 20
Product Groups: 38, 39

Date of Accounts	Aug 11	Aug 10	Aug 09
Working Capital	169	76	-37
Fixed Assets	240	229	222
Current Assets	740	815	956

Phoenix Foods Ltd

Brakey Road Weldon North Industrial Estate, Corby, NN17 5LU
Tel: 01536-200101 **Fax:** 01536-202218
E-mail: sales@phoenixfoods.co.uk
Website: http://www.phoenixfoods.co.uk
Bank(s): HSBC Bank plc
Directors: J. Kipling (Co Sec), G. Rutter (Chief Op Offcr), C. Wilding (Dir)
Managers: J. Riddy (Buyer), P. Tranter
Ultimate Holding Company: PHOENIX FOODS (HOLDINGS) LIMITED
Immediate Holding Company: PHOENIX FOODS LIMITED
Registration no: 01397554 **VAT No.:** GB 188 9042 21
Date established: 1978 **Turnover:** £10m - £20m
No.of Employees: 51 - 100 **Product Groups:** 20

Date of Accounts	Dec 11	Dec 10	Dec 09
Sales Turnover	12m	9m	7m
Pre Tax Profit/Loss	246	312	162
Working Capital	654	550	300
Fixed Assets	450	374	346
Current Assets	5m	3m	2m
Current Liabilities	366	341	202

Phoenix Shower Products

Unit 10 Corby Gate Business Park Prior Hall Road, Corby, NN17 5JG
Tel: 01536-205949 **Fax:** 01536-205361
E-mail: phoenixshowerpro@aol.com
Website: http://www.phoenixbathroomaccessories.com
Directors: P. Smith (Prop)
Immediate Holding Company: PHOENIX SHOWER PRODUCTS LIMITED
Registration no: 02862962 **VAT No.:** GB 638 2776 06
Date established: 1993 **No.of Employees:** 1 - 10 **Product Groups:** 36

Date of Accounts	Dec 11	Dec 10	Dec 09
Working Capital	31	34	27
Fixed Assets	19	13	12
Current Assets	78	73	58

Pilz Automation Technology

Oak House Medlicott Close, Corby, NN18 9NF
Tel: 01536-460766 **Fax:** 01536-460866
E-mail: sales@pilz.co.uk
Website: http://www.pilz.co.uk
Bank(s): National Westminster Bank Plc
Managers: S. Farrow (Chief Mgr)
Immediate Holding Company: PILZ AUTOMATION TECHNOLOGY UK LIMITED
Registration no: 03488963 **Date established:** 1997 **Turnover:** £2m - £5m
No.of Employees: 21 - 50 **Product Groups:** 37, 38, 40, 44, 49

Date of Accounts	Dec 11	Dec 10	Dec 09
Working Capital	43	33	23
Current Assets	44	34	23

Powdertech Ltd

5 Cockerell Road, Corby, NN17 5DU
Tel: 01536-400890 **Fax:** 01536-205999
E-mail: giles.a@powdertech.co.uk
Website: http://www.powdertech.co.uk
Bank(s): Barclays
Directors: G. Ashmead (Chief Op Offcr)
Immediate Holding Company: POWDERTECH LIMITED
Registration no: 02249909 **Date established:** 1988 **Turnover:** £2m - £5m
No.of Employees: 11 - 20 **Product Groups:** 32, 34, 46, 48

Date of Accounts	Aug 11	Aug 10	Aug 09
Working Capital	346	375	441
Fixed Assets	11	11	17
Current Assets	460	498	539

Pre Tech Tools

Unit 3 Brunel Court Earlstrees Industrial Estate, Corby, NN17 4UB
Tel: 01536-401336 **Fax:** 01536-401336
E-mail: pretech@fsmail.net
Website: http://www.brunelrd3.freeserve.co.uk
Directors: I. Ebbs (Prop)
Date established: 2002 **No.of Employees:** 1 - 10 **Product Groups:** 46

Premier Galvanising Ltd

Darwin Road Willowbrook East Industrial Estate, Corby, NN17 5XZ
Tel: 01536-409818 **Fax:** 01536-409722
E-mail: info@premiergalv.co.uk
Website: http://www.premiergalv.co.uk
Directors: A. Payne (Fin), R. Preston (Fab)
Managers: J. Deegan (Mktg Serv Mgr)
Immediate Holding Company: ASHBURY CHOCOLATES LIMITED
Registration no: 02799631 **Date established:** 2007
No.of Employees: 21 - 50 **Product Groups:** 46, 48

Date of Accounts	Dec 11	Dec 10	Dec 09
Sales Turnover	29m	32m	22m
Pre Tax Profit/Loss	-396	623	-720
Working Capital	-956	-86	-657
Fixed Assets	3m	3m	2m
Current Assets	8m	8m	7m
Current Liabilities	4m	4m	2m

Premier Motor Co.

Weldon Road, Corby, NN17 5UE
Tel: 01536-200427 **Fax:** 01536-264500
Directors: W. Masson (MD)
Managers: S. Woods (Sales Prom Mgr)
Turnover: £1m - £2m **No.of Employees:** 1 - 10 **Product Groups:** 38, 39, 45, 67, 85

Process Sensors Europe Ltd

Adelaide House Corby Gate Business Park, Corby, NN17 5JG
Tel: 01536-408066 **Fax:** 01536-407813
E-mail: syork@processsensors.com
Website: http://www.processsensors.co.uk
Directors: S. York (Dir)
Immediate Holding Company: PROCESS SENSORS (EUROPE) LIMITED
Registration no: 04136159 **Date established:** 2001
No.of Employees: 1 - 10 **Product Groups:** 38

Date of Accounts	Dec 11	Dec 10	Dec 09
Sales Turnover	N/A	1m	1m
Pre Tax Profit/Loss	N/A	-9	34
Working Capital	338	267	270
Fixed Assets	7	16	26
Current Assets	606	407	438
Current Liabilities	N/A	4	45

Pyramid Laboratories Ltd

Unit B Cavendish Courtyard Weldon North Industrial Estate, Corby, NN17 5DZ
Tel: 01536-401202 **Fax:** 01536-206321
Directors: J. Garner (Dir)
Immediate Holding Company: PYRAMID LABORATORIES LIMITED
Registration no: 02938949 **Date established:** 1994
No.of Employees: 1 - 10 **Product Groups:** 46, 48

Date of Accounts	Sep 11	Sep 10	Sep 09
Working Capital	-14	5	25
Fixed Assets	78	82	86
Current Assets	38	38	58

R P C Containers Ltd

4 Sallow Road Weldon North Industrial Estate, Corby, NN17 5JX
Tel: 01536-263488 **Fax:** 01536-272910
E-mail: v.dean@rpc-corby.co.uk
Website: http://www.rpc-containers.co.uk
Bank(s): National Westminster Bank Plc
Managers: I. Smith (Mats Contrlr), J. Taylor (I.T. Exec), J. Taylor (Tech Serv Mgr), V. Dean (Sales & Mktg Mg), Z. Garrod (Fin Mgr), I. McIntosh (Fin Mgr)
Ultimate Holding Company: RPC GROUP PLC
Immediate Holding Company: RPC CONTAINERS LIMITED
Registration no: 02786492 **Date established:** 1993
No.of Employees: 251 - 500 **Product Groups:** 30, 66

Date of Accounts	Mar 11	Mar 10	Mar 09
Sales Turnover	189m	175m	183m
Pre Tax Profit/Loss	14m	15m	-1m
Working Capital	21m	17m	-37m
Fixed Assets	81m	77m	79m
Current Assets	76m	66m	68m
Current Liabilities	17m	13m	14m

Recticel Corby

83-84 Manton Road Earlstrees Industrial Estate, Corby, NN17 4JL
Tel: 01536-402345 **Fax:** 01536-400524
E-mail: miller.chris@recticel.com
Website: http://www.recticel.com
Bank(s): HSBC, Victoria St, Nottingham
Managers: A. Smith (Sales & Mktg Mg), R. King (Plant), S. Moore (I.T. Exec), Z. Taylor
Immediate Holding Company: RECTICEL (UK) LTD
Registration no: 01099072 **VAT No.:** GB 408 7065 51
Turnover: £10m - £20m **No.of Employees:** 51 - 100 **Product Groups:** 29, 30, 31, 39, 42, 49

Rhophase Microwaves Ltd

13 Earlstrees Court Earlstrees Industrial Estate, Corby, NN17 4RH
Tel: 01536-263440 **Fax:** 01536-260764
E-mail: sales@rhophase.co.uk
Website: http://www.rhophase.co.uk
Directors: C. Kneizys (Co Sec)
Managers: R. Valentine (Chief Mgr)
Ultimate Holding Company: ROSENBERGER MICRO-COAX LIMITED
Immediate Holding Company: RHOPHASE MICROWAVE LIMITED
Registration no: 01823304 **VAT No.:** GB 396 0955 10
Date established: 1984 **Turnover:** £2m - £5m **No.of Employees:** 21 - 50
Product Groups: 37

Date of Accounts	Dec 11	Dec 10	Dec 09
Sales Turnover	2m	N/A	N/A
Pre Tax Profit/Loss	548	N/A	N/A
Working Capital	626	563	567
Fixed Assets	58	72	88
Current Assets	968	857	910
Current Liabilities	216	N/A	N/A

Roquette UK Ltd

Sallow Road Weldon North Industrial Estate, Corby, NN17 5JX
Tel: 01536-273000 **Fax:** 01536-263873
E-mail: chris.scarrott@roquette.com
Website: http://www.roquette.com
Bank(s): Barclays, Peterborough
Directors: C. Scarrott (Dir), K. Halloway (Sales), S. Price (Fin)
Managers: B. Sherriden (Tech Serv Mgr), N. Streatfield (Purch Mgr), J. Wilson (Personnel)
Ultimate Holding Company: ROQUETTE FRERES SA (FRANCE)
Immediate Holding Company: ROQUETTE UK LIMITED
Registration no: 01486339 **Date established:** 1980
Turnover: £125m - £250m **No.of Employees:** 101 - 250
Product Groups: 20, 31, 32

Date of Accounts	Dec 11	Dec 10	Dec 09
Sales Turnover	170m	141m	143m
Pre Tax Profit/Loss	10m	6m	6m
Working Capital	12m	7m	12m
Fixed Assets	45m	41m	30m
Current Assets	46m	42m	42m
Current Liabilities	3m	887	2m

Run Visual

Unit N Harlow House Shelton Road, Willowbrook East Industrial Estate, Corby, NN17 5XH
Tel: 01536-203330 **Fax:** 01536-402009
E-mail: info@runvisual.co.uk
Website: http://www.runvisual.co.uk
Directors: S. Smith (Prop)
Registration no: 05153054 **Date established:** 1995
Turnover: £500,000 - £1m **No.of Employees:** 1 - 10 **Product Groups:** 89

Date of Accounts	Aug 08	Aug 07	Aug 06
Working Capital	-44	-42	-67
Fixed Assets	47	56	77
Current Assets	31	35	54
Current Liabilities	74	77	121

Scandura

St James Road St James Industrial Estate, Corby, NN18 8AW
Tel: 01536-267121 **Fax:** 01536-266392
E-mail: info@scandura.co.uk
Website: http://www.scandura.co.uk
Directors: D. Mitchell (Fin)
Managers: A. Emery (Chief Mgr)
Ultimate Holding Company: UNITED INDUSTRIES GROUP
Immediate Holding Company: MOYER MANUFACTURING COMPANY LIMITED(THE)
Registration no: 00576712 **VAT No.:** GB 281 3294 58
Date established: 1957 **No.of Employees:** 11 - 20 **Product Groups:** 23, 25, 27, 30, 33, 40, 66

Wilfrid Smith Ltd

Elm House Medlicott Close, Corby, NN18 9NF
Tel: 01536-460020 **Fax:** 01536-462400
E-mail: info@wilfrid-smith.co.uk
Website: http://www.wilfrid-smith.co.uk
Directors: J. Walkey (MD)
Managers: S. Young
Immediate Holding Company: WILFRID SMITH GROUP LIMITED
Registration no: 03254193 **VAT No.:** GB 346 6866 14
Date established: 1996 **Turnover:** £5m - £10m **No.of Employees:** 1 - 10
Product Groups: 61

Date of Accounts	Dec 11	Dec 10	Dec 09
Sales Turnover	N/A	N/A	5m
Pre Tax Profit/Loss	N/A	N/A	502
Working Capital	492	477	341
Fixed Assets	62	67	42
Current Assets	2m	3m	2m
Current Liabilities	N/A	N/A	200

Speedy Assets Ltd

Unit 5 Cronin Road Weldon South Industrial Estate, Corby, NN18 8AQ
Tel: 01536-206306 **Fax:** 01536-264513
E-mail: simon.hilliard@speedyhire.co.uk
Website: http://www.speedyhire.co.uk
Managers: S. Hilliard (Mgr)
Immediate Holding Company: SPEEDY HIRE PLC
Registration no: 04529136 **Turnover:** £250,000 - £500,000
No.of Employees: 1 - 10 **Product Groups:** 35, 37, 38, 39, 45, 48, 83

Spirol Industries Ltd

17 Princewood Road Earlstrees Industrial Estate, Corby, NN17 4ET
Tel: 01536-444800 **Fax:** 01536-203415
E-mail: info@spirol.com
Website: http://www.spirol.com
Bank(s): HSBC Bank plc
Directors: A. Freeman (MD)
Managers: F. Pinchbeck (Personnel)
Ultimate Holding Company: SPIROL HOLDING CORP (USA)
Immediate Holding Company: SPIROL INDUSTRIES LIMITED
Registration no: 00675663 **Date established:** 1960
No.of Employees: 21 - 50 **Product Groups:** 30, 35, 36, 37, 38, 42, 46, 47, 66

Date of Accounts	Sep 08	Sep 09	Sep 10
Working Capital	2m	2m	3m
Fixed Assets	2m	2m	2m
Current Assets	3m	3m	3m

Tata Steel

PO Box 101, Corby, NN17 5UA
Tel: 01536-402121 **Fax:** 01536-404111
Website: http://www.tatasteel.com
Directors: J. Baxter (Fin), R. Blaauw (MD), K. Muirden (Sales)
Managers: R. Baillie (Purch Mgr), G. Brady (Tech Serv Mgr)
Ultimate Holding Company: TATA STEEL LIMITED (INDIA)
Immediate Holding Company: CORUS GROUP LIMITED
Registration no: 03811373 **VAT No.:** GB 238 7122 60
Date established: 1999 **Turnover:** £10m - £20m
No.of Employees: 501 - 1000 **Product Groups:** 34, 35

Technical Foam Services Ltd

57 Burkitt Road Earlstrees Industrial Estate, Corby, NN17 4DT
Tel: 01536-443000 **Fax:** 01536-443230
E-mail: info@technicalfoamservices.co.uk
Website: http://www.technicalfoamservices.co.uk
Bank(s): Barclays
Directors: D. Geddes (MD), H. Francis (Dir)
Immediate Holding Company: TECHNICAL FOAM SERVICES LIMITED
Registration no: 02448832 **VAT No.:** GB 550 8015 66
Date established: 1989 **Turnover:** £1m - £2m **No.of Employees:** 11 - 20
Product Groups: 29, 30, 48, 49

Date of Accounts	Dec 11	Dec 10	Dec 09
Working Capital	588	456	301
Fixed Assets	64	56	41
Current Assets	991	767	606

Technifast Ltd

Norfold Road, Corby, NN18 9QD
Tel: 01536-461140 **Fax:** 01536-461662
E-mail: sales@technifast.co.uk
Website: http://www.technifast.co.uk
Bank(s): HSBC
Directors: L. Speed (MD)
Immediate Holding Company: TECHNIFAST LTD.
Registration no: 02460440 **VAT No.:** GB 550 6965 25
Date established: 1990 **Turnover:** £1m - £2m **No.of Employees:** 11 - 20
Product Groups: 30, 35, 39, 42, 45, 46, 66

Date of Accounts	Dec 11	Dec 10	Dec 09
Working Capital	743	742	738
Fixed Assets	61	29	24
Current Assets	1m	1m	1m

The Nicholls Group

Enterprise Park Hunters Road, Weldon North Industrial Estate, Corby, NN17 5JE
Tel: 01536-400234 **Fax:** 01536-262750
E-mail: info@nichollsgroup.co.uk
Website: http://www.nichollsgroup.co.uk
Bank(s): Barclays - Uppingham
Directors: C. Dawtrey (Fin)
Immediate Holding Company: NICHOLLS ENGINEERING SERVICES LIMITED
Registration no: 01543431 **Date established:** 1981
No.of Employees: 11 - 20 **Product Groups:** 42, 44, 54

Date of Accounts	Feb 10	Feb 09	Feb 08
Working Capital	227	284	271
Fixed Assets	66	64	75
Current Assets	571	605	563

Unicorn Automation (Ndt) Limited
Unit K Cavendish Courtyard Weldon North Industrial Estate, Corby, NN17 5DZ
Tel: 01536-406664 **Fax:** 01536-266635
E-mail: enquiries@unicorn-automation.co.uk
Website: http://www.unicorn-automation.co.uk
Directors: A. McDougall (Dir), C. James (Co Sec), C. James (Dir), R. Green (Dir)
Immediate Holding Company: Unicorn Automation (Ndt) Ltd
Registration no: 02824838 **Date established:** 1991 **Turnover:** £1m - £2m
No.of Employees: 1 - 10 **Product Groups:** 85

Date of Accounts	Jun 09	Jun 08	Jun 07
Working Capital	2m	2m	2m
Fixed Assets	366	371	377
Current Assets	3m	2m	2m
Current Liabilities	N/A	41	N/A

Waste Recycling Group Ltd
Weldon Landfill Site Kettering Road, Weldon, Corby, NN17 3JG
Tel: 01536-406296 **Fax:** 01536-401557
Website: http://www.wrg.co.uk
Managers: N. Harrold (Mgr)
Ultimate Holding Company: FOMENTO DE CONSTRUCCIONES Y CONTRATAS SA (SPAIN)
Immediate Holding Company: FCC ENVIRONMENT (UK) LIMITED
Registration no: 02902416 **Date established:** 1994
No.of Employees: 1 - 10 **Product Groups:** 45

Date of Accounts	Dec 10	Dec 09	Dec 08
Sales Turnover	497m	553m	524m
Pre Tax Profit/Loss	12m	-16m	-19m
Working Capital	-117m	-227m	-217m
Fixed Assets	800m	826m	836m
Current Assets	85m	112m	115m
Current Liabilities	168m	188m	142m

Watford Control Instruments Ltd
Godwin Road, Corby, NN17 4DS
Tel: 01536-401345 **Fax:** 01536-401164
E-mail: sales@watfordcontrol.co.uk
Website: http://www.watfordcontrol.co.uk
Bank(s): Royal Bank of Scotland, Threadneedle St, London
Directors: C. Brown (MD), S. Brod (Ch)
Managers: P. Rogers (Sales Prom Mgr)
Registration no: 00434534 **VAT No.:** GB 576 8859 61
Date established: 1947 **Turnover:** £2m - £5m **No.of Employees:** 51 - 100
Product Groups: 37, 38

Date of Accounts	Dec 11	Dec 10	Dec 09
Working Capital	913	1m	880
Fixed Assets	197	219	380
Current Assets	1m	1m	1m

Watts Industrial Tyres plc
1 Priors Court Priors Haw Road, Corby, NN17 5JG
Tel: 01536-406973 **Fax:** 01536-443662
E-mail: andrewkear@watts-group.co.uk
Website: http://www.industrialtyre.com
Directors: D. Pearson (MD), J. Thursdon (MD)
Ultimate Holding Company: Watts Of Lydney Group Ltd
Immediate Holding Company: WATTS INDUSTRIAL TYRES LIMITED
Registration no: 01434811 **Date established:** 1979
Turnover: £500,000 - £1m **No.of Employees:** 1 - 10 **Product Groups:** 29, 68

D Welsh
Unit H Edison Courtyard Brunel Road, Earlstrees Industrial Estate, Corby, NN17 4LS
Tel: 01536-400601 **Fax:** 01536-400848
Managers: D. Welsh (Mgr)
Immediate Holding Company: D WELSH ENGINEERING LIMITED
Registration no: 07509312 **Date established:** 2011
No.of Employees: 1 - 10 **Product Groups:** 35

Wycliff Services Ltd
Godwin Road Earlstrees Industrial Estate, Corby, NN17 4DS
Tel: 01536-406500 **Fax:** 01536-406800
E-mail: peterd@wycliff-services.co.uk
Website: http://www.wycliff-services.co.uk
Directors: J. Harrison (Dir)
Immediate Holding Company: WYCLIFF SERVICES LIMITED
Registration no: 02972279 **VAT No.:** GB 638 6318 16
Date established: 1994 **Turnover:** £2m - £5m **No.of Employees:** 21 - 50
Product Groups: 48

Date of Accounts	Sep 11	Sep 10	Sep 09
Working Capital	150	196	85
Fixed Assets	549	562	538
Current Assets	999	956	692

Wydels Ltd
A Gaydon House Trevithick Road, Willowbrook East Industrial Estate, Corby, NN17 5XY
Tel: 01536-264064 **Fax:** 01536-264062
E-mail: enquiries@wydels.co.uk
Website: http://www.wydels.co.uk
Directors: I. Young (Dir)
Immediate Holding Company: WYDELS LIMITED
Registration no: 05697661 **Date established:** 2006
No.of Employees: 1 - 10 **Product Groups:** 36, 40

Date of Accounts	Mar 12	Mar 11	Mar 10
Working Capital	66	59	57
Fixed Assets	38	49	55
Current Assets	169	171	181

Daventry

A S D Metal Services Daventry
Alvis Way Royal Oak Industrial Estate, Daventry, NN11 8QQ
Tel: 01327-876021 **Fax:** 01327-872612
E-mail: spencer.bishop@asdmetals.co.uk
Website: http://www.asdplc.co.uk
Bank(s): Barclays Bank PLC
Managers: S. Bishop (Chief Mgr)
Immediate Holding Company: ASSOCIATED STEEL DISTRIBUTORS LTD
Registration no: 01370600 **Turnover:** £2m - £5m
No.of Employees: 21 - 50 **Product Groups:** 34

Agathon UK
Nene House Drayton Way, Drayton Fields Industrial Estate, Daventry, NN11 8EA
Tel: 01327-877036 **Fax:** 01327-872749
E-mail: sales@agathon.co.uk
Website: http://www.agathon.ch/en
Managers: M. Lucas (Sales Prom Mgr)
Ultimate Holding Company: RITCHIE BROS. AUCTIONEERS INC (USA)
Immediate Holding Company: RITCHIE BROS. AUCTIONEERS (UK) LIMITED
Registration no: 03874860 **VAT No.:** GB 387 6191 09
Date established: 1999 **Turnover:** £5m - £10m **No.of Employees:** 1 - 10
Product Groups: 46, 67

Date of Accounts	Dec 10	Dec 09	Dec 08
Sales Turnover	3m	13	4m
Pre Tax Profit/Loss	358	2m	2m
Working Capital	2m	2m	609
Fixed Assets	164	234	274
Current Assets	2m	2m	3m
Current Liabilities	283	529	778

Alpha Cure Ltd
Great Central Way Industrial Estate Great Central Way, Woodford Halse, Daventry, NN11 3PZ
Tel: 01327-263900 **Fax:** 01327-263902
E-mail: info@alpha-cure.com
Website: http://www.alpha-cure.com
Directors: M. Slater (Co Sec), S. Atherstone (Export), S. Haines (Sales), B. Rambaldini (I.T. Dir)
Managers: K. Atherstone (Tech Serv Mgr)
Ultimate Holding Company: ALPHA-CURE HOLDINGS LIMITED
Immediate Holding Company: ALPHA-CURE LIMITED
Registration no: 03191947 **Date established:** 1996
No.of Employees: 21 - 50 **Product Groups:** 67

Date of Accounts	Dec 11	Dec 10	Dec 09
Working Capital	896	753	671
Fixed Assets	458	439	426
Current Assets	2m	2m	2m

Amega Sciences plc
17 Lanchester Way Royal Oak Industrial Estate, Daventry, NN11 8PH
Tel: 01327-704444 **Fax:** 01327-871154
E-mail: admin@amega-sciences.com
Website: http://www.amega-sciences.com
Directors: J. Walton (Fin)
Managers: P. Ridley, L. Farrell (Sales Prom Mgr), V. Reardon (Purch Mgr)
Ultimate Holding Company: AMEGA SCIENCES HOLDINGS LIMITED
Immediate Holding Company: AMEGA SCIENCES PLC
Registration no: 01840633 **Date established:** 1984 **Turnover:** £5m - £10m
No.of Employees: 21 - 50 **Product Groups:** 66

Date of Accounts	Oct 11	Oct 10	Oct 09
Sales Turnover	9m	8m	6m
Pre Tax Profit/Loss	363	819	475
Working Capital	1m	1m	1m
Fixed Assets	1m	591	527
Current Assets	3m	3m	2m
Current Liabilities	483	526	326

A Amos
32 Lanchester Way Royal Oak Industrial Estate, Daventry, NN11 8PH
Tel: 01327-300720 **Fax:** 01327-705768
Directors: A. Amos (Prop)
Date established: 1986 **No.of Employees:** 1 - 10 **Product Groups:** 46

Ayrshire Metal Products Daventry Ltd
Royal Oak Way North Royal Oak Industrial Estate, Daventry, NN11 8NR
Tel: 01327-300990 **Fax:** 01327-300885
E-mail: sales@ayrshire.co.uk
Website: http://www.ayrshire.co.uk
Bank(s): The Royal Bank of Scotland
Directors: D. Pickerill (Fin), M. Wilson (Dir), P. Short (MD)
Managers: H. Nairn (Tech Serv Mgr), J. Stafford (Sales Prom Mgr)
Ultimate Holding Company: AYRSHIRE METAL PRODUCTS PUBLIC LIMITED COMPANY
Immediate Holding Company: AIRFRAME LIMITED
Registration no: 03513761 **Date established:** 1998
Turnover: £20m - £50m **No.of Employees:** 51 - 100 **Product Groups:** 34, 35, 48

Baughans Barrel Screens
The Old Pow Camp Boddington Road Byfield, Daventry, NN11 6XU
Tel: 01327-261810 **Fax:** 01327-263172
E-mail: sales@baughans.co.uk
Website: http://www.baughans.co.uk
Directors: A. Baughan (MD)
No.of Employees: 11 - 20 **Product Groups:** 39, 45

Best Years Ltd
PO Box 6898, Daventry, NN11 3WG
Tel: 01327-262189 **Fax:** 01327-262189
E-mail: sales@bestyears.co.uk
Website: http://www.bestyears.co.uk
Directors: G. Humphreys (Dir)
Immediate Holding Company: BEST YEARS LIMITED
Registration no: 03822300 **Date established:** 1999
Turnover: £250,000 - £500,000 **No.of Employees:** 1 - 10
Product Groups: 49

Date of Accounts	Mar 11	Mar 10	Mar 09
Working Capital	-44	-41	-12
Current Assets	60	62	60

Bodyshop Solutions (t/a Celette)
Stephenson Close Drayton Fields Industrial Estate, Daventry, NN11 8RF
Tel: 01327-300700 **Fax:** 01327-300586
E-mail: enquiries@celetteuk.com
Website: http://www.celetteuk.com
Directors: P. Donohoe (Sales)
Immediate Holding Company: BODY SHOP SOLUTIONS LIMITED
Registration no: 05158331 **VAT No.:** GB 284 6828 14
Date established: 2004 **Turnover:** £1m - £2m **No.of Employees:** 1 - 10
Product Groups: 39

Date of Accounts	Jul 11	Jul 10	Jul 09
Working Capital	252	206	139
Fixed Assets	116	148	166
Current Assets	511	497	513

Braunston Marina Ltd
The Wharf Braunston, Daventry, NN11 7JH
Tel: 01788-891373 **Fax:** 01788-891436
E-mail: info@braunstonmarina.co.uk
Website: http://www.braunstonmarina.co.uk
Bank(s): Barclays
Directors: T. Coghlan (MD)
Immediate Holding Company: BRAUNSTON MARINA LIMITED
Registration no: 02275577 **Date established:** 1988
Turnover: £250,000 - £500,000 **No.of Employees:** 11 - 20
Product Groups: 39

Date of Accounts	Dec 11	Dec 10	Dec 09
Working Capital	-146	-120	-145
Fixed Assets	685	704	724
Current Assets	212	249	242

C R C Commercial & Industrial Recruitment Ltd
1 Market Square, Daventry, NN11 4BH
Tel: 01327-878737 **Fax:** 01327-878586
E-mail: daventry@crconline.co.uk
Website: http://www.crconline.co.uk
Managers: P. Harris
Immediate Holding Company: CONTRACT RECRUITMENT CONSULTANTS LIMITED
Registration no: 06941820 **Date established:** 2009
Turnover: Up to £250,000 **No.of Employees:** 1 - 10 **Product Groups:** 80

Date of Accounts	Mar 11	Mar 10
Working Capital	3	-22
Fixed Assets	8	20
Current Assets	403	107

Cummins Ltd
Royal Oak Way South Royal Oak Industrial Estate, Daventry, NN11 8NU
Tel: 01327-886000 **Fax:** 01327-886100
E-mail: info@cummins.com
Website: http://www.cummins.com
Managers: J. Bousfield (Personnel), D. Boyles, C. Nunley (Comptroller), S. Pandita (Comptroller), P. Glover (Plant), D. Moore (Chief Mgr), J. Parry (I.T. Exec)
Ultimate Holding Company: CUMMINS INC (USA)
Immediate Holding Company: CUMMINS LTD.
Registration no: 00573951 **VAT No.:** GB 299 2238 18
Date established: 1956 **Turnover:** £125m - £250m
No.of Employees: 1001 - 1500 **Product Groups:** 37, 40, 68

Date of Accounts	Dec 11	Dec 10	Dec 09
Sales Turnover	1886m	1374m	802m
Pre Tax Profit/Loss	377m	239m	89m
Working Capital	443m	220m	336m
Fixed Assets	250m	234m	75m
Current Assets	1104m	683m	676m
Current Liabilities	239m	67m	26m

Doepke UK Ltd
3 Bentley Way Royal Oak Industrial Estate, Daventry, NN11 8QH
Tel: 01628-829133 **Fax:** 01628-829149
E-mail: sales@doepke.co.uk
Website: http://www.doepke.co.uk
Directors: S. Cranton (MD)
Ultimate Holding Company: DOEPKE SCHALTGERATE GMBH & CO KG (GERMANY)
Immediate Holding Company: DOEPKE UK LTD
Registration no: 01164338 **VAT No.:** GB 212 6439 86
Date established: 1974 **Turnover:** £500,000 - £1m
No.of Employees: 1 - 10 **Product Groups:** 37

Date of Accounts	Dec 11	Dec 10	Dec 09
Working Capital	513	305	153
Fixed Assets	260	263	228
Current Assets	1m	794	665

Emilen Ltd
4 Farndon Road Woodford Halse, Daventry, NN11 3TT
Tel: 01295-660033
E-mail: info@emilen.com
Website: http://www.emilen.com
Directors: J. Standen (Prop)
Immediate Holding Company: EMILEN LIMITED
Registration no: 05364267 **Date established:** 2005
No.of Employees: 1 - 10 **Product Groups:** 37, 44, 84

Date of Accounts	Feb 11	Feb 10	Feb 09
Sales Turnover	N/A	N/A	70
Pre Tax Profit/Loss	N/A	N/A	25
Working Capital	-6	-3	-5
Fixed Assets	6	5	5
Current Assets	1	4	13
Current Liabilities	N/A	N/A	19

Endeavour Speciality Chemicals Ltd
Unit 12 Low March Industrial Estate Low March, Daventry, NN11 4SD
Tel: 01327-310079 **Fax:** 01327-310701
E-mail: enquiries@endeavourchem.co.uk
Website: http://www.endeavourchem.co.uk
Directors: G. Parker (Co Sec), A. Hanrahan (MD)
Managers: J. Robinson (Sales Prom Mgr), D. Brown (Purch Mgr), K. Wootton, G. Cartwright (Ops Mgr), D. Jones (Chief Mgr)
Ultimate Holding Company: ROBINSON BROTHERS (RYDERS GREEN) LIMITED
Immediate Holding Company: ENDEAVOUR SPECIALITY CHEMICALS LIMITED
Registration no: 02563702 **Date established:** 1990 **Turnover:** £2m - £5m
No.of Employees: 21 - 50 **Product Groups:** 31

Date of Accounts	Dec 11	Dec 10	Dec 09
Sales Turnover	4m	3m	3m
Pre Tax Profit/Loss	143	286	119
Working Capital	2m	1m	1m
Fixed Assets	246	268	281
Current Assets	2m	2m	1m
Current Liabilities	104	145	101

Espera Scales
Unit 1 Stephenson Close Drayton Fields Industrial Estate, Daventry, NN11 8RF
Tel: 08450-567900 **Fax:** 08450-567901
E-mail: sales@espera.co.uk
Website: http://www.espera.com

see next page

Espera Scales - Cont'd

Directors: M. Korthauer (Dir), P. Kettell (Fin)
Managers: B. Grover (Serv Mgr)
Immediate Holding Company: ESPERA SCALES LTD
Registration no: 01697400 **Date established:** 1983
No.of Employees: 1 - 10 **Product Groups:** 38, 42

Date of Accounts	Dec 10	Dec 09	Dec 08
Working Capital	31	167	126
Fixed Assets	14	19	16
Current Assets	318	371	474

Excel G S Ltd

5 Daimler Close Royal Oak Industrial Estate, Daventry, NN11 8QJ
Tel: 01327-315889
E-mail: info@excel-gs.com
Directors: J. Malone (Dir)
Immediate Holding Company: EXCEL (GS) LIMITED
Registration no: 03827443 **Date established:** 1999
No.of Employees: 1 - 10 **Product Groups:** 32, 63

Date of Accounts	Aug 11	Aug 10	Aug 09
Working Capital	-47	-70	-40
Fixed Assets	72	69	40
Current Assets	319	324	329

Fagor Automation UK Ltd

Unit 2a Brunel Close Drayton Fields Industrial Estate, Daventry, NN11 8RB
Tel: 01327-300067 **Fax:** 01327-300880
E-mail: sales@fagorautomation.co.uk
Website: http://www.fagorautomation.co.uk
Managers: L. Drury (Mgr)
Ultimate Holding Company: FAGOR AUTOMATION S COOP LTD (SPAIN)
Immediate Holding Company: FAGOR AUTOMATION UK LTD
Registration no: 03457837 **Date established:** 1997
Turnover: Up to £250,000 **No.of Employees:** 1 - 10 **Product Groups:** 38

Date of Accounts	Dec 11	Dec 10	Dec 09
Sales Turnover	N/A	164	149
Pre Tax Profit/Loss	N/A	-26	-30
Working Capital	-221	-204	-179
Current Assets	90	71	86
Current Liabilities	N/A	16	9

Food Ingredients International Ltd

34 Staverton Road, Daventry, NN11 4HL
Tel: 01327-705444 **Fax:** 01327-704331
E-mail: fooding@aol.com
Website: http://www.foodingredientsinternational.co.uk
Directors: M. Smallwood (MD), A. Smallwood (Co Sec)
Immediate Holding Company: FOOD INGREDIENTS INTERNATIONAL LIMITED
Registration no: 04067827 **Date established:** 2000
Turnover: £500,000 - £1m **No.of Employees:** 1 - 10 **Product Groups:** 20, 31

Date of Accounts	Jul 11	Jul 10	Jul 09
Working Capital	233	205	79
Fixed Assets	1	1	1
Current Assets	650	590	649

foxstandpipes

9-11 Siddeley Way Royal Oak Industrial Estate, Daventry, NN11 8PA
Tel: 01327-311011 **Fax:** 01327-300216
E-mail: sales@kaver.co.uk
Website: http://foxstandpipes.co.uk
Directors: R. Bell (Dir)
Date established: 2009 **Turnover:** £250,000 - £500,000
No.of Employees: 1 - 10 **Product Groups:** 30, 35

General Carbide UK Ltd

Unit 6 Royal Oak Industrial Estate Royal Oak Industrial Estate, Daventry, NN11 8PL
Tel: 01327-300595 **Fax:** 01327-300862
E-mail: rod@generalcarbide.co.uk
Website: http://www.generalcarbide.co.uk
Managers: R. Print (Sales Prom Mgr)
Immediate Holding Company: GENC 2010 LIMITED
Registration no: 02355402 **VAT No.:** GB 532 0647 71
Date established: 1989 **Turnover:** £1m - £2m **No.of Employees:** 1 - 10
Product Groups: 34, 36, 42, 45, 46

Date of Accounts	Dec 11	Dec 10
Working Capital	-217	-126
Fixed Assets	192	197
Current Assets	426	269

Goliath Materials Handling

Unit 1 Oak House Royal Oak Way North, Royal Oak Industrial Estate, Daventry, NN11 8PQ
Tel: 01327-310330 **Fax:** 01327-310330
Directors: K. Horne (Prop)
Date established: 1987 **No.of Employees:** 1 - 10 **Product Groups:** 35, 39, 45

H E S Sales Ltd

Prospect Way Royal Oak Industrial Estate, Daventry, NN11 8PL
Tel: 01327-300322 **Fax:** 01327-311411
E-mail: daventry@hes-sales.com
Website: http://www.hes-sales.com
Bank(s): Barclays, High St
Managers: A. Moorhouse (Chief Mgr)
Immediate Holding Company: H.E.S. SALES LIMITED
Registration no: 05835529 **Date established:** 2006 **Turnover:** £2m - £5m
No.of Employees: 11 - 20 **Product Groups:** 29, 30, 36, 40, 45, 48, 66, 67, 68

Date of Accounts	Mar 11	Mar 10	Mar 09
Working Capital	528	440	356
Fixed Assets	60	60	86
Current Assets	991	799	813

Hymo Ltd

Grand Union Works Whilton Locks, Whilton, Daventry, NN11 2NH
Tel: 01604-661601 **Fax:** 01604-660166
E-mail: sales@hymo.ltd.uk
Website: http://www.hymo.ltd.uk
Bank(s): Svenska Handelsbanken, 3-5 Newgate St, London EC1A 7DA
Directors: R. Holmgren (MD)
Ultimate Holding Company: MARCO AB (SWEDEN)
Immediate Holding Company: HYMO LIMITED
Registration no: 00911607 **Date established:** 1967 **Turnover:** £5m - £10m
No.of Employees: 11 - 20 **Product Groups:** 40, 45, 67, 84

Date of Accounts	Dec 11	Dec 10	Dec 09
Working Capital	167	127	106
Current Assets	372	500	339

Integrated Business Systems Ltd

24 Cottesbrook Park Heartlands Business Park, Daventry, NN11 8YL
Tel: 01327-302999 **Fax:** 01327-302990
E-mail: sales@intergratedbsl.com
Website: http://www.intergratedbsl.com
Managers: S. Rayford (Tech Serv Mgr)
Immediate Holding Company: INTEGRATED BUSINESS SYSTEMS LIMITED
Registration no: 03923927 **Date established:** 2000
Turnover: Up to £250,000 **No.of Employees:** 1 - 10 **Product Groups:** 37, 67

Date of Accounts	Mar 11	Mar 10	Mar 09
Working Capital	27	12	-35
Fixed Assets	32	32	36
Current Assets	310	223	156

Intelligent Motion Control Ltd

4 Brunel Close Drayton Fields Industrial Estate, Daventry, NN11 8RB
Tel: 01327-307600 **Fax:** 01327-300319
E-mail: info@inmoco.co.uk
Website: http://www.inmoco.co.uk
Directors: V. Wailay (Fin)
Managers: G. Bush (Sales Prom Mgr)
Immediate Holding Company: INTELLIGENT MOTION CONTROL LIMITED
Registration no: 02142001 **VAT No.:** GB 467 3826 13
Date established: 1987 **Turnover:** £1m - £2m **No.of Employees:** 1 - 10
Product Groups: 37, 38, 46

Date of Accounts	Dec 11	Dec 10	Dec 09
Working Capital	592	317	540
Fixed Assets	703	684	734
Current Assets	1m	865	818

Isotron Limited

Brunel Close Drayton Fields Industrial Estate, Daventry, NN11 8RB
Tel: 01327-706111 **Fax:** 01327-300019
E-mail: assistance@isotron.com
Website: http://www.isotron.co.uk
Managers: A. Smith (Site Co-ord)
Registration no: 01771333 **Turnover:** £10m - £20m
No.of Employees: 21 - 50 **Product Groups:** 38, 42

Metokote UK

Hackwood Road High March Industrial Estate, Daventry, NN11 4ES
Tel: 01327-701400 **Fax:** 01327-300 141
E-mail: pkearns@metokote.com
Website: http://www.metokote.com
Directors: K. Vicente (Fin)
Managers: A. Freeman (Sales Prom Mgr), H. Williamson (Personnel), P. Kearns
Ultimate Holding Company: METOKOTE CORPORATION (USA)
Immediate Holding Company: METOKOTE UK LIMITED
Registration no: 03346979 **Date established:** 1997 **Turnover:** £5m - £10m
No.of Employees: 51 - 100 **Product Groups:** 46, 48

Date of Accounts	Oct 11	Oct 10	Oct 09
Sales Turnover	10m	8m	6m
Pre Tax Profit/Loss	185	59	-189
Working Capital	-1m	-2m	-2m
Fixed Assets	4m	4m	5m
Current Assets	3m	3m	2m
Current Liabilities	767	665	439

Mila Hardware

1 Brunel Close Drayton Fields Industrial Estate, Daventry, NN11 8RB
Tel: 01327-872511 **Fax:** 01327-872575
E-mail: sales@mila.co.uk
Website: http://www.mila.co.uk
Directors: P. Wreford (Fin), V. Sanders (Sales & Mktg)
Managers: D. Ward (Tech Serv Mgr), O. Burgess, L. Coldwell (Personnel)
Ultimate Holding Company: HEYWOOD WILLIAMS GROUP PLC
Immediate Holding Company: HWG 2006 LTD
Registration no: 01457413 **VAT No.:** GB 307 3411 92
Turnover: £20m - £50m **No.of Employees:** 101 - 250 **Product Groups:** 36

Date of Accounts	Dec 07	Dec 06	Dec 05
Working Capital	7350	7350	7350
Current Assets	7350	7350	7350
Total Share Capital	500	500	500

Octagon Products

3 Brindley Close Drayton Fields Industrial Estate, Daventry, NN11 8RP
Tel: 01327-877100 **Fax:** 01327-877063
E-mail: octagon@cropstorage.co.uk
Website: http://www.octagonproducts.co.uk
Directors: J. Madigan (Prop)
Turnover: Up to £250,000 **No.of Employees:** 1 - 10 **Product Groups:** 41

Palway Ltd

6 Macadam Close Drayton Fields Industrial Estate, Daventry, NN11 8RX
Tel: 01327-876387 **Fax:** 01327-872615
E-mail: jt@palway.com
Website: http://www.palway.com
Directors: P. Thorp (Fin), J. Thorp (MD)
Immediate Holding Company: PALWAY LIMITED
Registration no: 02071494 **Date established:** 1986
No.of Employees: 1 - 10 **Product Groups:** 38, 42

Date of Accounts	Dec 10	Dec 09	Dec 08
Working Capital	-75	-57	-34
Fixed Assets	1	4	57
Current Assets	138	133	68

Patrick Shoes Ltd

Broad March Long March Industrial Estate, Daventry, NN11 4HE
Tel: 01327-703841 **Fax:** 01327-300209
E-mail: mark@patrickshoes.co.uk
Website: http://www.patrickshoes.co.uk
Bank(s): Nat west
Directors: M. Englert (MD)
Immediate Holding Company: PATRICK SHOES LIMITED
Registration no: 01268368 **VAT No.:** 294 0363 55 **Date established:** 1976
Turnover: £2m - £5m **No.of Employees:** 11 - 20 **Product Groups:** 63

Date of Accounts	Jul 11	Jul 10	Jul 09
Working Capital	382	285	161
Fixed Assets	3m	3m	3m
Current Assets	2m	1m	1m

Phoenix County Metals Ltd

Great Central Way Industrial Estate Great Central Way, Woodford Halse, Daventry, NN11 3PZ
Tel: 01327-260581 **Fax:** 01327-261682
E-mail: paul@pcm-ltd.co.uk
Website: http://www.phoenixcountymetals.co.uk
Bank(s): Lloyds TSB Bank plc
Directors: J. Childs (Fin), P. Johnson (MD)
Ultimate Holding Company: DIAMOND LIBRA LIMITED
Immediate Holding Company: PHOENIX COUNTY METALS LIMITED
Registration no: 01849288 **VAT No.:** GB 408 6395 35
Date established: 1984 **Turnover:** £1m - £2m **No.of Employees:** 11 - 20
Product Groups: 34, 54

Date of Accounts	Jan 12	Jan 11	Jan 10
Working Capital	698	798	559
Fixed Assets	844	428	432
Current Assets	1m	1m	788

Planline International Ltd

3 Boddington Road Byfield, Daventry, NN11 6UP
Tel: 01327-264406 **Fax:** 01327-264406
E-mail: sales@planlineinternational.com
Website: http://www.planlineinternational.com
Directors: G. Gilbert (Dir), G. Gilbert (MD), R. Gilbert (Fin)
Immediate Holding Company: PLANLINE INTERNATIONAL LIMITED
Registration no: 04192473 **VAT No.:** GB 775 8126 94
Date established: 2001 **Turnover:** Up to £250,000
No.of Employees: 1 - 10 **Product Groups:** 25, 26, 28, 30, 35, 38, 44, 45, 49, 64, 67, 80

Date of Accounts	Mar 08	Mar 07	Mar 06
Working Capital	-9	-5	-2
Fixed Assets	10	8	5
Current Assets	31	25	20
Current Liabilities	40	30	21

Poli Film UK Ltd

7 Brunel Close Drayton Fields Industrial Estate, Daventry, NN11 8RB
Tel: 01327-876071 **Fax:** 01327-300005
E-mail: sales@poli-film.co.uk
Website: http://www.poli-film.de
Bank(s): Natwest
Directors: P. Beaver (Dir)
Ultimate Holding Company: POLI-FILM VERWALTUNGS GMBH (GERMANY)
Immediate Holding Company: POLI-FILM UK LIMITED
Registration no: 01254215 **VAT No.:** GB 289 7185 92
Date established: 1976 **No.of Employees:** 11 - 20 **Product Groups:** 30

Date of Accounts	Dec 11	Dec 10	Dec 09
Working Capital	2m	2m	2m
Fixed Assets	74	95	87
Current Assets	3m	3m	3m

Quick Axis Ltd

Unit 14 Gresley Close Drayton Fields Industrial Estate, Daventry, NN11 8RZ
Tel: 08454-502531 **Fax:** 08454-502532
E-mail: quickaxis@btconnect.com
Directors: A. Harper (Dir)
Immediate Holding Company: QUICK AXIS LIMITED
Registration no: 06618317 **Date established:** 2008
No.of Employees: 1 - 10 **Product Groups:** 46

Date of Accounts	Jun 12	Jun 11	Jun 10
Working Capital	-27	-19	-4
Fixed Assets	33	42	31
Current Assets	60	66	68

Retec Machine Tools Ltd

48 High March High March Industrial Estate, Daventry, NN11 4HB
Tel: 01327-312800 **Fax:** 01327-878080
E-mail: steve@retec.co.uk
Website: http://www.retec.co.uk
Directors: S. Cockerill (Dir)
Immediate Holding Company: RETEC MACHINE TOOLS LIMITED
Registration no: 02567683 **Date established:** 1990
No.of Employees: 1 - 10 **Product Groups:** 46

Date of Accounts	Dec 11	Dec 10	Dec 09
Working Capital	-200	-196	-252
Fixed Assets	11	14	19
Current Assets	121	8	3

Rugby Plastics Ltd

11 Lanchester Way Royal Oak Industrial Estate, Daventry, NN11 8PH
Tel: 01327-702668 **Fax:** 01327-300468
E-mail: sales@rugbyplastics.com
Website: http://www.rugbyplastics.com
Bank(s): Barclays
Directors: G. Barthus (MD), P. Barthus (Fin)
Immediate Holding Company: RUGBY PLASTICS LIMITED
Registration no: 00617049 **VAT No.:** GB 120 3922 14
Date established: 1958 **Turnover:** £1m - £2m **No.of Employees:** 11 - 20
Product Groups: 30, 42

Date of Accounts	Dec 11	Dec 10	Dec 08
Working Capital	-1	-17	-39
Fixed Assets	842	825	891
Current Assets	365	391	277
Current Liabilities	366	N/A	N/A

Saxon Lifts Ltd

Grand Union Works Whilton Locks, Whilton, Daventry, NN11 2NH
Tel: 01327-843355 **Fax:** 01327-843887
E-mail: mail@saxonlifts.com
Website: http://www.saxonlifts.com
Bank(s): HSBC Bank plc
Directors: B. Jacobsson (Co Sec), S. Roe (MD)
Immediate Holding Company: SAXON LIFTS LIMITED
Registration no: 02321700 **VAT No.:** GB 486 0822 28
Date established: 1988 **Turnover:** £2m - £5m **No.of Employees:** 11 - 20
Product Groups: 26, 45, 84

Date of Accounts	Dec 11	Dec 10	Dec 09
Working Capital	105	224	241
Fixed Assets	348	409	419
Current Assets	832	1m	815

Semperit Industrial Products Ltd

Cottesbrooke Park Heartlands Business Park, Daventry, NN11 8YL
Tel: 01327-313140 **Fax:** 01327-313149
E-mail: allison.runacres@semperit.co.uk
Website: http://semperit.at

Managers: A. Runacres (Sales Admin)
Ultimate Holding Company: SEMPERIT AG HOLDING (AUSTRIA)
Immediate Holding Company: SEMPERIT INDUSTRIAL PRODUCTS LIMITED
Registration no: 01954091 **VAT No.:** GB 363 4710 59
Date established: 1985 **Turnover:** £1m - £2m **No.of Employees:** 1 - 10
Product Groups: 29

Date of Accounts	Dec 11	Dec 10	Dec 09
Sales Turnover	1m	1m	1m
Pre Tax Profit/Loss	115	94	121
Working Capital	188	144	12
Fixed Assets	120	81	146
Current Assets	236	240	126
Current Liabilities	48	94	99

Slik Media

22 Cotters Brooke Park Heartlands Business Park, Daventry, NN11 8YL
Tel: 01327-315168 **Fax:** 01327-315705
E-mail: info@slikmedia.co.uk
Website: http://www.slikmedia.co.uk
Directors: T. Keen (Prop)
Immediate Holding Company: SLIK MEDIA LIMITED
Registration no: 04986683 **Date established:** 2003
No.of Employees: 1 - 10 **Product Groups:** 80

T & G Compressor Services

Brindley Close Drayton Fields Industrial Estate, Daventry, NN11 8RP
Tel: 01327-871081 **Fax:** 01327-311100
E-mail: tony@tgcompressors.co.uk
Website: http://www.tgcompressors.co.uk
Directors: T. Bristow (Prop)
No.of Employees: 1 - 10 **Product Groups:** 28, 40, 48

Tema Machinery Ltd

3 Great Central Way Woodford Halse, Daventry, NN11 3PZ
Tel: 01327-262600 **Fax:** 01327-262571
E-mail: sales@tema.co.uk
Website: http://www.tema.co.uk
Directors: H. Van Delden (Fin), K. Lyons (MD)
Ultimate Holding Company: STAFAG HOLDING AG (SWITZERLAND)
Immediate Holding Company: TEMA (MACHINERY) LIMITED
Registration no: 00694081 **Date established:** 1961 **Turnover:** £1m - £2m
No.of Employees: 11 - 20 **Product Groups:** 16, 30, 35, 36, 41, 42, 45, 84

Date of Accounts	Dec 11	Dec 10	Dec 09
Working Capital	1m	1m	1m
Fixed Assets	195	211	229
Current Assets	3m	1m	1m

Total Supplies Co. Ltd

17 Brunel Close Drayton Fields Industrial Estate, Daventry, NN11 8RB
Tel: 01327-312212 **Fax:** 01327-301991
E-mail: keith.parsons@totalsupplies.co.uk
Website: http://www.totalsupplies.co.uk
Directors: K. Parsons (Dir)
Immediate Holding Company: TOTAL SUPPLIES AND SERVICES COMPANY LIMITED
Registration no: 02765649 **Date established:** 1992
No.of Employees: 1 - 10 **Product Groups:** 38, 42

Date of Accounts	Mar 12	Mar 11	Mar 10
Working Capital	-6	-9	-20
Fixed Assets	19	22	25
Current Assets	48	58	62

Vistaplan International Ltd

High March High March Industrial Estate, Daventry, NN11 4QE
Tel: 01327-704767 **Fax:** 01327-300243
E-mail: sales@vistaplan.com
Website: http://www.vistaplan.com
Directors: D. Cartwright (MD)
Ultimate Holding Company: REDIWELD HOLDINGS LIMITED
Immediate Holding Company: VISTAPLAN INTERNATIONAL LIMITED
Registration no: 01308714 **Date established:** 1977 **Turnover:** £2m - £5m
No.of Employees: 21 - 50 **Product Groups:** 26, 29, 36, 38, 39, 44, 48, 49, 64, 66, 67, 81

Date of Accounts	Dec 11	Dec 10	Dec 09
Working Capital	358	400	469
Fixed Assets	188	193	211
Current Assets	532	579	595

Weldtech Services

17 James Watt Close Drayton Fields Industrial Estate, Daventry, NN11 8RJ
Tel: 01327-300508 **Fax:** 01327-300508
Directors: J. Vicmanis (Ptnr)
Immediate Holding Company: WELDTEC LIMITED
Registration no: 07994687 **Date established:** 2012
No.of Employees: 1 - 10 **Product Groups:** 35

Irthlingborough

Utile Engineering Co. Ltd

New Street, Irthlingborough, NN9 5UG
Tel: 01933-650216 **Fax:** 01933-652738
E-mail: sales@utileengineering.com
Website: http://www.utileengineering.com
Bank(s): Lloyds TSB Bank plc
Directors: J. Rainbow (Fin), T. Poole (Dir), N. Peck (Sales), R. Poole (Ch), T. Poole (MD)
Managers: J. Ainsworth (Works Gen Mgr), J. Rainbow (Accounts)
Ultimate Holding Company: 04672038
Immediate Holding Company: UTILE ENGINEERING CO. LIMITED(THE)
Registration no: 01656155 **VAT No.:** GB 119 8598 22
Date established: 1982 **Turnover:** £2m - £5m **No.of Employees:** 21 - 50
Product Groups: 40

Date of Accounts	Mar 12	Mar 11	Mar 10
Working Capital	741	779	522
Fixed Assets	21	35	43
Current Assets	2m	2m	1m

Kettering

A B L Perpack 1985 Ltd

7 Baron Avenue Telford Way Industrial Estate, Kettering, NN16 8UW
Tel: 01536-412744 **Fax:** 01536-412752
E-mail: christine@ablperpack.co.uk
Website: http://www.ablperpack.co.uk
Directors: D. Cohen (Mkt Research)
Managers: C. Ruff
Ultimate Holding Company: FLEXEMBAL SA (SWITZERLAND)
Immediate Holding Company: A.B.L. PERPACK (1985) LIMITED
Registration no: 01898805 **Date established:** 1985 **Turnover:** £1m - £2m
No.of Employees: 1 - 10 **Product Groups:** 30

Date of Accounts	Dec 11	Dec 10	Dec 09
Sales Turnover	1m	1m	2m
Pre Tax Profit/Loss	-4	13	-23
Working Capital	47	69	96
Fixed Assets	17	5	6
Current Assets	605	586	635
Current Liabilities	33	44	27

A G's Martial Arts & Aerobics Centre

Tailby House Bath Road, Kettering, NN16 8NL
Tel: 01536-513715 **Fax:** 01536-416118
E-mail: andyg@agufs.hotmail.co.uk
Directors: A. Gibney (Prop)
Ultimate Holding Company: E.A.TAILBY LIMITED
Immediate Holding Company: E. A. TAILBY COMPONENTS LIMITED
Registration no: 02940892 **Date established:** 1994
No.of Employees: 21 - 50 **Product Groups:** 89

Date of Accounts	Mar 12	Mar 11	Mar 10
Working Capital	250	173	140
Fixed Assets	98	94	68
Current Assets	413	285	220

Abbey Board

Cromwell House Altendiez Way, Burton Latimer, Kettering, NN15 5YZ
Tel: 01536-420055 **Fax:** 01536-421726
E-mail: julie.coles@abbey.dssp.com
Website: http://www.abbeycorrugated.co.uk
Bank(s): National Westminster Bank Plc
Managers: J. Coles (Personnel)
Immediate Holding Company: DAVID S. SMITH P.L.C.
Registration no: 00630681 **VAT No.:** GB 608 7163 35
Date established: 1972 **Turnover:** £20m - £50m
No.of Employees: 51 - 100 **Product Groups:** 27, 28, 30, 45, 49, 66, 84

Agora Services Ltd

1 Telford Way Telford Way Industrial Estate, Kettering, NN16 8UN
Tel: 01536-481629 **Fax:** 01536-410193
E-mail: sales@agoraservices.co.uk
Website: http://www.agoraservices.co.uk
Directors: C. Haycock (MD)
Immediate Holding Company: AGORA SERVICES LIMITED
Registration no: 03125254 **Date established:** 1995
Turnover: Up to £250,000 **No.of Employees:** 1 - 10 **Product Groups:** 35, 41, 42, 45, 48, 52, 54

Date of Accounts	Nov 11	Nov 10	Nov 09
Working Capital	106	83	89
Fixed Assets	1	5	15
Current Assets	122	101	127

The Alumasc Group plc

Station Road Burton Latimer, Kettering, NN15 5JP
Tel: 01536-383844 **Fax:** 01536-725069
E-mail: info@alumasc.co.uk
Website: http://www.alumasc.co.uk
Directors: P. Hooper (Grp Chief Exec)
Managers: T. Scarvaci (Tech Serv Mgr), A. Magson, C. Waples (Personnel)
Immediate Holding Company: THE ALUMASC GROUP PLC
Registration no: 01767387 **Date established:** 1983
Turnover: £75m - £125m **No.of Employees:** 1 - 10 **Product Groups:** 30

Date of Accounts	Jun 11	Jun 10	Jun 09
Sales Turnover	107m	93m	109m
Pre Tax Profit/Loss	5m	3m	2m
Working Capital	16m	17m	15m
Fixed Assets	36m	39m	42m
Current Assets	42m	39m	34m
Current Liabilities	6m	7m	7m

Antony G Cope

4 Watermill Close Desborough, Kettering, NN14 2XW
Tel: 01536-762804 **Fax:** 01536- 762804
Directors: A. Cope (Prop)
Date established: 1992 **No.of Employees:** 1 - 10 **Product Groups:** 35

Applied Dynamics International

1450 Montagu Court Kettering Parkway, Kettering Venture Park, Kettering, NN15 6XR
Tel: 01536-410077 **Fax:** 01536-410019
E-mail: debbie@adi.com
Website: http://www.adi.com
Managers: D. Beech (Admin Off)
Ultimate Holding Company: APPLIED DYNAMICS INTERNATIONAL INC (USA)
Immediate Holding Company: APPLIED DYNAMICS INTERNATIONAL LIMITED
Registration no: 01682794 **Date established:** 1982
Turnover: £250,000 - £500,000 **No.of Employees:** 1 - 10
Product Groups: 67

Date of Accounts	Dec 11	Dec 10	Dec 09
Working Capital	-20	-28	-6
Fixed Assets	1	1	3
Current Assets	232	163	130

Astwell Augers Ltd

A14 Huntingdon Road Thrapston, Kettering, NN14 4PT
Tel: 01832-735300 **Fax:** 01832-735533
E-mail: sales@astwell.co.uk
Website: http://www.astwell.co.uk
Bank(s): National Westminster Bank Plc
Directors: R. Jones (MD), H. Jones (Fin)
Immediate Holding Company: ASTWELL AUGERS LIMITED
Registration no: 01636698 **VAT No.:** GB 230 5374 91
Date established: 1982 **Turnover:** £500,000 - £1m
No.of Employees: 11 - 20 **Product Groups:** 41, 45

Date of Accounts	Oct 11	Oct 10	Oct 09
Working Capital	392	333	307
Fixed Assets	306	313	303
Current Assets	991	996	1m

Blandfords

Broughton Grange Business Centre Headlands, Kettering, NN15 6XA
Tel: 01536-483699 **Fax:** 01536-411505
E-mail: info@blandfords.net
Website: http://www.blandfords.net
Bank(s): National Westminster Bank Plc
Directors: P. Smith (Ptnr)
Immediate Holding Company: BLANDFORDS LLP
Registration no: OC315417 **VAT No.:** GB 119 7705 52
Date established: 2005 **No.of Employees:** 21 - 50 **Product Groups:** 52, 85

Date of Accounts	Oct 11	Oct 10	Oct 09
Working Capital	-61	181	146
Fixed Assets	150	129	166
Current Assets	313	763	290

Carrs Welding Technologies Ltd

Unit 2 Henson Park Henson Way, Telford Way Industrial Estate, Kettering, NN16 8PX
Tel: 01536-412828 **Fax:** 01536-310262
E-mail: phil@carrswelding.co.uk
Website: http://www.carrswelding.co.uk
Directors: P. Carr (MD)
Immediate Holding Company: CARR'S WELDING TECHNOLOGIES LIMITED
Registration no: 03921135 **Date established:** 2000
Turnover: £250,000 - £500,000 **No.of Employees:** 1 - 10
Product Groups: 37, 48, 84

Date of Accounts	Apr 12	Apr 11	Apr 10
Working Capital	129	68	8
Fixed Assets	485	467	464
Current Assets	359	242	138

Clan Marketing Co.

77 Harrington Road Loddington, Kettering, NN14 1JZ
Tel: 01536-711326 **Fax:** 01536-711326
E-mail: admin@clanmarketing.co.uk
Website: http://www.litterpicker.co.uk
Directors: B. Martin (Prop)
Immediate Holding Company: INTIMATE DETAILS LTD
Date established: 2006 **Turnover:** Up to £250,000
No.of Employees: 1 - 10 **Product Groups:** 49

Coding & Handling

52 Meeting Lane Burton Latimer, Kettering, NN15 5LS
Tel: 01536-721026 **Fax:** 01536-725056
Website: http://www.codingandhandling.co.uk
Directors: J. Manning (Prop)
Immediate Holding Company: CODEJET INTAM SERVICES LTD
Registration no: 04853154 **Date established:** 2003
Turnover: £250,000 - £500,000 **No.of Employees:** 1 - 10
Product Groups: 28, 32, 42, 44, 46, 80

Date of Accounts	Mar 10	Mar 09	Mar 08
Working Capital	-40	-44	-37
Fixed Assets	N/A	1	13
Current Assets	29	23	35

Countrywear Ltd

1b-1c Robinson Way Telford Way Industrial Estate, Kettering, NN16 8PT
Tel: 01536-481558 **Fax:** 01536-485218
E-mail: info@countrywearuk.com
Website: http://www.countrywearuk.com
Directors: J. Lillie (Prop)
Immediate Holding Company: COUNTRYWEAR LIMITED
Registration no: 04363226 **VAT No.:** GB 581 0408 60
Date established: 2002 **Turnover:** £250,000 - £500,000
No.of Employees: 1 - 10 **Product Groups:** 63

Date of Accounts	Mar 12	Mar 11	Mar 10
Working Capital	-46	11	16
Fixed Assets	35	32	19
Current Assets	133	199	189

County Footware

2270 Kettering Parkway Kettering Venture Park, Kettering, NN15 6XR
Tel: 01536-527201 **Fax:** 01536-411085
E-mail: mark.barron@pattersonmedical.com
Website: http://www.countyfootwear.com
Bank(s): Bank of Scotland
Managers: M. Barron (Mgr)
Immediate Holding Company: COUNTY FOOTWEAR LIMITED
Registration no: 03395131 **VAT No.:** GB 550 7985 14
Date established: 1997 **Turnover:** £2m - £5m **No.of Employees:** 51 - 100
Product Groups: 22, 38

Crawford Precision Engineering Ltd

Unit 5 Cross Court Industrial Estate, Kettering, NN16 9BN
Tel: 01536-417140 **Fax:** 01536-524059
E-mail: cpeng@globalnet.co.uk
Website: http://www.crawfordprecision.co.uk
Directors: J. Crawford (MD), K. Crawford (Fin)
Immediate Holding Company: CRAWFORD PRECISION ENGINEERING LIMITED
Registration no: 05348980 **Date established:** 2005
Turnover: £250,000 - £500,000 **No.of Employees:** 1 - 10
Product Groups: 35, 40, 41, 45

Date of Accounts	Feb 12	Feb 11	Feb 10
Working Capital	472	469	427
Fixed Assets	1	1	11
Current Assets	509	530	436

D R Harrod Tractors

Cranford Road Great Addington, Kettering, NN14 4BH
Tel: 01536-330422 **Fax:** 01933-460072
Directors: D. Harrod (Ptnr)
Immediate Holding Company: D.R. HARROD TRACTORS LLP
Registration no: OC301861 **Date established:** 2002
No.of Employees: 1 - 10 **Product Groups:** 41

Date of Accounts	Mar 11	Mar 10	Mar 07
Working Capital	30	34	28
Fixed Assets	51	39	20
Current Assets	39	42	39
Current Liabilities	N/A	N/A	10

Davies & Company

12 Beatrice Road, Kettering, NN16 9QS
Tel: 01536-513456 **Fax:** 01536-310080
E-mail: sales@equimat.co.uk
Website: http://www.equimat.co.uk
Directors: A. Gregory (MD), G. Martin (Fin)
Immediate Holding Company: DINKIE HEEL P.L.C.
Registration no: 00507461 **VAT No.:** GB 137 6241 71
Date established: 1988 **Turnover:** £2m - £5m **No.of Employees:** 1 - 10
Product Groups: 23

Dodson & Horrell Country Store

Spencer Street Ringstead, Kettering, NN14 4BX
Tel: 01933-461539 **Fax:** 01832-737 303
E-mail: rclark@dodsonandhorrell.com
Website: http://www.dodsonandhorrellcountrystore.co.uk
Bank(s): Lloyds TSB Bank plc
Managers: R. Clark (Mgr)
Immediate Holding Company: CLON COMMUNICATIONS LLP
Registration no: 02098720 **VAT No.:** GB 463 0619 57
Date established: 2008 **Turnover:** £20m - £50m
No.of Employees: 11 - 20 **Product Groups:** 62

Date of Accounts	Oct 11	Oct 10	Oct 09
Working Capital	-5	-21	-18
Fixed Assets	20	29	33
Current Assets	12	10	24

Doorway Services

2 High Street Rothwell, Kettering, NN14 6LE
Tel: 01536-418798 **Fax:** 01536-418798
E-mail: service@doorwayservices.org
Website: http://www.doorwayservices.co.uk
Directors: M. Shewry (Ptnr)
No.of Employees: 1 - 10 **Product Groups:** 35, 36, 37, 45, 66

Dunkelman & Son Ltd

Manor House Gold Street, Desborough, Kettering, NN14 2PF
Tel: 01536-760760 **Fax:** 020-7287 0933
E-mail: sales@dunkelman.com
Website: http://www.dunkelman.com
Bank(s): Barclays, London
Directors: J. Hummel (Co Sec), K. Burton (Sales), R. Holmes (Purch)
Managers: J. Smeathers (Tech Serv Mgr)
Immediate Holding Company: DUNKELMAN & SON LIMITED
Registration no: 00466486 **VAT No.:** GB 119 4552 66
Date established: 1949 **Turnover:** £5m - £10m
No.of Employees: 51 - 100 **Product Groups:** 22, 32

Date of Accounts	Jun 12	Jun 11	Jun 10
Sales Turnover	8m	7m	6m
Pre Tax Profit/Loss	676	715	396
Working Capital	3m	3m	2m
Fixed Assets	87	49	70
Current Assets	4m	4m	3m
Current Liabilities	349	473	421

The European Shoe Machinery Company Ltd

Iridium House 4 Kings Court, Kettering, NN15 6WJ
Tel: 01536-483583 **Fax:** 01536-482482
E-mail: info@tesmc.com
Website: http://www.tesmc.com
Directors: R. Petrozzi (MD)
Immediate Holding Company: THE EUROPEAN SHOE MACHINERY COMPANY LIMITED
Registration no: 03159789 **Date established:** 1996
No.of Employees: 1 - 10 **Product Groups:** 43

Date of Accounts	Jan 12	Jan 11	Jan 10
Working Capital	398	246	269
Fixed Assets	219	224	256
Current Assets	516	333	453

Eveden Ltd

Rothwell Road Desborough, Kettering, NN14 2PG
Tel: 01536-760282 **Fax:** 01536-762149
E-mail: info@eveden.com
Website: http://www.eveden.com
Directors: A. Thwaites (MD), G. Embley (Co Sec)
Ultimate Holding Company: EVEDEN GROUP LIMITED
Immediate Holding Company: EVEDEN LIMITED
Registration no: 00171167 **Date established:** 2020
Turnover: £50m - £75m **No.of Employees:** 251 - 500 **Product Groups:** 24

Date of Accounts	Jun 11	Jun 10	Jun 09
Sales Turnover	52m	50m	48m
Pre Tax Profit/Loss	4m	4m	4m
Working Capital	13m	11m	10m
Fixed Assets	5m	4m	4m
Current Assets	43m	37m	30m
Current Liabilities	6m	5m	4m

Fenland Hydrotech

7 Chancery Lane Thrapston, Kettering, NN14 4JL
Tel: 01832-734612 **Fax:** 01832-734780
E-mail: info@fenhydro.co.uk
Website: http://www.fenhydro.co.uk
Directors: S. Winpenny (MD), S. Winpenny (Fin)
Immediate Holding Company: FENLAND HYDROTECH CONSULTING ENGINEERS LTD
Registration no: 06397292 **Date established:** 2007
Turnover: £500,000 - £1m **No.of Employees:** 1 - 10 **Product Groups:** 54, 84

Filtercare

5 Alexandra Street Burton Latimer, Kettering, NN15 5SE
Tel: 01536-722049 **Fax:** 01536-398647
E-mail: filtercare@hotmail.com
Website: http://www.filtercare.co.uk
Directors: P. Cottell (Prop)
Immediate Holding Company: FILTERCARE ONLINE LIMITED
Registration no: 08151463 **Date established:** 2012
No.of Employees: 1 - 10 **Product Groups:** 38, 42

Flag Innovations

The White House 12 Milldale Road, Kettering, NN15 6QB
Tel: 01536-515471 **Fax:** 01536-515471
E-mail: sales@flag-innovations.com
Website: http://www.flag-innovations.com
Directors: R. Connolly (Prop)
No.of Employees: 1 - 10 **Product Groups:** 24, 30, 35, 49

G R P Material Supplies

Garrard Way Telford Way Industrial Estate, Kettering, NN16 8TD
Tel: 01536-525227 **Fax:** 01536-410950
E-mail: geoff.whitworth@grpms.co.uk
Website: http://www.grpms.co.uk
Managers: G. Whitworth
Immediate Holding Company: JGE CAR WASH LIMITED
Registration no: 02013484 **Date established:** 1986
No.of Employees: 1 - 10 **Product Groups:** 46, 48

Date of Accounts	Mar 11	Mar 10	Mar 09
Working Capital	-46	-26	-13
Fixed Assets	511	365	383
Current Assets	23	36	39

The Gammidge

Kettering Parkway Kettering Venture Park, Kettering, NN15 6EZ
Tel: 01536-415222 **Fax:** 01536-532970
E-mail: mail@gammidge.co.uk
Website: http://www.wranglerfootwear.co.uk
Bank(s): Barclays
Directors: J. Minney (MD), P. Brown (Co Sec)
Registration no: 00338212 **Turnover:** £2m - £5m
No.of Employees: 11 - 20 **Product Groups:** 22

Gotch Saunders & Surridge LLP (Chartered Architects and Quantity Surveyors)

35 Headlands, Kettering, NN15 7ES
Tel: 01536-513165 **Fax:** 01536-410226
E-mail: blg@gotch.co.uk
Website: http://www.gotch.co.uk
Bank(s): HSBC Bank plc
Directors: B. Gotch (Snr Part)
Immediate Holding Company: GOTCH, SAUNDERS & SURRIDGE LLP
Registration no: OC336029 **Date established:** 2008 **Turnover:** £1m - £2m
No.of Employees: 21 - 50 **Product Groups:** 84

Date of Accounts	Jun 11	Jun 10	Jun 09
Working Capital	1m	1m	2m
Fixed Assets	121	143	133
Current Assets	2m	2m	2m

Graham

Northfield Avenue, Kettering, NN16 9SJ
Tel: 01536-412259 **Fax:** 01933-441668
E-mail: adam.sibley@graham-group.co.uk
Website: http://www.jewson.co.uk
Managers: R. Williams (Mgr)
Ultimate Holding Company: SAINT-GOBAIN PLC
Immediate Holding Company: GRAHAM GROUP LTD
Registration no: 00066738 **No.of Employees:** 1 - 10 **Product Groups:** 66

Great Eastern Service Co.

143-149 Bath Road, Kettering, NN16 8NE
Tel: 01536-416390 **Fax:** 01536-416390
E-mail: johnt@greateasternservicecompany.co.uk
Directors: J. Taylor (MD)
Immediate Holding Company: FLOMATIC RENTALS LIMITED
Registration no: 02082091 **Date established:** 1986
No.of Employees: 1 - 10 **Product Groups:** 20, 40, 41

Date of Accounts	Dec 11	Dec 10	Nov 09
Working Capital	73	60	22
Fixed Assets	44	53	1
Current Assets	259	271	40

Hayway Tool & Hardware Company Ltd

Cunliffe Drive, Kettering, NN16 8LD
Tel: 01536-481114 **Fax:** 01536-483514
E-mail: sales@haywaytools.com
Website: http://www.haywaytools.com
Directors: J. Burton (Fin), N. Burton (MD)
Immediate Holding Company: HAYWAY TOOL AND HARDWARE COMPANY LIMITED(THE)
Registration no: 01638786 **VAT No.:** GB 360 0072 06
Date established: 1982 **Turnover:** £500,000 - £1m
No.of Employees: 1 - 10 **Product Groups:** 22, 24, 26, 30, 33, 35, 36, 37, 39, 40, 44, 45, 46, 47, 49, 66

Date of Accounts	Dec 11	Dec 10	Dec 09
Working Capital	202	208	221
Fixed Assets	3	5	5
Current Assets	312	315	313

Infrared Heater UK

Unit 2 Torridge Close Telford Way Industrial Estate, Kettering, NN16 8PY
Tel: 01536-525136 **Fax:** 01536-481569
E-mail: infraredheater@rackett.freeserve.co.uk
Website: http://www.infrared-heater-radiant-electric-gas-kerosene.co.uk
Directors: A. Harvey (Develop)
Registration no: 387766 **Date established:** 1999 **Turnover:** £1m - £2m
No.of Employees: 11 - 20 **Product Groups:** 33, 37, 40

J & S Interim & Management Consultancy Ltd

West Wing Glendon Hall, Kettering, NN14 1QE
Tel: 01536-711152 **Fax:** 01536-711152
E-mail: admin@jandsinterim.co.uk
Website: http://www.jandsinterim.co.uk
Directors: J. Scott (Dir), S. Scott (Dir)
Registration no: 04619148 **No.of Employees:** 1 - 10 **Product Groups:** 80

Date of Accounts	Mar 08	Mar 07	Mar 06
Working Capital	13	18	1
Fixed Assets	1	1	1
Current Assets	37	38	15
Current Liabilities	24	20	14

T James Electrical Ltd

30a Regent Street, Kettering, NN16 8QG
Tel: 01536-514254 **Fax:** 01536-411213
E-mail: enquiries@tjameselectrical.co.uk
Website: http://www.tjameselectrical.co.uk
Bank(s): NatWest
Directors: M. Himwood (Fin), S. Turner (MD), L. Turner (Fin)
Immediate Holding Company: T.JAMES(ELECTRICAL)LIMITED
Registration no: 00718697 **VAT No.:** GB 119 5542 64
Date established: 1962 **Turnover:** Up to £250,000
No.of Employees: 21 - 50 **Product Groups:** 52

Date of Accounts	Mar 09	Mar 08	Sep 11
Working Capital	204	128	287
Fixed Assets	235	187	179
Current Assets	1m	944	1m

Kettering Compressed Air Centre

Cunliffe Drive Industrial Estate Cunliffe Drive, Kettering, NN16 8LD
Tel: 01536-520339 **Fax:** 01536-310061
Website: http://www.compressorengineering.co.uk
Bank(s): National Westminster, Wellingborough
Directors: I. Pulley (Dir), I. Pulley (MD), L. Hearn (Dir), L. Pulley (Fin), L. Hearn (Eng Serv), M. George (Dir)
Managers: M. Green (Sales Prom Mgr), Green (Sales Prom Mgr), Pulley (Purch Mgr), D. Deakin (Sales Prom Mgr), W. Guthrie (Purch Mgr), V. Bates (Chief Acct)
Immediate Holding Company: HAYWAY TOOL AND HARDWARE COMPANY LIMITED(THE)
Registration no: 01504228 **Date established:** 1982 **Turnover:** £2m - £5m
No.of Employees: 11 - 20 **Product Groups:** 48

Date of Accounts	Dec 07	Dec 06	Dec 05
Working Capital	872	809	1130
Fixed Assets	267	142	N/A
Current Assets	1369	1149	1365
Current Liabilities	497	340	235

Lappset UK Ltd

Henson Way, Kettering, NN16 8PX
Tel: 01536-641261 **Fax:** 01536-521703
E-mail: uk@lappset.com
Website: http://www.lappset.com/global/en.iw3
Ultimate Holding Company: LAPPSET GROUP OY (FINLAND)
Registration no: 02480276 **Date established:** 1968
No.of Employees: 11 - 20 **Product Groups:** 26, 49, 52, 65

Date of Accounts	Dec 09	Dec 08	Dec 07
Working Capital	-680	-622	12
Fixed Assets	191	201	220
Current Assets	379	1m	861

Lee Dickens Ltd

The Old Water Mill Rushton Road, Desborough, Kettering, NN14 2QW
Tel: 01536-760156 **Fax:** 01536-762552
E-mail: mark.dickens@lee-dickens.co.uk
Website: http://www.lee-dickens.co.uk
Directors: M. Dickens (Fin)
Immediate Holding Company: LEE-DICKENS LIMITED
Registration no: 00735448 **Date established:** 1962 **Turnover:** £1m - £2m
No.of Employees: 21 - 50 **Product Groups:** 37, 38, 67

Date of Accounts	Apr 11	Apr 10	Apr 09
Sales Turnover	1m	1m	1m
Pre Tax Profit/Loss	-203	-143	31
Working Capital	793	941	1m
Fixed Assets	442	450	458
Current Assets	1m	1m	1m
Current Liabilities	69	71	70

Lee-Dickens Ltd

Rushton Rd Desborough, Kettering, NN14 2QW
Tel: 01536-760156 **Fax:** 01536-762552
E-mail: sales@lee-dickens.co.uk
Website: http://www.lee-dickens.co.uk
Bank(s): HSBC, Northampton
Managers: M. Dickens, J. Meadows, G. Dickens, G. Dickens (Mktg Serv Mgr), R. Gee (Intern Sales En)
Registration no: 00735448 **VAT No.:** GB 120 0270 46
Date established: 1962 **Turnover:** £2m - £5m **No.of Employees:** 21 - 50
Product Groups: 37, 38, 40, 44, 47, 67

Date of Accounts	Apr 08	Apr 07	Apr 06
Sales Turnover	1207	1268	1517
Pre Tax Profit/Loss	-174	-198	-161
Working Capital	980	1109	1311
Fixed Assets	455	482	477
Current Assets	1182	1242	1505
Current Liabilities	202	132	195
Total Share Capital	30	30	30
ROCE% (Return on Capital Employed)	-12.1	-12.4	-9.0
ROT% (Return on Turnover)	-14.4	-15.6	-10.6

Littlestone & Goodwin Ltd

Elgee Works Victoria Street Desborough, Kettering, NN14 2LX
Tel: 01536-760084 **Fax:** 01536-762550
E-mail: david.littlestone@littlestone.co.uk
Directors: A. Kirk (Sales), D. Littlestone (MD), S. Littlestone (Co Sec)
Immediate Holding Company: LITTLESTONE & GOODWIN.LIMITED
Registration no: 00315097 **Date established:** 1936 **Turnover:** £2m - £5m
No.of Employees: 1 - 10 **Product Groups:** 22, 61

Date of Accounts	Dec 11	Dec 10	Dec 09
Sales Turnover	N/A	N/A	4m
Pre Tax Profit/Loss	N/A	N/A	-254
Working Capital	1m	1m	1m
Fixed Assets	72	75	64
Current Assets	1m	1m	1m
Current Liabilities	N/A	N/A	129

Loake Shoemakers

Wood Street, Kettering, NN16 9SN
Tel: 01536-415411 **Fax:** 01536-410190
E-mail: mail@loake.co.uk
Website: http://www.loake.co.uk
Bank(s): HSBC
Directors: J. Perkins Cory (Sales), R. Sutton (Fin), D. Coker (Pers), A. Loake (MD), A. Cory (Mkt Research)
Immediate Holding Company: LOAKE BROTHERS LIMITED
Registration no: 00043081 **VAT No.:** GB 119 1503 94
Date established: 1995 **Turnover:** £10m - £20m
No.of Employees: 101 - 250 **Product Groups:** 22

Date of Accounts	Dec 11	Dec 10	Dec 09
Sales Turnover	16m	16m	13m
Pre Tax Profit/Loss	1m	1m	1m
Working Capital	11m	11m	10m
Fixed Assets	2m	2m	2m
Current Assets	12m	12m	11m
Current Liabilities	561	697	685

M W C Pipe Work & Fabrications

Unit 3 Orlingbury Road Isham, Kettering, NN14 1HW
Tel: 01536-722075 **Fax:** 01536-722075
Directors: M. Corstin (Prop)
Immediate Holding Company: GREEN BEAN DEVELOPMENT COMPANY LIMITED
Date established: 2010 **No.of Employees:** 1 - 10 **Product Groups:** 35, 46, 48, 49

Mobility For Life Kettering Ltd
19 Hampden Crescent, Kettering, NN16 0LA
Tel: 01536-412411
Directors: S. Rumney (MD)
Immediate Holding Company: MOBILITY FOR LIFE (KETTERING) LIMITED
Registration no: 06261286 **Date established:** 2007
Turnover: Up to £250,000 **No.of Employees:** 1 - 10 **Product Groups:** 26, 38, 39

Date of Accounts	May 11	May 10	May 09
Sales Turnover	36	57	44
Pre Tax Profit/Loss	-2	1	1
Working Capital	2	3	4
Current Assets	11	12	12

Mosaic Board Printers Ltd
Unit 1-2 Pytchley Lodge Industrial Estate Pytchley Lodge Road, Kettering, NN15 6JQ
Tel: 01536-312500 **Fax:** 01536-312555
E-mail: info@mosaic-boardprint.com
Website: http://www.mosaic-boardprint.com
Bank(s): HSBC Bank plc
Directors: G. Pearce (MD)
Immediate Holding Company: MOSAIC BOARD PRINTERS LIMITED
Registration no: 03203404 **Date established:** 1996
No.of Employees: 11 - 20 **Product Groups:** 27, 28, 49, 76

Date of Accounts	Aug 11	Aug 10	Aug 09
Working Capital	-63	-91	-147
Fixed Assets	566	588	651
Current Assets	491	393	358

O Kay Engineering Services Ltd
Eagle Avenue Magnetic Park, Desborough, Kettering, NN14 2WD
Tel: 01536-765010 **Fax:** 01536-765011
E-mail: postbox@okay.co.uk
Website: http://www.okay.co.uk
Directors: P. Goldblats (Fin), T. Kay (Dir)
Managers: A. Kay (I.T. Exec), D. Eastern (Prod Mgr), P. Goldblats (Comptroller), R. Woolman (Sales Prom Mgr), D. Webb (Accounts)
Registration no: 00777495 **Date established:** 1999 **Turnover:** £2m - £5m
No.of Employees: 1 - 10 **Product Groups:** 44, 45, 54

Date of Accounts	Oct 07	Oct 06	Oct 05
Working Capital	725	681	643
Fixed Assets	395	451	418
Current Assets	1831	1359	1595
Current Liabilities	1106	678	952
Total Share Capital	16	16	16

D W O'Brien Ltd
64 Trafalgar Road, Kettering, NN16 8DD
Tel: 01536-484495 **Fax:** 01536-410976
E-mail: sales@dwobrien.co.uk
Website: http://www.dwobrien.co.uk
Bank(s): Yorkshire Bank PLC
Directors: J. O'Brien (Ch), F. O'brien (Dir)
Managers: M. Truce, J. Coates (Comptroller), L. McStay (Comptroller)
Immediate Holding Company: D.W. O'BRIEN LIMITED
Registration no: 01099894 **VAT No.:** GB 121 5458 94
Date established: 1973 **Turnover:** £2m - £5m **No.of Employees:** 11 - 20
Product Groups: 46, 48

Date of Accounts	Aug 11	Aug 10	Aug 09
Working Capital	294	251	198
Fixed Assets	187	173	275
Current Assets	764	754	593

Pegasus Software Ltd
Orion House Orion Way, Kettering, NN15 6PE
Tel: 01536-495000 **Fax:** 01536-495001
E-mail: mailbox@pegasus.co.uk
Website: http://www.pegasus.co.uk
Bank(s): Barclays
Directors: G. Bisnought (Co Sec), S. Anderson (Dir)
Ultimate Holding Company: GOLDEN GATE CAPITAL (USA)
Immediate Holding Company: PEGASUS SOFTWARE LIMITED
Registration no: 01601542 **Date established:** 1981 **Turnover:** £5m - £10m
No.of Employees: 51 - 100 **Product Groups:** 44

Date of Accounts	May 11	May 10	May 09
Sales Turnover	6m	7m	7m
Pre Tax Profit/Loss	1m	1m	678
Working Capital	4m	3m	1m
Fixed Assets	3m	3m	3m
Current Assets	9m	6m	15m
Current Liabilities	3m	2m	3m

Pink & Jones
Britannia House Riley Road, Telford Way Industrial Estate, Kettering, NN16 8NN
Tel: 01604-714448 **Fax:** 01604-410584
E-mail: removals@pinkandjones.co.uk
Website: http://www.pinkandjones.co.uk
Bank(s): H.S.B.C.
Directors: J. Thompson (MD)
Ultimate Holding Company: ECLIPSE WEB LIMITED
Immediate Holding Company: ECLIPSE WEB LIMITED
Registration no: 00655579 **Date established:** 2005
Turnover: £10m - £20m **No.of Employees:** 21 - 50 **Product Groups:** 45, 72

Date of Accounts	Dec 11	Dec 10	Dec 09
Sales Turnover	20m	16m	15m
Pre Tax Profit/Loss	2m	1m	639
Working Capital	1m	27	226
Fixed Assets	6m	7m	5m
Current Assets	10m	8m	7m
Current Liabilities	2m	3m	2m

Prosaw Ltd
Telford Way Telford Way Industrial Estate, Kettering, NN16 8UN
Tel: 01536-410999 **Fax:** 01536-410080
E-mail: sales@prosaw.co.uk
Website: http://www.prosaw.co.uk
Bank(s): Barclays
Directors: G. Jenner (MD), P. Crick (Dir)
Immediate Holding Company: PROSAW LIMITED
Registration no: 01115014 **VAT No.:** GB 330 2990 76
Date established: 1973 **Turnover:** Up to £250,000
No.of Employees: 21 - 50 **Product Groups:** 37, 46

Date of Accounts	Dec 11	Dec 10	Dec 09
Working Capital	1m	1m	1m
Fixed Assets	62	50	431
Current Assets	2m	2m	2m

Quickpack UK Ltd
14 Linnell Way Telford Way Industrial Estate, Kettering, NN16 8PS
Tel: 01536-510910 **Fax:** 01536-410568
E-mail: quickpackuk@quickpack.com
Website: http://www.quickpack.com
Directors: J. Beattie (Co Sec), M. McGregor (Sales)
Ultimate Holding Company: Plus Holding SA (Switzerland)
Immediate Holding Company: Interdibipack Spa
Registration no: 01804796 **VAT No.:** GB 396 9360 93
Date established: 1998 **Turnover:** £500,000 - £1m
No.of Employees: 1 - 10 **Product Groups:** 42, 48

Date of Accounts	Jun 08	Jun 07	Jun 06
Working Capital	-72	-72	-46
Fixed Assets	28	28	N/A
Current Assets	2	7	40
Current Liabilities	74	79	86
Total Share Capital	21	21	21

R Lewin Scales
191 St Johns Road, Kettering, NN15 5AW
Tel: 01536-415574 **Fax:** 01536-416227
E-mail: reglewin@scaleman.freeserve.co.uk
Directors: R. Lewin (Prop), R. Lewing (Prop)
Date established: 1977 **No.of Employees:** 1 - 10 **Product Groups:** 38, 42

Rigid Containers Ltd (a subsidiary of Rigid Containers (Holdings) Ltd)
Stoke Albany Road Desborough, Kettering, NN14 2SR
Tel: 01536-760266 **Fax:** 01536-762714
E-mail: richardcoward@rigid.co.uk
Website: http://www.rigid.co.uk
Bank(s): Barclays
Directors: J. Freeman (Mkt Research), L. Maynard (Fin), R. Coward (MD)
Managers: C. Vickers (Tech Serv Mgr), S. Vincent (Buyer), J. Lawson (Personnel)
Ultimate Holding Company: VPK PACKAGING GROUP NV (BELGIUM)
Immediate Holding Company: RIGID CONTAINERS LIMITED
Registration no: 00290827 **Date established:** 1934
Turnover: £50m - £75m **No.of Employees:** 101 - 250
Product Groups: 27, 28

Date of Accounts	Dec 11	Dec 10	Dec 09
Sales Turnover	78m	67m	59m
Pre Tax Profit/Loss	3m	-2m	3m
Working Capital	1m	-2m	529
Fixed Assets	15m	15m	13m
Current Assets	27m	28m	21m
Current Liabilities	3m	3m	3m

Rotadyne Ready Rollers
Saxon House Henson Way, Telford Way Industrial Estate, Kettering, NN16 8PX
Tel: 01536-519300 **Fax:** 01536-411091
E-mail: kettering@rotadyne.co.uk
Website: http://www.rotadyne.co.uk
Managers: J. Walshe (Mgr)
Ultimate Holding Company: WALLS AND FLOORS LIMITED
Immediate Holding Company: WALLS AND FLOORS (KETTERING) LIMITED
Registration no: 02739202 **Date established:** 1987 **Turnover:** £2m - £5m
No.of Employees: 21 - 50 **Product Groups:** 29, 44

Date of Accounts	Mar 11	Mar 10	Mar 09
Sales Turnover	15m	12m	11m
Pre Tax Profit/Loss	903	335	540
Working Capital	6m	5m	5m
Fixed Assets	337	309	329
Current Assets	8m	7m	6m
Current Liabilities	649	528	490

Rothenberger UK Ltd
2 Kingsthorne Park Henson Way, Telford Way Industrial Estate, Kettering, NN16 8PX
Tel: 01536-310300 **Fax:** 01536-310600
E-mail: sales@rothenberger.co.uk
Website: http://www.rothenberger.com
Directors: J. Potter (MD), M. Phillips (Comm)
Managers: K. Clarke (Nat Sales Mgr), L. Wood (Mktg Serv Mgr)
Ultimate Holding Company: ROTHENBERGER AG (GERMANY)
Immediate Holding Company: ROTHENBERGER (U.K.) LIMITED
Registration no: 01023214 **Date established:** 1971
Turnover: £10m - £20m **No.of Employees:** 21 - 50 **Product Groups:** 46

Date of Accounts	Dec 11	Dec 10	Dec 09
Sales Turnover	16m	14m	13m
Pre Tax Profit/Loss	2m	1m	1m
Working Capital	3m	3m	2m
Fixed Assets	44	31	6
Current Assets	6m	5m	4m
Current Liabilities	2m	2m	1m

SATRA Technology Centre
Satra House Rockingham Road, Kettering, NN16 9JH
Tel: 01536-410000 **Fax:** 01536-410626
E-mail: equipsales@satra.co.uk
Website: http://www.satra.co.uk
Bank(s): National Westminster Bank Plc
Directors: P. Harris (Dir), R. Whittaker (Grp Chief Exec), R. Morgan (Co Sec), R. Turner (Grp Chief Exec)
Managers: J. Locke (Mktg Serv Mgr), K. Rason (I.T. Exec), M. Lucas (Personnel), S. Andrew (Purch Mgr)
Immediate Holding Company: Satra
Registration no: 03856296 **VAT No.:** GB 738 0227 41
Date established: 1999 **Turnover:** £5m - £10m
No.of Employees: 101 - 250 **Product Groups:** 38, 85

Date of Accounts	Dec 07	Dec 06	Dec 05
Sales Turnover	9101	8106	6823
Pre Tax Profit/Loss	227	-65	51
Working Capital	493	614	515
Fixed Assets	8090	6618	5771
Current Assets	3727	3669	3678
Current Liabilities	3234	3055	3162
Total Share Capital	5000	2000	2000
ROCE% (Return on Capital Employed)	2.6	-0.9	0.8
ROT% (Return on Turnover)	2.5	-0.8	0.7

Security Matters
1 Wellingborough Road Broughton, Kettering, NN14 1PD
Tel: 01536-790999 **Fax:** 01536-790710
Website: http://www.security-matters.co.uk
Directors: J. Hawkins (Prop)
No.of Employees: 11 - 20 **Product Groups:** 36, 39, 66

Sharnold Ltd
67 Spencer Street Burton Latimer, Kettering, NN15 5SQ
Tel: 01536-723524 **Fax:** 01536-420656
E-mail: sharnoldltd@btconnect.com
Website: http://www.sharnoldltd.co.uk
Directors: M. Chapman (Dir)
Immediate Holding Company: SHARNOLD LIMITED
Registration no: 00971095 **Date established:** 1970
Turnover: Up to £250,000 **No.of Employees:** 1 - 10 **Product Groups:** 46

Date of Accounts	Mar 12	Mar 11	Mar 10
Working Capital	-30	-32	-31
Fixed Assets	53	54	52
Current Assets	38	38	38

Sonic Security Services Ltd
Unit 3-5 Grange Road Workshops Grange Road, Geddington, Kettering, NN14 1AL
Tel: 01536-461200 **Fax:** 01536-461201
E-mail: delia@sonicsecurity.co.uk
Website: http://www.sonicsecurity.co.uk
Directors: D. Payne (Co Sec)
Immediate Holding Company: SONIC SECURITY SERVICES LIMITED
Registration no: 02779190 **Date established:** 1993
No.of Employees: 1 - 10 **Product Groups:** 26, 35, 36, 37, 38, 39, 40, 44, 48, 52, 54, 66, 67, 68, 80, 81, 83, 84

Date of Accounts	Dec 11	Dec 10	Dec 09
Working Capital	36	7	-29
Fixed Assets	25	33	41
Current Assets	153	186	214

Stanair Industrial Door Services Ltd
Unit 2 Henson Way Telford Way Industrial Estate, Kettering, NN16 8PX
Tel: 01536-482187 **Fax:** 01536-411799
E-mail: info@stanair.co.uk
Website: http://www.stanair.co.uk
Directors: M. Markham (MD), S. Markham (Fin)
Managers: M. Wall (Mktg Serv Mgr), P. Gregory
Immediate Holding Company: STANAIR INDUSTRIAL DOOR SERVICES LIMITED
Registration no: 01180826 **Date established:** 1974 **Turnover:** £1m - £2m
No.of Employees: 21 - 50 **Product Groups:** 35, 36

Date of Accounts	Aug 11	Aug 10	Aug 09
Working Capital	460	448	409
Fixed Assets	905	919	965
Current Assets	1m	1m	982

Standard Engineering Ltd
10 Garrard Way Telford Way Industrial Estate, Kettering, NN16 8TD
Tel: 01536-517070 **Fax:** 01536-410755
Website: http://www.standardgroup.co.uk
Directors: K. Malyon (Sales), K. Malyon (MD), I. Holiday (Fin), I. Holliday (Fin)
Managers: N. Stewart (Ops Mgr)
Ultimate Holding Company: STANDARD GROUP LIMITED
Immediate Holding Company: STANDARD ENGINEERING LIMITED
Registration no: 03731414 **Date established:** 1999
No.of Employees: 11 - 20 **Product Groups:** 43

Date of Accounts	Jul 11	Jul 10	Jul 09
Working Capital	464	329	189
Fixed Assets	55	68	71
Current Assets	709	755	582

Star Automation Uk Ltd
1A Vernon Court Henson Way, Telford Ind Est, Kettering, NN16 8PX
Tel: 01536-521884 **Fax:** 01536-512784
E-mail: sales@amtechuk.com
Website: http://star-europe.com
Managers: K. Dunham (Eng)
Date established: 1991 **No.of Employees:** 1 - 10 **Product Groups:** 42

Date of Accounts	Dec 07	Dec 06	Dec 05
Sales Turnover	508	N/A	N/A
Pre Tax Profit/Loss	-4	N/A	N/A
Working Capital	-147	-153	-52
Fixed Assets	20	37	35
Current Assets	489	272	580
Current Liabilities	636	425	632
Total Share Capital	200	200	200
ROCE% (Return on Capital Employed)	3.1		
ROT% (Return on Turnover)	-0.8		

Stellar Technik Ltd
1-3 Sterling Court Loddington, Kettering, NN14 1RZ
Tel: 01536-483467 **Fax:** 01536-483434
Directors: R. Scarr (Dir), J. Scarr (Fin)
Immediate Holding Company: STELLAR TECHNIK LIMITED
Registration no: 02957962 **Date established:** 1994
No.of Employees: 1 - 10 **Product Groups:** 46

Date of Accounts	Feb 11
Working Capital	-24
Fixed Assets	27
Current Assets	30

Sure-Can Ltd
Unit 6 Adam Business Centre Henson Way, Telford Way Industrial Estate, Kettering, NN16 8PX
Tel: 01536-411882 **Fax:** 01536-518086
E-mail: sales@sure-can.co.uk
Website: http://www.sure-can.co.uk
Directors: S. Lloyd (MD)
Immediate Holding Company: SURE-CAN LIMITED
Registration no: 04568323 **Date established:** 2002
No.of Employees: 11 - 20 **Product Groups:** 32, 34, 35, 36, 37, 40, 46

Date of Accounts	Mar 12	Mar 11	Mar 10
Working Capital	1m	1m	938
Fixed Assets	66	59	58
Current Assets	1m	1m	1m

E A Tailby Ltd
Tailby House Bath Road, Kettering, NN16 8NL
Tel: 01536-512639 **Fax:** 01536-414816
E-mail: info@tailby.com
Website: http://www.tailby.com
Bank(s): HSBC Bank plc
Directors: S. Tailby (MD)
Managers: P. Tailby (Comptroller)
Immediate Holding Company: E.A.TAILBY LIMITED
Registration no: 00526798 **VAT No.:** GB 120 1784 10
Date established: 1953 **Turnover:** £2m - £5m **No.of Employees:** 11 - 20
Product Groups: 22

see next page

E A Tailby Ltd - Cont'd

Date of Accounts	Mar 12	Mar 11	Mar 10
Working Capital	-39	-21	-3
Fixed Assets	249	278	286
Current Assets	2	14	23

Timsons Ltd

Perfecta Works Bath Road, Kettering, NN16 8NQ
Tel: 01536-411611 **Fax:** 01536-411666
E-mail: jeff.ward@timsons.com
Website: http://www.timsons.com
Bank(s): National Westminster
Directors: J. Walker (Sales & Mktg), J. Ward (MD), J. Burn (Fin)
Managers: R. Brown (Tech Serv Mgr), G. Piazza (Purch Mgr)
Ultimate Holding Company: E.A.T. (HOLDINGS) LIMITED
Immediate Holding Company: TIMSONS LIMITED
Registration no: 00514948 **VAT No.:** GB 120 2591 16
Date established: 1953 **Turnover:** £10m - £20m
No.of Employees: 101 - 250 **Product Groups:** 44

Date of Accounts	Mar 11	Mar 10	Mar 09
Sales Turnover	19m	5m	18m
Pre Tax Profit/Loss	756	-2m	346
Working Capital	3m	2m	3m
Fixed Assets	1m	1m	1m
Current Assets	7m	6m	8m
Current Liabilities	270	2m	1m

Topcoat Sprayers Finishers

Pytchley Lodge Industrial Estate Pytchley Lodge Road, Kettering, NN15 6JQ
Tel: 01536-312550 **Fax:** 01536-414305
E-mail: terry@topnotchjoinery.co.uk
Directors: T. Nolan (Ptnr)
Date established: 1998 **No.of Employees:** 1 - 10 **Product Groups:** 46, 48

Tripal International ltd

4 Orion Park Orion Way, Kettering, NN15 6PE
Tel: 0870-7706600 **Fax:** 0870-7706670
E-mail: enquiries@tripal.com
Website: http://www.tripal.com
Directors: M. Turner (Dir), S. Poole (Co Sec)
Immediate Holding Company: Tripal International ltd
Registration no: 05165152 **Date established:** 2004
Turnover: £10m - £20m **No.of Employees:** 1 - 10 **Product Groups:** 22

Date of Accounts	Mar 08	Mar 07	Mar 06
Working Capital	1035	963	1116
Fixed Assets	915	730	839
Current Assets	2541	1970	1807
Current Liabilities	1506	1006	690

Trumans Business Consulting

5 Rodewell House Well Lane, Kettering, NN14 6DQ
Tel: 07799-766821
E-mail: info@trumans-consulting.co.uk
Website: http://www.trumans-consulting.co.uk
Directors: S. Mitchell (Ptnr), S. Humphreys (Ptnr)
Registration no: 07199068 **Date established:** 2009 **Turnover:**
No.of Employees: Unknown **Product Groups:** 80

Versalift Distributors UK Ltd

1 Altendiez Way Burton Latimer, Kettering, NN15 5YT
Tel: 01536-721010 **Fax:** 01536-721111
E-mail: admin@versalift.co.uk
Website: http://www.versalift.co.uk
Directors: K. Swinfield (Sales & Mktg), S. Couling (MD)
Managers: C. Mahon (Chief Acct)
Ultimate Holding Company: O'FLAHERTY HOLDINGS LTD (EIRE)
Immediate Holding Company: VERSALIFT DISTRIBUTORS (U.K.) LIMITED
Registration no: 02888311 **Date established:** 1994
Turnover: £10m - £20m **No.of Employees:** 51 - 100 **Product Groups:** 39, 45, 67, 86

Date of Accounts	Dec 11	Dec 10	Dec 09
Sales Turnover	10m	10m	13m
Pre Tax Profit/Loss	330	-353	339
Working Capital	-2m	-2m	-2m
Fixed Assets	4m	4m	4m
Current Assets	8m	8m	6m
Current Liabilities	2m	2m	856

Volvo Trucks

Pytchley Lodge Road Industrial Estate Pytchley Lodge Road, Kettering, NN15 6JJ
Tel: 01536-516311 **Fax:** 01536-412386
E-mail: lisa.fisher@volvosouth.co.uk
Website: http://www.volvotrucks.co.uk
Managers: L. Fisher
Registration no: 00215909 **VAT No.:** GB 293 6582 19
Turnover: £20m - £50m **No.of Employees:** 21 - 50 **Product Groups:** 39

Vordale Ltd

Irthlingborough Road Little Addington, Kettering, NN14 4AS
Tel: 01933-652330 **Fax:** 01933-651592
Directors: M. Mullan (MD)
Registration no: 01628219 **Date established:** 1987
No.of Employees: 11 - 20 **Product Groups:** 43

Warren Measurement Systems

15 Berwick Way, Kettering, NN15 5XF
Tel: 01536-310722 **Fax:** 01536-310722
E-mail: heather@warrenmeasurement.co.uk
Website: http://www.warrenmeasurement.co.uk
Directors: H. Elmore (Prop)
Immediate Holding Company: WARREN MEASUREMENT SYSTEMS LTD
Registration no: 07170390 **Date established:** 2010
Turnover: Up to £250,000 **No.of Employees:** 1 - 10 **Product Groups:** 46

Date of Accounts	Feb 12	Feb 11
Working Capital	-3	N/A
Fixed Assets	1	1
Current Assets	18	19

Websight Solutions

254 Kingsley Avenue, Kettering, NN16 9EZ
Tel: 07766-207400 **Fax:** 0870-1224871
E-mail: sales@websight-solutions.com
Website: http://www.websight-solutions.com
Directors: J. Webb (Prop)
Date established: 1999 **No.of Employees:** 1 - 10 **Product Groups:** 44, 79

Weetabix Ltd (Head Office)

PO Box 5, Kettering, NN15 5JR
Tel: 01536-722181 **Fax:** 01536-726148
E-mail: richard.martin@weetabix.co.uk
Website: http://www.weetabix.co.uk
Bank(s): Barclays, Kettering
Directors: D. Revell (Sales), J. Evoy (Pers), R. Martin (Dir), L. Booth (Co Sec)
Ultimate Holding Company: LATIMER CAYMAN I LIMITED (CAYMAN ISLANDS)
Immediate Holding Company: WEETABIX LIMITED
Registration no: 00267687 **VAT No.:** GB 119 3924 60
Date established: 1932 **Turnover:** £250m - £500m
No.of Employees: 1001 - 1500 **Product Groups:** 20

Date of Accounts	Dec 11	Dec 08	Dec 09
Sales Turnover	335m	314m	322m
Pre Tax Profit/Loss	86m	77m	97m
Working Capital	631m	328m	421m
Fixed Assets	116m	137m	139m
Current Assets	686m	401m	487m
Current Liabilities	15m	16m	16m

Werma UK Ltd

First West Business Centre Linnell Way, Telford Way Industrial Estate, Kettering, NN16 8PS
Tel: 01536-522853 **Fax:** 01536-514810
E-mail: uksales@werma.co.uk
Website: http://www.werma.co.uk
Managers: P. Osborn (Sales Prom Mgr)
Immediate Holding Company: WERMA (U.K.) LIMITED
Registration no: 06117998 **Date established:** 2007
No.of Employees: 1 - 10 **Product Groups:** 40, 67

Date of Accounts	Dec 11	Dec 10	Dec 09
Working Capital	-305	-344	-247
Fixed Assets	21	35	46
Current Assets	659	522	359

Wicksteed Leisure Ltd

Digby Street, Kettering, NN16 8YJ
Tel: 01536-517028 **Fax:** 01536-410633
E-mail: sales@wicksteed.co.uk
Website: http://www.wicksteed.co.uk
Bank(s): Midland, West Bromwich
Directors: S. Rockingham (Mkt Research), S. Weatherell (Sales)
Managers: L. Hibbins (Buyer), R. Davies (Tech Serv Mgr), C. Kwah
Ultimate Holding Company: JARDENTOME LIMITED
Immediate Holding Company: WICKSTEED LEISURE LIMITED
Registration no: 00603152 **VAT No.:** GB 119 1066 90
Date established: 1958 **Turnover:** £20m - £50m
No.of Employees: 101 - 250 **Product Groups:** 36, 49

Date of Accounts	Dec 11	Dec 10	Dec 09
Sales Turnover	25m	27m	22m
Pre Tax Profit/Loss	605	3m	77
Working Capital	10m	10m	8m
Fixed Assets	3m	3m	4m
Current Assets	13m	13m	13m
Current Liabilities	741	2m	530

Winkhaus UK Ltd

2950 Kettering Parkway Kettering Ventu Kettering Venture Park, Kettering, NN15 6XZ
Tel: 01536-316016 **Fax:** 01536-416516
E-mail: sales@winkhaus.co.uk
Website: http://www.winkhaus.co.uk
Managers: A. Shelford
Ultimate Holding Company: AUG WINKHAUS GMBH & CO KG (GERMANY)
Immediate Holding Company: WINKHAUS (U.K.) LIMITED
Registration no: 02685723 **Date established:** 1992
Turnover: £10m - £20m **No.of Employees:** 21 - 50 **Product Groups:** 26, 35

Date of Accounts	Dec 11	Dec 10	Dec 09
Sales Turnover	12m	11m	11m
Pre Tax Profit/Loss	604	156	93
Working Capital	2m	2m	2m
Fixed Assets	283	369	477
Current Assets	5m	4m	3m
Current Liabilities	1m	1m	746

Northampton

3D Sports (a division of Kookaburra Reader Ltd)

3 Brakey Road Weldon North Industrial Estate, Corby, Northampton, NN17 5LU
Tel: 0845-6760099 **Fax:** 01536-209 211
E-mail: info@3dsports.co.uk
Website: http://www.3dsports.co.uk
Managers: B. Attwood (Mgr), R. Attwood (Chief Mgr)
Ultimate Holding Company: Victa Ltd
Immediate Holding Company: Alfred Reader & Co Ltd
Registration no: 01460168 **VAT No.:** GB 326 3587 47
Date established: 1985 **Turnover:** £1m - £2m **No.of Employees:** 1 - 10
Product Groups: 49

Date of Accounts	Jun 08	Jun 07	Jun 06
Working Capital	-14	-14	-14
Current Liabilities	14	14	14
Total Share Capital	10	10	10

A B G Rubber & Plastics Ltd

10 Skelty Close Brackmills Industrial Estate, Northampton, NN4 7PL
Tel: 01604-700880 **Fax:** 01604-766113
E-mail: sales@abgrp.co.uk
Website: http://www.abgrp.co.uk
Bank(s): Lloyds TSB Bank plc
Managers: K. Barford (Sales Prom Mgr)
Ultimate Holding Company: OADBY PLASTICS LIMITED
Immediate Holding Company: A.B.G. RUBBER & PLASTICS LIMITED
Registration no: 01202761 **VAT No.:** GB 195 7391 17
Date established: 1975 **Turnover:** £2m - £5m **No.of Employees:** 11 - 20
Product Groups: 29, 30, 31, 41, 48

Date of Accounts	Dec 11	Dec 10	Dec 09
Working Capital	766	679	569
Fixed Assets	267	169	183
Current Assets	1m	885	771

A H Allen Steel Services

Liliput Road Brackmills Industrial Estate, Northampton, NN4 7DT
Tel: 01604-762211 **Fax:** 01604-765525
E-mail: sales@aha-steel.co.uk
Website: http://www.aha-steel.co.uk
Bank(s): HSBC Bank plc
Directors: M. Mcbean (MD)
Ultimate Holding Company: BARRETT STEEL LIMITED
Immediate Holding Company: A.H.ALLEN STEEL SERVICES LIMITED
Registration no: 02761852 **VAT No.:** GB 623 8873 15
Date established: 1992 **Turnover:** £5m - £10m **No.of Employees:** 21 - 50
Product Groups: 66

Date of Accounts	Sep 08
Working Capital	1
Current Assets	1

A S L

Spring Hill Farm Harborough Road, Pitsford, Northampton, NN6 9AA
Tel: 01604-883300 **Fax:** 01604-883881
E-mail: sales@aslholdings.co.uk
Website: http://www.aslh.co.uk
Directors: B. Berry (MD)
Immediate Holding Company: C & F SERVICES LIMITED
Registration no: 04402008 **Date established:** 1996 **Turnover:** £2m - £5m
No.of Employees: 11 - 20 **Product Groups:** 44

Date of Accounts	Dec 07	Dec 06	Dec 05
Working Capital	-446	-254	-2
Fixed Assets	604	348	117
Current Assets	1068	986	991
Current Liabilities	1514	1240	993

A V O UK Ltd

Caswell Road Brackmills Industrial Estate, Northampton, NN4 7PW
Tel: 01604-708101 **Fax:** 01604-761030
E-mail: sales@avouk.com
Website: http://www.avouk.com
Directors: N. Killerby (MD)
Immediate Holding Company: AVO UK LIMITED
Registration no: 04182161 **Date established:** 2001 **Turnover:** £5m - £10m
No.of Employees: 1 - 10 **Product Groups:** 29, 35, 39, 48

Date of Accounts	Sep 11	Sep 10	Sep 09
Working Capital	658	647	636
Fixed Assets	28	35	29
Current Assets	793	820	805

Able Direct Centre Ltd

5 Mallard Close Earls Barton, Northampton, NN6 0LS
Tel: 01604-810781 **Fax:** 08704-442766
E-mail: sales@able-labels.co.uk
Website: http://www.able-labels.co.uk
Directors: M. Stather Lodge (Dir)
Ultimate Holding Company: OCM WEALTH MANAGEMENT LIMITED
Immediate Holding Company: ABLE-DIRECT CENTRE LIMITED
Registration no: 01104053 **Date established:** 1973 **Turnover:** £2m - £5m
No.of Employees: 21 - 50 **Product Groups:** 81

Date of Accounts	Apr 11	Apr 10	Apr 09
Working Capital	-432	-196	-17
Fixed Assets	589	488	145
Current Assets	196	125	209

Acam Instrumentation Ltd

23 Thomas Street, Northampton, NN1 3EN
Tel: 01604-628700 **Fax:** 01604-628700
E-mail: info@acamltd.co.uk
Website: http://www.acamltd.co.uk
Directors: J. Cottam (MD)
Immediate Holding Company: ACAM INSTRUMENTATION LIMITED
Registration no: 01543383 **VAT No.:** GB 314 9529 50
Date established: 1981 **Turnover:** Up to £250,000
No.of Employees: 1 - 10 **Product Groups:** 37, 38

Date of Accounts	Mar 11	Mar 10	Mar 09
Sales Turnover	217	239	260
Working Capital	-207	-178	-139
Fixed Assets	211	211	216
Current Assets	66	27	91

Access Irrigation Ltd

17 Yelvertoft Road Crick, Northampton, NN6 7XS
Tel: 01788-823811 **Fax:** 01788-824256
E-mail: sales@access-irrigation.co.uk
Website: http://www.access-irrigation.co.uk
Bank(s): National Westminster Bank Plc
Directors: M. Clarke (Fin), M. Pearce (MD)
Immediate Holding Company: ACCESS IRRIGATION LIMITED
Registration no: 01291598 **VAT No.:** GB 273 9355 29
Date established: 1976 **Turnover:** £1m - £2m **No.of Employees:** 11 - 20
Product Groups: 41, 51

Date of Accounts	Dec 11	Dec 10	Dec 09
Working Capital	168	62	63
Fixed Assets	43	146	138
Current Assets	247	164	156

Accuride International Ltd

Liliput Road Brackmills Industrial Estate, Northampton, NN4 7AS
Tel: 01604-761111 **Fax:** 01604-767190
E-mail: pbayles@accuride.com
Website: http://www.accuride-europe.com
Directors: P. Bayles (Eng Serv)
Managers: P. Weston (Fin Mgr), S. Witkowski (Mktg Serv Mgr), D. Evans, J. Armstrong
Ultimate Holding Company: ACCURIDE INTERNATIONAL INC (USA)
Immediate Holding Company: ACCURIDE INTERNATIONAL LIMITED
Registration no: 00352801 **VAT No.:** GB 290 7578 23
Date established: 1939 **Turnover:** £10m - £20m
No.of Employees: 21 - 50 **Product Groups:** 34, 35, 36, 39, 46, 48

Date of Accounts	Aug 11	Aug 10	Aug 09
Sales Turnover	11m	10m	10m
Pre Tax Profit/Loss	3m	2m	412
Working Capital	4m	3m	4m
Fixed Assets	4m	4m	5m
Current Assets	6m	5m	6m
Current Liabilities	631	537	488

Acme Neon

Fitzroy Terrace Grafton Street, Northampton, NN1 2NU
Tel: 01604-631068 **Fax:** 01604-631068
E-mail: colin@acmeneon.co.uk
Website: http://www.acmeneon.co.uk

Directors: C. Felce (Ptnr)
Date established: 1978 **Turnover:** Up to £250,000
No.of Employees: 1 - 10 **Product Groups:** 37, 49, 52, 65, 67, 84

Affero Ltd
62 Water Lane Wootton, Northampton, NN4 6HG
Tel: 01604-709106 **Fax:** 01604-705317
E-mail: info@affero.co.uk
Website: http://www.affero.co.uk
Directors: M. Kightley (Co Sec)
Immediate Holding Company: AFFERO LTD
Registration no: 04688855 **Date established:** 2003
No.of Employees: 1 - 10 **Product Groups:** 35, 39, 45

Date of Accounts	Mar 11	Mar 10	Mar 09
Working Capital	53	56	33
Fixed Assets	4	8	12
Current Assets	110	119	112

All Food Hygiene
91 Battalion Drive Wootton, Northampton, NN4 6RX
Tel: 07850-650955 **Fax:** 01604-677052
E-mail: info@foodhygiene.org
Website: http://www.foodhygiene.org
Directors: S. Vaughan (Prop)
Turnover: Up to £250,000 **No.of Employees:** 1 - 10 **Product Groups:** 86

Allen Lyman Office Equipment Ltd
213 Wellingborough Road, Northampton, NN1 4EF
Tel: 01604-639586 **Fax:** 01604-231249
E-mail: allenlyman@yahoo.co.uk
Website: http://www.allenlyman.com
Directors: G. Goodwin (MD)
Immediate Holding Company: ALLEN LYMAN OFFICE EQUIPMENT LIMITED
Registration no: 01284627 **VAT No.:** GB 294 0494 40
Date established: 1976 **Turnover:** £1m - £2m **No.of Employees:** 1 - 10
Product Groups: 26, 61

Date of Accounts	Mar 11	Mar 10	Mar 09
Working Capital	257	260	611
Fixed Assets	18	35	52
Current Assets	526	616	794

Alltyre Marketing Ltd
9-11 White House Industrial Estate Main Road, Earls Barton, Northampton, NN6 0HJ
Tel: 01604-811911 **Fax:** 01604-812951
E-mail: alltyre@alltyre.freeserve.co.uk
Website: http://www.alltyre.freeserve.co.uk
Directors: A. Sharpe (Dir)
Immediate Holding Company: ALLTYRE MARKETING LIMITED
Registration no: 01148023 **Date established:** 1973
No.of Employees: 1 - 10 **Product Groups:** 29

Date of Accounts	Jan 11	Jan 10	Jan 09
Working Capital	49	87	7
Fixed Assets	511	513	571
Current Assets	70	102	137

Amaacon Centre for Management & Marketing Education
Victory House 400 Pavilion Drive, Northampton Business Park, Northampton, NN4 7PA
Tel: 0844-800 7307 **Fax:** 01604-410 838
E-mail: enquiries@amaaconedu.com
Website: http://www.managementandmarketingcollege.com
Directors: A. Ashiru (Dir)
Registration no: 06411999 **Date established:** 2007
No.of Employees: 11 - 20 **Product Groups:** 86

Ambivent Ltd
Unit 1 Moulton Court Anglia Way, Moulton Park Industrial Estate, Northampton, NN3 6JA
Tel: 01604-645788 **Fax:** 01604-491178
E-mail: sales@ambivent.co.uk
Website: http://www.ambivent.co.uk
Directors: S. Dudson (MD), N. Mackman (Contracts), G. Nightingale (Design), S. Wootton (Fin)
Immediate Holding Company: AMBIVENT LIMITED
Registration no: 05133667 **Date established:** 2004
No.of Employees: 21 - 50 **Product Groups:** 40, 45, 48, 84

Date of Accounts	Dec 11	Dec 10	Dec 09
Working Capital	353	443	551
Fixed Assets	111	115	147
Current Assets	1m	2m	2m

AMK Drives & Controls Ltd
Moulton Park Business Centre Redhouse Road, Moulton Park Industrial Estate, Northampton, NN3 6AQ
Tel: 01604-497806 **Fax:** 01604-497809
E-mail: patrick.amk@talk21.com
Website: http://www.talk21.com
Directors: K. Muller Bauer (Fin)
Immediate Holding Company: HEALTH CARE RESPONSE LTD
Registration no: 02739814 **Date established:** 2009
Turnover: Up to £250,000 **No.of Employees:** 1 - 10 **Product Groups:** 37, 38

Date of Accounts	Dec 07	Dec 06	Dec 05
Working Capital	11	11	11
Current Assets	15	15	15
Current Liabilities	4	4	4
Total Share Capital	10	10	10

Anglia Television Ltd
77b Abington Street, Northampton, NN1 2BH
Tel: 01604-624343 **Fax:** 01604-629856
E-mail: northants@itv.com
Website: http://www.angliatv.co.uk
Directors: G. Creelman (MD)
Managers: K. Heidel ()
Ultimate Holding Company: ITV PLC
Immediate Holding Company: ANGLIA TELEVISION LIMITED
Registration no: 05959958 **Date established:** 2006
No.of Employees: 1 - 10 **Product Groups:** 89

Anitox
Anitox House 80 Main Road, Earls Barton, Northampton, NN6 0HJ
Tel: 01604-811228 **Fax:** 01604-811013
E-mail: james.burk@anitox.co.uk
Website: http://www.anitox.com
Directors: J. Birk (Co Sec), J. Burk (Co Sec)
Managers: R. York (Tech Serv Mgr), M. Walker (Mktg Serv Mgr)
Ultimate Holding Company: RIVERSIDE MICRO CAO FUND 1 LP (USA)
Immediate Holding Company: ANITOX LIMITED
Registration no: 02544185 **Date established:** 1990 **Turnover:** £5m - £10m
No.of Employees: 11 - 20 **Product Groups:** 07

Date of Accounts	Dec 11	Dec 10	Dec 09
Sales Turnover	N/A	7m	5m
Pre Tax Profit/Loss	N/A	357	60
Working Capital	910	922	864
Fixed Assets	845	692	519
Current Assets	2m	2m	2m
Current Liabilities	N/A	317	204

Applied Micro Sciences Ltd (Software Department)
102 Windingbrook Lane, Northampton, NN4 0XN
Tel: 01604-702407
E-mail: inbox@amssoft.co.uk
Website: http://www.amssoft.co.uk
Directors: C. Leong (Dir)
Immediate Holding Company: APPLIED MICRO SCIENCES LIMITED
Registration no: 01994895 **Date established:** 1986
Turnover: Up to £250,000 **No.of Employees:** 1 - 10 **Product Groups:** 44

Date of Accounts	Sep 11	Sep 10	Sep 09
Working Capital	-2	-1	7
Fixed Assets	3	2	3
Current Assets	9	20	15

Archive Attic Ltd
The Farm Office Grooms Lane, Creaton, Northampton, NN6 8NN
Tel: 01604-505050
E-mail: george@archiveattic.co.uk
Website: http://www.archiveattic.co.uk
Directors: G. Matts (MD), J. Matts (Ch)
Managers: G. Matts (Sales Prom Mgr)
Immediate Holding Company: LOC-BOX SELF STORAGE LIMITED
Registration no: 05001136 **Date established:** 2003
No.of Employees: 1 - 10 **Product Groups:** 26, 77, 80

Date of Accounts	Jan 11	Jan 10	Jan 09
Working Capital	-13	-5	-24
Fixed Assets	65	39	47
Current Assets	2	4	1

Armstrong Optical Ltd
31 Kacston House North Hampton Science Park, Moulton Park Industrial Estate, Northampton, NN3 6LG
Tel: 01604-654220 **Fax:** 01933-622226
E-mail: info@armstrongoptical.co.uk
Website: http://www.armstrongoptical.co.uk
Directors: I. Routledge (MD)
Immediate Holding Company: ARMSTRONG OPTICAL LIMITED
Registration no: 03406287 **VAT No.:** GB 695 9488 49
Date established: 1997 **Turnover:** Up to £250,000
No.of Employees: 1 - 10 **Product Groups:** 30, 38, 85

Date of Accounts	Sep 11	Sep 10	Sep 09
Working Capital	-33	19	23
Current Assets	25	104	129

Arnold Engineering Plastics Ltd
2 Regal Close Kings Park Road, Moulton Park Industrial Estate, Northampton, NN3 6LL
Tel: 01604-499651 **Fax:** 01604-790057
E-mail: info@arnold-aep.co.uk
Website: http://www.arnoldplastics.com
Bank(s): Lloyds TSB
Directors: K. Hackett (Sales & Mktg), P. Larkins (Dir), P. Larkin (MD), C. Howard (Fin)
Immediate Holding Company: ARNOLD ENGINEERING PLASTICS LIMITED
Registration no: 01082972 **VAT No.:** 408 6416 53 **Date established:** 1972
Turnover: £1m - £2m **No.of Employees:** 51 - 100 **Product Groups:** 26, 30, 40, 81

Date of Accounts	Mar 12	Mar 11	Mar 10
Working Capital	234	173	118
Fixed Assets	813	866	674
Current Assets	699	774	609

Arrowquint Ltd
Building 5 Hendrickson Site Wellingborough Road, Sywell, Northampton, NN6 0BN
Tel: 08450-655455 **Fax:** 01604-493814
E-mail: sales@arrowquint.co.uk
Website: http://www.arrowquint.co.uk
Directors: K. Horne (MD)
Managers: T. McHale (Sales Prom Mgr), G. Dawson
Ultimate Holding Company: STONEVALE DEVELOPMENTS LIMITED
Immediate Holding Company: ARROWQUINT LIMITED
Registration no: 01878050 **VAT No.:** GB 412 7837 53
Date established: 1985 **Turnover:** £500,000 - £1m
No.of Employees: 1 - 10 **Product Groups:** 30, 34, 37, 38, 39, 42, 43, 44, 51, 67, 84

Date of Accounts	Jan 04	Jan 05	Jan 06
Sales Turnover	69m	70m	67m
Pre Tax Profit/Loss	2m	3m	-2m
Working Capital	-476	7m	6m
Fixed Assets	9m	3m	2m
Current Assets	17m	28m	25m
Current Liabilities	5m	5m	4m

Artillus Illuminating Solutions Ltd
Unit 5 Bellman Gate Holcot Lane, Sywell, Northampton, NN6 0BL
Tel: 01604-678410 **Fax:** 01604-671335
E-mail: j.elliott@artillus.com
Website: http://www.artillus.com
Directors: T. Jaeger (Dir)
Immediate Holding Company: ARTILLUS ILLUMINATING SOLUTIONS LIMITED
Registration no: 04318364 **Date established:** 2001 **Turnover:** £1m - £2m
No.of Employees: 1 - 10 **Product Groups:** 25, 30, 37, 40, 49, 67

Date of Accounts	Nov 11	Nov 10	Nov 09
Working Capital	80	-0	31
Fixed Assets	7	5	7
Current Assets	205	140	80

Ashton Court Group Ltd
Thorpwood Management Centre Blisworth Road, Courteenhall, Northampton, NN7 2QB
Tel: 01604-864781 **Fax:** 01604-864611
E-mail: info@ashtoncourt.com
Website: http://www.ashtoncourt.com
Directors: G. Wishart (MD)
Immediate Holding Company: ASHTON COURT GROUP LIMITED
Registration no: 02657259 **Date established:** 1991
Turnover: £250,000 - £500,000 **No.of Employees:** 11 - 20
Product Groups: 44

Date of Accounts	Sep 11	Sep 10	Sep 09
Working Capital	197	207	215
Current Assets	338	331	548

Atlantechs Ltd
Building 15 The Royal Ordenance Depot Bridge Street, Weedon, Northampton, NN7 4PS
Tel: 01327-342484 **Fax:** 01327-341454
E-mail: info@atlantechseating.com
Website: http://www.atlantechseating.com
Directors: S. Bratt (Fin)
Managers: G. Bratt (Sales Prom Mgr), N. Carter
Immediate Holding Company: ATLANTECHS LIMITED
Registration no: 02465470 **Date established:** 1990
No.of Employees: 21 - 50 **Product Groups:** 39, 68

Date of Accounts	Jan 11	Jan 10	Jan 09
Working Capital	-34	-42	-41
Fixed Assets	36	43	50
Current Assets	213	211	176

AVK UK Ltd
8 Rushmills, Northampton, NN4 7YB
Tel: 01604-601188
Website: http://www.aquagasavk.co.uk
Managers: B. Green
Ultimate Holding Company: ASX 14,145 APS (DENMARK)
Immediate Holding Company: AVK UK LIMITED
Registration no: 01838290 **Date established:** 1984
Turnover: £20m - £50m **No.of Employees:** 51 - 100 **Product Groups:** 36

Date of Accounts	Sep 11	Sep 10	Sep 09
Sales Turnover	26m	27m	29m
Pre Tax Profit/Loss	518	537	735
Working Capital	3m	3m	3m
Fixed Assets	546	575	462
Current Assets	9m	9m	10m
Current Liabilities	2m	2m	2m

Avon Cosmetics Ltd Head Office
Nunn Mills Road, Northampton, NN1 5PA
Tel: 01604-232425 **Fax:** 01604-232444
E-mail: carol.stronach@avon.com
Website: http://www.avon.uk.com
Bank(s): HSBC Bank plc
Directors: S. Gilkes (Tech Serv), A. Gill (Pers), N. Clark (Mkt Research), A. Judge (Fin), A. Watts (Mkt Research)
Managers: R. Pinnock
Ultimate Holding Company: AVON PRODUCTS INC (USA)
Immediate Holding Company: AVON COSMETICS LIMITED
Registration no: 00592235 **VAT No.:** GB 623 7733 36
Date established: 1957 **Turnover:** £250m - £500m
No.of Employees: 501 - 1000 **Product Groups:** 63

Date of Accounts	Dec 11	Dec 10	Dec 09
Sales Turnover	312m	329m	317m
Pre Tax Profit/Loss	25m	4m	-7m
Working Capital	9m	-5m	-4m
Fixed Assets	79m	81m	81m
Current Assets	100m	92m	110m
Current Liabilities	34m	26m	36m

Azimex Fabrications Ltd
Cartwright Road, Northampton, NN2 6HF
Tel: 01604-717712 **Fax:** 01604-791087
E-mail: john@azimex.wannadoo.co.uk
Website: http://www.azimex.co.uk
Directors: A. Macleod (Fin), J. Addison (MD)
Immediate Holding Company: AZIMEX FABRICATIONS LIMITED
Registration no: 01558719 **VAT No.:** GB 336 2641 65
Date established: 1981 **Turnover:** £250,000 - £500,000
No.of Employees: 1 - 10 **Product Groups:** 48

Date of Accounts	Apr 11	Apr 10	Apr 09
Working Capital	52	47	67
Fixed Assets	3	3	3
Current Assets	176	134	131

B D E Northampton Ltd
14 The Business Centre Ross Road, Weedon Road Industrial Estate, Northampton, NN5 5AX
Tel: 01604-750380 **Fax:** 01604-750377
E-mail: sales@bdeltd.co.uk
Website: http://www.bdeltd.co.uk
Directors: B. Russell (Co Sec)
Managers: L. Cosby (District Mgr)
Immediate Holding Company: B.D.E. (NORTHAMPTON) LIMITED
Registration no: 01414112 **Date established:** 1979
Turnover: Up to £250,000 **No.of Employees:** 1 - 10 **Product Groups:** 34

Date of Accounts	Dec 11	Dec 10	Dec 09
Working Capital	131	110	108
Fixed Assets	164	164	164
Current Assets	295	236	210

B P X Electro Mechanical Co. Ltd
Unit 25-26 Ross Road Business Centre Ross Road, Weedon Road Industrial Estate, Northampton, NN5 5AX
Tel: 01604-759906 **Fax:** 01604-759916
E-mail: agoadby@bpx.co.uk
Website: http://www.bpx.co.uk
Managers: A. Goadby (Sales Off Mgr)
Registration no: 00863458 **Turnover:** £500,000 - £1m
No.of Employees: 1 - 10 **Product Groups:** 37, 38, 44, 67, 84

B S S
Riverside Way Bedford Road, Northampton, NN1 5NX
Tel: 01604-251400 **Fax:** 01604-620588
E-mail: admin@bss-group.co.uk
Website: http://www.bssuk.co.uk
Bank(s): HSBC Bank plc

see next page

***B S S** - Cont'd*

Managers: M. Pennell (District Mgr)
Immediate Holding Company: BUSINESS SUPPORT SERVICES UK LTD
Registration no: 03106393 **VAT No.:** GB 316 0004 22
Turnover: £500,000 - £1m **No.of Employees:** 11 - 20
Product Groups: 66, 83

Barker Shoes

Station Road Earls Barton, Northampton, NN6 0NT
Tel: 01604-810387 **Fax:** 01604-812350
E-mail: akalsi@btinternet.com
Website: http://www.barker-shoes.co.uk
Bank(s): National Westminster Bank Plc
Directors: K. Sharma (Co Sec), A. Kalsi (Ch)
Ultimate Holding Company: NEWBURY HOLDINGS LTD (CYPRUS)
Immediate Holding Company: BARKER SHOES LIMITED
Registration no: 00133893 **VAT No.:** GB 119 3057 81
Date established: 2014 **Turnover:** £10m - £20m
No.of Employees: 101 - 250 **Product Groups:** 22

Date of Accounts	Mar 11	Mar 10	Mar 09
Sales Turnover	15m	13m	13m
Pre Tax Profit/Loss	251	242	207
Working Capital	2m	3m	3m
Fixed Assets	3m	4m	3m
Current Assets	9m	9m	13m
Current Liabilities	3m	3m	8m

Biffa Waste Services Ltd

Welford Landfill Site Welford Quarry Portly Ford, Welford, Northampton, NN6 6JF
Tel: 01858-575722 **Fax:** 01858-575836
E-mail: marketing@biffa.co.uk
Website: http://www.biffa.co.uk
Directors: M. Bettington (MD), M. Bettington (MD)
Managers: D. Wright (District Mgr)
Immediate Holding Company: BIFFA WASTE SERVICES LIMITED
Registration no: 00946107 **Date established:** 1969
No.of Employees: 21 - 50 **Product Groups:** 32, 54

Date of Accounts	Mar 08	Mar 09	Apr 10
Sales Turnover	555m	574m	492m
Pre Tax Profit/Loss	23m	50m	30m
Working Capital	229m	271m	293m
Fixed Assets	371m	360m	378m
Current Assets	409m	534m	609m
Current Liabilities	50m	100m	115m

Black & Decker Ltd

Caswell Road Brackmills Industrial Estate, Northampton, NN4 7PW
Tel: 01604-768777 **Fax:** 01604-769066
Website: http://www.blackanddecker.com
Managers: L. Scott (Chief Buyer), P. Downing (), G. Snelling (), N. Dabvenprt (Mgr)
Ultimate Holding Company: STANLEY BLACK & DECKER CORPORATION (USA)
Immediate Holding Company: BLACK & DECKER
Registration no: 00291547 **Date established:** 1934 **Turnover:** £5m - £10m
No.of Employees: 51 - 100 **Product Groups:** 36, 37

Date of Accounts	Dec 10	Dec 09	Dec 08
Sales Turnover	23m	79m	100m
Pre Tax Profit/Loss	-3m	-19m	-10m
Working Capital	61m	131m	152m
Fixed Assets	296m	297m	299m
Current Assets	121m	198m	269m
Current Liabilities	2m	9m	8m

Blacks Leisure Group plc

Mansard Close Westgate Industrial Estate, Northampton, NN5 5DL
Tel: 01604-441111 **Fax:** 01604-441164
E-mail: enquiries@blacks.co.uk
Website: http://www.blacks.co.uk
Directors: P. Hartley (Fin)
Immediate Holding Company: BLACKS LEISURE GROUP PLC
Registration no: 00582190 **VAT No.:** GB 466 3662 23
Date established: 1957 **No.of Employees:** 1501 & over
Product Groups: 24, 61, 65

Date of Accounts	Feb 09	Feb 10	Feb 11
Sales Turnover	268m	241m	202m
Pre Tax Profit/Loss	-14m	-44m	-5m
Working Capital	16m	-24m	-10m
Fixed Assets	71m	55m	54m
Current Assets	63m	47m	43m
Current Liabilities	23m	33m	20m

Blue Water Marketing Ltd

1 Ferro Fields Brixworth Industrial Estate Brixworth, Northampton, NN6 9UA
Tel: 01604-889020
E-mail: reception@bluewatermarketing.co.uk
Website: http://www.bluewatermarketing.co.uk
Directors: M. Soames (Dir)
Immediate Holding Company: BLUEWATER MARKETING LIMITED
Registration no: 04955135 **Date established:** 2003
Turnover: £500,000 - £1m **No.of Employees:** 11 - 20 **Product Groups:** 81

Date of Accounts	Nov 11	Nov 10	Nov 09
Working Capital	9	-10	-33
Fixed Assets	10	12	153
Current Assets	83	46	74

Bourbon Fabi UK Ltd

North Portway Close Round Spinney Industrial Estate, Northampton, NN3 8RE
Tel: 01604-493126 **Fax:** 01604-644547
E-mail: rob.gunn@bourbonfabi.co.uk
Website: http://www.bourbonfabi.co.uk
Directors: B. Cornet (Co Sec), C. Bourbon (MD)
Immediate Holding Company: BOURBON AUTOMOTIVE PLASTICS NORTHAMPTON LIMITED
Registration no: 03385357 **VAT No.:** GB 695 7458 68
Date established: 1997 **Turnover:** £5m - £10m
No.of Employees: 101 - 250 **Product Groups:** 29, 30, 39, 87

Date of Accounts	Sep 11	Sep 10	Sep 09
Sales Turnover	10m	9m	9m
Pre Tax Profit/Loss	1m	-1m	-915
Working Capital	1m	62	1m
Fixed Assets	2m	2m	2m
Current Assets	5m	3m	3m
Current Liabilities	2m	893	485

Boxes Prestige Ltd

PO Box 111, Northampton, NN6 0JE
Tel: 01604-811971 **Fax:** 01604-811978
E-mail: oneill@boxesprestige.co.uk
Website: http://www.boxesgroup.co.uk
Directors: C. O'neill (Dir), P. Burgess (Dir), P. Burgess (MD)
Ultimate Holding Company: CLONDALKIN GROUP HOLDINGS BV (NETHERLANDS)
Immediate Holding Company: CLONDALKIN PHARMA & HEALTHCARE (NORTHAMPTON) LTD.
Registration no: 03088793 **Date established:** 1995
Turnover: £10m - £20m **No.of Employees:** 101 - 250
Product Groups: 27, 30

Date of Accounts	Dec 10	Dec 09	Dec 08
Sales Turnover	14m	11m	13m
Pre Tax Profit/Loss	583	44	667
Working Capital	-2m	-2m	-2m
Fixed Assets	3m	3m	4m
Current Assets	4m	3m	3m
Current Liabilities	494	702	1m

Boyall Graphics & Print Ltd

44 Tenter Road Moulton Park Industrial Estate Moulton Park Industrial Estate, Northampton, NN3 6AX
Tel: 01604-647465 **Fax:** 01604-790231
E-mail: sales@boyallgraphics.co.uk
Website: http://www.boyallgraphics.co.uk
Directors: H. Boyall (Co Sec), B. Boyall (MD)
Immediate Holding Company: BOYALL GRAPHICS & PRINT LIMITED
Registration no: 02752692 **Date established:** 1992
No.of Employees: 11 - 20 **Product Groups:** 23, 28

Date of Accounts	Dec 11	Dec 10	Dec 09
Working Capital	165	162	236
Fixed Assets	340	395	479
Current Assets	355	327	433

Brackmills Fabrications

17 Osyth Close Brackmills Industrial Estate, Northampton, NN4 7DY
Tel: 01604-677013 **Fax:** 01604-675125
E-mail: info@brackmillsfabrication.co.uk
Website: http://www.brackmillsfabrication.co.uk
Directors: S. Austin (Fin)
Immediate Holding Company: LIFTING SYSTEMS LTD.
Registration no: 05067191 **Date established:** 1994
No.of Employees: 21 - 50 **Product Groups:** 35, 40, 51, 66, 84

Date of Accounts	Dec 11	Dec 10	Dec 09
Working Capital	-323	-317	-190
Fixed Assets	858	636	509
Current Assets	886	610	541

Brampton Heath Golf Centre

Sandy Lane Church Brampton, Northampton, NN6 8AX
Tel: 01604-843939 **Fax:** 01604-843885
E-mail: info@bhgc.co.uk
Website: http://www.bhgc.co.uk
Directors: W. Rice (Prop)
Turnover: Up to £250,000 **No.of Employees:** 11 - 20 **Product Groups:** 24, 26, 69, 80, 81

F Brinklow & Co. Ltd

121 Clare Street, Northampton, NN1 3JA
Tel: 01604-636845 **Fax:** 01604-636862
E-mail: richard@fbrinklow.co.uk
Directors: R. Campin (MD)
Immediate Holding Company: F.BRINKLOW & COMPANY LIMITED
Registration no: 00525021 **VAT No.:** GB 119 9347 42
Date established: 1953 **Turnover:** Up to £250,000
No.of Employees: 1 - 10 **Product Groups:** 48

Date of Accounts	Mar 11	Mar 10	Mar 09
Working Capital	156	122	175
Fixed Assets	11	14	18
Current Assets	217	165	236

The British Pepper & Spice Company Ltd

Rhosili Road Brackmills Industrial Estate, Northampton, NN4 7AN
Tel: 01604-766461 **Fax:** 01604-763156
E-mail: sales@britishpepper.co.uk
Website: http://www.britishpepper.co.uk
Bank(s): National Westminster Bank Plc
Directors: I. James (Grp Chief Exec), I. Kelland (Mkt Research), R. Howard (Co Sec), J. Hedley (Fin)
Ultimate Holding Company: SHS GROUP LIMITED
Immediate Holding Company: THE BRITISH PEPPER & SPICE COMPANY LIMITED
Registration no: 03510819 **Date established:** 1998
Turnover: £20m - £50m **No.of Employees:** 101 - 250 **Product Groups:** 20

Date of Accounts	Dec 10	Dec 11	Jan 09
Sales Turnover	31m	33m	N/A
Pre Tax Profit/Loss	3m	2m	2m
Working Capital	9m	9m	8m
Fixed Assets	4m	5m	15m
Current Assets	18m	21m	13m
Current Liabilities	2m	1m	786

Brixworth Engineering

Creaton Road Brixworth, Northampton, NN6 9BW
Tel: 01604-880338 **Fax:** 01604-880252
E-mail: sales@benco.co.uk
Website: http://www.benco.co.uk
Directors: S. Muir (Fin)
Immediate Holding Company: J.A.P. NORTHAMPTON LIMITED
Registration no: 02602316 **Date established:** 1991
Turnover: £500,000 - £1m **No.of Employees:** 11 - 20
Product Groups: 07, 33, 39, 46, 48, 72

Date of Accounts	May 11	May 10	May 02
Working Capital	-1	-1	-1

Buck & Hickman Ltd

Unit 2 Chartergate Moulton Park, Moulton Park Industrial Estate, Northampton, NN3 6QF
Tel: 01604-797400 **Fax:** 01604-797401
E-mail: northampton@buckandhickman.com
Website: http://www.buckandhickman.com
Managers: C. McCulloch (District Mgr)
Ultimate Holding Company: TRAVIS PERKINS PLC
Immediate Holding Company: BOSTON (2011) LIMITED
Registration no: 06028304 **Date established:** 2006
No.of Employees: 1 - 10 **Product Groups:** 24, 29, 33, 36, 37, 41, 46

Date of Accounts	Dec 10	Mar 10	Mar 09
Working Capital	6m	6m	6m
Current Assets	27m	27m	27m

Butchers Pet Care

Crick, Northampton, NN6 7TZ
Tel: 01788-823711 **Fax:** 01788-822960
E-mail: reception@butcherspetcare.com
Website: http://www.butcherspetcare.com
Directors: D. Evans (Sales & Mktg), F. Powell (Fin)
Managers: M. Burrows (I.T. Exec), S. Alexander (Mktg Serv Mgr), C. Mallett, A. Wall (Personnel)
Ultimate Holding Company: F.W. BAKER LIMITED
Immediate Holding Company: BUTCHER'S PET CARE LIMITED
Registration no: 01716195 **Date established:** 1983
Turnover: £50m - £75m **No.of Employees:** 101 - 250
Product Groups: 20, 42, 61, 62

Date of Accounts	Jul 11	Jul 10	Jul 09
Sales Turnover	74m	72m	65m
Pre Tax Profit/Loss	4m	6m	5m
Working Capital	3m	9m	8m
Fixed Assets	24m	11m	2m
Current Assets	27m	23m	21m
Current Liabilities	6m	6m	5m

C E M The Wilde Group Ltd

Harlestone Firs Harlestone Road, Northampton, NN5 6UJ
Tel: 01604-586000 **Fax:** 01604-756700
E-mail: sales@cemfencing.co.uk
Website: http://www.cemfencing.co.uk
Directors: S. Wilde (Prop)
Managers: R. Marshal (Chief Acct)
Immediate Holding Company: CEM FENCING LTD.
Registration no: 04507769 **Date established:** 2002 **Turnover:** £5m - £10m
No.of Employees: 21 - 50 **Product Groups:** 30, 35, 52, 66

C M L Industrial Services

Lockington House Great Brington, Northampton, NN7 4HY
Tel: 01604-770383 **Fax:** 01604-770929
E-mail: cmlindustrialservices@hotmail.co.uk
Directors: C. Lacey (Ptnr)
Date established: 1981 **No.of Employees:** 1 - 10 **Product Groups:** 46

C P L Petroleum

Lodge Way Lodge Farm Industrial Estate, Northampton, NN5 7US
Tel: 01604-752531 **Fax:** 01604-587114
E-mail: corporate@cplindustries.co.uk
Website: http://www.cplpetroleum.co.uk
Managers: D. Pulling (Mgr)
Ultimate Holding Company: CPL INDUSTRIES HOLDINGS LIMITED
Immediate Holding Company: CPL PETROLEUM LIMITED
Registration no: 03003860 **VAT No.:** GB 721 5764 39
Date established: 1994 **Turnover:** £1m - £2m **No.of Employees:** 1 - 10
Product Groups: 66

Date of Accounts	Mar 12	Mar 11	Mar 10
Pre Tax Profit/Loss	N/A	878	904
Working Capital	31	30m	30m
Fixed Assets	26	26m	26m
Current Assets	57	56m	56m
Current Liabilities	26	246	253

Carlson Marketing Group UK Ltd

Belgrave House 1 Greyfriars, Northampton, NN1 2LQ
Tel: 020-8875 0875 **Fax:** 01604-230219
E-mail: sales@carlson-europe.com
Website: http://www.carlsonmarketing.co.uk
Bank(s): Citibank International plc
Directors: D. Perkind (Grp Chief Exec), S. Bal (I.T. Dir), S. Dall (I.T. Dir), J. Harman (Pres), A. Parris (Co Sec), F. Mccusker (Dep Pres), F. Mccusker (MD)
Immediate Holding Company: CARLSON MARKETING GROUP (U.K.) LIMITED
Registration no: 00648706 **VAT No.:** GB 536 6404 43
Date established: 1960 **Turnover:** £10m - £20m
No.of Employees: 51 - 100 **Product Groups:** 80, 81, 86

Date of Accounts	Dec 06	Dec 05	Dec 04
Pre Tax Profit/Loss	-800	-4220	660
Working Capital	72790	75370	N/A
Fixed Assets	2470	2470	6640
Current Assets	86790	86320	86590
Current Liabilities	14000	10950	11180
Total Share Capital	81910	81910	81910
ROCE% (Return on Capital Employed)	-1.1	-5.4	0.8

Central Fire Services

55 Redruth Close, Northampton, NN4 8PL
Tel: 07952-529505
Directors: D. Galashan (Prop)
Date established: 2004 **No.of Employees:** 1 - 10 **Product Groups:** 38, 42

Cereform Ltd

Barn Way Lodge Farm Industrial Estate, Northampton, NN5 7UW
Tel: 01604-755522 **Fax:** 01604-759343
E-mail: info@cereform.com
Website: http://www.cereform.com
Bank(s): National Westminster Bank Plc
Directors: R. Schofield (Fin), I. Smith (Fin), M. Turner (Mkt Research)
Managers: C. Demblon (Cust Serv Mgr)
Ultimate Holding Company: WITTINGTON INVESTMENTS LIMITED
Immediate Holding Company: CEREFORM LIMITED
Registration no: 00346958 **VAT No.:** GB 635 8313 34
Date established: 1938 **Turnover:** £50m - £75m
No.of Employees: 101 - 250 **Product Groups:** 20

Date of Accounts	Aug 08	Aug 09	Aug 10
Sales Turnover	59m	69m	70m
Pre Tax Profit/Loss	4m	3m	3m
Working Capital	18m	18m	18m
Fixed Assets	10m	8m	8m
Current Assets	27m	27m	28m
Current Liabilities	3m	3m	3m

Chartered Institution Of Wastes Management

9 Saxon Court St Peters Gardens, Northampton, NN1 1SX
Tel: 01604-620426 **Fax:** 01604-621339
E-mail: karen.wilkins@ciwm.co.uk
Website: http://www.ciwm.co.uk
Managers: J. Bent (Tech Serv Mgr), A. Currie, J. Diggins (Personnel), K. Wilkins, K. Webster (Fin Mgr)

Immediate Holding Company: INSTITUTE OF WASTES MANAGEMENT
Registration no: 00229724 **Date established:** 2028
Turnover: Up to £250,000 **No.of Employees:** 21 - 50 **Product Groups:** 87

Church & Co. Ltd

St James, Northampton, NN5 5JB
Tel: 01604-751251 **Fax:** 01604-754405
E-mail: info@church-footwear.com
Website: http://www.church-footwear.com
Bank(s): National Westminster Bank Plc
Directors: J. Mead (Mkt Research), S. Etheridge (Grp Chief Exec), H. Shah (Fin), H. Errington (Pers)
Managers: S. Munns (Purch Mgr), B. Humberstone (Cust Serv Mgr)
Ultimate Holding Company: PRADA SPA (ITALY)
Immediate Holding Company: CHURCH & CO. (FOOTWEAR) LIMITED
Registration no: 00529983 **VAT No.:** GB 294 1857 25
Date established: 1954 **Turnover:** £5m - £10m
No.of Employees: 251 - 500 **Product Groups:** 22, 24

Date of Accounts	Jan 11	Jan 10	Jan 08
Sales Turnover	N/A	N/A	6m
Pre Tax Profit/Loss	N/A	N/A	500
Working Capital	13	13	13
Current Assets	13	13	13

Civica UK Ltd

1 Sovereign Court South Portway Close, Round Spinney Industrial Estate, Northampton, NN3 8RH
Tel: 01604-798555 **Fax:** 01604-798505
E-mail: info@cavetab.co.uk
Website: http://www.cavetab.co.uk
Bank(s): HSBC, 123 Chancery La, London, WC2
Directors: I. Keers (MD)
Managers: K. Black (Sales Prom Mgr), J. Brown (Personnel), W. Doherty (Tech Serv Mgr), P. Marsh
Ultimate Holding Company: CORNWALL TOPCO LIMITED
Immediate Holding Company: CAVE TAB LIMITED
Registration no: 00948622 **VAT No.:** GB 222 2391 04
Date established: 1969 **Turnover:** £1m - £2m **No.of Employees:** 21 - 50
Product Groups: 26, 28, 49

Date of Accounts	Dec 10	Dec 09	Dec 08
Sales Turnover	1m	1m	2m
Pre Tax Profit/Loss	50	51	-224
Working Capital	318	273	199
Fixed Assets	24	32	63
Current Assets	447	435	611
Current Liabilities	63	107	275

Collingwood Lighting Ltd

Brooklands House Sywell Aerodrome, Sywell, Northampton, NN6 0BT
Tel: 01604-495151 **Fax:** 01604-495095
E-mail: sales@collingwoodgroup.com
Website: http://www.collingwoodlighting.com
Bank(s): HSBC Bank plc
Directors: P. Hampton (MD), R. Peters (Sales), J. Maeers (MD), G. Wilson (Fin)
Managers: W. Hilyard (Personnel), T. Darby (Sales Prom Mgr), A. Maloney (Purch Mgr), A. Garside, P. Hopkins
Ultimate Holding Company: COLLINGWOOD GROUP LIMITED
Immediate Holding Company: COLLINGWOOD LIGHTING LIMITED
Registration no: 00900626 **VAT No.:** GB 290 8834 26
Date established: 1967 **Turnover:** £5m - £10m
No.of Employees: 101 - 250 **Product Groups:** 37

Date of Accounts	Mar 11	Mar 10	Mar 09
Sales Turnover	9m	9m	N/A
Pre Tax Profit/Loss	730	463	632
Working Capital	2m	2m	2m
Fixed Assets	480	360	360
Current Assets	4m	3m	4m
Current Liabilities	635	386	342

Commercial Fire Services

17 Saffron Close, Northampton, NN4 0SG
Tel: 01604-768946 **Fax:** 01604-768946
Directors: R. Hayward (Prop)
Date established: 1991 **No.of Employees:** 1 - 10 **Product Groups:** 38, 42

Commrich Ltd

40 Forfar Street St James, Northampton, NN5 5BJ
Tel: 01604-457403 **Fax:** 0709-237 8859
E-mail: sales@commrich.net
Website: http://www.commrich.net
Directors: M. Ledger (Fin), R. Ledger (MD)
Immediate Holding Company: COMMRICH LIMITED
Registration no: 04332879 **Date established:** 2001
No.of Employees: 1 - 10 **Product Groups:** 44

Date of Accounts	Dec 10	Dec 09	Dec 07
Working Capital	2	4	4
Fixed Assets	N/A	N/A	1
Current Assets	4	4	7

Control Equipment Services Ltd

9 Staveley Way Brixworth Industrial Estate, Brixworth, Northampton, NN6 9EU
Tel: 01604-882372 **Fax:** 01604-883529
Website: http://www.cesl-services.co.uk
Registration no: 03690543 **Date established:** 1998
No.of Employees: 11 - 20 **Product Groups:** 37, 38, 44, 49

Counterline Ltd

4 Park Lane Harpole, Northampton, NN7 4BT
Tel: 01604-832100 **Fax:** 01604-832100
Website: http://www.counterline.co.uk
Directors: A. Hall (Sales)
Ultimate Holding Company: COUNTERLINE HOLDINGS LIMITED
Immediate Holding Company: COUNTERLINE LIMITED
Registration no: 05471587 **Date established:** 2005
No.of Employees: 1 - 10 **Product Groups:** 20, 40, 41

Date of Accounts	Jun 11	Jun 10	Jun 09
Sales Turnover	10m	7m	7m
Pre Tax Profit/Loss	130	165	515
Working Capital	1m	1m	1m
Fixed Assets	1m	1m	1m
Current Assets	5m	4m	4m
Current Liabilities	2m	2m	2m

Crockett & Jones Ltd

Perry Street, Northampton, NN1 4HN
Tel: 01604-631515 **Fax:** 01604-230037
E-mail: info@crockettandjones.com
Website: http://www.crockettandjones.com
Bank(s): Barclays
Directors: J. Jones (MD), J. Banks (Co Sec)
Managers: J. Bolden
Immediate Holding Company: CROCKETT AND JONES LIMITED
Registration no: 00451921 **VAT No.:** GB 119 3242 86
Date established: 1948 **Turnover:** £20m - £50m
No.of Employees: 101 - 250 **Product Groups:** 22

Date of Accounts	Feb 12	Feb 11	Feb 10
Sales Turnover	22m	20m	17m
Pre Tax Profit/Loss	3m	3m	2m
Working Capital	9m	8m	6m
Fixed Assets	2m	2m	2m
Current Assets	11m	10m	8m
Current Liabilities	2m	1m	2m

Curtis Instruments UK Ltd

5 Upper Priory Street Grafton Street Industrial Estate, Northampton, NN1 2PT
Tel: 01604-629755 **Fax:** 01604-629876
E-mail: sales@curtisinst.co.uk
Website: http://www.curtisinst.co.uk
Bank(s): Barclays
Directors: B. Langsford (MD)
Managers: D. Moran, A. Chapman (Sales Admin), C. Perry, J. Hancock (Fin Mgr)
Ultimate Holding Company: CURTIS INSTRUMENTS INC (USA)
Immediate Holding Company: CURTIS INSTRUMENTS (U.K.) LIMITED
Registration no: 01155844 **VAT No.:** GB 178 2358 36
Date established: 1974 **Turnover:** £5m - £10m **No.of Employees:** 21 - 50
Product Groups: 37, 38, 39, 40, 49

Date of Accounts	Nov 11	Nov 10	Nov 09
Sales Turnover	10m	9m	7m
Pre Tax Profit/Loss	725	492	78
Working Capital	3m	2m	3m
Fixed Assets	751	716	775
Current Assets	5m	4m	4m
Current Liabilities	803	524	383

D & D Marquee Hire

1 Devonshire Close Boughton, Northampton, NN2 8RY
Tel: 01604-821460 **Fax:** 01604-845696
E-mail: ddmarqueehire@aol.com
Website: http://www.ddmarquees.co.uk
Directors: A. Darlington (Prop)
Turnover: Up to £250,000 **No.of Employees:** 1 - 10 **Product Groups:** 24, 66, 83, 84

D L S Electronic Services Ltd

108 Northampton Lane North Moulton, Northampton, NN3 7QW
Tel: 01604-645921 **Fax:** 01604-645921
E-mail: dave@dlselec.com
Directors: S. Smith (Co Sec), D. Smith (Dir)
Immediate Holding Company: D.L.S. ELECTRONIC SERVICES LIMITED
Registration no: 02517071 **Date established:** 1990
No.of Employees: 1 - 10 **Product Groups:** 35, 39, 45

Date of Accounts	Jul 12	Jul 11	Jul 10
Working Capital	60	54	60
Fixed Assets	11	18	26
Current Assets	109	109	97

Dachser Transport UK Ltd

Oxwich Close Brackmills Industrial Estate, Northampton, NN4 7BH
Tel: 01604-666222 **Fax:** 01604-666239
E-mail: nick.lowe@dachser.com
Website: http://www.dachser.com
Bank(s): National Westminster Bank Plc
Directors: J. Goodman (Chief Op Offcr), N. Lowe (MD), S. Rowley (Co Sec)
Managers: M. Winpress (Sales & Mktg Mg), R. Remika (Export Sales Mg)
Ultimate Holding Company: DACHSER GMBH & CO KG (GERMANY)
Immediate Holding Company: DACHSER LIMITED
Registration no: 01195803 **VAT No.:** GB 281 6147 56
Date established: 1975 **Turnover:** £20m - £50m
No.of Employees: 21 - 50 **Product Groups:** 76

Date of Accounts	Dec 09	Dec 08	Dec 07
Sales Turnover	24m	N/A	N/A
Pre Tax Profit/Loss	580	394	777
Working Capital	1m	2m	2m
Fixed Assets	1m	1m	1m
Current Assets	5m	6m	4m
Current Liabilities	469	647	278

Datatrade Ltd

Unit 35 Cornwell Business Park Salthouse Road, Brackmills Industrial Estate, Northampton, NN4 7EX
Tel: 01604-666666 **Fax:** 01604-768666
E-mail: enquiries@datatrade.co.uk
Website: http://www.datatrade.co.uk
Bank(s): National Westminster
Directors: C. Lacey (Tech Serv), J. Clubb (Fin), P. Laplanche (Sales)
Managers: D. Hunt (Develop Mgr), J. Redrup (Personnel)
Ultimate Holding Company: DATATRADE HOLDINGS LIMITED
Immediate Holding Company: DATATRADE LIMITED
Registration no: 01491136 **VAT No.:** GB 336 1796 41
Date established: 1980 **Turnover:** £2m - £5m **No.of Employees:** 21 - 50
Product Groups: 44, 80

Date of Accounts	Sep 11	Sep 10	Sep 09
Sales Turnover	N/A	N/A	2m
Pre Tax Profit/Loss	N/A	N/A	140
Working Capital	83	66	106
Fixed Assets	65	63	64
Current Assets	889	759	952
Current Liabilities	N/A	N/A	495

Dickens Bros Ltd

69-71 Kettering Road, Northampton, NN1 4AP
Tel: 01604-636537 **Fax:** 01604-636537
E-mail: dickensbrothers@btinternet.com
Website: http://www.dickensbrothers.co.uk
Directors: B. Dickens (MD)
Immediate Holding Company: DICKENS BROTHERS LIMITED
Registration no: 00175216 **VAT No.:** GB 119 3759 49
Date established: 2021 **Turnover:** £250,000 - £500,000
No.of Employees: 1 - 10 **Product Groups:** 43

Date of Accounts	Nov 11	Nov 10	Nov 09
Working Capital	222	220	216
Fixed Assets	20	21	22
Current Assets	251	255	262

Direct Selling News Europe Ltd

Enterprise House 30 Billing Road, Northampton, NN1 5DQ
Tel: 0783-129 4148 **Fax:** 020-7497 3144
E-mail: kslater@dsneurope.com
Website: http://www.directsellingnews.com
Directors: R. Berry (Dir), R. Parker (MD)
Managers: K. Slater
Immediate Holding Company: DIRECT SELLING NEWS EUROPE, LTD.
Registration no: 06362498 **Date established:** 2007
No.of Employees: 1 - 10 **Product Groups:** 87

Date of Accounts	Dec 10	Dec 09	Dec 08
Working Capital	-308	35	-13
Fixed Assets	2	2	3
Current Assets	7	69	17
Current Liabilities	308	N/A	N/A

Dixey Instruments

5 High Street Brixworth, Northampton, NN6 9DD
Tel: 01604-882480 **Fax:** 01604-882488
E-mail: info@dixeyinstruments.com
Website: http://www.dixeyinstruments.com
Managers: E. Mcfall (Mgr)
Immediate Holding Company: DIXEY INSTRUMENTS LTD
Registration no: 07808419 **VAT No.:** GB 729 7290 00
Date established: 2011 **Turnover:** £250,000 - £500,000
No.of Employees: 1 - 10 **Product Groups:** 36, 37, 38

D-Pac Ltd

4 Sketty Close Brackmills Industrial Estate, Northampton, NN4 7PL
Tel: 01604-705600 **Fax:** 01604-708100
E-mail: sales@unipacpet.com
Website: http://www.unipacpet.com
Directors: R. Devani (MD)
Immediate Holding Company: D-PAC LIMITED
Registration no: 01861177 **VAT No.:** GB 449 3668 07
Date established: 1984 **Turnover:** £500,000 - £1m
No.of Employees: 11 - 20 **Product Groups:** 49

Date of Accounts	Mar 11	Mar 10	Mar 09
Working Capital	-12	-43	-65
Fixed Assets	761	772	786
Current Assets	325	273	252

Dr A J Burch - Harlestone Road Surgery

117 Harlestone Road, Northampton, NN5 7AQ
Tel: 01604-751832 **Fax:** 01604-756700
E-mail: sales@harlestonewoodengates.co.uk
Website: http://harlestonewoodengates.co.uk
Managers: M. Smith (Sales Admin)
Registration no: 02804618 **Date established:** 1985 **Turnover:**
No.of Employees: 21 - 50 **Product Groups:** 25

Dunlop Hiflex Fluid Power Ltd

2 Tenter Road Moulton Park Industrial Estate, Northampton, NN3 6PZ
Tel: 01604-499111 **Fax:** 01604-790305
E-mail: sales@hiflex-fluidpower.com
Website: http://www.dunlophiflex.com
Managers: M. Clark (Mgr)
Registration no: 01810238 **Date established:** 1984
No.of Employees: 1 - 10 **Product Groups:** 29, 30, 36, 67

Duo GB Ltd

4 Monks Pond Street, Northampton, NN1 2LF
Tel: 01604-230445 **Fax:** 01604-231389
E-mail: sales@duogb.co.uk
Website: http://www.leitner.co.uk
Directors: D. Crockford (MD)
Immediate Holding Company: DUOGB LIMITED
Registration no: 02362188 **VAT No.:** GB 581 3249 39
Date established: 1989 **Turnover:** £500,000 - £1m
No.of Employees: 1 - 10 **Product Groups:** 26, 81

Date of Accounts	Sep 11	Sep 10	Sep 09
Working Capital	29	34	24
Current Assets	81	86	106

E M P Intelligence Service

Springfield House 7 The Avenue, Dallington, Northampton, NN5 7AJ
Tel: 01604-755005 **Fax:** 01604-755104
E-mail: apollard@emp-is.com
Website: http://www.emp-is.com
Directors: A. Pollard (Prop)
Date established: 1994 **No.of Employees:** 1 - 10 **Product Groups:** 80

East Midlands Micro Imaging

Unit M22 K G House Kingsfield Close, Kings Heath Indl-Est, Northampton, NN5 7QS
Tel: 01604-644665 **Fax:** 01604- 643673
E-mail: sales@em-micro-imaging.co.uk
Website: http://www.em-micro-imaging.co.uk
Directors: A. Bateman (Dir), A. Forward (Sales)
Managers: M. Bateman (Mgr)
Registration no: 03969830 **VAT No.:** GB 289 8380 89
Date established: 2000 **Turnover:** £250,000 - £500,000
No.of Employees: 1 - 10 **Product Groups:** 27, 38, 44, 65, 80, 81

Encon Air Systems Ltd

31 Quarry Park Close Moulton Park Industrial Estate, Northampton, NN3 6QB
Tel: 01604-494187 **Fax:** 01604-645848
E-mail: info@encon-air.co.uk
Website: http://www.encon-air.co.uk
Directors: S. Dawson (Fin)
Immediate Holding Company: ENCON AIR SYSTEMS LIMITED
Registration no: 02063860 **VAT No.:** GB 443 8986 04
Date established: 1986 **Turnover:** £500,000 - £1m
No.of Employees: 1 - 10 **Product Groups:** 52, 54

Date of Accounts	Oct 11	Oct 10	Oct 09
Working Capital	394	355	343
Fixed Assets	55	57	45
Current Assets	841	830	649

Encore Personnel Services

4 College St Mews, Northampton, NN1 2QF
Tel: 01604-824170 **Fax:** 01604-250485
E-mail: northampton@encorepersonnel.co.uk
Website: http://www.encorepersonnal.co.uk
Managers: K. Haywood (Mgr)
Turnover: £10m - £20m **No.of Employees:** 1 - 10 **Product Groups:** 72, 80, 84, 86

Enigma Translation Ltd
2 Gibson Lane Dallington Park Road, Northampton, NN5 7PN
Tel: 01604-750799 **Fax:** 01604-750799
E-mail: enquiries@enigmatranslation.co.uk
Website: http://www.enigmatranslation.co.uk
Directors: G. Bowles (Fin)
Immediate Holding Company: ENIGMA TRANSLATION LIMITED
Registration no: 05113879 **Date established:** 2004
No.of Employees: 1 - 10 **Product Groups:** 80

Date of Accounts	Apr 11	Apr 10	Apr 08
Working Capital	2	-0	14
Fixed Assets	N/A	N/A	1
Current Assets	34	18	37
Current Liabilities	10	N/A	N/A

Eriks Hose Technology Ltd
12 Osyth Close Brackmills Industrial Estate, Northampton, NN4 7DY
Tel: 01604-762175 **Fax:** 01604-769915
E-mail: sales@fhsn.co.uk
Website: http://www.eriks-hose-technology.co.uk
Directors: M. Burgess (Dir)
Ultimate Holding Company: SHV HOLDINGS NV (NETHERLANDS)
Immediate Holding Company: ERIKS HOSE TECHNOLOGY LIMITED
Registration no: 03461760 **VAT No.:** GB 417 1439 65
Date established: 1997 **Turnover:** £2m - £5m **No.of Employees:** 1 - 10
Product Groups: 23, 27, 29, 30, 36

Date of Accounts	Dec 11	Dec 10	Dec 09
Sales Turnover	3m	4m	4m
Pre Tax Profit/Loss	-2m	-154	693
Working Capital	723	822	1m
Fixed Assets	193	2m	2m
Current Assets	2m	2m	2m
Current Liabilities	94	70	143

European Drives & Motor Repairs
9 Mansion Close Moulton Park Industrial Estate, Northampton, NN3 6RU
Tel: 01604-499777 **Fax:** 01604-492777
E-mail: malcolms@edmr.co.uk
Website: http://www.edmr.co.uk
Bank(s): HSBC Bank plc
Directors: M. Snell (MD)
Managers: D. Croft (), T. Libertucci (District Mgr), M. Beasley (Mgr), C. Rudge (Mgr)
Registration no: 00891601 **Date established:** 1988 **Turnover:** £2m - £5m
No.of Employees: 11 - 20 **Product Groups:** 37, 39, 48, 67

Date of Accounts	Aug 08	Aug 07	Aug 06
Working Capital	150	128	162
Fixed Assets	88	124	110
Current Assets	592	598	534
Current Liabilities	443	469	372
Total Share Capital	1	1	1

Exact Technology Ltd
10 Sketty Close Brackmills Industrial Estate, Northampton, NN4 7PL
Tel: 01604-768320 **Fax:** 01604-769619
E-mail: sales@exact-technology.com
Website: http://www.exact-technology.com
Directors: P. Miller (MD), R. Scowen (MD)
Managers: Z. Smyth (Admin Off), A. Baxendale (Mats Contrlr), B. Price (Sales Prom Mgr), R. Benad (Prod Mgr), W. Thompson (Tech Sales Mgr)
Registration no: 03828630 **VAT No.:** GB 738 7677 72
Date established: 1975 **Turnover:** £2m - £5m **No.of Employees:** 1 - 10
Product Groups: 43, 44

Date of Accounts	Dec 05
Working Capital	-162
Current Liabilities	162
Total Share Capital	100

Expert Developments Ltd
Unit 3 Bective Works Bective Road, Northampton, NN2 7TD
Tel: 01604-791339 **Fax:** 01604-791717
E-mail: info@expertdevelopments.com
Website: http://www.expertdevelopments.com
Directors: G. Whitehouse (MD)
Immediate Holding Company: EXPERT DEVELOPMENTS LIMITED
Registration no: 02573942 **VAT No.:** GB 576 4160 27
Date established: 1991 **Turnover:** £250,000 - £500,000
No.of Employees: 1 - 10 **Product Groups:** 48

Date of Accounts	Mar 11	Mar 10	Mar 09
Working Capital	44	1	-8
Fixed Assets	41	37	41
Current Assets	151	161	106

F F P Packaging Solutions Ltd
1-7 Tenter Road Moulton Park Industrial Estate, Northampton, NN3 6PZ
Tel: 01604-643535 **Fax:** 01604-492427
E-mail: info@ffpkg.co.uk
Website: http://www.ffpkg.co.uk
Bank(s): National Westminster
Directors: K. Berresford (Sales), P. Dundas (Fin)
Managers: R. Chudley, H. Thorpe (Personnel), I. Hedges
Immediate Holding Company: FFP PACKAGING SOLUTIONS LIMITED
Registration no: 00893217 **Date established:** 1966
Turnover: £10m - £20m **No.of Employees:** 101 - 250
Product Groups: 28, 30

Date of Accounts	Jan 11	Jan 10	Jan 09
Sales Turnover	19m	17m	18m
Pre Tax Profit/Loss	110	32	-2m
Working Capital	4m	4m	3m
Fixed Assets	5m	4m	5m
Current Assets	8m	7m	6m
Current Liabilities	1m	1m	800

Faber Blinds UK Ltd
Pond Wood Close Moulton Park Industrial Estate, Northampton, NN3 6RT
Tel: 01604-766251 **Fax:** 01604-768802
E-mail: sales.uk@faber.com
Website: http://www.faberblinds.co.uk
Directors: D. Harris (MD)
Managers: M. Abbott (Fin Mgr)
Ultimate Holding Company: HUNTER DOUGLAS NV (NETHERLANDS ANTILLES)
Immediate Holding Company: FABER BLINDS UK LIMITED
Registration no: 00716485 **VAT No.:** GB 119 2857 54
Date established: 1962 **Turnover:** £5m - £10m **No.of Employees:** 21 - 50
Product Groups: 24, 35

Date of Accounts	Dec 11	Dec 10	Dec 09
Sales Turnover	3m	7m	8m
Pre Tax Profit/Loss	-60	1m	360
Working Capital	4m	4m	2m
Fixed Assets	78	27	1m
Current Assets	5m	5m	4m
Current Liabilities	274	429	551

Festo Ltd
Applied Automation Centre 55 Caswell Road, Brackmills Industrial Estate, Northampton, NN4 7PY
Tel: 0800-626422 **Fax:** 01604-667001
E-mail: info_gb@festo.com
Website: http://www.festo.com
Bank(s): National Westminster Bank Plc
Directors: M. Gaffney (Fin), G. Wiles (MD)
Managers: S. Sands (Mktg Serv Mgr), S. Hersy (Personnel), S. Sands (Mktg Serv Mgr)
Ultimate Holding Company: FESTO AG (GERMANY)
Immediate Holding Company: FESTO LIMITED
Registration no: 00926749 **Date established:** 1968
Turnover: £20m - £50m **No.of Employees:** 51 - 100 **Product Groups:** 37, 38, 40, 84, 86

Date of Accounts	Dec 11	Dec 10	Dec 09
Sales Turnover	29m	26m	20m
Pre Tax Profit/Loss	5m	3m	983
Working Capital	6m	5m	3m
Fixed Assets	2m	2m	3m
Current Assets	14m	12m	8m
Current Liabilities	4m	3m	2m

Filtration Control Ltd
Unit B & C Longman Court Sketty Close, Brackmills Industrial Estate, Northampton, NN4 7PL
Tel: 01604-707750
E-mail: sales@filtrationcontrol.com
Website: http://www.filtrationcontrol.com
Directors: D. Norville (MD), M. Jones (Export), P. Hudson (Fin), D. Johnson (Tech Serv)
Managers: A. Muddiman (Purch Mgr)
Immediate Holding Company: FILTRATION CONTROL LTD.
Registration no: 02524269 **Date established:** 1990
Turnover: £10m - £20m **No.of Employees:** 51 - 100 **Product Groups:** 37, 42

Date of Accounts	Mar 11	Mar 10	Mar 09
Sales Turnover	16m	15m	N/A
Pre Tax Profit/Loss	866	607	128
Working Capital	119	-79	-507
Fixed Assets	551	682	806
Current Assets	6m	6m	5m
Current Liabilities	3m	2m	2m

1st Class Packaging Ltd
3 Kingsfield Business Park Gladstone Road, Northampton, NN5 7PP
Tel: 01604-750730 **Fax:** 01604-750530
E-mail: enquiries@1stclasspkg.co.uk
Website: http://www.1stclasspackaging.co.uk
Directors: C. Sigley (Co Sec), B. Hancock (Dir)
Ultimate Holding Company: PAPERLINX LIMITED (AUSTRALIA)
Immediate Holding Company: 1ST CLASS PACKAGING LIMITED
Registration no: 03313971 **Date established:** 1997 **Turnover:** £2m - £5m
No.of Employees: 11 - 20 **Product Groups:** 38, 42

Date of Accounts	Jun 11	Jun 10	Jun 09
Sales Turnover	5m	4m	4m
Pre Tax Profit/Loss	343	181	277
Working Capital	2m	1m	1m
Fixed Assets	5	9	12
Current Assets	3m	2m	2m
Current Liabilities	489	251	367

Foden Ibex Ltd
Ibex House Ferro Fields Scaldwell Road, Brixworth, Northampton, NN6 9UA
Tel: 01604-880605 **Fax:** 01604-880802
E-mail: sales@fodenibex.co.uk
Website: http://www.english-gaiter.co.uk
Bank(s): Barclays
Directors: M. Lee (MD)
Immediate Holding Company: FODEN IBEX LIMITED
Registration no: 00785332 **VAT No.:** GB 294 0065 63
Date established: 1963 **Turnover:** £2m - £5m **No.of Employees:** 11 - 20
Product Groups: 22, 23, 24, 49, 66

Date of Accounts	Dec 11	Dec 10	Dec 09
Working Capital	262	213	204
Fixed Assets	2m	2m	2m
Current Assets	368	348	322

Franklin Silencers Ltd
1 Grafton Place Grafton Street Industrial Estate, Northampton, NN1 2PS
Tel: 01604-626266 **Fax:** 01604-233757
E-mail: danny.weisenberger@franklinsilencers.co.uk
Website: http://www.franklinsilencers.co.uk
Bank(s): Lloyds TSB Bank plc
Directors: D. Weisenberger (MD), J. Bateman (Dir)
Immediate Holding Company: FRANKLIN SILENCERS LIMITED
Registration no: 00837346 **VAT No.:** GB 119 9399 23
Date established: 1965 **Turnover:** £1m - £2m **No.of Employees:** 21 - 50
Product Groups: 35, 39, 40

Date of Accounts	Mar 11	Mar 10	Mar 09
Working Capital	89	-23	20
Fixed Assets	842	887	985
Current Assets	790	581	569

Freeman Automotive UK Ltd
Upton Valley Way East Pineham, Northampton, NN4 9EF
Tel: 01604-583344 **Fax:** 01604-583744
E-mail: studio@ebcbrakes.com
Website: http://www.ebcbrakes.com
Managers: L. Lawson (Comptroller), N. Brown (Mktg Serv Mgr), N. Flemming
Immediate Holding Company: FREEMAN AUTOMOTIVE (UK) LTD
Registration no: 01690939 **Date established:** 1983
Turnover: £20m - £50m **No.of Employees:** 101 - 250 **Product Groups:** 68

Date of Accounts	Oct 11	Oct 10	Oct 09
Sales Turnover	27m	29m	29m
Pre Tax Profit/Loss	7m	9m	7m
Working Capital	15m	15m	7m
Fixed Assets	26m	13m	15m
Current Assets	24m	23m	19m
Current Liabilities	2m	2m	3m

Funke
387 Wellingborough Road, Northampton, NN1 4EY
Tel: 01604-239716 **Fax:** 01604-239719
Website: http://www.funke.de
Managers: D. Knightbridge (Mgr)
Immediate Holding Company: FUNKE GMBH
Date established: 1970 **Turnover:** £10m - £20m **No.of Employees:** 1 - 10
Product Groups: 40

Glass Northampton Ltd
25-29 Bailiff Street, Northampton, NN1 3DX
Tel: 01604-233343 **Fax:** 01604-233298
E-mail: admin@glass-northampton.co.uk
Website: http://www.glass-northampton.co.uk
Bank(s): Barclays
Directors: C. Brown (MD)
Managers: R. Duckett (Fin Mgr)
Ultimate Holding Company: GLASS NORTHAMPTON HOLDINGS LIMITED
Immediate Holding Company: GLASS NORTHAMPTON HOLDINGS LIMITED
Registration no: 03482159 **VAT No.:** GB 120 1626 28
Date established: 1997 **No.of Employees:** 21 - 50 **Product Groups:** 33, 35, 66

Date of Accounts	Dec 11	Dec 10	Dec 09
Working Capital	29	29	29
Fixed Assets	128	131	135
Current Assets	57	57	57

Grant Thornton UK LLP
Elgin House Billing Road, Northampton, NN1 5AU
Tel: 01604-623800 **Fax:** 01604-230486
E-mail: info@grant-thornton.co.uk
Website: http://www.grant-thornton.co.uk
Directors: S. Robinson (Ptnr), T. Blades (Snr Part)
Managers: J. Shepherd (Mktg Serv Mgr)
Immediate Holding Company: Grant Thornton UK Llp
Registration no: 02917818 **Date established:** 2009
Turnover: £50m - £75m **No.of Employees:** 51 - 100 **Product Groups:** 80

H2o Group
Foxhill Farm Stables Foxhill Road, West Haddon, Northampton, NN6 7BG
Tel: 01788-510529 **Fax:** 01788-510728
E-mail: mail@h2oplc.com
Website: http://www.the-wright-group.co.uk
Bank(s): National Westminster Bank Plc
Directors: A. Pridgeon (Dir), R. Allen (MD), A. Allen (Fin)
Managers: K. Leveland (Personnel), C. Leveland (Personnel)
Immediate Holding Company: WRL Ltd
Registration no: 03579679 **VAT No.:** GB 212 7546 80
Date established: 1998 **Turnover:** £2m - £5m **No.of Employees:** 21 - 50
Product Groups: 30, 36, 38, 40, 41, 51

Haddonstone Ltd
Forge House Church Lane, East Haddon, Northampton, NN6 8DB
Tel: 01604-770711 **Fax:** 01604-770027
E-mail: simons@haddonstone.co.uk
Website: http://www.haddonstone.com
Bank(s): National Westminster Bank Plc
Directors: A. Lowe (Sales), E. Lennox (Co Sec), S. Scott (Mkt Research)
Managers: G. Stoke-davy (Tech Serv Mgr)
Ultimate Holding Company: ADENWOOD LIMITED
Immediate Holding Company: ARCADIAN GARDEN FEATURES LIMITED
Registration no: 03878449 **VAT No.:** GB 443 8197 31
Date established: 1999 **Turnover:** £5m - £10m **No.of Employees:** 21 - 50
Product Groups: 30, 33, 35, 36, 40

Hako Machines Ltd
Eldon Close Crick, Northampton, NN6 7SL
Tel: 01788-823535 **Fax:** 01788-823969
E-mail: sales@hako.co.uk
Website: http://www.hako.co.uk
Directors: N. Meredith (MD), M. Woollven (Co Sec), J. Millar (Fin)
Managers: J. Veasey (Personnel), D. Forber (Sales & Mktg Mg)
Ultimate Holding Company: L POSSEHL & CO GMBH (GERMANY)
Immediate Holding Company: HAKO MACHINES LIMITED
Registration no: 01414225 **VAT No.:** GB 291 3978 03
Date established: 1979 **Turnover:** £10m - £20m
No.of Employees: 51 - 100 **Product Groups:** 37, 40

Date of Accounts	Dec 11	Dec 10	Dec 09
Sales Turnover	12m	11m	14m
Pre Tax Profit/Loss	-361	-119	114
Working Capital	22	610	767
Fixed Assets	1m	1m	1m
Current Assets	4m	4m	5m
Current Liabilities	586	530	550

Hamilton Plastic Packaging Ltd
18 Galowhill Road Brackmills Indl-Est, Northampton, NN4 7EE
Tel: 01604-766329 **Fax:** 01604-701790
E-mail: andrew.s@hamiltonpp.com
Website: http://www.hamiltonpp.com
Bank(s): Barclays
Directors: A. Sidders (MD), D. Endersby (Sales)
Managers: R. Burrows (Sec)
Immediate Holding Company: NMLAD LIMITED
Registration no: 01718892 **VAT No.:** GB 281 6193 49
Date established: 1983 **Turnover:** £1m - £2m **No.of Employees:** 11 - 20
Product Groups: 20, 30

Date of Accounts	Apr 10	Apr 09	Apr 08
Working Capital	226	192	249
Fixed Assets	209	266	324
Current Assets	484	423	497

Harltex Ltd
12 Norman-D-Gate Industrial Estate Norman-D-Gate, Northampton, NN1 5NT
Tel: 01604-632343 **Fax:** 01604-632344
E-mail: harltex@btconnect.com
Bank(s): TSB
Directors: H. Ainsworth (MD), R. Leader (Comm)
Immediate Holding Company: HARLTEX LIMITED
Registration no: 01895572 **VAT No.:** GB 420 7168 75
Date established: 1985 **No.of Employees:** 11 - 20 **Product Groups:** 29

Date of Accounts	Apr 12	Apr 11	Apr 10
Working Capital	954	803	341
Fixed Assets	63	80	93
Current Assets	1m	1m	611

Harting Ltd
Caswell Road Brackmills Industrial Estate, Northampton, NN4 7PW
Tel: 01604-827500 **Fax:** 01604-827548
E-mail: gb@harting.co.uk
Website: http://www.harting.com
Bank(s): Barclays

Directors: S. Asbury (Sales & Mktg), P. Hannon (MD)
Managers: V. Copeland (Personnel), T. Mayo (Tech Serv Mgr), D. Arnold (Chief Buyer), D. Iliffe
Ultimate Holding Company: HARTING KGAA (GERMANY)
Immediate Holding Company: HARTING UK LIMITED
Registration no: 01491158 **VAT No.:** GB 864 4452 09
Date established: 1980 **Turnover:** £20m - £50m
No.of Employees: 51 - 100 **Product Groups:** 30, 35, 37, 39, 44

Date of Accounts	Sep 11	Sep 10	Sep 09
Sales Turnover	21m	19m	15m
Pre Tax Profit/Loss	2m	992	112
Working Capital	4m	3m	3m
Fixed Assets	1m	990	965
Current Assets	7m	7m	5m
Current Liabilities	1m	2m	643

Harting Ltd
Caswell Road Brackmills Industrial Estate, Northampton, NN4 7PW
Tel: 01604-827500 **Fax:** 01604-706777
E-mail: gb@harting.com
Website: http://www.harting.co.uk
Bank(s): Barclays
Directors: K. Canham (Mkt Research), D. Franklin (Mkt Research), P. Hannon (MD)
Managers: S. Asbury (Sales Prom Mgr), T. Mayo (I.T. Exec)
Immediate Holding Company: Harting KGaA (Germany)
Registration no: 01491158 **VAT No.:** GB 864 4452 09
Date established: 1945 **Turnover:** £10m - £20m
No.of Employees: 101 - 250 **Product Groups:** 30, 35, 37, 39, 44

Hawes Signs Ltd
Sandfield Close Moulton Park Industrial Estate, Northampton, NN3 6EU
Tel: 01604-790000 **Fax:** 01604-790190
E-mail: info@hawes.co.uk
Website: http://www.hawes.co.uk
Bank(s): Lloyds TSB Bank plc
Directors: C. Hawes (Sales & Mktg), D. Thorpe (Fin)
Ultimate Holding Company: HAWES GROUP LIMITED
Immediate Holding Company: HAWES GROUP LIMITED
Registration no: 00469969 **VAT No.:** GB 227 0366 80
Date established: 1949 **Turnover:** £10m - £20m
No.of Employees: 101 - 250 **Product Groups:** 37, 49, 52

Date of Accounts	Dec 11	Dec 10	Dec 09
Sales Turnover	17m	16m	13m
Pre Tax Profit/Loss	107	-611	-3m
Working Capital	427	139	526
Fixed Assets	475	657	929
Current Assets	5m	7m	5m
Current Liabilities	2m	2m	1m

Haynes & Cann Ltd
1-9 Overstone Road, Northampton, NN1 3JL
Tel: 01604-626143 **Fax:** 01604-604721
E-mail: haynes.cann@btconnect.com
Directors: B. Keech (MD), R. Starmer (Co Sec)
Managers: L. Cushing (Admin Off)
Immediate Holding Company: HAYNES & CANN,LIMITED
Registration no: 00158033 **VAT No.:** GB 120 1239 35
Date established: 1919 **Turnover:** £500,000 - £1m
No.of Employees: 1 - 10 **Product Groups:** 24

Date of Accounts	Dec 07	Dec 06
Working Capital	488	494
Fixed Assets	145	154
Current Assets	710	682
Current Liabilities	222	188
Total Share Capital	279	279

Henderson Farbrications UK Ltd
Kings Park Road Moulton Park, Moulton Park Industrial Estate, Northampton, NN3 6LL
Tel: 01604-499200 **Fax:** 01604-492856
E-mail: info@hendfab.com
Website: http://www.hendfab.com
Bank(s): Barclays
Directors: S. O'looney (MD)
Managers: A. Lasbury (Tech Serv Mgr), S. Rivett (Fin Mgr)
Ultimate Holding Company: HENDERSON HOLDINGS UK LIMITED
Immediate Holding Company: HENDERSON HOLDINGS UK LIMITED
Registration no: 06729906 **Date established:** 2008 **Turnover:** £1m - £2m
No.of Employees: 21 - 50 **Product Groups:** 26, 35, 40, 48

Date of Accounts	Nov 11	Nov 10	Nov 09
Working Capital	798	539	232
Current Assets	843	578	248

Heritage Belt Company
Leo House The Business Centre Ross Road, Weedon Road Industrial Estate, Northampton, NN5 5AX
Tel: 01604-684700 **Fax:** 01604-684719
E-mail: info@regentbelt.co.uk
Website: http://www.regentbelt.co.uk
Bank(s): Lloyds TSB Bank plc
Directors: V. Luguterah (Prop)
Immediate Holding Company: REGENT BELT COMPANY LIMITED
Registration no: SC054983 **Date established:** 1974
Turnover: £5m - £10m **No.of Employees:** 11 - 20 **Product Groups:** 22, 66

Date of Accounts	Jul 11	Jul 10	Jul 09
Working Capital	34	-19	-2
Fixed Assets	266	220	148
Current Assets	358	311	255

Howes Percival Solicitors
Oxford House, Northampton, NN1 5PN
Tel: 01604-230400 **Fax:** 01604-620956
E-mail: law@howespercival.com
Website: http://www.howespercival.com
Directors: A. Mearns (Fin), G. Couldrake (Ptnr)
Managers: P. Ogram (Sales Admin), G. Merrington (Tech Serv Mgr)
Immediate Holding Company: HOWES PERCIVAL LLP
Registration no: OC322781 **VAT No.:** GB 119 5235 73
Date established: 2006 **Turnover:** £10m - £20m
No.of Employees: 51 - 100 **Product Groups:** 80

Date of Accounts	Apr 11	Apr 10	Apr 09
Sales Turnover	17m	18m	18m
Pre Tax Profit/Loss	4m	5m	4m
Working Capital	9m	9m	7m
Fixed Assets	1m	791	968
Current Assets	12m	12m	10m
Current Liabilities	3m	3m	2m

Huddle and Bliss
PO Box 742, Northampton, NN7 3WQ
Tel: 01604-832759 **Fax:** 01604-831903
E-mail: enquiries@huddleandbliss.com
Website: http://www.huddleandbliss.com
Registration no: 06801669 **Product Groups:** 24, 63, 65

I C S Security Solutions Ltd
Unit 1-2 J B J Business Park Northampton Road, Blisworth, Northampton, NN7 3DW
Tel: 01604-858565 **Fax:** 01604-859545
Directors: L. Goody (Co Sec), A. Good (MD)
Immediate Holding Company: ICS SECURITY SOLUTIONS LIMITED
Registration no: 04904184 **Date established:** 2003
No.of Employees: 11 - 20 **Product Groups:** 34, 40

Date of Accounts	Sep 11	Sep 10	Sep 09
Working Capital	320	306	284
Fixed Assets	107	133	98
Current Assets	1m	1m	998
Current Liabilities	389	396	414

Ideal Tanks & Pumps Ltd
The Gas Station Rugby Road, Lower Harlestone, Northampton, NN7 4ER
Tel: 01604-843359 **Fax:** 01604-843359
E-mail: admin@idealtanksandpumps.co.uk
Directors: M. Robinson (MD)
Immediate Holding Company: IDEAL TANKS & PUMPS LIMITED
Registration no: 00908631 **Date established:** 1967
No.of Employees: 1 - 10 **Product Groups:** 35, 42, 45

Date of Accounts	May 11	May 10	May 09
Working Capital	475	290	240
Fixed Assets	68	81	66
Current Assets	727	429	396

Igus (UK) Ltd
51A Caswell Road Brackmills Industrial Estate, Northampton, NN4 7PW
Tel: 01604-677240 **Fax:** 01604-677242
E-mail: sales_uk@igus.co.uk
Website: http://www.igus.co.uk
Bank(s): National Westminster Bank Plc
Directors: D. Chapman (Dir)
Managers: L. Wilkins (Product)
Ultimate Holding Company: Igus GmbH (Germany)
Registration no: 02600866 **Date established:** 1991 **Turnover:** £5m - £10m
No.of Employees: 21 - 50 **Product Groups:** 30, 35, 37, 45, 47, 48, 66

Date of Accounts	Dec 11	Dec 10	Dec 09
Sales Turnover	14m	11m	8m
Pre Tax Profit/Loss	2m	1m	432
Working Capital	2m	819	786
Fixed Assets	3m	3m	3m
Current Assets	5m	4m	3m
Current Liabilities	1m	1m	501

Independent Warranty Association
20 Billing Road, Northampton, NN1 5AW
Tel: 01604-604511 **Fax:** 01604-604512
E-mail: enquiries@iwa.biz
Website: http://www.iwa.biz
Bank(s): HSBC Bank plc
Directors: R. Hodgeson (Ptnr)
Registration no: 02953436 **VAT No.:** GB 581 4085 38
Turnover: £10m - £20m **No.of Employees:** 11 - 20 **Product Groups:** 82

Indespension Ltd
St Peters Way, Northampton, NN1 1SZ
Tel: 01604-259221 **Fax:** 01604-259223
E-mail: northampton@indespension.com
Website: http://www.indespension.com
Managers: D. Savage (Mgr)
Ultimate Holding Company: D.R.A. LTD
Immediate Holding Company: INDESPENSION LTD
Registration no: 02125263 **Date established:** 1987
Turnover: £20m - £50m **No.of Employees:** 1 - 10 **Product Groups:** 39

Date of Accounts	Jun 11	Jun 10	Jun 09
Sales Turnover	17m	15m	19m
Pre Tax Profit/Loss	550	192	137
Working Capital	2m	1m	2m
Fixed Assets	4m	5m	6m
Current Assets	8m	8m	8m
Current Liabilities	3m	527	783

Jackson Stops & Staff
20 Bridge Street, Northampton, NN1 1NR
Tel: 01604-632991 **Fax:** 01604-232613
E-mail: northampton@jackson-stops.co.uk
Website: http://www.jackson-stops.co.uk
Directors: Q. Jackson-Stops (Snr Part), R. Jones (Ptnr)
Managers: C. Wookey (Sales Prom Mgr)
Immediate Holding Company: PRESTON HOMES LIMITED
Registration no: 02072515 **Date established:** 2005
Turnover: Up to £250,000 **No.of Employees:** 11 - 20 **Product Groups:** 80

Date of Accounts	Mar 11	Mar 10	Mar 09
Sales Turnover	N/A	45	47
Pre Tax Profit/Loss	N/A	35	38
Working Capital	5	2	2
Current Assets	14	10	11
Current Liabilities	N/A	8	7

Jewson Ltd
31-33 St James Mill Road, Northampton, NN5 5JW
Tel: 01604-750707 **Fax:** 01604-756630
Website: http://www.jewson.co.uk
Bank(s): Barclays
Managers: S. Harm (District Mgr)
Ultimate Holding Company: COMPAGNIE DE SAINT GOBAIN (FRANCE)
Immediate Holding Company: JEWSON LIMITED
Registration no: 00348407 **VAT No.:** GB 497 7184 83
Date established: 1939 **Turnover:** £2m - £5m **No.of Employees:** 11 - 20
Product Groups: 66

Date of Accounts	Dec 11	Dec 10	Dec 09
Sales Turnover	1606m	1547m	1485m
Pre Tax Profit/Loss	18m	100m	45m
Working Capital	-345m	-250m	-349m
Fixed Assets	496m	387m	461m
Current Assets	657m	1005m	1320m
Current Liabilities	66m	120m	64m

Jewson Ltd
Spencer Bridge Road, Northampton, NN5 7DR
Tel: 01604-581214 **Fax:** 01604-759658
Website: http://www.jewson.co.uk
Managers: S. Kirwin (District Mgr)
Ultimate Holding Company: COMPAGNIE DE SAINT GOBAIN (FRANCE)
Immediate Holding Company: JEWSON LIMITED
Registration no: 00348407 **Date established:** 1939
Turnover: £500m - £1,000m **No.of Employees:** 1 - 10
Product Groups: 25, 66

Date of Accounts	Dec 11	Dec 10	Dec 09
Sales Turnover	1606m	1547m	1485m
Pre Tax Profit/Loss	18m	100m	45m
Working Capital	-345m	-250m	-349m
Fixed Assets	496m	387m	461m
Current Assets	657m	1005m	1320m
Current Liabilities	66m	120m	64m

Johnson & Starley Ltd
Rhosili Road Brackmills Industrial Estate, Northampton, NN4 7LZ
Tel: 01604-762881 **Fax:** 01604-767408
E-mail: info@johnsonandstarleyltd.co.uk
Website: http://www.johnsonandstarley.co.uk
Bank(s): Barclays
Directors: R. Haynes (Fin)
Managers: M. Millichamp (Tech Serv Mgr), A. Chinsang, C. Walsh (Purch Mgr)
Ultimate Holding Company: PETER GYLLENHAMMAR AB (SWEDEN)
Immediate Holding Company: JOHNSON & STARLEY LIMITED
Registration no: 00185924 **Date established:** 2022
Turnover: £10m - £20m **No.of Employees:** 51 - 100 **Product Groups:** 40, 52, 66

Date of Accounts	Jun 11	Jun 10	Jun 09
Sales Turnover	15m	15m	20m
Pre Tax Profit/Loss	2m	980	1m
Working Capital	7m	7m	6m
Fixed Assets	695	617	401
Current Assets	9m	8m	9m
Current Liabilities	668	386	2m

Karrimor Ltd
440 - 450 Cob Drive Swan Valley, Northampton, NN4 9BB
Tel: 0870-838 7300 **Fax:** 01254-893100
E-mail: info@sports-world.com
Website: http://www.karrimor.com
Managers: G. Bardsley (Sales Prom Mgr), M. Lee (I.T. Exec), N. Kennedy (Mgr), P. Rigby (Mgr)
Registration no: 05215974 **VAT No.:** GB 707 7863 05
Date established: 1952 **Turnover:** £10m - £20m **No.of Employees:** 1 - 10
Product Groups: 22, 24

Date of Accounts	Apr 08	Apr 07
Sales Turnover	1387	1853
Pre Tax Profit/Loss	N/A	24
Working Capital	909	1310
Fixed Assets	N/A	1
Current Assets	1068	1524
Current Liabilities	160	214
ROCE% (Return on Capital Employed)		1.8
ROT% (Return on Turnover)		1.3

Lab 3 Ltd
1 The Business Centre Ross Road, Weedon Road Industrial Estate, Northampton, NN5 5AX
Tel: 01604-581111 **Fax:** 0870-126 0350
E-mail: sales@lab3.co.uk
Website: http://www.lab3.co.uk
Bank(s): National Westminster Bank Plc
Directors: J. Short (Ch)
Ultimate Holding Company: THE SCIENTIFIC GROUP LIMITED
Immediate Holding Company: LAB 3 LIMITED
Registration no: 03956360 **Date established:** 2000 **Turnover:** £5m - £10m
No.of Employees: 21 - 50 **Product Groups:** 33, 38, 63, 65, 66

Date of Accounts	Dec 11	Dec 10	Dec 09
Sales Turnover	8m	8m	7m
Pre Tax Profit/Loss	640	749	427
Working Capital	2m	1m	1m
Fixed Assets	766	677	817
Current Assets	3m	3m	3m
Current Liabilities	667	696	524

Landmark Lifts Ltd
29 Charter Gate Quarry Park Close, Moulton Park Industrial Estate, Northampton, NN3 6QB
Tel: 01604-671007 **Fax:** 01604-495111
E-mail: enquiries@landmarklifts.co.uk
Website: http://www.landmarklifts.co.uk
Managers: D. Jones (Sales Prom Mgr)
Immediate Holding Company: LANDMARK LIFTS LIMITED
Registration no: 03493472 **Date established:** 1998 **Turnover:** £2m - £5m
No.of Employees: 11 - 20 **Product Groups:** 35, 39, 45

Date of Accounts	Mar 11	Mar 10	Mar 09
Sales Turnover	3m	3m	3m
Pre Tax Profit/Loss	312	667	254
Working Capital	647	512	50
Fixed Assets	76	55	32
Current Assets	1m	2m	976
Current Liabilities	504	759	557

LaserPerformance
Station Works Long Buckby, Northampton, NN6 7PF
Tel: 01327-841600 **Fax:** 01327-841651
E-mail: shop.uk@laserperformance.com
Website: http://www.lasersailing.com
Bank(s): Barclays
Directors: A. Hancock (Ch), M. Weiner (Fin), T. Coventry (MD)
Managers: P. Ewbank (I.T. Exec)
Ultimate Holding Company: Sina Ltd
Immediate Holding Company: Gavel Securities Ltd
Registration no: 00922893 **VAT No.:** GB 536 6541 33
Date established: 1967 **Turnover:** £10m - £20m
No.of Employees: 51 - 100 **Product Groups:** 39

Lennox Industries
Cornwell Business Park Salthouse Road, Brackmills, Northampton, NN4 7EX
Tel: 01604-669100 **Fax:** 01604-669150
E-mail: info.uk@lennoxeurope.com
Website: http://www.lennoxuk.com
Bank(s): Natwest, Northampton
Directors: A. Turbard (MD), B. Pestana (Sales), H. Longman (Fab), W. Burbidge (Fin), D. Birties (Dir), H. Bizios (Dir), P. Roorda (Fin)

see next page

Lennox Industries - Cont'd

Managers: J. Brunnock (Mktg Serv Mgr), L. Davis (Personnel), I. Roper (Sales & Mktg Mg), J. Brennock (Mktg Serv Mgr), R. James, S. Smith (Buyer), K. Bath (Comptroller)
Ultimate Holding Company: LENNOX INTERNATIONAL INC (USA)
Immediate Holding Company: DATATRADE LIMITED
Registration no: 00671868 **Date established:** 1980 **Turnover:** £5m - £10m
No.of Employees: 21 - 50 **Product Groups:** 37, 40, 52

Date of Accounts	Dec 06	Dec 05
Sales Turnover	6781	8130
Pre Tax Profit/Loss	-761	-1535
Working Capital	-2931	-2458
Fixed Assets	85	121
Current Assets	2313	3206
Current Liabilities	5244	5664
Total Share Capital	314	314
ROCE% (Return on Capital Employed)	26.7	65.7
ROT% (Return on Turnover)	-11.2	-18.9

Levcat Catering Equipment Ltd

7 Gate Lodge Close Round Spinney Industrial Estate, Northampton, NN3 8RJ
Tel: 01604-499881 **Fax:** 01604-499961
E-mail: lacatering@btconnect.com
Website: http://www.chinesecookers.com
Directors: C. Levett (MD)
Immediate Holding Company: LEVCAT CATERING EQUIPMENT LIMITED
Registration no: 07227190 **Date established:** 2010
Turnover: £500,000 - £1m **No.of Employees:** 1 - 10 **Product Groups:** 40

Date of Accounts	Mar 11
Working Capital	-2
Fixed Assets	4
Current Assets	49

Lifting Systems Ltd (A Division of Lifting Systems Ltd)

17 Osyth Close Brackmills Industrial Estate, Northampton, NN4 7DY
Tel: 01604-766777 **Fax:** 01604-766746
E-mail: info@lifting-systems.co.uk
Website: http://www.lifting-systems.co.uk
Bank(s): Barclays
Directors: S. Austin (Dir)
Managers: A. Fletcher (Chief Mgr)
Immediate Holding Company: LIFTING SYSTEMS LTD.
Registration no: 02995141 **VAT No.:** GB 623 7351 50
Date established: 1994 **Turnover:** £500,000 - £1m
No.of Employees: 21 - 50 **Product Groups:** 45, 48, 85

Date of Accounts	Dec 11	Dec 10	Dec 09
Working Capital	-323	-317	-190
Fixed Assets	858	636	509
Current Assets	886	610	541

Lindab Ltd

Unit 9-10 Carousel Way Riverside Business Park, Northampton, NN3 9HG
Tel: 01604-788350 **Fax:** 01604-788351
E-mail: sales@lindab.co.uk
Website: http://www.lindab.co.uk
Managers: M. Repo
Ultimate Holding Company: LINDAB INTERNATIONAL AB (SWEDEN)
Immediate Holding Company: LINDAB LIMITED
Registration no: 01641399 **Date established:** 1982
Turnover: £20m - £50m **No.of Employees:** 21 - 50 **Product Groups:** 36, 37, 48

Date of Accounts	Dec 11	Dec 10	Dec 09
Sales Turnover	51m	47m	49m
Pre Tax Profit/Loss	1m	-204	354
Working Capital	16m	-3m	-4m
Fixed Assets	16m	20m	22m
Current Assets	22m	20m	23m
Current Liabilities	1m	980	775

Llewellyn (Safety Advisors) Europe Ltd

Victory House 400 Pavilion Drive, Northampton Business Park, Northampton, NN4 7PA
Tel: 0845-6432852 **Fax:** 01604-521001
E-mail: enquiries@llewellyneurope.com
Website: http://www.llewellyneurope.com
Product Groups: 24, 54, 76, 80, 84, 86, 87

Date of Accounts	Sep 08	Sep 07	Sep 06
Working Capital	-5	-1	7
Fixed Assets	10	17	2
Current Assets	14	19	14
Current Liabilities	20	20	7

Logistics Works

Burrowdale Harborough Road, Maidwell, Northampton, NN6 9JA
Tel: 07771-806094
E-mail: enquiries@logisticsworks.co.uk
Website: http://www.logisticsworks.co.uk
Directors: C. Rabjohn (Prop)
Immediate Holding Company: LOGISTICS WORKS LIMITED
Registration no: 06688894 **Date established:** 2008
Turnover: Up to £250,000 **No.of Employees:** 1 - 10 **Product Groups:** 80, 84

Date of Accounts	Mar 12	Mar 11	Mar 10
Working Capital	56	52	44
Fixed Assets	1	N/A	N/A
Current Assets	84	77	69

Mann Electrical Services

3-4 Ryehill Court Lodge Farm Industrial Estate, Northampton, NN5 7EU
Tel: 01604-750202 **Fax:** 01604-750152
E-mail: projects@mannelectricalservices.co.uk
Website: http://www.mannelectricalservices.co.uk
Managers: R. Farmer (District Mgr)
Immediate Holding Company: MORGAN BENNETT GROUP
Registration no: 00844635 **VAT No.:** 272 6789 17 **Date established:** 1990
Turnover: £2m - £5m **No.of Employees:** 1 - 10 **Product Groups:** 52

Mawsley Machinery Ltd

Brixworth Industrial Estate Brixworth, Northampton, NN6 9UA
Tel: 01604-880621 **Fax:** 01604-881746
E-mail: sales@mawsley.com
Website: http://www.mawsley.com
Directors: K. Pearce (Dir)
Immediate Holding Company: MAWSLEY MACHINERY LIMITED
Registration no: 01522617 **Date established:** 1980
Turnover: £10m - £20m **No.of Employees:** 11 - 20 **Product Groups:** 45, 48, 67, 83

Date of Accounts	Mar 11	Mar 10	Mar 09
Pre Tax Profit/Loss	N/A	N/A	51
Working Capital	328	208	309
Fixed Assets	194	265	412
Current Assets	2m	1m	2m
Current Liabilities	N/A	N/A	142

Mediumz Ltd

Unit 12 Bondfield Avenue Industrial Estate, Northampton, NN2 7RD
Tel: 01604-710006
E-mail: info@mediumzltd.com
Website: http://www.mediumzltd.com
Directors: G. Griffiths (Dir)
Immediate Holding Company: MEDIUMZ LTD
Registration no: 05166061 **Date established:** 2004
No.of Employees: 1 - 10 **Product Groups:** 28, 37, 38

Date of Accounts	Mar 12	Mar 11	Mar 10
Working Capital	-1	-12	-9
Fixed Assets	35	18	14
Current Assets	79	53	55

Mercedes A M G

Morgan Drive Brixworth, Northampton, NN6 9GZ
Tel: 01604-880100 **Fax:** 01604-882800
E-mail: reception@mercedes-benz-hpe.com
Website: http://www.mercedes-amg-HPP.com
Bank(s): Lloyds TSB Bank plc
Directors: H. Maik (Prop)
Ultimate Holding Company: DAIMLER AKTIENGESELLSCHAFT (GERMANY)
Immediate Holding Company: MERCEDES AMG HIGH PERFORMANCE POWERTRAINS LIMITED
Registration no: 01760288 **VAT No.:** GB 387 6578 82
Date established: 1983 **Turnover:** £75m - £125m
No.of Employees: 501 - 1000 **Product Groups:** 39, 68

Date of Accounts	Dec 11	Dec 10	Dec 09
Sales Turnover	122m	82m	97m
Pre Tax Profit/Loss	5m	5m	5m
Working Capital	11m	-15m	-8m
Fixed Assets	100m	98m	101m
Current Assets	32m	25m	21m
Current Liabilities	6m	6m	18m

Millen Machine Tools Ltd

Hamilton House 126 St Georges Avenue, Northampton, NN2 6JF
Tel: 01604-721122 **Fax:** 01604- 721329
E-mail: harvey.millen@virgin.net
Directors: S. Hartman (Dir)
Immediate Holding Company: EDWIN MILLEN ESTATES LTD
Registration no: 00800156 **VAT No.:** GB 227 4099 57
Date established: 1964 **Turnover:** £1m - £2m **No.of Employees:** 1 - 10
Product Groups: 46, 67

Date of Accounts	Aug 11	Aug 10	Aug 09
Working Capital	730	1m	2m
Fixed Assets	2m	2m	1m
Current Assets	759	1m	2m

Modulex Systems Ltd

3 The Glades Grange Park, Northampton, NN4 5BS
Tel: 01604-684020 **Fax:** 01604-672161
E-mail: mxuk@modulex.co.uk
Website: http://www.modulex.co.uk
Bank(s): Danske Bank
Directors: J. Bellamy (MD), A. Jensen (Fin)
Managers: J. Murphy (Sales Prom Mgr)
Ultimate Holding Company: MODULEX AS (DENMARK)
Immediate Holding Company: MODULEX SYSTEMS LIMITED
Registration no: 01404746 **VAT No.:** GB 294 3711 43
Date established: 1978 **Turnover:** £1m - £2m **No.of Employees:** 21 - 50
Product Groups: 26, 37, 49

Date of Accounts	Dec 11	Dec 10	Dec 09
Sales Turnover	1m	2m	2m
Pre Tax Profit/Loss	65	101	33
Working Capital	832	787	721
Current Assets	940	1m	965
Current Liabilities	94	224	209

M T Associates

4 Harborough Road, Northampton, NN2 7AZ
Tel: 01604-711707 **Fax:** 01604-717991
Website: http://www.mtassociates.co.uk
Directors: M. Tew (Prop)
Date established: 2004 **No.of Employees:** 1 - 10 **Product Groups:** 35

N.I.M Ltd Engineering

Yardley House 100 Chase Park Road, Yardley Hastings, Northampton, NN7 1HF
Tel: 01604-696120 **Fax:** 01604-696122
E-mail: info@nimltdengineering.com
Website: http://www.nimltdengineering.com
Directors: L. Delany (MD)
No.of Employees: 1 - 10 **Product Groups:** 25, 33, 35

N R G Group Ltd

4 Rushmills, Northampton, NN4 7YB
Tel: 01604-732700 **Fax:** 01752-340173
Website: http://www.nrg-group.com
Directors: N. Palmer (MD)
Managers: H. Clayton (Mktg Serv Mgr)
Ultimate Holding Company: Ricoh Co. Ltd
Immediate Holding Company: Gestetner Holdings P.L.C.
Registration no: 02184499 **VAT No.:** GB 577 4168 05
Turnover: £1m - £2m **No.of Employees:** 251 - 500 **Product Groups:** 44

Date of Accounts	Mar 08	Mar 07	Mar 06
Sales Turnover	N/A	1372m	1022m
Pre Tax Profit/Loss	94000	35400	29300
Working Capital	1119m	273000	222500
Fixed Assets	445000	92000	100100
Current Assets	1246m	614100	528300
Current Liabilities	127000	341100	305800
Total Share Capital	50000	49700	49700
ROCE% (Return on Capital Employed)	6.0	9.7	9.1
ROT% (Return on Turnover)		2.6	2.9

Nemco Metals International Ltd

5 Pennard Close Brackmills Industrial Estate, Northampton, NN4 7BE
Tel: 01604-766181 **Fax:** 01276-61704
E-mail: fred.weyler@nemcometals.co.uk
Website: http://www.nemcometals.co.uk
Bank(s): National Westminster Bank Plc
Directors: F. Weyler (MD)
Managers: A. Hayhurst (Comm)
Ultimate Holding Company: WIELAND-WERKE AG (GERMANY)
Immediate Holding Company: WIELAND WERKE (U.K.) LIMITED
Registration no: 01182598 **VAT No.:** GB 523 1096 78
Date established: 1974 **Turnover:** £250,000 - £500,000
No.of Employees: 21 - 50 **Product Groups:** 34, 35, 36, 46

Date of Accounts	Sep 11	Sep 10	Sep 09
Sales Turnover	34m	28m	15m
Pre Tax Profit/Loss	2m	942	443
Working Capital	4m	4m	3m
Fixed Assets	2m	2m	2m
Current Assets	10m	9m	5m
Current Liabilities	1m	973	432

Nene Catering Equipment Ltd

19 Upper Priory Street Grafton Street Industrial Estate, Northampton, NN1 2PT
Tel: 01604-621555 **Fax:** 01604-621383
E-mail: gary@nenecateringequipment.co.uk
Directors: G. Adams (Dir), S. Lane (Co Sec)
Immediate Holding Company: NENE CATERING EQUIPMENT LIMITED
Registration no: 02934731 **Date established:** 1994
No.of Employees: 11 - 20 **Product Groups:** 20, 40, 41

Date of Accounts	Nov 10	Nov 09	Nov 08
Working Capital	35	61	123
Fixed Assets	35	44	55
Current Assets	412	306	400

Nene Storage Equipment Ltd

Nene House Station Road, Watford, Northampton, NN6 7XN
Tel: 01327-300456 **Fax:** 01327-300737
E-mail: enquiries@nene.co.uk
Website: http://www.nene.co.uk
Bank(s): Lloyds TSB
Directors: P. Fagan (MD)
Ultimate Holding Company: NENE GROUP PLC
Immediate Holding Company: NENE STORAGE EQUIPMENT LIMITED
Registration no: 01162468 **VAT No.:** 281 7914 34 **Date established:** 1974
Turnover: £5m - £10m **No.of Employees:** 11 - 20 **Product Groups:** 67

Date of Accounts	Dec 11	Dec 10	Dec 09
Sales Turnover	9m	7m	4m
Pre Tax Profit/Loss	492	-379	144
Working Capital	1m	749	1m
Fixed Assets	633	669	418
Current Assets	4m	3m	3m
Current Liabilities	705	355	219

The Networking Store Ltd

189 Main Road Duston, Northampton, NN5 6RD
Tel: 08443-573410 **Fax:** 08716-611524
E-mail: sales@network-cabling.co.uk
Website: http://www.network-cabling.co.uk/store
Directors: S. Pearson (MD)
Immediate Holding Company: THE NETWORKING STORE LIMITED
Registration no: 07184732 **Date established:** 2010
No.of Employees: 1 - 10 **Product Groups:** 37, 52, 67, 84

Date of Accounts	May 11
Working Capital	3
Current Assets	61

Norbert Dentressangle UK Ltd

Norbert House Lodge Way, Lodge Farm Industrial Estate, Northampton, NN5 7SL
Tel: 01604-737100 **Fax:** 01698-833122
E-mail: david.lynch@norbert-dentressangle.co.uk
Website: http://www.norbert-dentressangle.co.uk
Bank(s): Bank of Scotland
Directors: D. Lynch (Co Sec)
Ultimate Holding Company: NORBERT DENTRESSANGLE SA (FRANCE)
Immediate Holding Company: SALVESEN LOGISTICS LIMITED
Registration no: 00346268 **VAT No.:** GB 581 3791 23
Date established: 1938 **No.of Employees:** 101 - 250 **Product Groups:** 72, 77, 84

Date of Accounts	Dec 11	Dec 10	Dec 09
Pre Tax Profit/Loss	707	-1m	4m
Working Capital	195m	202m	208m
Fixed Assets	10	10	10
Current Assets	197m	202m	210m
Current Liabilities	430	148	2m

Northampton Gauging Services

Hillside Road Flore, Northampton, NN7 4NA
Tel: 01327-341598 **Fax:** 01327-342529
E-mail: n.gauge@virgin.net
Website: http://www.gaugingservices.co.uk
Directors: R. Clarke (Prop)
Date established: 1978 **No.of Employees:** 1 - 10 **Product Groups:** 38

Northampton Gun Co.

136 St James Road, Northampton, NN5 5LQ
Tel: 01604-751206 **Fax:** 01604-751206
E-mail: sales@northamptongun.co.uk
Website: http://www.northamptongun.co.uk
Managers: A. Gibbins (Mgr)
Date established: 1983 **No.of Employees:** 1 - 10 **Product Groups:** 36, 39, 40

Northampton & Midland Plating Co. Ltd

6 Connaught Street, Northampton, NN1 3BP
Tel: 01604-631372 **Fax:** 01604-604940
E-mail: nmpsupplier@googlemail.com
Website: http://www.nmpltd.co.uk
Directors: E. Patrick (Dir)
Immediate Holding Company: NORTHAMPTON AND MIDLAND PLATING COMPANY LIMITED
Registration no: 00433281 **Date established:** 1947
Turnover: £500,000 - £1m **No.of Employees:** 1 - 10 **Product Groups:** 46, 48

Date of Accounts	Apr 08	Apr 07	Apr 06
Working Capital	100	86	74
Fixed Assets	148	156	167
Current Assets	238	210	323
Current Liabilities	138	125	248
Total Share Capital	4	4	4

Northamptonshire Chamber Of Commerce
Opus House Anglia Way, Moulton Park Industrial Estate, Northampton, NN3 6JA
Tel: 01604-490490 **Fax:** 01604-670362
E-mail: membership@northants-chamber.co.uk
Website: http://www.northants-chamber.co.uk
Bank(s): HSBC
Directors: P. Griffiths (Grp Chief Exec)
Immediate Holding Company: NORTHAMPTONSHIRE CHAMBER OF COMMERCE
Registration no: 04043116 **Date established:** 2000
No.of Employees: 11 - 20 **Product Groups:** 87

Date of Accounts	Mar 12	Mar 11	Mar 10
Working Capital	-0	-0	-0

Northants Precision Grinding Ltd
12 Tenter Road Moulton Park Industrial Estate, Northampton, NN3 6PZ
Tel: 01604-648772 **Fax:** 01604-642851
E-mail: sales@northantsgrinding.co.uk
Website: http://www.northantsgrinding.co.uk
Directors: J. Madden (Fin)
Immediate Holding Company: NORTHANTS PRECISION GRINDING LIMITED
Registration no: 00725392 **Date established:** 1962
No.of Employees: 1 - 10 **Product Groups:** 46, 48

Date of Accounts	May 11	May 10	May 09
Working Capital	71	83	191
Fixed Assets	45	54	74
Current Assets	120	124	224

The Office Based In Town
Beckett House 14 Billing Road, Northampton, NN1 5AW
Tel: 01604-632779 **Fax:** 01595-696577
E-mail: sales@theoffice-uk.co.uk
Website: http://www.theoffice-uk.co.uk
Directors: G. Fuchs (Dir)
Immediate Holding Company: HARYL (1991) LIMITED
Registration no: 04478804 **VAT No.:** GB 620 1873 68
Date established: 1989 **Turnover:** Up to £250,000
No.of Employees: 1 - 10 **Product Groups:** 80

Date of Accounts	Mar 11	Mar 10	Mar 09
Working Capital	-49	-22	-44
Fixed Assets	2m	2m	2m
Current Assets	117	125	121

Opus Energy Ltd
Summerhouse Road Moulton Park Industrial Estate, Northampton, NN3 6BJ
Tel: 08453-302655
E-mail: contactus@opusenergy.com
Website: http://www.opusenergy.co.uk
Managers: K. Poulter (Mktg Serv Mgr)
Ultimate Holding Company: OPUS ENERGY GROUP LIMITED
Immediate Holding Company: OPUS ENERGY LIMITED
Registration no: 04382246 **Date established:** 2002
No.of Employees: 51 - 100 **Product Groups:** 18

Date of Accounts	Mar 12	Mar 11	Mar 10
Sales Turnover	207m	169m	151m
Pre Tax Profit/Loss	11m	13m	9m
Working Capital	19m	19m	16m
Fixed Assets	2m	616	341
Current Assets	40m	36m	34m
Current Liabilities	13m	15m	17m

Pager Call Systems Ltd
PO Box 240, Northampton, NN5 6WZ
Tel: 08456-444109 **Fax:** 08456-444108
E-mail: enquiries@pagercall.co.uk
Website: http://www.pagercall.co.uk
Managers: S. Department (Sales Prom Mgr)
Immediate Holding Company: PAGER CALL SYSTEMS LIMITED
Registration no: 06667049 **Date established:** 2008 **Turnover:** £1m - £2m
No.of Employees: 1 - 10 **Product Groups:** 37, 67

Date of Accounts	Aug 11	Aug 10	Aug 09
Working Capital	16	16	-2
Fixed Assets	1	N/A	N/A
Current Assets	68	72	35

Paladon Systems Ltd
Ferro Fields Brixworth, Northampton, NN6 9UA
Tel: 01604-880700 **Fax:** 01224-772868
E-mail: matthew.shepherd@paladonsystems.com
Website: http://www.paladonsystems.com
Bank(s): Midland
Managers: J. Grant (Develop Mgr), M. Shepherd (Mktg Serv Mgr)
Immediate Holding Company: PALADON SYSTEMS LIMITED
Registration no: 01592919 **VAT No.:** GB 336 4172 64
Date established: 1981 **Turnover:** £5m - £10m **No.of Employees:** 21 - 50
Product Groups: 37, 38

Date of Accounts	Sep 11	Sep 10	Sep 09
Working Capital	24	215	100
Fixed Assets	506	514	519
Current Assets	1m	1m	2m

Park Scientific Ltd
24 Low Farm Place Moulton Park Industrial Estate, Northampton, NN3 6HY
Tel: 01604-646495 **Fax:** 01604-648241
E-mail: andrew.lett@parkscientific.com
Website: http://www.parkscientific.com
Directors: M. Parry (Fin), A. Lett (MD)
Managers: P. Story (Warehouse Mgr)
Immediate Holding Company: PARK SCIENTIFIC LIMITED
Registration no: 01539971 **Date established:** 1981
Turnover: Up to £250,000 **No.of Employees:** 1 - 10 **Product Groups:** 31, 32, 66

Date of Accounts	Mar 10	Mar 09	Mar 08
Working Capital	82	159	124
Fixed Assets	6	11	15
Current Assets	278	340	472

Pavilion Textiles Ltd
17 Gate Lodge Close Round Spinney, Northampton, NN3 8RJ
Tel: 01604-741111 **Fax:** 01604-670611
E-mail: contact@paviliontextiles.com
Website: http://www.paviliontextiles.com
Directors: R. Sherburn (Co Sec), T. Fraser (Dir)
Registration no: 02370500 **No.of Employees:** 21 - 50 **Product Groups:** 23

Pianoforte Supplies Ltd
Simplex Works Ashton Road, Roade, Northampton, NN7 2LG
Tel: 01604-862441 **Fax:** 01604-862427
E-mail: davidm@psluk.co.uk
Website: http://www.psluk.co.uk
Bank(s): Barclays
Directors: C. Wilson (I.T. Dir), D. Mobbs (Co Sec), D. Mobbs (Fin), R. Howkins (Grp Chief Exec)
Managers: K. Betts (Purch Mgr), W. Mack (Sales & Mktg Mg), S. Conway (Personnel)
Immediate Holding Company: PIANOFORTE SUPPLIES LIMITED
Registration no: 01680544 **Date established:** 1982 **Turnover:** £2m - £5m
No.of Employees: 51 - 100 **Product Groups:** 29, 30, 34, 36, 39, 48, 66

Piroto Labelling Ltd
9 Pond Wood Close Moulton Park Industrial Estate, Northampton, NN3 6RT
Tel: 01604-646600 **Fax:** 01604-492090
E-mail: l.mann@piroto-labelling.com
Website: http://www.piroto-labelling.com
Bank(s): Bank Of Scotland
Directors: A. Mann (Fin), L. Mann (MD)
Managers: A. Harris, D. Cassidy (Tech Serv Mgr), B. Hadwin (Sales Admin)
Ultimate Holding Company: MANNERING EUROPE LIMITED
Immediate Holding Company: PIROTO LABELLING LIMITED
Registration no: 01092907 **VAT No.:** GB 228 1604 79
Date established: 1973 **Turnover:** £2m - £5m **No.of Employees:** 21 - 50
Product Groups: 27, 28, 30, 35

Date of Accounts	Dec 11	Dec 10	Dec 09
Working Capital	1m	1m	1m
Fixed Assets	364	377	384
Current Assets	2m	2m	2m

Pittam Fabrications
102 Bunting Road, Northampton, NN2 6EE
Tel: 01604-719669
Website: http://www.rogertarry.com
No.of Employees: 1 - 10 **Product Groups:** 35, 44, 52

Plastic ID
2 Redhouse Square, Duncan Close Moulton Park, Northampton, NN3 6WL
Tel: 0844-7361563 **Fax:** 0844-7362793
E-mail: sales@plastic-id.com
Website: http://www.plastic-id.com
Directors: S. Jones (MD)
Registration no: 6489739 **Date established:** 2008 **Turnover:**
No.of Employees: 1 - 10 **Product Groups:** 28, 30, 37, 38, 40, 44, 49, 81

Portman Asset Finance Ltd
18 Osyth Close Brackmills Industrial Estate, Northampton, NN4 7DY
Tel: 08448-008825 **Fax:** 0844-800 8826
E-mail: info@portmanassetfinance.co.uk
Website: http://www.portmanassetfinance.co.uk
Directors: A. Read (Dir)
Immediate Holding Company: PORTMAN ASSET FINANCE LIMITED
Registration no: 06226530 **Date established:** 2007 **Turnover:** £1m - £2m
No.of Employees: 1 - 10 **Product Groups:** 82

Date of Accounts	Sep 12	Sep 11	Sep 10
Sales Turnover	N/A	1m	572
Pre Tax Profit/Loss	N/A	311	104
Working Capital	560	268	116
Fixed Assets	44	52	50
Current Assets	890	414	194
Current Liabilities	N/A	135	63

Prestige Cutters
Pond Wood Close Moulton Park Industrial Estate, Northampton, NN3 6RT
Tel: 01604-790037 **Fax:** 01604-499287
Directors: J. Connor (Prop)
Immediate Holding Company: PRESTIGE CUTTERS LIMITED
Registration no: 04774768 **Date established:** 2003
No.of Employees: 1 - 10 **Product Groups:** 46

Date of Accounts	Apr 11	Apr 10	Apr 09
Working Capital	-36	-15	16
Fixed Assets	37	40	44
Current Assets	45	44	56

Alan Pritchard
28 Deancourt Drive, Northampton, NN5 6PY
Tel: 01604-583580 **Fax:** 01604-583580
E-mail: pritcharda2@sky.com
Directors: A. Pritchard (Prop)
Date established: 2000 **No.of Employees:** 1 - 10 **Product Groups:** 41

Pyramid Packaging & Finishing Solutions Ltd
1 Crofton Court Owl Close, Moulton Park Indl-Est, Northampton, NN3 6HZ
Tel: 01604-492662 **Fax:** 01604-492005
E-mail: pyramid.packaging@virgin.net
Directors: R. Field (MD)
Managers: M. Lester (Mgr)
Immediate Holding Company: PYRAMID PACKAGING & FINISHING SOLUTIONS LIMITED
Registration no: 04372978 **Date established:** 2002
No.of Employees: 1 - 10 **Product Groups:** 38, 42

Date of Accounts	Mar 10	Mar 09	Mar 08
Working Capital	42	27	23
Fixed Assets	2	4	3
Current Assets	60	49	60

Quinton Major Precision Ltd
Rhosili Road Brackmills Industrial Estate, Northampton, NN4 7JE
Tel: 01604-766400 **Fax:** 01604-769017
E-mail: enquiries@quinton-major.co.uk
Website: http://www.quinton-major.co.uk
Bank(s): National Westminster
Directors: F. Clark (Dir)
Immediate Holding Company: QUINTON MAJOR PRECISION LIMITED
Registration no: 01610411 **VAT No.:** GB 336 3835 47
Date established: 1982 **Turnover:** £2m - £5m **No.of Employees:** 21 - 50
Product Groups: 39, 48

Date of Accounts	Mar 11	Mar 10	Mar 09
Sales Turnover	N/A	2m	N/A
Pre Tax Profit/Loss	N/A	11	N/A
Working Capital	381	290	262
Fixed Assets	110	153	211
Current Assets	2m	1m	693
Current Liabilities	N/A	300	N/A

R G Engineering
54 Dunster Street, Northampton, NN1 3JY
Tel: 01604-639673 **Fax:** 01604-639673
E-mail: rgengineering@btopenworld.com
Directors: R. Grainger (MD)
Registration no: 00447046 **VAT No.:** GB 294 3672 27
Date established: 1976 **Turnover:** Up to £250,000
No.of Employees: 1 - 10 **Product Groups:** 30

R S M Castings Ltd
7 North Portway Close Round Spinney Industrial Estate, Northampton, NN3 8RQ
Tel: 01604-671333 **Fax:** 01604-491012
E-mail: sales@rsm-castings.co.uk
Website: http://www.rsm-castings.co.uk
Bank(s): National Westminster Bank Plc
Directors: K. Danns (Fab)
Managers: J. Bishop (Comptroller)
Immediate Holding Company: R S M CASTINGS LIMITED
Registration no: 01184461 **VAT No.:** GB 121 8536 85
Date established: 1974 **Turnover:** £2m - £5m **No.of Employees:** 51 - 100
Product Groups: 34

Date of Accounts	Dec 11	Dec 10	Dec 09
Sales Turnover	N/A	N/A	4m
Pre Tax Profit/Loss	N/A	N/A	-265
Working Capital	244	-43	-199
Fixed Assets	2m	2m	2m
Current Assets	2m	1m	922
Current Liabilities	216	222	151

Radio Structures Ltd
T R S Complex Gate Lodge Close, Round Spinney Industrial Estate, Northampton, NN3 8RJ
Tel: 01604-790005 **Fax:** 01604-790797
E-mail: sales@radiostructures.com
Website: http://www.radiostructures.com
Directors: E. Jones (Fin), G. Jones (Sales)
Immediate Holding Company: RADIO STRUCTURES LIMITED
Registration no: 01695386 **Date established:** 1983
No.of Employees: 1 - 10 **Product Groups:** 35, 37, 67, 79

Date of Accounts	Mar 12	Mar 11	Mar 10
Working Capital	226	171	136
Fixed Assets	132	133	134
Current Assets	312	280	275

Real World Designs Ltd
Unit 2-3 Adams House Northampton Science Park Kings Park Road, Moulton Park Industrial Estate, Northampton, NN3 6LG
Tel: 01604-654293
E-mail: sales@realworlddesigns.co.uk
Website: http://www.realworlddesigns.co.uk
Directors: R. Weatherley (MD)
Immediate Holding Company: REAL WORLD DESIGNS LIMITED
Registration no: 04719741 **Date established:** 2003
No.of Employees: 1 - 10 **Product Groups:** 37, 67

Date of Accounts	Mar 11	Mar 10	Mar 09
Working Capital	-26	25	-540
Fixed Assets	68	73	74
Current Assets	211	221	172

Redbreast Industrial Equipment Ltd
1 Staveley Way Brixworth Industrial Estate, Brixworth, Northampton, NN6 9EU
Tel: 01604-882088 **Fax:** 01604-882015
E-mail: sales@redbreastrobin.co.uk
Bank(s): Barclays
Directors: P. Finch (Comm), S. Hewson (Dir), D. Hewson (Fin)
Immediate Holding Company: REDBREAST INDUSTRIAL EQUIPMENT LIMITED
Registration no: 01773646 **VAT No.:** GB 387 6542 06
Date established: 1983 **Turnover:** £2m - £5m **No.of Employees:** 11 - 20
Product Groups: 37, 40

Date of Accounts	Dec 07	Dec 06	Dec 05
Working Capital	181	251	223
Fixed Assets	45	40	72
Current Assets	774	643	662
Current Liabilities	593	392	440
Total Share Capital	15	15	15

Reed Specialist Recruitment
7 Fish Street, Northampton, NN1 2AA
Tel: 01604-636644 **Fax:** 01604-629381
E-mail: northampton.employment@reed.co.uk
Website: http://www.reed.co.uk
Managers: E. Potts (District Mgr)
Ultimate Holding Company: REED GLOBAL LTD (MALTA)
Immediate Holding Company: REED EMPLOYMENT LIMITED
Registration no: 00669854 **Date established:** 1960
Turnover: £250m - £500m **No.of Employees:** 1 - 10 **Product Groups:** 80

Date of Accounts	Jun 11	Jun 10	Dec 07
Sales Turnover	618	450	287m
Pre Tax Profit/Loss	-2m	310	8m
Working Capital	23m	28m	28m
Fixed Assets	31	36	5m
Current Assets	28m	30m	74m
Current Liabilities	37	29	21m

Reldale Ltd
60 Dunster Street, Northampton, NN1 3JY
Tel: 01604-632438 **Fax:** 01604-632438
E-mail: enquiries@reldaleltd.co.uk
Website: http://www.reldaleltd.co.uk
Directors: N. Lawrence (Dir)
Immediate Holding Company: RELDALE LIMITED
Registration no: 01377309 **VAT No.:** GB 461 0825 66
Date established: 1978 **Turnover:** £250,000 - £500,000
No.of Employees: 1 - 10 **Product Groups:** 48

Date of Accounts	Mar 11	Mar 10	Mar 09
Working Capital	-24	-27	-15
Fixed Assets	5	6	6
Current Assets	85	76	85

Ridge Tool UK - Division Of Emerson
Ridge Tool PO Box 893, Crick, Northampton, NN6 7TY
Tel: 08082-389869 **Fax:** 0808-238 9904
E-mail: sales.uk@ridgid.com
Website: http://www.ridgid.eu

see next page

***Ridge Tool UK - Division Of Emerson** - Cont'd*

Directors: B. Reynolds (Sales)
Managers: J. Muckle (Mgr), K. Crimle (Contrlr)
Immediate Holding Company: RIDGE TOOL EUROPE N.V. (BELGIUM)
Registration no: 02294158 **Date established:** 1988
No.of Employees: 1 - 10 **Product Groups:** 40, 46

Rigiflex Extrusions Ltd

Ibex Barn Ferro Fields Scaldwell Road Industrial Estate, Brixworth, Northampton, NN6 9UA
Tel: 01604-880217 **Fax:** 01604-880129
E-mail: sales@rigiflexextrusions.co.uk
Website: http://www.rigiflexextrusions.com
Bank(s): National Westminster
Directors: T. Hawkins (Dir)
Immediate Holding Company: RIGIFLEX EXTRUSIONS LIMITED
Registration no: 02516792 **Date established:** 1990
Turnover: £500,000 - £1m **No.of Employees:** 11 - 20 **Product Groups:** 30

Date of Accounts	Mar 12	Mar 11	Mar 10
Working Capital	291	231	1m
Fixed Assets	148	151	155
Current Assets	625	482	1m

Robert Horne Group

Huntsman House Mansion Close, Moulton Park Industrial Estate, Northampton, NN3 6RU
Tel: 08444-777644 **Fax:** 023-8061 0005
E-mail: rh.eastleigh@roberthorne.co.uk
Website: http://www.roberthorne.co.uk
Managers: G. Dunne (Mgr)
Ultimate Holding Company: PAPERLINX LIMITED (AUSTRALIA)
Immediate Holding Company: ROBERT HORNE GROUP LIMITED
Registration no: 00584756 **VAT No.:** GB 235 7221 76
Date established: 1957 **No.of Employees:** 251 - 500 **Product Groups:** 66

Date of Accounts	Jun 11	Jun 10	Jun 09
Sales Turnover	303m	303m	301m
Pre Tax Profit/Loss	222	-6m	-313
Working Capital	61m	66m	71m
Fixed Assets	22m	23m	22m
Current Assets	126m	129m	137m
Current Liabilities	8m	5m	5m

Ronson Incorporated Ltd

Station Works Station Road Long Buckby, Northampton, NN6 7PF
Tel: 01327-841500 **Fax:** 01327-841501
Website: http://www.ronson.com
Directors: P. Hulme (Fin), S. Russell (MD)
Managers: M. Looney (Mktg Serv Mgr)
Ultimate Holding Company: AMY HOLDINGS LIMITED
Immediate Holding Company: RONSON INCORPORATED LIMITED
Registration no: 05701604 **VAT No.:** 424 4909 50 **Date established:** 2006
Turnover: £5m - £10m **No.of Employees:** 1 - 10 **Product Groups:** 62

Rooksmere Studios

Sywell Road Overstone, Northampton, NN6 0AG
Tel: 01604-495310 **Fax:** 01604-643382
E-mail: info@rooksmerestudios.com
Website: http://www.rooksmerestudios.com
Directors: M. Hutchinson (Prop)
Date established: 2002 **Turnover:** Up to £250,000
No.of Employees: 1 - 10 **Product Groups:** 89

Rushton Ablett Ltd

Arthur Street, Northampton, NN2 6DX
Tel: 01604-715474 **Fax:** 01604-791069
E-mail: ianf@rablett.co.uk
Website: http://www.jujujellies.co.uk
Directors: I. Ferris (MD)
Managers: D. Mason (Fin Mgr)
Immediate Holding Company: RUSHTON ABLETT LIMITED
Registration no: 02725688 **Date established:** 1992
Turnover: £10m - £20m **No.of Employees:** 21 - 50 **Product Groups:** 22

Date of Accounts	Dec 11	Mar 11	Mar 10
Sales Turnover	13m	15m	13m
Pre Tax Profit/Loss	2m	608	301
Working Capital	3m	2m	2m
Fixed Assets	116	164	188
Current Assets	6m	5m	4m
Current Liabilities	859	499	435

Russell Services

Rear of The Firs Queen Street, Weedon, Northampton, NN7 4RA
Tel: 01327-340847 **Fax:** 01327-340847
Website: http://www.russellservices.co.uk
Directors: D. Russell (Prop)
Date established: 1986 **No.of Employees:** 1 - 10 **Product Groups:** 46, 48

Ryan Plastics Ltd

Units 2-3 Mallard Close, Earls Barton, Northampton, NN6 0JF
Tel: 01604-811395 **Fax:** 01604-812872
E-mail: sales@ryanplastics.co.uk
Website: http://www.ryanplastics.co.uk
Directors: J. Ryan (MD)
Immediate Holding Company: RYAN PLASTICS LIMITED
Registration no: 03250598 **Date established:** 1996
Turnover: £500,000 - £1m **No.of Employees:** 1 - 10 **Product Groups:** 30, 48, 66

Date of Accounts	Sep 11	Sep 10	Sep 09
Working Capital	85	-25	80
Fixed Assets	204	176	70
Current Assets	207	44	134

S P X UK Ltd

Ironstone Way Brixworth, Northampton, NN6 9UD
Tel: 01327-303400 **Fax:** 01327-871625
E-mail: sales@servicesolutions.spx.com
Website: http://www.spx.com
Managers: A. Davies, S. Heath (Fin Mgr)
Ultimate Holding Company: SPX CORPORATION INC (USA)
Immediate Holding Company: SPX FLOW TECHNOLOGY LIMITED
Registration no: 02813467 **Date established:** 1993
Turnover: £20m - £50m **No.of Employees:** 21 - 50 **Product Groups:** 32, 33, 35, 36, 38, 39, 40, 41, 42, 43, 44, 45, 48, 66

Date of Accounts	Dec 11	Dec 10	Dec 09
Sales Turnover	40m	30m	43m
Pre Tax Profit/Loss	3m	-1m	4m
Working Capital	18m	15m	15m
Fixed Assets	2m	2m	3m
Current Assets	29m	26m	25m
Current Liabilities	3m	4m	3m

SANO TOOLS

8 Low Farm Place Moulton Park Industrial Estate, Northampton, NN3 6HY
Tel: 01604-947179 **Fax:** 01604-521070
E-mail: office@sanotools.com
Website: http://www.sanotools.com
Directors: B. Francis (Ptnr)
Immediate Holding Company: SPECTRUM LINGUISTICS & PERFORMANCE DEVELOPMENT LTD
Date established: 2010 **Turnover:** £250,000 - £500,000
No.of Employees: 1 - 10 **Product Groups:** 46

Sca Foam Products (Formerly Tuscarora)

Cornhill Close Lodge Farm Industrial Estate, Northampton, NN5 7UB
Tel: 01604-596800 **Fax:** 01604-759024
E-mail: jonathan.haddock@sca.com
Website: http://www.scafoamproducts.co.uk
Bank(s): National Westminster Bank Plc
Directors: A. Tillson (Fin), J. Haddock (Dir)
Managers: J. Adams (Mktg Serv Mgr), J. Cant (Sales Prom Mgr)
Immediate Holding Company: KIPPER PROPERTY LLP
Registration no: 00053913 **VAT No.:** GB 705 3135 70
Date established: 2007 **No.of Employees:** 51 - 100 **Product Groups:** 07, 27, 30, 84, 85

Scott Fowler Solicitors

Old Church Chambers 23-24 Sandhill Road, Northampton, NN5 5LH
Tel: 01604-750506 **Fax:** 01604-751960
E-mail: r.fowler@scott-fowler.co.uk
Website: http://www.scottfowler.com
Bank(s): Royal Bank of Scotland
Directors: R. Fowler (Ptnr)
Immediate Holding Company: LYNCREST PROPERTIES LIMITED
Registration no: 04733041 **Date established:** 1988
Turnover: £500,000 - £1m **No.of Employees:** 21 - 50 **Product Groups:** 80

Date of Accounts	Feb 12	Feb 11	Feb 10
Working Capital	-261	-269	-283
Fixed Assets	956	1m	1m
Current Assets	47	42	20

Setech Solutions Ltd

53A High Street Bugbrooke, Northampton, NN7 3PG
Tel: 01604-832623 **Fax:** 01604-832623
E-mail: info@setechsolutions.com
Website: http://www.setechsolutions.com
Directors: S. Evans (Dir)
Immediate Holding Company: SETECH SOLUTIONS LTD
Registration no: 05169254 **Date established:** 2004
No.of Employees: 1 - 10 **Product Groups:** 37, 38, 85

Date of Accounts	Jul 11	Jul 10	Jul 08
Working Capital	8	5	7
Current Assets	39	30	28

Shoosmiths

5 The Lakes, Northampton, NN4 7SH
Tel: 0370-086 3000 **Fax:** 01604-543543
E-mail: northampton@shoosmiths.co.uk
Website: http://www.shoosmiths.co.uk
Managers: K. Carter
Immediate Holding Company: BEVERLEY MEWS RESIDENTS COMPANY LTD
Registration no: 03523996 **Date established:** 1845
Turnover: £20m - £50m **No.of Employees:** 51 - 100 **Product Groups:** 80

Sidaplax-Plastic Suppliers Inc

7 Harrowden Road Brackmills Industrial Estate, Northampton, NN4 7EB
Tel: 01604-766699 **Fax:** 01604-766768
E-mail: barnard@sidaplax.co.uk
Website: http://www.sidaplax.com
Managers: C. Barnard (Chief Mgr)
Immediate Holding Company: SIDAPLAX-PLASTIC SUPPLIERS,INC.
Registration no: FC015744 **Date established:** 1990 **Turnover:** £2m - £5m
No.of Employees: 1 - 10 **Product Groups:** 30

Date of Accounts	Nov 06
Sales Turnover	6460
Pre Tax Profit/Loss	180
Working Capital	2250
Fixed Assets	150
Current Assets	2640
Current Liabilities	390
Total Share Capital	30
ROCE% (Return on Capital Employed)	7.5

Howard Smith Paper Ltd

Sovereign House Rhosili Road, Brackmills Industrial Estate, Northampton, NN4 7JE
Tel: 08456-082370 **Fax:** 08706-082373
E-mail: marketing@hspg.com
Website: http://www.hspg.com
Bank(s): Barclays, PO Box 544, 54 Lombard St, London EC3V 9EX
Directors: M. Lane Ley (MD), M. Lane-Ley (MD)
Ultimate Holding Company: PAPERLINX LIMITED (AUSTRALIA)
Immediate Holding Company: HOWARD SMITH PAPER LIMITED
Registration no: 00744570 **VAT No.:** GB 581 1902 47
Date established: 1962 **Turnover:** £125m - £250m
No.of Employees: 21 - 50 **Product Groups:** 27, 28, 61, 66

Date of Accounts	Jun 11	Jun 10	Jun 09
Working Capital	2m	2m	2m
Current Assets	2m	2m	2m

Solutions Group

2 Redbourn Park Liliput Road, Brackmills Industrial Estate, Northampton, NN4 7DT
Tel: 08456-444000 **Fax:** 01604-664561
E-mail: info@solutionsgroup-plc.com
Website: http://www.solutionsgroup-plc.com
Managers: D. Holmes (Tech Serv Mgr), G. Lester (Mgr), J. Osbourne, K. Aldred (Buyer), C. Cooper (Personnel)
Ultimate Holding Company: GL & JK INVESTMENTS LIMITED
Immediate Holding Company: SOLUTIONS GROUP (U.K.) PLC
Registration no: 02565454 **Date established:** 1990
Turnover: £10m - £20m **No.of Employees:** 51 - 100 **Product Groups:** 37

Date of Accounts	May 12	May 11	May 10
Sales Turnover	8m	14m	16m
Pre Tax Profit/Loss	222	197	189
Working Capital	2m	2m	1m
Fixed Assets	126	170	180
Current Assets	4m	5m	5m
Current Liabilities	757	578	2m

Springline Ltd

Pond Wood Close Moulton Park Industrial Estate, Northampton, NN3 6RT
Tel: 01604-644961 **Fax:** 01604-495090
E-mail: sales@springline.net
Website: http://www.springline.net
Directors: K. Tipping (Dir)
Immediate Holding Company: SPRING LINE LIMITED
Registration no: 01656991 **Date established:** 1982
Turnover: £250,000 - £500,000 **No.of Employees:** 11 - 20
Product Groups: 22, 43

Date of Accounts	Dec 11	Dec 10	Dec 09
Working Capital	177	162	131
Fixed Assets	105	107	122
Current Assets	313	307	235

Stagecoach Ltd

Rothersthorpe Avenue Rothersthorpe Avenue Ind Estate, Northampton, NN4 8UT
Tel: 01604-662266 **Fax:** 01604-702812
Website: http://www.stagecoachbus.com
Directors: S. Burd (MD), A. Whitnall (Co Sec)
Ultimate Holding Company: STAGECOACH GROUP PLC
Immediate Holding Company: STAGECOACH LIMITED
Registration no: 03092390 **Date established:** 1995
No.of Employees: 21 - 50 **Product Groups:** 72

Date of Accounts	Apr 11	Apr 10	Apr 09
Pre Tax Profit/Loss	-251	-240	-531
Working Capital	-13	203	412
Current Assets	2m	2m	2m

Stantone Mechanical Handling Ltd

3 Rothersthorpe Avenue Rothersthorpe Avenue Ind Estate, Northampton, NN4 8JW
Tel: 01604-761001 **Fax:** 01604-762318
E-mail: richard.barkworth@stantonemechanical.com
Website: http://www.stantonemechanical.com
Directors: R. Barkworth (Sales)
Immediate Holding Company: STANTONE MECHANICAL HANDLING LIMITED
Registration no: 00684018 **Date established:** 1961
No.of Employees: 1 - 10 **Product Groups:** 35, 39, 45

Date of Accounts	Feb 12	Feb 11	Feb 10
Working Capital	200	172	202
Fixed Assets	128	88	115
Current Assets	372	271	286

StanTronic Instruments

53A High Street Bugbrooke, Northampton, NN7 3PG
Tel: 01604-832521 **Fax:** 01604-832521
E-mail: info@stantronic.co.uk
Website: http://www.stantronic.co.uk
Managers: S. Evans (Chief Mgr)
Immediate Holding Company: STANTRONIC INSTRUMENTS (UK) LTD
Registration no: 07741130 **Date established:** 2011
No.of Employees: 1 - 10 **Product Groups:** 38

Stertil UK Ltd

Caswell Road Brackmills Industrial Estate, Northampton, NN4 7PW
Tel: 08707-700471 **Fax:** 01604-765181
E-mail: info@stertiluk.com
Website: http://www.stertiluk.com
Bank(s): National Westminster Bank Plc
Directors: M. Painter (MD), M. Paynter (MD)
Immediate Holding Company: STERTIL UK LTD.
Registration no: 01103855 **VAT No.:** GB 211 4025 32
Date established: 1973 **Turnover:** £10m - £20m
No.of Employees: 51 - 100 **Product Groups:** 25, 29, 30, 35, 36, 40, 45

Date of Accounts	Dec 11	Dec 10	Dec 09
Sales Turnover	16m	13m	16m
Pre Tax Profit/Loss	589	373	539
Working Capital	2m	1m	1m
Fixed Assets	129	152	173
Current Assets	5m	4m	4m
Current Liabilities	1m	936	1m

Stuart Buglass Ironwork Ltd

Clifford Mill house Little Houghton, Northampton, NN7 1AL
Tel: 01604-890366 **Fax:** 01604-890372
E-mail: sbuglass@aol.com
Website: http://www.stuartbuglass.co.uk
Directors: M. Milligan (MD)
Registration no: 02748591 **No.of Employees:** 1 - 10 **Product Groups:** 35, 36, 37

Studfast Studwelding Ltd

5 Low Farm Place Moulton Park Industrial Estate, Northampton, NN3 6HY
Tel: 01604-790901 **Fax:** 01604-492946
E-mail: sales.studfast@btconnect.com
Website: http://www.studfast-studwelding.com
Directors: P. Turland (Dir)
Immediate Holding Company: STUDFAST STUD WELDING LIMITED
Registration no: 02310404 **VAT No.:** GB 486 0661 26
Date established: 1988 **Turnover:** £500,000 - £1m
No.of Employees: 1 - 10 **Product Groups:** 48

Date of Accounts	Dec 11	Dec 10	Dec 09
Working Capital	103	86	110
Fixed Assets	49	21	28
Current Assets	248	181	204

Sunley Conference Centre

Nene College Campus Boughton Green Road, Northampton, NN2 7AN
Tel: 01604-892020 **Fax:** 01604-777201
E-mail: john.jones@northampton.ac.uk
Website: http://www.sunley-northampton.co.uk
Directors: J. Jones (MD)
Immediate Holding Company: UNIVERSITY COLLEGE NORTHAMPTON
Date established: 1971 **Turnover:** £1m - £2m **No.of Employees:** 11 - 20
Product Groups: 86

Sutch Lifting Equipment Ltd

18 Millbrook Close St James Mill Road, Northampton, NN5 5JF
Tel: 01604-751146 **Fax:** 01604-758062
E-mail: info@sutch.co.uk
Website: http://www.sutch.co.uk
Bank(s): National Westminster

Directors: M. Sutch (Co Sec), I. Sutch (MD)
Immediate Holding Company: SUTCH LIFTING EQUIPMENT LIMITED
Registration no: 03598569 **VAT No.:** GB 336 5406 60
Date established: 1998 **Turnover:** £500,000 - £1m
No.of Employees: 11 - 20 **Product Groups:** 23, 35, 39

Date of Accounts	Jul 12	Jul 11	Jul 10
Working Capital	115	52	25
Fixed Assets	87	90	86
Current Assets	482	460	363

Swift Duplication Ltd
11 Poppyfield Court, Northampton, NN3 8NG
Tel: 01604-401160
E-mail: paul@swiftduplication.com
Website: http://www.swiftduplication.com
Directors: P. Higgins (MD), P. Higgins (Dir)
Immediate Holding Company: SWIFT DUPLICATION LTD
Registration no: 06621378 **Date established:** 2008
Turnover: Up to £250,000 **No.of Employees:** 1 - 10 **Product Groups:** 44, 48

Date of Accounts	Jun 10	Jun 09
Working Capital	-1	2
Fixed Assets	1	1
Current Assets	27	40

T & K Precision Ltd
9-10 Gatelodge Close Round Spinney Industrial Estate, Northampton, NN3 8RJ
Tel: 01604-493101 **Fax:** 01604-493208
E-mail: sales@tkprecision.com
Website: http://www.tkprecision.com
Directors: T. Forster (Jt MD), P. Forster (MD), C. Forster (MD), T. Forster (MD)
Managers: G. Burgess (Works Gen Mgr)
Immediate Holding Company: T.& K.PRECISION LIMITED
Registration no: 00680126 **VAT No.:** GB 120 0188 31
Date established: 1961 **Turnover:** £1m - £2m **No.of Employees:** 1 - 10
Product Groups: 35, 39, 48, 61

Date of Accounts	Mar 12	Mar 11	Mar 10
Working Capital	1m	723	545
Fixed Assets	495	469	409
Current Assets	2m	1m	882

Tandler Precision Ltd
29 Ross Road Business Centre, Northampton, NN5 5AX
Tel: 01604-588056 **Fax:** 01604-588064
E-mail: sales@tandler.co.uk
Website: http://www.tandler.co.uk
Managers: S. Jarvis (Mktg Serv Mgr)
Ultimate Holding Company: Tandler GmbH
Registration no: 02397735 **Turnover:** £500,000 - £1m
No.of Employees: 1 - 10 **Product Groups:** 35, 67

Date of Accounts	Dec 11	Dec 10	Dec 09
Working Capital	225	234	185
Fixed Assets	168	200	207
Current Assets	378	414	326

Terex UK Ltd
Watford Village, Northampton, NN6 7XN
Tel: 01327-705621 **Fax:** 01327-871704
E-mail: adrian.hyde@terexce.com
Website: http://www.terex.co.uk
Directors: E. Cohen (Co Sec)
Managers: R. Davey (Chief Mgr)
Immediate Holding Company: International Machinery Company Ltd
Registration no: 00494347 **Turnover:** £20m - £50m
No.of Employees: 1 - 10 **Product Groups:** 51

Date of Accounts	Dec 07	Dec 06
Sales Turnover	39257	36485
Pre Tax Profit/Loss	-13544	-5131
Working Capital	-9641	-5310
Fixed Assets	225	340
Current Assets	42605	45234
Current Liabilities	52246	50544
Total Share Capital	1	1
ROCE% (Return on Capital Employed)	143.8	103.2
ROT% (Return on Turnover)	-34.5	-14.1

Texas Instruments Ltd
800 Pavilion Drive Northampton Business Park, Northampton, NN4 7YL
Tel: 01604-663000 **Fax:** 01604-663001
E-mail: m-cowles@ti.com
Website: http://www.ti.com
Directors: K. Pharoah (Co Sec), K. Lathaen (Pers), M. Cowles (MD), M. Cowles (MD)
Managers: C. Lawrence (Tech Serv Mgr)
Ultimate Holding Company: TEXAS INSTRUMENTS INC (USA)
Immediate Holding Company: TEXAS INSTRUMENTS LIMITED
Registration no: 00574102 **Date established:** 1956
Turnover: £20m - £50m **No.of Employees:** 51 - 100 **Product Groups:** 37

Date of Accounts	Dec 11	Dec 10	Dec 09
Sales Turnover	24m	19m	23m
Pre Tax Profit/Loss	6m	-189	4m
Working Capital	25m	20m	19m
Fixed Assets	2m	4m	5m
Current Assets	33m	24m	24m
Current Liabilities	7m	3m	2m

David Thomas Ltd
1 Gate Lodge Close Round Spinney Industrial Estate, Northampton, NN3 8RJ
Tel: 01604-646216 **Fax:** 01604-790366
E-mail: peterrolfe@davidthomas.com
Website: http://www.davidthomas.com
Directors: P. Rolfe (Dir)
Immediate Holding Company: DAVID THOMAS (CONTACT LENSES) LIMITED
Registration no: 01043189 **Date established:** 1972
No.of Employees: 11 - 20 **Product Groups:** 33, 38

Date of Accounts	Dec 11	Dec 10	Dec 09
Working Capital	332	368	309
Fixed Assets	705	624	481
Current Assets	907	901	604

3di Consulting Ltd
Unit 5 Adams House Northampton Science Park Kings Park Road, Moulton Park Industrial Estate, Northampton, NN3 6LG
Tel: 01604-654114 **Fax:** 01604-654117
E-mail: info@3di.co.uk
Website: http://www.3di.co.uk
Directors: T. Wye (MD)
Immediate Holding Company: 3DI CONSULTING LIMITED
Registration no: 05156642 **Date established:** 2004
No.of Employees: 1 - 10 **Product Groups:** 84

Date of Accounts	Jun 11	Jun 10	Jun 09
Working Capital	-1	-8	-0
Fixed Assets	14	15	44
Current Assets	52	18	79

Chris Thrift
23 High Street Wootton, Northampton, NN4 6LW
Tel: 01604-769213
E-mail: cd_thrift@hotmail.com
Directors: C. Thrift (Prop)
Date established: 2002 **No.of Employees:** 1 - 10 **Product Groups:** 35

Torquemeters
West Haddon Road Ravensthorpe, Northampton, NN6 8ET
Tel: 01604-770232 **Fax:** 01604-770778
E-mail: info@torquemeters.com
Website: http://www.torquemeters.com
Bank(s): The Royal Bank of Scotland
Directors: A. Delves (Sales & Mktg), B. Van Millingen (MD), M. Bennett (Co Sec)
Managers: P. Johnson (Prod Mgr)
Immediate Holding Company: TORQUEMETERS LIMITED
Registration no: 00492122 **VAT No.:** GB 119 8974 20
Date established: 1951 **Turnover:** £2m - £5m **No.of Employees:** 21 - 50
Product Groups: 35, 38

Date of Accounts	Mar 12	Mar 11	Mar 10
Working Capital	2m	2m	1m
Fixed Assets	969	879	1m
Current Assets	5m	4m	3m

Towerite Environmental Consultants
Old Road Lamport, Northampton, NN6 9HF
Tel: 01604-686772 **Fax:** 01604-686773
E-mail: info@towerite.co.uk
Website: http://www.towerite.co.uk
Directors: V. McKie (Co Sec)
Immediate Holding Company: TOWERITE LIMITED
Registration no: 02433029 **VAT No.:** GB 581 1176 50
Date established: 1989 **Turnover:** £2m - £5m **No.of Employees:** 1 - 10
Product Groups: 32, 42, 51

Date of Accounts	Dec 09	Dec 08	Dec 07
Working Capital	963	515	194
Fixed Assets	9	8	10
Current Assets	2m	949	589

Travis Perkins plc (incorporating Mersey Plastics)
Lodge Way House Lodge Way, Lodge Farm Industrial Estate, Northampton, NN5 7UG
Tel: 01604-752424 **Fax:** 0151-486 3031
E-mail: geoff.cooper@travisperkins.co.uk
Website: http://www.travisperkins.co.uk
Directors: G. Cooper (Grp Chief Exec), S. Finlay (MD)
Immediate Holding Company: TRAVIS PERKINS PLC
Registration no: 00824821 **VAT No.:** GB 408 5556 737
Date established: 1964 **Turnover:** Over £1,000m **No.of Employees:** 1 - 10
Product Groups: 30

Date of Accounts	Dec 10	Dec 09	Dec 08
Sales Turnover	3153m	2931m	3179m
Pre Tax Profit/Loss	197m	213m	146m
Working Capital	159m	248m	71m
Fixed Assets	2749m	2108m	2173m
Current Assets	1329m	1035m	718m
Current Liabilities	412m	109m	237m

Turbo Technics Ltd
2 Sketty Close Brackmills Industrial Estate Brackmills Industrial Estate, Northampton, NN4 7PL
Tel: 01604-705050 **Fax:** 01604-769668
E-mail: enquiries@turbotechnics.com
Website: http://www.turbotechnics.com
Directors: K. Kershaw (Co Sec), G. Kershaw (Ch & MD)
Managers: H. Bibby (Sales Prom), R. Yeoman
Immediate Holding Company: TURBO TECHNICS LIMITED
Registration no: 01678701 **Date established:** 1982 **Turnover:** £1m - £2m
No.of Employees: 1 - 10 **Product Groups:** 39, 40

Date of Accounts	Mar 11	Mar 10	Mar 09
Working Capital	194	243	299
Fixed Assets	628	329	243
Current Assets	1m	969	869

Verve Workspace
Verve House 4 Squirrels Lane, Northampton, NN5 6JH
Tel: 08450-697989 **Fax:** 08450-697999
E-mail: sales@verveworkspace.co.uk
Website: http://www.verveworkspace.co.uk
Directors: S. Allens (Prop)
Immediate Holding Company: VERVE WORKSPACE LTD
Registration no: 05183491 **Date established:** 2004
Turnover: £500,000 - £1m **No.of Employees:** 1 - 10 **Product Groups:** 67

Date of Accounts	Jul 11	Jul 10	Jul 09
Working Capital	-4	-2	25
Fixed Assets	93	16	N/A
Current Assets	79	71	97

Visa Energy GB Ltd
400 Pavilion Drive, Northampton, NN4 7PA
Tel: 01604-410838 **Fax:** 0844-800 7311
E-mail: enquiries@visaenergy.com
Website: http://www.visaenergy.com
Directors: A. Ash (MD)
Immediate Holding Company: VISA ENERGY GB LIMITED
Registration no: 06410219 **Date established:** 2007
No.of Employees: 21 - 50 **Product Groups:** 37, 38, 40, 67

Date of Accounts	Dec 11	Dec 10	Dec 09
Sales Turnover	154	N/A	99
Working Capital	14	5	2
Fixed Assets	1	1	1
Current Assets	14	30	26

Vision Products Europe Ltd
Unit 1 Redbourne Park Liliput Road Brackmills, Brackmills Industrial Estate, Northampton, NN4 7DT
Tel: 01604-662742 **Fax:** 0845-017 1011
E-mail: sales@vision-products.co.uk
Website: http://www.vision-products.co.uk
Managers: R. Stallyworthy
Immediate Holding Company: VISION PRODUCTS (EUROPE) LIMITED
Registration no: 05044512 **Date established:** 2004 **Turnover:** £5m - £10m
No.of Employees: 1 - 10 **Product Groups:** 38, 67

Date of Accounts	May 12	May 11	May 10
Sales Turnover	N/A	N/A	8m
Pre Tax Profit/Loss	N/A	N/A	157
Working Capital	587	605	540
Fixed Assets	45	52	66
Current Assets	2m	1m	2m
Current Liabilities	N/A	N/A	550

W H Shoebridge Ltd
109 Billing Road, Northampton, NN1 5HU
Tel: 01604-638099 **Fax:** 01604-628694
E-mail: wh.shoebridge@virgin.net
Website: http://www.shoebridges.com
Bank(s): National Westminster Bank Plc
Directors: L. Going (Dir), R. Shoebridge (MD)
Immediate Holding Company: SHOEBRIDGE ENGINEERING LIMITED
Registration no: 04584341 **VAT No.:** GB 120 2927 09
Date established: 2002 **Turnover:** £1m - £2m **No.of Employees:** 21 - 50
Product Groups: 48

Date of Accounts	Mar 12	Mar 11	Mar 10
Working Capital	71	5	-55
Fixed Assets	196	205	181
Current Assets	451	358	281

Walkerpack Ltd
Unit 34 Liliput Road Brackmills Industrial Estate, Northampton, NN4 7DT
Tel: 01604-760529 **Fax:** 01604-675641
E-mail: info@walkerpack.co.uk
Website: http://www.thewalkergroup.co.uk
Bank(s): HSBC Bank plc
Directors: L. Clarke (Fin), L. Moss (MD)
Managers: C. Farnsworth (Sales Prom Mgr), E. Oliver (Tech Serv Mgr), R. Farey
Immediate Holding Company: WALKER HOLDING LIMITED
Registration no: 00971654 **VAT No.:** GB 874 4440 09
Date established: 1970 **Turnover:** £5m - £10m
No.of Employees: 101 - 250 **Product Groups:** 76

Date of Accounts	Feb 08	Feb 11	Feb 10
Working Capital	998	1m	1m
Fixed Assets	319	246	270
Current Assets	1m	2m	2m
Current Liabilities	240	294	94

Jervis B Webb Co. Ltd (European Headquarters)
Cob Drive Swan Valley, Northampton, NN4 9BB
Tel: 01604-658150 **Fax:** 01604-656246
E-mail: info@jerviswebb.com
Website: http://www.jerviswebb.com
Directors: I. Mole (MD), R. Mole (Eng Serv)
Managers: T. Toolan (Transport)
Ultimate Holding Company: DAIFUKU COMPANY LIMITED (JAPAN)
Immediate Holding Company: JERVIS B.WEBB COMPANY LTD
Registration no: 00939789 **Date established:** 1968 **Turnover:** £5m - £10m
No.of Employees: 1 - 10 **Product Groups:** 30, 38, 39, 41, 42, 43, 44, 45, 46, 84

Date of Accounts	Dec 11	Dec 10	Dec 09
Working Capital	3m	4m	4m
Fixed Assets	7	10	14
Current Assets	4m	5m	6m

Wisden & Franklin Ltd
6-8 Osyth Close Brackmills Industrial Estate, Northampton, NN4 7DY
Tel: 01604-665760 **Fax:** 01604-705491
E-mail: info@wandf.com
Website: http://www.wandf.com
Bank(s): London Corporate Banking, PO Box 1516, 50 Pall Mall, London
Directors: D. Flitterman (MD), D. Slitterman (Dir), D. Hayes (Dir)
Managers: D. Russell (Works Gen Mgr)
Immediate Holding Company: WISDEN & FRANKLIN LIMITED
Registration no: 03067091 **VAT No.:** GB 661 2039 61
Date established: 1995 **Turnover:** £1m - £2m **No.of Employees:** 21 - 50
Product Groups: 27, 28, 30, 42, 48, 66, 81

Wrightrain Environmental Ltd
Foxhill Farm Stables Foxhill Road, West Haddon, Northampton, NN6 7BG
Tel: 01788-510529 **Fax:** 01788-510728
E-mail: sales@wrightrain.co.uk
Website: http://www.the-wright-group.co.uk
Directors: C. Hutchins (Grp Chief Exec), J. O'connor (Co Sec), M. Knight (MD), N. Farmer (MD), A. Allen (Fin)
Immediate Holding Company: WRIGHT RAIN ENVIRONMENTAL LIMITED
Registration no: 06867276 **VAT No.:** GB 730 1755 59
Date established: 2009 **Turnover:** £5m - £10m **No.of Employees:** 1 - 10
Product Groups: 41

XCAM Ltd
Unit 8 Grove Farm Grove Farm Lane, Moulton, Northampton, NN3 7TG
Tel: 01604-670729
E-mail: info@xcam.co.uk
Website: http://www.xcam.co.uk
Managers: D. Colebrook (Snr Eng)
Immediate Holding Company: XCAM LIMITED
Registration no: 03114535 **Date established:** 1995
No.of Employees: 1 - 10 **Product Groups:** 37, 38

Date of Accounts	Sep 11	Sep 10	Sep 09
Working Capital	72	56	58
Fixed Assets	31	28	9
Current Assets	217	209	109

Xtracs Ltd
Unit 9-12 Chapel Farm Hanslope Road, Hartwell, Northampton, NN7 2EU
Tel: 01908-511740 **Fax:** 01908-511729
E-mail: sales@xtracs.com
Website: http://www.xtracs.com
Directors: R. Falzon (Dir)
Immediate Holding Company: XTRACS LIMITED
Registration no: 04941654 **Date established:** 2003 **Turnover:** £1m - £2m
No.of Employees: 1 - 10 **Product Groups:** 26, 49

Date of Accounts	Mar 11	Mar 10	Mar 09
Working Capital	110	51	29
Fixed Assets	10	16	21
Current Assets	252	185	185

Rushden

Alimak Hek Ltd
Northampton Road, Rushden, NN10 6BW
Tel: 01933-354700 **Fax:** 01933-410600
E-mail: info.uk@alimakhek.com
Website: http://www.alimakhek.com
Directors: G. Paul (Co Sec)
Managers: M. Bednall (Mktg Serv Mgr), M. Irving (Fin Mgr)
Ultimate Holding Company: ALIMAK HEK GROUP AB (SWEDEN)
Immediate Holding Company: ALIMAK HEK LTD
Registration no: 00930125 **Date established:** 1968 **Turnover:** £5m - £10m
No.of Employees: 21 - 50 **Product Groups:** 45

Date of Accounts	Dec 11	Dec 10	Dec 09
Sales Turnover	12m	5m	6m
Pre Tax Profit/Loss	1m	732	934
Working Capital	3m	3m	3m
Fixed Assets	16	15	24
Current Assets	6m	5m	4m
Current Liabilities	1m	957	721

B L Pneumatics Ltd
Norris Way, Rushden, NN10 6BP
Tel: 01933-358822 **Fax:** 01933-410451
E-mail: sales@blpneumatics.co.uk
Website: http://www.blpneumatics.co.uk
Directors: M. Singlehurst (Dir), K. Deighton (Dir), H. Barnett (Dir)
Registration no: 01232236 **Date established:** 1975 **Turnover:** £1m - £2m
No.of Employees: 1 - 10 **Product Groups:** 30, 35, 36, 37, 38, 40, 45, 46, 48, 67, 84

Date of Accounts	Feb 12	Feb 11	Feb 10
Working Capital	203	183	150
Fixed Assets	32	33	36
Current Assets	329	338	268

C A J Services Ltd
Unit K Bury Close, Higham Ferrers, Rushden, NN10 8HQ
Tel: 01933-355001 **Fax:** 01933-355009
E-mail: mail@cajservices.co.uk
Website: http://www.cajservices.co.uk
Directors: C. Jackson (MD)
Immediate Holding Company: C.A.J. SERVICES LIMITED
Registration no: 04598007 **Date established:** 2002
No.of Employees: 1 - 10 **Product Groups:** 54

Date of Accounts	Nov 11	Nov 10	Nov 09
Working Capital	-341	-263	-300
Fixed Assets	2m	1m	838
Current Assets	752	362	429

Chamberlain Plastics Ltd
Bury Close Higham Ferrers, Rushden, NN10 8HQ
Tel: 01933-353875 **Fax:** 01933-410206
E-mail: sales@chamberlain-plastics.co.uk
Website: http://www.chamberlain-plastics.co.uk
Bank(s): Bank of Scotland
Directors: S. Boyd (MD), T. Mannion Butt (Co Sec)
Ultimate Holding Company: CAL GROUP LIMITED
Immediate Holding Company: CHAMBERLAIN PLASTICS LIMITED
Registration no: 03068482 **VAT No.:** GB 638 6169 07
Date established: 1995 **Turnover:** £2m - £5m **No.of Employees:** 11 - 20
Product Groups: 30, 48

Date of Accounts	Dec 10	Dec 09	Dec 08
Working Capital	401	632	957
Fixed Assets	86	125	158
Current Assets	656	898	1m

Cirgraphics Ltd
Victoria Road, Rushden, NN10 0AS
Tel: 01933-315005 **Fax:** 01933-318789
E-mail: enquiries@cirgraphics.com
Website: http://www.cirgraphics.com
Directors: K. Lewis (Dir)
Immediate Holding Company: CIRGRAPHICS LIMITED
Registration no: 01609913 **VAT No.:** GB 336 3554 55
Date established: 1982 **Turnover:** £500,000 - £1m
No.of Employees: 1 - 10 **Product Groups:** 38

Date of Accounts	Oct 11	Oct 10	Oct 09
Working Capital	199	171	168
Fixed Assets	2	1	2
Current Assets	227	198	196

D B Shoes Ltd
19-21 Irchester Road, Rushden, NN10 9XF
Tel: 01933-359217 **Fax:** 01933-410218
E-mail: enquiries@dbshoes.co.uk
Website: http://www.dbshoes.co.uk
Bank(s): Natwest
Directors: D. Denton (Fin), C. Denton (Dir)
Ultimate Holding Company: DENTON BROTHERS LIMITED
Immediate Holding Company: D.B. SHOES LIMITED
Registration no: 00163960 **Date established:** 2020 **Turnover:** £5m - £10m
No.of Employees: 21 - 50 **Product Groups:** 22

Date of Accounts	Dec 11	Dec 10	Dec 09
Working Capital	899	979	853
Fixed Assets	138	125	105
Current Assets	1m	1m	1m

D C V Engineering
32 Lodge Road, Rushden, NN10 9HA
Tel: 01933-411946 **Fax:** 01933-311426
Directors: D. Benn (Prop)
Immediate Holding Company: DCV PLANT SERVICES LTD
Registration no: 08179315 **Date established:** 2012
No.of Employees: 1 - 10 **Product Groups:** 41

Dawson Books Ltd
Unit C Brindley Close, Rushden, NN10 6DB
Tel: 01933-417500 **Fax:** 01933-417501
E-mail: enquiries@dawsonbooks.co.uk
Website: http://www.dawsonbooks.co.uk
Directors: P. Whittingham (Comm), N. Harknett (MD)
Managers: A. Benton, S. Welch (Mktg Serv Mgr), S. Welch (Mktg Serv Mgr), P. Whittingham, A. Benton, A. Darcy (Personnel), G. Hammond
Ultimate Holding Company: SMITHS NEWS PLC
Immediate Holding Company: DAWSON BOOKS LIMITED
Registration no: 06882367 **Date established:** 2009
Turnover: £20m - £50m **No.of Employees:** 101 - 250
Product Groups: 44, 64, 81, 84

Date of Accounts	Aug 11	Sep 10
Sales Turnover	38m	54m
Pre Tax Profit/Loss	290	705
Working Capital	-4m	-3m
Fixed Assets	5m	1m
Current Assets	6m	6m
Current Liabilities	622	2m

William Green & Son Ltd
Queen Street, Rushden, NN10 0AB
Tel: 01933-358734 **Fax:** 01933-410106
E-mail: greenson.shoes@btinternet.com
Website: http://www.grenson.co.uk
Managers: D. Taylor (Fin Mgr), S. Johnson (Mgr)
Immediate Holding Company: WILLIAM GREEN & SON LIMITED
Registration no: 05085681 **Date established:** 2004
Turnover: £250,000 - £500,000 **No.of Employees:** 21 - 50
Product Groups: 22

Date of Accounts	Mar 11	Mar 10	Mar 09
Sales Turnover	416	3m	4m
Pre Tax Profit/Loss	1m	-350	-383
Working Capital	1m	-125	675
Fixed Assets	42	222	144
Current Assets	2m	3m	2m
Current Liabilities	46	380	421

Grenson Shoes Ltd
Queen Street, Rushden, NN10 0AB
Tel: 01933-358734 **Fax:** 01933-410106
E-mail: customerservices@grenson.co.uk
Website: http://www.grenson.co.uk
Bank(s): National Westminster Bank Plc
Directors: T. Little (MD)
Immediate Holding Company: GRENSON SHOES LIMITED
Registration no: 00133802 **VAT No.:** GB 119 1555 75
Date established: 2014 **Turnover:** £5m - £10m **No.of Employees:** 21 - 50
Product Groups: 22

Date of Accounts	Mar 11	Mar 10	Mar 09
Working Capital	124	124	124
Current Assets	124	124	124

Hallmarque Associates Ltd
Cherry Tree 17 Prospect Avenue, Rushden, NN10 6DQ
Tel: 01933-386519
E-mail: admin@hallmarque-associates.co.uk
Website: http://www.hallmarque-associates.co.uk
Directors: I. Smith (MD)
Immediate Holding Company: HALLMARQUE ASSOCIATES LIMITED
Registration no: 05727397 **Date established:** 2006
No.of Employees: 1 - 10 **Product Groups:** 80, 84, 86

Date of Accounts	Mar 08	Mar 07
Working Capital	-1	N/A
Fixed Assets	1	1
Current Assets	12	12

Humanware Europe Ltd
Russell Smith House Unit 2 Bullmatt Business Centre, Rushden, NN10 6AR
Tel: 01933-415800 **Fax:** 01933-411209
E-mail: eu.sales@humanware.com
Website: http://www.humanware.com
Directors: C. Whithers Green (Fin)
Managers: A. Davis (Mktg Serv Mgr), P. Poulson, S. Firmin (Tech Serv Mgr)
Ultimate Holding Company: JOIMONT HOLDINGS (NEW ZEALAND)
Immediate Holding Company: HUMANWARE EUROPE LTD
Registration no: 02678026 **Date established:** 1992 **Turnover:** £1m - £2m
No.of Employees: 21 - 50 **Product Groups:** 38, 67

Date of Accounts	Dec 11	Dec 10	Dec 09
Working Capital	1m	977	853
Fixed Assets	94	157	171
Current Assets	3m	2m	2m

I T W Devcon
Unit 3 Shipton Way Express Business Park, Northampton Road, Rushden, NN10 6GL
Tel: 0870-4587388 **Fax:** 0870-4589077
E-mail: info@itwdevcon.eu.com
Website: http://www.itw-devcon.co.uk
Directors: R. Nightingale (MD)
Managers: P. Belm (Mktg Serv Mgr), P. Lansborough (I.T. Exec)
Ultimate Holding Company: I T W Inc (USA)
Immediate Holding Company: I.T.W. Ltd
Registration no: 01916457 **VAT No.:** GB 513 9543 46
Turnover: Up to £250,000 **No.of Employees:** 1 - 10 **Product Groups:** 30, 31, 32, 48

I T W Plexus (a division of I T W Ltd)
Unit 3 Shipton Way Express Business Park, Northampton Road, Rushden, NN10 6GL
Tel: 0870-4587588 **Fax:** 0870-4589077
E-mail: sales@itwplexus.co.uk
Website: http://www.itwplexus.co.uk
Managers: I. Lancey (Sales Prom Mgr), M. Scott (Nat Sales Mgr), P. Bellm (Comm)
Ultimate Holding Company: I T W (Inc) (USA)
Immediate Holding Company: I T W Ltd
Registration no: 00559693 **No.of Employees:** 11 - 20
Product Groups: 32, 66, 68

Johnson''s Mini Crusher Hire
41 The Hedges Higham Ferrers, Rushden, NN10 8AA
Tel: 01933-313395
E-mail: info@johnsonsminicrusherhire.co.uk
Website: http://www.johnsonsminicrusherhire.co.uk
No.of Employees: 1 - 10 **Product Groups:** 42, 45, 83

Kempston Controls Ltd
Shirley Road, Rushden, NN10 6BZ
Tel: 01933-411411 **Fax:** 01933-410211
E-mail: richard.regan@kempstoncontrols.co.uk
Website: http://www.kempstoncontrols.co.uk
Bank(s): Bank of Scotland, P.O. Box 267, 38 Threadneedle St, London EC2P 2EH
Directors: S. Couchman (MD), C. Barrowcliffe (Sales), R. Reagan (MD), R. Regan (MD), E. Regan (Fin)
Managers: A. Horn (Buyer), S. Robinson (I.T. Exec)
Immediate Holding Company: KEMPSTON CONTROLS LIMITED
Registration no: 04492893 **VAT No.:** GB 238 6568 25
Date established: 2002 **Turnover:** £2m - £5m **No.of Employees:** 21 - 50
Product Groups: 30, 37, 38, 40, 49, 67

Kingtools
Norris Way, Rushden, NN10 6BP
Tel: 01933-410900 **Fax:** 01933-350471
E-mail: dennis.dangerfield@kingtools.co.uk
Website: http://www.kingtools.co.uk
Directors: D. Dangerfield (Prop)
VAT No.: GB 638 4449 11 **Turnover:** £1m - £2m **No.of Employees:** 1 - 10
Product Groups: 30, 37, 67

Ladwa Engineering Ltd
Sanders Lodge Industrial Estate, Rushden, NN10 6BQ
Tel: 01933-359204 **Fax:** 01933-410583
E-mail: sales@ladwaengineering.com
Directors: A. Dilley (Dir)
Immediate Holding Company: LADWA (ENGINEERING) LIMITED
Registration no: 01107343 **Date established:** 1973
Turnover: £250,000 - £500,000 **No.of Employees:** 1 - 10
Product Groups: 48

Date of Accounts	Nov 11	Nov 10	Nov 09
Working Capital	273	229	252
Fixed Assets	41	50	61
Current Assets	375	332	340

Major International Ltd
Higham Business Park Bury Close, Higham Ferrers, Rushden, NN10 8HQ
Tel: 01933-356012 **Fax:** 01933-274168
E-mail: dbryant@majorint.com
Website: http://www.majorint.com
Directors: D. Bryant (Comm), M. Hollyman (Co Sec)
Immediate Holding Company: MAJOR INTERNATIONAL LIMITED
Registration no: 02440746 **Date established:** 1989 **Turnover:** £2m - £5m
No.of Employees: 11 - 20 **Product Groups:** 20, 62

Date of Accounts	Dec 11	Dec 10	Dec 09
Sales Turnover	N/A	N/A	5m
Pre Tax Profit/Loss	N/A	N/A	-58
Working Capital	1m	1m	1m
Fixed Assets	299	287	272
Current Assets	2m	2m	2m
Current Liabilities	N/A	N/A	401

Marriott Construction
Marriott House Brindley Close, Rushden, NN10 6EN
Tel: 01933-357511 **Fax:** 01933-356746
Website: http://www.kier.co.uk
Bank(s): National Westminster, Bedford
Directors: R. Mercy (Ch), R. Murphy (MD)
Managers: M. Dean (Personnel), D. Coleman (Mktg Serv Mgr), P. Foster (I.T. Exec)
Ultimate Holding Company: KIER GROUP PLC
Immediate Holding Company: MARRIOTT LIMITED
Registration no: 00931371 **Date established:** 1968 **Turnover:** £1m - £2m
No.of Employees: 51 - 100 **Product Groups:** 51

Millermatic Vending
32 High Street Wymington, Rushden, NN10 9LS
Tel: 01933-359189 **Fax:** 01933-359189
E-mail: sales@millermatic.co.uk
Website: http://www.millermatic.co.uk
Directors: D. Furlong (Snr Part)
Date established: 1977 **No.of Employees:** 1 - 10 **Product Groups:** 38, 42

Northedge Packaging Ltd
Unit A Higham Business Park Bury Close, Higham Ferrers, Rushden, NN10 8HQ
Tel: 01933-317208 **Fax:** 01933-312881
E-mail: info@north-edge.co.uk
Website: http://www.north-edge.co.uk
Directors: A. Marsh (Ptnr)
Immediate Holding Company: NORTHEDGE PACKAGING LIMITED
Registration no: 02246539 **Date established:** 1988
No.of Employees: 1 - 10 **Product Groups:** 38, 42

Date of Accounts	Apr 12	Apr 11	Apr 10
Working Capital	96	92	151
Fixed Assets	10	12	1
Current Assets	387	335	179

P C L Machinery
5 Elan Court Norris Way, Rushden, NN10 6BP
Tel: 01933-410707 **Fax:** 01933-410807
E-mail: sales@pclmachinery.co.uk
Website: http://www.pclmachinery.co.uk
Directors: B. Line (Prop)
Registration no: 02265073 **VAT No.:** GB 486 3813 14
Turnover: £500,000 - £1m **No.of Employees:** 1 - 10 **Product Groups:** 38, 42, 67, 84

Phoenix Industrial Packaging Ltd
Unit 5 Sanders Lodge Industrial Estate, Rushden, NN10 6BQ
Tel: 0844-2640600 **Fax:** 0844-2640601
E-mail: sales@phoenix-pkg.co.uk
Website: http://www.phoenix-pkg.co.uk
Directors: S. Hogston (Fin)
Registration no: 02973866 **Date established:** 1994
No.of Employees: 11 - 20 **Product Groups:** 38, 42

Date of Accounts	Oct 08	Oct 07	Oct 06
Working Capital	158	190	157
Fixed Assets	1206	1236	1308
Current Assets	716	896	573
Current Liabilities	558	705	416

Pro Active Asbestos Control Ltd
1 Dover Close, Rushden, NN10 0RQ
Tel: 01933-313999 **Fax:** 01933-357822
E-mail: info@proactiveasbestos.com
Website: http://www.proactiveasbestos.com
Directors: T. James (Fin)
Immediate Holding Company: PRO-ACTIVE ASBESTOS CONTROL LTD
Registration no: 06146641 **Date established:** 2007
Turnover: Up to £250,000 **No.of Employees:** 1 - 10 **Product Groups:** 54

Date of Accounts	Mar 11	Mar 10	Mar 09
Working Capital	35	4	-2
Fixed Assets	6	4	6
Current Assets	143	41	27

R P C Group plc Head Office (RPC Containers Ltd)
Sapphire House Crown Way, Rushden, NN10 6FB
Tel: 01933-416528 **Fax:** 01933-410083
E-mail: marketing@rpc-group.com
Website: http://www.rpc-group.com
Directors: P. Vervaat (Fin), R. Joyce (Co Sec)
Managers: D. Evans (Grp Purch Mgr), J. Pack (Mktg Serv Mgr)
Immediate Holding Company: RPC GROUP PLC
Registration no: 02578443 **Date established:** 1991
Turnover: Over £1,000m **No.of Employees:** 21 - 50 **Product Groups:** 30

Date of Accounts	Mar 12	Mar 11	Mar 10
Sales Turnover	1130m	819m	720m
Pre Tax Profit/Loss	60m	35m	19m
Working Capital	45m	-25m	42m
Fixed Assets	516m	518m	303m
Current Assets	365m	356m	244m
Current Liabilities	107m	107m	65m

Rock It Promotions
The Old Employment Exchange East Grove, Rushden, NN10 0AP
Tel: 01933-311179 **Fax:** 01933-413279
E-mail: sales@promoclothing.com
Website: http://www.promoclothing.com
Directors: A. Campen (Sales)
Turnover: £500,000 - £1m **No.of Employees:** 1 - 10 **Product Groups:** 23, 24, 49

Sanders & Sanders Ltd
Spencer Works Spencer Road, Rushden, NN10 6AE
Tel: 01933-353066 **Fax:** 01933-410355
E-mail: mail@sanders-uk.com
Website: http://www.sanders-uk.com
Bank(s): National Westminster
Directors: H. Sanders (MD), P. Andrews (Sales)
Managers: C. Woodhead, C. Greenhalf (Buyer)
Immediate Holding Company: SANDERS AND SANDERS LIMITED
Registration no: 00343139 **VAT No.:** GB 120 0388 23
Date established: 1938 **Turnover:** £2m - £5m **No.of Employees:** 51 - 100
Product Groups: 22

Date of Accounts	Feb 12	Feb 11	Feb 10
Sales Turnover	5m	3m	2m
Pre Tax Profit/Loss	289	77	-79
Working Capital	890	685	601
Fixed Assets	168	167	190
Current Assets	2m	1m	1m
Current Liabilities	221	205	138

Sargent Shoes Ltd
Portland Road, Rushden, NN10 0DQ
Tel: 01933-312065 **Fax:** 01933-410207
E-mail: p.sargent@alfred-sargent.co.uk
Website: http://www.alfred-sargent.co.uk
Bank(s): Lloyds TSB Bank plc
Directors: A. Sargent (Fab), P. Sargent (MD), P. Sargent (MD)
Managers: P. Elder (I.T. Exec), P. Elder (Fin Mgr), S. Tennant (Sales Prom Mgr)
Immediate Holding Company: ALFRED SARGENT & SONS LIMITED
Registration no: 06772438 **VAT No.:** GB 119 1197 75
Date established: 2008 **Turnover:** £2m - £5m **No.of Employees:** 51 - 100
Product Groups: 22

Date of Accounts	Dec 09
Working Capital	78
Fixed Assets	82
Current Assets	735

Stovart Ltd
Unit 7-10 Sanders Lodge Industrial Estate, Rushden, NN10 9BQ
Tel: 01933-355348 **Fax:** 01933-411511
E-mail: info@stovart.com
Website: http://www.stovart.com
Directors: I. Batten (MD)
Immediate Holding Company: STOVART LIMITED
Registration no: 03306147 **Date established:** 1997
Turnover: Up to £250,000 **No.of Employees:** 1 - 10 **Product Groups:** 48

Date of Accounts	Mar 11	Mar 09	Mar 08
Working Capital	86	46	127
Fixed Assets	100	165	12
Current Assets	167	131	202

Stromag Ltd
29 Wellingborough Road, Rushden, NN10 9YE
Tel: 01933-350407 **Fax:** 01933-358692
E-mail: sales@stromag.com
Website: http://www.stromag.ltd.uk
Bank(s): HSBC Bank plc
Directors: G. Glennon (MD), C. West (Co Sec)
Ultimate Holding Company: STROMAG HOLDING GMBH (GERMANY)
Immediate Holding Company: GKN STROMAG UK LTD
Registration no: 00888808 **Date established:** 1966 **Turnover:** £2m - £5m
No.of Employees: 11 - 20 **Product Groups:** 35, 37, 41, 43, 44, 45, 46

Date of Accounts	Dec 11	Dec 10	Dec 09
Sales Turnover	3m	N/A	N/A
Pre Tax Profit/Loss	562	N/A	N/A
Working Capital	1m	964	1m
Fixed Assets	51	46	50
Current Assets	1m	1m	1m
Current Liabilities	240	N/A	N/A

Sureweld UK Ltd
Sanders Lodge Industrial Estate, Rushden, NN10 6BQ
Tel: 01933-357005 **Fax:** 01933-357606
E-mail: info@surerweld.co.uk
Website: http://www.sureweld.co.uk
Directors: R. Papworth (MD)
Ultimate Holding Company: SUREWELD (HOLDINGS) LIMITED
Immediate Holding Company: SUREWELD (U.K.) LIMITED
Registration no: 01144518 **Date established:** 1973 **Turnover:** £1m - £2m
No.of Employees: 1 - 10 **Product Groups:** 37, 40, 46

Date of Accounts	Dec 11	Dec 10	Dec 09
Working Capital	222	263	345
Fixed Assets	6	8	8
Current Assets	437	495	541

Tampographic Ltd
1 Elan Court Norris Way, Rushden, NN10 6BP
Tel: 01933-358326 **Fax:** 01933-316478
E-mail: sales@tampographic.co.uk
Website: http://www.tampographic.co.uk
Directors: J. Morrison (MD)
Immediate Holding Company: TAMPOGRAPHIC SERVICES LIMITED
Registration no: 02138879 **VAT No.:** GB 445 6924 31
Date established: 1987 **Turnover:** £500,000 - £1m
No.of Employees: 1 - 10 **Product Groups:** 28, 32, 42, 44

Date of Accounts	Dec 11	Dec 10	Dec 09
Working Capital	76	63	48
Fixed Assets	81	84	86
Current Assets	91	78	59

Terminator Clothing
55a Moor Road, Rushden, NN10 9TP
Tel: 01933-411333 **Fax:** 01933-411333
E-mail: info@terminator.co.uk
Website: http://www.terminator.co.uk
Directors: J. Wright (Dir), T. Wright (Co Sec)
Immediate Holding Company: TERMINATOR CLOTHING LTD
Registration no: 03661013 **Date established:** 1998
Turnover: Up to £250,000 **No.of Employees:** 1 - 10 **Product Groups:** 24, 49

Date of Accounts	Oct 11	Oct 10	Oct 09
Working Capital	14	1	26
Fixed Assets	1	1	2
Current Assets	60	38	78

Trylon Ltd
Bury Close Higham Ferrers, Rushden, NN10 8HQ
Tel: 01933-411724 **Fax:** 01933-350357
E-mail: info@trylon.co.uk
Website: http://www.trylon.co.uk
Directors: G. Wilkinson (Dir), T. Bellamy (Co Sec)
Ultimate Holding Company: TRYLON COMMUNITY LIMITED
Immediate Holding Company: TRYLON,LIMITED
Registration no: 00387324 **Date established:** 1944
Turnover: £500,000 - £1m **No.of Employees:** 1 - 10 **Product Groups:** 33

Date of Accounts	Aug 11	Aug 10	Aug 09
Working Capital	173	205	219
Fixed Assets	13	16	19
Current Assets	215	246	258

World Rubber
The Cottage Upper Higham Lane, Rushden, NN10 0SU
Tel: 01933-627160 **Fax:** 01933-460095
E-mail: nickmason@worldrubber.co.uk
Website: http://www.worldrubber.co.uk
Directors: B. Mason (MD)
Immediate Holding Company: CARR BROTHERS (FARMERS) LIMITED
Registration no: 06390316 **Date established:** 2004
Turnover: £500,000 - £1m **No.of Employees:** 11 - 20
Product Groups: 29, 63, 66

Date of Accounts	Dec 10	Dec 09	Dec 08
Working Capital	-51	-51	-51
Current Liabilities	N/A	51	51

Towcester

A I S Solutions Ltd
Woods Lane Potterspury, Towcester, NN12 7PT
Tel: 01908-760775 **Fax:** 01908-888775
E-mail: mail@aisensors.com
Website: http://www.aisensors.com
Directors: P. Dennis (Dir)
Immediate Holding Company: A.I.S. SOLUTIONS LIMITED
Registration no: 06678073 **Date established:** 2008
No.of Employees: 1 - 10 **Product Groups:** 37, 38

Date of Accounts	Aug 11	Aug 10	Aug 09
Working Capital	8	7	-6
Fixed Assets	1	N/A	N/A
Current Assets	36	29	3

British Racing Drivers Club
B R D C Farm Silverstone Circuit, Silverstone, Towcester, NN12 8TN
Tel: 01327-850920 **Fax:** 01327-850930
E-mail: enquiries@brdc.co.uk
Website: http://www.brdc.co.uk
Managers: S. Pringle
Ultimate Holding Company: BRITISH RACING DRIVERS CLUB LIMITED(THE)
Immediate Holding Company: BRITISH RACING DRIVERS CLUB LIMITED(THE)
Registration no: 00257980 **Date established:** 1931
Turnover: £20m - £50m **No.of Employees:** 1 - 10 **Product Groups:** 39

Date of Accounts	Dec 11	Dec 10	Dec 09
Sales Turnover	56m	49m	39m
Pre Tax Profit/Loss	-5m	-2m	1m
Working Capital	-18m	-12m	8m
Fixed Assets	97m	105m	71m
Current Assets	6m	9m	24m
Current Liabilities	18m	16m	14m

Coldene
Unit 24 Burcote Wood Business Centre, Wood Burcote, Towcester, NN12 8TA
Tel: 01327-350070 **Fax:** 01327-350071
E-mail: sales@coldene.co.uk
Website: http://www.coldenecastorsandwheels.co.uk
Directors: C. Barton (Dir)
Immediate Holding Company: COLDENE CASTORS LIMITED
Registration no: 05551043 **Date established:** 2005
No.of Employees: 1 - 10 **Product Groups:** 30, 35, 39, 66

DISUK Limited
Silverstone Innovation Centre Silverstone Circuit, Silverstone, Towcester, NN12 8GX
Tel: 01327-856070 **Fax:** 01933-402938
E-mail: info@disuk.com
Website: http://www.disuk.com
Directors: P. Howard (MD)
Registration no: 05299207 **Date established:** 1989
Turnover: £500,000 - £1m **No.of Employees:** 1 - 10 **Product Groups:** 44

Illusion Race Paint
9 Home Farm Buildings Northampton Road, Stoke Bruerne, Towcester, NN12 7XU
Tel: 01604-864086
Website: http://www.illusionracepaint.co.uk
Directors: L. Frost (Prop)
Date established: 2003 **No.of Employees:** 1 - 10 **Product Groups:** 46, 48

Monarch Mobility Services
67 Meadow View Potterspury, Towcester, NN12 7PJ
Tel: 01908-543124
E-mail: sales@monarchmobility.co.uk
Website: http://www.monarchmobility.co.uk
Directors: M. Read (Prop)
Registration no: 04368629 **No.of Employees:** 1 - 10 **Product Groups:** 35, 39, 45

P R P Optoelectronics Ltd
Wood Burcote Way, Towcester, NN12 6TF
Tel: 01327-359135 **Fax:** 01327-359602
E-mail: vanessap@prpopto.co.uk
Website: http://www.prpopto.com
Bank(s): Lloyds
Directors: N. Lethby (Fin), P. Stark (Co Sec)
Managers: L. McHenry (Sales & Mktg Mg), R. Green, G. Plain
Immediate Holding Company: PRP OPTOELECTRONICS LIMITED
Registration no: 02383612 **VAT No.:** GB 536 3372 45
Date established: 1989 **Turnover:** £2m - £5m **No.of Employees:** 21 - 50
Product Groups: 37, 39

Date of Accounts	Sep 11	Sep 10	Sep 09
Working Capital	2m	2m	2m
Fixed Assets	288	292	289
Current Assets	3m	3m	2m

P V C Rainwear
Burcote Wood Business Centre Wood Burcote, Towcester, NN12 8TA
Tel: 01327-352222 **Fax:** 01327-359995
Website: http://www.pvcrainwear.com
Directors: G. Louther (Dir)
No.of Employees: 11 - 20 **Product Groups:** 22, 24

Pro-Align Ltd
The Old Orhard Towcester Road, Greens Norton, Towcester, NN12 8AN
Tel: 01327-323007 **Fax:** 01327-354529
E-mail: carl.potter@pro-align.co.uk
Website: http://www.pro-align.co.uk
Directors: P. Beaurain (MD)
Managers: C. Potter (Chief Mgr)
Registration no: 02572576 **No.of Employees:** 21 - 50 **Product Groups:** 39

Sandwell UK Ltd
Unit 2 Foundry Place Old Tiffield Road, Towcester, NN12 6FP
Tel: 01327-350205 **Fax:** 01327-350222
E-mail: sales@sandwell-uk.com
Website: http://www.sandwell-uk.com
Directors: S. McGrory (Fin)
Immediate Holding Company: SANDWELL UK LIMITED
Registration no: 04295201 **Date established:** 2001
No.of Employees: 11 - 20 **Product Groups:** 46, 48

Date of Accounts	Aug 11	Aug 10	Aug 09
Working Capital	288	236	189
Fixed Assets	144	85	107
Current Assets	379	305	235

Saul Research
51 Windsor Close, Towcester, NN12 6JB
Tel: 01327-353720 **Fax:** 01327-353720
E-mail: h@saulresearch.co.uk
Website: http://www.saulresearch.co.uk
Directors: P. Saul (MD), P. Saul (Prop)
No.of Employees: 1 - 10 **Product Groups:** 37, 38, 44, 67, 84

Robert Speck Ltd
Little Ridge Whittlebury Road, Silverstone, Towcester, NN12 8UD
Tel: 01327-857307 **Fax:** 01327-858166
E-mail: info@robertspeck.com
Website: http://www.robertspeck.com
Directors: M. Carpenter (Prop)
Immediate Holding Company: ROBERT SPECK LIMITED
Registration no: 00528241 **Date established:** 1954
No.of Employees: 1 - 10 **Product Groups:** 46, 47, 67

Date of Accounts	Mar 11	Mar 10	Mar 09
Working Capital	118	145	155
Fixed Assets	10	11	11
Current Assets	175	264	227

StrainSense Ltd
The Old Barn Woods Lane, Potterspury, Towcester, NN12 7PT
Tel: 01908-543038 **Fax:** 08700-940810
E-mail: sales@strainsense.co.uk
Website: http://www.strainsense.co.uk
Directors: A. Cross (MD), J. Cross (Fin)
Immediate Holding Company: STRAINSENSE LIMITED
Registration no: 04459986 **VAT No.:** GB 795 2044 15
Date established: 2002 **Turnover:** £500,000 - £1m
No.of Employees: 1 - 10 **Product Groups:** 37, 38, 39, 85

Date of Accounts	Mar 12	Mar 11	Mar 10
Working Capital	35	14	-77
Fixed Assets	6	6	6
Current Assets	255	211	138

T T S
Unit 3 West End Farm West End, Silverstone, Towcester, NN12 8UY
Tel: 01327-858212 **Fax:** 01327-858099
E-mail: richard@tts-performance.co.uk
Website: http://www.tts-performance.com
Directors: R. Albans (Prop)
Immediate Holding Company: SILVERSTONE COMMUNICATIONS LTD
Date established: 2006 **No.of Employees:** 1 - 10 **Product Groups:** 39, 40

Tanks Pumps & Equipment Ltd
26 The Slade Silverstone, Towcester, NN12 8UH
Tel: 01327-857676 **Fax:** 01327-857676
Directors: L. Bayliss (Co Sec)
Immediate Holding Company: TANKS PUMPS & EQUIPMENT LIMITED
Registration no: 03686771 **Date established:** 1998
No.of Employees: 1 - 10 **Product Groups:** 35, 42, 45

Date of Accounts	Dec 11	Dec 10	Dec 09
Working Capital	21	6	19
Fixed Assets	14	18	8
Current Assets	60	54	50

Technical Direct Ltd

York Farm Business Centre Watling Street, Towcester, NN12 8EU
Tel: 01327-830109 **Fax:** 01327-830969
E-mail: admin@technicaldirect.co.uk
Website: http://www.technicaldirect.co.uk
Directors: N. Rimmer (Dir)
Ultimate Holding Company: WOODBOURNE BOLBECK LIMITED
Immediate Holding Company: TECHNICAL DIRECT (UK) LIMITED
Registration no: 04478615 **Date established:** 2002
No.of Employees: 1 - 10 **Product Groups:** 37, 44

Date of Accounts	Jan 11	Jan 10	Jan 09
Working Capital	155	179	124
Fixed Assets	93	97	110
Current Assets	262	290	209

Timbercraft Cabinet Displays

Abercorn House York Farm Business Centre Watling Street, Towcester, NN12 8EU
Tel: 01327-830663 **Fax:** 01327-830963
E-mail: info@displaycases.co.uk
Website: http://www.displaycases.co.uk
Directors: D. Cooper (Prop)
Ultimate Holding Company: WOODBOURNE BOLBECK LIMITED
Immediate Holding Company: TECHNICAL DIRECT (UK) LIMITED
Registration no: 04478615 **Date established:** 2002
No.of Employees: 1 - 10 **Product Groups:** 26, 30, 33, 49

Date of Accounts	Jan 11	Jan 10	Jan 09
Working Capital	155	179	124
Fixed Assets	93	97	110
Current Assets	262	290	209

Weddel Swift Distribution Ltd (Randall Parker Food Group)

The Old Rectory Banbury Lane, Cold Higham, Towcester, NN12 8LR
Tel: 01327-830888 **Fax:** 01327-830868
E-mail: info@wsdepots.com
Website: http://www.wsdepots.com
Bank(s): Lloyds
Directors: R. Field (Grp Chief Exec)
Managers: J. Simon (Comptroller), E. Harmston (Personnel), S. Hulbert (Tech Serv Mgr)
Ultimate Holding Company: RANDALL PARKER FOOD GROUP LIMITED
Immediate Holding Company: WEDDEL SWIFT LIMITED
Registration no: 04021321 **Date established:** 2000
Turnover: £20m - £50m **No.of Employees:** 11 - 20 **Product Groups:** 61

Date of Accounts	Sep 11	Sep 10	Sep 09
Sales Turnover	48m	44m	57m
Pre Tax Profit/Loss	-197	95	683
Working Capital	3m	3m	3m
Fixed Assets	78	80	106
Current Assets	15m	13m	14m
Current Liabilities	4m	3m	3m

Zip Karts

Unit 1 Silverstone Tech Park, Silverstone Circuit, Towcester, NN12 8TN
Tel: 01327-855310 **Fax:** 01992-447327
E-mail: info@zipkart.com
Website: http://www.zipkart.com
Bank(s): Barclays
Directors: M. Hines (MD)
Immediate Holding Company: Zip Kart Ltd
Registration no: 02373526 **VAT No.:** GB 214 1344 13
Date established: 1989 **Turnover:** Up to £250,000
No.of Employees: 11 - 20 **Product Groups:** 39

Wellingborough

1st Direct Vehicle Rentals

3 Morris Close Park Farm Industrial Estate, Wellingborough, NN8 6XF
Tel: 01933-400002 **Fax:** 01933-274321
Website: http://www.europcar.co.uk
Managers: H. Auriemma (Mgr)
Immediate Holding Company: MAILSHOT LTD
Registration no: 02158135 **VAT No.:** GB 408 6023 72
Date established: 1987 **Turnover:** £2m - £5m **No.of Employees:** 1 - 10
Product Groups: 81

Ability Training

Kimbolton Road Chelveston, Wellingborough, NN9 6AN
Tel: 01933-624218 **Fax:** 01933-622393
E-mail: sales@jst-forktrucks.co.uk
Website: http://www.abilitytraining.co.uk
Directors: J. Kew (Dir)
Ultimate Holding Company: J.S.T. FORKLIFTS LIMITED
Immediate Holding Company: ABILITY TRAINING LIMITED
Registration no: 03484136 **Date established:** 1997
No.of Employees: 1 - 10 **Product Groups:** 35, 39, 45

Date of Accounts	Jun 11	Jun 10	Jun 09
Working Capital	-57	-66	-64
Fixed Assets	N/A	9	9
Current Assets	N/A	N/A	5

Airwair International Ltd

Cobbs Lane Wollaston, Wellingborough, NN29 7SW
Tel: 01933-663281 **Fax:** 01933-663848
E-mail: david.suddens@drmartens.com
Website: http://www.drmartens.co.uk
Directors: P. Humphrey (Pers), A. Wright (Fin)
Managers: A. Mason, F. Mitchell, D. Suddens, N. Harris (Tech Serv Mgr)
Ultimate Holding Company: R GRIGGS GROUP LIMITED
Immediate Holding Company: AIRWAIR INTERNATIONAL LIMITED
Registration no: 03009359 **Date established:** 1995
Turnover: £75m - £125m **No.of Employees:** 51 - 100 **Product Groups:** 61

Date of Accounts	Mar 12	Mar 11	Mar 10
Sales Turnover	90m	78m	52m
Pre Tax Profit/Loss	18m	12m	2m
Working Capital	7m	-11m	-25m
Fixed Assets	3m	1m	579
Current Assets	30m	21m	9m
Current Liabilities	2m	3m	2m

Aleph Europe Ltd

1 Newton Close Park Farm Industrial Estate, Wellingborough, NN8 6UW
Tel: 01933-679600 **Fax:** 01933-401165
E-mail: info@alepheurope.com
Website: http://www.alepheurope.com
Directors: T. Horinouchi (Dir)
Ultimate Holding Company: Nippon Aleph Corporation (Japan)
Immediate Holding Company: ALEPH EUROPE LIMITED
Registration no: 02174023 **VAT No.:** GB 486 3195 14
Date established: 1987 **Turnover:** £2m - £5m **No.of Employees:** 1 - 10
Product Groups: 37, 38, 40

Date of Accounts	Dec 07	Dec 06	Dec 05
Working Capital	321	312	299
Fixed Assets	13	15	11
Current Assets	662	682	395
Current Liabilities	341	369	96
Total Share Capital	50	50	50

A-Lift Crane Hire Ltd

Denham House 131 Main Road, Wilby, Wellingborough, NN8 2UB
Tel: 01933-222412 **Fax:** 01933-225584
E-mail: enquiries@aliftcranehire.co.uk
Website: http://www.aliftcranehire.co.uk
Directors: D. Robson (MD)
Immediate Holding Company: A-LIFT CRANE HIRE LIMITED
Registration no: 05076670 **Date established:** 2004
Turnover: £500,000 - £1m **No.of Employees:** 1 - 10 **Product Groups:** 83

Date of Accounts	Oct 11	Apr 10	Apr 09
Working Capital	127	171	120
Fixed Assets	593	308	306
Current Assets	470	293	203

Allen Concrete Ltd

35-37 Rixon Road Finedon Road Industrial Estate, Wellingborough, NN8 4BA
Tel: 01933-276848 **Fax:** 01933-442013
E-mail: info@allenconcrete.co.uk
Website: http://www.allenconcrete.co.uk
Bank(s): Barclays
Managers: N. Crowhurst (Sales Prom Mgr)
Ultimate Holding Company: TOPCRETE LIMITED
Immediate Holding Company: ALLEN (CONCRETE) LIMITED
Registration no: 02120862 **VAT No.:** GB 209 3411 88
Date established: 1987 **Turnover:** £2m - £5m **No.of Employees:** 11 - 20
Product Groups: 33

Date of Accounts	Feb 08	Feb 11	Feb 10
Working Capital	1m	1m	1m
Fixed Assets	3m	4m	4m
Current Assets	2m	2m	2m

Andromeda Products Ltd

6 Stanton Close Finedon Road Industrial Estate, Wellingborough, NN8 4HN
Tel: 01933-234448 **Fax:** 01933-234449
E-mail: sales@andromeda-ltd.co.uk
Website: http://www.andromeda-ltd.co.uk
Directors: P. Darcy (Fin)
Managers: A. D'Arcy (Sales Prom Mgr), C. D'Arcy (Sales Prom Mgr), M. Shooter (Sales Prom Mgr)
Ultimate Holding Company: ANDROMEDA PRODUCTS LIMITED
Registration no: 02336293 **VAT No.:** GB 554 1047 64
Date established: 1989 **Turnover:** £500,000 - £1m
No.of Employees: 1 - 10 **Product Groups:** 37

Date of Accounts	Mar 08	Mar 07	Mar 06
Sales Turnover	N/A	N/A	875
Pre Tax Profit/Loss	N/A	41	28
Working Capital	354	332	298
Fixed Assets	10	11	13
Current Assets	617	549	548
Current Liabilities	262	217	250
Total Share Capital	6	6	6
ROCE% (Return on Capital Employed)		11.9	9.0
ROT% (Return on Turnover)			3.2

B F Bassett & Findley Ltd

Talbot Road North, Wellingborough, NN8 1QS
Tel: 01933-224898 **Fax:** 01933-227731
E-mail: info@bassettandfindley.ltd.uk
Website: http://www.bassettandfindley.co.uk
Bank(s): HSBC Bank plc
Directors: J. Spencer (Fin)
Managers: K. McDermott (Sales Prom Mgr), L. Clipstone (Tech Serv Mgr), C. Shakespeare
Ultimate Holding Company: BASSETT & FINDLEY HOLDINGS LIMITED
Immediate Holding Company: SUNNY AFTERNOON LIMITED
Registration no: 00171730 **VAT No.:** GB 119 1807 74
Date established: 2020 **No.of Employees:** 21 - 50 **Product Groups:** 26, 35, 49, 52

Date of Accounts	Dec 09	Dec 08	Dec 07
Working Capital	830	1m	1m
Fixed Assets	144	168	179
Current Assets	1m	2m	2m

B I Engineering

Crane Close Denington Industrial Estate, Wellingborough, NN8 2QG
Tel: 01933-228012 **Fax:** 01933-441935
E-mail: enquiries@biengineering.co.uk
Website: http://www.btconect.com
Bank(s): Barclays
Directors: J. Macham (MD)
Managers: A. Dynes, C. King (Purch Mgr)
Immediate Holding Company: BOZEAT INDUSTRIAL LIMITED
Registration no: 03770579 **VAT No.:** GB 284 6657 15
Date established: 1975 **Turnover:** £2m - £5m
No.of Employees: 101 - 250 **Product Groups:** 39

Date of Accounts	Sep 11	Sep 10	Sep 09
Working Capital	668	515	539
Fixed Assets	N/A	1m	1m
Current Assets	2m	2m	2m

Scott Bader Co. Ltd

Wollaston Hall Wollaston, Wellingborough, NN29 7RL
Tel: 01933-663100 **Fax:** 01933-663028
E-mail: info@scottbader.com
Website: http://www.scottbader.com
Bank(s): National Westminster Bank Plc
Directors: A. Forester (Fin), P. Ayears (Purch)
Managers: G. Singh, S. Dyas (Mktg Serv Mgr)
Ultimate Holding Company: SCOTT BADER COMMONWEALTH LIMITED(THE)
Immediate Holding Company: SCOTT BADER UK LIMITED
Registration no: 04562724 **Date established:** 2002
Turnover: £50m - £75m **No.of Employees:** 101 - 250
Product Groups: 23, 30, 31, 32, 33, 52, 66

Date of Accounts	Dec 11	Dec 10	Dec 09
Sales Turnover	75m	65m	55m
Pre Tax Profit/Loss	971	528	3m
Working Capital	348	3m	2m
Fixed Assets	15m	13m	14m
Current Assets	23m	24m	19m
Current Liabilities	2m	2m	2m

Booker Cash & Carry Ltd

Equity House Irthlingborough Road, Wellingborough, NN8 1LT
Tel: 01933-371000 **Fax:** 01933-371010
Website: http://www.booker.co.uk
Directors: C. Wilson (Grp Chief Exec), J. Prentis (Fin), M. Chilton (Co Sec)
Ultimate Holding Company: BOOKER GROUP PLC
Immediate Holding Company: BOOKER CASH & CARRY LIMITED
Registration no: 05355306 **VAT No.:** GB 222 3640 04
Date established: 2005 **Turnover:** Over £1,000m
No.of Employees: 1501 & over **Product Groups:** 61

Date of Accounts	Mar 12	Mar 09	Mar 10
Sales Turnover	3736m	3094m	3285m
Pre Tax Profit/Loss	65m	34m	53m
Working Capital	404m	212m	248m
Fixed Assets	154m	398m	387m
Current Assets	1043m	638m	746m
Current Liabilities	59m	48m	56m

Brandcontact UK Ltd

19 Thames Road, Wellingborough, NN8 5WU
Tel: 01933-401820 **Fax:** 01933-401396
E-mail: bc@brandcontact.co.uk
Website: http://www.brandcontact.co.uk
Directors: N. Asodia (Fin)
Immediate Holding Company: BRANDCONTACT (UK) LIMITED
Registration no: 02903111 **VAT No.:** GB 638 3486 10
Date established: 1994 **Turnover:** £500,000 - £1m
No.of Employees: 1 - 10 **Product Groups:** 61

Date of Accounts	Apr 11	Apr 10	Apr 09
Working Capital	41	60	52
Fixed Assets	1	1	2
Current Assets	205	294	299

Bushboard Ltd

Rixon Road, Wellingborough, NN8 4BA
Tel: 01933-232200 **Fax:** 01933-232280
E-mail: washrooms@bushboard.co.uk
Website: http://www.bushboard.co.uk
Bank(s): Lloyds TSB Bank plc
Directors: M. Rees (Dir), N. Horton (Comm), D. Campden (Fin)
Ultimate Holding Company: INTERCEDE HOLDCO LIMITED
Immediate Holding Company: BUSHBOARD WASHROOM SYSTEMS LIMITED
Registration no: 02058476 **Date established:** 1986 **Turnover:** £5m - £10m
No.of Employees: 51 - 100 **Product Groups:** 26

Date of Accounts	Dec 11	Dec 10	Dec 09
Sales Turnover	8m	7m	7m
Pre Tax Profit/Loss	-3m	772	156
Working Capital	4m	3m	3m
Fixed Assets	128	146	146
Current Assets	4m	6m	12m
Current Liabilities	519	2m	526

C B Training

11 Eastlands Road Finedon, Wellingborough, NN9 5DZ
Tel: 01933-398028 **Fax:** 01933- 398028
E-mail: cbt@ntlworld.com
Directors: C. Brailey (Prop)
Date established: 2001 **No.of Employees:** 1 - 10 **Product Groups:** 35, 39, 45

Central Strapping Co.

109a Leyland Trading Estate, Wellingborough, NN8 1RT
Tel: 01933-443335 **Fax:** 01933-443336
E-mail: sales@central-strapping.co.uk
Directors: N. Bennett (Prop)
Immediate Holding Company: THE CENTRAL STRAPPING CO. LIMITED
Registration no: 03900058 **Date established:** 1999
No.of Employees: 1 - 10 **Product Groups:** 38, 42

CESAB Material Handling UK

10 Regent Park Park Farm Industrial Estate, Wellingborough, NN8 6GR
Tel: 01933-670462 **Fax:** 01933-679854
E-mail: marketing@cesab-forklifts.co.uk
Website: http://www.cesab-forklifts.co.uk
Directors: A. Bialetti (Sales & Mktg)
Managers: T. Stephens (Chief Mgr), M. Hobdey (Sales Prom Mgr), S. Siricusoa (Chief Mgr), P. Siracusa (Chief Mgr)
Ultimate Holding Company: TOYOTA INDUSTRIES CORP (JAPAN)
Immediate Holding Company: CESAB LIMITED
Registration no: 02570888 **VAT No.:** GB 547 6274 17
Date established: 1990 **Turnover:** £1m - £2m **No.of Employees:** 1 - 10
Product Groups: 45, 67, 83, 84

Date of Accounts	Mar 11	Mar 10	Mar 09
Sales Turnover	2m	1m	N/A
Pre Tax Profit/Loss	8	-17	N/A
Working Capital	43	35	49
Fixed Assets	28	29	32
Current Assets	683	839	1m
Current Liabilities	121	107	N/A

Chubb Electronic Security Ltd (Branch Office)

4 Dencora Business Park Booth Drive, Park Farm Industrial Estate, Wellingborough, NN8 6GR
Tel: 01933-671070 **Fax:** 01933-671079
E-mail: wellingborough@chubbsecurity.co.uk
Website: http://www.chubb.co.uk
Managers: D. Bolton (Sec), M. Ault (Ops Mgr)
Immediate Holding Company: CHUBB GROUP SECURITY LTD
Registration no: 00524469 **Date established:** 1999
Turnover: £500m - £1,000m **No.of Employees:** 51 - 100
Product Groups: 36, 40

Date of Accounts	Dec 11	Dec 10	Dec 09
Sales Turnover	61m	97m	89m
Pre Tax Profit/Loss	-9m	1m	1m
Working Capital	189	9m	8m
Fixed Assets	14m	15m	11m
Current Assets	129m	27m	19m
Current Liabilities	7m	10m	6m

Chubb Security Personel
Booth Drive Park Farm Industrial Estate, Wellingborough, NN8 6GR
Tel: 01933-671000 **Fax:** 01933-671116
E-mail: jackiegregory@chubb.co.uk
Website: http://www.chubb.co.uk
Directors: G. Broad (Sales), P. Rose (Fin)
Managers: J. Gregory (Mktg Serv Mgr)
Ultimate Holding Company: MARMON HOLDINGS INC (USA)
Immediate Holding Company: CHUBB GROUP SECURITY LTD
Registration no: 01062876 **Date established:** 1999
Turnover: £125m - £250m **No.of Employees:** 1501 & over
Product Groups: 81

Copeman Hart & Co. Ltd
Finedon Road Irthlingborough, Wellingborough, NN9 5TZ
Tel: 01933-652600 **Fax:** 01933-652288
E-mail: info@copemanhart.co.uk
Website: http://www.copemanhart.co.uk
Directors: E. Hart (MD)
Immediate Holding Company: COPEMAN HART & COMPANY LIMITED
Registration no: 00696548 **VAT No.:** GB 233 7239 69
Date established: 1961 **Turnover:** £250,000 - £500,000
No.of Employees: 1 - 10 **Product Groups:** 49

Date of Accounts	**Mar 12**	**Mar 11**	**Mar 10**
Working Capital	-29	129	41
Fixed Assets	12	4	168
Current Assets	146	161	178

Corus
12-14 Bridle Close Finedon Road Industrial Estate, Wellingborough, NN8 4RN
Tel: 01933-440123 **Fax:** 01933-440326
E-mail: sally.chisholm-lee@corusgroup.com
Website: http://www.corusgroup.com
Managers: R. Lee (Sales Prom Mgr), S. Chisholm-Lee (Chief Mgr), S. Chisholm Lee (Mgr)
Immediate Holding Company: CORUS GROUP LIMITED
Registration no: 03811373 **Date established:** 1999
No.of Employees: 11 - 20 **Product Groups:** 66

Cox Geo J Ltd
160 Alexandra Road, Wellingborough, NN8 1EH
Tel: 01933-224181 **Fax:** 01933-277892
E-mail: steve@georgecox.co.uk
Website: http://www.georgecox.co.uk
Directors: A. Waterfield (MD)
Managers: S. Collins (Mgr)
Immediate Holding Company: GEO.J.COX LTD
Registration no: 00286315 **VAT No.:** GB 119 1140 07
Turnover: £2m - £5m **No.of Employees:** 1 - 10 **Product Groups:** 22

Date of Accounts	**Mar 11**	**Mar 10**	**Mar 09**
Working Capital	287	286	232
Fixed Assets	504	497	500
Current Assets	446	439	338

Fenton Precision Engineering Ltd
Finedon Sidings Trading Estate Furnace Lane, Finedon, Wellingborough, NN9 5NY
Tel: 01536-723488 **Fax:** 01536-726642
E-mail: sales@fentonprecision.co.uk
Website: http://www.fentonprecision.co.uk
Directors: A. Atkins (MD)
Immediate Holding Company: FENTON PRECISION LTD
Registration no: 05129085 **Date established:** 2004 **Turnover:** £1m - £2m
No.of Employees: 21 - 50 **Product Groups:** 46, 48

Date of Accounts	**Sep 11**	**Sep 10**	**Sep 09**
Working Capital	-0	-0	-0

Foam Techniques Ltd
Booth Drive Park Farm Industrial Estate, Wellingborough, NN8 6GR
Tel: 01933-400096 **Fax:** 01933-400095
E-mail: vrelan@foamtechniques.co.uk
Website: http://www.foamtechniques.co.uk
Bank(s): Lloyds TSB Bank plc
Directors: V. Relan (Fin)
Managers: L. Eddie (Tech Serv Mgr), S. Thomas (Sales & Mktg Mg), G. Oliver
Immediate Holding Company: FOAM TECHNIQUES LIMITED
Registration no: 02078810 **VAT No.:** GB 443 8901 38
Date established: 1986 **Turnover:** £2m - £5m **No.of Employees:** 51 - 100
Product Groups: 23, 24, 27, 29, 30, 31, 32, 33, 39, 42, 49, 66, 76

Date of Accounts	**Mar 11**	**Mar 10**	**Mar 09**
Pre Tax Profit/Loss	N/A	N/A	73
Working Capital	1m	1m	1m
Fixed Assets	321	135	187
Current Assets	2m	2m	2m
Current Liabilities	N/A	N/A	144

Freeman Finance Ltd
24 Coulon Close Irchester, Wellingborough, NN29 7UW
Tel: 01933-318530
E-mail: info@leasingforbusiness.co.uk
Website: http://www.leasingforbusiness.co.uk
Directors: C. Lambrick (Fin), E. Lambrick (MD)
Immediate Holding Company: FREEMAN FINANCE LIMITED
Registration no: 05020165 **Date established:** 2004
Turnover: Up to £250,000 **No.of Employees:** 1 - 10 **Product Groups:** 82

Date of Accounts	**Dec 07**	**Mar 11**	**Mar 10**
Working Capital	-0	-3	-12
Fixed Assets	1	N/A	N/A
Current Assets	9	9	5

Gallay
Paterson Road Finedon Road Industrial Estate, Wellingborough, NN8 4BZ
Tel: 01933-224801 **Fax:** 01933-279902
E-mail: sales@gallay.co.uk
Website: http://www.gallay.co.uk
Bank(s): Barclays
Directors: S. Kenyon (Dir)
Managers: J. Richards (Purch Mgr), T. Hewitt (Sales & Mktg Mg)
Ultimate Holding Company: MCANDREW LIMITED
Immediate Holding Company: GALLAY LIMITED
Registration no: 03376867 **Date established:** 1997 **Turnover:** £5m - £10m
No.of Employees: 51 - 100 **Product Groups:** 39, 40

Date of Accounts	**Dec 11**	**Dec 10**	**Dec 09**
Sales Turnover	8m	9m	8m
Pre Tax Profit/Loss	1m	1m	2
Working Capital	4m	4m	3m
Fixed Assets	1m	855	909
Current Assets	5m	5m	4m
Current Liabilities	708	1m	184

Glenvale Packaging
Unit 3 Edison Close, Park Farm Industrial Estate, Wellingborough, NN8 6AH
Tel: 01933-673677 **Fax:** 01933-676728
E-mail: garrycoleman@glenvale-pkg.co.uk
Website: http://www.glenvale-pkg.co.uk
Directors: G. Coleman (Ptnr)
VAT No.: GB 576 7921 87 **Turnover:** £250,000 - £500,000
No.of Employees: 1 - 10 **Product Groups:** 35, 42, 67

Global Cutting Technologies Ltd
Unit 12 Trinity Centre Park Farm Industrial Estate, Wellingborough, NN8 6ZB
Tel: 01933-676060 **Fax:** 01933-273399
E-mail: sales@gct-online.co.uk
Website: http://www.gct-online.co.uk
Directors: R. Cosford (MD)
Immediate Holding Company: GLOBAL CUTTING TECHNOLOGIES LIMITED
Registration no: 03541855 **Date established:** 1998
No.of Employees: 1 - 10 **Product Groups:** 37, 42

Date of Accounts	**Sep 11**	**Sep 10**	**Sep 09**
Working Capital	237	171	154
Fixed Assets	21	6	1
Current Assets	683	527	272

Gomex Tools Ltd
Unit 1 Phoenix Court Everitt Close Denington Industrial Estate, Wellingborough, NN8 2QE
Tel: 01933-228185 **Fax:** 01933-229224
E-mail: info@gomex.co.uk
Website: http://www.gomex.co.uk
Managers: P. Newiadomy (Sales Prom Mgr)
Ultimate Holding Company: DUROC AB (SWEDEN)
Immediate Holding Company: GOMEX TOOLS LIMITED
Registration no: 00773907 **VAT No.:** GB 336 5382 48
Date established: 1963 **Turnover:** £250,000 - £500,000
No.of Employees: 1 - 10 **Product Groups:** 36

Date of Accounts	**Dec 11**	**Dec 10**	**Dec 09**
Sales Turnover	324	337	337
Pre Tax Profit/Loss	77	-20	-19
Working Capital	111	34	51
Fixed Assets	N/A	1	4
Current Assets	200	199	205
Current Liabilities	14	18	16

Gracey & Associates Ltd
Three Ways High Street, Chelveston, Wellingborough, NN9 6AS
Tel: 01933-624212 **Fax:** 01933-624608
E-mail: hire@gracey.com
Website: http://www.gracey.com
Directors: D. Murray (Fin), W. Gracey (MD)
Immediate Holding Company: GRACEY AND ASSOCIATES LIMITED
Registration no: 05294413 **Date established:** 2004
Turnover: £250,000 - £500,000 **No.of Employees:** 1 - 10
Product Groups: 38

Hampton Steel & Wire
London Road Denington Industrial Estate, Wellingborough, NN8 2DJ
Tel: 01933-233333 **Fax:** 01933-442701
E-mail: admin@hamptonsteel.co.uk
Website: http://www.hamptonsteel.co.uk
Bank(s): National Westminster Bank Plc
Managers: M. Johnson (Mgr)
Immediate Holding Company: FINDLAY DURHAM & BRODIE LTD
Registration no: 00513560 **VAT No.:** GB 694 4513 10
No.of Employees: 21 - 50 **Product Groups:** 34, 35

Hawkes Technical Ltd
Spencer Parade Stanwick, Wellingborough, NN9 6QJ
Tel: 01933-622492 **Fax:** 01933-624092
E-mail: info@hawkestechnical.com
Website: http://www.hawkestechnical.com
Directors: S. Underwood (Dir)
Immediate Holding Company: HAWKES TECHNICAL LIMITED
Registration no: 01228132 **Date established:** 1975 **Turnover:** £2m - £5m
No.of Employees: 11 - 20 **Product Groups:** 29, 42, 43, 44, 47, 48, 67

Date of Accounts	**Feb 08**	**Feb 11**	**Feb 10**
Working Capital	638	445	543
Fixed Assets	114	103	96
Current Assets	1m	1m	1m

Graham Holmes Astraseal Ltd
Astraseal House Paterson Road, Finedon Road Industrial Estate, Wellingborough, NN8 4EX
Tel: 01933-227233 **Fax:** 01933-228951
E-mail: info@astraseal.com
Website: http://www.astraseal.com
Directors: M. Naylor (Fin), R. Essam (Comm)
Managers: R. Fensom (Tech Serv Mgr), Z. Nedimovic (Sales & Mktg Mg), S. Warren (Purch Mgr)
Ultimate Holding Company: ASTRASEAL (HOLDINGS) LIMITED
Immediate Holding Company: GRAHAM HOLMES ASTRASEAL LIMITED
Registration no: 02593809 **Date established:** 1991
Turnover: £10m - £20m **No.of Employees:** 101 - 250
Product Groups: 30, 33

Date of Accounts	**Mar 11**	**Mar 10**	**Mar 09**
Sales Turnover	15m	17m	16m
Pre Tax Profit/Loss	-2m	5	-847
Working Capital	4m	5m	5m
Fixed Assets	5m	4m	4m
Current Assets	6m	8m	7m
Current Liabilities	642	722	498

I S E Fire Products & Services Ltd
16 Orlingbury Road Little Harrowden, Wellingborough, NN9 5BH
Tel: 01933-677125 **Fax:** 01536-420444
E-mail: sales@isefireproducts.co.uk
Website: http://www.isefireproducts.co.uk
Directors: S. Bates (Fin), N. Bates (MD)
Immediate Holding Company: ISE FIRE PRODUCTS & SERVICES LIMITED
Registration no: 03818395 **Date established:** 1999
Turnover: £500,000 - £1m **No.of Employees:** 11 - 20
Product Groups: 32, 40, 52, 86

Date of Accounts	**Sep 11**	**Sep 10**	**Sep 09**
Sales Turnover	N/A	861	847
Pre Tax Profit/Loss	N/A	162	205
Working Capital	177	124	155
Fixed Assets	373	400	193
Current Assets	333	258	283
Current Liabilities	N/A	90	93

Ideal Manufactures
Atlas House Burton Road, Finedon, Wellingborough, NN9 5HX
Tel: 01933-681616 **Fax:** 01933-681042
E-mail: enquiries@idealmanufacturing.com
Website: http://www.idealmanufacturing.com
Directors: M. Kalli (MD)
Immediate Holding Company: IDEAL CHEMICALS LIMITED
Registration no: 02231803 **Date established:** 1988
No.of Employees: 11 - 20 **Product Groups:** 32, 63

Jaybeam Ltd
Rutherford Drive Park Farm South, Wellingborough, NN8 6AX
Tel: 01933-408408 **Fax:** 01933-408404
E-mail: uk.sales@jaybeamwireless.com
Website: http://www.jaybeam.co.uk
Bank(s): National Westminster Bank Plc
Directors: J. Hartman (MD), S. Roberts (Co Sec), D. Heber Suffrin (Grp Chief Exec)
Managers: D. Jenkins (Purch Mgr), D. Watts (Chief Buyer)
Ultimate Holding Company: AMPHENOL CORPORATION INC (USA)
Registration no: 01008835 **Date established:** 1971
Turnover: £10m - £20m **No.of Employees:** 101 - 250
Product Groups: 35, 37

Date of Accounts	**Dec 07**	**Dec 06**
Sales Turnover	10m	7m
Pre Tax Profit/Loss	-1m	-751
Working Capital	66	319
Fixed Assets	12m	12m
Current Assets	3m	3m
Current Liabilities	500	357

K E B UK Ltd
6 Morris Close Park Farm Industrial Estate, Wellingborough, NN8 6XF
Tel: 01933-402220 **Fax:** 01933-400724
E-mail: info@keb-uk.co.uk
Website: http://www.keb-uk.co.uk
Directors: T. Skelton (MD)
Ultimate Holding Company: BRINKMANN GMBH & CO KG (GERMANY)
Immediate Holding Company: KEB (UK) LIMITED
Registration no: 02258366 **Date established:** 1988 **Turnover:** £2m - £5m
No.of Employees: 1 - 10 **Product Groups:** 35, 37, 38, 67

Date of Accounts	**Dec 11**	**Dec 10**	**Dec 09**
Working Capital	282	268	268
Fixed Assets	58	53	62
Current Assets	840	844	724

Krohne Ltd
Rutherford Drive Park Farm Industrial Estate, Wellingborough, NN8 6AE
Tel: 01933-408500 **Fax:** 01933-408501
E-mail: t.fawcett@krohne.com
Website: http://www.krohne.com
Directors: T. Fawcett (Dir), M. Keir (Fin)
Managers: M. Browning (Prod Mgr), T. McHugh (Mktg Serv Mgr), M. Hindmarch, D. Durkin (Personnel), P. Mutton (Tech Serv Mgr)
Ultimate Holding Company: LUDWIG KROHNE GMBH & CO KG (GERMANY)
Immediate Holding Company: KROHNE LIMITED
Registration no: 01254855 **Date established:** 1976
Turnover: £20m - £50m **No.of Employees:** 101 - 250 **Product Groups:** 38

Date of Accounts	**Dec 11**	**Dec 10**	**Dec 09**
Sales Turnover	23m	19m	19m
Pre Tax Profit/Loss	2m	922	624
Working Capital	1m	164	-444
Fixed Assets	4m	4m	5m
Current Assets	11m	9m	8m
Current Liabilities	1m	894	7m

John Lack Equipment
6 Denington Court Denington Industrial Estate, Wellingborough, NN8 2QR
Tel: 01933-441646 **Fax:** 01933-441476
E-mail: info@johnlack.com
Website: http://www.johnlack.com
Directors: J. Lack (Prop)
No.of Employees: 1 - 10 **Product Groups:** 28, 43, 44, 46, 48

Liquid Control Ltd
Stewarts Road Finedon Road Industrial Estate, Wellingborough, NN8 4RJ
Tel: 01933-277571 **Fax:** 01933-440273
E-mail: sales@liquidcontrol.co.uk
Website: http://www.liquidcontrol.co.uk
Bank(s): Barclays, Northampton
Directors: S. Bridgeman (Sales), K. Khadar (Co Sec), S. Lewis (Fin)
Managers: J. Thomas (Mktg Serv Mgr)
Ultimate Holding Company: GRACO INC (USA)
Immediate Holding Company: LIQUID CONTROL LIMITED
Registration no: 01010237 **Date established:** 1971 **Turnover:** £1m - £2m
No.of Employees: 11 - 20 **Product Groups:** 37, 40, 42, 47

Date of Accounts	**Dec 11**	**Dec 10**	**Dec 09**
Sales Turnover	N/A	N/A	2m
Pre Tax Profit/Loss	N/A	N/A	-132
Working Capital	307	268	312
Fixed Assets	449	425	439
Current Assets	853	754	583
Current Liabilities	N/A	N/A	98

Lonsdale Direct Solutions
Denington Road Denington Industrial Estate, Wellingborough, NN8 2RA
Tel: 01933-228855 **Fax:** 01933-442405
E-mail: info@lonsdaledirect.co.uk
Website: http://www.lonsdaledirect.co.uk
Bank(s): Barclays, Wellingborough
Directors: L. Hornby (MD), D. Lawrence (Fin)
Managers: D. Huckbody (Tech Serv Mgr), G. Kiernan (Mgr), D. Martin (Purch Mgr)
Ultimate Holding Company: ALIMTEAM LIMITED
Immediate Holding Company: LONSDALE PRINT SOLUTIONS LIMITED
Registration no: 00146517 **VAT No.:** GB 336 5344 56
Date established: 2017 **Turnover:** £5m - £10m
No.of Employees: 51 - 100 **Product Groups:** 27, 28

Date of Accounts	**Sep 11**	**Sep 10**	**Sep 09**
Sales Turnover	9m	9m	8m
Pre Tax Profit/Loss	131	315	293

see next page

***Lonsdale Direct Solutions** - Cont'd*

Working Capital	256	332	335
Fixed Assets	3m	3m	3m
Current Assets	3m	2m	3m
Current Liabilities	393	626	529

M C P Ltd

1-4 Nielson Road Finedon Road Industrial Estate, Wellingborough, NN8 4PE
Tel: 01933-225766 **Fax:** 01933-227814
E-mail: info@mcp-group.co.uk
Website: http://www.mcp-group.co.uk
Bank(s): H S B C
Managers: G. Morgan (Sales Prom Mgr), W. Gross (Prod Mgr), M. Harrower (Purch Mgr), N. Pennington (Prod Mgr)
Ultimate Holding Company: MCP GROUP SA (BELGIUM)
Immediate Holding Company: MCP ARAMAYO LIMITED
Registration no: 04526380 **VAT No.:** GB 227 2966 46
Date established: 2002 **Turnover:** £20m - £50m
No.of Employees: 101 - 250 **Product Groups:** 12, 31, 34, 37

Date of Accounts	Dec 07
Sales Turnover	7m
Pre Tax Profit/Loss	9m
Working Capital	589
Fixed Assets	27m
Current Assets	1m
Current Liabilities	168

M. & C. Services (Northampton) Ltd

Victory House Unit 5 Denington Road, Denington Industrial Estate, Wellingborough, NN8 2QH
Tel: 01933-272113 **Fax:** 01933-228347
Website: http://www.mandcservices.co.uk
Directors: S. Wood (Dir)
Registration no: 02728167 **Date established:** 1992
No.of Employees: 1 - 10 **Product Groups:** 35, 39, 45

Date of Accounts	Jul 08	Jul 07	Jul 06
Working Capital	210	234	199
Fixed Assets	1	1	2
Current Assets	240	270	257
Current Liabilities	29	37	59

Mac Systems

10 Vaux Road Finedon Road Industrial Estate, Wellingborough, NN8 4TG
Tel: 01933-441868 **Fax:** 01933-441869
E-mail: sales@macsystemsltd.co.uk
Website: http://www.macsystemsltd.co.uk
Directors: J. Mitchell (Dir)
Immediate Holding Company: BARTON PETROLEUM (HOLDINGS) LIMITED
Registration no: 05073551 **Date established:** 2004
Turnover: £75m - £125m **No.of Employees:** 11 - 20 **Product Groups:** 35, 36, 37, 39, 40, 49, 52

Machine Guard Solutions Ltd

86 Leyland Trading Estate, Wellingborough, NN8 1RT
Tel: 01933-226335 **Fax:** 01933-276501
E-mail: mgsolutions@btconnect.com
Website: http://www.machineguardsolutions.com
Directors: M. Convine (Dir)
Immediate Holding Company: MACHINE GUARD SOLUTIONS LIMITED
Registration no: 06534217 **VAT No.:** GB 787 5668 54
Date established: 2008 **No.of Employees:** 1 - 10 **Product Groups:** 37, 38, 40, 46, 54

Date of Accounts	Mar 12	Mar 11	Mar 10
Working Capital	68	55	48
Fixed Assets	188	205	222
Current Assets	109	130	134

Marco Beverage Systems Ltd

The Shire House Strixton, Wellingborough, NN29 7PA
Tel: 01933-666488 **Fax:** 01933-666968
E-mail: sales@marco-bev.co.uk
Website: http://www.marco-bev.co.uk
Directors: C. York (Sales)
Immediate Holding Company: TAYLORFITCH LIMITED
Registration no: 00085247 **Date established:** 2003
Turnover: £500,000 - £1m **No.of Employees:** 1 - 10 **Product Groups:** 20, 40, 42, 49, 62, 67

Date of Accounts	Mar 11	Mar 10	Mar 09
Working Capital	2	6	12
Fixed Assets	1	1	2
Current Assets	31	40	61

Maziak

1 Stanton Close Finedon Road Industrial Estate, Wellingborough, NN8 4HN
Tel: 01933-222000 **Fax:** 01536-411842
E-mail: j.maziak@maziak.co.uk
Website: http://www.kcas.co.uk
Bank(s): National Westminster
Directors: J. Maziak (MD)
Immediate Holding Company: MAZIAK HOLDINGS LIMITED
Registration no: 04182570 **VAT No.:** 551 0501 91 **Date established:** 2001
No.of Employees: 21 - 50 **Product Groups:** 52

Date of Accounts	Jan 12	Jan 11	Jan 10
Working Capital	-45	-45	-70
Fixed Assets	436	436	435
Current Assets	69	63	23

Microwave Services

1-2 Herriotts Lane, Wellingborough, NN8 4PT
Tel: 01933-442355 **Fax:** 01933-441885
Directors: P. Fletcher (Prop)
Date established: 1978 **No.of Employees:** 1 - 10 **Product Groups:** 36, 40

Motrax Motorcycle Accessories Ltd

230 Station Road Finedon, Wellingborough, NN9 5NT
Tel: 01933-418414 **Fax:** 01933- 418415
Website: http://www.motrax.co.uk
Directors: S. Franklin (Dir), P. Phillips (Fin), C. Sheagh (Fin), S. Sumner (Sales)
Managers: N. Vidler (Personnel), N. Usher, A. Kiani (Tech Serv Mgr)
Ultimate Holding Company: THOMAS SPORTS LIMITED
Immediate Holding Company: MOTRAX MOTORCYCLE ACCESSORIES LIMITED
Registration no: 02815574 **Date established:** 1993 **Turnover:** £5m - £10m
No.of Employees: 21 - 50 **Product Groups:** 24, 36, 39, 40

Date of Accounts	Dec 09	Dec 08	Dec 07
Sales Turnover	7m	8m	10m
Pre Tax Profit/Loss	2m	-21	2m
Working Capital	11m	9m	9m
Fixed Assets	96	184	265
Current Assets	12m	10m	11m
Current Liabilities	294	428	34

The Mug Barn

29-31 Main Street Little Harrowden, Wellingborough, NN9 5BA
Tel: 07812-998597
E-mail: contact@themugbarn.com
Website: http://www.themugbarn.com
Product Groups: 24, 63

Mykal Industries Ltd

Farnsworth House Morris Close, Park Farm Industrial Estate, Wellingborough, NN8 6XF
Tel: 01933-402822 **Fax:** 01933-402488
E-mail: enquiries@mykal.co.uk
Website: http://www.mykal.co.uk
Directors: P. Henderson (Grp Chief Exec), M. Core (Co Sec)
Managers: A. McIvor (Ops Mgr), M. Dent (Mktg Serv Mgr)
Immediate Holding Company: MYKAL INDUSTRIES LIMITED
Registration no: 02715843 **Date established:** 1992 **Turnover:** £2m - £5m
No.of Employees: 21 - 50 **Product Groups:** 23, 32, 39, 46

Date of Accounts	Dec 11	Dec 10	Dec 09
Working Capital	397	379	344
Fixed Assets	899	922	1m
Current Assets	1m	1m	1m

N P S Shoes Ltd

South Street Wollaston, Wellingborough, NN29 7RY
Tel: 01933-664207 **Fax:** 01933-664699
E-mail: info@nps-solovair.co.uk
Website: http://www.nps-solovair.co.uk
Bank(s): Co-operative
Managers: C. Castle (Chief Mgr), M. Hilson (Comptroller)
Immediate Holding Company: NPS (SHOES) LIMITED
Registration no: 05678953 **VAT No.:** GB 120 4002 51
Date established: 2006 **Turnover:** £2m - £5m **No.of Employees:** 21 - 50
Product Groups: 22

Date of Accounts	Mar 11	Mar 10	Mar 09
Working Capital	9	45	78
Fixed Assets	171	165	184
Current Assets	526	433	389

Nimlok Ltd

Nimlok House 45 Booth Drive, Park Farm Industrial Estate, Wellingborough, NN8 6NL
Tel: 01933-409409 **Fax:** 01933-409451
E-mail: info@nimlock.co.uk
Website: http://www.nimlock.co.uk
Directors: J. Roberts (Fin), T. Perutz (Ch)
Immediate Holding Company: P3 GROUP EUROPE LIMITED
Registration no: 00973784 **VAT No.:** GB 239 7575 17
Date established: 1970 **Turnover:** £10m - £20m
No.of Employees: 51 - 100 **Product Groups:** 26

Date of Accounts	Dec 11	Dec 10	Dec 09
Sales Turnover	21m	20m	18m
Pre Tax Profit/Loss	1m	1m	1m
Working Capital	4m	4m	4m
Fixed Assets	991	794	813
Current Assets	8m	7m	7m
Current Liabilities	2m	2m	2m

P E D Technologies Ltd

Brunel Close Park Farm Industrial Estate, Wellingborough, NN8 6QX
Tel: 01933-403777 **Fax:** 01933-403888
E-mail: sales@pafsystems.com
Website: http://www.insulatedcontainers.co.uk
Bank(s): National Westminster Bank Plc
Directors: B. Cheney (Dir)
Immediate Holding Company: PED TECHNOLOGIES LIMITED
Registration no: 01200846 **VAT No.:** GB 281 6727 38
Date established: 1975 **Turnover:** £2m - £5m **No.of Employees:** 11 - 20
Product Groups: 40, 42

Date of Accounts	Apr 12	Apr 11	Apr 10
Working Capital	3	45	29
Fixed Assets	100	99	95
Current Assets	598	651	532

Penhall Ltd

28 Huxley Close, Wellingborough, NN8 6AB
Tel: 01933-678851 **Fax:** 01933-674204
E-mail: bclark@penhall.com
Website: http://www.penhall.com
Directors: D. Kanghton (Dir), D. Knighton (Co Sec)
Immediate Holding Company: PENHALL LIMITED
Registration no: 02944862 **Date established:** 1994
No.of Employees: 1 - 10 **Product Groups:** 46

Date of Accounts	Sep 11	Sep 10	Sep 09
Working Capital	181	209	228
Fixed Assets	96	77	77
Current Assets	271	256	274

Penspell Ltd

1 Bradfield Road Finedon Road Industrial Estate, Wellingborough, NN8 4HB
Tel: 01933-443605 **Fax:** 01933-271489
E-mail: penspell@btclick.com
Website: http://www.penspell.co.uk
Directors: S. Pentlow (Prop), S. Pentlow (MD)
Immediate Holding Company: PENSPELL LIMITED
Registration no: 02556951 **VAT No.:** GB 551 0009 95
Date established: 1990 **Turnover:** £250,000 - £500,000
No.of Employees: 1 - 10 **Product Groups:** 30, 48

Date of Accounts	Dec 07
Working Capital	5
Fixed Assets	13
Current Assets	80
Current Liabilities	74

Pod Exhibition Systems

The Stables Lower Farm High Street, Irchester, Wellingborough, NN29 7AB
Tel: 01933-411159 **Fax:** 01933-411906
E-mail: info@pod-exhibition-systems.co.uk
Website: http://www.pod-exhibition-systems.co.uk
Directors: J. Plosky (Dir)
No.of Employees: 1 - 10 **Product Groups:** 26, 28, 30, 49, 81, 83

Powdat Enamellers Ltd

20-32 Sanders Road Finedon Road Industrial Estate, Wellingborough, NN8 4NL
Tel: 01933-445920 **Fax:** 01933-445924
E-mail: sales@powdat.co.uk
Website: http://www.powdat.co.uk
Bank(s): Barclays, Northampton
Directors: C. Mather (MD), A. Mather (Fin)
Immediate Holding Company: POWDAT ENAMELLERS LIMITED
Registration no: 01174701 **VAT No.:** GB 121 8133 10
Date established: 1974 **Turnover:** £1m - £2m **No.of Employees:** 11 - 20
Product Groups: 48

Date of Accounts	Mar 11	Mar 10	Mar 09
Sales Turnover	1m	943	1m
Pre Tax Profit/Loss	119	9	-69
Working Capital	120	77	165
Fixed Assets	471	394	337
Current Assets	442	342	379
Current Liabilities	140	78	141

R M R Control & Automation Ltd

2 Denington Court Denington Industrial Estate, Wellingborough, NN8 2QR
Tel: 01933-441110 **Fax:** 01933-441130
E-mail: sales@rmr.co.uk
Website: http://www.rmr.co.uk
Directors: R. Fowkes (MD), B. Wilson (Fin)
Immediate Holding Company: RMR CONTROL & AUTOMATION LIMITED
Registration no: 04647012 **VAT No.:** GB 336 5394 41
Date established: 2003 **Turnover:** £1m - £2m **No.of Employees:** 1 - 10
Product Groups: 85

Date of Accounts	Mar 12	Mar 11	Mar 10
Working Capital	189	179	135
Fixed Assets	51	60	69
Current Assets	362	389	255

RPC Containers Ltd

Grove Street Raunds, Wellingborough, NN9 6ED
Tel: 01933-623311 **Fax:** 01933-622126
E-mail: sales@rpc-oakham.co.uk
Website: http://www.rpc-containers.co.uk
Directors: R. Marsh (Grp Chief Exec)
Managers: N. Brittain (Purch Mgr), D. Wingrave, D. Baker (Sales & Mktg Mg), M. Stone, S. Fox (Cust Serv Mgr)
Ultimate Holding Company: RPC Group P.L.C.
Immediate Holding Company: RPC Group plc
Registration no: 02786492 **No.of Employees:** 101 - 250
Product Groups: 30, 66

Date of Accounts	Mar 08	Mar 07	Mar 06
Sales Turnover	198400	203500	201180
Pre Tax Profit/Loss	-1900	500	5100
Working Capital	-34800	-37100	-32250
Fixed Assets	83400	85700	83320
Current Assets	70600	70400	65380
Current Liabilities	105400	107500	97630
Total Share Capital	10000	10000	10000
ROCE% (Return on Capital Employed)	-3.9	1.0	10.0
ROT% (Return on Turnover)	-1.0	0.2	2.5

Saeloc Ltd

28 Huxley Close, Wellingborough, NN8 6AB
Tel: 01933-678000 **Fax:** 01933-678999
E-mail: sales@saeloc.co.uk
Website: http://www.saeloc.co.uk
Directors: D. Knighton (Fin), M. Clark (I.T. Dir)
Immediate Holding Company: SAELOC LIMITED
Registration no: 03782035 **Date established:** 1999
No.of Employees: 1 - 10 **Product Groups:** 38, 42

Date of Accounts	Mar 11	Mar 10	Mar 09
Working Capital	122	152	165
Fixed Assets	55	38	4
Current Assets	290	339	418

Santa Pod Raceway

Airfield Road Podington, Wellingborough, NN29 7XA
Tel: 01234-782828 **Fax:** 01234-782818
E-mail: info@santapod.com
Website: http://www.santapod.co.uk
Managers: D. Lloyd-Jones (Mgr)
Immediate Holding Company: TRAKBAK RACING LIMITED
Registration no: 03470065 **VAT No.:** GB 706 1275 58
Date established: 1997 **Turnover:** £1m - £2m **No.of Employees:** 1 - 10
Product Groups: 81

Date of Accounts	Dec 11	Dec 10	Dec 09
Working Capital	-542	-652	-584
Fixed Assets	993	1m	1m
Current Assets	595	396	409

Simon O'Neill Design + Promotions

27 Sanders Road Finedon Rd Ind Est, Wellingborough, NN8 4NL
Tel: 01933-442974 **Fax:** 01933-443786
E-mail: simon@sondp.com
Website: http://www.sondp.com
Directors: S. O'neill (Prop)
Managers: L. Mark (Mktg Serv Mgr), L. Sweeney (Sales Prom Mgr), S. Hagan (Mktg Serv Mgr)
Date established: 1990 **No.of Employees:** 1 - 10 **Product Groups:** 22, 24, 27, 28, 49, 81

SIPS UK Ltd

Unit 18 New Barn Farm Industrial Estate, Brick Kiln Road, Raunds, Wellingborough, NN9 6HY
Tel: 01933-622007 **Fax:** 01234-860171
E-mail: njp@sips.uk.com
Website: http://www.sips.uk.com
Product Groups: 25, 52, 66, 84

Date of Accounts	Dec 07
Working Capital	-29
Fixed Assets	75
Current Assets	115
Current Liabilities	143

Sloane Ltd

2-20 Booth Drive Park Farm Industrial Estate, Wellingborough, NN8 6GR
Tel: 01933-401555 **Fax:** 01933-400507
E-mail: info@sloanegroup.co.uk
Website: http://www.sloanegroup.co.uk
Bank(s): National Westminster
Directors: S. Woodhouse (MD)
Managers: T. Lambert (Develop Mgr), J. Williams (Tech Serv Mgr), M. Brown (Buyer), G. Phillips (Fin Mgr)

Ultimate Holding Company: BERKSHIRE HATHAWAY INC (USA)
Immediate Holding Company: SLOANE LIMITED
Registration no: 05048227 **VAT No.:** GB 232 9346 64
Date established: 2004 **Turnover:** £10m - £20m
No.of Employees: 21 - 50 **Product Groups:** 26, 35, 49

The Soft Group

177 Mill Road, Wellingborough, NN8 1PR
Tel: 01933-225672
E-mail: info@thesoftgroup.com
Website: http://www.thesoftgroup.com
Directors: V. Cox (MD)
Date established: 2003 **No.of Employees:** 1 - 10 **Product Groups:** 24, 49

Sonifex Ltd

61 Station Road Irthlingborough, Wellingborough, NN9 5QE
Tel: 01933-650700 **Fax:** 01933-650726
E-mail: sales@sonifex.co.uk
Website: http://www.sonifex.co.uk
Bank(s): HSBC
Directors: M. Brooke (MD), V. Chettle (Co Sec)
Immediate Holding Company: SONIFEX LIMITED
Registration no: 01717864 **VAT No.:** GB 119 8532 52
Date established: 1983 **Turnover:** £1m - £2m **No.of Employees:** 21 - 50
Product Groups: 37, 40, 85

Date of Accounts	Jul 11	Jul 10	Jul 09
Working Capital	2m	2m	2m
Fixed Assets	203	223	235
Current Assets	2m	2m	2m

Spray Craft Coatings Ltd

5 Parsons Hall High Street, Irchester, Wellingborough, NN29 7AB
Tel: 01933-357171 **Fax:** 01933-317825
E-mail: spraycraft.coatings@hotmail.co.uk
Directors: A. Ward (MD)
Immediate Holding Company: SPRAY-CRAFT COATINGS LIMITED
Registration no: 04332886 **Date established:** 2001
No.of Employees: 1 - 10 **Product Groups:** 46, 48

Date of Accounts	Mar 11	Mar 10	Mar 09
Working Capital	-10	-17	-2
Fixed Assets	6	7	9
Current Assets	35	29	35

Sprint Graphics

80 Station Road Irthlingborough, Wellingborough, NN9 5QE
Tel: 01933-651908 **Fax:** 01933-655688
E-mail: sales@sprintgraphics.co.uk
Website: http://www.spirtgraphics.co.uk
Directors: T. Driscoll (Prop), T. Driscoll (MD)
Managers: B. Trow (Mgr)
Immediate Holding Company: CENTRAL GARAGE (IRTHLINGBOROUGH) LIMITED
Registration no: 01086094 **Date established:** 1972
Turnover: Up to £250,000 **No.of Employees:** 1 - 10 **Product Groups:** 26, 27, 28, 30, 39, 40, 48, 49, 67, 81

Date of Accounts	Apr 11	Apr 10	Apr 09
Working Capital	1m	773	756
Fixed Assets	13	551	570
Current Assets	1m	976	949

Stribbons Ltd

99 Sanders Road Finedon Road Industrial Estate, Wellingborough, NN8 4NL
Tel: 01933-443446 **Fax:** 01933-443435
E-mail: sales@stribbons.co.uk
Website: http://www.stribbons.co.uk
Directors: T. Hall-Wright (Sales), A. Spaughton (Mkt Research), S. Curtis (Dir), G. Curtis (MD)
Immediate Holding Company: STRIBBONS LIMITED
Registration no: 05080009 **VAT No.:** GB 550 7578 27
Date established: 2004 **Turnover:** £2m - £5m **No.of Employees:** 1 - 10
Product Groups: 22, 23, 24, 27, 30, 35, 37, 49, 63, 66, 81

Date of Accounts	Dec 09	Dec 08	Dec 07
Working Capital	-24	375	331
Fixed Assets	913	984	1m
Current Assets	249	814	915

T S R Plastics Ltd

Station Road Finedon, Wellingborough, NN9 5NX
Tel: 01536-722333 **Fax:** 01536-725174
E-mail: carlo.tai@tsrplastics.co.uk
Website: http://www.b-line.uk.com
Directors: C. Tai (MD), I. Brookes (Sales)
Managers: C. Wright (Mgr)
Immediate Holding Company: T.S.R.PLASTICS LIMITED
Registration no: 00977074 **Date established:** 1970 **Turnover:** £5m - £10m
No.of Employees: 21 - 50 **Product Groups:** 30, 65

Date of Accounts	Mar 11	Mar 10	Mar 09
Working Capital	2m	2m	2m
Fixed Assets	934	873	920
Current Assets	3m	3m	3m

Tawi UK

4 Phoenix Court Everitt Close, Denington Indl-Est, Wellingborough, NN8 2QE
Tel: 01933-277260 **Fax:** 01933-277209
E-mail: simon.coles@tawi.co.uk
Website: http://www.tawi.co.uk
Directors: L. Emblad (Dir), M. Roberts (Co Sec)
Managers: A. Bellamy (Sales & Mktg Mg), A. Bellemy (Sales & Mktg Mg), P. Kempster (Sales Admin), M. Roberts (Chief Mgr), S. Coles (Sales Prom Mgr)
Ultimate Holding Company: TAWI INTERNATIONAL AB(SWEDEN)
Immediate Holding Company: TAWI UK LIMITED
Registration no: 03447931 **Date established:** 1997
Turnover: Up to £250,000 **No.of Employees:** 1 - 10 **Product Groups:** 36, 38, 39, 40, 44, 45, 48, 67, 84

Date of Accounts	Dec 11	Dec 10	Dec 09
Working Capital	318	309	418
Fixed Assets	30	36	25
Current Assets	448	370	455

Thomas H Loveday

Belgrade Centre Denington Road, Denington Industrial Estate, Wellingborough, NN8 2QH
Tel: 01933-652652 **Fax:** 01933-650454
E-mail: phl@loveson.co.uk
Website: http://www.loveson.co.uk
Directors: M. Loveday (MD), P. Kirby (Sales), S. Loveday (Co Sec)
Immediate Holding Company: THOMAS H.LOVEDAY,LIMITED
Registration no: 00164298 **Date established:** 2020 **Turnover:** £2m - £5m
No.of Employees: 1 - 10 **Product Groups:** 22, 35, 41, 63

Date of Accounts	Mar 09	Mar 08	Feb 07
Sales Turnover	2m	2m	N/A
Pre Tax Profit/Loss	-176	-42	N/A
Working Capital	27	337	367
Fixed Assets	159	25	37
Current Assets	2m	888	821
Current Liabilities	34	355	N/A

Tordoff Wellingborough Ltd

Unit C8 Baird Court Park Farm Industrial Estate, Wellingborough, NN8 6QJ
Tel: 01933-675457 **Fax:** 01933-675665
E-mail: obekuk@btconnect.com
Directors: G. Cobb (Dir), J. Bannell (Co Sec)
Immediate Holding Company: OBEK (U.K.) LIMITED
Registration no: 01814277 **VAT No.:** GB 243 6622 68
Date established: 1984 **Turnover:** £250,000 - £500,000
No.of Employees: 21 - 50 **Product Groups:** 48

Date of Accounts	Sep 08	Sep 07	Sep 06
Working Capital	142	24	35
Fixed Assets	N/A	163	203
Current Assets	146	153	125
Current Liabilities	4	129	89

Turnell & Odell Ltd

61-65 Sanders Road Finedon Road Industrial Estate, Wellingborough, NN8 4NL
Tel: 01933-222061 **Fax:** 01933-440073
E-mail: clive@toengineering.co.uk
Website: http://www.toengineering.co.uk
Bank(s): Barclays
Directors: S. Fyfe (Dir), C. Odell (Dir)
Managers: K. Rees (Tech Serv Mgr), D. Shortland (Prod Eng)
Immediate Holding Company: TURNELL AND ODELL LIMITED
Registration no: 00380198 **Date established:** 1943 **Turnover:** £1m - £2m
No.of Employees: 21 - 50 **Product Groups:** 48

Date of Accounts	Dec 11	Dec 10	Dec 09
Working Capital	109	87	4
Fixed Assets	222	250	215
Current Assets	1m	816	628
Current Liabilities	N/A	306	283

United Forktrucks 1992 Ltd

27 Trojan Centre Finedon Road Industrial Estate, Wellingborough, NN8 4ST
Tel: 01933-275522 **Fax:** 01933-275533
E-mail: wellingborough@unitedforktrucks.co.uk
Website: http://www.unitedforktrucks.co.uk
Managers: P. Scott (Mgr)
Immediate Holding Company: UNITED FORKTRUCKS (1992) LIMITED
Registration no: 02693495 **Date established:** 1992
No.of Employees: 1 - 10 **Product Groups:** 35, 39, 45

Date of Accounts	Apr 12	Apr 11	Apr 10
Sales Turnover	6m	7m	6m
Pre Tax Profit/Loss	83	184	-25
Working Capital	150	-84	-345
Fixed Assets	3m	3m	3m
Current Assets	1m	1m	1m
Current Liabilities	277	262	404

Vermeer UK

45-51 Rixon Road, Wellingborough, NN8 4BA
Tel: 01933-274400 **Fax:** 01933-274403
E-mail: sales@vermeeruk.co.uk
Website: http://www.vermeeruk.co.uk
Directors: L. Goodman (MD), C. Stott (Co Sec)
Registration no: 02242036 **VAT No.:** GB 638 4456 14
No.of Employees: 11 - 20 **Product Groups:** 45

Vredestein UK Ltd

Unit D Whittle Close Park Farm Industrial Estate, Wellingborough, NN8 6TY
Tel: 01933-677770 **Fax:** 01933-675329
E-mail: bettsm@vredestein.com
Website: http://www.vredestein.com
Directors: S. Jackson (MD), M. Betts (Fin)
Managers: J. McCleery, M. Thrower (Fin Mgr), T. Swanson (Sales Off Mgr)
Ultimate Holding Company: APOLLO TYRES LIMITED (INDIA)
Immediate Holding Company: VREDESTEIN (U.K.) LIMITED
Registration no: 00290012 **VAT No.:** GB 238 9471 25
Date established: 1934 **Turnover:** £10m - £20m
No.of Employees: 11 - 20 **Product Groups:** 29

Date of Accounts	Dec 08	Mar 12	Mar 11
Sales Turnover	16m	15m	14m
Pre Tax Profit/Loss	-711	728	548
Working Capital	-2m	-139	-859
Fixed Assets	12	20	12
Current Assets	4m	3m	3m
Current Liabilities	720	501	569

Wayman Engineering

16 Littledale, Wellingborough, NN8 5QW
Tel: 01933-677946 **Fax:** 01933-395874
Website: http://www.waymanengineering.com
Directors: D. Wayman (Fin), P. Wayman (MD)
Registration no: 03847448 **Turnover:** Up to £250,000
No.of Employees: 1 - 10 **Product Groups:** 36, 45, 46, 84

Westland Casting Co. Ltd

4-5 Vaux Road Finedon Road Industrial Estate, Wellingborough, NN8 4TG
Tel: 01933-276718 **Fax:** 01933-442185
E-mail: paul@westlandcasting.co.uk
Website: http://www.westlandcasting.co.uk
Bank(s): Lloyds TSB Bank plc
Directors: P. Borland (MD)
Ultimate Holding Company: RUGELEY METALS LIMITED
Immediate Holding Company: WESTLANDS CASTING CO LIMITED
Registration no: 00715801 **Date established:** 1962 **Turnover:** £1m - £2m
No.of Employees: 11 - 20 **Product Groups:** 34

Date of Accounts	Sep 11	Sep 10	Sep 09
Working Capital	292	269	207
Fixed Assets	114	111	115
Current Assets	718	581	358

Whitworth Holdings Ltd

Victoria Mills London Road, Wellingborough, NN8 2DT
Tel: 01933-443444 **Fax:** 01933-222523
E-mail: enquiries@whitworthbros.ltd.uk
Website: http://www.whitworthbros.ltd.uk
Directors: M. George (Ch), S. Large (Co Sec), T. Davies (Fin)
Managers: S. Mackrell (Chief Acct), S. Houghton (Tech Serv Mgr)
Ultimate Holding Company: PURE MAGIC INDUSTRIES LIMITED
Immediate Holding Company: WHITWORTHS HOLDINGS LIMITED
Registration no: 00300719 **VAT No.:** GB 120 2052 46
Date established: 1935 **Turnover:** £125m - £250m
No.of Employees: 101 - 250 **Product Groups:** 02, 20, 32, 41

Date of Accounts	Mar 11	Mar 10	Mar 09
Sales Turnover	128m	103m	107m
Pre Tax Profit/Loss	2m	6m	5m
Working Capital	36m	44m	35m
Fixed Assets	29m	20m	22m
Current Assets	67m	59m	53m
Current Liabilities	14m	3m	4m

Wittmann Battenfeld UK Ltd

53-61 Sanders Road Finedon Road Industrial Estate, Wellingborough, NN8 4NL
Tel: 01933-275777 **Fax:** 01933-270590
E-mail: sales@wittmann-group.co.uk
Website: http://www.wittmann-group.co.uk
Bank(s): Barclays
Directors: B. Hill (Dir)
Ultimate Holding Company: ADCURAM AG (GERMANY)
Immediate Holding Company: WITTMANN BATTENFELD UK LTD.
Registration no: 00630797 **VAT No.:** GB 338 0622 51
Date established: 1959 **Turnover:** £500m - £1,000m
No.of Employees: 11 - 20 **Product Groups:** 38, 42

Date of Accounts	Dec 11	Dec 10	Dec 09
Working Capital	64	26	-275
Fixed Assets	10	12	30
Current Assets	2m	945	1m

NORTHUMBERLAND

Alnwick

Hardy Advanced Composites
Willowburn Trading Estate, Alnwick, NE66 2PF
Tel: 01665-602550 **Fax:** 01665-602389
E-mail: chrisb@hardycomposites.co.uk
Website: http://www.hardycomposites.co.uk
Bank(s): HSBC Bank plc
Managers: C. Bond
Immediate Holding Company: HARDY ADVANCED COMPOSITES LIMITED
Registration no: 07854970 **Date established:** 2011 **Turnover:** £1m - £2m
No.of Employees: 21 - 50 **Product Groups:** 30, 33, 39, 49, 84

Hardy & Greys Ltd
Willowburn Trading Estate, Alnwick, NE66 2PF
Tel: 01665-602771 **Fax:** 01665-602389
E-mail: enquiries@hardygreys.com
Website: http://www.hardyfishing.com
Directors: R. Maudslay (MD), K. Brewster (Mkt Research), D. Douglas (Pers), I. Bell (Fin)
Managers: H. Collins (Purch Mgr)
Ultimate Holding Company: HARRIS & SHELDON GROUP LIMITED
Immediate Holding Company: HARDY & GREYS LIMITED
Registration no: 00229782 **Date established:** 2028
Turnover: £10m - £20m **No.of Employees:** 51 - 100 **Product Groups:** 49

Date of Accounts	Dec 11	Dec 10	Dec 09
Sales Turnover	13m	13m	13m
Pre Tax Profit/Loss	-859	-309	-567
Working Capital	8m	8m	7m
Fixed Assets	2m	2m	2m
Current Assets	10m	9m	8m
Current Liabilities	457	967	656

Jewson Ltd
Unit 2 Station Yard Wagonway Road, Alnwick, NE66 2NP
Tel: 01665-604218 **Fax:** 01665-510097
E-mail: tony.norton@jewson.co.uk
Website: http://www.jewson.co.uk
Directors: C. Kenward (Fin), P. Hindle (MD), T. Newman (Sales)
Managers: T. Norton (District Mgr)
Ultimate Holding Company: COMPAGNIE DE SAINT GOBAIN (FRANCE)
Immediate Holding Company: JEWSON LIMITED
Registration no: 00348407 **Date established:** 1939
Turnover: £500m - £1,000m **No.of Employees:** 1 - 10
Product Groups: 66

Date of Accounts	Dec 11	Dec 10	Dec 09
Sales Turnover	1606m	1547m	1485m
Pre Tax Profit/Loss	18m	100m	45m
Working Capital	-345m	-250m	-349m
Fixed Assets	496m	387m	461m
Current Assets	657m	1005m	1320m
Current Liabilities	66m	120m	64m

Thomas Sherriff & Co. Ltd
Hawthorn Close Lionheart Enterprise Park, Alnwick, NE66 2HT
Tel: 01665-603555 **Fax:** 01665-510558
Website: http://www.thomassherriff.co.uk
Managers: A. Hedgecock (Mgr)
Immediate Holding Company: THOMAS SHERRIFF AND COMPANY LIMITED
Registration no: 00906135 **Date established:** 1967
No.of Employees: 1 - 10 **Product Groups:** 41

Date of Accounts	Jan 12	Jan 11	Jan 10
Sales Turnover	24m	17m	19m
Pre Tax Profit/Loss	519	536	562
Working Capital	4m	3m	3m
Fixed Assets	1m	1m	1m
Current Assets	8m	8m	6m
Current Liabilities	239	292	480

Swarland Brick
Thrunton, Alnwick, NE66 4SD
Tel: 01665-574229 **Fax:** 01665-574400
E-mail: chris@swarlandbrick.fsnet.co.uk
Website: http://www.swarlandbrick.com
Directors: J. Blythe (MD), J. Blythe (Fin)
Immediate Holding Company: SWARLAND BRICK COMPANY LIMITED(THE)
Registration no: 00323991 **VAT No.:** 175 9014 51 **Date established:** 1937
Turnover: £1m - £2m **No.of Employees:** 1 - 10 **Product Groups:** 33

Date of Accounts	Mar 11	Mar 10	Mar 09
Working Capital	2m	2m	3m
Fixed Assets	208	223	242
Current Assets	2m	3m	3m

Ashington

A-Belco Ltd The A-Belco Group
Factory No1 Jubilee Industrial Estate Jubilee Industrial Estate, Ashington, NE63 8UG
Tel: 01670-813275 **Fax:** 01670-851141
E-mail: sales@cortem.co.uk
Website: http://www.a-belco.co.uk
Directors: B. Scott (Dir)
Managers: E. Slater
Ultimate Holding Company: A-BELCO PROPERTY LIMITED
Immediate Holding Company: A-BELCO (HOLDINGS) LIMITED
Registration no: 04212515 **VAT No.:** GB 621 0374 85
Date established: 2001 **Turnover:** Up to £250,000
No.of Employees: 51 - 100 **Product Groups:** 37

Date of Accounts	Mar 11	Mar 10	Mar 09
Working Capital	78	78	78
Fixed Assets	326	126	126
Current Assets	79	279	279
Current Liabilities	N/A	200	N/A

Alcan Smelting & Power UK
Lynemouth Smelter, Ashington, NE63 9YH
Tel: 01670-393811 **Fax:** 01670-393956
Website: http://www.alcan.com
Directors: W. Jones (MD)
Managers: J. Carr (Admin Off), A. Marchand (Purch Mgr)
Ultimate Holding Company: Alcan Aluminium Ltd (Canada)
Immediate Holding Company: British Alcan Aluminium (UK) Ltd
Registration no: 00750143 **Turnover:** £125m - £250m
No.of Employees: 1 - 10 **Product Groups:** 34

Arefco Special Products Ltd
Jubilee Industrial Estate, Ashington, NE63 8UA
Tel: 01670-819513 **Fax:** 01670-816132
E-mail: sales@arefco.co.uk
Website: http://www.arefco.co.uk
Bank(s): Barclays
Directors: B. Evans (Dir)
Managers: G. Burton, S. Mason (Fin Mgr), D. Love (Personnel), A. Tate (Prod Mgr)
Immediate Holding Company: AREFCO SPECIAL PRODUCTS LIMITED
Registration no: 04399251 **VAT No.:** GB 297 6128 17
Date established: 2002 **Turnover:** £2m - £5m **No.of Employees:** 21 - 50
Product Groups: 29, 30, 33, 36

Date of Accounts	Dec 11	Apr 11	Apr 10
Sales Turnover	N/A	N/A	3m
Pre Tax Profit/Loss	N/A	N/A	850
Working Capital	1m	1m	1m
Fixed Assets	465	462	508
Current Assets	2m	2m	2m
Current Liabilities	N/A	N/A	317

Culpitt Ltd
Jubilee Industrial Estate, Ashington, NE63 8UQ
Tel: 01670-814545 **Fax:** 01670-815248
E-mail: info@culpitt.com
Website: http://www.culpitt.com
Bank(s): HSBC Bank plc
Directors: S. Bilton (Dir), T. Wylie (Dir)
Managers: H. Pearson (Personnel), J. Ames (Tech Serv Mgr), S. Keogh
Ultimate Holding Company: DECOPAC INC (USA)
Immediate Holding Company: CULPITT LIMITED
Registration no: 00261326 **Date established:** 1931
Turnover: £10m - £20m **No.of Employees:** 101 - 250
Product Groups: 20, 23, 49

Date of Accounts	Dec 11	Dec 10	Dec 09
Sales Turnover	20m	17m	13m
Pre Tax Profit/Loss	2m	2m	1m
Working Capital	7m	7m	6m
Fixed Assets	4m	3m	3m
Current Assets	9m	10m	8m
Current Liabilities	1m	2m	978

Lintron Electronics Ltd
Unit 6b Wansbeck Business Park Rotary Parkway, Ashington, NE63 8QW
Tel: 01670-811888 **Fax:** 01670-858910
E-mail: info@lintron.co.uk
Website: http://www.lintron.co.uk
Directors: J. Magnusson (MD)
Ultimate Holding Company: LINTRON TECHNOLOGIES AB (SWEDEN)
Immediate Holding Company: LINTRON ELECTRONICS LIMITED
Registration no: 02248136 **Date established:** 1988 **Turnover:** £1m - £2m
No.of Employees: 11 - 20 **Product Groups:** 37

Date of Accounts	Dec 11	Dec 10	Dec 09
Working Capital	337	376	355
Fixed Assets	67	25	49
Current Assets	368	392	385

N E Attachments Ltd
Unit 11 Waterside Court North Seaton Industrial Estate, Ashington, NE63 0YG
Tel: 01670-858500 **Fax:** 01670-858500
E-mail: sales@neattachments.co.uk
Website: http://www.neattachments.co.uk
Directors: M. Wilson (MD)
Immediate Holding Company: N. E. ATTACHMENTS LIMITED
Registration no: 05227407 **Date established:** 2004
No.of Employees: 1 - 10 **Product Groups:** 35, 39, 45

Date of Accounts	Sep 11	Sep 10	Sep 09
Sales Turnover	N/A	125	60
Pre Tax Profit/Loss	N/A	34	6
Working Capital	24	31	16
Fixed Assets	33	39	34
Current Assets	31	38	20
Current Liabilities	N/A	7	3

The Store Forge
15 Lintonville Terrace, Ashington, NE63 9UN
Tel: 01670-522088 **Fax:** 01670-522088
E-mail: colwilkuk@aol.com
Directors: C. Wilkinson (Prop)
Date established: 1992 **No.of Employees:** 1 - 10 **Product Groups:** 26, 35

Thermacore Ltd
Unit 12 Wansbeck Business Park Rotary Parkway, Ashington, NE63 8QW
Tel: 01670-859500 **Fax:** 01670-859539
E-mail: info@thermacore.com
Website: http://www.thermacore-europe.com
Directors: J. Yates (MD)
Managers: J. Broadbent (Sales & Mktg Mg), C. Weightman, C. Barr, N. Gleghorn (Personnel)
Ultimate Holding Company: THERMACORE INC (USA)
Immediate Holding Company: THERMACORE EUROPE LIMITED
Registration no: 03501481 **Date established:** 1998 **Turnover:** £5m - £10m
No.of Employees: 51 - 100 **Product Groups:** 40

Date of Accounts	Dec 11	Dec 10	Dec 09
Sales Turnover	6m	8m	5m
Pre Tax Profit/Loss	381	902	461
Working Capital	1m	1m	1m
Fixed Assets	896	943	946
Current Assets	2m	4m	2m
Current Liabilities	480	1m	601

Turnbull (Electro Platers) Ltd
Factory BT 75-4 North Seaton Indl-Est, Ashington, NE63 0YB
Tel: 01670-854383 **Fax:** 01670-854593
Bank(s): Lloyds, Morpeth
Directors: J. Turnbull (Tech Serv), H. Turnbull (MD)
Managers: B. Graves (Chief Mgr), J. O'Neil (Gen Contact)
Immediate Holding Company: TURNBULL (ELECTRO PLATERS) LIMITED
Registration no: 01625538 **Date established:** 1982
Turnover: £250,000 - £500,000 **No.of Employees:** 21 - 50
Product Groups: 48

Date of Accounts	Dec 03	Mar 07	Mar 06
Working Capital	-47	-354	-337
Fixed Assets	200	133	155
Current Assets	174	190	149

Bedlington

Andrew Brown

5 Eden Court, Bedlington, NE22 5DG
Tel: 0774-513 3682
E-mail: info@ideal-cars.co.uk
Website: http://www.abpcservices.co.uk
Directors: A. Brown (Prop)
Date established: 2006 **Turnover:** Up to £250,000
No.of Employees: 1 - 10 **Product Groups:** 44, 48

Century Catering Equipment

35 Grange Park Avenue, Bedlington, NE22 7EG
Tel: 01670-825309 **Fax:** 01670-825309
E-mail: centurycatuk@yahoo.co.uk
Website: http://www.century-catering-equipment.co.uk
Directors: D. O'Neill (Prop)
Date established: 1997 **No.of Employees:** 1 - 10 **Product Groups:** 20, 40, 41

Falon Nameplates Ltd

10-13 Stephenson Court Barrington Industrial Estate Barrington Industrial Estate, Bedlington, NE22 7DN
Tel: 01670-530136 **Fax:** 01670-530102
E-mail: quotes@falon-nameplates.co.uk
Website: http://www.falon-nameplates.co.uk
Directors: F. More (Fin), K. More (MD)
Immediate Holding Company: FALON NAMEPLATES LIMITED
Registration no: 03633066 **Date established:** 1998
No.of Employees: 11 - 20 **Product Groups:** 49

Date of Accounts	Dec 11	Dec 10	Dec 09
Working Capital	37	32	-18
Fixed Assets	71	69	77
Current Assets	160	149	132

Hetheringtons Shoe Services Ltd

80 Front Street West, Bedlington, NE22 5UA
Tel: 01670-821505 **Fax:** 01670-821505
E-mail: hetheringtons.shoe.services@unicombox.co.uk
Website: http://www.unicombox.co.uk
Directors: S. Hetherington (MD)
Immediate Holding Company: HETHERINGTON SHOE SERVICES LIMITED
Registration no: 03048597 **VAT No.:** GB 633 6528 35
Date established: 1995 **Turnover:** Up to £250,000
No.of Employees: 1 - 10 **Product Groups:** 61

Date of Accounts	Mar 12	Mar 11	Mar 10
Working Capital	8	6	4
Fixed Assets	4	5	6
Current Assets	14	15	12

Millhouse Developments

Ravensworth House 1 Ravensworth Street, Bedlington, NE22 7JP
Tel: 01670-530616 **Fax:** 01670-829649
Directors: B. Sunley (Co Sec), M. Muter (MD)
Ultimate Holding Company: MILLHOUSE GROUP HOLDINGS LIMITED
Immediate Holding Company: MILLHOUSE DEVELOPMENTS LIMITED
Registration no: 01876733 **VAT No.:** GB 387 5748 88
Date established: 1985 **Turnover:** £2m - £5m **No.of Employees:** 1 - 10
Product Groups: 80

Date of Accounts	Mar 11	Mar 10	Mar 09
Working Capital	2m	361	530
Fixed Assets	26	238	243
Current Assets	4m	4m	5m

Moulded Packaging Solutions

Unit 2 Sleekburn Business Centre, West Sleekburn, Bedlington, NE22 7DD
Tel: 01670-522003 **Fax:** 01670-854559
E-mail: alan.charlton@mps-europe.com
Website: http://www.mps-europe.com
Directors: A. Charlton (MD)
Immediate Holding Company: MOULDED PACKAGING SOLUTIONS LTD
Registration no: 05923811 **Date established:** 2006
No.of Employees: 11 - 20 **Product Groups:** 30, 42, 48

Date of Accounts	Jan 12	Jan 11	Jan 10
Working Capital	-39	-148	-153
Fixed Assets	276	330	335
Current Assets	426	285	180
Current Liabilities	N/A	N/A	95

T T Electronics Welwyn Components Ltd

Welwyn Electronics Park, Bedlington, NE22 7AA
Tel: 01670-822181 **Fax:** 01670-829465
E-mail: info@welwyn-tt.com
Website: http://www.welwyn-tt.com
Directors: W. Sharp (Co Sec)
Ultimate Holding Company: TT ELECTRONICS PLC
Immediate Holding Company: WELWYN COMPONENTS LIMITED
Registration no: 00162480 **Date established:** 2020
Turnover: £20m - £50m **No.of Employees:** 101 - 250 **Product Groups:** 37

Date of Accounts	Dec 11	Dec 10	Dec 09
Sales Turnover	38m	25m	17m
Pre Tax Profit/Loss	3m	3m	424
Working Capital	5m	3m	2m
Fixed Assets	2m	3m	3m
Current Assets	15m	8m	7m
Current Liabilities	2m	1m	2m

Techflow Flexibles Ltd

Unit 4 Gooch Avenue Barrington Industrial Estate, Bedlington, NE22 7DQ
Tel: 01670-828844 **Fax:** 01670-827000
E-mail: sales@techflowflexibles.co.uk
Website: http://www.brazenlight.co.uk
Directors: G. Scott (MD)
Managers: A. Nicol (Tech Serv Mgr), A. Thompson (Eng Serv Mgr), P. McClintock (Comptroller)
Immediate Holding Company: TECHFLOW FLEXIBLES LIMITED
Registration no: 05704584 **Date established:** 2006 **Turnover:** £5m - £10m
No.of Employees: 21 - 50 **Product Groups:** 29, 30, 35, 36, 39, 40, 42, 45, 46, 52, 54, 66, 67, 68, 71, 80, 84

Date of Accounts	Aug 11	Aug 10	Aug 09
Sales Turnover	10m	10m	N/A
Pre Tax Profit/Loss	1m	1m	N/A
Working Capital	2m	1m	278
Fixed Assets	595	576	229
Current Assets	5m	4m	6m
Current Liabilities	2m	2m	N/A

Berwick Upon Tweed

Border Engines

East Ord Trading Estate Tweedmouth, Berwick Upon Tweed, TD15 2XF
Tel: 01289-305186 **Fax:** 01289-308993
Directors: B. Davidson (Dir)
Ultimate Holding Company: H.O. SHORT & SON LIMITED
Immediate Holding Company: CEREAL FOODS LIMITED
Date established: 2000 **No.of Employees:** 1 - 10 **Product Groups:** 35, 36, 39

Date of Accounts	Apr 11	Apr 10	Apr 05
Working Capital	1	1	1
Current Assets	4	4	4

D D S

3b Church Street, Berwick upon Tweed, TD15 1EE
Tel: 01289-306921 **Fax:** 01289-466000
E-mail: info@dds-uk.co.uk
Website: http://www.dds-uk.co.uk
Directors: C. Richardson (Ptnr)
Immediate Holding Company: PROHELP LIMITED
Date established: 2003 **Turnover:** Up to £250,000
No.of Employees: 1 - 10 **Product Groups:** 82

Frontier Agriculture Ltd

North Road Industrial Estate, Berwick Upon Tweed, TD15 1UN
Tel: 01289-330303 **Fax:** 01289-308145
E-mail: info@frontierag.co.uk
Website: http://www.frontierag.co.uk
Managers: A. Ainslie (Chief Mgr)
Immediate Holding Company: FRONTIER AGRICULTURE LIMITED
Registration no: 05288567 **VAT No.:** GB 183 8080 48
Date established: 2004 **Turnover:** £75m - £125m
No.of Employees: 21 - 50 **Product Groups:** 62

Date of Accounts	Jun 11	Jun 10	Jun 09
Sales Turnover	1402m	981m	1154m
Pre Tax Profit/Loss	39m	24m	30m
Working Capital	100m	77m	59m
Fixed Assets	29m	24m	26m
Current Assets	357m	217m	201m
Current Liabilities	32m	16m	23m

Graham

Tweedside Trading Estate Tweedmouth, Berwick Upon Tweed, TD15 2XF
Tel: 01289-306446 **Fax:** 01289-303554
Website: http://www.graham-group.co.uk
Managers: A. Spires (Mgr)
Ultimate Holding Company: H.O. SHORT & SON LIMITED
Immediate Holding Company: CEREAL FOODS LIMITED
Registration no: 00205369 **Date established:** 2000
Turnover: £20m - £50m **No.of Employees:** 1 - 10 **Product Groups:** 66

Date of Accounts	Apr 11	Apr 10	Apr 05
Working Capital	1	1	1
Current Assets	4	4	4

Jewson Ltd

Tweedside Trading Estate Tweedmouth, Berwick Upon Tweed, TD15 2XF
Tel: 01289-308877 **Fax:** 01289-330253
Website: http://www.jewson.co.uk
Managers: G. Noble (District Mgr), R. Holloway (District Mgr)
Ultimate Holding Company: COMPAGNIE DE SAINT GOBAIN (FRANCE)
Immediate Holding Company: JEWSON LIMITED
Registration no: 00348407 **VAT No.:** GB 497 7184 83
Date established: 1939 **Turnover:** £20m - £50m
No.of Employees: 11 - 20 **Product Groups:** 66

Date of Accounts	Dec 11	Dec 10	Dec 09
Sales Turnover	1606m	1547m	1485m
Pre Tax Profit/Loss	18m	100m	45m
Working Capital	-345m	-250m	-349m
Fixed Assets	496m	387m	461m
Current Assets	657m	1005m	1320m
Current Liabilities	66m	120m	64m

Keenweld Welding Supplies

Unit 7b East Ord Industrial Estate Tweedmouth, Berwick Upon Tweed, TD15 2XF
Tel: 01289-302649 **Fax:** 01289-302649
E-mail: keenweld@btinternet.com
Directors: C. Keenan (MD)
Immediate Holding Company: KEENWELD (WELDING SUPPLIES) LIMITED
Registration no: 04750333 **Date established:** 2003
No.of Employees: 1 - 10 **Product Groups:** 46

Date of Accounts	May 12	May 11	May 10
Working Capital	18	12	17
Fixed Assets	3	5	6
Current Assets	37	28	33

Lindisfarne Hotel

Green Lane Holy Island, Berwick Upon Tweed, TD15 2SQ
Tel: 01289-389273 **Fax:** 01289-389284
Website: http://www.thelindisfarnehotel.co.uk
Directors: S. Atkinson (Prop)
Immediate Holding Company: LINDISFARNE LIMITED
Registration no: 01214754 **Date established:** 1975
Turnover: £500,000 - £1m **No.of Employees:** 1 - 10 **Product Groups:** 21

Date of Accounts	Dec 11	Dec 10	Dec 09
Working Capital	109	112	156
Fixed Assets	444	451	463
Current Assets	269	315	290

W N Lindsay Stevedores Ltd

1 Dock Road Tweedmouth, Berwick Upon Tweed, TD15 2BG
Tel: 01289-306209 **Fax:** 01289-306101
E-mail: alanairving@wnlindsay.com
Directors: A. Irving (Dir), G. Lindsay (Dir), T. Nixon (Ch)
Immediate Holding Company: W.N. LINDSAY (STEVEDORES) LIMITED
Registration no: SC043806 **Date established:** 1966
Turnover: £250,000 - £500,000 **No.of Employees:** 1 - 10
Product Groups: 74

Date of Accounts	May 07	May 06
Working Capital	99	77
Fixed Assets	187	208
Current Assets	121	138
Current Liabilities	22	61

Mccreath Simpson & Prentice Ltd

Ordfield House Tweedside Trading Estate, Tweedmouth, Berwick Upon Tweed, TD15 2XZ
Tel: 01289-330022 **Fax:** 01289-333390
E-mail: nigelforster@mspagriculture.co.uk
Website: http://www.simpsonsmalt.co.uk
Directors: N. Foster (Fin), W. Foster (Fin), N. Forster (Fin), D. McCreath (Ch), A. Richardson (MD), M. Richardson (MD)
Managers: S. Richardson (Personnel), J. Stobbs (I.T. Exec)
Ultimate Holding Company: SIMPSONS MALT LIMITED
Immediate Holding Company: MCCREATH SIMPSON & PRENTICE LIMITED
Registration no: 01013406 **VAT No.:** GB 297 9571 82
Date established: 1971 **No.of Employees:** 21 - 50 **Product Groups:** 62

Date of Accounts	Jun 07	Dec 08	Jan 10
Working Capital	N/A	N/A	1m
Current Assets	N/A	N/A	1m

S A Mather

8 Holburn Cottages Holburn Village, Berwick Upon Tweed, TD15 2UJ
Tel: 01289-388428
Directors: S. Mather (Prop)
Date established: 1997 **No.of Employees:** 1 - 10 **Product Groups:** 26, 35

Middleton Agricultural Engineering

Ancroft Town Farm, Berwick Upon Tweed, TD15 2TB
Tel: 01289-387411
E-mail: scnichols@btconnect.com
Directors: G. Middleton (Prop)
Date established: 2006 **No.of Employees:** 1 - 10 **Product Groups:** 41

Servitir

17c Windmill Way West Ramparts Business Park, Berwick Upon Tweed, TD15 1TB
Tel: 08453-132212 **Fax:** 0845-313 2213
E-mail: info@servitir.com
Website: http://www.servitir.com
Managers: N. Renton
Ultimate Holding Company: CLIVEDEN SECURITIES LIMITED
Immediate Holding Company: ANCROFT TRACTORS LIMITED
Date established: 1979 **Turnover:** £2m - £5m **No.of Employees:** 1 - 10
Product Groups: 31

Date of Accounts	Mar 11	Mar 10
Working Capital	157	154
Fixed Assets	1m	1m
Current Assets	452	404

Thomas Waugh

Shoresdean, Berwick Upon Tweed, TD15 2NJ
Tel: 01289-387261
Directors: T. Waugh (Prop)
Date established: 1965 **No.of Employees:** 1 - 10 **Product Groups:** 41

Blyth

Aluline

1 Aldborough House Aldborough Street, Blyth, NE24 2EU
Tel: 01670-369603 **Fax:** 01670-359226
E-mail: design@aluline.co.uk
Website: http://www.aluline.co.uk
Directors: C. Clark (Mkt Research), W. Clark (MD), P. Abdo (Ch)
Managers: W. Clark (Mgr)
Immediate Holding Company: ALULINE LIMITED
Registration no: 03490498 **Date established:** 1998
Turnover: Up to £250,000 **No.of Employees:** 1 - 10 **Product Groups:** 30, 31, 32, 36, 41, 42, 52, 54

Date of Accounts	Dec 09	Dec 08	Dec 07
Working Capital	158	243	306
Fixed Assets	417	416	434
Current Assets	627	809	577

Hytorc Unex Ltd

24a Spencer Court Blyth Riverside Business Park, Blyth, NE24 5TW
Tel: 01670-363800 **Fax:** 01670-363803
E-mail: sales@hytorc.co.uk
Website: http://www.hytorc.co.uk
Managers: S. Simpson (Chief Mgr)
Ultimate Holding Company: HYTORC CORPORATION
Registration no: 02607411 **VAT No.:** GB 499 9422 71
Turnover: £2m - £5m **No.of Employees:** 1 - 10 **Product Groups:** 29, 35, 36, 37, 38, 39, 40, 46, 85

Date of Accounts	Dec 09	Dec 08	Dec 07
Working Capital	656	415	335
Fixed Assets	394	410	327
Current Assets	2m	1m	1m

It's A Wrap Northeast Ltd

Unit 14 Grasmere Way, Blyth Riverside Business Park, Blyth, NE24 4RR
Tel: 01670-543663 **Fax:** 01670-543663
E-mail: sales@itsawrap.org.uk
Website: http://www.itsawrap.org.uk
Directors: K. Donnelly (Dir), K. Donnelly (MD)
Immediate Holding Company: IT'S A WRAP (N.E) LIMITED
Registration no: 07142849 **Date established:** 2010
Turnover: £250,000 - £500,000 **No.of Employees:** 1 - 10
Product Groups: 67

Jewson Ltd

Spencer Road, Blyth, NE24 5TG
Tel: 01670-368111 **Fax:** 01670-360280
E-mail: paul.hind@jewson.co.uk
Website: http://www.jewson.co.uk
Directors: P. Hindle (MD)
Managers: P. Hind (District Mgr)
Ultimate Holding Company: COMPAGNIE DE SAINT GOBAIN (FRANCE)
Immediate Holding Company: JEWSON LIMITED
Registration no: 00348407 **VAT No.:** GB 497 7184 83
Date established: 1939 **Turnover:** £500m - £1,000m
No.of Employees: 1 - 10 **Product Groups:** 66

see next page

Jewson Ltd - Cont'd

Date of Accounts	Dec 11	Dec 10	Dec 09
Sales Turnover	1606m	1547m	1485m
Pre Tax Profit/Loss	18m	100m	45m
Working Capital	-345m	-250m	-349m
Fixed Assets	496m	387m	461m
Current Assets	657m	1005m	1320m
Current Liabilities	66m	120m	64m

Kingston Services
1 Cramlington Terrace, Blyth, NE24 4AQ
Tel: 01670-360027 **Fax:** 01670-360027
Directors: B. Thompson (Prop)
No.of Employees: 1 - 10 **Product Groups:** 38, 67

R Kirkland Blyth Ltd
62-66 Bridge Street, Blyth, NE24 2AP
Tel: 01670-352196 **Fax:** 01670-360238
E-mail: info@r-kirkland.co.uk
Website: http://www.r-kirkland.co.uk
Bank(s): HSBC
Directors: J. McGlen (MD), H. Mcglen (Fin)
Managers: C. McGlen
Immediate Holding Company: ROBERT KIRKLAND (BLYTH) LIMITED
Registration no: 01138871 **Date established:** 1973 **Turnover:** £2m - £5m
No.of Employees: 21 - 50 **Product Groups:** 52

Date of Accounts	May 11	May 10	May 09
Working Capital	493	589	375
Fixed Assets	719	797	802
Current Assets	1m	1m	971

N E Fire Ltd
PO Box 91, Blyth, NE24 9DB
Tel: 01670-569054 **Fax:** 01670-351506
E-mail: info@nefireextinguishers.com
Website: http://www.nefireextinguishers.com
Directors: J. Carling (MD)
Immediate Holding Company: N E FIRE LIMITED
Registration no: 07375742 **Date established:** 2010
Turnover: Up to £250,000 **No.of Employees:** 1 - 10 **Product Groups:** 40

Date of Accounts	Mar 11
Working Capital	-1
Fixed Assets	10
Current Assets	20

NaREC (New and Renewable Energy Centre)
Eddie Ferguson House Ridley Street, Blyth, NE24 3AG
Tel: 01670-359555 **Fax:** 01670-359666
E-mail: steve.abbott@narec.co.uk
Website: http://www.narec.co.uk
Managers: S. Abbott
Ultimate Holding Company: 04659351
Immediate Holding Company: NAREC DEVELOPMENT SERVICES LIMITED
Registration no: 05636283 **Date established:** 2005
No.of Employees: 51 - 100 **Product Groups:** 54, 85

Northumbria Engineering
Unit 16 Grasmere Way, Blyth Riverside Business Park, Blyth, NE24 4RR
Tel: 01670-540333 **Fax:** 01670-540333
E-mail: ian@northumbria-engineering.co.uk
Website: http://www.northumbria-engineering.co.uk
Directors: I. Pattison (MD)
No.of Employees: 1 - 10 **Product Groups:** 46

Optical Digital Media Ltd
6 Larch Grove Woodlands Glade Blyth, Blyth, NE24 3XU
Tel: 01670-364611 **Fax:** 01670-541564
E-mail: info@odm-ltd.co.uk
Website: http://www.odm-ltd.co.uk
Directors: G. Douds (Fin), J. Ouds (Dir), A. Hood (Dir), J. Douds (MD)
Immediate Holding Company: OPTICAL DIGITAL MEDIA LTD.
Registration no: 05282396 **Date established:** 2004 **Turnover:** £1m - £2m
No.of Employees: 1 - 10 **Product Groups:** 44

Date of Accounts	Nov 07	Nov 06	Nov 05
Working Capital	13	-12	6
Fixed Assets	2	N/A	1
Current Assets	20	15	16
Current Liabilities	7	27	10

R R Packaging Ltd
4 Ballast Hill, Blyth, NE24 2AU
Tel: 01670-546666 **Fax:** 01670-546555
E-mail: sales@rrpackaging.co.uk
Website: http://www.rrpackaging.co.uk
Directors: R. White (Dir)
Immediate Holding Company: R&R PACKAGING LIMITED
Registration no: 07660998 **Date established:** 2011
No.of Employees: 1 - 10 **Product Groups:** 07, 20, 23, 24, 25, 26, 27, 28, 29, 30, 31, 32, 33, 34, 35, 36, 37, 38, 39, 40, 41, 42, 43, 44, 45, 48, 49, 54, 61, 63, 64, 66, 67, 76, 80, 84, 85, 86, 87

Thomas Fuel Injection
Unit 25 Grasmere Way Blyth Riverside Business Park, Blyth, NE24 4RR
Tel: 01670-369252
Website: http://www.thomasfuelinjection.co.uk
Directors: I. Thomas (Prop)
Immediate Holding Company: THOMAS FUEL INJECTION LIMITED
Registration no: 07912781 **Date established:** 2012
No.of Employees: 1 - 10 **Product Groups:** 40

Travis Perkins plc
Spencer Road Blyth Riverside Business Park, Blyth, NE24 5TG
Tel: 01670-352126 **Fax:** 01670-351857
E-mail: blyth@travisperkins.co.uk
Website: http://www.travisperkins.co.uk
Managers: B. Berrow (Mgr)
Immediate Holding Company: TRAVIS PERKINS PLC
Registration no: 00824821 **Date established:** 1964
No.of Employees: 1 - 10 **Product Groups:** 08, 25, 66

Date of Accounts	Dec 11	Dec 10	Dec 09
Sales Turnover	4779m	3153m	2931m
Pre Tax Profit/Loss	270m	197m	213m
Working Capital	133m	159m	248m
Fixed Assets	2771m	2749m	2108m
Current Assets	1421m	1329m	1035m
Current Liabilities	473m	412m	109m

T E Watson & Son
Front Street, Blyth, NE24 4HN
Tel: 01670-823357 **Fax:** 01670-823357
Directors: G. Watson (Ptnr)
Date established: 1945 **No.of Employees:** 1 - 10 **Product Groups:** 26, 35

Widescope (Based In Blyth)
Ridley Street, Blyth, NE24 3AG
Tel: 01670-542854 **Fax:** 01670-542890
E-mail: helpdesk@widescope.net
Website: http://www.widescope.net
Directors: S. Bradley (Dir)
Immediate Holding Company: WIDESCOPE INTERNET LIMITED
Registration no: 06575310 **Date established:** 2008 **Turnover:** £1m - £2m
No.of Employees: 1 - 10 **Product Groups:** 44

Date of Accounts	Apr 11	Apr 10	Apr 09
Working Capital	1	1	N/A
Current Assets	2	2	2

Choppington

Pidra Ltd (HVAC)
Unit 23 Avebury Avenue, Choppington, NE62 5HE
Tel: 0191-267 7111 **Fax:** 0191-267 7222
E-mail: info@pidra.co.uk
Website: http://www.pidra.ltd.uk
Directors: J. Weightman (Fin)
Immediate Holding Company: PIDRA LIMITED
Registration no: 04055282 **VAT No.:** GB 747 2409 24
Date established: 2000 **Turnover:** £500,000 - £1m
No.of Employees: 1 - 10 **Product Groups:** 30, 33, 34, 35, 36, 37, 38, 39, 40, 42, 46, 52, 66, 84

Date of Accounts	Dec 11	Dec 10	Dec 09
Working Capital	-8	-35	10
Fixed Assets	40	36	2
Current Assets	172	145	27

Corbridge

Hexham Sealants Ltd
Station Yard Station Road, Corbridge, NE45 5AY
Tel: 01434-633344 **Fax:** 01434-633346
E-mail: sales@hexaflex.co.uk
Website: http://www.hexhamsealants.co.uk
Directors: R. Taylor (MD), B. Taylor (MD), R. Taylor (Ptnr)
VAT No.: GB 698 5576 54 **Turnover:** Up to £250,000
No.of Employees: 1 - 10 **Product Groups:** 52, 84

Cramlington

AMCourierServices
26 Easington Ave Hartford Green, Cramlington, NE23 3HR
Tel: 01670-735667 **Fax:** 01670-735667
E-mail: andrew@amcourierservices.co.uk
Website: http://www.amcourierservices.co.uk
Managers: A. Morrison (Comm), D. Morrison (Accounts)
Registration no: 06564271 **Date established:** 2005
No.of Employees: 1 - 10 **Product Groups:** 39, 72, 75, 76

B & B Attachments
Unit 39 Colbourne Crescent Nelson Park, Cramlington, NE23 1WB
Tel: 01670-737373 **Fax:** 01670-736286
E-mail: info@bandbattachments.com
Website: http://www.bandbattachments.com
Bank(s): HSBC Bank plc
Directors: J. Lambath (Chief Op Offcr), J. Lamberth (Chief Op Offcr)
Managers: A. Harrison (Comptroller), P. Weatheritt
Ultimate Holding Company: B & B ATTACHMENTS (HOLDINGS) LIMITED
Immediate Holding Company: B.& B. ATTACHMENTS LIMITED
Registration no: 01532448 **VAT No.:** GB 314 6962 51
Date established: 1980 **Turnover:** £5m - £10m **No.of Employees:** 21 - 50
Product Groups: 45

Date of Accounts	Dec 10	Dec 09	Dec 08
Sales Turnover	N/A	6m	8m
Pre Tax Profit/Loss	N/A	-371	-211
Working Capital	1m	-125	179
Fixed Assets	683	790	1m
Current Assets	3m	2m	3m
Current Liabilities	N/A	596	1m

C M P UK Ltd A Division Of British Engines Ltd
36 Nelson Way Nelson Park East, Cramlington, NE23 1WH
Tel: 0191-265 7411 **Fax:** 0191-265 0581
E-mail: enquiries@cmp-products.com
Website: http://www.cmp-products.com
Bank(s): HSBC Bank plc
Directors: M. McDermott (Fin)
Managers: G. Robertson (Mktg Serv Mgr), P. Wood (Sales Prom Mgr), R. Couch (Personnel), D. Morris, S. Read, J. Maciver (Tech Serv Mgr)
Immediate Holding Company: CMP MARKETING LIMITED
Registration no: 00174648 **VAT No.:** GB 555 8517 12
Date established: 2021 **Turnover:** £500,000 - £1m
No.of Employees: 101 - 250 **Product Groups:** 30, 35, 37, 38

Date of Accounts	Apr 11	Apr 12	May 09
Sales Turnover	510	555	455
Pre Tax Profit/Loss	53	128	97
Working Capital	56	118	231
Fixed Assets	2m	2m	2m
Current Assets	2m	2m	258
Current Liabilities	2m	2m	27

Fastrack Flooring (North) Ltd
Suite 10, Hubbway House Bassington Lane, Cramlington, NE23 8AD
Tel: 01670-700907 **Fax:** 01670-700911
E-mail: alan@rutherford1.freeserve.co.uk
Website: http://www.kellysearch.com/partners/fastrackflooringnorth.asp
Product Groups: 22, 23, 25, 27, 29, 30, 31, 32, 33, 35, 36, 37, 39, 40, 45, 48, 49, 52, 63, 66, 81, 83

Date of Accounts	Jun 08	Jun 07	Jun 06
Sales Turnover	327	479	321
Pre Tax Profit/Loss	30	7	10
Working Capital	-9	-39	2
Fixed Assets	9	39	11
Current Assets	37	93	47
Current Liabilities	46	132	45

F L T Fork Lift Trucks
Suite 10 Hubbway House Bassington Industrial Estate, Cramlington, NE23 8AD
Tel: 01670-730666 **Fax:** 01670-716700
E-mail: hd@flt.co.uk
Website: http://www.flt.co.uk
Directors: C. Bown (MD)
Immediate Holding Company: MATTINSON BEDROOMS LIMITED
Registration no: 04907762 **Date established:** 2003 **Turnover:** £2m - £5m
No.of Employees: 11 - 20 **Product Groups:** 39, 45, 67, 80

Jackel International Ltd
Dudley Lane, Cramlington, NE23 7RH
Tel: 0191-250 4400 **Fax:** 0191-250 1727
E-mail: mail@jackel.co.uk
Website: http://www.tommeetippee.co.uk
Bank(s): Lloyds TSB Bank plc
Directors: S. Parkin (MD)
Managers: M. Cook, L. Jackson (Personnel), L. Haswell, P. Dowson, R. Buckingham
Ultimate Holding Company: JAKE HOLDINGS LIMITED
Immediate Holding Company: JACKEL INTERNATIONAL LIMITED
Registration no: 01894022 **VAT No.:** GB 176 1481 54
Date established: 1985 **Turnover:** £20m - £50m
No.of Employees: 101 - 250 **Product Groups:** 22, 30, 49

Date of Accounts	Dec 11	Dec 10	Dec 09
Sales Turnover	46m	46m	45m
Pre Tax Profit/Loss	5m	2m	7m
Working Capital	26m	21m	20m
Fixed Assets	2m	2m	1m
Current Assets	101m	90m	72m
Current Liabilities	6m	5m	4m

Messer Cutting Systems
Northumberland Business Park West, Cramlington, NE23 7RH
Tel: 0191-250 4610 **Fax:** 0191-250 1471
E-mail: alan.cardwell@messer-cw.co.uk
Website: http://www.messer-cw.co.uk
Managers: A. Cardwell (Chief Mgr)
Ultimate Holding Company: MEC HOLDING GMBH (GERMANY)
Immediate Holding Company: MESSER GRIESHEIM LIMITED
Registration no: 00656079 **Date established:** 1960 **Turnover:** £2m - £5m
No.of Employees: 11 - 20 **Product Groups:** 46

Date of Accounts	Dec 11	Dec 10	Dec 09
Sales Turnover	3m	2m	2m
Pre Tax Profit/Loss	349	456	92
Working Capital	4m	4m	3m
Fixed Assets	25	31	23
Current Assets	4m	4m	4m
Current Liabilities	472	383	332

Pearson Spares & Service Ltd
Unit 1 Baker Road Nelson Park West, Cramlington, NE23 1WL
Tel: 01670-739061 **Fax:** 01670-739777
Directors: A. Storey (Dir)
Immediate Holding Company: PEARSON SPARES & SERVICE LIMITED
Registration no: 01894567 **Date established:** 1985
No.of Employees: 1 - 10 **Product Groups:** 46

Date of Accounts	Mar 11	Mar 10	Mar 09
Working Capital	15	15	21
Fixed Assets	1	1	1
Current Assets	57	72	60

Thomas Potter Ltd
Unit 1j Admiral Business Park Nelson Way Nelson Park West, Cramlington, NE23 1WG
Tel: 01670-591100 **Fax:** 01670-591101
E-mail: sales@thomaspotter.com
Website: http://www.thomaspotter.com
Bank(s): Barclays, North Shields
Directors: I. Malley (Dir)
Immediate Holding Company: THOMAS POTTER LIMITED
Registration no: 05970064 **Date established:** 2006 **Turnover:** £2m - £5m
No.of Employees: 11 - 20 **Product Groups:** 30, 35, 36, 66

Date of Accounts	May 11	May 10	May 09
Working Capital	386	185	475
Fixed Assets	19	10	6
Current Assets	835	684	705

Product Group
Unit 40a Colbourne Crescent Nelson Park, Cramlington, NE23 1WB
Tel: 01670-730784 **Fax:** 01670-734915
E-mail: product@theproductgroup.co.uk
Website: http://www.theproductgroup.co.uk
Directors: M. Cochran (Prop)
VAT No.: GB 499 8402 82 **Turnover:** £2m - £5m **No.of Employees:** 1 - 10
Product Groups: 80, 81, 84

Randstad Ltd
Randstad House Crow Hall Road Nelson Park East, Cramlington, NE23 1WH
Tel: 01670-735575 **Fax:** 01670-590739
E-mail: enquiries@randstadltd.co.uk
Website: http://www.randstadltd.co.uk
Bank(s): Allied Irish
Directors: M. Dowd (Fin), J. Dowd (Dir)
Immediate Holding Company: RANDSTAD LIMITED
Registration no: 01259594 **VAT No.:** GB 178 9813 03
Date established: 1976 **Turnover:** £2m - £5m **No.of Employees:** 21 - 50
Product Groups: 68

Date of Accounts	May 11	May 10	May 09
Working Capital	2m	2m	1m
Fixed Assets	2m	2m	831
Current Assets	2m	2m	2m

Renolit Cramlington Ltd
Station Road, Cramlington, NE23 8AQ
Tel: 01670-718222 **Fax:** 01670-590096
E-mail: cova.products@renolit.com
Website: http://www.renolit.com
Bank(s): National Westminster

Directors: S. Wilson (Fin), S. Wilson (Fin), D. Ritchie (Pers)
Managers: L. Hughes (Mktg Serv Mgr), N. Crate (Purch Mgr), M. Mcdonagh (Mktg Serv Mgr), D. Ritchie (Personnel), A. Lawton (Tech Serv Mgr), A. Lawton (Tech Serv Mgr), M. McDonagh (Sales Prom Mgr)
Ultimate Holding Company: JAKOB MULLER GMBH & CO KG (GERMANY)
Immediate Holding Company: RENOLIT (U.K.) LIMITED
Registration no: 01375539 **VAT No.:** GB 305 8450 69
Date established: 1978 **Turnover:** £10m - £20m
No.of Employees: 101 - 250 **Product Groups:** 30

Date of Accounts	Dec 11	Dec 10	Dec 09
Sales Turnover	9	12m	24m
Pre Tax Profit/Loss	5m	-325	2m
Working Capital	-4m	-6m	378
Fixed Assets	28m	28m	29m
Current Assets	33	701	10m
Current Liabilities	230	285	839

S & B E P S Ltd

Grieves Row Dudley, Cramlington, NE23 7PY
Tel: 0191-250 0818 **Fax:** 0191-250 0548
E-mail: darren.smith@sandbeps.com
Website: http://www.sandbeps.com
Directors: D. Davidson (Fin), D. Smith (MD), H. Smith (Co Sec), P. Banks (I.T. Dir)
Immediate Holding Company: S AND B EPS LIMITED
Registration no: 01646418 **Date established:** 1982
No.of Employees: 21 - 50 **Product Groups:** 30, 76

Date of Accounts	Apr 11	Apr 10	Apr 09
Working Capital	187	88	117
Fixed Assets	1m	1m	1m
Current Assets	2m	1m	1m
Current Liabilities	N/A	973	N/A

Shasun Pharma Soloutions Ltd

Sterling Place Dudley, Cramlington, NE23 7QG
Tel: 0191-250 0471 **Fax:** 0191-250 1514
E-mail: john.lindley@eu.rhodia.com
Website: http://www.shasun.com
Directors: S. Hampson (Dir), A. Murphy (Co Sec)
Ultimate Holding Company: RHODIA SA (FRANCE)
Immediate Holding Company: RHODIA PHARMA SOLUTIONS (HOLDINGS) LIMITED
Registration no: 03080257 **VAT No.:** GB 698 4987 38
Date established: 1995 **Turnover:** £20m - £50m
No.of Employees: 251 - 500 **Product Groups:** 32, 85

Date of Accounts	Dec 11	Dec 10	Dec 09
Pre Tax Profit/Loss	42	29	57
Working Capital	2m	2m	2m
Current Assets	2m	2m	2m

Storage Equipment Safety Service Ltd

South Nelson Road, Cramlington, NE23 1EG
Tel: 01670-736444 **Fax:** 01670-739903
E-mail: doreen@sess.co.uk
Website: http://www.sess.co.uk
Directors: M. Swan (Co Sec), D. Atchinson (Dir), D. Wheatley (Fin)
Managers: M. Pinel, A. Knox (Buyer), A. Raffle
Immediate Holding Company: STORAGE EQUIPMENT SAFETY SERVICE LIMITED
Registration no: 03309244 **VAT No.:** GB 687 0668 87
Date established: 1997 **No.of Employees:** 21 - 50 **Product Groups:** 26, 54, 81

Date of Accounts	Dec 08	Apr 12	Apr 11
Working Capital	-101	-127	-227
Fixed Assets	878	931	974
Current Assets	427	444	452

Truscott Catering Equipment Ltd

Unit 54c South Nelson Road South Nelson Industrial Estate, Cramlington, NE23 1WF
Tel: 01670-714440 **Fax:** 01670-715585
E-mail: sales@truscott-ce.com
Website: http://www.truscott-ce.com
Directors: J. Brown (Fin), R. Brown (MD)
Immediate Holding Company: TRUSCOTT CATERING EQUIPMENT LIMITED
Registration no: 03040802 **Date established:** 1995
No.of Employees: 1 - 10 **Product Groups:** 20, 40, 41

Date of Accounts	Jun 11	Jun 10	Jun 09
Working Capital	-13	-15	17
Fixed Assets	18	25	31
Current Assets	87	69	89

Victory Signs Newcastle Ltd

Unit 4 Rhodes Court, Cramlington, NE23 1WF
Tel: 01670-733155 **Fax:** 01670-733150
E-mail: info@victory-signs.co.uk
Website: http://www.victorysigns.co.uk
Directors: P. Wood (Co Sec)
Immediate Holding Company: VICTORY SIGNS (NEWCASTLE) LIMITED
Registration no: 02649208 **VAT No.:** GB 499 7849 45
Date established: 1991 **No.of Employees:** 1 - 10 **Product Groups:** 27, 28, 30, 33, 35, 36, 37, 38, 39, 40, 44, 47, 48, 49, 52, 65, 67, 68, 81, 84

Date of Accounts	Oct 11	Oct 10	Oct 09
Working Capital	116	90	72
Fixed Assets	53	66	69
Current Assets	320	249	276

Haltwhistle

Agma Ltd

Gemini Works Haltwhistle Industrial Estate, Haltwhistle, NE49 9HA
Tel: 01434-320598 **Fax:** 01434-321650
E-mail: mfranklin@agma.co.uk
Website: http://www.agma.co.uk
Bank(s): Barclays
Directors: M. Franklin (MD), W. Scott (Fin)
Managers: M. Routledge (Ops Mgr)
Ultimate Holding Company: LINCHEM LIMITED
Immediate Holding Company: AGMA LIMITED
Registration no: 00939450 **VAT No.:** GB 178 8923 01
Date established: 1968 **Turnover:** £2m - £5m **No.of Employees:** 21 - 50
Product Groups: 31, 32

Date of Accounts	Aug 11	Aug 10	Aug 09
Working Capital	977	839	718
Fixed Assets	100	88	110
Current Assets	1m	1m	1m

B L Scarth Ltd

33 Central Drive, Haltwhistle, NE49 9AX
Tel: 01434-322852 **Fax:** 01434-322852
E-mail: scarthbuilders@yahoo.com
Website: http://www.scarthbuilders.co.uk
Directors: B. Scarth (Dir), B. Scarth (Co Sec)
Immediate Holding Company: B. L. SCARTH LIMITED
Registration no: 06560654 **Date established:** 2008
Turnover: Up to £250,000 **No.of Employees:** 1 - 10 **Product Groups:** 25, 52

Date of Accounts	Mar 11	Mar 10	Mar 09
Sales Turnover	80	208	71
Pre Tax Profit/Loss	9	41	3
Working Capital	9	15	-2
Fixed Assets	24	21	25
Current Assets	29	86	14
Current Liabilities	15	39	13

Hexham

Border Counties Insurance Services

46 Priestpopple, Hexham, NE46 1PQ
Tel: 01434-603521 **Fax:** 01434-600047
E-mail: jlee@bordercounties.co.uk
Website: http://www.bordercounties.co.uk
Directors: J. Lee (MD)
Immediate Holding Company: BORDER COUNTIES FARMERS LTD
Registration no: 00149848 **Date established:** 1918 **Turnover:** £2m - £5m
No.of Employees: 1 - 10 **Product Groups:** 82, 87

Creative Coding Limited

8 Hencotes, Hexham, NE46 2EJ
Tel: 01434-610430 **Fax:** 01434-610401
E-mail: enquiries@creativecoding.co.uk
Website: http://www.creativecoding.co.uk
Directors: R. Hawkin (Mkt Research), P. Hawkin (MD)
Registration no: 04215492 **Date established:** 2001
Turnover: Up to £250,000 **No.of Employees:** 1 - 10 **Product Groups:** 44, 84

Date of Accounts	Mar 10	Mar 09	Mar 08
Working Capital	1	1	1
Fixed Assets	2	2	2
Current Assets	8	9	8
Current Liabilities	7	8	7

Davison Tyne Metal Ltd

Bridge End, Hexham, NE46 4JL
Tel: 01434-604211 **Fax:** 01434-602733
E-mail: enquiries@davisontynemetal.co.uk
Website: http://www.davisontynemetal.co.uk
Directors: I. Richardson (MD)
Immediate Holding Company: DAVISON TYNE METAL LIMITED
Registration no: 01696898 **VAT No.:** GB 393 3046 50
Date established: 1983 **Turnover:** £1m - £2m **No.of Employees:** 21 - 50
Product Groups: 17, 34, 35

Date of Accounts	May 12	May 11	May 10
Working Capital	1m	1m	1m
Fixed Assets	249	257	255
Current Assets	1m	1m	1m

Egger UK Ltd

Anick Grange Road, Hexham, NE46 4JS
Tel: 01434-602191 **Fax:** 01434-600122
E-mail: info@egger.co.uk
Website: http://www.egger.co.uk
Directors: B. Steinlechner (Dir), B. Livesey (MD)
Ultimate Holding Company: EGGER HOLZWERKSTOFFE GMBH (AUSTRIA)
Immediate Holding Company: EGGER (BARONY) LIMITED
Registration no: 03062157 **Date established:** 1995
Turnover: £20m - £50m **No.of Employees:** 501 - 1000
Product Groups: 25

Date of Accounts	Apr 11	Apr 10	Apr 09
Sales Turnover	N/A	N/A	545
Pre Tax Profit/Loss	116	-346	-598
Working Capital	21m	21m	19m
Fixed Assets	10m	10m	10m
Current Assets	21m	22m	22m
Current Liabilities	8	92	8

Northumbrian Surveys

Orchard House Catton, Hexham, NE47 9QR
Tel: 01434-683670 **Fax:** 01434-683940
E-mail: bdngeo@aol.com
Website: http://www.northumbrian-surveys.co.uk
Directors: B. Donolly (Dir)
No.of Employees: 1 - 10 **Product Groups:** 37, 54, 84

P D L Solutions Europe Ltd

1 Tanners Yard Tanners Yard, Hexham, NE46 3NY
Tel: 01434-609473 **Fax:** 01434-606292
E-mail: sales@polymer-distribution.com
Website: http://www.polymer-distribution.com
Directors: P. Charlton (MD)
Immediate Holding Company: POLYMER DISTRIBUTION LIMITED
Registration no: 03786656 **Date established:** 1999
Turnover: £250,000 - £500,000 **No.of Employees:** 1 - 10
Product Groups: 30

Date of Accounts	Jun 11	Jun 10	Jun 09
Working Capital	-119	-120	-126
Current Assets	25	47	55

Morpeth

Affinis LBD Ltd

Cavil Head Acklington, Morpeth, NE65 9DF
Tel: 01670-761966 **Fax:** 01670-761966
E-mail: sales@affinislbd.com
Website: http://www.affinislbd.com
Directors: I. Drant (MD), I. Grant (Dir), Y. Vickers (Dir)
Immediate Holding Company: AFFINIS LBD LTD.
Registration no: 05123540 **Date established:** 2004
Turnover: Up to £250,000 **No.of Employees:** 1 - 10 **Product Groups:** 80

Bristol Street Motors - Morpeth

Coopies Lane, Morpeth, NE61 6JW
Tel: 01670-519611 **Fax:** 01670-501432
Website: http://www.bristolstreetmotors.co.uk
Managers: C. Richardson (Sales Prom Mgr)
Ultimate Holding Company: TED JOHNSON (HOLDINGS) LTD.
Immediate Holding Company: STANNERS EQUIPMENT LIMITED
Registration no: 04214746 **VAT No.:** GB 555 9108 24
Date established: 1980 **No.of Employees:** 1 - 10 **Product Groups:** 68

Date of Accounts	Jun 11	Jun 10	Jun 09
Working Capital	1m	1m	1m
Fixed Assets	143	138	174
Current Assets	2m	2m	2m

The Coca Cola Enterprises

Abbey Well, Morpeth, NE61 6JF
Tel: 01670-513113 **Fax:** 01670-515821
E-mail: info@abbey-well.co.uk
Website: http://www.abbeywells.co.uk
Bank(s): Barclays
Managers: K. Smith (Chief Mgr)
Immediate Holding Company: WATERS & ROBSON HOLDINGS LIMITED
Registration no: 04676030 **VAT No.:** GB 177 0592 44
Date established: 2003 **Turnover:** £10m - £20m
No.of Employees: 21 - 50 **Product Groups:** 21

Date of Accounts	Dec 11	Dec 10	Dec 09
Pre Tax Profit/Loss	-10	-1	-0
Working Capital	-9	N/A	1
Fixed Assets	2m	2m	2m
Current Assets	N/A	N/A	1
Current Liabilities	9	N/A	N/A

Econofreeze Morpeth Ltd

78 Newgate Street, Morpeth, NE61 1BQ
Tel: 01670-515160 **Fax:** 01670-516702
Website: http://www.econofreeze.com
Directors: N. Wake (Sales), C. Wake (Dir)
Immediate Holding Company: ECONOFREEZE (MORPETH) LIMITED
Registration no: 01069913 **Date established:** 1972 **Turnover:** £1m - £2m
No.of Employees: 1 - 10 **Product Groups:** 26, 63

Date of Accounts	Dec 11	Dec 10	Dec 09
Sales Turnover	N/A	N/A	1m
Pre Tax Profit/Loss	N/A	N/A	96
Working Capital	328	354	362
Fixed Assets	29	23	25
Current Assets	364	410	461
Current Liabilities	N/A	N/A	32

English Furnishings

Unit 3 Coopies Field Coopies Lane, Morpeth, NE61 6JT
Tel: 01670-513773
Website: http://www.englishfurnishings.co.uk
Directors: J. English (Prop)
Immediate Holding Company: AUTOMINSTER LIMITED
Date established: 1984 **No.of Employees:** 1 - 10 **Product Groups:** 24, 26, 61

Date of Accounts	Nov 11	Nov 10	Nov 09
Working Capital	-10	10	20
Fixed Assets	3	3	9
Current Assets	35	56	60
Current Liabilities	19	20	19

Hydratight Morpeth

5 Coopies Field Coopies Lane, Morpeth, NE61 6JT
Tel: 01670-515432 **Fax:** 01670-513110
E-mail: philip.maxted@hydratight.com
Website: http://www.hydratight.com
Bank(s): HSBC Bank plc
Directors: N. Gemmell (Co Sec)
Managers: B. Williams (Tech Serv Mgr), J. Gill (Mgr)
Ultimate Holding Company: ACTUANT CORP (USA)
Immediate Holding Company: HYDRATIGHT OPERATIONS LIMITED
Registration no: 01385259 **Date established:** 1978
Turnover: £20m - £50m **No.of Employees:** 21 - 50 **Product Groups:** 36, 38, 40, 46, 48, 85

Date of Accounts	Aug 11	Aug 10	Aug 09
Sales Turnover	23m	42m	40m
Pre Tax Profit/Loss	8m	11m	-48
Working Capital	15m	8m	21m
Fixed Assets	N/A	4m	4m
Current Assets	15m	20m	29m
Current Liabilities	N/A	4m	4m

Intech Publicity

14 Bracken Ridge, Morpeth, NE61 3SY
Tel: 01670-519102 **Fax:** 01670-515815
E-mail: djw.intech@talktalk.net
Directors: D. Wilkinson (Prop), D. Wilkinson (Dir)
Turnover: Up to £250,000 **No.of Employees:** 1 - 10 **Product Groups:** 81

Jewson Ltd

Coopies Lane, Morpeth, NE61 6JN
Tel: 01670-519093 **Fax:** 01670-516028
Website: http://www.jewson.co.uk
Directors: P. Hindle (MD)
Managers: M. Baker (District Mgr)
Ultimate Holding Company: COMPAGNIE DE SAINT GOBAIN (FRANCE)
Immediate Holding Company: JEWSON LIMITED
Registration no: 00348407 **VAT No.:** GB 394 1212 63
Date established: 1939 **Turnover:** £2m - £5m **No.of Employees:** 1 - 10
Product Groups: 66

see next page

Jewson Ltd - Cont'd

Date of Accounts	Dec 11	Dec 10	Dec 09
Sales Turnover	1606m	1547m	1485m
Pre Tax Profit/Loss	18m	100m	45m
Working Capital	-345m	-250m	-349m
Fixed Assets	496m	387m	461m
Current Assets	657m	1005m	1320m
Current Liabilities	66m	120m	64m

Kennedy Watts LLP

13 Newgate Street, Morpeth, NE61 1AL
Tel: 01670-503378 **Fax:** 01670-503376
E-mail: d.mayhew@kwm.uk.com
Directors: D. Mayhew (Ptnr)
Immediate Holding Company: QUANTIS LIMITED
Registration no: 05173758 **Date established:** 2004
No.of Employees: 1 - 10 **Product Groups:** 35

Date of Accounts	Aug 11	Aug 10	Aug 09
Working Capital	134	113	133
Fixed Assets	N/A	1	1
Current Assets	186	163	191

Newtown Engineering Co.

Garleigh Road Rothbury, Morpeth, NE65 7RG
Tel: 01669-620755 **Fax:** 01669-620478
E-mail: enqs@newtownengineering.co.uk
Website: http://www.newtownengineering.co.uk
Directors: R. Edmondson (Ptnr)
Turnover: £250,000 - £500,000 **No.of Employees:** 1 - 10
Product Groups: 41

Northern Structures

Amble Industrial Estate Amble, Morpeth, NE65 0PE
Tel: 01665-710746 **Fax:** 01665-712738
E-mail: sales@northernstructures.co.uk
Website: http://www.northernstructures.co.uk
Bank(s): Barclays
Directors: A. Tremlett (Fin)
Immediate Holding Company: NORTHERN STRUCTURES LTD
Registration no: 01253968 **Date established:** 1976 **Turnover:** £1m - £2m
No.of Employees: 21 - 50 **Product Groups:** 35, 52

Date of Accounts	Sep 11	Sep 10	Sep 09
Working Capital	994	2m	1m
Fixed Assets	380	277	284
Current Assets	2m	2m	2m

Northumberland County Council

County Hall, Morpeth, NE61 2EF
Tel: 0845-6006400 **Fax:** 01670-533253
E-mail: s.stewart@northumberland.gov.uk
Website: http://www.northumberland.gov.uk
Bank(s): Cooperative
Directors: S. Stewart (Grp Chief Exec), S. Mason (Fin), M. Henderson (Grp Chief Exec)
Managers: S. Mason, J. Hamilton, G. Adams (Develop Mgr), G. Patterson, H. Elliott (Chief Acct), D. Brough (Projects)
No.of Employees: 21 - 50 **Product Groups:** 80, 84

Smith & Co (South Shields) Ltd

Morwick Mill Acklington, Morpeth, NE65 9DG
Tel: 01665-711112 **Fax:** 0191-455 2414
E-mail: j.r.collin@smith-and-co.co.uk
Website: http://www.smith-and-co.co.uk
Directors: J. Collin (MD), R. Collin (Ch)
Immediate Holding Company: Smith & Co.(South Shields)Limited
Registration no: 00846473 **VAT No.:** GB 176 0025 85
Date established: 1965 **Turnover:** £500,000 - £1m
No.of Employees: 1 - 10 **Product Groups:** 34, 36

Weldon Gun Room Murray Of Alnwcik

High Weldon Farm Longframlington, Morpeth, NE65 8AY
Tel: 01665-570011 **Fax:** 01665-570765
Directors: S. Jopson (Prop)
Date established: 1998 **No.of Employees:** 1 - 10 **Product Groups:** 36, 39, 40

West Scomac Catering Equipment Ltd

Hadston Industrial Estate Hadston, Morpeth, NE65 9YG
Tel: 01670-760082 **Fax:** 01670-761404
E-mail: sales@stellex.co.uk
Website: http://www.stellex.co.uk
Bank(s): Lloyds TSB
Managers: Chamberlain (Chief Mgr)
Ultimate Holding Company: WHITE BROS. (N CLE-ON-TYNE) LIMITED
Immediate Holding Company: STELLEX LIMITED
Registration no: 00329753 **VAT No.:** GB 137 5274 61
Date established: 1937 **Turnover:** £1m - £2m **No.of Employees:** 21 - 50
Product Groups: 40, 45

Date of Accounts	Dec 09	Dec 08	Dec 07
Working Capital	-35	-104	-99
Fixed Assets	305	329	353
Current Assets	670	643	1m

Prudhoe

Bespoke Concrete Products Ltd

Tynedale Works Princess Way, Prudhoe, NE42 6PL
Tel: 01661-839340 **Fax:** 01661-833923
E-mail: info@bespokeconcrete.co.uk
Website: http://www.bespokeconcrete.co.uk
Bank(s): National Westminster Bank Plc
Directors: M. Kay (MD)
Ultimate Holding Company: MAYMASK (8) LIMITED
Immediate Holding Company: BESPOKE CONCRETE PRODUCTS LIMITED
Registration no: 02773783 **VAT No.:** GB 605 5042 75
Date established: 1992 **Turnover:** £500,000 - £1m
No.of Employees: 21 - 50 **Product Groups:** 33

Date of Accounts	Mar 11	Mar 10	Mar 09
Working Capital	54	-5	-152
Fixed Assets	200	213	228
Current Assets	459	389	358

C J & L Fenwick

2 Station Industrial Estate Low Prudhoe, Prudhoe, NE42 6NP
Tel: 01661-833474 **Fax:** 01661-833474
Website: http://www.cjandlfenwick.co.uk
Directors: C. Fenwick (Prop)
Immediate Holding Company: MAINWARING LIMITED
Registration no: 04468506 **Date established:** 2003
Turnover: Up to £250,000 **No.of Employees:** 1 - 10 **Product Groups:** 35, 48

Date of Accounts	Jun 11	Jun 10	Jun 09
Working Capital	-70	-60	-104
Fixed Assets	401	411	398
Current Assets	189	184	126

Gladstone Packaging

Station Road Low Prudhoe, Prudhoe, NE42 6NP
Tel: 01661-830300 **Fax:** 01661-844443
Website: http://www.gladstonepackaging.com
Directors: A. Gladstone (Prop)
Date established: 1993 **No.of Employees:** 1 - 10 **Product Groups:** 38, 42

Hammerite Products Ltd

Eltringham Works, Prudhoe, NE42 6LP
Tel: 01661-830000 **Fax:** 01661-835760
E-mail: sales@hammerite.com
Website: http://www.hammerite.com
Bank(s): Barclays
Directors: R. Helbing (Dir)
Ultimate Holding Company: AKZO NOBEL NV (NETHERLANDS)
Immediate Holding Company: HAMMERITE PRODUCTS LIMITED
Registration no: 02781134 **VAT No.:** 439 4758 08 **Date established:** 1993
Turnover: £20m - £50m **No.of Employees:** 51 - 100 **Product Groups:** 31, 32

Date of Accounts	Dec 11	Dec 10	Dec 09
Sales Turnover	27m	23m	32m
Pre Tax Profit/Loss	128	34	6m
Working Capital	8m	7m	7m
Fixed Assets	4m	5m	5m
Current Assets	13m	12m	15m
Current Liabilities	2m	1m	2m

Premier Plating North East Ltd

Premier House Low Prudhoe, Prudhoe, NE42 6NP
Tel: 01661-831415 **Fax:** 01661-831416
E-mail: info@premierplating.co.uk
Website: http://www.premierplating.co.uk
Directors: I. Dixon (MD)
Immediate Holding Company: THE PREMIER PLATING COMPANY (NORTHEAST) LIMITED
Registration no: 04468506 **Date established:** 2002
No.of Employees: 1 - 10 **Product Groups:** 46, 48

Date of Accounts	Mar 12	Mar 11	Mar 10
Working Capital	67	61	42
Fixed Assets	60	56	50
Current Assets	122	127	99

Quantum Controls Ltd

6a Dukesway Low Prudhoe Industrial Estate, Prudhoe, NE42 6PQ
Tel: 01661-835566 **Fax:** 01661-833868
E-mail: sales@quantum-controls.co.uk
Website: http://www.quantum-controls.co.uk
Bank(s): Barclays, Gateshead, Tyne and Wear
Directors: K. Brown (Dir)
Managers: S. Greene (Sales Prom Mgr), K. Hall (Comptroller)
Ultimate Holding Company: QUANTUM CH LIMITED
Immediate Holding Company: QUANTUM CONTROLS LTD
Registration no: 04118204 **VAT No.:** GB 177 1169 50
Date established: 2000 **Turnover:** £2m - £5m **No.of Employees:** 21 - 50
Product Groups: 37

Date of Accounts	Jan 12	Jan 11	Jan 10
Working Capital	618	433	241
Fixed Assets	82	92	100
Current Assets	1m	1m	796
Current Liabilities	N/A	216	N/A

Red Alert

18 Prospect Terrace, Prudhoe, NE42 6JD
Tel: 07970-491092
E-mail: ray.woodhouse@virgin.net
Website: http://www.prudhoebusiness.co.uk/redalert.htm
Directors: R. Woodhouse (Prop)
Date established: 2003 **No.of Employees:** 1 - 10 **Product Groups:** 38, 42

Runhead Forge Ltd

Station Works Low Prudhoe, Prudhoe, NE42 6NP
Tel: 01661-832245 **Fax:** 01661-832230
Directors: J. Ostell (Fin)
Immediate Holding Company: RUNHEAD FORGE LIMITED
Registration no: 01903146 **Date established:** 1985
No.of Employees: 1 - 10 **Product Groups:** 26, 35

Date of Accounts	Sep 11	Sep 10	Sep 09
Working Capital	42	34	9
Fixed Assets	26	N/A	4
Current Assets	89	77	63

Wooler

M Fairnington

A Berwick Road, Wooler, NE71 6AH
Tel: 01668-282027 **Fax:** 01668-282439
Directors: M. Fairnington (Prop)
Date established: 1991 **No.of Employees:** 1 - 10 **Product Groups:** 41

NOTTINGHAMSHIRE

Mansfield

Ansini Ltd (ASG Group Ltd)
The Business Park Pleasley Vale, Mansfield, NG19 8RL
Tel: 01623-812333 **Fax:** 01623-812444
E-mail: info@ansini.co.uk
Website: http://www.ansini.co.uk
Bank(s): T.S.B.
Directors: A. Toothill (Fin)
Ultimate Holding Company: ASG GROUP ASSOCIATES LIMITED
Immediate Holding Company: ANSINI LIMITED
Registration no: 03120759 **Date established:** 1995
Turnover: £500,000 - £1m **No.of Employees:** 21 - 50
Product Groups: 30, 39, 48, 66

Date of Accounts	Feb 08	Feb 11	Feb 10
Working Capital	432	501	391
Fixed Assets	163	278	317
Current Assets	901	843	729

Bilbeck Merchants Ltd
159 Yorke Street Mansfield Woodhouse, Mansfield, NG19 9NU
Tel: 01623-651101 **Fax:** 01623-653387
E-mail: sales@bilbeck.com
Website: http://www.bilbeck.com
Bank(s): HSBC, Mansfield
Directors: C. Kose (Fin), D. Beck (MD)
Immediate Holding Company: BILBECK (MERCHANTS) LIMITED
Registration no: 00680944 **Date established:** 1961
Turnover: £10m - £20m **No.of Employees:** 21 - 50 **Product Groups:** 36, 66

Date of Accounts	Mar 11	Mar 10	Mar 09
Sales Turnover	17m	17m	19m
Pre Tax Profit/Loss	394	600	785
Working Capital	3m	3m	3m
Fixed Assets	847	898	953
Current Assets	5m	5m	5m
Current Liabilities	344	349	520

Bladen Box
Mill 1 The Business Park, Pleasley Vale, Mansfield, NG19 8RL
Tel: 01623-812047 **Fax:** 01623-812478
E-mail: info@bladenbox.com
Website: http://www.bladenbox.com
Directors: J. Bladen (Prop)
Immediate Holding Company: BLADEN BOX LIMITED
Registration no: 05126513 **Date established:** 2004
No.of Employees: 11 - 20 **Product Groups:** 38, 42

Date of Accounts	May 12	May 11	May 10
Working Capital	-66	-107	-70
Fixed Assets	179	108	71
Current Assets	209	225	136

Brodale Catering Equipment Ltd
10 King Edward Street Shirebrook, Mansfield, NG20 8AU
Tel: 01623-747593 **Fax:** 01623-744143
E-mail: catering@brodale.co.uk
Website: http://www.brodale.co.uk
Directors: K. Bradfield (Dir), K. Bromley (Dir)
Immediate Holding Company: BRODALE CATERING EQUIPMENT LIMITED
Registration no: 03349645 **Date established:** 1997
No.of Employees: 1 - 10 **Product Groups:** 20, 40, 41

Bubbles Showers & Bathrooms
Unit 3 Hallam Way Old Mill Lane Industrial Estate, Mansfield Woodhouse, Mansfield, NG19 9BG
Tel: 01623-661111
Website: http://www.bubbles-uk.com
Directors: T. Duffy (Ptnr)
Immediate Holding Company: BUBBLES SHOWERS AND BATHROOMS LTD
Registration no: 07078384 **Date established:** 2009
No.of Employees: 1 - 10 **Product Groups:** 26, 33, 36

Date of Accounts	Dec 11	Dec 10
Working Capital	316	401
Fixed Assets	454	39
Current Assets	355	448

Captive Closures
Burma Road Blidworth, Mansfield, NG21 0RT
Tel: 01623-491112 **Fax:** 01623-491113
E-mail: captive.mick@btconnect.com
Website: http://www.captiveclosures.com
Directors: L. Warrell (Ptnr)
Immediate Holding Company: CAPTIVE CLOSURES LLP
Registration no: OC325220 **VAT No.:** GB 598 3031 17
Date established: 2007 **Turnover:** £500,000 - £1m
No.of Employees: 11 - 20 **Product Groups:** 31, 48

Date of Accounts	Mar 11	Mar 10	Mar 09
Working Capital	79	75	81
Fixed Assets	189	194	187
Current Assets	187	203	159

Cassells Industrial Products
60 Littleworth, Mansfield, NG18 2SH
Tel: 01623-622439 **Fax:** 01623-420134
E-mail: sales@ciponline.co.uk
Website: http://www.ciponline.co.uk
Directors: W. Cassell (Sales), D. Cassell (Fin)
Immediate Holding Company: CASSELLS INDUSTRIAL PRODUCTS LIMITED
Registration no: 02981272 **Date established:** 1994
Turnover: £500,000 - £1m **No.of Employees:** 1 - 10 **Product Groups:** 36, 37, 46

Date of Accounts	Aug 11	Aug 10	Aug 09
Working Capital	73	57	50
Fixed Assets	13	4	10
Current Assets	279	287	208
Current Liabilities	83	103	49

Caunton Access Ltd
Arrowmax Buildings Langwith Road, Langwith Junction, Mansfield, NG20 9RN
Tel: 01636-636662 **Fax:** 0870-731 9109
E-mail: enquiries@cauntonaccess.com
Website: http://www.cauntonaccess.com
Directors: S. Brown (MD)
Immediate Holding Company: CAUNTON ACCESS LIMITED
Registration no: 06437322 **Date established:** 2007
Turnover: £500,000 - £1m **No.of Employees:** 1 - 10 **Product Groups:** 35

Date of Accounts	Nov 11	Nov 10	Nov 09
Working Capital	-10	19	48
Fixed Assets	36	11	11
Current Assets	168	33	113
Current Liabilities	179	14	64

Central Computer Management Ltd
Lower Oakham Way, Mansfield, NG18 5BY
Tel: 01623-622210 **Fax:** 01623-622128
E-mail: sjohnson@ccmlpay.com
Website: http://www.ccmlpay.co.uk
Bank(s): Barclays, Sheffield
Directors: S. Johnson (MD)
Immediate Holding Company: CENTRAL COMPUTER MANAGEMENT LIMITED
Registration no: 01514281 **VAT No.:** GB 351 8694 30
Date established: 1980 **Turnover:** £1m - £2m **No.of Employees:** 11 - 20
Product Groups: 80

Date of Accounts	Aug 11	Aug 10	Aug 09
Working Capital	167	186	177
Fixed Assets	19	10	16
Current Assets	279	364	364

Combined Energy Solutions Ltd
Hamilton House Kestral Road, Mansfield, NG18 5FT
Tel: 01623-422766 **Fax:** 01623-629479
E-mail: sales@combinedenergy.co.uk
Website: http://www.combinedenergysolutions.com
Directors: K. Farrimond (MD)
Managers: E. Staley
Ultimate Holding Company: BRIGGS & FORRESTER LIMITED
Immediate Holding Company: COMBINED ENERGY SOLUTIONS LIMITED
Registration no: 04371530 **Date established:** 2002
No.of Employees: 51 - 100 **Product Groups:** 35, 39, 45

Date of Accounts	Oct 11	Oct 10	Oct 09
Sales Turnover	9m	9m	10m
Pre Tax Profit/Loss	16	5	-1m
Working Capital	200	-366	-506
Fixed Assets	229	282	422
Current Assets	3m	3m	3m
Current Liabilities	1m	1m	1m

Crown Speciality Packaging UK Ltd
Crown Farm Way Forest Town, Mansfield, NG19 0FT
Tel: 01623-622651
Website: http://www.crowncork.com
Directors: C. Robinson (Dir)
Managers: N. Betts (Personnel), N. Allen (Fin Mgr)
Ultimate Holding Company: CROWN HOLDINGS INC (USA)
Immediate Holding Company: CROWN SPECIALITY PACKAGING UK LIMITED
Registration no: 02398420 **Date established:** 1989
Turnover: £50m - £75m **No.of Employees:** 101 - 250
Product Groups: 35, 48

Date of Accounts	Dec 11	Dec 10	Dec 09
Sales Turnover	69m	69m	62m
Pre Tax Profit/Loss	2m	2m	2m
Working Capital	11m	10m	8m
Fixed Assets	6m	6m	6m
Current Assets	24m	33m	28m
Current Liabilities	5m	16m	13m

D I P T Protrade
Unit 15 Maun Close, Mansfield, NG18 5GY
Tel: 01623-658615 **Fax:** 01623-620216
E-mail: steve.walton@protrade.co.uk
Website: http://www.protrade.co.uk
Managers: E. King (District Mgr)
No.of Employees: 1 - 10 **Product Groups:** 37

Dale Mansfield Ltd
Rotherham Road New Houghton, Mansfield, NG19 8TF
Tel: 01623-810659 **Fax:** 01623-811660
E-mail: enquiry@dale-mansfield.co.uk
Website: http://www.dale-mansfield.co.uk
Bank(s): The Yorkshire Bank
Directors: D. Potter (Co Sec)
Managers: I. Baker (Sales Prom Mgr), M. Slack (Purch Mgr)
Immediate Holding Company: DALE (MANSFIELD) LIMITED
Registration no: 02858338 **Date established:** 1993 **Turnover:** £2m - £5m
No.of Employees: 51 - 100 **Product Groups:** 40, 45, 48

Date of Accounts	Dec 11	Dec 10	Dec 09
Working Capital	1m	1m	992
Fixed Assets	1m	1m	1m
Current Assets	2m	2m	1m

W H Davis Ltd
Langwith Road Langwith Junction, Mansfield, NG20 9SA
Tel: 01623-741600 **Fax:** 01623-744474
E-mail: management@whdavis.co.uk
Website: http://www.whdavis.co.uk
Bank(s): HSBC Bank plc
Directors: T. Sharpe (Purch), M. Jackson (Dir)
Managers: D. Hazelton (Chief Acct), C. Charlesworth (Personnel)
Ultimate Holding Company: PORTCHESTER EQUITY LIMITED
Immediate Holding Company: W.H. DAVIS LIMITED
Registration no: 01797397 **VAT No.:** GB 401 6657 73
Date established: 1984 **Turnover:** £5m - £10m
No.of Employees: 101 - 250 **Product Groups:** 39, 45

Date of Accounts	Aug 09	Aug 08	Sep 11
Sales Turnover	15m	8m	8m
Pre Tax Profit/Loss	922	165	478
Working Capital	1m	3m	3m
Fixed Assets	2m	905	2m
Current Assets	3m	6m	5m
Current Liabilities	849	1m	498

Deanestor Ltd
Deanestor Building Warren Way, Forest Town, Mansfield, NG19 0FL
Tel: 01623-420041 **Fax:** 01623-420061
E-mail: general@deanestor.co.uk
Website: http://www.deanestor.co.uk
Directors: I. Bolton (Fin)
Managers: N. Shaw (Tech Serv Mgr), S. Williams (Chief Buyer), T. Darby (Personnel), A. Booth (Chief Acct), J. Berry (Sales & Mktg Mg)
Ultimate Holding Company: RYTON HOLDINGS LTD (GUERNSEY)
Immediate Holding Company: DEANESTOR PLC
Registration no: 02946819 **Date established:** 1994
Turnover: £10m - £20m **No.of Employees:** 101 - 250
Product Groups: 26, 28, 67

Date of Accounts	Dec 11	Jun 10	Jun 09
Sales Turnover	16m	13m	13m
Pre Tax Profit/Loss	492	1m	1m
Working Capital	4m	4m	3m
Fixed Assets	2m	2m	3m
Current Assets	7m	7m	5m
Current Liabilities	1m	1m	1m

Dunlop Slazenger International Ltd (Golf Division)

Unit A Brook Park East, Shirebrook, Mansfield, NG20 8RY
Tel: 08708-387310 **Fax:** 0870-838 7158
Website: http://www.dunlopsports.com
Managers: B. Leach
Ultimate Holding Company: SPORTS DIRECT INTERNATIONAL PLC
Immediate Holding Company: DUNLOP SLAZENGER LIMITED
Registration no: 02030941 **Date established:** 1986
Turnover: £20m - £50m **No.of Employees:** 51 - 100 **Product Groups:** 22, 24, 49, 65, 89

Date of Accounts	Dec 03	Dec 02	Apr 11
Working Capital	1	1	1
Current Assets	1	1	1

F C C Electrical Wholesalers Ltd

Hallam Way Old Mill Lane Industrial Estate, Mansfield Woodhouse, Mansfield, NG19 9BG
Tel: 01623-631200 **Fax:** 01623-420541
E-mail: terrysankey@fcc-electrical.co.uk
Website: http://www.fccelectrical.co.uk
Managers: T. Sankey (Chief Acct), G. Feltimo (District Mgr)
Ultimate Holding Company: CIRCUIT GROUP LIMITED
Immediate Holding Company: F C C ELECTRICAL WHOLESALERS LTD
Registration no: 00677498 **VAT No.:** GB 116 4405 00
Date established: 1960 **Turnover:** £5m - £10m **No.of Employees:** 21 - 50
Product Groups: 77

Date of Accounts	Dec 11	Dec 10	Dec 09
Working Capital	1m	1m	1m
Fixed Assets	429	448	449
Current Assets	2m	2m	2m

Fibresand International Ltd

Ash House Ransom Wood Business Park Southwell Road, Rainworth, Mansfield, NG21 0HJ
Tel: 01623-675305 **Fax:** 01623-675308
E-mail: enquiries@fibresand.com
Website: http://www.fibresand.com
Directors: M. Cannon (Ch)
Ultimate Holding Company: RANSOMWOOD ESTATES LIMITED
Immediate Holding Company: FIBRESAND INTERNATIONAL LIMITED
Registration no: 03761587 **VAT No.:** GB 728 6879 72
Date established: 1999 **Turnover:** £500,000 - £1m
No.of Employees: 1 - 10 **Product Groups:** 49, 85

Date of Accounts	Dec 11	Dec 10	Dec 09
Working Capital	66	123	-219
Fixed Assets	104	132	160
Current Assets	74	123	222

G S Print Ltd

Unit 4 Halls Workspace, Mansfield, NG18 5HF
Tel: 01623-427540 **Fax:** 01623-427541
E-mail: enquiries@gs-print.co.uk
Website: http://www.gs-print.co.uk
Directors: A. Ginever (Dir), A. Bagley (Fin)
Immediate Holding Company: G S PRINT LIMITED
Registration no: 02733132 **Date established:** 1992
No.of Employees: 1 - 10 **Product Groups:** 21, 22, 23, 24, 26, 27, 28, 30, 32, 33, 35, 36, 37, 38, 44, 49, 65, 75, 81

Date of Accounts	Jun 11	Jun 10	Jun 09
Working Capital	-11	-59	-38
Fixed Assets	206	212	219
Current Assets	56	77	111

Generator Associates Ltd

Glendale House Lime Tree Drive, Harlow Wood, Mansfield, NG18 4UZ
Tel: 01623-624005 **Fax:** 01623-635595
E-mail: sales@generatorassociates.com
Website: http://www.generatorassociates.com
Directors: R. Stevens (Dir)
Managers: C. Stevens (Mktg Serv Mgr)
Registration no: 05259639 **Date established:** 2005 **Turnover:** £1m - £2m
No.of Employees: 1 - 10 **Product Groups:** 37, 40, 52, 67, 83

Date of Accounts	Oct 07
Working Capital	-32
Fixed Assets	91
Current Assets	178
Current Liabilities	211

Glenair UK

40 Lower Oakham Way, Mansfield, NG18 5BY
Tel: 01623-638100 **Fax:** 01623-638111
E-mail: enquiries@glenair.co.uk
Website: http://www.glenair.co.uk
Bank(s): National Westminster Bank Plc
Directors: A. Coulson (Sales), A. Birks (MD), P. McGee (Fin)
Managers: K. Harding (Personnel), M. Fletcher (Tech Serv Mgr), T. Hall (Sales & Mktg Mg), C. Small
Ultimate Holding Company: GLENAIR INC. (USA)
Immediate Holding Company: GLENAIR UK LIMITED
Registration no: 01198102 **Date established:** 1975
Turnover: £50m - £75m **No.of Employees:** 251 - 500
Product Groups: 36, 37

Date of Accounts	Sep 11	Sep 10	Sep 09
Sales Turnover	73m	60m	60m
Pre Tax Profit/Loss	8m	2m	3m
Working Capital	31m	24m	23m
Fixed Assets	8m	9m	10m
Current Assets	47m	40m	39m
Current Liabilities	8m	6m	6m

Herbert Baggaley Construction Ltd

1 Melton Way, Mansfield, NG18 5FU
Tel: 01623-421421 **Fax:** 01623-420775
E-mail: contactus@baggaley.co.uk
Website: http://www.baggaley.co.uk
Bank(s): National Westminster Bank Plc
Directors: I. Baggaley (Grp Ch), M. Illingworth (Co Sec)
Managers: B. Dolby
Ultimate Holding Company: BAGGALEY GROUP LIMITED
Immediate Holding Company: HERBERT BAGGALEY CONSTRUCTION LIMITED
Registration no: 00271618 **VAT No.:** GB 458 2890 10
Date established: 1932 **Turnover:** £10m - £20m
No.of Employees: 51 - 100 **Product Groups:** 52

Date of Accounts	Dec 11	Dec 10	Jun 10
Sales Turnover	35m	17m	22m
Pre Tax Profit/Loss	-876	104	-1m
Working Capital	69	1m	1m
Fixed Assets	149	210	255
Current Assets	9m	10m	7m
Current Liabilities	5m	6m	3m

Hidentity Ltd

Unit 3 Victoria Street, Mansfield, NG18 5RR
Tel: 01623-429090 **Fax:** 01623-429090
E-mail: hide@hidentity.co.uk
Website: http://www.hidentity.co.uk
Managers: P. Gent (Mgr)
Immediate Holding Company: HIDENTITY LIMITED
Registration no: 05402856 **Date established:** 2005
Turnover: Up to £250,000 **No.of Employees:** 1 - 10 **Product Groups:** 26, 61, 63

Date of Accounts	Mar 11	Mar 10	Mar 09
Working Capital	37	15	-21
Fixed Assets	13	15	12
Current Assets	63	36	21

I E S P C A Ltd

The Millcourt Centre Pleasley Vale, Mansfield, NG19 8RL
Tel: 01623-819319 **Fax:** 01623-819329
E-mail: info@iespca.com
Website: http://www.iespca.com
Bank(s): Barclays
Directors: D. Mullen (Sales & Mktg), N. Power (Grp MD), N. Powell (MD)
Managers: K. Ryan (Eng Serv Mgr)
Ultimate Holding Company: IES INDUSTRIAL CONTROLS GROUP LIMITED
Immediate Holding Company: IES - PCA LIMITED
Registration no: 04410235 **VAT No.:** GB 740 9612 34
Date established: 2002 **Turnover:** £2m - £5m **No.of Employees:** 21 - 50
Product Groups: 37

Date of Accounts	Aug 10	Aug 09	Aug 08
Sales Turnover	N/A	2m	N/A
Pre Tax Profit/Loss	N/A	-170	N/A
Working Capital	-42	-79	53
Fixed Assets	266	299	357
Current Assets	730	802	2m
Current Liabilities	66	319	258

J H R Packaging Co. Ltd

Vernon Street Shirebrook, Mansfield, NG20 8SS
Tel: 01623-742291 **Fax:** 01623-748491
E-mail: jhr.packaging@btconnect.com
Website: http://www.jhrpackaging.co.uk
Directors: P. Etches (MD), J. Etches (Co Sec)
Immediate Holding Company: J.H.R. PACKAGING COMPANY LIMITED(THE)
Registration no: 01498869 **Date established:** 1980
No.of Employees: 11 - 20 **Product Groups:** 25, 45

Date of Accounts	Jun 11	Jun 10	Jun 09
Working Capital	184	163	154
Fixed Assets	81	90	99
Current Assets	264	232	242

Jonathan James Ltd

Carter Lane Shirebrook, Mansfield, NG20 8AH
Tel: 01623-746270 **Fax:** 01623-744304
E-mail: robert.nightingale@jonathan-james.co.uk
Website: http://www.jonathan-james.co.uk
Bank(s): National Westminster Bank Plc
Directors: J. Broughton (MD), J. Broughton (Dir), N. Goulding (Fin)
Managers: D. Thompson (Personnel)
Ultimate Holding Company: BROUGHTON BROTHERS LIMITED
Immediate Holding Company: JONATHAN JAMES (MANSFIELD) LIMITED
Registration no: 01104646 **VAT No.:** GB 401 5984 63
Date established: 1973 **Turnover:** £20m - £50m
No.of Employees: 21 - 50 **Product Groups:** 61

Date of Accounts	Jul 07	Jul 06	Jul 05
Sales Turnover	22m	24m	26m
Pre Tax Profit/Loss	55	10	-31
Working Capital	965	866	1m
Fixed Assets	367	436	173
Current Assets	4m	4m	5m
Current Liabilities	1m	2m	2m

KaMo UK (Trading Division Of KVM Energy Ltd)

I-Centre House Hamilton Way, Oakham Business Park, Mansfield, NG18 5BR
Tel: 01623-422006 **Fax:** 01623-422003
E-mail: info@kamouk.com
Website: http://www.kamouk.com
Directors: S. O'Brien (MD)
No.of Employees: 1 - 10 **Product Groups:** 36, 38, 40

Key Personnel Ltd

39 West Gate, Mansfield, NG18 1RX
Tel: 01623-420488 **Fax:** 01623-420531
E-mail: mansfield@key-personnel.co.uk
Website: http://www.key-personnel.co.uk
Managers: S. Jones (District Mgr)
Immediate Holding Company: KEY PERSONNEL SOLUTIONS LIMITED
Registration no: 07730331 **Date established:** 2011
No.of Employees: 1 - 10 **Product Groups:** 80, 86

Kingfisher Lighting Ltd

Ratcher Way Forest Town, Mansfield, NG19 0FS
Tel: 01623-415900 **Fax:** 01623-415910
E-mail: sales@kingfisherlighting.com
Website: http://www.kingfisherlighting.com
Bank(s): National Westminster Bank Plc
Directors: J. Harding (Co Sec), M. Harding (Dir), R. Rawson (Fin)
Managers: K. Eastern (Personnel)
Ultimate Holding Company: BLUE RIBAND ENTERPRISES LIMITED
Immediate Holding Company: KINGFISHER LIGHTING LIMITED
Registration no: 02236337 **VAT No.:** GB 509 1458 48
Date established: 1988 **Turnover:** £5m - £10m **No.of Employees:** 21 - 50
Product Groups: 37

Date of Accounts	Mar 11	Mar 10	Mar 09
Sales Turnover	8m	7m	8m
Pre Tax Profit/Loss	531	400	773
Working Capital	1m	1m	704
Fixed Assets	153	172	228
Current Assets	3m	3m	3m
Current Liabilities	703	573	855

Kobold Instruments Ltd

Unit 8-9 Brunts Business Centre Samuel Brunts Way, Mansfield, NG18 2AH
Tel: 01623-427701 **Fax:** 01623-427702
E-mail: klaus.kobold@kobold.com
Website: http://www.kobold.com
Directors: K. Kobold (Dir)
Managers: R. Gregory (Chief Mgr)
Immediate Holding Company: KOBOLD INSTRUMENTS LIMITED
Registration no: 02486586 **VAT No.:** GB 555 4916 18
Date established: 1990 **Turnover:** £500,000 - £1m
No.of Employees: 1 - 10 **Product Groups:** 38

Date of Accounts	Dec 11	Dec 10	Dec 09
Sales Turnover	881	N/A	N/A
Pre Tax Profit/Loss	52	N/A	N/A
Working Capital	408	369	318
Fixed Assets	1	2	3
Current Assets	518	461	393
Current Liabilities	62	N/A	N/A

L M Plastic

Mill 3 The Business Park, Pleasley Vale, Mansfield, NG19 8RL
Tel: 01623-818888
E-mail: rob@lmps.uk.com
Website: http://www.lmps.uk.com
Directors: R. Lubelski (MD)
Immediate Holding Company: L & M PLASTIC SOLUTIONS LIMITED
Registration no: 06079528 **Date established:** 2007
Turnover: Up to £250,000 **No.of Employees:** 1 - 10 **Product Groups:** 23, 26, 30, 32, 49

Date of Accounts	Feb 08	Feb 11	Feb 10
Working Capital	-17	-20	-26
Fixed Assets	1	6	7
Current Assets	1	5	5

Linney Group Ltd

Adamsway, Mansfield, NG18 4FL
Tel: 01623-450450 **Fax:** 01623-450451
E-mail: miles.linney@linney.co.uk
Website: http://www.linney.com
Bank(s): National Westminster Bank Plc
Directors: M. Linney (MD), R. Munro (Fin)
Managers: P. Stickland, M. Huffen (Tech Serv Mgr), I. Barradell
Immediate Holding Company: W.& J.LINNEY,LIMITED
Registration no: 00137552 **Date established:** 2014
Turnover: £50m - £75m **No.of Employees:** 251 - 500 **Product Groups:** 28

Date of Accounts	May 08	May 09	May 10
Sales Turnover	48m	56m	52m
Pre Tax Profit/Loss	1m	1m	1m
Working Capital	667	391	-252
Fixed Assets	15m	22m	21m
Current Assets	13m	13m	15m
Current Liabilities	4m	3m	5m

M G C Systems Ltd

Power Transmission House Redcliffe Road, Mansfield, NG18 2QH
Tel: 01623-635150 **Fax:** 01623-635125
E-mail: sales@mgcsystems.com
Website: http://www.mgcsystems.com
Directors: R. Darling (MD)
Managers: C. Waterfall (Sales Prom Mgr)
Registration no: 02221677 **VAT No.:** 509 1198 48 **Date established:** 1988
Turnover: £500,000 - £1m **No.of Employees:** 1 - 10 **Product Groups:** 35, 37

M K Powder Coatings

74-76 Station Road Shirebrook, Mansfield, NG20 8SZ
Tel: 01623-747491 **Fax:** 01623-747491
E-mail: mkmc28@aol.com
Directors: M. Kimberley (Ptnr)
No.of Employees: 1 - 10 **Product Groups:** 46, 48

M P R Electric Gates Ltd

Unit 23b Kings Mill Way, Mansfield, NG18 5ER
Tel: 01623-633241 **Fax:** 01623-634693
E-mail: mprelectricgates@talktalkbusiness.net
Website: http://www.electricgatesdirect.co.uk
Directors: M. Reddington (Dir)
Immediate Holding Company: M P R ELECTRIC GATES LIMITED
Registration no: 06288640 **Date established:** 2007
No.of Employees: 1 - 10 **Product Groups:** 25, 35, 36, 49, 67

Date of Accounts	May 11	May 10	May 09
Working Capital	265	204	122
Fixed Assets	43	36	22
Current Assets	358	304	221

Mandarin Creative Solutions Ltd

Carne Main Street, Blidworth, Mansfield, NG21 0QH
Tel: 0845-8330030 **Fax:** 0845-8330040
E-mail: studio@mandarincreates.com
Website: http://www.mandarincreates.com
Managers: S. Harvey (Comm)
Registration no: 05312050 **Date established:** 2004
Turnover: Up to £250,000 **No.of Employees:** 1 - 10 **Product Groups:** 81

Date of Accounts	Mar 08	Mar 07	Mar 06
Working Capital	53	36	22
Fixed Assets	21	21	4
Current Assets	72	67	57
Current Liabilities	18	31	35

Mansfield Anodisers Ltd

46 Hermitage Way, Mansfield, NG18 5ES
Tel: 01623-627700 **Fax:** 01623-628800
E-mail: info@mansfield-anodisers.co.uk
Website: http://www.mansfield-anodisers.co.uk
Directors: K. Carlisle (Fin)
Immediate Holding Company: MANSFIELD ANODISERS LIMITED
Registration no: 03698048 **Date established:** 1999
No.of Employees: 1 - 10 **Product Groups:** 46, 48

Date of Accounts	Dec 11	Dec 10	Dec 09
Working Capital	120	27	-5
Fixed Assets	91	88	67
Current Assets	303	217	149

Mansfield Gun Centre

10 Chesterfield Road North, Mansfield, NG19 7HH
Tel: 01623-653126 **Fax:** 01623-640773
E-mail: sales@mansfieldguncentre.co.uk
Website: http://www.mansfieldguncentre.co.uk

Directors: J. Harrold (Ptnr)
Date established: 1981 **No.of Employees:** 1 - 10 **Product Groups:** 36, 39, 40

Marlin Signs
84 Jenny Becketts Lane, Mansfield, NG18 4HS
Tel: 01623-650060 **Fax:** 01623-661321
E-mail: martin.sellars@btconnect.com
Website: http://www.marlinsigns.com
Directors: M. Sellars (Prop)
VAT No.: GB 738 0427 33 **Turnover:** £250,000 - £500,000
No.of Employees: 1 - 10 **Product Groups:** 40

N E Group
Edwinstowe House High Street, Edwinstowe, Mansfield, NG21 9PL
Tel: 01623-827900 **Fax:** 01623-824070
E-mail: phadley@nottsent.co.uk
Website: http://www.negroup.co.uk
Directors: R. Aston (Fin)
Managers: P. Hadley, S. Lankin (Personnel)
Ultimate Holding Company: ALKANE ENERGY PLC
Immediate Holding Company: NOTTINGHAMSHIRE ENTERPRISES
Registration no: 02408386 **Date established:** 1989 **Turnover:** £2m - £5m
No.of Employees: 21 - 50 **Product Groups:** 80, 83

Date of Accounts	Mar 11	Mar 10	Mar 09
Working Capital	-297	-178	560
Fixed Assets	2m	2m	2m
Current Assets	224	466	1m

Ohra
14 Johnson Drive, Mansfield, NG18 4BB
Tel: 01623-656043 **Fax:** 01623-656051
E-mail: meadows@ohra.de
Website: http://www.ohra.co.uk
Directors: R. Meadows (Prop)
Date established: 1999 **No.of Employees:** 1 - 10 **Product Groups:** 26, 35, 42, 45, 67

Quality Tempered Glass
Millennium Business Park Concorde Way, Mansfield, NG19 7JZ
Tel: 01623-416300 **Fax:** 01623-416303
E-mail: markd@qualitytempered.com
Website: http://www.independentglass.co.uk
Managers: M. Donson (Chief Mgr), K. jarvis (Chief Acct)
Ultimate Holding Company: WESTCROWNS LIMITED
Immediate Holding Company: INDEPENDENT GLASS COMPANY LIMITED
Registration no: 04181248 **Date established:** 2001 **Turnover:** £2m - £5m
No.of Employees: 51 - 100 **Product Groups:** 33

Raymond Crane Hire Ltd
Mill Way Old Mill Lane Industrial Estate, Mansfield Woodhouse, Mansfield, NG19 9BG
Tel: 01623-654221 **Fax:** 01623-420390
E-mail: philipraymond@fsmail.net
Website: http://www.raymondcranehire.co.uk
Directors: R. Morton (MD)
Immediate Holding Company: RAYMOND CRANE HIRE LIMITED
Registration no: 04397532 **VAT No.:** GB 345 8620 42
Date established: 2002 **Turnover:** £500,000 - £1m
No.of Employees: 11 - 20 **Product Groups:** 45

Date of Accounts	Jul 11	Jul 10	Jul 09
Working Capital	64	48	58
Fixed Assets	32	35	27
Current Assets	346	413	364

S D C Trailers Ltd
Bradder Way, Mansfield, NG18 5DQ
Tel: 01623-625354 **Fax:** 01623-626946
E-mail: paulbratton@sdctrailers.com
Website: http://www.sdctrailers.com
Bank(s): Northern Bank, Magerafelt
Directors: P. Bratton (MD), M. Cuskeran (Fin), C. McCauley (Fin)
Managers: A. Cooper (Purch Mgr)
Ultimate Holding Company: RETLAN MANUFACTURING LTD
Immediate Holding Company: SDC TRAILERS LIMITED
Registration no: NI015713 **VAT No.:** GB 598 4643 78
Date established: 1982 **Turnover:** £250m - £500m
No.of Employees: 51 - 100 **Product Groups:** 39

Date of Accounts	Mar 12	Mar 11	Mar 09
Sales Turnover	89m	81m	75m
Pre Tax Profit/Loss	2m	1m	2m
Working Capital	17m	15m	13m
Fixed Assets	20m	21m	22m
Current Assets	60m	61m	45m
Current Liabilities	5m	4m	5m

S D Products
The Broadway, Mansfield, NG18 2RL
Tel: 01623-655265 **Fax:** 01623-420689
E-mail: sales@sdproducts.co.uk
Website: http://www.sdproducts.co.uk
Directors: D. Lee (MD)
Immediate Holding Company: S.D. PRODUCTS LIMITED
Registration no: 01877045 **VAT No.:** GB 309 6834 37
Date established: 1985 **Turnover:** £1m - £2m **No.of Employees:** 1 - 10
Product Groups: 22, 30, 35, 36, 39, 42, 66

Date of Accounts	Mar 11	Mar 10	Mar 09
Working Capital	211	143	114
Fixed Assets	120	107	112
Current Assets	565	499	452

S L S Precision Engineers Ltd
1 Hermitage Way, Mansfield, NG18 5ES
Tel: 01623-456601 **Fax:** 01623-456602
E-mail: slsprec@aol.com
Website: http://www.sls-precision.co.uk
Directors: D. Lane (Co Sec), D. Sugg (MD)
Immediate Holding Company: S.L.S.PRECISION ENGINEERS LIMITED
Registration no: 01464556 **VAT No.:** GB 331 5581 71
Date established: 1979 **Turnover:** £500,000 - £1m
No.of Employees: 1 - 10 **Product Groups:** 42, 48

Date of Accounts	Nov 11	Nov 10	Nov 09
Working Capital	167	132	177
Fixed Assets	107	31	47
Current Assets	286	217	265

Sherwood Portable Acccomodation
Fourlanes New Mill Lane, Forest Town, Mansfield, NG19 0HH
Tel: 01623-428771 **Fax:** 01623-424964
E-mail: info@sherwoodcabins.co.uk
Website: http://www.sherwoodcabins.co.uk
Directors: J. Williams (Prop)
No.of Employees: 1 - 10 **Product Groups:** 25, 35, 51, 80, 83

Shop Equip Ltd
Park View North Street Langwith, Mansfield, NG20 9BN
Tel: 01623-741500 **Fax:** 01623-741505
E-mail: sales@shop-equip.com
Website: http://www.shop-equip.com
Directors: L. Noble (MD)
Ultimate Holding Company: MOSTYN LIMITED
Immediate Holding Company: SHOP-EQUIP LIMITED
Registration no: 02372059 **Date established:** 1989 **Turnover:** £2m - £5m
No.of Employees: 11 - 20 **Product Groups:** 26

Date of Accounts	Dec 11	Dec 10	Dec 09
Working Capital	657	673	237
Fixed Assets	685	722	761
Current Assets	1m	1m	1m

Stannah Lift Services Ltd
48 Bleak Hill Way, Mansfield, NG18 5EZ
Tel: 01623-631010 **Fax:** 01623-636182
Website: http://www.stannah.co.uk
Directors: A. Stannah (Dir)
Ultimate Holding Company: STANNAH LIFTS HOLDINGS LIMITED
Immediate Holding Company: STANNAH LIFT SERVICES LIMITED
Registration no: 01189799 **Date established:** 1974
No.of Employees: 21 - 50 **Product Groups:** 35, 39, 45

Date of Accounts	Dec 11	Dec 10	Dec 09
Sales Turnover	84m	82m	87m
Pre Tax Profit/Loss	191	2m	2m
Working Capital	12m	14m	15m
Fixed Assets	4m	4m	3m
Current Assets	21m	24m	24m
Current Liabilities	6m	6m	7m

Status Scientific Controls
Hermitage Lane Inudst Estate Kings Mill Way, Mansfield, NG18 5ER
Tel: 01623-651381 **Fax:** 01623-421063
E-mail: sales@status-scientific.com
Website: http://www.status-scientific.com
Bank(s): National Westminster Bank Plc
Directors: A. Kirk (Fin), W. Baxter (MD), K. Foster (Sales)
Ultimate Holding Company: RICHBLOOM HOLDINGS LIMITED
Immediate Holding Company: STATUS SCIENTIFIC CONTROLS LIMITED
Registration no: 02231611 **VAT No.:** GB 509 3507 51
Date established: 1988 **Turnover:** £1m - £2m **No.of Employees:** 21 - 50
Product Groups: 38

Date of Accounts	Dec 11	Dec 10	Dec 09
Sales Turnover	2m	2m	2m
Pre Tax Profit/Loss	507	398	167
Working Capital	358	373	539
Fixed Assets	16	12	10
Current Assets	1m	632	792
Current Liabilities	55	46	156

Steelworld Fabrication
Unit 7b Long Stoop Way Forest Town, Mansfield, NG19 0FQ
Tel: 01623-420444 **Fax:** 01623-420465
E-mail: glyn@steelworld.co.uk
Website: http://www.steelworld.co.uk
Bank(s): Barclays
Directors: R. Halsey (MD)
Ultimate Holding Company: STEELWORLD FABRICATIONS HOLDINGS LIMITED
Immediate Holding Company: STEELWORLD FABRICATIONS LTD
Registration no: 04085822 **Date established:** 2000 **Turnover:** £2m - £5m
No.of Employees: 11 - 20 **Product Groups:** 37, 44, 46, 48

Date of Accounts	Mar 11	Mar 10	Mar 09
Working Capital	-0	20	15
Fixed Assets	1	1	N/A
Current Assets	69	70	52

Stratstone Honda (part of Pendragon P.L.C.)
Southwell Road West, Mansfield, NG18 4TR
Tel: 01623-787776 **Fax:** 01623-788384
Directors: S. Meldrum (Dir)
Turnover: £50m - £75m **No.of Employees:** 51 - 100 **Product Groups:** 68

Tremic Tools Ltd
37 Hermitage Way, Mansfield, NG18 5ES
Tel: 01623-656405 **Fax:** 01623-421181
E-mail: tremic@tremictools.com
Bank(s): National Westminster Bank Plc
Directors: T. Webb (Dir)
Immediate Holding Company: TREMIC TOOLS LIMITED
Registration no: 02803786 **VAT No.:** GB 419 7893 01
Date established: 1993 **Turnover:** £500,000 - £1m
No.of Employees: 11 - 20 **Product Groups:** 30, 42, 44, 46, 48

Date of Accounts	Jul 11	Jul 10	Jul 09
Working Capital	-68	-24	-89
Fixed Assets	310	346	385
Current Assets	94	162	124

True2Life Ltd
Mansfield I-Centre Oakham Business Park, Hamilton Way, Mansfield, NG18 5BR
Tel: 01623-672083 **Fax:** 01623-600601
E-mail: sales@true2life.co.uk
Website: http://www.true2life.co.uk
Directors: D. Forrest (Dir)
Managers: R. Needham (Develop Mgr)
Registration no: 05439526 **Date established:** 2005
Turnover: Up to £250,000 **No.of Employees:** 1 - 10 **Product Groups:** 44, 87

Date of Accounts	Apr 07	Apr 06
Working Capital	-94	-80
Fixed Assets	7	5
Current Assets	19	18
Current Liabilities	113	98

TurnerFox Recruitment
18 Albert Street, Mansfield, NG18 1EB
Tel: 01623-656303 **Fax:** 01623-658891
E-mail: jobs@turnerfox.co.uk
Website: http://www.turnerfox.co.uk
Directors: C. Turner (Ptnr)
No.of Employees: 1 - 10 **Product Groups:** 80

Newark

Abbott & Co Newark Ltd
Newark Boiler Works Northern Road, Newark, NG24 2EJ
Tel: 01636-704208 **Fax:** 01636-705742
E-mail: henryp@air-receivers.co.uk
Website: http://www.air-receivers.co.uk
Bank(s): Lloyds, 37 Castlegate, Newark
Directors: H. Price (Dir), N. Vinter (Sales)
Ultimate Holding Company: ABBOTT AND COMPANY HOLDINGS LIMITED
Immediate Holding Company: ABBOTT & CO. (NEWARK) LIMITED
Registration no: 02833304 **Date established:** 1993
Turnover: £500,000 - £1m **No.of Employees:** 11 - 20
Product Groups: 35, 48

Date of Accounts	Sep 11	Sep 10	Sep 09
Working Capital	731	639	683
Fixed Assets	33	22	15
Current Assets	2m	1m	1m

Activ Web Design
8 Mayden House, Long Bennington Business Park Main Road, Long Bennington, Newark, NG23 5DJ
Tel: 0845-0940497 **Fax:** 0870-7515574
E-mail: info@activwebdesign.com
Website: http://www.activwebdesign.com/hu17/
Directors: I. Petrie (Develop)
Managers: B. Gardiner (District Mgr)
Registration no: 07079090 **Date established:** 2008
Turnover: Up to £250,000 **No.of Employees:** 1 - 10 **Product Groups:** 44

AEM Lifting Ltd
Ollerton Road Tuxford, Newark, NG22 0PQ
Tel: 01777-874928 **Fax:** 01777-871855
E-mail: hires@aemlifting.com
Website: http://www.aemlifting.com
Directors: A. Morris (MD)
Immediate Holding Company: A.E. MORRIS LIMITED
Registration no: 01858132 **Date established:** 1984
Turnover: Up to £250,000 **No.of Employees:** 1 - 10 **Product Groups:** 35, 39, 45

Date of Accounts	Nov 11	Nov 10	Nov 09
Sales Turnover	107	148	163
Pre Tax Profit/Loss	3	24	12
Working Capital	369	23	-111
Fixed Assets	2m	2m	2m
Current Assets	561	533	464
Current Liabilities	100	85	68

Agricultural Travel Bureau Ltd
14 Chain Lane, Newark, NG24 1AU
Tel: 01636-705612 **Fax:** 0870-4423291
E-mail: info@agritravel.co.uk
Website: http://www.agritravel.co.uk
Directors: G. Lewis (Co Sec)
Immediate Holding Company: AGRICULTURAL TRAVEL BUREAU LIMITED
Registration no: 01006704 **Date established:** 1971
Turnover: Up to £250,000 **No.of Employees:** 11 - 20 **Product Groups:** 69

Date of Accounts	Oct 09	Oct 08	Oct 07
Working Capital	-236	-85	-337
Fixed Assets	1m	1m	1m
Current Assets	202	303	286

Allied Packaging
Station Farm Main Street, Claypole, Newark, NG23 5BJ
Tel: 01636-626476 **Fax:** 01636-626476
Directors: D. Good (Ptnr)
Immediate Holding Company: FIVE BELLS INN LIMITED
Registration no: 04486984 **Date established:** 2002
No.of Employees: 1 - 10 **Product Groups:** 38, 42

Date of Accounts	Jul 11	Jul 10	Jul 09
Working Capital	-58	-11	15
Fixed Assets	86	83	93
Current Assets	86	137	169

The Barcode Warehouse
Telford Drive, Newark, NG24 2DX
Tel: 01636-602000 **Fax:** 01636-602001
E-mail: sales@thebarcodewarehouse.co.uk
Website: http://www.thebarcodewarehouse.co.uk
Directors: S. Jury (Co Sec), R. Lee (Ch), R. Staniforth (Fin)
Managers: A. Gray (Purch Mgr), C. Fearn (Sales Prom Mgr), C. Pugh (Tech Serv Mgr), J. Lee (Personnel)
Immediate Holding Company: THE BARCODE WAREHOUSE LIMITED
Registration no: 03842666 **Date established:** 1999
Turnover: £20m - £50m **No.of Employees:** 51 - 100 **Product Groups:** 23, 27, 28, 29, 30, 35, 42, 44, 49, 67

Date of Accounts	Apr 11	Apr 10	Apr 09
Sales Turnover	23m	20m	16m
Pre Tax Profit/Loss	269	157	642
Working Capital	-478	-711	-150
Fixed Assets	3m	3m	3m
Current Assets	6m	6m	4m
Current Liabilities	3m	3m	2m

Blagg & Johnson Ltd
Newark Business Park Brunel Drive, Newark, NG24 2EG
Tel: 01636-703137 **Fax:** 01636-701914
E-mail: info@blaggs.co.uk
Website: http://www.blaggs.co.uk
Bank(s): HSBC Bank plc

see next page

Blagg & Johnson Ltd - *Cont'd*
Directors: M. McGillian (Co Sec), C. Gray (Sales)
Managers: S. Prior (Purch Mgr), S. Prior (Prod Mgr)
Immediate Holding Company: BLAGG & JOHNSON LIMITED
Registration no: 01023248 **VAT No.:** GB 555 7964 89
Date established: 1971 **Turnover:** £5m - £10m **No.of Employees:** 21 - 50
Product Groups: 26, 34, 35, 36, 40, 45, 48, 49

Date of Accounts	Sep 11	Sep 10	Sep 09
Working Capital	589	475	675
Fixed Assets	195	279	352
Current Assets	1m	1m	1m

P M Bradley Fabrications Ltd
Unit HC Lodge Lane Industrial Estate Lodge Lane, Tuxford, Newark, NG22 0NL
Tel: 01777-871222 **Fax:** 01777-871922
E-mail: info@pmbfabrications.co.uk
Website: http://www.pmbfabrications.co.uk
Directors: C. Bradley (Fin), P. Bradley (MD)
Immediate Holding Company: P M BRADLEY FABRICATIONS LIMITED
Registration no: 04407341 **VAT No.:** GB 182 8876 13
Date established: 2002 **Turnover:** £250,000 - £500,000
No.of Employees: 1 - 10 **Product Groups:** 48

Date of Accounts	Mar 11	Mar 10	Mar 09
Working Capital	59	43	70
Fixed Assets	14	18	23
Current Assets	137	121	154

British Diamalt
Maltkiln Lane, Newark, NG24 1HN
Tel: 01753-614730 **Fax:** 01753-614740
E-mail: sales@diamalt.co.uk
Website: http://www.diamalt.co.uk
Bank(s): Barclays
Directors: R. Barron (MD)
Managers: L. Wilson (Accounts), J. Rushby (I.T. Exec)
Registration no: 02447222 **Date established:** 1989
Turnover: £10m - £20m **No.of Employees:** 51 - 100 **Product Groups:** 20

C F Parkinson Ltd
Telford Drive, Newark, NG24 2DX
Tel: 01636-672631 **Fax:** 01636-707542
E-mail: denise.clay@parkinsons.co.uk
Website: http://www.parkinsons.co.uk
Managers: D. Clay (District Mgr)
Ultimate Holding Company: C. F. PARKINSON (HOLDINGS) LIMITED
Immediate Holding Company: C.F. PARKINSON LIMITED
Registration no: 00456255 **Date established:** 1948
Turnover: £10m - £20m **No.of Employees:** 11 - 20 **Product Groups:** 35, 36, 39

Date of Accounts	Jan 11	Jan 10	Jan 09
Sales Turnover	9m	8m	N/A
Pre Tax Profit/Loss	176	18	205
Working Capital	255	443	-92
Fixed Assets	5m	4m	4m
Current Assets	3m	3m	3m
Current Liabilities	1m	911	842

C & G Hydraulic Services
4 Newark Storage Industrial Estate Bowbridge Road, Newark, NG24 4EQ
Tel: 01636-613113 **Fax:** 01636-613113
E-mail: cghydraulic@btconnect.com
Directors: G. Hewitt (Prop)
No.of Employees: 1 - 10 **Product Groups:** 32, 36, 40, 48

C M I Ltd
United House High Street, Collingham, Newark, NG23 7NG
Tel: 01636-892078 **Fax:** 01636-893037
E-mail: info@cmi.ltd.uk
Website: http://www.cmi.ltd.uk
Directors: C. Muirhead (MD)
Immediate Holding Company: C.M.I. LIMITED
Registration no: 01510044 **VAT No.:** GB 416 1383 72
Date established: 1980 **No.of Employees:** 1 - 10 **Product Groups:** 32, 66

Date of Accounts	Aug 12	Aug 11	Aug 10
Working Capital	574	570	548
Fixed Assets	105	106	103
Current Assets	820	886	1m
Current Liabilities	N/A	N/A	5

C & V Ceramics
The Old Bakehouse Sherwood Drive, New Ollerton, Newark, NG22 9PP
Tel: 01623-862633 **Fax:** 01623-862633
E-mail: info@candvhobbyceramics.co.uk
Website: http://www.candvhobbyceramics.co.uk
Directors: V. Ashley (Prop)
No.of Employees: 1 - 10 **Product Groups:** 14, 32, 49

Date of Accounts	May 11
Working Capital	13
Fixed Assets	5
Current Assets	13

A J Calladine Metal Finishing
Unit 4 Brailwood Close, Bilsthorpe, Newark, NG22 8UG
Tel: 01623-870372 **Fax:** 01623-870372
Directors: A. Calladine (Prop)
Date established: 1995 **No.of Employees:** 1 - 10 **Product Groups:** 46, 48

Carrick Fabrications
5 The Close, Newark, NG24 1NR
Tel: 01636-678370 **Fax:** 01636-678370
Directors: J. Gillespie (Prop)
Date established: 1998 **No.of Employees:** 1 - 10 **Product Groups:** 35

Conveyor Systems Nottingham Ltd
Chapel Lane Walesby, Newark, NG22 9NS
Tel: 01623-860878 **Fax:** 01623-860061
E-mail: consys@consys.co.uk
Website: http://www.consys.co.uk
Directors: J. Holmes (Fin), K. Langham (MD)
Managers: K. Taylor (Sales Prom Mgr)
Registration no: 01855403 **VAT No.:** GB 419 7565 18
Date established: 2000 **Turnover:** £1m - £2m **No.of Employees:** 1 - 10
Product Groups: 45

Date of Accounts	Aug 08	Aug 07	Aug 06
Working Capital	147	39	72
Fixed Assets	5	8	11
Current Assets	192	145	189
Current Liabilities	45	106	118

Curtain & Blind
16 Carter Gate, Newark, NG24 1UB
Tel: 01636-702102 **Fax:** 01609-781669
E-mail: info@bridz.co.uk
Website: http://www.curtainandblindnewark.co.uk
Directors: N. Spowage (Prop)
No.of Employees: 1 - 10 **Product Groups:** 25, 36, 40, 63

Derry Builders
London Road, Newark, NG24 1JP
Tel: 01636-614300 **Fax:** 01636-605387
E-mail: steve.burley@derry-bs.co.uk
Website: http://www.derry-bs.co.uk
Bank(s): National Westminster Bank Plc
Directors: S. Burley (Dir), M. Sheldon (Fin), M. Townsend (MD)
Managers: D. Martin (Tech Serv Mgr)
Ultimate Holding Company: BOWMER AND KIRKLAND LIMITED
Immediate Holding Company: DERRY BUILDING SERVICES LIMITED
Registration no: 01481063 **VAT No.:** GB 309 8654 29
Date established: 1980 **Turnover:** £20m - £50m
No.of Employees: 251 - 500 **Product Groups:** 38

Date of Accounts	Aug 11	Aug 10	Aug 09
Sales Turnover	43m	46m	50m
Pre Tax Profit/Loss	2m	1m	2m
Working Capital	7m	7m	6m
Fixed Assets	136	145	186
Current Assets	26m	26m	26m
Current Liabilities	7m	12m	2m

Dosco Overseas Engineering Ltd
Dosco Industrial Estate Ollerton Road, Tuxford, Newark, NG22 0PQ
Tel: 01777-870621 **Fax:** 01777-871580
E-mail: info@dosco.co.uk
Website: http://www.dosco.co.uk
Directors: P. Adrych (Sales), L. Holloway (Co Sec), M. Cain (Grp Chief Exec)
Managers: C. Player (Fin Mgr), P. Denton (Purch Mgr)
Ultimate Holding Company: BILLINGTON HOLDINGS PLC
Immediate Holding Company: DOSCO OVERSEAS ENGINEERING LIMITED
Registration no: 00567906 **Date established:** 1956
Turnover: £10m - £20m **No.of Employees:** 21 - 50 **Product Groups:** 45

Date of Accounts	Dec 11	Dec 10	Dec 09
Sales Turnover	10m	13m	8m
Pre Tax Profit/Loss	-2m	-596	-2m
Working Capital	4m	5m	5m
Fixed Assets	315	175	186
Current Assets	13m	9m	7m
Current Liabilities	4m	3m	1m

E C Walton & Co. Ltd
Old North Road Sutton-on-Trent, Newark, NG23 6QN
Tel: 01636-880100 **Fax:** 01636-822027
E-mail: waltons@waltons.co.uk
Website: http://www.waltons.co.uk
Directors: B. Walton (Jt MD), F. Kelly (Sales), H. Walton (Dir), I. Robertson (Mkt Research), N. Walton (Jt MD), R. Walton (Dir)
Managers: D. Wood (Ops Mgr), J. Fairhurst (), L. Dudley (Designer), N. Sharper (Buyer)
Ultimate Holding Company: Newark Group Ltd
Immediate Holding Company: E.C.WALTON & CO., LIMITED
Registration no: 05079585 **VAT No.:** GB 117 7576 49
Date established: 2004 **Turnover:** £5m - £10m **No.of Employees:** 1 - 10
Product Groups: 25

Date of Accounts	Dec 07	Dec 06	Dec 05
Sales Turnover	25698	27611	31620
Pre Tax Profit/Loss	-6807	3737	2865
Working Capital	1360	8473	6035
Fixed Assets	5195	5225	5030
Current Assets	6553	14827	10516
Current Liabilities	5193	6354	4481
Total Share Capital	38	38	38
ROCE% (Return on Capital Employed)	-103.9	27.3	25.9
ROT% (Return on Turnover)	-26.5	13.5	9.1

Egress Systems Ltd
The Old Wheelhouse Hall Farm Main Street, Kirklington, Newark, NG22 8NN
Tel: 01636-819256
E-mail: info@egress-sys.co.uk
Website: http://www.egress-sys.co.uk
Directors: C. Mouter (Dir)
Immediate Holding Company: EGRESS SYSTEMS LIMITED
Registration no: 04872869 **Date established:** 2003
Turnover: Up to £250,000 **No.of Employees:** 1 - 10 **Product Groups:** 44, 49, 83

Date of Accounts	Aug 11	Aug 10	Aug 09
Working Capital	79	43	38
Fixed Assets	20	12	11
Current Assets	142	70	73
Current Liabilities	29	N/A	N/A

Essential Electrical Services UK Llp
5 Staff House Brandon Road Stubton, Newark, NG23 5BY
Tel: 01636-626168
E-mail: essential.electrical@virgin.net
Website: http://www.essential-electrical-services.co.uk
Directors: J. Britten Crooks (Dir)
Immediate Holding Company: ESSENTIAL ELECTRICAL SERVICES (UK) LLP
Registration no: OC325842 **Date established:** 2007
Turnover: Up to £250,000 **No.of Employees:** 1 - 10 **Product Groups:** 38, 67, 85

Date of Accounts	May 11	May 10	Feb 09
Sales Turnover	24	41	47
Pre Tax Profit/Loss	15	25	30
Working Capital	4	3	N/A
Fixed Assets	2	3	4
Current Assets	8	5	4
Current Liabilities	2	2	3

F R Europe
Church House 3 Church Walk, Newark, NG24 1JS
Tel: 01636-610000 **Fax:** 01636-610106
E-mail: infonew@freurope.com
Website: http://www.freurope.com
Directors: A. Keiller (Dir)
Immediate Holding Company: CFR CONSULTING GROUP LIMITED
Registration no: 05756124 **Date established:** 2005
No.of Employees: 1 - 10 **Product Groups:** 80, 87

Flowserve
Hawton Lane New Balderton, Newark, NG24 3BU
Tel: 01636-494600 **Fax:** 01636-705991
E-mail: newark@flowserve.com
Website: http://www.flowserve.com
Bank(s): Barclays
Managers: A. Freer (Chief Mgr), S. Shah (I.T. Exec)
Ultimate Holding Company: PER AARSLEFF A/S (DENMARK)
Immediate Holding Company: CENTRUM PILE LIMITED
Registration no: 02741659 **VAT No.:** GB 605 4260 700 001
Date established: 2001 **Turnover:** £5m - £10m
No.of Employees: 251 - 500 **Product Groups:** 39, 40

Date of Accounts	Sep 11	Sep 10	Sep 09
Sales Turnover	2m	2m	2m
Pre Tax Profit/Loss	-1m	-1m	-1m
Working Capital	-7m	-7m	-7m
Fixed Assets	6m	7m	7m
Current Assets	1m	1m	1m
Current Liabilities	40	65	40

Fuller Engineering Design
40 Manor Drive Long Bennington, Newark, NG23 5GZ
Tel: 01400-282660 **Fax:** 01400-282717
E-mail: info@fullerengineeringdesign.co.uk
Website: http://www.fullerengineeringdesign.co.uk
Directors: B. Fuller (Prop)
Turnover: Up to £250,000 **No.of Employees:** 1 - 10 **Product Groups:** 44, 81, 85

G D M Lindex Ltd
The Courtyard Long Row, Newark, NG24 1RW
Tel: 01636-610030 **Fax:** 01636-610022
E-mail: sales@gdmlindex.co.uk
Website: http://www.gdmlindex.co.uk
Directors: L. Hendry (Co Sec)
Immediate Holding Company: GDM LINDEX LIMITED
Registration no: 01901830 **Date established:** 1985
No.of Employees: 1 - 10 **Product Groups:** 45, 61, 67

Date of Accounts	Apr 12	Apr 11	Apr 10
Working Capital	212	199	165
Fixed Assets	34	33	61
Current Assets	1m	1m	1m

Gainsborough Steel Services Ltd
Sylvan Way Balderton, Newark, NG24 3UT
Tel: 01427-616664 **Fax:** 01427-810274
E-mail: sales@gainsborough-steel.co.uk
Website: http://www.gainsborough-steel.co.uk
Bank(s): HSBC
Managers: D. Thompson (Sales Prom Mgr)
Ultimate Holding Company: BARRETT STEEL LIMITED
Immediate Holding Company: GAINSBOROUGH STEEL SERVICES LIMITED
Registration no: 02762748 **Date established:** 1992
Turnover: £10m - £20m **No.of Employees:** 21 - 50 **Product Groups:** 34

Date of Accounts	Sep 07
Sales Turnover	11m
Pre Tax Profit/Loss	504
Working Capital	1
Current Assets	1

Graff Of Newark Ltd
Woodhill Road Collingham, Newark, NG23 7NR
Tel: 01636-893036 **Fax:** 01636-893317
E-mail: sales@graffofnewark.co.uk
Website: http://www.graffofnewark.co.uk
Directors: A. Leonard (MD)
Immediate Holding Company: GRAFF OF NEWARK LIMITED
Registration no: 05632486 **VAT No.:** GB 385 2393 29
Date established: 2005 **Turnover:** £1m - £2m **No.of Employees:** 1 - 10
Product Groups: 37

Date of Accounts	Dec 10	Dec 09	Dec 08
Working Capital	-16	-21	-3
Current Assets	9	45	33

Hardchrome Plating & Grinding
Unit 195 Boughton Industrial Estate, Boughton, Newark, NG22 9LE
Tel: 01623-862314 **Fax:** 01623-862314
E-mail: f.poulton@hardchromeplating.co.uk
Website: http://www.hardchromeplating.co.uk
Managers: F. Poulton (Chief Mgr), F. Poulton (Mgr)
Immediate Holding Company: HARD CHROME PLATING AND GRINDING LIMITED
Registration no: 06736965 **Date established:** 2008
Turnover: Up to £250,000 **No.of Employees:** 1 - 10 **Product Groups:** 48

Date of Accounts	Nov 10	Nov 09
Working Capital	-79	-104
Fixed Assets	119	127
Current Assets	50	47

Heatherose Control Pannels
Unit 1 Oaktreehouse 3 Brunel Drive, Newark, NG24 2EG
Tel: 01636-702805 **Fax:** 01636-679376
Website: http://www.heatherrose.co.uk
Directors: J. Ross (Fin), P. Martin (Dir)
Immediate Holding Company: HEATHEROSE LIMITED
Registration no: 00964988 **Date established:** 1969
No.of Employees: 11 - 20 **Product Groups:** 36, 40

Date of Accounts	May 11	May 10	May 09
Working Capital	143	175	112
Fixed Assets	4	4	3
Current Assets	297	289	389

Henkel Ltd
Winthorpe Road, Newark, NG24 2AL
Tel: 01636-646711 **Fax:** 01636-605187
E-mail: eric.norman@uk.henkel.com
Website: http://www.henkel.com
Bank(s): Barclays
Directors: E. Norman (Prop), D. Pashley (Purch), E. Smith (Sales)
Ultimate Holding Company: HENKEL KGAA (GERMANY)
Immediate Holding Company: HENKEL LIMITED
Registration no: 00215496 **VAT No.:** 168 6045 44 **Date established:** 1926
Turnover: £20m - £50m **No.of Employees:** 21 - 50 **Product Groups:** 32

Date of Accounts	Dec 10	Dec 09	Dec 08
Sales Turnover	278m	275m	289m
Pre Tax Profit/Loss	168	2m	-100m
Working Capital	17m	-1m	-209m
Fixed Assets	144m	164m	307m
Current Assets	141m	165m	111m
Current Liabilities	17m	17m	12m

Hollybank Engineering Co. Ltd
Ollerton Road, Newark, NG22 0PQ
Tel: 01777-870925 **Fax:** 01777-870524
E-mail: info@hollybank.co.uk
Website: http://www.hollybank.co.uk
Bank(s): HSBC Bank plc
Directors: K. Garner (MD), P. Hart (Fin), S. Fewster (MD)
Managers: A. Hayward (Chief Mgr)
Ultimate Holding Company: Amco Corp. P.L.C.
Immediate Holding Company: Dosco Overseas Engineering Ltd
Registration no: 00520887 **VAT No.:** GB 125 7394 60
Date established: 1910 **Turnover:** £2m - £5m **No.of Employees:** 11 - 20
Product Groups: 45

Hoval Ltd
North Gate, Newark, NG24 1JN
Tel: 01636-672711 **Fax:** 01636-673532
E-mail: dhemington@hoval.co.uk
Website: http://www.hoval.co.uk
Bank(s): Barclays
Directors: A. Walker (MD), D. Hemington (Fin), I. Dagley (Sales & Mktg), K. Stones (I.T. Dir)
Managers: R. Bagley (Buyer)
Ultimate Holding Company: INTERHOVAL A G (SWITZERLAND)
Immediate Holding Company: HOVAL LIMITED
Registration no: 00592844 **Date established:** 1957
Turnover: £10m - £20m **No.of Employees:** 101 - 250
Product Groups: 35, 40, 45, 48

Date of Accounts	Mar 12	Mar 11	Mar 10
Sales Turnover	18m	14m	15m
Pre Tax Profit/Loss	105	168	503
Working Capital	3m	4m	4m
Fixed Assets	2m	2m	2m
Current Assets	9m	7m	7m
Current Liabilities	903	958	983

Jackson Electronics Ltd
Danethorpe Lane Danethorpe, Newark, NG24 2PD
Tel: 01636-705718 **Fax:** 01636-610120
E-mail: jdj@jacksonelectronics.co.uk
Website: http://www.jacksonelectronics.co.uk
Directors: J. Jackson (MD)
Immediate Holding Company: JACKSON ELECTRONICS LIMITED
Registration no: 03768092 **VAT No.:** GB 745 4006 48
Date established: 1999 **Turnover:** £500,000 - £1m
No.of Employees: 1 - 10 **Product Groups:** 37, 38, 54

Date of Accounts	Mar 11	Mar 10	Mar 09
Working Capital	2m	2m	2m
Fixed Assets	265	312	289
Current Assets	2m	2m	2m

Koppen & Lethem Ltd
3 Glenholm Park Brunel Drive, Newark, NG24 2EG
Tel: 01636-676794 **Fax:** 01636-671055
E-mail: helen@koppen-lethem.co.uk
Website: http://www.koppen-lethem.co.uk
Directors: H. Ponting (Fin)
Ultimate Holding Company: DOEDIJINS INTERNATIONAL HOLDINGS BV (HOLLAND)
Immediate Holding Company: KOPPEN & LETHEM LIMITED
Registration no: 01340895 **Date established:** 1977 **Turnover:** £2m - £5m
No.of Employees: 1 - 10 **Product Groups:** 36, 40, 45

Date of Accounts	Dec 11	Dec 10	Dec 09
Working Capital	526	461	723
Fixed Assets	22	9	13
Current Assets	1m	1m	1m

Lumineri
8 London Road Balderton, Newark, NG24 3AJ
Tel: 07875-715904 **Fax:** 0845-0946302
E-mail: info@lumineri.co.uk
Website: http://www.lumineri.co.uk
Directors: S. Ellis (Grp Chief Exec)
Date established: 2007 **Turnover:** Up to £250,000
No.of Employees: 1 - 10 **Product Groups:** 49

M L B Engineering
1a Belle Eau Park Bilsthorpe, Newark, NG22 8TX
Tel: 01623-871991 **Fax:** 01623-871991
E-mail: sales@mlbengineering.co.uk
Directors: M. Burrows (Prop)
Immediate Holding Company: MLB ENGINEERING SERVICES (1994) LTD
Registration no: 07992300 **Date established:** 2012
No.of Employees: 1 - 10 **Product Groups:** 26, 35

M L Furnaces Ltd
71a Boughton Industrial Estate Boughton, Newark, NG22 9LD
Tel: 01623-835611 **Fax:** 01623-860745
E-mail: sales@mlfurnaces.com
Website: http://www.mlfurnaces.com
Directors: M. Lockwood (MD)
Immediate Holding Company: M.L. FURNACES LIMITED
Registration no: 04497468 **Date established:** 2002
Turnover: £500,000 - £1m **No.of Employees:** 1 - 10 **Product Groups:** 40, 42, 46, 47, 48, 67

Date of Accounts	Oct 11	Oct 10	Oct 09
Working Capital	183	175	180
Fixed Assets	46	24	29
Current Assets	302	252	231

Mechfast Ltd
The Coach House Hexgreave Park Farnsfield, Newark, NG22 8LS
Tel: 01623-883000 **Fax:** 01623-883004
E-mail: sales@mechfast.co.uk
Website: http://www.mechfast.co.uk
Managers: N. Jeffery (Mgr)
Immediate Holding Company: MECHFAST LIMITED
Registration no: 01325919 **Date established:** 1977
Turnover: £250,000 - £500,000 **No.of Employees:** 1 - 10
Product Groups: 35

Date of Accounts	Dec 11	Dec 10	Dec 09
Working Capital	101	69	53
Fixed Assets	4	4	5
Current Assets	214	184	155

N S K Europe
Northern Road, Newark, NG24 2JF
Tel: 01636-643000 **Fax:** 01628-509808
E-mail: info-uk@nsk.com
Website: http://www.eu.nsk.com
Bank(s): HSBC Bank plc
Directors: N. Otsuka (Dir), T. Parker (Co Sec)
Ultimate Holding Company: NSK LTD (JAPAN)
Immediate Holding Company: NSK EUROPE LIMITED
Registration no: 02223191 **Date established:** 1988
No.of Employees: 1501 & over **Product Groups:** 35, 39, 45, 46

P A Freight
International Logistics Centre Farndon Road, Newark, NG24 4SP
Tel: 01636-605555 **Fax:** 01636-605321
E-mail: enquiries@pafreight.co.uk
Website: http://www.pafreight.co.uk
Directors: A. Morris (MD), L. Lewin (Co Sec)
Managers: C. Lawson (Personnel)
Immediate Holding Company: P.A. FREIGHT SERVICES (MIDLANDS) LIMITED
Registration no: 02327273 **Date established:** 1988
No.of Employees: 21 - 50 **Product Groups:** 76

Date of Accounts	Aug 11	Aug 10	Aug 09
Working Capital	7	-100	-89
Fixed Assets	671	873	850
Current Assets	505	450	593

Park Farm Design
5 Park Farm Main Street, Carlton-On-Trent, Newark, NG23 6NW
Tel: 01636-822221
E-mail: info@parkfarmdesign.co.uk
Website: http://www.parkfarmdesign.co.uk
Directors: L. Davenport (Prop)
Date established: 2008 **Turnover:** **No.of Employees:** 1 - 10
Product Groups: 25, 30, 33, 35, 36, 40, 52, 66

Pneu-Therm Ltd
Unit 14a Telford Drive Brunel Drive Industrial Estate, Newark, NG24 2DX
Tel: 01636-679415 **Fax:** 01636-678453
Website: http://www.pneutherm.com
Directors: C. Pearce (Dir)
Immediate Holding Company: PNEU-THERM LIMITED
Registration no: 04348546 **VAT No.:** GB 745 8096 01
Date established: 2002 **Turnover:** £2m - £5m **No.of Employees:** 1 - 10
Product Groups: 30, 36, 38, 40, 46, 47

Date of Accounts	Dec 11	Dec 10	Dec 09
Working Capital	262	205	222
Fixed Assets	108	37	42
Current Assets	373	320	320

Quality Chemical Co. (Quality Consultants)
Longridge School Lane, Eakring, Newark, NG22 0DE
Tel: 01623-871270 **Fax:** 01623-871270
E-mail: sales@qc-online.co.uk
Website: http://www.qc-online.co.uk
Directors: D. Brown (Prop)
Turnover: Up to £250,000 **No.of Employees:** 1 - 10 **Product Groups:** 24

R H Fabrications
Fosse Road East Stoke, Newark, NG23 5QH
Tel: 01636-525380 **Fax:** 01636-525380
E-mail: richardhardy1@googlemail.com
Directors: R. Hardy (Prop)
Date established: 2000 **No.of Employees:** 1 - 10 **Product Groups:** 35

Requip Supplies Ltd
PO Box 57, Newark, NG24 1LR
Tel: 01636-671520 **Fax:** 01636-611066
E-mail: sales@requip.co.uk
Website: http://www.requipsupplies.co.uk
Directors: P. Oakey (Fin), M. Oakey (Dir)
Immediate Holding Company: REQUIP SUPPLIES LIMITED
Registration no: 02609427 **Date established:** 1991
Turnover: £500,000 - £1m **No.of Employees:** 1 - 10 **Product Groups:** 34, 45, 67

Date of Accounts	Nov 11	Nov 10	Nov 09
Working Capital	811	604	562
Fixed Assets	20	23	23
Current Assets	2m	1m	1m

Samsons Fabrications
7 Lansbury Road Bilsthorpe, Newark, NG22 8RL
Tel: 01623-411250 **Fax:** 01623-411250
E-mail: hayleyj68@aol.com
Directors: V. Johnson (Prop)
Date established: 2001 **No.of Employees:** 1 - 10 **Product Groups:** 26, 35

Spikomat Ltd
Old Great North Road Sutton-on-Trent, Newark, NG23 6QS
Tel: 01636-821123 **Fax:** 01636-822038
E-mail: sales@skewers.co.uk
Website: http://www.skewers.co.uk
Directors: C. Nicholson (MD), M. Moulds (Fin)
Immediate Holding Company: SPIKOMAT LIMITED
Registration no: 03690563 **Date established:** 1998
No.of Employees: 1 - 10 **Product Groups:** 20, 40, 41

Date of Accounts	Jan 11	Jan 10	Jan 09
Working Capital	2m	1m	1m
Fixed Assets	96	109	123
Current Assets	2m	2m	2m

Stainbusters (Lincoln & Retford)
55 Linden Avenue Tuxford, Newark, NG22 0JR
Tel: 0800-137772 **Fax:** 01777-872183
E-mail: sales@stainbusters.co.uk
Website: http://www.stainbusters.co.uk
Directors: F. Hewitt (Fin), A. Hewitt (MD)
Immediate Holding Company: CITIE CLEANING SERVICES LIMITED
Registration no: 04607576 **Date established:** 2002
Turnover: Up to £250,000 **No.of Employees:** 1 - 10 **Product Groups:** 23

Date of Accounts	Mar 11	Mar 10	Mar 08
Working Capital	-15	-16	-4
Fixed Assets	20	21	26
Current Assets	3	6	19

Studweldpro UK Ltd
Ollerton Road Tuxford, Newark, NG22 0PQ
Tel: 01777-874500 **Fax:** 01777-874555
E-mail: sales@swpuk.com
Website: http://www.swpuk.com
Directors: E. Stocks (MD), M. Adams (Fin)
Managers: J. Gaughan (Tech Serv Mgr)
Immediate Holding Company: STUDWELDPRO - U.K. LIMITED
Registration no: 01307206 **VAT No.:** GB 295 3510 47
Date established: 1977 **Turnover:** £2m - £5m **No.of Employees:** 21 - 50
Product Groups: 35, 46

Date of Accounts	Dec 11	Dec 10	Dec 09
Working Capital	732	623	618
Fixed Assets	2m	2m	2m
Current Assets	2m	2m	2m

Sunpro Window Films
37 Pelham Street, Newark, NG24 4XD
Tel: 08712-305100
Website: http://www.sunprowindowfilms.co.uk
Managers: J. Mason
No.of Employees: 21 - 50 **Product Groups:** 27, 30

Timico Ltd
Beaconhill Park Cafferata Way, Newark, NG24 2TN
Tel: 08448-718100 **Fax:** 0844-871 8117
E-mail: enquiries@timico.co.uk
Website: http://www.timico.co.uk
Directors: J. Radford (Co Sec)
Managers: T. Davies, C. Morell (Mgr), D. Davies (Personnel), T. Bunn, S. Hodges, D. Sears
Immediate Holding Company: TIMICO LIMITED
Registration no: 04841830 **Date established:** 2003
Turnover: £20m - £50m **No.of Employees:** 51 - 100 **Product Groups:** 44, 67

Date of Accounts	Dec 11	Dec 10	Dec 09
Sales Turnover	24m	23m	22m
Pre Tax Profit/Loss	2m	1m	457
Working Capital	-88	-1m	1m
Fixed Assets	12m	10m	5m
Current Assets	5m	7m	5m
Current Liabilities	2m	2m	2m

UK Bar Services Ltd
Peacock Farm 28 Main Road Long Bennington, Newark, NG23 5EH
Tel: 01400-282878 **Fax:** 01400-282878
E-mail: info@ukbarservices.co.uk
Website: http://www.ukbarservices.co.uk
Directors: T. Birch (Dir)
Immediate Holding Company: UK BAR SERVICE LTD.
Registration no: 05520826 **Date established:** 2005
Turnover: £250,000 - £500,000 **No.of Employees:** 1 - 10
Product Groups: 40, 67, 69, 81, 89

Date of Accounts	Jul 09	Jul 07	Jul 06
Working Capital	-34	13	-1
Fixed Assets	3	4	4
Current Assets	15	13	5

UK Waste Solutions Ltd
Alexander House Cafferata Way, Newark, NG24 2TN
Tel: 01636-640744 **Fax:** 01636-640745
E-mail: garry.johnson@ukwsl.co.uk
Website: http://www.ukwsl.co.uk
Directors: G. Johnson (Dir), C. Giscombe (Pers)
Immediate Holding Company: UK WASTE SOLUTIONS LIMITED
Registration no: 04995890 **Date established:** 2004 **Turnover:** £5m - £10m
No.of Employees: 25 **Product Groups:** 26, 27, 29, 30, 32, 33, 34, 37, 54

Date of Accounts	Mar 11	Mar 10	Mar 09
Working Capital	1m	554	347
Fixed Assets	120	25	26
Current Assets	3m	2m	1m

Zella Instrumentation & Control Ltd
Unit 2 Cook House Brunel Drive, Newark, NG24 2FB
Tel: 01636-704370 **Fax:** 01636-640296
E-mail: sales@zella-instrumentation.co.uk
Website: http://www.zella.co.uk
Directors: G. Magson (Dir)
Immediate Holding Company: ZELLA INSTRUMENTATION & CONTROL LIMITED
Registration no: 01168284 **Date established:** 1974
Turnover: £500,000 - £1m **No.of Employees:** 1 - 10 **Product Groups:** 35, 36, 37, 38, 39, 40, 44, 67, 84

Date of Accounts	Dec 11	Dec 10	Dec 09
Working Capital	250	275	283
Fixed Assets	12	16	19
Current Assets	263	284	293

Zentec Ltd
Applefields Mansfield Road, Edingley, Newark, NG22 8BG
Tel: 01623-883146
E-mail: enquiries@zentec.co.uk
Website: http://www.zentec.co.uk
Directors: M. Tolliday (MD)
Immediate Holding Company: ZENTEC LIMITED
Registration no: 03818312 **Date established:** 1999
Turnover: £500,000 - £1m **No.of Employees:** 1 - 10 **Product Groups:** 71, 72, 74, 77, 80, 84, 85, 86

Date of Accounts	Sep 11	Sep 10	Sep 09
Working Capital	110	57	-2
Fixed Assets	1	1	N/A
Current Assets	186	96	13

Nottingham

3 D Group
465 Westdale Lane Mapperley, Nottingham, NG3 6DH
Tel: 0115-952 2772
E-mail: ddkeypro@hotmail.com
Website: http://www.3dgroupuk.com
Managers: D. Sanderson (Mgr)
Turnover: £250,000 - £500,000 **No.of Employees:** 1 - 10
Product Groups: 36, 52

A & E Plastic Fabrications Ltd
40 St. Peters Street Radford, Nottingham, NG7 3FF
Tel: 0115-978 0048 **Fax:** 0115-979 1351
E-mail: info@aaep.co.uk
Website: http://www.aeplastics.co.uk
Bank(s): Barclays
Directors: D. Carney (MD), R. Carney (Dir)
Immediate Holding Company: A. & E. Plastic Fabrications Ltd
Registration no: 01974925 **VAT No.:** GB 309 5490 48
Date established: 1986 **Turnover:** £500,000 - £1m
No.of Employees: 21 - 50 **Product Groups:** 48

A J Restoration Co. Ltd
Restoration House Second Avenue, Nottingham, NG6 8NE
Tel: 0115-927 7044 **Fax:** 0115-976 3476
E-mail: sales@ajrestoration.co.uk
Website: http://www.ajrestoration.co.uk
Bank(s): National Westminster Bank Plc
Directors: A. Andrew (Fin)
Registration no: 01310768 **Turnover:** £500,000 - £1m
No.of Employees: 11 - 20 **Product Groups:** 35, 37, 51, 52

Date of Accounts	Aug 04	Aug 03
Working Capital	24	-31
Fixed Assets	73	55
Current Assets	78	114
Current Liabilities	54	144
Total Share Capital	30	30

A L Dalton Ltd
Crossgate Drive Queens Drive Indl-Est, Nottingham, NG2 1LW
Tel: 0115-986 5201 **Fax:** 0115-986 2820
E-mail: sales@daltonsmachines.com
Website: http://www.daltonsmachines.com
Directors: A. Dalton (Dir), F. Dalton (MD)
Ultimate Holding Company: A L DALTON HOLDINGS LIMITED
Immediate Holding Company: A L DALTON LIMITED
Registration no: 00148767 **Date established:** 1917 **Turnover:** £5m - £10m
No.of Employees: 21 - 50 **Product Groups:** 40, 47

Date of Accounts	Dec 10	Dec 09	Dec 08
Working Capital	-379	-363	-187
Fixed Assets	953	939	1m
Current Assets	1m	959	1m

A N Wallis & Co. Ltd
Greasley Street, Nottingham, NG6 8NG
Tel: 0115-927 1721 **Fax:** 0115-875 6630
E-mail: info@an-wallis.com
Website: http://www.an-wallis.com
Bank(s): Lloyds TSB
Directors: D. Nesbitt (MD), M. Rimmington (Sales), S. Healy (Fin)
Managers: S. Mitchell (Ops Mgr)
Immediate Holding Company: A N WALLIS & COMPANY LIMITED
Registration no: 03972865 **Date established:** 2000
Turnover: £10m - £20m **No.of Employees:** 21 - 50 **Product Groups:** 34, 37

Date of Accounts	Dec 11	Dec 10	Dec 09
Sales Turnover	15m	12m	8m
Pre Tax Profit/Loss	369	384	111
Working Capital	1m	938	724
Fixed Assets	964	1m	1m
Current Assets	4m	3m	3m
Current Liabilities	535	600	447

A P P H Nottingham Ltd
Urban Road Kirkby-in-ashfield, Nottingham, NG17 8AP
Tel: 01623-754355 **Fax:** 01623-723904
E-mail: sales@beauforteng.co.uk
Website: http://www.apph.com
Bank(s): HSBC Bank plc
Managers: K. Wardle (Sales Prom Mgr), J. Clark (Chief Mgr), J. Clarke (Mgr), J. Monahan (Buyer), P. Jones (I.T. Exec)
Ultimate Holding Company: BBA AVIATION PLC
Immediate Holding Company: APPH NOTTINGHAM LIMITED
Registration no: 02125837 **VAT No.:** GB 183 3721 61
Date established: 1987 **Turnover:** £2m - £5m **No.of Employees:** 51 - 100
Product Groups: 39, 48, 85

A P S Security
173 Bennett Street Long Eaton, Nottingham, NG10 4HG
Tel: 0115-946 1510 **Fax:** 0115-973 1356
E-mail: apssec@aps-security.co.uk
Website: http://www.aps-security.co.uk
Directors: M. Warrilow (Dir)
Immediate Holding Company: ADVANCED PROTECTIVE SYSTEMS LTD
Registration no: 03260062 **Date established:** 1996
No.of Employees: 1 - 10 **Product Groups:** 36, 40, 52

A S G Enterprises Ltd
Unit 5 Shiptons Business Centre, Nottingham, NG7 7FN
Tel: 0115-841 3301 **Fax:** 0115-872 0462
E-mail: info@asg-enterprises.co.uk
Website: http://www.asg-enterprises.co.uk
Directors: Z. Ali (MD)
Immediate Holding Company: ASG ENTERPRISES LIMITED
Registration no: 06246522 **Date established:** 2007
Turnover: Up to £250,000 **No.of Employees:** 21 - 50 **Product Groups:** 81

Date of Accounts	Mar 11	Mar 10	Mar 09
Sales Turnover	N/A	N/A	222
Pre Tax Profit/Loss	N/A	N/A	4
Working Capital	8	-2	-6
Fixed Assets	4	5	4
Current Assets	28	9	3
Current Liabilities	N/A	N/A	9

Aalco Nottingham
Harrimans Lane Lenton Lane Industrial Estate, Nottingham, NG7 2SD
Tel: 0115-988 2600 **Fax:** 0115-988 2636
E-mail: nottingham@aalco.co.uk
Website: http://www.aalco.co.uk
Bank(s): National Westminster Bank Plc
Managers: A. Moreley, A. Gascoigne (Mgr), A. Simkiss (Purch Mgr), D. Meads (Sales Prom Mgr)
Ultimate Holding Company: MIMOSA HEALTHCARE HOLDINGS LIMITED
Immediate Holding Company: MIMOSA HEALTHCARE (BYRON & RUFFORD) LIMITED
Registration no: 01747048 **Date established:** 2004
Turnover: £125m - £250m **No.of Employees:** 21 - 50
Product Groups: 34, 35, 36, 66

Date of Accounts	Dec 09	Dec 08	May 11
Pre Tax Profit/Loss	N/A	-18	N/A
Working Capital	84	84	84
Current Assets	96	96	96
Current Liabilities	N/A	N/A	12

Abbco Grinding Equipment
Wilmot Lane Beeston, Nottingham, NG9 1ER
Tel: 0115-922 6060 **Fax:** 0115-922 6060
E-mail: imbanners@yahoo.co.uk
Directors: S. Bankcroft (Ptnr), S. Bancroft (Ptnr)
Immediate Holding Company: MYFORD (HOLDINGS) LIMITED
Registration no: 01014336 **Date established:** 1971
Turnover: Up to £250,000 **No.of Employees:** 1 - 10 **Product Groups:** 46

Absolute Cooling
Unit 6 Hackers Close East Bridgford, Nottingham, NG13 8PU
Tel: 01949-829000 **Fax:** 01949-829099
Website: http://www.absolutecooling.co.uk
Directors: P. Faulkner (Dir)
No.of Employees: 1 - 10 **Product Groups:** 40, 66

Access Training East Midlands Ltd
Cawley House 96 Cliff Road, Nottingham, NG1 1GW
Tel: 0115-958 7257 **Fax:** 0115-950 4684
E-mail: info@atem.co.uk
Website: http://www.atem.co.uk
Bank(s): National Westminster
Directors: D. Gibson (Chief Op Offcr)
Managers: W. Fisher, H. Elliott (Mktg Serv Mgr), M. Pepper, T. Royce (Tech Serv Mgr), A. Walker (Personnel)
Immediate Holding Company: ACCESS TRAINING (EAST MIDLANDS) LTD
Registration no: 05398372 **VAT No.:** GB 385 2391 33
Date established: 2005 **Turnover:** £1m - £2m **No.of Employees:** 51 - 100
Product Groups: 86

Date of Accounts	Jul 11	Jul 10	Jul 09
Working Capital	448	445	398
Current Assets	989	942	837

Advanex Europe
Glaisdale Drive East, Nottingham, NG8 4JY
Tel: 0115-929 3931 **Fax:** 0115-929 5773
E-mail: enquiries@advanexeurope.co.uk
Website: http://www.advanexeurope.co.uk
Bank(s): HSBC Bank plc
Directors: D. Blatherwick (Tech Serv), R. Hallam (Fin)
Managers: D. Betts (Chief Buyer), J. Poole
Ultimate Holding Company: ADVANEX GROUP INC (JAPAN)
Immediate Holding Company: KATO-ENTEX LIMITED
Registration no: 02853659 **Date established:** 1993 **Turnover:** £1m - £2m
No.of Employees: 51 - 100 **Product Groups:** 35, 36, 39, 66

Date of Accounts	Mar 12	Mar 10	Mar 09
Sales Turnover	N/A	3m	4m
Pre Tax Profit/Loss	N/A	-256	-299
Working Capital	N/A	2m	2m
Fixed Assets	N/A	1m	1m
Current Assets	N/A	2m	2m
Current Liabilities	N/A	207	188

Ailsen Ltd
Finch Close, Nottingham, NG7 2NN
Tel: 0115-986 9686 **Fax:** 0115-986 1430
E-mail: mail@ailsen.ltd.uk
Website: http://www.ailsen.ltd.uk
Bank(s): National Westminster Bank Plc
Directors: J. Hall (MD), P. Phillips (Fin)
Managers: D. Brittan (Tech Serv Mgr)
Ultimate Holding Company: PACKSTONE LIMITED
Immediate Holding Company: AILSEN LIMITED
Registration no: 01214933 **VAT No.:** GB 352 8317 54
Date established: 1975 **No.of Employees:** 21 - 50 **Product Groups:** 84

Date of Accounts	Dec 09	Dec 08	Dec 07
Working Capital	343	305	209
Fixed Assets	6	8	146
Current Assets	2m	2m	2m

Air Tube Services ltd
Commercial House 23 Meadow Road Netherfield, Nottingham, NG4 2FR
Tel: 0115-9611911
E-mail: sales@airtubeservices.co.uk
Website: http://www.airtubeservices.co.uk
Directors: M. Bright (MD)
Date established: 2008 **No.of Employees:** 3 **Product Groups:** 22, 30, 36, 42, 45, 48, 52, 81, 84

Date of Accounts	Apr 11	Apr 10	Apr 09
Working Capital	-0	11	7
Fixed Assets	4	6	2
Current Assets	22	30	13
Current Liabilities	N/A	13	4

Airport Bearing Co. Ltd
Unit 4d Blenheim Park Road, Nottingham, NG6 8YP
Tel: 0115-975 7571 **Fax:** 0115-927 3778
E-mail: sales@abco.co.uk
Website: http://www.abco.co.uk
Bank(s): National Westminster Bank Plc
Directors: A. Gibson (Dir)
Immediate Holding Company: AIRPORT BEARING COMPANY LIMITED
Registration no: 01581768 **Date established:** 1981 **Turnover:** £1m - £2m
No.of Employees: 11 - 20 **Product Groups:** 35

Date of Accounts	Oct 11	Oct 10	Oct 09
Working Capital	277	186	148
Fixed Assets	65	15	13
Current Assets	744	591	442

All Steel Fabrications Ltd
Thrumpton Avenue Long Eaton, Nottingham, NG10 2GB
Tel: 0115-946 1688 **Fax:** 0115-946 1688
E-mail: info@allsteelsculpture.com
Website: http://www.allsteelsculpture.com
Directors: P. Elliott (Dir)
Immediate Holding Company: ALL STEEL FABRICATIONS LIMITED
Registration no: 07623345 **Date established:** 2011
No.of Employees: 1 - 10 **Product Groups:** 35

Alpharail Ltd
Urban Road Kirkby-in-Ashfield, Nottingham, NG17 8AP
Tel: 01623-750214 **Fax:** 01623-756596
E-mail: mark.sipson@alpharail.co.uk
Website: http://www.alpharail.co.uk
Bank(s): HSBC, Derby
Directors: M. Sipson (Fin), P. Ball (Dir)
Managers: N. Wilkinson (Purch Mgr)
Immediate Holding Company: ALPHA RAIL LIMITED
Registration no: 04326396 **VAT No.:** GB 411 2477 88
Date established: 2001 **No.of Employees:** 21 - 50 **Product Groups:** 35

Date of Accounts	Mar 11	Mar 10	Mar 09
Working Capital	388	396	591
Fixed Assets	306	346	404
Current Assets	833	847	1m

Aluset Security Print
Chester House 2 Mansfield Road, Eastwood, Nottingham, NG16 3AQ
Tel: 01773-769317 **Fax:** 01773-716206
E-mail: sales@aluset.com
Website: http://www.aluset.com
Directors: M. Brady (Grp Chief Exec), B. Kenworthy (Dir), S. Thomas (Sales)
Managers: S. Thomas (Mktg Serv Mgr), S. Thomas (Mgr)
Registration no: 00002879 **VAT No.:** GB 454 5049 48
Turnover: £10m - £20m **No.of Employees:** 1 - 10 **Product Groups:** 28, 32

Anixter
Queens Bridge Road, Nottingham, NG2 1NB
Tel: 0115-986 0127 **Fax:** 0115-986 2574
E-mail: nottingham.sales@anixter.com
Website: http://www.axixter.com
Managers: P. West (Mgr)
Ultimate Holding Company: ANIXTER INTERNATIONAL INC (USA)
Immediate Holding Company: ANIXTER(U.K.)LIMITED
Registration no: 01017023 **VAT No.:** GB 462 0222 90
Date established: 1971 **No.of Employees:** 11 - 20 **Product Groups:** 35, 67

Date of Accounts	Dec 11	Dec 10	Dec 09
Sales Turnover	N/A	148	169
Pre Tax Profit/Loss	N/A	10	-8
Working Capital	-35	-17	-24
Fixed Assets	50	21	22
Current Assets	33	33	32
Current Liabilities	N/A	N/A	36

Annesley Woodhouse Working Mens Club
Forest Road Kirkby-in-Ashfield, Nottingham, NG17 9HW
Tel: 01623-752264
E-mail: gary.cain@ntlworld.com
Directors: G. Atkin (Ch)
No.of Employees: 1 - 10 **Product Groups:** 30, 49, 62

Anson Concise Ltd
1 Eagle Close Arnold, Nottingham, NG5 7FJ
Tel: 0115-926 0911 **Fax:** 0115-967 3398
E-mail: info@ansonconcise.co.uk
Website: http://www.ansonconcise.co.uk
Directors: C. Reynolds (Fin), P. Simpson (MD)
Immediate Holding Company: ANSON CONCISE LIMITED
Registration no: 03547142 **Date established:** 1998
No.of Employees: 1 - 10 **Product Groups:** 26

Date of Accounts	Mar 12	Mar 11	Mar 10
Working Capital	9	-9	-14
Fixed Assets	N/A	1	1
Current Assets	70	73	77

Apollo Windows Conservatories & Extensions
128 Coppice Road Arnold, Nottingham, NG5 7GT
Tel: 0115-920 9519 **Fax:** 0115-967 1906
Website: http://www.apollowindows-nottingham.co.uk
Directors: I. Hopkins (Dir)
Immediate Holding Company: THE WINDOW DEPOT LIMITED
Registration no: 02641606 **Date established:** 2001
No.of Employees: 1 - 10 **Product Groups:** 26, 35

Date of Accounts	May 11
Working Capital	-4
Fixed Assets	3
Current Assets	2

Arco East Midlands Ltd
PO Box 3, Nottingham, NG8 4GS
Tel: 0115-928 6411 **Fax:** 0115-928 9041
E-mail: nottingham.branch@arco.co.uk
Website: http://www.arco.co.uk
Directors: A. Adderson (Dir)
Managers: M. Bennie (Reg Sales Mgr)
Registration no: 00486220 **Date established:** 1950
Turnover: £20m - £50m **No.of Employees:** 21 - 50 **Product Groups:** 24, 29, 30, 40

Arden Winch & Co. Ltd
116 Station Road Beeston, Nottingham, NG9 2AY
Tel: 0115-925 8222 **Fax:** 0115-925 8444
E-mail: julie.cooke@ardenwinch.com
Website: http://www.ardenwinch.com
Directors: J. Cooke (Dir)
Immediate Holding Company: ARDEN WINCH & CO LIMITED
Registration no: 01253792 **VAT No.:** GB 172 2678 54
Date established: 1976 **Turnover:** £5m - £10m **No.of Employees:** 1 - 10
Product Groups: 49, 63, 66, 67

Date of Accounts	Dec 11	Dec 10	Dec 09
Working Capital	484	522	555
Fixed Assets	2m	2m	2m
Current Assets	1m	1m	1m

Arena Sun Control Systems Ltd
Private Road 2 Colwick Industrial Estate, Nottingham, NG4 2JR
Tel: 0115-961 8234 **Fax:** 0115-940 2472
E-mail: sales@arenasun.co.uk
Website: http://www.arena-blinds.com
Bank(s): Natwest
Directors: K. Dobson (Co Sec), S. Dalby (Comm), J. Risman (Grp Chief Exec), D. Lewis (Tech Serv), A. Thomas (Fin)
Managers: I. Galpin, A. Graham (Personnel)
Ultimate Holding Company: BELLOTTO HOLDINGS LIMITED
Immediate Holding Company: ARENA SUN CONTROL SYSTEMS LIMITED
Registration no: 03438260 **VAT No.:** GB 411 6682 62
Date established: 1997 **Turnover:** £10m - £20m
No.of Employees: 11 - 20 **Product Groups:** 24, 30, 35, 36

Date of Accounts	Sep 11	Sep 08	Sep 09
Sales Turnover	14m	14m	12m
Pre Tax Profit/Loss	-338	2m	312

Working Capital	10m	10m	11m
Fixed Assets	350	N/A	N/A
Current Assets	12m	12m	12m
Current Liabilities	764	668	423

Arrow Electrical Contractors
A9 Hartley Business Centre Hucknall Road, Nottingham, NG5 1FD
Tel: 0115-960 5550 **Fax:** 0115-985 6883
E-mail: scott@arrow-ec.co.uk
Website: http://www.arrowelectricalcontractors.co.uk
Directors: S. Warren (Fin)
Immediate Holding Company: ARROW ELECTRICAL CONTRACTORS LIMITED
Registration no: 05448123 **Date established:** 2005
No.of Employees: 1 - 10 **Product Groups:** 52, 67

Date of Accounts	May 10	May 09	May 08
Working Capital	-17	-20	-27
Fixed Assets	26	31	37
Current Assets	68	59	82

Artex Ltd
Pasture Lane Ruddington, Nottingham, NG11 6AE
Tel: 0115-940 5066 **Fax:** 0115-940 5240
E-mail: nathan.cole@bpb.com
Website: http://www.artex-rawlplug.co.uk
Directors: G. Chambers (MD), N. Cole (Fin), A. Turner (Mkt Research), C. Gardener (Sales)
Managers: L. Bentley (Fin Mgr), G. Burton-wareing (Personnel)
Ultimate Holding Company: COMPAGNIE DE SAINT GOBAIN (FRANCE)
Immediate Holding Company: ARTEX LIMITED
Registration no: 04140239 **Date established:** 2001
No.of Employees: 101 - 250 **Product Groups:** 66

Date of Accounts	Dec 11	Dec 10	Dec 09
Sales Turnover	55m	49m	54m
Pre Tax Profit/Loss	8m	3m	4m
Working Capital	-10m	-10m	-6m
Fixed Assets	91m	82m	74m
Current Assets	17m	10m	11m
Current Liabilities	10m	12m	8m

Artistic Upholstery Ltd
Bridge Street Long Eaton, Nottingham, NG10 4QQ
Tel: 0115-973 4481 **Fax:** 0115-946 1018
E-mail: sales@artisticupholstery.co.uk
Website: http://www.artisticupholstery.co.uk
Bank(s): HSBC, Long Eaton
Directors: A. Mitchell (Dir)
Immediate Holding Company: ARTISTIC UPHOLSTERY LIMITED
Registration no: 00474743 **VAT No.:** GB 125 2153 10
Date established: 1949 **Turnover:** £1m - £2m **No.of Employees:** 21 - 50
Product Groups: 26

Date of Accounts	Oct 11	Oct 10	Oct 09
Working Capital	137	130	128
Fixed Assets	230	243	227
Current Assets	493	480	414

Arup Ltd
The Frontage 11 Queen Street, Nottingham, NG1 2BL
Tel: 0115-948 4711 **Fax:** 0115-948 4185
E-mail: robin.lee@arup.com
Website: http://www.arup.com
Directors: R. Lee (Dir)
Immediate Holding Company: ARUP LIMITED
Registration no: 02461313 **Date established:** 1990
No.of Employees: 21 - 50 **Product Groups:** 44

Date of Accounts	Mar 11	Mar 10	Mar 09
Sales Turnover	3m	2m	N/A
Pre Tax Profit/Loss	582	416	N/A
Working Capital	819	-153	73
Fixed Assets	15m	16m	N/A
Current Assets	3m	497	73
Current Liabilities	538	610	N/A

Ashfield Extrusion Ltd
B Field Industrial Estate Clover Street, Kirkby-In-Ashfield, Nottingham, NG17 7LH
Tel: 01623-757333 **Fax:** 01623-751771
E-mail: ashfield.sales@btconnect.com
Website: http://www.ashfield-extrusion.co.uk
Bank(s): Barclays, High Wycombe
Directors: A. Bennett (Fin), B. Andrew (Fin), C. Davies (Dir)
Managers: K. Davies (Sales & Mktg Mg)
Ultimate Holding Company: ARKLOW ENGINEERING LIMITED
Immediate Holding Company: ASHFIELD EXTRUSION LIMITED
Registration no: 01809384 **Date established:** 1984 **Turnover:** £2m - £5m
No.of Employees: 51 - 100 **Product Groups:** 34, 35, 48

Date of Accounts	Dec 11	Dec 10	Dec 09
Sales Turnover	5m	N/A	N/A
Pre Tax Profit/Loss	372	N/A	N/A
Working Capital	2m	2m	2m
Fixed Assets	928	814	901
Current Assets	3m	3m	2m
Current Liabilities	465	N/A	N/A

Assystance IT Solutions
Mercury House Northgate, Nottingham, NG7 7FN
Tel: 0115-964 8222 **Fax:** 0115-964 8201
E-mail: ask@webstreamsolutions.com
Website: http://www.apexbusinessservicesltd.co.uk
Directors: C. Kelly (Prop), A. Johnson (Dir)
Managers: J. Tantum (Mgr)
Immediate Holding Company: Solutions4elearning Ltd
Registration no: 06090664 **Date established:** 2007
No.of Employees: 1 - 10 **Product Groups:** 44

Attenborough Dental Ltd
Viscosa House George Street, Nottingham, NG1 3BN
Tel: 0115-947 3562 **Fax:** 0115-950 9086
E-mail: info@attenborough.com
Website: http://www.attenborough.com
Bank(s): Barclays
Directors: E. Attenborough (MD), J. Attenborough (Co Sec)
Ultimate Holding Company: C & L E ATTENBOROUGH LIMITED
Immediate Holding Company: ATTENBOROUGH DENTAL LABORATORIES LTD
Registration no: 03985345 **VAT No.:** GB 116 2729 81
Date established: 2000 **Turnover:** £500,000 - £1m
No.of Employees: 21 - 50 **Product Groups:** 35, 38, 49, 67

Date of Accounts	Apr 11	Apr 10	Apr 09
Working Capital	20	5	4
Fixed Assets	34	27	27
Current Assets	107	63	46

Audiorent.Co.Uk
3 Kirkdale Gardens Long Eaton, Nottingham, NG10 3JA
Tel: 01332-242 248
E-mail: contact@audiorent.co.uk
Website: http://www.audiorent.co.uk
Managers: D. Booth (Chief Acct), I. Bradley (Mgr)
Date established: 2005 **No.of Employees:** 1 - 10 **Product Groups:** 37, 83, 89

Auto Sparks Ltd
80-88 Derby Road Sandiacre, Nottingham, NG10 5HU
Tel: 0115-949 7211 **Fax:** 0115-949 1955
E-mail: sales@autosparks.co.uk
Website: http://www.autosparks.co.uk
Directors: D. Johnson (Dir), D. Johnson (Dir)
Immediate Holding Company: AUTO-SPARKS LIMITED
Registration no: 02982858 **Date established:** 1994
No.of Employees: 21 - 50 **Product Groups:** 39

Date of Accounts	Oct 11	Oct 10	Oct 09
Working Capital	288	118	-198
Fixed Assets	1m	1m	1m
Current Assets	581	359	322

Autoreel Ltd
Palmer Drive Stapleford, Nottingham, NG9 7BW
Tel: 0115-939 0200 **Fax:** 0115-939 0201
E-mail: autoreel@autoreel.co.uk
Website: http://www.autoreel.co.uk
Bank(s): Bank of Scotland
Directors: D. Miller (Co Sec), P. Wheelhouse (MD)
Ultimate Holding Company: BRITISH DRILLING AND FREEZING COMPANY LIMITED
Immediate Holding Company: AUTOREEL LIMITED
Registration no: 01933665 **VAT No.:** 439 5265 26 **Date established:** 1985
Turnover: £1m - £2m **No.of Employees:** 11 - 20 **Product Groups:** 36, 45, 46, 47

Date of Accounts	Dec 11	Dec 10	Dec 09
Sales Turnover	1m	870	1m
Pre Tax Profit/Loss	131	12	113
Working Capital	168	257	239
Fixed Assets	18	28	39
Current Assets	488	397	527
Current Liabilities	128	37	85

B A S Castings Ltd
Wharf Road Industrial Estate Pinxton, Nottingham, NG16 6LE
Tel: 01773-812028 **Fax:** 01773-861948
E-mail: sales@bascastings.co.uk
Website: http://www.bascastings.co.uk
Bank(s): Barclays Bank PLC
Directors: S. Dilks (Sales), T. Henderson (Comm)
Managers: A. Smithurst (Sales Off Mgr)
Ultimate Holding Company: PRAYER INVESTMENTS LIMITED (CYPRUS)
Immediate Holding Company: BAS CASTINGS LIMITED
Registration no: 01137480 **VAT No.:** GB 158 2370 60
Date established: 1973 **Turnover:** £10m - £20m
No.of Employees: 51 - 100 **Product Groups:** 34, 36

Date of Accounts	Dec 11	Dec 10	Dec 09
Sales Turnover	11m	8m	7m
Pre Tax Profit/Loss	987	496	412
Working Capital	814	508	439
Fixed Assets	390	351	369
Current Assets	3m	2m	2m
Current Liabilities	460	282	260

B A S F plc (Agricultural Division)
Mere Way Ruddington Fields Business Park, Ruddington, Nottingham, NG11 6JS
Tel: 0161-485 6222 **Fax:** 0161-486 0891
E-mail: info.service@basf-plc.co.uk
Website: http://www.basf.com
Bank(s): National Westminster Bank Plc
Directors: H. Koerner (Co Sec), S. Hatton (Pers), W. Seufert (Pres)
Ultimate Holding Company: BASF SOCIETAS EUROPAEA (GERMANY)
Immediate Holding Company: BASF PUBLIC LIMITED COMPANY
Registration no: 00667980 **Date established:** 1960
Turnover: £500m - £1,000m **No.of Employees:** 251 - 500
Product Groups: 30, 31, 32, 61

Date of Accounts	Dec 11	Dec 10	Dec 09
Sales Turnover	571m	506m	368m
Pre Tax Profit/Loss	7m	10m	9m
Working Capital	-45m	-43m	-16m
Fixed Assets	93m	93m	55m
Current Assets	96m	106m	113m
Current Liabilities	13m	15m	22m

B B Drilling Ltd a division of British Drilling & Freezing Co. Ltd
Private Road No 3 Colwick Industrial Colwick Industrial Estate, Nottingham, NG4 2BB
Tel: 0115-940 0141 **Fax:** 0115-961 7388
E-mail: c.james@bdf.co.uk
Website: http://www.bdf.co.uk/drill
Bank(s): Bank of Scotland, Nottingham
Directors: P. Wheelhouse (MD)
Managers: A. Atkin (Personnel), H. Mew (Sales & Mktg Mg), D. Miller (Fin Mgr), D. Miller (Fin Mgr)
Ultimate Holding Company: BRITISH DRILLING AND FREEZING COMPANY LIMITED
Immediate Holding Company: B. B. DRILLING LIMITED
Registration no: 01342222 **Date established:** 1977
Turnover: £10m - £20m **No.of Employees:** 21 - 50 **Product Groups:** 51

B S S Austin Stroud (t/a Pegler and Louden)
Martin Close Bleneim Industrial Estate, Nottingham, NG6 8UW
Tel: 08708-507064 **Fax:** 08708-507065
E-mail: sales@bssuk.co.uk
Website: http://www.bssuk.co.uk
Bank(s): HSBC Bank plc
Directors: A. Firth (Dir)
Registration no: SC60987 **VAT No.:** GB 316 0004 22
No.of Employees: 21 - 50 **Product Groups:** 30, 33, 36, 37, 39, 40, 45

Badgemaster Ltd
Hazelford Way Newstead Industrial Estate, Newstead Village, Nottingham, NG15 0DQ
Tel: 01623-723112 **Fax:** 01623-723113
E-mail: customerservices@badgemaster.co.uk
Website: http://www.badgemaster.co.uk
Directors: V. Bancroft (Fin), J. Bancroft (MD)
Managers: M. Harrison (Personnel)
Immediate Holding Company: BADGEMASTER LIMITED
Registration no: 02730127 **Date established:** 1992 **Turnover:** £2m - £5m
No.of Employees: 51 - 100 **Product Groups:** 30

Date of Accounts	May 11	May 10	May 09
Working Capital	341	279	347
Fixed Assets	323	303	354
Current Assets	980	948	1m

Bagfast Ltd
Unit 2 Morris Court Colwick Industrial Estate, Nottingham, NG4 2JN
Tel: 0115-940 1658 **Fax:** 0115-961 1714
E-mail: sales@bagfast.com
Website: http://www.bagfast.com
Directors: R. Heppinstall (MD)
Immediate Holding Company: BAGFAST LIMITED
Registration no: 02282815 **VAT No.:** GB 305 1338 01
Date established: 1988 **Turnover:** £500,000 - £1m
No.of Employees: 1 - 10 **Product Groups:** 30, 41, 45, 48, 67, 84

Date of Accounts	Jul 11	Jul 10	Jul 09
Working Capital	-119	-117	-99
Fixed Assets	1	2	2
Current Assets	12	20	18
Current Liabilities	N/A	8	N/A

Bampton Packaging Ltd
Lenton Lane, Nottingham, NG7 2NR
Tel: 0115-957 8911 **Fax:** 0115-986 2984
E-mail: mike.brown@bamptonpackaging.co.uk
Website: http://www.bamptonpackaging.co.uk
Bank(s): The Royal Bank of Scotland
Directors: M. Brown (MD), S. Hallsworth (Co Sec), M. Higham (Sales), M. Brown (Fin)
Managers: J. Lacey (Purch Mgr)
Ultimate Holding Company: BAMPTON PACKAGING (HOLDINGS) LIMITED
Immediate Holding Company: BAMPTON PACKAGING LIMITED
Registration no: 00214769 **VAT No.:** GB 352 9292 39
Date established: 1926 **Turnover:** Up to £250,000
No.of Employees: 21 - 50 **Product Groups:** 23, 25, 27, 28, 30, 45, 48, 76, 84

Date of Accounts	Mar 11	Mar 10	Mar 09
Pre Tax Profit/Loss	N/A	N/A	-41
Working Capital	2m	2m	2m
Fixed Assets	130	159	150
Current Assets	3m	3m	3m
Current Liabilities	N/A	N/A	645

Barclay & Mathieson Ltd
Arnold Road, Nottingham, NG6 0EF
Tel: 0115-970 1171 **Fax:** 0115-942 2181
E-mail: nottingham@bmsteel.co.uk
Website: http://www.bmsteel.co.uk
Bank(s): The Royal Bank of Scotland
Managers: D. Watts (Mgr)
Ultimate Holding Company: STEMCOR HOLDINGS LIMITED
Immediate Holding Company: BARCLAY & MATHIESON LIMITED
Registration no: SC030987 **VAT No.:** GB 259 6926 05
Date established: 1955 **Turnover:** £10m - £20m
No.of Employees: 11 - 20 **Product Groups:** 34, 66

Date of Accounts	Dec 11	Dec 10	Dec 09
Sales Turnover	55m	48m	35m
Pre Tax Profit/Loss	2m	2m	-865
Working Capital	11m	13m	13m
Fixed Assets	19m	16m	18m
Current Assets	24m	25m	20m
Current Liabilities	4m	5m	713

Barnetts Confectioners Ltd
Stansfield Street, Nottingham, NG7 2AE
Tel: 0115-978 4642 **Fax:** 0115-944 9236
E-mail: sales@barnettconfectioners.co.uk
Website: http://www.barnettconfectioners.co.uk
Directors: R. Barnett (MD)
Immediate Holding Company: BARNETT CONFECTIONERS LIMITED
Registration no: 01063650 **VAT No.:** GB 117 8128 71
Date established: 1972 **Turnover:** £500,000 - £1m
No.of Employees: 1 - 10 **Product Groups:** 31

Date of Accounts	Dec 11	Dec 10	Dec 09
Working Capital	225	270	270
Fixed Assets	197	206	216
Current Assets	353	425	413

Basic Business Systems Ltd
Brookside Road Ruddington, Nottingham, NG11 6AT
Tel: 0115-940 5000 **Fax:** 0115-940 5450
E-mail: info@basic.co.uk
Website: http://www.basic.co.uk
Bank(s): Barclays
Directors: P. Smith (Dir)
Immediate Holding Company: BASIC BUSINESS SYSTEMS LIMITED
Registration no: 01459294 **VAT No.:** GB 309 7047 55
Date established: 1979 **No.of Employees:** 11 - 20 **Product Groups:** 44, 84

Date of Accounts	Mar 12	Mar 11	Mar 10
Working Capital	126	71	112
Fixed Assets	59	102	51
Current Assets	385	383	303

The Beck Company Ltd
Quorn Road, Nottingham, NG5 1DT
Tel: 0115-962 4121 **Fax:** 0115-969 1362
E-mail: info@thebeckco.com
Website: http://www.thebeckco.com
Bank(s): HSBC Bank plc
Directors: J. Ball (Dir)
Ultimate Holding Company: BILBECK (MERCHANTS) LIMITED
Immediate Holding Company: THE BECK COMPANY LIMITED
Registration no: 01250669 **VAT No.:** GB 118 6577 46
Date established: 1976 **Turnover:** £10m - £20m
No.of Employees: 21 - 50 **Product Groups:** 36, 66

Date of Accounts	Mar 11	Mar 10	Mar 09
Sales Turnover	13m	12m	N/A
Pre Tax Profit/Loss	387	575	767

see next page

***The Beck Company Ltd** - Cont'd*

Working Capital	2m	2m	2m
Fixed Assets	533	593	662
Current Assets	3m	4m	3m
Current Liabilities	254	245	433

Bed & Bath Company
2 Home Farm Cottage Staunton In The Vale, Nottingham, NG13 9PE
Tel: 01949-844441 **Fax:** 01949-844001
E-mail: julie.stone@bedandbath.co.uk
Website: http://www.bedandbath.co.uk
Directors: J. Lawrence (Dir), J. Stone (Prop), P. Evans (MD)
Managers: L. Merrifield (Accounts), T. Clarke (Sales Prom Mgr), E. Haxby (Purch Mgr)
Immediate Holding Company: BED & BATH (U.K.) LIMITED
Registration no: 01551578 **VAT No.:** GB 354 1159 69
Date established: 1981 **Turnover:** £1m - £2m **No.of Employees:** 1 - 10
Product Groups: 22, 24

Bemas Boiler Erectors Ltd
PO Box 28, Nottingham, NG10 2GA
Tel: 0115-972 8954 **Fax:** 0115-946 1857
E-mail: enquiries@bemasboilers.co.uk
Website: http://www.bemasboilers.co.uk
Directors: P. Weston (MD)
Immediate Holding Company: BEMAS BOILER ERECTORS LIMITED
Registration no: 01216601 **VAT No.:** GB 118 1760 80
Date established: 1975 **Turnover:** £500,000 - £1m
No.of Employees: 1 - 10 **Product Groups:** 48, 52

Date of Accounts	May 12	May 11	May 10
Working Capital	246	281	198
Fixed Assets	326	292	317
Current Assets	386	483	378

Berridge Painting Systems Ltd
Nottingham Road Beeston, Nottingham, NG9 6DR
Tel: 0115-925 8291 **Fax:** 0115-925 9157
E-mail: sales@berridge.co.uk
Website: http://www.berridge.co.uk
Directors: J. Herrod (Dir)
Ultimate Holding Company: SHEETFABS (NOTTINGHAM) LIMITED
Immediate Holding Company: BERRIDGE PAINTING SYSTEMS LIMITED
Registration no: 01844847 **Date established:** 1984 **Turnover:** £1m - £2m
No.of Employees: 1 - 10 **Product Groups:** 40, 46, 48

Date of Accounts	Oct 11	Oct 10	Oct 09
Working Capital	387	341	343
Fixed Assets	N/A	4	6
Current Assets	503	477	429

Biffa Waste Services Ltd
Private Road 2 Colwick Industrial Estate, Nottingham, NG4 2JR
Tel: 0115-961 6424 **Fax:** 01623-627958
E-mail: marketing@biffa.co.uk
Website: http://www.biffa.co.uk
Managers: D. Woodriff (Mgr)
Immediate Holding Company: BIFFA WASTE SERVICES LIMITED
Registration no: 00946107 **Date established:** 1969
No.of Employees: 1 - 10 **Product Groups:** 32, 54

Date of Accounts	Mar 08	Mar 09	Apr 10
Sales Turnover	555m	574m	492m
Pre Tax Profit/Loss	23m	50m	30m
Working Capital	229m	271m	293m
Fixed Assets	371m	360m	378m
Current Assets	409m	534m	609m
Current Liabilities	50m	100m	115m

Birchwood Price Tools
Park Lodge Road Giltbrook, Nottingham, NG16 2AR
Tel: 0115-938 9000 **Fax:** 0115-938 9010
E-mail: sales@birchwoodpricetools.com
Website: http://www.birchwoodpricetools.com
Bank(s): Barclays
Directors: P. Nieduszynski (MD)
Managers: R. Sedgwick (Sales Prom Mgr)
Registration no: 01132499 **VAT No.:** GB 450 0502 06
Date established: 2005 **Turnover:** £10m - £20m
No.of Employees: 51 - 100 **Product Groups:** 37, 40, 45, 61, 67, 83

Blugilt Holdings Ltd
Environment House 6 Union Road, Nottingham, NG3 1FH
Tel: 0115-901 3000 **Fax:** 0115-901 3100
Directors: A. Puri (Ch)
Turnover: £75m - £125m **No.of Employees:** 1 - 10 **Product Groups:** 30, 31

Date of Accounts	Dec 09	Dec 08	Dec 07
Pre Tax Profit/Loss	-1	180	-4
Working Capital	2m	2m	1m
Current Assets	2m	2m	1m
Current Liabilities	3	3	31

Blumax Metal Finishers Ltd
Unit 1 Brand Street, Nottingham, NG2 3GW
Tel: 0115-986 5776 **Fax:** 0115-985 0286
Directors: K. Blewitt (MD)
Immediate Holding Company: BLUMAX METAL FINISHERS LIMITED.
Registration no: 04256500 **Date established:** 2001
No.of Employees: 1 - 10 **Product Groups:** 46, 48

Date of Accounts	Jul 11	Jul 10	Jul 09
Working Capital	193	145	186
Fixed Assets	42	50	31
Current Assets	281	241	244

Boldon Drilling Ltd
Private Road 3 Colwick Industrial Estate, Nottingham, NG4 2BB
Tel: 0115-961 1250 **Fax:** 0115-961 7338
E-mail: drill@bds.co.uk
Website: http://www.bdf.co.uk/drill
Directors: P. Wheelhouse (MD)
Managers: K. Halliday (Buyer), D. Miller (Chief Acct), A. Atkin (Personnel)
Ultimate Holding Company: BRITISH DRILLING AND FREEZING COMPANY LIMITED
Immediate Holding Company: BOLDON DRILLING LIMITED
Registration no: 01056020 **Date established:** 1972 **Turnover:** £5m - £10m
No.of Employees: 11 - 20 **Product Groups:** 51

Bonzo Band
Harington Mills Block G Leopold Street, Long Eaton, Nottingham, NG10 4QE
Tel: 0115-946 0111 **Fax:** 0115-946 3617
E-mail: info@bonzoband.co.uk
Website: http://www.bonzoband.co.uk
Directors: M. White (MD)
Immediate Holding Company: BONZO BAND LIMITED
Registration no: 03467090 **Date established:** 1997
Turnover: £250,000 - £500,000 **No.of Employees:** 1 - 10
Product Groups: 38, 42

Date of Accounts	Nov 11	Nov 10	Nov 09
Working Capital	300	226	138
Fixed Assets	35	22	15
Current Assets	367	297	198

Boots UK Ltd
Thane Road, Nottingham, NG90 1BS
Tel: 0115-968 9172 **Fax:** 0115-949 2120
Website: http://www.boots.co.uk
Bank(s): National Westminster Bank Plc
Directors: N. Rudd (Ch), R. Fraser (I.T. Dir), R. Baker (Grp Chief Exec), P. Bateman (Pers), N. Usher (Dir), K. Piggott (Dir), I. Hunter (Mkt Research), A. Robson (Dir)
Managers: W. Cotton, P. Stoneham, D. Burley (Mgr)
Ultimate Holding Company: AB ACQUISITIONS HOLDINGS LTD (GIBRALTAR)
Immediate Holding Company: BOOTS UK LIMITED
Registration no: 00928555 **Date established:** 1968
Turnover: £250,000 - £500,000 **No.of Employees:** 1501 & over
Product Groups: 61

Date of Accounts	Mar 08	Mar 07	Mar 06
Sales Turnover	254	229	199
Pre Tax Profit/Loss	11	-21	3
Working Capital	18	7	28
Current Assets	27	22	28
Current Liabilities	9	15	N/A
ROCE% (Return on Capital Employed)	61.0	-306.8	
ROT% (Return on Turnover)	4.2	-9.2	1.3

B P X Electro Mechanical Co. Ltd
386 Haydn Road, Nottingham, NG5 1EA
Tel: 0115-970 4531 **Fax:** 0115-942 2240
E-mail: rcollins@bpx.co.uk
Website: http://www.bpx.co.uk
Directors: R. Collins (Dir)
Registration no: 00000863 **VAT No.:** GB 113 7064 03
Turnover: £10m - £20m **No.of Employees:** 1 - 10 **Product Groups:** 77

A Bratt & Son Ltd
Abbeyfield Road, Nottingham, NG7 2SZ
Tel: 0115-986 2221 **Fax:** 0115-986 1991
E-mail: sales@brattsladders.com
Website: http://www.brattsladders.com
Bank(s): Yorkshire Bank PLC
Directors: S. Bratt (MD)
Immediate Holding Company: A. BRATT & SON LIMITED
Registration no: 00822682 **VAT No.:** GB 116 2592 82
Date established: 1964 **Turnover:** £1m - £2m **No.of Employees:** 11 - 20
Product Groups: 25, 30

Date of Accounts	Oct 11	Oct 10	Oct 09
Working Capital	142	156	225
Fixed Assets	210	223	236
Current Assets	388	378	483

Brightwake Ltd
Sidings Road Lowmoor Industrial Estate, Kirkby-In-Ashfield, Nottingham, NG17 7JZ
Tel: 01623-751151 **Fax:** 01623-757636
E-mail: sales@brightwake.co.uk
Website: http://www.brightwake.co.uk
Directors: V. Allen (Dir)
Immediate Holding Company: BRIGHTWAKE LIMITED
Registration no: 01356034 **VAT No.:** GB 309 3579 42
Date established: 1978 **Turnover:** £10m - £20m
No.of Employees: 51 - 100 **Product Groups:** 23, 24, 31, 38, 48

Date of Accounts	Mar 11	Mar 10	Mar 09
Sales Turnover	13m	10m	N/A
Pre Tax Profit/Loss	721	661	367
Working Capital	2m	2m	2m
Fixed Assets	2m	1m	963
Current Assets	6m	4m	3m
Current Liabilities	1m	661	450

Brinsmoor Solutions Ltd
Unit 2 Aerial Way Hucknall, Nottingham, NG15 6DW
Tel: 0115-964 0961 **Fax:** 0115-964 1819
E-mail: brinsmoor@btconnect.com
Directors: G. Cresswell (Fin), S. Hadman (MD)
Immediate Holding Company: BRINSMOOR SOLUTIONS LIMITED
Registration no: 04026675 **Date established:** 2000
No.of Employees: 11 - 20 **Product Groups:** 30, 39, 40

Date of Accounts	Dec 11	Dec 10	Jul 10
Working Capital	-4	-4	-10
Fixed Assets	5	17	23
Current Assets	130	144	355

Britannia Lightning Prevectron Ltd
12 Longue Drive Calverton, Nottingham, NG14 6QF
Tel: 0115-847 7113 **Fax:** 0115-847 5185
E-mail: mike@prevectron.co.uk
Website: http://www.lightningconsultants.co.uk
Directors: M. Dutczak (MD)
Immediate Holding Company: BRITANNIA LIGHTNING PREVECTRON LIMITED
Registration no: 03802510 **Date established:** 1999
No.of Employees: 1 - 10 **Product Groups:** 37

Date of Accounts	Jul 11	Jul 10	Jul 09
Working Capital	85	69	63
Fixed Assets	8	11	15
Current Assets	160	82	126

British Geological Survey
Kingsley Dunham Centre Keyworth, Nottingham, NG12 5GG
Tel: 0115-936 3100 **Fax:** 0115-936 3200
E-mail: enquiries@bgs.ac.uk
Website: http://www.bgs.ac.uk
Directors: D. Ovedia (Mkt Research), A. Clowes (Fin), E. Johnston (Sales), J. Ludden (MD)
Managers: M. Squires, A. Clewes (Fin Mgr), J. Raynor (Sales Prom Mgr), I. Ainslie (I.T. Exec), J. Orr (Personnel)
Immediate Holding Company: IGS (INTERNATIONAL GEOSCIENCE SERVICES) LIMITED
Registration no: 02236749 **Date established:** 2010
No.of Employees: 251 - 500 **Product Groups:** 87

Date of Accounts	Dec 11
Working Capital	114
Fixed Assets	2
Current Assets	178

Broadbent & Co. Ltd
Unit 4 Colwick Business Park Private Road 2, Colwick Industrial Estate, Nottingham, NG4 2JR
Tel: 0115-940 0777 **Fax:** 0115-987 3744
E-mail: sales@broadbentandco.com
Website: http://www.broadbentandco.com
Directors: S. Broadbent (Dir)
Immediate Holding Company: BROADBENT & CO. LIMITED
Registration no: 02380769 **Date established:** 1989
Turnover: £500,000 - £1m **No.of Employees:** 1 - 10 **Product Groups:** 40, 52

Date of Accounts	May 11	May 10	May 09
Working Capital	73	57	69
Fixed Assets	42	25	24
Current Assets	271	249	239

Brooks Brothers Midlands Ltd
Willow Road Lenton Lane, Nottingham, NG7 2PR
Tel: 0115-993 1111 **Fax:** 0115-993 1151
E-mail: enquiries@brooksmidlands.co.uk
Website: http://www.brookstimber.uk.com
Bank(s): Bank of Scotland
Managers: M. Rose (Tech Serv Mgr), M. Osborne, M. Hall (Chief Mgr), N. Sheffield (Fin Mgr)
Ultimate Holding Company: GEORGE A. SHERRIFF LIMITED
Immediate Holding Company: BROOKS BROS.(MIDLANDS) LIMITED
Registration no: 02359574 **VAT No.:** GB 520 7152 82
Date established: 1989 **Turnover:** £10m - £20m
No.of Employees: 21 - 50 **Product Groups:** 25, 52, 66

Date of Accounts	Dec 11	Dec 10	Dec 09
Sales Turnover	11m	11m	9m
Pre Tax Profit/Loss	633	642	605
Working Capital	4m	4m	3m
Fixed Assets	2m	2m	2m
Current Assets	5m	5m	4m
Current Liabilities	358	429	360

Browne Jacobson
Mowbray House Castle Meadow Road, Nottingham, NG2 1BJ
Tel: 0115-976 6000 **Fax:** 0115-976 6000
E-mail: info@brownejacobson.com
Website: http://www.brownejacobson.com
Directors: P. Harrison (Fin), I. Blatherwick (Snr Part)
Managers: P. Harrison (Chief Acct), E. Henry (Personnel), R. Aucott, D. Simms (Tech Serv Mgr)
Immediate Holding Company: BROWNE JACOBSON LLP
Registration no: OC306448 **VAT No.:** GB 116 3962 70
Date established: 2003 **Turnover:** £20m - £50m
No.of Employees: 501 - 1000 **Product Groups:** 80

Date of Accounts	Apr 11	Apr 10	Apr 09
Sales Turnover	35m	33m	31m
Pre Tax Profit/Loss	10m	10m	6m
Working Capital	13m	10m	8m
Fixed Assets	1m	2m	2m
Current Assets	18m	15m	13m
Current Liabilities	4m	3m	2m

Bryson Packaging Ltd
Unit 34 Trent South Industrial Park, Nottingham, NG2 4EQ
Tel: 0115-950 8686 **Fax:** 0115-941 3821
E-mail: bryson2010@btconnect.com
Website: http://www.brysonpackaging.co.uk
Directors: L. Robinson (Prop)
Immediate Holding Company: BRYSON PACKAGING LIMITED
Registration no: 01216669 **Date established:** 1975
No.of Employees: 1 - 10 **Product Groups:** 38, 42

Date of Accounts	Dec 11	Dec 10	Dec 09
Working Capital	15	16	13
Fixed Assets	13	17	17
Current Assets	121	115	133

Buck & Hickman Ltd
Unit 2 Longwall Avenue, Queens Drive Industrial Estate, Nottingham, NG2 1NA
Tel: 0115-986 8282 **Fax:** 0115-986 8486
E-mail: nottingham@buckandhickman.com
Website: http://www.buckandhickman.com
Managers: A. Hunter (Sales Off Mgr), P. Farr (District Mgr)
Ultimate Holding Company: TRAVIS PERKINS PLC
Immediate Holding Company: BOSTON (2011) LIMITED
Registration no: 06028304 **Date established:** 2006
Turnover: £10m - £20m **No.of Employees:** 11 - 20 **Product Groups:** 23, 24, 33, 36, 37, 41, 42, 45, 46, 66, 67, 83

Date of Accounts	Dec 10	Mar 10	Mar 09
Working Capital	6m	6m	6m
Current Assets	27m	27m	27m

Bulwell Precision Engineers Ltd
Wharf Road Industrial Estate Pinxton, Nottingham, NG16 6LE
Tel: 01773-810102 **Fax:** 01773-861644
E-mail: chris.henson@bulwell.com
Website: http://www.bulwell.com
Bank(s): National Westminster Bank Plc
Directors: M. Edmonds (Fin), A. Lee (Fin), E. Jones (Chief Op Offcr), S. Beech (MD)
Managers: J. Dixon (Personnel), N. Allen
Ultimate Holding Company: NASMYTH GROUP LIMITED
Immediate Holding Company: BULWELL PRECISION ENGINEERS LIMITED
Registration no: 00568879 **VAT No.:** GB 716 6739 10
Date established: 1956 **Turnover:** £20m - £50m
No.of Employees: 101 - 250 **Product Groups:** 33, 34, 35, 36, 39, 48

Date of Accounts	Jan 12	Jan 11	Jan 10
Sales Turnover	20m	16m	16m
Pre Tax Profit/Loss	2m	759	382
Working Capital	6m	6m	4m
Fixed Assets	3m	3m	3m
Current Assets	16m	15m	14m
Current Liabilities	6m	5m	1m

Bulwell Tool & Plant Ltd
Unit 8 Thames Street, Nottingham, NG6 8HW
Tel: 0115-975 5990 **Fax:** 0115-927 8115
E-mail: info@bulwellforktrucks.co.uk
Website: http://www.bulwellforktrucks.co.uk
Directors: N. Salisbury (MD)
Immediate Holding Company: BULWELL TOOL & PLANT LIMITED
Registration no: 03740497 **Date established:** 1999
No.of Employees: 1 - 10 **Product Groups:** 45, 83

Date of Accounts	Apr 11	Apr 10	Apr 09
Working Capital	19	27	26
Fixed Assets	4	5	6
Current Assets	46	73	57
Current Liabilities	3	N/A	N/A

Bunny Appliance Warehouse Ltd
Appliance Warehouses Gotham Lane, Bunny, Nottingham, NG11 6QJ
Tel: 0115-984 4357 **Fax:** 0115-945 6001
E-mail: james@bunnyappliancewarehouse.co.uk
Website: http://www.bunnyappliancewarehouse.co.uk
Directors: P. Bysouth Kemp (Dir), J. Bysouth Kemp (Dir)
Ultimate Holding Company: BAW (HOLDINGS) LIMITED
Immediate Holding Company: BUNNY APPLIANCE WAREHOUSE LTD
Registration no: 03027841 **Date established:** 1995
Turnover: £20m - £50m **No.of Employees:** 21 - 50 **Product Groups:** 40, 63

Date of Accounts	Jul 11	Jul 10	Jul 09
Sales Turnover	25m	21m	20m
Pre Tax Profit/Loss	1m	161	3m
Working Capital	4m	3m	1m
Fixed Assets	256	1m	2m
Current Assets	10m	7m	4m
Current Liabilities	925	3m	865

Burgass Carrier Bags
2 Nether Street Beeston, Nottingham, NG9 2AT
Tel: 0115-943 1775 **Fax:** 0115-925 2775
E-mail: helen@carrier-bag.com
Website: http://www.carrier-bag.com
Directors: H. Wright (MD)
Managers: A. Howard (Chief Acct)
Registration no: 03604098 **No.of Employees:** 11 - 20 **Product Groups:** 30

Burt Bros Hosiery Ltd
A-C Willow Road, Nottingham, NG7 2TA
Tel: 0115-970 6133 **Fax:** 0115-942 0576
E-mail: hannahburt@burtbros.co.uk
Website: http://www.burtbros.co.uk
Bank(s): AIB Group
Directors: H. Burt (Fin), S. Burt (Sales), T. Lewis (Fin)
Ultimate Holding Company: A.C.GILL,LIMITED
Immediate Holding Company: BURT BROS.(HOSIERY)LIMITED
Registration no: 00451130 **Date established:** 1948
Turnover: £10m - £20m **No.of Employees:** 51 - 100 **Product Groups:** 24

Date of Accounts	Dec 11	Dec 10	Dec 09
Sales Turnover	17m	14m	15m
Pre Tax Profit/Loss	686	658	922
Working Capital	2m	2m	2m
Fixed Assets	4m	4m	4m
Current Assets	7m	8m	7m
Current Liabilities	727	862	2m

C & A Spraying Services
Adco Business Centre Bobbers Mill, Nottingham, NG8 5AH
Tel: 0115-979 1300 **Fax:** 0115-979 1300
E-mail: ashleykerry93@yahoo.com
Directors: A. Kerry (Prop)
Date established: 2002 **No.of Employees:** 1 - 10 **Product Groups:** 46, 48

C & H Precision Finishers Ltd
Precision House Derby Road, Sandiacre, Nottingham, NG10 5HU
Tel: 0115-939 4707 **Fax:** 0115-949 0146
E-mail: admin@chprecision.co.uk
Website: http://www.chprecision.co.uk
Managers: J. Oldershaw (Mgr), S. King (Chief Acct)
Ultimate Holding Company: AVINGTRANS PLC
Immediate Holding Company: C & H PRECISION FINISHERS LIMITED
Registration no: 02905047 **Date established:** 1994 **Turnover:** £2m - £5m
No.of Employees: 51 - 100 **Product Groups:** 46, 48, 85

Date of Accounts	May 11	May 10	May 09
Sales Turnover	3m	2m	3m
Pre Tax Profit/Loss	739	354	366
Working Capital	-37	-76	-116
Fixed Assets	621	590	642
Current Assets	1m	1m	637
Current Liabilities	247	404	206

Cad Academy Ltd
Sherwood House Gregory Boulevard, Nottingham, NG7 6LB
Tel: 0115-969 1114 **Fax:** 0115-969 1115
E-mail: info@microcad.co.uk
Website: http://www.graphite.co.uk
Directors: G. Gubas (MD), G. Gubas (Dir), K. Jackson (Ch)
Immediate Holding Company: OVC PROPERTIES LTD
Registration no: 05807810 **Date established:** 1999 **Turnover:** £1m - £2m
No.of Employees: 1 - 10 **Product Groups:** 44, 47, 86

Date of Accounts	Jun 09	Jun 08	Jun 07
Working Capital	-20	-1	1
Fixed Assets	14	18	14
Current Assets	59	103	49

Caljan Rite Hite Ltd
Moorbridge Road Bingham, Nottingham, NG13 8GG
Tel: 01949-838850 **Fax:** 01949-836953
E-mail: caljanritehite@caljanritehite.co.uk
Website: http://www.caljanritehite.co.uk
Directors: G. Sanderson (Co Sec), G. Sanderson (Fin), H. Olesen (Dir), M. Hilton (MD), M. Baugh (MD)
Immediate Holding Company: CALJAN RITE-HITE LIMITED
Registration no: 03223165 **Date established:** 1996
Turnover: £500,000 - £1m **No.of Employees:** 11 - 20
Product Groups: 45, 84

Date of Accounts	Dec 08	Dec 07	Dec 06
Working Capital	503	141	45
Fixed Assets	36	49	45
Current Assets	1593	3197	2877
Current Liabilities	1090	3056	2832
Total Share Capital	4000	3500	3500

Call Aid UK Ltd
50 Cornhill Road Carlton, Nottingham, NG4 1GE
Tel: 0115-940 0905 **Fax:** 0115-940 3369
E-mail: sales@callaiduk.com
Website: http://www.callaiduk.com
Directors: R. Gretton (MD), J. Gretton (Fin)
Immediate Holding Company: CALL AID UK LIMITED
Registration no: 03309012 **Date established:** 1997 **Turnover:** £1m - £2m
No.of Employees: 1 - 10 **Product Groups:** 37, 40, 63, 67

Date of Accounts	Jan 12	Jan 11	Jan 10
Working Capital	20	9	5
Fixed Assets	71	79	75
Current Assets	118	90	106

Canal Engineering Ltd
Lenton Lane, Nottingham, NG7 2PQ
Tel: 0115-986 6321 **Fax:** 0115-986 0211
E-mail: enquiries@canalengineering.co.uk
Website: http://www.canalengineering.co.uk
Managers: M. Dorey
Ultimate Holding Company: JOHN LORD HOLDINGS LIMITED
Immediate Holding Company: CANAL ENGINEERING LIMITED
Registration no: 04145340 **VAT No.:** GB 610 5096 75
Date established: 2001 **Turnover:** £10m - £20m
No.of Employees: 51 - 100 **Product Groups:** 48

Date of Accounts	Aug 11	Aug 10	Aug 09
Sales Turnover	N/A	6m	7m
Pre Tax Profit/Loss	N/A	96	13
Working Capital	799	659	529
Fixed Assets	382	518	619
Current Assets	2m	2m	2m
Current Liabilities	N/A	220	291

Canlin Castings Ltd
Eastview Terrace Langley Mill, Nottingham, NG16 4DF
Tel: 01773-715412 **Fax:** 01773-530434
E-mail: sales@canlincastings.co.uk
Website: http://www.canlincastings.co.uk
Directors: R. Canlin (Dir), A. Carlin (Dir)
Managers: M. Mogg
Immediate Holding Company: CANLIN CASTINGS LIMITED
Registration no: 00606574 **VAT No.:** GB 118 8627 47
Date established: 1958 **Turnover:** £500,000 - £1m
No.of Employees: 11 - 20 **Product Groups:** 34

Date of Accounts	Jun 11	Jun 10	Jun 09
Working Capital	274	237	232
Fixed Assets	271	269	300
Current Assets	686	543	471

Capatex Ltd
127 North Gate, Nottingham, NG7 7FZ
Tel: 0115-978 6111 **Fax:** 01933-664455
E-mail: sales@capatex.com
Website: http://www.capatex.com
Directors: G. Strauss (MD)
Immediate Holding Company: CAPATEX LIMITED
Registration no: 03025039 **Date established:** 1995
No.of Employees: 11 - 20 **Product Groups:** 22, 23, 24, 27, 29, 30, 32, 33, 35, 36, 37, 38, 39, 40, 42, 43, 45, 48, 49, 63, 65, 66, 67

Date of Accounts	May 10	May 09	May 08
Working Capital	936	912	865
Fixed Assets	103	124	146
Current Assets	2m	2m	1m

Castle Embroidering Ltd
Unit J Stonebridge Court Alfred Street South, Nottingham, NG3 2GY
Tel: 0115-947 2888 **Fax:** 0115-947 2888
E-mail: info@castle-embroidering.co.uk
Website: http://www.castle-embroidering.com
Directors: J. Flint (MD), H. Flint (Fin)
Immediate Holding Company: CASTLE EMBROIDERING LIMITED
Registration no: 04242451 **VAT No.:** GB 772 0818 26
Date established: 2001 **Turnover:** £250,000 - £500,000
No.of Employees: 1 - 10 **Product Groups:** 23, 49, 84

Date of Accounts	Jun 11	Jun 10	Jun 09
Working Capital	150	131	95
Fixed Assets	20	42	53
Current Assets	243	225	200

Castle Pumps Ltd
16 Farrington Way Eastwood, Nottingham, NG16 3BF
Tel: 0333-800 6006 **Fax:** 08451-664884
E-mail: sales@castlepumps.com
Website: http://www.castlepumps.com
Directors: K. Moore (MD)
Immediate Holding Company: CASTLE PUMPS LTD
Registration no: 06307240 **Date established:** 2007
Turnover: £500,000 - £1m **No.of Employees:** 1 - 10 **Product Groups:** 22, 23, 29, 30, 31, 33, 34, 35, 36, 37, 38, 39, 40, 41, 42, 43, 45, 46, 48, 49, 67, 68, 83

Date of Accounts	Jul 10	Jul 09	Jul 08
Working Capital	152	30	2
Fixed Assets	24	3	N/A
Current Assets	371	382	83

Cats Direct (Autospares (Sutton) Ltd)
Acton Road Long Eaton, Nottingham, NG10 1FR
Tel: 0115-983 5280 **Fax:** 0115-972 1112
E-mail: mail@cats-direct.com
Website: http://www.cats-direct-shop.co.uk
Managers: C. Brown (District Mgr)
Turnover: £5m - £10m **No.of Employees:** 101 - 250 **Product Groups:** 39, 40, 68

Central Soucre Ltd
Harris House Moorbridge Road Bingham, Nottingham, NG13 8GG
Tel: 01949-836622 **Fax:** 01949-836662
E-mail: ken.miller@central-source.co.uk
Website: http://www.cs-uk.com
Bank(s): Barclays Bedford
Directors: K. Miller (MD), K. Miller (Dir), J. Miller (Co Sec), J. Miller (Fin)
Managers: S. Holt (Accounts)
Immediate Holding Company: CENTRAL SOURCE LIMITED
Registration no: 02610384 **VAT No.:** GB 196 2534 40
Date established: 1991 **Turnover:** £1m - £2m **No.of Employees:** 11 - 20
Product Groups: 26, 30, 39, 40, 41, 45

Date of Accounts	May 12	May 11	May 10
Working Capital	317	292	212
Fixed Assets	70	106	130

Current Assets	633	673	696

Centralised Services Marketing Ltd
Piccadilly, Nottingham, NG6 9FN
Tel: 0115-927 9127 **Fax:** 0115-977 0744
E-mail: centser@btconnect.com
Website: http://www.centralisedservices.co.uk
Directors: D. Morley (Dir), W. Morley (MD)
Immediate Holding Company: CENTRALISED SERVICES (MARKETING) LIMITED
Registration no: 01426897 **VAT No.:** GB 352 6466 47
Date established: 1979 **Turnover:** £500,000 - £1m
No.of Employees: 1 - 10 **Product Groups:** 27, 28, 36

Date of Accounts	Apr 08	Apr 07	Apr 06
Working Capital	-43	-40	-19
Fixed Assets	14	16	19
Current Assets	26	30	51
Current Liabilities	69	70	70

Charnvel Ltd
Charnvel House Canterbury Road, Nottingham, NG8 1PQ
Tel: 0115-985 4000 **Fax:** 0115-985 5558
E-mail: maria.kirby@charnvel.co.uk
Website: http://www.charnvel.co.uk
Bank(s): National Westminster Bank Plc
Directors: S. Kirby (Dir), M. Kirby (Fin)
Managers: P. Stoves (Mgr)
Ultimate Holding Company: CHARNVEL (NOTTINGHAM) LIMITED
Immediate Holding Company: CHARNVEL LIMITED
Registration no: 02238866 **Date established:** 1988
Turnover: £500,000 - £1m **No.of Employees:** 11 - 20
Product Groups: 35, 37, 40, 67

Date of Accounts	May 11	May 10	May 09
Working Capital	2m	2m	2m
Fixed Assets	79	76	99
Current Assets	2m	2m	2m

Chinal Managment Services
215 University Boulevard Beeston, Nottingham, NG9 2GJ
Tel: 0115-922 5735 **Fax:** 0115-922 6142
E-mail: training@harrymitchell.fsbusiness.co.uk
Website: http://www.harrymitchell.co.uk
Directors: E. Chinal (Dir)
Immediate Holding Company: MANHAO FOUNDATION
Registration no: 00793926 **Date established:** 2011 **Turnover:** £2m - £5m
No.of Employees: 1 - 10 **Product Groups:** 80

Chronos B T H Ltd
Unit 1 Centurion Business Park, Nottingham, NG6 8WN
Tel: 0115-935 1351 **Fax:** 0115-960 6941
E-mail: ormp@premiertech.com
Website: http://www.chronosbth.com
Managers: P. Orme (Chief Mgr)
Ultimate Holding Company: PREMIER TECH LTD (CANADA)
Immediate Holding Company: CHRONOS BTH LIMITED
Registration no: 01715650 **Date established:** 1983 **Turnover:** £2m - £5m
No.of Employees: 21 - 50 **Product Groups:** 38, 45, 67

Date of Accounts	Feb 08	Feb 11	Feb 10
Sales Turnover	4m	4m	3m
Pre Tax Profit/Loss	417	-97	206
Working Capital	682	971	979
Fixed Assets	149	104	176
Current Assets	1m	2m	2m
Current Liabilities	292	727	347

Chubb Electronic Security Ltd
Oaktree House 2 Phoenix Place Phoenix Court, Nottingham, NG8 6BA
Tel: 0115-922 8338 **Fax:** 0115-943 6866
E-mail: nottingham@chubb.co.uk
Website: http://www.chubb.co.uk
Bank(s): National Westminster Bank Plc
Managers: D. Bolderson (District Mgr), C. Leivers (District Mgr)
Immediate Holding Company: Chubb Group Security Ltd
Registration no: 00524469 **No.of Employees:** 21 - 50
Product Groups: 36, 37, 40

Churchill Steeplejacks UK Ltd (Nottingham)
Unit 3 Brookside Road Ruddington, Nottingham, NG11 6AT
Tel: 0115-984 1600 **Fax:** 0115-984 1194
E-mail: wayne@churchsteeple.co.uk
Website: http://www.churchillrefurbishment.co.uk
Directors: S. Murry (MD), W. Murry (Sales), D. Murray (Dir)
Managers: A. Cabourn
Immediate Holding Company: CHURCHILL STEEPLEJACKS (U.K.) LIMITED
Registration no: 07332657 **Date established:** 2010
No.of Employees: 1 - 10 **Product Groups:** 84

City Electrical Factors Ltd
Unit 3 Saxondale Court Leen Drive Hucknall Lane, Nottingham, NG6 8AD
Tel: 0115-975 7317 **Fax:** 0115-975 7405
Website: http://www.cef.co.uk
Managers: L. Barks (District Mgr)
Ultimate Holding Company: CEF HOLDINGS LIMITED
Immediate Holding Company: CITY ELECTRICAL FACTORS LIMITED
Registration no: 00336408 **Date established:** 1938
Turnover: £250m - £500m **No.of Employees:** 1 - 10 **Product Groups:** 37, 40

Date of Accounts	Apr 11	Apr 10	Apr 09
Sales Turnover	439m	406m	444m
Pre Tax Profit/Loss	22m	26m	34m
Working Capital	53m	172m	164m
Fixed Assets	13m	17m	18m
Current Assets	179m	250m	227m
Current Liabilities	53m	23m	20m

Cleansmart Ltd
2 Phoenix Court Finch Close, Nottingham, NG7 2PU
Tel: 0115-824 0034
Website: http://www.cleansmartsupplies.co.uk
Directors: M. Flewitt (MD)
Immediate Holding Company: CLEANSMART LIMITED
Registration no: 05595775 **Date established:** 2005
No.of Employees: 1 - 10 **Product Groups:** 32, 40

Date of Accounts	Mar 11	Mar 10	Mar 09
Working Capital	27	-6	-19
Fixed Assets	53	60	66
Current Assets	175	125	87

Clippa Safe Ltd

Lanthwaite Road, Nottingham, NG11 8LD
Tel: 0115-921 1899 **Fax:** 0115-984 5554
E-mail: sales@clippasafe.co.uk
Website: http://www.clippasafe.co.uk
Bank(s): National Westminster Bank Plc
Directors: R. Cheetham (MD), G. Cheetham (MD), R. Cheetham (MD)
Managers: R. Scott (Sales Prom Mgr)
Immediate Holding Company: CLIPPASAFE LIMITED
Registration no: 00599132 **VAT No.:** GB 117 3023 13
Date established: 1958 **Turnover:** £2m - £5m **No.of Employees:** 21 - 50
Product Groups: 22

Date of Accounts	Jan 11	Jan 10	Jan 09
Working Capital	897	637	803
Fixed Assets	64	67	61
Current Assets	1m	1m	1m
Current Liabilities	N/A	3	N/A

Cole Fabrics plc

3 Ludlow Hill Road West Bridgford, Nottingham, NG2 6HF
Tel: 0115-923 6000 **Fax:** 0115-923 3274
E-mail: info@colefabrics.com
Website: http://www.colefabrics.com
Bank(s): Barclays
Directors: S. Forster (Co Sec)
Immediate Holding Company: COLE FABRICS PLC
Registration no: 02150561 **VAT No.:** GB 520 6300 01
Date established: 1987 **Turnover:** £5m - £10m
No.of Employees: 51 - 100 **Product Groups:** 23

Date of Accounts	Jan 12	Jan 11	Jan 10
Sales Turnover	9m	9m	10m
Pre Tax Profit/Loss	233	394	743
Working Capital	3m	3m	3m
Fixed Assets	639	698	751
Current Assets	4m	4m	4m
Current Liabilities	272	393	528

Colsalake Ltd

6 Eldon Road Industrial Estate Attenborough, Beeston, Nottingham, NG9 6DZ
Tel: 0115-943 1558 **Fax:** 0115-925 0990
E-mail: colsalakeltd@aol.com
Website: http://www.precisiongears.co.uk
Directors: D. Brailsford (MD)
Immediate Holding Company: COLSALAKE LIMITED
Registration no: 01676415 **VAT No.:** GB 385 2253 45
Date established: 1982 **No.of Employees:** 1 - 10 **Product Groups:** 35

Date of Accounts	Jun 12	Jun 11	Jun 10
Working Capital	65	106	123
Fixed Assets	31	37	44
Current Assets	137	207	185

Colwick Instruments Ltd

PO Box 8268, Nottingham, NG3 6AJ
Tel: 0115-962 2999 **Fax:** 0115-961 4582
E-mail: enquires@colwickinstruments.co.uk
Website: http://www.colwickinstruments.co.uk
Directors: D. Cameron (MD)
Immediate Holding Company: COLWICK INSTRUMENTS LIMITED
Registration no: 01460590 **VAT No.:** GB 309 8566 26
Date established: 1979 **No.of Employees:** 1 - 10 **Product Groups:** 31, 38

Date of Accounts	Dec 10	Dec 09	Dec 08
Working Capital	-19	-11	-2
Fixed Assets	2	1	2
Current Assets	24	33	34

Complete Tools & Fixings

Evans Yard Piccadilly, Nottingham, NG6 9FN
Tel: 0115-975 3761 **Fax:** 0115-975 3819
E-mail: info@completetools.co.uk
Website: http://www.comptools.co.uk
Directors: J. Wardell (Ptnr)
Immediate Holding Company: COMPLETE TOOLS AND FIXINGS LIMITED
Registration no: 06505890 **Date established:** 2008
No.of Employees: 1 - 10 **Product Groups:** 35, 48, 66

Date of Accounts	Mar 12	Mar 11	Mar 10
Working Capital	35	43	45
Fixed Assets	74	87	100
Current Assets	228	270	273

Conquer Pest Control Ltd

Chestnut Farm Chestnut Lane, Barton-In-Fabis, Nottingham, NG11 0AE
Tel: 0115-983 0735 **Fax:** 0115-983 1229
E-mail: info@conquerpestcontrol.co.uk
Website: http://www.conquerpestcontrol.co.uk
Directors: H. Mott (Dir)
Immediate Holding Company: CONQUER PEST CONTROL LIMITED
Registration no: 05860978 **Date established:** 2006
No.of Employees: 1 - 10 **Product Groups:** 52

Date of Accounts	Jul 11	Jul 10	Jul 09
Working Capital	-0	3	-2
Fixed Assets	64	41	37
Current Assets	136	124	108

Jim Cooper

71 Main Street Burton Joyce, Nottingham, NG14 5ED
Tel: 0115-931 2931
E-mail: jimwc66@aol.com
Website: http://www.jimcooper.co.uk
Directors: J. Cooper (Prop)
Immediate Holding Company: FUNKY FEET LTD
Date established: 2007 **No.of Employees:** 1 - 10 **Product Groups:** 36, 40

Cooper M E D C (Inc. Next Two)

2 Colliery Road Pinxton, Nottingham, NG16 6JF
Tel: 01773-864100 **Fax:** 01773-582800
E-mail: medc.admin@cooperindustries.com
Website: http://www.coopermedc.com
Managers: E. Boot (Admin Off)
Ultimate Holding Company: COOPER INDUSTRIES LTD (BERMUDA)
Immediate Holding Company: COOPER MEDC LIMITED
Registration no: 01202172 **VAT No.:** GB 127 5666 51
Date established: 1975 **Turnover:** £10m - £20m **No.of Employees:** 1 - 10
Product Groups: 37, 39, 40

Date of Accounts	Dec 11	Dec 10	Dec 09
Sales Turnover	23m	19m	19m
Pre Tax Profit/Loss	7m	5m	5m
Working Capital	4m	-1m	17m
Fixed Assets	2m	2m	2m
Current Assets	10m	6m	37m
Current Liabilities	4m	4m	3m

Cooper Parry

14 Park Row, Nottingham, NG1 6GR
Tel: 0115-958 0212 **Fax:** 0115-958 8800
E-mail: advice@cooperparry.com
Website: http://www.cooperparry.com
Directors: C. Shaw (Ch)
Ultimate Holding Company: COOPER PARRY LLP
Immediate Holding Company: COOPER PARRY WEALTH STRATEGIES LIMITED
Registration no: 04220777 **Date established:** 2001
Turnover: £500,000 - £1m **No.of Employees:** 1 - 10 **Product Groups:** 80, 82

Date of Accounts	Apr 12	Apr 11	Apr 10
Sales Turnover	1m	1m	921
Pre Tax Profit/Loss	20	-55	943
Working Capital	231	168	429
Fixed Assets	1m	1m	1m
Current Assets	397	637	1m
Current Liabilities	156	194	136

Copley Scientific Ltd

Colwick Quays Business Park Road No 2, Colwick, Nottingham, NG4 2JY
Tel: 0115-961 6229 **Fax:** 0115-961 7637
E-mail: sales@copleyscientific.co.uk
Website: http://www.copleyscientific.com
Bank(s): National Westminster Bank Plc
Directors: A. Copley (Dir)
Immediate Holding Company: COPLEY SCIENTIFIC LIMITED
Registration no: 01390012 **Date established:** 1978 **Turnover:** £2m - £5m
No.of Employees: 11 - 20 **Product Groups:** 38, 42

Date of Accounts	Dec 11	Dec 10	Dec 09
Working Capital	2m	1m	1m
Fixed Assets	648	640	685
Current Assets	3m	2m	2m

Cormans

Mancor House Bolsover Street, Hucknall, Nottingham, NG15 7TZ
Tel: 0115-963 2268 **Fax:** 0115-963 2062
Directors: M. Holland (MD), M. Wright (Fin)
Immediate Holding Company: S. CORMAN (CALVERTON) LIMITED
Registration no: 00364800 **Date established:** 1941
Turnover: Up to £250,000 **No.of Employees:** 1 - 10 **Product Groups:** 63

Date of Accounts	Jan 12	Jan 11	Jan 10
Sales Turnover	N/A	167	172
Pre Tax Profit/Loss	N/A	-45	12
Working Capital	16	16	61
Current Assets	47	41	83
Current Liabilities	N/A	25	21

Cornish Engineering Ltd

Popham Street, Nottingham, NG1 7JD
Tel: 0115-950 4944 **Fax:** 0115-950 4215
Directors: W. Lewin (MD), S. Davies (Fin)
Immediate Holding Company: CORNISH ENGINEERING,LIMITED
Registration no: 00386609 **VAT No.:** GB 116 3038 06
Date established: 1944 **Turnover:** Up to £250,000
No.of Employees: 1 - 10 **Product Groups:** 35, 84

Date of Accounts	Mar 12	Mar 11	Mar 10
Working Capital	660	619	604
Fixed Assets	4	4	3
Current Assets	709	653	651

Courtaulds

Box 54 Haydn Road, Nottingham, NG5 1DH
Tel: 0115-924 6100 **Fax:** 0115-924 6101
Website: http://www.prettypolly.co.uk
Directors: M. Ellis (Fin)
Ultimate Holding Company: SARA LEE CORPORATION (USA)
Immediate Holding Company: COURTAULDS LIMITED
Registration no: 03609524 **VAT No.:** GB 558 8297 79
Date established: 1998 **Turnover:** £2m - £5m **No.of Employees:** 51 - 100
Product Groups: 28, 61

Cresswell Sewing Machines

83 Mansfield Road Daybrook, Nottingham, NG5 6BH
Tel: 0115-926 7572 **Fax:** 0115-926 7572
Directors: G. Creswell (Prop)
Date established: 1999 **No.of Employees:** 1 - 10 **Product Groups:** 43

Cross Electrical Nottingham Ltd

Trace Works Debdale Lane, Keyworth, Nottingham, NG12 5HN
Tel: 0115-937 5121 **Fax:** 0115-937 5116
E-mail: david.rogers@cross-electrical.co.uk
Website: http://www.cross-electrical.co.uk
Directors: C. Ross (MD)
Immediate Holding Company: CROSS ELECTRICAL (NOTTINGHAM) LIMITED
Registration no: 01119059 **VAT No.:** GB 118 0530 05
Date established: 1973 **No.of Employees:** 1 - 10 **Product Groups:** 29, 30, 33, 35, 37, 38, 40, 42, 52, 66, 84

Date of Accounts	Jun 11	Jun 10	Jun 09
Working Capital	-41	-71	-137
Fixed Assets	250	235	257
Current Assets	246	200	181

Crusader Ltd

Oxford House Easthorpe Street, Ruddington, Nottingham, NG11 6LA
Tel: 0115-940 5550 **Fax:** 0115-940 6660
E-mail: info@crusaderltd.com
Website: http://www.crusaderltd.com
Bank(s): Bank of Scotland
Directors: K. Soden Barton (Dir), R. Evans (Asst MD)
Immediate Holding Company: CRUSADER LIMITED
Registration no: 02197455 **VAT No.:** GB 413 2321 10
Date established: 1987 **No.of Employees:** 21 - 50 **Product Groups:** 44

Date of Accounts	Mar 11	Mar 10	Mar 09
Working Capital	321	278	204
Fixed Assets	75	68	69
Current Assets	802	863	1m

Custom Frames

Mitre Studios Second Avenue Greasley Street, Nottingham, NG6 8NE
Tel: 0115-979 4604 **Fax:** 0115-976 4606
E-mail: studio@custom-frames.co.uk
Website: http://www.custom-frames.co.uk
Directors: A. Carlisle (MD)
Immediate Holding Company: CUSTOM FRAMES PICTURE FRAMING LIMITED
Registration no: 04676326 **Date established:** 2003
No.of Employees: 1 - 10 **Product Groups:** 25, 26, 30, 36

Date of Accounts	Mar 11	Mar 09	Mar 08
Working Capital	-30	-34	-36
Fixed Assets	34	41	45
Current Assets	43	-34	45

D G B Refrigeration Ltd

Unit 2 Salisbury Street, Nottingham, NG7 2BE
Tel: 0115-979 0260 **Fax:** 0115-942 3122
E-mail: gary@dgb-refrigeration.co.uk
Website: http://www.dgb-refrigeration.co.uk
Directors: G. Barlow (Dir)
Immediate Holding Company: DGB REFRIGERATION LIMITED
Registration no: 02888847 **Date established:** 1994
No.of Employees: 11 - 20 **Product Groups:** 40, 66

Date of Accounts	Jan 12	Jan 11	Jan 10
Working Capital	49	32	209
Fixed Assets	9	9	10
Current Assets	153	194	231

D & G Filters Ltd

Unit 2 Washdyke Lane Hucknall, Nottingham, NG15 6NH
Tel: 0115-953 3488 **Fax:** 0115-953 3788
E-mail: sales@d-gfilters.co.uk
Website: http://www.d-gfilters.co.uk
Directors: D. Faulkner (MD)
Immediate Holding Company: D & G FILTERS LIMITED
Registration no: 03510150 **Date established:** 1998
No.of Employees: 1 - 10 **Product Groups:** 38, 42

Date of Accounts	Mar 12	Mar 11	Mar 10
Working Capital	176	72	101
Fixed Assets	11	7	5
Current Assets	315	149	191

D S L Systems Ltd

Adbolton Hall Adbolton Lane, West Bridgford, Nottingham, NG2 5AS
Tel: 0115-981 3700 **Fax:** 0115-813702
E-mail: matthewswallow@dsl-systems.co.uk
Website: http://www.dsl-systems.com
Directors: M. Swallow (MD)
Immediate Holding Company: DSL SYSTEMS HOLDINGS LIMITED
Registration no: 05423261 **VAT No.:** GB 309 6533 51
Date established: 2005 **Turnover:** £500,000 - £1m
No.of Employees: 11 - 20 **Product Groups:** 84

Date of Accounts	Aug 11	Aug 10	Aug 09
Working Capital	-22	-21	-102
Fixed Assets	925	925	925

D S M Industrial Engineering Ltd

Nottingham Road Beeston, Nottingham, NG9 6DP
Tel: 0115-925 5927 **Fax:** 0115-925 8456
E-mail: enquiries@dsmstainlessproducts.co.uk
Website: http://www.dsmstainlessproducts.co.uk
Bank(s): The Royal Bank of Scotland
Directors: G. Davies (MD)
Ultimate Holding Company: GMVC INVESTMENTS LIMITED
Immediate Holding Company: DSM INDUSTRIAL ENGINEERING LIMITED
Registration no: 02743862 **VAT No.:** GB 610 4594 64
Date established: 1992 **Turnover:** £500,000 - £1m
No.of Employees: 11 - 20 **Product Groups:** 26

Date of Accounts	Oct 11	Oct 10	Oct 09
Working Capital	401	482	473
Fixed Assets	642	242	259
Current Assets	514	590	581

D42 Thermal Ltd

46 Cavendish Street Arnold, Nottingham, NG5 7DL
Tel: 07581-218299
E-mail: csmith@dept-42.co.uk
Website: http://www.d42thermal.co.uk
Managers: C. Smith
Registration no: 7413217 **Date established:** 2010 **Turnover:**
No.of Employees: 1 - 10 **Product Groups:** 29, 37, 38, 40

Dacrylate Paints Ltd

Lime Street Kirkby-In-Ashfield, Nottingham, NG17 8AL
Tel: 01623-753845 **Fax:** 01623-757151
E-mail: sales@dacrylate.co.uk
Website: http://www.dacrylate.co.uk
Bank(s): Barclays
Directors: S. Watkins (Co Sec), D. Eames (MD)
Ultimate Holding Company: DACRYLATE LIMITED
Immediate Holding Company: DACRYLATE PAINTS LIMITED
Registration no: 01744820 **VAT No.:** GB 116 6542 77
Date established: 1983 **Turnover:** £2m - £5m **No.of Employees:** 21 - 50
Product Groups: 32

Date of Accounts	Aug 11	Aug 10	Aug 09
Working Capital	2m	2m	1m
Fixed Assets	92	50	64
Current Assets	2m	2m	2m

Data Technologies Ltd

Gothic House Barker Gate, Nottingham, NG1 1JU
Tel: 0115-840 5500 **Fax:** 0870-122 0668
E-mail: enquiries@datatechnologies.co.uk
Website: http://www.datatechnologies.co.uk
Directors: A. Howard (Prop)
Immediate Holding Company: DATA TECHNOLOGIES LIMITED
Registration no: 02819888 **VAT No.:** GB 664 5136 30
Date established: 1993 **Turnover:** Up to £250,000
No.of Employees: 1 - 10 **Product Groups:** 44

Date of Accounts	Mar 11	Mar 10	Mar 05
Working Capital	17	17	102
Fixed Assets	106	106	5
Current Assets	19	17	103

Data Com Technology Ltd

45 Trent View Gardens Radcliffe-On-Trent, Nottingham, NG12 1AY
Tel: 0115-847 8756 **Fax:** 0115-933 3868
E-mail: simon_tomlinson@ntlworld.com
Website: http://www.datcomtechology.co.uk
Directors: S. Tomlinson (MD)
Immediate Holding Company: DATACOM TECHNOLOGY LTD
Registration no: 06390312 **Date established:** 2007
No.of Employees: 1 - 10 **Product Groups:** 37

Date of Accounts	Mar 11	Mar 10	Mar 09
Working Capital	N/A	-5	-5
Fixed Assets	3	5	6
Current Assets	34	62	38

John Deere Ltd
Harby Road Langar, Nottingham, NG13 9HT
Tel: 01949-860491 **Fax:** 01949-860490
E-mail: richardjohnson@johndeere.com
Website: http://www.johndeere.co.uk
Bank(s): Barclays
Directors: G. Day (Mkt Research), R. Johnson (MD), S. Baty (Co Sec)
Managers: M. Gardner (Personnel)
Ultimate Holding Company: DEERE & COMPANY (USA)
Immediate Holding Company: JOHN DEERE LIMITED
Registration no: SC028492 **Date established:** 1951
Turnover: £250m - £500m **No.of Employees:** 51 - 100
Product Groups: 41, 61, 67

Date of Accounts	Oct 11	Oct 10	Oct 09
Sales Turnover	479m	395m	409m
Pre Tax Profit/Loss	12m	15m	21m
Working Capital	44m	36m	25m
Fixed Assets	12m	12m	12m
Current Assets	738m	451m	347m
Current Liabilities	53m	38m	26m

D M S Ltd
Brookhill Industrial Estate Pinxton, Nottingham, NG16 6NT
Tel: 01773-534555 **Fax:** 01773-534666
E-mail: sales@dmsltd.com
Website: http://www.dmsltd.com
Directors: C. Minns (Sales)
Immediate Holding Company: DIRECT METERING SUPPLIES LIMITED
Registration no: 03652700 **VAT No.:** GB 745 6830 09
Date established: 1998 **No.of Employees:** 1 - 10 **Product Groups:** 33, 35, 36, 38, 41, 43, 49, 67

Djanogly City Academy Nottingham
Sherwood Rise Nottingham Road, Nottingham, NG7 7AR
Tel: 0115-942 4422 **Fax:** 0115-942 4034
E-mail: info@djanogly.notts.sch.uk
Website: http://www.djanogly.notts.sch.uk
Bank(s): HSBC Bank plc
Directors: N. Acres (Mkt Research), R. Dunmore (Co Sec), R. Kenyon (Dir), R. Potter (Head)
Managers: C. Edey (I.T. Exec)
Immediate Holding Company: DJANOGLY LEARNING TRUST
Registration no: 04544722 **Date established:** 2002
Turnover: £10m - £20m **No.of Employees:** 101 - 250 **Product Groups:** 86

Date of Accounts	Aug 11	Aug 10	Aug 09
Sales Turnover	13m	13m	13m
Pre Tax Profit/Loss	-308	-279	46
Working Capital	2m	2m	2m
Fixed Assets	19m	19m	20m
Current Assets	3m	3m	4m
Current Liabilities	1m	709	1m

Douglas Gill Ltd
429 Tamworth Road Long Eaton, Nottingham, NG10 3JT
Tel: 0115-973 5251 **Fax:** 0115-946 0855
E-mail: rod@douglasgill.co.uk
Website: http://www.douglasgill.co.uk
Directors: R. Gill (MD)
Immediate Holding Company: DOUGLAS GILL LIMITED
Registration no: 00498611 **VAT No.:** GB 125 3900 09
Date established: 1951 **Turnover:** £1m - £2m **No.of Employees:** 1 - 10
Product Groups: 23

Date of Accounts	Aug 11	Aug 10	Aug 09
Working Capital	775	887	1m
Fixed Assets	177	139	38
Current Assets	860	1m	1m

Drain Centre a division of Wolseley UK Ltd
Nottingham Science & Technology Park, Nottingham, NG7 2RG
Tel: 0115-925 2108 **Fax:** 0115-943 0349
E-mail: graham.helleywell@wolsley.co.uk
Website: http://www.plumbcenter.co.uk
Managers: G. Helleywell (Mgr)
Immediate Holding Company: WSV HOLDINGS LIMITED
Registration no: 03855020 **Date established:** 1989
No.of Employees: 1 - 10 **Product Groups:** 30, 31, 36, 39, 40, 42, 48, 66

Duresta Upholstery Ltd
Fields Farm Road Long Eaton, Nottingham, NG10 3FZ
Tel: 0115-973 7000 **Fax:** 0115-946 1028
E-mail: uksales@duresta.co.uk
Website: http://www.duresta.co.uk
Bank(s): Barclays, Cardiff
Directors: J. Moore (Sales), M. Cottam (Fin), C. Swann (Chief Op Offcr), C. Kenyon Brown (MD)
Managers: S. Wills, J. Atkinson (Purch Mgr), A. Gower
Immediate Holding Company: DURESTA UPHOLSTERY LIMITED
Registration no: 00341415 **VAT No.:** GB 133 4836 74
Date established: 1938 **Turnover:** £10m - £20m
No.of Employees: 101 - 250 **Product Groups:** 26

Date of Accounts	Dec 07	Jun 11	Jun 10
Sales Turnover	18m	16m	15m
Pre Tax Profit/Loss	2m	623	432
Working Capital	8m	8m	8m
Fixed Assets	532	208	348
Current Assets	11m	11m	11m
Current Liabilities	2m	962	N/A

Dynamite Baits Ltd
Wolds Farm The Fosse, Cotgrave, Nottingham, NG12 3HG
Tel: 0115-989 9060 **Fax:** 0115-989 4254
E-mail: info@dynamitebaits.com
Website: http://www.dynamitebaits.com
Managers: A. Sherwin, L. Brooks (Purch Mgr)
Immediate Holding Company: DYNAMITE BAITS LIMITED
Registration no: 04338458 **Date established:** 2001
Turnover: £250,000 - £500,000 **No.of Employees:** 51 - 100
Product Groups: 01, 20

Date of Accounts	Dec 11	Dec 10	Dec 09
Sales Turnover	7m	7m	N/A
Pre Tax Profit/Loss	-683	192	N/A
Working Capital	-92	809	454
Fixed Assets	1m	1m	1m
Current Assets	3m	2m	1m
Current Liabilities	404	199	N/A

E C S Engineering
Brookhill Industrial Estate Pinxton, Nottingham, NG16 6NS
Tel: 01773-860001 **Fax:** 01773-810003
E-mail: gjordan@ecsengineeringservices.com
Website: http://www.ecsengineering.com
Bank(s): Barclays, Mansfield
Directors: K. Robinson (Co Sec), P. Anderson (MD), G. Jordan (MD)
Managers: B. Godfrey (Mktg Serv Mgr), C. Kennedey (Purch Mgr)
Immediate Holding Company: ECS ENGINEERING SERVICES LTD.
Registration no: 02454269 **VAT No.:** GB 646 7106 31
Date established: 1989 **Turnover:** £5m - £10m
No.of Employees: 51 - 100 **Product Groups:** 85

Date of Accounts	Mar 12	Mar 11	Mar 10
Sales Turnover	10m	9m	10m
Pre Tax Profit/Loss	-140	212	458
Working Capital	49	121	-79
Fixed Assets	859	755	886
Current Assets	4m	3m	3m
Current Liabilities	2m	2m	2m

E C S Nottingham Ltd
Unit 17 Hazelford Way, Newstead Village, Nottingham, NG15 0DQ
Tel: 01623-720444 **Fax:** 01623-720445
E-mail: uksales@ecsnotts.co.uk
Website: http://www.ecsnottingham.co.uk
Directors: N. Fletcher (MD)
Managers: P. Sivorn (Fin Mgr), D. Gilbert (Buyer), R. Glen (Ops Mgr), R. Saxton (Mgr)
Immediate Holding Company: ECS (NOTTINGHAM) LIMITED
Registration no: 02639956 **Date established:** 1991 **Turnover:** £5m - £10m
No.of Employees: 21 - 50 **Product Groups:** 44, 80, 81

Date of Accounts	Aug 11	Aug 10	Aug 09
Sales Turnover	10m	N/A	N/A
Pre Tax Profit/Loss	83	N/A	N/A
Working Capital	168	166	148
Fixed Assets	305	298	337
Current Assets	4m	3m	2m
Current Liabilities	189	N/A	N/A

E R F Electrical Wholesalers Ltd
Salop Street Daybrook, Nottingham, NG5 6HD
Tel: 0115-920 3960 **Fax:** 0115-967 3866
E-mail: robincombellack@erfelectrical.co.uk
Website: http://www.erfelectrical.co.uk
Bank(s): Barclays
Directors: A. Smith (Fin)
Managers: V. Partridge (Tech Serv Mgr), C. Robins (Personnel), A. Laycock (Sales & Mktg Mg), J. Branley (Fin Mgr)
Immediate Holding Company: ERF ELECTRICAL WHOLESALERS LTD.
Registration no: 00911692 **VAT No.:** GB 116 2206 16
Date established: 1967 **Turnover:** £20m - £50m
No.of Employees: 11 - 20 **Product Groups:** 67

Date of Accounts	Dec 11	Dec 10	Dec 09
Sales Turnover	22m	21m	21m
Pre Tax Profit/Loss	20	117	40
Working Capital	1m	1m	1m
Fixed Assets	779	733	729
Current Assets	7m	6m	6m
Current Liabilities	492	468	662

Eagle Scientific Ltd
Regent House Lenton Street, Sandiacre, Nottingham, NG10 5DJ
Tel: 0115-949 1111 **Fax:** 0115-939 1144
E-mail: vijay.mehan@eagle-scientific.co.uk
Website: http://www.eagle-scientific.co.uk
Bank(s): National Westminster Bank Plc
Directors: V. Mehan (Dir)
Immediate Holding Company: EAGLE SCIENTIFIC LIMITED
Registration no: 01446445 **VAT No.:** GB 340 1561 00
Date established: 1979 **Turnover:** £5m - £10m **No.of Employees:** 21 - 50
Product Groups: 27, 28, 31, 32, 33, 38, 42, 47, 63, 64, 67

Date of Accounts	Mar 11	Mar 10	Mar 09
Sales Turnover	10m	8m	N/A
Pre Tax Profit/Loss	974	297	307
Working Capital	2m	901	904
Fixed Assets	754	765	789
Current Assets	5m	2m	3m
Current Liabilities	N/A	112	136

Emics Calibration Services
248 Radford Boulevard Radford, Nottingham, NG7 5QG
Tel: 0115-942 4748 **Fax:** 0115-942 4746
E-mail: garyswift@emics.co.uk
Website: http://www.emics.co.uk
Directors: G. Swift (Dir), S. Tingey (Dir), S. Moss (Co Sec)
Immediate Holding Company: E.M.I.C.S. Ltd
Registration no: 02999227 **Date established:** 1994
No.of Employees: 21 - 50 **Product Groups:** 38, 85

Date of Accounts	Dec 09	Dec 08	Dec 07
Working Capital	256	125	109
Fixed Assets	120	178	134
Current Assets	549	294	307

Equinox
5 Papplewick Lane Hucknall, Nottingham, NG15 7TN
Tel: 0115-964 1999 **Fax:** 0115-964 1999
E-mail: tmitford@btinternet.com
Directors: T. Mitford (Prop)
Immediate Holding Company: BROOKS MOBILITY LTD
Registration no: 06145811 **Date established:** 2007
No.of Employees: 1 - 10 **Product Groups:** 38, 42

ERIKS UK (Nottingham Service Centre)
Industrial Distribution Service Centre Unit 12 Robin Hood Industrial Estate, Nottingham, NG3 1GE
Tel: 0115-958 1312 **Fax:** 0115-958 1279
E-mail: nottingham@eriks.co.uk
Website: http://www.eriks.co.uk
Managers: J. Cole (Sales Admin)
Immediate Holding Company: GRAHAM ROBERTS PLASTICS LIMITED
Registration no: 00917112 **Date established:** 1969 **Turnover:** £5m - £10m
No.of Employees: 1 - 10 **Product Groups:** 66

Esprit Automation
Placketts Mill Church Drive, Sandiacre, Nottingham, NG10 5EE
Tel: 0115-939 1888
Website: http://www.esprit-automation.co.uk
Directors: G. Smith (MD)
Managers: G. McGuire (Sales Prom Mgr)
Immediate Holding Company: ESPRIT AUTOMATION LIMITED
Registration no: 02113853 **Date established:** 1987
No.of Employees: 21 - 50 **Product Groups:** 46

Date of Accounts	Mar 11	Mar 10	Mar 09
Working Capital	1m	1m	1m
Fixed Assets	212	125	183
Current Assets	3m	3m	3m

European Conveyor Systems
Pintail Close Netherfield, Nottingham, NG4 2SG
Tel: 0115-987 4363 **Fax:** 0115-987 6281
E-mail: sales@europeanconveyors.co.uk
Website: http://www.europeanconveyors.co.uk
Directors: J. Bower (Dir)
Ultimate Holding Company: EUROPEAN CONVEYOR SYSTEMS (HOLDINGS) LIMITED
Immediate Holding Company: EUROPEAN CONVEYOR SYSTEMS LIMITED
Registration no: 02726514 **Date established:** 1992 **Turnover:** £2m - £5m
No.of Employees: 11 - 20 **Product Groups:** 35, 39, 45

Date of Accounts	Dec 11	Jul 10	Jul 09
Sales Turnover	N/A	3m	4m
Pre Tax Profit/Loss	N/A	8	123
Working Capital	1m	1m	970
Fixed Assets	85	195	189
Current Assets	3m	3m	3m
Current Liabilities	N/A	909	1m

Eversheds
1 Royal Standard Place, Nottingham, NG1 6FZ
Tel: 0115-950 7000 **Fax:** 0115-950 7111
E-mail: nottingham@eversheds.com
Website: http://www.eversheds.com
Directors: C. Underwood (Fin), B. Hughes (Grp Chief Exec)
Ultimate Holding Company: ACORDIS BV (NETHERLANDS)
Immediate Holding Company: STG PREDECESSORS LIMITED
Registration no: OC304065 **VAT No.:** GB 109 4602 84
Date established: 2006 **No.of Employees:** 101 - 250 **Product Groups:** 80

Date of Accounts	Dec 11	Dec 10	Dec 09
Sales Turnover	28	1m	2m
Pre Tax Profit/Loss	-726	-678	-855
Working Capital	3m	4m	5m
Current Assets	3m	4m	7m
Current Liabilities	332	415	1m

Experian plc
Landmark House Experian Way Ng2 Business Park, Nottingham, NG80 1ZZ
Tel: 08700-121111 **Fax:** 0870-196 8200
E-mail: info@experian.com
Website: http://www.experian.co.uk
Bank(s): Barclays
Directors: C. Boundy (MD)
Ultimate Holding Company: EXPERIAN PLC (JERSEY)
Immediate Holding Company: EXPERIAN LIMITED
Registration no: 00653331 **VAT No.:** 503 1947 69 **Date established:** 1960
Turnover: £250m - £500m **No.of Employees:** 1501 & over
Product Groups: 80, 81

Date of Accounts	Mar 12	Mar 11	Mar 10
Sales Turnover	399m	376m	363m
Pre Tax Profit/Loss	198m	90m	29m
Working Capital	-244m	-207m	-281m
Fixed Assets	442m	382m	345m
Current Assets	192m	1260m	1247m
Current Liabilities	99m	95m	91m

F B S Prestige
Unit Blilac Grove Beeston, Nottingham, NG9 1PF
Tel: 0115-943 1111 **Fax:** 01254-690484
E-mail: info@fluorocarbon.co.uk
Website: http://www.fbsprestige.co.uk
Managers: M. Schinagl (Ops Mgr)
Immediate Holding Company: PFB HIRE LIMITED
Registration no: 01504061 **Date established:** 2010
Turnover: Up to £250,000 **No.of Employees:** 11 - 20 **Product Groups:** 36, 40, 41

Date of Accounts	Jul 12	Jul 11
Working Capital	-816	-851
Fixed Assets	3m	3m
Current Assets	312	-851

F W Mason & Sons Midland Ltd
Road 8 Colwick Industrial Estate, Nottingham, NG4 2EQ
Tel: 0115-911 3500 **Fax:** 0115-911 3555
E-mail: sales@masons-timber.co.uk
Website: http://www.masons-timber.co.uk
Directors: D. Mason (MD), F. Mason (Co Sec)
Immediate Holding Company: F.W.MASON & SONS(MIDLAND)LIMITED
Registration no: 00478566 **Date established:** 1950
Turnover: £10m - £20m **No.of Employees:** 1 - 10 **Product Groups:** 48

Fans & Spares Ltd
Unit 25 Whitemoor Court Industrial Estate Whitemoor Court, Nottingham, NG8 5BY
Tel: 0115-929 4104 **Fax:** 0115-929 2710
E-mail: nottingham@fansandspares.co.uk
Website: http://www.fansandspares.co.uk
Directors: N. Rapley (MD)
Immediate Holding Company: FANS & SPARES LTD
Registration no: 07240936 **Date established:** 2010 **Turnover:** £5m - £10m
No.of Employees: 1 - 10 **Product Groups:** 33, 39, 40, 48, 52

Faspak Containers Ltd
6 Ashville Close Queens Drive Industrial Estate, Nottingham, NG2 1LL
Tel: 0115-986 9391 **Fax:** 0115-986 8310
E-mail: diane@faspak.co.uk
Website: http://www.faspak.co.uk
Directors: D. Webber (MD)
Ultimate Holding Company: FASPAK LTD
Immediate Holding Company: FASPAK (CONTAINERS) LIMITED
Registration no: 01056603 **VAT No.:** GB 116 6570 72
Date established: 1972 **Turnover:** £2m - £5m **No.of Employees:** 11 - 20
Product Groups: 25, 30, 42, 85

Date of Accounts	Jul 11	Jul 10	Jul 09
Working Capital	211	358	469
Fixed Assets	2	16	24
Current Assets	410	577	710

Fastframe UK
Amber Drive Langley Mill, Nottingham, NG16 4BE
Tel: 01773-714777 **Fax:** 01773-534181
E-mail: pmoody@fastframeuk.com
Website: http://www.fastframeuk.com
Directors: P. Moody (Comm)
Immediate Holding Company: FAST FRAME UK MANUFACTURING LIMITED
Registration no: 06787883 **Date established:** 2009
No.of Employees: 21 - 50 **Product Groups:** 33, 35

Fibre Technology Ltd
Brookhill Industrial Estate Pinxton, Nottingham, NG16 6NT
Tel: 01773-580286 **Fax:** 01773-580287
E-mail: sales@fibretech.com
Website: http://www.fibretech.com
Managers: B. Irvine
Ultimate Holding Company: DYNAMIC-MATERIALS GROUP LIMITED
Immediate Holding Company: BOMANTON PROPERTIES (2006) LTD
Registration no: 01537119 **Date established:** 1981 **Turnover:** £1m - £2m
No.of Employees: 11 - 20 **Product Groups:** 34

Date of Accounts	Dec 11	Dec 10	Dec 09
Working Capital	64	64	64
Current Assets	64	64	64

1st Galaxy Fireworks Ltd (t/a Blue Moon (UK) Ltd)
The Pyro Plot Nottingham Road, Ravenshead, Nottingham, NG15 9HP
Tel: 01623-792121 **Fax:** 08704-430211
E-mail: lee@1stgalaxy.co.uk
Website: http://www.galaxy-fireworks.co.uk
Managers: L. Smith (Ops Mgr)
Immediate Holding Company: 1ST GALAXY FIREWORKS LIMITED
Registration no: 03842899 **Date established:** 1999
Turnover: £250,000 - £500,000 **No.of Employees:** 1 - 10
Product Groups: 32, 89

Date of Accounts	Feb 08	Feb 11	Feb 10
Working Capital	-22	-22	-31
Fixed Assets	79	69	79
Current Assets	129	79	83

Flexopack Ltd
Mallard Road Victoria Business Park, Netherfield, Nottingham, NG4 2PE
Tel: 0115-940 3939 **Fax:** 0115-940 3837
E-mail: sales@flexopack.co.uk
Website: http://www.flexopack.co.uk
Directors: J. Lewis (Co Sec), A. Lewis (MD)
Immediate Holding Company: FLEXOPACK LIMITED
Registration no: 02117982 **Date established:** 1987
Turnover: Up to £250,000 **No.of Employees:** 11 - 20 **Product Groups:** 30

Date of Accounts	May 11	May 10	May 09
Working Capital	-149	-174	-133
Fixed Assets	1m	1m	1m
Current Assets	925	995	759

Flitterman Investments Ltd
Michael House Rennie Hogg Road Riverside Business Park, Nottingham, NG2 1RX
Tel: 0115-985 2200 **Fax:** 0115-986 3271
E-mail: laurence.flitterman@outdoorscene.com
Website: http://www.outdoorscene.com
Directors: L. Flitterman (Dir)
Ultimate Holding Company: SECURITAS AB (SWEDEN)
Immediate Holding Company: FLITTERMAN INVESTMENTS LIMITED
Registration no: 00807062 **Date established:** 1964
No.of Employees: 1 - 10 **Product Groups:** 63

Date of Accounts	Mar 11	Mar 10	Mar 09
Working Capital	690	816	1m
Fixed Assets	2m	2m	2m
Current Assets	1m	1m	1m

F & M Steed Upholstery Ltd
Bonsall Street Long Eaton, Nottingham, NG10 2AL
Tel: 0115-973 4166 **Fax:** 0115-946 1845
E-mail: richard@steedupholstery.com
Website: http://www.steedupholstery.com
Directors: R. Steed (MD)
Immediate Holding Company: F. & M. STEED LIMITED
Registration no: 00850142 **Date established:** 1965 **Turnover:** £1m - £2m
No.of Employees: 51 - 100 **Product Groups:** 63

Date of Accounts	May 11	May 10	May 09
Working Capital	179	149	187
Fixed Assets	659	705	735
Current Assets	707	753	687

Focus Label Machinery Ltd
Kendryl Park Chapel Lane, Bingham, Nottingham, NG13 8GF
Tel: 01949-836223 **Fax:** 01949-836542
E-mail: sales@focuslabel.com
Website: http://www.focuslabel.com
Bank(s): National Westminster Bank Plc
Directors: D. Lee (Dir), A. Lee (Co Sec)
Immediate Holding Company: FOCUS LABEL MACHINERY LIMITED
Registration no: 02247753 **Date established:** 1988 **Turnover:** £1m - £2m
No.of Employees: 21 - 50 **Product Groups:** 28, 32, 42, 43, 44

Date of Accounts	May 11	May 10	May 09
Working Capital	2m	2m	3m
Fixed Assets	2m	2m	2m
Current Assets	3m	4m	4m

FOCUS Promotions Ltd
397b Tamworth Road Long Eaton, Nottingham, NG10 3JP
Tel: 0115-973 4457 **Fax:** 0115-946 1245
E-mail: sales@focus-promotions.co.uk
Website: http://www.focus-promotions.co.uk
Directors: T. Mayfield (Fin)
Immediate Holding Company: FOCUS PROMOTIONS LIMITED
Registration no: 06162335 **VAT No.:** GB 755 6314 20
Date established: 2007 **Turnover:** £500,000 - £1m
No.of Employees: 1 - 10 **Product Groups:** 20, 21, 22, 23, 24, 26, 27, 28, 30, 32, 33, 35, 36, 37, 38, 39, 44, 49, 64, 65, 80, 81

Date of Accounts	Mar 12	Mar 11	Mar 10
Working Capital	-2	1	-3
Fixed Assets	2	3	3
Current Assets	102	75	57

Food & Drug Analytical Services Ltd
Biocity Pennyfoot Street, Nottingham, NG1 1GF
Tel: 0115-912 4265 **Fax:** 0115-912 4267
E-mail: office@fdas.org
Website: http://www.fdas.org
Directors: T. Ray (Grp Chief Exec), S. Jones (Fin), L. Taylor (Tech Serv)
Managers: J. Evans
Registration no: 05034039 **No.of Employees:** 1 - 10 **Product Groups:** 85

Foster Industrial
Church Street Lenton, Nottingham, NG7 2FH
Tel: 0115-970 0598 **Fax:** 0115-942 3388
E-mail: richard@fosterindustrial.co.uk
Website: http://www.fosterindustrial.co.uk
Bank(s): HSBC Bank plc
Directors: R. Foster (MD)
Immediate Holding Company: FOSTER & COMPANY WELDTECH LIMITED
Registration no: 03756447 **VAT No.:** GB 117 0109 18
Date established: 1999 **Turnover:** £1m - £2m **No.of Employees:** 21 - 50
Product Groups: 18, 24, 29, 34, 35, 37, 45, 75

Date of Accounts	Dec 10	Dec 09	Dec 08
Working Capital	492	480	501
Fixed Assets	41	43	65
Current Assets	1m	920	903

Frametrade
Unit 3 Joshua Business Park Cromford Road, Langley Mill, Nottingham, NG16 4EW
Tel: 01773-714809 **Fax:** 01773-714276
Directors: J. Bansord (Prop)
Immediate Holding Company: FRAME TRADE UK LTD
Registration no: 04677642 **Date established:** 2003
No.of Employees: 11 - 20 **Product Groups:** 35

Date of Accounts	Jul 11	Jul 10	Jul 09
Working Capital	-61	1	-20
Fixed Assets	56	55	31
Current Assets	306	272	219

Frank Hand Galvanizers Ltd
7 Colwick Industrial Estate Colwick Industrial Estate, Nottingham, NG4 2AD
Tel: 0115-987 0508 **Fax:** 0115-940 0793
E-mail: enquiries@frankhand.co.uk
Website: http://www.frankhand.co.uk
Bank(s): National Westminster Bank Plc
Directors: S. Furman (Fin), A. Everington (Dir)
Immediate Holding Company: FRANK HAND (GALVANIZERS) LIMITED
Registration no: 00778603 **VAT No.:** GB 116 3957 63
Date established: 1963 **Turnover:** £500,000 - £1m
No.of Employees: 11 - 20 **Product Groups:** 46, 48

Date of Accounts	Oct 11	Oct 10	Oct 09
Working Capital	-115	-122	-131
Fixed Assets	457	468	487
Current Assets	319	312	312

G Underwood Ltd
13 Main Street Keyworth, Nottingham, NG12 5AA
Tel: 0115-937 6706 **Fax:** 0115-937 6806
E-mail: help@underwood.co.uk
Website: http://www.cablesforcomputers.com
Directors: G. Underwood (MD)
Immediate Holding Company: G. UNDERWOOD LIMITED
Registration no: 04734457 **VAT No.:** GB 274 2596 36
Date established: 2003 **Turnover:** £250,000 - £500,000
No.of Employees: 1 - 10 **Product Groups:** 34, 66

Date of Accounts	Apr 11	Apr 10	Apr 09
Working Capital	78	19	76
Fixed Assets	550	598	647
Current Assets	183	162	139

Games Workshop Ltd
Warhammer World Willow Road, Nottingham, NG7 2WS
Tel: 0115-916 8410 **Fax:** 0115-916 8008
E-mail: orders@games-workshop.co.uk
Website: http://www.games-workshop.com
Managers: T. Howard (Purch Mgr), H. Rapinet (Personnel), S. Brewin (Tech Serv Mgr), K. Rowntree (Comptroller), M. Wells
Ultimate Holding Company: GAMES WORKSHOP GROUP PLC
Immediate Holding Company: GAMES WORKSHOP LIMITED
Registration no: 01467092 **VAT No.:** GB 580 8534 21
Date established: 1979 **Turnover:** £75m - £125m
No.of Employees: 501 - 1000 **Product Groups:** 49, 65

Date of Accounts	May 09	May 10	May 11
Sales Turnover	69m	75m	77m
Pre Tax Profit/Loss	6m	12m	13m
Working Capital	7m	7m	3m
Fixed Assets	27m	24m	23m
Current Assets	24m	25m	19m
Current Liabilities	14m	15m	14m

Gee Tee Signs Ltd
Bestwood Road, Nottingham, NG6 8SS
Tel: 0115-976 1188 **Fax:** 0115-976 1213
E-mail: sales@geeteesigns.com
Website: http://www.geeteesigns.com
Bank(s): National Westminster Bank Plc
Directors: G. Snowden (I.T. Dir), K. Korpal (MD), T. Sharma (Sales & Mktg)
Managers: B. Howell
Immediate Holding Company: GEE-TEE SIGNS LIMITED
Registration no: 01724512 **VAT No.:** GB 309 2895 37
Date established: 1983 **Turnover:** £5m - £10m
No.of Employees: 51 - 100 **Product Groups:** 37

Date of Accounts	May 11	May 10	May 09
Sales Turnover	N/A	N/A	6m
Pre Tax Profit/Loss	N/A	N/A	28
Working Capital	726	893	860
Fixed Assets	145	178	186
Current Assets	2m	2m	2m
Current Liabilities	N/A	N/A	258

Gem Fabs
The Old Coachworks Portland Road, Hucknall, Nottingham, NG15 7SF
Tel: 0115-968 1927
E-mail: stuart@gemfabs.com
Website: http://www.gemfabs.com
Directors: S. Weightman (Ptnr)
Immediate Holding Company: PORTLAND STAINLESS STEEL LTD.
Date established: 2011 **No.of Employees:** 1 - 10 **Product Groups:** 35

Gill Insulation Notts Ltd
Unit 5 33 Ebury Road, Nottingham, NG5 1BB
Tel: 0115-962 6043 **Fax:** 0115-969 1688
E-mail: sales@gillins.com
Website: http://www.gillins.com
Directors: R. Drew (MD), A. Drew (Co Sec)
Ultimate Holding Company: LIBERTY2803 LIMITED
Immediate Holding Company: GILL CONTRACTS LIMITED
Registration no: 01994138 **VAT No.:** GB 567 8001 28
Date established: 1986 **Turnover:** £5m - £10m **No.of Employees:** 1 - 10
Product Groups: 52, 54

Gledhill Building Product
5 Bestwood Road Brookhill Industrial Estate, Pinxton, Nottingham, NG16 6NT
Tel: 01773-580684 **Fax:** 01773-581129
Website: http://www.gledhill.net
Directors: P. Holland (MD)
Managers: M. Causer (Mgr)
Immediate Holding Company: GLEDHILL BUILDING PRODUCTS LIMITED
Registration no: 04784515 **Date established:** 2003
Turnover: £10m - £20m **No.of Employees:** 1 - 10 **Product Groups:** 35, 42, 45

Date of Accounts	Sep 11	Sep 10	Sep 09
Sales Turnover	19m	17m	15m
Pre Tax Profit/Loss	334	-11	289
Working Capital	1m	1m	2m
Fixed Assets	3m	2m	1m
Current Assets	7m	7m	6m
Current Liabilities	3m	4m	3m

Global E M C UK Ltd
Prospect Close Lowmoor Business Park, Kirkby-In-Ashfield, Nottingham, NG17 7LF
Tel: 01623-755539 **Fax:** 01623-755719
E-mail: info@global-emc.co.uk
Website: http://www.global-emc.co.uk
Directors: G. Pitchford (MD)
Ultimate Holding Company: STRONGFIELD TECHNOLOGIES LIMITED
Immediate Holding Company: GLOBAL EMC UK LTD
Registration no: 02929032 **Date established:** 1994
Turnover: Up to £250,000 **No.of Employees:** 1 - 10 **Product Groups:** 32

Date of Accounts	May 11	May 10	May 09
Working Capital	-6	15	-4
Fixed Assets	13	8	19
Current Assets	294	129	93

P D Gough Co. Ltd
Old Foundry Common Lane, Watnall, Nottingham, NG16 1HD
Tel: 0115-938 2241 **Fax:** 0115-945 9162
E-mail: info@pdgough.com
Website: http://www.pdgough.com
Bank(s): Barclays
Directors: R. Brown (Fin)
Immediate Holding Company: P. D. GOUGH & CO. LIMITED
Registration no: 01888367 **Date established:** 1985
Turnover: £250,000 - £500,000 **No.of Employees:** 11 - 20
Product Groups: 68

Date of Accounts	Sep 11	Sep 10	Sep 09
Working Capital	23	67	160
Fixed Assets	189	195	201
Current Assets	125	219	279

Graingate
2 Lockwood Close, Nottingham, NG5 9JN
Tel: 0115-967 1888 **Fax:** 0115-967 1777
E-mail: enquiries@graingate.co.uk
Website: http://www.graingate.co.uk
Directors: S. Green (Dir)
Immediate Holding Company: GRAINGATE LIMITED
Registration no: 01539010 **VAT No.:** GB 352 6499 32
Date established: 1981 **Turnover:** £500,000 - £1m
No.of Employees: 1 - 10 **Product Groups:** 30, 66

Date of Accounts	Aug 11	Aug 10	Aug 09
Working Capital	-131	-124	-87
Fixed Assets	435	439	449
Current Assets	140	140	162

Greene Tweed & Co. Ltd
Mere Way Ruddington Fields Business Park, Ruddington, Nottingham, NG11 6JS
Tel: 0115-931 5777 **Fax:** 0115-931 5888
E-mail: info@greenetweed.com
Website: http://www.gtweed.com
Bank(s): National Westminster
Directors: A. Lane (Co Sec), M. Delfiner (Ch)
Ultimate Holding Company: GREENE TWEED OF DELAWARE INC (USA)
Immediate Holding Company: GREENE TWEED & CO LIMITED
Registration no: 01643349 **VAT No.:** GB 352 9044 58
Date established: 1982 **Turnover:** £20m - £50m
No.of Employees: 101 - 250 **Product Groups:** 29, 30

Date of Accounts	Mar 12	Mar 11	Mar 10
Sales Turnover	35m	N/A	N/A
Pre Tax Profit/Loss	3m	625	540
Working Capital	8m	4m	4m
Fixed Assets	8m	7m	7m
Current Assets	13m	9m	7m
Current Liabilities	1m	764	515

Grumpy Joe's Ltd
Redhill Marina Ratcliffe-on-Soar, Nottingham, NG11 0EB
Tel: 01509-670006 **Fax:** 01509-672606
E-mail: sales@grumpyjoe.co.uk
Website: http://www.grumpyjoe.co.uk
Managers: M. Cooper (Mgr)
Immediate Holding Company: GRUMPY JOES LIMITED
Registration no: 07438521 **Date established:** 2010
No.of Employees: 11 - 20 **Product Groups:** 26, 40

Date of Accounts	Mar 12
Working Capital	39
Fixed Assets	142
Current Assets	302

Gunn & Moore
Trent Lane Industrial Estate, Nottingham, NG2 4DS
Tel: 0115-985 3500 **Fax:** 0115-985 3501
E-mail: peterwright@unicorngroup.com
Website: http://www.unicorngroup.com
Bank(s): National Westminster Bank Plc

Directors: P. Wright (MD)
Ultimate Holding Company: UNICORN PRODUCTS LTD
Immediate Holding Company: HAROLD POTTER HOLDINGS LIMITED
Registration no: 02854683 **Date established:** 2004
Turnover: £250,000 - £500,000 **No.of Employees:** 21 - 50
Product Groups: 23, 36, 49

H P M Ltd

9 Ascot Industrial Estate Sandiacre, Nottingham, NG10 5DL
Tel: 0115-939 0716 **Fax:** 0115-949 1106
E-mail: sales@hpmltd.com
Website: http://www.hpmltd.com
Bank(s): HSBC Bank plc
Directors: B. Sood (Tech Serv), R. Shread (Comm)
Immediate Holding Company: H.P.M. LIMITED
Registration no: 02349003 **Date established:** 1989 **Turnover:** £1m - £2m
No.of Employees: 21 - 50 **Product Groups:** 29, 30, 66, 84

Date of Accounts	Apr 11	Apr 10	Apr 09
Working Capital	128	N/A	12
Fixed Assets	103	108	117
Current Assets	313	191	286

Hallam Plastics Ltd

Hallam Way Station Road Langley Mill, Nottingham, NG16 4AN
Tel: 01773-531151 **Fax:** 01773-533267
E-mail: enquiries@hallamplastics.co.uk
Website: http://www.hallamplastics.co.uk
Bank(s): Barclays
Directors: S. Lacey (MD)
Managers: S. Davies (Chief Acct), A. Boyle (Tech Sales Eng), K. Eyre (Buyer)
Ultimate Holding Company: BOWEDENE LIMITED
Immediate Holding Company: HALLAM PLASTICS LIMITED
Registration no: 01071839 **VAT No.:** GB 593 4368 07
Date established: 1972 **Turnover:** £5m - £10m
No.of Employees: 51 - 100 **Product Groups:** 30

Date of Accounts	Apr 11	Apr 10	Apr 09
Sales Turnover	6m	4m	5m
Pre Tax Profit/Loss	666	319	627
Working Capital	3m	3m	3m
Fixed Assets	912	905	944
Current Assets	4m	4m	3m
Current Liabilities	346	260	331

Hanson Concrete Products plc

Hoveringham Works Hoveringham Lane, Hoveringham, Nottingham, NG14 7JX
Tel: 01636-832000 **Fax:** 01636-832020
E-mail: enquiries@hanson.com
Website: http://www.hanson.com
Directors: R. Monro (Co Sec), T. Poole (Ch)
Immediate Holding Company: UKELLA LIMITED
Registration no: 07114362 **Date established:** 2011
Turnover: £10m - £20m **No.of Employees:** 21 - 50 **Product Groups:** 33

Harold Potter

Trent Lane, Nottingham, NG2 4DS
Tel: 0115-983 8111 **Fax:** 0115-983 8112
E-mail: info@haroldpotter.co.uk
Website: http://www.haroldpotter.co.uk
Directors: T. Calladine (MD)
Immediate Holding Company: HAROLD POTTER LIMITED
Registration no: 04207795 **Date established:** 2001
No.of Employees: 11 - 20 **Product Groups:** 23, 26, 29, 30, 35, 37, 38, 39, 41, 42, 43, 44, 45

Date of Accounts	Jun 11	Jun 10	Jun 09
Working Capital	104	175	187
Fixed Assets	127	157	101
Current Assets	603	671	439

Harsco Rail Ltd

Unit 1 Chewton Street Eastwood, Nottingham, NG16 3HB
Tel: 01773-539480 **Fax:** 01773-539481
E-mail: awardle@harsco.com
Website: http://www.harscorail.com
Bank(s): National Westminster Bank Plc
Directors: A. Wardle (MD), M. Emmerson (Fin)
Managers: C. Rowley (Chief Buyer), D. Mills, E. Niemann, P. Watson (Develop Mgr)
Ultimate Holding Company: HARSCO CORPORATION (USA)
Immediate Holding Company: HARSCO RAIL LIMITED
Registration no: 00977100 **Date established:** 1970
Turnover: £10m - £20m **No.of Employees:** 21 - 50 **Product Groups:** 45

Date of Accounts	Dec 11	Dec 10	Dec 09
Sales Turnover	19m	21m	25m
Pre Tax Profit/Loss	1m	1m	3m
Working Capital	11m	10m	13m
Fixed Assets	4m	4m	690
Current Assets	14m	13m	20m
Current Liabilities	2m	2m	3m

Harvey Quilting Ltd

11 Robin Hood Industrial Estate Alfred Street South, Nottingham, NG3 1GE
Tel: 0115-958 5777 **Fax:** 0115-950 3339
E-mail: tony@harveyquilting.co.uk
Website: http://www.harveyquilting.co.uk
Directors: A. Bailey (Sales), T. Bailey (MD)
Immediate Holding Company: HARVEY QUILTING LIMITED
Registration no: 03739303 **Date established:** 1999
No.of Employees: 11 - 20 **Product Groups:** 23, 43

Date of Accounts	Mar 11	Mar 10	Mar 09
Working Capital	18	15	10
Fixed Assets	15	12	13
Current Assets	110	110	94

Hayssensandiacre

101 Lilac Grove Beeston, Nottingham, NG9 1PF
Tel: 0115-967 8787 **Fax:** 0115-967 8707
E-mail: simon.lagoe@hayssensandiacre.com
Website: http://www.rose-forgrove.co.uk
Directors: S. Lagoe (MD), W. Ellis (Fin)
Managers: J. Press (Tech Serv Mgr), N. Algar, P. Middleton
Ultimate Holding Company: BARRY WEHMILLER INC (USA)
Immediate Holding Company: BARRY-WEHMILLER EUROPE (ST ALBANS) LIMITED
Registration no: 07232277 **Date established:** 1977
No.of Employees: 101 - 250 **Product Groups:** 38, 42

Date of Accounts	Sep 11	Sep 10	Sep 09
Sales Turnover	N/A	1m	7m
Pre Tax Profit/Loss	N/A	2m	-309
Working Capital	400	400	-2m
Fixed Assets	N/A	N/A	45
Current Assets	400	400	3m
Current Liabilities	N/A	N/A	465

Highland Print Services Highland Print

Unit 1-2 Stedfast Court 23 Watnall Road, Hucknall, Nottingham, NG15 7LD
Tel: 0115-964 0253 **Fax:** 0115-964 0651
E-mail: info@highlandprint.co.uk
Website: http://www.highlandprint.co.uk
Directors: G. Barnes (Prop)
No.of Employees: 1 - 10 **Product Groups:** 37, 64, 65, 66

Hildred Engineering Co. Ltd

Units 2 4 & 6 Parkway Court, Nottingham, NG8 4GN
Tel: 0115-928 2217 **Fax:** 0115-985 4998
E-mail: hildredengco@aol.com
Website: http://www.hildredengineering.co.uk
Directors: J. Hildred (MD)
Immediate Holding Company: HILDRED ENGINEERING CO LIMITED
Registration no: 02162196 **VAT No.:** GB 450 1868 56
Date established: 1987 **Turnover:** £500,000 - £1m
No.of Employees: 1 - 10 **Product Groups:** 46, 48

Date of Accounts	Mar 11	Mar 10	Mar 09
Working Capital	90	42	134
Fixed Assets	132	155	179
Current Assets	202	167	229

Hillarys Blinds Northern Ltd

Private Road No 2 Colwick Business Park, Colwick Industrial Estate, Nottingham, NG4 2JR
Tel: 0115-961 7420 **Fax:** 0115-961 4176
E-mail: enquiries@hillarys.co.uk
Website: http://www.hillarys.co.uk
Bank(s): National Westminster Bank Plc
Directors: D. Lewis (Dir), J. Risman (Grp Chief Exec), K. Dobson (Co Sec), S. Earith (Mkt Research)
Managers: B. Hitchcock (Sales Prom Mgr), J. Bond (I.T. Exec), S. Dolby (Sales Prom Mgr)
Ultimate Holding Company: Bellotto Holdings Ltd
Immediate Holding Company: HILLARYS BLINDS (HOLDINGS) LIMITED
Registration no: 02692951 **VAT No.:** GB 416 1682 62
Date established: 1992 **Turnover:** £75m - £125m
No.of Employees: 501 - 1000 **Product Groups:** 24, 27, 35, 36, 37

Hire Station Ltd

Fields Farm Road Long Eaton, Nottingham, NG10 3FZ
Tel: 0845-6045337 **Fax:** 0845-6688999
E-mail: hirestation.online@vpplc.com
Website: http://www.hirestation.co.uk
Managers: N. Lawton (Mgr)
Immediate Holding Company: VP plc
Registration no: 03428037 **Date established:** 2001
No.of Employees: 1 - 10 **Product Groups:** 35, 37, 39, 45

Holger Christiansen UK Ltd

Unit 7-8 Glaisdale Business Centre Glaisdale Parkway, Nottingham, NG8 4GP
Tel: 0115-928 0086 **Fax:** 0115-928 0033
Website: http://www.hcdk.com
Bank(s): National Westminster Bank Plc
Directors: K. Bloodworth (Fin)
Managers: P. Murray (Reg Mgr)
Ultimate Holding Company: ROBERT BOSCH GMBH (GERMANY)
Immediate Holding Company: HOLGER CHRISTIANSEN UK LIMITED
Registration no: 01841076 **VAT No.:** GB 416 1454 75
Date established: 1984 **Turnover:** £5m - £10m **No.of Employees:** 21 - 50
Product Groups: 39, 68

Date of Accounts	Dec 11	Dec 10	Dec 09
Sales Turnover	8m	9m	9m
Pre Tax Profit/Loss	185	277	228
Working Capital	2m	1m	1m
Fixed Assets	N/A	81	107
Current Assets	4m	4m	4m
Current Liabilities	716	317	130

Horizon Lifts Ltd

28 Main Street Awsworth, Nottingham, NG16 2QT
Tel: 0115-944 1020 **Fax:** 0115-944 1019
E-mail: info@horizonlifts.com
Website: http://www.horizonlifts.com
Directors: W. Staniland (MD)
Immediate Holding Company: HORIZON LIFTS LIMITED
Registration no: 02435813 **Date established:** 1989
No.of Employees: 1 - 10 **Product Groups:** 35, 39, 45

Date of Accounts	Nov 11	Nov 10	Nov 09
Working Capital	-4	-5	-7
Fixed Assets	89	89	90
Current Assets	411	329	307

House Of Brass

282-284 Huntingdon Street, Nottingham, NG1 3NA
Tel: 0115-947 5430
E-mail: sales@houseofbrass.co.uk
Website: http://www.houseofbrass.co.uk
Directors: B. Fakey (Prop)
Immediate Holding Company: HOUSE OF BRASS LIMITED
Registration no: 04901892 **Date established:** 2003
No.of Employees: 1 - 10 **Product Groups:** 35, 36

Date of Accounts	Sep 11	Sep 10	Sep 09
Working Capital	-20	-21	-35
Fixed Assets	66	68	69
Current Assets	26	20	17

G H Hurt & Son Ltd

65 High Road Chilwell, Beeston, Nottingham, NG9 4AJ
Tel: 0115-925 4080 **Fax:** 0115-925 5904
E-mail: info@ghhurt.com
Website: http://www.ghhurt.com
Bank(s): Barclays, Beeston
Directors: H. Hurt (MD)
Immediate Holding Company: G. H. HURT & SON LIMITED
Registration no: 02205013 **VAT No.:** GB 117 0667 81
Date established: 1987 **No.of Employees:** 11 - 20 **Product Groups:** 23, 43

Date of Accounts	Mar 12	Mar 11	Mar 10
Working Capital	15	74	75
Fixed Assets	135	136	34
Current Assets	59	102	95

Hydropath Holdings Ltd

Unit 7 The Midway, Nottingham, NG7 2TS
Tel: 0115-986 9966 **Fax:** 0115-986 9944
E-mail: sales@hydropath.com
Website: http://www.hydropath.com
Directors: D. Stefanini (Dir)
Ultimate Holding Company: HYDROPATH HOLDINGS LIMITED
Immediate Holding Company: HYDROPATH (U.K.) LIMITED
Registration no: 02760486 **Date established:** 1992
Turnover: £250,000 - £500,000 **No.of Employees:** 1 - 10
Product Groups: 30, 32, 38, 40, 42, 45, 51, 52, 54, 85

Date of Accounts	Apr 09	Apr 08
Working Capital	75	75
Current Assets	75	75

Hydrotechnik UK Ltd

Unit 10 Easter Park Lenton Lane, Nottingham, NG7 2PX
Tel: 0115-900 3550 **Fax:** 0115-970 5597
E-mail: info@hydrotechnik.co.uk
Website: http://www.hydrotechnik.co.uk
Directors: P. Ellis (Dir)
Immediate Holding Company: HYDROTECHNIK UK LIMITED
Registration no: 02551583 **VAT No.:** GB 538 6717 10
Date established: 1990 **Turnover:** £2m - £5m **No.of Employees:** 1 - 10
Product Groups: 38, 40, 42, 68

Date of Accounts	Dec 11	Dec 10	Dec 09
Working Capital	179	58	211
Fixed Assets	33	63	73
Current Assets	770	839	850

I Dress Myself T-shirt design & screen printing

32-40 Carrington Street, Nottingham, NG1 7FG
Tel: 0115-947 4140
E-mail: tees@idressmyself.co.uk
Website: http://www.idressmyself.co.uk
Directors: P. Conway (Prop)
Immediate Holding Company: NOTTINGHAM AND DISTRICT CITIZENS ADVICE BUREAU
Registration no: 02323141 **Date established:** 1988
Turnover: £500,000 - £1m **No.of Employees:** 1 - 10 **Product Groups:** 23, 24, 63

I G I Insurance

Market Square House St James's Street, Nottingham, NG1 6FG
Tel: 0115-941 1022 **Fax:** 0115-941 1316
E-mail: nottingham@igi.co.uk
Website: http://www.igi.co.uk
Directors: K. Wardell (MD), P. Nutting (Ch), S. Wallis (Fin)
Ultimate Holding Company: VATRYGGINGAFELAG ISLANDS HF (ICELAND)
Immediate Holding Company: PEDIGREE LIVESTOCK INSURANCE LIMITED
Registration no: 01229676 **Date established:** 1963
No.of Employees: 21 - 50 **Product Groups:** 82

Date of Accounts	Dec 07	Dec 06	Mar 06
Pre Tax Profit/Loss	751	-1615	-1459
Fixed Assets	17089	6042	5943
Current Assets	27539	15487	10350
Current Liabilities	19159	3737	2078
Total Share Capital	11500	7500	7500
ROCE% (Return on Capital Employed)	2.9	-9.1	-10.3

I T B Fabrications

Deakins Place, Nottingham, NG7 3FT
Tel: 0115-978 2100 **Fax:** 0115-978 2818
E-mail: ian@itbfabs.freeserve.co.uk
Website: http://www.itbfabs.freeserve.co.uk
Directors: I. Barnett (Dir)
Ultimate Holding Company: G B WILLBOND LIMITED
Immediate Holding Company: FULLRICH LIMITED
Registration no: 00467828 **Date established:** 1949
No.of Employees: 11 - 20 **Product Groups:** 35

Date of Accounts	Sep 11	Sep 10	Sep 09
Sales Turnover	14m	14m	13m
Pre Tax Profit/Loss	472	315	151
Working Capital	3m	2m	2m
Fixed Assets	542	807	1m
Current Assets	5m	4m	4m
Current Liabilities	708	642	339

Imp UK Ltd

Harby Road Langar, Nottingham, NG13 9HY
Tel: 01949-861020 **Fax:** 01949-861067
E-mail: enquiries@catensa.co.uk
Website: http://www.catensa.co.uk
Directors: M. Hopkins (Chief Op Offcr), D. Goff (Fin)
Managers: M. Turner, S. Lewis, J. O'Donnell
Ultimate Holding Company: FOSBELE INVESTMENTS SA (LUXEMBOURG)
Immediate Holding Company: I.M.P. (UK) LIMITED
Registration no: 02136627 **Date established:** 1987 **Turnover:** £5m - £10m
No.of Employees: 51 - 100 **Product Groups:** 23, 36

Date of Accounts	Dec 11	Dec 10	Dec 09
Sales Turnover	9m	8m	3m
Pre Tax Profit/Loss	194	208	-234
Working Capital	619	741	255
Fixed Assets	3m	2m	2m
Current Assets	3m	3m	2m
Current Liabilities	2m	1m	1m

In2connect Design & Marketing Ltd

Acton Grove Long Eaton, Nottingham, NG10 1FY
Tel: 0115-901 1100 **Fax:** 0115-901 1111
E-mail: info@in2connect.net
Website: http://www.in2connect.net
Directors: D. Whitaker (MD), P. Clay (Chief Op Offcr)
Managers: M. Bagnall (Purch Mgr), P. Richmond (I.T. Exec), R. Hayward (Sales Prom Mgr), S. McGivern (Sales Prom Mgr)
Immediate Holding Company: STEEL DECKING LIMITED
Registration no: 05302310 **VAT No.:** 796 4897 43 **Date established:** 2001
Turnover: £250,000 - £500,000 **No.of Employees:** 1 - 10
Product Groups: 33, 35

Date of Accounts	Mar 11	Mar 10	Mar 09
Pre Tax Profit/Loss	N/A	-6m	3m
Working Capital	N/A	N/A	-1
Fixed Assets	6m	6m	12m
Current Assets	N/A	N/A	10

Inchcape Accident Repair Centre
Derby Road, Nottingham, NG7 2GQ
Tel: 0115-942 1700 **Fax:** 0115-942 4489
E-mail: mark.pallett@ir.inchcape.co.uk
Website: http://www.inchcape-accident-repair.co.uk
Bank(s): National Westminster Bank Plc
Managers: M. Pallett (Chief Mgr)
Immediate Holding Company: INCHCAPE
VAT No.: GB 243 6111 93 **Turnover:** £5m - £10m
No.of Employees: 51 - 100 **Product Groups:** 68

Industrial Self Adhesives Ltd
Robey Close Linby, Nottingham, NG15 8AA
Tel: 0115-968 1895 **Fax:** 0115-963 2821
E-mail: sales@isatape.co.uk
Website: http://www.isatape.co.uk
Directors: A. Davies (Dir)
Immediate Holding Company: INDUSTRIAL SELF ADHESIVES LIMITED
Registration no: 01073820 **VAT No.:** GB 116 6141 95
Date established: 1972 **Turnover:** £1m - £2m **No.of Employees:** 1 - 10
Product Groups: 23, 27

Date of Accounts	May 12	May 11	May 10
Working Capital	145	150	172
Fixed Assets	85	96	138
Current Assets	558	589	559

Industrial Automation A Division Of Tew Engineering Ltd
6 The Midway, Nottingham, NG7 2TS
Tel: 0115-840 0500 **Fax:** 0115-840 5959
E-mail: sales@ind-auto.com
Website: http://www.ind-auto.com
Bank(s): HSBC Bank plc
Directors: A. Carus (Fin), M. Paradise (Chief Op Offcr)
Ultimate Holding Company: TEW HOLDINGS 2008 LIMITED
Immediate Holding Company: TEW ENGINEERING LIMITED
Registration no: 01134730 **Date established:** 1973 **Turnover:** £2m - £5m
No.of Employees: 21 - 50 **Product Groups:** 37, 38, 44, 45, 46, 47, 67, 84

Date of Accounts	Apr 12	Apr 11	Apr 10
Sales Turnover	10m	7m	7m
Pre Tax Profit/Loss	547	60	-7
Working Capital	1m	962	712
Fixed Assets	3m	3m	4m
Current Assets	5m	3m	3m
Current Liabilities	3m	1m	1m

Initial Electronic Security Systems Ltd
5 Churchill Park Colwick, Nottingham, NG4 2HF
Tel: 0115-987 9299 **Fax:** 0115-987 9697
Website: http://www.ies.uk.com
Directors: M. Smith (MD)
Managers: S. Thackery (Mgr)
Immediate Holding Company: Mitie Group plc
Registration no: 00715168 **Turnover:** £20m - £50m
No.of Employees: 1 - 10 **Product Groups:** 40

Insphire Ltd
Unit 5 Chase Park, Nottingham, NG2 4GT
Tel: 0115-979 3377 **Fax:** 0115-911 1447
E-mail: sales@insphire.com
Website: http://www.insphire.com
Managers: K. Miles
Immediate Holding Company: INSPHIRE LIMITED
Registration no: 03309635 **Date established:** 1997
No.of Employees: 21 - 50 **Product Groups:** 44

Date of Accounts	Mar 11	Mar 10	Mar 09
Working Capital	955	725	658
Fixed Assets	193	181	167
Current Assets	2m	1m	1m

Instrument Repair Service
35 Radcliffe Road West Bridgford, Nottingham, NG2 5FF
Tel: 0115-981 9988 **Fax:** 0115-945 5358
E-mail: info@irs-gb.com
Website: http://www.irs-gb.com
Directors: H. Glover (Fin)
Managers: A. Martin (Tech Serv Mgr)
Immediate Holding Company: INSTRUMENT REPAIR SERVICE LIMITED
Registration no: 02173913 **Date established:** 1987 **Turnover:** £1m - £2m
No.of Employees: 21 - 50 **Product Groups:** 38, 39

Date of Accounts	Oct 11	Oct 10	Oct 09
Working Capital	126	124	114
Current Assets	133	136	121

Iron Art
3 Standard Works St Bartholomews Road Wells Road, Nottingham, NG3 3AR
Tel: 0115-961 1299 **Fax:** 0115-961 1299
Directors: A. Cairns (Prop)
Date established: 2000 **No.of Employees:** 1 - 10 **Product Groups:** 26, 35

Itt Water Waste Water
Private Road 1 Colwick Industrial Estate, Nottingham, NG4 2AN
Tel: 0115-940 0111 **Fax:** 01202-631008
E-mail: sales@flyght.co.uk
Website: http://www.flygt.co.uk
Managers: A. Gawel (Mgr), A. Mawby (Chief Buyer), A. Barry (Sales Prom Mgr), B. Allen (Sales Prom Mgr), R. Randall (Eng)
Immediate Holding Company: ITT WATER & WASTEWATER UK LIMITED
Registration no: 00479504 **Date established:** 1950
Turnover: £50m - £75m **No.of Employees:** 1 - 10 **Product Groups:** 39, 40, 42, 45, 46

Date of Accounts	Dec 10	Dec 09	Dec 08
Sales Turnover	58m	60m	61m
Pre Tax Profit/Loss	2m	522	-3m
Working Capital	-1m	-2m	-3m
Fixed Assets	6m	7m	7m
Current Assets	16m	14m	17m
Current Liabilities	5m	4m	6m

J H P Training
Market Square House St James's Street, Nottingham, NG1 6FJ
Tel: 0115-950 5777 **Fax:** 0115-941 3287
E-mail: nottingham.business.centre@jhp-group.com
Website: http://www.jhptraining.com
Directors: J. Pitman (Ch)
Managers: Staw (Sales & Mktg Mg), C. Burn (Sales & Mktg Mg), C. Burns (Sales & Mktg Mg), D. Harris (Mgr)
Immediate Holding Company: JHP TRAINING LIMITED
Registration no: 03247918 **Date established:** 1996
Turnover: £50m - £75m **No.of Employees:** 21 - 50 **Product Groups:** 86

J Mcintyre Machinery Ltd
Mountstar 2 Harrimans Lane, Lenton Lane Industrial Estate, Nottingham, NG7 2SD
Tel: 0115-970 6530
Website: http://www.tardisrecycling.com
Managers: R. Morgan (Mgr)
Immediate Holding Company: J. Mcintyre (Machinery) Ltd
Registration no: 01220330 **Date established:** 1975
No.of Employees: 11 - 20 **Product Groups:** 36, 46

Jena Rotary Technology Ltd
Willow Drive Annesley, Nottingham, NG15 0DP
Tel: 01623-726010 **Fax:** 01623-726018
E-mail: sales@jena-tec.co.uk
Website: http://www.jena-tec.co.uk
Directors: P. Ward (MD)
Managers: C. Parker (Chief Acct)
Ultimate Holding Company: AVINGTRANS PLC
Immediate Holding Company: JENA ROTARY TECHNOLOGY LIMITED
Registration no: 02760232 **Date established:** 1992 **Turnover:** £2m - £5m
No.of Employees: 21 - 50 **Product Groups:** 35, 38, 48

Date of Accounts	May 11	May 10	May 09
Sales Turnover	3m	2m	2m
Pre Tax Profit/Loss	184	156	46
Working Capital	363	373	210
Fixed Assets	614	589	590
Current Assets	2m	2m	2m
Current Liabilities	321	155	112

Jewson Ltd
Mill Street, Nottingham, NG6 0JW
Tel: 0115-978 6151 **Fax:** 0115-942 3736
E-mail: iank.murray@jewson.co.uk
Website: http://www.jewson.co.uk
Managers: I. Murray (Mgr)
Ultimate Holding Company: COMPAGNIE DE SAINT GOBAIN (FRANCE)
Immediate Holding Company: JEWSON LIMITED
Registration no: 00348407 **VAT No.:** GB 394 1212 63
Date established: 1939 **Turnover:** £2m - £5m **No.of Employees:** 11 - 20
Product Groups: 66

Date of Accounts	Dec 11	Dec 10	Dec 09
Sales Turnover	1606m	1547m	1485m
Pre Tax Profit/Loss	18m	100m	45m
Working Capital	-345m	-250m	-349m
Fixed Assets	496m	387m	461m
Current Assets	657m	1005m	1320m
Current Liabilities	66m	120m	64m

Jewson Ltd
Private Road 1 Colwick Industrial Estate, Nottingham, NG4 2JQ
Tel: 0115-961 5459 **Fax:** 0115-961 3849
E-mail: jason.pick@jewson.co.uk
Website: http://www.jewson.co.uk
Managers: J. Pick (Chief Mgr)
Ultimate Holding Company: COMPAGNIE DE SAINT GOBAIN (FRANCE)
Immediate Holding Company: JEWSON LIMITED
Registration no: 00348407 **Date established:** 1939
No.of Employees: 11 - 20 **Product Groups:** 66

Date of Accounts	Dec 11	Dec 10	Dec 09
Sales Turnover	1606m	1547m	1485m
Pre Tax Profit/Loss	18m	100m	45m
Working Capital	-345m	-250m	-349m
Fixed Assets	496m	387m	461m
Current Assets	657m	1005m	1320m
Current Liabilities	66m	120m	64m

Josery Textiles Ltd
Unit 2 Benneworth Close, Hucknall, Nottingham, NG15 6EL
Tel: 0115-963 2200 **Fax:** 0115-964 0223
E-mail: enquiries@josery.co.uk
Website: http://www.josery.co.uk
Bank(s): National Westminster Bank Plc
Directors: T. Jones (Dir)
Immediate Holding Company: JOSERY TEXTILES LIMITED
Registration no: 00348088 **Date established:** 1939 **Turnover:** £1m - £2m
No.of Employees: 11 - 20 **Product Groups:** 24

Date of Accounts	Sep 11	Sep 09	Sep 08
Working Capital	2m	2m	2m
Fixed Assets	796	795	636
Current Assets	2m	2m	2m

K B L Fabrication & Engineering
Unit 5 Church View Business Park Church Street, Old Basford, Nottingham, NG6 0GA
Tel: 0115-942 2660 **Fax:** 0115-942 2689
Directors: K. Hussain (Prop)
Date established: 2002 **No.of Employees:** 1 - 10 **Product Groups:** 35

K R C S Group Ltd
Queens Court Lenton Lane, Nottingham, NG7 2NR
Tel: 0115-985 1797 **Fax:** 0115-986 0744
E-mail: info@krcs.co.uk
Website: http://www.krcs.co.uk
Directors: K. Woods (MD), C. Benner (Dir), R. Woods (Sales), P. Woods (Serv)
Managers: D. Hands (Develop Mgr)
Ultimate Holding Company: DEVELOPING INSIGHT LIMITED
Immediate Holding Company: KRCS (DIGITAL SOLUTIONS) LIMITED
Registration no: 02322420 **VAT No.:** GB 568 2367 10
Date established: 1988 **Turnover:** £2m - £5m **No.of Employees:** 21 - 50
Product Groups: 44

Date of Accounts	Dec 08	Dec 07	Jun 11
Sales Turnover	N/A	6m	N/A
Pre Tax Profit/Loss	N/A	50	N/A
Working Capital	-133	-105	-121
Fixed Assets	135	93	104
Current Assets	582	620	1m
Current Liabilities	N/A	725	N/A

Kappa Paper Recycling (Nottingham Depot)
Private Road 2 Colwick Industrial Estate, Nottingham, NG4 2JR
Tel: 0115-961 1753 **Fax:** 0115-940 0102
Website: http://www.kappa-paperrecycling.co.uk
Directors: C. Allen (MD)
Managers: M. Challans (Depot Mgr), G. Johnson (Sales Prom Mgr), G. Johnstone (Mgr)
Immediate Holding Company: Kappa SSK Ltd
Registration no: 00040681 **VAT No.:** GB 462 0709 62
Turnover: £250,000 - £500,000 **No.of Employees:** 1 - 10
Product Groups: 42, 66

Kaylee Transfers Ltd
PO Box 11, Nottingham, NG10 2DP
Tel: 0115-973 5247 **Fax:** 0115-946 0801
E-mail: sales@kaylee.uk.com
Website: http://www.kaylee.uk.com
Bank(s): Barclays
Directors: I. Hardiker (MD), R. Hardiker (MD)
Immediate Holding Company: KAYLEE TRANSFERS LIMITED
Registration no: 00461171 **VAT No.:** GB 125 5699 48
Date established: 1948 **Turnover:** £1m - £2m **No.of Employees:** 11 - 20
Product Groups: 23, 28, 84

Date of Accounts	Dec 11	Dec 10	Dec 09
Working Capital	801	784	810
Fixed Assets	307	313	366
Current Assets	2m	2m	1m

Knobs
Leone Works John Street, New Basford, Nottingham, NG7 7HL
Tel: 0115-942 0006 **Fax:** 0115-970 2106
E-mail: sales@knobs.uk.com
Website: http://www.knobs.uk.com
Bank(s): National Westminster Bank Plc
Directors: C. Hanley (Fin), R. Swann (MD), S. Swann (Ch)
Managers: E. Wilkinson (Sales Admin)
Ultimate Holding Company: ENCOMPASS GROUP LIMITED
Immediate Holding Company: KNOBS LIMITED
Registration no: 02140937 **VAT No.:** GB 462 6160 56
Date established: 1987 **Turnover:** £250,000 - £500,000
No.of Employees: 21 - 50 **Product Groups:** 30

Kompress Holdings Ltd
Unit 5 Little Tennis Street, Nottingham, NG2 4EL
Tel: 0115-958 1029 **Fax:** 0115-958 4180
E-mail: sales@kompress.com
Website: http://www.kompress.com
Directors: R. Litchfield (MD)
Managers: L. Riley (I.T. Exec)
Immediate Holding Company: KOMPRESS HOLDINGS LIMITED
Registration no: 01397261 **Date established:** 1978 **Turnover:** £5m - £10m
No.of Employees: 1 - 10 **Product Groups:** 35, 37, 46, 47

Date of Accounts	Dec 11	Dec 10	Dec 09
Working Capital	-147	-294	-119
Fixed Assets	631	864	1m
Current Assets	874	753	673

L A C Conveyors
Unit 3 Charles Park Industrial Estate Cinderhill Road, Nottingham, NG6 8RE
Tel: 0115-975 3300 **Fax:** 0115-975 3384
E-mail: sales@lacconveyors.co.uk
Website: http://www.lacconveyors.co.uk
Directors: C. Unwin (MD)
Registration no: 01807371 **VAT No.:** GB 385 4477 13
Turnover: £500,000 - £1m **No.of Employees:** 11 - 20 **Product Groups:** 39

Date of Accounts	Mar 08
Working Capital	19
Current Assets	144
Current Liabilities	125

L S Intimas
Fields Farm Road Long Eaton, Nottingham, NG10 3FZ
Tel: 0115-983 6000 **Fax:** 0115-946 8425
Bank(s): Barclays
Directors: J. Piercy (I.T. Dir), T. Laughton (Fin), A. Webster (MD), C. Duncumbe (Grp Chief Exec)
Immediate Holding Company: PIDCOCK MOTOR CYCLES LIMITED
Registration no: 01201567 **VAT No.:** GB 416 4638 50
Date established: 1975 **Turnover:** £50m - £75m
No.of Employees: 21 - 50 **Product Groups:** 24

Date of Accounts	Dec 07	Dec 06	Dec 05
Sales Turnover	19m	21m	22m
Pre Tax Profit/Loss	-4m	1m	546
Working Capital	23m	30m	33m
Fixed Assets	11m	8m	8m
Current Assets	36m	42m	43m
Current Liabilities	1m	5m	2m

Langley Mechanical Services Ltd
Unit 11 Linkmel Road, Eastwood, Nottingham, NG16 3RZ
Tel: 0114-276 6999 **Fax:** 01773-530235
E-mail: sales@langleymechanicalservices.co.uk
Website: http://www.langleymechanicalservices.co.uk
Directors: S. Whysall (Fin), A. Whysall (MD)
Ultimate Holding Company: LANGLEY MECHANICAL LIMITED
Immediate Holding Company: LANGLEY MECHANICAL LIMITED
Registration no: 05024238 **VAT No.:** GB 353 4651 56
Date established: 2004 **Turnover:** £1m - £2m **No.of Employees:** 1 - 10
Product Groups: 83

Date of Accounts	Dec 11	Dec 10	Dec 09
Fixed Assets	1m	1m	1m

Lawmax Electrical Contractors Ltd
Lawmax House 30-32 Nottingham Road, Stapleford, Nottingham, NG9 8AA
Tel: 0115-939 4248 **Fax:** 0115-939 9412
E-mail: sales@lawmaxelec.co.uk
Website: http://www.lawmaxelec.co.uk
Bank(s): National Westminster Bank Plc
Directors: C. Lawson (Fin), J. Maxwell (MD)
Immediate Holding Company: LAWMAX ELECTRICAL CONTRACTORS LIMITED
Registration no: 01385739 **VAT No.:** GB 309 4140 80
Date established: 1978 **Turnover:** £1m - £2m **No.of Employees:** 21 - 50
Product Groups: 52

Date of Accounts	Mar 11	Mar 10	Mar 09
Working Capital	1m	580	853
Fixed Assets	48	62	56
Current Assets	3m	2m	2m

Leaderflush Shapland
Milnhay Road Langley Mill, Nottingham, NG16 4AZ
Tel: 01773-530500 **Fax:** 01773-530040
E-mail: enquiries@leaderflushshapland.co.uk
Website: http://www.leaderflushshapland.co.uk
Bank(s): Barclays, Manchester

Directors: I. Hopkinson (MD)
Ultimate Holding Company: Sig plc
Immediate Holding Company: LS Group Ltd
Registration no: 03822835 **VAT No.:** GB 146 6958 25
Date established: 1999 **Turnover:** £250,000 - £500,000
No.of Employees: 101 - 250 **Product Groups:** 25, 30, 35, 47

Lear Corporation UK Ltd

Glaisdale Parkway, Nottingham, NG8 4GP
Tel: 0115-901 2200 **Fax:** 0115-928 9688
Website: http://www.lear.com
Bank(s): Citibank International plc
Directors: S. French (MD), P. Jefferson (Dir), J. Mccarthy (Co Sec)
Managers: K. Swain (Sales Prom Mgr), J. Lambert, S. Donaghue (Purch Mgr), N. Griffiths (Project Eng), D. Nicholas (Personnel), J. Taylor, J. Bryant, J. Davey, H. Christopher, D. Westley (Plant), C. Prance, P. Dilks (Mats Contrlr)
Ultimate Holding Company: LEAR CORPORATION (USA)
Immediate Holding Company: LEAR CORPORATION (UK) LIMITED
Registration no: 02818078 **VAT No.:** GB 694 2312 30
Date established: 1993 **Turnover:** £250,000 - £500,000
No.of Employees: 251 - 500 **Product Groups:** 39

Date of Accounts	Dec 10	Dec 09	Dec 08
Sales Turnover	215m	89m	157m
Pre Tax Profit/Loss	4m	-4m	-8m
Working Capital	5m	4m	6m
Fixed Assets	9m	6m	7m
Current Assets	75m	43m	48m
Current Liabilities	14m	9m	13m

Lee Beesley Ltd

Park Lane, Nottingham, NG6 0DT
Tel: 0115-927 2821 **Fax:** 0115-976 1041
E-mail: chutchinson@leebeesley.co.uk
Website: http://www.leebeesley.co.uk
Directors: A. Ford (MD), B. Roberts (Fin), P. McTearn (Dir), T. Savage (Dir)
Managers: C. Ford (Comm), C. Hutchinson (Mgr), R. Ford (Sales Prom Mgr)
Ultimate Holding Company: VINCI SA (FRANCE)
Immediate Holding Company: LEE BEESLEY HOLDINGS LIMITED
Registration no: 01234891 **VAT No.:** GB 520 7693 48
Date established: 1975 **Turnover:** £2m - £5m **No.of Employees:** 21 - 50
Product Groups: 44

Date of Accounts	Dec 07	Dec 06	Dec 05
Sales Turnover	3615	3592	2413
Pre Tax Profit/Loss	-269	254	-336
Working Capital	180	-194	-551
Fixed Assets	74	117	304
Current Assets	1211	2893	889
Current Liabilities	1031	3087	1440
ROCE% (Return on Capital Employed)	-105.9	-329.9	136.0
ROT% (Return on Turnover)	-7.4	7.1	-13.9

Leec Ltd

Private Road 7 Colwick Industrial Estate, Nottingham, NG4 2AJ
Tel: 0115-961 6222 **Fax:** 0115-961 6680
E-mail: general@leec.co.uk
Website: http://www.leec.co.uk
Bank(s): Lloyds TSB Bank plc
Directors: M. Kurby (Fin), P. Venners (MD), P. Martin (Sales), J. Leggott (Co Sec)
Managers: G. Land (Buyer), R. Venners, H. Erasmus (Fin Mgr)
Ultimate Holding Company: LEEC HOLDINGS LIMITED
Immediate Holding Company: LEEC LIMITED
Registration no: 01459141 **VAT No.:** GB 309 8056 49
Date established: 1979 **Turnover:** £5m - £10m
No.of Employees: 51 - 100 **Product Groups:** 26, 38, 42

Date of Accounts	Feb 11	Feb 10	Feb 09
Sales Turnover	5m	5m	6m
Pre Tax Profit/Loss	231	191	498
Working Capital	1m	3m	3m
Fixed Assets	1m	1m	1m
Current Assets	2m	4m	4m
Current Liabilities	160	405	720

Librex Ltd

Colwick Road, Nottingham, NG2 4BG
Tel: 0115-950 4664 **Fax:** 0115-958 6683
E-mail: sales@librex.co.uk
Website: http://www.librex.co.uk
Directors: M. Wright (Fin)
Managers: J. Hoyes
Ultimate Holding Company: JB HOLDINGS LIMITED
Immediate Holding Company: LIBREX EDUCATIONAL LIMITED
Registration no: 01260261 **VAT No.:** GB 118 2216 73
Date established: 1976 **Turnover:** £1m - £2m **No.of Employees:** 11 - 20
Product Groups: 26

Date of Accounts	Dec 11	Dec 10	Oct 09
Working Capital	-28	42	82
Fixed Assets	541	557	525
Current Assets	331	367	241

Alan Litman Ltd

Damad House 490 Radford Road, Nottingham, NG7 7EE
Tel: 0115-970 8992 **Fax:** 0115-942 0546
E-mail: cs@litmans.org
Website: http://www.litmans.org
Bank(s): National Westminster Bank Plc
Directors: C. Sherwin (MD), J. Prime (Co Sec)
Ultimate Holding Company: FB 43 LIMITED
Immediate Holding Company: ALAN LITMAN LIMITED
Registration no: 00532495 **VAT No.:** GB 116 4824 77
Date established: 1954 **Turnover:** £2m - £5m **No.of Employees:** 11 - 20
Product Groups: 23

Date of Accounts	Dec 09	Dec 08	Dec 07
Sales Turnover	N/A	N/A	4m
Pre Tax Profit/Loss	N/A	N/A	483
Working Capital	673	887	754
Fixed Assets	100	66	56
Current Assets	2m	2m	1m
Current Liabilities	N/A	N/A	639

Loxam Access Ltd

Unit 12a Glaisdale Point Glaisdale Parkway, Nottingham, NG8 4GP
Tel: 0115-900 8855 **Fax:** 0115-900 8880
E-mail: info@loxam-access.co.uk
Website: http://www.loxam-access.co.uk
Directors: B. Stead (MD)
Ultimate Holding Company: LOXAM HOLDING (FRANCE)
Immediate Holding Company: LOXAM ACCESS LIMITED
Registration no: 03988789 **Date established:** 2000
Turnover: £10m - £20m **No.of Employees:** 101 - 250
Product Groups: 35, 45, 83

Date of Accounts	Dec 11	Dec 10	Dec 09
Sales Turnover	10m	10m	10m
Pre Tax Profit/Loss	-60	-734	-1m
Working Capital	-6m	-5m	-6m
Fixed Assets	7m	6m	8m
Current Assets	3m	3m	3m
Current Liabilities	612	807	845

Luxfer Gas Cylinders

Private Road No 2 Colwick Industrial Estate, Nottingham, NG4 2BH
Tel: 0115-980 3800 **Fax:** 0115-980 3899
E-mail: david.rix@luxfer.net
Website: http://www.luxfercylinders.com
Bank(s): National Westminster Bank Plc
Directors: L. Seddon (Co Sec), D. Rix (MD), M. Vadher (Mkt Research)
Managers: D. Tordoff (Sales Prom Mgr), T. Bathgate (Tech Serv Mgr), S. Hartshaw (Personnel), G. Thompson (Fin Mgr), D. Weston (Purch Mgr)
Ultimate Holding Company: LUXFER HOLDINGS PLC
Immediate Holding Company: LUXFER GAS CYLINDERS LIMITED
Registration no: 03376625 **Date established:** 1997
Turnover: £20m - £50m **No.of Employees:** 101 - 250
Product Groups: 31, 35, 38, 40

Date of Accounts	Dec 11	Dec 10	Dec 09
Sales Turnover	48m	45m	38m
Pre Tax Profit/Loss	3m	3m	-281
Working Capital	6m	4m	1m
Fixed Assets	10m	10m	9m
Current Assets	13m	12m	10m
Current Liabilities	2m	2m	3m

M C T Services

3 Grey Street Kirkby-in-Ashfield, Nottingham, NG17 8GW
Tel: 01623-722339 **Fax:** 01623-722339
Directors: M. Pennington (Prop)
Date established: 1999 **No.of Employees:** 1 - 10 **Product Groups:** 46

M G Renewables

Lenton Business Centre Lenton Boulevard, Nottingham, NG7 2BY
Tel: 0115-978 3423
Website: http://www.mgrenewables.com
Directors: M. Dowd (Fin)
Immediate Holding Company: MG Renewables Ltd
Registration no: 06032214 **Date established:** 2006
No.of Employees: 1 - 10 **Product Groups:** 37, 40

M G Rubber Co. Ltd

Moorbridge Road Bingham Industrial Estate, Bingham, Nottingham, NG13 8GG
Tel: 01949-839112 **Fax:** 01949-831357
E-mail: sales@mgrubber.com
Website: http://www.mgrubber.com
Bank(s): Barclays
Directors: B. Rae (MD), W. Grimshaw (Dir)
Managers: K. Popplewell (Sales Prom Mgr)
Immediate Holding Company: M G RUBBER CO. LIMITED
Registration no: 05971436 **VAT No.:** GB 118 7657 43
Date established: 2006 **Turnover:** £5m - £10m
No.of Employees: 51 - 100 **Product Groups:** 24

Date of Accounts	Apr 11	Apr 10	Apr 09
Sales Turnover	N/A	N/A	4m
Pre Tax Profit/Loss	N/A	N/A	96
Working Capital	1m	1m	988
Fixed Assets	22	46	72
Current Assets	2m	2m	2m
Current Liabilities	N/A	N/A	204

M J Maillis UK Ltd

Monarch House Chrysalis Way, Eastwood, Nottingham, NG16 3RY
Tel: 01773-539000 **Fax:** 01773-539090
E-mail: info@mallis.co.uk
Website: http://www.maillis.co.uk
Bank(s): HSBC Bank Plc
Directors: G. Bowron (Co Sec), P. Davies (MD)
Managers: S. Hains (Tech Serv Mgr), A. Walker (Tech Sales Mgr), M. Sural (Purch Mgr)
Ultimate Holding Company: M.J. MAILLIS S.A. (GREECE)
Immediate Holding Company: M J MAILLIS (UK) LIMITED
Registration no: 03246586 **VAT No.:** GB 333 7102 88
Date established: 1996 **Turnover:** £10m - £20m
No.of Employees: 51 - 100 **Product Groups:** 30, 42, 45

Date of Accounts	Dec 11	Dec 10	Dec 09
Sales Turnover	20m	19m	16m
Pre Tax Profit/Loss	-1m	-3m	-3m
Working Capital	-11m	-14m	-12m
Fixed Assets	7m	7m	8m
Current Assets	7m	7m	7m
Current Liabilities	18m	5m	1m

M & R Refinishing Ltd

Private Road 4 Colwick Industrial Estate, Nottingham, NG4 2JT
Tel: 0115-940 0466 **Fax:** 0115-961 6809
E-mail: enquiries@mandrrefinishing.com
Website: http://www.mandrrefinishing.com
Directors: C. Ovendale (Fin), P. Whitehead (MD)
Ultimate Holding Company: M & R PROPERTY HOLDINGS LIMITED
Immediate Holding Company: M & R REFINISHING LIMITED
Registration no: 01847051 **Date established:** 1984
No.of Employees: 11 - 20 **Product Groups:** 46, 48

Date of Accounts	Dec 11	Dec 10	Dec 09
Working Capital	92	128	127
Fixed Assets	42	49	53
Current Assets	208	217	186

Machine Mart

211 Lower Parliament Street, Nottingham, NG1 1GN
Tel: 0115-956 1811 **Fax:** 08707-707811
E-mail: sales@machinemart.co.uk
Website: http://www.machinemart.co.uk
Directors: K. Stephenson (MD), K. Stevenson (MD), J. Williams (Fin)
Managers: I. Pinn (Buyer), M. Reed (Sales Prom Mgr), R. Bernard (Mktg Serv Mgr), R. Watson (I.T. Exec), V. Bhimami (Comptroller), A. Blair (Personnel)
Immediate Holding Company: MACHINE MART LIMITED
Registration no: 01555925 **VAT No.:** GB 306 5741 67
Date established: 1981 **Turnover:** £50m - £75m
No.of Employees: 251 - 500 **Product Groups:** 35, 36, 37, 40, 47

Date of Accounts	May 09	May 08	May 07
Sales Turnover	56m	61m	59m
Pre Tax Profit/Loss	9m	12m	9m
Working Capital	27m	20m	18m
Fixed Assets	5m	5m	5m
Current Assets	51m	45m	37m
Current Liabilities	21m	21m	15m

Malem Medical

10 Willow Holt Lowdham, Nottingham, NG14 7EJ
Tel: 0115-966 4440 **Fax:** 0115-966 4672
E-mail: malem@enterprise.net
Website: http://www.malem.co.uk
Directors: H. Malem (MD)
Immediate Holding Company: MALEM MEDICAL LIMITED
Registration no: 01730392 **Date established:** 1983 **Turnover:** £1m - £2m
No.of Employees: 11 - 20 **Product Groups:** 67

Malmic Lace Ltd

Malmic House Brookside Road, Ruddington, Nottingham, NG11 6AT
Tel: 0115-940 5151 **Fax:** 0115-984 5706
E-mail: info@malmiclace.co.uk
Website: http://www.malmiclace.co.uk
Bank(s): National Westminster
Directors: J. Wallis (Fin), M. Jaffe (Sales)
Ultimate Holding Company: WALLIS BROTHERS LIMITED
Immediate Holding Company: MALMIC LACE LIMITED
Registration no: 00819475 **VAT No.:** GB 116 5044 01
Date established: 1964 **Turnover:** £1m - £2m **No.of Employees:** 11 - 20
Product Groups: 23

Date of Accounts	Mar 11	Mar 10	Mar 09
Working Capital	-669	-617	-563
Fixed Assets	32	6	7
Current Assets	535	504	721

Maplin Electronics Ltd

86-88 Lower Parliament Street, Nottingham, NG1 1EH
Tel: 08432-277304 **Fax:** 0115-941 0247
E-mail: customercare@maplin.co.uk
Website: http://www.maplin.co.uk
Managers: D. Walker (Mgr)
Ultimate Holding Company: MONTAGU PRIVATE EQUITY LLP
Immediate Holding Company: MAPLIN ELECTRONICS LIMITED
Registration no: 01264385 **Date established:** 1976
Turnover: £125m - £250m **No.of Employees:** 1 - 10 **Product Groups:** 37, 61

Date of Accounts	Dec 11	Dec 08	Dec 09
Sales Turnover	205m	204m	204m
Pre Tax Profit/Loss	25m	32m	35m
Working Capital	118m	49m	75m
Fixed Assets	27m	28m	28m
Current Assets	207m	108m	142m
Current Liabilities	78m	51m	59m

Marsh Bellofram

9 Castle Park, Nottingham, NG2 1AH
Tel: 0115-993 3300 **Fax:** 0115-993 3301
E-mail: adaniels@marshbellofram.com
Website: http://www.marshbellofram.com
Bank(s): HSBC Bank
Directors: A. Daniels (Fin)
Ultimate Holding Company: BELLOFRAM CORPORATION INC (USA)
Immediate Holding Company: MARSH BELLOFRAM EUROPE LIMITED
Registration no: 00090604 **VAT No.:** GB 616 3074 95
Date established: 2006 **Turnover:** £2m - £5m **No.of Employees:** 11 - 20
Product Groups: 30, 36, 37, 38, 39, 40, 41, 42, 44, 45, 46, 48, 49, 66, 67

Date of Accounts	Dec 11	Dec 10	Dec 09
Working Capital	2m	1m	1m
Fixed Assets	923	913	907
Current Assets	2m	2m	2m

Marshall Agricultural Engineering

New Buildings Forest Lane, Papplewick, Nottingham, NG15 8FG
Tel: 0115-963 0011 **Fax:** 0115-963 0022
E-mail: howard@howardmarshalleng.co.uk
Managers: H. Marshall (Mgr)
Immediate Holding Company: J. WALSTER LIMITED
Registration no: 01889092 **Date established:** 1985
No.of Employees: 11 - 20 **Product Groups:** 41

Date of Accounts	Sep 11	Sep 10	Sep 09
Working Capital	3m	2m	2m
Fixed Assets	1	2	3
Current Assets	5m	4m	4m

Matrix Net Ltd

1 Nelson Street Long Eaton, Nottingham, NG10 1DB
Tel: 0115-946 4222 **Fax:** 0115-946 4232
E-mail: sales@matrixnet.co.uk
Website: http://www.matrixnet.co.uk
Directors: I. Clarke (Dir)
Immediate Holding Company: MATRIX NET LIMITED
Registration no: 03911410 **Date established:** 2000
No.of Employees: 1 - 10 **Product Groups:** 37, 40, 44

Date of Accounts	Feb 11	Feb 10	Feb 09
Working Capital	-2	15	33
Fixed Assets	151	152	153
Current Assets	97	145	172

Medoc Computers Ltd

Meadow House Meadow Lane, Nottingham, NG2 3HS
Tel: 0115-986 8786 **Fax:** 0115-986 8737
E-mail: info@medoc.co.uk
Website: http://www.medoc.com
Bank(s): Lloyds
Directors: L. Done (MD)
Managers: B. Timson
Immediate Holding Company: MEDOC COMPUTERS LIMITED
Registration no: 01583691 **VAT No.:** GB 352 7406 60
Date established: 1981 **Turnover:** £1m - £2m **No.of Employees:** 11 - 20
Product Groups: 44

Date of Accounts	Aug 11	Aug 10	Aug 09
Working Capital	258	330	286
Fixed Assets	181	194	226
Current Assets	613	687	645

Henry Mein Partnership

10-12 Clarendon Street, Nottingham, NG1 5HQ
Tel: 0115-947 6065 **Fax:** 0115-924 0136
E-mail: info@henrymein.co.uk
Website: http://www.henrymein.co.uk
Bank(s): Barclays
Managers: J. Heason (Sales Admin)
No.of Employees: 11 - 20 **Product Groups:** 84

Merrin Joinery
Kirkby in Ashfield, Nottingham, NG17 5GS
Tel: 07979-981345
E-mail: enquiries@merrinjoinery.com
Website: http://www.merrinjoinery.com
Managers: C. Merrin (Comm)
Registration no: 01638786 **Date established:** 2007
Turnover: Up to £250,000 **No.of Employees:** 1 - 10 **Product Groups:** 25

Metrum Information Storage Ltd
Oxford Street Long Eaton, Nottingham, NG10 1JR
Tel: 0118-973 3000 **Fax:** 0118-973 4363
E-mail: enquiries@metrum.co.uk
Website: http://www.metrum.co.uk
Directors: C. Beaton (MD), C. Beeton (MD), S. Wensley (MD), T. Lorkin (MD), K. Chatt (Fin)
Managers: G. Linb (Personnel), G. Limb (Chief Mgr), M. George (Mktg Serv Mgr)
Ultimate Holding Company: Metrum Information Storage Ltd
Immediate Holding Company: TDM Tape Services Ltd
Registration no: 02648290 **No.of Employees:** 11 - 20 **Product Groups:** 44

Microtech Filters Ltd
Alva Lodge Kirkby Lane, Pinxton, Nottingham, NG16 6HW
Tel: 01773-862345 **Fax:** 01773-863111
E-mail: info@microtechfilters.co.uk
Website: http://www.microtechfilters.co.uk
Bank(s): National Westminster Bank Plc
Directors: P. Moore (MD)
Managers: S. Bergin (Chief Buyer), M. Drewry (Chief Acct)
Immediate Holding Company: J PARKINSON HOLDINGS LIMITED
Registration no: 01852667 **Date established:** 1984
No.of Employees: 21 - 50 **Product Groups:** 33, 40, 42

Date of Accounts	Oct 11	Aug 10	Aug 09
Working Capital	587	624	614
Fixed Assets	74	360	346
Current Assets	811	624	865

Midland Box Co. Ltd
Field Indl-Est Clover Street, Kirkby-In-Ashfield, Nottingham, NG17 7LH
Tel: 01623-758758 **Fax:** 01623-757229
E-mail: enquiries@westpack.co.uk
Website: http://www.midlandbox.co.uk
Bank(s): HSBC Bank plc
Directors: A. Fox (MD), S. Turner (Dir), S. Turner (MD)
Managers: R. Draycott (Chief Mgr), C. Morris (Accounts)
Ultimate Holding Company: W.K.WEST,LIMITED
Immediate Holding Company: MIDLAND BOX COMPANY LIMITED
Registration no: 00309069 **VAT No.:** GB 118 6383 59
Date established: 1936 **Turnover:** £1m - £2m **No.of Employees:** 11 - 20
Product Groups: 27

Date of Accounts	Dec 10	Dec 09	Dec 08
Working Capital	210	160	229
Fixed Assets	132	158	174
Current Assets	624	673	739
Current Liabilities	N/A	N/A	444

Midland Catering Engineers
Private Road No 5, Nottingham, NG4 2JU
Tel: 0115-987 9686 **Fax:** 0115-961 3887
Directors: P. Isaacs (Prop)
Immediate Holding Company: MIDLAND CATERING ENGINEERS LIMITED
Registration no: 05193045 **Date established:** 2004
No.of Employees: 1 - 10 **Product Groups:** 20, 40, 41

Date of Accounts	Mar 11	Mar 10	Mar 09
Working Capital	151	102	67
Fixed Assets	71	47	56
Current Assets	210	138	144

Midland Filtration Ltd
11a West Avenue West Bridgford, Nottingham, NG2 7NL
Tel: 0115-982 0676 **Fax:** 0115-945 5836
E-mail: richard.johnson@midfilters.co.uk
Website: http://www.midfilters.co.uk
Bank(s): National Westminster Bank Plc
Directors: R. Johnson (Dir), R. Johnson (MD), W. Taylor (Sales), A. Godfrey (Fin)
Managers: K. Barber (Sales Admin)
Immediate Holding Company: MIDLAND FILTRATION LIMITED
Registration no: 01936235 **VAT No.:** GB 416 3203 90
Date established: 1985 **Turnover:** £1m - £2m **No.of Employees:** 21 - 50
Product Groups: 23, 24, 33, 34, 35, 39, 40, 42, 45, 48

Date of Accounts	May 11	May 10	May 09
Working Capital	81	66	62
Fixed Assets	73	81	86
Current Assets	673	680	599

Midland Gate Automation
16 Hawthorne Rise Awsworth, Nottingham, NG16 2RG
Tel: 0115-944 5856
Website: http://www.midlandgateautomation.co.uk
Directors: D. Greenham (Prop), D. Greenham (Fin)
Immediate Holding Company: MIDLAND GATE AUTOMATION LIMITED
Registration no: 04795291 **Date established:** 2003
No.of Employees: 1 - 10 **Product Groups:** 35, 40

Midland HR
Ruddington Hall Loughborough Road, Ruddington, Nottingham, NG11 6LL
Tel: 0115-945 6000 **Fax:** 0115-940 5286
E-mail: reception@midlandhr.co.uk
Website: http://www.midlandhr.co.uk
Directors: D. Mcgrath (MD), M. Doughty (Co Sec)
Ultimate Holding Company: MIDLAND SOFTWARE HOLDINGS LIMITED
Immediate Holding Company: MIDLAND SOFTWARE LIMITED
Registration no: 01852206 **Date established:** 1984
Turnover: £20m - £50m **No.of Employees:** 251 - 500 **Product Groups:** 44

Date of Accounts	Dec 11	Dec 10	Dec 09
Sales Turnover	27m	25m	21m
Pre Tax Profit/Loss	3m	5m	3m
Working Capital	3m	3m	2m
Fixed Assets	907	518	460
Current Assets	11m	12m	8m
Current Liabilities	7m	8m	5m

Midland Reprographics Ltd
The Old Church Main Street, Kimberley, Nottingham, NG16 2LL
Tel: 0115-938 2353 **Fax:** 0115-945 9748
E-mail: sales@midlandreprographics.com
Website: http://www.midlandreprographics.com
Directors: D. Laidler (MD)
Immediate Holding Company: MIDLAND REPROGRAPHICS LIMITED
Registration no: 02622758 **Date established:** 1991
No.of Employees: 1 - 10 **Product Groups:** 28, 38, 44, 64, 67

Date of Accounts	Jun 11	Jun 10	Jun 09
Working Capital	14	6	-8
Fixed Assets	4	N/A	N/A
Current Assets	97	88	81

Midland Stairlifts Ltd
11 Glebe Farm View Gedling, Nottingham, NG4 4NZ
Tel: 0115-961 3855 **Fax:** 0115-987 0285
E-mail: stephen.whitt@ntlworld.com
Website: http://www.ntlhome.com
Directors: S. Whitt (MD), J. Whitt (Co Sec)
Immediate Holding Company: MIDLAND STAIRLIFTS LIMITED
Registration no: 04488680 **Date established:** 2002
No.of Employees: 1 - 10 **Product Groups:** 35, 39, 45

Date of Accounts	Jul 11	Jul 10	Jul 09
Working Capital	29	36	31
Fixed Assets	17	7	9
Current Assets	51	58	54

Midland Wiper Manufacturing Co. Ltd
Fletcher Street Long Eaton, Nottingham, NG10 1JU
Tel: 0115-973 5187 **Fax:** 0115-946 2012
E-mail: office@midlandwiper.co.uk
Website: http://www.midlandwiper.co.uk
Bank(s): Barclays, Long Eaton
Directors: M. Smith (Sales), T. Smith (Dir)
Immediate Holding Company: MIDLAND WIPER MANUFACTURING COMPANY LIMITED
Registration no: 00138962 **VAT No.:** GB 125 6107 94
Date established: 2015 **Turnover:** £1m - £2m **No.of Employees:** 11 - 20
Product Groups: 23, 27, 66

Date of Accounts	Mar 12	Mar 11	Mar 10
Working Capital	179	175	121
Fixed Assets	142	115	122
Current Assets	658	634	539

Mighty
2 Colwick Quays Business Park Private Road 2, Colwick Industrial Estate, Nottingham, NG4 2JR
Tel: 0115-940 2222 **Fax:** 0115-940 2232
E-mail: mark.murphy@robert-prettie.co.uk
Website: http://www.robert-prettie.co.uk
Bank(s): Royal Bank of Scotland
Directors: M. Murphy (MD), A. Baker (MD)
Managers: J. Burton (Tech Serv Mgr), P. Neary, R. Griffiths (Comptroller)
Immediate Holding Company: BYTEM LTD
Registration no: 00948375 **Date established:** 2007
Turnover: £10m - £20m **No.of Employees:** 51 - 100 **Product Groups:** 52

Date of Accounts	Mar 08
Sales Turnover	48740
Pre Tax Profit/Loss	2990
Working Capital	8780
Fixed Assets	180
Current Assets	20960
Current Liabilities	12180
Total Share Capital	30
ROCE% (Return on Capital Employed)	33.4

Mills Computer Products International Ltd
7 Amber Drive Langley Mill, Nottingham, NG16 4BE
Tel: 01773-761246 **Fax:** 01773-531246
E-mail: enquiries@millsimage.co.uk
Website: http://www.millsimage.co.uk
Bank(s): Barclays, Dudley
Managers: J. Lewis, J. Allen (Sales & Mktg Mg), S. Skelton (Fin Mgr), A. Doherty (Warehouse Mgr)
Ultimate Holding Company: STARBO INVESTMENT LIMITED (HONG KONG)
Immediate Holding Company: MILLS COMPUTER PRODUCTS (INTERNATIONAL) LIMITED
Registration no: 03200492 **VAT No.:** GB 683 9313 06
Date established: 1996 **Turnover:** £5m - £10m **No.of Employees:** 21 - 50
Product Groups: 23

Date of Accounts	Dec 11	Dec 10	Dec 09
Sales Turnover	6m	5m	5m
Pre Tax Profit/Loss	434	728	443
Working Capital	2m	1m	865
Fixed Assets	135	137	18
Current Assets	3m	3m	2m
Current Liabilities	225	305	198

MINNI-DIE LIMITED
40 TRENT SOUTH INDUSTRIAL PARK LITTLE TENNIS STREET, NOTTINGHAM, NG2 4EQ
Tel: 0115-941 9009 **Fax:** 0115-050 3921
E-mail: sales@minni-die.co.uk
Website: http://www.minni-die.co.uk
Managers: B. Ash (Sales Prom Mgr), P. Marsh (Sales Prom Mgr)
Registration no: 06935453 **Date established:** 2009
No.of Employees: 1 - 10 **Product Groups:** 46

Minni-Die Ltd
Unit 40 Trent South Industrial Park Little Tennis Street, Nottingham, NG2 4EQ
Tel: 0115-941 9009 **Fax:** 0115-950 3921
E-mail: sales@minni-die.com
Website: http://www.parsellminni-die.com
Bank(s): HSBC Bank plc
Directors: C. Parsell (Fin)
Managers: B. Ash (Chief Mgr), G. Parsell (Sales Prom Mgr), P. Marsh (Works Gen Mgr)
Immediate Holding Company: Parsell Minni-Die Ltd
Registration no: 06935453 **VAT No.:** GB 610 5793 53
Turnover: £500,000 - £1m **No.of Employees:** 21 - 50
Product Groups: 36, 40, 42, 46

Mirabel Ltd
123 Mansfield Road Daybrook, Nottingham, NG5 6HT
Tel: 0115-967 0022 **Fax:** 0115-920 6875
E-mail: enquires@mirabeluk.com
Website: http://www.mirabel.co.uk
Bank(s): National Westminster
Directors: T. Briggs (MD), P. Cater (Sales)
Managers: R. Hudson, A. Pritchett (Sales Prom Mgr), W. Whitby (Mktg Serv Mgr)
Registration no: 03789076 **VAT No.:** GB 728 6341 20
Date established: 1925 **Turnover:** £5m - £10m **No.of Employees:** 21 - 50
Product Groups: 23, 84

Monarch Textiles
Prospect Close Lowmoor Business Park, Kirkby-in-Ashfield, Nottingham, NG17 7LF
Tel: 01623-750777 **Fax:** 01623-720779
E-mail: enquiry@monarch-textiles.co.uk
Website: http://www.monarch-safety.com
Bank(s): National Westminster Bank Plc
Directors: P. Curtis (MD), J. Peto (Snr Part), A. O'Dell (Sales)
Ultimate Holding Company: STRONGFIELD TECHNOLOGIES LIMITED
Immediate Holding Company: GLOBAL EMC INTERNATIONAL LIMITED
Registration no: 06373874 **VAT No.:** GB 598 6250 87
Date established: 2007 **Turnover:** Up to £250,000
No.of Employees: 51 - 100 **Product Groups:** 24

Date of Accounts	Jun 07	Jun 06
Working Capital	453	398
Fixed Assets	1460	1476
Current Assets	1630	1473
Current Liabilities	1177	1075
Total Share Capital	75	75

Morris Vermaport
14 Vickery Way Beeston, Nottingham, NG9 6RY
Tel: 0115-973 7500 **Fax:** 0115-973 7501
E-mail: peterf@morrisvermaport.co.uk
Website: http://www.morrisvermaport.co.uk
Bank(s): Lloyds TSB Bank plc
Directors: A. Wadell (Chief Op Offcr), P. Fox (Fin)
Managers: M. Fox (Tech Serv Mgr), I. Lilley (Develop Mgr)
Immediate Holding Company: MORRIS VERMAPORT LIMITED
Registration no: 03681149 **VAT No.:** GB 309 6619 41
Date established: 1998 **Turnover:** £5m - £10m
No.of Employees: 51 - 100 **Product Groups:** 45, 48

Date of Accounts	Jun 11	Jun 10	Jun 09
Sales Turnover	7m	7m	6m
Pre Tax Profit/Loss	309	85	-222
Working Capital	-332	-499	-159
Fixed Assets	654	763	404
Current Assets	2m	2m	1m
Current Liabilities	1m	1m	990

Murphy & Son
Alpine Street, Nottingham, NG6 0HQ
Tel: 0115-978 5494 **Fax:** 0115-924 4654
E-mail: sales@murphyandson.co.uk
Website: http://www.murphyandson.co.uk
Bank(s): Barclays
Directors: C. Fleming (MD)
Immediate Holding Company: HAYESSHELF NUMBER 1 LIMITED
Registration no: 03984360 **VAT No.:** GB 196 8782 88
Date established: 2000 **Turnover:** £2m - £5m **No.of Employees:** 51 - 100
Product Groups: 32, 84

Date of Accounts	Jun 11	Apr 10	Apr 09
Working Capital	1m	845	22
Fixed Assets	N/A	47	252
Current Assets	1m	2m	569

Myford Ltd
Wilmot Lane Chilwell Road, Beeston, Nottingham, NG9 1ER
Tel: 0115-925 4222 **Fax:** 0115-943 1299
E-mail: sales@myford.com
Website: http://www.myford.com
Bank(s): Midland
Directors: J. Moore (Fin), G. Davies (Co Sec), C. Moore (MD), C. Moore (Sales)
Managers: D. Wheat (Mktg Serv Mgr), J. Alvey (Sales Prom Mgr), M. Townsend (Sales Prom Mgr)
Immediate Holding Company: MYFORD (HOLDINGS) LIMITED
Registration no: 00328817 **VAT No.:** GB 116 8582 55
Date established: 1937 **Turnover:** £2m - £5m **No.of Employees:** 21 - 50
Product Groups: 46, 48

Date of Accounts	Sep 09	Sep 08	Sep 07
Sales Turnover	693	822	705
Pre Tax Profit/Loss	-149	-71	-115
Working Capital	1m	2m	2m
Fixed Assets	33	44	53
Current Assets	1m	2m	2m
Current Liabilities	44	42	32

National Auto Parts
Willow Road, Nottingham, NG7 2TA
Tel: 0115-973 8100 **Fax:** 0115-973 8101
E-mail: daveh@national-auto.co.uk
Website: http://www.national-auto.co.uk
Bank(s): Lloyds TSB
Directors: D. Houlden (MD), D. Holden (MD)
Managers: K. Hall (Chief Buyer), N. Barrett, L. Watson (), F. Clues (Fin Mgr), G. Walker (Sales & Mktg Mg), C. Parry (I.T. Exec), G. Walker (Mktg Serv Mgr)
Ultimate Holding Company: A.C.GILL,LIMITED
Immediate Holding Company: NOTTINGHAM TEXTILES LIMITED
Registration no: 00357290 **Date established:** 1939 **Turnover:** £5m - £10m
No.of Employees: 101 - 250 **Product Groups:** 39

Date of Accounts	Mar 11	Mar 10	Mar 09
Working Capital	-64	-123	5
Fixed Assets	583	525	569
Current Assets	834	479	654

Neil Hannah Partnership
PO Box 7352, Nottingham, NG12 3JP
Tel: 0870-6092615 **Fax:** 0115-989 9544
E-mail: info@neilhannahpartnership.co.uk
Website: http://www.neilhannahpartnership.co.uk
Directors: N. Hannah (Ptnr)
Registration no: 06795490 **Date established:** 2002
No.of Employees: 1 - 10 **Product Groups:** 80, 81

Newson Gale Ltd
Omega House Private Road 8, Colwick Industrial Estate, Nottingham, NG4 2JX
Tel: 0115-940 7500 **Fax:** 0115-940 7501
E-mail: groundit@newson-gale.co.uk
Website: http://newson-gale.co.uk
Managers: L. Middleton, S. Logan
Immediate Holding Company: NEWSON GALE LIMITED
Registration no: 02281932 **VAT No.:** GB 507 4800 60
Date established: 1988 **Turnover:** £2m - £5m **No.of Employees:** 21 - 50
Product Groups: 35, 37

Date of Accounts	Dec 11	Dec 10	Dec 09
Working Capital	1m	1m	816
Fixed Assets	100	92	58
Current Assets	2m	2m	1m

Nexor Ltd
Bell House Nottingham Science & Technology Park, Nottingham, NG7 2RL
Tel: 0115-952 0500 **Fax:** 0115-952 0519
E-mail: info@nexor.com
Website: http://www.nexor.com
Bank(s): National Westminster Bank Plc
Directors: N. Fasey (Fin)
Immediate Holding Company: NEXOR LIMITED
Registration no: 05152465 **VAT No.:** GB 567 8820 89
Date established: 2004 **Turnover:** £2m - £5m **No.of Employees:** 51 - 100
Product Groups: 44, 84

Date of Accounts	Mar 11	Mar 10	Mar 09
Sales Turnover	3m	3m	4m
Pre Tax Profit/Loss	-283	94	420
Working Capital	110	433	28
Fixed Assets	427	482	569
Current Assets	1m	2m	2m
Current Liabilities	833	1m	2m

Nofotec
Unit 5 Morris Court Private Road 3, Colwick Industrial Estate, Nottingham, NG4 2JN
Tel: 0115-987 6696 **Fax:** 0115-940 0070
E-mail: info@nofotec.co.uk
Website: http://www.nofotec.co.uk
Directors: D. Bush (MD), B. Bush (Fin)
Managers: P. Revill (Works Gen Mgr)
Immediate Holding Company: NOFOTEC COMPANY LIMITED
Registration no: 01593721 **VAT No.:** GB 416 2270 80
Date established: 1981 **Turnover:** £500,000 - £1m
No.of Employees: 1 - 10 **Product Groups:** 46, 84

Date of Accounts	Nov 08	Nov 07	Nov 06
Working Capital	-5	-53	13
Fixed Assets	62	167	178
Current Assets	104	79	80
Current Liabilities	109	133	68

Nottingham Building Society
Nottingham House 5-13 Upper Parliament Street, Nottingham, NG1 2BX
Tel: 0115-956 4256 **Fax:** 0115-948 3948
E-mail: sales-development@thenottingham.com
Website: http://www.thenottingham.com
Directors: D. Watts (Co Sec), A. Piranie (Fin)
Managers: P. Stanhope (Mktg Serv Mgr), D. Marlow
Ultimate Holding Company: NOTTINGHAM BUILDING SOCIETY
Immediate Holding Company: NOTTINGHAM PROPERTY SERVICES LIMITED
Registration no: 02272731 **Date established:** 1988 **Turnover:** £1m - £2m
No.of Employees: 101 - 250 **Product Groups:** 82

Date of Accounts	Dec 11	Dec 10	Dec 09
Sales Turnover	1m	1m	2m
Pre Tax Profit/Loss	-171	-190	-101
Working Capital	-1m	-2m	-1m
Fixed Assets	1m	1m	1m
Current Assets	59	105	224
Current Liabilities	95	86	52

Nottingham Electrical Distributors Ltd
Unit 6 Tennis Court Industrial Estate, Nottingham, NG2 4EW
Tel: 0115-950 5727 **Fax:** 0115-950 1963
E-mail: info@ned-sted.co.uk
Directors: M. Pykett (Dir)
Immediate Holding Company: NOTTINGHAM ELECTRICAL DISTRIBUTORS LIMITED
Registration no: 02610056 **VAT No.:** GB 568 0779 94
Date established: 1991 **Turnover:** £250,000 - £500,000
No.of Employees: 1 - 10 **Product Groups:** 77

Nottingham Evening Post
Castle Wharf House, Nottingham, NG1 7EU
Tel: 0115-948 2000 **Fax:** 0115-964 4032
Website: http://www.thisisnottingham.co.uk
Bank(s): National Westminster Bank Plc
Managers: A. Leys (Mgr), A. Jones (Sales Admin)
Immediate Holding Company: NORTHCLIFFE NEWSPAPER LTD
Registration no: 02915487 **VAT No.:** GB 749 7046 94
Turnover: £20m - £50m **No.of Employees:** 101 - 250 **Product Groups:** 28

Nottingham Pallet Racking Co.
Tall Trees House 12 Blackhill Drive, Carlton, Nottingham, NG4 3FT
Tel: 07973-336458 **Fax:** 0115-840 9850
E-mail: byronwood11@hotmail.com
Website: http://www.nottmusedracking.co.uk
Directors: T. Wood (Prop)
Date established: 1990 **No.of Employees:** 1 - 10 **Product Groups:** 26, 85

Nottingham Paper Bag Co. Ltd
Mundella Works Mundella Road, Nottingham, NG2 2EQ
Tel: 0115-986 1376 **Fax:** 0115-986 2018
E-mail: glyn@godfrey.co.uk
Website: http://www.thepaperman.net
Directors: G. Godfrey (MD)
Immediate Holding Company: NOTTINGHAM PAPER BAG COMPANY LIMITED(THE)
Registration no: 00282999 **Date established:** 1933
Turnover: Up to £250,000 **No.of Employees:** 1 - 10 **Product Groups:** 20, 27

Date of Accounts	Dec 11	Dec 10	Dec 08
Working Capital	5	-31	-32
Fixed Assets	25	24	29
Current Assets	47	30	34

Nottingham Platers Ltd
Southwark Street, Nottingham, NG6 0DB
Tel: 0115-978 4637 **Fax:** 0115-978 9754
E-mail: mail@chrome-platers.com
Website: http://www.chrome-platers.com
Bank(s): Barclays
Directors: J. Powell (Co Sec), M. Humphries (Dir)
Immediate Holding Company: NOTTINGHAM PLATERS LIMITED
Registration no: 01661536 **VAT No.:** GB 352 9895 09
Date established: 1982 **No.of Employees:** 21 - 50 **Product Groups:** 48

Date of Accounts	Oct 11	Oct 10	Oct 09
Working Capital	540	455	360
Fixed Assets	988	985	533
Current Assets	737	669	493

Nottingham Suspended Ceilings Ltd
Wright Street Netherfield, Nottingham, NG4 2PG
Tel: 0115-987 9880 **Fax:** 0115-940 0086
E-mail: enquiries@nsceilings.co.uk
Website: http://www.nsceilings.co.uk
Directors: M. Wells (Dir)
Immediate Holding Company: NOTTINGHAM SUSPENDED CEILINGS LIMITED
Registration no: 00746020 **VAT No.:** GB 117 3332 00
Date established: 1963 **Turnover:** £1m - £2m **No.of Employees:** 1 - 10
Product Groups: 35, 52

Date of Accounts	Mar 10	Mar 09	Mar 08
Working Capital	101	161	163
Fixed Assets	133	156	168
Current Assets	186	314	315

Nottingham Zinc Group Ltd
Byron Avenue Lowmoor Business Park, Kirkby-in-Ashfield, Nottingham, NG17 7LA
Tel: 01623-752107 **Fax:** 01623-721453
E-mail: blayne@nottinghamzincgroup.com
Website: http://www.nottinghamzincgroup.com
Bank(s): HSBC Bank plc
Directors: B. Flint (Dir), C. Thomas (Dir)
Ultimate Holding Company: NOTTINGHAM ZINC HOLDINGS LIMITED
Immediate Holding Company: NOTTINGHAM ZINC GROUP LIMITED
Registration no: 04362474 **VAT No.:** GB 385 1518 40
Date established: 2002 **Turnover:** £2m - £5m **No.of Employees:** 21 - 50
Product Groups: 48

Date of Accounts	Mar 12	Mar 11	Mar 09
Working Capital	-66	-114	208
Fixed Assets	519	504	626
Current Assets	491	510	622

Oakdene Automatic Transmissions
Freeth Street, Nottingham, NG2 3GT
Tel: 0115-986 6603 **Fax:** 0115-986 3511
E-mail: info@oakdenegarage.com
Website: http://www.oakdeneautomatictransmissions.co.uk
Directors: R. Dean (Prop)
Date established: 1985 **No.of Employees:** 1 - 10 **Product Groups:** 35, 45

Omega Red Group Ltd
Blenheim Industrial Estate Bulwell, Nottingham, NG6 8WA
Tel: 0115-877 6666 **Fax:** 0115-876 7744
E-mail: enquiries@omegaredgroup.com
Website: http://www.omegaredgroup.com
Bank(s): National Westminster Bank Plc
Directors: C. Watkins (MD)
Ultimate Holding Company: HYDRIADES IV LIMITED
Immediate Holding Company: OMEGA RED GROUP LIMITED
Registration no: 02197902 **VAT No.:** GB 496 4033 28
Date established: 1987 **Turnover:** £10m - £20m
No.of Employees: 21 - 50 **Product Groups:** 37, 38, 52, 84

Date of Accounts	Mar 11	Mar 10	Mar 09
Sales Turnover	16m	16m	15m
Pre Tax Profit/Loss	4m	4m	3m
Working Capital	5m	7m	4m
Fixed Assets	382	448	450
Current Assets	8m	11m	7m
Current Liabilities	2m	2m	2m

One Packaging Ltd
6 Moorbridge Road Bingham, Nottingham, NG13 8GG
Tel: 01949-837666 **Fax:** 01949-836366
E-mail: info@onepack.co.uk
Website: http://www.onepack.co.uk
Directors: G. Almond (MD)
Immediate Holding Company: ONE PACKAGING LIMITED
Registration no: 04823513 **Date established:** 2003
No.of Employees: 11 - 20 **Product Groups:** 38, 42

Date of Accounts	Jul 11	Jul 10	Jul 09
Working Capital	-119	-37	-25
Fixed Assets	182	131	96
Current Assets	1m	1m	969

Open Projects Ltd
Unit 6 Beeston Business Centre Technology Drive, Beeston, Nottingham, NG9 2ND
Tel: 0115-943 6421 **Fax:** 0115-922 0213
E-mail: info@openprojects.co.uk
Website: http://www.openprojects.co.uk
Directors: R. Gutteridge (MD)
Immediate Holding Company: OPEN-PROJECTS LIMITED
Registration no: 02422753 **Date established:** 1989
No.of Employees: 1 - 10 **Product Groups:** 44

Date of Accounts	Jan 12	Jan 11	Jan 10
Working Capital	485	304	182
Fixed Assets	4	1	1
Current Assets	580	381	224

Os2 Systems
14 Gedling Grove Arnold, Nottingham, NG5 7ES
Tel: 0115-926 8832
E-mail: sales@os2-systems.co.uk
Website: http://www.os2-systems.co.uk
Directors: S. Price (Prop)
Date established: 2006 **Turnover:** Up to £250,000
No.of Employees: 1 - 10 **Product Groups:** 44

P & A Finishes Ltd
Unit 13 Bailey Brook Business Centre Amber Drive, Langley Mill, Nottingham, NG16 4BE
Tel: 01773-768867 **Fax:** 01773-768867
E-mail: info@pandafinishes.co.uk
Directors: P. Harvey (MD)
Immediate Holding Company: P & A FINISHES LIMITED
Registration no: 05495720 **Date established:** 2005
No.of Employees: 1 - 10 **Product Groups:** 46, 48

Date of Accounts	Jun 11	Jun 10	Jun 09
Sales Turnover	N/A	56	52
Pre Tax Profit/Loss	N/A	-11	-9
Working Capital	-27	6	6
Current Assets	5	10	7

P R P Consulting
Gothic House Barker Gate, Nottingham, NG1 1JU
Tel: 0115-958 0403 **Fax:** 0115-948 3098
E-mail: sales@pr-principles.co.uk
Website: http://www.prpconsulting.co.uk
Directors: P. Woodall (Snr Part)
Immediate Holding Company: CLIFFORD SPINK ASSOCIATES LIMITED
Registration no: 02059044 **Date established:** 2003 **Turnover:** £1m - £2m
No.of Employees: 1 - 10 **Product Groups:** 80, 81

Date of Accounts	Mar 12	Mar 11	Mar 10
Working Capital	83	92	20
Fixed Assets	4	8	13
Current Assets	121	250	155

P & S Healthcare
Edward House King Edward Street, Hucknall, Nottingham, NG15 7JR
Tel: 0115-968 1188
E-mail: sales@pshealthcare.org.uk
Website: http://www.pshealthcare.co.uk
Directors: S. O'regan (Prop)
Ultimate Holding Company: F.J.BAMKIN & SON LIMITED
Immediate Holding Company: P & S HEALTHCARE LIMITED
Registration no: 05124930 **Date established:** 2004
No.of Employees: 21 - 50 **Product Groups:** 24

Date of Accounts	Mar 11	Mar 10	Mar 09
Working Capital	54	30	-1
Fixed Assets	3	3	N/A
Current Assets	86	70	35

Par Communications
Mile End Road Colwick, Nottingham, NG4 2BU
Tel: 0115-961 4744 **Fax:** 0115-940 0714
E-mail: roy.southworth@parjacks.co.uk
Website: http://www.parjacks.co.uk
Bank(s): Barclays
Directors: J. Fairbrother (Fin), R. Southworth (Dir)
Managers: N. Southworth (Prod Mgr), C. Lowe (Buyer)
Ultimate Holding Company: PAR COMMUNICATIONS (LEEDS) LIMITED
Immediate Holding Company: PAR COMMUNICATIONS LTD
Registration no: 00522418 **VAT No.:** GB 352 7889 14
Date established: 1953 **Turnover:** £1m - £2m **No.of Employees:** 21 - 50
Product Groups: 45

Date of Accounts	Dec 11	Dec 10	Dec 09
Working Capital	782	687	475
Fixed Assets	193	209	72
Current Assets	1m	1m	734

Paradise Windows
Pye Hill Road Jacksdale, Nottingham, NG16 5LR
Tel: 01773-606333 **Fax:** 01773-606444
Website: http://www.paradisewindows.co.uk
Managers: P. Hemstock (Mgr)
Date established: 2003 **No.of Employees:** 1 - 10 **Product Groups:** 25, 30, 35, 39

Parker & Farr Furniture Ltd
75 Derby Road Bramcote, Nottingham, NG9 3GY
Tel: 0115-925 2131 **Fax:** 0115-968 3129
E-mail: sales@parkerandfarr.co.uk
Website: http://www.parkerandfarr.co.uk
Bank(s): Barclays
Directors: J. Brooks (Co Sec)
Ultimate Holding Company: JDP FURNITURE GROUP LIMITED
Immediate Holding Company: PARKER & FARR FURNITURE LIMITED
Registration no: 04012084 **Date established:** 2000 **Turnover:** £1m - £2m
No.of Employees: 21 - 50 **Product Groups:** 23

Date of Accounts	Sep 08	Sep 09	Oct 10
Working Capital	-59	-364	340
Fixed Assets	7	5	3
Current Assets	745	484	466

Payne
Giltway Giltbrook, Nottingham, NG16 2GT
Tel: 0115-975 9000 **Fax:** 0115-975 9001
E-mail: nottingham@payne-worldwide.com
Website: http://www.payne-worldwide.com
Bank(s): National Westminster Bank Plc
Directors: A. Evans (Fin)
Managers: C. Tong (Tech Serv Mgr), P. Toner (Personnel), P. Bailey (Sales Prom Mgr), S. Hill, S. Browne (Mktg Serv Mgr), S. Turner (Mktg Serv Mgr)
Ultimate Holding Company: BUNZL PLC
Immediate Holding Company: FILTRONA UK LTD
Registration no: 00259345 **Turnover:** £20m - £50m
No.of Employees: 101 - 250 **Product Groups:** 27, 30, 36, 42, 66

Date of Accounts	Dec 07	Dec 06
Sales Turnover	415	415
Pre Tax Profit/Loss	-82	-27
Working Capital	-6562	-6239
Fixed Assets	7156	7181
Current Assets	1308	1409
Current Liabilities	7870	7648
Total Share Capital	100	100
ROCE% (Return on Capital Employed)	-13.8	-2.9
ROT% (Return on Turnover)	-19.8	-6.5

Pel Engineering Ltd
Unit A17 Ashforth Business Centre Ashforth Street, Nottingham, NG3 4BG
Tel: 0115-958 3022 **Fax:** 0115-958 3022
Website: http://www.plengineering.co.uk
Directors: J. Dewick (Fin), B. Eaton (MD)
Immediate Holding Company: PEL ENGINEERING LIMITED
Registration no: 03595907 **Date established:** 1998
No.of Employees: 1 - 10 **Product Groups:** 35, 39, 45

Date of Accounts	Jul 11	Jul 10	Jul 09
Working Capital	11	6	19
Fixed Assets	19	17	23
Current Assets	61	40	66

Pentam Composites
9 Martin Court Bleneim Industrial Estate, Nottingham, NG6 8US
Tel: 0115-979 4494 **Fax:** 0115-979 4495
E-mail: enquiries@pentam.co.uk
Website: http://www.pentam.co.uk
Directors: J. Mephan (Prop)
Immediate Holding Company: PENTAM COMPOSITES LIMITED
Registration no: 02970984 **Date established:** 1994
Turnover: £250,000 - £500,000 **No.of Employees:** 1 - 10
Product Groups: 30

see next page

Pentam Composites - *Cont'd*

Date of Accounts	Jan 12	Jan 11	Jan 10
Working Capital	118	107	95
Fixed Assets	104	114	125
Current Assets	208	161	147

W H Pettit & Co Long Eaton Ltd

Granville Works Bonsall Street, Long Eaton, Nottingham, NG10 2AH
Tel: 0115-973 2577 **Fax:** 0115-946 1212
Directors: S. Stocks (MD)
Immediate Holding Company: W.H.PETTIT & CO.(LONG EATON)LIMITED
Registration no: 00624607 **VAT No.:** GB 126 3366 79
Date established: 1959 **Turnover:** £250,000 - £500,000
No.of Employees: 1 - 10 **Product Groups:** 48

Date of Accounts	Apr 11	Apr 10	Apr 09
Working Capital	27	61	59
Fixed Assets	5	6	8
Current Assets	79	116	135

Philip Harris International Ltd

Pintail Close Victoria Business Park, Netherfield, Nottingham, NG4 2SG
Tel: 0115-907 4001 **Fax:** 0115-907 4002
E-mail: exportsales@philipharris.co.uk
Website: http://www.philipharris.co.uk
Bank(s): Lloyds TSB Bank plc
Directors: D. Nancom (MD), J. Foley (Sales & Mktg), P. Fisher (I.T. Dir), P. Isherwood (MD)
Managers: D. Marsh (Projects), C. Vail (Purch Mgr)
Ultimate Holding Company: Philip Harris Holdings P.L.C.
Immediate Holding Company: Findell Education Ltd
Registration no: 01119082 **No.of Employees:** 101 - 250
Product Groups: 28, 33, 38, 42, 47, 63

Phoneline

26 High Street Long Eaton, Nottingham, NG10 1LL
Tel: 0115-946 5656 **Fax:** 0115-946 4188
E-mail: jgcomms@msn.com
Directors: A. Odedra (Prop)
Registration no: 03674757 **Turnover:** £500,000 - £1m
No.of Employees: 1 - 10 **Product Groups:** 37

Pilkington UK Ltd

2-6 Mallard Road Victoria Business Park, Netherfield, Nottingham, NG4 2PE
Tel: 0115-940 0980 **Fax:** 0115-961 7993
E-mail: parker@pilkington.com
Website: http://www.pilkington.com
Managers: G. Pearson (District Mgr)
Ultimate Holding Company: NIPPON SHEET GLASS CO LTD (JAPAN)
Immediate Holding Company: PILKINGTON UNITED KINGDOM LIMITED
Registration no: 01417048 **Date established:** 1979
Turnover: Over £1,000m **No.of Employees:** 21 - 50 **Product Groups:** 66

Date of Accounts	Mar 12	Mar 11	Mar 10
Sales Turnover	263m	233m	218m
Pre Tax Profit/Loss	-16m	-19m	-63m
Working Capital	64m	78m	106m
Fixed Assets	117m	111m	108m
Current Assets	106m	124m	158m
Current Liabilities	10m	11m	14m

Plastech Print Ltd

Debdale Lane Keyworth, Nottingham, NG12 5HN
Tel: 0115-937 4041 **Fax:** 0115-937 3426
E-mail: sales@plastechprint.co.uk
Website: http://www.plastechprint.co.uk
Bank(s): National Westminster
Directors: P. Thomas (Fin)
Immediate Holding Company: PLASTECH PRINT LIMITED
Registration no: 02641590 **Date established:** 1991 **Turnover:** £1m - £2m
No.of Employees: 11 - 20 **Product Groups:** 23, 30, 49

Date of Accounts	Dec 10	Dec 09	Dec 08
Working Capital	42	108	145
Fixed Assets	47	53	53
Current Assets	138	216	269

Plastic Fabrications Ltd

Unit 1 Forest Street Kirkby-In-Ashfield, Nottingham, NG17 7DT
Tel: 01623-720400 **Fax:** 01623-720800
E-mail: dsharp@plasticfabs.co.uk
Website: http://www.plastic-fabrication.com
Directors: G. Hutchings (MD)
Immediate Holding Company: PLASTIC FABRICATIONS LIMITED
Registration no: 05501802 **Date established:** 2005
Turnover: Up to £250,000 **No.of Employees:** 1 - 10 **Product Groups:** 40, 48

Date of Accounts	Jul 11	Jul 10	Jul 09
Sales Turnover	N/A	81	71
Pre Tax Profit/Loss	N/A	1	N/A
Working Capital	-3	-1	-1
Fixed Assets	2	2	2
Current Assets	19	25	16
Current Liabilities	N/A	27	13

Plastic Strapping Company Ltd (Strapping Systems Division)

Glaisdale Drive East, Nottingham, NG8 4JJ
Tel: 0115-929 1212 **Fax:** 0115-929 0957
E-mail: sales@pscl.co.uk
Website: http://www.pscl.co.uk
Directors: T. Sandland (Sales), J. Sandland (MD)
Ultimate Holding Company: PLASTIC STRAPPING CO. LIMITED(THE)
Immediate Holding Company: PLASTIC STRAPPING CO. LIMITED(THE)
Registration no: 01442855 **Date established:** 1979 **Turnover:** £1m - £2m
No.of Employees: 21 - 50 **Product Groups:** 23, 30, 34, 35

Date of Accounts	Jul 11	Jul 10	Jul 09
Working Capital	389	374	332
Fixed Assets	145	149	156
Current Assets	670	636	570

Polestar Chromoworks Ltd

Wigman Road, Nottingham, NG8 3JA
Tel: 0115-900 8300 **Fax:** 0115-900 8320
E-mail: barry.hibbert@polestar-group.com
Website: http://www.polestar-group.com
Bank(s): Lloyds
Directors: B. Hibbert (Grp Chief Exec), C. Sparks (Fin)
Managers: R. Leonardi (Purch Mgr), J. Brooks (Sales Prom Mgr)
Immediate Holding Company: TERMINUS 37 LIMITED
Registration no: 00146470 **Date established:** 2017
Turnover: £10m - £20m **No.of Employees:** 51 - 100 **Product Groups:** 28

Date of Accounts	Sep 08
Pre Tax Profit/Loss	-17136
Total Share Capital	165

Pompadour Laboratories Ltd

Mount Street New Basford, Nottingham, NG7 7HF
Tel: 0115-978 1383 **Fax:** 0115-978 4598
E-mail: sales@pompadour.co.uk
Website: http://www.pompadour.co.uk
Directors: A. Barron (Dir), J. Barron (MD), J. Hunkin (Dir)
Immediate Holding Company: POMPADOUR LABORATORIES LIMITED
Registration no: 00447154 **Date established:** 1947 **Turnover:** £2m - £5m
No.of Employees: 21 - 50 **Product Groups:** 63

Date of Accounts	Dec 11	Dec 10	Dec 09
Sales Turnover	4m	4m	4m
Pre Tax Profit/Loss	262	248	180
Working Capital	1m	1m	2m
Fixed Assets	439	385	518
Current Assets	2m	2m	2m
Current Liabilities	141	162	150

Pork Farms Ltd

Queens Drive Industrial Estate, Nottingham, NG2 1LU
Tel: 0115-986 6541 **Fax:** 0115-986 1236
E-mail: enquiries@dorset-chilled-foods.co.uk
Website: http://www.pork-farms.co.uk
Managers: S. Stuart (Mgr)
Ultimate Holding Company: ELIOT LUXEMBOURG HOLDCO SARL (LUXEMBOURG)
Immediate Holding Company: PORK FARMS LIMITED
Registration no: 05998346 **VAT No.:** GB 168 7433 30
Date established: 2006 **Turnover:** £125m - £250m
No.of Employees: 251 - 500 **Product Groups:** 62

Date of Accounts	Mar 12	Mar 09	Mar 10
Sales Turnover	145m	130m	125m
Pre Tax Profit/Loss	-13m	-19m	-13m
Working Capital	4m	-72m	-84m
Fixed Assets	19m	24m	22m
Current Assets	36m	26m	24m
Current Liabilities	10m	13m	8m

Powder Process Design Services Ltd

PO Box 9738, Nottingham, NG10 9DG
Tel: 0845-0941248 **Fax:** 0845-0941249
E-mail: sales@powder-processing.co.uk
Website: http://www.powder-processing.co.uk
Directors: N. Thomas (MD)
Immediate Holding Company: POWDER PROCESS DESIGN SERVICES LTD
Registration no: 06497152 **Date established:** 2008 **Turnover:** £1m - £2m
No.of Employees: 1 - 10 **Product Groups:** 17, 45

Power-Lifts Ltd

Marlborough House 18 Marlborough Road, Woodthorpe, Nottingham, NG5 4FG
Tel: 0115-926 9996 **Fax:** 0115-966 1173
E-mail: info@powerlift.co.uk
Website: http://www.powerlift.co.uk
Directors: N. Roberts (Dir)
Immediate Holding Company: POWER-LIFTS LIMITED
Registration no: 03909248 **Date established:** 2000 **Turnover:** £1m - £2m
No.of Employees: 1 - 10 **Product Groups:** 26, 45, 84

Date of Accounts	Nov 11	Nov 10	Nov 09
Working Capital	30	-11	-27
Fixed Assets	158	162	164
Current Assets	180	276	242

Premier Solutions Nottingham Ltd

11 Ascot Industrial Estate Sandiacre, Nottingham, NG10 5DL
Tel: 0115-939 4122 **Fax:** 0115-949 0453
E-mail: info@premiersolutions.co.uk
Website: http://www.premiersolutions.co.uk
Directors: A. Gardner (Dir)
Immediate Holding Company: PREMIER SOLUTIONS (NOTTINGHAM) LIMITED
Registration no: 04410732 **VAT No.:** GB 118 1290 91
Date established: 2002 **Turnover:** £1m - £2m **No.of Employees:** 1 - 10
Product Groups: 38, 67

Date of Accounts	Dec 11	Dec 10	Dec 09
Working Capital	128	89	24
Fixed Assets	5	7	10
Current Assets	182	149	139

Price & Buckland Ltd

Benneworth Close Hucknall, Nottingham, NG15 6EL
Tel: 0115-964 0827 **Fax:** 0115-964 0769
E-mail: anthony.buckland@price-buckland.co.uk
Website: http://www.price-buckland.co.uk
Bank(s): Barclays
Directors: A. Buckland (Dir), N. Buckland (Mkt Research), G. Phillips (Dir), S. Creamer Acma (Fin)
Managers: S. Head (Personnel)
Immediate Holding Company: PRICE & BUCKLAND LIMITED
Registration no: 00636587 **VAT No.:** GB 117 3000 25
Date established: 1959 **Turnover:** £5m - £10m
No.of Employees: 51 - 100 **Product Groups:** 24

Date of Accounts	Dec 11	Dec 10	Dec 09
Sales Turnover	8m	8m	7m
Pre Tax Profit/Loss	536	900	1m
Working Capital	2m	2m	2m
Fixed Assets	1m	1m	1m
Current Assets	3m	3m	3m
Current Liabilities	112	327	441

Print 4 Ltd

Dabell Avenue, Nottingham, NG6 8WA
Tel: 0115-977 0064 **Fax:** 0115-977 0675
E-mail: june@print4.co.uk
Website: http://www.print4.co.uk
Directors: M. Boam (Dir), P. Clark (Dir), J. Ringham (Fin)
Managers: D. Graham (Mktg Serv Mgr)
Immediate Holding Company: PRINT 4 LIMITED
Registration no: 02652693 **Date established:** 1991 **Turnover:** £2m - £5m
No.of Employees: 21 - 50 **Product Groups:** 48

Date of Accounts	Mar 12	Mar 11	Mar 10
Working Capital	429	581	512
Fixed Assets	286	746	819
Current Assets	2m	2m	2m

Progress Rail Services UK Ltd

Osmaston Street Sandiacre, Nottingham, NG10 5AN
Tel: 0115-921 8218 **Fax:** 0115-541 8219
E-mail: melanie.wild@bbrail.com
Website: http://www.bbrail.com
Bank(s): National Westminster Bank Plc
Managers: G. Beeson (Personnel), H. Samrai (Fin Mgr), S. Kentfield (Comm), E. Holland (Tech Serv Mgr), V. Langham, M. Wild
Ultimate Holding Company: BALFOUR BEATTY PLC
Immediate Holding Company: BALFOUR BEATTY RAIL TRACK SYSTEMS LIMITED
Registration no: 02311350 **VAT No.:** GB 217 9672 35
Date established: 1988 **Turnover:** £20m - £50m
No.of Employees: 101 - 250 **Product Groups:** 34, 35, 39, 45, 48

Protectis Ltd

12a Hazel Street Bulwell, Nottingham, NG6 8EA
Tel: 0115-975 8820 **Fax:** 0115-975 8821
E-mail: info@protectis.co.uk
Website: http://www.protectis.co.uk
Bank(s): Barclays
Directors: M. Wiltshire (Fin)
Immediate Holding Company: PROTECTIS LIMITED
Registration no: 03204173 **VAT No.:** GB 678 8959 37
Date established: 1996 **Turnover:** £1m - £2m **No.of Employees:** 21 - 50
Product Groups: 33, 37, 52, 84

Date of Accounts	Mar 12	Mar 11	Mar 10
Working Capital	484	499	467
Fixed Assets	140	152	155
Current Assets	723	743	657

Quadrant Security Group Ltd

3a Attenborough Lane Beeston, Nottingham, NG9 5JN
Tel: 0115-925 2521 **Fax:** 01923-211590
E-mail: info@qsg.co.uk
Website: http://www.qsg.co.uk
Directors: N. Poultney (Fin)
Managers: W. Smith (Purch Mgr)
Ultimate Holding Company: SYNECTICS PLC
Immediate Holding Company: SECURITY DESIGN ASSOCIATES (1979) LIMITED
Registration no: SC069292 **VAT No.:** GB 417 0698 46
Date established: 1979 **Turnover:** £10m - £20m
No.of Employees: 51 - 100 **Product Groups:** 37

Date of Accounts	May 08
Working Capital	-682

Questmark Ltd

104 Derby Road Long Eaton, Nottingham, NG10 4LS
Tel: 0115-983 7700 **Fax:** 0115-946 7515
E-mail: lisa.bryers@questmark.co.uk
Website: http://www.questmark.co.uk
Directors: L. Mcmaster (Chief Op Offcr), L. Bryers (Fin)
Immediate Holding Company: QUESTMARK LIMITED
Registration no: 02868962 **Date established:** 1993
Turnover: £500,000 - £1m **No.of Employees:** 11 - 20
Product Groups: 37, 67, 79

Date of Accounts	Dec 11	Dec 10	Dec 09
Working Capital	82	97	59
Fixed Assets	120	213	263
Current Assets	1m	1m	888

R B Cranes Ltd

111 Station Road Selston, Nottingham, NG16 6FF
Tel: 01773-811400 **Fax:** 01773-580483
E-mail: info@rbcranes.co.uk
Website: http://www.rbcranes.co.uk
Directors: A. Langley (Grp Chief Exec)
Managers: A. Senior (Sales Prom Mgr)
Immediate Holding Company: LANGLEY HOLDINGS PLC
Registration no: 01251365 **VAT No.:** GB 660 6791 17
Date established: 1980 **Turnover:** £5m - £10m **No.of Employees:** 1 - 10
Product Groups: 45, 48

Date of Accounts	Dec 07	Dec 06	Dec 05
Sales Turnover	8316	7643	6825
Pre Tax Profit/Loss	1406	1061	744
Working Capital	-32	910	-164
Fixed Assets	267	300	N/A
Current Assets	4317	3335	1942
Current Liabilities	4349	2424	2105
ROCE% (Return on Capital Employed)	598.8	87.6	-455.1
ROT% (Return on Turnover)	16.9	13.9	10.9

R C S Filling Machines Ltd

Unit 1 Brand Street, Nottingham, NG2 3GW
Tel: 0115-985 1717 **Fax:** 0115-985 1948
E-mail: info@rcsfilling.com
Website: http://www.rcsfilling.com
Directors: D. Kirk (Fin), R. Gammon (MD)
Immediate Holding Company: RCS FILLING MACHINES LTD.
Registration no: 04336217 **Date established:** 2001
Turnover: £250,000 - £500,000 **No.of Employees:** 1 - 10
Product Groups: 42

Date of Accounts	Oct 11	Oct 10	Oct 09
Working Capital	48	61	73
Fixed Assets	18	18	21
Current Assets	85	103	116

R D A Projects Ltd

Innovation House Daleside Road, Nottingham, NG2 4DH
Tel: 0115-911 0243 **Fax:** 0115-911 0246
E-mail: richard@rdaprojects.co.uk
Website: http://www.rdaprojects.co.uk
Directors: R. Bates (Dir), A. Lancaster (Sales & Mktg)
Immediate Holding Company: R.D.A. PROJECTS LIMITED
Registration no: 03291291 **Date established:** 1996
No.of Employees: 1 - 10 **Product Groups:** 26, 35

Date of Accounts	Dec 11	Dec 10	Dec 09
Working Capital	569	167	166
Fixed Assets	190	195	212
Current Assets	1m	338	485

R G Foster

Bull Close Road, Nottingham, NG7 2UL
Tel: 0115-988 2222 **Fax:** 0115-985 1881
E-mail: russell@foster-tm.co.uk
Website: http://www.foster-tm.co.uk
Directors: R. Foster (Dir)
Ultimate Holding Company: TYNEMILL LIMITED
Immediate Holding Company: R.G. FOSTER TEXTILE MACHINERY LIMITED

Registration no: 01292470 **VAT No.:** GB 728 6451 13
Date established: 1976 **Turnover:** £2m - £5m **No.of Employees:** 1 - 10
Product Groups: 38, 40, 43

Date of Accounts	Apr 11	Apr 10	Apr 09
Working Capital	169	124	138
Fixed Assets	48	61	27
Current Assets	1m	929	886

R H Export Packers Ltd

Lenton Freight Terminal Lenton Lane, Nottingham, NG7 2NR
Tel: 0115-943 8034 **Fax:** 0115-943 8045
E-mail: sales@rhep.co.uk
Website: http://www.rhep.co.uk
Bank(s): Barclays
Directors: A. Baxter (Dir), A. Clark (Dir), T. Clarke (Dir)
Managers: R. Litchfield (I.T. Exec), T. Hastings (Chief Mgr)
Ultimate Holding Company: Rennies Freight Services Ltd
Immediate Holding Company: RH EXPORT PACKERS LIMITED
Registration no: 01191841 **VAT No.:** GB 117 4066 87
Date established: 1974 **Turnover:** £250,000 - £500,000
No.of Employees: 11 - 20 **Product Groups:** 25, 76

Date of Accounts	Dec 09	Dec 08	Dec 07
Sales Turnover	N/A	414	625
Pre Tax Profit/Loss	N/A	6	-5
Working Capital	112	112	73
Fixed Assets	N/A	N/A	35
Current Assets	112	114	73
Current Liabilities	N/A	2	N/A

R H Freight

Lenton Lane, Nottingham, NG7 2NR
Tel: 0115-943 8000 **Fax:** 0115-943 8045
Website: http://www.rhfreight.com
Directors: A. Baxter (Dir), I. Baxter (MD), S. Rafferty (Co Sec)
Managers: R. Lichfield (Tech Serv Mgr), L. Horne (Chief Mgr)
Ultimate Holding Company: RENNIES FREIGHT SERVICES LIMITED
Immediate Holding Company: RENNIE HOGG TRANSPORT LIMITED
Registration no: 00971509 **Date established:** 1970
Turnover: £10m - £20m **No.of Employees:** 101 - 250 **Product Groups:** 76

Date of Accounts	Dec 11	Dec 10	Dec 09
Sales Turnover	12m	10m	9m
Pre Tax Profit/Loss	-533	23	216
Working Capital	166	-382	-500
Fixed Assets	N/A	1m	2m
Current Assets	166	211	274
Current Liabilities	N/A	86	164

R S Components

Lenton Lane, Nottingham, NG7 2NR
Tel: 0115-986 6381 **Fax:** 0115-986 6604
E-mail: rsint@rs-components.com
Website: http://www.rswww.com
Managers: P. Quested (Mgr)
Ultimate Holding Company: UNIVERSITY OF NOTTINGHAM (UK)
Immediate Holding Company: UNIP MANAGEMENT LIMITED
Registration no: 02830029 **VAT No.:** GB 243 1640 91
Date established: 1997 **Turnover:** £250m - £500m
No.of Employees: 1 - 10 **Product Groups:** 67

Date of Accounts	Jul 99	Jul 98	Jul 04
Sales Turnover	6m	N/A	N/A
Pre Tax Profit/Loss	-1m	N/A	N/A
Working Capital	-1m	N/A	N/A
Current Assets	18m	11	N/A
Current Liabilities	2m	1	N/A

R V S Group

72 Lower Parliament Street, Nottingham, NG1 1EH
Tel: 0115-950 4334 **Fax:** 0115-950 6742
E-mail: mail@rvsgroup.co.uk
Website: http://www.rvsgroup.co.uk
Directors: D. Richardson (Dir)
Immediate Holding Company: R V S GROUP LIMITED
Registration no: 01618000 **Date established:** 1982 **Turnover:** £1m - £2m
No.of Employees: 11 - 20 **Product Groups:** 48, 67

Date of Accounts	Jun 11	Jun 10	Jun 09
Working Capital	163	217	186
Fixed Assets	16	13	16
Current Assets	356	473	344
Current Liabilities	N/A	130	158

Race Paint

15 Great Northern Road Eastwood, Nottingham, NG16 3PD
Tel: 01773-533072 **Fax:** 01773-533072
E-mail: racepaintuk@aol.com
Website: http://www.racepaintuk.com
Directors: T. Chambres (Prop)
No.of Employees: 1 - 10 **Product Groups:** 38, 39, 40, 68

Radford Supplies Ltd

Unit 2 Little Tennis Street White City Trading Estate, Nottingham, NG2 4EL
Tel: 0115-948 6990 **Fax:** 0115-948 6991
E-mail: sales@radfordjewellery.com
Website: http://www.radfordaccessories.com
Bank(s): National Westminster
Directors: M. Radford (Dir)
Managers: P. Walton (Ops Mgr), B. Francis (Chief Mgr)
Immediate Holding Company: RADFORD SUPPLIES LIMITED
Registration no: 01473372 **VAT No.:** 309 8004 68 **Date established:** 1980
Turnover: £1m - £2m **No.of Employees:** 21 - 50 **Product Groups:** 33, 49

Date of Accounts	Dec 11	Dec 10	Dec 09
Working Capital	1m	1m	1m
Fixed Assets	65	96	117
Current Assets	2m	2m	2m

Rake 'N' Lift & Co - Nottingham Rakes UK Rakes Specialists (Rake UK Rake Specialists)

33 Firs Road Edwalton, Nottingham, NG12 4BY
Tel: 07802-857103 **Fax:** 07802-857103
Directors: M. Garton-Smith (Prop)
Turnover: Up to £250,000 **No.of Employees:** 1 - 10 **Product Groups:** 25, 30, 41, 45, 66

Raleigh UK Ltd

Church Street Eastwood, Nottingham, NG16 3HT
Tel: 01773-532600 **Fax:** 01773-532601
E-mail: sales@raleigh.co.uk
Website: http://www.raleigh.co.uk
Directors: C. Bird (Fin), A. Graham (Fin), M. Gouldthorp (MD), P. Rickaby (Sales)
Managers: S. Wigley, B. Timson (Tech Serv Mgr), B. Hillsdon (Mktg Serv Mgr), F. Gallis (Personnel)
Ultimate Holding Company: RALEIGH CYCLE LIMITED (JERSEY)
Immediate Holding Company: RALEIGH UK LTD
Registration no: 00139076 **Date established:** 2015
Turnover: £20m - £50m **No.of Employees:** 101 - 250
Product Groups: 39, 68

Date of Accounts	Sep 11	Sep 10	Sep 09
Sales Turnover	36m	38m	33m
Pre Tax Profit/Loss	688	1m	1m
Working Capital	9m	9m	8m
Fixed Assets	240	241	393
Current Assets	18m	19m	17m
Current Liabilities	1m	2m	2m

Ramsey Butler Research

Beeston Marina Riverside Road, Beeston, Nottingham, NG9 1NA
Tel: 0781-426 6931
E-mail: benbutler@rbresearch.com
Website: http://www.rbresearch.com
Directors: B. Butler (Prop), B. Butler (MD)
Immediate Holding Company: BEESTON MARINA LIMITED
Registration no: 02192074 **Date established:** 1987
Turnover: Up to £250,000 **No.of Employees:** 1 - 10 **Product Groups:** 87

Date of Accounts	Dec 95	Dec 10	Dec 09
Working Capital	34	N/A	34
Current Assets	34	N/A	34

Recliner World

Unit 1 Queens Road, Nottingham, NG2 3AS
Tel: 0115-978 7373 **Fax:** 0115-978 3720
E-mail: customerservices@reclinerworld.co.uk
Website: http://www.reclinerworld.co.uk
Directors: J. Seagrave (Fin)
Managers: R. Seagrave (I.T. Exec)
Immediate Holding Company: Recliner World Ltd
Registration no: 03198175 **Date established:** 1996
No.of Employees: 1 - 10 **Product Groups:** 26

Date of Accounts	Oct 07	Oct 06	Oct 05
Working Capital	-122	-117	-60
Fixed Assets	26	26	30
Current Assets	97	237	375
Current Liabilities	220	354	434
Total Share Capital	1	1	1

Removals In Nottingham

252 Alfreton Road, Nottingham, NG7 5LS
Tel: 07850-157618
E-mail: vanmannotts@googlemail.com
Website: http://www.bg-removal.co.uk
Directors: J. Khan (Dir)
Date established: 2009 **Turnover:** **No.of Employees:** 1 - 10
Product Groups: 72, 80

Rexel Senate Electrical Wholesalers Ltd

Unit 12 Castle Park, Nottingham, NG2 1AH
Tel: 0115-986 0111 **Fax:** 0115-986 2841
E-mail: nottingham@rexelsenate.co.uk
Website: http://www.rexelsenate.co.uk
Managers: C. Meek (Mgr)
Ultimate Holding Company: REXEL LTD FRANCE
Registration no: 02588733 **VAT No.:** GB 587 2692 88
Turnover: £2m - £5m **No.of Employees:** 1 - 10 **Product Groups:** 77

Robinson Plastic Packaging Ltd

Lowmoor Road Kirkby-in-Ashfield, Nottingham, NG17 7JU
Tel: 01623-752869 **Fax:** 01623-751726
E-mail: sales@robinsonpackaging.com
Website: http://www.robinsonpackaging.com
Directors: J. Brook (Sales), N. Morley (Chief Op Offcr)
Managers: G. Halfpenny (Fin Mgr), S. Robertson (Sales & Mktg Mg), R. Bailey (Purch Mgr), N. Davidson (Fin Mgr)
Ultimate Holding Company: ROBINSON PLC
Immediate Holding Company: ROBINSON PLASTIC PACKAGING LIMITED
Registration no: 04964354 **Date established:** 2003 **Turnover:** £5m - £10m
No.of Employees: 101 - 250 **Product Groups:** 30

Date of Accounts	Dec 11	Dec 10	Dec 09
Sales Turnover	11m	10m	9m
Pre Tax Profit/Loss	1m	916	598
Working Capital	903	2m	2m
Fixed Assets	1m	1m	1m
Current Assets	4m	4m	3m
Current Liabilities	878	619	549

Rollstore

Chatsworth Avenue Long Eaton, Nottingham, NG10 2FL
Tel: 0115-946 3524
E-mail: sales@rollstore.co.uk
Website: http://www.rollstore.co.uk
Directors: R. Brown (Ptnr)
Immediate Holding Company: ROLLSTORE LIMITED
Registration no: 06540452 **Date established:** 2008
No.of Employees: 1 - 10 **Product Groups:** 35, 42, 45

Date of Accounts	Jun 11	Jun 10	Jun 09
Working Capital	161	6	1
Current Assets	288	59	79

Romax Technology Ltd

Rutherford House Nottingham Science & Technology, Nottingham, NG7 2PZ
Tel: 0115-951 8800 **Fax:** 0115-951 8801
E-mail: sales@romaxtech.com
Website: http://www.romaxtech.com
Bank(s): National Westminster
Directors: P. Poon (Dir), R. Irons (Fin), A. Poon (Co Sec)
Managers: S. Ackers (Tech Serv Mgr), J. Godden (Sales Admin)
Immediate Holding Company: ROMAX TECHNOLOGY LTD.
Registration no: 02345696 **VAT No.:** GB 526 2467 46
Date established: 1989 **Turnover:** £10m - £20m
No.of Employees: 51 - 100 **Product Groups:** 47

Date of Accounts	Mar 12	Mar 11	Mar 10
Sales Turnover	12m	13m	10m
Pre Tax Profit/Loss	-2m	723	1m
Working Capital	9m	2m	2m
Fixed Assets	653	1m	633
Current Assets	12m	6m	5m
Current Liabilities	3m	4m	3m

Roodsafe Ltd

Unit 21 Parklane B C, Old Basford, Nottingham, NG6 0DU
Tel: 0115-927 4111 **Fax:** 0115-927 4117
E-mail: info@roodsafe.com
Website: http://www.roodsafe.com
Directors: S. Rood (MD)
Registration no: 04119480 **Turnover:** £250,000 - £500,000
No.of Employees: 11 - 20 **Product Groups:** 40, 67, 86

Date of Accounts	Dec 07	Dec 06	Dec 05
Working Capital	6	39	9
Fixed Assets	25	27	1
Current Assets	169	115	30
Current Liabilities	163	76	21

Rose UK

Unit 13 Vision Business Park Firth Way, Nottingham, NG6 8GF
Tel: 0115-927 9542 **Fax:** 0115-976 1986
E-mail: rose@roseuksecurityservices.co.uk
Website: http://www.roseuksecurityservices.co.uk
Directors: D. Scriven (Dir)
Managers: R. Scriven (Personnel)
Immediate Holding Company: ROSE UK SERVICES LIMITED
Registration no: 04712285 **Date established:** 2003
Turnover: £500,000 - £1m **No.of Employees:** 1 - 10 **Product Groups:** 36, 81

Rossi Clothing

2 Victoria Park Way Netherfield, Nottingham, NG4 2PA
Tel: 0115-987 0319 **Fax:** 0115-987 3572
E-mail: margaret@rossi-clothing.co.uk
Website: http://www.rossi-clothing.co.uk
Directors: M. Kitchen (Fin), G. Marzano (MD)
Immediate Holding Company: ROSSI SPORTS LIMITED
Registration no: 03153558 **VAT No.:** GB 309 9513 42
Date established: 1996 **Turnover:** £2m - £5m **No.of Employees:** 1 - 10
Product Groups: 24, 63

Date of Accounts	Jan 09	Jan 08	Jan 07
Working Capital	538	750	800
Fixed Assets	N/A	5	35
Current Assets	575	819	854

Rowlson Industrial Sewing Engineers Ltd

Westbury Road, Nottingham, NG5 1EJ
Tel: 0115-979 1333 **Fax:** 0115-979 1444
E-mail: john.rowlson@rowlson.com
Website: http://www.rowlson.com
Directors: J. Rowlson (MD)
Immediate Holding Company: ROWLSON INDUSTRIAL SEWING ENGINEERS LIMITED
Registration no: 01329820 **Date established:** 1977
No.of Employees: 1 - 10 **Product Groups:** 43

Date of Accounts	Oct 11	Oct 10	Oct 09
Working Capital	169	206	215
Fixed Assets	10	13	16
Current Assets	312	310	314

Rushcliffe

Boundary Road West Bridgford, Nottingham, NG2 7BW
Tel: 0115-923 4921 **Fax:** 0115-974 8091
E-mail: sales@rushcliffe-school.co.uk
Website: http://www.leisurecentre.com
Managers: P. Abelett (Mgr)
Immediate Holding Company: THE RUSHCLIFFE SCHOOL ACADEMY TRUST
Registration no: 08128513 **Date established:** 2012
No.of Employees: 21 - 50 **Product Groups:** 25, 31, 63, 66

Date of Accounts	Mar 11	Mar 10	Mar 09
Working Capital	-303	-575	-834
Fixed Assets	883	942	1m
Current Assets	169	341	88

S Collins & Company Ltd

Ascot Road, Nottingham, NG8 5HD
Tel: 0115-942 5522 **Fax:** 0115-942 5405
E-mail: fcollins@proweb.co.uk
Website: http://www.collinscashandcarry.co.uk
Directors: F. Collins (MD)
Immediate Holding Company: S. COLLINS & CO. LIMITED
Registration no: 00484469 **VAT No.:** GB 116 4926 69
Date established: 1950 **Turnover:** £5m - £10m **No.of Employees:** 1 - 10
Product Groups: 61

Date of Accounts	Jan 12	Jan 11	Jan 10
Sales Turnover	5m	6m	7m
Pre Tax Profit/Loss	141	230	168
Working Capital	2m	2m	2m
Fixed Assets	1m	1m	1m
Current Assets	3m	3m	3m
Current Liabilities	400	527	504

S E B International Ltd

Unity Road Lowmoor Industrial Estate, Kirkby-In-Ashfield, Nottingham, NG17 7LE
Tel: 01623-754490 **Fax:** 01623-753477
E-mail: contact@sebinternational.com
Website: http://www.sebinternational.com
Directors: V. Storey (Fin)
Managers: B. Storey (Mgr)
Immediate Holding Company: S.E.B. INTERNATIONAL LIMITED
Registration no: 01022690 **VAT No.:** GB 126 4182 84
Date established: 1971 **Turnover:** £2m - £5m **No.of Employees:** 21 - 50
Product Groups: 30, 35, 36, 37, 38, 39, 45, 46

Date of Accounts	Aug 11	Aug 10	Aug 09
Working Capital	6m	6m	5m
Fixed Assets	259	258	280
Current Assets	7m	6m	6m

S E P Solutions Ltd

3 Abba Close Kimberley, Nottingham, NG16 2HT
Tel: 0115-938 9685 **Fax:** 0115-938 9686
E-mail: sales@sepsolutions.net
Website: http://www.sepsolutions.co.uk
Directors: P. Bebbington (Dir)
Immediate Holding Company: SEP SOLUTIONS LIMITED
Registration no: 04417142 **Date established:** 2002
Turnover: Up to £250,000 **No.of Employees:** 1 - 10 **Product Groups:** 37

Date of Accounts	Mar 12	Mar 11	Mar 10
Working Capital	17	28	26
Fixed Assets	2	2	1
Current Assets	32	37	32

S & G Fabrications
23 Salisbury Square, Nottingham, NG7 2AB
Tel: 0115-924 4603 **Fax:** 0115-942 2919
Directors: S. Briggs (Prop)
Date established: 1991 **No.of Employees:** 1 - 10 **Product Groups:** 26, 35

Safeway Security
Foxhall Business Centre Foxhall Road, Nottingham, NG7 6LH
Tel: 0800-389 7564 **Fax:** 01949-823764
E-mail: sales@safeway-security.co.uk
Website: http://www.safeway-security.co.uk
Directors: M. Donkin (MD)
Immediate Holding Company: SAFEWAY SECURITY LTD
Registration no: 06643937 **Date established:** 2008
Turnover: Up to £250,000 **No.of Employees:** 1 - 10 **Product Groups:** 37, 40, 67

Date of Accounts	Jul 11	Jul 10	Jul 09
Sales Turnover	31	N/A	N/A
Working Capital	1	N/A	N/A
Current Assets	2	N/A	N/A

Saint Ann's Sheet Metal Co. Ltd
Eagle Close Arnold, Nottingham, NG5 7FJ
Tel: 0115-926 9649 **Fax:** 0115-967 0698
E-mail: info@saintanns.co.uk
Website: http://www.saintanns.co.uk
Bank(s): National Westminster Bank Plc
Directors: C. Bloomer (Fin), D. Bloomer (MD)
Immediate Holding Company: SAINT ANNS SHEET METAL COMPANY LIMITED
Registration no: 03554665 **VAT No.:** GB 706 4747 28
Date established: 1998 **Turnover:** £500,000 - £1m
No.of Employees: 21 - 50 **Product Groups:** 48

Date of Accounts	May 12	May 11	May 10
Working Capital	127	166	146
Fixed Assets	715	661	665
Current Assets	542	696	757

Sallis Healthcare Ltd (Healthcare)
Waterford Street, Nottingham, NG6 0DH
Tel: 0115-978 7841 **Fax:** 0115-942 2272
E-mail: info@sallis.co.uk
Website: http://www.sallis.co.uk
Bank(s): National Westminster Bank Plc
Directors: P. Sallis (MD)
Managers: D. Pendlebury, K. Edwards (Purch Mgr), R. Sallis (Export Sales Mg)
Immediate Holding Company: SALLIS HEALTHCARE LIMITED
Registration no: 00402658 **VAT No.:** GB 117 1692 77
Date established: 1946 **Turnover:** £2m - £5m **No.of Employees:** 51 - 100
Product Groups: 24, 29, 38, 63

Date of Accounts	Sep 11	Sep 10	Sep 09
Working Capital	709	750	789
Fixed Assets	262	300	344
Current Assets	1m	1m	1m

Sandicliffe Motor Group
280 Nottingham Road, Nottingham, NG7 7DG
Tel: 0115-942 2100 **Fax:** 0115-949 0457
E-mail: info@sandicliffe.co.uk
Website: http://www.sandicliffe.co.uk
Managers: A. Worboys (Sales Prom Mgr)
Ultimate Holding Company: SANDICLIFFE MOTOR HOLDINGS LIMITED
Immediate Holding Company: SANDICLIFFE GARAGE LIMITED
Registration no: 00452840 **Date established:** 1948 **Turnover:** £5m - £10m
No.of Employees: 101 - 250 **Product Groups:** 68

Date of Accounts	Dec 11	Dec 10	Dec 09
Sales Turnover	10m	9m	9m
Pre Tax Profit/Loss	235	49	401
Working Capital	-935	12	167
Fixed Assets	27m	23m	24m
Current Assets	32m	32m	28m
Current Liabilities	33m	1m	1m

Richard Sankey & Son Ltd
Bennerley Road Bulwell, Nottingham, NG6 8PE
Tel: 0115-927 7335 **Fax:** 0115-977 0197
E-mail: info@rsankey.co.uk
Website: http://www.rsankey.co.uk
Bank(s): Merita Bank Ltd
Directors: I. Fraser (Grp Chief Exec), P. Kelly (Co Sec)
Managers: D. Hunter (Sales Prom Mgr), M. Fraser (Mktg Serv Mgr), M. Ravnkilde (Buyer), P. Wilson (Sales Prom Mgr)
Ultimate Holding Company: FISKARS OY AB (FINLAND)
Immediate Holding Company: RICHARD SANKEY & SON LIMITED
Registration no: 00074856 **VAT No.:** GB 450 1022 15
Date established: 2002 **Turnover:** £10m - £20m
No.of Employees: 101 - 250 **Product Groups:** 30, 40

Date of Accounts	Dec 07	Dec 06	Dec 05
Sales Turnover	18923	18881	15324
Pre Tax Profit/Loss	179	295	92
Working Capital	1774	2007	1853
Fixed Assets	3096	2891	3047
Current Assets	7296	6807	6152
Current Liabilities	5522	4800	4299
Total Share Capital	478	478	478
ROCE% (Return on Capital Employed)	3.7	6.0	1.9
ROT% (Return on Turnover)	0.9	1.6	0.6

Scientific Laboratory Supplies Ltd
22-23 Nottingham South & Wilford Industrial Estate, Nottingham, NG11 7EP
Tel: 0115-982 1111 **Fax:** 0115-982 5275
E-mail: plister@scientific-labs.co.uk
Website: http://www.scientificlabs.co.uk
Managers: P. Lister (Mgr)
Ultimate Holding Company: SLS GROUP LIMITED
Immediate Holding Company: SCIENTIFIC LABORATORY SUPPLIES LIMITED
Registration no: 02577009 **Date established:** 1991
No.of Employees: 21 - 50 **Product Groups:** 38, 42

Date of Accounts	Apr 11	Apr 10	Apr 09
Sales Turnover	23m	21m	19m
Pre Tax Profit/Loss	316	176	86
Working Capital	1m	1m	2m
Fixed Assets	393	419	298
Current Assets	9m	8m	7m
Current Liabilities	3m	3m	2m

Serif Europe Ltd
12 Nottingham South & Wilford Industrial Estate, Nottingham, NG11 7EP
Tel: 0115-914 2000 **Fax:** 0115-914 2020
E-mail: sales@serif.com
Website: http://www.serif.com
Bank(s): Nat West
Directors: G. Bates (MD), A. Hewson (Sales), M. Evans (Fin)
Managers: B. Cowan (Sales Admin), S. Richards (Personnel), G. Jonson (Tech Serv Mgr)
Ultimate Holding Company: SERIF GROUP LIMITED
Immediate Holding Company: SERIF (EUROPE) LIMITED
Registration no: 02117968 **VAT No.:** GB 450 1595 65
Date established: 1987 **Turnover:** £10m - £20m
No.of Employees: 101 - 250 **Product Groups:** 84

Date of Accounts	Dec 11	Dec 10	Dec 09
Sales Turnover	14m	14m	13m
Pre Tax Profit/Loss	1m	1m	948
Working Capital	6m	5m	6m
Fixed Assets	571	300	401
Current Assets	8m	7m	8m
Current Liabilities	1m	972	901

Servatruc Ltd
Church Street Old Basford, Nottingham, NG6 0GA
Tel: 0115-978 5504 **Fax:** 0115-942 2001
E-mail: christopher@servatruc.co.uk
Website: http://www.servatruc.co.uk
Directors: C. Rollinson (MD), M. Rollinson (I.T. Dir), E. Rollinson (Co Sec)
Immediate Holding Company: SERVATRUC LIMITED
Registration no: 00981587 **Date established:** 1970
No.of Employees: 1 - 10 **Product Groups:** 39, 40, 45, 48, 67

Date of Accounts	Jun 11	Jun 10	Jun 09
Working Capital	258	348	265
Fixed Assets	558	528	611
Current Assets	478	609	533

S F Group
Millennium Way West, Nottingham, NG8 6AS
Tel: 0115-975 8000 **Fax:** 0114-263 4141
E-mail: shodson@sfgroup.com
Website: http://www.sfguk.com
Directors: R. Young (Prop), T. Minnis (MD)
Managers: R. Warrick (Accounts), M. Hill (Mktg Serv Mgr), P. Tolley (Mgr), D. Gregson (I.T. Exec), T. Dimmock (District Mgr)
Immediate Holding Company: JENSON BRITTLE LTD
Registration no: 06876917 **Turnover:** £10m - £20m
No.of Employees: 21 - 50 **Product Groups:** 80

Sharp & Nickless Ltd
77 College Street Long Eaton, Nottingham, NG10 4NN
Tel: 0115-973 2169 **Fax:** 0115-973 2169
Website: http://www.sharpandnickless.co.uk
Directors: A. Hannabuss (Fin), J. Holbrook (MD)
Immediate Holding Company: SHARP & NICKLESS LIMITED
Registration no: 00182442 **Date established:** 2022
No.of Employees: 11 - 20 **Product Groups:** 20

Date of Accounts	Feb 08	Feb 11	Feb 10
Working Capital	-14	40	-53
Fixed Assets	162	156	159
Current Assets	115	104	99

Sheen Equipment
Greasley Street, Nottingham, NG6 8NG
Tel: 0115-927 2321 **Fax:** 0115-977 0671
Directors: H. Prichard (Prop)
Registration no: 01431484 **VAT No.:** GB 117 4076 84
Turnover: £500,000 - £1m **No.of Employees:** 1 - 10 **Product Groups:** 35, 36, 40, 41, 46

Date of Accounts	Dec 05
Working Capital	1039
Current Assets	1087
Current Liabilities	48
Total Share Capital	30

Sheetfabs Nottingham Ltd
Nottingham Road Attenborough, Beeston, Nottingham, NG9 6DR
Tel: 0115-925 8101 **Fax:** 0115-943 0872
E-mail: david@sheetfabs.co.uk
Website: http://www.sheetfabs.co.uk
Bank(s): Yorkshire Bank PLC
Directors: D. Mason (Dir), M. Herrod (Fin)
Managers: R. Sefton (Buyer)
Immediate Holding Company: SHEETFABS (NOTTINGHAM) LIMITED
Registration no: 00426392 **Date established:** 1946 **Turnover:** £2m - £5m
No.of Employees: 21 - 50 **Product Groups:** 26, 35, 36, 40, 45, 46, 48, 67

Date of Accounts	Dec 10	Dec 09	Dec 08
Working Capital	2m	2m	2m
Fixed Assets	617	616	751
Current Assets	3m	3m	2m

Sherwood Interiors Ltd
The Spire Egypt Road, Nottingham, NG7 7GD
Tel: 0115-942 7870 **Fax:** 0115-961 5505
E-mail: info@sherwoodinteriors.co.uk
Website: http://www.tvedt.co.uk
Directors: S. Kinsey (MD)
Ultimate Holding Company: TVEDT GROUP HOLDINGS LTD (JERSEY)
Immediate Holding Company: SHERWOOD INTERIORS LIMITED
Registration no: 02332687 **VAT No.:** GB 572 5162 42
Date established: 1989 **Turnover:** £5m - £10m **No.of Employees:** 11 - 20
Product Groups: 52

Date of Accounts	Dec 11	Dec 10	Dec 09
Sales Turnover	7m	N/A	8m
Pre Tax Profit/Loss	501	N/A	9
Working Capital	2m	2m	2m
Fixed Assets	26	34	60
Current Assets	4m	3m	3m
Current Liabilities	477	N/A	177

Showstoppers Ltd
7 Urban Road Kirkby-in-Ashfield, Nottingham, NG17 8AH
Tel: 01623-754985 **Fax:** 01623-754985
E-mail: webinfo@showstoppersltd.co.uk
Website: http://www.showstoppersltd.co.uk
Directors: A. Cooke (Fin), C. Hall (Dir)
Immediate Holding Company: SHOWSTOPPERS LIMITED
Registration no: 04385755 **Date established:** 2002
Turnover: Up to £250,000 **No.of Employees:** 1 - 10 **Product Groups:** 33, 49

Date of Accounts	Mar 11	Mar 10	Mar 09
Working Capital	1	-7	-4
Fixed Assets	22	14	18
Current Assets	35	31	35

Silicone Altimex Ltd
49 Pasture Road Stapleford, Nottingham, NG9 8HR
Tel: 0115-949 6890 **Fax:** 0115-949 6890
E-mail: enquiries@silalt.co.uk
Website: http://www.silalt.co.uk
Directors: G. Ridgway (I.T. Dir), J. Whitworth (Fin)
Ultimate Holding Company: FORESTCRAFT LIMITED
Immediate Holding Company: SILICONE-ALTIMEX LIMITED
Registration no: 01449832 **Date established:** 1979 **Turnover:** £2m - £5m
No.of Employees: 51 - 100 **Product Groups:** 29, 30, 31, 32, 33, 38, 42, 48, 49, 63, 67

Date of Accounts	Sep 10	Sep 09	Sep 08
Sales Turnover	N/A	N/A	4m
Pre Tax Profit/Loss	N/A	N/A	333
Working Capital	2m	2m	2m
Fixed Assets	418	440	366
Current Assets	2m	3m	3m
Current Liabilities	N/A	N/A	236

R Simon Dryers Ltd
Unit 1 Morris Court Private Road 3, Colwick Industrial Estate, Nottingham, NG4 2BD
Tel: 0115-961 6276 **Fax:** 0115-961 6351
E-mail: sales@simon-dryers.co.uk
Website: http://www.simon-dryers.co.uk
Bank(s): Midland
Directors: L. Johnson (Fin)
Ultimate Holding Company: TUMMERS BEHEER B.V (NETHERLANDS)
Immediate Holding Company: R. SIMON (DRYERS) LIMITED
Registration no: 02622705 **VAT No.:** GB 385 2354 39
Date established: 1991 **Turnover:** £2m - £5m **No.of Employees:** 11 - 20
Product Groups: 40, 41

Date of Accounts	Dec 11	Dec 10	Dec 09
Sales Turnover	3m	2m	1m
Pre Tax Profit/Loss	-201	134	1m
Working Capital	-401	-243	-358
Fixed Assets	70	73	78
Current Assets	596	933	212
Current Liabilities	179	597	117

Simpkin & Icke Holdings Ltd
Glaisdale Works Glaisdale Drive, Nottingham, NG8 4JU
Tel: 0115-929 2106 **Fax:** 0115-929 0446
E-mail: julie.icke@simpkin-and-icke.co.uk
Website: http://www.simpkin-and-icke.co.uk
Directors: C. Icke (Jt MD), C. Icke (Dir), D. Icke (Jt MD), J. Icke (Fin)
Immediate Holding Company: SIMPKIN & ICKE (HOLDINGS) LIMITED
Registration no: 00308946 **VAT No.:** 118 8929 31 **Date established:** 1936
Turnover: £2m - £5m **No.of Employees:** 11 - 20 **Product Groups:** 27

Date of Accounts	Dec 07	Dec 06	Dec 05
Working Capital	-244	-192	-96
Fixed Assets	1329	598	625
Current Assets	N/A	3	3
Current Liabilities	244	195	99
Total Share Capital	1	1	1

Simplex Knitting Ltd
Bye Pass Road Beeston, Nottingham, NG9 5HN
Tel: 0115-925 4980 **Fax:** 0115-943 0772
E-mail: enquiries@simplexknittingcompany.ltd.uk
Website: http://www.simplexknitting.co.uk
Bank(s): National Westminster
Directors: C. King (Co Sec), A. Stiegler (Ch)
Immediate Holding Company: SIMPLEX KNITTING COMPANY LIMITED
Registration no: 00517599 **VAT No.:** GB 116 7697 43
Date established: 1953 **Turnover:** £5m - £10m **No.of Employees:** 21 - 50
Product Groups: 23, 24

Date of Accounts	Aug 11	Aug 10	Aug 09
Working Capital	5m	6m	6m
Fixed Assets	2m	2m	2m
Current Assets	6m	6m	6m

Paul Smith Ltd
Riverside Building Riverside Way, Nottingham, NG2 1DP
Tel: 0115-986 8877 **Fax:** 0115-986 2649
E-mail: john.morley@paulsmith.co.uk
Website: http://www.paulsmith.co.uk
Directors: J. Morley (MD)
Managers: A. Long (Fin Mgr), L. Bingham (Tech Serv Mgr), M. Mitchell (Personnel)
Ultimate Holding Company: PAUL SMITH GROUP HOLDINGS LIMITED
Immediate Holding Company: PAUL SMITH FOUNDATION
Registration no: 03346635 **Date established:** 1997
Turnover: Up to £250,000 **No.of Employees:** 1 - 10 **Product Groups:** 61, 63

Date of Accounts	Jun 11	Jun 10	Jun 09
Pre Tax Profit/Loss	-0	-0	-0

Specialist Garment Braids (a division of S.G. Beal (Nottingham) Ltd)
Harrington Mills Leopold Street, Long Eaton, Nottingham, NG10 4QG
Tel: 0115-946 0666 **Fax:** 0115-946 2676
E-mail: sales@sgbraids.com
Website: http://www.sgbraids.com
Directors: A. Beal (Dir)
Immediate Holding Company: SIREN FURNITURE LIMITED
Registration no: 03908548 **Date established:** 2000
No.of Employees: 1 - 10 **Product Groups:** 23, 24, 63

Date of Accounts	Mar 11	Mar 10	Mar 09
Working Capital	-108	-199	-343
Fixed Assets	569	621	637
Current Assets	819	729	337

Speedo International Ltd
Ascot Road, Nottingham, NG8 5AJ
Tel: 0115-916 7000 **Fax:** 0115-910 5005
E-mail: speedoinfo@pentland.com
Website: http://www.speedo.com
Directors: C. Sneddon (Sales & Mktg), P. Campbell (Co Sec), P. Campbell (Fin)
Managers: R. Davies (Sales Prom Mgr)
Immediate Holding Company: SPEEDO INTERNATIONAL LIMITED
Registration no: 00227323 **VAT No.:** GB 116 2950 82
Date established: 2028 **Turnover:** £75m - £125m
No.of Employees: 101 - 250 **Product Groups:** 24

Date of Accounts	Dec 07	Dec 06	Dec 05
Sales Turnover	67400	67110	69450
Pre Tax Profit/Loss	-6420	2530	7240
Working Capital	3700	5210	4040
Fixed Assets	12280	17470	17520
Current Assets	47750	48930	42900
Current Liabilities	44050	43720	38860
Total Share Capital	19630	19630	19630
ROCE% (Return on Capital Employed)	-40.2	11.2	33.6
ROT% (Return on Turnover)	-9.5	3.8	10.4

Speedograph Richfield Ltd

1a Dalton Drive Arnold, Nottingham, NG5 7JR
Tel: 0115-926 4235 **Fax:** 0115-920 9912
E-mail: info@speedographrichfield.com
Website: http://www.speedographrichfield.com
Bank(s): HSBC
Directors: T. Ingle (Dir)
Managers: R. Benson (Chief Acct), D. Morton (Tech Serv Mgr)
Ultimate Holding Company: SPEEDOGRAPH LIMITED
Immediate Holding Company: THOS RICHFIELD AND SON LIMITED
Registration no: 02652763 **VAT No.:** GB 352 7069 52
Date established: 1991 **Turnover:** £2m - £5m **No.of Employees:** 11 - 20
Product Groups: 38, 39

Date of Accounts	Dec 11	Dec 10	Dec 09
Working Capital	67	127	129
Fixed Assets	N/A	4	6
Current Assets	68	198	161

SRCL

Eastcroft Incinerator The Incinerator Building, Incinerator Road, Nottingham, NG2 3AF
Tel: 0845-1242020 **Fax:** 0113-235 1286
E-mail: mwardle@srcl.com
Website: http://www.srcl.com
Product Groups: 30, 40, 42, 54

Standard Motor Products Europe Ltd

Unit 5b Little Oak Drive Annesley, Nottingham, NG15 0DR
Tel: 01623-886400 **Fax:** 01623-886500
E-mail: info@smpeurope.com
Website: http://www.smpeurope.com
Bank(s): Barclays, Old Market Square, Nottingham
Managers: A. Payton (Tech Serv Mgr), C. Morris (Purch Mgr), G. Logan (Mktg Serv Mgr), M. Donker (Fin Mgr), L. Kirkwood, V. Alexandra
Ultimate Holding Company: STANDARD MOTOR PRODUCTS HOLDINGS LIMITED
Immediate Holding Company: STANDARD MOTOR PRODUCTS EUROPE LIMITED
Registration no: 00955888 **VAT No.:** GB 598 6056 83
Date established: 1969 **Turnover:** £20m - £50m
No.of Employees: 51 - 100 **Product Groups:** 38, 39, 40

Date of Accounts	Dec 11	Dec 10	Dec 09
Sales Turnover	21m	21m	18m
Pre Tax Profit/Loss	1m	1m	811
Working Capital	8m	7m	5m
Fixed Assets	2m	1m	3m
Current Assets	13m	12m	10m
Current Liabilities	2m	2m	2m

Status Metrology Solutions Ltd

Measurement House Lenton Street, Sandiacre, Nottingham, NG10 5DX
Tel: 0115-939 2228 **Fax:** 0115-949 3355
E-mail: info@statusmetrology.com
Website: http://www.statusmetrology.com
Bank(s): HSBC Bank plc
Directors: A. Tillett (Dir)
Ultimate Holding Company: METROLOGY SOLUTIONS LIMITED
Immediate Holding Company: STATUS METROLOGY SOLUTIONS LTD
Registration no: 02859536 **VAT No.:** GB 610 6909 55
Date established: 1993 **Turnover:** £1m - £2m **No.of Employees:** 11 - 20
Product Groups: 44, 48, 85

Date of Accounts	Dec 11	Dec 10	Dec 09
Working Capital	149	122	123
Fixed Assets	67	19	15
Current Assets	324	327	233

Stora Enso UK Ltd

G4 Ash Tree Court Mellors Way Nottingham Business Park, Nottingham, NG8 6PY
Tel: 0115-964 7100 **Fax:** 0115-964 7170
E-mail: ian.jennings@storaenso.com
Website: http://www.storaenso.com
Directors: P. Watt (Sales)
Ultimate Holding Company: STORA ENSO OYJ {FINLAND}
Immediate Holding Company: STORA ENSO UK LIMITED
Registration no: 01294742 **Date established:** 1977 **Turnover:** £1m - £2m
No.of Employees: 11 - 20 **Product Groups:** 38, 42

Date of Accounts	Dec 11	Dec 10	Dec 09
Sales Turnover	6m	7m	13m
Pre Tax Profit/Loss	-8	317	393
Working Capital	3m	4m	5m
Fixed Assets	370	738	529
Current Assets	4m	5m	6m
Current Liabilities	332	513	523

Storer Refrigeration & Catering Manufacturers

Newstead Industrial Estate Brookfield Road, Arnold, Nottingham, NG5 7ER
Tel: 0115-920 0329 **Fax:** 0115-967 0676
E-mail: tedblake@supanet.com
Website: http://www.storersltd.com
Directors: G. Storer (Dir)
Ultimate Holding Company: STORER HOLDINGS LIMITED
Immediate Holding Company: STORER REFRIGERATION AND CATERING MANUFACTURERS LIMITED
Registration no: 02198808 **Date established:** 1987 **Turnover:** £5m - £10m
No.of Employees: 51 - 100 **Product Groups:** 40, 42, 52

Date of Accounts	Mar 11	Mar 10	Mar 09
Sales Turnover	7m	6m	N/A
Pre Tax Profit/Loss	14	24	127
Working Capital	135	168	164
Fixed Assets	230	160	190
Current Assets	3m	2m	2m
Current Liabilities	1m	1m	989

Strella Fabrics Ltd

Grant House Grant Street, Nottingham, NG7 3GS
Tel: 0115-955 4444 **Fax:** 0115-955 4500
E-mail: enquiries@strella-fabrics.ltd.uk
Website: http://www.strella-fabrics.ltd.uk
Bank(s): Royal Bank of Scotland
Directors: L. Strauss (Grp Chief Exec), O. Pellerey (Sales), L. Strauss (MD)
Immediate Holding Company: STRELLA FABRICS LIMITED
Registration no: 03411043 **VAT No.:** GB 694 8891 55
Date established: 1997 **Turnover:** £1m - £2m **No.of Employees:** 11 - 20
Product Groups: 23

Date of Accounts	Oct 07	Oct 06	Oct 05
Working Capital	1	N/A	17
Fixed Assets	2	9	17
Current Assets	893	761	755
Current Liabilities	892	761	739
Total Share Capital	50	50	50

W B Stubbs Hawksworth Ltd

Progress Works Hawksworth, Nottingham, NG13 9DF
Tel: 01949-850218 **Fax:** 01949-851255
Bank(s): National Westminster
Directors: C. Bradwell (MD)
Immediate Holding Company: W.B.STUBBS(HAWKSWORTH)LIMITED
Registration no: 00620673 **VAT No.:** GB 117 4734 72
Date established: 1959 **Turnover:** £2m - £5m **No.of Employees:** 21 - 50
Product Groups: 40, 41, 45

Date of Accounts	Dec 11	Dec 10	Dec 09
Working Capital	944	1m	1m
Fixed Assets	1m	1m	1m
Current Assets	1m	1m	1m

Sunspel Menswear Ltd

Cavendish House Canal Street, Long Eaton, Nottingham, NG10 4HP
Tel: 0115-973 5292 **Fax:** 0115-946 1378
E-mail: info@sunspel.com
Website: http://www.sunspel.com
Bank(s): HSBC
Directors: N. Brooke (Dir), N. Brookes (MD)
Ultimate Holding Company: THOMAS A. HILL LIMITED
Immediate Holding Company: SUNSPEL MENSWEAR LIMITED
Registration no: 01781094 **VAT No.:** GB 125 2425 03
Date established: 1983 **No.of Employees:** 21 - 50 **Product Groups:** 24

Date of Accounts	Jan 11	Jan 10	Jan 09
Working Capital	2m	1m	1m
Fixed Assets	89	101	102
Current Assets	2m	2m	1m

Swisstulle UK Ltd

P O Box 9955, Nottingham, NG4 9DY
Tel: 0115-841 4370 **Fax:** 0115-840 4370
E-mail: sales@swisstulle.co.uk
Website: http://www.swisstulle.co.uk
Bank(s): National Westminster Bank Plc
Directors: A. Illi (Ch), J. Roscalns (MD), J. Roskalns (MD)
Managers: N. Truman (Sales Prom Mgr)
Ultimate Holding Company: C W C
Immediate Holding Company: Swiss Net Co. Ltd
Registration no: 00045771 **VAT No.:** GB 116 3166 94
Date established: 2005 **Turnover:** £2m - £5m **No.of Employees:** 51 - 100
Product Groups: 23

Date of Accounts	Dec 07	Dec 06	Dec 05
Sales Turnover	N/A	N/A	2294
Pre Tax Profit/Loss	N/A	N/A	-274
Working Capital	498	975	928
Fixed Assets	727	764	599
Current Assets	1050	1230	1272
Current Liabilities	552	255	343
Total Share Capital	600	600	600
ROCE% (Return on Capital Employed)			-17.9
ROT% (Return on Turnover)			-11.9

Synshield Fabrications Ltd

434b Watnall Road Hucknall, Nottingham, NG15 6FQ
Tel: 0115-963 7465
E-mail: synshield@gmail.com
Directors: P. Bellamy (MD)
Immediate Holding Company: SYNSHIELD FABRICATIONS LIMITED
Registration no: 05171317 **Date established:** 2004
No.of Employees: 1 - 10 **Product Groups:** 35, 48, 52

Date of Accounts	Jul 11	Jul 10	Jul 09
Working Capital	-10	-11	-9
Fixed Assets	15	17	10
Current Assets	56	57	51

T R Fabrications

92 Meadow Road Netherfield, Nottingham, NG4 2FR
Tel: 0115-940 2030 **Fax:** 0115-940 2080
E-mail: info@trfabrications.co.uk
Website: http://www.trfabrications.co.uk
Directors: M. Rowley (Dir)
Immediate Holding Company: TR FABRICATIONS (NOTTM) LIMITED
Registration no: 06502067 **Date established:** 2008
No.of Employees: 1 - 10 **Product Groups:** 35

Date of Accounts	Mar 11	Mar 10	Mar 09
Working Capital	22	12	-23
Fixed Assets	154	166	178
Current Assets	86	70	83

Tascol Shore Engineering Ltd

3 Hill Crest Park Hoyle Road, Calverton, Nottingham, NG14 6QJ
Tel: 0115-965 6652 **Fax:** 0115-965 6653
E-mail: sales@tascol.co.uk
Website: http://www.tascol.co.uk
Directors: P. Shore (MD), S. Roy (Fin)
Immediate Holding Company: TASCOL SHORE ENGINEERING LIMITED
Registration no: 04207509 **Date established:** 2001
No.of Employees: 1 - 10 **Product Groups:** 38, 42

Date of Accounts	Mar 08	Mar 07	Mar 06
Working Capital	73	70	267
Fixed Assets	16	7	4
Current Assets	197	203	390
Current Liabilities	124	134	123

Teksol Training & Technology Ltd

17 New Eaton Road Stapleford, Nottingham, NG9 7EF
Tel: 0115-949 0497
E-mail: lizzie.taylor@teksol-gassafetytraining.com
Website: http://www.teksol-gassafetytraining.com
Directors: L. Taylor (MD)
Immediate Holding Company: TEKSOL TRAINING AND TECHNOLOGY LIMITED
Registration no: 03743058 **Date established:** 1999
No.of Employees: 1 - 10 **Product Groups:** 35, 37, 39, 84, 86

Date of Accounts	Mar 11	Mar 10	Mar 07
Working Capital	1	7	21
Fixed Assets	4	4	3
Current Assets	26	47	34

Tektroniks

Unit 21 High Hazles Road Cotgrave, Nottingham, NG12 3GZ
Tel: 0115-989 0090 **Fax:** 0115-989 0048
E-mail: info@tektroniks.co.uk
Website: http://www.tektroniks.co.uk
Directors: S. Smith (MD)
Immediate Holding Company: TEK TRONIKS LIMITED
Registration no: 02797409 **Date established:** 1993
No.of Employees: 1 - 10 **Product Groups:** 37, 38, 40, 67

Date of Accounts	Dec 11	Dec 10	Dec 09
Working Capital	202	133	203
Fixed Assets	65	50	86
Current Assets	487	326	352
Current Liabilities	N/A	75	43

Telbrook Ltd

7 Nottingham South & Wilford Industrial Estate, Nottingham, NG11 7EP
Tel: 0115-982 1133 **Fax:** 0115-937 4032
E-mail: charles@telbrook.co.uk
Website: http://www.telbrook.co.uk
Directors: C. Martin (Sales)
Immediate Holding Company: TELBROOK LIMITED
Registration no: 02825364 **Date established:** 1993
No.of Employees: 21 - 50 **Product Groups:** 46

Date of Accounts	Mar 11	Mar 10	Mar 09
Working Capital	-509	-354	-347
Fixed Assets	1m	760	744
Current Assets	1m	1m	976

Tennant Varipack

The Midway, Nottingham, NG7 2TS
Tel: 0115-988 1300 **Fax:** 0115-988 5310
E-mail: info@tennantpvc.co.uk
Website: http://www.tennantpvc.co.uk
Bank(s): Lloyds TSB
Directors: R. Tennant (Prop)
Managers: R. Campbell
Ultimate Holding Company: TENNANT GROUP LIMITED
Immediate Holding Company: TENNANT VARIPACK LIMITED
Registration no: 00903675 **VAT No.:** GB 284 7234 38
Date established: 1967 **No.of Employees:** 21 - 50 **Product Groups:** 30

Date of Accounts	Mar 09	Mar 08	Sep 11
Working Capital	-88	-12	-91
Fixed Assets	16	20	N/A
Current Assets	365	419	273
Current Liabilities	170	152	N/A

Termate

Leone Works John Street, New Basford, Nottingham, NG7 7HL
Tel: 0115-978 4652 **Fax:** 0115-970 2106
E-mail: sales@termate.com
Website: http://www.termate.com
Bank(s): National Westminster, Nottingham
Directors: R. Swann (Prop)
Managers: C. McConnell (Comptroller), D. McKain (Mktg Serv Mgr), D. Ward (Buyer)
Immediate Holding Company: TERMATE LIMITED
Registration no: 06720857 **VAT No.:** 450 1418 87 **Date established:** 2008
Turnover: £1m - £2m **No.of Employees:** 21 - 50 **Product Groups:** 37

The Wilson Organisation

Wilson House 1-3 Waverley Street, Nottingham, NG7 4HG
Tel: 0115-942 0111 **Fax:** 0115-942 0459
E-mail: info@wilorg.com
Website: http://www.wilorg.com
Bank(s): National Westminster
Directors: J. Steele (Fin)
Managers: T. Morgan (Personnel), H. Davies (Tech Serv Mgr), P. Briggs (Sales & Mktg Mg)
Immediate Holding Company: WILSON INSURANCE BROKING GROUP LIMITED
Registration no: 00862690 **VAT No.:** GB 695 1123 32
Date established: 1965 **Turnover:** £2m - £5m **No.of Employees:** 51 - 100
Product Groups: 82

Date of Accounts	Mar 11	Mar 10	Mar 09
Sales Turnover	4m	4m	4m
Pre Tax Profit/Loss	44	-190	-22
Working Capital	-61	-86	132
Fixed Assets	1m	1m	2m
Current Assets	2m	3m	3m
Current Liabilities	225	483	492

Thomas & Betts

Wilford Road, Nottingham, NG2 1EB
Tel: 0115-964 3700 **Fax:** 0115-986 0538
E-mail: martin.critchley@tnb.com
Website: http://www.tnb.com
Directors: E. Mills (Fin), J. Barlow (Pers)
Managers: E. Lucas, D. Waton (Mktg Serv Mgr), M. Singh (Plant), T. Barnett (Tech Serv Mgr)
Immediate Holding Company: THOMAS & BETTS HOLDINGS (U.K.)
Registration no: 02287881 **Date established:** 1988
Turnover: Up to £250,000 **No.of Employees:** 101 - 250
Product Groups: 27, 30, 36, 37, 39, 40, 42, 51, 67, 68

Thyssenkrupp Elevator UK Ltd

Traffic Street, Nottingham, NG2 1NF
Tel: 0115-986 8213 **Fax:** 0115-986 1549
E-mail: brian.marcus@tke-uk-thyssenkrupp.com
Website: http://www.thyssen-lifts.co.uk
Bank(s): National Westminster
Directors: B. Marcus (Contracts), P. Coleman (Fin), A. Sunderland (MD)
Managers: R. Graham (Personnel), T. Watson (Tech Serv Mgr)
Ultimate Holding Company: THYSSEN KRUPP AG (GERMANY)
Immediate Holding Company: THYSSENKRUPP ELEVATOR UK LIMITED
Registration no: 00688790 **VAT No.:** GB 450 1782 66
Date established: 1961 **Turnover:** £50m - £75m
No.of Employees: 501 - 1000 **Product Groups:** 48

see next page

***Thyssenkrupp Elevator UK Ltd** - Cont'd*

Date of Accounts	Sep 10	Sep 09	Sep 08
Sales Turnover	66m	94m	97m
Pre Tax Profit/Loss	-23m	-10m	-3m
Working Capital	6m	11m	14m
Fixed Assets	1m	2m	2m
Current Assets	31m	55m	57m
Current Liabilities	21m	10m	12m

Tools To Go

325 Hucknall Road, Nottingham, NG5 1FJ
Tel: 0115-962 0962 **Fax:** 0115-962 6659
Managers: M. Messon (Mgr)
Immediate Holding Company: TOOLS TO GO LIMITED
Registration no: 04552011 **Date established:** 2002
No.of Employees: 1 - 10 **Product Groups:** 37

Topaz Computer Systems Ltd

Chrysalis Way Langley Bridge, Eastwood, Nottingham, NG16 3RY
Tel: 01773-531551 **Fax:** 01773-716121
E-mail: info@topaz.co.uk
Website: http://www.topaz.co.uk
Directors: A. Stanley (Dir), G. Griffiths (MD), J. Griffiths (Co Sec)
Managers: E. Stanley (Sales Prom Mgr)
Immediate Holding Company: Safe Computing Holdings Ltd
Registration no: 02420422 **Turnover:** £2m - £5m
No.of Employees: 21 - 50 **Product Groups:** 44

Date of Accounts	Dec 07	Dec 06	Dec 05
Working Capital	-28	-22	-29
Fixed Assets	452	308	344
Current Assets	819	733	631
Current Liabilities	848	755	661
Total Share Capital	15	15	100

Total wall

Midland House 117 Trent Boulevard West Bridgford, Nottingham, NG2 5BN
Tel: 0115-982 0810 **Fax:** 0115-982 0830
E-mail: iwa@totalstone.co.uk
Website: http://www.totalstone.co.uk
Directors: I. Alcorn (Dir)
Date established: 1981 **Turnover:** £500,000 - £1m
No.of Employees: 11 - 20 **Product Groups:** 33

T Q C Ltd

Hooton Street, Nottingham, NG3 2NJ
Tel: 0115-950 3561 **Fax:** 0115-948 4642
E-mail: sales@tqc.co.uk
Website: http://www.tqc.co.uk
Bank(s): Barclays
Directors: M. Jones (Dir), K. Tupling (Co Sec), G. Murray (MD)
Immediate Holding Company: TQC LIMITED
Registration no: 01959944 **Date established:** 1985 **Turnover:** £2m - £5m
No.of Employees: 21 - 50 **Product Groups:** 38, 39, 40, 84

Date of Accounts	Sep 11	Sep 10	Sep 09
Working Capital	153	97	255
Fixed Assets	481	492	583
Current Assets	656	552	656

Trade Partners International

6 Reynolds Drive Wollaton, Nottingham, NG8 1HE
Tel: 07989-414051
E-mail: info@trade-partners.net
Website: http://www.trade-partners.net
Directors: T. Bradley (Dir), A. Bradley (Co Sec), A. Topham (Dir)
Immediate Holding Company: TRADE PARTNERS INTERNATIONAL LIMITED
Registration no: 06059139 **Date established:** 2007
Turnover: Up to £250,000 **No.of Employees:** 1 - 10 **Product Groups:** 29

Date of Accounts	Apr 08
Sales Turnover	237
Pre Tax Profit/Loss	1
Working Capital	29
Fixed Assets	2
Current Assets	124
Current Liabilities	95
ROCE% (Return on Capital Employed)	3.5

Travis Perkins plc

Crossgate Drive Queens Drive Industrial Estate, Nottingham, NG2 1LN
Tel: 0115-986 2691 **Fax:** 0115-986 1469
E-mail: colin.larking@travisperkins.co.uk
Website: http://www.travisperkins.co.uk
Managers: C. Larking (Mgr)
Immediate Holding Company: TRAVIS PERKINS PLC
Registration no: 00824821 **Date established:** 1964
No.of Employees: 21 - 50 **Product Groups:** 66

Date of Accounts	Dec 11	Dec 10	Dec 09
Sales Turnover	4779m	3153m	2931m
Pre Tax Profit/Loss	270m	197m	213m
Working Capital	133m	159m	248m
Fixed Assets	2771m	2749m	2108m
Current Assets	1421m	1329m	1035m
Current Liabilities	473m	412m	109m

Trent Concrete Ltd

Private Road 3 Colwick Industrial Estate, Nottingham, NG4 2BG
Tel: 0115-987 9747 **Fax:** 0115-987 9948
E-mail: anthony.orange@trentconcrete.co.uk
Website: http://www.trentconcrete.co.uk
Bank(s): Barclays, Nottingham
Directors: A. Orange (Comm), C. Jones (Contracts), D. Walker (Comm), J. Alexander (Co Sec), J. Alexander (Fin), P. King (Fab)
Managers: P. Smith (Purch Mgr), T. Orange
Ultimate Holding Company: Trent Concrete Ltd
Immediate Holding Company: TRENT CONCRETE LIMITED
Registration no: 01018733 **Date established:** 1971
Turnover: £10m - £20m **No.of Employees:** 101 - 250
Product Groups: 33, 35

Date of Accounts	Oct 08	Sep 07	Oct 06
Sales Turnover	11m	13m	11m
Pre Tax Profit/Loss	-460	880	610
Working Capital	-80	250	-500
Fixed Assets	4m	5m	3m
Current Assets	3m	3m	3m
Current Liabilities	3m	3m	4m
Total Share Capital	180	200	200

Trowell Plant Sales Ltd

111 Station Road Selston, Nottingham, NG16 6FF
Tel: 01773-580878 **Fax:** 01773-580881
E-mail: tpsl@btconnect.com
Website: http://www.trowellplant.com
Directors: P. Hodges (MD)
Immediate Holding Company: TROWELL PLANT SALES LIMITED
Registration no: 00958043 **VAT No.:** GB 117 0367 93
Date established: 1969 **Turnover:** £500,000 - £1m
No.of Employees: 1 - 10 **Product Groups:** 40, 45, 66, 67

Date of Accounts	Mar 12	Mar 11	Mar 10
Working Capital	93	79	62
Fixed Assets	1	1	N/A
Current Assets	268	251	141

Tyack Export Sales Services

52 Davies Road West Bridgford, Nottingham, NG2 5JA
Tel: 0115-981 1633 **Fax:** 0115-969 6030
E-mail: martin@exportsales.net
Website: http://www.exportsales.net
Directors: M. Tyack (Prop)
Managers: D. Tyack (Chief Mgr)
Turnover: £1m - £2m **No.of Employees:** 1 - 10 **Product Groups:** 35, 49, 61

V F Northern Europe Ltd

Park Road East Calverton, Nottingham, NG14 6GD
Tel: 0115-965 6565 **Fax:** 0115-965 7742
E-mail: info@scs.com
Website: http://www.vfc.com
Bank(s): Barclays
Directors: P. Emmerson (Dir)
Ultimate Holding Company: VF CORP (USA)
Immediate Holding Company: VF NORTHERN EUROPE LIMITED
Registration no: SC047368 **Date established:** 1970
Turnover: £20m - £50m **No.of Employees:** 101 - 250 **Product Groups:** 24

Date of Accounts	Dec 11	Dec 10	Dec 09
Sales Turnover	23m	20m	19m
Pre Tax Profit/Loss	4m	2m	2m
Working Capital	2m	-592	756
Fixed Assets	3m	3m	3m
Current Assets	45m	42m	35m
Current Liabilities	9m	7m	5m

Vantage Training Ltd

The Wharf Trent Lane, East Bridgford, Nottingham, NG13 8PF
Tel: 01949-21212 **Fax:** 01949- 829281
E-mail: info@vtl.co.uk
Website: http://www.vtl.co.uk
Directors: G. Lewis (MD)
Immediate Holding Company: VANTAGE TRAINING LIMITED
Registration no: 03034123 **Date established:** 1995
No.of Employees: 1 - 10 **Product Groups:** 86

Date of Accounts	Apr 11	Apr 10	Apr 09
Working Capital	263	254	212
Fixed Assets	12	14	18
Current Assets	288	332	228

The Vinyl Corporation

Decalcraft Park Awsworth Lane, Cossall, Nottingham, NG16 2SA
Tel: 0115-930 1133 **Fax:** 0115-944 1778
E-mail: dmtvc.march@btconnect.com
Website: http://www.thevinylcorporation.co.uk
Directors: D. March (MD)
Registration no: 03937900 **Date established:** 1984 **Turnover:** £1m - £2m
No.of Employees: 1 - 10 **Product Groups:** 39

Vision Express UK

Abbeyfield Road Lenton, Nottingham, NG7 2SP
Tel: 0115-986 5225 **Fax:** 0115-985 0974
Website: http://www.visionexpress.com
Directors: R. Beck (Fin)
Ultimate Holding Company: HAL TRUST (BERMUDA)
Immediate Holding Company: VISION EXPRESS (UK) LIMITED
Registration no: 02189907 **Date established:** 1987
Turnover: £125m - £250m **No.of Employees:** 101 - 250
Product Groups: 61

Date of Accounts	Dec 11	Dec 10	Dec 09
Sales Turnover	196m	191m	195m
Pre Tax Profit/Loss	14m	11m	19m
Working Capital	-19m	3m	2m
Fixed Assets	46m	42m	43m
Current Assets	36m	35m	34m
Current Liabilities	15m	14m	16m

Vista Signs

267 Nottingham Road, Nottingham, NG7 7DA
Tel: 0115-942 1511 **Fax:** 0115-942 2462
E-mail: sales@vista-signs.co.uk
Website: http://www.vista-signs.co.uk
Bank(s): Lloyds TSB Bank plc
Directors: S. Harrower (Dir), J. Christian (MD)
Managers: P. Rowe (Sales Prom Mgr)
Immediate Holding Company: VISTA SIGNS LIMITED
Registration no: 00843125 **Date established:** 1965
No.of Employees: 21 - 50 **Product Groups:** 39, 45

Date of Accounts	Dec 07	Dec 06	Dec 05
Working Capital	42	104	161
Fixed Assets	80	110	128
Current Assets	437	426	536
Current Liabilities	395	322	375
Total Share Capital	15	15	15

Visual Packaging Ltd

Easter Park Lenton Lane, Nottingham, NG7 2PX
Tel: 0115-978 8000 **Fax:** 0115-970 3770
E-mail: stw@visualpackaging.co.uk
Website: http://www.visualpackaging.co.uk
Directors: S. Webster (MD)
Immediate Holding Company: VISUAL PACKAGING (PLASTICS) LIMITED
Registration no: 02363620 **Date established:** 1989
No.of Employees: 11 - 20 **Product Groups:** 30, 38, 48

Date of Accounts	Jun 11	Jun 10	Jun 09
Working Capital	415	287	159
Fixed Assets	481	238	282
Current Assets	1m	1m	869

Vollmer UK Ltd

Unit 2 Orchard Park Industrial Estate Sandiacre, Nottingham, NG10 5BP
Tel: 0115-949 1040 **Fax:** 0115-949 0042
E-mail: admin@vollmer-uk.com
Website: http://www.vollmer-group.com
Bank(s): Barclays, Old Market Square, Nottingham
Directors: G. Hopkins (MD), P. Taylor (Fin)
Managers: R. Gough (Sales Admin)
Immediate Holding Company: VOLLMER UK LIMITED
Registration no: 00503995 **Date established:** 1952 **Turnover:** £2m - £5m
No.of Employees: 11 - 20 **Product Groups:** 46, 49

Date of Accounts	Dec 11	Dec 10	Dec 09
Working Capital	1m	1m	1m
Fixed Assets	185	211	212
Current Assets	2m	2m	2m

W J P Engineering Plastics Ltd

2 Albert Avenue, Nottingham, NG8 5BE
Tel: 0115-929 9555 **Fax:** 0115-929 0422
E-mail: sales@wjpengineeringplastics.co.uk
Website: http://www.wjpengineeringplastics.co.uk
Bank(s): National Westminster Bank Plc
Directors: G. Eley (MD)
Immediate Holding Company: W.J.P. ENGINEERING PLASTICS LIMITED
Registration no: 01102698 **Date established:** 1973
Turnover: £250,000 - £500,000 **No.of Employees:** 11 - 20
Product Groups: 30, 31, 33, 48

Date of Accounts	Apr 11	Apr 10	Apr 09
Working Capital	84	77	73
Fixed Assets	1	N/A	5
Current Assets	226	208	198

Watlow Ltd

Robey Close Linby, Nottingham, NG15 8AA
Tel: 0115-964 0777 **Fax:** 0115-964 0071
E-mail: ahalton@watlow.co.uk
Website: http://www.watlow.co.uk
Managers: D. Robson (Tech Serv Mgr), A. Halton (Comm), A. Halton (Comptroller)
Ultimate Holding Company: WATLOW ELECTRIC MANUFACTURING CO (USA)
Immediate Holding Company: WATLOW LIMITED
Registration no: 02152272 **Date established:** 1987 **Turnover:** £2m - £5m
No.of Employees: 11 - 20 **Product Groups:** 37, 38, 40

Date of Accounts	Dec 11	Dec 10	Dec 09
Sales Turnover	5m	4m	4m
Pre Tax Profit/Loss	241	393	38
Working Capital	2m	1m	2m
Fixed Assets	525	714	780
Current Assets	2m	2m	2m
Current Liabilities	237	223	70

Webro Cable & Connectors Ltd

Vision House Meadow Brooks Business Park Meadow Lane, Long Eaton, Nottingham, NG10 2GD
Tel: 0115-972 4483 **Fax:** 0115-946 1230
E-mail: info@webro.com
Website: http://www.webro.com
Directors: P. Edginton (Ptnr)
Ultimate Holding Company: WEBRO (LONG EATON) LIMITED
Immediate Holding Company: WEBRO (AGENCY SALES) LIMITED
Registration no: 02291826 **Date established:** 1988 **Turnover:** £5m - £10m
No.of Employees: 21 - 50 **Product Groups:** 35, 37, 44, 68

We-Ef Lighting Ltd

Unit 4 Canalside Indl-Est Kinoulton Road, Cropwell Bishop, Nottingham, NG12 3BE
Tel: 0115-989 0319 **Fax:** 07000-784982
E-mail: info.uk@we-ef.com
Website: http://www.we-ef.com
Directors: M. Hill (MD)
Managers: J. Davis (Sales Admin)
Immediate Holding Company: WE-EF LIGHTING LIMITED
Registration no: 03302236 **Date established:** 1997
No.of Employees: 1 - 10 **Product Groups:** 37, 67

Date of Accounts	Jun 11	Jun 10	Jun 07
Working Capital	248	219	360
Fixed Assets	64	61	52
Current Assets	597	332	653

Welbeck Sports

Unit 2 Benneworth Close Hucknall, Nottingham, NG15 6EL
Tel: 0115-963 2848 **Fax:** 0115-964 0223
E-mail: sales@welbecksports.co.uk
Website: http://www.welbecksports.co.uk
Directors: T. Jones (Dir)
Immediate Holding Company: PRICE & BUCKLAND LIMITED
Date established: 1959 **No.of Employees:** 11 - 20 **Product Groups:** 24, 28, 84

Welder Equipment Services Ltd

Redfield Road Lenton Lane Industrial Estate, Nottingham, NG7 2UJ
Tel: 0115-986 8181 **Fax:** 0115-985 1936
Website: http://www.wehireit.co.uk
Directors: R. Godley (MD)
Ultimate Holding Company: LINDE AG (GERMANY)
Immediate Holding Company: WELDER EQUIPMENT SERVICES LIMITED
Registration no: 01538861 **Date established:** 1981
Turnover: £500,000 - £1m **No.of Employees:** 11 - 20 **Product Groups:** 46

Date of Accounts	Dec 11	Dec 10	Dec 09
Sales Turnover	720	631	577
Pre Tax Profit/Loss	71	-44	-58
Working Capital	120	51	-19
Fixed Assets	258	379	395
Current Assets	274	209	191
Current Liabilities	69	37	19

Westbridge International Group Ltd

Westbridge House Holland Street, Nottingham, NG7 5DS
Tel: 0115-978 2254 **Fax:** 0115-942 0547
E-mail: sales@wbig.co.uk
Website: http://www.wbig.co.uk
Directors: G. Moxon (Fin), N. Rubins (Grp Chief Exec)
Managers: C. Tiffin (Sales Prom Mgr), D. Gill
Ultimate Holding Company: WESTBRIDGE INTERNATIONAL GROUP LIMITED
Immediate Holding Company: WESTBRIDGE INTERNATIONAL GROUP LIMITED

Registration no: 00954380 **VAT No.:** GB 385 3967 01
Date established: 1969 **Turnover:** £50m - £75m
No.of Employees: 21 - 50 **Product Groups:** 63

Date of Accounts	Feb 11	Feb 10	Feb 09
Sales Turnover	66m	60m	52m
Pre Tax Profit/Loss	-178	-212	2m
Working Capital	-4m	-4m	-2m
Fixed Assets	36m	35m	33m
Current Assets	14m	13m	11m
Current Liabilities	1m	1m	1m

Wheatcroft Garden Centre

Landmere Lane Edwalton, Nottingham, NG12 4DE
Tel: 0115-921 6061 **Fax:** 0115-984 1247
E-mail: coles@notcutts.co.uk
Website: http://www.notcutts.co.uk
Bank(s): Nat West
Managers: S. Cole (Mgr)
Immediate Holding Company: WHEATCROFT LIMITED
Registration no: 03820840 **Date established:** 1999
No.of Employees: 51 - 100 **Product Groups:** 26, 62

Date of Accounts	Dec 11	Dec 10	Dec 09
Working Capital	81	-233	-274
Fixed Assets	5m	5m	5m
Current Assets	379	204	270

Whitefields Secure Document Storage Ltd

Tithby Road Bingham, Nottingham, NG13 8GQ
Tel: 01949-831781 **Fax:** 01949-836500
E-mail: sales@wdstorage.co.uk
Website: http://www.wdstorage.co.uk
Managers: A. Hammond (Sales Prom Mgr)
Immediate Holding Company: WHITEFIELDS STORAGE LIMITED
Registration no: 04660968 **Date established:** 2003
No.of Employees: 1 - 10 **Product Groups:** 80

Date of Accounts	Mar 12	Mar 11	Mar 10
Working Capital	138	111	124
Fixed Assets	99	96	87
Current Assets	199	176	141

Whyte & Son Nottingham Ltd

Lincoln Street Old Basford, Nottingham, NG6 0FT
Tel: 0115-978 4264
Directors: C. Whyte (Dir)
Immediate Holding Company: WHYTE AND SON (NOTTINGHAM) LIMITED
Registration no: 00167829 **Date established:** 1920
No.of Employees: 21 - 50 **Product Groups:** 63

Date of Accounts	Jul 11	Jul 10	Jul 09
Working Capital	51	26	1m
Fixed Assets	2m	2m	673
Current Assets	87	73	1m

Wolseley UK Ltd

Unit 5 Centurion Way Riverside Industrial Estate, Nottingham, NG2 1RW
Tel: 0115-957 8200 **Fax:** 0115-957 8201
E-mail: sales@wolseley.co.uk
Website: http://www.pipecenter.co.uk
Managers: P. Dawson (Sales Admin), M. Morris (District Mgr)
Ultimate Holding Company: Wolseley Centres
Immediate Holding Company: Pipeline Center
Registration no: 00636445 **Turnover:** £75m - £125m
No.of Employees: 11 - 20 **Product Groups:** 66

Garth T Wright Fasteners

Colwickwood Works Colwick Road, Nottingham, NG2 4BG
Tel: 0115-958 8360 **Fax:** 0115-948 4967
E-mail: wright@wright-engineers.co.uk
Website: http://www.wright-engineers.co.uk
Directors: R. Wright (Prop)
Immediate Holding Company: ERIC NEWMAN ASSOCIATES LIMITED
Registration no: 05165701 **Date established:** 1968
Turnover: Up to £250,000 **No.of Employees:** 1 - 10 **Product Groups:** 35, 66

Date of Accounts	Dec 11	Dec 10	Dec 09
Working Capital	390	364	379
Fixed Assets	68	78	87
Current Assets	420	392	415

Z F Great Britain Ltd

Abbeyfield Road, Nottingham, NG7 2SX
Tel: 0115-986 9211 **Fax:** 0115-986 9261
E-mail: christopher.adcock@zf-group.co.uk
Website: http://www.zf-group.co.uk
Bank(s): Barclays
Directors: J. Lawrence (Fin), J. Poore (MD), C. Adcock (Dir)
Managers: C. Holland (Mktg Serv Mgr), G. Truckel (Sales Prom Mgr), J. Shaw (Sales Prom Mgr), J. Truckel (Sales Prom Mgr)
Ultimate Holding Company: ZF FRIEDRICHSHAFEN AG (GERMANY)
Immediate Holding Company: ZF SERVICES UK LIMITED
Registration no: 01137722 **VAT No.:** 118 2242 00 **Date established:** 1973
Turnover: £20m - £50m **No.of Employees:** 101 - 250
Product Groups: 35, 39

Date of Accounts	Dec 09	Dec 08	Dec 07
Sales Turnover	22m	23m	27m
Pre Tax Profit/Loss	-368	812	2m
Working Capital	7m	8m	10m
Fixed Assets	1m	1m	1m
Current Assets	10m	12m	13m
Current Liabilities	933	993	1m

Zouch Converters Ltd

Cumberland House 35 Park Row, Nottingham, NG1 6EE
Tel: 0115-988 6295 **Fax:** 0115-988 6215
E-mail: sales@zouchconverters.co.uk
Website: http://www.zouchconverters.co.uk
Immediate Holding Company: ZOUCH CONVERTERS LIMITED
Registration no: 05342950 **Date established:** 2005
Turnover: £500,000 - £1m **No.of Employees:** 1 - 10 **Product Groups:** 27, 30

Date of Accounts	Mar 11	Mar 10	Mar 09
Working Capital	-1	-19	-32
Fixed Assets	3	3	1
Current Assets	167	130	58

Retford

A D A Assessment Solutions Ltd

Firs Farm House Bilby, Retford, DN22 8JB
Tel: 01777-711141 **Fax:** 01777-711144
E-mail: info@improver.co.uk
Website: http://www.improver.co.uk
Directors: A. Darbyshire (Dir)
Immediate Holding Company: ADA ASSESSMENT SOLUTIONS LIMITED
Registration no: 04185122 **VAT No.:** GB 593 3770 09
Date established: 2001 **Turnover:** £250,000 - £500,000
No.of Employees: 1 - 10 **Product Groups:** 44

Date of Accounts	Mar 11	Mar 10	Mar 08
Working Capital	-58	-55	-54
Fixed Assets	72	79	94
Current Assets	3	4	6

A S Supplies

3 West Carr Industrial Estate Stirling Road, Retford, DN22 7SN
Tel: 01777-706793 **Fax:** 01777-706794
E-mail: sales@assupplies-retford.co.uk
Website: http://www.assupplies-retford.co.uk
Directors: P. Slinger (Prop)
Date established: 1978 **No.of Employees:** 1 - 10 **Product Groups:** 35

Aqua Services

29 Southfield Rise North Leverton, Retford, DN22 0AY
Tel: 01777-708140 **Fax:** 01777-860140
E-mail: maquaserve@aol.com
Directors: J. Marshall (Prop)
Date established: 1996 **No.of Employees:** 1 - 10 **Product Groups:** 36, 40

Atherton Materials Handling Ltd

Access Road Common Lane, Ranskill, Retford, DN22 8LW
Tel: 01777-817000 **Fax:** 01777-817665
E-mail: enquiries@amhltd.co.uk
Website: http://www.amhltd.co.uk
Bank(s): Barclays
Directors: D. Atherton (MD)
Managers: K. Atherton (Sales Admin)
Immediate Holding Company: ATHERTON CONVEYORS LIMITED
Registration no: 04218516 **VAT No.:** GB 974 3194 92
Date established: 2001 **Turnover:** £1m - £2m **No.of Employees:** 11 - 20
Product Groups: 29, 30, 33, 34, 35, 36, 41, 42, 45, 46, 54, 61, 67, 83, 84

Date of Accounts	Mar 10	Mar 09	Mar 08
Working Capital	24	34	185
Fixed Assets	49	162	130
Current Assets	151	346	442

L Baines & Son

Stanford Works Church Lane, Clarborough, Retford, DN22 9NA
Tel: 01777-702994 **Fax:** 01777-711108
Directors: M. Baines (Prop)
Date established: 1960 **No.of Employees:** 1 - 10 **Product Groups:** 41

Beeversales Agricultural Components Ltd

11 Randall Park Way, Retford, DN22 7WF
Tel: 01777-700611 **Fax:** 01777-701799
E-mail: sales@beeversales.com
Website: http://www.beeversales.com
Directors: R. Beevers (MD), I. Beevers (Fin)
Immediate Holding Company: BEEVERSALES AGRICULTURAL COMPONENTS LIMITED
Registration no: 01977278 **VAT No.:** GB 365 1492 46
Date established: 1986 **Turnover:** £1m - £2m **No.of Employees:** 1 - 10
Product Groups: 41, 67

Date of Accounts	Mar 12	Mar 11	Mar 10
Working Capital	402	163	373
Fixed Assets	622	398	190
Current Assets	857	744	834
Current Liabilities	N/A	N/A	90

Builder Center Ltd

New Street, Retford, DN22 6EG
Tel: 01777-705111 **Fax:** 01777-710863
E-mail: sales@buildcenter.co.uk
Website: http://www.buildcenter.co.uk
Managers: L. Harthen (District Mgr)
Ultimate Holding Company: WOLSELEY PLC (JERSEY)
Immediate Holding Company: BUILD CENTER LIMITED
Registration no: 00462397 **Date established:** 1948 **Turnover:** £2m - £5m
No.of Employees: 11 - 20 **Product Groups:** 36, 44, 66, 83

Date of Accounts	Jul 09
Working Capital	78
Current Assets	78

Engineering Services Humber Ltd

West Carr Road, Retford, DN22 7SW
Tel: 01777-861000 **Fax:** 01777-861020
E-mail: info@engineeringservices.co.uk
Website: http://www.engineeringservices.co.uk
Directors: S. Thorneloe (Fin)
Immediate Holding Company: ENGINEERING SERVICES (HUMBER) LIMITED
Registration no: 00800916 **Date established:** 1964
No.of Employees: 21 - 50 **Product Groups:** 30, 31, 42, 48

Horse Rug Service

Greenfields Grove, Retford, DN22 0RN
Tel: 01777-702918 **Fax:** 01777-706029
E-mail: info@greenfields-stud.co.uk
Website: http://www.greenfields-stud.co.uk
Directors: B. Duncalf (Ptnr)
Date established: 2003 **No.of Employees:** 1 - 10 **Product Groups:** 41, 65

Icon Polymer Group Ltd

Victoria Works Thrumpton Lane, Retford, DN22 6HH
Tel: 01777-714300 **Fax:** 01777-709739
E-mail: info@iconpolymer.com
Website: http://www.iconpolymer.com
Directors: T. Pryce (MD)
Immediate Holding Company: ICON POLYMER GROUP LIMITED
Registration no: 05264971 **Date established:** 2004
Turnover: Up to £250,000 **No.of Employees:** 251 - 500
Product Groups: 22, 23, 27, 29, 66

Date of Accounts	Sep 11	Sep 10	Sep 09
Sales Turnover	19m	19m	18m
Pre Tax Profit/Loss	663	935	629
Working Capital	2m	2m	1m
Fixed Assets	10m	11m	11m
Current Assets	7m	7m	6m
Current Liabilities	1m	1m	2m

J-Flex Rubber Products

Unit 1 London Road Business Park, Retford, DN22 6HG
Tel: 01777-712400 **Fax:** 01777-712409
E-mail: sales@j-flex.co.uk
Website: http://www.j-flex.co.uk
Bank(s): National Westminster Bank Plc
Directors: J. Kirk (Co Sec), J. Kirk (MD)
Immediate Holding Company: CLOCKPRESS LIMITED
Registration no: 02448048 **Date established:** 1989 **Turnover:** £2m - £5m
No.of Employees: 11 - 20 **Product Groups:** 29

Date of Accounts	Apr 11	Apr 10	Apr 09
Working Capital	159	126	72
Fixed Assets	45	46	69
Current Assets	1m	912	750

Latty International Ltd (in association with Latty International - France)

Westfield Road, Retford, DN22 7BT
Tel: 01777-708836 **Fax:** 01777-707474
E-mail: sales@latty.co.uk
Website: http://www.latty.com
Directors: M. Francis (Fin)
Managers: J. Crowe (Sales Prom Mgr)
Immediate Holding Company: LATTY INTERNATIONAL LTD
Registration no: 02574066 **VAT No.:** GB 570 9408 28
Date established: 1991 **Turnover:** £1m - £2m **No.of Employees:** 1 - 10
Product Groups: 23, 29, 30, 34

Date of Accounts	Dec 11	Dec 10	Dec 09
Sales Turnover	780	N/A	N/A
Pre Tax Profit/Loss	12	N/A	N/A
Working Capital	47	33	103
Fixed Assets	7	9	13
Current Assets	415	325	273
Current Liabilities	47	N/A	N/A

Lawson Road Planing Ltd

Unit 8-10 Rossington Business Park West Carr Road, Retford, DN22 7SW
Tel: 01777-860081 **Fax:** 01777-860082
E-mail: enquiries@lawsonroadplaning.co.uk
Website: http://www.lawsonroadplaning.co.uk
Directors: J. Lawson (MD)
Immediate Holding Company: LAWSON SURFACING LIMITED
Registration no: 04258251 **Date established:** 2001 **Turnover:** £2m - £5m
No.of Employees: 11 - 20 **Product Groups:** 45, 48, 83

Date of Accounts	Mar 09	Mar 08	Mar 07
Working Capital	-76	21	-87
Fixed Assets	177	216	200
Current Assets	447	737	511

M & D Industrial Doors

63 Ordsall Park Road, Retford, DN22 7PB
Tel: 01777-709507
Managers: D. Shaw (Mgr), D. Shaw (Mgr)
Date established: 1991 **No.of Employees:** 1 - 10 **Product Groups:** 26, 35

M H Design

6 Willand Court Retford, Retford, DN22 7GD
Tel: 01777-704967 **Fax:** 01777-719517
E-mail: mark@mhdesign.co.uk
Website: http://www.mhdesign.co.uk
Directors: M. Henshaw (Prop)
Immediate Holding Company: M H DESIGN SOLUTIONS LIMITED
Registration no: 07186197 **Date established:** 2010
No.of Employees: 1 - 10 **Product Groups:** 33, 35, 36, 45, 46

Date of Accounts	Mar 11
Working Capital	-10
Fixed Assets	11
Current Assets	3

Polyurethane Products Ltd

Stirling Road West Carr Industrial Estate, Retford, DN22 7SN
Tel: 01777-712500 **Fax:** 01777-707001
E-mail: wynn.crorkin@poly-products.co.uk
Website: http://www.poly-products.co.uk
Bank(s): Fortis
Directors: N. Williams (Sales), W. Crorkin (MD)
Managers: K. Mason (I.T. Exec)
Immediate Holding Company: TRELLEBORG PPL LIMITED
Registration no: 04226233 **VAT No.:** GB 772 7383 00
Date established: 2001 **Turnover:** £5m - £10m
No.of Employees: 51 - 100 **Product Groups:** 29

Ray Small Contractors

Church Lane East Drayton, Retford, DN22 0LH
Tel: 01777-248245 **Fax:** 01777-248171
Directors: R. Small (Ptnr)
Immediate Holding Company: RAY SMALL CONTRACTORS LIMITED
Registration no: 03684153 **Date established:** 1998
No.of Employees: 1 - 10 **Product Groups:** 41

Date of Accounts	Dec 07	Apr 11	Apr 10
Working Capital	860	110	292
Fixed Assets	10	35	37
Current Assets	926	182	360

Tarmac Ltd

Bellmoor Quarry, Retford, DN22 8SG
Tel: 01777-713500 **Fax:** 01777-860546
E-mail: stuart.haines@tarmac.co.uk
Website: http://www.tarmac.co.uk
Directors: S. Haines (Dir)
Managers: S. Noble (Intern Sales En), M. Jackson (Sales Prom Mgr)
Ultimate Holding Company: ANGLO AMERICAN PLC
Immediate Holding Company: TARMAC LIMITED
Registration no: 00453791 **Date established:** 1948
No.of Employees: 51 - 100 **Product Groups:** 14, 31, 33

Date of Accounts	Dec 10	Dec 09	Dec 08
Sales Turnover	1069m	1247m	1566m
Pre Tax Profit/Loss	75m	-47m	-29m

see next page

Tarmac Ltd - Cont'd

Working Capital	-24m	25m	2m
Fixed Assets	1244m	1391m	1434m
Current Assets	321m	431m	447m
Current Liabilities	93m	168m	213m

The Management Edge

Lowfield House Smeath Lane Clarborough, Retford, DN22 9JN
Tel: 01777-703316
E-mail: colin@themanagementedge.co.uk
Website: http://www.themanagementedge.co.uk
Directors: C. Reed (MD), C. Reed (Prop), J. Reed (Prop)
Date established: 2011 **Turnover:** Up to £250,000 **No.of Employees:** 2
Product Groups: 80, 86

Valentino's Pizzeria

12 Churchgate, Retford, DN22 6PQ
Tel: 01777-860808
Managers: M. Ghazello (Mgr)
Date established: 2001 **No.of Employees:** 1 - 10 **Product Groups:** 38, 42

West Retford Hotel

24 North Road, Retford, DN22 7XG
Tel: 01777-706333 **Fax:** 01777-709951
E-mail: andrew.lavin@westretfordhotel.co.uk
Website: http://www.regalhotels.co.uk
Bank(s): National Westminster Bank Plc
Managers: A. Lavin (Chief Mgr), H. Rann (Chief Acct)
Immediate Holding Company: WEST RETFORD HOTEL LIMITED
Registration no: 05372392 **VAT No.:** GB 614 8836 22
Date established: 2005 **Turnover:** £1m - £2m **No.of Employees:** 51 - 100
Product Groups: 69

Date of Accounts	Feb 11	Feb 10	Feb 09
Sales Turnover	2m	2m	2m
Pre Tax Profit/Loss	310	346	229
Working Capital	-40	-86	-168
Fixed Assets	5m	5m	5m
Current Assets	326	181	141
Current Liabilities	148	24	163

Steve Wilkinson

Gamston Airfield Gamston, Retford, DN22 0QL
Tel: 01777-838007
E-mail: sales@wilkeng.com
Directors: S. Wilkinson (Prop)
Immediate Holding Company: DOVETAIL JOINERY SERVICES LIMITED
Registration no: 04901979 **Date established:** 2003
No.of Employees: 1 - 10 **Product Groups:** 35

Date of Accounts	Mar 12	Mar 11	Mar 10
Working Capital	-6	-18	-12
Fixed Assets	16	20	25
Current Assets	82	42	97

Southwell

Advanex Europe Ltd

Mill Park Industrial Estate Station Road, Southwell, NG25 0ET
Tel: 01636-815555 **Fax:** 01636-817725
E-mail: sales@advanexeurope.co.uk
Website: http://www.advanexeurope.co.uk
Bank(s): Barclays
Directors: P. Clifford (MD)
Managers: C. Moss (Sales Admin), N. Hardy (Comptroller), A. Reast
Ultimate Holding Company: ADVANEX GROUP INC (JAPAN)
Immediate Holding Company: ADVANEX EUROPE LIMITED
Registration no: 02301464 **VAT No.:** GB 509 2682 38
Date established: 1988 **Turnover:** £10m - £20m
No.of Employees: 51 - 100 **Product Groups:** 66

Date of Accounts	Mar 10	Mar 09	Mar 11
Sales Turnover	7m	9m	11m
Pre Tax Profit/Loss	163	468	2m
Working Capital	3m	2m	4m
Fixed Assets	3m	3m	3m
Current Assets	4m	4m	6m
Current Liabilities	493	425	1m

R J Consultancy Southwell Ltd

25 Dornoch Avenue, Southwell, NG25 0EU
Tel: 01636-812856
E-mail: info@rjconsultancy.co.uk
Website: http://www.rjconsultancy.co.uk
Directors: J. Bull (MD)
Immediate Holding Company: RJ CONSULTANCY (SOUTHWELL) LTD
Registration no: 04947016 **Date established:** 2003
No.of Employees: 1 - 10 **Product Groups:** 80

Date of Accounts	Oct 11	Oct 10	Oct 09
Working Capital	22	3	4
Fixed Assets	1	N/A	N/A
Current Assets	48	30	27

Sutton In Ashfield

A F Switchgear Ltd

Nunn Brook Road Huthwaite, Sutton In Ashfield, NG17 2HU
Tel: 01623-555600 **Fax:** 01623-555800
E-mail: sales@afswitchgear.co.uk
Website: http://www.afswitchgear.co.uk
Directors: R. Thompson (Sales), I. Foster (MD), J. Bosworth (Fin)
Managers: S. Armiger
Ultimate Holding Company: A.F. SWITCHGEAR (HOLDINGS) LIMITED
Immediate Holding Company: A F SWITCHGEAR LIMITED
Registration no: 01179371 **Date established:** 1974
Turnover: £10m - £20m **No.of Employees:** 51 - 100 **Product Groups:** 37

Date of Accounts	Dec 11	Dec 10	Dec 09
Sales Turnover	19m	14m	17m
Pre Tax Profit/Loss	2m	493	785
Working Capital	4m	3m	3m
Fixed Assets	277	351	481
Current Assets	8m	8m	7m
Current Liabilities	1m	525	815

Abacus Lighting Ltd

Oddicroft Lane, Sutton In Ashfield, NG17 5FT
Tel: 01623-511111 **Fax:** 01623-552133
E-mail: sales@abacuslighting.com
Website: http://www.abacuslighting.com
Bank(s): Barclays
Directors: A. Morris Richardson (MD), E. Whitehead (Fin)
Managers: I. Smith (Sales & Mktg Mg), S. Kokuciak, P. Bullock (Purch Mgr), A. Brannan (Tech Serv Mgr)
Ultimate Holding Company: ABACUS HOLDINGS LIMITED
Immediate Holding Company: ABACUS HOLDINGS LIMITED
Registration no: 00943023 **Date established:** 1968
Turnover: £20m - £50m **No.of Employees:** 101 - 250
Product Groups: 26, 33, 35, 36, 37, 39, 48, 52

Date of Accounts	Dec 11	Dec 10	Dec 09
Sales Turnover	30m	29m	28m
Pre Tax Profit/Loss	-1m	-97	829
Working Capital	-2m	830	479
Fixed Assets	7m	5m	3m
Current Assets	10m	11m	9m
Current Liabilities	3m	3m	2m

Anderworth Engineering

40 Forest Road, Sutton In Ashfield, NG17 3BB
Tel: 01623-553277
Directors: A. Wordsworth (Prop)
No.of Employees: 1 - 10 **Product Groups:** 35

B J H Engineering

Reform Street Industrial Estate Reform Street, Sutton In Ashfield, NG17 5DB
Tel: 01623-842022 **Fax:** 01623-844156
E-mail: bjh@aol.com
Directors: S. Cotterill (Dir)
Date established: 1983 **No.of Employees:** 1 - 10 **Product Groups:** 35

Date of Accounts	Nov 11	Nov 10	Nov 09
Working Capital	100	63	58
Fixed Assets	18	10	13
Current Assets	163	117	114

B R C Ltd

Station Road, Sutton In Ashfield, NG17 5FR
Tel: 01623-555111 **Fax:** 01623-440932
E-mail: paul.wilcoxson@brc.ltd.uk
Website: http://www.brc-reinforcement.co.uk
Managers: P. Wilcoxson (Site Co-ord), E. Willet
Immediate Holding Company: BRC LIMITED
Registration no: 06662824 **Date established:** 2008
No.of Employees: 21 - 50 **Product Groups:** 25, 29, 30, 31, 32, 33, 34, 35, 36, 45, 66

Date of Accounts	Dec 11	Dec 10	Dec 09
Sales Turnover	124m	105m	79m
Pre Tax Profit/Loss	689	1m	515
Working Capital	19m	11m	-2m
Fixed Assets	22m	23m	25m
Current Assets	40m	26m	18m
Current Liabilities	917	3m	4m

E W Barnard Ltd

14 Alfreton Road, Sutton In Ashfield, NG17 1FW
Tel: 01623-555527 **Fax:** 01623-443781
E-mail: r.barnard@btconnect.com
Website: http://www.barnard-confectionery.co.uk
Directors: R. Barnard (Dir)
Ultimate Holding Company: E.W.BARNARD (HOLDINGS) LIMITED
Immediate Holding Company: E.W.BARNARD LIMITED
Registration no: 00711766 **Date established:** 1961
No.of Employees: 11 - 20 **Product Groups:** 20, 62

Date of Accounts	Dec 11	Dec 10	Dec 09
Working Capital	303	308	243
Fixed Assets	53	55	63
Current Assets	616	691	640

Bestblinds

23 Pleasley Road Skegby, Sutton In Ashfield, NG17 3BS
Tel: 01623-552797 **Fax:** 01623-455264
E-mail: bestblinds@business.com
Website: http://www.bestblinds-of-mansfield.com
Directors: R. Jordan (Prop)
Immediate Holding Company: ONLINE BESTBLINDS / AQUASURE LTD
Date established: 2011 **No.of Employees:** 1 - 10 **Product Groups:** 24, 35, 63

Boneham & Turner Ltd

Oddicroft Lane, Sutton In Ashfield, NG17 5FS
Tel: 01623-445450 **Fax:** 01623-621645
E-mail: sales@boneham.co.uk
Website: http://www.boneham.co.uk
Bank(s): National Westminster Bank Plc
Directors: A. Nicklin (Ch), C. Boneham (Sales), N. Boneham (Dir)
Managers: P. Boneham (Mktg Serv Mgr), T. Chadburn (Purch Mgr)
Immediate Holding Company: BONEHAM & TURNER LIMITED
Registration no: 00151276 **VAT No.:** GB 116 4089 81
Date established: 2018 **No.of Employees:** 21 - 50 **Product Groups:** 34, 35, 42, 46, 48

Date of Accounts	Jul 11	Jul 10	Jul 09
Working Capital	1m	1m	1m
Fixed Assets	2m	2m	2m
Current Assets	2m	2m	1m
Current Liabilities	N/A	N/A	103

Border Precision Tools & Plastics Ltd

13a Hamilton Road, Sutton In Ashfield, NG17 5LD
Tel: 01623-441218 **Fax:** 01623-441218
E-mail: borderplastics@btconnect.com
Website: http://www.borderplastics.co.uk
Directors: S. Walters (Dir), S. Walters (Fin)
Immediate Holding Company: BORDER PRECISION PLASTICS LIMITED
Registration no: 05370837 **Date established:** 2005
No.of Employees: 1 - 10 **Product Groups:** 29, 30, 48

Date of Accounts	Mar 11	Mar 10	Mar 09
Working Capital	16	10	6
Fixed Assets	20	25	33
Current Assets	42	28	20

Buckley Lamb Ltd

Eastfield Side, Sutton In Ashfield, NG17 4JW
Tel: 01623-550350 **Fax:** 01623-440384
E-mail: sales@buckleylamb.co.uk
Website: http://www.buckleylamb.co.uk
Bank(s): National Westminster Bank Plc
Directors: R. Lamb (Dir), K. Lamb (Fin)
Immediate Holding Company: BUCKLEY LAMB LIMITED
Registration no: 01372935 **VAT No.:** GB 309 3756 46
Date established: 1978 **Turnover:** £2m - £5m **No.of Employees:** 21 - 50
Product Groups: 24

Date of Accounts	Jun 11	Jun 10	Jun 09
Sales Turnover	3m	N/A	N/A
Pre Tax Profit/Loss	44	N/A	N/A
Working Capital	308	332	467
Fixed Assets	62	42	69
Current Assets	1m	1m	1m
Current Liabilities	124	138	N/A

BWF Tec GmbH & Co.

Unit 4 Orchard Court Nunn Brook Road, Huthwaite, Sutton In Ashfield, NG17 2HZ
Tel: 01908-516177 **Fax:** 01908-290468
E-mail: bwf-envirotec@bwf-group.de
Website: http://www.bwf-group.de
Directors: A. Neite (Chief Op Offcr), S. Grant (MD)
Managers: K. Wells (Sales Prom Mgr), T. Jennings (Sales Prom Mgr), D. Lund (Fin Mgr)
Immediate Holding Company: B W F Kunststoffe
Registration no: 03137458 **Turnover:** £2m - £5m
No.of Employees: 11 - 20 **Product Groups:** 30, 42, 49

Cable Tec Ltd (Phone-A-Hose)

Kirkby Folly Road, Sutton In Ashfield, NG17 5HN
Tel: 01623-440398 **Fax:** 01623-440142
E-mail: sales@cable-tec.co.uk
Website: http://www.cable-tec.co.uk
Directors: J. Worley (MD)
Immediate Holding Company: CABLE-TEC CABLES & CONTROLS LIMITED
Registration no: 02289383 **Date established:** 1988
No.of Employees: 1 - 10 **Product Groups:** 35, 39, 41

Date of Accounts	Sep 11	Sep 10	Sep 09
Working Capital	57	31	74
Fixed Assets	74	85	77
Current Assets	555	403	393

Components Direct

Nunn Close Huthwaite, Sutton In Ashfield, NG17 2HW
Tel: 01623-788400 **Fax:** 01623-788488
E-mail: sales@comdir.co.uk
Website: http://www.comdir.co.uk
Directors: I. Barnes (MD), S. Cusick (Fin)
Managers: A. Mitchell (Sales & Mktg Mg)
Immediate Holding Company: COMPONENTS DIRECT LIMITED
Registration no: 03867593 **Date established:** 1999 **Turnover:** £1m - £2m
No.of Employees: 51 - 100 **Product Groups:** 30, 32, 35, 36, 39, 42, 66

Crown Aerosols UK

Oddicroft Lane, Sutton In Ashfield, NG17 5FS
Tel: 01623-555555
E-mail: jbarnett@crowncork.com
Website: http://www.crowncork.com
Managers: J. Morris (Sales Prom Mgr), J. Barnett (Plant), C. Chadwick (Comptroller)
Immediate Holding Company: BONEHAM & TURNER LIMITED
Registration no: 00151276 **Date established:** 2018
No.of Employees: 1 - 10 **Product Groups:** 35, 45

Date of Accounts	Jul 11	Jul 10	Jul 09
Working Capital	1m	1m	1m
Fixed Assets	2m	2m	2m
Current Assets	2m	2m	1m
Current Liabilities	N/A	N/A	103

Getinge UK Ltd

Orchard Way, Sutton In Ashfield, NG17 1JU
Tel: 01623-510033 **Fax:** 01623-440456
E-mail: stephen.parrish@getinge.com
Website: http://www.getinge.com
Bank(s): National Westminster
Directors: G. Russell (Fin), N. Satchell (MD)
Managers: R. William (Personnel), A. Lloyd (Purch Mgr), M. Hill (Sales Prom Mgr), M. Berry (Tech Serv Mgr)
Ultimate Holding Company: GETINGE AB (SWEDEN)
Immediate Holding Company: GETINGE UK LTD
Registration no: 00671115 **Date established:** 1960
Turnover: £10m - £20m **No.of Employees:** 101 - 250
Product Groups: 24, 42, 85

Date of Accounts	Dec 11	Dec 10	Dec 09
Sales Turnover	18m	20m	19m
Pre Tax Profit/Loss	3m	2m	3m
Working Capital	16m	15m	14m
Fixed Assets	360	395	405
Current Assets	22m	20m	17m
Current Liabilities	2m	3m	2m

Imoress Sutton

Coxmoor Road, Sutton In Ashfield, NG17 5LA
Tel: 01623-518458 **Fax:** 01623-518031
Website: http://www.impressgroup.com
Directors: S. Clarke (Sales & Mktg), A. Cook (MD)
Managers: D. Horton (Plant), N. Harding (Purch Mgr), T. Russell (I.T. Exec), D. Horton (Mgr), S. Willcox, S. Willcox (Personnel)
Immediate Holding Company: Impress UK Holding 2 Ltd
Registration no: 00186479 **No.of Employees:** 101 - 250
Product Groups: 35, 45

Inpress

Forest Works Coxmoor Road, Sutton In Ashfield, NG17 5LA
Tel: 01623-512012
Website: http://www.alcan.com
Directors: D. Horton (Dir), T. Kilbride (Fin)
Managers: K. McGinn, A. Cantwell (Personnel), S. Cox (Comptroller), A. Pearce (Tech Serv Mgr)
Date established: 1922 **No.of Employees:** 101 - 250 **Product Groups:** 35, 42, 45

Date of Accounts	Dec 07
Sales Turnover	60680
Pre Tax Profit/Loss	5590
Working Capital	9840
Fixed Assets	9050
Current Assets	42780
Current Liabilities	32940
Total Share Capital	170
ROCE% (Return on Capital Employed)	29.6

Jet Press Ltd
Nunn Close Huthwaite, Sutton In Ashfield, NG17 2HW
Tel: 01623-551800 **Fax:** 01623-551175
E-mail: sales@jetpress.com
Website: http://www.jetpress.com
Bank(s): Barclays, Nottingham
Directors: A. Mitchell (Sales & Mktg), S. Cusick (Pers), I. Barnes (MD), J. Miller (Chief Op Offcr)
Managers: S. Morley (Tech Serv Mgr)
Immediate Holding Company: JET PRESS LIMITED
Registration no: 01884896 **VAT No.:** GB 509 4994 09
Date established: 1985 **Turnover:** £5m - £10m **No.of Employees:** 21 - 50
Product Groups: 27, 30, 35, 36, 39, 66

Date of Accounts	Apr 11	Apr 10	Apr 09
Sales Turnover	7m	6m	6m
Pre Tax Profit/Loss	1m	542	783
Working Capital	2m	2m	2m
Fixed Assets	998	962	1m
Current Assets	3m	3m	3m
Current Liabilities	529	241	172

Knowles
County Estate Nunn Brook Road, Huthwaite, Sutton In Ashfield, NG17 2HU
Tel: 01623-441474 **Fax:** 01623-440779
E-mail: arthur.knowles@knowlespto.com
Website: http://www.knowlespto.com
Directors: A. Knowles (Ptnr)
Ultimate Holding Company: A.F. SWITCHGEAR (HOLDINGS) LIMITED
Immediate Holding Company: BARIS GROUP LIMITED
Registration no: 06408854 **Date established:** 2002 **Turnover:** £5m - £10m
No.of Employees: 1 - 10 **Product Groups:** 35, 45

Date of Accounts	Jan 12	Jan 11	Jan 10
Sales Turnover	N/A	6m	10m
Pre Tax Profit/Loss	N/A	138	771
Working Capital	N/A	N/A	152
Fixed Assets	N/A	N/A	68
Current Assets	N/A	N/A	2m
Current Liabilities	N/A	N/A	1m

Maun Industries
Hamilton Road, Sutton In Ashfield, NG17 5LD
Tel: 01623-554599 **Fax:** 01623-557203
E-mail: sales@maun-industries.co.uk
Website: http://www.maun-industries.co.uk
Bank(s): National Westminster Bank Plc
Directors: E. Thomas (MD)
Managers: K. Bardens (Sales Prom Mgr)
Ultimate Holding Company: EMLIST LIMITED
Immediate Holding Company: MAUN INDUSTRIES,LIMITED
Registration no: 00384684 **VAT No.:** GB 458 2413 44
Date established: 1944 **No.of Employees:** 21 - 50 **Product Groups:** 40, 45, 46

Date of Accounts	Dec 11	Dec 10	Dec 09
Working Capital	4m	4m	3m
Fixed Assets	582	586	682
Current Assets	5m	4m	4m

Maun Motors Van & Truck Sales
Common Road Huthwaite, Sutton In Ashfield, NG17 2NB
Tel: 01623-554747 **Fax:** 01623-443225
E-mail: sales@maunmotors.co.uk
Website: http://www.maunmotors.co.uk
Directors: D. Kennedy (Prop)
Registration no: 02904597 **Date established:** 1994
Turnover: £75m - £125m **No.of Employees:** 1 - 10 **Product Groups:** 68

Mitchell Power Systems
Fulwood Road South, Sutton In Ashfield, NG17 2JZ
Tel: 01623-550550 **Fax:** 01623-551617
E-mail: andrew.lamb@mitchells.co.uk
Website: http://www.mitchells.co.uk
Bank(s): Barclays
Directors: A. Lamb (Sales), W. Sharp (Fin)
Ultimate Holding Company: TURNER & CO. (GLASGOW) LIMITED.
Immediate Holding Company: MITCHELL DIESEL LIMITED
Registration no: 01179564 **Date established:** 1974
Turnover: £20m - £50m **No.of Employees:** 51 - 100 **Product Groups:** 40

Date of Accounts	Mar 08	Mar 09	Mar 10
Sales Turnover	39m	39m	38m
Pre Tax Profit/Loss	4m	3m	3m
Working Capital	12m	15m	16m
Fixed Assets	2m	1m	1m
Current Assets	21m	22m	23m
Current Liabilities	3m	2m	2m

North Midland Construction Plc
Nunn Close Huthwaite, Sutton In Ashfield, NG17 2HW
Tel: 01623-515008 **Fax:** 01623-440071
E-mail: robert.moyle@northmid.co.uk
Website: http://www.northmid.co.uk
Directors: M. Garratt (Fin)
Managers: S. Ainley, M. Thornett (Mktg Serv Mgr), N. Walmsley (Personnel), R. Booth (Tech Serv Mgr), R. Moyle
Immediate Holding Company: NORTH MIDLAND CONSTRUCTION PUBLIC LIMITED COMPANY
Registration no: 00425188 **Date established:** 1946
Turnover: £20m - £50m **No.of Employees:** 51 - 100 **Product Groups:** 51

Date of Accounts	Dec 11	Dec 10	Dec 09
Sales Turnover	167m	165m	144m
Pre Tax Profit/Loss	-783	4m	2m
Working Capital	10m	10m	9m
Fixed Assets	11m	12m	11m
Current Assets	55m	52m	47m
Current Liabilities	8m	9m	9m

Norton Lea International Ltd
Phoenix House Mansfield Road, Sutton In Ashfield, NG17 4HR
Tel: 01623-551150 **Fax:** 01623-440483
Website: http://www.leainternational.co.uk
Bank(s): Barclays
Directors: B. Lea (Co Sec), I. Lea (Dir)
Ultimate Holding Company: TRANSCOM LIMITED (BAHAMAS)
Immediate Holding Company: THE LEADING MODELMAKING COMPANY LIMITED
Registration no: 06424668 **VAT No.:** GB 419 7501 44
Date established: 2007 **Turnover:** £500,000 - £1m
No.of Employees: 11 - 20 **Product Groups:** 35, 83

Date of Accounts	May 03	May 02	May 01
Sales Turnover	256	N/A	N/A
Pre Tax Profit/Loss	21	N/A	N/A
Working Capital	-272	-309	-476
Fixed Assets	236	252	261
Current Assets	354	126	346
Current Liabilities	625	435	822
ROCE% (Return on Capital Employed)	-59.5		
ROT% (Return on Turnover)	8.4		

Plastic Moulding Solutions
19 Leander Close, Sutton In Ashfield, NG17 5BF
Tel: 01623-452639 **Fax:** 01623-487356
E-mail: tomowil@btinternet.com
Website: http://www.plasticmouldingsolutions.co.uk
Managers: R. Tomlinson
Turnover: Up to £250,000 **No.of Employees:** 1 - 10 **Product Groups:** 80

Preconomy
Orchard Way, Sutton In Ashfield, NG17 1JU
Tel: 01623-554211 **Fax:** 01623-514057
E-mail: ngiles@preconomy.com
Website: http://www.preconomy.com
Bank(s): Yorkshire Bank PLC
Directors: N. Giles (MD), P. Ramsay (Fin)
Immediate Holding Company: PRECONOMY LIMITED
Registration no: 03904224 **VAT No.:** GB 117 6713 70
Date established: 2000 **Turnover:** £2m - £5m **No.of Employees:** 21 - 50
Product Groups: 30, 42, 48

Date of Accounts	Dec 11	Dec 10	Dec 09
Sales Turnover	4m	3m	2m
Pre Tax Profit/Loss	92	969	-561
Working Capital	200	153	269
Fixed Assets	666	504	633
Current Assets	1m	862	1m
Current Liabilities	399	366	474

Premier Trophies
42-44 Outram Street, Sutton In Ashfield, NG17 4FS
Tel: 01623-512849 **Fax:** 01623-480443
Directors: D. Toon (Ptnr)
Date established: 1975 **Turnover:** Up to £250,000
No.of Employees: 1 - 10 **Product Groups:** 33, 49, 65

Prestige Blinds
Redcliffe Street, Sutton In Ashfield, NG17 4ET
Tel: 01623-430170
E-mail: info@prestige-blinds.com
Website: http://www.prestige-blinds.com
Directors: D. Saxton (Prop)
Immediate Holding Company: PRESTIGE BLINDS LTD.
Registration no: 04363710 **Date established:** 2002
No.of Employees: 1 - 10 **Product Groups:** 25, 30, 63, 66

Date of Accounts	Jan 11	Jan 10	Jan 08
Working Capital	177	195	191
Fixed Assets	1	1	1
Current Assets	324	231	275

Quantum Clothing Group
North Street Huthwaite, Sutton In Ashfield, NG17 2PE
Tel: 01623-447200 **Fax:** 01623-447201
E-mail: carl.pate@quantumclothing.com
Website: http://www.quantumclothing.com
Directors: C. Pate (Fin)
Managers: S. Chesterman (Tech Serv Mgr)
Ultimate Holding Company: BRAMHOPE GROUP HOLDINGS LIMITED
Immediate Holding Company: QUANTUM CLOTHING GROUP LIMITED
Registration no: 00001812 **Date established:** 1965
Turnover: £75m - £125m **No.of Employees:** 101 - 250
Product Groups: 24, 63

Date of Accounts	Apr 08	Apr 09	Apr 10
Sales Turnover	84m	77m	81m
Pre Tax Profit/Loss	4m	-2m	-2m
Working Capital	14m	15m	23m
Fixed Assets	11m	7m	7m
Current Assets	31m	34m	40m
Current Liabilities	6m	7m	10m

Quickits Limited
Unit 3 Drakehouse Court, Hamilton Road, Sutton In Ashfield, NG17 5LD
Tel: 01623-515545 **Fax:** 01623-515546
E-mail: enquiries@quickits-online.co.uk
Website: http://www.quickits-online.co.uk
Directors: R. Smith (Dir)
Registration no: 05260560 **Date established:** 2003
No.of Employees: 1 - 10 **Product Groups:** 36, 37, 38

R T B Nationwide Express Couriers
9 New Hucknall Waye Huthwaite, Sutton In Ashfield, NG17 2SS
Tel: 01623-513651 **Fax:** 01623-513651
E-mail: rcbnationwide@sky.com
Directors: R. Bestick (Ptnr)
Date established: 2007 **Turnover:** Up to £250,000
No.of Employees: 1 - 10 **Product Groups:** 72

Reader Grout & Equipment
Prospect Court Nunn Close, Huthwaite, Sutton In Ashfield, NG17 2HW
Tel: 01623-518350 **Fax:** 01623-518351
E-mail: mike.smith@readergrout.co.uk
Website: http://www.readergrout.co.uk
Bank(s): Barclays
Directors: M. Fowles-Smith (Dir)
Ultimate Holding Company: LANGLEY HOLDINGS PLC
Immediate Holding Company: READER GROUT & EQUIPMENT LIMITED
Registration no: 03025049 **VAT No.:** GB 439 5293 21
Date established: 1995 **Turnover:** £20m - £50m
No.of Employees: 11 - 20 **Product Groups:** 33, 45

Regal Fire Ltd
Alfreton Road, Sutton In Ashfield, NG17 1JB
Tel: 01623-510068 **Fax:** 01623-510068
E-mail: enquiry@regalfire.co.uk
Website: http://www.regalfire.co.uk
Directors: P. Coupe (MD)
Immediate Holding Company: REGAL FIRE LIMITED
Registration no: 04546561 **Date established:** 2002
Turnover: Up to £250,000 **No.of Employees:** 1 - 10 **Product Groups:** 38, 42

Date of Accounts	Oct 11	Oct 10	Oct 09
Working Capital	-19	-28	-35
Fixed Assets	29	35	41
Current Assets	69	48	46

Rotork Valvekits
Brookside Way Huthwaite, Sutton In Ashfield, NG17 2NL
Tel: 01623-446776 **Fax:** 01623-440214
E-mail: sales@rotork.com
Website: http://www.rotork.com
Bank(s): Barclays
Managers: C. Mellins (Chief Mgr)
Ultimate Holding Company: ROTORK PLC
Immediate Holding Company: A. S. D. WHOLESALE LIMITED
Registration no: 03215737 **VAT No.:** GB 458 2504 41
Date established: 1995 **Turnover:** £5m - £10m **No.of Employees:** 21 - 50
Product Groups: 65

Date of Accounts	Apr 11	Apr 10	Apr 09
Sales Turnover	8m	9m	8m
Pre Tax Profit/Loss	265	279	296
Working Capital	752	649	559
Fixed Assets	1m	1m	1m
Current Assets	2m	2m	1m
Current Liabilities	161	140	139

Sky Plas Ltd
Eastfield Side, Sutton In Ashfield, NG17 4JR
Tel: 01623-553527 **Fax:** 01623-556737
E-mail: sales@skyplastics.demon.co.uk
Website: http://www.skyplastics.co.uk
Directors: C. Stainwright (MD)
Immediate Holding Company: SKY PLAS LIMITED
Registration no: 06959198 **VAT No.:** GB 117 1895 63
Date established: 2009 **Turnover:** Up to £250,000
No.of Employees: 1 - 10 **Product Groups:** 30, 48, 66

Date of Accounts	Jun 12	Jun 11	Jun 10
Working Capital	97	61	29
Fixed Assets	5	7	9
Current Assets	131	90	58

Storage City Ltd
Export Drive Fulwood I E, Huthwaite, Sutton In Ashfield, NG17 6AF
Tel: 01623-441440 **Fax:** 01623-516819
E-mail: mso@storagecity.co.uk
Website: http://www.storagecity.co.uk
Bank(s): National Westminster
Directors: M. Oldershaw (MD), J. Howard (MD)
Managers: S. Hobb (Sales & Mktg Mg)
Ultimate Holding Company: 02522080
Immediate Holding Company: STORAGE CITY LIMITED
Registration no: 01726230 **VAT No.:** GB 420 8677 49
Date established: 1983 **Turnover:** £50m - £75m
No.of Employees: 11 - 20 **Product Groups:** 40

Date of Accounts	Dec 09	Dec 08	Dec 07
Working Capital	103	132	116
Fixed Assets	34	36	36
Current Assets	130	178	216
Current Liabilities	8	14	21

Tibshelf Garden Products Ltd
Unit 1 Reform Street Industrial Estate Reform Street, Sutton In Ashfield, NG17 5DB
Tel: 01623-443331
E-mail: info@greenhousesgalore.co.uk
Website: http://www.greenhousesgalore.co.uk
Directors: A. Pope (Fin), A. Pope (MD)
Immediate Holding Company: TIBSHELF GARDEN PRODUCTS LIMITED
Registration no: 04279792 **Date established:** 2001
No.of Employees: 1 - 10 **Product Groups:** 26, 35

Date of Accounts	Oct 11	Oct 10	Oct 09
Working Capital	25	36	46
Fixed Assets	13	15	21
Current Assets	88	98	96

Townscape Products Ltd
Fulwood Road South, Sutton In Ashfield, NG17 2JZ
Tel: 01623-513355 **Fax:** 01623-440267
E-mail: sales@townscape-products.co.uk
Website: http://www.townscape-products.co.uk
Bank(s): National Westminster
Directors: J. Goss (MD), J. Goss (MD), Y. Davies (Fin)
Managers: D. Larthwell (Tech Serv Mgr)
Immediate Holding Company: TOWNSCAPE PRODUCTS LIMITED
Registration no: 01162845 **VAT No.:** GB 509 4690 29
Date established: 1974 **Turnover:** £2m - £5m **No.of Employees:** 21 - 50
Product Groups: 26, 33

Date of Accounts	Mar 11	Mar 10	Mar 09
Working Capital	695	540	838
Fixed Assets	1m	1m	1m
Current Assets	1m	979	1m

Uvi Nottingham
Phoenix House Mansfield Road, Sutton In Ashfield, NG17 4HR
Tel: 01623-528620 **Fax:** 08706-093702
Website: http://www.uvigroup.com
Directors: T. Pepper (Dir)
No.of Employees: 11 - 20 **Product Groups:** 35, 49, 80, 84

The Vector Studio
44 High Oakham Close, Sutton In Ashfield, NG17 4JS
Tel: 07931-934479
E-mail: thevectorstudio@hotmail.com
Website: http://www.thevectorstudio.co.uk
Directors: J. Cooke (Ptnr), J. Slaney (Ptnr)
No.of Employees: 1 - 10 **Product Groups:** 81

Worksop

A D H Flooring Ltd
1a Shepherds Avenue, Worksop, S81 0JD
Tel: 01909-489915 **Fax:** 01909-470094
E-mail: contact@adhf.co.uk
Website: http://www.adhf.co.uk
Directors: A. Harper (MD)
Immediate Holding Company: A.D.H. FLOORING LIMITED
Registration no: 06083739 **Date established:** 2007
No.of Employees: 1 - 10 **Product Groups:** 29, 30, 33, 52

Date of Accounts	Feb 08	Feb 11	Feb 10
Working Capital	-28	-8	-18
Fixed Assets	32	9	16

see next page

***A D H Flooring Ltd** - Cont'd*

Current Assets	29	24	26

Ashley Engineering Electrical Ltd
95 Gateford Road, Worksop, S80 1UD
Tel: 01909-487474 **Fax:** 01909-500341
E-mail: mhannon@ashleyengineeringelectrical.co.uk
Website: http://www.ashleyengineering.com
Bank(s): National Westminster Bank Plc
Directors: M. Hannon (Dir), G. Boyce (Dir)
Immediate Holding Company: ASHLEY ENGINEERING (ELECTRICAL) LIMITED
Registration no: 03000944 **VAT No.:** GB 651 6137 48
Date established: 1994 **Turnover:** £500,000 - £1m
No.of Employees: 21 - 50 **Product Groups:** 52

Date of Accounts	Mar 08	Mar 07	Mar 06
Working Capital	340	278	501
Fixed Assets	286	234	166
Current Assets	1558	1137	1073
Current Liabilities	1217	859	572
Total Share Capital	12	12	12

Canning Conveyor Co. Ltd
Sandy Lane Industrial Estate Sandy Lane, Worksop, S80 1TN
Tel: 01909-486166 **Fax:** 01909-500638
E-mail: andrew.canning@canningconveyor.co.uk
Website: http://www.canningconveyor.co.uk
Directors: A. Canning (MD), J. Hibbert (Co Sec)
Managers: J. Fores (Purch Mgr), M. Bateman (Mgr), J. Canning (Mgr), M. Nelthorpe (Mgr), C. Neithorpe (Prod Mgr), E. Canning (Mgr)
Registration no: 00858193 **VAT No.:** GB 439 5298 11
Date established: 1965 **Turnover:** £5m - £10m **No.of Employees:** 21 - 50
Product Groups: 22, 29, 30, 39, 41, 45, 67, 84

Date of Accounts	Aug 11	Aug 10	Aug 09
Sales Turnover	7m	5m	6m
Pre Tax Profit/Loss	466	272	147
Working Capital	2m	2m	2m
Fixed Assets	2m	1m	1m
Current Assets	4m	3m	3m
Current Liabilities	378	399	255

Cinch Connectors Ltd
Shireoaks Road, Worksop, S80 3HA
Tel: 01909-474131 **Fax:** 01909-478321
E-mail: info@cinchuk.com
Website: http://www.cinchuk.com
Bank(s): HSBC Bank plc
Directors: S. Martin (Fin)
Managers: H. Pearson (Personnel), J. Elton (Purch Mgr), J. Waterfall (Tech Serv Mgr), P. Connelley
Ultimate Holding Company: BEL FUSE INC (USA)
Immediate Holding Company: CINCH CONNECTORS LIMITED
Registration no: 02178707 **VAT No.:** GB 458 2332 44
Date established: 1987 **Turnover:** £5m - £10m
No.of Employees: 51 - 100 **Product Groups:** 30, 37, 39, 67

Date of Accounts	Dec 11	Dec 10	Dec 09
Sales Turnover	7m	7m	7m
Pre Tax Profit/Loss	358	484	416
Working Capital	2m	2m	1m
Fixed Assets	953	1m	1m
Current Assets	4m	3m	3m
Current Liabilities	434	458	494

Cognitronics Ltd
Claylands Avenue, Worksop, S81 7DJ
Tel: 01909-477272 **Fax:** 01909-486260
E-mail: phil@cognitronics.co.uk
Website: http://www.cognitronics.co.uk
Bank(s): Lloyds
Directors: J. Bottreill (Sales), P. Spotswood (MD)
Immediate Holding Company: COGNITRONICS LIMITED
Registration no: 01296618 **VAT No.:** 174 1764 54 **Date established:** 1977
Turnover: £2m - £5m **No.of Employees:** 11 - 20 **Product Groups:** 44, 49

Date of Accounts	Mar 08	Sep 11	Sep 10
Working Capital	569	632	661
Fixed Assets	84	43	34
Current Assets	1m	1m	1m

D D C Outsourcing Solutions
The Data Solution Centre Manton Wood, Worksop, S80 2RS
Tel: 01909-488600 **Fax:** 01909-488700
E-mail: enquiries@ddcos.com
Website: http://www.ddcos.com
Bank(s): HSBC
Directors: L. Ancliff (Fin), T. Webb (Develop), C. Gray (MD)
Managers: J. Colyer (Personnel), L. Cotterill
Immediate Holding Company: CGF MARKETING SERVICES LIMITED
Registration no: 02151319 **VAT No.:** 608 0018 79 **Date established:** 1987
Turnover: £1m - £2m **No.of Employees:** 51 - 100 **Product Groups:** 44, 79

Date of Accounts	Dec 11	Dec 10	Dec 09
Working Capital	506	386	299
Fixed Assets	100	101	91
Current Assets	1m	1m	1m

Louis Demery & Sons Ltd
67a Newcastle Avenue, Worksop, S80 1LX
Tel: 01909-500358 **Fax:** 01909-500637
E-mail: ldsltd@btconnect.com
Directors: J. Demery (Prop)
Immediate Holding Company: LOUIS DEMERY & SONS LIMITED
Registration no: 00428622 **VAT No.:** GB 172 5612 69
Date established: 1947 **Turnover:** £1m - £2m **No.of Employees:** 1 - 10
Product Groups: 67

Date of Accounts	Mar 12	Mar 11	Mar 10
Working Capital	6	26	98
Fixed Assets	1	1	1
Current Assets	84	212	196

Eurovalve UK Ltd
Unit 1 Dukeries Way, Worksop, S81 7DW
Tel: 01909-530444 **Fax:** 01909-530044
E-mail: sales@eurovalve.co.uk
Website: http://www.eurovalve.co.uk
Directors: N. Pond (Dir)
Immediate Holding Company: EUROVALVE (U.K.) LIMITED
Registration no: 03545461 **Date established:** 1998
No.of Employees: 1 - 10 **Product Groups:** 36, 37, 38

Date of Accounts	Apr 12	Apr 11	Apr 10
Working Capital	581	461	404
Fixed Assets	58	52	37
Current Assets	1m	949	910

Hadfield C N C & Electronics Company Ltd
15 Retford Road, Worksop, S80 2PT
Tel: 01909-500760 **Fax:** 01909-542800
E-mail: service@hcnc.co.uk
Website: http://www.hcnc.co.uk
Directors: M. Hadfield (MD), J. Davies (Co Sec), J. Davies (Fin)
Managers: P. Justice (Mktg Serv Mgr)
Immediate Holding Company: HADFIELD CNC & ELECTRONICS CO. LTD.
Registration no: 03499279 **Date established:** 1998
Turnover: £500,000 - £1m **No.of Employees:** 1 - 10 **Product Groups:** 37, 48

Date of Accounts	Mar 10	Mar 09	Mar 08
Working Capital	292	348	345
Fixed Assets	4	4	4
Current Assets	293	351	383

Imagenta Moulding plc
Unit 2 Coach Crescent, Shireoaks, Worksop, S81 8AD
Tel: 01909-472210 **Fax:** 01909-472211
E-mail: sales@imagentaplc.co.uk
Website: http://www.imagentaplc.co.uk
Managers: J. Abdullah (Chief Mgr), K. Kibble (Ops Mgr), K. Mason (Admin Off), B. Thompson (Sales Prom Mgr)
Immediate Holding Company: IMAGENTA MOULDING PLC
Registration no: 03747766 **Date established:** 1999 **Turnover:** £2m - £5m
No.of Employees: 21 - 50 **Product Groups:** 66

Date of Accounts	Sep 11	Sep 10	Sep 09
Sales Turnover	2m	2m	1m
Pre Tax Profit/Loss	28	4	22
Working Capital	135	190	80
Fixed Assets	820	791	704
Current Assets	702	781	429
Current Liabilities	140	169	65

J Dowd Electrical Solutions Ltd
40 Church Walk, Worksop, S80 2EJ
Tel: 01909-476428 **Fax:** 01909-532626
E-mail: james@dowd959.freeserve.co.uk
Website: http://www.jdowdelectricalservices.com
Directors: J. Dowd (Prop)
Immediate Holding Company: J DOWD ELECTRICAL SERVICES LIMITED
Registration no: 05329910 **VAT No.:** GB 286 6236 27
Date established: 2005 **Turnover:** £5m - £10m **No.of Employees:** 1 - 10
Product Groups: 52

Date of Accounts	Apr 10	Apr 09	Apr 08
Working Capital	-223	-131	-113
Fixed Assets	69	87	87
Current Assets	80	74	89

Klingspor Abrasives Ltd
31-33 Retford Road, Worksop, S80 2PU
Tel: 01909-504400 **Fax:** 01909-504405
E-mail: louisa.widderson@klingspor.co.uk
Website: http://www.klingspor.co.uk
Bank(s): Lloyds
Directors: L. Widdowson (Fin), O. Ter Jung (Sales), R. Shiers (Co Sec)
Managers: C. Taylor (Sales Prom Mgr), C. McGuire (Mktg Serv Mgr)
Ultimate Holding Company: KLINGSPOR AG (GERMANY)
Immediate Holding Company: KLINGSPOR ABRASIVES LIMITED
Registration no: SC026372 **Date established:** 1948
Turnover: £5m - £10m **No.of Employees:** 21 - 50 **Product Groups:** 33, 36

Date of Accounts	Dec 11	Dec 10	Dec 09
Sales Turnover	8m	7m	7m
Pre Tax Profit/Loss	909	655	351
Working Capital	2m	2m	2m
Fixed Assets	24	33	25
Current Assets	3m	3m	3m
Current Liabilities	587	455	311

Markham Sheffield Ltd
Lawn Road Carlton-in-Lindrick, Worksop, S81 9LB
Tel: 01909-730861 **Fax:** 01909-733584
E-mail: sales@markham-sheffield.co.uk
Website: http://www.markham-sheffield.co.uk
Directors: G. Wrigglesworth (Sales)
Ultimate Holding Company: BECCA HOLDINGS LIMITED
Immediate Holding Company: MARKHAM (SHEFFIELD) LIMITED
Registration no: 00488431 **VAT No.:** GB 125 8811 65
Date established: 1950 **Turnover:** £2m - £5m **No.of Employees:** 1 - 10
Product Groups: 40, 45

Date of Accounts	Dec 11	Dec 10	Dec 09
Working Capital	334	293	228
Fixed Assets	249	278	321
Current Assets	502	406	337

Mckenna Group Ltd
Lawn Road Carlton-in-Lindrick, Worksop, S81 9LB
Tel: 01909-541414 **Fax:** 01909-541415
E-mail: enquiries@mckennagroup.co.uk
Website: http://www.mckennagroup.co.uk
Bank(s): Barclays, Bridgegate, Rotherham
Directors: D. Mckenna (Dir), L. Anderson (Fin)
Managers: K. Collins (Personnel), L. Gwitera
Ultimate Holding Company: BECCA HOLDINGS LIMITED
Immediate Holding Company: MCKENNA PRECISION CASTINGS LIMITED
Registration no: 01713320 **VAT No.:** GB 308 9597 16
Date established: 1983 **Turnover:** £2m - £5m **No.of Employees:** 21 - 50
Product Groups: 34, 38

Date of Accounts	Apr 11	Apr 10	Apr 09
Sales Turnover	N/A	3m	N/A
Pre Tax Profit/Loss	N/A	-268	-436
Working Capital	1m	2m	2m
Fixed Assets	814	908	960
Current Assets	2m	2m	3m
Current Liabilities	N/A	134	153

Medicare Systems Ltd
Old Brewery Yard Unit 4 Kilton Road, Worksop, S80 2DE
Tel: 01909-542828
E-mail: info@medicaresystems.co.uk
Website: http://www.medicaresystems.co.uk
Directors: M. Timoney (MD)
Immediate Holding Company: MEDICARE SYSTEMS LIMITED
Registration no: 04812539 **Date established:** 2003
No.of Employees: 11 - 20 **Product Groups:** 37, 38

Date of Accounts	Aug 11	Aug 10	Aug 09
Working Capital	112	150	88
Fixed Assets	50	31	28
Current Assets	352	289	194

Midland Steel Equipment
16 King Street Creswell, Worksop, S80 4ER
Tel: 01909-721090 **Fax:** 01909-723593
E-mail: enquiries@midlandsteelequipment.co.uk
Website: http://www.midlandsteelequipment.co.uk
Directors: M. Buxton (Fin), M. Buxton (MD)
Immediate Holding Company: MIDLAND STEEL EQUIPMENT LIMITED
Registration no: 04403703 **VAT No.:** GB 295 2897 02
Date established: 2002 **Turnover:** £250,000 - £500,000
No.of Employees: 1 - 10 **Product Groups:** 26

Date of Accounts	Jul 11	Jul 10	Jul 09
Sales Turnover	N/A	N/A	336
Working Capital	-4	-4	-13
Fixed Assets	6	6	8
Current Assets	65	65	37

Monition Ltd
Bondhay Complex Whitwell Common, Worksop, S80 3EH
Tel: 01909-722000
E-mail: sales@monition.com
Website: http://www.monition.com
Directors: M. Burrows (MD)
Immediate Holding Company: MONITION LIMITED
Registration no: 02218477 **Date established:** 1988
No.of Employees: 21 - 50 **Product Groups:** 38, 84, 85

Date of Accounts	Jan 11	Jan 10	Jan 09
Working Capital	393	418	235
Fixed Assets	193	153	174
Current Assets	588	804	561

Pandrol UK Ltd
Bone Mill Lane, Worksop, S81 7AX
Tel: 01909-476101 **Fax:** 01909-500004
E-mail: reception@pandrol.com
Website: http://www.pandrol.com
Bank(s): Barclays
Directors: D. Ross (Fin), D. Webster (MD)
Managers: D. Hampton
Ultimate Holding Company: DELACHAUX SA (FRANCE)
Immediate Holding Company: PANDROL UK LIMITED
Registration no: 00397784 **VAT No.:** GB 232 6951 62
Date established: 1945 **Turnover:** £20m - £50m
No.of Employees: 101 - 250 **Product Groups:** 39

Date of Accounts	Dec 11
Working Capital	75
Current Assets	75

Pressure Engineering International Ltd
Retford Road, Worksop, S80 2PU
Tel: 01909-535400
Directors: S. Plant (Dir)
Ultimate Holding Company: LANGLEY HOLDINGS PLC
Immediate Holding Company: PRESSURE ENGINEERING INTERNATIONAL LIMITED
Registration no: 05167433 **Date established:** 2004 **Turnover:** £2m - £5m
No.of Employees: 11 - 20 **Product Groups:** 35, 39, 40

R Ekin Fabrications
Claylands Avenue, Worksop, S81 7BQ
Tel: 01909-472638 **Fax:** 01909-472638
Directors: K. Morris (Ptnr)
Immediate Holding Company: LINDRICK CONSTRUCTION SERVICES LIMITED
Registration no: 06234941 **Date established:** 2007
No.of Employees: 1 - 10 **Product Groups:** 35

Date of Accounts	Oct 11	Oct 10	Oct 09
Sales Turnover	N/A	N/A	1m
Pre Tax Profit/Loss	N/A	N/A	15
Working Capital	-17	-16	-13
Fixed Assets	15	13	16
Current Assets	134	102	93
Current Liabilities	N/A	N/A	52

Robinson Healthcare Ltd
Lawn Road Carlton In Lindrick, Carlton-in-Lindrick, Worksop, S81 9LB
Tel: 01909-735000 **Fax:** 01246-559929
E-mail: leigh.thomasson@robinsonhealthcare.com
Website: http://www.robinsonhealthcare.com
Directors: R. Hall (Chief Op Offcr), M. Richardson (Sales), L. Thomasson (MD), G. Smith (Fin)
Managers: J. Lee (Personnel), R. Ibbotson (Mktg Serv Mgr), T. Johnson (Tech Serv Mgr)
Ultimate Holding Company: ROBINSON HEALTHCARE HOLDINGS LTD
Immediate Holding Company: ROBINSON HEALTHCARE LIMITED
Registration no: 03773211 **VAT No.:** GB 458 1616 35
Date established: 1999 **Turnover:** £10m - £20m
No.of Employees: 101 - 250 **Product Groups:** 23, 24, 27, 30, 31, 32, 38, 40, 43, 63

Date of Accounts	Jun 11	Jun 10	Jun 09
Sales Turnover	20m	19m	20m
Pre Tax Profit/Loss	135	790	2m
Working Capital	6m	5m	3m
Fixed Assets	3m	6m	6m
Current Assets	9m	8m	8m
Current Liabilities	1m	950	1m

Ryton Arms Ltd
Osberton Hall Osberton, Worksop, S81 0UF
Tel: 01777-860222 **Fax:** 01909-530231
E-mail: sales@rytonarms.co.uk
Website: http://www.rytonarms.co.uk
Directors: M. Yates (Fin)
Ultimate Holding Company: FORMAREA (SALES) LIMITED
Immediate Holding Company: FEE PROPERTY DEVELOPMENTS LIMITED
Date established: 1987 **No.of Employees:** 1 - 10 **Product Groups:** 36, 39, 40

Date of Accounts	Jun 06
Working Capital	-95
Current Liabilities	95

S W Fabrications
Whitwell Common, Worksop, S80 3EH
Tel: 01246-812900 **Fax:** 01246-812900
E-mail: swfabss@hotmail.co.uk

Directors: S. Webley (Prop)
Immediate Holding Company: SAFAPOND DIRECT LTD
Registration no: 04441667 **Date established:** 2010
No.of Employees: 1 - 10 **Product Groups:** 35

Date of Accounts	Jun 11	Jun 10	Jun 09
Working Capital	9	-8	-9
Fixed Assets	13	8	9
Current Assets	61	39	26
Current Liabilities	30	N/A	N/A

Seafield Logistics Ltd

Unit 1 The Point Coach Road, Shireoaks, Worksop, S81 8BW
Tel: 01909-475561 **Fax:** 01909-501043
E-mail: sales@seafield.co.uk
Website: http://www.seafield.co.uk
Bank(s): National Westminster Bank Plc
Directors: M. Strong (MD), M. Kirkman (Fin)
Managers: N. Holt (Mktg Serv Mgr), J. Gregory (Personnel), J. Hunt (Tech Serv Mgr)
Ultimate Holding Company: BALLAUGH HOLDINGS LTD (BVI)
Immediate Holding Company: SEAFIELD LOGISTICS LIMITED
Registration no: 04816206 **Date established:** 2003
No.of Employees: 101 - 250 **Product Groups:** 48, 72, 77, 84

Date of Accounts	Jun 11	Jun 10	Jun 09
Sales Turnover	30m	24m	23m
Pre Tax Profit/Loss	124	241	151
Working Capital	90	176	-1m
Fixed Assets	1m	849	2m
Current Assets	7m	7m	3m
Current Liabilities	2m	2m	1m

Select Scales Ltd

36 Skinner Street Creswell, Worksop, S80 4JH
Tel: 01909-722960 **Fax:** 01909-724057
E-mail: sales@selectscales.co.uk
Website: http://www.selectscales.co.uk
Directors: I. Webster (MD)
Immediate Holding Company: SELECT SCALES LIMITED
Registration no: 04533210 **Date established:** 2002
No.of Employees: 1 - 10 **Product Groups:** 38, 42

Date of Accounts	Sep 11	Sep 10	Sep 09
Working Capital	-7	-25	-58
Fixed Assets	47	53	59
Current Assets	118	110	94

Sellec Special Cables Ltd

Dukeries Way, Worksop, S81 7DW
Tel: 01909-483539 **Fax:** 01909-500181
E-mail: sales@sellec.com
Website: http://www.sellec.com
Directors: K. Methley (Dir)
Immediate Holding Company: SELLEC (SPECIAL CABLES) LIMITED
Registration no: 01770724 **VAT No.:** 390 9294 19 **Date established:** 1983
Turnover: £2m - £5m **No.of Employees:** 1 - 10 **Product Groups:** 37

Date of Accounts	Dec 11	Dec 10	Dec 09
Sales Turnover	3m	2m	2m
Pre Tax Profit/Loss	287	176	118
Working Capital	309	262	223
Fixed Assets	27	36	37
Current Assets	1m	1m	992
Current Liabilities	463	140	106

Smiths Flour Mills Ltd

PO Box 3, Worksop, S80 1QY
Tel: 01909-472216 **Fax:** 01909-480212
E-mail: reception@smiths-flour-mills.co.uk
Website: http://www.smiths-flour-mills.co.uk
Directors: S. Mackay (MD)
Ultimate Holding Company: CORNDON LIMITED
Immediate Holding Company: SMITHS FLOUR MILLS LIMITED
Registration no: 05998367 **Date established:** 2006
Turnover: £50m - £75m **No.of Employees:** 51 - 100 **Product Groups:** 20, 32

Date of Accounts	Mar 09	Mar 08	Apr 10
Sales Turnover	70m	65m	65m
Pre Tax Profit/Loss	1m	-2m	2m
Working Capital	2m	2m	3m
Fixed Assets	23m	24m	22m
Current Assets	10m	11m	10m
Current Liabilities	1m	821	1m

T E P Fabrications

Old Colliery Yard Southfield Lane, Whitwell, Worksop, S80 3LH
Tel: 01909-721726
Directors: T. Pollard (Prop)
Immediate Holding Company: PHOENIX PLANT & MACHINERY LTD
Date established: 2010 **No.of Employees:** 1 - 10 **Product Groups:** 35

Date of Accounts	Mar 11	Mar 10
Working Capital	47	-23
Fixed Assets	23	17
Current Assets	102	60

K H Taylor Ltd

Sheffield Road Blyth, Worksop, S81 8HF
Tel: 01909-590000 **Fax:** 01909-591713
E-mail: khtaylor@lineone.net
Website: http://www.kh-taylor.co.uk
Directors: K. Taylor (MD)
Immediate Holding Company: K.H. TAYLOR LIMITED
Registration no: 01076125 **VAT No.:** GB 126 4277 73
Date established: 1972 **Turnover:** £500,000 - £1m
No.of Employees: 1 - 10 **Product Groups:** 20

Date of Accounts	Jun 11	Jun 10	Jun 09
Working Capital	486	633	182
Fixed Assets	2m	2m	2m
Current Assets	827	1m	1m

Ulma Packaging

4 Woodland Court Coach CR, Shireoaks, Worksop, S81 8AD
Tel: 01909-506504 **Fax:** 01909-506509
E-mail: info@ulmapackaging.co.uk
Website: http://www.ulmapackaging.com
Directors: D. Patterson (Dir)
Date established: 2002 **No.of Employees:** 11 - 20 **Product Groups:** 38, 42

Wilkinson Hardware Stores Ltd

JK House Roebuck Way, Worksop, S80 3YY
Tel: 01909-505505 **Fax:** 01909-505777
E-mail: communications@wilko.co.uk
Website: http://www.wilko.co.uk
Directors: S. Mitchell (MD), K. Swan (Dir), K. Swann (Dir), G. Brown (Dir), I. White (Co Sec)
Managers: S. Gunn (Mktg Serv Mgr)
Immediate Holding Company: WILKINSON HARDWARE STORES,LIMITED
Registration no: 00365335 **Date established:** 1941
Turnover: Over £1,000m **No.of Employees:** 1 - 10 **Product Groups:** 61

Date of Accounts	Jan 09	Jan 10	Jan 11
Sales Turnover	1449m	1556m	1559m
Pre Tax Profit/Loss	29m	65m	61m
Working Capital	-36m	-21m	-11m
Fixed Assets	252m	256m	266m
Current Assets	149m	175m	191m
Current Liabilities	78m	105m	99m

Worksop Galvanising Ltd (Wedge Group Galvanizing)

Claylands Avenue, Worksop, S81 7BQ
Tel: 01909-486384 **Fax:** 01909-482540
E-mail: david.leverton@wegge-galv.co.uk
Website: http://www.wedge-galv.co.uk
Bank(s): National Westminster Bank Plc
Managers: D. Brownbridge (Buyer), P. Robinson (Sales Prom Mgr), B. Calvert (Chief Mgr), M. Storey
Immediate Holding Company: IRIZAR U.K. LIMITED
Registration no: 03473145 **Date established:** 2011
No.of Employees: 21 - 50 **Product Groups:** 48

Date of Accounts	Dec 11
Working Capital	-173
Fixed Assets	1
Current Assets	454

OXFORDSHIRE

Abingdon

A S Scientific Products Ltd
2 Barton Lane, Abingdon, OX14 3NB
Tel: 01235-533060 **Fax:** 01235-554125
E-mail: enquiries@asscientific.co.uk
Website: http://www.asscientific.co.uk
Bank(s): National Westminster Bank Plc
Directors: P. Wiggins (MD)
Managers: A. Lister (Fin Mgr), D. Matthews (Purch Mgr)
Ultimate Holding Company: 06007115
Immediate Holding Company: A.S. SCIENTIFIC PRODUCTS LIMITED
Registration no: 01289082 **VAT No.:** GB 196 0272 54
Date established: 1976 **Turnover:** £2m - £5m **No.of Employees:** 21 - 50
Product Groups: 36, 38, 40, 42, 48, 52, 84, 85

Date of Accounts	Nov 11	Nov 10	Nov 09
Working Capital	717	524	634
Fixed Assets	136	1m	1m
Current Assets	1m	994	1m

A W Grace & Son Ltd
Unit 124 Culham No1 Site Culham, Abingdon, OX14 3DA
Tel: 01235-531462 **Fax:** 01235-534021
E-mail: info@awgrace.co.uk
Website: http://www.awgrace.co.uk
Directors: C. Grace (Prop)
Immediate Holding Company: A W GRACE & SON LIMITED
Registration no: 03210432 **Date established:** 1996
Turnover: £250,000 - £500,000 **No.of Employees:** 11 - 20
Product Groups: 48

Date of Accounts	Aug 11	Aug 10	Aug 09
Working Capital	18	20	40
Fixed Assets	91	82	104
Current Assets	109	124	117

Abingdon Access Ltd
33 West St Helen Street, Abingdon, OX14 5DY
Tel: 08453-373415
E-mail: info@abingdonaccess.com
Website: http://www.abingdonaccess.com
Directors: T. Coles (MD)
Immediate Holding Company: ABINGDON ACCESS LIMITED
Registration no: 07598068 **Date established:** 2011
No.of Employees: 1 - 10 **Product Groups:** 36, 40, 52

Date of Accounts	Apr 12
Working Capital	-38
Fixed Assets	52
Current Assets	21

Abingdon Fork Trucks
26a High Street Drayton, Abingdon, OX14 4JL
Tel: 01235-847777 **Fax:** 01235-847727
E-mail: davidwoodwards@live.co.uk
Directors: D. Woodward (Prop), D. Woodwards (Prop)
Date established: 2004 **No.of Employees:** 1 - 10 **Product Groups:** 35, 39, 45

Achilles Group Ltd
30 Milton Park Milton, Abingdon, OX14 4SH
Tel: 01235-820813 **Fax:** 01235-821093
E-mail: enquiries@achilles.com
Website: http://www.achilles.co.uk
Directors: A. Wilkinson (Co Sec)
Immediate Holding Company: ACHILLES INFORMATION LIMITED
Registration no: SC137975 **Date established:** 1992
Turnover: £20m - £50m **No.of Employees:** 101 - 250 **Product Groups:** 80

Date of Accounts	Apr 12	Apr 11	Apr 10
Sales Turnover	26m	21m	19m
Pre Tax Profit/Loss	458	2m	3m
Working Capital	-4m	-5m	-6m
Fixed Assets	8m	9m	9m
Current Assets	9m	6m	4m
Current Liabilities	9m	8m	7m

Adhectic Ltd
Phoenix House Radley Road Industrial Estate, Abingdon, OX14 3RY
Tel: 01235-520738 **Fax:** 01235-525554
E-mail: sales@adhectic.co.uk
Website: http://www.adhectic.co.uk
Managers: A. Haynes (Chief Mgr)
Immediate Holding Company: ADHECTIC LIMITED
Registration no: 00642897 **Date established:** 1959 **Turnover:** £1m - £2m
No.of Employees: 1 - 10 **Product Groups:** 25, 32, 61, 66

Date of Accounts	Mar 11	Mar 10	Mar 09
Sales Turnover	N/A	1m	N/A
Pre Tax Profit/Loss	N/A	59	N/A
Working Capital	177	176	171
Fixed Assets	28	33	3
Current Assets	476	436	354
Current Liabilities	N/A	64	N/A

Akzo Nobel Coatings Ltd
136 Milton Park Milton, Abingdon, OX14 4SB
Tel: 01235-862226 **Fax:** 01235-862236
E-mail: cr@akzonobel.com
Website: http://www.sikkenscr.co.uk
Managers: S. Dixon
Ultimate Holding Company: AKZO NOBEL NV (NETHERLANDS)
Immediate Holding Company: AKZO NOBEL COATINGS LIMITED
Registration no: 03124411 **Date established:** 1995
Turnover: £20m - £50m **No.of Employees:** 51 - 100 **Product Groups:** 28, 32, 68

Date of Accounts	Dec 11	Dec 10	Dec 09
Sales Turnover	25m	28m	28m
Pre Tax Profit/Loss	-4m	-2m	-3m
Working Capital	-5m	-3m	-988
Fixed Assets	N/A	N/A	168
Current Assets	18m	15m	13m
Current Liabilities	3m	4m	2m

All Labels Ltd
Unit S1 North Kingston Business Park, Kingston Bagpuize, Abingdon, OX13 5AS
Tel: 01865-821841 **Fax:** 01865-821840
E-mail: sales@all-labels.net
Website: http://www.all-labels.net
Directors: H. Rogers (MD), D. Rogers (Fin)
Immediate Holding Company: ALL LABELS LIMITED
Registration no: 04042082 **VAT No.:** GB 750 0034 86
Date established: 2000 **Turnover:** £1m - £2m **No.of Employees:** 1 - 10
Product Groups: 27, 28, 30, 35, 36, 49

Date of Accounts	Apr 12	Apr 11	Apr 10
Working Capital	77	67	31
Fixed Assets	75	73	79
Current Assets	155	158	83

All Makes Ltd
39 Milton Park Milton, Abingdon, OX14 4RT
Tel: 01235-821122 **Fax:** 01235-821133
E-mail: richardh@allmakes.co.uk
Website: http://www.allmakes4x4.com
Bank(s): HSBC
Directors: E. Prescot (Sales), R. Howe (Dir)
Managers: J. Chowns (Chief Acct), M. Hand (Tech Serv Mgr)
Ultimate Holding Company: ALLMAKES 4 X 4 LIMITED
Immediate Holding Company: ALLMAKES LIMITED
Registration no: 01314091 **VAT No.:** GB 332 7847 44
Date established: 1977 **Turnover:** £20m - £50m
No.of Employees: 51 - 100 **Product Groups:** 45, 68

Date of Accounts	Dec 11	Dec 10	May 10
Sales Turnover	33m	18m	27m
Pre Tax Profit/Loss	825	491	495
Working Capital	6m	5m	5m
Fixed Assets	779	823	857
Current Assets	15m	13m	14m
Current Liabilities	837	882	808

Basildon Chemical Co. Ltd / KCC
Kimber Road, Abingdon, OX14 1RZ
Tel: 01235-526677 **Fax:** 01235-524334
E-mail: sales@baschem.co.uk
Website: http://www.baschem.co.uk
Bank(s): Lloyds TSB Bank plc
Directors: I. Watling (MD)
Managers: G. Castle, R. Pritchard (Mktg Serv Mgr), N. Surman (Sales Prom Mgr), C. Cox (Mktg Serv Mgr), N. Surman (Mktg Serv Mgr), R. Blackwell (Mgr)
Registration no: 01016104 **VAT No.:** GB 199 0774 12
Turnover: £10m - £20m **No.of Employees:** 65 **Product Groups:** 20, 27, 31, 32, 45, 62, 66, 68, 85

Date of Accounts	Dec 11	Jun 11	Jun 10
Sales Turnover	9m	16m	15m
Pre Tax Profit/Loss	747	2m	822
Working Capital	4m	4m	4m
Fixed Assets	4m	4m	2m
Current Assets	7m	6m	6m
Current Liabilities	2m	665	350

Bookpoint Ltd
130 Milton Park Milton, Abingdon, OX14 4SB
Tel: 01235-400400 **Fax:** 01235-400445
E-mail: pubeasy@bookpoint.co.uk
Website: http://www.bookpoint.co.uk
Bank(s): Bank of Scotland, London
Directors: P. De Cacqueray (Fin), T. Hely Hutchinson (Dir)
Managers: M. Wright, N. Yates (Admin Off), J. Perkins (Personnel)
Ultimate Holding Company: LAGARDERE SCA (FRANCE)
Immediate Holding Company: BOOKPOINT LIMITED
Registration no: 00978415 **VAT No.:** GB 532 5829 40
Date established: 1970 **Turnover:** £10m - £20m
No.of Employees: 251 - 500 **Product Groups:** 64

Date of Accounts	Dec 11	Dec 10	Dec 09
Sales Turnover	16m	16m	18m
Pre Tax Profit/Loss	5m	-588	-269
Working Capital	-6m	-6m	-4m
Fixed Assets	13m	6m	5m
Current Assets	6m	5m	4m
Current Liabilities	2m	3m	3m

Bowman International Ltd
Unit 10 Isis Court Wyndyke Furlong, Abingdon, OX14 1DZ
Tel: 01235-462500 **Fax:** 01235-811234
E-mail: enquiries@bowman.co.uk
Website: http://www.bowman.co.uk
Bank(s): Barclays
Directors: S. Hancock (Dir)
Immediate Holding Company: BOWMAN INTERNATIONAL LIMITED
Registration no: 02750164 **VAT No.:** GB 614 5538 45
Date established: 1992 **Turnover:** £2m - £5m **No.of Employees:** 11 - 20
Product Groups: 29, 30, 33, 34, 35, 37, 39, 66

Date of Accounts	Sep 11	Sep 10	Sep 09
Working Capital	2m	1m	1m
Fixed Assets	2m	2m	1m
Current Assets	3m	3m	2m

British Franchise Association
85f Milton Park Milton, Abingdon, OX14 4RY
Tel: 01235-820470 **Fax:** 01235-832 158
E-mail: mailroom@thebfa.org
Website: http://www.thebfa.org
Managers: B. Smart
Immediate Holding Company: BRITISH FRANCHISE ASSOCIATION
Registration no: 01341267 **Date established:** 1977 **Turnover:** £1m - £2m
No.of Employees: 1 - 10 **Product Groups:** 87

Date of Accounts	Sep 11	Sep 10	Sep 09
Sales Turnover	1m	1m	1m
Pre Tax Profit/Loss	-47	-7	-73
Working Capital	768	872	895
Fixed Assets	121	63	48
Current Assets	1m	1m	1m
Current Liabilities	188	94	144

Cellmark
Blacklands Way, Abingdon, OX14 1DY
Tel: 01235-528000 **Fax:** 01235-554830
E-mail: info@cellmark.co.uk
Website: http://www.cellmark.co.uk
Directors: R. Derbyshire (Chief Op Offcr)
Managers: J. Pulling (Tech Serv Mgr), S. Edwards (Purch Mgr)
Immediate Holding Company: ORCHID CELLMARK LTD
Registration no: 04045527 **VAT No.:** GB 582 3236 42
Date established: 2000 **Turnover:** £20m - £50m
No.of Employees: 101 - 250 **Product Groups:** 31

Date of Accounts	Dec 11	Dec 10	Dec 09
Sales Turnover	26m	26m	19m
Pre Tax Profit/Loss	2m	5m	978
Working Capital	7m	10m	7m
Fixed Assets	4m	2m	2m
Current Assets	11m	14m	9m
Current Liabilities	2m	3m	1m

Crowcon Detection Instrument Ltd
Unit 2 2-6 Blacklands Way, Abingdon, OX14 1DY
Tel: 01235-557700 **Fax:** 01235-553062
E-mail: sales@crowcon.com
Website: http://www.crowcon.com
Bank(s): Barclays
Directors: W. Reef (MD), S. Kukula (Tech Serv), N. Rossiter (Fab), A. Stamper (MD), K. Worthington (Fin), P. Dunn (Sales & Mktg)
Managers: M. Osbourne (Purch Mgr), L. Jones (Accounts), G. Franklin, D. Riddle (Develop Mgr)
Ultimate Holding Company: HALMA PUBLIC LIMITED COMPANY
Immediate Holding Company: CROWCON DETECTION INSTRUMENTS LIMITED

Registration no: 00978878 **VAT No.:** GB 194 2701 59
Date established: 1970 **Turnover:** £20m - £50m
No.of Employees: 101 - 250 **Product Groups:** 38, 40, 45

Date of Accounts	Mar 08	Mar 09	Apr 10
Sales Turnover	25m	27m	27m
Pre Tax Profit/Loss	3m	3m	4m
Working Capital	438	2m	2m
Fixed Assets	3m	3m	2m
Current Assets	10m	11m	11m
Current Liabilities	2m	2m	1m

Desso Ltd

9 Hitching Court Blacklands Way, Abingdon, OX14 1RB
Tel: 01235-554848 **Fax:** 01494-680020
E-mail: chext@desso.com
Website: http://www.desso.com
Managers: C. Hext (Comptroller), L. Gladwell (Sales Prom Mgr)
Ultimate Holding Company: DESSO GROUP BV (THE NETHERLANDS)
Immediate Holding Company: DESSO LIMITED
Registration no: 02622045 **Date established:** 1991
Turnover: £10m - £20m **No.of Employees:** 1 - 10 **Product Groups:** 23

Date of Accounts	Dec 11	Dec 10	Dec 09
Sales Turnover	17m	16m	13m
Pre Tax Profit/Loss	25	223	194
Working Capital	938	752	632
Fixed Assets	105	134	168
Current Assets	4m	4m	3m
Current Liabilities	773	798	380

E S Technology

Unit H1-H2 Kingston Business Park, Kingston Bagpuize, Abingdon, OX13 5FB
Tel: 01865-821818 **Fax:** 01865-821044
E-mail: sales@estechnology.co.uk
Website: http://www.estechnology.co.uk
Directors: T. Millard (Dir)
Registration no: 02105199 **Date established:** 1987 **Turnover:** £1m - £2m
No.of Employees: 11 - 20 **Product Groups:** 28, 37, 38, 39, 42, 44, 47, 48, 49, 85

Graham

Drayton Road, Abingdon, OX14 5HX
Tel: 01235-524326 **Fax:** 01235-554675
E-mail: gordoncree@graham-group.co.uk
Website: http://www.jewson.co.uk
Managers: G. Murrell (Mgr)
Ultimate Holding Company: SAINT-GOBAIN PLC
Immediate Holding Company: GRAHAM GROUP LTD
Registration no: 00066738 **Date established:** 1980
No.of Employees: 21 - 50 **Product Groups:** 66

Halver Ltd

Pearith Farm Long Wittenham, Abingdon, OX14 4PS
Tel: 01235-511666 **Fax:** 01235-811566
E-mail: info@halver.com
Website: http://www.halver.com
Directors: B. Gerrath (Fin), K. Gerrath (MD)
Immediate Holding Company: HALVER LIMITED
Registration no: 03021455 **VAT No.:** GB 630 9223 60
Date established: 1995 **Turnover:** £1m - £2m **No.of Employees:** 1 - 10
Product Groups: 39

Date of Accounts	Mar 11	Mar 10	Mar 09
Working Capital	615	520	468
Fixed Assets	111	126	48
Current Assets	769	757	724

Hutton Engineering Precision Ltd

Nuffield Way, Abingdon, OX14 1RX
Tel: 01235-520284 **Fax:** 01235-559001
E-mail: karim.sekkat@oxeng.co.uk
Website: http://www.huttonengineering.co.uk
Directors: K. Sekkat (MD)
Managers: L. Hindmarch Sekkat (Personnel)
Ultimate Holding Company: ERASMA COMPANY LTD
Immediate Holding Company: HUTTON ENGINEERING (PRECISION) LIMITED
Registration no: 03769653 **VAT No.:** GB 348 4463 34
Date established: 1999 **Turnover:** £2m - £5m **No.of Employees:** 21 - 50
Product Groups: 48

Date of Accounts	Jan 11	Jan 10	Jan 09
Sales Turnover	8m	4m	N/A
Pre Tax Profit/Loss	1m	370	N/A
Working Capital	3m	2m	2m
Fixed Assets	409	457	663
Current Assets	5m	3m	3m
Current Liabilities	726	420	N/A

I M I Cornelius

39-41 Nuffield Way, Abingdon, OX14 1AE
Tel: 01235-555123 **Fax:** 01235-555456
Website: http://www.corneliusuk.com
Bank(s): Barclays, Abingdon
Directors: A. Samples (Fin), A. Rudd (I.T. Dir)
Managers: D. Matthewman (Personnel), D. Plant (Tech Serv Mgr), P. Kelly (Prod Mgr), V. Clarke (Prod Mgr)
Ultimate Holding Company: IMI PLC
Immediate Holding Company: OBJEX (INVESTMENTS) LTD
Registration no: 01668782 **Turnover:** £10m - £20m
No.of Employees: 21 - 50 **Product Groups:** 30, 40, 66

J Curtis & Sons Ltd

Thrupp Lane Radley, Abingdon, OX14 3NG
Tel: 01235-524545 **Fax:** 01235-524545
Directors: J. Macdonald (MD)
Immediate Holding Company: J, CURTIS & SONS LIMITED
Registration no: 00461922 **VAT No.:** GB 195 2149 49
Date established: 1948 **Turnover:** £1m - £2m **No.of Employees:** 1 - 10
Product Groups: 14

Date of Accounts	Dec 11	Dec 10	Dec 09
Working Capital	6m	6m	6m
Fixed Assets	8m	8m	8m
Current Assets	7m	7m	7m

Linde Hydraulics Ltd

12-13 Eyston Way, Abingdon, OX14 1TR
Tel: 01235-522828 **Fax:** 01235-554036
E-mail: enquiries@lindehydraulics.co.uk
Website: http://www.lindehydraulics.co.uk
Bank(s): HSBC
Directors: D. Bowman (Co Sec), J. Chapman (Dir)
Ultimate Holding Company: SUPERLIFT HOLDINGS SARL (LUXEMBOURG)
Immediate Holding Company: LINDE HYDRAULICS LIMITED
Registration no: 00976342 **Date established:** 1970 **Turnover:** £2m - £5m
No.of Employees: 11 - 20 **Product Groups:** 38, 40

Date of Accounts	Dec 11	Dec 10	Dec 09
Sales Turnover	4m	4m	3m
Pre Tax Profit/Loss	389	198	221
Working Capital	6m	5m	5m
Fixed Assets	429	460	518
Current Assets	6m	6m	6m
Current Liabilities	376	538	463

Machining Centre Ltd

Pembroke Lane Milton, Abingdon, OX14 4EA
Tel: 01235-831343 **Fax:** 01235-834708
E-mail: sales@machiningcentre.co.uk
Website: http://www.machiningcentre.co.uk
Bank(s): Barclays, Abingdon
Directors: J. Harris (MD)
Immediate Holding Company: THE MACHINING CENTRE LIMITED
Registration no: 01346481 **VAT No.:** GB 311 4187 95
Date established: 1978 **Turnover:** £1m - £2m **No.of Employees:** 11 - 20
Product Groups: 35, 48

Date of Accounts	Feb 08	Feb 10	Feb 09
Working Capital	-84	-177	-167
Fixed Assets	277	174	228
Current Assets	284	346	307

Mepc Milton Park Ltd

99 Milton Park Milton, Abingdon, OX14 4RY
Tel: 01235-865555 **Fax:** 01235-865560
E-mail: enquiries@miltonpark.co.uk
Website: http://www.miltonpark.co.uk
Bank(s): Barclays
Directors: R. De Blaby (Grp Chief Exec)
Ultimate Holding Company: BT Pension Scheme
Immediate Holding Company: MEPC MILTON PARK LIMITED
Registration no: 01772924 **Date established:** 1983 **Turnover:** £1m - £2m
No.of Employees: 11 - 20 **Product Groups:** 80

Date of Accounts	Dec 11	Dec 10	Dec 09
Sales Turnover	2m	2m	2m
Pre Tax Profit/Loss	1m	689	958
Working Capital	12m	11m	18m
Fixed Assets	5m	5m	5m
Current Assets	13m	12m	19m
Current Liabilities	1m	714	441

Merkko Enterprises

Unit S12-S12a Kingston Business Park Kingston Bagpuize, Abingdon, OX13 5AS
Tel: 01865-820090 **Fax:** 01865-821864
E-mail: ianduckitt@merkko.co.uk
Website: http://www.merkko.com
Directors: I. Duckitt (MD)
Immediate Holding Company: MERKKO ENTERPRISES LIMITED
Registration no: 05772944 **Date established:** 2006 **Turnover:** £2m - £5m
No.of Employees: 1 - 10 **Product Groups:** 30, 33, 35, 39, 40, 66, 83

Date of Accounts	Jun 11	Jun 10	Jun 09
Sales Turnover	2m	2m	1m
Pre Tax Profit/Loss	-35	-61	-189
Working Capital	-580	-559	-487
Fixed Assets	40	54	47
Current Assets	908	735	498
Current Liabilities	955	942	777

Michel Hurel Transport UK Ltd

3 Vineyard Chambers Vineyard, Abingdon, OX14 3PX
Tel: 01235-536070 **Fax:** 01235-557430
E-mail: sales@michel-hurel.co.uk
Website: http://www.michel-hurel.co.uk
Directors: B. Hallo (MD)
Ultimate Holding Company: MICHEL HUREL HOLDINGS LIMITED
Immediate Holding Company: MICHEL HUREL TRANSPORT U.K. LIMITED
Registration no: 01993017 **VAT No.:** GB 438 4425 41
Date established: 1986 **Turnover:** £2m - £5m **No.of Employees:** 1 - 10
Product Groups: 76

Date of Accounts	Mar 11	Mar 10	Mar 09
Sales Turnover	5m	5m	7m
Pre Tax Profit/Loss	99	12	478
Working Capital	771	736	794
Fixed Assets	36	46	37
Current Assets	1m	2m	2m
Current Liabilities	265	417	529

Miele

Fairacres Marcham Road, Abingdon, OX14 1TW
Tel: 01235-554455 **Fax:** 01235-554477
E-mail: info@miele.co.uk
Website: http://www.miele.co.uk
Bank(s): Barclays Bank Ltd
Managers: S. Grantham (District Mgr)
Ultimate Holding Company: MIELE BETEILIGUNG GMBH (GERMANY)
Immediate Holding Company: MIELE COMPANY LIMITED
Registration no: 00769014 **Date established:** 1963
Turnover: £75m - £125m **No.of Employees:** 251 - 500
Product Groups: 26, 33, 38, 40

Date of Accounts	Dec 11	Dec 10	Dec 09
Sales Turnover	111m	110m	112m
Pre Tax Profit/Loss	170	-2m	-4m
Working Capital	13m	11m	7m
Fixed Assets	23m	24m	25m
Current Assets	35m	32m	28m
Current Liabilities	9m	7m	4m

Milton Electrical Services Ltd

Unit 120 C Milton Park, Milton, Abingdon, OX14 4SA
Tel: 01235-861777
E-mail: info@miltonelectrical.co.uk
Website: http://www.miltonelectrical.co.uk
Directors: F. Napper (MD)
Immediate Holding Company: CARBON COLOUR COMPANY LIMITED
Registration no: 04269072 **Date established:** 1995
No.of Employees: 1 - 10 **Product Groups:** 37, 52, 67, 84

Date of Accounts	Apr 11	Apr 10	Apr 09
Sales Turnover	1m	1m	1m
Pre Tax Profit/Loss	173	-53	212
Working Capital	504	348	564
Fixed Assets	116	100	71
Current Assets	658	471	679
Current Liabilities	77	73	94

Motan Ltd

10 Blacklands Way, Abingdon, OX14 1RD
Tel: 01235-550011 **Fax:** 01235-550033
E-mail: sales.ltd@motan.com
Website: http://www.motan.co.uk
Directors: A. Gibbons (Sales), D. Brown (Dir), D. Sturgess (Tech Serv), H. Roch (MD), U. Eberhardt (Dir)
Managers: C. Moodey
Ultimate Holding Company: MOTAN HOLDING GMBH (GERMANY)
Immediate Holding Company: MOTAN LIMITED
Registration no: 02066417 **VAT No.:** GB 423 7863 39
Date established: 1986 **Turnover:** £2m - £5m **No.of Employees:** 1 - 10
Product Groups: 38, 42, 45

Date of Accounts	Dec 09	Dec 08	Dec 07
Working Capital	461	428	533
Fixed Assets	19	32	29
Current Assets	1m	884	1m

Nord Gear Ltd

11 Barton Lane, Abingdon, OX14 3NB
Tel: 01235-534404 **Fax:** 01235-534414
E-mail: info@nord-uk.com
Website: http://www.nord.com
Directors: A. Stephenson (MD)
Immediate Holding Company: NORD GEAR LIMITED
Registration no: 02970420 **VAT No.:** 641 6898 07 **Date established:** 1994
Turnover: £10m - £20m **No.of Employees:** 21 - 50 **Product Groups:** 35, 37

Date of Accounts	Dec 11	Dec 10	Dec 09
Sales Turnover	11m	8m	8m
Pre Tax Profit/Loss	446	83	147
Working Capital	-400	-755	-884
Fixed Assets	1m	1m	2m
Current Assets	3m	3m	2m
Current Liabilities	3m	545	502

Nuffield Press Ltd

21 Nuffield Way, Abingdon, OX14 1RL
Tel: 01235-554422 **Fax:** 01235-535445
E-mail: paulw@nuffield.co.uk
Website: http://www.nuffield.co.uk
Bank(s): Barclays, Oxford
Directors: P. Kennelly (MD), P. Kennerley (MD), P. Wilson (Fin)
Managers: P. Warne (Purch Mgr), R. Cooper (I.T. Exec)
Immediate Holding Company: THE NUFFIELD PRESS LIMITED
Registration no: 02692772 **Date established:** 1992 **Turnover:** £5m - £10m
No.of Employees: 51 - 100 **Product Groups:** 28

Date of Accounts	Dec 07	Dec 06	Dec 05
Sales Turnover	7609	7498	8506
Pre Tax Profit/Loss	8	130	425
Working Capital	384	120	-1
Fixed Assets	2669	2983	2612
Current Assets	2715	2496	2676
Current Liabilities	2332	2377	2677
Total Share Capital	492	492	492
ROCE% (Return on Capital Employed)	0.3	4.2	16.3
ROT% (Return on Turnover)	0.1	1.7	5.0

O C Z Technology

25 Milton Park Milton, Abingdon, OX14 4SH
Tel: 01235-824900 **Fax:** 01235-821141
E-mail: james@oxsemi.com
Website: http://www.oxsemi.com
Bank(s): Cootes
Directors: A. Tout (Dir)
Immediate Holding Company: PLX TECHNOLOGY LIMITED
Registration no: 02733820 **VAT No.:** GB 596 3927 81
Date established: 1992 **Turnover:** £10m - £20m
No.of Employees: 21 - 50 **Product Groups:** 37

Date of Accounts	Dec 08	Dec 07	Dec 06
Sales Turnover	22m	42m	27m
Pre Tax Profit/Loss	-6m	-2m	-2m
Working Capital	5m	10m	11m
Fixed Assets	4m	3m	3m
Current Assets	9m	17m	18m
Current Liabilities	4m	8m	7m
Total Share Capital	208	208	208

Oxford Fencing Supplies

Kingston Business Park Kingston Bagpuize, Abingdon, OX13 5AS
Tel: 01865-820904 **Fax:** 01865-820803
E-mail: info@oxfordfencing.co.uk
Website: http://www.oxfordfencing.co.uk
Directors: P. Whittington (Prop)
Turnover: £1m - £2m **No.of Employees:** 1 - 10 **Product Groups:** 23, 25, 35, 49, 66

Oxford Instruments

Tubney Wood, Abingdon, OX13 5QX
Tel: 01865-393200 **Fax:** 01865-393333
E-mail: plasma.technology@oxinst.co.uk
Website: http://www.oxford-instruments.com
Bank(s): Barclays
Directors: S. Johnson-Brett (Co Sec), J. Lewis-crosby (Tech Serv), K. Boyd (Fin), C. Flint (Pers), L. Sheppard (Grp Mktg)
Managers: I. Wright
Immediate Holding Company: OXFORD INSTRUMENTS PLC
Registration no: 00775598 **VAT No.:** GB 596 1170 25
Date established: 1963 **Turnover:** £250m - £500m
No.of Employees: 101 - 250 **Product Groups:** 47

Date of Accounts	Mar 12	Mar 11	Mar 10
Sales Turnover	337m	262m	212m
Pre Tax Profit/Loss	36m	27m	18m
Working Capital	47m	37m	30m
Fixed Assets	126m	83m	85m
Current Assets	159m	126m	112m
Current Liabilities	82m	58m	37m

Oxford Law & Computing Ltd

Tatham House Northcourt Lane, Abingdon, OX14 1PN
Tel: 01235-203690 **Fax:** 01235-553379
E-mail: rjb@oxfordlaw.co.uk
Website: http://www.oxfordlaw.co.uk

see next page

***Oxford Law & Computing Ltd** - Cont'd*

Directors: R. Brockbank (MD)
Immediate Holding Company: OXFORD LAW AND COMPUTING LIMITED
Registration no: 01584098 **Date established:** 1981
Turnover: Up to £250,000 **No.of Employees:** 1 - 10 **Product Groups:** 28, 44, 84

Date of Accounts	Mar 08	Mar 07	Mar 06
Working Capital	-1	-8	18
Fixed Assets	2	1	2
Current Assets	41	16	46
Current Liabilities	42	24	28
Total Share Capital	9	9	9

Oxford Padprint Techniques

Unit 5 Radley Road Industrial Estate, Abingdon, OX14 3RY
Tel: 01235-535551 **Fax:** 01235-535551
E-mail: sales@oxfordpadprint.co.uk
Website: http://www.oxfordpadprint.co.uk
Managers: S. Holdsworth (Prod Mgr)
Immediate Holding Company: OXFORD PADPRINT TECHNIQUES LIMITED
Registration no: 03197836 **Date established:** 1996
Turnover: £250,000 - £500,000 **No.of Employees:** 1 - 10
Product Groups: 28, 38, 49, 65, 80

Date of Accounts	Jun 11	Jun 10	Jun 09
Sales Turnover	N/A	269	302
Pre Tax Profit/Loss	N/A	101	141
Working Capital	590	304	230
Fixed Assets	41	228	240
Current Assets	646	345	278
Current Liabilities	N/A	39	46

Oxford Software (a division of Applied Systems (Oxford) Ltd)

Clockhouse Barn Sugworth Lane, Radley, Abingdon, OX14 2HX
Tel: 0845-1300332 **Fax:** 0845-1300334
E-mail: enquiry@oxfordsoftware.com
Website: http://www.oxfordsoftware.com
Bank(s): Lloyds, Abingdon
Directors: N. Malden (Develop), D. Hancock (MD)
Ultimate Holding Company: Oxford Software
Registration no: 01580187 **VAT No.:** GB 490 6506 37
Turnover: £1m - £2m **No.of Employees:** 21 - 50 **Product Groups:** 44

Penlon Ltd

Abingdon Science Park Barton Lane, Abingdon, OX14 3PH
Tel: 01235-547000 **Fax:** 01235-547021
E-mail: alison.tarrant@penlon.com
Website: http://www.penlon.com
Bank(s): Bank of Scotland, St. Andrew Square, Edinburgh
Directors: A. Tarrant (Pers)
Ultimate Holding Company: INTERMED LIMITED
Immediate Holding Company: PENLON LIMITED
Registration no: 03228364 **VAT No.:** GB 663 5805 19
Date established: 1996 **Turnover:** £20m - £50m
No.of Employees: 101 - 250 **Product Groups:** 67

Date of Accounts	Dec 11	Dec 10	Dec 09
Sales Turnover	21m	32m	33m
Pre Tax Profit/Loss	10m	52	798
Working Capital	29m	18m	17m
Fixed Assets	1m	3m	3m
Current Assets	33m	28m	24m
Current Liabilities	2m	3m	1m

John Penny Woodworking Machinery Ltd

16 Napier Court Barton Lane, Abingdon, OX14 3YT
Tel: 01235-531700 **Fax:** 01235-522772
E-mail: john.penny@btconnect.com
Website: http://www.john-penny.co.uk
Directors: J. Penny (MD)
Immediate Holding Company: JOHN PENNY WOODWORKING MACHINERY LIMITED
Registration no: 02188357 **Date established:** 1987
No.of Employees: 1 - 10 **Product Groups:** 46

Date of Accounts	Apr 11	Apr 10	Apr 09
Working Capital	160	161	186
Fixed Assets	1	1	4
Current Assets	274	260	316

Pro Laser

100 Ock Street, Abingdon, OX14 5DH
Tel: 01235-550522 **Fax:** 01235-550499
E-mail: info@prolaser.co.uk
Website: http://www.prolaser.co.uk
Directors: J. Green (Dir)
Immediate Holding Company: OXFORD LEASING AND FINANCE LIMITED
Registration no: 02127864 **Date established:** 1987
Turnover: £250,000 - £500,000 **No.of Employees:** 1 - 10
Product Groups: 37, 38, 44, 46, 48, 54, 85, 87

Production Tools Oxon Ltd

Unit H 3 Southern Zone Kingston Business Park, Kingston Bagpuize, Abingdon, OX13 5FB
Tel: 01865-821021 **Fax:** 01865-821116
E-mail: simon.fathers@ptoxon.co.uk
Website: http://www.ptoxon.co.uk
Directors: S. Fathers (MD)
Immediate Holding Company: PRODUCTION TOOLS (OXON) LIMITED
Registration no: 03173604 **VAT No.:** GB 663 4872 09
Date established: 1996 **Turnover:** Up to £250,000
No.of Employees: 1 - 10 **Product Groups:** 48

Date of Accounts	Mar 11	Mar 10	Mar 09
Working Capital	14	-127	-122
Fixed Assets	254	258	263
Current Assets	98	107	97

PV Crystalox Solar PLC

Brook House 174 Milton Park, Abingdon, OX14 4SE
Tel: 01235-437160 **Fax:** 01235-770111
E-mail: info@crystalox.com
Website: http://www.crystalox.com
Bank(s): National Westminster Bank Plc
Directors: B. Garrard (I.T. Dir), I. Dorrity (Mkt Research), P. Finnegan (Fin), R. Greaves (Dir)
Managers: G. Young (Buyer), S. Alldham (I.T. Exec)
Ultimate Holding Company: Crystalox (Holdings) Ltd
Immediate Holding Company: Crystalox Solar Ltd
Registration no: 06019466 **VAT No.:** GB 348 6283 26
Turnover: £75m - £125m **No.of Employees:** 21 - 50 **Product Groups:** 40, 42, 46

R M plc

183 Milton Park Trading Estate Milton, Abingdon, OX14 4SE
Tel: 08450-700300 **Fax:** 01235-826999
E-mail: info@rm.com
Website: http://www.rm.com
Bank(s): Barclays
Directors: T. Sweeney (Grp Chief Exec), M. Greig (Dir), J. Govan (Dir), T. Pearson (Grp Chief Exec)
Immediate Holding Company: RM PLC
Registration no: 01749877 **VAT No.:** 630 8236 56 **Date established:** 1983
Turnover: £250m - £500m **No.of Employees:** 501 - 1000
Product Groups: 80

Date of Accounts	Nov 11	Sep 10	Sep 09
Sales Turnover	351m	380m	347m
Pre Tax Profit/Loss	-23m	24m	16m
Working Capital	26m	29m	21m
Fixed Assets	49m	68m	69m
Current Assets	114m	138m	119m
Current Liabilities	72m	75m	71m

Roger Askew Photography

14 Winterborne Road, Abingdon, OX14 1AJ
Tel: 01235-538542
E-mail: roger@rogeraskewphotography.co.uk
Website: http://www.rogeraskewphotography.co.uk
Directors: R. Askew (Prop)
Date established: 2003 **No.of Employees:** 1 - 10 **Product Groups:** 81

S.C.L Mobile Communications

38 Swinburne Road, Abingdon, OX14 2HD
Tel: 0800-0856377 **Fax:** 01235-527003
E-mail: sclmobilecom@aol.co.uk
Website: http://www.sclmobilecommunications.co.uk
Managers: S. Lewis (Chief Acct)
Date established: 2001 **Turnover:** Up to £250,000
No.of Employees: 1 - 10 **Product Groups:** 22, 37, 38, 44, 48, 49, 61, 67, 79, 83, 84

S K M Enviros

D5 Culham Science Centre, Abingdon, OX14 3DB
Tel: 01865-408280 **Fax:** 01865-407582
E-mail: information@globalskm.com
Website: http://www.enviros.com
Directors: P. Portlock (MD)
Ultimate Holding Company: CARILLION PLC
Immediate Holding Company: RAE UK LIMITED
Registration no: 01721409 **VAT No.:** GB 604 2396 61
Date established: 2004 **Turnover:** £20m - £50m **No.of Employees:** 1 - 10
Product Groups: 54

Date of Accounts	Mar 11	Mar 10	Mar 09
Working Capital	83	29	11
Fixed Assets	1	1	N/A
Current Assets	119	61	54
Current Liabilities	35	N/A	N/A

Serac UK

23 The Quadrant, Abingdon, OX14 3YS
Tel: 01235-537222 **Fax:** 01235-537815
E-mail: info@serac-uk.com
Website: http://www.serac-group.com
Directors: M. Titera (Sales), A. Graffin (Ch)
Managers: C. Van Kiele, A. Gardener (Tech Serv Mgr)
Immediate Holding Company: SERAC UK
Registration no: FC020628 **VAT No.:** GB 685 6517 90
Date established: 1997 **Turnover:** £20m - £50m **No.of Employees:** 1 - 10
Product Groups: 42, 48

Sitesafe UK Ltd

Lodge Hill, Abingdon, OX14 2JD
Tel: 01865-326553 **Fax:** 01865-326552
E-mail: info@sitesafe.uk.com
Website: http://www.sitesafe.uk.com
Directors: R. Hopkins (Dir)
Immediate Holding Company: SITESAFE UK LTD.
Registration no: 02506273 **Date established:** 1990
Turnover: Up to £250,000 **No.of Employees:** 1 - 10 **Product Groups:** 86

Date of Accounts	Jul 11	Jul 10	Jul 09
Working Capital	1	-2	-16
Fixed Assets	11	14	19
Current Assets	31	57	43

Marc Smith

Unit S3 Kingston Business Park, Kingston Bagpuize, Abingdon, OX13 5FE
Tel: 01865-820920 **Fax:** 01865-821092
E-mail: marc@marcsmithkitchens.com
Website: http://www.marcsmithkitchens.com
Directors: M. Smith (Prop)
No.of Employees: 1 - 10 **Product Groups:** 26

Syndicut Communications

6 Lombard Street, Abingdon, OX14 5BJ
Tel: 01235-466060 **Fax:** 01235-528339
E-mail: info@syndicut.com
Website: http://www.syndicut.com
Directors: N. Bromage (Dir), R. Watts (Fin)
Immediate Holding Company: SYNDICUT COMMUNICATIONS LTD
Registration no: 04382669 **Date established:** 2002
Turnover: £250,000 - £500,000 **No.of Employees:** 1 - 10
Product Groups: 81

Date of Accounts	May 11	May 10	May 09
Working Capital	3	48	49
Fixed Assets	N/A	3	3
Current Assets	116	150	138

Syntagm Ltd

10 Oxford Road, Abingdon, OX14 2DS
Tel: 01235-522859 **Fax:** 01235-554449
E-mail: info@syntagm.co.uk
Website: http://www.syntagm.co.uk
Directors: W. Hudson (MD)
Immediate Holding Company: SYNTAGM LIMITED
Registration no: 01895345 **Date established:** 1985
Turnover: Up to £250,000 **No.of Employees:** 1 - 10 **Product Groups:** 86

Date of Accounts	May 11	May 10	May 09
Working Capital	30	33	22
Fixed Assets	3	3	4
Current Assets	43	50	44

Textra

8 Station Yard Steventon, Abingdon, OX13 6RX
Tel: 01235-823100 **Fax:** 0870-241 4950
E-mail: sales@textra.co.uk
Website: http://www.textra.co.uk
Directors: T. Mackinnon (Co Sec), P. Mackinnon (Dir)
Immediate Holding Company: TEXTRA LIMITED
Registration no: 01075237 **Date established:** 1972 **Turnover:** £2m - £5m
No.of Employees: 1 - 10 **Product Groups:** 23, 63

Date of Accounts	Apr 12	Apr 11	Apr 10
Working Capital	271	289	297
Fixed Assets	1	1	2
Current Assets	293	311	328

Vtech Electronics UK plc

Napier Court Barton Lane, Abingdon, OX14 3YT
Tel: 01235-555545 **Fax:** 01235-546805
E-mail: steve_mason@vtech.com
Website: http://www.vtechuk.com
Bank(s): National Westminster
Directors: C. Richardson (Mkt Research), G. Canning (Sales), S. Mason (Co Sec), S. Mason (Co Sec)
Managers: R. Purves (Tech Serv Mgr)
Ultimate Holding Company: VTECH HOLDINGS LIMITED
Immediate Holding Company: VTECH ELECTRONICS EUROPE PLC
Registration no: 02178243 **VAT No.:** GB 479 2775 87
Date established: 1987 **Turnover:** £20m - £50m
No.of Employees: 21 - 50 **Product Groups:** 65

Date of Accounts	Mar 12	Mar 11	Mar 10
Sales Turnover	46m	42m	35m
Pre Tax Profit/Loss	983	1m	3m
Working Capital	8m	7m	6m
Fixed Assets	22	20	36
Current Assets	12m	11m	10m
Current Liabilities	3m	3m	3m

Michael Weinig UK Ltd

5 Blacklands Way, Abingdon, OX14 1DY
Tel: 01235-557600 **Fax:** 01235-538070
E-mail: sales@weinig.co.uk
Website: http://www.weinig.com
Directors: P. Reeves (Fin)
Managers: E. Kent (Chief Acct)
Ultimate Holding Company: WEINIG INTERNATIONAL AG (GERMANY)
Immediate Holding Company: MICHAEL WEINIG (UK) LIMITED
Registration no: 01617754 **Date established:** 1982 **Turnover:** £5m - £10m
No.of Employees: 11 - 20 **Product Groups:** 47, 67

Date of Accounts	Dec 11	Dec 10	Dec 09
Sales Turnover	9m	8m	5m
Pre Tax Profit/Loss	795	812	-280
Working Capital	626	145	-557
Fixed Assets	133	118	132
Current Assets	5m	5m	3m
Current Liabilities	1m	1m	1m

Bampton

P D Hook Hatcheries Ltd

Cote, Bampton, OX18 2EG
Tel: 01993-850261 **Fax:** 01993-851441
E-mail: sales@pdhook.co.uk
Website: http://www.pdhook.co.uk
Directors: M. Wannell (Fin), N. Boyle (Tech Serv), J. Hook (MD), S. Povey (Sales)
Managers: J. Newman (Personnel)
Ultimate Holding Company: P. D. HOOK (GROUP) LIMITED
Immediate Holding Company: P.D.HOOK(HATCHERIES)LIMITED
Registration no: 00777937 **Date established:** 1963
Turnover: £75m - £125m **No.of Employees:** 21 - 50 **Product Groups:** 41

Date of Accounts	Oct 11	Oct 10	Oct 09
Sales Turnover	95m	85m	76m
Pre Tax Profit/Loss	4m	4m	3m
Working Capital	5m	3m	1m
Fixed Assets	9m	10m	10m
Current Assets	19m	16m	17m
Current Liabilities	2m	3m	4m

Techno Weld Ltd

81 New Road, Bampton, OX18 2NP
Tel: 01993-851028 **Fax:** 01993-851036
E-mail: enquiries@techno-weld.co.uk
Website: http://www.techno-weld.co.uk
Directors: G. Newman (Dir)
Immediate Holding Company: TECHNO-WELD LIMITED
Registration no: 02880964 **Date established:** 1993
Turnover: Up to £250,000 **No.of Employees:** 1 - 10 **Product Groups:** 46

Date of Accounts	May 11	May 10	May 09
Sales Turnover	N/A	5	5
Pre Tax Profit/Loss	N/A	5	N/A
Working Capital	-98	-100	-105
Current Assets	4	2	4

Zeriba

2 Hill View Lew, Bampton, OX18 2BA
Tel: 01993-850009
E-mail: hayres@zeriba.co.uk
Website: http://www.chlorideupssales.co.uk
Directors: H. Ayres (Fin)
Immediate Holding Company: ZERIBA LIMITED
Registration no: 06136552 **Date established:** 2007
Turnover: Up to £250,000 **No.of Employees:** 1 - 10 **Product Groups:** 37, 44

Date of Accounts	May 11	May 09	May 08
Working Capital	-2	-0	-1
Fixed Assets	N/A	2	1
Current Assets	1	5	N/A

Banbury

A 1 Egg Packers Ltd
34 The Rydes Bodicote, Banbury, OX15 4EJ
Tel: 01295-252172 **Fax:** 01295-277223
Directors: J. Cox (Dir)
Immediate Holding Company: A 1 EGG PACKERS LIMITED
Registration no: 00846852 **Date established:** 1965
No.of Employees: 1 - 10 **Product Groups:** 38, 42

Date of Accounts	Dec 11	Dec 10	Dec 09
Working Capital	61	61	58
Current Assets	276	199	247

A G Products
4-5 North Bar Street, Banbury, OX16 0TB
Tel: 01295-259608 **Fax:** 01295-271787
E-mail: steve@agproducts.co.uk
Website: http://www.agproducts.co.uk
Directors: S. Gold (Ptnr)
VAT No.: GB 704 9851 20 **Turnover:** £250,000 - £500,000
No.of Employees: 1 - 10 **Product Groups:** 49

A & R Handling
Home Farm Works Clifton Road, Deddington, Banbury, OX15 0TP
Tel: 01869-336248 **Fax:** 01869-336248
Directors: A. Cross (Prop)
Immediate Holding Company: T & H HANDLING LIMITED
Registration no: 02689785 **Date established:** 1992
No.of Employees: 1 - 10 **Product Groups:** 35, 39, 45

ABC Information Services Ltd
12 St Marys Road Adderbury, Banbury, OX17 3HB
Tel: 01295-811543
E-mail: info@abcis.co.uk
Website: http://www.abcis.co.uk
Directors: P. Ely (MD)
Immediate Holding Company: ABC INFORMATION SERVICES LIMITED
Registration no: 04972347 **Date established:** 2003
Turnover: £250,000 - £500,000 **No.of Employees:** 1 - 10
Product Groups: 44

Date of Accounts	Nov 11	Nov 10	Nov 09
Working Capital	-2	-1	1
Current Assets	2	N/A	1

Alternative Gifts
The Innovation Centre Mewburn Road, Banbury, OX16 9PA
Tel: 0870-2006272 **Fax:** 0870-2006282
E-mail: info@alt-gifts.com
Website: http://www.alt-gifts.com
Directors: J. Vincent (MD)
Managers: J. Edwards (Mktg Serv Mgr)
Registration no: 06596199 **Date established:** 1999
Turnover: Up to £250,000 **No.of Employees:** 1 - 10 **Product Groups:** 49

AW Glass
Unit 6 Swan Industrial Estate Gatteridge Street, Banbury, OX16 5DH
Tel: 01295-278772 **Fax:** 01295-265169
E-mail: awglassltd@btconnect.com
Directors: K. Wench (Fin)
Immediate Holding Company: AW GLASS LIMITED
Registration no: 06060845 **Date established:** 2007
Turnover: Up to £250,000 **No.of Employees:** 1 - 10 **Product Groups:** 33, 35, 63, 66

Date of Accounts	Jan 10	Jan 09	Jan 08
Sales Turnover	169	134	42
Pre Tax Profit/Loss	-9	-18	-13
Working Capital	-13	-24	-1
Fixed Assets	5	6	8
Current Assets	23	32	17
Current Liabilities	22	14	4

Bag 'N' Box Man
Unit 1 West Street Shutford, Banbury, OX15 6PH
Tel: 01295-788522 **Fax:** 01295-788523
E-mail: sales@bagnboxman.co.uk
Website: http://www.bagnboxman.co.uk
Managers: M. Harvey (Mgr)
Immediate Holding Company: THE BAG 'N' BOX MAN LIMITED
Registration no: 04726550 **Date established:** 2003
No.of Employees: 1 - 10 **Product Groups:** 38, 42

Date of Accounts	Apr 11	Apr 10	Apr 09
Working Capital	100	117	96
Fixed Assets	7	15	28
Current Assets	193	233	194

Banbury Nameplates Ltd
Dashwood Road, Banbury, OX16 5HD
Tel: 01295-267638 **Fax:** 01295-271745
E-mail: sales@banburynameplates.co.uk
Website: http://www.banburynameplates.co.uk
Directors: M. Lucas (Fin), J. Lucas (Dir)
Immediate Holding Company: BANBURY NAMEPLATES LIMITED
Registration no: 01304472 **VAT No.:** GB 294 1648 34
Date established: 1977 **Turnover:** £500,000 - £1m
No.of Employees: 1 - 10 **Product Groups:** 28, 30

Date of Accounts	Nov 11	Nov 10	Nov 09
Working Capital	91	81	62
Fixed Assets	55	43	48
Current Assets	136	112	104

Banbury Plastic Fittings Ltd BPF
13 Overfield Thorpe Way, Banbury, OX16 4XR
Tel: 01295-264800 **Fax:** 01295-264901
E-mail: jason@bpfittings.co.uk
Website: http://www.bpfittings.co.uk
Directors: J. Kidd (Dir), J. Stead (Dir)
Immediate Holding Company: BANBURY PLASTIC FITTINGS LIMITED
Registration no: 03935890 **VAT No.:** GB 748 2855 92
Date established: 2000 **Turnover:** £500,000 - £1m
No.of Employees: 1 - 10 **Product Groups:** 23, 26, 29, 30, 31, 35, 36, 37, 39, 44, 46, 47, 48, 63, 66

Barry Callebaut UK Ltd
Wildmere Road, Banbury, OX16 3UU
Tel: 01295-224700 **Fax:** 01295-224780
E-mail: andy_fleming@barry-callebaut.com
Website: http://www.barry-callebaut.com
Managers: A. Fleming
Ultimate Holding Company: BARRY CALLEBAUT AG (SWITZERLAND)
Immediate Holding Company: BARRY CALLEBAUT MANUFACTURING (UK) LIMITED
Registration no: 01156841 **Date established:** 1974
Turnover: £125m - £250m **No.of Employees:** 101 - 250
Product Groups: 20

Date of Accounts	Aug 11	Aug 10	Aug 09
Sales Turnover	204m	213m	193m
Pre Tax Profit/Loss	2m	1m	1m
Working Capital	7m	10m	8m
Fixed Assets	20m	19m	19m
Current Assets	27m	27m	33m
Current Liabilities	9m	1m	9m

Bearing Traders Ltd
10 Penhill Industrial Park Beaumont Road, Banbury, OX16 1RW
Tel: 01295-251111 **Fax:** 01295-256006
E-mail: bnsales@bearingtraders.com
Website: http://www.bearingtraders.com
Managers: M. Castle (District Mgr)
Immediate Holding Company: BEARING TRADERS LIMITED
Registration no: 01994643 **Date established:** 1986
No.of Employees: 1 - 10 **Product Groups:** 35, 36

Date of Accounts	Apr 11	Apr 10	Apr 09
Sales Turnover	N/A	N/A	4m
Pre Tax Profit/Loss	N/A	N/A	60
Working Capital	-10	-52	-61
Fixed Assets	91	111	115
Current Assets	1m	911	965
Current Liabilities	N/A	N/A	525

P R Booth
Hall Farm Buildings Hortons Lane, Milcombe, Banbury, OX15 4RG
Tel: 01295-721453 **Fax:** 01295-721453
Directors: P. Booth (Prop)
Date established: 1969 **No.of Employees:** 1 - 10 **Product Groups:** 41

Brady Corporation Ltd
Wildmere Industrial Estate Wildmere Road, Banbury, OX16 3JU
Tel: 01295-228200 **Fax:** 01295-228100
E-mail: peter_sephton@bradycorp.com
Website: http://www.bradycorp.com
Bank(s): ABN Amrow Bank
Directors: P. Sephton (Dir), D. Mathieson (Fin)
Managers: H. Scares (Personnel), S. Maxwell (I.T. Exec), P. Ingleby (Product), C. Kelly (Personnel), R. Foster (Sales & Mktg Mg)
Ultimate Holding Company: BRADY CORP (USA)
Immediate Holding Company: BRADY CORPORATION LIMITED
Registration no: 04201763 **VAT No.:** GB 747 8798 54
Date established: 2001 **Turnover:** £50m - £75m
No.of Employees: 51 - 100 **Product Groups:** 28, 30, 40, 42, 44, 49, 67

Date of Accounts	Jul 11	Jul 10	Jul 09
Sales Turnover	51m	54m	52m
Pre Tax Profit/Loss	351	473	7m
Working Capital	12m	7m	13m
Fixed Assets	29m	33m	35m
Current Assets	28m	22m	27m
Current Liabilities	5m	5m	4m

British Valve & Actuator Association
Unit 9 Manor Park, Banbury, OX16 3TB
Tel: 01295-221270 **Fax:** 01295-268965
E-mail: enquiry@bvaa.org.uk
Website: http://www.bvaa.org.uk
Directors: R. Bartlett (Dir)
Immediate Holding Company: BRITISH VALVE AND ACTUATOR ASSOCIATION LIMITED
Registration no: 01141396 **VAT No.:** GB 240 9494 54
Date established: 1973 **Turnover:** Up to £250,000
No.of Employees: 1 - 10 **Product Groups:** 36, 38

Date of Accounts	Mar 12	Mar 11	Mar 10
Working Capital	146	115	109
Fixed Assets	12	8	12
Current Assets	270	280	177

C P L Petroleum
Station Approach, Banbury, OX16 5AB
Tel: 01295-268422 **Fax:** 01295-255350
E-mail: marketing@gb-oils.co.uk
Website: http://www.cplpetroleum.co.uk
Managers: V. Coull (Mgr)
Ultimate Holding Company: CPL INDUSTRIES HOLDINGS LIMITED
Immediate Holding Company: CPL PETROLEUM LIMITED
Registration no: 03003860 **Date established:** 1994 **Turnover:** £1m - £2m
No.of Employees: 1 - 10 **Product Groups:** 66

Date of Accounts	Mar 12	Mar 11	Mar 10
Pre Tax Profit/Loss	N/A	878	904
Working Capital	31	30m	30m
Fixed Assets	26	26m	26m
Current Assets	57	56m	56m
Current Liabilities	26	246	253

Caplugs Ltd
Unit 5 Overfield Thorpe Way, Banbury, OX16 4XR
Tel: 01295-263753 **Fax:** 01295-263788
E-mail: support@caplugs.co.uk
Website: http://www.caplugs.co.uk
Directors: P. Mutton (MD)
Ultimate Holding Company: MARK IV LIMITED
Immediate Holding Company: CAPLUGS LIMITED
Registration no: 02488919 **Date established:** 1990 **Turnover:** £1m - £2m
No.of Employees: 1 - 10 **Product Groups:** 27, 29, 30, 35, 40, 48

Date of Accounts	Feb 08	Feb 11	Feb 10
Sales Turnover	N/A	770	N/A
Pre Tax Profit/Loss	N/A	35	N/A
Working Capital	68	202	175
Fixed Assets	187	151	163
Current Assets	238	308	301
Current Liabilities	N/A	48	N/A

Cherwell Industrial Doors
Milner House Thorpe Way, Banbury, OX16 4SP
Tel: 01295-256698 **Fax:** 01295-276636
E-mail: info@cherwelldoors.com
Website: http://www.cherwelldoors.com
Directors: A. Beddows (Co Sec)
Immediate Holding Company: CHERWELL INDUSTRIAL DOORS LIMITED
Registration no: 05718117 **Date established:** 2006
No.of Employees: 1 - 10 **Product Groups:** 26, 35

Date of Accounts	Apr 12	Feb 11	Feb 10
Working Capital	-20	-20	3
Fixed Assets	39	23	21
Current Assets	86	61	57

Cherwell Valley Silos Ltd
Twyford, Banbury, OX17 3AA
Tel: 01295-811441 **Fax:** 01295-811228
E-mail: roger.wertheimer@cherwellvalleysilos.co.uk
Website: http://www.cherwellvalleysilos.co.uk
Bank(s): National Westminster Bank Plc
Directors: B. Mills (Sales), C. Wertheimer (Co Sec)
Ultimate Holding Company: K.J. CHERRY & SONS LIMITED
Immediate Holding Company: CHERWELL VALLEY SILOS LIMITED
Registration no: 00696016 **VAT No.:** GB 443 8828 22
Date established: 1961 **Turnover:** £20m - £50m
No.of Employees: 101 - 250 **Product Groups:** 62, 72

Date of Accounts	Jun 11	Jun 10	Jun 09
Sales Turnover	48m	43m	35m
Pre Tax Profit/Loss	7	293	-33
Working Capital	-3m	-2m	-2m
Fixed Assets	6m	6m	5m
Current Assets	5m	5m	5m
Current Liabilities	3m	3m	4m

Cleenol Group Ltd
Neville House Beaumont Road, Banbury, OX16 1RB
Tel: 01295-251721 **Fax:** 01295-269561
E-mail: md@cleenol.co.uk
Website: http://www.cleenol.co.uk
Bank(s): HSBC Bank plc
Directors: R. Greaves (MD), J. Childerstone (Fin)
Managers: A. Duffy (Purch Mgr), P. Alsworth
Ultimate Holding Company: CLEENOL HOLDINGS LIMITED
Immediate Holding Company: CLEENOL GROUP LIMITED
Registration no: 00635803 **VAT No.:** GB 119 4183 71
Date established: 1959 **Turnover:** £5m - £10m
No.of Employees: 101 - 250 **Product Groups:** 31, 32, 63, 66

Date of Accounts	Oct 11	Oct 10	Oct 09
Sales Turnover	8m	8m	8m
Pre Tax Profit/Loss	-42	78	179
Working Capital	199	346	440
Fixed Assets	2m	2m	2m
Current Assets	3m	2m	3m
Current Liabilities	367	254	350

Connectors & Switchgear Ltd
25 Chacombe Road Middleton Cheney, Banbury, OX17 2QS
Tel: 01295-710505 **Fax:** 01295-712667
E-mail: roy.beckham@connectorsandswitchgear.co.uk
Website: http://www.connectorsandswitchgear.co.uk
Directors: R. Beckham (Dir)
Immediate Holding Company: CONNECTORS & SWITCHGEAR LIMITED
Registration no: 00991314 **VAT No.:** GB 121 2646 11
Date established: 1970 **Turnover:** £1m - £2m **No.of Employees:** 21 - 50
Product Groups: 37

Date of Accounts	Dec 11	Dec 10	Dec 09
Working Capital	1m	861	677
Fixed Assets	470	351	403
Current Assets	1m	1m	936

Copernica Ltd
Unit 5 Wates Way The Acre Estate, Banbury, OX16 3TS
Tel: 01295-220110 **Fax:** 01295-255325
E-mail: bcox@copernica.co.uk
Website: http://www.copernica.co.uk
Directors: M. Wilkinson (Sales & Mktg), B. Cox (Fin)
Immediate Holding Company: COPERNICA LIMITED
Registration no: 05260568 **Date established:** 2004 **Turnover:** £1m - £2m
No.of Employees: 1 - 10 **Product Groups:** 44, 84

Date of Accounts	Sep 11	Sep 10	Sep 09
Working Capital	-70	-93	-140
Fixed Assets	46	40	28
Current Assets	334	296	235

Corsair Engineering Ltd
Beaumont Close, Banbury, OX16 1SH
Tel: 01295-267021 **Fax:** 01295-270396
E-mail: sales@corsairengineering.co.uk
Website: http://www.corsairengineering.co.uk
Bank(s): Barclays
Directors: A. Sahajpal (MD)
Immediate Holding Company: CORSAIR ENGINEERING LIMITED
Registration no: 04671849 **VAT No.:** GB 215 9266 58
Date established: 2003 **Turnover:** £2m - £5m **No.of Employees:** 21 - 50
Product Groups: 40

Date of Accounts	Dec 11	Dec 10	Dec 09
Working Capital	147	72	N/A
Fixed Assets	13	17	N/A
Current Assets	607	348	N/A

Dar Lighting Ltd
Wildmere Road, Banbury, OX16 3JZ
Tel: 01295-672200 **Fax:** 01295-271743
E-mail: sales@darlighting.co.uk
Website: http://www.darlighting.co.uk
Bank(s): Yorkshire Bank PLC
Directors: D. Hidson (Fin), J. McNair (Sales), T. Bulgarelli (Fin), N. Cosgrove-Mcguirk (MD)
Managers: A. Buck (Tech Serv Mgr), Y. Piper (Personnel)
Ultimate Holding Company: DAR LIGHTING LIMITED
Immediate Holding Company: DAR LUMINAIRES LIMITED
Registration no: 01005785 **VAT No.:** GB 222 5308 02
Date established: 1971 **Turnover:** £5m - £10m
No.of Employees: 101 - 250 **Product Groups:** 37

Date of Accounts	Jun 11	Jun 10	Jun 09
Working Capital	535	535	535
Current Assets	545	545	545
Current Liabilities	10	10	10

Demag Cranes & Components Ltd
Beaumont Rd, Banbury, OX16 1QZ
Tel: 01295-676100 **Fax:** 01295-226106
E-mail: help@demagcranes.com
Website: http://www.demagcranes.com

see next page

Demag Cranes & Components Ltd - Cont'd

Directors: A. Clarke (MD), P. Bartlett (Sales)
Managers: G. Baird (Serv Mgr), O. Birlenbach (Fin Mgr), D. Smith (Mktg Serv Mgr)
Ultimate Holding Company: Demag Cranes AG, Dusseldorf
Registration no: 02450667 **VAT No.:** GB 536 4524 43
Date established: 1969 **No.of Employees:** 101 - 250 **Product Groups:** 35, 37, 38, 39, 41, 43, 45, 48, 52, 67, 71, 74, 84, 85, 86

Date of Accounts	Sep 11	Sep 10	Sep 09
Pre Tax Profit/Loss	750	N/A	900
Working Capital	-2m	-2m	N/A
Fixed Assets	6m	6m	6m
Current Assets	750	N/A	N/A
Current Liabilities	3m	N/A	N/A

Digiwise Security

Barford Road Bloxham, Banbury, OX15 4FF
Tel: 01295-724155 **Fax:** 01295-722801
E-mail: info@digiwise-uk.co.uk
Website: http://www.digiwise-uk.co.uk
Directors: J. Decreek (MD)
Immediate Holding Company: REMOTE-LEARNER UK LIMITED
Registration no: 05205281 **Date established:** 2011 **Turnover:** £1m - £2m
No.of Employees: 1 - 10 **Product Groups:** 37, 40, 67

Elite Surface Finishing Ltd

6 Overfield Thorpe Way, Banbury, OX16 4XR
Tel: 01295-255668 **Fax:** 01295-253775
E-mail: elite.sf@virgin.net
Directors: P. Burbidge (Fin), A. Burbidge (MD)
Immediate Holding Company: ELITE SURFACE FINISHING LIMITED
Registration no: 03018799 **Date established:** 1995
No.of Employees: 1 - 10 **Product Groups:** 46, 48

Date of Accounts	Mar 12	Mar 11	Mar 10
Working Capital	122	76	51
Fixed Assets	178	175	165
Current Assets	250	172	100

Ellacotts LLP

23 West Bar Street, Banbury, OX16 9SA
Tel: 01295-250401 **Fax:** 01295-271480
E-mail: derek@jbaccounts.co.uk
Website: http://www.jbaccounts.co.uk
Directors: D. Boughton (Ptnr)
Immediate Holding Company: JONES BOUGHTON LIMITED
Registration no: 05533332 **Date established:** 2005
No.of Employees: 51 - 100 **Product Groups:** 80, 81, 87

Date of Accounts	Jan 12	Jan 11	Jan 10
Working Capital	184	494	45
Fixed Assets	N/A	N/A	42
Current Assets	191	552	126

Emward Fastenings Ltd (division of Belfin Group)

Beaumont Close, Banbury, OX16 1TG
Tel: 01295-701206 **Fax:** 01295-701262
E-mail: sales@emward.co.uk
Website: http://www.emwardfastenings.com
Directors: M. McInerney (Fin), G. Bellazzi (MD)
Immediate Holding Company: EMWARD FASTENINGS LIMITED
Registration no: 01223883 **Date established:** 1975 **Turnover:** £2m - £5m
No.of Employees: 1 - 10 **Product Groups:** 35, 36, 66

Date of Accounts	Dec 11	Dec 10	Dec 09
Working Capital	340	64	-811
Fixed Assets	1m	1m	1m
Current Assets	484	515	362

Encase Ltd

Beaumont Road, Banbury, OX16 1RE
Tel: 01295-752900 **Fax:** 01295-752910
E-mail: info@encase.co.uk
Website: http://www.encase.co.uk
Bank(s): HSBC Bank plc
Directors: G. Button (Fin), M. Costa (MD)
Managers: D. Hainesworth (Sales Prom Mgr), J. Hayden (Tech Serv Mgr), M. Hartley (Mktg Serv Mgr), S. Miller (Purch Mgr), D. Wood (Personnel)
Ultimate Holding Company: CANADIAN OVERSEAS PACKAGING INDUSTRIES LTD (CANADA)
Immediate Holding Company: ENCASE LIMITED
Registration no: 00852604 **VAT No.:** GB 408 5650 50
Date established: 1965 **Turnover:** £20m - £50m
No.of Employees: 101 - 250 **Product Groups:** 27

Date of Accounts	Jun 12	Jun 11	Jun 10
Sales Turnover	33m	32m	26m
Pre Tax Profit/Loss	1m	138	186
Working Capital	1m	-1m	-2m
Fixed Assets	5m	5m	6m
Current Assets	12m	14m	12m
Current Liabilities	2m	2m	2m

Fiddes Payne

4 Network Eleven Thorpe Way, Banbury, OX16 4XS
Tel: 01295-253888 **Fax:** 01295-269166
E-mail: info@fiddespayne.co.uk
Website: http://www.fiddespayne.co.uk
Bank(s): National Westminster
Directors: C. White (Ptnr)
Immediate Holding Company: FIDDES PAYNE LIMITED
Registration no: 02678291 **VAT No.:** GB 589 5524 82
Date established: 1992 **Turnover:** £10m - £20m
No.of Employees: 51 - 100 **Product Groups:** 20, 41

Date of Accounts	Jun 08	Jul 10	Jul 11
Sales Turnover	7m	10m	12m
Pre Tax Profit/Loss	-651	-5	610
Working Capital	570	2m	2m
Fixed Assets	712	818	719
Current Assets	3m	4m	4m
Current Liabilities	109	247	317

Fired Earth Ltd

Twyford Mill Oxford Road, Adderbury, Banbury, OX17 3SX
Tel: 01295-812088 **Fax:** 01295-810832
E-mail: enquiries@firedearth.com
Website: http://www.firedearth.com
Bank(s): Barclays
Directors: S. Smith (Fin)
Managers: G. Blythe (Purch Mgr), R. Rees (Sales Prom Mgr), K. Lowe (Mktg Serv Mgr)
Ultimate Holding Company: AGA RANGEMASTER GROUP PLC
Immediate Holding Company: FIRED EARTH LIMITED
Registration no: 01733704 **VAT No.:** GB 348 8583 04
Date established: 1983 **Turnover:** £5m - £10m
No.of Employees: 101 - 250 **Product Groups:** 33, 84

Date of Accounts	Dec 11	Dec 10
Sales Turnover	15m	N/A
Pre Tax Profit/Loss	-1m	N/A
Working Capital	-2m	8m
Fixed Assets	1m	168
Current Assets	6m	8m
Current Liabilities	2m	N/A

Fountain Forestry Ltd

Fountains Blenheim Court, Banbury, OX16 5BH
Tel: 01295-750000 **Fax:** 01295-753253
E-mail: lisa.burton@fountainsplc.com
Website: http://www.fountainforestry.com
Directors: R. Haddon (Grp Chief Exec)
Ultimate Holding Company: FOUNTAINS HOLDINGS 1 LIMITED
Immediate Holding Company: FG REALISATIONS NO. 2 LIMITED
Registration no: 04090138 **Date established:** 2000 **Turnover:** £2m - £5m
No.of Employees: 51 - 100 **Product Groups:** 80, 86, 89

Date of Accounts	Aug 10	Sep 09	Sep 08
Sales Turnover	3m	3m	3m
Pre Tax Profit/Loss	482	437	588
Working Capital	3m	2m	2m
Fixed Assets	127	174	145
Current Assets	6m	5m	7m
Current Liabilities	3m	3m	5m

Gem Tool Hire & Sales Ltd

England House Beaumont Road, Banbury, OX16 1TF
Tel: 01295-252288 **Fax:** 01295-272052
E-mail: office@gemtools.co.uk
Website: http://www.gem-tools.co.uk
Registration no: 01800399 **Turnover:** £500,000 - £1m
No.of Employees: 21 - 50 **Product Groups:** 30, 33, 35, 36, 37, 40, 41, 45, 66, 67, 83

Date of Accounts	Sep 11	Sep 10	Sep 09
Working Capital	501	484	482
Fixed Assets	1m	1m	1m
Current Assets	975	943	948

Glass Slipper Interactive

1st Floor Coach House, Manor Farm Business Park Appletree Road, Chipping Warden, Banbury, OX17 1LH
Tel: 01295-724568
E-mail: david@glassslipperinteractive.com
Website: http://www.glassslipperinteractive.com
Directors: D. Taylor (MD)
Date established: 2004 **Turnover:** Up to £250,000
No.of Employees: 1 - 10 **Product Groups:** 44, 61, 80

Glazeparts UK Ltd

Wildmere Road Daventry Road Industrial Estate, Banbury, OX16 3JU
Tel: 01295-264533 **Fax:** 01295-266699
E-mail: mark.nelson@glazpart.co.uk
Website: http://www.glazpart.co.uk
Directors: M. Nelson (Co Sec)
Ultimate Holding Company: GLAZPART HOLDINGS LIMITED
Immediate Holding Company: GLAZEPARTS (U.K.) LIMITED
Registration no: 02338656 **VAT No.:** GB 408 6578 27
Date established: 1989 **Turnover:** £5m - £10m **No.of Employees:** 1 - 10
Product Groups: 30

Graham

Marley Way, Banbury, OX16 2RD
Tel: 01295-250822 **Fax:** 01295-257466
E-mail: carl.guntrip@graham-group.co.uk
Website: http://www.graham-group.co.uk
Managers: C. Guntrip (District Mgr)
Immediate Holding Company: GRAHAM BUILDERS MERCHANTS LIMITED
Registration no: 00066738 **Date established:** 2000
Turnover: Up to £250,000 **No.of Employees:** 1 - 10 **Product Groups:** 66

Hanley Precision Tools

Unit 21b Wildmere Industrial Estate, Banbury, OX16 3JU
Tel: 01295-264223 **Fax:** 01295-268927
E-mail: sales@glazpart.co.uk
Website: http://www.glazpart.com
Directors: M. Nelson (Fin)
Immediate Holding Company: GLAZPART (HOLDING) CO.
Turnover: £500,000 - £1m **No.of Employees:** 51 - 100
Product Groups: 30, 42, 48, 67, 84

Hawkins Roofing

Unit 9a Thorpe Way, Banbury, OX16 4SP
Tel: 01295-252363 **Fax:** 01295-251008
E-mail: info@hawkins-roofing.co.uk
Website: http://www.hawkins-roofing.co.uk
Bank(s): Barclays
Directors: M. Hawkins (Dir)
Managers: J. Baker, L. Hawkins (Personnel)
Immediate Holding Company: HAWKINS GROUP OF COMPANIES LIMITED
Registration no: 04304081 **VAT No.:** GB 408 6590 37
Date established: 2001 **Turnover:** £1m - £2m **No.of Employees:** 51 - 100
Product Groups: 48

Date of Accounts	Nov 10	Nov 09	Nov 08
Working Capital	844	648	428
Fixed Assets	460	475	535
Current Assets	2m	2m	1m

Headway Music Audio Ltd

Headway House Walnut Tree Lane St Thomas Street, Deddington, Banbury, OX15 0SY
Tel: 01869-338404 **Fax:** 01869-338395
E-mail: sales@headwaymusicaudio.com
Website: http://www.headwaymusicaudio.com
Directors: J. Littler (Dir)
Immediate Holding Company: HEADWAY MUSIC AUDIO LTD
Registration no: 05685289 **Date established:** 2006
Turnover: Up to £250,000 **No.of Employees:** 1 - 10 **Product Groups:** 37, 38

Date of Accounts	Jan 12	Jan 11	Jan 10
Working Capital	27	32	32
Fixed Assets	15	10	11
Current Assets	46	51	53

Heraeus Amba Ltd

Thorpe Way, Banbury, OX16 4ST
Tel: 01295-272666 **Fax:** 01295-272611
E-mail: craig.wenlock@heraeus.com
Website: http://www.heraeusamba.co.uk
Bank(s): Lloyds TSB Bank plc
Directors: C. Wenlock (MD), N. Spilker (Fin)
Managers: J. Watts (Tech Serv Mgr), R. Berry, R. McClean (Sales Prom Mgr)
Ultimate Holding Company: HERAEUS HOLDING GMBH (GERMANY)
Immediate Holding Company: HERAEUS AMBA LIMITED
Registration no: 01637954 **VAT No.:** GB 336 4906 45
Date established: 1982 **Turnover:** £5m - £10m
No.of Employees: 51 - 100 **Product Groups:** 37

Date of Accounts	Dec 11	Dec 10	Dec 09
Sales Turnover	8m	7m	6m
Pre Tax Profit/Loss	1m	1m	768
Working Capital	5m	4m	4m
Fixed Assets	1m	824	936
Current Assets	6m	5m	4m
Current Liabilities	633	447	366

High Profile

9 Haslemere Way, Banbury, OX16 5RW
Tel: 01295-267966 **Fax:** 01295-272477
E-mail: sales@high-profile.co.uk
Website: http://www.high-profile.co.uk
Managers: R. Hope Jones (Chief Mgr)
Immediate Holding Company: HIGH PROFILE PLASTIC PRODUCTS LIMITED
Registration no: 05670385 **Date established:** 2006 **Turnover:** £2m - £5m
No.of Employees: 21 - 50 **Product Groups:** 24, 25, 29, 49, 65, 81

Date of Accounts	Feb 12	Feb 11	Feb 10
Working Capital	183	154	38
Fixed Assets	208	213	210
Current Assets	888	856	783

Hospitality Search International Ltd

8 West Bar Street, Banbury, OX16 9RR
Tel: 01295-279696 **Fax:** 01295-279697
E-mail: sales@hospitalitysearch.co.uk
Website: http://www.hospitalitysearch.co.uk
Directors: P. Graham (Fin), A. Graham (MD)
Immediate Holding Company: HOSPITALITY SEARCH INTERNATIONAL LIMITED
Registration no: 03061599 **Date established:** 1995
No.of Employees: 1 - 10 **Product Groups:** 80

Date of Accounts	Jul 11	Jul 10	Jul 09
Working Capital	55	68	55
Fixed Assets	227	227	228
Current Assets	113	126	105

Integrate HR Ltd

Bloxham Mill Barford Road, Bloxham, Banbury, OX15 4FF
Tel: 01295-722833 **Fax:** 0870-4602968
E-mail: sales@integratehr.com
Website: http://www.integratehr.com
Directors: J. White (Chief Op Offcr), S. Knight (Tech Serv)
Registration no: 04494697 **Date established:** 2002
No.of Employees: 1 - 10 **Product Groups:** 44, 80

Karcher UK Ltd

Kärcher House Beaumont Road, Banbury, OX16 1TB
Tel: 01295-752000 **Fax:** 01295-266436
E-mail: enquiries@karcher.co.uk
Website: http://www.karcher.co.uk
Bank(s): Barclays, Bayetisch Vereinsbank & Banque Nationale De Paris
Directors: C. McKay (Sales & Mktg), M. Venner (Fin), N. Scott (Sales), S. Keeping (MD)
Managers: K. McGuinness (Personnel)
Ultimate Holding Company: ALFRED KARCHER GMBH & CO KG (GERMANY)
Immediate Holding Company: KARCHER (U.K.) LIMITED
Registration no: 01350233 **VAT No.:** GB 294 2363 45
Date established: 1978 **Turnover:** £50m - £75m
No.of Employees: 101 - 250 **Product Groups:** 32, 39, 40, 83

Date of Accounts	Dec 11	Dec 10	Dec 09
Sales Turnover	66m	63m	59m
Pre Tax Profit/Loss	30	515	-3m
Working Capital	6m	6m	-304
Fixed Assets	2m	3m	3m
Current Assets	14m	12m	11m
Current Liabilities	2m	2m	2m

L V D UK Ltd

Unit 3 Wildmere Road, Banbury, OX16 3JU
Tel: 01295-676800 **Fax:** 01295-262980
E-mail: j.goodwin@lvduk.com
Website: http://www.lvdgroup.com
Directors: C. Phillips (MD)
Ultimate Holding Company: L V D COMPANY NV (BELGIUM)
Immediate Holding Company: LVD PULLMAX LTD.
Registration no: 01608880 **Date established:** 1982
No.of Employees: 1 - 10 **Product Groups:** 42, 44, 46

Date of Accounts	Dec 11	Dec 10	Dec 09
Working Capital	224	175	341
Fixed Assets	62	85	108
Current Assets	1m	693	861

Lambourne Agricultural Consultants Ltd

Grange Barn Birds Lane, Epwell, Banbury, OX15 6LQ
Tel: 01295-788006 **Fax:** 01295-788006
E-mail: enquiry@ruralagriculturalconsultants.co.uk
Directors: M. Stack (Co Sec)
Immediate Holding Company: LAMBOURNE AGRICULTURAL CONSULTANTS LIMITED
Registration no: 05358041 **Date established:** 2005
Turnover: Up to £250,000 **No.of Employees:** 1 - 10 **Product Groups:** 80, 84

Date of Accounts	Mar 11	Mar 10	Mar 09
Sales Turnover	28	43	39
Pre Tax Profit/Loss	-4	4	-2
Working Capital	2	5	N/A
Fixed Assets	N/A	N/A	1
Current Assets	3	10	7
Current Liabilities	1	5	3

Laser Lines Ltd
Beaumont Close, Banbury, OX16 1TH
Tel: 01295-672500 **Fax:** 01295-672550
E-mail: info@laserlines.co.uk
Website: http://www.laserlines.co.uk
Bank(s): National Westminster Bank Plc
Directors: M. Turner (Sales), R. Wilkin (MD), S. Hall (Fin)
Ultimate Holding Company: LASER LINES LIMITED
Immediate Holding Company: LASER LINES (UK) LIMITED
Registration no: 04021637 **VAT No.:** GB 284 5083 43
Date established: 2000 **Turnover:** £2m - £5m **No.of Employees:** 11 - 20
Product Groups: 37, 38, 42, 44, 45, 46, 47, 48

Date of Accounts	Jul 11	Jul 10	Jul 09
Working Capital	415	415	2m
Fixed Assets	N/A	N/A	35
Current Assets	415	415	3m

Lincoln Industrial Ltd
Unit 2 Canada Close, Banbury, OX16 2RT
Tel: 01295-256611 **Fax:** 01295-275771
E-mail: sales@lincolnindustrial.co.uk
Website: http://www.lincolnindustrial.com
Directors: H. Kannegiesser (MD)
Ultimate Holding Company: THE HARBOUR GROUP LIMITED
Immediate Holding Company: LINCOLN INDUSTRIAL LIMITED
Registration no: 03306746 **Date established:** 1997 **Turnover:** £1m - £2m
No.of Employees: 1 - 10 **Product Groups:** 40, 84

Date of Accounts	Dec 11	Dec 10	Dec 09
Sales Turnover	1m	1m	847
Pre Tax Profit/Loss	156	206	90
Working Capital	1m	934	784
Fixed Assets	N/A	1	2
Current Assets	1m	1m	914
Current Liabilities	77	92	73

The Little Green Agency
The Old Chapel Milcombe, Banbury, OX15 4RP
Tel: 01295-721701 **Fax:** 01295-721701
E-mail: mail@little-green-agency.com
Website: http://www.little-green-agency.com
Directors: P. De Noratti (Ptnr)
Date established: 2008 **No.of Employees:** 1 - 10 **Product Groups:** 81

Lloyds Commercial Finance Ltd
1 Brookhill Way, Banbury, OX16 3EL
Tel: 01295-272272 **Fax:** 01295-272246
E-mail: marketing@alexlawrie.com
Website: http://www.ltsbcf.co.uk
Bank(s): Lloyds TSB Bank plc
Directors: P. Saunders (Dir), S. Featherstone (MD), T. Ettershank (MD)
Managers: G. Hall (Mgr)
Ultimate Holding Company: Lloyds Banking Group plc
Immediate Holding Company: LLOYDS TSB COMMERCIAL FINANCE LIMITED
Registration no: 00733011 **Date established:** 1962
Turnover: £125m - £250m **No.of Employees:** 251 - 500
Product Groups: 82

Main Consultants Ltd
Bloxham Mill Barford Road, Bloxham, Banbury, OX15 4FF
Tel: 01295-724590 **Fax:** 01295-722801
E-mail: steve.hilling@mainconsultants.co.uk
Website: http://www.main-consultants.com
Directors: A. Hardiman (Fin), S. Hilling (MD)
Immediate Holding Company: MAIN CONSULTANTS LIMITED
Registration no: 03303801 **Date established:** 1997
Turnover: Up to £250,000 **No.of Employees:** 21 - 50 **Product Groups:** 88

Date of Accounts	Apr 11	Apr 10	Apr 09
Working Capital	-1	-1	-4
Fixed Assets	N/A	2	3
Current Assets	1	4	2
Current Liabilities	N/A	4	N/A

Matchett Group
Unit 1 Somerville Court Aynho Road, Adderbury, Banbury, OX17 3NS
Tel: 01295-814200 **Fax:** 01295-272108
E-mail: enquiries@matchettgroup.com
Website: http://www.matchettgroup.com
Directors: P. Thomas (MD)
Immediate Holding Company: ZONE FITTED FURNITURE LIMITED
Registration no: 01221570 **VAT No.:** GB 284 5988 94
Date established: 2011 **Turnover:** £2m - £5m **No.of Employees:** 1 - 10
Product Groups: 44, 86

Date of Accounts	Dec 11
Working Capital	61
Current Assets	164
Current Liabilities	97

Mettex Electrical Ltd
Beaumont Close, Banbury, OX16 1TG
Tel: 01295-250826 **Fax:** 01295-268643
E-mail: gill@mettex.com
Website: http://www.mettex.com
Bank(s): Barclays
Managers: G. Fearon (Mgr)
Registration no: 01138730 **VAT No.:** GB 200 3544 26
Date established: 1974 **Turnover:** £2m - £5m **No.of Employees:** 21 - 50
Product Groups: 35, 36, 37, 39, 67

Date of Accounts	Mar 08	Mar 07	Mar 06
Working Capital	645	587	354
Fixed Assets	1114	1172	1156
Current Assets	1270	1189	827
Current Liabilities	626	601	473
Total Share Capital	6	6	6

Morgan Sindall
2 Canalside House Tramway Road, Banbury, OX16 5RH
Tel: 01295-817950 **Fax:** 01295-817951
Website: http://www.bluestone.plc.uk
Managers: G. Lucas (Mgr)
Ultimate Holding Company: MORGAN SINDALL PLC
Immediate Holding Company: MORGAN ASHURST PLC
Registration no: 06327165 **Turnover:** £50m - £75m
No.of Employees: 21 - 50 **Product Groups:** 52, 80

Motoman Robotics UK Ltd
Unit 2 Johnson Park Wildmere Road, Banbury, OX16 3JU
Tel: 01295-272755 **Fax:** 01295-267127
E-mail: davewalsh@motoman.co.uk
Website: http://www.motoman.co.uk
Bank(s): S-E-Banken
Directors: D. Walsh (Sales), J. Dangelillo (MD), J. Jarhall (Co Sec)
Ultimate Holding Company: YASKAWA ELECTRIC CORP (JAPAN)
Immediate Holding Company: YASKAWA UK LIMITED
Registration no: 01475387 **Date established:** 1980 **Turnover:** £2m - £5m
No.of Employees: 21 - 50 **Product Groups:** 45, 46

Date of Accounts	Feb 12	Feb 11	Feb 10
Sales Turnover	N/A	5m	4m
Pre Tax Profit/Loss	N/A	206	9
Working Capital	999	995	852
Fixed Assets	61	43	39
Current Assets	4m	4m	3m
Current Liabilities	N/A	434	311

Moulding Investments Ltd
Cyroma House Beaumont Road, Banbury, OX16 1RJ
Tel: 01295-273775 **Fax:** 01684-560862
E-mail: stuart@wyvernmouldings.co.uk
Website: http://www.wyvernmouldings.co.uk
Directors: A. Grant (Fin), M. Falkingham (MD)
Immediate Holding Company: MOULDING INVESTMENTS LIMITED
Registration no: 04459605 **VAT No.:** GB 299 1620 26
Date established: 2002 **Turnover:** £250,000 - £500,000
No.of Employees: 1 - 10 **Product Groups:** 30, 66

Date of Accounts	Jun 11	Jun 10	Jun 09
Working Capital	202	183	72
Fixed Assets	130	149	168
Current Assets	232	237	130

Norbar Torque Tools Ltd
Beaumont Road, Banbury, OX16 1XJ
Tel: 01295-270333 **Fax:** 01295-753643
E-mail: enquiry@norbar.com
Website: http://www.norbar.com
Bank(s): HSBC Bank plc
Directors: C. Rohll (Comm), P. Brodey (Sales & Mktg), N. Brodey (MD), C. Brodey (Fin)
Managers: T. Marine (Tech Serv Mgr), W. Stewart-lee (Personnel), M. Houson (Purch Mgr)
Ultimate Holding Company: NORBAR TORQUE TOOLS HOLDINGS LIMITED
Immediate Holding Company: NORBAR TORQUE TOOLS LIMITED
Registration no: 00380480 **VAT No.:** GB 119 1060 05
Date established: 1943 **Turnover:** £20m - £50m
No.of Employees: 101 - 250 **Product Groups:** 36, 37, 38, 39, 40, 85

Date of Accounts	Dec 11	Dec 10	Dec 09
Sales Turnover	25m	21m	17m
Pre Tax Profit/Loss	2m	2m	735
Working Capital	7m	7m	6m
Fixed Assets	3m	3m	3m
Current Assets	12m	11m	8m
Current Liabilities	2m	2m	788

Otmoors Gunsmiths
Hudson Street Deddington, Banbury, OX15 0SW
Tel: 01869-338558
E-mail: otmoors@hotmail.co.uk
Website: http://www.otmoors.co.uk
Directors: G. Robottom (Prop)
Registration no: 03350344 **Date established:** 1997
No.of Employees: 1 - 10 **Product Groups:** 36, 39, 40

Payne Security Ltd
Wildmere Road, Banbury, OX16 3JU
Tel: 01295-265601 **Fax:** 01295-251109
E-mail: markpalmer@payne-worldwide.com
Website: http://www.payne-security.com
Bank(s): National Westminster
Directors: S. Jones (MD)
Managers: S. Jones (Personnel), L. Lewis (Buyer), P. Gill (Chief Mgr), M. Palmer (Mgr), P. James (Comptroller)
Ultimate Holding Company: ALEXANDER INDUSTRIAL SUPPLIES (ESSEX) LIMITED
Immediate Holding Company: PAYNE SECURITY LIMITED
Registration no: 03131037 **VAT No.:** GB 536 5132 55
Date established: 1995 **Turnover:** £5m - £10m
No.of Employees: 51 - 100 **Product Groups:** 30, 40, 42, 44

Date of Accounts	May 11	May 10	May 09
Sales Turnover	7m	7m	7m
Pre Tax Profit/Loss	393	547	53
Working Capital	4m	3m	3m
Fixed Assets	2m	3m	3m
Current Assets	5m	4m	4m
Current Liabilities	668	586	437

Penguin Swimming Pools Ltd
5a Thorpe Close, Banbury, OX16 4SW
Tel: 01295-269091 **Fax:** 01295-266881
E-mail: mail@penguinpools.co.uk
Website: http://www.penguinpools.co.uk
Bank(s): Lloyds, Bovey Tracey, Devon
Directors: G. Davis (Dir)
Immediate Holding Company: PENGUIN SWIMMING POOLS LIMITED
Registration no: 02755674 **VAT No.:** GB 585 7815 85
Date established: 1992 **Turnover:** £1m - £2m **No.of Employees:** 21 - 50
Product Groups: 52

Date of Accounts	Dec 11	Dec 10	Dec 09
Working Capital	309	337	242
Fixed Assets	88	65	47
Current Assets	1m	1m	1m

Permanent Shuttering Systems Ltd
Stonewold House Upper Tadmarton, Banbury, OX15 5SG
Tel: 01295-788699 **Fax:** 0560-152 9429
E-mail: info_pss@btconnect.com
Website: http://www.shutteringsystems.com
Managers: R. Vurnell (Mgr)
Immediate Holding Company: PERMANENT SHUTTERING SYSTEMS LIMITED
Registration no: 02796755 **VAT No.:** GB 660 9254 28
Date established: 1993 **Turnover:** £500,000 - £1m
No.of Employees: 1 - 10 **Product Groups:** 33, 52

Date of Accounts	Apr 11	Apr 10	Apr 09
Working Capital	-6	-9	-3
Fixed Assets	2	2	3
Current Assets	38	34	31

Plymovent Limited
Beaumont House Beaumont Road, Banbury, OX16 1RH
Tel: 01295-259311 **Fax:** 01295-271750
E-mail: info@plymovent.co.uk
Website: http://www.plymovent.co.uk
Directors: T. Ashall (MD)
Managers: B. Darvell (Purch Mgr), D. Juhlin
Registration no: 01405906 **VAT No.:** GB 294 3808 28
Turnover: £2m - £5m **No.of Employees:** 1 - 10 **Product Groups:** 29, 30, 40, 42, 46, 52, 54, 66, 68

Date of Accounts	Dec 10	Dec 09	Dec 08
Sales Turnover	1m	982	1m
Pre Tax Profit/Loss	41	146	-88
Working Capital	476	513	275
Fixed Assets	1	4	9
Current Assets	644	688	450
Current Liabilities	100	103	98

Security & Protection Agency Ltd
Mercia House 51 South Bar Street, Banbury, OX16 9AB
Tel: 08456-431811 **Fax:** 01295-201209
E-mail: info@security-protection-agency.com
Website: http://www.security-protection-agency.com
Directors: T. Butt (Prop), L. O'Neill (Fin)
Immediate Holding Company: SECURITY AND PROTECTION AGENCY LIMITED
Registration no: 06533449 **Date established:** 2008
Turnover: Up to £250,000 **No.of Employees:** 1 - 10 **Product Groups:** 80, 81

Date of Accounts	Apr 11	Apr 10	Apr 09
Sales Turnover	N/A	N/A	15
Pre Tax Profit/Loss	N/A	N/A	-20
Working Capital	-1	-2	-21
Fixed Assets	1	1	N/A
Current Assets	2	4	15
Current Liabilities	N/A	N/A	36

Selecto Part UK Ltd
Top Farm House Shenington, Banbury, OX15 6LZ
Tel: 01295-670734 **Fax:** 01295-678170
E-mail: info@selecto-part.co.uk
Website: http://www.selecto-part.co.uk
Directors: M. Coles (Fin), R. Coles (MD)
Immediate Holding Company: SELECTO-PART UK LIMITED
Registration no: 03556846 **VAT No.:** GB 704 9895 00
Date established: 1998 **No.of Employees:** 1 - 10 **Product Groups:** 30

Date of Accounts	May 10	May 05
Sales Turnover	4	N/A
Pre Tax Profit/Loss	1	N/A
Working Capital	N/A	1
Current Assets	4	11
Current Liabilities	4	N/A

Sensor Technology Ltd
Apollo Park Ironstone Lane, Wroxton, Banbury, OX15 6AY
Tel: 01869-238400 **Fax:** 01869-238401
E-mail: info@sensors.co.uk
Website: http://www.sensors.co.uk
Managers: M. Ingham (Sales Eng)
Immediate Holding Company: SENSOR TECHNOLOGY LIMITED
Registration no: 01242171 **VAT No.:** GB 294 0460 57
Date established: 1976 **Turnover:** £500,000 - £1m
No.of Employees: 1 - 10 **Product Groups:** 37, 38, 85

Date of Accounts	Mar 12	Mar 11	Mar 10
Working Capital	-2m	-2m	-642
Fixed Assets	2	3	6
Current Assets	178	182	228

Seton (Brady Corporation Ltd)
14 Wildmere Road Wildmere Industrial Estate, Banbury, OX16 3JU
Tel: 0800-585501 **Fax:** 01295- 268233
E-mail: info@seton.co.uk
Website: http://www.seton.co.uk
Managers: M. Waite
Ultimate Holding Company: HELLA KGAA HUECK & CO (GERMANY)
Immediate Holding Company: VACS LTD.
Registration no: 04190853 **VAT No.:** GB 408 6174 51
Date established: 1997 **Turnover:** £5m - £10m **No.of Employees:** 1 - 10
Product Groups: 24, 30, 33, 36, 37, 38, 40, 45, 49, 51, 63, 67, 68, 80, 83, 84, 85

Date of Accounts	May 11	May 10	May 09
Sales Turnover	7m	7m	7m
Pre Tax Profit/Loss	393	547	53
Working Capital	4m	3m	3m
Fixed Assets	2m	3m	3m
Current Assets	5m	4m	4m
Current Liabilities	668	586	437

Snowcard Insurance Services Ltd
Long Barn 1st Floor Office Appletree Road, Chipping Warden, Banbury, OX17 1LH
Tel: 01295-660836 **Fax:** 01327-263227
E-mail: enquiries@snowcard.co.uk
Website: http://www.snowcard.co.uk
Directors: R. Dadson (Dir)
Immediate Holding Company: SNOWCARD INSURANCE SERVICES LIMITED
Registration no: 02491373 **Date established:** 1990
No.of Employees: 1 - 10 **Product Groups:** 82

Date of Accounts	Apr 12	Apr 11	Apr 10
Working Capital	N/A	-11	5
Fixed Assets	60	74	53
Current Assets	77	71	91

Stabilus
Unit 4 Canada Close, Banbury, OX16 2RT
Tel: 01295-700100 **Fax:** 01295-700106
E-mail: info@uk.stabilus.com
Website: http://www.stabilus.com
Managers: B. Ayliff (Chief Mgr)
Ultimate Holding Company: STAB DEVELOPMENT SARL (LUXEMBOURG)
Immediate Holding Company: STABILUS LIMITED
Registration no: 02269075 **Date established:** 1988
Turnover: £500,000 - £1m **No.of Employees:** 1 - 10 **Product Groups:** 35, 39, 40, 66

Date of Accounts	Sep 11	Sep 10	Sep 09
Sales Turnover	996	766	501
Pre Tax Profit/Loss	546	271	140

see next page

***Stabilus** - Cont'd*

Working Capital	11m	11m	11m
Fixed Assets	N/A	N/A	3
Current Assets	11m	11m	11m
Current Liabilities	146	130	89

Swan Foundry Banbury Ltd
Swan Close Road, Banbury, OX16 5AL
Tel: 01295-263134 **Fax:** 01295-270461
E-mail: info@swangroup.co.uk
Website: http://www.swangroup.co.uk
Bank(s): National Westminster Bank
Directors: M. Phillips (MD)
Managers: L. Remmer (Personnel)
Immediate Holding Company: SWAN FOUNDRY (BANBURY) LIMITED
Registration no: 00430927 **Date established:** 1947 **Turnover:** £2m - £5m
No.of Employees: 21 - 50 **Product Groups:** 34

Date of Accounts	Jul 11	Jul 10	Jul 09
Working Capital	-77	-170	-202
Fixed Assets	421	482	546
Current Assets	1m	900	915

Swan Generators Ltd
Unit 6 Thorpe Close, Banbury, OX16 4SW
Tel: 01295-261601 **Fax:** 01295-271352
E-mail: standby@swangenerators.co.uk
Website: http://www.swangenerators.co.uk
Directors: S. Arthur (Co Sec)
Immediate Holding Company: SWAN GENERATORS LIMITED
Registration no: 03344577 **VAT No.:** GB 688 0346 06
Date established: 1997 **Turnover:** £1m - £2m **No.of Employees:** 1 - 10
Product Groups: 37, 48, 52, 83

Date of Accounts	Mar 11	Mar 10	Mar 09
Working Capital	713	764	742
Fixed Assets	37	22	27
Current Assets	1m	993	1m

Tepco Engineering International
13 Overfield Thorpe Way, Banbury, OX16 4XR
Tel: 01295-264200 **Fax:** 01295-264901
E-mail: sales@tepcoengineering.co.uk
Website: http://www.tepcoengineering.co.uk
Directors: J. Stead (Dir), J. Stead (Prop)
Managers: M. Jones (Comm)
Immediate Holding Company: TEPCO ENGINEERING (INTERNATIONAL) LIMITED
Registration no: 05865634 **Date established:** 2006
Turnover: £250,000 - £500,000 **No.of Employees:** 1 - 10
Product Groups: 30, 34, 35, 36, 66

Date of Accounts	Jun 11	Jun 10	Jun 09
Working Capital	-6	5	N/A
Fixed Assets	N/A	1	2
Current Assets	33	47	74
Current Liabilities	N/A	N/A	57

Thames Valley Catering Equipment
11 Strawberry Hill Bloxham, Banbury, OX15 4NW
Tel: 01295-722250 **Fax:** 01295-721126
E-mail: info@thamesvalleycatering.co.uk
Website: http://www.thamesvalleycatering.co.uk
Directors: S. Wratten (MD)
No.of Employees: 1 - 10 **Product Groups:** 20, 40, 41

The Ashcroft Clinic
Hudson Street Deddington, Banbury, OX15 0SW
Tel: 01869-338854 **Fax:** 01869-338854
E-mail: mail@ashcroftclinic.com
Website: http://www.ashcroftclinic.com
Directors: R. Stovell (Prop)
Registration no: 03350344 **VAT No.:** GB 336 0794 50
Date established: 1997 **Turnover:** Up to £250,000
No.of Employees: 1 - 10 **Product Groups:** 38

The Bin Company
Bloxham Business Centre Barford Road, Bloxham, Banbury, OX15 4FF
Tel: 08456-023630 **Fax:** 01494-441166
E-mail: info@thebincompany.com
Website: http://www.thebincompany.com
Directors: S. Albon (MD)
Immediate Holding Company: REMOTE-LEARNER UK LIMITED
Registration no: 04593968 **Date established:** 2011
No.of Employees: 1 - 10 **Product Groups:** 38, 42

Date of Accounts	Nov 10	Nov 09	Nov 08
Working Capital	174	153	136
Fixed Assets	25	6	8
Current Assets	243	203	198

The Enormous Handkerchief Co.
Canada Close, Banbury, OX16 2RT
Tel: 01295-702481 **Fax:** 01295-702499
E-mail: info@presentsformen.com
Website: http://www.enormoushandkerchief.co.uk
Directors: J. Hudson (Ptnr)
Ultimate Holding Company: VESCOM GROEP B V (NETHERLANDS)
Immediate Holding Company: ROYCE LINGERIE LIMITED
Date established: 1991 **No.of Employees:** 1 - 10 **Product Groups:** 24

Date of Accounts	Dec 11	Dec 10	Dec 09
Working Capital	70	-64	-65
Current Assets	734	733	456

Toby Electronics Ltd
Beaumont Road, Banbury, OX16 1TU
Tel: 01295-271777 **Fax:** 01295-271744
E-mail: info@toby.co.uk
Website: http://www.toby.co.uk
Bank(s): Yorkshire Bank
Directors: B. Molyneux (Fin), J. Portlock (Sales), T. Portlock (MD)
Managers: P. Donnelly (Purch Mgr)
Immediate Holding Company: TOBY ELECTRONICS LIMITED
Registration no: 01713516 **VAT No.:** GB 387 5522 17
Date established: 1983 **Turnover:** £5m - £10m **No.of Employees:** 21 - 50
Product Groups: 37, 44, 47

Date of Accounts	Mar 11	Mar 10	Mar 09
Sales Turnover	7m	5m	6m
Pre Tax Profit/Loss	444	227	536
Working Capital	1m	2m	1m
Fixed Assets	1m	1m	1m
Current Assets	3m	2m	2m
Current Liabilities	412	245	299

Tomita UK Ltd
Fortway House, Banbury, OX16 4SP
Tel: 01295-277317 **Fax:** 01295-278889
E-mail: sales@tomita.co.uk
Website: http://www.tomita.co.uk
Directors: K. Tomita (Dir)
Immediate Holding Company: TOMITA U.K. LIMITED
Registration no: 02575058 **Date established:** 1991 **Turnover:** £2m - £5m
No.of Employees: 1 - 10 **Product Groups:** 29, 30

Date of Accounts	Dec 11	Dec 10	Dec 09
Sales Turnover	3m	3m	4m
Pre Tax Profit/Loss	-96	45	-262
Working Capital	421	517	465
Fixed Assets	6	8	15
Current Assets	941	1m	805
Current Liabilities	68	34	47

Tradewinds UK Ltd
2 Lombard Way, Banbury, OX16 4TD
Tel: 01295-278866 **Fax:** 01295-278855
E-mail: richard.fairhurst@tradewindsworldwide.co.uk
Website: http://www.tradewindsworldwide.co.uk
Bank(s): HSBC Bank plc
Directors: A. Paul (MD), A. Poole (Fin), R. Brower (Sales), R. Fairhurst (Dir)
Managers: S. Jelfs (Accounts)
Immediate Holding Company: TRADEWINDS WORLDWIDE LIMITED
Registration no: 01487838 **VAT No.:** GB 436 7480 30
Date established: 1980 **Turnover:** £5m - £10m **No.of Employees:** 11 - 20
Product Groups: 29, 68

Treadplates Carpet Fitting Accessories
Unit 3-4 Brailes Industrial Estate Winderton Road, Lower Brailes, Banbury, OX15 5JW
Tel: 01608-685414 **Fax:** 01608-685665
E-mail: sales@treadplates.co.uk
Website: http://www.treadplates.co.uk
Directors: S. Edwards (Prop)
Immediate Holding Company: TREADPLATES LIMITED
Registration no: 08073272 **Date established:** 2012
No.of Employees: 1 - 10 **Product Groups:** 35, 36

Tube & Bracket Co. Ltd
8 Canada Close, Banbury, OX16 2RT
Tel: 01295-277791 **Fax:** 01295-268654
E-mail: sales@tubeandbracket.com
Website: http://www.tubeandbracket.com
Directors: N. Tyler (MD)
No.of Employees: 11 - 20 **Product Groups:** 26, 45, 47

Uniform Express Ltd
Unit 5 Haslemere Way, Banbury, OX16 5TY
Tel: 01295-709774 **Fax:** 01295-701724
E-mail: sales@uniformexpress.co.uk
Website: http://www.uniformexpress.co.uk
Bank(s): Barclays
Directors: K. Dodd (Fin), A. Beavis (Sales), D. McPherson (Prop)
Immediate Holding Company: UNIFORM EXPRESS LIMITED
Registration no: 05117913 **VAT No.:** 421 6898 37 **Date established:** 2004
Turnover: £2m - £5m **No.of Employees:** 21 - 50 **Product Groups:** 24

Date of Accounts	Dec 11	Dec 10	Dec 09
Working Capital	2m	518	500
Fixed Assets	133	181	164
Current Assets	3m	2m	2m

Wagner Spraytech
2 Main Road Middleton Cheney, Banbury, OX17 2ND
Tel: 01295-714200 **Fax:** 01295-710100
E-mail: enquiries@wagnerspraytech.co.uk
Website: http://www.wagner-group.com
Managers: I. Pocock (Cust Serv Mgr)
Ultimate Holding Company: Wagner International AG (CHE)
Immediate Holding Company: WAGNER SPRAYTECH (UK) LIMITED
Registration no: 01390423 **VAT No.:** GB 306 1313 11
Date established: 1978 **Turnover:** £2m - £5m **No.of Employees:** 1 - 10
Product Groups: 40, 42, 46, 48, 67

Date of Accounts	Jan 12	Jan 11	Jan 10
Working Capital	121	74	49
Fixed Assets	17	25	34
Current Assets	250	189	118

Weatherwise Canopies & Covers
Thorpe Lane, Banbury, OX16 4UT
Tel: 01295-253097 **Fax:** 01295-253097
E-mail: weatherwise@fsbdial.co.uk
Directors: E. Woodruff (Snr Part)
Managers: S. Woodruff (Mgr), S. Woodruff (Sales Admin)
Immediate Holding Company: PETER HAINES ENGINEERS LIMITED
Registration no: 04396162 **VAT No.:** 121 0923 21 **Date established:** 2002
Turnover: £250,000 - £500,000 **No.of Employees:** 1 - 10
Product Groups: 45

Date of Accounts	Apr 11	Apr 10	Apr 09
Working Capital	435	351	374
Fixed Assets	421	324	335
Current Assets	939	807	704

Webs Ltd
Ashborne House Waterperry Court Middleton Road, Banbury, OX16 4QG
Tel: 01295-277272 **Fax:** 01295-264070
E-mail: enquiries@websint.com
Website: http://www.websint.com
Directors: F. Saunders (MD), S. Pickin (Tech Serv)
Managers: M. Gibbs (Sales Admin)
Immediate Holding Company: WEBS LIMITED
Registration no: 03267938 **Date established:** 1996
Turnover: £500,000 - £1m **No.of Employees:** 1 - 10 **Product Groups:** 38, 42, 54, 84, 85

Date of Accounts	Dec 10	Dec 09	Dec 08
Working Capital	37	55	123
Fixed Assets	14	12	7
Current Assets	82	132	217

C Young Wrappings Ltd
The Chalet Main Road, Broughton, Banbury, OX15 5DZ
Tel: 01295-262186 **Fax:** 01295-262186
Directors: C. Bate (Dir), L. Bate (Fin)
Immediate Holding Company: C. YOUNG (WRAPPINGS) LIMITED
Registration no: 01209633 **Date established:** 1975
No.of Employees: 1 - 10 **Product Groups:** 38, 42

Date of Accounts	May 12	May 11	May 10
Working Capital	6	10	18
Fixed Assets	2	2	2
Current Assets	164	146	170

Bicester

A C G Labels
Hall Farm Main Street, Fringford, Bicester, OX27 8DP
Tel: 01869-277059 **Fax:** 01869-277060
Website: http://www.acglabels.co.uk
Directors: A. Thomas (Prop)
Immediate Holding Company: I & H THOMAS LIMITED
Registration no: 02548498 **Date established:** 1990
Turnover: Up to £250,000 **No.of Employees:** 1 - 10 **Product Groups:** 27, 30, 35, 49

Abac Air Compressors
Unit 11 Granville Way, Bicester, OX26 4JT
Tel: 01869-326226 **Fax:** 01869-326216
E-mail: enquiries@abac.co.uk
Website: http://www.abac.co.uk
Bank(s): Barclays, City Branch
Directors: M. Palici (MD)
Managers: V. Blower (Mgr)
Ultimate Holding Company: ATLAS COPCO AB (SWEDEN)
Immediate Holding Company: ABAC (UK) LIMITED
Registration no: 02592182 **Date established:** 1991 **Turnover:** £2m - £5m
No.of Employees: 11 - 20 **Product Groups:** 31, 38, 40, 42, 48, 67, 68, 83

Date of Accounts	Dec 09	Dec 08	Dec 07
Sales Turnover	5m	6m	6m
Pre Tax Profit/Loss	30	182	56
Working Capital	629	407	453
Fixed Assets	917	953	1m
Current Assets	2m	2m	3m
Current Liabilities	215	356	393

Air Control Associates
Unit D3a Telford Road, Bicester, OX26 4LD
Tel: 0845-8801959 **Fax:** 01869-321704
E-mail: joe@acaltd.co.uk
Website: http://www.acaltd.com
Product Groups: 26, 30, 33, 35, 37, 38, 40, 42, 44, 52, 66, 80, 83, 84, 86, 87

Date of Accounts	Dec 99	Dec 98	Dec 97
Working Capital	48	14	-6
Fixed Assets	7	13	28
Current Assets	214	170	130
Current Liabilities	167	157	135

Andura Coatings Ltd
20 Murdock Road, Bicester, OX26 4PP
Tel: 01869-240374 **Fax:** 01869-240375
E-mail: info@andura.co.uk
Website: http://www.andura.com
Directors: R. Mckillop (Fin)
Ultimate Holding Company: BAY-BAL UK LIMITED
Immediate Holding Company: BAY-BAL SPECIALIST COATING LIMITED
Registration no: 01939457 **VAT No.:** GB 623 7640 43
Date established: 1985 **Turnover:** £1m - £2m **No.of Employees:** 11 - 20
Product Groups: 30, 32

Date of Accounts	Mar 11	Mar 10	Mar 09
Working Capital	170	77	244
Fixed Assets	62	95	89
Current Assets	548	512	619

Aston Windows Europe Ltd
Unit 2 Lakeside Farm Middle Aston, Bicester, OX25 5PP
Tel: 01869-347241 **Fax:** 01869-347777
E-mail: sales@astonwindows.com
Website: http://www.astonwindows.com
Directors: J. America (MD)
Immediate Holding Company: ASTON WINDOWS LIMITED
Registration no: 04796639 **Date established:** 2003
No.of Employees: 1 - 10 **Product Groups:** 26, 35

Atlas M T S Ltd
Unit 9 Granville Way, Bicester, OX26 4JT
Tel: 01869-365440 **Fax:** 01869-354765
E-mail: chris.hazelby@ametek.com
Website: http://www.atlas-mts.com
Directors: C. Hazelby (MD), P. Gibbon (MD)
Immediate Holding Company: SIDALLS BICESTER LIMITED
Date established: 1982 **No.of Employees:** 1 - 10 **Product Groups:** 38, 67, 85

Date of Accounts	Mar 08	Mar 07	Mar 05
Sales Turnover	N/A	N/A	72
Pre Tax Profit/Loss	N/A	N/A	-20
Working Capital	-74	-2	-60
Fixed Assets	82	53	4
Current Assets	17	22	N/A
Current Liabilities	N/A	N/A	4

Beans Skiing Equipment
86 Sheep Street, Bicester, OX26 6LP
Tel: 01869-246451 **Fax:** 01869-240412
E-mail: info@beansonline.co.uk
Website: http://www.beansonline.co.uk
Directors: C. Bean (Prop)
Immediate Holding Company: KELMAC LIMITED
Registration no: 02893226 **Date established:** 1994
No.of Employees: 1 - 10 **Product Groups:** 22, 24, 35, 40, 49, 61, 65

Brand Protect Ltd
Stonecroft Chambers Somerton Road, Ardley, Bicester, OX27 7PF
Tel: 01869-346160 **Fax:** 01869-346148
E-mail: advice@bptm.co.uk
Website: http://www.bptm.co.uk
Directors: B. Whyatt (Ptnr)
Immediate Holding Company: BRAND PROTECT LIMITED
Registration no: 07151387 **Date established:** 2010
No.of Employees: 1 - 10 **Product Groups:** 80

Date of Accounts	Nov 11	Nov 10
Working Capital	-42	46
Fixed Assets	116	2

Current Assets	155	192

Brita Water Filter Systems Ltd

Brita House Granville Way, Bicester, OX26 4JT
Tel: 01932-770599 **Fax:** 0870-487 0999
E-mail: professional@brita.co.uk
Website: http://www.brita.co.uk
Managers: A. Gilbert (Mktg Serv Mgr), D. Banfield (Sales Prom Mgr)
Ultimate Holding Company: Brita Wasser-Filter-Systeme GmbH (Germany)
Immediate Holding Company: BRITA WATER FILTER SYSTEMS LIMITED
Registration no: 02700375 **Date established:** 1992
Turnover: £20m - £50m **No.of Employees:** 1 - 10 **Product Groups:** 41

Date of Accounts	Dec 09	Dec 08	Dec 07
Sales Turnover	38m	38m	38m
Pre Tax Profit/Loss	2m	2m	1m
Working Capital	7m	6m	5m
Fixed Assets	6m	6m	6m
Current Assets	16m	16m	15m
Current Liabilities	6m	6m	5m

Calpeda Ltd

8 Wedgwood Road Industrial Estate, Bicester, OX26 4UL
Tel: 01869-241441 **Fax:** 01869-240681
E-mail: pumps@calpeda.co.uk
Website: http://www.calpeda.co.uk
Bank(s): Barclays
Directors: K. Hall (MD), D. White (Fin)
Ultimate Holding Company: CALPEDA SPA (ITALY)
Immediate Holding Company: CALPEDA LIMITED
Registration no: 01568643 **Date established:** 1981 **Turnover:** £1m - £2m
No.of Employees: 11 - 20 **Product Groups:** 39, 40, 45, 46

Date of Accounts	Dec 11	Dec 10	Dec 09
Working Capital	2m	1m	1m
Fixed Assets	571	653	693
Current Assets	2m	2m	2m

Capita

Unit E7-E10 Telford Road, Bicester, OX26 4UP
Tel: 01869-245711 **Fax:** 01869-240982
E-mail: diane.aloia@capita.co.uk
Website: http://www.capita-tds.co.uk
Bank(s): Lloyds TSB Bank plc
Directors: D. Aloia (Dir)
Managers: G. Christopides (Fin Mgr)
Ultimate Holding Company: BELL AND HOWELL CHICAGO
Immediate Holding Company: BELL AND HOWELL LTD
Registration no: 00702043 **VAT No.:** GB 199 1334 35
Turnover: £2m - £5m **No.of Employees:** 51 - 100 **Product Groups:** 27, 38

Cherwell Laboratories Ltd

7-8 Launton Business Centre Murdock Road, Bicester, OX26 4XB
Tel: 01869-355500 **Fax:** 01869-355545
E-mail: karen.munson@cherwell-labs.co.uk
Website: http://www.cherwell-labs.co.uk
Bank(s): Bank of Scotland
Directors: L. Whittard (Ch), A. Whittard (MD)
Managers: A. Whittard
Registration no: 01159518 **VAT No.:** GB 121 6903 94
Date established: 1974 **Turnover:** £2m - £5m **No.of Employees:** 51 - 100
Product Groups: 31, 38, 42

Date of Accounts	Feb 12	Feb 11	Feb 10
Sales Turnover	4m	3m	3m
Pre Tax Profit/Loss	352	311	272
Working Capital	801	708	476
Fixed Assets	591	405	321
Current Assets	2m	1m	1m
Current Liabilities	157	141	194

Chiltern Invadex Ltd

126 Churchill Road, Bicester, OX26 4XD
Tel: 01869-363100 **Fax:** 01869-365588
E-mail: sales@chilterninvadex.co.uk
Website: http://www.chilterninvadex.co.uk
Directors: M. Benyon (Prop)
Managers: N. Holland (Purch Mgr), J. Barnes
Immediate Holding Company: CHILTERN INVADEX LIMITED
Registration no: 06050608 **Date established:** 2007
No.of Employees: 21 - 50 **Product Groups:** 38, 66, 67

Date of Accounts	Feb 08
Pre Tax Profit/Loss	87
Working Capital	-1m
Fixed Assets	2m
Current Assets	3m
Current Liabilities	2m

Coating Consultant

31 Churchill Road, Bicester, OX26 4TR
Tel: 01869-327577 **Fax:** 01869-327577
E-mail: info@coatingconsultant.co.uk
Website: http://www.coatingconsultant.co.uk
Directors: B. Blue (Prop)
Date established: 1995 **No.of Employees:** 1 - 10 **Product Groups:** 46, 48

E P Barrus

Granville Way, Bicester, OX26 4UR
Tel: 01869-363636 **Fax:** 01869-363660
E-mail: robert.muir@barrus.co.uk
Website: http://www.barrus.co.uk
Bank(s): Barclays, Bicester
Directors: T. Glen (Fin), R. Muir (MD)
Managers: A. Walden (Personnel), K. Clarke (Mktg Serv Mgr), D. Cosland, D. Hansford (Tech Serv Mgr)
Ultimate Holding Company: E. P. B. HOLDINGS LIMITED
Immediate Holding Company: E. P. B. HOLDINGS LIMITED
Registration no: 03398788 **Date established:** 1997
Turnover: £20m - £50m **No.of Employees:** 101 - 250
Product Groups: 29, 37, 40, 41

Date of Accounts	Sep 11	Sep 10	Sep 09
Sales Turnover	39m	39m	35m
Pre Tax Profit/Loss	775	389	686
Working Capital	8m	7m	7m
Fixed Assets	3m	3m	3m
Current Assets	18m	17m	15m
Current Liabilities	4m	3m	3m

Fineapply Water Treatment Equipment

77 Heyford Park Camp Road, Upper Heyford, Bicester, OX25 5HD
Tel: 01869-238070 **Fax:** 01869-238071
E-mail: robertgnicoll@aol.com
Website: http://www.fineapply.co.uk
Directors: R. Nicoll (Co Sec)
Managers: C. Wiles (I.T. Exec)
Ultimate Holding Company: ZETA COMPLIANCE GROUP PLC
Immediate Holding Company: ZETA COMPLIANCE SERVICES LIMITED
Registration no: 03351062 **Date established:** 1997 **Turnover:** £2m - £5m
No.of Employees: 1 - 10 **Product Groups:** 84

Date of Accounts	May 11	May 10	May 09
Working Capital	535	407	384
Fixed Assets	145	143	145
Current Assets	571	511	485

Golden River Traffic Ltd

Unit A4 Telford Road, Bicester, OX26 4LD
Tel: 01869-362800 **Fax:** 01869-246858
E-mail: sales@goldenriver.com
Website: http://www.goldenriver.com
Bank(s): Barclays
Directors: I. Wood Smith (Dir), N. Lanigan (MD)
Ultimate Holding Company: CLEARVIEW TRAFFIC GROUP LIMITED
Immediate Holding Company: GOLDEN RIVER LIMITED
Registration no: 01187716 **Date established:** 1974 **Turnover:** £5m - £10m
No.of Employees: 21 - 50 **Product Groups:** 38, 39, 44

Date of Accounts	Mar 11	Mar 10	Mar 09
Working Capital	1	649	649
Current Assets	1	650	650
Current Liabilities	N/A	1	1

Huber+Suhner (UK) Ltd

Telford Road, Bicester, OX26 4LA
Tel: 01869-364100 **Fax:** 01869-249046
E-mail: info.uk@hubersuhner.co.uk
Website: http://www.hubersuhner.co.uk
Bank(s): Lloyds TSB Bank plc
Directors: A. Thomas (Dir), H. Magnay (Mkt Research), M. Frizzell (Fin), P. Harris (MD)
Ultimate Holding Company: HUBER AND SUHNER AG (SWITZERLAND)
Immediate Holding Company: Huber & Suhner AG (CHE)
Registration no: 00902205 **VAT No.:** GB 233 5713 77
Date established: 1995 **Turnover:** £20m - £50m
No.of Employees: 101 - 250 **Product Groups:** 30, 35, 37, 38

Date of Accounts	Dec 09	Dec 08	Dec 07
Sales Turnover	21m	17m	15m
Pre Tax Profit/Loss	3m	2m	984
Working Capital	6m	4m	5m
Fixed Assets	2m	2m	2m
Current Assets	9m	8m	7m
Current Liabilities	2m	1m	989

Ice Cool Services Ltd

B9 Telford Road, Bicester, OX26 4LD
Tel: 01869-247947 **Fax:** 01869-253368
E-mail: sales@icecoolservices.com
Website: http://www.icecoolservices.com
Directors: B. Gough (Dir), B. Jennings (Sales)
Immediate Holding Company: ICE COOL SERVICES LIMITED
Registration no: 01354447 **Date established:** 1978 **Turnover:** £1m - £2m
No.of Employees: 21 - 50 **Product Groups:** 40, 67

Date of Accounts	Mar 11	Mar 10	Mar 09
Working Capital	537	504	476
Fixed Assets	118	109	118
Current Assets	1m	1m	1m

J H Chandeliers

8 Lerwick Croft, Bicester, OX26 4XL
Tel: 01869-240101 **Fax:** 01869-240101
Directors: J. Hall (Prop)
No.of Employees: 1 - 10 **Product Groups:** 37, 67

J N J Electronics

The Garth Launton Road, Bicester, OX26 6PS
Tel: 01869-323327 **Fax:** 01869-323328
E-mail: mail@jnjelectronics.co.uk
Website: http://www.jnjelectronics.co.uk
Directors: J. Redgard (Dir)
Immediate Holding Company: JNJ ELECTRONICS LIMITED
Registration no: 04979976 **Date established:** 2003
No.of Employees: 1 - 10 **Product Groups:** 34, 38, 67

Date of Accounts	Nov 11	Nov 10	Nov 08
Working Capital	1	1	5
Current Assets	8	13	56

Knife Wizard

A2 Murdock Road, Bicester, OX26 4PP
Tel: 01869-357700 **Fax:** 01869-357758
E-mail: enquiries@knifewizard.co.uk
Website: http://www.knifewizard.co.uk
Directors: C. Woodcock (Prop)
Immediate Holding Company: KNIFE WIZARD LIMITED
Registration no: 04438040 **Date established:** 2002
No.of Employees: 1 - 10 **Product Groups:** 36, 41, 67

Date of Accounts	May 11	May 10	May 09
Working Capital	66	93	57
Fixed Assets	9	8	8
Current Assets	151	179	125

M W Video Systems Ltd

64 North Street Fritwell, Bicester, OX27 7QR
Tel: 01869-345222 **Fax:** 01869-346002
E-mail: sales@mwvideo.com
Website: http://www.mwvideo.com
Directors: E. Glassey (MD)
Immediate Holding Company: M W VIDEO SYSTEMS LIMITED
Registration no: 01468924 **Date established:** 1979 **Turnover:** £1m - £2m
No.of Employees: 1 - 10 **Product Groups:** 37, 44

Date of Accounts	Dec 10	Dec 09	Dec 08
Working Capital	67	42	53
Fixed Assets	5	6	6
Current Assets	280	203	206

Middle Aston House Ltd

Middle Aston, Bicester, OX25 5PT
Tel: 01869-340361 **Fax:** 01869-340659
E-mail: training@pera.com
Website: http://www.middleastonhouse.co.uk
Directors: A. Smith (Dir)
Ultimate Holding Company: PERA INTERNATIONAL
Immediate Holding Company: MIDDLE ASTON HOUSE LIMITED
Registration no: 02507306 **Date established:** 1990 **Turnover:** £1m - £2m
No.of Employees: 21 - 50 **Product Groups:** 80, 86, 89

Date of Accounts	Dec 10	Dec 09	Dec 08
Sales Turnover	2m	1m	2m
Pre Tax Profit/Loss	237	115	355
Working Capital	1m	1m	910
Fixed Assets	3m	3m	3m
Current Assets	3m	3m	3m
Current Liabilities	87	66	97

Morley's

Arkwright Road, Bicester, OX26 4UU
Tel: 01869-320320 **Fax:** 01869-320312
E-mail: sales@morleys.co.uk
Website: http://www.morleys.co.uk
Directors: C. Gilbert (MD)
Ultimate Holding Company: MORLEYS STORES LIMITED
Immediate Holding Company: PRINCIPAL FURNITURE LTD.
Registration no: 00242437 **Date established:** 1995 **Turnover:** £5m - £10m
No.of Employees: 21 - 50 **Product Groups:** 26, 49, 67, 83

Nationwide Access Ltd

35 Heyford Park Camp Road, Upper Heyford, Bicester, OX25 5HD
Tel: 01869-233666 **Fax:** 01869-233999
E-mail: marketing@nationwideaccess.co.uk
Website: http://www.nationwideaccess.co.uk
Directors: H. Walters (Mkt Research)
Managers: D. Johnston (Mgr)
Ultimate Holding Company: Lavendon Group plc
Immediate Holding Company: Zooom Holdings UK Ltd
Registration no: 04405299 **Turnover:** £20m - £50m
No.of Employees: 1 - 10 **Product Groups:** 45, 83

The Oneida Shop

30 Pingle Drive, Bicester, OX26 6WD
Tel: 01869-324789 **Fax:** 01869-324789
Managers: N. Harland (Mgr)
Date established: 1995 **No.of Employees:** 1 - 10 **Product Groups:** 20, 40, 41

OPEN MIND Technologies UK Ltd

Unit 1-2 Telford Road, Bicester, OX26 4LD
Tel: 01869-290003 **Fax:** 01869-369429
E-mail: adrian.smith@openmind-tech.com
Website: http://www.openmind-tech.com
Directors: A. Smith (MD)
Immediate Holding Company: OPEN MIND TECHNOLOGIES UK LIMITED
Registration no: 03969959 **Date established:** 2000
No.of Employees: 1 - 10 **Product Groups:** 41, 42, 43, 67

Date of Accounts	Dec 11	Dec 10	Dec 09
Sales Turnover	1m	565	671
Pre Tax Profit/Loss	117	-62	9
Working Capital	-42	-150	-77
Fixed Assets	28	24	13
Current Assets	455	272	284
Current Liabilities	85	54	24

Oxford Preservation Services

20 Ashdene Road, Bicester, OX26 2BH
Tel: 01869-252423 **Fax:** 01869-327333
E-mail: michaelong@talk21.com
Website: http://www.oxfordpreservationservices.co.uk
Managers: M. Long (Mgr)
No.of Employees: 1 - 10 **Product Groups:** 14, 30, 32, 52

P A Turney Ltd

Middleton Stoney, Bicester, OX25 4AB
Tel: 01869-343333 **Fax:** 01869-343540
E-mail: maggie.benstead@paturney.com
Website: http://www.paturney.co.uk
Bank(s): National Westminster Bank Plc
Directors: N. Houghton (Fin), P. Turney (MD)
Managers: M. Grice, N. Barker (Grp Sales Mgr)
Immediate Holding Company: P.A.TURNEY LIMITED
Registration no: 00607154 **VAT No.:** GB 119 9110 73
Date established: 1958 **Turnover:** £20m - £50m
No.of Employees: 21 - 50 **Product Groups:** 67

Date of Accounts	Dec 11	Dec 10	Dec 09
Sales Turnover	27m	25m	23m
Pre Tax Profit/Loss	242	160	258
Working Capital	3m	2m	2m
Fixed Assets	2m	2m	2m
Current Assets	9m	7m	7m
Current Liabilities	813	1m	1m

P W Resistance Welding Products Ltd

Unit 10 Bicester Park Charbridge Way, Bicester, OX26 4SS
Tel: 01869-253688 **Fax:** 01869-240249
E-mail: sales@pwrwp.co.uk
Website: http://www.pwrwp.co.uk
Directors: C. Brent-Smith (Ch), I. Brent-Smith (MD), T. Renahan (Sales)
Managers: T. Renahan (Sales Prom Mgr), J. Mansfield (Purch Mgr), M. Webb (Sales Prom Mgr), W. Lewis (Fin Mgr)
Immediate Holding Company: PW RESISTANCE WELDING PRODUCTS LIMITED
Registration no: 01784726 **VAT No.:** GB 119 1148 88
Date established: 1984 **Turnover:** £1m - £2m **No.of Employees:** 1 - 10
Product Groups: 35, 37, 39, 45, 46, 67

Date of Accounts	Mar 10	Mar 09	Mar 08
Sales Turnover	N/A	1m	1m
Pre Tax Profit/Loss	N/A	5	44
Working Capital	68	70	61
Fixed Assets	34	29	34
Current Assets	394	490	547
Current Liabilities	N/A	N/A	29

Pallas Connections Ltd

Unit 1 Field Farm Business Centre Launton, Bicester, OX26 5EL
Tel: 01869-277053 **Fax:** 01869-277058
E-mail: hornby@pallasconnections.co.uk
Website: http://www.pallasconnections.co.uk
Directors: A. Hornby (Fin)
Immediate Holding Company: PALLAS CONNECTIONS LIMITED
Registration no: 02812892 **VAT No.:** GB 623 5707 47
Date established: 1993 **Turnover:** £250,000 - £500,000
No.of Employees: 1 - 10 **Product Groups:** 37

Date of Accounts	Apr 11	Apr 10	Apr 09
Working Capital	36	14	17
Fixed Assets	1	2	2
Current Assets	65	48	61

Powerfactor Ltd
8 Pear Tree Farm Townsend, Marsh Gibbon, Bicester, OX27 0EY
Tel: 01869-278585 **Fax:** 01869-278989
E-mail: sales@powerfactor.co.uk
Website: http://www.powerfactor.co.uk
Directors: D. Stonell (Dir), D. Stonell (Fin)
Immediate Holding Company: POWER FACTOR LIMITED
Registration no: 03179311 **VAT No.:** GB 663 4711 33
Date established: 1996 **No.of Employees:** 1 - 10 **Product Groups:** 37

Date of Accounts	Apr 11	Apr 10	Apr 09
Working Capital	-3	-7	-11
Fixed Assets	9	12	15
Current Assets	67	33	22

Prestige Industrial Pipework Equipment
Unit L10 Telford Road, Bicester, OX26 4LD
Tel: 01869-324424 **Fax:** 01869-323273
E-mail: sales@pipe-ltd.com
Website: http://www.pipe-ltd.com
Managers: K. Smith (Admin Off)
Immediate Holding Company: P.I.P.E. LIMITED
Registration no: 02710714 **VAT No.:** 536 5465 28 **Date established:** 1992
Turnover: £1m - £2m **No.of Employees:** 1 - 10 **Product Groups:** 29, 36, 37, 46

Date of Accounts	Mar 11	Mar 10	Mar 09
Working Capital	62	70	61
Fixed Assets	84	55	24
Current Assets	697	616	696

Quadraco Ltd
C1 Telford Road, Bicester, OX26 4LD
Tel: 01869-608708 **Fax:** 01869-608789
E-mail: brian.tovey@quadraco.com
Website: http://www.quadraco.com
Directors: A. Stevens (Co Sec), B. Tovey (MD)
Managers: S. Martin (Comptroller), B. Holloway, E. Gamble (Chief Acct)
Immediate Holding Company: QUADRACO LIMITED
Registration no: 04203438 **Date established:** 2001 **Turnover:** £5m - £10m
No.of Employees: 21 - 50 **Product Groups:** 26, 49, 61

Date of Accounts	Dec 10	Dec 09	Dec 08
Working Capital	1m	917	991
Fixed Assets	97	91	109
Current Assets	2m	1m	1m

Ravensburger Ltd
1 Avonbury Business Park Howes Lane, Bicester, OX26 2UB
Tel: 01869-363800 **Fax:** 01869-363815
E-mail: sales@ravensburger.com
Website: http://www.ravensburger.com
Bank(s): National Westminster
Directors: T. Hall (MD), A. Wood (Co Sec)
Managers: B. Bramwell (Mktg Serv Mgr), C. Reeves (Tech Serv Mgr), D. Scott (Sales Prom Mgr)
Ultimate Holding Company: RAVENSBURGER AKTIENGESELLSCHAFT (GERMANY
Immediate Holding Company: RAVENSBURGER LIMITED
Registration no: 00817350 **VAT No.:** GB 241 6641 76
Date established: 1964 **Turnover:** £10m - £20m
No.of Employees: 11 - 20 **Product Groups:** 49

Date of Accounts	Dec 11	Dec 10	Dec 09
Sales Turnover	11m	11m	8m
Pre Tax Profit/Loss	481	557	-151
Working Capital	1m	1m	72
Fixed Assets	51	1	14
Current Assets	6m	7m	5m
Current Liabilities	2m	2m	1m

Revolution Engineering Supplies Ltd
Pear Tree Farm Industrial Units Bicester Road, Marsh Gibbon, Bicester, OX27 0GB
Tel: 01869-278579 **Fax:** 01869-278965
E-mail: office@revolution-eng.co.uk
Website: http://www.revolution-eng.co.uk
Directors: A. Lynch (MD)
Immediate Holding Company: REVOLUTION ENGINEERING SUPPLIES LIMITED
Registration no: 05466397 **Date established:** 2005
No.of Employees: 1 - 10 **Product Groups:** 22, 23, 29, 30, 34, 35, 36, 37, 38, 39, 40, 42, 43, 46, 48, 49, 63, 66, 68

Date of Accounts	Jun 11	Jun 10	Jun 09
Working Capital	N/A	N/A	-0
Current Assets	107	102	96

Roecraft Wrought Ironwork
63 Wedgewood Road, Bicester, OX26 4UL
Tel: 01869-240254 **Fax:** 01869-240254
Directors: D. Pratt (Prop)
Date established: 1985 **No.of Employees:** 1 - 10 **Product Groups:** 26, 35

Sci-Net
Unit 5 Lakeside Farm Middle Aston, Bicester, OX25 5PP
Tel: 01869-349949 **Fax:** 01869-340063
E-mail: solutions@sci-net.co.uk
Website: http://www.sci-net.co.uk
Bank(s): Bank of Scotland
Directors: D. Ferguson (MD)
Registration no: 03624389 **VAT No.:** GB 194 8586 03
Date established: 1973 **Turnover:** £500,000 - £1m
No.of Employees: 11 - 20 **Product Groups:** 44

Date of Accounts	Aug 07	Aug 06	Aug 05
Working Capital	-17	-9	43
Fixed Assets	182	196	19
Current Assets	200	202	125
Current Liabilities	217	212	82

Singles That Mingle Ltd
Park House The Lane, Chesterton, Bicester, OX26 1UX
Tel: 07810-544326
E-mail: links@singlesthatmingle.co.uk
Website: http://www.singlesthatmingle.co.uk
Directors: S. Payne (Fin)
Immediate Holding Company: SINGLES THAT MINGLE LTD
Registration no: 07904678 **Date established:** 2012
No.of Employees: 1 - 10 **Product Groups:** 69

Supporter Datacare
3012 Heyford Park Camp Road, Upper Heyford, Bicester, OX25 5HF
Tel: 01869-233771 **Fax:** 01869-233066
E-mail: info@datacareltd.com
Website: http://www.datacareltd.com
Directors: J. Clarke (MD), J. Jasper (Dir)
Managers: J. Lazenby (I.T. Exec)
Ultimate Holding Company: Supporta plc
Immediate Holding Company: DATACARE BUSINESS SYSTEMS LIMITED
Registration no: 01529016 **Date established:** 1980 **Turnover:** £1m - £2m
No.of Employees: 21 - 50 **Product Groups:** 44, 77

Date of Accounts	Mar 08	Mar 07	Mar 06
Sales Turnover	2169	1916	1666
Pre Tax Profit/Loss	267	372	358
Working Capital	771	436	175
Fixed Assets	371	446	497
Current Assets	1851	891	654
Current Liabilities	1080	455	479
Total Share Capital	3	3	3
ROCE% (Return on Capital Employed)	23.4	42.1	53.4
ROT% (Return on Turnover)	12.3	19.4	21.5

Tract Ltd
Mckay Trading Estate Station Approach, Bicester, OX26 6BF
Tel: 01869-326300 **Fax:** 01869-323430
E-mail: info@tract.ltd.uk
Website: http://www.tract.co.uk
Bank(s): National Westminster, London
Directors: R. Hughes (MD), M. Allan (Sales)
Managers: K. Davison (Sales Prom Mgr), S. Merrick (Sec), M. Henderson (I.T. Exec), A. Todd (Purch Mgr), M. Parrott (Sales Prom Mgr)
Ultimate Holding Company: HILL TOP HOLDINGS LIMITED
Immediate Holding Company: TRACT LIMITED
Registration no: 01263274 **VAT No.:** 195 9463 08 **Date established:** 1976
Turnover: £2m - £5m **No.of Employees:** 21 - 50 **Product Groups:** 26

Date of Accounts	Dec 09	Dec 08	Dec 07
Sales Turnover	N/A	3m	N/A
Pre Tax Profit/Loss	N/A	43	N/A
Working Capital	231	345	152
Fixed Assets	111	141	181
Current Assets	1m	1m	1m
Current Liabilities	N/A	587	N/A

Turney Group
P A Turney Ltd Middleton Stoney, Bicester, OX25 4AB
Tel: 01869-343333 **Fax:** 01869-343540
E-mail: nigel.barker@paturney.com
Website: http://www.turneygroup.com
Registration no: 00607154 **No.of Employees:** 51 - 100
Product Groups: 41, 61, 66, 67

Turney-Agriforce
Lords Farm, Bicester, OX27 7HL
Tel: 01869-354840 **Fax:** 01869-353964
E-mail: paul.turney@paturney.com
Website: http://www.turneyagriforce.com
Directors: P. Turney (MD)
Date established: 2005 **No.of Employees:** 11 - 20 **Product Groups:** 41

Burford

Emmeti UK Ltd
Unit 6 Tannery Yard Witney Street, Burford, OX18 4DW
Tel: 01993-824900 **Fax:** 01993-824990
E-mail: sales@emmeti.co.uk
Website: http://www.emmeti.co.uk
Managers: K. Finch (Ops Mgr)
Immediate Holding Company: EMMETI UK LTD
Registration no: 05162683 **Date established:** 2004
No.of Employees: 1 - 10 **Product Groups:** 36, 37, 38

Date of Accounts	Dec 11	Dec 10	Dec 09
Working Capital	179	110	-60
Fixed Assets	36	21	6
Current Assets	2m	2m	1m

Carterton

5a's Power Tools & Plant Hire
15-18 Viscount Industrial Estate Station Road, Brize Norton, Carterton, OX18 3QQ
Tel: 01993-851111 **Fax:** 01993-850011
Website: http://www.5as.co.uk
Directors: B. Cooper (Fin), R. Adams (Dir)
Date established: 1998 **No.of Employees:** 1 - 10 **Product Groups:** 37

E & S Environmental Services Ltd
10 Viscount Industrial Estate Station Road Brize Norton, Carterton, OX18 3QQ
Tel: 01993-852419 **Fax:** 01993-852152
E-mail: info@eandsgroup.co.uk
Website: http://www.eandsgroup.co.uk
Directors: S. Clarke (Fin), E. Clarke (Dir)
Managers: M. Jordan (Tech Serv Mgr)
Ultimate Holding Company: ADLER & ALLAN HOLDINGS LIMITED
Immediate Holding Company: E & S ENVIRONMENTAL SERVICES LIMITED
Registration no: 05288826 **Date established:** 2004 **Turnover:** £5m - £10m
No.of Employees: 21 - 50 **Product Groups:** 40

Date of Accounts	Dec 08	Sep 11	Sep 10
Sales Turnover	N/A	5m	5m
Pre Tax Profit/Loss	N/A	424	853
Working Capital	-155	-211	427
Fixed Assets	480	2m	915
Current Assets	576	3m	2m
Current Liabilities	N/A	3m	386

Monarch Fire UK Ltd
The Office Suite 32 Stoneleigh Drive, Carterton, OX18 1ED
Tel: 01993-841660 **Fax:** 01993-841660
E-mail: info@monarchfire.co.uk
Website: http://www.monarchire.co.uk
Directors: S. Shorten (Fin), D. Shorten (MD)
Immediate Holding Company: MONARCH FIRE (UK) LIMITED
Registration no: 04583254 **Date established:** 2002
No.of Employees: 1 - 10 **Product Groups:** 38, 42

Date of Accounts	Nov 11	Nov 10	Nov 09
Working Capital	-8	-6	-5
Fixed Assets	11	14	18
Current Assets	22	19	29

Perfect Bindery Solutions LLP
Unit 4 Broadshires Way, Carterton, OX18 1AD
Tel: 01993-840077 **Fax:** 01993-840096
E-mail: steve@binderysolutions.co.uk
Website: http://www.binderysolutions.co.uk
Directors: S. Giddins (Ptnr)
Immediate Holding Company: PERFECT BINDERY SOLUTIONS LLP
Registration no: OC344872 **Date established:** 2009
No.of Employees: 1 - 10 **Product Groups:** 44, 67

Date of Accounts	Mar 11	Mar 10
Working Capital	-31	-26
Fixed Assets	14	13
Current Assets	276	232

S M B Bearings Ltd
8 West Oxfordshire Industrial Park Wavers Ground, Brize Norton, Carterton, OX18 3YJ
Tel: 01993-842555 **Fax:** 01993-842666
E-mail: sales@smbbearings.com
Website: http://www.smbbearings.com
Directors: C. Johnson (Dir)
Immediate Holding Company: SMB BEARINGS LIMITED
Registration no: 02623650 **VAT No.:** GB 596 2011 40
Date established: 1991 **Turnover:** £1m - £2m **No.of Employees:** 1 - 10
Product Groups: 30, 35, 49

Date of Accounts	Nov 11	Nov 10	Nov 09
Working Capital	339	188	775
Fixed Assets	404	413	17
Current Assets	723	716	938
Current Liabilities	N/A	70	N/A

Chinnor

Fire Safety Services Ltd
Sanderum House Oakley Road, Chinnor, OX39 4TW
Tel: 0845-388 1596 **Fax:** 01865-890085
E-mail: info@firesafetyadvisor.co.uk
Website: http://www.firesafetyadvisor.co.uk
Directors: P. Jolley (Dir)
Registration no: 03757758 **No.of Employees:** 1 - 10 **Product Groups:** 84

Date of Accounts	Mar 08	Mar 07	Mar 06
Working Capital	1	N/A	-5
Fixed Assets	10	2	1
Current Assets	20	21	15
Current Liabilities	19	21	20

M P S Personalised Products
1 Orchard Way, Chinnor, OX39 4UD
Tel: 01844-354450 **Fax:** 01844-354450
E-mail: info@mpspersonalisedproducts.co.uk
Website: http://www.mpspersonalisedclothing.co.uk
Directors: M. Purdy (Dir)
Turnover: Up to £250,000 **No.of Employees:** 1 - 10 **Product Groups:** 24, 63

Chipping Norton

K Allen
10 London Road, Chipping Norton, OX7 5AX
Tel: 01608-643798 **Fax:** 01608-646660
Directors: K. Allen (Prop)
Date established: 1979 **No.of Employees:** 1 - 10 **Product Groups:** 36, 39, 40

Allshred Ltd
PO Box 240, Chipping Norton, OX7 9BA
Tel: 0800-389 5155
E-mail: admin@allshred.co.uk
Website: http://www.allshred.co.uk
Directors: I. Mackay (MD)
Immediate Holding Company: ALLSHRED LIMITED
Registration no: 05638572 **Date established:** 2005
Turnover: Up to £250,000 **No.of Employees:** 1 - 10 **Product Groups:** 27, 80

Date of Accounts	Apr 12	Apr 11	Apr 10
Working Capital	-24	-37	-59
Fixed Assets	35	44	55
Current Assets	40	43	43

Analysco Ltd
11 Woodlands Close Milton-Under-Wychwood, Chipping Norton, OX7 6LS
Tel: 01993-831792 **Fax:** 01993-226874
E-mail: contact@analysco.co.uk
Website: http://www.analysco.co.uk
Directors: C. Jackson (Prop)
Registration no: 05754846 **Turnover:** Up to £250,000
No.of Employees: 1 - 10 **Product Groups:** 67

Brathalyzer Direct
The Old Farmhouse Kingham Road, Churchill, Chipping Norton, OX7 6NE
Tel: 01608-658935 **Fax:** 01608-658935
E-mail: contactus@breathalyserdirect.co.uk
Website: http://www.breathalyserdirect.co.uk
Directors: M. Butterworth (Prop)
Immediate Holding Company: UK BREATHALYZER SHOP LTD
Registration no: 06442887 **Date established:** 2007
No.of Employees: 1 - 10 **Product Groups:** 40

British Fluid Power Association Ltd
Cheriton House 17 Cromwell Park Banbury Road, Chipping Norton, OX7 5SR
Tel: 01608-647900 **Fax:** 01608-647919
E-mail: enquiries@bfpa.co.uk
Website: http://www.bfpa.co.uk
Directors: I. Morris (Dir)
Immediate Holding Company: BRITISH FLUID POWER ASSOCIATION LIMITED

Registration no: 00823988 **VAT No.:** GB 443 9115 54
Date established: 1964 **Turnover:** £250,000 - £500,000
No.of Employees: 1 - 10 **Product Groups:** 38, 40, 46, 67, 87

Date of Accounts	Dec 11	Dec 10	Dec 09
Working Capital	185	166	158
Fixed Assets	237	118	120
Current Assets	278	309	206

Cochranes Of Oxford Ltd
Grove Farm Barns High Street, Shipton-under-Wychwood, Chipping Norton, OX7 6DG
Tel: 01993-832868 **Fax:** 01993-832578
E-mail: tom@cochranes.co.uk
Website: http://www.cochranes.co.uk
Directors: J. Cochrane (MD), J. Monjack (Sales), T. Cochrane (MD), M. Cochrane (Dir)
Managers: Cochrane (I.T. Exec), T. Cockran (Mgr), G. Grayson (Accounts)
Immediate Holding Company: COCHRANES OF OXFORD LIMITED
Registration no: 00722590 **Date established:** 1962
Turnover: £500,000 - £1m **No.of Employees:** 1 - 10 **Product Groups:** 28, 49

Date of Accounts	Nov 10	Nov 09	Nov 08
Working Capital	406	377	347
Fixed Assets	22	19	18
Current Assets	495	429	416

Cotswold Tool & Plant Hire
3 Station Road, Chipping Norton, OX7 5HX
Tel: 01608-644227 **Fax:** 01608-645321
Directors: D. Coleman (Prop)
Immediate Holding Company: COTSWOLD TOOL AND PLANT HIRE LIMITED
Registration no: 03335816 **Date established:** 1997
No.of Employees: 1 - 10 **Product Groups:** 45, 83

Date of Accounts	May 11	May 10	May 09
Working Capital	206	152	142
Fixed Assets	683	714	737
Current Assets	295	237	234

E M C Plastics UK Ltd
Unit 3b Wychwood Business Centre Shipton-under-Wychwood, Chipping Norton, OX7 6XU
Tel: 01993-832000 **Fax:** 01993-831444
E-mail: sales@emc-uk.com
Website: http://www.emc-uk.com
Directors: D. Slater (MD)
Immediate Holding Company: E.M.C. PLASTICS UK LIMITED
Registration no: 03058991 **VAT No.:** GB 663 2600 52
Date established: 1995 **Turnover:** Up to £250,000
No.of Employees: 1 - 10 **Product Groups:** 28, 37, 38, 85

Date of Accounts	May 11	May 10	May 09
Sales Turnover	136	228	229
Pre Tax Profit/Loss	-28	-24	-12
Working Capital	-84	-54	-34
Fixed Assets	101	104	113
Current Assets	47	75	83
Current Liabilities	59	48	25

Hydac Technology Ltd
Woodstock Road Charlbury, Chipping Norton, OX7 3ES
Tel: 01608-811211 **Fax:** 01608-811259
E-mail: george.muscat@hydac.co.uk
Website: http://www.hydacuk.com
Bank(s): Lloyds TSB Bank plc
Directors: G. Muscat (MD)
Managers: A. Wixon (Tech Supp Mgr), B. Johnson (Mktg Serv Mgr), L. Fern
Immediate Holding Company: HYDAC TECHNOLOGY LIMITED
Registration no: 01261214 **Date established:** 1976 **Turnover:** £5m - £10m
No.of Employees: 51 - 100 **Product Groups:** 33, 35, 36, 38, 39, 40, 42, 45, 46, 67

Ie-Ndt Manufacturer
Unit C Heath Farm Swerford, Chipping Norton, OX7 4BN
Tel: 01608-683985 **Fax:** 01608-683476
E-mail: enquiries@ie-ndt.co.uk
Website: http://www.ie-ndt.co.uk
Directors: L. Kowol (Prop)
Immediate Holding Company: IE-NDT LIMITED
Registration no: 04131610 **VAT No.:** GB 226 9008 67
Date established: 2000 **Turnover:** £1m - £2m **No.of Employees:** 1 - 10
Product Groups: 27, 37, 38

Date of Accounts	Dec 11	Dec 10	Dec 09
Working Capital	70	76	58
Fixed Assets	1	3	4
Current Assets	207	131	132

Isis Fluid Control Ltd
Station Yard The Leys, Chipping Norton, OX7 5HZ
Tel: 01608-645755 **Fax:** 01608-645532
E-mail: sales@isis-fluid.com
Website: http://www.isis-fluid.co.uk
Bank(s): Barclays
Directors: P. Wright (MD)
Managers: K. Augar (Chief Acct), J. Millard (Sales & Mktg Mg)
Immediate Holding Company: ISIS FLUID CONTROL LIMITED
Registration no: 02613241 **VAT No.:** GB 596 1448 06
Date established: 1991 **Turnover:** £2m - £5m **No.of Employees:** 21 - 50
Product Groups: 36, 38, 39, 40

Date of Accounts	Dec 11	Aug 10	Aug 09
Working Capital	957	571	613
Fixed Assets	59	101	102
Current Assets	3m	2m	2m

Knollands
Station Road, Chipping Norton, OX7 5HX
Tel: 0845-094 5603 **Fax:** 01295- 688261
E-mail: wayne@knollands.co.uk
Website: http://www.knollands.co.uk
Directors: W. Clark (Prop)
Date established: 1994 **Turnover:** **No.of Employees:** 1 - 10
Product Groups: 30

Manor Veterinary Exports Ltd
Manor Farm Ascott Under Wychwood, Ascott-under-Wychwood, Chipping Norton, OX7 6AL
Tel: 01993-830278 **Fax:** 01993-830395
E-mail: johngrippervet@compuserve.com
Website: http://www.manorveterinaryexports.com
Directors: A. Gripper (Fin)
Immediate Holding Company: MANOR VETERINARY EXPORTS LIMITED
Registration no: 05304463 **VAT No.:** GB 336 1963 48
Date established: 2004 **Turnover:** Up to £250,000
No.of Employees: 1 - 10 **Product Groups:** 63

Date of Accounts	Nov 11	Nov 10	Nov 09
Working Capital	85	54	35
Fixed Assets	N/A	N/A	5
Current Assets	132	124	77

New Barn Garage
Nineacres Lane Charlbury, Chipping Norton, OX7 3QZ
Tel: 01608-813001 **Fax:** 01608-813001
E-mail: new.barn@btconnect.com
Website: http://www.newbarngarage.co.uk
Directors: P. Sullivan (Prop)
Date established: 1962 **No.of Employees:** 1 - 10 **Product Groups:** 39

Oxford Plastic Systems Ltd
T2 Enstone Airfield Enstone, Chipping Norton, OX7 4NP
Tel: 01608-678888 **Fax:** 01608-678899
E-mail: sales@oxfordplastics.com
Website: http://www.oxfordplastics.com
Directors: B. Whiteley (Co Sec), A. Whiteley (Co Sec), C. Whiteley (MD)
Managers: P. Braddy (Sales Prom Mgr), S. Gentis (Mktg Serv Mgr), P. Creighton (Eng Serv Mgr), S. Gee (Import Mgr)
Immediate Holding Company: OXFORD PLASTIC SYSTEMS LIMITED
Registration no: 01956653 **VAT No.:** GB 448 5168 23
Date established: 1985 **Turnover:** £10m - £20m
No.of Employees: 21 - 50 **Product Groups:** 29, 30, 39, 66

Date of Accounts	Mar 11	Mar 10	Mar 09
Sales Turnover	11m	9m	10m
Pre Tax Profit/Loss	869	381	339
Working Capital	947	316	92
Fixed Assets	3m	2m	3m
Current Assets	4m	3m	3m
Current Liabilities	2m	1m	2m

The Roof Light Co. Ltd
Unit 8 Wychwood Business Centre, Shipton-under-Wychwood, Chipping Norton, OX7 6XU
Tel: 01993-830613
E-mail: info@therooflightcompany.co.uk
Website: http://www.therooflightcompany.co.uk
Directors: V. King (Dir)
No.of Employees: 21 - 50 **Product Groups:** 26, 35

Spearhead Training
19 Cheriton House Cromwell Park Banbury Road, Chipping Norton, OX7 5SR
Tel: 01608-644144 **Fax:** 01608-649680
E-mail: info@spearhead-training.co.uk
Website: http://www.spearhead-training.co.uk
Directors: D. Stone (MD)
Immediate Holding Company: SPEARHEAD TRAINING GROUP LIMITED
Registration no: 01559442 **VAT No.:** GB 335 3725 60
Date established: 1981 **No.of Employees:** 1 - 10 **Product Groups:** 80, 81, 86

Date of Accounts	Sep 11	Sep 10	Sep 09
Working Capital	51	11	-4
Fixed Assets	8	10	16
Current Assets	134	92	67

Didcot

Abingdon Freight Forwarding Agency Ltd
Park 34 Collett, Didcot, OX11 7WB
Tel: 01235-817334 **Fax:** 01235-750040
E-mail: roy.woodward@affa.co.uk
Website: http://www.affa.co.uk
Bank(s): Lloyds TSB Bank plc
Directors: R. Woodward (MD)
Managers: T. Woodward (Sales & Mktg Mg), M. Wilkinson (Tech Serv Mgr)
Ultimate Holding Company: ABINGDON FREIGHT HOLDINGS LIMITED
Immediate Holding Company: ABINGDON FREIGHT FORWARDING AGENCY LIMITED
Registration no: 01129767 **VAT No.:** GB 195 4866 11
Date established: 1973 **Turnover:** £2m - £5m **No.of Employees:** 11 - 20
Product Groups: 48, 72, 76

Date of Accounts	Jan 11	Jan 10	Jan 09
Working Capital	21	-58	-92
Fixed Assets	37	64	106
Current Assets	1m	840	851
Current Liabilities	N/A	285	298

Action Sealtite
Unit 14 Moorbrook Park, Didcot, OX11 7HP
Tel: 01235-512500 **Fax:** 01235-512666
E-mail: info@actionsealtite.com
Website: http://www.actionsealtite.com
Bank(s): Lloyds TSB Bank plc
Directors: K. Davies (Sales)
Managers: H. Robinson
Immediate Holding Company: ACTION-SEALTITE LIMITED
Registration no: 01610309 **VAT No.:** GB 336 4113 80
Date established: 1982 **Turnover:** £2m - £5m **No.of Employees:** 11 - 20
Product Groups: 35, 36

Date of Accounts	Apr 08	Apr 07	Apr 06
Working Capital	370	360	363
Fixed Assets	21	14	23
Current Assets	1263	1377	1209
Current Liabilities	893	1017	846
Total Share Capital	1	1	1

Allenfield Precision Engineering Ltd
Richs Sidings Broadway, Didcot, OX11 8AG
Tel: 01235-816880 **Fax:** 01235-811848
E-mail: sales@allenfield.co.uk
Website: http://www.allenfield.co.uk
Directors: J. Davies (Dir)
Immediate Holding Company: ALLENFIELD PRECISION ENGINEERING LIMITED
Registration no: 00864487 **VAT No.:** GB 199 0608 29
Date established: 1965 **Turnover:** Up to £250,000
No.of Employees: 1 - 10 **Product Groups:** 48

Date of Accounts	Nov 11	Nov 10	Nov 09
Working Capital	168	148	124
Fixed Assets	5	6	7
Current Assets	216	196	153

Biffa Waste Services Ltd
Gooch Drive, Didcot, OX11 7PR
Tel: 0800-601601 **Fax:** 01235- 813881
E-mail: marketing@biffa.co.uk
Website: http://www.biffa.co.uk
Directors: M. Bellington (MD)
Ultimate Holding Company: THAMES CRYOGENICS LIMITED
Immediate Holding Company: BIFFA WASTE SERVICES LIMITED
Registration no: 00946107 **Date established:** 1969
No.of Employees: 51 - 100 **Product Groups:** 32, 54

Date of Accounts	Mar 08	Mar 09	Apr 10
Sales Turnover	555m	574m	492m
Pre Tax Profit/Loss	23m	50m	30m
Working Capital	229m	271m	293m
Fixed Assets	371m	360m	378m
Current Assets	409m	534m	609m
Current Liabilities	50m	100m	115m

Fives Stein
4a Churchward Southmead Industrial Park, Didcot, OX11 7HB
Tel: 01235-811111 **Fax:** 01235-817676
E-mail: alan.hendry@fivesgroup.com
Website: http://www.fivesgroup.com
Bank(s): The Royal Bank of Scotland
Directors: A. Hendry (Sales), M. Hawkins (Co Sec), E. Knowles (Co Sec)
Ultimate Holding Company: FL INVESTCO (FRANCE)
Immediate Holding Company: FIVES STEIN LIMITED
Registration no: 02814647 **VAT No.:** GB 630 5202 88
Date established: 1993 **Turnover:** £10m - £20m
No.of Employees: 21 - 50 **Product Groups:** 45, 46

Date of Accounts	Dec 11	Dec 10	Dec 09
Sales Turnover	11m	9m	8m
Pre Tax Profit/Loss	238	158	92
Working Capital	2m	2m	3m
Fixed Assets	427	210	203
Current Assets	4m	3m	3m
Current Liabilities	1m	927	421

Harwell Oxford +
551 South Becquerel Avenue, Didcot, OX11 0TB
Tel: 01235-841999 **Fax:** 01235-832287
E-mail: sales@scientifics.com
Website: http://www.harwelloxford.com
Bank(s): Clydesdale
Directors: D. Watson (Sales), A. Gibson (MD)
Managers: N. Sturrock (Personnel), J. Barratt (I.T. Exec), M. Barke (Purch Mgr)
Immediate Holding Company: Atesta Ltd
Registration no: SC196706 **VAT No.:** GB 742 9496 95
Turnover: £1m - £2m **No.of Employees:** 51 - 100 **Product Groups:** 85

Kingston Blinds
8 Foxhall Road, Didcot, OX11 7AA
Tel: 01235-814553 **Fax:** 01235-511308
E-mail: neil@kingstonblinds.co.uk
Website: http://www.kingstonblinds.co.uk
Directors: N. Kingston (Prop)
No.of Employees: 1 - 10 **Product Groups:** 24, 30, 35, 36, 37, 39, 49, 63, 66

Oxford Lasers Ltd
Moorbrook Park, Didcot, OX11 7HP
Tel: 01235-810088 **Fax:** 01235-810060
E-mail: alan.ferguson@oxfordlasers.com
Website: http://www.oxfordlasers.com
Bank(s): Barclays, Oxford
Directors: A. Ferguson (Dir), A. Kearsley (Fin), J. Baker (Dir)
Ultimate Holding Company: OXFORD LASERS GROUP LIMITED
Immediate Holding Company: OXFORD LASERS LIMITED
Registration no: 01332714 **VAT No.:** GB 196 1825 34
Date established: 1977 **Turnover:** £2m - £5m **No.of Employees:** 21 - 50
Product Groups: 37, 85

Date of Accounts	Dec 11	Dec 10	Dec 09
Working Capital	696	393	258
Fixed Assets	136	149	156
Current Assets	1m	987	1m

Qudos Technology Ltd
Rutherford Appleton Laboratory Chilton, Harwell Science & Innovation Campus, Didcot, OX11 0QX
Tel: 01235-445468 **Fax:** 01235-445445
E-mail: enquiries@qudostechnology.co.uk
Website: http://www.qudostechnology.co.uk
Directors: T. Barlow (Snr Part)
Ultimate Holding Company: QUDOS MICRO AND NANO TECHNOLOGY LTD
Immediate Holding Company: QUDOS TECHNOLOGY LIMITED
Registration no: 01876439 **Date established:** 1985
Turnover: £500,000 - £1m **No.of Employees:** 1 - 10 **Product Groups:** 37

Date of Accounts	Dec 11	Dec 10	Dec 09
Working Capital	-7	15	14
Fixed Assets	27	31	36
Current Assets	174	227	204

Redbox Fire Control Ltd
Unit 3 The Cobden Centre Hawksworth, Didcot, OX11 7HL
Tel: 01235-810000 **Fax:** 023-8077 6131
E-mail: mail@redboxfire.co.uk
Website: http://www.redboxfire.co.uk
Directors: C. Webb (MD)
Date established: 1987 **No.of Employees:** 1 - 10 **Product Groups:** 39, 40, 67, 68, 84, 86

The Toolpost
Unit 7 Hawksworth, Didcot, OX11 7HR
Tel: 01235-511101 **Fax:** 01235-811185
E-mail: peter@toolpost.co.uk
Website: http://www.toolpost.co.uk
Directors: E. Hemsley (Fin), P. Hemsley (MD)
Immediate Holding Company: TOOLPOST LIMITED
Registration no: 03424720 **Date established:** 1997
No.of Employees: 1 - 10 **Product Groups:** 33, 36, 40, 47, 67

TVH Industrial Products
1a Hawksworth Southmead Park, Didcot, OX11 7HR
Tel: 01235-511001 **Fax:** 01235-519529
E-mail: sale@tvhydraulics.co.uk
Website: http://www.tvhuk.co.uk
Directors: P. Dunn (Prop)
Date established: 1989 **No.of Employees:** 1 - 10 **Product Groups:** 29, 30

Date of Accounts	Oct 11	Oct 10	Oct 09
Sales Turnover	N/A	2m	2m
Pre Tax Profit/Loss	N/A	-26	-148
Working Capital	289	-73	-20
Fixed Assets	2m	2m	2m
Current Assets	616	462	413
Current Liabilities	N/A	71	74

Faringdon

Alser UK Ltd
6 Pioneer Road, Faringdon, SN7 7BU
Tel: 01367-242635 **Fax:** 01367-242807
E-mail: info@alser.co.uk
Website: http://www.alser.co.uk
Bank(s): Barclays
Directors: N. Pritchard (Fin), V. Harris (Co Sec), R. Harris (Dir)
Managers: K. Davidson
Immediate Holding Company: ALSER (UK) LIMITED
Registration no: 02249407 **VAT No.:** GB 522 0925 76
Date established: 1988 **Turnover:** £2m - £5m **No.of Employees:** 21 - 50
Product Groups: 26, 52

Date of Accounts	Apr 12	Apr 11	Apr 10
Sales Turnover	4m	N/A	N/A
Pre Tax Profit/Loss	242	N/A	N/A
Working Capital	566	690	696
Fixed Assets	134	80	121
Current Assets	1m	1m	1m
Current Liabilities	138	N/A	N/A

Boston Retail Products
PO Box 3564, Faringdon, SN7 9AR
Tel: 08707-706680 **Fax:** 08707-706681
E-mail: sales@bostonretail.com
Website: http://www.bostonretail.com
Managers: J. Wickham (Mgr)
Ultimate Holding Company: WORLEY PARSONS LTD (AUSTRALIA)
Immediate Holding Company: WORLEY PARSONS EUROPE LIMITED
Registration no: 02775255 **Date established:** 1991 **Turnover:** £5m - £10m
No.of Employees: 1 - 10 **Product Groups:** 66

Bray Group Ltd
Olive House 1 Regal Way, Faringdon, SN7 7BX
Tel: 01367-240736 **Fax:** 01367-242625
E-mail: info@bray-healthcare.com
Website: http://www.bray.co.uk
Bank(s): Barclays
Directors: C. Hobbs (MD)
Ultimate Holding Company: BRAY HOLDINGS LIMITED
Immediate Holding Company: BRAY GROUP LIMITED
Registration no: 01396401 **Date established:** 1978 **Turnover:** £2m - £5m
No.of Employees: 51 - 100 **Product Groups:** 24, 29, 30

Date of Accounts	Dec 11	Dec 10	Dec 09
Working Capital	493	304	384
Fixed Assets	603	613	637
Current Assets	1m	895	1m

Challow Products
7 Old Saw Mills Road, Faringdon, SN7 7DS
Tel: 01367-240091 **Fax:** 01367-242516
E-mail: office@challowproducts.co.uk
Website: http://www.challowproducts.co.uk
Managers: M. Draper (Mgr)
Immediate Holding Company: SEVERN VALLEY WOODWORKS LTD
Turnover: £5m - £10m **No.of Employees:** 1 - 10 **Product Groups:** 25

Clearway Sales & Promotional Products
PO Box 2779, Faringdon, SN7 7BZ
Tel: 01367-242400 **Fax:** 01367-244299
E-mail: enquiry@clearwaykeyrings.co.uk
Website: http://www.clearwaykeyrings.co.uk
Managers: M. Lewickyj (Admin Off)
Registration no: 05166224 **No.of Employees:** 1 - 10 **Product Groups:** 49

D P L Engineering Ltd
27 High Street Stanford In The Vale, Faringdon, SN7 8LH
Tel: 01367-718910 **Fax:** 01367-718910
E-mail: info@dplengineering.co.uk
Website: http://www.dplengineering.co.uk
Directors: D. Leech (Dir)
Immediate Holding Company: DPL ENGINEERING LIMITED
Registration no: 04928872 **Date established:** 2003
Turnover: Up to £250,000 **No.of Employees:** 1 - 10 **Product Groups:** 46, 48

Date of Accounts	Sep 11	Sep 10	Sep 09
Working Capital	21	2	9
Fixed Assets	4	6	8
Current Assets	43	24	24

Edicron Ltd
The Rac Building Park Road, Faringdon, SN7 7BP
Tel: 01367-243030 **Fax:** 01367-243131
E-mail: sales@edicron.co.uk
Website: http://www.edicron.com
Directors: P. Cruh (MD)
Ultimate Holding Company: ETABLISSEMENT VADEMEX
Immediate Holding Company: EDICRON LIMITED
Registration no: 02774947 **VAT No.:** GB 618 1189 40
Date established: 1992 **Turnover:** £500,000 - £1m
No.of Employees: 1 - 10 **Product Groups:** 37, 47, 67

Date of Accounts	Dec 10	Dec 08	Dec 07
Working Capital	-777	-788	-768
Fixed Assets	3	3	4
Current Assets	77	67	60
Current Liabilities	N/A	20	27

Rogers Gardenstone
Sands Hill Sandshill, Faringdon, SN7 7PQ
Tel: 01367-240112 **Fax:** 01367-242980
Website: http://www.rogersgardenstone.co.uk
Directors: P. Hurley (MD)
Immediate Holding Company: ROGERS CONCRETE LIMITED
Registration no: 01118977 **VAT No.:** GB 311 4607 02
Date established: 1973 **Turnover:** £1m - £2m **No.of Employees:** 1 - 10
Product Groups: 33

Specialist Xpress
9 Market Place, Faringdon, SN7 7HL
Tel: 01367-240077 **Fax:** 01367-240066
E-mail: info@specialistxpress.com
Website: http://www.specialistxpress.com
Managers: I. Kenworthy (Sales Admin), A. Sheppard (Mgr)
Immediate Holding Company: MARRIOTT BROWN LIMITED
Registration no: 04888356 **Date established:** 2003
No.of Employees: 1 - 10 **Product Groups:** 35

Date of Accounts	Sep 11	Sep 10	Sep 08
Working Capital	30	19	15
Current Assets	48	33	28

Storage Solutions Ltd
Unit 7 White Horse Business Park Ware Road, Stanford In The Vale, Faringdon, SN7 8NY
Tel: 01367-711800 **Fax:** 01367-711809
E-mail: sales@storagesolutions.co.uk
Website: http://www.storagesolutions.co.uk
Directors: P. Sully (MD)
Immediate Holding Company: STORAGE SOLUTIONS LIMITED
Registration no: 02834206 **Date established:** 1993
No.of Employees: 1 - 10 **Product Groups:** 25, 26, 29, 30, 33, 35, 36, 39, 40, 41, 43, 45, 46, 47, 49, 67, 72, 77, 84, 85

Date of Accounts	Aug 11	Aug 10	Aug 09
Working Capital	134	30	84
Fixed Assets	448	453	481
Current Assets	577	504	314

Sub Micron Ltd
21-23 High Street Stanford In The Vale, Faringdon, SN7 8LH
Tel: 01367-718018 **Fax:** 01367-718018
E-mail: sales@submicron.co.uk
Website: http://www.submicron.co.uk
Directors: E. Popkiss (MD)
Immediate Holding Company: SUB MICRON LIMITED
Registration no: 04531065 **VAT No.:** GB 618 2714 42
Date established: 2002 **Turnover:** Up to £250,000
No.of Employees: 1 - 10 **Product Groups:** 29, 37

Date of Accounts	Jul 11	Jul 10	Jul 09
Working Capital	169	144	136
Fixed Assets	5	5	9
Current Assets	217	189	179

Henley On Thames

Adnet Ltd
3 Manor Farm Barns High Street, Nettlebed, Henley On Thames, RG9 5DA
Tel: 01491-642133 **Fax:** 01491-642144
E-mail: info@adnet.ltd.uk
Website: http://www.adnet.ltd.uk
Directors: C. Bartlett (Fin)
Immediate Holding Company: ADNET LIMITED
Registration no: 02939908 **VAT No.:** GB 603 9788 15
Date established: 1994 **Turnover:** £500,000 - £1m
No.of Employees: 1 - 10 **Product Groups:** 44, 67, 86

Date of Accounts	Dec 11	Dec 10	Dec 09
Working Capital	-3	1	4
Fixed Assets	4	8	11
Current Assets	198	175	236

Breathe Marketing Ltd Geoff Hocking
Royal House Station Road, Henley On Thames, RG9 1AZ
Tel: 01491-575057 **Fax:** 01491-575067
E-mail: geoff@breathe4u.com
Website: http://www.breathe4u.com
Directors: G. Hocking (Prop), G. Hocking (Dir)
Immediate Holding Company: BREATHE MARKETING LIMITED
Registration no: 04772930 **Date established:** 2003
Turnover: Up to £250,000 **No.of Employees:** 1 - 10 **Product Groups:** 28, 44, 81, 84

Date of Accounts	May 11	May 10	May 09
Working Capital	-3	1	-3
Fixed Assets	5	N/A	4
Current Assets	37	46	47

Burlington Entry Systems Ltd
Unit 9 Van Alloys Industrial Estate Busgrove Lane, Stoke Row, Henley On Thames, RG9 5QW
Tel: 01491-680501 **Fax:** 01491-680540
E-mail: accounts@came.co.uk
Website: http://www.came.co.uk
Directors: H. Wynn Jones (Fin)
Registration no: 02208732 **Date established:** 1987
No.of Employees: 1 - 10 **Product Groups:** 26, 35

Date of Accounts	Mar 10	Mar 09	Mar 08
Working Capital	286	358	281
Fixed Assets	N/A	N/A	1
Current Assets	398	485	382

Channel Advantage Ltd
The Old Dairy Stonor, Henley On Thames, RG9 6HF
Tel: 01491-639100 **Fax:** 01491-639166
E-mail: rlipscombe@channel-advantage.co.uk
Website: http://www.channeladvantage.co.uk
Directors: S. Lane (Mkt Research), C. Pearson (MD), R. Lipscombe (MD), T. Hall (MD)
Managers: T. Hall
Immediate Holding Company: CHANNEL ADVANTAGE LIMITED
Registration no: 03016118 **Date established:** 1995 **Turnover:** £2m - £5m
No.of Employees: 1 - 10 **Product Groups:** 81

Date of Accounts	Mar 11	Mar 10	Mar 09
Working Capital	1m	896	841
Fixed Assets	39	96	119
Current Assets	1m	2m	2m

Courtiers Investment Services Limited
Hart Street, Henley On Thames, RG9 2AU
Tel: 01491-578368 **Fax:** 01491-572294
E-mail: info@courtiers.co.uk
Website: http://www.courtiers.co.uk
Bank(s): The Royal Bank of Scotland
Directors: G. Reynolds (MD), J. Shepperd (MD)
Immediate Holding Company: Courtiers Investment Services Ltd
Registration no: 01387954 **VAT No.:** GB 669 2553 96
Date established: 1995 **Turnover:** £1m - £2m **No.of Employees:** 11 - 20
Product Groups: 82

Date of Accounts	Mar 10	Mar 09	Mar 08
Sales Turnover	4m	3m	3m
Pre Tax Profit/Loss	953	609	627
Working Capital	660	367	332
Fixed Assets	89	112	166
Current Assets	1m	742	800
Current Liabilities	758	337	436

Dalton I D Ltd
Dalton House Newtown Road, Henley On Thames, RG9 1HG
Tel: 01491-419000 **Fax:** 0800-731 1957
E-mail: sales@dalton.co.uk
Website: http://www.dalton.co.uk
Directors: A. Matthews (Fin), D. Brierley (MD)
Managers: A. Rance (Buyer)
Immediate Holding Company: RUSCOMBE HOMES LTD
Registration no: 00432210 **VAT No.:** GB 194 8082 31
Date established: 1947 **Turnover:** £2m - £5m **No.of Employees:** 21 - 50
Product Groups: 30, 38, 41

Date of Accounts	Jun 10	Jun 09	Jun 08
Working Capital	-61	-106	-32
Fixed Assets	2m	2m	2m
Current Assets	90	35	14

Engis UK Ltd
Unit 9 Centenary Business Park Station Road, Henley On Thames, RG9 1DS
Tel: 01491-411117 **Fax:** 01491-412252
E-mail: sales@engis.uk.com
Website: http://www.engis.uk.com
Directors: J. Wellings (MD)
Ultimate Holding Company: ENGIS CORPORATION (USA)
Immediate Holding Company: ENGIS (UK) LIMITED
Registration no: 02739754 **Date established:** 1992 **Turnover:** £1m - £2m
No.of Employees: 1 - 10 **Product Groups:** 33, 46

Date of Accounts	Mar 11	Mar 10	Mar 09
Working Capital	-318	-333	-224
Fixed Assets	5	N/A	N/A
Current Assets	1m	721	890

Fast Systems Ltd
Dalton House Newtown Road, Henley On Thames, RG9 1HG
Tel: 01491-419200 **Fax:** 01384-252160
E-mail: sales@scalewatcher.co.uk
Website: http://www.fastpress.co.uk
Directors: P. Dalglish (Dir)
Immediate Holding Company: FAST SYSTEMS LIMITED
Registration no: 01744352 **Date established:** 1983
No.of Employees: 1 - 10 **Product Groups:** 40, 47, 67

Date of Accounts	Dec 11	Dec 10	Dec 09
Working Capital	632	766	744
Fixed Assets	10	12	15
Current Assets	790	952	883

Ferroalloy Trading Company UK Limited
Unit 3, The Business Centre Greys Green Rotherfield Greys, Henley On Thames, RG9 4QG
Tel: 0118-986 4310 **Fax:** 0118-986 4310
E-mail: ftcuk@ymail.com
Website: http://www.ftc-uk.com
Directors: B. Pourkomailian (Grp Chief Exec)
Registration no: 06959230 **Date established:** 2009
Turnover: £500,000 - £1m **No.of Employees:** 1 - 10 **Product Groups:** 14, 33, 34, 66

Henley Business School
Greenlands Hambleden, Henley On Thames, RG9 3AU
Tel: 01491-571454 **Fax:** 01491-571635
E-mail: jilly.birks@henley.com
Website: http://www.henley.reading.ac.uk
Bank(s): Barclays
Directors: D. Savage (Co Sec)
Managers: J. Board
Ultimate Holding Company: UNIVERSITY OF READING
Immediate Holding Company: HENLEY MANAGEMENT COLLEGE LIMITED(THE)
Registration no: 01576378 **Date established:** 1981
Turnover: £500,000 - £1m **No.of Employees:** 251 - 500
Product Groups: 86

Date of Accounts	Jul 11	Jul 10	Jul 09
Sales Turnover	661	6m	8m
Pre Tax Profit/Loss	16	-2m	-320
Working Capital	-2m	-2m	89
Current Assets	18	1m	1m
Current Liabilities	2m	1m	820

Houdret & Co. Ltd
Courtyard Suite 21-23 Hart Street, Henley On Thames, RG9 2AR
Tel: 01491-573512 **Fax:** 01491-579793
E-mail: helen.herridge@houdret.co.uk
Website: http://www.houdretandcompany.org
Directors: H. Herridge (Fin)
Immediate Holding Company: HOUDRET & COMPANY LIMITED
Registration no: 01117071 **Date established:** 1973
Turnover: £250,000 - £500,000 **No.of Employees:** 1 - 10
Product Groups: 61

Date of Accounts	May 09	May 08	Nov 11
Working Capital	117	87	365
Fixed Assets	45	59	23
Current Assets	1m	1m	2m

Invesco Perpetual
Perpetual Park Drive, Henley On Thames, RG9 1HH
Tel: 01491-417000 **Fax:** 01491-416000
E-mail: enquiry@invescoperpetual.co.uk
Website: http://www.invescoperpetual.co.uk
Directors: M. Perman (Co Sec), R. White (Mkt Research)
Managers: C. Newman (Sales Prom Mgr), C. Newman (Sales Prom Mgr)
No.of Employees: 501 - 1000 **Product Groups:** 82

Marsden Weighing Machine Group
Anvil House Tuns Lane, Henley On Thames, RG9 1SA
Tel: 08451-307330 **Fax:** 08451-307440
E-mail: sales@marsdengroup.co.uk
Website: http://www.marsden-weighing.co.uk
Bank(s): Barclays
Directors: S. Tooher (Prop)
Ultimate Holding Company: MARSDEN GROUP HOLDINGS LIMITED
Immediate Holding Company: MARSDEN WEIGHING MACHINE GROUP LIMITED
Registration no: 01014815 **VAT No.:** GB 757 2558 00
Date established: 1971 **Turnover:** £2m - £5m **No.of Employees:** 21 - 50
Product Groups: 38, 48, 83

Date of Accounts	Dec 11	Dec 10	Dec 09
Working Capital	2m	1m	1m
Fixed Assets	230	154	105
Current Assets	2m	2m	2m

Projex Design
Unit 1 Van Alloys Industrial Estate Busgrove Lane, Stoke Row, Henley On Thames, RG9 5QB
Tel: 01491-682757 **Fax:** 01491-681778
E-mail: andy@projexdesign.co.uk
Website: http://www.projexdesign.co.uk
Directors: A. Packman (Dir)
Turnover: Up to £250,000 **No.of Employees:** 1 - 10 **Product Groups:** 81

Signals Ltd
Broadgates Market Place, Henley On Thames, RG9 2AA
Tel: 01491-571812 **Fax:** 0161-287 5511
E-mail: info@signals.co.uk
Website: http://www.signals.co.uk
Bank(s): HSBC Bank plc
Directors: J. Precey (Fin)
Managers: A. Paines
Immediate Holding Company: SIGNALS LIMITED
Registration no: 03568955 **VAT No.:** GB 748 4185 04
Date established: 1998 **Turnover:** £2m - £5m **No.of Employees:** 11 - 20
Product Groups: 37, 39, 40

Date of Accounts	Mar 11	Mar 10	Mar 09
Working Capital	128	82	92
Fixed Assets	71	92	108
Current Assets	318	347	235

Simpson Associates
8 Friday Street, Henley On Thames, RG9 1AH
Tel: 01491-576221 **Fax:** 01491-410129
E-mail: mail@simpsoneng.com
Website: http://simpsoneng.com
Bank(s): Lloyds TSB
Directors: M. Ellis (Ptnr)
Immediate Holding Company: SIMPSON ASSOCIATES CONSULTING ENGINEERS LLP
Registration no: OC351954 **VAT No.:** GB 438 2240 63
Date established: 2010 **Turnover:** Up to £250,000
No.of Employees: 21 - 50 **Product Groups:** 54, 80, 81, 84

Date of Accounts	Mar 11
Working Capital	850
Fixed Assets	85
Current Assets	1m

David Somerset Skincare
PO Box 8, Henley On Thames, RG9 6YZ
Tel: 01491-578080
E-mail: info@somersets.com
Website: http://www.somersets.com
Directors: D. Collas (MD), D. Collas (Prop)
Turnover: £250,000 - £500,000 **No.of Employees:** 1 - 10
Product Groups: 32

Stuart Turner Ltd
Market Place, Henley On Thames, RG9 2AD
Tel: 01491-572655 **Fax:** 01491-573704
E-mail: pumps@stuart-turner.co.uk
Website: http://www.stuart-turner.co.uk
Bank(s): National Westminster
Directors: J. Leverton (Fin), M. Harris (Fin)
Managers: J. Plomer (Personnel), S. Collingworth (Buyer), C. Goswell (Tech Serv Mgr)
Immediate Holding Company: STUART TURNER LIMITED
Registration no: 00088368 **VAT No.:** GB 199 0987 92
Date established: 2006 **Turnover:** £10m - £20m
No.of Employees: 21 - 50 **Product Groups:** 30, 39, 40, 41

Date of Accounts	Sep 11	Sep 10	Sep 09
Sales Turnover	15m	14m	13m
Pre Tax Profit/Loss	3m	3m	2m
Working Capital	10m	9m	8m
Fixed Assets	5m	5m	5m
Current Assets	13m	11m	10m
Current Liabilities	1m	1m	777

Videcom International Ltd
Newtown Road, Henley On Thames, RG9 1HG
Tel: 01491-578427 **Fax:** 01491-579368
E-mail: info@videcom.com
Website: http://www.videcom.com
Bank(s): National Westminster Bank Plc
Managers: Z. Maines (Comptroller)
Ultimate Holding Company: VIDECOM TRAVEL SYSTEMS LIMITED
Immediate Holding Company: VIDECOM INTERNATIONAL LIMITED
Registration no: 01277790 **Date established:** 1976 **Turnover:** £1m - £2m
No.of Employees: 11 - 20 **Product Groups:** 37, 44, 67

Date of Accounts	Mar 11	Mar 10	Mar 09
Working Capital	692	923	969
Fixed Assets	142	151	220
Current Assets	844	1m	1m

Windfall Brands Ltd
Northfield House Northfield End, Henley On Thames, RG9 2JG
Tel: 01491-845 620 **Fax:** 01491-412 929
E-mail: info@windfalldrinks.com
Website: http://www.windfalldrinks.com
Product Groups: 20, 21, 62

Date of Accounts	Sep 08	Sep 07	Sep 06
Working Capital	5	4	17
Fixed Assets	14	11	3
Current Assets	85	113	89
Current Liabilities	80	109	73

Kidlington

T J Beaver
32-34 The Moors, Kidlington, OX5 2AJ
Tel: 01865-372328 **Fax:** 01865-372328
Directors: T. Beaver (Prop)
Date established: 1968 **No.of Employees:** 1 - 10 **Product Groups:** 26, 35

Daniels Healthcare Ltd
14 Station Field Industrial Estate, Kidlington, OX5 1JD
Tel: 01865-371841 **Fax:** 01442-826880
E-mail: info@daniels.co.uk
Website: http://www.daniels.co.uk
Bank(s): Barclays, London
Directors: G. Paxton (Co Sec), W. Hatton (Dir), S. Hazlett (Chief Op Offcr), H. Simler (MD), E. Lanyon (Comm), S. Picillo (Pers)
Managers: P. Collins (Fin Mgr), L. Criag (Personnel), L. Smith (Tech Serv Mgr), D. Dewet (I.T. Exec)
Ultimate Holding Company: DANIELS HEALTHCARE GROUP LIMITED
Immediate Holding Company: DANIELS HEALTHCARE LIMITED
Registration no: 01389430 **VAT No.:** GB 418 9297 13
Date established: 1978 **Turnover:** £1m - £2m **No.of Employees:** 51 - 100
Product Groups: 30

Date of Accounts	Sep 11	Sep 10	Sep 09
Sales Turnover	2m	2m	2m
Pre Tax Profit/Loss	247	2m	1m
Working Capital	-173	-498	-826
Fixed Assets	2m	2m	2m
Current Assets	3m	3m	3m
Current Liabilities	786	713	778

Dynamix Technology Ltd
17 Station Field Industrial Estate Banbury Road, Kidlington, OX5 1JD
Tel: 01608-730988 **Fax:** 01608-730988
E-mail: enquiries@dynamixtechnology.com
Website: http://www.dynamixtechnology.com
Directors: L. Brew (Fin), P. Swanson (MD)
Registration no: 02789259 **Date established:** 1993
Turnover: Up to £250,000 **No.of Employees:** 1 - 10 **Product Groups:** 86

Date of Accounts	Feb 10	Feb 09	Feb 08
Working Capital	7	8	8
Current Assets	10	11	13

Elsevier Publishers Ltd
The Boulevard Langford Lane, Kidlington, OX5 1GB
Tel: 01865-843000 **Fax:** 01865-843010
E-mail: gavin.howe@rbi.co.uk
Website: http://www.elsevier.co.uk
Directors: T. Coorey (I.T. Dir)
Managers: G. Howe (Personnel), A. Kitson, D. Lomas (Comptroller)
Ultimate Holding Company: REED ELSEVIER GROUP PLC
Immediate Holding Company: ELSEVIER LIMITED
Registration no: 01982084 **Date established:** 1986
Turnover: £250m - £500m **No.of Employees:** 501 - 1000
Product Groups: 28, 80

Date of Accounts	Dec 11	Dec 10	Dec 09
Sales Turnover	444m	417m	396m
Pre Tax Profit/Loss	203m	152m	146m
Working Capital	140m	71m	11m
Fixed Assets	119m	136m	153m
Current Assets	523m	372m	352m
Current Liabilities	302m	262m	294m

G N Resound UK Ltd
Building A Kirtlington Business Centre, Kirtlington, Kidlington, OX5 3JA
Tel: 01869-352800 **Fax:** 01869-343466
E-mail: info@gnresound.co.uk
Website: http://www.gnresound.co.uk
Bank(s): Unibank
Directors: J. Van Huyssteen (Dir)
Managers: J. Svimberska (Personnel)
Ultimate Holding Company: GN STORE NORD A/S (DENMARK)
Immediate Holding Company: GN RESOUND LTD
Registration no: 02984645 **VAT No.:** GB 685 6499 66
Date established: 1994 **Turnover:** £10m - £20m
No.of Employees: 101 - 250 **Product Groups:** 37, 67

Date of Accounts	Dec 11	Dec 10	Dec 09
Sales Turnover	20m	18m	19m
Pre Tax Profit/Loss	2m	-273	347
Working Capital	8m	6m	8m
Fixed Assets	2m	2m	1m
Current Assets	11m	13m	10m
Current Liabilities	1m	1m	1m

Hartwell Ford
Oxford Motor Park Langford Lane, Kidlington, OX5 1FH
Tel: 08443-247430 **Fax:** 01865-290301
E-mail: f01gm@hartwell.co.uk
Website: http://www.hartwell.co.uk
Managers: M. Williams (Chief Acct), Y. Cubbage (Chief Mgr)
Immediate Holding Company: Hartwell Holdings Ltd
Registration no: 00155302 **No.of Employees:** 51 - 100
Product Groups: 68

Date of Accounts	Nov 11	Nov 10	Nov 09
Sales Turnover	255m	271m	252m
Pre Tax Profit/Loss	7m	6m	5m
Working Capital	179m	174m	164m
Fixed Assets	2m	2m	5m
Current Assets	219m	224m	207m
Current Liabilities	31m	39m	33m

Homegoods
7 Fairfax Centre, Kidlington, OX5 2PA
Tel: 01865-436010 **Fax:** 01865-433360
E-mail: sales@homegoods.co.uk
Website: http://www.homegoods.co.uk
Directors: M. Felton (Prop)
Date established: 1998 **No.of Employees:** 11 - 20 **Product Groups:** 36, 40

Inchcape plc
Oxford Motor Park Langford Lane, Kidlington, OX5 1HT
Tel: 08451-255900 **Fax:** 01865-849415
E-mail: iukhq@inchcape.com
Website: http://www.inchcape.co.uk
Bank(s): National Westminster Bank Plc
Managers: R. Armstrong (Mgr)
Ultimate Holding Company: INCHCAPE PLC
Immediate Holding Company: INCHCAPE UK LIMITED
Registration no: 03695690 **Date established:** 1999
Turnover: £500m - £1,000m **No.of Employees:** 11 - 20
Product Groups: 68

Indukey UK Ltd
11 Begbroke Lane Begbroke, Kidlington, OX5 1RN
Tel: 01865-841882 **Fax:** 01865-373102
E-mail: info@indukey.co.uk
Website: http://www.indukey.co.uk
Directors: M. van der Linden (MD), M. Van Der Linden (Fin)
Immediate Holding Company: INDUKEY UK LIMITED
Registration no: 05398908 **Date established:** 2005
Turnover: Up to £250,000 **No.of Employees:** 1 - 10 **Product Groups:** 44

Date of Accounts	Mar 07	Mar 06
Working Capital	-9	-5
Fixed Assets	2	2
Current Assets	14	11
Current Liabilities	23	N/A

Industrial Design Ltd
7 Lakesmere Close, Kidlington, OX5 1LG
Tel: 08701-283835 **Fax:** 08701-314307
E-mail: james.ward@industrialdesign.ltd.uk
Website: http://www.industrialdesign.ltd.uk
Directors: J. Ward (Dir), M. Fikuart (MD)
Immediate Holding Company: INDUSTRIAL DESIGN LIMITED
Registration no: 04588322 **Date established:** 2002
No.of Employees: 1 - 10 **Product Groups:** 38, 40, 52, 67, 84

Date of Accounts	Nov 10	Nov 09	Nov 08
Working Capital	54	47	52
Fixed Assets	3	6	7
Current Assets	227	147	196

Intertronics
Unit 17 Station Field Industrial Estate, Kidlington, OX5 1JD
Tel: 01865-842842 **Fax:** 01865-842172
E-mail: enquiries@intertronics.co.uk
Website: http://www.intertronics.co.uk
Bank(s): National Westminster Bank Plc
Directors: L. Brew (Fin), P. Swanson (MD)
Registration no: 01835617 **VAT No.:** GB 391 6244 43
No.of Employees: 11 - 20 **Product Groups:** 27, 32

K C I Medical
K C I House The Langford Business Park Langford Locks, Kidlington, OX5 1GF
Tel: 01865-840600 **Fax:** 01865-840626
E-mail: wburns@kci-medical.com
Website: http://www.kci-medical.com
Bank(s): National Westminster Bank Plc
Directors: W. Burns (Dir)
Managers: C. Priestley, P. McGrane (Comptroller)
Ultimate Holding Company: KINETIC CONCEPTS INC (USA)
Immediate Holding Company: KCI MEDICAL LIMITED
Registration no: 01130981 **VAT No.:** GB 423 6348 60
Date established: 1973 **Turnover:** £20m - £50m
No.of Employees: 101 - 250 **Product Groups:** 26

Date of Accounts	Dec 10	Dec 09	Dec 08
Sales Turnover	26m	31m	30m
Pre Tax Profit/Loss	870	1m	3m
Working Capital	11m	9m	8m
Fixed Assets	15m	16m	16m
Current Assets	13m	13m	15m
Current Liabilities	790	2m	4m

M T G Property Services Ltd
PO Box 321, Kidlington, OX5 9AB
Tel: 01865-378183 **Fax:** 07771-681139
E-mail: info@mtg-ps.com
Website: http://www.mtg-ps.com
Directors: T. Marshall (MD), D. Marshall (Sales), D. Marshell (Sales), T. Marsall (MD)
Managers: C. Washbrock (Mktg Serv Mgr)
No.of Employees: 1 - 10 **Product Groups:** 80

Date of Accounts	Oct 06	Oct 05
Working Capital	-15	-5
Fixed Assets	3	2
Current Assets	2	7
Current Liabilities	17	12

Mechadyne International Ltd
Park Farm Technology Centre Akeman Street, Kirtlington, Kidlington, OX5 3JQ
Tel: 01869-350903 **Fax:** 01869-351302
E-mail: info@mechadyne-int.com
Website: http://www.mechadyne-int.com
Directors: R. Miles (Dir)
Ultimate Holding Company: MECHADYNE HOLDINGS LIMITED
Immediate Holding Company: MECHADYNE INTERNATIONAL LIMITED
Registration no: 01834088 **Date established:** 1984
Turnover: £250,000 - £500,000 **No.of Employees:** 11 - 20
Product Groups: 81, 85

Date of Accounts	Dec 11	Dec 10	Dec 09
Sales Turnover	687	400	817
Pre Tax Profit/Loss	-140	-589	-343
Working Capital	167	200	495
Fixed Assets	3	8	15
Current Assets	301	380	549
Current Liabilities	65	106	34

Molyslip Atlantic Ltd
Unit A1 Danebrook Court Langford Lane, Kidlington, OX5 1LQ
Tel: 01865-370032 **Fax:** 01865-372030
E-mail: enquiries@molyslip.co.uk
Website: http://www.molyslip.co.uk
Directors: J. Wills (Dir)
Immediate Holding Company: MOLYSLIP ATLANTIC LIMITED
Registration no: 02664511 **VAT No.:** GB 578 2951 91
Date established: 1991 **No.of Employees:** 1 - 10 **Product Groups:** 31, 32, 66

Date of Accounts	May 12	May 11	May 10
Working Capital	458	404	299
Fixed Assets	705	633	633
Current Assets	522	477	368

Moss Plastic Parts Ltd

Langford Locks, Kidlington, OX5 1HX
Tel: 01865-841100 **Fax:** 01865-370135
E-mail: sales@mossplastics.com
Website: http://www.mossplastics.com
Bank(s): National Westminster Bank Plc
Directors: M. Fish (MD), M. Ibberson (Fin), J. Green (Co Sec)
Managers: A. Mooney (Personnel), K. Berry (Purch Mgr), D. Decrease (Mktg Serv Mgr), M. Williams (Tech Serv Mgr)
Ultimate Holding Company: FILTRONA PLC
Immediate Holding Company: MOSS PLASTIC PARTS LIMITED
Registration no: 00547495 **VAT No.:** GB 194 5510 51
Date established: 1955 **Turnover:** £20m - £50m
No.of Employees: 251 - 500 **Product Groups:** 27, 30, 39, 66

Date of Accounts	Dec 11	Dec 10	Dec 09
Sales Turnover	37m	33m	26m
Pre Tax Profit/Loss	8m	5m	2m
Working Capital	18m	12m	9m
Fixed Assets	16m	16m	15m
Current Assets	32m	24m	19m
Current Liabilities	5m	3m	2m

The Oxford Duplication Centre

29 Banbury Road, Kidlington, OX5 1AQ
Tel: 01865-457000
E-mail: info@theduplicationcentre.co.uk
Website: http://www.theduplicationcentre.co.uk
Managers: C. Foulsham (Comm)
Date established: 2004 **Turnover:** £250,000 - £500,000
No.of Employees: 1 - 10 **Product Groups:** 44

Walters OEP Ltd

Unit 5 Oxonian Park, Langford Rocks, Kidlington, OX5 1FP
Tel: 01993-886205 **Fax:** 01993-886210
E-mail: sales@oep.co.uk
Website: http://www.oep.co.uk
Managers: R. Atkinson (Sales Prom Mgr)
Turnover: £2m - £5m **No.of Employees:** 21 - 50 **Product Groups:** 37, 38, 44

Date of Accounts	Mar 08	Mar 07	Dec 05
Pre Tax Profit/Loss	N/A	125	N/A
Working Capital	-553	-558	-305
Fixed Assets	780	827	305
Current Liabilities	554	558	305
ROCE% (Return on Capital Employed)		46.4	

Watling J C B Ltd

8 Station Field Industrial Estate, Kidlington, OX5 1JD
Tel: 01865-856200 **Fax:** 01865-856202
Website: http://www.watling.co.uk
Managers: S. Cocks (Mgr)
Ultimate Holding Company: HAJCO 199 LIMITED
Immediate Holding Company: WATLING JCB LIMITED
Registration no: 01245540 **Date established:** 1976
No.of Employees: 1 - 10 **Product Groups:** 42, 45

Date of Accounts	Dec 11	Dec 10	Dec 09
Sales Turnover	85m	59m	42m
Pre Tax Profit/Loss	2m	1m	531
Working Capital	4m	3m	3m
Fixed Assets	2m	2m	1m
Current Assets	16m	12m	9m
Current Liabilities	3m	3m	2m

Oxford

AC Disco Light & Pa Hire

Leyshon Road Wheatley, Oxford, OX33 1XF
Tel: 01865-875519
E-mail: contact@acdisco.com
Website: http://www.acdisco.com
Directors: J. Walton (Ptnr)
Date established: 2003 **No.of Employees:** 1 - 10 **Product Groups:** 37, 83

Amey plc

The Sherard Building Edmund Halley Road, Oxford, OX4 4DQ
Tel: 01865-713100 **Fax:** 01865-713300
E-mail: enquiries@amey.co.uk
Website: http://www.amey.co.uk
Directors: A. Nelson (Fin), D. Lloyd (Tech Serv), M. Ewell (Grp Chief Exec)
Ultimate Holding Company: FERROVIAL SA (SPAIN)
Immediate Holding Company: AMEY PLC
Registration no: 02379479 **Date established:** 1989
Turnover: £500m - £1,000m **No.of Employees:** 101 - 250
Product Groups: 72

Date of Accounts	Dec 11	Dec 10	Dec 09
Pre Tax Profit/Loss	27m	107m	386m
Working Capital	-117m	-137m	35m
Fixed Assets	201m	200m	200m
Current Assets	181m	188m	240m
Current Liabilities	700	40m	773

Anthony Walters Architectural Metal Work

91 Southend Garsington, Oxford, OX44 9DJ
Tel: 01865-361777 **Fax:** 01865-361332
E-mail: info@architectural-metalwork.com
Website: http://www.metalwork.uk.net
Directors: A. Walters (MD)
Registration no: 02757850 **Turnover:** £500,000 - £1m
No.of Employees: 1 - 10 **Product Groups:** 35

Autologic Diagnostics

Autologic House London Road, Wheatley, Oxford, OX33 1JH
Tel: 01865-870050 **Fax:** 01865-870051
E-mail: info@autologic.com
Website: http://www.autologic-diagnostics.com
Directors: I. Jones (Dir)
Managers: S. Adams (Tech Serv Mgr), K. Poffley (Mktg Serv Mgr), A. Fernandez (Sales Admin), N. Lepine (Sales Prom Mgr), A. Betteley (Eng Serv Mgr), J. Livingston (Fin Mgr)
Ultimate Holding Company: AUTOLOGIC DIAGNOSTICS HOLDINGS LIMITED
Immediate Holding Company: DIAGNOS LIMITED
Registration no: 03856565 **Date established:** 1999 **Turnover:** £5m - £10m
No.of Employees: 51 - 100 **Product Groups:** 44

Date of Accounts	Dec 11	Dec 10	Dec 09
Working Capital	10m	5m	3m
Fixed Assets	N/A	125	92
Current Assets	10m	7m	4m
Current Liabilities	N/A	N/A	2

Boult Wade Tennant Limited

First Floor Chatsworth House East Point Business Park, Sandy Lane West, Oxford, OX4 6LB
Tel: 01865-910160 **Fax:** 01865-910161
E-mail: boult@boult.com
Website: http://www.boult.com
Directors: N. Tucker (Ptnr), A. Hays (Ptnr), M. Spencer (Ptnr), F. Hide (Ptnr)
Registration no: 05408039 **Date established:** 1992
No.of Employees: 1 - 10 **Product Groups:** 44, 80, 87

Cab Glass Doors

Unit 13 Monument Business Park Warpsgrove Lane, Chalgrove, Oxford, OX44 7RW
Tel: 01865-891143 **Fax:** 01865-890033
E-mail: cab.glassdoors@virgin.net
Website: http://www.cab-glassdoors.co.uk
Directors: W. Fogden (Prop)
Immediate Holding Company: CULTURE VULTURE DIRECT LIMITED
Date established: 2002 **No.of Employees:** 1 - 10 **Product Groups:** 26, 30, 33, 40, 42, 67

Date of Accounts	Jan 11	Jan 10	Jan 09
Working Capital	N/A	N/A	-45
Fixed Assets	N/A	N/A	5
Current Assets	1	101	80
Current Liabilities	1	100	N/A

Canby Ltd

27 Park End Street, Oxford, OX1 1HU
Tel: 08452-770122 **Fax:** 01865-794673
E-mail: sales@canby.co.uk
Website: http://www.canby.co.uk
Managers: A. Mackrell (Mgr)
Immediate Holding Company: CANBY LTD
Registration no: 04445071 **Date established:** 2002
No.of Employees: 1 - 10 **Product Groups:** 02, 22, 23, 24, 43, 49, 66

Date of Accounts	Aug 11	Aug 10	Aug 09
Sales Turnover	1m	N/A	N/A
Pre Tax Profit/Loss	40	N/A	N/A
Working Capital	71	98	116
Fixed Assets	3	5	7
Current Assets	317	353	255
Current Liabilities	72	N/A	N/A

Cap Coder Ltd

Unit 42 Monument Business Park Warpsgrove Lane, Chalgrove, Oxford, OX44 7RW
Tel: 01865-891466 **Fax:** 01865-891292
E-mail: sales@capcoder.co.uk
Website: http://www.capcoder.co.uk
Bank(s): HSBC Bank plc
Directors: L. Bates (Dir)
Managers: S. Drake, J. Storey (Comptroller)
Immediate Holding Company: CAP CODER LIMITED
Registration no: 02101507 **VAT No.:** GB 285 1533 52
Date established: 1987 **Turnover:** £500,000 - £1m
No.of Employees: 11 - 20 **Product Groups:** 40, 42, 47

Date of Accounts	Apr 12	Apr 11	Apr 10
Working Capital	79	46	56
Fixed Assets	99	112	30
Current Assets	574	384	648

Carrier Refrigeration & Retail Systems Ltd

Meridian House Sandy Lane West, Littlemore, Oxford, OX4 6LB
Tel: 01865-337700 **Fax:** 01865-337799
E-mail: tracy.noble@carrier.utc.com
Website: http://www.carrier.com
Managers: C. Butler (Comptroller), L. Clarkson (Sales & Mktg Mg), T. Noble (Personnel), J. Buckingham (Tech Serv Mgr), H. Humphreys, T. Noble (Personnel)
Ultimate Holding Company: UNITED TECHNOLOGIES CORP INC (USA)
Immediate Holding Company: CARRIER REFRIGERATION UK LIMITED
Registration no: 00943308 **VAT No.:** GB 222 4236 06
Date established: 1968 **Turnover:** £20m - £50m
No.of Employees: 21 - 50 **Product Groups:** 40, 42, 48, 52, 77

Date of Accounts	Nov 10	Nov 09	Nov 08
Sales Turnover	42m	27m	39m
Pre Tax Profit/Loss	-1m	-4m	-4m
Working Capital	-9m	-8m	2m
Fixed Assets	3m	397	532
Current Assets	26m	19m	20m
Current Liabilities	5m	3m	3m

Ceramic Stove Co.

4 Earl Street, Oxford, OX2 0JA
Tel: 01865-245077 **Fax:** 01865-245077
E-mail: info@ceramicstove.com
Website: http://www.ceramicstove.com
Directors: N. Hills (Dir)
Immediate Holding Company: AAK EUROPE LIMITED
Registration no: 02551081 **Date established:** 1990
No.of Employees: 1 - 10 **Product Groups:** 40

Date of Accounts	Mar 11	Mar 10	Mar 07
Working Capital	1	-11	-1
Fixed Assets	1	1	2
Current Assets	3	2	18
Current Liabilities	N/A	N/A	17

Citizens Advice Bureau

95-96 St Aldgates, Oxford, OX1 1DA
Tel: 08444-111444 **Fax:** 01865-202715
E-mail: warren@cab-glassdoors.co.uk
Website: http://www.adviceguide.org.uk
Directors: Y. Davies (Grp Chief Exec)
Immediate Holding Company: OXFORD CITIZENS ADVICE BUREAU
Date established: 1997 **Turnover:** £500,000 - £1m
No.of Employees: 1 - 10 **Product Groups:** 33, 40

Date of Accounts	Mar 12	Mar 11	Mar 10
Sales Turnover	453	525	471
Pre Tax Profit/Loss	9	15	-460
Working Capital	108	95	76
Fixed Assets	5	12	21
Current Assets	248	184	165
Current Liabilities	140	89	89

Connell Marketing Associates

View Farm Barn Windmill Hill, Great Milton, Oxford, OX44 7NW
Tel: 01844-279070 **Fax:** 01844-279646
E-mail: david@connellmarketing.com
Website: http://www.connellmarketing.com
Directors: D. Connell (Prop)
Immediate Holding Company: PROLINX LIMITED
Registration no: 03379531 **VAT No.:** GB 434 6380 51
Date established: 1997 **Turnover:** £10m - £20m **No.of Employees:** 1 - 10
Product Groups: 44, 49, 80, 81

Conservation Resources UK Ltd

Unit 2 Ashville Way Cowley, Oxford, OX4 6TU
Tel: 01865-747755 **Fax:** 01865-747035
E-mail: conservarts@aol.com
Website: http://www.conservation-resources.co.uk
Directors: S. Ball (Dir)
Immediate Holding Company: CONSERVATION RESOURCES (U.K.) LIMITED
Registration no: 01573306 **VAT No.:** GB 340 6092 81
Date established: 1981 **No.of Employees:** 1 - 10 **Product Groups:** 26, 27, 32, 38

Date of Accounts	Dec 11	Dec 10	Dec 09
Working Capital	-25	-29	-37
Fixed Assets	21	25	30
Current Assets	102	116	118

Creative Home Supplies Ltd (CHS LImited)

32 The Lion Brewery St Thomas Street, Oxford, OX1 1JE
Tel: 01865-200278 **Fax:** 01865-200278
E-mail: cs@chs-limited.co.uk
Website: http://www.chs-limited.co.uk
Directors: O. Oznurlu (Fin)
Registration no: 06581817 **Date established:** 2006
Turnover: Up to £250,000 **No.of Employees:** 1 - 10 **Product Groups:** 30

DiskEng Advanced Data Recovery Services

John Eccles House Robert Robinson Avenue, Oxford Science Park, Oxford, OX4 4GP
Tel: 01865-469468 **Fax:** 01865-426036
E-mail: data.recovery@diskeng.com
Website: http://www.diskeng.com
Managers: A. Aly (Mgr), R. Mears (Mgr)
Registration no: 04471593 **Date established:** 2002
Turnover: Up to £250,000 **No.of Employees:** 1 - 10 **Product Groups:** 44

Drennan International Ltd

Bocardo Court Temple Road, Oxford, OX4 2EX
Tel: 01865-748989 **Fax:** 01865-748565
E-mail: sales@drennan.co.uk
Website: http://www.drennan.co.uk
Directors: F. Drennan (Co Sec), P. Brownlow (Dir)
Immediate Holding Company: DRENNAN INTERNATIONAL LIMITED
Registration no: 01420261 **Date established:** 1979 **Turnover:** £5m - £10m
No.of Employees: 101 - 250 **Product Groups:** 49

Date of Accounts	Dec 11	Dec 10	Dec 09
Sales Turnover	9m	9m	9m
Pre Tax Profit/Loss	822	165	454
Working Capital	5m	5m	5m
Fixed Assets	2m	2m	2m
Current Assets	6m	6m	7m
Current Liabilities	1m	569	1m

Ebbon Dacs Ltd

Faringdon Road Cumnor, Oxford, OX2 9QY
Tel: 01865-866810 **Fax:** 01865-860501
E-mail: info@ebbon-dacs.com
Website: http://www.ebbon-dacs.com
Directors: A. Wilson (Sales), P. Holmes (Fin), R. Pilkington (Dir), G. Forbes (Fin)
Managers: L. Rogers (Personnel)
Ultimate Holding Company: FAIRVIEW ANSTALT (LIECHTENSTEIN)
Immediate Holding Company: EBBON-DACS LIMITED
Registration no: 00722865 **Date established:** 1962 **Turnover:** £2m - £5m
No.of Employees: 21 - 50 **Product Groups:** 81

Date of Accounts	Nov 11	Nov 10	Nov 09
Sales Turnover	4m	4m	3m
Pre Tax Profit/Loss	658	-237	-937
Working Capital	656	143	179
Fixed Assets	321	356	528
Current Assets	1m	602	762
Current Liabilities	611	363	314

Electrocomponents plc

8050 Alec Issigonis Way Oxford Business Park North, Oxford, OX4 2HW
Tel: 01865-204000 **Fax:** 01865-207400
E-mail: simon.boddie@electrocomponents.com
Website: http://www.electrocomponents.com
Bank(s): HSBC Bank plc
Directors: I. Watson (Pers), R. Boynett (I.T. Dir), S. Boddie (Fin), I. Mason (Grp Chief Exec)
Ultimate Holding Company: ELECTROCOMPONENTS PUBLIC LIMITED COMPANY
Immediate Holding Company: ELECTROCOMPONENTS U.K. LIMITED
Registration no: 01648115 **VAT No.:** GB 243 1640 91
Date established: 1982 **Turnover:** Up to £250,000
No.of Employees: 51 - 100 **Product Groups:** 30, 85

Date of Accounts	Mar 12	Mar 11	Mar 10
Sales Turnover	4	N/A	N/A
Pre Tax Profit/Loss	63m	44m	41m
Working Capital	-37m	-51m	-35m
Fixed Assets	552m	558m	579m
Current Assets	6m	11m	14m
Current Liabilities	665	N/A	667

Euro Controls

Unit 54 Monument Business Park Warpsgrove Lane, Chalgrove, Oxford, OX44 7RW
Tel: 01865-400526 **Fax:** 01865-400524
E-mail: jodie@eurocontrols.co.uk
Website: http://www.eurocontrols.com
Directors: L. Watts (Prop)
Immediate Holding Company: EURO CONTROLS (UK) LTD.
Registration no: 03182808 **VAT No.:** GB 448 5277 18
Date established: 1996 **Turnover:** £500,000 - £1m
No.of Employees: 1 - 10 **Product Groups:** 40, 45, 66

Date of Accounts	Mar 11	Mar 10	Mar 09
Working Capital	93	104	112
Fixed Assets	6	6	11

Current Assets	258	255	250

Executive Fire Protection
26 Kelburne Road, Oxford, OX4 3SJ
Tel: 01865-771133 **Fax:** 01865-431119
E-mail: info@executivefire.co.uk
Website: http://www.executivefire.co.uk
Directors: J. Keown (Dir), K. Robinson (Co Sec)
Immediate Holding Company: EXECUTIVE FIRE PROTECTION LTD
Registration no: 04367147 **Date established:** 2002
No.of Employees: 1 - 10 **Product Groups:** 38, 42

Date of Accounts	Mar 08	Mar 07	Mar 06
Working Capital	136	82	51
Fixed Assets	59	46	38
Current Assets	208	147	92
Current Liabilities	72	64	41

F M A Systems Ltd
Unit 37 Monument Business Park Warpsgrove Lane, Chalgrove, Oxford, OX44 7RW
Tel: 01865-891682 **Fax:** 01865-891685
E-mail: sales@fma-systems.com
Website: http://www.fma-systems.com
Directors: C. Scott (MD)
Immediate Holding Company: F.M.A. SYSTEMS LIMITED
Registration no: 01738504 **VAT No.:** GB 413 1662 86
Date established: 1983 **Turnover:** £1m - £2m **No.of Employees:** 1 - 10
Product Groups: 44

Date of Accounts	Dec 11	Dec 10	Dec 09
Working Capital	161	149	188
Fixed Assets	6	6	7
Current Assets	292	280	347

Greens Steel Frame Building Ltd
Milton Pools Farm Great Milton, Oxford, OX44 7JE
Tel: 01844-278507 **Fax:** 01844-278438
E-mail: raysfish@yahoo.co.uk
Website: http://www.greens-sfb.co.uk
Directors: R. Green (MD)
Immediate Holding Company: GREENS STEEL FRAME BUILDINGS LIMITED
Registration no: 01673390 **Date established:** 1982
Turnover: £500,000 - £1m **No.of Employees:** 1 - 10 **Product Groups:** 35

Date of Accounts	Jan 11	Jan 10	Jan 09
Sales Turnover	N/A	932	795
Pre Tax Profit/Loss	N/A	104	129
Working Capital	671	656	598
Fixed Assets	23	28	20
Current Assets	723	820	642
Current Liabilities	N/A	134	41

Gresso Ltd
Wheatley Business Centre Old London Road, Wheatley, Oxford, OX3 1YW
Tel: 01865-522889
E-mail: enquiry@gresso.eu
Website: http://www.gresso.eu
Managers: A. Hale (Sales Prom Mgr)
Registration no: 06976356 **Date established:** 2009 **Turnover:**
No.of Employees: 1 - 10 **Product Groups:** 37, 39, 84

F Gutkind
Suite F8 Oxford Centre For Innovation, Oxford, OX2 0JX
Tel: 01865-812031 **Fax:** 01865-249261
E-mail: info@fgutkind.com
Website: http://www.fgutkind.com
Directors: J. Clemence (Dir), R. Willis (MD), R. Willis (Prop)
Immediate Holding Company: GLOBAL ENGAGE LIMITED
Registration no: 00334102 **VAT No.:** GB 243 4046 88
Date established: 2009 **Turnover:** £2m - £5m **No.of Employees:** 1 - 10
Product Groups: 31, 32

Date of Accounts	Apr 05
Sales Turnover	50
Pre Tax Profit/Loss	3
Working Capital	53
Current Assets	57
Current Liabilities	5

J Guy
23 London Road Wheatley, Oxford, OX33 1YJ
Tel: 01865-873311
Directors: J. Guy (Prop)
Date established: 1992 **No.of Employees:** 1 - 10 **Product Groups:** 35

Hartwell plc
Faringdon Road Cumnor, Oxford, OX2 9RE
Tel: 01865-866000 **Fax:** 01865-866010
E-mail: georgina.forbes@hartwell.co.uk
Website: http://www.hartwell.co.uk
Directors: G. Forbes (Co Sec), P. Holmes (Fin)
Managers: A. Hancox (Purch Mgr), M. Cannon (Tech Serv Mgr), L. Brooker (Sales & Mktg Mg)
Ultimate Holding Company: FAIRVIEW ANSTALT (LIECHTENSTEIN)
Immediate Holding Company: HARTWELL PLC
Registration no: 00155302 **VAT No.:** GB 194 3655 35
Date established: 2019 **Turnover:** £250m - £500m
No.of Employees: 21 - 50 **Product Groups:** 68

Date of Accounts	Nov 11	Nov 10	Nov 09
Sales Turnover	255m	271m	252m
Pre Tax Profit/Loss	7m	6m	5m
Working Capital	179m	174m	164m
Fixed Assets	2m	2m	5m
Current Assets	219m	224m	207m
Current Liabilities	31m	39m	33m

Image Science Ltd
Unit 17 Monument Business Park Warpsgrove Lane, Chalgrove, Oxford, OX44 7RW
Tel: 01865-400867 **Fax:** 01865-400869
E-mail: sales@image-science.co.uk
Website: http://www.image-science.co.uk
Directors: K. Urben (Dir)
Immediate Holding Company: IMAGE SCIENCE LIMITED
Registration no: 02596476 **Date established:** 1991
Turnover: £500,000 - £1m **No.of Employees:** 1 - 10 **Product Groups:** 38, 45, 47, 67, 85

Date of Accounts	Apr 11	Apr 10	Apr 09
Working Capital	1m	1m	1m
Fixed Assets	1	1	1
Current Assets	2m	1m	1m

Jewson Ltd
3 Lamarsh Road, Oxford, OX2 0HF
Tel: 01865-249821 **Fax:** 01865-241831
Website: http://www.hirepoint.co.uk
Directors: C. Kenward (Fin), P. Hindle (MD), T. Newman (Sales)
Managers: D. Harrod (District Mgr), S. Bayliff (Mgr)
Ultimate Holding Company: COMPAGNIE DE SAINT GOBAIN (FRANCE)
Immediate Holding Company: JEWSON LIMITED
Registration no: 00348407 **VAT No.:** GB 394 1212 63
Date established: 1939 **Turnover:** £500m - £1,000m
No.of Employees: 1 - 10 **Product Groups:** 25, 29, 30, 52, 66

Date of Accounts	Dec 11	Dec 10	Dec 09
Sales Turnover	1606m	1547m	1485m
Pre Tax Profit/Loss	18m	100m	45m
Working Capital	-345m	-250m	-349m
Fixed Assets	496m	387m	461m
Current Assets	657m	1005m	1320m
Current Liabilities	66m	120m	64m

Lancelyn Theatre Supplies
Electric Avenue Ferry Hinksey Road, Oxford, OX2 0BY
Tel: 01865-722468 **Fax:** 01865-728791
E-mail: reg@lancelynoxford.co.uk
Website: http://www.lancelynoxford.co.uk
Bank(s): Barclays
Managers: R. Berry (Chief Mgr)
VAT No.: GB 195 5314 45 **Turnover:** £1m - £2m **No.of Employees:** 11 - 20
Product Groups: 24, 26, 37

Lodge Furniture Ltd
PO Box 61, Oxford, OX33 1WQ
Tel: 08452-570254 **Fax:** 0870-165 6856
E-mail: judithh@lodge.co.uk
Website: http://www.lodgefurniture.co.uk
Directors: J. Heaton (Dir)
Registration no: 5580006 **Date established:** 2006
Turnover: £500,000 - £1m **No.of Employees:** 1 - 10 **Product Groups:** 25, 26

M F Hydraulics Ltd
Pony Road Cowley, Oxford, OX4 2RD
Tel: 01865-715757 **Fax:** 01865-748140
E-mail: mike@mfhydraulics.co.uk
Website: http://www.mfhydraulics.co.uk
Bank(s): Lloyds
Directors: M. Ford (MD)
Ultimate Holding Company: CENTRAL ENGINEERING & HYDRAULIC SERVICES LIMITED
Immediate Holding Company: M. F. HYDRAULICS LIMITED
Registration no: 01689586 **VAT No.:** GB 348 5734 24
Date established: 1982 **Turnover:** £1m - £2m **No.of Employees:** 11 - 20
Product Groups: 30

Date of Accounts	Mar 11	Mar 10	Mar 09
Working Capital	247	351	407
Fixed Assets	55	41	53
Current Assets	1m	1m	1m

Manches
Unit 9400 Alec Issigonis Way Oxford Business Park North, Oxford, OX4 2HN
Tel: 01865-722106 **Fax:** 01865-201012
E-mail: info@manches.com
Website: http://www.manches.com
Bank(s): Lloyds TSB.
Directors: N. Webb (Mkt Research), R. Smith (Snr Part)
Managers: T. Reid, J. Wise (Personnel), K. Collis
Registration no: OC305898 **Turnover:** £20m - £50m
No.of Employees: 101 - 250 **Product Groups:** 80

Manor House Stoves
Wheatley Road Garsington, Oxford, OX44 9DY
Tel: 01865-361505 **Fax:** 01865-361311
E-mail: info@manorhousestoves.co.uk
Website: http://www.manorhousestoves.co.uk
Directors: D. Lane (Prop)
Date established: 1977 **No.of Employees:** 1 - 10 **Product Groups:** 40

Maryland Joinery
Marylands Farm Chiselhampton, Oxford, OX44 7XD
Tel: 01865-890890 **Fax:** 01865-890890
E-mail: info@marylandsjoinery.co.uk
Website: http://www.marylandsjoinery.co.uk
Directors: T. Fullbrook (Ptnr)
No.of Employees: 1 - 10 **Product Groups:** 25, 26, 52, 63

Date of Accounts	Apr 08	Apr 07	Apr 06
Working Capital	-60	-57	-64
Fixed Assets	53	62	69
Current Assets	56	45	44
Current Liabilities	117	103	108
Total Share Capital	1	1	1

M-CAL Performance Technology Ltd
Po Box 346 Carterton, Oxford, OX18 9AL
Tel: 01993-844483 **Fax:** 01993-843843
E-mail: sales@m-cal.com
Website: http://www.m-cal.com
Registration no: 05667008 **No.of Employees:** 1 - 10 **Product Groups:** 30, 37, 38, 39, 40, 84

Date of Accounts	Dec 08	Dec 07	Dec 06
Sales Turnover	N/A	N/A	53
Pre Tax Profit/Loss	N/A	N/A	1
Working Capital	-13	-16	N/A
Fixed Assets	1	1	2
Current Assets	5	5	10
Current Liabilities	18	21	11
ROCE% (Return on Capital Employed)			106.3
ROT% (Return on Turnover)			2.7

N A G Ltd
Wilkinson House Jordan Hill Banbury Road, Oxford, OX2 8DR
Tel: 01865-511245 **Fax:** 01865-310139
E-mail: support@nag.co.uk
Website: http://www.nag.co.uk
Bank(s): HSBC
Directors: S. Shayler (MD), S. Hague (MD)
Managers: I. Reid (Sales & Mktg Mg), I. Reid (Sales & Mktg Mg), P. Mitchell (Tech Serv Mgr), K. Jenkins (Purch Mgr)
Immediate Holding Company: NAG LIMITED
Registration no: 03969095 **VAT No.:** GB 195 9078 11
Date established: 2000 **Turnover:** £5m - £10m
No.of Employees: 51 - 100 **Product Groups:** 28, 44, 67

Date of Accounts	Apr 11	Apr 10	Apr 09
Pre Tax Profit/Loss	-0	N/A	-0
Working Capital	3	3	3
Current Assets	3	3	3

News Quest Oxfordshire Ltd
Osney Mead Newspaper House, Oxford, OX2 0EJ
Tel: 01865-425262 **Fax:** 01865-425554
E-mail: s@thisisoxfordshire.co.uk
Website: http://www.thisisoxfordshire.co.uk
Bank(s): HSBC Bank plc
Directors: S. Donald (MD)
Managers: S. Harding
Immediate Holding Company: NEWSQUEST (OXFORDSHIRE & WILTSHIRE) LIMITED
Registration no: 03223511 **Date established:** 1996
Turnover: £20m - £50m **No.of Employees:** 101 - 250 **Product Groups:** 28

Date of Accounts	Dec 07
Sales Turnover	50610
Pre Tax Profit/Loss	1180
Working Capital	-58830
Fixed Assets	100260
Current Assets	6190
Current Liabilities	65020
ROCE% (Return on Capital Employed)	2.8

Nicholas Hunter Ltd
17 Chiltern Business Centre Garsington Road, Oxford, OX4 6NG
Tel: 01865-777365 **Fax:** 01865-200051
E-mail: office@nicholashunter.com
Website: http://www.nicholashunter.com
Directors: N. Hunter (MD)
Immediate Holding Company: NICHOLAS HUNTER LIMITED
Registration no: 01332924 **Date established:** 1977
No.of Employees: 1 - 10 **Product Groups:** 30, 44, 49, 65, 81

Date of Accounts	Jul 12	Jul 11	Jul 10
Working Capital	20	-5	-7
Fixed Assets	5	6	8
Current Assets	62	47	55

Oxbridge
Old Fruiterers Yard Osney Mead, Oxford, OX2 0ES
Tel: 01865-246510 **Fax:** 01865-794305
E-mail: oxbridge@btconnect.com
Directors: M. Keenan (Ptnr)
Immediate Holding Company: T.G. WEST & SON LIMITED
Registration no: 01324040 **VAT No.:** GB 410 7885 54
Date established: 1954 **No.of Employees:** 1 - 10 **Product Groups:** 20

Date of Accounts	Apr 11	Apr 10	Apr 09
Working Capital	-34	-37	24
Fixed Assets	84	87	87
Current Assets	23	34	53

Oxford Electronics
5 Kendall Crescent, Oxford, OX2 8NE
Tel: 01865-510131 **Fax:** 01865-311911
E-mail: sales@oxford-electronics.co.uk
Website: http://www.oxford-electronics.co.uk
Directors: J. Dooey (Ptnr)
Date established: 1980 **No.of Employees:** 1 - 10 **Product Groups:** 52

Oxford Glass
Unit 1 Botley Works North Hinksey Lane, Oxford, OX2 0LX
Tel: 01865-242450 **Fax:** 01865-243536
E-mail: sales@oxfordglass.co.uk
Website: http://www.oxfordglass.co.uk
Directors: S. Thomson (Ptnr)
No.of Employees: 1 - 10 **Product Groups:** 26, 33, 52, 63, 66

Oxford Innovation Ltd
Oxford Centre For Innovation New Road, Oxford, OX1 1BY
Tel: 01865-261480 **Fax:** 01865-261401
E-mail: enquiries@oxin.co.uk
Website: http://www.oxin.co.uk
Directors: D. Kingham (MD), M. Henry (Co Sec)
Managers: J. Willett (Develop Mgr)
Ultimate Holding Company: Oxford Trust
Immediate Holding Company: SQW Group Ltd
Registration no: 02177191 **VAT No.:** GB 537 1610 59
Date established: 1987 **Turnover:** £5m - £10m
No.of Employees: 51 - 100 **Product Groups:** 80

Date of Accounts	Mar 10	Mar 09	Mar 08
Sales Turnover	7m	6m	7m
Pre Tax Profit/Loss	495	610	1m
Working Capital	2m	1m	1m
Fixed Assets	316	956	1m
Current Assets	3m	2m	3m
Current Liabilities	833	773	2m

Oxford Ironmongery
64 Botley Road, Oxford, OX2 0BT
Tel: 01865-247949 **Fax:** 01865-794743
E-mail: info@oxfordironmongery.com
Website: http://www.oxfordironmongery.com
Directors: J. Newman (Dir)
Immediate Holding Company: OXFORD IRONMONGERY LTD
Registration no: 06024404 **Date established:** 2006
No.of Employees: 1 - 10 **Product Groups:** 36, 66

Date of Accounts	Jan 11	Jan 10	Jan 09
Sales Turnover	N/A	N/A	316
Working Capital	-7	-16	-20
Fixed Assets	42	40	40
Current Assets	66	51	49

Oxford Projects Ltd
Unit 1a Newtec Place Magdalen Road, Oxford, OX4 1RE
Tel: 01865-201815 **Fax:** 01865-242520
E-mail: info@oxfordprojects.co.uk
Website: http://www.oxfordprojects.co.uk
Directors: S. Kendall (Dir)
Immediate Holding Company: OXFORD PROJECTS LIMITED
Registration no: 02962401 **Date established:** 1994
Turnover: £250,000 - £500,000 **No.of Employees:** 1 - 10
Product Groups: 86

Date of Accounts	Dec 11	Dec 10	Dec 09
Working Capital	67	93	89
Fixed Assets	1	3	3
Current Assets	105	121	117

Oxford University Press
Great Clarendon Street, Oxford, OX2 6DP
Tel: 01865-556767 **Fax:** 01865-556646
E-mail: info@oxonpress.com
Website: http://www.oup.co.uk
Bank(s): Barclays
Directors: H. Reece (Grp Chief Exec), K. Jury (Mkt Research), T. Maahar (Sales), R. Boming (MD), P. Marshall (MD), J. Williams (Pers)
Managers: H. Rozier (Purch Mgr), K. Brown (Comptroller), D. Smith (I.T. Exec), J. Williams (Personnel)
Immediate Holding Company: OXFORD PRESS LIMITED
Registration no: 03072256 **Date established:** 1995
Turnover: £500m - £1,000m **No.of Employees:** 501 - 1000
Product Groups: 28, 64, 80

Pirtek Oxford
5 Driftway Centre Pony Road, Cowley, Oxford, OX4 2RD
Tel: 01865-711323 **Fax:** 01865-711257
E-mail: info@pirtek.co.uk
Website: http://www.pirtek.co.uk
Directors: A. Lucas (Dir)
Registration no: 3509698 **Date established:** 1993 **Turnover:** £10m - £20m
No.of Employees: 1 - 10 **Product Groups:** 30, 36, 84

Red Lion 49 Ltd (t/a Solid State Logic)
Spring Hill Road Begbroke, Oxford, OX5 1RU
Tel: 01865-842300 **Fax:** 01865-842118
E-mail: sales@solidstatelogic.com
Website: http://www.solid-state-logic.com
Directors: A. Davis (MD), C. Smith (Co Sec), N. Feldman (Mkt Research), P. Guerinet (Sales)
Managers: M. Hepworth (I.T. Exec)
Registration no: 05362730 **VAT No.:** 718 2880 17 **Date established:** 1970
Turnover: £20m - £50m **No.of Employees:** 101 - 250 **Product Groups:** 37

Date of Accounts	Dec 07	Dec 06
Sales Turnover	20168	17543
Pre Tax Profit/Loss	-350	426
Working Capital	375	756
Fixed Assets	3244	3671
Current Assets	6186	5530
Current Liabilities	5811	4774
Total Share Capital	3023	3023
ROCE% (Return on Capital Employed)	-9.7	9.6
ROT% (Return on Turnover)	-1.7	2.4

Reed Accountancy Personnel Ltd
8 High Street, Oxford, OX1 4AB
Tel: 01865-794797 **Fax:** 01865-248805
E-mail: oxford@reed.co.uk
Website: http://www.reed.co.uk
Directors: J. Reed (MD)
Managers: B. Babbley (District Mgr), G. Macdonald (Mgr), S. Badley (Comm)
Immediate Holding Company: Reed Personnel Services Ltd
Registration no: 00973629 **Date established:** 1992
Turnover: £75m - £125m **No.of Employees:** 1 - 10 **Product Groups:** 80

Reed Specialist Recruitment
8 High Street, Oxford, OX1 4AB
Tel: 01865-793600 **Fax:** 01865-798077
E-mail: sam.hawkins@reedglobal.co.uk
Website: http://www.reed.co.uk
Managers: S. Hawkins (Mgr)
Ultimate Holding Company: REED GLOBAL LTD (MALTA)
Immediate Holding Company: REED EMPLOYMENT LIMITED
Registration no: 00669854 **Date established:** 1960
Turnover: £500m - £1,000m **No.of Employees:** 1 - 10
Product Groups: 80

Date of Accounts	Jun 11	Jun 10	Dec 07
Sales Turnover	618	450	287m
Pre Tax Profit/Loss	-2m	310	8m
Working Capital	23m	28m	28m
Fixed Assets	31	36	5m
Current Assets	28m	30m	74m
Current Liabilities	37	29	21m

Renelec Chalgrove Ltd
Unit 43 Monument Industrial Park Warpsgrove Lane, Chalgrove, Oxford, OX44 7RW
Tel: 01865-891955 **Fax:** 01865-891950
E-mail: mail@renelec-chalgrove.co.uk
Website: http://www.renelec-chalgrove.co.uk
Directors: J. Skeen (Dir), S. Couse (Dir), R. Kennedy (Fin)
Managers: C. Jones, A. Barrett
Ultimate Holding Company: RENELEC GROUP LIMITED
Immediate Holding Company: RENELEC CHALGROVE LIMITED
Registration no: 03060329 **Date established:** 1995
Turnover: £10m - £20m **No.of Employees:** 11 - 20 **Product Groups:** 52

Date of Accounts	Sep 11	Sep 10	Sep 09
Sales Turnover	11m	9m	8m
Pre Tax Profit/Loss	50	12	-4
Working Capital	911	892	893
Fixed Assets	22	9	8
Current Assets	4m	4m	3m
Current Liabilities	579	529	627

Seal Seam Ltd
Orpwoods Farm Thame Road, Great Milton, Oxford, OX44 7JD
Tel: 01844-279377 **Fax:** 01844-278477
E-mail: frank@seal-seam.co.uk
Website: http://www.seal-seam.co.uk
Directors: F. Brackenbury (MD)
Immediate Holding Company: SEAL SEAM LIMITED
Registration no: 00780724 **Date established:** 1963
Turnover: Up to £250,000 **No.of Employees:** 1 - 10 **Product Groups:** 23, 24, 28, 29, 30, 32, 35, 39, 49, 63, 66, 81

Date of Accounts	Apr 11	Apr 10	Apr 09
Working Capital	23	10	9
Fixed Assets	2	7	12
Current Assets	61	29	31

Sharp Laboratories Of Europe Ltd
Oxford Science Park Edmund Halley Road, Oxford, OX4 4GB
Tel: 01865-747711 **Fax:** 01865-747717
E-mail: reception@sharp.co.uk
Website: http://www.sle.sharp.co.uk
Bank(s): National Westminster
Directors: S. Bold (Dir)
Managers: S. Jones (Fin Mgr), D. Hiller (Tech Serv Mgr)
Ultimate Holding Company: SHARP CORP (JAPAN)
Immediate Holding Company: SHARP LABORATORIES OF EUROPE, LTD.
Registration no: 02459180 **Date established:** 1990
Turnover: £10m - £20m **No.of Employees:** 101 - 250
Product Groups: 40, 44

Date of Accounts	Mar 12	Mar 11	Mar 10
Sales Turnover	13m	14m	14m
Pre Tax Profit/Loss	609	2m	1m
Working Capital	11m	14m	13m
Fixed Assets	7m	8m	8m
Current Assets	12m	16m	15m
Current Liabilities	576	1m	1m

Shoreheat Holburn Ltd
Unit 34 Botley Works North Hinksey Lane, Oxford, OX2 0LX
Tel: 01865-791671 **Fax:** 01865- 791635
Website: http://www.shoreheat.co.uk
Directors: G. Holton (MD)
Managers: S. Mitchell (Sales Prom Mgr), D. Nicholl (Mgr), M. O'Dea (Mgr), D. Nichol (Mgr)
Immediate Holding Company: SHOREHEAT LIMITED
Registration no: 01566154 **VAT No.:** GB 484 6088 12
Date established: 1981 **Turnover:** £5m - £10m **No.of Employees:** 1 - 10
Product Groups: 36, 38, 40

Shout Business Promotions
94 London Road Headington, Oxford, OX3 9FN
Tel: 0800-019 0967 **Fax:** 01494-481433
Directors: N. Ingram (Prop)
Immediate Holding Company: QBEEBIES LTD
Registration no: 06212235 **Date established:** 2011
Turnover: Up to £250,000 **No.of Employees:** 1 - 10 **Product Groups:** 49

Date of Accounts	Dec 08	Dec 07	Mar 11
Sales Turnover	219	203	2
Pre Tax Profit/Loss	26	-13	-36
Working Capital	76	16	3
Fixed Assets	14	47	N/A
Current Assets	101	62	3
Current Liabilities	25	45	N/A

Software Imaging International Ltd
9400 Garsington Road Oxford Business Park, Oxford Business Park North, Oxford, OX4 2HN
Tel: 01865-786000 **Fax:** 01865-786001
E-mail: oemsales@softwareimaging.com
Website: http://www.grattan.co.uk
Directors: J. Guy (Ch), K. Jampole (Dir), P. Lismer (Grp Chief Exec)
Managers: C. Cox (I.T. Exec), I. Anderson (Personnel)
Ultimate Holding Company: Software Imaging Group Ltd
Immediate Holding Company: Software Imaging Group Ltd
Registration no: 04253839 **VAT No.:** GB 630 6844 43
Date established: 1983 **Turnover:** £5m - £10m **No.of Employees:** 1 - 10
Product Groups: 44

Date of Accounts	Jan 10	Jan 09	Jan 08
Sales Turnover	2m	7m	8m
Pre Tax Profit/Loss	-5m	2m	2m
Working Capital	-2m	3m	2m
Fixed Assets	N/A	N/A	1
Current Assets	75	6m	5m
Current Liabilities	2m	3m	2m

Sandy Steele
16-17 St Ebbes Street, Oxford, OX1 1PT
Tel: 01865-773437
E-mail: sandylsteele@hotmail.com
Website: http://www.oxford-acupuncture.co.uk
Directors: S. Steele (Prop)
No.of Employees: 1 - 10 **Product Groups:** 88

Symm & Co. Ltd
Osney Mead, Oxford, OX2 0EQ
Tel: 01865-254900 **Fax:** 01865-254935
E-mail: mailbox@symm.co.uk
Website: http://www.symmgroup.com
Bank(s): National Westminster Bank Plc
Directors: M. Wittet (Fin)
Ultimate Holding Company: SYMM GROUP LIMITED
Immediate Holding Company: SYMM & COMPANY LIMITED
Registration no: 00258950 **Date established:** 1931
Turnover: £20m - £50m **No.of Employees:** 21 - 50 **Product Groups:** 52, 84

Date of Accounts	Mar 11	Mar 10	Mar 09
Sales Turnover	23m	22m	N/A
Pre Tax Profit/Loss	-757	1m	2m
Working Capital	3m	3m	2m
Fixed Assets	425	389	534
Current Assets	7m	7m	8m
Current Liabilities	941	2m	3m

Timbmet Ltd
Kemp House Chawley Park Cumnor Hill, Cumnor, Oxford, OX2 9PH
Tel: 01865-862223 **Fax:** 01865-864367
E-mail: marko.bjelic@timbmet.com
Website: http://www.timbmet.com
Bank(s): Barclays
Directors: J. Dobson (Fin)
Managers: W. Gillard (Personnel), S. Way, M. Bjelic, A. Shyam, J. Chambers
Ultimate Holding Company: TIMBMET HOLDINGS LIMITED
Immediate Holding Company: TIMBMET LIMITED
Registration no: 03009353 **VAT No.:** GB 195 0976 24
Date established: 1995 **Turnover:** £75m - £125m
No.of Employees: 51 - 100 **Product Groups:** 08, 25, 48

Date of Accounts	Mar 11	Mar 10	Mar 09
Sales Turnover	87m	82m	95m
Pre Tax Profit/Loss	297	-1m	-8m
Working Capital	9m	4m	4m
Fixed Assets	27m	30m	31m
Current Assets	37m	32m	37m
Current Liabilities	17m	16m	18m

Truck & Trailer Components Ltd
Unipart House Garsington Road, Cowley, Oxford, OX4 2PG
Tel: 01865-383999 **Fax:** 0800-361677
E-mail: ttc@unipart.co.uk
Website: http://www.ttcuk.co.uk
Directors: J. Gratrex (Pers), C. Powell (Tech Serv), A. Mourgue (Fin)
Managers: D. Miller (Mgr)
Ultimate Holding Company: UNIPART GROUP OF COMPANIES LIMITED
Immediate Holding Company: TRUCK & TRAILER COMPONENTS LIMITED
Registration no: 01865675 **VAT No.:** GB 448 5763 09
Date established: 1984 **Turnover:** £10m - £20m
No.of Employees: 51 - 100 **Product Groups:** 68

Unicol Engineering
Green Road Headington, Oxford, OX3 8EU
Tel: 01865-767676 **Fax:** 01865-767677
E-mail: sales@unicol.com
Website: http://www.unicol.com
Bank(s): Lloyds
Directors: D. Johnson (MD)
Immediate Holding Company: UNICOL ENGINEERING
Registration no: 01988697 **Date established:** 1986
No.of Employees: 21 - 50 **Product Groups:** 26, 37, 38, 49, 67

UPSMart
PO Box 1498, Oxford, OX3 3BY
Tel: 08447-365980 **Fax:** 01865-543110
E-mail: info@upsmart.co.uk
Website: http://www.upsmart.co.uk
No.of Employees: 1 - 10 **Product Groups:** 37, 44, 67

Vicon Motion Systems Ltd
Unit 14 7 West Way, Oxford, OX2 0JB
Tel: 01865-261800 **Fax:** 01865-240527
E-mail: sales@vicon.com
Website: http://www.vicon.com
Bank(s): National Westminster
Directors: J. Morris (Dir)
Ultimate Holding Company: OMG PLC
Immediate Holding Company: VICON MOTION SYSTEMS LIMITED
Registration no: 01801446 **VAT No.:** GB 768 3518 91
Date established: 1984 **Turnover:** £10m - £20m
No.of Employees: 51 - 100 **Product Groups:** 40, 83

Date of Accounts	Sep 11	Sep 10	Sep 09
Sales Turnover	13m	15m	11m
Pre Tax Profit/Loss	5m	3m	2m
Working Capital	14m	10m	9m
Fixed Assets	2m	2m	1m
Current Assets	17m	13m	11m
Current Liabilities	1m	2m	971

Waldner Ltd
7400 The Quorum Alec Issigonis Way Oxford Business Park North, Oxford, OX4 2JZ
Tel: 01865-788170 **Fax:** 01844-338716
E-mail: info@waldner.co.uk
Website: http://www.waldner.co.uk
Directors: K. Kreuzer (Dir), S. Springer (Co Sec)
Ultimate Holding Company: WALDNER LABOREINRICHTUNGEN VERWALTUNGS GMBH (GERMANY)
Immediate Holding Company: WALDNER LIMITED
Registration no: 02388661 **Date established:** 1989
Turnover: £250,000 - £500,000 **No.of Employees:** 11 - 20
Product Groups: 26, 42, 67

Date of Accounts	Jun 11	Jun 10	Jun 09
Working Capital	202	136	73
Fixed Assets	36	17	25
Current Assets	1m	2m	2m

Thame

Advanced Labelling Systems Ltd
Unit B Bandet Way, Thame, OX9 3SJ
Tel: 01844-213177 **Fax:** 01844-217188
E-mail: sales@als-eu.com
Website: http://www.als-eu.com
Directors: N. Donaldson (MD), P. Donaldson (Sales), V. Donaldson (Fin)
Immediate Holding Company: ADVANCED LABELLING SYSTEMS LIMITED
Registration no: 03334270 **Date established:** 1997
Turnover: £500,000 - £1m **No.of Employees:** 11 - 20
Product Groups: 27, 42, 43, 44

Date of Accounts	Apr 11	Apr 10	Apr 09
Working Capital	1m	1m	1m
Fixed Assets	39	38	19
Current Assets	2m	2m	2m

Angus Fire
Thame Park Road, Thame, OX9 3RT
Tel: 01844-265000 **Fax:** 01844-265156
E-mail: general.enquiries@kiddeuk.co.uk
Website: http://www.angusfire.co.uk
Bank(s): Barclays
Directors: C. Boon (Sales), L. Guest (Fin), P. Williams (MD)
Managers: B. Keeble (Mktg Serv Mgr), N. Hanson (Personnel), C. Thorp (Tech Serv Mgr), I. Ross (Purch Mgr)
Ultimate Holding Company: WILLIAMS P.L.C.
Immediate Holding Company: KIDDE UK
Registration no: 00714186 **VAT No.:** GB 348 3570 38
Turnover: £20m - £50m **No.of Employees:** 101 - 250
Product Groups: 32, 33, 38, 39, 40

Atlet Ltd
Jane Morbey Road, Thame, OX9 3RR
Tel: 01844-215501 **Fax:** 01844-216492
E-mail: sales@atlet.co.uk
Website: http://www.atlet.com
Bank(s): National Westminster Bank Plc
Ultimate Holding Company: NISSAN MOTOR CO LTD (JAPAN)
Immediate Holding Company: Atlet AB (Sweden)
Registration no: 00958167 **Date established:** 1969
Turnover: £20m - £50m **No.of Employees:** 101 - 250 **Product Groups:** 45

Date of Accounts	Dec 09	Dec 08	Dec 07
Sales Turnover	23m	23m	22m
Pre Tax Profit/Loss	1m	1m	1m
Working Capital	5m	4m	3m
Fixed Assets	5m	6m	5m
Current Assets	9m	7m	7m
Current Liabilities	2m	2m	2m

D A F Trucks Ltd
Eastern-By-Pass, Thame, OX9 3FB
Tel: 01844-261111 **Fax:** 01844-217111
E-mail: ray.ashworth@daftrucks.com
Website: http://www.daftrucks.co.uk
Bank(s): ABN AMRO Bank NV

Directors: R. Ashworth (MD), S. Moore (Fin)
Managers: T. Pain, E. Graham (Personnel)
Ultimate Holding Company: PACCAR INC (USA)
Immediate Holding Company: DAF TRUCKS LIMITED
Registration no: 02815777 **VAT No.:** GB 630 5369 52
Date established: 1993 **Turnover:** £20m - £50m
No.of Employees: 101 - 250 **Product Groups:** 39, 45, 68

Date of Accounts	Dec 11	Dec 10	Dec 09
Sales Turnover	17m	17m	17m
Pre Tax Profit/Loss	5m	1m	-3m
Working Capital	17m	7m	8m
Fixed Assets	89	79	108
Current Assets	23m	17m	25m
Current Liabilities	3m	7m	12m

Diagnostic Reagents Ltd
Wenman Road, Thame, OX9 3NY
Tel: 01844-212426 **Fax:** 01844-216162
E-mail: sales@diagen.co.uk
Website: http://www.diagen.co.uk
Directors: A. Denson (MD)
Immediate Holding Company: DIAGNOSTIC REAGENTS LIMITED
Registration no: 00704871 **VAT No.:** GB 194 3432 55
Date established: 1961 **No.of Employees:** 1 - 10 **Product Groups:** 31

Date of Accounts	Dec 10	Dec 09	Dec 08
Working Capital	383	590	490
Fixed Assets	217	244	278
Current Assets	741	667	588

Duntech Irrigation Services Ltd
12 Yeates Close, Thame, OX9 3AR
Tel: 01844-215411 **Fax:** 08712-435165
E-mail: contact@duntech-irrigation.com
Website: http://www.duntech-irrigation.com
Directors: A. Enticknap (Dir)
Immediate Holding Company: DUNTECH IRRIGATION SERVICES LIMITED
Registration no: 01789740 **Date established:** 1984
Turnover: Up to £250,000 **No.of Employees:** 1 - 10 **Product Groups:** 36, 41, 42, 51, 67

Date of Accounts	Feb 11	Feb 10	Feb 09
Sales Turnover	120	N/A	N/A
Pre Tax Profit/Loss	37	N/A	N/A
Working Capital	14	8	9
Fixed Assets	3	2	2
Current Assets	25	22	22
Current Liabilities	8	N/A	N/A

Glencore Grain UK Ltd
Warren House Bell Lane, Thame, OX9 3AL
Tel: 01844-261261 **Fax:** 01844-216301
E-mail: info@grainman.co.uk
Website: http://www.glencore.co.uk
Directors: E. Mostert (Fin), S. Pujara (Co Sec)
Ultimate Holding Company: GLENCORE INTERNATIONAL AG (SWITZERLAND)
Immediate Holding Company: GLENCORE GRAIN UK LTD.
Registration no: 00481296 **Date established:** 1969
Turnover: £250m - £500m **No.of Employees:** 21 - 50 **Product Groups:** 20

Date of Accounts	Dec 11	Dec 10	Dec 09
Sales Turnover	356m	293m	163m
Pre Tax Profit/Loss	2m	6m	2m
Working Capital	12m	10m	6m
Fixed Assets	773	367	244
Current Assets	53m	114m	31m
Current Liabilities	2m	18m	3m

A R Green
30 Towersey Drive, Thame, OX9 3NR
Tel: 01844-212347
Directors: A. Green (Ptnr)
Date established: 1987 **No.of Employees:** 1 - 10 **Product Groups:** 35

H C Pearce & Sons Ltd
Aylesbury Road, Thame, OX9 3AS
Tel: 01844-212034 **Fax:** 01844-261358
E-mail: info@hcpearce.co.uk
Website: http://www.hcpearce.co.uk
Bank(s): Barclays, Bradford
Managers: C. Behrens (Chief Mgr)
Immediate Holding Company: Francis Willey (British Wools 1935) Ltd
Registration no: 00436868 **VAT No.:** GB 195 4845 19
Turnover: £5m - £10m **No.of Employees:** 11 - 20 **Product Groups:** 23

Hickman Shearer
7 Buttermarket, Thame, OX9 3EW
Tel: 01844-215755 **Fax:** 01844-214549
E-mail: philip@hickman-shearer.co.uk
Website: http://www.hickman-shearer.co.uk
Directors: P. Davies (Dir)
Immediate Holding Company: MG PARTNERSHIP LTD
Registration no: 05018709 **Date established:** 2012
Turnover: £500,000 - £1m **No.of Employees:** 1 - 10 **Product Groups:** 61

Date of Accounts	Mar 11	Mar 10	Mar 09
Working Capital	119	148	159
Current Assets	722	405	322

Interfood Technology Ltd
Unit 11-12 Thame Park Business Centre Wenman Road, Thame, OX9 3XA
Tel: 01844-217676 **Fax:** 01844-217681
E-mail: mbishop@interfoodtechnology.com
Website: http://www.interfoodtechnology.com
Directors: J. Sydenham (Fin), M. Bishop (MD)
Ultimate Holding Company: POLY-CLIP BETEILIGUNGS GMBH (GERMANY)
Immediate Holding Company: INTERFOOD TECHNOLOGY LTD.
Registration no: 03800145 **Date established:** 1999
Turnover: £20m - £50m **No.of Employees:** 21 - 50 **Product Groups:** 20, 40, 41

Date of Accounts	Dec 11	Dec 10	Dec 09
Sales Turnover	21m	22m	14m
Pre Tax Profit/Loss	1m	2m	772
Working Capital	4m	3m	3m
Fixed Assets	535	422	250
Current Assets	11m	10m	9m
Current Liabilities	3m	4m	4m

International Precision Products
Unit 1a Station Yard, Thame, OX9 3UH
Tel: 01844-217678 **Fax:** 01844-215495
E-mail: ask@ippbv.com
Website: http://www.ippbv.com
Directors: M. Wolff (Sales)
Immediate Holding Company: INTERNATIONAL PRECISION PRODUCTS
Registration no: FC008055 **Date established:** 1974 **Turnover:** £2m - £5m
No.of Employees: 1 - 10 **Product Groups:** 37, 38, 39

Date of Accounts	Dec 07	Dec 06	Dec 05
Pre Tax Profit/Loss	413	368	224
Working Capital	2195	1904	1828
Fixed Assets	213	235	255
Current Assets	3455	3609	3678
Current Liabilities	1260	1705	1850
Total Share Capital	227	227	227
ROCE% (Return on Capital Employed)	17.2	17.2	10.8

Kidde Products
Wenman Road, Thame, OX9 3RT
Tel: 01524-264000 **Fax:** 01844-265156
E-mail: charles.boon@kiddeuk.co.uk
Website: http://www.kiddeuk.co.uk
Directors: C. Ibbotson (Pers), L. Guest (Fin)
Managers: A. Barton, C. Boon (Chief Mgr), C. Thorp (Tech Serv Mgr)
No.of Employees: 101 - 250 **Product Groups:** 38, 42

Kubota UK Ltd
7 Dormer Road, Thame, OX9 3UN
Tel: 01844-268000 **Fax:** 01844-216685
E-mail: yukio.sakai@kubota.co.uk
Website: http://www.kubota.co.uk
Bank(s): Barclays
Directors: T. Suzuki (MD)
Managers: A. Dymott (Tech Serv Mgr), D. Nash (Transport), C. Dillingham (Personnel), L. Law, D. Roberts (Mktg Serv Mgr)
Ultimate Holding Company: KUBOTA CORP (JAPAN)
Immediate Holding Company: KUBOTA (U.K.) LIMITED
Registration no: 01299429 **Date established:** 1977
Turnover: £75m - £125m **No.of Employees:** 51 - 100
Product Groups: 37, 41, 45

Date of Accounts	Dec 11	Dec 10	Dec 09
Sales Turnover	125m	98m	74m
Pre Tax Profit/Loss	9m	6m	2m
Working Capital	52m	46m	42m
Fixed Assets	248	257	331
Current Assets	84m	73m	65m
Current Liabilities	4m	5m	4m

Lucy Switchgear
Howland Road, Thame, OX9 3UJ
Tel: 01844-267267 **Fax:** 01844-267223
E-mail: info@lucyswitchgear.com
Website: http://www.lucyswitchgear.com
Bank(s): HSBC Bank plc
Managers: C. Levick (Chief Mgr)
Ultimate Holding Company: W LUCY & CO LTD
Registration no: 00051908 **No.of Employees:** 251 - 500
Product Groups: 37, 48, 67

Nordson UK Ltd
Wenman Road, Thame, OX9 3SW
Tel: 01844-264500 **Fax:** 01844-215358
E-mail: salesoxf@uk.nordson.com
Website: http://www.nordson.com
Bank(s): Fortis
Directors: P. Mcmahon (Fin)
Managers: D. Griffiths (Div Mgr), P. Brown (Tech Serv Mgr), A. Byram (Sales Prom Mgr), J. Palazzo (Chief Mgr), S. Hankin, S. Slade
Ultimate Holding Company: Nordson Corporation
Immediate Holding Company: Nordson Corp (USA)
Registration no: 01056577 **VAT No.:** GB 195 1238 55
Date established: 1972 **Turnover:** Over £1,000m
No.of Employees: 11 - 20 **Product Groups:** 37, 42, 43, 44, 47, 67

Optical Filters
Unit 13-14 Thame Park Business Centre Wenman Road, Thame, OX9 3XA
Tel: 01844-260377 **Fax:** 01844-260355
E-mail: information@opticalfilters.co.uk
Website: http://www.opticalfilters.co.uk
Bank(s): Lloyds TSB Bank plc
Directors: K. Whitney (Fin)
Managers: R. Rickman (Chief Mgr), K. Merritt (Mktg Serv Mgr), S. Poole (Personnel), K. Whytock (Buyer)
Ultimate Holding Company: SEASPARKLE INVESTMENTS SA (LIBERIA)
Immediate Holding Company: OPTICAL FILTERS LIMITED
Registration no: 02289077 **VAT No.:** GB 537 3354 41
Date established: 1988 **Turnover:** £2m - £5m **No.of Employees:** 21 - 50
Product Groups: 37, 38

Date of Accounts	Dec 11	Dec 10	Dec 09
Working Capital	686	669	664
Fixed Assets	250	265	102
Current Assets	1m	1m	1m

Primary Designs Ltd
Unit 10 Thame Park Business Centre Wenman Road, Thame, OX9 3XA
Tel: 01844-216057 **Fax:** 01844-216058
E-mail: patbarrett@primarydesigns.co.uk
Website: http://www.primarydesigns.co.uk
Directors: P. Barrett (Dir)
Immediate Holding Company: PRIMARY DESIGNS LIMITED
Registration no: 03522410 **Date established:** 1998
No.of Employees: 11 - 20 **Product Groups:** 35, 36, 39, 40, 46, 48, 68

Date of Accounts	Sep 11	Sep 10	Sep 09
Working Capital	562	518	585
Fixed Assets	186	57	47
Current Assets	898	703	689

The Shield Group
60 London Road Milton Common, Thame, OX9 2JL
Tel: 01844-278666 **Fax:** 01844-278664
E-mail: service@theshieldgroup.co.uk
Website: http://www.theshieldgroup.co.uk
Directors: J. Partington (Prop)
No.of Employees: 1 - 10 **Product Groups:** 32, 38, 52, 71

Sill Lighting UK Ltd
3 Thame Park Business Centre Wenman Road, Thame, OX9 3XA
Tel: 01844-260006 **Fax:** 01844-260760
E-mail: sales@sill-uk.com
Website: http://www.sill-uk.com
Managers: R. Bohannon (Chief Mgr)
Immediate Holding Company: SILL LIGHTING (UK) LIMITED
Registration no: 04288961 **Date established:** 2001 **Turnover:** £1m - £2m
No.of Employees: 1 - 10 **Product Groups:** 35, 37, 39

Specialised Latex Services Ltd
7 Lupton Road, Thame, OX9 3SE
Tel: 01844-212489 **Fax:** 01844-212489
E-mail: sales@specialisedlatex.co.uk
Website: http://www.specialisedlatex.co.uk
Bank(s): Bank of Scotland
Directors: A. Spouse (MD), G. Spouse (Sales), J. Spouse (Fin)
Immediate Holding Company: SPECIALISED LATEX SERVICES LIMITED
Registration no: 01125581 **VAT No.:** 208 9875 22 **Date established:** 1973
Turnover: £500,000 - £1m **No.of Employees:** 11 - 20
Product Groups: 24, 29

Date of Accounts	Jul 11	Jul 10	Jul 09
Working Capital	274	280	256
Fixed Assets	319	308	309
Current Assets	493	538	569

Spruced Up Ltd
26 Park Street, Thame, OX9 3HP
Tel: 01844-343783
E-mail: info@spruced-up.co.uk
Website: http://www.spruced-up.co.uk
Directors: R. Jeffries (MD)
Immediate Holding Company: SPRUCED-UP LIMITED
Registration no: 04978609 **Date established:** 2003
Turnover: Up to £250,000 **No.of Employees:** 1 - 10 **Product Groups:** 25, 35, 49, 52

Date of Accounts	Nov 11	Nov 10	Nov 09
Sales Turnover	231	231	N/A
Pre Tax Profit/Loss	39	19	N/A
Working Capital	12	12	-11
Fixed Assets	3	5	12
Current Assets	37	34	36
Current Liabilities	25	14	12

Systech Instruments Ltd
17 Thame Business Park, Thame, OX9 3XA
Tel: 01844-216838 **Fax:** 01844-217220
E-mail: b.cummings@systechillinois.com
Website: http://www.systechillinois.com
Bank(s): Lloyds TSB Bank plc
Directors: B. Cummings (Dir), S. Hanks (Fin)
Immediate Holding Company: SYSTECH INSTRUMENTS LIMITED
Registration no: 02591191 **VAT No.:** GB 596 3929 77
Date established: 1991 **Turnover:** £1m - £2m **No.of Employees:** 11 - 20
Product Groups: 38, 39, 41, 45, 67

Date of Accounts	Dec 11	Dec 10	Jun 09
Working Capital	1m	877	2m
Fixed Assets	880	1m	676
Current Assets	1m	2m	2m

Thame Energy Systems 1998 Ltd
39 North Street, Thame, OX9 3BJ
Tel: 01844-218705 **Fax:** 01844-218748
E-mail: joe@thame-energy.com
Website: http://www.thame-energy.com
Directors: W. Richardson (Prop)
Immediate Holding Company: THAME ENERGY SYSTEMS (1998) LIMITED
Registration no: 03665544 **Date established:** 1998
Turnover: £250,000 - £500,000 **No.of Employees:** 1 - 10
Product Groups: 40, 41, 45, 66

Date of Accounts	Mar 11	Mar 10	Mar 09
Working Capital	52	12	35
Fixed Assets	1	1	N/A
Current Assets	169	107	168

Wharton Electronics Ltd
Unit 15 Thame Park Business Centre Wenman Road, Thame, OX9 3XA
Tel: 01844-260567 **Fax:** 01844-218855
E-mail: sales@wharton.co.uk
Website: http://www.wharton.co.uk
Bank(s): National Westminster Bank Plc
Directors: E. Wharton (MD)
Immediate Holding Company: WHARTON ELECTRONICS LIMITED
Registration no: 04221564 **Date established:** 2001 **Turnover:** £2m - £5m
No.of Employees: 11 - 20 **Product Groups:** 49

Date of Accounts	Jun 11	Jun 10	Jun 09
Working Capital	158	137	132
Fixed Assets	177	176	198
Current Assets	955	744	810

Zilog (UK)
Suite 4- First Floor Oxford House Oxford Road, Thame, OX9 2AH
Tel: 01844-263600 **Fax:** 01844-263601
E-mail: thame@avnet-memec.eu
Website: http://www.zilog.com
Directors: P. Grace (Dir)
Managers: C. Dennis (Sales Prom Mgr)
Ultimate Holding Company: Zilog Inc (USA)
Registration no: 01283368 **Date established:** 1976
Turnover: £250,000 - £500,000 **No.of Employees:** 1 - 10
Product Groups: 37, 44

Wallingford

The Aroma Company Europe Ltd
Hilliard House Lester Way, Wallingford, OX10 9TA
Tel: 01491-835510
E-mail: info@aromaco.co.uk
Website: http://www.aromaco.co.uk
Directors: V. Lord (MD)
Immediate Holding Company: THE AROMA COMPANY (EUROPE) LTD.
Registration no: 03252112 **Date established:** 1996
Turnover: Up to £250,000 **No.of Employees:** 1 - 10 **Product Groups:** 81

see next page

***The Aroma Company Europe Ltd** - Cont'd*

Date of Accounts	Mar 12	Mar 11	Mar 10
Working Capital	159	173	172
Fixed Assets	20	23	34
Current Assets	198	268	442

Brapack Ltd
Brapack Building Moreton Avenue, Wallingford, OX10 9DE
Tel: 01491-834600 **Fax:** 01491-825409
E-mail: sales@brapack.com
Website: http://www.bratack.com
Bank(s): HSBC Bank plc
Directors: J. Ayres (MD), K. Thomas (Dir), R. Ayres (Dir), S. Ayres (Sales)
Immediate Holding Company: BRAPACK LIMITED
Registration no: 01446173 **VAT No.:** GB 314 3623 88
Date established: 1979 **Turnover:** £1m - £2m **No.of Employees:** 11 - 20
Product Groups: 32, 66

Date of Accounts	Aug 07	Aug 06	Aug 05
Working Capital	58	157	233
Fixed Assets	858	883	910
Current Assets	542	536	619

Bromag Structures Ltd
2 Mill Lane Benson, Wallingford, OX10 6SA
Tel: 01491-838808
E-mail: jo@bromag.co.uk
Website: http://www.bromag.co.uk
Directors: R. Hine (Ch), L. Hilton (Co Sec)
Immediate Holding Company: BROMAG STRUCTURES LIMITED
Registration no: 00915197 **Date established:** 1967
No.of Employees: 1 - 10 **Product Groups:** 35

Date of Accounts	Dec 11	Dec 10	Dec 09
Working Capital	521	493	464
Fixed Assets	721	727	730
Current Assets	553	549	536

Buffalo Timber Buildings
Ipsden, Wallingford, OX10 6BS
Tel: 01491-837682 **Fax:** 01491-825418
E-mail: sales@buffalo-fence.co.uk
Website: http://www.buffalo-fence.co.uk
Directors: C. Sherlock (Fin), V. Demerest (MD)
Immediate Holding Company: BUFFALO FENCE LIMITED
Registration no: 01107290 **Date established:** 1973 **Turnover:** £1m - £2m
No.of Employees: 11 - 20 **Product Groups:** 25, 30, 33, 35, 40, 52

Date of Accounts	Jul 09	Jul 08	Apr 07
Working Capital	101	231	273
Fixed Assets	58	87	115
Current Assets	289	401	777

Cesol Tiles Ltd
11 Bushell Business Park Lester Way, Wallingford, OX10 9DD
Tel: 01491-833662 **Fax:** 01491-825147
E-mail: caroline@cesol.co.uk
Website: http://www.cesol.co.uk
Directors: C. Hicks (Dir)
Immediate Holding Company: CESOL TILES LIMITED
Registration no: 01630406 **Date established:** 1982
Turnover: Up to £250,000 **No.of Employees:** 1 - 10 **Product Groups:** 30, 31, 33, 35, 66

Date of Accounts	Aug 11	Aug 10	Aug 09
Working Capital	-26	-26	-26
Current Assets	13	13	13

Clean Machine Ltd
2 St Peters Place, Wallingford, OX10 0BG
Tel: 01491-825600 **Fax:** 01491-825400
E-mail: sales@machinesthatclean.com
Website: http://www.machinesthatclean.com
Directors: I. Monk (MD)
Immediate Holding Company: CLEAN MACHINE LIMITED
Registration no: 03777363 **Date established:** 1999
Turnover: Up to £250,000 **No.of Employees:** 1 - 10 **Product Groups:** 27, 29, 30, 32, 39, 40, 49, 63, 68

Date of Accounts	Dec 11	Dec 10	Dec 09
Sales Turnover	N/A	N/A	247
Pre Tax Profit/Loss	N/A	N/A	6
Working Capital	-14	-17	-41
Fixed Assets	51	57	66
Current Assets	76	89	69
Current Liabilities	N/A	N/A	69

Douglas Delabie Ltd
Henderson House Hithercroft Road, Wallingford, OX10 9DG
Tel: 01491-824449 **Fax:** 01491-825727
E-mail: info@douglasdelabie.co.uk
Website: http://www.douglasdelabie.co.uk
Bank(s): National Westminster Bank Plc
Directors: J. Williams (Comm), R. Stammers (MD)
Managers: J. Lake (Comptroller)
Immediate Holding Company: DOUGLAS DELABIE LIMITED
Registration no: 01764854 **VAT No.:** GB 362 9031 60
Date established: 1983 **Turnover:** £1m - £2m **No.of Employees:** 11 - 20
Product Groups: 36

Date of Accounts	Dec 11	Dec 10	Dec 09
Working Capital	913	952	1m
Fixed Assets	110	26	44
Current Assets	2m	1m	2m

Fischer Fixings UK Ltd
Whitely Road, Wallingford, OX10 9AT
Tel: 01491-827900 **Fax:** 01491-827953
E-mail: sales@fischer.co.uk
Website: http://www.fischer.co.uk
Bank(s): Lloyds
Directors: R. Weik (MD)
Ultimate Holding Company: FISCHER HOLDING GMBH & CO KG (GERMANY)
Immediate Holding Company: FISCHER FIXINGS UK LIMITED
Registration no: 00959713 **Date established:** 1969
Turnover: £10m - £20m **No.of Employees:** 21 - 50 **Product Groups:** 35, 36, 66

Date of Accounts	Dec 11	Dec 10	Dec 09
Sales Turnover	14m	13m	13m
Pre Tax Profit/Loss	-553	-1m	-2m
Working Capital	2m	-1m	-176
Fixed Assets	2m	2m	2m
Current Assets	4m	4m	4m
Current Liabilities	1m	964	948

Fondera Ltd
Unit 7a Beadle Trading Estate Hithercroft Road, Wallingford, OX10 9EZ
Tel: 01491-836222 **Fax:** 01491-836776
E-mail: fonderaltd@aol.com
Website: http://www.fondera.co.uk
Directors: C. Devall (Sales), A. Devall (Fin)
Managers: C. Jenkins (Mgr), R. Hindley, S. Jenkins (Mgr)
Immediate Holding Company: FONDERA LIMITED
Registration no: 01113341 **VAT No.:** GB 200 1683 22
Date established: 1973 **Turnover:** £500,000 - £1m
No.of Employees: 1 - 10 **Product Groups:** 39

Date of Accounts	Jul 09	Jul 08	Jul 07
Working Capital	49	62	8
Fixed Assets	299	270	284
Current Assets	191	249	180

Fugro Ltd
Fugro House Hithercroft Road, Wallingford, OX10 9RB
Tel: 01491-820700 **Fax:** 01491-820 599
E-mail: uk@geos.com
Website: http://www.fugro-geoconsulting.com
Bank(s): Lloyds TSB Bank plc
Directors: P. Power (MD)
Managers: M. Silver (Mktg Serv Mgr), H. Green (Personnel), D. Simpson (Comptroller), G. Dew
Ultimate Holding Company: FUGRO NV (NETHERLANDS)
Immediate Holding Company: FUGRO LIMITED
Registration no: 03167161 **Date established:** 1996 **Turnover:** £1m - £2m
No.of Employees: 251 - 500 **Product Groups:** 38, 67

Date of Accounts	Dec 11	Dec 10	Dec 09
Sales Turnover	3m	1m	N/A
Pre Tax Profit/Loss	425	352	N/A
Working Capital	565	260	7
Fixed Assets	7	N/A	N/A
Current Assets	957	728	7
Current Liabilities	221	185	N/A

Liquid Solutions Ltd
1 Datchet Green,Brightwell-Cum-Sotwell, Wallingford, OX10 0QB
Tel: 01491-839993 **Fax:** 01491-839993
E-mail: info@liquidsolutions.co.uk
Website: http://www.liquidsolutions.co.uk
Directors: P. Argyll (Prop)
Registration no: 06112388 **Date established:** 2002
No.of Employees: 1 - 10 **Product Groups:** 20, 40, 41

M M R Ltd
Wallingford House 46 High Street, Wallingford, OX10 0DB
Tel: 01491-824999 **Fax:** 01491-824666
E-mail: info@mmr-research.com
Website: http://www.mmr-research.com
Directors: C. Rogers (Dir)
Managers: H. Barlobe
Immediate Holding Company: MATHEMATICAL MARKET RESEARCH LIMITED
Registration no: 02304169 **Date established:** 1988
Turnover: £10m - £20m **No.of Employees:** 51 - 100 **Product Groups:** 81

Date of Accounts	Mar 12	Mar 11	Mar 10
Sales Turnover	13m	12m	8m
Pre Tax Profit/Loss	1m	1m	518
Working Capital	3m	3m	2m
Fixed Assets	126	106	68
Current Assets	6m	14m	10m
Current Liabilities	2m	2m	1m

Motor Marine
40 Borough Avenue, Wallingford, OX10 0TB
Tel: 01491-834785 **Fax:** 01491-834785
E-mail: info@collegecruisers.com
Directors: A. Strong (Prop)
Immediate Holding Company: MOTOR MARINE LIMITED
Registration no: 01580636 **Date established:** 1981
Turnover: Up to £250,000 **No.of Employees:** 1 - 10 **Product Groups:** 35, 36, 39

Presentation Display Ltd
Unit 3 Ayres Yard Station Road, Wallingford, OX10 0JZ
Tel: 01491-825588 **Fax:** 01491-826106
E-mail: presentation@f2s.com
Directors: J. Partridge (MD), P. Partridge (Dir)
Immediate Holding Company: PRESENTATION DISPLAY LIMITED
Registration no: 01521831 **Date established:** 1980
Turnover: £500,000 - £1m **No.of Employees:** 1 - 10 **Product Groups:** 26, 40, 67

Date of Accounts	Nov 07	Nov 06	Nov 05
Working Capital	68	99	107
Fixed Assets	18	18	22
Current Assets	230	209	188
Current Liabilities	163	109	81

Raceparts
Unit 3 Rockfort Industrial Estate, Wallingford, OX10 9DA
Tel: 01491-822000 **Fax:** 01491-822009
E-mail: sales@raceparts.co.uk
Website: http://www.raceparts.co.uk
Directors: P. Bloore (Dir)
Ultimate Holding Company: RACEPARTS GROSVENOR LIMITED
Immediate Holding Company: RACEPARTS LIMITED
Registration no: 02587687 **VAT No.:** GB 292 6900 37
Date established: 1991 **No.of Employees:** 1 - 10 **Product Groups:** 39

Date of Accounts	Sep 11	Sep 10	Sep 09
Working Capital	-2	-2	-2
Fixed Assets	2	2	2
Current Assets	3	71	159

G Stow plc
Lupton Road, Wallingford, OX10 9BS
Tel: 01491-834445 **Fax:** 01491-827640
E-mail: admin@gstowplc.com
Website: http://www.gstowplc.com
Directors: J. Smith (Co Sec), T. Lapper (Chief Op Offcr)
Immediate Holding Company: G. STOW PLC
Registration no: 02645390 **Date established:** 1991 **Turnover:** £2m - £5m
No.of Employees: 21 - 50 **Product Groups:** 51

Date of Accounts	Dec 11	Dec 10	Dec 09
Sales Turnover	5m	3m	4m
Pre Tax Profit/Loss	218	-197	75
Working Capital	2m	1m	2m
Fixed Assets	324	274	241
Current Assets	2m	2m	2m
Current Liabilities	262	238	291

Swaggers
51 St Martins Street, Wallingford, OX10 0AJ
Tel: 01491-824022 **Fax:** 01491-613039
E-mail: info@swaggers.co.uk
Website: http://www.swaggers.co.uk
Directors: M. Edis (Prop)
Date established: 2001 **Turnover:** £250,000 - £500,000
No.of Employees: 1 - 10 **Product Groups:** 22, 24, 63

Ulka Scintilla Pumps Ltd
24 Hazel Grove, Wallingford, OX10 0TA
Tel: 01491-202010 **Fax:** 01491-201888
E-mail: graham@irrisupplies.com
Product Groups: 30, 37, 38, 39, 40

Verco Ltd
Hithercroft Road, Wallingford, OX10 9DG
Tel: 01491-839966 **Fax:** 01491-835656
E-mail: sales@ver.co.uk
Website: http://www.ver.co.uk
Bank(s): Lloyds TSB Bank plc
Directors: J. Fogden (MD), B. Mack (Purch)
Managers: S. Hughes (Fin Mgr), J. Spence (Personnel), C. Jones (Sales Prom Mgr), N. Wilson (Personnel), C. Jones (Sales & Mktg Mg)
Ultimate Holding Company: VERTICAL CABINET COMPANY LIMITED
Immediate Holding Company: VERCO LIMITED
Registration no: 01829633 **VAT No.:** GB 434 5749 34
Date established: 1984 **Turnover:** £2m - £5m **No.of Employees:** 21 - 50
Product Groups: 40

Date of Accounts	Sep 11	Sep 10	Sep 09
Sales Turnover	5m	4m	3m
Pre Tax Profit/Loss	82	-99	-496
Working Capital	753	672	771
Current Assets	2m	2m	1m
Current Liabilities	179	161	110

H R Wallingford Ltd
Howbery Park, Wallingford, OX10 8BA
Tel: 01491-835381 **Fax:** 01491-832233
E-mail: info@hrwallingford.co.uk
Website: http://www.hrwallingford.co.uk
Directors: J. Ormston (Grp Chief Exec), J. Smallman (MD)
Managers: J. Harrop (Mktg Serv Mgr), M. Keevil (Tech Serv Mgr), K. Powell (Sales Prom Mgr)
Ultimate Holding Company: HR WALLINGFORD GROUP LIMITED
Immediate Holding Company: WALLINGFORD LIMITED
Registration no: 02959991 **VAT No.:** GB 570 0397 52
Date established: 1994 **Turnover:** £20m - £50m
No.of Employees: 101 - 250 **Product Groups:** 44, 54, 84

Wantage

Antigo Breakers
Cobweb Buildings The Lane, Lyford, Wantage, OX12 0EE
Tel: 01235-869021 **Fax:** 01235-869022
E-mail: mailbox@antigobreakers.co.uk
Website: http://www.antigobreakers.co.uk
Directors: S. Woolaston (MD)
Immediate Holding Company: ANTIGO BREAKERS LIMITED
Registration no: 04745945 **Date established:** 2003
No.of Employees: 1 - 10 **Product Groups:** 14, 45, 48, 51, 52, 54, 67, 83

Date of Accounts	Dec 11	Dec 10	Jun 09
Working Capital	-7	27	160
Fixed Assets	N/A	68	81
Current Assets	19	217	326

Brick Kiln Paint Specialists
New Road Childrey, Wantage, OX12 9PG
Tel: 01235-751647 **Fax:** 01235-751575
Website: http://www.brickkilngroup.co.uk
Directors: J. Matthews (Prop)
Registration no: 03641643 **Date established:** 1987 **Turnover:** £2m - £5m
No.of Employees: 11 - 20 **Product Groups:** 46, 48

Date of Accounts	Oct 08	Oct 07	Oct 06
Sales Turnover	N/A	2441	2566
Pre Tax Profit/Loss	N/A	350	618
Working Capital	792	590	622
Fixed Assets	359	379	365
Current Assets	1156	824	972
Current Liabilities	364	235	351
ROCE% (Return on Capital Employed)		36.1	62.6
ROT% (Return on Turnover)		14.3	24.1

C M S Industries
Grove Technology Park Downsview Road, Wantage, OX12 9FA
Tel: 01235-773370 **Fax:** 01235-773371
E-mail: sales@cmsindustries.com
Website: http://www.cmsindustries.com
Bank(s): National Westminster Bank Plc
Directors: S. Liquerish (Dir)
Immediate Holding Company: WORLDWIDE BUSINESS SOLUTIONS (GROUP) LTD
Registration no: 03272358 **VAT No.:** GB 537 3093 43
Date established: 2008 **Turnover:** £5m - £10m **No.of Employees:** 11 - 20
Product Groups: 26, 29, 36, 39, 40

Date of Accounts	Jun 08	Jun 07	Jun 06
Working Capital	1097	856	762
Fixed Assets	437	477	502
Current Assets	2523	2129	1493
Current Liabilities	1426	1273	731
Total Share Capital	4	4	5

Crown Packaging
Downsview Road, Wantage, OX12 9BP
Tel: 01235-772929 **Fax:** 01905-762357
E-mail: jenny@crowncork.com
Website: http://www.crowncork.com

Directors: N. Wakely (Fin), J. Simpson (MD)
Managers: S. Reed
Ultimate Holding Company: CROWN HOLDINGS INC (USA)
Immediate Holding Company: CARNAUDMETALBOX OVERSEAS LTD.
Registration no: 00455814 **Date established:** 1948 **Turnover:** £5m - £10m
No.of Employees: 251 - 500 **Product Groups:** 30, 35

Date of Accounts	Dec 11	Dec 10	Dec 09
Sales Turnover	6m	N/A	N/A
Pre Tax Profit/Loss	6m	N/A	1m
Working Capital	26m	20m	20m
Fixed Assets	9m	9m	9m
Current Assets	26m	20m	20m
Current Liabilities	31	28	33

Deca Materials Handling Ltd
13 Adkin Way, Wantage, OX12 9HN
Tel: 01235-770022 **Fax:** 01235-770027
E-mail: info@budgetft.co.uk
Website: http://www.deca-mh.co.uk
Directors: J. Slight (MD), I. Slight (Fin)
Immediate Holding Company: DECA MATERIALS HANDLING LIMITED
Registration no: 02298851 **VAT No.:** GB 532 5746 44
Date established: 1988 **Turnover:** Up to £250,000
No.of Employees: 1 - 10 **Product Groups:** 45, 48, 67

Date of Accounts	Dec 10	Dec 09	Dec 08
Working Capital	-1	9	13
Fixed Assets	15	18	11
Current Assets	33	44	38

EMS Physio Ltd
Unit 20 Grove Technology Park Downsview Road, Wantage, OX12 9FE
Tel: 01235-772272 **Fax:** 01235-763518
E-mail: sales@emsphysio.co.uk
Website: http://www.emsphysio.co.uk
Bank(s): Barclays
Directors: J. Greenham (MD)
Managers: G. Kent (Comptroller), D. Wilton, P. Bennett (Sales Admin)
Immediate Holding Company: EMS PHYSIO LTD
Registration no: 00601612 **VAT No.:** GB 198 9150 11
Date established: 1958 **Turnover:** £2m - £5m **No.of Employees:** 21 - 50
Product Groups: 37, 38, 49

Date of Accounts	Mar 11	Mar 10	Mar 09
Working Capital	2m	1m	2m
Fixed Assets	2m	2m	2m
Current Assets	2m	2m	2m

Kosran E C V UK Ltd
No 6 The Glenmore Centre Grove Technology Park, Wantage, OX12 9FA
Tel: 08707-875687 **Fax:** 0870-787 5633
E-mail: sales@kosran.com
Website: http://www.kosran.com
Directors: P. Sheeran (MD)
Immediate Holding Company: KOSRAN ECV (UK) LIMITED
Registration no: NI041596 **Date established:** 2001
No.of Employees: 1 - 10 **Product Groups:** 36, 68, 81

Date of Accounts	Sep 07	Sep 06	Sep 04
Working Capital	-740	-459	N/A
Fixed Assets	30	33	N/A
Current Assets	1m	320	N/A

M I D Engineering
Saddleworth House South Street, Letcombe Regis, Wantage, OX12 9JY
Tel: 01235-771114 **Fax:** 01235-771114
Website: http://www.mid-engineering.co.uk
Directors: M. Doman (Ptnr)
Date established: 2001 **No.of Employees:** 1 - 10 **Product Groups:** 41

M J C Services
17 Fettiplace, Wantage, OX12 7EN
Tel: 01235-767717 **Fax:** 01235-767717
E-mail: mjcforklifts@btinternet.com
Website: http://www.mjcservices.co.uk
Directors: M. Crossley (Prop)
No.of Employees: 1 - 10 **Product Groups:** 45, 48, 67, 71, 83, 86

Macdermid Autotype Ltd
Grove Road, Wantage, OX12 7BZ
Tel: 01235-771111 **Fax:** 01235-771196
E-mail: info@macdermidautotype.com
Website: http://www.macdermidautotype.com
Bank(s): National Westminster Bank Plc
Directors: D. Curtis (Fin), J. Braham (MD)
Managers: B. Proctor (Tech Serv Mgr), D. Parker (Mktg Serv Mgr), G. Braham (Sales Prom Mgr), S. Osbourne, J. Elliot (Personnel), J. Cruickshank (Purch Mgr), J. Edge
Ultimate Holding Company: MACDERMID HOLDINGS LLC (USA)
Immediate Holding Company: MACDERMID AUTOTYPE LIMITED
Registration no: 00192795 **Date established:** 2023
Turnover: £20m - £50m **No.of Employees:** 251 - 500
Product Groups: 27, 28, 30, 31, 44, 49

Date of Accounts	Dec 11	Dec 10	Dec 09
Sales Turnover	40m	40m	31m
Pre Tax Profit/Loss	7m	6m	4m
Working Capital	9m	10m	8m
Fixed Assets	4m	4m	5m
Current Assets	15m	17m	13m
Current Liabilities	3m	4m	2m

Matthews Land Group
Bybrook House Old Manor Court, Letcombe Regis, Wantage, OX12 9JL
Tel: 01235-770224 **Fax:** 01235-770224
E-mail: c.matthews513@btinternet.com
Website: http://www.matthewslandgroup.com
No.of Employees: 1 - 10 **Product Groups:** 23, 25, 33, 35, 41, 45, 49, 52, 66

Date of Accounts	Mar 07	Apr 06
Working Capital	-20	-40
Fixed Assets	46	41
Current Assets	33	27
Current Liabilities	53	67

Meadow Foods
Unit 11-12 Manor Road Farm Barn Manor Road, Wantage, OX12 8NE
Tel: 01235-774010 **Fax:** 01235-774011
E-mail: r.middleton@meadowfoods.com
Website: http://www.meadowfoods.com
Directors: R. Middleton (Dir)
Immediate Holding Company: ARLA FOODS UK PLC
Registration no: 02143253 **Date established:** 1992
Turnover: £50m - £75m **No.of Employees:** 1 - 10 **Product Groups:** 62, 85

Peter Allen Feeders
Unit 3 Elms Farm Grove Road, Grove, Wantage, OX12 7PD
Tel: 01235-772161 **Fax:** 01235-768650
E-mail: sales@allen-trading.co.uk
Website: http://www.peterallenfeeders.co.uk
Directors: P. Allan (Prop), P. Allen (Prop)
Immediate Holding Company: PETER ALLEN FEEDERS LIMITED
Registration no: 07115277 **Date established:** 2010
No.of Employees: 1 - 10 **Product Groups:** 41

R J C Construction
Unit 15 W & G Industrial Estate Faringdon Road, East Challow, Wantage, OX12 9TF
Tel: 01235-763964 **Fax:** 01235-763964
E-mail: roly@rjcconstruction.fsnet.co.uk
Website: http://www.rjc-construction.co.uk
Directors: R. Crook (Prop)
No.of Employees: 1 - 10 **Product Groups:** 34, 36, 45, 48, 52, 66

Smart Type
6 Springfield Road, Wantage, OX12 8ES
Tel: 01235-771377
E-mail: sarahcollinsuk@hotmail.com
Website: http://www.smarttype.co.uk
Directors: S. Collins (Prop)
No.of Employees: 1 - 10 **Product Groups:** 80

Velox Ltd
Units 1-4 Manor Road Farm Barn Manor Road, Wantage, OX12 8NE
Tel: 01235-770133 **Fax:** 01235-770122
E-mail: sales@veloxgrills.com
Website: http://www.veloxgrills.com
Directors: J. Gould (Fin)
Immediate Holding Company: SILESIA UK LIMITED
Registration no: 02692983 **Date established:** 1992
No.of Employees: 1 - 10 **Product Groups:** 20, 40, 67

Date of Accounts	Mar 12	Mar 11	Mar 10
Working Capital	-70	-69	-51
Fixed Assets	1	1	1
Current Assets	14	13	44

W B S Group Consulting
Grove Business Centre Grove Technology Park, Wantage, OX12 9FF
Tel: 01235-227434 **Fax:** 01235-227434
E-mail: info@wwbsgroup.com
Website: http://www.wbsgroup.com
Directors: J. Turnbull (Prop)
Immediate Holding Company: WBS GROUP LIMITED
Registration no: 03971691 **Date established:** 2000
No.of Employees: 1 - 10 **Product Groups:** 80, 86

Date of Accounts	Apr 12	Apr 11	Apr 10
Sales Turnover	N/A	N/A	202
Pre Tax Profit/Loss	N/A	N/A	-31
Working Capital	-115	-175	-262
Current Assets	81	76	26
Current Liabilities	59	133	137

Williams F1
Williams Grand Prix Engineer Grove, Wantage, OX12 0DQ
Tel: 01235-777700 **Fax:** 01235-764705
E-mail: enquiries@williamsf1.com
Website: http://www.williamsf1.com
Directors: L. Evans (Fin), F. Williams (Prop)
Managers: N. Salter (Personnel), M. Jones, C. Taylor (Tech Serv Mgr)
Immediate Holding Company: THE WILLIAMS F1 TEAM FOUNDATION
Registration no: 07136191 **VAT No.:** GB 292 5593 25
Date established: 2010 **Turnover:** £125m - £250m
No.of Employees: 251 - 500 **Product Groups:** 39

Date of Accounts	Dec 09	Nov 08	Nov 07
Sales Turnover	108m	126m	67m
Pre Tax Profit/Loss	5m	9m	-21m
Working Capital	-6m	-7m	-15m
Fixed Assets	38m	41m	42m
Current Assets	35m	21m	12m
Current Liabilities	29m	9m	10m

Watlington

A Y Fabrication
Unit 7E Lys Mill Farm, Howe Road, Watlington, OX49 5EP
Tel: 07527-028755 **Fax:** 01993-708477
E-mail: jo@certainexhibitions.co.uk
Product Groups: 26, 33, 34, 35, 36, 48, 49, 52, 63, 66

Accuvac Prototypes Ltd
Unit F2 Watlington Industrial Estate Cuxham Road, Watlington, OX49 5LU
Tel: 01491-613161 **Fax:** 01491-613161
E-mail: enquiries@accuvac.co.uk
Website: http://www.accuvac.co.uk
Directors: C. Newell (MD), D. Mells (Fin)
Immediate Holding Company: ACCUVAC PROTOTYPES LIMITED
Registration no: 01695493 **Date established:** 1983
Turnover: Up to £250,000 **No.of Employees:** 1 - 10 **Product Groups:** 28, 30, 48, 49, 66

Date of Accounts	Oct 11	Oct 10	Oct 09
Sales Turnover	131	116	145
Pre Tax Profit/Loss	27	18	35
Working Capital	40	49	58
Fixed Assets	2	N/A	6
Current Assets	95	95	117
Current Liabilities	25	11	28

C P Steel Processing Ltd
61 Shirburn Road, Watlington, OX49 5BZ
Tel: 01491-614683 **Fax:** 01491-614573
E-mail: sales@downhills.co.uk
Website: http://www.downhills.co.uk
Bank(s): Lloyds TSB Bank plc
Directors: J. Downhill (Fin)
Immediate Holding Company: C P STEEL PROCESSING LIMITED
Registration no: 04748368 **VAT No.:** GB 226 3458 66
Date established: 2003 **Turnover:** £2m - £5m **No.of Employees:** 11 - 20
Product Groups: 34, 35

Date of Accounts	Oct 11	Oct 10	Oct 09
Sales Turnover	N/A	N/A	3m
Pre Tax Profit/Loss	N/A	N/A	79
Working Capital	357	283	214
Fixed Assets	42	92	139
Current Assets	1m	963	764
Current Liabilities	N/A	N/A	125

J B K S Architects Ltd
Suite 1 Parkwood Stud Aston Park, Aston Rowant, Watlington, OX49 5SP
Tel: 01844-350101 **Fax:** 01844-281813
E-mail: ks@jbks.co.uk
Website: http://www.jbks.co.uk
Directors: K. Sampson (Dir)
Registration no: 05157563 **Date established:** 2005
No.of Employees: 1 - 10 **Product Groups:** 84

Real Organic Foods
Couching House Couching Street, Watlington, OX49 5PX
Tel: 01491-615280 **Fax:** 01491-615289
E-mail: info@realorganic.co.uk
Website: http://www.realorganic.co.uk
Directors: D. Morgan (Prop)
Ultimate Holding Company: SONICWALL INC (USA)
Immediate Holding Company: AVENTAIL EUROPE LIMITED
Registration no: 3951990 **Date established:** 1999
No.of Employees: 1 - 10 **Product Groups:** 20

Date of Accounts	Dec 09	Dec 08	Dec 07
Sales Turnover	165	380	545
Pre Tax Profit/Loss	9	18	15
Working Capital	-7	-42	-65
Fixed Assets	213	243	258
Current Assets	3	16	10
Current Liabilities	10	58	76

Selling Sciences
20 High Street, Watlington, OX49 5PY
Tel: 01491-614962 **Fax:** 01491-613367
E-mail: sales@sellingsciences.com
Website: http://www.sellingsciences.com
Directors: J. Judd (Co Sec)
Managers: C. Hayden (Sales Admin)
Immediate Holding Company: MUSIC & TRAVEL TOUR CONSULTANTS LIMITED
Registration no: 02509331 **Date established:** 2001
Turnover: Up to £250,000 **No.of Employees:** 1 - 10 **Product Groups:** 86

Date of Accounts	Oct 11	Oct 10	Oct 09
Sales Turnover	N/A	N/A	1m
Pre Tax Profit/Loss	N/A	N/A	197
Working Capital	246	244	264
Fixed Assets	1	1	2
Current Assets	467	406	477
Current Liabilities	N/A	N/A	162

Technical Moulding Projects
Unit 3-6 Watlington Industrial Estate Cuxham Road, Watlington, OX49 5LU
Tel: 01491-613539 **Fax:** 01491-612096
E-mail: tmp@techmouldproj.demon.co.uk
Website: http://www.techmouldproj.demon.co.uk
Directors: R. Plumridge (Ptnr)
VAT No.: 491 8818 02 **Date established:** 1988 **Turnover:** £500,000 - £1m
No.of Employees: 11 - 20 **Product Groups:** 30, 48

Witney

Airdri Ltd
Technology House Oakfield Industrial Estate Eynsham, Witney, OX29 4AQ
Tel: 01865-882330 **Fax:** 01865-881647
E-mail: sales@airdri.com
Website: http://www.airdri.com
Bank(s): Barclays, 93 Baker Street, London W1A 4SD
Directors: P. Phillips (MD), G. Davies (Fin), P. Philipps (MD)
Managers: G. Davies (Fin Mgr), P. Stockton (Sales Admin)
Immediate Holding Company: AIRDRI LIMITED
Registration no: 01156251 **VAT No.:** GB 209 0960 70
Date established: 1974 **Turnover:** £5m - £10m **No.of Employees:** 21 - 50
Product Groups: 26, 36, 38, 40, 66, 84

Date of Accounts	Dec 11	Dec 10	Dec 09
Sales Turnover	10m	9m	9m
Pre Tax Profit/Loss	1m	2m	1m
Working Capital	4m	3m	3m
Fixed Assets	2m	2m	2m
Current Assets	5m	5m	4m
Current Liabilities	491	693	338

Algar Electrical Motors Ltd
Southfield Place Eynsham, Witney, OX29 4PB
Tel: 01865-880588 **Fax:** 01865-883918
E-mail: algar@eynsham.co.uk
Website: http://www.algar-ltd.co.uk
Directors: B. Gardner (MD)
Immediate Holding Company: ALGAR (ELECTRIC MOTORS) LIMITED
Registration no: 01405271 **VAT No.:** GB 311 5934 79
Date established: 1978 **Turnover:** £250,000 - £500,000
No.of Employees: 1 - 10 **Product Groups:** 48, 52, 67

Date of Accounts	Feb 12	Feb 11	Feb 10
Working Capital	-46	-22	16
Fixed Assets	289	290	294
Current Assets	96	108	123

Ambic Equipment Ltd
Unit 1 Parkside Avenue Two, Witney, OX28 4YF
Tel: 01993-776555 **Fax:** 01993-779039
E-mail: enquiries@ambic.co.uk
Website: http://www.ambic.co.uk
Directors: D. Stewart (MD), M. Tyler (Fin)
Ultimate Holding Company: SKELLERUP HOLDINGS LTD (NEW ZEALAND)
Immediate Holding Company: AMBIC EQUIPMENT LIMITED
Registration no: 01381911 **VAT No.:** GB 311 5337 00
Date established: 1978 **Turnover:** £2m - £5m **No.of Employees:** 1 - 10
Product Groups: 41, 67

Date of Accounts	Jun 11	Jun 10	Jun 09
Working Capital	2m	2m	2m
Fixed Assets	677	550	598
Current Assets	2m	2m	2m

Amiantus Ltd
New Yatt Business Centre New Yatt, Witney, OX29 6TJ
Tel: 01993-868899 **Fax:** 01993-869080
E-mail: admin@amiantus.co.uk
Website: http://www.amiantus.co.uk
Directors: R. Pearce (MD)
No.of Employees: 1 - 10 **Product Groups:** 54, 85

Date of Accounts	Dec 07	Dec 06
Working Capital	-12	-19
Fixed Assets	7	6
Current Assets	65	32
Current Liabilities	76	52

S C Ayling
Unit 2 Newland, Witney, OX28 3JH
Tel: 01993-700113 **Fax:** 01993-708615
E-mail: s.ayling@btconnect.com
Website: http://www.scayling.co.uk
Directors: S. Ayling (Prop)
Immediate Holding Company: S C AYLING LTD
Registration no: 06409693 **Date established:** 2007
No.of Employees: 1 - 10 **Product Groups:** 30

Date of Accounts	Dec 11	Dec 10	Dec 09
Working Capital	-79	-94	-102
Fixed Assets	148	173	105
Current Assets	94	90	70

Bartington Instruments Ltd
5 Thorney Leys Business Park, Witney, OX28 4GE
Tel: 01993-706565 **Fax:** 01993-774813
E-mail: tessa.evans@bartington.com
Website: http://www.bartington.com
Directors: T. Evans (MD)
Managers: K. McDermott (Buyer), L. Letourneur
Immediate Holding Company: BARTINGTON INSTRUMENTS LIMITED
Registration no: 01938710 **VAT No.:** GB 348 7637 12
Date established: 1985 **Turnover:** £1m - £2m **No.of Employees:** 21 - 50
Product Groups: 38

Date of Accounts	Sep 11	Sep 10	Sep 09
Working Capital	704	785	637
Fixed Assets	232	134	152
Current Assets	875	1m	790

Basics
7 Eagle Industrial Estate Church Green, Witney, OX28 4YR
Tel: 01993-706708 **Fax:** 01993-709097
E-mail: info@basictableware.com
Website: http://www.basictableware.com
Directors: M. Higgins (Prop)
Date established: 2001 **No.of Employees:** 1 - 10 **Product Groups:** 20, 40, 41

Beautiful Linen Hire
Unit 7 Park Farm Estate, Northmoor, Witney, OX29 5AZ
Tel: 01865-300444 **Fax:** 01865-300777
E-mail: sales@beautiful-group.com
Website: http://www.beautiful-linen.com
Directors: C. Clinkard (MD)
No.of Employees: 1 - 10 **Product Groups:** 83

Bicester Products Squash Court Manufacturers Ltd
55 West End, Witney, OX28 1NJ
Tel: 01993-774426 **Fax:** 01993-779569
E-mail: sales@squashcourts.co.uk
Website: http://www.squashcourts.co.uk
Directors: A. Fish (MD)
Managers: G. Williams (Contracts Mgr), S. Young (Accounts)
Immediate Holding Company: Bicester Products Ltd
Registration no: 01526206 **VAT No.:** GB 434 5018 73
Turnover: £250,000 - £500,000 **No.of Employees:** 1 - 10
Product Groups: 25

Bowles Trading Co
Old Rectory Church Hanborough, Witney, OX29 8AB
Tel: 01993-883383
Managers: P. Bowles (Mgr)
No.of Employees: 1 - 10 **Product Groups:** 37, 67

British Motor Heritage Ltd
Cotswold Business Park Range Road, Witney, OX29 0YB
Tel: 01993-707200 **Fax:** 01993-707222
E-mail: info@bmh-ltd.com
Website: http://www.bmh-ltd.com
Directors: J. Yae (MD)
Managers: J. Pollard (Tech Serv Mgr), M. Davies (Sales Prom Mgr), D. Jane (Transport)
Immediate Holding Company: BRITISH MOTOR HERITAGE LIMITED
Registration no: 00243547 **VAT No.:** GB 239 3549 38
Date established: 2029 **No.of Employees:** 21 - 50 **Product Groups:** 39

Date of Accounts	Dec 11	Dec 10	Dec 09
Working Capital	570	475	392
Fixed Assets	1m	1m	1m
Current Assets	2m	2m	2m

C W Headdress Ltd
7 Witan Park Avenue Two, Witney, OX28 4FH
Tel: 01993-703515 **Fax:** 01993-775904
E-mail: steve.cossey@christygroup.com
Website: http://www.cwheaddress.com
Bank(s): HSBC Bank plc
Directors: G. Panons (Grp)
Managers: J. Smith (Chief Mgr), S. Cossey (Mgr), P. Watton (Buyer)
Ultimate Holding Company: FORMERLY H LIMITED
Immediate Holding Company: C W HEADDRESS LIMITED
Registration no: 03165540 **VAT No.:** GB 663 4629 18
Date established: 1996 **Turnover:** £500,000 - £1m
No.of Employees: 11 - 20 **Product Groups:** 24

Date of Accounts	Dec 10	Dec 09	Dec 08
Sales Turnover	656	1m	1m
Pre Tax Profit/Loss	-82	-95	25
Working Capital	-1	231	323
Fixed Assets	160	10	13
Current Assets	508	1m	944
Current Liabilities	5	11	12

Certikin International Ltd
Witan Park Avenue Two, Witney, OX28 4FJ
Tel: 01993-778855 **Fax:** 01993-778620
E-mail: info@certikin.co.uk
Website: http://www.certikin.co.uk
Bank(s): National Westminster
Directors: I. Danne (Fin), N. Murray (MD)
Managers: M. Shepherd (Purch Mgr), R. Way (Tech Sales Mgr), S. Thorne (Tech Serv Mgr), C. Saunders (Mktg Serv Mgr), D. Murray (Personnel)
Ultimate Holding Company: FLUIDRA S A (SPAIN)
Immediate Holding Company: CERTIKIN INTERNATIONAL LIMITED
Registration no: 03047290 **VAT No.:** GB 630 9686 20
Date established: 1995 **Turnover:** £20m - £50m
No.of Employees: 51 - 100 **Product Groups:** 33, 36, 42, 52

Date of Accounts	Dec 11	Dec 10	Dec 09
Sales Turnover	27m	27m	25m
Pre Tax Profit/Loss	1m	2m	1m
Working Capital	5m	4m	4m
Fixed Assets	924	923	1m
Current Assets	12m	11m	10m
Current Liabilities	1m	1m	1m

Colour Tech Oxford Ltd
Unit 9 154 Newland, Witney, OX28 3JH
Tel: 01993-700908 **Fax:** 01993-708788
Directors: D. Horseman (MD), S. Horseman (Co Sec)
Immediate Holding Company: COLOUR TECH OXFORD LIMITED
Registration no: 04213544 **Date established:** 2001
No.of Employees: 1 - 10 **Product Groups:** 46, 48

Date of Accounts	May 11	May 10	May 09
Working Capital	-5	-6	-8
Fixed Assets	5	7	8
Current Assets	14	16	12

Complete Presentation Ltd
Unit 12 Nimrod De Havilland Way, Witney, OX29 0YG
Tel: 01993-890960 **Fax:** 01993-890961
E-mail: info@cp-group.co.uk
Website: http://www.complete-presentation.co.uk
Directors: C. Piper (MD)
Immediate Holding Company: COMPLETE PRESENTATION LIMITED
Registration no: 05921177 **Date established:** 2006
No.of Employees: 1 - 10 **Product Groups:** 23, 24, 26, 28, 30, 49, 81, 83

Date of Accounts	Sep 11	Sep 10	Sep 09
Working Capital	-147	-126	-149
Fixed Assets	142	148	162
Current Assets	34	58	39

Corndell Furniture Company Ltd
5 Windrush Park Road, Witney, OX29 7DZ
Tel: 01993-776545 **Fax:** 01993-774052
E-mail: enquiries@corndell.co.uk
Website: http://www.corndell.co.uk
Directors: B. Ahern (MD)
Managers: L. Woodley (Buyer)
Immediate Holding Company: CORNDELL FURNITURE COMPANY LIMITED
Registration no: 01123436 **Date established:** 1973
Turnover: £20m - £50m **No.of Employees:** 101 - 250 **Product Groups:** 26

Date of Accounts	Dec 11	Dec 10	Jul 09
Sales Turnover	12m	22m	14m
Pre Tax Profit/Loss	-14	-445	-116
Working Capital	242	244	555
Fixed Assets	202	248	288
Current Assets	3m	4m	4m
Current Liabilities	517	623	1m

Cotswold Tool & Press
Bromag Industrial Estate Minster Lovell, Witney, OX29 0SR
Tel: 01993-772923 **Fax:** 01993-779615
E-mail: sales@ctap.co.uk
Website: http://www.ctap.co.uk
Directors: M. Jones (MD)
Managers: C. Reynolds (Sales Admin)
Immediate Holding Company: COTSWOLD TOOL AND PRESS LIMITED
Registration no: 01181327 **Date established:** 1974 **Turnover:** £1m - £2m
No.of Employees: 1 - 10 **Product Groups:** 46, 48

Date of Accounts	Jan 12	Jan 11	Jan 10
Working Capital	72	70	51
Fixed Assets	152	166	194
Current Assets	354	375	236

Desktop Engineering Ltd
6-7 Bankside Hanborough Business Park, Long Hanborough, Witney, OX29 8LJ
Tel: 01993-883555 **Fax:** 01993-883201
E-mail: info@dte.co.uk
Website: http://www.dte.co.uk
Bank(s): Barclays Bank
Directors: J. Haines Gadd (Fin), G. Haines (MD)
Ultimate Holding Company: DTE SOLUTIONS LIMITED
Immediate Holding Company: CENIT LIMITED
Registration no: 03238823 **Date established:** 1996 **Turnover:** £1m - £2m
No.of Employees: 11 - 20 **Product Groups:** 44, 86

Date of Accounts	Dec 11	Dec 10	Dec 09
Working Capital	-218	-235	-180
Fixed Assets	N/A	1	N/A
Current Assets	104	93	144

Encon Insulations Ltd
Stanton Harcourt Industrial Estate Stanton Harcourt, Witney, OX29 5UU
Tel: 01865-734500 **Fax:** 01865-734518
E-mail: witney@encon.co.uk
Website: http://www.encon.co.uk
Directors: M. Self (Dir)
Ultimate Holding Company: WOLSELEY PLC (JERSEY)
Immediate Holding Company: ENCON INSULATION LIMITED
Registration no: 01377342 **VAT No.:** GB 399 2893 75
Date established: 1978 **No.of Employees:** 11 - 20 **Product Groups:** 33

Formula Systems (a division of Airdri Ltd)
Technology House Oakfield Industrial Estate, Eynsham, Witney, OX29 4AQ
Tel: 01865-882442 **Fax:** 01865-881647
E-mail: sales@formula-systems.com
Website: http://www.formula-systems.com
Bank(s): Barclays
Managers: J. Curzon (Mgr)
Ultimate Holding Company: AIRDRI LIMITED
Immediate Holding Company: FORMULA SYSTEMS LIMITED
Registration no: 01768135 **VAT No.:** GB 209 0960 70
Date established: 1983 **Turnover:** £5m - £10m **No.of Employees:** 21 - 50
Product Groups: 37, 38, 40, 45, 67, 84, 85

Date of Accounts	Dec 99	Dec 10	Dec 08
Working Capital	18	18	18
Current Assets	18	18	18

Francis Lovel & Co.
Downs Road, Witney, OX29 0RF
Tel: 01993-864949 **Fax:** 01993-864919
E-mail: sales@francislovel.com
Website: http://www.francislovel.com
Directors: F. Lovel (Prop)
Immediate Holding Company: FRANCIS LOVEL & CO LIMITED
Registration no: 05076305 **Date established:** 2004 **Turnover:** £1m - £2m
No.of Employees: 1 - 10 **Product Groups:** 36, 39, 40

Date of Accounts	Aug 11	Aug 10	Aug 09
Working Capital	207	227	166
Fixed Assets	127	34	40
Current Assets	921	899	803

G S M Industrial Graphics Ltd
Unit 25-26 Avenue One, Witney, OX28 4BZ
Tel: 01993-776511 **Fax:** 01993-778238
E-mail: info@gsmgroup.co.uk
Website: http://www.gsmgroup.co.uk
Bank(s): National Westminster Bank Plc
Directors: A. Barwood (Fin)
Managers: D. Souch (Purch Mgr), A. Farthing (Chief Mgr), C. Walker (Fin Mgr)
Ultimate Holding Company: G S M GROUP LIMITED
Immediate Holding Company: G S M INDUSTRIAL GRAPHICS LIMITED
Registration no: 04236571 **VAT No.:** GB 685 6585 73
Date established: 2001 **Turnover:** £5m - £10m
No.of Employees: 51 - 100 **Product Groups:** 35, 36, 39, 48, 49

Date of Accounts	May 11	May 10	May 09
Sales Turnover	11m	9m	7m
Pre Tax Profit/Loss	844	233	225
Working Capital	2m	1m	971
Fixed Assets	608	518	660
Current Assets	5m	3m	3m
Current Liabilities	2m	2m	1m

Global 360
Newman Court, Witney, OX29 7LY
Tel: 01993-700111 **Fax:** 01993-776057
E-mail: global.360@btinternet.com
Website: http://www.globalthreesixty.co.uk
Directors: P. Harflett (Prop)
Immediate Holding Company: GLOBAL 360 LTD
Registration no: 06681754 **Date established:** 2008
No.of Employees: 1 - 10 **Product Groups:** 61, 71, 72, 75, 76, 79, 80

Hexagon Computers Ltd
9 Fenlock Court Blenheim Office Park, Long Hanborough, Witney, OX29 8LN
Tel: 01993-883626 **Fax:** 01993-883980
E-mail: steve.barnett@hexagoncomputers.com
Website: http://www.hexagoncomputers.co.uk
Directors: S. Barnett (Fin)
Immediate Holding Company: HEXAGON COMPUTERS LIMITED
Registration no: 03193628 **VAT No.:** GB 663 4984 95
Date established: 1996 **Turnover:** £500,000 - £1m
No.of Employees: 1 - 10 **Product Groups:** 67

Date of Accounts	May 11	May 10	May 09
Sales Turnover	N/A	504	511
Pre Tax Profit/Loss	N/A	18	10
Working Capital	-242	408	375
Fixed Assets	469	3	3
Current Assets	51	581	603
Current Liabilities	N/A	113	150

Hytec Information Security
9-10 Oasis Park Stanton Harcourt Road, Eynsham, Witney, OX29 4TP
Tel: 01865-881616 **Fax:** 01865-887444
E-mail: alan.hunt@hytec.co.uk
Website: http://www.hytec.co.uk
Directors: A. Hunt (Dir), D. Bryant (Fin)
Ultimate Holding Company: OLM GROUP LIMITED
Immediate Holding Company: HYTEC INFORMATION SECURITY LIMITED
Registration no: 04551277 **VAT No.:** GB 462 1275 64
Date established: 2002 **Turnover:** £2m - £5m **No.of Employees:** 1 - 10
Product Groups: 37, 38, 44, 48, 52, 67, 81

Date of Accounts	Mar 08	Jun 10	Jun 09
Sales Turnover	1m	N/A	2m
Pre Tax Profit/Loss	-211	N/A	-131
Working Capital	-279	-67	-172
Fixed Assets	155	3	11
Current Assets	513	391	327
Current Liabilities	642	N/A	310

Icon Computing Services
Mill Street, Witney, OX28 6DG
Tel: 01993-776737 **Fax:** 0870-054 8530
E-mail: info@icon-cs.com
Website: http://www.icon-cs.com
Directors: P. Parry (Prop)
Turnover: Up to £250,000 **No.of Employees:** 1 - 10 **Product Groups:** 44, 80, 84

J S P Ltd
Worsham Mill Worsham, Witney, OX29 0TA
Tel: 01993-824000 **Fax:** 01993-824422
E-mail: sales@jsp.co.uk
Website: http://www.jsp.co.uk
Bank(s): Midland, Manchester
Directors: M. Johnstone (Grp Chief Exec), P. Dizier (Sales), C. Murray (Co Sec)
Managers: A. Payne (Fin Mgr), R. Ellis (Tech Serv Mgr), D. Nicholson, S. Hartwell (Personnel), J. Simpson
Immediate Holding Company: JSP LIMITED
Registration no: 00791380 **VAT No.:** GB 597 8797 37
Date established: 1964 **Turnover:** £20m - £50m
No.of Employees: 101 - 250 **Product Groups:** 67

Date of Accounts	Dec 11	Dec 10	Dec 09
Sales Turnover	28m	27m	28m
Pre Tax Profit/Loss	2m	1m	2m

Working Capital	11m	11m	10m
Fixed Assets	6m	4m	4m
Current Assets	18m	18m	18m
Current Liabilities	2m	1m	2m

K N F Neuberger UK Ltd

Avenue Two Station Lane Industrial Estate, Witney, OX28 4FA
Tel: 01993-778373 **Fax:** 01993-775148
E-mail: info@knf.co.uk
Website: http://www.knf.co.uk
Directors: S. Barwick (MD)
Immediate Holding Company: KNF NEUBERGER U.K. LIMITED
Registration no: 01388157 **Date established:** 1978 **Turnover:** £2m - £5m
No.of Employees: 11 - 20 **Product Groups:** 31, 39, 40, 42, 67, 83

Date of Accounts	Dec 11	Dec 10	Dec 09
Working Capital	924	733	593
Fixed Assets	213	215	236
Current Assets	1m	1m	816
Current Liabilities	N/A	N/A	183

Kaydee Web Design

62B High Street, Witney, OX28 6HJ
Tel: 0844-8709621 **Fax:** 01993-775090
E-mail: design@kaydee.net
Website: http://www.kaydee.net
Directors: K. Drewett (MD)
Date established: 2000 **No.of Employees:** 1 - 10 **Product Groups:** 44

Kilkenny & Gomm Ltd

14 Hanborough Business Park Long Hanborough, Witney, OX29 8LH
Tel: 01865-883380 **Fax:** 01865-883380
E-mail: e-mail@kilkennygomm.com
Website: http://www.kilkennygomm.com
Directors: G. Kilkenny (MD)
Immediate Holding Company: KILKENNY & GOMM LIMITED
Registration no: 04473685 **Date established:** 2002
Turnover: Up to £250,000 **No.of Employees:** 1 - 10 **Product Groups:** 52

Date of Accounts	Jun 11	Jun 10	Jun 09
Working Capital	234	271	251
Fixed Assets	7	6	9
Current Assets	323	271	296

Lovell Johns Ltd

10 Hanborough Business Park Long Hanborough, Witney, OX29 8RU
Tel: 01993-883161 **Fax:** 01993-883096
E-mail: sales@lovelljohns.com
Website: http://www.lovelljohns.com
Bank(s): National Westminster
Directors: B. Wootton (Fin), D. Stephens (MD)
Ultimate Holding Company: AVUSA LTD (SOUTH AFRICA)
Immediate Holding Company: LOVELL JOHNS LIMITED
Registration no: 01214692 **VAT No.:** GB 196 0947 25
Date established: 1975 **Turnover:** £1m - £2m **No.of Employees:** 11 - 20
Product Groups: 81

Date of Accounts	Mar 11	Mar 10	Mar 09
Sales Turnover	1m	1m	2m
Pre Tax Profit/Loss	-154	-144	13
Working Capital	-671	-451	-318
Fixed Assets	97	30	41
Current Assets	321	438	863
Current Liabilities	85	115	253

Low Power Radio Solutions Ltd

Two Rivers Industrial Estate Station Lane, Witney, OX28 4BH
Tel: 01993-709418 **Fax:** 01993-705415
E-mail: sales@lprs.co.uk
Website: http://www.lprs.co.uk
Directors: J. Sharples (MD)
Immediate Holding Company: LOW POWER RADIO SOLUTIONS LIMITED
Registration no: 01921587 **VAT No.:** GB 434 5928 34
Date established: 1985 **Turnover:** £500,000 - £1m
No.of Employees: 1 - 10 **Product Groups:** 37

Date of Accounts	Dec 11	Dec 10	Dec 09
Working Capital	119	72	96
Fixed Assets	11	4	1
Current Assets	390	344	315

Meech Static Eliminators Ltd

Unit 2 Network Point Range Road, Witney, OX29 0YN
Tel: 01993-706700 **Fax:** 01993-776977
E-mail: sales@meech.com
Website: http://www.meech.com
Directors: C. Francis (MD), S. Gray (Co Sec)
Managers: E. Graham (Sales Prom Mgr), E. Grant (Mktg Serv Mgr)
Ultimate Holding Company: MEECH INTERNATIONAL LIMITED
Immediate Holding Company: MEECH STATIC ELIMINATORS LIMITED
Registration no: 01525004 **Date established:** 1907 **Turnover:** £2m - £5m
No.of Employees: 21 - 50 **Product Groups:** 27, 30, 37, 40, 42, 43, 44, 67

Date of Accounts	Sep 11	Sep 10	Sep 09
Working Capital	958	688	544
Fixed Assets	2m	2m	2m
Current Assets	2m	1m	1m

N D S L Ltd

Unit 2 Oakfield Industrial Estate Eynsham, Witney, OX29 4TS
Tel: 01865-884288 **Fax:** 01865-884289
E-mail: sales@ndsl.co.uk
Website: http://www.ndsl.co.uk
Directors: R. Willcock (Dir), D. Brown (Dir), J. Laurie (Dir)
Managers: P. Taberham (Sales Prom Mgr)
Ultimate Holding Company: NDSL GROUP LIMITED
Immediate Holding Company: NDSL LIMITED
Registration no: 02677280 **Date established:** 1992 **Turnover:** £1m - £2m
No.of Employees: 1 - 10 **Product Groups:** 38

Date of Accounts	Dec 10	Dec 09	Dec 08
Sales Turnover	1m	1m	846
Pre Tax Profit/Loss	315	237	591
Working Capital	2m	2m	2m
Fixed Assets	1	2	2
Current Assets	2m	2m	2m
Current Liabilities	61	100	49

O G M Ltd

Stanton Harcourt Road Eynsham, Witney, OX29 4JB
Tel: 01865-880444 **Fax:** 01865-883838
E-mail: sales@ogm.uk.com
Website: http://www.ogm.uk.com
Bank(s): Barclays
Directors: V. Whiteman (Fin), A. Beale (Sales), P. Wightman (MD)
Managers: W. Holden (Purch Mgr), C. Collins (Sales Admin)
Immediate Holding Company: OGM LIMITED
Registration no: 07419225 **Date established:** 2010 **Turnover:** £5m - £10m
No.of Employees: 51 - 100 **Product Groups:** 30, 35, 37, 38, 39, 48, 49, 66

Date of Accounts	Oct 11
Fixed Assets	2

Oasis Fashions Limited

The Triangle Stanton Harcourt Industrial Estate, Stanton Harcourt, Witney, OX29 5UT
Tel: 01865-874700 **Fax:** 01865-734898
E-mail: help@oasis-stores.co.uk
Website: http://www.oasis-stores.com
Directors: D. Lovelock (MD), M. Bennett (Ch), R. Glanville (MD), V. Scott (MD)
Managers: R. French (I.T. Exec), P. Parson (I.T. Exec)
Immediate Holding Company: Coast Ltd
Registration no: 06822219 **Turnover:** £50m - £75m
No.of Employees: 251 - 500 **Product Groups:** 61

Date of Accounts	Jan 10
Sales Turnover	132m
Pre Tax Profit/Loss	-20m
Working Capital	-4m
Fixed Assets	18m
Current Assets	23m
Current Liabilities	5m

Oxford Cartographers

Oasis Park Stanton Harcourt Road, Eynsham, Witney, OX29 4TP
Tel: 01865-882884 **Fax:** 01865-882925
E-mail: info@oxfordcartographers.com
Website: http://www.oxfordcartographers.com
Directors: P. Treadwell (Sales), P. Watson (MD)
Immediate Holding Company: Cook Hammond & Kell Ltd
Turnover: Up to £250,000 **No.of Employees:** 1 - 10 **Product Groups:** 28, 49, 81

Oxford Insulation Cladding

Unit 9 Oakfield Industrial Estate Eynsham, Witney, OX29 4TH
Tel: 01865-882662 **Fax:** 01865-883925
E-mail: ddavies@oicltd.freeserve.co.uk
Website: http://www.insulationcladding.co.uk
Directors: D. Davies (MD)
Immediate Holding Company: PHOTOTECHNIQUES LIMITED
Date established: 2002 **Turnover:** Up to £250,000
No.of Employees: 1 - 10 **Product Groups:** 30, 33, 84

Date of Accounts	Oct 09	Oct 08	Oct 06
Working Capital	28	17	8
Fixed Assets	7	3	14
Current Assets	40	27	19

Oxon Fastening Systems Ltd

Academic House Oakfield Industrial Estate, Eynsham, Witney, OX29 4AJ
Tel: 01865-884022 **Fax:** 01865-884033
E-mail: dave@oxonfasteningsystems.ltd.uk
Website: http://www.oxonfasteningsystems.ltd.uk
Directors: T. Dixon (Dir), D. Dixon (MD)
Immediate Holding Company: OXON FASTENING SYSTEMS LIMITED
Registration no: 03701256 **Date established:** 1999
No.of Employees: 11 - 20 **Product Groups:** 30, 33, 35, 36, 37, 38, 39, 40, 41, 46, 47, 48, 49, 65, 66, 67, 68, 83

Date of Accounts	Mar 12	Mar 11	Mar 10
Working Capital	1m	1m	985
Fixed Assets	453	262	259
Current Assets	1m	1m	1m

Oxon Packaging

Unit 4b Stanton Harcourt Industrial Estate Stanton Harcourt, Witney, OX29 5UX
Tel: 01865-731422 **Fax:** 01865-731423
E-mail: oxpac@hotmail.com
Directors: C. Burnett (Prop)
Date established: 2000 **No.of Employees:** 1 - 10 **Product Groups:** 38, 42

F J Payne & Son Ltd

Oakfield Industrial Estate Eynsham, Witney, OX29 4AW
Tel: 01865-882299 **Fax:** 01865-882309
E-mail: sales@fjpayne.com
Website: http://www.fjpayne.com
Directors: T. Payne (MD), F. Payne (Fin)
Immediate Holding Company: F.J. PAYNE & SON LIMITED
Registration no: 03260974 **Date established:** 1996
No.of Employees: 1 - 10 **Product Groups:** 39, 48, 84

Date of Accounts	Dec 11	Dec 10	Dec 09
Working Capital	100	100	80
Fixed Assets	12	15	20
Current Assets	151	142	117

Pelltech Ltd

Station Lane, Witney, OX28 4YS
Tel: 01993-776451 **Fax:** 01993-771606
E-mail: enquiries@pelltech.co.uk
Website: http://www.pelltech.co.uk
Directors: M. Hatt (MD)
Immediate Holding Company: PELLTECH LIMITED
Registration no: 01096529 **VAT No.:** GB 195 1965 24
Date established: 1973 **No.of Employees:** 1 - 10 **Product Groups:** 27, 28, 38, 44

Date of Accounts	Dec 11	Dec 10	Dec 09
Working Capital	-432	-280	-322
Fixed Assets	40	19	24
Current Assets	1m	967	891

Pro Polishers

Unit F1 New Yatt Business Centre New Yatt, Witney, OX29 6TJ
Tel: 01993-868806 **Fax:** 01993-868853
Directors: G. Bowerman (Dir)
Date established: 1996 **No.of Employees:** 1 - 10 **Product Groups:** 46, 48

Production Quest Ltd

Rowan Court North Leigh Business Park Nursery Road, North Leigh, Witney, OX29 6SW
Tel: 01993-883366 **Fax:** 01993-881123
E-mail: stewart.perry@bakerhughes.com
Website: http://www.bakerhughes.com
Managers: S. Perry (Prod Mgr)
Ultimate Holding Company: BAKER HUGHES INC (USA)
Immediate Holding Company: PRODUCTIONQUEST LIMITED
Registration no: 04710491 **VAT No.:** GB 532 5087 58
Date established: 2003 **Turnover:** £1m - £2m **No.of Employees:** 11 - 20
Product Groups: 38, 40

Raaco GB Ltd

Wenrisc House Meadow Court High Street, Witney, OX28 6ER
Tel: 01993-776333 **Fax:** 01993-776444
E-mail: gbmail@raaco.com
Website: http://www.raaco.com
Directors: P. Damberg (MD)
Ultimate Holding Company: RACCO HOLDING APS (DENMARK)
Immediate Holding Company: RAACO GREAT BRITAIN LIMITED
Registration no: 00674244 **VAT No.:** GB 232 6219 86
Date established: 1960 **Turnover:** £1m - £2m **No.of Employees:** 1 - 10
Product Groups: 22, 26, 30, 35, 39

Date of Accounts	Dec 11	Dec 10	Dec 09
Sales Turnover	2m	2m	1m
Pre Tax Profit/Loss	-7	45	49
Working Capital	141	146	111
Current Assets	319	372	333
Current Liabilities	170	157	128

Red Technology

E-Commerce House Oakfield Industrial Estate, Eynsham, Witney, OX29 4AG
Tel: 01865-880800 **Fax:** 01865-880865
E-mail: info@redtechnology.com
Website: http://www.redtechnology.com
Directors: J. Candy (Develop)
Managers: W. Brodeur
Immediate Holding Company: RED TECHNOLOGY SOLUTIONS LIMITED
Registration no: 05970219 **Date established:** 2006
No.of Employees: 21 - 50 **Product Groups:** 44, 79, 84

Date of Accounts	Dec 11	Dec 10	Dec 09
Working Capital	1m	68	454
Fixed Assets	105	77	69
Current Assets	2m	802	854

Regent Hose & Hydraulics Ltd

2 Minster Industrial Estate Downs Road, Witney, OX29 0QS
Tel: 01993-778278 **Fax:** 01993-779018
E-mail: sales@monarchhose.co.uk
Website: http://www.monarchhose.co.uk
Managers: C. Demczak (District Mgr), G. Wright (Mgr)
Immediate Holding Company: REGENT HOSE AND HYDRAULICS LIMITED
Registration no: 01599363 **VAT No.:** GB 348 5324 43
Date established: 1981 **Turnover:** £1m - £2m **No.of Employees:** 1 - 10
Product Groups: 29, 30

Richards Engineering

Unit 4-5 Frasers Yard Oakfield Industrial Estate, Eynsham, Witney, OX29 4TR
Tel: 01865-882778 **Fax:** 01865-882778
Directors: S. Richards (Prop)
Date established: 1991 **No.of Employees:** 1 - 10 **Product Groups:** 35

S J Wharton Ltd

Downs Road, Witney, OX29 0RF
Tel: 01993-779630 **Fax:** 01993-706602
E-mail: sales@sjwharton.co.uk
Website: http://www.sjwharton.co.uk
Directors: M. Wharton (MD)
Immediate Holding Company: S.J.WHARTON LIMITED
Registration no: 00375144 **Date established:** 1942
No.of Employees: 1 - 10 **Product Groups:** 22, 24, 27, 29, 30, 31, 32, 33, 34, 35, 36, 37, 38, 39, 40, 41, 42, 45, 46, 47, 48, 61, 63, 66, 67, 83

Date of Accounts	Oct 11	Oct 10	Oct 09
Working Capital	51	46	49
Fixed Assets	1	3	6
Current Assets	121	118	126

Sandawana Castings Ltd

Unit 4 Bromag Industrial Estate Minster Lovell, Witney, OX29 0SR
Tel: 01993-775862 **Fax:** 01993-776692
E-mail: gary.ashton@wlucy.co.uk
Website: http://www.sandawana.co.uk
Bank(s): HSBC
Directors: G. Ashton (Fin)
Ultimate Holding Company: W.L. SHAREHOLDING COMPANY LIMITED
Immediate Holding Company: SANDAWANA CASTINGS LIMITED
Registration no: 01753431 **VAT No.:** GB 348 9034 32
Date established: 1983 **Turnover:** £2m - £5m **No.of Employees:** 21 - 50
Product Groups: 34, 36, 45

Date of Accounts	Dec 11	Dec 10	Dec 09
Sales Turnover	N/A	3m	N/A
Pre Tax Profit/Loss	N/A	216	N/A
Working Capital	992	711	453
Fixed Assets	1m	1m	1m
Current Assets	2m	1m	766
Current Liabilities	N/A	278	N/A

Selectronic Ltd

Book End, Witney, OX29 0YE
Tel: 01993-778000 **Fax:** 01993-772512
E-mail: sales@selectronic.co.uk
Website: http://www.selectronic.co.uk
Bank(s): HSBC Bank plc
Directors: K. Stark (MD), K. Dry (Sales), D. Borrett (MD)
Ultimate Holding Company: SELECTRONIC GROUP LIMITED
Immediate Holding Company: SELECTRONIC LIMITED
Registration no: 01465562 **VAT No.:** GB 332 7590 55
Date established: 1979 **Turnover:** £5m - £10m **No.of Employees:** 21 - 50
Product Groups: 37, 38, 44

Date of Accounts	Nov 11	Nov 10	Nov 09
Working Capital	1m	998	891
Fixed Assets	94	108	103
Current Assets	2m	2m	2m

Siemens Magnet Technology

Wharf Road Eynsham, Witney, OX29 4BP
Tel: 01865-880880 **Fax:** 01865-850176
Website: http://www.omt.co.uk
Bank(s): National Westminster Bank Plc

see next page

Siemens Magnet Technology - Cont'd
Managers: S. Mobley, M. Roberts, M. Atallah (Purch Mgr)
Ultimate Holding Company: SIEMENS
Registration no: 00566186 **VAT No.:** GB 532 5920 54
Date established: 1989 **Turnover:** £75m - £125m
No.of Employees: 251 - 500 **Product Groups:** 37, 67

Slater Plastics Ltd
7 Hanborough Business Park Lodge Road, Long Hanborough, Witney, OX29 8LH
Tel: 01993-881486 **Fax:** 01993-883070
E-mail: info@slaterplastics.com
Website: http://www.slaterplastics.com
Directors: A. Tognola (Dir)
Immediate Holding Company: SLATER PLASTICS LIMITED
Registration no: 06894671 **VAT No.:** GB 630 8704 49
Date established: 2009 **Turnover:** £250,000 - £500,000
No.of Employees: 1 - 10 **Product Groups:** 37, 38

Date of Accounts	Jul 11	Jul 10
Working Capital	-5	-5
Fixed Assets	18	24
Current Assets	79	75

Smurfit Kappa Sheet Feeding Ltd
Windrush Park Road, Witney, OX29 7EX
Tel: 01993-771188 **Fax:** 01993-701201
Website: http://www.smurfitkappa.co.uk
Managers: S. Acum (Comptroller), S. Earnshaw (Comptroller), M. Disbury (Ops Mgr)
Registration no: 01017013 **Turnover:** £1m - £2m
No.of Employees: 51 - 100 **Product Groups:** 27

Solar Solutions Direct
4a Lombard Street Eynsham, Witney, OX29 4HT
Tel: 01865-880722
E-mail: office@solsol.co.uk
Website: http://www.solsol.co.uk
Directors: D. Taylor (MD)
Immediate Holding Company: SOLAR SOLUTIONS DIRECT LIMITED
Registration no: 05149556 **Date established:** 2004
No.of Employees: 1 - 10 **Product Groups:** 37, 52

Date of Accounts	Sep 11	Sep 10	Sep 09
Working Capital	-121	-97	-128
Fixed Assets	5	8	10
Current Assets	74	60	59

Systemair - Villavent Ltd
Avenue Two Station Lane, Witney, OX28 4YL
Tel: 01993-778481 **Fax:** 01993-779962
E-mail: sales@villavent.co.uk
Website: http://www.villavent.co.uk
Bank(s): Handelsbanken
Directors: N. Rapley (MD)
Ultimate Holding Company: SYSTEMAIR AB (SWEDEN)
Immediate Holding Company: VILLAVENT LIMITED
Registration no: 01839460 **VAT No.:** 410 7322 01 **Date established:** 1984
Turnover: £2m - £5m **No.of Employees:** 11 - 20 **Product Groups:** 23, 36, 40

Date of Accounts	Apr 12	Apr 11	Apr 10
Sales Turnover	3m	3m	4m
Pre Tax Profit/Loss	-188	32	161
Working Capital	-267	61	286
Fixed Assets	650	693	628
Current Assets	2m	1m	1m
Current Liabilities	229	160	258

Technirack Systems Ltd
Witney Road Standlake, Witney, OX29 7PR
Tel: 01993-893602 **Fax:** 01993-893601
Website: http://www.technirack.co.uk
Directors: A. Holliday (Co Sec), A. Holliday (Fin)
Immediate Holding Company: TECHNIRACK SYSTEMS LIMITED
Registration no: 01222502 **Date established:** 1975
No.of Employees: 1 - 10 **Product Groups:** 26, 35

Date of Accounts	Dec 07	Dec 06	Dec 05
Working Capital	23	55	54
Fixed Assets	4	4	4
Current Assets	137	123	242
Current Liabilities	114	68	187
Total Share Capital	2	2	2

Vigortronix Ltd
16 De Havilland Way Windrush Park, Witney, OX29 0YG
Tel: 01993-777570 **Fax:** 01993-777580
E-mail: sales@vigortronix.com
Website: http://www.vigortronix.com
Directors: B. Hallett (MD)
Registration no: 06630112 **Date established:** 2006 **Turnover:** £1m - £2m
No.of Employees: 11 - 20 **Product Groups:** 37

Vsw/Atom Tech Limited
Nursery Road North Leigh Business Park, Witney, OX29 6SN
Tel: 01993-880005 **Fax:** 01993-880060
Website: http://www.vsw.co.uk
Directors: M. Brayford (MD), E. Bergstrand (Fin)
Immediate Holding Company: Vsw/Atom Tech Ltd
Registration no: 02603130 **No.of Employees:** 11 - 20 **Product Groups:** 65

W S I Internet Consulting
Leafield Technical Centre Langley, Witney, OX29 9EF
Tel: 01993-871000
E-mail: carl@wsi-internetmarketing.co.uk
Website: http://www.wsi-internet-marketing.co.uk
Directors: C. Scholfield (Ptnr)
Immediate Holding Company: FORMTECH COMPOSITE LIMITED
Registration no: 05284802 **Date established:** 2008
No.of Employees: 1 - 10 **Product Groups:** 44, 79

Walker Machinery
Lindsay Farm High Cogges, Witney, OX29 6UN
Tel: 01993-772255 **Fax:** 01993-771007
E-mail: sales@walkermachinery.fsnet.co.uk
Website: http://www.walkermachinery.fsnet.co.uk
Directors: J. Walker (Prop)
Immediate Holding Company: WALKER ENTERPRISES (PRODUCTIONS) LIMITED
Registration no: 04688425 **Date established:** 2003
Turnover: £500,000 - £1m **No.of Employees:** 1 - 10 **Product Groups:** 39, 41, 45

Date of Accounts	Oct 11	Aug 10	Aug 09
Working Capital	158	150	113
Fixed Assets	100	89	95
Current Assets	311	304	219

Wehrle Environmental
A6 Spinners Court 53 West End, Witney, OX28 1NH
Tel: 01993-849300 **Fax:** 01993-849309
E-mail: info@wehrle-env.co.uk
Website: http://www.wehrle-env.co.uk
Directors: E. Muhle (Dir)
Managers: A. Robinson (Chief Mgr), T. Robins (Mgr)
Immediate Holding Company: WEHRLE ENVIRONMENTAL LIMITED
Registration no: 06780201 **Date established:** 2008
No.of Employees: 1 - 10 **Product Groups:** 41, 42, 54, 84

Date of Accounts	Dec 09	Jun 11
Sales Turnover	N/A	113
Pre Tax Profit/Loss	N/A	8
Working Capital	N/A	5
Fixed Assets	N/A	2
Current Assets	N/A	27
Current Liabilities	N/A	8

Windrush Guns Ltd
PO Box 127, Witney, OX28 6FX
Tel: 01993-703035 **Fax:** 01993-771014
Directors: I. Petty (MD), S. Petty (Fin)
No.of Employees: 1 - 10 **Product Groups:** 36, 39, 40

Date of Accounts	Sep 07	Sep 06
Working Capital	-3	-3
Current Liabilities	3	3
Total Share Capital	10	10

Witney Plant Hire Ltd
Unit 7-8 Avenue Three Station Lane, Witney, OX28 4BP
Tel: 01993-708020 **Fax:** 01993-708020
E-mail: david.johns@witneyplanthire.com
Website: http://www.witneyplanthire.com
Directors: D. Johns (MD)
Immediate Holding Company: WITNEY PLANT HIRE LIMITED
Registration no: 03950126 **Date established:** 2000
No.of Employees: 1 - 10 **Product Groups:** 83

Date of Accounts	Mar 11	Mar 10	Mar 09
Working Capital	-286	-222	-260
Fixed Assets	3m	2m	2m
Current Assets	518	374	324

Witney Welding
Farley Lane Stonesfield, Witney, OX29 8HB
Tel: 01993-891198 **Fax:** 08701-365412
Website: http://www.witneywelding.co.uk
Directors: P. Bullock (Dir)
Date established: 2002 **No.of Employees:** 1 - 10 **Product Groups:** 35

Wychwood Water Systems Ltd
Unit K County Park Avenue Two, Witney, OX28 4YD
Tel: 01993-892211 **Fax:** 01993-832212
E-mail: sales@wychwood-water.com
Website: http://www.wychwood-water.com
Directors: P. Wood (MD)
Immediate Holding Company: WYCHWOOD WATER SYSTEMS LIMITED
Registration no: 03307144 **Date established:** 1997
No.of Employees: 11 - 20 **Product Groups:** 32, 40, 41, 42, 52, 54, 85

Date of Accounts	Mar 11	Mar 10	Mar 09
Working Capital	10	-23	63
Fixed Assets	107	94	94
Current Assets	523	286	388

Woodstock

Writersworld Ltd
2 Bear Close FL Bear Close, Woodstock, OX20 1JX
Tel: 01993-812500
E-mail: enquiries@writersworld.co.uk
Website: http://www.writersworld.co.uk
Managers: G. Cook (Mgr)
Immediate Holding Company: WRITERSWORLD LIMITED
Registration no: 04367863 **Date established:** 2002
Turnover: £250m - £500m **No.of Employees:** 1 - 10 **Product Groups:** 28, 44, 64, 80, 81, 82, 86, 87

Date of Accounts	Feb 11	Feb 10	Feb 08
Working Capital	1	1	1
Current Assets	1	1	1

SHROPSHIRE

Bridgnorth

A S K Supplies Ltd
5 Stretton Close, Bridgnorth, WV16 5DB
Tel: 01746-768164 **Fax:** 01746-766835
E-mail: sales@asksupplies.co.uk
Website: http://www.asksupplies.co.uk
Directors: T. Gluyas (Fin)
Managers: K. Gluyas (Admin Off)
Immediate Holding Company: A.S.K. SUPPLIES LIMITED
Registration no: 03733678 **Date established:** 1999
No.of Employees: 1 - 10 **Product Groups:** 26, 35

Date of Accounts	Sep 11	Jun 10	Jun 09
Working Capital	-5	-3	4
Fixed Assets	N/A	1	1
Current Assets	7	8	18

A.V.B. Mills Ltd (John Mills Hydraulic Press Division)
Aldenham Business Park Muckley Cross, Bridgnorth, WV16 4RR
Tel: 01746-714418 **Fax:** 01746-714419
E-mail: sales@avbmills.com
Website: http://www.avbmills.co.uk
Directors: V. Jones (MD), M. Jeffcoat (Dir)
Ultimate Holding Company: A B Birch Ltd
Registration no: 02855870 **Turnover:** £500,000 - £1m
No.of Employees: 1 - 10 **Product Groups:** 42, 43, 45, 46, 47, 48, 67

Date of Accounts	Aug 08	Aug 07	Aug 06
Sales Turnover	113	167	186
Pre Tax Profit/Loss	15	19	25
Working Capital	37	25	19
Fixed Assets	2	1	2
Current Assets	76	71	61
Current Liabilities	39	46	43
ROCE% (Return on Capital Employed)	38.3	73.0	118.9
ROT% (Return on Turnover)	13.2	11.7	13.2

Coram Showers Ltd
Unit 3 Stanmore Industrial Estate, Bridgnorth, WV15 5HP
Tel: 01746-766466 **Fax:** 01746-764140
E-mail: sales@coram.co.uk
Website: http://www.coram.co.uk
Directors: M. Dain (Fin), P. Dimeloe (MD), G. Jones (Fin), K. McCormick (Sales)
Managers: T. Sweet (Personnel), C. Rautleuy (Mktg Serv Mgr), A. Welsh (Tech Serv Mgr), R. Parks (Purch Mgr)
Ultimate Holding Company: CORAM NV (BELGIUM)
Immediate Holding Company: CORAM SHOWERS LIMITED
Registration no: 00589581 **Date established:** 1957
Turnover: £10m - £20m **No.of Employees:** 51 - 100 **Product Groups:** 30, 33, 36, 63, 66

Date of Accounts	Dec 11	Dec 10	Dec 09
Sales Turnover	10m	10m	12m
Pre Tax Profit/Loss	-198	-184	943
Working Capital	6m	7m	7m
Fixed Assets	1m	1m	1m
Current Assets	8m	8m	8m
Current Liabilities	975	923	1m

Craven Dunnill & Co. Ltd
Stourbridge Road, Bridgnorth, WV15 6AS
Tel: 01746-761611 **Fax:** 01746-767007
E-mail: sales@cravendunnill.co.uk
Website: http://www.cravendunnill.co.uk
Directors: P. Weeks (Fin), P. Howells (MD)
Managers: S. Whitehurst
Immediate Holding Company: CRAVEN DUNNILL & CO.LIMITED
Registration no: 00006028 **Date established:** 1972 **Turnover:** £5m - £10m
No.of Employees: 51 - 100 **Product Groups:** 30, 31, 33, 35

Date of Accounts	Dec 11	Dec 10	Dec 09
Sales Turnover	8m	7m	8m
Pre Tax Profit/Loss	245	169	80
Working Capital	1m	1m	1m
Fixed Assets	1m	1m	1m
Current Assets	3m	2m	2m
Current Liabilities	677	575	441

Mark Dady Associates Ltd
25 Salop Street, Bridgnorth, WV16 5BH
Tel: 01746-766455 **Fax:** 01746-769455
E-mail: mailbox@markdadyassociates.co.uk
Website: http://www.markdadyassociates.co.uk
Directors: M. Dady (Prop)
Immediate Holding Company: MARK DADY ASSOCIATES LTD
Registration no: 06770938 **Date established:** 2008
No.of Employees: 1 - 10 **Product Groups:** 35

Date of Accounts	Dec 10	Dec 09
Working Capital	-34	-39
Fixed Assets	34	39
Current Assets	26	69

Danagri - 3 S Ltd
The Livestock & Auction Centre Unit 8 Wenlock Road, Bridgnorth, WV16 4QR
Tel: 01746-762777 **Fax:** 01746-764777
E-mail: info@danagri-3s.com
Website: http://www.danagri-3s.com
Directors: M. Unitt (MD)
Immediate Holding Company: DANAGRI - 3S LIMITED
Registration no: 01736387 **Date established:** 1983 **Turnover:** £1m - £2m
No.of Employees: 1 - 10 **Product Groups:** 61

Date of Accounts	Dec 11	Dec 10	Dec 09
Working Capital	420	402	301
Fixed Assets	46	23	27
Current Assets	761	876	518

Davro Iron & Steel Co. Ltd
Ridgewell Works Stourbridge Road, Wootton, Bridgnorth, WV15 6ED
Tel: 01746-780242 **Fax:** 01746-780930
E-mail: simon.evans@davrosteel.co.uk
Website: http://www.davrosteel.co.uk
Bank(s): Lloyds TSB Bank plc
Directors: S. Evans (Co Sec), R. Evans (Sales), L. Beddall (Sales), M. Nielan (Fin)
Immediate Holding Company: DAVRO IRON AND STEEL COMPANY LIMITED(THE)
Registration no: 00471310 **VAT No.:** GB 655 1271 45
Date established: 1949 **Turnover:** £20m - £50m
No.of Employees: 21 - 50 **Product Groups:** 34, 48, 66, 77

Date of Accounts	Mar 11	Mar 10	Mar 09
Sales Turnover	26m	12m	N/A
Pre Tax Profit/Loss	218	56	163
Working Capital	808	735	713
Fixed Assets	3m	3m	3m
Current Assets	12m	6m	6m
Current Liabilities	525	131	594

Digwood Ltd
Alveley Industrial Estate Alveley, Bridgnorth, WV15 6HG
Tel: 01746-780468 **Fax:** 01746-780371
E-mail: sales@digwood.com
Website: http://www.digwood.com
Managers: R. Evans (Sales Prom Mgr)
Immediate Holding Company: DIGWOODS LIMITED
Registration no: 02313986 **Date established:** 1988 **Turnover:** £1m - £2m
No.of Employees: 1 - 10 **Product Groups:** 45, 67

Date of Accounts	Mar 12	Mar 11	Mar 10
Working Capital	116	120	82
Fixed Assets	26	33	48
Current Assets	250	354	262

Filtermist International Ltd
Stourbridge Road Industrial Estate Faraday Drive, Bridgnorth, WV15 5BA
Tel: 01746-765361 **Fax:** 01746-766882
E-mail: sales@filtermist.com
Website: http://www.filtermist.com
Bank(s): Barclays, Wolverhampton
Directors: R. Woodward (Sales), R. Taft (I.T. Dir), M. Stansfield (MD)
Managers: L. Berry, V. Williams (Fin Mgr)
Ultimate Holding Company: FILTERMIST LIMITED
Immediate Holding Company: FILTERMIST INTERNATIONAL LIMITED
Registration no: 03312267 **Date established:** 1997 **Turnover:** £5m - £10m
No.of Employees: 21 - 50 **Product Groups:** 40, 42

Date of Accounts	Dec 11	Dec 10	Dec 09
Sales Turnover	9m	6m	2m
Pre Tax Profit/Loss	3m	2m	203
Working Capital	1m	3m	2m
Fixed Assets	3m	3m	4m
Current Assets	3m	5m	3m
Current Liabilities	563	606	131

Grainger & Worrall Ltd
Unit 1-7 Stanmore Industrial Estate, Bridgnorth, WV15 5HP
Tel: 01746-768250 **Fax:** 01746-768251
E-mail: jlewis@gwcast.co.uk
Website: http://www.gwcast.co.uk
Bank(s): National Westminster Bank Plc
Directors: A. Weston (Fin), A. Wesson (Fin), J. Grainger (MD)
Managers: S. Coyle (Personnel), B. Jones (Tech Serv Mgr), R. Plant (Buyer)
Ultimate Holding Company: GRAINGER HOLDINGS LIMITED
Immediate Holding Company: GRAINGER & WORRALL LIMITED
Registration no: 00980487 **Date established:** 1970
Turnover: £20m - £50m **No.of Employees:** 251 - 500 **Product Groups:** 46

Date of Accounts	May 11	May 10	May 09
Sales Turnover	21m	15m	19m
Pre Tax Profit/Loss	729	491	162
Working Capital	-237	-182	-4
Fixed Assets	4m	2m	3m
Current Assets	8m	6m	5m
Current Liabilities	1m	649	734

Hickman Steels International Ltd
Po Box 6, Bridgnorth, WV16 5JJ
Tel: 01746-762 750 **Fax:** 01746-767299
E-mail: mikemansfield@hickmansteels.com
Website: http://www.hickmansteels.com
Directors: M. Mansfield (MD), B. Mansfield Hickman (MD)
Immediate Holding Company: Bridgnorth Steels Ltd
Registration no: 07043449 **Date established:** 1978 **Turnover:** £1m - £2m
No.of Employees: 1 - 10 **Product Groups:** 66

Date of Accounts	Mar 08	Mar 07	Mar 06
Working Capital	382	343	393
Fixed Assets	N/A	1	2
Current Assets	585	592	568
Current Liabilities	203	250	175
Total Share Capital	9	9	9

F L Hitchman
Unit 46 Ditton Priors Trading Estate Station Road, Ditton Priors, Bridgnorth, WV16 6SS
Tel: 01746-712242 **Fax:** 01746-712055
E-mail: enquiries@aquaroll.com
Website: http://www.aquaroll.com
Managers: K. Clarke (Chief Mgr)
Immediate Holding Company: F. L. HITCHMAN LIMITED
Registration no: 07964238 **Date established:** 2012
No.of Employees: 1 - 10 **Product Groups:** 30

P L Jones & Son
57 St Marys Street, Bridgnorth, WV16 4DR
Tel: 01746-763261 **Fax:** 01746-763261
Directors: P. Jones (Prop)
Date established: 1964 **No.of Employees:** 1 - 10 **Product Groups:** 36

Kecol Pumping Systems Ltd
Faraday Drive, Bridgnorth, WV15 5BJ
Tel: 01746-764311 **Fax:** 01746-763375
E-mail: sales@kecol.co.uk
Website: http://www.kecol.co.uk
Bank(s): Barclays, Queen Sq, Wolverhampton
Registration no: 06405042 **Date established:** 1973
No.of Employees: 21 - 50 **Product Groups:** 40, 41, 42, 83, 84

Date of Accounts	Oct 11	Oct 10	Oct 09
Working Capital	181	106	88
Fixed Assets	21	17	23
Current Assets	334	310	189

L A Plant Hire Ltd
Stone Haven Halfway House Lane, Eardington, Bridgnorth, WV16 5JP
Tel: 01746-711497 **Fax:** 01746-711497
Directors: T. Hill (MD)
Immediate Holding Company: L A PLANT HIRE LIMITED
Registration no: 04858629 **Date established:** 2003
No.of Employees: 1 - 10 **Product Groups:** 45, 72, 83

Date of Accounts	Aug 10	Aug 09	Aug 08
Working Capital	-990	-1m	-1m
Fixed Assets	765	841	933
Current Assets	119	61	95

Ladders and Access Lynton Engineering S/B Ltd
April Cottage Broad Lanes, Six Ashes, Bridgnorth, WV15 6EG
Tel: 01746-781587
E-mail: info@laddersandaccess.com
Website: http://www.laddersandaccess.com
No.of Employees: 1 - 10 **Product Groups:** 25, 35, 66

Laser Sport International Ltd
Building 19 Stanmore Industrial Estate, Bridgnorth, WV15 5HR
Tel: 01746-767186 **Fax:** 01746-761312
E-mail: christine.reddihough@lasersport.biz
Website: http://www.lasersport.biz
Directors: I. Reddihough (MD)
Immediate Holding Company: LASERSPORT INTERNATIONAL LIMITED
Registration no: 03946026 **Date established:** 2000
Turnover: £500,000 - £1m **No.of Employees:** 11 - 20 **Product Groups:** 36

Date of Accounts	Mar 11	Mar 10	Mar 09
Working Capital	8	6	13
Current Assets	178	177	195

Leonardt Ltd
New Road Highley, Bridgnorth, WV16 6NN
Tel: 01746-861203 **Fax:** 0121-615 3352
E-mail: info@leonardt.com
Website: http://www.leonardt.com
Bank(s): HSBC Bank plc, Shrewsbury
Directors: S. Askey (Dir), P. Meredith (Co Sec), P. Meredith (Fin), N. Parkin (Sales), N. Parkin (Dir), C. Sherwood (Works)
Immediate Holding Company: LEONARDT LIMITED
Registration no: 05714731 **Date established:** 2006
No.of Employees: 21 - 50 **Product Groups:** 35, 48, 49

Date of Accounts	Mar 12	Mar 11	Mar 10
Working Capital	378	429	500
Fixed Assets	523	433	412
Current Assets	2m	2m	2m

Manuscript Pen Co. Ltd
New Road Highley, Bridgnorth, WV16 6NN
Tel: 01746-861236 **Fax:** 01746-862737
E-mail: malissa@calligraphy.co.uk
Website: http://www.calligraphy.co.uk
Directors: C. Stockbridge (Mkt Research), J. Bryan (Fin), M. Chappell (Sales), N. Stockbridge (MD), L. Jones (Works), M. Stockbridge (Dir)
Managers: S. Walford (Purch Mgr)
Ultimate Holding Company: HIGHLEY PENS LIMITED
Immediate Holding Company: MANUSCRIPT PEN COMPANY LTD
Registration no: 02414044 **Date established:** 1989
Turnover: £500,000 - £1m **No.of Employees:** 21 - 50 **Product Groups:** 49

Date of Accounts	Dec 11	Dec 10	Dec 09
Working Capital	1m	1m	1m
Fixed Assets	206	167	172
Current Assets	1m	1m	1m

Modern Systems Electronics Ltd
Aldenham Mill Muckley Cross, Acton Round, Bridgnorth, WV16 4RR
Tel: 01746-714112 **Fax:** 01746-714113
E-mail: ian@modernsys.co.uk
Website: http://www.modernsys.co.uk
Directors: I. Stones (MD)
Immediate Holding Company: MODERN SYSTEMS (ELECTRONICS) LIMITED
Registration no: 03379549 **Date established:** 1997
Turnover: £250,000 - £500,000 **No.of Employees:** 1 - 10
Product Groups: 38, 84

Date of Accounts	Nov 11	Nov 10	Nov 09
Working Capital	2	12	-1
Fixed Assets	5	6	7
Current Assets	57	79	40

Novelis Foil & Technical Products
Stourbridge Road, Bridgnorth, WV15 6AW
Tel: 01746-713000 **Fax:** 01746-761860
E-mail: jane.hyde@novelis.com
Website: http://www.novelis.com
Directors: E. Faust (Fin), M. Adams (Fin)
Managers: J. Hyde, M. Stanley (Tech Serv Mgr), T. Harrold (Buyer), L. Nary (Personnel)
Ultimate Holding Company: A.L. PACKAGING (SWITZERLAND)
Immediate Holding Company: ALCAN PACKAGING
Registration no: 00279596 **Turnover:** £75m - £125m
No.of Employees: 251 - 500 **Product Groups:** 34

A Seedhouse & Son
Hallon Forge Workshop Hallon, Worfield, Bridgnorth, WV15 5JZ
Tel: 01746-716247 **Fax:** 01746-716113
E-mail: is290774@yahoo.co.uk
Directors: I. Seedhouse (Ptnr)
Date established: 1953 **No.of Employees:** 1 - 10 **Product Groups:** 41

Shiloh Computers Ltd
Smithfield Centre Whitburn Street, Bridgnorth, WV16 4QT
Tel: 01746-760780 **Fax:** 01746-768710
E-mail: support@shilohcomputers.com
Website: http://www.shilohcomputers.com
Bank(s): Barclays
Directors: P. Harris (MD), R. Harris (Co Sec)
Immediate Holding Company: JENTECH COMPUTERS LIMITED
Registration no: 01972117 **VAT No.:** GB 478 9069 81
Date established: 1985 **Turnover:** Up to £250,000
No.of Employees: 11 - 20 **Product Groups:** 44, 67

Date of Accounts	Mar 11	Mar 10	Mar 09
Sales Turnover	N/A	N/A	18
Working Capital	-95	-96	-96
Current Assets	13	13	19
Current Liabilities	N/A	N/A	4

Simple Simon Packaging
1 Severn Valley Industrial Estate Knowle Sands, Bridgnorth, WV16 5JL
Tel: 01746-767333 **Fax:** 01746-768660
Directors: D. Sproson (Ptnr)
Immediate Holding Company: SIMPLE SIMON PACKAGING LIMITED
Registration no: 08111267 **Date established:** 2012
No.of Employees: 1 - 10 **Product Groups:** 38, 42

The Taylor Winfield Corporation
Lasyard House Underhill Street, Bridgnorth, WV16 4BB
Tel: 01746-766500 **Fax:** 01746-769050
Managers: P. Cooke (Chief Mgr)
Immediate Holding Company: THE CIVIL ENGINEERING CONTRACTORS ASSOCIATION (MIDLANDS) LIMITED
Date established: 1997 **No.of Employees:** 1 - 10 **Product Groups:** 45, 46, 48, 84

Bucknell

Gordon Morris Agricultural Engineers
Bedstone Road, Bucknell, SY7 0AQ
Tel: 01547-530600
Directors: G. Morris (Prop)
Date established: 1991 **No.of Employees:** 1 - 10 **Product Groups:** 41

Church Stretton

Jacob UK Ltd
Unit 2 Laundry Bank Watling Street South, Church Stretton, SY6 6PH
Tel: 01694-722841 **Fax:** 01694-723473
E-mail: sales@jacob-uk.com
Website: http://www.jacob-uk.com
Directors: J. West (MD)
Ultimate Holding Company: FR JACOB SOHNE GMBH & CO (GERMANY)
Immediate Holding Company: JACOB (UK) LIMITED
Registration no: 04104231 **VAT No.:** GB 762 7262 19
Date established: 2000 **Turnover:** £1m - £2m **No.of Employees:** 1 - 10
Product Groups: 36, 40

Date of Accounts	Dec 11	Dec 10	Dec 09
Working Capital	416	293	220
Fixed Assets	9	4	5
Current Assets	756	597	667

John H Teague
Lane End Soudley, Church Stretton, SY6 7HQ
Tel: 01694-723267
Directors: J. Teague (Prop)
Date established: 1971 **No.of Employees:** 1 - 10 **Product Groups:** 41

Craven Arms

Border Holdings UK Ltd
The Grove, Craven Arms, SY7 8DA
Tel: 01588-672711 **Fax:** 01588-672660
E-mail: info@britpart.co.uk
Website: http://www.britpart.com
Directors: A. Overs (Co Sec), D. Beddow (MD)
Immediate Holding Company: BORDER HOLDINGS (U.K.) LTD.
Registration no: 01664243 **VAT No.:** GB 307 2884 54
Date established: 1982 **Turnover:** £50m - £75m
No.of Employees: 101 - 250 **Product Groups:** 39

Date of Accounts	Mar 12	Mar 11	Mar 10
Sales Turnover	51m	48m	43m
Pre Tax Profit/Loss	8m	7m	7m
Working Capital	32m	27m	22m
Fixed Assets	7m	6m	6m
Current Assets	44m	38m	29m
Current Liabilities	7m	6m	2m

C & W Specialist Equipment Ltd
Leintwardine, Craven Arms, SY7 0NB
Tel: 01547-540654 **Fax:** 01547-540412
E-mail: sales.service@cw-spec.com
Website: http://www.cw-spec.com
Directors: M. Cremer (Co Sec), N. Cremer (MD)
Immediate Holding Company: C. & W. SPECIALIST EQUIPMENT LIMITED
Registration no: 02171963 **Date established:** 1987
Turnover: £500,000 - £1m **No.of Employees:** 1 - 10 **Product Groups:** 38, 85

Date of Accounts	Sep 11	Sep 10	Sep 09
Working Capital	169	137	102
Fixed Assets	27	34	45
Current Assets	302	252	166
Current Liabilities	13	N/A	N/A

Clear View Chimneys
Church View 3 Hand Causeway, Clun, Craven Arms, SY7 8JN
Tel: 01588-640910
Directors: M. Oliver (MD)
No.of Employees: 1 - 10 **Product Groups:** 40

Reo UK Ltd
Unit 2-4 Callow Hill Road, Craven Arms, SY7 8NT
Tel: 01588-676167 **Fax:** 01588-672718
E-mail: main@reo.co.uk
Website: http://www.reo.co.uk
Directors: S. Hughes (MD), J. Hughes (Fin)
Immediate Holding Company: REO (U.K.) LIMITED
Registration no: 02415988 **VAT No.:** GB 489 3483 88
Date established: 1989 **Turnover:** £500,000 - £1m
No.of Employees: 1 - 10 **Product Groups:** 37, 38

Date of Accounts	Dec 11	Dec 10	Dec 09
Working Capital	368	285	256
Fixed Assets	22	10	14
Current Assets	967	870	637

Ellesmere

A B P
The Abattoir Hordley, Ellesmere, SY12 9BL
Tel: 01939-270333 **Fax:** 01939-270405
Website: http://www.abpltd.com
Bank(s): Barclays
Managers: S. Jones (Tech Serv Mgr), L. Walford (Personnel), J. Lees (Ops Mgr), K. Saywell (Comptroller)
Immediate Holding Company: ANGLO BEEF PROCESSORS
Registration no: 05215145 **VAT No.:** GB 158 9489 00
Date established: 2004 **No.of Employees:** 501 - 1000 **Product Groups:** 20

Cargotec UK Ltd
Cargotec Industrial Park, Ellesmere, SY12 9TW
Tel: 01691-623100 **Fax:** 01691-623022
E-mail: enquiries.uk@hiab.com
Website: http://www.cargotec.com
Directors: I. Leppanen (MD), I. Lettanen (MD)
Managers: D. Bolland (Tech Serv Mgr), M. Cornwall (Purch Mgr), A. Johnson (Chief Acct)
Ultimate Holding Company: CARGOTEC OYJ (FINLAND)
Immediate Holding Company: CARGOTEC UK LIMITED
Registration no: 02117024 **Date established:** 1987
Turnover: £50m - £75m **No.of Employees:** 21 - 50 **Product Groups:** 39

Date of Accounts	Dec 11	Dec 10	Dec 09
Sales Turnover	69m	57m	35m
Pre Tax Profit/Loss	892	127	-119
Working Capital	25m	26m	27m
Fixed Assets	27m	26m	26m
Current Assets	37m	35m	45m
Current Liabilities	4m	3m	4m

E T C Sawmills Ltd
Cargotec Industrial Park, Ellesmere, SY12 9JW
Tel: 01691-622441 **Fax:** 01691-623468
E-mail: info@etcsawmills.co.uk
Website: http://www.etcsawmills.co.uk
Bank(s): HSBC Bank plc
Directors: R. Evans (Fin), C. Heskins (MD)
Managers: A. Williams (Personnel), T. Wakefield (Sales Prom Mgr)
Ultimate Holding Company: PENARTH COMMERCIAL PROPERTIES (HOLDINGS) LIMITED
Immediate Holding Company: E.T.C. SAW MILLS LIMITED
Registration no: 01433784 **VAT No.:** GB 451 7544 46
Date established: 1979 **Turnover:** £5m - £10m
No.of Employees: 101 - 250 **Product Groups:** 08, 25, 66

Date of Accounts	Feb 08	Feb 11	Feb 10
Sales Turnover	11m	10m	8m
Pre Tax Profit/Loss	1m	1m	671
Working Capital	3m	2m	2m
Fixed Assets	3m	3m	3m
Current Assets	6m	6m	4m
Current Liabilities	1m	2m	472

Fabdec Ltd
Grange Road, Ellesmere, SY12 9DG
Tel: 01691-622811 **Fax:** 01691-627222
E-mail: reception@fabdec.com
Website: http://www.fabdec.com
Bank(s): National Westminster Bank Plc
Directors: G. Egar (Fin), G. Haddad (Sales & Mktg), C. Powell (MD)
Managers: S. Billington (Tech Serv Mgr), G. Elner (Purch Mgr)
Ultimate Holding Company: FABDEC HOLDINGS LIMITED
Immediate Holding Company: FABDEC LIMITED
Registration no: 00675981 **Date established:** 1960
Turnover: £10m - £20m **No.of Employees:** 51 - 100 **Product Groups:** 35, 40, 48

Date of Accounts	Dec 11	Dec 10	Dec 09
Sales Turnover	17m	14m	14m
Pre Tax Profit/Loss	2m	881	791
Working Capital	5m	4m	4m
Fixed Assets	827	703	584
Current Assets	8m	7m	7m
Current Liabilities	851	557	696

Newstyle Fabrication Ltd
1 St Johns Close, Ellesmere, SY12 0HL
Tel: 01691-622494 **Fax:** 01691-773303
Directors: J. Dyke (Fin)
Immediate Holding Company: NEWSTYLE FABRICATIONS LIMITED
Registration no: 01987993 **Date established:** 1986
No.of Employees: 1 - 10 **Product Groups:** 35

Date of Accounts	Feb 08	Feb 11	Feb 10
Working Capital	1m	2m	2m
Fixed Assets	18	8	10
Current Assets	1m	2m	2m

Ridgway Holdings International Ltd (Ridgway Holdings International Ltd)
The Laurels Dudleston Heath, Ellesmere, SY12 9LD
Tel: 01691-770171 **Fax:** 01691-690699
E-mail: sales@ridgwayrentals.com
Website: http://www.ridgway-holdings.co.uk
Immediate Holding Company: RIDGWAY HOLDINGS INTERNATIONAL LTD
Registration no: 03209914 **Date established:** 1996
No.of Employees: 1 - 10 **Product Groups:** 45, 67, 83

Date of Accounts	Apr 08	Apr 07	Apr 06
Pre Tax Profit/Loss	1178	N/A	N/A
Working Capital	-2293	-2278	-1674
Fixed Assets	13583	10839	7847
Current Assets	1274	1718	980
Current Liabilities	3566	3996	2654
ROCE% (Return on Capital Employed)	10.4		

Ludlow

Benchmark Instruments Ltd
Orleton Road Ludlow Business Park, Ludlow, SY8 1XF
Tel: 01584-872404 **Fax:** 01584-877274
E-mail: sales@benchmark-bpl.com
Website: http://www.benchmarkinstruments.com
Managers: A. Roberts (Works Gen Mgr)
Immediate Holding Company: BENCHMARK INSTRUMENTS LIMITED
Registration no: 03243344 **VAT No.:** GB 678 9697 36
Date established: 1996 **Turnover:** £250,000 - £500,000
No.of Employees: 1 - 10 **Product Groups:** 38

Date of Accounts	Sep 11	Sep 10	Sep 09
Sales Turnover	366	N/A	571
Pre Tax Profit/Loss	-1	N/A	30
Working Capital	29	28	-57
Fixed Assets	4	5	222
Current Assets	98	119	131
Current Liabilities	22	N/A	63

Biffa Waste Services Ltd
Ludlow Council Dept Coder Road, Ludlow Business Park, Ludlow, SY8 1XE
Tel: 01584-878448 **Fax:** 01584-874951
E-mail: marketing@biffa.co.uk
Website: http://www.biffa.co.uk
Managers: I. Hancock (Mgr)
Immediate Holding Company: BIFFA WASTE SERVICES LIMITED
Registration no: 00946107 **Date established:** 1969
Turnover: £500,000 - £1m **No.of Employees:** 21 - 50 **Product Groups:** 54

Date of Accounts	Mar 08	Mar 09	Apr 10
Sales Turnover	555m	574m	492m
Pre Tax Profit/Loss	23m	50m	30m
Working Capital	229m	271m	293m
Fixed Assets	371m	360m	378m
Current Assets	409m	534m	609m
Current Liabilities	50m	100m	115m

BYPY Hydraulics & Transmissions Ltd
Lingen Road Ludlow Business Park, Ludlow, SY8 1XD
Tel: 01584-873012 **Fax:** 01584-876647
E-mail: sales@bypy.co.uk
Website: http://www.bypy.co.uk
Directors: I. Teece (MD), R. Summers (MD), A. Bridge (MD)
Managers: R. Rowley (Tech Eng), N. Askew (Tech Sales Mgr), C. Davies (Purch Mgr), R. Summers (Sales Prom Mgr), M. Rowley (Tech Eng)
Immediate Holding Company: HYDRAULICS AND TRANSMISSIONS LIMITED
Registration no: 06110656 **Date established:** 2007 **Turnover:** £2m - £5m
No.of Employees: 11 - 20 **Product Groups:** 35, 38, 40, 67

Date of Accounts	Dec 11	Dec 10	Dec 09
Working Capital	-395	-468	-588
Fixed Assets	937	953	967
Current Assets	2m	2m	2m

John Godrich
Pellow House Old Street, Ludlow, SY8 1NU
Tel: 01584-873153 **Fax:** 01584-872424
E-mail: johngodrich@johngodrich.co.uk
Website: http://www.johngodrich.co.uk
Directors: J. Godrich (Prop)
Immediate Holding Company: CREDIT MACHINES LIMITED
Registration no: 01424135 **VAT No.:** GB 135 8230 78
Date established: 1979 **Turnover:** £500,000 - £1m
No.of Employees: 1 - 10 **Product Groups:** 38

Harrier Fluid Power Ltd
Parys Road Ludlow Business Park, Ludlow, SY8 1XY
Tel: 01584-876033 **Fax:** 01584-876044
E-mail: sales@harrieronline.co.uk
Website: http://www.harrieronline.co.uk
Directors: T. Cole (Fin), M. Parsonage (Dir), S. Parsonage (MD)
Immediate Holding Company: HARRIER FLUID POWER LIMITED
Registration no: 03174819 **VAT No.:** 682 2498 09 **Date established:** 1996
Turnover: £500,000 - £1m **No.of Employees:** 1 - 10 **Product Groups:** 40, 42, 45

Date of Accounts	May 11	May 10	May 09
Working Capital	162	144	116
Fixed Assets	560	558	564
Current Assets	907	708	645

Information Strategies Key Intangible Value
2 Corve View Culmington, Ludlow, SY8 2DD
Tel: 0701-702 6815 **Fax:** 07017-026814
E-mail: iskiv@iskiv.net
Website: http://www.iskiv.net/
Directors: I. Silderstein (Ptnr)
Managers: I. Silberstein (Consultant)
Immediate Holding Company: Information Strategies Key Intangible Value Ltd
Registration no: 05347895 **Date established:** 2005
Turnover: Up to £250,000 **No.of Employees:** 1 - 10 **Product Groups:** 61, 81

Interflex Hose & Bellows Ltd
Orleton Road Ludlow Business Pk, Ludlow, SY8 1XF
Tel: 01584-878500 **Fax:** 01584-878115
E-mail: enquiries@interflex.co.uk
Website: http://www.interflex.co.uk
Directors: L. Urmston (Dir)
Managers: T. Urmston (Sales Prom)
Registration no: 02143702 **VAT No.:** GB 467 8413 13
Date established: 1987 **Turnover:** £250,000 - £500,000
No.of Employees: 1 - 10 **Product Groups:** 23, 29, 30, 35, 36, 38, 39, 40, 45, 66, 84

Date of Accounts	Jun 07	Jun 06
Working Capital	60	52
Fixed Assets	3	3
Current Assets	163	127
Current Liabilities	103	75

Kingfisher Leisurewear Ltd
Unit 12b-12c Orleton Road, Ludlow Business Park, Ludlow, SY8 1XF
Tel: 01584-877661 **Fax:** 01584-876399
E-mail: sales@kingflw.com
Website: http://www.kingflw.com
Directors: P. Mason (Dir), T. Guard (Chief Op Offcr), A. Mitchell (MD), S. Mason (Fin)
Immediate Holding Company: KINGFISHER LEISUREWEAR LIMITED
Registration no: 03264965 **Date established:** 1996 **Turnover:** £2m - £5m
No.of Employees: 21 - 50 **Product Groups:** 23, 24

Date of Accounts	Dec 11	Dec 10	Dec 09
Sales Turnover	N/A	4m	N/A
Pre Tax Profit/Loss	N/A	283	N/A
Working Capital	-521	-357	-428
Fixed Assets	1m	845	948
Current Assets	647	749	561
Current Liabilities	N/A	490	N/A

Mcconnel Ltd
Temeside Works, Ludlow, SY8 1JL
Tel: 01584-873131 **Fax:** 01584-876463
E-mail: gdavies@mcconnel.com
Website: http://www.mcconnel.com
Directors: E. Madden (Fin), G. Davies (MD)
Managers: M. Dyson (Tech Serv Mgr), W. Brown (Mktg Serv Mgr), J. Walters (Purch Mgr), C. Davies (Sales Prom Mgr), W. Goodall (Personnel)
Ultimate Holding Company: ALAMO GROUP INC (USA)
Immediate Holding Company: MCCONNEL LIMITED
Registration no: 00305192 **Date established:** 1935
Turnover: £10m - £20m **No.of Employees:** 51 - 100 **Product Groups:** 41, 67

Date of Accounts	Dec 11	Dec 10	Dec 09
Sales Turnover	23m	21m	20m
Pre Tax Profit/Loss	4m	3m	4m
Working Capital	24m	21m	19m
Fixed Assets	1m	1m	1m
Current Assets	28m	25m	21m
Current Liabilities	1m	911	884

Mercia Flexibles
Orleton Road Ludlow Business Park, Ludlow, SY8 1XF
Tel: 01584-874999 **Fax:** 01584-874007
E-mail: enquiries@merciaflexibles.co.uk
Website: http://www.merciaflexibles.co.uk
Directors: T. Urmston (MD)
Managers: T. Urmston (Sales Prom Mgr)
Registration no: 02143702 **Turnover:** Up to £250,000
No.of Employees: 1 - 10 **Product Groups:** 23, 29, 30, 35, 36, 38, 39, 40, 45, 84

Pearce Engineering
Fishmore Road Fishmore, Ludlow, SY8 3DP
Tel: 01584-876016 **Fax:** 01584-876016
E-mail: shop@pearcecycles.co.uk
Website: http://www.pearcecycles.co.uk
Directors: L. Pearce (Ptnr)
Date established: 1990 **No.of Employees:** 1 - 10 **Product Groups:** 41

J A Rowson
Church Farm Stoke St Milborough, Ludlow, SY8 2EJ
Tel: 01584-823640
E-mail: rowson@themail.co.uk
Website: http://www.themail.co.uk
Directors: J. Rowson (Prop)
Date established: 1959 **No.of Employees:** 1 - 10 **Product Groups:** 35

Square Two Lubrication Ltd
Unit 12 Orleton Road, Ludlow Business Park, Ludlow, SY8 1XF
Tel: 01584-874220 **Fax:** 0870-011 3324
E-mail: lube@s2lube.com
Website: http://www.s2lube.com
Directors: H. Mcevaddy (MD)
Immediate Holding Company: SQUARE TWO MOBILITY LIMITED
Registration no: 05257263 **VAT No.:** GB 694 6512 02
Date established: 2004 **Turnover:** Up to £250,000
No.of Employees: 1 - 10 **Product Groups:** 31, 32, 35, 36, 39, 40, 42, 45, 48, 49, 66, 68

Date of Accounts	Oct 11	Oct 10	Oct 09
Working Capital	-1	N/A	N/A
Fixed Assets	3	3	4
Current Assets	16	19	15

Unifire & Security Ltd
Unit 3 Head Office Station Yard Bromfield, Ludlow, SY8 2BT
Tel: 01432-353400 **Fax:** 01432-378414
E-mail: peter@unifire.co.uk
Website: http://www.uni-fire.co.uk
Directors: P. Pritchard (Prop)
Immediate Holding Company: UNIFIRE & SECURITY LIMITED
Registration no: 06099549 **Date established:** 2007
No.of Employees: 1 - 10 **Product Groups:** 38, 42

Date of Accounts	May 11	May 10	May 09
Working Capital	168	95	38
Fixed Assets	56	47	46
Current Assets	291	252	140

Lydbury North

David Williams
2 Church Close, Lydbury North, SY7 8AU
Tel: 01588-680625
Directors: D. Williams (Prop)
Date established: 1979 **No.of Employees:** 1 - 10 **Product Groups:** 35

Market Drayton

Depicton Ltd
Unit 3-5 Maer Lane Industrial Estate Llewellyn Roberts Way, Market Drayton, TF9 1QS
Tel: 01630-655800 **Fax:** 01630-653258
E-mail: sales@depicton.com
Website: http://www.depicton.com
Bank(s): National Westminster Bank Plc
Directors: C. Grey (Dir)
Immediate Holding Company: DEPICTON LIMITED
Registration no: 02554811 **VAT No.:** GB 368 2172 41
Date established: 1990 **Turnover:** £1m - £2m **No.of Employees:** 21 - 50
Product Groups: 27, 28, 30

Date of Accounts	Dec 11	Dec 10	Dec 09
Working Capital	423	389	432
Fixed Assets	954	1m	1m
Current Assets	960	917	866

Isoform Ltd
Maer Lane Industrial Estate Llewellyn Roberts Way, Market Drayton, TF9 1QS
Tel: 01630-652772 **Fax:** 01630-652518
E-mail: info@isoform.co.uk
Website: http://www.isoform.co.uk
Directors: P. Morris (Dir)
Immediate Holding Company: ISOFORM LIMITED
Registration no: 02018711 **VAT No.:** GB 322 6658 59
Date established: 1986 **No.of Employees:** 1 - 10 **Product Groups:** 29, 46

Date of Accounts	May 12	May 11	May 10
Working Capital	2m	2m	2m
Fixed Assets	89	93	98
Current Assets	2m	2m	2m

Leyfos Plastics
Unit D1 Rosehill Industrial, Stoke Heath, Market Drayton, TF9 2JU
Tel: 01630-638557 **Fax:** 01630-638651
E-mail: sales@leyfos.co.uk
Website: http://www.leyfos.com
Directors: J. Wyncherley (Dir), J. Wycherley (MD), M. Wycherley (Dir), D. Wycherley (Co Sec)
Immediate Holding Company: LEYFOS PLASTICS LIMITED
Registration no: 01064533 **Date established:** 1972
Turnover: £500,000 - £1m **No.of Employees:** 1 - 10 **Product Groups:** 32, 48

Date of Accounts	Aug 09	Aug 08	Aug 07
Working Capital	180	624	451
Fixed Assets	92	233	273
Current Assets	513	969	749

Muller Dairy (UK) Ltd
Shrewsbury Road, Market Drayton, TF9 3SQ
Tel: 01630-692000 **Fax:** 01630-692001
E-mail: consumers@muller.co.uk
Website: http://www.muller.co.uk
Bank(s): Bayerishche Verbinsbank
Directors: D. Grey (Chief Op Offcr), H. Green (Purch), S. Gilliland (Grp Chief Exec), S. Jones (I.T. Dir), C. Smith (Sales)
Managers: M. Paxton, A. Oakes (Tech Serv Mgr), C. McDonough (Mktg Serv Mgr)
Registration no: 02092691 **VAT No.:** GB 687 9095 63
Turnover: £500m - £1,000m **No.of Employees:** 1001 - 1500
Product Groups: 20

Date of Accounts	Dec 09	Dec 08	Dec 07
Sales Turnover	401m	398m	468m
Pre Tax Profit/Loss	37m	19m	45m
Working Capital	44m	20m	242m
Fixed Assets	234	224	391
Current Assets	117m	93m	327m
Current Liabilities	71m	71m	84m

P H Structures
Unit C13 Rosehill Industrial Estate Rosehill Road, Stoke Heath, Market Drayton, TF9 2JU
Tel: 01630-638773 **Fax:** 01630-685840
Directors: S. Hewitt (Prop)
Date established: 1994 **No.of Employees:** 1 - 10 **Product Groups:** 35

Porkfarms Ltd
Maer Lane, Market Drayton, TF9 3AL
Tel: 01630-652271 **Fax:** 01630-657644
Bank(s): Midland
Managers: K. Tye (Personnel), J. Morris (Purch Mgr), L. Macleod (Chief Mgr), R. Hinton (Fin Mgr)
Ultimate Holding Company: ELIOT LUXEMBOURG HOLDCO SARL (LUXEMBOURG)
Immediate Holding Company: PORK FARMS LIMITED
Registration no: 05998346 **VAT No.:** GB 168 7433 30
Date established: 2006 **Turnover:** £20m - £50m
No.of Employees: 251 - 500 **Product Groups:** 20

Date of Accounts	Mar 12	Mar 09	Mar 10
Sales Turnover	145m	130m	125m
Pre Tax Profit/Loss	-13m	-19m	-13m
Working Capital	4m	-72m	-84m
Fixed Assets	19m	24m	22m
Current Assets	36m	26m	24m
Current Liabilities	10m	13m	8m

Precolor Sales Ltd (Precolor Tank Division)
Newport Road, Market Drayton, TF9 2AA
Tel: 01630-657281 **Fax:** 01630-655545
E-mail: enquiries@precolor.co.uk
Website: http://www.precolortankdivision.co.uk
Bank(s): Lloyds TSB Bank plc
Managers: S. Barker (Mgr)
Immediate Holding Company: PRECOLOR SALES LIMITED
Registration no: 01224981 **VAT No.:** GB 280 3161 83
Date established: 1975 **Turnover:** £1m - £2m **No.of Employees:** 11 - 20
Product Groups: 30, 37, 38, 40, 41, 42, 48, 66

Date of Accounts	Aug 11	Aug 10	Aug 09
Working Capital	422	397	370
Fixed Assets	100	103	107
Current Assets	621	521	536

Stapling & Nailing Supplies
1 Church Farm Ashley, Market Drayton, TF9 4QT
Tel: 01630-673511 **Fax:** 01630-673525
E-mail: info@mytoolkit.co.uk
Website: http://www.mytoolkit.co.uk
Managers: S. Pollock (Mgr)
Immediate Holding Company: MYTOOLKIT LTD
Date established: 2012 **No.of Employees:** 1 - 10 **Product Groups:** 35

T & M Glass Fibre Mouldings
Unit 3 Sutton Road, Tern Hill, Market Drayton, TF9 2JH
Tel: 01630-638383 **Fax:** 01630-638383
E-mail: seanmalkin@hotmail.com
Directors: S. Malkim (Prop)
Immediate Holding Company: T. & M. GLASS FIBRE MOULDING
VAT No.: GB 592 6865 86 **Date established:** 1992
Turnover: Up to £250,000 **No.of Employees:** 1 - 10 **Product Groups:** 30

Much Wenlock

Boiler Spares International Ltd
Unit 23 Sheinwood Farm Sheinton Road, Much Wenlock, TF13 6NR
Tel: 01952-728605 **Fax:** 01952-728013
Website: http://www.boiler-spares.com
Directors: S. Marandola (Fin), C. Marandola (MD)
Immediate Holding Company: BOILER SPARES INTERNATIONAL LIMITED
Registration no: 02897712 **Date established:** 1994
Turnover: Up to £250,000 **No.of Employees:** 1 - 10 **Product Groups:** 40, 61, 66

Date of Accounts	Mar 08	Mar 07	Mar 06
Working Capital	-13	-1	7
Fixed Assets	4	5	5
Current Assets	21	50	27
Current Liabilities	33	51	20

Landowner Liquid Fertilizers Ltd
Farley, Much Wenlock, TF13 6NX
Tel: 01952-727754 **Fax:** 01952-727755
E-mail: info@landowner.co.uk
Website: http://www.qlf.co.uk
Directors: W. Boon (Fin)
Immediate Holding Company: LANDOWNER CROP NUTRITION (MIDLANDS) LTD.
Registration no: 02496478 **Date established:** 1990 **Turnover:** £2m - £5m
No.of Employees: 1 - 10 **Product Groups:** 62, 66

Date of Accounts	Sep 11	Sep 10	Sep 09
Working Capital	3	3	3
Current Assets	11	11	11
Current Liabilities	8	8	8

Lightsource Event Technology Ltd
Fox Studio King Street, Much Wenlock, TF13 6BL
Tel: 01952-727715 **Fax:** 08704-204316
E-mail: lights@lightsource.co.uk
Website: http://www.lightsource.co.uk
Directors: R. Cumberland (Dir)
Immediate Holding Company: BIZ PRESENTATIONS LIMITED
Registration no: 02989290 **VAT No.:** GB 404 2296 81
Date established: 1994 **Turnover:** Up to £250,000
No.of Employees: 1 - 10 **Product Groups:** 81, 83

Date of Accounts	Oct 11	Oct 10	Oct 09
Sales Turnover	20	21	19
Pre Tax Profit/Loss	8	10	8
Working Capital	-1	-1	-1
Fixed Assets	2	3	3
Current Assets	4	3	3
Current Liabilities	3	3	2

Lime Green Products Ltd
Coates Kilns Stretton Road, Much Wenlock, TF13 6DG
Tel: 01952-728611 **Fax:** 01952-728361
E-mail: sales@lime-green.co.uk
Website: http://www.lime-green.co.uk
Managers: M. Cooperthwaite (Mgr)
Immediate Holding Company: LIME GREEN PRODUCTS LTD
Registration no: 04409990 **Date established:** 2002
No.of Employees: 1 - 10 **Product Groups:** 33

Date of Accounts	Mar 12	Mar 11	Mar 10
Working Capital	83	34	12
Fixed Assets	171	187	151
Current Assets	224	222	165

Quality Liquid Feeds Ltd
Farley, Much Wenlock, TF13 6NX
Tel: 01952-727754 **Fax:** 01952-727755
E-mail: info@qlf.co.uk
Website: http://www.qlf.co.uk
Directors: W. Boon (MD)
Managers: S. Jackson (Mgr)
Registration no: 02655770 **Turnover:** £250,000 - £500,000
No.of Employees: 1 - 10 **Product Groups:** 20

Date of Accounts	Sep 07	Sep 06	Sep 05
Working Capital	-263	-164	-105
Fixed Assets	498	431	361
Current Assets	402	372	415
Current Liabilities	665	536	520

Wenlock Packinging Ltd
12 Stretton Road, Much Wenlock, TF13 6AS
Tel: 01952-727073 **Fax:** 01952-727101
E-mail: martin@mjwj.enta.net
Website: http://www.wenlockpackaging.co.uk
Directors: M. Jones (MD), M. Jones (Prop)
Immediate Holding Company: WENLOCK PACKAGING LIMITED
Registration no: 04385762 **Date established:** 2002
No.of Employees: 1 - 10 **Product Groups:** 38, 42

Date of Accounts	Mar 11	Mar 10	Mar 09
Working Capital	101	106	116
Fixed Assets	9	4	5
Current Assets	252	257	261

Newport

E-Vend UK
PO Box 104, Newport, TF10 0AA
Tel: 08700-052633 **Fax:** 0870-005 2644
E-mail: submissions@e-vend-uk.com
Website: http://www.e-vend-uk.com
Managers: M. Dove (Sales Prom Mgr)
Date established: 2000 **Turnover:** £250,000 - £500,000
No.of Employees: 1 - 10 **Product Groups:** 49

Mirage Eyewear Ltd
Midgley Court Salters Lane, Newport, TF10 7BG
Tel: 01952-820963 **Fax:** 01952-820412
E-mail: contact@mirage-eyewear.co.uk
Website: http://www.mirage-eyewear.co.uk
Managers: A. Newton (Chief Acct), R. Newton (Mgr)
Immediate Holding Company: MIRAGE EYEWEAR (1993) LIMITED
Registration no: 02753790 **Date established:** 1992
No.of Employees: 1 - 10 **Product Groups:** 37, 38, 65

Date of Accounts	Oct 11	Oct 10	Oct 09
Working Capital	198	207	220
Fixed Assets	N/A	N/A	1
Current Assets	338	318	336

Tibberton Engineering Services
The Workshop Tibberton Grange, Tibberton, Newport, TF10 8PE
Tel: 01952-541692
Directors: J. Collins (Prop)
Date established: 1990 **No.of Employees:** 1 - 10 **Product Groups:** 41

Oswestry

A - Z Engineering Ltd
Station Road Whittington, Oswestry, SY11 4DA
Tel: 01691-662204 **Fax:** 01691-670113
E-mail: sales@azltd.co.uk
Website: http://www.azltd.co.uk
Bank(s): Natwest, Oswestry
Directors: R. Jones (Dir)
Immediate Holding Company: A - Z ENGINEERING LIMITED
Registration no: 03860114 **VAT No.:** GB 159 0748 41
Date established: 1999 **Turnover:** £250,000 - £500,000
No.of Employees: 11 - 20 **Product Groups:** 48

Date of Accounts	Dec 11	Dec 10	Dec 09
Working Capital	62	50	-4
Fixed Assets	184	225	172
Current Assets	252	208	179

Aluroll Ltd
Mile Oak Industrial Estate Maesbury Road, Oswestry, SY10 8GA
Tel: 01691-679257 **Fax:** 01691-671482
E-mail: enquiry@aluroll.co.uk
Website: http://www.aluroll.co.uk
Directors: M. Evans (MD), R. Elwin (Fin)
Immediate Holding Company: ALUROLL LIMITED
Registration no: 05212026 **Date established:** 2004
No.of Employees: 1 - 10 **Product Groups:** 26, 35

Date of Accounts	Sep 11	Sep 10	Sep 09
Working Capital	305	5	184
Fixed Assets	291	278	34
Current Assets	750	638	557

Beacon Systems Ltd
16 Upper Brook Street, Oswestry, SY11 2TB
Tel: 01691-657960 **Fax:** 01691-670462
E-mail: admin@moulsonpp.co.uk
Website: http://www.moulsonpp.co.uk
Directors: H. Pontefract (MD)
Immediate Holding Company: BEACON SYSTEMS LIMITED
Registration no: 03389545 **VAT No.:** GB 335 3163 76
Date established: 1997 **Turnover:** £1m - £2m **No.of Employees:** 1 - 10
Product Groups: 31, 32, 40, 41, 42, 80, 84

Date of Accounts	Jun 12	Jun 11	Jun 10
Working Capital	63	46	33
Fixed Assets	4	4	5
Current Assets	68	52	39

Border Fabrications
Cambrian Buildings Coney Green, Oswestry, SY11 2JL
Tel: 01691-650268 **Fax:** 01691-650268
Directors: T. Hillidge (Prop)
Immediate Holding Company: 119 ABBEVILLE ROAD LIMITED
Registration no: 04540587 **Date established:** 2002
No.of Employees: 1 - 10 **Product Groups:** 35

The Bridge Coffee Company Ltd
Unit 8 Whittington Business Park Park Green, Whittington, Oswestry, SY11 4ND
Tel: 01691-659999
E-mail: sales@bridge-coffee.co.uk
Website: http://www.bridge-coffee.co.uk
Directors: M. Derham (MD)
Immediate Holding Company: THE BRIDGE COFFEE COMPANY LIMITED
Registration no: 05066590 **Date established:** 2004
Turnover: Up to £250,000 **No.of Employees:** 1 - 10 **Product Groups:** 20, 21, 26, 30, 36, 40, 62, 67

Date of Accounts	Mar 12	Mar 11	Mar 10
Working Capital	-11	-7	-10
Fixed Assets	15	15	20
Current Assets	21	18	22

Richard Burbidge Ltd
Whittington Road, Oswestry, SY11 1HZ
Tel: 01691-655131 **Fax:** 01691-657694
E-mail: info@richardburbidge.co.uk
Website: http://www.richardburbidge.com
Bank(s): National Westminster Bank Plc
Directors: R. Lincoln (Fin), C. Davies (Co Sec), S. Underhill (Grp Chief Exec)
Managers: H. Costello, K. Williams (Tech Serv Mgr), J. Burbidge, A. Tovey (Chief Buyer)
Ultimate Holding Company: RIPAT LIMITED
Immediate Holding Company: RICHARD BURBIDGE LIMITED
Registration no: 02037421 **VAT No.:** GB 159 1050 77
Date established: 1986 **Turnover:** £20m - £50m
No.of Employees: 101 - 250 **Product Groups:** 25

Date of Accounts	Sep 08	Oct 09	Oct 10
Sales Turnover	58m	46m	30m
Pre Tax Profit/Loss	-1m	4m	-10m
Working Capital	23m	24m	16m
Fixed Assets	10m	10m	2m
Current Assets	31m	30m	23m
Current Liabilities	4m	4m	4m

G L Evans
Plas Du Llanrhaeadr Ym Mochnant, Oswestry, SY10 0BQ
Tel: 01691-860331
Directors: G. Evans (Prop)
Date established: 1980 **No.of Employees:** 1 - 10 **Product Groups:** 41

Furniture Design
Unit 15 Rednal Industrial Estate West Felton, Oswestry, SY11 4HS
Tel: 01691-611864
E-mail: info@chrisnanglefurniture.co.uk
Website: http://www.chrisnanglefurniture.co.uk
Managers: C. Nangle (Mgr)
Date established: 2000 **Turnover:** Up to £250,000
No.of Employees: 1 - 10 **Product Groups:** 26

GB Simms & Associates Engineers
6 Firs Close St Martins, Oswestry, SY11 3LT
Tel: 01691-778377 **Fax:** 01691-770267
E-mail: gordon.simms@sky.com
Directors: G. Simms (Prop)
No.of Employees: 1 - 10 **Product Groups:** 35

Globestock Ltd
Mile Oak Industrial Estate Maesbury Road, Oswestry, SY10 8GA
Tel: 01691-654966 **Fax:** 01691-661726
E-mail: info@globestock.co.uk
Website: http://www.globestock.co.uk
Directors: B. Swinstead (Fin), V. Lewis (Dir)
Ultimate Holding Company: EVANS ENTERPRISES LIMITED
Immediate Holding Company: GLOBESTOCK LIMITED
Registration no: 01641128 **VAT No.:** GB 372 3950 43
Date established: 1982 **Turnover:** £500,000 - £1m
No.of Employees: 1 - 10 **Product Groups:** 40, 67

Date of Accounts	Mar 11	Mar 10	Mar 09
Working Capital	459	463	431
Fixed Assets	43	46	31
Current Assets	566	513	493

Hire2higher
Glovers Meadow, Oswestry, SY10 8NH
Tel: 01691-654000 **Fax:** 01691-654111
E-mail: info@hire2higher.co.uk
Website: http://www.hire2higher.co.uk
Directors: C. Lloyd (MD)
Immediate Holding Company: BRIGHT STAR UNIVERSE LIMITED
Registration no: 04313698 **Date established:** 2011
No.of Employees: 1 - 10 **Product Groups:** 36, 39, 45, 83

R G Jones
Garth Y Gelynen Penybontfawr, Oswestry, SY10 0PQ
Tel: 01691-860520
Directors: G. Jones (Prop)
No.of Employees: 1 - 10 **Product Groups:** 41

Lloyds Animal Feeds Ltd
Morton, Oswestry, SY10 8BH
Tel: 01691-830741 **Fax:** 01691-831052
E-mail: steveh@lloydsanimalfeed.com
Website: http://www.lloydsfeeds.com
Directors: W. Lloyd (MD)
Ultimate Holding Company: LAF HOLDINGS LIMITED
Immediate Holding Company: LLOYD'S (ANIMAL) FEEDS LIMITED
Registration no: 00820148 **Date established:** 1964
Turnover: £50m - £75m **No.of Employees:** 21 - 50 **Product Groups:** 20

Date of Accounts	Mar 11	Mar 10	Mar 09
Sales Turnover	62m	56m	63m
Pre Tax Profit/Loss	2m	2m	3m
Working Capital	9m	9m	7m
Fixed Assets	984	1m	1m
Current Assets	16m	15m	13m
Current Liabilities	740	420	699

Mist Air Environmental
Hillcrest Pen-Y-Bont, Oswestry, SY10 9JF
Tel: 01691-828487 **Fax:** 01691-828499
E-mail: info@mist-air.co.uk
Website: http://www.mist-air.co.uk
Directors: M. Carter (MD)
Immediate Holding Company: MIST-AIR ENVIRONMENTAL SYSTEMS LIMITED
Registration no: 03767548 **Date established:** 1999
No.of Employees: 11 - 20 **Product Groups:** 38, 42

Premier Bodies Ltd
Old Ifton Colliery St Martins, Oswestry, SY11 3DA
Tel: 01691-773737 **Fax:** 01691-773891
E-mail: info@premierbodies.co.uk
Website: http://www.premier-bodies.co.uk
Directors: A. Hurdsman (Fin), J. Stockton (Mkt Research)
Immediate Holding Company: PREMIER BODIES LTD
Registration no: 03527650 **Date established:** 1998
No.of Employees: 1 - 10 **Product Groups:** 35, 36, 42, 45, 48, 67

Date of Accounts	Mar 12	Mar 11	Mar 10
Working Capital	39	5	73
Fixed Assets	225	242	187
Current Assets	325	333	316

Pressing Solutions
3 Queens Close, Oswestry, SY11 2JA
Tel: 01691-670891
E-mail: sales@pressingsolutions.co.uk
Website: http://www.pressingsolutions.co.uk
Directors: E. Watson (Dir)
Immediate Holding Company: MIL-TEK (ENVIRONMENTAL) LTD
Registration no: 03274632 **Date established:** 1996
No.of Employees: 1 - 10 **Product Groups:** 38, 42

Date of Accounts	Nov 11	Nov 10	Nov 09
Working Capital	-8	-5	6
Fixed Assets	6	6	7
Current Assets	36	36	35

Taylor Precision Plastics Ltd
Mile Oak Industrial Estate Maesbury Road, Oswestry, SY10 8GA
Tel: 01691-679516 **Fax:** 01691-670538
E-mail: sales@cvrollers.co.uk
Website: http://www.cvrollers.co.uk
Bank(s): Lloyds TSB
Directors: K. Taylor (Dir)
Immediate Holding Company: C V ROLLERS (TPP) LIMITED
Registration no: 00893261 **Date established:** 1966
Turnover: £500,000 - £1m **No.of Employees:** 11 - 20
Product Groups: 30, 35

Date of Accounts	Mar 11	Mar 10	Mar 09
Working Capital	153	120	110
Fixed Assets	51	16	57
Current Assets	237	210	159

Technocover
Whittington Road, Oswestry, SY11 1HZ
Tel: 01691-653251 **Fax:** 01691-658222
E-mail: terry.bratten@technocover.com
Website: http://www.jonesofoswestry.com
Directors: J. Jones (Comm)
Managers: J. Lewis (I.T. Exec), P. Murphy (Sales Prom Mgr), S. Horton (Mktg Serv Mgr), T. Bratten (Mktg Serv Mgr), J. Mitten (Personnel)

Immediate Holding Company: RICHARD BURBIDGE LIMITED
Registration no: 02037421 **VAT No.:** GB 351 7500 74
Date established: 1986 **Turnover:** £50m - £75m **No.of Employees:** 1 - 10
Product Groups: 33

Uplec Industries Ltd
Oakhurst Hall Oakhurst Road, Oswestry, SY10 7BZ
Tel: 01691-650422 **Fax:** 01691-658553
E-mail: enquiries@uplec.co.uk
Website: http://www.uplec.co.uk
Directors: R. Parry (MD)
Immediate Holding Company: UPLEC INDUSTRIES LIMITED
Registration no: 01665166 **VAT No.:** GB 377 7801 10
Date established: 1982 **Turnover:** £500,000 - £1m
No.of Employees: 1 - 10 **Product Groups:** 37, 38

Date of Accounts	Aug 10	Aug 09	Aug 08
Working Capital	-100	-68	77
Fixed Assets	448	463	478
Current Assets	230	276	261

Shifnal

Adfield Harvey Ltd
The Granary Beckbury, Shifnal, TF11 9DG
Tel: 01952-752500 **Fax:** 01952-752510
E-mail: info@adfield.co.uk
Website: http://www.adfield.co.uk
Bank(s): Barclays
Directors: I. Field (MD)
Immediate Holding Company: ADFIELD-HARVEY LIMITED
Registration no: 01180823 **VAT No.:** GB 300 2094 28
Date established: 1974 **Turnover:** £1m - £2m **No.of Employees:** 11 - 20
Product Groups: 28, 80, 81

Date of Accounts	Dec 11	Dec 10	Dec 09
Working Capital	-5	-24	-59
Fixed Assets	112	133	146
Current Assets	184	187	354
Current Liabilities	8	N/A	N/A

Keith Davies
Hem Manor Farm Hem Lane, The Hem, Shifnal, TF11 9PT
Tel: 01952-463840
Directors: K. Davies (Prop)
Date established: 1990 **No.of Employees:** 1 - 10 **Product Groups:** 41

R W Evans Transport Ltd
Hilton Bank, Shifnal, TF11 8RH
Tel: 01952-691666 **Fax:** 01952-691466
Directors: F. Evans (MD)
Immediate Holding Company: R.W.EVANS(TRANSPORT)LIMITED
Registration no: 00982259 **Date established:** 1970
Turnover: £250,000 - £500,000 **No.of Employees:** 1 - 10
Product Groups: 41

Date of Accounts	Jun 11	Jun 10	Jun 07
Working Capital	-10	-4	-2
Fixed Assets	173	173	173
Current Assets	12	23	30
Current Liabilities	1	1	1

Seymour Manufacturing International Smi Ltd
Sutton Hall Farm Sutton Maddock, Shifnal, TF11 9NQ
Tel: 01952-730630 **Fax:** 01952-730330
E-mail: enquiries@seymour-mi.com
Website: http://www.seymour-mi.com
Directors: B. Seymour (Dir), D. Humphries (Co Sec)
Managers: R. Morris
Immediate Holding Company: SEYMOUR MANUFACTURING INTERNATIONAL LIMITED
Registration no: 02322042 **Date established:** 1988
No.of Employees: 11 - 20 **Product Groups:** 40

Date of Accounts	Jun 09	Feb 12	Feb 11
Working Capital	445	337	358
Fixed Assets	79	78	93
Current Assets	670	559	487

Wrekin Construction
Lamledge Lane, Shifnal, TF11 8BE
Tel: 01952-468080 **Fax:** 01952-468081
E-mail: postmaster@wrekin.co.uk
Website: http://www.wrekin.co.uk
Bank(s): National Westminster Bank Plc
Directors: N. Ibbotson (Fin), J. Worthington (Grp Chief Exec), P. Greenwood (Dir)
Immediate Holding Company: Wrekin Group P.L.C.
Registration no: 00536615 **Date established:** 2008
Turnover: £50m - £75m **No.of Employees:** 51 - 100 **Product Groups:** 51

Shrewsbury

A T Wilde & Son Ltd
Station Yard Station Road, Dorrington, Shrewsbury, SY5 7LH
Tel: 01743-718777 **Fax:** 01694-723945
E-mail: enquiries@atwildeplantparts.co.uk
Website: http://www.atwildeplantparts.co.uk
Directors: K. Wilde (Dir)
Immediate Holding Company: A.T. WILDE AND SON LIMITED
Registration no: 01842765 **Date established:** 1984
Turnover: £500,000 - £1m **No.of Employees:** 11 - 20
Product Groups: 36, 39, 41, 45, 48, 52, 54, 67, 71, 82, 83, 84, 87

Date of Accounts	May 11	May 10	May 09
Working Capital	1m	1m	1m
Fixed Assets	18	22	1
Current Assets	1m	1m	1m

Alexon Appliances
14 Carlton Close Bicton Heath, Shrewsbury, SY3 5JA
Tel: 01743-246153
E-mail: dave-trow@hotmail.co.uk
Directors: D. Trow (Prop)
No.of Employees: 1 - 10 **Product Groups:** 43

Anticorrosion Engineering Ltd
4 Langley Drive Bayston Hill, Shrewsbury, SY3 0PR
Tel: 01743-871164
E-mail: chris@anticorr.com
Website: http://www.anticorr.com
Directors: C. Googan (MD)
Immediate Holding Company: ANTICORROSION ENGINEERING LIMITED
Registration no: 04097491 **Date established:** 2000
No.of Employees: 1 - 10 **Product Groups:** 46, 48

Date of Accounts	Nov 11	Nov 10	Nov 07
Working Capital	74	65	54
Fixed Assets	1	1	2
Current Assets	107	99	70

B M L Hayley
BML House Harlescott Lane, Shrewsbury, SY1 3AY
Tel: 01743-452000 **Fax:** 01743-452024
E-mail: info@bml-hayley.co.uk
Website: http://www.bmltd.co.uk
Bank(s): The Royal Bank of Scotland
Directors: S. Hughes (MD), S. Hughes (MD)
Ultimate Holding Company: HAYLEY GROUP PUBLIC LIMITED COMPANY
Immediate Holding Company: BEARING MAN LIMITED
Registration no: 02399424 **Date established:** 1989 **Turnover:** £5m - £10m
No.of Employees: 11 - 20 **Product Groups:** 35, 66

Date of Accounts	May 11	May 10	May 09
Sales Turnover	9m	7m	7m
Pre Tax Profit/Loss	777	159	142
Working Capital	1m	1m	1m
Fixed Assets	77	94	111
Current Assets	3m	3m	3m
Current Liabilities	605	319	247

B B N International
Clay House Harnage, Cressage, Shrewsbury, SY5 6EF
Tel: 08453-655061
E-mail: sales@bbnint.co.uk
Website: http://www.bbnint.co.uk
Directors: B. Nimmo (Prop)
Immediate Holding Company: BBN INTERNATIONAL LIMITED
Registration no: 05637424 **Date established:** 2005
No.of Employees: 1 - 10 **Product Groups:** 37

Date of Accounts	Mar 11	Mar 10	Mar 09
Working Capital	25	-6	20
Fixed Assets	3	1	1
Current Assets	129	18	44

B F Interactive B.F.Group
128 Frankwell, Shrewsbury, SY3 8JX
Tel: 01743-270444 **Fax:** 01743-368381
E-mail: mitch@bfgroup.co.uk
Website: http://www.bfgroup.co.uk
Directors: S. Mitchell (Prop)
Immediate Holding Company: BF INTERACTIVE UK LIMITED
Registration no: 06459285 **Date established:** 2007 **Turnover:** £1m - £2m
No.of Employees: 1 - 10 **Product Groups:** 26, 37

Border Windows
Unit A The Old Creamery Aston Road, Wem, Shrewsbury, SY4 5BA
Tel: 01939-233655
E-mail: info@borderwindows.co.uk
Directors: A. Reynolds (Prop)
No.of Employees: 1 - 10 **Product Groups:** 26, 35

Browns of Wem Ltd
Four Lane Ends Wem, Shrewsbury, SY4 5UQ
Tel: 01939-232382 **Fax:** 01939-234032
E-mail: info@brownsofwem.co.uk
Website: http://www.brownsofwem.com
Bank(s): Barclays
Directors: N. Jefferies (Dir), V. Evens (Dir)
Immediate Holding Company: BROWNS OF WEM (DEVELOPMENTS) LIMITED
Registration no: 00843735 **Date established:** 1965 **Turnover:** £2m - £5m
No.of Employees: 21 - 50 **Product Groups:** 25, 35

Date of Accounts	Mar 11	Mar 10	Mar 09
Working Capital	-95	-94	-94
Fixed Assets	425	425	425
Current Assets	1	2	N/A

C H Welding Services
Cartmel Drive, Shrewsbury, SY1 3TB
Tel: 0781-441 9193
E-mail: chweldingservices@googlemail.com
Website: http://www.chweldingservices.com
Directors: C. Hitchin (Fin)
Immediate Holding Company: S.F.K. LIMITED
Date established: 1987 **No.of Employees:** 1 - 10 **Product Groups:** 34, 35, 48, 49, 66

Date of Accounts	Mar 11	Mar 10	Mar 09
Working Capital	6	16	58
Fixed Assets	32	38	45
Current Assets	56	78	142

C S S Mobile
PO Box 18, Shrewsbury, SY3 8JY
Tel: 07790-672720
E-mail: purchasing@cssmobile.net
Website: http://www.cssmobile.net
Directors: W. Barns (Prop)
Immediate Holding Company: RADFIELD HOME CARE LTD
Registration no: 05941894 **Date established:** 2007
No.of Employees: 1 - 10 **Product Groups:** 37, 44, 67

Date of Accounts	Oct 11	Oct 10	Oct 09
Working Capital	64	47	30
Fixed Assets	5	5	2
Current Assets	89	61	49

Carbon-monoxide-detectors.co.uk
18 Wellmeadow Gardens, Shrewsbury, SY3 8UP
Tel: 01743-369544
E-mail: gedbrookes@ntlworld.com
Website: http://www.carbon-monoxide-detectors.co.uk
Directors: G. Brooks (MD)
No.of Employees: 1 - 10 **Product Groups:** 31, 38, 67

Central Fire Control
Unit 1-4 Trench Hall Farm Tilley Green, Wem, Shrewsbury, SY4 5PJ
Tel: 01939-232211 **Fax:** 01939-232211
Directors: M. Buttery (MD)
Registration no: OC323363 **Date established:** 2006
No.of Employees: 1 - 10 **Product Groups:** 38, 42

Chalet World Ski
1 Bellstone, Shrewsbury, SY1 1HU
Tel: 01743-231199
E-mail: sales@chaletworldski.co.uk
Website: http://www.chaletworld.co.uk
Directors: Q. Morgan (Ptnr), Q. Morgan (Dir)
Managers: L. Rowe
Ultimate Holding Company: GALLIERS HOMES LIMITED
Immediate Holding Company: GRAYSAND CONSTRUCTION LIMITED
Registration no: 03084776 **Date established:** 1987
No.of Employees: 1 - 10 **Product Groups:** 69

Cherry Green Services
Yew Tree Cottage Lower Road Harmer Hill, Harmer Hill, Shrewsbury, SY4 3ED
Tel: 0845-017 0925
E-mail: enquiries@cherrygreenaccess.co.uk
Website: http://www.cherrygreenaccess.co.uk
Directors: A. Newlove (Dir), J. Bertolini (Fin)
Immediate Holding Company: CHERRY GREEN SERVICES LIMITED
Registration no: 06276433 **Date established:** 2007
Turnover: Up to £250,000 **No.of Employees:** 1 - 10 **Product Groups:** 45, 83

Christmas Stockholders Ltd
Ainsdale Drive, Shrewsbury, SY1 3TL
Tel: 01743-462515 **Fax:** 01743-464430
Bank(s): Barclays
Directors: D. Christmas (MD)
Immediate Holding Company: CHRISTMAS STOCKHOLDERS LIMITED
Registration no: 01060397 **VAT No.:** GB 162 1138 01
Date established: 1972 **Turnover:** £5m - £10m **No.of Employees:** 21 - 50
Product Groups: 34, 36, 66

Date of Accounts	Sep 11	Sep 10	Sep 09
Sales Turnover	7m	7m	6m
Pre Tax Profit/Loss	691	495	207
Working Capital	4m	4m	4m
Fixed Assets	2m	2m	2m
Current Assets	5m	6m	4m
Current Liabilities	263	148	169

Condover Forge
Unit 97a Condover Industrial Estate Dorrington, Shrewsbury, SY5 7NH
Tel: 01743-872152
Directors: H. Criton (Prop)
Date established: 1998 **No.of Employees:** 1 - 10 **Product Groups:** 35

D K L Technical Rubber Products Ltd
Unit E19-E20 Wem Industrial Estate Soulton Road, Wem, Shrewsbury, SY4 5SD
Tel: 01939-234656 **Fax:** 01939-235246
Directors: S. Mansfield (Fin)
Immediate Holding Company: D.K.L. TECHNICAL RUBBER PRODUCTS LIMITED
Registration no: 02220939 **Date established:** 1988
Turnover: £250,000 - £500,000 **No.of Employees:** 1 - 10
Product Groups: 29

Date of Accounts	Mar 12	Mar 11	Mar 10
Working Capital	58	37	48
Fixed Assets	8	28	13
Current Assets	90	94	75

Dead Good Undies
Delta House 264 Monkmoor Road, Shrewsbury, SY2 5ST
Tel: 01743-247246
E-mail: info@deadgoodundies.com
Website: http://www.deadgoodundies.com
Directors: A. Davies (Prop)
Immediate Holding Company: ARH GROUP LIMITED
Registration no: 04743639 **Date established:** 1994
Turnover: Up to £250,000 **No.of Employees:** 1 - 10 **Product Groups:** 23, 24

Date of Accounts	Jun 11	Jun 10	Jun 09
Sales Turnover	12m	10m	9m
Pre Tax Profit/Loss	421	444	619
Working Capital	2m	1m	1m
Fixed Assets	982	910	960
Current Assets	4m	3m	3m
Current Liabilities	666	543	585

Dechra Veterinary Products Ltd
West Pavilion Sansaw Business Park, Hadnall, Shrewsbury, SY4 4AS
Tel: 01939-211200 **Fax:** 01939-211201
E-mail: info@dechra.com
Website: http://www.dechra.com
Managers: B. Parmenter
Immediate Holding Company: DECHRA VETERINARY PRODUCTS LIMITED
Registration no: 05385888 **Date established:** 2005
No.of Employees: 21 - 50 **Product Groups:** 61

Date of Accounts	Dec 07	Jun 11	Jun 10
Sales Turnover	11m	32m	18m
Pre Tax Profit/Loss	239	596	149
Working Capital	362	729	302
Fixed Assets	N/A	63	35
Current Assets	2m	13m	8m
Current Liabilities	614	2m	2m

Denro Power Services Ltd
Battlefield Enterprise Park, Shrewsbury, SY1 3JE
Tel: 01743-440033 **Fax:** 01743-440034
E-mail: sales@denro.co.uk
Website: http://www.denro.co.uk
Directors: D. Rogers (Dir), L. Rogers (Co Sec)
Immediate Holding Company: DENRO POWER SERVICES LIMITED
Registration no: 07097428 **Date established:** 2009
No.of Employees: 1 - 10 **Product Groups:** 83

Date of Accounts	Dec 11	Dec 10
Working Capital	-36	-29
Fixed Assets	45	42
Current Assets	98	105

Doncaster Shrewsbury Ltd
Whitchurch Road, Shrewsbury, SY1 4DP
Tel: 01743-454300 **Fax:** 01743-450125
E-mail: sward@doncasters.com
Website: http://www.doncasters.com
Bank(s): Lloyds TSB
Managers: D. Harvie (Chief Mgr)
Registration no: 00720207 **VAT No.:** GB 239 6880 17
Turnover: £20m - £50m **No.of Employees:** 251 - 500
Product Groups: 34, 39, 40, 48

Dumbstruck
94 Abbots Road Monk Moore, Shrewsbury, SY2 5QG
Tel: 01743-464965 **Fax:** 05602-049802
E-mail: debsk39@hotmail.com
Website: http://www.dumbstruck-design.co.uk
Directors: D. Kenyon (Prop)
No.of Employees: 1 - 10 **Product Groups:** 26, 34, 35, 48, 49, 66

Eagle Engineering Co
98a Condover Industrial Estate Dorrington, Shrewsbury, SY5 7NH
Tel: 01743-718587 **Fax:** 01743-718587
Directors: D. Francis (Dir)
Date established: 1973 **No.of Employees:** 1 - 10 **Product Groups:** 35

Engineered Timber Solutions Ltd
Unit 2 Rodenhurst Business Park Rodington, Shrewsbury, SY4 4QU
Tel: 01952-771170 **Fax:** 01952-770073
Website: http://www.etstrusses.co.uk
Directors: P. Sankey (MD)
Immediate Holding Company: ENGINEERED TIMBER SOLUTIONS LIMITED
Registration no: 04855981 **Date established:** 2003
No.of Employees: 11 - 20 **Product Groups:** 35, 66

Date of Accounts	Dec 11	Dec 10	Dec 09
Working Capital	142	222	141
Fixed Assets	57	9	27
Current Assets	479	508	254

Euro Manufacturing & Marketing Ltd
11-13 High Street Wem, Shrewsbury, SY4 5AA
Tel: 01939-235073 **Fax:** 01939-235074
E-mail: peter@eurogroup.gb.com
Website: http://www.eurogroup.gb.com
Directors: J. Bailey (Dir), P. Bailey (MD), P. Bailey (Prop)
Managers: S. Brooks (Sec)
Immediate Holding Company: EURO MANUFACTURING & MARKETING LIMITED
Registration no: 02723871 **Date established:** 1992
No.of Employees: 11 - 20 **Product Groups:** 68

Date of Accounts	Dec 10	Dec 09	Dec 08
Working Capital	46	50	53
Fixed Assets	5	6	6
Current Assets	323	320	312

Europa Fastenings
Unit 9c Leaton Industrial Estate Bomere Heath, Shrewsbury, SY4 3AP
Tel: 01939-291199 **Fax:** 01939-291299
E-mail: stephen@europafastenings.co.uk
Website: http://www.europafastenings.co.uk
Directors: S. Cowan (Dir)
Ultimate Holding Company: AMASON SERVICES LTD
Immediate Holding Company: AMAZON SERVICES LTD
Registration no: 03064302 **Turnover:** £500,000 - £1m
No.of Employees: 1 - 10 **Product Groups:** 35, 66

Furrows
The Shrewsbury Garage Benbow Business Park Harlescott Lane, Shrewsbury, SY1 3EQ
Tel: 01743-454444 **Fax:** 01743-236009
E-mail: shrewsbury@furrows.co.uk
Website: http://www.furrows.co.uk
Managers: K. Lloyd (Mktg Serv Mgr), K. Pyatt, R. Smith (Mgr), P. Pragg (Personnel)
Ultimate Holding Company: FURROWS HOLDINGS LIMITED
Immediate Holding Company: FURROWS LIMITED
Registration no: 00149772 **VAT No.:** GB 404 1295 88
Date established: 2018 **Turnover:** £50m - £75m
No.of Employees: 21 - 50 **Product Groups:** 39, 40, 68, 82

Date of Accounts	Dec 11	Dec 10	Dec 09
Sales Turnover	71m	74m	72m
Pre Tax Profit/Loss	568	1m	937
Working Capital	5m	7m	8m
Fixed Assets	2m	3m	3m
Current Assets	26m	26m	23m
Current Liabilities	4m	1m	1m

G M E Structures Ltd
E11-E14 Wem Industrial Estate Soulton Road, Wem, Shrewsbury, SY4 5SD
Tel: 01939-233023 **Fax:** 01939-234059
E-mail: sales@gme-structures.com
Website: http://www.gme-structures.com
Directors: A. Greaves (MD), T. Greaves (Fin)
Immediate Holding Company: GME STRUCTURES LIMITED
Registration no: 04484689 **Date established:** 2002
No.of Employees: 11 - 20 **Product Groups:** 35, 36, 39, 48, 51, 52, 66

Date of Accounts	Aug 10	Aug 09	Aug 08
Working Capital	146	113	132
Fixed Assets	148	187	234
Current Assets	572	637	663

Greenhous Group Ltd
Collina House Holsworth Park Oxon Business Park, Bicton Heath, Shrewsbury, SY3 5HJ
Tel: 01743-352244 **Fax:** 01743-357230
E-mail: sales@greenhouse.co.uk
Website: http://www.greenhous.co.uk
Directors: D. Passant (Dir)
Ultimate Holding Company: GREENHOUS GROUP (HOLDINGS) LIMITED
Immediate Holding Company: GREENHOUS LIMITED
Registration no: 00747073 **Date established:** 1963
Turnover: £500,000 - £1,000m **No.of Employees:** 1 - 10
Product Groups: 68

Gresolvent Ltd
Unit C1a Wem Industrial Estate Soulton Road, Wem, Shrewsbury, SY4 5SD
Tel: 01939-232326 **Fax:** 01939-232386
E-mail: gresolvent@btconnect.com
Website: http://www.gresolvent.co.uk
Directors: T. Booth (Fin)
Date established: 1991 **No.of Employees:** 1 - 10 **Product Groups:** 31, 32, 49, 63

Gwaza Ltd
Ennerdale Road, Shrewsbury, SY1 3NR
Tel: 01743-461371 **Fax:** 01743-463732
E-mail: sales@gwaza.co.uk
Website: http://www.gwaza.co.uk
Directors: V. Edwards (MD), N. Weston (Fin)
Managers: C. Oaks (Mgr)
Immediate Holding Company: FARMPOWER INTERNATIONAL LTD
Registration no: 04459357 **Date established:** 2002
Turnover: £250,000 - £500,000 **No.of Employees:** 11 - 20
Product Groups: 67

Date of Accounts	Dec 11	Dec 10	Dec 09
Working Capital	7	-8	346
Fixed Assets	346	353	N/A
Current Assets	22	3	362

Hermes Data Communications International Ltd
Hermes House Samuel Court Oxon Business Park, Bicton Heath, Shrewsbury, SY3 5DD
Tel: 01743-235555 **Fax:** 01743-271717
E-mail: fiona.m@hermes.uk.com
Website: http://www.hermes.uk.com
Bank(s): Barclays
Directors: G. Steer (Tech Serv)
Managers: K. Harrison
Immediate Holding Company: HERMES DATACOMMUNICATIONS INTERNATIONAL LIMITED
Registration no: 02478340 **VAT No.:** GB 489 2571 96
Date established: 1990 **Turnover:** £10m - £20m
No.of Employees: 21 - 50 **Product Groups:** 37

Date of Accounts	Dec 11	Dec 10	Dec 09
Sales Turnover	17m	17m	15m
Pre Tax Profit/Loss	2m	1m	647
Working Capital	1m	-59	-381
Fixed Assets	1m	1m	1m
Current Assets	5m	5m	3m
Current Liabilities	2m	3m	2m

Honeywell Control Systems Ltd
7 Albert Road, Shrewsbury, SY1 4JB
Tel: 01743-245062
Website: http://www.honeywell.com/uk
Ultimate Holding Company: HONEYWELL INTERNATIONAL INC (USA)
Immediate Holding Company: HONEYWELL CONTROL SYSTEMS LIMITED
Registration no: 00217803 **Date established:** 2026
Turnover: £250m - £500m **No.of Employees:** 1 - 10 **Product Groups:** 38, 39, 68

Date of Accounts	Dec 11	Dec 10	Dec 09
Sales Turnover	335m	348m	340m
Pre Tax Profit/Loss	16m	16m	2m
Working Capital	123m	111m	66m
Fixed Assets	13m	14m	16m
Current Assets	247m	227m	169m
Current Liabilities	47m	37m	33m

Hughes Fabrications
Cliffdale Cottage Weston Road, Minsterley, Shrewsbury, SY5 0JJ
Tel: 01588-650147 **Fax:** 01588-650147
E-mail: jonhughesfabs@aol.com
Product Groups: 34, 35, 36, 40, 48, 49, 52, 66

Bob Johnson Engineers Ltd
10b Shoplatch, Shrewsbury, SY1 1HL
Tel: 01743-350893 **Fax:** 01743-233619
E-mail: info@bjse.co.uk
Website: http://www.bjse.co.uk
Directors: B. Johnson (Dir)
Immediate Holding Company: BOB JOHNSON ENGINEERS LIMITED
Registration no: 06140212 **Date established:** 2007
No.of Employees: 1 - 10 **Product Groups:** 35

Date of Accounts	Mar 12	Mar 11	Mar 10
Working Capital	55	43	30
Fixed Assets	43	42	46
Current Assets	114	114	96

Kingsland Polymers Ltd
1 Brassey Road, Shrewsbury, SY3 7FA
Tel: 01743-249103 **Fax:** 01743-340123
E-mail: info@kingslandpolymers.co.uk
Website: http://www.kingslandpolymers.co.uk
Managers: C. Padmore (Mgr)
Immediate Holding Company: KINGSLAND POLYMERS LIMITED
Registration no: 03765588 **Date established:** 1999
No.of Employees: 1 - 10 **Product Groups:** 31, 33

Date of Accounts	May 11	May 10	May 09
Working Capital	149	128	66
Fixed Assets	34	52	77
Current Assets	1m	1m	1m

Longden Engineering
The Farriers Annscroft, Shrewsbury, SY5 8AN
Tel: 01743-860131 **Fax:** 01743-860315
Website: http://www.longdenengineering.co.uk
Managers: J. Rowe (Mgr)
Immediate Holding Company: SHROPSHIRE PARTNERS IN CARE
Registration no: 04586309 **VAT No.:** GB 434 0316 90
Date established: 2003 **Turnover:** Up to £250,000
No.of Employees: 1 - 10 **Product Groups:** 48

Date of Accounts	Apr 11	Apr 10	Apr 08
Working Capital	33	26	5
Fixed Assets	937	937	470
Current Assets	52	42	100

Mercian Masterplan Ltd
Drury Lane Rodington, Shrewsbury, SY4 4RG
Tel: 01952-770167 **Fax:** 01952-770965
E-mail: sales@mercianmasterplan.com
Website: http://www.mercianmasterplan.com
Directors: C. Armstrong (MD)
Ultimate Holding Company: HOLDWORTH LIMITED
Immediate Holding Company: MERCIAN MASTERPLAN LIMITED
Registration no: 01300666 **Date established:** 1977 **Turnover:** £2m - £5m
No.of Employees: 1 - 10 **Product Groups:** 35, 83

Date of Accounts	Nov 11	Nov 10	Nov 09
Working Capital	164	107	199
Fixed Assets	939	986	914
Current Assets	314	223	527

Modern Fire Extinguisher Services Ltd
Unit 62 Atcham Business Park Atcham, Shrewsbury, SY4 4UG
Tel: 01743-761186 **Fax:** 01743-761246
E-mail: info@modern-fire.co.uk
Website: http://www.modern-fire.co.uk
Directors: K. Hotchkiss (MD)
Immediate Holding Company: MODERN FIRE EXTINGUISHER SERVICES LIMITED
Registration no: 02843145 **Date established:** 1993
No.of Employees: 1 - 10 **Product Groups:** 38, 42

Date of Accounts	Mar 11	Mar 10	Mar 09
Working Capital	31	14	6
Fixed Assets	12	8	13
Current Assets	78	85	68

Morris Lubricants
38 -41 Castle Foregate, Shrewsbury, SY1 2EL
Tel: 01743-232200 **Fax:** 01743-353584
E-mail: info@morris-lubricants.co.uk
Website: http://www.morrislubricants.co.uk
Directors: J. Shelton (Co Sec), A. Goddard (MD)
Managers: N. Taylor (Tech Serv Mgr)
Immediate Holding Company: MORRIS LUBRICANTS LIMITED
Registration no: 05148521 **Date established:** 2004
Turnover: £20m - £50m **No.of Employees:** 101 - 250
Product Groups: 31, 32, 39, 42, 66

Morsafe Supplies
192 Monkmoor Road, Shrewsbury, SY2 5BH
Tel: 01743-356318 **Fax:** 01743-350875
Directors: M. Plant (Prop)
Turnover: Up to £250,000 **No.of Employees:** 1 - 10 **Product Groups:** 24, 38, 39, 40, 65

N T M-GB Ltd
Harlescott Lane, Shrewsbury, SY1 3AG
Tel: 01743-465400 **Fax:** 01743-465222
Website: http://www.ntm.fi
Directors: P. Westley (MD)
Ultimate Holding Company: AB NARPES TRA & METALL-OY NARPION PUU JA METALLI (FINLA
Immediate Holding Company: NTM-GB LIMITED
Registration no: 04984293 **Date established:** 2003
No.of Employees: 1 - 10 **Product Groups:** 39, 45

Date of Accounts	Dec 11	Dec 10	Dec 09
Working Capital	205	436	276
Fixed Assets	335	8	127
Current Assets	2m	1m	1m

Nasus Mechanical Handling
Unit 3-4 Monkmoor Trading Estate Monkmoor Road, Shrewsbury, SY2 5TZ
Tel: 01743-355496 **Fax:** 01743-235443
E-mail: service@nasus.co.uk
Website: http://www.nasus.co.uk
Directors: S. McNally (Fin)
Managers: D. Brow (Serv Mgr)
Immediate Holding Company: NMH (2011) LIMITED
Registration no: 01873525 **Date established:** 1984
Turnover: £500,000 - £1m **No.of Employees:** 1 - 10 **Product Groups:** 35, 39, 45

Date of Accounts	Oct 11	Oct 10	Oct 09
Working Capital	188	106	142
Fixed Assets	N/A	25	31
Current Assets	208	226	251

Pennants Buildings
Tankerville Lodge Tankerville, Pennerley, Shrewsbury, SY5 0NB
Tel: 01743-792774 **Fax:** 01743-792088
E-mail: antonhy@tankervilefreeserev.co.uk
Website: http://www.pennantbuildings.co.uk
Directors: A. Thorton (Prop)
No.of Employees: 1 - 10 **Product Groups:** 35

Price Fallows Fabrications Ltd
40-41 Ennerdale Road, Shrewsbury, SY1 3LD
Tel: 01743-448344 **Fax:** 01743-444025
E-mail: postmaster@pricefallows.co.uk
Website: http://www.pricefallows.co.uk
Bank(s): Barclays
Directors: R. Price (MD), A. Price (Ptnr)
Managers: W. Price, S. Bonen
Immediate Holding Company: PRICE FALLOWS FABRICATIONS LIMITED
Registration no: 07145361 **VAT No.:** GB 377 7091 15
Date established: 2010 **Turnover:** £250,000 - £500,000
No.of Employees: 11 - 20 **Product Groups:** 48

Date of Accounts	Dec 11	Dec 10
Working Capital	65	57
Current Assets	324	250

Provq Ltd
Unit 32a Atcham Business Park Atcham, Shrewsbury, SY4 4UG
Tel: 01743-762055 **Fax:** 01743-709011
E-mail: info@provq.com
Website: http://www.provq.com
Directors: B. Stockton (Dir)
Immediate Holding Company: PROVQ LIMITED
Registration no: 05559332 **Date established:** 2005
No.of Employees: 1 - 10 **Product Groups:** 80

Date of Accounts	Nov 11	Nov 10	Nov 09
Working Capital	139	104	85
Fixed Assets	89	42	34
Current Assets	304	253	232

RhinoCo Technology
3B Vernon Drive, shrewsbury, SY1 3TF
Tel: 0845-6445421 **Fax:** 0845-6445431
E-mail: sales@rhinoco.co.uk
Website: http://www.rhinoco.co.uk
Managers: k. naylor (Sales Admin)
Registration no: BR009958 **Date established:** 1978 **Turnover:**
No.of Employees: Unknown **Product Groups:** 37, 38, 40, 67

S K M Enviros
Enviros House Sitka Drive, Shrewsbury, SY2 6LG
Tel: 01743-284800 **Fax:** 01743-245558
E-mail: enquiries@enviros.com
Website: http://www.skm.com
Directors: D. Cattermole (Pers)
Managers: H. Francis (Sales Admin), A. Hibbert (Tech Serv Mgr), C. Dawson (Sales Admin)
Ultimate Holding Company: ALASKA PROPERTY GROUP LIMITED
Immediate Holding Company: ALASKA PROPERTIES LIMITED
Registration no: 01721409 **VAT No.:** GB 685 1974 87
Date established: 1997 **Turnover:** Up to £250,000
No.of Employees: 51 - 100 **Product Groups:** 34, 54, 84

Salop Design & Engineering
Brixton Way, Shrewsbury, SY1 3LB
Tel: 01743-450501 **Fax:** 01743-440904
E-mail: info@salopdesign.co.uk
Website: http://www.salopdesign.co.uk
Bank(s): Barclays
Directors: B. Russell (Fin), R. Homden (MD), R. Homden (MD)
Ultimate Holding Company: R.A. HOMDEN LIMITED
Immediate Holding Company: SALOP DESIGN & ENGINEERING LIMITED
Registration no: 00895927 **VAT No.:** GB 159 8838 00
Date established: 1967 **Turnover:** £2m - £5m **No.of Employees:** 51 - 100
Product Groups: 46, 48

Date of Accounts	Mar 11	Mar 10	Mar 09
Pre Tax Profit/Loss	N/A	N/A	-395
Working Capital	1m	1m	2m
Fixed Assets	1m	2m	2m
Current Assets	2m	2m	2m
Current Liabilities	N/A	N/A	130

Sciquip Ltd
Merrington Business Park Bomere Heath, Shrewsbury, SY4 3QJ
Tel: 01939-291200 **Fax:** 01939-291100
E-mail: info@sciquip.co.uk
Website: http://www.sciquip.co.uk
Directors: M. Brooksbank (MD)
Immediate Holding Company: SCIQUIP LIMITED
Registration no: 04253055 **Date established:** 2001
No.of Employees: 1 - 10 **Product Groups:** 42, 67

Date of Accounts	Dec 11	Dec 10	Dec 09
Working Capital	166	66	224
Fixed Assets	4	5	6
Current Assets	617	483	502

Scott & Newman Ltd
4 Longbow Close, Shrewsbury, SY1 3GZ
Tel: 01743-452040 **Fax:** 01743-452044
E-mail: ro@snpots.co.uk
Website: http://www.scottandnewman.co.uk
Directors: R. Owen (MD)
Immediate Holding Company: SCOTT & NEWMAN LIMITED
Registration no: 01112043 **Date established:** 1973
Turnover: £20m - £50m **No.of Employees:** 11 - 20 **Product Groups:** 62

Date of Accounts	Jun 11	Jun 10	Jun 09
Sales Turnover	22m	N/A	12m
Pre Tax Profit/Loss	886	N/A	400
Working Capital	2m	997	991
Fixed Assets	132	166	146
Current Assets	4m	2m	2m
Current Liabilities	612	N/A	342

Smithers Rapra Technology
Smither Rapra Shawbury, Shrewsbury, SY4 4NR
Tel: 01939-250383 **Fax:** 01939-251118
E-mail: info@rapra.net
Website: http://www.rapra.net
Directors: M. McColl (Fin), S. Ankers (Fin), S. Vinter (Chief Op Offcr), K. Foster (Pers)
Managers: L. Gauld
Ultimate Holding Company: THE SMITHERS GROUP INC (USA)
Immediate Holding Company: SMITHERS RAPRA AND SMITHERS PIRA LIMITED
Registration no: 05761324 **Date established:** 2006 **Turnover:** £5m - £10m
No.of Employees: 51 - 100 **Product Groups:** 85

Date of Accounts	Dec 11	Dec 10	Dec 09
Sales Turnover	7m	8m	9m
Pre Tax Profit/Loss	-541	311	248
Working Capital	-8	246	347
Fixed Assets	673	689	717
Current Assets	2m	3m	2m
Current Liabilities	1m	2m	2m

Sporting & General Supply Co Shrewsbury
91 Belle Vue Road, Shrewsbury, SY3 7LY
Tel: 01743-350991 **Fax:** 01743-350991
Website: http://www.sportingandgeneralsupply.com
Directors: S. Godfrey (Prop)
Immediate Holding Company: SPORTING AND GENERAL SUPPLY (SHREWSBURY) LIMITED
Registration no: 00964414 **Date established:** 1969
No.of Employees: 1 - 10 **Product Groups:** 36, 39, 40

Date of Accounts	Jun 11	Jun 10	Jun 09
Working Capital	40	41	48
Fixed Assets	3	2	3
Current Assets	67	64	66
Current Liabilities	7	N/A	N/A

Steel Design Fabrications
Painsbrook Lane Hadnall, Shrewsbury, SY4 4BA
Tel: 01939-210246 **Fax:** 01939-210246
E-mail: info@steeldesignfabrications.com
Website: http://www.steeldesignfabrications.co.uk
Directors: S. Jones (Prop)
Immediate Holding Company: STEEL DESIGN FABRICATIONS LIMITED
Registration no: 06681702 **Date established:** 2008
No.of Employees: 1 - 10 **Product Groups:** 35, 81

Date of Accounts	Aug 11	Aug 10	Aug 09
Working Capital	-0	-7	9
Fixed Assets	14	17	20
Current Assets	24	27	26

Structural Glass Solutions Ltd
Unit 9-10 Harlescott Barns Harlescott Lane, Shrewsbury, SY1 3SZ
Tel: 01743-461122 **Fax:** 01743-461123
E-mail: jdr@glassolutions.co.uk
Website: http://www.structuralglass.co.uk
Directors: J. Roberts (Dir)
Immediate Holding Company: STRUCTURAL GLASS SOLUTIONS LIMITED
Registration no: 04556596 **Date established:** 2002 **Turnover:** £1m - £2m
No.of Employees: 1 - 10 **Product Groups:** 30, 33, 35, 52, 66

Date of Accounts	Dec 11	Dec 10	Dec 09
Working Capital	104	102	50
Fixed Assets	7	9	17
Current Assets	561	745	532

Warwick Wright Financial Services Ltd
Suite 1 Canon Court West Abbey Lawn, Shrewsbury, SY2 5DE
Tel: 08452-604560
E-mail: info@warwickwright.com
Website: http://www.warwickwright.com
Directors: D. Masters (MD)
Managers: D. Masters (Chief Mgr)
Ultimate Holding Company: PENDRAGON CORPORATE SERVICES LIMITED
Immediate Holding Company: WARWICK-WRIGHT FINANCIAL SERVICES LIMITED
Registration no: 02101591 **Date established:** 1987
No.of Employees: 1 - 10 **Product Groups:** 82

Date of Accounts	Dec 08	Dec 07	Dec 06
Working Capital	38	50	41
Fixed Assets	15	17	23
Current Assets	55	64	53
Current Liabilities	17	14	12
Total Share Capital	56	56	56

Welfix Fixings & Fasteners
192 Monkmoor Road, Shrewsbury, SY2 5BH
Tel: 01743-344766 **Fax:** 01743-350875
E-mail: info@welfix.co.uk
Website: http://www.welfix.co.uk
Directors: W. Leader (Prop)
Date established: 1994 **Turnover:** £250,000 - £500,000
No.of Employees: 1 - 10 **Product Groups:** 35, 66

Window & Door Security Systems Ltd
Unit 28a Atcham Industrial Estate Atcham, Shrewsbury, SY4 4UG
Tel: 01743-761555 **Fax:** 01743-761586
E-mail: sales@windowanddoorsecurity.co.uk
Website: http://www.windowanddoorsecurity.co.uk
Directors: J. Davies (Dir), S. Harbage (MD)
Immediate Holding Company: WINDOW & DOOR SECURITY SYSTEMS LIMITED
Registration no: 04736509 **Date established:** 2003
No.of Employees: 1 - 10 **Product Groups:** 81

Date of Accounts	Jun 10	Jun 09	Jun 08
Working Capital	-20	-27	-29
Fixed Assets	7	9	12
Current Assets	85	65	92

Telford

3 C L Ltd
Stafford Park 16, Telford, TF3 3BS
Tel: 01952-290941 **Fax:** 01952-290943
E-mail: info@3cl.com
Website: http://www.3cl.com
Bank(s): Yorkshire Bank PLC
Directors: M. Farmer (Fin), G. Wickes (MD), G. Wicks (Dir), S. Clarke (Sales)
Managers: M. Farmer
Ultimate Holding Company: T.H.W. DODD (AIR CONDITIONING) LIMITED
Immediate Holding Company: CLOSED CIRCUIT COOLING LIMITED
Registration no: 02060506 **VAT No.:** GB 351 6143 77
Date established: 1979 **Turnover:** £5m - £10m **No.of Employees:** 21 - 50
Product Groups: 40, 52

Date of Accounts	Dec 11	Dec 10	Dec 09
Working Capital	-356	-66	-252
Fixed Assets	684	365	390
Current Assets	659	1m	2m

A D P Dealer Services UK Ltd
Unit 3 Stafford Park 1, Telford, TF3 3BD
Tel: 01952-292433 **Fax:** 01952-292260
E-mail: steve_johnson@adp.com
Website: http://www.adpdsi.com
Managers: S. Johnson (Mktg Serv Mgr)
Ultimate Holding Company: AUTOMATIC DATA PROCESSING INC (USA)
Immediate Holding Company: ADP DEALER SERVICES UK LIMITED
Registration no: 01281651 **Date established:** 1976
No.of Employees: 21 - 50 **Product Groups:** 44, 68

Date of Accounts	Jun 11	Jun 10	Jun 09
Sales Turnover	63m	67m	76m
Pre Tax Profit/Loss	6m	22m	3m
Working Capital	6m	16m	276
Fixed Assets	23m	8m	8m
Current Assets	37m	44m	34m
Current Liabilities	26m	24m	28m

A Y Fabrications
Unit B4 Hortonwood 10 10 Hortonwood, Telford, TF1 7ES
Tel: 01952-605526 **Fax:** 01952-605526
Directors: S. Allen (Prop)
Date established: 1977 **No.of Employees:** 1 - 10 **Product Groups:** 35

Acoustafoam Ltd
Unit D Halesfield 10, Telford, TF7 4QP
Tel: 01952-581340 **Fax:** 01952-581455
E-mail: mike@acoustafoam.com
Website: http://www.acoustafoam.com
Bank(s): Barclays
Directors: M. Tranter (MD)
Managers: J. Burgess (Chief Acct), C. Goldsbough (Purch Mgr)
Immediate Holding Company: ACOUSTA FOAM LIMITED
Registration no: 01494707 **Date established:** 1980 **Turnover:** £5m - £10m
No.of Employees: 21 - 50 **Product Groups:** 29, 30, 31, 33, 39, 52, 54

Date of Accounts	Dec 11	Dec 10	Dec 09
Working Capital	161	202	180
Fixed Assets	1m	1m	1m
Current Assets	678	549	438

AGA Rayburn
PO Box 30, Telford, TF8 7DX
Tel: 01952-642000 **Fax:** 01952- 243138
E-mail: info@aga-web.co.uk
Website: http://www.aga-rayburn.co.uk
Bank(s): Lloyds TSB Bank plc
Managers: M. Newby (Mgr)
Ultimate Holding Company: GLYNWED INTERNATIONAL GROUP P.L.C.
Immediate Holding Company: AGALINKS
No.of Employees: 101 - 250 **Product Groups:** 40

Airgonomics Ltd
Unit 17 Queensway Link Industrial Estate Stafford Park, Telford, TF3 3DN
Tel: 01952-299920 **Fax:** 01952-290063
E-mail: sales@airgonomics.co.uk
Website: http://www.airgonomics.co.uk
Directors: J. Ellis (Dir)
Immediate Holding Company: AIRGONOMICS LIMITED
Registration no: 02741375 **VAT No.:** GB 632 0324 87
Date established: 1992 **Turnover:** £500,000 - £1m
No.of Employees: 1 - 10 **Product Groups:** 35, 37, 39, 40, 44, 45, 48, 67, 84

Date of Accounts	Sep 11	Sep 10	Sep 09
Working Capital	57	94	88
Fixed Assets	8	11	14
Current Assets	77	138	109

Alcoa Fastening Systems Ltd
Unit C Stafford Park 7, Telford, TF3 3BQ
Tel: 01952-207700 **Fax:** 01952-207701
E-mail: marcuslokier@alcoa.com
Website: http://www.alcoa.com
Managers: J. Sahadew (Mktg Serv Mgr), L. Dalton (Personnel), W. Waterstone (Comptroller), M. Lokier (Ops Mgr), R. Jones (Tech Serv Mgr), W. Will
Ultimate Holding Company: ALCOA INC (USA)
Immediate Holding Company: ALCOA FASTENING SYSTEMS LIMITED
Registration no: 01736094 **Date established:** 1983
No.of Employees: 51 - 100 **Product Groups:** 39

Date of Accounts	Dec 11	Dec 10	Dec 09
Sales Turnover	23m	18m	15m
Pre Tax Profit/Loss	3m	2m	783
Working Capital	5m	3m	3m
Fixed Assets	4m	4m	4m
Current Assets	9m	8m	7m
Current Liabilities	2m	3m	3m

Alumasc Interior Building Products Ltd
Unit C1 Halesfield 19, Telford, TF7 4QT
Tel: 01952-580590 **Fax:** 01952-587805
E-mail: sales@pendock.co.uk
Website: http://www.pendock.co.uk
Bank(s): Barclays
Directors: D. Coleman (Fin), M. Taylor (Sales & Mktg), M. Leaf (MD), R. Cooke (Fin), C. Langley (Mkt Research)
Managers: P. Wainer (Sales Prom Mgr)
Ultimate Holding Company: THE ALUMASC GROUP PLC
Immediate Holding Company: ALUMASC INTERIOR BUILDING PRODUCTS LIMITED
Registration no: 03758186 **Date established:** 1999 **Turnover:** £5m - £10m
No.of Employees: 21 - 50 **Product Groups:** 30, 35, 36, 37

Ambroplastics Ltd
Chamber House Halesfield 13, Telford, TF7 4PL
Tel: 01952-684922 **Fax:** 01952-581414
E-mail: info@ambro.co.uk
Website: http://www.ambro.co.uk
Bank(s): Barclays
Directors: P. Caudle (MD), T. Teichmann (Co Sec)
Ultimate Holding Company: AMBRO TEN TEN LIMITED
Immediate Holding Company: AMBROPLASTICS LIMITED
Registration no: 00731878 **VAT No.:** GB 202 9683 67
Date established: 1962 **Turnover:** £2m - £5m **No.of Employees:** 21 - 50
Product Groups: 27, 30

Date of Accounts	Dec 11	Dec 10	Dec 09
Working Capital	1m	1m	567
Fixed Assets	108	141	502
Current Assets	2m	2m	1m

Ampacet UK
Unit F1 21 Halesfield Industrial Estate, Telford, TF7 4NX
Tel: 01952-581814 **Fax:** 01952-581815
Website: http://www.ampacet.com
Directors: G. Giusto (Fin), H. Sartori (Dir)
Ultimate Holding Company: AMPACET CORP (USA)
Immediate Holding Company: AMPACET UK LIMITED
Registration no: 04868378 **Date established:** 2003
Turnover: £10m - £20m **No.of Employees:** 1 - 10 **Product Groups:** 32

Date of Accounts	Dec 11	Dec 10	Dec 09
Sales Turnover	13m	N/A	N/A
Pre Tax Profit/Loss	495	N/A	N/A
Working Capital	1m	883	521
Fixed Assets	598	610	568
Current Assets	4m	3m	2m
Current Liabilities	581	N/A	N/A

Andrews Mobility Solutions
Unit 22 St Georges Road Industrial Estate Donnington, Telford, TF2 7QZ
Tel: 01952-613131
Website: http://www.andrewsmobilitysolutions.co.uk
Directors: A. James (Prop)
No.of Employees: 1 - 10 **Product Groups:** 26, 38, 39

Apex Fabrications
Unit 18 Heath Hill Industrial Estate, Dawley, Telford, TF4 2RH
Tel: 01952-505671
Directors: A. Short (Prop)
Immediate Holding Company: APEX FABRICATIONS LLP
Registration no: OC302993 **Date established:** 2002
Turnover: Up to £250,000 **No.of Employees:** 1 - 10 **Product Groups:** 35

Date of Accounts	Mar 11	Mar 10	Mar 09
Sales Turnover	N/A	N/A	99
Pre Tax Profit/Loss	N/A	N/A	57
Working Capital	-1	-13	1
Fixed Assets	33	38	30
Current Assets	15	6	17
Current Liabilities	8	9	1

Ashtead Plant Hire Co. Ltd

St Georges Road Donnington, Telford, TF2 7RA
Tel: 01952-620320 **Fax:** 01952-610708
E-mail: telford@aplant.com
Website: http://www.aplant.com
Directors: B. Trueman (Prop), P. Lewis (MD)
Managers: B. Trueman (Chief Mgr), B. Truman (Sales Prom Mgr), J. Newell (District Mgr)
Ultimate Holding Company: FOMENTO DE CONSTRUCCIONES Y CONTRATAS SA (SPAIN)
Immediate Holding Company: TELFORD & WREKIN SERVICES LIMITED
Registration no: 04088472 **VAT No.:** GB 209 5687 37
Date established: 2000 **Turnover:** £10m - £20m **No.of Employees:** 1 - 10
Product Groups: 83

Asta Development plc

10 Pearson Road Central Park, Telford, TF2 9TX
Tel: 01952-293491 **Fax:** 01952-293494
E-mail: sales@astadev.com
Website: http://www.astadev.com
Directors: M. Mccullen (Dir), P. Bamforth (MD)
Managers: R. Omerod (Sales Prom)
Ultimate Holding Company: ELECO PUBLIC LIMITED COMPANY
Immediate Holding Company: ASTA DEVELOPMENT PLC
Registration no: 02021387 **Date established:** 1986 **Turnover:** £5m - £10m
No.of Employees: 11 - 20 **Product Groups:** 44

Date of Accounts	Jun 10	Jun 09	Jun 08
Sales Turnover	4m	4m	5m
Pre Tax Profit/Loss	471	631	1m
Working Capital	2m	2m	2m
Fixed Assets	140	193	232
Current Assets	4m	4m	4m
Current Liabilities	1m	1m	1m

B A C Corrosion Control Ltd

Unit C10-C11 Stafford Park 11, Telford, TF3 3AY
Tel: 01952-208500 **Fax:** 01952-290325
E-mail: sales@bacgroup.com
Website: http://www.bacgroup.com
Bank(s): Lloyds TSB Bank plc
Managers: D. Marsden (Fin Mgr), C. Coley (Purch Mgr), N. Dalby (Mktg Serv Mgr), S. Goring (Ops Mgr)
Ultimate Holding Company: MIRDOC HOLDING AB (SWEDEN)
Immediate Holding Company: BAC CORROSION CONTROL LIMITED
Registration no: 01394643 **VAT No.:** GB 304 6896 45
Date established: 1978 **Turnover:** £10m - £20m
No.of Employees: 21 - 50 **Product Groups:** 31, 32, 34, 35, 37, 38, 39, 46, 52, 67, 84

Date of Accounts	Dec 11	Dec 10	Dec 09
Working Capital	1m	906	1m
Fixed Assets	533	564	281
Current Assets	2m	2m	2m

Besblock Ltd

Halesfield 21, Telford, TF7 4NF
Tel: 01952-586778 **Fax:** 01952-585224
E-mail: info@besblock.co.uk
Website: http://www.besblock.co.uk
Bank(s): Barclays
Directors: J. Huxley (MD)
Immediate Holding Company: BESBLOCK LIMITED
Registration no: 01059042 **VAT No.:** GB 159 3394 35
Date established: 1972 **Turnover:** £5m - £10m **No.of Employees:** 21 - 50
Product Groups: 33

Date of Accounts	Apr 12	Apr 11	Apr 10
Working Capital	3m	3m	3m
Fixed Assets	2m	2m	2m
Current Assets	4m	4m	4m

Bischof & Klein UK Ltd

Unit C Hortonwood 2, Telford, TF1 7XX
Tel: 01952-606848 **Fax:** 01952-606698
E-mail: info.uk@bk-international.com
Website: http://www.bk-international.com
Bank(s): HSBC
Directors: D. Plumb (Fin), G. Eickholt (MD)
Managers: C. Harrison (Personnel), M. Waldron (Tech Serv Mgr), N. Keating (Sales Prom Mgr)
Ultimate Holding Company: KLEIN AND GUNTHER VERMOGENSVERWALTUNG GMBH
Immediate Holding Company: BISCHOF & KLEIN (UK) LIMITED
Registration no: 01372782 **Date established:** 1978
Turnover: £10m - £20m **No.of Employees:** 101 - 250 **Product Groups:** 25

Date of Accounts	Dec 11	Dec 10	Dec 09
Sales Turnover	18m	19m	15m
Pre Tax Profit/Loss	317	195	-473
Working Capital	142	11	-897
Fixed Assets	5m	5m	5m
Current Assets	6m	6m	5m
Current Liabilities	899	978	2m

Blockleys Brick Ltd

Sommerfeld Road Trench Lock, Telford, TF1 5RY
Tel: 01952-251933 **Fax:** 01952-265377
E-mail: sales@blockleys.com
Website: http://www.blockleys.com
Bank(s): Barclays, Wellington
Directors: C. Robinson (MD)
Managers: D. Evans (Comm), C. Duncan
Ultimate Holding Company: MICHELMERSH BRICK HOLDINGS PLC
Immediate Holding Company: MICHELMERSH BRICK UK LIMITED
Registration no: 02527552 **VAT No.:** GB 549 6645 93
Date established: 1990 **Turnover:** £20m - £50m
No.of Employees: 21 - 50 **Product Groups:** 33

Date of Accounts	Dec 11	Dec 10	Dec 09
Sales Turnover	24m	7m	9m
Pre Tax Profit/Loss	549	-7m	-169
Working Capital	-11m	-12m	-3m
Fixed Assets	10m	11m	8m
Current Assets	16m	14m	9m
Current Liabilities	4m	44	3m

Borgers Ltd

Hortonwood 30, Telford, TF1 7LJ
Tel: 01952-670345 **Fax:** 01952-670123
E-mail: info@borgers-group.com
Website: http://www.borgers-group.com
Bank(s): Barclays
Directors: K. Kuve (MD)
Managers: A. Rogers (Tech Serv Mgr), R. Lockley (Personnel), R. Plant (Buyer), F. Stephen (Fin Mgr)
Ultimate Holding Company: BORGERS AG (GERMANY)
Immediate Holding Company: BORGERS LIMITED
Registration no: 02149178 **VAT No.:** GB 478 8245 92
Date established: 1987 **Turnover:** £10m - £20m
No.of Employees: 51 - 100 **Product Groups:** 23, 33, 39, 68, 85

Date of Accounts	Dec 11	Dec 10	Dec 09
Sales Turnover	15m	12m	11m
Pre Tax Profit/Loss	310	-501	-2m
Working Capital	-24	401	-1m
Fixed Assets	2m	3m	5m
Current Assets	4m	3m	3m
Current Liabilities	1m	737	487

Busch UK Ltd

Hortonwood 3035, Telford, TF1 7YB
Tel: 01952-678700 **Fax:** 01952-677423
E-mail: sales@busch-gvt.co.uk
Website: http://www.busch.co.uk
Directors: A. Busch (Grp Chief Exec), I. Graves (MD)
Managers: D. Underwood (Tech Serv Mgr), M. Sumnall (Sales & Mktg Mg), P. Smith (Sales Eng), M. Kelly-Jones (Mktg Serv Mgr)
Ultimate Holding Company: BUSCH BETEILIGUNGSVERWALTUNG GMBH (GERMANY)
Immediate Holding Company: BUSCH (UK) LIMITED
Registration no: 01007314 **VAT No.:** GB 218 7097 47
Date established: 1971 **Turnover:** £10m - £20m
No.of Employees: 51 - 100 **Product Groups:** 39, 40, 48, 67

Date of Accounts	Dec 11	Dec 10	Dec 09
Sales Turnover	15m	12m	10m
Pre Tax Profit/Loss	818	697	531
Working Capital	8m	8m	7m
Fixed Assets	3m	2m	2m
Current Assets	11m	10m	10m
Current Liabilities	1m	1m	1m

C & L Fabrication Ltd

Unit D3 Hortonwood 10, Telford, TF1 7ES
Tel: 01952-676666 **Fax:** 01952-677760
E-mail: info@clfabrication.co.uk
Website: http://www.clfabrication.co.uk
Directors: T. Cumming (MD)
Immediate Holding Company: C & L FABRICATION LIMITED
Registration no: 05295934 **Date established:** 2004
No.of Employees: 1 - 10 **Product Groups:** 42, 48, 54, 84

Date of Accounts	Nov 07	Nov 06	Nov 05
Working Capital	30	41	-1
Fixed Assets	26	31	10
Current Assets	225	207	18
Current Liabilities	195	166	19

Capricorn Mouldings Ltd

Unit C4 Stafford Park 11, Telford, TF3 3AY
Tel: 01952-201090 **Fax:** 01952-222744
E-mail: info@capricornmouldings.co.uk
Website: http://www.capricornmouldings.co.uk
Directors: T. Stones (MD)
Immediate Holding Company: CAPRICORN MOULDINGS LIMITED
Registration no: 01707498 **VAT No.:** GB 377 8356 00
Date established: 1983 **Turnover:** £500,000 - £1m
No.of Employees: 1 - 10 **Product Groups:** 30

Date of Accounts	Mar 12	Mar 11	Mar 10
Working Capital	224	192	245
Fixed Assets	94	106	70
Current Assets	369	284	297

Carbonation Techniques Ltd

Halesfield Business Park Halesfield 8, Telford, TF7 4QN
Tel: 01952-583901 **Fax:** 01952-583901
E-mail: info@carbotech.co.uk
Website: http://www.carbotech.co.uk
Directors: W. Sharpe (Fin)
Immediate Holding Company: CARBONATION TECHNIQUES LIMITED
Registration no: 05108888 **VAT No.:** GB 835 1349 32
Date established: 2004 **No.of Employees:** 1 - 10 **Product Groups:** 42, 48, 67

Date of Accounts	Apr 12	Apr 11	Apr 10
Working Capital	39	20	30
Fixed Assets	5	7	7
Current Assets	160	67	79

Castlebridge Plant

Ketley Business Park Ketley, Telford, TF1 5JD
Tel: 01952-254422 **Fax:** 01952-254433
E-mail: scornes@scottishcoal.co.uk
Website: http://www.castlebridgeplant.co.uk/
Directors: S. Cornes (Dir)
Immediate Holding Company: TELFORD AND THE WREKIN CITIZENS ADVICE BUREAUX
Registration no: 03844929 **Date established:** 1999
Turnover: £500,000 - £1m **No.of Employees:** 11 - 20
Product Groups: 45, 48

Date of Accounts	Mar 11	Mar 10	Mar 09
Sales Turnover	681	669	691
Pre Tax Profit/Loss	96	64	162
Working Capital	490	403	314
Fixed Assets	1	2	2
Current Assets	504	425	327

Cedo Ltd

Unit 11 Halesfield 11, Telford, TF7 4LZ
Tel: 01952-272727 **Fax:** 01952-274102
E-mail: info@cedo.com
Website: http://www.cedo.com
Directors: D. Quagliariello (Sales)
Managers: C. Chunsi (Tech Serv Mgr), J. Vaghela, J. McComasky
Ultimate Holding Company: CEDO HOLDINGS LIMITED
Immediate Holding Company: CEDO LIMITED
Registration no: 00934776 **VAT No.:** GB 504 8043 72
Date established: 1968 **Turnover:** £75m - £125m
No.of Employees: 251 - 500 **Product Groups:** 27, 30, 43

Date of Accounts	Dec 11	Dec 10	Dec 09
Sales Turnover	100m	89m	86m
Pre Tax Profit/Loss	7m	6m	8m
Working Capital	24m	18m	13m
Fixed Assets	3m	4m	4m
Current Assets	55m	45m	36m
Current Liabilities	4m	4m	5m

Chequer Foods Ltd

Halesfield 14, Telford, TF7 4QR
Tel: 01952-680404 **Fax:** 01952-684164
E-mail: cfsales@chequer.co.uk
Website: http://www.chequer.co.uk
Bank(s): Lloyds TSB Bank plc
Directors: M. Greenwood (Dir)
Managers: T. Yorke (Comptroller), V. Jackson (Personnel), J. Hall (Buyer), V. Dykes (Develop Mgr)
Ultimate Holding Company: MELDREW INVESTMENTS BV (NETHERLANDS)
Immediate Holding Company: CHEQUER FOODS LIMITED
Registration no: 00744256 **Date established:** 1962
Turnover: £10m - £20m **No.of Employees:** 101 - 250
Product Groups: 20, 21, 48, 84

Date of Accounts	Mar 09	Mar 10	Apr 11
Sales Turnover	16m	16m	17m
Pre Tax Profit/Loss	-754	74	419
Working Capital	1m	1m	2m
Fixed Assets	2m	1m	2m
Current Assets	5m	5m	5m
Current Liabilities	749	647	773

Cobra Seats Ltd

Units D1-D2 Halesfield 23, Telford, TF7 4NY
Tel: 01952-684020 **Fax:** 01952-581772
E-mail: sales@cobraseats.com
Website: http://www.cobraseats.com
Bank(s): Natwest Bank Ltd
Directors: M. Dunsford (MD), A. Dunsford (Fin)
Immediate Holding Company: COBRA SEATS LIMITED
Registration no: 01370248 **VAT No.:** GB 304 6449 70
Date established: 1978 **Turnover:** £1m - £2m **No.of Employees:** 21 - 50
Product Groups: 39

Date of Accounts	May 11	May 10	May 09
Working Capital	232	123	192
Fixed Assets	173	190	223
Current Assets	645	735	966

Control Techniques

4 Stafford Park 4, Telford, TF3 3BA
Tel: 01952-213700 **Fax:** 01952-213701
E-mail: dave.baston@emerson.com
Website: http://www.controltechniques.com
Bank(s): HSBC Bank plc
Managers: S. Prinsloo (Mgr)
Ultimate Holding Company: SHROPSHIRE CHAMBER OF COMMERCE AND ENTERPRISE LIMITED
Immediate Holding Company: SHROPSHIRE CHAMBER OF INDUSTRY AND COMMERCE LIMITED
Registration no: 06430811 **Date established:** 1995
No.of Employees: 21 - 50 **Product Groups:** 37, 38, 46

W Corbett & Co Galvanizing Ltd

New Alexandra Works Haldane Halesfield 1, Telford, TF7 4QQ
Tel: 01952-412777 **Fax:** 01952-412888
E-mail: mstatham@wcorbett.co.uk
Website: http://www.wcorbett.co.uk
Directors: M. Statham (MD)
Immediate Holding Company: W. CORBETT & CO. (GALVANIZING) LIMITED
Registration no: 00490482 **VAT No.:** GB 160 9477 48
Date established: 1951 **Turnover:** £5m - £10m **No.of Employees:** 1 - 10
Product Groups: 48

Date of Accounts	Mar 12	Mar 11	Mar 10
Sales Turnover	10m	9m	10m
Pre Tax Profit/Loss	710	270	215
Working Capital	1m	348	303
Fixed Assets	4m	4m	4m
Current Assets	4m	3m	3m
Current Liabilities	928	404	741

Cortec Ltd

6 Knightsbridge Cresent Stirchley, Telford, TF3 1BN
Tel: 01952-591224 **Fax:** 01952-594383
Directors: G. Davies (MD)
Immediate Holding Company: CORTEC LIMITED
Registration no: 01506104 **Date established:** 1980
No.of Employees: 1 - 10 **Product Groups:** 46, 48

Date of Accounts	Mar 10	Mar 09	Mar 08
Working Capital	N/A	4	2
Current Assets	1	8	6

Craemer UK Ltd

Craemer House Hortonwood 1, Telford, TF1 7GN
Tel: 01952-607800 **Fax:** 01952-607801
E-mail: sales@craemer.com
Website: http://www.craemer.com
Directors: S. Brandenburg (MD)
Managers: S. Poppitt
Ultimate Holding Company: CRAEMER HOLDINGS GMBH (GERMANY)
Immediate Holding Company: CRAEMER UK LIMITED
Registration no: 02574815 **Date established:** 1991
Turnover: £10m - £20m **No.of Employees:** 21 - 50 **Product Groups:** 30, 45

Date of Accounts	Dec 11	Dec 10	Dec 09
Sales Turnover	17m	16m	13m
Pre Tax Profit/Loss	361	422	1m
Working Capital	2m	930	602
Fixed Assets	9m	9m	10m
Current Assets	4m	3m	3m
Current Liabilities	1m	1m	600

D M S Engineering Services

32 Beverley Road Oakengates, Telford, TF2 6SD
Tel: 01952-409836 **Fax:** 01952-410873
E-mail: mikesarchet@blueyonder.co.uk
Directors: M. Sarchet (Prop)
VAT No.: GB 404 2500 11 **No.of Employees:** 1 - 10 **Product Groups:** 35, 48

Damstahl Stainless Ltd

Halesfield 4, Telford, TF7 4AP
Tel: 01952-583999 **Fax:** 01952-583958
E-mail: bw@damstahl.com
Website: http://www.damstahl.co.uk
Bank(s): Unibank, London

Managers: P. Cooper
Ultimate Holding Company: DAMSTAHL A/S (DENMARK)
Immediate Holding Company: DAMSTAHL STAINLESS LIMITED
Registration no: 02610843 **Date established:** 1991 **Turnover:** £5m - £10m
No.of Employees: 11 - 20 **Product Groups:** 34, 35, 36, 66

Date of Accounts	Dec 11	Dec 10	Dec 09
Sales Turnover	9m	9m	8m
Pre Tax Profit/Loss	-780	242	182
Working Capital	-751	4	-285
Fixed Assets	21	46	93
Current Assets	3m	4m	4m
Current Liabilities	137	208	134

Dekura Ltd
Unit G Stafford Park 18, Telford, TF3 3BN
Tel: 01952-201631 **Fax:** 01952-290010
E-mail: enquiries@dekura.co.uk
Website: http://www.dekura.co.uk
Directors: R. Morris (MD)
Managers: J. Mccluskey (Ops Mgr)
Ultimate Holding Company: EPWIN GROUP LIMITED
Immediate Holding Company: DEKURA LIMITED
Registration no: 02333227 **Date established:** 1989 **Turnover:** £2m - £5m
No.of Employees: 51 - 100 **Product Groups:** 30, 42

Denso Manufacturing UK Ltd
Queensway Campus, Telford, TF1 7FS
Tel: 01952-608400 **Fax:** 01952-675222
Website: http://www.denso-europe.com
Directors: M. Hayward (MD)
Ultimate Holding Company: DENSO CORPORATION (JAPAN)
Immediate Holding Company: DENSO MANUFACTURING UK LTD.
Registration no: 02502865 **Date established:** 1990
Turnover: £125m - £250m **No.of Employees:** 501 - 1000
Product Groups: 38, 40, 68

Date of Accounts	Mar 11	Mar 10	Mar 09
Sales Turnover	174m	171m	197m
Pre Tax Profit/Loss	-779	-2m	-14m
Working Capital	10m	10m	5m
Fixed Assets	50m	51m	56m
Current Assets	55m	42m	29m
Current Liabilities	13m	12m	10m

Depureco
Unit 36 B 4 Business Development Centre Stafford Park 4, Telford, TF3 3BA
Tel: 01952-290590 **Fax:** 01952-290752
E-mail: enquiries@depureco.co.uk
Website: http://www.depureco.co.uk
Managers: R. Jones (Mgr)
Registration no: 37866990 **No.of Employees:** 1 - 10 **Product Groups:** 36, 39, 40, 42, 45, 46, 66, 68, 83

Discount Domains Ltd
PO Box 95, Telford, TF2 8SU
Tel: 01952-670044 **Fax:** 01952-582227
E-mail: sales@discountdomainsuk.com
Website: http://www.discountdomains.ltd.uk
Directors: C. McDonnell (MD)
Immediate Holding Company: DISCOUNT DOMAINS LIMITED
Registration no: 04470102 **Date established:** 2002
Turnover: £250,000 - £500,000 **No.of Employees:** 1 - 10
Product Groups: 44, 80

Date of Accounts	Mar 11	Mar 10	Mar 09
Working Capital	-28	-28	-30
Fixed Assets	39	56	54
Current Assets	81	71	66

Door Loading Services UK Ltd
Unit 12 Horton Court Hortonwood 50, Telford, TF1 7GY
Tel: 01952-676600 **Fax:** 01952-676100
E-mail: info@doorloadingservices.co.uk
Website: http://www.doorloadingservices.co.uk
Managers: R. Mcyoung (Mgr)
Immediate Holding Company: DOOR LOADING SERVICES UK LTD
Registration no: 06499450 **Date established:** 2008
Turnover: Up to £250,000 **No.of Employees:** 1 - 10 **Product Groups:** 35

Date of Accounts	Feb 11	Feb 10	Feb 09
Working Capital	-50	-51	-8
Fixed Assets	34	9	9
Current Assets	75	70	75

E C T
Unit 38 Business Development Centre Stafford Park 4, Telford, TF3 3BA
Tel: 01952-200013
E-mail: joe@ect1.co.uk
Website: http://www.ect1.co.uk
Directors: J. Azzopardi (Prop)
Immediate Holding Company: MESL ELECTRICAL SERVICES LIMITED
Registration no: 07443981 **Date established:** 2010
Turnover: Up to £250,000 **No.of Employees:** 1 - 10 **Product Groups:** 37, 39, 48

Date of Accounts	Nov 11
Working Capital	2
Current Assets	8

E N T A Group Ltd
European Headquaters Stafford Park 6, Telford, TF3 3AT
Tel: 01952-428888 **Fax:** 0870-7709500
E-mail: sales@enta.com
Website: http://www.entagroup.com
Directors: J. Abberton (Dir), J. Tsai (MD)
Managers: D. Perks (Sales Prom Mgr), H. Nguyed (I.T. Exec), M. Mulvihill (Purch Mgr), S. Hutchinson (Mktg Serv Mgr)
Immediate Holding Company: ENTA UK LIMITED
Registration no: 05959142 **VAT No.:** GB 549 6630 09
Date established: 1990 **Turnover:** £75m - £125m
No.of Employees: 51 - 100 **Product Groups:** 44

E W A B Engineering Ltd
16 Stafford Park, Telford, TF3 3BS
Tel: 01952-239220 **Fax:** 01952-239258
E-mail: glyn.punter@ewab.com
Website: http://www.ewab.com
Bank(s): Svenskahandels Banken
Directors: M. Hickman (Fin), G. Punter (MD)
Ultimate Holding Company: EWAB HOLDING AG (SWITZERLAND)
Immediate Holding Company: EWAB ENGINEERING LIMITED
Registration no: 02060506 **Date established:** 1986 **Turnover:** £2m - £5m
No.of Employees: 11 - 20 **Product Groups:** 45, 84

Date of Accounts	Dec 11	Dec 10	Dec 09
Working Capital	-356	-66	-252
Fixed Assets	684	365	390
Current Assets	659	1m	2m

Entanet International Ltd
Stafford Park 6, Telford, TF3 3AT
Tel: 03331-010600 **Fax:** 01952-419922
E-mail: sales@enta.net
Website: http://www.enta.net
Directors: J. Tsai (Co Sec)
Managers: D. Bus (Tech Serv Mgr), K. Fuller (Mktg Serv Mgr), D. Perks (Sales Prom Mgr), A. Yeo, R. Hope (Purch Mgr), C. Lee (Personnel)
Ultimate Holding Company: ENTA UK LIMITED
Immediate Holding Company: ENTA TECHNOLOGIES LIMITED
Registration no: 02526028 **Date established:** 1990
Turnover: £75m - £125m **No.of Employees:** 51 - 100
Product Groups: 37, 44, 79

Date of Accounts	Oct 11	Oct 10	Oct 09
Sales Turnover	113m	99m	84m
Pre Tax Profit/Loss	509	408	370
Working Capital	3m	3m	3m
Fixed Assets	2m	3m	3m
Current Assets	21m	17m	15m
Current Liabilities	6m	2m	3m

Epson Telford Ltd
Hortonwood 30, Telford, TF1 7YD
Tel: 08449-410021 **Fax:** 01952-284797
E-mail: kevin.browne@epson-telford-ltd.co.uk
Website: http://www.epson.co.uk
Directors: A. Moffat (Fin), K. Browne (MD)
Managers: P. Pemberton (Tech Serv Mgr), R. Meredith
Ultimate Holding Company: SEIKO EPSON CORP (JAPAN)
Immediate Holding Company: EPSON TELFORD LIMITED
Registration no: 02090005 **Date established:** 1987
Turnover: £50m - £75m **No.of Employees:** 501 - 1000
Product Groups: 44

Date of Accounts	Mar 11	Mar 10	Mar 09
Sales Turnover	51m	49m	45m
Pre Tax Profit/Loss	839	2m	2m
Working Capital	21m	20m	18m
Fixed Assets	15m	16m	17m
Current Assets	28m	26m	22m
Current Liabilities	2m	1m	2m

ERIKS UK (Telford Service Centre)
Unit 9 Horton Court, Telford, TF1 7GY
Tel: 01952-606696 **Fax:** 01952-670333
E-mail: telford@eriks.co.uk
Website: http://www.eriks.co.uk
Managers: G. Dalton (District Mgr)
Immediate Holding Company: WYKO HOLDINGS LTD
Registration no: 00917112 **No.of Employees:** 1 - 10 **Product Groups:** 48

Evershed Robotics Ltd
Unit D1 Hortonwood 10, Telford, TF1 7ES
Tel: 01952-608020 **Fax:** 01952-608388
E-mail: les@evershedrobotics.com
Website: http://www.evershedrobotics.com
Directors: L. Clarke (MD)
Immediate Holding Company: EVERSHED ROBOTICS LIMITED
Registration no: NI029014 **VAT No.:** GB 617 5273 37
Date established: 1994 **Turnover:** £500,000 - £1m
No.of Employees: 1 - 10 **Product Groups:** 45

Date of Accounts	Sep 11	Sep 10	Sep 09
Working Capital	74	49	31
Current Assets	382	245	312

Flexi Plan Partitions Ltd
Unit J1 Halesfield 19, Telford, TF7 4QT
Tel: 01952-586126 **Fax:** 01952-581174
E-mail: flexplanpartitions@btopenworld.com
Directors: K. Maughan (MD)
Immediate Holding Company: FLEXI-PLAN PARTITIONS LIMITED
Registration no: 01077956 **VAT No.:** GB 160 6773 59
Date established: 1972 **Turnover:** £500,000 - £1m
No.of Employees: 1 - 10 **Product Groups:** 35, 52

Fruit Of The Loom Ltd
Fruit of The Loom House Halesfield 10, Telford, TF7 4QP
Tel: 01952-587123 **Fax:** 01952-581898
E-mail: leonard@ftlte.fruit.com
Website: http://www.fruitoftheloom.co.uk
Bank(s): ABN AMRO Bank NV
Managers: L. Marbury I I I
Ultimate Holding Company: BERKSHIRE HATHAWAY INC (USA)
Immediate Holding Company: FRUIT OF THE LOOM INVESTMENTS LIMITED
Registration no: 02459406 **VAT No.:** GB 549 4058 21
Date established: 1990 **Turnover:** £50m - £75m
No.of Employees: 51 - 100 **Product Groups:** 24

Date of Accounts	Dec 11	Dec 10	Dec 09
Pre Tax Profit/Loss	17m	-208	-120
Working Capital	-2m	-2m	-2m
Fixed Assets	8m	8m	8m

G E M Engineering Services
Unit B9 Tweedale Industrial Estate Madeley, Telford, TF7 4JR
Tel: 01952-588525 **Fax:** 01952-588525
Directors: G. Murrell (Prop)
Date established: 1976 **Turnover:** Up to £250,000
No.of Employees: 1 - 10 **Product Groups:** 48

G K N Auto Structure Ltd
PO Box 20, Telford, TF1 6RE
Tel: 01952-244321 **Fax:** 01952-428131
Website: http://www.gkn.com
Bank(s): Barclays
Directors: N. Williams (MD), W. Hoey (Fin), D. Short (Pers)
Ultimate Holding Company: GKN PLC
Immediate Holding Company: GKN AUTOSTRUCTURES LIMITED
Registration no: 00600230 **VAT No.:** GB 100 3286 30
Date established: 1958 **Turnover:** £50m - £75m
No.of Employees: 501 - 1000 **Product Groups:** 37, 39, 45, 48

Date of Accounts	Dec 11	Dec 10	Dec 09
Sales Turnover	60m	52m	39m
Pre Tax Profit/Loss	3m	-3m	-8m
Working Capital	31m	14m	16m
Fixed Assets	4m	3m	3m
Current Assets	51m	28m	27m
Current Liabilities	5m	4m	3m

Gefran UK
7 Pearson Road Central Park, Telford, TF2 9TX
Tel: 01952-291361 **Fax:** 08452-604556
E-mail: mark@gefran.co.uk
Website: http://www.gefran.co.uk
Directors: M. Macdonell (Dir), R. Barron (Co Sec)
Managers: M. McDonal (Chief Mgr)
Ultimate Holding Company: FP042030
Immediate Holding Company: GEFRAN UK LIMITED
Registration no: 03494468 **Date established:** 1998
Turnover: £500,000 - £1m **No.of Employees:** 1 - 10 **Product Groups:** 37, 38, 44, 84

Date of Accounts	Dec 09	Dec 08	Dec 07
Working Capital	-2m	-995	-57
Fixed Assets	238	267	27
Current Assets	962	619	834

Gibson Greetings International Ltd
Gibson House Hortonwood 30, Telford, TF1 7YF
Tel: 01952-608333 **Fax:** 01952-608363
Website: http://www.gibson-greetings.co.uk
Bank(s): The Royal Bank of Scotland
Directors: A. Paterson (Sales), C. Miles (MD), K. Vaux (Dir), V. Jackson (Pers)
Ultimate Holding Company: Gibson Greetings Inc, Cincinnati, Ohio 45237, USA
Immediate Holding Company: GIBSON GREETINGS INTERNATIONAL LIMITED
Registration no: FC016299 **VAT No.:** GB 528 7592 06
Date established: 1991 **Turnover:** £20m - £50m
No.of Employees: 101 - 250 **Product Groups:** 27

Gilgen Door Systems Ltd
Halesfield 4, Telford, TF7 4AP
Tel: 08700-005235 **Fax:** 0870-000 5234
E-mail: info@gilgendoorsystems.co.uk
Website: http://www.gilgendoorsystems.co.uk
Bank(s): National Westminster
Managers: G. Davies, H. Kaur, N. Hamer (Fin Mgr), H. Jones (Mktg Serv Mgr)
Ultimate Holding Company: KABA HOLDING AG (SWITZERLAND)
Immediate Holding Company: GILGEN DOOR SYSTEMS UK LIMITED
Registration no: 03762371 **VAT No.:** GB 736 6734 06
Date established: 1999 **Turnover:** £10m - £20m
No.of Employees: 51 - 100 **Product Groups:** 25

Date of Accounts	Dec 11	Jun 10	Jun 09
Sales Turnover	21m	17m	21m
Pre Tax Profit/Loss	-2m	-779	-424
Working Capital	378	1m	2m
Fixed Assets	353	406	607
Current Assets	5m	5m	6m
Current Liabilities	1m	2m	2m

Gra-Bern Electrical
Unit 26 Tweedale Court, Madeley, Telford, TF7 4JZ
Tel: 01952-586038 **Fax:** 01952-583365
E-mail: enquiries@gra-bern.co.uk
Website: http://www.gra-bern.co.uk
Directors: G. Brown (Ptnr)
Registration no: 02046716 **VAT No.:** GB 289 4164 18
Turnover: £500,000 - £1m **No.of Employees:** 11 - 20 **Product Groups:** 52

Grange Fencing Ltd
Halesfield 21, Telford, TF7 4PA
Tel: 01952-586460 **Fax:** 01952-684461
E-mail: sales@grangefen.co.uk
Website: http://www.grangefen.co.uk
Directors: S. Drake (Fin)
Managers: A. Barrett (Sales Prom Mgr), C. Baugh, D. Edwards (Tech Serv Mgr), B. Main (Mktg Serv Mgr), L. Cleaver
Ultimate Holding Company: GEORGE HILL HOLDINGS LIMITED
Immediate Holding Company: GRANGE FENCING ERECTORS LIMITED
Registration no: 01109071 **Date established:** 1973
Turnover: £20m - £50m **No.of Employees:** 51 - 100 **Product Groups:** 25, 35

Date of Accounts	Sep 11	Sep 10	Sep 09
Working Capital	1	1	1
Current Assets	1	1	1

Hager Engineering Ltd
50 Horton Wood, Telford, TF1 7FT
Tel: 01952-677899 **Fax:** 01952-676935
E-mail: info@hager.co.uk
Website: http://www.hager.com
Bank(s): National Westminster Bank Plc
Directors: M. Herre (MD), K. Overmass (Dir), P. Hird (Sales), P. Davies (MD), K. Jones (Dir), C. Leak (Fin), B. Davies (MD)
Managers: P. Oliver (Commun Mgr), N. Smith (Mktg Serv Mgr), P. Pickerill (I.T. Exec), M. Newton (Sales Prom Mgr), M. Edwards (Purch Mgr)
Ultimate Holding Company: HAGER INVESTMENT SA (LUXEMBOURG)
Immediate Holding Company: HAGER ENGINEERING LIMITED
Registration no: 02777167 **VAT No.:** GB 357 4762 23
Date established: 1993 **Turnover:** £10m - £20m
No.of Employees: 101 - 250 **Product Groups:** 30, 37, 40, 49, 67

Date of Accounts	Dec 09	Dec 08	Dec 07
Sales Turnover	34m	38m	37m
Pre Tax Profit/Loss	965	1m	398
Working Capital	841	-293	-2m
Fixed Assets	3m	4m	4m
Current Assets	20m	18m	14m
Current Liabilities	5m	6m	5m

Hexagon Metrology Hexagon AB
Halesfield 13, Telford, TF7 4PL
Tel: 01952-681300 **Fax:** 01952-681311
E-mail: peter.freer@hexagonmetrology.com
Website: http://www.hexmet.co.uk
Bank(s): Lloyds TSB Bank plc
Directors: P. Freer (Dir)
Managers: J. Drover (Sales Prom Mgr), N. Ward (Tech Serv Mgr), P. Heighway (Sales Admin), S. Bagri (Comptroller)

see next page

Hexagon Metrology Hexagon AB - Cont'd

Ultimate Holding Company: HEXAGON AB (SWEDEN)
Immediate Holding Company: HEXAGON METROLOGY LIMITED
Registration no: 01523574 **VAT No.:** GB 351 6877 32
Date established: 1980 **Turnover:** £10m - £20m
No.of Employees: 51 - 100 **Product Groups:** 38

Date of Accounts	Dec 11	Dec 10	Dec 09
Sales Turnover	16m	13m	11m
Pre Tax Profit/Loss	-151	410	430
Working Capital	2m	2m	2m
Fixed Assets	3m	2m	2m
Current Assets	11m	8m	5m
Current Liabilities	2m	2m	1m

Hi Tech Access Covers Ltd

Walcot, Telford, TF6 5ER
Tel: 01952-740222 **Fax:** 01952-740331
E-mail: sales@htacovers.co.uk
Website: http://www.wrekinfabs.co.uk
Directors: S. Reynolds (MD), L. Walker (Co Sec)
Ultimate Holding Company: HILAN ENGINEERING LIMITED
Immediate Holding Company: HI TECH ACCESS COVERS LIMITED
Registration no: 03130910 **Date established:** 1995
No.of Employees: 21 - 50 **Product Groups:** 35

Date of Accounts	Nov 08	Sep 11	Sep 10
Working Capital	41	96	-32
Fixed Assets	62	39	44
Current Assets	322	422	305

Hitherbest Ltd

Heath Hill Court Heath Hill Industrial Estate, Dawley, Telford, TF4 2RH
Tel: 01952-632100 **Fax:** 01952-632109
E-mail: fredr@hitherbest.uk.com
Website: http://www.hitherbest.co.uk
Bank(s): Lloyds TSB Bank plc
Directors: L. Williams (Fin), L. Slattery (Co Sec), C. Evans (MD)
Managers: F. Richards, I. Davidson (Sales Prom Mgr)
Immediate Holding Company: HITHERBEST LIMITED
Registration no: 01923890 **VAT No.:** GB 433 9288 30
Date established: 1985 **Turnover:** £2m - £5m **No.of Employees:** 21 - 50
Product Groups: 48

Date of Accounts	Jan 12	Jan 11	Jan 10
Working Capital	759	541	366
Fixed Assets	811	931	971
Current Assets	1m	873	649

Horton Automatics Ltd

Unit A Hortonwood 31, Telford, TF1 7YZ
Tel: 01952-670169 **Fax:** 01952-670181
E-mail: sales@horton-automatics.ltd.uk
Website: http://www.horton-automatics.ltd.uk
Bank(s): Barclays, Telford
Directors: T. O'Keeffe (Sales), C. Gaite (Chief Op Offcr)
Managers: J. Kelly (Buyer), M. Hickman (Fin Mgr)
Ultimate Holding Company: SANWA SHUTTER CORP (JAPAN)
Immediate Holding Company: HORTON AUTOMATICS LIMITED
Registration no: 02324269 **VAT No.:** GB 489 1980 84
Date established: 1988 **Turnover:** £2m - £5m **No.of Employees:** 21 - 50
Product Groups: 35

Date of Accounts	Dec 11	Dec 10	Dec 09
Sales Turnover	4m	4m	4m
Pre Tax Profit/Loss	460	612	170
Working Capital	3m	2m	2m
Fixed Assets	57	46	41
Current Assets	4m	3m	2m
Current Liabilities	383	358	291

House Commercial & Industrial ACCESS EQUIPMENT OPERATOR SERVICES

The Rock, Telford, TF3 5DE
Tel: 01952-503860
E-mail: enquiries@accessoperator.co.uk
Website: http://www.accessoperator.co.uk
No.of Employees: 1 - 10 **Product Groups:** 45, 67, 83

Hymix Ltd

Unit C10-C11 Stafford Park 11, Telford, TF3 3AY
Tel: 01952-200900 **Fax:** 01952-200901
E-mail: mail@hymix.com
Website: http://www.hymix.com
Directors: N. Humpish (MD), K. Humpish (Co Sec)
Managers: D. Weaving (Mats Contrlr), C. Humpish (Personnel)
Ultimate Holding Company: HYMIX HOLDINGS LIMITED
Immediate Holding Company: HYMIX LIMITED
Registration no: 02061079 **VAT No.:** GB 499 6494 61
Date established: 1986 **Turnover:** £2m - £5m **No.of Employees:** 21 - 50
Product Groups: 45

Date of Accounts	Nov 10	Nov 09	Nov 08
Working Capital	45	41	14
Current Assets	561	202	124

I C International

Gower Street Trading Estate St Georges, Telford, TF2 9HW
Tel: 01952-620206 **Fax:** 01952-620456
E-mail: sales@ic-international.com
Website: http://www.ic-international.com
Bank(s): Lloyds TSB Bank plc
Directors: M. Illman (MD)
Immediate Holding Company: I C INTERNATIONAL LIMITED
Registration no: 02606715 **VAT No.:** GB 549 7432 08
Date established: 1991 **Turnover:** £1m - £2m **No.of Employees:** 21 - 50
Product Groups: 23, 24, 30, 33, 39, 40, 46, 66

Date of Accounts	Dec 11	Dec 10	Dec 09
Working Capital	-92	-44	-82
Fixed Assets	94	97	92
Current Assets	79	143	90

Industrial Bearings Ltd

Orleton Lane Wellington, Telford, TF1 2BG
Tel: 01952-222100 **Fax:** 01952-244121
Website: http://www.nbcgroup.co.uk
Directors: J. Thornton (MD)
Immediate Holding Company: Campion Holdings Ltd
Registration no: 00807250 **Date established:** 1964
No.of Employees: 51 - 100 **Product Groups:** 35, 67

Interspiro Ltd

7 Hawksworth Road Central Park, Telford, TF2 9TU
Tel: 01952-200190 **Fax:** 01952-299805
E-mail: infouk@interspiro.com
Website: http://www.interspiro.com/uk
Bank(s): HSBC, Princes & Poultry St, London
Directors: T. Evans (Fin)
Managers: W. Shillam (Sales Prom Mgr)
Ultimate Holding Company: OCENCO INC (USA)
Immediate Holding Company: INTERSPIRO LIMITED
Registration no: 01194705 **VAT No.:** GB 224 1308 10
Date established: 1974 **Turnover:** £2m - £5m **No.of Employees:** 11 - 20
Product Groups: 24, 35, 40, 86

Date of Accounts	Aug 11	Aug 10	Aug 09
Working Capital	501	447	157
Fixed Assets	11	13	22
Current Assets	854	891	918

Jardine Leisure

Dale End Coalbrookdale, Telford, TF8 7DS
Tel: 01952-432908 **Fax:** 01952-432909
E-mail: info@jardineleisure.co.uk
Website: http://www.jardineleisure.co.uk
Directors: B. Smith (Ptnr), B. Smith (Prop), M. Robinson (Ptnr)
Immediate Holding Company: JARDINE LEISURE LTD
Registration no: 05632286 **VAT No.:** GB 467 8797 66
Date established: 2005 **Turnover:** £1m - £2m **No.of Employees:** 1 - 10
Product Groups: 26

Jewson Ltd

Stafford Park 13, Telford, TF3 3AZ
Tel: 01952-290841 **Fax:** 01952-291092
Website: http://www.jewson.co.uk
Managers: M. Hoult (Mgr)
Ultimate Holding Company: COMPAGNIE DE SAINT GOBAIN (FRANCE)
Immediate Holding Company: JEWSON LIMITED
Registration no: 00348407 **Date established:** 1939
Turnover: £500m - £1,000m **No.of Employees:** 11 - 20
Product Groups: 66

Date of Accounts	Dec 11	Dec 10	Dec 09
Sales Turnover	1606m	1547m	1485m
Pre Tax Profit/Loss	18m	100m	45m
Working Capital	-345m	-250m	-349m
Fixed Assets	496m	387m	461m
Current Assets	657m	1005m	1320m
Current Liabilities	66m	120m	64m

Joseph Ash Galvanising

Stafford Park 6, Telford, TF3 3AT
Tel: 01952-290201 **Fax:** 01952-290113
E-mail: grahamm@josephash.co.uk
Website: http://www.josephash.co.uk
Managers: D. Hanson (Chief Mgr)
Immediate Holding Company: ENTAMEDIA LIMITED
Registration no: 05959142 **Date established:** 2003
Turnover: £75m - £125m **No.of Employees:** 21 - 50 **Product Groups:** 48

Date of Accounts	Oct 11	Oct 10	Oct 09
Sales Turnover	113m	99m	84m
Pre Tax Profit/Loss	509	408	370
Working Capital	3m	3m	3m
Fixed Assets	2m	3m	3m
Current Assets	21m	17m	15m
Current Liabilities	6m	2m	3m

K N Wheels Ltd

Beverley Road Off Holyhead Road, Ketley, Telford, TF1 5DS
Tel: 01952-614402 **Fax:** 01952-613757
E-mail: sales@knwheels.co.uk
Website: http://www.knwheels.co.uk
Bank(s): HSBC Bank plc
Directors: C. Brown (Fab), D. Belt (MD), G. Powick (Sales), J. Brown (Dir), R. Brown (Dir)
Immediate Holding Company: KN Wheels Ltd
Registration no: 00680243 **VAT No.:** GB 100 4475 22
Date established: 1961 **Turnover:** £2m - £5m **No.of Employees:** 21 - 50
Product Groups: 39

Date of Accounts	Mar 08	Mar 07	Mar 06
Working Capital	106	93	138
Fixed Assets	453	456	414
Current Assets	684	745	779
Current Liabilities	578	652	641

Kaba Door Systems

Halesfield 4, Telford, TF7 4AP
Tel: 08700-005235 **Fax:** 01952-682101
E-mail: marketing@kcb.kaba.com
Website: http://www.kaba.co.uk
Directors: A. Starkey (Chief Op Offcr), P. Faerber (MD), P. Andrews (Fin), K. Way (Sales & Mktg), K. Wearing (Sales), D. Ratcliffe (Co Sec)
Managers: D. Kerry (Mktg Serv Mgr)
Ultimate Holding Company: KABA HOLDING AG (SWITZERLAND)
Immediate Holding Company: GILGEN DOOR SYSTEMS UK LIMITED
Registration no: 03762371 **VAT No.:** GB 158 2370 60
Date established: 1999 **Turnover:** £10m - £20m **No.of Employees:** 1 - 10
Product Groups: 25, 33, 35, 36, 48, 52, 66

Date of Accounts	Jun 09	Jun 08	Jun 07
Sales Turnover	21m	25m	24m
Pre Tax Profit/Loss	-424	-325	-36
Working Capital	2m	3m	3m
Fixed Assets	607	825	887
Current Assets	6m	8m	9m
Current Liabilities	2m	2m	2m

Kendall Electrical Services Telford Ltd

Stafford Park 6, Telford, TF3 3AT
Tel: 01952-290830 **Fax:** 01952-291027
E-mail: sales@kendall-group.co.uk
Website: http://www.kendall-group.co.uk
Bank(s): Lloyds TSB Bank plc
Directors: K. Kendall (MD), M. Kendall (Fin)
Immediate Holding Company: KENDALL ELECTRICAL SERVICES (TELFORD) LIMITED
Registration no: 00980214 **VAT No.:** GB 594 1754 11
Date established: 1970 **Turnover:** £1m - £2m **No.of Employees:** 21 - 50
Product Groups: 52

Date of Accounts	Dec 10	Dec 09	Dec 08
Working Capital	-314	-213	-141
Fixed Assets	480	480	405
Current Assets	153	300	466

G Leddington Electrical Ltd

15 Church Parade, Telford, TF2 6EX
Tel: 01952-615958 **Fax:** 01952-620473
E-mail: info@leddingtons.co.uk
Directors: G. Leddington (MD)
Immediate Holding Company: G. LEDDINGTON (ELECTRICAL) LIMITED
Registration no: 01564475 **VAT No.:** GB 161 8391 57
Date established: 1981 **Turnover:** £250,000 - £500,000
No.of Employees: 1 - 10 **Product Groups:** 52

Date of Accounts	Jul 11	Jul 10	Jul 09
Working Capital	90	122	105
Fixed Assets	1	14	28
Current Assets	152	278	231

Lewis & Mason Plastics

Unit 10 Stafford Park 12, Telford, TF3 3BJ
Tel: 01952-210322 **Fax:** 01952-292647
E-mail: sales@airsystemcontrols.co.uk
Website: http://www.lewis-mason-plastics.co.uk
Directors: W. Cooper (MD)
Registration no: 03509855 **Turnover:** £250,000 - £500,000
No.of Employees: 1 - 10 **Product Groups:** 30

Link 51 Ltd

Link House Halesfield 6, Telford, TF7 4LN
Tel: 01952-682251 **Fax:** 01952-682452
E-mail: services@wagon-storage.com
Website: http://www.link51.co.uk
Directors: K. Stapleford (Fin)
Immediate Holding Company: LINK 51 LIMITED
Registration no: 04440478 **Date established:** 2002
Turnover: £50m - £75m **No.of Employees:** 251 - 500
Product Groups: 26, 30, 35, 36, 49, 67

Link Lockers

Link House Halesfield 6, Telford, TF7 4LN
Tel: 0800-073 0300 **Fax:** 01952-684312
E-mail: sales@linklockers.co.uk
Website: http://www.linklockers.co.uk
Directors: S. Woodhouse (MD), S. Johnson (MD), J. Decae (Sales), G. Notley (MD), C. O"connor (MD)
Managers: P. Jackson (Mktg Serv Mgr), J. Robinson (Buyer), P. Jackson (Sales & Mktg Mg), K. Acock, A. Rowe (Fin Mgr), K. Acock (Personnel)
Ultimate Holding Company: WHITTAN SCOTTISH LIMITED PARTNERSHIP (UK)
Immediate Holding Company: WHITTAN GROUP LIMITED
Registration no: 04436871 **Date established:** 2005
Turnover: £125m - £250m **No.of Employees:** 101 - 250
Product Groups: 26, 35, 36, 49

Date of Accounts	Mar 11	Mar 10	Mar 09
Pre Tax Profit/Loss	-26	-607	-41
Working Capital	21m	16m	18m
Fixed Assets	16m	16m	16m
Current Assets	22m	18m	19m
Current Liabilities	848	644	688

Lissan Harper International Ltd

Unit B4 Stafford Park 4, Telford, TF3 3BA
Tel: 01952-292408 **Fax:** 01952-292419
E-mail: info@lissan-harper.co.uk
Website: http://www.lissanharper.co.uk
Bank(s): National Westminster Bank Plc
Directors: N. Kapur (Dir)
Immediate Holding Company: LISSAN HARPER INTERNATIONAL LIMITED
Registration no: 04366321 **VAT No.:** GB 791 1230 47
Date established: 2002 **Turnover:** £2m - £5m **No.of Employees:** 11 - 20
Product Groups: 22

Date of Accounts	May 11	May 10	May 09
Working Capital	2m	2m	1m
Fixed Assets	87	64	203
Current Assets	2m	2m	2m

Logitech Electronics Ltd

121 Trench Road Trench, Telford, TF2 7DP
Tel: 01952-677416 **Fax:** 01952-605857
E-mail: sales@logitechelectronics.co.uk
Website: http://www.logitechelectronics.co.uk
Managers: H. Pickering (Sales Prom Mgr)
Immediate Holding Company: LOGITECH ELECTRONICS HOLDINGS LIMITED
Registration no: 07713159 **VAT No.:** GB 433 9152 55
Date established: 2011 **Turnover:** £500,000 - £1m
No.of Employees: 1 - 10 **Product Groups:** 37, 38, 39, 40, 45, 67, 84

Date of Accounts	Mar 10	Mar 09	Mar 08
Working Capital	746	759	654
Fixed Assets	485	485	485
Current Assets	862	901	784

Lyndex Recycling Ltd

Stafford Park 10, Telford, TF3 3BP
Tel: 01952-290333 **Fax:** 01952-290229
E-mail: info@lyndexrecycling.com
Website: http://www.lyndexrecycling.com
Directors: B. Carson (Dir)
Immediate Holding Company: LYNDEX RECYCLING SYSTEMS LIMITED
Registration no: 05488915 **VAT No.:** GB 377 8011 34
Date established: 2005 **Turnover:** £5m - £10m **No.of Employees:** 1 - 10
Product Groups: 46

Date of Accounts	Jun 11	Jun 10	Jun 09
Working Capital	678	642	524
Fixed Assets	75	74	76
Current Assets	3m	2m	2m

Lyreco UK Ltd

Unit 5 Deer Park Court, Donnington Wood, Telford, TF2 7NB
Tel: 01952-293000 **Fax:** 08450-762698
E-mail: info@lyreco.com
Website: http://www.lyreco.co.uk
Bank(s): Barclays
Directors: D. Full (Fin), C. Chater (Sales)
Managers: S. Renton (Personnel), J. Mason (Tech Serv Mgr), D. Cowley, C. Gibbons, C. Keane (Mktg Serv Mgr)
Ultimate Holding Company: LYRECO SA (FRANCE)
Immediate Holding Company: LYRECO UK LIMITED
Registration no: 00442696 **Date established:** 1947
Turnover: £250m - £500m **No.of Employees:** 501 - 1000
Product Groups: 27

Date of Accounts	Dec 11	Dec 10	Dec 09
Sales Turnover	255m	277m	300m
Pre Tax Profit/Loss	15m	16m	16m

Working Capital	62m	81m	69m
Fixed Assets	17m	18m	18m
Current Assets	103m	129m	119m
Current Liabilities	7m	8m	9m

M P I Ltd

Suite 1 Syer House Stafford Court, Telford, TF3 3BD
Tel: 01952-290862 **Fax:** 01952-290864
E-mail: info@mpiltd.co.uk
Website: http://www.mpi.ltd.uk
Directors: J. Herbert (Sales)
Ultimate Holding Company: M.P.I. (HERTS) LIMITED
Immediate Holding Company: M.P.I. LIMITED
Registration no: 02746209 **Date established:** 1992
No.of Employees: 1 - 10 **Product Groups:** 80

Date of Accounts	Sep 11	Sep 10	Sep 09
Sales Turnover	21m	19m	21m
Pre Tax Profit/Loss	313	402	1m
Working Capital	2m	2m	1m
Fixed Assets	759	827	902
Current Assets	6m	5m	5m
Current Liabilities	889	603	1m

Magiboards Ltd

Unit F Stafford Park 12, Telford, TF3 3BJ
Tel: 01952-292111 **Fax:** 01952-292280
E-mail: sales@magiboards.com
Website: http://www.magiboards.com
Bank(s): Barclays
Managers: J. Horton (Chief Mgr)
Immediate Holding Company: MAGIBOARDS LIMITED
Registration no: 05534989 **VAT No.:** GB 594 2542 21
Date established: 2005 **Turnover:** £1m - £2m **No.of Employees:** 11 - 20
Product Groups: 26, 28, 38, 49

Date of Accounts	Dec 11	Dec 10	Dec 09
Working Capital	-34	-58	-1
Fixed Assets	16	42	55
Current Assets	262	244	314

Magna's Specialist Confectioners

Magna House Stafford Park 3, Telford, TF3 3BH
Tel: 01952-290952 **Fax:** 01952-290380
E-mail: pmchale@magna.co.uk
Website: http://www.magna.co.uk
Bank(s): Barclays
Directors: P. McHale (MD), A. Mchale (Fin)
Managers: B. Clay, L. Cullen (Mktg Serv Mgr), L. Cullen (Mktg Serv Mgr), N. Davey (Tech Serv Mgr), F. Hamer, F. Hamer (Personnel), J. Christain (Purch Mgr)
Immediate Holding Company: MAGNA SPECIALIST CONFECTIONERS LIMITED
Registration no: 01050340 **VAT No.:** GB 159 2362 53
Date established: 1972 **Turnover:** £20m - £50m
No.of Employees: 101 - 250 **Product Groups:** 20

Date of Accounts	Apr 11	Apr 09	Apr 09
Sales Turnover	49m	43m	43m
Pre Tax Profit/Loss	64	758	758
Working Capital	3m	-192	-192
Fixed Assets	15m	13m	13m
Current Assets	9m	5m	5m
Current Liabilities	3m	2m	2m

Making Computers Easy I.T - Visulizing

Unit 38 Abbeyfields, Randlay, Telford, TF3 - 2AL
Tel: 07765-061174 **Fax:** 07765-061174
E-mail: making.computers.easy.it.visual@googlemail.com
Website: http://itvisualmakingcomputerseasy.synthasite.com/
Directors: K. Gray (MD)
Date established: 1998 **No.of Employees:** 1 - 10 **Product Groups:** 44, 86

Makita Manufacturing Europe Ltd

Hortonwood 7, Telford, TF1 7YX
Tel: 01952-677688 **Fax:** 01952-677678
E-mail: sales@mmemakita.com
Website: http://www.mmemakita.com
Directors: P. Harris (MD), M. Cope (Fin)
Managers: R. Annett (Personnel)
Ultimate Holding Company: MAKITA CORPORATION (JAPAN)
Immediate Holding Company: MAKITA MANUFACTURING EUROPE LIMITED
Registration no: 02427964 **VAT No.:** GB 549 4401 34
Date established: 1989 **Turnover:** £50m - £75m
No.of Employees: 501 - 1000 **Product Groups:** 37

Date of Accounts	Mar 12	Mar 11	Mar 10
Sales Turnover	112m	71m	45m
Pre Tax Profit/Loss	6m	855	2m
Working Capital	60m	56m	56m
Fixed Assets	10m	10m	10m
Current Assets	73m	71m	63m
Current Liabilities	3m	2m	1m

Maxell Europe Ltd (Maxell Europe Ltd)

Apley, Telford, TF1 6DA
Tel: 01952-522222 **Fax:** 01952-522391
E-mail: warnerc@eu.maxell.com
Website: http://www.maxell.eu
Managers: H. Bailey (Buyer), A. Broad (Tech Serv Mgr), D. Phillips (Develop Mgr), I. Jaimeson (Personnel), S. Shagauchi (Mgr)
Ultimate Holding Company: HITACHI LTD (JAPAN)
Immediate Holding Company: MAXELL EUROPE LIMITED
Registration no: 01485997 **VAT No.:** GB 245 7047 59
Date established: 1980 **Turnover:** £125m - £250m
No.of Employees: 51 - 100 **Product Groups:** 44, 89

Date of Accounts	Mar 11	Mar 10	Mar 09
Sales Turnover	119m	122m	122m
Pre Tax Profit/Loss	-9m	-2m	1m
Working Capital	28m	27m	37m
Fixed Assets	4m	4m	6m
Current Assets	59m	61m	70m
Current Liabilities	3m	4m	13m

Mercian Lifting Gear UK Ltd

15 Trench Lock 3 Sommerfeld Road, Telford, TF1 5ST
Tel: 01952-261851 **Fax:** 01952-222028
Website: http://www.mercian.co.uk
Managers: T. Bailey (Mgr)
Immediate Holding Company: MERCIAN LIFTING GEAR (UK) LIMITED
Registration no: 02774600 **Date established:** 1992
No.of Employees: 1 - 10 **Product Groups:** 35, 39, 45

Date of Accounts	Feb 12	Feb 11	Feb 10
Working Capital	167	122	250
Fixed Assets	61	76	133
Current Assets	332	269	391

Merrythought Ltd

Merrythought Village Dale End, Coalbrookdale, Telford, TF8 7NJ
Tel: 01952-433116 **Fax:** 01952-432054
E-mail: contact@merrythought.co.uk
Website: http://www.merrythought.co.uk
Bank(s): Barclays
Directors: S. Holmes (Dir)
Managers: J. Hall-gough
Immediate Holding Company: MERRYTHOUGHT TOYS LIMITED
Registration no: 05978427 **VAT No.:** GB 161 5806 69
Date established: 2006 **Turnover:** £2m - £5m **No.of Employees:** 21 - 50
Product Groups: 49, 65

Midland Alloy Windows Co. Ltd

Stafford Park 17, Telford, TF3 3DG
Tel: 01952-290961 **Fax:** 01952-290441
E-mail: info@midlandalloy.com
Website: http://www.midlandalloy.com
Bank(s): National Westminster Bank Plc
Directors: P. Beirne (Dir)
Ultimate Holding Company: MIDLAND ALLOY HOLDINGS LIMITED
Immediate Holding Company: MIDLAND ALLOY LIMITED
Registration no: 02674601 **VAT No.:** GB 594 0422 41
Date established: 1992 **Turnover:** £1m - £2m **No.of Employees:** 21 - 50
Product Groups: 33, 34, 35, 36, 37, 39, 44, 48, 49

Date of Accounts	Dec 11	Dec 10	Dec 09
Working Capital	442	476	203
Fixed Assets	74	94	153
Current Assets	1m	847	534

Midland Computers Ltd

Unit 4 Sovereign Park Halesfield 24, Telford, TF7 4NZ
Tel: 01952-588688 **Fax:** 01952-588555
E-mail: sales@midlandcomputers.com
Website: http://www.midlandcomputers.com
Directors: C. Bickerton (MD), K. Bickerton (Fin), H. Corcoran (Sales)
Managers: N. Dodd (Sales Prom Mgr), A. Davies, I. Cox (Eng Serv Mgr)
Immediate Holding Company: MIDLAND COMPUTERS LTD.
Registration no: 03857880 **Date established:** 1999 **Turnover:** £5m - £10m
No.of Employees: 21 - 50 **Product Groups:** 44, 67

Date of Accounts	Sep 11	Sep 10	Sep 09
Working Capital	810	666	615
Fixed Assets	119	154	165
Current Assets	1m	868	886

Mobile Base Co Shropshire Ltd

Unit E1 Stafford Park 15, Telford, TF3 3BB
Tel: 01952-200018 **Fax:** 01952-291119
Directors: G. Sabin (Dir)
Immediate Holding Company: THE MOBILE BASE COMPANY (SHROPSHIRE) LIMITED
Registration no: 02803133 **VAT No.:** GB 594 3902 12
Date established: 1993 **Turnover:** Up to £250,000
No.of Employees: 1 - 10 **Product Groups:** 26

Date of Accounts	Mar 11	Mar 10	Mar 09
Working Capital	281	278	305
Fixed Assets	16	21	13
Current Assets	295	292	347

MOCAP Ltd

Hortonwood 35, Telford, TF1 7YW
Tel: 01952-670247 **Fax:** 01952-670241
E-mail: sales@mocap.co.uk
Website: http://www.mocap.com
Bank(s): The Royal Bank of Scotland
Managers: T. Grigg
Ultimate Holding Company: PACOM LLC (USA)
Immediate Holding Company: PACOM LIMITED
Registration no: 02182694 **VAT No.:** GB 478 8756 67
Date established: 1987 **No.of Employees:** 51 - 100 **Product Groups:** 27, 28, 29, 30, 38, 40, 46, 48, 66

Date of Accounts	Dec 11	Dec 10	Dec 09
Working Capital	740	86	113
Fixed Assets	1m	1m	1m
Current Assets	2m	737	692

Moresecure Ltd

PO Box 34, Telford, TF7 4EH
Tel: 01952-683900 **Fax:** 01952-683982
E-mail: sales@moresecureint.co.uk
Website: http://www.moresecureint.com
Bank(s): National Westminster
Directors: C. O'connor (MD)
Managers: M. Butcher (Personnel), M. Butcher (Personnel), K. Pressel (Fin Mgr), K. Pressel (Fin Mgr), S. Johnson (I.T. Exec)
Immediate Holding Company: MORE SECURE LIMITED
Registration no: 05977038 **Date established:** 2006
Turnover: £10m - £20m **No.of Employees:** 21 - 50 **Product Groups:** 26, 49

Date of Accounts	Mar 11	Mar 10	Mar 09
Working Capital	66	-20	-19
Fixed Assets	4	1	1
Current Assets	214	62	56

Motivation Traffic Control Ltd

Unit 5 Horton Court Hortonwood 50, Telford, TF1 7XZ
Tel: 01952-670390 **Fax:** 01952-670379
E-mail: info@motivation-tc.co.uk
Website: http://www.motivation-tc.co.uk
Directors: A. Jaques (Co Sec), D. Perkins (Dir)
Ultimate Holding Company: ASSA ABLOY AB (PUBL) (SWEDEN)
Immediate Holding Company: MOTIVATION (TRAFFIC CONTROL) LIMITED
Registration no: 02242049 **VAT No.:** GB 494 0601 49
Date established: 1988 **Turnover:** £250,000 - £500,000
No.of Employees: 1 - 10 **Product Groups:** 35, 39, 40, 49, 51, 52

Date of Accounts	Dec 11	Dec 10	Dec 09
Sales Turnover	508	420	503
Pre Tax Profit/Loss	58	-13	28
Working Capital	740	722	731
Fixed Assets	3	3	4
Current Assets	970	939	929
Current Liabilities	188	171	42

N B C Group Ltd

Crown Works Orleton Lane, Wellington, Telford, TF1 2BG
Tel: 01952-222300 **Fax:** 01952-641325
E-mail: enquiries.kell04@nbcgroup.co.uk
Website: http://www.nbcgroup.co.uk
Bank(s): Lloyds TSB Bank plc
Managers: K. Read (Chief Mgr), D. Lowe (Purch Mgr), B. Horne (Comptroller), L. Milton
Ultimate Holding Company: CAMPION HOLDINGS LIMITED
Immediate Holding Company: NBC GROUP LIMITED
Registration no: 01373154 **VAT No.:** GB 304 6860 66
Date established: 1978 **Turnover:** £5m - £10m **No.of Employees:** 21 - 50
Product Groups: 35, 36

Date of Accounts	Jul 11	Jul 10	Jul 09
Sales Turnover	9m	8m	8m
Pre Tax Profit/Loss	588	12	-398
Working Capital	4m	4m	4m
Fixed Assets	446	449	473
Current Assets	7m	6m	6m
Current Liabilities	2m	2m	1m

N C S

8 Pearson Road Central Park, Telford, TF2 9TX
Tel: 01952-210243 **Fax:** 08707-267168
E-mail: david.aspinall@ncsjob.co.uk
Website: http://www.ncsjob.co.uk
Directors: D. Aspinall (MD)
Date established: 2003 **Turnover:** £5m - £10m **No.of Employees:** 1 - 10
Product Groups: 52, 80

Pelloby Engineering Ltd

Halesfield 19, Telford, TF7 4QT
Tel: 01952-586626 **Fax:** 01952-587871
E-mail: sales@pelloby.com
Website: http://www.pelloby.com
Bank(s): Lloyds TSB Bank plc
Directors: A. Casewell (Chief Op Offcr), G. Hickman (MD), S. Pinson (Fin)
Managers: S. Smith (Purch Mgr)
Immediate Holding Company: PELLOBY ENGINEERING LIMITED
Registration no: 03954513 **Date established:** 2000 **Turnover:** £2m - £5m
No.of Employees: 21 - 50 **Product Groups:** 39, 45, 48

Date of Accounts	Jul 11	Jul 10	Jul 09
Working Capital	-122	-30	-59
Current Assets	N/A	N/A	366

Pometon Ltd

5 Queensway Link Industrial Estate, Telford, TF3 3DN
Tel: 01952-299777 **Fax:** 01952-299008
E-mail: sales@pometon.demon.co.uk
Website: http://www.pometon.demon.co.uk
Directors: S. Fletcher (Co Sec)
Immediate Holding Company: POMETON LIMITED
Registration no: 03263909 **VAT No.:** GB 687 6353 82
Date established: 1996 **Turnover:** £2m - £5m **No.of Employees:** 1 - 10
Product Groups: 33, 34

Date of Accounts	Dec 11	Dec 10	Dec 09
Working Capital	655	413	315
Fixed Assets	48	29	38
Current Assets	1m	1m	1m

Pooler L M T Ltd

Lower Grounds Farm Shirlowe, Telford, TF6 6LT
Tel: 01952-770189 **Fax:** 01952-770762
E-mail: info@pooler-lmt.com
Website: http://www.pooler-lmt.com
Directors: R. Pooler (Dir)
Immediate Holding Company: POOLER-LMT LIMITED
Registration no: 03682805 **Date established:** 1998
No.of Employees: 1 - 10 **Product Groups:** 35, 39, 45

Date of Accounts	Dec 11	Dec 10	Dec 09
Working Capital	-225	-180	-106
Fixed Assets	177	194	113
Current Assets	25	16	506

Pro Vac Engineering

Unit 11 Halesfield 18, Telford, TF7 4PP
Tel: 01952-587276 **Fax:** 01952-585157
E-mail: sales@provacuum.com
Website: http://www.provacengineering.com
Directors: C. Turrell (Co Sec), N. Sutherland (MD)
Managers: C. Deakin (Mgr)
Immediate Holding Company: PRO-VACUUM LIMITED
Registration no: 06662416 **VAT No.:** 594 0083 37 **Date established:** 1982
Turnover: £500,000 - £1m **No.of Employees:** 1 - 10 **Product Groups:** 46, 48

Date of Accounts	Jun 08	Jun 07	Jun 06
Working Capital	466	257	220
Fixed Assets	15	82	91
Current Assets	586	495	438
Current Liabilities	120	238	217

Profile 22 Systems Ltd

Stafford Park 6, Telford, TF3 3AT
Tel: 01952-290910 **Fax:** 01952-290460
E-mail: mail@profile22.co.uk
Website: http://www.profile22.co.uk
Bank(s): National Westminster
Directors: R. McGlennon (Sales), D. Rigley (MD)
Managers: N. Stanley (Tech Serv Mgr), A. O'Connor (Personnel), L. Turner (Fin Mgr), A. Maybury (Purch Mgr)
Ultimate Holding Company: EPWIN GROUP LIMITED
Immediate Holding Company: PROFILE 22 SYSTEMS LIMITED
Registration no: 02467789 **Date established:** 1990
Turnover: £75m - £125m **No.of Employees:** 21 - 50 **Product Groups:** 30

Date of Accounts	Nov 10	Nov 09	Nov 08
Sales Turnover	25m	27m	24m
Pre Tax Profit/Loss	1m	690	636
Working Capital	653	-514	-2m
Fixed Assets	2m	2m	3m
Current Assets	5m	3m	6m
Current Liabilities	3m	2m	2m

Proto Precision Engineering

Unit 28 Heath Hill Industrial Estate Dawley, Telford, TF4 2RH
Tel: 01952-506227 **Fax:** 01952-506227
Directors: C. Thomas (Prop)
Date established: 1967 **Turnover:** Up to £250,000
No.of Employees: 1 - 10 **Product Groups:** 48

Ptex Supplies
11 Poplar Drive Wellington, Telford, TF1 3NG
Tel: 01952-223860 **Fax:** 01952-223860
Directors: P. Teckoe (Prop)
Date established: 1993 **No.of Employees:** 1 - 10 **Product Groups:** 35

R T I T B
Access House Halesfield 17, Telford, TF7 4PW
Tel: 01952-520200 **Fax:** 01952-520201
E-mail: laura_nelson@rtitb.co.uk
Website: http://www.rtitb.co.uk
Directors: L. Nelson (Chief Op Offcr), L. Williams (Fin), R. Hughes (Sales)
Ultimate Holding Company: CAPITB TRUST
Immediate Holding Company: RTITB LIMITED
Registration no: 03671395 **Date established:** 1998
Turnover: £500,000 - £1m **No.of Employees:** 21 - 50
Product Groups: 38, 45, 67, 86

Date of Accounts	Mar 12	Mar 11	Mar 10
Sales Turnover	N/A	731	1m
Pre Tax Profit/Loss	-25	-32	22
Working Capital	33	88	-6
Fixed Assets	1m	1m	1m
Current Assets	142	192	487
Current Liabilities	N/A	2	185

Ra'Alloy Ramps Ltd
Unit B8 Hortonwood 10, Telford, TF1 7ES
Tel: 01952-677877 **Fax:** 01952-677883
E-mail: stuart@raalloy.co.uk
Website: http://www.raalloy.co.uk
Directors: L. Corfield (Fin)
Managers: S. Reynolds (Sales Prom Mgr)
Immediate Holding Company: RA'ALLOY RAMPS LIMITED
Registration no: 06799607 **Date established:** 2009
Turnover: £250,000 - £500,000 **No.of Employees:** 1 - 10
Product Groups: 35, 39, 45

Date of Accounts	Jul 11	Jul 10	Jul 09
Working Capital	10	4	-2
Fixed Assets	63	24	11
Current Assets	333	181	67
Current Liabilities	12	N/A	N/A

Reepol C B P Ltd
Unit G4 Court Works Industrial Estate Bridgnorth Road, Madeley, Telford, TF7 4JB
Tel: 01952-588575 **Fax:** 01952-587886
E-mail: sales@reepol.com
Website: http://www.reepol.co.uk
Directors: P. Mcgarry (MD)
Immediate Holding Company: REEPOL CHEMICAL BUILDING PRODUCTS LIMITED
Registration no: 02101866 **VAT No.:** 478 8573 75 **Date established:** 1987
No.of Employees: 1 - 10 **Product Groups:** 32, 33

Date of Accounts	Oct 11	Oct 10	Oct 09
Working Capital	263	274	293
Fixed Assets	13	20	24
Current Assets	434	448	503

Respol Industrial Flooring
Overley, Telford, TF6 5HD
Tel: 01952-740400 **Fax:** 01952-740711
E-mail: david@respol.co.uk
Website: http://www.respol.co.uk
Bank(s): National Westminster
Directors: D. Clark (Snr Part), J. Turley (Fin)
Immediate Holding Company: RESPOL REFURB LIMITED
Registration no: 02386288 **VAT No.:** GB 433 9673 27
Date established: 1989 **Turnover:** £1m - £2m **No.of Employees:** 11 - 20
Product Groups: 29, 31, 32, 33, 52

Date of Accounts	Mar 12	Mar 11	Mar 10
Working Capital	-1	-1	-1
Current Liabilities	1	1	1

Ricoh UK Products Ltd
Priorslee, Telford, TF2 9NS
Tel: 01952-290090 **Fax:** 01952-290288
E-mail: enquiries@ricoh-rpl.com
Website: http://www.ricoh-europe.com
Bank(s): Barclays
Directors: T. Tokura (MD), R. Baggott (Fin)
Managers: S. Griffiths (Personnel), L. Walker (Purch Mgr), G. Dunn (Tech Serv Mgr)
Ultimate Holding Company: RICOH COMPANY LIMITED (JAPAN)
Immediate Holding Company: RICOH UK HOLDINGS LIMITED
Registration no: 02736947 **VAT No.:** GB 386 3014 52
Date established: 1992 **Turnover:** £125m - £250m
No.of Employees: 501 - 1000 **Product Groups:** 44

Date of Accounts	Mar 11	Mar 10	Mar 09
Pre Tax Profit/Loss	4m	23m	N/A
Working Capital	1	1	N/A
Fixed Assets	19m	19m	19m
Current Assets	1	1	N/A

Rowan Telmac Ltd
Rowan House Hortonwood 33, Telford, TF1 7EX
Tel: 01952-677705 **Fax:** 01952-605600
E-mail: sales@rowantelmac.co.uk
Website: http://www.rowantelmac.co.uk
Directors: R. Mallard (MD), H. Mallard (Fin), M. Mallard (Co Sec)
Ultimate Holding Company: ROWAN TELMAC HOLDINGS LIMITED
Immediate Holding Company: ROWAN-TELMAC LIMITED
Registration no: 02166825 **VAT No.:** GB 478 8916 71
Date established: 1987 **Turnover:** £2m - £5m **No.of Employees:** 21 - 50
Product Groups: 48

Date of Accounts	Sep 11	Sep 10	Sep 09
Working Capital	1m	1m	962
Fixed Assets	1m	168	68
Current Assets	3m	3m	2m

Rsa Cutting Systems Ltd
Unit 1 Tweedale Court Industrial Estate, Madeley, Telford, TF7 4JZ
Tel: 01952-585183 **Fax:** 01952-580511
E-mail: rsa.gb@rsa.de
Website: http://www.rsa.de
Managers: M. King (Sales Prom Mgr)
Immediate Holding Company: RSA CUTTING & DEBURRING SYSTEMS LIMITED
Registration no: 02276746 **VAT No.:** GB 489 4696 66
Date established: 1988 **Turnover:** £500,000 - £1m
No.of Employees: 1 - 10 **Product Groups:** 46, 49

Date of Accounts	Dec 10	Dec 09	Dec 08
Working Capital	-236	-119	50
Fixed Assets	2	3	7
Current Assets	460	283	273

Runtime UK Ltd
Unit 20 Business Development Centre Stafford Park 4, Telford, TF3 3BA
Tel: 01952-290000
E-mail: andy@runtimeuk.com
Website: http://www.runtimeuk.com
Directors: D. Smith (Fin), A. Smith (MD)
Immediate Holding Company: RUNTIME (UK) LTD
Registration no: 03575339 **VAT No.:** GB 723 3716 48
Date established: 1998 **Turnover:** £250,000 - £500,000
No.of Employees: 1 - 10 **Product Groups:** 28, 44

Date of Accounts	Jun 08	Jun 07	Jun 06
Working Capital	-18	-11	-4
Fixed Assets	3	5	1
Current Assets	17	21	24
Current Liabilities	35	32	28

S M P Security Ltd
Unit 5-6 Halesfield 24, Telford, TF7 4NZ
Tel: 01952-585673 **Fax:** 01952-582816
E-mail: sales@smpsecurity.co.uk
Website: http://www.smpsecurity.co.uk
Bank(s): Bank of Wales
Directors: P. Skitt (Grp Chief Exec)
Immediate Holding Company: S.M.P. SECURITY LIMITED
Registration no: 01174536 **VAT No.:** 162 6352 71 **Date established:** 1974
Turnover: £2m - £5m **No.of Employees:** 21 - 50 **Product Groups:** 36

Date of Accounts	Dec 11	Dec 10	Dec 09
Working Capital	427	488	421
Fixed Assets	865	860	869
Current Assets	1m	1m	1m

S P Holding Services
Upper Coalmoor Farm Horsehay, Telford, TF4 2PX
Tel: 01952-501155 **Fax:** 01952-506655
E-mail: info@spholding.co.uk
Website: http://www.spholding.co.uk
Directors: T. Holding (Fin), S. Holding (MD)
Managers: C. Parry (Personnel), A. Campbell, J. Deakin (Tech Serv Mgr)
Immediate Holding Company: S P HOLDING SERVICES LIMITED
Registration no: 03464899 **Date established:** 1997
No.of Employees: 51 - 100 **Product Groups:** 35, 54, 83

Date of Accounts	Mar 12	Mar 11	Mar 10
Working Capital	-244	-700	-594
Fixed Assets	4m	4m	3m
Current Assets	907	670	896

Salop Sand & Gravel Supply Co. Ltd
Station Road Admaston, Telford, TF5 0AN
Tel: 01952-254101 **Fax:** 01952-223932
E-mail: info@gravel.co.uk
Website: http://www.gravel.co.uk
Directors: R. Parton (MD)
Immediate Holding Company: SALOP SAND & GRAVEL SUPPLY COMPANY LIMITED
Registration no: 00681822 **VAT No.:** GB 159 3690 31
Date established: 1961 **Turnover:** £1m - £2m **No.of Employees:** 1 - 10
Product Groups: 14

Date of Accounts	Dec 11	Dec 10	Dec 09
Working Capital	3m	3m	2m
Fixed Assets	2m	2m	1m
Current Assets	6m	8m	5m

Sawmatic
Commercial Way Oakengates, Telford, TF2 6SG
Tel: 01952-615489 **Fax:** 01952-613469
E-mail: neil@sawmatic.co.uk
Website: http://www.sawmatic.com
Bank(s): Barclays
Directors: N. Major (Ptnr)
VAT No.: GB 304 6991 51 **Date established:** 1979 **Turnover:** £1m - £2m
No.of Employees: 11 - 20 **Product Groups:** 36, 37, 46

Schneider
Stafford Park 5, Telford, TF3 3BL
Tel: 08706-088608 **Fax:** 0870-608 8606
Website: http://www.schneider-electric.com
Directors: S. Coop (MD)
Managers: M. Berelowitz, P. Ward
Ultimate Holding Company: SCHNEIDER ELECTRIC SA (FRANCE)
Immediate Holding Company: MERLIN GERIN LIMITED
Registration no: 02756203 **VAT No.:** GB 301 4285 05
Date established: 1992 **No.of Employees:** 1 - 10 **Product Groups:** 26, 28, 29, 30, 31, 33, 35, 36, 37, 38, 39, 40, 44, 45, 46, 49, 67, 84

Senoplast UK Ltd
3 Landau Court Tan Bank, Wellington, Telford, TF1 1HE
Tel: 01952-243999 **Fax:** 01952-260044
E-mail: post@senoplast.co.uk
Website: http://www.senoplast.co.uk
Managers: R. Cooper (Sales Prom Mgr)
Immediate Holding Company: SENOPLAST (UK) LIMITED
Registration no: 01811681 **Date established:** 1984
Turnover: £10m - £20m **No.of Employees:** 1 - 10 **Product Groups:** 30, 66

Date of Accounts	Mar 11	Mar 10	Mar 09
Working Capital	114	188	271
Fixed Assets	89	95	107
Current Assets	293	378	495

Ses Sterling Ltd
Unit 2 Harcourt Business, Telford, TF7 4PW
Tel: 01952-686196 **Fax:** 01952-684286
E-mail: sales@ses-sterling.com
Website: http://www.ses-sterling.com
Directors: G. Driver (MD), P. Seymour (Co Sec)
Immediate Holding Company: S.E.S. STERLING LIMITED
Registration no: 00943499 **VAT No.:** GB 199 3205 36
Date established: 1968 **Turnover:** £1m - £2m **No.of Employees:** 1 - 10
Product Groups: 30, 36, 37

Date of Accounts	Dec 09	Dec 08	Dec 07
Sales Turnover	N/A	N/A	2m
Pre Tax Profit/Loss	N/A	N/A	81
Working Capital	415	499	553
Fixed Assets	1m	1m	1m
Current Assets	735	893	850
Current Liabilities	N/A	N/A	72

Silgel Ltd (a division Of Multiosorb Technologies)
Stafford Park 6, Telford, TF3 3A
Tel: 01952-236300 **Fax:** 01952-236 301
E-mail: sales@multisorb.co.uk
Website: http://www.multisorb.com
Registration no: 04183185 **No.of Employees:** 21 - 50
Product Groups: 38, 42

Smartwater Technolgy
Nedge Hill Technology Park, Telford, TF3 3WY
Tel: 01952-204104 **Fax:** 0870-242 4561
E-mail: enquiries@smartwater.com
Website: http://www.smartwater.com
Directors: M. Owen (Cust Serv)
Managers: D. Reynolds (Mktg Serv Mgr), R. Harris (Tech Serv Mgr), M. Pearson, N. Wilkinson (Personnel)
Registration no: 02875523 **No.of Employees:** 21 - 50 **Product Groups:** 81

Date of Accounts	Jun 08	Jun 07	Feb 06
Working Capital	1433	561	261
Fixed Assets	250	285	304
Current Assets	2262	1065	635
Current Liabilities	829	505	374

Solar Inks Ltd
Unit E3 Halesfield 23, Telford, TF7 4NY
Tel: 01952-680066 **Fax:** 01952-680088
E-mail: info@solarinks.com
Website: http://www.solarinks.com
Directors: J. Mack (MD)
Immediate Holding Company: SOLAR INKS LTD
Registration no: 05104479 **Date established:** 2004
No.of Employees: 1 - 10 **Product Groups:** 32

Date of Accounts	Apr 11	Apr 10	Apr 09
Working Capital	240	230	182
Fixed Assets	114	67	41
Current Assets	398	373	320

Speedy Signs Ltd
Unit E5 Halesfield 5, Telford, TF7 4QJ
Tel: 01952-586677 **Fax:** 01952-586380
Directors: N. Gutteridge (MD)
Registration no: 04725999 **No.of Employees:** 1 - 10 **Product Groups:** 24, 37, 49

Stadco Telford
Queensway Hortonwood, Telford, TF1 7LL
Tel: 01952-222111 **Fax:** 01952-222050
E-mail: t_daimon@ogihara.co.uk
Website: http://www.stadco.co.uk
Bank(s): Lloyds TSB Bank plc
Directors: J. McCormick (Fin)
Managers: J. Witcombe, R. Macera (Plant), G. Bearman (Tech Serv Mgr)
Ultimate Holding Company: THAI SUMMIT AUTOPARTS INDUSTRY LTD (THAILAND)
Immediate Holding Company: OGIHARA EUROPE LIMITED
Registration no: 02982561 **Date established:** 1994 **Turnover:** £2m - £5m
No.of Employees: 51 - 100 **Product Groups:** 39

Date of Accounts	Mar 11	Mar 10	Mar 09
Sales Turnover	3m	32m	35m
Pre Tax Profit/Loss	-3m	-8m	-3m
Working Capital	-10m	-22m	-16m
Fixed Assets	N/A	15m	19m
Current Assets	6m	5m	11m
Current Liabilities	1m	1m	751

Staircase & Balustrades Ltd
Slaney Street Oakengates, Telford, TF2 6ET
Tel: 01952-610370 **Fax:** 01952- 610370
Directors: C. Snell (MD), H. Snell (Fin)
Immediate Holding Company: STAIRCASES & BALUSTRADES LTD
Registration no: 00990519 **Date established:** 1970
No.of Employees: 1 - 10 **Product Groups:** 35

Staubli UK Ltd
Lodge Park Hortonwood 30, Telford, TF1 7ET
Tel: 01952-604984
E-mail: p.stone@staubli.com
Website: http://www.staubli.com
Bank(s): Credit Lyonnais
Directors: P. Stone (MD)
Managers: P. Stone (Chief Mgr)
Ultimate Holding Company: FP033781
Immediate Holding Company: STAUBLI (UK) LIMITED
Registration no: 02321549 **Date established:** 1988 **Turnover:** £2m - £5m
No.of Employees: 21 - 50 **Product Groups:** 45, 84

Date of Accounts	Dec 09	Dec 08	Dec 07
Sales Turnover	N/A	5m	5m
Pre Tax Profit/Loss	N/A	143	-356
Working Capital	1m	919	914
Fixed Assets	58	83	190
Current Assets	2m	2m	2m
Current Liabilities	N/A	279	289

Strata Creative
171 Holyhead Road Wellington, Telford, TF1 2DP
Tel: 01952-222757 **Fax:** 01952-243176
E-mail: studio@stratacreative.co.uk
Website: http://www.stratacreative.co.uk
Directors: L. Edwards (Dir)
Date established: 1988 **No.of Employees:** 1 - 10 **Product Groups:** 37, 44, 49, 80, 81, 84, 89

Swanstone
Unit 9 Cedar Court Halesfield 17, Telford, TF7 4PF
Tel: 01952-400050 **Fax:** 01952-400060
E-mail: sales@swanstone-uk.com
Website: http://www.swanstone-uk.com
Directors: C. Pitchford (MD)
Immediate Holding Company: SWANSTONE LIMITED
Registration no: 02774832 **Date established:** 1992
Turnover: £500,000 - £1m **No.of Employees:** 1 - 10 **Product Groups:** 30, 33, 36, 37, 42, 44, 46, 48, 66

Date of Accounts	Jan 11	Jan 10	Jan 09
Working Capital	103	63	98
Fixed Assets	34	44	95
Current Assets	380	223	247

T D S Midlands Ltd
2 Vineyard Road Wellington, Telford, TF1 1HA
Tel: 01952-221441 **Fax:** 01952-221451
E-mail: daniel.leech@tdsmidlands.co.uk
Website: http://www.tdsmidlands.co.uk
Directors: D. Leech (Prop)
Immediate Holding Company: T.D.S. MIDLANDS LIMITED
Registration no: 02754878 **Date established:** 1992
Turnover: £500,000 - £1m **No.of Employees:** 1 - 10 **Product Groups:** 33, 35, 44, 81, 84

Date of Accounts	Sep 11	Sep 10	Sep 09
Sales Turnover	615	529	531
Pre Tax Profit/Loss	169	118	115
Working Capital	-9	-26	-31
Fixed Assets	24	28	33
Current Assets	240	121	126
Current Liabilities	232	142	144

Tamlite
Unit 12 Stafford Park 12, Telford, TF3 3BJ
Tel: 01952-292566 **Fax:** 01952-292978
E-mail: mnorthwood@tamlite.co.uk
Website: http://www.tamlite.com
Bank(s): HSBC
Managers: M. Northwood (Mgr)
Immediate Holding Company: PETER GRANT PAPERS LIMITED
Registration no: 01329787 **VAT No.:** 272 7453 45 **Date established:** 1977
Turnover: £20m - £50m **No.of Employees:** 21 - 50 **Product Groups:** 37

Date of Accounts	Dec 11	Dec 10	Dec 09
Sales Turnover	24m	23m	22m
Pre Tax Profit/Loss	-1m	225	960
Working Capital	-2m	-186	188
Fixed Assets	4m	4m	5m
Current Assets	9m	9m	9m
Current Liabilities	5m	4m	5m

Tamtec Electronics
Stafford Park 12, Telford, TF3 3BJ
Tel: 01952-299399 **Fax:** 01952-299300
Website: http://www.teeco.com
Managers: D. Billingham (Mgr)
Immediate Holding Company: SASHPOINT LIMITED
Registration no: 01329787 **Date established:** 2003
Turnover: £20m - £50m **No.of Employees:** 1 - 10 **Product Groups:** 37

Date of Accounts	Dec 11	Dec 10	Dec 09
Sales Turnover	24m	23m	22m
Pre Tax Profit/Loss	-1m	225	960
Working Capital	-2m	-186	188
Fixed Assets	4m	4m	5m
Current Assets	9m	9m	9m
Current Liabilities	5m	4m	5m

Telcoat Ltd
Unit C4 Halesfield 23, Telford, TF7 4NY
Tel: 01952-684186 **Fax:** 01952-680012
E-mail: telfordsheet@aol.com
Directors: J. Wright (Fin), J. Wright (Dir)
Immediate Holding Company: TELCOAT LIMITED
Registration no: 01599946 **VAT No.:** GB 351 6393 54
Date established: 1981 **No.of Employees:** 1 - 10 **Product Groups:** 48

Date of Accounts	Aug 11	Aug 10	Aug 09
Working Capital	258	284	298
Fixed Assets	319	332	354
Current Assets	377	433	483

Telford Extrusions
Stafford Park 6, Telford, TF3 3AT
Tel: 01952-293229 **Fax:** 01952-292752
E-mail: mail@profile22.com
Website: http://www.profile22.com
Directors: R. Ross (Fin), D. Wrigley (MD)
Managers: R. McGlennan (Sales Prom Mgr), K. Leese (Mktg Serv Mgr), N. Stanley (Tech Serv Mgr), A. Maybury, A. O'Connor (Personnel)
Immediate Holding Company: ENTAMEDIA LIMITED
Registration no: 05959142 **VAT No.:** GB 668 4611 07
Date established: 2003 **Turnover:** £75m - £125m
No.of Employees: 101 - 250 **Product Groups:** 30

Date of Accounts	Oct 11	Oct 10	Oct 09
Sales Turnover	113m	99m	84m
Pre Tax Profit/Loss	509	408	370
Working Capital	3m	3m	3m
Fixed Assets	2m	3m	3m
Current Assets	21m	17m	15m
Current Liabilities	6m	2m	3m

Telford Plastics Ltd
Unit 2 Shropshire Court Halesfield 2, Telford, TF7 4QH
Tel: 01952-583641 **Fax:** 01952-680242
E-mail: sales@telfordplastics.com
Website: http://www.telfordplastics.com
Directors: D. Hodgin (MD)
Immediate Holding Company: TELFORD PLASTICS LIMITED
Registration no: 03034495 **VAT No.:** GB 377 7256 09
Date established: 1995 **Turnover:** £250,000 - £500,000
No.of Employees: 21 - 50 **Product Groups:** 30, 48

Date of Accounts	Aug 11	Aug 10	Aug 09
Working Capital	123	49	25
Current Assets	601	505	343

Telford Pressure Castings
Halesfield 8, Telford, TF7 4QN
Tel: 01952-586984 **Fax:** 01952-586711
E-mail: john.deeming@landsecurity.co.uk
Website: http://www.telfordpressurecastings.co.uk
Bank(s): HSBC
Directors: A. Mckeoun (MD)
Immediate Holding Company: SPECIALIST SCHOOLS SERVICES LTD
Registration no: 02472720 **VAT No.:** GB 497 6585 70
Date established: 2012 **Turnover:** £2m - £5m **No.of Employees:** 11 - 20
Product Groups: 34

Tesa Technology UK Ltd
Metrology House Halesfield 13, Telford, TF7 4PL
Tel: 01952-681349 **Fax:** 01952-681391
E-mail: tesa-uk@hexagonmetrology.com
Website: http://www.tesabs.co.uk
Managers: D. Brisco
Ultimate Holding Company: HEXAGON AB (SWEDEN)
Immediate Holding Company: TESA TECHNOLOGY UK LIMITED
Registration no: 00378534 **VAT No.:** GB 196 8086 11
Date established: 1943 **Turnover:** £1m - £2m **No.of Employees:** 1 - 10
Product Groups: 34, 37, 38, 39, 45, 46, 49, 65, 67, 84, 85

Date of Accounts	Dec 11	Dec 10	Dec 09
Sales Turnover	2m	1m	2m
Pre Tax Profit/Loss	-16	-142	38
Working Capital	-288	-274	-135
Fixed Assets	N/A	2	5
Current Assets	1m	833	1m
Current Liabilities	142	146	130

Ticona UK Ltd
Grosvenor House Hollinswood Road, Central Park, Telford, TF2 9TW
Tel: 01952-213400 **Fax:** 01952-213423
E-mail: info@ticona.com
Website: http://www.ticona.com
Directors: S. Kemp (MD)
Ultimate Holding Company: CELANESE CORPORATION (U.S.A)
Immediate Holding Company: TICONA UK LIMITED
Registration no: 03429561 **Date established:** 1997
Turnover: Up to £250,000 **No.of Employees:** 1 - 10 **Product Groups:** 23, 30, 31, 66

Date of Accounts	Dec 11	Dec 10	Dec 09
Sales Turnover	187	138	151
Pre Tax Profit/Loss	196	-147	-2
Working Capital	3m	707	134
Fixed Assets	906	915	63
Current Assets	3m	1m	626
Current Liabilities	82	164	148

Tinson Training Ltd
11 Ewart Road Donnington, Telford, TF2 7LP
Tel: 07940-419397
E-mail: enquiries@btinson.co.uk
Website: http://www.tinsontraining.co.uk
Directors: B. Tinson (Dir), C. Gregory (Fin)
Immediate Holding Company: TINSON TRAINING LTD
Registration no: 06489097 **Date established:** 2008
No.of Employees: 1 - 10 **Product Groups:** 86

Date of Accounts	May 11	May 10
Working Capital	18	6
Fixed Assets	2	2
Current Assets	33	17

Tollgate Products
Heslop Halesfield 21, Telford, TF7 4NX
Tel: 01952-520130 **Fax:** 01952-586605
E-mail: e.sneade@tollgateproducts.co.uk
Website: http://www.tollgateproducts.co.uk
Directors: E. Sneade (Fin)
Ultimate Holding Company: TOLLGATE PRODUCTS HOLDINGS LIMITED
Immediate Holding Company: TOLLGATE PRODUCTS LIMITED
Registration no: 01461701 **Date established:** 1979 **Turnover:** £2m - £5m
No.of Employees: 21 - 50 **Product Groups:** 30, 35, 36, 63, 66

Date of Accounts	Oct 11	Oct 10	Oct 09
Working Capital	614	674	447
Fixed Assets	156	174	185
Current Assets	1m	961	919

Transicon Ltd
Unit 1 Hortonwood 2, Telford, TF1 7GW
Tel: 01952-605515 **Fax:** 01952-605628
E-mail: office@transicon.co.uk
Website: http://www.transicon.co.uk
Directors: P. Blake (MD), R. Cotsford (Sales & Mktg), G. Palmer (Dir)
Managers: D. Turpin (Buyer), L. Blake (Fin Mgr)
Ultimate Holding Company: GW 1130 LIMITED
Immediate Holding Company: TRANSICON LTD.
Registration no: 02481862 **Date established:** 1990
No.of Employees: 21 - 50 **Product Groups:** 37, 44, 48

Date of Accounts	Dec 11	Dec 10	Dec 09
Working Capital	252	191	208
Fixed Assets	510	548	506
Current Assets	702	1m	479

Tranter Lowe
66 High Street Dawley, Telford, TF4 2HD
Tel: 01952-505896 **Fax:** 01952-507788
E-mail: m.lowe@tranterlowe.co.uk
Website: http://www.tranterlowe.co.uk
Directors: P. Lowe (Ptnr)
Immediate Holding Company: TRANTER LOWE (DAWLEY) LTD
Registration no: 06545641 **VAT No.:** GB 160 1008 26
Date established: 2008 **Turnover:** £500,000 - £1m
No.of Employees: 1 - 10 **Product Groups:** 80, 82

V A Technology Ltd
Versatile Technology Centre Halesfield 9, Telford, TF7 4QW
Tel: 01952-585252 **Fax:** 01952-585288
E-mail: sales@vatech.co.uk
Website: http://www.vatech.co.uk
Directors: J. Byrne (MD)
Managers: S. Burgen
Immediate Holding Company: V A TECHNOLOGY LIMITED
Registration no: 02316924 **Date established:** 1988
Turnover: £10m - £20m **No.of Employees:** 51 - 100 **Product Groups:** 35, 39, 45

Date of Accounts	Jul 11	Jul 10	Jul 09
Sales Turnover	12m	9m	10m
Pre Tax Profit/Loss	3m	3m	3m
Working Capital	9m	8m	6m
Fixed Assets	2m	2m	2m
Current Assets	15m	14m	10m
Current Liabilities	5m	5m	3m

Valco Cincinnati
Unit 8 Hortonwood 32, Telford, TF1 7YN
Tel: 01952-677911 **Fax:** 01952-677945
E-mail: sales@valco.co.uk
Website: http://www.valco.co.uk
Bank(s): Barclays
Directors: G. Amend (Ch), J. Chambers (Co Sec), R. Taylor (Dir)
Immediate Holding Company: VALCO CINCINNATI LIMITED
Registration no: 02232599 **Date established:** 1988 **Turnover:** £5m - £10m
No.of Employees: 11 - 20 **Product Groups:** 42

Date of Accounts	Dec 11	Dec 10	Dec 09
Working Capital	862	658	698
Fixed Assets	114	123	97
Current Assets	3m	4m	3m

Vargus Tooling Ltd
Halesfield 4, Telford, TF7 4AP
Tel: 01952-583222 **Fax:** 01952-583383
E-mail: asm@vargustooling.co.uk
Website: http://www.vargustooling.co.uk
Managers: A. Smith (Chief Mgr)
Immediate Holding Company: VARGUS TOOLING UK LIMITED
Registration no: 04976911 **Date established:** 2003 **Turnover:** £1m - £2m
No.of Employees: 1 - 10 **Product Groups:** 46

Date of Accounts	Dec 11	Dec 10	Dec 09
Sales Turnover	2m	1m	1m
Pre Tax Profit/Loss	62	10	-116
Working Capital	77	15	5
Current Assets	892	846	760
Current Liabilities	62	34	29

Ventel Sheet Metal Ltd
Unit B2 Halesfield 5, Telford, TF7 4QJ
Tel: 01952-588095 **Fax:** 01952-684663
E-mail: ventel@bumbledog.co.uk
Website: http://www.ventel.co.uk
Directors: J. Beddow (Fin)
Immediate Holding Company: VENTEL SHEET METAL LIMITED
Registration no: 02047021 **VAT No.:** GB 434 0874 56
Date established: 1986 **No.of Employees:** 11 - 20 **Product Groups:** 35, 36, 48

Date of Accounts	Sep 11	Sep 10	Sep 09
Working Capital	87	92	115
Fixed Assets	16	19	22
Current Assets	150	180	220

Veolia Enviromental Services
Waste Service Centre Dog In The Lane, Little Wenlock, Telford, TF6 5AR
Tel: 01952-630459 **Fax:** 01952-630219
E-mail: john.twyford@veolia.co.uk
Website: http://www.onyxgroup.co.uk
Managers: J. Twyford (Mgr)
Immediate Holding Company: ONYX ENVIRONMENTAL GROUP
Registration no: 00997695 **Turnover:** £2m - £5m
No.of Employees: 21 - 50 **Product Groups:** 39, 54

W J Capper Transport Ltd
Orchard House Springhill, Wellington, Telford, TF1 3NA
Tel: 01952-251888 **Fax:** 01952-243108
E-mail: mike@wjcapper.com
Website: http://www.palletforce.com
Directors: M. Capper (MD), M. Capper (MD)
Immediate Holding Company: W.J.CAPPER TRANSPORT LIMITED
Registration no: 01081887 **Date established:** 1972 **Turnover:** £1m - £2m
No.of Employees: 21 - 50 **Product Groups:** 77

Date of Accounts	Dec 11	Dec 10	Dec 09
Working Capital	589	492	342
Fixed Assets	125	149	219
Current Assets	1m	1m	932

Webster-Wilkinson Ltd
Unit A Halesfield 10, Telford, TF7 4QP
Tel: 01952-585701 **Fax:** 01952-581901
E-mail: sales@webster-wilkinson.com
Website: http://www.webster-wilkinson.com
Bank(s): HSBC
Directors: M. Webster (Dir)
Ultimate Holding Company: MELRACE LIMITED
Immediate Holding Company: WEBSTER-WILKINSON LIMITED
Registration no: 00892102 **VAT No.:** GB 159 2898 12
Date established: 1966 **Turnover:** £5m - £10m
No.of Employees: 51 - 100 **Product Groups:** 33, 35

Date of Accounts	Dec 11	Dec 10	Dec 09
Sales Turnover	N/A	N/A	6m
Pre Tax Profit/Loss	N/A	N/A	590
Working Capital	706	663	795
Fixed Assets	511	616	451
Current Assets	2m	2m	2m
Current Liabilities	N/A	N/A	411

West Mercia Mechanical Services
10 Arrow Road, Telford, TF5 0LF
Tel: 01952-247007 **Fax:** 01952-247007
E-mail: sales@autoelectrics.net
Website: http://www.autoelectrics.net
Directors: K. Morgan (Prop)
Date established: 1995 **Turnover:** Up to £250,000
No.of Employees: 1 - 10 **Product Groups:** 39

Windsor Life Assurance
Winsdor House Telford Centre, Town Centre, Telford, TF3 4NB
Tel: 0800-073 1777 **Fax:** 08707-091111
E-mail: graham.singleton@adminre.co.uk
Website: http://www.windsor-life.com
Bank(s): HSBC
Directors: G. Singleton (Grp Chief Exec), J. Yates (MD), P. Shakespeare (Co Sec), R. Howe (Dir), W. Wilson (Dir)
Managers: D. Taylor (I.T. Exec)
Ultimate Holding Company: SWISS REINSURANCE CO (SWITZERLAND).
Immediate Holding Company: WINDSOR LIFE ASSURANCE COMPANY LIMITED
Registration no: 00754167 **VAT No.:** GB 647 8719 84
Date established: 1963 **Turnover:** £250m - £500m
No.of Employees: 501 - 1000 **Product Groups:** 82

Date of Accounts	Dec 10	Dec 09	Dec 08
Pre Tax Profit/Loss	58m	2m	502
Fixed Assets	9038m	16771m	16m
Current Assets	8963m	319m	257
Current Liabilities	684m	626m	631

Winlock Security Ltd
Halesfield 8, Telford, TF7 4ES
Tel: 01952-680178 **Fax:** 01952-684355
E-mail: sales@winlock.co.uk
Website: http://www.winlock.co.uk
Bank(s): Lloyds TSB Bank plc
Directors: P. Dupre Smith (MD)
Managers: D. Britnell, D. Clark (Fin Mgr)
Ultimate Holding Company: LOWE AND FLETCHER LIMITED
Immediate Holding Company: WINLOCK SECURITY LIMITED
Registration no: 02204121 **Date established:** 1987 **Turnover:** £5m - £10m
No.of Employees: 101 - 250 **Product Groups:** 36

see next page

Winlock Security Ltd - Cont'd

Date of Accounts	Dec 11	Dec 10	Dec 09
Sales Turnover	7m	8m	8m
Pre Tax Profit/Loss	-235	-120	-201
Working Capital	267	444	405
Fixed Assets	102	187	313
Current Assets	3m	3m	2m
Current Liabilities	95	1m	825

Wrap Film Systems Ltd

Hortonwood 45, Telford, TF1 7FA
Tel: 01952-678800 **Fax:** 01494-656801
E-mail: adrian.brown@wrapfilm.com
Website: http://www.wrapfilm.com
Directors: A. Brown (MD)
Managers: R. Tucker (Purch Mgr), A. Brierly (Fin Mgr), C. Morgan (Mktg Serv Mgr), J. crook (Nat Sales Mgr), A. Haden (Tech Serv Mgr), S. Drummond (Personnel)
Ultimate Holding Company: REYNOLDS CONSUMER PRODUCTS (UK) LIMITED
Immediate Holding Company: REYNOLDS SUBCO (UK) LIMITED
Registration no: 03322218 **VAT No.:** GB 287 9879 61
Date established: 1997 **Turnover:** £5m - £10m
No.of Employees: 251 - 500 **Product Groups:** 30

Date of Accounts	Dec 11	Dec 10	Dec 09
Sales Turnover	N/A	N/A	10m
Pre Tax Profit/Loss	32	-54	2m
Working Capital	894	862	4m
Current Assets	904	909	5m
Current Liabilities	10	47	1m

Wrekin Circuits Ltd

Unit 29 30 Hortonwood 33, Telford, TF1 7EX
Tel: 01952-670011 **Fax:** 01952-606565
E-mail: sales@wrekin-circuits.co.uk
Website: http://www.wrekin-circuits.co.uk
Bank(s): HSBC
Directors: D. Brown (Fab), S. Blower (MD)
Managers: J. Purdon (Tech Serv Mgr), P. Adlam, A. Morris (Sales & Mktg Mg)
Immediate Holding Company: WREKIN CIRCUITS LIMITED
Registration no: 02567175 **VAT No.:** GB 560 3898 22
Date established: 1990 **Turnover:** £2m - £5m **No.of Employees:** 21 - 50
Product Groups: 37, 44, 48

Date of Accounts	Sep 11	Sep 10	Sep 09
Working Capital	74	22	-15
Fixed Assets	541	526	613
Current Assets	713	609	538
Current Liabilities	274	203	N/A

Wrekin Shell Moulding

Halesfield 21, Telford, TF7 4NX
Tel: 01952-580946 **Fax:** 01952-582546
E-mail: enquiries@dynafluid.com
Website: http://www.dynafluid.com
Directors: M. Ellis (MD), D. Oakes (Co Sec)
Managers: C. Cooper (Sales & Mktg Mg)
Immediate Holding Company: WREKIN SHELL MOULDINGS LIMITED
Registration no: 02710581 **Date established:** 1992 **Turnover:** £2m - £5m
No.of Employees: 21 - 50 **Product Groups:** 46

Date of Accounts	Feb 08	Feb 11	Feb 10
Pre Tax Profit/Loss	345	N/A	N/A
Working Capital	669	728	929
Fixed Assets	1m	1m	1m
Current Assets	1m	1m	1m
Current Liabilities	147	N/A	N/A

P L Wyatt

26 Paradise Coalbrookdale, Telford, TF8 7NP
Tel: 01952-432685 **Fax:** 01952-433883
E-mail: beckywyatt1@hotmail.co.uk
Directors: P. Wyatt (Prop)
Date established: 2000 **No.of Employees:** 1 - 10 **Product Groups:** 37, 40, 48

Xebec Tech Ltd

Print House Halesfield 17, Telford, TF7 4PW
Tel: 01952-586000 **Fax:** 01952-680111
E-mail: info@xebectech.com.tw
Website: http://www.xebectech.com
Directors: H. Dhulashia (MD), M. Dhulashia (Fin)
Ultimate Holding Company: CAPITB TRUST
Immediate Holding Company: COMPUPACK LIMITED
Registration no: 03729820 **Date established:** 1999 **Turnover:** £1m - £2m
No.of Employees: 1 - 10 **Product Groups:** 38, 42

Date of Accounts	Mar 11	Mar 10	Mar 09
Working Capital	74	74	100
Fixed Assets	147	147	159
Current Assets	121	121	187

Whitchurch

5 Star Bar Catering Supplies

53 Green End, Whitchurch, SY13 1AJ
Tel: 01948-662720 **Fax:** 01948-662720
E-mail: supertourer@aol.com
Directors: P. Jones (Prop)
Date established: 1983 **No.of Employees:** 1 - 10 **Product Groups:** 20, 40, 41

Down To Earth

Bronington Park School Lane, Bronington, Whitchurch, SY13 3HN
Tel: 01948-780377 **Fax:** 01948-780677
E-mail: down.2earth@btconnect.com
Website: http://www.contemparymetalwork.co.uk
Directors: P. Rogers (Ptnr)
Date established: 1966 **No.of Employees:** 1 - 10 **Product Groups:** 26, 35

H West Prees Ltd

Lower Heath Prees, Whitchurch, SY13 2BT
Tel: 01948-840465 **Fax:** 01948-841055
E-mail: info@harrywest.co.uk
Website: http://www.harrywest.co.uk
Bank(s): Barclays
Directors: B. Shone (Co Sec), J. Whitfield (Pers), T. Soan (Sales & Mktg), J. West (MD)
Managers: J. Llewellyn
Immediate Holding Company: HARRY WEST (PREES) LIMITED
Registration no: 01261082 **VAT No.:** GB 280 4711 69
Date established: 1976 **Turnover:** £2m - £5m **No.of Employees:** 21 - 50
Product Groups: 35, 41, 52

Date of Accounts	May 11	May 10	May 09
Working Capital	959	1m	442
Fixed Assets	392	435	577
Current Assets	2m	2m	2m

Roger Needham & Sons Ltd

Unit 2a-2b Waymills Industrial Estate Waymills, Whitchurch, SY13 1TT
Tel: 01948-662629 **Fax:** 01948-665045
E-mail: sales@needham-group.com
Website: http://www.needham-group.com
Directors: D. Needham (MD)
Immediate Holding Company: ROGER NEEDHAM & SONS LIMITED
Registration no: 00741700 **VAT No.:** GB 278 3086 30
Date established: 1962 **Turnover:** £2m - £5m **No.of Employees:** 1 - 10
Product Groups: 32, 48, 49

Date of Accounts	Nov 11	Nov 10	Nov 09
Working Capital	309	307	325
Fixed Assets	112	121	118
Current Assets	608	484	477

R B Lewis & Co.

Wherley Rough Garage Lower Heath, Prees, Whitchurch, SY13 2BH
Tel: 01948-840886 **Fax:** 01948-840109
E-mail: lewis@liftrucks78.freeserve.co.uk
Website: http://www.liftrucks78.freeserve.co.uk
Directors: R. Lewis (Prop)
Date established: 1980 **No.of Employees:** 1 - 10 **Product Groups:** 35, 39, 45

Scanlans Plant Hire Ltd

Waymills, Whitchurch, SY13 1RT
Tel: 01948-665149 **Fax:** 01948-667263
E-mail: scanlansplant@tiscali.co.uk
Website: http://www.scanlansgroup.co.uk
Managers: C. Hughes (Mgr)
Registration no: 03848590 **Date established:** 1999
No.of Employees: 1 - 10 **Product Groups:** 14, 31, 72, 83

The Wooden Gate Timber Products

Pear Tree Farm Broadhay Lane Lower Heath, Prees, Whitchurch, SY13 2BJ
Tel: 01948-841844 **Fax:** 01782-512374
E-mail: sales@woodengatecompany.co.uk
Website: http://www.woodengatecompany.co.uk
Directors: S. Scarle (Prop)
Immediate Holding Company: THE WOODEN GATE COMPANY LTD
Registration no: 05948319 **Date established:** 2006
No.of Employees: 1 - 10 **Product Groups:** 26, 35

Date of Accounts	Mar 11	Mar 10	Mar 09
Working Capital	-60	-60	-19
Fixed Assets	40	49	56
Current Assets	64	65	64

Wyatt Bros Water Services Ltd

Waymills Industrial Estate Waymills, Whitchurch, SY13 1TT
Tel: 01948-662526 **Fax:** 01948-667560
E-mail: info@wyattbros.com
Website: http://www.wyattbros.com
Directors: J. Wyatt (MD)
Immediate Holding Company: WYATT BROS. (WATER SERVICES) LIMITED
Registration no: 04593196 **Date established:** 2002
No.of Employees: 11 - 20 **Product Groups:** 30, 32, 35, 36, 37, 38, 39, 40, 42, 45, 48, 51, 52, 54, 66, 67, 76, 80, 82, 84, 85

Date of Accounts	Mar 11	Mar 10	Mar 09
Sales Turnover	N/A	1m	N/A
Pre Tax Profit/Loss	N/A	72	N/A
Working Capital	728	83	512
Fixed Assets	564	960	572
Current Assets	780	557	547
Current Liabilities	N/A	97	N/A

SOMERSET

Axbridge

Weston Catering Supplies
Mendip Industrial Estate Mendip Road, Rooksbridge, Axbridge, BS26 2UG
Tel: 01934-750367 **Fax:** 01934-750686
E-mail: westcatering@hotmail.com
Website: http://www.westoncateringsupplies.co.uk
Directors: R. Wright (Prop)
Immediate Holding Company: SAFE CYLINDER STORAGE LTD
Registration no: 06169658 **Date established:** 2007
No.of Employees: 1 - 10 **Product Groups:** 20, 40, 41

Date of Accounts	Jun 11	Jun 10	Jun 09
Working Capital	-35	-50	-44
Fixed Assets	7	7	9
Current Assets	71	46	43

Bridgwater

Ashtead Plant Hire Co. Ltd
Wylds Road, Bridgwater, TA6 4BH
Tel: 01278-423153 **Fax:** 01278-444299
E-mail: sales@aplant.com
Website: http://www.aplant.com
Managers: P. Lewis (Depot Mgr), T. Andrews (Mgr)
Registration no: 00444569 **VAT No.:** GB 221 5687 37
Turnover: £125m - £250m **No.of Employees:** 1 - 10 **Product Groups:** 72, 83

A-Tanks
Unit 1 Durleigh Farm Enmore Road, Durleigh, Bridgwater, TA5 2AW
Tel: 01278-455655 **Fax:** 05603-446613
E-mail: donb@a-tanks.co.uk
Website: http://www.a-tanks.co.uk
Directors: D. Baker (Prop)
No.of Employees: 1 - 10 **Product Groups:** 38, 42, 48, 51, 54

AXIS First
Axis House 53-55 St Mary Street, Bridgwater, TA6 3EQ
Tel: 01278-421020 **Fax:** 01278-451198
E-mail: sales@axisfirst.co.uk
Website: http://www.systemsaxis.co.uk
Bank(s): Lloyds
Directors: C. Craven (Dir), D. Pike (MD)
Immediate Holding Company: AXIS FIRST LIMITED
Registration no: 01595904 **VAT No.:** GB 515 8599 12
Date established: 1981 **Turnover:** £1m - £2m **No.of Employees:** 21 - 50
Product Groups: 44

B F F Nonwovens
Bath Road, Bridgwater, TA6 4NZ
Tel: 01278-428500 **Fax:** 01278-429499
E-mail: enquiries@bff-technicalfabrics.co.uk
Website: http://www.bff-technicalfabrics.co.uk
Directors: A. Brownlow (MD), C. Burhop (Fin)
Managers: A. Hardwidge, M. Lendon (Cust Serv Mgr), K. Labuschagne (Tech Serv Mgr)
Immediate Holding Company: BFF NONWOVENS LIMITED
Registration no: 04573423 **Date established:** 2002
Turnover: £10m - £20m **No.of Employees:** 51 - 100 **Product Groups:** 23, 24, 27, 63

Date of Accounts	Mar 12	Mar 11	Mar 10
Sales Turnover	12m	9m	8m
Pre Tax Profit/Loss	3m	911	570
Working Capital	2m	851	496
Fixed Assets	1m	1m	984
Current Assets	4m	3m	3m
Current Liabilities	1m	950	508

David Bearman
Brunswick House Woolavington Hill, Woolavington, Bridgwater, TA7 8HG
Tel: 01278-685250
E-mail: info@davidbearman.co.uk
Website: http://www.davidbearman.co.uk
Directors: D. Bearman (Prop)
Immediate Holding Company: DAVID BEARMAN LIMITED
Registration no: 06383922 **Date established:** 2007
No.of Employees: 1 - 10 **Product Groups:** 35

Date of Accounts	Sep 11	Sep 10	Sep 09
Working Capital	-16	-12	-21
Fixed Assets	63	71	81
Current Assets	21	35	22

Bish Bosh Sound
1 Frederick Road, Bridgwater, TA6 4NF
Tel: 01278-434198
E-mail: info@bishboshsound.co.uk
Website: http://www.bishboshsound.co.uk
Directors: J. Hedges (Prop)
No.of Employees: 1 - 10 **Product Groups:** 37, 61, 67, 83

Bond Gun Accessories Ltd
33 Tynte Road, Bridgwater, TA6 4LA
Tel: 01278-427345
E-mail: sales@bgaltd.co.uk
Website: http://www.bgaltd.co.uk
Directors: C. Bond (Fin), J. Bond (MD)
Immediate Holding Company: BOND GUN ACCESSORIES LIMITED
Registration no: 04627848 **Date established:** 2003
Turnover: Up to £250,000 **No.of Employees:** 1 - 10 **Product Groups:** 36, 39, 40

Date of Accounts	Jan 12	Jan 11	Jan 10
Working Capital	-4	1	14
Current Assets	13	17	14

Bradford Building Supplies Ltd
139 Bristol Road, Bridgwater, TA6 4AQ
Tel: 01278-422654 **Fax:** 01278-450574
E-mail: bbs.bridgwater@bradford.co.uk
Website: http://www.bradfords.co.uk
Managers: K. Williams (Mgr)
Immediate Holding Company: BRADFORDS BUILDING SUPPLIES LIMITED
Registration no: 00278994 **VAT No.:** GB 453 8510 46
Date established: 1933 **Turnover:** £20m - £50m **No.of Employees:** 1 - 10
Product Groups: 66

Date of Accounts	Apr 11	Apr 10	Apr 09
Sales Turnover	135m	130m	140m
Pre Tax Profit/Loss	4m	6m	3m
Working Capital	16m	10m	18m
Fixed Assets	39m	39m	43m
Current Assets	42m	41m	41m
Current Liabilities	6m	6m	6m

C R C Industries
Ambersil House Wylds Road, Bridgwater, TA6 4DD
Tel: 01278-424200 **Fax:** 01502-501491
E-mail: salesuk@crcind.com
Website: http://www.ambersil.com
Bank(s): HSBC Bank plc
Directors: G. Churchard (MD), P. Best (Fin), W. Mcalistar (MD), W. McAlister (MD)
Managers: K. Charles-Neal (Mktg Serv Mgr), W. MacCallister (Chief Mgr)
Immediate Holding Company: AUTOMOTIVE CLEANING CHEMICALS LTD
Registration no: 01873880 **VAT No.:** GB 491 1046 64
Date established: 1984 **Turnover:** £2m - £5m **No.of Employees:** 21 - 50
Product Groups: 32, 66

Date of Accounts	Dec 09	Dec 08	Dec 07
Sales Turnover	8m	8m	7m
Pre Tax Profit/Loss	618	979	821
Working Capital	2m	9m	2m
Fixed Assets	6m	569	595
Current Assets	3m	10m	4m
Current Liabilities	531	672	752

Classic Iron
11 Middle Street Puriton, Bridgwater, TA7 8AU
Tel: 01278-685308 **Fax:** 01278-685308
Directors: M. Edwards (Prop)
Date established: 1999 **No.of Employees:** 1 - 10 **Product Groups:** 26, 35

D S D Buildings Ltd
Kings Acre Shearston North Petherton, Bridgwater, TA6 6PL
Tel: 01278-663829 **Fax:** 01278-588084
E-mail: sales@dsdbuildings.co.uk
Website: http://www.dsdbuildings.co.uk
Directors: B. Cossey (MD), D. Cossey (Fin)
Immediate Holding Company: D S D BUILDINGS LIMITED
Registration no: 05345284 **Date established:** 2005
No.of Employees: 1 - 10 **Product Groups:** 25, 35, 52, 66

Date of Accounts	Jan 12	Jan 11	Jan 10
Working Capital	-14	-18	-30
Fixed Assets	38	40	26
Current Assets	25	58	16

Decomatic
Unit 6 Robins Drive, Bridgwater, TA6 4DL
Tel: 01278-444151 **Fax:** 01278-422411
E-mail: sales@decomatic.com
Website: http://www.decomatic.com
Directors: S. Fletcher (MD)
Registration no: 13837934 **VAT No.:** GB 185 9246 23
Turnover: £1m - £2m **No.of Employees:** 1 - 10 **Product Groups:** 30

Deltaform Ltd
Brue Avenue, Bridgwater, TA6 5YE
Tel: 01278-410160 **Fax:** 01278-410161
E-mail: sales@deltaform.co.uk
Website: http://www.deltaform.co.uk
Directors: I. Chedzey (Dir), R. Adams (Dir), S. Jones (Dir)
Managers: G. Barnden (Mktg Serv Mgr)
Immediate Holding Company: DELTAFORM LIMITED
Registration no: 02743951 **VAT No.:** GB 586 3106 31
Date established: 1992 **Turnover:** £20m - £50m
No.of Employees: 101 - 250 **Product Groups:** 20, 30, 48, 49

Date of Accounts	Apr 11	Apr 10	Apr 09
Sales Turnover	25m	26m	19m
Pre Tax Profit/Loss	187	2m	711
Working Capital	-1m	-1m	-1m
Fixed Assets	5m	5m	4m
Current Assets	8m	7m	5m
Current Liabilities	5m	5m	3m

Drain Centre Civils
Unit 26 Carvers Mill Business Park Wylds Road, Bridgwater, TA6 4BH
Tel: 01278-451884 **Fax:** 01278-451914
E-mail: stuart.martin@wolseley.co.uk
Website: http://www.draincentre.co.uk
Managers: S. Martin (District Mgr)
Immediate Holding Company: COSYBED LIMITED
Registration no: 01723828 **VAT No.:** GB 595 4236 12
Date established: 1983 **Turnover:** £1m - £2m **No.of Employees:** 1 - 10
Product Groups: 30, 35, 36, 39, 40, 42, 48, 66

Exchange
Express Park Bristol Road, Bridgwater, TA6 4RR
Tel: 01278-459997 **Fax:** 01278-457779
Website: http://www.expresspark.co.uk/theexchange
Directors: L. Moore (Prop)
Immediate Holding Company: DATECH LIMITED
Registration no: 05839789 **Date established:** 2001
No.of Employees: 21 - 50 **Product Groups:** 69, 81

Date of Accounts	Dec 11	Dec 10	Dec 09
Working Capital	-118	-28	-27
Fixed Assets	48	89	131
Current Assets	92	201	295

W Gadsby & Son Ltd
Gadsby House Huntworth Business Park, Bridgwater, TA6 6TS
Tel: 01278-437123 **Fax:** 01278-458561
E-mail: info@gadsby.co.uk
Website: http://www.gadsby.co.uk
Bank(s): Lloyds TSB Bank plc
Directors: P. Gadsby (MD)
Immediate Holding Company: W. GADSBY AND SON LIMITED
Registration no: 00528221 **VAT No.:** GB 586 0573 15
Date established: 1954 **Turnover:** Up to £250,000
No.of Employees: 11 - 20 **Product Groups:** 64

Date of Accounts	May 11	May 10	May 09
Working Capital	356	414	727
Fixed Assets	129	116	137
Current Assets	1m	660	1m

Gerber Juice Company Ltd
Mallard Court Express Park Bristol Road, Bridgwater, TA6 4RN
Tel: 01278-441600 **Fax:** 01278-441777
E-mail: info@gerberjuice.com
Website: http://www.gerberjuice.com
Bank(s): HSBC, Holborn Circus, London
Directors: M. Millard (Comm)
Managers: D. Fisher (Tech Serv Mgr), R. Peak (Comptroller), S. Wishart, J. Staunton (Personnel)
Ultimate Holding Company: QUADRIGA INTERNATIONAL LTD (BVI)
Immediate Holding Company: GERBER JUICE COMPANY LIMITED
Registration no: 00161079 **VAT No.:** GB 243 0215 14
Date established: 2019 **Turnover:** £250m - £500m
No.of Employees: 501 - 1000 **Product Groups:** 20, 21

see next page

Gerber Juice Company Ltd - Cont'd

Date of Accounts	Dec 11	Dec 10	Dec 09
Sales Turnover	300m	264m	300m
Pre Tax Profit/Loss	8m	7m	11m
Working Capital	27m	13m	17m
Fixed Assets	65m	66m	62m
Current Assets	124m	94m	101m
Current Liabilities	33m	26m	29m

Hydrax Ltd
Wylds Road, Bridgwater, TA6 4BH
Tel: 01278-727600 **Fax:** 01278-727601
E-mail: sales@hydrax.co.uk
Website: http://www.hydrax.co.uk
Bank(s): Lloyds TSB Bank plc
Directors: B. Eden (MD), R. Eden (Dir)
Immediate Holding Company: HYDRAX LIMITED
Registration no: 01757914 **Date established:** 1983 **Turnover:** £1m - £2m
No.of Employees: 21 - 50 **Product Groups:** 40, 45, 46, 48, 52

Date of Accounts	Apr 12	Apr 11	Apr 10
Working Capital	647	635	685
Fixed Assets	27	14	17
Current Assets	1m	1m	955

Jasun Filtration Ltd
Riverside House Parrett Way, Bridgwater, TA6 5LB
Tel: 01278-452277 **Fax:** 01278-450873
E-mail: colin@jfilters.com
Website: http://www.jfilters.com
Directors: C. Hitch (Sales), G. Bentley (MD)
Immediate Holding Company: JASUN ENVIROCARE PLC
Registration no: 01078501 **VAT No.:** GB 218 1271 87
Date established: 1972 **Turnover:** £5m - £10m
No.of Employees: 51 - 100 **Product Groups:** 35, 40, 42, 67

Date of Accounts	Dec 11	Dec 10	Dec 09
Sales Turnover	7m	5m	4m
Pre Tax Profit/Loss	558	490	318
Working Capital	-208	-231	392
Fixed Assets	3m	3m	2m
Current Assets	2m	2m	1m
Current Liabilities	1m	725	185

Johnson Elevanja Ltd
Bath Road, Bridgwater, TA6 4YQ
Tel: 01278-456411 **Fax:** 01278-429949
E-mail: sales@jbrakes.com
Website: http://www.elevanja.com
Bank(s): HSBC Bank plc
Directors: J. Gibbons (Dir)
Ultimate Holding Company: MANUFAX HOLDINGS INC (CANADA)
Immediate Holding Company: MANUFAX LIMITED
Registration no: 02790594 **Date established:** 1993 **Turnover:** £1m - £2m
No.of Employees: 11 - 20 **Product Groups:** 35, 37, 48

Date of Accounts	Oct 11	Oct 10	Oct 09
Working Capital	209	86	730
Fixed Assets	256	257	258
Current Assets	251	145	790

Kellands Plant Sales Ltd
Salmon Parade, Bridgwater, TA6 5JY
Tel: 01278-451601 **Fax:** 01278-446381
E-mail: sales@kellandsplantsales.co.uk
Website: http://www.kellands.com
Bank(s): National Westminster Bank Plc
Directors: G. Bagwell (MD), H. Mear (Co Sec)
Managers: S. Ameer-ali (Personnel)
Immediate Holding Company: KELLANDS (HOLDINGS) LIMITED
Registration no: 00434982 **VAT No.:** GB 130 3477 02
Date established: 1947 **Turnover:** £10m - £20m
No.of Employees: 21 - 50 **Product Groups:** 67

Date of Accounts	Dec 11	Dec 10	Dec 09
Sales Turnover	14m	13m	10m
Pre Tax Profit/Loss	610	443	299
Working Capital	2m	2m	2m
Fixed Assets	3m	3m	3m
Current Assets	5m	3m	3m
Current Liabilities	429	492	241

Madregal Designs Ltd
Unit 8 Suprema Business Park Suprema Avenue, Edington, Bridgwater, TA7 9LF
Tel: 01278-723483 **Fax:** 01278-723285
E-mail: info@madregaldesigns.com
Website: http://www.madregaldesigns.com
Directors: A. James (Dir)
Immediate Holding Company: MADREGAL DESIGNS LIMITED
Registration no: 06344086 **Date established:** 2007
No.of Employees: 1 - 10 **Product Groups:** 26, 35

Date of Accounts	Aug 08	Mar 11	Mar 10
Working Capital	-62	-46	-42
Fixed Assets	66	46	55
Current Assets	36	52	60

Mayflower Hydraulics
Castlefields Trading Estate Symons Way, Bridgwater, TA6 4DR
Tel: 01278-450226 **Fax:** 01278-446678
Website: http://www.promoster.co.uk
Directors: J. Vincent (Co Sec), S. Vincent (Ptnr)
Immediate Holding Company: MAYFLOWER HYDRAULICS LIMITED
Registration no: 01517429 **VAT No.:** GB 469 6725 74
Date established: 1980 **Turnover:** Up to £250,000
No.of Employees: 1 - 10 **Product Groups:** 48

Date of Accounts	Sep 99	Sep 02	Sep 01
Working Capital	2	2	2
Current Assets	2	2	2

Micron Bio-Systems
Bath Road, Bridgwater, TA6 4NZ
Tel: 01278-427272
E-mail: info@micronbio-systems.co.uk
Website: http://www.micronbio-systems.co.uk
Managers: L. Llamas
Immediate Holding Company: STERLING MATERIALS LIMITED
Registration no: 03423831 **Date established:** 2004
No.of Employees: 1 - 10 **Product Groups:** 20

Date of Accounts	Mar 11	Mar 10	Mar 09
Working Capital	7	65	98
Fixed Assets	43	49	21
Current Assets	392	482	302
Current Liabilities	N/A	145	81

Neal Hamlin
Unit 13 Station Yard Wellington Road, Bridgwater, TA6 5HA
Tel: 01278-445326
E-mail: neal@nealhamlin.co.uk
Website: http://www.nealhamlin.co.uk
Directors: N. Hamlin (Prop)
Date established: 1979 **No.of Employees:** 1 - 10 **Product Groups:** 26, 35

One Stop Pony Shop
Poole House Thorngrove, Middlezoy, Bridgwater, TA7 0PD
Tel: 01823-690001 **Fax:** 01823-690001
E-mail: sales@onestopponyshop.co.uk
Website: http://www.onestopponyshop.co.uk
Directors: A. Braddock (Prop)
No.of Employees: 1 - 10 **Product Groups:** 24, 49, 63, 65

Portakabin Ltd (Bristol Hire Centre)
The Drove, Bridgwater, TA6 4AG
Tel: 01278-445665 **Fax:** 01278-445646
E-mail: toby.sidebotham@portakabin.com
Website: http://www.portakabin.com
Managers: T. Sidebotham
Immediate Holding Company: PORTAKABIN LIMITED
Registration no: 00685303 **Date established:** 1961
Turnover: £500,000 - £1m **No.of Employees:** 11 - 20 **Product Groups:** 35

Date of Accounts	Jun 11	Jun 10	Jun 09
Sales Turnover	171m	174m	202m
Pre Tax Profit/Loss	27m	26m	30m
Working Capital	35m	25m	8m
Fixed Assets	104m	103m	113m
Current Assets	79m	76m	67m
Current Liabilities	27m	35m	29m

Sedgemoor Fire Prevention Ltd
Winters Barn Bush Lane, Spaxton, Bridgwater, TA5 1AH
Tel: 01278-671627 **Fax:** 01278-671355
E-mail: philip.granville@btopenworld.com
Website: http://www.sedgemoorfire.com
Directors: P. Granville (MD)
Immediate Holding Company: SEDGEMOOR FIRE PREVENTION LIMITED
Registration no: 04490789 **Date established:** 2002
No.of Employees: 1 - 10 **Product Groups:** 38, 42

Date of Accounts	Oct 11	Oct 10	Oct 09
Working Capital	244	222	214
Fixed Assets	50	56	49
Current Assets	293	267	264

Siton Film Converters
6 Robins Drive, Bridgwater, TA6 4DL
Tel: 01278-444202 **Fax:** 01278-451117
Directors: A. Meek (Prop)
Date established: 1993 **No.of Employees:** 1 - 10 **Product Groups:** 38, 42

Technical Woodmachinery Sales Bridgwater Ltd
22 Axe Road Colley Lane Industrial Estate, Bridgwater, TA6 5LN
Tel: 01278-455622 **Fax:** 01278-451905
E-mail: info@twsbridgwater.co.uk
Website: http://www.twsbridgwater.co.uk
Directors: J. Self (MD)
Immediate Holding Company: TECHNICAL WOODMACHINERY SALES (BRIDGWATER) LIMITED
Registration no: 01988381 **Date established:** 1986
No.of Employees: 1 - 10 **Product Groups:** 46

Date of Accounts	Jul 11	Jul 10	Jul 09
Working Capital	437	446	433
Fixed Assets	21	23	25
Current Assets	506	512	514

Travis Perkins plc
Bristol Road, Bridgwater, TA6 4DT
Tel: 01278-457371 **Fax:** 01278-457561
E-mail: steve.marsh@travisperkins.co.uk
Website: http://www.travisperkins.co.uk
Bank(s): HSBC
Managers: S. Marsh (District Mgr)
Immediate Holding Company: TRAVIS PERKINS PLC
Registration no: 00824821 **Date established:** 1964
Turnover: £10m - £20m **No.of Employees:** 21 - 50 **Product Groups:** 66

Date of Accounts	Dec 11	Dec 10	Dec 09
Sales Turnover	4779m	3153m	2931m
Pre Tax Profit/Loss	270m	197m	213m
Working Capital	133m	159m	248m
Fixed Assets	2771m	2749m	2108m
Current Assets	1421m	1329m	1035m
Current Liabilities	473m	412m	109m

Trelleborg Sealing Solutions
Dunball Industrial Estate Dunball, Bridgwater, TA6 4TP
Tel: 01278-686800 **Fax:** 01278-686848
E-mail: frank.shaw@trelleborg.com
Website: http://www.trelleborg.com
Managers: R. Seetenby (Fin Mgr), F. Shaw (Chief Mgr), K. Wegg (Purch Mgr)
No.of Employees: 101 - 250 **Product Groups:** 38, 42

Bruton

Redlynch Agricultural Engineering
Redlynch, Bruton, BA10 0NH
Tel: 01749-812628 **Fax:** 01749-812881
E-mail: redlynchtractors@btconnect.com
Website: http://www.redlynchtractors.co.uk
Directors: N. Heal (MD), L. Rowe (Co Sec)
Immediate Holding Company: REDLYNCH AGRICULTURAL ENGINEERING LIMITED
Registration no: 03316370 **Date established:** 1997
No.of Employees: 1 - 10 **Product Groups:** 41

Date of Accounts	Nov 11	Nov 10	Nov 09
Working Capital	2m	1m	1m
Fixed Assets	635	651	871
Current Assets	4m	2m	2m

Burnham On Sea

Bridgwater Electronics Ltd
Unit 9 Westmans Trading Estate Love Lane, Burnham On Sea, TA8 1EY
Tel: 01278-789552 **Fax:** 01278-789782
E-mail: sales@bridgwater-electronics.co.uk
Website: http://www.bridgwater-electronics.co.uk
Directors: C. Palmer (MD)
Immediate Holding Company: BRIDGWATER ELECTRONICS LIMITED
Registration no: 03808342 **Date established:** 1999
No.of Employees: 1 - 10 **Product Groups:** 37, 39, 67, 68

Date of Accounts	Jun 11	Jun 10	Jun 09
Working Capital	15	12	23
Fixed Assets	6	7	7
Current Assets	25	20	51

Castle Cary

Clanville Sawmills Ltd (t/a Jonathon Cruse & Gass)
Clanville, Castle Cary, BA7 7PQ
Tel: 01963-350881 **Fax:** 01963-351562
E-mail: admin@clanvillesawmills.co.uk
Website: http://www.clanvillesawmills.co.uk
Bank(s): National Westminster Bank Plc
Directors: A. Chambers (Dir), W. Hazell (Dir)
Immediate Holding Company: CLANVILLE SAWMILLS LIMITED
Registration no: 00426828 **VAT No.:** GB 129 9234 48
Date established: 1947 **Turnover:** £1m - £2m **No.of Employees:** 11 - 20
Product Groups: 25, 29, 30, 35, 42, 45, 48, 66, 67, 76

Date of Accounts	Dec 11	Dec 10	Dec 09
Working Capital	369	372	468
Fixed Assets	440	416	321
Current Assets	554	538	600

Snell 2000 Ltd
Torbay Road Trading Estate Torbay Road, Castle Cary, BA7 7DT
Tel: 01963-351616 **Fax:** 01963-351818
E-mail: info@snell2000.com
Website: http://www.snellstonesystems.com
Directors: E. Snell (Fin), T. Snell (MD)
Immediate Holding Company: SNELL 2000 LIMITED
Registration no: 03339815 **Date established:** 1997
No.of Employees: 1 - 10 **Product Groups:** 45

Date of Accounts	Apr 11	Apr 10	Apr 09
Working Capital	-40	-48	-47
Current Assets	29	20	25

Tyre Renewals Ltd
Torbay Road, Castle Cary, BA7 7DT
Tel: 01963-350470 **Fax:** 01963-350503
E-mail: michael.rees@tyre-renewals.co.uk
Website: http://www.tyre-renewals.co.uk
Bank(s): National Westminster Bank Plc
Directors: M. Rees (Dir)
Immediate Holding Company: TYRE RENEWALS LIMITED
Registration no: 00921415 **VAT No.:** GB 378 7292 96
Date established: 1967 **Turnover:** Up to £250,000
No.of Employees: 11 - 20 **Product Groups:** 29

Date of Accounts	Oct 11	Oct 10	Oct 09
Working Capital	-5	12	-161
Fixed Assets	1m	1m	1m
Current Assets	583	607	590

Chard

Airstream Copywriting Services
ACS House Windsor Crescent, Chard, TA20 2HG
Tel: 01460-239388 **Fax:** 01460-239388
E-mail: copywriteruk@aol.com
Website: http://www.copywriter.uk.com
Directors: D. Carter (Prop)
Date established: 1996 **Turnover:** Up to £250,000
No.of Employees: 1 - 10 **Product Groups:** 81

Bodycote Heat Treatments Ltd
Leach Road Chard Business Park, Chard, TA20 1FA
Tel: 01460-67957 **Fax:** 01460-67962
E-mail: john.morris@bodycote.com
Website: http://www.bodycote.com
Bank(s): HSBC, Manchester
Managers: J. Morris (Works Gen Mgr)
Ultimate Holding Company: BODYCOTE PLC
Immediate Holding Company: BODYCOTE HEAT TREATMENTS LIMITED
Registration no: 01025652 **Date established:** 1971 **Turnover:** £5m - £10m
No.of Employees: 21 - 50 **Product Groups:** 48

Date of Accounts	Dec 11	Dec 10	Dec 09
Sales Turnover	37m	33m	31m
Pre Tax Profit/Loss	6m	4m	-10m
Working Capital	13m	11m	7m
Fixed Assets	40m	42m	46m
Current Assets	21m	18m	15m
Current Liabilities	5m	5m	5m

Brecknell Willis & Co. Ltd
PO Box 10, Chard, TA20 2DE
Tel: 01460-64941 **Fax:** 01460-66122
E-mail: enquiries@brecknellwillis.com
Website: http://www.brecknell-willis.co.uk
Directors: M. Perfect (Dir)
Managers: D. Steel (Tech Serv Mgr), S. Pearce, L. Barrett
Ultimate Holding Company: FANDSTAN ELECTRIC GROUP LIMITED
Immediate Holding Company: BRECKNELL, WILLIS & CO. LIMITED
Registration no: 00306444 **Date established:** 1935
Turnover: £20m - £50m **No.of Employees:** 101 - 250
Product Groups: 35, 37, 45, 46

Date of Accounts	Dec 11	Dec 10	Dec 09
Sales Turnover	38m	41m	37m
Pre Tax Profit/Loss	4m	4m	4m
Working Capital	10m	12m	11m
Fixed Assets	7m	3m	3m
Current Assets	23m	27m	25m
Current Liabilities	7m	10m	10m

Brecknell Willis Composites Ltd
Unit 1 Millfield, Chard, TA20 2BB
Tel: 01460-68111 **Fax:** 01460-66057
E-mail: mike@bwcomposites.co.uk
Website: http://www.bwcomposites.co.uk
Directors: M. Casemore (MD)
Managers: B. Madry, R. Turner (Admin Off)
Ultimate Holding Company: FANDSTAN ELECTRIC GROUP LIMITED
Immediate Holding Company: BRECKNELL WILLIS COMPOSITES LIMITED
Registration no: 03150185 **Date established:** 1996 **Turnover:** £1m - £2m
No.of Employees: 21 - 50 **Product Groups:** 30, 39

Date of Accounts	Dec 11	Dec 10	Dec 09
Sales Turnover	3m	3m	3m
Pre Tax Profit/Loss	682	556	284
Working Capital	1m	978	586
Fixed Assets	411	410	454
Current Assets	2m	2m	1m
Current Liabilities	194	294	201

C & D South West
Kingfisher Works Millfield, Chard, TA20 2BB
Tel: 01460-64701 **Fax:** 01460-64702
E-mail: sales@cdsw.co.uk
Website: http://www.cdsw.co.uk
Directors: C. Hammond (MD)
Immediate Holding Company: C & D SOUTH WEST LTD
Registration no: 05150159 **Date established:** 2004
No.of Employees: 11 - 20 **Product Groups:** 77

Date of Accounts	Jun 11	Jun 10	Jun 09
Working Capital	106	37	39
Fixed Assets	280	247	190
Current Assets	495	291	252

Chuckleprint
Unit 7 Crimchard Business Centre, Chard, TA20 1JT
Tel: 01460-65145 **Fax:** 01460-65145
E-mail: dee.mear@gmail.com
Directors: D. Mear (Ptnr)
VAT No.: GB 323 2672 79 **Date established:** 1980
Turnover: Up to £250,000 **No.of Employees:** 1 - 10 **Product Groups:** 23

Clegg
Pulleys Barn Wambrook, Chard, TA20 3DF
Tel: 01460-62583 **Fax:** 01460-62583
Directors: A. Clegg (Prop)
Date established: 1988 **No.of Employees:** 1 - 10 **Product Groups:** 26, 35

Coker Engineering Ltd
Millfield Close, Chard, TA20 2DJ
Tel: 01460-67162 **Fax:** 01460-61210
E-mail: sales@cokerengineering.com
Website: http://www.cokerengineering.com
Directors: S. Throup (Dir), M. Throup (MD)
Immediate Holding Company: COKER ENGINEERING LIMITED
Registration no: 02871670 **VAT No.:** GB 634 4023 69
Date established: 1993 **Turnover:** £250,000 - £500,000
No.of Employees: 11 - 20 **Product Groups:** 48

Date of Accounts	Dec 11	Dec 10	Dec 09
Working Capital	522	349	424
Fixed Assets	37	43	52
Current Assets	667	484	493

Craftwurks
Winsham, Chard, TA20 4JU
Tel: 01460-30088
E-mail: simon@craftwurks.co.uk
Website: http://www.craftwurks.co.uk
Directors: S. Hebditch (Prop)
Immediate Holding Company: INSPIRED METAL LTD
Date established: 2012 **No.of Employees:** 1 - 10 **Product Groups:** 26, 35

Doncasters
Beeching Close, Chard, TA20 1BB
Tel: 01460-62892 **Fax:** 01460-67702
E-mail: pholt@doncasters.com
Website: http://www.doncasters.com
Directors: V. Halsey (Pers), P. Thompson (I.T. Dir), N. Booth (Fin)
Managers: P. Holt, M. Sunshine, C. Hubery, D. Gill (Tech Serv Mgr), M. Murphy (Personnel)
Immediate Holding Company: PRESTON ELECTRONICS (CHARD) LIMITED
Registration no: 00975764 **Date established:** 1989 **Turnover:** £5m - £10m
No.of Employees: 101 - 250 **Product Groups:** 34, 39, 66

Epak Electronics Ltd
8 Millfield, Chard, TA20 2BB
Tel: 01460-61791 **Fax:** 01460-67833
E-mail: sales@epakelectronics.com
Website: http://www.epakelectronics.com
Directors: N. Blamey (MD)
Immediate Holding Company: EPAK ELECTRONICS LIMITED
Registration no: 01229882 **VAT No.:** GB 284 7432 34
Date established: 1975 **Turnover:** £2m - £5m **No.of Employees:** 1 - 10
Product Groups: 37, 38, 47

Date of Accounts	Dec 11	Dec 10	Dec 09
Working Capital	70	69	91
Fixed Assets	196	202	206
Current Assets	208	228	216

J S J Solutions
Unit 2a Furnham Close, Chard, TA20 1DA
Tel: 01460-61550 **Fax:** 01460-61312
E-mail: sales@jsjsolutions.co.uk
Website: http://www.jsjsolutions.co.uk
Managers: G. Smillie (Mgr)
Date established: 2005 **No.of Employees:** 11 - 20 **Product Groups:** 35

Metal Tech Precision Ltd
Yonder Hill Chard Junction, Chard, TA20 4QR
Tel: 01460-221737 **Fax:** 01460-221747
E-mail: info@metal-tech.com
Website: http://www.metal-tech.com
Directors: S. Hill (MD), J. Hill (Fin)
Managers: D. Grinter, S. Blake, V. Barnes (Sales Admin)
Immediate Holding Company: METALTECH PRECISION LTD
Registration no: 03840106 **Date established:** 1999 **Turnover:** £5m - £10m
No.of Employees: 51 - 100 **Product Groups:** 35, 36, 37, 46, 48, 52, 84, 87

Date of Accounts	Oct 11	Oct 10	Oct 09
Sales Turnover	6m	5m	5m
Pre Tax Profit/Loss	403	197	374
Working Capital	360	47	293
Fixed Assets	3m	3m	3m
Current Assets	2m	2m	1m
Current Liabilities	344	406	195

N C Welding & Electrical Services Ltd
Devonia Furnham Road, Chard, TA20 1BE
Tel: 01460-68668
Website: http://www.ncweldingandelectrical.com
Directors: N. Crabb (Ptnr)
Immediate Holding Company: N C WELDING & ELECTRICAL SERVICES LIMITED
Registration no: 07217340 **Date established:** 2010
No.of Employees: 1 - 10 **Product Groups:** 35

Numatic International
Millfield Industrial Estate Millfield, Chard, TA20 2GB
Tel: 01460-68600 **Fax:** 01460-68458
E-mail: sales@numatic.co.uk
Website: http://www.numatic.co.uk
Bank(s): Barclays
Directors: C. Duncan (MD)
Managers: K. Porter (Tech Serv Mgr), M. Watson (Buyer), S. Whitlock (Fin Mgr), J. Evans (Sales & Mktg Mg), G. Attridge (Personnel)
Immediate Holding Company: NUMATIC INTERNATIONAL LIMITED
Registration no: 00773331 **Date established:** 1963
Turnover: £75m - £125m **No.of Employees:** 501 - 1000
Product Groups: 40

Date of Accounts	Dec 11	Dec 10	Dec 09
Sales Turnover	111m	105m	98m
Pre Tax Profit/Loss	5m	5m	5m
Working Capital	25m	23m	16m
Fixed Assets	30m	30m	30m
Current Assets	43m	43m	41m
Current Liabilities	7m	6m	6m

Phoenix Engineering Company Ltd
Phoenix Works Coombe Street, Chard, TA20 1JE
Tel: 01460-63531 **Fax:** 01460-67388
E-mail: service@phoenixeng.co.uk
Website: http://www.phoenixeng.co.uk
Directors: T. Jennings (Comm), S. Jennings (Dir), J. Jennings (Fin)
Managers: P. Gidley (Purch Mgr), B. Love (Buyer)
Ultimate Holding Company: JENNINGS INDUSTRIES LIMITED
Immediate Holding Company: PHOENIX ENGINEERING COMPANY LIMITED
Registration no: 00086564 **Date established:** 2005 **Turnover:** £5m - £10m
No.of Employees: 51 - 100 **Product Groups:** 42, 45

Date of Accounts	Sep 11	Sep 10	Sep 09
Working Capital	4m	4m	3m
Fixed Assets	86	105	106
Current Assets	5m	5m	4m

T P Timber Products
1 East Street, Chard, TA20 1EP
Tel: 01460-65655
Directors: P. Adams (Ptnr)
No.of Employees: 1 - 10 **Product Groups:** 35

Cheddar

Gerrard Hellier
Windy Ridge Sharpham Road, Cheddar, BS27 3DR
Tel: 01934-742886 **Fax:** 01934-742886
Directors: G. Hellier (Prop)
Date established: 1995 **No.of Employees:** 1 - 10 **Product Groups:** 26, 35

Date of Accounts	Oct 11	Oct 10	Oct 09
Sales Turnover	N/A	66	59
Pre Tax Profit/Loss	N/A	4	1
Working Capital	2	5	4
Fixed Assets	3	3	4
Current Assets	17	16	18
Current Liabilities	N/A	2	1

K P Food Machinery
7 Winchester Farm Draycott Road, Cheddar, BS27 3RP
Tel: 01934-741200 **Fax:** 01749-841588
E-mail: food@machinery23.fsnet.co.uk
Website: http://www.machinery23.fsnet.co.uk
Directors: K. Penny (Prop)
Date established: 2001 **No.of Employees:** 1 - 10 **Product Groups:** 20, 40, 41

Norset Office Supplies Ltd (t/a Lanier (South West))
Tween Town, Cheddar, BS27 3JD
Tel: 01934-742184 **Fax:** 01934-743986
E-mail: sales@laniersouthwest.co.uk
Website: http://www.laniersouthwest.co.uk
Directors: C. Smith (Prop), C. Smith (MD), M. Smith (MD)
Managers: S. Smith (Sales Admin)
Ultimate Holding Company: FINEFRONT LIMITED
Immediate Holding Company: NORSET OFFICE SUPPLIES LIMITED
Registration no: 02480181 **Date established:** 1990
Turnover: £500,000 - £1m **No.of Employees:** 1 - 10 **Product Groups:** 37, 44, 79

Date of Accounts	Dec 10	Dec 09	Dec 08
Working Capital	29	33	10
Fixed Assets	24	21	26
Current Assets	173	183	153

Palletech Welding
Unit 16 Winchester Farm Draycott Road, Cheddar, BS27 3RP
Tel: 01934-613223 **Fax:** 01934-613223
Directors: M. Stanton (Prop)
Date established: 2002 **No.of Employees:** 1 - 10 **Product Groups:** 26, 35

Ruption Bikes (t/a Split Second Imports)
Cheddar Business Park Wedmore Road, Cheddar, BS27 3EB
Tel: 01934-743888 **Fax:** 01934-743073
E-mail: sales@ruption.co.uk
Website: http://www.rupton.com
Directors: R. Hill (MD)
Managers: A. Bishop (Sales Prom Mgr)
Registration no: 03236050 **VAT No.:** GB 586 2556 05
Turnover: £1m - £2m **No.of Employees:** 1 - 10 **Product Groups:** 39, 68

Date of Accounts	Jun 10	Jun 09	Jun 08
Working Capital	693	439	524
Fixed Assets	114	60	29
Current Assets	1m	1m	1m
Current Liabilities	N/A	N/A	64

Crewkerne

M D Broom
Fairview Clapton Gate, Crewkerne, TA18 8PP
Tel: 01460-76669 **Fax:** 01460-76669
Directors: M. Broom (Prop)
Date established: 1991 **No.of Employees:** 1 - 10 **Product Groups:** 41

Cronite Castings Ltd
Blacknell Lane, Crewkerne, TA18 7YA
Tel: 01460-270300 **Fax:** 01460-72643
E-mail: nmanley@cronitecastings.com
Website: http://www.ase.com
Bank(s): Barclays, Walsall
Directors: N. Manley (MD)
Ultimate Holding Company: SAFE SA (FRANCE)
Immediate Holding Company: CRONITE CASTINGS LIMITED
Registration no: 00805297 **Date established:** 1964
Turnover: £10m - £20m **No.of Employees:** 101 - 250
Product Groups: 34, 36, 66

Date of Accounts	Dec 11	Dec 10	Dec 09
Sales Turnover	18m	13m	12m
Pre Tax Profit/Loss	1m	327	-302
Working Capital	3m	2m	2m
Fixed Assets	1m	1m	1m
Current Assets	7m	7m	5m
Current Liabilities	727	404	392

D C Services
Ashcombe Cottage Wayford, Crewkerne, TA18 8QJ
Tel: 01460-30553 **Fax:** 01460-30553
E-mail: dc-services@btconnect.com
Website: http://www.dc-services.co.uk
Directors: T. Bonfield (Prop)
Date established: 2000 **No.of Employees:** 1 - 10 **Product Groups:** 46

Euroquartz Ltd
Blacknell Lane, Crewkerne, TA18 7HE
Tel: 01460-230000 **Fax:** 01460-230001
E-mail: info@euroquartz.co.uk
Website: http://www.euroquartz.co.uk
Bank(s): Barclays
Directors: A. Treble (Fin)
Immediate Holding Company: EUROQUARTZ LIMITED
Registration no: 01773012 **Date established:** 1983 **Turnover:** £2m - £5m
No.of Employees: 21 - 50 **Product Groups:** 37

Date of Accounts	Dec 11	Dec 10	Dec 09
Working Capital	1m	1m	768
Fixed Assets	245	278	342
Current Assets	2m	2m	2m

I Q D Frequency Products Ltd
Station Road, Crewkerne, TA18 8AR
Tel: 01460-270200 **Fax:** 01460-72578
E-mail: info@cmac.com
Website: http://www.cmac.com/mt
Bank(s): National Westminster Bank Plc
Directors: D. Ralph (Dir)
Ultimate Holding Company: IQD GROUP LIMITED
Immediate Holding Company: IQD FREQUENCY PRODUCTS LIMITED
Registration no: 06478545 **VAT No.:** GB 187 3951 20
Date established: 2008 **Turnover:** £5m - £10m **No.of Employees:** 21 - 50
Product Groups: 37, 38

Date of Accounts	May 11	May 10	May 09
Sales Turnover	N/A	N/A	8m
Pre Tax Profit/Loss	N/A	N/A	231
Working Capital	118	18	-25
Fixed Assets	681	727	612
Current Assets	2m	2m	1m
Current Liabilities	N/A	N/A	395

Merriott Plastics Ltd
Eden Works Blacknell Lane, Crewkerne, TA18 7HE
Tel: 01460-72457 **Fax:** 01460-74481
E-mail: sales@merriott.com
Website: http://www.merriott.com
Bank(s): Lloyds TSB
Directors: A. Lawrence (Co Sec), I. Low (Chief Op Offcr)
Immediate Holding Company: MERRIOTT PLASTICS LIMITED
Registration no: 03496165 **Date established:** 1998 **Turnover:** £5m - £10m
No.of Employees: 51 - 100 **Product Groups:** 30, 37

Date of Accounts	Mar 11	Mar 10	Mar 09
Sales Turnover	9m	8m	N/A
Pre Tax Profit/Loss	1m	854	587
Working Capital	2m	2m	1m
Fixed Assets	1m	785	484
Current Assets	4m	3m	2m
Current Liabilities	474	430	258

Rod Page Woodturning
11 Southmead Crescent, Crewkerne, TA18 8DH
Tel: 01460-271426
E-mail: rod@rodpage-woodturner.co.uk
Website: http://rodpage-woodturner.co.uk

see next page

Rod Page Woodturning - Cont'd

Directors: R. Page (Prop)
Product Groups: 25, 36, 37, 48, 65

Rotalink Ltd

Cropmead, Crewkerne, TA18 7HQ
Tel: 01460-72000 **Fax:** 01460-74278
E-mail: info@rotalink.com
Website: http://www.rotalink.com
Bank(s): National Westminster Bank Plc
Directors: R. Hazell (Fin), M. Hazell (MD), P. Magee (Fin)
Managers: S. Nicol (Mktg Serv Mgr), D. Auton (Buyer), I. Redman (Tech Serv Mgr)
Ultimate Holding Company: OVAL (259) LIMITED
Immediate Holding Company: ROTALINK LIMITED
Registration no: 00313872 **VAT No.:** GB 585 9601 94
Date established: 1936 **Turnover:** £5m - £10m
No.of Employees: 51 - 100 **Product Groups:** 35, 37, 38, 46, 49

Date of Accounts	Sep 11	Sep 10	Sep 09
Sales Turnover	8m	9m	7m
Pre Tax Profit/Loss	2m	2m	2m
Working Capital	6m	5m	6m
Fixed Assets	867	517	595
Current Assets	7m	7m	7m
Current Liabilities	678	1m	1m

W & J Tod

Unit 8 Cropmead, Crewkerne, TA18 7HQ
Tel: 01460-77666 **Fax:** 01460-78001
E-mail: info@tods.co.uk
Website: http://www.tods.co.uk
Bank(s): National Westminster, Milton Keynes
Directors: S. Finch (MD), P. Louch (Fin)
Managers: P. Sweetland (Tech Serv Mgr)
Immediate Holding Company: W & J TOD HOLDINGS LIMITED
Registration no: 02514416 **VAT No.:** GB 429 0504 66
Date established: 1990 **Turnover:** £10m - £20m
No.of Employees: 101 - 250 **Product Groups:** 30, 39

Date of Accounts	Mar 08	Sep 11	Sep 10
Sales Turnover	14m	16m	13m
Pre Tax Profit/Loss	890	1m	14
Working Capital	136	778	-507
Fixed Assets	2m	2m	2m
Current Assets	5m	6m	5m
Current Liabilities	1m	3m	2m

Dulverton

N J Bawden

Brushford, Dulverton, TA22 9AR
Tel: 01398-323162
Directors: N. Bawden (Prop)
Date established: 1975 **No.of Employees:** 1 - 10 **Product Groups:** 41

Exmore Metalcraft

Unit 1b Barns Close Indl-Est Barns Close, Dulverton, TA22 9DZ
Tel: 07779-062850
Directors: P. Warren (Prop)
Date established: 2003 **No.of Employees:** 1 - 10 **Product Groups:** 35, 46, 49

Frome

Aggregate Industries

Marston House Marston Bigot, Frome, BA11 5DU
Tel: 01373-451001 **Fax:** 01373-836501
E-mail: sue.spicer@aggregate.com
Website: http://www.aggregate.com
Directors: K. White (Co Sec), L. Quinn (Div)
Managers: S. Spicer (Sales Admin)
Immediate Holding Company: RECYCLED ROCK AND AGGREGATE LIMITED
Registration no: 03060314 **Date established:** 1995
Turnover: £125m - £250m **No.of Employees:** 51 - 100
Product Groups: 45, 51, 84

Date of Accounts	Mar 11	Mar 10	Mar 07
Pre Tax Profit/Loss	2	N/A	18
Working Capital	N/A	53	53
Current Assets	1	53	56
Current Liabilities	1	N/A	3

Building Additions Ltd

Southgate Commerce Park, Frome, BA11 2RY
Tel: 01373-454577 **Fax:** 01373-454578
E-mail: sales@buildingadditions.co.uk
Website: http://www.buildingadditions.co.uk
Bank(s): HSBC Bank plc
Directors: A. Ferris (MD), A. Regan (Sales)
Immediate Holding Company: BUILDING ADDITIONS LIMITED
Registration no: 03369691 **VAT No.:** GB 692 0350 44
Date established: 1997 **Turnover:** £1m - £2m **No.of Employees:** 11 - 20
Product Groups: 25, 30

Date of Accounts	Jul 11	Jul 10	Jul 09
Sales Turnover	N/A	N/A	2m
Pre Tax Profit/Loss	N/A	N/A	188
Working Capital	51	25	60
Fixed Assets	15	19	23
Current Assets	330	411	520
Current Liabilities	N/A	N/A	228

Butler Tanner & Dennis Ltd

Caxton Road, Frome, BA11 1NF
Tel: 01373-451500 **Fax:** 01373-451333
E-mail: enquiries@butlertanneranddennis.com
Website: http://www.butlertanneranddennis.com
Bank(s): HSBC Bank plc
Directors: K. Sarney (MD)
Immediate Holding Company: BUTLER, TANNER & DENNIS LIMITED
Registration no: 06633222 **VAT No.:** GB 137 4186 63
Date established: 2008 **Turnover:** £20m - £50m
No.of Employees: 101 - 250 **Product Groups:** 28, 81

Date of Accounts	Dec 10	Dec 09
Sales Turnover	13m	15m
Pre Tax Profit/Loss	-841	-3m
Working Capital	-2m	-643
Fixed Assets	6m	4m
Current Assets	4m	4m
Current Liabilities	979	844

Carley Engineering Ltd

Carley Works Garsdale, Frome, BA11 1PR
Tel: 01373-452231 **Fax:** 01373-451139
Directors: K. Jeffries (Fin), M. Stockting (Dir)
Immediate Holding Company: CARLEY ENGINEERING LIMITED
Registration no: 06899291 **VAT No.:** GB 302 5427 00
Date established: 2009 **Turnover:** £2m - £5m **No.of Employees:** 11 - 20
Product Groups: 48

Date of Accounts	Jul 11	Jul 10
Working Capital	343	180
Fixed Assets	70	4
Current Assets	791	449

Cellar Management Services

43 Innox Hill, Frome, BA11 2LN
Tel: 01373-452778 **Fax:** 01373-452778
Directors: F. Howard Coles (Prop)
No.of Employees: 1 - 10 **Product Groups:** 20, 40, 41

Davies & Davies Crockery Hire

Monksham Farm Marston Bigot, Frome, BA11 5BR
Tel: 01373-836177
E-mail: racheltwigger@yahoo.com
Website: http://www.davies-davies-crockeryhire.com
Directors: R. Twigger (Snr Part)
Immediate Holding Company: LAND & MINERAL MANAGEMENT LIMITED
Registration no: 02757573 **Date established:** 1992
No.of Employees: 1 - 10 **Product Groups:** 20, 40, 41

Ian Fellows Ltd

The Old Tannery Lower Keyford, Frome, BA11 4AR
Tel: 01373-473161 **Fax:** 01373-451609
E-mail: sales@ianfellows.co.uk
Website: http://www.ianfellows.co.uk
Directors: A. Fowler (Chief Op Offcr)
Ultimate Holding Company: MARCO HOLDING COMPANY LIMITED
Immediate Holding Company: IAN FELLOWS LIMITED
Registration no: 01399030 **Date established:** 1978 **Turnover:** £1m - £2m
No.of Employees: 1 - 10 **Product Groups:** 38

Date of Accounts	Mar 11	Nov 09	Nov 08
Working Capital	65	55	112
Fixed Assets	43	54	64
Current Assets	251	207	253
Current Liabilities	113	97	110

Fork Truck Services

36 Summer Hill, Frome, BA11 1LT
Tel: 01373-466427 **Fax:** 01373-303936
Website: http://www.forktruckservices.co.uk
Directors: D. Seviour (Dir)
Immediate Holding Company: FORK TRUCK SERVICES (FROME) LIMITED
Registration no: 04689369 **Date established:** 2003
No.of Employees: 1 - 10 **Product Groups:** 35, 39, 45

Date of Accounts	Mar 11	Mar 10	Mar 09
Working Capital	8	9	12
Fixed Assets	1	2	2
Current Assets	27	24	26

Frome Tool & Gauge Ltd

Manor Road Marston Trading Estate, Frome, BA11 4BL
Tel: 01373-462226 **Fax:** 01373-452123
E-mail: michael.west@frometoolandguage.co.uk
Bank(s): HSBC Bank plc
Directors: A. Hazel (Dir), M. West (Ch)
Managers: F. Farley (Buyer)
Immediate Holding Company: FROME TOOL & GAUGE LTD
Registration no: 01647491 **Date established:** 1982 **Turnover:** £1m - £2m
No.of Employees: 21 - 50 **Product Groups:** 38, 46, 48

Date of Accounts	Jun 11	Jun 10	Jun 09
Working Capital	265	203	170
Fixed Assets	236	245	237
Current Assets	457	326	334

Guitarbitz Guitar Shop

C5 Southgate Commerce Park, Frome, BA11 2RY
Tel: 08452-222603
E-mail: sales@guitarbitz.com
Website: http://www.guitarbitz.com
Directors: D. Kenwood (Co Sec)
Registration no: 05086329 **Date established:** 2004
Turnover: £250,000 - £500,000 **No.of Employees:** 1 - 10
Product Groups: 49

Date of Accounts	Mar 08	Mar 07	Mar 06
Working Capital	23	27	15
Fixed Assets	9	2	2
Current Assets	73	61	66
Current Liabilities	50	34	51

Jewson Ltd

Station Approach, Frome, BA11 1RE
Tel: 01373-463459 **Fax:** 01373-463459
Website: http://www.jewson.co.uk
Managers: S. Desbrough (Mgr)
Ultimate Holding Company: COMPAGNIE DE SAINT GOBAIN (FRANCE)
Immediate Holding Company: JEWSON LIMITED
Registration no: 00348407 **Date established:** 1939 **Turnover:** £2m - £5m
No.of Employees: 1 - 10 **Product Groups:** 66

Date of Accounts	Dec 11	Dec 10	Dec 09
Sales Turnover	1606m	1547m	1485m
Pre Tax Profit/Loss	18m	100m	45m
Working Capital	-345m	-250m	-349m
Fixed Assets	496m	387m	461m
Current Assets	657m	1005m	1320m
Current Liabilities	66m	120m	64m

L J H Group Ltd

Leigh Road Chantry, Frome, BA11 3LR
Tel: 01373-836451 **Fax:** 01373-836879
E-mail: sales@ljhgroup.co.uk
Website: http://www.ljhgroup.co.uk
Bank(s): Royal Bank of Scotland
Directors: A. Moss (MD), D. Lloyd (Dir), S. Hall (Fin), W. Elliot (MD), W. Elliott (MD)
Managers: G. Moore (Personnel)
Ultimate Holding Company: AM SERVICES (UK) LTD
Immediate Holding Company: L.J.H. GROUP LIMITED
Registration no: 01237248 **VAT No.:** 164 2288 03 **Date established:** 1975
Turnover: £1m - £2m **No.of Employees:** 21 - 50 **Product Groups:** 42, 45

Date of Accounts	Jun 11	Jun 10	Jun 09
Working Capital	211	41	-49
Fixed Assets	93	147	198
Current Assets	959	2m	918

R H Ling

82 Forest Road, Frome, BA11 2TQ
Tel: 01373-467592 **Fax:** 01373-467592
E-mail: ling1931@btinternet.com
Directors: R. Ling (Prop)
Date established: 1984 **No.of Employees:** 1 - 10 **Product Groups:** 36, 40

M I M Catering Equipment

Ridgeway Nunney, Frome, BA11 4NU
Tel: 01373-836772 **Fax:** 01373-836557
E-mail: mimcateringequip@btinternet.com
Directors: P. Garrod (Prop)
Date established: 1986 **No.of Employees:** 1 - 10 **Product Groups:** 20, 40, 41

Micron Gauges Ltd

1-3 Keyford Court Marston Trading Estate, Frome, BA11 4BD
Tel: 01373-461584 **Fax:** 01373-461585
E-mail: sales@microngauges.co.uk
Website: http://www.microngauges.co.uk
Bank(s): HSBC Bank plc
Directors: G. Latham (Dir), R. Willis (Dir), S. Latham (Dir)
Registration no: 02029565 **Date established:** 1986
Turnover: Up to £250,000 **No.of Employees:** 11 - 20 **Product Groups:** 37

Date of Accounts	Dec 07	Dec 06	Dec 05
Working Capital	-8	33	60
Fixed Assets	81	113	146
Current Assets	79	94	163
Current Liabilities	87	62	103

Mistover Ltd

2a Frome Road Beckington, Frome, BA11 6TD
Tel: 01373-830190 **Fax:** 08700- 517311
E-mail: info@mistover.co.uk
Website: http://www.mistover.co.uk
Directors: J. Noon (MD), M. Noon (Ptnr), I. Hodson (Fin), M. Noon (Sales), J. Noon (Dir)
Managers: I. Hodson (I.T. Exec)
Immediate Holding Company: MISTOVER LIMITED
Registration no: 04357533 **Date established:** 2002
Turnover: Up to £250,000 **No.of Employees:** 1 - 10 **Product Groups:** 54, 84, 86

Date of Accounts	Jan 11	Jan 10	Jan 09
Working Capital	4	1	-2
Fixed Assets	1	1	2
Current Assets	24	15	10

Mullett & Company UK Ltd

Raven Hill Leys Lane, Frome, BA11 2JT
Tel: 01373-455665 **Fax:** 01373-455667
E-mail: mulletts@mullettand.co.uk
Website: http://www.mullettand.co.uk
Directors: F. Kennard (Fin), J. Kennard (MD)
Immediate Holding Company: MULLETT AND COMPANY UK LIMITED
Registration no: 03554204 **VAT No.:** GB 712 9721 38
Date established: 1998 **Turnover:** Up to £250,000
No.of Employees: 1 - 10 **Product Groups:** 32

Date of Accounts	Jun 11	Jun 10	Jun 09
Sales Turnover	107	119	138
Pre Tax Profit/Loss	9	-0	-6
Working Capital	-0	-5	-5
Fixed Assets	1	N/A	N/A
Current Assets	31	33	41
Current Liabilities	5	6	5

Oakville Care Centre Ltd

3 Badcox, Frome, BA11 3BQ
Tel: 01373-455415 **Fax:** 01373-461438
E-mail: customerservices@oakvillecarecentre.co.uk
Website: http://www.oakvillecarecentre.co.uk
Directors: R. Lymer (Dir)
Immediate Holding Company: OAKVILLE CARE CENTRE LIMITED
Registration no: 07222952 **Date established:** 2010
No.of Employees: 1 - 10 **Product Groups:** 39, 45, 67, 85

Date of Accounts	Jun 11
Working Capital	13
Current Assets	31

S P Engineering Motorcycle Exhausts & Accessories Ltd

Unit 5 Keyford Court Manor Furlong, Frome, BA11 4BD
Tel: 01373-474740 **Fax:** 01373-471417
E-mail: sales@spengineering.co.uk
Website: http://www.spengineering.co.uk
Directors: D. Pepler (Ptnr)
Immediate Holding Company: SP ENGINEERING (FROME) LIMITED
Registration no: 05742334 **Date established:** 2006
Turnover: Up to £250,000 **No.of Employees:** 1 - 10 **Product Groups:** 45, 48

Date of Accounts	Mar 12	Mar 11	Mar 10
Sales Turnover	98	269	182
Pre Tax Profit/Loss	31	32	9
Working Capital	29	25	17
Fixed Assets	9	5	6
Current Assets	58	80	65
Current Liabilities	8	16	8

J W Singer

10 Handlemaker Road, Frome, BA11 4RW
Tel: 01373-462201 **Fax:** 01373-473156
E-mail: miles.denning@jwsinger.com
Website: http://www.jwsinger.com
Directors: M. Denning (Chief Op Offcr)
Managers: R. Treasure (Purch Mgr), P. Jones (Personnel), S. Giles (Comm), M. Macmichael, L. Rose (Personnel), K. McNeil (Chief Acct)

Ultimate Holding Company: TYCO
Registration no: 01841522 **Turnover:** £10m - £20m
No.of Employees: 51 - 100 **Product Groups:** 34, 40

Somerset Storage Ltd

The Retreat, Frome, BA11 5JU
Tel: 01373-467575
E-mail: info@somersetstorage.co.uk
Website: http://www.somersetstorage.co.uk
Managers: T. Thomas (Mgr)
Immediate Holding Company: SOMERSET STORAGE LIMITED
Registration no: 04674822 **Date established:** 2003
No.of Employees: 1 - 10 **Product Groups:** 35, 45, 67, 77

Date of Accounts	Mar 12	Mar 11	Mar 10
Working Capital	217	23	182
Fixed Assets	989	1m	679
Current Assets	384	242	302

T H White

Vallis Road, Frome, BA11 3EN
Tel: 01373-465941 **Fax:** 01373-462654
E-mail: reb@thwhite.co.uk
Website: http://www.thwhite.co.uk
Managers: R. Bennett (Mgr), D. Sobey (Buyer), D. Sobey
Immediate Holding Company: T. H. WHITE LIMITED
Registration no: 00519868 **Date established:** 1953
No.of Employees: 21 - 50 **Product Groups:** 41

Glastonbury

Avalon Plastics Ltd

Morland Road Morlands Enterprise Park, Glastonbury, BA6 9FZ
Tel: 08703-891998 **Fax:** 01458-834384
E-mail: enquiries@avalonplastics.co.uk
Website: http://www.avalonplastics.co.uk
Bank(s): Barclays, Bristol
Directors: H. Jones (Fin), K. Butler (MD), K. Jones (I.T. Dir)
Managers: P. Routley (Personnel), P. Christian, S. Dyer (Tech Sales Mgr)
Ultimate Holding Company: BECKERY PROPERTIES LIMITED
Immediate Holding Company: AVALON PLASTICS LIMITED
Registration no: 04932732 **Date established:** 2003
Turnover: £10m - £20m **No.of Employees:** 101 - 250
Product Groups: 30, 66

Date of Accounts	Nov 11	Nov 10	Nov 09
Sales Turnover	11m	10m	8m
Pre Tax Profit/Loss	-112	-18	207
Working Capital	-410	-24	356
Fixed Assets	2m	2m	2m
Current Assets	4m	4m	3m
Current Liabilities	3m	2m	2m

Castle Welding & Fabrication Ltd

Sabre Engineering Works West Pennard, Glastonbury, BA6 8ND
Tel: 01749-890666 **Fax:** 01749-890673
E-mail: julian@castlewelding.co.uk
Website: http://www.castlewelding.co.uk
Directors: J. Wittleton (MD)
Immediate Holding Company: CASTLE WELDING AND FABRICATION LIMITED
Registration no: 04600171 **Date established:** 2002
No.of Employees: 1 - 10 **Product Groups:** 26, 35

Date of Accounts	Dec 11	Dec 10	Dec 09
Working Capital	-166	-171	-161
Fixed Assets	558	561	560
Current Assets	64	61	93

Date Palm Developments

Ham Street Baltonsborough, Glastonbury, BA6 8QG
Tel: 01458-851000 **Fax:** 01458-850999
E-mail: avril.brackpool@datepalm.co.uk
Website: http://www.datepalm.co.uk
Directors: A. Brackpool (MD)
Ultimate Holding Company: ST JULIENS LIMITED
Immediate Holding Company: D.P.D. LIMITED
Registration no: 03851847 **VAT No.:** 701 0172 06 **Date established:** 1999
Turnover: £1m - £2m **No.of Employees:** 21 - 50 **Product Groups:** 07, 31, 41, 42

Date of Accounts	Nov 10	Nov 09	Nov 08
Working Capital	529	342	275
Fixed Assets	217	250	282
Current Assets	1m	788	701

R J Draper & Co. Ltd

PO Box 3, Glastonbury, BA6 8YA
Tel: 01458-831420 **Fax:** 01458-835355
E-mail: info@draper-of-glastonbury.com
Website: http://www.draper-of-glastonbury.com
Bank(s): Lloyds
Directors: N. Draper (MD)
Immediate Holding Company: R.J.DRAPER & COMPANY,LIMITED
Registration no: 00369371 **VAT No.:** GB 130 0365 28
Date established: 1941 **Turnover:** £5m - £10m **No.of Employees:** 11 - 20
Product Groups: 22

Date of Accounts	Apr 12	Apr 11	Apr 10
Working Capital	-682	-658	-668
Fixed Assets	780	785	789
Current Assets	364	300	242
Current Liabilities	900	N/A	N/A

Expressions Display Ltd

The Homestead Newtown, West Pennard, Glastonbury, BA6 8NN
Tel: 01458-832702 **Fax:** 01458-832712
E-mail: sales@expressionsdisplay.co.uk
Website: http://www.expressionsdisplay.co.uk
Directors: N. Hewitt-Cooper (Dir)
Immediate Holding Company: EXPRESSIONS DISPLAY LIMITED
Registration no: 05050680 **Date established:** 2004
Turnover: £250,000 - £500,000 **No.of Employees:** 1 - 10
Product Groups: 26

Date of Accounts	Mar 11	Mar 10	Mar 09
Sales Turnover	N/A	N/A	397
Pre Tax Profit/Loss	N/A	N/A	79
Working Capital	3	1	12
Fixed Assets	N/A	1	2
Current Assets	45	44	86
Current Liabilities	N/A	N/A	41

Glastonbury Spring Water Co.

Park Corner Farm Park Corner, Glastonbury, BA6 8JY
Tel: 01458-834344 **Fax:** 01458-833360
E-mail: sales@glastonburyspringwater.com
Website: http://www.glastonburyspringwater.com
Directors: C. Tucker (Dir)
Ultimate Holding Company: PARK CORNER HOLDINGS LIMITED
Immediate Holding Company: GLASTONBURY SPRING WATER COMPANY LIMITED
Registration no: 02302169 **Date established:** 1988
No.of Employees: 11 - 20 **Product Groups:** 21, 36, 40

Date of Accounts	Jul 11	Jul 10	Jul 09
Working Capital	-56	83	21
Fixed Assets	671	582	552
Current Assets	225	287	196

E J Godwin Peat Industries Ltd

St Marys Road Meare, Glastonbury, BA6 9SP
Tel: 01458-860644 **Fax:** 01458-860587
E-mail: ejgodwin@btinternet.com
Website: http://www.ejgodwin.biz
Directors: A. Rowland (Dir)
Immediate Holding Company: E.J. GODWIN (PEAT INDUSTRIES) LIMITED
Registration no: 00317585 **VAT No.:** GB 130 1938 02
Date established: 1936 **Turnover:** £2m - £5m **No.of Employees:** 1 - 10
Product Groups: 25, 32, 41

Date of Accounts	Jul 11	Jul 10	Jul 09
Working Capital	2m	1m	2m
Fixed Assets	2m	2m	2m
Current Assets	3m	3m	3m

Middleton Engineering Ltd

Ashcott Road Meare, Glastonbury, BA6 9SU
Tel: 01458-860264 **Fax:** 01458-860311
E-mail: admin@middletonengineering.co.uk
Website: http://www.middletonengineering.co.uk
Bank(s): Lloyds TSB Bank plc
Directors: J. Middleton (Fin), M. Smith (I.T. Dir)
Managers: S. Young (Fin Mgr), D. Rossiter (Buyer)
Immediate Holding Company: MIDDLETON ENGINEERING LIMITED
Registration no: 01952788 **VAT No.:** GB 436 9012 53
Date established: 1985 **Turnover:** £1m - £2m **No.of Employees:** 21 - 50
Product Groups: 44, 46

Date of Accounts	Jan 12	Jan 11	Jan 10
Working Capital	1m	1m	879
Fixed Assets	1m	1m	1m
Current Assets	2m	2m	1m

J R Porter & Son Saw Specialists Ltd

Stileway, Glastonbury, BA6 9SH
Tel: 01458-860259 **Fax:** 01458-860731
Directors: J. Porter (MD)
Immediate Holding Company: J.R. PORTER & SON (SAW SPECIALISTS) LIMITED
Registration no: 01933887 **Date established:** 1985
Turnover: Up to £250,000 **No.of Employees:** 1 - 10 **Product Groups:** 48

Date of Accounts	Oct 11	Oct 10	Oct 09
Working Capital	-6	1	6
Fixed Assets	4	6	9
Current Assets	28	31	28

Sequoien Community Interest Company

91 Bere Lane, Glastonbury, BA6 8BE
Tel: 01458-833256
Directors: S. Markert Emans (Fin)
Immediate Holding Company: SEQUOIEN COMMUNITY INTEREST COMPANY
Registration no: 06073429 **Date established:** 2007
No.of Employees: 1 - 10 **Product Groups:** 35, 36, 39

Highbridge

Amcor Flexibles Baricol

No 1 Gass Close Isleport Business Park, Highbridge, TA9 4JT
Tel: 01278-793232 **Fax:** 01278-794996
E-mail: sales@amcor.com
Website: http://www.amcor.com
Directors: L. Asp (Dir), S. Embleton Smith (Co Sec)
Immediate Holding Company: FLEXTRUS LIMITED
Registration no: 06371607 **Date established:** 2007
Turnover: £10m - £20m **No.of Employees:** 1 - 10 **Product Groups:** 30, 31

Date of Accounts	Dec 11	Dec 10	Dec 09
Sales Turnover	12m	12m	12m
Pre Tax Profit/Loss	110	539	625
Working Capital	2m	2m	2m
Fixed Assets	787	935	635
Current Assets	4m	5m	5m
Current Liabilities	245	534	738

Amesbury & Puddy

The Forge Church Street, Mark, Highbridge, TA9 4NF
Tel: 01278-641224 **Fax:** 01278-641601
E-mail: amesbury.puddy@hotmail.co.uk
Directors: P. Boobyer (Prop)
Date established: 1958 **No.of Employees:** 1 - 10 **Product Groups:** 41

Jo Bird & Co. Ltd

Factory Lane Bason Bridge, Highbridge, TA9 4RN
Tel: 01278-785546 **Fax:** 01278-780541
E-mail: jobird@btinternet.com
Website: http://www.jobird.co.uk
Bank(s): Lloyds TSB Bank plc
Directors: G. Atkins (MD)
Immediate Holding Company: JO BIRD AND COMPANY LIMITED
Registration no: 01583922 **VAT No.:** GB 437 0836 46
Date established: 1981 **Turnover:** £1m - £2m **No.of Employees:** 11 - 20
Product Groups: 26, 30, 39, 40, 67, 74, 84

Date of Accounts	May 12	May 11	May 10
Working Capital	447	315	243
Fixed Assets	52	37	56
Current Assets	946	655	488

Cooper B Line Ltd

Commerce Way, Highbridge, TA9 4AQ
Tel: 01278-783371 **Fax:** 01278-789037
E-mail: sales@cooperbline.co.uk
Website: http://www.cooperbline.co.uk
Bank(s): National Westminster Bank Plc
Directors: D. Olive (Fin), N. Thompson (MD)
Managers: G. Day (Purch Mgr), J. Day (Sales Prom Mgr), S. Brady (Mktg Serv Mgr), T. Milburn (Tech Serv Mgr), E. Bartlett (Personnel)
Ultimate Holding Company: COOPER INDUSTRIES PUBLIC LIMITED COMPANY
Immediate Holding Company: COOPER B-LINE LIMITED
Registration no: 00619241 **VAT No.:** GB 130 0195 27
Date established: 1959 **Turnover:** £5m - £10m
No.of Employees: 101 - 250 **Product Groups:** 26, 35, 36, 66

Date of Accounts	Dec 11	Dec 10	Dec 09
Sales Turnover	7m	10m	9m
Pre Tax Profit/Loss	-2m	-1m	-251
Working Capital	-6m	-4m	-3m
Fixed Assets	4m	3m	3m
Current Assets	3m	3m	3m
Current Liabilities	282	408	294

Delta Civil Engineering Group Holdings Ltd

Newtown Road, Highbridge, TA9 3HX
Tel: 01278-764100 **Fax:** 01278-764111
E-mail: civils@deltace.com
Website: http://www.deltace.com
Managers: M. Lill (Mktg Serv Mgr), P. Spencer (Admin Off)
Immediate Holding Company: DELTA CIVIL ENGINEERING GROUP (HOLDINGS) LIMITED
Registration no: 00974498 **Date established:** 1970 **Turnover:** £5m - £10m
No.of Employees: 21 - 50 **Product Groups:** 51

Date of Accounts	Jan 11	Jan 10	Jan 09
Sales Turnover	5m	7m	6m
Pre Tax Profit/Loss	262	410	223
Working Capital	478	475	261
Fixed Assets	739	647	487
Current Assets	2m	2m	2m
Current Liabilities	577	346	769

Dirt Driver Ltd

Ham Road Brent Knoll, Highbridge, TA9 4BJ
Tel: 01278-785425 **Fax:** 01278-781790
E-mail: info@dirtdriver.co.uk
Website: http://www.dirtdriver.co.uk
Directors: N. Driver (MD)
Immediate Holding Company: DIRT DRIVER LIMITED
Registration no: 01041712 **Date established:** 1972
No.of Employees: 1 - 10 **Product Groups:** 38, 42

Date of Accounts	Mar 11	Mar 10	Mar 09
Working Capital	334	352	404
Fixed Assets	72	87	100
Current Assets	516	533	543

Fans & Blowers Ltd

Walrow Industrial Estate Commerce Way, Highbridge, TA9 4AG
Tel: 01278-784004 **Fax:** 01278-792848
E-mail: jmn@fansandblowers.com
Website: http://www.fansandblowers.com
Bank(s): Barclays
Directors: B. Dawes (Sales), J. Newey (MD)
Managers: D. Keates (Sales Prom Mgr), K. Paice (Buyer)
Ultimate Holding Company: JAMSWEENEY LIMITED
Immediate Holding Company: FANS & BLOWERS LIMITED
Registration no: 05071200 **VAT No.:** GB 564 5099 18
Date established: 2004 **Turnover:** £2m - £5m **No.of Employees:** 21 - 50
Product Groups: 39, 40, 66

Date of Accounts	Mar 11	Mar 10	Mar 09
Working Capital	136	97	-21
Fixed Assets	541	507	380
Current Assets	1m	1m	946

Flextrus

1 Gass Close, Highbridge, TA9 4JT
Tel: 01278-793232 **Fax:** 01278-794996
E-mail: info@flextrus.com
Website: http://www.flextrus.com
Directors: C. Gorst (Sales & Mktg)
Managers: S. Embleton-Smith (Chief Mgr), A. Harvey (Purch Mgr), S. Embleton Smith (Chief Mgr), D. Loader (Comptroller)
Immediate Holding Company: FLEXTRUS LIMITED
Registration no: 06371607 **Date established:** 2007
Turnover: £10m - £20m **No.of Employees:** 21 - 50 **Product Groups:** 30, 31, 48

Date of Accounts	Dec 11	Dec 10	Dec 09
Sales Turnover	12m	12m	12m
Pre Tax Profit/Loss	110	539	625
Working Capital	2m	2m	2m
Fixed Assets	787	935	635
Current Assets	4m	5m	5m
Current Liabilities	245	534	738

M P G Forktrucks Ltd

Commerce Way, Highbridge, TA9 4AG
Tel: 01278-788250 **Fax:** 01278-788676
E-mail: mpgforktrucks@btconnect.com
Directors: M. Denham (MD)
Immediate Holding Company: MPG FORKTRUCKS LIMITED
Registration no: 05401707 **Date established:** 2005
No.of Employees: 1 - 10 **Product Groups:** 39, 40, 45

Date of Accounts	Mar 11	Mar 10	Mar 09
Working Capital	-57	-67	-58
Fixed Assets	57	67	77
Current Assets	19	24	24

Quick Sign

Quick Sign House Evercreech Way Walrow Industrial Estate, Highbridge, TA9 4AR
Tel: 01278-787268 **Fax:** 01278-787268
E-mail: sales@quick-sign.co.uk
Website: http://www.quick-sign.co.uk
Directors: N. Burke (Prop)
Date established: 1988 **Turnover:** Up to £250,000
No.of Employees: 1 - 10 **Product Groups:** 28, 39, 49, 52, 81

S & D Replacement Tanks
15 Old Pawlett Road West Huntspill, Highbridge, TA9 3RH
Tel: 01278-792685
E-mail: sanddtanks@hotmail.co.uk
Website: http://www.sanddtanks.co.uk
Directors: R. Smith (Prop)
Date established: 1995 **No.of Employees:** 1 - 10 **Product Groups:** 35, 42, 45

Wedlock Electronic Services
Wellfield House Vole Road, Mark, Highbridge, TA9 4NZ
Tel: 01278-641317 **Fax:** 01278-641181
E-mail: john@microwavemarketing.co.uk
Website: http://www.microwavemarketing.co.uk
Directors: J. Wedlock (Prop)
Date established: 1978 **No.of Employees:** 1 - 10 **Product Groups:** 36, 40

Ilminster

Baker Engineering
Ashwell Farm Ashwell, Ilminster, TA19 9DX
Tel: 01460-55757 **Fax:** 01460-55757
E-mail: bakereng@tiscali.co.uk
Directors: M. Baker (Prop)
Registration no: 03718688 **Date established:** 1999
No.of Employees: 1 - 10 **Product Groups:** 41

Dido Industrial Bearings Europe Ltd (Sintered Products Division)
Winterhay Lane Winterhay, Ilminster, TA19 9PH
Tel: 01460-53221 **Fax:** 01460-57832
E-mail: davidlambert@daidoeurope.com
Website: http://www.daidoeurope.com
Directors: D. Ireland (Co Sec), K. Kogure (Fin)
Managers: N. Green (Personnel), C. Sheehan (Purch Mgr), D. Lambert, D. Lambert (Sales Prom Mgr), S. Caubman (Tech Serv Mgr)
Ultimate Holding Company: DAIDO METAL CO. LTD (JAPAN)
Immediate Holding Company: DAIDO INDUSTRIAL BEARINGS EUROPE LIMITED
Registration no: 03616334 **VAT No.:** GB 712 7213 67
Date established: 1998 **Turnover:** £10m - £20m
No.of Employees: 101 - 250 **Product Groups:** 35, 39, 40

Date of Accounts	Dec 11	Dec 10	Dec 09
Sales Turnover	15m	11m	11m
Pre Tax Profit/Loss	109	48	-605
Working Capital	-2m	-1m	-796
Fixed Assets	6m	6m	6m
Current Assets	8m	6m	5m
Current Liabilities	369	277	492

Electric Mobility Euro Ltd
Canal Way, Ilminster, TA19 9DL
Tel: 01460-258100 **Fax:** 01460-258125
E-mail: sales@electricmobility.co.uk
Website: http://www.electricmobility.co.uk
Directors: S. Flowers (Dir)
Managers: A. Hearn (Comptroller), A. Stockford, L. Tuffin (Mktg Serv Mgr)
Immediate Holding Company: ELECTRIC MOBILITY EURO LIMITED
Registration no: 02419231 **VAT No.:** GB 363 2063 76
Date established: 1989 **Turnover:** £5m - £10m **No.of Employees:** 21 - 50
Product Groups: 39

Date of Accounts	Dec 11	Dec 10	Dec 09
Sales Turnover	8m	8m	9m
Pre Tax Profit/Loss	86	170	579
Working Capital	3m	3m	3m
Fixed Assets	2m	2m	2m
Current Assets	5m	5m	5m
Current Liabilities	171	116	348

Golledge Electronics Ltd
Eaglewood Park Dillington, Ilminster, TA19 9DQ
Tel: 01460-256100 **Fax:** 01460-256101
E-mail: sales@golledge.com
Website: http://www.golledge.com
Directors: J. Golledge (Co Sec), D. Newton (Sales), J. Golledge (MD)
Immediate Holding Company: GOLLEDGE ELECTRONICS LIMITED
Registration no: 02525681 **Date established:** 1990 **Turnover:** £1m - £2m
No.of Employees: 11 - 20 **Product Groups:** 17, 37, 38

Date of Accounts	Aug 11	Aug 10	Aug 09
Working Capital	2m	2m	1m
Fixed Assets	73	77	93
Current Assets	3m	3m	2m

Gooch & Housego plc
Dowlish Ford, Ilminster, TA19 0PF
Tel: 01460-256440 **Fax:** 01460-256441
E-mail: sales@goochandhousego.com
Website: http://www.goochandhousego.com
Bank(s): National Westminster
Directors: A. Boteler (Fin), P. Heal (Co Sec)
Managers: N. Felts (Mktg Serv Mgr), A. Hepple (Sales Prom Mgr), C. Bache (Tech Serv Mgr), G. Jones, J. Furbey (Purch Mgr), M. Hendrick (Personnel)
Ultimate Holding Company: GOOCH & HOUSEGO PLC
Immediate Holding Company: GOOCH & HOUSEGO PLC
Registration no: 00526832 **VAT No.:** GB 130 3539 06
Date established: 1953 **Turnover:** £50m - £75m
No.of Employees: 51 - 100 **Product Groups:** 33, 38, 48

Date of Accounts	Sep 11	Sep 10	Sep 09
Sales Turnover	61m	45m	36m
Pre Tax Profit/Loss	9m	5m	1m
Working Capital	18m	11m	7m
Fixed Assets	47m	34m	35m
Current Assets	38m	23m	20m
Current Liabilities	11m	5m	3m

Loxston Garden Machinery
New Road Seavington, Ilminster, TA19 0QU
Tel: 01460-242562 **Fax:** 01460-241680
E-mail: info@loxston.co.uk
Website: http://www.loxston.co.uk
Directors: P. Loxston (Prop)
Immediate Holding Company: LOXSTON GROUNDCARE LIMITED
Registration no: 02937554 **Date established:** 1994
No.of Employees: 1 - 10 **Product Groups:** 67

Date of Accounts	Nov 11	Nov 10	Nov 09
Working Capital	52	62	72
Fixed Assets	40	22	25
Current Assets	277	283	295

Minsterstone Ltd
Harts Close, Ilminster, TA19 9DJ
Tel: 01460-52277 **Fax:** 01460-57865
E-mail: sales@minsterstone.ltd.uk
Website: http://www.minsterstone.ltd.uk
Bank(s): Lloyds
Directors: L. Chamberlain (Fin), V. Chamberlain (MD)
Immediate Holding Company: MINSTERSTONE LIMITED
Registration no: 03005647 **VAT No.:** GB 634 6578 14
Date established: 1995 **No.of Employees:** 11 - 20 **Product Groups:** 33

Date of Accounts	Feb 08	Feb 11	Feb 10
Working Capital	8	-166	-47
Fixed Assets	14	1	10
Current Assets	247	296	268

Powermatic Ltd
The Factory Hort Bridge Hort Bridge, Ilminster, TA19 9PS
Tel: 01460-53535 **Fax:** 01460-52341
E-mail: info@powermatic.co.uk
Website: http://www.powermatic.co.uk
Directors: P. Brompton (MD), N. Lumber (Fin)
Managers: F. Brant (Sales Admin)
Ultimate Holding Company: STAMM INTERNATIONAL CORP (USA)
Immediate Holding Company: POWRMATIC LIMITED
Registration no: 00657482 **VAT No.:** GB 291 0407 79
Date established: 1960 **Turnover:** £5m - £10m
No.of Employees: 51 - 100 **Product Groups:** 35, 40

Date of Accounts	Jun 12	Jun 11	Jun 10
Sales Turnover	9m	9m	7m
Pre Tax Profit/Loss	207	459	-799
Working Capital	4m	5m	4m
Fixed Assets	2m	2m	856
Current Assets	5m	7m	5m
Current Liabilities	211	270	127

Snell Engineering
Rose Mills Industrial Estate Hort Bridge, Ilminster, TA19 9PS
Tel: 01460-54961 **Fax:** 01460-54961
Directors: P. Snell (Prop)
Immediate Holding Company: KAYMAR (SOUTH WEST) LIMITED
Registration no: 01657118 **Date established:** 1982
Turnover: Up to £250,000 **No.of Employees:** 1 - 10 **Product Groups:** 35

Date of Accounts	Dec 87	Dec 86
Sales Turnover	130	103
Pre Tax Profit/Loss	-14	-8
Fixed Assets	18	20
Current Assets	34	31

Langport

Moplant
Riverbridge Bow Street, Langport, TA10 9YA
Tel: 01458-253300 **Fax:** 01458-253996
E-mail: sales@moplant.co.uk
Website: http://www.moplant.co.uk
Managers: J. Jones (Site Co-ord)
Registration no: 00984247 **VAT No.:** GB 504 1762 75
Turnover: £500,000 - £1m **No.of Employees:** 1 - 10 **Product Groups:** 29, 30

R J Reed
Bineham Cottages Knole, Langport, TA10 9JG
Tel: 01458-241910
Directors: R. Reed (Prop)
Date established: 2004 **No.of Employees:** 1 - 10 **Product Groups:** 35

Martock

Evamix Aggregates (a division of Paull & Co.)
Coat Road, Martock, TA12 6EX
Tel: 01935-825252 **Fax:** 01935-822721
Directors: R. Davies (Dir)
Immediate Holding Company: YEO PAULL LIMITED
Registration no: 00048482 **Date established:** 1996 **Turnover:** £1m - £2m
No.of Employees: 1 - 10 **Product Groups:** 14

Date of Accounts	Dec 11	Dec 10	Dec 09
Working Capital	95	97	108
Fixed Assets	1m	1m	1m
Current Assets	150	145	162

Hoistway Ltd
Parrett Works, Martock, TA12 6AE
Tel: 01935-823369 **Fax:** 01935-823441
E-mail: ian.dufall@hoistway.co.uk
Website: http://www.hoistway.co.uk
Directors: I. Dufall (MD)
Immediate Holding Company: HOISTWAY LTD.
Registration no: 04266972 **Date established:** 2001
No.of Employees: 11 - 20 **Product Groups:** 35, 39, 45

Date of Accounts	Mar 12	Mar 11	Mar 10
Working Capital	172	76	-3
Fixed Assets	48	16	26
Current Assets	456	364	277

Neals Coatings Ltd
7 Oakland Court, Martock, TA12 6HP
Tel: 01935-826030 **Fax:** 01935-823974
E-mail: info@nealscoatings.co.uk
Website: http://www.nealscoatings.co.uk
Directors: G. Neal (MD)
Immediate Holding Company: NEALS COATINGS LTD
Registration no: 01992543 **Date established:** 1986
No.of Employees: 1 - 10 **Product Groups:** 46, 48

Date of Accounts	Apr 11	Apr 10	Apr 09
Working Capital	72	48	46
Fixed Assets	12	11	8
Current Assets	174	176	122

S F M
9 Bancombe Court, Martock, TA12 6HB
Tel: 01935-822285 **Fax:** 01935-826199
E-mail: admin@sfmtechnology.co.uk
Website: http://www.sfmtechnology.co.uk
Directors: R. Whittington (Dir), K. Tridgell (Sales)
Ultimate Holding Company: KTRW ENGINEERING (DEVELOPMENTS) LIMITED
Immediate Holding Company: SFM TECHNOLOGY LIMITED
Registration no: 01900440 **VAT No.:** GB 429 1444 53
Date established: 1985 **Turnover:** £2m - £5m **No.of Employees:** 21 - 50
Product Groups: 41, 67

Date of Accounts	Dec 11	Dec 10	Dec 09
Sales Turnover	N/A	4m	5m
Pre Tax Profit/Loss	N/A	470	338
Working Capital	2m	2m	2m
Fixed Assets	250	348	409
Current Assets	3m	3m	3m
Current Liabilities	N/A	738	973

S & W Polytunnel UK Ltd
2 Great Western Road, Martock, TA12 6HB
Tel: 01935-822979 **Fax:** 01935-822919
Directors: B. Hall (MD)
Immediate Holding Company: S & W POLYTUNNEL (UK) LIMITED
Registration no: 01398231 **Date established:** 1978
Turnover: Up to £250,000 **No.of Employees:** 1 - 10 **Product Groups:** 26, 35

Date of Accounts	Feb 11	Feb 10	Feb 09
Sales Turnover	22	24	21
Pre Tax Profit/Loss	-6	N/A	-5
Working Capital	-239	-234	-235
Fixed Assets	4	4	5
Current Assets	5	9	11
Current Liabilities	1	1	N/A

Merriott

Ernest B Westman Ltd
43 Lower Street, Merriott, TA16 5NL
Tel: 01823-321844 **Fax:** 01823-321876
E-mail: ebw@dircon.co.uk
Website: http://ebwestman.co.uk
Directors: P. Westman (MD), T. Westman (Fin)
Immediate Holding Company: ERNST.B.WESTMAN.LIMITED
Registration no: 00100073 **VAT No.:** GB 243 9314 64
Date established: 2008 **No.of Employees:** 1 - 10 **Product Groups:** 12, 31, 34, 35, 36, 40, 48, 66

Date of Accounts	Oct 11	Oct 10	Oct 09
Working Capital	60	66	64
Fixed Assets	1	1	2
Current Assets	79	141	98

Minehead

Mr J White
Burgundy Road, Minehead, TA24 5QJ
Tel: 01643-704137 **Fax:** 01643-704137
E-mail: jeremy@jeremywhite23.wanadoo.co.uk
Directors: J. White (Prop)
Date established: 2002 **No.of Employees:** 1 - 10 **Product Groups:** 35

Shepton Mallet

Brittons Ltd
Waterlip Works Cranmore, Shepton Mallet, BA4 4RW
Tel: 01749-880371 **Fax:** 01749-880347
E-mail: tm-jenkinson@brittons-uk.com
Website: http://www.britons-uk.com
Directors: J. Bridges (Fin), S. Spencer (Dir), T. Jenkinson (MD)
Managers: T. Jenkinson (Chief Mgr), J. Stott (Admin Off)
Immediate Holding Company: BRITTONS LIMITED
Registration no: 05185338 **Date established:** 2004
Turnover: £500,000 - £1m **No.of Employees:** 1 - 10 **Product Groups:** 37, 48

Date of Accounts	Dec 07
Total Share Capital	20

Ernest A Candy
Sandstones Lamyatt, Shepton Mallet, BA4 6NP
Tel: 01749-813451
Directors: A. Candy (Prop)
Date established: 1987 **No.of Employees:** 1 - 10 **Product Groups:** 41

A Connock
Unit 4 Lower Charlton Trading Estate, Shepton Mallet, BA4 5QE
Tel: 01749-345390 **Fax:** 01749-344493
Directors: G. Connock (Prop)
Immediate Holding Company: MCNULTY PARTNERSHIP LIMITED
Registration no: 04675029 **Date established:** 2006
No.of Employees: 1 - 10 **Product Groups:** 41

Date of Accounts	Aug 11	Aug 10	Aug 09
Working Capital	-37	3	-5
Fixed Assets	44	41	39
Current Assets	35	70	45

Delacamp UK Ltd
1 Mendip Avenue, Shepton Mallet, BA4 4PE
Tel: 01749-822100 **Fax:** 01749-347209
E-mail: info@delacamp.com
Website: http://www.delacamp.com

Directors: R. Day (Dir)
Managers: J. Travers (Tech Serv Mgr)
Ultimate Holding Company: H DELACAMP GMBH & CO KG (GERMANY)
Immediate Holding Company: DELACAMP U.K. LIMITED
Registration no: 03015569 **Date established:** 1995 **Turnover:** £5m - £10m
No.of Employees: 21 - 50 **Product Groups:** 30, 32, 44, 48, 64, 67

Date of Accounts	Dec 11	Dec 10	Dec 09
Sales Turnover	6m	7m	8m
Pre Tax Profit/Loss	210	593	743
Working Capital	955	1m	1m
Fixed Assets	1m	1m	1m
Current Assets	2m	2m	3m
Current Liabilities	243	400	432

Framptons Ltd

76 Charlton Road, Shepton Mallet, BA4 5PD
Tel: 01749-341000 **Fax:** 01749-344997
E-mail: enquiries@framptons.ltd.uk
Website: http://www.framptons.ltd.uk
Directors: I. Harvey (MD)
Managers: E. Frampton (Mgr)
Ultimate Holding Company: FRAMPTON HOLDINGS LIMITED
Immediate Holding Company: FRAMPTON HOLDINGS LIMITED
Registration no: 02479836 **VAT No.:** GB 130 1566 13
Date established: 1990 **Turnover:** Up to £250,000
No.of Employees: 1 - 10 **Product Groups:** 20, 31, 62

Date of Accounts	Jun 08	Jun 09	Jun 10
Sales Turnover	N/A	20m	25m
Pre Tax Profit/Loss	102	398	866
Working Capital	138	-287	-29
Fixed Assets	1m	4m	5m
Current Assets	312	5m	6m
Current Liabilities	26	874	1m

O V Garland & Sons Ltd

The Forge Dark Lane, North Wootton, Shepton Mallet, BA4 4AQ
Tel: 01749-890288 **Fax:** 01749-890288
Directors: G. Garland (Dir)
Immediate Holding Company: O.V. GARLAND AND SONS LIMITED
Registration no: 01041591 **Date established:** 1972
No.of Employees: 1 - 10 **Product Groups:** 41

Date of Accounts	Apr 11	Apr 10	Apr 09
Working Capital	78	84	80
Fixed Assets	13	13	8
Current Assets	222	198	173

Metso Minerals Ltd

23 Brewmaster Buildings Charlton Trading Estate, Shepton Mallet, BA4 5QE
Tel: 01749-333555 **Fax:** 01749-345117
Website: http://www.metso.com
Managers: S. Watts (Comptroller), S. Watts (Ops Mgr)
No.of Employees: 11 - 20 **Product Groups:** 42, 45

E H Nicholls

Windmill Farm Wagon & Horses Hill, Doulting, Shepton Mallet, BA4 4ND
Tel: 07703-322205
Directors: E. Nicholls (Prop)
Date established: 1981 **No.of Employees:** 1 - 10 **Product Groups:** 26, 35

Ray Weeks Services Ltd

Unit 1 Leighton Lane Industrial Estate Evercreech, Shepton Mallet, BA4 6LQ
Tel: 01749-831584 **Fax:** 01749-831585
E-mail: ray@rwservices5.fsnet.co.uk
Website: http://www.rwservices5.fsnet.co.uk
Directors: R. Weeks (MD)
Immediate Holding Company: RAY WEEKS SERVICES LIMITED
Registration no: 04705587 **Date established:** 2003
No.of Employees: 1 - 10 **Product Groups:** 20, 40, 41

Date of Accounts	Mar 08	Mar 07	Mar 06
Working Capital	25	-6	-6
Fixed Assets	14	17	21
Current Assets	111	73	70
Current Liabilities	86	79	76

Kenn Wagg Business Support

34 Waterlip, Shepton Mallet, BA4 4RN
Tel: 01749-880596
E-mail: info@kennwagg.co.uk
Website: http://www.kennwagg.co.uk
Managers: K. Wagg (Consultant)
Date established: 1985 **Turnover:** Up to £250,000
No.of Employees: 1 - 10 **Product Groups:** 80

Somerton

Fabricoat Steel Fabricators

Unit 4 East Lydford East Lydford, Somerton, TA11 7HA
Tel: 01963-240099 **Fax:** 01963-240099
E-mail: paul.molton@btconnect.com
Managers: P. Malton (Mgr)
Date established: 2004 **No.of Employees:** 1 - 10 **Product Groups:** 35

Foundrax Engineering Products Limited

Wessex Park, Somerton, TA11 6SB
Tel: 01458-274888 **Fax:** 01458-274880
E-mail: sales@foundrax.co.uk
Website: http://www.foundrax.co.uk
Directors: A. Allston (MD), C. Austin (MD), L. Austin (Dir)
Managers: V. Stanley (Sales Admin)
Immediate Holding Company: Foundrax Engineering Products Ltd
Registration no: 00460583 **VAT No.:** GB 336 6365 43
Date established: 1948 **No.of Employees:** 11 - 20 **Product Groups:** 38

Date of Accounts	Mar 10	Mar 09	Mar 08
Working Capital	44	112	75
Fixed Assets	102	48	72
Current Assets	362	354	377

Mobile Welding Supplies Ltd

Meadow Lea Langport Road, Somerton, TA11 6HX
Tel: 01458-273774 **Fax:** 01458-273774
Website: http://www.mobileweldingsupplies.co.uk
Directors: O. Baxter (MD)
Immediate Holding Company: MOBILE WELDING SUPPLIES LIMITED
Registration no: 04774593 **Date established:** 2003
No.of Employees: 1 - 10 **Product Groups:** 46

Date of Accounts	Mar 11	Mar 10	Mar 09
Working Capital	25	16	12
Fixed Assets	4	5	6
Current Assets	44	47	36
Current Liabilities	15	N/A	N/A

South Petherton

Probiotics International Ltd

Lopenhead, South Petherton, TA13 5JH
Tel: 01460-243230 **Fax:** 0121-779 3110
E-mail: info@protexin.com
Website: http://www.protexin.com
Bank(s): Barclays
Directors: T. Lewis (MD)
Ultimate Holding Company: TITHEBARN LIMITED
Immediate Holding Company: THE HEALTHY BOWELS COMPANY LIMITED
Registration no: 03850471 **VAT No.:** GB 164 2401 92
Date established: 1999 **Turnover:** £5m - £10m
No.of Employees: 51 - 100 **Product Groups:** 09, 20, 31, 32, 38, 41, 54, 61, 62, 63, 84

Date of Accounts	Dec 11	Dec 10	Dec 09
Working Capital	108	43	18
Fixed Assets	N/A	26	29
Current Assets	108	678	702
Current Liabilities	N/A	135	180

Stoke Sub Hamdon

Dennis Greenham

Television Shop Great Street, Norton sub Hamdon, Stoke Sub Hamdon, TA14 6SQ
Tel: 01935-881287 **Fax:** 01935-881287
Directors: M. Greenham (Prop)
Date established: 1950 **No.of Employees:** 1 - 10 **Product Groups:** 43

Southcombe Brothers Ltd

Off Great Field Lane, Stoke Sub Hamdon, TA14 6QD
Tel: 01935-823567 **Fax:** 01935-822918
E-mail: sales@southcombe.com
Website: http://www.southcombe.co.uk
Bank(s): Lloyds TSB
Managers: C. Southcombe (Mktg Serv Mgr), D. Evans (Chief Acct), J. Dawkins (Sales Prom Mgr)
Immediate Holding Company: SOUTHCOMBE BROTHERS LIMITED
Registration no: 00372391 **VAT No.:** GB 186 2830 43
Date established: 1942 **Turnover:** £2m - £5m **No.of Employees:** 51 - 100
Product Groups: 24

Date of Accounts	Dec 11	Dec 10	Dec 09
Sales Turnover	N/A	N/A	4m
Pre Tax Profit/Loss	N/A	N/A	19
Working Capital	1m	1m	1m
Fixed Assets	900	977	974
Current Assets	2m	2m	2m
Current Liabilities	N/A	N/A	147

Street

Avalon Guns Of Street

191 High Street, Street, BA16 0NE
Tel: 01458-841504 **Fax:** 01458-840020
E-mail: info@avalon-guns.com
Website: http://www.avalon-guns.com
Directors: A. Whitemore (Dir)
Immediate Holding Company: AVALON GUNS LIMITED
Registration no: 05683439 **Date established:** 2006
No.of Employees: 1 - 10 **Product Groups:** 36, 39, 40

Date of Accounts	Mar 11	Mar 10	Mar 09
Working Capital	-179	-266	-404
Fixed Assets	1m	1m	1m
Current Assets	462	576	689

Morlands Glastonbury

3 Creeches Lane Walton, Street, BA16 9RR
Tel: 01458-446969 **Fax:** 01458-840108
E-mail: morlandsltd@btconnect.com
Website: http://www.morlandssheepskin.co.uk
Directors: A. Stalbow (Ch)
Ultimate Holding Company: G.R. HOLDINGS P.L.C.
Registration no: 01640988 **VAT No.:** GB 437 0483 53
Date established: 1870 **Turnover:** £1m - £2m **No.of Employees:** 1 - 10
Product Groups: 22, 24

Rogers Agriculture

Bramble Hill Works Bramble Hill, Walton, Street, BA16 9RQ
Tel: 01458-448389 **Fax:** 01458-443572
Directors: M. Rogers (Prop)
Date established: 1989 **No.of Employees:** 1 - 10 **Product Groups:** 41

Taunton

A 2 B Stairlifts

Unit 3 Cipher House Culmhead Business Centre, Culmhead, Taunton, TA3 7DY
Tel: 01823-601605
E-mail: sales@a2bstairlifts.com
Website: http://www.a2bstairlifts.com
Directors: G. Stevens (Prop)
Immediate Holding Company: A2B STAIRLIFTS LIMITED
Registration no: 07707087 **Date established:** 2011
No.of Employees: 1 - 10 **Product Groups:** 35, 39, 45

Advance Fixings

69 Staplegrove Road, Taunton, TA1 1DG
Tel: 01823-338391
E-mail: sales@advancefixings.com
Website: http://www.advancefixings.com
Directors: P. Beaumont (Ptnr)
Date established: 1989 **No.of Employees:** 1 - 10 **Product Groups:** 35

Air Duct Fabrication & Maintenance

20 High Street Wiveliscombe, Taunton, TA4 2JX
Tel: 01984-623844 **Fax:** 01984-623844
Directors: R. Anderson (Prop)
Date established: 1976 **No.of Employees:** 1 - 10 **Product Groups:** 37, 40, 48

Biffa Waste Services Ltd

Canal Road, Taunton, TA1 1PL
Tel: 01823-324442 **Fax:** 01823-353308
Website: http://www.biffa.co.uk
Managers: R. Potter (Mgr)
Immediate Holding Company: BIFFA WASTE SERVICES LIMITED
Registration no: 00946107 **VAT No.:** 537 9116 27 **Date established:** 1969
Turnover: £20m - £50m **No.of Employees:** 1 - 10 **Product Groups:** 54

Date of Accounts	Mar 08	Mar 09	Apr 10
Sales Turnover	555m	574m	492m
Pre Tax Profit/Loss	23m	50m	30m
Working Capital	229m	271m	293m
Fixed Assets	371m	360m	378m
Current Assets	409m	534m	609m
Current Liabilities	50m	100m	115m

Booking Services International Ltd

B S I House Blackbrook Park Avenue, Taunton, TA1 2PF
Tel: 01823-444644 **Fax:** 01823-444648
E-mail: enquiries@bsi.co.uk
Website: http://www.bsi.co.uk
Directors: W. Brice (Co Sec), T. Elswood (MD)
Managers: T. Burn (Mktg Serv Mgr), M. Conebeer (Tech Serv Mgr)
Ultimate Holding Company: CAPITA PLC
Immediate Holding Company: BSI GROUP LIMITED
Registration no: 03005596 **Date established:** 1995
Turnover: £50m - £75m **No.of Employees:** 101 - 250 **Product Groups:** 69

Date of Accounts	Dec 11	Jun 10	Jun 09
Pre Tax Profit/Loss	N/A	4m	1m
Working Capital	-2m	-3m	-3m
Fixed Assets	3m	3m	3m
Current Assets	3m	1m	8m
Current Liabilities	3	3	1

Branchflowers UK

Paradise Close Cothelstone, Taunton, TA4 3DT
Tel: 01823-432000 **Fax:** 01823-430500
E-mail: info@batmanuk.com
Website: http://www.batmanuk.com
Directors: G. Branchflower (Prop)
No.of Employees: 1 - 10 **Product Groups:** 37, 38, 39, 68

Brendon Powerwashers

Station Road Wiveliscombe, Taunton, TA4 2LX
Tel: 01984-624500 **Fax:** 01984-624501
E-mail: sales@powerwashers.co.uk
Website: http://www.powerwashers.co.uk
Directors: C. Hendy (Dir)
Registration no: 02291340 **VAT No.:** GB 515 7035 63
Turnover: £2m - £5m **No.of Employees:** 11 - 20 **Product Groups:** 46

Bridge Tyres

Bridge House Crescent Car Park, Taunton, TA1 4ED
Tel: 01823-334494 **Fax:** 01823-336433
E-mail: michael@bridgetyres.co.uk
Website: http://www.bridgetyres.co.uk
Directors: M. Potter (Prop)
Immediate Holding Company: BRIDGE TYRES LTD
Registration no: 06669593 **Date established:** 2008
No.of Employees: 1 - 10 **Product Groups:** 35, 39, 48

Date of Accounts	Aug 10	Aug 09
Working Capital	-34	-23
Fixed Assets	6	7
Current Assets	23	27

Camellia Contracts

Unit 3 & 10 Walronds Park, Isle Brewers, Taunton, TA3 6QP
Tel: 01460-281848 **Fax:** 01460-281868
E-mail: jporter.camellia@btconnect.com
Website: http://www.camellia-grp.co.uk
Directors: J. Porter (Fin)
Managers: T. Hodson (Ops Mgr)
Immediate Holding Company: CAMELLIA CONTRACTS LIMITED
Registration no: 05360278 **VAT No.:** GB 469 7569 72
Date established: 2005 **Turnover:** Up to £250,000
No.of Employees: 11 - 20 **Product Groups:** 30, 48

Date of Accounts	Feb 12	Feb 11	Feb 10
Working Capital	45	149	323
Fixed Assets	181	191	208
Current Assets	247	340	556

Canopies South West Quantock Windows

Corner House 120a Normandy Drive, Taunton, TA1 2LE
Tel: 01823-254843 **Fax:** 08450-171984
E-mail: canopiessw@btconnect.com
Website: http://www.canopiessouthwest.co.uk
Directors: S. Wase (Ptnr)
No.of Employees: 1 - 10 **Product Groups:** 24, 30, 35, 66

D & I Pearce Ltd

Clean Moor Wiveliscombe, Taunton, TA4 2AG
Tel: 01984-623382 **Fax:** 01984-623382
E-mail: ian.pearce@paspecialists.co.uk
Website: http://www.paspecialists.co.uk
Directors: I. Pearce (MD)
No.of Employees: 1 - 10 **Product Groups:** 37, 83

David Ormerod Hearing Aid Specialists Ltd

50 St James Street, Taunton, TA1 1JR
Tel: 01823-257529
Managers: G. Monks
Immediate Holding Company: DAVID ORMEROD HEARING CENTRES LIMITED

see next page

***David Ormerod Hearing Aid Specialists Ltd** - Cont'd*

Registration no: 00823009 **Date established:** 1964
Turnover: £20m - £50m **No.of Employees:** 1 - 10 **Product Groups:** 22, 37

Date of Accounts	Sep 10	Sep 09	Sep 08
Sales Turnover	33m	27m	28m
Pre Tax Profit/Loss	6m	1m	-3m
Working Capital	4m	1m	-124
Fixed Assets	3m	4m	4m
Current Assets	14m	10m	7m
Current Liabilities	6m	7m	5m

Devon & Somerset Fire Protection Ltd

5 Thornash Close Monkton Heathfield, Taunton, TA2 8PQ
Tel: 01823-412996 **Fax:** 01823-412996
E-mail: colinsmith@dsfire.co.uk
Website: http://www.dsfire.co.uk
Directors: C. Smith (MD), P. Smith (Fin)
Immediate Holding Company: DEVON AND SOMERSET FIRE PROTECTION LIMITED
Registration no: 04502491 **Date established:** 2002
Turnover: Up to £250,000 **No.of Employees:** 1 - 10 **Product Groups:** 38, 42

Date of Accounts	Aug 12	Aug 11	Aug 10
Working Capital	3	-6	-2
Fixed Assets	3	3	4
Current Assets	3	2	8

Eriks (Industrial Distribution Service Centre)

Venture Way Unit 3 The Venture Eleven, Priorswood Industrial Estate, Taunton, TA2 8DG
Tel: 01823-271221 **Fax:** 0121-508 6009
E-mail: taunton@eriks.co.uk
Website: http://www.eriks.co.uk
Managers: J. Clement (Chief Mgr)
Immediate Holding Company: WYKO HOLDINGS LTD
Registration no: 03142338 **Turnover:** £500m - £1,000m
No.of Employees: 1 - 10 **Product Groups:** 30, 35, 66

F B H Associates Ltd

Hi Point House Thomas Street, Taunton, TA2 6HB
Tel: 01823-335292 **Fax:** 01823-332104
E-mail: info@fbh.co.uk
Website: http://www.fbh.co.uk
Directors: N. Westwater (MD)
Immediate Holding Company: FBH ASSOCIATES LIMITED
Registration no: 02619902 **Date established:** 1991
No.of Employees: 1 - 10 **Product Groups:** 44

Date of Accounts	Jul 11	Jul 10	Jul 09
Working Capital	230	208	224
Fixed Assets	9	11	10
Current Assets	488	413	371

Food Hygiene Training - South West

8 Pope Close, Taunton, TA1 4YE
Tel: 07768-600037
E-mail: info@foodhygienetraining-southwest.co.uk
Website: http://www.foodhygienetraining-southwest.co.uk
Directors: D. Robinson (Prop)
Date established: 2008 **Turnover:** Up to £250,000
No.of Employees: 1 - 10 **Product Groups:** 86

Friendberry Ltd

Kingswood Stogumber, Taunton, TA4 3TP
Tel: 01984-656310 **Fax:** 01984-656667
E-mail: karen@friendberry.co.uk
Website: http://www.friendberry.co.uk
Directors: J. Scarborough (Dir), K. Lewis (Fin)
Immediate Holding Company: FRIENDBERRY LIMITED
Registration no: 01585618 **VAT No.:** GB 357 3681 28
Date established: 1981 **Turnover:** £250,000 - £500,000
No.of Employees: 1 - 10 **Product Groups:** 86

Date of Accounts	Jan 11	Jan 10	Jan 09
Working Capital	-17	-15	-15
Fixed Assets	36	36	40
Current Assets	44	55	48

Hawkins Agri Ltd

Unit 3b Roughmoor Williton Industrial Estate, Taunton, TA4 4RF
Tel: 01984-633900 **Fax:** 01984-633030
E-mail: ian.parsons@hawkins-agri.co.uk
Website: http://www.hawkins-agri.co.uk
Managers: I. Parsons (Depot Mgr)
Immediate Holding Company: HAWKINS AGRI LIMITED
Registration no: 04829133 **Date established:** 2003
No.of Employees: 1 - 10 **Product Groups:** 41

Date of Accounts	Dec 11	Dec 10	Dec 09
Working Capital	1m	894	887
Fixed Assets	514	575	544
Current Assets	2m	2m	3m

Howard Filter Systems

East Skirdle Waterrow, Taunton, TA4 2AY
Tel: 01984-623112 **Fax:** 01984-624770
E-mail: info@howard-filters.co.uk
Website: http://www.howard-filters.co.uk
Directors: M. Howard (Dir)
Immediate Holding Company: HOWARD FILTER SYSTEMS LIMITED
Registration no: 02585436 **VAT No.:** GB 569 9289 60
Date established: 1991 **Turnover:** Up to £250,000
No.of Employees: 1 - 10 **Product Groups:** 42

Date of Accounts	Jun 12	Jun 11	Jun 10
Sales Turnover	N/A	N/A	45
Pre Tax Profit/Loss	N/A	N/A	6
Working Capital	11	17	16
Current Assets	18	30	23
Current Liabilities	N/A	N/A	3

Jewson Ltd

Priory Way, Taunton, TA1 2BB
Tel: 01823-337121 **Fax:** 01823-322897
E-mail: richard.ayres@jewson.co.uk
Website: http://www.jewson.co.uk
Managers: R. Ayres (Mgr)
Ultimate Holding Company: COMPAGNIE DE SAINT GOBAIN (FRANCE)
Immediate Holding Company: JEWSON LIMITED
Registration no: 00348407 **Date established:** 1939 **Turnover:** £2m - £5m
No.of Employees: 11 - 20 **Product Groups:** 66

Date of Accounts	Dec 11	Dec 10	Dec 09
Sales Turnover	1606m	1547m	1485m
Pre Tax Profit/Loss	18m	100m	45m
Working Capital	-345m	-250m	-349m
Fixed Assets	496m	387m	461m
Current Assets	657m	1005m	1320m
Current Liabilities	66m	120m	64m

Marshalsea Hydraulics Ltd

Venture Way Priorswood Industrial Estate, Taunton, TA2 8DE
Tel: 01823-331081 **Fax:** 01823-323382
E-mail: andrew@marshalsea.co.uk
Website: http://www.marshalsea.co.uk
Directors: A. Revans (Fin)
Ultimate Holding Company: BIFOLD GROUP LIMITED
Immediate Holding Company: MARSHALSEA HYDRAULICS LIMITED
Registration no: 00246258 **VAT No.:** GB 585 9034 06
Date established: 1930 **Turnover:** £1m - £2m **No.of Employees:** 51 - 100
Product Groups: 36, 40

Date of Accounts	Aug 08	Aug 09	Aug 10
Working Capital	1m	2m	2m
Fixed Assets	1m	797	615
Current Assets	3m	3m	3m

Martec International Ltd

40 High Street, Taunton, TA1 3PN
Tel: 01823-333469 **Fax:** 01823-332423
E-mail: info@martec-international.com
Website: http://www.martec-international.com
Directors: B. Hume (Fin), B. Hume (MD)
Immediate Holding Company: MARTEC HOLDINGS LIMITED
Registration no: 03270701 **VAT No.:** GB 728 7669 78
Date established: 1996 **Turnover:** £2m - £5m **No.of Employees:** 1 - 10
Product Groups: 80, 86

Date of Accounts	Mar 11	Mar 10	Mar 08
Working Capital	26	26	-118
Fixed Assets	127	127	315
Current Assets	26	26	1

Matravers Engineering Ltd

Isle Moor Works Fivehead, Taunton, TA3 6PA
Tel: 01460-281544 **Fax:** 01460-281735
E-mail: info@matravers.co.uk
Website: http://www.matravers.co.uk
Bank(s): Lloyds TSB Bank plc
Directors: N. Ball (Dir)
Managers: T. Churchill (Chief Mgr)
Immediate Holding Company: MATRAVERS ENGINEERING LIMITED
Registration no: 02460600 **VAT No.:** GB 570 2046 71
Date established: 1990 **No.of Employees:** 21 - 50 **Product Groups:** 35, 45

Date of Accounts	Dec 11	Dec 10	Dec 09
Working Capital	398	312	328
Fixed Assets	222	257	284
Current Assets	589	452	588

Mobility 4 U

3 Crown Walk High Street, Taunton, TA1 3PU
Tel: 01823-333133
Website: http://mobility-4-u.com
Directors: M. Talley (Prop)
No.of Employees: 1 - 10 **Product Groups:** 26, 38, 39

Parsons Brinckerhoff

Riverside Chambers Castle Street, Taunton, TA1 4AP
Tel: 01823-281190 **Fax:** 01823-424401
E-mail: info@pbworld.com
Website: http://www.pbworld.co.uk
Managers: L. Sydenham (Mgr)
Ultimate Holding Company: BALFOUR BEATTY PLC
Immediate Holding Company: PARSONS BRINCKERHOFF LTD
Registration no: 02554514 **Date established:** 1990
No.of Employees: 11 - 20 **Product Groups:** 84

Petropipe International Ltd

Greenway Monkton Heathfield, Taunton, TA2 8NH
Tel: 01823-413289 **Fax:** 01823-413287
E-mail: sales@petropipe.co.uk
Website: http://www.petropipe.co.uk
Directors: A. Webb (MD)
Immediate Holding Company: PETROPIPE INTERNATIONAL LIMITED
Registration no: 02979899 **Date established:** 1994
No.of Employees: 1 - 10 **Product Groups:** 36, 37, 38

Date of Accounts	Mar 11	Mar 10	Mar 09
Working Capital	-7	-3	414
Fixed Assets	5	6	4
Current Assets	293	608	768
Current Liabilities	N/A	153	130

Protel Associates Ltd

PO Box 761, Taunton, TA4 3WY
Tel: 08442-412990 **Fax:** 0870-066 7035
E-mail: info@protelprojects.com
Website: http://www.protelprojects.com
Directors: T. Hough (MD)
Immediate Holding Company: PROTEL ASSOCIATES LIMITED
Registration no: 03499257 **VAT No.:** GB 669 8336 74
Date established: 1998 **Turnover:** £500,000 - £1m
No.of Employees: 11 - 20 **Product Groups:** 80, 81

Date of Accounts	Mar 12	Mar 11	Mar 10
Working Capital	-67	-77	-37
Fixed Assets	91	122	108
Current Assets	193	191	238

Quantock Engineering Co.

Unit 3 The Brewery Golden Hill, Wiveliscombe, Taunton, TA4 2NY
Tel: 01984-623850 **Fax:** 01984-624588
E-mail: info@quantockengineering.co.uk
Website: http://www.quantockengineering.co.uk
Directors: M. Anderson (Ptnr)
Immediate Holding Company: QUANTOCK PLASTICS LIMITED
Registration no: 01499185 **Date established:** 1980
No.of Employees: 1 - 10 **Product Groups:** 35, 39, 45

Race & Marine

Unit 2 Riverside Works Bathpool, Taunton, TA1 2DX
Tel: 01823-282662 **Fax:** 01823-282662
E-mail: steve@racemarine.co.uk
Website: http://www.racemarine.co.uk
Directors: S. Causley (MD), R. Causley (Fin)
Immediate Holding Company: RACE & MARINE LIMITED
Registration no: 04257374 **Date established:** 2001
Turnover: Up to £250,000 **No.of Employees:** 1 - 10 **Product Groups:** 35, 36, 39

Date of Accounts	Feb 12	Feb 11	Feb 10
Working Capital	22	31	33
Fixed Assets	3	4	2
Current Assets	83	100	90

Rexquote Ltd

Broadgauge Business Park Westridge Way, Bishops Lydeard, Taunton, TA4 3RU
Tel: 01823-433398 **Fax:** 01823-433378
E-mail: sales@rexquote.co.uk
Website: http://www.rexquote.co.uk
Directors: D. Hooper (MD), K. Hollands (Fin)
Ultimate Holding Company: REXQUOTE LTD
Immediate Holding Company: ROADRAILER LTD
Registration no: 01984091 **Date established:** 1986 **Turnover:** £5m - £10m
No.of Employees: 21 - 50 **Product Groups:** 45

Date of Accounts	Jun 08
Pre Tax Profit/Loss	433
Working Capital	-401
Fixed Assets	998
Current Assets	2m
Current Liabilities	280

Royale Products

16 Ilminster Road, Taunton, TA1 2DR
Tel: 01823-335702 **Fax:** 01823-326869
Website: http://www.royaleproducts.co.uk
Directors: D. Millard (Prop)
Date established: 1990 **No.of Employees:** 1 - 10 **Product Groups:** 36, 40

T M Safety Signs

Unit 2 Nightingale Farm Units West Hatch, Taunton, TA3 5RH
Tel: 01823-481040 **Fax:** 01823-481043
E-mail: info@tmsafetysigns.com
Website: http://www.tmsafetysigns.com
Directors: C. Nagle (MD)
No.of Employees: 1 - 10 **Product Groups:** 30, 49, 68

Taunton Heating & Plumbing

Unit 11 The Venture Eleven Venture Way, Priorswood Industrial Estate, Taunton, TA2 8DG
Tel: 01823-278887 **Fax:** 01823-353999
E-mail: tauntonplumbing@btconnect.com
Website: http://www.tauntonplumbingandheating.co.uk
Directors: C. Newton (Ptnr)
Immediate Holding Company: TAUNTON HEATING & PLUMBING LIMITED
Registration no: 07818975 **Date established:** 2011
No.of Employees: 1 - 10 **Product Groups:** 40, 42, 52

Taunton Landrover

138 Bridgwater Road Bathpool, Taunton, TA2 8BN
Tel: 01823-412559 **Fax:** 01823-412733
E-mail: steve.whitefield@tauntonlandrover.co.uk
Website: http://www.tauntonlandrover.co.uk
Bank(s): Lloyds TSB
Directors: A. Barrett (MD), N. Perry (Fin)
Managers: S. Whitefield (District Mgr), G. Wallace (Sales Prom Mgr), S. Whitefield
Ultimate Holding Company: Helston Garages Group Ltd
Immediate Holding Company: Helston Garages Ltd
Registration no: 01235626 **Turnover:** £10m - £20m
No.of Employees: 21 - 50 **Product Groups:** 68

Date of Accounts	Dec 07	Dec 06	Dec 05
Sales Turnover	15216	13306	13611
Pre Tax Profit/Loss	317	250	335
Working Capital	1726	1398	422
Fixed Assets	1997	2105	2883
Current Assets	4308	5175	3720
Current Liabilities	2582	3777	3298
Total Share Capital	10	10	10
ROCE% (Return on Capital Employed)	8.5	7.1	10.1
ROT% (Return on Turnover)	2.1	1.9	2.5

Taunton Lifting Services

Ivy Farm Capland Hatch Beauchamp, Taunton, TA3 6TR
Tel: 01823-481111 **Fax:** 01823-480682
E-mail: tonymgreen@fsmail.net
Directors: A. Green (Prop)
Registration no: 04979174 **Date established:** 2003
No.of Employees: 1 - 10 **Product Groups:** 35, 39, 45

Taylorwest

178 Cheddon Road, Taunton, TA2 7AN
Tel: 08451-085758 **Fax:** 01823-451514
E-mail: info@taylorwest.co.uk
Website: http://www.taylorwest.co.uk
Directors: J. Taylor (Prop)
Immediate Holding Company: TAYLOR WEST
Registration no: 00308697 **Date established:** 1935
No.of Employees: 1 - 10 **Product Groups:** 26, 35

Date of Accounts	Jan 93	Jan 92	Jan 91
Sales Turnover	27	160	164
Pre Tax Profit/Loss	3	-1	-11
Working Capital	10	N/A	N/A
Fixed Assets	18	29	35
Current Assets	21	29	36

Vapormatt Ltd

Monarch Centre Venture Way, Priorswood Industrial Est, Taunton, TA2 8DE
Tel: 01823-257976 **Fax:** 01823-336446
E-mail: ryan.ashworth@vapormatt.co.uk
Website: http://www.vapormatt.com
Directors: M. Teague (Sales), T. Ashworth (Tech Serv), R. Ashworth (MD)
Registration no: 01479677 **Date established:** 1981 **Turnover:** £2m - £5m
No.of Employees: 21 - 50 **Product Groups:** 32, 33, 39, 40, 42, 45, 46, 47, 48, 54

Date of Accounts	Apr 11	Apr 10	Apr 09
Sales Turnover	4m	3m	3m
Pre Tax Profit/Loss	3	-36	63
Working Capital	724	674	654
Fixed Assets	120	162	202
Current Assets	2m	2m	1m
Current Liabilities	1m	652	487

Weavo Fencing Products Ltd
Station Works Hatch Beauchamp, Taunton, TA3 6SH
Tel: 01823-480571 **Fax:** 01823-480175
E-mail: sales@weavo.com
Website: http://www.weavo.co.uk
Directors: D. Marks (MD)
Immediate Holding Company: WEAVO (FENCING) PRODUCTS LIMITED
Registration no: 01478144 **VAT No.:** GB 336 7044 58
Date established: 1980 **Turnover:** £500,000 - £1m
No.of Employees: 1 - 10 **Product Groups:** 25

Date of Accounts	Mar 11	Mar 10	Mar 09
Working Capital	580	583	558
Fixed Assets	189	210	215
Current Assets	812	712	688
Current Liabilities	200	N/A	N/A

West Country Guns
9 The Square Wiveliscombe, Taunton, TA4 2JT
Tel: 01984-623829
E-mail: sales@westcountryguns.com
Website: http://www.westcountryguns.com
Managers: S. Hartman (Mgr)
Date established: 1991 **No.of Employees:** 1 - 10 **Product Groups:** 36, 39, 40

West Taunton Powder Coating
Ford Road Wiveliscombe, Taunton, TA4 2RE
Tel: 01984-624122 **Fax:** 01984-624122
E-mail: info@westtauntonpowdercoating.co.uk
Website: http://www.westtauntonpowdercoating.co.uk
Directors: L. Mccarthy (Prop)
Immediate Holding Company: COTLEIGH BREWERY LIMITED
Registration no: 04758308 **Date established:** 2003
No.of Employees: 1 - 10 **Product Groups:** 46, 48

Date of Accounts	Jun 11	Jun 10	Jun 09
Working Capital	-449	-431	-308
Fixed Assets	851	904	966
Current Assets	187	198	220

Western Fix It Engineering Ltd
Venture Way Priorswood Industrial Estate, Taunton, TA2 8DG
Tel: 01823-282385 **Fax:** 01823-331087
E-mail: sales@westernfix-itengineering.com
Website: http://www.westernfix-itengineering.co.uk
Bank(s): National Westminster
Directors: G. Norris (Fin), R. Norris (MD)
Ultimate Holding Company: C.S.WILLIAMS(TAUNTON)LIMITED
Immediate Holding Company: WESTERN FIX-IT ENGINEERING LIMITED
Registration no: 04477439 **Date established:** 2002
Turnover: £500,000 - £1m **No.of Employees:** 11 - 20 **Product Groups:** 48

Date of Accounts	Aug 11	Aug 10	Aug 09
Working Capital	161	91	81
Fixed Assets	327	375	401
Current Assets	402	365	406

Western Provident Association Ltd
Rivergate House Blackbrook Park Avenue, Taunton, TA1 2PE
Tel: 01823-625000 **Fax:** 01823-623050
E-mail: mcd@wpa.org.uk
Website: http://www.wpa.org.uk
Bank(s): National Westminster Bank Plc
Directors: R. Johnson (Co Sec), J. Stainton (MD), J. Stainton (Grp Chief Exec)
Managers: M. Chambers (Comptroller), M. Woods (Personnel)
Immediate Holding Company: WESTERN PROVIDENT ASSOCIATION LIMITED
Registration no: 00475557 **VAT No.:** GB 567 6817 88
Date established: 1949 **Turnover:** £75m - £125m
No.of Employees: 251 - 500 **Product Groups:** 82

Date of Accounts	Dec 10	Dec 09	Dec 08
Pre Tax Profit/Loss	13m	16m	-11m
Fixed Assets	10m	181m	163m
Current Assets	213m	36m	46m
Current Liabilities	5m	9m	3m

Templecombe

Greenbest Ltd
Unit 2 The Marsh, Henstridge, Templecombe, BA8 0TF
Tel: 01963-364788 **Fax:** 01963-364789
E-mail: info@greenbest.co.uk
Website: http://www.greenbest.co.uk
Directors: T. Le Mesurier (Dir), T. Lemesurier (Co Sec)
Immediate Holding Company: GREENBEST LTD
Registration no: 03626337 **Date established:** 1998
Turnover: £250,000 - £500,000 **No.of Employees:** 11 - 20
Product Groups: 02, 07, 11, 20, 24, 30, 32, 41, 42, 66, 67, 84, 85, 87

Date of Accounts	Dec 11	Dec 10	Dec 09
Working Capital	-76	-65	-26
Fixed Assets	324	293	97
Current Assets	807	898	810

Newton Steelstock Ltd
Gibbs Marsh Trading Estate Landshire Lane, Henstridge, Templecombe, BA8 0QG
Tel: 01963-363763 **Fax:** 01963-362887
E-mail: ian.lockyer@newtonsteel.com
Website: http://www.newtonsteel.com
Bank(s): National Westminster Bank Plc
Directors: I. Lockier (MD), I. Lockyer (MD), R. Newell (Co Sec), G. Wait (Jt MD), C. Vining (Ch)
Managers: J. Wakefield (Sales Prom Mgr), J. James (Purch Mgr)
Immediate Holding Company: NEWTON STEEL STOCK LIMITED
Registration no: 02008285 **VAT No.:** GB 429 2712 49
Date established: 1986 **Turnover:** £20m - £50m
No.of Employees: 51 - 100 **Product Groups:** 66

Date of Accounts	Jan 08	Jan 07
Sales Turnover	38860	28517
Pre Tax Profit/Loss	3162	3857
Working Capital	2143	48
Fixed Assets	4857	5061
Current Assets	18167	15470
Current Liabilities	16023	15422
Total Share Capital	91	91
ROCE% (Return on Capital Employed)	45.2	75.5
ROT% (Return on Turnover)	8.1	13.5

S P C International
1-3 Station Road, Templecombe, BA8 0JR
Tel: 01963-370504 **Fax:** 01963-370101
E-mail: info@spcint.com
Website: http://www.spcint.com
Bank(s): National Westminster Bank Plc
Directors: H. Ajibola (Fin), W. Moore (I.T. Dir), T. Spall (Tech Serv), J. Hemphill (MD), C. Lindsell (Sales), B. Orr (Co Sec)
Managers: J. Rose, G. Disbery (Ops Mgr), C. Robinson (Purch Mgr), R. Brett (Site Co-ord)
Immediate Holding Company: SPC INTERNATIONAL LTD
Registration no: 02447928 **VAT No.:** GB 710 5916 55
Date established: 1989 **No.of Employees:** 101 - 250 **Product Groups:** 44

Thales Templecombe Group
Ocean House Throop Road, Templecombe, BA8 0DH
Tel: 01963-370551 **Fax:** 01963-372200
E-mail: sales@tms-ltd.com
Website: http://www.thalesgroup.co.uk
Directors: J. Standen (MD), M. Seabrook (Co Sec)
Managers: S. Holt (Personnel), P. Leonard (Comptroller), S. Musgrave
Ultimate Holding Company: THALES SA (FRANCE)
Immediate Holding Company: THALES UNDERWATER SYSTEMS LIMITED
Registration no: 03084140 **Date established:** 1995
Turnover: £125m - £250m **No.of Employees:** 501 - 1000
Product Groups: 37, 38, 39

Date of Accounts	Dec 11	Dec 10	Dec 09
Sales Turnover	135m	124m	122m
Pre Tax Profit/Loss	16m	12m	8m
Working Capital	91m	77m	62m
Fixed Assets	13m	14m	18m
Current Assets	213m	181m	154m
Current Liabilities	93m	89m	79m

Watchet

Badcock & Evered
Washford Mill Washford, Watchet, TA23 0JY
Tel: 01984-640412 **Fax:** 01984-640160
E-mail: enquiries@badcockevered.co.uk
Directors: N. Short (Dir)
Immediate Holding Company: BADCOCK & EVERED,LIMITED
Registration no: 00219128 **Date established:** 2027 **Turnover:** £2m - £5m
No.of Employees: 21 - 50 **Product Groups:** 62

Date of Accounts	Jun 12	Jun 11	Jun 10
Working Capital	-5	-7	-780
Fixed Assets	760	760	760
Current Assets	5	7	7

Lush Designs
2 Goodings Roadwater, Watchet, TA23 0RS
Tel: 01984-640168 **Fax:** 01984-640168
E-mail: info@lushdesigns.co.uk
Website: http://www.lushdesigns.co.uk
Directors: A. Flind (Prop)
Date established: 2005 **Turnover:** Up to £250,000
No.of Employees: 1 - 10 **Product Groups:** 44

Mike Reynolds Industrial Fabrics
31 Five Bells Five Bells, Watchet, TA23 0HZ
Tel: 01984-631858 **Fax:** 05603-278525
E-mail: mike@industrialfabricsuk.com
Website: http://www.industrialfabricsuk.com
Directors: M. Reynolds (Prop)
No.of Employees: 1 - 10 **Product Groups:** 23, 24, 29, 35, 42, 45

St Regis Paper Co. Ltd
Wansbourh Paper Mills, Watchet, TA23 0AY
Tel: 01984-631456 **Fax:** 01984- 634123
E-mail: info@stregis.co.uk
Website: http://www.stregis.co.uk
Bank(s): National Westminster
Directors: A. Wakeman (Fin)
Managers: D. Foulds (Chief Mgr), L. Seldon (Buyer), J. Graddon (Personnel), C. Nicol (Chief Mgr), C. Nickle (Mgr), A. Wakeman (Comptroller), M. Stedman
Ultimate Holding Company: DS SMITH PLC
Immediate Holding Company: DS SMITH INTERNATIONAL LTD
Registration no: 00518152 **VAT No.:** 479 5202 22 **Date established:** 1898
Turnover: £20m - £50m **No.of Employees:** 101 - 250 **Product Groups:** 27

Wellington

Art In Lighting
Kyrle House Ashbrittle, Wellington, TA21 0LJ
Tel: 01823-672224 **Fax:** 01823-673372
Directors: J. Hunter (Prop)
No.of Employees: 1 - 10 **Product Groups:** 37, 67

F & R Products Ltd
Unit 12 Blackdown Business Park Sylvan Road, Wellington, TA21 8ST
Tel: 01823-663281 **Fax:** 01823-664378
E-mail: sales@fandrproducts.co.uk
Website: http://www.fandrproducts.co.uk
Directors: C. Waller (Dir)
Immediate Holding Company: F AND R PRODUCTS LIMITED
Registration no: 07896559 **VAT No.:** GB 753 3377 23
Date established: 2012 **Turnover:** £250,000 - £500,000
No.of Employees: 1 - 10 **Product Groups:** 30, 31, 36, 40, 42, 46, 48

Fox Brothers & Company Ltd Fox Bros & Co.
Tonedale Mill Wardleworth Way, Wellington, TA21 0BA
Tel: 01823-662271 **Fax:** 01823-666963
E-mail: info@foxflannel.com
Website: http://www.foxflannel.com
Bank(s): HSBC
Directors: D. Cordeaux (MD)
Immediate Holding Company: FOX BROTHERS & CO LTD
Registration no: 03274591 **VAT No.:** 742 4705 40 **Date established:** 1996
Turnover: £1m - £2m **No.of Employees:** 21 - 50 **Product Groups:** 23

Date of Accounts	Mar 11	Mar 10	Mar 09
Working Capital	425	103	-607
Fixed Assets	31	18	9
Current Assets	739	331	236

Idoneus Ltd
1st Floor Office Suite 5-7 South Street, Wellington, TA21 8NR
Tel: 01823-666886
E-mail: helpdesk@idoneus.co.uk
Website: http://www.idoneus.co.uk
Directors: L. O'sullivan (MD)
Immediate Holding Company: IDONEUS LIMITED
Registration no: 05956663 **Date established:** 2006
Turnover: Up to £250,000 **No.of Employees:** 1 - 10 **Product Groups:** 44

Date of Accounts	Oct 11	Oct 10	Oct 09
Working Capital	22	17	-4
Fixed Assets	N/A	1	1
Current Assets	25	27	21

Inspirit
Unit 3 The Courtyard 9 Mantle Street, Wellington, TA21 8AR
Tel: 01823-669778 **Fax:** 01823-669778
E-mail: geoffredstone@aol.com
Website: http://www.inspirituphostery.co.uk
Managers: G. Redstone (Mgr)
No.of Employees: 1 - 10 **Product Groups:** 24, 26

Limab UK
Unit 3I Westpark, Chelston, Wellington, TA21 9AD
Tel: 01823-668633
E-mail: john.miller@limab.co.uk
Website: http://www.limab.co.uk
Directors: J. Miller (Fin), J. Miller (Dir)
Immediate Holding Company: LIMAB (UK) LIMITED
Registration no: 06289838 **Date established:** 2007
No.of Employees: 1 - 10 **Product Groups:** 38

Date of Accounts	Dec 11	Dec 10	Dec 09
Working Capital	92	56	22
Fixed Assets	29	6	8
Current Assets	261	209	110

M K Test Systems Ltd
Orchard Court West Buckland, Wellington, TA21 9LE
Tel: 01823-661100 **Fax:** 01823-661160
E-mail: jason@mktest.com
Website: http://www.mktest.com
Bank(s): Barclays
Directors: P. Threlfall (Co Sec), J. Evans (Sales), M. Threlfall (Dir)
Managers: L. Robson (Sales Prom Mgr)
Ultimate Holding Company: 06777534
Immediate Holding Company: M.K. TEST SYSTEMS LTD.
Registration no: 02706775 **VAT No.:** GB 927 1266 23
Date established: 1992 **Turnover:** £2m - £5m **No.of Employees:** 11 - 20
Product Groups: 37, 38

Motalines Bolts & Fixings
Castle Road Chelston Business Park, Wellington, TA21 9JQ
Tel: 01823-661066 **Fax:** 01823-666099
E-mail: sales@motalines.co.uk
Website: http://www.motalines.co.uk
Directors: R. Lines (Prop)
Date established: 2004 **No.of Employees:** 1 - 10 **Product Groups:** 35

Mr Modshelf Ltd
Unit 1 Greenham Business Park, Greenham, Wellington, TA21 0LR
Tel: 01823-672640 **Fax:** 01823-673338
E-mail: mrmodshelf@hotmail.com
Website: http://www.modularshelving.co.uk
Directors: D. Luke (Dir)
Immediate Holding Company: MR MODSHELF LIMITED
Registration no: 03592857 **Date established:** 1998
No.of Employees: 1 - 10 **Product Groups:** 20, 40, 41

Date of Accounts	Jul 11	Jul 10	Jul 09
Working Capital	57	71	63
Fixed Assets	43	32	43
Current Assets	143	142	168

Parquip Of Somerset
Unit 1 Monument View Summerfield Avenue, Chelston Business Park, Wellington, TA21 9ND
Tel: 01823-669205 **Fax:** 01823-669205
E-mail: sales@parquip.co.uk
Website: http://www.parquip.co.uk
Directors: N. Parsons (Prop)
Date established: 2007 **Turnover:** Up to £250,000
No.of Employees: 1 - 10 **Product Groups:** 30

Pritex
Station Mills, Wellington, TA21 8NN
Tel: 01823-664271 **Fax:** 01823-660023
E-mail: iwilliams@pritex.co.uk
Website: http://www.pritex.co.uk
Bank(s): National Westminster Bank Plc
Directors: I. Williams (Sales)
Managers: A. Harvey (Purch Mgr), L. Hansford (Personnel)
Ultimate Holding Company: STEINHOFF INTERNATIONAL HOLDINGS LTD (SOUTH AFRICA)
Immediate Holding Company: PRITEX LIMITED
Registration no: 00618659 **VAT No.:** GB 129 9305 51
Date established: 1959 **Turnover:** £20m - £50m
No.of Employees: 101 - 250 **Product Groups:** 26, 29, 30, 49

Date of Accounts	Jun 11	Jun 10	Jun 09
Sales Turnover	23m	19m	14m
Pre Tax Profit/Loss	2m	429	372
Working Capital	2m	2m	2m
Fixed Assets	1m	1m	1m
Current Assets	7m	6m	6m
Current Liabilities	870	435	2m

Proco S T S
Castle Road Chelston Business Park, Wellington, TA21 9JQ
Tel: 01823-663535 **Fax:** 01823-663373
E-mail: info@proco-sts.com
Website: http://www.proco-sts.com

see next page

Proco S T S - Cont'd

Directors: P. Hyde (MD)
Managers: S. Par (Fin Mgr), R. Daw
No.of Employees: 11 - 20 **Product Groups:** 42, 48

Relyon Ltd

Station Mills, Wellington, TA21 8NN
Tel: 01823-667501 **Fax:** 01823-666079
E-mail: enquries@reylon.co.uk
Website: http://www.relyon.co.uk
Directors: A. Chapman (Fin), A. Murdoch (MD), M. Ashcroft (Co Sec)
Ultimate Holding Company: STEINHOFF INTERNATIONAL HOLDINGS LTD (SOUTH AFRICA)
Immediate Holding Company: RELYON LIMITED
Registration no: 00470381 **Date established:** 1949
Turnover: £20m - £50m **No.of Employees:** 251 - 500 **Product Groups:** 26

Date of Accounts	Jun 11	Jun 10	Jun 09
Sales Turnover	31m	36m	35m
Pre Tax Profit/Loss	2m	382	-37
Working Capital	4m	4m	3m
Fixed Assets	9m	9m	10m
Current Assets	10m	8m	9m
Current Liabilities	2m	1m	1m

Seals & Mounts Ltd

Unit 1h Castle Road, Chelston Business Park, Wellington, TA21 9JQ
Tel: 01823-660033
E-mail: sales@sealsandmounts.co.uk
Website: http://www.sealsandmounts.co.uk
Directors: A. Giblett (Dir)
Immediate Holding Company: SEALS AND MOUNTS LIMITED
Registration no: 03922395 **Date established:** 2000
No.of Employees: 1 - 10 **Product Groups:** 38, 42

Date of Accounts	Dec 11	Dec 10	Dec 09
Working Capital	66	49	21
Fixed Assets	10	6	6
Current Assets	179	159	126

Sirus Microtech

Unit 2 Greenham Business Park Greenham, Wellington, TA21 0LR
Tel: 01823-660665 **Fax:** 01823-665321
E-mail: sales@speciality-textiles.com
Website: http://www.sirusmicrotech.com
Directors: A. Smith (MD), K. Waterman Smith (Fin), K. Waterman-Smith (Fin)
Managers: J. Gosling (Purch Mgr)
Immediate Holding Company: SIRUS MICROTECH LIMITED
Registration no: 01910263 **VAT No.:** GB 429 0172 65
Date established: 1985 **Turnover:** £250,000 - £500,000
No.of Employees: 1 - 10 **Product Groups:** 30

Date of Accounts	May 11	May 10	May 09
Working Capital	60	27	27
Fixed Assets	7	5	6
Current Assets	160	124	88

Swallofield plc

Swallowfield House, Wellington, TA21 8NL
Tel: 01823-662241 **Fax:** 01823-663642
E-mail: scp@swallowfield.com
Website: http://www.swallowfield.com
Bank(s): National Westminster Bank Plc
Managers: M. Warren, S. Golding (Tech Serv Mgr), V. Caryer, J. Fletcher, P. Ambridge (Personnel)
Ultimate Holding Company: SWALLOWFIELD PLC
Immediate Holding Company: SWALLOWFIELD PLC
Registration no: 01975376 **VAT No.:** GB 429 2206 64
Date established: 1986 **Turnover:** £20m - £50m
No.of Employees: 251 - 500 **Product Groups:** 31, 48

Tradestock Ltd

Pool Works Poole, Wellington, TA21 9HW
Tel: 01823-661717 **Fax:** 01823-666543
E-mail: sales@tradestockltd.co.uk
Website: http://www.tradestockltd.co.uk
Bank(s): National Westminster Bank Plc
Directors: K. Nye (MD)
Immediate Holding Company: TRADESTOCK LIMITED
Registration no: 04012477 **VAT No.:** GB 753 5718 13
Date established: 2000 **Turnover:** £2m - £5m **No.of Employees:** 21 - 50
Product Groups: 30

Date of Accounts	Dec 11	Dec 10	Dec 09
Sales Turnover	N/A	6m	8m
Pre Tax Profit/Loss	N/A	260	377
Working Capital	8	695	612
Fixed Assets	2m	378	449
Current Assets	1m	3m	3m
Current Liabilities	N/A	1m	2m

Westco Bilanciai

Unit 4b Westpark, Chelston, Wellington, TA21 9AD
Tel: 01823-662355 **Fax:** 01823-662017
E-mail: dclark@westcoweigh.co.uk
Website: http://www.westcoweigh.co.uk
Bank(s): Barclays, Taunton
Directors: D. Clark (Dir)
Ultimate Holding Company: BILANCIAI INTERNATIONAL SRL LTD (ITALY)
Immediate Holding Company: WESTCO BILANCIAI LIMITED
Registration no: 01157746 **VAT No.:** GB 013 3154 20
Date established: 1974 **Turnover:** £500,000 - £1m
No.of Employees: 11 - 20 **Product Groups:** 38

Date of Accounts	Dec 11	Dec 10	Dec 09
Working Capital	487	467	501
Fixed Assets	70	32	35
Current Assets	914	827	817

Wells

J W G Blunt

Barnaby Roughmoor Lane, Westbury sub Mendip, Wells, BA5 1HQ
Tel: 01749-870666 **Fax:** 01749-870666
Directors: J. Blunt (Prop)
Date established: 1981 **No.of Employees:** 1 - 10 **Product Groups:** 26, 35

Garden Dreams

The Stoneworks West Horrington, Wells, BA5 3EH
Tel: 01749-677777 **Fax:** 01749-346679
E-mail: mail@garden-dreams.net
Website: http://www.garden-dreams.net
Directors: P. Carpenter (Dir), S. Gibson (Dir)
Immediate Holding Company: Cargib Ltd
Registration no: 06096116 **Date established:** 2007
No.of Employees: 1 - 10 **Product Groups:** 33

Date of Accounts	Mar 08
Working Capital	3
Fixed Assets	3
Current Assets	18
Current Liabilities	14

P B T International

Haydon, Wells, BA5 3EF
Tel: 01749-685685 **Fax:** 01749-834834
E-mail: sales@xinia.com
Website: http://www.xinia.com
Directors: G. Thompson (Tech Serv), J. Fry (Fin)
Managers: C. Clifford (Personnel), R. Broadwater (Purch Mgr), R. Thompson (Mktg Serv Mgr)
Immediate Holding Company: P.B.T. INTERNATIONAL LIMITED
Registration no: 01805267 **Date established:** 1984 **Turnover:** £5m - £10m
No.of Employees: 51 - 100 **Product Groups:** 44

Date of Accounts	Jun 11	Jun 10	Jun 09
Sales Turnover	6m	6m	5m
Pre Tax Profit/Loss	341	538	362
Working Capital	507	427	192
Fixed Assets	3m	3m	2m
Current Assets	2m	2m	2m
Current Liabilities	983	933	909

Precision Applications Ltd

Unit 20 Lodge Hill Industrial Estate Station Road, Westbury Sub Mendip, Wells, BA5 1EY
Tel: 01749-870525 **Fax:** 01749-870525
E-mail: info@precisionapplications.com
Website: http://www.precisionapplications.com
Directors: M. Bishop (Co Sec)
Ultimate Holding Company: ONECHECK LIMITED
Immediate Holding Company: PRECISION APPLICATIONS LIMITED
Registration no: 02464204 **Date established:** 1990
No.of Employees: 11 - 20 **Product Groups:** 44

Date of Accounts	Mar 12	Mar 11	Mar 10
Working Capital	61	39	151
Fixed Assets	13	15	19
Current Assets	413	436	455

Redwood Stone

The Stoneworks West Horrington, Haydon, Wells, BA5 3EH
Tel: 01749-677777 **Fax:** 01749-671177
E-mail: mail@redwoodstone.com
Website: http://www.redwoodstone.com
Directors: T. Redwood (Dir)
Immediate Holding Company: REDWOOD FOLLY & GARDEN LIMITED
Registration no: 06133232 **Date established:** 2007 **Turnover:** £1m - £2m
No.of Employees: 1 - 10 **Product Groups:** 33

Date of Accounts	Dec 11	Dec 10	Dec 09
Working Capital	51	69	61
Fixed Assets	10	13	14
Current Assets	112	187	178

Shoon Trading Ltd

Southover, Wells, BA5 1UH
Tel: 01749-686868 **Fax:** 01749-686860
E-mail: info@shoon.com
Website: http://www.shoon.com
Directors: S. Sanders (Dir)
Immediate Holding Company: SHOON LIMITED
Registration no: 01628262 **Date established:** 1982
Turnover: £10m - £20m **No.of Employees:** 11 - 20 **Product Groups:** 24, 49

Date of Accounts	Jan 09	Jan 10	Jan 11
Sales Turnover	N/A	18m	18m
Pre Tax Profit/Loss	-1m	-325	-577
Working Capital	3m	3m	2m
Fixed Assets	1m	933	748
Current Assets	5m	5m	5m
Current Liabilities	1m	949	1m

Tweedie Evans Consulting

The Old Chapel 35a Southover, Wells, BA5 1UH
Tel: 01749-677760 **Fax:** 01749-679345
E-mail: info@tecon.co.uk
Website: http://www.tecon.co.uk
Directors: R. Evans (Dir)
Registration no: 5186011 **Date established:** 2004 **Turnover:**
No.of Employees: 1 - 10 **Product Groups:** 54, 84, 85

Wincanton

A F M Food Machinery Ltd

6 Hill Close BAYFORD HILL, Wincanton, BA9 9NF
Tel: 01963-33211 **Fax:** 01963-34012
E-mail: afmfoodmachinery@freezone.co.uk
Website: http://www.afmfoodmachinery.com
Directors: A. Mann (MD), P. Mann (Sales), I. Mann (Co Sec)
Immediate Holding Company: A.F.M. Food Machinery Ltd
Registration no: 02013451 **Date established:** 1986
Turnover: Up to £250,000 **No.of Employees:** 1 - 10 **Product Groups:** 20, 48

Date of Accounts	Jul 08	Jul 07	Jul 06
Sales Turnover	149	146	197
Pre Tax Profit/Loss	25	25	7
Working Capital	-17	22	14
Fixed Assets	13	13	13
Current Assets	34	70	55
Current Liabilities	37	N/A	8

Nicholas Bray & Son Ltd

PO Box 4279, Wincanton, BA9 0AB
Tel: 01963-364240 **Fax:** 01963-364240
E-mail: sales@nicholasbray.co.uk
Website: http://www.nicholasbray.com
Directors: J. Austin (Sales), L. Austin (Co Sec), E. Austin (MD)
Immediate Holding Company: Nicholas Bray & Son (2008) Ltd
Registration no: 01371013 **VAT No.:** GB 323 2349 86
Date established: 1978 **Turnover:** £250,000 - £500,000
No.of Employees: 1 - 10 **Product Groups:** 29, 41

Date of Accounts	Oct 07	Oct 06	Oct 05
Working Capital	110	73	24
Fixed Assets	21	11	17
Current Assets	151	124	115
Current Liabilities	41	51	91
Total Share Capital	1	1	1

Bridge Motors Ltd

Silver Street, Wincanton, BA9 9AN
Tel: 01963-33313 **Fax:** 01963-33924
E-mail: enquiries@bridgemotorswincanton.co.uk
Website: http://www.bridgemotorswincanton.co.uk
Directors: C. Williams (Dir)
Immediate Holding Company: BRIDGE MOTORS (WINCANTON) LIMITED
Registration no: 00670264 **Date established:** 1960
No.of Employees: 1 - 10 **Product Groups:** 29, 39, 68

Date of Accounts	Mar 11	Mar 10	Mar 07
Working Capital	319	323	308
Fixed Assets	11	13	19
Current Assets	407	407	407

Henshaw Inflatables Ltd

7 The Tythings Commercial Centre, Wincanton, BA9 9RZ
Tel: 01963-33237 **Fax:** 01963-34578
E-mail: mail@henshaw.co.uk
Website: http://www.henshaw.co.uk
Directors: C. Hornidge (MD)
Managers: C. King (Prod Mgr), J. Carey
Immediate Holding Company: HENSHAW INFLATABLES LIMITED
Registration no: 02506266 **VAT No.:** GB 543 4088 48
Date established: 1990 **Turnover:** £1m - £2m **No.of Employees:** 21 - 50
Product Groups: 29, 39

Date of Accounts	Oct 11	Oct 10	Oct 09
Working Capital	522	570	497
Fixed Assets	204	188	189
Current Assets	1m	1m	957

Millside Holdings Ltd

Clear Springs Farm Stoke Trister, Wincanton, BA9 9PQ
Tel: 01963-32994 **Fax:** 01963-33220
E-mail: sales@nightsiniron.com
Website: http://www.nightsiniron.com
Managers: C. Bower (Mgr)
Registration no: 04943165 **Date established:** 1993
No.of Employees: 1 - 10 **Product Groups:** 26, 35

Powerguards Inc Ramping Systems Ltd

Bennetts Mead Southgate Road, Wincanton, BA9 9EB
Tel: 01963-31206 **Fax:** 01963-31904
E-mail: powerguardsinc@beeb.net
Website: http://www.rampsforaccess.co.uk
Directors: M. Baker (Prop)
Immediate Holding Company: POWERGUARDS INCORPORATING RAMPING SYSTEMS LTD.
Registration no: 03850641 **Date established:** 1999
No.of Employees: 1 - 10 **Product Groups:** 35, 40, 67

Date of Accounts	Jun 11	Jun 10	Jun 09
Working Capital	56	103	90
Fixed Assets	60	71	67
Current Assets	175	204	185

Toolex Ltd

Wessex Way Wincanton Business Park, Wincanton, BA9 9RP
Tel: 01963-31199 **Fax:** 01963-31205
E-mail: heinz@toolex.co.uk
Website: http://www.toolex.co.uk
Directors: D. Forster (Co Sec), H. Forster (MD)
Immediate Holding Company: TOOLEX LIMITED
Registration no: 00949993 **Date established:** 1969 **Turnover:** £1m - £2m
No.of Employees: 1 - 10 **Product Groups:** 36, 46

Date of Accounts	Dec 11	Dec 10	Dec 09
Working Capital	401	387	381
Fixed Assets	108	117	138
Current Assets	630	579	530

Yeovil

B A E Systems

Lupin Way Alvington, Yeovil, BA22 8UZ
Tel: 01935-445000 **Fax:** 01935-443111
E-mail: nicky.donovan@baesystems.com
Website: http://www.baesystems.com
Directors: S. Moxham (Fin), P. Burke (Dir)
Managers: I. Dicker, N. Edwards (Purch Mgr), M. Ashley, A. Margrett (Personnel)
Ultimate Holding Company: BAE SYSTEMS PLC
Immediate Holding Company: TERRINGTON SYSTEMS LIMITED
Registration no: 01001553 **Date established:** 1986
Turnover: £20m - £50m **No.of Employees:** 101 - 250 **Product Groups:** 44

Date of Accounts	Dec 10	Dec 09	Dec 08
Sales Turnover	37m	34m	37m
Pre Tax Profit/Loss	7m	1m	3m
Working Capital	6m	13m	11m
Fixed Assets	2	1m	1m
Current Assets	6m	24m	23m
Current Liabilities	N/A	10m	10m

B & C Designs

77 Combe Park, Yeovil, BA21 3BE
Tel: 01935-478187 **Fax:** 01935-478187
Website: http://www.customleather.co.uk
Directors: P. Bagg (Ptnr)
Date established: 1984 **No.of Employees:** 1 - 10 **Product Groups:** 24

Bonsoir of London Ltd

Boundary Way Lufton Trading Estate, Lufton, Yeovil, BA22 8HZ
Tel: 01935-473330 **Fax:** 01935-470520
E-mail: peter@bonsoir-london.co.uk
Website: http://www.bonsoirdirect.com
Bank(s): HSBC Bank plc

Directors: J. Prenn (Ch), B. Methven (Co Sec)
Managers: J. Smith (Comptroller), P. Rodgers (Ops Mgr), P. Rogers (Ops Mgr)
Ultimate Holding Company: AUTOLOGIC HOLDINGS PLC
Immediate Holding Company: BONSOIR OF LONDON LIMITED
Registration no: 02958778 **VAT No.:** GB 221 9338 76
Date established: 1994 **No.of Employees:** 11 - 20 **Product Groups:** 24

Date of Accounts	Dec 10	Dec 09	Dec 08
Sales Turnover	2m	2m	2m
Pre Tax Profit/Loss	2m	-3m	-8m
Working Capital	10m	7m	7m
Fixed Assets	5m	5m	9m
Current Assets	10m	7m	7m
Current Liabilities	194	178	219

Bowshers Electrical

19 Buckland Road Pen Mill Trading Estate, Yeovil, BA21 5HA
Tel: 01935-423926 **Fax:** 01935-432865
E-mail: enquiries@bowshers-electrical.co.uk
Website: http://www.bowshers-electrical.co.uk
Bank(s): National Westminster Bank Plc
Directors: M. New (Dir), P. New (MD)
Immediate Holding Company: BOWSHERS ELECTRICAL SERVICES LIMITED
Registration no: 01049578 **Date established:** 1972
Turnover: £500,000 - £1m **No.of Employees:** 21 - 50 **Product Groups:** 52

Date of Accounts	Apr 12	Apr 11	Apr 10
Working Capital	691	513	537
Fixed Assets	31	56	62
Current Assets	1m	705	722

Cavity Trays Ltd

Boundary Avenue Lufton Trading Estate, Lufton, Yeovil, BA22 8HU
Tel: 01935-474769 **Fax:** 01935-428223
E-mail: enquiries@cavitytrays.co.uk
Website: http://www.cavitytrays.com
Bank(s): National Westminster Bank Plc
Directors: I. Leary (Sales), J. Shillabeer (MD)
Managers: P. Holbrook (Prod Mgr)
Immediate Holding Company: CAVITY TRAYS LIMITED,
Registration no: 00766755 **Date established:** 1963 **Turnover:** £2m - £5m
No.of Employees: 21 - 50 **Product Groups:** 30, 31, 35, 40, 66

Date of Accounts	Oct 11	Oct 10	Oct 09
Sales Turnover	N/A	N/A	4m
Pre Tax Profit/Loss	N/A	N/A	448
Working Capital	2m	1m	957
Fixed Assets	475	441	349
Current Assets	3m	2m	1m
Current Liabilities	N/A	N/A	364

Custom Timber Buildings Ltd

Bracketts Farm Higher Halstock Leigh, Yeovil, BA22 9QX
Tel: 01935-891195 **Fax:** 01935-891028
E-mail: custom.buildings@gmail.com
Website: http://www.customtimberbuildingsltd.co.uk
Managers: N. Williams (Admin Off)
Immediate Holding Company: CUSTOM TIMBER BUILDING LIMITED
Registration no: 04004508 **Date established:** 2000
Turnover: Up to £250,000 **No.of Employees:** 1 - 10 **Product Groups:** 25, 35

Date of Accounts	Dec 11	Dec 10	Dec 09
Working Capital	-32	-28	9
Fixed Assets	5	6	6
Current Assets	121	-28	103

Garador Ltd

PO Box 5, Yeovil, BA20 2EJ
Tel: 01935-443700 **Fax:** 01935-443744
E-mail: alan.bacon@garador.co.uk
Website: http://www.garador.co.uk
Directors: A. Bacon (Fin)
Managers: J. Fowler (Tech Serv Mgr), P. Eddleston (Mktg Serv Mgr), R. Williams (Purch Mgr), S. Stallard (Sales Prom Mgr), V. Goodby (Personnel)
Ultimate Holding Company: HORMANN KG FREISEN (GERMANY)
Immediate Holding Company: GARADOR LIMITED
Registration no: 02225871 **VAT No.:** GB 730 4220 83
Date established: 1988 **Turnover:** £10m - £20m
No.of Employees: 101 - 250 **Product Groups:** 25, 30, 35

Date of Accounts	Dec 11	Dec 10	Dec 09
Sales Turnover	17m	18m	15m
Pre Tax Profit/Loss	1m	2m	758
Working Capital	7m	5m	3m
Fixed Assets	9m	10m	10m
Current Assets	8m	7m	5m
Current Liabilities	740	745	681

Honeywell Aerospace

Bunford Lane, Yeovil, BA20 2YD
Tel: 01935-475181 **Fax:** 01935-427600
E-mail: gary.simpson@honeywell.com
Website: http://www.honeywell.com
Bank(s): National Westminster Bank Plc
Managers: M. Tutcher, A. Jones (Purch Mgr), G. Simpson, M. Stringer (Fin Mgr), S. Sturtidant (Personnel)
Immediate Holding Company: HONEYWELL INTERNATIONAL UK LTD
Registration no: 00406281 **Turnover:** £125m - £250m
No.of Employees: 501 - 1000 **Product Groups:** 33, 34, 39, 40

J Haynes Ltd (t/a Haynes Publishing)

High Street Sparkford, Yeovil, BA22 7JJ
Tel: 01963-440635 **Fax:** 01963-440001
E-mail: sales@haynes.co.uk
Website: http://www.haynes.co.uk
Bank(s): Barclays
Directors: J. Haynes (MD)
Ultimate Holding Company: HAYNES PUBLISHING GROUP PUBLIC LIMITED COMPANY
Immediate Holding Company: J.H. HAYNES & CO. LIMITED
Registration no: 01449587 **VAT No.:** GB 323 6351 79
Date established: 1979 **Turnover:** £10m - £20m
No.of Employees: 51 - 100 **Product Groups:** 28, 64

Date of Accounts	May 11	May 10	May 09
Sales Turnover	10m	11m	12m
Pre Tax Profit/Loss	879	291	305
Working Capital	7m	7m	7m
Fixed Assets	438	551	699
Current Assets	10m	9m	10m
Current Liabilities	1m	978	914

Jewson Ltd

30 Oxford Road Pen Mill Trading Estate, Yeovil, BA21 5HR
Tel: 01935-427411 **Fax:** 01935-431826
E-mail: kevan.downey@jewson.co.uk
Website: http://www.jewson.co.uk
Managers: K. Downey (District Mgr)
Ultimate Holding Company: COMPAGNIE DE SAINT GOBAIN (FRANCE)
Immediate Holding Company: JEWSON LIMITED
Registration no: 00348407 **VAT No.:** GB 497 7184 83
Date established: 1939 **Turnover:** £500m - £1,000m
No.of Employees: 1 - 10 **Product Groups:** 66

Date of Accounts	Dec 11	Dec 10	Dec 09
Sales Turnover	1606m	1547m	1485m
Pre Tax Profit/Loss	18m	100m	45m
Working Capital	-345m	-250m	-349m
Fixed Assets	496m	387m	461m
Current Assets	657m	1005m	1320m
Current Liabilities	66m	120m	64m

L S UK Rewinds

Buckland Road Pen Mill Trading Estate, Yeovil, BA21 5EA
Tel: 01935-476255 **Fax:** 01935-433627
E-mail: rewind@rgillard.wannado.co.uk
Directors: T. Harris (Dir), C. Sexton (Dir)
Managers: R. Gillard (District Mgr)
Immediate Holding Company: A E W LTD (SHEFFIELD)
Registration no: 01968355 **VAT No.:** GB 109 4320 94
Turnover: £500,000 - £1m **No.of Employees:** 1 - 10 **Product Groups:** 35, 37

Linescan

Bartlett Court 2 Sea King Road, Lynx Trading Estate, Yeovil, BA20 2NZ
Tel: 01935-471440 **Fax:** 01935-475285
E-mail: enquiries@linescan.co.uk
Website: http://www.linescan.co.uk
Managers: R. Panou (Mgr)
Immediate Holding Company: UNIVERSAL ENGINEER
Registration no: 01517579 **VAT No.:** GB 736 9199 84
Date established: 1980 **Turnover:** £1m - £2m **No.of Employees:** 11 - 20
Product Groups: 44, 81

M R D Refrigeration

5 Kenmore Drive, Yeovil, BA21 4BG
Tel: 01935-421602
Directors: M. Dodge (Prop)
Date established: 1984 **No.of Employees:** 1 - 10 **Product Groups:** 36, 40

Mentor Plating Ltd

2 -3 Mead Avenue Houndstone Business Park, Yeovil, BA22 8RT
Tel: 01935-471575 **Fax:** 01935-471575
Directors: T. Rowles (MD)
Immediate Holding Company: MENTOR PLATING LIMITED
Registration no: 03950964 **Date established:** 2000
No.of Employees: 1 - 10 **Product Groups:** 46, 48

Date of Accounts	Mar 11	Mar 10	Mar 09
Working Capital	29	-10	N/A
Fixed Assets	25	28	21
Current Assets	103	41	38

Miles Hardware Ltd

55-57 Glenthorne Avenue, Yeovil, BA21 4PN
Tel: 01935-421281 **Fax:** 01935-434153
E-mail: michaelmiles@mtmc.co.uk
Website: http://www.mtmc.co.uk
Directors: M. Miles (MD)
Immediate Holding Company: MILES HARDWARE (YEOVIL) LIMITED
Registration no: 01871026 **Date established:** 1984
No.of Employees: 1 - 10 **Product Groups:** 37

Date of Accounts	Mar 12	Mar 11	Mar 10
Working Capital	53	40	67
Fixed Assets	104	114	123
Current Assets	294	299	282

L H Nichols Ltd

Nautilus Works Reckleford, Yeovil, BA21 4EL
Tel: 01935-476288 **Fax:** 01935-431474
E-mail: office@lhnichols.com
Website: http://www.lhnichols.com
Directors: M. White (Dir)
Immediate Holding Company: L. H. NICHOLS LIMITED
Registration no: 00544627 **VAT No.:** GB 185 9799 79
Date established: 1955 **Turnover:** £1m - £2m **No.of Employees:** 11 - 20
Product Groups: 22

Date of Accounts	Dec 11	Dec 10	Dec 09
Sales Turnover	1m	1m	1m
Pre Tax Profit/Loss	90	61	10
Working Capital	2m	2m	2m
Fixed Assets	224	200	201
Current Assets	3m	2m	2m
Current Liabilities	669	595	456

Perrys Recycling

Rimpton Road Marston Magna, Yeovil, BA22 8DL
Tel: 01935-850111 **Fax:** 01935-851555
E-mail: info@perrys-recycling.co.uk
Website: http://www.perrys-recycling.co.uk
Bank(s): Natwest
Directors: C. Perry (MD), S. Perry (Dir)
Managers: P. Nugent (Sales Prom Mgr), I. Lambert (Fin Mgr)
Ultimate Holding Company: PERRYS HOLDINGS LIMITED
Immediate Holding Company: PERRYS HOLDINGS LIMITED
Registration no: 05997102 **Date established:** 2006 **Turnover:** £5m - £10m
No.of Employees: 21 - 50 **Product Groups:** 27, 30, 33, 42, 44, 54, 66, 80

Date of Accounts	Dec 11	Dec 10	Dec 09
Sales Turnover	8m	8m	6m
Pre Tax Profit/Loss	676	1m	422
Working Capital	3m	3m	2m
Fixed Assets	5m	5m	5m
Current Assets	4m	5m	3m
Current Liabilities	236	523	244

Preston Storage

High Farm Industrial Estate Bernards Way, Yeovil, BA20 2FH
Tel: 01935-444640 **Fax:** 01935-434258
E-mail: dawn.jones@prestonstorage.co.uk
Website: http://www.prestonstorage.co.uk
Managers: D. Jones (Admin Off)
Ultimate Holding Company: HORMANN KG FREISEN (GERMANY)
Immediate Holding Company: CLASSIC MOULDINGS (U.K.) LTD.
Date established: 1992 **No.of Employees:** 1 - 10 **Product Groups:** 36, 39, 77

Pro Atria

Old Exchange South Cadbury, Yeovil, BA22 7ET
Tel: 01963-441311
E-mail: tima@proatria.com
Website: http://www.proginetuk.co.uk
Directors: T. Adams (MD)
Immediate Holding Company: PRO:ATRIA LIMITED
Registration no: 04213930 **Date established:** 2001
Turnover: £500,000 - £1m **No.of Employees:** 1 - 10 **Product Groups:** 44

Date of Accounts	Sep 11	Sep 10	Sep 09
Working Capital	3	-23	-2
Fixed Assets	3	2	3
Current Assets	23	13	57

F W Sibley Ltd

36 Goldcroft, Yeovil, BA21 4DH
Tel: 01935-423671 **Fax:** 01935-433407
E-mail: dillonharris@tiscali.co.uk
Website: http://www.fwsibley.com
Directors: K. Harris (Dir)
Immediate Holding Company: F.W. SIBLEY (1980) LIMITED
Registration no: 01514582 **Date established:** 1980
Turnover: Up to £250,000 **No.of Employees:** 1 - 10 **Product Groups:** 36, 63

Date of Accounts	Aug 11	Aug 10	Aug 09
Working Capital	-13	-6	-9
Fixed Assets	2	N/A	N/A
Current Assets	27	17	16

Sparkford Sawmills Ltd

Sparkford, Yeovil, BA22 7LH
Tel: 01963-440414 **Fax:** 01963-440982
E-mail: info@sparkford.com
Website: http://www.sparkford.com
Bank(s): Barclays
Directors: C. Minto (Fin), N. Lee (MD)
Immediate Holding Company: SPARKFORD SAWMILLS LIMITED
Registration no: 01009137 **VAT No.:** GB 186 1686 29
Date established: 1971 **Turnover:** £2m - £5m **No.of Employees:** 11 - 20
Product Groups: 25, 52

Date of Accounts	Mar 11	Mar 10	Mar 09
Working Capital	-184	-143	-94
Fixed Assets	409	416	428
Current Assets	121	164	217

Town & Country Retail

Tor View Farm Galhampton, Yeovil, BA22 7AE
Tel: 01963-440443 **Fax:** 01963-440654
Website: http://www.town-countryretail.co.uk
Managers: N. Wynn (Mgr)
No.of Employees: 1 - 10 **Product Groups:** 41

UVFish Ltd

3 Font Villas West Coker, Yeovil, BA22 9BY
Tel: 01935-804205 **Fax:** 0870-4798648
E-mail: enquiries@uvfish.co.uk
Website: http://www.uvfish.co.uk
Directors: L. Gilham (MD)
Registration no: 05546091 **Date established:** 2005
Turnover: Up to £250,000 **No.of Employees:** 1 - 10 **Product Groups:** 44

Wessex Industrial Doors Yeovil Ltd

Artillery Road Lufton, Yeovil, BA22 8RP
Tel: 01935-473708 **Fax:** 01935-479413
E-mail: enquiries@wessexindustrialdoors.com
Website: http://www.wessexindustrialdoors.com
Directors: D. Gould (MD), S. Gould (Co Sec)
Immediate Holding Company: WESSEX INDUSTRIAL DOORS (YEOVIL) LIMITED
Registration no: 01634450 **Date established:** 1982
No.of Employees: 11 - 20 **Product Groups:** 26, 35

Date of Accounts	May 11	May 10	May 09
Working Capital	95	93	207
Fixed Assets	48	57	63
Current Assets	254	264	419

Wessex Packaging

Watercombe Park Lynx Trading Estate, Yeovil, BA20 2HL
Tel: 01935-474217 **Fax:** 08707-707364
E-mail: sales@wessexpkg.co.uk
Website: http://www.wessexpkg.co.uk
Directors: P. Barter (Ptnr)
Immediate Holding Company: TEMPAK UK LTD
Registration no: 06052978 **Date established:** 2007
No.of Employees: 11 - 20 **Product Groups:** 38, 42

Woodfinishes Ltd

Units 11-13 Yeovil Small Business Centre Houndstone Business Park, Yeovil, BA22 8WA
Tel: 01935-432841 **Fax:** 01935- 432841
E-mail: info@woodfinishes-ltd.co.uk
Website: http://www.woodfinishesonline.co.uk
Directors: G. Chapman (Fin), P. Chapman (MD)
Immediate Holding Company: WOODFINISHES LIMITED
Registration no: 04181455 **Date established:** 2001
Turnover: £250,000 - £500,000 **No.of Employees:** 1 - 10
Product Groups: 46, 48

Date of Accounts	Dec 11	Dec 10	Dec 09
Working Capital	40	15	25
Fixed Assets	20	23	13
Current Assets	268	147	144

Yeovil Gear Services Ltd

Oxford Road Pen Mill Trading Estate, Yeovil, BA21 5HR
Tel: 01935-428473 **Fax:** 01935-432765
E-mail: sales@gearservice.co.uk
Directors: J. Flannery (MD)
Immediate Holding Company: YEOVIL GEAR SERVICES LIMITED
Registration no: 03753663 **VAT No.:** GB 323 2969 56
Date established: 1999 **Turnover:** Up to £250,000
No.of Employees: 1 - 10 **Product Groups:** 33, 35, 38, 66

see next page

***Yeovil Gear Services Ltd** - Cont'd*

Date of Accounts	Dec 11	Dec 10	Dec 09
Working Capital	39	68	53
Fixed Assets	1	13	30
Current Assets	70	107	88

Yeovil Hydraulics

14 Gazelle Road Lynx Trading Estate, Yeovil, BA20 2PJ
Tel: 01935-472233 **Fax:** 01935-431211
E-mail: enquiries@yeovilhydraulics.co.uk
Website: http://www.yeovilhydraulics.co.uk
Directors: S. Vincent (Dir), J. Vincent (Ptnr)
Managers: C. Massey (Sales Prom Mgr)
Ultimate Holding Company: V.G.G. Group Ltd
Registration no: 01809021 **Turnover:** Up to £250,000
No.of Employees: 1 - 10 **Product Groups:** 29, 30, 31, 32, 33, 34, 35, 36, 37, 38, 39, 40, 41, 45, 46, 48, 61, 67, 68, 83, 84

Yeovil Spraying 2000

Unit 13a The Old Sawmills Halves Lane, East Coker, Yeovil, BA22 9JJ
Tel: 01935-864240 **Fax:** 01935-864075
Directors: M. Bennyworth (Prop)
Date established: 1987 **No.of Employees:** 1 - 10 **Product Groups:** 46, 48

Y P H Waste Management Ltd

Artillery Road Lufton, Yeovil, BA22 8RP
Tel: 01935-412211 **Fax:** 01935-411963
Website: http://www.yph.co.uk
Bank(s): National Westminster Bank Plc
Directors: N. Timmis (MD)
Ultimate Holding Company: ABBEY MANOR GROUP LIMITED
Immediate Holding Company: YPH WASTE MANAGEMENT LTD
Registration no: 00859184 **VAT No.:** GB 185 5486 23
Date established: 1965 **Turnover:** £500,000 - £1m
No.of Employees: 11 - 20 **Product Groups:** 54

Date of Accounts	Dec 11	Mar 11	Mar 10
Sales Turnover	19m	31m	25m
Pre Tax Profit/Loss	549	-3m	306
Working Capital	911	682	3m
Fixed Assets	2m	2m	2m
Current Assets	6m	7m	7m
Current Liabilities	886	490	773

STAFFORDSHIRE

Burntwood

Astrapac Midlands Ltd
Mount Road, Burntwood, WS7 0AJ
Tel: 01543-677262 **Fax:** 01543-672718
E-mail: sales@astrapac.co.uk
Website: http://www.astrapac.co.uk
Directors: C. Tutt (MD)
Immediate Holding Company: ASTRAPAC (MIDLANDS) LIMITED
Registration no: 01157477 **Date established:** 1974
Turnover: £500,000 - £1m **No.of Employees:** 1 - 10 **Product Groups:** 42, 67

Date of Accounts	Jan 12	Jan 11	Jan 10
Working Capital	19	-2	-0
Fixed Assets	11	15	13
Current Assets	161	165	159

Burntwood Spray Booth & Systems
Prospect Road, Burntwood, WS7 0BU
Tel: 01543-685565 **Fax:** 01543-684931
E-mail: spraybooths@unitech.co.uk
Website: http://www.burntwoodspraybooths.co.uk
Bank(s): Barclays
Directors: C. Bottomer (Dir), M. Street (MD), N. Imlah (MD)
Managers: R. Ebdon (Sales Prom Mgr), S. Groord (Mgr), M. Jones (Purch Mgr)
Immediate Holding Company: Unitech Industries Ltd
Registration no: 04585675 **Date established:** 2002
No.of Employees: 101 - 250 **Product Groups:** 40, 46

ECO Hydraulic Presses Ltd
Unit 1 Stanley Business Park Prospect Road, Burntwood, WS7 0AL
Tel: 01543-671011 **Fax:** 01543-676266
E-mail: ehp@edbroemt.co.uk
Website: http://www.edbroemt.co.uk
Directors: P. Rigby (MD)
Turnover: £250,000 - £500,000 **No.of Employees:** 10 **Product Groups:** 42, 43, 46

Date of Accounts	Sep 11	Sep 10
Working Capital	-3	N/A
Fixed Assets	4	N/A
Current Assets	3	2

Emak UK Ltd
Unit 8 Zone 4, Burntwood Business Park, Burntwood, WS7 3XD
Tel: 01543-687660 **Fax:** 01543-670721
E-mail: nturner@emak.co.uk
Website: http://www.emak.co.uk
Directors: N. Turner (MD)
Immediate Holding Company: EMAK UK LIMITED
Registration no: 01306606 **Date established:** 1977 **Turnover:** £2m - £5m
No.of Employees: 11 - 20 **Product Groups:** 37, 41

Date of Accounts	Dec 11	Dec 10	Dec 09
Sales Turnover	3m	3m	3m
Pre Tax Profit/Loss	47	-158	-38
Working Capital	546	532	645
Fixed Assets	61	47	57
Current Assets	3m	2m	2m
Current Liabilities	186	147	135

Gemdoors
24 Meadway Street, Burntwood, WS7 4TW
Tel: 07969-745377
E-mail: jackie.richardson1@ntlworld.com
Directors: J. Richardson (Ptnr)
Date established: 2002 **No.of Employees:** 1 - 10 **Product Groups:** 26, 35

Hytec Mouldings Ltd
Unit 2e Ring Road Zone 2 Burntwood Business Park Burntwood Business Park, Burntwood, WS7 3JQ
Tel: 01543-687200 **Fax:** 01543-673392
E-mail: peterlucas@hytecplastics.com
Website: http://www.hytecplastics.com
Bank(s): Lloyds TSB Bank plc
Directors: P. Lucas (Tech Serv), K. Troman (Fin)
Managers: H. James (Accounts), Cooper (Purch Mgr)
Immediate Holding Company: HYTEC PLASTIC MOULDINGS LIMITED
Registration no: 01868729 **Date established:** 1984 **Turnover:** £2m - £5m
No.of Employees: 21 - 50 **Product Groups:** 30

Date of Accounts	Mar 08	Mar 07	Mar 06
Working Capital	123	104	171
Fixed Assets	310	373	387
Current Assets	1m	858	1m

In-Tech Solutions UK Ltd
65 Park Road Hammerwich, Burntwood, WS7 0EE
Tel: 01543-672774
E-mail: annette.james@in-techsolutions.co.uk
Website: http://www.in-techsolutions.co.uk
Directors: J. James (MD)
Immediate Holding Company: IN-TECH SOLUTIONS (UK) LIMITED
Registration no: 05722054 **Date established:** 2006
Turnover: £500,000 - £1m **No.of Employees:** 1 - 10 **Product Groups:** 44

Date of Accounts	Oct 11	Oct 10	Oct 09
Working Capital	683	549	365
Current Assets	897	827	572

Maier UK Ltd
Attwood Road Chasewater Heaths Business Park, Burntwood Business Park, Burntwood, WS7 3GJ
Tel: 01543-277460 **Fax:** 01543-278752
E-mail: andrho@muk.maier.es
Website: http://www.maier.es
Bank(s): Barclays Bank
Directors: A. Gonzalez (Fin), A. Rhodes (Dir)
Managers: P. McArdle (Sales & Mktg Mg)
Immediate Holding Company: MAIER U.K. LIMITED
Registration no: 03758650 **VAT No.:** GB 747 3411 32
Date established: 1999 **Turnover:** £10m - £20m
No.of Employees: 51 - 100 **Product Groups:** 30, 48

Date of Accounts	Dec 11	Dec 10	Dec 09
Sales Turnover	17m	19m	15m
Pre Tax Profit/Loss	543	837	-1m
Working Capital	3m	265	4m
Fixed Assets	5m	6m	7m
Current Assets	6m	5m	8m
Current Liabilities	1m	2m	1m

Metal Products Arden Ltd
Prospect Road, Burntwood, WS7 0AE
Tel: 01543-682627 **Fax:** 01543-671901
E-mail: matthew.maiden@metalproducts.co.uk
Website: http://www.metalproducts.co.uk
Bank(s): HSBC Bank plc, Lichfield
Directors: C. Hobday (Fin), M. Stanley (MD)
Managers: S. Hart (Works Gen Mgr), M. Maiden (Tech Serv Mgr)
Immediate Holding Company: METAL PRODUCTS (ARDEN) LIMITED
Registration no: 00626621 **Date established:** 1959 **Turnover:** £1m - £2m
No.of Employees: 51 - 100 **Product Groups:** 45

Date of Accounts	Apr 12	Apr 11	Apr 10
Working Capital	1m	890	822
Fixed Assets	98	111	146
Current Assets	2m	2m	1m

Mizkan Europe
New Road, Burntwood, WS7 0AB
Tel: 01543-685555 **Fax:** 01543-677149
E-mail: reception@mizkan.co.uk
Website: http://www.mizkan.co.uk
Bank(s): National Westminster Bank Plc
Managers: A. Cartwright (Chief Mgr), G. Skett (I.T. Exec), L. Jackson (Comptroller)
Ultimate Holding Company: MIZKAN ASSET CO LTD (JAPAN)
Immediate Holding Company: MIZKAN EUROPE LIMITED
Registration no: 03508450 **Date established:** 1998
Turnover: £10m - £20m **No.of Employees:** 51 - 100 **Product Groups:** 20

Date of Accounts	Feb 12	Feb 11	Feb 10
Sales Turnover	14m	14m	14m
Pre Tax Profit/Loss	-189	63	568
Working Capital	3m	4m	4m
Fixed Assets	5m	4m	4m
Current Assets	6m	6m	7m
Current Liabilities	950	609	857

Performance Feeders
Lavender House Station Road, Hammerwich, Burntwood, WS7 0JZ
Tel: 01543-454055 **Fax:** 01543-454047
E-mail: enquiries@performancefeeders.co.uk
Website: http://www.performancefeeders.co.uk
Directors: R. Pelari (MD)
No.of Employees: 1 - 10 **Product Groups:** 37, 45, 84

Prestige Iron Craft
34a Baker Street, Burntwood, WS7 4QD
Tel: 01543-302850
Directors: D. Baggott (Prop)
Date established: 2001 **No.of Employees:** 1 - 10 **Product Groups:** 26, 35

Pruftechnik Ltd
Unit 2A Plant Lane Business Park, Plant Lane, Burntwood, WS7 3JQ
Tel: 01543-448350 **Fax:** 01543-275472
E-mail: info@pruftechnik.co.uk
Website: http://www.pruftechnik.co.uk
Bank(s): HSBC Bank plc
Directors: P. Poste (Sales & Mktg)
Ultimate Holding Company: Pruftechnik AG (Germany)
Registration no: 02942599 **Turnover:** £2m - £5m
No.of Employees: 21 - 50 **Product Groups:** 38, 85

Date of Accounts	Dec 09	Dec 08	Dec 07
Working Capital	1m	733	738
Fixed Assets	526	541	129
Current Assets	2m	2m	2m

R & G Industrial Supplies Ltd
Plot U6 Prospect Road, Burntwood, WS7 0AL
Tel: 01543-679274 **Fax:** 01543-675469
E-mail: sales@rgindustrial.co.uk
Website: http://www.rgindustrial.co.uk
Directors: G. Sanders (Dir)
Immediate Holding Company: R & G INDUSTRIAL SUPPLIES LTD
Registration no: 06380106 **Date established:** 2007 **Turnover:** £2m - £5m
No.of Employees: 1 - 10 **Product Groups:** 35, 66

Date of Accounts	Oct 10	Oct 09	Oct 08
Working Capital	2	3	1
Fixed Assets	2	3	2
Current Assets	46	37	30

Staffordshire Industrial Doors Ltd
Prospect Road, Burntwood, WS7 0AE
Tel: 01543-317304 **Fax:** 01543-317305
E-mail: chris.bate@siddoors.com
Website: http://www.siddoors.com
Directors: C. Bate (MD)
Immediate Holding Company: STAFFORDSHIRE INDUSTRIAL DOORS LIMITED
Registration no: 04095675 **Date established:** 2000
Turnover: £250,000 - £500,000 **No.of Employees:** 1 - 10
Product Groups: 26, 35

Date of Accounts	Oct 11	Oct 10	Oct 09
Working Capital	9	11	12
Fixed Assets	5	6	7
Current Assets	53	60	59

UK Sewing Machines Service
9 Knight Road, Burntwood, WS7 1PX
Tel: 01543-675886 **Fax:** 01543-672479
E-mail: elsonfamily@hotmail.co.uk
Directors: D. Elson (Prop)
Date established: 1979 **No.of Employees:** 1 - 10 **Product Groups:** 43

White Interiors Ltd
19 Tean Close, Burntwood, WS7 9JS
Tel: 01543-672279 **Fax:** 01543-677377
Website: http://www.whiteinteriors.co.uk
Directors: A. White (Fin)
Immediate Holding Company: W. AND A. WHITE INTERIORS LIMITED
Registration no: 02564634 **Date established:** 1990
No.of Employees: 1 - 10 **Product Groups:** 24, 25, 52, 66

Date of Accounts	Dec 10	Dec 09	Dec 08
Working Capital	-6	-5	16
Fixed Assets	16	22	6
Current Assets	43	49	41

Burton on Trent

A&A Lifting and Safety Ltd
28 Churchward Drive Stretton, Burton on Trent, DE13 0AU
Tel: 01785-318239
E-mail: sales@aslifting.co.uk
Website: http://www.aalifting.co.uk
Managers: A. Swann (Sales Admin)
Registration no: 7157498 **Date established:** 2010 **Turnover:**
No.of Employees: 1 - 10 **Product Groups:** 35, 40, 45, 52

A&S Lifting and Safety Ltd
28 Churchward Drive Stretton, Burton On Trent, DE13 0AU
Tel: 07530-040476
E-mail: sales@aslifting.co.uk
Website: http://www.aslifting.co.uk

see next page

***A&S Lifting and Safety Ltd** - Cont'd*

Directors: A. Swann (MD)
Date established: 2010 **Turnover:** **No.of Employees:** 1 - 10
Product Groups: 35, 37, 39, 45, 48, 67, 83, 84, 85, 86

Abiljo Excavator Services Ltd

Unit 315 Fauld Industrial Estate Tutbury, Burton On Trent, DE13 9HS
Tel: 01283-815544 **Fax:** 01283-812961
E-mail: sales@abiljo.ltd.uk
Website: http://www.abiljo.ltd.uk
Bank(s): National Westminster Bank Plc
Directors: A. Walker (Dir), M. Walker (Dir)
Immediate Holding Company: ABILJO EXCAVATOR SERVICES LIMITED
Registration no: 01427164 **VAT No.:** GB 353 4115 80
Date established: 1979 **Turnover:** £2m - £5m **No.of Employees:** 21 - 50
Product Groups: 45, 67

Date of Accounts	Dec 11	Dec 10	Dec 09
Working Capital	-586	-668	-564
Fixed Assets	894	888	931
Current Assets	974	869	817

Arca Ltd

237 Branston Road, Burton On Trent, DE14 3BT
Tel: 01283-531126 **Fax:** 01283-568228
E-mail: info@arca.org.uk
Website: http://www.arca.org.uk
Directors: C. Gilchrist (Dir), T. Jago (Grp Chief Exec)
Immediate Holding Company: ASBESTOS REMOVAL CONTRACTORS ASSOCIATION
Registration no: 01972620 **VAT No.:** GB 318 4785 33
Date established: 1985 **Turnover:** £1m - £2m **No.of Employees:** 1 - 10
Product Groups: 87

Ashberry UK Ltd

Park Hollow Farm Hoar Cross, Lower Hoar Cross Road, Burton On Trent, DE13 8RE
Tel: 01283-575659 **Fax:** 01283-575260
E-mail: enquiries@ashberryuk.com
Website: http://www.ashberryuk.com
Product Groups: 46, 48

Date of Accounts	Mar 10	Mar 09	Mar 08
Working Capital	179	224	215
Fixed Assets	14	20	23
Current Assets	201	268	381

Automatic Peeler Co. (Speedpeel)

Premier House 146 Field Lane, Burton On Trent, DE13 0NN
Tel: 01283-565819 **Fax:** 01283-565819
E-mail: sales@autopeel.com
Website: http://www.autopeel.com
Directors: G. Jeffrey (MD)
Registration no: 02284251 **Date established:** 1988 **Turnover:** £2m - £5m
No.of Employees: 1 - 10 **Product Groups:** 40, 41, 84

Bell Equipment UK

Unit 6c Graycar Business Park Barton Turns Barton Under, Barton Under Needwood, Burton On Trent, DE13 8EN
Tel: 01283-712862 **Fax:** 01283-712687
E-mail: general@uk.bellequipment.com
Website: http://www.bellequipment.co.uk
Bank(s): Nedbank S.A.
Directors: M. Wells (Fin), N. Paynter (Dir)
Managers: D. Evans (Personnel), N. Learoyd (Sales Prom Mgr), C. Arkle (Purch Mgr)
Ultimate Holding Company: BELL EQUIPMENT LTD (SOUTH AFRICA)
Immediate Holding Company: BELL EQUIPMENT UK LIMITED
Registration no: 03591436 **VAT No.:** GB 715 1264 62
Date established: 1998 **Turnover:** £20m - £50m
No.of Employees: 21 - 50 **Product Groups:** 39, 41, 45, 46, 67, 68

Date of Accounts	Dec 11	Dec 10	Dec 09
Sales Turnover	33m	23m	17m
Pre Tax Profit/Loss	1m	-2m	-655
Working Capital	5m	4m	5m
Fixed Assets	63	56	88
Current Assets	15m	16m	16m
Current Liabilities	2m	3m	2m

Bisbell Magnetic Products Ltd

Hillfield Lane Stretton, Burton On Trent, DE13 0BN
Tel: 01283-531000 **Fax:** 01283-534000
E-mail: sales@bisbellmagnets.com
Website: http://www.bisbellmagnets.com
Bank(s): Barclays
Directors: W. Lloyd Morris (MD)
Immediate Holding Company: BISBELL MAGNETIC PRODUCTS LIMITED
Registration no: 01015802 **VAT No.:** GB 125 2446 92
Date established: 1971 **Turnover:** £1m - £2m **No.of Employees:** 11 - 20
Product Groups: 37

Date of Accounts	Dec 11	Dec 10	Dec 09
Working Capital	447	372	362
Fixed Assets	347	345	356
Current Assets	599	619	516

Box-It

Rolleston Park Tutbury, Burton On Trent, DE13 9HQ
Tel: 01283-815748 **Fax:** 01283-521416
E-mail: sales@boxit-nm.co.uk
Website: http://www.boxit-nm.co.uk
Directors: H. McDonald (MD)
Managers: V. Holmes (Sales Prom Mgr)
Registration no: 05338185 **Date established:** 2005
Turnover: Up to £250,000 **No.of Employees:** 1 - 10 **Product Groups:** 80

Roger Bullivant Ltd

Walton Road Drakelow, Burton On Trent, DE15 9UA
Tel: 01283-511115 **Fax:** 01283-540826
E-mail: marketing@roger-bullivant.co.uk
Website: http://www.roger-bullivant.co.uk
Directors: R. Brown (MD), R. Bullivant. (Ch), S. Powell (Pers)
Immediate Holding Company: ROGER BULLIVANT LIMITED
Registration no: 07681731 **VAT No.:** GB 354 5361 54
Date established: 2011 **Turnover:** £75m - £125m
No.of Employees: 501 - 1000 **Product Groups:** 51, 52

Burton Hydraulics & Pneumatics

Paget Street, Burton On Trent, DE14 3TQ
Tel: 01283-532745 **Fax:** 01283-530637
E-mail: sales@burtonhydraulics.co.uk
Website: http://www.burton-hydraulics.co.uk
Directors: K. Mee (Sales)
Immediate Holding Company: BURTON HYDRAULICS AND PNEUMATICS LIMITED
Registration no: 01289122 **VAT No.:** GB 345 8054 49
Date established: 1976 **Turnover:** £500,000 - £1m
No.of Employees: 1 - 10 **Product Groups:** 29, 30, 67

Date of Accounts	Mar 12	Mar 11	Mar 10
Working Capital	20	26	-9
Fixed Assets	42	43	33
Current Assets	334	343	256

Burton Rubber Co. Ltd

Crown Industrial Estate Anglesey Road, Burton On Trent, DE14 3NX
Tel: 01283-567717 **Fax:** 01283-511462
E-mail: enquiries@burtonrubberco.com
Website: http://www.burtonrubberco.com
Bank(s): The Royal Bank of Scotland
Directors: C. Insley (I.T. Dir)
Immediate Holding Company: BURTON RUBBER CO. LIMITED
Registration no: 01248892 **VAT No.:** GB 289 1153 38
Date established: 1976 **Turnover:** £2m - £5m **No.of Employees:** 21 - 50
Product Groups: 29

Date of Accounts	Mar 11	Mar 10	Mar 09
Working Capital	-55	-87	-91
Fixed Assets	53	66	67
Current Assets	671	503	421

Burton Stove Enamelling

Unit 14 Anderstaff Industrial Estate Hawkins Lane, Burton On Trent, DE14 1QH
Tel: 01283-561195 **Fax:** 01283-561195
E-mail: t-j.burgess@sky.com
Directors: T. Burgess (Ptnr)
Date established: 1973 **No.of Employees:** 1 - 10 **Product Groups:** 46, 48

C E S Environments Instruments Ltd

Bretby Business Park Bretby, Burton On Trent, DE15 0YZ
Tel: 01283-216334 **Fax:** 01283-550939
E-mail: dcormack@eec1.com
Website: http://www.cesei.co.uk
Bank(s): Barclays, Maidenhead
Directors: R. Allen (Dir)
Immediate Holding Company: CES ENVIRONMENTAL INSTRUMENTS LTD.
Registration no: 02970174 **VAT No.:** GB 301 9541 85
Date established: 1994 **Turnover:** £2m - £5m **No.of Employees:** 11 - 20
Product Groups: 40, 42, 54

Date of Accounts	Nov 11	Nov 10	Nov 09
Working Capital	13	6	28
Fixed Assets	167	191	158
Current Assets	219	169	140

C G P Chemicals Ltd

The Old Dairy Bladon Paddocks Newton Road, Newton Solney, Burton On Trent, DE15 0TQ
Tel: 01283-511101 **Fax:** 01283-511102
E-mail: sales@cgpchemicals.co.uk
Website: http://www.cgpchemicals.co.uk
Directors: C. Grantham (MD)
Ultimate Holding Company: C.G. POLYMER ENGINEERING LIMITED
Immediate Holding Company: ADVANCED BONDING SOLUTIONS LTD
Registration no: 02229086 **VAT No.:** GB 507 6565 34
Date established: 1988 **No.of Employees:** 1 - 10 **Product Groups:** 29, 31, 32, 37, 48, 66, 68

Date of Accounts	Mar 11	Mar 10	Mar 08
Working Capital	-0	-0	115
Fixed Assets	N/A	N/A	20
Current Assets	N/A	N/A	168

Cape Warwick Ltd

Shaw House Shaw Lane, Kings Bromley, Burton On Trent, DE13 7JQ
Tel: 01543-472443 **Fax:** 01543-472461
E-mail: tom@colorprouk.com
Website: http://www.cape-warwick.co.uk
Directors: M. Kinnersley (Comm)
Immediate Holding Company: CAPE WARWICK LTD
Registration no: 02621564 **Date established:** 1991
No.of Employees: 1 - 10 **Product Groups:** 26, 30, 45

Date of Accounts	Apr 12	Apr 11	Apr 10
Working Capital	188	203	198
Fixed Assets	31	27	34
Current Assets	238	293	291

Clayton Equipment Ltd

Second Avenue Centrum One Hundred, Burton On Trent, DE14 2WF
Tel: 08701-129191 **Fax:** 01283-814772
E-mail: steve.gretton@claytonequipment.co.uk
Website: http://www.clayton-equipment.co.uk
Directors: S. Gretton (MD), R. Overton (Fin), D. Goma (Co Sec)
Ultimate Holding Company: PUNCH TAVERNS PLC
Immediate Holding Company: CLAYTON EQUIPMENT LIMITED
Registration no: 05095086 **Date established:** 2004
No.of Employees: 21 - 50 **Product Groups:** 39

Date of Accounts	Feb 12	Feb 11	Feb 10
Working Capital	414	421	353
Fixed Assets	165	187	208
Current Assets	2m	2m	2m

Crestchic Ltd

Second Ave, Burton On Trent, DE14 2WF
Tel: 01283-531645 **Fax:** 01283-510103
E-mail: sales@crestchic.co.uk
Website: http://www.crestchic.co.uk
Bank(s): Bank of Scotland
Managers: D. Robinson, J. Gould (Prod Mgr), J. Gould (Chief Mgr), D. Gould (Sales Prom Mgr), P. Hinchcliffe (Purch Mgr)
Registration no: 01772456 **VAT No.:** GB 880 9851 77
Date established: 1983 **Turnover:** £5m - £10m **No.of Employees:** 21 - 50
Product Groups: 37, 38, 85

Date of Accounts	Dec 11	Dec 10	Dec 09
Sales Turnover	13m	10m	9m
Pre Tax Profit/Loss	2m	2m	3m
Working Capital	1m	2m	3m
Fixed Assets	6m	6m	6m
Current Assets	7m	6m	5m
Current Liabilities	856	533	1m

Croboride Engineering Ltd

Little Burton West, Burton On Trent, DE14 1PP
Tel: 01283-511188 **Fax:** 01283-530845
E-mail: office@croboride.co.uk
Website: http://www.croboride.co.uk
Directors: M. Billings (Dir)
Immediate Holding Company: CROBORIDE ENGINEERING LIMITED
Registration no: 02319062 **VAT No.:** GB 507 8233 49
Date established: 1988 **Turnover:** £500,000 - £1m
No.of Employees: 1 - 10 **Product Groups:** 48

Date of Accounts	Dec 11	Dec 10	Dec 09
Working Capital	11	9	10
Fixed Assets	265	260	238
Current Assets	166	159	149

Daifuku Europe Ltd

Office FF 14 Imex Business Centre Shobnall Road, Burton On Trent, DE14 2AU
Tel: 01283-500005 **Fax:** 01283-500015
E-mail: john_liptrot.europe@ha.daifuku.co.jp
Website: http://www.daifukuafa.co.uk
Managers: J. Liptrot (Mgr)
Ultimate Holding Company: DAIFUKU COMPANY LIMITED (JAPAN)
Immediate Holding Company: DAIFUKU EUROPE LIMITED
Registration no: 02424830 **Date established:** 1989
No.of Employees: 1 - 10 **Product Groups:** 35, 39, 45

Date of Accounts	Dec 08
Sales Turnover	28m
Pre Tax Profit/Loss	270
Working Capital	1m
Fixed Assets	98
Current Assets	12m
Current Liabilities	3m

Darley Ltd

Wellington Road, Burton On Trent, DE14 2AD
Tel: 01283-564936 **Fax:** 01283-545688
E-mail: mailbox@darley.co.uk
Website: http://www.darleylimited.co.uk
Directors: J. Alton (Dir), R. Cotton (Purch), S. Blake (Sales), A. Barlow (Fin)
Ultimate Holding Company: DARLEY MANAGED HOLDINGS LIMITED
Immediate Holding Company: DARLEY LIMITED
Registration no: 00405648 **VAT No.:** GB 616 6856 14
Date established: 1946 **Turnover:** £10m - £20m
No.of Employees: 51 - 100 **Product Groups:** 27, 28

Date of Accounts	Apr 11	Apr 10	Apr 09
Sales Turnover	11m	11m	11m
Pre Tax Profit/Loss	38	276	448
Working Capital	4m	4m	2m
Fixed Assets	793	919	2m
Current Assets	7m	7m	6m
Current Liabilities	206	254	578

Delstron Systems Ltd

Paget Street, Burton On Trent, DE14 3TQ
Tel: 01283-565120 **Fax:** 01283-541859
E-mail: sjcardwell@delstron.co.uk
Website: http://www.delstron.co.uk
Directors: S. Cardwell (Dir)
Immediate Holding Company: DELSTRON SYSTEMS LIMITED
Registration no: 02666003 **Date established:** 1991
Turnover: £500,000 - £1m **No.of Employees:** 11 - 20 **Product Groups:** 48

Date of Accounts	Dec 11	Dec 10	Dec 09
Working Capital	481	269	245
Fixed Assets	201	177	180
Current Assets	720	384	344

Ditech Ltd

3.6 Archers Alrewas Road Kings Bromley, Burton On Trent, DE13 7HW
Tel: 01543-473633 **Fax:** 01543-573634
E-mail: enquiries@ditechltd.co.uk
Website: http://www.ditechltd.co.uk
Directors: P. Fairfield (Dir)
Immediate Holding Company: DITECH LIMITED
Registration no: 02829238 **Date established:** 1993
Turnover: £250,000 - £500,000 **No.of Employees:** 1 - 10
Product Groups: 35, 48

Date of Accounts	Jun 11	Jun 10	Jun 09
Working Capital	29	-22	1
Fixed Assets	34	34	31
Current Assets	128	66	96

Doncasters Group Ltd

Millennium Court First Avenue, Burton On Trent, DE14 2WH
Tel: 01332-864900 **Fax:** 01332-864888
E-mail: info@doncasters.com
Website: http://www.doncasters.com
Bank(s): National Westminster Bank Plc
Directors: H. Jackson (Fin)
Managers: B. Hollis (Tech Serv Mgr), C. Gamble (Mktg Serv Mgr), M. Schurch, T. Jesrai, E. Pugh (Personnel), L. Hall
Ultimate Holding Company: DUBAI HOLDING LLC (DUBAI)
Immediate Holding Company: DONCASTERS UK HOLDINGS LIMITED
Registration no: 03468793 **VAT No.:** GB 389 1553 14
Date established: 1997 **Turnover:** £500m - £1,000m
No.of Employees: 21 - 50 **Product Groups:** 34, 48

Date of Accounts	Dec 11	Dec 10	Dec 09
Pre Tax Profit/Loss	-16m	-24m	-21m
Working Capital	-3m	-3m	3m
Fixed Assets	216m	216m	216m
Current Assets	50m	50m	59m
Current Liabilities	N/A	N/A	30m

Duslasst Bot Ltd

Steel Fabs Industrial Estate Victoria Crescent, Burton On Trent, DE14 2QA
Tel: 01283-531536 **Fax:** 01283-516297
Website: http://www.duslasst.co.uk
Managers: B. Partington (Mgr)
Immediate Holding Company: DUSLASST LIMITED
Registration no: 03158125 **Date established:** 1996
No.of Employees: 1 - 10 **Product Groups:** 46, 48

Date of Accounts	Jun 11	Jun 10	Jun 09
Working Capital	-76	-77	-38
Fixed Assets	N/A	N/A	25
Current Assets	55	73	136

E X M

Unit 7 Sidings Industrial Estate Wetmore Road, Burton On Trent, DE14 1SB
Tel: 01283-509142 **Fax:** 01283- 509242
E-mail: dhedley@exmltd.co.uk
Website: http://www.exmltd.co.uk
Directors: D. Hedley (Prop)
Immediate Holding Company: E.X.M. LTD
Registration no: 03749243 **Date established:** 1999
Turnover: Up to £250,000 **No.of Employees:** 1 - 10 **Product Groups:** 37, 38, 67

Date of Accounts	Mar 06
Working Capital	1
Fixed Assets	1
Current Assets	29
Current Liabilities	29

G Evans

1 Northside Business Park Hawkins Lane, Burton On Trent, DE14 1DB
Tel: 01283-537313
E-mail: g.evans12@talk21.com
Website: http://www.hotmail
Directors: G. Evans (Prop)
Date established: 1993 **No.of Employees:** 1 - 10 **Product Groups:** 35

Frazer Nash Consultancy Ltd

Cayman House First Avenue Centrum One Hundred, Centrum One Hundred, Burton On Trent, DE14 2WN
Tel: 01283-517789 **Fax:** 01283-564469
E-mail: info@fnc.co.uk
Website: http://www.fnc.co.uk
Directors: A. Milton (MD)
Ultimate Holding Company: BABCOCK INTERNATIONAL GROUP PLC
Immediate Holding Company: FRAZER-NASH CONSULTANCY LIMITED
Registration no: 02562870 **Date established:** 1990 **Turnover:** £2m - £5m
No.of Employees: 251 - 500 **Product Groups:** 44, 54, 80, 84, 85, 86

Date of Accounts	Mar 12	Mar 11	Mar 10
Sales Turnover	43m	38m	35m
Pre Tax Profit/Loss	6m	5m	4m
Working Capital	14m	7m	122m
Fixed Assets	2m	2m	2m
Current Assets	24m	19m	22m
Current Liabilities	7m	9m	7m

T Giusti Ltd

Briggs House Derby Street, Burton On Trent, DE14 2LH
Tel: 01283-566661 **Fax:** 01933-272363
E-mail: sales@tgiusti.briggsplc.co.uk
Website: http://www.giusti.co.uk
Bank(s): Barclays
Directors: G. Cure (MD), J. Andrews (Ch), G. Cure (Grp Chief Exec), G. Cure (Prop), N. Proud (Dir)
Managers: P. Blackwell (Mgr), D. George (Sales Prom Mgr), A. Charles (Accounts)
Immediate Holding Company: T. GIUSTI LIMITED
Registration no: 00322670 **Date established:** 1937
Turnover: £10m - £20m **No.of Employees:** 51 - 100 **Product Groups:** 35, 41, 42, 84

Date of Accounts	Mar 11	Mar 10	Mar 09
Working Capital	N/A	N/A	2m
Fixed Assets	N/A	N/A	23
Current Assets	N/A	N/A	2m

Heritage Restoration Services Ltd

42 West Street, Burton On Trent, DE15 0BW
Tel: 01283-546266 **Fax:** 01283-546266
E-mail: enquiries@heritagerestorationservices.com
Website: http://www.heritagerestorationservices.com
Directors: D. Keyte (Dir), A. Keyte (Fin)
Immediate Holding Company: HERITAGE RESTORATION SERVICES LTD
Registration no: 03895203 **Date established:** 1999
Turnover: Up to £250,000 **No.of Employees:** 1 - 10 **Product Groups:** 48

Date of Accounts	Dec 10	Dec 09	Dec 08
Working Capital	-8	2	-14
Fixed Assets	7	5	6
Current Assets	N/A	9	1

Geo Hodges & Son Ltd

82 Horninglow Street, Burton On Trent, DE14 1PN
Tel: 01283-565461 **Fax:** 01283-510338
E-mail: contracts@hodges.co.uk
Website: http://www.hodges.co.uk
Bank(s): The Royal Bank of Scotland
Directors: G. Jones (MD), C. Seager (Co Sec)
Managers: P. Anslo (I.T. Exec), M. Clarke (Buyer), C. Seagar (Comptroller), P. Anslo (Tech Serv Mgr)
Ultimate Holding Company: HODGES HOLDINGS LIMITED
Immediate Holding Company: GEO.HODGES & SON LIMITED
Registration no: 00269991 **VAT No.:** GB 616 9512 31
Date established: 1932 **Turnover:** £2m - £5m **No.of Employees:** 21 - 50
Product Groups: 18, 25, 51, 52, 84

Date of Accounts	Oct 11	Oct 10	Oct 09
Sales Turnover	4m	4m	6m
Pre Tax Profit/Loss	14	70	174
Working Capital	18	67	69
Fixed Assets	182	181	168
Current Assets	539	953	902
Current Liabilities	237	383	367

Hodgson & Hodgson Group Ltd

Crown Industrial Estate Anglesey Road, Burton On Trent, DE14 3PA
Tel: 01283-493800 **Fax:** 01283-510186
E-mail: info@hodgsongroup.co.uk
Website: http://www.acoustic.co.uk
Managers: R. Plews (Ops Mgr)
Ultimate Holding Company: APPROVED ACOUSTIC APPLICATIONS LIMITED
Immediate Holding Company: HODGSON & HODGSON GROUP LIMITED
Registration no: 01574452 **Date established:** 1981
Turnover: £10m - £20m **No.of Employees:** 251 - 500
Product Groups: 23, 27, 30

Date of Accounts	Mar 11	Mar 10	Mar 09
Sales Turnover	14m	14m	21m
Pre Tax Profit/Loss	-27	-481	224
Working Capital	122	65	266
Fixed Assets	4m	5m	5m
Current Assets	5m	5m	5m
Current Liabilities	3m	3m	3m

Iceni Productions Ltd Advertising/Broadcast/Corporate/Video Production

The Studio Bell House Lane, Anslow, Burton on trent, DE13 9PA
Tel: 01283-5678 15 **Fax:** 01283-792993
E-mail: studio@iceni.tv
Website: http://www.iceni-tv.co.uk
Directors: C. Bentley (Dir), A. Jepson (Dir)
Registration no: 04173833 **Date established:** 2001
Turnover: £500,000 - £1m **No.of Employees:** 1 - 10 **Product Groups:** 89

Industrial Cranes & Parts

Unit 38 Imex Business Centre Shobnall Road, Burton On Trent, DE14 2AU
Tel: 01283-566332 **Fax:** 01283-544519
E-mail: sales@industrialcranesandparts.com
Website: http://www.industrialcranesandparts.com
Directors: M. Hull (Prop)
Ultimate Holding Company: THE BUSINESS FORT PLC
Immediate Holding Company: FORTRESS SERVICE GROUP PLC
Registration no: 06585699 **Date established:** 2003
No.of Employees: 1 - 10 **Product Groups:** 35, 39, 45

Date of Accounts	Mar 09	Sep 08	Sep 07
Sales Turnover	3m	9m	N/A
Pre Tax Profit/Loss	160	574	N/A
Working Capital	-193	-385	-241
Fixed Assets	792	820	559
Current Assets	2m	3m	2m
Current Liabilities	2m	3m	N/A

J H P Training

Britannia House Station Street, Burton On Trent, DE14 1AX
Tel: 01283-537057 **Fax:** 01283-515071
E-mail: sales@jhptraining.com
Website: http://www.jhptraining.com
Directors: S. Williams (MD)
Managers: K. Collins (Mgr), N. Keating (Mgr)
Immediate Holding Company: JHP Group Ltd
Registration no: 03247918 **Date established:** 1983
No.of Employees: 11 - 20 **Product Groups:** 86

J T Leavesley Group

Ryknield House Alrewas, Burton On Trent, DE13 7AB
Tel: 01283-791555 **Fax:** 01283-791500
E-mail: johndaubney@leavesley.com
Website: http://www.leavesleygroup.co.uk
Managers: M. Tolley
Ultimate Holding Company: J.T. LEAVESLEY LIMITED
Immediate Holding Company: J. T. LEAVESLEY (ALREWAS) LIMITED
Registration no: 00931247 **Date established:** 1968 **Turnover:** £5m - £10m
No.of Employees: 1 - 10 **Product Groups:** 26, 37, 39, 49

Date of Accounts	Apr 12	Apr 11	Apr 10
Sales Turnover	16m	19m	19m
Pre Tax Profit/Loss	225	157	219
Working Capital	346	-1m	382
Fixed Assets	25m	27m	28m
Current Assets	6m	6m	7m
Current Liabilities	1m	2m	1m

Keg Watch Ltd

PO Box 5935, Burton On Trent, DE13 0YL
Tel: 01283-741274 **Fax:** 01283-741374
E-mail: info@kegwatch.co.uk
Website: http://www.kegwatch.co.uk
Directors: C. Sarson (Co Sec)
Immediate Holding Company: KEGWATCH LIMITED
Registration no: 04088146 **Date established:** 2000
No.of Employees: 1 - 10 **Product Groups:** 20, 40, 41

Date of Accounts	Mar 12	Mar 11	Mar 10
Working Capital	212	250	255
Fixed Assets	173	172	175
Current Assets	416	399	440

Key Diesel

12 Derwent Park Hawkins Lane, Burton On Trent, DE14 1QA
Tel: 01283-537958 **Fax:** 01283-517425
E-mail: kieran@keydiesel.co.uk
Directors: K. Key (Prop)
Date established: 1968 **No.of Employees:** 1 - 10 **Product Groups:** 40

L H Group Services Ltd

Graycar Business Park Barton Turn, Barton under Needwood, Burton On Trent, DE13 8EN
Tel: 01283-722600 **Fax:** 01283-722622
E-mail: michael.isaac@lh-group.co.uk
Website: http://www.lh-group.co.uk
Directors: G. Lee (MD), G. Leech (MD)
Managers: S. Millington (Mktg Serv Mgr), D. Benham (Tech Serv Mgr)
Ultimate Holding Company: L H GROUP HOLDINGS LIMITED
Immediate Holding Company: L H GROUP SERVICES LIMITED
Registration no: 01394005 **VAT No.:** GB 331 5969 46
Date established: 1978 **Turnover:** £20m - £50m
No.of Employees: 101 - 250 **Product Groups:** 40, 48

Date of Accounts	Dec 11	Dec 10	Dec 09
Sales Turnover	30m	23m	22m
Pre Tax Profit/Loss	2m	399	138
Working Capital	3m	1m	2m
Fixed Assets	2m	2m	2m
Current Assets	12m	7m	7m
Current Liabilities	2m	1m	2m

Lanxess Ltd

Lichfield Road Branston, Burton On Trent, DE14 3WH
Tel: 01283-714200 **Fax:** 01283-714201
E-mail: kim.oconnor@lanxess.com
Website: http://www.lanxess.co.uk
Bank(s): National Westminster Bank Plc
Directors: K. O'connor (MD), M. Newson (Co Sec), S. Kentesber (Sales)
Managers: C. Flett (Fin Mgr), R. Warren (Tech Serv Mgr)
Ultimate Holding Company: LANXESS AG (GERMANY)
Immediate Holding Company: LANXESS LIMITED
Registration no: 03498959 **VAT No.:** GB 642 4694 27
Date established: 1998 **Turnover:** £10m - £20m
No.of Employees: 11 - 20 **Product Groups:** 31

Date of Accounts	Dec 10	Dec 09	Dec 08
Sales Turnover	18m	19m	18m
Pre Tax Profit/Loss	1m	1m	1m

Working Capital	9m	8m	6m
Fixed Assets	5m	5m	6m
Current Assets	11m	11m	9m
Current Liabilities	802	1m	1m

Leavesley Container Services Ltd

A38 Lichfield Road Branston, Burton On Trent, DE14 3HD
Tel: 01283-537382 **Fax:** 01283-511740
E-mail: malcolma@leavesley-containers.com
Website: http://www.leavesley-containers.com
Managers: R. Maison (Chief Mgr)
Ultimate Holding Company: ETEX GROUP SA (BELGIUM)
Immediate Holding Company: MARLEY ETERNIT LIMITED
Registration no: 00486100 **VAT No.:** GB 806 6135 41
Date established: 1950 **Turnover:** £125m - £250m
No.of Employees: 1 - 10 **Product Groups:** 45, 48, 76

Date of Accounts	Dec 11	Dec 10	Dec 09
Sales Turnover	129m	115m	103m
Pre Tax Profit/Loss	5m	2m	-3m
Working Capital	24m	27m	5m
Fixed Assets	84m	91m	87m
Current Assets	48m	46m	37m
Current Liabilities	12m	10m	10m

Lichfield International Freight Terminal Ltd

Wellington Road, Burton On Trent, DE14 2TG
Tel: 01283-511888 **Fax:** 01283-511900
E-mail: rfr@lichfieldinternational.co.uk
Website: http://www.lichfieldinternational.co.uk
Directors: P. Partington (Fin), R. Webster (MD)
Managers: C. Bonsell (Sales Prom Mgr), M. Jackson (Tech Serv Mgr)
Immediate Holding Company: LICHFIELD INTERNATIONAL FREIGHT TERMINAL LIMITED
Registration no: 02852323 **Date established:** 1993
Turnover: £500,000 - £1m **No.of Employees:** 21 - 50 **Product Groups:** 77

Date of Accounts	Oct 10	Oct 09	Oct 08
Working Capital	-411	-364	-416
Fixed Assets	3m	3m	3m
Current Assets	884	892	893

Lorien Resourcing Ltd

Millennium Court First Avenue, Burton On Trent, DE14 2WH
Tel: 01543-444244 **Fax:** 01543-444215
E-mail: engineering.solutions@lorien.co.uk
Website: http://www.lorienresourcing.co.uk
Bank(s): Barclays Bank
Directors: J. Kelly (MD)
Ultimate Holding Company: LORIEN LIMITED
Immediate Holding Company: LORIEN RESOURCING LIMITED
Registration no: 01333388 **VAT No.:** GB 613 0779 54
Date established: 1977 **Turnover:** £5m - £10m
No.of Employees: 51 - 100 **Product Groups:** 41, 48, 54, 80, 84

Date of Accounts	Jan 12	Jan 11	Jan 10
Sales Turnover	203m	204m	165m
Pre Tax Profit/Loss	3m	3m	2m
Working Capital	4m	4m	3m
Fixed Assets	466	731	964
Current Assets	48m	56m	47m
Current Liabilities	24m	29m	26m

Lorlec Ltd

Horninglow Road North, Burton On Trent, DE13 0SF
Tel: 01283-531191 **Fax:** 01283-538113
E-mail: accounts@lorlec.com
Website: http://www.lorlec.com
Directors: E. Lord (Fin), B. Lord (MD)
Immediate Holding Company: LORLEC LIMITED
Registration no: 02236833 **Date established:** 1988
Turnover: £500,000 - £1m **No.of Employees:** 1 - 10 **Product Groups:** 48

Date of Accounts	Nov 11	Nov 10	Nov 09
Working Capital	22	1	8
Fixed Assets	38	38	41
Current Assets	182	155	128

M H C Industrials Ltd

Wetmore Road, Burton On Trent, DE14 1QN
Tel: 01283-564651 **Fax:** 01283-511526
E-mail: sales@mhcind.co.uk
Website: http://www.mhcind.co.uk
Directors: M. Cherry (MD)
Registration no: 00578666 **Turnover:** £250,000 - £500,000
No.of Employees: 1 - 10 **Product Groups:** 47

Date of Accounts	Apr 06	Apr 05	Apr 02
Working Capital	4	10	33
Fixed Assets	12	15	25
Current Assets	18	25	49

Malrex Fabrications Ltd

Unit 6-7 H C M Industrial Estate Wetmore Road, Burton On Trent, DE14 1QR
Tel: 01283-511278 **Fax:** 01283-516870
E-mail: malrex@btconnect.com
Directors: K. Tunnicliffe (Fin), M. Tunnicliffe (MD)
Immediate Holding Company: MALREX FABRICATIONS LIMITED
Registration no: 03140235 **Date established:** 1995
Turnover: £500,000 - £1m **No.of Employees:** 11 - 20
Product Groups: 35, 42, 45

Date of Accounts	Dec 11	Dec 10	Dec 09
Sales Turnover	N/A	768	621
Pre Tax Profit/Loss	N/A	47	-10
Working Capital	97	94	86
Fixed Assets	9	11	13
Current Assets	188	234	167
Current Liabilities	N/A	83	24

Marley Eternit Ltd

Lichfield Road Branston Industrial Estate, Branston, Burton On Trent, DE14 3HD
Tel: 01283-722222 **Fax:** 01283-722242
E-mail: info@marleyeternit.co.uk
Website: http://www.marleyeternit.co.uk
Bank(s): Lloyds TSB
Directors: D. Speakman (Fin), M. Turner (MD)
Managers: N. Downes (Sales Prom Mgr), R. Bishop (Mktg Serv Mgr), J. Blair-park (Mgr), K. Clark (Purch Mgr)
Ultimate Holding Company: ETEX GROUP SA (BELGIUM)
Immediate Holding Company: ETERNIT UK LIMITED
Registration no: 00217768 **Date established:** 2026
Turnover: £10m - £20m **No.of Employees:** 101 - 250
Product Groups: 33, 52

see next page

***Marley Eternit Ltd** - Cont'd*

Date of Accounts	Dec 11	Dec 10	Dec 09
Sales Turnover	529	15m	31m
Pre Tax Profit/Loss	-213	-294	-3m
Working Capital	23m	23m	23m
Fixed Assets	7m	6m	17m
Current Assets	23m	24m	27m
Current Liabilities	335	312	522

Mid Anglia Engineering Ltd
Wetmore Road, Burton On Trent, DE14 1SN
Tel: 01283-563616 **Fax:** 01283-511135
E-mail: info@midanglia.com
Website: http://www.midanglia.com
Bank(s): National Westminster Bank Plc
Directors: M. Logue (Co Sec), K. Logue (Ch)
Immediate Holding Company: MID-ANGLIA ENGINEERING LIMITED
Registration no: 01268804 **VAT No.:** GB 289 1857 02
Date established: 1976 **Turnover:** £500,000 - £1m
No.of Employees: 11 - 20 **Product Groups:** 28, 35, 37, 38, 39, 40, 42, 46, 47, 67, 84

Date of Accounts	May 11	May 10	May 09
Working Capital	88	166	233
Fixed Assets	11	12	15
Current Assets	191	235	335

Molson Coors Brewers Ltd
137 High Street, Burton On Trent, DE14 1JZ
Tel: 01283-511000 **Fax:** 01937-832324
Website: http://www.fa-carling.co.uk
Bank(s): Lloyds TSB Bank plc
Managers: A. Hulme (Chief Mgr)
Ultimate Holding Company: MOLSON COORS BREWING COMPANY (U.S.A)
Immediate Holding Company: COORS BREWERS LIMITED
Registration no: 06824686 **Date established:** 2009
Turnover: £500m - £1,000m **No.of Employees:** 1501 & over
Product Groups: 21

Ornamental Gates
School House Newchurch, Hoar Cross, Burton On Trent, DE13 8RH
Tel: 01283-575586
Directors: S. Hartshorn (Prop)
Date established: 1994 **No.of Employees:** 1 - 10 **Product Groups:** 26, 35

Palletforce Plc
Callister Way, Burton On Trent, DE14 2SY
Tel: 08450-944441 **Fax:** 0845-643 5421
E-mail: sales@palletforce.com
Website: http://www.palletforce.com
Directors: M. Conroy (Grp Chief Exec)
Managers: H. Findlay (Personnel), D. Holland (Mktg Serv Mgr), D. Hughes (Tech Serv Mgr), N. Carpenter (Fin Mgr)
Immediate Holding Company: PALLETFORCE PLC
Registration no: 04088035 **Date established:** 2000
Turnover: £10m - £20m **No.of Employees:** 21 - 50 **Product Groups:** 77

Date of Accounts	Aug 11	Aug 10	Aug 09
Sales Turnover	13m	10m	8m
Pre Tax Profit/Loss	2m	2m	1m
Working Capital	5m	4m	3m
Fixed Assets	734	831	842
Current Assets	9m	8m	7m
Current Liabilities	3m	3m	2m

Paragon Pattern & Tool
Northside Business Park Hawkins Lane, Burton On Trent, DE14 1DB
Tel: 01283-512276 **Fax:** 01283-517767
E-mail: sales@paragon-patterns.co.uk
Website: http://www.paragon-patterns.co.uk
Directors: S. Mabbott (Ptnr)
Ultimate Holding Company: COOPER HOLDINGS (TAMWORTH AND BURTON) LIMITED
Immediate Holding Company: TRENTSIDE PROPERTY CO (BURTON) LIMITED
Registration no: 02583059 **Date established:** 1982 **Turnover:** £1m - £2m
No.of Employees: 11 - 20 **Product Groups:** 46

Date of Accounts	Oct 11	Oct 10	Oct 09
Working Capital	-2	14	21
Fixed Assets	49	49	49
Current Assets	6	37	44

Pipe Center
33 Hawkins Lane, Burton On Trent, DE14 1PT
Tel: 01283-567334 **Fax:** 01283-510207
E-mail: enquiries@pipelinecenter.co.uk
Website: http://www.pipelinecentre.co.uk
Directors: M. White (Fin)
Managers: K. Barratt (District Mgr)
Ultimate Holding Company: BRITISH FITTINGS GROUP P.L.C.
Registration no: 00797026 **Turnover:** £500,000 - £1m
No.of Employees: 1 - 10 **Product Groups:** 30, 34, 35, 36, 40

Date of Accounts	Jun 11	Jun 10	Jun 09
Sales Turnover	87m	96m	96m
Pre Tax Profit/Loss	-2m	5m	5m
Working Capital	-2m	1m	4m
Fixed Assets	36m	34m	26m
Current Assets	34m	33m	45m
Current Liabilities	9m	7m	9m

Plasplugs
Main Line Industrial Estate Wetmore Road, Burton On Trent, DE14 1SD
Tel: 0800-840 6820 **Fax:** 01283-531246
E-mail: neale.turner@plasplugs.com
Website: http://www.plasplugs.com
Bank(s): National Westminster
Directors: S. Turner (MD), N. Turner (Grp Chief Exec)
Managers: G. Hindley (Export Sales Mg), P. Boyce (Sales & Mktg Mg), D. Turner (I.T. Exec), V. Britain (Purch Mgr)
Immediate Holding Company: TURNER INTL LTD
Registration no: 01085038 **VAT No.:** 127 2551 83 **Date established:** 2009
Turnover: £10m - £20m **No.of Employees:** 11 - 20 **Product Groups:** 36

Product Publicity
Unit D Rhino Business Park Fauld Industrial Estate, Burton On Trent, DE13 9HS
Tel: 01283-815 893 **Fax:** 01283-812 992
E-mail: sales@productpublicity.com
Website: http://www.productpublicity.com

Directors: R. Guest (MD)
Managers: T. Guest (Serv Mgr)
Turnover: £500,000 - £1m **No.of Employees:** 1 - 10 **Product Groups:** 30, 49

Pugh & Sanders Ltd
Unit 2-4 Moseley Street, Burton On Trent, DE14 1DW
Tel: 01283-510824 **Fax:** 01283-511403
E-mail: sales@pughandsanders.co.uk
Website: http://www.pughandsanders.co.uk
Directors: J. Pugh (Dir), W. Pugh (Fin)
Immediate Holding Company: PUGH & SANDERS LIMITED
Registration no: 02287354 **VAT No.:** GB 507 7753 28
Date established: 1988 **Turnover:** £500,000 - £1m
No.of Employees: 11 - 20 **Product Groups:** 35, 66

Date of Accounts	Sep 11	Sep 10	Sep 09
Working Capital	130	86	114
Fixed Assets	69	35	28
Current Assets	968	794	674
Current Liabilities	N/A	N/A	176

Renold Chain UK Sales plc (UK Sales)
Derby Turning Building Derby Road, Burton On Trent, DE14 1RS
Tel: 01283-512940 **Fax:** 01283-512628
E-mail: enquiry@renold.com
Website: http://www.renold.com
Bank(s): Lloyds
Directors: J. Probert (Sales)
Managers: J. Mather (Mgr), D. Turner (Mktg Serv Mgr), P. Camwell (Purch Mgr)
Immediate Holding Company: RYKNELD METALS LIMITED
Registration no: 00182382 **VAT No.:** GB 145 1238 90
Date established: 1975 **No.of Employees:** 21 - 50 **Product Groups:** 35, 45

Date of Accounts	Aug 10	Aug 09	Aug 08
Working Capital	595	518	699
Fixed Assets	316	297	9
Current Assets	750	620	972

Reynolds Boughton
Unit 9 Graycar Business Park Barton Turn, Barton under Needwood, Burton On Trent, DE13 8EN
Tel: 01283-711771 **Fax:** 01283- 711669
E-mail: ceh@reynoldsboughton.com
Website: http://www.reynoldsboughton.com
Bank(s): Barclays
Directors: P. Maidstone (Fin), A. Burley (Sales & Mktg)
Managers: R. Elliot (Purch Mgr), C. Higgs
Ultimate Holding Company: T.T.BOUGHTON & SONS LIMITED
Immediate Holding Company: REYNOLDS BOUGHTON LIMITED
Registration no: 00418439 **VAT No.:** GB 207 6677 47
Date established: 1946 **Turnover:** £5m - £10m **No.of Employees:** 21 - 50
Product Groups: 39, 40

Date of Accounts	Aug 09	Aug 08	Aug 07
Sales Turnover	7m	N/A	N/A
Pre Tax Profit/Loss	-51	390	404
Working Capital	255	1m	986
Fixed Assets	741	431	525
Current Assets	1m	2m	2m
Current Liabilities	371	582	404

Riverside At Branston
Riverside Drive Branston, Burton On Trent, DE14 3EP
Tel: 01283-511234 **Fax:** 01283-511441
E-mail: riverside.branston@oldenglishinns.co.uk
Website: http://www.oldenglishinns.co.uk
Bank(s): National Westminster, Burton O
Managers: J. Tiebalel (Chief Mgr)
Immediate Holding Company: OLD ENGLISH PUB CO P.L.C.
Registration no: 03023704 **VAT No.:** GB 701 5146 79
Turnover: £1m - £2m **No.of Employees:** 11 - 20 **Product Groups:** 35, 66

Robinson Instruments Ltd (c/o Gaitronics Ltd)
Brunel Drive Stretton, Burton On Trent, DE13 0BZ
Tel: 01283-500500 **Fax:** 01283-500400
E-mail: sales@hipotronics.com
Website: http://www.high-voltage-hubbell.com
Directors: G. Lupton (Tech Serv)
Managers: D. Hilder (Sales Prom Mgr), J. Jackson (Ops Mgr), T. Fawcett (Site Co-ord), D. Hider (Sales Prom Mgr)
Ultimate Holding Company: Hubbell Inc.
Immediate Holding Company: Hubbell Ltd
Registration no: 00917257 **VAT No.:** GB 419 5300 64
Turnover: £2m - £5m **No.of Employees:** 101 - 250 **Product Groups:** 37, 38, 47

Date of Accounts	Dec 04	Dec 03
Sales Turnover	525	712
Pre Tax Profit/Loss	34	-472
Working Capital	608	641
Fixed Assets	12	28
Current Assets	948	1021
Current Liabilities	340	380
Total Share Capital	1389	1389
ROCE% (Return on Capital Employed)	5.5	-70.6
ROT% (Return on Turnover)	6.6	-66.3

Rumenco Ltd
Derby Road Stretton, Burton On Trent, DE13 0DW
Tel: 01283-511211 **Fax:** 01283-546152
E-mail: info@rumenco.co.uk
Website: http://www.rumenco.co.uk
Directors: N. Duncalf (Fin), N. Duncass (Fin), N. Lyon (MD)
Managers: R. Walters (Tech Serv Mgr), S. Glover (Personnel)
Immediate Holding Company: RUMENCO LIMITED
Registration no: 04016333 **Date established:** 2000
Turnover: £20m - £50m **No.of Employees:** 51 - 100 **Product Groups:** 20

Date of Accounts	Jun 11	Jun 10	Jun 09
Sales Turnover	29m	26m	24m
Pre Tax Profit/Loss	2m	4m	650
Working Capital	5m	4m	3m
Fixed Assets	2m	2m	2m
Current Assets	9m	10m	5m
Current Liabilities	2m	2m	1m

Rykneld Metals Ltd
Derby Road, Burton On Trent, DE14 1RS
Tel: 01283-562745 **Fax:** 01283-562745

Directors: G. Hill (Dir), K. Varley (Fin)
Immediate Holding Company: RYKNELD METALS LIMITED
Registration no: 01224749 **VAT No.:** GB 284 1658 38
Date established: 1975 **Turnover:** £1m - £2m **No.of Employees:** 1 - 10
Product Groups: 66

Date of Accounts	Aug 11	Aug 10	Aug 09
Working Capital	603	595	518
Fixed Assets	549	316	297
Current Assets	948	750	620

S M Barrett Construction Ltd
Daisy Bank Cottage Thorney Lanes, Newborough, Burton On Trent, DE13 8RY
Tel: 01283-821500 **Fax:** 01283-821500
E-mail: smbconsltd@aol.com
Website: http://www.smbarrett.co.uk
Directors: S. Barrett (MD)
Immediate Holding Company: S M BARRETT CONSTRUCTION LIMITED
Registration no: 03215147 **Date established:** 1996
No.of Employees: 1 - 10 **Product Groups:** 25, 35

Date of Accounts	Jun 11	Jun 10	Jun 08
Working Capital	-9	-20	-32
Fixed Assets	15	20	25
Current Assets	36	20	18

Shinwatec Ltd
Unit 3 Barberry Court Parkway, Centrum One Hundred, Burton On Trent, DE14 2UE
Tel: 01283-845848 **Fax:** 01283-845849
Directors: M. Nakamura (MD)
Ultimate Holding Company: SHINWA CO LTD (JAPAN)
Immediate Holding Company: SHINWATEC LIMITED
Registration no: 03237940 **Date established:** 1996
No.of Employees: 1 - 10 **Product Groups:** 37, 38, 48

Date of Accounts	Dec 11	Dec 10	Dec 09
Working Capital	-94	-94	211
Fixed Assets	2	1	N/A
Current Assets	381	732	2m

Specialist Tube Supplies Ltd
PO Box 6705, Burton On Trent, DE15 0ZS
Tel: 0870-2406301 **Fax:** 0870-2406302
E-mail: info@specialisttubesupplies.co.uk
Website: http://www.specialisttubesupplies.co.uk
Directors: T. Reeves (Dir)
Registration no: 4987605 **Date established:** 2004 **Turnover:** £2m - £5m
No.of Employees: 1 - 10 **Product Groups:** 34, 36

Stone LST Direct
100-105 Victoria CR, Burton On Trent, DE14 2QF
Tel: 01283-501090 **Fax:** 01283-501098
E-mail: info@stonell.com
Website: http://www.originalstoneco.co.uk
Directors: T. Rudd (MD)
Managers: M. Gerrard (Sales Prom Mgr)
Registration no: 03905146 **Date established:** 1972 **Turnover:** £5m - £10m
No.of Employees: 11 - 20 **Product Groups:** 14, 33

T A S Engineering Ltd
Unit 1 Millers Lane, Burton On Trent, DE14 2NS
Tel: 01283-529149 **Fax:** 01283-561096
E-mail: info@thinkant.co.uk
Website: http://www.thinkant.co.uk
Directors: G. Davies (Dir), A. Davies (Fin)
Immediate Holding Company: TAS ENGINEERING LTD
Registration no: 06333469 **Date established:** 2007
No.of Employees: 1 - 10 **Product Groups:** 35

Date of Accounts	Aug 11	Aug 10	Aug 09
Working Capital	-22	-26	-32
Fixed Assets	44	61	80
Current Assets	144	115	111

T & H Quality Fabrications
Unit 10 Burton Enterprise Park Hawkins Lane, Burton On Trent, DE14 1QG
Tel: 01283-517795
Directors: O. Hawcroft (Prop)
Date established: 1991 **No.of Employees:** 1 - 10 **Product Groups:** 35

The Webb Group (Findell P.L.C.)
Queen Street, Burton On Trent, DE14 3LP
Tel: 01283-566311 **Fax:** 01283-506301
E-mail: joe.mcnicholas@thewebbgroup.co.uk
Website: http://www.webbivorydm.com
Bank(s): Barclays
Managers: J. Mcnicholas
Ultimate Holding Company: FINDEL P.L.C.
Immediate Holding Company: CHOICES UK GROUP LIMITED
Registration no: 06286783 **Date established:** 2007
Turnover: £50m - £75m **No.of Employees:** 51 - 100 **Product Groups:** 61

Date of Accounts	Dec 08	Mar 08	Apr 10
Sales Turnover	55m	46m	56m
Pre Tax Profit/Loss	3m	-8m	-8m
Working Capital	-9m	-11m	-19m
Fixed Assets	4m	3m	5m
Current Assets	39m	19m	16m
Current Liabilities	34m	N/A	3m

Thurco Engineering
The Gatehouse Victoria Crescent, Burton On Trent, DE14 2QA
Tel: 01283-548195 **Fax:** 01283-511040
E-mail: sales@thurco.com
Website: http://www.thurco.com
Directors: G. Prescott (Dir), J. Prescott (Co Sec)
Immediate Holding Company: THURCO ENGINEERING COMPANY LIMITED
Registration no: 01028106 **Date established:** 1971
No.of Employees: 21 - 50 **Product Groups:** 35, 39, 45

Date of Accounts	Jun 11	Jun 10	Jun 09
Working Capital	-624	-524	-441
Fixed Assets	315	324	335
Current Assets	246	636	475

Vodafone Ltd
14 Underhill Walk, Burton On Trent, DE14 1DE
Tel: 07717-274813 **Fax:** 01283-560555
E-mail: info@vodafone.co.uk
Website: http://www.vodafone.co.uk

Directors: A. Mcdougall (MD)
Managers: A. Mcdougal (Mgr)
Ultimate Holding Company: VODAFONE GROUP PUBLIC LIMITED COMPANY
Immediate Holding Company: VODAFONE LIMITED
Registration no: 01471587 **Date established:** 1980
No.of Employees: 1 - 10 **Product Groups:** 37, 47, 52, 79, 84

Date of Accounts	Mar 12	Mar 11	Mar 10
Sales Turnover	5364m	5163m	4801m
Pre Tax Profit/Loss	-61m	-169m	-323m
Working Capital	1265m	966m	741m
Fixed Assets	5665m	5941m	6250m
Current Assets	5402m	3764m	3003m
Current Liabilities	954m	989m	945m

W H Mason & Son Ltd

The Old Sawmills Wetmore Road, Burton On Trent, DE14 1QN
Tel: 01283-564651 **Fax:** 01283-511526
E-mail: sales@justwood.com
Website: http://www.justwood.com
Directors: M. Cherry (Dir)
Immediate Holding Company: W.H. MASON & SON (TIMBER MERCHANTS) LIMITED
Registration no: 00511718 **VAT No.:** GB 125 2925 80
Date established: 1952 **Turnover:** £500,000 - £1m
No.of Employees: 1 - 10 **Product Groups:** 25, 48, 65

Date of Accounts	Apr 11	Apr 10	Apr 09
Working Capital	-148	-141	-113
Fixed Assets	377	381	384
Current Assets	83	74	60

W T Parker Ltd

24-28 Moor Street, Burton On Trent, DE14 3SX
Tel: 01283-542661 **Fax:** 01283-536189
E-mail: contracting@wtparker.co.uk
Website: http://www.wtparker.co.uk
Bank(s): Barclays
Directors: R. Pizzey (Co Sec), S. Smyth (MD)
Ultimate Holding Company: W.T. PARKER GROUP LTD.
Immediate Holding Company: W.T. PARKER LTD.
Registration no: 01270585 **Date established:** 1976
Turnover: £20m - £50m **No.of Employees:** 21 - 50 **Product Groups:** 37, 38, 52, 84

Date of Accounts	Feb 12	Feb 11	Feb 10
Sales Turnover	41m	34m	30m
Pre Tax Profit/Loss	2m	1m	2m
Working Capital	7m	6m	6m
Fixed Assets	417	253	138
Current Assets	15m	14m	9m
Current Liabilities	2m	3m	699

Walkerworld Steel Fabricators

451 Stanton Road, Burton On Trent, DE15 9RS
Tel: 01283-515439 **Fax:** 01283-517554
Directors: A. Sawdon (Prop)
Date established: 1998 **No.of Employees:** 1 - 10 **Product Groups:** 35

The Welly Shop Ltd

Fourth Avenue Centrum One Hundred, Burton On Trent, DE14 2WL
Tel: 01989-730217 **Fax:** 01989-730217
E-mail: sales@thewellyshop.com
Website: http://www.thewellyshop.com
Directors: D. Bridgford (MD)
Immediate Holding Company: THE DRYBOOT COMPANY LTD
Registration no: 05055741 **Date established:** 2004
No.of Employees: 1 - 10 **Product Groups:** 22

Wilo UK Ltd

Second Avenue Centrum One Hundred, Burton On Trent, DE14 2WJ
Tel: 01283-523000 **Fax:** 01283-523099
E-mail: sales@wilo.co.uk
Website: http://www.wilo.co.uk
Bank(s): Midland
Directors: G. Mannus (MD), R. Harden (Dir)
Managers: G. Wheatley (Tech Serv Mgr), L. Blakemore (Mktg Serv Mgr)
Ultimate Holding Company: WILO SE (GERMANY)
Immediate Holding Company: WILO (U.K.) LTD
Registration no: 01944189 **Date established:** 1985
No.of Employees: 21 - 50 **Product Groups:** 39, 40

Date of Accounts	Dec 11	Dec 10	Dec 09
Sales Turnover	16m	15m	N/A
Pre Tax Profit/Loss	358	319	-525
Working Capital	-64	-427	-304
Fixed Assets	1m	1m	1m
Current Assets	6m	5m	5m
Current Liabilities	2m	2m	1m

Cannock

A B Dust Control Ltd

Unit 6 Morston Court, Cannock, WS11 8JB
Tel: 01543-431370 **Fax:** 01543-570238
E-mail: david@abdustcontrol.com
Website: http://www.abdustcontrol.com
Directors: D. Bennetts (Dir), A. Bennett (MD), G. Bennett (Co Sec)
Managers: D. Bennett (Tech Serv Mgr), S. Edwards (Mktg Serv Mgr)
Immediate Holding Company: A.B. DUST CONTROL LIMITED
Registration no: 01586118 **VAT No.:** 361 8801 48 **Date established:** 1981
Turnover: Up to £250,000 **No.of Employees:** 1 - 10 **Product Groups:** 40, 42

Date of Accounts	Feb 08	Feb 11	Feb 10
Working Capital	27	-1	5
Fixed Assets	10	7	9
Current Assets	498	341	631

A Plus Training

52 Meadowsweet Way, Cannock, WS12 2GS
Tel: 01543-278082 **Fax:** 01543-279722
E-mail: info@chase901.fsnet.co.uk
Website: http://www.chase901.fsnet.co.uk
Directors: P. Askey (Prop)
Immediate Holding Company: A PLUS TRAINING (MIDLANDS) LIMITED
Registration no: 06510551 **Date established:** 2008
No.of Employees: 1 - 10 **Product Groups:** 35, 39, 45

Date of Accounts	Mar 12	Mar 11	Mar 10
Working Capital	-9	-10	-10
Fixed Assets	10	10	11
Current Assets	3	2	N/A

A T P Automatic Transmission Parts UK Ltd

Victoria Street Hednesford, Cannock, WS12 1BU
Tel: 01543-870330 **Fax:** 01543-426581
E-mail: alanrichards@atp-group.com
Website: http://www.atp-group.com
Directors: A. Smart (MD), M. Green (Co Sec)
Ultimate Holding Company: ATP INDUSTRIES GROUP LTD
Immediate Holding Company: A.T.P. AUTOMATIC TRANSMISSION PARTS (U.K.) LIMITED
Registration no: 01189741 **Date established:** 1974 **Turnover:** £5m - £10m
No.of Employees: 1 - 10 **Product Groups:** 35, 68

Adroit Modular Buildings plc

Delta Way, Cannock, WS11 0BE
Tel: 01543-404040 **Fax:** 01543-404114
E-mail: sales@elliott-algeco.com
Website: http://adroitmodular.com
Bank(s): HSBC Bank plc
Managers: A. Bacon (Purch Mgr)
Ultimate Holding Company: ADROIT GROUP LIMITED
Immediate Holding Company: ADROIT MODULAR BUILDINGS PLC
Registration no: 00668542 **Date established:** 1960
Turnover: £500m - £1,000m **No.of Employees:** 11 - 20
Product Groups: 25, 30, 33, 35, 39, 52, 66, 69, 80, 83, 84

Date of Accounts	Sep 09	Sep 08	Sep 07
Sales Turnover	3m	6m	3m
Pre Tax Profit/Loss	446	-279	-110
Working Capital	-1m	-131	-80
Fixed Assets	2m	2m	2m
Current Assets	3m	1m	939
Current Liabilities	239	294	188

Allsigns Express

5 Shorade Industrial Units New Street, Bridgtown, Cannock, WS11 0DH
Tel: 01543-500226 **Fax:** 01543-500227
Directors: S. Coate (Dir)
Managers: S. Cope (Mgr)
No.of Employees: 1 - 10 **Product Groups:** 37, 49

Amelec Ltd

101 Moreton Street, Cannock, WS11 5HN
Tel: 01543-466191 **Fax:** 01543-467339
E-mail: info@amelec.co.uk
Website: http://www.amelec.co.uk
Directors: P. Pearson (Co Sec)
Immediate Holding Company: AMELEC LIMITED
Registration no: 02030724 **VAT No.:** GB 435 5562 44
Date established: 1986 **Turnover:** £250,000 - £500,000
No.of Employees: 1 - 10 **Product Groups:** 37, 67

Date of Accounts	Mar 12	Mar 11	Mar 10
Working Capital	25	39	54
Fixed Assets	18	19	20
Current Assets	248	174	141

Apol Installations & Sales Ltd

Unit 20 Longford Industrial Estate Longford Road, Cannock, WS11 0DG
Tel: 01543-466696 **Fax:** 01543-462488
E-mail: apol@btinternet.com
Website: http://www.apolinstallations.co.uk
Directors: J. Knott (Co Sec), J. Knott (Fin), P. Holmes (MD)
Immediate Holding Company: APOL INSTALLATIONS & SALES LIMITED
Registration no: 01988104 **Date established:** 1986
No.of Employees: 11 - 20 **Product Groups:** 35, 45

Date of Accounts	Jan 08	Jan 07	Jan 06
Working Capital	-62	-81	-46
Fixed Assets	51	58	73
Current Assets	288	275	352
Current Liabilities	350	356	399
Total Share Capital	N/A	N/A	50

Arkrite Fencing Manufacturers Ltd

Progress Drive, Cannock, WS11 0JE
Tel: 01543-577677 **Fax:** 01543-574446
E-mail: arkrite@btconnect.com
Bank(s): Barclays
Directors: T. Timmins (MD)
Managers: J. Jones
Immediate Holding Company: ARKRITE FENCING MANUFACTURERS LIMITED
Registration no: 01145068 **VAT No.:** GB 101 2667 17
Date established: 1973 **Turnover:** £250,000 - £500,000
No.of Employees: 21 - 50 **Product Groups:** 34, 35

Date of Accounts	Nov 11	Nov 10	Nov 09
Working Capital	1m	1m	2m
Fixed Assets	341	346	252
Current Assets	2m	2m	2m

Avon Engineered Rubber Stafford

Belsize Close Norton Canes, Cannock, WS11 9TQ
Tel: 01543-270002 **Fax:** 01543-278046
E-mail: steve.huckfield@stafford-rubber.co.uk
Website: http://www.avon-group.co.uk
Bank(s): Midland
Directors: H. Challinor (Fin), S. Huckfield (MD)
Managers: J. Clouston, M. Brandrick (Buyer), P. Williams (Tech Serv Mgr), J. Brugden
Immediate Holding Company: STAFFORD RUBBER COMPANY LIMITED
Registration no: 01197511 **VAT No.:** GB 112 6226 14
Date established: 1975 **Turnover:** £5m - £10m
No.of Employees: 51 - 100 **Product Groups:** 29

Date of Accounts	Jan 07	Jan 06	Jan 05
Pre Tax Profit/Loss	N/A	-322	-618
Working Capital	-262	-176	-700
Fixed Assets	588	747	2m
Current Assets	1m	1m	2m
Current Liabilities	N/A	816	1m

Awe Precision Ltd

Unit 6-7 Wynns Venture Centre Broad Street, Cannock, WS11 0XL
Tel: 01543-467774 **Fax:** 01543-467750
E-mail: info@aweprecision.co.uk
Website: http://www.aweprecision.co.uk
Directors: J. Birch (Fin)
Immediate Holding Company: AWE PRECISION LIMITED
Registration no: 02965185 **Date established:** 1994
No.of Employees: 1 - 10 **Product Groups:** 46

Date of Accounts	Sep 07	Sep 06	Sep 05
Working Capital	12	-13	-2
Fixed Assets	27	26	48
Current Assets	159	134	133
Current Liabilities	147	147	135

B I Composites Ltd

Green Lane, Cannock, WS11 0JW
Tel: 01543-466021 **Fax:** 01543-574157
E-mail: hbhachu@bi-composites.co.uk
Website: http://www.bi-group.com
Managers: H. Bhachu (Ops Mgr)
Ultimate Holding Company: NATIONAL INDUSTRIES GROUP (HOLDING) SAK (KUWAIT)
Immediate Holding Company: BI COMPOSITES LIMITED
Registration no: 04034953 **Date established:** 2000
Turnover: £10m - £20m **No.of Employees:** 101 - 250
Product Groups: 29, 30, 66

Date of Accounts	Nov 11	Nov 10	Nov 09
Sales Turnover	8m	7m	6m
Pre Tax Profit/Loss	-305	-1m	-2m
Working Capital	975	926	-1m
Fixed Assets	520	723	899
Current Assets	3m	3m	2m
Current Liabilities	683	826	413

Briggs Equipment UK Ltd

Orbital 7 Orbital Way, Cannock, WS11 8XW
Tel: 01543-437800 **Fax:** 01543-437801
E-mail: richard.close@briggsequipment.co.uk
Website: http://www.briggsequipment.co.uk
Directors: R. Close (MD)
Managers: S. Rowlands (Tech Serv Mgr), A. Wharton
Ultimate Holding Company: SAMMONS ENTERPRISES INC (USA)
Immediate Holding Company: BRIGGS EQUIPMENT UK LIMITED
Registration no: 05895588 **Date established:** 2006
Turnover: £75m - £125m **No.of Employees:** 101 - 250
Product Groups: 35, 39, 45

Date of Accounts	Dec 11	Dec 10	Dec 09
Sales Turnover	93m	79m	88m
Pre Tax Profit/Loss	2m	-268	-5m
Working Capital	4m	7m	11m
Fixed Assets	86m	74m	70m
Current Assets	37m	39m	34m
Current Liabilities	13m	17m	10m

Burntwood Fasteners Ltd

Martindale Hawks Green Business Park, Cannock, WS11 7XN
Tel: 01543-572731 **Fax:** 01543-572735
E-mail: sales@burntwoodfasteners.co.uk
Website: http://www.burntwoodfasteners.co.uk
Directors: D. Sleigh (Sales), J. Elston (Fin), C. Sleigh (Prop)
Ultimate Holding Company: TROYCE LIMITED
Immediate Holding Company: BURNTWOOD FASTENERS LIMITED
Registration no: 01460388 **VAT No.:** GB 333 9392 43
Date established: 1979 **Turnover:** £500,000 - £1m
No.of Employees: 11 - 20 **Product Groups:** 35, 66

Date of Accounts	Dec 11	Dec 10	Dec 09
Working Capital	628	599	630
Fixed Assets	313	346	238
Current Assets	1m	1m	1m

Cannock Chemicals Ltd

99a North Street, Cannock, WS11 0AZ
Tel: 01543-571762 **Fax:** 01543-466011
E-mail: sales@thepolishingshop.co.uk
Website: http://www.thepolishingshop.co.uk
Directors: M. Malpass (Dir)
Immediate Holding Company: CANNOCK CHEMICALS LIMITED
Registration no: 01643201 **Date established:** 1982
No.of Employees: 11 - 20 **Product Groups:** 32, 34, 46, 48, 66

Date of Accounts	Sep 11	Sep 10	Sep 09
Working Capital	919	897	837
Fixed Assets	125	167	108
Current Assets	2m	2m	1m

Central Cables

Unit 8 Brindley Business Park Chaseside Drive, Hednesford, Cannock, WS11 7GD
Tel: 01543-422477 **Fax:** 01543-422420
E-mail: sales@centralcables.co.uk
Website: http://www.centralcables.co.uk
Directors: M. Chaney (Co Sec), M. Tinker (Dir)
Immediate Holding Company: CENTRAL CABLES LIMITED
Registration no: 02390122 **VAT No.:** GB 489 6872 62
Date established: 1989 **Turnover:** £1m - £2m **No.of Employees:** 1 - 10
Product Groups: 37

Date of Accounts	Oct 11	Oct 10	Oct 09
Working Capital	350	328	313
Fixed Assets	8	4	5
Current Assets	920	813	811

Chase Chamber Of Commerce

Park South Park Plaza, Heath Hayes, Cannock, WS12 2DB
Tel: 08450-710191 **Fax:** 01543-441698
E-mail: info@chase-chamber.com
Website: http://www.chase-chamber.com
Managers: C. Plant
Ultimate Holding Company: EAST MERCIA CHAMBER OF COMMERCE & INDUSTRY
Registration no: 04196701 **VAT No.:** GB 100 6255 26
Date established: 2001 **Turnover:** £2m - £5m **No.of Employees:** 1 - 10
Product Groups: 87

Chase Garage Doors Ltd

Unit 5 Littleton Business Park Littleton Drive, Cannock, WS12 4TR
Tel: 01543-467175 **Fax:** 01543-467175
E-mail: sales@chasegaragedoors.co.uk
Website: http://www.chasegaragedoors.co.uk
Directors: N. Duggan (Dir)
Immediate Holding Company: CHASE GARAGE DOORS LIMITED
Registration no: 04742722 **Date established:** 2003
No.of Employees: 1 - 10 **Product Groups:** 25, 30, 33, 35

Date of Accounts	Jul 11	Jul 10	Jul 07
Working Capital	22	41	44
Fixed Assets	13	10	11
Current Assets	77	100	115

Chillton Agricultural Equipment Ltd
Hyssop Close, Cannock, WS11 7XB
Tel: 01543-462787 **Fax:** 01543-462765
E-mail: anthony.johnson@chilton.com
Website: http://www.chillton.com
Directors: A. Johnson (MD)
Immediate Holding Company: MX (HANDLING EQUIPMENT) UK LIMITED
Registration no: 01011485 **Date established:** 1971 **Turnover:** £1m - £2m
No.of Employees: 11 - 20 **Product Groups:** 41, 45

Date of Accounts	Dec 11	Dec 10	Dec 09
Working Capital	1m	994	928
Fixed Assets	50	57	64
Current Assets	2m	2m	2m

Classic Stairlift Services Ltd
40 Beverley Hill Hednesford, Cannock, WS12 1QL
Tel: 0800-731 8842 **Fax:** 01543-424237
Website: http://www.stairlifts.fsnet.co.uk
Directors: P. Nicholson (Prop)
Immediate Holding Company: CLASSIC STAIRLIFTS LIMITED
Registration no: 07051784 **Date established:** 2009
No.of Employees: 1 - 10 **Product Groups:** 35, 39, 45

Date of Accounts	Dec 10
Working Capital	2
Fixed Assets	10
Current Assets	5

Coex Hubris Ltd
24-25 Rumer Hill Business Estate Rumer Hill Road, Cannock, WS11 0ET
Tel: 01543-574923 **Fax:** 01543-572129
E-mail: sales@coexhubris.co.uk
Website: http://www.coexhubris.co.uk
Directors: R. Lutwyche (MD)
Immediate Holding Company: COEX-HUBRIS LIMITED
Registration no: 02734780 **Date established:** 1992
No.of Employees: 1 - 10 **Product Groups:** 22, 28, 30, 49, 64, 66, 80

Date of Accounts	Dec 11	Dec 10	Dec 09
Working Capital	350	284	718
Fixed Assets	8	12	27
Current Assets	396	354	760

Condensate systems Ltd
2 Delta Way Business Centre Longford Road, Cannock, WS11 0LJ
Tel: 01543-378402 **Fax:** 01543-578202
E-mail: sales@oil-water.com
Website: http://www.oil-water.com
Directors: R. Turner (MD)
Immediate Holding Company: CONDENSATE SYSTEMS LIMITED
Registration no: 05844056 **Date established:** 2006
No.of Employees: 1 - 10 **Product Groups:** 36, 38, 40, 42, 67, 86

Date of Accounts	Jun 11	Jun 10	Jun 09
Working Capital	45	19	-6
Fixed Assets	3	1	N/A
Current Assets	155	101	52

Custom Spinnings
Unit 408 Chase Enterprise Centre Rugeley Road, Hednesford, Cannock, WS12 0QW
Tel: 01543-879714
Directors: A. Gee (Prop)
Immediate Holding Company: SWITCH ON SECURITY LIMITED
Registration no: 06714752 **Date established:** 2009
No.of Employees: 1 - 10 **Product Groups:** 35

Date of Accounts	Mar 11	Mar 10
Working Capital	18	-68
Current Assets	254	148

D P R Engineering
Unit 11 Prospect Business Park Longford Road, Cannock, WS11 0LG
Tel: 01543-577910 **Fax:** 01543-572306
E-mail: info@dprengineering.co.uk
Website: http://www.dprengineering.co.uk
Managers: L. Parkes (Chief Mgr)
Turnover: £250,000 - £500,000 **No.of Employees:** 1 - 10
Product Groups: 45, 46, 48, 66

Electrium Sales Ltd
Lakeside Plaza Walkmill Way, Cannock, WS11 0XE
Tel: 01543-455000 **Fax:** 01543-455001
E-mail: barry.glew@electrium.co.uk
Website: http://www.electrium.co.uk
Bank(s): Lloyds TSB Bank plc
Directors: B. Glew (MD)
Ultimate Holding Company: SIEMENS AG (GERMANY)
Immediate Holding Company: ELECTRIUM SALES LIMITED
Registration no: 02226729 **VAT No.:** GB 100 0992 22
Date established: 1988 **Turnover:** £50m - £75m
No.of Employees: 101 - 250 **Product Groups:** 30, 35, 37

Date of Accounts	Sep 11	Sep 10	Sep 09
Sales Turnover	100m	111m	114m
Pre Tax Profit/Loss	-4m	-15m	11m
Working Capital	13m	17m	31m
Fixed Assets	10m	6m	11m
Current Assets	75m	69m	81m
Current Liabilities	7m	20m	5m

Elite Engineered Products Ltd
Unit 11a Brookfield Drive, Cannock, WS11 0JN
Tel: 01543-220112 **Fax:** 01543-505416
E-mail: george@eepl.co.uk
Website: http://www.eepl.co.uk
Bank(s): Barclays
Directors: G. Dartan (Dir)
Immediate Holding Company: ELITE ENGINEERED PRODUCTS LIMITED
Registration no: 03581367 **Date established:** 1998
Turnover: £500,000 - £1m **No.of Employees:** 11 - 20
Product Groups: 30, 35, 36, 48

Date of Accounts	Aug 11	Aug 10	Aug 09
Working Capital	80	20	1
Fixed Assets	295	299	343
Current Assets	547	566	494

Exidor Ltd
Progress Drive, Cannock, WS11 0JE
Tel: 01543-578661 **Fax:** 01543-570050
E-mail: sales@exidor.co.uk
Website: http://www.exidor.co.uk
Bank(s): HSBC Bank plc
Directors: G. Deakin (Fin), N. Taylor (Sales & Mktg)
Managers: D. Foster (Buyer), M. White
Ultimate Holding Company: CHAMBERLIN PLC
Immediate Holding Company: EXIDOR LIMITED
Registration no: 00253697 **Date established:** 1931 **Turnover:** £5m - £10m
No.of Employees: 51 - 100 **Product Groups:** 35, 36, 66

Date of Accounts	Mar 12	Mar 11	Mar 10
Sales Turnover	5m	3m	3m
Pre Tax Profit/Loss	263	65	-108
Working Capital	985	1m	1m
Fixed Assets	1m	1m	1m
Current Assets	2m	3m	2m
Current Liabilities	260	277	214

Fire Direct
Tradmark House Hyssop Close, Cannock, WS11 7FA
Tel: 01543-466355
E-mail: firedirect@supanet.com
Directors: B. Baggot (Prop), R. Baggett (Prop)
Immediate Holding Company: VEHICLE ALLOCATIONS LTD
Date established: 2010 **No.of Employees:** 1 - 10 **Product Groups:** 38, 42

Fuel Conservation Services Ltd
Unit 1 Anglesey Business Park Littleworth Road, Hednesford, Cannock, WS12 1NR
Tel: 01543-871787 **Fax:** 01543-425757
E-mail: michael.myatt@fcs-ltd.com
Website: http://www.fcs-ltd.com
Bank(s): Barclays
Directors: M. Myatt (MD), P. Havelock (Dir)
Ultimate Holding Company: FCS INVESTMENTS LIMITED
Immediate Holding Company: FUEL CONSERVATION SERVICES LIMITED
Registration no: 01545906 **VAT No.:** GB 369 7083 09
Date established: 1981 **Turnover:** £1m - £2m **No.of Employees:** 21 - 50
Product Groups: 33

Date of Accounts	Dec 11	Dec 10	Dec 09
Working Capital	211	115	39
Fixed Assets	121	97	72
Current Assets	1m	743	454

Thomas Gameson & Sons Ltd
PO Box 1, Cannock, WS11 0AX
Tel: 01543-504191 **Fax:** 01543-462482
E-mail: lawrence@gameson.co.uk
Directors: L. Gameson (Prop)
Immediate Holding Company: THOMAS GAMESON & SONS,LIMITED
Registration no: 00066322 **VAT No.:** GB 100 1117 63
Date established: 2000 **Turnover:** £1m - £2m **No.of Employees:** 1 - 10
Product Groups: 48

Date of Accounts	Mar 11	Mar 10	Mar 09
Working Capital	290	209	210
Fixed Assets	85	82	108
Current Assets	426	444	442

Hawkins Mcgowan
10-12 Wolverhampton Road, Cannock, WS11 1AH
Tel: 01543-503296 **Fax:** 01543-572727
E-mail: hb@hawkinsmcgowan.co.uk
Website: http://www.hawkinsmcgowan.co.uk
Directors: G. Williams (Ptnr), H. Butterworth (Snr Part), H. Butterworth (Ptnr)
Date established: 1990 **Turnover:** Up to £250,000
No.of Employees: 1 - 10 **Product Groups:** 84

E H Humphries Norton Ltd
Great Western House 35 Martindale, Cannock, WS11 7XN
Tel: 01543-466766 **Fax:** 01543-504845
E-mail: enquiries@ehhumphries.co.uk
Website: http://www.ehhumphries.co.uk
Directors: D. Weldon (MD), K. Morgan (Co Sec)
Immediate Holding Company: E.H.HUMPHRIES(NORTON)LIMITED
Registration no: 00667336 **VAT No.:** GB 100 4794 06
Date established: 1960 **Turnover:** £2m - £5m **No.of Employees:** 21 - 50
Product Groups: 52

Date of Accounts	Oct 11	Oct 10	Oct 09
Working Capital	243	223	284
Fixed Assets	73	53	54
Current Assets	2m	1m	1m

Hydraline Engineering Ltd
Unit 33 Martindale, Cannock, WS11 7XN
Tel: 01543-502578 **Fax:** 01543-573884
E-mail: sales@hydralineltd.co.uk
Website: http://www.hydraline.co.uk
Directors: K. Bevington (Fin)
Immediate Holding Company: HYDRALINE ENGINEERING LIMITED
Registration no: 02875548 **Date established:** 1993
No.of Employees: 1 - 10 **Product Groups:** 35, 36, 37, 38, 39, 40, 41, 42, 43, 44, 45, 46, 47, 48, 51, 61, 63, 66, 67, 68, 83, 84, 85, 86

Date of Accounts	Dec 11	Dec 10	Dec 09
Working Capital	29	-37	136
Fixed Assets	91	204	224
Current Assets	105	68	171

I C E Installations
246 Cannock Road Heath Hayes, Cannock, WS12 3HA
Tel: 01543-271630 **Fax:** 01543-271630
E-mail: iceinstalations@tiscalli.co.uk
Directors: A. Greenwood (Prop)
No.of Employees: 1 - 10 **Product Groups:** 37, 67

I G M Robotic Systems Ltd
Unit 4 Littleton Drive, Cannock, WS12 4TR
Tel: 01543-462931 **Fax:** 01543-462836
E-mail: sales@igm.at
Website: http://www.igm.at
Directors: D. Richards (MD)
Ultimate Holding Company: THE GLOBAL WELDING TECHNOLOGIES AG (AUSTRIA)
Immediate Holding Company: I G M ROBOTIC SYSTEMS LIMITED
Registration no: 02292447 **Date established:** 1988
Turnover: £500,000 - £1m **No.of Employees:** 1 - 10 **Product Groups:** 44, 45

Date of Accounts	Dec 11	Dec 10	Dec 09
Sales Turnover	N/A	963	579
Pre Tax Profit/Loss	N/A	189	41
Working Capital	350	117	-68
Fixed Assets	68	18	10
Current Assets	426	179	142
Current Liabilities	N/A	39	27

Industrial Forklift Services
22 Cottage Close Hednesford, Cannock, WS12 1BS
Tel: 01543-876835 **Fax:** 01543-876835
Directors: D. Forrester (Prop)
Date established: 1994 **No.of Employees:** 1 - 10 **Product Groups:** 35, 39, 45

Jeavons & Wright Ltd
Hawkins Drive, Cannock, WS11 0XT
Tel: 01922-411004 **Fax:** 01922-411005
E-mail: jeavons.wrightltd@btopenworld.com
Directors: L. Jeavons (Co Sec)
Immediate Holding Company: JEAVONS AND WRIGHT LIMITED
Registration no: 01256459 **Date established:** 1976
No.of Employees: 1 - 10 **Product Groups:** 41

Date of Accounts	Apr 12	Apr 11	Apr 10
Working Capital	392	375	318
Fixed Assets	963	963	967
Current Assets	570	564	510

John Bennett Tool Makers
Unit 10 Delta Way Business Centre Longford Road, Cannock, WS11 0BE
Tel: 01543-500567 **Fax:** 01543-500567
E-mail: jbtoolmkr@aol.com
Directors: J. Bennett (Prop)
Immediate Holding Company: PENGRAVE INVESTMENTS LIMITED
Registration no: 02184178 **Date established:** 1987
No.of Employees: 1 - 10 **Product Groups:** 36

Mick Jones
13 Cannock Wood Industrial Estate Cannock Wood Street, Cannock, WS12 0PL
Tel: 01543-423462 **Fax:** 01543-877136
E-mail: mick@jones3272.fsnet.co.uk
Directors: S. Jones (Ptnr)
Ultimate Holding Company: ATP INDUSTRIES GROUP LTD
Immediate Holding Company: ATP AUTOMOTIVE TRANSMISSION REMANUFACTURING SPECIALISTS LTD
Date established: 1969 **No.of Employees:** 1 - 10 **Product Groups:** 45, 67, 83

Date of Accounts	Apr 11	Apr 10	Apr 09
Sales Turnover	N/A	6m	6m
Pre Tax Profit/Loss	N/A	269	89
Working Capital	677	114	-1m
Fixed Assets	148	155	176
Current Assets	3m	3m	3m
Current Liabilities	N/A	616	1m

Laser Process Ltd
Upper Keys Business Park Keys Park Road, Hednesford, Cannock, WS12 2GE
Tel: 01543-495000 **Fax:** 01543-495001
E-mail: sales@laserprocess.co.uk
Website: http://www.laserprocess.co.uk
Bank(s): Barclays
Directors: D. Lindsey (MD)
Managers: S. Murphy (Purch Mgr), Y. Dodd, J. Moore (Mktg Serv Mgr), K. Price (Tech Serv Mgr)
Ultimate Holding Company: DSM GROUP LIMITED
Immediate Holding Company: LASER PROCESS LIMITED
Registration no: 02591981 **VAT No.:** GB 537 0639 40
Date established: 1991 **Turnover:** £2m - £5m **No.of Employees:** 21 - 50
Product Groups: 33, 35, 45, 46, 48

Date of Accounts	Jun 11	Jun 10	Jun 09
Working Capital	-31	55	45
Fixed Assets	1m	423	253
Current Assets	1m	1m	914

Loprint
74 View Street Hednesford, Cannock, WS12 4JQ
Tel: 01543-451962 **Fax:** 01543-451962
E-mail: info@loprint.co.uk
Website: http://www.loprint.co.uk
Directors: S. Marsden (Prop)
Date established: 2002 **No.of Employees:** 1 - 10 **Product Groups:** 44

M G & J P Guns
103 Hednesford Road Heath Hayes, Cannock, WS12 3HL
Tel: 01543-275548
Managers: M. Lockamore (Mgr)
Date established: 1978 **No.of Employees:** 1 - 10 **Product Groups:** 36, 39, 40

M T Mechanical Handling Ltd
Unit 3 Beechwood Business Park Burdock Close, Cannock, WS11 7GB
Tel: 01543-573125 **Fax:** 01543-674590
E-mail: sales@mtmechanical.co.uk
Website: http://www.mtmechanical.co.uk
Directors: B. Taylor (Prop)
Immediate Holding Company: M.T. MECHANICAL HANDLING LIMITED
Registration no: 06803417 **Date established:** 2009
No.of Employees: 1 - 10 **Product Groups:** 35, 39, 45

Date of Accounts	Dec 11	Dec 10	Dec 09
Working Capital	-48	-97	-112
Fixed Assets	236	279	289
Current Assets	33	33	29

Measurement & Control Technology Ltd
4 Weston Close, Cannock, WS11 7YX
Tel: 01543-495780 **Fax:** 01543-495785
E-mail: info@mct-ltd.co.uk
Website: http://www.mct-ltd.co.uk
Directors: B. Mapley (Fin), D. Mapley (Dir)
Immediate Holding Company: MEASUREMENT & CONTROL TECHNOLOGY LIMITED
Registration no: 04486610 **Date established:** 2002
Turnover: Up to £250,000 **No.of Employees:** 1 - 10 **Product Groups:** 37, 38

Date of Accounts	Jul 11	Jul 10	Jul 09
Working Capital	2	2	1
Fixed Assets	1	1	1
Current Assets	14	17	12

Metal Finishing Supplies Ltd
99a North Street, Cannock, WS11 0AZ
Tel: 01543-505771 **Fax:** 01543-466011
E-mail: malcolmmalpass@metalfinishing.com
Website: http://www.thepolishingshop.co.uk

Directors: M. Malpass (MD)
Immediate Holding Company: METAL FINISHING SUPPLIES LIMITED
Registration no: 00916729 **Date established:** 1967
No.of Employees: 1 - 10 **Product Groups:** 46, 48

Date of Accounts	Sep 11	Sep 10	Sep 09
Working Capital	546	511	524
Fixed Assets	22	27	30
Current Assets	705	616	627

Midland Air Tools Ltd

Unit 1 Apex Business Park Walsall Road, Norton Canes, Cannock, WS11 9PU
Tel: 01543-276119 **Fax:** 01543-276612
E-mail: sales@midlandairtools.co.uk
Website: http://www.midlandairtools.co.uk
Directors: C. Brown (Sales), R. Green (MD)
Immediate Holding Company: MIDLAND AIR TOOLS LIMITED
Registration no: 01641376 **Date established:** 1982
Turnover: £500,000 - £1m **No.of Employees:** 1 - 10 **Product Groups:** 35, 40, 45, 48, 67

Date of Accounts	Dec 07	Apr 11	Apr 10
Working Capital	42	64	46
Fixed Assets	3	1	1
Current Assets	226	204	173

Midland Saw Service

Unit 10 Cock Sparrow Lane, Cannock, WS12 4PB
Tel: 01543-572390 **Fax:** 01543-572390
Directors: A. Green (Ptnr)
Date established: 2005 **No.of Employees:** 1 - 10 **Product Groups:** 46, 48

Mikron Engineering Ltd

Unit 2-3 Progress Business Centre Brookfield Drive, Cannock, WS11 0JN
Tel: 01543-467716 **Fax:** 01543-467718
E-mail: allautomatic@btinternet.com
Directors: E. Evans (Fin), M. Evans (MD)
Immediate Holding Company: MIKRON ENGINEERING LIMITED
Registration no: 01904516 **Date established:** 1985
No.of Employees: 1 - 10 **Product Groups:** 35, 45

Date of Accounts	May 11	May 10	May 09
Working Capital	28	29	-29
Fixed Assets	72	75	123
Current Assets	84	78	82

The Motorhouse

Watling Street, Cannock, WS11 1SL
Tel: 01543-506060 **Fax:** 01543-509320
E-mail: enquiries@motorhouse2000ltd.co.uk
Website: http://www.themotorhouse.co.uk
Bank(s): Royal Bank of Scotland, Colmore Row, Birmingham, B3 2AP
Directors: C. Bowen (MD)
Managers: S. Campbell (Mktg Serv Mgr), S. Butterley (Ops Mgr), S. Butterly (Mgr)
Immediate Holding Company: THE MOTORHOUSE (INVESTMENT HOLDINGS) LIMITED
Registration no: 07429529 **VAT No.:** GB 661 5542 37
Date established: 2010 **Turnover:** £125m - £250m
No.of Employees: 51 - 100 **Product Groups:** 68

Murphy Group

Hawks Green Lane, Cannock, WS11 7LH
Tel: 01543-466711 **Fax:** 01543-572877
E-mail: cannock@murphygroup.co.uk
Website: http://www.murphygroup.co.uk
Managers: S. Blackmore (District Mgr)
Ultimate Holding Company: MARYLAND LIMITED (ISLE OF MAN)
Immediate Holding Company: J. MURPHY & SONS LIMITED
Registration no: 00492042 **Date established:** 1951 **Turnover:** £5m - £10m
No.of Employees: 51 - 100 **Product Groups:** 51

Date of Accounts	Dec 10	Dec 09	Dec 08
Sales Turnover	401m	408m	445m
Pre Tax Profit/Loss	23m	25m	35m
Working Capital	142m	125m	118m
Fixed Assets	36m	37m	30m
Current Assets	210m	192m	193m
Current Liabilities	31m	30m	28m

Norton Aluminium Ltd

Norton Green Lane Norton Canes, Cannock, WS11 9PS
Tel: 01543-279329 **Fax:** 01543-275855
E-mail: henry@nortal.co.uk
Website: http://www.nortal.co.uk
Bank(s): Lloyds TSB Bank plc
Directors: R. Bray (Fin), R. Williamson (Dir), H. Dickinson (Dir), L. Tranter (Fin)
Immediate Holding Company: NAL REALISATIONS (STAFFORDSHIRE) LIMITED
Registration no: 00505253 **VAT No.:** GB 100 4644 25
Date established: 1952 **Turnover:** £20m - £50m
No.of Employees: 51 - 100 **Product Groups:** 34, 66

Date of Accounts	Sep 11	Sep 10	Sep 09
Sales Turnover	24m	21m	14m
Pre Tax Profit/Loss	287	585	103
Working Capital	2m	2m	4m
Fixed Assets	2m	1m	2m
Current Assets	9m	8m	7m
Current Liabilities	2m	551	911

P C B Portal UK Ltd

Centric House Keys Business Village Keys Park Road, Hednesford, Cannock, WS12 2HA
Tel: 01543-274030 **Fax:** 08450-267883
E-mail: sales@pcbportal.com
Website: http://www.pcbportal.com
Managers: D. Holton (Mgr)
Immediate Holding Company: PCB PORTAL (UK) LIMITED
Registration no: 07277800 **Date established:** 2010
No.of Employees: 21 - 50 **Product Groups:** 37, 44, 47, 61, 66

Parker Hannifin UK plc (Climate & Industrial Controls Group)

Walkmill Lane, Cannock, WS11 0LR
Tel: 01543-456000 **Fax:** 01543-456001
E-mail: parkercicgroup@parker.com
Website: http://www.parker.com
Managers: A. Cook, A. Quinn
Ultimate Holding Company: Parker Hannifin Corporation, Ohio USA
Registration no: 00425892 **Turnover:** £250m - £500m
No.of Employees: 251 - 500 **Product Groups:** 36, 38, 39, 40, 63, 66, 68

Pneumatic Services

5 Anglesey Business Park Littleworth Road, Hednesford, Cannock, WS12 1NR
Tel: 01543-879959 **Fax:** 01543-871043
E-mail: info@pswspraybooths.co.uk
Website: http://www.pswspraybooths.co.uk
Directors: I. Stone (MD)
Immediate Holding Company: ZAP CONTROLS TECHNOLOGY LIMITED
Date established: 2011 **No.of Employees:** 1 - 10 **Product Groups:** 38, 42

Date of Accounts	Aug 11	Aug 10	Aug 09
Working Capital	-2	-5	-5
Current Assets	31	32	10

Polysoude Welding Equipment

4 Littleton Business Park Littleton Drive, Cannock, WS12 4TR
Tel: 01543-466969 **Fax:** 01543- 462836
E-mail: info@polysoude.com
Website: http://www.polysoude.com
Managers: M. Courtney (Mgr)
Immediate Holding Company: FIRECLASS UK LIMITED
Registration no: 06012333 **Date established:** 2005
No.of Employees: 1 - 10 **Product Groups:** 46

Protek Electronics Ltd (Protek Electronics Ltd)

Phoenix House Phoenix Road, Cannock, WS11 7LR
Tel: 01543-467575 **Fax:** 01543-467575
E-mail: sales@protekuk.co.uk
Website: http://www.protekuk.co.uk
Bank(s): HSBC
Directors: G. Birkedale (Sales)
Immediate Holding Company: PROTEK ELECTRONICS LIMITED
Registration no: 03647163 **Date established:** 1998
Turnover: £250,000 - £500,000 **No.of Employees:** 11 - 20
Product Groups: 37, 38

Date of Accounts	Dec 11	Dec 10	Dec 09
Working Capital	214	132	137
Fixed Assets	15	19	22
Current Assets	724	471	575

Pyroban Envirosafe Ltd

Unit 4 Littleton Business Park Littleton Drive, Cannock, WS12 4TR
Tel: 01543-570048 **Fax:** 01543-574577
E-mail: sales@pyroban.com
Website: http://www.pyroban.com
Directors: P. Behdad (MD)
Ultimate Holding Company: PYROBAN GROUP LIMITED
Immediate Holding Company: PYROBAN ENVIROSAFE LIMITED
Registration no: 03131901 **Date established:** 1995
Turnover: £250,000 - £500,000 **No.of Employees:** 1 - 10
Product Groups: 38, 42

Date of Accounts	Dec 11	Jun 11	Jun 10
Sales Turnover	243	358	241
Pre Tax Profit/Loss	34	-18	-95
Working Capital	-17	-44	-41
Fixed Assets	4	6	10
Current Assets	170	145	75
Current Liabilities	48	33	30

R L S Tooling Ltd

Unit 11-12 Apex Business Park Walsall Road, Norton Canes, Cannock, WS11 9PU
Tel: 01543-271808 **Fax:** 01543-277571
E-mail: info@rlstooling.co.uk
Website: http://www.rlstooling.co.uk
Directors: R. Smith (MD)
Immediate Holding Company: RLS TOOLING LIMITED
Registration no: 02332638 **Date established:** 1989
No.of Employees: 11 - 20 **Product Groups:** 46

Date of Accounts	Feb 12	Feb 11	Feb 10
Working Capital	-39	-6	-13
Fixed Assets	358	285	190
Current Assets	405	356	306

R V J Engineering

Cannock Chase Enterprise Centre West Cannock Way Hednesford, Cannock, WS12 0QU
Tel: 01543-425264 **Fax:** 01543-512451
E-mail: rvj.com@virgin.net
Website: http://www.geocities.com/rvjengineering
Directors: R. Astle (Prop)
No.of Employees: 1 - 10 **Product Groups:** 39, 48, 85

Roundway Services

Progress Drive, Cannock, WS11 0JE
Tel: 01543-467011 **Fax:** 01543-467012
E-mail: sangerbenton@yahoo.co.uk
Directors: B. Sanger (Dir)
Immediate Holding Company: ROUNDWAY SERVICES LIMITED
Registration no: 03473453 **Date established:** 1997
No.of Employees: 1 - 10 **Product Groups:** 72

Date of Accounts	May 11	May 10	May 09
Working Capital	-80	-99	-45
Fixed Assets	47	66	76
Current Assets	232	250	268

S & H Systems Design & Installation Ltd

Unit 1 Beechwood Business Park Burdock Close, Cannock, WS11 7GB
Tel: 01543-462620 **Fax:** 01543-432630
E-mail: paul@s-and-h-systems.com
Website: http://www.s-and-h-systems.com
Bank(s): Barclays, Wolverhampton
Directors: P. Bunn (MD)
Immediate Holding Company: S & H SYSTEMS DESIGN AND INSTALLATION LIMITED
Registration no: 02255528 **VAT No.:** GB 489 4375 86
Date established: 1988 **Turnover:** £1m - £2m **No.of Employees:** 11 - 20
Product Groups: 37

Date of Accounts	May 11	May 10	May 09
Working Capital	181	203	314
Fixed Assets	19	25	33
Current Assets	266	311	535

Securefast PLC

Unit 6 Cedars Business Centre Avon Road, Cannock, WS11 1QJ
Tel: 01543-501600 **Fax:** 01902-609327
E-mail: sales@securefast.co.uk
Website: http://www.securefast.co.uk
Bank(s): Lloyds TSB Bank plc
Directors: D. Crawley (MD)
Managers: K. Farrell (Purch Mgr), C. Davis (Comptroller)
Immediate Holding Company: SECUREFAST PLC
Registration no: 02397020 **Date established:** 1989 **Turnover:** £5m - £10m
No.of Employees: 11 - 20 **Product Groups:** 36, 39

Date of Accounts	Mar 12	Mar 11	Mar 10
Sales Turnover	8m	7m	7m
Pre Tax Profit/Loss	149	19	105
Working Capital	571	381	304
Fixed Assets	868	975	1m
Current Assets	3m	3m	3m
Current Liabilities	318	189	255

Space Creations UK Ltd

Third Floor Falcon Point Park Plaza Heath Hayes, Heath Hayes, Cannock, WS12 2DE
Tel: 01543-572565 **Fax:** 01543-504987
E-mail: sales@spacecreationsuk.com
Website: http://www.spacecreationsuk.com
Directors: R. Clover (Co Sec)
Registration no: 04625885 **No.of Employees:** 1 - 10 **Product Groups:** 25, 26, 35, 52

Date of Accounts	Jan 08	Jan 07	Jan 06
Working Capital	18	-67	-24
Fixed Assets	34	46	27
Current Assets	1042	752	687
Current Liabilities	1024	819	711

Stakapal Ltd

Bettys Lane Norton Canes, Cannock, WS11 9NZ
Tel: 01543-278123 **Fax:** 01543-279543
Website: http://www.stakapal.co.uk
Directors: S. Burns Mace (MD), N. Betteley (MD)
Managers: S. Law (Buyer), J. Madden
Immediate Holding Company: STAKAPAL LIMITED
Registration no: 00913155 **Date established:** 1967
No.of Employees: 21 - 50 **Product Groups:** 26

Date of Accounts	Dec 11	Dec 10	Dec 09
Working Capital	1m	3m	3m
Fixed Assets	2m	2m	2m
Current Assets	2m	3m	3m

Star Installation Ltd

Unit B Progress Business Centre, Cannock, WS11 0JR
Tel: 01543-574146 **Fax:** 01543-469312
E-mail: roger@starinstallation.co.uk
Website: http://www.starinstallation.co.uk
Directors: R. Harrison (MD), V. Harrison (Co Sec)
Managers: S. Potts (Contracts Mgr)
Immediate Holding Company: STAR INSTALLATION (CONTRACTORS) LIMITED
Registration no: 02031122 **Date established:** 1986
Turnover: Up to £250,000 **No.of Employees:** 21 - 50 **Product Groups:** 52, 54, 84

Date of Accounts	Oct 11	Oct 10	Oct 09
Working Capital	535	476	429
Fixed Assets	144	120	135
Current Assets	1m	918	1m

Synatel Instrumentation Ltd

Walsall Road Norton Canes, Cannock, WS11 9TB
Tel: 01543-277003 **Fax:** 01543-271217
E-mail: sales@synatel.co.uk
Website: http://www.synatel.co.uk
Bank(s): Midland
Directors: A. Morris (Sales & Mktg), V. Bahal (Dir)
Managers: L. Elson (Purch Mgr), S. Wright (Tech Serv Mgr)
Immediate Holding Company: SYNATEL INSTRUMENTATION LIMITED
Registration no: 01495116 **VAT No.:** 592 6046 25 **Date established:** 1980
No.of Employees: 21 - 50 **Product Groups:** 37, 38

Date of Accounts	May 11	May 10	May 09
Working Capital	609	535	474
Fixed Assets	463	513	538
Current Assets	870	750	718

T K A Body Stampings Ltd

Wolverhampton Road, Cannock, WS11 1LY
Tel: 01543-466664 **Fax:** 01543-466665
E-mail: les.lees@tka-bs.thyssenkrupp.com
Website: http://www.thyssenkrupp.com
Bank(s): Barclays, Birmingham
Directors: L. Lees (Dir), B. Francis (Ch & MD), L. Lees (Fin)
Managers: A. Mitchell (Sales & Mktg Mg), V. Senney (I.T. Exec), S. Bolton (Personnel)
Ultimate Holding Company: THYSSEN KRUPP AG (GERMANY)
Immediate Holding Company: THYSSENKRUPP AUTOMOTIVE UK LTD
Registration no: 00024190 **Date established:** 1887
Turnover: £20m - £50m **No.of Employees:** 501 - 1000
Product Groups: 39, 48

Date of Accounts	Sep 10	Sep 09	Sep 08
Sales Turnover	294m	249m	353m
Pre Tax Profit/Loss	15m	-33m	13m
Working Capital	-4m	-38m	-45m
Fixed Assets	71m	76m	88m
Current Assets	88m	79m	96m
Current Liabilities	12m	7m	15m

Till Jig & Tool

Unit 9 Cock Sparrow Lane, Cannock, WS12 4PB
Tel: 01543-574346 **Fax:** 01543-574346
E-mail: ljtill@tilljigtool.fsnet.co.uk
Directors: L. Till (Prop)
Registration no: 00463177 **Date established:** 1949
No.of Employees: 1 - 10 **Product Groups:** 35, 45

Tube Polishing & Engineering

Conduit Road Norton Canes, Cannock, WS11 9TJ
Tel: 01543-275111 **Fax:** 01543-275462
E-mail: info@tube-polishing.co.uk
Website: http://www.tube-polishing.co.uk
Directors: M. Allen (Ptnr)
Ultimate Holding Company: W. E. SMITH HOLDINGS LIMITED
Immediate Holding Company: SITE CLEAR SOLUTIONS LTD
Registration no: 05463836 **Date established:** 2007
No.of Employees: 1 - 10 **Product Groups:** 46, 48

Date of Accounts	Oct 11	Oct 10	Oct 09
Working Capital	73	79	85
Fixed Assets	85	85	91
Current Assets	190	145	210

Waste & Hygiene Solutions Ltd
Unit 22 Rumer Hill Business Estate Rumer Hill Road, Cannock, WS11 0ET
Tel: 01543-500950 **Fax:** 01543-500956
E-mail: info@waste-hygiene.co.uk
Website: http://www.waste-hygiene.co.uk
Directors: I. Allen (Fin), R. Daley (MD)
Immediate Holding Company: WASTE & HYGIENE SOLUTIONS LIMITED
Registration no: 05021799 **Date established:** 2004
No.of Employees: 1 - 10 **Product Groups:** 38, 42

Date of Accounts	Jan 11	Jan 10	Jan 09
Working Capital	10	6	12
Fixed Assets	1	5	7
Current Assets	58	45	52

Weeden P S C
Anglesey Business Park Littleworth Road, Hednesford, Cannock, WS12 1NR
Tel: 01543-423838 **Fax:** 01543-871541
E-mail: enquiries@weedonpsc.com
Website: http://www.weedonpsc.com
Directors: D. Lawrence (Fin), J. Weedon (MD)
Immediate Holding Company: ZAP CONTROLS TECHNOLOGY LIMITED
Date established: 2011 **No.of Employees:** 51 - 100 **Product Groups:** 27, 42, 45, 67

Date of Accounts	Aug 11	Aug 10	Aug 09
Working Capital	-2	-5	-5
Current Assets	31	32	10

Westgate Stainless & Alloys Ltd
Unit 17 Morgans Business Park Bettys Lane, Norton Canes, Cannock, WS11 9UU
Tel: 01543-448956 **Fax:** 01543-448920
E-mail: sales@westgatestainless.com
Website: http://www.westgatestainless.com
Directors: A. Hattersley (MD)
Immediate Holding Company: WESTGATE STAINLESS AND ALLOYS LIMITED
Registration no: 05722924 **Date established:** 2006 **Turnover:** £5m - £10m
No.of Employees: 11 - 20 **Product Groups:** 66

Date of Accounts	May 11	May 10	May 09
Working Capital	393	340	395
Fixed Assets	24	21	14
Current Assets	865	959	782

R A Wood Adhesive Tapes Ltd
Unit 29 Umer Hill Road, Cannock, WS11 0ET
Tel: 01543-578331 **Fax:** 01543-572301
E-mail: sales@rawood.co.uk
Website: http://www.rawood.co.uk
Directors: R. Wood (MD)
Managers: C. Ward (Purch Mgr), A. Mullett (I.T. Exec), M. Hill (Sales Prom Mgr)
Ultimate Holding Company: TAPES TWO LIMITED
Immediate Holding Company: R.A. WOOD ADHESIVE TAPES LIMITED
Registration no: 02620425 **Date established:** 1991 **Turnover:** £5m - £10m
No.of Employees: 101 - 250 **Product Groups:** 23, 27, 30, 33, 37, 47, 66

Date of Accounts	Jun 09	Jun 08	Jun 07
Sales Turnover	10m	N/A	N/A
Pre Tax Profit/Loss	21	14	23
Working Capital	72	95	51
Fixed Assets	308	281	276
Current Assets	5m	4m	3m
Current Liabilities	2m	2m	1m

Zambelli Ltd
Bridgtown Business Centre North Street, Cannock, WS11 0XJ
Tel: 01543-462120 **Fax:** 01543-462120
Directors: J. Passerini Zambelli (Co Sec)
Ultimate Holding Company: ZAMBELLI srL(ITALY)
Immediate Holding Company: ZAMBELLI LIMITED
Registration no: 03070862 **Date established:** 1995
No.of Employees: 1 - 10 **Product Groups:** 38, 42

Date of Accounts	Dec 10	Dec 09	Dec 07
Working Capital	296	296	291
Fixed Assets	N/A	N/A	1
Current Assets	1m	838	1m

Zap Controls Ltd
Unit 100 Anglesey Business Park Littleworth Road, Hednesford, Cannock, WS12 1NR
Tel: 01543-879444 **Fax:** 01543-879333
E-mail: mail@zap-uk.com
Website: http://www.zap-uk.com
Directors: B. Gunton (Grp Chief Exec)
Immediate Holding Company: BGMG LIMITED
Registration no: 02533103 **VAT No.:** 776 1332 23 **Date established:** 1990
Turnover: £500,000 - £1m **No.of Employees:** 1 - 10 **Product Groups:** 84

Date of Accounts	Jul 06	Jul 05	Jul 04
Working Capital	484	460	443
Fixed Assets	89	91	117
Current Assets	783	619	743

Leek

Adams Foods Ltd
Sunnyhills Road, Leek, ST13 5SP
Tel: 01538-399111 **Fax:** 01538-399918
E-mail: sales@adamsfoods.com
Website: http://www.adamsfoods.com
Directors: C. Terry (Co Sec), I. Toal (MD), S. Whitfield (Sales)
Managers: D. Neil (Tech Serv Mgr), H. Turner
Ultimate Holding Company: IRISH DAIRY BOARD CO-OPERATIVE LTD (EIRE)
Immediate Holding Company: ADAMS FOODS LIMITED
Registration no: 00362221 **Date established:** 1940
Turnover: £250m - £500m **No.of Employees:** 101 - 250
Product Groups: 20, 62

Date of Accounts	Dec 11	Jan 09	Jan 10
Sales Turnover	322m	253m	233m
Pre Tax Profit/Loss	-1m	2m	7m
Working Capital	-4m	-9m	-4m
Fixed Assets	31m	29m	29m
Current Assets	93m	40m	54m
Current Liabilities	15m	6m	7m

F Ball & Co. Ltd
Churnetside Business Park Station Road, Cheddleton, Leek, ST13 7RS
Tel: 01538-361633 **Fax:** 01538-361622
E-mail: mail@f-ball.co.uk
Website: http://www.f-ball.co.uk
Directors: J. Hibbert (Sales), G. Ball (Ch), A. Beasley (Fin), I. King (Fin)
Managers: J. Sargent (Tech Serv Mgr), R. Harris (Mktg Serv Mgr), L. Hulson (Personnel), B. Pepper (Purch Mgr)
Immediate Holding Company: F.BALL AND CO. LIMITED
Registration no: 00282893 **VAT No.:** GB 217 8697 24
Date established: 1933 **Turnover:** £20m - £50m
No.of Employees: 51 - 100 **Product Groups:** 42

Date of Accounts	Dec 11	Dec 10	Dec 09
Sales Turnover	37m	35m	35m
Pre Tax Profit/Loss	2m	3m	4m
Working Capital	11m	10m	9m
Fixed Assets	21m	22m	21m
Current Assets	15m	13m	14m
Current Liabilities	3m	2m	3m

L M Bateman & Co. Ltd
Island Works Cheddleton, Leek, ST13 7HN
Tel: 01538-361326 **Fax:** 01538-360803
E-mail: sales@lmbateman.co.uk
Website: http://www.lmbateman.co.uk
Bank(s): National Westminster Bank Plc
Directors: I. Bryne (Sales), I. Byrne (Sales), J. Smith (Fin)
Managers: K. Fletcher (Purch Mgr), S. Jewsbury (Tech Serv Mgr), J. Smith (Personnel)
Immediate Holding Company: L.M. BATEMAN & COMPANY LIMITED
Registration no: 01400024 **VAT No.:** GB 318 9348 30
Date established: 1978 **Turnover:** £10m - £20m
No.of Employees: 101 - 250 **Product Groups:** 38

Date of Accounts	Jan 12	Jan 11	Jan 10
Sales Turnover	12m	11m	9m
Pre Tax Profit/Loss	339	278	129
Working Capital	1m	866	703
Fixed Assets	933	939	900
Current Assets	4m	4m	3m
Current Liabilities	475	420	1m

Collcap Packaging Ltd
Unit R Brooklands Way Basford Lane Industrial Estate, Leek, ST13 7QF
Tel: 01538-388344 **Fax:** 01538-398041
E-mail: sales@collcap.co.uk
Website: http://www.collcap.com
Directors: J. Mcdermott (Dir)
Managers: N. Kinson (Chief Mgr), D. Brunt (Fin Mgr)
Immediate Holding Company: COLLCAP PACKAGING LIMITED
Registration no: 02788868 **Date established:** 1993
Turnover: £10m - £20m **No.of Employees:** 21 - 50 **Product Groups:** 38, 42

Date of Accounts	Feb 08	Feb 11	Feb 10
Sales Turnover	N/A	12m	8m
Pre Tax Profit/Loss	600	519	230
Working Capital	566	2m	1m
Fixed Assets	2m	953	836
Current Assets	2m	5m	3m
Current Liabilities	344	247	202

Coms Co.
Pickwood Hall, Leek, ST13 5BZ
Tel: 0800-369 9123 **Fax:** 01538-388238
Website: http://www.commsco.com
Directors: S. Chauveau (Prop)
Immediate Holding Company: COMSCO LIMITED
Registration no: 06946652 **Date established:** 2009
No.of Employees: 1 - 10 **Product Groups:** 37, 39, 67

Dendrite Fabrications
18 Gordon Close, Leek, ST13 8NZ
Tel: 01538-384789 **Fax:** 01538-384789
E-mail: jasonbanks@worldonline.co.uk
Directors: J. Banks (Prop)
Turnover: Up to £250,000 **No.of Employees:** 1 - 10 **Product Groups:** 35, 48

Direct Developments Engineering Ltd
Unit 7 Churnet Works Harrison Way Cheddleton, Leek, ST13 7EF
Tel: 01538-361949
Directors: T. Fowler (Eng Serv)
No.of Employees: 21 - 50 **Product Groups:** 36, 40

Don Construction Products Ltd
Station Road Churnetside Business Park, Cheddleton, Leek, ST13 7RS
Tel: 01538-361799 **Fax:** 01538-361899
E-mail: info@donconstruction.com
Website: http://www.dcp-int.com
Directors: I. King (Fin), J. Igoe (MD)
Ultimate Holding Company: F.BALL AND CO. LIMITED
Immediate Holding Company: DON CONSTRUCTION PRODUCTS LIMITED
Registration no: 03311330 **VAT No.:** GB 684 3850 04
Date established: 1997 **Turnover:** £1m - £2m **No.of Employees:** 1 - 10
Product Groups: 31, 32, 33, 52

Date of Accounts	Dec 11	Dec 10	Dec 09
Working Capital	548	478	335
Fixed Assets	108	106	110
Current Assets	654	628	627

David Foster Photography & Video
14 Moorfields, Leek, ST13 5LU
Tel: 01538-386403
E-mail: admin@weddingsstorybook.co.uk
Website: http://www.davidandbeverleyfosterphotography.co.uk
Directors: D. Foster (Ptnr)
Date established: 1985 **No.of Employees:** 1 - 10 **Product Groups:** 81

Hall Engineering 2008 Ltd
Station Works Station Street, Leek, ST13 8BP
Tel: 01538-399566 **Fax:** 0560-115 7477
E-mail: halleng@btconnect.com
Website: http://www.hallengandfab.co.uk
Directors: D. Hall (Dir)
Immediate Holding Company: HALL ENGINEERING (2008) LIMITED
Registration no: 06707856 **Date established:** 2008
No.of Employees: 1 - 10 **Product Groups:** 41

Date of Accounts	Sep 11	Sep 10	Sep 09
Working Capital	12	50	34
Fixed Assets	28	7	4
Current Assets	120	103	76

Kelcoat Engineering Plastics Ltd
Barnfield Road Industrial Estate, Leek, ST13 5QG
Tel: 01538-383547 **Fax:** 01538-387918
E-mail: simonb@kelcoat.co.uk
Website: http://www.kelcoat.co.uk
Directors: C. Butterworth (Co Sec), S. Butterworth (Dir)
Immediate Holding Company: KELCOAT ENGINEERING PLASTICS LIMITED
Registration no: 00849189 **VAT No.:** GB 279 3195 19
Date established: 1965 **Turnover:** £250,000 - £500,000
No.of Employees: 1 - 10 **Product Groups:** 32, 48

Date of Accounts	May 11	May 10	May 09
Working Capital	-11	-11	11
Fixed Assets	19	19	23
Current Assets	96	108	123

Kemex Direct Ltd
Unit 6 Town Yard Business Park Station Street, Leek, ST13 8BP
Tel: 01538-388664 **Fax:** 01538-388665
E-mail: sales@kemex.co.uk
Website: http://www.kemex.co.uk
Directors: D. Alcock (Fin), A. Alcock (Dir)
Immediate Holding Company: KEMEX DIRECT LIMITED
Registration no: 03885971 **Date established:** 1999
No.of Employees: 1 - 10 **Product Groups:** 38, 42

Date of Accounts	Dec 11	Dec 10	Dec 09
Working Capital	15	12	11
Current Assets	104	81	48

Charles Leek & Sons Ltd
Springfield Works Ashbourne Road, Leek, ST13 5AY
Tel: 01538-382066 **Fax:** 01538-373153
E-mail: sales@leekgears.co.uk
Website: http://www.leekgears.co.uk
Bank(s): National Westminster Bank Plc
Directors: A. Leek (Dir)
Immediate Holding Company: CHARLES LEEK & SONS LIMITED
Registration no: 00163422 **VAT No.:** GB 278 3850 19
Date established: 2020 **Turnover:** £250,000 - £500,000
No.of Employees: 11 - 20 **Product Groups:** 25, 35

Date of Accounts	Oct 11	Oct 10	Oct 09
Working Capital	132	115	112
Fixed Assets	294	275	287
Current Assets	209	167	162

Leek Tools & Fasteners
Unit 8 Brooklands Way Basford Lane, Leek, ST13 7DT
Tel: 01538-385005 **Fax:** 01538-386007
Directors: S. Bolton (Dir)
Immediate Holding Company: LEEK TOOLS AND FASTENERS LTD
Registration no: 04638967 **Date established:** 2003
Turnover: Up to £250,000 **No.of Employees:** 1 - 10 **Product Groups:** 37

Date of Accounts	Dec 11	Dec 10	Dec 09
Sales Turnover	N/A	140	113
Pre Tax Profit/Loss	N/A	-3	-9
Working Capital	9	13	17
Fixed Assets	1	1	N/A
Current Assets	30	35	39
Current Liabilities	N/A	10	9

Leek United Building Society
50 St Edward Street, Leek, ST13 5DL
Tel: 01538-384151 **Fax:** 01538-399179
E-mail: finance@leekunited.co.uk
Website: http://www.leekunited.co.uk
Directors: K. Griffiths (Fin)
Managers: S. Bolton (Tech Serv Mgr), D. Wilson (Personnel), B. Gronneberg, L. Harrison, M. Platt
Ultimate Holding Company: LEEK UNITED BUILDING SOCIETY
Immediate Holding Company: LEEK UNITED HOME LOANS LIMITED
Registration no: 02277333 **Date established:** 1988
Turnover: Up to £250,000 **No.of Employees:** 51 - 100
Product Groups: 82

Date of Accounts	Dec 11	Dec 10	Dec 09
Sales Turnover	13	29	39
Pre Tax Profit/Loss	8	22	24
Working Capital	272	266	248
Current Assets	279	313	757
Current Liabilities	7	9	10

Marling Leek Ltd
Marling Mills Nelson Street, Leek, ST13 6BB
Tel: 01538-384108 **Fax:** 01538-387350
E-mail: sales@marling.co.uk
Website: http://www.marling.co.uk
Bank(s): National Westminster Bank Plc
Directors: A. Banks (Fin), E. Cooper (Comm), E. Cooper (Comm)
Managers: M. Greenwood (I.T. Exec), T. Shaw (Fin Mgr), A. Lancaster (Buyer), E. Keats (Personnel)
Ultimate Holding Company: COMITEX HOLDING NV (NETHERLANDS ANTILLES)
Immediate Holding Company: MARLING LEEK LIMITED
Registration no: 00762306 **VAT No.:** GB 274 1764 46
Date established: 1963 **Turnover:** £2m - £5m **No.of Employees:** 51 - 100
Product Groups: 23, 35, 39, 40

Date of Accounts	Dec 11	Dec 10	Dec 09
Sales Turnover	N/A	N/A	4m
Pre Tax Profit/Loss	N/A	N/A	-909
Working Capital	-516	795	1m
Fixed Assets	78	366	464
Current Assets	2m	5m	3m
Current Liabilities	N/A	N/A	119

O K Coal
49 Tittesworth Estate Blackshaw Moor, Leek, ST13 8TS
Tel: 01538-300427
E-mail: roger@oldkingcoal.co.uk
Website: http://www.okcoal.biz
Directors: R. Ellis (Prop)
Date established: 1982 **No.of Employees:** 1 - 10 **Product Groups:** 38, 42

Pinewood Drapilux UK Ltd
Albert Street, Leek, ST13 8AH
Tel: 01538-399153 **Fax:** 01538-373235
E-mail: sales@pinewood-fabrics.com
Website: http://www.pinewood-fabrics.com

Directors: M. Hambleton (MD), M. Hambleton (Sales)
Managers: D. Pattinfon (Purch Mgr), T. Minor
Ultimate Holding Company: SW HOLDING GMBH (GERMANY)
Immediate Holding Company: PINEWOOD FABRICS LIMITED
Registration no: 00555015 **VAT No.:** GB 278 3450 35
Date established: 1955 **Turnover:** £1m - £2m **No.of Employees:** 1 - 10
Product Groups: 24

Date of Accounts	Dec 07	Dec 06	Dec 05
Fixed Assets	244	244	244

G Richards

19 Russell Street, Leek, ST13 5JF
Tel: 01538-371774
Directors: G. Richards (Prop)
Date established: 1987 **No.of Employees:** 1 - 10 **Product Groups:** 26, 35

Supersport Leisure Shirts Ltd

Hope Silk Mills Macclesfield Road, Leek, ST13 8JZ
Tel: 01538-386226 **Fax:** 01538-399692
E-mail: sales@supersport.co.uk
Website: http://www.supersport.co.uk
Bank(s): Lloyds TSB
Directors: J. Allen (MD), S. Allen (Fin)
Managers: R. Degg (Fin Mgr)
Immediate Holding Company: SUPERSPORT (LEISURE SHIRTS) LIMITED
Registration no: 02010532 **VAT No.:** GB 435 5563 42
Date established: 1986 **Turnover:** £1m - £2m **No.of Employees:** 21 - 50
Product Groups: 24

Date of Accounts	Jan 11	Jan 10	Jan 09
Working Capital	672	719	811
Fixed Assets	437	489	519
Current Assets	740	791	880

Tractive Power Ltd

Unit 1, The Old Saw Mill Abbey Green Road, Leek, ST13 8SA
Tel: 01538-399000 **Fax:** 0560-116 9921
E-mail: info@tractivepower.com
Website: http://www.tractivepower.com
Directors: B. RATCLIFFE (Dir)
Registration no: 6467773 **Date established:** 2008
Turnover: £250,000 - £500,000 **No.of Employees:** 1 - 10
Product Groups: 45, 61

Lichfield

A F S Systems Ltd

9 Tamworth Road, Lichfield, WS14 9EY
Tel: 01543-264034 **Fax:** 01543-414367
E-mail: royeversham@arrowfire.co.uk
Website: http://www.arrowfire.co.uk
Directors: R. Eversham (Dir)
Immediate Holding Company: ARROW FIRE SYSTEMS LIMITED
Registration no: 03666007 **VAT No.:** GB 478 2222 37
Date established: 1998 **Turnover:** £250,000 - £500,000
No.of Employees: 1 - 10 **Product Groups:** 38, 40

Adhesive Applications Ltd

2 Richmond Drive, Lichfield, WS14 9SZ
Tel: 01543-255149 **Fax:** 01543-255149
E-mail: info@adhesiveapplications.com
Website: http://www.adhesiveapplications.com
Directors: P. Dancer (MD)
Immediate Holding Company: ADHESIVE APPLICATIONS LTD
Registration no: 04949781 **Date established:** 2003
No.of Employees: 1 - 10 **Product Groups:** 32, 47, 66

Adstorm

Charter House Sandford Street, Lichfield, WS13 6QA
Tel: 08456-444567
E-mail: enquiries@adstorm.co.uk
Website: http://www.adstorm.co.uk
Directors: R. Frost (Dir)
Immediate Holding Company: ADSTORM LTD
Registration no: 06392421 **Date established:** 2007
Turnover: £500,000 - £1m **No.of Employees:** 1 - 10 **Product Groups:** 44

Date of Accounts	Oct 11	Oct 10	Oct 09
Working Capital	27	120	53
Fixed Assets	9	10	10
Current Assets	107	166	179

Antiference Ltd

Fradley Distribution Park Wood End Lane, Fradley, Lichfield, WS13 8NE
Tel: 01675-465487 **Fax:** 01675-463478
E-mail: trevor.paintain@antiference.co.uk
Website: http://www.antiference.co.uk
Directors: J. Martin (MD), C. Mathews (Fin), T. Paintain (MD)
Managers: C. Sayers (Sales Prom Mgr), I. Denham (Gen Contact), I. Southam (Purch Mgr), K. Wright (Buyer), P. Blackaby (I.T. Exec)
Ultimate Holding Company: OC304887
Immediate Holding Company: ANTIFERENCE LIMITED
Registration no: 00336260 **VAT No.:** GB 645 2294 35
Date established: 1938 **Turnover:** £2m - £5m **No.of Employees:** 1 - 10
Product Groups: 37

B G Furnace Consultants

South Staffs Freight Terminal Lynn Lane, Shenstone, Lichfield, WS14 0ED
Tel: 01543-483030 **Fax:** 01543-483035
E-mail: bgfurnaces@btconnect.com
Website: http://www.bgfurnaces.co.uk
Directors: G. Jones (Prop)
Immediate Holding Company: SOUTH STAFFS FREIGHT TERMINAL LIMITED
Date established: 1996 **No.of Employees:** 1 - 10 **Product Groups:** 40, 42, 46

Date of Accounts	Jul 11	Jul 10	Jul 09
Working Capital	587	399	458
Fixed Assets	102	121	121
Current Assets	587	520	522

Blum Novotest Ltd

33 Townfields, Lichfield, WS13 8AA
Tel: 01543-257111 **Fax:** 01543-251746
E-mail: info@blum-novotest.co.uk
Website: http://www.blum-novotest.co.uk
Directors: D. Mold (Dir)
Immediate Holding Company: BLUM-NOVOTEST LTD.
Registration no: 03811409 **Date established:** 1999
No.of Employees: 1 - 10 **Product Groups:** 37, 38, 46, 85

Date of Accounts	Dec 11	Dec 10	Dec 09
Working Capital	44	103	74
Fixed Assets	5	3	2
Current Assets	67	116	88

Boxmart Ltd

Unit 1c Ringway Industrial Estate Eastern Avenue, Lichfield, WS13 7SF
Tel: 01543-411574 **Fax:** 01543-258952
E-mail: enquiries@boxmart.co.uk
Website: http://www.boxmart.co.uk
Directors: J. Offord (MD)
Immediate Holding Company: BOX - MART LIMITED
Registration no: 05108698 **Date established:** 2004
No.of Employees: 1 - 10 **Product Groups:** 23, 25, 27

Date of Accounts	Dec 11	Dec 10	Dec 09
Working Capital	162	128	107
Fixed Assets	N/A	1	5
Current Assets	541	415	312

C D R Forklift Training

33 Garrick Road, Lichfield, WS13 7DR
Tel: 01543-411305 **Fax:** 01543-411046
E-mail: info@cdr-training.co.uk
Website: http://www.cdr-training.co.uk
Directors: C. Reid (Ptnr)
Date established: 2004 **Turnover:** Up to £250,000
No.of Employees: 1 - 10 **Product Groups:** 86

C & G Mowers Service & Repairs Ltd

4c Wiltell Works Upper St John Street, Lichfield, WS14 9DX
Tel: 01543-414108 **Fax:** 01543-414108
E-mail: rob@cgmowers.co.uk
Website: http://www.cgmowers.co.uk
Directors: R. Cox (MD)
Immediate Holding Company: C & G MOWERS LTD
Registration no: 04866059 **Date established:** 2003
No.of Employees: 1 - 10 **Product Groups:** 41

Date of Accounts	Sep 11	Sep 10	Sep 08
Working Capital	18	30	10
Fixed Assets	14	16	15
Current Assets	49	58	36

Cadlogic Ltd

3 Greenhill, Lichfield, WS13 6DY
Tel: 01543-419886 **Fax:** 01543-419860
E-mail: steve.tew@cadlogic.com
Website: http://www.cadlogic.com
Directors: S. Tew (MD)
Immediate Holding Company: CADLOGIC LIMITED
Registration no: 02246940 **VAT No.:** GB 486 7595 75
Date established: 1988 **Turnover:** £250,000 - £500,000
No.of Employees: 1 - 10 **Product Groups:** 44

Date of Accounts	Jun 12	Jun 11	Jun 10
Sales Turnover	N/A	N/A	337
Pre Tax Profit/Loss	N/A	N/A	70
Working Capital	6	1	1
Current Assets	44	60	50
Current Liabilities	N/A	N/A	32

City Personnel Lichfield Ltd

Energy House Lombard Street, Lichfield, WS13 6DP
Tel: 01543-252237 **Fax:** 01543-418409
E-mail: business@citypersonnel-lichfield.com
Website: http://www.citypersonnel-lichfield.com
Directors: D. Ryall (MD), S. Ryall (MD)
Immediate Holding Company: CITY PERSONNEL (LICHFIELD) LIMITED
Registration no: 03559453 **Date established:** 1998
Turnover: £250,000 - £500,000 **No.of Employees:** 1 - 10
Product Groups: 80, 81

Date of Accounts	Jun 07	Jun 06
Working Capital	47	45
Fixed Assets	4	4
Current Assets	81	64
Current Liabilities	33	19
Total Share Capital	20	20

Crusader Abrasives Ltd

Unit 24 Crossfield Industrial Estate Crossfield Road, Lichfield, WS13 6RJ
Tel: 01543-263632 **Fax:** 01543-415787
Directors: P. Walton (Fin), T. Walton (MD)
Immediate Holding Company: CRUSADER ABRASIVES LIMITED
Registration no: 01901906 **Date established:** 1985
Turnover: Up to £250,000 **No.of Employees:** 1 - 10 **Product Groups:** 33, 36

Date of Accounts	Apr 10	Apr 09	Apr 08
Working Capital	-4	8	12
Fixed Assets	33	35	30
Current Assets	56	64	66

Curtain & Home

Windsor Park Trent Valley Road, Lichfield, WS13 6EU
Tel: 01543-410077 **Fax:** 01543-410077
E-mail: ronster@breathemail.net
Directors: J. Lippett (Prop)
Immediate Holding Company: CURTAIN & HOME LIMITED
Registration no: 07855227 **Date established:** 2011
No.of Employees: 1 - 10 **Product Groups:** 24, 52

Dengensha Europe Ltd

Unit 8 Birchbrook Industrial Park Lynn Lane, Shenstone, Lichfield, WS14 0DJ
Tel: 01543-481844 **Fax:** 01543-481851
E-mail: mail@dengensha.co.uk
Website: http://www.dengensha.co.uk
Directors: J. Mason (Fin)
Ultimate Holding Company: DENGENSHA MFG CO LTD (JAPAN)
Immediate Holding Company: DENGENSHA EUROPE LIMITED
Registration no: 03191563 **Date established:** 1996
No.of Employees: 1 - 10 **Product Groups:** 35, 45, 46, 47, 67

Date of Accounts	Mar 12	Mar 11	Mar 10
Working Capital	1m	1m	1m
Fixed Assets	80	134	120
Current Assets	2m	1m	1m

Duoform Precision Ltd

7 Birchbrook Industrial Park Lynn Lane, Shenstone, Lichfield, WS14 0DJ
Tel: 01543-480338 **Fax:** 01543-480128
E-mail: enquiries@duoform.co.uk
Website: http://www.duoform.co.uk
Directors: G. Wood (MD)
Managers: J. Reader (Mgr), D. Sheldon (Mgr)
Immediate Holding Company: DUOFORM PRECISION LIMITED
Registration no: 01918729 **VAT No.:** GB 389 3001 43
Date established: 1985 **Turnover:** £500,000 - £1m
No.of Employees: 1 - 10 **Product Groups:** 42, 48

Date of Accounts	Jun 07	Jun 06
Working Capital	209	210
Fixed Assets	4	5
Current Assets	403	287
Current Liabilities	194	77

G Brookes

Unit 34 Birchbrook Industrial Park Lynn Lane, Shenstone, Lichfield, WS14 0DJ
Tel: 01543-480060 **Fax:** 01543-481606
E-mail: info@gbrookes.co.uk
Website: http://www.gbrookes.co.uk
Directors: L. Hall (MD)
Immediate Holding Company: G BROOKES & CO LIMITED
Registration no: 02360953 **VAT No.:** GB 113 6136 09
Date established: 1989 **No.of Employees:** 1 - 10 **Product Groups:** 35, 44, 49, 65, 67, 81

Date of Accounts	Apr 12	Apr 11	Apr 10
Working Capital	111	128	110
Fixed Assets	19	25	13
Current Assets	233	284	284

G F P Engineering Ltd

Europa Way Britannia Enterprise Park, Lichfield, WS14 9TZ
Tel: 01543-263121 **Fax:** 01543-418873
E-mail: gfpeng@btconnect.com
Website: http://www.gfpengineering.f9.co.uk
Directors: C. Fox (MD)
Managers: R. Fox (Comm)
Immediate Holding Company: G.F.P.ENGINEERING LIMITED
Registration no: 00940891 **Date established:** 1968
Turnover: £250,000 - £500,000 **No.of Employees:** 1 - 10
Product Groups: 30

Date of Accounts	Dec 09	Dec 08	Dec 07
Sales Turnover	439	499	410
Pre Tax Profit/Loss	16	27	26
Working Capital	47	49	32
Fixed Assets	13	6	8
Current Assets	99	97	116
Current Liabilities	10	18	23

G K Marketing Services Ltd

Unit 21-22 Crossfield Industrial Estate Crossfield Road, Lichfield, WS13 6RJ
Tel: 01543-414130 **Fax:** 01543-250660
E-mail: sales@gkmktg.com
Website: http://www.gkmktg.com
Bank(s): National Westminster Bank Plc
Directors: G. King (MD)
Immediate Holding Company: G K MARKETING SERVICES LIMITED
Registration no: 02288908 **VAT No.:** GB 486 7544 92
Date established: 1988 **Turnover:** £500,000 - £1m
No.of Employees: 11 - 20 **Product Groups:** 28, 48

Date of Accounts	Oct 11	Oct 10	Oct 09
Working Capital	19	-1	-9
Fixed Assets	22	28	23
Current Assets	206	181	163
Current Liabilities	N/A	N/A	9

Geometrix

Unit 10 Shires Industrial Estate Essington Close, Lichfield, WS14 9AZ
Tel: 01543-452424 **Fax:** 01543-453012
E-mail: email@geometrix.co.uk
Website: http://www.geometrix.co.uk
Directors: J. Cook (Dir)
Immediate Holding Company: CHARTER MANAGEMENT LIMITED
Registration no: 00229474 **VAT No.:** GB 100 0300 77
Date established: 2002 **Turnover:** £1m - £2m **No.of Employees:** 1 - 10
Product Groups: 27, 30, 36, 38, 49, 64

Date of Accounts	Dec 09	Dec 08	Dec 07
Working Capital	-116	21	56
Fixed Assets	351	369	443
Current Assets	287	436	421

GEZE UK Ltd

Blenheim Way Fradley Park, Lichfield, WS13 8SY
Tel: 01543-443000 **Fax:** 01543-443001
E-mail: info.uk@geze.com
Website: http://www.geze.co.uk
Directors: A. Hall (MD)
Ultimate Holding Company: GEZE GMBH (GERMANY)
Immediate Holding Company: GEZE LIMITED
Registration no: 03218141 **VAT No.:** GB 529 3264 37
Date established: 1996 **Turnover:** £1m - £2m **No.of Employees:** 51 - 100
Product Groups: 35, 36, 37, 40

Date of Accounts	Jun 11	Jun 10	Jun 09
Working Capital	-1	61	61
Current Assets	13	61	63
Current Liabilities	14	N/A	N/A

GKN Sinter Metals Ltd

P.O. Box 3 Trent Valley Road, Lichfield, WS136HF
Tel: 01543-403000 **Fax:** 01543-403001
E-mail: info@gknsintermetals.co.uk
Website: http://www.gknsintermetals.co.uk
Bank(s): Lloyds TSB Bank plc
Directors: C. Granger (Dir), D. Rank (Fin), D. Clarkson (Chief Op Offcr), J. Spruell (Grp Chief Exec), S. Hollidge (Sales)
Managers: A. Henstock (Comptroller), A. Lloyd-Jones (Tech Serv Mgr), B. Bishop (Publicity), B. Johnson, D. Murray (Sales Prom Mgr), D. Roache (Personnel), J. Best (Quality Control), J. Wood (Transport), M. Khanna (Quality Control), M. Rowe (Safety), M. Smith (Maint), P. Adams (Drawing Office), R. Cornick (Lab Mgr), R. Lloyd (Personnel), S. Jones (Estimating), W. Thompson
Ultimate Holding Company: GKN plc
Immediate Holding Company: GKN Sinter Metals Holdings Ltd
Registration no: 00387190 **VAT No.:** GB 100 3286 30
Date established: 1944 **Turnover:** £2m - £5m
No.of Employees: 101 - 250 **Product Groups:** 34, 35, 42, 66

see next page

***GKN Sinter Metals Ltd** - Cont'd*

Date of Accounts	Dec 07
Pre Tax Profit/Loss	2580
Working Capital	24420
Current Assets	24530
Current Liabilities	110
Total Share Capital	1690
ROCE% (Return on Capital Employed)	10.6

I X R Systems Ltd (International Xray & Radar Systems)
9 Paskin Close Fradley, Lichfield, WS13 8NZ
Tel: 01283-792003 **Fax:** 01283-792004
E-mail: mike@ixrs.co.uk
Website: http://www.kellysearch.com/partners/ixsystems.asp
Directors: M. Davis (MD)
Immediate Holding Company: IXR SYSTEMS LIMITED
Registration no: 04232503 **Date established:** 2001
No.of Employees: 1 - 10 **Product Groups:** 20, 22, 24, 25, 26, 27, 29, 30, 31, 33, 34, 35, 37, 38, 39, 40, 42, 44, 48, 54, 66, 67, 84, 85, 86

Date of Accounts	Jun 11	Jun 10	Jun 09
Working Capital	-5	-5	-1
Fixed Assets	5	7	1
Current Assets	37	18	19

Douglas Jackson Ltd
23 Lichfield Business Village The Friary, Lichfield, WS13 6QG
Tel: 08456-209720 **Fax:** 08456-209721
E-mail: mail@douglas-jackson.com
Website: http://www.douglas-jackson.com
Directors: M. Ansell (Dir)
Immediate Holding Company: DOUGLAS JACKSON LIMITED
Registration no: 06091414 **Date established:** 2007 **Turnover:** £1m - £2m
No.of Employees: 1 - 10 **Product Groups:** 80

Date of Accounts	Mar 11	Mar 09	Mar 08
Working Capital	28	18	1
Fixed Assets	1	N/A	N/A
Current Assets	64	56	30
Current Liabilities	23	26	23

Jackson Lift Services
16 Titan Way Britannia Enterprise Park, Lichfield, WS14 9TT
Tel: 01543-262850 **Fax:** 01543-258809
E-mail: dgardner@jacksonlifts.com
Website: http://www.jacksonlifts.com
Managers: D. Gardner
Registration no: 02795309 **No.of Employees:** 1 - 10 **Product Groups:** 48

Jackson Services
16 Titan Way Britannia Enterprise Park, Lichfield, WS14 9TT
Tel: 01543-257235 **Fax:** 01543-258809
Managers: A. Knowle (Mgr)
No.of Employees: 1 - 10 **Product Groups:** 45, 48, 67

Jofemar UK
Unit 39 Britannia Way, Britannia Enterprise Park, Lichfield, WS14 9UY
Tel: 01543-251253 **Fax:** 01543-251259
E-mail: sales@jofemar.com
Website: http://www.jofemar.com
Managers: C. Matthews (Tech Serv Mgr)
Immediate Holding Company: JOFEMAR UK LIMITED
Registration no: 05647024 **VAT No.:** GB 580 7186 23
Date established: 2005 **Turnover:** £1m - £2m **No.of Employees:** 1 - 10
Product Groups: 61

Date of Accounts	Dec 11	Dec 10	Dec 09
Working Capital	44	66	80
Fixed Assets	2	3	3
Current Assets	167	190	193

K & H Toolmakers
Chesterfield Farm Ashcroft Lane, Lichfield, WS14 0EH
Tel: 01543-480184 **Fax:** 01543-480184
Directors: J. Kinson (Prop)
Date established: 1980 **No.of Employees:** 1 - 10 **Product Groups:** 36

L S C Group
Lincoln House Wellington Crescent, Fradley Park, Lichfield, WS13 8RZ
Tel: 01543-446800 **Fax:** 01543-446900
E-mail: careers@lsc.co.uk
Website: http://www.lsc.co.uk
Bank(s): Bank of Scotland
Managers: D. Fleet (Mgr), N. Hawkes, M. Hughes (Tech Serv Mgr), K. Werrett (Mktg Serv Mgr)
Ultimate Holding Company: BABCOCK INTERNATIONAL GROUP PLC
Immediate Holding Company: LSC GROUP HOLDINGS LIMITED
Registration no: 03533640 **Date established:** 1998
Turnover: £500,000 - £1m **No.of Employees:** 101 - 250
Product Groups: 44, 84

Date of Accounts	Mar 12	Mar 11	Mar 10
Pre Tax Profit/Loss	N/A	1m	N/A
Working Capital	1m	1m	N/A
Fixed Assets	3m	3m	3m
Current Assets	1m	1m	N/A

Bob Lane Woodturners
Unit 1 White House Farm Old London Road, Lichfield, WS14 9QW
Tel: 01543-483148 **Fax:** 01543-481245
E-mail: sales@theturner.co.uk
Website: http://www.theturner.co.uk
Directors: R. Lane (Prop)
Date established: 1988 **Turnover:** Up to £250,000
No.of Employees: 1 - 10 **Product Groups:** 25

Learning Impact International Ltd
Johnson Suite Lichfield House 32 Bore Street, Lichfield, WS13 6LL
Tel: 08454-503851 **Fax:** 0121-359 0138
E-mail: contact@learningimpact.co.uk
Website: http://www.learningimpact.co.uk
Managers: J. Farrall (Sales Admin)
Immediate Holding Company: LEARNING IMPACT INTERNATIONAL LIMITED
Registration no: 02907160 **VAT No.:** GB 753 7163 22
Date established: 1994 **Turnover:** £500,000 - £1m
No.of Employees: 1 - 10 **Product Groups:** 86

Date of Accounts	Jun 11	Jun 10	Jun 09
Working Capital	44	55	201
Fixed Assets	3	5	8
Current Assets	104	55	242

Linford-Bridgeman Ltd
Quonians Lane, Lichfield, WS13 7LB
Tel: 01543-414234 **Fax:** 01543-258250
E-mail: stuart.carter@linford.com
Website: http://www.linford.com
Bank(s): Barclays, Midland, National Westminster
Directors: S. Carter (MD), D. Linford (Ch), C. Hall (Co Sec), R. Pearson (MD), M. Thompson (Chief Op Offcr), P. Lee (Dir), S. Linford (Grp Chief Exec)
Managers: M. Perks (Mktg Serv Mgr), J. Babington, R. Newman
Ultimate Holding Company: F. & E.V. LINFORD LIMITED
Immediate Holding Company: LINFORD GROUP LIMITED
Registration no: 00998029 **Date established:** 1970
Turnover: £20m - £50m **No.of Employees:** 101 - 250 **Product Groups:** 52

Date of Accounts	Sep 10	Sep 09	Sep 08
Sales Turnover	36m	35m	39m
Pre Tax Profit/Loss	120	-759	587
Working Capital	201	228	895
Fixed Assets	679	714	804
Current Assets	8m	9m	12m
Current Liabilities	503	505	863

Lion Industries UK Ltd
9-10 Titan Way Britannia Enterprise Park, Lichfield, WS14 9TT
Tel: 01543-251560 **Fax:** 01543-251395
E-mail: info@lionindustries.co.uk
Website: http://www.lionindustries.co.uk
Directors: A. Dundas (Co Sec), D. Dundas (MD)
Immediate Holding Company: LION INDUSTRIES UK LIMITED
Registration no: 02831653 **VAT No.:** GB 426 9187 25
Date established: 1993 **Turnover:** £500,000 - £1m
No.of Employees: 1 - 10 **Product Groups:** 40, 46, 49

Date of Accounts	Dec 11	Dec 10	Dec 09
Working Capital	97	124	112
Fixed Assets	7	11	15
Current Assets	277	277	270

Netzsch Mastermix Ltd
23 Lombard Street, Lichfield, WS13 6DP
Tel: 01543-418938 **Fax:** 01543-418926
E-mail: nmx@netzsch-mastermix.co.uk
Website: http://www.netzsch-grinding.com
Directors: D. Tomlinson (MD)
Ultimate Holding Company: ERICH NETZSCH GMBH & CO HOLDING KG (GERM
Immediate Holding Company: NETZSCH MASTERMIX LIMITED
Registration no: 01421775 **Date established:** 1979
No.of Employees: 11 - 20 **Product Groups:** 07, 20, 23, 29, 32, 33, 40, 41, 42, 43, 46, 47, 48, 67

Date of Accounts	Jun 12	Jun 11	Jun 10
Working Capital	428	424	532
Fixed Assets	23	12	19
Current Assets	1m	1m	873

Norcan Ltd
Eastern Avenue, Lichfield, WS13 7SG
Tel: 01543-256616 **Fax:** 01543-263208
E-mail: simonpargeter@norcan.co.uk
Website: http://www.norcan.co.uk
Directors: S. Garner (Dir), N. Pargeter (Fin), S. Pargeter (MD), J. Pargeter (MD), S. Pargeter (Dir)
Ultimate Holding Company: CHARTER MANUFACTURING INTERNATIONAL LIMITED
Immediate Holding Company: NORCAN LIMITED
Registration no: 01133530 **VAT No.:** GB 101 4799 87
Date established: 1973 **Turnover:** £500,000 - £1m
No.of Employees: 1 - 10 **Product Groups:** 38

Date of Accounts	May 09	May 08	May 07
Working Capital	68	75	436
Fixed Assets	389	400	79
Current Assets	143	195	585

Norgren Ltd
Box 22 Eastern Avenue, Lichfield, WS13 6SB
Tel: 01543-265000 **Fax:** 01543-265854
E-mail: enquiry@norgren.com
Website: http://www.norgren.com
Directors: W. North (Fin), W. Hambleton (Pers)
Managers: J. McKinnon, S. Brunt (Purch Mgr)
Ultimate Holding Company: IMI PLC
Immediate Holding Company: IMI NORGREN (EXPORT) LIMITED
Registration no: 00624476 **VAT No.:** GB 405 2868 56
Date established: 1959 **Turnover:** £125m - £250m
No.of Employees: 251 - 500 **Product Groups:** 30, 35, 36, 37, 38, 39, 40, 42, 44, 45, 46, 48, 67, 84

Date of Accounts	Dec 10	Dec 09	Dec 08
Pre Tax Profit/Loss	60	96	161
Working Capital	3m	3m	3m
Current Assets	3m	3m	3m
Current Liabilities	17	27	46

N T N Bearings UK Ltd
11 Wellington Crescent Fradley Park Fradley Park, Lichfield, WS13 8RZ
Tel: 01543-445000 **Fax:** 01543-445035
E-mail: lex.browning@ntn-europe.com
Website: http://www.ntn-europe.com
Bank(s): Lloyds TSB
Directors: L. Browning (MD), T. Rate (Co Sec)
Managers: J. Sargent (Personnel), J. Chambers, M. Wooldridge (Sales Prom Mgr), A. Roberts (Tech Serv Mgr)
Ultimate Holding Company: N T N CORP (JAPAN)
Immediate Holding Company: NTN BEARINGS (UK) LIMITED
Registration no: 00816672 **VAT No.:** GB 100 3546 30
Date established: 1964 **Turnover:** £50m - £75m
No.of Employees: 21 - 50 **Product Groups:** 30, 34, 35, 39

Date of Accounts	Mar 12	Mar 11	Mar 10
Sales Turnover	54m	49m	36m
Pre Tax Profit/Loss	2m	2m	522
Working Capital	11m	10m	9m
Fixed Assets	2m	2m	2m
Current Assets	23m	20m	18m
Current Liabilities	12m	2m	1m

Palletways UK Ltd
Fradley Distribution Park Wood End Lane, Fradley, Lichfield, WS13 8NE
Tel: 01543-418000 **Fax:** 01543-418111
E-mail: reception@palletways.com
Website: http://www.palletways.com
Directors: T. Olsson (Tech Serv), R. Gittins (Sales), J. Wilson (Grp Chief Exec)
Managers: M. Summers (Personnel), P. Komuro (Mktg Serv Mgr), S. Hundleby
Ultimate Holding Company: PALLETWAYS GROUP LIMITED
Immediate Holding Company: PALLETWAYS (UK) LIMITED
Registration no: 02918303 **Date established:** 1994
Turnover: £75m - £125m **No.of Employees:** 101 - 250
Product Groups: 35, 39, 45, 68, 72, 76, 77, 80, 84

Date of Accounts	May 11	May 10	May 09
Sales Turnover	117m	112m	113m
Pre Tax Profit/Loss	7m	8m	6m
Working Capital	2m	3m	3m
Fixed Assets	1m	533	529
Current Assets	16m	16m	14m
Current Liabilities	4m	4m	3m

Pink'D Up Design & Wedding Photography
68 Blackberry Avenue, Lichfield, WS14 9GS
Tel: 01543-262331
E-mail: design@pinkdup.co.uk
Website: http://www.pinkdup.co.uk
Directors: A. Stuart (Dir), A. Stuart (Prop)
Date established: 2007 **Turnover:** Up to £250,000
No.of Employees: 1 - 10 **Product Groups:** 81

Process Heating Services Ltd
12 Noddington Avenue Whittington, Lichfield, WS14 9NQ
Tel: 01543-432661 **Fax:** 01543-432782
E-mail: sales@processheatingservices.com
Website: http://www.processheatingservices.com
Directors: T. Banks (MD), D. Banks (Fin)
Immediate Holding Company: PROCESS HEATING SERVICES LIMITED
Registration no: 05517161 **VAT No.:** GB 555 0595 32
Date established: 2005 **No.of Employees:** 1 - 10 **Product Groups:** 37, 40, 42, 66

Date of Accounts	Sep 11	Sep 10	Sep 09
Working Capital	9	16	7
Fixed Assets	1	1	N/A
Current Assets	77	73	45

Pure Beauty Online
PO Box 4880, Lichfield, WS14 4DA
Tel: 0121-314 7039
E-mail: shop@pure-beauty.co.uk
Website: http://www.pure-beauty.co.uk
Directors: C. Whittaker (Prop), G. Whittaker (Prop)
Date established: 2003 **No.of Employees:** 1 - 10 **Product Groups:** 61

S C A Packaging Ltd (Factory, UK Central Office)
Kirby House Lynn Lane, Shenstone, Lichfield, WS14 0DZ
Tel: 01543-482482 **Fax:** 01543-482400
E-mail: display.uk@sca.com
Website: http://www.sca.com
Managers: B. Ryan (Site Co-ord)
Ultimate Holding Company: SVENSKA CELLULOSA AB (SWEDEN)
Immediate Holding Company: DS SMITH CORRUGATED PACKAGING LIMITED
Registration no: 00053913 **Date established:** 1997
Turnover: £250m - £500m **No.of Employees:** 51 - 100
Product Groups: 27, 49, 66

Date of Accounts	Dec 10	Dec 09	Dec 08
Sales Turnover	125m	129m	332m
Pre Tax Profit/Loss	8m	-15m	-62m
Working Capital	269m	277m	290m
Fixed Assets	51m	54m	75m
Current Assets	297m	297m	411m
Current Liabilities	6m	5m	22m

S L P Consultants
4 The Beech Tree Elmhurst Business Park, Elmhurst, Lichfield, WS13 8EX
Tel: 01543-257799
E-mail: office@slpconsultants.co.uk
Directors: S. Pountney (Ptnr)
Immediate Holding Company: TOTAL ASSURANCE LIMITED
Date established: 2012 **No.of Employees:** 1 - 10 **Product Groups:** 35

The Sales Recruitment Network (West Midlands)
49 Birmingham Road, Lichfield, WS13 6PG
Tel: 01543-410717 **Fax:** 01543-308615
E-mail: w.midlands@tsrn.co.uk
Website: http://www.tsrn.co.uk
Managers: F. Sneddon (Mgr)
No.of Employees: 1 - 10 **Product Groups:** 80

SCA Newtec
Nutec Mill Eastern Avenue, Lichfield, WS13 7SE
Tel: 01543-306306 **Fax:** 01543-306307
E-mail: enquiries@scanutec.com
Website: http://www.scanutec.com/index.html
Bank(s): National Westminster Bank Plc
Directors: H. Tailor (Fin), T. Drake (Ch)
Managers: A. Elvis (Export Sales Mg)
Ultimate Holding Company: E.B.S.
Immediate Holding Company: Provimi Ltd
Registration no: 01262691 **VAT No.:** GB 289 2374 17
Turnover: £20m - £50m **No.of Employees:** 51 - 100 **Product Groups:** 20, 63

Shenstone Mechanical Services
Unit 17 Birchbrook Industrial Park Lynn Lane, Shenstone, Lichfield, WS14 0DJ
Tel: 01543-481392 **Fax:** 01543-481269
Website: http://www.shenstoneforklifts.co.uk
Directors: A. Wright (Fin), J. Knight (MD)
Immediate Holding Company: SHENSTONE MECHANICAL SERVICES LIMITED
Registration no: 02768162 **Date established:** 1992
No.of Employees: 1 - 10 **Product Groups:** 35, 39, 45

Date of Accounts	Mar 12	Mar 11	Mar 10
Working Capital	-0	6	49
Fixed Assets	13	16	21
Current Assets	62	45	60

Solomon & Whitehead Ltd
Lynn Lane Shenstone, Lichfield, WS14 0DX
Tel: 01543-480696 **Fax:** 01543-481619
E-mail: gbj@fineartgroup.co.uk
Website: http://www.fineartgroup.co.uk

Bank(s): HSBC
Directors: A. Birch (Fin), G. Jones (MD)
Immediate Holding Company: SOLOMON & WHITEHEAD LIMITED
Registration no: 07510362 **VAT No.:** GB 346 0656 55
Date established: 2011 **Turnover:** £1m - £2m **No.of Employees:** 21 - 50
Product Groups: 28

Date of Accounts	Dec 07	Dec 06	Dec 05
Sales Turnover	N/A	N/A	1157
Pre Tax Profit/Loss	N/A	N/A	-182
Working Capital	214	311	505
Fixed Assets	237	260	283
Current Assets	646	762	1034
Current Liabilities	432	451	529
ROCE% (Return on Capital Employed)			-23.1
ROT% (Return on Turnover)			-15.8

Sony Centre Galleria
Unit 1c Three Spires Shopping Centre, Lichfield, WS13 6NG
Tel: 01543-415486 **Fax:** 01543-418444
Website: http://www.sonycentres.co.uk
Managers: P. Sillence (District Mgr)
Ultimate Holding Company: SEAMAP LTD
Immediate Holding Company: ALERTBIND LTD
Registration no: 00377588 **Date established:** 2005
No.of Employees: 1 - 10 **Product Groups:** 36, 40

Newcastle

A B Connectors Ltd
324 Liverpool Road, Newcastle, ST5 9DY
Tel: 01782-636444 **Fax:** 01782-636444
E-mail: sales@ttabconnectors.com
Website: http://www.ttabconnectors.com
Directors: C. Green (Sales)
Ultimate Holding Company: TT ELECTRONICS PLC
Immediate Holding Company: AB CONNECTORS LIMITED
Registration no: 01914199 **Date established:** 1985
No.of Employees: 1 - 10 **Product Groups:** 36, 40

Date of Accounts	Dec 10	Dec 09	Dec 08
Sales Turnover	19m	16m	21m
Pre Tax Profit/Loss	468	257	788
Working Capital	4m	3m	3m
Fixed Assets	4m	5m	5m
Current Assets	7m	7m	10m
Current Liabilities	846	976	1m

Adgifts Online Ltd
17 Barracks Square, Newcastle, ST5 1LG
Tel: 08701-430700 **Fax:** 01782-715431
E-mail: sales@adgiftsonline.com
Website: http://www.adgiftsonline.com
Directors: A. Altham (Ptnr), A. Altham (Prop), T. Altham (Prop)
Managers: S. Vuckovic (Accounts), L. Greenhalgh
Immediate Holding Company: ADGIFTSONLINE LIMITED
Registration no: 03573281 **Date established:** 1998
Turnover: Up to £250,000 **No.of Employees:** 1 - 10 **Product Groups:** 49, 65, 81

Date of Accounts	Mar 11	Mar 10	Mar 09
Working Capital	-118	-105	-140
Fixed Assets	44	65	86
Current Assets	36	58	21

Affordable Appliances
81 High Street Silverdale, Newcastle, ST5 6LY
Tel: 01782-711966
Website: http://affordable-appliances.net/
Directors: L. Everall (Prop)
No.of Employees: 1 - 10 **Product Groups:** 43

Alcontrol Onsite Services
Unit 5 Loomer Road Indl-Est Loomer Road, Newcastle, ST5 7LB
Tel: 01782-576590 **Fax:** 01782-576599
E-mail: info@shieldon-siteservices.co.uk
Website: http://www.alcontrol.com
Directors: M. Timms (Dir), M. Timms (MD)
Managers: J. Alexander (Purch Mgr), J. Alexander
Ultimate Holding Company: THE CORBETT GROUP LIMITED
Immediate Holding Company: NEWCASTLE-UNDER-LYME STADIUM LIMITED
Registration no: 01061978 **Date established:** 1972
No.of Employees: 51 - 100 **Product Groups:** 38, 54, 84

Date of Accounts	Mar 11	Mar 10	Mar 09
Sales Turnover	18	18	18
Pre Tax Profit/Loss	16	18	-3
Working Capital	-130	-142	-157
Fixed Assets	325	325	275
Current Assets	N/A	6	11
Current Liabilities	8	8	5

Andritz Ltd (a division of Baker-Hughes Ltd)
R & B Technology Centre Speedwell Road, Parkhouse East, Newcastle, ST5 7RG
Tel: 01782-565656 **Fax:** 01782-566130
E-mail: environ.uk@andritz.com
Website: http://www.andritz.com
Directors: A. Stanley (Jt MD), J. Shelley (Jt MD), M. Weeks (Dir)
Managers: C. Machin (Purch Mgr), A. Lawton (Sales Prom Mgr), A. Swindles (Sales Prom Mgr), T. Barber (Sales Prom Mgr)
Ultimate Holding Company: ANDRITZ AG (AUSTRIA)
Immediate Holding Company: Baker-Hughes Ltd
Registration no: 02937921 **Date established:** 1994 **Turnover:** £5m - £10m
No.of Employees: 21 - 50 **Product Groups:** 41, 42

Date of Accounts	Dec 09	Dec 08	Dec 07
Sales Turnover	7m	6m	10m
Pre Tax Profit/Loss	-38	-244	738
Working Capital	3m	3m	3m
Fixed Assets	86	109	155
Current Assets	5m	5m	5m
Current Liabilities	695	980	N/A

Ashbrook Simon Hartley Ltd
10-11 Brindley Court Dalewood Road, Lymedale Business Park, Newcastle, ST5 9QH
Tel: 01782-578650 **Fax:** 01782-260534
E-mail: enquiries@as-h.com
Website: http://www.as-h.com
Bank(s): J P Morgan Bank (London)
Directors: M. Gibson (Dir), A. Hurlstone (Pers), D. Lake (Fin), M. Moston (Sales)
Managers: H. Williams, S. Burns (Prod Mgr), N. Sidhu (Tech Serv Mgr)
Ultimate Holding Company: ASHBROOK SIMON-HARTLEY LP (USA)
Immediate Holding Company: ASHBROOK SIMON-HARTLEY LIMITED
Registration no: 05259072 **VAT No.:** GB 854 2053 40
Date established: 2004 **Turnover:** £10m - £20m
No.of Employees: 51 - 100 **Product Groups:** 41, 42, 44, 48, 54, 67

Date of Accounts	Dec 11	Dec 10	Dec 09
Sales Turnover	13m	10m	14m
Pre Tax Profit/Loss	-215	-259	-86
Working Capital	1m	903	1m
Fixed Assets	696	946	1m
Current Assets	7m	5m	6m
Current Liabilities	2m	2m	2m

Autobrite-Direct
Unit 1 Valley Park Watermills Road, Newcastle, ST5 6AT
Tel: 01782-563319
E-mail: autobrite@tiscali.co.uk
Website: http://www.autobritedirect.co.uk
Directors: M. Moss (Prop)
Managers: M. Keen (Mgr)
Registration no: 01720888 **Date established:** 1983
No.of Employees: 1 - 10 **Product Groups:** 32, 39, 68

AWS Electronics Group Ltd
Croft Road Industrial Estate, Newcastle, ST5 0TW
Tel: 01782-799034 **Fax:** 01782-753207
E-mail: info@aws-electronics.co.uk
Website: http://www.aws-electronics.co.uk
Directors: P. Deehan (MD), C. Clues (I.T. Dir)
Managers: C. Boeman (Purch Mgr), T. Tucker (Purch Mgr), M. Howitt (Mgr), M. Keen (I.T. Exec), M. Allen
Ultimate Holding Company: AWS GROUP HOLDINGS LTD
Immediate Holding Company: AWS ELECTRONICS GROUP LIMITED
Registration no: 05626347 **VAT No.:** GB 280 1079 78
Date established: 2005 **Turnover:** £5m - £10m **No.of Employees:** 1 - 10
Product Groups: 37, 44, 48, 67, 85

Date of Accounts	Jun 11	Jun 10	Jun 09
Sales Turnover	40m	32m	33m
Pre Tax Profit/Loss	2m	1m	144
Working Capital	-2m	-3m	-4m
Fixed Assets	6m	7m	7m
Current Assets	14m	11m	9m
Current Liabilities	4m	3m	3m

Axair Fans UK Ltd
Lowfield Drive Centre 500, Wolstanton, Newcastle, ST5 0UU
Tel: 01782-349430 **Fax:** 01782-349439
E-mail: grant.edwards@axair-fans.co.uk
Website: http://www.axair-fans.co.uk
Directors: G. Edwards (MD)
Immediate Holding Company: AXAIR FANS UK LIMITED
Registration no: 02701642 **VAT No.:** GB 592 6736 00
Date established: 1992 **Turnover:** £1m - £2m **No.of Employees:** 1 - 10
Product Groups: 49

Date of Accounts	Mar 11	Mar 10	Mar 09
Working Capital	528	1m	1m
Fixed Assets	73	30	26
Current Assets	1m	2m	1m

B & J Engineering Stoke-On-Trent Ltd
Unit 7 Brampton Sidings Industrial Estate Hempstalls Lane, Newcastle, ST5 0SR
Tel: 01782-632132 **Fax:** 01782-628591
E-mail: julie@bj-engineering.co.uk
Website: http://www.bj-engineering.co.uk
Directors: J. Plant (MD)
Immediate Holding Company: B & J ENGINEERING (STOKE-ON-TRENT) LIMITED
Registration no: 04440810 **VAT No.:** GB 368 0565 32
Date established: 2002 **Turnover:** Up to £250,000
No.of Employees: 1 - 10 **Product Groups:** 48

Date of Accounts	Jul 11	Jul 10	Jul 09
Working Capital	406	318	309
Fixed Assets	217	228	165
Current Assets	510	420	413

B R F Site Services & Engineering
High Carr Works Talke Road, Chesterton, Newcastle, ST5 7AL
Tel: 01782-564725 **Fax:** 01782- 562727
Directors: B. Fletcher (Ptnr)
Date established: 1985 **No.of Employees:** 1 - 10 **Product Groups:** 35

Bricesco Ltd (British Ceramic Service Co. Ltd)
Lymedale Business Centre Hooters Hall Road, Lymedale Business Park, Newcastle, ST5 9QF
Tel: 01782-567300 **Fax:** 01782-344601
E-mail: richard.bridgewater@bricesco.co.uk
Website: http://www.bricesco.co.uk
Bank(s): Barclays, Newcastle under Lyme
Directors: R. Bridgewater (MD)
Immediate Holding Company: BRICESCO LIMITED
Registration no: 06035964 **VAT No.:** GB 655 1329 40
Date established: 2006 **Turnover:** £10m - £20m
No.of Employees: 11 - 20 **Product Groups:** 40, 45

Date of Accounts	Mar 11	Mar 10	Mar 09
Working Capital	-208	-191	-209
Fixed Assets	668	674	643
Current Assets	561	374	841

Beacon Engineering
Apedale Road, Newcastle, ST5 6BH
Tel: 01782-565810 **Fax:** 01782-565810
E-mail: beden33@hotmail.com
Directors: K. Rockett (Prop)
Immediate Holding Company: CAVANAGH DEVELOPMENTS LIMITED
Registration no: 03550701 **Date established:** 1998
No.of Employees: 1 - 10 **Product Groups:** 35, 42, 45

Date of Accounts	Mar 11	Mar 10	Mar 09
Working Capital	-79	-79	-79
Fixed Assets	106	106	106
Current Assets	20	20	20

George Birchall Group Management Ltd
Environment House Turner Crescent, Newcastle, ST5 7JZ
Tel: 01782-566885 **Fax:** 01782-561533
E-mail: sales@birchall.co.uk
Website: http://www.birchall.co.uk
Directors: I. Birchall (Dir), G. Birchall (Co Sec), A. Birchall (Tech Serv), G. Taylor (Fin)
Managers: G. Gornall (Buyer)
Immediate Holding Company: GEORGE BIRCHALL GROUP MANAGEMENT LIMITED
Registration no: 02465114 **Date established:** 1990
Turnover: £20m - £50m **No.of Employees:** 51 - 100 **Product Groups:** 52

Date of Accounts	Mar 12	Mar 11	Mar 10
Sales Turnover	37m	36m	24m
Pre Tax Profit/Loss	295	-687	-769
Working Capital	5m	4m	4m
Fixed Assets	910	983	1m
Current Assets	14m	12m	10m
Current Liabilities	1m	1m	899

BOCM Pauls Ltd
Speedwell Road Parkhouse Industrial Estate East, Newcastle, ST5 7RF
Tel: 01782-565565 **Fax:** 01782-564609
E-mail: info@bocmpauls.co.uk
Website: http://www.bocmpauls.co.uk
Managers: E. Carey (Ops Mgr)
Ultimate Holding Company: AGRICOLA GROUP LIMITED
Immediate Holding Company: BOCM PAULS LTD
Registration no: 00062904 **Date established:** 1999
Turnover: £10m - £20m **No.of Employees:** 21 - 50 **Product Groups:** 20

Date of Accounts	Dec 11	Dec 10	Dec 09
Sales Turnover	495m	425m	401m
Pre Tax Profit/Loss	8m	11m	4m
Working Capital	80m	75m	61m
Fixed Assets	73m	70m	67m
Current Assets	155m	149m	130m
Current Liabilities	7m	8m	6m

Bri-Ton Fine Foods Ltd
Rowhurst Close, Newcastle, ST5 6BE
Tel: 01782-561422
Website: http://www.bri-ton.co.uk
Directors: T. Bailey (MD), R. Arnold (Dir)
Immediate Holding Company: BRI-TON FINE FOODS LIMITED
Registration no: 01056729 **Date established:** 1972
Turnover: £250,000 - £500,000 **No.of Employees:** 11 - 20
Product Groups: 20, 62

Date of Accounts	May 11	May 10	May 09
Working Capital	-172	-248	1m
Fixed Assets	870	794	302
Current Assets	1m	1m	2m

Broxap Cloakroom Furniture
Rowhurst Close Rowhurst Indl-Est, Newcastle, ST5 6BD
Tel: 08448-004085 **Fax:** 01782-565357
E-mail: enquiries@broxap.com
Website: http://www.broxap.com
Directors: R. Lee (MD), J. Lee (Ch)
Managers: S. Lee-Saint (Mgr)
Ultimate Holding Company: BROXAP HOLDINGS LIMITED
Immediate Holding Company: BROXAP LIMITED
Registration no: 02583752 **VAT No.:** GB 592 5264 20
Date established: 1991 **Turnover:** £20m - £50m **No.of Employees:** 1 - 10
Product Groups: 33

Date of Accounts	Dec 10	Dec 09	Nov 08
Sales Turnover	42m	44m	38m
Pre Tax Profit/Loss	717	649	881
Working Capital	280	5m	293
Fixed Assets	9m	7m	5m
Current Assets	10m	13m	13m
Current Liabilities	2m	2m	6m

Caltherm UK Ltd
Rowhurst Industrial Estate, Newcastle, ST5 6BD
Tel: 01782-563865 **Fax:** 01782-561607
E-mail: admin@caltherm.co.uk
Website: http://www.caltherm.co.uk
Bank(s): National Westminster Bank Plc
Directors: A. Mountford (Co Sec)
Managers: D. Burton (Purch Mgr), I. Dawson (Tech Serv Mgr)
Immediate Holding Company: CALTHERM U.K. LIMITED
Registration no: 01411420 **VAT No.:** GB 318 9640 34
Date established: 1979 **Turnover:** £1m - £2m **No.of Employees:** 21 - 50
Product Groups: 40, 46, 67

Date of Accounts	Sep 11	Sep 10	Sep 09
Working Capital	123	98	106
Fixed Assets	127	141	99
Current Assets	578	524	401

CLS Wiring Systems 2000 Limited
Lymedale Small Firms Centre Dalewood Road, Lymedale Business Park, Newcastle, ST5 9QH
Tel: 01782-566400 **Fax:** 01782-565577
E-mail: sales@clswiring2000.co.uk
Website: http://www.clswiring2000.co.uk
Managers: R. Salt (Mgr)
Registration no: 04091983 **Date established:** 1999
No.of Employees: 11 - 20 **Product Groups:** 35

Computer People (Ajilon Group)
Med Ic3 Building Keele University Science Park, Keele, Newcastle, ST5 5NP
Tel: 01782-558000 **Fax:** 01782-558010
E-mail: ruthhamlett@computerpeople.co.uk
Website: http://www.computorpeople.co.uk
Bank(s): National Westminster Bank Plc
Managers: R. Hamlett
Immediate Holding Company: KPG COMPUTER HOLDINGS LIMITED
Registration no: 02378928 **VAT No.:** GB 451 9191 43
Date established: 1989 **No.of Employees:** 51 - 100 **Product Groups:** 80

D & K Motorcycle Sales Ltd

Swift House Liverpool Road, Newcastle, ST5 9JJ
Tel: 01782-861100 **Fax:** 01782-858433
E-mail: sales@dkmotorcycles.co.uk
Website: http://www.dkmotorcycles.co.uk
Managers: E. Mcdonald (Chief Mgr)
Immediate Holding Company: D K MOTORCYCLES LLP
Registration no: OC334576 **Date established:** 2008
No.of Employees: 51 - 100 **Product Groups:** 39, 40, 61, 68

Desmi Ltd

Norman House Unit 6a Rosevale Business Park, Newcastle, ST5 7UB
Tel: 01782-566900 **Fax:** 01782-563666
E-mail: desmi_ltd@desmi.com
Website: http://www.desmi.com
Bank(s): National Westminster Bank Plc
Directors: R. Flegg (MD), S. Withington (MD)
Ultimate Holding Company: DESMI A/S (DENMARK)
Immediate Holding Company: DESMI LIMITED
Registration no: 01389329 **VAT No.:** GB 318 8927 19
Date established: 1978 **Turnover:** £1m - £2m **No.of Employees:** 11 - 20
Product Groups: 39, 40

Date of Accounts	Dec 11	Dec 10	Dec 09
Working Capital	718	560	592
Fixed Assets	805	774	792
Current Assets	1m	2m	2m

Dupre Minerals

Spencroft Road, Newcastle, ST5 9JE
Tel: 01782-383000 **Fax:** 01782-636982
E-mail: info@dupreminerals.com
Website: http://www.dupreminerals.com
Bank(s): National Westminster, Hanley
Directors: R. Baylay (Sales), P. Tindall (Fin)
Managers: M. Officer (Personnel), S. Hill (Buyer)
Ultimate Holding Company: GOODWIN PLC
Immediate Holding Company: DUPRE MINERALS LIMITED
Registration no: 00632213 **Date established:** 1959 **Turnover:** £5m - £10m
No.of Employees: 21 - 50 **Product Groups:** 14, 17, 32, 33, 46

Date of Accounts	Apr 11	Apr 10	Apr 09
Sales Turnover	9m	6m	6m
Pre Tax Profit/Loss	824	446	44
Working Capital	169	838	915
Fixed Assets	933	226	163
Current Assets	5m	4m	3m
Current Liabilities	328	113	125

Edmundson Electrical Ltd

Spencroft Road, Newcastle, ST5 9JD
Tel: 01782-622234 **Fax:** 01782-711024
E-mail: newcastle_lime.150@eel.co.uk
Website: http://www.edmundson-electrical.co.uk/
Managers: A. Cotton (District Mgr)
Ultimate Holding Company: BLACKFRIARS CORP (USA)
Immediate Holding Company: EDMUNDSON ELECTRICAL LIMITED
Registration no: 02667012 **VAT No.:** GB 338 2468 41
Date established: 1991 **No.of Employees:** 21 - 50 **Product Groups:** 77

Date of Accounts	Dec 11	Dec 10	Dec 09
Sales Turnover	1023m	852m	788m
Pre Tax Profit/Loss	57m	53m	45m
Working Capital	256m	225m	184m
Fixed Assets	17m	3m	4m
Current Assets	439m	358m	298m
Current Liabilities	59m	38m	37m

F A B Systems Ltd

Unit 5 Newcastle Enterprise Centre High Street, Knutton, Newcastle, ST5 6BX
Tel: 01782-646593 **Fax:** 01782-659123
E-mail: mark@fabsystemsltd.co.uk
Website: http://www.fabsystemsltd.co.uk
Directors: M. Richards (MD)
Immediate Holding Company: F.A.B SYSTEMS LIMITED
Registration no: 04399374 **Date established:** 2002
Turnover: £250,000 - £500,000 **No.of Employees:** 21 - 50
Product Groups: 30

Date of Accounts	Mar 12	Mar 11	Mar 10
Working Capital	-0	-1	3
Fixed Assets	3	2	N/A
Current Assets	30	70	63
Current Liabilities	29	23	20

Fairey Industrial Ceramics

Lymedale Cross Lower Milehouse Lane, Newcastle, ST5 9BT
Tel: 01782-664420 **Fax:** 01782-664490
E-mail: filtersales@faireyceramics.com
Website: http://www.faireyceramics.com
Bank(s): National Westminster Bank Plc
Directors: T. Kelly (MD)
Ultimate Holding Company: LEONI AG (GERMANY)
Immediate Holding Company: LEONI PENSION TRUSTEES LIMITED
Registration no: 03928193 **Date established:** 2000 **Turnover:** £5m - £10m
No.of Employees: 51 - 100 **Product Groups:** 33, 36, 41, 42

Fans & Spares Ltd

Unit 2 Rosevale Road Parkhouse Industrial Estate West, Newcastle, ST5 7EF
Tel: 01782-579076 **Fax:** 01782-563592
E-mail: angi@systemair.co.uk
Website: http://www.fansandspares.co.uk
Managers: A. Gibson (Mgr)
Immediate Holding Company: FANS & SPARES LTD
Registration no: 07240936 **VAT No.:** GB 300 0687 11
Date established: 2010 **No.of Employees:** 1 - 10 **Product Groups:** 33, 39, 40, 48, 52

Date of Accounts	Apr 12	Apr 11	Apr 10
Sales Turnover	16m	14m	9m
Pre Tax Profit/Loss	763	-2m	-41
Working Capital	2m	1m	845
Fixed Assets	893	970	921
Current Assets	6m	6m	3m
Current Liabilities	619	665	273

Faraday Technology Ltd

Units 22-26 Croft Road Industrial Estate, Newcastle, ST5 0TW
Tel: 01782-661501 **Fax:** 01782-630101
E-mail: steve.farmer@faradaytech.co.uk
Website: http://www.faradaytech.co.uk
Directors: B. Lovatt (MD), S. Farmer (Fin)
Managers: A. Frost (Sales Prom Mgr), D. Simpson (Purch Mgr), A. Lewis (I.T. Exec), J. Holt (Sales Off Mgr), M. Pepper (Purch Mgr), N. Lewis (I.T. Exec), B. Pinxton (Sales Prom Mgr)
Immediate Holding Company: FARADAY TECHNOLOGY LIMITED
Registration no: 01854493 **VAT No.:** GB 402 0424 23
Date established: 1984 **Turnover:** £2m - £5m **No.of Employees:** 1 - 10
Product Groups: 37, 38

Date of Accounts	Nov 07	Nov 06	Nov 05
Working Capital	136	173	289
Fixed Assets	77	98	98
Current Assets	415	468	724
Current Liabilities	280	295	434

Fedex

Parkhouse Road East Parkhouse Industrial Estate East, Newcastle, ST5 7RB
Tel: 08456-000068 **Fax:** 01782-563302
E-mail: sales@anc.co.uk
Website: http://www.fedexuk.net
Managers: C. Groves (Mgr)
Ultimate Holding Company: FEDEX CORP (USA)
Immediate Holding Company: FEDEX UK LIMITED
Registration no: 01541168 **Date established:** 1981
Turnover: £125m - £250m **No.of Employees:** 251 - 500
Product Groups: 72, 76, 79

Date of Accounts	May 11	May 10	May 09
Sales Turnover	190m	182m	184m
Pre Tax Profit/Loss	16m	10m	7m
Working Capital	31m	24m	19m
Fixed Assets	23m	20m	18m
Current Assets	70m	61m	52m
Current Liabilities	22m	21m	17m

1st S G R

Garden Street, Newcastle, ST5 1BW
Tel: 0800-298 1979 **Fax:** 01782-614633
E-mail: sgrltd@btconnect.com
Website: http://www.sgr-glasscentre.co.uk
Directors: N. Pyatt (MD), M. Platt (Dir)
Immediate Holding Company: SAFETY GLASS REPLACEMENTS LIMITED
Registration no: 00316872 **Date established:** 1936
No.of Employees: 1 - 10 **Product Groups:** 26, 35

Date of Accounts	Jun 11	Jun 10	Jun 09
Working Capital	340	380	473
Fixed Assets	13	16	19
Current Assets	419	459	527

Fit-Lock Systems Ltd

Unit 3a Aspect Court Cannel Row, Silverdale, Newcastle, ST5 6SS
Tel: 01782-626450 **Fax:** 01782-614197
E-mail: sales@fitlocksystems.com
Website: http://www.fitlocksystems.com
Directors: N. Cruddos (MD)
Immediate Holding Company: FIT-LOCK SYSTEMS LIMITED
Registration no: 03091603 **VAT No.:** GB 639 0169 31
Date established: 1995 **No.of Employees:** 1 - 10 **Product Groups:** 35, 36

Date of Accounts	Aug 11	Aug 10	Aug 09
Working Capital	886	857	685
Fixed Assets	844	915	951
Current Assets	2m	2m	1m
Current Liabilities	N/A	600	N/A

Inspired Film & Video

I C 2 Building Keele University Science Park, Keele, Newcastle, ST5 5NH
Tel: 01782-613675 **Fax:** 01782-442834
E-mail: info@inspiredfilmandvideo.co.uk
Website: http://www.inspiredfilmandvideo.co.uk
Directors: D. Stubbs (MD)
Immediate Holding Company: INSPIRED FILM AND VIDEO LIMITED
Registration no: 05919449 **Date established:** 2006
No.of Employees: 1 - 10 **Product Groups:** 81, 89

Date of Accounts	Dec 10	Dec 09	Dec 08
Working Capital	20	15	16
Fixed Assets	3	7	11
Current Assets	33	25	21

Interdri Engineering Services

Unit 503 Lowfield Drive Centre 500, Wolstanton, Newcastle, ST5 0UU
Tel: 01782-633622 **Fax:** 01782-208122
E-mail: steve-hemmings@interdrieng.com
Website: http://www.interdrieng.com
Bank(s): HSBC
Directors: S. Hemmings (Prop)
Managers: K. Hemmings (Sales Prom Mgr)
Immediate Holding Company: INTERDRI MECHANICAL SERVICES LIMITED
Registration no: 08029605 **Date established:** 2012
Turnover: £250,000 - £500,000 **No.of Employees:** 11 - 20
Product Groups: 45

Date of Accounts	Jan 08	Jan 07	Jan 06
Working Capital	-18	-22	68
Fixed Assets	10	13	22
Current Assets	351	309	446
Current Liabilities	369	331	378
Total Share Capital	8	8	12

Intergas Ltd

Intergas House Speedwell Road, Parkhouse Industrial Estate East, Newcastle, ST5 7RG
Tel: 01782-565556 **Fax:** 01782-562882
E-mail: lhayes@intergasmail.com
Website: http://www.intergas.co.uk
Directors: L. Hayes (Dir)
Managers: F. Stanaway (Purch Mgr), G. Ellis (Personnel), I. Harding (Sales Prom Mgr), D. Millward (Chief Mgr)
Immediate Holding Company: STUART BOWLER HOLDINGS LIMITED
Registration no: 02679619 **Date established:** 1983 **Turnover:** £2m - £5m
No.of Employees: 21 - 50 **Product Groups:** 13, 31

Date of Accounts	Dec 10	Dec 09	Dec 08
Sales Turnover	71m	75m	69m
Pre Tax Profit/Loss	14m	48m	-5m
Working Capital	-171	-9m	-8m
Fixed Assets	162m	158m	165m
Current Assets	53m	36m	32m
Current Liabilities	4m	5m	5m

Internet Central Ltd

The Innovation Centre University of Keele, Keele, Newcastle, ST5 5NB
Tel: 01782-667788 **Fax:** 01782-667799
E-mail: sales@ic.co.uk
Website: http://www.netcentral.co.uk
Directors: M. Hyslop (MD), P. Ashley (Co Sec)
Ultimate Holding Company: GOODWIN PLC
Immediate Holding Company: INTERNET CENTRAL LIMITED
Registration no: 03079542 **Date established:** 1995 **Turnover:** £2m - £5m
No.of Employees: 11 - 20 **Product Groups:** 44, 79

Date of Accounts	Apr 11	Apr 10	Apr 09
Sales Turnover	2m	2m	2m
Pre Tax Profit/Loss	84	145	156
Working Capital	813	722	643
Fixed Assets	168	206	195
Current Assets	1m	1m	1m
Current Liabilities	132	163	184

J T Price & Co.

Holditch Road, Newcastle, ST5 9JG
Tel: 01782-562311 **Fax:** 01782-565654
Website: http://www.westlygroup.com
Directors: J. Salisbury (MD)
Managers: M. Richards (Fin Mgr)
Immediate Holding Company: SWEETMORE ENGINEERING HOLDINGS LTD
Registration no: 00160464 **VAT No.:** GB 318 8980 15
Date established: 1919 **Turnover:** £2m - £5m **No.of Employees:** 1 - 10
Product Groups: 34

Johnsons Photopia Ltd

Hempstalls Lane, Newcastle, ST5 0SW
Tel: 01782-753300 **Fax:** 01782-753399
E-mail: info@johnsons-photopia.co.uk
Website: http://www.johnsons-photopia.co.uk
Directors: T. Harrison (Fin), D. Harper (Chief Op Offcr)
Managers: M. Castle (Tech Serv Mgr), C. Calder (Mktg Serv Mgr)
Ultimate Holding Company: JOHNSONS PHOTOPIA GROUP LIMITED
Immediate Holding Company: JOHNSONS PHOTOPIA LIMITED
Registration no: 00365586 **Date established:** 1941 **Turnover:** £5m - £10m
No.of Employees: 51 - 100 **Product Groups:** 61

Date of Accounts	Dec 11	Dec 10	Dec 09
Sales Turnover	6m	7m	9m
Pre Tax Profit/Loss	332	555	1m
Working Capital	3m	3m	4m
Fixed Assets	23	53	93
Current Assets	4m	4m	5m
Current Liabilities	346	271	565

Langley Alloys Ltd

The Wharf 504-506 Lowfield Dr, Newcastle, ST5 0UU
Tel: 01782-610250 **Fax:** 01782-612219
E-mail: info@langleyalloys.com
Website: http://www.langleyalloys.com
Bank(s): Royal Bank of Scotland, Liverpool
Directors: J. Halliday (Ch)
Managers: I. McWirtler (Sales Prom Mgr)
Registration no: 03059791 **VAT No.:** GB 576 2202 47
Turnover: £5m - £10m **No.of Employees:** 21 - 50 **Product Groups:** 34, 35, 48

Latham International Ltd

Rowhurst Close Rowhurst Industrial Estate, Newcastle, ST5 6BD
Tel: 01782-565364 **Fax:** 01782-564886
E-mail: info@lathaminternational.com
Website: http://www.lathaminternational.com
Bank(s): Barclays
Directors: P. Latham (Dir)
Immediate Holding Company: LATHAM INTERNATIONAL LIMITED
Registration no: 02291707 **VAT No.:** GB 488 8783 57
Date established: 1988 **Turnover:** £2m - £5m **No.of Employees:** 11 - 20
Product Groups: 25, 29, 32, 35, 40, 41, 42, 45, 48, 54

Date of Accounts	Sep 11	Sep 10	Sep 09
Working Capital	853	511	40
Fixed Assets	113	349	378
Current Assets	2m	1m	1m

Leoni Wiring Systems Ltd

Lower Milehouse Lane, Newcastle, ST5 9BT
Tel: 01782-563366 **Fax:** 01782-604895
E-mail: gordon.clowes@leoni.com
Website: http://www.leoni.com
Bank(s): Barclays
Directors: G. Clowes (Fin), J. Grinrod (MD)
Managers: A. Gross (Comm), P. Smith (Mktg Serv Mgr)
Ultimate Holding Company: LEONI AG (GERMANY)
Immediate Holding Company: LEONI WIRING SYSTEMS U.K. LIMITED
Registration no: 03918171 **Date established:** 2000
Turnover: £125m - £250m **No.of Employees:** 101 - 250
Product Groups: 37

Date of Accounts	Dec 11	Dec 10	Dec 09
Sales Turnover	188m	153m	95m
Pre Tax Profit/Loss	21m	14m	755
Working Capital	47m	32m	22m
Fixed Assets	11m	11m	10m
Current Assets	110m	71m	45m
Current Liabilities	61m	38m	21m

Metanodic Engineers Ltd

Holditch Road, Newcastle, ST5 9JA
Tel: 01782-562231
E-mail: sales@metanodic-engineers.co.uk
Website: http://www.curtismixers.co.uk
Bank(s): HSBC
Directors: C. Miller (MD)
Immediate Holding Company: METANODIC (ENGINEERS) LIMITED
Registration no: 00460566 **Date established:** 1948
No.of Employees: 11 - 20 **Product Groups:** 36, 48

Date of Accounts	Dec 11	Dec 10	Dec 09
Working Capital	111	185	73
Fixed Assets	2m	2m	2m
Current Assets	234	329	151

Newlyme Controls Ltd

37-39 George Street, Newcastle, ST5 1JU
Tel: 01782-611144 **Fax:** 01782-619908
E-mail: info@newlyme.com
Website: http://www.newlyme.com
Bank(s): Barcleys

Directors: P. Cheetham (Dir), S. Jones (MD)
Managers: P. Littlejohn (Purch Mgr)
Ultimate Holding Company: Newlyme Controls Ltd
Registration no: 04978989 **VAT No.:** GB 278 7954 84
Date established: 2003 **Turnover:** £1m - £2m **No.of Employees:** 11 - 20
Product Groups: 37

Orbit Distribution Ltd
Unit 2 Lymedale Business Centre Hooters Hall Road, Lymedale Business Park, Newcastle, ST5 9QF
Tel: 01782-564757 **Fax:** 01782-561089
E-mail: info@orbitdistribution.co.uk
Website: http://www.orbitdistribution.co.uk
Managers: D. Mulliner (Sales Prom Mgr)
Immediate Holding Company: ORBIT DISTRIBUTION LIMITED
Registration no: 04070240 **Date established:** 2000 **Turnover:** £1m - £2m
No.of Employees: 11 - 20 **Product Groups:** 37, 44, 84

Date of Accounts	May 11	May 10	May 09
Working Capital	-4	-0	-4
Fixed Assets	38	22	26
Current Assets	679	498	418

Regina Industries Ltd
Brookhouse Road Parkhouse Industrial Estate West, Newcastle, ST5 7RU
Tel: 01782-565646 **Fax:** 01782-565610
E-mail: mbeardmore@regina.co.uk
Website: http://www.regina.co.uk
Bank(s): National Westminster Bank Plc
Directors: J. Goulding (Fin), M. Beardmore (MD)
Managers: C. Bester
Immediate Holding Company: REGINA INDUSTRIES LIMITED
Registration no: 00469468 **VAT No.:** GB 268 8985 35
Date established: 1949 **Turnover:** £2m - £5m **No.of Employees:** 21 - 50
Product Groups: 29, 30, 33, 42, 48, 66

Date of Accounts	Dec 11	Dec 10	Dec 09
Working Capital	458	447	437
Fixed Assets	1m	1m	1m
Current Assets	606	596	585

Richard Baker Harrison Ltd
Marsh Trees House Marsh Parade, Newcastle, ST5 1BT
Tel: 01782-622666 **Fax:** 01782-622655
E-mail: sales@whitson.co.uk
Website: http://www.whitson.co.uk
Bank(s): Bank of Wales PLC
Directors: D. Stuart (Sales), T. Smith (Co Sec)
Ultimate Holding Company: RICHARD BAKER,HARRISON LIMITED
Immediate Holding Company: WHITFIELD INTERNATIONAL LIMITED
Registration no: 02457767 **VAT No.:** GB 536 8567 05
Date established: 1990 **Turnover:** £5m - £10m **No.of Employees:** 11 - 20
Product Groups: 14, 31, 33, 42, 45, 67

Date of Accounts	Dec 10	Dec 08	Dec 07
Working Capital	50	50	-475
Fixed Assets	N/A	N/A	525
Current Assets	50	50	N/A

Scientific & Technical Gases Services
Units 1 & 2 Speedwell Road, Parkhouse Industrial Estate East, Newcastle, ST5 7RG
Tel: 01782-566897 **Fax:** 01782-564906
E-mail: info@stgas.eu
Website: http://www.stgas.eu
Directors: A. Addison (Dir)
Ultimate Holding Company: TWO WOLVES HOLDINGS LIMITED
Immediate Holding Company: SCIENTIFIC AND TECHNICAL GASES (SERVICES) LIMITED
Registration no: 06146208 **Date established:** 2007
No.of Employees: 1 - 10 **Product Groups:** 31, 38

SL Electrotech (inst) Ltd
Unit 6Loomer Road, Newcastle, ST5 7QQ
Tel: 01782-454126 **Fax:** 01782-564127
E-mail: info@slelectrotech.co.uk
Website: http://www.slelectrotech.co.uk
Directors: B. Pardoe (MD), H. Rai Thakral (MD)
Managers: K. Thakral (Fin Mgr)
Immediate Holding Company: S.L. Electrotech Ltd
Registration no: 01404654 **VAT No.:** GB 318 9327 38
Date established: 1978 **Turnover:** £250,000 - £500,000
No.of Employees: 1 - 10 **Product Groups:** 81

Date of Accounts	Dec 09	Dec 08	Dec 07
Working Capital	-6	-16	-27
Fixed Assets	1	2	1
Current Assets	5	8	3

T L P Ltd
Excellence House Dalewood Road, Lymedale Business Park, Newcastle, ST5 9QH
Tel: 01782-566030 **Fax:** 01782-566390
E-mail: sales@tlpgroup.co.uk
Website: http://www.tlpgroup.co.uk
Directors: A. Bowers (Fin), M. Bowyers (Dir), A. Jamieson (Fin)
Managers: A. Hudson
Ultimate Holding Company: PALLET EXPRESS SYSTEMS LIMITED
Immediate Holding Company: TLP LIMITED
Registration no: 02351060 **Date established:** 1989
No.of Employees: 21 - 50 **Product Groups:** 76

Date of Accounts	Apr 11	Apr 10	Apr 09
Working Capital	178	241	301
Fixed Assets	31	19	13
Current Assets	484	520	600

Vacucom Ltd
Unit 4b Aspect Court Cannel Row, Silverdale, Newcastle, ST5 6SS
Tel: 01782-660007 **Fax:** 01782-660009
E-mail: sales@vacucom.co.uk
Website: http://www.vacucom.co.uk
Directors: S. Cox (Dir)
Immediate Holding Company: VACUCOM LIMITED
Registration no: 03217160 **VAT No.:** GB 659 7965 55
Date established: 1996 **Turnover:** £500,000 - £1m
No.of Employees: 1 - 10 **Product Groups:** 40, 42, 45

Whitchem Ltd
23 Albert Street, Newcastle, ST5 1JP
Tel: 01782-711777 **Fax:** 01782-717290
E-mail: enquiries@whitchem.co.uk
Website: http://www.whitchem.co.uk
Bank(s): Bank of Scotland
Directors: C. Hawley (Fin)
Ultimate Holding Company: WHITFIELD CHEMICAL GROUP LIMITED
Immediate Holding Company: WHITCHEM LIMITED
Registration no: 02523537 **VAT No.:** GB 642 8301 52
Date established: 1990 **Turnover:** £10m - £20m
No.of Employees: 21 - 50 **Product Groups:** 32, 66

Date of Accounts	Dec 11	Dec 10	Dec 09
Sales Turnover	14m	12m	10m
Pre Tax Profit/Loss	892	736	536
Working Capital	1m	864	855
Fixed Assets	63	74	56
Current Assets	4m	3m	3m
Current Liabilities	1m	792	728

X-Traweld Ltd
Ebenezer House Ryecroft, Newcastle, ST5 2BE
Tel: 01782-374453 **Fax:** 01782-374453
Website: http://www.xtraweld.co.uk
Directors: G. Durston (MD)
Immediate Holding Company: X-TRAWELD SERVICES LTD
Registration no: 04654810 **Date established:** 2003
No.of Employees: 1 - 10 **Product Groups:** 35, 48, 66, 84

Date of Accounts	Apr 11	Apr 10	Apr 09
Working Capital	192	68	98
Fixed Assets	101	98	100
Current Assets	463	246	270

Rugeley

A D Certified Lifting Services Ltd
Unit 2 Riverside Power Station Road, Rugeley, WS15 2YR
Tel: 01889-576115 **Fax:** 01889-578953
E-mail: antoinette.woodward@adcertifiedlifting.co.uk
Website: http://www.adcertifiedlifting.co.uk
Directors: K. Raybould (MD)
Immediate Holding Company: A.D. CERTIFIED LIFTING SERVICES LIMITED
Registration no: 01500998 **VAT No.:** GB 345 9071 44
Date established: 1980 **Turnover:** £1m - £2m **No.of Employees:** 1 - 10
Product Groups: 45, 48, 84

Date of Accounts	Jul 11	Jul 10	Jul 09
Working Capital	9	13	49
Fixed Assets	8	19	16
Current Assets	107	108	135

A & R Electronic Developments Ltd
Unit A1 Trent Business Park Power Station Road, Rugeley, WS15 2WB
Tel: 01889-574980 **Fax:** 01889-574975
E-mail: rsol@arelectronics.co.uk
Website: http://arelectronics.co.uk
Directors: R. Soltysik (MD)
Immediate Holding Company: A. & R. ELECTRONIC DEVELOPMENTS LIMITED
Registration no: 02671135 **VAT No.:** GB 642 9677 02
Date established: 1991 **Turnover:** £1m - £2m **No.of Employees:** 1 - 10
Product Groups: 37, 44, 81, 84

Date of Accounts	Dec 11	Dec 10	Dec 09
Working Capital	404	998	956
Fixed Assets	632	12	13
Current Assets	461	1m	1m

Ability To Help
2 Pinetrees, Rugeley, WS15 1EQ
Tel: 01889-586673
E-mail: ability2help@aol.com
Directors: S. Mitchell (Prop)
Immediate Holding Company: SCOT MITCHELL LIMITED
Date established: 2002 **No.of Employees:** 1 - 10 **Product Groups:** 35, 39, 45

Date of Accounts	Jun 12	Jun 11	Jun 10
Sales Turnover	N/A	165	146
Pre Tax Profit/Loss	N/A	55	45
Working Capital	15	46	64
Fixed Assets	14	1	2
Current Assets	96	106	117
Current Liabilities	N/A	12	10

Aquacast Fabrications Ltd
Unit 3 Towers Business Park Wheelhouse Road, Rugeley, WS15 1UZ
Tel: 01889-572620 **Fax:** 01889-572629
E-mail: sales@aquacastltd.com
Website: http://www.aquacastltd.com
Directors: S. Hulse (MD)
Ultimate Holding Company: H & H PROPERTIES (RUGELEY) LIMITED
Immediate Holding Company: AQUACAST (FABRICATIONS) LIMITED
Registration no: 02962470 **Date established:** 1994
No.of Employees: 11 - 20 **Product Groups:** 34, 45, 52

Date of Accounts	Dec 11	Dec 10	Dec 09
Working Capital	37	24	36
Fixed Assets	86	99	77
Current Assets	749	789	600
Current Liabilities	320	N/A	245

Armitage Shanks Ltd (Ideal Standard)
Old Road Armitage, Rugeley, WS15 4KK
Tel: 01543-490253 **Fax:** 01543-491677
E-mail: merrickj1@aseur.com
Website: http://www.armitageshanks.co.uk
Bank(s): Lloyds TSB Bank plc
Directors: G. McFarlane (Fin), P. Cooper (Dir), P. Cooper (MD), P. Frankish (Mkt Research)
Managers: D. Papworth, P. Williamson, R. Moss (Commun Mgr), E. Ridgeway (Purch Mgr)
Ultimate Holding Company: Ideal Standard Holdings (BC) UK Ltd
Immediate Holding Company: ARMITAGE SHANKS LIMITED
Registration no: 00120158 **VAT No.:** GB 763 9284 90
Date established: 1912 **Turnover:** £2m - £5m **No.of Employees:** 21 - 50
Product Groups: 25, 30, 33, 36, 39, 63, 66

Date of Accounts	Dec 09	Dec 08	Dec 07
Sales Turnover	2m	2m	3m
Pre Tax Profit/Loss	2m	2m	1m
Working Capital	12m	11m	9m
Fixed Assets	3m	4m	5m
Current Assets	13m	11m	9m
Current Liabilities	578	820	357

Armitage Shanks
Armitage, Rugeley, WS15 4BT
Tel: 01543-490253 **Fax:** 01543-491677
E-mail: arm-idealinfo@idealstandard.com
Website: http://www.armitage-shanks.co.uk
Directors: S. Whitehead (MD)
Ultimate Holding Company: American Standard Inc
Registration no: 00120158 **Turnover:** £20m - £50m
No.of Employees: 101 - 250 **Product Groups:** 25, 30, 33, 36, 42

Barn Galleries
Parchfields Farm Trent Valley, Rugeley, WS15 3HB
Tel: 01889-586030 **Fax:** 01889-586030
Directors: M. Pope (Prop)
Immediate Holding Company: HITEC ENTERPRISES UK LIMITED
Registration no: 03209523 **Date established:** 1996
No.of Employees: 1 - 10 **Product Groups:** 35

Beckart Environmental International Ltd
62 Upper Way Upper Longdon, Rugeley, WS15 1QA
Tel: 01543-493189 **Fax:** 0870-383 5292
E-mail: enquiries@beckart.co.uk
Website: http://www.beckart.co.uk
Directors: B. Jones (Ptnr)
Immediate Holding Company: BECKART ENVIRONMENTAL INTERNATIONAL LIMITED
Registration no: 02686892 **Date established:** 1992
Turnover: £250,000 - £500,000 **No.of Employees:** 1 - 10
Product Groups: 32, 40, 42

Date of Accounts	Dec 11	Dec 10	Dec 09
Working Capital	89	96	86
Fixed Assets	N/A	N/A	1
Current Assets	143	142	133

Boommm Marketing Media Management
2 Penk Drive North, Rugeley, WS15 2XY
Tel: 01889-584972 **Fax:** 01889-800530
E-mail: postmaster@boommm.com
Website: http://www.boommm.com
Directors: P. Pallister (Fin), J. Pallister (MD)
Immediate Holding Company: BOO MARKETING & MEDIA MANAGEMENT LIMITED
Registration no: 04226250 **Date established:** 2001
Turnover: Up to £250,000 **No.of Employees:** 1 - 10 **Product Groups:** 81

Date of Accounts	May 11	May 10	May 06
Working Capital	-2	-8	-5
Fixed Assets	2	1	6
Current Assets	31	5	11

Digbits Ltd
1 Towers Business Park Wheelhouse Road, Rugeley, WS15 1UZ
Tel: 01889-503020 **Fax:** 01889-503021
E-mail: karen@digbits.co.uk
Website: http://www.digbits.co.uk
Directors: J. Clay (Dir)
Immediate Holding Company: DIGBITS LIMITED
Registration no: 02615482 **Date established:** 1991
No.of Employees: 11 - 20 **Product Groups:** 36, 39, 41, 42, 44, 45, 47, 48, 67, 68

Date of Accounts	Dec 11	Dec 10	Dec 09
Working Capital	-51	-17	55
Fixed Assets	2m	2m	2m
Current Assets	630	661	569

E G S Technologies
Unit 6 Waterside Business Park Wheelhouse Road, Rugeley, WS15 1LJ
Tel: 01889-583220 **Fax:** 07092-012948
E-mail: r.shapton@egstec.co.uk
Website: http://www.egstech.co.uk
Managers: R. Shapton
No.of Employees: 1 - 10 **Product Groups:** 38, 44, 80

Date of Accounts	Mar 12	Mar 11	Jan 10
Sales Turnover	N/A	N/A	509
Pre Tax Profit/Loss	N/A	N/A	-38
Working Capital	264	102	-24
Fixed Assets	24	21	26
Current Assets	377	274	232
Current Liabilities	N/A	N/A	82

E D L Lighting Ltd
Redbrook Lane, Rugeley, WS15 1QU
Tel: 01889-582112 **Fax:** 01889-584012
E-mail: sales@edl-lighting.co.uk
Website: http://www.edl-lighting.co.uk
Bank(s): HSBC
Directors: D. Taylor (Dir), J. Taylor (Fin)
Managers: W. Allen (Purch Mgr), N. Murray (Sales Prom Mgr)
Immediate Holding Company: EDL LIGHTING LIMITED
Registration no: 03772991 **VAT No.:** 738 8179 83 **Date established:** 1999
Turnover: £250,000 - £500,000 **No.of Employees:** 11 - 20
Product Groups: 37, 84

Date of Accounts	Sep 11	Sep 10	Sep 09
Working Capital	156	208	179
Fixed Assets	50	62	67
Current Assets	287	322	296

G Evans Services Ltd
Towers Business Park, Rugeley, WS15 1UZ
Tel: 01889-582096 **Fax:** 01889-570917
E-mail: online@gevans.co.uk
Website: http://www.gevans.co.uk
Directors: J. Gough (MD)
Managers: D. Farraday
Ultimate Holding Company: GOUGH GROUP HOLDINGS LIMITED
Immediate Holding Company: G.EVANS SERVICES LIMITED
Registration no: 03549255 **Date established:** 1998 **Turnover:** £2m - £5m
No.of Employees: 21 - 50 **Product Groups:** 52

Date of Accounts	Mar 11	Mar 10	Mar 09
Working Capital	994	738	588
Fixed Assets	40	80	1m
Current Assets	2m	3m	1m

Fleximas Ltd
Ashtree House Ashbrook Lane, Abbots Bromley, Rugeley, WS15 3DW
Tel: 01283-841800 **Fax:** 01283-841801
E-mail: enquiry@flexibulk.co.uk
Website: http://www.flexibulk.co.uk

see next page

Fleximas Ltd - *Cont'd*
Managers: S. Hendon (Mgr)
Registration no: 01361777 **VAT No.:** GB 554 9571 07
Date established: 1978 **Turnover:** £2m - £5m **No.of Employees:** 1 - 10
Product Groups: 23, 24, 29, 30, 41, 49, 61, 63, 66, 67

Injectaplas Ltd
Station Road, Rugeley, WS15 3HA
Tel: 01889-583335 **Fax:** 01889-583612
Website: http://www.plasticwheels.com
Directors: C. Wheelan (Prop)
Immediate Holding Company: INJECTAPLAS LIMITED
Registration no: 04628580 **VAT No.:** GB 599 4460 11
Date established: 2003 **Turnover:** £1m - £2m **No.of Employees:** 1 - 10
Product Groups: 30, 39

Date of Accounts	Dec 11	Dec 10	Dec 09
Working Capital	98	81	52
Fixed Assets	3	5	38
Current Assets	240	274	253

I S O Covers Ltd
Trent Valley Trading Estate Station Road, Rugeley, WS15 2HQ
Tel: 01889-574333 **Fax:** 01889-574111
E-mail: sales@isocovers.com
Website: http://www.isocovers.com
Bank(s): Nat West
Directors: J. Greaves (MD)
Immediate Holding Company: ISO COVERS LIMITED
Registration no: 05272904 **VAT No.:** GB 687 5869 52
Date established: 2004 **Turnover:** £250,000 - £500,000
No.of Employees: 21 - 50 **Product Groups:** 23, 33

Date of Accounts	Dec 11	Dec 10	Dec 09
Working Capital	338	340	364
Fixed Assets	25	30	34
Current Assets	586	547	629
Current Liabilities	61	40	83

Krypton Chemicals UK Ltd
Ashtree House Ashbrook Lane, Abbots Bromley, Rugeley, WS15 3DW
Tel: 01283-841805 **Fax:** 01283-841801
E-mail: enquiries@kryptonchemicals.co.uk
Website: http://www.kryptonchemicals.co.uk
Directors: S. Hendun (Dir)
Ultimate Holding Company: FLEXIBULK LIMITED
Immediate Holding Company: KRYPTON CHEMICALS UK LTD
Registration no: 03218949 **Date established:** 1996
No.of Employees: 1 - 10 **Product Groups:** 29, 30, 31, 33, 49, 52

L J W Air Conditioning Ltd
2 Post Office Lane, Rugeley, WS15 2UP
Tel: 01889-582422 **Fax:** 01889-583423
E-mail: paul@ljw.co.uk
Website: http://www.ljw.co.uk
Directors: L. Simkin (Fin), P. Simkin (MD)
Immediate Holding Company: LJW AIR CONDITIONING LTD.
Registration no: 03128237 **Date established:** 1995
Turnover: £250,000 - £500,000 **No.of Employees:** 1 - 10
Product Groups: 40

Date of Accounts	Dec 11	Dec 10	Dec 09
Working Capital	36	25	28
Fixed Assets	19	5	5
Current Assets	182	74	83

Langbow Ltd
222 Wolseley Court Towers Plaza Wheelhouse Road, Rugeley, WS15 1UW
Tel: 01889-575380 **Fax:** 01889-578872
E-mail: sales@langbow.com
Website: http://www.langbow.com
Directors: S. Hodson (Dir)
Immediate Holding Company: LANGBOW LIMITED
Registration no: 01147149 **VAT No.:** GB 112 1923 17
Date established: 1973 **Turnover:** £1m - £2m **No.of Employees:** 1 - 10
Product Groups: 46

Date of Accounts	Mar 12	Sep 10	Sep 09
Working Capital	167	193	212
Fixed Assets	20	33	46
Current Assets	241	344	272

Lyburn Supplies Ltd
Unit 36 Trent Valley Trading Estate Station Road, Rugeley, WS15 2HQ
Tel: 01889-577993 **Fax:** 01889-578638
E-mail: enquiries@lyburn.co.uk
Website: http://www.lyburn.co.uk
Directors: C. Willis (Sales), K. Willis (Sales)
Managers: F. Critchlow (Fin Mgr), T. Parr
Immediate Holding Company: LYBURN SUPPLIES LIMITED
Registration no: 05393425 **Date established:** 2005
No.of Employees: 11 - 20 **Product Groups:** 38, 42

Date of Accounts	Sep 11	Sep 10	Sep 09
Working Capital	-175	-240	-256
Fixed Assets	283	254	239
Current Assets	1m	1m	1m

Midland Pipeline Supplies Ltd
92 Old Eaton Road, Rugeley, WS15 2HA
Tel: 01889-585054 **Fax:** 01889-585194
Directors: M. Sanders (MD)
Immediate Holding Company: MIDLAND PIPELINE SUPPLIES LIMITED
Registration no: 02813095 **Date established:** 1993
No.of Employees: 1 - 10 **Product Groups:** 36, 37, 38

Date of Accounts	Jul 11	Jul 10	Jul 09
Working Capital	22	-28	-2
Fixed Assets	1	2	2
Current Assets	304	51	66

Paragon Lift Co. Ltd
PO Box 4878, Rugeley, WS15 9BB
Tel: 0121-693 1452 **Fax:** 0121-605 5554
Website: http://www.paragonlifts.co.uk
Directors: I. Ali (Co Sec), L. Embarba (Dir), R. Scrivens (MD)
Immediate Holding Company: PARAGON LIFT COMPANY LIMITED
Registration no: 03037875 **Date established:** 1995
No.of Employees: 1 - 10 **Product Groups:** 35, 39, 45

Date of Accounts	Aug 08	Aug 07	Aug 06
Working Capital	14	14	12
Fixed Assets	10	5	6
Current Assets	58	56	49
Current Liabilities	44	41	37

Rugeley Guns & Tackle
5 Market Square, Rugeley, WS15 2BL
Tel: 01889-579002
Directors: W. Probert (Prop)
Date established: 1983 **No.of Employees:** 1 - 10 **Product Groups:** 36, 39, 40

Smith Metal Centre
Power Station Road, Rugeley, WS15 2HS
Tel: 01889-576117 **Fax:** 01889-583976
E-mail: whitec@smithmetal.com
Website: http://www.smithmetal.com
Managers: M. Underhill (Site Co-ord)
Registration no: 03485838 **VAT No.:** GB 706 1581 51
No.of Employees: 1 - 10 **Product Groups:** 30, 34, 49, 66

Spraybooth Maintenance Services
14 Thorn Close, Rugeley, WS15 1TA
Tel: 01889-583908 **Fax:** 01889-583908
E-mail: office@spraybooth21.fsnet.co.uk
Website: http://www.spraybooth21.fsnet.co.uk
Directors: J. Whitehouse (Prop)
Immediate Holding Company: SPRAY BOOTH MAINTENANCE SERVICES LIMITED
Registration no: 04691980 **Date established:** 2003
No.of Employees: 1 - 10 **Product Groups:** 38, 42

Date of Accounts	Mar 11	Mar 10	Mar 09
Working Capital	52	58	57
Fixed Assets	12	N/A	N/A
Current Assets	83	91	92

Ultra Electronics Ltd (P M E S)
Towers Business Park Wheelhouse Road, Rugeley, WS15 1UZ
Tel: 01889-503300 **Fax:** 01889-572929
E-mail: enquiries@pmes.com
Website: http://www.ultra-electronics.com
Bank(s): The Royal Bank of Scotland
Directors: D. Sammons (Fin), J. Blogh (Dir)
Ultimate Holding Company: ULTRA ELECTRONICS HOLDINGS PLC
Immediate Holding Company: ULTRA ELECTRONICS LIMITED
Registration no: 02830644 **VAT No.:** GB 642 9909 07
Date established: 1993 **Turnover:** £10m - £20m
No.of Employees: 101 - 250 **Product Groups:** 37, 38, 45, 67

Date of Accounts	Dec 11	Dec 10	Dec 09
Sales Turnover	379m	313m	286m
Pre Tax Profit/Loss	59m	19m	24m
Working Capital	37m	-27m	15m
Fixed Assets	70m	76m	73m
Current Assets	208m	135m	160m
Current Liabilities	79m	68m	58m

Westley Controls
5 Market Square, Rugeley, WS15 2BL
Tel: 01889-586521 **Fax:** 01889- 575149
E-mail: westleycontrols@aol.com
Directors: A. Hill (MD)
Immediate Holding Company: WESTLEY PACKAGING MACHINERY LTD
Registration no: 01531528 **VAT No.:** GB 592 6085 15
Turnover: £250,000 - £500,000 **No.of Employees:** 1 - 10
Product Groups: 37, 38, 44

Stafford

A & A Automatics Ltd
4 Shop Lane Brewood, Stafford, ST19 9EB
Tel: 0845-466 7294 **Fax:** 0845-466 7295
E-mail: anthony@aaautomatics.wanadoo.co.uk
Website: http://www.aaautomatics.co.uk
Registration no: 04381685 **Date established:** 1990
Turnover: £500,000 - £1m **Product Groups:** 25, 30, 33, 35, 36, 45

Acorn Packaging Ltd
Unit 17c-17f Raleigh Hall Industrial Estate, Eccleshall, Stafford, ST21 6JL
Tel: 01785-851859 **Fax:** 01785-851831
E-mail: info@acornpackaging.com
Website: http://www.acornpackaging.com
Directors: K. Coffey (MD)
Immediate Holding Company: ACORN PACKAGING LIMITED
Registration no: 03082512 **Date established:** 1995
No.of Employees: 1 - 10 **Product Groups:** 28, 36, 67

Alpha Manufacturing Ltd
Pasturefields Lane Hixon, Stafford, ST18 0PS
Tel: 01889-270098 **Fax:** 01889-272042
E-mail: rob.eley@alphamanufacturing.co.uk
Website: http://www.alphamanufacturing.co.uk
Managers: R. Eley (Sales Prom Mgr), K. Barnacle (Personnel), T. Donkin (Purch Mgr), N. Andrews (Tech Serv Mgr), J. Aukim (Mktg Serv Mgr), J. Holyhead (Fin Mgr)
Immediate Holding Company: ALPHA MANUFACTURING HIXON LIMITED
Registration no: 02963616 **Date established:** 1994 **Turnover:** £5m - £10m
No.of Employees: 51 - 100 **Product Groups:** 34, 48

Date of Accounts	Aug 11	Aug 10	Aug 09
Sales Turnover	8m	6m	6m
Pre Tax Profit/Loss	232	-254	-57
Working Capital	266	60	335
Fixed Assets	1m	1m	2m
Current Assets	2m	2m	2m
Current Liabilities	441	421	503

Altecnic Ltd
Unit D C 3 Mustang Drive, Stafford, ST16 1GW
Tel: 01785-218200 **Fax:** 01785-218201
E-mail: sales@altecnic.co.uk
Website: http://www.altecnic.co.uk
Directors: A. Sherwin (MD)
Ultimate Holding Company: CALELLI SPA (ITALY)
Immediate Holding Company: ALTECNIC LIMITED
Registration no: 02095101 **Date established:** 1987
Turnover: £20m - £50m **No.of Employees:** 51 - 100 **Product Groups:** 29

Date of Accounts	Dec 11	Dec 10	Dec 09
Sales Turnover	29m	30m	28m
Pre Tax Profit/Loss	1m	1m	1m
Working Capital	4m	3m	2m
Fixed Assets	8m	8m	8m
Current Assets	16m	16m	14m
Current Liabilities	3m	4m	2m

Areva T&D UK Ltd
St Leonards Works St Leonards Avenue, Stafford, ST17 4LX
Tel: 01785-257111 **Fax:** 01785-257893
Website: http://www.areva.com
Directors: M. Williams (Fin)
Registration no: 02612364 **No.of Employees:** 1001 - 1500
Product Groups: 37, 80, 84

Areva T & D UK
Lichfield Road, Stafford, ST17 4LL
Tel: 01785-257111
Website: http://www.areva.com
No.of Employees: 501 - 1000 **Product Groups:** 37, 80, 84

B B Lift Engineers
Mount Pleasant Barn Acton Gate, Stafford, ST17 0RA
Tel: 01785-240576 **Fax:** 01785-240576
E-mail: brookes@bblifts.wannadoo.co.uk
Directors: T. Brookes (Prop)
Date established: 1989 **No.of Employees:** 1 - 10 **Product Groups:** 35, 39, 45

B H Holt & Sons Ltd
Wells Farm Bradley, Stafford, ST18 9EE
Tel: 01785-780250 **Fax:** 01785-780122
E-mail: mark@holtgb.com
Website: http://www.holtgb.com
Directors: L. Holt (Co Sec)
Immediate Holding Company: B.H. HOLT AND SONS LIMITED
Registration no: 03511774 **Date established:** 1998
No.of Employees: 1 - 10 **Product Groups:** 41, 45, 67

Date of Accounts	Mar 11	Mar 10	Mar 09
Working Capital	136	194	237
Fixed Assets	678	555	535
Current Assets	1m	696	1m
Current Liabilities	N/A	10	N/A

Bath Master Ltd
9 Silvester Way, Stafford, ST17 0PR
Tel: 01785-663377
Website: http://www.bathrepairs.net
Directors: S. Cooper (Fin), H. Cooper (MD)
Immediate Holding Company: BATHMASTER LTD
Registration no: 04717663 **Date established:** 2003
No.of Employees: 1 - 10 **Product Groups:** 46, 48

Date of Accounts	May 11	May 10	May 06
Working Capital	1	2	-0
Fixed Assets	1	1	2
Current Assets	9	12	3
Current Liabilities	N/A	10	N/A

Bostik Ltd
Common Road, Stafford, ST16 3EH
Tel: 01785-272727 **Fax:** 01785-257236
Website: http://www.bostik.com
Bank(s): HSBC, Leicester
Directors: T. Davidson (MD), K. Charlesworth (Fin), J. Boyle (Fin)
Managers: P. Hudson, L. Birch (Personnel), D. Marsden (Purch Mgr), P. Derby (I.T. Exec)
Ultimate Holding Company: TOTAL SAFETY INC (USA)
Immediate Holding Company: BOSTIK LIMITED
Registration no: 00068328 **VAT No.:** GB 113 7537 83
Date established: 2000 **Turnover:** £75m - £125m
No.of Employees: 251 - 500 **Product Groups:** 27, 29, 30, 31, 32, 33, 35, 37, 66

Date of Accounts	Dec 11	Dec 10	Dec 09
Sales Turnover	126m	124m	124m
Pre Tax Profit/Loss	4m	6m	2m
Working Capital	5m	6m	-592
Fixed Assets	52m	62m	59m
Current Assets	45m	45m	39m
Current Liabilities	10m	8m	9m

Broadcrown Holdings plc
Airfield Industrial Estate Hixon, Stafford, ST18 0PF
Tel: 01889-272200 **Fax:** 01889-272220
E-mail: info@broadcrown.co.uk
Website: http://www.broadcrown.co.uk
Bank(s): Royal Bank of Scotland
Directors: D. Borgman (MD)
Immediate Holding Company: BROADCROWN HOLDINGS PLC
Registration no: 03444600 **VAT No.:** 765 3387 01 **Date established:** 1997
Turnover: £50m - £75m **No.of Employees:** 101 - 250
Product Groups: 37, 52

Date of Accounts	Dec 11	Dec 10	Dec 09
Sales Turnover	57m	47m	37m
Pre Tax Profit/Loss	965	1m	442
Working Capital	10m	10m	10m
Fixed Assets	1m	1m	1m
Current Assets	29m	35m	26m
Current Liabilities	6m	4m	4m

C E P Ceilings Ltd
Common Road Industrial Estate Verulam Road, Stafford, ST16 3EA
Tel: 01785-223435 **Fax:** 01785-251309
E-mail: steven.ross@cepgroup.co.uk
Website: http://www.cepceilings.com
Directors: S. Ross (Fin)
Managers: A. Nichols (Sales Prom Mgr), P. Steadman (I.T. Exec)
Ultimate Holding Company: CEP REALITY LIMITED
Immediate Holding Company: CEP CEILINGS LIMITED
Registration no: 03244274 **VAT No.:** GB 670 3179 39
Date established: 1996 **No.of Employees:** 21 - 50 **Product Groups:** 33, 35, 40

Date of Accounts	Dec 11	Dec 10	Dec 09
Working Capital	1m	1m	979
Fixed Assets	90	124	158
Current Assets	2m	2m	2m
Current Liabilities	146	240	N/A

Carpet Time
47-49 Gaol Road, Stafford, ST16 3AR
Tel: 01785-252707 **Fax:** 01785-252707
E-mail: carpettime1@hotmail.co.uk
Website: http://www.carpettime.co.uk

Directors: S. Winfer (Prop)
Turnover: Up to £250,000 **No.of Employees:** 1 - 10 **Product Groups:** 23, 29, 40, 63

Chartley Coffee
Unit 22 Jupiter Business Park Airfield Industrial Estate, Hixon, Stafford, ST18 0PA
Tel: 01889-271600 **Fax:** 01889-500771
E-mail: enquiries@chartleycoffee.co.uk
Website: http://www.chartleycoffee.co.uk
Directors: O. Antcliff (Ptnr)
Immediate Holding Company: TATE & TATE LIMITED
Registration no: 03710630 **Date established:** 1999
No.of Employees: 1 - 10 **Product Groups:** 20, 40, 62, 63

Childcare Business Solutions
18 Kestrel Close, Stafford, ST17 0AY
Tel: 01785-211125 **Fax:** 01785-211125
E-mail: info@childcarebusinesssolutions.co.uk
Website: http://www.childcarebusinesssolutions.co.uk
Directors: J. Horsford (Dir), A. Horsford (Fin)
Registration no: 6058579 **Date established:** 2007
Turnover: Up to £250,000 **No.of Employees:** 1 - 10 **Product Groups:** 80, 81

Compact Data Management Ltd
6 Leons Way Tollgate Drive, Tollgate Industrial Estate, Stafford, ST16 3HS
Tel: 01785-220846 **Fax:** 01785-220876
E-mail: accounts@compact.uk.com
Website: http://www.compact.uk.com
Bank(s): HSBC Ban
Directors: S. Pearson (MD)
Immediate Holding Company: COMPACT DATA MANAGEMENT LIMITED
Registration no: 02740496 **VAT No.:** GB 669 9186 62
Date established: 1992 **Turnover:** £1m - £2m **No.of Employees:** 11 - 20
Product Groups: 44, 81

Date of Accounts	Sep 11	Sep 10	Sep 09
Working Capital	-2	-5	-5
Fixed Assets	7	9	15
Current Assets	75	83	88

Coperative Retail Logistics
Raleigh Hall Industrial Estate Eccleshall, Stafford, ST21 6JL
Tel: 01785-850831 **Fax:** 01785-851850
Website: http://www.acc-distribution.co.uk
Bank(s): Co-operative
Managers: D. Swain (), D. Swain, M. Shaw (I.T. Exec), P. Green (District Mgr), C. Packston (Sales Admin), J. Thomas (Trng Mgr)
Registration no: 01699460 **VAT No.:** GB 369 8554 84
Date established: 1983 **Turnover:** £20m - £50m
No.of Employees: 101 - 250 **Product Groups:** 62

Craig Tilsley & Son Ltd
Unit 7 Moorfields Industrial Estate, Cotes Heath, Stafford, ST21 6QY
Tel: 01782-791524 **Fax:** 01782-791316
Website: http://www.craigtilsley.co.uk
Directors: C. Tilsley (Dir)
Immediate Holding Company: CRAIG TILSLEY & SON LIMITED
Registration no: 02444912 **Date established:** 1989
No.of Employees: 11 - 20 **Product Groups:** 35, 36, 39

Date of Accounts	Dec 11	Dec 10	Dec 09
Working Capital	102	84	91
Fixed Assets	26	16	21
Current Assets	288	244	248

Daro Engineering Stafford Ltd
Unit 7a & 7b Dewick Depot Cannock Road, Brocton, Stafford, ST17 0SU
Tel: 01785-660391 **Fax:** 01785-665347
E-mail: office@daroengineering.co.uk
Website: http://www.daroengineering.co.uk
Bank(s): National Westminster Bank Plc
Directors: D. Brown (MD)
Immediate Holding Company: DARO ENGINEERING (STAFFORD) LIMITED
Registration no: 02492614 **VAT No.:** GB 369 8082 06
Date established: 1990 **Turnover:** £1m - £2m **No.of Employees:** 11 - 20
Product Groups: 48

Date of Accounts	Jul 11	Jul 10	Jul 09
Working Capital	84	75	84
Fixed Assets	75	87	101
Current Assets	300	257	231

De Dietrich Process Systems Ltd
Tollgate Drive Barlaston, Tollgate Industrial Estate, Stafford, ST16 3HS
Tel: 01785-609900 **Fax:** 01785-609899
E-mail: sales@ddpsltd.co.uk
Website: http://www.ddpsltd.co.uk
Bank(s): Midland Bank P.L.C, Durham
Directors: M. Bowen (Co Sec)
Managers: P. Riley (Nat Sales Mgr), R. Carter (Ops Mgr)
Ultimate Holding Company: FINANCIERE DE JAEGERTHAL
Immediate Holding Company: DE DIETRICH PROCESS SYSTEMS LIMITED
Registration no: 02838099 **VAT No.:** 592 7822 02 **Date established:** 1993
Turnover: £2m - £5m **No.of Employees:** 21 - 50 **Product Groups:** 33

Date of Accounts	Dec 11	Dec 10	Dec 09
Sales Turnover	4m	5m	3m
Pre Tax Profit/Loss	156	29	-1m
Working Capital	3m	3m	3m
Fixed Assets	54	111	167
Current Assets	4m	3m	4m
Current Liabilities	710	237	1m

E J P Agricultural Engineers
The Grange Shebdon, Stafford, ST20 0PX
Tel: 01785-280388 **Fax:** 01785-280388
Directors: E. Prinold (Prop)
Immediate Holding Company: NORTH SHROPSHIRE GRASS TRACK CAR CLUB LIMITED
Date established: 1979 **No.of Employees:** 1 - 10 **Product Groups:** 41

Date of Accounts	Oct 11	Oct 10	Oct 09
Working Capital	26	23	18
Fixed Assets	N/A	N/A	1
Current Assets	28	24	20

Elster Kromschroder
Ulster Buidling Tollgate Drive, Tollgate Industrial Estate, Stafford, ST16 3AF
Tel: 01785-275342 **Fax:** 01527-888821
E-mail: p.morris@kromschroder.co.uk
Website: http://www.jeavonsltd.co.uk
Bank(s): Deutsche Bank AG
Directors: P. Morris (Dir)
Immediate Holding Company: AUTOMATED WATER & EFFLUENT LIMITED
Registration no: 01966794 **Date established:** 1982
No.of Employees: 11 - 20 **Product Groups:** 35, 36, 38

Date of Accounts	Aug 11	Aug 10	Aug 09
Working Capital	644	557	425
Fixed Assets	74	77	76
Current Assets	964	897	738

E M S-Chemie UK Ltd
Darfin House Priestly Court Gillette Close, Staffordshire Technology Park, Stafford, ST18 0LQ
Tel: 01785-283739 **Fax:** 01785-607570
E-mail: welcome@uk.emsgrivory.com
Website: http://www.emschem.com
Directors: R. Williams (Fin)
Ultimate Holding Company: EMS-CHEMIE HOLDING AG (SWITZERLAND)
Immediate Holding Company: EMS-CHEMIE (UK) LTD
Registration no: 00568534 **Date established:** 1956
Turnover: £10m - £20m **No.of Employees:** 1 - 10 **Product Groups:** 23, 24, 30, 33

Date of Accounts	Dec 11	Dec 10	Dec 09
Sales Turnover	16m	13m	10m
Pre Tax Profit/Loss	626	685	370
Working Capital	3m	2m	2m
Fixed Assets	28	33	35
Current Assets	6m	5m	4m
Current Liabilities	584	564	238

First Impressions Europe Ltd
Cedar House 14 Hurstmead Drive, Stafford, ST17 4RX
Tel: 01785-623183 **Fax:** 01785-623184
E-mail: info@firstimpressionseurope.com
Website: http://www.firstimpressionseurope.com
Directors: M. Davis (MD), H. Davis (Fin)
Immediate Holding Company: FIRST IMPRESSIONS (EUROPE) LIMITED
Registration no: 04319975 **Date established:** 2001
Turnover: £250,000 - £500,000 **No.of Employees:** 1 - 10
Product Groups: 23, 24, 49, 63, 65, 81

Date of Accounts	Nov 11	Nov 10	Nov 09
Working Capital	-0	4	18
Fixed Assets	N/A	1	1
Current Assets	13	24	43

Formseal Ltd
Gorse Lane Knightley, Stafford, ST20 0JP
Tel: 01785-284808 **Fax:** 01785-284809
E-mail: info@formseal.co.uk
Website: http://www.formseal.co.uk
Directors: A. Wych (MD), M. Galaszia (Fin)
Immediate Holding Company: FORMSEAL LIMITED
Registration no: 02115493 **Date established:** 1987
Turnover: £500,000 - £1m **No.of Employees:** 1 - 10 **Product Groups:** 29, 30, 33, 35, 36, 49, 66

Date of Accounts	Jul 11	Jul 10	Jul 09
Working Capital	367	335	282
Fixed Assets	47	47	35
Current Assets	561	505	424

G N T Ltd
Mulberry House High Green, Brewood, Stafford, ST19 9BD
Tel: 01902-851 808 **Fax:** 01384-236929
E-mail: info@gnt.co.uk
Website: http://www.gnt.co.uk
Directors: B. Hall (MD), M. Griffith (Dir), W. Hall (MD)
Managers: P. Turley (Eng), F. Greening (Accounts)
Immediate Holding Company: G.N.T Ltd
Registration no: 01895522 **Turnover:** £1m - £2m
No.of Employees: 1 - 10 **Product Groups:** 44, 46, 84

Date of Accounts	Aug 08	Aug 07	Aug 06
Working Capital	155	195	190
Fixed Assets	8	N/A	33
Current Assets	185	297	237
Current Liabilities	30	101	46

George Bate Gumakers Stafford Ltd
7 Market Square, Stafford, ST16 2JN
Tel: 01785-244191 **Fax:** 01785-220181
E-mail: sales@bateofengland.co.uk
Website: http://www.bateofengland.co.uk
Directors: N. Cross (Dir)
Immediate Holding Company: GEORGE BATE GUNMAKERS (STAFFORD) LTD
Registration no: 01271275 **Date established:** 1976
No.of Employees: 1 - 10 **Product Groups:** 36, 39, 40

Date of Accounts	Mar 11	Mar 10	Mar 09
Working Capital	25	27	14
Fixed Assets	4	5	7
Current Assets	130	170	160

Goldstyle Limousines
84 Sidney Avenue, Stafford, ST17 4EN
Tel: 0791-528 2346
E-mail: ron@goldstylelimousines.co.uk
Website: http://www.goldstylelimousines.co.uk
Directors: R. Goldby (Prop)
Date established: 2006 **No.of Employees:** 1 - 10 **Product Groups:** 72

Industrial Electric Elements Ltd
Unit 7b Tollgate Industrial Park Beaconside, Tollgate Industrial Estate, Stafford, ST16 3HS
Tel: 01785-212561 **Fax:** 01785-259224
E-mail: sales@indelecelements.co.uk
Website: http://www.indelecelements.co.uk
Directors: D. Sheard (MD)
Immediate Holding Company: INDUSTRIAL ELECTRIC ELEMENTS LIMITED
Registration no: 04799505 **Date established:** 2003
Turnover: £500,000 - £1m **No.of Employees:** 1 - 10 **Product Groups:** 37, 40, 45, 46, 66

Date of Accounts	Jun 11	Jun 10	Jun 09
Working Capital	62	14	40
Fixed Assets	178	237	296
Current Assets	284	228	336

John Moore Tractor Parts Ltd
Ladford Covert Seighford, Stafford, ST18 9QG
Tel: 01785-282705 **Fax:** 01785-282664
E-mail: shirley.moore@johnmoore.co.uk
Website: http://www.johnmoore.co.uk
Directors: N. Moore (Dir)
Immediate Holding Company: JOHN MOORE (TRACTOR PARTS) LIMITED
Registration no: 01715561 **Date established:** 1983
Turnover: £500,000 - £1m **No.of Employees:** 11 - 20
Product Groups: 39, 40, 41, 42, 45, 66, 67, 68, 83, 84

Date of Accounts	Mar 11	Mar 10	Mar 09
Working Capital	2m	1m	1m
Fixed Assets	4m	4m	4m
Current Assets	2m	2m	2m

B E Jones
Unit F Weston House Salt Works Lane, Weston, Stafford, ST18 0JE
Tel: 01889-270709 **Fax:** 01889-270709
Directors: B. Jones (Prop)
Immediate Holding Company: KINGSTONE CIVIL ENGINEERING LIMITED
Registration no: 05597225 **Date established:** 2002
No.of Employees: 1 - 10 **Product Groups:** 26, 35

Date of Accounts	Mar 11	Mar 10	Mar 09
Working Capital	42	53	68
Fixed Assets	383	342	363
Current Assets	540	646	584

Kershaw & Co. Ltd
Hixon Industrial Estate Church Lane, Hixon, Stafford, ST18 0PY
Tel: 01889-270556 **Fax:** 01889-271295
E-mail: sales@kershaw-engineering.co.uk
Website: http://www.kershaw-engineering.co.uk
Directors: A. Kershaw (MD), M. Kershaw (Fin)
Immediate Holding Company: KERSHAW & CO. LIMITED
Registration no: 01970264 **VAT No.:** GB 435 5859 21
Date established: 1985 **Turnover:** Up to £250,000
No.of Employees: 1 - 10 **Product Groups:** 35

Date of Accounts	Jan 12	Jan 11	Jan 10
Working Capital	283	256	340
Fixed Assets	385	443	396
Current Assets	352	306	394

Kirklands Catering Equipment Ltd
North Walls, Stafford, ST16 3AD
Tel: 01785-259960 **Fax:** 01785-252266
Managers: J. Norman (District Mgr)
Immediate Holding Company: STAFFORDSHIRE BLIND
Registration no: 04154438 **Date established:** 2001
Turnover: Up to £250,000 **No.of Employees:** 1 - 10 **Product Groups:** 20, 40, 41

Kuhmichel Abrasiv Ltd
Friars Mill Friars Terrace, Stafford, ST17 4AU
Tel: 01785-252200 **Fax:** 01785-252100
E-mail: uk@kuhmichel.com
Website: http://www.kuhmichel.com
Directors: R. Scholtens (Dir)
Immediate Holding Company: KUHMICHEL ABRASIV LIMITED
Registration no: 06179029 **VAT No.:** GB 747 6132 21
Date established: 2007 **Turnover:** Up to £250,000
No.of Employees: 1 - 10 **Product Groups:** 14, 31, 33, 34, 40

Date of Accounts	Dec 11	Dec 10	Dec 09
Working Capital	1m	918	834
Fixed Assets	128	121	115
Current Assets	3m	2m	2m

MaxMax Ltd
Beech Grove Wootton, Eccleshall, Stafford, ST21 6HU
Tel: 0845-6066853 **Fax:** 01785-226767
E-mail: sales@maxmaxltd.com
Website: http://www.maxmaxltd.com
Registration no: 05268230 **Product Groups:** 22, 24, 36, 37, 38, 40, 41, 63, 66, 67

Mena Engineering UK Ltd
Unit 70 Elms Business Park Main Road, Great Haywood, Stafford, ST18 0RJ
Tel: 01889-883111 **Fax:** 01889-883222
E-mail: neil@menaengineering.co.uk
Website: http://www.menaengineering.co.uk
Directors: M. Elmore (MD)
Immediate Holding Company: MENA ENGINEERING (UK) LIMITED
Registration no: 04630711 **Date established:** 2003
Turnover: £500,000 - £1m **No.of Employees:** 1 - 10 **Product Groups:** 35

Date of Accounts	Jan 10	Jan 09	Jan 08
Sales Turnover	N/A	435	N/A
Working Capital	-24	-19	-2
Fixed Assets	28	38	44
Current Assets	49	83	79

Midway Material Handling
7 Pinewood Drive Little Haywood, Stafford, ST18 0NX
Tel: 01889-882014 **Fax:** 01889-882014
Directors: D. Kitson (Prop)
Date established: 1975 **No.of Employees:** 1 - 10 **Product Groups:** 35, 39, 45

N G W Fabrications Ltd
Unit 1l Airfield Industrial Estate, Hixon, Stafford, ST18 0PF
Tel: 01889-270003 **Fax:** 01782-373225
E-mail: ngwfabrications@aol.com
Website: http://www.ngwfabrications.fnet.co.uk
Directors: N. Warrilow (MD)
Immediate Holding Company: NGW FABRICATIONS LIMITED
Registration no: 06437238 **Date established:** 2007
No.of Employees: 1 - 10 **Product Groups:** 35

Date of Accounts	Nov 11	Nov 10	Nov 09
Working Capital	108	-1	-31
Fixed Assets	62	69	80
Current Assets	290	86	62

Nirvana Engineering Stafford Ltd
Dewick Depot Cannock Road, Brocton, Stafford, ST17 0SU
Tel: 01785-660700 **Fax:** 01785-661299
E-mail: russell.shaw@nirvana-engineering.com
Website: http://www.nirvana-engineering.com
Bank(s): Barclays

see next page

***Nirvana Engineering Stafford Ltd** - Cont'd*

Directors: R. Parkinson (Fin), R. Shaw (MD)
Ultimate Holding Company: MECHAN CONTROLS PLC
Immediate Holding Company: NIRVANA ENGINEERING (STAFFORD) LIMITED
Registration no: 02029584 **VAT No.:** GB 319 3469 42
Date established: 1986 **Turnover:** £1m - £2m **No.of Employees:** 11 - 20
Product Groups: 26, 30, 35, 46

Date of Accounts	Dec 11	Dec 10	Dec 09
Sales Turnover	2m	2m	1m
Pre Tax Profit/Loss	350	414	265
Working Capital	2m	2m	1m
Fixed Assets	53	51	59
Current Assets	2m	2m	1m
Current Liabilities	141	182	122

Noble Gates Ltd

Ivy House Farm Whiston, Penkridge, Stafford, ST19 5QH
Tel: 01785-714148 **Fax:** 01785-714148
E-mail: sales@noblegates.com
Website: http://www.noblegates.com
Directors: J. Noble (Fin), P. Noble (MD)
Immediate Holding Company: NOBLE GATES LIMITED
Registration no: 04467756 **Date established:** 2002
No.of Employees: 1 - 10 **Product Groups:** 26, 35

Date of Accounts	Jun 11	Jun 10	Jun 09
Working Capital	-0	-0	-1
Fixed Assets	14	19	25
Current Assets	38	40	42

P C D Maltron Ltd

Castle Fields New Port Road, Stafford, ST16 1BU
Tel: 08452-303265 **Fax:** 0845-230 3266
E-mail: sales@maltron.com
Website: http://www.maltron.com
Directors: P. Hobday (MD)
Immediate Holding Company: P.C.D. MALTRON LIMITED
Registration no: 01309051 **VAT No.:** GB 347 3443 51
Date established: 1977 **Turnover:** Up to £250,000
No.of Employees: 1 - 10 **Product Groups:** 44

Date of Accounts	Dec 10	Dec 09	Dec 08
Working Capital	92	105	101
Fixed Assets	2	2	1
Current Assets	120	133	134

Precious Washers Stafford Ltd

Unit 24 Wolseley Court, Staffordshire Technology Park, Stafford, ST18 0GA
Tel: 01785-227722 **Fax:** 01785-227744
E-mail: info@preciouswashers.co.uk
Website: http://www.preciouswashers.co.uk
Directors: D. Newton (MD)
Immediate Holding Company: PRECIOUS WASHERS (STAFFORD) LTD
Registration no: 07261362 **Date established:** 2010
No.of Employees: 1 - 10 **Product Groups:** 39, 40

Date of Accounts	Apr 11
Working Capital	-0
Current Assets	23

Rack & Shelf Labels

2809 Sharman Way, Gnosall, Stafford, ST20 0LX
Tel: 08448-009288 **Fax:** 08448-009289
E-mail: info@rackandshelflabels.co.uk
Website: http://www.rackandshelflabels.co.uk
Directors: R. Greeves (Dir)
Registration no: 05867871 **Date established:** 2006 **Turnover:**
No.of Employees: 1 - 10 **Product Groups:** 49

Red Products Ltd

Pagefields Summer Hill, Milwich, Stafford, ST18 0EL
Tel: 01889-505788
Website: http://www.redproducts.co.uk
Directors: K. Mayer (Dir)
Immediate Holding Company: RED PRODUCTS LIMITED
Registration no: 02857149 **Date established:** 1993
No.of Employees: 1 - 10 **Product Groups:** 38, 42

Date of Accounts	Jul 11	Jul 10	Jul 09
Working Capital	25	22	-5
Fixed Assets	5	5	6
Current Assets	45	45	67

Rowley Engineering Co. Ltd

Tollgate Industrial Estate, Stafford, ST16 3HS
Tel: 01785-223831 **Fax:** 01785-222764
E-mail: sales@roweng.com
Website: http://www.roweng.com
Directors: B. James (Dir), M. Watton (Dir), A. James (MD)
Immediate Holding Company: ROWLEY ENGINEERING COMPANY LIMITED
Registration no: 00997122 **Date established:** 1970
No.of Employees: 11 - 20 **Product Groups:** 26, 35

Date of Accounts	Mar 11	Mar 10	Mar 09
Working Capital	-98	-72	47
Fixed Assets	429	438	436
Current Assets	274	209	344

Sandmaster Ltd

Airfield Industrial Estate Hixon, Stafford, ST18 0PF
Tel: 01889-270695 **Fax:** 01889-271161
E-mail: james@sandmaster.com
Website: http://www.sandmaster.com
Bank(s): Royal Bank of Scotland
Directors: J. Morris Adams (Dir)
Ultimate Holding Company: SANDMASTER (UK) HOLDINGS LIMITED
Immediate Holding Company: SANDMASTER (UK) HOLDINGS LIMITED
Registration no: 06404070 **VAT No.:** GB 295 4243 39
Date established: 2007 **Turnover:** £5m - £10m
No.of Employees: 101 - 250 **Product Groups:** 33

Date of Accounts	Dec 11	Dec 10	Dec 09
Sales Turnover	10m	10m	8m
Pre Tax Profit/Loss	229	844	636
Working Capital	820	158	439
Fixed Assets	5m	5m	5m
Current Assets	3m	3m	3m
Current Liabilities	804	1m	2m

Schott UK Ltd

Drummond Road, Stafford, ST16 3EL
Tel: 01785-223166 **Fax:** 01785-223522
E-mail: info.uk@schott.com
Website: http://www.schott.com/uk
Bank(s): HSBC
Directors: A. Jones (Fin), J. Meadows (MD)
Managers: K. Walker (Tech Serv Mgr)
Ultimate Holding Company: SCHOTT AG (GERMANY)
Immediate Holding Company: SCHOTT UK LIMITED
Registration no: 01251097 **VAT No.:** GB 695 4391 89
Date established: 1976 **Turnover:** £2m - £5m **No.of Employees:** 21 - 50
Product Groups: 33

Date of Accounts	Sep 11	Sep 10	Sep 09
Sales Turnover	4m	4m	3m
Pre Tax Profit/Loss	-464	191	337
Working Capital	840	532	605
Fixed Assets	822	836	872
Current Assets	3m	2m	2m
Current Liabilities	513	347	140

Siebec UK Ltd

Unit 3 St Albans Business Park St Albans Road Industrial Estate, Stafford, ST16 3DR
Tel: 01785-227700 **Fax:** 01785-246006
E-mail: sales@siebec.co.uk
Website: http://www.siebec.com
Managers: N. Davies (Chief Mgr)
Immediate Holding Company: SIEBEC UK LIMITED
Registration no: 03142535 **Date established:** 1996
No.of Employees: 1 - 10 **Product Groups:** 33, 40, 41, 42

Date of Accounts	Dec 11	Dec 10	Dec 09
Working Capital	77	-15	-21
Fixed Assets	5	6	6
Current Assets	327	259	300

Simona UK Ltd

Unit 11 Telford Drive Tollgate Industrial Estate, Stafford, ST16 3ST
Tel: 01785-222444 **Fax:** 01785-222080
E-mail: sales@simona-uk.com
Website: http://www.simona.de
Directors: P. Eliades (Prop), L. Anderson (Co Sec)
Ultimate Holding Company: SIMONA AG (GERMANY)
Immediate Holding Company: SIMONA U.K. LIMITED
Registration no: 02439650 **Date established:** 1989
Turnover: £10m - £20m **No.of Employees:** 21 - 50 **Product Groups:** 30, 31

Date of Accounts	Dec 11	Dec 10	Dec 09
Sales Turnover	10m	10m	10m
Pre Tax Profit/Loss	209	197	104
Working Capital	983	758	3m
Fixed Assets	9	25	45
Current Assets	4m	4m	3m
Current Liabilities	563	690	616

Spiro Gills Thermal Products Ltd

St Albans Road Industrial Estate, Stafford, ST16 3DR
Tel: 01785-254554 **Fax:** 01785-259501
E-mail: steve.mottershead@spiro-gills.com
Website: http://www.spiro-gills.com
Directors: M. Lawrence (Co Sec), S. Mottershead (MD)
Managers: J. Freeman (Buyer), P. Hallam (Mktg Serv Mgr)
Immediate Holding Company: SPIRO-GILLS THERMAL PRODUCTS LTD
Registration no: 06529436 **Date established:** 2008
No.of Employees: 21 - 50 **Product Groups:** 36, 37, 40, 48, 66

Date of Accounts	Mar 09	Jun 11	Jun 10
Pre Tax Profit/Loss	277	N/A	N/A
Working Capital	582	105	264
Fixed Assets	356	268	308
Current Assets	3m	1m	1m
Current Liabilities	1m	N/A	N/A

Stafford Audi

Hurricane Close, Stafford, ST16 1GZ
Tel: 01785-250444 **Fax:** 01785-259444
E-mail: sales@staffordaudi.co.uk
Website: http://www.stafford.audi.co.uk
Managers: A. Coley (Sales Prom Mgr), A. Leigh (Comm), D. Poole (Mktg Serv Mgr), P. Druley (Chief Mgr)
No.of Employees: 21 - 50 **Product Groups:** 61

Stafford Couriers

1 North Avenue, Stafford, ST16 1NP
Tel: 01785-600113 **Fax:** 01785-600113
E-mail: stafford.couriers@ntlworld.com
Directors: P. Cope (Prop)
No.of Employees: 1 - 10 **Product Groups:** 79

Stafford Engineering Services Ltd

Gainsborough Works St Patricks Place, Stafford, ST16 2PN
Tel: 01785-220900 **Fax:** 01785-244897
E-mail: seswatkin@aol.com
Website: http://www.staffordengineering.co.uk
Bank(s): HSBC
Directors: C. Allsobrook (Ptnr), D. Watkin (Fin)
Immediate Holding Company: STAFFORD ENGINEERING SERVICES LIMITED
Registration no: 03911624 **VAT No.:** 747 9144 96 **Date established:** 2000
Turnover: £250,000 - £500,000 **No.of Employees:** 11 - 20
Product Groups: 46

Date of Accounts	Mar 11	Mar 10	Mar 09
Working Capital	27	-1	-3
Fixed Assets	56	75	73
Current Assets	180	172	157

Staffordshire Newspapers Ltd

The Publishing Centre Derby Street, Stafford, ST16 2DT
Tel: 01785-257700 **Fax:** 01785-253287
E-mail: mike.richardson@staffordshirenewspapers.co.uk
Website: http://www.staffordshirenewsletter.co.uk
Bank(s): Lloyds TSB Bank plc
Directors: M. Richardson (MD), J. Bannister (Co Sec)
Managers: A. Wynne, P. Whitelock, P. Lawrence (I.T. Exec)
Ultimate Holding Company: YATTENDON GROUP PLC
Immediate Holding Company: STAFFORDSHIRE NEWSPAPERS LTD.
Registration no: 00142592 **VAT No.:** GB 318 8490 32
Date established: 2016 **Turnover:** £2m - £5m **No.of Employees:** 21 - 50
Product Groups: 28

Date of Accounts	Dec 11	Dec 08	Dec 09
Sales Turnover	9m	9m	8m
Pre Tax Profit/Loss	181	-3m	-126
Working Capital	-4	556	391
Fixed Assets	16m	16m	16m
Current Assets	2m	2m	1m
Current Liabilities	1m	607	646

The Full Range At The Stove Barn

Sandon Lane Milwich, Stafford, ST18 0EG
Tel: 01889-505100 **Fax:** 01889-505598
Website: http://www.thefullrange.com
Directors: H. Hocknell (Ptnr)
Immediate Holding Company: THE FULL RANGE (MILWICH) LIMITED
Registration no: 07149488 **Date established:** 2011
No.of Employees: 1 - 10 **Product Groups:** 40

Tox Pressotechnik

Unit 21 Stafford Business Village Dyson Way, Staffordshire Technology Park, Stafford, ST18 0TW
Tel: 01785-887903 **Fax:** 01785-887027
E-mail: sales@tox-uk.com
Website: http://www.tox-uk.com
Managers: G. Hennessey (Sales Prom Mgr)
Immediate Holding Company: STONEFORGE GAMING LTD
Registration no: 02857928 **VAT No.:** GB 639 8259 87
Date established: 2011 **Turnover:** £500,000 - £1m
No.of Employees: 1 - 10 **Product Groups:** 35, 40, 46

Date of Accounts	Mar 11	Mar 10
Working Capital	4	1
Current Assets	20	19

Traction Equipment Stafford Ltd

Glover Street, Stafford, ST16 2NY
Tel: 01785-223355 **Fax:** 01785-211074
E-mail: call@tractionequipment.co.uk
Website: http://www.tractionequipment.co.uk
Directors: T. Bloomar (Ch)
Immediate Holding Company: TRACTION EQUIPMENT (STAFFORD) LIMITED
Registration no: 01048352 **Date established:** 1972
Turnover: £500,000 - £1m **No.of Employees:** 11 - 20
Product Groups: 35, 45, 72, 83

Date of Accounts	May 11	May 10	May 09
Working Capital	545	572	518
Fixed Assets	1m	1m	1m
Current Assets	691	666	656

Unitec Ceramics Ltd

Doxey, Stafford, ST16 1DZ
Tel: 01785-223122 **Fax:** 01785-212259
E-mail: sales@ucm-group.com
Website: http://www.ucm-group.com
Bank(s): Bank of Scotland
Directors: A. Gould (Fin), B. Davies (Mkt Research), J. Brundell (Dir)
Ultimate Holding Company: Universal Ceramic Materials P.L.C.
Immediate Holding Company: Ucm Group Ltd
Registration no: 02765381 **VAT No.:** GB 428 946 06
Date established: 1992 **Turnover:** £5m - £10m **No.of Employees:** 21 - 50
Product Groups: 31, 32, 33, 42, 48

Date of Accounts	Dec 07	Dec 06	Dec 05
Sales Turnover	5814	4400	4632
Pre Tax Profit/Loss	802	1447	1625
Working Capital	852	-708	1254
Fixed Assets	856	2337	2697
Current Assets	3646	2078	1883
Current Liabilities	2794	2786	629
ROCE% (Return on Capital Employed)	47.0	88.8	41.1
ROT% (Return on Turnover)	13.8	32.9	35.1

Viking Garden Buildings

Greyfriars Place, Stafford, ST16 2SD
Tel: 01785-252277 **Fax:** 01782-207645
E-mail: vikinggb@hotmail.com
Website: http://www.vikinggardenbuildings.com
Directors: D. Tippett (Dir)
Immediate Holding Company: PEACH PROPERTY COMPANY LLP
Registration no: 05110039 **Date established:** 2008
No.of Employees: 1 - 10 **Product Groups:** 33, 35, 66

Date of Accounts	Jun 11	Jun 10	Jun 09
Working Capital	-5	1	1
Fixed Assets	156	160	165
Current Assets	30	37	42

Web2View

Kate Salsbury 40 Aldersleigh Drive, Wildwood, Stafford, ST17 4RY
Tel: 01785-665845
E-mail: kate@web2view.co.uk
Website: http://www.web2view.co.uk
Directors: K. Salsbury (Prop)
Date established: 2006 **Turnover:** £250,000 - £500,000
No.of Employees: 11 - 20 **Product Groups:** 44

Stoke On Trent

4-Tec Fabrications

Unit 1 Cockshute Industrial Estate Shelton New Road, Stoke On Trent, ST4 7AW
Tel: 01782-263645 **Fax:** 01782-744351
E-mail: fourtecfabs@aol.com
Website: http://www.4tecsteelfabrications.com
Bank(s): National Westminster Bank Plc
Directors: M. Bourne (MD)
Immediate Holding Company: FOUR-TEC FABRICATIONS LIMITED
Registration no: 01866440 **VAT No.:** GB 402 0506 21
Date established: 1984 **Turnover:** £1m - £2m **No.of Employees:** 21 - 50
Product Groups: 48

Date of Accounts	Apr 11	Apr 10	Apr 09
Working Capital	94	144	130
Fixed Assets	72	70	72
Current Assets	317	380	366

A C M S Packaging Ltd

Unit 29 Blythe Park Cresswell Lane Cresswell, Stoke On Trent, ST11 9RD
Tel: 01782-388999 **Fax:** 01782-397323
E-mail: sales@acms-mkt.com
Directors: S. Hoad (Sales), S. Hold (Dir)
Immediate Holding Company: ACMS PACKAGING LIMITED
Registration no: 05914704 **Date established:** 2006
No.of Employees: 1 - 10 **Product Groups:** 38, 42

Date of Accounts	Sep 12	Sep 11	Sep 10
Working Capital	-3	-1	N/A
Fixed Assets	30	30	13

Current Assets	179	324	183

A M Fabrications Stoke-On-Trent Ltd

7 Britannia Park Industrial Estate North Road, Stoke On Trent, ST6 2PZ
Tel: 01782-269990 **Fax:** 01782-205177
E-mail: sales@amfabs.co.uk
Directors: S. Ward (Fin)
Immediate Holding Company: A.M. FABRICATIONS (S-O-T) LIMITED
Registration no: 03286058 **Date established:** 1996
Turnover: £250,000 - £500,000 **No.of Employees:** 11 - 20
Product Groups: 37, 40, 48

Date of Accounts	Dec 11	Dec 10	Dec 09
Sales Turnover	N/A	412	599
Pre Tax Profit/Loss	N/A	-47	2
Working Capital	13	32	78
Fixed Assets	18	12	14
Current Assets	128	142	197
Current Liabilities	16	32	19

A R Brown Mcfarlane & Company Ltd

Ladywell Works New Century Street, Stoke On Trent, ST1 5QH
Tel: 01782-289909 **Fax:** 01782-289804
E-mail: sales@brownmac.co.uk
Website: http://www.brownmac.com
Bank(s): Bank of Scotland, Glasgow
Directors: I. Johnson (Sales), L. Morris (Pers)
Ultimate Holding Company: A.R.BROWN,MCFARLANE & COMPANY, LIMITED
Immediate Holding Company: A.R.BROWN,MCFARLANE & COMPANY, LIMITED
Registration no: SC015906 **Date established:** 1930
Turnover: £10m - £20m **No.of Employees:** 51 - 100 **Product Groups:** 34

Date of Accounts	Mar 11	Mar 10	Mar 09
Sales Turnover	54m	37m	56m
Pre Tax Profit/Loss	2m	-362	3m
Working Capital	10m	9m	11m
Fixed Assets	6m	6m	4m
Current Assets	27m	18m	25m
Current Liabilities	2m	907	2m

A S D Metal Services plc

Berry Hill Road Berryhill Trading Estate, Stoke On Trent, ST4 2NL
Tel: 01782-220600 **Fax:** 01782-220609
E-mail: stoke@asdmetalservices.co.uk
Website: http://www.asdmetalservices.co.uk
Directors: A. Macdonald (Dir), M. Joyce (Fin)
Ultimate Holding Company: KLOCKNER UK HOLDINGS LTD
Immediate Holding Company: ASD METAL SERVICES LIMITED
Registration no: 02680562 **VAT No.:** GB 176 2423 63
Date established: 1992 **No.of Employees:** 1 - 10 **Product Groups:** 66

A S D Metal Services plc

Tunstall Road Biddulph, Stoke On Trent, ST8 6JZ
Tel: 01782-515152 **Fax:** 01782-522240
E-mail: lturtle@asdmetalservices.co.uk
Website: http://www.asdplc.co.uk
Bank(s): National Westminster Bank Plc
Managers: L. Turtle (Chief Mgr)
Ultimate Holding Company: BALLI KLOCKNER
Immediate Holding Company: ASD METAL SERVICES LIMITED
Registration no: 02680562 **Date established:** 1992
Turnover: £20m - £50m **No.of Employees:** 11 - 20 **Product Groups:** 34, 35

A W G Saw & Tool

185 King Street, Stoke On Trent, ST4 3ER
Tel: 01782-335000 **Fax:** 01782-320991
E-mail: awkgreen@aol.com
Directors: A. Green (Prop)
Date established: 1999 **No.of Employees:** 1 - 10 **Product Groups:** 46, 48

Aalco

Unit F Brown Lees Road Industrial Estate Forge Way, Knypersley, Stoke On Trent, ST8 7DN
Tel: 01782-375700 **Fax:** 01782-375701
E-mail: info@aalco.co.uk
Website: http://www.aalco.co.uk
Bank(s): National Westminster
Managers: C. Hellawell (Chief Mgr)
Ultimate Holding Company: UK STEELSTOCK LTD
Immediate Holding Company: AMARI METALS LTD
Registration no: 03551533 **Date established:** 2001
Turnover: £125m - £250m **No.of Employees:** 11 - 20
Product Groups: 34, 35, 36, 66

Active Industrial Services

The Genisis Centre North Staffs Enterprise Centre Innovation Way, Stoke On Trent, ST6 4BF
Tel: 08702-430969 **Fax:** 0870-243 0970
E-mail: warrington@advance-industrial.co.uk
Website: http://www.active-industrial.co.uk
Directors: T. Millband (MD), K. Maher (Fin)
Ultimate Holding Company: ACTIVE INDUSTRIAL SERVICES GROUP LIMITED
Immediate Holding Company: ACTIVE INDUSTRIAL ENGINEERING LIMITED
Registration no: 06312932 **Date established:** 2007
Turnover: £500,000 - £1m **No.of Employees:** 21 - 50
Product Groups: 40, 48, 72

Date of Accounts	Dec 11	Dec 10	Dec 09
Sales Turnover	N/A	384	551
Pre Tax Profit/Loss	N/A	-124	7
Working Capital	78	-6	-234
Fixed Assets	115	82	N/A
Current Assets	596	200	447
Current Liabilities	N/A	41	25

Addstone Cast Stone

Addstone Way Off Anchor Road, Stoke On Trent, ST3 5BL
Tel: 01785-878402 **Fax:** 01785-819958
E-mail: admin1@addstone.co.uk
Website: http://www.addstone.co.uk
Directors: J. Adams (MD)
Managers: J. Adams (Sales Prom Mgr)
Immediate Holding Company: ADDSTONE LIMITED
Registration no: 05783970 **Date established:** 2006 **Turnover:** £1m - £2m
No.of Employees: 1 - 10 **Product Groups:** 33

Aerosol & Fluid Technology Ltd

8 Berry Hill Road Berryhill Trading Estate, Stoke On Trent, ST4 2NL
Tel: 01782-285700 **Fax:** 01782-284700
E-mail: sales@aft-ltd.com
Website: http://www.aft-ltd.com
Directors: J. Harding (Co Sec), G. Rduch (MD), S. Moore (Co Sec)
Managers: A. Wardle (Sales Prom Mgr)
Immediate Holding Company: AEROSOL AND FLUID TECHNOLOGY LIMITED
Registration no: 03106936 **Date established:** 1995
No.of Employees: 11 - 20 **Product Groups:** 32, 54, 63

Date of Accounts	Mar 11	Mar 10	Mar 09
Working Capital	946	456	10
Fixed Assets	284	249	263
Current Assets	3m	2m	1m

Aerotherm Ltd

Unit 1 Portland Works Sutherland Road, Stoke On Trent, ST3 1HS
Tel: 01782-599157 **Fax:** 01782-317757
E-mail: sales@aerotherm.co.uk
Website: http://www.aerotherm.co.uk
Directors: D. Taylor (Dir)
Immediate Holding Company: AEROTHERM LIMITED
Registration no: 06578690 **Date established:** 2008
No.of Employees: 1 - 10 **Product Groups:** 40, 41, 48, 52

Alfatex UK Ltd

Office 27 Chatterley Whitfield Enterprise Park Chatterley, Stoke On Trent, ST6 8UW
Tel: 08456-030516 **Fax:** 01782-815161
E-mail: info@alfatex.co.uk
Website: http://www.alfatex.co.uk
Managers: S. Franklin (Sales Admin)
Immediate Holding Company: ALFATEX UK LTD
Registration no: 05606322 **Date established:** 2005
No.of Employees: 1 - 10 **Product Groups:** 22, 23, 24, 26, 27, 29, 30, 32, 35, 37, 38, 39, 42, 45, 46, 49, 52, 63, 66, 67, 68, 85

Date of Accounts	Dec 10	Dec 08	Dec 07
Working Capital	-110	-29	-37
Fixed Assets	N/A	N/A	1
Current Assets	90	143	55

Alliance Technical Services Ltd

38 Hampton Street Joiners Square Industrial Estate, Stoke On Trent, ST1 3EX
Tel: 01782-206264 **Fax:** 01782-825878
E-mail: sales@alliancetechnicalservices.com
Website: http://www.alliancetechnicalservices.com
Directors: D. Lowe (MD)
Immediate Holding Company: ALLIANCE TECHNICAL SERVICES LIMITED
Registration no: 03666978 **Date established:** 1998
No.of Employees: 1 - 10 **Product Groups:** 52

Date of Accounts	Nov 11	Nov 10	Nov 09
Working Capital	-11	-4	10
Fixed Assets	16	20	16
Current Assets	71	41	56

Alpha Pest Control Ltd

67 Heron Street, Stoke On Trent, ST4 3AR
Tel: 01782-343536 **Fax:** 01782-336366
E-mail: info@alphapest.co.uk
Website: http://www.alphapest.co.uk
Directors: M. Flynn (Dir), S. Cooper (Fin)
Immediate Holding Company: ALPHA PEST CONTROL LIMITED
Registration no: 02972314 **Date established:** 1994
No.of Employees: 11 - 20 **Product Groups:** 52

Date of Accounts	Mar 11	Mar 10	Mar 09
Working Capital	168	143	105
Fixed Assets	227	207	115
Current Assets	258	199	149

Alphatech International

70 Tarragon Drive, Stoke On Trent, ST3 7YE
Tel: 01782-388430 **Fax:** 01782-388432
E-mail: sales@alphatech-int.co.uk
Website: http://www.alphatech-int.co.uk
Directors: M. Murray (MD), M. Murray (Fin)
Immediate Holding Company: ALPHATECH INTERNATIONAL LTD
Registration no: 03528234 **VAT No.:** GB 729 9868 56
Date established: 1998 **Turnover:** £1m - £2m **No.of Employees:** 1 - 10
Product Groups: 38, 40

Date of Accounts	Dec 11	Dec 10	Dec 09
Working Capital	48	48	48
Fixed Assets	2	3	2
Current Assets	63	51	64
Current Liabilities	3	1	N/A

Alton Precision Engineering Ltd

Unit 27a Chemical Lane, Stoke On Trent, ST6 4PB
Tel: 01782-813735 **Fax:** 01782-813752
E-mail: altonpre@clara.co.uk
Website: http://www.clara.co.uk
Bank(s): Barclays
Directors: I. Walker (Dir), J. Walker (Fin)
Immediate Holding Company: ALTON PRECISION ENGINEERING LIMITED
Registration no: 02171235 **VAT No.:** GB 478 7508 91
Date established: 1987 **Turnover:** £500,000 - £1m
No.of Employees: 11 - 20 **Product Groups:** 48

Date of Accounts	Oct 11	Oct 10	Oct 09
Working Capital	160	101	66
Fixed Assets	365	282	256
Current Assets	480	342	256

Anderson Engineering Solutions

Unit 1 Reginald Street, Stoke On Trent, ST6 1DU
Tel: 01782-822322 **Fax:** 01782-822233
E-mail: info@aesolutions.co.uk
Website: http://www.aesolutions.co.uk
Directors: C. Anderson (Dir), L. Anderson (Fin)
Immediate Holding Company: ANDERSON ENGINEERING SOLUTIONS LIMITED
Registration no: 04775044 **Date established:** 2003
No.of Employees: 1 - 10 **Product Groups:** 35, 39

Date of Accounts	Dec 11	Dec 10	Dec 09
Working Capital	97	54	40
Fixed Assets	43	18	22
Current Assets	366	205	187

Andrews Sykes Hire Ltd

290 Leek Road, Stoke On Trent, ST4 2EJ
Tel: 01782-263864 **Fax:** 01782-208340
E-mail: mark.dobson@andrews-sykes.com
Website: http://www.andrews-sykes.com
Managers: M. Dobson (District Mgr)
Immediate Holding Company: ANDREWS SYKES HIRE LIMITED
Registration no: 02985657 **VAT No.:** GB 100 4295 24
Date established: 1994 **Turnover:** £20m - £50m **No.of Employees:** 1 - 10
Product Groups: 40

Date of Accounts	Dec 11	Dec 10	Dec 09
Sales Turnover	35m	36m	34m
Pre Tax Profit/Loss	10m	10m	8m
Working Capital	8m	6m	2m
Fixed Assets	7m	7m	9m
Current Assets	33m	35m	35m
Current Liabilities	7m	7m	5m

Auto Vent Stoke On Trent Ltd

Sandbach Road, Stoke On Trent, ST6 2DG
Tel: 01782-281505 **Fax:** 01782-202483
E-mail: sales@auto-vent.co.uk
Website: http://www.autovent.co.uk
Bank(s): Barclays, Hanley
Directors: L. Gray (Dir)
Immediate Holding Company: AUTO-VENT (STOKE-ON-TRENT) LTD
Registration no: 00469582 **VAT No.:** GB 278 3143 44
Date established: 1949 **Turnover:** £250,000 - £500,000
No.of Employees: 11 - 20 **Product Groups:** 35, 36, 40, 45, 48

Date of Accounts	Dec 11	Dec 10	Dec 09
Working Capital	113	140	128
Fixed Assets	75	55	61
Current Assets	372	240	274

Autobox

101-107 Uttoxeter Road, Stoke On Trent, ST3 1PF
Tel: 01782-313492 **Fax:** 01782-593131
E-mail: sales@auto-box.co.uk
Website: http://www.auto-box.co.uk
Directors: N. Pickin (Ptnr)
No.of Employees: 1 - 10 **Product Groups:** 31, 35, 39, 68

Aynsley China Ltd

Sutherland Road, Stoke On Trent, ST3 1HZ
Tel: 01782-339400 **Fax:** 01782-339401
E-mail: admin@aynsley.co.uk
Website: http://www.aynsley.co.uk
Directors: J. Sharkey (Fin), J. Maguire (MD)
Managers: J. Wallis (Sales Prom Mgr), M. Bisson (Comptroller), M. Holmes (Ops Mgr)
Ultimate Holding Company: FOSSGATE LIMITED (ISLE OF MAN)
Immediate Holding Company: AYNSLEY CHINA LIMITED
Registration no: 00277828 **VAT No.:** GB 478 7788 59
Date established: 1933 **Turnover:** £2m - £5m **No.of Employees:** 21 - 50
Product Groups: 33

Date of Accounts	Mar 12	Mar 11	Mar 10
Sales Turnover	4m	4m	3m
Pre Tax Profit/Loss	-203	-262	-357
Working Capital	2m	2m	2m
Fixed Assets	2m	2m	2m
Current Assets	3m	3m	3m
Current Liabilities	186	278	312

B H W Ceramics Ltd

Adelaide Street, Stoke On Trent, ST6 2BD
Tel: 01782-813855 **Fax:** 01782-575647
E-mail: info@bhwceramics.co.uk
Website: http://www.bhwceramics.co.uk
Directors: J. Flower (Fin)
Immediate Holding Company: B.H.W. CERAMICS LIMITED
Registration no: 01137724 **Date established:** 1973
Turnover: £10m - £20m **No.of Employees:** 1 - 10 **Product Groups:** 33

Date of Accounts	Dec 11	Dec 10	Dec 09
Working Capital	498	697	640
Fixed Assets	648	613	649
Current Assets	569	820	794

B I S Trent Rosettes

Unit 2 Railway Enterprise Centre Shelton New Road, Stoke On Trent, ST4 7SH
Tel: 01782-279797 **Fax:** 01782-279797
E-mail: bistrent@gmail.com
Directors: C. Davies (Prop)
VAT No.: GB 307 4072 83 **No.of Employees:** 1 - 10 **Product Groups:** 23

W G Ball Ltd

Longton Mill Anchor Road, Stoke On Trent, ST3 1JW
Tel: 01782-313956 **Fax:** 01782-598148
E-mail: sales@wgball.com
Website: http://www.wgball.com
Bank(s): National Westminster Bank Plc
Directors: J. Bull (MD)
Managers: D. Gurskyj (Mgr)
Immediate Holding Company: W.G.BALL LIMITED
Registration no: 00539046 **VAT No.:** GB 278 4524 27
Date established: 1954 **Turnover:** £1m - £2m **No.of Employees:** 11 - 20
Product Groups: 32

Date of Accounts	Sep 11	Sep 10	Sep 09
Working Capital	1m	1m	1m
Fixed Assets	224	243	258
Current Assets	2m	2m	2m

Beaufort Road Forage Co. Ltd

14 Oswald Avenue, Stoke On Trent, ST3 5HW
Tel: 01782-313421 **Fax:** 01782-313421
Website: http://www.beaufortforage-packaging.co.uk
Directors: R. Newton (MD)
Immediate Holding Company: BEAUFORT ROAD FORAGE CO. LIMITED(THE)
Registration no: 00378874 **Date established:** 1943
No.of Employees: 1 - 10 **Product Groups:** 38, 42

Date of Accounts	Mar 11	Mar 10	Mar 09
Working Capital	6	2	3
Fixed Assets	1	1	1
Current Assets	18	14	12
Current Liabilities	3	1	N/A

D Bennett
Campbell Road, Stoke On Trent, ST4 4DX
Tel: 01782-747166 **Fax:** 01782-744299
E-mail: enquiries@davidbennettceramicservices.co.uk
Directors: D. Bennett (Prop)
Immediate Holding Company: ROBERT HYDE AND SON (HOLDINGS) LIMITED
Registration no: 01940080 **Date established:** 1985
No.of Employees: 1 - 10 **Product Groups:** 36, 40

Binder Fastener Systems UK Ltd
Nile Street, Stoke On Trent, ST6 2BA
Tel: 01782-525780 **Fax:** 01782-813207
E-mail: david@binderuk.com
Website: http://www.binderuk.com
Directors: D. Antrobus (Chief Op Offcr)
Immediate Holding Company: BINDER FASTENER SYSTEMS (U.K.) LIMITED
Registration no: 02653396 **Date established:** 1991
Turnover: Up to £250,000 **No.of Employees:** 1 - 10 **Product Groups:** 23, 30

Date of Accounts	Dec 11	Dec 10	Dec 09
Working Capital	243	258	181
Fixed Assets	32	8	38
Current Assets	321	336	198

Brighthouse Ltd
7 Stafford Street, Stoke On Trent, ST1 1JW
Tel: 01782-215589
E-mail: customer.relations@brighthouse.co.uk
Website: http://www.brighthouse.co.uk
Managers: D. Lad (Mgr)
Ultimate Holding Company: VISION CAPITAL PARTNERS VI B LP
Immediate Holding Company: BRIGHTHOUSE LIMITED
Registration no: 06073794 **Date established:** 2007
No.of Employees: 1 - 10 **Product Groups:** 36, 40

Date of Accounts	Mar 12	Mar 11	Mar 10
Sales Turnover	266m	228m	197m
Pre Tax Profit/Loss	29m	25m	20m
Working Capital	57m	49m	68m
Fixed Assets	171m	161m	123m
Current Assets	97m	87m	98m
Current Liabilities	29m	26m	22m

Brison Gates
69 Stoke Old Road, Stoke On Trent, ST4 6ER
Tel: 01782-611807
Directors: B. Wilson (Prop)
Date established: 1999 **No.of Employees:** 1 - 10 **Product Groups:** 26, 35

James M Brown Ltd
Boving Works Napier Street, Stoke On Trent, ST4 4NX
Tel: 01782-744171 **Fax:** 01782-744473
E-mail: sales@jamesmbrown.co.uk
Website: http://www.jamesmbrown.co.uk
Directors: N. Simcock (Co Sec)
Managers: J. Perrie (Sales Prom Mgr)
Ultimate Holding Company: TENNANTS CONSOLIDATED LIMITED
Immediate Holding Company: JAMES M.BROWN LIMITED
Registration no: 00382434 **Date established:** 1943
Turnover: £10m - £20m **No.of Employees:** 51 - 100 **Product Groups:** 31, 32

Date of Accounts	Dec 11	Dec 10	Dec 09
Sales Turnover	16m	15m	12m
Pre Tax Profit/Loss	3m	2m	1m
Working Capital	7m	8m	7m
Fixed Assets	7m	5m	5m
Current Assets	8m	10m	9m
Current Liabilities	557	677	593

Bry-Kol Developments Ltd
10 Newcastle Street Burslem, Stoke On Trent, ST6 3QF
Tel: 01782-577991 **Fax:** 01782-577511
E-mail: lorraine@bry-kol.co.uk
Website: http://www.bry-kol.co.uk
Directors: L. Taylor (Fin), A. Smith (MD), S. Fryer (Comm)
Ultimate Holding Company: THERMIDOR LIMITED
Immediate Holding Company: BRY-KOL (DEVELOPMENTS) LIMITED
Registration no: 01369228 **Date established:** 1978 **Turnover:** £5m - £10m
No.of Employees: 21 - 50 **Product Groups:** 39, 40, 42, 52, 66

Date of Accounts	Dec 11	Dec 10	Dec 09
Working Capital	250	194	109
Fixed Assets	129	137	98
Current Assets	1m	1m	588

Buck & Hickman Ltd
Lymevale Court Lyme Drive Parklands, Stoke On Trent, ST4 6NW
Tel: 01782-616427 **Fax:** 01782-286355
E-mail: stoke@buckandhickman.com
Website: http://buckandhickman.com
Managers: D. Wicks (Sales Prom Mgr)
Ultimate Holding Company: TRAVIS PERKINS PLC
Immediate Holding Company: BOSTON (2011) LIMITED
Registration no: 06028304 **Date established:** 2006
No.of Employees: 1 - 10 **Product Groups:** 24, 29, 30, 36, 37, 41, 46

Date of Accounts	Dec 10	Mar 10	Mar 09
Working Capital	6m	6m	6m
Current Assets	27m	27m	27m

Building Adhesives Ltd
Longton Road, Stoke On Trent, ST4 8JB
Tel: 01782-591100 **Fax:** 01782-591101
E-mail: info@building-adhesives.com
Website: http://www.building-adhesives.com
Bank(s): National Westminster Bank Plc
Directors: A. Beasley (Fin)
Managers: R. Henson, E. Aust (Personnel), P. Vickers
Ultimate Holding Company: ARDEX LUXEMBOURG HOLDING SARL (LUXEMBOURG)
Immediate Holding Company: BUILDING ADHESIVES LIMITED
Registration no: 00742637 **VAT No.:** GB 278 4754 10
Date established: 1962 **Turnover:** £20m - £50m
No.of Employees: 101 - 250 **Product Groups:** 30, 32, 33

Date of Accounts	Dec 11	Dec 10	Dec 09
Sales Turnover	30m	32m	36m
Pre Tax Profit/Loss	3m	7m	7m
Working Capital	11m	12m	12m
Fixed Assets	22m	20m	20m
Current Assets	18m	18m	19m
Current Liabilities	3m	4m	5m

Bullock & Bosson
Unit 6 Victoria Road, Stoke On Trent, ST4 2HS
Tel: 01782-747222 **Fax:** 01782-746200
E-mail: sales@bullockandbosson.co.uk
Website: http://www.bullockandbosson.co.uk
Directors: S. Blyth (Co Sec)
Immediate Holding Company: BULLOCK AND BOSSON LIMITED
Registration no: 04109617 **VAT No.:** GB 370 6622 57
Date established: 2000 **Turnover:** £1m - £2m **No.of Employees:** 1 - 10
Product Groups: 26, 38, 48, 49, 64, 67

Burgess Dorling & Leigh Ltd
Middleport Pottery Port Street, Stoke On Trent, ST6 3PE
Tel: 01782-577866 **Fax:** 01782-575529
E-mail: info@burleigh.co.uk
Website: http://www.burleigh.co.uk
Bank(s): National Westminster Bank Plc
Directors: G. Biggs (MD), W. Dorling (Fin)
Managers: P. Deighton (Factory Mgr)
Ultimate Holding Company: HILCO TRADING LLC (UNITED STATES OF AMERICA)
Immediate Holding Company: BURGESS DORLING & LEIGH LIMITED
Registration no: 03820303 **VAT No.:** GB 278 4867 94
Date established: 1999 **Turnover:** £500,000 - £1m
No.of Employees: 51 - 100 **Product Groups:** 33, 63

Date of Accounts	Dec 11	Dec 10	Aug 09
Sales Turnover	2m	677	N/A
Pre Tax Profit/Loss	-89	125	N/A
Working Capital	-706	-927	-583
Fixed Assets	190	500	2m
Current Assets	542	247	466
Current Liabilities	112	29	N/A

C K Tech Serve Ltd
56 Fallow Field, Stoke On Trent, ST3 3EJ
Tel: 01782-448556 **Fax:** 01889-570020
E-mail: info@cktechserve.co.uk
Website: http://www.cktechserve.co.uk
Directors: C. Harrison (Dir)
Immediate Holding Company: C K TECH SERVE LIMITED
Registration no: 05601690 **Date established:** 2005
Turnover: Up to £250,000 **No.of Employees:** 1 - 10 **Product Groups:** 44, 48

Date of Accounts	Nov 11	Nov 10	Nov 09
Working Capital	-2	2	16
Fixed Assets	8	12	18
Current Assets	26	39	27

C P L Petroleum
Jamage Industrial Estate Talke Pits, Stoke On Trent, ST7 1XW
Tel: 01782-770600 **Fax:** 01782-774920
E-mail: j.carnell@cplpetroleum.co.uk
Website: http://www.cplpetroleum.co.uk
Managers: J. Carnell (Mgr)
Ultimate Holding Company: CPL INDUSTRIES HOLDINGS LIMITED
Immediate Holding Company: CPL PETROLEUM LIMITED
Registration no: 03003860 **Date established:** 1994
No.of Employees: 21 - 50 **Product Groups:** 66

Date of Accounts	Mar 12	Mar 11	Mar 10
Pre Tax Profit/Loss	N/A	878	904
Working Capital	31	30m	30m
Fixed Assets	26	26m	26m
Current Assets	57	56m	56m
Current Liabilities	26	246	253

C S G Ltd
Brook House Dodsleigh Lane Leigh, Stoke On Trent, ST10 4SJ
Tel: 01889-502473
E-mail: info@csgdms.com
Website: http://www.csgdms.com
Directors: L. Ingram (Dir)
Immediate Holding Company: CSG LIMITED
Registration no: 04904089 **Date established:** 2003
No.of Employees: 1 - 10 **Product Groups:** 44, 67

Date of Accounts	Oct 11	Oct 10	Oct 09
Working Capital	65	51	21
Fixed Assets	21	21	22
Current Assets	148	160	112

Camthorne Industrial Rubber Services Ltd
3 Campbell Road, Stoke On Trent, ST4 4DX
Tel: 01782-745588 **Fax:** 01782-745589
E-mail: sales@camthorne.co.uk
Website: http://www.camthorne.co.uk
Bank(s): National Westminster Bank Plc
Directors: A. Mcintyre (MD)
Ultimate Holding Company: CAMTHORNE HOLDINGS LIMITED
Immediate Holding Company: CAMTHORNE INDUSTRIAL RUBBER SERVICES LIMITED
Registration no: 01343959 **VAT No.:** GB 318 8893 10
Date established: 1977 **No.of Employees:** 11 - 20 **Product Groups:** 23, 29, 30, 36, 66

Date of Accounts	Sep 11	Sep 10	Sep 09
Working Capital	3	-10	-38
Fixed Assets	19	24	42
Current Assets	153	119	330

Casburt T M S
Park Hall Longton, Stoke On Trent, ST3 5XA
Tel: 01782-332511 **Fax:** 01782-501501
E-mail: info@casburt.com
Website: http://www.casburt.com
Directors: J. Prince (Co Sec), P. Caswell (MD)
Immediate Holding Company: CASBURT TMS LIMITED
Registration no: 04019268 **Date established:** 2000 **Turnover:** £2m - £5m
No.of Employees: 1 - 10 **Product Groups:** 41, 42

Date of Accounts	Sep 10	Sep 09	Sep 08
Working Capital	23	46	134
Fixed Assets	13	47	62
Current Assets	684	771	650

Castle Kilns Ltd
Unit 6 Trent House Dunning Street, Stoke On Trent, ST6 5AP
Tel: 01782-821500 **Fax:** 01782-819700
E-mail: sales@castlekilns.com
Website: http://www.castlekilns.com
Directors: D. Williams (Sales), K. Latocha (Dir)
Immediate Holding Company: CASTLE KILNS LIMITED
Registration no: 06856685 **Date established:** 2009
Turnover: £500,000 - £1m **No.of Employees:** 1 - 10 **Product Groups:** 40, 42, 46

Date of Accounts	Mar 11	Mar 10	Apr 09
Sales Turnover	276	352	N/A
Pre Tax Profit/Loss	1	7	N/A
Working Capital	3	1	N/A
Fixed Assets	5	6	N/A
Current Assets	63	46	N/A
Current Liabilities	N/A	6	N/A

Caterham Fireplaces
Unit 5-6 Trentside Business Park, Stoke On Trent, ST4 4EU
Tel: 01782-410880 **Fax:** 01782-410908
E-mail: trudi@caterhamgranite.com
Website: http://www.caterhamfireplaces.com
Directors: D. Wenger (Works)
Immediate Holding Company: CATERHAM MARBLE AND GRANITE LIMITED
Registration no: 03077360 **VAT No.:** GB 660 9796 89
Date established: 1995 **No.of Employees:** 21 - 50 **Product Groups:** 33, 66

Date of Accounts	Mar 08	Mar 09	Apr 10
Working Capital	1m	1m	1m
Fixed Assets	469	299	193
Current Assets	2m	2m	2m
Current Liabilities	N/A	4	N/A

Cavers Wall China Ltd
Berry Hill Road Berryhill Trading Estate, Stoke On Trent, ST4 2PQ
Tel: 01782-652800 **Fax:** 01782-652801
E-mail: sales@caverswallchina.co.uk
Website: http://www.caverswallchina.co.uk
Directors: T. Johnson (MD)
Ultimate Holding Company: T AND J HOLDINGS LIMITED
Immediate Holding Company: CAVERSWALL CHINA COMPANY LIMITED
Registration no: 02890913 **Date established:** 1994
Turnover: £500,000 - £1m **No.of Employees:** 11 - 20 **Product Groups:** 33

Date of Accounts	Mar 12	Mar 11	Mar 10
Working Capital	62	-17	13
Fixed Assets	2	1	1
Current Assets	233	185	188

Ceramic Industry Certification Scheme Ltd
Queens Road, Stoke On Trent, ST4 7LQ
Tel: 0151-707 1309 **Fax:** 01782-764363
E-mail: info@cicsltd.com
Website: http://www.cicsltd.com
Managers: T. Watts (Ops Mgr)
Ultimate Holding Company: BRITISH CERAMIC RESEARCH LIMITED
Immediate Holding Company: BRITISH CERAMIC RESEARCH ASSOCIATION
Registration no: 02293170 **VAT No.:** GB 278 3606 30
Date established: 1988 **Turnover:** £10m - £20m **No.of Employees:** 1 - 10
Product Groups: 54, 80, 84, 85

Churchill China UK Ltd
Marlborough Works High Street, Stoke On Trent, ST6 5NZ
Tel: 01782-577566 **Fax:** 01782-847617
E-mail: adrian.botterell@churchillchina.plc.uk
Website: http://www.churchill1795.com
Directors: A. Botterell (Dir), D. Taylor (Fin), I. Hicks (Tech Serv), A. Basnett (Pers), M. Philpott (Dir)
Ultimate Holding Company: CHURCHILL CHINA PLC
Immediate Holding Company: CHURCHILL CHINA PLC
Registration no: 02709505 **Date established:** 1992
Turnover: £20m - £50m **No.of Employees:** 101 - 250
Product Groups: 27, 30, 33, 36, 49, 63, 65, 67, 83

Date of Accounts	Dec 11	Dec 10	Dec 09
Sales Turnover	42m	44m	42m
Pre Tax Profit/Loss	3m	2m	2m
Working Capital	16m	15m	16m
Fixed Assets	16m	18m	18m
Current Assets	24m	23m	24m
Current Liabilities	6m	6m	5m

Cipher Graphics
1 Ohio Grove Hot Lane Industrial Etate, Hot Lane Industrial Estate, Stoke On Trent, ST6 2BL
Tel: 01782-525500 **Fax:** 01782-525505
Website: http://www.cipher-graphics.co.uk
Directors: J. Sherwood (Ptnr)
Immediate Holding Company: CIPHER GRAPHICS LIMITED
Registration no: 03424748 **Date established:** 1997
No.of Employees: 1 - 10 **Product Groups:** 28, 44, 49

Clayton Ceramics International Ltd
Oldfields Business Park Galveston Grove, Stoke On Trent, ST4 3PE
Tel: 01782-501805 **Fax:** 01782-325588
E-mail: claytan.int@btconnect.com
Website: http://www.claytangroup.com
Managers: E. Beardmore (Mgr)
Ultimate Holding Company: HALLMARK INVESTMENT COMPANY LTD
Immediate Holding Company: HALLMARK INVESTMENT COMPANY LTD
Registration no: 04115888 **Date established:** 2000
Turnover: £250,000 - £500,000 **No.of Employees:** 1 - 10
Product Groups: 33, 63

Date of Accounts	Apr 11	Apr 10	Apr 09
Working Capital	-86	-178	-65
Fixed Assets	870	765	828
Current Assets	489	400	462

Combustion Lining Ltd
Jacaidam Works Walley Street, Stoke On Trent, ST6 2AH
Tel: 01782-822712 **Fax:** 01782-823920
E-mail: info@combustionlinings.com
Website: http://www.combustionlinings.com
Directors: J. Hurst (MD)
Registration no: 00845600 **VAT No.:** GB 278 3882 06
Turnover: Up to £250,000 **No.of Employees:** 1 - 10 **Product Groups:** 33

Connextions Logistics Ltd
Link House Bute Street, Stoke On Trent, ST4 3PR
Tel: 01782-339559 **Fax:** 01782-339561
Website: http://www.connextions.co.uk
Bank(s): Barclays
Directors: S. Sutton (Fin), C. Riley (Chief Op Offcr)
Ultimate Holding Company: SUTTON VENTURE GROUP LIMITED
Immediate Holding Company: CONNEXTIONS LOGISTICS LIMITED
Registration no: 04328513 **VAT No.:** GB 592 6138 20
Date established: 2001 **Turnover:** £500,000 - £1m
No.of Employees: 11 - 20 **Product Groups:** 72, 77

J Copestake & Sons
Unit 8 Prospect Way Knypersley, Stoke On Trent, ST8 7PL
Tel: 01782-511732
Directors: J. Copestake (Prop)
Immediate Holding Company: J. COPESTAKE & SONS LIMITED
Registration no: 07190640 **Date established:** 2010
No.of Employees: 1 - 10 **Product Groups:** 35

Copper Alloys Ltd
Glendale Street, Stoke On Trent, ST6 2EP
Tel: 01782-816888 **Fax:** 01782-790111
E-mail: sales@copperalloys.net
Website: http://www.copperalloys.net
Directors: S. Gregory (Dir)
Managers: B. Turner (Sales & Mktg Mg)
Immediate Holding Company: COPPER ALLOYS LIMITED
Registration no: 03976687 **Date established:** 2000
Turnover: £250,000 - £500,000 **No.of Employees:** 21 - 50
Product Groups: 34, 36, 48

Date of Accounts	Dec 08	Jun 12	Jun 11
Working Capital	-62	178	43
Fixed Assets	1m	440	595
Current Assets	2m	2m	2m
Current Liabilities	1m	N/A	812

D E S E M Lifts
Bradwell Works Davenport Street, Stoke On Trent, ST6 4LL
Tel: 01782-811055 **Fax:** 01782-811056
E-mail: info@desem.co.uk
Website: http://www.desem.co.uk
Directors: D. Martin (MD)
Turnover: Up to £250,000 **No.of Employees:** 1 - 10 **Product Groups:** 35, 39, 45

Date of Accounts	May 09	May 08	May 07
Working Capital	24	129	35
Fixed Assets	12	15	18
Current Assets	135	353	218

D R B Safety Barriers
Unit 27 Longbridge Hayes Industrial Estate Chemical Lane, Stoke On Trent, ST6 4PB
Tel: 01782-836080 **Fax:** 01782-833030
E-mail: sales@drbsafetybarriers.co.uk
Website: http://www.drbsafetybarriers.co.uk
Directors: A. Oakley (Prop)
Immediate Holding Company: G & P VEHICLE COLLECTION AND DELIVERY SERVICE LIMITED
Date established: 1999 **Turnover:** Up to £250,000
No.of Employees: 1 - 10 **Product Groups:** 25, 45

Date of Accounts	Mar 11	Mar 10	Mar 09
Working Capital	197	195	201
Fixed Assets	116	123	134
Current Assets	310	250	269

D S Smith Recycling PLC
Campbell Road, Stoke On Trent, ST4 4RW
Tel: 01782-849985 **Fax:** 01782-412660
E-mail: enquire@recyclesevernsd.demon.co.uk
Website: http://www.dssmithrecycling.com
Managers: M. Jones (Mgr)
Ultimate Holding Company: DS SMITH PLC
Immediate Holding Company: ST. REGIS PAPER COMPANY LTD
Registration no: 02878780 **Turnover:** £1m - £2m
No.of Employees: 11 - 20 **Product Groups:** 27, 28, 49, 85

G W Dale Diesel Engineer Ltd
139 Newcastle Street, Stoke On Trent, ST6 3QJ
Tel: 01782-837824 **Fax:** 01782-839550
Directors: J. Dale (MD)
Immediate Holding Company: G.W.DALE(DIESEL ENGINEER)LIMITED
Registration no: 00814308 **Date established:** 1964
No.of Employees: 11 - 20 **Product Groups:** 35, 36, 39

Date of Accounts	Sep 11	Sep 10	Sep 09
Working Capital	249	245	238
Fixed Assets	26	30	33
Current Assets	314	322	302

Richard Dawkes
Unit 25 Bedford Street, Stoke On Trent, ST1 4PZ
Tel: 07779-300582
E-mail: richard@richarddawkes.co.uk
Website: http://www.richarddawkes.co.uk
Directors: R. Dawkes (Prop)
Immediate Holding Company: BEGIN AGAIN LIMITED
Date established: 2010 **No.of Employees:** 1 - 10 **Product Groups:** 28, 31, 64, 81

The Diamond Metal Finishing Company Ltd
6 Newfields Industrial Estate High Street, Stoke On Trent, ST6 5PD
Tel: 01782-822442 **Fax:** 01782-839125
E-mail: stevependo@aol.com
Website: http://www.diamondmetalfinishing.co.uk
Directors: K. Pendleton (Co Sec), S. Pendleton (Dir)
Immediate Holding Company: THE DIAMOND METAL FINISHING COMPANY LIMITED
Registration no: 00398214 **VAT No.:** GB 278 6011 46
Date established: 1945 **Turnover:** £1m - £2m **No.of Employees:** 21 - 50
Product Groups: 48

Date of Accounts	Jun 11	Jun 10	Jun 09
Sales Turnover	N/A	1m	906
Pre Tax Profit/Loss	N/A	21	-121
Working Capital	-8	-87	-90
Fixed Assets	164	169	184
Current Assets	492	341	226
Current Liabilities	N/A	79	61

Diaphragm Pumps Ltd
Unit 1 Willow Row, Stoke On Trent, ST3 2PU
Tel: 01782-332235 **Fax:** 01782-332240
E-mail: pumps@dpumps.com
Website: http://www.diaphragmpumps.co.uk
Directors: R. Buddin (MD)
Immediate Holding Company: DIAPHRAGM PUMPS LIMITED
Registration no: 03502876 **VAT No.:** GB 705 0655 59
Date established: 1998 **No.of Employees:** 11 - 20 **Product Groups:** 29, 40, 41, 67

Date of Accounts	Feb 11	Feb 10	Feb 09
Working Capital	989	380	270
Fixed Assets	17	15	21
Current Assets	2m	900	613

Distinctive Design
Oldmill Street, Stoke On Trent, ST4 2RP
Tel: 01782-844629 **Fax:** 01782-849334
Directors: J. Davies (Prop), T. Davies (Prop)
Date established: 2003 **No.of Employees:** 1 - 10 **Product Groups:** 35, 46, 49

Drain Centre (a division of Wolseley UK)
Weston Coyney Road, Stoke On Trent, ST3 5JT
Tel: 01782-311311 **Fax:** 01782-343400
E-mail: customerservices@wolseley.co.uk
Website: http://www.draincentre.co.uk
Managers: B. Moore (District Mgr)
Immediate Holding Company: GLYNWEDD INTERNATIONAL
Registration no: 00636445 **No.of Employees:** 1 - 10 **Product Groups:** 30, 36, 39, 40, 48, 66

Easat Antennas Ltd
Goodwin House Leek Road, Stoke On Trent, ST1 3NR
Tel: 01782-208028 **Fax:** 01782-208060
E-mail: rgoodwin@goodwingroup.com
Website: http://www.easet.co.uk
Directors: R. Goodwin (MD)
Ultimate Holding Company: GOODWIN PLC
Immediate Holding Company: EASAT ANTENNAS LTD.
Registration no: 02044226 **Date established:** 1986 **Turnover:** £5m - £10m
No.of Employees: 11 - 20 **Product Groups:** 37

Date of Accounts	Apr 11	Apr 10	Apr 09
Sales Turnover	7m	7m	4m
Pre Tax Profit/Loss	1m	1m	592
Working Capital	1m	1m	53
Fixed Assets	90	63	59
Current Assets	4m	3m	3m
Current Liabilities	2m	1m	2m

Electro Wind Ltd
1a High Street Newchapel, Stoke On Trent, ST7 4PU
Tel: 01782-776321 **Fax:** 01782-776422
E-mail: sales@electro-wind.co.uk
Website: http://www.electro-wind.co.uk
Bank(s): Lloyds TSB
Directors: L. Cooper (Sales & Mktg), R. Stanley Cooper (Fin)
Managers: G. Baxter
Ultimate Holding Company: ELECTRO WIND (HOLDINGS) LIMITED
Immediate Holding Company: ELECTRO WIND LIMITED
Registration no: 01408881 **VAT No.:** 318 9709 24 **Date established:** 1979
Turnover: £2m - £5m **No.of Employees:** 21 - 50 **Product Groups:** 37, 52

Date of Accounts	Feb 08	Feb 11	Feb 10
Working Capital	563	406	500
Fixed Assets	154	80	98
Current Assets	1m	889	870

Elite Papers Ltd
Unit 5 Little Row Fenton Industrial Estate, Stoke On Trent, ST4 2SQ
Tel: 01782-749200 **Fax:** 01782-749300
E-mail: sales@elitepapers.com
Website: http://www.elitepapers.com
Directors: M. Mason (Fin), G. Mason (MD)
Immediate Holding Company: ELITE PAPERS LIMITED
Registration no: 02631558 **Date established:** 1991
Turnover: Up to £250,000 **No.of Employees:** 1 - 10 **Product Groups:** 27

Date of Accounts	Sep 11	Sep 10	Sep 09
Sales Turnover	N/A	157	130
Pre Tax Profit/Loss	N/A	20	-10
Working Capital	35	37	15
Fixed Assets	2	1	1
Current Assets	71	93	40
Current Liabilities	N/A	8	4

Envisiontec
Spedding Road Fenton Industrial Estate, Fenton, Stoke On Trent, ST4 2ST
Tel: 01782-418030 **Fax:** 01782-418033
E-mail: enquiries@envisiontec.com
Website: http://www.envisiontec.com
Product Groups: 30, 32, 37, 47, 48, 67, 81

Eriks UK
Unit 2 Etruria Trading Estate, Stoke On Trent, ST4 6JQ
Tel: 01782-633444 **Fax:** 01782-717439
E-mail: stoke@eriks.co.uk
Website: http://www.eriks.co.uk
Managers: M. Tilston (District Mgr)
No.of Employees: 1 - 10 **Product Groups:** 29, 36

F W B Products Ltd
Whieldon Road, Stoke On Trent, ST4 4JE
Tel: 01782-744333 **Fax:** 01782-744577
E-mail: sales@fwb.co.uk
Website: http://www.fwb.co.uk
Bank(s): National Westminster, Burslem
Directors: P. Meehan (Fin), C. Siddle (Sales)
Managers: J. Barnsley (Buyer), S. Jervis (Mktg Serv Mgr), J. Ford (Comm), M. Cox (Tech Serv Mgr), A. Burrows (Personnel)
Ultimate Holding Company: FWB HOLDINGS LIMITED
Immediate Holding Company: F.W.B. PRODUCTS LIMITED
Registration no: 01660947 **VAT No.:** GB 278 8080 17
Date established: 1982 **Turnover:** £10m - £20m
No.of Employees: 51 - 100 **Product Groups:** 36, 63, 66, 67

Date of Accounts	Dec 11	Dec 10	Dec 09
Sales Turnover	17m	16m	17m
Pre Tax Profit/Loss	206	137	4
Working Capital	4m	3m	1m
Fixed Assets	258	363	438
Current Assets	8m	7m	7m
Current Liabilities	392	387	657

Farrs Ltd
Unit 5 Milton Road, Stoke On Trent, ST1 6LE
Tel: 01782-544440 **Fax:** 01782-544440
E-mail: sales@farrsplaster.co.uk
Website: http://www.farrsplasterltd.co.uk
Directors: B. Hollins (Prop), S. Hollins (Fin)
Immediate Holding Company: FARRS LIMITED
Registration no: 04454299 **Date established:** 2002
Turnover: £250,000 - £500,000 **No.of Employees:** 1 - 10
Product Groups: 33

Date of Accounts	Aug 11	Aug 10	Aug 09
Working Capital	-30	-37	-0
Fixed Assets	11	12	18
Current Assets	78	61	73

Fegg Hayes Pottery Ltd
2-4 Beaumont Road, Stoke On Trent, ST6 6BE
Tel: 01782-838328 **Fax:** 01782-826378
E-mail: info@fegghayespottery.co.uk
Website: http://www.fegghayespottery.co.uk
Directors: A. Johnson (Ptnr)
Immediate Holding Company: FEGG HAYES POTTERY LIMITED
Registration no: 01234380 **Date established:** 1975
Turnover: Up to £250,000 **No.of Employees:** 1 - 10 **Product Groups:** 02, 14, 20, 26, 31, 32, 33, 44, 62, 66

Date of Accounts	Dec 11	Dec 10	Dec 09
Working Capital	385	431	383
Fixed Assets	964	956	963
Current Assets	613	684	654

Ferro Great Britain Ltd (Ceramic Glaze Specialties Group)
Nile Street, Stoke On Trent, ST6 2BQ
Tel: 01782-820400 **Fax:** 01782-820402
E-mail: latimer@ferro.co.uk
Website: http://www.ferro.com
Bank(s): HSBC Bank plc
Managers: K. Davies
Ultimate Holding Company: FERRO CORPORATION (USA)
Immediate Holding Company: FERRO (GREAT BRITAIN) LIMITED
Registration no: 00244654 **Date established:** 2029
Turnover: £10m - £20m **No.of Employees:** 21 - 50 **Product Groups:** 32, 34

Date of Accounts	Dec 10	Dec 09	Dec 08
Sales Turnover	13m	10m	16m
Pre Tax Profit/Loss	423	38	1m
Working Capital	11m	12m	12m
Fixed Assets	4m	4m	5m
Current Assets	14m	15m	16m
Current Liabilities	766	431	415

Filter & Press Cloth Co. Ltd
26 Town Road Hillchurch Street, Stoke On Trent, ST1 2EX
Tel: 01782-281819 **Fax:** 01782-281819
Bank(s): Co-Operative
Directors: D. Ralphs (MD), R. Ralphs (Dir)
Managers: M. Ralphs (Sales Prom Mgr)
Immediate Holding Company: FILTER AND PRESS CLOTH COMPANY LIMITED (THE)
Registration no: 00764624 **VAT No.:** GB 278 3671 19
Date established: 1963 **Turnover:** £250,000 - £500,000
No.of Employees: 11 - 20 **Product Groups:** 23, 24, 40, 42, 43

Date of Accounts	Jun 08
Working Capital	107
Fixed Assets	36
Current Assets	116
Current Liabilities	9
Total Share Capital	6

Flametec Ltd
Newstead Trading Estate Trentham, Stoke On Trent, ST4 8HT
Tel: 01782-657331 **Fax:** 01782-644600
E-mail: tepsolutions@turner-eps.co.uk
Website: http://www.flametec.co.uk
Bank(s): Barclays, Swindon
Managers: D. Perks (Project Eng), G. Munro (Sales Prom Mgr), P. Fairehurst (Sales Prom Mgr)
Ultimate Holding Company: Turner & Company (Glasgow) Ltd
Registration no: 02107949 **VAT No.:** GB 459 6868 74
Date established: 1987 **Turnover:** £1m - £2m **No.of Employees:** 11 - 20
Product Groups: 37, 40, 42, 67

Fletcher Moorland Ltd
Elenora Street, Stoke On Trent, ST4 1QG
Tel: 01782-411021 **Fax:** 01782-744470
E-mail: diane@fletchermoorland.co.uk
Website: http://www.fletchermoorland.co.uk
Directors: M. Fletcher (Ch), D. Mansell (Dir), M. Fletcher (MD), B. Fletcher (MD), R. Fletcher (MD), J. Fletcher (Co Sec)
Managers: I. Powell (I.T. Exec), A. Mansell (Sales Prom Mgr)
Ultimate Holding Company: FLETCHER BICKERTON HOLDINGS LIMITED
Immediate Holding Company: FLETCHER MOORLAND LIMITED
Registration no: 02984467 **Date established:** 1994 **Turnover:** £1m - £2m
No.of Employees: 21 - 50 **Product Groups:** 35, 37, 38, 40, 45, 46, 48, 49

Date of Accounts	Sep 10	Sep 09	Sep 08
Working Capital	738	669	704
Fixed Assets	150	123	124
Current Assets	1m	1m	1m

Fords Of Blythe Bridge Ltd
203 Grindley Lane Blythe Bridge, Stoke On Trent, ST11 9JS
Tel: 01782-392125 **Fax:** 01782-396622
E-mail: robert.ford@blythebridge30.fsbusiness.co.uk
Website: http://www.blythebridge30.fsbusiness.co.uk
Bank(s): Lloyds TSB Bank plc
Directors: R. Ford (Dir), R. Croft (Chief Est)
Managers: B. Parish
Immediate Holding Company: FORDS OF BLYTHE BRIDGE LIMITED
Registration no: 01273930 **VAT No.:** GB 280 5892 34
Date established: 1976 **Turnover:** £2m - £5m **No.of Employees:** 21 - 50
Product Groups: 52

Date of Accounts	Mar 11	Mar 10	Mar 09
Working Capital	1m	1m	2m
Fixed Assets	1m	1m	463
Current Assets	3m	2m	3m
Current Liabilities	N/A	1	N/A

Fuchs Lubricants UK plc
New Century Street Hanley, Stoke On Trent, ST1 5HU
Tel: 01782-203700 **Fax:** 01782-202072
E-mail: richard.halhead@fuchs-oil.com
Website: http://www.fuchs-oil.com
Bank(s): HSBC Bank plc
Directors: R. Halhead (MD)
Managers: P. Taylor (Purch Mgr), R. Barrett (Mktg Serv Mgr), S. McClurg (Personnel), A. Bacon (Tech Serv Mgr)

see next page

***Fuchs Lubricants UK plc** - Cont'd*
Ultimate Holding Company: FUCHS PETROLUB AG (GERMANY)
Immediate Holding Company: FUCHS LUBRICANTS (UK) PLC
Registration no: 02412689 **VAT No.:** GB 280 5261 69
Date established: 1989 **Turnover:** £75m - £125m
No.of Employees: 251 - 500 **Product Groups:** 31, 32, 36, 39, 42, 66

Date of Accounts	Dec 11	Dec 10	Dec 09
Sales Turnover	100m	84m	97m
Pre Tax Profit/Loss	10m	10m	7m
Working Capital	19m	15m	18m
Fixed Assets	50m	53m	56m
Current Assets	35m	28m	29m
Current Liabilities	5m	5m	5m

Global Ceramic Materials Ltd
Milton Works Diamond Crescent, Stoke On Trent, ST2 7PX
Tel: 01782-537297 **Fax:** 01782-537867
E-mail: info@globalcm.co.uk
Website: http://www.globalcm.co.uk
Directors: J. Matthews (Fin), A. Brindley (Chief Op Offcr), S. Smith (Fin), D. Slinn (Sales)
Managers: A. Michelle (Personnel)
Ultimate Holding Company: VION HOLDING NV (NETHERLANDS)
Immediate Holding Company: GLOBAL CERAMIC MATERIALS LIMITED
Registration no: 03306838 **VAT No.:** GB 677 6982 58
Date established: 1997 **Turnover:** £5m - £10m **No.of Employees:** 21 - 50
Product Groups: 14, 17

Date of Accounts	Dec 11	Dec 10	Dec 09
Sales Turnover	7m	6m	5m
Pre Tax Profit/Loss	673	101	-139
Working Capital	2m	2m	2m
Fixed Assets	3m	3m	3m
Current Assets	3m	3m	2m
Current Liabilities	180	251	121

Godstone Curtainwalling Ltd
Mossdale Godstone, Leigh, Stoke On Trent, ST10 4QB
Tel: 01889-502501 **Fax:** 01889-502501
Directors: J. Rowley (Fin), L. Rowley (MD)
Immediate Holding Company: GODSTONE CURTAINWALLING LIMITED
Registration no: 03371644 **Date established:** 1997
No.of Employees: 21 - 50 **Product Groups:** 26, 35

Date of Accounts	Aug 10	Aug 09	Aug 08
Working Capital	260	508	371
Fixed Assets	323	51	72
Current Assets	329	604	483

Goodwin International Ltd
Ivy House Foundry, Stoke On Trent, ST1 3NR
Tel: 01782-220000 **Fax:** 01782-208060
E-mail: pashley@goodwingroup.com
Website: http://www.goodwin.co.uk
Bank(s): National Westminster
Directors: C. Jenkins (Sales), P. Ashley (Co Sec)
Managers: K. Salt (Buyer), M. Officer (Personnel), P. Tennakoon (Tech Serv Mgr)
Ultimate Holding Company: GOODWIN PLC
Immediate Holding Company: GOODWIN INTERNATIONAL LIMITED
Registration no: 00468115 **Date established:** 1949
Turnover: £20m - £50m **No.of Employees:** 51 - 100 **Product Groups:** 34, 40

Date of Accounts	Apr 11	Apr 10	Apr 09
Sales Turnover	37m	36m	47m
Pre Tax Profit/Loss	3m	6m	9m
Working Capital	-1m	284	176
Fixed Assets	3m	2m	2m
Current Assets	25m	16m	15m
Current Liabilities	4m	3m	4m

Gough Engineering Ltd
Newstead Industrial Trading Estate, Stoke On Trent, ST4 8GE
Tel: 01782-654770 **Fax:** 01782-654771
E-mail: info@goughengineering.com
Website: http://www.goughengineering.com
Directors: S. Harding (MD)
Immediate Holding Company: GOUGH & CO (ENGINEERING) LIMITED
Registration no: 04454556 **Date established:** 2002 **Turnover:** £2m - £5m
No.of Employees: 21 - 50 **Product Groups:** 29, 35, 41, 42

Date of Accounts	Dec 11	Dec 10	Dec 09
Working Capital	-217	-142	44
Fixed Assets	122	173	200
Current Assets	584	527	555

Grange Steels Ltd
Tunstall Road Biddulph, Stoke On Trent, ST8 6JZ
Tel: 01782-510210 **Fax:** 01782-510211
E-mail: grangesteels@asdmetalservices.co.uk
Website: http://www.asdplc.co.uk
Directors: C. Jones (Dir)
Ultimate Holding Company: KLOCKNER & CO AG (GERMANY)
Immediate Holding Company: GRANGE STEELS LIMITED
Registration no: 00255680 **Date established:** 1931 **Turnover:** £1m - £2m
No.of Employees: 1 - 10 **Product Groups:** 31

The Greenhouse People Ltd
Blythe Park Cresswell, Stoke On Trent, ST11 9RD
Tel: 01782-388811 **Fax:** 01782-388818
E-mail: info@thegreenhousepeople.co.uk
Website: http://www.thegreenhousepeople.co.uk
Directors: A. Breeze (Co Sec)
Managers: G. Smith (Mktg Serv Mgr), J. Durose (Tech Serv Mgr)
Immediate Holding Company: THE GREENHOUSE PEOPLE LTD
Registration no: 04980265 **Date established:** 2003
No.of Employees: 21 - 50 **Product Groups:** 26, 35

Date of Accounts	Dec 11	Dec 10	Dec 09
Working Capital	2m	940	644
Fixed Assets	562	421	356
Current Assets	3m	1m	1m

Greer I G S
Unit 9 Oldham Street, Joiners Square Industrial Estate, Stoke On Trent, ST1 3EY
Tel: 01782-215900
E-mail: enquiries@greerigs.co.uk
Website: http://www.greerigs.co.uk
Directors: D. Greer (Prop)
No.of Employees: 1 - 10 **Product Groups:** 81, 82

G V R Products Ltd
8 Snow Hill, Stoke On Trent, ST1 4LT
Tel: 01782-205599 **Fax:** 01782-205599
E-mail: sales@gvrproducts.co.uk
Website: http://www.gvrproducts.co.uk
Directors: G. Reddy (Dir)
Immediate Holding Company: GVR PRODUCTS LIMITED
Registration no: 04295824 **Date established:** 2001
Turnover: Up to £250,000 **No.of Employees:** 1 - 10 **Product Groups:** 38

Date of Accounts	Mar 11	Mar 10	Mar 09
Working Capital	-177	-235	-211
Fixed Assets	125	107	108
Current Assets	19	39	27

H & E Smith
Britannic Works Broom Street, Stoke On Trent, ST1 2ER
Tel: 01782-281617 **Fax:** 01782-269882
E-mail: fred@hesmith.co.uk
Website: http://www.hesmith.co.uk
Bank(s): Barclays
Directors: F. Smith (Prop), F. Smith (MD)
Immediate Holding Company: H. & E.SMITH LIMITED
Registration no: 00444404 **VAT No.:** GB 279 0528 33
Date established: 1947 **Turnover:** £1m - £2m **No.of Employees:** 21 - 50
Product Groups: 33

Date of Accounts	Mar 12	Mar 11	Mar 10
Working Capital	204	188	280
Fixed Assets	94	140	116
Current Assets	409	580	552

H & H Commercial Truck Services Ltd
Sneyd Industrial Estate, Stoke On Trent, ST6 2NT
Tel: 01782-575522 **Fax:** 01782-812913
E-mail: martynhancock@handhcommercials.co.uk
Website: http://www.trucksales.me.uk
Directors: M. Hancock (Fin)
Immediate Holding Company: H. AND H. COMMERCIAL TRUCK SERVICES LIMITED
Registration no: 01471245 **Date established:** 1980
Turnover: £500,000 - £1m **No.of Employees:** 1 - 10 **Product Groups:** 39, 45, 68, 72, 80, 82

Date of Accounts	Dec 10	Dec 09	Dec 08
Working Capital	-222	-199	-136
Fixed Assets	570	580	633
Current Assets	381	571	273

Ham Baker Pipelines Ltd
Garner Street Etruria, Stoke On Trent, ST4 7BH
Tel: 01782-202300 **Fax:** 01782-203639
E-mail: sbailie@hambaker.co.uk
Website: http://www.hambaker.co.uk
Directors: S. Bailey (MD), S. Mallen (Export), M. Hindley (Fin)
Managers: A. Singh (), S. Bailie (Mgr), C. Baker ()
Ultimate Holding Company: WTB HOLDINGS LIMITED
Immediate Holding Company: HAM BAKER LIMITED
Registration no: 04407970 **Date established:** 2002
Turnover: £10m - £20m **No.of Employees:** 101 - 250
Product Groups: 30, 67

Date of Accounts	Dec 10	Dec 09	Dec 08
Sales Turnover	14m	22m	29m
Pre Tax Profit/Loss	-3m	133	2m
Working Capital	-2m	-992	-352
Fixed Assets	9m	10m	10m
Current Assets	7m	9m	14m
Current Liabilities	3m	5m	7m

Harman Electronic Services
1 Perth Street, Stoke On Trent, ST4 3PJ
Tel: 01782-598662 **Fax:** 01782-598662
Website: http://www.btinternet.com
Directors: R. Harman (Prop)
No.of Employees: 1 - 10 **Product Groups:** 37, 84

Harsco
Park Lane, Stoke On Trent, ST4 3JP
Tel: 0161-223 3151 **Fax:** 01782-335164
E-mail: lpattyson@sgb.co.uk
Website: http://www.sgb.co.uk
Managers: L. Pattyson (Mgr), L. Banford (Mgr)
Immediate Holding Company: HARSCO INFRASTRUCTURE SERVICES LIMITED
Registration no: 00276562 **Date established:** 1933
No.of Employees: 11 - 20 **Product Groups:** 35, 52, 83

Heath Filtration Ltd
PO Box 1, Stoke On Trent, ST6 1BY
Tel: 01782-838591 **Fax:** 01782-835508
E-mail: info@heathfiltration.com
Website: http://www.heathfiltration.com
Bank(s): Lloyds TSB Bank plc
Directors: R. Heath (MD)
Immediate Holding Company: HEATH FILTRATION LIMITED
Registration no: 03603099 **VAT No.:** GB 280 6240 72
Date established: 1998 **Turnover:** £2m - £5m **No.of Employees:** 51 - 100
Product Groups: 23, 24, 40, 42

Date of Accounts	Oct 11	Oct 10	Oct 09
Working Capital	522	482	472
Fixed Assets	198	209	117
Current Assets	2m	1m	1m

Heraeus Silica & Metals Ltd
Cinderhill Industrial Estate, Stoke On Trent, ST3 5LB
Tel: 01782-599423 **Fax:** 01782-599802
E-mail: sales@4hml.com
Website: http://www.4hml.com
Directors: W. Chivers (Fin), G. Amison (Sales)
Ultimate Holding Company: HERAEUS HOLDING GMBH (GERMANY)
Immediate Holding Company: HERAEUS MATERIALS LIMITED
Registration no: 03556192 **VAT No.:** GB 709 0636 39
Date established: 1998 **Turnover:** £2m - £5m **No.of Employees:** 1 - 10
Product Groups: 32

Date of Accounts	Dec 11	Dec 10	Dec 09
Sales Turnover	6m	4m	2m
Pre Tax Profit/Loss	469	137	63
Working Capital	2m	2m	2m
Fixed Assets	73	77	60
Current Assets	3m	3m	2m
Current Liabilities	318	324	178

hpi building services Stoke
Leigh House Leigh Lane, Longbridge Hayes, Stoke On Trent, ST6 4PB
Tel: 01782-577022 **Fax:** 01782-575492
E-mail: cad@hpistoke.co.uk
Website: http://www.hpibuildingservices.co.uk
Product Groups: 38, 40, 52, 84

Hudson Of England Ltd
Sutherland Works Normacot Road, Stoke On Trent, ST3 1PP
Tel: 01782-319256 **Fax:** 01782-343300
E-mail: sales@hudsonandmiddleton.co.uk
Website: http://www.hudsonandmiddleton.co.uk
Bank(s): National Westminster Bank Plc
Directors: H. Smith (Dir), C. Hollingshead (Fin), M. Shirley (MD), M. Shirley (MD)
Immediate Holding Company: HUDSONS OF ENGLAND LTD
Registration no: 07632753 **VAT No.:** GB 280 3231 88
Date established: 2011 **Turnover:** £1m - £2m **No.of Employees:** 51 - 100
Product Groups: 33

Date of Accounts	Mar 07	Mar 06
Working Capital	-669	-511
Fixed Assets	60	54
Current Assets	835	771
Current Liabilities	1503	1282
Total Share Capital	120	120

John Hyde Engineering Ltd
Hyde Park Trading Estate City Road, Stoke On Trent, ST4 1DS
Tel: 01782-744261 **Fax:** 01782-747377
E-mail: john.hyde@johnhydeengineering.co.uk
Website: http://www.johnhydeengineering.co.uk
Directors: G. Hume (Dir), J. Hyde (MD)
Managers: W. Burrows (Chief Acct)
Ultimate Holding Company: ROBERT HYDE AND SON (HOLDINGS) LIMITED
Immediate Holding Company: JOHN HYDE ENGINEERING LIMITED
Registration no: 02305498 **Date established:** 1988 **Turnover:** £1m - £2m
No.of Employees: 21 - 50 **Product Groups:** 48

Date of Accounts	Jul 11	Jul 10	Jul 09
Working Capital	460	437	507
Current Assets	2m	1m	973

Hygan Products Ltd
Kingscroft Works Stoke Old Road, Stoke On Trent, ST4 6ES
Tel: 01782-613936 **Fax:** 01782-711614
E-mail: sales@hygan.com
Website: http://www.hygan.com
Directors: J. Hewitt (MD)
Immediate Holding Company: HYGAN PRODUCTS LIMITED
Registration no: 00736011 **VAT No.:** 278 7253 17 **Date established:** 1962
No.of Employees: 1 - 10 **Product Groups:** 33, 45, 47, 49, 63

Date of Accounts	Sep 11	Sep 10	Sep 09
Working Capital	125	93	106
Fixed Assets	2	1	1
Current Assets	207	158	180

I & P Lifting Gear Ltd
237 Scotia Road, Stoke On Trent, ST6 4PS
Tel: 01782-814411 **Fax:** 01782-575510
E-mail: info@iandplifting.co.uk
Website: http://www.iandplifting.co.uk
Bank(s): HSBC
Directors: G. Dean (MD)
Ultimate Holding Company: I. & P. LIFTING GEAR (HIRE) LIMITED
Immediate Holding Company: I. & P.LIFTING GEAR LIMITED
Registration no: 00898575 **VAT No.:** GB 479 7796 60
Date established: 1967 **Turnover:** £500,000 - £1m
No.of Employees: 11 - 20 **Product Groups:** 35, 45, 48, 84

Date of Accounts	Jun 11	Jun 10	Jun 09
Working Capital	491	503	543
Fixed Assets	211	219	224
Current Assets	679	659	686

Image Composites Ltd
Unit 3 Monarch Works Elswick Road, Fenton Industrial Estate, Stoke On Trent, ST4 2SH
Tel: 01782-411611 **Fax:** 01782-411888
E-mail: info@imagecomposites.co.uk
Website: http://www.imagecomposites.co.uk
Directors: J. Edgoose (Dir)
Ultimate Holding Company: MOORLAND COMPOSITES LTD
Immediate Holding Company: IMAGE COMPOSITES LIMITED
Registration no: 01300156 **Date established:** 1977
Turnover: £500,000 - £1m **No.of Employees:** 21 - 50 **Product Groups:** 30

Date of Accounts	Mar 08	Sep 11	Sep 10
Working Capital	105	244	190
Fixed Assets	203	495	493
Current Assets	314	576	427

Industrial & Construction Plant Ltd
Clarence Road, Stoke On Trent, ST3 1AZ
Tel: 01782-316791 **Fax:** 01782-599411
E-mail: linda@icpkramer.co.uk
Directors: L. Ward (Fin)
Ultimate Holding Company: LT HOLDINGS LIMITED
Immediate Holding Company: INDUSTRIAL & CONSTRUCTION PLANT LIMITED
Registration no: 00560220 **VAT No.:** GB 687 8901 67
Date established: 1956 **Turnover:** £2m - £5m **No.of Employees:** 1 - 10
Product Groups: 48

Date of Accounts	Mar 11	Mar 10	Mar 09
Working Capital	-602	-596	-382
Fixed Assets	3m	4m	4m
Current Assets	695	613	705

Intergrated Ducting Systems
Garner Street Etruria, Stoke On Trent, ST4 7BH
Tel: 08450-720241 **Fax:** 0845-007 2242
E-mail: leg@wtbgroup.com
Website: http://www.ids-access.co.uk
Directors: G. Armstrong (Chief Op Offcr)
Managers: A. Day (Mktg Serv Mgr), A. Daye (Mktg Serv Mgr)
Immediate Holding Company: SIMON-HARTLEY LIMITED
Registration no: 03628320 **Date established:** 2001 **Turnover:** £2m - £5m
No.of Employees: 1 - 10 **Product Groups:** 30

Date of Accounts	Dec 10	Dec 09	Dec 08
Sales Turnover	202	N/A	170
Working Capital	201	201	201
Current Assets	201	201	201

Internet Business Solutions
Trentham Business Quarter Bellringer Road, Trentham, Stoke On Trent, ST4 8GB
Tel: 0845-4567617
E-mail: neil@netbizsolutions.co.uk
Website: http://www.netbizsolutions.co.uk
Directors: N. Erlam (Prop), N. Erlam (MD)
Immediate Holding Company: Internet Business Solutions Ltd
Registration no: 05164137 **Date established:** 2004
No.of Employees: 21 - 50 **Product Groups:** 44

Date of Accounts	Nov 09	Nov 08	Nov 07
Working Capital	-20	-23	-61
Fixed Assets	73	29	22
Current Assets	164	71	17

J G Fenn Ltd
West Court Campbell Road, Stoke On Trent, ST4 4FB
Tel: 01782-315782 **Fax:** 01782-344060
E-mail: sales@fenns.co.uk
Website: http://www.fenns.co.uk
Bank(s): HSBC P.L.C.
Directors: L. Harris (Pers), P. Harris (MD)
Managers: M. Harris (Sales Prom Mgr), F. Hodgkinson (Fin Mgr), K. Deville (Tech Serv Mgr), R. Bradbury (Mktg Serv Mgr)
Ultimate Holding Company: J G FENN HOLDINGS LIMITED
Immediate Holding Company: J.G. FENN LIMITED
Registration no: 00100566 **Date established:** 2008
Turnover: £10m - £20m **No.of Employees:** 21 - 50 **Product Groups:** 23, 26, 27, 28, 30, 32, 33, 35, 37, 38, 42, 44, 49

Date of Accounts	Dec 11	Dec 10	Dec 09
Working Capital	1m	1m	1m
Fixed Assets	206	201	144
Current Assets	3m	3m	3m

J H P Training Ltd
London House London Road, Stoke On Trent, ST4 1NB
Tel: 01782-848999 **Fax:** 01782-744845
E-mail: stoke.business.centre@jhp-group.com
Website: http://www.jhptraining.com
Managers: V. Bebbington (Contracts Mgr)
Immediate Holding Company: JHP TRAINING LIMITED
Registration no: 03247918 **Date established:** 1996
No.of Employees: 11 - 20 **Product Groups:** 86

J P R Engineering Services Ltd
North Street, Stoke On Trent, ST4 7SA
Tel: 01782-744675 **Fax:** 01782-411780
E-mail: reception@jpr-engineering.com
Website: http://www.jpr-engineering.com
Directors: R. Davenport (Jt MD), J. Moran (MD), P. Williams (Jt MD)
Managers: L. Bailey (Accounts)
Immediate Holding Company: JPR ENGINEERING SERVICES LIMITED
Registration no: 01087200 **VAT No.:** GB 279 6557 93
Date established: 1972 **Turnover:** £5m - £10m **No.of Employees:** 1 - 10
Product Groups: 37

Date of Accounts	Jan 12	Jan 11	Jan 10
Sales Turnover	8m	7m	8m
Pre Tax Profit/Loss	125	-212	-331
Working Capital	849	871	1m
Fixed Assets	81	90	107
Current Assets	2m	2m	2m
Current Liabilities	324	358	379

J & T Group (Storage Division)
153 Victoria Street, Stoke On Trent, ST4 6HA
Tel: 01782-349440 **Fax:** 01782-349449
E-mail: sales@storagebins.co.uk
Website: http://www.storagebins.co.uk
Directors: J. Dale (MD)
Immediate Holding Company: J&T GROUP LIMITED
Registration no: 02334401 **VAT No.:** GB 533 2551 68
Date established: 1989 **Turnover:** £500,000 - £1m
No.of Employees: 1 - 10 **Product Groups:** 26, 30, 35, 36, 39, 45, 66, 67

Date of Accounts	Nov 11	Nov 10	Nov 09
Working Capital	186	247	241
Fixed Assets	27	22	4
Current Assets	249	301	294

Jackmark Engineering Ltd
Scott Lidgett Road, Stoke On Trent, ST6 4NQ
Tel: 01782-825555 **Fax:** 01782-834169
E-mail: graham@jackmark.f9.co.uk
Website: http://www.jackmark.com
Directors: K. Tudor-jackson (MD), G. Sutton (Dir)
Managers: P. Griffiths (Tech Serv Mgr)
Immediate Holding Company: JACKMARK ENGINEERING LIMITED
Registration no: 01870994 **VAT No.:** GB 402 0948 86
Date established: 1984 **Turnover:** £1m - £2m **No.of Employees:** 21 - 50
Product Groups: 38

Date of Accounts	Jul 11	Jul 10	Jul 09
Working Capital	357	695	657
Fixed Assets	213	230	250
Current Assets	712	951	1m

Jacksons Power Transmission Ltd
Canal Lane, Stoke On Trent, ST6 4PA
Tel: 01782-825400 **Fax:** 01782-835643
E-mail: sales@jacksonspower.co.uk
Website: http://www.jacksonspower.co.uk
Directors: P. Jackson (MD)
Immediate Holding Company: JACKSONS POWER TRANSMISSION LIMITED
Registration no: 02078538 **Date established:** 1986
No.of Employees: 1 - 10 **Product Groups:** 35, 38, 45, 48, 84

Date of Accounts	Jul 11	Jul 10	Jul 09
Working Capital	228	104	111
Fixed Assets	82	104	123
Current Assets	1m	1m	1m

Jarrobs Ltd
Units 1-5 Excalibur Industrial Estate Fields Road, Alsager, Stoke On Trent, ST7 2LX
Tel: 01270-878711 **Fax:** 01270-882464
E-mail: sales@jarrobs.co.uk
Website: http://www.jarrobs.co.uk
Bank(s): National Westminster Plc, Alsager
Directors: C. Robinson (Purch), J. Robinson (MD), R. Robinson Senior (Fin), R. Robinson (Sales)
Managers: J. Pace
Immediate Holding Company: JARROBS LIMITED
Registration no: 01287633 **VAT No.:** GB 280 5691 44
Date established: 1976 **Turnover:** £2m - £5m **No.of Employees:** 51 - 100
Product Groups: 48

Date of Accounts	Jan 12	Jan 11	Jan 10
Working Capital	159	505	417
Fixed Assets	866	666	842
Current Assets	1m	1m	1m

Johnson Progress Ltd
Victoria Works Victoria Road, Stoke On Trent, ST4 2QR
Tel: 01782-847911 **Fax:** 01782-744420
E-mail: sales@spwgroup.co.uk
Website: http://www.spwgroup.co.uk
Bank(s): Midland
Directors: B. Gnyla (Dir), P. Smith (Fin)
Immediate Holding Company: JOHNSON PROGRESS LIMITED
Registration no: 06550537 **VAT No.:** 592 6227 21 **Date established:** 2008
Turnover: £5m - £10m **No.of Employees:** 21 - 50 **Product Groups:** 23, 41, 42

Johnson Tiles Ltd
Harewood Street, Stoke On Trent, ST6 5JZ
Tel: 01782-575575 **Fax:** 01782-577377
E-mail: info@johnson-tiles.com
Website: http://www.johnson-tiles.com
Bank(s): Lloyds TSB Bank plc
Directors: I. Crowther (Sales), M. Birks (Fin), A. Moult (Admin), S. Dixon (MD), A. Sadler (Sales)
Managers: N. Whitehurst (Tech Serv Mgr), A. Adam, R. Wade
Ultimate Holding Company: NORCROS GROUP (HOLDINGS) LTD
Registration no: 00566694 **VAT No.:** GB 278 4006 49
Date established: 1901 **Turnover:** £50m - £75m
No.of Employees: 101 - 250 **Product Groups:** 32, 33, 66

Date of Accounts	Mar 08
Sales Turnover	50850
Pre Tax Profit/Loss	5730
Working Capital	24320
Current Assets	24320
Total Share Capital	50010

Keeling & Walker Ltd
Whieldon Road, Stoke On Trent, ST4 4JA
Tel: 01782-744136 **Fax:** 01782-744126
E-mail: sales@keelingwalker.co.uk
Website: http://www.keelingwalker.co.uk
Bank(s): Barclays
Directors: H. Brown (Fin), S. Lipiec (MD)
Managers: D. Moore (Buyer)
Ultimate Holding Company: AMCO INVESTMENTS LIMITED
Immediate Holding Company: KEELING & WALKER,LIMITED
Registration no: 00144119 **VAT No.:** GB 278 6759 87
Date established: 2016 **Turnover:** £20m - £50m
No.of Employees: 21 - 50 **Product Groups:** 31, 32, 33, 35

Date of Accounts	Dec 11	Dec 10	Dec 09
Sales Turnover	26m	22m	12m
Pre Tax Profit/Loss	2m	2m	819
Working Capital	2m	1m	804
Fixed Assets	1m	1m	1m
Current Assets	4m	3m	3m
Current Liabilities	838	1m	598

Kiln Control Services
60 Nile Street, Stoke On Trent, ST6 2BH
Tel: 01782-826799 **Fax:** 01782-826610
E-mail: sales@kilncontrolservices.co.uk
Website: http://www.kilncontrolservices.co.uk
Directors: S. Walton (Dir)
No.of Employees: 1 - 10 **Product Groups:** 40, 46

Kilns & Furnaces Ltd
Cinderhill Industrial Estate Weston Coyney Road, Longton, Stoke On Trent, ST3 5JU
Tel: 01782-344270 **Fax:** 01782-344279
E-mail: sales@kilns.co.uk
Website: http://www.kilns.co.uk
Directors: P. Ellis (Fin), K. Pedley (MD)
Immediate Holding Company: Ceramic Drying Systems Ltd
Registration no: 04298428 **VAT No.:** GB 278 7132 29
Date established: 2001 **Turnover:** £2m - £5m **No.of Employees:** 1 - 10
Product Groups: 40, 42, 45, 46, 48

Date of Accounts	Dec 07	Dec 06	Dec 05
Working Capital	104	75	82
Fixed Assets	8	11	11
Current Assets	416	233	228
Current Liabilities	312	158	146

Koch Glitsch
King Street, Stoke On Trent, ST4 2LT
Tel: 01782-744561 **Fax:** 01782-744630
E-mail: info@kochglitsch.com
Website: http://www.kochglitsch.com
Bank(s): Lloyds TSB
Directors: D. Britton (Fin), M. Mcduire (MD), D. Britton (MD), B. Hughes (Sales & Mktg)
Managers: T. Butler (I.T. Exec), M. Ricketts (Personnel), M. Stevenson (Personnel), T. Butler (Systems Mgr), D. Holbrook (Purch Mgr)
Ultimate Holding Company: KOCH INDUSTRIES INC (USA)
Immediate Holding Company: KOCH CHEMICAL TECHNOLOGY GROUP LIMITED
Registration no: 03321082 **VAT No.:** GB 116 8278 58
Date established: 1997 **Turnover:** £50m - £75m
No.of Employees: 51 - 100 **Product Groups:** 34

Date of Accounts	Dec 11	Dec 10	Dec 09
Sales Turnover	66m	57m	56m
Pre Tax Profit/Loss	-4m	2m	2m
Working Capital	7m	13m	12m
Fixed Assets	89m	3m	4m
Current Assets	23m	27m	22m
Current Liabilities	6m	9m	8m

L & M Ltd
Unit 1 Ribble Industrial Estate Newport Lane, Stoke On Trent, ST6 3BB
Tel: 01782-839555 **Fax:** 01782-839571
E-mail: support@lmcateringequipment.co.uk
Website: http://www.lmcateringequipment.co.uk
Directors: M. Bonfiglio (MD)
Ultimate Holding Company: TIMEWILD LIMITED
Immediate Holding Company: L & M LIMITED
Registration no: 01486512 **Date established:** 1980
No.of Employees: 11 - 20 **Product Groups:** 20, 40, 41

Date of Accounts	May 11	May 10
Working Capital	24	N/A
Current Assets	30	N/A

The Ladder Man
City Ladder Works Victoria Road, Fenton, Stoke On Trent, ST4 2HS
Tel: 0800-197 3839 **Fax:** 01782-410172
E-mail: info@theladderman.co.uk
Website: http://www.theladderman.co.uk
Directors: N. Dewey (MD)
Managers: L. Roberts (Transport)
Registration no: 00826542 **VAT No.:** GB 278 4402 41
Turnover: £250,000 - £500,000 **No.of Employees:** 1 - 10
Product Groups: 23, 25, 35, 36, 66, 83

Leamar Fire Systems Ltd
154 Chatterley Drive Kidsgrove Kidsgrove, Stoke On Trent, ST7 4LL
Tel: 01782-775149 **Fax:** 01782-775149
E-mail: sales@leamarfire.com
Website: http://www.leamarfire.com
Directors: L. Prince (Dir)
Registration no: 05279391 **Date established:** 2004
Turnover: £250,000 - £500,000 **No.of Employees:** 1 - 10
Product Groups: 35, 37, 40, 52, 67

Date of Accounts	Nov 07	Nov 06	Nov 05
Working Capital	-28	N/A	14
Fixed Assets	12	4	4
Current Assets	30	36	28
Current Liabilities	58	36	14

Longrange Systems UK Ltd
Link House Leek Road, Stoke On Trent, ST2 7AH
Tel: 01782-544700 **Fax:** 01782-544810
E-mail: tony@lrspagers.co.uk
Website: http://www.longrangesystems.co.uk
Directors: B. McKenzie (Fin), A. McKenzie (Dir)
Immediate Holding Company: LONGRANGE SYSTEMS UK LTD
Registration no: 02346462 **Date established:** 1989 **Turnover:** £1m - £2m
No.of Employees: 1 - 10 **Product Groups:** 37, 67

Date of Accounts	Feb 12	Feb 11	Feb 10
Working Capital	397	364	366
Fixed Assets	21	13	10
Current Assets	695	570	539

Longton Light Alloys Ltd
Foxley Lane, Stoke On Trent, ST2 7EH
Tel: 01782-536615 **Fax:** 01782-533415
E-mail: info@pugmills.com
Website: http://www.gladstone-engineering.com
Bank(s): Lloyds TSB
Directors: Bailey (Dir)
Immediate Holding Company: LONGTON LIGHT ALLOYS INCORPORATING GLADSTONE ENGINEERING COMPANY LIMIT
Registration no: 01374211 **VAT No.:** GB 318 8521 47
Date established: 1978 **Turnover:** £500,000 - £1m
No.of Employees: 11 - 20 **Product Groups:** 34, 42, 45, 48

Date of Accounts	Jun 11	Jun 10	Jun 09
Working Capital	471	422	398
Fixed Assets	59	62	64
Current Assets	652	543	543

Mcevoy Foods Ltd
International House Bellringer Road Trentham Lakes South, Stoke On Trent, ST4 8LJ
Tel: 01782-647040 **Fax:** 01782-647050
E-mail: howard@mcevoyfoods.co.uk
Website: http://www.mcevoyfoods.co.uk
Directors: H. Mcevoy (MD)
Immediate Holding Company: MCEVOY FOODS INTERNATIONAL LIMITED
Registration no: 03049469 **Date established:** 1995
No.of Employees: 1 - 10 **Product Groups:** 82

Date of Accounts	Aug 11	Aug 10	Aug 09
Working Capital	6	57	101
Fixed Assets	36	48	33
Current Assets	668	606	690

Mahle Industrial Filteration UK Ltd
Navigation Road, Stoke On Trent, ST6 3RU
Tel: 01782-575611 **Fax:** 01782-577001
E-mail: salesuk@amafiltergroup.com
Website: http://www.amafiltergroup.com
Bank(s): Den Norske Bank, London
Directors: J. Chapman (MD)
Managers: M. McAthey (Fin Mgr), N. Thomas (Sales Prom Mgr), P. Mountford (Purch Mgr), J. O'Neil (Personnel)
Ultimate Holding Company: MAHLE GMBH (GERMANY)
Immediate Holding Company: MAHLE INDUSTRIAL FILTRATION (UK) LTD.
Registration no: 02584430 **VAT No.:** GB 278 5335 25
Date established: 1991 **Turnover:** £5m - £10m **No.of Employees:** 21 - 50
Product Groups: 41, 42, 45

Date of Accounts	Dec 11	Dec 10	Dec 09
Sales Turnover	6m	6m	7m
Pre Tax Profit/Loss	128	576	2m
Working Capital	2m	2m	2m
Fixed Assets	451	407	430
Current Assets	5m	4m	4m
Current Liabilities	2m	961	792

Maplin Electronics Ltd
39-45 London Road, Stoke On Trent, ST4 1NB
Tel: 08432-277316 **Fax:** 01782-749997
E-mail: customercare@maplin.co.uk
Website: http://www.maplin.co.uk
Directors: K. Pacy (MD)
Ultimate Holding Company: MONTAGU PRIVATE EQUITY LLP
Immediate Holding Company: MAPLIN ELECTRONICS LIMITED
Registration no: 01264385 **Date established:** 1976
Turnover: £125m - £250m **No.of Employees:** 11 - 20
Product Groups: 37, 61

Date of Accounts	Dec 11	Dec 08	Dec 09
Sales Turnover	205m	204m	204m
Pre Tax Profit/Loss	25m	32m	35m

see next page

***Maplin Electronics Ltd** - Cont'd*

Working Capital	118m	49m	75m
Fixed Assets	27m	28m	28m
Current Assets	207m	108m	142m
Current Liabilities	78m	51m	59m

Max Frank Ltd
Whittle Road, Stoke On Trent, ST3 7HF
Tel: 01782-598041 **Fax:** 01782-315056
E-mail: info@maxfrank.co.uk
Website: http://www.maxfrank.co.uk
Directors: S. Miles (Fin)
Managers: S. James (Sales Prom Mgr), M. Atkins, K. Stevenson
Immediate Holding Company: MAX FRANK LIMITED
Registration no: 06309165 **Date established:** 2007
Turnover: £250,000 - £500,000 **No.of Employees:** 21 - 50
Product Groups: 30, 33, 45, 66

Date of Accounts	Dec 11	Dec 10	Dec 09
Working Capital	-739	-2m	-2m
Fixed Assets	603	655	832
Current Assets	1m	1m	945

Metal Proving Services
Goodwin House Leek Road, Stoke On Trent, ST1 3NR
Tel: 01782-206208 **Fax:** 01782-208060
Website: http://www.goodwingroup.com
Directors: S. Berks (Dir)
No.of Employees: 1 - 10 **Product Groups:** 34, 35, 46

Metalcraft Fabrication
Unit R Brunswick Industrial Estate Davenport Street, Stoke On Trent, ST6 4HS
Tel: 01782-822255
Directors: D. Arnold (Prop)
Registration no: 02528898 **Date established:** 1990
No.of Employees: 1 - 10 **Product Groups:** 26, 35

Metaref
Spedding Road Fenton Industrial Estate, Stoke On Trent, ST4 2SN
Tel: 01782-412111 **Fax:** 01782-744267
E-mail: enquiries@metaref.co.uk
Website: http://www.metaref.co.uk
Managers: A. Martin (Chief Mgr)
Immediate Holding Company: WALTHER TROWAL LIMITED
Registration no: 01329058 **VAT No.:** GB 561 0079 67
Date established: 1977 **Turnover:** £2m - £5m **No.of Employees:** 21 - 50
Product Groups: 33

Date of Accounts	Mar 12	Mar 11	Mar 10
Working Capital	1m	1m	906
Fixed Assets	916	1m	1m
Current Assets	2m	1m	1m

Michelin Tyre plc
Campbell Road, Stoke On Trent, ST4 4EY
Tel: 01782-402000 **Fax:** 01782-402253
E-mail: info@michelin.com
Website: http://www.michelin.co.uk
Managers: B. Bell (Sales Prom Mgr), P. Marsh (Site Co-ord), P. Niblett (Commun Mgr)
Ultimate Holding Company: COMPAGNIE GENERALE DES ETABLISSEMENTS MICHELIN (FRANCE)
Immediate Holding Company: MICHELIN TYRE PUBLIC LIMITED COMPANY
Registration no: 00084559 **Date established:** 2005
Turnover: £500m - £1,000m **No.of Employees:** 501 - 1000
Product Groups: 28, 29

Date of Accounts	Dec 11	Dec 10	Dec 09
Sales Turnover	962m	828m	737m
Pre Tax Profit/Loss	39m	33m	9m
Working Capital	149m	121m	120m
Fixed Assets	154m	155m	157m
Current Assets	451m	380m	351m
Current Liabilities	29m	26m	24m

Micronics Filtration Ltd
Sandbach Road, Stoke On Trent, ST6 2DR
Tel: 01782-284385 **Fax:** 01782-284987
E-mail: dave.phillips@micronicsinc.com
Website: http://www.micronicsinc.com
Directors: L. Hughes (Dir)
Immediate Holding Company: MICRONICS FILTRATION LIMITED
Registration no: 03091528 **Date established:** 1995
No.of Employees: 11 - 20 **Product Groups:** 38, 42

Date of Accounts	Dec 11	Dec 10	Dec 09
Working Capital	589	408	298
Fixed Assets	81	69	84
Current Assets	1m	959	615

Midas Engineering Services Ltd
Unit 8 Bradwell Works Davenport Street, Stoke On Trent, ST6 4LL
Tel: 01782-825489
E-mail: chris.mk1@ntlworld.com
Directors: C. Martin (MD), E. Jepson (Fin)
Immediate Holding Company: MIDAS ENGINEERING SERVICES LIMITED
Registration no: 04478700 **Date established:** 2002
No.of Employees: 1 - 10 **Product Groups:** 29, 36, 48, 52

Date of Accounts	Jul 11	Jul 10	Jul 08
Working Capital	-1	9	8
Fixed Assets	1	1	2
Current Assets	17	21	17

Milton Aluminium Casting Ltd
43 Millrise Road, Stoke On Trent, ST2 7BN
Tel: 01782-534176 **Fax:** 01782-545410
E-mail: richard@castspiralstairs.com
Directors: R. Harding (MD)
Immediate Holding Company: MILTON NON-FERROUS CASTING CO. LIMITED
Registration no: 00747439 **VAT No.:** GB 278 9594 78
Date established: 1963 **Turnover:** Up to £250,000
No.of Employees: 1 - 10 **Product Groups:** 34

Date of Accounts	Jan 08	Jan 07	Jan 06
Working Capital	-6	21	70
Fixed Assets	80	82	84
Current Assets	67	70	113
Current Liabilities	72	48	44

Mitras Composites UK Ltd
New Street Biddulph Moor, Stoke On Trent, ST8 7NL
Tel: 01782-375450 **Fax:** 01782-522652
E-mail: sales@mitras-composites.co.uk
Website: http://www.meterboxes.co.uk
Bank(s): Lloyds
Directors: J. Edgoose (Dir)
Ultimate Holding Company: MOORLAND COMPOSITES LTD
Immediate Holding Company: MITRAS COMPOSITES UK LIMITED
Registration no: 00364912 **VAT No.:** GB 682 2100 64
Date established: 1941 **Turnover:** £2m - £5m **No.of Employees:** 51 - 100
Product Groups: 30, 66

Date of Accounts	Sep 11	Sep 10	Sep 09
Sales Turnover	3m	8m	7m
Pre Tax Profit/Loss	924	559	420
Working Capital	5m	4m	4m
Fixed Assets	1m	1m	985
Current Assets	7m	6m	6m
Current Liabilities	585	685	440

Mobile Applications Ltd
14 Chemical Lane, Stoke On Trent, ST6 4PB
Tel: 01782-790824 **Fax:** 01782-790825
E-mail: sales@mobileapplicationsltd.co.uk
Website: http://www.mobileapplicationsltd.com
Directors: G. Dix (Dir)
Immediate Holding Company: MOBILE APPLICATIONS LIMITED
Registration no: 01567231 **VAT No.:** 319 3607 56 **Date established:** 1981
Turnover: £1m - £2m **No.of Employees:** 1 - 10 **Product Groups:** 34, 37, 47

Date of Accounts	Oct 11	Oct 10	Oct 09
Working Capital	51	66	89
Fixed Assets	244	267	279
Current Assets	148	179	188

Moorland Compound
New Street, Biddulph Moor, Stoke On Trent, ST8 7NL
Tel: 01782-375450 **Fax:** 01782-522652
E-mail: sales@mitras-composites.co.uk
Website: http://www.mitras-composites.co.uk
Directors: B. Moore (MD), M. Davis (MD)
Immediate Holding Company: Moorland Composites Ltd
Registration no: 04341556 **Date established:** 2001
No.of Employees: 1 - 10 **Product Groups:** 30, 33

More Training Centre Ltd
49a-51 Clive Street, Stoke On Trent, ST6 6DA
Tel: 01782-835327 **Fax:** 01782-831920
E-mail: info@moretrain.co.uk
Website: http://www.moretrain.co.uk
Directors: D. Owens (Fin), P. Owens (MD)
Immediate Holding Company: MORE TRAINING LIMITED
Registration no: 04740382 **Date established:** 2003
Turnover: £500,000 - £1m **No.of Employees:** 11 - 20 **Product Groups:** 87

Date of Accounts	Dec 11	Dec 10	Dec 09
Working Capital	-35	-39	-58
Fixed Assets	41	50	58
Current Assets	59	44	45

Morris Bros Ltd
Phoenix Works 215 Scotia Road, Stoke On Trent, ST6 4HB
Tel: 01782-834242 **Fax:** 01782-575686
E-mail: sales@morrisbrothers.com
Website: http://www.morrisbrothers.com
Directors: D. Walker (Dir)
Immediate Holding Company: MORRIS BROTHERS (TUNSTALL) LIMITED
Registration no: 00461974 **VAT No.:** GB 278 8715 00
Date established: 1948 **Turnover:** £1m - £2m **No.of Employees:** 21 - 50
Product Groups: 38

Date of Accounts	Apr 11	Apr 10	Apr 09
Working Capital	500	605	695
Fixed Assets	701	740	796
Current Assets	1m	1m	1m

N G Autos
Sutherland Street, Stoke On Trent, ST4 4HS
Tel: 01782-869966
Directors: N. Griffiths (Prop)
Immediate Holding Company: CYL-PRESS LIMITED
Date established: 1980 **No.of Employees:** 1 - 10 **Product Groups:** 35, 84

Nassau Industrial Doors Ltd
Jubilee House Dewsbury Road Fenton Industrial Estate, Stoke On Trent, ST4 2TB
Tel: 01782-418700 **Fax:** 01782-418720
E-mail: info@nassau.co.uk
Website: http://www.nassau.co.uk
Directors: J. Woolley (Co Sec), T. Salmon (MD)
Immediate Holding Company: NASSAU INDUSTRIAL DOORS LIMITED
Registration no: 02905100 **Date established:** 1994
No.of Employees: 11 - 20 **Product Groups:** 26, 35

Date of Accounts	Dec 11	Dec 10	Dec 09
Working Capital	212	211	208
Fixed Assets	177	178	181
Current Assets	1m	883	953

New Haden Pumps Ltd
New Haden Works Draycott Cross Road, Cheadle, Stoke On Trent, ST10 2NW
Tel: 01538-757900 **Fax:** 01538-757999
E-mail: carole.edwards@nhpumps.com
Website: http://www.nhpumps.com
Bank(s): Barclays
Directors: P. Warman (Sales), C. Edwards (Co Sec)
Managers: L. Manning (Ops Mgr), N. Beech (Personnel)
Ultimate Holding Company: NEW HADEN PUMPING SOLUTIONS LIMITED
Immediate Holding Company: NEW HADEN PUMPS LIMITED
Registration no: 00826997 **VAT No.:** GB 125 8864 44
Date established: 1964 **Turnover:** £2m - £5m **No.of Employees:** 21 - 50
Product Groups: 39, 40, 41, 42, 43, 45, 46

Date of Accounts	Dec 11	Dec 10	Dec 09
Working Capital	760	682	611
Fixed Assets	74	203	195
Current Assets	2m	1m	1m

Newstead
Newstead Industrial Trading Estate, Stoke On Trent, ST4 8HX
Tel: 01782-658411 **Fax:** 01782-642823
E-mail: marketing@biffa.co.uk
Website: http://www.biffa.co.uk
Managers: A. Bakes (Site Co-ord)
Ultimate Holding Company: WASTEINVESTMENTS LLP
Immediate Holding Company: NEWSTEAD WINDOW GROUP LIMITED
Registration no: 03724055 **Date established:** 1999
No.of Employees: 1 - 10 **Product Groups:** 32, 54

Norman Rhead Precast
Addstone Way Off Anchor Road, Stoke On Trent, ST3 5BL
Tel: 01782-599770 **Fax:** 01782-599771
E-mail: james.adams@normanrhead.co.uk
Website: http://www.normanrhead.co.uk
Directors: D. Rushden (Dir)
Managers: P. Stephenson (Mgr), N. Brooks (Sales Prom Mgr), J. Adams (Mgr)
Registration no: 00568517 **VAT No.:** GB 279 2811 28
Turnover: £1m - £2m **No.of Employees:** 1 - 10 **Product Groups:** 33, 66

North Staffordshire Warm Zone
Innitiative House 103 Campbell Road, Stoke On Trent, ST4 4DE
Tel: 01782-479099 **Fax:** 01782-749471
E-mail: nswz@stoke.gov.uk
Website: http://www.nswz.co.uk
Managers: S. Thorley
Date established: 2007 **No.of Employees:** 11 - 20 **Product Groups:** 33

North Staffs Pipes Services Ltd
23 High Street Cheadle, Stoke On Trent, ST10 1AA
Tel: 01538-757177 **Fax:** 01538-757177
Directors: S. Parrish (MD)
Immediate Holding Company: NORTH STAFFS PIPE SERVICES LIMITED
Registration no: 01065514 **VAT No.:** GB 592 7227 16
Date established: 1972 **Turnover:** £500,000 - £1m
No.of Employees: 1 - 10 **Product Groups:** 52

Date of Accounts	Sep 11	Sep 10	Sep 09
Working Capital	161	182	210
Fixed Assets	106	97	84
Current Assets	344	346	368

Northwood Food Machinery Ltd
6 Campbell Road, Stoke On Trent, ST4 4DX
Tel: 01782-749515 **Fax:** 01782-749516
E-mail: michael.southwick@northwoodfoodmachinery.co.uk
Website: http://www.northwoodfoodmachinery.co.uk
Directors: M. Southwick (Co Sec)
Immediate Holding Company: NORTHWOOD FOOD MACHINERY LIMITED
Registration no: 02300936 **Date established:** 1988
No.of Employees: 1 - 10 **Product Groups:** 20, 40, 41

Date of Accounts	Oct 11	Oct 10	Oct 09
Working Capital	95	76	111
Fixed Assets	9	11	4
Current Assets	158	134	154

J Oldham & Co. Ltd
Tearne House Hollington, Stoke On Trent, ST10 4HR
Tel: 01889-507353 **Fax:** 01889-507212
E-mail: enquiries@joldham.co.uk
Website: http://www.joldham.co.uk
Bank(s): NWB Plc, 25 Market Place, Uttoxeter, ST14 5HX
Directors: J. Oldham (MD), N. Oldham (Dir), R. Oldham (MD)
Immediate Holding Company: J. OLDHAM & CO. (STONEMASONS) LIMITED
Registration no: 00634514 **VAT No.:** GB 125 6063 88
Date established: 1959 **Turnover:** £1m - £2m **No.of Employees:** 21 - 50
Product Groups: 14, 33, 52

Date of Accounts	Apr 08
Working Capital	4
Current Assets	13
Current Liabilities	10

Open Logistix Systems Ltd
1 Lyme Vale Court Lyme Drive, Parklands, Stoke On Trent, ST4 6NW
Tel: 01782-627489 **Fax:** 01782-621630
E-mail: stewart.murray@openlogistixsystems.co.uk
Directors: S. Murray (MD)
Immediate Holding Company: OPEN LOGISTIX SYSTEMS LIMITED
Registration no: 04270083 **Date established:** 2001
No.of Employees: 11 - 20 **Product Groups:** 44

Date of Accounts	Mar 10	Jan 09	Feb 12
Sales Turnover	N/A	N/A	566
Pre Tax Profit/Loss	N/A	N/A	2m
Working Capital	544	596	2m
Fixed Assets	209	24	N/A
Current Assets	1m	1m	2m

Otto Bock Health Care plc
Limb Fitting Centre Haywood Hospital, Stoke On Trent, ST6 7AG
Tel: 01782-812499
Website: http://www.ottobock.com
Directors: A. Russell (Prop)
Managers: A. Russell (District Mgr)
Immediate Holding Company: OTTO BOCK HEALTHCARE PLC
Registration no: 01271967 **Date established:** 1976
No.of Employees: 1 - 10 **Product Groups:** 38, 67

Owen Industrial Filtration
Strongford House Old Road Barlaston, Stoke On Trent, ST12 9EW
Tel: 01782-372477 **Fax:** 01782-372477
E-mail: dowen.oifl@btinternet.com
Website: http://www.oifl.co.uk
Directors: D. Owen (MD)
Immediate Holding Company: OWEN INDUSTRIAL FILTRATION LIMITED
Registration no: 03531544 **Date established:** 1998
Turnover: Up to £250,000 **No.of Employees:** 1 - 10 **Product Groups:** 29, 30, 31, 33, 40, 41, 42, 61, 85

Date of Accounts	Mar 11	Mar 10	Mar 09
Working Capital	2	N/A	6
Fixed Assets	5	6	5
Current Assets	91	102	65
Current Liabilities	N/A	26	N/A

P J Welding
King Street, Stoke On Trent, ST4 3DJ
Tel: 01782-315512 **Fax:** 01782-315512

Directors: J. Dreja (Prop)
Date established: 1975 **No.of Employees:** 1 - 10 **Product Groups:** 26, 35

Parnham Tractors Ltd
Leek Road Waterhouses, Stoke On Trent, ST10 3HS
Tel: 01538-308436 **Fax:** 01538-308751
E-mail: info@parnhamtractors.co.uk
Website: http://www.parnhamtractors.co.uk
Directors: R. Hardy (MD), D. Robotham (Fin)
Immediate Holding Company: PARNHAM TRACTORS LIMITED
Registration no: 01268821 **Date established:** 1976
No.of Employees: 1 - 10 **Product Groups:** 41

Date of Accounts	Jan 12	Jan 11	Jan 10
Working Capital	30	58	63
Fixed Assets	175	166	166
Current Assets	769	699	645

Patterns & Dies Ltd
Bute Street, Stoke On Trent, ST4 3PW
Tel: 01782-343700 **Fax:** 01782-343800
E-mail: csharratt@patterns-dies.co.uk
Website: http://www.patterns-dies.co.uk
Bank(s): National Westminster
Directors: C. Sharratt (MD)
Ultimate Holding Company: PATTERNS & DIES (HOLDINGS) LIMITED
Immediate Holding Company: PATTERNS & DIES LIMITED
Registration no: 00938324 **VAT No.:** 278 9708 89 **Date established:** 1968
Turnover: £1m - £2m **No.of Employees:** 11 - 20 **Product Groups:** 33, 48

Date of Accounts	Aug 11	Aug 10	Aug 09
Working Capital	108	322	285
Fixed Assets	211	176	205
Current Assets	504	659	667

E J Payne Ltd
1-3 Belgrave Road, Stoke On Trent, ST3 4PR
Tel: 01782-312534 **Fax:** 01782-599868
E-mail: sales@ejpayne.com
Website: http://www.ejpayne.com
Directors: A. Payne (MD)
Immediate Holding Company: E. J. PAYNE LIMITED
Registration no: 02273892 **VAT No.:** GB 670 3110 75
Date established: 1988 **Turnover:** £500,000 - £1m
No.of Employees: 1 - 10 **Product Groups:** 38, 40, 42, 45, 47, 67

Date of Accounts	Dec 11	Dec 10	Dec 09
Working Capital	-20	-54	-37
Fixed Assets	133	152	161
Current Assets	172	193	272

Plasterscene Plaster Ware
18 Christchurch Street, Stoke On Trent, ST4 3AD
Tel: 01782-844481 **Fax:** 01782-879848
E-mail: susanlovatt5056@msn.com
Directors: S. Lovett (Prop), L. Yewdell (Prop), S. Lovatt (Prop)
Date established: 1996 **No.of Employees:** 1 - 10 **Product Groups:** 52

Podmores Engineers Ltd
H Great Fenton Business Park Grove Road, Stoke On Trent, ST4 4LZ
Tel: 01782-747478 **Fax:** 01782-416606
E-mail: info@podmores-systems.com
Website: http://www.podmores-systems.com
Bank(s): HSBC
Directors: A. Gough (MD)
Immediate Holding Company: PODMORES (ENGINEERS) LIMITED
Registration no: 04415376 **VAT No.:** GB 787 5157 79
Date established: 2002 **Turnover:** £1m - £2m **No.of Employees:** 11 - 20
Product Groups: 33, 37, 38, 40, 41, 42, 45, 46, 47, 48, 67, 84

Date of Accounts	Apr 11	Apr 10	Apr 09
Working Capital	9	-2	62
Fixed Assets	37	45	47
Current Assets	258	237	328

Portmeirion Group Ltd
London Road, Stoke On Trent, ST4 7QQ
Tel: 01782-744721 **Fax:** 01782-744061
E-mail: splimbley@portmeiriongroup.com
Website: http://www.portmeiriongroup.com
Bank(s): Lloyds
Managers: S. Plimbley (Mktg Serv Mgr)
Ultimate Holding Company: PORTMEIRION GROUP PUBLIC LIMITED COMPANY
Immediate Holding Company: PORTMEIRION ENTERPRISES LIMITED
Registration no: 01952972 **VAT No.:** GB 488 1529 09
Date established: 1985 **Turnover:** £20m - £50m
No.of Employees: 501 - 1000 **Product Groups:** 33

Date of Accounts	Dec 11	Dec 10	Dec 09
Pre Tax Profit/Loss	4m	-22	1m
Working Capital	-4m	-4m	-2m
Fixed Assets	7m	7m	5m
Current Assets	N/A	483	33
Current Liabilities	N/A	N/A	56

Potclays Ltd
Albion Works Brickkiln Lane, Stoke On Trent, ST4 7BP
Tel: 01782-219816 **Fax:** 01782-286506
E-mail: sales@potclays.co.uk
Website: http://www.potclays.co.uk
Bank(s): Barclays
Directors: R. Otter (Mkt Research), M. Eagles (Co Sec)
Managers: L. Clewlow (Purch Mgr), M. Winkle, J. Noake
Immediate Holding Company: POTCLAYS LIMITED
Registration no: 00364976 **VAT No.:** GB 279 3840 16
Date established: 1941 **Turnover:** £2m - £5m **No.of Employees:** 21 - 50
Product Groups: 32, 66

Date of Accounts	Dec 11	Dec 10	Dec 09
Working Capital	270	253	213
Fixed Assets	407	421	432
Current Assets	614	655	590

Potteries Die Company Ltd
136 Knypersley Road Norton, Stoke On Trent, ST6 8JD
Tel: 01782-534348 **Fax:** 01782-535297
E-mail: rkd@potteriesdie.co.uk
Website: http://www.potteriesdie.co.uk
Bank(s): Barclays
Directors: E. Keeling (Fin), R. Dunleavy (MD)
Ultimate Holding Company: PDC PRECISION ENGINEERS LIMITED
Immediate Holding Company: POTTERIES DIE COMPANY LIMITED(THE)
Registration no: 00317610 **VAT No.:** GB 278 8210 30
Date established: 1936 **Turnover:** £1m - £2m **No.of Employees:** 11 - 20
Product Groups: 46

Date of Accounts	Oct 11	Oct 10	Oct 09
Working Capital	256	263	297
Fixed Assets	55	63	71
Current Assets	361	371	388

Potteries Power Transmission Ltd
32 Hartshill Road, Stoke On Trent, ST4 7QU
Tel: 01782-844144 **Fax:** 01782-745222
E-mail: david@ppt-ltd.co.uk
Website: http://www.ppt-ltd.co.uk
Directors: D. Hodgson (MD)
Immediate Holding Company: POTTERIES POWER TRANSMISSION LIMITED
Registration no: 01189386 **VAT No.:** GB 280 2504 84
Date established: 1974 **Turnover:** £1m - £2m **No.of Employees:** 1 - 10
Product Groups: 35, 37, 40

Date of Accounts	Oct 11	Oct 10	Oct 09
Working Capital	-41	-53	-83
Fixed Assets	176	179	192
Current Assets	508	550	369

Practicon Ltd
The Old School House Chapel Lane, Rode Heath, Stoke On Trent, ST7 3SD
Tel: 01270-876211 **Fax:** 01270-878887
E-mail: sales@practicon.co.uk
Website: http://www.practicon.co.uk
Bank(s): National Westminster Bank Plc
Directors: A. Taylor (MD)
Managers: J. Goodwin (Sales Prom Mgr), M. James (Tech Serv Mgr)
Immediate Holding Company: PRACTICON LIMITED
Registration no: 01366391 **Date established:** 1978 **Turnover:** £1m - £2m
No.of Employees: 21 - 50 **Product Groups:** 38, 45

Date of Accounts	Mar 12	Mar 11	Mar 10
Working Capital	657	418	407
Fixed Assets	219	208	188
Current Assets	2m	849	733

Precision Engineering Products Chesterton Ltd
Hanley Road, Stoke On Trent, ST1 6LF
Tel: 01782-202053 **Fax:** 01782-285667
E-mail: tsteveton@aol.com
Website: http://www.members.aol.com/pepltd
Directors: M. Steventon (MD), T. Steventon (MD)
Managers: E. Steventon (Chief Mgr)
Immediate Holding Company: PRECISION ENGINEERING PRODUCTS (CHESTERTON) LIMITED
Registration no: 01031152 **VAT No.:** GB 278 6673 00
Date established: 1971 **No.of Employees:** 1 - 10 **Product Groups:** 37, 84

Date of Accounts	Jun 10	Jun 09	Jun 08
Working Capital	-7	-0	1
Fixed Assets	2	3	4
Current Assets	21	27	26

Prohire plc
React House Spedding Road, Fenton Industrial Estate, Stoke On Trent, ST4 2ST
Tel: 08708-501200 **Fax:** 08708-501201
E-mail: enquiries@prohire.plc.uk
Website: http://www.prohire.plc.uk
Bank(s): National Westminster
Directors: A. Morley (Sales), D. Barlow (Grp Chief Exec), L. Bedson (Fin)
Managers: T. Mansbridge (Tech Serv Mgr)
Ultimate Holding Company: PGCH LIMITED
Immediate Holding Company: PROHIRE PLC
Registration no: 01388495 **VAT No.:** GB 695 9556 26
Date established: 1978 **Turnover:** £10m - £20m
No.of Employees: 21 - 50 **Product Groups:** 72

Date of Accounts	Mar 12	Mar 11	Mar 10
Sales Turnover	19m	18m	17m
Pre Tax Profit/Loss	1m	2m	2m
Working Capital	9m	8m	5m
Fixed Assets	1m	2m	3m
Current Assets	22m	20m	17m
Current Liabilities	4m	3m	3m

Promtek Ltd
Fisher Street Brindley Ford, Stoke On Trent, ST8 7QJ
Tel: 01782-375600 **Fax:** 01782-375605
E-mail: pwilliams@promtek.com
Website: http://www.promtek.com
Bank(s): Barclays
Directors: C. Williams (MD)
Immediate Holding Company: PROMTEK LIMITED
Registration no: 02275192 **VAT No.:** GB 290 0123 02
Date established: 1988 **Turnover:** £1m - £2m **No.of Employees:** 11 - 20
Product Groups: 35, 38, 84

Date of Accounts	Apr 11	Apr 10	Apr 09
Working Capital	1m	1m	1m
Fixed Assets	42	63	63
Current Assets	1m	1m	1m

Protective Tapes UK Ltd
23a Hamil Road, Stoke On Trent, ST6 1AJ
Tel: 01782-833560 **Fax:** 01782-833550
E-mail: sales@protective-tapes.co.uk
Website: http://www.protective-tapes.co.uk
Bank(s): Barclays, Manchester
Directors: Y. Hayes (MD)
Managers: D. Miller (Sales Prom Mgr), K. Oakley
Immediate Holding Company: PROTECTIVE TAPES (U.K.) LIMITED
Registration no: 01706334 **VAT No.:** GB 173 439 68
Date established: 1983 **Turnover:** £1m - £2m **No.of Employees:** 11 - 20
Product Groups: 23, 27

Date of Accounts	Apr 12	Apr 11	Apr 10
Working Capital	69	12	-56
Fixed Assets	94	85	95
Current Assets	1m	1m	923

Pump House Farm Stables
Chance Hall Lane Scholar Green, Stoke On Trent, ST7 3ST
Tel: 01270-873072
E-mail: phfsbask2000@yahoo.co.uk
Website: http://www.phfs.co.uk
Directors: S. Baskerville (Ptnr)
Immediate Holding Company: PUMP HOUSE FARM SUPPLIES LIMITED
Registration no: 05738167 **Date established:** 2006
No.of Employees: 1 - 10 **Product Groups:** 36, 40, 66

Date of Accounts	Mar 12	Mar 11	Mar 09
Working Capital	-87	-91	-50
Fixed Assets	97	109	86
Current Assets	44	62	36

Q E D Project Engineering Ltd
10 Nile Street, Stoke On Trent, ST6 2AF
Tel: 01782-575612 **Fax:** 01782-833010
E-mail: neil.bott@qedprojects.com
Website: http://www.qedprojects.com
Directors: J. Howard (MD)
Immediate Holding Company: Q.E.D. PROJECT ENGINEERING LIMITED
Registration no: 01386086 **Date established:** 1978
Turnover: £500,000 - £1m **No.of Employees:** 1 - 10 **Product Groups:** 51

Date of Accounts	Aug 11	Aug 10	Aug 09
Sales Turnover	N/A	510	531
Working Capital	128	135	228
Fixed Assets	28	29	31
Current Assets	283	238	228

Qed Recruitment Ltd
10 Nile Street, Stoke On Trent, ST6 2AF
Tel: 01782-575612 **Fax:** 0870-762 2152
E-mail: rth@qedprojects.com
Website: http://www.qedprojects.com
Directors: N. Bott (MD)
Immediate Holding Company: QED RECRUITMENT LIMITED
Registration no: 05226123 **Date established:** 2004
No.of Employees: 1 - 10 **Product Groups:** 80

Qualfab Engineering
Clarence Road, Stoke On Trent, ST3 1AZ
Tel: 01782-342442 **Fax:** 01782- 342442
Directors: E. Chitt (Prop)
Ultimate Holding Company: LT HOLDINGS LIMITED
Immediate Holding Company: INDUSTRIAL & CONSTRUCTION PLANT LIMITED
Registration no: 00560220 **Date established:** 1956
No.of Employees: 1 - 10 **Product Groups:** 35

Date of Accounts	Mar 11	Mar 10	Mar 09
Working Capital	337	337	337
Fixed Assets	14	14	14
Current Assets	337	337	337

R G Bassett & Sons Ltd
Transport House Tittensor, Stoke On Trent, ST12 9HD
Tel: 01782-372251 **Fax:** 01782-371028
E-mail: info@bassett-group.co.uk
Website: http://www.bassett-group.co.uk
Directors: L. Bassett (Fin)
Managers: C. Bassett, M. Lean (Comptroller)
Immediate Holding Company: R G BASSETT & SONS LIMITED
Registration no: 02269632 **Date established:** 1988 **Turnover:** £5m - £10m
No.of Employees: 51 - 100 **Product Groups:** 72, 77

Date of Accounts	Mar 12	Mar 11	Mar 10
Sales Turnover	8m	7m	7m
Pre Tax Profit/Loss	226	144	138
Working Capital	798	641	658
Fixed Assets	2m	2m	2m
Current Assets	2m	2m	2m
Current Liabilities	359	283	252

R G Trade Supplies Ltd
Foley Street, Stoke On Trent, ST4 3DR
Tel: 01782-599125 **Fax:** 01782-335367
E-mail: info@rgteng.co.uk
Website: http://www.rgtengineering.co.uk
Directors: G. Hill (MD), R. Hill (MD)
Immediate Holding Company: R.G. TRADE SUPPLIES AND ENGINEERING LIMITED
Registration no: 01119121 **Date established:** 1973
No.of Employees: 21 - 50 **Product Groups:** 34, 35, 36, 39, 41, 48, 49, 68, 81, 85

Date of Accounts	Oct 11	Oct 10	Oct 09
Working Capital	216	299	236
Fixed Assets	281	202	187
Current Assets	538	548	471

Rackline Ltd
Oaktree Lane Talke Pits, Stoke On Trent, ST7 1RX
Tel: 01782-777666 **Fax:** 01782-777444
E-mail: lindsay.khan@rackline.com
Website: http://www.rackline.co.uk
Bank(s): Barclays
Directors: T. Goodwin (Comm), L. Khan (MD), S. Knobbs (Fin), S. Lister (Fin)
Managers: A. Cartwright (Purch Mgr)
Immediate Holding Company: RACKLINE LIMITED
Registration no: 04697883 **VAT No.:** GB 419 6167 35
Date established: 2003 **Turnover:** £5m - £10m
No.of Employees: 51 - 100 **Product Groups:** 26, 45, 49

Date of Accounts	Dec 11	Dec 10	Dec 09
Sales Turnover	9m	7m	7m
Pre Tax Profit/Loss	397	86	233
Working Capital	-313	-286	-138
Fixed Assets	1m	1m	2m
Current Assets	2m	2m	2m
Current Liabilities	1m	1m	644

Radway Control Systems Ltd
Unit 1 West Avenue Kidsgrove, Stoke On Trent, ST7 1TR
Tel: 01782-776622 **Fax:** 01782-785409
E-mail: email@radway.co.uk
Website: http://www.radway.co.uk
Directors: D. Allen (Dir)
Immediate Holding Company: RADWAY CONTROL SYSTEMS LIMITED
Registration no: 02953969 **Date established:** 1994
No.of Employees: 1 - 10 **Product Groups:** 37, 49

Date of Accounts	Jul 11	Jul 10	Jul 09
Working Capital	227	227	230
Fixed Assets	4	5	4
Current Assets	367	367	317

Rakeway
Unit J Brookhouse Way Cheadle, Stoke On Trent, ST10 1SR
Tel: 01538-750500
Website: http://www.rakeway.co.uk

see next page

***Rakeway** - Cont'd*

Directors: N. Richardson (MD)
Immediate Holding Company: RAKEWAY LIMITED
Registration no: 05032310 **Date established:** 2004
No.of Employees: 1 - 10 **Product Groups:** 36, 44, 48

Date of Accounts	May 12	May 11	May 10
Working Capital	-21	-25	-28
Fixed Assets	61	71	79
Current Assets	84	72	81

Robin Engineering Services Ltd

Unit 12 203 Grindley Lane Blythe Bridge, Stoke On Trent, ST11 9JS
Tel: 01782-392989 **Fax:** 01782-398798
E-mail: robinengineering@aol.com
Website: http://www.robinengineering.com
Directors: J. Pegg (Fin), B. Milnes (MD)
Immediate Holding Company: ROBIN ENGINEERING SERVICES LIMITED
Registration no: 04759281 **Date established:** 2003
Turnover: Up to £250,000 **No.of Employees:** 1 - 10 **Product Groups:** 35, 39, 45

Date of Accounts	May 11	May 10	May 09
Working Capital	-3	-2	N/A
Current Assets	N/A	1	1

Robinson Wire Cloth Ltd

1 Rebecca Street, Stoke On Trent, ST4 1AG
Tel: 01782-412521 **Fax:** 01782-412766
E-mail: info@wirecloth.uk.com
Website: http://www.wirecloth.uk.com
Directors: C. Ellis (Jt MD), C. Ellis (Dir), E. Ellis (Jt MD), E. Ellis (Fin)
Managers: L. Fox (Sales Prom Mgr)
Immediate Holding Company: ROBINSON WIRE CLOTH LIMITED
Registration no: 01436881 **VAT No.:** GB 319 0806 65
Date established: 1979 **No.of Employees:** 1 - 10 **Product Groups:** 29, 32, 33, 34, 35, 36, 41, 42, 45, 46, 47

Date of Accounts	Oct 11	Oct 10	Oct 09
Working Capital	317	253	258
Fixed Assets	76	81	86
Current Assets	377	305	296

Ross Microwave Oven Repairs Ltd

17-23 Waterloo Road, Stoke On Trent, ST6 2EH
Tel: 01782-838462 **Fax:** 01782-838462
Directors: B. Ross (MD)
Date established: 1973 **No.of Employees:** 1 - 10 **Product Groups:** 36, 40

S & L Engine Services

Railway Passage, Stoke On Trent, ST3 1BY
Tel: 01782-599245 **Fax:** 01782-599441
E-mail: slengineservices@btconnect.com
Directors: G. Lewis (Prop)
Immediate Holding Company: AYSHFORD CHINA LIMITED
Registration no: 01397046 **Date established:** 1978
Turnover: Up to £250,000 **No.of Employees:** 1 - 10 **Product Groups:** 35, 36, 39

Date of Accounts	Mar 11	Mar 10	Mar 09
Sales Turnover	N/A	50	61
Pre Tax Profit/Loss	N/A	-2	-3
Working Capital	-2	-4	-2
Fixed Assets	4	4	4
Current Assets	19	19	27
Current Liabilities	1	N/A	N/A

S W G Process Engineering Ltd

Gibson Street, Stoke On Trent, ST6 6AQ
Tel: 01782-824399 **Fax:** 01782-834015
E-mail: richard.shufflebottom@vibrodynamics.co.uk
Website: http://www.vibrodynamics.co.uk
Directors: R. Shufflebottom (Dir)
Immediate Holding Company: SWG PROCESS ENGINEERING LIMITED
Registration no: 02104495 **Date established:** 1987
Turnover: £500,000 - £1m **No.of Employees:** 1 - 10 **Product Groups:** 34, 35, 36, 37, 42, 45, 67

Date of Accounts	Dec 11	Dec 10	Dec 09
Working Capital	45	43	64
Fixed Assets	59	59	59
Current Assets	80	92	104

Salt Coachpainting Ltd

Sandbach Road, Stoke On Trent, ST6 2DG
Tel: 01782-213164 **Fax:** 01782-206538
E-mail: philevans660@googlemail.com
Directors: P. Evans (MD), D. Evans (Fin)
Immediate Holding Company: SALT COACHPAINTING LIMITED
Registration no: 03585701 **Date established:** 1998
No.of Employees: 1 - 10 **Product Groups:** 46, 48

Date of Accounts	Mar 12	Mar 11	Mar 10
Working Capital	67	63	84
Fixed Assets	1	1	1
Current Assets	90	89	106

Sandvik Heating Technology

Festival Park, Stoke On Trent, ST1 5UR
Tel: 01782-224800 **Fax:** 01782-224820
E-mail: info.ukstoke@kanthal.com
Website: http://www.kanthal.com
Managers: D. Burton (Chief Mgr)
Ultimate Holding Company: SANDVIK AB (SWEDEN)
Immediate Holding Company: KANTHAL ELECTROHEAT LIMITED
Registration no: 00679649 **VAT No.:** GB 263 3005 93
Date established: 1961 **Turnover:** £10m - £20m **No.of Employees:** 1 - 10
Product Groups: 33, 34, 35, 37, 40, 47

Scientific Glass Laboratories Ltd

Canal Lane, Stoke On Trent, ST6 4PQ
Tel: 01782-816237 **Fax:** 01782-575637
E-mail: sales@scientificglass.co.uk
Website: http://www.scientificglass.co.uk
Directors: P. Ruane (Fin), M. Ruane (MD)
Immediate Holding Company: SCIENTIFIC GLASS LABORATORIES LIMITED
Registration no: 00886418 **VAT No.:** GB 279 1916 19
Date established: 1966 **Turnover:** £1m - £2m **No.of Employees:** 1 - 10
Product Groups: 63

Date of Accounts	Mar 12	Mar 11	Mar 10
Working Capital	264	244	175
Fixed Assets	188	195	201
Current Assets	643	660	600

Signal Fire

63 Meaford Road Barlaston, Stoke On Trent, ST12 9EE
Tel: 01782-373742 **Fax:** 01782-373742
Directors: J. Davison (Prop)
Immediate Holding Company: SIGNAL FIRE & SAFETY LIMITED
Registration no: 04942381 **Date established:** 2003
No.of Employees: 1 - 10 **Product Groups:** 38, 42

Signs Express

Unit 3 Crabtree Close Fenton Industrial Estate, Stoke On Trent, ST4 2SW
Tel: 01782-416930 **Fax:** 01782-416931
E-mail: stokeontrent@signsexpress.co.uk
Website: http://www.signsexpress.co.uk
Directors: C. Gallon (Prop)
Immediate Holding Company: SIGNS EXPRESS LIMITED
Registration no: 02375913 **Date established:** 1989
No.of Employees: 1 - 10 **Product Groups:** 30, 39, 40, 80, 81, 84

Simpson & Co Number Plates Engraving & Copier Consumables

Unit 7 Cleveland Trading Estate College Road, Stoke On Trent, ST1 4DQ
Tel: 01782-212705 **Fax:** 01782-281158
E-mail: simpson.dawson@ntlworld.com
Directors: R. Dawson (Ptnr)
Date established: 1963 **Turnover:** £250,000 - £500,000
No.of Employees: 1 - 10 **Product Groups:** 28, 30, 39, 48, 49

Slave To Design

9 Oldham Street Joiners Square Industrial Estate, Stoke On Trent, ST1 3EY
Tel: 01782-207884 **Fax:** 01782-207884
E-mail: info@slavetodesign.com
Website: http://www.slavetodesign.com
Directors: I. Butcher (Prop)
Registration no: 05948928 **Date established:** 2006
Turnover: Up to £250,000 **No.of Employees:** 1 - 10 **Product Groups:** 81

Date of Accounts	Sep 07
Working Capital	-1
Fixed Assets	1
Current Assets	2
Current Liabilities	2

Soco System UK Ltd

Unit 18 Palmerston Street Joiners Square Industrial Estate, Stoke On Trent, ST1 3EU
Tel: 01782-274100 **Fax:** 01782-272696
E-mail: info@socosystem.co.uk
Website: http://www.socosystem.co.uk
Directors: P. Bangs (Co Sec)
Ultimate Holding Company: SOCO SYSTEM A/S (DENMARK)
Immediate Holding Company: SOCO SYSTEM (U.K.) LIMITED
Registration no: 02556578 **VAT No.:** GB 536 9859 84
Date established: 1990 **Turnover:** £1m - £2m **No.of Employees:** 1 - 10
Product Groups: 42, 45, 84

Date of Accounts	Sep 11	Sep 10	Sep 09
Sales Turnover	1m	1m	1m
Pre Tax Profit/Loss	-9	-33	-183
Working Capital	25	34	67
Current Assets	509	370	300
Current Liabilities	181	53	18

Sovereign Planned Services

Unit 3d Brown Lees Road Industrial Estate Knypersley, Stoke On Trent, ST8 7DN
Tel: 01782-510600 **Fax:** 01782-510700
E-mail: sales@sovpsl.com
Website: http://www.sovpsl.co.uk
Managers: A. Whalley (Mgr)
Registration no: 03491534 **No.of Employees:** 11 - 20
Product Groups: 30, 40, 48, 52, 68, 84

Date of Accounts	Apr 08	Apr 07	Apr 06
Working Capital	132	158	185
Fixed Assets	68	34	47
Current Assets	544	441	482
Current Liabilities	412	283	297

Spectrum Services

5-13 High Street Tunstall, Stoke On Trent, ST6 5TE
Tel: 01782-575592 **Fax:** 01782-811464
E-mail: enquiries@spectrum-services.com
Website: http://www.spectrum-services.com
Directors: J. Ryszka (Prop)
Date established: 1986 **No.of Employees:** 1 - 10 **Product Groups:** 43

Staffordshire Hydraulic Services Ltd

Mount Road Kidsgrove, Stoke On Trent, ST7 4AZ
Tel: 01782-771225 **Fax:** 01782-777087
E-mail: sales@staffshydraulics.co.uk
Website: http://www.staffshydraulics.co.uk
Bank(s): Barclays Bank
Directors: B. Thompson (MD), M. Thompson (Co Sec)
Immediate Holding Company: STAFFORDSHIRE HYDRAULIC SERVICES LIMITED
Registration no: 01258035 **Date established:** 1976 **Turnover:** £1m - £2m
No.of Employees: 21 - 50 **Product Groups:** 30, 35, 36, 37, 38, 39, 40, 42, 45, 52, 66, 67, 85

Date of Accounts	Jun 11	Jun 10	Jun 09
Working Capital	2m	1m	1m
Fixed Assets	246	256	249
Current Assets	3m	2m	2m

Steelite International plc

Orme Street, Stoke On Trent, ST6 3RB
Tel: 01782-821000 **Fax:** 01782-819926
E-mail: sales@steelite.com
Website: http://www.steelite.com
Bank(s): The Royal Bank of Scotland
Directors: R. Poole (Fin), K. Oakes (Sales)
Managers: A. Bennett (Tech Serv Mgr)
Ultimate Holding Company: STEELITE INTERNATIONAL HOLDINGS LIMITED
Immediate Holding Company: STEELITE INTERNATIONAL PLC
Registration no: 01697123 **Date established:** 1983
Turnover: £50m - £75m **No.of Employees:** 251 - 500
Product Groups: 33, 49

Date of Accounts	Dec 11	Dec 10	Dec 09
Sales Turnover	66m	61m	52m
Pre Tax Profit/Loss	8m	8m	5m
Working Capital	43m	41m	39m
Fixed Assets	723	890	1m
Current Assets	54m	51m	47m
Current Liabilities	7m	7m	6m

Stoke Galvanising Ltd

Nevada Lane Hot Lane, Hot Lane Industrial Estate, Stoke On Trent, ST6 2BN
Tel: 01782-811226 **Fax:** 01782-836686
Directors: N. Garratt (Fin)
Ultimate Holding Company: WIDNES GALVANISING LIMITED
Immediate Holding Company: STOKE GALVANISING LIMITED
Registration no: 02313414 **Date established:** 1988
No.of Employees: 11 - 20 **Product Groups:** 46, 48

Date of Accounts	Jun 11	Jun 10	Jun 09
Working Capital	780	684	641
Fixed Assets	135	137	116
Current Assets	1m	1m	1m
Current Liabilities	N/A	11	N/A

Stoke On Trent Workshops

211 City Road, Stoke On Trent, ST4 2PN
Tel: 01782-233900 **Fax:** 01782- 234900
E-mail: sales@stokeworkshops.co.uk
Website: http://www.stokeworkshops.co.uk
Bank(s): Co-Op, Stafford
Directors: M. Thompson (Dir)
Managers: M. Thompson (Sales Prom Mgr), M. Richards (Chief Mgr), M. Green (Prod Mgr), R. Bisson (Sales Prom Mgr)
Ultimate Holding Company: STOKE-ON-TRENT CITY COUNCIL
Immediate Holding Company: STOKE WORKSHOPS LIMITED
VAT No.: GB 280 0653 77 **Date established:** 2009
Turnover: £500,000 - £1m **No.of Employees:** 21 - 50
Product Groups: 49, 66

Surface Technology

Town House Farm Alsager Road, Audley, Stoke On Trent, ST7 8JQ
Tel: 01782-722147 **Fax:** 01782-729239
E-mail: brian.bailey@surface-tech.co.uk
Directors: B. Bailey (Dir)
Immediate Holding Company: VILLAGE INDUSTRIES LIMITED
Date established: 1986 **No.of Employees:** 1 - 10 **Product Groups:** 29, 30, 32, 40, 52

Date of Accounts	Jun 11	Jun 10	Jun 07
Working Capital	3	-1	-6
Fixed Assets	10	11	16
Current Assets	14	15	15

Systems Technology Consultants Ltd

PO Box 5, Stoke On Trent, ST1 4PZ
Tel: 01782-286300 **Fax:** 01782-280036
E-mail: sytech@sytech-consultants.com
Website: http://www.sytech-consultants.com
Directors: E. Blazier (Fin)
Immediate Holding Company: SYSTEMS TECHNOLOGY CONSULTANTS LIMITED
Registration no: 03301898 **VAT No.:** 338 4028 59 **Date established:** 1997
Turnover: £250,000 - £500,000 **No.of Employees:** 1 - 10
Product Groups: 44, 80

Date of Accounts	Oct 11	Jul 10	Jul 09
Working Capital	41	83	53
Fixed Assets	15	20	3
Current Assets	128	154	88

T S Fabrication & Welding

1 Navigation Road, Stoke On Trent, ST6 3BL
Tel: 01782-577667 **Fax:** 01782-577667
Directors: T. Howell (Prop)
Date established: 2003 **No.of Employees:** 1 - 10 **Product Groups:** 35

T W Fixings

53 Chatsworth Drive Werrington, Stoke On Trent, ST9 0PA
Tel: 01782-304104 **Fax:** 01782-305003
E-mail: twfixings@fsnet.com
Website: http://www.fixings.fsnet.co.uk
Directors: T. Warrington (Prop)
Date established: 1990 **No.of Employees:** 1 - 10 **Product Groups:** 35

Tarmac Quarry Products Ltd (Silomate)

Croxden Quarry Freehay, Cheadle, Stoke On Trent, ST10 1RH
Tel: 01538-722393 **Fax:** 01538-723980
E-mail: hughmcguigan@tarmac.co.uk
Website: http://www.tarmac.co.uk
Managers: H. Mcguigan (Mgr)
Ultimate Holding Company: ANGLO AMERICAN PLC
Immediate Holding Company: TARMAC LTD
Registration no: 00368254 **No.of Employees:** 21 - 50 **Product Groups:** 33

Taylormade Castings Ltd

Cobridge Road, Stoke On Trent, ST1 5JP
Tel: 01782-261537 **Fax:** 01782-261262
E-mail: g.taylor@taylormade-castings.co.uk
Bank(s): Barclays
Directors: M. Leese (Fin), G. Taylor (Dir)
Ultimate Holding Company: TAYLOR'S FOUNDRY LIMITED
Immediate Holding Company: TAYLORMADE CASTINGS LIMITED
Registration no: 01319501 **VAT No.:** GB 304 7758 52
Date established: 1977 **No.of Employees:** 21 - 50 **Product Groups:** 34, 66

Date of Accounts	Nov 11	Nov 10	Nov 09
Working Capital	801	774	692
Fixed Assets	300	309	358
Current Assets	1m	1m	1m

Tekdata Distribution Ltd

Technology House Crown Road, Stoke On Trent, ST1 5NJ
Tel: 01782-274255 **Fax:** 01782-665511
E-mail: info@tekdata.co.uk
Website: http://www.tekdata.co.uk
Bank(s): Barclays
Directors: G. Cooper (Fin)
Ultimate Holding Company: DCC PUBLIC LIMITED COMPANY
Immediate Holding Company: TEKDATA DISTRIBUTION LIMITED
Registration no: 04991487 **VAT No.:** GB 836 9242 04
Date established: 2003 **Turnover:** £5m - £10m **No.of Employees:** 21 - 50
Product Groups: 37, 44, 61, 67, 79

Date of Accounts	Mar 11	Mar 10	Mar 09
Sales Turnover	9m	9m	7m
Pre Tax Profit/Loss	533	652	679

Working Capital	1m	959	455
Fixed Assets	1m	1m	2m
Current Assets	4m	3m	3m
Current Liabilities	333	279	658

Terrafix Ltd
Unit 23c Newfields Industrial Estate High Street, Stoke On Trent, ST6 5PD
Tel: 01782-577015 **Fax:** 01782-835667
E-mail: enquiries@terrafix.co.uk
Website: http://www.terrafix.co.uk
Bank(s): National Westminster Bank Plc
Directors: C. Theaker (Tech Serv), R. Mason (I.T. Dir), C. Rosson (Mkt Research), C. Green (MD), C. Green (Sales), D. Adams (Fin)
Managers: C. Smith
Ultimate Holding Company: LAND NAVIGATION SYSTEMS LIMITED
Immediate Holding Company: TERRAFIX LIMITED
Registration no: 01650825 **VAT No.:** GB 646 9325 09
Date established: 1982 **Turnover:** £5m - £10m
No.of Employees: 51 - 100 **Product Groups:** 37, 44, 79, 86

Date of Accounts	Jun 11	Jun 10	Jun 09
Sales Turnover	9m	10m	9m
Pre Tax Profit/Loss	442	1m	2m
Working Capital	3m	3m	733
Fixed Assets	61	28	29
Current Assets	5m	4m	4m
Current Liabilities	957	592	2m

Thames Lubricants Ltd
Garner Street, Stoke On Trent, ST4 7DE
Tel: 01782-745678 **Fax:** 01782-848437
E-mail: sales@thameslubricants.co.uk
Website: http://www.thameslubricants.co.uk
Directors: J. Salt (Fin)
Immediate Holding Company: THAMES LUBRICANTS LIMITED
Registration no: 03516425 **Date established:** 1998
Turnover: £500,000 - £1m **No.of Employees:** 1 - 10 **Product Groups:** 31, 39, 66

Date of Accounts	May 11	May 10	May 09
Working Capital	-70	-68	-55
Fixed Assets	235	216	214
Current Assets	204	174	174

Thunderbolt Test & Maintenance Ltd
Unit 82 Shelton Enterprise Centre Bedford Street, Stoke On Trent, ST1 4PZ
Tel: 01782-251776 **Fax:** 01782-833555
E-mail: info@thunderbolt-tm.co.uk
Website: http://www.thunderbolttm.com
Directors: M. Heffernan (MD)
Immediate Holding Company: THUNDERBOLT TEST AND MAINTENANCE LIMITED
Registration no: 03131516 **Date established:** 1995
Turnover: £250,000 - £500,000 **No.of Employees:** 1 - 10
Product Groups: 84

Date of Accounts	Nov 10	Nov 09	Nov 08
Sales Turnover	455	494	597
Pre Tax Profit/Loss	-15	-19	20
Working Capital	-27	-10	6
Fixed Assets	29	27	31
Current Assets	134	102	146
Current Liabilities	2	10	17

Timberwise UK plc
47 The Green Cheadle, Stoke On Trent, ST10 1XS
Tel: 01782-599921 **Fax:** 0161-962 7610
E-mail: stoke@timberwise.co.uk
Website: http://www.timberwise.co.uk
Managers: J. Holt (Mgr)
Immediate Holding Company: TIMBERWISE (UK) LIMITED
Registration no: 03230356 **Date established:** 1996
No.of Employees: 11 - 20 **Product Groups:** 07, 32, 52

Torque Fast Calibration
Calibration House Canal Lane, Stoke On Trent, ST6 4NZ
Tel: 01782-835473 **Fax:** 01782-837562
E-mail: sales@torquefast.co.uk
Website: http://www.torquefast.co.uk
Managers: A. Windsor (Sales Admin)
Immediate Holding Company: TORQUE FAST CALIBRATION LIMITED
Registration no: 02768370 **Date established:** 1992
Turnover: £500,000 - £1m **No.of Employees:** 1 - 10 **Product Groups:** 38, 85

Date of Accounts	Sep 11	Sep 10	Sep 09
Working Capital	18	31	41
Fixed Assets	30	20	7
Current Assets	88	71	69

Total Bakery Engineers Ltd
Unit 3b Brown Lees Road Industrial Estate Forge Way, Knypersley, Stoke On Trent, ST8 7DN
Tel: 01782-511118 **Fax:** 01782-511129
E-mail: sales@totalbakeryengineers.co.uk
Website: http://www.totalbakeryengineers.co.uk
Directors: J. Ball (MD)
Immediate Holding Company: TOTAL BAKERY ENGINEERS LIMITED
Registration no: 02039170 **Date established:** 1986
No.of Employees: 1 - 10 **Product Groups:** 41

Date of Accounts	Aug 11	Aug 10	Aug 09
Working Capital	43	37	35
Fixed Assets	174	201	210
Current Assets	171	145	241

Trolleymanplus
5 Close Lane Alsager, Stoke On Trent, ST7 2JR
Tel: 01270-874582 **Fax:** 01270-874582
E-mail: solutions@trolleymanplus.co.uk
Website: http://www.trolleymanplus.co.uk
Managers: G. Clarke
Turnover: Up to £250,000 **No.of Employees:** 1 - 10 **Product Groups:** 36, 40, 45

Turner E P S Ltd
Newstead Industrial Trading Estate, Stoke On Trent, ST4 8HT
Tel: 01782-657331 **Fax:** 01782-644600
E-mail: jack.caldwell@turner-eps.co.uk
Website: http://www.turner-eps.co.uk
Bank(s): National Westminster Bank Plc
Directors: J. Caldwell (Chief Op Offcr)
Managers: A. Watson (Sales Prom Mgr), T. Charles (Chief Acct), M. Woodward, J. Withers (Mktg Serv Mgr)
Ultimate Holding Company: TURNER & CO. (GLASGOW) LIMITED
Immediate Holding Company: TILSLEY & LOVATT LIMITED
Registration no: 00400016 **VAT No.:** GB 278 3074 37
Date established: 1945 **Turnover:** £1m - £2m **No.of Employees:** 51 - 100
Product Groups: 37, 39, 40, 48, 66, 67, 68

Date of Accounts	Mar 08	Mar 09	Mar 10
Sales Turnover	10m	10m	12m
Pre Tax Profit/Loss	837	2m	879
Working Capital	680	2m	3m
Fixed Assets	253	260	N/A
Current Assets	5m	5m	4m
Current Liabilities	1m	1m	561

Twyford Bathrooms
Lawton Road Alsager, Stoke On Trent, ST7 2DF
Tel: 01270-879777 **Fax:** 01270-873864
E-mail: michaelconlon@twyfordbathrooms.com
Website: http://www.twyfordbathrooms.com
Directors: M. Conlon (MD)
Managers: S. Kenway (Personnel), K. Wood (Purch Mgr), J. Blackburn, M. Winfield (Mktg Serv Mgr)
Ultimate Holding Company: SOFIA I S+üRL (LUXEMBOURG)
Immediate Holding Company: TWYFORD BATHROOMS
Registration no: 00546129 **Date established:** 1955
Turnover: £50m - £75m **No.of Employees:** 251 - 500
Product Groups: 25, 30, 33, 36, 66

Date of Accounts	Dec 11	Dec 10	Dec 09
Sales Turnover	59m	64m	60m
Pre Tax Profit/Loss	6m	-8m	-7m
Working Capital	25m	27m	29m
Fixed Assets	3m	4m	4m
Current Assets	47m	53m	48m
Current Liabilities	8m	11m	3m

Venturi Jet Pumps Ltd
Venturi House 66 Edensor Road, Stoke On Trent, ST3 2QE
Tel: 01782-599800 **Fax:** 01782-599009
E-mail: sales@venturipumps.com
Website: http://www.venturipumps.co.uk
Directors: P. Emmett (Dir)
Immediate Holding Company: VENTURI JET PUMPS LIMITED
Registration no: 03654492 **VAT No.:** GB 715 4003 75
Date established: 1998 **Turnover:** £250,000 - £500,000
No.of Employees: 1 - 10 **Product Groups:** 34, 39, 40, 42, 67

Date of Accounts	Mar 12	Mar 11	Mar 10
Working Capital	224	133	138
Fixed Assets	53	50	52
Current Assets	309	175	192

Veolia Water Solutions & Technologies
Whittle Road, Stoke On Trent, ST3 7QD
Tel: 01782-599000 **Fax:** 01782-599001
E-mail: ian.ronson@veoliawater.com
Website: http://www.veoliawaterst.co.uk
Bank(s): HSBC Bank plc
Managers: S. Kettle (Fin Mgr), I. Ronson (Site Co-ord)
Ultimate Holding Company: VIVENDI UNIVERSAL S.A.
Immediate Holding Company: VIVENDI WATER SYSTEMS LTD
Registration no: 00327847 **VAT No.:** GB 207 8034 79
Turnover: £5m - £10m **No.of Employees:** 51 - 100 **Product Groups:** 29, 40, 42, 45

Vizual Management Solutions Ltd
24a Stanley Street, Stoke On Trent, ST6 6BW
Tel: 01782-812767 **Fax:** 01782-839682
E-mail: info@vizualms.co.uk
Website: http://www.time-attendance.co.uk
Directors: A. Dent (Fin), P. Mart (MD)
Immediate Holding Company: VIZUAL MANAGEMENT SOLUTIONS LIMITED
Registration no: 05343714 **Date established:** 2005
No.of Employees: 1 - 10 **Product Groups:** 40, 44

Date of Accounts	Mar 12	Mar 11	Mar 10
Working Capital	71	33	73
Current Assets	296	288	284

Vulcan Refractories Ltd
Brookhouse Industrial Estate Cheadle, Stoke On Trent, ST10 1PN
Tel: 01538-752238 **Fax:** 01538-753349
E-mail: nicholas@vulcan-refractories.co.uk
Website: http://www.vulcan-refractories.co.uk
Bank(s): National Westminster Bank Plc
Directors: N. Zienkowicz (MD), M. Clarke (Co Sec)
Immediate Holding Company: VULCAN REFRACTORIES LIMITED
Registration no: 00952421 **VAT No.:** GB 126 1391 90
Date established: 1969 **Turnover:** £2m - £5m **No.of Employees:** 51 - 100
Product Groups: 33, 35, 37, 40, 46, 48, 67

Date of Accounts	Dec 11	Mar 11	Mar 10
Working Capital	493	509	410
Fixed Assets	659	581	579
Current Assets	707	844	941

W I R S Wolverhampton Ltd
Unit 10 Crabtree Close Fenton Industrial Estate, Stoke On Trent, ST4 2SW
Tel: 01782-848547 **Fax:** 01782-411492
E-mail: stokesales@wirs.co.uk
Website: http://www.wirs.com
Directors: P. Marsh (Comm)
Immediate Holding Company: WIRS (WOLVERHAMPTON) LIMITED
Registration no: 02088761 **Date established:** 1987
No.of Employees: 1 - 10 **Product Groups:** 46

Date of Accounts	Sep 11	Sep 10	Sep 09
Working Capital	2m	2m	2m
Fixed Assets	816	836	862
Current Assets	3m	2m	2m

W L Mets Ltd
The Cottage Stores Stone Road, Tittensor, Stoke On Trent, ST12 9HA
Tel: 01782-374111 **Fax:** 01782-373488
E-mail: gordonhutch@wlmetals.co.uk
Website: http://www.wlmetals.co.uk
Directors: G. Hutchinson (Dir)
Immediate Holding Company: WLMETS LIMITED
Registration no: 02316568 **VAT No.:** GB 478 7776 66
Date established: 1988 **Turnover:** £1m - £2m **No.of Employees:** 1 - 10
Product Groups: 34, 35, 36, 37, 48

Date of Accounts	Apr 12	Apr 09	Apr 10
Working Capital	-42	10	-14
Fixed Assets	87	90	84
Current Assets	258	329	425

W Moorcroft Ltd
Sandbach Road Burslem, Stoke On Trent, ST6 2DQ
Tel: 01782-820500 **Fax:** 01782-820502
E-mail: enquiries@moorcroft.com
Website: http://www.moorcroft.com
Bank(s): National Westminster, Burslem
Directors: E. Adams (MD)
Managers: H. Hughs (Comptroller), C. Edwards
Ultimate Holding Company: W. MOORCROFT HOLDINGS LIMITED
Immediate Holding Company: W. MOORCROFT LIMITED
Registration no: 00128500 **VAT No.:** 670 3149 48 **Date established:** 2013
Turnover: £5m - £10m **No.of Employees:** 101 - 250 **Product Groups:** 33

Date of Accounts	Aug 11	Aug 10	Aug 08
Sales Turnover	6m	6m	5m
Pre Tax Profit/Loss	333	549	866
Working Capital	136	337	732
Fixed Assets	3m	2m	2m
Current Assets	2m	2m	2m
Current Liabilities	1m	732	639

W W R D UK Ltd
Wedgwood Drive Barlaston, Stoke On Trent, ST12 9ER
Tel: 01782-204141 **Fax:** 01782-204402
E-mail: pierre.devillemejane@wwrd.com
Website: http://www.wwrd.com
Directors: M. Downie (Co Sec), P. Wedgwood (Dir), T. O'Riley (MD), A. O'Reilly (Grp Chief Exec), P. De Villemejane (Grp Chief Exec), M. Campbell (Pers), C. Mackay (Fin)
Managers: C. Jackson (Mktg Serv Mgr), I. Turner (Purch Mgr), D. Gillfillan (Purch Mgr)
Ultimate Holding Company: WATERFORD WEDGWOOD PUBLIC LIMITED COMPANY
Immediate Holding Company: WATERFORD WEDGWOOD AUSTRALIA LIMITED
Registration no: 00047676 **Date established:** 1996
Turnover: £20m - £50m **No.of Employees:** 251 - 500 **Product Groups:** 33

Walkers Nonsuch Ltd
Calverley Street, Stoke On Trent, ST3 1QS
Tel: 01782-321525 **Fax:** 01782-599449
E-mail: sales@walkers-nonsuch.co.uk
Website: http://www.walkers-nonsuch.co.uk
Bank(s): Barclays, Longton
Directors: A. Hill (Chief Op Offcr), E. Walker (Factory), I. Walker (MD), C. Kennerley (Sales)
Managers: E. Rae
Immediate Holding Company: WALKER'S NONSUCH LIMITED
Registration no: 00186454 **VAT No.:** GB 278 3745 16
Date established: 2022 **Turnover:** £2m - £5m **No.of Employees:** 21 - 50
Product Groups: 20

Date of Accounts	Mar 11	Mar 10	Mar 09
Working Capital	2m	1m	1m
Fixed Assets	617	693	755
Current Assets	2m	2m	2m

B Whaleleys
Phoenix Ridge Greenway Hall Road, Light Oaks, Stoke On Trent, ST2 7NA
Tel: 01782-533959 **Fax:** 01782-533959
E-mail: bazandmuts@sky.com
Website: http://www.bwhalleymaintenance.co.uk
Directors: B. Whalley (Prop)
Date established: 1979 **No.of Employees:** 1 - 10 **Product Groups:** 26, 35

White Wear UK
12 Herbert Road, Stoke On Trent, ST3 4QR
Tel: 01782-501141
Website: http://www.univer.co.uk
Directors: L. Bootherstone (Prop)
Registration no: 06698342 **Date established:** 2008
No.of Employees: 1 - 10 **Product Groups:** 36, 40

William Mellard & Sons
River Works Campbell Road, Stoke On Trent, ST4 4RN
Tel: 01782-744777 **Fax:** 01782-744512
E-mail: simon.mellard@mellard.co.uk
Website: http://www.mellard.co.uk
Bank(s): National Westminster Bank Plc
Directors: S. Mellard (MD), J. Mellard (Fin)
Immediate Holding Company: WILLIAM MELLARD & SONS LIMITED
Registration no: 04189746 **VAT No.:** GB 278 8194 02
Date established: 2001 **Turnover:** £2m - £5m **No.of Employees:** 11 - 20
Product Groups: 34, 48, 77

Date of Accounts	Mar 12	Mar 11	Mar 10
Working Capital	-20	45	-8
Fixed Assets	1m	1m	1m
Current Assets	2m	2m	2m

Zepher UK Ltd
31 Grange Street, Stoke On Trent, ST6 2JH
Tel: 01260-272800 **Fax:** 01260-272444
E-mail: pbates@zepher-uk.com
Website: http://www.zepher-uk.com
Directors: P. Bates (Mkt Research), P. Bate (Dir)
Immediate Holding Company: ZEPHER UK LIMITED
Registration no: 04200139 **Date established:** 2001
Turnover: £500,000 - £1m **No.of Employees:** 1 - 10 **Product Groups:** 40

Stone

Autobar
Unit 1a Whitebridge Industrial Estate Whitebridge Lane, Stone, ST15 8LQ
Tel: 01785-815551 **Fax:** 01785-815248
Website: http://www.springbank.co.uk
Directors: M. Greenwood (Co Sec)
Ultimate Holding Company: CHARTERHOUSE CAPITAL PARTNERS VII FUND
Immediate Holding Company: SPRINGBANK INDUSTRIES LIMITED
Registration no: 01806287 **Date established:** 1984 **Turnover:** £2m - £5m
No.of Employees: 51 - 100 **Product Groups:** 38, 42

Date of Accounts	Mar 08	Mar 09	Mar 10
Sales Turnover	3m	3m	N/A
Pre Tax Profit/Loss	554	404	N/A
Working Capital	1m	1m	1m
Fixed Assets	56	N/A	N/A
Current Assets	2m	1m	1m

Bibby Scientific Ltd
Beacon Road, Stone, ST15 0SA
Tel: 01785-812121 **Fax:** 01785-813748
E-mail: info@bibby-scientific.com
Website: http://www.bibby-scientific.com
Directors: L. Eager (Fin), P. Rinaldi (Fin), J. Heffernan (Grp Chief Exec)
Managers: R. Skehens (Mktg Serv Mgr), A. Burke (Chief Buyer), C. Felley (Tech Serv Mgr), D. Henry (Personnel), S. Falthouse (Purch Mgr), M. Firkin (Personnel), G. Brookes, C. Selly (I.T. Exec)
Ultimate Holding Company: NOVA BOXER LP (GUERNSEY)
Immediate Holding Company: BIBBY SCIENTIFIC LIMITED
Registration no: 06381141 **Date established:** 2007
No.of Employees: 101 - 250 **Product Groups:** 29, 30, 33, 42, 63, 66

Date of Accounts	Sep 11	Sep 10	Sep 09
Sales Turnover	18m	18m	17m
Pre Tax Profit/Loss	-19m	15m	-3m
Working Capital	-28m	-18m	-27m
Fixed Assets	32m	41m	41m
Current Assets	21m	25m	17m
Current Liabilities	3m	2m	839

Bullet Sound Co.
Unit 2 Brookside Business Park Cold Meece, Stone, ST15 0RZ
Tel: 01785-761761 **Fax:** 01785-761761
E-mail: sale@bulletsound.com
Website: http://www.bulletsound.com
Directors: D. Turner (Prop)
VAT No.: GB 695 3720 04 **No.of Employees:** 1 - 10 **Product Groups:** 83

C C B Marketing & Promotion Ltd
Caernarvon House 4 Caernarvon Avenue, Stone, ST15 8YW
Tel: 01785-816444 **Fax:** 01785-815569
E-mail: info@ccbmarketing.co.uk
Website: http://www.ccbmarketing.com
Directors: H. Fynney (Fin), C. Bell (MD)
Immediate Holding Company: CCB MARKETING & PROMOTION LIMITED
Registration no: 04052508 **Date established:** 2000
Turnover: £250,000 - £500,000 **No.of Employees:** 1 - 10
Product Groups: 81

Date of Accounts	Mar 11	Mar 10	Mar 09
Working Capital	-1	-2	-2
Fixed Assets	1	2	3
Current Assets	N/A	9	6

Croner Reward
Reward House Diamond Way, Stone Business Park, Stone, ST15 0SD
Tel: 01785-813566 **Fax:** 01785-817007
E-mail: enquiries@wolterskluwer.co.uk
Website: http://www.croner-reward.co.uk
Managers: I. James (Sales & Mktg Mg), R. Whitehurst (Mktg Serv Mgr), S. Holmes (I.T. Exec), S. Bancoft, V. Copeland
Ultimate Holding Company: INSTEM PLC
Immediate Holding Company: INSTEM LSS LIMITED
Registration no: 01273492 **Date established:** 1998 **Turnover:** £2m - £5m
No.of Employees: 21 - 50 **Product Groups:** 80

D A W Enterprises Ltd (t/a Scalemaster)
Unit 6 Emerald Way, Stone Business Park, Stone, ST15 0SR
Tel: 01785-811636 **Fax:** 01785-811511
E-mail: info@scalemaster.co.uk
Website: http://www.scalemaster.co.uk
Managers: K. Tomlinson (Sales Admin), S. Robinson (Sec)
Immediate Holding Company: Alex Christian Ltd
Registration no: 02066656 **VAT No.:** GB 367 9766 80
Turnover: £1m - £2m **No.of Employees:** 1 - 10 **Product Groups:** 41

Daystate Ltd
Birch House Lane Swynnerton, Stone, ST15 0QQ
Tel: 01782-791755 **Fax:** 01782-791617
E-mail: office@daystate.com
Website: http://www.daystate.com
Directors: M. Marocchi (MD)
Immediate Holding Company: DAYSTATE LIMITED
Registration no: 01395286 **Date established:** 1978
No.of Employees: 11 - 20 **Product Groups:** 36, 39, 40

Date of Accounts	Dec 11	Dec 10	Dec 09
Working Capital	546	455	282
Fixed Assets	52	29	53
Current Assets	1m	1m	827

Dunoon
Unit 5 Walton Industrial Estate Beacon Road, Stone, ST15 0RY
Tel: 01785-817414 **Fax:** 01785-812322
E-mail: sales@dunoonmugs.co.uk
Website: http://www.dunoonmugs.co.uk
Bank(s): HSBC Bank plc
Directors: P. Smith (Sales & Mktg), C. Tunnicliffe (Co Sec)
Managers: B. Bagshaw (Chief Acct)
Immediate Holding Company: DUNOON CERAMICS HOLDINGS LIMITED
Registration no: 06846695 **VAT No.:** GB 264 7749 19
Date established: 2009 **Turnover:** £1m - £2m
No.of Employees: 101 - 250 **Product Groups:** 33

Date of Accounts	Mar 12	Mar 11	Mar 10
Working Capital	750	499	1
Fixed Assets	1m	1m	1m
Current Assets	814	506	10

Finder plc
Opal Way Stone Business Park, Stone, ST15 0SS
Tel: 01785-818100 **Fax:** 01785-815500
E-mail: enquiries@findel.co.uk
Website: http://www.findernet.com
Bank(s): Royal Bank of Scotland PLC
Directors: J. Stanford (MD)
Managers: J. Smith, T. Waller (Sales Prom Mgr), J. Gillen (Chief Acct)
Ultimate Holding Company: FINDER SPA (ITALY)
Immediate Holding Company: FINDER PUBLIC LIMITED COMPANY
Registration no: 02728832 **Date established:** 1992 **Turnover:** £2m - £5m
No.of Employees: 11 - 20 **Product Groups:** 37, 49

Date of Accounts	Dec 11	Dec 10	Dec 09
Sales Turnover	4m	4m	3m
Pre Tax Profit/Loss	738	466	363
Working Capital	1m	909	757
Fixed Assets	535	551	554
Current Assets	2m	2m	2m
Current Liabilities	481	386	320

G Mondini Ltd
Unit E Whitebridge Lane, Stone, ST15 8LY
Tel: 01785-812512 **Fax:** 01785-819512
E-mail: info@gmondini.co.uk
Website: http://www.gmondini.co.uk
Directors: A. Bickerton (MD)
Immediate Holding Company: G. MONDINI (UK) LIMITED
Date established: 2005 **No.of Employees:** 1 - 10 **Product Groups:** 38, 42

Date of Accounts	Dec 11	Jun 10	Jun 09
Working Capital	1m	944	533
Fixed Assets	14	46	6
Current Assets	2m	1m	1m

H & F Lift Trucks
Old Joules Works Newcastle Street, Stone, ST15 8JU
Tel: 01785-812176 **Fax:** 01785-812245
E-mail: sales@hflifttrucks.co.uk
Website: http://www.hflifttrucks.co.uk
Directors: T. Fitchett (Prop)
Ultimate Holding Company: RUBICON PARTNERS INDUSTRIES LLP
Immediate Holding Company: HAMMERSLEY & FITCHETT HOLDINGS LIMITED
Registration no: 03893264 **Date established:** 1999 **Turnover:** £5m - £10m
No.of Employees: 11 - 20 **Product Groups:** 45

Date of Accounts	Dec 11	Dec 10	Dec 09
Fixed Assets	200	200	200

Hammersley & Fitchet
Old Joules Works Newcastle Street, Stone, ST15 8JU
Tel: 01785-812176 **Fax:** 01785-812245
E-mail: sales@hflifttrucks.co.uk
Website: http://www.hflifttrucks.co.uk
Directors: T. Fitchet (Prop)
Immediate Holding Company: HAMMERSLEY & FITCHETT HOLDINGS LIMITED
Registration no: 03893264 **Date established:** 1999
No.of Employees: 11 - 20 **Product Groups:** 35, 39, 45

Date of Accounts	Dec 11	Dec 10	Dec 09
Fixed Assets	200	200	200

P E Hines & Sons Ltd
Whitebridge Lane, Stone, ST15 8LU
Tel: 01785-814921 **Fax:** 01785-818808
E-mail: barry.rowley@iclweb.com
Website: http://www.hines.co.uk
Directors: B. Rowley (Fin)
Immediate Holding Company: P.E. HINES & SONS LIMITED
Registration no: 02644272 **VAT No.:** GB 278 5434 23
Date established: 1991 **Turnover:** £2m - £5m **No.of Employees:** 1 - 10
Product Groups: 14, 17, 32, 33

Date of Accounts	Sep 11	Sep 10	Sep 09
Working Capital	644	595	608
Fixed Assets	14	12	5
Current Assets	879	933	886

H T S Direct Ltd
Units 17-18 Emerald Way, Stone Business Park, Stone, ST15 0SR
Tel: 01785-816747 **Fax:** 01543-462789
E-mail: sales@hts-direct.co.uk
Website: http://www.hts-direct.co.uk
Managers: C. Richards (Mgr)
Immediate Holding Company: HTS DIRECT LIMITED
Registration no: 04604710 **Date established:** 2002
No.of Employees: 1 - 10 **Product Groups:** 35, 38, 39, 40, 45, 65, 67, 68

Date of Accounts	Dec 11	Dec 10	Dec 09
Working Capital	142	45	86
Fixed Assets	143	3	3
Current Assets	207	200	184

Industrial Floor Treatments Stone Ltd
Emerald Way Stone Business Park, Stone, ST15 0SR
Tel: 01785-819800 **Fax:** 01785-816767
E-mail: enquiries@iftstone.co.uk
Website: http://www.iftstone.co.uk
Directors: J. White (Co Sec)
Immediate Holding Company: INDUSTRIAL FLOOR TREATMENTS (STONE) LIMITED
Registration no: 05217471 **Date established:** 2004
Turnover: £250,000 - £500,000 **No.of Employees:** 1 - 10
Product Groups: 52

Date of Accounts	Oct 11	Oct 10	Oct 09
Working Capital	-3	8	-6
Fixed Assets	9	11	5
Current Assets	86	37	41
Current Liabilities	14	14	N/A

Instem-Lss Ltd
2 Diamond Way Stone Business Park, Stone, ST15 0SD
Tel: 01785-825600 **Fax:** 01785-825625
E-mail: info@instem-lss.com
Website: http://www.instem-lss.com
Directors: J. McLauchlan (Grp Chief Exec)
Managers: N. Donaldson (Sales Prom Mgr), N. Goldsmith, H. Pal (Tech Serv Mgr), J. Jones (Mktg Serv Mgr)
Ultimate Holding Company: INSTEM PLC
Immediate Holding Company: INSTEM LSS LIMITED
Registration no: 03548215 **Date established:** 1998 **Turnover:** £2m - £5m
No.of Employees: 51 - 100 **Product Groups:** 44

Date of Accounts	Dec 11	Dec 10	Dec 08
Sales Turnover	4m	4m	9m
Pre Tax Profit/Loss	1m	2m	815
Working Capital	8m	8m	6m
Fixed Assets	332	267	990
Current Assets	16m	14m	12m
Current Liabilities	3m	2m	5m

MCP Group
8 Whitebridge Industrial Estate Whitebridge Lane, Stone, ST15 8LQ
Tel: 01785-815651 **Fax:** 01785-812115
E-mail: info@mcp-group.co.uk
Website: http://www.mcp-group.com
Bank(s): National Westminster Bank Plc
Directors: I. Cadell (Ch), I. Mclean (Fin), S. Scott (MD)
Managers: B. Bennett (Mktg Serv Mgr), N. Crook (I.T. Exec), S. Scoff (Mgr)
Ultimate Holding Company: Mining & Chemical Products Ltd
Immediate Holding Company: M. C. P. Ltd
Registration no: 01538706 **VAT No.:** GB 227 2966 46
Date established: 1997 **Turnover:** £5m - £10m **No.of Employees:** 21 - 50
Product Groups: 42, 46

Owlett Jaton
Opal Way Stone Business Park, Stone, ST15 0SW
Tel: 01785-811300 **Fax:** 01785-811718
E-mail: info@owlett-jaton.com
Website: http://www.owlett-jaton.com
Directors: S. Davies (Fin), J. Barker (Purch), G. Hopwood (MD)
Managers: K. Benton (Tech Serv Mgr), A. Lowrie
Ultimate Holding Company: BLACKFRIARS CORP (USA)
Immediate Holding Company: OWLETT-JATON LIMITED
Registration no: 03112228 **VAT No.:** GB 219 2348 67
Date established: 1995 **Turnover:** £2m - £5m
No.of Employees: 101 - 250 **Product Groups:** 35

Protectorglaze Ltd
Highbury House 15 The Woodlands Cold Meece, Stone, ST15 0YA
Tel: 01785-761888 **Fax:** 01785-760536
E-mail: sales@protectorglaze.com
Website: http://www.protectorglaze.com
Directors: R. Hayne (MD), F. Alcorn (Fin)
Immediate Holding Company: PROTECTALL INTERNATIONAL LIMITED
Registration no: 05107680 **Date established:** 2004
Turnover: Up to £250,000 **No.of Employees:** 1 - 10 **Product Groups:** 30, 52

Date of Accounts	Aug 09	Aug 08	Aug 07
Sales Turnover	183	204	88
Pre Tax Profit/Loss	-2	6	2
Working Capital	-2	6	2
Current Assets	34	48	15

Research Associates UK Ltd
29 The Avenue, Stone, ST15 8DG
Tel: 01785-813164 **Fax:** 01785-813268
E-mail: info@research-associates.co.uk
Website: http://www.research-associates.co.uk
Directors: L. Brace (Fin), R. Brace (MD)
Immediate Holding Company: RESEARCH ASSOCIATES (UK) LIMITED
Registration no: 04289608 **VAT No.:** GB 781 6309 16
Date established: 2001 **Turnover:** £250,000 - £500,000
No.of Employees: 1 - 10 **Product Groups:** 81

Date of Accounts	Aug 11	Aug 10	Aug 07
Working Capital	101	65	109
Fixed Assets	2	3	N/A
Current Assets	140	96	138

SciLabware
Beacon Road, Stone, ST15 0SA
Tel: 01785-812121 **Fax:** 0844-936 0232
E-mail: enquiries@scilabware.com
Website: http://www.scilabware.com
Managers: E. Wynn
Immediate Holding Company: SCILABWARE LIMITED
Registration no: 07723574 **Date established:** 2011 **Turnover:** £1m - £2m
No.of Employees: 51 - 100 **Product Groups:** 28, 33, 45, 48, 61, 63, 65

Date of Accounts	Dec 11
Sales Turnover	1m
Pre Tax Profit/Loss	809
Working Capital	607
Current Assets	5m
Current Liabilities	704

Switchtec Ltd
Brooms Road Stone Business Park, Stone, ST15 0SH
Tel: 01785-818600 **Fax:** 01785-811900
E-mail: sales@switchtec.co.uk
Website: http://www.switchtec.co.uk
Bank(s): Royal Bank of Scotland, Uttoxeter
Directors: J. Lester (MD), J. Plows (Sales)
Ultimate Holding Company: SWITCHTEC COMPONENTS LIMITED
Immediate Holding Company: SWITCHTEC LIMITED
Registration no: 01613368 **Date established:** 1982 **Turnover:** £2m - £5m
No.of Employees: 11 - 20 **Product Groups:** 37, 38, 40, 49

Date of Accounts	Dec 11	Dec 10	Dec 09
Working Capital	887	821	771
Fixed Assets	77	35	28
Current Assets	1m	1m	951

Touchstone Lighting Components Ltd
Unit 21-22 Emerald Way, Stone Business Park, Stone, ST15 0SR
Tel: 01785-817123 **Fax:** 01785-817120
E-mail: gary.stone@touchstonelighting.co.uk
Website: http://www.touchstonelighting.co.uk
Directors: G. Stone (MD), R. Wafaquani Hamilton (Fin), H. Stone (Dir)
Managers: R. Stone
Ultimate Holding Company: ITEM HOLDINGS LIMITED
Immediate Holding Company: TOUCHSTONE LIGHTING COMPONENTS LTD.
Registration no: 03518127 **Date established:** 1998 **Turnover:** £1m - £2m
No.of Employees: 11 - 20 **Product Groups:** 37, 67

Date of Accounts	Mar 12	Apr 11	Apr 10
Sales Turnover	1m	1m	1m
Pre Tax Profit/Loss	N/A	198	153
Working Capital	192	172	165
Fixed Assets	8	10	5
Current Assets	454	474	389
Current Liabilities	N/A	115	78

UK Safes Ltd
Unit 41 Whitebridge Estate Whitebridge Lane, Stone, ST15 8LQ
Tel: 01785-812902 **Fax:** 01785-812902
E-mail: sales@uksafes.co.uk
Website: http://www.uksafes.co.uk
Directors: B. George (Co Sec), G. Bailey (Dir), G. Bailey (MD)
Immediate Holding Company: U.K. SAFES LIMITED
Registration no: 03235800 **VAT No.:** GB 670 8958 91
Date established: 1996 **Turnover:** Up to £250,000
No.of Employees: 1 - 10 **Product Groups:** 36

Date of Accounts	Sep 10	Sep 09	Sep 08
Working Capital	-59	-71	-72
Fixed Assets	6	7	8
Current Assets	63	61	67

Tamworth

A T Services
Unit C Apollo Lichfield Road Industrial Estate, Tamworth, B79 7TA
Tel: 01827-68306 **Fax:** 01827-60359
E-mail: adt889@hotmail.com
Website: http://www.atservices.co.uk
Directors: A. Tunnah (Prop)
Immediate Holding Company: SUPRAJIT EUROPE LIMITED
Registration no: 02613471 **Date established:** 2006 **Turnover:** £5m - £10m
No.of Employees: 1 - 10 **Product Groups:** 35

Altelec Electrical Services
12 Nemesia, Tamworth, B77 4EL
Tel: 07944-544790
E-mail: info@altelec.co.uk
Website: http://www.altelec.co.uk
Directors: D. Hateley (Prop)
No.of Employees: 1 - 10 **Product Groups:** 37, 52, 84

Applied Vibration Ltd
48-50 Sandy Way Amington Industrial Estate, Tamworth, B77 4DS
Tel: 01827-318020 **Fax:** 01827-51059
E-mail: sales@appliedvibration.co.uk
Website: http://www.appliedvibration.co.uk
Directors: D. Wilkes (Dir)
Immediate Holding Company: APPLIED VIBRATION LIMITED
Registration no: 01260592 **Date established:** 1976 **Turnover:** £1m - £2m
No.of Employees: 1 - 10 **Product Groups:** 42, 45, 46

Date of Accounts	Jun 11	Jun 10	Jun 09
Working Capital	48	27	50
Fixed Assets	28	25	33
Current Assets	276	240	241

ARGO Services
Hillside Kingsbury, Tamworth, B78 2NH
Tel: 01827-874444
E-mail: enquiries@argoservices.co.uk
Website: http://www.argoservices.co.uk
Date established: 1977 **No.of Employees:** 1 - 10 **Product Groups:** 40

Arrow Imaging Ltd
Unit 34 Pebble Close, Tamworth, B77 4RD
Tel: 01827-310350 **Fax:** 01827-313880
E-mail: nick.hawkes@arrow-imaging.co.uk
Website: http://www.arrow-imaging.co.uk
Bank(s): Barclays
Directors: J. Scott (Dir), Scott (MD), K. Scott (MD), N. Hawkes (Dir)
Immediate Holding Company: SALA IMAGING LIMITED
Registration no: 02034790 **VAT No.:** GB 444 6776 19
Date established: 1986 **Turnover:** £1m - £2m **No.of Employees:** 21 - 50
Product Groups: 27, 44, 80, 81

Date of Accounts	Dec 09	Dec 08	Dec 07
Working Capital	847	886	687
Fixed Assets	227	290	390
Current Assets	1m	1m	1m

Auto Engineering Supplies Ltd
Unit 7 Forties Wilnecote, Tamworth, B77 5DG
Tel: 01827-286161 **Fax:** 01827-286042
E-mail: lguest@autoengsupplies.co.uk
Website: http://www.autoengsupplies.co.uk
Directors: M. O'connell (MD)
Ultimate Holding Company: R.F. HOLDINGS LIMITED
Immediate Holding Company: AUTO ENGINEERING SUPPLIES LIMITED
Registration no: 02966006 **VAT No.:** GB 614 4834 46
Date established: 1994 **Turnover:** £1m - £2m **No.of Employees:** 21 - 50
Product Groups: 27, 29, 48

Date of Accounts	Apr 11	Apr 10	Apr 09
Working Capital	260	230	307
Fixed Assets	45	37	54
Current Assets	428	331	404

Axiom GB Ltd
Mica Close, Tamworth, B77 4DR
Tel: 01827-61212 **Fax:** 01827-67272
E-mail: info@axiomgb.com
Website: http://www.axiomgb.com
Directors: A. Nickson (Fin)
Immediate Holding Company: AXIOM GB LIMITED
Registration no: 03787813 **Date established:** 1999
No.of Employees: 1 - 10 **Product Groups:** 38, 42

Date of Accounts	Dec 11	Dec 10	Dec 09
Working Capital	24	7	235
Fixed Assets	37	49	73
Current Assets	244	151	235

Bearings International Ltd
7 Hall Court Bridge Street, Polesworth, Tamworth, B78 1DT
Tel: 01827-330749 **Fax:** 01827-330038
Website: http://www.bearingsinternational.com
Directors: K. Foxall (MD)
Immediate Holding Company: BEARINGS (INTERNATIONAL) LIMITED
Registration no: 03053077 **Date established:** 1995
No.of Employees: 1 - 10 **Product Groups:** 35, 45

Date of Accounts	May 11	May 10	May 09
Working Capital	4	2	7
Fixed Assets	8	8	9
Current Assets	692	604	534

Russell Benussi Associates
3 Pebble Close, Tamworth, B77 4RD
Tel: 01827-68008 **Fax:** 01827-69265
E-mail: sales@benussi.com
Website: http://www.benussi.com
Directors: J. Benussi (Snr Part)
Immediate Holding Company: RUSSELL BENUSSI ASSOCIATES LIMITED
Registration no: 03892397 **VAT No.:** GB 486 9533 87
Date established: 1999 **Turnover:** £500,000 - £1m
No.of Employees: 1 - 10 **Product Groups:** 36, 42, 45

Date of Accounts	Oct 11	Oct 10	Oct 09
Working Capital	109	105	24
Fixed Assets	99	112	125
Current Assets	564	414	573

Biffa Waste Services Ltd
Rush Lane Dosthill, Tamworth, B77 1LT
Tel: 01827-289170 **Fax:** 01827-261089
Website: http://www.biffa.co.uk
Directors: M. Bettington (MD)
Managers: M. Massey (Site Co-ord)
Immediate Holding Company: BIFFA WASTE SERVICES LIMITED
Registration no: 00946107 **Date established:** 1969
No.of Employees: 1 - 10 **Product Groups:** 32, 54

Date of Accounts	Mar 08	Mar 09	Apr 10
Sales Turnover	555m	574m	492m
Pre Tax Profit/Loss	23m	50m	30m
Working Capital	229m	271m	293m
Fixed Assets	371m	360m	378m
Current Assets	409m	534m	609m
Current Liabilities	50m	100m	115m

Bright Fire
16 Cedar Drive, Tamworth, B79 8QL
Tel: 01827-705522
E-mail: playnow@hotmail.co.uk
Directors: R. Wheeler (Prop)
No.of Employees: 1 - 10 **Product Groups:** 38, 42

W Brighton Handrails (Handrails)
55 Quarry Hill Wilnecote, Tamworth, B77 5BW
Tel: 01827-284488 **Fax:** 01827-250907
E-mail: wbrightonhandrails@ntlworld.com
Website: http://www.marleyrail.com
Directors: W. Brighton (Prop)
Date established: 1976 **No.of Employees:** 1 - 10 **Product Groups:** 30

Brimalk Ltd
Unit 8 Apollo Park Lichfield Road Industrial Estate, Tamworth, B79 7TA
Tel: 01827-51550 **Fax:** 01827-51188
E-mail: sales@brimalk.co.uk
Website: http://brimalk.co.uk
Directors: J. Aucote (Dir)
Immediate Holding Company: BRIMALK LIMITED
Registration no: 02147045 **Date established:** 1987
Turnover: £250,000 - £500,000 **No.of Employees:** 1 - 10
Product Groups: 38, 44, 52

Date of Accounts	Aug 11	Aug 10	Aug 09
Working Capital	9	-8	-7
Fixed Assets	31	41	32
Current Assets	160	133	114

Brown & Holmes Tamworth Ltd
Apollo Lichfield Road Industrial Estate, Tamworth, B79 7TA
Tel: 01827-63591 **Fax:** 01827-54322
E-mail: cbaker@brownandholmes.co.uk
Website: http://www.brownandholmes.co.uk
Bank(s): Natwest
Directors: C. Baker (Dir), K. Ward (Fin)
Managers: S. Smith (Purch Mgr)
Immediate Holding Company: BROWN & HOLMES (TAMWORTH) LIMITED
Registration no: 04598626 **VAT No.:** GB 109 3681 67
Date established: 2002 **Turnover:** £2m - £5m **No.of Employees:** 21 - 50
Product Groups: 38, 46, 48

Date of Accounts	Mar 12	Mar 11	Mar 10
Working Capital	80	-124	-135
Fixed Assets	578	352	427
Current Assets	2m	2m	911

C & L Distribution Ltd
Unit 4 Lakeside Industrial Park Fazeley, Tamworth, B78 3NT
Tel: 01827-251333 **Fax:** 01827-282333
E-mail: admin@candl-distribution.ltd.uk
Website: http://www.candl-distribution.ltd.uk
Directors: C. Duckett (Dir)
Immediate Holding Company: C & L DISTRIBUTION LIMITED
Registration no: 01819292 **Date established:** 1984
Turnover: £500,000 - £1m **No.of Employees:** 11 - 20 **Product Groups:** 27

Date of Accounts	Dec 11	Dec 10	Dec 09
Working Capital	12	-10	51
Fixed Assets	212	236	242
Current Assets	287	308	345

C P L Petroleum
Piccadilly Way Kingsbury, Tamworth, B78 2EA
Tel: 01827-872266 **Fax:** 01902-490789
E-mail: julie.aldridge@cplpetroleum.co.uk
Website: http://www.emooil.co.uk
Managers: J. Aldridge (Depot Mgr)
Ultimate Holding Company: CPL INDUSTRIES HOLDINGS LIMITED
Immediate Holding Company: CPL PETROLEUM LIMITED
Registration no: 03003860 **VAT No.:** GB 7215 764 39
Date established: 1994 **No.of Employees:** 1 - 10 **Product Groups:** 66

Date of Accounts	Mar 12	Mar 11	Mar 10
Pre Tax Profit/Loss	N/A	878	904
Working Capital	31	30m	30m
Fixed Assets	26	26m	26m
Current Assets	57	56m	56m
Current Liabilities	26	246	253

Cew
Unit 1 Lichfield Trading Estate Lagrange, Tamworth, B79 7XD
Tel: 01827-66657 **Fax:** 01827-66639
E-mail: simon.collins@cewdes.co.uk
Website: http://www.electricaldistributors.co.uk
Directors: S. Collins (Prop)
Immediate Holding Company: COVENTRY ELECTRICAL WHOLESALERS LIMITED
Registration no: 03654113 **Date established:** 1998
No.of Employees: 1 - 10 **Product Groups:** 36, 40

Clear Solutions
9 Mariner, Tamworth, B79 7UL
Tel: 01827-63273 **Fax:** 01827-63273
E-mail: janvincent@cds.co.uk
Managers: J. Vince (Mgr)
Date established: 2003 **No.of Employees:** 1 - 10 **Product Groups:** 36

Crown Computing Ltd
Tamworth Business Park Amber Close Amington, Tamworth, B77 4RP
Tel: 01827-309800 **Fax:** 01827-309810
E-mail: sales@crowncomputing.co.uk
Website: http://www.crowncomputing.co.uk
Bank(s): Barclays
Directors: M. Hawkesford (MD)
Immediate Holding Company: CROWN COMPUTING LIMITED
Registration no: 02186297 **Date established:** 1987 **Turnover:** £2m - £5m
No.of Employees: 51 - 100 **Product Groups:** 44

Date of Accounts	Dec 11	Dec 10	Dec 09
Sales Turnover	5m	5m	4m
Pre Tax Profit/Loss	739	569	-57
Working Capital	2m	2m	1m
Fixed Assets	2m	2m	2m
Current Assets	4m	3m	2m
Current Liabilities	2m	1m	1m

Disklabs Ltd
Unit 6 & 7 Mercian Park Felspar Road, Tamworth, B77 4DP
Tel: 01827-50000 **Fax:** 01827-66666
E-mail: website@disklabsforensics.co.uk
Website: http://www.disklabs.com
Directors: S. Steggles (Dir)
Immediate Holding Company: DISKLABS LIMITED
Registration no: 03441987 **Date established:** 1997 **Turnover:** £1m - £2m
No.of Employees: 11 - 20 **Product Groups:** 44

Date of Accounts	Sep 11	Sep 10	Sep 09
Working Capital	108	78	-36
Fixed Assets	83	90	71
Current Assets	249	273	203

Dovetail Building Developments Ltd
Bonehill Farm Bonehill Road, Tamworth, B78 3HP
Tel: 0121-311 2900 **Fax:** 01827-311827
E-mail: sales@dovetailgreenhouses.co.uk
Website: http://www.dovetailgreenhouses.co.uk
Directors: D. Beasley (Fin)
Immediate Holding Company: Roger Beasley Enterprises Ltd
Registration no: 02658463 **Date established:** 2003
No.of Employees: 1 - 10 **Product Groups:** 26, 35

Date of Accounts	Dec 08	Dec 07	Dec 06
Working Capital	38	22	26
Fixed Assets	7	9	9
Current Assets	102	98	102
Current Liabilities	63	76	75

Eurolok Ltd
Tame Park Vanguard, Wilnecote, Tamworth, B77 5DY
Tel: 01827-287439 **Fax:** 01827-287485
E-mail: lee.davies@eurolok.co.uk
Website: http://www.eurolok.co.uk
Bank(s): Barclays Bank PLC
Directors: L. Davies (MD), M. Evans (Sales), N. Hodson (Sales)
Ultimate Holding Company: DAVICO INDUSTRIAL LIMITED
Immediate Holding Company: EUROLOK LIMITED
Registration no: 01566614 **VAT No.:** GB 620 0599 67
Date established: 1981 **No.of Employees:** 21 - 50 **Product Groups:** 30, 35, 39

European Metals Recycling Ltd
Trinity Road Kingsbury, Tamworth, B78 2LB
Tel: 01827-872281 **Fax:** 01827-874347
Website: http://www.emrltd.com
Managers: D. Wright (Mgr)
Immediate Holding Company: EUROPEAN METAL RECYCLING LIMITED
Registration no: 02954623 **Date established:** 1994
Turnover: £10m - £20m **No.of Employees:** 1 - 10 **Product Groups:** 42, 66

Date of Accounts	Dec 11	Dec 10	Dec 09
Sales Turnover	3032m	2431m	1843m
Pre Tax Profit/Loss	116m	155m	91m
Working Capital	414m	371m	167m
Fixed Assets	518m	483m	480m
Current Assets	1027m	717m	557m
Current Liabilities	124m	118m	185m

Euroteck Systems UK Ltd
Unit 6-7 Kepler, Tamworth, B79 7XE
Tel: 01827-312455 **Fax:** 01827-312548
E-mail: sales@euroteck.co.uk
Website: http://www.euroteck.co.uk
Directors: G. Wehrle (Fin), C. Sampson (MD)
Immediate Holding Company: EUROTECK SYSTEMS UK LIMITED
Registration no: 04475290 **Date established:** 2002 **Turnover:** £2m - £5m
No.of Employees: 1 - 10 **Product Groups:** 37, 38, 39, 46, 48, 67, 83, 85

Date of Accounts	Sep 11	Sep 10	Sep 09
Working Capital	77	28	-9
Fixed Assets	25	19	10
Current Assets	311	249	104

Foseco International Limited
Drayton Manor Business Park, Tamworth, B78 3TL
Tel: 01827-289999 **Fax:** 01827-250806
Website: http://www.foseco.co.uk
Bank(s): HSBC Bank plc
Directors: P. Dean (Fin)
Managers: E. O'Halloran
Registration no: 00468147 **No.of Employees:** 51 - 100
Product Groups: 32, 33, 42, 46

Fospat Industrial Ltd
Hints Road Mile Oak, Tamworth, B78 3PQ
Tel: 01827-288188 **Fax:** 01827-251444
E-mail: ha.frend@fospat.com
Website: http://www.fospat.com
Directors: H. Frend (Grp Chief Exec), H. Frend (MD), S. Frend (Fin)
Managers: M. Sadler (Sales Prom Mgr), K. Faukes (Quality Control)
Immediate Holding Company: FOSPAT INDUSTRIAL LIMITED
Registration no: 03143595 **Date established:** 1996 **Turnover:** £1m - £2m
No.of Employees: 1 - 10 **Product Groups:** 32, 38, 42, 49

Date of Accounts	Mar 08	Mar 07	Mar 06
Working Capital	29	6	24
Fixed Assets	107	129	124
Current Assets	364	378	345
Current Liabilities	335	371	320
Total Share Capital	80	80	80

Fosroc Ltd
Drayton Manor Business Park Coleshill Road, Tamworth, B78 3TL
Tel: 01827-262 2222 **Fax:** 01827- 262444
E-mail: info@fosrocuk.com
Website: http://www.fosroc.com

see next page

Fosroc Ltd - Cont'd

Directors: G. Kenick (Co Sec)
Managers: W. Zakers
Ultimate Holding Company: JMH FZCO (UNITED ARAB EMIRATES)
Immediate Holding Company: FOSROC LIMITED
Registration no: 04589343 **Date established:** 2002
Turnover: £10m - £20m **No.of Employees:** 51 - 100 **Product Groups:** 32, 66

Date of Accounts	Dec 11	Dec 10	Dec 09
Sales Turnover	17m	17m	18m
Pre Tax Profit/Loss	-2m	-803	-163
Working Capital	3m	4m	6m
Fixed Assets	311	405	409
Current Assets	5m	7m	8m
Current Liabilities	2m	1m	1m

Furness Controls Ltd

4 The Pavilions Amber Close, Tamworth, B77 4RP
Tel: 01827-59950 **Fax:** 01827-59540
E-mail: sales@furness-controls.com
Website: http://www.furness-controls.com
Bank(s): The Royal Bank of Scotland
Managers: S. Hedge (Div Mgr)
Immediate Holding Company: FURNESS CONTROLS LIMITED
Registration no: 00826592 **VAT No.:** GB 190 3319 75
Date established: 1964 **Turnover:** £2m - £5m **No.of Employees:** 11 - 20
Product Groups: 38, 85

Date of Accounts	Dec 11	Dec 10	Dec 09
Working Capital	2m	2m	1m
Fixed Assets	298	203	250
Current Assets	2m	2m	2m

G M B Associates

Unit 5 Ariane, Tamworth, B79 7XF
Tel: 01827-57561 **Fax:** 01827-61832
E-mail: sales@gmbassociates.co.uk
Website: http://www.gmbassociates.co.uk
Directors: G. Bayles (Prop)
VAT No.: GB 377 5461 18 **Date established:** 1983
Turnover: £500,000 - £1m **No.of Employees:** 1 - 10 **Product Groups:** 12, 14, 17, 25, 29, 30, 31, 33, 34, 35, 36, 37, 38, 39, 40, 43, 45, 46, 48, 49, 51, 66, 68, 84

Garrick Ridgway Engineering Ltd

4 Gerard Litchfield Road, Tamworth, B79 7UW
Tel: 01827-54347 **Fax:** 01827-52717
E-mail: garrickridgeway@aol.com
Directors: B. Jones (MD)
Immediate Holding Company: C.J. ENGINEERING (TOOLMAKERS) LIMITED
Registration no: 01082609 **Date established:** 1972
Turnover: Up to £250,000 **No.of Employees:** 1 - 10 **Product Groups:** 41, 66

Date of Accounts	Jul 11	Jul 10	Jul 09
Working Capital	27	27	27
Current Assets	33	33	33

Giant Buyer

207 Long Street Dordon, Tamworth, B78 1PZ
Tel: 08456-434850
E-mail: nick@giantbuyer.com
Website: http://www.giantbuyer.com
Managers: N. Carter (Mktg Serv Mgr)
No.of Employees: 11 - 20 **Product Groups:** 37, 38, 40, 67

Gills Cables Ltd

25 Apollo, Tamworth, B79 7TA
Tel: 01827-304777 **Fax:** 01827-314568
E-mail: petergreensmith@gillscables.com
Website: http://www.suprajit.com
Bank(s): Barclays, Leeds
Directors: K. Jones (Co Sec), P. Greensmith (Dir), R. Crozier (Comm)
Immediate Holding Company: SUPRAJIT EUROPE LIMITED
Registration no: 05695359 **VAT No.:** GB 109 8200 84
Date established: 2006 **Turnover:** £2m - £5m **No.of Employees:** 21 - 50
Product Groups: 30, 35, 39, 41, 68

Date of Accounts	Mar 11	Mar 10	Mar 09
Sales Turnover	3m	3m	4m
Pre Tax Profit/Loss	-146	-181	-511
Working Capital	501	568	656
Fixed Assets	390	621	862
Current Assets	1m	2m	2m
Current Liabilities	183	359	322

Gold & Wassall Hinges Ltd (U.K. Dept)

Castleworks Staffs Moor Industrial Estate Lichfield Road, Tamworth, B79 7TH
Tel: 01827-63391 **Fax:** 01827- 310819
E-mail: sales@goldwassallhinges.co.uk
Website: http://www.goldwassallhinges.co.uk
Bank(s): Lloyds TSB Bank plc
Directors: T. Fellows (Dir), C. Fellows (Chief Op Offcr)
Managers: M. Wilson (Comptroller)
Immediate Holding Company: GOLD & WASSALL (HINGES) LIMITED
Registration no: 00150925 **VAT No.:** GB 109 8081 66
Date established: 2018 **Turnover:** £2m - £5m **No.of Employees:** 51 - 100
Product Groups: 35, 36, 48, 49

Date of Accounts	Mar 11	Mar 10	Mar 09
Sales Turnover	4m	4m	N/A
Pre Tax Profit/Loss	220	172	238
Working Capital	2m	2m	2m
Fixed Assets	2m	2m	2m
Current Assets	3m	3m	3m
Current Liabilities	269	287	336

R W Greeff A division of Univar Ltd

Tame Park Vanguard, Wilnecote, Tamworth, B77 5DY
Tel: 01827-255200 **Fax:** 01827-255255
E-mail: rwgreeff@univareurope.com
Website: http://www.rwgreef.co.uk
Bank(s): HSBC, London EC3
Directors: K. Rowland (Grp Chief Exec), M. Hughes (MD)
Managers: R. Masterson, J. Whitehurst (Ops Mgr), A. Fletcher, K. Rowling (Mgr)
Ultimate Holding Company: Univar
Registration no: 00139876 **VAT No.:** GB 557 1803 34
Turnover: £20m - £50m **No.of Employees:** 21 - 50 **Product Groups:** 27, 29, 30, 31, 32, 33, 37, 41, 66

Heidelberg Graphic Equipment UK

Centurion Park Watling Street, Wilnecote, Tamworth, B77 5PN
Tel: 01827-262777 **Fax:** 01827-266209
Website: http://www.heidelberg.com
Bank(s): Lloyds TSB Bank plc
Directors: G. Clarke (MD), G. Moorhead (Div)
Managers: J. Hovnett (Serv Mgr), M. Summers (Sales Prom Mgr)
Registration no: 01177224 **VAT No.:** GB 228 0793 55
Turnover: £5m - £10m **No.of Employees:** 51 - 100 **Product Groups:** 44

Heuft Ltd

Ninian Park Ninian Way Wilnecote, Tamworth, B77 5ES
Tel: 01827-255800 **Fax:** 01827-716146
E-mail: uk@heuft.com
Website: http://www.heuft.com
Bank(s): Lloyds TSB Bank plc
Directors: D. Metcalf (MD)
Immediate Holding Company: HEUFT LIMITED
Registration no: 01940284 **VAT No.:** GB 418 6748 21
Date established: 1985 **Turnover:** £2m - £5m **No.of Employees:** 11 - 20
Product Groups: 37, 38, 41, 42, 80

Date of Accounts	Oct 11	Oct 10	Oct 09
Working Capital	-621	-434	-763
Fixed Assets	53	45	48
Current Assets	863	767	437

Hurricane Protective Clothing

Unit 2 Claymore Wilnecote, Tamworth, B77 5DQ
Tel: 01827-250808 **Fax:** 01827-250808
E-mail: hurricane@mgrubber.com
Managers: P. Grice (Mgr)
Immediate Holding Company: M.G. RUBBER CO. LTD
Registration no: 01754500 **Turnover:** £5m - £10m
No.of Employees: 11 - 20 **Product Groups:** 24

I C E Management Consultants

6 Coleshill Street Fazeley, Tamworth, B78 3RA
Tel: 01827-287256 **Fax:** 01827-251063
E-mail: p-wilkes@project-advice.com
Website: http://www.project-advice.com
Directors: P. Wilkes (Snr Part)
Immediate Holding Company: I.C.E. (MATERIALS HANDLING) LIMITED
Registration no: 01204748 **Date established:** 1975
Turnover: £250,000 - £500,000 **No.of Employees:** 1 - 10
Product Groups: 80

Date of Accounts	Mar 11	Mar 10	Mar 03
Working Capital	83	83	27
Fixed Assets	1	1	2
Current Assets	95	99	36

Impreglon UK Ltd

Kingsbury Link Trinity Road, Piccadilly, Tamworth, B78 2EX
Tel: 01827-871400 **Fax:** 01827-871401
E-mail: info@impreglon.co.uk
Website: http://www.impreglon.co.uk
Directors: G. Williams (MD), C. Moore (Dir)
Managers: A. George (Purch Mgr)
Immediate Holding Company: Impreglon SE
Registration no: 02028357 **Date established:** 1986
No.of Employees: 11 - 20 **Product Groups:** 30, 32, 48

Date of Accounts	Dec 11	Dec 10	Dec 09
Working Capital	142	145	163
Fixed Assets	2m	2m	2m
Current Assets	589	628	613

Integra Products

High Point Sandy Hill Park Sandy Way, Tamworth, B77 4DU
Tel: 01543-267100 **Fax:** 01543-267104
E-mail: john.martin@integra-products.co.uk
Website: http://www.integra-products.co.uk
Directors: C. Matthews (Fin), J. Martin (Dir)
Managers: J. Worth (Sales & Mktg Mgr), P. Blackaby (Tech Serv Mgr), P. Marsh
Ultimate Holding Company: RUBICON PARTNERS INDUSTRIES LLP
Immediate Holding Company: ANTIFERENCE LIMITED
Registration no: 00336260 **Date established:** 1938 **Turnover:** £2m - £5m
No.of Employees: 11 - 20 **Product Groups:** 24, 25, 30, 36, 63

Date of Accounts	Dec 11	Dec 10	Dec 09
Sales Turnover	N/A	3m	3m
Pre Tax Profit/Loss	N/A	746	866
Working Capital	494	7m	7m
Fixed Assets	48	43	25
Current Assets	2m	8m	8m
Current Liabilities	N/A	370	459

Invotec Circuits Tamworth Ltd

Hedging Lane Dosthill, Wilnecote, Tamworth, B77 5HH
Tel: 01827-263000 **Fax:** 01254-583373
E-mail: john.ennis@invotecgroup.com
Website: http://www.invotecgroup.com
Bank(s): Barclays
Directors: M. Pike (Fin), J. Ennis (MD), M. Bowman (Sales & Mktg)
Managers: P. Moreton, C. Rudlin (Buyer), C. Morris (Personnel)
Ultimate Holding Company: INVOTEC GROUP LIMITED
Immediate Holding Company: INVOTEC CIRCUITS TAMWORTH LIMITED
Registration no: 01994112 **VAT No.:** GB 326 0410 04
Date established: 1986 **Turnover:** £20m - £50m
No.of Employees: 101 - 250 **Product Groups:** 37

Date of Accounts	Dec 11	Dec 10	Dec 09
Sales Turnover	22m	21m	18m
Pre Tax Profit/Loss	2m	2m	2m
Working Capital	11m	9m	7m
Fixed Assets	4m	3m	4m
Current Assets	15m	14m	14m
Current Liabilities	2m	3m	4m

J C S Tools Ltd

200 Tamworth Road Two Gates, Tamworth, B77 1EA
Tel: 01827-281725 **Fax:** 01827-285434
E-mail: penny@jcstoolsltd.co.uk
Website: http://www.jcstoolsltd.co.uk
Directors: G. Scaldwell (Dir)
Managers: P. Smith (Sales Admin)
Immediate Holding Company: J.C.S.TOOLS LIMITED
Registration no: 01092436 **VAT No.:** GB 112 1600 41
Date established: 1973 **No.of Employees:** 1 - 10 **Product Groups:** 35, 46, 48

Date of Accounts	Dec 11	Dec 10	Dec 09
Working Capital	70	115	106
Fixed Assets	22	20	23
Current Assets	121	166	154

J V M Castings Ltd

Borman Lichfield Road Industrial Estate, Tamworth, B79 7TA
Tel: 01827-64096 **Fax:** 01827-69497
E-mail: sales@jvmcastings.com
Website: http://www.jvmcastings.com
Bank(s): Lloyds TSB Bank plc
Managers: J. West
Immediate Holding Company: JVM CASTINGS LIMITED
Registration no: 02677990 **Date established:** 1992
Turnover: £20m - £50m **No.of Employees:** 51 - 100 **Product Groups:** 22, 34

Date of Accounts	Mar 12	Mar 11	Mar 10
Sales Turnover	51m	45m	36m
Pre Tax Profit/Loss	-78	-568	-724
Working Capital	1m	3m	3m
Fixed Assets	8m	7m	5m
Current Assets	17m	14m	11m
Current Liabilities	7m	4m	3m

Komet Ltd

Unit 4 Clico Business Park Hamel House, Tamworth, B77 4DU
Tel: 01827-302518 **Fax:** 01827-300486
E-mail: info.uk@kometgroup.com
Website: http://www.kometgroup.com
Directors: S. Kirk (MD)
Ultimate Holding Company: KOMET GROUP HOLDING GMBH (GERMANY)
Immediate Holding Company: KOMET (UK) LIMITED
Registration no: 02788684 **Date established:** 1993
Turnover: £500,000 - £1m **No.of Employees:** 1 - 10 **Product Groups:** 46

Date of Accounts	Dec 11	Dec 10	Dec 09
Working Capital	417	315	296
Fixed Assets	68	67	76
Current Assets	617	656	623

Percy Lane Products Ltd

Lichfield Road, Tamworth, B79 7TL
Tel: 01827-63821 **Fax:** 01827-310159
E-mail: main@percy-lane.co.uk
Website: http://www.percy-lane.co.uk
Bank(s): Lloyds TSB Bank plc
Directors: P. Wright (Fin), J. Whetton (Sales), G. Fowler (Grp Chief Exec), A. Fowler (Fin)
Managers: P. Clay (Tech Serv Mgr), B. Hughes (Buyer)
Ultimate Holding Company: L&P 176 LIMITED
Immediate Holding Company: PERCY LANE LIMITED
Registration no: 04273769 **Date established:** 2001
Turnover: £10m - £20m **No.of Employees:** 101 - 250
Product Groups: 35, 36, 39, 45

Lawrence Industries Ltd

Lawrence House Apollo Lichfield Road Industrial Estate, Tamworth, B79 7TA
Tel: 01827-314151 **Fax:** 01827-314152
E-mail: sales@l-i.co.uk
Website: http://www.l-i.co.uk
Bank(s): Barclays
Directors: B. Meddings (Fin), C. Henn Allen (MD)
Ultimate Holding Company: PHIPPS & COMPANY LIMITED
Immediate Holding Company: LAWRENCE INDUSTRIES LIMITED
Registration no: 02878866 **Date established:** 1993
Turnover: £10m - £20m **No.of Employees:** 11 - 20 **Product Groups:** 14, 17, 23, 31, 32, 33

Date of Accounts	Mar 11	Mar 10	Mar 09
Sales Turnover	12m	12m	N/A
Pre Tax Profit/Loss	2m	2m	2m
Working Capital	3m	3m	3m
Fixed Assets	356	356	374
Current Assets	5m	5m	4m
Current Liabilities	804	698	538

Leader Chuck Systems Ltd

PO Box 16050, Tamworth, B77 9JP
Tel: 01827-700000 **Fax:** 01827-707777
E-mail: information@leaderchuck.com
Website: http://www.leaderchuck.com
Directors: M. Jones (MD)
Immediate Holding Company: LEADER CHUCK SYSTEMS LIMITED
Registration no: 02671693 **VAT No.:** GB 584 5006 37
Date established: 1991 **Turnover:** £500,000 - £1m
No.of Employees: 1 - 10 **Product Groups:** 36, 46

Date of Accounts	Dec 10	Dec 09	Dec 08
Working Capital	-0	19	23
Fixed Assets	14	18	26
Current Assets	207	135	250
Current Liabilities	N/A	2	N/A

Lutze Ltd

Unit 3 Sandy Hill Park Sandy Way, Tamworth, B77 4DU
Tel: 01827-313330 **Fax:** 01827-313332
E-mail: sales.gb@lutze.co.uk
Website: http://www.lutze.co.uk
Bank(s): Lloyds TSB
Directors: N. Broad (Dir)
Ultimate Holding Company: FRIEDRICH LUTZE GMBH & CO (GERMANY)
Immediate Holding Company: LUTZE LIMITED
Registration no: 02815561 **VAT No.:** GB 585 3397 00
Date established: 1993 **Turnover:** £500,000 - £1m
No.of Employees: 11 - 20 **Product Groups:** 35, 37

Date of Accounts	Dec 11	Dec 10	Dec 09
Working Capital	875	756	685
Fixed Assets	51	49	28
Current Assets	1m	1m	915

Madewell Products Ltd

Sandy Way Amington Industrial Estate, Tamworth, B77 4DS
Tel: 01827-305960 **Fax:** 01827-305961
E-mail: sales@madewellproducts.co.uk
Website: http://www.madewellproducts.co.uk
Bank(s): Co-op
Directors: E. Jeffreys (MD), R. Gibson (Ch), S. Gibson (Fin)
Managers: M. Gibson (Software Mgr), J. Patlow (Sales Admin)
Registration no: 02202222 **VAT No.:** GB 313 6622 81
Date established: 1987 **Turnover:** £1m - £2m **No.of Employees:** 21 - 50
Product Groups: 26, 34, 35

Date of Accounts	Jun 09	Jun 08	Jun 07
Working Capital	461	569	592
Fixed Assets	707	768	762
Current Assets	706	939	1m

Maydown International Tools Ltd
Mercury Park Amber Close, Tamworth, B77 4RP
Tel: 01827-309700 **Fax:** 01827-309719
E-mail: sales@maydown.co.uk
Website: http://www.maydown.co.uk
Directors: P. Stevens (MD)
Immediate Holding Company: MAYDOWN HOLDINGS LIMITED
Registration no: 01545596 **Date established:** 1981
No.of Employees: 1 - 10 **Product Groups:** 46

Date of Accounts	Mar 12	Mar 11	Mar 10
Working Capital	352	334	216
Fixed Assets	134	66	58
Current Assets	791	735	539

Microprise Ltd
Unit 3 Claymore Wilnecote, Tamworth, B77 5DQ
Tel: 01827-261554 **Fax:** 01827-261552
E-mail: sales@microprise.co.uk
Website: http://www.gaugemakers.com
Directors: Y. Margetts (Fin)
Immediate Holding Company: MICROPRISE LIMITED
Registration no: 02484017 **Date established:** 1990
No.of Employees: 1 - 10 **Product Groups:** 38, 45, 48, 67, 85

Date of Accounts	Mar 11	Mar 10	Mar 09
Working Capital	24	-53	-66
Fixed Assets	52	63	71
Current Assets	199	82	100

Midlands Electrical Specialists Ltd
3 Ariane, Tamworth, B79 7XF
Tel: 01827-63293 **Fax:** 01827-55588
E-mail: info@mesltd.com
Website: http://www.mesltd.com
Directors: L. Hyde (Dir), G. Hyde (MD)
Immediate Holding Company: MIDLANDS ELECTRICAL SPECIALISTS LIMITED
Registration no: 01195913 **VAT No.:** GB 112 6268 95
Date established: 1975 **Turnover:** £1m - £2m **No.of Employees:** 21 - 50
Product Groups: 52

Date of Accounts	Mar 11	Mar 10	Mar 09
Working Capital	78	44	32
Fixed Assets	47	61	49
Current Assets	269	163	266

Mitsubishi Carbide (M M C Hardmetal UK Ltd)
5-7 Galena Close, Tamworth, B77 4AS
Tel: 01827-312312 **Fax:** 01827-312314
E-mail: sales@mitsubishicarbide.co.uk
Website: http://www.mitsubishicarbide.com
Bank(s): Mitsubish Bank of Tokyo
Directors: S. Woodman (Fin)
Managers: M. Drayton (Sales & Mktg Mg)
Ultimate Holding Company: MITSUBISHI MATERIALS CORPORATION (JAPAN)
Immediate Holding Company: MMC HARDMETAL UK LIMITED
Registration no: 00897899 **Date established:** 1967
Turnover: £10m - £20m **No.of Employees:** 21 - 50 **Product Groups:** 36, 46

Date of Accounts	Dec 10	Dec 09	Dec 08
Sales Turnover	8m	8m	10m
Pre Tax Profit/Loss	327	-197	287
Working Capital	751	502	663
Fixed Assets	55	85	82
Current Assets	3m	3m	5m
Current Liabilities	485	248	411

Mormet Alloys Ltd
Tamworth Road Two Gates, Tamworth, B77 1EA
Tel: 01827-285555 **Fax:** 01827-286286
E-mail: colinmccoy@mormet.co.uk
Website: http://www.mormet.co.uk
Bank(s): Barclays, Tamworth
Directors: C. Mccoy (Dir), H. Hollins (Dir)
Ultimate Holding Company: MORMET (ALLOYS) LIMITED
Immediate Holding Company: MORMET LIMITED
Registration no: 01272778 **VAT No.:** GB 687 8974 40
Date established: 1976 **No.of Employees:** 11 - 20 **Product Groups:** 34, 66

Date of Accounts	Sep 11	Sep 10	Sep 09
Working Capital	9	9	9
Current Assets	9	9	9

National Windscreens Ltd
Bolehall House Amington Road, Tamworth, B77 3PA
Tel: 01827-304160 **Fax:** 01827-304161
E-mail: info@nationalwindscreens.co.uk
Website: http://www.nationalwindscreens.co.uk
Directors: M. Beresford Dutton (MD), P. Marsden (Comm), M. Beresford-dutton (MD), M. Dutton (MD)
Managers: R. Walters (Comm), G. Huxley (Comm), B. Dubber (Sales Prom Mgr)
Ultimate Holding Company: NATIONAL WINDSCREENS (REPLACEMENTS) LIMITED
Immediate Holding Company: NATIONAL WINDSCREENS (REPLACEMENTS) LIMITED
Registration no: 01612587 **Date established:** 1982
Turnover: £20m - £50m **No.of Employees:** 51 - 100 **Product Groups:** 39

Date of Accounts	May 10	May 09	May 08
Sales Turnover	12m	N/A	N/A
Pre Tax Profit/Loss	63	N/A	N/A
Working Capital	194	26	29
Fixed Assets	72	92	64
Current Assets	4m	2m	2m
Current Liabilities	1m	N/A	N/A

Nautic Steels Ltd
Claymore Tame Valley Industrial Estate, Wilnecote, Tamworth, B77 5DQ
Tel: 01827-281111 **Fax:** 01827-281444
E-mail: sales@nautic.co.uk
Website: http://www.nautic.co.uk
Bank(s): Lloyds TSB Bank plc
Directors: E. Shawsman (Fin)
Managers: E. Shortman (Fin Mgr), J. Tan (Purch Mgr), S. Rowland (Tech Serv Mgr)
Ultimate Holding Company: NAUTIC STEELS (HOLDINGS) LIMITED
Immediate Holding Company: NAUTIC STEELS LIMITED
Registration no: 02302004 **VAT No.:** GB 486 8587 69
Date established: 1988 **Turnover:** £10m - £20m
No.of Employees: 51 - 100 **Product Groups:** 36

Date of Accounts	Dec 11	Dec 10	Dec 09
Sales Turnover	12m	9m	8m
Pre Tax Profit/Loss	2m	307	138
Working Capital	4m	3m	2m
Current Assets	10m	7m	7m
Current Liabilities	558	168	64

Neuteq Europe
38 Sandy Way Amington Industrial Estate, Tamworth, B77 4DS
Tel: 01827-313644 **Fax:** 01827-311793
E-mail: sales@neuteq-europe.co.uk
Website: http://www.neuteq-europe.co.uk
Directors: M. Hendel (Sales), M. Edge (Co Sec)
Managers: A. Garatt
Immediate Holding Company: NEUTEQ EUROPE LIMITED
Registration no: 05506845 **Date established:** 2005
No.of Employees: 11 - 20 **Product Groups:** 46

Date of Accounts	Jul 11	Jul 10	Jul 09
Working Capital	778	620	388
Fixed Assets	183	123	134
Current Assets	2m	2m	916

O W L Electronics Ltd
PO Box 1330, Tamworth, B77 1AW
Tel: 08456-430212 **Fax:** 01827-60579
E-mail: info@o-w-l.co.uk
Website: http://www.o-w-l.co.uk
Directors: S. Phipps (Dir)
Immediate Holding Company: O.W.L. ELECTRONICS LIMITED
Registration no: 03695590 **VAT No.:** GB 729 3410 36
Date established: 1999 **Turnover:** £1m - £2m **No.of Employees:** 1 - 10
Product Groups: 37, 39, 40, 44, 45, 48, 67, 68, 81, 84, 89

Date of Accounts	Sep 11	Sep 10	Sep 09
Working Capital	12	13	6
Fixed Assets	2	3	2
Current Assets	35	33	31

Optical Coating Technologies Ltd
Unit 8 Lagrange Lichfield Road Industrial Estate, Tamworth, B79 7XD
Tel: 01827-63489 **Fax:** 01827-51918
E-mail: octwebsite@aol.com
Website: http://www.optical-coatings.com
Product Groups: 30, 31, 32, 38, 39, 40, 42, 44, 45, 46, 48, 49

Date of Accounts	Dec 11	Dec 10	Dec 09
Working Capital	523	407	285
Fixed Assets	21	20	38
Current Assets	818	661	426

Paddock Gear Engineering Ltd
2 Kingsbury Link Trinity Road, Piccadilly, Tamworth, B78 2EX
Tel: 01827-875566 **Fax:** 01827-875880
E-mail: j.marklew@paddockgear.co.uk
Website: http://www.paddockgear.co.uk
Directors: D. Marklew (MD), J. Marklew (Fin)
Managers: P. Spencer (Works Gen Mgr)
Immediate Holding Company: PADDOCK GEAR & ENGINEERING LIMITED
Registration no: 03791210 **Date established:** 1999
No.of Employees: 21 - 50 **Product Groups:** 35, 45

Date of Accounts	Dec 11	Dec 10	Dec 09
Working Capital	-536	-273	20
Fixed Assets	64	81	101
Current Assets	56	118	140

Pedrollo Distribution
9 Cavendish Lichfield Road Industrial Estate, Tamworth, B79 7XH
Tel: 01827-313000 **Fax:** 01827-313008
E-mail: sales@pedrollo.co.uk
Website: http://www.pedrollo.co.uk
Directors: C. Biglin (Dir), J. Snowdon (Fin)
Managers: M. Goodall (Mgr)
Immediate Holding Company: PEDROLLO DISTRIBUTION LIMITED
Registration no: 02829921 **Date established:** 1993
No.of Employees: 1 - 10 **Product Groups:** 33, 36, 37, 38, 39, 40, 41, 47, 66, 67

Date of Accounts	Dec 10	Dec 09	Dec 08
Working Capital	324	248	186
Fixed Assets	21	22	25
Current Assets	537	405	424

Petit Forestier
Birch Coppice Industrial Estate Watling Street, Dordon, Tamworth, B78 1SZ
Tel: 01827-263100 **Fax:** 01827-289071
E-mail: enquiries@petitforestier.co.uk
Website: http://www.petitforestier.co.uk
Directors: E. Forestier (Fin), V. Lachambre (Fin)
Managers: G. Robinson
Ultimate Holding Company: SYLVE INVEST SAS (BELGIUM)
Immediate Holding Company: PETIT FORESTIER UK LIMITED
Registration no: 01775955 **Date established:** 1983
Turnover: £20m - £50m **No.of Employees:** 51 - 100 **Product Groups:** 72, 82

Date of Accounts	Dec 11	Dec 10	Dec 09
Sales Turnover	39m	42m	47m
Pre Tax Profit/Loss	90	410	-94
Working Capital	-20m	-22m	-21m
Fixed Assets	78m	70m	71m
Current Assets	13m	11m	17m
Current Liabilities	1m	1m	4m

Powelectrics Ltd
2 Sandy Hill Park Sandy Way, Tamworth, B77 4DU
Tel: 01827-310666 **Fax:** 01827-310999
E-mail: sales@powelectrics.co.uk
Website: http://www.powelectrics.co.uk
Bank(s): National Westminster Bank Plc
Directors: P. John (Dir)
Immediate Holding Company: POWELECTRICS LIMITED
Registration no: 02549947 **VAT No.:** GB 377 5254 23
Date established: 1990 **Turnover:** £500,000 - £1m
No.of Employees: 11 - 20 **Product Groups:** 37, 38, 39, 40, 45, 67, 81

Date of Accounts	Dec 11	Dec 10	Dec 09
Working Capital	-12	59	-125
Fixed Assets	22	13	13
Current Assets	543	326	234

Precision Technologies International Ltd
22 Mariner, Tamworth, B79 7UL
Tel: 01827-54371 **Fax:** 01827- 310406
E-mail: sales@ptiltd.co.uk
Website: http://www.ptiltd.co.uk
Bank(s): United Bank of Kuwait
Directors: S. Maclean (Fin), B. Pinfield (MD), P. Walker (Tech Serv)
Ultimate Holding Company: PRECISION ENGINEERING SOLUTIONS LIMITED
Immediate Holding Company: PRECISION TECHNOLOGIES INTERNATIONAL LIMITED
Registration no: 04155600 **VAT No.:** GB 765 3441 21
Date established: 2001 **Turnover:** £5m - £10m
No.of Employees: 51 - 100 **Product Groups:** 35, 38

Date of Accounts	Apr 12	Apr 11	Apr 10
Working Capital	-27	-468	-749
Fixed Assets	706	774	930
Current Assets	1m	2m	2m

Press & Shear Machinery Ltd
Unit 12-14 Ninian Park Ninian Way, Wilnecote, Tamworth, B77 5ES
Tel: 01827-250000 **Fax:** 01827-250022
E-mail: sales@pressandshear.com
Website: http://www.pressandshear.com
Bank(s): Lloyds, Birmingham
Managers: C. Britton (Sales Admin)
Immediate Holding Company: PRESS & SHEAR MACHINERY LIMITED
Registration no: 02748787 **VAT No.:** GB 580 4688 14
Date established: 1992 **Turnover:** £2m - £5m **No.of Employees:** 11 - 20
Product Groups: 46

Date of Accounts	Sep 11	Sep 10	Sep 09
Working Capital	275	304	9
Fixed Assets	91	113	139
Current Assets	907	805	655

Pugh & Sanders
Unit 2 Ariane, Tamworth, B79 7XF
Tel: 01827-313707
Website: http://www.pughandsanders.co.uk
Managers: J. Griffin (Mgr)
Date established: 2004 **No.of Employees:** 1 - 10 **Product Groups:** 35

Pure Water Storage Ltd
Trickley Coppice Farm Coppice Lane, Middleton, Tamworth, B78 2BU
Tel: 0121-323 4000 **Fax:** 0121-323 4000
E-mail: jason@purewaterstorage.co.uk
Website: http://www.purewaterstorage.co.uk
Directors: L. Hall (Fin), J. Hall (Dir)
Immediate Holding Company: PUREWATER STORAGE LIMITED
Registration no: 04355472 **Date established:** 2002
No.of Employees: 11 - 20 **Product Groups:** 35, 42, 45

Date of Accounts	Mar 11	Mar 10	Mar 09
Working Capital	143	126	120
Fixed Assets	64	48	52
Current Assets	364	308	291

RPC Recycle Ltd
18 Apollo Lichfield Road Industrial Estate, Tamworth, B79 7TA
Tel: 0844-357 7077 **Fax:** 0844-357 9491
E-mail: charlotte@rpcrecycle.com
Website: http://www.rpcrecycle.com
Product Groups: 37, 54, 67

Satellite Industries
Satellite House Lichfield Trading Estate Lagrange, Tamworth, B79 7XD
Tel: 01827-723999 **Fax:** 01827-62644
E-mail: info@satelliteindustries.com
Website: http://www.satelliteindustries.com
Directors: J. Babcock (Co Sec), T. Hilde (Dir)
Managers: D. Cartwright (District Mgr)
Immediate Holding Company: SATELLITE INDUSTRIES GB LIMITED
Registration no: 03004731 **Date established:** 1994
No.of Employees: 1 - 10 **Product Groups:** 30, 36, 66

Date of Accounts	Dec 11	Dec 10	Dec 09
Working Capital	-70	-85	-121
Fixed Assets	21	25	32
Current Assets	210	82	110

Shopmobility
5th Floor In The Car Park George Street, Tamworth, B79 7LG
Tel: 01827-709392
Managers: A. Coleman (Mgr)
Immediate Holding Company: MM RETAIL ONE LTD
Date established: 2011 **No.of Employees:** 1 - 10 **Product Groups:** 38, 67

Simpson Strong-Tie International Inc
Cardinal Point Winchester Road, Tamworth, B78 3HG
Tel: 01827-255600 **Fax:** 01827-255616
E-mail: info@strongtie.com
Website: http://www.strongtie.co.uk
Bank(s): Barclays
Directors: S. Davis (Fin), M. Paulson (MD)
Managers: C. Sanders (Mktg Serv Mgr), A. Burke (Personnel), M. Loveless (Tech Serv Mgr), M. Foster (Prod Mgr)
Immediate Holding Company: SIMPSON STRONG-TIE INTERNATIONAL, INC.
Registration no: FC017716 **VAT No.:** GB 642 8221 50
Date established: 1994 **Turnover:** £1m - £2m **No.of Employees:** 51 - 100
Product Groups: 25, 33, 34, 35, 37, 41, 45, 46, 66

Smurfit Kappa Preprint
Mariner, Tamworth, B79 7TB
Tel: 01827-306400 **Fax:** 01827-306401
Website: http://www.uk.smurfitgroup.com
Managers: J. Mcallister (Chief Mgr), K. Pickett
Registration no: 01017013 **Date established:** 1982
No.of Employees: 11 - 20 **Product Groups:** 28

Smurfit Kappa Recycling
Birch Coppice Industrial Estate Watling Street, Dordon, Tamworth, B78 1SZ
Tel: 01827-892100 **Fax:** 01827-330400
E-mail: recycling.uk@smurfitkappa.co.uk
Website: http://www.smurfitkappa.co.uk
Managers: M. Challons (Mktg Serv Mgr)
Immediate Holding Company: CUMBRIA WASTE MANAGEMENT LTD
Registration no: 03162439 **No.of Employees:** 21 - 50 **Product Groups:** 27

S P I (Materials) Ltd
38 Amber Close Amington Industrial Estate, Tamworth, B77 4RP
Tel: 01827-305351 **Fax:** 01827-63686
E-mail: sales@spi-mail.com
Website: http://www.spi-online.com
Directors: M. Holt (Dir)
Registration no: 03533716 **Date established:** 2004
No.of Employees: 1 - 10 **Product Groups:** 36, 46

Date of Accounts	Sep 08	Sep 07	Sep 06
Pre Tax Profit/Loss	691	660	N/A
Working Capital	529	777	460
Fixed Assets	148	112	84
Current Assets	6379	4242	4216
Current Liabilities	5850	3466	3756
ROCE% (Return on Capital Employed)	102.0	74.2	

Stainless Tube & Needle Co. Ltd
66 Fazeley Road, Tamworth, B78 3JN
Tel: 01827-51162 **Fax:** 01827-65559
E-mail: robert.gold@stncoltd.co.uk
Website: http://www.stncoltd.co.uk
Bank(s): Lloyds
Directors: R. Gold (Fin), R. Perry (MD)
Immediate Holding Company: STAINLESS TUBE & NEEDLE COMPANY LIMITED
Registration no: 02374498 **VAT No.:** GB 486 9010 22
Date established: 1989 **Turnover:** £250,000 - £500,000
No.of Employees: 11 - 20 **Product Groups:** 66

Date of Accounts	Jul 11	Jul 10	Jul 09
Sales Turnover	497	416	417
Pre Tax Profit/Loss	34	4	4
Working Capital	107	84	79
Fixed Assets	8	10	11
Current Assets	186	146	139
Current Liabilities	44	28	24

Strong's Plastic Products Ltd
18 Silica Road Amington Industrial Estate, Tamworth, B77 4DT
Tel: 01827-302490 **Fax:** 01827-54999
E-mail: estelle@strongs.co.uk
Website: http://www.strongs.co.uk
Bank(s): Lloyds TSB Bank plc
Directors: B. Strong (MD)
Managers: E. Green (Fin Mgr)
Immediate Holding Company: STRONG'S PLASTIC PRODUCTS LIMITED
Registration no: 01877530 **VAT No.:** GB 425 3736 54
Date established: 1985 **Turnover:** £2m - £5m **No.of Employees:** 21 - 50
Product Groups: 30, 31, 39, 42, 48

Date of Accounts	Apr 11	Apr 10	Apr 09
Sales Turnover	3m	3m	3m
Pre Tax Profit/Loss	200	351	355
Working Capital	366	272	150
Fixed Assets	570	468	372
Current Assets	1m	915	712
Current Liabilities	218	282	169

Tamworth Heat Treatment Company Ltd
7 Darwell Park Mica Close, Tamworth, B77 4DR
Tel: 01827-318030 **Fax:** 01827-318039
E-mail: sales@tamworth-heat.co.uk
Website: http://www.tamworth-heat.co.uk
Directors: A. Crilly (Co Sec)
Managers: M. Whitehouse (Comm)
Immediate Holding Company: TAMWORTH HEAT TREATMENT LIMITED
Registration no: 01827957 **Date established:** 1984
No.of Employees: 11 - 20 **Product Groups:** 46, 48

Date of Accounts	Jun 11	Jun 10	Jun 09
Working Capital	106	-159	-231
Fixed Assets	1m	2m	2m
Current Assets	633	452	442

Tamworth Steel Stockholders Ltd
Gagarin Apollo, Tamworth, B79 7TA
Tel: 01827-61531 **Fax:** 01827- 310078
E-mail: sales@tamworthsteel.co.uk
Website: http://www.tamworthsteel.co.uk
Bank(s): National Westminster P.L.C.
Directors: J. Ratledge (Dir), J. Ratledge (MD)
Immediate Holding Company: TAMWORTH STEEL STOCKHOLDERS LIMITED
Registration no: 01109834 **VAT No.:** GB 111 7047 15
Date established: 1973 **Turnover:** £5m - £10m **No.of Employees:** 21 - 50
Product Groups: 66

Date of Accounts	Mar 11	Mar 10	Mar 09
Sales Turnover	7m	6m	N/A
Pre Tax Profit/Loss	509	79	309
Working Capital	1m	2m	2m
Fixed Assets	3m	2m	2m
Current Assets	4m	4m	3m
Current Liabilities	434	267	400

Thal UK Ltd
Satellite House Lichfield Trading Estate Lagrange, Tamworth, B79 7XD
Tel: 01827-723999 **Fax:** 01827-62644
E-mail: info@satellite-thal.com
Website: http://www.satellite-thal.com
Directors: T. Hilde (Dir), J. Babcock (Co Sec), J. Trelfa (Dir)
Managers: D. Cartwright (District Mgr), A. Willetts (Sales Prom Mgr)
Ultimate Holding Company: COLLIN (HOLDINGS) PLC
Immediate Holding Company: SATELLITE INDUSTRIES GB LIMITED
Registration no: 03004731 **VAT No.:** GB 580 3616 44
Date established: 1994 **Turnover:** £1m - £2m **No.of Employees:** 1 - 10
Product Groups: 36, 40, 83

Date of Accounts	Dec 11	Dec 10	Dec 09
Working Capital	-70	-85	-121
Fixed Assets	21	25	32
Current Assets	210	82	110

Thermal Clad Ltd
Unit 64 Tolsons Enterprise Park, Fazeley, Tamworth, B78 3QD
Tel: 01827-259972 **Fax:** 01827-282175
E-mail: enquiries@thermal-clad.co.uk
Website: http://www.thermal-clad.co.uk
Directors: K. Cartridge (MD)
Immediate Holding Company: THERMAL CLAD LIMITED
Registration no: 05305582 **Date established:** 2004
Turnover: £250,000 - £500,000 **No.of Employees:** 1 - 10
Product Groups: 30, 33, 40, 52, 66

Date of Accounts	Dec 11	Dec 10	Dec 09
Working Capital	16	22	-1
Fixed Assets	27	32	31
Current Assets	267	153	164

Trisport Ltd
38 Amber Close Tamworth Business Park, Tamworth, B77 4RP
Tel: 01827-56544 **Fax:** 01827-53181
E-mail: info@trisportgolf.com
Website: http://www.trisportgolf.com
Directors: R. Dupont (Fin)
Managers: B. Adams, L. Rowe, A. Lovell (Fin Mgr), E. Lucas
Ultimate Holding Company: PRIDE MANUFACTURING COMPANY LLC (USA)
Immediate Holding Company: TRISPORT LIMITED
Registration no: 03807486 **VAT No.:** GB 580 4014 67
Date established: 1999 **Turnover:** £10m - £20m
No.of Employees: 11 - 20 **Product Groups:** 22, 35

Date of Accounts	Dec 11	Dec 10	Dec 09
Sales Turnover	12m	14m	11m
Pre Tax Profit/Loss	2m	3m	2m
Working Capital	17m	15m	17m
Fixed Assets	5m	5m	6m
Current Assets	18m	16m	18m
Current Liabilities	532	791	697

Tube Fins Ltd
N Riverside Industrial Estate Atherstone Street, Fazeley, Tamworth, B78 3SD
Tel: 01827-251234 **Fax:** 01827-286612
E-mail: bob@tubefins.co.uk
Bank(s): Barclays, Lincoln
Directors: W. Zonta (Co Sec)
Managers: B. Mason (Ops Mgr)
Ultimate Holding Company: DYNAMIC TECHNOLOGIES SPA (ITALY)
Immediate Holding Company: TUBE FINS LIMITED
Registration no: 01021223 **Date established:** 1971 **Turnover:** £1m - £2m
No.of Employees: 11 - 20 **Product Groups:** 36, 40

Date of Accounts	Dec 11	Dec 10	Dec 09
Sales Turnover	2m	2m	1m
Pre Tax Profit/Loss	241	158	178
Working Capital	1m	906	790
Fixed Assets	36	26	29
Current Assets	1m	1m	1m
Current Liabilities	147	184	71

Tyndale Flooring
Unit 13 Mercian Park Mercian Park, Tamworth, B77 4DP
Tel: 01827-311321 **Fax:** 01827-311638
E-mail: steve.gledhill@tyndalemidlands.com
Website: http://www.tyndaleflooring.com
Managers: S. Gledhill (Chief Mgr)
No.of Employees: 11 - 20 **Product Groups:** 23, 31

Vanriet UK Ltd
Riverside Industrial Estate Frazeley, Tamworth, B78 3RL
Tel: 01827-288871 **Fax:** 01827-250810
E-mail: sales@vanriet.co.uk
Website: http://www.vanriet.co.uk
Bank(s): Barclays
Directors: T. Van Riet (MD), P. Farmery (Dir), T. Van Riet (Fin)
Managers: G. Wilkins (Purch Mgr), S. Groves (Admin Off), B. Fleming (Sales Prom Mgr), D. Welsh (Eng)
Immediate Holding Company: VANRIET (U.K.) LIMITED
Registration no: 02316657 **Date established:** 1988
Turnover: £500,000 - £1m **No.of Employees:** 11 - 20 **Product Groups:** 45

Date of Accounts	Dec 11	Dec 10	Dec 09
Sales Turnover	931	760	882
Pre Tax Profit/Loss	N/A	-145	-200
Working Capital	33	25	62
Fixed Assets	28	36	44
Current Assets	402	280	378
Current Liabilities	318	187	194

Vesuvius UK
Coleshill Road, Tamworth, B78 3TL
Tel: 01827-262021 **Fax:** 01827-250806
E-mail: r.brown@foseco.com
Website: http://www.foseco.co.uk
Directors: R. Sykes (MD)
Ultimate Holding Company: COOKSON GROUP PLC
Immediate Holding Company: 7 DAY CATERING LIMITED
Registration no: 00054713 **Date established:** 1990
Turnover: £20m - £50m **No.of Employees:** 101 - 250
Product Groups: 14, 17, 32, 33

Date of Accounts	May 11	May 10	May 09
Sales Turnover	61m	55m	32m
Pre Tax Profit/Loss	2m	1m	615
Working Capital	4m	2m	1m
Fixed Assets	60	91	112
Current Assets	12m	11m	6m
Current Liabilities	4m	4m	3m

Uttoxeter

B C Bell
14 Barnwell Close Stramshall, Uttoxeter, ST14 5AW
Tel: 01889-562480
Directors: B. Bell (Prop)
Immediate Holding Company: BELL CONSTRUCTION (UK) LIMITED
Registration no: 04559670 **Date established:** 2002
No.of Employees: 1 - 10 **Product Groups:** 35

Date of Accounts	Oct 11	Oct 10	Oct 09
Working Capital	-6	-12	-14
Fixed Assets	27	13	18
Current Assets	21	13	16

Brian Belcher & Son
64 Howitt Cresent, Uttoxeter, ST14 7AU
Tel: 01889-566245 **Fax:** 01889-566245
E-mail: b.belcher@btconnect.com
Directors: B. Belcher (Prop)
Date established: 1982 **No.of Employees:** 1 - 10 **Product Groups:** 38, 42

Compco Alternatives
Unit 102 Marchington Industrial Estate Stubby Lane, Marchington, Uttoxeter, ST14 8LP
Tel: 01283-820009
Directors: D. Johnstone (Prop)
No.of Employees: 1 - 10 **Product Groups:** 29

Fox's Biscuits
Dove Valley Bakeries Cheadle Road, Uttoxeter, ST14 7BT
Tel: 01889-563131 **Fax:** 01889-565379
E-mail: info@elkes-biscuits.co.uk
Website: http://www.northernfoods.com
Directors: K. Hand (MD)
Ultimate Holding Company: NORTHERN FOODS P.L.C.
Immediate Holding Company: NORTHERN FOODS GROCERY GROUP LTD
Registration no: 02415575 **VAT No.:** GB 168 7433 30
Turnover: £20m - £50m **No.of Employees:** 501 - 1000
Product Groups: 20

J C B Earthmovers Ltd
Lakeside Works Dentstone Road, Rocester, Uttoxeter, ST14 5JP
Tel: 01889-590312 **Fax:** 01889-591287
E-mail: loadall@jcb.com
Website: http://www.jcb.com
Directors: J. Patterson (Dir), A. Bamford (Dir)
Managers: M. Mcclurg
Ultimate Holding Company: TRANSMISSIONS & ENGINEERING SERVICES BV (NETHERLANDS)
Immediate Holding Company: J.C.B.EARTHMOVERS LIMITED
Registration no: 00934508 **Date established:** 1968
Turnover: £75m - £125m **No.of Employees:** 1501 & over
Product Groups: 45

Date of Accounts	Dec 10	Dec 09	Dec 08
Sales Turnover	116m	90m	144m
Pre Tax Profit/Loss	13m	7m	10m
Working Capital	15m	16m	17m
Fixed Assets	9m	10m	10m
Current Assets	46m	39m	38m
Current Liabilities	4m	3m	3m

R Jeffrey
36 Church Street, Uttoxeter, ST14 8AD
Tel: 01889-568636 **Fax:** 01889-500407
Directors: R. Jeffrey (Prop)
Immediate Holding Company: UTTOXETER ACCOUNTING SERVICES LTD
Registration no: 04859377 **Date established:** 2003
No.of Employees: 1 - 10 **Product Groups:** 41

Date of Accounts	Sep 11	Sep 10	Sep 09
Working Capital	-0	N/A	N/A
Current Assets	N/A	N/A	1

Professional Vehicle Services Ltd
2 Sorrel Close, Uttoxeter, ST14 8UP
Tel: 01889-560501 **Fax:** 01889-560506
E-mail: sales@pvsl.org.uk
Website: http://www.pvsl.net
Directors: C. Turner (Fin), K. Turner (MD)
Immediate Holding Company: PROFESSIONAL VEHICLE SERVICES LIMITED
Registration no: 04153601 **Date established:** 2001
No.of Employees: 1 - 10 **Product Groups:** 82

Date of Accounts	Nov 11	Nov 10	Nov 09
Working Capital	4	7	-1
Fixed Assets	1	1	1
Current Assets	12	21	18

Red Dog Photography
31 Cheadle Road, Uttoxeter, ST14 7BX
Tel: 01889-569232
E-mail: duncan@reddogphoto.co.uk
Website: http://www.reddogphoto.co.uk
Directors: D. Rob (Prop)
Date established: 2004 **Turnover:** Up to £250,000
No.of Employees: 1 - 10 **Product Groups:** 81

Trenchex Garden Machinery
Dovefields Dovefields Industrial Estate, Uttoxeter, ST14 8HU
Tel: 01889-565155 **Fax:** 01889-563140
E-mail: enquiries@trenchex.com
Website: http://www.lawn-king.co.uk
Directors: T. Skeldon (MD), L. Uston (Purch)
Managers: J. Chapman
Immediate Holding Company: TRENCHEX POWER PRODUCTS LIMITED
Registration no: 01330079 **Date established:** 1977 **Turnover:** £5m - £10m
No.of Employees: 11 - 20 **Product Groups:** 39, 41, 49, 67

Date of Accounts	Oct 11	Oct 10	Oct 09
Sales Turnover	6m	6m	7m
Pre Tax Profit/Loss	-550	68	71
Working Capital	608	1m	1m
Fixed Assets	199	222	244
Current Assets	2m	2m	2m
Current Liabilities	44	64	67

Tuffa UK Ltd
Dovefields Industrial Estate Derby Road, Uttoxeter, ST14 8SW
Tel: 01889-567700
E-mail: sales@tuffa.co.uk
Website: http://www.tuffa.co.uk
Directors: J. Shenton (Fin), R. Shenton (MD)
Managers: D. Boulton (Sales Prom Mgr), J. Shenton (Purch Mgr)
Immediate Holding Company: TUFFA UK LIMITED
Registration no: 05444911 **Date established:** 2005
No.of Employees: 21 - 50 **Product Groups:** 35, 42, 45

Date of Accounts	Jul 11	Jul 10	Jul 09
Working Capital	417	225	384
Fixed Assets	457	294	103
Current Assets	955	1m	935

Weighing Machine Services
Unit 1 Stubby Lane Marchington, Uttoxeter, ST14 8LP
Tel: 01283-820817 **Fax:** 01283-820924
E-mail: sales@weighingms.com
Website: http://www.weighingms.com
Directors: C. Boyle (Ptnr), P. Price (Prop)
Date established: 1979 **No.of Employees:** 1 - 10 **Product Groups:** 38, 42

SUFFOLK

Beccles

A J T's Ltd
Brook Farm Halesworth Road, Redisham, Beccles, NR34 8NF
Tel: 01986-781505 **Fax:** 01986-781505
Directors: J. Smith (Dir)
Immediate Holding Company: A. J. T'S. LTD.
Registration no: 05892136 **Date established:** 2006
No.of Employees: 1 - 10 **Product Groups:** 41

Date of Accounts	Jul 11	Jul 10	Jul 08
Working Capital	-10	-2	7
Current Assets	46	53	60
Current Liabilities	9	4	8

Brett Snowling
40 Cedar Drive Worlingham, Beccles, NR34 7EW
Tel: 01502-717730 **Fax:** 01502-717730
Website: http://www.brettsnowling.com
Directors: B. Snowling (Prop)
Date established: 1986 **Turnover:** Up to £250,000
No.of Employees: 1 - 10 **Product Groups:** 37, 52

Broadwater Mouldings Ltd
Benacre Road Ellough, Beccles, NR34 7XD
Tel: 01502-719310 **Fax:** 01379-384150
E-mail: sales@broadwater.co.uk
Website: http://www.broadwater.co.uk
Bank(s): Barclays, Framlingham
Directors: M. Barker (Fin)
Managers: A. Crisp (Purch Mgr), N. Thompson (Sales Admin), N. Thompson (Personnel)
Ultimate Holding Company: P.H. BETTS (HOLDINGS) LIMITED
Immediate Holding Company: BROADWATER MOULDINGS LIMITED
Registration no: 01025838 **VAT No.:** GB 334 0520 02
Date established: 1971 **Turnover:** £5m - £10m
No.of Employees: 51 - 100 **Product Groups:** 30

Date of Accounts	Jan 12	Jan 11	Jan 10
Sales Turnover	8m	7m	6m
Pre Tax Profit/Loss	582	408	497
Working Capital	2m	2m	3m
Fixed Assets	2m	343	180
Current Assets	3m	3m	4m
Current Liabilities	363	568	272

C P I William Clowes Ltd
Copland Way Ellough, Beccles, NR34 7TL
Tel: 01502-712884 **Fax:** 01502-717003
E-mail: thumphrey@cpibooks.co.uk
Website: http://www.cpibooks.co.uk
Bank(s): Barclays
Directors: S. Armes (MD), D. Browne (Sales), M. Robson (Co Sec)
Managers: A. Cray (Purch Mgr), T. Humphrey, J. Cooper (Fin Mgr), M. Tyson
Ultimate Holding Company: CAMERON FRANCE HOLDING SAS (FRANCE)
Immediate Holding Company: CPI WILLIAM CLOWES LTD
Registration no: 03369829 **VAT No.:** GB 688 8025 83
Date established: 1997 **Turnover:** £10m - £20m
No.of Employees: 101 - 250 **Product Groups:** 28

Date of Accounts	Mar 11	Mar 10	Mar 09
Sales Turnover	13m	12m	11m
Pre Tax Profit/Loss	592	-136	-278
Working Capital	-3m	-3m	-3m
Fixed Assets	4m	5m	5m
Current Assets	4m	3m	2m
Current Liabilities	393	1m	1m

Classic British Lighting
Unit 20 Common Road Aldeby, Beccles, NR34 0BL
Tel: 01502-678100
Directors: R. Derham (Prop)
No.of Employees: 1 - 10 **Product Groups:** 37, 67

Electroplate UK Ltd
Unit 8c Ellough Industrial Estate Ellough, Beccles, NR34 7TD
Tel: 01502-470045 **Fax:** 01502-470045
Website: http://www.electroplateuk.com
Directors: M. Barber (Fin), R. Goff (MD)
Immediate Holding Company: ELECTROPLATE (UK) LIMITED
Registration no: 04185305 **Date established:** 2001
No.of Employees: 1 - 10 **Product Groups:** 46, 48

Date of Accounts	Sep 11	Sep 10	Sep 09
Working Capital	39	-13	8
Fixed Assets	35	44	25
Current Assets	122	113	110

Jim Laws Lighting
West End West End Lodge, Wrentham, Beccles, NR34 7NH
Tel: 01502-675264
Directors: J. Laws (Prop)
No.of Employees: 1 - 10 **Product Groups:** 37, 67

M A P Services
Sandpit Lane Ellough, Beccles, NR34 7TH
Tel: 01502-710850 **Fax:** 01502-710850
Directors: M. Pipe (Ptnr)
Date established: 1996 **No.of Employees:** 1 - 10 **Product Groups:** 41

M & H Plastics
London Road, Beccles, NR34 8TS
Tel: 01502-715518 **Fax:** 01502-712581
E-mail: sales@mhplastics.com
Website: http://www.mhplastics.com
Bank(s): Co-Operative
Directors: M. Bryant (Fin), S. Chidgey (Sales), M. Last (Fin), D. Muttitt (Fin), D. Duffield (MD)
Managers: S. Smith (Purch Mgr), V. John (Mktg Serv Mgr), S. Kels (Personnel), H. Joshua (Personnel), S. Twitchett (Tech Serv Mgr), S. Catchpole (Mktg Serv Mgr)
Ultimate Holding Company: MAYNARD & HARRIS GROUP LIMITED
Immediate Holding Company: TRUCK & PLANT ENGINEERING LIMITED
Registration no: 05088875 **VAT No.:** GB 628 7724 07
Date established: 1998 **Turnover:** £50m - £75m
No.of Employees: 501 - 1000 **Product Groups:** 30, 32, 66

P C E Automation Ltd
Site 3 Ellough Airfield, Ellough, Beccles, NR34 7TE
Tel: 01502-713287 **Fax:** 01502-716679
E-mail: info@pce-automation.co.uk
Website: http://www.pce-automation.co.uk
Bank(s): Natwest
Directors: T. Cook (Dir)
Immediate Holding Company: P.C.E. AUTOMATION LIMITED
Registration no: 03801408 **VAT No.:** 105 3731 05 **Date established:** 1999
Turnover: £2m - £5m **No.of Employees:** 21 - 50 **Product Groups:** 38

Date of Accounts	Dec 11	Dec 10	Dec 09
Working Capital	675	567	470
Fixed Assets	72	65	69
Current Assets	1m	1m	1m

Project Design Services East Anglia Ltd
32 Blyburgate, Beccles, NR34 9TB
Tel: 01502-564892 **Fax:** 01502-531658
E-mail: info@projectdesign.co.uk
Website: http://www.projectdesign.co.uk
Directors: L. Newman (Fin), S. Smith (Sales), S. Smith (MD), G. Manning (MD)
Immediate Holding Company: PROJECT DESIGN SERVICES (EAST ANGLIA) LIMITED
Registration no: 01701950 **Date established:** 1983 **Turnover:** £1m - £2m
No.of Employees: 1 - 10 **Product Groups:** 44, 80

Date of Accounts	Mar 11	Mar 10	Mar 09
Working Capital	84	77	148
Fixed Assets	10	19	22
Current Assets	308	267	485

Regal Tanks Ltd
Benacre Road Ellough, Beccles, NR34 7XD
Tel: 01502-710100 **Fax:** 01502-710103
E-mail: info@regaltanks.co.uk
Website: http://www.regaltanks.co.uk
Directors: N. Elger (MD), T. Underwood (Co Sec)
Immediate Holding Company: REGAL TANKS LIMITED
Registration no: 07019037 **Date established:** 2009
No.of Employees: 1 - 10 **Product Groups:** 35, 42, 45

Route V J Horticultural
Unit 10 Common Lane North, Beccles, NR34 9BN
Tel: 01502-716450 **Fax:** 01502-715006
E-mail: battztastic@aol.com
Directors: D. Batterton (Prop)
Immediate Holding Company: A. TAYLOR AND SON (EASTERN) LIMITED
Registration no: 00367883 **Date established:** 1941
No.of Employees: 1 - 10 **Product Groups:** 41

Rowan Marine
Wherry Dyke Geldeston, Beccles, NR34 0LY
Tel: 01508-518598 **Fax:** 01508-518598
Directors: I. Ansell (Ptnr)
Date established: 1994 **No.of Employees:** 1 - 10 **Product Groups:** 35, 36, 39

R Tilney & Son
17 Smallgate, Beccles, NR34 9AB
Tel: 01502-712105 **Fax:** 01502-712105
Directors: R. Tilney (Prop)
Date established: 1983 **No.of Employees:** 1 - 10 **Product Groups:** 36, 39, 40

Travis Perkins plc
The Quay Fen Lane, Beccles, NR34 9BH
Tel: 01502-712421 **Fax:** 01502-711110
E-mail: paul.george@travisperkins.co.uk
Website: http://www.travisperkins.co.uk
Managers: P. George (District Mgr)
Immediate Holding Company: TRAVIS PERKINS PLC
Registration no: 00824821 **Date established:** 1964
No.of Employees: 11 - 20 **Product Groups:** 66

Date of Accounts	Dec 11	Dec 10	Dec 09
Sales Turnover	4779m	3153m	2931m
Pre Tax Profit/Loss	270m	197m	213m
Working Capital	133m	159m	248m
Fixed Assets	2771m	2749m	2108m
Current Assets	1421m	1329m	1035m
Current Liabilities	473m	412m	109m

Brandon

Abels Moving Services Ltd
Wimbledon Avenue, Brandon, IP27 0NZ
Tel: 01842-816600 **Fax:** 01842-813613
E-mail: enquiries@abels.co.uk
Website: http://www.abels.co.uk
Bank(s): National Westminster
Managers: J. Dods
Immediate Holding Company: ABELS INTERNATIONAL MOVING SERVICES LIMITED
Registration no: 06339559 **VAT No.:** GB 719 9751 84
Date established: 2007 **Turnover:** £5m - £10m
No.of Employees: 51 - 100 **Product Groups:** 72, 76

Chase Plastics Ltd
Mile End Works London Road, Brandon, IP27 0NE
Tel: 01842-810751 **Fax:** 01842-814738
E-mail: stephen@chase-plastics.co.uk
Website: http://www.chase-plastics.co.uk
Bank(s): Lloyds, Thetford
Directors: S. Chase (MD), J. Baker (Fin)
Ultimate Holding Company: OMAR GROUP LIMITED
Immediate Holding Company: CHASE PLASTICS LIMITED
Registration no: 01593735 **VAT No.:** GB 106 5117 07
Date established: 1981 **Turnover:** Up to £250,000
No.of Employees: 11 - 20 **Product Groups:** 30, 31, 48

Date of Accounts	Dec 11	Dec 10	Dec 09
Working Capital	-19	-157	-280
Fixed Assets	2m	2m	2m
Current Assets	941	802	567

Corus
Fengate Drove Weeting, Brandon, IP27 0PW
Tel: 01842-816200 **Fax:** 01842-813019
E-mail: alan.snow@corusgroup.com
Website: http://www.corusgroup.com
Managers: A. Snow (Chief Mgr), A. Snow (Mgr), D. Reece (Chief Mgr), T. Page (Chief Mgr)
Ultimate Holding Company: British Steel P.L.C.
Immediate Holding Company: CORUS GROUP LIMITED
Registration no: 03811373 **Date established:** 1999
Turnover: £250m - £500m **No.of Employees:** 11 - 20
Product Groups: 66, 77

Double Quick Anglia Ltd
Unit 7-8 New Court London Road Industrial Estate Wimbledon Avenue, Brandon, IP27 0NZ
Tel: 01842-811811 **Fax:** 01842-814751
E-mail: steven.double@btconnect.com
Website: http://www.double-quick.co.uk
Directors: S. Double (Dir)
Immediate Holding Company: DOUBLE QUICK (ANGLIA) LIMITED
Registration no: 03681304 **Date established:** 1998
Turnover: £500,000 - £1m **No.of Employees:** 1 - 10 **Product Groups:** 40, 66

Date of Accounts	Dec 11	Dec 10	Dec 09
Working Capital	32	49	62
Fixed Assets	8	11	14
Current Assets	245	225	217

Glazing Vision Ltd
36 Wimbledon Avenue, Brandon, IP27 0NZ
Tel: 01842-815581 **Fax:** 01842-815515
E-mail: david@glazing-vision.co.uk
Website: http://www.glazing-vision.co.uk
Directors: D. Hewlett (Fin)
Immediate Holding Company: GLAZING VISION LIMITED
Registration no: 02987024 **Date established:** 1994 **Turnover:** £2m - £5m
No.of Employees: 51 - 100 **Product Groups:** 25, 30, 33, 35, 37, 52, 66

Date of Accounts	Apr 10	Apr 09	Apr 08
Sales Turnover	N/A	6m	5m
Pre Tax Profit/Loss	N/A	195	946
Working Capital	675	545	1m
Fixed Assets	479	184	220
Current Assets	3m	2m	3m
Current Liabilities	N/A	1m	2m

Lignacite Ltd
Norfolk House High Street, Brandon, IP27 0AX
Tel: 01842-810678 **Fax:** 01842-814602
E-mail: info@lignacite.co.uk
Website: http://www.lignacite.co.uk
Bank(s): Barclays
Directors: G. De Lotbiniere (MD)
Managers: B. Edwards (Sales Admin)
Ultimate Holding Company: LIGNACITE LIMITED
Immediate Holding Company: LIGNACITE (BRANDON) LIMITED
Registration no: 02928931 **Date established:** 1994
Turnover: £10m - £20m **No.of Employees:** 21 - 50 **Product Groups:** 33

Niagri Engineering Ltd
1 Station Road Lakenheath, Brandon, IP27 9AA
Tel: 01842-862500 **Fax:** 01842-862501
E-mail: info@niagri.co.uk
Website: http://www.niagri.co.uk
Directors: A. Nicholson (MD)
Immediate Holding Company: NIAGRI ENGINEERING CO. LTD
Registration no: 03444026 **Date established:** 1997
No.of Employees: 11 - 20 **Product Groups:** 41, 61, 67

Date of Accounts	Jan 12	Jan 11	Jan 10
Working Capital	713	651	528
Fixed Assets	133	127	150
Current Assets	1m	1m	947

Omar Park Homes Ltd
London Road, Brandon, IP27 0NE
Tel: 01842-810673 **Fax:** 01842-814328
E-mail: info@omar.co.uk
Website: http://www.omar.co.uk
Bank(s): Lloyds TSB Bank plc
Managers: D. Westmoreland
Ultimate Holding Company: OMAR GROUP LIMITED
Immediate Holding Company: OMAR HOMES LIMITED
Registration no: 00848969 **VAT No.:** GB 299 9378 64
Date established: 1965 **Turnover:** £20m - £50m
No.of Employees: 101 - 250 **Product Groups:** 39, 80

Date of Accounts	Apr 12	Apr 11	Apr 10
Sales Turnover	12m	10m	11m
Pre Tax Profit/Loss	757	-254	196
Working Capital	482	-22	25
Fixed Assets	331	461	611
Current Assets	3m	2m	2m
Current Liabilities	1m	421	568

Solo Product Finishing
4 Highbury Road, Brandon, IP27 0ND
Tel: 01842-813355 **Fax:** 01842-813377
Website: http://www.powdercoatingsuffolk.com
Directors: M. Oneill (Dir)
Ultimate Holding Company: PETANI LTD
Immediate Holding Company: SOLO PRODUCT FINISHING LIMITED
Registration no: 01906084 **Date established:** 1985
No.of Employees: 1 - 10 **Product Groups:** 46, 48

Date of Accounts	May 11	May 10	May 08
Working Capital	5	10	10
Fixed Assets	9	11	18
Current Assets	78	52	80

Universal Diesel Services
Mundford Road Garage Weeting, Brandon, IP27 0PL
Tel: 01842-811794
Directors: P. Markell (Prop)
Immediate Holding Company: NU-SPAN FLOORING LIMITED
Date established: 2012 **No.of Employees:** 1 - 10 **Product Groups:** 40

Bungay

Nursey Of Bungay
12 Upper Olland Street, Bungay, NR35 1BQ
Tel: 01986-892821 **Fax:** 01986-892823
E-mail: sales@nurseysheepskin.co.uk
Website: http://www.nurseysheepskin.co.uk
Bank(s): HSBC Bank plc
Directors: T. Nursey (MD)
Immediate Holding Company: NURSEY & SON LIMITED
Registration no: 00580809 **VAT No.:** GB 105 2249 11
Date established: 1957 **Turnover:** £500,000 - £1m
No.of Employees: 11 - 20 **Product Groups:** 22, 24

Date of Accounts	Mar 11	Mar 10	Mar 09
Working Capital	428	606	465
Fixed Assets	228	228	224
Current Assets	511	656	499

Utilux UK Ltd
Hillside Road East, Bungay, NR35 1JX
Tel: 01986-895611 **Fax:** 01986-895280
E-mail: sales@utilux.co.uk
Website: http://www.utiluxeurope.com
Bank(s): Barclays
Directors: G. Bushnell (MD), P. Preston (Co Sec)
Managers: S. Dennant (Fin Mgr), H. Brown (Sales Prom Mgr), N. Baxter (Buyer)
Ultimate Holding Company: TEXTRON INC (USA)
Immediate Holding Company: KLAUKE UK LTD
Registration no: 00996894 **VAT No.:** GB 105 1801 20
Date established: 1970 **Turnover:** £2m - £5m **No.of Employees:** 11 - 20
Product Groups: 37

Date of Accounts	Dec 11	Dec 10	Dec 09
Sales Turnover	6m	5m	3m
Pre Tax Profit/Loss	370	361	-7
Working Capital	2m	2m	1m
Fixed Assets	403	399	416
Current Assets	3m	3m	2m
Current Liabilities	293	189	122

Bures

Foxhall Solutions Ltd
Foxhall The Croft, Bures, CO8 5JB
Tel: 01787-228402 **Fax:** 01787-227942
E-mail: info@foxhallsolutions.com
Website: http://www.foxhallsolutions.com
Directors: G. Hill (MD), L. Hughes (Fin)
Immediate Holding Company: FOXHALL SOLUTIONS LIMITED
Registration no: 03827278 **Date established:** 1999
Turnover: £250,000 - £500,000 **No.of Employees:** 1 - 10
Product Groups: 44

Date of Accounts	Mar 11	Mar 10	Mar 09
Working Capital	-3	-14	-32
Fixed Assets	4	5	6
Current Assets	91	67	58

Master Farm Services GB Ltd
Bures Park Colne Road, Bures, CO8 5DJ
Tel: 01787-228450 **Fax:** 01787-229146
E-mail: enquiries@masterfarm.co.uk
Website: http://www.masterfarm.co.uk
Directors: W. Ingram (MD)
Immediate Holding Company: MASTER FARM SERVICES (G.B.) LIMITED
Registration no: 02245261 **VAT No.:** GB 497 7335 88
Date established: 1988 **No.of Employees:** 1 - 10 **Product Groups:** 67

Date of Accounts	Nov 11	Nov 10	Nov 09
Working Capital	1m	852	848
Fixed Assets	118	153	43
Current Assets	1m	1m	999

Bury St Edmunds

A S K Group
2 Northgate Avenue, Bury St Edmunds, IP32 6BB
Tel: 01284-777900 **Fax:** 01284-764025
E-mail: reception@translate.co.uk
Website: http://www.askgroup.co.uk
Bank(s): Barclays
Directors: K. Barter (Pers), G. Keens (MD)
Managers: J. Wright (Tech Serv Mgr)
Immediate Holding Company: ASK PRINT LIMITED
Registration no: 07311203 **VAT No.:** GB 706 7178 26
Date established: 2010 **Turnover:** £1m - £2m **No.of Employees:** 11 - 20
Product Groups: 80

Akro Ltd
16 Blackberry Way Red Lodge, Bury St Edmunds, IP28 8TE
Tel: 0870-190 4091
E-mail: kelvin.phillips@akroservices.com
Website: http://www.akroservices.com
Directors: K. Phillips (Dir), M. Barlow (Co Sec)
Immediate Holding Company: AKRO LIMITED
Registration no: 05254949 **Date established:** 2004
No.of Employees: 1 - 10 **Product Groups:** 20, 40, 41

Date of Accounts	Jul 11	Jul 10	Jul 09
Working Capital	79	46	27
Fixed Assets	435	307	286
Current Assets	272	174	150

John Allan Aquariums Ltd
Eastern Way, Bury St Edmunds, IP32 7AB
Tel: 01284-755051 **Fax:** 01284-750960
E-mail: tradeenquiries@johnallanaquariums.com
Website: http://www.johnallanaquariums.com
Directors: B. Wallis (Fin), A. Riley (MD)
Immediate Holding Company: JOHN ALLAN AQUARIUMS LIMITED
Registration no: 00815958 **Date established:** 1964 **Turnover:** £1m - £2m
No.of Employees: 11 - 20 **Product Groups:** 33

Date of Accounts	Aug 11	Aug 10	Aug 09
Working Capital	314	399	401
Fixed Assets	59	69	177
Current Assets	590	743	660

Alphamatic Machine Tools
Eastern Way, Bury St Edmunds, IP32 7AB
Tel: 01284-701555 **Fax:** 01284-701530
Directors: P. Collier (Dir)
Immediate Holding Company: ALPHAMATIC LIMITED
Registration no: 03476220 **Date established:** 1997
No.of Employees: 1 - 10 **Product Groups:** 46

Date of Accounts	Mar 11	Mar 10	Mar 09
Working Capital	-169	-167	-167
Fixed Assets	11	14	17
Current Assets	18	19	19
Current Liabilities	N/A	N/A	186

AMOT (Roper Industries Ltd)
Western Way, Bury St Edmunds, IP33 3SZ
Tel: 01284-762222 **Fax:** 01284-760256
E-mail: info@amot.com
Website: http://www.amot.com
Bank(s): Barclays
Directors: M. Park (Chief Op Offcr), J. Chmiel (Ptnr), M. Parks (Chief Op Offcr), J. Davis (Fin)
Managers: H. Caine (Personnel), G. Turner (Fin Mgr), M. Orvis (Tech Serv Mgr), J. Ford (I.T. Exec), T. Condliffe (Chief Buyer)
Ultimate Holding Company: ROPER INDUSTRIES
Immediate Holding Company: AMOT INVESTMENTS LTD
Registration no: 02509935 **VAT No.:** GB 571 0884 35
Date established: 1960 **Turnover:** £10m - £20m
No.of Employees: 101 - 250 **Product Groups:** 36

Apex Belting Ltd
9 Boldero Road, Bury St Edmunds, IP32 7BS
Tel: 01284-752486 **Fax:** 01284-750542
E-mail: sales@apexbelting.co.uk
Website: http://www.apexbelting.co.uk
Bank(s): National Westminster Bank Plc
Directors: J. West (Fin), S. Pimbley (MD)
Ultimate Holding Company: APEX BELTING LIMITED
Immediate Holding Company: APEX CONVEYOR BELTING LIMITED
Registration no: 01961599 **VAT No.:** GB 443 0028 94
Date established: 1985 **Turnover:** £1m - £2m **No.of Employees:** 11 - 20
Product Groups: 23, 29, 30, 33, 35, 45, 48

Date of Accounts	Feb 12	Feb 11	Feb 10
Working Capital	1	1m	1m
Fixed Assets	N/A	73	84
Current Assets	1	2m	2m

Arco East Anglia Ltd
Easlea Road, Bury St Edmunds, IP32 7BY
Tel: 01284-773030 **Fax:** 01284-750529
E-mail: burystedmunds.banch@arco.co.uk
Website: http://www.arco.co.uk
Managers: J. Jacob (Mgr), P. Walsh (District Mgr), T. Smith (Mgr)
Registration no: 00486220 **No.of Employees:** 11 - 20
Product Groups: 24, 29, 30, 40

Armantini Processing Ltd
Hardings Farm Hardings Lane Norton, Bury St Edmunds, IP31 3NW
Tel: 01359-244631 **Fax:** 01359-259261
E-mail: armantiniprocessing@hotmail.com
Website: http://www.armantinigroup.com
Directors: S. Weldon (MD)
Immediate Holding Company: ARMANTINI PROCESSING LIMITED
Registration no: 06273457 **Date established:** 2007
Turnover: Up to £250,000 **No.of Employees:** 1 - 10 **Product Groups:** 66

Date of Accounts	Jun 11	Jun 09	Jun 08
Working Capital	-22	-12	-21
Fixed Assets	28	14	15
Current Assets	15	30	15

Avelair Compressors Ltd
Fred Castle Way Rougham Industrial Estate, Rougham, Bury St Edmunds, IP30 9ND
Tel: 01359-272828 **Fax:** 01359-272829
E-mail: info@avelair.co.uk
Website: http://www.avelair.co.uk
Bank(s): HSBC Bank plc
Directors: D. Wood (MD)
Immediate Holding Company: AVELAIR LIMITED
Registration no: 02800984 **VAT No.:** GB 637 7172 19
Date established: 1993 **Turnover:** £1m - £2m **No.of Employees:** 11 - 20
Product Groups: 40, 48

Date of Accounts	Apr 11	Apr 10	Apr 09
Working Capital	283	259	277
Fixed Assets	115	106	119
Current Assets	700	560	643

Mike Ayres Design Ltd
Unit 8 Shepherds Grove, Stanton, Bury St Edmunds, IP31 2AR
Tel: 01359-251551 **Fax:** 01359-251707
E-mail: enquiries@mikeayresdesign.co.uk
Website: http://www.mikeayresdesign.co.uk
Bank(s): Lloyds TSB Bank plc
Directors: M. Ayres (MD)
Managers: K. Whitmore, W. Carter (Admin Off)
Registration no: 03583876 **VAT No.:** GB 637 7036 27
Date established: 1998 **Turnover:** £1m - £2m **No.of Employees:** 11 - 20
Product Groups: 26, 28, 49, 65, 67, 84, 86

Date of Accounts	Dec 11	Dec 10	Dec 09
Working Capital	508	484	414
Fixed Assets	72	79	90
Current Assets	701	755	656

Baker Construction
3 The Courtyard Lamdin Road, Bury St Edmunds, IP32 6NU
Tel: 01284-700585 **Fax:** 01284-756535
E-mail: info@baker-construction.co.uk
Website: http://www.baker-construction.co.uk
Directors: J. Baker (Ch), D. Clarke (Fin), T. Whiting (Sales)
Immediate Holding Company: BAKER HOMES LIMITED
Registration no: 04303484 **VAT No.:** GB 299 8420 96
Date established: 2001 **Turnover:** £1m - £2m **No.of Employees:** 51 - 100
Product Groups: 52

Date of Accounts	Dec 09	Dec 08	Dec 07
Sales Turnover	520	4m	2m
Pre Tax Profit/Loss	-177	-341	-98
Working Capital	393	570	909
Current Assets	2m	2m	4m
Current Liabilities	456	447	487

Baker Tilly
Abbottsgate House Hollow Road, Bury St Edmunds, IP32 7FA
Tel: 01284-763311 **Fax:** 01284-704203
E-mail: stephen.duffety@bakertilly.co.uk
Website: http://www.bakertilly.co.uk
Directors: S. Duffety (Ptnr)
Immediate Holding Company: NEARLIFE LIMITED
Registration no: 03077999 **Date established:** 2005
Turnover: £75m - £125m **No.of Employees:** 51 - 100
Product Groups: 44, 80, 81, 82, 86

Date of Accounts	Apr 11	Apr 10	Apr 08
Working Capital	26	69	83
Fixed Assets	555	526	519
Current Assets	35	79	92

Barconwood Ltd
Unit 2a Woolpit Business Park Windmill Avenue, Woolpit, Bury St Edmunds, IP30 9UP
Tel: 01359-242490 **Fax:** 01359-242468
E-mail: sales@barconwood.co.uk
Website: http://www.barconwood.co.uk
Bank(s): Barclays, Market Place, Stowmarket, Suffolk
Directors: E. Cardozo (MD)
Ultimate Holding Company: EDADCA LIMITED
Immediate Holding Company: BARCONWOOD LIMITED
Registration no: 01864052 **VAT No.:** GB 410 6453 88
Date established: 1984 **No.of Employees:** 21 - 50 **Product Groups:** 26, 49

Date of Accounts	Sep 11	Sep 10	Sep 09
Working Capital	33	68	74
Fixed Assets	8	10	6
Current Assets	451	470	413

Biffa Waste Services Ltd
Chapel Pond Hill, Bury St Edmunds, IP32 7HT
Tel: 01284-731048 **Fax:** 01284-731091
E-mail: info@biffawasteservices.co.uk
Website: http://www.biffa.co.uk
Directors: R. Shivers (I.T. Dir)
Immediate Holding Company: BIFFA WASTE SERVICES LIMITED
Registration no: 00946107 **Date established:** 1969 **Turnover:** £2m - £5m
No.of Employees: 11 - 20 **Product Groups:** 54

Date of Accounts	Mar 08	Mar 09	Apr 10
Sales Turnover	555m	574m	492m
Pre Tax Profit/Loss	23m	50m	30m
Working Capital	229m	271m	293m
Fixed Assets	371m	360m	378m
Current Assets	409m	534m	609m
Current Liabilities	50m	100m	115m

Buzprint
72 Nowton Road, Bury St Edmunds, IP33 2BU
Tel: 01284-767575 **Fax:** 08452-991680
E-mail: sales@buzprint.co.uk
Website: http://www.buzprint.co.uk
Directors: D. Fuller (Prop)
Date established: 2006 **Turnover:** Up to £250,000
No.of Employees: 1 - 10 **Product Groups:** 28

Cardinal Detecto
Unit 17-18 Mercers Road, Bury St Edmunds, IP32 7HX
Tel: 01284-703117 **Fax:** 01284-703559
E-mail: sales@detectoscale.co.uk
Website: http://www.detectoscale.com
Directors: B. Spink (Dir)
No.of Employees: 1 - 10 **Product Groups:** 38, 42

C B C Services
Unit 22 Stanton, Bury St Edmunds, IP31 2AR
Tel: 01359-251924 **Fax:** 01359-251924
Directors: A. Clements (Ptnr)
Date established: 1987 **No.of Employees:** 1 - 10 **Product Groups:** 46, 48

Claas UK Ltd
Saxham Business Park Little Saxham, Bury St Edmunds, IP28 6QZ
Tel: 01284-763100 **Fax:** 01284-769839
E-mail: clive.last@claas.com
Website: http://www.claasuk.com
Bank(s): National Westminster Bank Plc
Managers: T. Tyrell
Ultimate Holding Company: CLAAS KGAA (GERMANY)
Immediate Holding Company: CLAAS HOLDINGS LIMITED
Registration no: 01500636 **VAT No.:** GB 460 4971 41
Date established: 1980 **Turnover:** Up to £250,000
No.of Employees: 51 - 100 **Product Groups:** 41

Date of Accounts	Sep 11	Sep 10	Sep 09
Pre Tax Profit/Loss	5m	5m	7m
Working Capital	71	3m	3m
Fixed Assets	27m	27m	28m
Current Assets	71	3m	3m
Current Liabilities	N/A	N/A	7

Classic Catering Equipment
Eika House Hawthorn Walk, Beck Row, Bury St Edmunds, IP28 8UD
Tel: 01638-711877 **Fax:** 01638- 711877
Directors: S. Seaman (Prop)
Date established: 1999 **No.of Employees:** 1 - 10 **Product Groups:** 20, 40, 41

Criterion Ices
Manor Farm Creamery Pakenham Road, Thurston, Bury St Edmunds, IP31 3QJ
Tel: 01359-230208 **Fax:** 01359-232838
E-mail: enquiries@criterion-ices.co.uk
Website: http://www.criterion-ices.co.uk
Directors: P. Myatt (MD)
Immediate Holding Company: CRITERION ICES LIMITED
Registration no: 02808106 **Date established:** 1993
Turnover: £250,000 - £500,000 **No.of Employees:** 11 - 20
Product Groups: 20

Date of Accounts	May 11	May 10	May 09
Working Capital	242	180	205
Fixed Assets	368	395	380
Current Assets	545	403	399

Curtain Girls Ltd
1 Sentinel Works Northgate Avenue, Bury St Edmunds, IP32 6AZ
Tel: 01284-374455 **Fax:** 01284-766160
E-mail: info@curtaingirls.co.uk
Website: http://www.curtaingirls.co.uk
Directors: J. Fiddian (Dir)
Immediate Holding Company: THE CURTAIN GIRLS LIMITED
Registration no: 03461784 **Date established:** 1997 **Turnover:** £2m - £5m
No.of Employees: 11 - 20 **Product Groups:** 23, 24

Date of Accounts	Oct 08	Oct 07	Mar 11
Working Capital	-70	-63	-93
Fixed Assets	5	3	1
Current Assets	60	43	31

Design Interface Ltd
Thurston Grange Thurston End, Hawkedon, Bury St Edmunds, IP29 4LQ
Tel: 01284-789608 **Fax:** 01284-789617
E-mail: enquiries@design-interface.com
Website: http://www.design-interface.com
Directors: D. Phillips (MD), T. Phillips (Fin)
Immediate Holding Company: DESIGN INTERFACE LIMITED
Registration no: 03492501 **Date established:** 1998
Turnover: Up to £250,000 **No.of Employees:** 1 - 10 **Product Groups:** 84

Date of Accounts	Jan 12	Jan 11	Jan 10
Working Capital	231	224	244
Fixed Assets	3	3	5
Current Assets	244	236	255

DocuPrint Ltd
64-65 Eastern Way, Bury St Edmunds, IP32 7AB
Tel: 01284-748560 **Fax:** 01284-764033
E-mail: sales@docuprint.co.uk
Website: http://www.docuprint.co.uk
Managers: I. Jones (Ops Mgr)
Ultimate Holding Company: AVAD GROUP LIMITED
Immediate Holding Company: DOCUPRINT LIMITED
Registration no: 05193752 **VAT No.:** GB 699 9642 41
Date established: 2004 **Turnover:** £1m - £2m **No.of Employees:** 21 - 50
Product Groups: 28, 44, 48

Date of Accounts	Dec 11	Dec 10	Dec 09
Working Capital	24	-42	9
Fixed Assets	590	666	687
Current Assets	374	539	536

Eastern Transformer Ltd
Overland Industrial Park Sudbury Road, Little Whelnetham, Bury St Edmunds, IP30 0UL
Tel: 01284-388033 **Fax:** 01284-386969
E-mail: info@ete.co.uk
Website: http://www.ete.co.uk
Bank(s): National Westminster Bank Plc
Directors: B. Tapping (MD)
Managers: S. Gardiner (Sales Prom Mgr)
Immediate Holding Company: EASTERN TRANSFORMERS & EQUIPMENT LIMITED
Registration no: 02086903 **VAT No.:** GB 410 5263 01
Date established: 1987 **Turnover:** £1m - £2m **No.of Employees:** 21 - 50
Product Groups: 37

Date of Accounts	Jun 11	Jun 10	Jun 09
Working Capital	N/A	-6	1
Fixed Assets	66	43	42
Current Assets	549	575	397

Eden Speciality Metal Trading Division Of Marmon Group Ltd (Marmon Group USA)
Field Road Mildenhall, Bury St Edmunds, IP28 7AR
Tel: 08707-258803 **Fax:** 01638-718342
E-mail: info@eden-industries.co.uk
Website: http://www.eden-industries.co.uk
Managers: F. Diviney (Admin Off)
No.of Employees: 51 - 100 **Product Groups:** 26

ERIKS UK (Bury St. Edmunds Service Centre)
Unit 8 Chamberlayne Road, Bury St Edmunds, IP32 7EY
Tel: 01284-769656 **Fax:** 01284-769526
E-mail: alex.lawrence@eriks.co.uk
Website: http://www.eriks.co.uk
Managers: A. Lawrence (Mgr)
Immediate Holding Company: WYKO HOLDINGS LTD
Registration no: 00917112 **Turnover:** £250m - £500m
No.of Employees: 1 - 10 **Product Groups:** 66

Excel Powder Coating Ltd
Unit 15 Chiswick Avenue, Mildenhall, Bury St Edmunds, IP28 7AY
Tel: 01638-510993 **Fax:** 01638-515089
E-mail: info@excel-powder-coatings.co.uk
Website: http://www.excel-powder-coatings.co.uk
Directors: W. Bradley (MD)
Immediate Holding Company: EXCEL POWDER COATINGS LIMITED
Registration no: 04139849 **Date established:** 2001
No.of Employees: 11 - 20 **Product Groups:** 37, 48, 67, 85

Date of Accounts	Dec 11	Dec 10	Dec 09
Working Capital	98	63	51
Fixed Assets	20	25	33
Current Assets	182	129	96

Forcemicro Ltd
Grove Lane Elmswell, Bury St Edmunds, IP30 9HN
Tel: 01359-244060 **Fax:** 01359-244062
E-mail: mail@forcemicro.co.uk
Website: http://www.forcemicro.co.uk
Directors: N. Marsh (Dir)
Immediate Holding Company: FORCEMICRO LIMITED
Registration no: 02236645 **Date established:** 1988
Turnover: Up to £250,000 **No.of Employees:** 1 - 10 **Product Groups:** 77

Date of Accounts	Jan 12	Jan 11	Jan 10
Working Capital	518	560	488
Fixed Assets	19	22	30
Current Assets	551	614	619

A J Fry Catering Equipment
Kenny Hill, Bury St Edmunds, IP28 8DS
Tel: 01353-675509 **Fax:** 01353-675509
Directors: T. Fry (Prop)
Date established: 1996 **No.of Employees:** 1 - 10 **Product Groups:** 20, 40, 41

G E Baker UK Ltd (t/a Quality Equipment)
The Heath Woolpit, Bury St Edmunds, IP30 9RN
Tel: 01359-240529 **Fax:** 01359-242086
E-mail: baker@quality-equipment.co.uk
Website: http://www.quality-equipment.co.uk
Directors: G. Baker (Dir), J. Baker (MD)
Immediate Holding Company: G.E. BAKER (U.K.) LIMITED
Registration no: 01406947 **Date established:** 1978 **Turnover:** £1m - £2m
No.of Employees: 21 - 50 **Product Groups:** 35, 38, 41

Date of Accounts	Dec 11	Dec 10	Dec 09
Working Capital	143	227	209
Fixed Assets	322	131	98
Current Assets	496	690	688

Gardenitems Ltd
2 Peckham Street, Bury St Edmunds, IP33 1SY
Tel: 0845-5190081
E-mail: service@gardenitems.co.uk
Website: http://www.gardenitems.co.uk
Directors: D. McHardy (Sales)
Managers: A. McLardy (Product), D. Watson (Sales Admin), M. Spinks
Registration no: 04516269 **Turnover:** Up to £250,000
No.of Employees: 1 - 10 **Product Groups:** 30, 33, 42

Goldring Products Ltd
8 Greyfriars Road, Bury St Edmunds, IP32 7DX
Tel: 01284-701101 **Fax:** 01284-750040
E-mail: sales@goldring.co.uk
Directors: N. Spence (Fin), G. Mcclelland (MD), J. Gay (MD)
Managers: J. Rudman (Works Gen Mgr), E. I'Anson (Buyer), H. Foreman (Sales Prom Mgr)
Ultimate Holding Company: ARMOUR GROUP PLC
Immediate Holding Company: GOLDRING PRODUCTS LIMITED
Registration no: 01243730 **VAT No.:** GB 299 7886 55
Date established: 1976 **Turnover:** £2m - £5m **No.of Employees:** 1 - 10
Product Groups: 26, 37

Date of Accounts	Aug 06	Aug 05	Aug 04
Sales Turnover	N/A	767	2m
Pre Tax Profit/Loss	N/A	55	441
Working Capital	113	113	771
Fixed Assets	N/A	N/A	5
Current Assets	113	113	1m
Current Liabilities	N/A	N/A	254

Colin Green & Associates
2 Brunwyn Close, Bury St Edmunds, IP32 7LL
Tel: 01284-704721 **Fax:** 01284-750859
E-mail: colin@greenassociates.co.uk
Website: http://www.greenassociates.co.uk
Directors: C. Green (Prop)
Date established: 1995 **No.of Employees:** 1 - 10 **Product Groups:** 42, 45

Greene King Brewing & Retailing Ltd
Westgate Brewery, Bury St Edmunds, IP33 1QT
Tel: 01284-763222 **Fax:** 01284-706502
E-mail: lindsaykeswick@greeneking.co.uk
Website: http://www.greeneking.co.uk
Bank(s): Lloyds TSB Bank plc
Directors: R. Anand (Dir), D. Just (Purch), G. Williams (Sales & Mktg), J. Adams (MD), L. Keswick (Co Sec), M. Chadwick (I.T. Dir), P. Lloyd (Mkt Research), T. Bridge (Ch)
Immediate Holding Company: GREENE KING BREWING AND RETAILING LIMITED
Registration no: 03298903 **VAT No.:** GB 514 9182 46
Date established: 1997 **Turnover:** £500m - £1,000m
No.of Employees: 1501 & over **Product Groups:** 20, 21, 62

Date of Accounts	May 08
Sales Turnover	711300
Pre Tax Profit/Loss	-64900
Working Capital	196800
Fixed Assets	1623m
Current Assets	884800
Current Liabilities	688000
Total Share Capital	830000
ROCE% (Return on Capital Employed)	-3.6

Griffith Elder & Co. Ltd
1 Oaklands Park, Bury St Edmunds, IP33 2RW
Tel: 01284-763616 **Fax:** 01284-700822
E-mail: sales@griffith-elder.com
Website: http://www.griffith-elder.com
Directors: Y. Elder (Fn), D. Elder (MD)
Immediate Holding Company: GRIFFITH ELDER AND COMPANY LIMITED
Registration no: 01561511 **Date established:** 1981 **Turnover:** £1m - £2m
No.of Employees: 1 - 10 **Product Groups:** 38, 39, 41, 44, 67, 83

Date of Accounts	Aug 11	Aug 10	Aug 09
Working Capital	282	241	215
Fixed Assets	16	21	22
Current Assets	593	515	604

H & M Automotive UK Ltd
70 Fred Dannatt Road Mildenhall, Bury St Edmunds, IP28 7RD
Tel: 01638-640100 **Fax:** 01638-781111
E-mail: sales@hmauto.com
Website: http://www.hmauto.com
Directors: S. Hall (Fin), H. Margison (Sales)
Managers: C. McKechnie, K. Mckechnie
Immediate Holding Company: H & M AUTOMOTIVE (UK) LIMITED
Registration no: 04681653 **Date established:** 2003
No.of Employees: 11 - 20 **Product Groups:** 35, 36, 37, 39, 40, 42, 66, 67, 68

Date of Accounts	Mar 11	Mar 10	Mar 09
Working Capital	531	567	155
Fixed Assets	126	88	42
Current Assets	1m	1m	495

H R P Ltd
Rougham Industrial Estate Rougham, Bury St Edmunds, IP30 9XA
Tel: 01359-270888 **Fax:** 01359-271132
E-mail: ralph.alliston@hrponline.co.uk
Website: http://www.hrponline.co.uk
Bank(s): Barclays
Directors: A. Pilgrim (MD), R. Alliston (Sales), K. Curtis (Ch), D. Allway (Mkt Research)
Managers: C. Smithson (Admin Off), G. Beardsley (I.T. Exec)
Immediate Holding Company: HRP LIMITED
Registration no: 00832237 **Date established:** 1964
Turnover: £20m - £50m **No.of Employees:** 251 - 500
Product Groups: 29, 38, 40, 52, 66

Date of Accounts	Dec 09	Dec 08	Dec 07
Sales Turnover	46m	53m	58m
Pre Tax Profit/Loss	651	985	1m
Working Capital	6m	6m	5m
Fixed Assets	3m	3m	3m
Current Assets	17m	23m	22m
Current Liabilities	3m	3m	5m

Haldo Developments Ltd
Haldo House Western Way, Bury St Edmunds, IP33 3SP
Tel: 01284-754043 **Fax:** 01284-767260
E-mail: info@haldo.com
Website: http://www.haldo.com

see next page

***Haldo Developments Ltd** - Cont'd*

Bank(s): National Westminster Bank Plc
Directors: A. Hall (Fin), I. Smith (Dir), R. Wildridge (MD)
Managers: J. Manganiello (Mktg Serv Mgr), T. Meanwell (Sales Admin)
Immediate Holding Company: HALDO DEVELOPMENTS LIMITED
Registration no: 00940159 **VAT No.:** GB 102 3516 27
Date established: 1968 **Turnover:** £2m - £5m **No.of Employees:** 21 - 50
Product Groups: 23, 24, 26, 27, 28, 29, 30, 32, 33, 35, 36, 37, 38, 39, 40, 44, 45, 49, 51, 52, 68, 81, 84

Date of Accounts	Dec 11	Dec 10	Dec 09
Working Capital	-253	-137	98
Fixed Assets	999	1m	1m
Current Assets	221	491	536

Helmsman (W.B. Bawn Ltd)

Northern Way, Bury St Edmunds, IP32 6NH
Tel: 01284-727600 **Fax:** 01284-727601
E-mail: sales@helmsman.co.uk
Website: http://www.helmsman.co.uk
Bank(s): Lloyds TSB Bank plc
Directors: P. Birr (Sales & Mktg), J. Young (Co Sec)
Managers: J. Scopes, R. Linton (Factory Mgr), K. Palfrey (I.T. Exec), I. Munnings (Fin Mgr), S. Gibson, K. Palfrey (Tech Serv Mgr)
Ultimate Holding Company: W B BAWN GROUP LIMITED
Immediate Holding Company: W.B. BAWN & CO. LTD
Registration no: 01244870 **Date established:** 1976 **Turnover:** £5m - £10m
No.of Employees: 51 - 100 **Product Groups:** 26, 49

Herga Electric

Northern Way, Bury St Edmunds, IP32 6NN
Tel: 01284-701422 **Fax:** 01284-753112
E-mail: info@herga.com
Website: http://www.herga.com
Bank(s): HSBC
Directors: J. Burgess (Fin), R. Chatham (MD)
Managers: G. Trezise (Purch Mgr), K. Lambert (Sales Eng), N. Forge (Tech Serv Mgr)
Immediate Holding Company: HERGA ELECTRIC LIMITED
Registration no: 00533707 **VAT No.:** GB 103 1454 27
Date established: 1954 **Turnover:** £2m - £5m
No.of Employees: 101 - 250 **Product Groups:** 37, 40

Date of Accounts	May 11	May 10	May 09
Working Capital	1m	1m	1m
Fixed Assets	129	161	229
Current Assets	2m	2m	2m

Hi Flow Valves Ltd

31 Hampstead Avenue Mildenhall, Bury St Edmunds, IP28 7AS
Tel: 01638-711500 **Fax:** 01638-711521
E-mail: andy.filkins@hi-flow.co.uk
Website: http://www.hi-flow.co.uk
Directors: P. Ashworth (Dir)
Managers: A. Filkins (Chief Mgr)
Immediate Holding Company: HI-FLOW VALVES LIMITED
Registration no: 02894057 **Date established:** 1994 **Turnover:** £2m - £5m
No.of Employees: 1 - 10 **Product Groups:** 36, 37, 38

Date of Accounts	Dec 07	Dec 06	Mar 06
Sales Turnover	2579	2560	3123
Pre Tax Profit/Loss	57	45	221
Working Capital	807	758	721
Fixed Assets	375	381	382
Current Assets	1540	1512	1739
Current Liabilities	733	754	1018
ROCE% (Return on Capital Employed)	4.9	4.0	20.0
ROT% (Return on Turnover)	2.2	1.8	7.1

Industrial Boiler Services Ltd

Manor Farm Great Whelnetham, Bury St Edmunds, IP30 0UQ
Tel: 01284-386878 **Fax:** 01284-724274
E-mail: info@industrialboilerservices.com
Website: http://www.industrialboilerservices.com
Directors: G. Oxley (MD), P. Osborn (Fin)
Immediate Holding Company: INDUSTRIAL BOILER SERVICES LIMITED
Registration no: 03953762 **Date established:** 2000
No.of Employees: 1 - 10 **Product Groups:** 37, 40, 48

Date of Accounts	Mar 11	Mar 10	Mar 09
Working Capital	-57	-145	-75
Fixed Assets	155	187	216
Current Assets	228	204	307
Current Liabilities	136	128	81

Invision UK

Unit 5 Woodland Business Park Rougham Industrial Estate, Rougham, Bury St Edmunds, IP30 9ND
Tel: 01359-270280 **Fax:** 01359-270281
Website: http://www.invisionuk.com
Directors: S. Beahan (Prop)
No.of Employees: 11 - 20 **Product Groups:** 37

J E B Engineering Design Ltd

Hampstead Avenue Mildenhall, Bury St Edmunds, IP28 7AS
Tel: 01638-718435 **Fax:** 01638-717962
E-mail: info@jebeng.com
Website: http://www.jebeng.com
Bank(s): National Westminster Bank Plc
Directors: J. Brown (Dir), J. Mann (Fin)
Managers: R. Smith, S. Davis (Buyer), S. Starling (Personnel), C. Salway (Tech Serv Mgr)
Ultimate Holding Company: J.E.B. ENGINEERING DESIGN LIMITED
Immediate Holding Company: J.E.B. ENGINEERING DESIGN LIMITED
Registration no: 01079733 **VAT No.:** GB 103 6142 21
Date established: 1972 **Turnover:** £1m - £2m
No.of Employees: 101 - 250 **Product Groups:** 46

Date of Accounts	Oct 11	Oct 10	Oct 09
Sales Turnover	17m	14m	13m
Pre Tax Profit/Loss	-2m	-2m	-734
Working Capital	-246	-2m	-6m
Fixed Assets	14m	16m	8m
Current Assets	13m	12m	7m
Current Liabilities	8m	10m	7m

J K H Drainage Units Ltd

Hampstead Avenue Mildenhall, Bury St Edmunds, IP28 7AS
Tel: 01638-713795 **Fax:** 01638-716313
E-mail: brian@jkhdrainageunits.co.uk
Website: http://www.jkhdrainageunits.co.uk
Directors: B. Prince (Dir)
Managers: L. Cianter (Tech Serv Mgr)
Immediate Holding Company: J.K.H.DRAINAGE UNITS LIMITED
Registration no: 00965953 **VAT No.:** GB 213 2672 94
Date established: 1969 **Turnover:** £1m - £2m **No.of Employees:** 21 - 50
Product Groups: 30, 33

Date of Accounts	Dec 11	Dec 10	Dec 09
Working Capital	606	499	419
Fixed Assets	422	458	505
Current Assets	1m	895	770

Jack Sealey Ltd

Kempson Way, Bury St Edmunds, IP32 7AR
Tel: 01284-757500 **Fax:** 01284-703534
E-mail: sales@sealey.co.uk
Website: http://www.sealey.co.uk
Bank(s): Barclays, Sudbury
Directors: M. Sweetman (MD), P. Sealey (Fin)
Ultimate Holding Company: SEALEY (UK) LIMITED
Immediate Holding Company: JACK SEALEY LIMITED
Registration no: 01329173 **VAT No.:** GB 521 1864 71
Date established: 1977 **Turnover:** £20m - £50m
No.of Employees: 251 - 500 **Product Groups:** 39

Date of Accounts	Apr 11	Apr 10	Apr 09
Sales Turnover	50m	46m	42m
Pre Tax Profit/Loss	5m	5m	4m
Working Capital	28m	26m	23m
Fixed Assets	10m	9m	10m
Current Assets	39m	38m	36m
Current Liabilities	7m	8m	10m

Keith Mount Liming Ltd

Unit A8 Risby Business Park Newmarket Road, Risby, Bury St Edmunds, IP28 6RD
Tel: 01284-811729 **Fax:** 01284-811590
E-mail: info@mountliming.co.uk
Website: http://www.mountliming.co.uk
Directors: A. Mount (Dir)
Immediate Holding Company: KEITH MOUNT (LIMING) LIMITED
Registration no: 02698194 **Date established:** 1992
Turnover: £500,000 - £1m **No.of Employees:** 1 - 10 **Product Groups:** 14, 33, 61

Date of Accounts	Jun 11	Jun 10	Jun 09
Working Capital	161	151	195
Fixed Assets	277	209	79
Current Assets	216	237	249

M C Integ Ltd

Integ Yard Rougham Industrial Estate, Rougham, Bury St Edmunds, IP30 9ND
Tel: 01359-270610 **Fax:** 01359-270458
E-mail: info@mc-integ.co.uk
Website: http://www.mc-integ.co.uk
Directors: J. Frost (MD), K. Pengelly (Sales), S. Borley (Tech Serv)
Managers: K. Andrews
Immediate Holding Company: M.C. INTEG LIMITED
Registration no: 01768415 **Date established:** 1983 **Turnover:** £1m - £2m
No.of Employees: 11 - 20 **Product Groups:** 35, 42, 45

Date of Accounts	Oct 11	Oct 10	Oct 09
Working Capital	256	243	222
Fixed Assets	15	21	23
Current Assets	719	808	1m

M R P Trucks & Trolleys

40 Horringer Road, Bury St Edmunds, IP33 2DR
Tel: 01284-766300 **Fax:** 01284-766500
E-mail: michael@mrptruckstrolleys.co.uk
Website: http://www.mrptruckstrolleys.co.uk
Directors: M. Popham (MD)
VAT No.: GB 410 5700 05 **Turnover:** £250,000 - £500,000
No.of Employees: 1 - 10 **Product Groups:** 35, 40, 45

Mamelok Holdings Ltd

Northern Way, Bury St Edmunds, IP32 6NJ
Tel: 01284-762291 **Fax:** 01284-703689
E-mail: sales@mamelok.com
Website: http://www.mamelok.com
Bank(s): Barclays
Directors: R. Gage (Fin)
Immediate Holding Company: CONNAUGHT LAWRENCE LTD
Registration no: 02563632 **VAT No.:** GB 213 7392 75
Date established: 1990 **Turnover:** £1m - £2m **No.of Employees:** 11 - 20
Product Groups: 27, 28, 49, 65

Date of Accounts	Dec 08	Dec 07	Dec 05
Working Capital	-46	-46	N/A
Fixed Assets	203	203	203
Current Liabilities	46	46	N/A
Total Share Capital	10	10	10

Marshall Bury St Edmunds

Moreton Hall Retail Park Bedingfeld Way, Bury St Edmunds, IP32 7BT
Tel: 01284-767344 **Fax:** 01284-702557
Website: http://www.marshallweb.co.uk
Bank(s): Lloyds TSB Bank plc
Managers: T. Littlewood (Sales Prom Mgr)
Ultimate Holding Company: MARSHALL OF CAMBRIDGE (HOLDINGS) LTD
Immediate Holding Company: MARSHALL OF CAMBRIDGE (MOTOR HOLDINGS) LTD
Registration no: 00295579 **Turnover:** £20m - £50m
No.of Employees: 11 - 20 **Product Groups:** 68

Metro Eyewear

The Beehive The Street, Herringswell, Bury St Edmunds, IP28 6ST
Tel: 01638-552404 **Fax:** 01638-751615
E-mail: info@metroeyewear.co.uk
Website: http://www.metroeyewear.co.uk
Directors: V. Hicks (Prop)
Immediate Holding Company: EYECOVER LIMITED
Registration no: 04773906 **Date established:** 2003
No.of Employees: 1 - 10 **Product Groups:** 38, 65

Miles Waterscapes Ltd

School House Farm Norton Road, Great Ashfield, Bury St Edmunds, IP31 3HJ
Tel: 01359-242356 **Fax:** 01359-241781
E-mail: contact@miles-water.com
Website: http://www.miles-water.com
Bank(s): Lloyds TSB Bank plc
Directors: R. Orford (MD)
Managers: J. Mellish (Char Surv), A. Woodiss (Sales Admin)
Immediate Holding Company: MILES WATERSCAPES LIMITED
Registration no: 01844904 **VAT No.:** GB 496 7077 90
Date established: 1984 **Turnover:** £2m - £5m **No.of Employees:** 21 - 50
Product Groups: 33, 35, 51, 84

Date of Accounts	Sep 11	Sep 10	Sep 09
Working Capital	-171	-87	-156
Fixed Assets	545	299	322
Current Assets	873	1m	459

Monkey Puzzle House - Residential Recording Studio

Monkey Puzzle House Heath Road, Woolpit, Bury St Edmunds, IP30 9RJ
Tel: 01359-245050 **Fax:** 01359-245060
E-mail: studio@monkeypuzzlehouse.com
Website: http://www.monkeypuzzlehouse.com
Date established: 2006 **No.of Employees:** 1 - 10 **Product Groups:** 89

Norfolk Greenhouses Ltd

Chiswick Avenue Mildenhall, Bury St Edmunds, IP28 7AZ
Tel: 01638-713418 **Fax:** 01638-714715
E-mail: info@norfolk-greenhouses.co.uk
Website: http://www.norfolk-greenhouses.co.uk
Directors: K. Waters (MD)
Immediate Holding Company: NORFOLK GREENHOUSES LIMITED
Registration no: 01338257 **VAT No.:** GB 304 8251 81
Date established: 1977 **No.of Employees:** 1 - 10 **Product Groups:** 30

Date of Accounts	Dec 11	Dec 10	Dec 09
Working Capital	64	127	207
Fixed Assets	2m	2m	2m
Current Assets	473	631	480

Nova Comex Ltd

51 Blackbird Drive, Bury St Edmunds, IP32 7DS
Tel: 01284-731018 **Fax:** 020-7183 1188
E-mail: info@novacomex.com
Website: http://www.novacomex.com
Directors: D. Zang (Dir)
Immediate Holding Company: MARIPOSA WEDDINGS LTD
Registration no: 05557147 **Date established:** 2010
Turnover: £500,000 - £1m **No.of Employees:** 1 - 10 **Product Groups:** 61

Date of Accounts	Sep 07
Working Capital	26
Current Assets	51
Current Liabilities	25

O K International Europe Ltd

Shepherds Grove Industrial Estate Stanton, Bury St Edmunds, IP31 2AR
Tel: 01359-250705 **Fax:** 01359-250165
E-mail: sales@okinteurope.co.uk
Website: http://www.okcorp.com
Managers: P. Herron (Sales Prom Mgr)
Immediate Holding Company: O/K INTERNATIONAL (EUROPE) LIMITED
Registration no: 01659848 **VAT No.:** GB 368 4204 44
Date established: 1982 **Turnover:** £1m - £2m **No.of Employees:** 1 - 10
Product Groups: 42, 45

Date of Accounts	May 11	May 10	May 09
Sales Turnover	N/A	1m	2m
Pre Tax Profit/Loss	N/A	-3	-86
Working Capital	-8	124	116
Fixed Assets	26	35	43
Current Assets	618	622	727
Current Liabilities	N/A	498	601

Oak Tree Ltd

Park Farm Business Centre Fornham Park, Fornham St Genevieve, Bury St Edmunds, IP28 6TS
Tel: 01284-763040 **Fax:** 01284-752891
E-mail: info@oaktree-training.co.uk
Website: http://www.oaktree-training.co.uk
Directors: S. Crowe (MD)
Immediate Holding Company: OAK TREE MANAGEMENT & TRAINING LTD
Registration no: 03961023 **Date established:** 2000
No.of Employees: 11 - 20 **Product Groups:** 86

Date of Accounts	Mar 12	Mar 11	Mar 10
Working Capital	125	105	101
Fixed Assets	7	13	18
Current Assets	255	236	189

C Olley & Sons Ltd

Iberia House 36 Southgate Avenue, Mildenhall, Bury St Edmunds, IP28 7AT
Tel: 01638-712076 **Fax:** 01638-717304
E-mail: info@olleycork.co.uk
Website: http://www.olleycork.co.uk
Directors: S. Littlechild (Fin)
Immediate Holding Company: C.OLLEY & SONS,LIMITED
Registration no: 00148506 **VAT No.:** GB 460 4890 41
Date established: 2017 **Turnover:** £2m - £5m **No.of Employees:** 1 - 10
Product Groups: 02, 22, 25, 27, 29, 30, 31, 32, 38, 39, 40, 42, 47, 49, 52, 61, 66, 67

Date of Accounts	Jan 12	Jan 11	Jan 10
Working Capital	57	56	63
Fixed Assets	218	222	232
Current Assets	98	86	86

Omiran Ltd

Units 1-2 James Carter Road, Mildenhall, Bury St Edmunds, IP28 7DE
Tel: 01638-716748 **Fax:** 01638-716779
E-mail: sales@omiran.co.uk
Website: http://www.omiran.co.uk
Directors: J. Taylor-Brown (MD), H. Taylor Brown (Co Sec)
Immediate Holding Company: OMIRAN LIMITED
Registration no: 02279903 **VAT No.:** GB 521 1196 86
Date established: 1988 **Turnover:** £1m - £2m **No.of Employees:** 1 - 10
Product Groups: 37, 44

Date of Accounts	Dec 10	Dec 09	Dec 08
Working Capital	59	103	91
Fixed Assets	2	2	2
Current Assets	93	148	116

On Demand Technology

5 Eastern Way, Bury St Edmunds, IP32 7AB
Tel: 01284-749105 **Fax:** 01284-749074
E-mail: juliant@ondemandtechnology.co.uk
Website: http://www.ondemandtechnology.co.uk

Directors: J. Thompson (MD)
Immediate Holding Company: ON DEMAND TECHNOLOGY LTD
Registration no: 05449430 **Date established:** 2005
Turnover: £500,000 - £1m **No.of Employees:** 1 - 10 **Product Groups:** 61, 81

Date of Accounts	May 11	May 10	May 09
Working Capital	-124	-117	-19
Fixed Assets	140	54	47
Current Assets	91	105	124

Orbital Food Machinery

Chapel Pond Hill, Bury St Edmunds, IP32 7HT
Tel: 01284-725255 **Fax:** 01284-725335
E-mail: sales@orbitalfoods.com
Website: http://www.orbitalfoods.com
Directors: T. Townsend (Dir)
Immediate Holding Company: ORBITAL FOOD MACHINERY LIMITED
Registration no: 04572741 **Date established:** 2002
No.of Employees: 11 - 20 **Product Groups:** 20, 40, 41

Date of Accounts	Jul 11	Jul 10	Jul 09
Working Capital	527	175	285
Current Assets	1m	512	302

P C Design Systems

Alpaca View The Green, Rougham, Bury St Edmunds, IP30 9JP
Tel: 01284-388588 **Fax:** 01284-388589
E-mail: waterworldwatersofteners@hotmail.com
Website: http://www.waterworldwatersoftners.co.uk
Managers: S. Copping (Mgr)
Immediate Holding Company: WATERWORLD SOLUTIONS LTD
Registration no: 06010370 **No.of Employees:** 1 - 10 **Product Groups:** 38, 42

The Pine House Company

Spinney Garage Ixworth Road, Stowlangtoft, Bury St Edmunds, IP31 3JS
Tel: 01359-235030 **Fax:** 01359-235030
E-mail: information@thepinehousecompany.co.uk
Website: http://www.thepinehousecompany.co.uk
Directors: S. Coe (Prop)
Date established: 2002 **No.of Employees:** 1 - 10 **Product Groups:** 26

Pipe Center

118a Newmarket Road, Bury St Edmunds, IP33 3TG
Tel: 01284-753046 **Fax:** 01284-750042
E-mail: robert.burt@wolseley.co.uk
Website: http://www.centres.co.uk
Managers: T. Halls (District Mgr)
Ultimate Holding Company: BRITISH FITTINGS GROUP P.L.C.
Registration no: 00546685 **Turnover:** £2m - £5m
No.of Employees: 1 - 10 **Product Groups:** 30, 35

Date of Accounts	Jun 11	Jun 10	Jun 09
Sales Turnover	87m	96m	96m
Pre Tax Profit/Loss	-2m	5m	5m
Working Capital	-2m	1m	4m
Fixed Assets	36m	34m	26m
Current Assets	34m	33m	45m
Current Liabilities	9m	7m	9m

Promaxx Print-Yourself Products

Denny Bros Ltd Kempson Way, Bury St Edmunds, IP32 7AR
Tel: 01284-829701 **Fax:** 01284-705575
E-mail: info@promaxx.co.uk
Website: http://www.promaxx.co.uk
Registration no: 01696899 **Date established:** 1996
No.of Employees: 51 - 100 **Product Groups:** 27

Proteus Equipment Ltd

P O Box 33, Bury St Edmunds, IP33 2RS
Tel: 01284-753954 **Fax:** 01284-701369
E-mail: info@proteusequipment.com
Website: http://www.proteusequipment.com
Directors: E. Kelly (MD)
Immediate Holding Company: PROTEUS EQUIPMENT LIMITED
Registration no: 02087313 **Date established:** 1987
No.of Employees: 11 - 20 **Product Groups:** 40, 45, 66, 83

Date of Accounts	Jun 11	Jun 10	Jun 09
Working Capital	1m	877	844
Fixed Assets	968	966	946
Current Assets	2m	1m	1m

Quality Castings Slough Ltd

Northern Way, Bury St Edmunds, IP32 6NW
Tel: 01284-755941 **Fax:** 01284-761770
E-mail: mail@qualitycastings.co.uk
Website: http://www.qualitycastings.co.uk
Bank(s): National Westminster
Directors: K. Bonsor (MD), M. Cleverden (Fin), M. Cleverdon (Fin)
Managers: J. Kennedy, D. Ball
Ultimate Holding Company: SAXHAM INVESTMENTS LTD (GUERNSEY)
Immediate Holding Company: QUALITY CASTINGS(SLOUGH)LIMITED
Registration no: 00634519 **VAT No.:** GB 102 6621 15
Date established: 1959 **Turnover:** £2m - £5m **No.of Employees:** 21 - 50
Product Groups: 34

Date of Accounts	Aug 11	Aug 10	Aug 09
Working Capital	1m	1m	1m
Fixed Assets	368	406	316
Current Assets	2m	2m	2m

R D Castings Ltd

Leyton Avenue Mildenhall, Bury St Edmunds, IP28 7BL
Tel: 01638-717944 **Fax:** 01638-716590
E-mail: sales@rdcastings.co.uk
Website: http://www.rdcastings.co.uk
Directors: A. Pateman (Sales), M. Pateman (I.T. Dir), R. Pateman (MD), J. Pateman (Dir)
Immediate Holding Company: R.D. CASTINGS LIMITED
Registration no: 01284002 **Date established:** 1976
No.of Employees: 21 - 50 **Product Groups:** 46

Date of Accounts	Oct 11	Oct 10	Oct 09
Working Capital	422	230	254
Fixed Assets	937	958	881
Current Assets	723	495	499

R G Carter Projects Ltd

30 Out Westgate, Bury St Edmunds, IP33 3PA
Tel: 01284-753355 **Fax:** 01284-753099
E-mail: mail@rgcarter-projects.co.uk
Website: http://www.rgcarter.com
Directors: T. Atkins (MD)
Ultimate Holding Company: RG CARTER GROUP LIMITED
Immediate Holding Company: R.G. CARTER PROJECTS LIMITED
Registration no: 01916420 **Date established:** 1985
Turnover: £75m - £125m **No.of Employees:** 51 - 100 **Product Groups:** 52

Date of Accounts	Dec 11	Dec 10	Dec 09
Sales Turnover	73m	80m	59m
Pre Tax Profit/Loss	2m	4m	5m
Working Capital	10m	8m	5m
Fixed Assets	852	683	3m
Current Assets	30m	32m	28m
Current Liabilities	10m	12m	14m

Robinson Young Ltd

Equis House 4 Eastern Way, Bury St Edmunds, IP32 7AB
Tel: 01284-766261 **Fax:** 01284-701105
E-mail: info@ry.tm
Website: http://www.robinsonyoung.co.uk
Directors: A. Pritchett (Sales), M. Robinson (MD), M. Morris (Fin), K. Sterling (Sales)
Managers: S. Golby (Personnel), E. Young (Tech Serv Mgr), K. Day, L. Shore
Ultimate Holding Company: ROBINSON YOUNG HOLDINGS LIMITED
Immediate Holding Company: ROBINSON YOUNG LIMITED
Registration no: 01067101 **VAT No.:** GB 105 7740 81
Date established: 1972 **Turnover:** £50m - £75m
No.of Employees: 101 - 250 **Product Groups:** 77

Date of Accounts	Dec 11	Dec 10	Dec 09
Sales Turnover	59m	60m	61m
Pre Tax Profit/Loss	535	297	244
Working Capital	4m	3m	3m
Fixed Assets	709	624	365
Current Assets	21m	19m	20m
Current Liabilities	10m	7m	8m

Kenneth Robson Equipment Ltd

5 Tewkesbury Place Great Barton, Bury St Edmunds, IP31 2TP
Tel: 01284-787330 **Fax:** 01284-788002
Directors: K. Robson (Fin)
Immediate Holding Company: KENNETH ROBSON EQUIPMENT LIMITED
Registration no: 01222673 **Date established:** 1975 **Turnover:** £1m - £2m
No.of Employees: 1 - 10 **Product Groups:** 45, 51, 83

Date of Accounts	Dec 11	Dec 10	Dec 09
Working Capital	187	184	186
Fixed Assets	N/A	N/A	1
Current Assets	257	235	237

Saxon Catering Equipment Services

91 Falcon Way Beck Row, Bury St Edmunds, IP28 8EL
Tel: 07909-522208 **Fax:** 01638-716356
Directors: D. Pangborn (Prop)
Date established: 1999 **No.of Employees:** 1 - 10 **Product Groups:** 20, 40, 41

Scootertech Ltd

13 Barns & Stables Timworth Green, Timworth, Bury St Edmunds, IP31 1HS
Tel: 01284-729180
Website: http://www.scootertech.co.uk
Directors: L. Makowski (Fin)
Managers: K. Parfry (Mgr)
Immediate Holding Company: SCOOTERTECH LIMITED
Registration no: 04846111 **Date established:** 2003
No.of Employees: 1 - 10 **Product Groups:** 39, 40

Date of Accounts	Jul 11	Jul 10	Jul 09
Working Capital	35	21	22
Fixed Assets	20	24	14
Current Assets	84	97	94

Sensortek

PO Box 222, Bury St Edmunds, IP28 6EE
Tel: 01284-728150 **Fax:** 01284-728155
E-mail: sales@sensortek.co.uk
Website: http://www.sensortek.co.uk
Managers: C. Hilder (Chief Mgr)
Registration no: 02552995 **Date established:** 1983
Turnover: £250,000 - £500,000 **No.of Employees:** 1 - 10
Product Groups: 37, 38

Service Partitions Ltd

2nd Floor Freedom House 5 Abbeyfields, Bury St Edmunds, IP33 1AQ
Tel: 01842-811339 **Fax:** 01842-812066
E-mail: sales@servicegroupinteriors.com
Website: http://www.servicegroupinteriors.com
Directors: W. Kirkham (Dir)
Immediate Holding Company: SERVICE PARTITIONS LIMITED
Registration no: 00976836 **VAT No.:** GB 102 3510 39
Date established: 1970 **Turnover:** £1m - £2m **No.of Employees:** 1 - 10
Product Groups: 35

Date of Accounts	Jul 11	Jul 10	Jul 09
Working Capital	124	170	172
Fixed Assets	17	23	16
Current Assets	184	251	230

Shelbourne Reynolds Engineering Ltd

Shepherds Grove Industrial Estate Stanton, Bury St Edmunds, IP31 2AR
Tel: 01359-250415 **Fax:** 01359-250464
E-mail: info@shelbourne.com
Website: http://www.shelbourne.com
Bank(s): National Westminster
Directors: N. Smith (Sales)
Managers: C. Bloomfield (Fin Mgr), R. Whalebelly (Tech Serv Mgr), B. Christosoro (Purch Mgr)
Ultimate Holding Company: RUSSIAN SHELBOURNE LIMITED
Immediate Holding Company: SHELBOURNE REYNOLDS ENGINEERING LIMITED
Registration no: 01055939 **VAT No.:** GB 102 0080 53
Date established: 1972 **Turnover:** £10m - £20m
No.of Employees: 51 - 100 **Product Groups:** 41, 46, 48

Date of Accounts	Sep 11	Sep 10	Sep 09
Sales Turnover	15m	14m	13m
Pre Tax Profit/Loss	2m	3m	2m
Working Capital	4m	5m	4m
Fixed Assets	1m	1m	1m
Current Assets	6m	6m	6m
Current Liabilities	386	566	999

Strain Measurement Devices

Bury Road Chedburgh, Bury St Edmunds, IP29 4UQ
Tel: 01284-852000 **Fax:** 01284-852371
E-mail: william.easlea@smdsensors.co.uk
Website: http://www.smdsensors.co.uk
Bank(s): Barclays Bank Plc
Directors: J. Walton (Fin), W. Easlea (Dir)
Managers: C. Bowman (Tech Serv Mgr)
Ultimate Holding Company: INTERNATIONAL SENSOR HOLDINGS INC (USA)
Immediate Holding Company: STRAIN MEASUREMENT DEVICES LIMITED
Registration no: 01610732 **VAT No.:** GB 368 4139 29
Date established: 1982 **Turnover:** £1m - £2m **No.of Employees:** 21 - 50
Product Groups: 38

Date of Accounts	Dec 11	Dec 10	Dec 09
Working Capital	1m	843	740
Fixed Assets	137	128	150
Current Assets	1m	1m	1m

Suffolk Agri-Centre Ltd

Fen Road Pakenham, Bury St Edmunds, IP31 2JS
Tel: 01359-232155 **Fax:** 01359-232337
E-mail: office@suffagri.co.uk
Website: http://www.suffagri.co.uk
Directors: D. Eley (Dir)
Immediate Holding Company: SUFFOLK AGRI CENTRE LIMITED
Registration no: 04715310 **Date established:** 2003 **Turnover:** £2m - £5m
No.of Employees: 11 - 20 **Product Groups:** 41

Date of Accounts	Apr 12	Apr 11	Apr 10
Working Capital	86	92	35
Fixed Assets	68	86	115
Current Assets	971	889	1m

Sunsquare Ltd

Unit 5a Barton Business Centre Barton Road, Bury St Edmunds, IP32 7BE
Tel: 08452-263172 **Fax:** 08452-263173
E-mail: sales@sunsquare.co.uk
Website: http://www.sunsquare.co.uk
Directors: J. Seldis (MD)
Managers: M. Lambert (Tech Sales Mgr), T. Hawkins (Chief Acct)
Immediate Holding Company: SUNSQUARE LIMITED
Registration no: 05018021 **Date established:** 2004
No.of Employees: 11 - 20 **Product Groups:** 26, 35

Date of Accounts	Jan 12	Jan 11	Jan 10
Working Capital	-88	-92	72
Fixed Assets	324	234	240
Current Assets	365	272	321

Swift Medical Trolleys Ltd

7 Micklesmere Drive, Bury St Edmunds, IP31 2UJ
Tel: 01359-233248 **Fax:** 01359-233317
E-mail: info@swiftmedicaltrolleys.co.uk
Website: http://www.swiftmedicaltrolleys.co.uk
Directors: L. Garner (Dir), J. Bartl (Dir)
Registration no: 07003461 **Date established:** 2009
Turnover: Up to £250,000 **No.of Employees:** 1 - 10 **Product Groups:** 26, 37

Thales Optronics Ltd

Dettingen House Dettingen Way, Bury St Edmunds, IP33 3TU
Tel: 01284-750599 **Fax:** 01284-750598
E-mail: andy.coe@uk.thalesgroup.com
Website: http://www.thalesgroup-optronics.com
Managers: A. Coe
Ultimate Holding Company: THALES SA (FRANCE)
Immediate Holding Company: THALES OPTRONICS (BURY ST. EDMUNDS) LIMITED
Registration no: 01127352 **Date established:** 1973
Turnover: Up to £250,000 **No.of Employees:** 51 - 100
Product Groups: 75

Date of Accounts	Dec 11	Dec 10	Dec 09
Sales Turnover	31	93	311
Pre Tax Profit/Loss	-3m	-555	-604
Working Capital	755	3m	3m
Fixed Assets	N/A	164	221
Current Assets	5m	4m	4m
Current Liabilities	1m	512	711

Total Locker Service

Brunel Eastern Court 13 Eastern Way, Bury St Edmunds, IP32 7AB
Tel: 01284-718773 **Fax:** 01284-750758
E-mail: admin@total-locker-service.co.uk
Website: http://www.total-locker-service.co.uk
Directors: A. Rivett (Dir)
Immediate Holding Company: GAWE PROPERTIES LIMITED
Registration no: 01805308 **Date established:** 2005
No.of Employees: 1 - 10 **Product Groups:** 26, 36, 44, 49, 67

Date of Accounts	Mar 08	Sep 11	Sep 10
Working Capital	167	182	181
Fixed Assets	48	11	21
Current Assets	208	199	204

Towergate Insurance

Blenheim House New Market Road, Bury St Edmunds, IP33 3SB
Tel: 01284-756565 **Fax:** 01284-725200
E-mail: burystedmunds@towergate.co.uk
Website: http://www.towergateinsurance.co.uk
Directors: D. Clark (Co Sec)
Managers: P. Whittaker, J. Yandle (Comptroller), I. True
Ultimate Holding Company: TOWERGATE PARTNERSHIP LIMITED
Immediate Holding Company: THE BECKETT GROUP LIMITED
Registration no: 01946377 **Date established:** 1985
No.of Employees: 51 - 100 **Product Groups:** 82

Date of Accounts	Dec 07	Dec 06	Dec 05
Pre Tax Profit/Loss	632	13m	30
Working Capital	1000	705	-2m
Fixed Assets	50	345	2m
Current Assets	1000	705	1m
Current Liabilities	N/A	N/A	442

Tranilamp Ltd

Sharon Road, Bury St Edmunds, IP33 3TZ
Tel: 01284-767055 **Fax:** 01284-701921
E-mail: sales@tranilamp.co.uk
Website: http://www.tranilamp.co.uk
Directors: J. Putnam (MD)
Immediate Holding Company: TRANILAMP LIMITED
Registration no: 00751750 **VAT No.:** GB 102 0205 59
Date established: 1963 **No.of Employees:** 1 - 10 **Product Groups:** 37, 38

Date of Accounts	Mar 11	Mar 10	Mar 09
Working Capital	263	281	283
Fixed Assets	612	175	187
Current Assets	311	327	319

R C Treatt & Co. Ltd

Northern Way, Bury St Edmunds, IP32 6NL
Tel: 01284-702500 **Fax:** 01284-703809
E-mail: marketing@rctreatt.com
Website: http://www.treatt.com
Bank(s): H S B C
Directors: R. Hope (Fin), A. Haines (Pers), P. Gash (Tech Serv), H. Bovill (MD), G. Bovill (Mkt Research)
Ultimate Holding Company: TREATT PLC
Immediate Holding Company: R.C.TREATT & CO.LIMITED
Registration no: 00131429 **VAT No.:** GB 428 0796 33
Date established: 2013 **Turnover:** £20m - £50m
No.of Employees: 101 - 250 **Product Groups:** 20, 31, 32, 66

Date of Accounts	Sep 11	Sep 10	Sep 09
Sales Turnover	47m	45m	41m
Pre Tax Profit/Loss	3m	4m	4m
Working Capital	17m	17m	13m
Fixed Assets	6m	6m	6m
Current Assets	27m	27m	21m
Current Liabilities	3m	2m	2m

Tripp Batt & Co. Ltd

Hepworth Road Stanton, Bury St Edmunds, IP31 2BT
Tel: 01359-250268 **Fax:** 01359-251603
E-mail: a.tunbridge@trippbatt.com
Website: http://www.trippbatt.co.uk
Directors: A. Tunbridge (Dir)
Ultimate Holding Company: CON MECH GROUP LIMITED
Immediate Holding Company: TRIPP BATT & CO LIMITED
Registration no: 02205462 **Date established:** 1987 **Turnover:** £2m - £5m
No.of Employees: 11 - 20 **Product Groups:** 41

Date of Accounts	Dec 11	Dec 10	Dec 09
Sales Turnover	N/A	N/A	2m
Pre Tax Profit/Loss	N/A	N/A	24
Working Capital	70	136	193
Fixed Assets	106	85	73
Current Assets	348	277	322
Current Liabilities	N/A	N/A	49

Veronalder Ltd

Unit 16 Chamberlayne Road Moreton Hall Industrial Estate, Bury St Edmunds, IP32 7EY
Tel: 01284-769565 **Fax:** 01284-768102
E-mail: gill@veronalder.co.uk
Website: http://www.veronalder.co.uk
Directors: J. Drury (MD), G. Drury (Fin)
Ultimate Holding Company: Veronalder Holdings Ltd
Immediate Holding Company: VERONALDER HOLDINGS LIMITED
Registration no: 02421612 **VAT No.:** GB 321 4234 08
Date established: 1989 **Turnover:** £1m - £2m **No.of Employees:** 1 - 10
Product Groups: 35, 36

Date of Accounts	Jul 07	Jan 12	Jan 11
Sales Turnover	624	N/A	N/A
Pre Tax Profit/Loss	45	N/A	N/A
Working Capital	-36	-129	-129
Fixed Assets	61	129	129
Current Assets	170	N/A	N/A
Current Liabilities	17	N/A	N/A

Virbac Ltd

Unit 16 Woolpit, Bury St Edmunds, IP30 9UP
Tel: 01359-243243 **Fax:** 01359-243200
E-mail: enquiries@virbac.co.uk
Website: http://www.virbac.co.uk
Ultimate Holding Company: VIRBAC SA (FRANCE)
Immediate Holding Company: VIRBAC LIMITED
Registration no: 01069800 **Date established:** 1972
Turnover: £20m - £50m **No.of Employees:** 11 - 20 **Product Groups:** 07

Date of Accounts	Dec 11	Dec 10	Dec 09
Sales Turnover	22m	20m	19m
Pre Tax Profit/Loss	280	1m	1m
Working Capital	3m	4m	4m
Fixed Assets	73	61	20
Current Assets	10m	8m	9m
Current Liabilities	4m	3m	3m

W E Instrumentation Ltd

Unit 15 Chamberlayne Road, Bury St Edmunds, IP32 7EY
Tel: 01284-704805 **Fax:** 01284-762932
E-mail: sales@we-instrumentation.co.uk
Website: http://www.we-instrumentation.co.uk
Directors: L. Elliott (Sales)
Immediate Holding Company: W.E. INSTRUMENTATION LIMITED
Registration no: 03026484 **VAT No.:** GB 443 0784 56
Date established: 1995 **Turnover:** £1m - £2m **No.of Employees:** 1 - 10
Product Groups: 38, 44

Date of Accounts	Mar 12	Mar 11	Mar 10
Working Capital	331	324	280
Fixed Assets	15	17	21
Current Assets	729	780	658

Wardsflex Ltd

Unit 22 James Carter Road, Mildenhall, Bury St Edmunds, IP28 7DE
Tel: 01638-778666 **Fax:** 01638-716863
E-mail: sales@wardsflex.co.uk
Website: http://www.wardsflex.co.uk
Directors: A. Pollard (MD)
Immediate Holding Company: WARDSFLEX LIMITED
Registration no: 07026072 **VAT No.:** GB 637 7977 74
Date established: 2009 **Turnover:** £1m - £2m **No.of Employees:** 1 - 10
Product Groups: 30, 34, 36, 37, 38, 40, 45, 46, 67

Date of Accounts	Dec 11	Dec 10
Working Capital	120	118
Fixed Assets	25	31
Current Assets	194	167

West Suffolk Leisurewear

82a-82c James Carter Road Mildenhall, Bury St Edmunds, IP28 7DE
Tel: 01638-717172 **Fax:** 01638-717028
E-mail: sales@wsluk.com
Website: http://www.wsluk.com
Directors: N. Thompson (Prop)
No.of Employees: 1 - 10 **Product Groups:** 23, 24, 63, 65

Witton Chemical Co. Ltd

Southgate Avenue Mildenhall, Bury St Edmunds, IP28 7AT
Tel: 01638-716001 **Fax:** 01638-717658
E-mail: ukoffice@witton.com
Website: http://www.witton.com
Bank(s): Barclays, Bedford
Directors: M. Rainer (Pers)
Managers: B. Knight (Fin Mgr), C. Smith (Sales Prom Mgr), N. McLoud
Immediate Holding Company: WITTON CHEMICAL CO.LIMITED
Registration no: 00740947 **VAT No.:** GB 103 5310 31
Date established: 1962 **Turnover:** £5m - £10m **No.of Employees:** 21 - 50
Product Groups: 31, 32, 66

Date of Accounts	Mar 11	Mar 10	Mar 09
Working Capital	587	146	192
Fixed Assets	2m	2m	3m
Current Assets	2m	2m	1m

Eye

Advanced Aluminium Design Ltd

Unit 19-20 Fortress Close Brome Industrial Park Airfield Industrial Estate, Eye, IP23 7HN
Tel: 01379-870071 **Fax:** 01379-870112
E-mail: sales@aadl.co.uk
Website: http://www.aadl.co.uk
Directors: K. Jones (Dir)
Immediate Holding Company: ADVANCED ALUMINIUM DESIGN LIMITED
Registration no: 05300430 **Date established:** 2004
No.of Employees: 1 - 10 **Product Groups:** 34, 46, 48

Date of Accounts	Dec 11	Dec 10	Dec 09
Working Capital	-67	-67	-56
Fixed Assets	218	185	193
Current Assets	247	210	162

Bartrums Group Ltd

Langton Green, Eye, IP23 7HN
Tel: 01379-870693 **Fax:** 01379-870942
E-mail: info@bartrums.com
Website: http://www.bartrums.com
Bank(s): Barclays
Directors: D. Gunson (Fin), S. Potter (Dir)
Managers: M. Gomersall (Transport)
Ultimate Holding Company: THE BARTRUM GROUP LIMITED
Immediate Holding Company: BARTRUMS HAULAGE AND STORAGE LIMITED
Registration no: 01370486 **VAT No.:** GB 571 1681 44
Date established: 1978 **Turnover:** £10m - £20m
No.of Employees: 21 - 50 **Product Groups:** 45, 87

Date of Accounts	Dec 11	Dec 10	Dec 09
Sales Turnover	17m	18m	15m
Pre Tax Profit/Loss	262	395	475
Working Capital	-4m	-3m	-2m
Fixed Assets	7m	7m	5m
Current Assets	4m	4m	3m
Current Liabilities	2m	520	502

Eleco Timber Frame Ltd (Eleco PLC)

Oaksmere Business Park Eye Airfield Industrial Estate, Yaxley, Eye, IP23 8BW
Tel: 01379-783465 **Fax:** 01379-783659
E-mail: stramit@eleco.com
Website: http://www.eleco.com
Directors: J. Ketteley (Dir), L. O'hara (Dir), B. Shum (Sales & Mktg), P. Taylor (MD)
Managers: J. Fox (Chief Mgr), I. Allen (I.T. Exec), D. White (Tech Serv Mgr)
Ultimate Holding Company: ELECO PUBLIC LIMITED COMPANY
Immediate Holding Company: ELECO TIMBER FRAME LIMITED
Registration no: 01473781 **Date established:** 1980 **Turnover:** £2m - £5m
No.of Employees: 1 - 10 **Product Groups:** 25, 30

Date of Accounts	Jun 10	Jun 09	Jun 08
Sales Turnover	4m	3m	8m
Pre Tax Profit/Loss	-1m	-1m	-2
Working Capital	-391	1m	2m
Fixed Assets	509	622	744
Current Assets	5m	5m	5m
Current Liabilities	266	125	367

Epr Eye Ltd

Eye Power Station Eye Airfield Industrial Estate, Eye, IP23 7DH
Tel: 01379-871100 **Fax:** 01379-871376
Website: http://www.eprl.co.uk
Directors: E. Wilkinson (Grp Chief Exec)
Ultimate Holding Company: Meif Renewable Energy (Holdings) Ltd
Immediate Holding Company: Fibrowatt Ltd
Registration no: 02234141 **Date established:** 1988 **Turnover:** £5m - £10m
No.of Employees: 21 - 50 **Product Groups:** 37, 54, 67

Carl Humphrey

Ipswich Road Brome, Eye, IP23 8AW
Tel: 01379-870666 **Fax:** 01379-871333
Website: http://www.humphreygroup.co.uk
Directors: C. Humphrey (Prop)
Ultimate Holding Company: PPT (EDM) HOLDINGS LIMITED
Immediate Holding Company: PREMIER PRECISION TOOLING LIMITED
Date established: 1996 **No.of Employees:** 11 - 20 **Product Groups:** 40, 45

Kitchen Engineering

The Old Hospital Low Road, Denham, Eye, IP21 5ET
Tel: 01379-871235 **Fax:** 01379- 871235
Directors: J. Kitchen (Prop)
Date established: 2000 **No.of Employees:** 1 - 10 **Product Groups:** 41

Mellis Welding Supplies

Willow Cottage The Common, Mellis, Eye, IP23 8DS
Tel: 01379-783289 **Fax:** 01379-788119
E-mail: trevor.bennett@hotmail.co.uk
Directors: P. Bennett (Co Sec), T. Bennett (MD)
Immediate Holding Company: MELLIS WELDING SUPPLIES LIMITED
Registration no: 01972093 **Date established:** 1985
Turnover: Up to £250,000 **No.of Employees:** 1 - 10 **Product Groups:** 46

Date of Accounts	Dec 11	Dec 10	Dec 09
Sales Turnover	181	157	175
Pre Tax Profit/Loss	-0	N/A	-1
Working Capital	82	82	81
Fixed Assets	4	4	5
Current Assets	128	129	127
Current Liabilities	3	5	7

Pac 3000 Ltd

Lawrence House Magdalen Street, Eye, IP23 7AJ
Tel: 01379-872710 **Fax:** 01379-872717
E-mail: lisa.rule@pac3000.com
Website: http://www.pac3000.com
Directors: L. Rule (Fin)
Immediate Holding Company: PAC 3000 LIMITED
Registration no: 02533989 **Date established:** 1990
No.of Employees: 1 - 10 **Product Groups:** 38, 42

Date of Accounts	Dec 11	Dec 10	Dec 09
Working Capital	46	24	-20
Fixed Assets	68	68	87
Current Assets	563	728	795

Permastore Ltd

Eye Airfield, Eye, IP23 7HS
Tel: 01379-870723 **Fax:** 01379-870530
E-mail: sales@permastore.com
Website: http://www.permastore.com
Bank(s): Barclays
Directors: R. Cole (Sales), P. Harrop (I.T. Dir), I. Henry (Fin), B. Atkinson (Sales), A. Gare (MD)
Managers: J. Halstone (Personnel), T. Dempster, A. Laughlin (Purch Mgr), K. Woods (Tech Serv Mgr)
Ultimate Holding Company: PERMASTORE GROUP LIMITED
Immediate Holding Company: PERMASTORE LIMITED
Registration no: 00257009 **VAT No.:** GB 450 6919 40
Date established: 1931 **Turnover:** £20m - £50m
No.of Employees: 101 - 250 **Product Groups:** 35

Date of Accounts	Mar 09	Mar 10	Mar 11
Sales Turnover	31m	23m	20m
Pre Tax Profit/Loss	6m	3m	2m
Working Capital	5m	6m	1m
Fixed Assets	3m	2m	3m
Current Assets	11m	12m	10m
Current Liabilities	1m	607	313

Bruce Starke & Co. Ltd

Langton Green, Eye, IP23 7HN
Tel: 01379-870209 **Fax:** 01379-871232
E-mail: info@bruce-starke.com
Website: http://www.bruce-starke.com
Bank(s): HSBC Bank plc
Directors: J. Mateboer (MD), J. Parry (Fin)
Ultimate Holding Company: MD MATTING SYSTEMS BV (NETHERLANDS)
Immediate Holding Company: BRUCE, STARKE & CO. LIMITED
Registration no: 00290045 **VAT No.:** GB 246 3300 87
Date established: 1934 **Turnover:** £1m - £2m **No.of Employees:** 11 - 20
Product Groups: 23

Date of Accounts	Dec 11	Dec 10	Dec 09
Working Capital	1m	1m	1m
Fixed Assets	911	934	953
Current Assets	1m	1m	1m

Watts Off Highway

Building 1 A140 Ipswich Road, Brome, Eye, IP23 8AW
Tel: 01379-870880 **Fax:** 01379-871436
E-mail: diss@watts-tyres.co.uk
Website: http://www.watts-tyres.co.uk
Directors: D. Pearson (MD), T. Dillage (Grp Chief Exec)
Immediate Holding Company: Watts of Lidney Group
Registration no: 01434811 **No.of Employees:** 1 - 10 **Product Groups:** 29, 68

Wrightfield Ltd

Progress Way, Eye, IP23 7HU
Tel: 01379-872800 **Fax:** 01379-872801
E-mail: sales@wrightfield.co.uk
Website: http://www.wrightfield.co.uk
Directors: J. Wilby (Dir), P. Rose (Fin)
Managers: M. Rose (Sales Prom Mgr)
Immediate Holding Company: WRIGHTFIELD LIMITED
Registration no: 02347731 **Date established:** 1989
Turnover: £250,000 - £500,000 **No.of Employees:** 21 - 50
Product Groups: 20, 41, 45

Date of Accounts	Mar 10	Mar 09	Mar 08
Working Capital	-222	-221	-290
Fixed Assets	1m	1m	1m
Current Assets	663	558	672

Felixstowe

Actaris Development UK Ltd

Langer Road, Felixstowe, IP11 2ER
Tel: 01394-694000 **Fax:** 01394-276030
E-mail: csaunders@actaris.co.uk
Website: http://www.felixstowe.actaris.com
Directors: M. Gowers (MD), I. Mundford (Co Sec)
Ultimate Holding Company: ITRON INC (USA)
Immediate Holding Company: ACTARIS DEVELOPMENT UK II LIMITED
Registration no: 05396135 **VAT No.:** 785 3949 68 **Date established:** 2005
Turnover: £20m - £50m **No.of Employees:** 1 - 10 **Product Groups:** 18

Date of Accounts	Dec 10	Dec 09	Dec 08
Pre Tax Profit/Loss	5m	23m	17m
Working Capital	5m	-39	-31m
Fixed Assets	68m	73m	107m
Current Assets	5m	132	109

Brinor International Shipping & Forwarding Ltd

Cliff House Hamilton Gardens, Felixstowe, IP11 7DH
Tel: 01394-274511 **Fax:** 01394-270695
E-mail: info@brinor.com
Website: http://www.brinor.com
Bank(s): Barclays
Directors: M. Bahr (MD), M. Varley (Fin)
Ultimate Holding Company: BRINOR (HOLDINGS) LIMITED
Immediate Holding Company: BRINOR (HOLDINGS) LIMITED
Registration no: 01758831 **VAT No.:** GB 344 4076 65
Date established: 1983 **Turnover:** £20m - £50m
No.of Employees: 51 - 100 **Product Groups:** 35, 36, 37, 39, 40, 45, 64, 71, 72, 76, 77

Date of Accounts	Apr 11	Apr 10	Apr 09
Sales Turnover	21m	19m	20m
Pre Tax Profit/Loss	264	146	158

Working Capital	3m	3m	2m
Fixed Assets	882	771	916
Current Assets	6m	7m	6m
Current Liabilities	844	940	884

Combat Alexander

1 Langer Park Industrial Estate Holland Road, Felixstowe, IP11 2DB
Tel: 01394-671763 **Fax:** 01394-671797
E-mail: sales@combatalexander.co.uk
Website: http://www.combatalexander.co.uk
Directors: A. Clegg (Prop)
Date established: 1991 **No.of Employees:** 1 - 10 **Product Groups:** 37, 67

Cory Logistics

Cory House Haven Exchange, Felixstowe, IP11 2QX
Tel: 01394-674822 **Fax:** 01394-673740
E-mail: sales@cory.co.uk
Website: http://www.cory.co.uk
Bank(s): National Westminster Bank Plc
Directors: J. Vanbergen (Dir), M. Harrison (MD)
Ultimate Holding Company: Powell Duffryn P.L.C.
Immediate Holding Company: Powell Duffryn Shipping Ltd
Registration no: 05105859 **VAT No.:** GB 244 0497 69
Turnover: £50m - £75m **No.of Employees:** 21 - 50 **Product Groups:** 45, 71, 72, 74, 75, 76, 77, 84

Cosco UK Ltd

Walton House Trinity Terminal Oysterbed Road, Felixstowe, IP11 4SS
Tel: 01394-673399 **Fax:** 01394-673554
E-mail: felixstowe@cosco.co.uk
Website: http://www.cosco.co.uk
Managers: B. Packham (), T. Ramsey (Mgr), F. Whittaker (Export Sales Mg)
Immediate Holding Company: COSCO (UK) LIMITED
Registration no: 02216271 **VAT No.:** GB 494 2167 29
Date established: 1988 **Turnover:** £5m - £10m **No.of Employees:** 1 - 10
Product Groups: 74, 76

Damco Sea & Air UK Ltd

Suite 22 Orwell House Ferry Lane, Felixstowe, IP11 3AQ
Tel: 01394-675989 **Fax:** 01394-674208
E-mail: paul.gallagher@damco.com
Website: http://www.damco.com
Bank(s): HSBC
Managers: P. Gallagher, G. Bastion (Purch Mgr), N. Hunt (Sales Prom Mgr), G. Pearce (Comptroller), Y. Mozhaeva (Mktg Serv Mgr)
Ultimate Holding Company: AP MOLLER MAERSK A/S (DENMARK)
Immediate Holding Company: DAMCO UK LIMITED
Registration no: 01847748 **VAT No.:** GB 506 4175 63
Date established: 1984 **Turnover:** £125m - £250m
No.of Employees: 51 - 100 **Product Groups:** 74

Date of Accounts	Dec 11	Dec 10	Dec 09
Sales Turnover	96m	140m	151m
Pre Tax Profit/Loss	-1m	-3m	-287
Working Capital	9m	10m	12m
Fixed Assets	259	267	271
Current Assets	35m	42m	34m
Current Liabilities	13m	13m	9m

Denholm International Freight

96 Langer Road, Felixstowe, IP11 2EG
Tel: 01394-696940 **Fax:** 01394-271147
E-mail: jalexander@dbforwarding.co.uk
Website: http://www.denholm-forwarding.co.uk
Directors: G. Hanson (Co Sec)
Managers: B. King (District Mgr)
Ultimate Holding Company: J. & J. DENHOLM LTD
Immediate Holding Company: DENHOLM BARWIL LTD
Registration no: 00269198 **No.of Employees:** 11 - 20
Product Groups: 72, 74

Dolphin East Anglia

PO Box 136, Felixstowe, IP11 9WW
Tel: 01394-277100
Website: http://www.dolphinstairliftseastanglia.co.uk
Directors: P. Smith (Dir)
Immediate Holding Company: DOLPHIN STAIRLIFTS (EAST ANGLIA) LIMITED
Registration no: 05296200 **Date established:** 2004
No.of Employees: 1 - 10 **Product Groups:** 35, 39, 45

Date of Accounts	Nov 10	Nov 09	Nov 08
Working Capital	15	40	-28
Fixed Assets	37	25	28
Current Assets	128	87	98

George Baker Shipping Ltd

Unit 4 Parker Avenue, Felixstowe, IP11 4HF
Tel: 01394-676367 **Fax:** 01394-673667
E-mail: enquiries@georgebakershipping.com
Website: http://www.georgebakershipping.com
Directors: N. Farmer (Fin), G. Baker (MD), L. Baker (Dir)
Managers: D. Pulley (Tech Serv Mgr)
Immediate Holding Company: GEORGE BAKER (SHIPPING) LIMITED
Registration no: 01613385 **Date established:** 1982 **Turnover:** £5m - £10m
No.of Employees: 21 - 50 **Product Groups:** 75, 76, 80

Date of Accounts	Jan 12	Jan 11	Jan 10
Sales Turnover	8m	N/A	N/A
Pre Tax Profit/Loss	468	N/A	N/A
Working Capital	931	646	420
Fixed Assets	92	85	108
Current Assets	6m	4m	4m
Current Liabilities	4m	N/A	N/A

Imorex

Dooley Road, Felixstowe, IP11 3HG
Tel: 01394-607740 **Fax:** 01394-607767
E-mail: info@imorex.co.uk
Website: http://www.imorex.co.uk
Directors: A. Nunn (Dir)
Managers: B. Blythe, D. Abblitt (Sales Prom Mgr)
Immediate Holding Company: IMOREX SHIPPING SERVICES LIMITED
Registration no: 01127998 **Date established:** 1973 **Turnover:** £1m - £2m
No.of Employees: 21 - 50 **Product Groups:** 76

Date of Accounts	Aug 11	Aug 10	Aug 09
Working Capital	4	14	-54
Fixed Assets	214	92	87
Current Assets	1m	844	789

Its Training Services

Cliff House Hamilton Gardens, Felixstowe, IP11 7EJ
Tel: 08456-123344 **Fax:** 01394-458501
E-mail: info@itstraining.co.uk
Website: http://www.itstraining.co.uk
Managers: S. Edson
Immediate Holding Company: ITS TRAINING LTD
Registration no: 04504655 **Date established:** 2002 **Turnover:** £2m - £5m
No.of Employees: 21 - 50 **Product Groups:** 86

Date of Accounts	Aug 11	Aug 10	Aug 09
Working Capital	-69	-68	-67

Charles Kendall Freight Ltd

Suite 10 Unit 3 Orwell House Ferry Lane, Felixstowe, IP11 3QL
Tel: 01394-673797 **Fax:** 01394-675235
E-mail: ssutton@charleskendallfreight.com
Website: http://www.charleskendallfreight.com
Managers: H. Hilyard
Ultimate Holding Company: CHARLES KENDALL GROUP LIMITED
Immediate Holding Company: CHARLES KENDALL FREIGHT LIMITED
Registration no: 00540121 **Date established:** 1954
No.of Employees: 1 - 10 **Product Groups:** 76

Date of Accounts	Dec 11	Dec 10	Dec 09
Sales Turnover	19m	21m	20m
Pre Tax Profit/Loss	445	248	107
Working Capital	3m	2m	2m
Current Assets	13m	9m	7m
Current Liabilities	167	150	95

Martlesham Metalcraft

Old Station Yard Station Road, Trimley St Mary, Felixstowe, IP11 0UB
Tel: 01394-670584
Directors: A. Fincham (Prop)
No.of Employees: 1 - 10 **Product Groups:** 26, 35

New Alliance Services Ltd

403A Trelawny House The Dock, Felixstowe, IP11 3EQ
Tel: 01394-676212 **Fax:** 01394-676423
Directors: M. Gamble (MD), C. Cotton (Fin)
Immediate Holding Company: NEW ALLIANCE SERVICES LIMITED
Registration no: 01578488 **Date established:** 1981
Turnover: £250,000 - £500,000 **No.of Employees:** 1 - 10
Product Groups: 72, 74, 76, 77, 82

Date of Accounts	Sep 11	Sep 10	Sep 09
Working Capital	245	232	229
Fixed Assets	10	12	16
Current Assets	425	437	394

Norfolk Line Ltd

10 Mansfield Park, Felixstowe, IP11 0BF
Tel: 01473-654800 **Fax:** 01394-603608
E-mail: felixstowe@norfolkline.com
Website: http://www.norfolklinelogistics.com
Bank(s): Barclays
Directors: D. Spencer (Fin), E. Green (MD), T. Woldbye (MD)
Managers: D. Oldham (I.T. Exec), S. Dolmor (Mktg Serv Mgr), T. Dexter (Personnel)
Ultimate Holding Company: A P MOLLER FINANCE SA (SWITZERLAND)
Immediate Holding Company: DFDS LOGISTICS LIMITED
Registration no: 00786104 **VAT No.:** GB 105 2372 12
Date established: 1963 **Turnover:** £75m - £125m
No.of Employees: 251 - 500 **Product Groups:** 72, 74, 76, 77

Date of Accounts	Dec 09	Dec 08	Dec 07
Sales Turnover	106m	106m	103m
Pre Tax Profit/Loss	2m	2m	3m
Working Capital	14m	10m	8m
Fixed Assets	9m	11m	12m
Current Assets	32m	30m	27m
Current Liabilities	9m	8m	9m

P D Logistics

Parker Avenue, Felixstowe, IP11 4HF
Tel: 01394-675541 **Fax:** 01394-675371
E-mail: sales@pglogistics.com
Website: http://www.pdlogistics.com
Bank(s): National Westminster Bank Plc
Directors: N. Warmisham (Dir)
Managers: M. Dodd (Mgr)
Ultimate Holding Company: Brookfield Ports UK Ltd
Immediate Holding Company: PD Portco Ltd
Registration no: 01422772 **Date established:** 2003 **Turnover:** £2m - £5m
No.of Employees: 21 - 50 **Product Groups:** 77

Date of Accounts	Dec 11	Dec 10	Jun 09
Working Capital	65m	57m	48m
Current Assets	78m	70m	61m

Penta GB Ltd

Unit 9 Schneider Close, Felixstowe, IP11 3SS
Tel: 01394-674912 **Fax:** 01394-674917
E-mail: jason@pentagb.co.uk
Website: http://www.pentagb.co.uk
Directors: J. Stokes (MD)
Immediate Holding Company: PENTA (GB) LIMITED
Registration no: 04628217 **Date established:** 2003 **Turnover:** £1m - £2m
No.of Employees: 11 - 20 **Product Groups:** 45, 72, 74, 75, 76

Date of Accounts	Dec 11	Dec 10	Dec 09
Working Capital	-215	-101	-62
Fixed Assets	461	268	289
Current Assets	809	611	444

R J J Freight Ltd

R J J House Haven Exchange South, Felixstowe, IP11 2QE
Tel: 01394-673466 **Fax:** 01394-673031
E-mail: hazel.usher@rjjfreight.co.uk
Website: http://www.rjjfreight.co.uk
Directors: H. Usher (Fin)
Immediate Holding Company: R J J FREIGHT LIMITED
Registration no: 02812754 **VAT No.:** GB 751 0081 71
Date established: 1993 **Turnover:** £10m - £20m
No.of Employees: 11 - 20 **Product Groups:** 76

Date of Accounts	Dec 11	Dec 10	Dec 09
Working Capital	223	208	123
Fixed Assets	357	364	473
Current Assets	2m	2m	2m

World Transport Agency Ltd (Branch)

Unit 5 Suite 17 Orwell House Ferry Lane, Felixstowe, IP11 3QU
Tel: 01394-673247 **Fax:** 01394-673721
E-mail: leanne.cartwright@wta.co.uk
Website: http://www.estron-group.com
Bank(s): HSBC
Managers: L. Cartwright (Sales Prom Mgr), M. White
Ultimate Holding Company: SOMMER HOLDINGS LTD
Immediate Holding Company: WORLD TRANSPORT AGENCY LIMITED
Registration no: 00129014 **VAT No.:** GB 235 9766 24
Date established: 2013 **Turnover:** £50m - £75m
No.of Employees: 21 - 50 **Product Groups:** 72, 76

Date of Accounts	Jun 11	Jun 10	Jun 09
Sales Turnover	58m	48m	48m
Pre Tax Profit/Loss	2m	1m	2m
Working Capital	3m	3m	3m
Fixed Assets	146	227	311
Current Assets	10m	10m	9m
Current Liabilities	872	477	754

Halesworth

Easitron Ltd

The Forge Linstead, Halesworth, IP19 0AA
Tel: 01986-785457 **Fax:** 01986-785457
Directors: J. Doy (Dir), V. Doy (Co Sec)
Immediate Holding Company: EASITRON LIMITED
Registration no: 02840640 **Date established:** 1993
No.of Employees: 1 - 10 **Product Groups:** 26, 35

Date of Accounts	Oct 11	Oct 10	Oct 09
Working Capital	-17	3	-3
Fixed Assets	45	29	31
Current Assets	40	48	43

Herrco Cosmetics

5-7 Broadway Drive, Halesworth, IP19 8QR
Tel: 01986-874149 **Fax:** 01986-874664
E-mail: info@herrco.co.uk
Website: http://www.herrco.co.uk
Directors: S. Herrmann (Fin)
Managers: D. Herrmann
Immediate Holding Company: HERRCO COSMETICS LIMITED
Registration no: 06822192 **Date established:** 2009
Turnover: £250,000 - £500,000 **No.of Employees:** 21 - 50
Product Groups: 31, 32, 48, 63

Date of Accounts	Mar 12	Mar 11	Mar 10
Working Capital	1m	765	382
Fixed Assets	748	550	409
Current Assets	2m	2m	901

J S T UK Ltd

Blyth Road, Halesworth, IP19 8EW
Tel: 01986-874131 **Fax:** 01986-874276
E-mail: sales@jst.co.uk
Website: http://www.jst.co.uk
Bank(s): Lloyds TSB Bank plc
Directors: T. Boughtwood (Co Sec)
Managers: S. Titchiner, L. Hull, J. Watts, P. Raven (Buyer)
Ultimate Holding Company: JST MFG CO LTD (JAPAN)
Immediate Holding Company: J.S.T. (U.K.) LIMITED
Registration no: 01617265 **VAT No.:** GB 372 9958 94
Date established: 1982 **Turnover:** £5m - £10m **No.of Employees:** 21 - 50
Product Groups: 37

Date of Accounts	Mar 11	Mar 10	Mar 09
Sales Turnover	10m	8m	N/A
Pre Tax Profit/Loss	2m	692	3m
Working Capital	28m	27m	25m
Fixed Assets	5m	5m	6m
Current Assets	30m	28m	26m
Current Liabilities	974	644	1m

Nortique

58 Thoroughfare, Halesworth, IP19 8AR
Tel: 01986-875656
E-mail: nortique@nortique.co.uk
Website: http://www.nortique.co.uk
Directors: C. Davies (Prop), M. Rowley (Prop)
Turnover: Up to £250,000 **No.of Employees:** 1 - 10 **Product Groups:** 25, 26, 32, 52

A Richardson & Sons

32 Quay Street, Halesworth, IP19 8ER
Tel: 01986-872520 **Fax:** 01986-872520
Directors: V. Richardson (Ptnr)
Date established: 1945 **No.of Employees:** 1 - 10 **Product Groups:** 36, 39, 40

V M Marketing Orthotics International

St Peter's Church Ubbeston, Halesworth, IP19 0EX
Tel: 01986-798120 **Fax:** 01986-798040
E-mail: info@vmmarketing.co.uk
Website: http://www.vmmarketing.co.uk
Directors: J. Vander-Molen (MD)
Date established: 1987 **No.of Employees:** 1 - 10 **Product Groups:** 22, 26, 38, 67

Viking Optical Ltd

Blyth Road Industrial Estate, Halesworth, IP19 8EN
Tel: 01986-875315 **Fax:** 01986-874788
E-mail: enquiries@vikingoptical.co.uk
Website: http://www.vikingoptical.co.uk
Bank(s): Midland
Managers: T. Strivens (Sales Prom Mgr)
Immediate Holding Company: VIKING OPTICAL LIMITED
Registration no: 01956767 **VAT No.:** GB 428 0560 62
Date established: 1985 **Turnover:** £1m - £2m **No.of Employees:** 21 - 50
Product Groups: 33, 38

Date of Accounts	Mar 11	Mar 10	Mar 09
Working Capital	790	681	974
Fixed Assets	76	95	96
Current Assets	1m	1m	1m

Haverhill

ABSCO Materials
42 Hollands Road, Haverhill, CB9 8SA
Tel: 01440-709709 **Fax:** 01440-709708
E-mail: enquiries@abscomaterials.com
Website: http://www.abscomaterials.com
Directors: T. Bayley (Ptnr)
Immediate Holding Company: EXCEL ASSOCIATES (UK) LIMITED
Date established: 1997 **No.of Employees:** 1 - 10 **Product Groups:** 17, 31, 34, 61, 66

Alphatech Ltd
Green House Homefield Road, Haverhill, CB9 8QP
Tel: 01440-714709 **Fax:** 01440-714706
E-mail: info@alphatech.co.uk
Website: http://www.alphatech.co.uk
Managers: S. Mathews (Comm)
Immediate Holding Company: ALPHATECH LIMITED
Registration no: 03300283 **Date established:** 1997
Turnover: £500,000 - £1m **No.of Employees:** 1 - 10 **Product Groups:** 38, 40, 85

Date of Accounts	Jan 12	Jan 11	Jan 10
Working Capital	22	12	-18
Fixed Assets	411	441	453
Current Assets	211	217	198

Ardex UK Ltd
Homefield Road, Haverhill, CB9 8QP
Tel: 01440-714939 **Fax:** 01440-716660
E-mail: info@ardex.co.uk
Website: http://www.ardex.co.uk
Bank(s): Lloyds TSB Bank plc
Directors: C. Knight (Fin), C. Knight (Fin), L. Kidd (Sales & Mktg), P. Bell (MD)
Managers: T. Biaene (Tech Serv Mgr)
Ultimate Holding Company: ARDEX LUXEMBOURG HOLDING SARL (LUXEMBOURG)
Immediate Holding Company: ARDEX UK LIMITED
Registration no: 00668297 **Date established:** 1960
Turnover: £10m - £20m **No.of Employees:** 51 - 100 **Product Groups:** 32, 33

Date of Accounts	Dec 11	Dec 10	Dec 09
Sales Turnover	19m	18m	18m
Pre Tax Profit/Loss	3m	3m	2m
Working Capital	4m	4m	4m
Fixed Assets	3m	4m	4m
Current Assets	7m	7m	6m
Current Liabilities	2m	1m	1m

Atlantis Water Treatment
3a Homefield Road, Haverhill, CB9 8QP
Tel: 01440-761500 **Fax:** 01440-705010
E-mail: mail@atlantis-uk.com
Website: http://www.atlantis-uk.com
Directors: N. Kent (Fin), J. Parr (MD)
Immediate Holding Company: ATLANTIS WATER TREATMENT LIMITED
Registration no: 03701510 **Date established:** 1999
No.of Employees: 1 - 10 **Product Groups:** 38, 42

Date of Accounts	Jun 11	Jun 10	Jun 09
Working Capital	34	35	33
Fixed Assets	11	17	9
Current Assets	79	95	97

Terence Barker Ltd
Barker House Phoenix Road, Haverhill, CB9 7AE
Tel: 01440-712905 **Fax:** 01440-715460
E-mail: sales@tbtanks.co.uk
Website: http://www.tbtanks.co.uk
Bank(s): Barclays Bank
Directors: J. Holt (Dir)
Ultimate Holding Company: ASSA ABLOY AB (PUBL) (SWEDEN)
Immediate Holding Company: TERENCE BARKER LIMITED
Registration no: 00988738 **VAT No.:** 213 453 20 **Date established:** 1970
Turnover: Up to £250,000 **No.of Employees:** 11 - 20 **Product Groups:** 30, 33, 35, 42, 45, 48, 52, 66, 77, 84

Date of Accounts	Sep 11	Sep 10	Sep 09
Working Capital	13	115	2
Fixed Assets	3m	3m	3m
Current Assets	367	387	414

Cowell & Cooper Ltd
Unit 10 Homefield Road, Haverhill, CB9 8QP
Tel: 01440-715870 **Fax:** 01440-709353
E-mail: enquiries@cowellandcooper.co.uk
Website: http://www.cowellandcooper.co.uk
Bank(s): Barclays
Directors: S. White (Fab)
Immediate Holding Company: COWELL AND COOPER,LIMITED
Registration no: 00429687 **Date established:** 1947 **Turnover:** £2m - £5m
No.of Employees: 11 - 20 **Product Groups:** 35

Date of Accounts	Feb 12	Feb 11	Feb 10
Working Capital	-79	-38	-40
Fixed Assets	1m	1m	1m
Current Assets	521	606	546

D B Sheetmetals Ltd
8 Piperell Way, Haverhill, CB9 8PH
Tel: 01440-706218 **Fax:** 01440-760268
E-mail: info@dbsheetmetals.co.uk
Website: http://www.dbsheetmetals.co.uk
Directors: C. Law (Co Sec)
Immediate Holding Company: D.B. SHEETMETALS LIMITED
Registration no: 02227768 **VAT No.:** GB 493 1109 54
Date established: 1988 **Turnover:** £1m - £2m **No.of Employees:** 21 - 50
Product Groups: 32, 34, 35, 36, 46, 48, 84

Date of Accounts	Mar 12	Mar 11	Mar 10
Working Capital	-23	-51	-92
Fixed Assets	267	318	385
Current Assets	339	358	384

Delstar Engineering Ltd
Homefield Road, Haverhill, CB9 8QP
Tel: 01440-762518 **Fax:** 01440-703820
E-mail: general@delstar.co.uk
Website: http://www.delstar.co.uk
Bank(s): HSBC Bank plc
Directors: K. Golding (MD), N. Scott (Co Sec)
Ultimate Holding Company: STAGE TECHNOLOGIES GROUP LIMITED
Immediate Holding Company: DELSTAR ENGINEERING LIMITED
Registration no: 01345698 **VAT No.:** GB 299 8387 68
Date established: 1977 **Turnover:** £2m - £5m **No.of Employees:** 21 - 50
Product Groups: 48, 85

Date of Accounts	Mar 12	Mar 11	Mar 10
Working Capital	1m	1m	852
Fixed Assets	134	150	198
Current Assets	3m	2m	2m

Edmolift UK Ltd
Blois Meadow Business Centre Blois Road, Steeple Bumpstead, Haverhill, CB9 7BN
Tel: 01440-730640 **Fax:** 01440-730004
E-mail: info@edmolift.co.uk
Website: http://www.edmolift.co.uk
Bank(s): National Westminster Bank Plc
Directors: D. Papani (Sales), D. Dicker (Fin)
Immediate Holding Company: EDMOLIFT UK LTD.
Registration no: 02456741 **VAT No.:** GB 538 5586 04
Date established: 1990 **Turnover:** £2m - £5m **No.of Employees:** 11 - 20
Product Groups: 26, 40, 45, 67

Date of Accounts	Aug 11	Aug 10	Aug 09
Working Capital	728	772	843
Fixed Assets	712	662	686
Current Assets	1m	1m	1m

Everlac GB Ltd
Moonhall Business Park Helions Bumpstead Road, Haverhill, CB9 7AA
Tel: 01440-766360 **Fax:** 01440-768897
E-mail: admin@everlac.co.uk
Website: http://www.everlac.co.uk
Bank(s): Barclays
Directors: D. Wilson (Comm)
Immediate Holding Company: EVERLAC (G.B.) LIMITED
Registration no: 01483035 **VAT No.:** GB 360 3521 85
Date established: 1980 **Turnover:** £1m - £2m **No.of Employees:** 11 - 20
Product Groups: 30, 32, 33

Date of Accounts	Dec 11	Dec 10	Dec 09
Working Capital	399	358	443
Fixed Assets	146	189	252
Current Assets	1m	1m	1m

F S M Manufacturing Ltd
Sturmer Road, Haverhill, CB9 7UU
Tel: 01440-762561 **Fax:** 01440-706251
E-mail: sales@f-s-m.co.uk
Website: http://www.f-s-m.co.uk
Bank(s): Barclays
Directors: C. Fellows (MD)
Immediate Holding Company: FSM MANUFACTURING LIMITED
Registration no: 01453287 **VAT No.:** GB 344 4512 71
Date established: 1979 **Turnover:** £1m - £2m **No.of Employees:** 21 - 50
Product Groups: 34, 35, 36, 40, 44, 46, 48, 52, 66, 84

Date of Accounts	Sep 11	Sep 10	Sep 09
Working Capital	306	356	309
Fixed Assets	556	268	338
Current Assets	656	790	703

Farmpartcentres
2 Homefield Road, Haverhill, CB9 8QP
Tel: 01440-704329 **Fax:** 01440-714260
E-mail: sales@farmparts.co.uk
Website: http://www.farmparts.co.uk
Directors: R. Lander (Ptnr)
Immediate Holding Company: BEAPHAR LIMITED
Registration no: 04139534 **Date established:** 1973
No.of Employees: 1 - 10 **Product Groups:** 41, 45, 67

Date of Accounts	Mar 12	Mar 11	Mar 10
Working Capital	598	580	510
Fixed Assets	9	N/A	25
Current Assets	899	807	616

Fibrefab Ltd
Boundary Road Sturmer, Haverhill, CB9 7YH
Tel: 01440-718800 **Fax:** 01440-712542
E-mail: sales@fibrefab.com
Website: http://www.fibrefab.com
Directors: A. Bishop (Fin)
Managers: G. Earyes (Purch Mgr), R. Smith (Tech Serv Mgr)
Ultimate Holding Company: SILBURY INVESTMENTS LTD (JERSEY)
Immediate Holding Company: FIBREFAB LIMITED
Registration no: 02734823 **Date established:** 1992
Turnover: £250,000 - £500,000 **No.of Employees:** 51 - 100
Product Groups: 33, 37, 44, 45, 52, 67, 84, 85

Date of Accounts	Dec 11	Dec 10	Dec 09
Sales Turnover	18m	17m	17m
Pre Tax Profit/Loss	575	393	262
Working Capital	2m	2m	2m
Fixed Assets	344	448	553
Current Assets	6m	6m	7m
Current Liabilities	427	622	413

Fire Security Sprinkler Installations Ltd
Homefield Road, Haverhill, CB9 8QP
Tel: 01440-705815 **Fax:** 01440-704352
E-mail: info@firesecurity.co.uk
Website: http://www.firesecurity.co.uk
Bank(s): Barclays, Bury St Edmunds
Directors: R. Pipe (Dir), S. Jesson (Fin)
Ultimate Holding Company: ASHTON YORK LIMITED
Immediate Holding Company: FIRE SECURITY (SPRINKLER INSTALLATIONS) LIMITED
Registration no: 01051511 **VAT No.:** GB 239 2332 68
Date established: 1972 **Turnover:** £500,000 - £1m
No.of Employees: 11 - 20 **Product Groups:** 40, 52

Date of Accounts	Mar 12	Mar 11	Mar 10
Working Capital	598	580	510
Fixed Assets	9	N/A	25
Current Assets	899	807	616

G T Vision Ltd
Hazel Stub Depot Camps Road, Haverhill, CB9 9AF
Tel: 01440-714737 **Fax:** 01440-709421
E-mail: eurosales@gt-vision.com
Website: http://www.gxoptical.com
Directors: M. Town (Dir), I. Baldwin (Sales)
Immediate Holding Company: GT VISION LTD
Registration no: 04974093 **Date established:** 2003 **Turnover:** £1m - £2m
No.of Employees: 11 - 20 **Product Groups:** 32, 65

Date of Accounts	Jan 12	Jan 11	Jan 10
Working Capital	91	84	69
Fixed Assets	43	31	17
Current Assets	318	302	289

Glassfusion Ltd
20 Rookwood Way, Haverhill, CB9 8PB
Tel: 01440-703769 **Fax:** 01440-708329
E-mail: info@glassfusion.ltd.uk
Website: http://www.glassfusion.ltd.uk
Directors: C. Briggs (MD)
Immediate Holding Company: GLASSFUSION LIMITED
Registration no: 01041385 **VAT No.:** GB 102 3802 26
Date established: 1972 **Turnover:** £500,000 - £1m
No.of Employees: 1 - 10 **Product Groups:** 33, 40, 63

Date of Accounts	Jan 12	Jan 11	Jan 10
Working Capital	-95	-13	-9
Fixed Assets	274	280	286
Current Assets	51	81	63

Graysons Freight Services Ltd
4 Hollands Road, Haverhill, CB9 8PP
Tel: 01440-762558 **Fax:** 01440-707119
E-mail: sales@graysons.net
Website: http://www.graysons.net
Directors: J. Fleming (MD)
Immediate Holding Company: GRAYSONS FREIGHT SERVICES LIMITED
Registration no: 01493008 **VAT No.:** GB 360 2186 78
Date established: 1980 **Turnover:** £1m - £2m **No.of Employees:** 1 - 10
Product Groups: 45

Date of Accounts	Jun 11	Jun 10	Jun 09
Working Capital	-124	-184	-213
Fixed Assets	4	8	11
Current Assets	241	341	321

D Gurteen & Sons Ltd
PO Box 1, Haverhill, CB9 8AZ
Tel: 01440-702601 **Fax:** 01440-703394
E-mail: sales@gurteen.co.uk
Website: http://www.gurteen.co.uk
Bank(s): Lloyds TSB Bank plc
Directors: D. Howard (Sales), J. Smart (Dir)
Managers: R. Brown (Tech Serv Mgr), G. Simpkin
Immediate Holding Company: D.GURTEEN & SONS,LIMITED
Registration no: 00236462 **VAT No.:** GB 102 3849 00
Date established: 2029 **Turnover:** £10m - £20m
No.of Employees: 21 - 50 **Product Groups:** 24

Date of Accounts	Jun 11	Jun 10	Jun 09
Sales Turnover	10m	9m	8m
Pre Tax Profit/Loss	512	819	-239
Working Capital	7m	6m	6m
Fixed Assets	93	80	561
Current Assets	7m	7m	7m
Current Liabilities	360	275	1m

Herbert Partnering Solutions Ltd,
Smithfield House Rookwood Way, Haverhill, CB9 8PD.
Tel: 01440-765380 **Fax:** 01440-713331
E-mail: info@herbertpsl.com
Website: http://www.herbertindustrial.com
Bank(s): Bank of Scotland
Directors: S. Tomlinson (Grp Chief Exec)
Managers: S. Stuttard (Sales Prom Mgr)
Immediate Holding Company: W M T Holdings P.L.C.
Registration no: 07342092 **Date established:** 1965
No.of Employees: 21 - 50 **Product Groups:** 42

Herbert Retail Ltd
Rookwood Way, Haverhill, CB9 8PD
Tel: 01440-711400 **Fax:** 01440-710469
E-mail: sales@herbertgroup.com
Website: http://www.herbertgroup.com
Directors: M. Brown (Dir), R. Herbert (MD), R. Herbert (Dir), M. Brown (MD), T. Cramphorn (Fin)
Managers: S. Hale (Buyer), T. Nickels (Mktg Serv Mgr), C. Evans (Sales Prom Mgr), G. Welch (Purch Mgr)
Immediate Holding Company: HERBERT RETAIL LIMITED
Registration no: 00103897 **VAT No.:** GB 700 2860 78
Date established: 2009 **Turnover:** £10m - £20m
No.of Employees: 101 - 250 **Product Groups:** 38, 42, 44, 48

Date of Accounts	Mar 10	Mar 09	Mar 08
Sales Turnover	13m	18m	23m
Pre Tax Profit/Loss	1m	504	1m
Working Capital	4m	4m	3m
Fixed Assets	257	356	448
Current Assets	6m	6m	7m
Current Liabilities	749	656	1m

International Flavours & Fragrances Ltd
Duddery Hill, Haverhill, CB9 8LG
Tel: 01440-715000 **Fax:** 01440-762199
E-mail: philip.gardner@iff.com
Website: http://www.ifs.com
Bank(s): Barclays
Directors: P. Gardner (Fin), D. Whitaker (Sales & Mktg)
Managers: L. Bleazey
Ultimate Holding Company: INTERNATIONAL FLAVORS AND FRAGRANCES INC (USA)
Immediate Holding Company: INTERNATIONAL FLAVOURS & FRAGRANCES I.F.F.(GREAT BRITAIN)LIMITED
Registration no: 00214174 **VAT No.:** GB 220 3102 44
Date established: 2026 **Turnover:** £75m - £125m
No.of Employees: 101 - 250 **Product Groups:** 20

Date of Accounts	Dec 11	Dec 10	Dec 09
Sales Turnover	110m	122m	123m
Pre Tax Profit/Loss	13m	13m	17m
Working Capital	84m	87m	85m
Fixed Assets	12m	15m	12m
Current Assets	112m	124m	112m
Current Liabilities	28m	8m	6m

L M K Thermosafe
Unit 9-10 Moonhall Business Park Helions Bumpstead Road, Haverhill, CB9 7AA
Tel: 01440-707141 **Fax:** 01440-713344
E-mail: sales@drumheating.com
Website: http://www.drumheating.com

Managers: I. Heaters
Immediate Holding Company: LMK THERMOSAFE LIMITED
Registration no: 03959310 **VAT No.:** GB 759 6388 64
Date established: 2000 **No.of Employees:** 1 - 10 **Product Groups:** 36, 37, 40

Date of Accounts	Mar 11	Mar 10	Mar 09
Working Capital	530	413	446
Fixed Assets	335	296	232
Current Assets	712	600	563

Lynvale Ltd

Lime Grove Estate Falconer Road, Haverhill, CB9 7XU
Tel: 01440-766975 **Fax:** 0870-160 9256
E-mail: info@lynvale.co.uk
Website: http://www.lynvale.co.uk
Directors: S. Baxendale (MD)
Immediate Holding Company: LYNVALE LIMITED
Registration no: 06006717 **Date established:** 2006
Turnover: £500,000 - £1m **No.of Employees:** 11 - 20 **Product Groups:** 27

Date of Accounts	Nov 11	Nov 10	Nov 09
Working Capital	-108	-22	-45
Fixed Assets	155	113	82
Current Assets	214	237	106

Mansol Preforms Ltd

1 Hollands Road, Haverhill, CB9 8PX
Tel: 01440-702371 **Fax:** 01440-712512
E-mail: info@mansol-preforms.com
Website: http://www.mansol-preforms.com
Bank(s): Barclays
Directors: D. Cherry (MD), J. Cherry (Fin)
Managers: P. Hill (Sales Admin)
Ultimate Holding Company: MANSOL HOLDINGS LIMITED
Immediate Holding Company: MANSOL (PREFORMS) LIMITED
Registration no: 00536059 **VAT No.:** GB 386 0197 33
Date established: 1954 **Turnover:** £500,000 - £1m
No.of Employees: 21 - 50 **Product Groups:** 33, 37

Date of Accounts	Jun 11	Jun 10	Jun 09
Working Capital	1m	754	467
Fixed Assets	914	793	809
Current Assets	1m	975	550

Marchant Manufacturing Co. Ltd

Piperell Way, Haverhill, CB9 8QW
Tel: 01440-705351 **Fax:** 01440-762593
E-mail: philipmarchant@marchant.co.uk
Website: http://www.marchant.co.uk
Bank(s): National Westminster Bank Plc
Directors: J. Marchant (Fin), P. Marchant (Ch), S. Parrett (MD), S. Marchant (Sales)
Immediate Holding Company: MARCHANT MANUFACTURING CO,LIMITED
Registration no: 00277794 **VAT No.:** GB 246 3520 73
Date established: 1933 **Turnover:** £10m - £20m
No.of Employees: 101 - 250 **Product Groups:** 27, 30, 32, 66, 76

Date of Accounts	Jan 09	Jan 10	Feb 11
Sales Turnover	12m	12m	10m
Pre Tax Profit/Loss	204	326	-750
Working Capital	681	576	-420
Fixed Assets	2m	1m	2m
Current Assets	4m	4m	3m
Current Liabilities	2m	3m	2m

Qualitape Ltd

1 Sarah Court Piperell Way, Haverhill, CB9 8PS
Tel: 01440-710747 **Fax:** 01440-763526
E-mail: sales@qualitape.co.uk
Website: http://www.qualitape.co.uk
Directors: G. Speller (MD)
Registration no: 03023302 **Date established:** 2000
Turnover: £10m - £20m **No.of Employees:** 1 - 10 **Product Groups:** 38, 42

Date of Accounts	May 08	May 07	May 06
Working Capital	51	52	59
Fixed Assets	43	49	42
Current Assets	409	381	377
Current Liabilities	358	328	318

Snap Display Systems East Anglia Ltd

Hazel Stubb Depot Camps Road Burton End, Haverhill, CB9 9AF
Tel: 01440-714381 **Fax:** 01440-706758
E-mail: sales@snapdisplays.co.uk
Website: http://www.snapdisplaysystems.com
Directors: C. Hawkins (MD)
Immediate Holding Company: SNAP DISPLAY SYSTEMS (EAST ANGLIA) LIMITED
Registration no: 02058536 **Date established:** 1986
Turnover: Up to £250,000 **No.of Employees:** 1 - 10 **Product Groups:** 25, 26, 27, 30, 35, 49, 52, 66, 81, 83, 84

Date of Accounts	Mar 11	Mar 10	Mar 09
Working Capital	-88	-58	-56
Fixed Assets	781	773	776
Current Assets	17	44	44

Taylor's Foundry Ltd

31 Hollands Road, Haverhill, CB9 8PU
Tel: 01440-702870 **Fax:** 01440-763454
E-mail: sales@taylorsfoundry.co.uk
Website: http://www.taylorsfoundry.co.uk
Bank(s): Barclays
Directors: J. Robinson (MD), J. Robinson (Sales)
Managers: G. Taylor (), D. Warman (Accounts), J. Robinson (Purch Mgr), J. Robinson (Tech Serv Mgr), G. Taylor (Tech Serv Mgr)
Registration no: 00463430 **VAT No.:** 103 2288 13 **Date established:** 1946
No.of Employees: 22 **Product Groups:** 34, 48, 66

Date of Accounts	Nov 11	Nov 10	Nov 09
Working Capital	600	648	394
Fixed Assets	281	287	294
Current Assets	1m	1m	937

Teletherm

11 Raymond Court Piperell Way, Haverhill, CB9 8PH
Tel: 01440-713313 **Fax:** 01440-709903
E-mail: teletherm@btconnect.com
Directors: K. Small (Dir)
Immediate Holding Company: TELETHERM LIMITED
Registration no: 06309051 **Date established:** 2007
No.of Employees: 1 - 10 **Product Groups:** 38, 67

Date of Accounts	Jul 11
Working Capital	1
Fixed Assets	8
Current Assets	1

Test Plugs Ltd

12 Falklands Road, Haverhill, CB9 0EA
Tel: 01440-704201 **Fax:** 01440-763121
E-mail: sales@test-plugs.com
Website: http://www.test-plugs.com
Directors: D. Howell (Dir)
Immediate Holding Company: TEST PLUGS LIMITED
Registration no: 01232637 **VAT No.:** GB 249 4199 27
Date established: 1975 **Turnover:** £250,000 - £500,000
No.of Employees: 1 - 10 **Product Groups:** 38

Date of Accounts	Dec 11	Dec 10	Dec 09
Working Capital	350	335	318
Fixed Assets	19	31	39
Current Assets	419	423	416

U C M Ltd

United House Falconer Road, Haverhill, CB9 7XU
Tel: 01440-760300 **Fax:** 01440-760301
E-mail: sales@ucmmanufacturing.co.uk
Website: http://www.ucmmanufacturing.co.uk
Directors: P. Mullens (Dir)
Immediate Holding Company: LAS VEGAS LIMITED
Registration no: 04939365 **Date established:** 2011
No.of Employees: 21 - 50 **Product Groups:** 35

Date of Accounts	Dec 11	Dec 10	Dec 09
Working Capital	415	375	629
Fixed Assets	13	35	48
Current Assets	652	874	982

Ipswich

Adaptive Images

Felaw Maltings 44 Felaw Street, Ipswich, IP2 8SJ
Tel: 01473-406646
E-mail: enquiries@adaptive-image.co.uk
Website: http://www.adaptive-image.co.uk
Managers: C. Simpson (Mgr)
Date established: 2004 **Turnover:** £250,000 - £500,000
No.of Employees: 1 - 10 **Product Groups:** 23

Akron

Unit 1 Penny Corner, Ipswich, IP1 5AP
Tel: 01473-461042 **Fax:** 01473-462924
E-mail: cterry@akronproducts.co.uk
Website: http://www.akronproducts.co.uk
Bank(s): Barclays, St Albans, Herts, AL1 3AN
Directors: S. Rees (Tech Serv), A. Scottgreen (Fin), K. Chittock (Sales & Mktg)
Managers: A. Scott Green (Ops Mgr)
Immediate Holding Company: HUNTLEIGH TECHNOLOGY P.L.C.
Registration no: 00942245 **VAT No.:** GB 299 7444 87
Turnover: £2m - £5m **No.of Employees:** 21 - 50 **Product Groups:** 26, 37, 38, 67

Alstons Cabinets Ltd

Nacton Road, Ipswich, IP3 9QL
Tel: 01473-725571 **Fax:** 01473-270732
E-mail: david.alston@alstons.co.uk
Website: http://www.alstons.co.uk
Bank(s): Lloyds TSB Bank plc
Directors: I. Bickers (Dir), J. Broad (Sales), J. Alston (MD), A. Alston (Ch), Bickers (Fin), D. Alston (Dir)
Managers: I. Bickers (Accounts), D. Alston (Sales Prom Mgr)
Ultimate Holding Company: 00734913
Immediate Holding Company: ALSTONS (CABINETS) LIMITED
Registration no: 00347641 **Date established:** 1938
Turnover: £10m - £20m **No.of Employees:** 101 - 250 **Product Groups:** 26

Date of Accounts	Jun 09	Jun 08	Jun 07
Sales Turnover	11m	12m	14m
Pre Tax Profit/Loss	-2m	-2m	-378
Working Capital	2m	3m	4m
Fixed Assets	5m	6m	7m
Current Assets	4m	5m	5m
Current Liabilities	889	650	524

Andrews Reprographics Ltd

Khartoum House 361 Woodbridge Road, Ipswich, IP4 4ET
Tel: 01473-711345 **Fax:** 01473-723151
E-mail: info@andrewsbiz.co.uk
Website: http://www.andrewsbiz.co.uk
Directors: S. Banks (MD)
Immediate Holding Company: ANDREWS REPROGRAPHICS LIMITED
Registration no: 01488009 **Date established:** 1980
No.of Employees: 1 - 10 **Product Groups:** 48, 67

Date of Accounts	Dec 11	Dec 10	Dec 09
Working Capital	-24	-21	-30
Fixed Assets	2	2	3
Current Assets	18	33	17

Anglian Energy Services

109 Newton Road, Ipswich, IP3 8HQ
Tel: 01473-614446 **Fax:** 01473-620443
E-mail: marcus@anglianenergy.co.uk
Website: http://www.aessprinklers.co.uk
Directors: M. Horner (Snr Part), M. Hornor (Prop), M. Horner (Prop)
Immediate Holding Company: AES NATIONAL LIMITED
Date established: 2011 **Turnover:** £250m - £500m
No.of Employees: 11 - 20 **Product Groups:** 40, 52, 84

Anglian Nutrition Products Co.

Crockatt Road Lady Lane Industrial Estate, Hadleigh, Ipswich, IP7 6RD
Tel: 01473-822121 **Fax:** 01473-822156
E-mail: mail@anupco.com
Website: http://www.anupco.com
Bank(s): Lloyds TSB
Managers: L. Greenfield (Admin Off), D. Maher (Chief Mgr)
Immediate Holding Company: Castyne Ltd
Registration no: 02760721 **VAT No.:** 289 6970 78 **Date established:** 1992
Turnover: £2m - £5m **No.of Employees:** 11 - 20 **Product Groups:** 20, 31, 63

Anvil Tool Company

PO Box 259, Ipswich, IP1 6RH
Tel: 01473-431226 **Fax:** 01473-431228
E-mail: mail@anvil-trading.com
Website: http://www.anvil-trading.com
Managers: C. Green (Chief Mgr), C. Green (Sales Prom Mgr)
Date established: 2002 **Turnover:** Up to £250,000
No.of Employees: 1 - 10 **Product Groups:** 33, 66

Archant Suffolk

30 Lower Brook Street, Ipswich, IP4 1AN
Tel: 01473-230023 **Fax:** 01473-324776
E-mail: jane.berry@archant.co.uk
Website: http://www.archant.co.uk
Directors: P. Swallow (MD), M. Farahar (Fin), S. McCreery (MD)
No.of Employees: 101 - 250 **Product Groups:** 28

Aries Power Solutions Ltd

Oaklands Flordon Road Creeting St Mary, Ipswich, IP6 8NH
Tel: 01449-720842 **Fax:** 01449-722846
E-mail: info@ariesgen.co.uk
Website: http://www.generating-sets.co.uk
Managers: K. Denny (Mgr)
Ultimate Holding Company: STAINES AND GOLDING LIMITED
Immediate Holding Company: ARIES POWER SOLUTIONS LIMITED
Registration no: 05541786 **VAT No.:** GB 867 1602 13
Date established: 2005 **Turnover:** £5m - £10m **No.of Employees:** 11 - 20
Product Groups: 37, 38, 39, 40, 48, 52, 67, 83

Date of Accounts	Sep 11	Sep 10	Sep 09
Working Capital	112	118	293
Fixed Assets	50	46	48
Current Assets	879	726	791

Ashe Converting Equipment Ltd

Bluestem Road Ransomes Industrial Estate, Ipswich, IP3 9RR
Tel: 01473-710912 **Fax:** 01473-719137
E-mail: sales@ashe.co.uk
Website: http://www.ashe.co.uk
Bank(s): Lloyds TSB Bank plc
Directors: J. Godbold (MD)
Managers: W. Daniels, K. Fordham (Chief Eng), C. Bunyan (Purch Mgr), M. Godbold
Immediate Holding Company: ASHE CONTROLS LIMITED
Registration no: 01154966 **VAT No.:** GB 285 3092 46
Date established: 1974 **Turnover:** £5m - £10m
No.of Employees: 51 - 100 **Product Groups:** 43, 44

Date of Accounts	Sep 11	Sep 10	Sep 09
Sales Turnover	6m	N/A	N/A
Pre Tax Profit/Loss	172	N/A	N/A
Working Capital	849	693	700
Fixed Assets	659	687	564
Current Assets	4m	3m	2m
Current Liabilities	2m	N/A	N/A

Associated British Ports

Old Custom House Common Quay Key Street, Ipswich, IP4 1BY
Tel: 01473-231010 **Fax:** 01473-230914
E-mail: ipswich@abports.co.uk
Website: http://www.abports.co.uk
Bank(s): National Westminster Bank Plc
Managers: A. Macfarlane
Ultimate Holding Company: ABP (JERSEY) LIMITED
Immediate Holding Company: ASSOCIATED BRITISH PORTS HOLDINGS LIMITED
Registration no: 01612178 **Date established:** 1982
Turnover: £10m - £20m **No.of Employees:** 101 - 250
Product Groups: 71, 74, 77

Date of Accounts	Dec 11	Dec 09	Dec 08
Sales Turnover	423m	402m	424m
Pre Tax Profit/Loss	307m	192m	204m
Working Capital	212m	410m	263m
Fixed Assets	1716m	1668m	1761m
Current Assets	294m	503m	337m
Current Liabilities	68m	79m	57m

Auremac

7 Bucklesham Road Kirton, Ipswich, IP10 0NX
Tel: 01394-448134 **Fax:** 01394-448518
E-mail: sales@auremac.com
Website: http://www.auremac.com
Directors: K. Mcgrane (Prop)
No.of Employees: 1 - 10 **Product Groups:** 37, 84

Axter Ltd

Unit 3 West Road Ransomes Europark, Ipswich, IP3 9SX
Tel: 01473-724056 **Fax:** 01473-232118
E-mail: info@axterltd.co.uk
Website: http://www.axter.co.uk
Bank(s): National Westminster Bank Plc
Directors: P. Wilcox Moore (MD)
Immediate Holding Company: AXTER LIMITED
Registration no: 01446923 **Date established:** 1979 **Turnover:** £2m - £5m
No.of Employees: 11 - 20 **Product Groups:** 30, 31, 32, 35

Date of Accounts	Dec 11	Dec 10	Dec 09
Working Capital	222	210	180
Fixed Assets	24	25	39
Current Assets	1m	1m	1m

B D K Industrial Products Ltd (Adhesive Technology Specialists)

Levington Park Bridge Road, Levington, Ipswich, IP10 0JE
Tel: 01473-659059 **Fax:** 01473-659104
E-mail: sales@bdk.uk.com
Website: http://www.bdk.uk.com
Directors: N. Falconer (MD)
Immediate Holding Company: B. D. K. INDUSTRIAL PRODUCTS LIMITED
Registration no: 00621647 **Date established:** 1959 **Turnover:** £5m - £10m
No.of Employees: 51 - 100 **Product Groups:** 23, 27, 28, 29, 30, 31, 32, 33, 34, 35, 37, 38, 39, 40, 42, 44, 48, 49, 64, 65, 66, 67, 68, 80

Date of Accounts	Jul 11	Jul 10	Jul 09
Working Capital	1m	1m	1m
Fixed Assets	753	659	707
Current Assets	3m	2m	2m

B S P International Foundations Ltd
Claydon Industrial Park Gipping Road, Claydon, Ipswich, IP6 0BZ
Tel: 01473-830431 **Fax:** 01473-832019
E-mail: jwakeling@bspif.co.uk
Website: http://www.bsp-if.com
Bank(s): National Westminster Bank Plc
Managers: J. Wakeling, R. Maidstone (Purch Mgr), R. Melton (Sales Prom Mgr)
Ultimate Holding Company: TEX HOLDINGS PLC
Immediate Holding Company: BSP INTERNATIONAL FOUNDATIONS LIMITED
Registration no: 00194713 **VAT No.:** GB 434 7275 43
Date established: 2023 **Turnover:** £5m - £10m **No.of Employees:** 21 - 50
Product Groups: 40, 45, 46, 54

Date of Accounts	Dec 11	Dec 10	Dec 09
Sales Turnover	7m	4m	6m
Pre Tax Profit/Loss	615	74	219
Working Capital	2m	2m	1m
Fixed Assets	153	144	190
Current Assets	3m	2m	3m
Current Liabilities	544	262	958

Barnes Group Ltd
6 Bermuda Road Ransoms Euro Park, Ransomes Industrial Estate, Ipswich, IP3 9RU
Tel: 01473-272222 **Fax:** 01473-272955
E-mail: nfayers@barnesconstruction.co.uk
Website: http://www.barnesgroup.co.uk
Bank(s): Lloyds TSB Bank plc
Directors: N. Fayers (Prop), N. Fayres (MD), N. Fayers (MD), W. Barnes (Ch)
Managers: R. Baddeley (I.T. Exec), S. Tutton (Sales Admin), C. Bruce (Mktg Serv Mgr)
Immediate Holding Company: THE BARNES GROUP LIMITED
Registration no: 01359667 **VAT No.:** GB 299 8992 51
Date established: 1978 **Turnover:** £20m - £50m
No.of Employees: 51 - 100 **Product Groups:** 48, 51, 52, 80, 84

Date of Accounts	Sep 11	Sep 10	Sep 09
Sales Turnover	54m	47m	41m
Pre Tax Profit/Loss	998	525	836
Working Capital	1m	2m	1m
Fixed Assets	3m	2m	2m
Current Assets	15m	16m	12m
Current Liabilities	6m	6m	4m

Biffa Waste Services
Paper Mill Lane Bramford, Ipswich, IP8 4DE
Tel: 01473-830564 **Fax:** 01473-832169
E-mail: richard.hill@biffa.co.uk
Website: http://www.biffa.co.uk
Managers: R. Hill (District Mgr)
Registration no: 00099057 **No.of Employees:** 1 - 10 **Product Groups:** 54, 72, 83

Bitmen Products Ltd
Unit 35 Claydon Business Park Great Blakenham, Ipswich, IP6 0NL
Tel: 01473-830030 **Fax:** 01954-231512
E-mail: dave@bitmen.co.uk
Website: http://www.tex-engineering.co.uk
Bank(s): National Westminster Bank PLC
Directors: A. Ogden (Fin), C. Parker (Fin), D. Ogden (Dir)
Immediate Holding Company: HOSS (HUGHES OIL SPILL SERVICES) LIMITED
Registration no: 02575929 **Date established:** 2003
Turnover: £250,000 - £500,000 **No.of Employees:** 11 - 20
Product Groups: 23, 35, 40, 45, 66, 67

Date of Accounts	Mar 11
Working Capital	-19
Fixed Assets	2
Current Assets	11

Boardley & Roberts Ltd
Plummers Dell Gipping Road, Great Blakenham, Ipswich, IP6 0JG
Tel: 01473-830272 **Fax:** 01473-830274
E-mail: sales@boardley-roberts.co.uk
Website: http://www.boardley-roberts.co.uk
Bank(s): Lloyds TSB Bank plc
Directors: R. Boardley (MD)
Immediate Holding Company: BOARDLEY AND ROBERTS LIMITED
Registration no: 01234517 **VAT No.:** GB 285 3739 22
Date established: 1975 **Turnover:** £1m - £2m **No.of Employees:** 11 - 20
Product Groups: 48

Date of Accounts	Dec 11	Dec 10	Dec 09
Working Capital	221	183	107
Fixed Assets	215	194	211
Current Assets	595	501	429

Bolton Aerospace Ltd
PO Box 22, Ipswich, IP2 0EG
Tel: 01473-252127 **Fax:** 01473-218229
E-mail: gyoung@boltonmetals.com
Website: http://www.boltonmetals.com
Bank(s): National Westminster
Directors: G. Young (Dir), N. Bridges (Co Sec)
Managers: G. Stokes (Buyer)
Ultimate Holding Company: BOLTON METALS INC (BAHAMAS)
Immediate Holding Company: BOLTON AEROSPACE LTD.
Registration no: 05832146 **VAT No.:** GB 340 1992 70
Date established: 2006 **Turnover:** £10m - £20m
No.of Employees: 101 - 250 **Product Groups:** 34, 48

Date of Accounts	Dec 11	Dec 10	Apr 10
Sales Turnover	24m	13m	14m
Pre Tax Profit/Loss	2m	474	-256
Working Capital	3m	2m	2m
Fixed Assets	2m	2m	2m
Current Assets	11m	9m	7m
Current Liabilities	1m	320	172

J L Bragg Ipswich Ltd
34 Boss Hall Road, Ipswich, IP1 5BN
Tel: 01473-748345 **Fax:** 01473-749889
E-mail: bragg@charcoal.uk.com
Website: http://www.charcoal.uk.com
Directors: J. Briggs (Co Sec), V. Briggs (Dir)
Immediate Holding Company: J.L.BRAGG (IPSWICH) LIMITED
Registration no: 01029805 **Date established:** 1971
Turnover: Up to £250,000 **No.of Employees:** 1 - 10 **Product Groups:** 20, 31

Date of Accounts	May 11	May 10	May 09
Working Capital	43	42	42
Fixed Assets	46	37	33
Current Assets	106	107	86

Brunswick Electrical Services Ltd
173 Brunswick Road, Ipswich, IP4 4DB
Tel: 01473-728352
E-mail: info@bre-services.com
Website: http://www.bre-services.com
Directors: S. Pasley (MD)
Immediate Holding Company: BRUNSWICK ELECTRICAL SERVICES LIMITED
Registration no: 07100422 **Date established:** 2009
No.of Employees: 1 - 10 **Product Groups:** 37, 84, 85

Date of Accounts	Dec 11	Dec 10
Working Capital	4	-2
Fixed Assets	6	8
Current Assets	33	33

C K Chemicals
Unit 16 Lady Lane Industrial Estate Hadleigh, Ipswich, IP7 6BQ
Tel: 01473-822836 **Fax:** 01473-824044
E-mail: sales@ckchemicals.co.uk
Website: http://www.ckchemicals.co.uk
Managers: S. Byford (Chief Mgr)
Immediate Holding Company: C.K. CHEMICALS LTD.
Registration no: 02157681 **Date established:** 1987
Turnover: £500,000 - £1m **No.of Employees:** 1 - 10 **Product Groups:** 32

Date of Accounts	Apr 12	Apr 11	Apr 10
Working Capital	455	453	300
Fixed Assets	222	207	172
Current Assets	686	687	447

Cash Register Supply Co.
94-96 Rushmere Road, Ipswich, IP4 4JY
Tel: 01473-723515 **Fax:** 01473-405631
E-mail: sales@crs-ipswich.co.uk
Website: http://www.crs-ipswich.co.uk
Directors: R. Randall (Ptnr)
Date established: 1975 **Turnover:** £250,000 - £500,000
No.of Employees: 1 - 10 **Product Groups:** 40, 44, 67

Celotex Ltd
Lady Lane Industrial Estate Hadleigh, Ipswich, IP7 6BA
Tel: 01473-822093 **Fax:** 01473-822093
E-mail: info@celotex.co.uk
Website: http://www.celotex.co.uk
Bank(s): Lloyds TSB Bank plc
Directors: C. King (Mkt Research), M. Goddard (Fin), P. Reid (Sales), R. Crisp (Mkt Research)
Managers: G. Wymer (Tech Serv Mgr), A. Penner (Personnel), B. Finlayson (Buyer)
Ultimate Holding Company: AAC CAPITAL PARTNERS HOLDING BV (NETHERLANDS)
Immediate Holding Company: CELOTEX LIMITED
Registration no: 02183896 **Date established:** 1987
Turnover: £50m - £75m **No.of Employees:** 101 - 250
Product Groups: 30, 33

Date of Accounts	Aug 11	Aug 10	Aug 09
Sales Turnover	70m	57m	55m
Pre Tax Profit/Loss	3m	1m	4m
Working Capital	20m	15m	14m
Fixed Assets	10m	10m	11m
Current Assets	29m	23m	20m
Current Liabilities	2m	1m	2m

Richard Ching & Son Ltd
34 Lady Lane Industrial Estate Hadleigh, Ipswich, IP7 6BQ
Tel: 01473-823484 **Fax:** 01473-827252
E-mail: sales@ching.co.uk
Website: http://www.ching.co.uk
Bank(s): Barclays, Sudbury
Directors: S. Harrington (MD)
Immediate Holding Company: RICHARD CHING AND SON LIMITED
Registration no: 00334826 **VAT No.:** GB 102 0125 57
Date established: 1937 **Turnover:** £500,000 - £1m
No.of Employees: 11 - 20 **Product Groups:** 23, 28, 48, 49

Date of Accounts	Sep 11	Sep 10	Sep 09
Working Capital	222	215	233
Fixed Assets	149	157	165
Current Assets	317	300	306

Conway Real Wood Ltd
1 Beardmore Park Martlesham Heath, Ipswich, IP5 3RX
Tel: 01473-610878 **Fax:** 01473-621537
Website: http://www.conwaypine.com
Managers: H. Rush (Mgr)
Ultimate Holding Company: CONWAY PINE HOLDINGS LIMITED
Immediate Holding Company: CONWAY PINE LIMITED
Registration no: 02286703 **Date established:** 1988 **Turnover:** £5m - £10m
No.of Employees: 1 - 10 **Product Groups:** 26, 37

Date of Accounts	Mar 11	Mar 10	Mar 09
Sales Turnover	N/A	N/A	6m
Pre Tax Profit/Loss	N/A	N/A	-320
Working Capital	-60	346	969
Fixed Assets	118	129	159
Current Assets	799	1m	1m
Current Liabilities	N/A	N/A	275

Cookson & Zinn PTL Ltd
Station Road Works Station Road, Hadleigh, Ipswich, IP7 5PN
Tel: 01473-825200 **Fax:** 01473-828446
E-mail: andrew.golding@czltd.com
Website: http://www.czltd.com
Bank(s): HSBC Bank plc
Directors: G. Lee (MD), A. Golding (Fin)
Managers: C. Smith (Quality Control), J. Seaman
Ultimate Holding Company: FRANKLIN FUELING SYSTEMS LIMITED
Immediate Holding Company: COOKSON AND ZINN (PTL) LIMITED
Registration no: 03879913 **VAT No.:** GB 344 5521 65
Date established: 1999 **Turnover:** £2m - £5m **No.of Employees:** 21 - 50
Product Groups: 35, 37, 41, 45

Date of Accounts	Dec 11	Dec 10	Mar 09
Sales Turnover	7m	4m	N/A
Pre Tax Profit/Loss	-52	-251	162
Working Capital	295	316	235
Fixed Assets	356	362	420
Current Assets	2m	2m	2m
Current Liabilities	424	408	496

Cory Brothers Shipping Agency Ltd
60 Landseer Road, Ipswich, IP3 0BG
Tel: 01473-217979 **Fax:** 01473-219456
E-mail: mark.hexley@cory.co.uk
Website: http://www.cory.co.uk
Managers: M. Hexley (Mgr)
Ultimate Holding Company: BRAEMAR SHIPPING SERVICES PLC
Immediate Holding Company: CORY BROTHERS SHIPPING AGENCY LIMITED
Registration no: 04717201 **VAT No.:** GB 244 0497 69
Date established: 2003 **No.of Employees:** 1 - 10 **Product Groups:** 39

Date of Accounts	Feb 12	Feb 12	Feb 11
Sales Turnover	30m	30m	28m
Pre Tax Profit/Loss	2m	2m	949
Working Capital	-2m	-2m	-2m
Fixed Assets	5m	5m	6m
Current Assets	12m	12m	13m
Current Liabilities	3m	3m	3m

Cosmic Automotives
Duke Street, Ipswich, IP3 0AF
Tel: 07906-967262 **Fax:** 01473-226263
Website: http://www.kingavon.co.uk
Bank(s): HSBC Bank plc
Directors: T. Munro (MD), N. Rowles (Sales)
Managers: A. Rumbell (Sales Prom Mgr), N. Sherman (Purch Mgr), S. Barrow (Mktg Serv Mgr)
Immediate Holding Company: HEMSCOTT P.L.C.
Registration no: 01325578 **VAT No.:** GB 751 0206 77
Date established: 2005 **Turnover:** £5m - £10m **No.of Employees:** 21 - 50
Product Groups: 39, 68

Crane Business Services & Utilities Ltd (Divisional Head Office)
Crane House Epsilon Terrace West Road, Ipswich, IP3 9FJ
Tel: 01473-277300 **Fax:** 01473-270301
E-mail: enquiries@crane-ltd.co.uk
Website: http://www.cranefs.com
Bank(s): National Westminster Bank Plc
Directors: P. Richardson (Dir), L. Collen (Pers), D. Pye (Sales), P. Cansdale (Fin)
Managers: S. Shand-brown (Mktg Serv Mgr), J. Lumsden
Ultimate Holding Company: CRANE CO. (USA)
Immediate Holding Company: CRANE LIMITED
Registration no: 00098677 **Date established:** 2008
Turnover: £75m - £125m **No.of Employees:** 51 - 100
Product Groups: 36, 38

Date of Accounts	Dec 11	Dec 10	Dec 09
Sales Turnover	106m	106m	106m
Pre Tax Profit/Loss	13m	15m	41m
Working Capital	49m	38m	33m
Fixed Assets	63m	65m	64m
Current Assets	76m	69m	65m
Current Liabilities	13m	18m	19m

Creative Cosmetics Ltd
7 Riverside Industrial Park Rapier Street, Ipswich, IP2 8JX
Tel: 01473-685599 **Fax:** 01473-680727
E-mail: enquiries@creativecosmetics.com
Website: http://www.creativecosmetics.com
Bank(s): HSBC Bank plc
Directors: A. Major (MD)
Immediate Holding Company: CREATIVE COSMETICS LIMITED
Registration no: 02150738 **VAT No.:** GB 460 4505 70
Date established: 1987 **Turnover:** £2m - £5m **No.of Employees:** 11 - 20
Product Groups: 31, 32

Date of Accounts	Dec 11	Dec 10	Dec 09
Working Capital	310	256	241
Fixed Assets	258	270	285
Current Assets	451	489	355

D G Design & Graphics
11 Industrial Centre Gower Street, Ipswich, IP2 8EX
Tel: 01473-681077 **Fax:** 01473-690604
E-mail: dgdesigngraphics@aol.com
Website: http://www.dgdesign-graphics.co.uk
Directors: D. Goodchild (Prop)
Date established: 1991 **Turnover:** Up to £250,000
No.of Employees: 1 - 10 **Product Groups:** 28, 30, 49, 65, 67, 68, 80, 81

Decco Ltd
Chapel Lane Great Blakenham, Ipswich, IP6 0JW
Tel: 01473-830601 **Fax:** 01473-832023
E-mail: andy.birrell@decco.co.uk
Website: http://www.decco.co.uk
Directors: A. Birrell (MD)
Managers: J. Dodson (Asst Gen Mgr)
Ultimate Holding Company: NEWBURY INVESTMENTS BV (NETHERLANDS)
Immediate Holding Company: DECCO LIMITED
Registration no: 00417021 **Date established:** 1946
No.of Employees: 21 - 50 **Product Groups:** 35, 36

Date of Accounts	Dec 11	Dec 10	Dec 09
Sales Turnover	94m	90m	88m
Pre Tax Profit/Loss	-485	5m	4m
Working Capital	21m	17m	14m
Fixed Assets	1m	3m	2m
Current Assets	34m	32m	30m
Current Liabilities	4m	5m	4m

Diversified Optical Ltd
116 Bucklesham Road, Ipswich, IP3 8TU
Tel: 01473-273737 **Fax:** 01473-272227
E-mail: plwright@compuserve.com
Website: http://www.diop.com
Directors: L. Kessler (Dir), L. Fantozzi (Dir), P. Wright (Dir)
Ultimate Holding Company: Diversified Optical Product Inc
Registration no: 01760639 **VAT No.:** 390 5460 48 **Date established:** 1983
Turnover: £250,000 - £500,000 **No.of Employees:** 1 - 10
Product Groups: 38

Douglas Hosking Furniture
Springbank Farm Monument Farm Lane, Foxhall, Ipswich, IP10 0AQ
Tel: 01473-631644 **Fax:** 01473-631655
E-mail: sales@douglashosking.com
Website: http://www.douglashosking.com
Directors: D. Hosking (Prop)
Immediate Holding Company: DOUGLAS HOSKING PROPERTIES LIMITED

Registration no: 03635325 **VAT No.:** GB 299 9993 44
Date established: 2002 **Turnover:** Up to £250,000
No.of Employees: 1 - 10 **Product Groups:** 26

Doves Clothing Co

4 Castle Meadows Offton, Ipswich, IP8 4RQ
Tel: 01473-658702
No.of Employees: 1 - 10 **Product Groups:** 24, 28, 84

Dowding & Mills Engineering Services Ltd

10 Blue Stem Road Ransomes Industrial Estate, Ipswich, IP3 9RR
Tel: 01473-717071 **Fax:** 01473-717075
E-mail: vince.clarke@dowdingandmills.com
Website: http://www.dowdingandmills.com
Managers: V. Clarke (District Mgr)
Immediate Holding Company: ASHE CONTROLS LIMITED
Registration no: SC028056 **Date established:** 1974
No.of Employees: 21 - 50 **Product Groups:** 37, 44, 45, 48, 84, 85

Date of Accounts	Sep 11	Sep 10	Sep 09
Sales Turnover	6m	N/A	N/A
Pre Tax Profit/Loss	172	N/A	N/A
Working Capital	849	693	700
Fixed Assets	659	687	564
Current Assets	4m	3m	2m
Current Liabilities	2m	N/A	N/A

Dynawest Plastics Ltd

Jaylyn House Elton Park Hadleigh Road, Ipswich, IP2 0DG
Tel: 01473-230248 **Fax:** 01473-230256
E-mail: rbj-ross@dynawest.co.uk
Website: http://www.dynawest.co.uk
Directors: A. Beckett (Fin), R. Ross (MD)
Immediate Holding Company: DYNAWEST LIMITED
Registration no: 01513481 **Date established:** 1980
No.of Employees: 1 - 10 **Product Groups:** 23, 25, 30, 45

Date of Accounts	Mar 12	Mar 11	Mar 10
Working Capital	430	413	328
Fixed Assets	15	17	15
Current Assets	950	694	559

E Rand & Sons

Chapel Lane Great Blakenham, Ipswich, IP6 0JY
Tel: 01473-832833 **Fax:** 01473-832834
E-mail: sales@rand.uk.com
Website: http://www.rand.uk.com
Bank(s): Midland
Directors: J. Clarke (Sales), S. Sim (MD), S. Sims (MD)
Ultimate Holding Company: E. RAND & SONS (HOLDINGS) LIMITED
Immediate Holding Company: E. RAND & SONS (HOLDINGS) LIMITED
Registration no: 00333973 **VAT No.:** GB 344 5643 51
Date established: 1937 **Turnover:** Up to £250,000
No.of Employees: 21 - 50 **Product Groups:** 37, 39, 40

Date of Accounts	Jan 12	Jan 11	Jan 10
Pre Tax Profit/Loss	N/A	2	19
Working Capital	61	43	39
Fixed Assets	344	345	346
Current Assets	70	52	48
Current Liabilities	N/A	8	9

Eastern Structures Ltd

Cliff Road Dock Estate, Ipswich, IP3 0AX
Tel: 01473-215888 **Fax:** 01473-288589
E-mail: info@easternstructures.co.uk
Website: http://www.easternstructures.co.uk
Directors: D. Pack (Dir)
Immediate Holding Company: EASTERN STRUCTURES LIMITED
Registration no: 05344609 **Date established:** 2005
No.of Employees: 1 - 10 **Product Groups:** 35

Date of Accounts	Mar 11	Mar 10	Mar 09
Working Capital	19	-19	-299
Fixed Assets	N/A	N/A	300
Current Assets	383	347	256

Edu-Fax Ltd

PO Box 94, Ipswich, IP7 9AH
Tel: 01473-652 822 **Fax:** 01473-652 822
E-mail: info@edu-fax.com
Website: http://www.edu-fax.com
Turnover: Up to £250,000 **No.of Employees:** 1 - 10 **Product Groups:** 28, 61, 86

H Erben Ltd

Lady Lane Hadleigh, Ipswich, IP7 6AS
Tel: 01473-823011 **Fax:** 01473-828252
E-mail: mail@erben.co.uk
Website: http://www.erben.co.uk
Bank(s): Bank of Scotland
Directors: J. Erben (Co Sec), S. Shand Brown (Dir)
Ultimate Holding Company: H. ERBEN HOLDINGS LIMITED
Immediate Holding Company: H.ERBEN LIMITED
Registration no: 00538781 **VAT No.:** GB 638 0114 62
Date established: 1954 **Turnover:** £20m - £50m
No.of Employees: 11 - 20 **Product Groups:** 21, 42, 48

Date of Accounts	Dec 11	Dec 10	Dec 09
Sales Turnover	25m	19m	N/A
Pre Tax Profit/Loss	428	408	N/A
Working Capital	915	586	590
Fixed Assets	1m	960	232
Current Assets	7m	5m	4m
Current Liabilities	897	769	N/A

Eversheds

Franciscan House 51 Princes Street, Ipswich, IP1 1UR
Tel: 01473-284428 **Fax:** 01473-233666
E-mail: lorrainegouch@eversheds.com
Website: http://www.eversheds.com
Managers: K. Smithers (Mgr)
Immediate Holding Company: EVERSHEDS LLP
Registration no: OC304065 **Date established:** 2003
No.of Employees: 51 - 100 **Product Groups:** 80

Factair Ltd

49 Boss Hall Road, Ipswich, IP1 5BN
Tel: 01473-746400 **Fax:** 01473-747123
E-mail: enquiries@factair.co.uk
Website: http://www.factair.co.uk
Bank(s): Bank of Scotland
Directors: C. Wakeman (MD)
Ultimate Holding Company: FACTAIR HOLDINGS LIMITED
Immediate Holding Company: FACTAIR LIMITED
Registration no: 01122611 **VAT No.:** GB 102 6321 27
Date established: 1973 **Turnover:** £2m - £5m **No.of Employees:** 21 - 50
Product Groups: 29, 31, 38, 40, 42, 45

Date of Accounts	Dec 11	Dec 10	Dec 09
Working Capital	2m	2m	2m
Fixed Assets	156	170	183
Current Assets	3m	3m	2m

Fork Rent plc

289-297 Felixstowe Road, Ipswich, IP3 9BS
Tel: 01473-727674 **Fax:** 01473-723862
E-mail: accounts@fork-rent.co.uk
Website: http://www.4ajcb.com
Directors: T. Nicholls (Fin), G. Nicholls (Dir)
Immediate Holding Company: FORK RENT PLC
Registration no: 01403858 **Date established:** 1978
Turnover: £10m - £20m **No.of Employees:** 51 - 100 **Product Groups:** 45, 83

Date of Accounts	Mar 12	Mar 11	Mar 10
Sales Turnover	15m	11m	8m
Pre Tax Profit/Loss	4m	2m	1m
Working Capital	-10m	-7m	-5m
Fixed Assets	40m	28m	19m
Current Assets	6m	3m	2m
Current Liabilities	2m	197	401

Fox's Stainless

Foxs Marina The Strand, Wherstead, Ipswich, IP2 8NJ
Tel: 01473-689111 **Fax:** 01473-601737
E-mail: foxs@foxsmarina.com
Website: http://www.foxsmarina.com
Directors: A. Ramm (Co Sec), G. Rowbothan (MD), M. Westmoreland (MD), R. Catchpole (Dir), R. Matthews (Ch), R. Catchtole (MD)
Managers: N. Gratton (Comm), R. Wheatley (I.T. Exec), R. Catchpole, S. Addy (Purch Mgr)
Ultimate Holding Company: FOX'S HOLDINGS LIMITED
Immediate Holding Company: FOX'S MARINA IPSWICH LIMITED
Registration no: 01883642 **VAT No.:** GB 407 0148 88
Date established: 1985 **Turnover:** £2m - £5m **No.of Employees:** 51 - 100
Product Groups: 39

Date of Accounts	Dec 09	Dec 08	Dec 07
Sales Turnover	N/A	N/A	5m
Pre Tax Profit/Loss	N/A	N/A	-28
Working Capital	641	727	312
Fixed Assets	553	558	543
Current Assets	2m	2m	2m
Current Liabilities	N/A	N/A	1m

Franklin Fueling Systems

Olympus Close, Ipswich, IP1 5LN
Tel: 01473-243300 **Fax:** 01473-243301
E-mail: sdewild@upp.co.uk
Website: http://www.upp.co.uk
Directors: A. Golding (Dir), J. Boundry (Co Sec)
Managers: C. McFee (Mktg Serv Mgr), G. Owens
Immediate Holding Company: FRANKLIN FUELING SYSTEMS LIMITED
Registration no: 02631843 **Date established:** 1991
Turnover: £10m - £20m **No.of Employees:** 11 - 20 **Product Groups:** 31, 84

Date of Accounts	Dec 11	Dec 10	Mar 10
Sales Turnover	14m	11m	25m
Pre Tax Profit/Loss	2m	-716	898
Working Capital	2m	2m	2m
Fixed Assets	2m	2m	3m
Current Assets	5m	5m	8m
Current Liabilities	2m	1m	2m

G & M Power Plant Ltd

31 Anson Road Martlesham Heath, Ipswich, IP5 3RG
Tel: 01473-662777 **Fax:** 01473-662785
E-mail: gandm@gmpp.co.uk
Website: http://www.gmpp.co.uk
Bank(s): National Westminster Bank Plc
Directors: R. Pollard (MD)
Managers: G. Chadwick (Sales Prom Mgr)
Immediate Holding Company: G & M POWER PLANT LIMITED
Registration no: 04094653 **VAT No.:** GB 861 3793 06
Date established: 2000 **Turnover:** £5m - £10m **No.of Employees:** 21 - 50
Product Groups: 37, 48, 52, 67, 84

Date of Accounts	Mar 12	Mar 11	Mar 10
Sales Turnover	7m	4m	6m
Pre Tax Profit/Loss	229	-182	114
Working Capital	254	17	-24
Fixed Assets	199	232	260
Current Assets	2m	850	2m
Current Liabilities	882	343	371

Gas Fired Products UK Ltd Space Ray

4-6 Chapel Lane Claydon, Ipswich, IP6 0JL
Tel: 01473-830551 **Fax:** 01473-832055
E-mail: info@spaceray.co.uk
Website: http://www.spaceray.co.uk
Ultimate Holding Company: GAS FIRED PRODUCTS INC (USA)
Registration no: 00812608 **Date established:** 1964
No.of Employees: 11 - 20 **Product Groups:** 46

Genesis P R Ltd

The Coach House Ipswich Road, Holbrook, Ipswich, IP9 2QR
Tel: 01473-326400 **Fax:** 01473-326409
E-mail: info@genesispr.co.uk
Website: http://www.genesispr.co.uk
Directors: C. Arbuthnot (MD)
Immediate Holding Company: GENESIS PR LTD.
Registration no: 05090589 **Date established:** 2004
Turnover: Up to £250,000 **No.of Employees:** 1 - 10 **Product Groups:** 80, 81

Date of Accounts	Mar 11	Mar 10	Mar 09
Working Capital	27	49	54
Fixed Assets	21	31	4
Current Assets	86	124	117

Genevac Ltd

6 Farthing Road, Ipswich, IP1 5AP
Tel: 01473-240000 **Fax:** 01473-461176
E-mail: info@genevac.com
Website: http://www.genevac.com
Bank(s): Lloyds TSB Bank plc
Directors: C. Grant (Dir)
Managers: E. Rosebridge (Comptroller), R. Darrington (Sales & Mktg Mg), J. Bland (Prod Mgr)
Ultimate Holding Company: SP LAB EQUIPMENT LLC (UNITED STATES OF AMERICA)
Immediate Holding Company: GENEVAC LIMITED
Registration no: 02456835 **VAT No.:** GB 571 0225 75
Date established: 1990 **Turnover:** £5m - £10m
No.of Employees: 51 - 100 **Product Groups:** 42

Date of Accounts	Mar 11	Mar 10	Mar 09
Sales Turnover	8m	8m	7m
Pre Tax Profit/Loss	2m	2m	1m
Working Capital	14m	14m	14m
Fixed Assets	150	182	44
Current Assets	16m	16m	17m
Current Liabilities	912	1m	1m

Geoquip Water Soloutions

7 The Sovereign Centre Farthing Road, Ipswich, IP1 5AP
Tel: 01473-463546 **Fax:** 01473-462146
E-mail: info@geoquipservices.co.uk
Website: http://www.geoquipwatersolutions.com
Directors: M. Deed (Dir)
Ultimate Holding Company: GQS HOLDINGS LTD
Immediate Holding Company: SOVEREIGN PUMPS INTERNATIONAL LIMITED
Registration no: 03304502 **Date established:** 1997
No.of Employees: 1 - 10 **Product Groups:** 40

Date of Accounts	Mar 11	Mar 10	Mar 07
Working Capital	121	156	156
Current Assets	121	156	156

Gill Insulation Eastern Ltd

39 Boss Hall Road, Ipswich, IP1 5BN
Tel: 01473-462822 **Fax:** 01473-241153
E-mail: jon@gilleastern.co.uk
Directors: J. Wright (Dir)
Ultimate Holding Company: WOLSELEY PLC (JERSEY)
Immediate Holding Company: GILL INSULATION EASTERN LIMITED
Registration no: 01985419 **VAT No.:** GB 567 8001 28
Date established: 1986 **Turnover:** £1m - £2m **No.of Employees:** 1 - 10
Product Groups: 52, 84

Date of Accounts	Jul 11	Jul 10	Jul 09
Sales Turnover	2m	2m	2m
Pre Tax Profit/Loss	153	167	235
Working Capital	1m	1m	933
Fixed Assets	6	N/A	N/A
Current Assets	2m	2m	2m
Current Liabilities	196	310	232

Global Hangers Ltd

2 Latimer Cottage Holbrook, Ipswich, IP9 2PL
Tel: 01473-780999 **Fax:** 01473-780990
E-mail: sales@globalhangers.com
Website: http://www.globalhangers.com
Directors: J. Marriott (Dir), J. Marriott (MD)
Immediate Holding Company: GLOBAL HANGERS LIMITED
Registration no: 03914978 **Date established:** 2000
No.of Employees: 1 - 10 **Product Groups:** 38, 42

Golden Triangle Properties

6 Stone Street Court, Stone Street, Hadleigh, Ipswich, IP7 6DN
Tel: 01473-810249 **Fax:** 01787-269791
E-mail: info@goldentriangleproperties.com
Website: http://www.goldentriangleproperties.com
Directors: R. Brand (Dir), E. Wheeler Brand (Fin)
Registration no: 05741373 **Date established:** 2006
No.of Employees: 1 - 10 **Product Groups:** 61

Date of Accounts	Mar 10	Mar 09	Mar 08
Working Capital	13	2	8
Fixed Assets	8	3	N/A
Current Assets	61	73	58

Grain Terminal Ipswich Ltd

Powell Duffryn House Cliff Quay, Ipswich, IP3 0BG
Tel: 01473-250461 **Fax:** 01473-233212
Website: http://www.ipswichgrainterminal.com
Bank(s): Lloyds TSB Bank plc
Directors: P. Simmonds (Dir)
Ultimate Holding Company: NIDERA HANDELSCOMPAGNIE BV (NETHERLANDS)
Immediate Holding Company: GRAIN TERMINAL (IPSWICH) LIMITED(THE)
Registration no: 00297744 **VAT No.:** GB 368 4067 28
Date established: 1935 **Turnover:** £2m - £5m **No.of Employees:** 11 - 20
Product Groups: 62

Date of Accounts	Sep 11	Sep 10	Sep 09
Sales Turnover	3m	3m	2m
Pre Tax Profit/Loss	349	83	-231
Working Capital	44	155	-31
Fixed Assets	347	476	628
Current Assets	640	732	202
Current Liabilities	324	271	174

Green Carrier PTS Ltd

10 Cliff Road, Ipswich, IP3 0AY
Tel: 01473-282600 **Fax:** 01473-287521
E-mail: sales@greencarrier-pts.co.uk
Website: http://www.greencarrier-pts.co.uk
Bank(s): Lloyds TSB Bank plc
Directors: D. Waugh (Sales)
Managers: C. Cook
Ultimate Holding Company: GREENCARRIER PTS LIMITED
Immediate Holding Company: GREENCARRIER PTS LIMITED
Registration no: 01488473 **VAT No.:** GB 344 4287 52
Date established: 1980 **Turnover:** £5m - £10m **No.of Employees:** 21 - 50
Product Groups: 72

Date of Accounts	Mar 12	Mar 11	Mar 10
Working Capital	925	614	530
Fixed Assets	304	452	527
Current Assets	2m	2m	1m

Guardian Energy Ltd

Knatton Mews 10 Turret Lane, Ipswich, IP4 1DL
Tel: 01473-217400 **Fax:** 01473-298502
E-mail: contactus@guardianenergy.co.uk
Website: http://www.guardianenergy.co.uk

see next page

Guardian Energy Ltd - *Cont'd*

Directors: E. Cumberland (MD)
Ultimate Holding Company: GUARDIAN ENERGY HOLDINGS LIMITED
Immediate Holding Company: GUARDIAN ENERGY LIMITED
Registration no: 04824075 **Date established:** 2003
No.of Employees: 1 - 10 **Product Groups:** 54

Date of Accounts	Mar 11	Mar 10	Mar 09
Working Capital	10	9	10
Fixed Assets	N/A	1	N/A
Current Assets	31	29	23

H T G Trading Ltd

Hillview Church Road, Otley, Ipswich, IP6 9NP
Tel: 01473-890522 **Fax:** 01473-890758
E-mail: malcolm.paxman@hubbard.co.uk
Website: http://www.hubbard.co.uk
Directors: M. Paxman (Dir)
Ultimate Holding Company: SAINTS CAPITAL CHAMONIX LP (USA)
Immediate Holding Company: HTG TRADING LIMITED
Registration no: 01828642 **VAT No.:** GB 103 2015 48
Date established: 1984 **Turnover:** £10m - £20m
No.of Employees: 51 - 100 **Product Groups:** 40, 42

Date of Accounts	Dec 11	Dec 10	Dec 09
Sales Turnover	10m	11m	9m
Pre Tax Profit/Loss	768	870	339
Working Capital	5m	5m	4m
Fixed Assets	7	19	32
Current Assets	9m	8m	7m
Current Liabilities	865	635	734

Hadleigh Castings Ltd

Pond Hall Road Hadleigh, Ipswich, IP7 5PW
Tel: 01473-827281 **Fax:** 01473-827879
E-mail: info@hadleighcastings.com
Website: http://www.hadleighcastings.com
Directors: D. Hart (Fin), N. Morsman (Tech Sales), C. Warnes (MD)
Managers: C. Lock, T. Garrity (Tech Serv Mgr)
Immediate Holding Company: HADLEIGH CASTINGS LIMITED
Registration no: 00965267 **VAT No.:** GB 570 5532 47
Date established: 1969 **Turnover:** £5m - £10m
No.of Employees: 101 - 250 **Product Groups:** 34

Date of Accounts	Dec 11	Dec 10	Dec 09
Sales Turnover	7m	6m	5m
Pre Tax Profit/Loss	304	279	159
Working Capital	903	701	488
Fixed Assets	2m	2m	2m
Current Assets	2m	2m	1m
Current Liabilities	567	352	390

Hodgson & Hodgson Acoustic Consultancy Devision

Aldham House Lady Lane Industrial Estate, Hadleigh, Ipswich, IP7 6BQ
Tel: 01473-824452 **Fax:** 01473-824408
E-mail: adc@acoustic.co.uk
Website: http://www.acoustic.co.uk
Directors: N. Grundy (Dir)
Immediate Holding Company: W J GREEN LIMITED
Registration no: 01618335 **Date established:** 2001
Turnover: £500,000 - £1m **No.of Employees:** 1 - 10 **Product Groups:** 52, 54

Date of Accounts	Oct 11	Oct 10	Oct 09
Working Capital	55	31	18
Fixed Assets	58	45	50
Current Assets	299	276	256

Impact Fork Trucks Ltd

Unit 105 Claydon Business Park Great Blakenham, Ipswich, IP6 0NL
Tel: 01473-833300 **Fax:** 01473-833022
E-mail: enquiries@impact-toyota.com
Website: http://www.impact-handling.com
Managers: B. Milton (Mgr)
Ultimate Holding Company: EQSTRA HOLDINGS LTD (SOUTH AFRICA)
Immediate Holding Company: IMPACT FORK TRUCKS LIMITED
Registration no: 02550150 **Date established:** 1990
No.of Employees: 11 - 20 **Product Groups:** 35, 39, 45

Date of Accounts	Jun 11	Jun 10	Jun 09
Sales Turnover	26m	26m	32m
Pre Tax Profit/Loss	820	293	-3m
Working Capital	-21m	-3m	-13m
Fixed Assets	27m	24m	28m
Current Assets	8m	8m	10m
Current Liabilities	25m	3m	4m

Ipswich Packaging Services Ltd

Sheep Drift Farm Waldringfield Road, Brightwell, Ipswich, IP10 0BJ
Tel: 01473-613359 **Fax:** 01473-613357
E-mail: sales@ipswich-packaging.com
Website: http://www.ipswich-packaging.com
Directors: E. Boulton (MD)
Date established: 1995 **No.of Employees:** 1 - 10 **Product Groups:** 38, 42

Ipswich Polycarbonate

Unit 23-24 Brookhouse Business Park Brunel Road, Hadleigh Road Industrial Estate, Ipswich, IP2 0EF
Tel: 01473-287779 **Fax:** 01473-288690
E-mail: eamon@falconwindows.com
Directors: E. Sheppard (Prop)
Immediate Holding Company: ELECTRONIC DREAM PLANT LIMITED
Date established: 2009 **No.of Employees:** 1 - 10 **Product Groups:** 30, 48

Ipswich & Sudbury Enterprise Agency

Felaw Maltings 44 Felaw Street, Ipswich, IP2 8SJ
Tel: 01473-407001 **Fax:** 01473-407301
Website: http://www.suffolkenterprise.co.uk
Directors: P. Celerier (Fin), R. Bingham (Dir), A. Seagers (Dir), M. Bax (MD)
Managers: G. Fretwell, C. Donaldson, J. McLeod
Immediate Holding Company: IPSWICH ENTERPRISE AGENCY LIMITED
Registration no: 01690882 **VAT No.:** GB 521 4293 73
Date established: 1983 **Turnover:** £500,000 - £1m
No.of Employees: 1 - 10 **Product Groups:** 54, 86

Ironway Ltd

Chattisham Place Chattisham, Ipswich, IP8 3QD
Tel: 01473-652770 **Fax:** 01473- 652118
E-mail: johneverett@live.co.uk
Directors: B. Everett (Fin), J. Everett (MD)
Immediate Holding Company: IRONWAY LIMITED
Registration no: 01666769 **Date established:** 1982
No.of Employees: 1 - 10 **Product Groups:** 26, 35

Date of Accounts	Mar 11	Mar 10	Mar 09
Working Capital	-13	-6	-7
Current Assets	2	2	1
Current Liabilities	N/A	2	N/A

J Breheny Contractors Ltd

Flordon Road Creeting St Mary, Ipswich, IP6 8NH
Tel: 01449-720282 **Fax:** 01449-721593
E-mail: j.breheny@breheny.co.uk
Website: http://www.breheny.co.uk
Bank(s): Barclays
Managers: J. Breheny
Ultimate Holding Company: BREHENY GROUP LIMITED
Immediate Holding Company: J.BREHENY CONTRACTORS LIMITED
Registration no: 00753976 **Date established:** 1963
Turnover: £50m - £75m **No.of Employees:** 251 - 500
Product Groups: 51, 52, 54

Date of Accounts	Mar 12	Mar 11	Mar 10
Sales Turnover	62m	60m	57m
Pre Tax Profit/Loss	260	264	319
Working Capital	2m	3m	3m
Fixed Assets	8m	7m	7m
Current Assets	18m	18m	19m
Current Liabilities	2m	2m	3m

K D M International Ltd

The Havens Ransomes Europark, Ipswich, IP3 9SJ
Tel: 01473-276900 **Fax:** 01473-276911
E-mail: sales@kdm.co.uk
Website: http://www.kdm.co.uk
Bank(s): Barclays
Directors: A. Walshe (MD), D. Spilling (Co Sec)
Managers: K. Sheppard (Tech Serv Mgr)
Immediate Holding Company: KDM INTERNATIONAL LIMITED
Registration no: 01210564 **VAT No.:** GB **Date established:** 1975
Turnover: £10m - £20m **No.of Employees:** 11 - 20 **Product Groups:** 66

Date of Accounts	Dec 11	Dec 10	Dec 09
Sales Turnover	18m	19m	14m
Pre Tax Profit/Loss	444	477	272
Working Capital	3m	2m	2m
Fixed Assets	2m	2m	2m
Current Assets	5m	5m	3m
Current Liabilities	899	1m	557

Kays Electronics

85 Cavendish Street, Ipswich, IP3 8AX
Tel: 01473-214040 **Fax:** 01473-214060
E-mail: enquiries@kayselectronics.com
Website: http://www.kayselectronics.com
Directors: M. Noble (Dir)
Immediate Holding Company: KAYS ELECTRONICS LIMITED
Registration no: 01090192 **VAT No.:** GB 104 0343 35
Date established: 1973 **Turnover:** £250,000 - £500,000
No.of Employees: 1 - 10 **Product Groups:** 37, 48

Date of Accounts	Dec 11	Dec 10	Dec 09
Working Capital	10	1	-8
Fixed Assets	203	205	207
Current Assets	19	22	26

R E H Kennedy Ltd

Whitehouse Road, Ipswich, IP1 5LT
Tel: 01473-240044 **Fax:** 01473-240098
E-mail: enquiries@rehkennedy.co.uk
Website: http://www.rehkennedy.co.uk
Bank(s): Barclays, Cardiff
Directors: J. Ruffles (MD), R. Langham (Dir), L. Nixon (Fin)
Immediate Holding Company: R.E.H. KENNEDY LIMITED
Registration no: 05306486 **VAT No.:** GB 133 4836 74
Date established: 2004 **Turnover:** £1m - £2m **No.of Employees:** 21 - 50
Product Groups: 26

Date of Accounts	Apr 11	Apr 10	Apr 08
Working Capital	77	5	56
Fixed Assets	527	541	599
Current Assets	381	427	477

Lever Press Ltd

12 Goddard Road, Ipswich, IP1 5NP
Tel: 01473-461464 **Fax:** 01473-240118
E-mail: sales@leverpress.co.uk
Website: http://www.leverpress.co.uk
Managers: J. Mitchell (Mgr)
Immediate Holding Company: LEVERPRESS LIMITED
Registration no: 01657905 **VAT No.:** GB 368 4392 17
Date established: 1982 **Turnover:** £500,000 - £1m
No.of Employees: 1 - 10 **Product Groups:** 27, 28, 81

Date of Accounts	Oct 11	Oct 10	Oct 09
Working Capital	-1	34	86
Fixed Assets	16	21	25
Current Assets	51	182	488

Liquid Line

109 Newton Road, Ipswich, IP3 8HQ
Tel: 01473-274427 **Fax:** 01473-279696
Directors: G. Poolie (Ptnr)
No.of Employees: 1 - 10 **Product Groups:** 40, 66

M G C Lamps

Unit 1 The Sovereign Centre Farthing Road, Ipswich, IP1 5AP
Tel: 01473-466300 **Fax:** 01473-240081
E-mail: sales@mgc-lamps.com
Website: http://www.mgc-lamps.com
Directors: J. Grieg (MD), J. Revell (Fin)
Immediate Holding Company: M.G.C. LAMPS LIMITED
Registration no: 01264315 **Date established:** 1976
No.of Employees: 21 - 50 **Product Groups:** 37

Date of Accounts	Mar 11	Mar 10	Mar 09
Working Capital	978	1m	981
Fixed Assets	243	301	253
Current Assets	3m	3m	2m

M R M International Generators Ltd

PO Box 78, Ipswich, IP9 2WZ
Tel: 01473-310000 **Fax:** 01473-310011
E-mail: sales@mrmint.co.uk
Website: http://www.mrmint.co.uk
Directors: R. Wright (Prop)
Immediate Holding Company: M.R.M. INTERNATIONAL GENERATORS LIMITED
Registration no: 02004738 **VAT No.:** GB 443 0999 35
Date established: 1986 **Turnover:** £2m - £5m **No.of Employees:** 1 - 10
Product Groups: 37, 46

Date of Accounts	Mar 12	Mar 11	Mar 10
Working Capital	1	7	-0
Fixed Assets	2	3	4
Current Assets	147	187	174

Master Chemical Europe Ltd

Unit 33 Maitland Road Lion Barn Industrial Estate Needham Market, Ipswich, IP6 8NZ
Tel: 01449-726800 **Fax:** 01449-721719
E-mail: info@masterchemical.co.uk
Website: http://www.masterchemical.com
Bank(s): Barclays
Directors: R. Lucas (Chief Op Offcr)
Ultimate Holding Company: MASTER CHEMICAL CORPORATION INC (USA)
Immediate Holding Company: MASTER CHEMICAL EUROPE LTD.
Registration no: 02509745 **VAT No.:** GB 571 0298 48
Date established: 1990 **Turnover:** £1m - £2m **No.of Employees:** 11 - 20
Product Groups: 31, 42, 46

Date of Accounts	Dec 11	Dec 10	Dec 09
Working Capital	855	737	735
Fixed Assets	15	25	56
Current Assets	2m	1m	1m

Medi Plinth Equipment Ltd

7 Holywells Road, Ipswich, IP3 0DL
Tel: 01473-212010 **Fax:** 01473-214165
E-mail: mail@medi-plinth.co.uk
Website: http://www.medi-plinth.co.uk
Bank(s): Natwest
Managers: T. Bigden (Chief Mgr)
Ultimate Holding Company: HEALTH-CARE EQUIPMENT AND SUPPLIES CO LTD
Immediate Holding Company: MEDI-PLINTH EQUIPMENT LIMITED
Registration no: 06204253 **VAT No.:** GB 638 0493 28
Date established: 2007 **Turnover:** £1m - £2m **No.of Employees:** 21 - 50
Product Groups: 83

Date of Accounts	Jun 11	Jun 10	Jun 09
Sales Turnover	1m	2m	2m
Pre Tax Profit/Loss	8	10	40
Working Capital	109	78	43
Fixed Assets	N/A	26	56
Current Assets	596	540	500
Current Liabilities	84	129	141

Mid Suffolk Welding Supplies

42 Upper Cavendish Street, Ipswich, IP3 8BS
Tel: 01473-711900
Directors: A. Tricker (Prop)
Date established: 1982 **No.of Employees:** 1 - 10 **Product Groups:** 46

Miracle Mills Ltd

Knightsdale Road, Ipswich, IP1 4LE
Tel: 01473-742325 **Fax:** 01473-462773
E-mail: info@cristy-turner.com
Website: http://www.miracle-mills.co.uk
Bank(s): Barclays
Directors: A. Gosling (Dir), R. Gosling (MD)
Ultimate Holding Company: Gosling Group Ltd
Immediate Holding Company: Christy Turner Ltd
Registration no: 01970038 **Date established:** 1985 **Turnover:** £2m - £5m
No.of Employees: 21 - 50 **Product Groups:** 41, 42, 47

Date of Accounts	Dec 09	Dec 08	Dec 07
Working Capital	N/A	N/A	5
Current Assets	N/A	N/A	5

Morrison Freight Ltd

Morrison House Addison Way, Great Blakenham, Ipswich, IP6 0RL
Tel: 01473-836500 **Fax:** 01473-836599
E-mail: sales@morrison.com
Website: http://www.morrison.com
Managers: W. Gordon
Ultimate Holding Company: MORRISON FREIGHT HOLDINGS LIMITED
Immediate Holding Company: MORRISON FREIGHT LIMITED
Registration no: 02444973 **Date established:** 1989 **Turnover:** £5m - £10m
No.of Employees: 11 - 20 **Product Groups:** 44

Date of Accounts	Mar 12	Mar 11	Mar 10
Sales Turnover	8m	7m	7m
Pre Tax Profit/Loss	354	194	253
Working Capital	512	300	252
Fixed Assets	35	56	90
Current Assets	2m	2m	2m
Current Liabilities	568	485	573

Mr Stainless

Suffolk Yacht Harbour Levington, Ipswich, IP10 0LN
Tel: 01473-659295 **Fax:** 01473-659336
E-mail: sales@mrstainless.co.uk
Website: http://www.mrstainless.co.uk
Directors: M. Wingar (Prop)
Immediate Holding Company: ENIGMACLAUSE LIMITED
Registration no: 06503052 **Date established:** 1999
No.of Employees: 1 - 10 **Product Groups:** 35

New Seal Gasket Ltd

9 Boss Hall Road, Ipswich, IP1 5BN
Tel: 01473-461141 **Fax:** 01473-240915
E-mail: ipswich@new-seal.co.uk
Website: http://www.burgmann.co.uk
Managers: B. Stephenson (District Mgr)
Immediate Holding Company: NEW-SEAL GASKET LTD
Registration no: 07635152 **VAT No.:** GB 222 3844 85
Date established: 2011 **No.of Employees:** 1 - 10 **Product Groups:** 22, 23, 29, 30

Date of Accounts	Dec 11	Sep 10	Sep 09
Sales Turnover	3m	N/A	N/A
Pre Tax Profit/Loss	305	N/A	N/A
Working Capital	645	369	277
Fixed Assets	118	408	407
Current Assets	1m	935	666
Current Liabilities	192	N/A	N/A

O O C L UK Branch

Oocl House Bridge Road, Levington, Ipswich, IP10 0NE
Tel: 01473-659000 **Fax:** 01473-654269
E-mail: jodie.crown@oocl.com
Website: http://www.oocl.com
Bank(s): Lloyds TSB Bank plc
Managers: J. Crown (Fin Mgr)
Ultimate Holding Company: ORIENT OVERSEAS (INTERNATIONAL) LTD (HONG KONG)

Immediate Holding Company: KENWAKE LIMITED
Registration no: 01473779 **VAT No.:** GB 515 1803 74
Date established: 1980 **Turnover:** £500,000 - £1m
No.of Employees: 51 - 100 **Product Groups:** 74

Parburch Medical Developments
PO Box 740, Ipswich, IP1 9ET
Tel: 01394-448664 **Fax:** 01394-448601
E-mail: pob.parker@fogless.co.uk
Website: http://www.Parburchmedical.co.uk
Directors: R. Parker (MD)
Immediate Holding Company: PARBURCH MEDICAL DEVELOPMENTS LIMITED
Registration no: 01797802 **VAT No.:** GB 390 6940 29
Date established: 1984 **Turnover:** £500,000 - £1m
No.of Employees: 1 - 10 **Product Groups:** 38

Date of Accounts	Apr 11	Apr 10	Apr 09
Working Capital	28	16	11
Fixed Assets	38	41	40
Current Assets	66	47	46

Patmore Water Softeners
120 Spring Road, Ipswich, IP4 2RR
Tel: 0800-0327670 **Fax:** 01473-719444
E-mail: tcpatmore@aol.com
Website: http://www.patmorewatersofteners.co.uk
Directors: T. Patmore (Prop)
Date established: 2000 **No.of Employees:** 1 - 10 **Product Groups:** 38, 42

Patmore Water Softeners
150 Spring Road, Ipswich, IP4 5NR
Tel: 01473-713600 **Fax:** 01473-719444
E-mail: tcpatmore@aol.com
Website: http://www.patmorewatersofteners.co.uk
Directors: T. Patmore (Prop)
Immediate Holding Company: PATMORE SOFTENERS LIMITED
Registration no: 04743835 **Date established:** 2003
No.of Employees: 1 - 10 **Product Groups:** 38, 42

Penn Packaging Ltd
Harkstead Hall Barn Harkstead, Ipswich, IP9 1DB
Tel: 01473-893990 **Fax:** 01473-893995
E-mail: info@penn-packaging.co.uk
Website: http://www.penn-packaging.co.uk
Directors: M. Goodwin (Dir)
Immediate Holding Company: PENN PACKAGING LIMITED
Registration no: 03158573 **Date established:** 1996
No.of Employees: 1 - 10 **Product Groups:** 38, 42

Date of Accounts	Mar 11	Mar 10	Mar 09
Pre Tax Profit/Loss	N/A	20	N/A
Working Capital	-131	-145	-150
Fixed Assets	10	1	1
Current Assets	41	71	100

Pix Europe Ltd
Unit 24 Farthing Road Industrial Estate, Ipswich, IP1 5AP
Tel: 01473-744612 **Fax:** 01473-744613
E-mail: info@pixeuro.com
Website: http://www.pixeuro.com
Directors: R. Sethi (Prop)
Immediate Holding Company: PIX EUROPE LIMITED
Registration no: 03665031 **Date established:** 1998
Turnover: £10m - £20m **No.of Employees:** 21 - 50 **Product Groups:** 29, 30, 35, 68

Date of Accounts	Mar 11	Mar 10
Sales Turnover	13m	9m
Pre Tax Profit/Loss	445	38
Working Capital	866	944
Fixed Assets	2m	2m
Current Assets	8m	6m
Current Liabilities	2m	2m

Plants Of Distinction
Abacus House Station Yard, Needham Market, Ipswich, IP6 8AS
Tel: 01449-721720 **Fax:** 01449-721722
E-mail: sales@plantsofdistinction.co.uk
Directors: T. Tostevin (Ptnr)
Immediate Holding Company: ANGUS TRAVEL LIMITED
Registration no: 03305045 **Date established:** 1997
No.of Employees: 1 - 10 **Product Groups:** 02

Date of Accounts	Mar 11	Mar 10	Mar 07
Working Capital	N/A	N/A	-7
Fixed Assets	1	N/A	1
Current Assets	7	8	6

Plescon Security Products
Unit 9 Sterling Complex Farthing Road, Ipswich, IP1 5AP
Tel: 01473-745375 **Fax:** 01473-747252
E-mail: info@plescon.co.uk
Website: http://www.plescon.co.uk
Directors: G. Broadhead (Dir), H. Morphew (Co Sec)
Managers: H. Morphew (Chief Mgr), T. Haywood (Tech Eng)
Ultimate Holding Company: PLESCON LIMITED
Immediate Holding Company: PLESCON SECURITY PRODUCTS LIMITED
Registration no: 02012544 **VAT No.:** GB 299 9964 51
Date established: 1986 **Turnover:** £1m - £2m **No.of Employees:** 1 - 10
Product Groups: 52

Date of Accounts	Dec 10	Dec 09	Dec 08
Working Capital	240	217	-61
Fixed Assets	46	54	72
Current Assets	422	386	397

Pound Gates
St Vincent House 1 Cutler Street, Ipswich, IP1 1UQ
Tel: 01473-346046 **Fax:** 01473-231591
E-mail: info@poundgates.com
Website: http://www.poundgates.com
Directors: R. Thacker (Sales)
Managers: A. Bath, M. Chandler (Comptroller), R. Attleton (Mktg Serv Mgr), R. Appleton (Mktg Serv Mgr), S. Connelly (Tech Serv Mgr)
Immediate Holding Company: POUND GATES AND COMPANY LIMITED
Registration no: 03097866 **Date established:** 1995 **Turnover:** £1m - £2m
No.of Employees: 21 - 50 **Product Groups:** 82

Date of Accounts	Mar 11	Mar 10	Mar 09
Sales Turnover	N/A	2m	N/A
Pre Tax Profit/Loss	N/A	105	83
Working Capital	651	716	761
Fixed Assets	57	76	N/A
Current Assets	2m	2m	2m
Current Liabilities	N/A	88	34

Poundfield Products Ltd
Grove Farm Creeting St Peter, Ipswich, IP6 8QG
Tel: 01449-723150 **Fax:** 01449-723151
E-mail: sales@poundfield.com
Website: http://www.poundfield.com
Directors: M. Jardine (MD), M. Snowling (Co Sec)
Managers: R. Faulkner
Immediate Holding Company: POUNDFIELD PRODUCTS LIMITED
Registration no: 02714196 **Date established:** 1992 **Turnover:** £5m - £10m
No.of Employees: 21 - 50 **Product Groups:** 30, 33, 35, 66

Date of Accounts	Dec 11	Dec 10	Dec 09
Sales Turnover	6m	6m	7m
Pre Tax Profit/Loss	-32	85	613
Working Capital	38	238	4
Fixed Assets	4m	4m	4m
Current Assets	2m	2m	2m
Current Liabilities	522	458	493

Pre-Serve UK Ltd
PO Box 11 Pinewood, Ipswich, IP8 3TP
Tel: 01394-421321 **Fax:** 01394-420679
Website: http://www.pre-serve.co.uk
Directors: T. Williams (MD)
Immediate Holding Company: PRE-SERVE (UK) LIMITED
Registration no: 04533355 **Date established:** 2002
No.of Employees: 1 - 10 **Product Groups:** 20, 32

Ransomes Jacobsen Ltd
West Road Ransomes Industrial Estate, Ipswich, IP3 9TT
Tel: 01473-270000 **Fax:** 01473-276300
E-mail: sales@ransomesjacobsen.com
Website: http://www.ransomesjacobsen.com
Directors: R. Comely (Mkt Research), R. Hall-roberts (Fin), I. Rooke (Tech Serv), D. Withers (MD), R. Price (Sales)
Managers: C. Mellelieu (Personnel)
Ultimate Holding Company: TEXTRON INC (USA)
Immediate Holding Company: RANSOMES JACOBSEN LIMITED
Registration no: 01070731 **Date established:** 1972
Turnover: £50m - £75m **No.of Employees:** 251 - 500 **Product Groups:** 39

Date of Accounts	Dec 11	Dec 10	Dec 09
Sales Turnover	63	67m	53m
Pre Tax Profit/Loss	N/A	3m	-923
Working Capital	28	28m	24m
Fixed Assets	21	21m	28m
Current Assets	38	36m	30m
Current Liabilities	1	1m	1m

Regent Publicity Ltd (Sales Office)
Felaw Maltings Felaw Street, Ipswich, IP2 8SJ
Tel: 01473-407080 **Fax:** 01273-820144
E-mail: sales@regentpublicity.co.uk
Website: http://www.regentpublicity.co.uk
Directors: B. Rudland (Dir)
Immediate Holding Company: REGENT PUBLICITY LIMITED
Registration no: 01635271 **Date established:** 1982 **Turnover:** £1m - £2m
No.of Employees: 1 - 10 **Product Groups:** 22, 27, 28, 30, 33, 44, 49, 81

Date of Accounts	Dec 11	Jun 10	Jun 09
Working Capital	21	14	11
Fixed Assets	19	6	7
Current Assets	322	223	201

Robert C Scutt Ltd
Maitland Road Lion Barn Industrial Estate, Needham Market, Ipswich, IP6 8NZ
Tel: 01449-722274 **Fax:** 01449-723311
E-mail: info@rcscutt.co.uk
Directors: D. Goward (MD)
Ultimate Holding Company: BTS GROUP LIMITED
Immediate Holding Company: ROBERT C.SCUTT LIMITED
Registration no: 00554492 **Date established:** 1955
No.of Employees: 21 - 50 **Product Groups:** 40, 66

Date of Accounts	Mar 11	Mar 10	Mar 09
Working Capital	655	690	649
Fixed Assets	149	135	143
Current Assets	2m	1m	1m

Rose Health Care
60 St Matthews Street, Ipswich, IP1 3EP
Tel: 01473-258508 **Fax:** 01473-258508
E-mail: bobjenkins@btconnect.com
Website: http://www.rosehealthcare.biz
Directors: B. Jenkins (MD)
No.of Employees: 1 - 10 **Product Groups:** 38, 67

Ruskin Lifting Engineers Ltd
84-86 Foxhall Road, Ipswich, IP3 8HN
Tel: 01473-253424 **Fax:** 01473-217233
E-mail: ruskin@ruskin.co.uk
Website: http://www.ruskin.co.uk
Directors: C. Sharp (MD), B. Marriage (Fin)
Immediate Holding Company: RUSKIN LIFTING ENGINEERS LIMITED
Registration no: 00505072 **Date established:** 1952
No.of Employees: 1 - 10 **Product Groups:** 35, 39, 45

Date of Accounts	Feb 08	Feb 11	Feb 10
Working Capital	91	59	7
Fixed Assets	7	3	4
Current Assets	153	87	57

S C H Supplies Ltd
Woodlands Holbrook, Ipswich, IP9 2PT
Tel: 01473-328272 **Fax:** 01473-327177
E-mail: sales@schsupplies.co.uk
Website: http://www.schsupplies.co.uk
Directors: A. Rodwell (MD)
Managers: J. Free
Immediate Holding Company: S.C.H. SUPPLIES LIMITED
Registration no: 00997908 **Date established:** 1970
No.of Employees: 11 - 20 **Product Groups:** 41

Date of Accounts	Dec 11	Dec 10	Dec 09
Working Capital	232	226	199
Fixed Assets	126	126	122
Current Assets	377	342	304

S C S Ltd
Multifreight House Cromwell Court, Ipswich, IP1 1XB
Tel: 01473-212421 **Fax:** 01473-212110
E-mail: sales@multifreight.com
Website: http://www.multifreight.com
Bank(s): Midland P.L.C., Ipswich
Directors: D. Nunn (Fin), M. Rattigan (Tech Serv), T. Clayton (Dir)
Immediate Holding Company: SCS LIMITED
Registration no: 02917939 **VAT No.:** GB 623 4385 48
Date established: 1994 **Turnover:** £1m - £2m **No.of Employees:** 11 - 20
Product Groups: 84

Date of Accounts	Mar 12	Mar 11	Mar 10
Working Capital	67	84	83
Fixed Assets	N/A	N/A	1
Current Assets	521	551	517

S F Services
Foxtail Road Ransomes Europark, Ipswich, IP3 9RT
Tel: 01473-725161 **Fax:** 01473-271601
E-mail: alanhutchings@blockfoil.com
Website: http://www.sfhotfoil.com
Immediate Holding Company: Blockfoil
Date established: 1980 **Turnover:** £500m - £1,000m
No.of Employees: 1 - 10 **Product Groups:** 27, 28, 34, 42, 44, 46

S G System Products Ltd
Unit 22 Wharfedale Road, Ipswich, IP1 4JP
Tel: 01473-240055 **Fax:** 01473-461616
E-mail: sales@sgsystems.co.uk
Website: http://www.handrails.co.uk
Directors: H. Watson (Dir)
Immediate Holding Company: S G SYSTEM PRODUCTS LIMITED
Registration no: 03314816 **VAT No.:** GB 688 5942 62
Date established: 1997 **Turnover:** £500,000 - £1m
No.of Employees: 1 - 10 **Product Groups:** 33, 35, 36

Date of Accounts	Jun 11	Jun 10	Jun 09
Working Capital	54	78	83
Fixed Assets	N/A	1	3
Current Assets	145	152	229

S Sacker Claydon Ltd
Gipping Road Great Blakenham, Ipswich, IP6 0JB
Tel: 01473-830373 **Fax:** 01473-832535
E-mail: adriandodds@sackers.co.uk
Website: http://www.sackers.co.uk
Directors: A. Dodds (Dir), D. Dodds (Jt MD)
Immediate Holding Company: S. SACKER (CLAYDON) LIMITED
Registration no: 01526052 **Date established:** 1980
Turnover: £10m - £20m **No.of Employees:** 51 - 100 **Product Groups:** 66

Savio
Broom Hill Road, Ipswich, IP1 4EH
Tel: 01473-215441 **Fax:** 01473-215441
E-mail: savio.uk@btinternet.com
Website: http://www.savio.it
Registration no: 06289272 **Turnover:** £50m - £75m
No.of Employees: 251 - 500 **Product Groups:** 36

Score Europe Ltd
Unit 8 Alpha Business Park 20 White House Road, Ipswich, IP1 5LT
Tel: 01473-242460 **Fax:** 01473-747644
E-mail: mike.billington@score-group.com
Website: http://www.score-group.com
Directors: M. Billington (Dir)
Ultimate Holding Company: SCORE GROUP PLC
Immediate Holding Company: SCORE (EUROPE) LIMITED
Registration no: SC094003 **VAT No.:** GB 498 5817 74
Date established: 1985 **Turnover:** £2m - £5m **No.of Employees:** 1 - 10
Product Groups: 38, 84

Date of Accounts	Sep 10	Sep 11	Oct 08
Sales Turnover	64m	61m	67m
Pre Tax Profit/Loss	5m	3m	7m
Working Capital	10m	9m	7m
Fixed Assets	4m	3m	4m
Current Assets	34m	31m	28m
Current Liabilities	12m	9m	10m

Scotts Co. Ltd
Paper Mill Lane Bramford, Ipswich, IP8 4BZ
Tel: 01473-830492
Website: http://www.scottsinternational.com
Directors: A. Van-Winden (Fin), J. Wyatt (MD)
Managers: J. Crowe (Sales Prom Mgr), N. Fraser
Registration no: 02924130 **VAT No.:** GB 637 9190 07
Turnover: £20m - £50m **No.of Employees:** 1 - 10 **Product Groups:** 32

Shade & Shelter Ltd
Unit 1-2 Perry Barn Burstall Lane, Sproughton, Ipswich, IP8 3DJ
Tel: 01473-656040 **Fax:** 01473-652837
E-mail: sales@marqueecovers.co.uk
Website: http://www.marqueeframes.co.uk
Product Groups: 35, 66, 67

Signs Express
6 Greenwich Close Landseer Road, Ipswich, IP3 0DD
Tel: 01473-281414 **Fax:** 01473-281456
E-mail: ipswich@signsexpress.co.uk
Website: http://www.signsexpress.co.uk
Directors: N. Dawes (MD), L. Dawes (Fin)
Immediate Holding Company: SIGNS EXPRESS LIMITED
Registration no: 02375913 **Date established:** 1989
No.of Employees: 1 - 10 **Product Groups:** 30, 39, 40, 80, 81, 84

Skar Precision Mouldings Ltd
Unit 3 Lady Lane Industrial Estate Hadleigh, Ipswich, IP7 6AZ
Tel: 01473-828000 **Fax:** 01473-828001
E-mail: sales@skar.co.uk
Website: http://www.skar.co.uk
Bank(s): Barclays
Directors: K. Gant (Fin)
Managers: M. Shuttlewood (Buyer)
Ultimate Holding Company: ASPIRE PLASTICS LIMITED
Immediate Holding Company: SKAR PRECISION MOULDINGS LIMITED
Registration no: 00949310 **VAT No.:** 103 5122 32 **Date established:** 1969
Turnover: £2m - £5m **No.of Employees:** 21 - 50 **Product Groups:** 30

Date of Accounts	Dec 11	Dec 10	Dec 09
Working Capital	615	686	171
Fixed Assets	1m	1m	1m

see next page

Skar Precision Mouldings Ltd - *Cont'd*

Current Assets	2m	2m	967

Southern Counties Fuels
Lanseer Road, Ipswich, IP3 0DB
Tel: 01473-225020 **Fax:** 01473-885030
E-mail: jonathan@scf.co.uk
Website: http://www.scf.co.uk
Managers: S. Scott (Mgr)
Ultimate Holding Company: DCC PUBLIC LIMITED COMPANY
Immediate Holding Company: SOUTHERN COUNTIES FUELS LIMITED
Registration no: 00903234 **Date established:** 1967
No.of Employees: 11 - 20 **Product Groups:** 31, 32, 39

Date of Accounts	Mar 12	Mar 11	Mar 10
Working Capital	20m	20m	20m
Current Assets	20m	20m	20m

Space-Ray UK
4-6 Chapel Lane Claydon, Ipswich, IP6 0JL
Tel: 01473-830551 **Fax:** 01473-832055
E-mail: info@spaceray.co.uk
Website: http://www.spaceray.co.uk
Directors: D. Oakley (MD)
Immediate Holding Company: GAS FIRED PRODUCTS INC (USA)
Registration no: 00812608 **VAT No.:** GB 102 5893 84
Date established: 1968 **Turnover:** £1m - £2m **No.of Employees:** 1 - 10
Product Groups: 40, 41, 46

Speedy Hire Ltd
Unit 5 Farthing Road, Ipswich, IP1 5AP
Tel: 01473-461083 **Fax:** 01473-240532
E-mail: martyn.watson@speedyservices.com
Website: http://www.speedyservice.com
Managers: M. Watson (Depot Mgr)
Ultimate Holding Company: ULC CO.
Immediate Holding Company: HEWDEN STUART LTD
Registration no: SC046005 **No.of Employees:** 1 - 10 **Product Groups:** 35, 37, 38, 39, 45, 48, 83

Steadfast Anglia Ltd
Unit 2 Columba Orion Avenue, Great Blakenham, Ipswich, IP6 0LW
Tel: 01473-834144 **Fax:** 01473-834145
E-mail: info@steadfastanglia.co.uk
Website: http://www.steadfastanglia.co.uk
Directors: C. Smith (Dir)
Immediate Holding Company: STEADFAST (ANGLIA) LIMITED
Registration no: 04161232 **Date established:** 2001
No.of Employees: 11 - 20 **Product Groups:** 23, 40, 49

Date of Accounts	Apr 11	Apr 10	Apr 09
Working Capital	66	144	85
Fixed Assets	40	50	50
Current Assets	228	278	230
Current Liabilities	N/A	N/A	145

Stelmax Ltd
21-23 Gloster Road Martlesham Heath, Ipswich, IP5 3RD
Tel: 01473-626651 **Fax:** 01473-610651
E-mail: stelmaxltd@aol.com
Website: http://www.stelmax.co.uk
Directors: G. Martin (MD)
Immediate Holding Company: STELMAX LIMITED
Registration no: 00654307 **VAT No.:** GB 104 5060 22
Date established: 1960 **Turnover:** £500,000 - £1m
No.of Employees: 1 - 10 **Product Groups:** 30, 32, 48, 66

Date of Accounts	Sep 11	Sep 10	Sep 09
Working Capital	136	129	126
Fixed Assets	22	27	32
Current Assets	233	215	170

Suffolk Fastener Ipswich Ltd
38 Boss Hall Road, Ipswich, IP1 5BN
Tel: 01473-740600 **Fax:** 01473-462871
E-mail: sales@suffolkfasteners.com
Website: http://www.suffolkfasteners.com
Directors: T. Digby (Fin)
Immediate Holding Company: SUFFOLK FASTENERS (IPSWICH) LTD
Registration no: 02622546 **Date established:** 1991
No.of Employees: 1 - 10 **Product Groups:** 29, 30, 35, 66

Date of Accounts	Nov 11	Nov 10	Nov 09
Working Capital	27	16	19
Fixed Assets	3	7	9
Current Assets	66	55	50

T T G Baron
Folly Lane Copdock, Ipswich, IP8 3JQ
Tel: 01473-730055 **Fax:** 01473-730169
E-mail: info@ttgbaron.co.uk
Website: http://www.ttgbaron.co.uk
Directors: M. Brown (Prop)
Immediate Holding Company: TTG BARON PROPERTIES LIMITED
Registration no: 03209399 **Date established:** 1996
No.of Employees: 1 - 10 **Product Groups:** 23, 24, 27, 49, 65

Date of Accounts	Mar 12	Mar 11	Mar 10
Working Capital	-126	-183	-185
Fixed Assets	1m	1m	2m
Current Assets	258	288	415

Thompson & Morgan UK Ltd
Poplar Lane Copdock, Ipswich, IP8 3BU
Tel: 01473-695200 **Fax:** 01473-680199
E-mail: phansord@thompson-morgan.com
Website: http://www.thompson-morgan.com
Bank(s): Barclays
Directors: K. Lewis (Fin)
Managers: A. Tokely (Purch Mgr), M. Smith (I.T. Exec), P. Hansord, S. Gittins (Export Sales Mg), C. Mills, C. Dixey, C. Mills (Personnel), O. Lockhart (Tech Serv Mgr), V. Ager (Mktg Serv Mgr)
Ultimate Holding Company: THOMPSON & MORGAN GROUP HOLDINGS LIMITED
Immediate Holding Company: THOMPSON & MORGAN (GROUP) LIMITED
Registration no: 02860589 **VAT No.:** GB 637 8510 20
Date established: 1993 **Turnover:** Up to £250,000
No.of Employees: 101 - 250 **Product Groups:** 02

Date of Accounts	Jun 11	Jun 10	Jun 09
Sales Turnover	72	170	N/A
Pre Tax Profit/Loss	-618	-475	-460

Working Capital	-2m	-1m	-724
Fixed Assets	6	6	6
Current Assets	556	556	556

Titchmarsh & Goodwin Ltd
Trinity Works Back Hamlet, Ipswich, IP3 8AL
Tel: 01473-252158 **Fax:** 01473-210948
E-mail: info@titchmarsh-goodwin.co.uk
Website: http://www.titchmarsh-goodwin.co.uk
Bank(s): HSBC
Directors: P. Goodwin (Dir)
Immediate Holding Company: TITCHMARSH AND GOODWIN
Registration no: 00840316 **VAT No.:** GB 102 8033 22
Date established: 1965 **Turnover:** Up to £250,000
No.of Employees: 21 - 50 **Product Groups:** 26

Toptech Europe Ltd
PO Box 627, Ipswich, IP8 3WZ
Tel: 01473-373400 **Fax:** 0871-218 6814
E-mail: info@toptech.co.uk
Website: http://www.toptech.co.uk
Managers: S. Goldspink (Sales Prom Mgr)
Immediate Holding Company: TOPTECH EUROPE LIMITED
Registration no: 06650756 **Date established:** 2008
Turnover: £500,000 - £1m **No.of Employees:** 1 - 10 **Product Groups:** 39

Date of Accounts	Dec 11	Dec 10	Dec 09
Working Capital	-64	-24	4
Fixed Assets	10	14	N/A
Current Assets	44	37	49

Total Butler Ltd
Vopak Terminal Landseer Road, Ipswich, IP3 0DE
Tel: 01473-288444 **Fax:** 01473-230059
E-mail: ipswitchdepot@totalbutler.co.uk
Website: http://www.totalbutler.co.uk
Directors: S. Palmer (MD)
Managers: R. Parsons (Mgr), M. Drysdale (Depot Mgr)
Ultimate Holding Company: FP035365
Immediate Holding Company: TOTAL BUTLER LIMITED
Registration no: 01162536 **Date established:** 1974
No.of Employees: 1 - 10 **Product Groups:** 31, 66

Uniport Business Systems Ltd
Unit 80 Claydon Business Park Great Blakenham, Ipswich, IP6 0NL
Tel: 01473-281155 **Fax:** 01473-280943
E-mail: pfg@uniport.co.uk
Website: http://www.uniport.co.uk
Bank(s): National Westminster
Directors: P. Griffiths (MD), C. Griffiths (Co Sec)
Managers: N. Webbster (I.T. Exec), W. Brown (Sales Admin)
Immediate Holding Company: UNIPORT BUSINESS SYSTEMS LIMITED
Registration no: 02500939 **VAT No.:** 571 1180 66 **Date established:** 1990
Turnover: Up to £250,000 **No.of Employees:** 11 - 20 **Product Groups:** 44

Date of Accounts	Mar 11	Mar 10	Mar 09
Working Capital	13	10	N/A
Fixed Assets	13	51	N/A
Current Assets	79	98	N/A
Current Liabilities	47	N/A	N/A

Used Trucks Ltd
Cardinal Court 35-37 St. Peters Street, Ipswich, IP1 1XF
Tel: 01473-261772 **Fax:** 01473-261770
E-mail: info@usedtrucks.ltd.uk
Website: http://www.usedtrucks.ltd.uk
Directors: J. Addison (MD), M. Cooper (Co Sec)
Immediate Holding Company: Seven Asset Ltd
Registration no: 04245372 **VAT No.:** GB 781 7737 87
Date established: 2000 **Turnover:** £1m - £2m **No.of Employees:** 1 - 10
Product Groups: 39, 45, 67, 68, 72

Date of Accounts	Sep 09	Sep 08	Sep 07
Sales Turnover	633	2m	1m
Pre Tax Profit/Loss	-135	11	82
Working Capital	-129	5	-5
Current Assets	75	177	434
Current Liabilities	71	163	435

Vacuum Reflex
West Road Ransomes Europark, Ipswich, IP3 9SX
Tel: 01473-725176 **Fax:** 01473-271941
E-mail: vacuumreflex@compuserve.com
Website: http://www.vacuum-reflex.com
Directors: P. Curtis (MD), A. Odell (Sales), J. Peto (Fin)
Managers: I. Hart (I.T. Exec), J. Eaton (Prod Mgr), J. Eaton (Mgr)
Ultimate Holding Company: Albashow Ltd
Registration no: 02983710 **VAT No.:** GB 598 6250 87
Date established: 2000 **Turnover:** £1m - £2m **No.of Employees:** 1 - 10
Product Groups: 22, 24, 38, 39, 40

Volspec Ltd
Woolverstone, Ipswich, IP9 1AS
Tel: 01473-780144 **Fax:** 01473-780174
E-mail: sales@volspec.co.uk
Website: http://www.volspec.co.uk
Directors: P. Mott (Dir)
Ultimate Holding Company: VOLSPEC (HOLDINGS) LIMITED
Immediate Holding Company: VOLSPEC LIMITED
Registration no: 01137688 **Date established:** 1973
No.of Employees: 1 - 10 **Product Groups:** 35, 36, 39

Date of Accounts	Apr 12	Apr 11	Apr 10
Working Capital	1m	1m	1m
Fixed Assets	103	110	104
Current Assets	2m	2m	2m

West Engineering Ltd
Olympus Close, Ipswich, IP1 5LN
Tel: 01473-467930 **Fax:** 01473-467931
E-mail: info@westengineering.co.uk
Website: http://www.westengineering.co.uk
Bank(s): Lloyds TSB
Directors: E. West (Fin), D. Smith (MD), R. Grobler (Dir)
Immediate Holding Company: WEST ENGINEERING LIMITED
Registration no: 04618506 **Date established:** 2002
Turnover: Up to £250,000 **No.of Employees:** 21 - 50 **Product Groups:** 35, 36, 39

Date of Accounts	Mar 12	Mar 11	Mar 10
Sales Turnover	N/A	N/A	81
Pre Tax Profit/Loss	N/A	N/A	-21

Working Capital	31	17	-4
Fixed Assets	13	13	14
Current Assets	82	26	14
Current Liabilities	N/A	N/A	2

Wilms Heating Equipment
4 Hill Farm Barns Ashbocking Road, Henley, Ipswich, IP6 0SA
Tel: 01473-785911 **Fax:** 01473-785921
E-mail: sales@wilms.co.uk
Website: http://www.wilms.co.uk
Directors: M. Storey (Dir)
Ultimate Holding Company: BRITISH FLOWPLANT GROUP
Registration no: 01238568 **VAT No.:** GB 631 9586 18
Date established: 1997 **Turnover:** £1m - £2m **No.of Employees:** 1 - 10
Product Groups: 40, 46

Yarwood Editorial Services
9 Willow Walk Needham Market, Ipswich, IP6 8DT
Tel: 01449-720558
E-mail: yarwood-editorial-services@phonecoop.coop
Managers: K. Yarwood
Turnover: Up to £250,000 **No.of Employees:** 1 - 10 **Product Groups:** 80, 81

Leiston

Beacon Lights
Beacon House Eastlands Industrial Estate, Leiston, IP16 4LL
Tel: 01728-833800 **Fax:** 08700-410421
E-mail: info@beaconlights.co.uk
Directors: P. Smith (Ptnr)
Immediate Holding Company: UNITEG SOLUTIONS LIMITED
Registration no: 02697978 **Date established:** 1992
Turnover: £500,000 - £1m **No.of Employees:** 1 - 10 **Product Groups:** 37, 67

Date of Accounts	Apr 95	Apr 11	Apr 10
Working Capital	7	N/A	N/A
Current Assets	10	N/A	N/A

Cable Accessories Ltd
Masterlord Industrial Park Station Road, Leiston, IP16 4JD
Tel: 01728-832799 **Fax:** 01728-831726
E-mail: sales@cableaccessories.com
Website: http://www.cableaccessories.com
Directors: J. Teehan (Co Sec), H. Brewell (Dir)
Immediate Holding Company: CABLE ACCESSORIES LIMITED
Registration no: 04196490 **VAT No.:** GB 772 6574 95
Date established: 2001 **Turnover:** £2m - £5m **No.of Employees:** 1 - 10
Product Groups: 36, 37, 39, 40, 47, 67, 68

Date of Accounts	Sep 11	Sep 10	Sep 09
Working Capital	70	80	81
Fixed Assets	43	40	23
Current Assets	619	720	606
Current Liabilities	N/A	340	276

D I G Engineering Ltd
Master Lord Industrial Estate, Leiston, IP16 4JD
Tel: 01728-832755 **Fax:** 01728-832764
E-mail: ivant@dig-group.co.uk
Website: http://www.dig-group.co.uk
Bank(s): HSBC Bank plc
Directors: I. Turner (Fin)
Ultimate Holding Company: D.I.G. (HOLDINGS) LIMITED
Immediate Holding Company: D.I.G. TUBE MANIPULATION & FABRICATION LIMITED
Registration no: 02317274 **VAT No.:** GB 632 1016 93
Date established: 1988 **No.of Employees:** 21 - 50 **Product Groups:** 44

Date of Accounts	Oct 11	Oct 10	Oct 09
Working Capital	203	217	217
Current Assets	227	246	250

Howarth Winterbrook Ltd
Key Building Eastlands Road, Leiston, IP16 4LL
Tel: 01728-833822 **Fax:** 01728-833855
E-mail: vicwoodgate@winterbrook.co.uk
Website: http://www.winterbrook.co.uk
Directors: V. Woodgate (MD)
Immediate Holding Company: UNITEG SOLUTIONS LIMITED
Registration no: 02001242 **VAT No.:** GB 390 6121 65
Date established: 1992 **Turnover:** £2m - £5m **No.of Employees:** 1 - 10
Product Groups: 20, 61, 62

Date of Accounts	Apr 95	Apr 11	Apr 10
Working Capital	7	N/A	N/A
Current Assets	10	N/A	N/A

Lowestoft

A 1 Productions Ltd
135 Yarmouth Road, Lowestoft, NR32 4AF
Tel: 01502-568616
E-mail: tom@a1productions.co.uk
Website: http://www.a1productions.co.uk
Directors: T. Tailford (MD)
Registration no: NF003140 **Date established:** 2008
Turnover: Up to £250,000 **No.of Employees:** 1 - 10 **Product Groups:** 44, 81

A K D Engineering Ltd
Horn Hill, Lowestoft, NR33 0PX
Tel: 01502-527800 **Fax:** 01502-527848
E-mail: sales@akd-engineering.co.uk
Website: http://www.akd-engineering.co.uk
Bank(s): Lloyds TSB Bank plc
Directors: F. Pallett (Sales), M. Perkins (Fin), M. Jones (MD)
Managers: L. Mitchell (Personnel), R. Anderson (Comptroller), T. Flegg (Buyer), C. Moore
Ultimate Holding Company: CAMELLIA PUBLIC LIMITED COMPANY
Immediate Holding Company: A.K.D.ENGINEERING LIMITED
Registration no: 00542907 **VAT No.:** GB 104 9386 69
Date established: 1955 **Turnover:** £2m - £5m **No.of Employees:** 51 - 100
Product Groups: 48

Date of Accounts	Dec 11	Dec 10	Dec 09
Sales Turnover	7m	6m	11m
Pre Tax Profit/Loss	-592	-321	868
Working Capital	682	35	286
Fixed Assets	2m	2m	2m
Current Assets	3m	2m	3m
Current Liabilities	428	706	2m

Automotive Cleaning Chemcials
4 Hadenham Road, Lowestoft, NR33 7NF
Tel: 01502-588133 **Fax:** 01502-501491
E-mail: alan.cook@acc-limited.co.uk
Website: http://www.acc-ltd.co.uk
Managers: A. Cook (Tech Serv Mgr)
Ultimate Holding Company: CALEDONIA INVESTMENTS PLC
Immediate Holding Company: AMBER CHEMICAL COMPANY LIMITED(THE)
Registration no: 01873880 **Date established:** 1984 **Turnover:** £2m - £5m
No.of Employees: 1 - 10 **Product Groups:** 35, 45

East Anglian Radio Services
4 High Beech, Lowestoft, NR32 2RY
Tel: 01502-568021 **Fax:** 07050-600176
E-mail: sales@eastanglianradio.com
Website: http://www.eastanglianradio.com
Managers: P. Johnson (Prod Mgr)
No.of Employees: 1 - 10 **Product Groups:** 37, 44, 83

Eastern Hardware Co. Ltd
Hamilton Road, Lowestoft, NR32 1XF
Tel: 01502-573257 **Fax:** 01502-586235
E-mail: eastern_hardware@btconnect.com
Bank(s): Barclays, Lowestoft
Directors: S. Beckett (Fin)
Ultimate Holding Company: PETER COLBY COMMERCIALS LIMITED
Immediate Holding Company: EASTERN HARDWARE COMPANY LIMITED
Registration no: 00391590 **VAT No.:** GB 104 9308 89
Date established: 1944 **Turnover:** £500,000 - £1m
No.of Employees: 11 - 20 **Product Groups:** 48

Date of Accounts	Sep 11	Sep 10	Sep 09
Sales Turnover	970	1m	782
Pre Tax Profit/Loss	101	105	67
Working Capital	195	121	93
Fixed Assets	30	10	12
Current Assets	297	301	229
Current Liabilities	71	64	39

Ecoflue
Copperfields Beach Road, Kessingland, Lowestoft, NR33 7RW
Tel: 01502-741388
E-mail: ecoflue@aol.com
Website: http://www.ecoflue.co.uk
Directors: J. Block (Prop)
Immediate Holding Company: ECOFLUE LIMITED
Registration no: 05597422 **Date established:** 2005
No.of Employees: 1 - 10 **Product Groups:** 33, 52

Date of Accounts	Aug 11	Aug 10	Aug 09
Working Capital	-4	-1	1
Fixed Assets	8	10	18
Current Assets	53	39	36

Elmdale Welding & Engineering Supplies Ltd
3 Sunhaven Industrial Estate Whapload Road, Lowestoft, NR32 1UE
Tel: 01502-562230 **Fax:** 01502-573963
E-mail: info@elmdale.co.uk
Website: http://www.elmdale.co.uk
Managers: M. Zandbergn (Mgr)
Immediate Holding Company: ELMDALE WELDING AND ENGINEERING SUPPLIES LIMITED
Registration no: 02018707 **Date established:** 1986
No.of Employees: 1 - 10 **Product Groups:** 46

Date of Accounts	Mar 11	Mar 10	Mar 09
Working Capital	526	463	436
Fixed Assets	150	185	172
Current Assets	1m	1m	1m

Energy Related Supplies Ltd
South Elmham Terrace, Lowestoft, NR33 9NQ
Tel: 01502-516836 **Fax:** 01502-500010
E-mail: ers@energyrelated.freeserve.co.uk
Directors: S. Dores (Prop)
Immediate Holding Company: ENERGY RELATED SUPPLIES LIMITED
Registration no: 01808510 **VAT No.:** GB 390 6950 26
Date established: 1984 **Turnover:** £1m - £2m **No.of Employees:** 1 - 10
Product Groups: 36, 61

Date of Accounts	Sep 11	Sep 10	Sep 09
Working Capital	359	289	342
Fixed Assets	125	534	530
Current Assets	382	509	477

Essex & Suffolk Water plc
Rectory Road, Lowestoft, NR33 0TL
Tel: 08457-820111 **Fax:** 01245-212345
E-mail: contactus@eswater.co.uk
Website: http://www.eswater.co.uk
Directors: J. Cuthbert (MD)
Ultimate Holding Company: SUEZ LYONNAISE - DES - EAUX
Registration no: 02635436 **Turnover:** £75m - £125m
No.of Employees: 1 - 10 **Product Groups:** 18

John Grose Group Ltd
Whapload Road, Lowestoft, NR32 1NN
Tel: 01502-565353 **Fax:** 01502-554767
E-mail: alistairleath@johngrose.co.uk
Website: http://www.johngrose.co.uk
Bank(s): HSBC Bank plc
Directors: D. Meade (Co Sec), P. Smith (Dir), A. Leith (MD)
Managers: D. Reed (Personnel), D. Ryder (Parts Mgr), J. Price (Sales & Mktg Mg), R. Snelham (Tech Serv Mgr)
Immediate Holding Company: JOHN GROSE GROUP LIMITED
Registration no: 01491537 **VAT No.:** GB 336 1738 55
Date established: 1980 **Turnover:** £75m - £125m
No.of Employees: 21 - 50 **Product Groups:** 39, 68

Date of Accounts	Dec 11	Dec 10	Dec 09
Sales Turnover	124m	118m	109m
Pre Tax Profit/Loss	2m	3m	3m
Working Capital	4m	5m	4m
Fixed Assets	13m	12m	12m
Current Assets	27m	29m	29m
Current Liabilities	2m	2m	3m

Harrod UK Ltd
1-3 Pinbush Road, Lowestoft, NR33 7NL
Tel: 01502-583515 **Fax:** 01502-582456
E-mail: sales@harrod.uk.com
Website: http://www.harrod.uk.com
Bank(s): HSBC Bank plc
Directors: C. Harrod (MD)
Managers: H. Simpson (Personnel), D. Bowling (Purch Mgr), L. Saunders (Mktg Serv Mgr)
Immediate Holding Company: HARROD UK LIMITED
Registration no: 00875029 **VAT No.:** GB 104 8573 75
Date established: 1966 **Turnover:** £10m - £20m
No.of Employees: 101 - 250 **Product Groups:** 23, 49, 52

Date of Accounts	Dec 11	Dec 10	Dec 09
Sales Turnover	12m	12m	12m
Pre Tax Profit/Loss	578	577	833
Working Capital	3m	3m	3m
Fixed Assets	2m	2m	2m
Current Assets	4m	4m	4m
Current Liabilities	458	390	507

Intuitive Solution
4 Suffolk Road, Lowestoft, NR32 1DZ
Tel: 01502-587613 **Fax:** 01502-514875
E-mail: enquiries@intuitivesolution.net
Website: http://www.intuitivesolution.net
Managers: I. Solution (Mgr)
Immediate Holding Company: L.R. GODFREY (LOWESTOFT) LIMITED
Date established: 1978 **No.of Employees:** 1 - 10 **Product Groups:** 44

Date of Accounts	Jan 11	Jan 10	Jan 09
Working Capital	411	196	56
Fixed Assets	34	7	10
Current Assets	1m	794	441

J M E Ltd
Electron House Old Nelson Street, Lowestoft, NR32 1EQ
Tel: 01502-500969 **Fax:** 01502-511932
E-mail: info@jme.co.uk
Website: http://www.jme.co.uk
Bank(s): National Westminster Bank Plc
Directors: P. Marjoribanks (MD), C. Wright (Fin)
Managers: M. Gale (Prod Mgr), S. Jennings (Develop Mgr)
Immediate Holding Company: JME LTD
Registration no: 02056386 **VAT No.:** GB 443 0172 87
Date established: 1986 **Turnover:** £1m - £2m **No.of Employees:** 21 - 50
Product Groups: 37, 38

Date of Accounts	Nov 11	Nov 10	Nov 09
Working Capital	2m	2m	2m
Fixed Assets	877	871	463
Current Assets	3m	3m	3m

L E C Marine Klyne Ltd
5 Cumberland Place, Lowestoft, NR32 1UQ
Tel: 01502-516971 **Fax:** 01502-516970
E-mail: enquire@lecmarine-klyne.co.uk
Website: http://www.lecmarine-klyne.com
Bank(s): National Westminster Bank Plc
Directors: M. Sawyer (MD), J. Anniss (Co Sec)
Immediate Holding Company: L.E.C. MARINE (KLYNE) LIMITED
Registration no: 05347674 **VAT No.:** GB 105 7823 77
Date established: 2005 **Turnover:** £10m - £20m
No.of Employees: 21 - 50 **Product Groups:** 37, 39, 48, 52, 80, 84

Date of Accounts	Oct 11	Oct 10	Oct 09
Working Capital	160	104	67
Fixed Assets	32	32	29
Current Assets	485	393	362

Lowestoft Tool Hire
Pearl Works Alexandra Road, Lowestoft, NR32 1PL
Tel: 01502-589291 **Fax:** 01502-501712
Directors: J. Dodsworth (Ptnr)
Immediate Holding Company: TENVILLE PRODUCTS LIMITED
Registration no: 01858161 **Date established:** 2003
No.of Employees: 1 - 10 **Product Groups:** 40, 46, 83

Date of Accounts	Jan 11	Jan 10	Jan 07
Working Capital	-0	4	1
Fixed Assets	1	N/A	1
Current Assets	19	27	17

M P Eastern Ltd
Trinity Road, Lowestoft, NR32 1XJ
Tel: 01502-573047 **Fax:** 01502-587419
E-mail: sales@mpeastern.co.uk
Directors: M. Edwards (Fin), R. Guise (MD)
Immediate Holding Company: M.P. (EASTERN) LIMITED
Registration no: 01918058 **Date established:** 1985
No.of Employees: 11 - 20 **Product Groups:** 46, 48

Date of Accounts	May 11	May 10	May 09
Working Capital	710	661	623
Fixed Assets	516	403	331
Current Assets	1m	1m	1m

Marine Electrics
Wildes Street, Lowestoft, NR32 1XH
Tel: 01502-518606 **Fax:** 01502-508169
E-mail: clivepickess@yahoo.co.uk
Directors: C. Pickess (Ptnr)
Immediate Holding Company: MARINE ELECTRICS LIMITED
Registration no: 02702168 **Date established:** 1992
No.of Employees: 11 - 20 **Product Groups:** 35, 36, 39

Date of Accounts	Apr 11	Apr 10	Apr 09
Working Capital	6	-18	-57
Fixed Assets	49	53	57
Current Assets	100	131	91

Middleton Heat Treatments Ltd
305 Whapload Road, Lowestoft, NR32 1UL
Tel: 01502-561721 **Fax:** 01502-517712
E-mail: mail@middleton-heat.co.uk
Website: http://www.middleton-heat.co.uk
Directors: S. Middleton (Dir)
Immediate Holding Company: MIDDLETON HEAT TREATMENTS LIMITED
Registration no: 02243676 **Date established:** 1988
No.of Employees: 1 - 10 **Product Groups:** 46, 48

Date of Accounts	Sep 11	Sep 10	Sep 09
Working Capital	203	111	99
Fixed Assets	75	80	60
Current Assets	320	188	173

Mobile M I G Ltd
Unit 4 Arnold Street, Lowestoft, NR32 1PU
Tel: 01502-512970 **Fax:** 01502-512971
E-mail: sales@mobilemig.co.uk
Website: http://www.mobilemig.co.uk
Directors: R. Kirkwood (MD)
Immediate Holding Company: MOBILE MIG LIMITED
Registration no: 04703846 **Date established:** 2003
Turnover: Up to £250,000 **No.of Employees:** 1 - 10 **Product Groups:** 26, 35

Date of Accounts	Mar 12	Mar 11	Mar 10
Sales Turnover	N/A	N/A	121
Pre Tax Profit/Loss	N/A	N/A	36
Working Capital	72	68	90
Fixed Assets	11	14	13
Current Assets	118	124	130
Current Liabilities	44	N/A	15

Nexen Lift Trucks Ltd
Riverside Road, Lowestoft, NR33 0TU
Tel: 01502-532211 **Fax:** 01502-508273
E-mail: info@nexenlifttrucks.com
Website: http://www.nexenlifttrucks.com
Directors: T. Mason (MD), S. Bowkett (Fin)
Managers: M. Edwards (Parts Mgr)
Ultimate Holding Company: WAVENEY FORK TRUCKS LIMITED
Immediate Holding Company: NEXEN LIFT TRUCKS LIMITED
Registration no: 04533784 **Date established:** 2002
No.of Employees: 21 - 50 **Product Groups:** 35, 39, 45

Date of Accounts	Jun 11	Jun 10	Jun 09
Working Capital	-2m	-383	-78
Fixed Assets	2m	85	39
Current Assets	1m	1m	1m

Norbert Dentressangle
Mobbs Way, Lowestoft, NR32 3BN
Tel: 01502-562911 **Fax:** 01502-511543
E-mail: derek.samuels@norbert-dentressangle.com
Website: http://www.norbertdentressangle.com
Managers: D. Samuels (Site Co-ord)
Registration no: SC007173 **Turnover:** £2m - £5m
No.of Employees: 51 - 100 **Product Groups:** 39, 72, 84

Polgain Ltd Peter Colby Commercials Ltd
1 Crown Score, Lowestoft, NR32 1JH
Tel: 01502-532880 **Fax:** 01502-539804
E-mail: info@polgain.co.uk
Website: http://www.polgain.co.uk
Managers: A. Bond (Chief Mgr)
Ultimate Holding Company: PETER COLBY COMMERCIALS LIMITED
Immediate Holding Company: POLGAIN LIMITED
Registration no: 03367952 **Date established:** 1997
Turnover: £500,000 - £1m **No.of Employees:** 11 - 20
Product Groups: 35, 37, 40, 48, 84

Date of Accounts	Sep 11	Sep 10	Sep 09
Sales Turnover	2m	1m	671
Pre Tax Profit/Loss	367	52	-54
Working Capital	102	-252	-279
Fixed Assets	234	193	124
Current Assets	593	442	183
Current Liabilities	241	116	15

R J Pryce & Company
Trinity Road, Lowestoft, NR32 1XJ
Tel: 01502-574141 **Fax:** 01502-501213
E-mail: sales@rjpryce.co.uk
Website: http://www.rjpryce.co.uk
Directors: D. Pryce (MD), J. Pryce (Fin)
Immediate Holding Company: R.J. PRYCE & CO. LIMITED
Registration no: 00559151 **VAT No.:** GB 104 6463 92
Date established: 1955 **Turnover:** £1m - £2m **No.of Employees:** 11 - 20
Product Groups: 35, 66

Date of Accounts	Dec 11	Dec 10	Dec 09
Working Capital	1m	957	886
Fixed Assets	534	563	595
Current Assets	1m	1m	1m

Small & Co Marine & Engineering Ltd
The Dry Dock 50 Commercial Road, Lowestoft, NR32 2TE
Tel: 01502-585709 **Fax:** 01502-581141
E-mail: paulk@smallandco.co.uk
Website: http://www.smallandco.co.uk
Bank(s): National Westminster Bank Plc
Directors: P. Kirby (MD), C. Kirby (Fin)
Immediate Holding Company: SMALL & CO MARINE & ENGINEERING LIMITED
Registration no: 02888294 **VAT No.:** GB 640 3983 37
Date established: 1994 **Turnover:** £2m - £5m **No.of Employees:** 21 - 50
Product Groups: 34, 35, 39, 41, 48

Date of Accounts	Sep 11	Sep 10	Sep 09
Working Capital	696	774	877
Fixed Assets	258	174	154
Current Assets	1m	1m	1m

Solar Energy Alliance Ltd
9 Battery Green Road, Lowestoft, NR32 1DE
Tel: 01502-512340 **Fax:** 01502-561399
E-mail: info@solarenergyalliance.com
Website: http://www.solarenergyalliance.com
Directors: C. King (Fin), C. Goodings (MD)
Immediate Holding Company: SOLAR ENERGY ALLIANCE LTD
Registration no: 06391061 **VAT No.:** GB 711 6535 56
Date established: 2007 **Turnover:** £500,000 - £1m
No.of Employees: 1 - 10 **Product Groups:** 37

Date of Accounts	Oct 11	Oct 10	Oct 09
Working Capital	210	84	51
Fixed Assets	147	148	4
Current Assets	674	290	161

Starfrost UK Ltd
Starfrost House Newcombe Road, Lowestoft, NR32 1XA
Tel: 01502-562206 **Fax:** 01502-584104
E-mail: sales@starfrost.co.uk
Website: http://www.starfrost.com

see next page

Starfrost UK Ltd - Cont'd
Bank(s): Lloyds TSB
Directors: K. Baillie (Fin), N. Hards (Fab), N. Winney (MD)
Managers: H. Bullman (Tech Serv Mgr), L. Allgrove (Mktg Serv Mgr), G. Bocking (Personnel)
Ultimate Holding Company: STAR REFRIGERATION LIMITED
Immediate Holding Company: STARFROST (UK) LIMITED
Registration no: 03124205 **VAT No.:** 394 2543 35 **Date established:** 1995
Turnover: £2m - £5m **No.of Employees:** 11 - 20 **Product Groups:** 40, 84

Date of Accounts	Dec 11	Dec 10	Dec 09
Sales Turnover	4m	4m	3m
Pre Tax Profit/Loss	39	86	8
Working Capital	566	574	540
Fixed Assets	21	19	19
Current Assets	2m	1m	989
Current Liabilities	552	489	292

System Control Solutions Ltd
7 Barley Way, Lowestoft, NR33 7NH
Tel: 01502-516864 **Fax:** 01502-501023
E-mail: rscales@scslow.co.uk
Website: http://www.scslow.co.uk
Directors: R. Scales (MD)
Immediate Holding Company: SYSTEM CONTROL SOLUTIONS LIMITED
Registration no: 01873729 **VAT No.:** GB 410 6727 77
Date established: 1984 **No.of Employees:** 1 - 10 **Product Groups:** 35, 37, 38

Date of Accounts	Mar 11	Mar 10	Mar 09
Working Capital	35	28	57
Fixed Assets	5	13	22
Current Assets	159	105	197

Waveney Rush Industry
The Old Maltings Caldecott Road, Lowestoft, NR32 3PH
Tel: 01502-538777 **Fax:** 01502-538477
E-mail: anna@waveneyrush.co.uk
Website: http://www.waveneyrush.co.uk
Directors: A. Toulson (Dir)
Registration no: 3940100 **Date established:** 1947
Turnover: Up to £250,000 **No.of Employees:** 1 - 10 **Product Groups:** 63

Date of Accounts	Dec 11	Dec 10	Dec 09
Working Capital	121	43	66
Fixed Assets	60	96	99
Current Assets	181	80	96

Westgate Fastenings
5-6 Cumberland Place, Lowestoft, NR32 1UQ
Tel: 01502-560061 **Fax:** 01502-517505
Managers: P. Newrick (Mgr)
Date established: 1987 **No.of Employees:** 1 - 10 **Product Groups:** 35

Witham Oil & Paint Lowestoft Ltd
Waveney Works Stanley Road, Lowestoft, NR33 9ND
Tel: 01502-563434 **Fax:** 01502-500010
E-mail: tony.baker@withamgroup.co.uk
Website: http://www.withamgroup.co.uk
Managers: J. Turner (Tech Serv Mgr), T. Baker (Ops Mgr), I. Haynes
Ultimate Holding Company: WITHAM GROUP HOLDINGS LIMITED
Immediate Holding Company: WITHAM OIL & PAINT (LOWESTOFT) LIMITED
Registration no: 02117373 **Date established:** 1987 **Turnover:** £1m - £2m
No.of Employees: 11 - 20 **Product Groups:** 31, 32

Date of Accounts	Mar 11	Mar 10	Mar 09
Working Capital	155	263	230
Fixed Assets	138	109	105
Current Assets	1m	897	788

Wrought Iron Specialists
North East Suffolk Business Centre Pinbush Road, Lowestoft, NR33 7NQ
Tel: 01502-585822 **Fax:** 01502-511834
E-mail: davidbwroughtiron@btinternet.com
Website: http://www.wroughtironspecialistslowestoft.co.uk
Directors: D. Burdett (Prop)
Immediate Holding Company: FLOOR SURFACES LIMITED
Registration no: 06423185 **Date established:** 2007
No.of Employees: 1 - 10 **Product Groups:** 26, 35

Zephyr Products
10 Battery Green Road, Lowestoft, NR32 1DE
Tel: 01502-572233 **Fax:** 01502-516700
E-mail: info@zephyrproducts.co.uk
Website: http://www.zephyrproducts.co.uk
Directors: D. Baldrey (Dir), D. Baldry (Dir)
Immediate Holding Company: ZEPHYR PRODUCTS LIMITED
Registration no: 02262564 **Date established:** 1988
No.of Employees: 1 - 10 **Product Groups:** 30, 35, 36

Date of Accounts	Dec 10	Dec 09	Dec 08
Working Capital	-27	41	3
Fixed Assets	12	16	N/A
Current Assets	60	245	75

Newmarket

Allied Mechanic Services Ltd (a division of Makers (UK) Ltd
Depot Road, Newmarket, CB8 0AL
Tel: 01638-661062 **Fax:** 01638-666538
E-mail: info@alliedservices.co.uk
Website: http://www.alliedservices.co.uk
Bank(s): Lloyds TSB Bank plc
Directors: A. Smith (Fin), N. Smith (Dir), P. Vickers (Dir)
Ultimate Holding Company: DAVID JARVIS (HOLDINGS) LIMITED
Immediate Holding Company: NEWMARKET PLANT HIRE LIMITED
Registration no: 02189826 **VAT No.:** GB 360 3854 58
Date established: 1987 **Turnover:** £2m - £5m **No.of Employees:** 21 - 50
Product Groups: 52

Date of Accounts	Jan 12	Jan 11	Jan 10
Working Capital	14	14	14
Current Assets	14	14	14

Anglian Precision Ltd
Unit 4 Lanwades Business Park Kennett, Newmarket, CB8 7PN
Tel: 01638-552111 **Fax:** 01638-552701
E-mail: sales@anglianprecision.co.uk
Website: http://www.anglianprecision.co.uk
Directors: S. Wallace (MD)
Immediate Holding Company: ANGLIAN PRECISION LIMITED
Registration no: 02866160 **Date established:** 1993
No.of Employees: 1 - 10 **Product Groups:** 46

Date of Accounts	Oct 11	Oct 10	Oct 09
Working Capital	189	244	233
Fixed Assets	41	50	66
Current Assets	290	326	314

B G Europa UK Ltd
Giffords Road Clopton, Wickhambrook, Newmarket, CB8 8PQ
Tel: 01440-821155 **Fax:** 01440-821156
E-mail: parts@bgeuropa.co.uk
Website: http://www.bgeuropa.co.uk
Directors: A. Pettingale (MD)
Immediate Holding Company: BG EUROPA (UK) LIMITED
Registration no: 02215504 **VAT No.:** GB 496 8151 02
Date established: 1988 **Turnover:** £1m - £2m **No.of Employees:** 1 - 10
Product Groups: 45

Date of Accounts	Dec 11	Dec 10	Dec 09
Working Capital	930	895	901
Fixed Assets	82	93	112
Current Assets	1m	1m	1m

B S A S Telecoms Ltd
Systems House Chippenham Hill, Moulton, Newmarket, CB8 7PL
Tel: 01638-552888 **Fax:** 01638-552892
E-mail: info@bsas.co.uk
Website: http://www.bsas.co.uk
Directors: A. Ebbsworth (MD)
Immediate Holding Company: BSAS (TELECOMS) LIMITED
Registration no: 04129178 **Date established:** 2000
No.of Employees: 21 - 50 **Product Groups:** 80

Date of Accounts	Nov 11	Nov 10	Nov 09
Working Capital	79	53	57
Fixed Assets	39	39	53
Current Assets	291	288	232

Beehive Coils Ltd
Studlands Park Industrial Estate, Newmarket, CB8 7AU
Tel: 01638-664134 **Fax:** 01638-661623
E-mail: info@beehivecoils.co.uk
Website: http://www.beehivecoils.co.uk
Bank(s): Barclays, High Street
Directors: M. Bartram (Dir), P. Turnbull (Chief Op Offcr), R. Bartram (MD)
Managers: C. Key, E. Copeman (Sales Prom Mgr)
Ultimate Holding Company: GEM INDUSTRIAL PRODUCTS LIMITED
Immediate Holding Company: BEEHIVE COILS LIMITED
Registration no: 00926489 **VAT No.:** GB 102 2666 13
Date established: 1968 **Turnover:** £2m - £5m **No.of Employees:** 51 - 100
Product Groups: 36, 40

Date of Accounts	Mar 11	Mar 10	Mar 09
Working Capital	1m	1m	1m
Current Assets	4m	3m	2m

H.E. & B.S. Benson Ltd
1 Laureate Industrial Estate School Road, Exning Road, Newmarket, CB8 0AR
Tel: 01638-663535 **Fax:** 01638-667434
E-mail: sales@hebsbenson.co.uk
Website: http://www.hebsbenson.co.uk
Bank(s): Barclays
Directors: D. Price (MD)
Managers: G. Atkins, M. Goodrham (Prod Mgr)
Registration no: 00717293 **VAT No.:** GB 102 0988 01
Turnover: £1m - £2m **No.of Employees:** 21 - 50 **Product Groups:** 37, 39, 67

Date of Accounts	Dec 07	Dec 06	Dec 05
Working Capital	374	367	359
Fixed Assets	94	79	66
Current Assets	463	461	508
Current Liabilities	89	94	148

Bronkhorst UK Ltd
1 Willie Snaith Road, Newmarket, CB8 7TG
Tel: 01223-833222 **Fax:** 01223-837683
E-mail: sales@bronkhorst.co.uk
Website: http://www.bronkhorst.co.uk
Managers: N. Pearce (Sales Prom Mgr)
Immediate Holding Company: BRONKHORST (UK) LIMITED
Registration no: 04376245 **VAT No.:** GB 793 3251 17
Date established: 2002 **No.of Employees:** 11 - 20 **Product Groups:** 36, 38, 40, 44, 67

Date of Accounts	Dec 11	Dec 10	Dec 09
Sales Turnover	N/A	5m	5m
Pre Tax Profit/Loss	N/A	301	212
Working Capital	873	948	800
Fixed Assets	90	113	26
Current Assets	1m	2m	1m
Current Liabilities	N/A	336	252

C & T Harnesses Ltd
Unit 2 Lanwades Business Park Kennett, Newmarket, CB8 7PN
Tel: 01638-751511 **Fax:** 01638-751965
E-mail: michael.cornwell@ctharnesses.com
Website: http://www.ctharnesses.com
Bank(s): Royal Bank of Scotland, Cambridge
Directors: M. Cornwell (MD)
Immediate Holding Company: C & T HARNESSES LIMITED
Registration no: 01740465 **Date established:** 1983
Turnover: £500,000 - £1m **No.of Employees:** 11 - 20 **Product Groups:** 37

Date of Accounts	Nov 11	Nov 10	Nov 09
Working Capital	359	382	403
Fixed Assets	3	3	3
Current Assets	460	456	455

Calbarrie Cambridge Ltd
Kennett Cottages Kennett, Newmarket, CB8 7QH
Tel: 01638-555150
E-mail: cambridge@calbarrie.com
Directors: J. Keyworth (Fin), M. Keyworth (MD)
Immediate Holding Company: CALBARRIE (CAMBRIDGE) LIMITED
Registration no: 05333894 **Date established:** 2005
No.of Employees: 1 - 10 **Product Groups:** 38, 42

Date of Accounts	Jan 12	Jan 11	Jan 10
Working Capital	-19	-26	-34
Fixed Assets	21	22	30
Current Assets	43	19	46

Cannon Textile Care
46 Exeter Road, Newmarket, CB8 8LR
Tel: 01638-663144 **Fax:** 01638-660056
E-mail: shaun.willett@ocs.co.uk
Website: http://www.cannonhygiene.com
Managers: S. Willett (Ops Mgr), T. Lusher (Chief Mgr)
Ultimate Holding Company: UFAC HOLDINGS LIMITED (IRELAND)
Immediate Holding Company: UFAC (U.K.) LIMITED
Registration no: 01276803 **Date established:** 1976
Turnover: £500,000 - £1m **No.of Employees:** 51 - 100
Product Groups: 23, 83

Date of Accounts	Mar 11	Mar 10	Mar 09
Working Capital	479	460	402
Fixed Assets	169	98	79
Current Assets	2m	2m	1m

Caps Cases Ltd
Studlands Park Industrial Estate, Newmarket, CB8 7AU
Tel: 01638-667326 **Fax:** 01638-667407
E-mail: sales@capscases.co.uk
Website: http://www.capscases.co.uk
Bank(s): Lloyds TSB Bank plc
Directors: T. Bissett (MD)
Ultimate Holding Company: TRADEGREAT LIMITED
Immediate Holding Company: CAPS CASES LIMITED
Registration no: 01636565 **Date established:** 1982
No.of Employees: 51 - 100 **Product Groups:** 26, 27

Date of Accounts	Oct 11	Oct 10	Oct 09
Sales Turnover	16m	14m	12m
Pre Tax Profit/Loss	409	67	70
Working Capital	192	-432	-494
Fixed Assets	2m	3m	3m
Current Assets	5m	4m	3m
Current Liabilities	2m	2m	1m

Cobham Antenna Systems, Microwave Antennas
Lambda House Cheveley, Newmarket, CB8 9RG
Tel: 01638-731888 **Fax:** 01638-731999
E-mail: antennasystems.ma@cobham.com
Website: http://www.european-antennas.co.uk
Bank(s): Barclays
Directors: B. Phillips (MD), M. Ware (Develop), C. Walker (Tech Serv)
Managers: S. Blades (Sales Prom), D. Spraggins (Buyer), P. Cornell (Mktg Serv Mgr)
Ultimate Holding Company: Cobham P.L.C.
Immediate Holding Company: Chelton Group
Registration no: 02547237 **Date established:** 1991 **Turnover:** £5m - £10m
No.of Employees: 21 - 50 **Product Groups:** 37

Coutts Arken Display Ltd
Unit 10 Studlands Park Avenue, Newmarket, CB8 7EA
Tel: 01638-565600 **Fax:** 01638-662770
E-mail: info@arken-pop.com
Website: http://www.arken-pop.com
Bank(s): Barclays
Directors: T. Scutt (MD)
Immediate Holding Company: C. A. Coutts Retail Ltd
Registration no: 01079247 **VAT No.:** GB 386 9550 95
Turnover: £2m - £5m **No.of Employees:** 51 - 100 **Product Groups:** 26, 30, 36, 37, 39, 45

Date of Accounts	Feb 08
Sales Turnover	12230
Pre Tax Profit/Loss	920
Working Capital	1440
Fixed Assets	2600
Current Assets	4920
Current Liabilities	3480
Total Share Capital	100
ROCE% (Return on Capital Employed)	22.8

D A G Corrugated Packaging
69 St Johns Avenue, Newmarket, CB8 8DE
Tel: 01638-667630 **Fax:** 01638-667630
Website: http://www.gradwick.fsnet.co.uk
Directors: D. Gradwick (Prop)
Date established: 1974 **No.of Employees:** 1 - 10 **Product Groups:** 38, 42

D S Smith Packaging Ltd
Fordham Road, Newmarket, CB8 7TX
Tel: 01638-722100 **Fax:** 01638-722101
E-mail: richard.caunt@dssp.com
Website: http://www.dssmith-packaging.com
Bank(s): National Westminster Bank Plc
Directors: G. Cox (MD)
Ultimate Holding Company: DS SMITH PLC
Immediate Holding Company: DS SMITH PACKAGING LIMITED
Registration no: 00630681 **VAT No.:** GB 599 3782 63
Date established: 1959 **Turnover:** £20m - £50m
No.of Employees: 101 - 250 **Product Groups:** 27

Date of Accounts	Apr 11	Apr 10	Apr 09
Sales Turnover	513m	427m	434m
Pre Tax Profit/Loss	17m	29m	18m
Working Capital	22m	24m	30m
Fixed Assets	125m	127m	137m
Current Assets	123m	116m	104m
Current Liabilities	15m	21m	19m

Dialight Europe
Exning Road, Newmarket, CB8 0AX
Tel: 01638-665161 **Fax:** 01638-561735
E-mail: sales@dialight.com
Website: http://www.blpcomp.com
Directors: N. Rowlan (Fin)
Managers: M. Rogers (Tech Serv Mgr), V. Matthews (Personnel), D. Richardson, R. Genders (Mktg Serv Mgr)
Ultimate Holding Company: DIALIGHT PLC
Immediate Holding Company: DIALIGHT EUROPE LIMITED
Registration no: 00186538 **Date established:** 2022
Turnover: £20m - £50m **No.of Employees:** 51 - 100 **Product Groups:** 37, 39, 40, 51, 52

Date of Accounts	Dec 11	Dec 10	Dec 09
Sales Turnover	29m	23m	19m
Pre Tax Profit/Loss	-2m	901	1m
Working Capital	683	3m	5m
Fixed Assets	6m	5m	2m
Current Assets	24m	18m	9m
Current Liabilities	1m	577	222

Encon Insulations Ltd
Unit 13 Studlands Park Industrial Estate, Newmarket, CB8 7AU
Tel: 01638-667208 **Fax:** 01638-664081
E-mail: i.blackwell@encon.co.uk
Website: http://www.encon.co.uk
Directors: P. Kirk (Fin)
Managers: J. Pease (Mgr)
Ultimate Holding Company: WOLSELEY PLC (JERSEY)
Immediate Holding Company: ENCON INSULATION LIMITED
Registration no: 01377342 **Date established:** 1978 **Turnover:** £5m - £10m
No.of Employees: 11 - 20 **Product Groups:** 30, 33, 66, 84

Fastec Engineering Ltd
8 Studlands Business Centre Studlands Park Avenue, Newmarket, CB8 7SS
Tel: 01638-660186 **Fax:** 01638-667374
E-mail: sales@fastecengineering.co.uk
Website: http://www.fastecengineering.co.uk
Directors: J. Williams (MD), R. Stokes (Fin)
Managers: D. Sparmer (Fin Mgr), A. Maynard (Tech Serv Mgr), S. Robertson
Immediate Holding Company: FASTEC RACING LIMITED
Registration no: 07940896 **Date established:** 2012 **Turnover:** £1m - £2m
No.of Employees: 21 - 50 **Product Groups:** 35, 48, 65

Date of Accounts	Jun 08	Jun 07	Jun 06
Working Capital	-89	-74	N/A
Fixed Assets	594	543	257
Current Assets	747	535	423
Current Liabilities	837	610	423
Total Share Capital	2	2	2

G E Aviation
Exning Road, Newmarket, CB8 0AU
Tel: 01638-663381 **Fax:** 01638-660628
E-mail: will.green@ge.com
Website: http://www.electroniccomponents.geaviationsystems.com
Bank(s): Lloyds TSB Bank plc
Directors: W. Green (MD)
Managers: S. Huggins (Purch Mgr), S. Riches (Develop Mgr), J. Eyles (Fin Mgr)
Ultimate Holding Company: SMITHS GROUP P.L.C.
Immediate Holding Company: SMITHS AEROSPACE
Registration no: 01047586 **VAT No.:** GB 226 6019 77
Turnover: £5m - £10m **No.of Employees:** 51 - 100 **Product Groups:** 37, 38, 39, 44, 45, 85

Gibson Saddlers Ltd
Queensbury Road, Newmarket, CB8 9AX
Tel: 01638-662330 **Fax:** 01638-666467
E-mail: gibson-saddlers@genie.co.uk
Website: http://www.gibson-saddlers.com
Bank(s): Barclays
Directors: K. Butcher (MD)
Immediate Holding Company: GIBSON SADDLERS LIMITED
Registration no: 00539509 **VAT No.:** GB 103 0724 29
Date established: 1954 **Turnover:** £1m - £2m **No.of Employees:** 11 - 20
Product Groups: 41, 63

Date of Accounts	Jan 12	Jan 11	Jan 10
Working Capital	172	169	163
Fixed Assets	51	33	32
Current Assets	359	373	367

GR3 Ltd
Units 5E & 5F Lynx Business Court, Newmarket, CB8 7NY
Tel: 01638-721296 **Fax:** 01638-721561
E-mail: info@gr3.co.uk
Website: http://www.gr3.co.uk
Product Groups: 33, 35, 52

Date of Accounts	Jul 07	Jul 06	Jul 05
Working Capital	331	308	116
Fixed Assets	204	117	115
Current Assets	753	729	647
Current Liabilities	422	421	531

H P B Management Ltd
24 Old Station Road, Newmarket, CB8 8EH
Tel: 01638-660066 **Fax:** 01638-660213
E-mail: info@hpb.co.uk
Website: http://www.hpb.co.uk
Directors: G. Baber (Prop), J. Baber (MD), R. Coe (Tech Serv), R. Halls (Fin)
Managers: R. Coe (Comptroller), R. Ogden (Personnel), J. Lay (Personnel)
Ultimate Holding Company: HPB HOLDINGS LIMITED (ISLE OF MAN)
Immediate Holding Company: HPB MANAGEMENT LIMITED
Registration no: 01581593 **Date established:** 1981 **Turnover:** £5m - £10m
No.of Employees: 51 - 100 **Product Groups:** 80, 82

Date of Accounts	Dec 11	Dec 10	Dec 09
Sales Turnover	10m	10m	9m
Pre Tax Profit/Loss	71	-215	-304
Working Capital	1m	746	917
Fixed Assets	49	49	49
Current Assets	2m	2m	3m
Current Liabilities	331	306	238

Mr Fothergills Seeds Ltd
Gazeley Road Kentford, Newmarket, CB8 7QB
Tel: 01638-751161 **Fax:** 01638-554083
E-mail: katherine.watt@mr-fothergills.co.uk
Website: http://www.mr-fothergills.co.uk
Bank(s): Barclays
Directors: D. Carey (Sales)
Managers: K. Watt
Immediate Holding Company: MR. FOTHERGILL'S SEEDS LIMITED
Registration no: 01710774 **VAT No.:** GB 390 5718 35
Date established: 1983 **Turnover:** £20m - £50m
No.of Employees: 101 - 250 **Product Groups:** 02, 07, 20, 62

Date of Accounts	Jun 11	Jun 10	Jun 09
Sales Turnover	25m	22m	18m
Pre Tax Profit/Loss	2m	2m	2m
Working Capital	8m	6m	4m
Fixed Assets	2m	2m	1m
Current Assets	16m	13m	11m
Current Liabilities	2m	3m	2m

Musks Ltd
Goodwin House Goodwin Business Park Willie Snaith Road, Newmarket, CB8 7SQ
Tel: 01638-662626 **Fax:** 01638-662424
E-mail: office@musks.com
Website: http://www.musks.com
Managers: E. Sheen (Sales & Mktg Mg)
Ultimate Holding Company: MUSKS FOOD GROUP LIMITED
Immediate Holding Company: MUSKS LIMITED
Registration no: 02782780 **Date established:** 1993 **Turnover:** £1m - £2m
No.of Employees: 1 - 10 **Product Groups:** 20

Date of Accounts	Apr 12	Apr 11	Apr 10
Sales Turnover	N/A	1m	N/A
Pre Tax Profit/Loss	N/A	-1	N/A
Working Capital	145	138	160
Fixed Assets	82	120	121
Current Assets	229	234	275
Current Liabilities	N/A	16	N/A

Pre Tec Engineering
1 Goodwin Business Park Willie Snaith Road, Newmarket, CB8 7SQ
Tel: 01638-561256 **Fax:** 01638-561227
E-mail: robert.bellamy@virgin.net
Directors: R. Bellamy (Prop)
Date established: 1993 **No.of Employees:** 1 - 10 **Product Groups:** 36

Sata UK Ltd
2 Enterprise Court 15 Studlands Park, Newmarket, CB8 7EP
Tel: 01638-666966 **Fax:** 0845-603 7086
E-mail: info@sata.com
Website: http://www.sata.com
Directors: M. Stephens (MD)
Immediate Holding Company: SATA UK LIMITED
Registration no: 05838058 **Date established:** 2006
No.of Employees: 1 - 10 **Product Groups:** 46, 48

Date of Accounts	Dec 11	Dec 10	Dec 09
Sales Turnover	411	403	383
Pre Tax Profit/Loss	27	26	25
Working Capital	106	84	62
Fixed Assets	7	9	11
Current Assets	145	121	97
Current Liabilities	N/A	38	35

Simpsons Of Newmarket
4 Mill Hill, Newmarket, CB8 0JB
Tel: 01638-667066 **Fax:** 01638-667066
E-mail: admin@simpsonsofnewmarket.co.uk
Website: http://www.simpsonsofnewmarket.co.uk
Directors: B. Simpson (Prop)
Date established: 1997 **No.of Employees:** 1 - 10 **Product Groups:** 36, 39, 40

Sionics Ltd
341 Exning Road, Newmarket, CB8 0AT
Tel: 01638-662822 **Fax:** 01638-662833
E-mail: info@sionics.co.uk
Website: http://www.sionics.co.uk
Directors: S. Coulson (MD)
Immediate Holding Company: SIONICS LIMITED
Registration no: 05769067 **Date established:** 2006
No.of Employees: 21 - 50 **Product Groups:** 37, 48, 81, 84

Date of Accounts	Apr 12	Apr 11	Apr 10
Working Capital	-93	-46	-82
Fixed Assets	333	246	185
Current Assets	151	226	79

Stratech Scientific Ltd.
7 Acorn Business Centre Oaks Drive, Newmarket, CB8 7SY
Tel: 01638-782600 **Fax:** 01638-782606
E-mail: info@stratech.co.uk
Website: http://www.stratech.co.uk
Managers: L. Scicluna (Mktg Serv Mgr)
Registration no: 01690218 **Date established:** 1983
No.of Employees: 1 - 10 **Product Groups:** 85

Tattersalls Ltd
Terrace House 125 High Street, Newmarket, CB8 9BT
Tel: 01638-665931 **Fax:** 01638-660850
E-mail: sales@tattersalls.com
Website: http://www.tattersalls.com
Directors: J. George (Mkt Research), J. George (Mkt Research), P. Ryan (Fin)
Managers: F. Rowland (Tech Serv Mgr)
Immediate Holding Company: TATTERSALLS LIMITED
Registration no: 00791113 **Date established:** 1964
Turnover: £10m - £20m **No.of Employees:** 21 - 50 **Product Groups:** 01

Date of Accounts	Jun 11	Jun 10	Jun 09
Sales Turnover	18m	17m	18m
Pre Tax Profit/Loss	4m	2m	3m
Working Capital	17m	15m	15m
Fixed Assets	44m	44m	45m
Current Assets	34m	28m	28m
Current Liabilities	3m	3m	4m

U F A C UK Ltd
Waterwitch House 46 Exeter Road, Newmarket, CB8 8RX
Tel: 01638-665923 **Fax:** 01638-667756
E-mail: mail@ufacuk.com
Website: http://www.ufacuk.com
Directors: R. Jones (MD)
Ultimate Holding Company: UFAC HOLDINGS LIMITED (IRELAND)
Immediate Holding Company: UFAC (U.K.) LIMITED
Registration no: 01239779 **Date established:** 1976
No.of Employees: 1 - 10 **Product Groups:** 20, 62

Date of Accounts	Mar 11	Mar 10	Mar 09
Working Capital	479	460	402
Fixed Assets	169	98	79
Current Assets	2m	2m	1m

Saxmundham

A S I Ltd
Alliance House Snape, Saxmundham, IP17 1SW
Tel: 01728-688555 **Fax:** 01728-688950
E-mail: info@a-s-i.co.uk
Website: http://www.a-s-i.co.uk
Directors: E. King (MD)
Registration no: 01021792 **VAT No.:** GB 102 0398 22
Turnover: £1m - £2m **No.of Employees:** 1 - 10 **Product Groups:** 36

Cico Chimney Linings Ltd
North End Wood Hinton Road, Darsham, Saxmundham, IP17 3QS
Tel: 01986-784044 **Fax:** 01986-784763
E-mail: cico@chimney-problems.co.uk
Website: http://www.chimney-problems.co.uk
Managers: P. Haime
Immediate Holding Company: CICO CHIMNEY LININGS (NORFOLK & SUFFOLK) LIMITED
Registration no: 06144031 **VAT No.:** GB 372 9559 11
Date established: 2007 **Turnover:** £1m - £2m **No.of Employees:** 1 - 10
Product Groups: 33, 35, 40, 52, 84

Date of Accounts	Mar 11	Mar 10	Mar 09
Working Capital	-21	-29	-29
Fixed Assets	2	3	1
Current Assets	12	16	58

Grafo Products Ltd
St Old Good Depot St Johns Road, Saxmundham, IP17 1BE
Tel: 01986-873127 **Fax:** 01986-872850
E-mail: info@grafoproducts.fsnet.co.uk
Website: http://www.grafoproducts.co.uk
Directors: G. Coles (MD)
Immediate Holding Company: GRAFO-PRODUCTS LIMITED
Registration no: 03089657 **Date established:** 1995
Turnover: £250,000 - £500,000 **No.of Employees:** 1 - 10
Product Groups: 32, 52

Date of Accounts	Feb 08	Feb 11	Feb 10
Sales Turnover	584	441	317
Pre Tax Profit/Loss	26	135	-2
Working Capital	81	175	79
Fixed Assets	78	77	68
Current Assets	243	306	244
Current Liabilities	86	81	67

Tenza Technologies Ltd
Carlton Park Industrial Estate Carlton, Saxmundham, IP17 2NL
Tel: 01728-602811 **Fax:** 01728-604108
E-mail: adrian.smith@tenzatech.com
Website: http://www.tenzatech.com
Bank(s): Barclays, Market Place, Macclesfield
Directors: M. Urquart (Co Sec)
Managers: P. Wren (I.T. Exec), E. Pollard (Personnel), L. Greer (Prod Mgr), J. Edwards (Purch Mgr), A. Smith (Chief Mgr)
Ultimate Holding Company: BRIGHTBOROUGH CAPITAL LIMITED
Immediate Holding Company: TENZA TECHNOLOGIES LIMITED
Registration no: 02027635 **VAT No.:** GB 637 7187 06
Date established: 1986 **Turnover:** £20m - £50m
No.of Employees: 51 - 100 **Product Groups:** 27, 28, 30

Date of Accounts	Sep 11	Sep 10	Sep 09
Sales Turnover	20m	18m	15m
Pre Tax Profit/Loss	47	605	509
Working Capital	3m	3m	2m
Fixed Assets	358	356	530
Current Assets	10m	9m	7m
Current Liabilities	4m	4m	3m

V I P Garden Machines
Croft Farm Farnham Road, Snape, Saxmundham, IP17 1QW
Tel: 01728-688457
Directors: D. Abbott (Prop)
Date established: 1988 **No.of Employees:** 1 - 10 **Product Groups:** 36

S Wright
Grove Farm Rendham Road, Saxmundham, IP17 2AA
Tel: 01728-604466 **Fax:** 01728-604466
Directors: S. Wright (Prop)
No.of Employees: 1 - 10 **Product Groups:** 41

Stowmarket

Aspall Cyder
Cyder House Aspall, Stowmarket, IP14 6PD
Tel: 01728-860510 **Fax:** 01728-861031
E-mail: info@aspall.co.uk
Website: http://www.aspall.co.uk
Bank(s): C. Hoare & Co
Directors: B. Chevallier Guild (MD)
Managers: S. Rose (Buyer), C. Maskell (Fin Mgr), D. Ilston (Tech Serv Mgr), T. Johnson (Ops Mgr), H. Ramnought (Mktg Serv Mgr)
Immediate Holding Company: ASPALL CYDER LIMITED
Registration no: 02032494 **VAT No.:** GB 102 2264 17
Date established: 1986 **Turnover:** £5m - £10m
No.of Employees: 51 - 100 **Product Groups:** 20, 21

Date of Accounts	Apr 08	Apr 09	Apr 10
Sales Turnover	N/A	N/A	9m
Pre Tax Profit/Loss	N/A	N/A	209
Working Capital	280	-42	509
Fixed Assets	2m	1m	1m
Current Assets	694	694	1m
Current Liabilities	295	486	688

Baby Point Ltd
Unit 15 Tomo Business Park Tomo Road, Stowmarket, IP14 5EP
Tel: 01449-770607 **Fax:** 01449-678444
E-mail: sales@babypoint.co.uk
Website: http://www.babypoint.co.uk
Directors: J. Grainger (MD)
Immediate Holding Company: BABY POINT LIMITED
Registration no: 02960406 **Date established:** 1994
Turnover: £250,000 - £500,000 **No.of Employees:** 1 - 10
Product Groups: 26

Date of Accounts	Aug 11	Aug 10	Aug 09
Working Capital	27	27	31
Fixed Assets	38	38	41
Current Assets	84	79	84

Bosch Lawn & Garden Ltd
Suffolk Works, Stowmarket, IP14 1EY
Tel: 01449-742000 **Fax:** 01449-742008
Website: http://www.bosch.co.uk
Bank(s): Bank of Scotland

see next page

Bosch Lawn & Garden Ltd - *Cont'd*
Directors: F. Toma (MD)
Ultimate Holding Company: ROBERT BOSCH GMBH (GERMANY)
Immediate Holding Company: BOSCH LAWN AND GARDEN LIMITED
Registration no: 03073491 **VAT No.:** GB 571 4741 37
Date established: 1995 **Turnover:** £125m - £250m
No.of Employees: 501 - 1000 **Product Groups:** 37, 40, 41

Date of Accounts	Dec 11	Dec 10	Dec 09
Sales Turnover	155m	139m	148m
Pre Tax Profit/Loss	-16m	-7m	2m
Working Capital	-11m	353	6m
Fixed Assets	6m	9m	9m
Current Assets	38m	33m	30m
Current Liabilities	15m	13m	2m

Bright Acres Hire Or Buy
Unit 19 Charles Industrial Estate Stowupland Road, Stowmarket, IP14 5AH
Tel: 01449-612632 **Fax:** 01449-770541
E-mail: d.macdonald@brightacres.co.uk
Website: http://www.brightacreshire.co.uk
Directors: D. Macdonald (Ptnr)
No.of Employees: 1 - 10 **Product Groups:** 45, 83

Ceva Network Logistics Ltd
Norwich Road Mendlesham, Stowmarket, IP14 5NA
Tel: 01449-766401 **Fax:** 01449-767881
E-mail: darren.williams@cevalogistics.com
Website: http://www.cevalogistics.com
Managers: D. Williams (Chief Mgr)
Ultimate Holding Company: CEVA GROUP PLC
Immediate Holding Company: CEVA NETWORK LOGISTICS LIMITED
Registration no: 03723307 **Date established:** 1999 **Turnover:** £2m - £5m
No.of Employees: 101 - 250 **Product Groups:** 77

Date of Accounts	Dec 11	Dec 10	Dec 09
Pre Tax Profit/Loss	20m	N/A	N/A
Working Capital	1	538	538
Fixed Assets	852	852	852
Current Assets	1	676	676

Climax Molybdenum UK Ltd
Needham Road, Stowmarket, IP14 2AE
Tel: 01449-674431 **Fax:** 01449-675972
E-mail: pinchley@phelpsdodge.com
Website: http://www.climaxmolybdenum.com
Bank(s): National Westminster
Directors: A. Armour (Sales), J. Stapleton (Co Sec)
Ultimate Holding Company: FREEPORT MCMORAN COPPER & GOLD INC (USA)
Immediate Holding Company: CLIMAX MOLYBDENUM U.K. LIMITED
Registration no: 00359564 **VAT No.:** GB 390 5841 36
Date established: 1940 **Turnover:** £10m - £20m
No.of Employees: 51 - 100 **Product Groups:** 31, 32, 34

Date of Accounts	Dec 10	Dec 09	Dec 08
Sales Turnover	12m	8m	15m
Pre Tax Profit/Loss	3m	251	9m
Working Capital	16m	14m	13m
Fixed Assets	3m	3m	3m
Current Assets	17m	14m	17m
Current Liabilities	752	309	2m

Consilium ltd
The Old Stables, Onehouse Hall Lower Road, Onehouse, Stowmarket, IP14 3BY
Tel: 01449-676435 **Fax:** 01449-676436
E-mail: info@consilium.co.uk
Website: http://www.consilium.europa.eu
Directors: B. Stuart-Barker (Prop)
Registration no: 03620926 **VAT No.:** GB 608 3802 47
Turnover: £500,000 - £1m **No.of Employees:** 1 - 10 **Product Groups:** 81, 89

D & D Buckle Trading Co.
Unit 17 Tomo Business Park Tomo Road, Stowmarket, IP14 5AY
Tel: 01449-613091 **Fax:** 01449-677606
Directors: D. Buckle (Prop)
Immediate Holding Company: BACTON TRANSPORT SERVICES LIMITED
Date established: 1991 **No.of Employees:** 1 - 10 **Product Groups:** 37

Date of Accounts	Jun 11	Jun 10	Jun 09
Working Capital	471	479	416
Fixed Assets	429	358	398
Current Assets	1m	1m	783
Current Liabilities	193	203	50

Flame Skill
25 Combs Lane, Stowmarket, IP14 2DA
Tel: 01449-677118 **Fax:** 01449-771303
E-mail: sales@flameskill.co.uk
Website: http://www.flameskill.co.uk
Directors: P. Finch (Prop)
Date established: 2001 **No.of Employees:** 1 - 10 **Product Groups:** 38, 42

GECS Cleaning GE Computer Services
3 Church View Wyverstone, Stowmarket, IP14 4SQ
Tel: 01449-781603
E-mail: glen@gecscleaning.co.uk
Website: http://www.gecscleaning.co.uk
Directors: G. Hudson (Prop)
Turnover: Up to £250,000 **No.of Employees:** 1 - 10 **Product Groups:** 32, 44, 52

Peter Hall
Southview Cottage Walsham Road, Finningham, Stowmarket, IP14 4JN
Tel: 01449-781523
E-mail: info@silverandglass.com
Website: http://www.designsuk.freeserve.co.uk
Directors: P. Hall (Prop)
No.of Employees: 1 - 10 **Product Groups:** 46, 48

Ironoak Forge Ltd
Hollybush Farm Buxhall, Stowmarket, IP14 3DP
Tel: 01449-737076
Website: http://www.ironoakforge.co.uk
Directors: M. Chaplin (Fin), G. Chaplin (MD)
Immediate Holding Company: IRONOAK LIMITED
Registration no: 01457285 **Date established:** 1979
No.of Employees: 1 - 10 **Product Groups:** 26, 35

Date of Accounts	Jan 12	Jan 11	Jan 10
Working Capital	18	18	16
Fixed Assets	N/A	1	1
Current Assets	31	30	25

Lingwood Food Services
Unit 7-9 Tomo Business Park Tomo Road, Stowmarket, IP14 5EP
Tel: 01449-771202 **Fax:** 01449-771203
E-mail: sales@lingwood.net
Website: http://www.lingwood.net
Directors: I. Hope (Dir)
Ultimate Holding Company: LINGWOOD HOLDINGS LIMITED
Immediate Holding Company: LINGWOOD FOOD SERVICES LIMITED
Registration no: 03295706 **Date established:** 1996
No.of Employees: 1 - 10 **Product Groups:** 20, 40, 41

Date of Accounts	Dec 11	Dec 10	Dec 09
Working Capital	427	302	141
Fixed Assets	105	60	50
Current Assets	970	851	352

Mendabath (U.K.) Limited
72 Thirlmere Drive, Stowmarket, IP14 1SR
Tel: 0800-3284324
E-mail: info@mendabath.co.uk
Website: http://www.mendabath.co.uk
Directors: G. Baison (Prop)
Registration no: 01718642 **Date established:** 1998
No.of Employees: 1 - 10 **Product Groups:** 46, 48

Micro Solutions
Whitings Farm Mendlesham, Stowmarket, IP14 5RR
Tel: 01449-766700 **Fax:** 08704-869727
E-mail: micro.solutions@btinternet.com
Website: http://www.ukf.net
Directors: S. Hewitt (Prop)
Date established: 1986 **Turnover:** Up to £250,000
No.of Employees: 1 - 10 **Product Groups:** 37, 84

Orion Manufacturing Ltd
Unit 4 Tomo Industrial Estate Tomo Road, Stowmarket, IP14 5AY
Tel: 01449-614014 **Fax:** 01449-614015
E-mail: info@omltd.net
Website: http://www.omltd.net
Directors: H. Lennard (Fin), S. Redmond (MD)
Immediate Holding Company: NEWLAND PROPERTY LEASING LIMITED
Registration no: 03007838 **Date established:** 1995
No.of Employees: 1 - 10 **Product Groups:** 20, 40, 41

Date of Accounts	Jan 11	Jan 10	Jan 09
Working Capital	60	59	289
Fixed Assets	550	574	375
Current Assets	72	69	299

Q K Honeycomb Products Ltd
Creeting Road, Stowmarket, IP14 5AS
Tel: 01449-612145 **Fax:** 01449-677604
E-mail: sales@qkhoneycomb.co.uk
Website: http://www.qkhoneycomb.co.uk
Bank(s): National Westminster, Colchester
Directors: J. Field (MD)
Managers: D. Hindley (Chief Acct), J. Durrant (Sales Prom Mgr)
Ultimate Holding Company: TEX HOLDINGS PLC
Immediate Holding Company: QK HONEYCOMB PRODUCTS LIMITED
Registration no: 00835004 **VAT No.:** GB 368 4026 42
Date established: 1965 **Turnover:** £2m - £5m **No.of Employees:** 51 - 100
Product Groups: 25, 27, 30

Date of Accounts	Dec 11	Dec 10	Dec 09
Sales Turnover	4m	4m	4m
Pre Tax Profit/Loss	-153	-235	-389
Working Capital	521	544	480
Fixed Assets	1m	1m	1m
Current Assets	1m	1m	1m
Current Liabilities	125	164	115

Skyline I F E Ltd
The Old School Church Lane, Little Stonham, Stowmarket, IP14 5JL
Tel: 01449-711011 **Fax:** 01449-711680
E-mail: lorrainel@skyline-ife.co.uk
Website: http://www.skyline-ife.com
Bank(s): Lloyds TSB Bank plc
Directors: L. Leech (Chief Op Offcr)
Immediate Holding Company: SKYLINE IFE LIMITED
Registration no: 01508607 **VAT No.:** GB 344 4812 59
Date established: 1980 **Turnover:** £500,000 - £1m
No.of Employees: 11 - 20 **Product Groups:** 89

Date of Accounts	Jul 12	Jul 11	Jul 10
Working Capital	327	561	471
Fixed Assets	309	199	154
Current Assets	470	933	873

Tank Change Ltd
Maycroft Walsham Road, Finningham, Stowmarket, IP14 4JG
Tel: 01449-781210 **Fax:** 01449-781790
E-mail: perry@tankchange.co.uk
Website: http://www.tankchange.co.uk
Directors: T. Brown (MD), P. Brown (Dir)
Immediate Holding Company: TANK CHANGE LIMITED
Registration no: 03836683 **Date established:** 1999
No.of Employees: 1 - 10 **Product Groups:** 35, 42, 45

Date of Accounts	Dec 11	Dec 10	Dec 09
Working Capital	116	147	149
Fixed Assets	278	20	24
Current Assets	281	368	420

Tomlinson Groundcare
Hall Orchard Buxhall, Stowmarket, IP14 3DL
Tel: 01449-736060 **Fax:** 01449-737070
E-mail: info@tomlinsongroundcare.co.uk
Website: http://www.tomlinsongroundcare.co.uk
Directors: R. Tomlinson (Prop)
Turnover: Up to £250,000 **No.of Employees:** 1 - 10 **Product Groups:** 30, 35, 37, 40, 41, 42

V I P
Stonham Aspal, Stowmarket, IP14 6AX
Tel: 01473-890285 **Fax:** 01473-890764
E-mail: sales@weatherwriter.co.uk
Website: http://www.weatherwriter.com
Directors: V. Allen (Ptnr)
VAT No.: GB 103 8525 92 **Turnover:** £250,000 - £500,000
No.of Employees: 1 - 10 **Product Groups:** 27, 49

Sudbury

A F T Trenchers Ltd
16-17 Addison Road, Sudbury, CO10 2YW
Tel: 01787-311811 **Fax:** 01787-310888
E-mail: info@trenchers.co.uk
Website: http://www.trenchers.co.uk
Bank(s): Barclays
Directors: H. Jurgens (MD)
Immediate Holding Company: A.F.T. TRENCHERS LIMITED
Registration no: 04168993 **VAT No.:** GB 102 5746 00
Date established: 2001 **Turnover:** £1m - £2m **No.of Employees:** 11 - 20
Product Groups: 45

Date of Accounts	Jun 11	Jun 10	Jun 09
Working Capital	827	635	471
Fixed Assets	19	21	29
Current Assets	953	859	650

Advantay Ltd
Vantage House Woodhall Business Park, Sudbury, CO10 1WH
Tel: 01787-314070 **Fax:** 08709-089321
E-mail: info@advantay.co.uk
Website: http://www.advantay.co.uk
Directors: M. Durrant (MD)
Immediate Holding Company: ADVANTAY LIMITED
Registration no: 04678329 **Date established:** 2003
Turnover: £250,000 - £500,000 **No.of Employees:** 1 - 10
Product Groups: 36, 38

Date of Accounts	Mar 12	Mar 11	Mar 10
Working Capital	246	221	163
Fixed Assets	18	14	10
Current Assets	552	477	421

Anglia Composites
Stour Valley Business Centre Brundon Lane, Sudbury, CO10 7GB
Tel: 01787-377322 **Fax:** 01787-377433
E-mail: info@angliacomposites.co.uk
Website: http://www.angliacomposites.co.uk
Directors: K. Bareham (Dir)
Immediate Holding Company: NAUGHTY HAMPER LIMITED
Date established: 2012 **No.of Employees:** 1 - 10 **Product Groups:** 30

Date of Accounts	Nov 10	Nov 09	Nov 08
Working Capital	-11	-8	-9
Fixed Assets	2	3	7
Current Assets	61	35	39

Anglia Labels Sales Ltd
Bull Lane Industrial Estate Bull Lane, Acton, Sudbury, CO10 0BD
Tel: 01787-379118 **Fax:** 01787-378840
E-mail: sales@anglialabels.co.uk
Website: http://www.anglialabels.co.uk
Bank(s): Barclays Bank PLC
Directors: N. Marshall (Fin), R. Grindell (MD)
Managers: I. Woodhead (Sales Prom Mgr)
Immediate Holding Company: ANGLIA LABELS (SALES) LIMITED
Registration no: 01478524 **Date established:** 1980 **Turnover:** £1m - £2m
No.of Employees: 11 - 20 **Product Groups:** 23, 27, 49

Date of Accounts	May 11	May 10	May 09
Working Capital	304	221	200
Fixed Assets	386	116	68
Current Assets	592	480	350

British Gaskets Ltd
Bulmer Road Industrial Estate Bulmer Road, Sudbury, CO10 7HJ
Tel: 01787-881188 **Fax:** 01787-880595
E-mail: andrew.thurlbourn@britishgaskets.co.uk
Website: http://www.british-gaskets.co.uk
Bank(s): Bank of Scotland
Directors: A. Thurlbourn (Dir)
Ultimate Holding Company: MASTER INDUSTRIES JERSEY LTD (JERSEY)
Immediate Holding Company: BRITISH GASKETS LIMITED
Registration no: 00431728 **Date established:** 1947 **Turnover:** £5m - £10m
No.of Employees: 21 - 50 **Product Groups:** 29, 30

Date of Accounts	Nov 11	Nov 10	Nov 09
Sales Turnover	11m	10m	7m
Pre Tax Profit/Loss	705	312	57
Working Capital	878	473	370
Fixed Assets	2m	2m	1m
Current Assets	5m	4m	3m
Current Liabilities	1m	2m	2m

C J Ironcraft Ltd
Waldingfield Aerodrome Great Waldingfield, Sudbury, CO10 0RE
Tel: 01787-373917
Directors: P. Kelling (Prop)
Immediate Holding Company: C J IRONCRAFT LIMITED
Registration no: 07913747 **Date established:** 2012
No.of Employees: 1 - 10 **Product Groups:** 26, 35

C M T S
Unit 7 The Cloisters Church Field Road, Sudbury, CO10 2YR
Tel: 01787-468685 **Fax:** 01787-468687
E-mail: sales@cmts.co.uk
Website: http://www.cmts.co.uk
Directors: G. Eade (MD)
Immediate Holding Company: C.M.T.S. LIMITED
Registration no: 01835866 **Date established:** 1984
Turnover: £500,000 - £1m **No.of Employees:** 1 - 10 **Product Groups:** 67

Date of Accounts	Mar 12	Mar 11	Mar 10
Working Capital	187	159	140
Fixed Assets	N/A	12	27
Current Assets	260	228	194

Cubitt Theobald Ltd
St Catherines Road Long Melford, Sudbury, CO10 9JU
Tel: 01787-371002 **Fax:** 01787-880625
E-mail: george_cubitt@cubitt.co.uk
Website: http://www.cubitt.co.uk

Directors: G. Cubitt (Prop)
Ultimate Holding Company: LAKETONS LIMITED
Immediate Holding Company: CUBITT THEOBALD LIMITED
Registration no: 00391366 **VAT No.:** GB 103 5120 36
Date established: 1944 **Turnover:** £5m - £10m
No.of Employees: 51 - 100 **Product Groups:** 52

Date of Accounts	**Oct 11**	**Oct 10**	**Oct 09**
Sales Turnover	10m	11m	11m
Pre Tax Profit/Loss	10	15	5
Working Capital	161	109	47
Fixed Assets	214	247	288
Current Assets	3m	3m	2m
Current Liabilities	1m	767	371

Dallmer Ltd
4 Norman Way High Street, Lavenham, Sudbury, CO10 9PY
Tel: 01787-248244 **Fax:** 01787-248246
E-mail: info@dallmer.de
Website: http://www.dallmer.de
Managers: J. Purser (Chief Mgr)
Immediate Holding Company: DALLMER LIMITED
Registration no: 03235118 **Date established:** 1996
No.of Employees: 1 - 10 **Product Groups:** 29, 30, 36

Date of Accounts	**Dec 11**	**Dec 10**	**Dec 09**
Working Capital	454	346	288
Fixed Assets	10	12	20
Current Assets	744	535	746

DuPont Animal Health Solutions (Head Office)
Windham Road Chilton Industrial Estate, Sudbury, CO10 2XD
Tel: 01787-377305 **Fax:** 01787-310846
E-mail: biosecurity@gbr.dupont.com
Website: http://www.ahs.dupont.com
Bank(s): Barclays
Managers: A. Atkinson (Personnel), A. Ward (I.T. Exec), A. Deeks (Mktg Serv Mgr), D. Stockford (Plant), P. Giles (Purch Mgr)
Immediate Holding Company: PLASART LIMITED
Registration no: 00690279 **VAT No.:** GB 285 3516 42
Date established: 1971 **Turnover:** £10m - £20m
No.of Employees: 21 - 50 **Product Groups:** 32

Date of Accounts	**Jun 11**	**Jun 10**	**Jun 09**
Working Capital	-2	-1	-1
Fixed Assets	2	3	4
Current Assets	49	51	48

Essex Gate Systems
High Lodge Boxford Lane, Boxford, Sudbury, CO10 5JX
Tel: 01787-211779
E-mail: info@essexgates.com
Website: http://www.essexgates.com
Directors: L. Palmer (Prop)
Immediate Holding Company: ESSEX GATE SYSTEMS LIMITED
Registration no: 04440618 **Date established:** 2002
Turnover: Up to £250,000 **No.of Employees:** 1 - 10 **Product Groups:** 35

Fleetwood Group Holdings Ltd
Hall Street Long Melford, Sudbury, CO10 9JP
Tel: 0870-7740008 **Fax:** 0870-7740009
E-mail: fleetwoodcaravans@dial.pipex.com
Website: http://www.fleetwoodcaravans.co.uk
Directors: B. Peljhan (Dir), D. Webb (Dir), R. Allen (Comm), R. Emrich (MD)
Ultimate Holding Company: Kabe (Sweden)
Immediate Holding Company: FLEETWOOD GROUP HOLDINGS LIMITED
Registration no: 04604741 **VAT No.:** GB 529 4036 45
Date established: 2002 **Turnover:** £5m - £10m **No.of Employees:** 1 - 10
Product Groups: 39

Date of Accounts	**Dec 08**	**Dec 07**	**Dec 06**
Pre Tax Profit/Loss	-11	-16	-30
Working Capital	-77	-74	-566
Fixed Assets	762	769	777
Current Assets	N/A	N/A	5
Current Liabilities	3	3	3

Gainsborough Silk Weaving Co. Ltd
Gainsborough Silk Ltd Alexandra Road, Sudbury, CO10 2XH
Tel: 01787-372081 **Fax:** 01787-881785
E-mail: sales@gainsborough.co.uk
Website: http://www.gainsborough.co.uk
Bank(s): Barclays
Directors: N. Thomas (Sales), S. Hobson (Fin), N. Thomas (Sales)
Managers: D. Sargeant (Mgr), D. Sargent (Sales Admin)
Immediate Holding Company: THE GAINSBOROUGH SILK WEAVING COMPANY LIMITED
Registration no: 05016402 **VAT No.:** GB 102 2618 24
Date established: 2004 **No.of Employees:** 11 - 20 **Product Groups:** 23, 63

Date of Accounts	**Feb 08**	**Feb 11**	**Feb 10**
Working Capital	113	-8	80
Fixed Assets	599	478	579
Current Assets	461	347	371

Gatewrights
Ryes Farm Little Henny, Sudbury, CO10 7EA
Tel: 01787-882988 **Fax:** 01787-460880
Directors: F. Chappell (Ptnr)
Date established: 2003 **No.of Employees:** 1 - 10 **Product Groups:** 26, 35

The Grating Company Ltd
1-2 Warner Way Chilton Industrial Estate, Sudbury, CO10 2GG
Tel: 01787-319922 **Fax:** 01787-310562
E-mail: info@gratingcompany.co.uk
Website: http://www.gratingcompany.co.uk
Directors: L. Heseltine (MD), N. Heseltine (Fin)
Immediate Holding Company: S H L INTERNATIONAL LIMITED
Registration no: 03273772 **Date established:** 1996 **Turnover:** £1m - £2m
No.of Employees: 1 - 10 **Product Groups:** 30, 41

Date of Accounts	**Dec 10**	**Dec 09**	**Dec 08**
Working Capital	-56	-43	-29
Fixed Assets	N/A	5	5
Current Assets	96	109	127
Current Liabilities	152	152	156

Horsemat Limited (East Anglian Sealing Co. Ltd)
Unit 4 The Old Stables Goldingham Hall, Bulmer, Sudbury, CO10 7ER
Tel: 01787-880433 **Fax:** 0871-4338858
E-mail: sales@horsemat.co.uk
Website: http://www.horsemat.co.uk

Directors: S. Cant (MD)
Registration no: 05738280 **Turnover:** £5m - £10m
No.of Employees: 1 - 10 **Product Groups:** 23, 29, 49, 65, 66

Lee Packaging Ltd
Bull Lane Industrial Estate Bull Lane, Acton, Sudbury, CO10 0BD
Tel: 01787-372874 **Fax:** 01787-376707
E-mail: sales@leepackaging.co.uk
Website: http://www.leecreative.com
Bank(s): Barclays
Directors: D. Orr (Fin), D. Orr (Co Sec)
Managers: A. Roberts (Sales Prom Mgr)
Immediate Holding Company: LEE PACKAGING LIMITED
Registration no: 01526549 **VAT No.:** GB 299 8835 67
Date established: 1980 **Turnover:** £1m - £2m **No.of Employees:** 11 - 20
Product Groups: 27, 30, 49

Date of Accounts	**Mar 08**	**Mar 07**	**Mar 06**
Working Capital	-151	-153	-183
Fixed Assets	214	70	82
Current Assets	445	356	295
Current Liabilities	596	508	478
Total Share Capital	2	2	1

Mactenn Systems Ltd
1 Bull Lane Acton, Sudbury, CO10 0BD
Tel: 01787-882422 **Fax:** 01787-882433
E-mail: sales@mactenn.com
Website: http://www.mactenn.com
Bank(s): Barclays Bank Plc
Directors: M. Crawley (MD), M. Petsola (Dir), C. Cullimore (Dir), L. Suckling (Dir)
Registration no: 02962738 **VAT No.:** GB 650 8893 06
Date established: 1994 **Turnover:** £1m - £2m **No.of Employees:** 11 - 20
Product Groups: 32, 35, 36, 38, 40, 41, 42, 44, 45, 67, 84

Date of Accounts	**Mar 08**
Sales Turnover	1254
Working Capital	396
Fixed Assets	26
Current Assets	670
Current Liabilities	274
Total Share Capital	34

P Tuckwell Ltd
2 Chilton Industrial Estate Windham Road, Chilton Industrial Estate, Sudbury, CO10 2XD
Tel: 01787-374100 **Fax:** 01787-374105
E-mail: sudbury@tuckwell.co.uk
Website: http://www.tuckwell.co.uk
Managers: W. Waterer (Mgr)
Immediate Holding Company: P. TUCKWELL LIMITED
Registration no: 01189939 **Date established:** 1974
No.of Employees: 1 - 10 **Product Groups:** 41

Date of Accounts	**Nov 11**	**Nov 10**	**Nov 09**
Sales Turnover	43m	33m	34m
Pre Tax Profit/Loss	2m	945	1m
Working Capital	4m	4m	4m
Fixed Assets	2m	819	825
Current Assets	15m	14m	12m
Current Liabilities	3m	3m	3m

Phillips Engineering Ltd
Bulmer Road Industrial Estate Bulmer Road, Sudbury, CO10 7HJ
Tel: 01787-373549 **Fax:** 01787-880276
E-mail: phillips.engineering@o2.co.uk
Website: http://www.o2.co.uk
Directors: N. Phillips (Prop)
Immediate Holding Company: PHILLIPS ENGINEERING LIMITED
Registration no: 07867472 **VAT No.:** GB 299 8017 04
Date established: 2011 **Turnover:** Up to £250,000
No.of Employees: 1 - 10 **Product Groups:** 48

Quansboro Plastics Ltd
Acton Place Industrial Estate Acton, Sudbury, CO10 0BB
Tel: 01787-377207 **Fax:** 01787-311515
E-mail: quansboro@supanet.com
Website: http://www.quansboro.co.uk
Directors: L. Wilshere (MD), F. Wilshere (Fin)
Immediate Holding Company: QUANSBORO PLASTICS LTD
Registration no: 01298935 **VAT No.:** GB 299 6401 13
Date established: 1977 **Turnover:** £500,000 - £1m
No.of Employees: 1 - 10 **Product Groups:** 30

Date of Accounts	**Mar 12**	**Mar 11**	**Mar 10**
Working Capital	-26	-1	-5
Fixed Assets	41	20	30
Current Assets	91	119	149
Current Liabilities	81	86	N/A

E M Richford Ltd
Curzon Road, Sudbury, CO10 2XW
Tel: 01787-375241 **Fax:** 01787-310179
E-mail: andrew@richstamp.co.uk
Website: http://www.richstamp.co.uk
Bank(s): HSBC, Holborn Circus
Directors: B. Richford (Co Sec), A. Richford (MD)
Managers: R. Brewster (Tech Serv Mgr), E. Tatham (Sales Prom Mgr), J. Wright (Fin Mgr)
Immediate Holding Company: E.M.RICHFORD,LIMITED
Registration no: 00151054 **Date established:** 2018 **Turnover:** £5m - £10m
No.of Employees: 51 - 100 **Product Groups:** 27, 28, 32, 42, 44, 49

Date of Accounts	**Dec 11**	**Dec 10**	**Dec 09**
Sales Turnover	8m	9m	6m
Pre Tax Profit/Loss	595	-67	26
Working Capital	4m	3m	3m
Fixed Assets	1m	1m	2m
Current Assets	5m	5m	4m
Current Liabilities	386	154	285

S R L Technical Services Ltd
Holbrook House Holbrook Hall Park, Little Waldingfield, Sudbury, CO10 0TH
Tel: 01787-247595 **Fax:** 01787-248420
E-mail: eric.knight@soundresearch.co.uk
Website: http://www.soundresearch.co.uk
Bank(s): Lloyds TSB
Directors: D. Clarke (Dir), S. Woods (Co Sec), E. Knight (Dir)
Managers: J. Bendy (Tech Supp Mgr), R. Pike
Immediate Holding Company: SRL TECHNICAL SERVICES LTD
Registration no: 00907694 **VAT No.:** 103 6407 11 **Date established:** 1967
Turnover: £1m - £2m **No.of Employees:** 21 - 50 **Product Groups:** 54, 85

Date of Accounts	**Aug 11**	**Aug 10**	**Aug 09**
Working Capital	725	812	1m
Fixed Assets	305	321	356

Current Assets	997	1m	2m

Scorpian Coatings
Sommet Mill Green, Edwardstone, Sudbury, CO10 5PU
Tel: 01787-211111
E-mail: a.mayers@scorpiancoatings.com
Website: http://www.scorpiancoatings.com
Directors: A. Mayers (Prop)
Immediate Holding Company: A R MAYERS LIMITED
Registration no: 04813751 **Date established:** 2003
No.of Employees: 1 - 10 **Product Groups:** 46, 48

Date of Accounts	**Jun 11**	**Jun 09**	**Jun 08**
Working Capital	-10	-17	-15
Fixed Assets	9	9	10
Current Assets	N/A	2	4

J Scott & Son Ltd
69 Richard Burn Way, Sudbury, CO10 1SY
Tel: 01787-310873 **Fax:** 01787- 310873
Managers: G. Gordon (Mgr)
No.of Employees: 1 - 10 **Product Groups:** 20, 40, 41

Date of Accounts	**Aug 07**	**Aug 06**
Working Capital	5	48
Fixed Assets	21	30
Current Assets	381	456
Current Liabilities	376	408

Scribe Gifts Cogrid LLP
Borehagate ,King Street, Sudbury, CO10 2EG
Tel: 01787-373306
E-mail: online@scribegifts.co.uk
Website: http://www.scribegifts.com
Managers: T. Coverdale (Mgr)
Date established: 2006 **Turnover:** Up to £250,000
No.of Employees: 1 - 10 **Product Groups:** 33, 36, 49

Siemens Healthcare
Chilton Industrial Estate Northern Road, Sudbury, CO10 2XQ
Tel: 01787-880022 **Fax:** 01787-880033
E-mail: gerard.gent@siemens.com
Website: http://www.siemens.com
Directors: G. Gent (Co Sec), D. Goodey (Fin)
Ultimate Holding Company: SIEMENS AG (GERMANY)
Immediate Holding Company: SIEMENS HEALTHCARE DIAGNOSTICS MANUFACTURING LTD
Registration no: 01915763 **Date established:** 1985
Turnover: £50m - £75m **No.of Employees:** 251 - 500
Product Groups: 38, 67

Date of Accounts	**Sep 11**	**Sep 10**	**Sep 09**
Sales Turnover	64m	64	60
Pre Tax Profit/Loss	3m	6	6
Working Capital	39m	37	32
Fixed Assets	2m	2	2
Current Assets	41m	48	39
Current Liabilities	2m	6	3

Skyview Systems Ltd
Skyview House 9 Churchfield Road, Sudbury, CO10 2YA
Tel: 01787-883138 **Fax:** 01787-883139
E-mail: sales@skyview.co.uk
Website: http://www.skyview.co.uk
Directors: M. Hart (Fin), N. Hart (MD)
Ultimate Holding Company: SKYVIEW (HOLDINGS) LIMITED
Immediate Holding Company: SKYVIEW SYSTEMS LIMITED
Registration no: 02535682 **VAT No.:** GB 594 5191 09
Date established: 1990 **Turnover:** £500,000 - £1m
No.of Employees: 1 - 10 **Product Groups:** 38, 39, 40, 42, 44, 48, 54, 67, 71, 85

Date of Accounts	**Feb 08**	**Feb 11**	**Feb 10**
Working Capital	-31	-32	-39
Fixed Assets	400	364	385
Current Assets	246	343	342

Specflue Ltd
8 Curzon Road Chilton Industrial Estate, Sudbury, CO10 2XW
Tel: 01787-880333 **Fax:** 01787-880555
E-mail: sales@specflue.com
Website: http://www.specflue.com
Bank(s): HSBC P.L.C.
Directors: A. Williams (Fin), G. Perrins (Fin), J. Fry (MD), J. Fry (Dir)
Managers: M. Inkpen (Personnel), T. Saunders (Tech Serv Mgr), L. Jones (Mktg Serv Mgr)
Immediate Holding Company: SPECFLUE LIMITED
Registration no: 02716331 **VAT No.:** GB 594 9258 80
Date established: 1992 **Turnover:** £10m - £20m
No.of Employees: 21 - 50 **Product Groups:** 35, 36, 52

Date of Accounts	**Dec 11**	**Dec 10**	**Dec 09**
Sales Turnover	16m	13m	11m
Pre Tax Profit/Loss	1m	950	1m
Working Capital	3m	3m	2m
Fixed Assets	2m	2m	2m
Current Assets	5m	4m	4m
Current Liabilities	1m	756	820

Spraybake Ltd
Milner Road Chilton Industrial Estate, Sudbury, CO10 2XG
Tel: 01787-888650 **Fax:** 01787-882305
E-mail: sales@spraybake.co.uk
Website: http://www.spraybake.co.uk
Bank(s): Lloyds TSB Bank plc
Directors: P. Grocott (Dir)
Immediate Holding Company: SPRAYBAKE LIMITED
Registration no: 05322305 **VAT No.:** GB 239 9422 32
Date established: 2004 **Turnover:** £5m - £10m **No.of Employees:** 11 - 20
Product Groups: 39, 40, 46

Date of Accounts	**Mar 11**	**Mar 10**	**Mar 09**
Working Capital	-239	-281	-260
Fixed Assets	457	455	477
Current Assets	338	483	376

Spraybooth Technology Ltd
8 Ballingdon Hill Industrial Estate Ballingdon Hill, Sudbury, CO10 2DX
Tel: 01787-313550 **Fax:** 01787-313542
E-mail: enquiries@sprayboothtechnology.co.uk
Website: http://www.sprayboothtechnology.co.uk

see next page

***Spraybooth Technology Ltd** - Cont'd*

Directors: R. Arthur (Dir)
Managers: J. Ellis (Fin Mgr)
Immediate Holding Company: SPRAYBOOTH TECHNOLOGY LIMITED
Registration no: 02783840 **Date established:** 1993
No.of Employees: 11 - 20 **Product Groups:** 38, 42

Date of Accounts	Apr 11	Apr 10	Apr 09
Working Capital	7	160	333
Fixed Assets	129	98	105
Current Assets	1m	1m	842

Sudbury Picture Frames

Unit 9 Drury Drive, Sudbury, CO10 1WH
Tel: 01787-376014 **Fax:** 01787-376014
E-mail: admin@sudbury-picture-frames.co.uk
Website: http://www.sudbury-picture-frames.co.uk
Directors: W. Hayward (Prop)
Turnover: Up to £250,000 **No.of Employees:** 1 - 10 **Product Groups:** 25, 26, 30, 36, 48

Suffolk Steel Stockholders Ltd

Woodhall Business Park, Sudbury, CO10 1WH
Tel: 01787-370015 **Fax:** 01787-379109
Bank(s): National Westminster Bank Plc
Directors: D. Jakeman (Dir)
Immediate Holding Company: SUFFOLK STEEL STOCKHOLDERS LIMITED
Registration no: 01507752 **VAT No.:** GB 344 4828 44
Date established: 1980 **Turnover:** £1m - £2m **No.of Employees:** 11 - 20
Product Groups: 66

Date of Accounts	Aug 11	Aug 10	Aug 09
Working Capital	354	337	299
Fixed Assets	342	364	350
Current Assets	813	721	656

T D C Document Management

Unit 3 Gable End Courtyard Hall Street, Long Melford, Sudbury, CO10 9JT
Tel: 01787-319090 **Fax:** 01787-319988
E-mail: j.daultrey.tdc@virgin.net
Website: http://www.tdcdocumentmanagement.co.uk
Directors: J. Daultrey (Prop)
Date established: 1993 **No.of Employees:** 1 - 10 **Product Groups:** 27, 38, 44, 72, 80, 81

Thermalair Ltd

Unit 1 Milner Road Chilton Road Industrial Estate, Sudbury, CO10 2XG
Tel: 01787-888659 **Fax:** 01359-271445
E-mail: enquiries@thermalair.co.uk
Website: http://www.thermalair.co.uk
Directors: P. Grocott (MD)
Immediate Holding Company: THERMALAIR LIMITED
Registration no: 01676950 **VAT No.:** GB 368 4347 22
Date established: 1982 **Turnover:** £500,000 - £1m
No.of Employees: 1 - 10 **Product Groups:** 40, 48, 52, 66

Date of Accounts	Oct 07	Mar 11	Mar 10
Sales Turnover	939	N/A	N/A
Pre Tax Profit/Loss	124	N/A	N/A
Working Capital	253	138	411
Fixed Assets	37	10	12
Current Assets	417	226	521
Current Liabilities	86	N/A	N/A

The Unique Paper Company Ltd

Unit 8 Inca Business Park Bull Lane, Acton, Sudbury, CO10 0BB
Tel: 01787-312199 **Fax:** 01787-312189
E-mail: sales@theuniquepapercompany.co.uk
Website: http://www.theuniquepapercompany.co.uk
Managers: M. Smart (Chief Acct)
Immediate Holding Company: THE UNIQUE PAPER COMPANY LIMITED
Registration no: 05328849 **Date established:** 2005
No.of Employees: 1 - 10 **Product Groups:** 27, 32, 49

Date of Accounts	Jan 12	Jan 11	Jan 10
Working Capital	5	9	-91
Fixed Assets	516	240	232
Current Assets	801	976	1m

Vanners Ltd

The Mill Shop Weavers Lane, Sudbury, CO10 1BB
Tel: 01787-372396 **Fax:** 01787-310674
E-mail: info@vanners.com
Website: http://vanners.com
Bank(s): HSBC
Directors: R. Stevenson (MD)
Ultimate Holding Company: SILK INDUSTRIES LIMITED
Immediate Holding Company: VANNERS TIES LIMITED
Registration no: 02322023 **VAT No.:** GB 527 3954 24
Date established: 1988 **Turnover:** £1m - £2m **No.of Employees:** 51 - 100
Product Groups: 23, 63

W Attwood Ltd (established 1894)

Milner Road Chilton Industrial Estate, Sudbury, CO10 2XG
Tel: 01787-373666 **Fax:** 01787-312353
E-mail: w.attwood@biasbinding.co.uk
Website: http://www.biasbinding.co.uk
Directors: M. Attwood (Dir)
Immediate Holding Company: W. ATTWOOD LIMITED
Registration no: 00187833 **VAT No.:** GB 102 0776 16
Date established: 2023 **Turnover:** £1m - £2m **No.of Employees:** 1 - 10
Product Groups: 23, 63

Date of Accounts	Dec 11	Dec 10	Dec 09
Working Capital	253	227	207
Fixed Assets	368	370	380
Current Assets	290	258	232

Stephen Walters & Sons Ltd

Sudbury Silk Mills, Sudbury, CO10 2XB
Tel: 01787-372266 **Fax:** 01787-880126
E-mail: sales@stephenwalters.co.uk
Website: http://www.stephenwalters.co.uk
Bank(s): Lloyds
Directors: N. Currie (Co Sec), B. Crabtree (Sales), M. James (Fin)
Ultimate Holding Company: WALTERS HOLDINGS LIMITED
Immediate Holding Company: STEPHEN WALTERS & SONS LIMITED
Registration no: 00060209 **VAT No.:** GB 102 0226 51
Date established: 1999 **Turnover:** £5m - £10m
No.of Employees: 101 - 250 **Product Groups:** 23, 63

Date of Accounts	Mar 12	Mar 11	Mar 10
Sales Turnover	8m	7m	6m
Pre Tax Profit/Loss	326	92	483
Working Capital	2m	2m	2m
Fixed Assets	1m	1m	1m
Current Assets	6m	7m	5m
Current Liabilities	428	243	224

Woodbridge

Allfarm Installations Ltd

Unit 5 & 6 Fullers Business Centre Riverside View, Wickham Market, Woodbridge, IP13 0TA
Tel: 01728-746200 **Fax:** 01728-747666
E-mail: mail@allfarmuk.com
Directors: C. Bloomfield (Fin)
Managers: S. Dickons (Sales Prom Mgr)
Immediate Holding Company: ALLFARM INSTALLATIONS LIMITED
Registration no: 03634649 **Date established:** 1998
No.of Employees: 1 - 10 **Product Groups:** 41

Date of Accounts	Dec 11	Dec 10	Dec 09
Working Capital	-10	-44	-94
Fixed Assets	11	8	6
Current Assets	225	242	218

Amarinth Ltd

Bentwaters Parks Rendlesham, Woodbridge, IP12 2TW
Tel: 01394-462120 **Fax:** 01394-462130
E-mail: enquiries@amarinth.com
Website: http://www.amarinth.com
Directors: D. Cutler (Fin), S. Buckley (Sales & Mktg), O. Brigginshaw (MD)
Managers: K. Gray (Ops Mgr)
Immediate Holding Company: AMARINTH LIMITED
Registration no: 04525158 **Date established:** 2002 **Turnover:** £2m - £5m
No.of Employees: 21 - 50 **Product Groups:** 67

Date of Accounts	Dec 11	Dec 10	Dec 09
Working Capital	2m	965	810
Fixed Assets	485	504	493
Current Assets	6m	3m	2m

Bone-Dry Organic Carpet & Upholstery Cleaning

Jacksons Farm Laxfield Road, Dennington, Woodbridge, IP13 8AS
Tel: 01728-638899
E-mail: carpets@bonedrycleaning.com
Website: http://www.bonedrycleaning.com
Turnover: Up to £250,000 **No.of Employees:** 1 - 10 **Product Groups:** 23, 32, 52

Cogent Technology Ltd

Dock Lane Melton, Woodbridge, IP12 1PE
Tel: 01394-445566 **Fax:** 01394-380604
E-mail: sales@cogent-technology.co.uk
Website: http://www.cogent-technology.co.uk
Directors: N. Slator (MD)
Managers: M. Charlesworth (Eng Serv Mgr), R. Stainer, J. Logan (Purch Mgr), L. Caraccio
Immediate Holding Company: COGENT TECHNOLOGY LIMITED
Registration no: 01855453 **VAT No.:** GB 521 0690 83
Date established: 1984 **Turnover:** £2m - £5m **No.of Employees:** 51 - 100
Product Groups: 84

Date of Accounts	Sep 11	Sep 10	Sep 09
Working Capital	548	428	391
Fixed Assets	543	526	449
Current Assets	2m	2m	1m

Dangerspot Books Ltd

Old Bank House High Street, Laxfield, Woodbridge, IP13 8DX
Tel: 01986-798613 **Fax:** 01986-798172
E-mail: hedley@dangerspot.co.uk
Website: http://www.dangerspot.co.uk
Directors: J. Roberts (Fin), H. Griffin (MD)
Immediate Holding Company: DANGERSPOT BOOKS LTD
Registration no: 04807888 **Date established:** 2003
Turnover: Up to £250,000 **No.of Employees:** 1 - 10 **Product Groups:** 28

Date of Accounts	Jun 11	Jun 10	Jun 09
Sales Turnover	N/A	13	9
Pre Tax Profit/Loss	N/A	-0	-2
Working Capital	-10	-27	-27
Fixed Assets	N/A	20	20
Current Assets	21	N/A	N/A
Current Liabilities	32	N/A	N/A

Electronic Terminations Ltd

High Street Wickham Market, Woodbridge, IP13 0RF
Tel: 01728-748111 **Fax:** 01728-748222
E-mail: barrie@grouproland.com
Website: http://www.electronic-terminations.com
Directors: B. Emerson (MD)
Immediate Holding Company: ELECTRONIC TERMINATIONS LIMITED
Registration no: 01309058 **VAT No.:** GB 299 7051 09
Date established: 1977 **Turnover:** £500,000 - £1m
No.of Employees: 1 - 10 **Product Groups:** 37

Date of Accounts	Jul 11	Jul 10	Jul 09
Sales Turnover	N/A	N/A	635
Pre Tax Profit/Loss	N/A	N/A	173
Working Capital	387	120	2m
Fixed Assets	20	9	10
Current Assets	722	528	2m
Current Liabilities	N/A	N/A	100

G F C Lighting LLP

10 Sandy Lane Iken, Woodbridge, IP12 2HE
Tel: 01728-687840
E-mail: sales@gfclighting.co.uk
Website: http://www.gfclighting.co.uk
Directors: C. Thompson (Prop)
Immediate Holding Company: GFC LIGHTING LLP
Registration no: OC323445 **Date established:** 2006
No.of Employees: 1 - 10 **Product Groups:** 37, 67

Date of Accounts	Mar 11	Mar 10	Mar 09
Working Capital	-28	-32	-18
Fixed Assets	14	19	5
Current Assets	1	N/A	11

GAH Heating Products Ltd

Building 846 Bentwaters Park, Rendlesham, Woodbridge, IP12 2TW
Tel: 01394-421160 **Fax:** 01394-421170
E-mail: mail@gah.co.uk
Website: http://www.gah.co.uk
Bank(s): HSBC Bank plc
Directors: G. Gooch (Sales), J. Reader (MD)
Ultimate Holding Company: H E B Boilers Ltd
Immediate Holding Company: G A H Refridgeration
Registration no: 02815253 **VAT No.:** GB 637 7949 79
Turnover: Up to £250,000 **No.of Employees:** 11 - 20 **Product Groups:** 40

Grayston Bros

Station Road Laxfield, Woodbridge, IP13 8HQ
Tel: 01986-798225 **Fax:** 01986-798225
Directors: N. Grayston (Ptnr)
Date established: 1900 **No.of Employees:** 1 - 10 **Product Groups:** 41

Hatcher Components Ltd

Broadwater Road Framlingham, Woodbridge, IP13 9LL
Tel: 01728-723675 **Fax:** 01728-724475
E-mail: info@hatchercomp.co.uk
Website: http://www.hatchercomp.co.uk
Bank(s): Barclays
Directors: B. Getley (MD), M. Barker (Fin)
Managers: L. Wink (Buyer)
Ultimate Holding Company: P.H. BETTS (HOLDINGS) LIMITED
Immediate Holding Company: HATCHER COMPONENTS LIMITED
Registration no: 01025842 **Date established:** 1971 **Turnover:** £5m - £10m
No.of Employees: 51 - 100 **Product Groups:** 39

Date of Accounts	Jan 12	Jan 11	Jan 10
Working Capital	1m	934	907
Fixed Assets	631	628	643
Current Assets	2m	2m	1m

Hedley Griffin Films

PO Box 274, Woodbridge, IP13 8WX
Tel: 01986-798613 **Fax:** 01986-798172
E-mail: hedley@hedleygriffinfilms.com
Website: http://www.hedleygriffinfilms.com
Directors: H. Griffin (Prop)
No.of Employees: 1 - 10 **Product Groups:** 89

Kesgrave Aggregates

Dan's Meadow Bealings Road, Martlesham, Woodbridge, IP12 4RW
Tel: 01394-386751 **Fax:** 01394-386752
E-mail: sales@kesgraveaggregates.co.uk
Website: http://www.kesgraveaggregates.co.uk
Directors: A. Garrard (Prop)
Date established: 1982 **No.of Employees:** 1 - 10 **Product Groups:** 14, 25, 66

L E & P Tuckwell Ltd

Shop Street Worlingworth, Woodbridge, IP13 7HU
Tel: 01728-628325
E-mail: hubbardr42@yahoo.co.uk
Website: http://www.tuckwell.co.uk
Directors: T. Tooley (Sales), D. Tuckwell (Co Sec), O. Poulson (Sales)
Managers: R. Hubbard (Transport), S. King (Fin Mgr), T. Glover (Mktg Serv Mgr)
Immediate Holding Company: P. TUCKWELL LIMITED
Registration no: 01189939 **Date established:** 1974
Turnover: £20m - £50m **No.of Employees:** 21 - 50 **Product Groups:** 41

Date of Accounts	Nov 11	Nov 10	Nov 09
Sales Turnover	43m	33m	34m
Pre Tax Profit/Loss	2m	945	1m
Working Capital	4m	4m	4m
Fixed Assets	2m	819	825
Current Assets	15m	14m	12m
Current Liabilities	3m	3m	3m

Micronizing UK Ltd

Off Saxtead Road Framlingham, Woodbridge, IP13 9PT
Tel: 01728-723435 **Fax:** 01728-724359
E-mail: info@micronizing.com
Website: http://www.micronizing.com
Directors: R. Newton (MD)
Immediate Holding Company: MICRONIZING INTERNATIONAL LIMITED
Registration no: 03111135 **Date established:** 1995
No.of Employees: 1 - 10 **Product Groups:** 41, 67, 84

Date of Accounts	Mar 11	Mar 10	Mar 03
Fixed Assets	561	561	561

National Farm Research Unit

25 Fore Street Framlingham, Woodbridge, IP13 9DY
Tel: 01728-621364 **Fax:** 01728-622510
E-mail: nfru@nfru.co.uk
Website: http://www.nfru.co.uk
Bank(s): Barclays
Directors: K. Garroch (MD), J. Williams (Sales & Mktg)
Immediate Holding Company: Precision Prospecting Ltd
Registration no: 02977800 **VAT No.:** GB 571 4866 17
Date established: 1994 **Turnover:** £500,000 - £1m
No.of Employees: 21 - 50 **Product Groups:** 81, 84

Notcutts Ltd

Garden Centre 74 Cumberland Street, Woodbridge, IP12 4AF
Tel: 01394-445400 **Fax:** 01394-445440
E-mail: reception@nottcutts.co.uk
Website: http://www.notcutts.co.uk
Directors: C. Notcutts (Dir), C. Moss (Fin)
Ultimate Holding Company: NOTCUTTS GROUP LIMITED
Immediate Holding Company: NOTCUTTS LIMITED
Registration no: 00393104 **Date established:** 1945
Turnover: £50m - £75m **No.of Employees:** 51 - 100 **Product Groups:** 07

Date of Accounts	Aug 09	Aug 08	Feb 12
Sales Turnover	57m	37m	58m
Pre Tax Profit/Loss	3m	271	3m
Working Capital	7m	3m	-6m
Fixed Assets	42m	29m	49m
Current Assets	16m	9m	15m
Current Liabilities	5m	1m	3m

Paragon Parts Ltd

Unit 22 Red House Farm Marlborough Road, Saxtead, Woodbridge, IP13 9RD
Tel: 01728-685886 **Fax:** 01728-685088
E-mail: sales@paragonparts.co.uk
Website: http://www.paragonparts.co.uk

Directors: J. Handley (MD)
Immediate Holding Company: PARAGON PARTS (HOLDINGS) LIMITED
Registration no: 04121713 **Date established:** 2000
No.of Employees: 1 - 10 **Product Groups:** 46

Date of Accounts	Sep 11	Sep 10	Sep 09
Working Capital	-150	-150	-150
Fixed Assets	113	113	113
Current Liabilities	150	N/A	N/A

Pinnacle Stainless Ltd

Hall Farm Barns Hasketon, Woodbridge, IP13 6JJ
Tel: 01473-738759 **Fax:** 01473-738456
Directors: E. Barton (Fin), W. Foster (MD)
Immediate Holding Company: PINNACLE STAINLESS LIMITED
Registration no: 04852518 **Date established:** 2003
Turnover: £250,000 - £500,000 **No.of Employees:** 1 - 10
Product Groups: 20, 40, 41

Date of Accounts	Apr 11	Apr 10	Apr 09
Sales Turnover	N/A	381	481
Working Capital	8	26	35
Fixed Assets	59	73	87
Current Assets	74	105	109

Plastics For Games Ltd

1 Riverside View Wickham Market, Woodbridge, IP13 0TA
Tel: 01728-745300 **Fax:** 01728-745309
E-mail: sales@plasticsforgames.co.uk
Website: http://www.p4g.co.uk
Directors: D. Kibble (MD), I. Kibble (Sales)
Immediate Holding Company: PLASTICS FOR GAMES LIMITED
Registration no: 02262037 **VAT No.:** GB 466 1958 12
Date established: 1988 **Turnover:** £1m - £2m **No.of Employees:** 1 - 10
Product Groups: 28, 49

Date of Accounts	Dec 11	Dec 10	Dec 09
Working Capital	196	203	181
Fixed Assets	415	397	389
Current Assets	418	416	331

Precision Prospecting Ltd

25 Fore Street Framlingham, Woodbridge, IP13 9DY
Tel: 01728-622500 **Fax:** 01728-622510
E-mail: info@nfru.co.uk
Website: http://www.precisionprospecting.com
Directors: J. Cunnell (Co Sec), J. Williams (Sales & Mktg), K. Garroch (MD), K. Garroch (MD)
Immediate Holding Company: PRECISION PROSPECTING (IRELAND) LIMITED
Registration no: 03594460 **Date established:** 1998
Turnover: Up to £250,000 **No.of Employees:** 21 - 50 **Product Groups:** 81

Date of Accounts	Mar 11	Mar 10	Mar 09
Working Capital	N/A	N/A	-162
Current Liabilities	N/A	N/A	1

Resolve Enviromental Solutions Ltd

Unit 17b Seven Acres Business Park Newbourne Road, Waldringfield, Woodbridge, IP12 4PS
Tel: 01473-736000 **Fax:** 01473-736001
E-mail: info@resolveenvironmental.co.uk
Website: http://www.resolveenvironmental.co.uk
Directors: S. Willing (Fin)
Immediate Holding Company: PARTY SHOES LTD
Registration no: 06515157 **Date established:** 2011
Turnover: Up to £250,000 **No.of Employees:** 1 - 10 **Product Groups:** 40, 85

Robush Ltd

Gull Farm Grundisburgh, Woodbridge, IP13 6RN
Tel: 01473-738569 **Fax:** 01728-748332
E-mail: sales@robush.co.uk
Website: http://www.robush.co.uk
Directors: B. Cummings (MD)
Immediate Holding Company: ROBUSH LIMITED
Registration no: 02291741 **VAT No.:** GB 571 2851 40
Date established: 1988 **Turnover:** £250,000 - £500,000
No.of Employees: 1 - 10 **Product Groups:** 29, 35

Date of Accounts	Dec 11	Dec 10	Dec 09
Working Capital	-105	-57	-97
Fixed Assets	134	152	184
Current Assets	403	409	366
Current Liabilities	N/A	182	N/A

Roland Plastics Ltd

High Street Wickham Market, Woodbridge, IP13 0RF
Tel: 01728-747777 **Fax:** 01728-748222
E-mail: maggie@rolandplastics.com
Website: http://www.rolandplastics.com
Bank(s): Barclays, P.O.Box 1504, Southend on Sea, SS2 6XX
Directors: P. Turner (Ptnr), M. Buck (Jt MD), B. Emerson (Co Sec)
Managers: A. Ewing (Personnel)
Ultimate Holding Company: MVOC LLC (USA)
Immediate Holding Company: ROLAND PLASTICS LIMITED
Registration no: 01894926 **VAT No.:** GB 427 9446 21
Date established: 1985 **Turnover:** £1m - £2m **No.of Employees:** 21 - 50
Product Groups: 30, 35, 37, 39, 66

Date of Accounts	Mar 11	Mar 10	Mar 09
Sales Turnover	1m	1m	2m
Pre Tax Profit/Loss	105	-87	-197
Working Capital	394	246	198
Fixed Assets	342	369	509
Current Assets	553	650	639
Current Liabilities	33	102	42

Seckford Wines

Dock Lane Melton, Woodbridge, IP12 1PE
Tel: 01394-446622 **Fax:** 01394-446633
E-mail: sales@seckfordwines.co.uk
Website: http://www.seckfordwines.co.uk
Directors: I. Pv (Ch), R. Harvey Jones (Co Sec)
Immediate Holding Company: SECKFORD WINES LIMITED
Registration no: 01924614 **Date established:** 1985
Turnover: £10m - £20m **No.of Employees:** 11 - 20 **Product Groups:** 21, 62

Date of Accounts	Sep 11	Sep 10	Sep 09
Sales Turnover	20m	18m	11m
Pre Tax Profit/Loss	555	278	-96
Working Capital	3m	3m	2m
Fixed Assets	636	641	663
Current Assets	5m	5m	4m
Current Liabilities	795	1m	596

Sheds & Cabins Kesgrave Aggregates

Dan's Meadow Bealings Road, Martlesham, Woodbridge, IP12 4RW
Tel: 01394-386751 **Fax:** 01394-386752
E-mail: dans_meadow@hotmail.co.uk
Website: http://www.shedsandcabins.co.uk
Managers: C. Garrard (Mgr)
No.of Employees: 1 - 10 **Product Groups:** 25, 33, 35, 41, 66

Sierra Space Heating

Bridge Works Mill Lane, Hasketon, Woodbridge, IP13 6HE
Tel: 01473-738317 **Fax:** 01473-738316
E-mail: chris@sierraheating.co.uk
Website: http://www.sierraheating.co.uk
Directors: C. Mittell (MD)
Immediate Holding Company: SIERRA SPACE HEATING LIMITED
Registration no: 03009206 **VAT No.:** GB 638 1001 70
Date established: 1995 **Turnover:** £250,000 - £500,000
No.of Employees: 1 - 10 **Product Groups:** 40, 41

Date of Accounts	Dec 11	Dec 10	Dec 09
Sales Turnover	N/A	396	548
Working Capital	145	120	120
Fixed Assets	1	2	2
Current Assets	195	226	233

Structural Inspection Design Services

5 Ransom Road, Woodbridge, IP12 4JU
Tel: 01394-389044
Directors: J. Leming (Ptnr)
Immediate Holding Company: GEMSTONES EDUCATION LTD
Date established: 2011 **No.of Employees:** 1 - 10 **Product Groups:** 35

Stuart Clay Traps Ltd

3 Wilford Bridge Road Melton, Woodbridge, IP12 1RB
Tel: 01394-385567 **Fax:** 01394-387757
E-mail: sales@stuartsgunsandtackle.com
Website: http://www.stuartsgunsandtackle.com
Directors: A. Clarke (MD)
Immediate Holding Company: STUART CLAY TRAPS LIMITED
Registration no: 01833562 **Date established:** 1984
No.of Employees: 1 - 10 **Product Groups:** 36, 39, 40

Date of Accounts	Dec 11	Dec 10	Dec 09
Working Capital	46	62	43
Fixed Assets	1	1	1
Current Assets	183	186	177

Synergy Audio

23-25 Well Close Square Framlingham, Woodbridge, IP13 9DT
Tel: 01728-724207
E-mail: rob@synergyaudio.co.uk
Website: http://www.synergyaudio.co.uk
Directors: R. Quin (Dir)
Immediate Holding Company: SYNERGY AUDIO LIMITED
Registration no: 04300952 **Date established:** 2001
No.of Employees: 1 - 10 **Product Groups:** 37, 83, 89

Date of Accounts	Mar 12	Mar 11	Mar 10
Working Capital	97	82	50
Fixed Assets	26	33	41
Current Assets	165	124	90

Technicraft Anglia Ltd

Wilford Bridge Road Melton, Woodbridge, IP12 1RB
Tel: 01394-385213 **Fax:** 01394-387914
E-mail: nigel@technicraft.co.uk
Website: http://www.technicraft.co.uk
Bank(s): Lloyds, Woodbridge
Directors: N. Webb (MD), C. Webb (Fin)
Managers: P. Keal (Tech Serv Mgr)
Ultimate Holding Company: TECHNICRAFT (NCW) LIMITED
Immediate Holding Company: TECHNICRAFT (ANGLIA) LIMITED
Registration no: 01125747 **VAT No.:** GB 104 2291 18
Date established: 1973 **Turnover:** £500,000 - £1m
No.of Employees: 21 - 50 **Product Groups:** 48

Date of Accounts	Dec 11	Dec 10	Dec 09
Working Capital	1m	988	701
Fixed Assets	1m	1m	1m
Current Assets	1m	1m	832

Thurlow Nunn Standen Ltd

61 The Street Melton, Woodbridge, IP12 1PL
Tel: 01394-382801 **Fax:** 01394-384330
E-mail: accounts@tnsgroup.co.uk
Website: http://www.tnsgroup.co.uk
Managers: A. Brown (District Mgr)
Ultimate Holding Company: GEORGE THURLOW AND SONS (HOLDINGS) LIMITED
Immediate Holding Company: THURLOW NUNN STANDEN LIMITED
Registration no: 05310718 **Date established:** 2004
No.of Employees: 21 - 50 **Product Groups:** 41

Date of Accounts	Dec 11	Dec 10	Dec 09
Sales Turnover	40m	34m	34m
Pre Tax Profit/Loss	859	837	710
Working Capital	3m	2m	2m
Fixed Assets	607	593	580
Current Assets	9m	7m	5m
Current Liabilities	4m	2m	2m

Trulock & Harris

Unit 1 & 2 Ore Trading Estate Woodbridge Road Framlingham, Woodbridge, IP13 9LL
Tel: 01728-724776
Website: http://www.trulockandharris.com
Directors: J. Harris (Dir)
Date established: 2003 **No.of Employees:** 1 - 10 **Product Groups:** 36, 39, 40

Richard Western Ltd

The Durbans Apsey Green, Framlingham, Woodbridge, IP13 9RP
Tel: 01728-723224 **Fax:** 01728-724291
E-mail: sales@richard-western.co.uk
Website: http://www.richard-western.co.uk
Bank(s): Lloyds TSB
Directors: A. Western (Fab), M. Roberts (Co Sec), M. Murray (Sales & Mktg), R. Western (MD)
Immediate Holding Company: RICHARD WESTERN LIMITED
Registration no: 01296660 **VAT No.:** GB 334 1222 05
Date established: 1977 **Turnover:** £2m - £5m **No.of Employees:** 21 - 50
Product Groups: 39, 41

Date of Accounts	Jan 11	Jan 10	Sep 08
Working Capital	660	663	611
Fixed Assets	417	453	431
Current Assets	2m	1m	2m

Woodbridge Wrought Iron

24 Peterhouse Crescent, Woodbridge, IP12 4HT
Tel: 01394-387971
E-mail: tom.moye.blacksmiths@btinternet.com
Directors: T. Moye (Prop)
Date established: 1992 **No.of Employees:** 1 - 10 **Product Groups:** 26, 35

SURREY

Addlestone

Broadway Malyan Ltd
3 Weybridge Business Park Addlestone Road, Addlestone, KT15 2BW
Tel: 01932-845599 **Fax:** 01932-856206
E-mail: man@broadwaymalyan.com
Website: http://www.broadwaymalyan.com
Bank(s): Barclays
Directors: J. Oliver (Fin), J. Turner (Dir)
Managers: L. Smith, A. Davies (Tech Serv Mgr)
Ultimate Holding Company: BROADWAY MALYAN HOLDINGS LIMITED
Immediate Holding Company: BROADWAY MALYAN HOLDINGS LIMITED
Registration no: 05418411 **VAT No.:** GB 529 9346 05
Date established: 2005 **Turnover:** £20m - £50m
No.of Employees: 101 - 250 **Product Groups:** 84

Date of Accounts	Apr 11	Apr 10	Apr 09
Sales Turnover	41m	32m	51m
Pre Tax Profit/Loss	686	-2m	236
Working Capital	8m	6m	6m
Fixed Assets	1m	2m	3m
Current Assets	20m	19m	20m
Current Liabilities	4m	4m	6m

C N C Systems
40 Redwoods, Addlestone, KT15 1JN
Tel: 01932-830492 **Fax:** 01932-828011
Website: http://www.cncsystemsltd.co.uk
Directors: M. Salt (Prop)
Date established: 2001 **No.of Employees:** 1 - 10 **Product Groups:** 46

Centura Foods Ltd
Bourne Business Park Dashwood Lang Road, Addlestone, KT15 2HJ
Tel: 01932-265000 **Fax:** 01784-437096
Website: http://www.charnwood.com
Bank(s): Barclays, Lombard St, London, EC3
Managers: L. Scurr (Sales Admin)
Ultimate Holding Company: Tomkins P.L.C.
Immediate Holding Company: Rank House McDougell Ltd
Registration no: 00062450 **VAT No.:** GB 674 0729 21
Turnover: £20m - £50m **No.of Employees:** 51 - 100 **Product Groups:** 20

Chep UK Ltd
Addlestone Road, Addlestone, KT15 2UP
Tel: 01932-850085 **Fax:** 01932-850144
Website: http://www.chep.com
Directors: K. Porritt (Fin)
Managers: L. Mitchell (Personnel)
Ultimate Holding Company: BRAMBLES LIMITED (AUSTRALIA)
Immediate Holding Company: CHEP UK LIMITED
Registration no: 00197807 **Date established:** 2024
Turnover: £250m - £500m **No.of Employees:** 501 - 1000
Product Groups: 26, 45

Date of Accounts	Jun 11	Jun 10	Jun 09
Sales Turnover	291m	273m	273m
Pre Tax Profit/Loss	68m	66m	47m
Working Capital	-549	3m	4m
Fixed Assets	219m	191m	160m
Current Assets	62m	60m	56m
Current Liabilities	37m	36m	33m

Computer Solutions Ltd
1A New Haw Road, Addlestone, KT15 2BZ
Tel: 01932-829460 **Fax:** 01932-840603
E-mail: sales@computer-solutions.co.uk
Website: http://www.computer-solutions.co.uk
Directors: C. Shears (Fin), C. Stephens (MD)
Managers: M. Wollen (Admin Off)
Registration no: 01451477 **Date established:** 1979
Turnover: £500,000 - £1m **No.of Employees:** 1 - 10 **Product Groups:** 44

Date of Accounts	Sep 09	Sep 08	Sep 07
Sales Turnover	N/A	N/A	550
Pre Tax Profit/Loss	N/A	N/A	72
Working Capital	121	98	84
Fixed Assets	1	1	3
Current Assets	208	196	177
Current Liabilities	N/A	N/A	33

Dentsply (Head Office)
Building 1 Aviator Park Station Road, Addlestone, KT15 2PG
Tel: 01932-853422 **Fax:** 01932-840168
E-mail: jane.groves@dentsply.com
Website: http://www.dentsply.co.uk
Bank(s): HSBC Bank plc
Directors: S. Douglas (Pers), S. Ringrose (Sales), G. Campbell (MD), P. Frith (Co Sec)
Managers: M. Rutherford (Tech Serv Mgr), J. Sainter (Mktg Serv Mgr), O. Humphreys (Fin Mgr)
Ultimate Holding Company: DENTSPLY INTERNATIONAL INC (USA)
Immediate Holding Company: DENTSPLY LIMITED
Registration no: FC013038 **VAT No.:** GB 223 8471 30
Date established: 1985 **Turnover:** £20m - £50m
No.of Employees: 51 - 100 **Product Groups:** 63, 67, 82

Date of Accounts	Dec 06
Sales Turnover	41m
Pre Tax Profit/Loss	-11
Working Capital	-9m
Fixed Assets	104m
Current Assets	13m
Current Liabilities	21m

Duplo International Ltd
Automated Precision House Hamm Moor Lane, Addlestone, KT15 2SD
Tel: 01932-263900 **Fax:** 01372-460252
E-mail: enquiries@duplointernational.com
Website: http://www.duplointernational.com
Bank(s): Lloyds TSB Bank plc
Directors: G. Nutting (Fin), R. Greenhalgh (Ch), T. Lock (MD)
Managers: J. Doyle (Personnel), J. Brewer (Tech Serv Mgr), P. Jolly (Mktg Serv Mgr)
Ultimate Holding Company: DUPLO INTERNATIONAL GROUP LIMITED
Immediate Holding Company: DUPLO INTERNATIONAL LIMITED
Registration no: 02300316 **VAT No.:** GB 493 6818 00
Date established: 1988 **Turnover:** £20m - £50m
No.of Employees: 51 - 100 **Product Groups:** 28, 30, 42, 44, 48, 67, 83

Date of Accounts	May 12	May 11	May 10
Sales Turnover	28m	29m	27m
Pre Tax Profit/Loss	156	567	1m
Working Capital	9m	10m	10m
Fixed Assets	712	249	240
Current Assets	18m	19m	22m
Current Liabilities	2m	2m	1m

K K Balers Ltd
Victory Park Road, Addlestone, KT15 2AX
Tel: 01932-852423 **Fax:** 01932-847170
E-mail: sales@kkbalers.com
Website: http://www.kkbalers.com
Directors: J. Lawton (MD)
Immediate Holding Company: KK BALERS LIMITED
Registration no: 02785753 **VAT No.:** GB 584 6754 90
Date established: 1993 **Turnover:** £1m - £2m **No.of Employees:** 1 - 10
Product Groups: 42, 45, 46

Date of Accounts	Apr 11	Apr 10	Apr 09
Working Capital	212	207	165
Fixed Assets	18	21	27
Current Assets	665	678	621

K K Water Purification Ltd
Victory Park Road, Addlestone, KT15 2AX
Tel: 01932-858170 **Fax:** 01932-847170
E-mail: sales@kkbalers.com
Website: http://www.kkgroupint.com
Directors: B. Pullen (Sales), J. Lawton (MD), P. Wadsworth (Sales), S. Massingham (Sales)
Managers: D. Richardson (Admin Off)
Immediate Holding Company: K.K. WATER PURIFICATION LTD.
Registration no: 02487583 **VAT No.:** GB 530 2286 79
Date established: 1990 **Turnover:** £2m - £5m **No.of Employees:** 11 - 20
Product Groups: 36, 37

Date of Accounts	Apr 08
Working Capital	346
Fixed Assets	5
Current Assets	451
Current Liabilities	105

K R Microwaves
16 Langshott Close Woodham, Addlestone, KT15 3SE
Tel: 01932-343975 **Fax:** 01932-348084
Directors: K. Roberts (Prop)
Date established: 1988 **No.of Employees:** 1 - 10 **Product Groups:** 36, 40

Lattice Semi Conductor Ltd
Rivermead House Hamm Moor Lane, Addlestone, KT15 2SF
Tel: 01932-825700 **Fax:** 01932-825701
E-mail: jackie.black@latticesemi.com
Website: http://www.latticesemi.com
Managers: J. Black (Admin Off)
Ultimate Holding Company: LATTICE SEMICONDUCTORS CORP (USA)
Immediate Holding Company: LATTICE SEMICONDUCTOR UK LTD.
Registration no: 02899981 **Date established:** 1994
Turnover: £500,000 - £1m **No.of Employees:** 1 - 10 **Product Groups:** 37, 44

Date of Accounts	Dec 11	Dec 10	Dec 09
Sales Turnover	913	913	897
Pre Tax Profit/Loss	59	55	11
Working Capital	182	135	94
Fixed Assets	6	12	14
Current Assets	276	187	135
Current Liabilities	52	48	35

Michael Page Ltd
1 Dashwood Lang Road Bourne Business Park, Addlestone, KT15 2QW
Tel: 01932-264000 **Fax:** 01932-264089
E-mail: slough@accountancyadditions.com
Website: http://www.michaelpage.com
Bank(s): HSBC, London
Directors: K. Stagg (Co Sec)
Managers: S. Puckett
Ultimate Holding Company: MICHAEL PAGE INTERNATIONAL PLC
Immediate Holding Company: MICHAEL PAGE LIMITED
Registration no: 01609138 **Date established:** 1982
Turnover: £20m - £50m **No.of Employees:** 51 - 100 **Product Groups:** 80, 87

Date of Accounts	Dec 10	Dec 09	Dec 08
Working Capital	2	2	2
Current Assets	8m	8m	8m

Pandrol International Ltd
63 Station Road, Addlestone, KT15 2AR
Tel: 01932-834500 **Fax:** 01932-850858
E-mail: vincentlunel@pandrol.com
Website: http://www.pandrol.com
Directors: V. Lunel (Co Sec)
Ultimate Holding Company: DELACHAUX SA (FRANCE)
Immediate Holding Company: PANDROL INTERNATIONAL LIMITED
Registration no: 00398548 **Date established:** 1945
Turnover: Up to £250,000 **No.of Employees:** 21 - 50 **Product Groups:** 39

Date of Accounts	Dec 11	Dec 10	Dec 09
Pre Tax Profit/Loss	34m	18m	12m
Working Capital	-50m	-45m	-42m
Fixed Assets	186m	171m	147m
Current Assets	3m	2m	2m

SAP Motor Factors
29-33 Brighton Road, Addlestone, KT15 1PG
Tel: 01932-857921
E-mail: inquires@sapmotorparts.com
Website: http://www.sapmotorparts.com
Directors: J. Channel (Dir), P. Hayter (MD)
Immediate Holding Company: Surrey Brake & Exhaust Services Group Ltd
Registration no: 01677659 **Date established:** 1982
Turnover: £500,000 - £1m **No.of Employees:** 1 - 10 **Product Groups:** 68

Tensid UK Ltd
70a Wheatash Road, Addlestone, KT15 2ES
Tel: 01932-564133 **Fax:** 01932-562046
E-mail: info@tensid.com
Website: http://www.tensid.com
Directors: R. Turk (MD)
Managers: A. Parkinson, M. Bowler, M. Carbery (Mktg Serv Mgr)
Immediate Holding Company: TENSID UK LTD
Registration no: 02308378 **VAT No.:** GB 492 9620 12
Date established: 1988 **Turnover:** £1m - £2m **No.of Employees:** 1 - 10
Product Groups: 32, 40

Date of Accounts	Dec 11	Dec 10	Dec 09
Working Capital	89	41	247
Fixed Assets	7	12	35
Current Assets	267	213	442

TT Signs
206 Station Road, Addlestone, KT15 2PH
Tel: 08702-009191 **Fax:** 01932-702549
E-mail: sales@ttsigns.co.uk
Website: http://www.ttsigns.co.uk
No.of Employees: 1 - 10 **Product Groups:** 30, 39, 40

You Choose
22 Broomfield Road New Haw, Addlestone, KT15 3BN
Tel: 0800-970 5252 **Fax:** 01932-429321
E-mail: tim@youchoose.uk.com
Website: http://www.youchoose.uk.com

Directors: T. Cork (MD), L. Hurren (Fin)
Immediate Holding Company: YOU CHOOSE (THE INDEPENDENT WINDOW BROKERS) LIMITED
Registration no: 04400352 **Date established:** 2002
No.of Employees: 1 - 10 **Product Groups:** 30, 33, 35, 36, 40

Date of Accounts	Mar 11	Mar 10	Mar 09
Working Capital	9	39	83
Fixed Assets	3	4	6
Current Assets	51	53	106

Ashtead

Downsoft Ltd
Downsway Woodview Close, Ashtead, KT21 1HA
Tel: 01372-272422 **Fax:** 01372-276122
E-mail: carol@downsoft.co.uk
Website: http://www.downsoft.co.uk
Directors: C. Dare (MD)
Immediate Holding Company: DOWNSOFT LIMITED
Registration no: 01673031 **VAT No.:** GB 367 5568 07
Date established: 1982 **Turnover:** Up to £250,000
No.of Employees: 1 - 10 **Product Groups:** 28, 37, 44, 65, 89

Date of Accounts	May 11	May 10	May 09
Sales Turnover	9	13	17
Pre Tax Profit/Loss	-2	-1	-2
Working Capital	-7	-5	-3
Fixed Assets	4	5	4
Current Assets	2	2	1
Current Liabilities	8	7	4

Fitex Curtain & Blinds
6 Craddocks Parade, Ashtead, KT21 1QL
Tel: 01372-275037 **Fax:** 01372-271500
E-mail: info@fit-ex.com
Website: http://www.fitex.com
Directors: D. Jones (Prop)
Immediate Holding Company: FIT-EX LIMITED
Registration no: 05126751 **Date established:** 2004
No.of Employees: 1 - 10 **Product Groups:** 36, 63

Date of Accounts	Apr 11	Apr 10	Apr 09
Working Capital	-4	15	-18
Fixed Assets	38	1	4
Current Assets	80	78	74

J G Shelton & Co. Ltd
The Warren, Ashtead, KT21 2SH
Tel: 01372-278422 **Fax:** 01372-279338
E-mail: tracy.bennett@jg-shelton.co.uk
Website: http://www.jg-shelton.co.uk
Directors: T. Bennett (Co Sec)
Immediate Holding Company: J.G.SHELTON & CO. LIMITED
Registration no: 00749620 **VAT No.:** GB 209 9318 48
Date established: 1963 **Turnover:** £1m - £2m **No.of Employees:** 1 - 10
Product Groups: 40

Date of Accounts	Mar 11	Mar 10	Mar 09
Working Capital	-316	89	39
Fixed Assets	1m	680	692
Current Assets	537	718	344

Bagshot

Caspian Food Services Ltd
2 High Street, Bagshot, GU19 5AE
Tel: 01276-474344 **Fax:** 01276-479849
E-mail: lhawes@caspianuk.com
Website: http://www.flame-grilled.co.uk
Directors: M. Gray (Fin)
Ultimate Holding Company: CASPIAN UK GROUP LIMITED
Immediate Holding Company: CASPIAN FOOD SERVICES LIMITED
Registration no: 01450855 **Date established:** 1979
Turnover: £20m - £50m **No.of Employees:** 1 - 10 **Product Groups:** 69

Date of Accounts	Jan 09	Jan 10	Jan 11
Sales Turnover	32m	34m	33m
Pre Tax Profit/Loss	4m	1m	1m
Working Capital	4m	3m	3m
Fixed Assets	9m	9m	9m
Current Assets	14m	13m	13m
Current Liabilities	5m	4m	4m

Delavale Engineering Ltd
Goodalls Yard 9-13 Guildford Road, Bagshot, GU19 5JJ
Tel: 01276-476571 **Fax:** 01276-471602
E-mail: sales@delavale.co.uk
Directors: S. Burrows (MD)
Immediate Holding Company: DELAVALE ENGINEERING LIMITED
Registration no: 01359340 **VAT No.:** GB 211 6202 26
Date established: 1978 **Turnover:** £500,000 - £1m
No.of Employees: 1 - 10 **Product Groups:** 35, 48

Date of Accounts	Sep 11	Sep 10	Sep 09
Working Capital	88	68	29
Fixed Assets	77	97	116
Current Assets	135	130	103

Nampack Paper Holdings Ltd
Windlebrook House Guildford Road, Bagshot, GU19 5NG
Tel: 01276-452266 **Fax:** 01276-453376
Directors: C. Bruce (Fin), I. Willis (Non Exec), J. Leek (Non Exec), J. Monks (Grp Chief Exec), J. Grainger (Ch), L. Taviansky (Fin), P. Ryan (Non Exec)
Ultimate Holding Company: NAMPAK LTD (SOUTH AFRICA)
Immediate Holding Company: NAMPAK PAPER HOLDINGS LIMITED
Registration no: 00360964 **VAT No.:** GB 733 5728 24
Date established: 1940 **Turnover:** £5m - £10m **No.of Employees:** 1 - 10
Product Groups: 82

Robin Instruments Ltd
PO Box 541, Bagshot, GU19 5XB
Tel: 01276-451365 **Fax:** 01276-474103
E-mail: sales@robin-instruments.co.uk
Website: http://www.robin-instruments.co.uk
Directors: R. Norman (MD), J. Norman (MD)
Managers: C. Brown (Sales Admin)
Registration no: 01779108 **Turnover:** Up to £250,000
No.of Employees: 1 - 10 **Product Groups:** 38, 42, 54

Date of Accounts	Mar 08	Mar 07	Mar 06
Working Capital	-5	-15	-21
Fixed Assets	1	1	3
Current Assets	60	21	14
Current Liabilities	65	35	36

Rubbair Door Ltd (Rubbair Door Inc)
Half Moon Street, Bagshot, GU19 5AL
Tel: 01276-479911 **Fax:** 01276-453333
E-mail: sales@rubbair.com
Website: http://www.rubbair.co.uk
Directors: G. Harris (Co Sec)
Managers: B. Harris (Mgr)
Immediate Holding Company: RUBBAIR DOOR LIMITED
Registration no: 04017030 **Date established:** 2000
Turnover: £250,000 - £500,000 **No.of Employees:** 1 - 10
Product Groups: 35, 40

Date of Accounts	Dec 11	Dec 10	Dec 09
Working Capital	102	71	78
Fixed Assets	1	3	3
Current Assets	372	283	240
Current Liabilities	N/A	N/A	145

Banstead

Costello Security
21 Nork Way, Banstead, SM7 1PB
Tel: 08452-608830 **Fax:** 08452-608831
E-mail: info@costellosecurity.co.uk
Website: http://www.costellosecurity.co.uk
Directors: G. Costello (Prop)
Immediate Holding Company: COSTELLO SECURITY LIMITED
Registration no: 07733229 **Date established:** 2011
No.of Employees: 1 - 10 **Product Groups:** 35, 36, 48

Betchworth

A G C Welding & Steel Fabrications Ltd
Unit 2 Old Barley Mow Works Old Reigate Road, Betchworth, RH3 7LW
Tel: 01737-841169
Directors: A. Jackman (Co Sec)
Immediate Holding Company: A.G.C. WELDING & STEEL FABRICATIONS LIMITED
Registration no: 05400698 **Date established:** 2005
No.of Employees: 1 - 10 **Product Groups:** 35, 52

Date of Accounts	Mar 12	Mar 11	Mar 10
Working Capital	46	19	19
Fixed Assets	16	10	11
Current Assets	78	46	50

Chertsey Plant Hire Ltd
Station Road Buckland, Betchworth, RH3 7BX
Tel: 01737-844622 **Fax:** 01737-844623
E-mail: mail@chertseyplanthire.co.uk
Website: http://www.chertseyplanthire.co.uk
Directors: G. Balle (Dir), M. O'Halloran (Co Sec)
Immediate Holding Company: CHERTSEY PLANT HIRE LIMITED
Registration no: 02922551 **VAT No.:** GB 635 9336 17
Date established: 1994 **Turnover:** £2m - £5m **No.of Employees:** 1 - 10
Product Groups: 36, 39, 40, 41, 42, 44, 45, 54, 83

Date of Accounts	Mar 11	Mar 10	Mar 09
Working Capital	-608	36	177
Fixed Assets	4m	3m	3m
Current Assets	1m	1m	1m

Electromec Services
56 Oakdene Road Brockham, Betchworth, RH3 7JX
Tel: 01737-843078 **Fax:** 01737-843285
E-mail: electromecservices@btinternet.com
Directors: J. Stevens (Prop)
Immediate Holding Company: ELECTROMEC SERVICES LIMITED
Registration no: 06446585 **Date established:** 2007
No.of Employees: 1 - 10 **Product Groups:** 35, 36, 39

Date of Accounts	Mar 11	Mar 10	Mar 09
Working Capital	-37	-34	-26
Fixed Assets	18	37	34
Current Assets	17	37	44

Les Tuileries Ltd
The Cart Shed Stoney Croft Farm, Betchworth, RH3 7EY
Tel: 01306-888028 **Fax:** 01306-881252
E-mail: info@ltinteriordesign.co.uk
Website: http://www.ltinteriordesign.co.uk
Directors: P. Allen (MD)
Immediate Holding Company: LES TUILERIES LIMITED
Registration no: 06349259 **Date established:** 2007
No.of Employees: 1 - 10 **Product Groups:** 37, 52, 86

Date of Accounts	Aug 11	Aug 10	Aug 09
Working Capital	-18	-12	-17
Fixed Assets	6	10	14
Current Assets	7	8	4

Camberley

A M D
A M D House Frimley Business Park, Frimley, Camberley, GU16 7SL
Tel: 01276-803299 **Fax:** 01276-683781
E-mail: sale@amd.com
Website: http://www.amd.com
Directors: A. Buxton (Sales), D. Hooks (Mkt Research), K. Smith (Dir)
Managers: D. Everitt (Sales Admin)
Ultimate Holding Company: ADVANCED MICRO DEVICES INC (USA)
Immediate Holding Company: ADVANCED MICRO DEVICES (U.K.) LIMITED
Registration no: 03049168 **Date established:** 1973 **Turnover:** £5m - £10m
No.of Employees: 21 - 50 **Product Groups:** 37, 44, 48

Date of Accounts	Dec 09	Dec 08	Dec 07
Sales Turnover	6m	9m	8m
Pre Tax Profit/Loss	-1m	90	265
Working Capital	1m	2m	1m
Fixed Assets	26	62	146
Current Assets	2m	2m	2m
Current Liabilities	436	437	511

A T M Parts
11-12 Admiralty Way, Camberley, GU15 3DT
Tel: 01276-607200 **Fax:** 01276-609040
E-mail: info@atm-parts.com
Website: http://www.atm-parts.com
Directors: S. Froome (MD)
Managers: M. Fifield (Ops Mgr), S. Weeks (Sales & Mktg Mg)
Ultimate Holding Company: MAINET LIMITED
Immediate Holding Company: ATM PARTS COMPANY LIMITED
Registration no: 02848103 **Date established:** 1993 **Turnover:** £2m - £5m
No.of Employees: 21 - 50 **Product Groups:** 37, 44

Date of Accounts	Mar 11	Mar 10	Mar 09
Sales Turnover	5m	3m	6m
Pre Tax Profit/Loss	-55	-524	693
Working Capital	1m	2m	2m
Fixed Assets	55	84	200
Current Assets	2m	2m	3m
Current Liabilities	96	85	371

Abtech Ltd
6 White Hart Parade Blackwater, Camberley, GU17 9AA
Tel: 0870-801 0080 **Fax:** 0870-801 0090
E-mail: sales@abtechbasements.co.uk
Website: http://www.abtechbasements.co.uk
Product Groups: 51, 52

Date of Accounts	Dec 07	Dec 06
Working Capital	562	489
Fixed Assets	144	147
Current Assets	1990	1946
Current Liabilities	1428	1457

Amazon Filters Ltd
Unit 1k Albany Park, Camberley, GU16 7PG
Tel: 01276-670600 **Fax:** 01276-670101
E-mail: sales@amazonfilters.co.uk
Website: http://www.amazonfilters.co.uk
Bank(s): H S B C
Directors: J. Kirby (Sales), J. Kirby (Dir)
Managers: S. Mann, R. Pappadakis (Personnel), K. Wickert (Mktg Serv Mgr), A. Witherington (Tech Serv Mgr), S. Northedge (Fin Mgr)
Immediate Holding Company: AMAZON FILTERS LIMITED
Registration no: 01318147 **VAT No.:** GB 292 6332 48
Date established: 1977 **Turnover:** £10m - £20m
No.of Employees: 51 - 100 **Product Groups:** 27, 33, 34, 35, 36, 37, 38, 39, 40, 41, 42, 44, 45, 47, 48, 67

Date of Accounts	Feb 08	Feb 11	Feb 10
Sales Turnover	N/A	12m	10m
Pre Tax Profit/Loss	1m	2m	1m
Working Capital	1m	3m	2m
Fixed Assets	2m	2m	2m
Current Assets	3m	5m	4m
Current Liabilities	776	690	880

Amer Sports UK & Ireland Ltd
Theta Lyon Way, Frimley, Camberley, GU16 7ER
Tel: 01276-404800 **Fax:** 01294-316 255
E-mail: amer.communications@amersports.com
Website: http://www.amersports.com
Directors: M. White (MD)
Managers: A. Karey (Ops Mgr), C. White (I.T. Exec), D. Wright (Sales & Mktg Mg), J. Ballerdie (Mktg Serv Mgr), A. Mcpherson (Accounts)
Immediate Holding Company: Amer Group Ltd
Registration no: SC036215 **Turnover:** £20m - £50m
No.of Employees: 1 - 10 **Product Groups:** 49

Apex Security Ltd
Suite 116 Frimley House 5 The Parade, Frimley, Camberley, GU16 7QJ
Tel: 0800-281083 **Fax:** 01202- 419198
E-mail: sales@apexsecurity.co.uk
Website: http://www.apexsecurity.co.uk
Managers: A. Warner (Mgr)
Immediate Holding Company: APEX SECURITY LIMITED
Registration no: 04382135 **Date established:** 2002
No.of Employees: 1 - 10 **Product Groups:** 26, 35

Date of Accounts	Mar 11	Mar 10	Mar 09
Sales Turnover	143	139	116
Pre Tax Profit/Loss	2	-4	-10
Working Capital	-1	-3	1
Fixed Assets	1	2	2
Current Assets	30	23	19
Current Liabilities	13	9	7

Arc Control Systems
Leafy Oak Farm Workshops Cobbetts Lane, Blackwater, Camberley, GU17 9LW
Tel: 01252-890294 **Fax:** 01252-890294
E-mail: richard.foster@arc-controls.co.uk
Website: http://www.arc-controls.co.uk
Directors: R. Foster (Dir)
No.of Employees: 11 - 20 **Product Groups:** 37, 40, 48

Date of Accounts	Sep 11	Sep 10	Sep 09
Sales Turnover	744	793	652
Pre Tax Profit/Loss	116	165	150
Working Capital	133	181	160
Fixed Assets	21	3	4
Current Assets	262	348	309
Current Liabilities	67	94	84

Arrow Lift Engineers Ltd
181 Upper Chobham Road, Camberley, GU15 1EH
Tel: 01276-27516
E-mail: info@arrowlifts.co.uk
Website: http://www.arrowlifts.co.uk
Directors: I. Phillips (Dir)
Immediate Holding Company: ARROW LIFT ENGINEERS LIMITED
Registration no: 03563387 **Date established:** 1998
No.of Employees: 1 - 10 **Product Groups:** 45, 48, 67

Date of Accounts	May 11	May 10	May 09
Working Capital	-37	-47	-52
Fixed Assets	41	60	77
Current Assets	272	256	237

Ascot Wholesale Ltd
5 Leafy Oak Farm Cobbetts Lane, Blackwater, Camberley, GU17 9LW
Tel: 01252-875555 **Fax:** 01252-876666
E-mail: mike@ascotwholesale.co.uk
Website: http://www.ascotwholesale.co.uk
Directors: M. Taylor (Dir)
Immediate Holding Company: ASCOT WHOLESALE LIMITED
Registration no: 05397915 **Date established:** 2005
No.of Employees: 11 - 20 **Product Groups:** 20, 21, 22, 23, 30, 32, 33, 36, 37, 38, 40, 42, 44, 49, 52, 62, 63, 67, 81

Date of Accounts	Jun 11	Jun 10	Jun 09
Working Capital	-114	-119	-120
Fixed Assets	158	166	179
Current Assets	391	369	441

B M S Sheet Metal Ltd
99 Deepcut Bridge Road Deepcut, Camberley, GU16 6SD
Tel: 01252-835409 **Fax:** 01252-834708
E-mail: sales@bmssheetmetal.co.uk
Website: http://www.bmssheetmetal.co.uk
Directors: S. Mcculley (Dir)
Immediate Holding Company: B.M.S. (SHEET METAL) LIMITED
Registration no: 00847555 **Date established:** 1965
Turnover: £500,000 - £1m **No.of Employees:** 1 - 10 **Product Groups:** 48

Date of Accounts	May 11	May 10	May 09
Working Capital	38	84	77
Fixed Assets	8	7	10
Current Assets	113	149	141

Bayphase Ltd
St Georges House Knoll Road, Camberley, GU15 3SY
Tel: 01276-682828 **Fax:** 01276-63334
E-mail: sales@bayphase.com
Website: http://www.bayphase.com
Directors: G. Eyre (MD), P. Eyre (Fin)
Immediate Holding Company: BAYPHASE LIMITED
Registration no: 02023879 **Date established:** 1986 **Turnover:** £2m - £5m
No.of Employees: 1 - 10 **Product Groups:** 84

Date of Accounts	Jun 11	Jun 10	Jun 09
Working Capital	284	197	27
Fixed Assets	53	59	50
Current Assets	405	264	125

Beaver Services
39 Rideway Close, Camberley, GU15 2NX
Tel: 01276-20440 **Fax:** 01276-20467
E-mail: rcjohnson@ntlworld.com
Directors: R. Johnson (Prop)
Date established: 1987 **No.of Employees:** 1 - 10 **Product Groups:** 43

Camberley Catering Equipment
208 Frimley Road, Camberley, GU15 2QJ
Tel: 01276-681919 **Fax:** 01276-686254
E-mail: sales@silesia.co.uk
Website: http://www.silesia.co.uk
Directors: G. Lowe (Dir)
Registration no: 00525004 **Turnover:** £500,000 - £1m
No.of Employees: 1 - 10 **Product Groups:** 40, 67

Date of Accounts	Apr 08	Apr 07	Apr 06
Working Capital	-8	-13	-35
Fixed Assets	48	59	52
Current Assets	41	47	60
Current Liabilities	49	60	95

Camberley Precision Sheet Metal Ltd
Unit 10 Standard Works Bridge Road, Camberley, GU15 2QR
Tel: 01276-64112 **Fax:** 01276-64125
E-mail: john@camberleyprecision.co.uk
Website: http://www.camberleyprecision.co.uk
Bank(s): National Westminster Bank Plc
Managers: J. Mckinnon (Mgr)
Immediate Holding Company: CAMBERLEY PRECISION SHEETMETAL LIMITED
Registration no: 05963810 **VAT No.:** GB 296 0410 60
Date established: 2006 **Turnover:** £500,000 - £1m
No.of Employees: 11 - 20 **Product Groups:** 48

Date of Accounts	Mar 11	Mar 10	Mar 09
Working Capital	240	105	-42
Fixed Assets	289	333	376
Current Assets	704	399	376

Concrete Society
Riverside House 4 Meadows Business Park Station Approach, Blackwater, Camberley, GU17 9AB
Tel: 01276-607140 **Fax:** 01276-607141
E-mail: enquiries@concrete.org.uk
Website: http://www.concrete.org.uk
Directors: K. Calverley (MD)
Immediate Holding Company: CONCRETE SOCIETY LIMITED(THE)
Registration no: 00884419 **Date established:** 1966 **Turnover:** £1m - £2m
No.of Employees: 11 - 20 **Product Groups:** 87

Date of Accounts	Dec 11	Dec 10	Dec 09
Working Capital	46	46	46
Current Assets	46	46	46

Courtridge Ltd (t/a Javelin Plastics)
Unit 1m Albany Park, Camberley, GU16 7PF
Tel: 01276-64446 **Fax:** 01276-691174
E-mail: enquiries@javelinplastics.co.uk
Website: http://www.javelinplastics.co.uk
Bank(s): National Westminster Bank Plc
Directors: E. Moore (Co Sec), L. Reading (Jt MD), M. Crowe (Jt MD), R. Allaway (Tech Serv), R. Allaway (I.T. Dir)
Managers: S. Pigdin (I.T. Exec)
Ultimate Holding Company: COURTRIDGE HOLDINGS LIMITED
Immediate Holding Company: JAVELIN PLASTICS LIMITED
Registration no: 01745181 **VAT No.:** GB 384 2862 26
Date established: 1983 **Turnover:** £2m - £5m **No.of Employees:** 51 - 100
Product Groups: 30, 48

Date of Accounts	Sep 11	Sep 10	Sep 09
Sales Turnover	10m	N/A	N/A
Pre Tax Profit/Loss	325	N/A	N/A
Working Capital	357	432	453
Fixed Assets	428	374	210
Current Assets	4m	4m	3m
Current Liabilities	2m	2m	922

Crest Lifts
Linsford Business Park Linsford Lane, Mytchett, Camberley, GU16 6DL
Tel: 01252-521400 **Fax:** 01252-520468
E-mail: sales@crestlifts.com
Website: http://www.crestlifts.com
Managers: N. Winslade (Admin Off)
Immediate Holding Company: CREST LIFTS LIMITED
Registration no: 02220215 **Date established:** 1988
No.of Employees: 11 - 20 **Product Groups:** 35, 39, 45

Date of Accounts	Dec 11	Dec 10	Dec 09
Working Capital	161	50	-37
Fixed Assets	52	53	42
Current Assets	987	297	295

D D Hire
67 London Road Blackwater, Camberley, GU17 0AB
Tel: 01276-31132 **Fax:** 01276- 600818
E-mail: steve@ddhire.co.uk
Website: http://www.ddhire.co.uk
Directors: S. De Merist (MD)
Immediate Holding Company: TWINEROSE LIMITED
Registration no: 04553867 **Date established:** 1974
No.of Employees: 11 - 20 **Product Groups:** 22, 23, 24, 25, 31, 33, 35, 36, 37, 38, 39, 40, 41, 42, 45, 46, 47, 48, 49, 51, 52, 63, 66, 67, 72, 76, 81, 83, 84

Date of Accounts	Dec 11	Dec 10	Dec 09
Working Capital	246	218	118
Fixed Assets	829	871	993
Current Assets	641	504	485

Data Dialogue
3 Admiralty Way, Camberley, GU15 3DT
Tel: 01276-36377 **Fax:** 01252-541615
E-mail: sales@datadialogue.co.uk
Website: http://www.datadialogue.co.uk
Bank(s): National Westminster
Directors: P. Boxall (MD)
Immediate Holding Company: DATA DIALOGUE LIMITED
Registration no: 02789248 **VAT No.:** GB 492 8647 94
Date established: 1993 **Turnover:** £500,000 - £1m
No.of Employees: 21 - 50 **Product Groups:** 44

Date of Accounts	Jul 99	Jul 11	Jul 10
Current Assets	N/A	14	N/A
Current Liabilities	N/A	14	N/A

Diamond Management Services LLP
Diamond House 149 Frimley Road, Camberley, GU15 2PS
Tel: 01276-702500 **Fax:** 01276-692903
E-mail: info@dms-management.com
Website: http://www.dms-management.com
Directors: S. Colvin (Co Sec), R. Colvin (Ptnr)
Immediate Holding Company: DIAMOND MANAGEMENT SERVICES LLP
Registration no: OC315100 **Date established:** 2005
Turnover: £250,000 - £500,000 **No.of Employees:** 1 - 10
Product Groups: 80

Date of Accounts	Mar 11	Mar 10	Mar 09
Sales Turnover	N/A	309	326
Pre Tax Profit/Loss	N/A	160	148
Working Capital	18	86	100
Fixed Assets	4	3	5
Current Assets	67	98	115
Current Liabilities	N/A	12	10

Dionex UK Ltd
Unit 4 Albany Court Albany Park, Camberley, GU16 7QL
Tel: 01276-691722 **Fax:** 01276-691837
E-mail: info-uk@dionex.com
Website: http://www.dionex.com
Bank(s): Barclays
Directors: A. Raby (MD)
Managers: J. Brugnoli (Sales Off Mgr)
Ultimate Holding Company: THERMO FISHER SCIENTIFIC INC (USA)
Immediate Holding Company: DIONEX (UK) LIMITED
Registration no: 01478505 **Date established:** 1980
Turnover: £10m - £20m **No.of Employees:** 21 - 50 **Product Groups:** 31, 33, 38, 41, 42

Date of Accounts	Dec 11	Jun 11	Jun 10
Sales Turnover	6m	12m	10m
Pre Tax Profit/Loss	-685	-660	-911
Working Capital	1m	2m	2m
Fixed Assets	58	56	40
Current Assets	5m	7m	7m
Current Liabilities	2m	2m	2m

Embers Fireplaces
221 Frimley Green Road Frimley Green, Camberley, GU16 6LA
Tel: 01252-837837 **Fax:** 01252-837837
E-mail: info@embersfireplaces.co.uk
Website: http://www.embersfireplaces.co.uk
Directors: S. Burton (Prop)
Immediate Holding Company: B M H (HEATING) LIMITED
Registration no: 03533647 **Date established:** 1998
No.of Employees: 1 - 10 **Product Groups:** 35, 40, 52

Date of Accounts	May 12	May 11	May 10
Working Capital	-37	-26	-31
Current Assets	84	109	100

Engineering Services Crondall Ltd
M Linsford Industrial Park Linsford Lane, Mytchett, Camberley, GU16 6DJ
Tel: 01252-372373 **Fax:** 01252-370797
E-mail: keith@gme.co.uk
Website: http://www.gme.co.uk
Directors: K. Chandler (Dir), A. Chandler (Fin)
Immediate Holding Company: ENGINEERING SERVICES (CRONDALL) LIMITED
Registration no: 02343704 **Date established:** 1989
No.of Employees: 1 - 10 **Product Groups:** 38, 42

Date of Accounts	Jan 12	Jan 11	Jan 10
Working Capital	1	N/A	2
Fixed Assets	1	2	1
Current Assets	11	16	10

Erif UK Ltd
Prospect House 6 Archipelago Lyon Way, Frimley, Camberley, GU16 7ER
Tel: 08458-877999 **Fax:** 01276-601337
E-mail: tim@erif.co.uk
Website: http://www.erif.co.uk
Bank(s): National Westminster Bank Plc
Directors: P. Holdway (MD)
Managers: D. Kelly (Sales Prom Mgr), T. Dyer (Mgr), S. Hedges (Personnel)
Immediate Holding Company: ERIF (UK) LTD.
Registration no: 02692091 **VAT No.:** GB 530 1802 92
Date established: 1992 **Turnover:** £2m - £5m **No.of Employees:** 11 - 20
Product Groups: 37, 38, 40, 52, 81

Date of Accounts	Mar 08	Mar 07	Mar 06
Working Capital	-63	227	291
Fixed Assets	148	118	163
Current Assets	1467	1207	1271
Current Liabilities	1529	980	980
Total Share Capital	57	57	57

Eurocell Building Plastics Ltd
Unit 18 Nelson Way, Camberley, GU15 3DH
Tel: 01276-671901 **Fax:** 01276-671896
Website: http://www.eurocell.co.uk
Managers: J. Boulton (Mgr)
Ultimate Holding Company: TESSENDERLO CHEMIE NV (BELGIUM)
Immediate Holding Company: EUROCELL BUILDING PLASTICS LIMITED
Registration no: 03071407 **Date established:** 1995
Turnover: £50m - £75m **No.of Employees:** 1 - 10 **Product Groups:** 30

Date of Accounts	Dec 11	Dec 10	Dec 09
Sales Turnover	82m	80m	68m
Pre Tax Profit/Loss	4m	5m	4m
Working Capital	15m	12m	7m
Fixed Assets	3m	3m	5m
Current Assets	29m	29m	20m
Current Liabilities	4m	4m	3m

Flags & Standards Ltd
Evanlode 5 Bramble Bank Frimley Green, Camberley, GU16 6PN
Tel: 01252-835225 **Fax:** 020-8363 3377
E-mail: sales@flagsandstandards.com
Website: http://www.flagsandstandards.co.uk
Directors: A. Gardner (Prop), S. Gardner (Dir)
Immediate Holding Company: FLAGS AND STANDARDS LIMITED
Registration no: 02946141 **Date established:** 1994
Turnover: Up to £250,000 **No.of Employees:** 1 - 10 **Product Groups:** 49

Date of Accounts	Jul 07	Jul 06
Working Capital	-35	-43
Fixed Assets	3	4
Current Assets	12	13
Current Liabilities	46	56

Flickers Ltd
Cottage Farm Cobbetts Lane, Blackwater, Camberley, GU17 9LW
Tel: 01252-860403 **Fax:** 01252-860404
E-mail: info@flickers.co.uk
Website: http://www.flickers.co.uk
Directors: A. Phillips (MD)
Immediate Holding Company: FLICKERS LIMITED
Registration no: 02311328 **Date established:** 1988
No.of Employees: 1 - 10 **Product Groups:** 32, 36, 67

Date of Accounts	Oct 11	Oct 10	Oct 09
Working Capital	4	3	3
Fixed Assets	1	2	2
Current Assets	11	13	15

H T S Hocker
Unit 3 Lawrence Way, Camberley, GU15 3DL
Tel: 08702-426056 **Fax:** 08702-426057
E-mail: sales@roderhts.com
Website: http://www.roderhts.com
Directors: G. Hills (Dir)
Turnover: £10m - £20m **No.of Employees:** 11 - 20 **Product Groups:** 24

Hamilton Frazer Ltd
7 Ravenstone Road, Camberley, GU15 1SN
Tel: 01276-23903 **Fax:** 08444-150701
E-mail: sales@seastore.co.uk
Website: http://www.seatstore.co.uk
Directors: D. Begley (MD), S. Davies (Fin)
Immediate Holding Company: HAMILTON FRAZER LIMITED
Registration no: 03214111 **Date established:** 1996
Turnover: £500,000 - £1m **No.of Employees:** 1 - 10 **Product Groups:** 26

Date of Accounts	Jun 09	Jun 08	Jun 07
Sales Turnover	N/A	357	441
Pre Tax Profit/Loss	N/A	45	61
Working Capital	104	99	93
Fixed Assets	11	13	27
Current Assets	137	141	144
Current Liabilities	N/A	11	20

Holiday Autos UK & Ireland Ltd
Holiday Autos House Pembroke Broadway, Camberley, GU15 3XD
Tel: 0870-400 0000 **Fax:** 0870-400 4470
E-mail: brianm@holidayautos.co.uk
Website: http://www.holidayautos.com
Directors: I. Call (Sales), M. Hart (MD), E. Kamm (Fin), B. Murphy (MD), M. Cunlisse (Mkt Research)
Ultimate Holding Company: SOVEREIGN HOLDINGS INC (USA)
Immediate Holding Company: HOLIDAY AUTOS U.K. AND IRELAND LIMITED
Registration no: 03292373 **Date established:** 1996
Turnover: £20m - £50m **No.of Employees:** 51 - 100 **Product Groups:** 72

Date of Accounts	Dec 10	Dec 09	Dec 08
Sales Turnover	43m	52m	57m
Pre Tax Profit/Loss	-4m	-2m	7m
Working Capital	26m	30m	33m
Current Assets	121m	82m	66m
Current Liabilities	14m	14m	19m

Humiseal Europe Ltd (Head Office)
Albany Park, Camberley, GU16 7PH
Tel: 01276-691100 **Fax:** 01276-691227
E-mail: dgreenman@chasecorp.com
Website: http://www.humiseal.com
Bank(s): Lloyds TSB Bank plc
Directors: D. Greenman (MD)
Ultimate Holding Company: CHASE CORPORATION INC (USA)
Immediate Holding Company: HUMISEAL EUROPE LIMITED
Registration no: 01480710 **VAT No.:** GB 347 3761 37
Date established: 1980 **Turnover:** £5m - £10m **No.of Employees:** 11 - 20
Product Groups: 31, 32, 37

Date of Accounts	Aug 11	Aug 10	Aug 09
Sales Turnover	5m	4m	3m
Pre Tax Profit/Loss	2m	2m	1m

Working Capital	8m	7m	5m
Fixed Assets	479	180	208
Current Assets	9m	8m	6m
Current Liabilities	316	477	252

Ideal Scaffolding Southern Ltd
32a Sturt Road Frimley Green, Camberley, GU16 6HY
Tel: 01252-660666 **Fax:** 01252-645170
E-mail: sales@ideal-scaffolding.com
Website: http://www.ideal-scaffolding.com
Directors: D. Lee (MD)
Immediate Holding Company: IDEAL SCAFFOLDING (SOUTHERN) LTD
Registration no: 05458411 **Date established:** 2005
No.of Employees: 1 - 10 **Product Groups:** 35, 52, 66, 83

Date of Accounts	Jul 11	Jul 10	Jul 09
Working Capital	72	96	19
Fixed Assets	51	65	40
Current Assets	203	220	116

Integrated Data Cabling Ltd
103 Mytchett Road Mytchett, Camberley, GU16 6ES
Tel: 01252-370023 **Fax:** 01252-372157
E-mail: warren.stokes@idcuk.co.uk
Website: http://www.idcuk.co.uk
Directors: W. Stokes (Fin), W. Stokes (MD), R. Stokes (Ch), L. Stokes (Co Sec)
Managers: B. Silverman (Sales Prom Mgr)
Immediate Holding Company: INTEGRATED DATA CABLING LIMITED
Registration no: 02553187 **Date established:** 1990 **Turnover:** £2m - £5m
No.of Employees: 11 - 20 **Product Groups:** 37, 44, 67, 84

Date of Accounts	Mar 08	Mar 07
Working Capital	104	154
Fixed Assets	48	59
Current Assets	1099	768
Current Liabilities	995	614
Total Share Capital	100	100

Kalsep UK
Unit 2f Albany Park Frimley Park, Camberley, GU16 7PL
Tel: 01276-675675 **Fax:** 01276-676276
E-mail: ggregory@kalsep.co.uk
Website: http://www.kalsep.co.uk
Directors: L. Wickham (Co Sec)
Managers: G. Gregory (Chief Mgr), J. Tomlinson (Mktg Serv Mgr)
Immediate Holding Company: KALSEP UK LIMITED
Registration no: 05449538 **Date established:** 2005 **Turnover:** £2m - £5m
No.of Employees: 1 - 10 **Product Groups:** 41, 42

Date of Accounts	Sep 11	Sep 10	Sep 09
Working Capital	90	142	134
Fixed Assets	7	5	9
Current Assets	403	367	602
Current Liabilities	N/A	N/A	319

Keyte Bearings
10 Doman Road York Town Industrial Estate, Camberley, GU15 3DF
Tel: 01276-670063 **Fax:** 01276-27180
E-mail: sales@keytebearings.co.uk
Website: http://www.keytebearings.co.uk
Managers: J. Fuller (Chief Mgr)
Date established: 1940 **No.of Employees:** 51 - 100 **Product Groups:** 35

L Teq Ltd
Lapwing 440 Frimley Business Park, Frimley, Camberley, GU16 7SG
Tel: 01276-686566 **Fax:** 01276-686550
E-mail: sales@lteq.com
Website: http://www.lteq.com
Directors: D. Bookham (I.T. Dir), D. Harper (Sales), N. Powney (Mkt Research)
Managers: J. Mason (Mktg Serv Mgr)
Ultimate Holding Company: OMNIGLOBE NETWORKS INC (CANADA)
Registration no: 01690210 **Date established:** 1983 **Turnover:** £2m - £5m
No.of Employees: 21 - 50 **Product Groups:** 37, 39

Date of Accounts	Dec 07	Mar 07	Mar 06
Sales Turnover	3510	4221	4452
Pre Tax Profit/Loss	10	232	284
Working Capital	1199	1187	955
Fixed Assets	32	34	33
Current Assets	3276	1952	2467
Current Liabilities	2077	765	1512
Total Share Capital	50	50	50
ROCE% (Return on Capital Employed)	0.8	19.0	28.7
ROT% (Return on Turnover)	0.3	5.5	6.4

Lanode Ltd
420 Frimley Business Park Frimley, Camberley, GU16 7SG
Tel: 01276-677220 **Fax:** 01276-677221
E-mail: sales@lanode.com
Website: http://www.lanode.com
Managers: N. Howarth (Mktg Serv Mgr)
Immediate Holding Company: LANODE LIMITED
Registration no: 02702078 **Date established:** 1992
No.of Employees: 1 - 10 **Product Groups:** 67

Date of Accounts	Mar 12	Mar 11	Mar 10
Working Capital	1m	994	922
Fixed Assets	26	31	6
Current Assets	1m	1m	1m

Logic
7 Priory Court Tuscam Way, Camberley, GU15 3YX
Tel: 01276-64371 **Fax:** 01276-691273
E-mail: logicelectronics@btinternet.com
Website: http://www.logicelectronics.co.uk
Directors: F. Ribton (MD)
Immediate Holding Company: Jauch Quartz U.K. (Components Division) Ltd
Registration no: 01997178 **Date established:** 1986 **Turnover:** £1m - £2m
No.of Employees: 1 - 10 **Product Groups:** 67

The Makaton Charity
46 London Road Blackwater, Camberley, GU17 0AA
Tel: 01276-606760 **Fax:** 01276-36725
E-mail: info@makaton.org
Website: http://www.makaton.org
Managers: N. Wren (Mktg Serv Mgr), L. Nelhams (Fin Mgr), L. Schwartz
Immediate Holding Company: THE MAKATON CHARITY
Registration no: 06280108 **VAT No.:** GB 591 7835 96
Date established: 2007 **No.of Employees:** 21 - 50 **Product Groups:** 49, 86

Date of Accounts	Jun 11	Jun 10	Jun 09
Sales Turnover	1m	1m	1m
Pre Tax Profit/Loss	25	58	24

Working Capital	399	332	269
Fixed Assets	437	467	449
Current Assets	654	606	465
Current Liabilities	219	215	139

Melitzer Safety Equipment
7 Frimley Road, Camberley, GU15 3EN
Tel: 01276-65474 **Fax:** 01276-62880
E-mail: j.angove@tiscali.co.uk
Directors: M. White (MD)
Managers: J. Angos (Mgr), J. Angove (Mgr)
Registration no: 01858338 **Date established:** 1971
Turnover: £500,000 - £1m **No.of Employees:** 1 - 10 **Product Groups:** 22, 24, 38, 40, 49, 63, 67, 68

Micro Electronic Services
3 Admiralty Way, Camberley, GU15 3DT
Tel: 01276-36349 **Fax:** 01252-541615
E-mail: pboxall@microelec.co.uk
Website: http://www.microelec.co.uk
Bank(s): National Westminster
Directors: C. Bird (Sales), P. Boxall (MD), M. Godding (Fin)
Managers: I. Murphy (Tech Serv Mgr)
Immediate Holding Company: MICRO ELECTRONIC SERVICES LTD
Registration no: 02278708 **VAT No.:** GB 492 8647 94
Date established: 1988 **Turnover:** £1m - £2m **No.of Employees:** 21 - 50
Product Groups: 48

Date of Accounts	Dec 11	Dec 10	Dec 09
Working Capital	39	-6	52
Fixed Assets	71	63	30
Current Assets	367	377	345

Pool Vac Ltd
229 London Road, Camberley, GU15 3EY
Tel: 01276-25252 **Fax:** 01276-21796
E-mail: poolvac@web-hq.com
Directors: G. Clay (MD)
Immediate Holding Company: POOL-VAC LTD
Registration no: 00695810 **Date established:** 1961
Turnover: Up to £250,000 **No.of Employees:** 1 - 10 **Product Groups:** 52

Pro-Touch Solutions Ltd
Unit 1 Albany Park, Camberley, GU16 7QQ
Tel: 01276-684400 **Fax:** 01276-681585
E-mail: sales@protouch.co.uk
Website: http://www.protouch.co.uk
Directors: T. Quarry (MD)
Immediate Holding Company: PRO TOUCH MANUFACTURING LIMITED
Registration no: 03794579 **VAT No.:** GB 755 1539 21
Date established: 1999 **Turnover:** £2m - £5m **No.of Employees:** 21 - 50
Product Groups: 35, 37, 44, 49, 81, 83

Date of Accounts	Dec 10	Dec 09	Dec 08
Sales Turnover	N/A	N/A	5m
Pre Tax Profit/Loss	N/A	N/A	170
Working Capital	547	558	661
Fixed Assets	43	38	28
Current Assets	1m	1m	1m
Current Liabilities	N/A	N/A	265

Projects Department Ltd
26 Woodlands Road, Camberley, GU15 3NA
Tel: 01276-681423 **Fax:** 01276-537170
E-mail: info@projectsdepartment.com
Website: http://www.projectsdepartment.com
Directors: P. Daffarn (MD)
Immediate Holding Company: PROJECTS DEPARTMENT LIMITED
Registration no: 03811095 **Date established:** 1999
No.of Employees: 1 - 10 **Product Groups:** 36, 37, 38, 45, 52, 67, 80, 84

Date of Accounts	Aug 11	Aug 10	Aug 09
Working Capital	115	67	8
Fixed Assets	3	5	2
Current Assets	186	156	75

Prontaprint Ltd
9 Helix Business Park, Camberley, GU15 2QT
Tel: 01276-681373 **Fax:** 01276-683800
E-mail: sales@prontaprint-online.com
Website: http://www.prontaprint.com
Directors: J. Earl (MD), K. Skitt (Dir)
Ultimate Holding Company: NAPG LIMITED
Immediate Holding Company: PRONTAPRINT LIMITED
Registration no: 00998213 **Date established:** 1970
No.of Employees: 1 - 10 **Product Groups:** 44

Date of Accounts	Dec 09	Dec 08	Dec 07
Sales Turnover	5m	6m	4m
Pre Tax Profit/Loss	450	1m	640
Working Capital	2m	2m	671
Fixed Assets	359	498	385
Current Assets	3m	3m	2m
Current Liabilities	288	111	377

Prospect 360
Intertec House 1 Tomlins Avenue, Frimley, Camberley, GU16 8LJ
Tel: 01276-691199
E-mail: data@prospect360.co.uk
Website: http://www.prospect360.co.uk
Directors: V. Mishra (Dir)
Immediate Holding Company: INTERTEC DATA SOLUTIONS LIMITED
Registration no: 04802191 **Date established:** 2003
No.of Employees: 1 - 10 **Product Groups:** 81

Date of Accounts	Jun 11	Jun 10	Jun 09
Working Capital	40	6	4
Fixed Assets	4	4	1
Current Assets	127	49	35

Quest Welding Services
R Linsford Business Park Linsford Lane, Mytchett, Camberley, GU16 6DL
Tel: 01252-377698 **Fax:** 01252-373251
Directors: E. Bateman (Prop)
Immediate Holding Company: QUEST WELDING SERVICES LIMITED
Registration no: 02048319 **Date established:** 1986
No.of Employees: 1 - 10 **Product Groups:** 46

Reed Accountancy Personnel Ltd
33c Obelisk Way, Camberley, GU15 3SG
Tel: 01276-693580 **Fax:** 01276-28693
E-mail: rapcamberley@reed.co.uk
Website: http://www.reed.co.uk
Managers: M. Gourley (Mgr)
Immediate Holding Company: REED PERSONNEL SERVICES LTD
Registration no: 00973629 **Date established:** 1960
Turnover: £125m - £250m **No.of Employees:** 1 - 10 **Product Groups:** 80

Reed Specialist Recruitment
33 Obelisk Way, Camberley, GU15 3SG
Tel: 01276-691547 **Fax:** 01276-693571
E-mail: camberley@reed.co.uk
Website: http://www.reed.co.uk
Managers: M. Gourley (Comm)
Ultimate Holding Company: REED GLOBAL LTD (MALTA)
Immediate Holding Company: REED EMPLOYMENT LIMITED
Registration no: 00669854 **Date established:** 1960
Turnover: £75m - £125m **No.of Employees:** 1 - 10 **Product Groups:** 80

Date of Accounts	Jun 11	Jun 10	Dec 07
Sales Turnover	618	450	287m
Pre Tax Profit/Loss	-2m	310	8m
Working Capital	23m	28m	28m
Fixed Assets	31	36	5m
Current Assets	28m	30m	74m
Current Liabilities	37	29	21m

Rugged Systems
Marlin House 459 London, Camberley, GU15 3JA
Tel: 01276-686707 **Fax:** 01276-854109
Website: http://www.rugged-systems.com
Managers: C. Harrington (Sales Prom Mgr)
Ultimate Holding Company: SOLID STATE PLC
Immediate Holding Company: RUGGED SYSTEMS LIMITED
Registration no: 03548691 **Date established:** 1998 **Turnover:** £5m - £10m
No.of Employees: 1 - 10 **Product Groups:** 37, 44, 67

Date of Accounts	Mar 12	Mar 11	Mar 10
Sales Turnover	N/A	4m	N/A
Pre Tax Profit/Loss	N/A	102	N/A
Working Capital	70	64	-100
Fixed Assets	N/A	5	72
Current Assets	70	1m	683
Current Liabilities	N/A	410	N/A

S C Johnson Ltd
Frimley Green Road Frimley, Camberley, GU16 7AJ
Tel: 01276-852000 **Fax:** 01276-852121
E-mail: m.patrick.james.obrien@scjohnson.com
Website: http://www.scjohnson.co.uk
Directors: P. O'Brien (Dir)
Ultimate Holding Company: SC JOHNSON & SON INC (USA)
Immediate Holding Company: SC JOHNSON LTD
Registration no: 04166155 **VAT No.:** 358 8677 85 **Date established:** 2001
Turnover: £125m - £250m **No.of Employees:** 251 - 500
Product Groups: 30, 36

Date of Accounts	Jun 10	Jun 09	Jun 08
Sales Turnover	131m	129m	115m
Pre Tax Profit/Loss	2m	-3m	114
Working Capital	24m	20m	20m
Fixed Assets	7m	9m	12m
Current Assets	44m	40m	48m
Current Liabilities	7m	6m	14m

S G S UK Ltd
217-221 London Road, Camberley, GU15 3EY
Tel: 01276-697877 **Fax:** 01276-697696
E-mail: theresa.fairbrass@sgs.com
Website: http://www.sgs.co.uk
Bank(s): National Westminster, Bracknell
Managers: M. Anscomb
Ultimate Holding Company: SGS SA (SWITZERLAND)
Immediate Holding Company: SGS UNITED KINGDOM LIMITED
Registration no: 01193985 **Date established:** 1974
Turnover: £20m - £50m **No.of Employees:** 51 - 100 **Product Groups:** 51, 54, 80, 82, 84

Date of Accounts	Dec 11	Dec 10	Dec 09
Sales Turnover	101m	90m	97m
Pre Tax Profit/Loss	19m	7m	10m
Working Capital	8m	8m	12m
Fixed Assets	32m	27m	22m
Current Assets	34m	29m	35m
Current Liabilities	20m	18m	14m

Sandhurst Engineering Ltd
8 Doman Road Yorktown Industrial Estate, Camberley, GU15 3DF
Tel: 01276-684989 **Fax:** 01276-691404
E-mail: sales@sandhursteng.co.uk
Website: http://www.sandhursteng.co.uk
Directors: D. Howarth (MD), K. Howarth (Co Sec), P. Howarth (Fin), A. Howarth (MD)
Managers: A. Howath (Sales & Mktg Mg), A. Howarth (Sales & Mktg Mg), P. Howarth (Sec)
Immediate Holding Company: SANDHURST ENGINEERING LIMITED
Registration no: 02027194 **VAT No.:** GB 314 7845 50
Date established: 1978 **Turnover:** £250,000 - £500,000
No.of Employees: 1 - 10 **Product Groups:** 48

Date of Accounts	Aug 11	Aug 10	Aug 09
Working Capital	5	1	-19
Fixed Assets	7	9	11
Current Assets	81	74	45

Sheet Tech Fabrications
6 Doman Road, Camberley, GU15 3DF
Tel: 01276-684800 **Fax:** 01276-20696
Website: http://www.sheettech.fsnet.co.uk
Directors: C. Dottson (Ptnr)
Immediate Holding Company: THERMAL PERIMETER HEATING SYSTEMS LIMITED
Registration no: 06984781 **VAT No.:** GB 384 4039 43
Date established: 2001 **Turnover:** £1m - £2m **No.of Employees:** 11 - 20
Product Groups: 48

Date of Accounts	Jul 11	Jul 10	Jul 09
Working Capital	32	34	55
Current Assets	105	75	152

Specialist Electronics Services Ltd
25 Craven Court Stanhope Road, Camberley, GU15 3BS
Tel: 01276-63483 **Fax:** 01276-63327
E-mail: info@sesltd.com
Website: http://www.sesltd.com
Bank(s): The Royal Bank of Scotland

see next page

Specialist Electronics Services Ltd - Cont'd

Directors: M. Mabin (Dir)
Managers: B. Dolman, P. Crate (Tech Serv Mgr), G. Ellis (Purch Mgr)
Ultimate Holding Company: CURTISS WRIGHT CORPORATION (U.S.A)
Immediate Holding Company: SPECIALIST ELECTRONICS SERVICES LIMITED
Registration no: 02595180 **VAT No.:** GB 572 6845 09
Date established: 1991 **Turnover:** £2m - £5m **No.of Employees:** 21 - 50
Product Groups: 36, 37, 38, 39, 68, 84

Date of Accounts	Dec 11	Dec 10	May 10
Sales Turnover	6m	2m	N/A
Pre Tax Profit/Loss	375	-32	N/A
Working Capital	1m	629	691
Fixed Assets	92	54	415
Current Assets	4m	2m	2m
Current Liabilities	1m	851	N/A

Andreas Stihl Ltd

Stihl House Stanhope Road, Camberley, GU15 3YT
Tel: 01276-20202 **Fax:** 01276- 670510
E-mail: info@stihl.co.uk
Website: http://www.stihl.co.uk
Managers: E. Dell, D. Spencer (Tech Serv Mgr), N. Burroughs (Fin Mgr), N. Burroughs (Fin Mgr), S. Larter-conway (Mktg Serv Mgr), S. Parkin (Nat Sales Mgr)
Ultimate Holding Company: STIHL HOLDING KG (GERMANY)
Immediate Holding Company: ANDREAS STIHL LIMITED
Registration no: 01376302 **Date established:** 1978
Turnover: £50m - £75m **No.of Employees:** 51 - 100 **Product Groups:** 37, 67

Date of Accounts	Dec 11	Dec 10	Dec 09
Sales Turnover	64m	61m	59m
Pre Tax Profit/Loss	4m	7m	5m
Working Capital	11m	13m	11m
Fixed Assets	6m	5m	5m
Current Assets	22m	24m	20m
Current Liabilities	3m	3m	3m

Strebel Ltd

Unit 1f Albany Park, Camberley, GU16 7PB
Tel: 01276-685422 **Fax:** 01276-685405
E-mail: info@strebel.co.uk
Website: http://www.strebel.co.uk
Bank(s): Barclays
Directors: A. Parker (MD), D. Thorneycroft (MD)
Managers: P. Kitchen
Ultimate Holding Company: GEBE GMBH (AUSTRIA)
Immediate Holding Company: STREBEL LIMITED
Registration no: 01197182 **Date established:** 1975 **Turnover:** £2m - £5m
No.of Employees: 21 - 50 **Product Groups:** 40

Date of Accounts	Dec 11	Dec 10	Dec 09
Working Capital	369	666	566
Fixed Assets	65	69	78
Current Assets	2m	2m	2m

TCB-Arrow Ltd

Watchmoor House Watchmoor Road, Camberley, GU15 3AQ
Tel: 01276-679394 **Fax:** 01276-679055
E-mail: sales@tcb-arrow.co.uk
Website: http://www.tcb-arrow.co.uk
No.of Employees: 21 - 50 **Product Groups:** 26, 29, 30, 31, 36, 37, 38, 39, 40, 42, 44, 48, 66, 67, 84

Date of Accounts	Mar 08	Mar 07	Mar 06
Working Capital	462	414	591
Fixed Assets	256	304	157
Current Assets	1032	1168	1090
Current Liabilities	569	753	499

Telindus Ltd

Centurion Watchmoor Park, Camberley, GU15 3YL
Tel: 01276-406100 **Fax:** 01276-406101
E-mail: info@telindus.co.uk
Website: http://www.telindus.co.uk
Bank(s): National Westminster Bank Plc
Directors: J. Dunn (I.T. Dir), P. Amer (Fin), P. Dowdeswell (Co Sec)
Managers: S. Broughton (Sales Admin), M. Greenwood, H. Jinks (Accounts)
Ultimate Holding Company: BELGACOM NV (BELGIUM)
Immediate Holding Company: TELINDUS SURVEILLANCE SOLUTIONS LTD
Registration no: 01596440 **Date established:** 1981 **Turnover:** £2m - £5m
No.of Employees: 101 - 250 **Product Groups:** 37, 44

Date of Accounts	Dec 11	Dec 10	Dec 09
Sales Turnover	61m	41m	44
Pre Tax Profit/Loss	-1m	-2m	-1
Working Capital	-2m	-5m	N/A
Fixed Assets	5m	5m	2
Current Assets	27m	13m	12
Current Liabilities	12m	7m	8

Vincent & Rymill

Wharf Road Frimley Green, Camberley, GU16 6PT
Tel: 01252-834242 **Fax:** 01252-838989
Website: http://www.vincentrymill.co.uk
Directors: T. Vincent (Ptnr)
Immediate Holding Company: BOB POTTER LEISURE LIMITED
Registration no: 01400585 **Date established:** 1977
No.of Employees: 1 - 10 **Product Groups:** 35

Date of Accounts	Jan 12	Jan 11	Jan 04
Working Capital	-6	-6	-6
Current Liabilities	6	6	N/A

Xstrahl Ltd

Watchmoor Park The Coliseum, Camberley, GU15 3YL
Tel: 01276-462696 **Fax:** 01276-684 205
E-mail: support@xstrahl.com
Website: http://www.xstrahl.com
Directors: M. Robinson (MD)
Immediate Holding Company: XSTRAHL LIMITED
Registration no: 03105256 **VAT No.:** GB 569 9323 86
Date established: 1995 **Turnover:** £1m - £2m **No.of Employees:** 1 - 10
Product Groups: 37

Date of Accounts	Sep 11	Sep 10	Sep 09
Working Capital	2m	1m	1m
Fixed Assets	178	188	179
Current Assets	3m	2m	2m

Zhender Group UK Ltd

Unit 4 Watchmoor Point, Camberley, GU15 3AD
Tel: 01252-515151 **Fax:** 01276-605801
Website: http://www.bisque.co.uk
Directors: N. Coston (Tech Serv), D. Gosden (Fin), T. Twohig (MD)
Managers: C. Walley, C. Flower (Tech Serv Mgr), J. Pattberg
Ultimate Holding Company: ZEHNDER GROUP AG (SWITZERLAND)
Immediate Holding Company: ZEHNDER GROUP UK LIMITED
Registration no: 02296696 **Date established:** 1988 **Turnover:** £5m - £10m
No.of Employees: 21 - 50 **Product Groups:** 36, 40

Date of Accounts	Dec 11	Dec 10	Dec 09
Sales Turnover	26m	25m	26m
Pre Tax Profit/Loss	112	5m	-270
Working Capital	3m	3m	1m
Fixed Assets	3m	3m	3m
Current Assets	10m	10m	12m
Current Liabilities	2m	2m	2m

Carshalton

Burns Iron Work Ltd

33c William Street, Carshalton, SM5 2RB
Tel: 07958-519299 **Fax:** 020-8647 2683
Website: http://www.burnsironwork.com
Directors: D. Burns (MD), P. Burns (Fin)
Immediate Holding Company: BURNS IRONWORK LIMITED
Registration no: 04454366 **Date established:** 2002
Turnover: Up to £250,000 **No.of Employees:** 1 - 10 **Product Groups:** 26, 35

Date of Accounts	Mar 12	Mar 11	Mar 10
Sales Turnover	45	59	38
Pre Tax Profit/Loss	2	11	-4
Working Capital	4	16	6
Fixed Assets	15	17	20
Current Assets	5	20	9
Current Liabilities	1	N/A	1

P W Merkle Ltd

18 Oakhurst Rise, Carshalton, SM5 4AG
Tel: 020-8642 5755 **Fax:** 020-8646 3000
E-mail: sales@pw-merkle.co.uk
Website: http://www.pw-merkle.co.uk
Directors: J. French (Dir)
Immediate Holding Company: P.W. MERKLE LIMITED
Registration no: 00344980 **VAT No.:** GB 243 6804 62
Date established: 1938 **Turnover:** £1m - £2m **No.of Employees:** 1 - 10
Product Groups: 36, 42, 43, 44, 46

Date of Accounts	Mar 11	Mar 10	Mar 09
Working Capital	24	32	41
Current Assets	143	93	98

Model Railway Developments

6 The Square, Carshalton, SM5 3BN
Tel: 08456-441101 **Fax:** 020-8773 0442
Directors: H. Carr (Prop)
Registration no: 06759884 **Date established:** 2008
No.of Employees: 1 - 10 **Product Groups:** 35

S T R Designers & Lithographic Printers

Vellum Mill 76a Mill Lane, Carshalton, SM5 2JR
Tel: 020-8647 9790 **Fax:** 020-8669 2140
E-mail: studio@str.uk.com
Website: http://www.str.uk.com
Directors: S. Ladbrook (Ptnr)
Registration no: 2214220 **Date established:** 1979 **Turnover:**
No.of Employees: 1 - 10 **Product Groups:** 44, 64, 81, 86

Caterham

Arctic Paper UK Ltd

Quadrant House 47 Croydon Road, Caterham, CR3 6PB
Tel: 01883-331800 **Fax:** 01883-330560
E-mail: info@arcticpaper.com
Website: http://www.arcticpaper.com
Directors: S. Andreasson (Fin), G. Colyer (MD)
Immediate Holding Company: ARCTIC PAPER UK LIMITED
Registration no: 01756276 **Date established:** 1983 **Turnover:** £1m - £2m
No.of Employees: 1 - 10 **Product Groups:** 27

Date of Accounts	Dec 11	Dec 10	Dec 09
Sales Turnover	1m	1m	1m
Pre Tax Profit/Loss	279	159	156
Working Capital	232	440	320
Current Assets	387	564	406
Current Liabilities	134	113	84

The Beautiful Box Company

10 Adair Gardens, Caterham, CR3 5GD
Tel: 07802-624428
E-mail: laura@thebeautifulboxco.co.uk
Website: http://www.thebeautifulboxco.co.uk
Directors: L. Madgwick (Prop)
Immediate Holding Company: GRANIQUE DESIGNS LTD
Date established: 2012 **No.of Employees:** 1 - 10 **Product Groups:** 28

Caterham Cars Ltd

32 Station Avenue, Caterham, CR3 6LB
Tel: 01883-333700 **Fax:** 01883-333707
E-mail: andynoble@caterham.co.uk
Website: http://www.caterham.co.uk
Bank(s): HSBC Bank plc
Directors: A. Noble (Sales)
Ultimate Holding Company: CATERHAM ENTERPRISES LIMITED
Immediate Holding Company: CATERHAM CARS LTD.
Registration no: 01171408 **Date established:** 1974
Turnover: £10m - £20m **No.of Employees:** 11 - 20 **Product Groups:** 39

Date of Accounts	Dec 11	Dec 10	Dec 09
Sales Turnover	19m	20m	15m
Pre Tax Profit/Loss	1m	1m	201
Working Capital	2m	2m	221
Fixed Assets	1m	822	796
Current Assets	6m	6m	7m
Current Liabilities	2m	3m	3m

Express Skip Here

Unit 2 Paddock Barn Farm Godstone Road, Caterham, CR3 6SF
Tel: 020-8649 9676 **Fax:** 020-8666 9471
E-mail: baldskip@yahoo.co.uk
Website: http://www.expressskips.co.uk
Directors: K. Harvey (Prop)
No.of Employees: 1 - 10 **Product Groups:** 45, 67, 83

Home County Fire Protection

138 Stafford Road, Caterham, CR3 6JE
Tel: 01883-370997 **Fax:** 01883-342540
E-mail: bw.ford@ntlworld.com
Directors: B. Ford (MD), L. Fleming (Fin), L. Fleming (Dir)
Immediate Holding Company: HOME COUNTY FIRE & SECURITY LIMITED
Registration no: 03688636 **Date established:** 1998
No.of Employees: 1 - 10 **Product Groups:** 38, 42

Date of Accounts	Dec 10	Dec 09	Dec 08
Working Capital	4	7	-10
Fixed Assets	10	11	14
Current Assets	58	45	37

J A M Design Screen Print

143a Croydon Road, Caterham, CR3 6PF
Tel: 01883-343444 **Fax:** 01883-343444
E-mail: jim.rimmington@btinternet.com
Directors: J. Rimmington (Prop)
Date established: 1988 **Turnover:** Up to £250,000
No.of Employees: 1 - 10 **Product Groups:** 23, 27, 28, 39, 40

Linden Homes Ltd

Linden House Guards Avenue, Caterham, CR3 5XL
Tel: 01883-334400 **Fax:** 01883-348108
E-mail: steve.bangs@lindenhomes.co.uk
Website: http://www.lindenhomes.co.uk
Directors: C. Rogers (Fin), S. Bangs (MD), E. Nesbitt (Sales & Mktg)
Managers: S. Nash (Chief Buyer)
Immediate Holding Company: LINDEN HOMES LIMITED
Registration no: 00762318 **Date established:** 1963
No.of Employees: 51 - 100 **Product Groups:** 51, 52

Date of Accounts	Aug 11	Aug 10	Aug 09
Working Capital	-35	35	61
Fixed Assets	1m	1m	1m
Current Assets	310	322	334

M & P Electrical

41 Croydon Road, Caterham, CR3 6PD
Tel: 01883-340930
E-mail: sales@mp-electrical.co.uk
Website: http://www.mp-electrical.co.uk
Directors: D. Gaule (Prop), D. Gaule (Prop)
Immediate Holding Company: WINGATE HOLDINGS LIMITED
Registration no: 03872950 **Date established:** 1999
No.of Employees: 1 - 10 **Product Groups:** 37, 40, 67

Mojocom Systems Ltd

Birchwood Cottage Woldingham Road, Woldingham, Caterham, CR3 7LR
Tel: 01883-349922 **Fax:** 01883-332841
E-mail: info@mojocom.co.uk
Website: http://www.mojocom.co.uk
Directors: J. Wickham (MD)
Immediate Holding Company: MOJOCOM SYSTEMS LIMITED
Registration no: 02213499 **Date established:** 1988
Turnover: Up to £250,000 **No.of Employees:** 1 - 10 **Product Groups:** 37, 67

Date of Accounts	Mar 11	Mar 10	Mar 09
Sales Turnover	N/A	33	39
Pre Tax Profit/Loss	N/A	4	7
Working Capital	-4	-1	1
Current Assets	4	5	8
Current Liabilities	N/A	1	1

Pickerings Lift Europe

409-411 Croydon Road, Caterham, CR3 6PP
Tel: 01883-341850 **Fax:** 01883-341842
E-mail: gary.rains@pickerings.co.uk
Website: http://www.pickerings.co.uk
Managers: G. Rains (Reg Mgr)
Registration no: 03217853 **No.of Employees:** 11 - 20
Product Groups: 35, 39, 45

Chris Shiplee Associates

33 High Street, Caterham, CR3 5UE
Tel: 01883-341223
Directors: C. Shiplee (Ptnr)
Date established: 2001 **No.of Employees:** 1 - 10 **Product Groups:** 35

Stone Labels Ltd

37 Nelson Road, Caterham, CR3 5PP
Tel: 01883-373373 **Fax:** 01883-373737
E-mail: andy@stonelabels.co.uk
Website: http://www.stonelabels.co.uk
Directors: A. Catford (MD), S. Catford (Fin)
Immediate Holding Company: STONE LABELS LIMITED
Registration no: 01857556 **VAT No.:** 318 2282 69 **Date established:** 1984
Turnover: Up to £250,000 **No.of Employees:** 1 - 10 **Product Groups:** 27, 28, 30

Date of Accounts	Dec 11	Dec 10	Dec 09
Sales Turnover	155	155	188
Working Capital	24	27	35
Fixed Assets	7	8	10
Current Assets	42	47	65

Universal Food Service Equipment Ltd

13-17 Station Avenue, Caterham, CR3 6LB
Tel: 01883-341800 **Fax:** 01883-341794
E-mail: roger@universalfse.co.uk
Website: http://www.baronprofessional.com
Directors: R. Flanagan (MD)
Immediate Holding Company: UNIVERSAL FOOD SERVICE EQUIPMENT LIMITED
Registration no: 04219013 **Date established:** 2001
Turnover: £500,000 - £1m **No.of Employees:** 1 - 10 **Product Groups:** 20, 40, 41

Date of Accounts	Oct 11	Oct 10	Oct 09
Sales Turnover	N/A	N/A	577
Pre Tax Profit/Loss	N/A	N/A	55

Working Capital	-15	-37	N/A
Fixed Assets	16	19	N/A
Current Assets	321	286	266
Current Liabilities	N/A	N/A	60

Chertsey

A D P Ltd

40-48 Pyrcroft Road, Chertsey, KT16 9JT
Tel: 08452-300237 **Fax:** 08452-302371
E-mail: sales@adp-es.co.uk
Website: http://www.uk.adp.com
Bank(s): Barclays
Directors: D. Mcguire (MD)
Managers: P. White, M. Smith (Tech Serv Mgr)
Ultimate Holding Company: AUTOMATIC DATA PROCESSING INC (USA)
Immediate Holding Company: ADP LIMITED
Registration no: 01761559 **Date established:** 1983
Turnover: £20m - £50m **No.of Employees:** 251 - 500
Product Groups: 44, 80

Date of Accounts	Jun 11	Jun 10	Jun 09
Pre Tax Profit/Loss	-4m	-380	-1m
Working Capital	N/A	-37m	-36m
Fixed Assets	N/A	622	626
Current Liabilities	N/A	46	42

Assured Transport Solutions Ltd

Building 116, Royal Armament R&D Establishment, Chobham Lane, Chertsey, KT16 0EE
Tel: 0844-249 4950 **Fax:** 01344-874070
E-mail: sales@assuredtransport.co.uk
Website: http://www.assuredtransport.co.uk
Directors: F. Guest (Dir)
Registration no: 04362719 **Date established:** 1995
No.of Employees: 1 - 10 **Product Groups:** 72

Compass Group plc

Compass House Guildford Street, Chertsey, KT16 9BQ
Tel: 01932-573000 **Fax:** 01932-569956
Website: http://www.compass-group.com
Bank(s): National Westminster Bank Plc
Directors: J. Kingston (Pers), D. Blakemore (Fin)
Managers: R. Cousins, O. Cock
Ultimate Holding Company: COMPASS GROUP PLC
Registration no: 04083914 **VAT No.:** GB 466 4777 01
Date established: 2000 **Turnover:** Over £1,000m
No.of Employees: 101 - 250 **Product Groups:** 69

Date of Accounts	Sep 11	Sep 10	Sep 09
Sales Turnover	15833m	14468m	13444m
Pre Tax Profit/Loss	958m	913m	773m
Working Capital	-515m	-487m	-549m
Fixed Assets	5935m	5502m	5091m
Current Assets	3475m	2752m	2550m
Current Liabilities	2615m	1979m	2036m

Conrico Service Centre

Hanworth Lane, Chertsey, KT16 9LA
Tel: 01932-581090 **Fax:** 01932-567032
E-mail: jwood@conrico.com
Website: http://www.conrico.com
Bank(s): Lloyds TSB Bank plc
Directors: P. Benzimra (Co Sec)
Managers: G. Beacham (Comptroller), P. Govier
Ultimate Holding Company: REGENT TRUST COMPANY LTD (JERSEY)
Immediate Holding Company: CONRICO INTERNATIONAL LTD
Registration no: 01886151 **VAT No.:** GB 413 3615 85
Date established: 1985 **Turnover:** £20m - £50m
No.of Employees: 21 - 50 **Product Groups:** 61, 68

Date of Accounts	Dec 10	Dec 09	Dec 08
Sales Turnover	23m	25m	19m
Pre Tax Profit/Loss	470	1m	-1m
Working Capital	4m	4m	3m
Fixed Assets	3m	4m	4m
Current Assets	11m	13m	21m
Current Liabilities	2m	5m	3m

Construction Health & Safety Group

St Anns Road, Chertsey, KT16 9DG
Tel: 01932-561871 **Fax:** 01932-560193
E-mail: info@chsg.co.uk
Website: http://www.chfg.co.uk
Managers: W. Emery (Chief Mgr)
Immediate Holding Company: CONSTRUCTION HEALTH AND SAFETY GROUP
Registration no: 01573103 **VAT No.:** GB 221 4344 09
Date established: 1981 **Turnover:** Up to £250,000
No.of Employees: 1 - 10 **Product Groups:** 86

Date of Accounts	Dec 11	Dec 10	Dec 09
Sales Turnover	244	242	219
Pre Tax Profit/Loss	-108	-140	-93
Working Capital	608	222	346
Fixed Assets	283	777	793
Current Assets	690	285	386
Current Liabilities	76	57	39

Crest Nicholson

Crest House Pyrcroft Road, Chertsey, KT16 9GN
Tel: 01932-580555 **Fax:** 0870-336 3990
E-mail: info@crestnicholson.com
Website: http://www.crestnicholson.com
Bank(s): National Westminster Bank Plc
Directors: P. Bergin (Fin)
Managers: I. Johnson (Chief Buyer), S. Stone, M. Gibbons (Tech Serv Mgr), H. Saunders, J. Cookson (Personnel)
Ultimate Holding Company: CREST NICHOLSON HOLDINGS LIMITED
Immediate Holding Company: CREST NICHOLSON PLC
Registration no: 01040616 **VAT No.:** GB 138 0886 49
Date established: 1972 **Turnover:** £250m - £500m
No.of Employees: 251 - 500 **Product Groups:** 80

Date of Accounts	Oct 11	Oct 10	Oct 09
Sales Turnover	319m	N/A	N/A
Pre Tax Profit/Loss	-15m	-6m	7m
Working Capital	239m	169m	176m
Fixed Assets	53m	9m	10m
Current Assets	637m	499m	534m
Current Liabilities	136m	6m	4m

Distrupol

119 Guildford Street, Chertsey, KT16 9AL
Tel: 01932-566033 **Fax:** 01932-560363
E-mail: info@distrupol.com
Website: http://www.distrupol.com
Bank(s): National Westminster Bank Plc
Directors: G. Moore (Grp Chief Exec)
Managers: E. Clarke (Comptroller), R. Orme (Sales Prom Mgr), S. Backhouse (Tech Serv Mgr)
Ultimate Holding Company: ELLIS & EVERARD P.L.C.
Immediate Holding Company: ELLIS & EVERARD (UK HOLDINGS) LTD
Registration no: 00754472 **Turnover:** £50m - £75m
No.of Employees: 21 - 50 **Product Groups:** 30, 31, 32

Gulmay Ltd

St. Anns House St. Anns Road, Chertsey, KT16 9EH
Tel: 01932-570600 **Fax:** 01932-568700
E-mail: sales@gulmay.co.uk
Website: http://www.gulmay.co.uk
Bank(s): National Westminster Bank Plc
Directors: J. Hall (MD), J. Duncan (Fin)
Immediate Holding Company: Gulmay Holdings Ltd
Registration no: 01264416 **VAT No.:** GB 321 5380 89
Date established: 1976 **Turnover:** £5m - £10m **No.of Employees:** 21 - 50
Product Groups: 37

Date of Accounts	Mar 10	Mar 09	Mar 08
Sales Turnover	5m	6m	6m
Pre Tax Profit/Loss	871	1m	2m
Working Capital	4m	4m	4m
Fixed Assets	95	114	112
Current Assets	4m	4m	5m
Current Liabilities	219	215	467

K M Products Europe Ltd

Unit B The Forum, Chertsey, KT16 9JX
Tel: 01932-571991 **Fax:** 01932-571994
E-mail: sales@kmpuk.com
Website: http://www.kmpuk.com
Directors: N. Smith (Dir)
Ultimate Holding Company: KMP HOLDINGS LIMITED
Immediate Holding Company: KM PRODUCTS EUROPE LIMITED
Registration no: 02768670 **VAT No.:** GB 584 4681 06
Date established: 1992 **Turnover:** £5m - £10m **No.of Employees:** 1 - 10
Product Groups: 40, 42

Date of Accounts	Dec 11	Dec 10	Dec 09
Sales Turnover	10m	9m	8m
Pre Tax Profit/Loss	820	480	431
Working Capital	2m	1m	914
Fixed Assets	951	968	977
Current Assets	7m	6m	5m
Current Liabilities	353	409	515

Longs Ltd

Hanworth Lane Business Park, Chertsey, KT16 9LZ
Tel: 01932-561241 **Fax:** 01932-567391
E-mail: sales@longs.co.uk
Website: http://www.longs.co.uk
Bank(s): Lloyds
Directors: M. Green (Fin), P. Green (Dir)
Ultimate Holding Company: LONGS HOLDINGS LIMITED
Immediate Holding Company: LONGS LIMITED
Registration no: 00068496 **VAT No.:** GB 211 3892 87
Date established: 2000 **Turnover:** £5m - £10m **No.of Employees:** 11 - 20
Product Groups: 29, 38

Date of Accounts	Dec 11	Dec 10	Dec 09
Working Capital	842	966	839
Fixed Assets	1m	1m	1m
Current Assets	1m	1m	1m

M K Packaging

Fairview Woodlands Close, Ottershaw, Chertsey, KT16 0QR
Tel: 01932-875232 **Fax:** 01932-875493
Directors: M. Kane (Prop)
Date established: 1994 **No.of Employees:** 1 - 10 **Product Groups:** 38, 42

Metrode Products Ltd

Hanworth Lane, Chertsey, KT16 9LL
Tel: 01932-566721 **Fax:** 01932-565168
E-mail: info@metrode.com
Website: http://www.metrode.com
Bank(s): HSBC Bank plc
Directors: M. Chalmers (Fin)
Managers: P. Frost (Chief Mgr)
Immediate Holding Company: METRODE PRODUCTS LIMITED
Registration no: 00769971 **VAT No.:** GB 211 5690 89
Date established: 1963 **Turnover:** £10m - £20m
No.of Employees: 51 - 100 **Product Groups:** 35

Date of Accounts	Dec 10	Dec 09	Dec 08
Sales Turnover	17m	18m	18m
Pre Tax Profit/Loss	2m	2m	4m
Working Capital	5m	10m	8m
Fixed Assets	7m	6m	6m
Current Assets	12m	13m	12m
Current Liabilities	622	793	986

Patterson Products Ltd

Ford Road, Chertsey, KT16 8HG
Tel: 01932-570016 **Fax:** 01932-570084
E-mail: andrew@patterson.co.uk
Website: http://www.golfbuggy.org
Directors: A. Shelton (MD)
Immediate Holding Company: PATTERSON PRODUCTS LIMITED
Registration no: 04532741 **VAT No.:** GB 591 6749 94
Date established: 2002 **Turnover:** £250,000 - £500,000
No.of Employees: 1 - 10 **Product Groups:** 48

Date of Accounts	Feb 12	Feb 11	Feb 10
Sales Turnover	417	468	N/A
Pre Tax Profit/Loss	87	83	N/A
Working Capital	-16	-38	-83
Fixed Assets	75	88	104
Current Assets	34	19	26
Current Liabilities	36	31	N/A

M S Pellew

50 London Street, Chertsey, KT16 8AJ
Tel: 01932-563807
Directors: M. Pellew (Prop)
Date established: 1960 **No.of Employees:** 1 - 10 **Product Groups:** 26, 35

Portman Travel

Rutherwyk House Guildford Street, Chertsey, KT16 9AY
Tel: 01932-797100 **Fax:** 01256-330774
E-mail: marketing@portmantravel.com
Website: http://www.portmantravel.com
Directors: D. Canavan (Fin)
Managers: J. Hook (Mktg Serv Mgr), J. Odriscoll (Personnel), L. Welsh (Mktg Serv Mgr), D. Bishop, J. Baldwin (Tech Serv Mgr)
Ultimate Holding Company: SUPER SELECTOR SARL
Immediate Holding Company: PORTMAN TRAVEL LIMITED
Registration no: 00620104 **VAT No.:** GB 440 5907 59
Date established: 1959 **Turnover:** £500,000 - £1m
No.of Employees: 51 - 100 **Product Groups:** 69

Date of Accounts	Dec 11	Dec 10	Dec 09
Sales Turnover	260m	257m	239m
Pre Tax Profit/Loss	4m	4m	2m
Working Capital	14m	13m	15m
Fixed Assets	6m	5m	4m
Current Assets	27m	30m	29m
Current Liabilities	2m	3m	2m

R G L Promotions

3 Riversdell Close, Chertsey, KT16 9JW
Tel: 01932-561070 **Fax:** 01932-562831
Directors: P. Erasmus (Prop)
No.of Employees: 1 - 10 **Product Groups:** 24, 49

RAVIAN GB LIMITED

3000 HILLSWOOD DRIVE, Chertsey, KT16 0RS
Tel: 020-7000 1949 **Fax:** 020-7000 1953
E-mail: mail@ravian-gb.co.uk
Website: http://www.ravian-gb.co.uk
Managers: I. SMETHURST (Chief Mgr)
Registration no: 05444043 **Date established:** 2005 **Turnover:** £1m - £2m
No.of Employees: 1 - 10 **Product Groups:** 35, 36, 40, 42

Regus Management Ltd

3000 Hillswood Drive, Chertsey, KT16 0RS
Tel: 01932-895000 **Fax:** 01932-895001
E-mail: enquiries@regus.com
Website: http://www.regus.com
Bank(s): Lloyds
Directors: R. Lobo (Dir), T. Regan (Co Sec), T. Regan (Fin), U. Short (Mkt Research), M. Dixon (MD), A. Gibbons (Sales)
Managers: M. Brockington
Immediate Holding Company: REGUS MANAGEMENT LIMITED
Registration no: 02307313 **Date established:** 1988
Turnover: £20m - £50m **No.of Employees:** 51 - 100 **Product Groups:** 80

Date of Accounts	Dec 09	Dec 08	Dec 07
Sales Turnover	N/A	20m	N/A
Pre Tax Profit/Loss	-11m	12m	3m
Working Capital	510	9m	51m
Fixed Assets	2m	16m	12m
Current Assets	3m	24m	52m
Current Liabilities	2m	2m	N/A

Stanhope Seta Ltd

London Street, Chertsey, KT16 8AP
Tel: 01932-564391 **Fax:** 01932-568363
E-mail: sales@stanhope-seta.co.uk
Website: http://www.stanhope-seta.co.uk
Bank(s): Barclays
Directors: G. Verity (Dir), M. Verity (MD)
Managers: C. Morrison (Mktg Serv Mgr), B. Powell (Product), G. Daily (Tech Serv Mgr)
Ultimate Holding Company: GUILLEMOT CORPORATION SA (FRANCE)
Immediate Holding Company: STANHOPE-SETA LIMITED
Registration no: 00361699 **Date established:** 1940
Turnover: £10m - £20m **No.of Employees:** 51 - 100 **Product Groups:** 38, 42

Date of Accounts	Jul 11	Jul 10	Jul 09
Sales Turnover	13m	10m	N/A
Pre Tax Profit/Loss	474	532	403
Working Capital	3m	4m	3m
Fixed Assets	1m	1m	1m
Current Assets	7m	6m	6m
Current Liabilities	2m	226	1m

Thorpe Park Ski Shop

Staines Road, Chertsey, KT16 8PN
Tel: 0870-4444466 **Fax:** 01932-566367
E-mail: admin@thorpepark.com
Website: http://www.thorpepark.com
Bank(s): National Westminster
Directors: M. Collins (Co Sec), J. Robinson (Dir)
Managers: P. Ronchetti (Chief Mgr)
Ultimate Holding Company: Pearsons
Turnover: £10m - £20m **No.of Employees:** 101 - 250 **Product Groups:** 89

Treadstone

Unit 3 Hersham Farm Longcross Road, Longcross, Chertsey, KT16 0DN
Tel: 01932-873741 **Fax:** 01932-873741
E-mail: info@treadstone.co.uk
Website: http://www.treadstone.co.uk
Managers: T. Hessian (Mgr)
Registration no: 03538313 **Date established:** 2002
No.of Employees: 1 - 10 **Product Groups:** 27, 30, 35, 66

Trident Honda

Guildford Road Ottershaw, Chertsey, KT16 0NZ
Tel: 01932-874411 **Fax:** 01932-874931
E-mail: info@tridentgarages.co.uk
Website: http://www.tridentgarages.co.uk
Bank(s): Barclays, Guildford
Directors: C. Roberts (Fin), C. Roberts (Fin), R. Roberts (MD)
Managers: C. Arthurs (Sales Prom Mgr), C. Gale
Immediate Holding Company: TRIDENT GARAGES LIMITED
Registration no: 00764299 **VAT No.:** GB 211 4200 40
Date established: 1963 **Turnover:** £20m - £50m
No.of Employees: 51 - 100 **Product Groups:** 68

Date of Accounts	Dec 11	Dec 10	Dec 09
Sales Turnover	25m	28m	28m
Pre Tax Profit/Loss	-129	-4	251
Working Capital	-626	-513	-301
Fixed Assets	5m	5m	5m
Current Assets	2m	3m	3m
Current Liabilities	481	800	873

V M C Ltd
Trafalgar Works Station Road, Chertsey, KT16 8BE
Tel: 01932-563434 **Fax:** 01932-566598
E-mail: info@vmclimited.co.uk
Website: http://www.vmclimited.co.uk
Bank(s): Barclays
Directors: J. Taylor (Dir), P. Taylor (MD), S. Powel (Pers)
Immediate Holding Company: V.M.C.LIMITED
Registration no: 00502468 **Date established:** 1951
No.of Employees: 11 - 20 **Product Groups:** 48

Date of Accounts	Feb 11	Feb 10	Feb 09
Working Capital	29	13	23
Fixed Assets	43	39	41
Current Assets	71	36	42

Wacker Chemicals
120-122 Bridge Road, Chertsey, KT16 8LA
Tel: 01932-445006
E-mail: info.uk@wacker.com
Website: http://www.wacker.com
Managers: A. Thoren (Sales Admin)
Immediate Holding Company: PWG SCREEN MEDIA LTD
Date established: 2005 **No.of Employees:** 1 - 10 **Product Groups:** 32, 35, 68

Date of Accounts	May 11	May 10	May 09
Sales Turnover	N/A	N/A	43
Pre Tax Profit/Loss	N/A	N/A	8
Working Capital	1	13	-49
Current Assets	4	24	16
Current Liabilities	N/A	N/A	3

Xstratek Ltd
Bramshill Manor Guildford Road, Ottershaw, Chertsey, KT16 0QN
Tel: 01932-454040 **Fax:** 01932-454045
E-mail: enquiries@xshire.com
Website: http://www.xshire.com
Managers: S. Dyke (Mgr)
Immediate Holding Company: XSTRATEK LIMITED
Registration no: 07516359 **Date established:** 2011
No.of Employees: 1 - 10 **Product Groups:** 37, 83

Chessington

John Artis Ltd
Cox Lane, Chessington, KT9 1SF
Tel: 020-8391 5544 **Fax:** 020-8391 4595
E-mail: orders@john-artis.ltd.uk
Website: http://www.johnartis.co.uk
Bank(s): Barclays, Luton, Beds
Directors: C. Weeden (Fin), I. Jelley (Sales)
Managers: S. Huntington (Tech Serv Mgr)
Ultimate Holding Company: ARTWARE TRADING LIMITED
Immediate Holding Company: JOHN ARTIS LIMITED
Registration no: 01201735 **VAT No.:** GB 711 1963 60
Date established: 1975 **Turnover:** £5m - £10m **No.of Employees:** 11 - 20
Product Groups: 33

Date of Accounts	May 08	Mar 11	Mar 10
Sales Turnover	N/A	8m	8m
Pre Tax Profit/Loss	982	651	638
Working Capital	3m	4m	4m
Fixed Assets	291	110	134
Current Assets	5m	6m	5m
Current Liabilities	694	702	686

Avnet
Cox Lane, Chessington, KT9 1SJ
Tel: 020-8286 5000 **Fax:** 020-8286 5056
E-mail: sales@belmirco.eu.com
Website: http://www.adequatinterim.fr
Directors: G. Watt (MD)
Managers: S. Nicholls
Ultimate Holding Company: BELL MICROPRODUCTS INC
Immediate Holding Company: BELL MICROPRODUCTS LIMITED
Registration no: 03969946 **Date established:** 2000
Turnover: £500m - £1,000m **No.of Employees:** 251 - 500
Product Groups: 44

Date of Accounts	Dec 09	Dec 08	Dec 07
Sales Turnover	620m	620m	699m
Pre Tax Profit/Loss	9m	-4m	5m
Working Capital	57m	55m	62m
Fixed Assets	16m	17m	18m
Current Assets	161m	158m	166m
Current Liabilities	14m	11m	15m

Bishops Move Overseas
Unit 5 Davis Road Industrial Park Davis Road, Chessington, KT9 1TQ
Tel: 020-8391 8200 **Fax:** 020-7498 0749
E-mail: birmingham.manager@bishopsmove.com
Website: http://www.bishopsmove.com
Bank(s): The Royal Bank of Scotland
Directors: C. Marshell (Fin), N. Bishop (MD), P. Bishop (I.T. Dir), C. Marshall (Sales & Mktg), C. Shaddock (Fin)
Managers: P. Bishop (I.T. Exec), N. Bishop
Ultimate Holding Company: 00226302
Immediate Holding Company: BISHOP'S MOVE (CHICHESTER) LIMITED
Registration no: 00386710 **VAT No.:** GB 653 1529 44
Date established: 1944 **Turnover:** £10m - £20m
No.of Employees: 11 - 20 **Product Groups:** 72

Blueprint Dental Equipment Ltd
15B Oakcroft Road, Chessington, KT9 1RH
Tel: 0845-0036274 **Fax:** 0845-0036275
E-mail: info@blueprintdental.co.uk
Website: http://www.blueprintdental.co.uk
Directors: S. Bowler (Dir), S. Mir (Dir)
Registration no: 05055354 **Turnover:** £500,000 - £1m
No.of Employees: 11 - 20 **Product Groups:** 26, 38

Date of Accounts	Mar 08	Mar 07	Mar 06
Working Capital	58	7	36
Fixed Assets	21	11	2
Current Assets	58	50	143
Current Liabilities	N/A	44	108
Total Share Capital	1	1	1

Compressed Air Centre Ltd
104 Roebuck Road, Chessington, KT9 1JX
Tel: 020-8974 2626 **Fax:** 020-8974 2882
E-mail: info@compressedair.co.uk
Website: http://www.compressedair.co.uk
Directors: N. Rummens (MD)
Ultimate Holding Company: COMPRESSED AIR CENTRE HOLDINGS LIMITED
Immediate Holding Company: COMPRESSED AIR CENTRE LIMITED
Registration no: 02712449 **VAT No.:** GB 611 8711 60
Date established: 1992 **Turnover:** £1m - £2m **No.of Employees:** 1 - 10
Product Groups: 40

Date of Accounts	Jun 12	Jun 11	Jun 10
Working Capital	532	529	530
Fixed Assets	510	492	503
Current Assets	911	910	890

Crown Air Conditioning Ltd
57 Hemsby Road, Chessington, KT9 2DY
Tel: 08712-183030
E-mail: enquiries@crownac.co.uk
Website: http://www.crownac.co.uk
Directors: M. Brown (MD)
Immediate Holding Company: CROWN AIR CONDITIONING LIMITED
Registration no: 06434997 **Date established:** 2007
No.of Employees: 1 - 10 **Product Groups:** 35, 38, 40

Date of Accounts	Nov 11	Nov 10	Nov 09
Working Capital	19	19	54
Fixed Assets	4	4	N/A
Current Assets	55	55	68
Current Liabilities	36	N/A	N/A

Digico UK Ltd
Unit 10, Chessington, KT9 2QL
Tel: 01372-845600 **Fax:** 01372-845656
E-mail: info@digiconsoles.com
Website: http://www.digico.biz
Bank(s): Barclays
Directors: C. Parritt (Fin), D. Webster (Mkt Research), J. Gordon (MD)
Ultimate Holding Company: DIGICO EUROPE LIMITED
Immediate Holding Company: DIGICO UK LIMITED
Registration no: 04336508 **VAT No.:** GB 216 9735 43
Date established: 2001 **Turnover:** £10m - £20m
No.of Employees: 21 - 50 **Product Groups:** 37

Date of Accounts	Dec 11	Dec 10	Dec 09
Sales Turnover	21m	19m	13m
Pre Tax Profit/Loss	6m	5m	2m
Working Capital	7m	7m	3m
Fixed Assets	275	295	298
Current Assets	13m	11m	7m
Current Liabilities	3m	3m	2m

Europa Navaids Ltd
69 Angus Close, Chessington, KT9 2BN
Tel: 020-8391 0545
E-mail: vincentvoy@hotmail.co.uk
Directors: V. Jakomin (MD), V. Jakomin (Prop)
Immediate Holding Company: EUROPA NAVAIDS LIMITED
Registration no: 02080730 **VAT No.:** GB 493 6838 91
Date established: 1986 **Turnover:** Up to £250,000
No.of Employees: 1 - 10 **Product Groups:** 37, 39, 84

F L D Chemicals Ltd
Oakcroft Road, Chessington, KT9 1RH
Tel: 020-8391 2331 **Fax:** 020-8974 2850
E-mail: info@fld.co.uk
Website: http://www.fld.co.uk
Directors: M. Laird (Dir)
Immediate Holding Company: FLD CHEMICALS LIMITED
Registration no: 01815750 **Date established:** 1984
Turnover: £20m - £50m **No.of Employees:** 11 - 20 **Product Groups:** 14, 20, 27, 29, 30, 31, 32, 33, 34, 37, 39, 42, 48, 51, 52, 67, 76, 84, 85

Date of Accounts	Jul 11	Jul 10	Jul 09
Working Capital	10	17	16
Fixed Assets	1	1	2
Current Assets	100	101	68

Fabris Lane Ltd
1 Lion Park Avenue, Chessington, KT9 1ST
Tel: 020-8974 1642 **Fax:** 020-8974 1672
E-mail: rod.lane@fabrislane.co.uk
Website: http://www.fabrislane.com
Bank(s): Bank of Wales PLC
Directors: S. Drury (Fin), T. Downes (Co Sec), R. Lane (Dir)
Managers: C. Mitcham (Personnel)
Ultimate Holding Company: THREE HUNDRED LTD.
Immediate Holding Company: THREE HUNDRED LTD.
Registration no: 06192393 **VAT No.:** GB 609 2654 35
Date established: 2007 **Turnover:** £10m - £20m
No.of Employees: 51 - 100 **Product Groups:** 38

Date of Accounts	Sep 10	Sep 09	Sep 08
Sales Turnover	16m	16m	N/A
Pre Tax Profit/Loss	-371	-3m	-690
Working Capital	2m	1m	-2m
Fixed Assets	476	3m	11m
Current Assets	4m	5m	1
Current Liabilities	2m	2m	82

Intram Barwell Ltd
Barwell Business Park Leatherhead Road, Chessington, KT9 2NY
Tel: 020-8391 7500 **Fax:** 020-8974 1629
E-mail: enquiries@ibl.co.uk
Website: http://www.ibl.co.uk
Directors: A. Penfold (Dir), A. Smith (Co Sec), I. Simpson (Ch)
Managers: M. Brown (Personnel), G. Lamport (I.T. Exec), M. Manning (Purch Mgr), P. Saunders (Mktg Serv Mgr), B. Saunders (Sales Admin)
Ultimate Holding Company: IBL Holdings Ltd
Immediate Holding Company: I B L Holdings Ltd
Registration no: 04601794 **VAT No.:** GB 391 5037 53
Date established: 2002 **Turnover:** £5m - £10m **No.of Employees:** 11 - 20
Product Groups: 37

Date of Accounts	Dec 07	Dec 06	Dec 05
Sales Turnover	N/A	7m	8m
Pre Tax Profit/Loss	-36	-64	-13
Working Capital	266	255	226
Fixed Assets	171	219	307
Current Assets	4m	3m	3m
Current Liabilities	4m	3m	3m
Total Share Capital	275	275	275

Leybold Vacuum
Unit 3 Silverglade Business Park Leatherhead Road, Chessington, KT9 2QL
Tel: 01372-737300 **Fax:** 01372-737301
E-mail: sales.uk.in@oerlikon.com
Website: http://www.leybold.com
Bank(s): Barclays
Managers: V. Crewpick (Mgr)
Ultimate Holding Company: OC OERLIKON CORPORATION AG (SWITZERLAND)
Immediate Holding Company: OERLIKON LEYBOLD VACUUM UK LTD
Registration no: 00668677 **VAT No.:** GB 205 6026 03
Date established: 1960 **Turnover:** £2m - £5m **No.of Employees:** 11 - 20
Product Groups: 36, 38, 40, 42, 67

Date of Accounts	Dec 11	Dec 10	Dec 09
Sales Turnover	3m	2m	2m
Pre Tax Profit/Loss	241	74	-199
Working Capital	827	669	625
Fixed Assets	44	30	39
Current Assets	1m	868	833
Current Liabilities	284	187	197

Michael Rennison Associates
29 Station Road, Chessington, KT9 1AX
Tel: 020-8397 4352 **Fax:** 020-8397 4352
Directors: M. Rennison (Head)
Date established: 1996 **No.of Employees:** 1 - 10 **Product Groups:** 35

Mid Surrey Windings Ltd
Unit D Oakcroft Works Oakcroft Road, Chessington, KT9 1RH
Tel: 020-8397 8559 **Fax:** 020-8397 8493
E-mail: sales@mid-surreywindings.co.uk
Website: http://www.mid-surreywindings.co.uk
Directors: C. Smith (Dir)
Immediate Holding Company: MID-SURREY WINDINGS LIMITED
Registration no: 04330939 **Date established:** 2001
Turnover: £250,000 - £500,000 **No.of Employees:** 1 - 10
Product Groups: 37

Date of Accounts	Nov 09	Nov 08	Nov 07
Sales Turnover	344	349	303
Pre Tax Profit/Loss	2	18	5
Working Capital	30	35	19
Fixed Assets	12	5	7
Current Assets	95	126	122
Current Liabilities	24	31	48

Mollart Engineering
106 Roebuck Road, Chessington, KT9 1EU
Tel: 020-8391 2282 **Fax:** 020-8391 6626
E-mail: info@mollart.com
Website: http://www.mollart.com
Bank(s): National Westminster
Directors: G. Mollart (MD), I. Petitt (Sales)
Ultimate Holding Company: MOLLART HOLDINGS LIMITED
Immediate Holding Company: MOLLART ENGINEERING LIMITED
Registration no: 01563799 **VAT No.:** GB 391 5679 13
Date established: 1981 **Turnover:** £10m - £20m
No.of Employees: 51 - 100 **Product Groups:** 46

Date of Accounts	Mar 11	Mar 10	Mar 09
Sales Turnover	13m	10m	12m
Pre Tax Profit/Loss	549	88	76
Working Capital	912	676	704
Fixed Assets	3m	3m	4m
Current Assets	6m	4m	6m
Current Liabilities	2m	588	1m

P F C Corofil (a division of Pre-formed Components Ltd)
Unit 3-4 King Georges Trading Estate Davis Road, Chessington, KT9 1TT
Tel: 020-8391 0533 **Fax:** 020-8391 2723
E-mail: sales@pfc-corofil.com
Website: http://www.pfc-corofil.com
Managers: C. Irvine (Mgr)
Registration no: 01743333 **No.of Employees:** 1 - 10 **Product Groups:** 52

P J Installation Southern Ltd
25 Wolsey Way, Chessington, KT9 1XQ
Tel: 020-8397 3003 **Fax:** 020-8288 8814
E-mail: tinaselway@pjinstallation.com
Directors: T. Selway (Dir)
Immediate Holding Company: PJ INSTALLATIONS (SOUTHERN) LIMITED
Registration no: 05790905 **Date established:** 2006
No.of Employees: 21 - 50 **Product Groups:** 35, 40, 52

Date of Accounts	Apr 08	Apr 07
Working Capital	97	15
Fixed Assets	68	67
Current Assets	284	321
Current Liabilities	188	307

Preformed Components Ltd
Unit 3-4 King Georges Trading Estate Davis Road, Chessington, KT9 1TT
Tel: 020-8391 0533 **Fax:** 020-8391 4328
E-mail: sales@pfc-corofil.com
Website: http://www.pfc-corofil.com
Directors: J. Gerrard (MD), J. Guerard (Fin), N. Difato (Sales), K. Irvine (Ch), G. Ashley (MD)
Managers: C. Irvin (Mgr)
Ultimate Holding Company: WOLSELEY PLC (JERSEY)
Immediate Holding Company: PRE-FORMED COMPONENTS LIMITED
Registration no: 00716672 **Date established:** 1962 **Turnover:** £2m - £5m
No.of Employees: 1 - 10 **Product Groups:** 27, 30, 32, 33

Date of Accounts	Jul 11	Jul 10	Jul 09
Sales Turnover	3m	3m	3m
Pre Tax Profit/Loss	21	-14	276
Working Capital	994	987	1m
Fixed Assets	86	79	49
Current Assets	1m	1m	1m
Current Liabilities	109	92	98

Reltex Relief Supplies Ltd
Canvas Works Cox Lane, Chessington, KT9 1SG
Tel: 020-8397 4373
Website: http://www.reltex.net
Directors: B. Prosser (Dir)
Immediate Holding Company: RELTEX RELIEF SUPPLIES LIMITED
Registration no: 03721047 **Date established:** 1999
No.of Employees: 1 - 10 **Product Groups:** 24, 30

Date of Accounts	Mar 11	Mar 10	Mar 09
Working Capital	1m	1m	1m
Fixed Assets	5	4	3

Current Assets	2m	4m	2m

Service Graphics Ltd
Unit E1-E4 Barwell Business Park Leatherhead Road, Chessington, KT9 2NY
Tel: 020-8877 6600 **Fax:** 020-8871 3521
E-mail: steve.benson@servicegraphics.co.uk
Website: http://www.servicegraphics.co.uk
Bank(s): National Westminster
Directors: B. Brown (MD), S. Benson (Dir)
Ultimate Holding Company: ST IVES PLC
Immediate Holding Company: SERVICE GRAPHICS LIMITED
Registration no: 04332146 **Date established:** 2001
Turnover: Up to £250,000 **No.of Employees:** 251 - 500
Product Groups: 28

Date of Accounts	Jul 09	Jul 10	Aug 07
Sales Turnover	1m	1m	860
Pre Tax Profit/Loss	-142	58	221
Working Capital	228	15	113
Fixed Assets	37	N/A	113
Current Assets	453	15	529
Current Liabilities	89	N/A	190

Siderise Insulation Ltd
15c Oakcroft Road, Chessington, KT9 1RH
Tel: 020-8391 3650 **Fax:** 01656-812509
E-mail: sales@siderise.com
Website: http://www.siderise.co.uk
Managers: M. Carrick
Ultimate Holding Company: SIDERISE (HOLDINGS) LIMITED
Immediate Holding Company: SIDERISE INSULATION LIMITED
Registration no: 02370350 **Date established:** 1989 **Turnover:** £2m - £5m
No.of Employees: 1 - 10 **Product Groups:** 14, 30, 33

Date of Accounts	Dec 11	Dec 10	Dec 09
Working Capital	727	600	465
Fixed Assets	409	496	530
Current Assets	2m	1m	1m

Starpoint Electrics Ltd
Units 1-5 King George's Trading Estate Davis Road, Chessington, KT9 1TT
Tel: 020-8391 7700 **Fax:** 020-8391 7760
E-mail: sales@starpoint.uk.com
Website: http://www.starpoint.uk.com
Directors: C. Crossman (I.T. Dir), B. Marchini (MD), D. Fryer (Fin), R. Stevens (Sales)
Immediate Holding Company: Starpoint Developments Ltd
Registration no: 00922239 **VAT No.:** GB 216 3631 85
Date established: 1967 **Turnover:** £10m - £20m
No.of Employees: 51 - 100 **Product Groups:** 44

Date of Accounts	Dec 09	Dec 08	Dec 07
Sales Turnover	612	943	15m
Pre Tax Profit/Loss	48	370	-2m
Working Capital	402	1m	2m
Fixed Assets	35	58	312
Current Assets	477	2m	5m
Current Liabilities	40	69	184

Tradex Instruments Ltd
Unit C Davis Road, Chessington, KT9 1TY
Tel: 020-8391 0136 **Fax:** 020-8397 1924
E-mail: info@tradexinstruments.com
Website: http://www.tradexinstruments.com
Directors: J. Graham (Dir)
Immediate Holding Company: TRADEX INSTRUMENTS LIMITED
Registration no: 00689522 **VAT No.:** GB 216 6048 77
Date established: 1961 **Turnover:** £500,000 - £1m
No.of Employees: 1 - 10 **Product Groups:** 35, 48

Date of Accounts	Nov 11	Nov 10	Nov 09
Working Capital	193	244	345
Fixed Assets	524	527	530
Current Assets	228	275	420

Visuals Engineers
55 Selwood Road, Chessington, KT9 1PT
Tel: 020-8397 1567 **Fax:** 020-8287 8618
E-mail: visuals@bigfoot.com
Directors: A. Moss (Prop)
No.of Employees: 1 - 10 **Product Groups:** 37, 80, 84

Cobham

Alder Networks Ltd
7 Gavell Road, Cobham, KT11 1AL
Tel: 01932-866866
E-mail: sales@aldernetworks.co.uk
Website: http://www.aldernetworks.co.uk
Directors: M. Aldridge (MD), D. Aldridge (Co Sec)
Immediate Holding Company: ALDER NETWORKS LTD
Registration no: 04891787 **Date established:** 2003
No.of Employees: 1 - 10 **Product Groups:** 37

Date of Accounts	Sep 11	Sep 10	Sep 09
Working Capital	N/A	-0	N/A
Current Assets	5	3	4

The Berkeley Group Holdings Ltd
Berkeley House 19 Portsmouth Road, Cobham, KT11 1JG
Tel: 01932-868555 **Fax:** 01932-868667
E-mail: robert.perrins@berkeleygroup.co.uk
Website: http://www.berkeleygroup.co.uk
Bank(s): Barclays
Directors: R. Stearn (Co Sec), R. Perrins (MD)
Managers: N. Simpkin, N. Hodson
Immediate Holding Company: BERKELEY GROUP PLC(THE)
Registration no: 01454064 **Date established:** 1979
Turnover: £500m - £1,000m **No.of Employees:** 101 - 250
Product Groups: 52

Date of Accounts	Apr 12	Apr 11	Apr 10
Sales Turnover	N/A	743m	N/A
Pre Tax Profit/Loss	235m	136m	57m
Working Capital	571m	895m	194m
Fixed Assets	1471m	114m	1507m
Current Assets	733m	1976m	328m
Current Liabilities	127m	616m	106m

Burvills
The Forge Cossins Farm Downside Road, Downside, Cobham, KT11 3LZ
Tel: 01932-589666 **Fax:** 01932-589669
E-mail: chris.clarkson@burvills.co.uk
Website: http://www.burvills.co.uk
Directors: D. Weston (Fin), C. Clarkson (MD)
Immediate Holding Company: S. BURVILL & SON LIMITED
Registration no: 03430300 **Date established:** 1997
Turnover: £500,000 - £1m **No.of Employees:** 11 - 20
Product Groups: 35, 46, 49

Date of Accounts	Sep 11	Sep 10	Sep 09
Working Capital	207	81	186
Fixed Assets	84	89	64
Current Assets	533	473	415

Cedar Nursery Ltd
Horsley Road, Cobham, KT11 3JX
Tel: 01932-862473 **Fax:** 01932-867152
E-mail: sales@landscaping.co.uk
Website: http://www.landscaping.co.uk
Managers: A. Clark (Chief Mgr)
Immediate Holding Company: CEDAR NURSERY LIMITED
Registration no: SC165971 **Date established:** 1996
No.of Employees: 1 - 10 **Product Groups:** 30, 33, 36

Date of Accounts	Oct 11	Oct 10	Oct 09
Working Capital	-10	-13	-0
Fixed Assets	104	103	104
Current Assets	12	4	17

Coolicious Frozen Yogurt Taste Trends Ltd
53-57 High Street, Cobham, KT11 3DP
Tel: 08453-377017 **Fax:** 0845-337 7307
E-mail: admin@tastetrends.co.uk
Website: http://www.coolicious.com
Directors: R. Drane (MD), M. Blake (Sales)
No.of Employees: 1 - 10 **Product Groups:** 62

Melbry Events Ltd
Vine House 41 Portsmouth Road, Cobham, KT11 1JQ
Tel: 0845-234 8002 **Fax:** 01932-868 447
E-mail: theeventsteam@melbryevents.co.uk
Website: http://www.melbryevents.co.uk
Directors: A. Hurley (Dir), M. Hurley (Dir)
Date established: 1997 **No.of Employees:** 1 - 10 **Product Groups:** 89

Mundays Solicitors
Cedar House Portsmouth Road, Cobham, KT11 1AN
Tel: 01932-590500 **Fax:** 01932-590220
E-mail: enq@mundays.co.uk
Website: http://www.mundays.co.uk
Directors: V. Toon (Snr Part)
Immediate Holding Company: MUNDAYS LLP
Registration no: OC313856 **Date established:** 2005
Turnover: £5m - £10m **No.of Employees:** 51 - 100 **Product Groups:** 80

Date of Accounts	Jul 11	Jul 10	Jul 09
Sales Turnover	9m	10m	11m
Pre Tax Profit/Loss	3m	3m	3m
Working Capital	2m	2m	2m
Fixed Assets	381	377	598
Current Assets	4m	4m	5m
Current Liabilities	633	582	626

Proteome Sciences plc
Coveham House Downside Bridge Road, Cobham, KT11 3EP
Tel: 01932-865065 **Fax:** 01932-868696
E-mail: steven.harris@proteomics.com
Website: http://www.proteomics.com
Directors: C. Pearce (Dir), J. Malthouse (Fin)
Immediate Holding Company: PROTEOME SCIENCES PLC
Registration no: 02879724 **Date established:** 1993 **Turnover:** £1m - £2m
No.of Employees: 1 - 10 **Product Groups:** 31

Date of Accounts	Dec 11	Dec 10	Dec 09
Sales Turnover	1m	10m	1m
Pre Tax Profit/Loss	-5m	5m	-4m
Working Capital	-2m	2m	-14m
Fixed Assets	6m	6m	5m
Current Assets	5m	10m	996
Current Liabilities	7m	7m	14m

R & D Marketings Ltd
11a Anyards Road, Cobham, KT11 2LW
Tel: 01932-866600 **Fax:** 01932-866688
E-mail: ruth@demista.co.uk
Website: http://www.demista.co.uk
Directors: R. Perl (Dir)
Registration no: 02722250 **No.of Employees:** 1 - 10 **Product Groups:** 33, 40, 66

Tozer Seeds Ltd
Pyports Downside Bridge Road, Cobham, KT11 3EH
Tel: 01932-862059 **Fax:** 01932-868973
E-mail: info@tozerseeds.com
Website: http://www.tozerseeds.com
Directors: P. Dawson (Dir)
Ultimate Holding Company: A.L.TOZER LIMITED
Immediate Holding Company: A.L.TOZER LIMITED
Registration no: 00391270 **Date established:** 1944
Turnover: £10m - £20m **No.of Employees:** 21 - 50 **Product Groups:** 02

Date of Accounts	Jun 11	Jun 10	Jun 09
Sales Turnover	10m	10m	9m
Pre Tax Profit/Loss	353	580	151
Working Capital	3m	3m	2m
Fixed Assets	1m	1m	1m
Current Assets	5m	5m	5m
Current Liabilities	315	269	288

Coulsdon

Beatons Caterers
90 Keston Avenue, Coulsdon, CR5 1HN
Tel: 01737-557444 **Fax:** 01737-557709
E-mail: beatonscaterers@aol.com
Website: http://www.beatonscaterers.com
Directors: A. Mazzola (Prop)
Date established: 1980 **No.of Employees:** 1 - 10 **Product Groups:** 69

Bryson Products
Unit D Redlands, Coulsdon, CR5 2HT
Tel: 020-8660 9119 **Fax:** 020-8660 8306
E-mail: sales@bryson.co.uk
Directors: M. Reiner (Prop)
Managers: C. Reiner (Tech Serv Mgr), D. Reiner (Mktg Serv Mgr)
Date established: 1973 **No.of Employees:** 21 - 50 **Product Groups:** 35

Control Energy Costs Ltd
Tollers Farm Drive Road, Coulsdon, CR5 1BN
Tel: 01737-556631 **Fax:** 01737-553601
E-mail: c.cleanthi@cec.uk.com
Website: http://www.cc.uk.com
Bank(s): National Westminster Bank Plc
Directors: C. Cleanthi (MD), P. Ager (Dir)
Managers: M. Hitchens (Personnel), M. Stephenson
Immediate Holding Company: CONTROL ENERGY COSTS LIMITED
Registration no: 01549615 **Date established:** 1981 **Turnover:** £1m - £2m
No.of Employees: 21 - 50 **Product Groups:** 54

Date of Accounts	Aug 11	Aug 10	Aug 09
Sales Turnover	2m	2m	2m
Pre Tax Profit/Loss	30	583	535
Working Capital	3m	3m	5m
Fixed Assets	2m	2m	2m
Current Assets	3m	5m	5m
Current Liabilities	403	553	699

Croylek Ltd
23 Ullswater Crescent, Coulsdon, CR5 2UY
Tel: 020-8668 1481 **Fax:** 020-8763 0750
E-mail: sales@croylek.co.uk
Website: http://www.croylek.co.uk
Bank(s): National Westminster Bank Plc
Directors: M. Kosky (MD), M. Kosky (Fin)
Ultimate Holding Company: APEX GLOBAL SERVICES LIMITED
Immediate Holding Company: CROYLEK LIMITED
Registration no: 00824514 **VAT No.:** GB 217 9364 46
Date established: 1964 **Turnover:** £2m - £5m **No.of Employees:** 21 - 50
Product Groups: 27, 29, 30, 32, 33, 37, 48

Date of Accounts	Dec 11	Dec 10	Dec 09
Working Capital	860	681	466
Fixed Assets	547	595	573
Current Assets	2m	2m	1m

Davuka
2c The Wend, Coulsdon, CR5 2AX
Tel: 020-8660 2854 **Fax:** 020-8645 2556
E-mail: info@davuka.co.uk
Website: http://www.decorative-coving.co.uk
Directors: D. Warner (MD)
Immediate Holding Company: DAVUKA GRP LIMITED
Registration no: 04649533 **Date established:** 2003
Turnover: £250,000 - £500,000 **No.of Employees:** 1 - 10
Product Groups: 30

Date of Accounts	Jan 12	Jan 11	Jan 10
Working Capital	59	66	63
Fixed Assets	1	1	1
Current Assets	155	132	126

G T Shooting
53 Chipstead Valley Road, Coulsdon, CR5 2RB
Tel: 020-8660 6843 **Fax:** 020-8660 6843
E-mail: sales@gtshooting.co.uk
Website: http://www.gtshooting.co.uk
Directors: T. Hammond (Prop)
Date established: 1992 **No.of Employees:** 1 - 10 **Product Groups:** 36, 39, 40

Iskra UK Ltd
Unit A6, Redlands, Ullswater Crescent,, Coulsdon, CR5 2HT
Tel: 020-8668 7141 **Fax:** 020-8668 3108
E-mail: sales@iskra-agency.co.uk
Website: http://www.iskra-ae.com
Directors: D. Curtis (Co Sec), I. Vipotnik (MD)
Managers: S. Blackburn (Sales Prom Mgr)
Ultimate Holding Company: ISKRA AVTOELEKRIKA DD (SLOVENIA)
Registration no: 02692859 **Date established:** 1992
Turnover: £10m - £20m **No.of Employees:** 1 - 10 **Product Groups:** 37, 38, 40

Date of Accounts	Dec 09	Dec 08	Dec 07
Sales Turnover	11m	18m	13m
Pre Tax Profit/Loss	38	377	175
Working Capital	538	556	755
Fixed Assets	434	487	455
Current Assets	4m	6m	6m
Current Liabilities	280	763	687

Outlook Stockholders Ltd
Woodcote Grove Farm Woodcote Grove, Coulsdon, CR5 2QQ
Tel: 020-8668 9656 **Fax:** 020-8668 5111
E-mail: leslefevre@msn.com
Website: http://www.outlookmetalstock.com
Directors: L. Lefevre (MD)
Immediate Holding Company: OUTLOOK STOCKHOLDERS LIMITED
Registration no: 01597293 **VAT No.:** GB 367 3305 49
Date established: 1981 **Turnover:** £500,000 - £1m
No.of Employees: 1 - 10 **Product Groups:** 30, 34, 66

Date of Accounts	Oct 10	Oct 09	Oct 08
Working Capital	4	7	8
Fixed Assets	1	1	1
Current Assets	82	91	125

Perfectair Ltd
Smitham House 127 Brighton Road, Coulsdon, CR5 2XB
Tel: 020-8668 4561 **Fax:** 020- 86602306
Directors: P. Terry (MD), D. Terry (Fin)
Immediate Holding Company: PERFECTAIR LIMITED
Registration no: 07523646 **VAT No.:** GB 443 1456 68
Date established: 2011 **Turnover:** £500,000 - £1m
No.of Employees: 1 - 10 **Product Groups:** 38, 40, 42, 51, 52, 54, 66, 84

Ricoh UK Ltd
Ricoh House 15 Ullswater Crescent, Coulsdon, CR5 2HR
Tel: 020-8763 1010 **Fax:** 020-8763 1110
Website: http://www.ricoh.co.uk

see next page

***Ricoh UK Ltd** - Cont'd*

Directors: R. Hewitt (Fin)
Managers: D. Bray (Mgr)
Ultimate Holding Company: RICOH COMPANY LIMITED (JAPAN)
Immediate Holding Company: RICOH UK LIMITED
Registration no: 01271033 **Date established:** 1976
Turnover: £50m - £75m **No.of Employees:** 101 - 250
Product Groups: 44, 64, 67, 83

S G Estimating Ltd

150a Brighton Road, Coulsdon, CR5 2YY
Tel: 020-8763 8503 **Fax:** 020-8763 8502
E-mail: info@sgestimating.co.uk
Website: http://www.sgestimating.co.uk
Directors: S. Gesese (MD)
Immediate Holding Company: S. G. ESTIMATING LIMITED
Registration no: 05750751 **Date established:** 2006
Turnover: Up to £250,000 **No.of Employees:** 1 - 10 **Product Groups:** 84

Date of Accounts	Mar 12	Mar 11	Mar 10
Working Capital	13	-2	-3
Fixed Assets	N/A	4	9
Current Assets	42	38	26

Cranleigh

A & A Wines Ltd

13 Manfield Park, Cranleigh, GU6 8PT
Tel: 01483-274666 **Fax:** 01483-268460
E-mail: info@aawines.co.uk
Website: http://www.aawines.co.uk
Directors: A. Connor (Dir)
Immediate Holding Company: A & A WINES LIMITED
Registration no: 01836130 **Date established:** 1984 **Turnover:** £1m - £2m
No.of Employees: 1 - 10 **Product Groups:** 61

Date of Accounts	Dec 11	Dec 10	Dec 09
Working Capital	404	430	456
Fixed Assets	57	58	53
Current Assets	631	673	706

Andrin Electronic Components

Mead House Little Mead Industrial Estate Little Mead, Cranleigh, GU6 8ND
Tel: 01483-267735 **Fax:** 01483-267565
E-mail: kngra@aol.com
Directors: K. Graham (Ptnr)
Immediate Holding Company: DL OFFICE SUPPLIES LIMITED
Registration no: 04380614 **Date established:** 2002
Turnover: Up to £250,000 **No.of Employees:** 1 - 10 **Product Groups:** 33, 37, 38, 44, 67

Date of Accounts	Mar 11	Mar 10	Mar 09
Working Capital	186	62	46
Fixed Assets	45	35	40
Current Assets	551	386	315

Centriplant Rebuilds & Tank Co. Ltd

Little Mead Industrial Estate Alfold Road, Cranleigh, GU6 8ND
Tel: 01483-271507 **Fax:** 01483-278183
E-mail: sales@centriplant.co.uk
Website: http://www.centriplant.co.uk
Directors: M. Williams (MD)
Ultimate Holding Company: EVEDAN LIMITED
Immediate Holding Company: EVEDAN LIMITED
Registration no: 01356785 **VAT No.:** GB 296 2877 02
Date established: 1978 **Turnover:** £1m - £2m **No.of Employees:** 11 - 20
Product Groups: 35, 41

Date of Accounts	Dec 11	Dec 10	Dec 09
Working Capital	-24	34	84
Fixed Assets	3m	3m	3m
Current Assets	136	194	217

Cevac Ltd

Hildene The Village, Ewhurst, Cranleigh, GU6 7PG
Tel: 01483-272001 **Fax:** 01483-273233
E-mail: sales@cevac.co.uk
Website: http://www.cevac.co.uk
Directors: G. Pratt (Fin)
Immediate Holding Company: CEVAC LIMITED
Registration no: 02786595 **Date established:** 1993
Turnover: Up to £250,000 **No.of Employees:** 1 - 10 **Product Groups:** 40, 66

Date of Accounts	May 11	May 10	May 09
Working Capital	166	183	181
Fixed Assets	22	6	5
Current Assets	368	370	332

Cozens Smith (t/a Cozens-Smith)

Unit 4 Cranleigh Works, Cranleigh, GU6 8SB
Tel: 01483-273131 **Fax:** 01483-268238
Directors: P. Sparkes (MD)
Immediate Holding Company: SPARKS WELDING LTD
Registration no: 03158399 **VAT No.:** GB 644 7071 36
Date established: 1996 **Turnover:** Up to £250,000
No.of Employees: 1 - 10 **Product Groups:** 35, 48

Cranleigh Freight Services Ltd

Building 68 Dunsfold Park Stovolds Hill, Cranleigh, GU6 8TB
Tel: 01483-201330 **Fax:** 01483-272124
E-mail: info@cranleigh.co.uk
Website: http://www.cranleigh.co.uk
Directors: N. Fox (Fin)
Managers: M. Kerney (Tech Serv Mgr), B. Young (Sales & Mktg Mg)
Immediate Holding Company: CRANLEIGH FREIGHT SERVICES LIMITED
Registration no: 01465323 **VAT No.:** GB 296 1943 20
Date established: 1979 **Turnover:** £10m - £20m
No.of Employees: 101 - 250 **Product Groups:** 72, 74, 75, 76, 77, 79, 84

Date of Accounts	Dec 11	Dec 10	Dec 09
Sales Turnover	15m	15m	14m
Pre Tax Profit/Loss	-38	278	138
Working Capital	-71	493	547
Fixed Assets	3m	2m	1m
Current Assets	3m	3m	2m
Current Liabilities	495	426	514

Cranleigh Systems

Unit 14 Littlemead Industrial Estate, Cranleigh, GU6 8ND
Tel: 01483-272111 **Fax:** 01483-277772
E-mail: ian.lucus@cranleighgroup.com
Website: http://www.crangroup.co.uk
Bank(s): Lloyds TSB Bank plc
Directors: D. Smith (Dir)
Managers: I. Lucas (Sales Admin), P. Prociuk (Tech Serv Mgr), I. Lucus (Sales Admin), P. Francis (Sales Prom Mgr)
Ultimate Holding Company: ION GEOPHYSICAL CORPORATION (USA)
Immediate Holding Company: I/O MARINE SYSTEMS LIMITED
Registration no: 02672793 **Date established:** 1991 **Turnover:** £2m - £5m
No.of Employees: 21 - 50 **Product Groups:** 37

Date of Accounts	Dec 10	Dec 09	Dec 08
Sales Turnover	5m	5m	4m
Pre Tax Profit/Loss	327	359	38
Working Capital	2m	2m	1m
Fixed Assets	179	209	226
Current Assets	4m	4m	4m
Current Liabilities	247	193	287

Eli-Chem Resins UK Ltd

Astra House Astra Works, The Common, Cranleigh, GU6 8RE
Tel: 01483-266636 **Fax:** 01483-266650
E-mail: sales@elichem.co.uk
Website: http://www.elichem.co.uk
No.of Employees: 1 - 10 **Product Groups:** 29, 30, 31, 32

Date of Accounts	Mar 08	Mar 07	Mar 06
Working Capital	24	14	3
Fixed Assets	3	3	4
Current Assets	211	147	119
Current Liabilities	186	133	116
Total Share Capital	1	1	1

Etheringtons Electrical Services Ltd

46 Dunsfold Park Stovolds Hill, Cranleigh, GU6 8TB
Tel: 01483-200769 **Fax:** 01483-200714
E-mail: etherington@dsl.pipex.com
Website: http://www.etheringtons.co.uk
Bank(s): Lloyds TSB Bank plc
Directors: M. Dagger (Co Sec), M. Dagger (Dir), M. Bowdidth (MD), M. Bowditch (Fin)
Immediate Holding Company: ETHERINGTONS ELECTRICAL & MECHANICAL SERVICES LIMITED
Registration no: 04509114 **VAT No.:** GB 213 0904 12
Date established: 2002 **Turnover:** £500,000 - £1m
No.of Employees: 11 - 20 **Product Groups:** 52

Date of Accounts	Dec 10	Dec 09	Dec 08
Working Capital	-9	-14	-25
Fixed Assets	39	46	51
Current Assets	87	111	137

G H L Liftrucks Ltd

Unit 10 Hewitts Industrial Estate, Elmbridge Road, Cranleigh, GU6 8LW
Tel: 01483-276101 **Fax:** 01483-277430
E-mail: surrey@forktrucks.co.uk
Website: http://www.forktrucks.co.uk
Directors: D. Alger (MD)
Managers: J. Pinder ()
Registration no: 01379041 **Turnover:** £2m - £5m
No.of Employees: 21 - 50 **Product Groups:** 45

Date of Accounts	Dec 09	Dec 08	Dec 07
Sales Turnover	11m	15m	16m
Pre Tax Profit/Loss	44	248	904
Working Capital	621	256	391
Fixed Assets	2m	2m	2m
Current Assets	3m	3m	4m
Current Liabilities	768	1m	1m

Jewson Ltd

The Common, Cranleigh, GU6 8RY
Tel: 01483-273511 **Fax:** 01483-267392
E-mail: paul.williams@jewson.co.uk
Website: http://www.jewson.co.uk
Managers: P. Williams (Mgr)
Ultimate Holding Company: COMPAGNIE DE SAINT GOBAIN (FRANCE)
Immediate Holding Company: JEWSON LIMITED
Registration no: 00348407 **Date established:** 1939
Turnover: £500m - £1,000m **No.of Employees:** 11 - 20
Product Groups: 66

Date of Accounts	Dec 11	Dec 10	Dec 09
Sales Turnover	1606m	1547m	1485m
Pre Tax Profit/Loss	18m	100m	45m
Working Capital	-345m	-250m	-349m
Fixed Assets	496m	387m	461m
Current Assets	657m	1005m	1320m
Current Liabilities	66m	120m	64m

The Luke Design

71 Smithbrook Kilns, Cranleigh, GU6 8JJ
Tel: 01483-267532
E-mail: loopme@theloopdesign.com
Website: http://thelukedesign.com
Directors: P. Lawrence (Snr Part)
Immediate Holding Company: BURRELL BLAIN WILSON ASSOCIATES LIMITED
Date established: 1994 **Turnover:** £1m - £2m **No.of Employees:** 1 - 10
Product Groups: 81

Keith Payne Products Ltd

Unit 3-4 Hewitts Industrial Estate Elmbridge Road, Cranleigh, GU6 8LN
Tel: 01483-276000 **Fax:** 01483-278167
E-mail: sales@keithpayneproducts.com
Website: http://www.keithpayneproducts.com
Bank(s): Barclays
Directors: K. Payne (MD)
Immediate Holding Company: KEITH PAYNE PRODUCTS LIMITED
Registration no: 01354449 **Date established:** 1978 **Turnover:** £1m - £2m
No.of Employees: 11 - 20 **Product Groups:** 23, 25, 27, 29, 30, 33, 36, 37, 39, 40, 49, 66, 68

Date of Accounts	Apr 11	Apr 10	Apr 09
Working Capital	874	340	384
Fixed Assets	13	26	41
Current Assets	1m	606	513

R & G Products

Unit 28 Alfold Business Centre Loxwood Road, Alfold, Cranleigh, GU6 8HP
Tel: 01273-490051 **Fax:** 01403-752261
E-mail: gill@randgproducts.co.uk
Website: http://www.randgproducts.co.uk

Directors: G. Henshaw (Dir)
No.of Employees: 1 - 10 **Product Groups:** 30, 44, 79

Redemtech (UK) Limited

132 Dunsfold Park Stovolds Hill, Cranleigh, GU6 8TB
Tel: 0870-6000085 **Fax:** 08706-000 041
E-mail: info@redemtech.co.uk
Website: http://www.redemtech.co.uk
Directors: R. Gue (MD)
Registration no: 04354614 **No.of Employees:** 51 - 100
Product Groups: 44

Date of Accounts	Mar 07	Mar 06
Working Capital	297	242
Fixed Assets	82	95
Current Assets	798	636
Current Liabilities	501	394
Total Share Capital	210	210

Sparks Welding Ltd

Unit 4 Cranleigh Works, Cranleigh, GU6 8SB
Tel: 01483-273131
Directors: P. Sparks (MD)
Immediate Holding Company: SPARKES WELDING LTD.
Registration no: 03158399 **Date established:** 1996
Turnover: £250,000 - £500,000 **No.of Employees:** 1 - 10
Product Groups: 35

Date of Accounts	Mar 11	Mar 10	Mar 09
Sales Turnover	326	214	297
Pre Tax Profit/Loss	11	10	-8
Working Capital	-3	-11	-54
Fixed Assets	19	22	24
Current Assets	69	25	22
Current Liabilities	22	12	26

Croydon

A B M Electrical Distributors Ltd

63 London Road, Croydon, CR0 2RF
Tel: 020-8681 2025 **Fax:** 020-8688 3332
E-mail: info@abmelectricaldistributors.co.uk
Website: http://www.abmelectricaldistributors.co.uk
Directors: H. Shah (Prop)
Immediate Holding Company: ABM ELECTRICAL DISTRIBUTORS LIMITED
Registration no: 02821410 **VAT No.:** GB 629 9228 03
Date established: 1993 **Turnover:** Up to £250,000
No.of Employees: 1 - 10 **Product Groups:** 67

Date of Accounts	Sep 11	Sep 10	Sep 09
Working Capital	229	204	203
Fixed Assets	21	2	3
Current Assets	471	498	360

A J G Waters Equipment Ltd

PO Box 1853, Croydon, CR9 7AW
Tel: 020-8689 9994 **Fax:** 020-8689 1715
E-mail: sales@watersequip.co.uk
Website: http://www.watersequip.co.uk
Directors: J. Sells (Fin)
Immediate Holding Company: AJG WATERS (EQUIPMENT) LIMITED
Registration no: 02647577 **Date established:** 1991
Turnover: £500,000 - £1m **No.of Employees:** 1 - 10 **Product Groups:** 36, 37, 40, 42, 46, 48, 66, 84

Date of Accounts	Dec 11	Dec 10	Dec 09
Working Capital	87	58	51
Fixed Assets	9	12	15
Current Assets	141	109	110

Ace Precision Engineers

Unit 5 Tait Road Industrial Estate, Croydon, CR0 2DP
Tel: 020-8683 0487 **Fax:** 020-8684 4583
E-mail: lumir@talktalk.net
Website: http://www.aceprecisionengineering.co.uk
Directors: L. Povada (Prop)
Immediate Holding Company: PRESTIGE COACHWORKS (SURREY) LIMITED
Registration no: 07136196 **VAT No.:** GB 220 2505 27
Date established: 2010 **Turnover:** Up to £250,000
No.of Employees: 1 - 10 **Product Groups:** 48

Adec Marine Ltd

4 Masons Avenue, Croydon, CR0 9XS
Tel: 020-8686 9717 **Fax:** 020-8680 9912
E-mail: sales@adecmarine.co.uk
Website: http://www.adecmarine.co.uk
Directors: M. Barling (MD)
Immediate Holding Company: ADEC MARINE LIMITED
Registration no: 01859493 **VAT No.:** GB 574 3589 04
Date established: 1984 **Turnover:** £500,000 - £1m
No.of Employees: 1 - 10 **Product Groups:** 32, 39, 40, 74

Date of Accounts	Dec 11	Dec 10	Dec 09
Working Capital	326	284	258
Fixed Assets	6	8	11
Current Assets	640	626	672

Agrolon Ltd

Wettern House Dingwall Road, Croydon, CR0 0XH
Tel: 020-8681 6978 **Fax:** 020-8681 3605
E-mail: potato@agrolon.co.uk
Directors: J. Castella (MD), J. Subietas (Dir), R. Bennett (Co Sec)
Immediate Holding Company: AGROLON LIMITED
Registration no: 00558076 **Date established:** 1955
No.of Employees: 1 - 10 **Product Groups:** 02, 61

Date of Accounts	Jun 11	Jun 10	Jun 09
Working Capital	746	781	791
Fixed Assets	314	314	315
Current Assets	753	807	908
Current Liabilities	6	7	6

Aircraft Unit Engineering Co. Ltd

10 Silver Wing Industrial Esthoratius Way, Croydon, CR0 4RU
Tel: 020-8686 7755 **Fax:** 020-8681 3837
E-mail: office@aircraftunit.com
Website: http://www.btinternet.com

Directors: B. Sheerim (Prop), B. Sheerin (MD)
Managers: P. Donovan
Immediate Holding Company: Aircraft Unit Engineering Co.Limited
Registration no: 00675083 **VAT No.:** GB 229 2024 86
Date established: 1960 **Turnover:** £1m - £2m **No.of Employees:** 1 - 10
Product Groups: 39, 46, 48, 81

Akrobat Creative Marketing Ltd

19 Ledbury Place, Croydon, CR0 1ET
Tel: 020-8688 6026 **Fax:** 020-8680 4083
Website: http://www.akrobat.co.uk
Directors: K. Bearne (Prop)
Immediate Holding Company: AKROBAT LIMITED
Registration no: 02778233 **VAT No.:** GB 625 6361 40
Date established: 1993 **Turnover:** £500,000 - £1m
No.of Employees: 1 - 10 **Product Groups:** 81

Date of Accounts	Jan 12	Jan 11	Jan 10
Working Capital	54	47	54
Current Assets	63	48	55

Allparts Zone

Unit 2 Tramsheds Industrial Estate Coomber Way, Croydon, CR0 4TQ
Tel: 020-8684 8181 **Fax:** 020-8689 3622
E-mail: sales@allpartszone.co.uk
Website: http://www.allpartszone.com
Bank(s): National Westminster Bank Plc
Directors: A. Desai (Dir), T. Singh (MD)
Immediate Holding Company: FINELIST GROUP P.L.C.
Registration no: 01968355 **VAT No.:** GB 589 2301 20
Turnover: £500m - £1,000m **No.of Employees:** 21 - 50
Product Groups: 68

Date of Accounts	Apr 02
Working Capital	148
Current Assets	206
Current Liabilities	59

Arrow Fastener UK Ltd

Unit 5 Z K Park 23 Commerce Way, Croydon, CR0 4ZS
Tel: 020-8686 9180 **Fax:** 020-8686 9197
E-mail: johnmilton@arrowfastener.com
Website: http://www.arrowfastener.com
Bank(s): Barclays, Edgware Rd, Marble Arch Business Centre
Directors: J. Milton (Dir)
Managers: J. Milton (Purch Mgr), S. McEniry (Mgr), S. Smith (Accounts), N. Roberts (Sales Prom Mgr)
Ultimate Holding Company: MASCO CORP INC (USA)
Immediate Holding Company: ARROW FASTENER (UK) LIMITED
Registration no: 01191953 **VAT No.:** GB 394 6180 25
Date established: 1974 **Turnover:** £2m - £5m **No.of Employees:** 11 - 20
Product Groups: 32, 35, 36, 37, 66

Date of Accounts	Dec 10	Dec 09	Dec 08
Sales Turnover	2m	2m	3m
Pre Tax Profit/Loss	294	202	998
Working Capital	11m	11m	11m
Fixed Assets	73	58	70
Current Assets	11m	11m	11m
Current Liabilities	95	81	88

Asbestos Aware

102-116 Windmill Road, Croydon, CR0 2XQ
Tel: 0208-6654212 **Fax:** 0208-6654201
E-mail: andy@srbc.biz
Website: http://www.asbestosaware.co.uk
Product Groups: 85

Assa Abloy Security Solutions

Unit 3-4 Z K Park 23 Commerce Way, Croydon, CR0 4ZS
Tel: 020-8688 5191 **Fax:** 020-8688 0285
E-mail: sales@assaabloy.co.uk
Website: http://www.assa.co.uk
Bank(s): National Westminster Bank Plc
Directors: D. Wigglesworth (MD), J. Little (Fin)
Managers: A. Carter (Mktg Serv Mgr), G. Bishop (I.T. Exec)
Immediate Holding Company: ASSA ABLOY LTD
Registration no: 02066014 **VAT No.:** GB 765 3581 05
Turnover: £5m - £10m **No.of Employees:** 21 - 50 **Product Groups:** 35, 36, 39, 40, 44, 49, 52, 66

Barclays Car Insurance

Bedford Park, Croydon, CR9 2XX
Tel: 08706-001211 **Fax:** 020-8681 5458
E-mail: mail@barclays.co.uk
Website: http://www.barclays.co.uk
Directors: K. Hinkley (MD), C. Milson (Dir)
Managers: D. Coles (Cust Serv Mgr)
Ultimate Holding Company: BARCLAYS PLC
Immediate Holding Company: BARCLAYS GROUP HOLDINGS LTD
Registration no: 00973765 **Turnover:** £250,000 - £500,000
No.of Employees: 1 - 10 **Product Groups:** 82

Baur Test Equipment Ltd

Unit C1 Connaught Business Centre Imperial Way, Croydon, CR0 4RR
Tel: 020-8661 0957 **Fax:** 020-8642 4801
E-mail: sales@baurtest.com
Website: http://www.baurtest.com
Directors: M. Webb (Fin)
Ultimate Holding Company: BAUR PRUEF-U MESSTECHNIK GMBH (AUSTRIA)
Immediate Holding Company: BAUR TEST EQUIPMENT LIMITED
Registration no: 02266530 **VAT No.:** GB 452 5831 47
Date established: 1988 **No.of Employees:** 1 - 10 **Product Groups:** 38, 67, 85

Date of Accounts	Dec 11	Dec 10	Dec 09
Sales Turnover	N/A	N/A	862
Pre Tax Profit/Loss	N/A	N/A	-18
Working Capital	296	223	168
Fixed Assets	18	13	26
Current Assets	3m	317	437
Current Liabilities	N/A	N/A	16

Bayard Packaging Ltd

Unit 46 Silver Wing Industrial Estate Imperial Way, Croydon, CR0 4RR
Tel: 020-8688 7778 **Fax:** 020-8692 3851
E-mail: sales@bayardpackaging.co.uk
Website: http://www.polythene-envelopes.com
Directors: P. Fox (MD)
Immediate Holding Company: BAYARD PACKAGING LIMITED
Registration no: 01691991 **Date established:** 1983
Turnover: £500,000 - £1m **No.of Employees:** 1 - 10 **Product Groups:** 30

Date of Accounts	May 11	May 10	May 09
Working Capital	41	64	71
Fixed Assets	23	14	16
Current Assets	151	149	190
Current Liabilities	N/A	76	N/A

Bishop Pipe Freezing Ltd Pipefreezing & Hot Tapping

58a Shirley Road, Croydon, CR0 7EP
Tel: 0800-132750 **Fax:** 020- 86545459
E-mail: bishop@pipefreezingsales.com
Website: http://www.pipefreezingsales.com
Directors: C. Bishop (MD)
Ultimate Holding Company: BISHOP GROUP SERVICES LIMITED
Immediate Holding Company: CYRIL W. BISHOP ENGINEERING SERVICES LIMITED
Registration no: 04365375 **Date established:** 2002
No.of Employees: 1 - 10 **Product Groups:** 30, 35, 36, 37, 38, 39, 40, 41, 42, 46, 47, 48, 51, 52, 54, 80, 84, 85

C D L 1992 Co. Ltd

29 Grafton Road, Croydon, CR0 3RP
Tel: 020-8680 3077 **Fax:** 020-8686 9225
E-mail: office@cdlco.fsnet.co.uk
Website: http://www.cdl-exhibition-contractors.com
Directors: R. Searl (Dir)
Immediate Holding Company: CDL (1992) COMPANY LIMITED
Registration no: 02734001 **Date established:** 1992
Turnover: £500,000 - £1m **No.of Employees:** 1 - 10 **Product Groups:** 26, 81

Date of Accounts	Jul 11	Jul 10	Jul 09
Sales Turnover	N/A	521	N/A
Pre Tax Profit/Loss	N/A	-65	N/A
Working Capital	-16	41	26
Fixed Assets	16	21	129
Current Assets	152	142	157
Current Liabilities	N/A	52	N/A

Car Cooling

5 Farm Lane, Croydon, CR0 8AQ
Tel: 08456-525356
E-mail: sales@carcooling.co.uk
Website: http://www.carcooling.co.uk
Turnover: Up to £250,000 **No.of Employees:** 1 - 10 **Product Groups:** 40, 66

Centronic Ltd

Centronic House King Henrys Drive, New Addington, Croydon, CR9 0BG
Tel: 01689-808000 **Fax:** 01689-841822
E-mail: info@centronic.co.uk
Website: http://www.centronic.co.uk
Bank(s): National Westminster Bank Plc
Directors: L. Howard (Dir)
Ultimate Holding Company: CENTRONIC HOLDINGS LIMITED
Immediate Holding Company: CENTRONIC LIMITED
Registration no: 00469940 **VAT No.:** GB 611 9334 59
Date established: 1949 **Turnover:** £5m - £10m
No.of Employees: 51 - 100 **Product Groups:** 35, 37, 38, 45, 48, 54, 84

Date of Accounts	Jan 12	Jan 11	Jan 10
Sales Turnover	8m	7m	5m
Pre Tax Profit/Loss	262	655	-451
Working Capital	2m	2m	2m
Fixed Assets	789	560	544
Current Assets	4m	3m	3m
Current Liabilities	515	476	265

Chromalox UK Ltd

20-28 Whitehorse Road, Croydon, CR0 2JA
Tel: 020-8665 8900 **Fax:** 020-8689 0571
E-mail: uksales@chromalox.com
Website: http://www.chromalox.com
Bank(s): Barclays
Directors: F. Mohammed (Fin)
Ultimate Holding Company: JP MORGAN CHASE & CO (USA)
Immediate Holding Company: CHROMALOX (UK) LIMITED
Registration no: 04325451 **Date established:** 2001
Turnover: £10m - £20m **No.of Employees:** 21 - 50 **Product Groups:** 37, 38, 40

Date of Accounts	Sep 11	Sep 10	Sep 09
Sales Turnover	10m	10m	13m
Pre Tax Profit/Loss	477	421	-1m
Working Capital	-2m	-3m	-3m
Fixed Assets	202	214	262
Current Assets	5m	4m	4m
Current Liabilities	2m	221	245

Complete Signs

226 High Street, Croydon, CR9 1DF
Tel: 0800-376 0244 **Fax:** 0870-870 7332
E-mail: sales@completesigns.co.uk
Website: http://www.completesigns.co.uk
Directors: M. Johnson (MD)
Managers: M. Johnson (Sales Prom Mgr)
Immediate Holding Company: FREEDOM GREECE LTD
Registration no: 06960360 **Date established:** 2010
No.of Employees: 1 - 10 **Product Groups:** 39, 40, 49

Construction Industry Accountancy Ltd

Airport House Purley Way, Croydon, CR0 0XZ
Tel: 020-8651 5050 **Fax:** 01342-836798
E-mail: admin@cisvat.co.uk
Website: http://www.theconstructionshop.com
Directors: M. Mcconomy (Dir)
Immediate Holding Company: CONSTRUCTACCOUNTS LIMITED
Registration no: 04655066 **Date established:** 2003
Turnover: Up to £250,000 **No.of Employees:** 1 - 10 **Product Groups:** 22, 24, 25, 26, 30, 35, 36, 37, 40, 41, 42, 45, 47, 66, 67, 83

Date of Accounts	Mar 11	Mar 10	Mar 09
Working Capital	6	18	8
Fixed Assets	N/A	12	15
Current Assets	7	19	10

Currys

12 Trojan Way Purley Way, Croydon, CR0 4XL
Tel: 08445-616263 **Fax:** 020-8686 8136
Website: http://www.currys.co.uk
Managers: A. Fuller (Mgr)
Ultimate Holding Company: DIXONS RETAIL PLC
Immediate Holding Company: CURRYS GROUP LIMITED
Registration no: 00222379 **Date established:** 2027
No.of Employees: 21 - 50 **Product Groups:** 36, 40

Date of Accounts	May 08	May 09	May 10
Working Capital	13	13m	13m
Current Assets	13	13m	13m

D M C Business Machines plc (Northwest)

59 Imperial Way, Croydon, CR0 4RR
Tel: 0800-413953 **Fax:** 0161-861 7888
E-mail: service@dmcplc.co.uk
Website: http://www.dmcplc.info
Directors: J. Hill (MD), J. Hill (MD)
Managers: B. Bignell (Personnel), D. Kelly (Sales Prom Mgr), K. Streatfield (Tech Serv Mgr), M. Cowan (Purch Mgr)
Immediate Holding Company: D.M.C. BUSINESS MACHINES PLC
Registration no: 02559122 **Date established:** 1990
No.of Employees: 51 - 100 **Product Groups:** 44

Date of Accounts	Feb 12	Feb 11	Feb 10
Sales Turnover	29m	23m	16m
Pre Tax Profit/Loss	898	525	101
Working Capital	3m	2m	2m
Fixed Assets	95	92	83
Current Assets	6m	6m	6m
Current Liabilities	1m	914	1m

Dernier & Hamlyn Ltd

Unit 5 Jaycee House 214 Purley Way, Croydon, CR0 4XG
Tel: 020-8760 0900 **Fax:** 020-8760 0955
E-mail: info@dernier-hamlyn.com
Website: http://www.dernier-hamlyn.com
Bank(s): Barclays
Directors: J. Quantrill (Dir)
Immediate Holding Company: DERNIER & HAMLYN LIMITED
Registration no: 04061729 **Date established:** 2000 **Turnover:** £2m - £5m
No.of Employees: 11 - 20 **Product Groups:** 33, 37, 49

Date of Accounts	Feb 12	Feb 11	Feb 10
Working Capital	381	573	545
Fixed Assets	10	32	55
Current Assets	1m	1m	1m

Direct Line Insurance plc

3 Edridge Road, Croydon, CR9 1AG
Tel: 020-8686 3313 **Fax:** 020-8256 5202
Website: http://www.directline.com
Directors: P. Geddes (Grp Chief Exec), A. Court (Grp Chief Exec), P. Fish (Sales), N. Mcluskie (Dir), I. Chippingdale (Ch), G. Ross (MD), J. Wallace (Mkt Research), P. Hutchings (Dir)
Managers: G. Hedger (Mktg Serv Mgr)
Ultimate Holding Company: THE ROYAL BANK OF SCOTLAND GROUP PUBLIC LIMITED COMPANY
Immediate Holding Company: DIRECT LINE LIFE INSURANCE COMPANY LIMITED
Registration no: 02199286 **Date established:** 1987
Turnover: £500m - £1,000m **No.of Employees:** 51 - 100
Product Groups: 80, 82

Date of Accounts	Dec 08	Dec 07	Dec 06
Sales Turnover	N/A	N/A	2m
Pre Tax Profit/Loss	N/A	N/A	5m
Working Capital	N/A	369	130m
Current Assets	N/A	369	132m
Current Liabilities	N/A	N/A	1m

Earth Anchors Ltd

15 Campbell Road, Croydon, CR0 2SQ
Tel: 020-8684 9601 **Fax:** 020-8684 2230
E-mail: enquiries@earth-anchors.com
Website: http://www.earth-anchors.com
Directors: P. Bennett (Dir), L. Harris (Co Sec)
Immediate Holding Company: EARTH ANCHORS LIMITED
Registration no: 00842961 **VAT No.:** GB 219 7862 28
Date established: 1965 **Turnover:** Up to £250,000
No.of Employees: 1 - 10 **Product Groups:** 26, 36

Date of Accounts	May 12	May 11	May 10
Working Capital	195	225	245
Fixed Assets	193	204	216
Current Assets	412	439	479

Electro Inductors Ltd

Unit 3 19-25 Neville Road, Croydon, CR0 2DS
Tel: 020-8684 6100 **Fax:** 020-8684 6109
E-mail: sales@aluminium-inductors.co.uk
Website: http://www.aluminium-inductors.co.uk
Directors: B. Martindale (MD)
Immediate Holding Company: ELECTRO-INDUCTORS LIMITED
Registration no: 00426442 **Date established:** 1946
Turnover: Up to £250,000 **No.of Employees:** 1 - 10 **Product Groups:** 37

Date of Accounts	Mar 11	Mar 10	Mar 09
Sales Turnover	188	95	188
Pre Tax Profit/Loss	32	-16	15
Working Capital	54	37	60
Fixed Assets	2	2	3
Current Assets	95	53	80
Current Liabilities	15	10	18

Elite Heating Ltd

Henderson Works Henderson Road, Croydon, CR0 2QG
Tel: 020-8664 9099 **Fax:** 020-8664 8699
E-mail: shaun@eliteheating.com
Website: http://www.eliteheatingservice.co.uk
Directors: S. Ottmann (MD)
Managers: D. Owen (Mgr)
Immediate Holding Company: ELITE HEATING LIMITED
Registration no: 04416410 **Date established:** 2002
No.of Employees: 1 - 10 **Product Groups:** 40

Date of Accounts	Mar 10	Mar 09	Mar 08
Working Capital	-134	-74	-128
Fixed Assets	9	10	123
Current Assets	132	219	188

European Metals Recycling Ltd

Endeavour Way, Croydon, CR0 4TR
Tel: 020-8683 3499 **Fax:** 020-8684 5911
Website: http://www.elrltd.com
Managers: T. Bells (Mgr)
Immediate Holding Company: EUROPEAN METAL RECYCLING LIMITED
Registration no: 02954623 **Date established:** 1994
Turnover: £10m - £20m **No.of Employees:** 1 - 10 **Product Groups:** 42, 66

see next page

European Metals Recycling Ltd - *Cont'd*

Date of Accounts	Dec 11	Dec 10	Dec 09
Sales Turnover	3032m	2431m	1843m
Pre Tax Profit/Loss	116m	155m	91m
Working Capital	414m	371m	167m
Fixed Assets	518m	483m	480m
Current Assets	1027m	717m	557m
Current Liabilities	124m	118m	185m

Euro-Tech Export Ltd

518 Purley Way, Croydon, CR0 4RE
Tel: 020-8760 7300 **Fax:** 020-8680 8120
E-mail: sales@eurotech.co.uk
Website: http://www.eurotech.co.uk
Directors: C. Smallwood (MD)
Immediate Holding Company: EURO-TECH (EXPORT) LIMITED
Registration no: 01613039 **Date established:** 1982 **Turnover:** £2m - £5m
No.of Employees: 11 - 20 **Product Groups:** 33, 35, 37, 38, 39, 44, 61, 67, 68

Date of Accounts	Apr 11	Apr 10	Apr 09
Working Capital	536	523	475
Fixed Assets	3	4	4
Current Assets	766	762	682

First Stop Computer Group Ltd

15-18 Progress Business Park Progress Way, Croydon, CR0 4XD
Tel: 020-8688 4432 **Fax:** 020-8688 1226
E-mail: sales@firststoptraining.co.uk
Website: http://www.firststop.co.uk
Directors: M. McCabe (Ch), S. Gallagher (Prop), S. Djadali (Dir), S. Gallagher (MD), P. Rutter (Dir)
Immediate Holding Company: R V K TRUCK ENGINEERING LIMITED
Registration no: 05577139 **Date established:** 1992
Turnover: £250,000 - £500,000 **No.of Employees:** 1 - 10
Product Groups: 44, 80, 82, 86

Forde Fire Protection Ltd

84 Sumner Road, Croydon, CR0 3LJ
Tel: 020-8686 4455 **Fax:** 020-8686 2888
Directors: R. Forde (MD)
No.of Employees: 21 - 50 **Product Groups:** 38, 42

Freightline International Ltd

288a High Street, Croydon, CR0 1NG
Tel: 020-8680 1255 **Fax:** 020-8681 1545
E-mail: info@freightline-international.co.uk
Website: http://www.freightline-international.co.uk
Directors: L. Felstead (Fin), T. Felstead (MD)
Immediate Holding Company: FREIGHTLINE INTERNATIONAL LIMITED
Registration no: 01230544 **VAT No.:** GB 219 4570 56
Date established: 1975 **Turnover:** £1m - £2m **No.of Employees:** 1 - 10
Product Groups: 39, 45, 61, 72, 74, 75, 76

Date of Accounts	Mar 11	Mar 10	Mar 09
Sales Turnover	N/A	N/A	1m
Pre Tax Profit/Loss	N/A	N/A	28
Working Capital	146	70	7
Fixed Assets	40	40	44
Current Assets	580	569	328
Current Liabilities	N/A	N/A	23

G M T Electrical Services Ltd

93-95 Gloucester Road, Croydon, CR0 2DN
Tel: 020-8683 0464 **Fax:** 020-8664 9775
Directors: F. Brown (Fin)
Immediate Holding Company: GMT ELECTRICAL SERVICES LIMITED
Registration no: 02061432 **Date established:** 1986
Turnover: £250,000 - £500,000 **No.of Employees:** 1 - 10
Product Groups: 84

Date of Accounts	Oct 11	Oct 10	Oct 09
Sales Turnover	493	460	451
Pre Tax Profit/Loss	56	43	34
Working Capital	-36	-25	-18
Fixed Assets	220	229	240
Current Assets	117	96	111
Current Liabilities	34	40	29

Gibson Hanson Graphics Ltd

2nd Floor Amp House Dingwall Road, Croydon, CR0 2LX
Tel: 020-8260 1200 **Fax:** 020-8260 1212
E-mail: clare.stead@gibsonhanson.co.uk
Directors: K. Vaux (Fin), J. Charlton (MD)
Managers: D. Reid (Tech Serv Mgr)
Ultimate Holding Company: AMERICAN GREETINGS CORPORATION (USA)
Immediate Holding Company: GIBSON HANSON GRAPHICS LIMITED
Registration no: 03220599 **Date established:** 1996
Turnover: £50m - £75m **No.of Employees:** 21 - 50 **Product Groups:** 27, 33, 35, 49

Date of Accounts	Feb 12	Feb 08	Feb 11
Sales Turnover	N/A	59m	N/A
Pre Tax Profit/Loss	N/A	10m	N/A
Working Capital	40m	40m	40m
Current Assets	40m	40m	40m

Glanville Metal Spinning Co. Ltd

Tait Road, Croydon, CR0 2DT
Tel: 020-8689 6339 **Fax:** 020-8689 6388
E-mail: gmsc@btconnect.com
Website: http://www.metalspinning7.co.uk
Directors: M. Knight (Co Sec)
Immediate Holding Company: GLANVILLE METAL SPINNING COMPANY LIMITED
Registration no: 00535493 **Date established:** 1954
Turnover: £250,000 - £500,000 **No.of Employees:** 1 - 10
Product Groups: 46, 48

Date of Accounts	Jul 11	Jul 10	Jul 09
Working Capital	38	14	29
Fixed Assets	23	20	11
Current Assets	112	92	96

GlasTechnik ltd

Btech 4 Meridian Centre Vulcan Way, New Addington, Croydon, CR0 9UG
Tel: 01689-848535 **Fax:** 01724-764352
E-mail: info@glastechnik.co.uk
Website: http://www.glastechnik.co.uk
Directors: A. Lambert (Head)
Registration no: 04793662 **VAT No.:** GB 613 7081 60
Turnover: £250,000 - £500,000 **No.of Employees:** 1 - 10
Product Groups: 33, 36, 38, 39, 63, 67

Goddard Perry Consulting Ltd

6th Floor Corinthian House 17 Lansdowne Road, Croydon, CR0 2BX
Tel: 020-8603 3700 **Fax:** 020-8649 8831
E-mail: contact@goddardperry.com
Website: http://www.mkpltd.co.uk
Directors: S. Goddard (MD)
Ultimate Holding Company: GODDARD PERRY HOLDINGS LIMITED
Immediate Holding Company: MICHAEL KIRK AND PARTNERS LIMITED
Registration no: 02121038 **Date established:** 1987 **Turnover:** £1m - £2m
No.of Employees: 21 - 50 **Product Groups:** 82

Date of Accounts	Dec 10	Jul 10	Jul 09
Sales Turnover	N/A	N/A	1m
Pre Tax Profit/Loss	N/A	N/A	186
Working Capital	N/A	51	68
Fixed Assets	N/A	N/A	115
Current Assets	25	231	290
Current Liabilities	N/A	N/A	160

H R Denne Ltd

Unit G 09 Lombard House, Croydon, CR0 3JP
Tel: 01293-514723 **Fax:** 020-7358 1090
E-mail: sales@hrdenne.com
Website: http://www.hrdenne.com
Directors: B. Mckee (MD)
Ultimate Holding Company: R. ELWOOD AND COMPANY LIMITED
Immediate Holding Company: H R DENNE LIMITED
Registration no: FC016912 **Date established:** 1992 **Turnover:** £1m - £2m
No.of Employees: 11 - 20 **Product Groups:** 24

Date of Accounts	Oct 99	Oct 98	Oct 03
Sales Turnover	N/A	N/A	1m
Pre Tax Profit/Loss	84	86	19
Working Capital	449	399	103
Fixed Assets	65	50	571
Current Assets	2m	1m	788
Current Liabilities	458	262	46

Harris & Bailey Ltd

50 Hastings Road, Croydon, CR9 6BR
Tel: 020-8654 3181 **Fax:** 020-8656 9369
E-mail: mail@harris-bailey.co.uk
Website: http://www.harris-bailey.co.uk
Bank(s): Barclays
Directors: T. Hayman (MD), C. Simpson (Fin), B. Richardson (Ch), C. Simpson (Fin)
Managers: D. Gasson
Immediate Holding Company: HARRIS & BAILEY LIMITED
Registration no: 00129871 **VAT No.:** GB 217 9506 52
Date established: 2013 **Turnover:** £10m - £20m
No.of Employees: 51 - 100 **Product Groups:** 66

Date of Accounts	Mar 12	Mar 11	Mar 10
Sales Turnover	14m	13m	12m
Pre Tax Profit/Loss	804	371	43
Working Capital	8m	8m	8m
Fixed Assets	2m	2m	2m
Current Assets	9m	9m	9m
Current Liabilities	494	324	388

H T Z Ltd

Vulcan Way New Addington, Croydon, CR0 9UG
Tel: 01689-843345 **Fax:** 01689-841792
E-mail: james.bagshawe@htz.biz
Website: http://www.htz.biz
Bank(s): Co-op
Directors: J. Bagshawe (Dir)
Managers: S. Carey, T. Le-vine (Tech Serv Mgr), L. Boateng
Immediate Holding Company: HOOK & TUCKER ZENYX LIMITED
Registration no: 00714824 **Date established:** 1962 **Turnover:** £2m - £5m
No.of Employees: 21 - 50 **Product Groups:** 37, 38

Date of Accounts	Mar 11	Mar 10	Mar 09
Working Capital	257	234	240
Fixed Assets	330	330	330
Current Assets	304	283	308

Impact Food Service Sales

38 Lynton Road, Croydon, CR0 3QX
Tel: 020-8684 2909 **Fax:** 020-8684 8066
Directors: M. Connor (Prop)
Date established: 1999 **No.of Employees:** 1 - 10 **Product Groups:** 20, 40, 41

It Bromley & Croydon

87 Bramble Close, Croydon, CR0 8JL
Tel: 020-8777 2921 **Fax:** 08700-940896
E-mail: sales@itcroydon.co.uk
Website: http://www.itcroydon.co.uk
Directors: D. Lees (Ch), D. Leese (Prop), A. Lees (Ptnr)
Registration no: 06022878 **Date established:** 2006
No.of Employees: 1 - 10 **Product Groups:** 44

J T Davies & Sons Ltd

7 Aberdeen Road, Croydon, CR0 1EQ
Tel: 020-8681 3222 **Fax:** 020-8760 0390
E-mail: sales@mayorsworder.co.uk
Website: http://www.jtdavies.co.uk
Directors: J. Lewis (Dir), M. Davies (MD), M. Everett (Dir)
Ultimate Holding Company: MAT Davies Holdings Ltd
Immediate Holding Company: M.A.T. Davies Holdings Ltd
Registration no: 00117575 **VAT No.:** GB 232 1839 81
Turnover: £10m - £20m **No.of Employees:** 21 - 50 **Product Groups:** 69

Jewson Ltd

24-26 Lower Addiscombe Road, Croydon, CR0 6AA
Tel: 020-8688 2164 **Fax:** 020-8666 0197
Website: http://www.jewson.co.uk
Managers: J. Griffin (District Mgr)
Ultimate Holding Company: COMPAGNIE DE SAINT GOBAIN (FRANCE)
Immediate Holding Company: JEWSON LIMITED
Registration no: 00348407 **Date established:** 1939
Turnover: £500m - £1,000m **No.of Employees:** 1 - 10
Product Groups: 66

Date of Accounts	Dec 11	Dec 10	Dec 09
Sales Turnover	1606m	1547m	1485m
Pre Tax Profit/Loss	18m	100m	45m
Working Capital	-345m	-250m	-349m
Fixed Assets	496m	387m	461m
Current Assets	657m	1005m	1320m
Current Liabilities	66m	120m	64m

Knightsbridge Property Services Ltd

Airport House Purley Way, Croydon, CR0 0XZ
Tel: 020-8253 4588 **Fax:** 020-8287 3737
E-mail: enquiries@kpsltd.co.uk
Website: http://www.knightsbridgepropertyservices.co.uk
Directors: J. Millman (Prop), J. Millman (Ch)
Immediate Holding Company: KNIGHTSBRIDGE PROPERTY SERVICES LIMITED
Registration no: 02659811 **Date established:** 1991
Turnover: £250m - £500m **No.of Employees:** 21 - 50 **Product Groups:** 52

Date of Accounts	Jul 11	Jul 10	Jul 09
Sales Turnover	4m	4m	4m
Pre Tax Profit/Loss	191	231	107
Working Capital	548	484	426
Fixed Assets	80	81	74
Current Assets	1m	1m	1m
Current Liabilities	N/A	217	397

LA Fitness Ltd

33 Imperial Way Purley Way, Croydon, CR0 4RR
Tel: 08431-701020 **Fax:** 020-8667 1527
E-mail: sale@lafitness.co.uk
Website: http://www.lafitness.co.uk
Managers: C. Llyod
Ultimate Holding Company: MOP ACQUISITIONS (LAF) LIMITED
Immediate Holding Company: L A FITNESS LIMITED
Registration no: 03224406 **Date established:** 1996
No.of Employees: 1 - 10 **Product Groups:** 69

Date of Accounts	Oct 11	Jul 10	Jul 09
Pre Tax Profit/Loss	3m	3m	2m
Working Capital	60m	57m	54m
Fixed Assets	5m	5m	5m
Current Assets	60m	57m	54m
Current Liabilities	N/A	N/A	1

Laboratory News

Davis House Robert Street, Croydon, CR0 1QQ
Tel: 020-8253 8600 **Fax:** 020-8253 4609
E-mail: admin@metropolis.co.uk
Website: http://www.metropolis.co.uk
Managers: D. Moon (Comm)
Immediate Holding Company: ANNOUNCEMENT LIMITED
Date established: 2004 **No.of Employees:** 1 - 10 **Product Groups:** 30, 37, 44

Level Developments Ltd

Spencer Place 97-99 Gloucester Road, Croydon, CR0 2DN
Tel: 020-8684 1400 **Fax:** 020-8684 1422
E-mail: sales@leveldevelopments.com
Website: http://www.leveldevelopments.com
Bank(s): Bank of Scotland
Directors: L. Jones (MD), M. Jones (MD)
Managers: K. Murphy (Sales Admin)
Immediate Holding Company: LEVEL DEVELOPMENTS LIMITED
Registration no: 02179307 **VAT No.:** GB 468 7021 29
Date established: 1987 **Turnover:** £500,000 - £1m
No.of Employees: 21 - 50 **Product Groups:** 33, 36, 38, 39, 45

Date of Accounts	Nov 11	Nov 10	Nov 09
Sales Turnover	2m	1m	890
Pre Tax Profit/Loss	373	288	114
Working Capital	392	312	184
Fixed Assets	415	343	355
Current Assets	622	505	316
Current Liabilities	86	88	37

Lyn Plan Upholstery Ltd

43 Imperial Way, Croydon, CR9 4LP
Tel: 020-8681 1833 **Fax:** 020-8680 5727
E-mail: sales@lynplan.com
Website: http://www.lynplan.com
Directors: A. England (MD)
Managers: T. Mason
Immediate Holding Company: LYNPLAN LIMITED
Registration no: 00963634 **VAT No.:** GB 691 4919 00
Date established: 1969 **Turnover:** £2m - £5m **No.of Employees:** 51 - 100
Product Groups: 26

Date of Accounts	Dec 09	Dec 08	Dec 07
Working Capital	-181	-195	-253
Fixed Assets	540	567	597
Current Assets	546	536	542

Mansell Construction Services Ltd

Roman House, Croydon, BR9 6BU
Tel: 020-8654 8191 **Fax:** 020-8655 3916
E-mail: mailbox@mansell.plc.uk
Website: http://www.constructingcommunities.com
Bank(s): Midland; Barclays; National Westminster; Lloyds
Directors: G. Garvin (Grp Mktg), S. Waite (MD), J. Wickerson (Ch)
Ultimate Holding Company: BALFOUR BEATTY PLC
Immediate Holding Company: MANSELL CONSTRUCTION SERVICES LIMITED
Registration no: 01197246 **Date established:** 1975
No.of Employees: 101 - 250 **Product Groups:** 52

Date of Accounts	Dec 11	Dec 10	Dec 09
Sales Turnover	868m	772m	859m
Pre Tax Profit/Loss	14m	15m	20m
Working Capital	86m	85m	102m
Fixed Assets	37m	38m	32m
Current Assets	379m	383m	366m
Current Liabilities	232m	258m	248m

Maplin Electronics Ltd

166 North End, Croydon, CR9 1SE
Tel: 08432-277338 **Fax:** 020-8686 5462
E-mail: customercare@maplin.co.uk
Website: http://www.maplin.co.uk
Managers: S. Head (Mgr)
Ultimate Holding Company: MONTAGU PRIVATE EQUITY LLP
Immediate Holding Company: MAPLIN ELECTRONICS LIMITED
Registration no: 01264385 **Date established:** 1976
Turnover: £125m - £250m **No.of Employees:** 21 - 50
Product Groups: 37, 61

Date of Accounts	Dec 11	Dec 08	Dec 09
Sales Turnover	205m	204m	204m
Pre Tax Profit/Loss	25m	32m	35m
Working Capital	118m	49m	75m
Fixed Assets	27m	28m	28m
Current Assets	207m	108m	142m
Current Liabilities	78m	51m	59m

Mascot Letting Agent
1 Holmesdale Road, Croydon, CR0 2LR
Tel: 020-8665 6683 **Fax:** 020-8665 6683
E-mail: mascot.croydon@btinternet.com
Managers: F. Jakhura (Mgr)
Immediate Holding Company: SPJ COMPUTER SERVICES LIMITED
Registration no: 05817399 **Date established:** 1995
Turnover: Up to £250,000 **No.of Employees:** 1 - 10 **Product Groups:** 80

Date of Accounts	Dec 11	Dec 10	Dec 09
Sales Turnover	98	85	98
Pre Tax Profit/Loss	6	13	28
Working Capital	-8	-5	-11
Fixed Assets	75	79	76
Current Assets	N/A	6	11
Current Liabilities	6	5	4

Mitsubishi Electric Europe BV Power Systems Group (Engineering Division)
7th Floor Stephenson House 2 Cherry Orchard Road, Croydon, CR0 6BA
Tel: 020-8686 9551 **Fax:** 020-8688 2035
E-mail: tetsuya.shinohara@crd.meuk.mee.com
Website: http://www.mitsubishielectric.co.uk
Directors: T. Shinohara (MD)
Managers: M. Freeman (Tech Serv Mgr), S. Langdon
Immediate Holding Company: PULSE LEISURE LIMITED
Registration no: FC019156 **Date established:** 2011
Turnover: Over £1,000m **No.of Employees:** 51 - 100 **Product Groups:** 37

Modern Labelling Methods Ltd
38 Fullerton Road, Croydon, CR0 6JD
Tel: 020-8656 9659 **Fax:** 020-8656 7979
E-mail: tlemon@modernlabellingmethods.co.uk
Website: http://www.modernlabelingmethods.co.uk
Directors: T. Lemon (MD), T. Lemon (Ptnr), B. Hutchins (Fin)
Immediate Holding Company: MODERN LABELLING METHODS LIMITED
Registration no: 05532200 **Date established:** 2005 **Turnover:** £2m - £5m
No.of Employees: 1 - 10 **Product Groups:** 28, 42

Date of Accounts	Aug 07	Aug 06	Dec 05
Sales Turnover	42	363	N/A
Pre Tax Profit/Loss	19	-68	N/A
Working Capital	34	29	-8
Fixed Assets	200	204	321
Current Assets	54	44	234
Current Liabilities	20	15	242
Total Share Capital	15	15	15
ROCE% (Return on Capital Employed)	8.3	-29.4	
ROT% (Return on Turnover)	46.4	-18.8	

Mondial Assistance Ltd
Mondial House 102 George Street, Croydon, CR9 1AJ
Tel: 020-8681 2525 **Fax:** 020-8688 0577
E-mail: anthony_lancaster@mondial-assistance.co.uk
Website: http://www.mondial-assistance.co.uk
Directors: A. Lancaster (Dir)
Managers: M. Hynd (Comptroller), S. Kirby (Mktg Serv Mgr), J. Totten, M. Stapley (Personnel), L. Taylor
Ultimate Holding Company: ALLIANZ SE (GERMANY)
Immediate Holding Company: MONDIAL ASSISTANCE (UK) LIMITED
Registration no: 01710361 **Date established:** 1983
Turnover: £20m - £50m **No.of Employees:** 251 - 500 **Product Groups:** 72

Date of Accounts	Dec 11	Dec 10	Dec 09
Sales Turnover	49m	49m	49m
Pre Tax Profit/Loss	6m	9m	10m
Working Capital	26m	31m	27m
Fixed Assets	3m	3m	4m
Current Assets	97m	101m	109m
Current Liabilities	55m	54m	63m

National Abrasives Ltd
67 Imperial Way, Croydon, CR0 4RR
Tel: 020-8633 1880 **Fax:** 020-8633 1881
E-mail: stephen@national-abrasives.co.uk
Website: http://www.national-abrasives.com
Directors: S. Furnell (MD)
Immediate Holding Company: FURNELL ABRASIVES LTD
Date established: 2004 **No.of Employees:** 11 - 20 **Product Groups:** 24, 33, 35, 49

Date of Accounts	Sep 11	Sep 10	Sep 09
Working Capital	-5	27	-31
Fixed Assets	273	179	130
Current Assets	610	505	459

Nicholson Plastics Ltd
20b Lansdowne Road, Croydon, CR0 2BX
Tel: 020-8760 0930 **Fax:** 020- 86881811
Website: http://www.nicholsonplastics.co.uk
Managers: M. Blezard (Mgr)
Ultimate Holding Company: GODDARD PERRY HOLDINGS LIMITED
Immediate Holding Company: SERENITY FLEX & REWARD LIMITED
Registration no: 05647242 **Date established:** 2007
Turnover: £250,000 - £500,000 **No.of Employees:** 1 - 10
Product Groups: 33, 35

Date of Accounts	Dec 11	Dec 10	Jul 09
Sales Turnover	258	340	218
Pre Tax Profit/Loss	-60	-64	-65
Working Capital	-305	-245	-198
Fixed Assets	1	1	18
Current Assets	61	114	41
Current Liabilities	24	24	14

Office Team
Unit 4 500 Purley Way, Croydon, CR0 4NZ
Tel: 020-8774 3422 **Fax:** 020-8640 2905
E-mail: info@officeteam.co.uk
Website: http://www.officeteam.co.uk
Directors: M. Ewart-smith (Fin), P. Maynard (Co Sec)
Managers: A. Borrell (Sales Prom Mgr), D. Hayes (Tech Serv Mgr), J. Whiteway, D. Worthington (Personnel), A. Griffiths (Purch Mgr), K. De Silva (Mktg Serv Mgr)
Ultimate Holding Company: OSG HOLDINGS LIMITED
Immediate Holding Company: STAT-PLUS LIMITED
Registration no: 02595313 **Date established:** 1991
Turnover: £75m - £125m **No.of Employees:** 101 - 250
Product Groups: 64

Date of Accounts	Dec 10	Dec 09	Dec 08
Sales Turnover	N/A	17m	26m
Pre Tax Profit/Loss	220	3m	4m
Working Capital	2	5m	10m
Fixed Assets	N/A	N/A	744
Current Assets	2	19m	15m
Current Liabilities	N/A	N/A	2m

Power Tech Lighting
Airport House Purley Way, Croydon, CR0 0XZ
Tel: 020-8781 6959 **Fax:** 020-8781 6981
Managers: P. Dear (Mgr)
Immediate Holding Company: POWERTEC LIGHTING LIMITED
Registration no: 02992590 **Date established:** 1994
No.of Employees: 1 - 10 **Product Groups:** 37, 67

Date of Accounts	Mar 11	Mar 10	Mar 09
Working Capital	67	75	81
Fixed Assets	11	13	15
Current Assets	101	103	101

Preform Management Ltd T/A Croydon Power Tool Centre
79 Gloucester Road, Croydon, CR0 2DN
Tel: 020-8683 0550 **Fax:** 020-8684 7507
E-mail: croydonpowertools@yahoo.co.uk
Directors: D. Gabriel (Dir), D. Gabriel (MD), J. Watts (Sales)
Managers: N. Grayson (Mgr)
Immediate Holding Company: PRESTIGE COACHWORKS (SURREY) LIMITED
Registration no: 02660648 **VAT No.:** GB 574 3432 37
Date established: 2010 **Turnover:** £500,000 - £1m
No.of Employees: 1 - 10 **Product Groups:** 37

Pure Foods Systems Ltd
4 Coomber Way, Croydon, CR0 4TQ
Tel: 020-8401 6730 **Fax:** 020-8395 3071
E-mail: sales@purefoodssystems.co.uk
Website: http://www.purefoodssystems.co.uk
Directors: N. Mattey (Sales)
Registration no: 03217647 **Date established:** 1995
Turnover: £500,000 - £1m **No.of Employees:** 1 - 10 **Product Groups:** 20, 21

Purina Pet Care
St Georges House Park Lane, Croydon, CR9 1NR
Tel: 020-8949 6100 **Fax:** 020-8255 5709
E-mail: info@compass-group.co.uk
Website: http://www.nestle.com
Bank(s): Barclays
Directors: M. Stripe (Pers), E. Legge (Fin), D. Bruce (Tech Serv)
Managers: I. Deschamps
Ultimate Holding Company: NESTLE SA (SWITZERLAND)
Immediate Holding Company: NESTLE PURINA PETCARE (U.K.) LIMITED
Registration no: 00121700 **VAT No.:** 528 0478 39 **Date established:** 2012
Turnover: £250m - £500m **No.of Employees:** 1001 - 1500
Product Groups: 20

Date of Accounts	Dec 11	Dec 10	Dec 09
Sales Turnover	468m	457m	451m
Pre Tax Profit/Loss	26m	32m	33m
Working Capital	17m	4m	40m
Fixed Assets	121m	114m	104m
Current Assets	103m	124m	118m
Current Liabilities	47m	57m	54m

R.J. Lifts & Escalators Ltd
2 Orchard Way, Croydon, CR0 7NG
Tel: 020-8776 2453 **Fax:** 020-8776 2453
E-mail: mail@rjliftsltd.co.uk
Website: http://www.rjliftandtestingservices.co.uk
Registration no: 04603684 **Turnover:** Up to £250,000
No.of Employees: 1 - 10 **Product Groups:** 35, 39, 45

Date of Accounts	Mar 08	Mar 07	Mar 06
Working Capital	-2	7	5
Fixed Assets	15	8	7
Current Assets	28	37	37
Current Liabilities	30	29	32

Reed Accountancy Personnel Ltd
52 George Street, Croydon, CR0 1PB
Tel: 020-8680 4034 **Fax:** 020-8686 5413
Website: http://www.reed.co.uk
Managers: K. O'Reilly (Mgr)
Immediate Holding Company: REED PERSONNEL SERVICES LTD
Registration no: 00973629 **Turnover:** £125m - £250m
No.of Employees: 1 - 10 **Product Groups:** 80

Reed Employment Ltd
52 George Street, Croydon, CR0 1PB
Tel: 020-8688 3498 **Fax:** 020-8681 6558
E-mail: croydon@reed.co.uk
Website: http://www.reedemployment.co.uk
Managers: L. Douglas (Mgr)
Ultimate Holding Company: REED GLOBAL LTD (MALTA)
Immediate Holding Company: REED EMPLOYMENT LIMITED
Registration no: 00669854 **Date established:** 1960
Turnover: £75m - £125m **No.of Employees:** 1 - 10 **Product Groups:** 80

Date of Accounts	Jun 11	Jun 10	Dec 07
Sales Turnover	618	450	287m
Pre Tax Profit/Loss	-2m	310	8m
Working Capital	23m	28m	28m
Fixed Assets	31	36	5m
Current Assets	28m	30m	74m
Current Liabilities	37	29	21m

Reed Insurance
52 George Street, Croydon, CR0 1PB
Tel: 020-8256 1340 **Fax:** 020-8649 8584
E-mail: atcroydon@reed.co.uk
Website: http://www.reed.co.uk
Directors: A. Pattel (Prop)
Managers: L. Douglas (Mgr), L. Widows (Mgr)
Immediate Holding Company: L&E Title Group Ltd
Registration no: 04459633 **Date established:** 2006
Turnover: £125m - £250m **No.of Employees:** 1 - 10 **Product Groups:** 80

Alex Reid Ltd
128-130 Beddington Lane, Croydon, CR0 4YZ
Tel: 08456-344454 **Fax:** 020-8683 4335
E-mail: sales@alexreid.co.uk
Website: http://www.alexreid.co.uk
Bank(s): National Westminster Bank Plc
Managers: N. Burdenshaw (Mgr), L. House (Personnel), T. Stacey (Sales Prom Mgr)
Ultimate Holding Company: JOHNSON SERVICE GROUP PLC
Immediate Holding Company: ALEX REID LIMITED
Registration no: 01025547 **Date established:** 1971
Turnover: £10m - £20m **No.of Employees:** 11 - 20 **Product Groups:** 32, 35, 40, 45, 66, 67

Date of Accounts	Dec 11	Dec 10	Dec 09
Sales Turnover	12m	14	15m
Pre Tax Profit/Loss	10	-1	-201
Working Capital	-905	-1	-288
Fixed Assets	154	N/A	205
Current Assets	5m	4	4m
Current Liabilities	409	1	493

Remys Ltd
Unit 6 ZK Park 23 Commerce Way, Croydon, CR0 4ZS
Tel: 020-8680 2191 **Fax:** 020-8681 3514
E-mail: mail@remys.co.uk
Website: http://www.remys.co.uk
Bank(s): Nat West
Directors: A. Shah (MD), A. Shah (Prop)
Immediate Holding Company: REMY'S LIMITED
Registration no: 01782856 **VAT No.:** GB 407 3245 75
Date established: 1984 **Turnover:** £5m - £10m **No.of Employees:** 11 - 20
Product Groups: 63

Date of Accounts	Apr 12	Apr 11	Apr 10
Working Capital	-223	184	1m
Fixed Assets	11m	9m	8m
Current Assets	3m	3m	4m

Riches & Blythin Architects
Albany House 82 South End, Croydon, CR0 1DQ
Tel: 020-8686 7373 **Fax:** 020-8680 4434
E-mail: richesandblythin@aol.com
Directors: D. Barbour (Prop), D. Barbour (Snr Part)
Immediate Holding Company: M.W. (CROYDON) LIMITED
Registration no: 02070513 **Date established:** 1986
Turnover: Up to £250,000 **No.of Employees:** 1 - 10 **Product Groups:** 84

Roberts & Burling Roofing Supplies Ltd
120 Beddington Lane, Croydon, CR0 4YZ
Tel: 020-8689 0481 **Fax:** 020-8689 3063
E-mail: bmcroydon@robertsandburling.co.uk
Directors: C. Chalcraft (Fin), R. Monro (Co Sec)
Ultimate Holding Company: SIG PLC
Immediate Holding Company: ROBERTS & BURLING ROOFING SUPPLIES LIMITED
Registration no: 02655587 **Date established:** 1991
No.of Employees: 1 - 10 **Product Groups:** 30, 31, 33, 35

Sanico Building Services Ltd
17-21 George Street, Croydon, CR0 1LA
Tel: 07833-118 149 **Fax:** 020-8407 2032
E-mail: info@sanico.co.uk
Website: http://www.sanico.co.uk
Directors: D. Voronsov (MD)
Registration no: 04672687 **Date established:** 2003
Turnover: £250,000 - £500,000 **No.of Employees:** 11 - 20
Product Groups: 52

Date of Accounts	Mar 09	Mar 08	Mar 07
Sales Turnover	78	106	25
Pre Tax Profit/Loss	-29	6	6
Working Capital	5	22	N/A
Fixed Assets	1	1	1
Current Assets	12	24	2
Current Liabilities	N/A	2	2

Serco Ltd
Unit 3 123 Beddington Lane, Croydon, CR9 4NX
Tel: 020-8665 9098 **Fax:** 020-8665 9954
E-mail: cliff.jones@serco.com
Website: http://www.serco.com
Directors: B. Moustin (Fin)
Managers: C. Jones (Mgr)
Ultimate Holding Company: SERCO GROUP PLC
Immediate Holding Company: SERCO LIMITED
Registration no: 00242246 **Date established:** 2029
No.of Employees: 21 - 50 **Product Groups:** 38, 67

Date of Accounts	Dec 11	Dec 10	Dec 09
Sales Turnover	1762m	1820m	1760m
Pre Tax Profit/Loss	48m	100m	39m
Working Capital	154m	119m	242m
Fixed Assets	571m	494m	516m
Current Assets	556m	584m	765m
Current Liabilities	312m	368m	374m

Shoreheat
Unit 4 Commerce Trade Park 4 Commerce Way, Croydon, CR0 4YN
Tel: 020-8688 7438 **Fax:** 020- 86800663
Website: http://www.shoreheat.co.uk
Directors: G. Holton (MD)
Managers: M. Burgess (District Mgr), M. Burgess (Mgr), R. Terry (Sales Prom Mgr)
Immediate Holding Company: SHOREHEAT LIMITED
Registration no: 01566154 **Date established:** 1981 **Turnover:** £5m - £10m
No.of Employees: 1 - 10 **Product Groups:** 40, 54

Siesta Cork Tile Co.
Tait Road Industrial Estate 21 Tait Road, Croydon, CR0 2DP
Tel: 020-8683 4055 **Fax:** 020-8683 4480
E-mail: info@siestacorktile.co.uk
Website: http://www.siestacorktile.co.uk
Directors: R. Bacon (Ptnr)
Registration no: 01420008 **VAT No.:** GB 218 0671 76
Date established: 1969 **Turnover:** £500,000 - £1m
No.of Employees: 1 - 10 **Product Groups:** 22, 25, 29, 31, 39, 49, 66

Sigma Aerospace Ltd
12 Imperial Way, Croydon, CR9 4LE
Tel: 020-8688 7777 **Fax:** 020-8688 6603
E-mail: enquiries@sigmaaerospace.com
Website: http://www.sigmaaerospace.com
Bank(s): Bank of Scotland
Directors: P. Bryant (Co Sec), T. Brown (Mkt Research), S. Jones (MD), P. Bryant (Fin), D. Jackson (Dir), B. Merrikin (MD)
Managers: S. Stevens (Sec), A. Thomas (Sales Prom), N. Geall, A. Dare (Sales Prom Mgr)

see next page

Sigma Aerospace Ltd - Cont'd

Ultimate Holding Company: VECTOR AEROSPACE CORP (CANADA)
Immediate Holding Company: VECTOR AEROSPACE ENGINE SERVICES UK LIMITED
Registration no: 03496478 **Date established:** 1998
Turnover: £20m - £50m **No.of Employees:** 101 - 250
Product Groups: 38, 39

Signsmiths Ltd

Unit 8 Enterprise Close, Croydon, CR0 3RZ
Tel: 020-8689 4056 **Fax:** 020-8633 9554
E-mail: info@signsmiths.biz
Website: http://www.signsmiths.biz
Directors: A. Smith (Prop)
Immediate Holding Company: SIGNSMITHS LTD
Registration no: 07178313 **VAT No.:** GB 218 5912 55
Date established: 2010 **Turnover:** £2m - £5m **No.of Employees:** 1 - 10
Product Groups: 39

Date of Accounts	Mar 11
Working Capital	-1
Fixed Assets	31
Current Assets	47

Simply Enabling

84 Alderton Road, Croydon, CR0 6HJ
Tel: 020-8654 0808
E-mail: info@simplyenabling.com
Website: http://www.simplyenabling.com
Directors: K. Duignan (MD)
Date established: 1982 **No.of Employees:** 1 - 10 **Product Groups:** 80

Sir Frederick Snow & Partners Ltd

17 Lansdowne Road, Croydon, CR0 2BX
Tel: 020-8604 8999 **Fax:** 020-8604 8877
E-mail: post@fsnow.co.uk
Website: http://www.snow.co.uk
Bank(s): Barclays
Directors: G. Ramsay (Co Sec), P. Martin (MD), S. Smith (Sales & Mktg)
Ultimate Holding Company: ASSOCIATED CONSULTING ENGINEERS (HOLDINGS) SA (LUX.)
Immediate Holding Company: SNOW CONSULTING LTD.
Registration no: 02571263 **VAT No.:** 494 5318 23 **Date established:** 1991
Turnover: £2m - £5m **No.of Employees:** 21 - 50 **Product Groups:** 80

Date of Accounts	Dec 11	Dec 10	Dec 09
Sales Turnover	3m	3m	3m
Pre Tax Profit/Loss	172	245	127
Working Capital	1m	1m	876
Fixed Assets	39	50	74
Current Assets	2m	2m	2m
Current Liabilities	222	331	364

Southern Welders

14 Valentyne Close New Addington, Croydon, CR0 0JU
Tel: 020-8409 0002
Directors: T. Daubeney (Dir)
Date established: 1997 **No.of Employees:** 1 - 10 **Product Groups:** 26, 35

Speedy Asset Services

Unit C Pioneers Industrial Park Beddington Farm Road, Croydon, CR0 4XB
Tel: 020-8683 4900 **Fax:** 020-8683 4924
E-mail: gary.joyice@speedyservices.com
Website: http://www.speedyservices.com
Managers: P. Bodycomb (Depot Mgr)
Ultimate Holding Company: SPEEDY HIRE PLC
Immediate Holding Company: SPEEDY LIFTING LIMITED
Registration no: 04529136 **Date established:** 2002
No.of Employees: 1 - 10 **Product Groups:** 35, 39, 45

Date of Accounts	Sep 11	Sep 10	Sep 09
Sales Turnover	415	285	351
Pre Tax Profit/Loss	213	194	244
Working Capital	-74	-59	142
Fixed Assets	4m	4m	4m
Current Assets	75	31	301
Current Liabilities	118	82	147

Spyra Distribution

112 Beddington Lane, Croydon, CR0 4TD
Tel: 020-8665 1155 **Fax:** 020-8665 1122
E-mail: sales@spyradistribution.co.uk
Website: http://www.spyradistribution.co.uk
Directors: S. Bailey (Sales), J. Seales (MD)
Date established: 2006 **Turnover:** £250,000 - £500,000
No.of Employees: 1 - 10 **Product Groups:** 22

Stonewest Ltd

Lamberts Place St James's Road, Croydon, CR9 2HX
Tel: 020-8684 6646 **Fax:** 020-8684 9323
E-mail: info@stonewest.co.uk
Website: http://www.stonewest.co.uk
Bank(s): Barclays
Directors: G. Bright (Co Sec)
Managers: B. Byrne (Personnel)
Ultimate Holding Company: STONEWEST CAPITAL LIMITED
Immediate Holding Company: CROYDON REALISATIONS LIMITED
Registration no: 02946968 **VAT No.:** GB 650 1987 32
Date established: 1994 **Turnover:** £10m - £20m
No.of Employees: 101 - 250 **Product Groups:** 52

Date of Accounts	May 10	May 09	May 08
Sales Turnover	13m	19m	21m
Pre Tax Profit/Loss	-394	224	668
Working Capital	687	1m	1m
Fixed Assets	148	203	182
Current Assets	8m	9m	10m
Current Liabilities	2m	2m	2m

Summit Elevators Ltd

Unit 19 Vulcan Business Centre Vulcan Way, New Addington, Croydon, CR0 9UG
Tel: 01689-848455 **Fax:** 01689-848844
Website: http://www.summitelevators.co.uk
Directors: C. Coelho (Sales), R. Doswell (Fin)
Immediate Holding Company: SUMMIT ELEVATORS LIMITED
Registration no: 03306900 **Date established:** 1997
No.of Employees: 1 - 10 **Product Groups:** 35, 39, 45

Date of Accounts	Mar 11	Mar 10	Mar 09
Working Capital	116	112	68
Fixed Assets	81	106	136
Current Assets	264	333	341

Superdrug Stores plc

118 Beddington Lane, Croydon, CR0 4TB
Tel: 020-8684 7000 **Fax:** 020-8684 6102
E-mail: edith.shih@superdrugs.com
Website: http://www.superdrug.com
Directors: A. Lyne (Tech Serv), J. Wat (MD), J. Mackie (Pers), G. Smith (Fin), S. Jebson (Comm)
Managers: G. Mason, D. Jarvis
Ultimate Holding Company: HUTCHISON WHAMPOA LIMITED (HONG KONG)
Immediate Holding Company: SUPERDRUG STORES PLC
Registration no: 00807043 **VAT No.:** 777 9471 60 **Date established:** 1964
Turnover: Over £1,000m **No.of Employees:** 101 - 250
Product Groups: 61

Date of Accounts	Dec 11	Dec 08	Dec 09
Sales Turnover	1049m	1075m	1075m
Pre Tax Profit/Loss	6m	-7m	-234
Working Capital	27m	11m	28m
Fixed Assets	124m	148m	130m
Current Assets	389m	394m	432m
Current Liabilities	83m	63m	73m

Surgical Instrument Group Holdings Ltd

89a Gloucester Road, Croydon, CR0 2DN
Tel: 020-8683 1103 **Fax:** 020-8683 1105
E-mail: iansleeper@sighltd.com
Website: http://www.sighltd.com
Directors: I. Sleeper (Fin)
Immediate Holding Company: SURGICAL INSTRUMENTS GROUP HOLDINGS LIMITED
Registration no: 03134118 **Date established:** 1995
Turnover: £500,000 - £1m **No.of Employees:** 1 - 10 **Product Groups:** 38, 67

Date of Accounts	Dec 11	Dec 10	Dec 09
Sales Turnover	768	699	N/A
Pre Tax Profit/Loss	11	36	N/A
Working Capital	147	160	191
Fixed Assets	174	80	21
Current Assets	316	321	298
Current Liabilities	11	30	N/A

Toroid Technology Ltd

50 Mill Lane Purley Way, Croydon, CR0 4AA
Tel: 020-8686 8646 **Fax:** 020-8686 7177
E-mail: toroids@toroid-tech.com
Website: http://www.toroid-tech.com
Directors: T. Richards (Fin), P. Richards (MD)
Immediate Holding Company: TOROID TECHNOLOGY LIMITED
Registration no: 01468296 **VAT No.:** GB 344 6225 64
Date established: 1979 **Turnover:** £1m - £2m **No.of Employees:** 1 - 10
Product Groups: 37, 38

Date of Accounts	Mar 11	Mar 10	Mar 09
Working Capital	263	246	238
Fixed Assets	40	45	50
Current Assets	287	267	298

Vendtrade

13 Imperial Way, Croydon, CR0 4RR
Tel: 020-8401 6730 **Fax:** 020-8395 3071
E-mail: info@purefoodsystems.co.uk
Website: http://www.purefoodsystems.co.uk
Directors: D. Mattey (Ptnr)
Managers: M. Mattey (Mgr)
Turnover: Up to £250,000 **No.of Employees:** 11 - 20 **Product Groups:** 49, 61, 62, 67

L E Went

Unit 17 Tait Road, Croydon, CR0 2DT
Tel: 020-8684 0204 **Fax:** 020-8684 0847
Website: http://www.lewentltd.co.uk
Directors: I. Went (Prop)
Immediate Holding Company: L.E. WENT LTD
Registration no: 00806860 **No.of Employees:** 1 - 10 **Product Groups:** 38, 42

John C Wheeler International Ltd

4 Newman Road, Croydon, CR0 3JX
Tel: 020-8310 2032 **Fax:** 020-8312 1913
E-mail: info@johncwheeler.co.uk
Website: http://www.wheelerlogistics.co.uk
Directors: P. Paterson (Fin), D. Patterson (MD)
Immediate Holding Company: JOHN C. WHEELER INTERNATIONAL LIMITED
Registration no: 01722828 **VAT No.:** GB 435 4628 45
Date established: 1983 **Turnover:** £2m - £5m **No.of Employees:** 1 - 10
Product Groups: 72, 76, 77

Date of Accounts	Oct 09	Oct 08	Oct 07
Working Capital	-148	-149	-83
Fixed Assets	82	81	84
Current Assets	130	450	475

Winwood Lifts

34 North Downs Road New Addington, Croydon, CR0 0LB
Tel: 01689-848222 **Fax:** 01689- 848222
Directors: P. Winwood (Prop)
Immediate Holding Company: WINWOOD LIFTS LTD
Registration no: 05461850 **Date established:** 2005
No.of Employees: 1 - 10 **Product Groups:** 35, 39, 45

Date of Accounts	Mar 08	Mar 07	Mar 06
Working Capital	-1	-3	6
Fixed Assets	10	14	11
Current Assets	17	14	13
Current Liabilities	17	17	8

Zotefoams plc

675 Mitcham Road, Croydon, CR9 3AL
Tel: 020-8664 1600 **Fax:** 020-8664 1616
E-mail: info@zotefoams.com
Website: http://www.zotefoams.com
Directors: P. Van Rheenen (Sales & Mktg), D. Stirling (MD), C. Hurst (Fin)
Managers: M. Walshe, M. Richards (Tech Serv Mgr), F. Gray (Personnel)
Immediate Holding Company: ZOTEFOAMS PLC
Registration no: 02714645 **Date established:** 1992
Turnover: £20m - £50m **No.of Employees:** 101 - 250
Product Groups: 30, 42

Date of Accounts	Dec 11	Dec 10	Dec 09
Sales Turnover	44m	40m	32m
Pre Tax Profit/Loss	5m	6m	3m
Working Capital	11m	11m	9m
Fixed Assets	32m	33m	28m
Current Assets	20m	18m	15m
Current Liabilities	7m	4m	3m

Dorking

Auto Imagination

The Courtyard Ranmore Manor Crocknorth Road, Dorking, RH5 6SX
Tel: 01483-284114
Website: http://www.autoimagination.com
Directors: N. Butler (Prop)
Turnover: Up to £250,000 **No.of Employees:** 1 - 10 **Product Groups:** 39

Bales Worldwide Ltd

Bales House Junction Road, Dorking, RH4 3HL
Tel: 01306-732732 **Fax:** 01306-740048
E-mail: enquiries@balesworldwide.com
Website: http://www.balesworldwide.com
Directors: A. McArdle (Co Sec), I. Fenton (Dir), V. Thorn (Pers)
Managers: M. Kesby (Mktg Serv Mgr), E. Shorts
Ultimate Holding Company: VIRGIN GROUP HOLDINGS LTD (BVI)
Immediate Holding Company: BALES WORLDWIDE LIMITED
Registration no: 00441920 **Date established:** 1947
Turnover: £10m - £20m **No.of Employees:** 21 - 50 **Product Groups:** 69

Date of Accounts	Dec 09	Dec 08	Dec 07
Sales Turnover	11m	N/A	N/A
Pre Tax Profit/Loss	-183	368	367
Working Capital	1m	1m	1m
Fixed Assets	775	1m	969
Current Assets	4m	5m	6m
Current Liabilities	98	210	313

Broanmain

Forge Works Horsham Road, Mid Holmwood, Dorking, RH5 4EJ
Tel: 01306-885888 **Fax:** 01306-885889
E-mail: info@broanmain.co.uk
Website: http://www.broanmain.co.uk
Bank(s): HSBC
Directors: J. Davis (Fin), W. Davis (MD), W. Davis (MD)
Managers: R. McManus (Sales Prom Mgr)
Immediate Holding Company: BROANMAIN LIMITED
Registration no: 01155816 **Date established:** 1974 **Turnover:** £1m - £2m
No.of Employees: 21 - 50 **Product Groups:** 29, 30, 48

Date of Accounts	Sep 11	Sep 10	Sep 09
Working Capital	134	97	48
Fixed Assets	474	135	168
Current Assets	507	417	381

Carville Ltd

Station Road, Dorking, RH4 1HQ
Tel: 01306-881681 **Fax:** 01306-876265
E-mail: sales@carville.co.uk
Website: http://www.carville.co.uk
Bank(s): HSBC, Guildford
Directors: K. Patel (Fin), P. Robinson (MD), R. Fraser (Dir)
Immediate Holding Company: CARVILLE LIMITED
Registration no: 02806578 **Date established:** 1993
No.of Employees: 21 - 50 **Product Groups:** 30, 48, 66

Date of Accounts	Dec 11	Dec 10	Dec 09
Working Capital	518	469	679
Fixed Assets	1m	1m	1m
Current Assets	755	689	1m

The Chefshop

2 Woodhams Farmhouse Honeywood Lane, Okewood Hill, Dorking, RH5 5PY
Tel: 01306-628035 **Fax:** 01306-628035
E-mail: spinchin@aol.com
Directors: S. Pinchin (Ptnr)
Immediate Holding Company: THE CHEFSHOP LTD
Registration no: 05972113 **Date established:** 2006
No.of Employees: 1 - 10 **Product Groups:** 20, 40, 41

Clinical Engineering Consultants Ltd

2 Harlow House Dukes Road, Newdigate, Dorking, RH5 5BY
Tel: 01306-631681 **Fax:** 01306-631688
E-mail: cec.co@lineone.net
Website: http://www.cec-ltd.co.uk
Directors: B. Green (Fin), P. Green (Dir)
Immediate Holding Company: CLINICAL ENGINEERING CONSULTANTS LIMITED
Registration no: 02115087 **Date established:** 1987
Turnover: Up to £250,000 **No.of Employees:** 1 - 10 **Product Groups:** 26, 39

Date of Accounts	Mar 12	Mar 11	Mar 10
Working Capital	102	94	97
Fixed Assets	N/A	1	1
Current Assets	128	118	119

Communication Eleven CB Radio

Hill View Mid-Holmwood Lane, Mid Holmwood, Dorking, RH5 4HD
Tel: 01306-881137 **Fax:** 01306-881137
E-mail: sales@4x4cb.com
Website: http://www.4x4cb.com
Directors: J. Aitken (Prop)
No.of Employees: 1 - 10 **Product Groups:** 37, 67

Complete Interiors

Firtree House Horsham Road, Dorking, RH5 4LQ
Tel: 01306-712614 **Fax:** 01306-876427
E-mail: info@completeinteriors.co.uk
Website: http://www.completeinteriors.co.uk
Directors: N. Wright (MD)
Registration no: 01148827 **Date established:** 1973
Turnover: £250,000 - £500,000 **No.of Employees:** 1 - 10
Product Groups: 33, 35, 37, 40, 42, 52, 63, 66

Data Loop Ltd

Beare Green Court, Dorking, RH5 4SL
Tel: 01306-711088 **Fax:** 01306-713108
E-mail: sales@data-loop.co.uk
Website: http://www.data-loop.co.uk

Directors: D. Lord (MD), N. Lord (Mkt Research)
Registration no: 00872252 **VAT No.:** GB 216 1660 88
Date established: 1966 **Turnover:** £500,000 - £1m
No.of Employees: 1 - 10 **Product Groups:** 30, 31, 33, 37, 38, 39, 40, 42, 44, 61, 67, 88

Date of Accounts	Jun 11	Jun 10	Jun 09
Working Capital	-88	-10	-1
Fixed Assets	12	13	15
Current Assets	86	135	110

DIY Marquees
Unit 15, Havenbury Estate Station Road, Dorking, RH4 1ES
Tel: 01306-876767
E-mail: sales@diymarquees.co.uk
Website: http://www.marquees-for-sale.co.uk
Product Groups: 24, 83, 84

F N C Ltd
Stonebridge House Dorking Business Park, Dorking, RH4 1HJ
Tel: 01306-885050 **Fax:** 01306-886464
E-mail: a.milton@fnc.co.uk
Website: http://www.fnc.co.uk
Directors: A. Milton (MD), R. Burge (Co Sec)
Ultimate Holding Company: BABCOCK INTERNATIONAL GROUP PLC
Immediate Holding Company: FNC LIMITED
Registration no: 03277619 **Date established:** 1996
Turnover: £20m - £50m **No.of Employees:** 1 - 10 **Product Groups:** 44, 54, 80, 84, 85, 86

Farm Supplies Dorking Ltd
Ansell Road, Dorking, RH4 1QW
Tel: 01306-880456 **Fax:** 01306-876869
E-mail: sales@fslandservices.co.uk
Website: http://www.fslandservices.co.uk
Directors: J. Hall (MD)
Immediate Holding Company: FARM SUPPLIES (DORKING) LIMITED
Registration no: 00598458 **VAT No.:** GB 209 7075 58
Date established: 1958 **Turnover:** £500,000 - £1m
No.of Employees: 1 - 10 **Product Groups:** 22, 24, 26, 35, 40, 41, 48, 63, 66, 67

Date of Accounts	Dec 11	Dec 10	Dec 09
Working Capital	21	27	27
Fixed Assets	194	195	196
Current Assets	140	143	131

Flo-Code UK Ltd
Gable End Holmbury St Mary Holmbury St Mary, Dorking, RH5 6LQ
Tel: 01306-731863 **Fax:** 01306-731864
E-mail: sales@flo-codeuk.com
Website: http://www.flo-codeuk.com
Directors: B. Steele Turner (Dir), K. Steele Turner (Co Sec)
Immediate Holding Company: FLO-CODE (UK) LIMITED
Registration no: 05011555 **Date established:** 2004
No.of Employees: 1 - 10 **Product Groups:** 27

Date of Accounts	Jan 11	Jan 10	Jan 09
Working Capital	42	39	31
Fixed Assets	2	2	2
Current Assets	67	63	50

Fountain Softeners
Surrey Hills Business Park Sheephouse Lane, Wotton, Dorking, RH5 6QT
Tel: 01306-889090 **Fax:** 01306-889977
E-mail: sales@fountainsofteners.co.uk
Website: http://www.fountainsofteners.co.uk
Directors: A. Rolland (Dir)
Date established: 2004 **No.of Employees:** 1 - 10 **Product Groups:** 38, 42

Henri Picard & Frere
8 Pixham Court Pixham Lane, Dorking, RH4 1PG
Tel: 020-8949 3142 **Fax:** 020-8949 3142
E-mail: sales@picard.co.uk
Website: http://www.picard.co.uk
Directors: A. Hill (MD)
Registration no: 00645590 **VAT No.:** GB 243 4174 79
Turnover: £500,000 - £1m **No.of Employees:** 1 - 10 **Product Groups:** 30, 31, 33, 35, 36, 37, 38, 42, 45, 46, 47, 48, 49, 67

Date of Accounts	Dec 08	Dec 07	Dec 06
Working Capital	58	57	57
Fixed Assets	4	5	5
Current Assets	64	67	64
Current Liabilities	7	10	7
Total Share Capital	52	52	52

C & D King Ltd
15 Havenbury Industrial Estate, Dorking, RH4 1ES
Tel: 01306-876767 **Fax:** 01306-887479
E-mail: kings@lineone.net
Website: http://www.moleskins.co.uk
Directors: King (Dir)
Ultimate Holding Company: CITYREALM LIMITED
Immediate Holding Company: C & D KING LIMITED
Registration no: 01774732 **Date established:** 1983
No.of Employees: 1 - 10 **Product Groups:** 24

Date of Accounts	Mar 11	Mar 10	Mar 09
Working Capital	251	185	119
Fixed Assets	1	2	3
Current Assets	308	321	173

Komori Currency Technology
Unit 2 & 3 Tillingbourne Court Dorking Business Park, Dorking, RH4 1HJ
Tel: 01306-876331 **Fax:** 01306-876380
E-mail: info@komoricurrency.co.uk
Website: http://www.komoricurrency.co.uk
Directors: B. Flutter (MD)
Ultimate Holding Company: KOMORI CORPORATION (JAPAN)
Immediate Holding Company: KOMORI U.K. LIMITED
Registration no: 01792090 **Date established:** 1984
Turnover: £20m - £50m **No.of Employees:** 1 - 10 **Product Groups:** 44

Date of Accounts	Mar 10	Mar 09	Mar 08
Sales Turnover	22m	40m	50m
Pre Tax Profit/Loss	751	1m	3m
Working Capital	7m	7m	6m
Fixed Assets	455	775	880
Current Assets	21m	32m	32m
Current Liabilities	6m	5m	5m

Kuoni Travel Ltd
Kuoni House Deepdene Avenue, Dorking, RH5 4AZ
Tel: 01306-740888 **Fax:** 01306-744288
E-mail: holidays@kuoni.co.uk
Website: http://www.kuoni.co.uk
Bank(s): Natwest Bank, Dorking, Surrey
Directors: D. Jones (MD), M. Norman (Fin)
Managers: N. Wilkinson (Mktg Serv Mgr), J. Day (Sales Admin), P. Beagles (Tech Serv Mgr), L. Ellett-carty (Personnel)
Ultimate Holding Company: KUONI TRAVEL HOLDINGS LTD (SWITZERLAND)
Immediate Holding Company: KUONI TRAVEL LIMITED
Registration no: 00395623 **VAT No.:** GB 239 2614 58
Date established: 1945 **Turnover:** £250m - £500m
No.of Employees: 251 - 500 **Product Groups:** 69

Date of Accounts	Dec 11	Dec 10	Dec 09
Sales Turnover	300m	315m	327m
Pre Tax Profit/Loss	-6m	-15m	-7m
Working Capital	-24m	-24m	-24m
Fixed Assets	42m	50m	67m
Current Assets	107m	117m	63m
Current Liabilities	56m	56m	58m

M B Production Engineering Ltd
Sturtwood Farm Partridge Lane Newdigate, Dorking, RH5 5EE
Tel: 01306-631113 **Fax:** 01306-631114
E-mail: michaelbuttle@btconnect.com
Website: http://www.mbengineering.co.uk
Directors: M. Buttle (Prop)
Immediate Holding Company: M.B. (PRODUCTION) ENGINEERING LIMITED
Registration no: 02923006 **Date established:** 1994
Turnover: Up to £250,000 **No.of Employees:** 1 - 10 **Product Groups:** 34, 35, 48, 49, 66

Date of Accounts	Apr 11	Apr 10	Apr 09
Working Capital	3	4	18
Fixed Assets	13	12	8
Current Assets	28	30	68
Current Liabilities	5	11	27

Newdigate Veterinary Surgery
Cudworth Lane Newdigate, Dorking, RH5 5BH
Tel: 01306-631012 **Fax:** 01306-631013
E-mail: admin@baringsfield.co.uk
Website: http://www.baringsfield.co.uk
Directors: P. Edmondson (Prop)
Immediate Holding Company: THE JIREH TRUST
Registration no: 02492985 **Date established:** 1990
Turnover: Up to £250,000 **No.of Employees:** 1 - 10 **Product Groups:** 38, 67

David Owens
The Courtyard Dunley Hill Ranmore Common Road, Dorking, RH5 6SX
Tel: 01483-285556 **Fax:** 01483-285556
E-mail: info@ornamentalblacksmith.co.uk
Website: http://www.ornamentalblacksmith.co.uk
Directors: D. Owens (Prop)
Ultimate Holding Company: CONTRACTING SOLUTIONS (NEW MEDIA) LIMITED
Immediate Holding Company: NETPRACTISE LIMITED
Registration no: 05134877 **Date established:** 2004
Turnover: £500,000 - £1m **No.of Employees:** 1 - 10 **Product Groups:** 26, 35

Date of Accounts	Jan 10	Jan 09	Jan 08
Sales Turnover	N/A	N/A	888
Pre Tax Profit/Loss	N/A	N/A	-1
Working Capital	113	138	98
Fixed Assets	9	12	9
Current Assets	896	915	449
Current Liabilities	N/A	N/A	169

Power & Water Systems Consultants Ltd
1 Paper Mews 330 High Street, Dorking, RH4 2TU
Tel: 07980-985170 **Fax:** 01491-410780
E-mail: info@pwsc.co.uk
Website: http://www.pwsc.co.uk
Directors: L. Wyatt (Fin), T. Wyatt (MD)
Registration no: 02043425 **Date established:** 1986
Turnover: Up to £250,000 **No.of Employees:** 1 - 10 **Product Groups:** 38, 85

Date of Accounts	Mar 07	Mar 06
Working Capital	-9	-2
Fixed Assets	3	2
Current Assets	2	2
Current Liabilities	10	4
Total Share Capital	2	2

Prosips Ltd
Greens Farm Rusper Road, Newdigate, Dorking, RH5 5BE
Tel: 01306-631488 **Fax:** 01306-631492
E-mail: nick@prosips.com
Website: http://www.prosips.com
Product Groups: 30, 33, 35, 39, 42, 43, 45, 46, 47, 67

Date of Accounts	Jun 07	Jun 06
Working Capital	10	18
Fixed Assets	N/A	4
Current Assets	15	26
Current Liabilities	5	7
Total Share Capital	10	10

Safe Security Services Ltd
The Atrium Curtis Road, Dorking, RH4 1XA
Tel: 0845-8382448 **Fax:** 0845-8382449
E-mail: info@safesecurityservices.co.uk
Website: http://www.safesecurityservices.co.uk
Managers: C. Waylett (Mktg Serv Mgr), C. Winchester (Ops Mgr)
Registration no: 05055106 **Turnover:** £1m - £2m
No.of Employees: 11 - 20 **Product Groups:** 36

Date of Accounts	Jul 08	Jul 07	Jul 06
Working Capital	96	36	52
Fixed Assets	19	20	2
Current Assets	238	127	87
Current Liabilities	142	91	35

Symbiant Consulting Limited
P.O. Box 563, Dorking, RH5 4XX
Tel: 01306-621036 **Fax:** 020-8338 0728
E-mail: sales@chamoisdirect.com
Website: http://www.symbiantconsulting.co.uk
Product Groups: 22, 23, 66

Robert Wynter & Partners
Abinger House Surrey Hills Business Park, Wotton, Dorking, RH5 6QT
Tel: 01306-879875 **Fax:** 01306-741799
E-mail: wyntereast@aol.com
Directors: B. Wynter (Snr Part)
Date established: 1998 **No.of Employees:** 1 - 10 **Product Groups:** 35

Date of Accounts	Mar 10	Mar 09	Mar 08
Working Capital	108	120	148
Fixed Assets	14	14	16
Current Assets	177	162	199
Current Liabilities	11	24	42

East Molesey

Graham Builders Merchants Ltd
160b Walton Road, East Molesey, KT8 0HP
Tel: 020-8941 6181 **Fax:** 020-8941 4169
Website: http://www.graham-group.co.uk
Managers: D. Loman (Mgr)
Ultimate Holding Company: COMPAGNIE DE SAINT GOBAIN (FRANCE)
Immediate Holding Company: GRAHAM BUILDERS MERCHANTS LIMITED
Registration no: 00066738 **Date established:** 2000
No.of Employees: 1 - 10 **Product Groups:** 66

Date of Accounts	Dec 08
Working Capital	8
Current Assets	8

Medicom UK Ltd
Thames Side House Hurst Road, East Molesey, KT8 9EY
Tel: 020-8481 8100 **Fax:** 020-8481 8105
E-mail: enquiries@medicomgroup.com
Website: http://www.medicomgroup.com
Bank(s): The Royal Bank of Scotland
Directors: G. Hayburn (MD)
Ultimate Holding Company: MEDICOM INTERNATIONAL LIMITED
Immediate Holding Company: MEDICOM (UK) LIMITED
Registration no: 01527313 **Date established:** 1980 **Turnover:** £5m - £10m
No.of Employees: 11 - 20 **Product Groups:** 28

Date of Accounts	Dec 11	Dec 10	Dec 09
Sales Turnover	8m	4m	3m
Pre Tax Profit/Loss	2m	822	551
Working Capital	2m	825	631
Fixed Assets	72	17	19
Current Assets	4m	2m	1m
Current Liabilities	2m	555	521

Planet Television UK & Ireland Ltd
7 Feltham Avenue, East Molesey, KT8 9BJ
Tel: 020-8974 6050
E-mail: media@planet-television.com
Website: http://www.planet-television.com
Directors: P. Kirby (MD)
Immediate Holding Company: PLANET VIDEO PRODUCTIONS LIMITED
Registration no: 02196490 **Date established:** 1987
No.of Employees: 21 - 50 **Product Groups:** 37, 44, 81, 89

Date of Accounts	Mar 12	Mar 11	Mar 10
Sales Turnover	4	6	19
Pre Tax Profit/Loss	-4	-12	-29
Working Capital	-4	N/A	143
Fixed Assets	337	337	2
Current Assets	6	7	151

Pyramid Engineering & Manufacturing Co. Ltd
8 Palace Road, East Molesey, KT8 9DL
Tel: 020-8979 4814 **Fax:** 020- 89794814
Directors: D. Meyer (I.T. Dir), M. Meyer (Fin)
Immediate Holding Company: PYRAMID ENGINEERING AND MANUFACTURING COMPANY LIMITED
Registration no: 00718660 **Date established:** 1962
Turnover: Up to £250,000 **No.of Employees:** 1 - 10 **Product Groups:** 42

Date of Accounts	May 07	May 06
Working Capital	8	10
Fixed Assets	N/A	1
Current Assets	21	22
Current Liabilities	13	12
Total Share Capital	3	3

Stokvis Energy Systems
96r Walton Road, East Molesey, KT8 0DL
Tel: 020-8783 3050 **Fax:** 08707-707767
E-mail: info@stokvisboilers.com
Website: http://www.stokvisboilers.com
Managers: A. Dimbleby
No.of Employees: 1 - 10 **Product Groups:** 40, 66, 67

Egham

Air Action Couriers
International Distribution Centre Crabtree Road, Thorpe, Egham, TW20 8RS
Tel: 01784-222880 **Fax:** 01784-222881
E-mail: des@airaction.com
Website: http://www.airaction.com
Bank(s): National Westminster Bank Plc
Directors: D. Flitterman (Fin), D. Lyons (MD)
Managers: D. Still (Export Sales Mg), S. Mills (I.T. Exec)
Ultimate Holding Company: C J Bourne (Asset Management) Ltd
Immediate Holding Company: Air Action Ltd
Registration no: 01347436 **VAT No.:** GB 222 3236 11
Date established: 1996 **Turnover:** £2m - £5m **No.of Employees:** 21 - 50
Product Groups: 76

Brakes
Alpha Way Thorpe Industrial Park, Thorpe, Egham, TW20 8RT
Tel: 01784-485050 **Fax:** 01784-485040
Website: http://www.brake.co.uk
Bank(s): The Royal Bank of Scotland

see next page

***Brakes** - Cont'd*

Managers: J. Smith (Chief Mgr)
Ultimate Holding Company: CUCINA LUX INVESTMENTS LTD
Immediate Holding Company: BRAKE BROS LTD
Registration no: 05532896 **VAT No.:** GB 268 5442 31
Date established: 1873 **Turnover:** £10m - £20m
No.of Employees: 101 - 250 **Product Groups:** 62

Bunce Sheet Metal Work Services

Unit B5 Crabtree Road Thorpe Industrial Estate, Egham, TW20 8RN
Tel: 01784-433556 **Fax:** 01784-433555
E-mail: sales@buncesheetmetal.co.uk
Website: http://www.buncesheetmetal.co.uk
Directors: W. Bunce (Snr Part)
Ultimate Holding Company: RAHMQVIST INTERNATIONAL SA (LUXEMBOURG)
Immediate Holding Company: RAHMQVIST UK LTD.
Registration no: 01243491 **Date established:** 1976 **Turnover:** £2m - £5m
No.of Employees: 1 - 10 **Product Groups:** 48

Date of Accounts	Dec 11	Dec 10	Dec 09
Sales Turnover	2m	2m	2m
Pre Tax Profit/Loss	-82	-73	-51
Working Capital	139	218	286
Fixed Assets	2	6	6
Current Assets	567	519	587
Current Liabilities	243	217	211

C D N Consular Services Ltd

Runnymede House 96-97 High Street, Egham, TW20 9HQ
Tel: 01784-221720 **Fax:** 01784-250945
E-mail: sales@cdn-consular.co.uk
Website: http://www.cdn.co.uk
Directors: N. Beard (Ptnr)
Managers: S. Sturcke
Immediate Holding Company: CDN CONSULAR SERVICES LIMITED
Registration no: 07147017 **Date established:** 2010 **Turnover:** £2m - £5m
No.of Employees: 21 - 50 **Product Groups:** 80

Date of Accounts	Jun 11
Working Capital	-2m
Fixed Assets	2m
Current Assets	810

C H G Meridian UK Ltd

Unit 2 Alpha Way, Thorpe Industrial Estate, Egham, TW20 8RZ
Tel: 01784-470701 **Fax:** 01784-439183
E-mail: stefan.ertel@chg-meridian.com
Website: http://www.chg-meridian.com
Directors: D. Harmon (Dir), P. McCord (Dir), S. Ertel (Sales), S. Swiatek (Sales), F. Emmery (Fin), T. Bolton (Dir), B. Ofria (Dir)
Ultimate Holding Company: CHG-MERIDIAN DEUTSCHE COMPUTER LEASING AG (GERMANY)
Immediate Holding Company: CHG-MERIDIAN (HOLDINGS) UK LIMITED
Registration no: 04040776 **Date established:** 2000 **Turnover:** £5m - £10m
No.of Employees: 21 - 50 **Product Groups:** 44

Date of Accounts	Dec 10	Dec 09	Dec 08
Fixed Assets	25m	25m	22m

Cardiff Property plc

56 Station Road, Egham, TW20 9LF
Tel: 01784-437444 **Fax:** 01784-439157
E-mail: webmaster@cardiff-property.com
Website: http://www.cardiff-property.com
Directors: R. Wollenberg (Ch), D. Whitaker (Fin), J. Wollenberg (MD)
Managers: A. Anderson (Chief Buyer)
Ultimate Holding Company: CARDIFF PROPERTY PUBLIC LIMITED COMPANY(THE)
Immediate Holding Company: CARDIFF PROPERTY PUBLIC LIMITED COMPANY(THE)
Registration no: 00022705 **Date established:** 1986
Turnover: £500,000 - £1m **No.of Employees:** 1 - 10 **Product Groups:** 80

Date of Accounts	Sep 11	Sep 10	Sep 09
Sales Turnover	546	793	1m
Pre Tax Profit/Loss	788	500	-656
Working Capital	5m	5m	6m
Fixed Assets	11m	10m	11m
Current Assets	6m	6m	7m
Current Liabilities	522	585	689

Cemex UK Operations Ltd

Coldharbour Lane Thorpe, Egham, TW20 8TD
Tel: 01932-568833 **Fax:** 01388-450056
E-mail: john.metcalfe@cemex.co.uk
Website: http://www.cemex.co.uk
Directors: J. Metcalfe (MD)
Managers: J. Metcalf (Comm)
Immediate Holding Company: R M C Group P.L.C.
Registration no: 00658390 **Turnover:** Up to £250,000
No.of Employees: 1 - 10 **Product Groups:** 37

Cemex UK Operations Limited

CEMEX House Coldharbour Lane, Thorpe, Egham, TW20 8TD
Tel: 01932-568833 **Fax:** 0115-943 1966
E-mail: webmanager.hbm@cemex.co.uk
Website: http://www.cemex.co.uk
Bank(s): National Westminster, London
Directors: F. Parker (MD)
Managers: T. Charles (Sales Prom Mgr)
Immediate Holding Company: RMC P.L.C.
Registration no: 00658390 **Turnover:** £20m - £50m
No.of Employees: 11 - 20 **Product Groups:** 33, 52

Donland Engineering Ltd

Foundation House Stoneylands Road, Egham, TW20 9QR
Tel: 01784-436151 **Fax:** 01784-436038
E-mail: e@donlandeng.co.uk
Bank(s): HSBC
Directors: J. Johnson (Dir), I. Johnson (MD)
Immediate Holding Company: DONLAND ENGINEERING(SOUTHERN)LIMITED
Registration no: 01163263 **VAT No.:** 211 5389 86 **Date established:** 1974
Turnover: £2m - £5m **No.of Employees:** 21 - 50 **Product Groups:** 52

Date of Accounts	Dec 11	Dec 10	Dec 09
Working Capital	490	478	472
Fixed Assets	233	233	233
Current Assets	501	494	528

Dropsa UK Ltd

6 Egham Business Village Crabtree Road, Egham, TW20 8RB
Tel: 01784-431177 **Fax:** 01784-438598
E-mail: sales@dropsa.com
Website: http://www.dropsa.com
Directors: S. Divisi (MD)
Immediate Holding Company: DROPSA UK LIMITED
Registration no: 01576128 **VAT No.:** GB 340 7495 54
Date established: 1981 **Turnover:** £1m - £2m **No.of Employees:** 1 - 10
Product Groups: 36, 38, 40, 45, 49, 66, 67, 84

Date of Accounts	Dec 11	Dec 10	Dec 09
Working Capital	29	123	190
Fixed Assets	341	350	338
Current Assets	869	785	423

Freeway Transport

Unit 5 8 Delta Way Thorpe Industrial Estate, Egham, TW20 8RN
Tel: 01784-473000 **Fax:** 01784- 473000
Website: http://www.freewaytransport.net
Directors: S. Wilbraham (Co Sec)
Ultimate Holding Company: RAHMQVIST INTERNATIONAL SA (LUXEMBOURG)
Immediate Holding Company: RAHMQVIST UK LTD.
Registration no: 01243491 **Date established:** 1976 **Turnover:** £2m - £5m
No.of Employees: 1001 - 1500 **Product Groups:** 26, 77

Date of Accounts	Dec 11	Dec 10	Dec 09
Sales Turnover	2m	2m	2m
Pre Tax Profit/Loss	-82	-73	-51
Working Capital	139	218	286
Fixed Assets	2	6	6
Current Assets	567	519	587
Current Liabilities	243	217	211

Genius Reserve Executive Search Ltd

Bank House 81 St Judes Road, Englefield Green, Egham, TW20 0DF
Tel: 01784-439930 **Fax:** 01784-439931
E-mail: info@geniusreserve.com
Website: http://www.geniusreserve.com
Managers: P. Fourie
Immediate Holding Company: GENIUS RESERVE LIMITED
Registration no: 04448955 **Date established:** 2002
Turnover: £500,000 - £1m **No.of Employees:** 1 - 10 **Product Groups:** 80

Date of Accounts	May 11	May 10	May 09
Sales Turnover	751	376	575
Pre Tax Profit/Loss	278	-6	220
Working Capital	316	201	262
Fixed Assets	14	22	30
Current Assets	443	223	309
Current Liabilities	124	18	45

Hamilton Sundstrand International Corporation

Kingfisher House 160-162 High Street, Egham, TW20 9HP
Tel: 01784-414600 **Fax:** 01784-438092
E-mail: alison.doran@hs.utc.com
Website: http://www.hamiltonsundstrand.com
Directors: M. Ryan (Dir)
Managers: B. Worsham ()
Ultimate Holding Company: United Technologies Corporation (USA)
Immediate Holding Company: Hamilton Sundstrand (USA)
Registration no: FC009425 **Turnover:** Over £1,000m
No.of Employees: 1 - 10 **Product Groups:** 38, 39, 40

Kerry Foods Ltd

Thorpe Lea Manor Thorpe Lea Road, Egham, TW20 8HY
Tel: 01784-430777 **Fax:** 01784-479597
E-mail: enquiries@kerryfoods.co.uk
Website: http://www.kerrygroup.com
Bank(s): National Westminster Bank Plc
Directors: B. Mehigan (Fin)
Ultimate Holding Company: KERRY GROUP PUBLIC LIMITED COMPANY
Immediate Holding Company: KERRY HOLDINGS (U.K.) LIMITED
Registration no: 01663249 **VAT No.:** GB 635 8381 17
Date established: 1982 **Turnover:** £250m - £500m
No.of Employees: 101 - 250 **Product Groups:** 20, 62

Date of Accounts	Dec 11	Dec 10	Dec 09
Pre Tax Profit/Loss	30m	-4m	-6m
Working Capital	-8m	-56m	-46m
Fixed Assets	252m	252m	252m
Current Assets	2	2	2m
Current Liabilities	1m	1m	921

Mega-Quartz UK Ltd

25 Boshers Gardens, Egham, TW20 9NZ
Tel: 01784-437072 **Fax:** 01784-435793
E-mail: moundn@aol.com
Website: http://www.megaquartz.co.uk
Directors: N. Mound (MD), J. Barnes (Fin)
Immediate Holding Company: MEGA-QUARTZ UK LTD
Registration no: 04763012 **VAT No.:** GB 382 4871 27
Date established: 2003 **Turnover:** Up to £250,000
No.of Employees: 1 - 10 **Product Groups:** 38, 49

Date of Accounts	Jul 11	Jul 10	Jul 09
Working Capital	84	60	45
Fixed Assets	1	1	2
Current Assets	127	91	71

Moore Bowman Services Ltd

2 Glebe Road, Egham, TW20 8BT
Tel: 01784-452387 **Fax:** 01784-458500
Directors: A. Bennett (Fin), R. Moore (MD)
Immediate Holding Company: MOORE BOWMAN SERVICES LIMITED
Registration no: 00968969 **Date established:** 1969
Turnover: Up to £250,000 **No.of Employees:** 1 - 10 **Product Groups:** 46

Date of Accounts	Mar 11	Mar 10	Mar 09
Working Capital	-128	-122	-117
Fixed Assets	50	51	52
Current Assets	51	40	27

October21

Ashling Green Road, Thorpe, Egham, TW20 8QT
Tel: 08448-841921 **Fax:** 0870-896 5521
E-mail: design@october21.net
Website: http://www.october21.net
Directors: S. Harries (Dir)
Immediate Holding Company: OCTOBER 21 LTD
Registration no: 06094323 **Date established:** 2007
Turnover: Up to £250,000 **No.of Employees:** 1 - 10 **Product Groups:** 81

Date of Accounts	Mar 11	Mar 10	Mar 09
Working Capital	-5	1	9
Fixed Assets	1	1	2
Current Assets	17	24	25

Otto Bock Healthcare plc

32 Parsonage Road Englefield Green, Egham, TW20 0LD
Tel: 01784-744900 **Fax:** 01784-744901
E-mail: philip.yates@ottobock.com
Website: http://www.ottobock.co.uk
Bank(s): Barclays
Directors: A. Maclean (Sales & Mktg), G. Bates (Fin), P. Yates (MD)
Managers: G. Norris (Mktg Serv Mgr), N. Ward (Personnel)
Ultimate Holding Company: OTTO BOCK HOLDING GMBH & CO KG (GERMANY)
Immediate Holding Company: OTTO BOCK HEALTHCARE PLC
Registration no: 01271967 **VAT No.:** GB 228 4212 81
Date established: 1976 **Turnover:** £20m - £50m
No.of Employees: 101 - 250 **Product Groups:** 38

Date of Accounts	Dec 11	Dec 10	Dec 09
Sales Turnover	20m	21m	22m
Pre Tax Profit/Loss	1m	913	856
Working Capital	3m	2m	2m
Fixed Assets	2m	2m	3m
Current Assets	8m	7m	7m
Current Liabilities	2m	2m	1m

Rahmqvist UK Ltd

Crabtree Road Thorpe Industrial Estate, Egham, TW20 8RN
Tel: 01784-439888 **Fax:** 01784-471419
E-mail: tony.cracknell@rahmqvist.com
Website: http://www.rahmqvist.com
Directors: T. Cracknell (Mkt Research)
Ultimate Holding Company: RAHMQVIST INTERNATIONAL SA (LUXEMBOURG)
Immediate Holding Company: RAHMQVIST UK LTD.
Registration no: 01243491 **VAT No.:** GB 335 4214 80
Date established: 1976 **Turnover:** £2m - £5m **No.of Employees:** 1 - 10
Product Groups: 27

Date of Accounts	Dec 11	Dec 10	Dec 09
Sales Turnover	2m	2m	2m
Pre Tax Profit/Loss	-82	-73	-51
Working Capital	139	218	286
Fixed Assets	2	6	6
Current Assets	567	519	587
Current Liabilities	243	217	211

Rock-It Cargo Ltd

Thorpe Industrial Estate Delta Way, Egham, TW20 8RX
Tel: 01784-431301 **Fax:** 01784-471052
E-mail: chrisw@rock-it.co.uk
Website: http://www.rock-itcargo.co.uk
Directors: C. Wright (MD), J. Mcnally (Co Sec), I. Haynes (Dir)
Managers: A. Durrant (Chief Mgr), C. Wright (Sales Prom Mgr)
Ultimate Holding Company: CALERA LLC (USA)
Immediate Holding Company: ROCK-IT CARGO LIMITED
Registration no: 01414774 **VAT No.:** GB 413 4140 04
Date established: 1979 **Turnover:** £10m - £20m
No.of Employees: 21 - 50 **Product Groups:** 76

Date of Accounts	Dec 10	Dec 09	Dec 08
Sales Turnover	15m	12m	N/A
Pre Tax Profit/Loss	391	504	2m
Working Capital	981	4m	4m
Fixed Assets	4m	29	43
Current Assets	3m	6m	7m
Current Liabilities	603	486	834

Royal Holloway & Bedford New College

Egham Hill, Egham, TW20 0EX
Tel: 01784-434455 **Fax:** 01784-437520
E-mail: tony.greenwood@rhul.ac.uk
Website: http://www.rhul.ac.uk
Bank(s): National Westminster Bank Plc
Directors: T. Greenwood (Dir), L. Gibbs (Tech Serv), J. Strudley (Co Sec), G. Robinson (Fin), J. Grimmer (Pers)
Immediate Holding Company: ROYAL HOLLOWAY ENTERPRISE LIMITED
Registration no: 02667639 **Date established:** 1991
Turnover: £250,000 - £500,000 **No.of Employees:** 501 - 1000
Product Groups: 54, 81, 84, 85, 86

Date of Accounts	Jul 11	Jul 10	Jul 09
Sales Turnover	317	552	389
Pre Tax Profit/Loss	16	28	20
Working Capital	50	37	16
Current Assets	280	368	342
Current Liabilities	24	38	36

S M P Playgrounds

Ten Acre Lane, Egham, TW20 8RJ
Tel: 01784-489100 **Fax:** 01784-431067
E-mail: sales@smp.co.uk
Website: http://www.smp.co.uk
Bank(s): HSBC
Directors: S. Sylvester (MD)
Ultimate Holding Company: APOLLO INVESTMENT CORPORATION (UNITED STATES)
Immediate Holding Company: S.M.P. (PLAYGROUNDS) LIMITED
Registration no: 00908021 **VAT No.:** GB 207 8538 51
Date established: 1967 **Turnover:** £10m - £20m
No.of Employees: 21 - 50 **Product Groups:** 26, 29, 49, 65

Date of Accounts	Dec 11	Dec 10	Dec 09
Sales Turnover	13m	12m	11m
Pre Tax Profit/Loss	1m	1m	575
Working Capital	3m	3m	9m
Fixed Assets	109	156	144
Current Assets	5m	4m	10m
Current Liabilities	1m	1m	841

Seabourne Forwarding Group

International Distribution Centre Crabtree Road, Thorpe, Egham, TW20 8RS
Tel: 01784-222800 **Fax:** 01784-222801
E-mail: info@seabourne-group.com
Website: http://www.seabourne-group.com
Directors: D. Flitterman (MD), D. Hayes (Co Sec)
Ultimate Holding Company: C J BOURNE (ASSET MANAGEMENT) LIMITED
Immediate Holding Company: CHACALLI-DE DECKER LTD.
Registration no: 00864285 **Date established:** 1996 **Turnover:** £1m - £2m
No.of Employees: 51 - 100 **Product Groups:** 79

Date of Accounts	Dec 11	Dec 10	Jun 09
Pre Tax Profit/Loss	N/A	N/A	-35
Working Capital	-126	-122	-181

Current Assets	44	36	32
Current Liabilities	N/A	N/A	5

Spectris plc
35-51 Station Road, Egham, TW20 9NP
Tel: 01784-470470 **Fax:** 01784-470848
E-mail: headoffice@spectris.com
Website: http://www.spectris.com
Bank(s): National Westminster Bank Plc
Directors: R. Stephens (Co Sec)
Managers: C. Watson, J. Ibison, R. Martin, S. Wadham (Commun Mgr)
Immediate Holding Company: SPECTRIS PLC
Registration no: 02025003 **Date established:** 1986
Turnover: Over £1,000m **No.of Employees:** 21 - 50 **Product Groups:** 82

Date of Accounts	Dec 11	Dec 10	Dec 09
Sales Turnover	1106m	902m	787m
Pre Tax Profit/Loss	166m	120m	54m
Working Capital	134m	117m	52m
Fixed Assets	924m	582m	530m
Current Assets	439m	391m	313m
Current Liabilities	210m	272m	203m

Thames Wire Co.
Unit 1 Omega Way, Egham, TW20 8RD
Tel: 01784-479949
Website: http://www.thameswire.co.uk
Directors: N. Duke (MD), Y. Duke (Fin)
No.of Employees: 11 - 20 **Product Groups:** 35, 48

Verbatim Ltd
Prestige House 23-26 High Street, Egham, TW20 9DU
Tel: 01784-439781 **Fax:** 01784-470760
E-mail: info@verbatim-europe.com
Website: http://www.verbatim-europe.com
Managers: M. Oreilly
Ultimate Holding Company: MITSUBISHI CHEMICAL HOLDINGS CORPORATION (JAPAN)
Immediate Holding Company: VERBATIM LIMITED
Registration no: 01669496 **Date established:** 1982
Turnover: £250m - £500m **No.of Employees:** 21 - 50
Product Groups: 37, 44, 67

Visual-q Ltd
The Corner House Willow Walk, Englefield Green, Egham, TW20 0DQ
Tel: 01784-477780
E-mail: tgates@visual-q.co.uk
Website: http://www.visual-q.co.uk
Directors: C. Gates (Fin), T. Gates (Dir), T. Gates (MD)
Immediate Holding Company: VISUAL-Q LIMITED
Registration no: 04510103 **Date established:** 2002
Turnover: £250,000 - £500,000 **No.of Employees:** 1 - 10
Product Groups: 44, 67

Epsom

Abgene Limited
Abgene House Blenheim Road, Epsom, KT19 9AP
Tel: 01372-723456 **Fax:** 01372-741414
E-mail: sales@abgene.com
Website: http://www.abgene.com
Directors: G. Cerroni (MD), J. Kennedy (Fin)
Managers: P. Blazeby (Lab Mgr)
Ultimate Holding Company: MAXINGVEST AG (GERMANY)
Registration no: 05556241 **Date established:** 2000
Turnover: £50m - £75m **No.of Employees:** 1 - 10 **Product Groups:** 30

Acre (Air Conditioning & Refrigeration) Ltd
Suite 120 Reaver House 12 East Street, Epsom, KT17 1HX
Tel: 0800-9709122
E-mail: info@acresolutions.co.uk
Website: http://www.acresolutions.co.uk
Product Groups: 37, 38, 39, 40, 52, 66, 83, 84

All Four Seasons Ltd
6 Stoneleigh Park Road, Epsom, KT19 0QT
Tel: 020-8224 6597 **Fax:** 020-8224 6156
E-mail: info@allfourseasons.co.uk
Website: http://www.allfourseasons.co.uk
Directors: A. Skanes (Dir)
Immediate Holding Company: ALL FOUR SEASONS LIMITED
Registration no: 02002724 **Date established:** 1986 **Turnover:** £1m - £2m
No.of Employees: 1 - 10 **Product Groups:** 40, 52, 84

Date of Accounts	Mar 12	Mar 11	Mar 10
Working Capital	-12	7	40
Fixed Assets	21	21	20
Current Assets	154	111	184

Bunzl Catering Supplies Ltd (a division of Bunzl Disposables Europe Ltd)
Epsom Chase 1 Hook Road, Epsom, KT19 8TY
Tel: 01372-736300 **Fax:** 01372-736301
E-mail: reception.epsom@bunzlcatering.co.uk
Website: http://www.bunzlcatering.co.uk
Bank(s): Barclays, 63 Colmore Row, Birmingham
Directors: P. Hussey (Co Sec), A. Mooney (Fin), P. Wilcox (Mkt Research), P. Budge (MD), M. Johnson (MD), R. Abrahams (Purch)
Managers: L. Belcher (Personnel), J. Rogers (Tech Serv Mgr), J. Newell (I.T. Exec)
Ultimate Holding Company: BUNZL PUBLIC LIMITED COMPANY
Immediate Holding Company: CENTRAL CATERING SUPPLIES LIMITED
Registration no: 03888254 **Date established:** 1999
Turnover: Over £1,000m **No.of Employees:** 51 - 100 **Product Groups:** 20, 24, 27, 29, 30, 40, 49

Bytes Software Services
15-17 Chessington Road Ewell, Epsom, KT17 1TS
Tel: 020-8786 1500 **Fax:** 020-8393 6622
E-mail: tellmemore@bytes.co.uk
Website: http://www.bytes.co.uk
Directors: K. Richardson (Fin), N. Murphy (MD)
Ultimate Holding Company: ALLIED ELECTRONICS CORPORATION LTD (SOUTH AFRICA)
Immediate Holding Company: BYTES SOFTWARE SERVICES LIMITED
Registration no: 01616977 **VAT No.:** GB 367 3987 94
Date established: 1982 **Turnover:** £125m - £250m
No.of Employees: 101 - 250 **Product Groups:** 44

Date of Accounts	Feb 08	Feb 11	Feb 10
Sales Turnover	111m	148m	129m
Pre Tax Profit/Loss	3m	4m	4m
Working Capital	8m	17m	14m
Fixed Assets	629	379	376
Current Assets	21m	39m	27m
Current Liabilities	8m	13m	7m

Cognex
Unit 7-8 First Quarter Blenheim Road, Epsom, KT19 9QN
Tel: 01372-754100 **Fax:** 01372-754150
E-mail: sales@cognex.co.uk
Website: http://www.cognex.com
Directors: P. Neve (Dir)
Managers: L. Simpson (Public Relation)
Registration no: 07410692 **Date established:** 1998
No.of Employees: 1 - 10 **Product Groups:** 38, 44

Dagenham Motors Ltd
East Street, Epsom, KT17 1HF
Tel: 01372-804000 **Fax:** 01372-804041
E-mail: pete.parker@polar-motor.co.uk
Website: http://www.dagenhammotors.co.uk
Directors: B. Grant (Dir), C. Hayden (Ch), M. Lumbard (Reg Sales)
Managers: P. Parker (Chief Mgr), S. Bigwood (Sales Prom Mgr), S. Thurgood (Serv Mgr)
Ultimate Holding Company: FORD MOTOR COMPANY (USA)
Immediate Holding Company: DAGENHAM MOTORS LIMITED
Registration no: 01560525 **Date established:** 1981
Turnover: £20m - £50m **No.of Employees:** 11 - 20 **Product Groups:** 68

Date of Accounts	Dec 09	Dec 08	Dec 07
Working Capital	20m	20m	20m
Fixed Assets	32	32	32
Current Assets	20m	20m	20m

Epsom Downs Racecourse
Entrance Pavillian Epsom Downs, Epsom, KT18 5LQ
Tel: 01372-726311 **Fax:** 01372-748253
E-mail: epsom@thejockeyclub.co.uk
Website: http://www.epsomdowns.co.uk
Managers: C. Woodcock (Mktg Serv Mgr), P. White (Sales Prom Mgr), C. Beaumont, L. Bulmer (Personnel)
Registration no: 00868241 **VAT No.:** GB 629 9719 81
Turnover: £10m - £20m **No.of Employees:** 21 - 50 **Product Groups:** 69

Epsom Quality Line
Roy Richmond Way, Epsom, KT19 9AF
Tel: 01372-731703 **Fax:** 01372-731740
E-mail: steve.whiteway@epsomcoaches.com
Website: http://www.epsomcoaches.com
Bank(s): Barclays
Directors: N. Mandvia (Fin)
Managers: G. Hughes (Mktg Serv Mgr), J. Ball (Personnel), J. Ball (Mgr)
Immediate Holding Company: H.R. RICHMOND LIMITED
Registration no: 00281992 **VAT No.:** GB 608 9390 14
Date established: 1933 **Turnover:** £2m - £5m
No.of Employees: 101 - 250 **Product Groups:** 69, 72

Date of Accounts	Oct 11	Oct 10	Oct 09
Sales Turnover	16m	14m	14m
Pre Tax Profit/Loss	251	-180	951
Working Capital	-2m	-1m	-441
Fixed Assets	8m	7m	7m
Current Assets	1m	1m	2m
Current Liabilities	850	805	1m

Esher Scaffolding
19 Trotter Way, Epsom, KT19 7EW
Tel: 020-8408 0851
Managers: F. Withers (Mgr)
No.of Employees: 1 - 10 **Product Groups:** 35, 48, 52, 66

Flairlight
12 Hillcrest Close, Epsom, KT18 5JY
Tel: 01372-807661 **Fax:** 01372-807660
E-mail: mike@flairlight.co.uk
Website: http://www.flairlight.co.uk
Directors: M. Eddowes (MD)
Registration no: 05392140 **Turnover:** £250,000 - £500,000
No.of Employees: 1 - 10 **Product Groups:** 38, 67, 84

Date of Accounts	Mar 08	Mar 07	Mar 06
Working Capital	61	49	8
Fixed Assets	4	5	4
Current Assets	185	165	144
Current Liabilities	124	117	136

National Counties Building Society
30 Church Street, Epsom, KT17 4NL
Tel: 01372-742211 **Fax:** 01372-745607
E-mail: info@ncbs.co.uk
Website: http://www.ncbs.co.uk
Directors: J. Milton (Grp Chief Exec)
Ultimate Holding Company: NATIONAL COUNTIES BUILDING SOCIETY
Immediate Holding Company: NATIONAL COUNTIES ESTATE AGENTS LIMITED
Registration no: FP021396 **Date established:** 1986 **Turnover:** £5m - £10m
No.of Employees: 51 - 100 **Product Groups:** 82

Date of Accounts	Dec 11	Dec 10	Dec 09
Working Capital	-12	-12	-12

Nationwide Filter Co. Ltd
Unit 16 First Quarter Blenheim Road, Epsom, KT19 9QN
Tel: 01372-728548 **Fax:** 01372-742831
E-mail: info@nationwidefilters.com
Website: http://www.nationwidefilters.com
Directors: R. Cross (MD)
No.of Employees: 1 - 10 **Product Groups:** 38, 42

Date of Accounts	Mar 08	Mar 07	Mar 06
Sales Turnover	4498	4144	3913
Pre Tax Profit/Loss	219	171	140
Working Capital	937	2198	2219
Fixed Assets	156	228	290
Current Assets	3847	3497	5503
Current Liabilities	2910	1300	3284
Total Share Capital	27	2	27
ROCE% (Return on Capital Employed)	20.0	7.1	5.6
ROT% (Return on Turnover)	4.9	4.1	3.6

Nikko Electronics Ltd
358 Kingston Road, Epsom, KT19 0DT
Tel: 020-8393 7774 **Fax:** 020-8393 7395
E-mail: hicham@nikko-electronics.co.uk
Website: http://www.dalbani.co.uk
Directors: H. Dalbani (MD), I. Dalbani (Fin)
Immediate Holding Company: NIKKO ELECTRONICS LTD
Registration no: 01761975 **Date established:** 1983
Turnover: £500,000 - £1m **No.of Employees:** 1 - 10 **Product Groups:** 33, 37

Date of Accounts	Feb 08	Feb 11	Feb 10
Working Capital	103	2	40
Fixed Assets	6	7	5
Current Assets	582	284	284

North East Surrey College Of Technology
Nescot W52 Reigate Road Ewell, Epsom, KT17 3DS
Tel: 020-8394 1731 **Fax:** 020-8394 3030
E-mail: reception@nescot.ac.uk
Website: http://www.nescot.ac.uk
Directors: A. Eatan (Fin), D. Smith (Grp Chief Exec)
Managers: J. Udy (Mktg Serv Mgr), I. Gibins (Tech Serv Mgr), D. Patterson (Personnel)
Immediate Holding Company: NORTH EAST SURREY COLLEGE OF TECHNOLOGY TRUST
Registration no: 02566775 **Date established:** 1990
No.of Employees: 1501 & over **Product Groups:** 86

Date of Accounts	Jul 11	Jul 10	Jul 09
Working Capital	33	33	58
Current Assets	33	33	58

1 Stop Data Ltd
46 High Street Ewell, Epsom, KT17 1RW
Tel: 020-8786 9111 **Fax:** 020-8786 9115
E-mail: info@1stopdata.com
Website: http://www.1stopdata.com
Directors: P. Murphy (MD)
Immediate Holding Company: ONE STOP DATA LIMITED
Registration no: 04176935 **Date established:** 2001
No.of Employees: 11 - 20 **Product Groups:** 81

Date of Accounts	Jun 11	Jun 10	Jun 09
Working Capital	-54	-79	198
Fixed Assets	250	257	11
Current Assets	338	204	398

Reed
57 High Street, Epsom, KT19 8DH
Tel: 01372-743522 **Fax:** 01372-722552
E-mail: epsom.employment@reed.co.uk
Website: http://www.reed.co.uk
Managers: A. Freeman (Mgr)
Ultimate Holding Company: REED GLOBAL LTD (MALTA)
Immediate Holding Company: REED EMPLOYMENT LIMITED
Registration no: 00669854 **Date established:** 1960
Turnover: £250m - £500m **No.of Employees:** 1 - 10 **Product Groups:** 80

Date of Accounts	Jun 11	Jun 10	Dec 07
Sales Turnover	618	450	287m
Pre Tax Profit/Loss	-2m	310	8m
Working Capital	23m	28m	28m
Fixed Assets	31	36	5m
Current Assets	28m	30m	74m
Current Liabilities	37	29	21m

Sale Point Systems
103 Great Tattenhams, Epsom, KT18 5RB
Tel: 01737-355321 **Fax:** 01403-784994
E-mail: sales@salepointsystems.co.uk
Website: http://www.salepointsystems.co.uk
Directors: P. Harper (Prop)
Date established: 1983 **No.of Employees:** 1 - 10 **Product Groups:** 38, 42

Sartorius Ltd
Longmead Business Centre Blenheim Road, Epsom, KT19 9QQ
Tel: 01372-737102 **Fax:** 01372-729927
E-mail: uk.weighing@sartorius.com
Website: http://www.sartorius.com
Directors: T. Richardson (Dir)
Managers: I. Hargrave (Comptroller)
Ultimate Holding Company: SARTORIUS AG (GERMANY)
Immediate Holding Company: SARTORIUS MECHATRONICS UK LIMITED
Registration no: 01126814 **Date established:** 1973 **Turnover:** £5m - £10m
No.of Employees: 51 - 100 **Product Groups:** 38, 67

Date of Accounts	Dec 11	Dec 10	Dec 09
Sales Turnover	8m	9m	8m
Pre Tax Profit/Loss	-128	308	-66
Working Capital	278	2m	1m
Fixed Assets	1m	160	187
Current Assets	2m	3m	3m
Current Liabilities	2m	1m	871

Seeability
1a Hook Road, Epsom, KT19 8FQ
Tel: 01372-755000 **Fax:** 01372-755001
E-mail: enquiries@seeability.org
Website: http://www.seeability.org
Bank(s): Lloyds TSB
Directors: B. Newcombe (Fin), D. Scott-Ralphs (Grp Chief Exec)
Managers: A. Dunbar (Personnel), M. Mannisi (Tech Serv Mgr), J. McGann
Ultimate Holding Company: THE ROYAL SCHOOL FOR THE BLIND
Immediate Holding Company: SEE-ABILITY LIMITED
Registration no: 02780575 **VAT No.:** GB 235 5661 58
Date established: 1993 **No.of Employees:** 21 - 50 **Product Groups:** 88

Skyscrapers UK Ltd
81 Cheam Road, Epsom, KT17 3EG
Tel: 020-8786 7456 **Fax:** 020-8786 7456
E-mail: info@skyscrapersuk.com
Website: http://www.skyscrapersuk.com
Directors: C. Georgiou (Dir)
Immediate Holding Company: SKYSCRAPERS UK LIMITED
Registration no: 02616604 **Date established:** 1991
Turnover: Up to £250,000 **No.of Employees:** 1 - 10 **Product Groups:** 35, 39, 45

Date of Accounts	Jun 11	Jun 09	Jun 08
Sales Turnover	N/A	101	95
Working Capital	85	53	40
Fixed Assets	15	11	14
Current Assets	104	73	61

Stulz UK Ltd Epsom
First Quarter Blenheim Road, Epsom, KT19 9QN
Tel: 01372-749666 **Fax:** 01372-739444
E-mail: sales@stulz.co.uk
Website: http://www.stulz.co.uk
Directors: C. Webber (Sales)
Managers: D. Siveter (Mgr)
Immediate Holding Company: STULZ U.K. LIMITED
Registration no: 02113767 **Date established:** 1987 **Turnover:** £5m - £10m
No.of Employees: 21 - 50 **Product Groups:** 38, 40, 43, 52, 66, 84

Date of Accounts	Dec 11	Dec 10	Dec 09
Sales Turnover	10m	16m	10m
Pre Tax Profit/Loss	570	2m	602
Working Capital	3m	3m	2m
Fixed Assets	375	360	282
Current Assets	5m	6m	4m
Current Liabilities	683	1m	967

Suburban Grills & Railings
7 The Looe Reigate Road, Epsom, KT17 3BZ
Tel: 020-8786 8114 **Fax:** 020-8786 8114
E-mail: andysub@tiscali.co.uk
Website: http://www.railings-gates.com
Directors: A. Jones (Prop)
Date established: 2001 **No.of Employees:** 1 - 10 **Product Groups:** 26, 35

Thermo Fisher Scientific
Abgene House Blenheim Road, Epsom, KT19 9AP
Tel: 01372-723456 **Fax:** 01372-741873
E-mail: info@thermofisher.com
Website: http://www.thermofisherscientific.com
Bank(s): Barclays
Directors: J. Kennedy (Fin), R. Higginbotham (Pers)
Managers: G. Maynell (Site Co-ord), K. Fairfax (Chief Mgr), J. Wolstenholme (Mktg Serv Mgr)
Ultimate Holding Company: MAXINGVEST AG (GERMANY)
Immediate Holding Company: TCHIBO COFFEE INTERNATIONAL LIMITED
Registration no: 07112358 **Date established:** 1963
No.of Employees: 51 - 100 **Product Groups:** 38

Date of Accounts	Dec 10	Dec 09	Dec 08
Sales Turnover	20m	20m	22m
Pre Tax Profit/Loss	997	2m	3m
Working Capital	12m	12m	11m
Fixed Assets	5m	4m	3m
Current Assets	15m	15m	18m
Current Liabilities	1m	2m	2m

Toyota GB plc
Great Burgh Burgh Heath, Epsom, KT18 5UX
Tel: 01737-363633 **Fax:** 01737-778820
E-mail: info@toyota.com
Website: http://www.ltl.uk.com
Managers: R. Balshaw
Ultimate Holding Company: TOYOTA MOTOR CORPORATION (JAPAN)
Immediate Holding Company: LEXUS (GB) LIMITED
Registration no: 02484623 **Date established:** 1990
Turnover: Over £1,000m **No.of Employees:** 501 - 1000
Product Groups: 80

Date of Accounts	Mar 12	Mar 11	Mar 10
Sales Turnover	1363m	1455m	1533m
Pre Tax Profit/Loss	-35m	3m	-3m
Working Capital	-12m	14m	10m
Fixed Assets	38m	44m	43m
Current Assets	436m	436m	465m
Current Liabilities	128m	147m	168m

David Tyrrell Food & Hospitality
481 Chessington Road, Epsom, KT19 9JH
Tel: 020-8397 3030 **Fax:** 020-8397 4747
E-mail: davidtyrrell@foodhospitality.co.uk
Website: http://www.foodhospitality.co.uk
Directors: D. Tyrrell (Prop)
Registration no: 05425646 **Date established:** 2005
Turnover: Up to £250,000 **No.of Employees:** 1 - 10 **Product Groups:** 24, 37, 69, 83, 89

UK Awnings
Conservatory Blinds Limited 8-10 Ruxley Lane Ewell, Epsom, KT19 0JD
Tel: 020-8394 0011 **Fax:** 020-8394 0022
E-mail: info@uk-awnings.com
Website: http://www.uk-awnings.com
No.of Employees: 1 - 10 **Product Groups:** 24, 35, 63, 66

W E C S Precision Ltd
Blenheim Road, Epsom, KT19 9BE
Tel: 01372-741633 **Fax:** 01372-740539
E-mail: npooles@wecsprecision.com
Bank(s): National Westminster
Directors: N. Pooles (Prop)
Immediate Holding Company: WECS PRECISION LIMITED
Registration no: 05114474 **VAT No.:** GB 210 4551 17
Date established: 2004 **Turnover:** £500,000 - £1m
No.of Employees: 11 - 20 **Product Groups:** 48

Date of Accounts	Mar 11	Mar 10	Mar 09
Working Capital	261	100	7
Fixed Assets	536	581	669
Current Assets	555	621	516

Esher

George Alexander & Partners
Thames Mews Portsmouth Road, Esher, KT10 9AD
Tel: 01372-466406 **Fax:** 01372-466476
Directors: G. Alexander (Snr Part)
Date established: 1995 **No.of Employees:** 1 - 10 **Product Groups:** 35

Ashley & Co.
129 Ember Lane, Esher, KT10 8EH
Tel: 020-8398 0700 **Fax:** 020-8398 9493
E-mail: info@taxreturn.co.uk
Website: http://www.taxreturn.co.uk
Directors: P. Kearsley (Prop)
Registration no: 03846050 **Date established:** 1999
No.of Employees: 1 - 10 **Product Groups:** 80

Chelsea Artisans Ltd
Unit C2 Sandown Industrial Park Mill Road, Esher, KT10 8BL
Tel: 01372-469301 **Fax:** 01372-470590
E-mail: jeremyj@chelsea-artisans.co.uk
Website: http://www.chelsea-artisans.co.uk
Bank(s): Lloyds TSB Bank plc
Directors: C. McIntee (Dir), J. John (Dir)
Immediate Holding Company: CHELSEA ARTISANS LIMITED
Registration no: 02770898 **VAT No.:** GB 584 6466 95
Date established: 1992 **No.of Employees:** 21 - 50 **Product Groups:** 14, 30, 33

Date of Accounts	Jan 10	Jan 09	Jan 08
Working Capital	408	408	95
Fixed Assets	153	74	105
Current Assets	849	1m	569

Dairy Crest
Claygate House Littleworth Road, Esher, KT10 9PN
Tel: 01372-472200 **Fax:** 01372-476111
Website: http://www.dairycrest.co.uk
Directors: M. Allen (Grp Chief Exec)
Ultimate Holding Company: DAIRY CREST GROUP PLC
Immediate Holding Company: DAIRY CREST UK LIMITED
Registration no: 06679840 **Date established:** 2008
No.of Employees: 251 - 500 **Product Groups:** 20

Date of Accounts	Mar 12	Mar 11	Mar 10
Pre Tax Profit/Loss	7m	5m	N/A
Fixed Assets	229m	229m	229m
Current Assets	12m	5m	N/A

Empire
4 Rose Cottages Station Road, Claygate, Esher, KT10 9DJ
Tel: 0701-071 4766 **Fax:** 01372-466158
Directors: S. Wiltshire (Prop)
No.of Employees: 1 - 10 **Product Groups:** 36, 52, 81

Safetymark Consultancy Services
Sydney Cottages Elm Road, Claygate, Esher, KT10 0EJ
Tel: 01372-462277 **Fax:** 01372-462288
E-mail: admin@safetymark.net
Website: http://www.safetymark.net
Directors: M. Snelling (Dir)
Date established: 1999 **No.of Employees:** 1 - 10 **Product Groups:** 30, 32, 80

Thyssenkrupp V D M UK Ltd
VDM House 111 Hare Lane, Claygate, Esher, KT10 0QY
Tel: 01372-467137 **Fax:** 01372-466388
Website: http://www.thyssenkruppvdm.com
Directors: S. Fuller (Co Sec)
Ultimate Holding Company: THYSSEN KRUPP AG (GERMANY)
Immediate Holding Company: THYSSENKRUPP VDM UK LIMITED
Registration no: 00490646 **VAT No.:** GB 211 7786 66
Date established: 1951 **Turnover:** Up to £250,000
No.of Employees: 1 - 10 **Product Groups:** 34, 35, 36

Date of Accounts	Sep 11	Sep 10	Sep 09
Sales Turnover	72	1m	3m
Pre Tax Profit/Loss	1m	615	857
Working Capital	5m	4m	4m
Fixed Assets	7	26	55
Current Assets	6m	5m	5m
Current Liabilities	175	194	371

Farnham

A V A Ltd
Unit 1 Monkton Park, Farnham, GU9 9PA
Tel: 01252-733040 **Fax:** 01252-722958
E-mail: srpentony@avamountings.co.uk
Website: http://www.ava-antivibrationmountings.co.uk
Bank(s): Barclays
Directors: A. Pentony (Ch), M. Pentony (MD), S. Pentony (Dir)
Managers: A. Hoare (Purch Mgr), J. Hudson (Sales Prom Mgr), A. Hoare (Accounts)
Immediate Holding Company: A.V.A.Limited
Registration no: 00252941 **Date established:** 1930 **Turnover:** £1m - £2m
No.of Employees: 51 - 100 **Product Groups:** 29, 38, 39

Date of Accounts	Mar 12	Mar 11	Mar 10
Working Capital	458	432	428
Fixed Assets	30	44	48
Current Assets	717	593	618

Acorn Ironmongery Ltd
Unit C The Factory Dippenhall, Farnham, GU10 5DW
Tel: 01252-820858 **Fax:** 01252-820878
E-mail: info@acornfarnham.co.uk
Website: http://www.acornfarnham.co.uk
Directors: S. Faulkner (Fin), G. Faulkner (MD)
Immediate Holding Company: ACORN IRONMONGERY LIMITED
Registration no: 04402642 **Date established:** 2002
No.of Employees: 1 - 10 **Product Groups:** 25, 26, 30, 33, 35, 36, 37, 38, 39, 40, 49, 66

Date of Accounts	Mar 11	Mar 10	Mar 09
Working Capital	101	99	66
Fixed Assets	2	11	25
Current Assets	276	274	300

Adco UK Ltd
The Factory Dippenhall, Farnham, GU10 5DW
Tel: 01252-725100 **Fax:** 01252-725900
Website: http://www.adco.co.uk
Directors: S. Climpson (Dir)
Registration no: 03693695 **Date established:** 1999
Turnover: £500,000 - £1m **No.of Employees:** 1 - 10 **Product Groups:** 32, 37, 66

Advantage Business Group Ltd
The Barbican East Street, Farnham, GU9 7TB
Tel: 01252-738500 **Fax:** 01252-717065
E-mail: enquiries@advantage-business.co.uk
Website: http://www.advantage-business.co.uk
Directors: D. Percival (Dir), P. Kirane (Mkt Research), P. Kirrane (Mkt Research)
Managers: R. Symon (I.T. Exec)
Immediate Holding Company: ADVANTAGE BUSINESS GROUP LIMITED
Registration no: 06975109 **Date established:** 2009
Turnover: £10m - £20m **No.of Employees:** 51 - 100 **Product Groups:** 44, 54, 84, 85

Date of Accounts	Mar 08	Dec 06	Dec 05
Sales Turnover	N/A	17477	15313
Pre Tax Profit/Loss	-335	680	-183
Working Capital	-661	1630	1233
Fixed Assets	2078	464	367
Current Assets	N/A	5026	3739
Current Liabilities	661	3396	2506
Total Share Capital	1106	1106	1106
ROCE% (Return on Capital Employed)	-23.6	32.5	-11.4
ROT% (Return on Turnover)		3.9	-1.2

Aero Support Ltd
PO Box 483, Farnham, GU9 8NY
Tel: 0845-4563778 **Fax:** 0845-6443779
E-mail: sales@aerosupport.aero
Website: http://www.aerosupport.aero
Directors: C. Snelgrove (MD)
Registration no: 04598726 **Date established:** 2002
No.of Employees: 1 - 10 **Product Groups:** 37, 44

Date of Accounts	Apr 10	Apr 09	Apr 08
Working Capital	56	40	48
Fixed Assets	11	10	13
Current Assets	100	83	99
Current Liabilities	30	N/A	N/A

Anglia Transformers Ltd
Grange Road Tongham, Farnham, GU10 1DJ
Tel: 01252-782089 **Fax:** 01252-782913
E-mail: sales@angliatransformers.co.uk
Website: http://www.angliatransformers.co.uk
Bank(s): The Co-operative Bank PLC
Directors: N. Garrett (MD)
Immediate Holding Company: ANGLIA TRANSFORMERS LIMITED
Registration no: 00833248 **Date established:** 1965 **Turnover:** £1m - £2m
No.of Employees: 11 - 20 **Product Groups:** 37

Date of Accounts	Sep 11	Sep 10	Sep 09
Working Capital	142	140	150
Fixed Assets	33	31	36
Current Assets	178	167	195

Anville Instruments
Bramble Orchard Folly Lane North, Farnham, GU9 0HX
Tel: 01252-351030 **Fax:** 01252-323492
E-mail: sales@anvilleinstruments.com
Website: http://www.anvilleinstruments.com
Directors: D. Truin (Dir)
Immediate Holding Company: ANVILLE INSTRUMENTS LIMITED
Registration no: 02563700 **Date established:** 1990 **Turnover:** £1m - £2m
No.of Employees: 1 - 10 **Product Groups:** 38, 44

Date of Accounts	Oct 07	Apr 11	Apr 10
Working Capital	-78	60	83
Fixed Assets	259	5	5
Current Assets	56	146	234

Arcadia Irrigation UK
Kennel Cottage Hawthorn Lane, Rowledge, Farnham, GU10 4DJ
Tel: 01252-714986 **Fax:** 01252-821563
E-mail: sales@arcadiairrigation.co.uk
Website: http://www.arcadiairrigation.co.uk
Directors: P. Berphoud (Prop)
Date established: 1984 **Turnover:** Up to £250,000
No.of Employees: 1 - 10 **Product Groups:** 40, 41

Ave UK Ltd
Unit 4 Riverside Industrial Park, Farnham, GU9 7UG
Tel: 01252-733200 **Fax:** 01252-733480
E-mail: sales@aveuk.net
Website: http://www.aveuk.net
Directors: S. Bradley (Sales & Mktg)
Immediate Holding Company: AVE UK LTD
Registration no: 02411963 **Date established:** 1989
No.of Employees: 1 - 10 **Product Groups:** 38, 42

Date of Accounts	Dec 11	Dec 10	Dec 09
Working Capital	-85	-72	-53
Fixed Assets	246	258	170
Current Assets	81	43	186

B B S Ltd
Unit B Grovebell Industrial Estate Wrecclesham Road Wrecclesham, Farnham, GU10 4PL
Tel: 01252-727755 **Fax:** 01252-727766
E-mail: enquiries@magimix-spares.co.uk
Website: http://www.magimix-spares.co.uk
Directors: B. Frost (MD)
Immediate Holding Company: B.B.S. LIMITED
Registration no: 02747961 **Date established:** 1992
No.of Employees: 1 - 10 **Product Groups:** 40

Date of Accounts	Mar 11	Mar 10	Mar 09
Working Capital	69	53	52
Fixed Assets	23	42	35
Current Assets	316	301	226

C M K Sales
18 Upper Hale Road, Farnham, GU9 0NS
Tel: 01252-711278
E-mail: christine.mckelvey1@yahoo.co.uk
Directors: C. Mckelvey (Ptnr)
Date established: 1988 **No.of Employees:** 1 - 10 **Product Groups:** 46

CIBA Vision
Guildford Road Industrial Estate Guildford Road, Farnham, GU9 9PZ
Tel: 01252-712222 **Fax:** 01252-733207
Website: http://www.cibavision.com
Managers: R. Rees (Mgr)
No.of Employees: 11 - 20 **Product Groups:** 37, 38, 65

D & M Engineering Ltd
2-4 Poyle Road Tongham, Farnham, GU10 1DS
Tel: 01252-782838 **Fax:** 01252-781168
E-mail: dmeng@sagehost.co.uk
Website: http://www.dm-eng.co.uk

Directors: P. Brown (MD)
Immediate Holding Company: D & M ENGINEERING LIMITED
Registration no: 02706103 **Date established:** 1992
Turnover: £250,000 - £500,000 **No.of Employees:** 11 - 20
Product Groups: 33, 46, 48

Date of Accounts	Sep 11	Sep 10	Sep 09
Working Capital	55	19	45
Fixed Assets	42	35	42
Current Assets	183	96	145

D R S Technoli UK Ltd

Lynwood House Farnham Trading Estate, Farnham, GU9 9NN
Tel: 01252-730500 **Fax:** 01252-730530
E-mail: sales@drsuk.org
Website: http://www.drs.com
Bank(s): HSBC Bank plc
Directors: D. Ward (MD), N. Refold (Fin)
Managers: B. McNeill (Purch Mgr), D. Woods (Tech Serv Mgr), J. Goodwin (Personnel)
Ultimate Holding Company: FINMECCANICA SPA (ITALY)
Immediate Holding Company: TACTICAL SYSTEMS LIMITED
Registration no: 02898780 **VAT No.:** GB 449 4182 28
Date established: 1994 **Turnover:** Up to £250,000
No.of Employees: 51 - 100 **Product Groups:** 37, 44

Date of Accounts	Jun 11	Jun 10	Jun 09
Sales Turnover	71	81	75
Pre Tax Profit/Loss	54	66	59
Working Capital	21	11	-2
Current Assets	37	30	17
Current Liabilities	16	18	20

Dimar Ltd

18 East Street, Farnham, GU9 7SD
Tel: 01252-719997 **Fax:** 01252-719998
E-mail: enquiries@dimar.co.uk
Website: http://www.dimar.co.uk
Directors: M. Skouras (Dir)
Immediate Holding Company: DIMAR LTD
Registration no: 07859163 **Date established:** 2011 **Turnover:** £5m - £10m
No.of Employees: 1 - 10 **Product Groups:** 34, 48

Date of Accounts	Jun 08	Jun 07	Jun 06
Working Capital	-216	-433	-317
Fixed Assets	978	1012	1019
Current Assets	1595	1304	2267
Current Liabilities	1811	1738	2584

Direct Cleaning Services Southern Ltd

Unit 8 Romans Business Park East Street, Farnham, GU9 7SX
Tel: 01252-718884 **Fax:** 01252-718994
E-mail: info@dcssurrey.co.uk
Website: http://www.dcssurrey.co.uk
Directors: M. Gilliam (MD)
Immediate Holding Company: DIRECT CLEANING SERVICES (SOUTHERN) LIMITED
Registration no: 07593297 **Date established:** 2011
No.of Employees: 1 - 10 **Product Groups:** 32, 44, 52, 64, 80

Farnham Castle Briefings Ltd

Farnham Castle, Farnham, GU9 0AG
Tel: 01252-721194 **Fax:** 01252-711283
E-mail: info@farnhamcastle.com
Website: http://www.farnhamcastle.com
Directors: J. Twiss (Grp Chief Exec), P. Evans (Co Sec)
Ultimate Holding Company: FARNHAM CASTLE
Immediate Holding Company: FARNHAM CASTLE BRIEFINGS LIMITED
Registration no: 04127900 **Date established:** 2000 **Turnover:** £1m - £2m
No.of Employees: 1 - 10 **Product Groups:** 69, 80, 81, 83, 86, 89

Date of Accounts	Sep 11	Sep 10	Sep 09
Sales Turnover	1m	1m	2m
Pre Tax Profit/Loss	-82	-33	-124
Working Capital	-156	-331	-359
Fixed Assets	755	790	607
Current Assets	203	155	154
Current Liabilities	225	199	212

Farnham Fencing

9 Arthur Close, Farnham, GU9 8PE
Tel: 01252-725582 **Fax:** 01252-725582
Website: http://www.farnham-fencing.co.uk
Directors: D. Birney (Prop)
No.of Employees: 1 - 10 **Product Groups:** 26, 35

Flexible Handling Systems

15 Weywood Lane, Farnham, GU9 9DP
Tel: 01252-314344 **Fax:** 01252-314344
E-mail: info@flexiblehandling.co.uk
Website: http://www.flexiblehandling.co.uk
Managers: M. Gillard (Sales Admin)
No.of Employees: 1 - 10 **Product Groups:** 37, 45, 67

Gillespie UK Ltd

Silvertree Coxbridge Business Park, Farnham, GU10 5EH
Tel: 01252-747825 **Fax:** 0871-429 8062
E-mail: pamgarratt@gillespieuk.co.uk
Website: http://www.gillespieuk.co.uk
Directors: M. Treacy (MD)
Managers: G. Mackee (Comptroller), J. Beitch (Mktg Serv Mgr)
Ultimate Holding Company: TVEDT GROUP HOLDINGS LTD (JERSEY)
Immediate Holding Company: GILLESPIE (UK) LIMITED
Registration no: 02332696 **Date established:** 1989
No.of Employees: 11 - 20 **Product Groups:** 33

Date of Accounts	Dec 11	Dec 10	Dec 09
Working Capital	-2m	-1m	-1m
Fixed Assets	20	38	54
Current Assets	549	904	838

Grantham Tool Sharpening

98 The Street Wrecclesham, Farnham, GU10 4QR
Tel: 01252-724833
Directors: A. Grantham (Prop)
Date established: 1958 **No.of Employees:** 1 - 10 **Product Groups:** 36

Greycar Ltd

Greycar House 5 Ferns Mead, Farnham, GU9 7XP
Tel: 01252-821937 **Fax:** 01252-734071
E-mail: info@greycar.com
Website: http://www.greycar.com
Directors: J. Leech (MD)
Registration no: 5862987 **Date established:** 2006
Turnover: Up to £250,000 **No.of Employees:** 1 - 10 **Product Groups:** 24

Date of Accounts	Sep 09	Sep 08
Working Capital	-21	-16
Current Assets	22	19

Halcyon Solutions

Lawday Link, Farnham, GU9 0BS
Tel: 01252-715765 **Fax:** 01252-715765
E-mail: mike.hearsey@btinternet.com
Website: http://www.halcyon-solutions.co.uk
Directors: M. Hearsey (Prop)
VAT No.: GB 664 5114 40 **Date established:** 1995
No.of Employees: 1 - 10 **Product Groups:** 37, 38, 40, 42, 46, 54, 84

International Process Technologies Ltd

Farnham Trading Estate, Farnham, GU9 9NY
Tel: 01252-736800 **Fax:** 01252-724503
E-mail: sales@plascoat.com
Website: http://www.plascoat.com
Bank(s): Bank of Scotland
Directors: C. Dunnett (MD), G. Elkin (Fin), K. Bilham (Fin)
Immediate Holding Company: INTERNATIONAL PROCESS TECHNOLOGIES LIMITED
Registration no: 03139509 **VAT No.:** GB 211 3232 32
Date established: 1995 **Turnover:** £20m - £50m
No.of Employees: 21 - 50 **Product Groups:** 32

Date of Accounts	Dec 10	Dec 09	Dec 08
Sales Turnover	24m	21m	25m
Pre Tax Profit/Loss	2m	1m	1m
Working Capital	2m	2m	1m
Fixed Assets	5m	6m	6m
Current Assets	6m	6m	7m
Current Liabilities	2m	2m	2m

Kinetrol Ltd

Farnham Trading Estate, Farnham, GU9 9NW
Tel: 01252-733838 **Fax:** 01252-713042
E-mail: sales@kinetrol.com
Website: http://www.kinetrol.com
Bank(s): Fortis Bank
Directors: B. Morgan (Co Sec), J. Nash (MD)
Managers: G. Burton (Sales & Mktg Mg), R. Cox (Works Gen Mgr), S. Creighton-kelly (Tech Serv Mgr)
Immediate Holding Company: KINETROL LIMITED
Registration no: 00598619 **VAT No.:** GB 320 4054 16
Date established: 1958 **Turnover:** £20m - £50m
No.of Employees: 101 - 250 **Product Groups:** 38, 40

Date of Accounts	Sep 11	Sep 10	Sep 09
Sales Turnover	22m	19m	22m
Pre Tax Profit/Loss	3m	3m	4m
Working Capital	12m	10m	10m
Fixed Assets	6m	7m	4m
Current Assets	14m	12m	13m
Current Liabilities	1m	1m	2m

Molek UK

Molex House, Farnham, GU9 7XX
Tel: 01252-720720 **Fax:** 01252-720721
E-mail: mxuk@molex.com
Website: http://www.molex.com
Directors: G. Faughnan (Sales), G. Graham (MD)
Managers: K. Scott (Serv Mgr), D. McCoy (Personnel)
Ultimate Holding Company: MOLEX INC (USA)
Immediate Holding Company: MOLEX ELECTRONICS LIMITED
Registration no: 01432862 **Date established:** 1979 **Turnover:** £5m - £10m
No.of Employees: 1 - 10 **Product Groups:** 37, 39, 67

Multigerm Ltd

Sandy Farm Sands Road, The Sands, Farnham, GU10 1PX
Tel: 01252-783374 **Fax:** 01252-782567
E-mail: smith@mgerm.demon.co.uk
Website: http://www.mgerm.demon.co.uk
Directors: A. Smith (Dir), B. Smith (MD), B. Smith (Dir), A. Smith (Co Sec)
Immediate Holding Company: MULTIGERM UK ENTERPRISES LTD
Registration no: 03399865 **Date established:** 1997
Turnover: Up to £250,000 **No.of Employees:** 1 - 10 **Product Groups:** 62

Date of Accounts	Oct 11	Oct 10	Oct 09
Working Capital	-159	-129	-98
Fixed Assets	30	33	37
Current Assets	21	24	32

Numa

Mead House Bentley, Farnham, GU10 5HY
Tel: 01420-22918 **Fax:** 01420-22865
E-mail: info@numahammers.com
Website: http://www.numahammers.com
Managers: C. Beare (Mgr)
Ultimate Holding Company: O F AHLMARK AND COMPANY AB - SWEDEN
Registration no: 01153003 **Date established:** 1973
Turnover: £20m - £50m **No.of Employees:** 1 - 10 **Product Groups:** 36

On-Track Recruitment & Training Ltd

23 Long Garden Walk, Farnham, GU9 7HX
Tel: 01252-727887 **Fax:** 01252-737243
E-mail: info@ontrackrecruitment.co.uk
Website: http://www.ontrackrecruitment.co.uk
Directors: S. Cripps (MD)
Immediate Holding Company: ON TRACK RECRUITMENT AND TRAINING LIMITED
Registration no: 03948864 **Date established:** 2000
Turnover: £250,000 - £500,000 **No.of Employees:** 1 - 10
Product Groups: 80

Date of Accounts	Mar 12	Mar 11	Mar 10
Sales Turnover	425	395	270
Pre Tax Profit/Loss	87	76	1
Working Capital	217	170	243
Fixed Assets	181	184	186
Current Assets	289	244	289
Current Liabilities	52	54	27

Opus Telecommunications Ltd

The Hopkiln Bentley, Farnham, GU10 5LZ
Tel: 01420-567600 **Fax:** 01420-567616
E-mail: mark.castle@opustelecom.co.uk
Website: http://www.opustelecom.co.uk
Directors: M. Castle (Sales)
Immediate Holding Company: OPUS TELECOMMUNICATIONS LIMITED
Registration no: 06397656 **Date established:** 2007
Turnover: £250,000 - £500,000 **No.of Employees:** 11 - 20
Product Groups: 37, 52

P H S Water Logic

Unit 4 Dares Farm Farnham Road, Ewshot, Farnham, GU10 5BB
Tel: 01252-852260
Website: http://www.phs.co.uk
Managers: A. Mason (Sales Admin)
No.of Employees: 21 - 50 **Product Groups:** 40, 66

Plascoat

Farnham Trading Estate, Farnham, GU9 9NY
Tel: 01252-736800 **Fax:** 01252-724503
E-mail: sales@plascoat.com
Website: http://www.plascoat.com
Bank(s): Bank of Scotland
Directors: K. Bilham (Fin), P. Benson (Dir), C. Dunnett (MD)
Managers: D. Wilson (Purch Mgr)
Ultimate Holding Company: INTERNATIONAL PROCESS TECHNOLOGIES LIMITED
Immediate Holding Company: INTERNATIONAL PROCESS TECHNOLOGIES LIMITED
Registration no: 03139509 **VAT No.:** GB 211 3232 32
Date established: 1995 **Turnover:** £20m - £50m
No.of Employees: 21 - 50 **Product Groups:** 29, 30, 32

Date of Accounts	Dec 11	Dec 10	Dec 09
Sales Turnover	26m	24m	21m
Pre Tax Profit/Loss	2m	2m	1m
Working Capital	3m	2m	2m
Fixed Assets	6m	5m	6m
Current Assets	7m	6m	6m
Current Liabilities	2m	2m	2m

Polar Seal Tapes & Conversions

Guildford Road Trading Estate Guildford Road, Farnham, GU9 9PZ
Tel: 01252-726000 **Fax:** 01252-728125
E-mail: sales@polarseal.net
Website: http://www.polarseal.net
Bank(s): National Westminster Bank Plc
Directors: F. Rich (Snr Part)
Immediate Holding Company: CASTLE PRODUCTIONS (FARNHAM) LIMITED
Registration no: 02334480 **Date established:** 1989 **Turnover:** £2m - £5m
No.of Employees: 11 - 20 **Product Groups:** 24, 27, 30, 66

Protean Electric Limited

Silvertree Unit 10B Coxbridge Business Park, Alton Road, Farnham, GU10 5EH
Tel: 01252-741800 **Fax:** 01252-741801
E-mail: info@proteanelectric.com
Website: http://www.pmlflightlink.com
Directors: M. Boughtwood (MD), S. Brockway (Dir), J. Henry (Fin)
Managers: C. Newman (Nat Sales Mgr)
Immediate Holding Company: Qed Group Ltd
Registration no: 06747884 **Date established:** 1901 **Turnover:** £2m - £5m
No.of Employees: 21 - 50 **Product Groups:** 35, 37, 38, 39, 67

Sign A Rama

Unit 5 Farnham Business Centre Dogflud Way, Farnham, GU9 7UP
Tel: 01252-821932 **Fax:** 01252-734140
E-mail: farnham@signarama.co.uk
Website: http://www.aldershotsigns.co.uk
Directors: M. Ralf (Prop)
Immediate Holding Company: ABSOLUTE SIGNS LTD
Registration no: 07106075 **Date established:** 2011
Turnover: Up to £250,000 **No.of Employees:** 1 - 10 **Product Groups:** 27, 28, 30, 37, 39, 40, 49

Southco Manufacturing Ltd

Farnham Trading Estate, Farnham, GU9 9PL
Tel: 01252-714422 **Fax:** 0845-117 9445
E-mail: info@southco.com
Website: http://www.southco.com
Bank(s): Barclays
Directors: S. Austin (Pers)
Managers: D. Kelly (Serv Mgr), P. Reichle (Mktg Serv Mgr), K. Cumley, P. Testeil (Mgr), R. Kitchen (Purch Mgr), C. Roberts (Ops Mgr), S. Hunt (Tech Serv Mgr)
Ultimate Holding Company: SOUTH CHESTER TUBE COMPANY (USA)
Immediate Holding Company: SOUTHCO MANUFACTURING LIMITED
Registration no: 04328069 **VAT No.:** GB 152 9211 81
Date established: 2001 **Turnover:** £10m - £20m
No.of Employees: 51 - 100 **Product Groups:** 35, 36, 39, 66

Date of Accounts	Dec 11	Dec 10	Dec 09
Sales Turnover	72m	65m	54m
Pre Tax Profit/Loss	7m	5m	4m
Working Capital	14m	8m	635
Fixed Assets	25m	27m	29m
Current Assets	23m	25m	21m
Current Liabilities	4m	4m	4m

Spraying Systems Ltd

Farnham Business Park Weydon Lane, Farnham, GU9 8QT
Tel: 01252-727200 **Fax:** 01252-712211
E-mail: info.uk@spray.com
Website: http://www.spray.com
Managers: J. Mcgarrey (Mgr)
Ultimate Holding Company: SPRAYING SYSTEMS CO (USA)
Immediate Holding Company: SPRAYING SYSTEMS LIMITED
Registration no: 02794373 **VAT No.:** GB 602 6134 83
Date established: 1993 **Turnover:** £500,000 - £1m
No.of Employees: 1 - 10 **Product Groups:** 30, 36

Date of Accounts	Dec 11	Dec 10	Dec 09
Working Capital	259	250	108
Fixed Assets	19	38	65
Current Assets	562	491	521

Stemmer Imaging

The Old Barn Grange Court, Tongham, Farnham, GU10 1DW
Tel: 01252-780000 **Fax:** 01252-780001
E-mail: sales@stemmer-imaging.co.uk
Website: http://www.stemmer-imaging.co.uk
Directors: D. Hern (MD)
Managers: S. Hearn, S. Barker (Fin Mgr)
Immediate Holding Company: STEMMER IMAGING LIMITED
Registration no: 03370750 **Date established:** 1997 **Turnover:** £5m - £10m
No.of Employees: 21 - 50 **Product Groups:** 37, 38, 44

Date of Accounts	Jun 11	Jun 10	Jun 09
Working Capital	1m	692	500
Fixed Assets	151	61	54
Current Assets	2m	2m	2m

Surrey Blinds

Rangefield Court Farnham Trading Estate, Farnham, GU9 9NP
Tel: 0800-862 0707
E-mail: sales@surreyblinds.co.uk
Website: http://www.surreyblindsandshutters.co.uk
Directors: C. de Carteret (Ptnr)
Date established: 2009 **Turnover:** Up to £250,000
No.of Employees: 1 - 10 **Product Groups:** 24, 25, 30, 35

Surrey Translation Bureau Ltd (Surrey Language Centre)

Sandford House 39 West Street, Farnham, GU9 7DX
Tel: 01252-733999 **Fax:** 01252-733773
E-mail: john@surreylanguage.co.uk
Website: http://www.surreylanguage.co.uk
Bank(s): Barclays
Directors: J. Cooke (Dir)
Immediate Holding Company: STB LIMITED
Registration no: 05033482 **VAT No.:** GB 715 7859 01
Date established: 2004 **Turnover:** £1m - £2m **No.of Employees:** 11 - 20
Product Groups: 80

Date of Accounts	Mar 11	Mar 10	Mar 09
Working Capital	93	70	35
Fixed Assets	156	159	164
Current Assets	214	134	152

T G H Electrical Systems Ltd

84 Oxenden Road Tongham, Farnham, GU10 1AJ
Tel: 01252-343998 **Fax:** 01252- 330279
Directors: G. Potter (Dir)
No.of Employees: 1 - 10 **Product Groups:** 36, 40

Touch Vision Ltd

6 The Riverside Dogflud Way, Farnham, GU9 7SS
Tel: 01252-823850 **Fax:** 01252-711702
E-mail: info@touchvision.tv
Website: http://www.touchvision.tv
Bank(s): National Westminster
Directors: N. Findjan (Fin)
Ultimate Holding Company: MEDIAZEST PLC
Immediate Holding Company: TOUCH VISION LIMITED
Registration no: 01227519 **VAT No.:** GB 709 9491 91
Date established: 1975 **Turnover:** £5m - £10m **No.of Employees:** 11 - 20
Product Groups: 37

Date of Accounts	Dec 08	Mar 12	Mar 11
Sales Turnover	4m	3m	2m
Pre Tax Profit/Loss	9	12	132
Working Capital	142	-15	55
Fixed Assets	75	97	32
Current Assets	1m	682	963
Current Liabilities	216	347	41

Westway Composites

Unit H The Factory Dippenhall, Farnham, GU10 5DW
Tel: 01252-820200 **Fax:** 01252-820217
E-mail: paul@westway.co.uk
Website: http://www.westway.co.uk
Directors: P. Denton (MD)
VAT No.: GB 413 5205 94 **Date established:** 1985
No.of Employees: 1 - 10 **Product Groups:** 30

Date of Accounts	Dec 02	Dec 01	Dec 00
Sales Turnover	683	650	N/A
Pre Tax Profit/Loss	70	6	N/A
Working Capital	149	95	110
Fixed Assets	142	154	137
Current Assets	267	213	235
Current Liabilities	118	119	125
Total Share Capital	1	1	1
ROCE% (Return on Capital Employed)	24.1	2.4	
ROT% (Return on Turnover)	10.3	0.9	

Godalming

A V S Fencing Supplies Ltd

Avs Trading Park Unit 1 Chapel Lane, Milford, Godalming, GU8 5HE
Tel: 01483-410960 **Fax:** 01483-860867
E-mail: admin@avsfencing.co.uk
Website: http://www.avsfencing.co.uk
Managers: M. Whiting (Mgr)
Immediate Holding Company: AVS FENCING SUPPLIES LIMITED
Registration no: 02818962 **Date established:** 1993
No.of Employees: 11 - 20 **Product Groups:** 23, 25, 30, 33, 35, 36, 39, 41, 49, 66

Date of Accounts	Dec 11	Dec 10	Dec 09
Sales Turnover	12m	11m	10m
Pre Tax Profit/Loss	149	24	245
Working Capital	333	-128	-113
Fixed Assets	271	205	237
Current Assets	2m	2m	2m
Current Liabilities	352	811	915

A3 Printers

Dover House Witley, Godalming, GU8 5QZ
Tel: 01428-682546 **Fax:** 01428-684900
E-mail: sales@a3p.co.uk
Website: http://www.action-t-shirts.co.uk
Directors: A. Adler (Fin), O. Smith (MD)
Immediate Holding Company: UNIVERSAL COMPREHENSIVE SERVICES LIMITED
Registration no: 00957166 **Date established:** 1969
No.of Employees: 1 - 10 **Product Groups:** 23, 24, 49

Date of Accounts	Aug 11	Aug 10	Aug 09
Working Capital	-36	-14	-35
Fixed Assets	25	28	31
Current Assets	40	32	41

Absolute Security Surrey

5 Langham Park Catteshall Lane, Godalming, GU7 1NG
Tel: 01483-791500 **Fax:** 01483-791540
E-mail: info@absolutesecurity.co.uk
Website: http://www.absolutesecurity.co.uk
Directors: A. Rees (Prop)
Immediate Holding Company: ABSOLUTE SECURITY SYSTEMS LIMITED
Registration no: 04024536 **Date established:** 2000
No.of Employees: 11 - 20 **Product Groups:** 35, 37, 38, 81

Date of Accounts	Jun 11	Jun 10	Jun 09
Working Capital	-478	-473	-494
Fixed Assets	1m	1m	1m
Current Assets	377	471	462

Action T-Shirt

4 Cramhurst Lane Witley, Godalming, GU8 5QZ
Tel: 01428-682546 **Fax:** 01428-684900
E-mail: sales@action-t-shirts.co.uk
Website: http://www.the-t-shirt-site.com
Product Groups: 24, 49, 63

Altius Consulting

Mill Pool House Mill Lane, Godalming, GU7 1EY
Tel: 01483-418628 **Fax:** 01438-418680
E-mail: info@altiusconsulting.com
Website: http://www.altiusconsulting.com
Directors: J. Cowle (Fin)
Immediate Holding Company: ALTIUS CONSULTING LIMITED
Registration no: 02748906 **Date established:** 1992
No.of Employees: 21 - 50 **Product Groups:** 80

Date of Accounts	Dec 11	Dec 10	Dec 09
Working Capital	363	389	348
Fixed Assets	26	45	44
Current Assets	848	1m	1m

Axtell Plant Hire

Station Approach Wormley, Godalming, GU8 5TB
Tel: 01428-685987 **Fax:** 01428-685978
E-mail: enquiries@axtell.info
Website: http://www.grabtrucks.com
Directors: A. Axtell (Ptnr)
Managers: S. Newdick (Sales Prom Mgr), P. Chapman (Chief Acct)
Immediate Holding Company: NESS UK LIMITED
Date established: 2009 **No.of Employees:** 11 - 20 **Product Groups:** 14, 33, 39, 41, 45, 51, 52, 83

Date of Accounts	May 11	May 10
Sales Turnover	68	N/A
Working Capital	-34	33
Current Assets	2	33

C-Mi Lab plc

Catteshall Mill Catteshall Road, Godalming, GU7 1NJ
Tel: 01483-527119 **Fax:** 0845-026 7681
E-mail: adamt@cmilabsplc.com
Website: http://www.cmilabsplc.com
Directors: D. Hobson (MD)
Managers: A. Trussler (Mgr), K. Clark (Mktg Serv Mgr), T. Leopoldo (Accounts)
Immediate Holding Company: C - MI LABS LIMITED
Registration no: 03164249 **Date established:** 1996
No.of Employees: 1 - 10 **Product Groups:** 44

Date of Accounts	Mar 11	Mar 10	Mar 09
Sales Turnover	N/A	N/A	3m
Pre Tax Profit/Loss	N/A	N/A	1
Working Capital	-70	-68	-61
Current Assets	N/A	N/A	1
Current Liabilities	N/A	N/A	51

Dunelm Aviation Plant & Machinery Ltd

1 Miltons Yard Petworth Road, Witley, Godalming, GU8 5LH
Tel: 01428-682801 **Fax:** 01428-682902
E-mail: sales@dunelmaviation.co.uk
Website: http://www.btinternet.com
Directors: R. Allan (Fin)
Immediate Holding Company: DUNELM AVIATION, PLANT AND MACHINERY LIMITED
Registration no: 01883303 **Date established:** 1985
Turnover: £500,000 - £1m **No.of Employees:** 1 - 10 **Product Groups:** 33, 39

Date of Accounts	May 11	May 10	May 09
Sales Turnover	924	993	1m
Pre Tax Profit/Loss	-46	10	26
Working Capital	-88	-21	-13
Fixed Assets	359	365	371
Current Assets	487	998	965
Current Liabilities	12	23	34

English Chain Co. Ltd

24 Brighton Road, Godalming, GU7 1NS
Tel: 08453-303446 **Fax:** 08453-303226
E-mail: sales@englishchain.co.uk
Website: http://www.englishchain.co.uk
Managers: I. Olson (Mgr)
Ultimate Holding Company: EUROCHAIN HOLDINGS LTD (CHANNEL ISLANDS)
Immediate Holding Company: ENGLISH CHAIN COMPANY LIMITED
Registration no: 00427960 **Date established:** 1947 **Turnover:** £5m - £10m
No.of Employees: 1 - 10 **Product Groups:** 30, 35, 36, 39

Date of Accounts	Dec 11	Dec 10	Dec 09
Working Capital	690	681	649
Fixed Assets	416	417	433
Current Assets	1m	1m	1m

Fordway Solutions Ltd

Hambledon House Catteshall Lane, Godalming, GU7 1JJ
Tel: 01483-528200 **Fax:** 01483-528203
E-mail: sales@fordway.com
Website: http://www.fordway.com
Bank(s): The Royal Bank of Scotland
Directors: G. Parris (Fin), R. Blanford (MD)
Managers: P. Banfield (Mktg Serv Mgr)
Immediate Holding Company: FORDWAY SOLUTIONS LIMITED
Registration no: 02640206 **VAT No.:** GB 572 8005 43
Date established: 1991 **Turnover:** £5m - £10m **No.of Employees:** 21 - 50
Product Groups: 44, 80

Date of Accounts	Aug 11	Aug 10	Aug 09
Sales Turnover	10m	8m	4m
Pre Tax Profit/Loss	385	377	-171
Working Capital	1m	1m	1m
Fixed Assets	347	262	296
Current Assets	3m	2m	2m
Current Liabilities	779	581	579

Hawco

The Wharf Abbey Mill Business Park, Lower Eashing, Godalming, GU7 2QN
Tel: 01483-869000 **Fax:** 01204-675010
E-mail: info@hawco.co.uk
Website: http://www.hawco.co.uk
Bank(s): National Westminster Bank Plc
Managers: W. Root (Mgr)
Ultimate Holding Company: DIPLOMA PLC
Immediate Holding Company: HAWCO LIMITED
Registration no: 00764905 **VAT No.:** GB 358 8073 20
Date established: 1963 **Turnover:** £1m - £2m **No.of Employees:** 21 - 50
Product Groups: 37, 38

Jewson Ltd

2 Chalk Road, Godalming, GU7 3HH
Tel: 01483-414682 **Fax:** 01483-860249
Website: http://www.jewson.co.uk
Managers: M. Cushing (District Mgr)
Ultimate Holding Company: COMPAGNIE DE SAINT GOBAIN (FRANCE)
Immediate Holding Company: JEWSON LIMITED
Registration no: 00348407 **VAT No.:** GB 497 7184 33
Date established: 1939 **Turnover:** £2m - £5m **No.of Employees:** 21 - 50
Product Groups: 66

Date of Accounts	Dec 11	Dec 10	Dec 09
Sales Turnover	1606m	1547m	1485m
Pre Tax Profit/Loss	18m	100m	45m
Working Capital	-345m	-250m	-349m
Fixed Assets	496m	387m	461m
Current Assets	657m	1005m	1320m
Current Liabilities	66m	120m	64m

Kallo Foods Ltd

Coopers Place Combe Lane, Wormley, Godalming, GU8 5SZ
Tel: 01428-685100 **Fax:** 01428-685800
E-mail: sales@kallofoods.com
Website: http://www.kallofoods.com
Bank(s): National Westminster Bank Plc
Directors: J. Heemskerk (Fin), P. Yeates (Sales), S. Schaafsma (Dir), P. Cairns (Dir), A. Dent (Mkt Research), D. Kleerekoper (MD)
Managers: J. Merchant (I.T. Exec)
Ultimate Holding Company: FP002275
Immediate Holding Company: KALLO FOODS LIMITED
Registration no: 02893019 **Date established:** 1994
Turnover: £20m - £50m **No.of Employees:** 21 - 50 **Product Groups:** 85

Date of Accounts	Dec 09	Dec 08	Dec 07
Sales Turnover	41m	39m	33m
Pre Tax Profit/Loss	188	3m	3m
Working Capital	9m	8m	10m
Fixed Assets	11m	12m	7m
Current Assets	17m	18m	18m
Current Liabilities	2m	4m	3m

Kea Developments

Henley House Summers Lane, Hurtmore, Godalming, GU7 2RR
Tel: 01483-421199
Directors: P. Hogg (MD)
Date established: 2001 **No.of Employees:** 1 - 10 **Product Groups:** 38, 42

Messagemaker Displays Ltd

2 Miltons Yard Petworth Road, Witley, Godalming, GU8 5LH
Tel: 08450-212340 **Fax:** 08703-305733
E-mail: paulb@messagemaker.co.uk
Website: http://www.messagemaker.co.uk
Directors: H. Filer (Dir), P. Bubb (Mkt Research)
Immediate Holding Company: MESSAGEMAKER DISPLAYS LIMITED
Registration no: 03726273 **Date established:** 1999
No.of Employees: 1 - 10 **Product Groups:** 37, 38, 49

Date of Accounts	Feb 08	Feb 11	Feb 10
Working Capital	-11	-12	-12
Fixed Assets	24	13	14
Current Assets	208	321	165

Nationwide Maintenance Ltd

Huxley House Catteshall Lane Weyside Park, Godalming, GU7 1XE
Tel: 01483-428674 **Fax:** 01483-426987
E-mail: csykes@nationmaint.co.uk
Website: http://www.nationmaint.co.uk
Directors: C. Sykes (Fin)
Managers: S. Ketteringham (Tech Serv Mgr), C. Gillingham (Personnel)
Ultimate Holding Company: EUROPA SUPPORT SERVICES LIMITED
Immediate Holding Company: EUROPA NATIONWIDE TECHNICAL SERVICES LIMITED
Registration no: 03409815 **Date established:** 1997
Turnover: £20m - £50m **No.of Employees:** 51 - 100 **Product Groups:** 52

Date of Accounts	Dec 11	Dec 10	Sep 09
Sales Turnover	27m	36m	31m
Pre Tax Profit/Loss	640	889	642
Working Capital	5m	4m	4m
Fixed Assets	217	278	159
Current Assets	11m	12m	12m
Current Liabilities	1m	2m	2m

Olema Engineering

The Orchards Chiddingfold Road, Dunsfold, Godalming, GU8 4PB
Tel: 01483-200700 **Fax:** 01483-200700
E-mail: mail@olemaengineering.co.uk
Website: http://www.olemaengineering.co.uk
Directors: W. Goodal (Prop)
Date established: 2002 **No.of Employees:** 1 - 10 **Product Groups:** 35

Powersource Projects Ltd

Powerpro House Capital Park Combe Lane, Wormley, Godalming, GU8 5TJ
Tel: 01428-684980 **Fax:** 01428-667979
E-mail: sales@power-source-pro.co.uk
Website: http://www.power-source-pro.co.uk
Directors: R. Millar (MD)
Immediate Holding Company: POWERSOURCE PROJECTS LIMITED
Registration no: 04102249 **VAT No.:** GB 742 7265 27
Date established: 2000 **Turnover:** £2m - £5m **No.of Employees:** 1 - 10
Product Groups: 37, 40, 67

Date of Accounts	Dec 11	Mar 11	Mar 10
Sales Turnover	9m	8m	8m
Pre Tax Profit/Loss	302	281	282
Working Capital	90	51	46
Fixed Assets	34	39	37
Current Assets	1m	1m	1m
Current Liabilities	548	288	415

Stable Micro Systems

Vienna Court Lammas Road, Godalming, GU7 1YL
Tel: 01483-427345 **Fax:** 01483-427600
E-mail: sales@stablemicrosystems.com
Website: http://www.stablemicrosystems.com

Directors: M. Proto (MD), A. McLachlan (Co Sec)
Managers: M. Batehup (Tech Serv Mgr)
Immediate Holding Company: STABLE MICRO SYSTEMS LIMITED
Registration no: 01702660 **Date established:** 1983 **Turnover:** £2m - £5m
No.of Employees: 21 - 50 **Product Groups:** 38, 67

Date of Accounts	Mar 12	Mar 11	Mar 10
Working Capital	2m	2m	1m
Fixed Assets	1m	1m	1m
Current Assets	3m	3m	2m

Symbio
Unit 8 Coopers Place Combe Lane, Wormley, Godalming, GU8 5SZ
Tel: 01428-685762 **Fax:** 01428-685702
E-mail: info@symbio.co.uk
Website: http://www.symbio.co.uk
Managers: P. Gearing (Mgr)
Registration no: 02534746 **Date established:** 1990
Turnover: £250,000 - £500,000 **No.of Employees:** 1 - 10
Product Groups: 42, 54

Total Soft Water
24 Church Road Milford, Godalming, GU8 5JD
Tel: 01483-421318
E-mail: kshrimptin@softwatershop.com
Website: http://www.totalsoftwater.com
Directors: K. Shrimptin (MD)
Immediate Holding Company: ADRECK DIAGNOSTICS LIMITED
Date established: 2000 **No.of Employees:** 1 - 10 **Product Groups:** 38, 42

Date of Accounts	Mar 09	Mar 08	Sep 11
Working Capital	15	-1	4
Fixed Assets	2	1	5
Current Assets	51	22	85

Tracklink UK Ltd
Unit 5 Miltons Yard Petworth Road, Witley, Godalming, GU8 5LH
Tel: 01428-685124
E-mail: paul@tklink.co.uk
Website: http://www.tklink.co.uk
Directors: P. Mccleave (MD)
Immediate Holding Company: TRACKLINK UK LIMITED
Registration no: 04486879 **Date established:** 2002
No.of Employees: 1 - 10 **Product Groups:** 37, 38, 39

Date of Accounts	Mar 11	Mar 10	Mar 09
Working Capital	91	24	12
Current Assets	442	237	168

Triad Group plc
Huxley House Weyside Park Catteshall Lane, Godalming, GU7 1XE
Tel: 01483-860222 **Fax:** 01483-860198
E-mail: enquiries@triad.co.uk
Website: http://www.triad.co.uk
Bank(s): Bank of Scotland
Directors: A. Fulton (Dir)
Managers: M. Daniels (Tech Serv Mgr), N. Burrows (Comptroller)
Immediate Holding Company: TRIAD GROUP PLC
Registration no: 02285049 **Date established:** 1988
Turnover: £10m - £20m **No.of Employees:** 51 - 100 **Product Groups:** 44, 80, 81, 85

Date of Accounts	Mar 12	Mar 11	Mar 10
Sales Turnover	19m	23m	27m
Pre Tax Profit/Loss	-76	-920	-613
Working Capital	1m	740	1m
Fixed Assets	291	484	892
Current Assets	4m	5m	6m
Current Liabilities	1m	2m	3m

Van Tongeren International Ltd
Van Tongeren House 84a High Street, Godalming, GU7 1DU
Tel: 01483-428082 **Fax:** 01483-417741
E-mail: info@van-tongeren.com
Website: http://www.vantongeren.co.uk
Directors: M. Besley (Dir)
Immediate Holding Company: VAN TONGEREN INTERNATIONAL LIMITED
Registration no: 01018378 **Date established:** 1971 **Turnover:** £5m - £10m
No.of Employees: 1 - 10 **Product Groups:** 46

Date of Accounts	Dec 07	Jun 11	Jun 10
Sales Turnover	5m	8m	11m
Pre Tax Profit/Loss	155	258	2m
Working Capital	805	2m	2m
Fixed Assets	38	14	26
Current Assets	4m	7m	10m
Current Liabilities	2m	3m	4m

Village Gate Automation
2 Nugent Close Dunsfold, Godalming, GU8 4NW
Tel: 01483-200898
E-mail: kevin-shreeve@villagegateautomation.co.uk
Website: http://www.villagegateautomation.co.uk
Directors: K. Shreeve (Prop)
No.of Employees: 1 - 10 **Product Groups:** 26, 35

Watco UK Ltd
Watco House Filmer Grove, Godalming, GU7 3AL
Tel: 01483-425000 **Fax:** 01483-428888
E-mail: sales@watco.co.uk
Website: http://www.watco.co.uk
Directors: E. Southern (Dir), E. Suthon (MD), C. Binks (Fin), A. Barbier (Mkt Research)
Managers: D. Van Sippart (Tech Serv Mgr)
Ultimate Holding Company: RPM INTERNATIONAL INC (USA)
Immediate Holding Company: WATCO UK LIMITED
Registration no: 00459144 **VAT No.:** GB 413 2086 91
Date established: 1948 **Turnover:** £5m - £10m **No.of Employees:** 21 - 50
Product Groups: 30, 31, 32

Date of Accounts	May 12	May 11	May 10
Sales Turnover	10m	9m	10m
Pre Tax Profit/Loss	2m	2m	3m
Working Capital	5m	4m	5m
Fixed Assets	4m	4m	4m
Current Assets	10m	6m	9m
Current Liabilities	884	938	704

Godstone

Able Engraving & Design
Unit D1-D2 Haysbridge Business Centre Brickhouse Lane, South Godstone, Godstone, RH9 8JW
Tel: 01342-843211 **Fax:** 01342-844209
E-mail: a.douglas@able-engraving.co.uk
Website: http://www.able-engraving.co.uk
Directors: A. Douglas (Prop)
Turnover: £250,000 - £500,000 **No.of Employees:** 1 - 10
Product Groups: 25, 28, 30, 32, 33, 35, 36, 44, 46, 47, 48, 49, 65

Bluebell Blinds ltd
Wickens Place Godstone Hill, Godstone, RH9 8AP
Tel: 01733-239416 **Fax:** 01406-380482
E-mail: info@blindfix.co.uk
Website: http://blindfix.co.uk
Directors: K. Wheeler (Prop), N. Douglas (Co Sec)
Managers: A. Douglas (Chief Mgr)
Registration no: 05237369 **VAT No.:** GB 602 4666 60
No.of Employees: 1 - 10 **Product Groups:** 35

Chatfield Applied Research Laboratories Ltd
Newton House Byers Lane, South Godstone, Godstone, RH9 8JH
Tel: 01342-893344 **Fax:** 01342-893542
E-mail: chrischatfield@paintsealanttest.co.uk
Directors: D. Chatfield (Ch), D. Chatfield (Fin), C. Chatfield (MD)
Immediate Holding Company: CHATFIELD APPLIED RESEARCH LABORATORIES LIMITED(THE)
Registration no: 00723949 **VAT No.:** GB 217 8256 54
Date established: 1962 **Turnover:** £250,000 - £500,000
No.of Employees: 1 - 10 **Product Groups:** 85

Date of Accounts	Jul 08	Jul 07	Jul 06
Working Capital	55	109	50
Fixed Assets	377	381	385
Current Assets	136	138	65
Current Liabilities	81	29	16

Electrical Express Ltd
Units D3-4 Haysbridge Business Centre Brickhouse Lane, South Godstone, Godstone, RH9 8JW
Tel: 01342-844445 **Fax:** 01342-844401
Directors: P. Brain (MD)
Immediate Holding Company: ELECTRICAL EXPRESS (EUROPE) LIMITED
Registration no: 03104758 **Date established:** 1995
No.of Employees: 1 - 10 **Product Groups:** 37, 67

Date of Accounts	Feb 11	Feb 10	Feb 09
Working Capital	365	359	232
Current Assets	942	732	467

Freeman Hire & Sales Ltd
Unit O Lambs Business Park Terracotta Road, South Godstone, Godstone, RH9 8LJ
Tel: 01342-892121 **Fax:** 01342-892725
E-mail: info@freeman-hire.co.uk
Website: http://www.freemanhire.com
Directors: P. Freeman (MD)
Immediate Holding Company: FREEMAN HIRE & SALES LIMITED
Registration no: 06222287 **Date established:** 2007
No.of Employees: 1 - 10 **Product Groups:** 36, 45, 67

Date of Accounts	Mar 11	Mar 10	Mar 09
Working Capital	-88	-99	-89
Fixed Assets	93	104	123
Current Assets	37	43	31

Raisin Social
34 Crowhurst Mead, Godstone, RH9 8BF
Tel: 01883-731173 **Fax:** 01883-731174
E-mail: info@raisin-social.com
Website: http://www.raisin-social.com
Directors: S. Halliday (Prop)
Registration no: 02065170 **VAT No.:** GB 444 0865 50
Turnover: £10m - £20m **No.of Employees:** 11 - 20 **Product Groups:** 21, 61

Date of Accounts	Dec 07
Pre Tax Profit/Loss	192
Working Capital	773
Fixed Assets	111
Current Assets	8578
Current Liabilities	7805
Total Share Capital	100
ROCE% (Return on Capital Employed)	21.8

Spantech Products Ltd
10 Beech Gardens Crawley Down, South Godstone, Godstone, RH9 8HB
Tel: 01342-893239 **Fax:** 01342-892584
E-mail: spantech@auptag.com
Website: http://www.spantech.co.uk
Directors: C. Narain (MD)
Immediate Holding Company: SPANTECH PRODUCTS LIMITED
Registration no: 01808903 **VAT No.:** GB 404 5221 00
Date established: 1984 **Turnover:** £250,000 - £500,000
No.of Employees: 1 - 10 **Product Groups:** 38

Date of Accounts	Jun 11	Jun 10	Jun 09
Working Capital	163	124	55
Fixed Assets	139	142	149
Current Assets	274	249	130

Steel The Scene
Unit 1 Parkwood Industrial Estate Byers Lane, South Godstone, Godstone, RH9 8JJ
Tel: 01342-893237 **Fax:** 01342-894521
E-mail: sets@steelthescene.co.uk
Website: http://www.steelthescene.co.uk
Directors: B. Ashwick (Ptnr)
Turnover: £250,000 - £500,000 **No.of Employees:** 1 - 10
Product Groups: 26, 45, 52, 81, 83, 89

Toogood Industrial
Haysbridge Business Centre Brickhouse Lane, South Godstone, Godstone, RH9 8JW
Tel: 01342-844188 **Fax:** 01342-844220
E-mail: office@toogood.co.uk
Website: http://www.toogood.co.uk
Directors: P. Toogood (Prop), C. Bess-Stanley (Purch), B. Stanley (Dir)
Immediate Holding Company: TOOGOOD INDUSTRIAL LIMITED
Registration no: 04995631 **VAT No.:** GB 424 9999 95
Date established: 2003 **Turnover:** Up to £250,000
No.of Employees: 1 - 10 **Product Groups:** 30, 33, 34, 35

Date of Accounts	Dec 10	Dec 09	Dec 08
Sales Turnover	194	208	266
Pre Tax Profit/Loss	25	12	47
Working Capital	-33	-48	-57
Fixed Assets	39	50	63
Current Assets	51	56	68
Current Liabilities	55	53	25

Guildford

A V Pound & Company Ltd
Sussex House The Pines Trading Estate, Guildford, GU3 3BH
Tel: 01483-280900 **Fax:** 01483-280901
E-mail: info@chemoxpound.com
Website: http://www.avpound.com
Directors: F. Pound (MD), G. Pound (MD), G. Pound (Co Sec)
Ultimate Holding Company: COMPANY ADMINISTRATORS LIMITED
Immediate Holding Company: A.V. POUND (ASIA) LIMITED
Registration no: 01905875 **Date established:** 1985 **Turnover:** £5m - £10m
No.of Employees: 11 - 20 **Product Groups:** 31

Abbotsford Associates
39 Marlyns Drive, Guildford, GU4 7LT
Tel: 01483-303638 **Fax:** 01483-303638
Directors: D. Boshier (Ptnr)
Date established: 1994 **No.of Employees:** 1 - 10 **Product Groups:** 35

Allianz Insurance plc
57 Ladymead, Guildford, GU1 1DB
Tel: 01483-568161 **Fax:** 01483-300952
E-mail: a.torrance@cornhill.co.uk
Website: http://www.allianz.co.uk
Directors: A. Torrance (Grp Chief Exec)
Ultimate Holding Company: ALLIANZ HOLDINGS PLC
Immediate Holding Company: ALLIANZ INSURANCE PLC
Registration no: 00084638 **Date established:** 2005
Turnover: Over £1,000m **No.of Employees:** 501 - 1000
Product Groups: 82

Date of Accounts	Dec 11	Dec 10	Dec 09
Pre Tax Profit/Loss	137m	97m	143m
Fixed Assets	2574m	2657m	2738m
Current Assets	1086m	1131m	1107m
Current Liabilities	577m	3003m	443m

Amadeus Design & Build
4 Howard Buildings Burpham Lane, Guildford, GU4 7NB
Tel: 0870-734 6154 **Fax:** 01483- 455511
E-mail: team@amadeusdbl.com
Website: http://www.amadeusdbl.co.uk
Directors: D. Ellis (Dir), C. Ellis (Dir)
Date established: 2003 **No.of Employees:** 1 - 10 **Product Groups:** 52

Arrow Group Industries
6 Quarry Street, Guildford, GU1 3UR
Tel: 01483-455004
E-mail: mike.scull@arrowshed.com
Website: http://www.arrowsheds.com
Directors: M. Skull (Dir)
Immediate Holding Company: LLOYD DAVIES SURVEYORS AND VALUERS GUILDFORD LIMITED
Registration no: 06226410 **Date established:** 2007
No.of Employees: 1 - 10 **Product Groups:** 35

Date of Accounts	Apr 11	Apr 10	Apr 09
Working Capital	-22	-28	-1
Fixed Assets	19	37	56
Current Assets	61	145	146

Ash Fabrications
5 Peterborough Road, Guildford, GU2 9SY
Tel: 01483-565119 **Fax:** 01483-565119
Directors: A. Habgood (Prop)
Date established: 1993 **No.of Employees:** 1 - 10 **Product Groups:** 26, 35

Beacon Electrical Co. Ltd
285 Stoughton Road, Guildford, GU2 9PR
Tel: 01483-562271 **Fax:** 01483-579233
E-mail: beacon-guildford@rhelectric.co.uk
Website: http://www.rhelectric.co.uk
Managers: G. Dwyer (Mgr)
Immediate Holding Company: R & H GROUP - SWINDON
Registration no: 00246059 **No.of Employees:** 1 - 10 **Product Groups:** 35, 37, 45, 67

Birchgrove Products
Unit 3c Merrow Business Park Merrow Lane, Guildford, GU4 7WA
Tel: 01483-533400 **Fax:** 01483-533700
E-mail: sales@birchgrove.co.uk
Website: http://www.birchgrove.co.uk
Directors: A. Bradshaw (MD)
Immediate Holding Company: BIRCHGROVE PRODUCTS LIMITED
Registration no: 02306473 **Date established:** 1988
Turnover: £250,000 - £500,000 **No.of Employees:** 1 - 10
Product Groups: 30, 40, 65, 67

Date of Accounts	Mar 11	Mar 10	Mar 09
Sales Turnover	N/A	N/A	334
Working Capital	-154	-155	-147
Fixed Assets	141	141	141
Current Assets	435	430	456

Boc Gases Ltd
The Priestley Centre 10 Priestley Road, Surrey Research Park, Guildford, GU2 7XY
Tel: 01483-579857 **Fax:** 0800-136601
E-mail: specialproducts@uk.gases.boc.com
Website: http://www.boc.com
Directors: J. Filer (Dir), S. Thornton (Mkt Research), T. Haywood (Public Relation), R. Chatterton (Mkt Research), P. Richardson (Safety), G. Brown (Mkt Research), C. Lambert (Fin), B. Beecroft (MD), A. Wiper (Comm), J. Ford (Cust Serv)
Managers: C. Douglass (Comm), J. Romer (District Mgr)
Ultimate Holding Company: LINDE AG (GERMANY)
Immediate Holding Company: BOC LIMITED
Registration no: 00337663 **VAT No.:** GB 226 5565 55
Date established: 1938 **Turnover:** £500m - £1,000m
No.of Employees: 21 - 50 **Product Groups:** 31, 32

Date of Accounts	Dec 11	Dec 10	Dec 08
Sales Turnover	726m	691m	721m
Pre Tax Profit/Loss	122m	125m	67m
Working Capital	409m	278m	-219m
Fixed Assets	480m	492m	538m
Current Assets	724m	578m	371m
Current Liabilities	64m	68m	73m

Britannic Technologies Ltd
Britannic House Merrow Business Park, Guildford, GU4 7WA
Tel: 01483-242526 **Fax:** 0845-050 1001
E-mail: enquiries@btlnet.co.uk
Website: http://www.btlnet.co.uk
Directors: R. Dendle (MD)
Managers: J. Sharpe (Sales Prom Mgr), C. Winnan
Ultimate Holding Company: BRITANNIC GROUP (HOLDINGS) LIMITED
Immediate Holding Company: BRITANNIC TELECOM COMPANY LIMITED
Registration no: 04409227 **Date established:** 2002 **Turnover:** £5m - £10m
No.of Employees: 51 - 100 **Product Groups:** 37, 38, 48

C T C National Cyclists Organisation
Parklands Railton Road, Guildford, GU2 9JX
Tel: 08447-368450 **Fax:** 01483-426994
E-mail: kevin.mayne@ctc.org.uk
Website: http://www.ctc.org.uk
Directors: C. McKinley (Chief Op Offcr), G. Seabright (Dir), K. Mayne (Grp Chief Exec)
Managers: D. Dowling, S. Cherry (Sales Admin)
Ultimate Holding Company: CYCLISTS TOURING CLUB.
Immediate Holding Company: CYCLISTS TOURING CLUB (NORTHERN) LIMITED
Registration no: 01101957 **Date established:** 1973
Turnover: £250,000 - £500,000 **No.of Employees:** 51 - 100
Product Groups: 87

Date of Accounts	Sep 11	Sep 10	Sep 09
Pre Tax Profit/Loss	10	-0	-1
Working Capital	69	59	59
Current Assets	70	61	61
Current Liabilities	1	1	1

The Cast Iron Company Ltd
Home Farm Shere Road, Albury, Guildford, GU5 9BL
Tel: 01483-203388 **Fax:** 01483-229088
E-mail: info@castiron.co.uk
Website: http://www.castiron.co.uk
Directors: J. Smith (Prop)
Immediate Holding Company: THE CAST IRON COMPANY LIMITED
Registration no: 02413240 **Date established:** 1989
No.of Employees: 1 - 10 **Product Groups:** 26, 35

Date of Accounts	Sep 11	Sep 10	Sep 09
Working Capital	261	81	218
Fixed Assets	9	N/A	N/A
Current Assets	814	283	571
Current Liabilities	276	99	144

Chemox Pound Ltd
Sussex House 11 The Pines Trading Estate Broad Street, Guildford, GU3 3BH
Tel: 01483-450660 **Fax:** 01483-450770
E-mail: andrew.stone@chemox.co.uk
Website: http://www.chemoxpound.com
Bank(s): National Westminster Bank Plc
Directors: A. Stone (Dir), D. Barnby (Co Sec)
Ultimate Holding Company: HOBART ENTERPRISES LIMITED (ISLE OF MAN)
Immediate Holding Company: CHEMOX LIMITED
Registration no: 01707005 **Date established:** 1983
Turnover: £10m - £20m **No.of Employees:** 11 - 20 **Product Groups:** 31, 32, 34

Date of Accounts	Dec 10	Dec 09	Dec 08
Sales Turnover	12m	9m	8m
Pre Tax Profit/Loss	826	583	517
Working Capital	2m	1m	748
Fixed Assets	77	42	64
Current Assets	4m	3m	2m
Current Liabilities	1m	1m	821

Cleansorb Ltd
Unit 1J Merrow Business Centre, Merrow Lane, Guildford, GU4 7WA
Tel: 01483-300107 **Fax:** 01483-300109
E-mail: contact@cleansorb.com
Website: http://www.cleansorb.com
Directors: R. Harris (Dir), I. McKay (Dir)
Registration no: 02974002 **VAT No.:** GB 664 6466 04
Date established: 1994 **Turnover:** £5m - £10m **No.of Employees:** 1 - 10
Product Groups: 32, 45, 51, 66

Date of Accounts	Mar 12	Mar 11	Mar 10
Working Capital	1m	2m	1m
Fixed Assets	672	544	471
Current Assets	1m	2m	1m

Clin-Tech Ltd
Unit G Perram Works Merrow Lane, Guildford, GU4 7BN
Tel: 01483-301902 **Fax:** 01483-301907
E-mail: info@clin-tech.co.uk
Website: http://www.clin-tech.co.uk
Directors: M. Childerstone (MD)
Immediate Holding Company: CLIN-TECH LIMITED
Registration no: 00929040 **VAT No.:** GB 205 5876 58
Date established: 1968 **Turnover:** Up to £250,000
No.of Employees: 1 - 10 **Product Groups:** 31, 32, 66

Date of Accounts	Jan 12	Jan 11	Jan 09
Working Capital	5	5	5
Current Assets	5	5	5

Corporate Multimedia Solutions
The Old Barn Guildford Road, Normandy, Guildford, GU3 2AU
Tel: 01483-237723
E-mail: webenquiries@corporatemultimedia.com
Website: http://www.corporatemultimedia.com
Directors: M. Hudson (Dir)
Date established: 1996 **Turnover:** £500,000 - £1m
No.of Employees: 1 - 10 **Product Groups:** 89

Detica Ltd
Chancellor Court Occam Road, Surrey Research Park, Guildford, GU2 7YP
Tel: 01483-816000 **Fax:** 01483-816144
E-mail: queries@detica.com
Website: http://www.detica.com
Directors: C. Conway (Vice Ch), M. Gradden (Fin), M. Sutherland (MD)
Managers: N. Wilding (Mktg Serv Mgr)
Ultimate Holding Company: BAE SYSTEMS PLC
Immediate Holding Company: DETICA HOLDINGS LIMITED
Registration no: 05116710 **Date established:** 2004 **Turnover:** £1m - £2m
No.of Employees: 501 - 1000 **Product Groups:** 44, 84

Date of Accounts	Dec 10	Dec 09	Dec 08
Pre Tax Profit/Loss	159	206	28m
Working Capital	28m	28m	27m
Current Assets	67m	67m	66m
Current Liabilities	N/A	N/A	428

Doble Powertest
Unit 5 Weyvern Park Portsmouth Road, Peasmarsh, Guildford, GU3 1NA
Tel: 01483-514120 **Fax:** 01483-514149
E-mail: rheywood@doble.com
Website: http://www.doble.com
Managers: R. Heywood (Mgr)
No.of Employees: 21 - 50 **Product Groups:** 38, 85

F G Barnes
Moorfield Road Slyfield Industrial Estate, Guildford, GU1 1RT
Tel: 01483-885885 **Fax:** 01483-885888
E-mail: enquiries@fg-barnes.co.uk
Website: http://www.fg-barnes.co.uk
Bank(s): H.S.B.C
Directors: J. Ross (Pers)
Managers: D. Marshall (Tech Serv Mgr), S. Goodchild (Chief Mgr)
Ultimate Holding Company: F.G.BARNES & SONS,LIMITED
Immediate Holding Company: F G BARNES (MAIDSTONE) LIMITED
Registration no: 04548410 **VAT No.:** GB 211 2914 06
Date established: 2002 **Turnover:** £10m - £20m
No.of Employees: 51 - 100 **Product Groups:** 68

Date of Accounts	Dec 11	Dec 10	Dec 09
Sales Turnover	13m	13m	13m
Pre Tax Profit/Loss	-541	-175	19
Working Capital	-48	57	230
Fixed Assets	46	79	81
Current Assets	2m	3m	3m
Current Liabilities	673	233	1m

Fike Protection Systems Ltd
4 The Moorfield Centre Moorfield Road, Slyfield Industrial Estate, Guildford, GU1 1RA
Tel: 01483-457584 **Fax:** 01483-456235
E-mail: sales@fike.com
Website: http://www.fike.com
Directors: S. Stanley (Fin), M. Austin (MD)
Managers: P. Lovelock
Immediate Holding Company: FIKE PROTECTION SYSTEMS LIMITED
Registration no: 03622173 **Date established:** 1998 **Turnover:** £5m - £10m
No.of Employees: 11 - 20 **Product Groups:** 33, 40

Date of Accounts	Dec 11	Dec 10	Dec 09
Sales Turnover	N/A	N/A	6m
Pre Tax Profit/Loss	N/A	N/A	-87
Working Capital	945	657	237
Fixed Assets	62	50	61
Current Assets	3m	3m	3m
Current Liabilities	N/A	N/A	426

G D K Air Conditioning
22-23 Enterprise Estate Moorfield Road, Guildford, GU1 1RB
Tel: 01483-570953 **Fax:** 01483-894162
E-mail: sales@gdkltd.co.uk
Website: http://www.gdkairconditioning.co.uk
Directors: D. Willey (MD)
Managers: I. Springer (Mgr), S. Peterson (Mgr)
Ultimate Holding Company: GDK AIR CONDITIONING LIMITED
Immediate Holding Company: GDK AIR CONDITIONING LIMITED
Registration no: 04584181 **Date established:** 2002 **Turnover:** £1m - £2m
No.of Employees: 1 - 10 **Product Groups:** 52

Date of Accounts	Apr 11	Apr 10	Apr 09
Working Capital	52	40	17
Fixed Assets	20	23	37
Current Assets	169	120	91

Geo Language Services
2a St Mary's Terrace Mill Lane, Guildford, GU1 3TZ
Tel: 01483-577750 **Fax:** 01483-431815
E-mail: help@geolanguages.co.uk
Website: http://www.geolanguages.co.uk
Directors: G. Poole (Fin)
Immediate Holding Company: GEO LANGUAGE SERVICES LTD
Registration no: 05813388 **Date established:** 2006
No.of Employees: 1 - 10 **Product Groups:** 80

Date of Accounts	May 11	May 10	May 09
Working Capital	111	15	-5
Fixed Assets	10	5	5
Current Assets	369	172	112

George Abbot School
Woodruff Avenue, Guildford, GU1 1XX
Tel: 01483-888000 **Fax:** 01483-888001
E-mail: office@georgeabbot.surrey.sch.uk
Website: http://www.georgeabbot.surrey.sch.uk
Managers: D. Moloney
Immediate Holding Company: GEORGE ABBOT SCHOOL ACADEMY TRUST
Registration no: 07649091 **Date established:** 2011
No.of Employees: 101 - 250 **Product Groups:** 41

George Weil & Sons Ltd
Old Portsmouth Road Peasmarsh, Guildford, GU3 1LZ
Tel: 01483-565800 **Fax:** 01483-565807
E-mail: esales@georgeweil.com
Website: http://www.georgeweil.com
Managers: J. Barrell (Sales Prom Mgr)
Immediate Holding Company: FIBRECRAFTS LIMITED
Registration no: 03738838 **Date established:** 1999
No.of Employees: 1 - 10 **Product Groups:** 23, 27, 32, 66

Guildford Shades (t/a Guildford Shades)
Keens Lane, Guildford, GU3 3JS
Tel: 01483-232394 **Fax:** 01483- 236420
E-mail: sales@guildfordshades.co.uk
Website: http://www.guildfordshades.co.uk
Directors: B. Ross (MD), S. Ross (Dir)
Immediate Holding Company: MARQUEES LIMITED
Registration no: 00283650 **VAT No.:** GB 413 8023 85
Date established: 1934 **Turnover:** £1m - £2m **No.of Employees:** 1 - 10
Product Groups: 23

Date of Accounts	Sep 11	Sep 10	Sep 09
Working Capital	54	227	184
Fixed Assets	N/A	85	97
Current Assets	117	348	287

H S O P Text Processing Services
Shortlands Snowdenham Lane, Bramley, Guildford, GU5 0AT
Tel: 01483-892287
Directors: I. Hamilton (Prop)
Date established: 1977 **Turnover:** Up to £250,000
No.of Employees: 1 - 10 **Product Groups:** 44

H2O Heaven
Unit A St James House Bedford Road, Guildford, GU1 4SJ
Tel: 01483-576881 **Fax:** 07720-953144
E-mail: sales@h2oheaven.com
Website: http://www.h2oheaven.com
Directors: Coakley (MD)
Ultimate Holding Company: STACKHOUSE POLAND HOLDINGS LTD
Immediate Holding Company: RHB INSURANCE SERVICES LIMITED
Registration no: 04281378 **Date established:** 1984 **Turnover:** £5m - £10m
No.of Employees: 1 - 10 **Product Groups:** 32, 38, 52, 66

Date of Accounts	Dec 11	Dec 10	Dec 09
Sales Turnover	8m	8m	7m
Pre Tax Profit/Loss	2m	2m	1m
Working Capital	240	383	159
Fixed Assets	3m	3m	3m
Current Assets	6m	7m	6m
Current Liabilities	6m	6m	5m

Heat Profile
Unit 1 Walnut Tree Park Walnut Tree Close, Guildford, GU1 4TR
Tel: 01483-537000 **Fax:** 01483-537500
E-mail: sales@heatprofile.co.uk
Website: http://www.heatprofile.co.uk
Directors: P. Kilkenny (MD), I. Mitchell (Sales)
Ultimate Holding Company: CHANTELLE SA (FRANCE)
Immediate Holding Company: CHANTELLE LINGERIE LIMITED
Registration no: 01897006 **Date established:** 1986
Turnover: £500,000 - £1m **No.of Employees:** 1 - 10 **Product Groups:** 40

Date of Accounts	Dec 11	Dec 10	Dec 09
Working Capital	901	907	890
Fixed Assets	8	34	59
Current Assets	1m	1m	1m

Honey Brothers Ltd
New Pond Road Peasmarsh, Guildford, GU3 1JR
Tel: 01483-561362 **Fax:** 01483-535608
E-mail: sales@honeybros.com
Website: http://www.honeybros.com
Directors: M. Day (MD), B. Honey (Co Sec)
Immediate Holding Company: HONEY BROTHERS LIMITED
Registration no: 06298752 **Date established:** 2007 **Turnover:** £1m - £2m
No.of Employees: 11 - 20 **Product Groups:** 67

Date of Accounts	Mar 11	Mar 10	Mar 09
Working Capital	232	181	132
Fixed Assets	489	447	37
Current Assets	894	730	592

Hutton & Rostron Ltd
Netley House Gomshall Road, Gomshall, Guildford, GU5 9HA
Tel: 01483-203221 **Fax:** 01483-202911
E-mail: james@handr.co.uk
Website: http://www.handr.co.uk
Directors: J. Hutton (MD)
Immediate Holding Company: HUTTON + ROSTRON LIMITED
Registration no: 01884622 **Date established:** 1985
No.of Employees: 1 - 10 **Product Groups:** 80

Inline London
Unit 3 Bridge Park Merrow Lane, Guildford, GU4 7BF
Tel: 08450-770045 **Fax:** 08450-770046
E-mail: info@inlinelondon.co.uk
Website: http://www.inlinelondon.co.uk
Directors: N. Thomas (MD)
Registration no: 02757936 **Date established:** 2004
No.of Employees: 1 - 10 **Product Groups:** 23, 24, 26, 38, 63, 67

Ip Test Ltd
15 The Pines Trading Estate Broad Street, Guildford, GU3 3BH
Tel: 01483-567218 **Fax:** 01483- 506054
E-mail: sales@iptest.com
Website: http://www.iptest.com
Bank(s): Lloyds TSB Bank plc
Directors: A. Middleton (Co Sec), D. Furse (MD), D. Newth (MD), R. Denyer (Dir)
Managers: A. Simmons (Personnel)
Immediate Holding Company: IP TEST LIMITED
Registration no: 05822155 **Date established:** 2006 **Turnover:** £1m - £2m
No.of Employees: 21 - 50 **Product Groups:** 38

Date of Accounts	Dec 11	Dec 10	Dec 09
Working Capital	654	201	151
Fixed Assets	15	25	40
Current Assets	1m	2m	325

Jewson Ltd
Walnut Tree Close, Guildford, GU1 4UB
Tel: 01483-560066 **Fax:** 01483-532711
Website: http://www.jewson.co.uk

Managers: P. Daley (Mgr)
Ultimate Holding Company: COMPAGNIE DE SAINT GOBAIN (FRANCE)
Immediate Holding Company: JEWSON LIMITED
Registration no: 00348407 **VAT No.:** GB 394 1212 63
Date established: 1939 **Turnover:** £2m - £5m
No.of Employees: 1501 & over **Product Groups:** 66

Date of Accounts	Dec 11	Dec 10	Dec 09
Sales Turnover	1606m	1547m	1485m
Pre Tax Profit/Loss	18m	100m	45m
Working Capital	-345m	-250m	-349m
Fixed Assets	496m	387m	461m
Current Assets	657m	1005m	1320m
Current Liabilities	66m	120m	64m

Key Cleaning Services
35 Harts Gardens, Guildford, GU2 9QB
Tel: 01483-531038
E-mail: info@keycleaning.co.uk
Website: http://www.keycleaning.co.uk
Directors: M. Burgess (Ptnr)
Date established: 2000 **No.of Employees:** 1 - 10 **Product Groups:** 32, 48, 52, 63, 80

The Knob Connection
13 Tunsgate, Guildford, GU1 3QT
Tel: 01483-565122 **Fax:** 01483-565122
E-mail: sales@knobconnection.com
Website: http://www.knobconnection.com
Directors: M. Cousin (Prop)
Date established: 2001 **No.of Employees:** 1 - 10 **Product Groups:** 35, 36

Kuju Entertainment Ltd
Suite 2 River House Broadford Park Business Centre Broadford Park, Shalford, Guildford, GU4 8EP
Tel: 01483-409950 **Fax:** 01483-571662
E-mail: admin@kuju.com
Website: http://www.kuju.com
Managers: A. Walter (Asst Gen Mgr)
Ultimate Holding Company: CATALIS SE NETHERLANDS
Immediate Holding Company: KUJU PLC
Registration no: 04335012 **Date established:** 2001
Turnover: £10m - £20m **No.of Employees:** 11 - 20 **Product Groups:** 44

Date of Accounts	Dec 11	Dec 10	Dec 09
Pre Tax Profit/Loss	-12	-0	2
Working Capital	-18	-6	1m
Fixed Assets	4m	4m	4m
Current Assets	N/A	N/A	1m
Current Liabilities	18	6	5

Laytons Solicitors
Tempus Court Onslow Street, Guildford, GU1 4SS
Tel: 01483-407000 **Fax:** 01483-407070
E-mail: will.slater@laytons.com
Website: http://www.laytons.com
Directors: W. Slater (Snr Part)
Managers: Z. Melville-harris, J. Carter (Chief Acct)
Immediate Holding Company: LUMESSE CORPORATE LIMITED
Registration no: 04296658 **Date established:** 2001
Turnover: £10m - £20m **No.of Employees:** 21 - 50 **Product Groups:** 80

Lion In The Sun
PO Box 1034, Guildford, GU5 0XG
Tel: 01483-890070 **Fax:** 0870-751 7085
E-mail: info@lioninthesun.com
Website: http://www.lioninthesun.com
Directors: C. Sanders (Dir)
Registration no: 04879454 **No.of Employees:** 1 - 10 **Product Groups:** 24, 32

Manitowoc Foodservice UK Limited Enodis UK Food Service
Ashbourne House The Guildway, Old Portsmouth Road, Guildford, GU3 1LR
Tel: 01483-464900 **Fax:** 01483-464905
E-mail: fsuk.info@manitowoc.com
Website: http://www.enodisuk.com
Ultimate Holding Company: Enodis plc
Immediate Holding Company: Enodis plc
Registration no: 02656967 **No.of Employees:** 101 - 250
Product Groups: 40, 67

Marrick Commercial Interiors
Bridge Park Merrow Lane, Guildford, GU4 7BF
Tel: 01483-306500 **Fax:** 01483-455378
E-mail: info@marrickgroup.co.uk
Website: http://www.marrickcommercialinteriors.co.uk
Directors: D. Taylor (Prop)
No.of Employees: 1 - 10 **Product Groups:** 25, 26, 27, 30, 33, 35, 37, 38, 40, 52, 61, 66, 67, 81, 84, 87

Mickle Laboratory Engineering Co. Ltd
Goose Green Gomshall, Guildford, GU5 9LJ
Tel: 01483-202178 **Fax:** 01483-202178
E-mail: anthony@micklelab.co.uk
Website: http://www.micklelab.co.uk
Directors: A. Mickle (MD)
Immediate Holding Company: MICKLE LABORATORY ENGINEERING CO. LIMITED
Registration no: 01413483 **VAT No.:** GB 296 4452 24
Date established: 1979 **Turnover:** Up to £250,000
No.of Employees: 1 - 10 **Product Groups:** 42

Date of Accounts	Feb 11	Feb 10	Feb 09
Sales Turnover	100	N/A	N/A
Working Capital	232	279	296
Fixed Assets	137	138	141
Current Assets	379	358	409
Current Liabilities	N/A	72	N/A

N B S Technologies
B1 Moorfield Point Moorfield Road Slyfield Industrial Estate, Guildford, GU1 1RU
Tel: 01483-563200 **Fax:** 01932-351382
E-mail: sales@nbstech.com
Website: http://www.nbstech.com
Managers: P. Barton (Prod Mgr)
Ultimate Holding Company: BROOKFIELD ASSET MANAGEMENT INC (CANADA)
Immediate Holding Company: NBS TECHNOLOGIES LIMITED
Registration no: 03500404 **VAT No.:** GB 689 2424 93
Date established: 1998 **Turnover:** £2m - £5m **No.of Employees:** 11 - 20
Product Groups: 28, 30, 37, 40, 44

Date of Accounts	Sep 11	Sep 10	Sep 09
Sales Turnover	3m	5m	4m
Pre Tax Profit/Loss	51	286	156
Working Capital	924	910	700
Fixed Assets	51	20	28
Current Assets	2m	2m	2m
Current Liabilities	140	302	275

New Level Recruitment
32-34 London Road, Guildford, GU1 2AB
Tel: 08452-701640 **Fax:** 0870-891 3120
E-mail: jo@newlevelrecruitment.com
Website: http://www.newlevelrecruitment.com
Directors: J. Mack (Dir)
Immediate Holding Company: NEW LEVEL RECRUITMENT LIMITED
Registration no: 05374578 **Date established:** 2005
No.of Employees: 1 - 10 **Product Groups:** 54, 80, 84

Date of Accounts	Feb 12	Feb 11	Feb 10
Working Capital	-4	-16	-5
Fixed Assets	N/A	N/A	3
Current Assets	6	2	29

Nynas Ltd
116 London Road, Guildford, GU1 1TN
Tel: 01483-506953 **Fax:** 01483-506954
Website: http://www.nynas.com
Directors: K. Lloyd Sherlock (Co Sec), M. Ward (Co Sec), T. Larney (MD)
Managers: D. Moore (Sales Prom Mgr), P. Vann (Chief Mgr)
Immediate Holding Company: NYNAS NAPHTHENICS LIMITED
Registration no: 02450786 **VAT No.:** GB 641 4722 54
Date established: 1989 **Turnover:** £500,000 - £1m
No.of Employees: 1 - 10 **Product Groups:** 31, 32, 66

Openbet Retail
Bishopsgate House Broadford Park, Shalford, Guildford, GU4 8ED
Tel: 01483-293900 **Fax:** 01483-533333
E-mail: solutions@openbet.com
Website: http://www.openbetretail.com
Bank(s): HSBC Bank plc
Directors: C. Rowlands (Fin), M. Randall (Fin), L. Warrington (Pers)
Managers: G. Blackburne (Purch Mgr), C. Stansfield (Personnel), R. Irvin (Tech Serv Mgr), S. Underwood (Sales & Mktg Mg)
Ultimate Holding Company: VITRUVIAN PARTNERS LLP
Immediate Holding Company: OPENBET RETAIL LIMITED
Registration no: 02730742 **Date established:** 1992
Turnover: £10m - £20m **No.of Employees:** 51 - 100 **Product Groups:** 37, 39, 44

Date of Accounts	Nov 09	Nov 08	Jun 11
Sales Turnover	13m	22m	15m
Pre Tax Profit/Loss	1m	-1m	-113
Working Capital	9m	6m	-8m
Fixed Assets	9m	8m	737
Current Assets	13m	13m	8m
Current Liabilities	4m	4m	3m

Ornate Products
Tilsey Farm Horsham Road, Bramley, Guildford, GU5 0LN
Tel: 01483-277000 **Fax:** 01483-475134
E-mail: ornateproducts@aol.com
Website: http://www.ornateproducts.co.uk
Directors: A. Clamp (Dir)
VAT No.: GB 414 0453 94 **Date established:** 1986
No.of Employees: 1 - 10 **Product Groups:** 33, 65

P P A Energy
1 Frederick Sanger Road Surrey Research Park, Guildford, GU2 7YD
Tel: 01483-544944 **Fax:** 01483-544955
E-mail: marketing@ppaenergy.co.uk
Website: http://www.ppaenergy.co.uk
Directors: C. Lucas (Dir)
Managers: N. Pinto
Immediate Holding Company: PPA ENERGY DEVELOPMENTS LIMITED
Registration no: 07367794 **Date established:** 2010
No.of Employees: 11 - 20 **Product Groups:** 37, 84

Petroplan
91 Walnut Tree Close, Guildford, GU1 4UQ
Tel: 01483-881500 **Fax:** 01483-881501
E-mail: info@petroplan.com
Website: http://www.petroplan.com
Bank(s): Royal Bank of Scotland
Directors: R. Williams (Fin)
Immediate Holding Company: PETROPLAN LIMITED
Registration no: 01266770 **VAT No.:** GB 215 1085 05
Date established: 1976 **Turnover:** £50m - £75m
No.of Employees: 21 - 50 **Product Groups:** 80

Date of Accounts	Dec 11	Dec 10	Dec 09
Sales Turnover	88m	56m	49m
Pre Tax Profit/Loss	652	210	104
Working Capital	1m	745	501
Fixed Assets	76	79	166
Current Assets	20m	12m	9m
Current Liabilities	13m	1m	673

Philips Electronics UK Ltd
Philips Centre Guildford Business Park, Guildford, GU2 8XH
Tel: 08706-010101
Website: http://www.philips.com
Directors: G. Prior (MD), M. Conroy (Sales), N. Mesher (Sales)
Ultimate Holding Company: KONINKLIJKE PHILIPS ELECTRONICS NV (NETHERLANDS)
Immediate Holding Company: PHILIPS ELECTRONICS UK LIMITED
Registration no: 00446897 **Date established:** 1947
Turnover: £500m - £1,000m **No.of Employees:** 1 - 10
Product Groups: 40

Date of Accounts	Dec 09	Dec 08	Dec 07
Sales Turnover	736m	827m	813m
Pre Tax Profit/Loss	30m	4m	33m
Working Capital	27m	12m	-162m
Fixed Assets	449m	395m	546m
Current Assets	274m	283m	388m
Current Liabilities	72m	60m	N/A

Premier Fund Managers Ltd
1 Eastgate Court High Street, Guildford, GU1 3DE
Tel: 01483-306090 **Fax:** 01483-300845
E-mail: info@premierfunds.co.uk
Website: http://www.premierfunds.co.uk
Directors: K. Strange (Div), M. Burgess (Pers), S. Wilson (Sales & Mktg), N. Macpherson (Fin), M. O'shea (Grp Chief Exec)
Ultimate Holding Company: PREMIER ASSET MANAGEMENT GROUP LTD
Immediate Holding Company: PREMIER FUND MANAGERS LIMITED
Registration no: 02274227 **Date established:** 1988 **Turnover:** £5m - £10m
No.of Employees: 51 - 100 **Product Groups:** 80

Date of Accounts	Sep 11	Sep 10	Sep 09
Sales Turnover	7m	8m	5m
Pre Tax Profit/Loss	-199	337	-247
Working Capital	1m	1m	1m
Current Assets	3m	3m	3m
Current Liabilities	732	838	865

Premier Supply Co.
Perram Works Merrow Lane, Guildford, GU4 7BN
Tel: 01483-534346 **Fax:** 01483-303992
E-mail: info@premiersupply.co.uk
Website: http://www.premiersupply.co.uk
Bank(s): National Westminster Bank Plc
Managers: G. Mancey (Chief Mgr)
Ultimate Holding Company: D.S. JOHNSTON (HOLDINGS) LTD
Immediate Holding Company: JOHNSTON & CO. (HOLDINGS) LTD
Registration no: 00692835 **VAT No.:** GB 211 4920 06
Date established: 1993 **Turnover:** £2m - £5m **No.of Employees:** 11 - 20
Product Groups: 40, 68

Q V S Electrical Wholsale
Unit 9 Quadrum Park Old Portsmouth Road, Peasmarsh, Guildford, GU3 1LU
Tel: 01483-569559 **Fax:** 01483-570090
E-mail: guildford@qvsdirect.co.uk
Website: http://www.qvsdirect.co.uk
Directors: P. Brain (Prop)
Date established: 2004 **No.of Employees:** 1 - 10 **Product Groups:** 36, 40

R2 Proofreading
9 Old Farm Road, Guildford, GU1 1QN
Tel: 01483-533895
E-mail: enquiries@r2proofreading.co.uk
Website: http://www.r2proofreading.co.uk
Directors: R. Rayment (Prop)
Date established: 2007 **No.of Employees:** 1 - 10 **Product Groups:** 80

Reed Computing Cmptr Recruitment Consultancy
17 Woodbridge Road, Guildford, GU1 4PU
Tel: 01483-569061 **Fax:** 01483-567288
E-mail: saleseastcomputing@reed.co.uk
Website: http://www.reed.co.uk
Directors: R. Frodin (MD)
Ultimate Holding Company: REED PERSONNEL SERVICES P.L.C.
Registration no: 00669854 **Turnover:** £125m - £250m
No.of Employees: 21 - 50 **Product Groups:** 80

Reed Specialist Recruitment
51-53 High Street, Guildford, GU1 3DY
Tel: 01483-529900 **Fax:** 01483-529901
E-mail: guildford@reed.co.uk
Website: http://www.reed.co.uk
Managers: S. Stone (Mgr)
Ultimate Holding Company: REED GLOBAL LTD (MALTA)
Immediate Holding Company: REED EMPLOYMENT LIMITED
Registration no: 00669854 **Date established:** 1960
Turnover: £75m - £125m **No.of Employees:** 1 - 10 **Product Groups:** 80

Date of Accounts	Jun 11	Jun 10	Dec 07
Sales Turnover	618	450	287m
Pre Tax Profit/Loss	-2m	310	8m
Working Capital	23m	28m	28m
Fixed Assets	31	36	5m
Current Assets	28m	30m	74m
Current Liabilities	37	29	21m

Reneuron
10 Nugent Road Surrey Research Park, Guildford, GU2 7AF
Tel: 01483-302560 **Fax:** 01483-534864
E-mail: info@reneuron.com
Website: http://www.reneuron.com
Managers: M. Hunt
Ultimate Holding Company: RENEURON GROUP PLC
Immediate Holding Company: RENEURON LIMITED
Registration no: 03375897 **Date established:** 1997
Turnover: Up to £250,000 **No.of Employees:** 11 - 20 **Product Groups:** 31

Date of Accounts	Mar 12	Mar 11	Mar 10
Sales Turnover	40	29	31
Pre Tax Profit/Loss	-6m	-6m	-3m
Working Capital	-52m	-47m	1m
Fixed Assets	2m	2m	2m
Current Assets	1m	971	2m
Current Liabilities	436	349	290

Royal Surrey County Hospital Charitable Fund
Egerton Road, Guildford, GU2 7XX
Tel: 01483-464146 **Fax:** 01483-406899
Website: http://www.royalsurrey.nhs.uk
Directors: C. Langley (Dir)
Date established: 1990 **No.of Employees:** 1 - 10 **Product Groups:** 30, 38, 67

SafeInside
Unit 9 Clasford Farm Stables Aldershot Road, Guildford, GU3 3HQ
Tel: 01483-237393
E-mail: info@safeinside.co.uk
Website: http://www.safeinside.co.uk
Directors: M. Sebo (Prop)
Turnover: £250,000 - £500,000 **No.of Employees:** 1 - 10
Product Groups: 36, 37, 39, 66

Sanofi Aventis
1 Onslow Street, Guildford, GU1 4YS
Tel: 01483-505515 **Fax:** 01483-354320
E-mail: nigel.brooksby@sanofi-synthelabo.com
Website: http://www.sanofi.com
Managers: N. Brooksby (Mgr)
Ultimate Holding Company: SANOFI-AVENTIS SA (FRANCE)
Immediate Holding Company: SANOFI-AVENTIS UK HOLDINGS LIMITED
Registration no: 03203829 **VAT No.:** GB 572 8546 09
Date established: 1996 **Turnover:** £500m - £1,000m
No.of Employees: 251 - 500 **Product Groups:** 66

Date of Accounts	Dec 11	Dec 10	Dec 09
Pre Tax Profit/Loss	-16m	41m	-49m
Working Capital	-262m	-262m	-261m
Fixed Assets	704m	720m	678m
Current Assets	1438m	134	134

Solimarco
15 Harvey Road, Guildford, GU1 3SG
Tel: 01483-304967
E-mail: admin@solimarco.net
Website: http://www.solimarco.net
Directors: M. Bourne (Dir), M. Bourn (Snr Part)
Registration no: 05681762 **Date established:** 2006
Turnover: Up to £250,000 **No.of Employees:** 1 - 10 **Product Groups:** 80

Space Air Conditiong plc
1 Opus Park Moorfield Road, Slyfield Industrial Estate, Guildford, GU1 1SZ
Tel: 01483-504883 **Fax:** 01483-574835
E-mail: info@spaceair.co.uk
Website: http://www.spaceair.co.uk
Directors: B. Stone (Dir), M. Burby (Fin), N. Afram (MD)
Managers: E. Callaghan (Tech Serv Mgr), B. Fernandez (Personnel), L. Ford (Mktg Serv Mgr)
Immediate Holding Company: SPACE AIRCONDITIONING PLC
Registration no: 01313460 **Date established:** 1977
Turnover: £10m - £20m **No.of Employees:** 51 - 100 **Product Groups:** 30, 39, 40, 66

Date of Accounts	Dec 11	Dec 10	Dec 09
Sales Turnover	19m	21m	19m
Pre Tax Profit/Loss	-419	261	-316
Working Capital	841	1m	974
Fixed Assets	872	943	929
Current Assets	4m	4m	5m
Current Liabilities	2m	2m	2m

Stephenson Plastics
The Workshop Piccards Farm Sandy Lane, Guildford, GU3 1HD
Tel: 01483-565277 **Fax:** 01483-505047
E-mail: roger.may@stephensonplastics.com
Website: http://www.stephensonplastics.com
Directors: R. May (MD)
VAT No.: GB 335 4371 64 **Date established:** 1978
Turnover: Up to £250,000 **No.of Employees:** 1 - 10 **Product Groups:** 30, 66

Date of Accounts	Mar 08	Mar 07
Sales Turnover	154	84
Pre Tax Profit/Loss	41	-18
Working Capital	1	-17
Fixed Assets	10	12
Current Assets	39	10
Current Liabilities	38	27
ROCE% (Return on Capital Employed)	361.1	368.3
ROT% (Return on Turnover)	26.5	-22.0

T & R Holdings Ltd
Woodbridge Meadows, Guildford, GU1 1BJ
Tel: 01483-568281 **Fax:** 01483-504961
Website: http://www.transformers.co.uk
Directors: A. Cowley (Fin)
Managers: G. Gumbrell (Buyer), R. Newman
Ultimate Holding Company: T & R HOLDINGS (INVESTMENTS) LIMITED
Immediate Holding Company: T & R Holdings Ltd.
Registration no: 01781368 **Date established:** 1983
Turnover: Up to £250,000 **No.of Employees:** 51 - 100
Product Groups: 36, 40

Date of Accounts	Dec 11	Dec 10	Dec 09
Sales Turnover	75	433	407
Pre Tax Profit/Loss	210	168	270
Working Capital	2m	1m	1m
Fixed Assets	8m	8m	8m
Current Assets	2m	2m	2m
Current Liabilities	314	380	364

T & R Test Equipment Ltd
15-16 Woodbridge Meadows Guilford, Guildford, GU1 1BJ
Tel: 01483-207428 **Fax:** 01483-235759
E-mail: info@trtest.com
Website: http://www.trtest.com
Bank(s): Nat West
Directors: P. Cole (Dir)
Immediate Holding Company: T. & R. TEST EQUIPMENT LIMITED
Registration no: 01539633 **VAT No.:** GB 591 7768 85
Date established: 1981 **Turnover:** £1m - £2m **No.of Employees:** 11 - 20
Product Groups: 38

Date of Accounts	Dec 11	Dec 10	Dec 09
Working Capital	869	764	619
Fixed Assets	18	16	11
Current Assets	1m	1m	830

Times Review Series Of Newspapers
Stoke Mill Woking Road, Guildford, GU1 1QA
Tel: 01483-508700 **Fax:** 01483-508851
Website: http://www.getsurrey.co.uk
Bank(s): National Westminster Bank Plc
Directors: C. Roberts (Dir), J. Cattell (Fin), N. Profit (Mkt Research)
Managers: N. Ashton (Mktg Serv Mgr)
Ultimate Holding Company: Guardian Media Group P.L.C.
VAT No.: GB 145 774 45 **Date established:** 1904 **Turnover:** £10m - £20m
No.of Employees: 51 - 100 **Product Groups:** 28

Torque Leader (manufactured by M H H Engineering Co. Ltd)
The Tannery Tannery Lane Gosden Common, Bramley, Guildford, GU5 0AB
Tel: 01483-892772 **Fax:** 01483-898536
E-mail: d.parsley@torqueleader.co.uk
Website: http://www.torqueleader.com
Bank(s): lloyds TSB Bank plc, Guildford Branch
Directors: P. Hare (Fin), P. Hare (Fin), G. Allen (MD), D. Parsley (MD), D. Jackson (Sales & Mktg)
Managers: J. Ellera (Personnel), A. Horton (Tech Serv Mgr), T. Elliott (I.T. Exec), D. Giddins (Buyer), D. Giddins (Buyer)
Ultimate Holding Company: GEDORE WERKZEUGFABRIK OTTO DOWIDAT KG (GERMANY)
Immediate Holding Company: M.H.H.ENGINEERING COMPANY LIMITED
Registration no: 00333313 **VAT No.:** GB 211 6880 79
Date established: 1937 **Turnover:** £5m - £10m
No.of Employees: 51 - 100 **Product Groups:** 36, 37, 38, 40, 46, 85

Date of Accounts	Dec 11	Dec 10	Dec 09
Sales Turnover	6m	5m	4m
Pre Tax Profit/Loss	933	520	303
Working Capital	4m	3m	3m
Fixed Assets	2m	2m	2m
Current Assets	4m	4m	4m
Current Liabilities	245	223	174

Transym Computer Services Limited
Chapel House 1 Chapel Street, Guildford, GU1 3UH
Tel: 01483-538330
E-mail: sales@transym.com
Website: http://www.transym.com
Managers: M. Allen (Sales Prom)
Registration no: 01723514 **Date established:** 1985
No.of Employees: 1 - 10 **Product Groups:** 44

U O P Ltd
Liongate Ladymead, Guildford, GU1 1AT
Tel: 01483-304848 **Fax:** 01483-304863
E-mail: mike.brown@uop.com
Website: http://www.uop.com
Directors: G. Davies (Fin), J. Woodcock (Dir)
Managers: E. Allan (Personnel), N. Porter (Tech Serv Mgr)
Ultimate Holding Company: HONEYWELL INTERNATIONAL INC (USA)
Immediate Holding Company: UOP LIMITED
Registration no: 00521570 **Date established:** 1953
Turnover: £75m - £125m **No.of Employees:** 101 - 250
Product Groups: 38, 42

Date of Accounts	Dec 11	Dec 10	Dec 09
Sales Turnover	86m	98m	108m
Pre Tax Profit/Loss	19m	24m	25m
Working Capital	119m	100m	78m
Fixed Assets	11m	12m	12m
Current Assets	142m	131m	119m
Current Liabilities	18m	20m	26m

Unico Components Ltd
Unit 2b Henley Business Park Pirbright Road, Normandy, Guildford, GU3 2DX
Tel: 01483-237621 **Fax:** 01483-237081
E-mail: sales@unico.uk.com
Website: http://www.unico.uk.com
Directors: D. Goldon (Dir)
Immediate Holding Company: UNICO COMPONENTS LIMITED
Registration no: 00992448 **VAT No.:** GB 212 0959 90
Date established: 1970 **Turnover:** £2m - £5m **No.of Employees:** 1 - 10
Product Groups: 36

Date of Accounts	Sep 11	Sep 10	Sep 09
Working Capital	103	156	129
Fixed Assets	5	27	53
Current Assets	362	379	407

Unisto Ltd
Postford Mill Mill Lane, Chilworth, Guildford, GU4 8RT
Tel: 01483-209100 **Fax:** 01483-209109
E-mail: sales@unisto.co.uk
Website: http://www.unisto.co.uk
Bank(s): Barclays
Directors: D. Miller (Sales & Mktg), D. Spry (Dir)
Managers: M. Fielder (Sales Admin), C. Munday (Comptroller), P. Stoffel ()
Ultimate Holding Company: Rofima AG (Switzerland)
Immediate Holding Company: Unisto AG (Switzerland)
Registration no: 00333367 **Date established:** 1926 **Turnover:** £2m - £5m
No.of Employees: 11 - 20 **Product Groups:** 27, 30, 35, 36, 37, 42, 45, 49

Date of Accounts	Dec 11	Dec 10	Dec 09
Working Capital	715	460	488
Fixed Assets	320	335	339
Current Assets	2m	2m	1m

Waiter's Friend Company Ltd
Unit 12 Quadrum Park Old Portsmouth Road, Peasmarsh, Guildford, GU3 1LU
Tel: 01483-560695 **Fax:** 01483-458080
E-mail: sales@waitersfriend.com
Website: http://www.waitersfriend.com
Directors: R. Fenner (MD)
Immediate Holding Company: THE WAITER'S FRIEND COMPANY LIMITED
Registration no: 03966847 **Date established:** 2000 **Turnover:** £1m - £2m
No.of Employees: 1 - 10 **Product Groups:** 22, 36, 40, 41, 42, 49, 62, 65, 67, 81

Date of Accounts	Mar 12	Mar 11	Mar 10
Working Capital	85	129	130
Fixed Assets	9	12	18
Current Assets	220	278	249

Water Softener Services
7 Enterprise Park Moorfield Road, Guildford, GU1 1RB
Tel: 01483-539693 **Fax:** 01483-889548
E-mail: enquiries@watersofteners.fsnet.co.uk
Website: http://www.watersofteners.fsnet.co.uk
Directors: R. Sargent (Prop)
Date established: 1985 **No.of Employees:** 1 - 10 **Product Groups:** 38, 42

Wieland Electric Ltd
1 The Riverside Business Centre Walnut Tree Close, Guildford, GU1 4UG
Tel: 01483-531213 **Fax:** 01483-505029
E-mail: sales@wieland-electric.com
Website: http://www.wieland-electric.com
Directors: M. Redfern (MD)
Managers: A. Woods, G. Wicks (Personnel), H. Giffard
Ultimate Holding Company: WIELAND HOLDING GMBH (GERMANY)
Immediate Holding Company: WIELAND ELECTRIC LIMITED
Registration no: 02349613 **Date established:** 1989 **Turnover:** £5m - £10m
No.of Employees: 21 - 50 **Product Groups:** 37

Date of Accounts	Dec 11	Dec 10	Dec 09
Sales Turnover	N/A	9m	9m
Pre Tax Profit/Loss	N/A	220	445
Working Capital	1m	885	1m
Fixed Assets	66	50	67
Current Assets	2m	3m	3m
Current Liabilities	N/A	450	281

Wilson Electrical Ltd
Unit 8 Midleton Industrial Estate, Guildford, GU2 8XW
Tel: 01483-502602 **Fax:** 01483-454722
E-mail: guildford@wilsonelectrical.com
Website: http://www.wilsonelectrical.com
Directors: A. Powell (MD)
Managers: F. McDonald (Chief Acct)
Immediate Holding Company: WILSON ELECTRICAL DISTRIBUTORS LIMITED
Registration no: 01479269 **VAT No.:** GB 289 7094 95
Date established: 1980 **Turnover:** £10m - £20m
No.of Employees: 11 - 20 **Product Groups:** 52

Date of Accounts	Mar 12	Mar 11	Mar 10
Sales Turnover	14m	13m	11m
Pre Tax Profit/Loss	692	536	402
Working Capital	2m	2m	2m
Fixed Assets	568	498	133
Current Assets	5m	5m	4m
Current Liabilities	930	695	581

Wood & Floors Com
6 Yew Tree Drive, Guildford, GU1 1PD
Tel: 0783-534 4146
E-mail: info@woodandfloors.com
Website: http://www.woodandfloors.com
Directors: P. Tearaszkiewicz (Prop)
Date established: 1984 **Turnover:** Up to £250,000
No.of Employees: 1 - 10 **Product Groups:** 25

Wrightsons British Tags
Unit 6 Quadrum Park Old Portsmouth Road, Peasmarsh, Guildford, GU3 1LU
Tel: 01483-569237
E-mail: mail@britishtags.co.uk
Website: http://www.britishtags.co.uk
Managers: A. Culloden (Admin Off)
Immediate Holding Company: WRIGHTSONS BRITISH TAGS LIMITED
Registration no: 00654801 **Date established:** 1960 **Turnover:** £1m - £2m
No.of Employees: 1 - 10 **Product Groups:** 27, 30, 49

Date of Accounts	Dec 11	Dec 10	Dec 09
Sales Turnover	N/A	2m	1m
Pre Tax Profit/Loss	N/A	36	-20
Working Capital	655	599	562
Fixed Assets	470	477	478
Current Assets	1m	922	809
Current Liabilities	N/A	41	25

Haslemere

A M G Electronics
Scotlands Midhurst Road, Haslemere, GU27 2PT
Tel: 01428-658775 **Fax:** 01428-658438
E-mail: sales@c-ducer.com
Website: http://www.c-ducer.com
Directors: A. French (Prop)
Immediate Holding Company: OBJECTS D'ART HASLEMERE LIMITED
Registration no: 07080600 **Date established:** 2009
Turnover: Up to £250,000 **No.of Employees:** 1 - 10 **Product Groups:** 37, 49, 67, 84

Date of Accounts	Mar 11	Mar 10	Mar 09
Sales Turnover	35	33	33
Pre Tax Profit/Loss	5	6	5
Working Capital	2	7	7
Fixed Assets	2	1	1
Current Assets	12	14	14
Current Liabilities	8	2	5

Bufton Plant Hire
Windfallwood Common, Haslemere, GU27 3BX
Tel: 01428-707437
Directors: P. Searle (Ptnr)
No.of Employees: 1 - 10 **Product Groups:** 45, 67, 83

Clement Windows Ltd
Clement House Weydown Road, Haslemere, GU27 1HR
Tel: 01428-643393 **Fax:** 01428-644436
E-mail: info@clementwg.co.uk
Website: http://www.clementwg.co.uk
Bank(s): Barclays
Directors: K. Tomkin (Fin)
Ultimate Holding Company: CLEMENT HOLDINGS LIMITED
Immediate Holding Company: CLEMENT HOLDINGS LIMITED
Registration no: 02612693 **VAT No.:** GB 211 3337 18
Date established: 1991 **Turnover:** £2m - £5m **No.of Employees:** 51 - 100
Product Groups: 33, 35

Date of Accounts	Mar 12	Mar 11	Mar 10
Sales Turnover	4m	4m	6m
Pre Tax Profit/Loss	84	-214	-687
Working Capital	-103	-211	-35
Fixed Assets	1m	2m	2m
Current Assets	1m	1m	682
Current Liabilities	817	874	518

Crown Memorials Ltd
Hamilton House 39 Kings Road, Haslemere, GU27 2QA
Tel: 01428-641941 **Fax:** 01428-641881
E-mail: info@crownmemorials.co.uk
Website: http://www.crownmemorials.co.uk
Directors: A. White (Fin), G. Priestman (MD)
Immediate Holding Company: Bridgwater Bros. Holdings Ltd
Registration no: 01594090 **No.of Employees:** 1 - 10 **Product Groups:** 33

Date of Accounts	Sep 09	Sep 08	Sep 07
Sales Turnover	694	705	639
Pre Tax Profit/Loss	66	46	-11
Working Capital	224	201	233
Fixed Assets	79	96	120
Current Assets	411	396	423
Current Liabilities	26	27	14

Moodies Leisure Ltd
Blair House Three Gates Lane, Haslemere, GU27 2LD
Tel: 01428-644310 **Fax:** 01428-661620
E-mail: info@moodies.co.uk
Website: http://www.moodies.co.uk
Directors: D. Moodie (MD)
Immediate Holding Company: Moodies (Leisure) Ltd
Registration no: 01452517 **No.of Employees:** 1 - 10 **Product Groups:** 45

Date of Accounts	Oct 07	Oct 06	Oct 05
Working Capital	-86	-86	-51
Fixed Assets	111	98	94
Current Assets	13	16	29
Current Liabilities	99	102	80
Total Share Capital	30	30	30

Paint Services Group Ltd
Weydown Road, Haslemere, GU27 1BT
Tel: 01428-651246 **Fax:** 01428-661471
E-mail: info@paintservices.com
Website: http://www.paintservices.com
Bank(s): Barclays
Directors: A. Swayne (Fin)
Managers: K. Odell (Mgr)
Ultimate Holding Company: GRAYTONE LIMITED
Immediate Holding Company: PAINT SERVICES GROUP LIMITED
Registration no: 00447039 **Date established:** 1947 **Turnover:** £5m - £10m
No.of Employees: 21 - 50 **Product Groups:** 32, 46

Date of Accounts	Mar 11	Mar 10	Mar 09
Sales Turnover	N/A	6m	7m
Pre Tax Profit/Loss	N/A	104	108
Working Capital	1m	770	671
Fixed Assets	35	74	107
Current Assets	3m	3m	3m
Current Liabilities	N/A	991	1m

Road Runner Electronic Products
Scotlands Close, Haslemere, GU27 3AE
Tel: 01428-653300 **Fax:** 01428-653300
Website: http://www.rrunner.co.uk
Directors: T. Brine (Dir)
No.of Employees: 1 - 10 **Product Groups:** 30, 47, 67

T P L Logistics Management
Lakeside House Hindhead Road, Haslemere, GU27 3PJ
Tel: 01428-647900 **Fax:** 01428-647907
E-mail: info@tpl-logistics-management.co.uk
Website: http://www.tpl-logistics-management.co.uk
Directors: R. Wileman (Comm), D. Orme (Co Sec), J. Wileman (MD)
Registration no: 02354358 **No.of Employees:** 1 - 10 **Product Groups:** 80

Hindhead

Grayshott Pottery
School Road Grayshott, Hindhead, GU26 6LR
Tel: 01428-604404 **Fax:** 01428-604944
E-mail: sales@grayshottpottery.com
Website: http://www.grayshottpottery.com
Bank(s): National Westminster Bank Plc
Directors: C. Greenaway (MD)
Immediate Holding Company: DARTINGTON POTTERY LIMITED
Registration no: 07801896 **VAT No.:** GB 188 5192 22
Date established: 2011 **Turnover:** £1m - £2m **No.of Employees:** 21 - 50
Product Groups: 33

Horley

A T Stone Ltd
Unit 15 Gatwick Business Park Kennel Lane, Hookwood, Horley, RH6 0AH
Tel: 01293-784501 **Fax:** 01923-824413
E-mail: info@atstone.co.uk
Website: http://www.atstone.co.uk
Directors: A. Mudd (MD)
Immediate Holding Company: AT STONE LIMITED
Registration no: 05833372 **Date established:** 2006
No.of Employees: 1 - 10 **Product Groups:** 14, 33

Date of Accounts	Jan 10	Jan 09	Jan 08
Working Capital	-11	-24	3
Fixed Assets	7	10	13
Current Assets	94	51	78

Alexander Engineering & Sons Ltd
Unit 2 Brittleware Farm, Charlwood, Horley, RH6 0EB
Tel: 01293-862265 **Fax:** 01403-243226
E-mail: nicolawalkey@yahoo.co.uk
Website: http://www.alexanderstanley.com
Directors: N. Walkey (Co Sec)
Immediate Holding Company: ALEXANDER ENGINEERING & SONS LIMITED
Registration no: 07948780 **Date established:** 2012
Turnover: £250,000 - £500,000 **No.of Employees:** 1 - 10
Product Groups: 45, 48, 67, 83, 86

Date of Accounts	Mar 08
Sales Turnover	589
Pre Tax Profit/Loss	41
Working Capital	-64
Fixed Assets	150
Current Assets	133
Current Liabilities	197
Total Share Capital	1
ROCE% (Return on Capital Employed)	48.1

Ascendit Lifts Ltd
4c-4d Gatwick Metro Centre Balcombe Road, Horley, RH6 9GA
Tel: 01293-785185 **Fax:** 01293-785485
E-mail: info@ascenditlifts.co.uk
Website: http://www.ascenditlifts.co.uk
Directors: L. Barratt (Fin), A. Barratt (MD)
Immediate Holding Company: ASCENDIT LIFTS LIMITED
Registration no: 03493530 **Date established:** 1998
No.of Employees: 21 - 50 **Product Groups:** 35, 39, 45

Date of Accounts	Jan 12	Jan 11	Jan 10
Working Capital	427	482	441
Fixed Assets	229	189	199
Current Assets	791	822	871

Bay Engraving
Unit 1k Vallance By-Ways Lowfield Heath Road, Charlwood, Horley, RH6 0BT
Tel: 01293-863063 **Fax:** 01293-863296
E-mail: a.watts@bayengravingltd.com
Website: http://www.bayengravingltd.com
Directors: A. Watts (Dir)
No.of Employees: 1 - 10 **Product Groups:** 25, 28, 30, 33, 36, 37, 38, 39, 44, 45, 46, 47, 48, 49, 63, 65, 67, 81

Date of Accounts	Mar 08	Mar 07	Mar 06
Working Capital	-2	1	-1
Fixed Assets	22	25	27
Current Assets	27	27	23
Current Liabilities	29	26	24

C N C Vacuum Processes Ltd
Hunters Lodge Balcombe Road, Horley, RH6 9SJ
Tel: 01293-822660 **Fax:** 01293-822661
E-mail: john@cncvacuum.co.uk
Website: http://www.cncvacuumprocesses.co.uk
Directors: J. Dye (Fin)
Immediate Holding Company: C.N.C. VACUUM PROCESSES LIMITED
Registration no: 01592411 **VAT No.:** GB 412 4712 88
Date established: 1981 **Turnover:** £500,000 - £1m
No.of Employees: 1 - 10 **Product Groups:** 48

Date of Accounts	Dec 11	Dec 10	Dec 09
Working Capital	42	75	86
Fixed Assets	73	89	78
Current Assets	107	115	143

The Computastat Group Ltd
Smallmead House Smallmead, Horley, RH6 9LW
Tel: 01293-773221 **Fax:** 01293-786747
E-mail: sales@computastat-group.co.uk
Website: http://www.computastat-group.co.uk
Directors: B. Ballard (Dir)
Registration no: 02223638 **Turnover:** £2m - £5m
No.of Employees: 1 - 10 **Product Groups:** 28

Date of Accounts	Dec 07	Dec 06	Dec 05
Sales Turnover	2180	2100	N/A
Pre Tax Profit/Loss	226	185	N/A
Working Capital	224	141	144
Fixed Assets	23	15	13
Current Assets	895	775	684
Current Liabilities	670	634	540
ROCE% (Return on Capital Employed)	91.3	118.3	
ROT% (Return on Turnover)	10.4	8.8	

Cova Security Gates Ltd
Bonehurst Road, Horley, RH6 8RB
Tel: 01293-820528 **Fax:** 01293-776348
E-mail: sales@covasecuritygates.com
Website: http://www.covasecuritygates.com
Directors: G. Cowan (MD), J. Tettmar (Sales & Mktg), M. Volpin (Dir)
Registration no: 02108888 **Date established:** 1987 **Turnover:** £2m - £5m
No.of Employees: 11 - 20 **Product Groups:** 29, 35, 36, 39, 40, 49, 68

Date of Accounts	May 09	May 08	May 07
Working Capital	750	522	325
Fixed Assets	424	433	420
Current Assets	2m	2m	1m

Drill Service Horley Ltd
23 Albert Road, Horley, RH6 7HR
Tel: 01293-774911 **Fax:** 01293-820463
E-mail: sales@drill-service.co.uk
Website: http://www.drill-service.co.uk
Bank(s): Royal Bank of Scotland
Directors: G. Howell (MD), W. Prangle (Sales)
Immediate Holding Company: DRILL SERVICE (HORLEY) LIMITED
Registration no: 00696597 **VAT No.:** GB 210 0690 23
Date established: 1961 **Turnover:** £1m - £2m **No.of Employees:** 11 - 20
Product Groups: 33, 36, 37, 38, 45, 46, 48, 67

Date of Accounts	Jun 12	Jun 11	Jun 10
Working Capital	849	751	732
Fixed Assets	845	854	852
Current Assets	1m	978	1m

Fire Protection Services
24 The Street Charlwood, Horley, RH6 0BY
Tel: 01293-862647 **Fax:** 01293-862613
E-mail: info@fpssurrey.co.uk
Website: http://www.fpssurrey.co.uk
Directors: L. Page (Prop)
Date established: 1999 **No.of Employees:** 1 - 10 **Product Groups:** 38, 42

G V S Assist Ltd
Plough Road Smallfield, Horley, RH6 9JW
Tel: 08455-040466 **Fax:** 01342-437799
E-mail: sales@gvs.co.uk
Website: http://www.gvs.co.uk
Directors: D. Mann (MD)
Immediate Holding Company: GENERAL VENDING SERVICES LIMITED
Registration no: 03061186 **Date established:** 1995
Turnover: £10m - £20m **No.of Employees:** 101 - 250
Product Groups: 37, 40, 49

Date of Accounts	Jun 11	Jun 10	Jun 09
Sales Turnover	14m	14m	14m
Pre Tax Profit/Loss	2m	2m	2m
Working Capital	3m	3m	2m
Fixed Assets	919	924	1m
Current Assets	6m	5m	6m
Current Liabilities	2m	2m	2m

Just Metal UK Ltd
Unit 3C Gonville Works Redehall Road, Smallfield, Horley, RH6 9QL
Tel: 01342-844892 **Fax:** 01342-844 892
E-mail: info@justmetal.co.uk
Website: http://www.justmetal.co.uk
Directors: P. Catlin (Dir)
Immediate Holding Company: JUST METAL UK LIMITED
Registration no: 06933589 **Date established:** 2009
No.of Employees: 1 - 10 **Product Groups:** 35

Date of Accounts	Mar 11	Mar 10
Working Capital	-31	-39
Fixed Assets	45	46
Current Assets	37	46

Langdale Bros
Weatherhill Works Hathersham Close, Smallfield, Horley, RH6 9JE
Tel: 01342-843164 **Fax:** 01342-843164
E-mail: langdalebros@aol.com
Website: http://www.langdalebros.co.uk
Directors: S. Langdale (Ptnr)
VAT No.: GB 312 9604 74 **Turnover:** £250,000 - £500,000
No.of Employees: 1 - 10 **Product Groups:** 46

Joseph Lewis Furniture & Interiors
Mayfield Court 56 Massetts Road, Horley, RH6 7DS
Tel: 01483-266855
E-mail: joseph@joseph-lewis.co.uk
Website: http://www.joseph-lewis.co.uk
Directors: J. Lewis (Prop)
No.of Employees: 1 - 10 **Product Groups:** 26, 30

Longman Gates
Unit 2 Hornecourt Manor Farm Hornecourt Hill, Horne, Horley, RH6 9LB
Tel: 01342-844846 **Fax:** 01342-844846
E-mail: info@longmangates.co.uk
Website: http://www.longmangates.co.uk
Directors: R. Longman (Prop)
Date established: 1998 **Turnover:** Up to £250,000
No.of Employees: 1 - 10 **Product Groups:** 25, 35, 36, 66

Marlborough Communications Ltd
Dovenby Hall Balcombe Road, Horley, RH6 9UU
Tel: 01293-775071 **Fax:** 01293-820781
E-mail: enquiries@marlboroughcomms.com
Website: http://www.marlboroughcomms.com
Directors: S. Lydiate (Fin), S. Lydiate (Co Sec), D. Allery (MD)
Managers: T. Brown (Tech Serv Mgr)
Ultimate Holding Company: MARLBOROUGH COMMUNICATIONS (HOLDINGS) LIMITED
Immediate Holding Company: MARLBOROUGH COMMUNICATIONS LIMITED
Registration no: 01507639 **VAT No.:** GB 339 9882 87
Date established: 1980 **Turnover:** £10m - £20m
No.of Employees: 21 - 50 **Product Groups:** 37

Date of Accounts	Sep 11	Sep 10	Sep 09
Sales Turnover	14m	22m	17m
Pre Tax Profit/Loss	2m	4m	1m
Working Capital	925	4m	3m
Fixed Assets	145	240	148
Current Assets	3m	6m	8m
Current Liabilities	1m	2m	3m

Meatec
Unit 7 Charlwood Place Charlwood, Horley, RH6 0EB
Tel: 01293-863791 **Fax:** 01293-863298
E-mail: info@meatec.co.uk
Website: http://www.meatec.co.uk
Directors: N. Tomlinson (Co Sec)
Immediate Holding Company: MEATEC LTD
Registration no: 01817600 **Date established:** 1984
Turnover: Up to £250,000 **No.of Employees:** 1 - 10 **Product Groups:** 41

Date of Accounts	Jul 11	Jul 10	Jul 09
Sales Turnover	171	N/A	N/A
Pre Tax Profit/Loss	62	N/A	N/A
Working Capital	43	54	55
Fixed Assets	10	13	17
Current Assets	79	86	98
Current Liabilities	31	N/A	N/A

Millennium & Copthorne Hotels plc
Victoria House Victoria Road, Horley, RH6 7AF
Tel: 01293-772288 **Fax:** 01293-772345
E-mail: marketing@mill-cop.com
Website: http://www.millenniumhotels.com
Bank(s): National Westminster
Directors: A. Bushnell (Fin)
Ultimate Holding Company: HONG LEONG INVESTMENT HOLDINGS PTE LTD (REP SINGAPORE)
Immediate Holding Company: MILLENNIUM & COPTHORNE HOTELS PLC
Registration no: 03004377 **VAT No.:** GB 644 6995 88
Date established: 1994 **Turnover:** £500m - £1,000m
No.of Employees: 1501 & over **Product Groups:** 69

Date of Accounts	Dec 11	Dec 10	Dec 09
Sales Turnover	821m	744m	654m
Pre Tax Profit/Loss	193m	129m	82m
Working Capital	273m	121m	13m
Fixed Assets	2747m	2756m	2486m
Current Assets	574m	430m	270m
Current Liabilities	188m	254m	239m

Mindex Ltd
6 Gatwick Metro Centre Balcombe Road, Horley, RH6 9GA
Tel: 01293-408123 **Fax:** 01293-408125
E-mail: sales@mindex.co.uk
Website: http://www.mindex-ltd.co.uk
Directors: J. Nichols (MD), E. Nichols (Fin)
Immediate Holding Company: MINDEX LIMITED
Registration no: 01800799 **VAT No.:** GB 395 2309 37
Date established: 1984 **Turnover:** £1m - £2m **No.of Employees:** 1 - 10
Product Groups: 40, 61, 67

Date of Accounts	Jun 11	Jun 10	Jun 09
Working Capital	64	20	5
Fixed Assets	5	8	3
Current Assets	601	532	435

Niagara Therapy UK Ltd
Middleton House 49 High Street, Horley, RH6 7RJ
Tel: 01293-787040 **Fax:** 01293-782006
E-mail: irvin@niagarahealthcare.co.uk
Website: http://www.niagarahealthcare.co.uk
Directors: I. Milsom (MD), T. Ellis (Fin)
Managers: C. Stone (), M. Dougall, M. Dougall (Personnel)
Ultimate Holding Company: NHC Holdings Ltd
Immediate Holding Company: Niagara Healthcare Ltd
Registration no: 01397622 **Date established:** 1978
No.of Employees: 11 - 20 **Product Groups:** 38, 67

P M Ironwork

Unit 23 Charlwood Place Norwood Hill Road, Charlwood, Horley, RH6 0EB
Tel: 01737-226811 **Fax:** 01293-863875
E-mail: sales@pmironwork.co.uk
Website: http://www.pmironwork.co.uk
Directors: P. Martin (Prop)
Immediate Holding Company: P.M. IRONWORK LTD
Registration no: 06543174 **Date established:** 2008
No.of Employees: 1 - 10 **Product Groups:** 26, 35

Date of Accounts	Mar 11	Mar 10	Mar 09
Working Capital	-1	2	-5
Fixed Assets	7	9	13
Current Assets	80	76	80

Roband Electronics plc

Charlwood Works Lowfield Heath Road, Charlwood, Horley, RH6 0BU
Tel: 01293-843000 **Fax:** 01293-843001
E-mail: postroom@roband.co.uk
Website: http://www.roband.co.uk
Bank(s): Lloyds
Directors: A. Gold (MD)
Managers: A. Morely (Tech Serv Mgr), C. Wain-heapy, P. Lacy
Immediate Holding Company: ROBAND ELECTRONICS PLC
Registration no: 00566699 **Date established:** 1956 **Turnover:** £2m - £5m
No.of Employees: 51 - 100 **Product Groups:** 37, 84

Date of Accounts	May 11	May 10	May 09
Sales Turnover	4m	3m	2m
Pre Tax Profit/Loss	249	-296	187
Working Capital	1m	1m	2m
Fixed Assets	3m	3m	3m
Current Assets	3m	3m	3m
Current Liabilities	1m	1m	1m

K T A Smith

Brookside Antlands Lane, Shipley Bridge, Horley, RH6 9TE
Tel: 01293-776005 **Fax:** 01293-823584
Directors: K. Smith (Prop)
Date established: 1985 **No.of Employees:** 1 - 10 **Product Groups:** 35

Sporting Surface Supplies Ltd

Hathersham Lane Smallfield, Horley, RH6 9JG
Tel: 01342-843663 **Fax:** 01342-844180
E-mail: info@sportingsurfacesupplies.com
Website: http://www.sportingsurfacesupplies.com
Directors: R. Rumble (Ch), S. Rumble (Dir)
Ultimate Holding Company: HURSTRIDGE LIMITED
Immediate Holding Company: SPORTING SURFACE SUPPLIES LIMITED
Registration no: 02688081 **Date established:** 1992
Turnover: £500,000 - £1m **No.of Employees:** 11 - 20
Product Groups: 33, 41, 49

Date of Accounts	Jun 11	Jun 10	Jun 09
Working Capital	79	80	132
Fixed Assets	51	76	105
Current Assets	272	272	314

T A Boxall & Co. Ltd

20 Balcombe Road, Horley, RH6 9HR
Tel: 01293-820133 **Fax:** 01293-776139
E-mail: admin@taboxall.co.uk
Website: http://www.taboxall.co.uk
Bank(s): Barclays
Directors: R. Ransley (Dir)
Managers: L. Beavan (Personnel)
Immediate Holding Company: T.A. BOXALL & COMPANY LIMITED
Registration no: 01519047 **Date established:** 1980 **Turnover:** £2m - £5m
No.of Employees: 51 - 100 **Product Groups:** 52

Date of Accounts	Dec 11	Dec 10	Dec 09
Working Capital	848	760	835
Fixed Assets	71	93	141
Current Assets	2m	1m	1m

T & M Plant Hire Ltd

Woodside The Close, Horley, RH6 9EB
Tel: 01293-774500 **Fax:** 01293-776400
E-mail: terry@tandmplanthire.com
Website: http://www.bowser-hire.com
Directors: T. Beasley (MD)
Immediate Holding Company: T & M PLANT HIRE LIMITED
Registration no: 03146496 **Date established:** 1996 **Turnover:** £1m - £2m
No.of Employees: 1 - 10 **Product Groups:** 39, 72, 83, 84

Date of Accounts	Apr 11	Apr 10	Apr 09
Sales Turnover	N/A	N/A	1m
Pre Tax Profit/Loss	N/A	N/A	66
Working Capital	-407	28	-7
Fixed Assets	1m	946	741
Current Assets	591	439	305
Current Liabilities	N/A	286	222

Technical Graphics

Suite 1 Gatwick House Peeks Brook Lane, Horley, RH6 9ST
Tel: 020-8668 4646 **Fax:** 020-8668 7747
E-mail: tholding@techgraf.co.uk
Website: http://www.techgraf.co.uk
Directors: T. Holding (Dir), D. Dyson (Fin)
Immediate Holding Company: TECHNICAL GRAPHICS LIMITED
Registration no: 06231403 **VAT No.:** GB 656 6412 22
Date established: 2007 **Turnover:** £2m - £5m **No.of Employees:** 1 - 10
Product Groups: 44, 48, 84

Date of Accounts	Mar 11	Mar 10	Mar 09
Working Capital	-0	7	28
Fixed Assets	1	1	2
Current Assets	71	78	107

Village Engineering

Unit 8 Betchworth Works Ifield Road, Charlwood, Horley, RH6 0DZ
Tel: 01293-863048 **Fax:** 01293-862841
E-mail: sales@villageengineering.co.uk
Website: http://www.villageengineering.co.uk
Directors: R. Marner (Prop)
Date established: 1988 **Turnover:** Up to £250,000
No.of Employees: 1 - 10 **Product Groups:** 34, 35, 46, 48, 49, 51, 66, 85

Kenley

M Criscuolo & Co. Ltd

Crisco House 169 Godstone Road, Kenley, CR8 5BL
Tel: 020-8660 7949 **Fax:** 020-8668 5334
E-mail: sales@crisco.co.uk
Website: http://www.crisco.co.uk
Directors: J. Criscuolo (Dir)
Immediate Holding Company: M.CRISCUOLO & CO.,LIMITED
Registration no: 00253903 **VAT No.:** GB 232 3148 01
Date established: 1931 **Turnover:** Up to £250,000
No.of Employees: 1 - 10 **Product Groups:** 30

Date of Accounts	Dec 11	Dec 10	Dec 09
Sales Turnover	N/A	N/A	181
Pre Tax Profit/Loss	N/A	N/A	11
Working Capital	-65	-84	-86
Fixed Assets	176	179	182
Current Assets	67	43	67
Current Liabilities	96	86	63

Optical Surfaces Ltd

Godstone Road, Kenley, CR8 5AA
Tel: 020-8668 6126 **Fax:** 020-8660 7743
E-mail: sales@optisurf.com
Website: http://www.optisurf.com
Bank(s): National Westminster Bank Plc
Directors: W. Harris (MD)
Immediate Holding Company: OPTICAL SURFACES LIMITED
Registration no: 02641133 **VAT No.:** GB 528 7876 89
Date established: 1991 **Turnover:** £1m - £2m **No.of Employees:** 11 - 20
Product Groups: 38

Date of Accounts	Dec 11	Dec 10	Dec 09
Sales Turnover	931	2m	2m
Pre Tax Profit/Loss	43	485	300
Working Capital	615	715	505
Fixed Assets	43	51	53
Current Assets	844	910	669
Current Liabilities	206	192	146

Right Ideas

19 Hayes Lane, Kenley, CR8 5LE
Tel: 020-8668 8991 **Fax:** 020-8660 0985
E-mail: sales@rightideas.co.uk
Website: http://www.rightideas.co.uk
Directors: B. Evans (Ptnr)
Date established: 1982 **Turnover:** £2m - £5m **No.of Employees:** 1 - 10
Product Groups: 49

Scanprobe Techniques Ltd

11 Bushey Close, Kenley, CR8 5AU
Tel: 020-3253 2001 **Fax:** 01883-626813
E-mail: sales@scanprobe.com
Website: http://www.scanprobe.com
Directors: J. Barry (MD)
Managers: E. Sterry (Fin Mgr)
Immediate Holding Company: SCANPROBE TECHNIQUES LIMITED
Registration no: 02682996 **Date established:** 1992 **Turnover:** £1m - £2m
No.of Employees: 11 - 20 **Product Groups:** 37, 38, 40, 47

Date of Accounts	Jun 11	Jun 10	Jun 09
Working Capital	1m	946	812
Fixed Assets	107	96	111
Current Assets	2m	1m	1m

Secom plc

Secom House 52 Godstone Road, Kenley, CR8 5JF
Tel: 020-8645 5400 **Fax:** 020-8660 8937
Website: http://www.secom.plc.uk
Directors: P. Simpson (Fin), M. Pakezawa (MD), J. White (Sales & Mktg), A. Gover (Chief Op Offcr), M. Takezawa (MD)
Managers: D. Senech-Soler (Mktg Serv Mgr)
Ultimate Holding Company: SECOM CO LTD (JAPAN)
Immediate Holding Company: SECOM PLC
Registration no: 02585807 **VAT No.:** GB 445 8383 22
Date established: 1991 **Turnover:** £20m - £50m
No.of Employees: 51 - 100 **Product Groups:** 35, 36, 37, 38, 39, 40, 44, 52, 67, 81, 83

Date of Accounts	Dec 11	Dec 10	Dec 09
Sales Turnover	40m	39m	35m
Pre Tax Profit/Loss	2m	2m	272
Working Capital	14m	13m	11m
Fixed Assets	14m	5m	6m
Current Assets	27m	24m	22m
Current Liabilities	11m	10m	10m

Turner Electronics

Turner House 11 Roke Close, Kenley, CR8 5NL
Tel: 020-8668 0821 **Fax:** 020-8668 2782
E-mail: aj-turner@turnerelectronics.co.uk
Website: http://www.turnerelectronics.co.uk
Directors: D. Turner (Fin), A. Turner (Dir)
Immediate Holding Company: TURNER ELECTRONICS LIMITED
Registration no: 01405403 **VAT No.:** GB 407 3470 68
Date established: 1978 **Turnover:** £1m - £2m **No.of Employees:** 1 - 10
Product Groups: 46

Kingston Upon Thames

Adnor Ltd

Mill Place, Kingston Upon Thames, KT1 2RL
Tel: 020-8549 4728 **Fax:** 020-8549 8989
E-mail: sales@adnor.co.uk
Website: http://www.adnor.co.uk
Directors: N. Doran (Dir), I. Doran (Co Sec)
Immediate Holding Company: ADNOR LTD.
Registration no: 00867945 **VAT No.:** GB 216 0133 19
Date established: 1965 **Turnover:** £250,000 - £500,000
No.of Employees: 1 - 10 **Product Groups:** 48

Date of Accounts	Dec 11	Dec 10	Dec 09
Working Capital	154	152	119
Fixed Assets	229	207	229
Current Assets	227	221	162

Albany Blind Company

The Albany Boathouse Lower Ham Road, Kingston Upon Thames, KT2 5BB
Tel: 020-8549 5436 **Fax:** 020-8549 5332
E-mail: peter@albany-blind.co.uk
Website: http://www.albany-blind.com
Directors: C. Burchett (Fin), T. Creed Miles (Dir)
Ultimate Holding Company: CREED-MILES & SON LIMITED
Immediate Holding Company: ALBANY BLIND COMPANY LIMITED
Registration no: 01634193 **VAT No.:** GB 318 3477 49
Date established: 1982 **Turnover:** Up to £250,000
No.of Employees: 1 - 10 **Product Groups:** 24, 30, 35

Date of Accounts	Jun 11	Jun 10	Jun 09
Working Capital	3	3	3
Current Assets	3	3	3

Anderson Hearn Keene Ltd

5 Bridle Close, Kingston Upon Thames, KT1 2JW
Tel: 020-8541 4222 **Fax:** 020-8541 4518
E-mail: david.hearn@andersonhearnkeene.co.uk
Website: http://www.andersonhearnkeene.co.uk
Directors: D. Hearn (MD)
Managers: B. Richardson
Immediate Holding Company: ANDERSON HEARN KEENE LIMITED
Registration no: 02999672 **VAT No.:** GB 652 7762 14
Date established: 1994 **Turnover:** £500,000 - £1m
No.of Employees: 11 - 20 **Product Groups:** 81

Date of Accounts	Dec 11	Dec 10	Dec 09
Working Capital	129	185	347
Fixed Assets	4	5	5
Current Assets	242	456	525

Arrow Plastics Ltd

Arrow Works 65 Hampden Road, Kingston Upon Thames, KT1 3HQ
Tel: 020-8546 6258 **Fax:** 020-8541 4654
E-mail: mail@arrow-plastics.co.uk
Website: http://www.arrow-plastics.co.uk
Directors: M. Wombwell (MD), S. Croucher (Fin)
Managers: C. Scott
Immediate Holding Company: ARROW PLASTICS LIMITED
Registration no: 04727143 **Date established:** 2003
No.of Employees: 51 - 100 **Product Groups:** 30, 48, 66

Date of Accounts	Dec 11	Dec 10	Dec 09
Working Capital	459	394	397
Fixed Assets	361	391	327
Current Assets	1m	2m	1m

Bay Ridge UK Ltd

44 Kingston Hill Place, Kingston Upon Thames, KT2 7QY
Tel: 020-8546 8902 **Fax:** 020-8549 2200
E-mail: office@bayridge-uk.com
Website: http://www.bayridge-uk.com
Directors: D. Caowki (Prop)
Immediate Holding Company: Bay Ridge UK Ltd
Registration no: 04790464 **Date established:** 2006
No.of Employees: 1 - 10 **Product Groups:** 22, 24, 63

Chamber Of Commerce Kingston

3 Kingsmill Business Park Chapel Mill Road, Kingston Upon Thames, KT1 3GZ
Tel: 020-8481 0450 **Fax:** 020-8481 0460
E-mail: info@in-thebox.co.uk
Website: http://www.in-thebox.co.uk
Directors: L. Gagliani (Grp Chief Exec)
Immediate Holding Company: Z1 TECHNOLOGY SERVICES LTD
Registration no: 06481851 **Date established:** 2008
No.of Employees: 1 - 10 **Product Groups:** 87

Date of Accounts	Oct 11
Working Capital	1
Current Assets	1

Databac Group

1 The Ashway Centre Elm Crescent, Kingston Upon Thames, KT2 6HH
Tel: 020-8546 9826 **Fax:** 020-8547 1026
E-mail: enquiries@databac.com
Website: http://www.databac.com
Directors: L. Richards (Co Sec)
Managers: A. Picard (Chief Mgr)
Immediate Holding Company: DATABAC GROUP LIMITED
Registration no: 01829889 **Date established:** 1984 **Turnover:** £1m - £2m
No.of Employees: 11 - 20 **Product Groups:** 28, 30

Date of Accounts	Mar 11	Mar 10	Mar 09
Working Capital	278	291	336
Fixed Assets	683	683	672
Current Assets	476	480	547

Easy Ramps Ltd

7 Union Street, Kingston Upon Thames, KT1 1RP
Tel: 01784-818181 **Fax:** 01784-818182
E-mail: sales@easyramps.co.uk
Website: http://www.easyramps.co.uk
Managers: R. Hawkins, D. Alexiev (Mgr)
Registration no: 06752251 **Turnover:** £1m - £2m
No.of Employees: 1 - 10 **Product Groups:** 23, 29, 30, 35, 39, 45, 48, 67, 71, 76, 83

Hine Systems

85 Richmond Park Road, Kingston upon Thames, KT2 6AF
Tel: 07773-135910
E-mail: andy@hinesystems.com
Website: http://www.hinesystems.com
Directors: A. Hine (Prop), A. Hine (Grp Chief Exec)
Immediate Holding Company: HINE SYSTEMS LIMITED
Registration no: 06207296 **Date established:** 2007
No.of Employees: 1 - 10 **Product Groups:** 44, 80

Date of Accounts	Mar 10	Mar 09	Mar 08
Working Capital	46	12	40
Current Assets	71	22	53

Hospitality & Leisure Manpower

8 Lower Teddington Road, Kingston Upon Thames, KT1 4ER
Tel: 020-8977 4419 **Fax:** 020-8977 5519
E-mail: hlm@halm.co.uk
Website: http://www.halm.co.uk
Directors: A. Battersby (Fin), D. Battersby (MD)
Managers: C. Downing (Comm), P. Hallan (Ops Mgr)
Immediate Holding Company: HOSPITALITY AND LEISURE MANPOWER LIMITED
Registration no: 02448148 **Date established:** 1989
Turnover: £250,000 - £500,000 **No.of Employees:** 1 - 10
Product Groups: 86

Date of Accounts	Mar 11	Mar 10	Mar 09
Working Capital	-192	-51	42
Fixed Assets	N/A	N/A	1
Current Assets	38	75	409

Images For Industry Ltd

58 Eaton Drive, Kingston Upon Thames, KT2 7QX
Tel: 020-8123 9360
E-mail: sales@imagesforindustry.co.uk
Website: http://www.imagesforindustry.co.uk
Directors: M. Pincham (Fin), A. Pincham (MD)
Immediate Holding Company: IMAGES FOR INDUSTRY LIMITED
Registration no: 03519388 **Date established:** 1998
Turnover: Up to £250,000 **No.of Employees:** 1 - 10 **Product Groups:** 81

Date of Accounts	Mar 11	Mar 10	Mar 09
Sales Turnover	6	15	17
Pre Tax Profit/Loss	-8	-2	2
Working Capital	-34	-26	-25
Fixed Assets	6	6	6
Current Assets	1	3	5
Current Liabilities	1	2	2

Maplin Electronics Ltd

2-6 Alderman Judge Mall Eden Walk Shopping Centre, Kingston Upon Thames, KT1 1BS
Tel: 08432-277340
E-mail: customercare@maplin.co.uk
Website: http://www.maplin.co.uk
Ultimate Holding Company: MONTAGU PRIVATE EQUITY LLP
Immediate Holding Company: MAPLIN ELECTRONICS LIMITED
Registration no: 01264385 **Date established:** 1976
Turnover: £125m - £250m **No.of Employees:** 1 - 10 **Product Groups:** 37, 61

Date of Accounts	Dec 11	Dec 08	Dec 09
Sales Turnover	205m	204m	204m
Pre Tax Profit/Loss	25m	32m	35m
Working Capital	118m	49m	75m
Fixed Assets	27m	28m	28m
Current Assets	207m	108m	142m
Current Liabilities	78m	51m	59m

Metapraxis Ltd

Kingstons House Coombe Road, Kingston upon Thames, KT2 7AB
Tel: 020-8541 2700 **Fax:** 020-8546 2105
E-mail: info@metapraxis.com
Website: http://www.metapraxis.com
Directors: R. Bittlestone (Ch), J. Bittlestone (Co Sec)
Immediate Holding Company: METAPRAXIS LIMITED
Registration no: 01412766 **Date established:** 1979 **Turnover:** £1m - £2m
No.of Employees: 11 - 20 **Product Groups:** 80

Date of Accounts	Jun 11	Jun 10	Jun 09
Sales Turnover	2m	2m	2m
Pre Tax Profit/Loss	122	-40	-261
Working Capital	1m	1m	1m
Fixed Assets	23	15	12
Current Assets	2m	2m	2m
Current Liabilities	526	449	593

Minatol Ltd

Mandarin House 4 Manorgate Road, Kingston Upon Thames, KT2 7UB
Tel: 020-8549 9222 **Fax:** 020-8547 1635
E-mail: sales@minatol.co.uk
Website: http://www.minatol.co.uk
Bank(s): National Westminster, Kingston Hill
Directors: C. Warnock (Ch), R. Abel (Sales), R. Cann (MD)
Immediate Holding Company: MINATOL LIMITED
Registration no: 00239771 **VAT No.:** GB 218 1949 52
Date established: 2029 **Turnover:** £2m - £5m **No.of Employees:** 21 - 50
Product Groups: 24, 25, 27, 30, 49

Date of Accounts	Apr 11	Apr 10	Apr 09
Working Capital	611	576	557
Fixed Assets	994	1m	990
Current Assets	2m	2m	2m

Panels Plus Ltd

22-24 Mill Place, Kingston Upon Thames, KT1 2RJ
Tel: 020-8399 6343 **Fax:** 020-8399 6343
E-mail: sales@panelsplusltd.com
Website: http://www.panelsplusltd.com
Directors: K. Hyams (Dir)
Immediate Holding Company: PANELS PLUS LIMITED
Registration no: 04781340 **Date established:** 2003
Turnover: Up to £250,000 **No.of Employees:** 1 - 10 **Product Groups:** 25, 26, 33, 66

Date of Accounts	Mar 12	Mar 11	Mar 10
Working Capital	253	209	160
Fixed Assets	18	7	27
Current Assets	288	251	184

Plant Handling Ltd

7 Union Street, Kingston Upon Thames, KT1 1RP
Tel: 01784-818181 **Fax:** 01784-818182
E-mail: sales@phl.co.uk
Website: http://www.phl.co.uk
Directors: J. Sharma (Co Sec), R. Hawkins (MD)
Immediate Holding Company: PLANT HANDLING LIMITED
Registration no: 05438341 **VAT No.:** GB 530 3643 76
Date established: 2005 **Turnover:** £2m - £5m **No.of Employees:** 1 - 10
Product Groups: 39, 45, 48, 67

Date of Accounts	Apr 11	Apr 10	Apr 09
Working Capital	283	210	62
Fixed Assets	58	66	33
Current Assets	1m	1m	580

Poddymeter Ltd

Unit 2 Park Works Borough Road, Kingston Upon Thames, KT2 6BD
Tel: 020-8546 9311 **Fax:** 020-8547 2325
E-mail: clive.nicholls@poddymeter.co.uk
Website: http://www.poddymeter.co.uk
Bank(s): Barclays, Watford
Directors: C. Nicholls (MD)
Immediate Holding Company: PODDYMETER LIMITED
Registration no: 02447176 **VAT No.:** GB 563 8097 13
Date established: 1989 **Turnover:** £1m - £2m **No.of Employees:** 11 - 20
Product Groups: 38

Date of Accounts	Dec 11	Dec 10	Dec 09
Sales Turnover	610	603	N/A
Pre Tax Profit/Loss	65	62	N/A

Working Capital	140	118	101
Fixed Assets	8	8	9
Current Assets	221	232	225
Current Liabilities	70	65	N/A

Preisser UK Ltd

37 Dickerage Road, Kingston Upon Thames, KT1 3SR
Tel: 020-8336 1290 **Fax:** 020-8336 1651
E-mail: sales@preisser.co.uk
Website: http://www.preisser.co.uk
Directors: S. Lucas (MD)
Immediate Holding Company: PREISSER UK LIMITED
Registration no: 03798628 **VAT No.:** GB 731 5665 34
Date established: 1999 **Turnover:** £1m - £2m **No.of Employees:** 1 - 10
Product Groups: 37, 38, 39, 44, 45, 47, 49, 67, 85

Date of Accounts	Jun 11	Jun 10	Jun 09
Working Capital	133	131	128
Fixed Assets	4	6	8
Current Assets	214	279	349

Reed Accountancy Personnel Ltd

70 Clarence Street, Kingston Upon Thames, KT1 1NN
Tel: 020-8547 3505 **Fax:** 020-8547 1425
E-mail: rapkingston@reed.co.uk
Website: http://www.reed.co.uk
Managers: S. Thomas (Mgr)
Immediate Holding Company: REED PERSONNEL SERVICES LTD
Registration no: 00973629 **Date established:** 1961
Turnover: £125m - £250m **No.of Employees:** 1 - 10 **Product Groups:** 80

Reed Specialist Recruitment

68 Clarence Street, Kingston Upon Thames, KT1 1NN
Tel: 020-8549 9381 **Fax:** 020-8541 5704
E-mail: kingston.employment@reed.co.uk
Website: http://www.reed.co.uk
Directors: C. Dyos (Reg MD)
Ultimate Holding Company: REED GLOBAL LTD (MALTA)
Immediate Holding Company: REED EMPLOYMENT LIMITED
Registration no: 00669854 **Date established:** 1960
No.of Employees: 1 - 10 **Product Groups:** 80

Date of Accounts	Jun 11	Jun 10	Dec 07
Sales Turnover	618	450	287m
Pre Tax Profit/Loss	-2m	310	8m
Working Capital	23m	28m	28m
Fixed Assets	31	36	5m
Current Assets	28m	30m	74m
Current Liabilities	37	29	21m

Robert Marshall Marketing Consultants

194 Richmond Road, Kingston Upon Thames, KT2 5HE
Tel: 020-8546 1711 **Fax:** 020-8974 6120
E-mail: robmarshall123@btinternet.com
Directors: R. Marshall (Prop)
VAT No.: GB 318 2858 42 **Date established:** 1981
Turnover: Up to £250,000 **No.of Employees:** 1 - 10 **Product Groups:** 81

Rohm Great Britain Ltd

12 Ashway Centre Elm Crescent, Kingston Upon Thames, KT2 6HH
Tel: 020-8549 6647 **Fax:** 020-8541 1783
E-mail: rohm@rohmgb.co.uk
Website: http://www.rohm.co.uk
Directors: B. Long (MD)
Managers: R. Lydon (Sales Prom Mgr)
Immediate Holding Company: ROHM (GREAT BRITAIN) LIMITED
Registration no: 00629431 **Date established:** 1959 **Turnover:** £2m - £5m
No.of Employees: 1 - 10 **Product Groups:** 30, 46

Date of Accounts	Dec 08
Working Capital	187
Fixed Assets	595
Current Assets	698
Current Liabilities	511
Total Share Capital	5

Tadius Tech Ltd

Tir Na N'Og Coombe Ridings, Kingston Upon Thames, KT2 7JT
Tel: 020-8439 7626 **Fax:** 020-8439 7631
E-mail: trond@radius.co.uk
Website: http://www.radius.co.uk
Directors: T. Thorman (MD)
Immediate Holding Company: RADIUS TECH LIMITED
Registration no: 05377746 **VAT No.:** GB 731 1729 54
Date established: 2005 **Turnover:** £500,000 - £1m
No.of Employees: 1 - 10 **Product Groups:** 37, 38, 52, 67, 80

Date of Accounts	Mar 11	Mar 10	Mar 09
Working Capital	31	7	77
Fixed Assets	6	7	9
Current Assets	419	391	353

The Bentall Centre

Bentalls Shopping Centre Wood Street, Kingston Upon Thames, KT1 1TP
Tel: 020-8541 5066 **Fax:** 020-8541 5077
E-mail: bentallsonline@bentalls.co.uk
Website: http://www.thebentallcentre-shopping.com
Managers: R. Ritchie
Immediate Holding Company: THE BENTALL CENTRE TRADERS ASSOCIATION (KINGSTON) LIMITED
Registration no: 02707254 **VAT No.:** GB 215 9750 53
Date established: 1992 **Turnover:** £500,000 - £1m
No.of Employees: 1 - 10 **Product Groups:** 61

Date of Accounts	Nov 11	Nov 10	Nov 09
Sales Turnover	639	648	645
Pre Tax Profit/Loss	38	-7	84
Working Capital	205	167	174
Current Assets	469	492	436
Current Liabilities	233	220	214

Unipetrol UK Ltd

6 Canbury Business Centre Canbury Park Road, Kingston Upon Thames, KT2 6LX
Tel: 020-8255 8051 **Fax:** 020- 85463500
E-mail: leos.gal@unipetrol.co.uk
Website: http://www.seznam.cz
Directors: L. Gal (Dir)
Immediate Holding Company: WJS MUSIC LIMITED
Registration no: 00307697 **Date established:** 2008
Turnover: Up to £250,000 **No.of Employees:** 1 - 10 **Product Groups:** 61, 66

Date of Accounts	Dec 06	Dec 05
Sales Turnover	70	90
Pre Tax Profit/Loss	30	60

Working Capital	40	10
Current Assets	40	20
Total Share Capital	100	100
ROT% (Return on Turnover)	42.9	66.7

Wolterskluwer UK Ltd

145 London Road, Kingston Upon Thames, KT2 6SR
Tel: 020-8547 3333 **Fax:** 020-8547 2638
E-mail: info@wolterskluwer.co.uk
Website: http://www.wolterskluwer.co.uk
Bank(s): National Westminster Bank Plc
Managers: C. Wolse
Ultimate Holding Company: WOLTERS KLUWER NV (NETHERLANDS)
Immediate Holding Company: WOLTERS KLUWER HOLDINGS (UK) PLC
Registration no: 01329311 **VAT No.:** GB 710 9357 45
Date established: 1977 **No.of Employees:** 251 - 500 **Product Groups:** 28, 81

Date of Accounts	Dec 11	Dec 10	Dec 09
Pre Tax Profit/Loss	-3m	-5m	-41
Working Capital	-102m	-102m	-92m
Fixed Assets	144m	146m	142m
Current Assets	63m	73m	81m
Current Liabilities	423	1m	2m

Leatherhead

Amag UK Ltd (AMAG & Rolling GmbH)

Beckley Lodge Leatherhead Road, Bookham, Leatherhead, KT23 4RN
Tel: 01372-450661 **Fax:** 01372-450833
E-mail: brian@amag.co.uk
Website: http://www.amag.at
Managers: B. Parish (Chief Mgr)
Ultimate Holding Company: CONSTANTIA PACKAGING AG (AUSTRIA)
Immediate Holding Company: AMAG U.K. LIMITED
Registration no: 01561503 **Date established:** 1981
Turnover: £250,000 - £500,000 **No.of Employees:** 1 - 10
Product Groups: 34, 35, 40

Date of Accounts	Dec 11	Dec 10	Dec 09
Sales Turnover	480	433	411
Pre Tax Profit/Loss	36	32	30
Working Capital	64	54	52
Fixed Assets	13	18	3
Current Assets	145	121	119
Current Liabilities	75	64	64

Applied Photophysics Ltd

Unit 21 Leatherhead Trade Park Station Road, Leatherhead, KT22 7AG
Tel: 01372-386537 **Fax:** 01372-386477
E-mail: sales@photophysics.com
Website: http://www.photophysics.com
Bank(s): Barclays
Directors: D. Gregson (MD), P. Johnson (Co Sec)
Ultimate Holding Company: INVESTROP LTD (JERSEY)
Immediate Holding Company: APPLIED PHOTOPHYSICS LIMITED
Registration no: 01006739 **VAT No.:** GB 564 2354 43
Date established: 1971 **Turnover:** £5m - £10m **No.of Employees:** 21 - 50
Product Groups: 38

Date of Accounts	Jan 12	Jan 11	Jan 10
Sales Turnover	5m	5m	4m
Pre Tax Profit/Loss	295	385	302
Working Capital	968	853	855
Fixed Assets	487	498	163
Current Assets	2m	2m	1m
Current Liabilities	391	411	331

Ashtead Plant Hire Co. Ltd

130 Kingston Road, Leatherhead, KT22 7PU
Tel: 01372-379844 **Fax:** 01372-378681
E-mail: leatherheadth@aplant.com
Website: http://www.aplant.com
Bank(s): Lloyds TSB Bank plc
Managers: S. Sparrow (Mgr)
Ultimate Holding Company: Ashtead Group P.L.C.
Registration no: 00444569 **Turnover:** £20m - £50m
No.of Employees: 11 - 20 **Product Groups:** 83

Bookham Guns

Barracks Farm Cobham Road, Fetcham, Leatherhead, KT22 9TP
Tel: 01372-362072 **Fax:** 01372-362073
E-mail: jwproctor1940@aol.com
Directors: J. Proctor (Ptnr)
Immediate Holding Company: PROCTOR & SON ENGINEERING LTD
Registration no: 05062847 **Date established:** 2004
No.of Employees: 1 - 10 **Product Groups:** 36, 39, 40

Date of Accounts	Mar 11	Mar 10	Mar 08
Working Capital	107	78	44
Fixed Assets	14	23	9
Current Assets	134	94	73

Bpa Consulting Ltd

Dorset House Regent Park Kingston Road, Leatherhead, KT22 7PL
Tel: 01306-875500 **Fax:** 01306-888179
E-mail: bpa@bpaconsulting.com
Website: http://www.bpaconsulting.com
Directors: M. Hutton (MD)
Ultimate Holding Company: BPA GROUP LIMITED
Immediate Holding Company: BPA CONSULTING LIMITED
Registration no: 03173626 **VAT No.:** GB 644 7559 06
Date established: 1996 **Turnover:** £1m - £2m **No.of Employees:** 1 - 10
Product Groups: 84

Date of Accounts	Dec 11	Dec 10	Dec 09
Working Capital	85	89	103
Fixed Assets	12	15	N/A
Current Assets	120	117	130

Buchanan & Curwen Holdings Ltd

Fairfield Works Upper Fairfield Road, Leatherhead, KT22 7HJ
Tel: 01372-373481 **Fax:** 01372-377458
E-mail: buchanans@b-and-c.co.uk
Website: http://www.b-and-c.co.uk
Directors: N. Morris (MD), N. Morris (MD)
Ultimate Holding Company: BUCHANAN & CURWEN GROUP LIMITED
Immediate Holding Company: BUCHANAN & CURWEN (HOLDINGS) LIMITED

see next page

Buchanan & Curwen Holdings Ltd - Cont'd
Registration no: 00266706 **VAT No.:** GB 235 5695 41
Date established: 1932 **Turnover:** £250,000 - £500,000
No.of Employees: 1 - 10 **Product Groups:** 52

Date of Accounts	Oct 10	Oct 09	Oct 08
Sales Turnover	N/A	N/A	495
Pre Tax Profit/Loss	-11	1m	-331
Working Capital	11	22	-154
Fixed Assets	N/A	N/A	417
Current Assets	22	22	451
Current Liabilities	11	N/A	71

C P Kelco Ltd
Cleeve Court Cleeve Road, Leatherhead, KT22 7UD
Tel: 01372-369400 **Fax:** 01372-369401
E-mail: malcolm.laws@cpkelco.com
Website: http://www.cpkelco.com
Directors: N. Wilson (MD)
Ultimate Holding Company: J M HUBER CORP (USA)
Immediate Holding Company: CP KELCO UK LIMITED
Registration no: 03969110 **Date established:** 2000
Turnover: £20m - £50m **No.of Employees:** 1 - 10 **Product Groups:** 20, 31, 32

Date of Accounts	Dec 11	Dec 10	Dec 09
Sales Turnover	34m	35m	34m
Pre Tax Profit/Loss	-440	2m	-1m
Working Capital	6m	18m	16m
Current Assets	8m	19m	20m
Current Liabilities	605	486	348

Cavendish French Ltd
22 Church Road Bookham, Leatherhead, KT23 3PW
Tel: 01372-459944 **Fax:** 01372-459384
E-mail: sales@cavendishfrench.com
Website: http://www.cavendishfrench.com
Directors: R. Haynes (Dir)
Immediate Holding Company: CAVENDISH FRENCH LIMITED
Registration no: 02953447 **VAT No.:** GB 345 9797 95
Date established: 1994 **Turnover:** £500,000 - £1m
No.of Employees: 1 - 10 **Product Groups:** 33, 49, 65

Date of Accounts	Dec 11	Dec 10	Dec 09
Working Capital	234	236	300
Fixed Assets	82	86	29
Current Assets	341	369	352

Denny's Uniforms
1 Cleeve Court Cleeve Road, Leatherhead, KT22 7UD
Tel: 01372-377904 **Fax:** 01372-362920
E-mail: sales@dennys.co.uk
Website: http://www.dennys.co.uk
Bank(s): Lloyds TSB
Directors: J. Jubert (Fin), N. Jubert (MD)
Managers: C. Tipper (Export Sales Mg)
Immediate Holding Company: Wood Harris
Turnover: Up to £250,000 **No.of Employees:** 21 - 50 **Product Groups:** 24

Digiscans
Unit 25 Brook Willow Farm Woodlands Road, Leatherhead, KT22 0AN
Tel: 01372-841071
E-mail: info@digiscanltd.com
Website: http://www.digiscans.co.uk
Managers: C. Ashley (Mgr)
Date established: 1982 **No.of Employees:** 1 - 10 **Product Groups:** 44

Robert Dyas Holdings Ltd
Cleeve Court Cleeve Road, Leatherhead, KT22 7SD
Tel: 01372-361444 **Fax:** 01372-361094
E-mail: enquiries@robertdyas.co.uk
Website: http://www.robertdyas.co.uk
Directors: P. Green (Comm), G. Coles (Grp Chief Exec), M. Emerson (Fin)
Managers: C. Collins (Personnel), W. Woods, P. McDermott
Ultimate Holding Company: CLEEVE COURT HOLDINGS LIMITED
Immediate Holding Company: ROBERT DYAS HOLDINGS LIMITED
Registration no: 04041884 **VAT No.:** GB 216 0936 78
Date established: 2000 **Turnover:** £75m - £125m
No.of Employees: 51 - 100 **Product Groups:** 61

Date of Accounts	Mar 12	Mar 09	Mar 10
Sales Turnover	106m	108m	108m
Pre Tax Profit/Loss	186	-10m	3m
Working Capital	5m	5m	4m
Fixed Assets	7m	16m	8m
Current Assets	23m	36m	23m
Current Liabilities	4m	10m	5m

Eveready Hire
Ashtead House Crouch Industrial Estate Barnett Wood Lane, Leatherhead, KT22 7DG
Tel: 01372-383337 **Fax:** 01372-383351
E-mail: eddie@leander-construction.co.uk
Website: http://www.evereadyhire.com
Directors: E. Shepherd (Dir)
Ultimate Holding Company: LEANDER HOLDINGS (UK) LIMITED
Immediate Holding Company: EVEREADY HIRE LIMITED
Registration no: 04548026 **Date established:** 2002 **Turnover:** £2m - £5m
No.of Employees: 1 - 10 **Product Groups:** 30, 33, 35, 36, 37, 40, 41, 42, 45, 46, 47, 67, 83

Date of Accounts	Sep 11	Sep 10	Sep 09
Sales Turnover	3m	3m	2m
Pre Tax Profit/Loss	256	154	46
Working Capital	-788	-654	-1m
Fixed Assets	2m	2m	2m
Current Assets	803	823	698
Current Liabilities	698	402	682

Hunter & Hyland Ltd
201-205 Kingston Road, Leatherhead, KT22 7PB
Tel: 01372-378511 **Fax:** 01372-370038
E-mail: enquiries@hunterandhyland.co.uk
Website: http://www.hunterandhyland.co.uk
Bank(s): Lloyds TSB Bank plc
Directors: J. Moon (MD), S. Moon (Fin)
Managers: A. Woodward (Chief Mgr), J. Moon (Personnel)
Immediate Holding Company: HUNTER & HYLAND LIMITED
Registration no: 01534353 **VAT No.:** GB 235 5787 36
Date established: 1980 **Turnover:** £1m - £2m **No.of Employees:** 21 - 50
Product Groups: 63

Date of Accounts	Jan 12	Jan 11	Jan 10
Working Capital	2m	2m	1m
Fixed Assets	233	213	226
Current Assets	2m	2m	2m

K B R
Hill Park Court Springfield Drive, Leatherhead, KT22 7NL
Tel: 01372-865000 **Fax:** 01372-864400
Website: http://www.kbr.com
Directors: S. Nicholson (Dir), I. Smith (Co Sec)
Ultimate Holding Company: KBR INC (USA)
Immediate Holding Company: KBR (ASPIRE SERVICES) LIMITED
Registration no: 05704218 **Date established:** 2006
Turnover: £50m - £75m **No.of Employees:** 1501 & over
Product Groups: 80, 84

Date of Accounts	Dec 11	Dec 10	Dec 09
Sales Turnover	69m	67m	69m
Pre Tax Profit/Loss	1m	1m	2m
Working Capital	710	2m	4m
Current Assets	9m	13m	13m
Current Liabilities	7m	10m	8m

Kingsmead
Unit 34 Bookham Industrial Estate Bookham, Leatherhead, KT23 3EU
Tel: 01372-459678 **Fax:** 01372-454894
E-mail: graham@kingmead.com
Website: http://www.kingsmead.com
Bank(s): Barclays
Directors: G. Storey (Prop)
Immediate Holding Company: CARRINGTON GREEN LIMITED
Registration no: 07127923 **VAT No.:** GB 395 2672 18
Date established: 2010 **Turnover:** £1m - £2m **No.of Employees:** 11 - 20
Product Groups: 27, 28

Date of Accounts	Mar 08	Mar 07	Mar 06
Working Capital	36	-66	54
Fixed Assets	198	244	59
Current Assets	321	285	370
Current Liabilities	285	350	316
Total Share Capital	14	14	14

L O T - Oriel Ltd
Unit 1 Mole Business Park Randalls Road, Leatherhead, KT22 7BA
Tel: 01372-378822 **Fax:** 01372-375353
E-mail: info@lotoriel.co.uk
Website: http://www.lotoriel.co.uk
Directors: C. Budleigh (Fin), D. Want (MD), J. Green (Sales)
Ultimate Holding Company: QUANTUM DESIGN HOLDING GMBH & CO KG (GERMANY)
Immediate Holding Company: L.O.T.-ORIEL LIMITED
Registration no: 01259082 **Date established:** 1976
Turnover: £500,000 - £1m **No.of Employees:** 1 - 10 **Product Groups:** 37, 38

Date of Accounts	Sep 11	Sep 10	Sep 09
Working Capital	538	579	558
Fixed Assets	70	66	77
Current Assets	1m	1m	1m

Leatherhead Food Research
Randalls Road, Leatherhead, KT22 7RY
Tel: 01372-376761 **Fax:** 01372-386228
E-mail: enquiries@lfra.co.uk
Website: http://www.leatherheadfood.com
Bank(s): Barclays
Directors: M. Incles (Sales & Mktg), J. Gordon Smith (Fin), J. Gordon-smith (Fin)
Managers: P. Berryman, I. Dawson (Tech Serv Mgr)
Ultimate Holding Company: LEATHERHEAD INTERNATIONAL LIMITED
Immediate Holding Company: LEATHERHEAD FOOD INTERNATIONAL LIMITED
Registration no: 03420548 **VAT No.:** GB 609 0859 27
Date established: 1997 **Turnover:** £5m - £10m
No.of Employees: 101 - 250 **Product Groups:** 54, 80, 81, 84, 85, 87

Date of Accounts	Dec 11	Dec 10	Dec 09
Sales Turnover	9m	9m	9m
Pre Tax Profit/Loss	-261	1m	2m
Working Capital	-2m	-1m	-1m
Fixed Assets	9m	9m	9m
Current Assets	3m	3m	3m
Current Liabilities	4m	4m	4m

Lektron Networks Power & Controls
Stable View 55 Dorking Road, Bookham, Leatherhead, KT23 4PY
Tel: 01372-458252 **Fax:** 01372-458122
E-mail: jason.watts@lektron.co.uk
Website: http://www.lektron.co.uk
Directors: J. Watts (Ptnr)
No.of Employees: 11 - 20 **Product Groups:** 37, 84, 85

Oldham Lighting Projects Ltd
Claudgen House Eastwick Road, Bookham, Leatherhead, KT23 4DT
Tel: 01372-459999 **Fax:** 01372-459559
E-mail: sales@oldhamlighting.co.uk
Website: http://www.oldhamlighting.co.uk
Directors: C. Richardson (MD)
Ultimate Holding Company: OLDHAM LIGHTING PROJECTS LIMITED
Immediate Holding Company: OLDHAM LIGHTING PROJECTS LIMITED
Registration no: 07188484 **Date established:** 2010 **Turnover:** £1m - £2m
No.of Employees: 1 - 10 **Product Groups:** 37

Date of Accounts	Sep 11	Sep 10
Working Capital	11	2
Fixed Assets	39	N/A
Current Assets	260	45

Partminer Worldwide Inc
14 High Street, Leatherhead, KT22 8AN
Tel: 01372-384999 **Fax:** 01372-384998
E-mail: pginimav@partminer.com
Website: http://www.partminer.com
Directors: B. Ally (Co Sec)
Managers: M. Wollenberg (Sales Prom Mgr), P. Ginimav (Sales Prom Mgr)
Immediate Holding Company: PARTMINER LTD.
Registration no: 03879809 **Date established:** 1999
Turnover: £500,000 - £1m **No.of Employees:** 1 - 10 **Product Groups:** 37, 67

Date of Accounts	Dec 10	Dec 09	Dec 08
Sales Turnover	722	678	3m
Pre Tax Profit/Loss	36	-62	89
Working Capital	75	46	92
Fixed Assets	3	6	2
Current Assets	163	123	274
Current Liabilities	67	51	71

Photo Me (International) plc
Church Road Bookham, Leatherhead, KT23 3EU
Tel: 01372-453399 **Fax:** 01372-459064
E-mail: info@photo-me.co.uk
Website: http://www.photo-me.co.uk
Bank(s): Lloyds, 39 Threadneedle St, London EC2R 8AU
Directors: G. Macfarlane (Dir)
Ultimate Holding Company: PHOTO - ME INTERNATIONAL P L C
Immediate Holding Company: PHOTO - ME INTERNATIONAL P L C
Registration no: 00735438 **VAT No.:** GB 212 0297 13
Date established: 1962 **Turnover:** £125m - £250m
No.of Employees: 51 - 100 **Product Groups:** 49, 61, 81

Date of Accounts	Apr 11	Apr 10	Apr 09
Sales Turnover	220m	223m	211m
Pre Tax Profit/Loss	18m	12m	-5m
Working Capital	29m	19m	12m
Fixed Assets	81m	85m	100m
Current Assets	98m	84m	78m
Current Liabilities	37m	31m	34m

Pira
Cleeve Road, Leatherhead, KT22 7RU
Tel: 01372-802000 **Fax:** 01372-802238
E-mail: info@pira-international.com
Website: http://www.pira-international.com
Directors: R. Wilkinson (Co Sec), J. Roeck (MD)
Managers: P. Squires (Sales Prom Mgr), H. Bunce (Personnel), P. Thursby (Purch Mgr), C. Britchford (Tech Serv Mgr), R. Leigh (Mktg Serv Mgr)
Ultimate Holding Company: THE SMITHERS GROUP INC (USA)
Immediate Holding Company: SMITHERS INFORMATION LIMITED
Registration no: 03858209 **Date established:** 1999 **Turnover:** £5m - £10m
No.of Employees: 51 - 100 **Product Groups:** 20, 28, 80, 81, 84

Date of Accounts	Dec 11	Dec 10	Dec 09
Sales Turnover	9m	8m	7m
Pre Tax Profit/Loss	-249	397	-10
Working Capital	760	874	733
Fixed Assets	2m	2m	4m
Current Assets	3m	3m	3m
Current Liabilities	2m	1m	1m

Puma UK Trustees Ltd
Challenge Court Barnett Wood Lane, Leatherhead, KT22 7LW
Tel: 01372-360255 **Fax:** 01372-362081
E-mail: info-uk@puma.com
Website: http://www.puma.com
Directors: T. Ward (MD)
Managers: K. Middleton (Transport)
Immediate Holding Company: PUMA PREMIER LTD
Registration no: 05347587 **Date established:** 2005 **Turnover:** £5m - £10m
No.of Employees: 1 - 10 **Product Groups:** 22

Date of Accounts	Dec 07
Sales Turnover	8m
Pre Tax Profit/Loss	-5m
Working Capital	-10m
Fixed Assets	196m
Current Assets	3m
Current Liabilities	391

Verint Systems Inc
Kings Court Kingston Road, Leatherhead, KT22 7SL
Tel: 01372-869000 **Fax:** 01372-869005
E-mail: sales@witness.com
Website: http://verint.com
Bank(s): HSBC, Crawley
Directors: D. Parcell (Dir), K. Mercer (Dir), N. Discombe (Grp Chief Exec), P. Fante (Co Sec)
Managers: J. Jagger (I.T. Exec), S. Lucas (Mgr), T. Goodwin (Mktg Serv Mgr)
Immediate Holding Company: Verint WS Holdings Ltd
Registration no: 02563800 **Date established:** 1990
Turnover: £20m - £50m **No.of Employees:** 101 - 250
Product Groups: 37, 38, 44, 67, 85

Date of Accounts	Dec 05
Sales Turnover	27100
Pre Tax Profit/Loss	1391
Working Capital	34928
Fixed Assets	3747
Current Assets	48146
Current Liabilities	13218
Total Share Capital	75
ROCE% (Return on Capital Employed)	3.6

Wassen International Ltd
Unit 14 Mole Business Park Randalls Road, Leatherhead, KT22 7BA
Tel: 01372-379828 **Fax:** 01372-376599
E-mail: info@wassen.com
Website: http://www.wassen.com
Bank(s): Barclays
Directors: M. Barber (Dir)
Ultimate Holding Company: WASSEN GROUP HOLDINGS LIMITED
Immediate Holding Company: EFAMOL LIMITED
Registration no: 04624258 **Date established:** 2002 **Turnover:** £2m - £5m
No.of Employees: 11 - 20 **Product Groups:** 31

Date of Accounts	Sep 10	Sep 09	Sep 08
Sales Turnover	4m	4m	4m
Pre Tax Profit/Loss	260	261	213
Working Capital	2m	2m	1m
Fixed Assets	27	34	49
Current Assets	4m	3m	3m
Current Liabilities	910	554	662

Wood Harris Ltd (t/a Denny's)
1 Cleeve Court Cleeve Road, Leatherhead, KT22 7UD
Tel: 01372-377904 **Fax:** 01372-362920
E-mail: sales@dennys.co.uk
Website: http://www.dennys.co.uk
Bank(s): Lloyds TSB
Directors: D. Green (Sales)
Ultimate Holding Company: H.SEDGWICK LIMITED
Immediate Holding Company: DENNY'S UNIFORMS LIMITED
Registration no: 00423051 **VAT No.:** 219 6129 59 **Date established:** 1946
Turnover: £5m - £10m **No.of Employees:** 21 - 50 **Product Groups:** 24

Date of Accounts	Oct 11	Oct 10	Oct 09
Sales Turnover	8m	7m	7m
Pre Tax Profit/Loss	493	215	61
Working Capital	2m	1m	1m
Fixed Assets	163	205	231
Current Assets	3m	2m	2m
Current Liabilities	640	448	187

Xmark Media Ltd
Old Village Hall The Street, Effingham, Leatherhead, KT24 5JS
Tel: 01372-750555 **Fax:** 01372-750666
E-mail: info@xmarkmedia.com
Website: http://www.xmarkmedia.com
Directors: L. Devreux (MD), L. Devereux (MD)
Immediate Holding Company: XMARK MEDIA LTD
Registration no: 03013100 **VAT No.:** GB 358 7364 14
Date established: 1995 **Turnover:** £250,000 - £500,000
No.of Employees: 1 - 10 **Product Groups:** 81

Date of Accounts	Mar 11	Mar 10	Mar 09
Working Capital	-78	-84	-76
Fixed Assets	5	5	5
Current Assets	21	29	40
Current Liabilities	11	11	11

Lightwater

Indigo I T Ltd
92 Guildford Road, Lightwater, GU18 5RP
Tel: 01483-472200 **Fax:** 01483-472299
E-mail: sales@indigo-it.com
Website: http://www.indigo-it.com
Directors: T. Galvin (MD), C. Galvin (Fin)
Immediate Holding Company: INDIGO I.T. LTD
Registration no: 04404474 **Date established:** 2002
No.of Employees: 1 - 10 **Product Groups:** 44

Date of Accounts	Mar 11	Mar 10	Mar 09
Working Capital	-115	-118	3
Fixed Assets	156	186	3
Current Assets	85	122	248

KFS Service Ltd
The Avenue, Lightwater, GU18 5RF
Tel: 01276-479404 **Fax:** 01276-479504
E-mail: enquiry@kfsservice.co.uk
Website: http://kfsservice.co.uk
Managers: N. Holden (Chief Mgr)
Registration no: 06585930 **Date established:** 2008
Turnover: £250,000 - £500,000 **No.of Employees:** 1 - 10
Product Groups: 40, 48, 67

National Door Co.
Pyramid House 52 Guildford Road, Lightwater, GU18 5SD
Tel: 01276-451555 **Fax:** 01276-453666
E-mail: info@nationaldomes.com
Website: http://www.nationaldomelightcompany.co.uk
Directors: B. Newman (Co Sec)
No.of Employees: 11 - 20 **Product Groups:** 30, 38, 40, 66

Lingfield

Alice Soundtech plc
Unit 34d Hobbs Indl-Est Newchapel, Lingfield, RH7 6HN
Tel: 01342-833500 **Fax:** 01342-833350
E-mail: sales@alice.co.uk
Website: http://www.alice.co.uk
Bank(s): Barclays, Crawley
Directors: R. Gemmell Smith (Fin), A. Gemmell-Smith (Ch)
Immediate Holding Company: TRANSMISSION SYSTEMS LTD
Registration no: 01754206 **VAT No.:** GB 394 9262 08
Date established: 1983 **Turnover:** £1m - £2m **No.of Employees:** 11 - 20
Product Groups: 37

Date of Accounts	Apr 11	Apr 10	Apr 09
Working Capital	29	29	46
Fixed Assets	276	337	326
Current Assets	165	163	181

Autoculture Ltd
Unit 2 Pond Farm Ray Lane, Lingfield, RH7 6JG
Tel: 01342-837591 **Fax:** 01342-835486
E-mail: sales@autoculture.co.uk
Website: http://www.autoculture.co.uk
Directors: M. Searle (MD), S. Searle (Ptnr)
Immediate Holding Company: AUTOCULTURE LIMITED
Registration no: 03954047 **VAT No.:** GB 210 6267 04
Date established: 2000 **Turnover:** £500,000 - £1m
No.of Employees: 1 - 10 **Product Groups:** 30, 39, 49, 67

Biffa Waste Services Ltd
Unit 38 Hobbs Industrial Estate Newchapel, Lingfield, RH7 6HN
Tel: 0800-601601 **Fax:** 01342- 836645
Website: http://www.biffa.co.uk
Managers: J. Gilmour (Mgr)
Immediate Holding Company: BIFFA WASTE SERVICES LIMITED
Registration no: 00946107 **Date established:** 1969
No.of Employees: 11 - 20 **Product Groups:** 32, 54

Date of Accounts	Mar 08	Mar 09	Apr 10
Sales Turnover	555m	574m	492m
Pre Tax Profit/Loss	23m	50m	30m
Working Capital	229m	271m	293m
Fixed Assets	371m	360m	378m
Current Assets	409m	534m	609m
Current Liabilities	50m	100m	115m

C J T Bathrooms
Unit 41d Hobbs Industrial Estate, Newchapel, Lingfield, RH7 6HN
Tel: 01342-832624 **Fax:** 01342-832279
E-mail: cjtbathrooms@btconnect.com
Website: http://www.cjtbathrooms.co.uk
Directors: J. Crowhurst (Prop)
Turnover: £250,000 - £500,000 **No.of Employees:** 1 - 10
Product Groups: 26, 30

D S Developments
Unit 41a Hobbs Industrial Estate Newchapel, Lingfield, RH7 6HN
Tel: 01342-835444 **Fax:** 01342-832277
E-mail: enquiries@dsdevelopments.co.uk
Website: http://www.dsdevelopments.co.uk
Directors: D. Shepherd (Dir)
Date established: 2000 **Turnover:** Up to £250,000
No.of Employees: 1 - 10 **Product Groups:** 37

Elion Electronics
54 High Street Dormansland, Lingfield, RH7 6PY
Tel: 01342-832212
Website: http://www.elionelectronics.com
Directors: S. Kent (Prop)
No.of Employees: 1 - 10 **Product Groups:** 37

Extra Space Industries
Unit 27 Hobbs Industrial Estate Newchapel, Lingfield, RH7 6HN
Tel: 01342-830040 **Fax:** 01342-836978
E-mail: enquiries@extraspace.co.uk
Website: http://www.extraspace.co.uk
Directors: A. Hall (Chief Op Offcr)
Registration no: 02024573 **VAT No.:** GB 407 8314 57
Date established: 1986 **Turnover:** £2m - £5m **No.of Employees:** 1 - 10
Product Groups: 25, 35, 83

Date of Accounts	Mar 08	Mar 07	Mar 06
Working Capital	470	175	160
Fixed Assets	152	437	261
Current Assets	1058	1046	901
Current Liabilities	588	871	742

Foremost Coatings
Unit 40 Hobbs Industrial Estate Newchapel, Lingfield, RH7 6HN
Tel: 01342-833455 **Fax:** 01342-832623
E-mail: david@foremostcoatings.co.uk
Website: http://www.foremostcoatings.co.uk
Directors: C. Skillett (Prop)
Immediate Holding Company: FOREMOST COATINGS LIMITED
Registration no: 08018452 **VAT No.:** GB 492 5381 24
Date established: 2012 **Turnover:** Up to £250,000
No.of Employees: 1 - 10 **Product Groups:** 48

Maidenbower Sheet Metal Ltd
The Barn Stantons Hall Farm Eastbourne Road, Blindley Heath, Lingfield, RH7 6LG
Tel: 01342-837144 **Fax:** 01342-837956
E-mail: martin@maidenbowersheetmetal.co.uk
Directors: M. Goody (MD)
Immediate Holding Company: MAIDENBOWER SHEETMETAL LIMITED
Registration no: 03358714 **Date established:** 1997
No.of Employees: 1 - 10 **Product Groups:** 37, 40, 48

Date of Accounts	Mar 12	Mar 11	Mar 10
Working Capital	-141	-152	-135
Fixed Assets	25	21	27
Current Assets	300	214	313

Mitcham

21St Century Technology Plc
Drake Road, Mitcham, CR4 4HQ
Tel: 08448-717990 **Fax:** 0870-160 1748
E-mail: info@toad.co.uk
Website: http://www.21stplc.com
Directors: N. Grimmond (MD)
Managers: M. Johnston (I.T. Exec)
Ultimate Holding Company: 21ST CENTURY TECHNOLOGY PLC
Immediate Holding Company: 21ST CENTURY TECHNOLOGY PLC
Registration no: 02974642 **Date established:** 1994
Turnover: £10m - £20m **No.of Employees:** 1 - 10 **Product Groups:** 36, 37, 39

Date of Accounts	Dec 11	Dec 10	Dec 09
Sales Turnover	14m	11m	10m
Pre Tax Profit/Loss	1m	860	691
Working Capital	5m	4m	1m
Fixed Assets	5m	5m	8m
Current Assets	9m	7m	4m
Current Liabilities	2m	2m	2m

Aldridge Print Group
Unit 9 Mitcham Industrial Estate Streatham Road, Mitcham, CR4 2AP
Tel: 020-8239 4100 **Fax:** 020-8239 4120
E-mail: aldridges@apgprint.com
Website: http://www.apgprint.com
Bank(s): National Westminster Bank Plc
Directors: J. Sheehan (Sales), R. Aldridge (MD), S. Aldridge (Co Sec), S. Aldridge (Fin)
Managers: C. Hamlin (Prod Mgr), M. Capon (I.T. Exec)
Immediate Holding Company: ALDRIDGE PRINT GROUP LIMITED
Registration no: 03923817 **VAT No.:** GB 372 8131 54
Date established: 2000 **Turnover:** £5m - £10m
No.of Employees: 51 - 100 **Product Groups:** 28

Date of Accounts	Aug 10	Aug 09	Aug 08
Sales Turnover	449	8m	N/A
Pre Tax Profit/Loss	258	53	2
Working Capital	-151	-835	-233
Fixed Assets	3m	5m	3m
Current Assets	19	3m	15
Current Liabilities	59	1m	N/A

Ats Automated Training Systems Ltd
Unit 1 Astral Building Wandle Technology Park - Mill Green Road, Mitcham, CR4 4HZ
Tel: 020-8648 4000 **Fax:** 020-8648 4388
E-mail: info@atstraining.co.uk
Website: http://www.atstraining.co.uk
Directors: J. Cooper (MD), L. Krokidis (Fin)
Immediate Holding Company: ATS AUTOMATED TRAINING SYSTEMS LTD
Registration no: 03765378 **VAT No.:** GB 341 1000 34
Date established: 1999 **Turnover:** Up to £250,000
No.of Employees: 1 - 10 **Product Groups:** 86

Date of Accounts	Jun 11	Jun 10	Jun 09
Working Capital	49	56	92
Current Assets	123	138	197

B & D Clays & Chemicals Ltd
10 Wandle Way, Mitcham, CR4 4NB
Tel: 020-8640 9221 **Fax:** 020-8648 5033
E-mail: sales@bdclays.co.uk
Website: http://www.catlitters.co.uk
Directors: J. Trotter (Dir), P. Harrison (Dir)
Managers: D. Parr (Sales Prom Mgr)
Immediate Holding Company: B. & D. CLAYS AND CHEMICALS LIMITED
Registration no: 01181514 **VAT No.:** GB 219 2577 52
Date established: 1974 **Turnover:** £1m - £2m **No.of Employees:** 1 - 10
Product Groups: 31, 32, 33

Date of Accounts	Jun 11	Jun 10	Jun 09
Sales Turnover	1m	1m	1m
Pre Tax Profit/Loss	150	132	129
Working Capital	37	19	-82
Fixed Assets	2m	1m	1m
Current Assets	365	344	404
Current Liabilities	172	160	112

W E Baxter Ltd
10 Osier Way, Mitcham, CR4 4NF
Tel: 020-8685 1234 **Fax:** 020-8640 2781
E-mail: sales@we-baxter.co.uk
Website: http://www.we-baxter.co.uk
Directors: S. Fuller (MD)
Ultimate Holding Company: CAMERON FRANCE HOLDING SAS (FRANCE)
Immediate Holding Company: W.E.BAXTER LIMITED
Registration no: 00027884 **Date established:** 1988 **Turnover:** £1m - £2m
No.of Employees: 11 - 20 **Product Groups:** 30, 44

Date of Accounts	Mar 11	Mar 10	Mar 09
Sales Turnover	2m	2m	1m
Pre Tax Profit/Loss	-103	-146	33
Working Capital	206	302	411
Fixed Assets	40	19	21
Current Assets	582	736	687
Current Liabilities	62	62	38

Boxall Engineering Ltd
Unit 50 Grace Business Centre 23 Willow Lane, Mitcham, CR4 4TU
Tel: 020-8648 8468 **Fax:** 020-8648 4162
E-mail: info@boxall-industrial.co.uk
Website: http://www.boxall-industrial.co.uk
Directors: I. Boxall (MD), J. Hamilton (Co Sec)
Immediate Holding Company: BOXALL ENGINEERING LIMITED
Registration no: 00792047 **VAT No.:** GB 574 2812 32
Date established: 1964 **Turnover:** £250,000 - £500,000
No.of Employees: 1 - 10 **Product Groups:** 46

Date of Accounts	Apr 11	Apr 10	Apr 09
Working Capital	138	122	147
Fixed Assets	114	120	125
Current Assets	203	186	214

Carclo Technical Plastic Ltd
47 Wates Way, Mitcham, CR4 4HR
Tel: 020-8685 0500 **Fax:** 020-8640 4715
E-mail: enquiriesm@carclo-plc.com
Website: http://www.carclo-plc.com
Bank(s): National Westminster
Directors: M. Day (Sales), P. Ward (MD), R. Ottaway (Fin)
Managers: B. Graham (Buyer)
Immediate Holding Company: Carclo P.L.C.
Registration no: 01786038 **Date established:** 1984 **Turnover:** £5m - £10m
No.of Employees: 101 - 250 **Product Groups:** 29, 30, 32, 48, 67

Date of Accounts	Mar 08	Mar 07	Mar 06
Sales Turnover	34631	19221	19504
Pre Tax Profit/Loss	-1200	-1082	-2562
Working Capital	8381	8659	2591
Fixed Assets	13915	14728	4651
Current Assets	17213	16034	6976
Current Liabilities	8831	7375	4385
Total Share Capital	1000	1000	1000
ROCE% (Return on Capital Employed)	-5.4	-4.6	-35.4
ROT% (Return on Turnover)	-3.5	-5.6	-13.1

Chrisanne Ltd
110-112 Morden Road, Mitcham, CR4 4XB
Tel: 020-8646 8531 **Fax:** 020-8646 8271
E-mail: sales@chrisanne.com
Website: http://www.chrisanne.com
Bank(s): National Westminster
Managers: K. Vince (Mgr)
Immediate Holding Company: CHRISANNE LIMITED
Registration no: 01979551 **Date established:** 1986
No.of Employees: 51 - 100 **Product Groups:** 24

Date of Accounts	Dec 11	Dec 10	Dec 09
Working Capital	663	566	552
Fixed Assets	155	173	192
Current Assets	2m	1m	1m

Comar Architectural Aluminium Systems
Unit 5, The Willow Centre 17 Willow Lane, Mitcham, CR4 4NX
Tel: 020-8685 9685 **Fax:** 020-8646 5096
E-mail: info@parksidegroup.co.uk
Website: http://www.comar-alu.co.uk
Bank(s): Barclays
Directors: D. Cook (Dir)
Ultimate Holding Company: Parkside Group Ltd
Registration no: 00921619 **Turnover:** £5m - £10m
No.of Employees: 21 - 50 **Product Groups:** 26, 30, 35, 52

Concrete Repairs Ltd
Cathite House 23a Willow Lane, Mitcham, CR4 4TU
Tel: 020-8288 4848 **Fax:** 020-8288 4847
E-mail: mail@concrete-repairs.co.uk
Website: http://www.concrete-repairs.co.uk
Bank(s): HSBC Bank plc
Directors: A. Rimoldi (MD), J. Drewett (Mkt Research), S. Patel (Fin)
Managers: A. Marsh, S. Blakeway (Tech Serv Mgr), S. O'Sullivan
Ultimate Holding Company: CENTURA GROUP LIMITED
Immediate Holding Company: CONCRETE REPAIRS LIMITED
Registration no: 00781062 **Date established:** 1963
Turnover: £20m - £50m **No.of Employees:** 251 - 500 **Product Groups:** 51

Date of Accounts	Jun 11	Jun 10	Jun 09
Sales Turnover	25m	29m	29m
Pre Tax Profit/Loss	213	526	452
Working Capital	949	781	480
Fixed Assets	302	303	429
Current Assets	9m	9m	8m
Current Liabilities	6m	6m	5m

Crown Tools & Fixings
Unit 49 Grace Business Centre 23 Willow Lane, Mitcham, CR4 4TU
Tel: 020-8648 3000 **Fax:** 020-8648 3001
E-mail: sales@crowntools.co.uk
Website: http://www.crowntools.co.uk
Directors: D. Hyslop (MD), D. Howell (Fin)
Immediate Holding Company: CROWN TOOLS & FIXINGS LIMITED
Registration no: 02268128 **VAT No.:** GB 452 5430 65
Date established: 1988 **Turnover:** £250,000 - £500,000
No.of Employees: 1 - 10 **Product Groups:** 26, 30, 33, 35, 36, 37, 66

Date of Accounts	Jun 11	Jun 10	Jun 09
Working Capital	207	263	133
Fixed Assets	8	11	15
Current Assets	269	263	246

Direct Cleaning Supplies
10 Bunting Close, Mitcham, CR4 4ND
Tel: 020-8687 5555 **Fax:** 020-8640 3374
E-mail: ian@forestdalebs.co.uk
Managers: I. Cheeseman (Mgr)
Immediate Holding Company: DIRECT CLEANING SUPPLY LTD
Registration no: 01552298 **VAT No.:** GB 237 5791 33
Turnover: £1m - £2m **No.of Employees:** 11 - 20 **Product Groups:** 63, 66

Economos UK Ltd
Unit B2 Connaught Business Centre 22 Willow Lane, Mitcham, CR4 4NA
Tel: 020-8648 0252 **Fax:** 020-8648 0248
Website: http://www.economos.com
No.of Employees: 51 - 100 **Product Groups:** 29, 31, 48

Eden Joinery
7a 260 Church Road, Mitcham, CR4 3BW
Tel: 020-8685 9989
E-mail: edenjoinery@ntlworld.com
Directors: T. Eden (Prop)
Date established: 2001 **No.of Employees:** 1 - 10 **Product Groups:** 35, 36

Glamox Luxo Lighting Ltd
Unit 1 Abbey Industrial Estate 24 Willow Lane, Mitcham, CR4 4NA
Tel: 020-8687 3370 **Fax:** 020-8274 3501
E-mail: romana.berzolla@glamoxluxo.com
Website: http://www.luxo.co.uk
Bank(s): Den Norske, London
Directors: J. Savory (MD)
Managers: S. Pye (Purch Mgr), R. Berzolla (Sales Admin)
Ultimate Holding Company: LUXO ASA (NORWAY)
Immediate Holding Company: GLAMOX LUXO LIGHTING LIMITED
Registration no: 00670006 **VAT No.:** GB 205 3553 92
Date established: 1960 **Turnover:** £5m - £10m **No.of Employees:** 21 - 50
Product Groups: 37

Date of Accounts	Dec 09	Dec 08	Dec 07
Sales Turnover	6m	5m	5m
Pre Tax Profit/Loss	223	233	167
Working Capital	190	-44	-214
Fixed Assets	45	60	1
Current Assets	1m	2m	2m
Current Liabilities	268	296	227

Iimage Retrieval UK Ltd
Wandle House Riverside Drive, Mitcham, CR4 4BU
Tel: 020-8288 1212
E-mail: sales@iiri.co.uk
Website: http://www.imageretrieval.co.uk
Directors: D. Jenkins (Dir), K. Jenkins (Co Sec)
Immediate Holding Company: IIMAGE RETRIEVAL (U.K.) LIMITED
Registration no: 03093647 **Date established:** 1995
No.of Employees: 1 - 10 **Product Groups:** 44, 67

Date of Accounts	Dec 11	Dec 10	Dec 09
Working Capital	49	48	51
Fixed Assets	120	133	140
Current Assets	125	180	146

Kitchen Worktops London
Unit 3 Abbey Industrial Estate 24 Willow Lane, Mitcham, CR4 4NA
Tel: 020-8685 1555 **Fax:** 020-8685 1777
E-mail: business@dostone.co.uk
Website: http://www.dostone.co.uk
Directors: A. Banowicz (MD)
Immediate Holding Company: KITCHEN WORKTOPS LONDON LTD
Registration no: 07159502 **Date established:** 2010
Turnover: £500,000 - £1m **No.of Employees:** 1 - 10 **Product Groups:** 14, 26, 33, 48, 52, 63, 65, 66, 67, 69

K M F
297 Tamworth Lane, Mitcham, CR4 1DD
Tel: 020-8646 6488 **Fax:** 020-8685 9564
E-mail: terrys@kmfprecision.co.uk
Website: http://www.kmfprecision.co.uk
Directors: M. Cherifi (Prop)
Immediate Holding Company: KMF CATERING LIMITED
Registration no: 04485856 **Date established:** 2002
No.of Employees: 1 - 10 **Product Groups:** 20, 40, 41

Date of Accounts	Jul 11	Jul 10	Jul 09
Working Capital	-13	-14	-9
Fixed Assets	2	2	3
Current Assets	39	39	32

Lock Studios Ltd
32 Wates Way, Mitcham, CR4 4HR
Tel: 020-8648 2381 **Fax:** 020-8646 0542
Directors: M. Foss (Fin), M. Foss (Dir)
Managers: P. Clark (Mgr)
Immediate Holding Company: LOCK STUDIOS LIMITED
Registration no: 00843963 **VAT No.:** GB 235 7119 67
Date established: 1965 **Turnover:** Up to £250,000
No.of Employees: 1 - 10 **Product Groups:** 23, 27, 28, 30, 49, 52, 84

Date of Accounts	Mar 08	Mar 07	Mar 06
Working Capital	26	26	29
Fixed Assets	4	5	7
Current Assets	98	95	106
Current Liabilities	72	69	77

Lombard Grill & Gate
4 Eagle Trading Estate 29 Willow Lane, Mitcham, CR4 4UY
Tel: 020-8687 0844 **Fax:** 020-8640 4108
Managers: P. Collins (Mgr)
Date established: 1995 **No.of Employees:** 21 - 50 **Product Groups:** 26, 35

Open Date Equipment Ltd
Unit 8 9 Puma Trade Park 145 Morden Road, Mitcham, CR4 4DG
Tel: 020-8655 4999 **Fax:** 020-8655 4990
E-mail: francess@opendate.com
Website: http://www.opendate.com
Bank(s): National Westminster Bank Plc
Directors: F. Sinclair (Dir), G. Cowlard (Grp Chief Exec)
Managers: D. White (Sales Prom Mgr)
Immediate Holding Company: OPEN DATE EQUIPMENT LIMITED
Registration no: 01158619 **VAT No.:** GB 223 8898 31
Date established: 1974 **Turnover:** £2m - £5m **No.of Employees:** 21 - 50
Product Groups: 30, 44, 48

Date of Accounts	Jan 11	Jan 10	Jan 09
Sales Turnover	3m	2m	2m
Pre Tax Profit/Loss	494	215	-92
Working Capital	2m	1m	1m
Fixed Assets	117	137	145
Current Assets	2m	2m	1m
Current Liabilities	68	63	124

P G T Ceewrite Ltd
Falcon Business Centre 2-4 Willow Lane, Mitcham, CR4 4NA
Tel: 020-8648 9461 **Fax:** 020-8685 9638
E-mail: sales@pgt-uk.co.uk
Website: http://www.pgtechnology.co.uk
Bank(s): National Westminster
Directors: M. Hill (MD)
Immediate Holding Company: PGT CEEWRITE LIMITED
Registration no: 07359593 **VAT No.:** 218 4854 48 **Date established:** 2010
Turnover: £1m - £2m **No.of Employees:** 21 - 50 **Product Groups:** 38, 46, 48

Date of Accounts	Jan 12	Jan 11
Sales Turnover	5m	N/A
Pre Tax Profit/Loss	75	N/A
Working Capital	432	N/A
Fixed Assets	1m	N/A
Current Assets	2m	N/A
Current Liabilities	667	N/A

Parkside Group Ltd
5 Willow Business Centre 17 Willow Lane, Mitcham, CR4 4NX
Tel: 020-8685 9685 **Fax:** 020-8646 5096
E-mail: peterd@parksidegroup.co.uk
Website: http://www.comar-alu.co.uk
Directors: P. Dziurzynski (MD), D. Trussell (Dir), M. Hayward (Chief Op Offcr)
Managers: A. Davey (Mktg Serv Mgr), L. Alexander (Fin Mgr)
Immediate Holding Company: PARKSIDE GROUP LIMITED(THE)
Registration no: 00921619 **Date established:** 1967
Turnover: £10m - £20m **No.of Employees:** 51 - 100 **Product Groups:** 35

Date of Accounts	Dec 11	Dec 10	Dec 09
Sales Turnover	16m	16m	16m
Pre Tax Profit/Loss	-39	-198	-66
Working Capital	8m	8m	8m
Fixed Assets	826	995	1m
Current Assets	11m	10m	9m
Current Liabilities	910	909	714

Plastico Ltd
100 Morden Road, Mitcham, CR4 4DA
Tel: 020-8646 0456 **Fax:** 020-8646 5440
E-mail: sales@plastico.co.uk
Website: http://www.plastico.co.uk
Bank(s): Barclays
Directors: C. Wiggins (Grp Chief Exec)
Managers: A. Knight (Personnel), J. Sinclair (Comptroller), K. Lowe, W. Wignall (Buyer)
Ultimate Holding Company: D.GREEN & CO.(STOKE NEWINGTON)LIMITED
Immediate Holding Company: PLASTICO LIMITED
Registration no: 01858859 **VAT No.:** GB 407 4842 52
Date established: 1984 **Turnover:** £10m - £20m
No.of Employees: 101 - 250 **Product Groups:** 24, 29, 30, 63

Date of Accounts	Mar 11	Mar 10	Mar 09
Sales Turnover	12m	12m	12m
Pre Tax Profit/Loss	338	124	114
Working Capital	817	558	393
Fixed Assets	933	1m	1m
Current Assets	4m	3m	3m
Current Liabilities	1m	815	379

Renlon Ltd
Unit 12 Boundary Business Court 92-94 Church Road, Mitcham, CR4 3TD
Tel: 020-8687 4000 **Fax:** 020-8687 4040
E-mail: robins@renlon.com
Website: http://www.renlon.com
Directors: M. Vowles (Fin), R. Scibilia (MD)
Managers: C. Carter (Mktg Serv Mgr)
Immediate Holding Company: RENLON HOLDINGS LIMITED
Registration no: 03356307 **VAT No.:** GB 468 6897 66
Date established: 1997 **Turnover:** £2m - £5m **No.of Employees:** 1 - 10
Product Groups: 32, 52

Date of Accounts	Apr 12	Apr 11	Apr 10
Working Capital	87	87	87
Current Assets	103	151	167

Secure Vision UK Ltd
Sandham Hous Boundary Business Court, Mitcham, CR4 3TD
Tel: 020-8687 5320 **Fax:** 020-8687 5561
E-mail: sales@securvision.co.uk
Website: http://www.securevision.co.uk
Directors: B. Baines (MD), N. Baines (Ch)
Managers: G. Mayne (Projects), S. Baines (Eng)
Ultimate Holding Company: BROOKVEX TECHNICAL SERVICES LIMITED
Immediate Holding Company: SECURE VISION U.K. LIMITED
Registration no: 03182801 **Date established:** 1996
No.of Employees: 1 - 10 **Product Groups:** 37, 40, 52, 79

Date of Accounts	Mar 11	Mar 10	Apr 09
Sales Turnover	N/A	3m	2m
Pre Tax Profit/Loss	N/A	-644	N/A
Working Capital	-1m	-390	-195
Fixed Assets	19	25	32
Current Assets	2m	2m	601
Current Liabilities	N/A	504	N/A

Shelley Engineering Redhill Ltd
Unit 31-33 Grace Business Centre 23 Willow Lane, Mitcham, CR4 4TU
Tel: 020-8685 0302 **Fax:** 020-8687 0572
E-mail: mail@shelleyengineering.co.uk
Website: http://www.shelleyengineering.co.uk
Bank(s): Lloyds TSB Bank plc
Directors: J. Law (Dir), R. Melody (Dir), D. Butcher (MD)
Immediate Holding Company: SHELLEY ENGINEERING (REDHILL) LIMITED
Registration no: 05720051 **VAT No.:** GB 339 8685 94
Date established: 2006 **Turnover:** £2m - £5m **No.of Employees:** 21 - 50
Product Groups: 35, 48

Date of Accounts	Mar 11	Mar 10	Mar 09
Working Capital	309	189	270
Fixed Assets	9	16	24
Current Assets	746	583	597

SKF Economos U.K. Ltd Mitcham Branch
Unit B2, Connaught Business Centre 22 Willow Lane, Mitcham, CR4 4NA
Tel: 020-8648 0252 **Fax:** 020-8648 0248
E-mail: mitcham@economos.com
Website: http://www.economos.co.uk
Directors: R. Kumra (MD), P. Chambers (MD)
Product Groups: 29, 30, 33, 40, 42, 48

Smith & Prince Ltd (CPA Electrical)
92 Church Road, Mitcham, CR4 3TD
Tel: 020-8408 7200 **Fax:** 020-8646 8348
E-mail: sales@smithprince.co.uk
Website: http://www.smithprince.co.uk
Directors: R. Whorrod (MD), D. Burrell (Admin), M. Mumford (Sales)
Ultimate Holding Company: OXALIS GROUP LIMITED
Immediate Holding Company: OXALIS LIGHTING LIMITED
Registration no: 00874571 **VAT No.:** GB 216 2048 00
Date established: 1966 **Turnover:** £500,000 - £1m
No.of Employees: 1 - 10 **Product Groups:** 37, 39, 52

Date of Accounts	Dec 10	Dec 09	Mar 09
Working Capital	-37	137	81
Fixed Assets	39	15	20
Current Assets	127	232	217

Super Sharp Saw Service
174 London Road, Mitcham, CR4 3LD
Tel: 020-8648 2154 **Fax:** 020-8648 2154
Directors: E. Thomas (Ptnr)
Immediate Holding Company: POS CUSTOMISED DISPLAYS LIMITED
Registration no: 03951133 **Date established:** 2000
Turnover: Up to £250,000 **No.of Employees:** 1 - 10 **Product Groups:** 36, 37, 41, 47

Utopia Windows
4a Wandle Trading Estate Goat Road, Mitcham, CR4 4HW
Tel: 020-8640 1991 **Fax:** 05600-751974
E-mail: sales@utopiawindows.co.uk
Website: http://www.utopiawindows.co.uk
Directors: R. Noekes (MD)
Registration no: 00728977 **Date established:** 1962
No.of Employees: 1 - 10 **Product Groups:** 30, 33, 35, 36, 52

Date of Accounts	Apr 08	Apr 07	Apr 06
Sales Turnover	N/A	121	131
Pre Tax Profit/Loss	N/A	10	20
Working Capital	25	30	20
Fixed Assets	21	16	25
Current Assets	60	39	39
Current Liabilities	35	9	19
ROCE% (Return on Capital Employed)		22.5	44.3
ROT% (Return on Turnover)		8.4	15.2

Willow Powder Coating
Unit 11 Eagle Trading Estate Willow Lane, Mitcham, CR4 4UY
Tel: 020-8646 7169 **Fax:** 020-8646 7169
E-mail: r.pink@willowpc.co.uk
Website: http://www.willowpowdercoating.co.uk
Directors: B. Pink (Prop)
Immediate Holding Company: WILLOW POWDER COATING LIMITED
Registration no: 06116567 **Date established:** 2007
Turnover: £250,000 - £500,000 **No.of Employees:** 1 - 10
Product Groups: 46, 48

Date of Accounts	Mar 11	Mar 10	Mar 09
Sales Turnover	315	287	292
Pre Tax Profit/Loss	98	103	122
Working Capital	-27	-21	-19
Fixed Assets	49	51	45
Current Assets	103	109	83
Current Liabilities	112	120	86

Morden

Associated Painting Services Ltd
Unit 3 193 Garth Road, Morden, SM4 4LZ
Tel: 020-8330 3322 **Fax:** 020-8330 3355
E-mail: tobyjcharris@hotmail.com
Website: http://www.associatedpaint.co.uk
Directors: T. Harris (MD)
Immediate Holding Company: ASSOCIATED PAINTING SERVICES LIMITED
Registration no: 02720800 **Date established:** 1992
No.of Employees: 1 - 10 **Product Groups:** 46, 48

Date of Accounts	May 09	Mar 12	Mar 11
Working Capital	36	47	37
Fixed Assets	14	8	10
Current Assets	96	79	95

Bajwa Steel
50 Central Road, Morden, SM4 5RP
Tel: 0800-077 8929
E-mail: bajwasteel@hotmail.co.uk
Website: http://www.bajwasteel.com
Managers: S. Mohammed (Mgr)
Immediate Holding Company: BAJWA STEEL LTD
Registration no: 07573906 **Date established:** 2011
No.of Employees: 1 - 10 **Product Groups:** 35, 49, 66

Curtis Plumbing Heating Services
2 Pollard Court, Morden, SM4 6EH
Tel: 0783-623 5999 **Fax:** 020-8150 6313
E-mail: info@cphs.co.uk
Website: http://www.curtisphs.co.uk

Directors: P. Curtis (Prop)
Registration no: 06886624 **Date established:** 2009
Turnover: Up to £250,000 **No.of Employees:** 1 - 10 **Product Groups:** 37, 40, 52

Electro Refrigeration
Unit 5 193 The Garth Road Industrial Centre Garth Road, Morden, SM4 4LZ
Tel: 020-3277 1090 **Fax:** 020-8684 1899
E-mail: info@electroref.co.uk
Website: http://www.electroref.co.uk
Directors: C. Miller (MD), L. Tillyer (Dir), B. McNelan (Dir)
Immediate Holding Company: ELECTRO REFRIGERATION SERVICES LIMITED
Registration no: 02920030 **Date established:** 1994 **Turnover:** £1m - £2m
No.of Employees: 21 - 50 **Product Groups:** 41

Date of Accounts	Dec 11	Dec 10	Dec 09
Working Capital	76	132	135
Fixed Assets	50	59	59
Current Assets	82	139	148

H P C Health Line
158 The Garth Road Industrial Centre Garth Road, Morden, SM4 4LZ
Tel: 020-8335 3636 **Fax:** 020-8335 0300
E-mail: sales@hanfare.co.uk
Website: http://www.hanfare.co.uk
Bank(s): HSBC Bank plc
Directors: S. Pritchard (Dir)
Immediate Holding Company: HPC HEALTHLINE UK LIMITED
Registration no: 02000388 **VAT No.:** GB 562 0645 54
Date established: 1986 **Turnover:** £20m - £50m
No.of Employees: 21 - 50 **Product Groups:** 24, 29

Date of Accounts	Dec 11	Dec 10	Dec 09
Sales Turnover	47m	41m	37m
Pre Tax Profit/Loss	3m	3m	3m
Working Capital	5m	3m	3m
Fixed Assets	2m	2m	1m
Current Assets	20m	18m	14m
Current Liabilities	6m	6m	4m

Edward Holt Manufacturing
Beverley Trading Estate Garth Road, Morden, SM4 4LU
Tel: 020-8335 3919 **Fax:** 020-8335 3920
Website: http://www.edwardholt.freeserve.co.uk
Directors: J. Mayersbeth (Dir)
Date established: 2001 **No.of Employees:** 1 - 10 **Product Groups:** 37

Kay Optical Servicing
89b London Road, Morden, SM4 5HP
Tel: 020-8648 8822 **Fax:** 020-8687 2021
E-mail: info@kayoptical.co.uk
Website: http://www.kayoptical.co.uk
Directors: T. Kay (Prop)
VAT No.: GB 217 1232 06 **Turnover:** £1m - £2m **No.of Employees:** 1 - 10
Product Groups: 48

Paul Mark Ventilation Ltd
Unit 12 193 Garth Road Industrial Centre, Morden, SM4 4LZ
Tel: 020-8335 4125 **Fax:** 020-8335 4103
Website: http://www.ductworkuk.com
Directors: R. Steines (Dir)
Immediate Holding Company: PAULMARK VENTILATION LIMITED
Registration no: 02786248 **Date established:** 1993
No.of Employees: 1 - 10 **Product Groups:** 37, 40, 48

Date of Accounts	Sep 11	Sep 10	Sep 09
Working Capital	51	98	-19
Fixed Assets	23	30	51
Current Assets	134	187	64

Project Coin Machines Ltd
Athena House 88 London Road, Morden, SM4 5AZ
Tel: 020-8664 3400 **Fax:** 020-8664 3449
E-mail: rajah@projectcoin.co.uk
Website: http://www.projectcoin.co.uk
Directors: A. Boulton (Fin), R. Beneducci (MD), A. Bolton (MD)
Managers: T. Bonanno, R. Ramabhandran
Immediate Holding Company: PROJECT COIN MACHINES LIMITED
Registration no: 01410815 **Date established:** 1979
No.of Employees: 21 - 50 **Product Groups:** 20, 40, 41

Date of Accounts	Nov 10	Nov 09	Nov 08
Working Capital	258	894	2m
Fixed Assets	63	83	63
Current Assets	2m	2m	2m

Sillette Sonic Ltd
2 Beverley Trading Estate Garth Road, Morden, SM4 4LU
Tel: 020-8337 7543 **Fax:** 020-8330 9014
E-mail: sales@sillette.co.uk
Website: http://www.sillette.co.uk
Directors: G. Print (Dir)
Immediate Holding Company: SILLETTE SONIC LIMITED
Registration no: 02723900 **Date established:** 1992
No.of Employees: 1 - 10 **Product Groups:** 35, 36, 39

Date of Accounts	Sep 11	Sep 10	Sep 09
Working Capital	293	269	279
Fixed Assets	1	10	19
Current Assets	338	311	324

T C Services
Unit 3 Garth Road 1-7 Amenity Way, Morden, SM4 4NJ
Tel: 020-8335 3779 **Fax:** 020-8335 3633
Managers: C. Button (Mgr)
No.of Employees: 1 - 10 **Product Groups:** 40, 66

New Malden

Adams & Adams Ltd
Adams House Dickerage Lane, New Malden, KT3 3SF
Tel: 020-8949 1121 **Fax:** 020-8336 1126
E-mail: adamsnewmalden@aol.com
Directors: M. Adams (Dir)
Immediate Holding Company: ADAMS & ADAMS LIMITED
Registration no: 00381172 **VAT No.:** GB 215 9251 71
Date established: 1943 **Turnover:** £250,000 - £500,000
No.of Employees: 1 - 10 **Product Groups:** 77, 80

Date of Accounts	Feb 12	Feb 11	Feb 10
Working Capital	546	632	396
Fixed Assets	5m	6m	6m
Current Assets	657	767	565

C & S Processing
Rear of 5-19 Coombe Road, New Malden, KT3 4PX
Tel: 020-8336 1037 **Fax:** 020-8336 1037
E-mail: sales@csprocessing.co.uk
Website: http://www.csprocessing.co.uk
Directors: C. Found (Dir)
Immediate Holding Company: C & S PROCESSING LIMITED
Registration no: 05727870 **Date established:** 2006
No.of Employees: 1 - 10 **Product Groups:** 37, 48

Date of Accounts	Sep 11	Sep 10	Sep 09
Working Capital	49	28	16
Fixed Assets	106	94	101
Current Assets	147	146	153

The Character Group plc
86-88 Coombe Road, New Malden, KT3 4QS
Tel: 020-8949 5898 **Fax:** 020-8336 2585
E-mail: jon.diver@thecharacter.com
Website: http://www.character-online.com
Directors: J. Diver (Grp Mktg), J. Diver (Dir)
Managers: A. Chadwick (Personnel), D. Hindle (Tech Serv Mgr), K. Shah
Immediate Holding Company: THE CHARACTER GROUP PLC
Registration no: 03033333 **Date established:** 1995
Turnover: £75m - £125m **No.of Employees:** 11 - 20 **Product Groups:** 49, 65, 81

Date of Accounts	Aug 11	Aug 10	Aug 09
Sales Turnover	95m	85m	69m
Pre Tax Profit/Loss	9m	8m	-2m
Working Capital	-253	4m	10m
Fixed Assets	8m	2m	2m
Current Assets	40m	42m	32m
Current Liabilities	27m	23m	16m

Dresser-Rand UK Ltd
C I Tower St Georges Square High Street, New Malden, KT3 4DN
Tel: 020-8336 7300 **Fax:** 020-8336 0773
Website: http://www.dresser-rand.com
Managers: A. Drake (Mgr)
Ultimate Holding Company: DRESSER RAND INC (USA)
Immediate Holding Company: DRESSER -RAND (U.K.) LIMITED
Registration no: 00759945 **Date established:** 1963
No.of Employees: 1 - 10 **Product Groups:** 37, 40

Date of Accounts	Dec 11	Dec 10	Dec 09
Sales Turnover	25m	38m	51m
Pre Tax Profit/Loss	5m	6m	11m
Working Capital	24m	22m	19m
Fixed Assets	379	406	446
Current Assets	42m	42m	38m
Current Liabilities	6m	5m	4m

Jukebox Showroom Limited
Britannia Chambers 181/185 High Street, New Malden, KT3 4BH
Tel: 07769-588551 **Fax:** 020-8992 8480
E-mail: steve@jukeboxshowroom.co.uk
Website: http://www.jukeboxshowroom.co.uk
Directors: R. Winfield (Dir), S. Winfield (Dir)
Registration no: 00395359 **Date established:** 2009
No.of Employees: 1 - 10 **Product Groups:** 37

Lazer Systems
36 Lawrence Avenue, New Malden, KT3 5LY
Tel: 020-8401 6818 **Fax:** 020-8401 6818
E-mail: lazersystems@blueyonder.co.uk
Website: http://www.lazersystems.co.uk
Directors: S. Lasenby (Dir)
Immediate Holding Company: RADIOVISOR LIMITED
Registration no: 03292214 **Date established:** 1996
No.of Employees: 1 - 10 **Product Groups:** 37, 38, 67

Date of Accounts	Mar 12	Mar 11	Mar 10
Working Capital	10	21	15
Current Assets	51	32	33

Lyquidity Solutions Ltd
PO Box 504, New Malden, KT3 9FP
Tel: 020-7043 2777 **Fax:** 0870-137 3744
E-mail: info@lyquidity.com
Website: http://www.lyquidity.com
Directors: S. Seddon (Dir)
Immediate Holding Company: LYQUIDITY SOLUTIONS LIMITED
Registration no: 04226794 **Date established:** 2001
Turnover: Up to £250,000 **No.of Employees:** 11 - 20 **Product Groups:** 44

Date of Accounts	Jun 11	Jun 10	Jun 09
Sales Turnover	N/A	N/A	34
Working Capital	2	1	5
Current Assets	4	3	5

Northrop Grumman Sperry Marine
Burlington House 118 Burlington Road, New Malden, KT3 4NR
Tel: 020-8329 2000 **Fax:** 020-8329 2415
E-mail: paul.woodman@sperry.ngc.com
Website: http://www.northropgrumman.com
Directors: P. Woodman (Fin)
Managers: C. Bruce, P. Farrington, L. Shippy (Personnel)
Ultimate Holding Company: NORTHROP GRUMMAN CORPORATION (USA)
Immediate Holding Company: NORTHROP GRUMMAN SPERRY MARINE LIMITED
Registration no: 03879775 **Date established:** 1999
Turnover: £75m - £125m **No.of Employees:** 101 - 250
Product Groups: 39, 84

Date of Accounts	Dec 11	Dec 10	Dec 09
Sales Turnover	99m	113m	120m
Pre Tax Profit/Loss	-7m	-2m	2m
Working Capital	10m	14m	17m
Fixed Assets	45	46	54
Current Assets	70m	100m	149m
Current Liabilities	26m	24m	17m

The P P & D Complete Printing Service
99 Burlington Road, New Malden, KT3 4LR
Tel: 020-8949 5231 **Fax:** 020-8949 4358
E-mail: waconroy@btinternet.com
Website: http://www.ppanddprints.co.uk
Managers: W. Conroy (Mgr)
No.of Employees: 1 - 10 **Product Groups:** 27, 28, 49, 81

Saipem Ltd
Saipem House Station Road, New Malden, KT3 6JJ
Tel: 020-8296 5000 **Fax:** 020-8296 5100
Website: http://www.e-m-c.co.uk
Directors: E. Van Stijn (Fin), M. Villa (Co Sec), S. Porcari (MD)
Managers: I. Stapleton (Tech Serv Mgr), J. Soares (Personnel)
Immediate Holding Company: SAIPEM LIMITED
Registration no: 07195109 **Date established:** 2010
No.of Employees: 251 - 500 **Product Groups:** 51

Star Graphics
37-39 Rookwood Avenue, New Malden, KT3 4LY
Tel: 07956-261567 **Fax:** 020-8605 1011
Directors: T. Engert (Dir)
Immediate Holding Company: LINKBYTE LIMITED
Registration no: 05034343 **Date established:** 2011
No.of Employees: 1 - 10 **Product Groups:** 35, 37, 49, 80, 81

Tam Leisure New Malden Ltd
180 Kingston Road, New Malden, KT3 3RD
Tel: 020-8949 5435 **Fax:** 020-8336 1418
E-mail: sales@tamleisure.net
Website: http://www.just-camping.co.uk
Directors: J. Roberts West (Co Sec), K. West (MD)
Immediate Holding Company: TAM LEISURE NEW MALDEN LIMITED
Registration no: 05857143 **VAT No.:** GB 217 1205 09
Date established: 2006 **Turnover:** £2m - £5m **No.of Employees:** 1 - 10
Product Groups: 39, 40

Date of Accounts	Jul 11	Jul 10	Jul 09
Working Capital	27	-34	-97
Fixed Assets	191	199	211
Current Assets	440	443	372

Triple A International
18 Lawrence Avenue, New Malden, KT3 5LY
Tel: 020-8335 3135 **Fax:** 020-8337 8297
E-mail: sales@aaa.co.uk
Website: http://www.aaa.co.uk
Directors: D. Mortimer (MD)
Immediate Holding Company: TRIPLE A GROUP LIMITED
Registration no: 02470325 **Date established:** 1990
Turnover: Up to £250,000 **No.of Employees:** 1 - 10 **Product Groups:** 80

Date of Accounts	Oct 11	Oct 10	Oct 09
Working Capital	-13	-13	-13

Vac Electric
98 Burlington Road, New Malden, KT3 4NT
Tel: 020-8949 4232 **Fax:** 020-8942 4833
Website: http://www.brightnet.co.uk
Directors: N. Huntley (Prop)
Date established: 1957 **No.of Employees:** 1 - 10 **Product Groups:** 43

L E Went Ltd
52-56 Burlington Road, New Malden, KT3 4NU
Tel: 020-8949 0626 **Fax:** 020-8715 1116
E-mail: iew.paint@virgin.net
Website: http://www.pgen.net
Directors: I. Went (MD), J. Went (Fin)
Ultimate Holding Company: L.E. WENT LIMITED
Immediate Holding Company: L.E. WENT LIMITED
Registration no: 00806860 **Date established:** 1964 **Turnover:** £1m - £2m
No.of Employees: 11 - 20 **Product Groups:** 39

Date of Accounts	Dec 10	Dec 09	Dec 08
Working Capital	-98	-22	-34
Fixed Assets	711	727	730
Current Assets	464	460	489

Oxted

Distributed Technology Ltd
63 Bluehouse Lane, Oxted, RH8 0AP
Tel: 01883-716161 **Fax:** 01883-716865
E-mail: sales@dtl-connectors.co.uk
Website: http://www.dtl-connectors.co.uk
Directors: C. Walford (Co Sec), D. Walford (MD), D. Woolford (Dir), H. Woolford (Dir)
Immediate Holding Company: DISTRIBUTED TECHNOLOGY LIMITED
Registration no: 05469710 **Date established:** 2005
Turnover: £500,000 - £1m **No.of Employees:** 1 - 10 **Product Groups:** 37, 47

Date of Accounts	Dec 03
Sales Turnover	684
Pre Tax Profit/Loss	-28
Working Capital	122
Fixed Assets	45
Current Assets	463
Current Liabilities	341
Total Share Capital	70
ROCE% (Return on Capital Employed)	-16.8

Flatau Dick UK Ltd
22 Tally Road, Oxted, RH8 0TG
Tel: 01883-730707 **Fax:** 01883-717100
E-mail: bob@flataudick.co.uk
Website: http://www.flataudick.co.uk
Directors: B. Harvey (MD)
Immediate Holding Company: FLATAU DICK (UK) LIMITED
Registration no: 05370125 **Date established:** 2005
Turnover: £500,000 - £1m **No.of Employees:** 1 - 10 **Product Groups:** 66

Date of Accounts	Apr 11	Apr 10	Apr 09
Working Capital	49	142	171
Fixed Assets	1	2	4
Current Assets	400	303	394

Rex Bousfield Ltd
18-20 Fairviews, Oxted, RH8 9BD
Tel: 01883-717033 **Fax:** 01883-717890
E-mail: jeff.thompson@bousfield.com
Website: http://www.bousfieldltd.co.uk
Directors: M. Ellis (Co Sec), J. Thompson (MD)
Managers: B. Dalton, M. Walker (Tech Serv Mgr), K. White (Mktg Serv Mgr)
Immediate Holding Company: REX BOUSFIELD LIMITED
Registration no: 00331922 **Date established:** 1937
Turnover: £10m - £20m **No.of Employees:** 21 - 50 **Product Groups:** 39

see next page

***Rex Bousfield Ltd** - Cont'd*

Date of Accounts	Mar 11	Mar 10	Mar 09
Sales Turnover	16m	16m	16m
Pre Tax Profit/Loss	365	150	484
Working Capital	2m	2m	1m
Fixed Assets	3m	3m	3m
Current Assets	5m	5m	5m
Current Liabilities	685	911	1m

Tillrolls Direct

Orchard Cottage Farm Red Lane, Oxted, RH8 0RT
Tel: 01883-723130 **Fax:** 01883-731444
E-mail: enquiries@tillrollsdirect.co.uk
Website: http://www.tillrollsdirect.co.uk
Directors: D. Taylor (MD)
Immediate Holding Company: TILL ROLLS DIRECT LIMITED
Registration no: 05708031 **Date established:** 2006
Turnover: £500,000 - £1m **No.of Employees:** 1 - 10 **Product Groups:** 27

Purley

Azurra Mosaics

PO Box 2801, Purley, CR8 1WX
Tel: 08450-908110 **Fax:** 0845-862 8110
E-mail: brian@mosaics.co.uk
Website: http://www.mosaics.co.uk
Directors: B. Mercer (Ptnr)
Date established: 1999 **No.of Employees:** 1 - 10 **Product Groups:** 33, 49, 64

Creative Web Mall UK

33, Banstead Road, Purley, CR8 3EB
Tel: 020-7193 7303
E-mail: uk@creativewebmall.com
Website: http://www.creativewebmall.co.uk
Directors: S. Surana (Dir)
Date established: 2003 **Turnover:** Up to £250,000
No.of Employees: 51 - 100 **Product Groups:** 44

Firstassist Services Ltd

32-42 High Street, Purley, CR8 2PP
Tel: 020-8763 3333 **Fax:** 020-8668 1262
E-mail: corporate.info@firstassist.co.uk
Website: http://www.capita.co.uk
Bank(s): National Westminster Bank Plc
Directors: N. Davidson (Fin), J. Powell (MD)
Managers: S. Schoeman (Tech Serv Mgr), I. Sparks, G. Handford (Personnel), H. Roberts (Purch Mgr)
Ultimate Holding Company: CAPITA PLC
Immediate Holding Company: FIRSTASSIST SERVICES LIMITED
Registration no: 01404718 **VAT No.:** GB 244 0498 67
Date established: 1978 **Turnover:** £5m - £10m
No.of Employees: 101 - 250 **Product Groups:** 82

Date of Accounts	Dec 11	Dec 10	Dec 09
Sales Turnover	16m	17m	18m
Pre Tax Profit/Loss	2m	-2m	-210
Working Capital	-5m	-7m	2m
Fixed Assets	47	80	761
Current Assets	10m	7m	6m
Current Liabilities	4m	3m	4m

K C S Contractor Services

Capella Court Brighton Road, Purley, CR8 2PG
Tel: 020-8660 2444 **Fax:** 020-8668 8196
E-mail: sales@kcsconnect.com
Website: http://www.kcsconnect.com
Directors: D. McErlain (Dir)
Ultimate Holding Company: BERTELSMANN AG (GERMANY)
Immediate Holding Company: CREDIT SOLUTIONS LIMITED
Registration no: 01019844 **Date established:** 1990
Turnover: Up to £250,000 **No.of Employees:** 1 - 10 **Product Groups:** 40, 44, 80

Date of Accounts	Dec 11	Dec 10	Sep 09
Sales Turnover	N/A	N/A	16m
Pre Tax Profit/Loss	-2m	-2m	-182
Working Capital	-12m	-11m	-2m
Fixed Assets	9m	9m	7m
Current Assets	585	4m	5m
Current Liabilities	4	83	7m

Leaf Accounts Plus

Lansdowne Road, Purley, CR8 2PE
Tel: 07960-618027
E-mail: leafaccountsplus@gmail.com
Website: http://www.leafaccountsplus.com
Directors: A. Khan (Prop)
Date established: 2005 **No.of Employees:** 1 - 10 **Product Groups:** 80

P R W Machinery Ltd

Merley 16 Copse Hill, Purley, CR8 4LH
Tel: 020-8651 0928 **Fax:** 020-8651 0930
E-mail: info@prwmachinery.co.uk
Website: http://www.prwmachinery.co.uk
Directors: R. Tuck (MD), J. Tuck (Fin)
Immediate Holding Company: P.R.W. MACHINERY LIMITED
Registration no: 01617073 **Date established:** 1982
Turnover: Up to £250,000 **No.of Employees:** 1 - 10 **Product Groups:** 38, 42

Date of Accounts	Feb 08	Feb 11	Feb 10
Sales Turnover	207	111	175
Pre Tax Profit/Loss	34	-5	10
Working Capital	6	-11	-11
Fixed Assets	24	6	12
Current Assets	102	28	38
Current Liabilities	88	10	17

Stoakes Systems Ltd

1 Banstead Road, Purley, CR8 3EB
Tel: 020-8660 7667 **Fax:** 020-8660 5707
E-mail: mailbox@stoakes.co.uk
Website: http://www.stoakes.co.uk
Directors: M. Day (Sales & Mktg), R. Stoakes (MD)
Ultimate Holding Company: ASTRALITE LIMITED
Immediate Holding Company: STOAKES SYSTEMS LIMITED
Registration no: 00931500 **VAT No.:** GB 574 2666 17
Date established: 1968 **Turnover:** £2m - £5m **No.of Employees:** 1 - 10
Product Groups: 35

Date of Accounts	Mar 11	Mar 10	Mar 09
Sales Turnover	4m	5m	8m
Pre Tax Profit/Loss	486	816	1m
Working Capital	891	841	1m
Current Assets	1m	2m	2m
Current Liabilities	363	727	886

Transformation 4 Life

62 Reedham Drive, Purley, CR8 4DS
Tel: 07802-436159 **Fax:** 020-8668 2215
E-mail: louisdesouza@gmail.com
Website: http://www.weightlossonthego.com
Directors: L. De Souza (Prop)
Date established: 2006 **Turnover:** Up to £250,000
No.of Employees: 1 - 10 **Product Groups:** 61

Y D T Medical

92 Hartley Down, Purley, CR8 4EB
Tel: 020-8763 9777 **Fax:** 020-8763 9444
E-mail: info@ydtlimited.com
Website: http://www.ydtlimited.com
Directors: J. Yorke (Prop)
Registration no: 04182437 **Turnover:** £250,000 - £500,000
No.of Employees: 1 - 10 **Product Groups:** 07, 24, 26, 27, 28, 29, 30, 31, 32, 37, 38, 48, 63, 66, 67, 68, 80, 82, 83, 84, 85

Redhill

A E L Crystals Ltd

Unit 28 Salbrook Road Industrial Estate Salbrook Road, Salfords, Redhill, RH1 5GJ
Tel: 01293-789200 **Fax:** 01293-524888
E-mail: info@aelcrystals.co.uk
Website: http://www.aelcrystals.co.uk
Directors: C. Edwards (Fin), S. Mellors (Sales)
Immediate Holding Company: A E L CRYSTALS LIMITED
Registration no: 02596247 **Date established:** 1991 **Turnover:** £2m - £5m
No.of Employees: 1 - 10 **Product Groups:** 33, 37, 38, 49

Date of Accounts	Jun 11	Jun 10	Jun 09
Working Capital	249	242	242
Fixed Assets	30	39	33
Current Assets	845	1m	796
Current Liabilities	278	N/A	N/A

AdoptSMT UK Ltd

Unit 30, Salbrook Road Industrial Estate Salbrook Road, Salfords, Redhill, RH1 5GJ
Tel: 01293-827 880 **Fax:** 01293-774 632
E-mail: sales@alternativesmt.com
Website: http://www.alternativesmt.com
Directors: P. Fraiman (MD)
Immediate Holding Company: Alternativesmt Ltd
Registration no: 06642980 **Date established:** 2008
No.of Employees: 1 - 10 **Product Groups:** 48

Date of Accounts	Aug 07	Aug 06
Working Capital	424	446
Fixed Assets	49	67
Current Assets	1777	1530
Current Liabilities	1353	1084
Total Share Capital	10	10

Allstore Services Ltd

14 Oak Lodge Drive, Redhill, RH1 5EB
Tel: 01293-776755 **Fax:** 01293-776705
E-mail: ian@allstoreuk.co.uk
Website: http://www.allstoreuk.co.uk
Directors: S. Cunningham Brown (Fin), I. Cunningham (MD)
Immediate Holding Company: ALLSTORE SERVICES LIMITED
Registration no: 04576567 **Date established:** 2002
Turnover: £500,000 - £1m **No.of Employees:** 1 - 10 **Product Groups:** 25, 26, 30, 33, 35, 39, 44, 45, 49, 52, 67, 83

Date of Accounts	Oct 10	Oct 09	Oct 08
Sales Turnover	658	355	811
Pre Tax Profit/Loss	-32	42	84
Working Capital	-34	-9	-11
Fixed Assets	8	10	13
Current Assets	159	113	178
Current Liabilities	45	67	79

Armstrong Holden Brooke Pullen Ltd

Ormside House 21 Ormside Way, Redhill, RH1 2BA
Tel: 01737-378100 **Fax:** 01737-378140
E-mail: salesuk@armlink.com
Website: http://www.holdenbrookepullen.com
Bank(s): Barclays, Manchester
Directors: B. Ross (MD), M. Sherman (Dir)
Managers: N. Lloyd (Buyer), S. Howlett (I.T. Exec)
Immediate Holding Company: Howard Anderson Ltd
Registration no: 07261626 **Date established:** 1950
Turnover: £10m - £20m **No.of Employees:** 11 - 20 **Product Groups:** 40, 45

Axa Assistance UK Ltd

106-118 Station Road, Redhill, RH1 1PR
Tel: 08706-090023 **Fax:** 0870-609 0024
E-mail: bob.ewers@axa-assistance.co.uk
Website: http://www.axa-assistance.co.uk
Directors: B. Ewers (MD)
Ultimate Holding Company: AXA SA (FRANCE)
Immediate Holding Company: AXA ASSISTANCE (U.K.) LIMITED
Registration no: 02638890 **Date established:** 1991 **Turnover:** £5m - £10m
No.of Employees: 251 - 500 **Product Groups:** 82, 88

Date of Accounts	Dec 11	Dec 10	Dec 09
Sales Turnover	10m	14m	14m
Pre Tax Profit/Loss	465	281	839
Working Capital	3m	2m	1m
Fixed Assets	266	908	1m
Current Assets	13m	11m	13m
Current Liabilities	6m	8m	7m

Beronworth Standby Systems Ltd

Systems House 32a Ifold Road, Redhill, RH1 6EG
Tel: 01737-767291 **Fax:** 01737-767484
E-mail: enquiries@beronworth.com
Website: http://www.beronworth.com
Directors: C. Da Silva Skinner (Co Sec), R. Burch (MD)
Immediate Holding Company: BERONWORTH STANDBY SYSTEMS LIMITED
Registration no: 01921401 **VAT No.:** GB 425 1070 92
Date established: 1985 **Turnover:** Up to £250,000
No.of Employees: 1 - 10 **Product Groups:** 37, 67

Date of Accounts	Mar 11	Mar 10	Mar 09
Sales Turnover	N/A	N/A	113
Pre Tax Profit/Loss	N/A	N/A	19
Working Capital	-31	-17	-13
Fixed Assets	20	1	1
Current Assets	52	61	80
Current Liabilities	N/A	N/A	23

Biffa Waste Services

Patteson Court Landfill Cormongers Lane, Nutfield, Redhill, RH1 4ER
Tel: 01737-765122 **Fax:** 01737-765042
E-mail: info@biffa.co.uk
Website: http://www.biffa.co.uk
Managers: A. Jenner (Mgr)
Ultimate Holding Company: BIFFA LTD
Immediate Holding Company: RECLAMATION & DISPOSAL LTD
Registration no: 01032104 **Turnover:** £1m - £2m
No.of Employees: 11 - 20 **Product Groups:** 54

Bragman Flett Ltd

34 Holmethorpe Avenue, Redhill, RH1 2NL
Tel: 01737-779200 **Fax:** 01737-779600
E-mail: bragman.flett@btopenworld.com
Website: http://www.bragmanflett.co.uk
Directors: K. Jacobs (Prop)
Immediate Holding Company: BRAGMAN FLETT LIMITED
Registration no: 02079603 **VAT No.:** GB 437 3557 35
Date established: 1986 **Turnover:** £250,000 - £500,000
No.of Employees: 1 - 10 **Product Groups:** 48

Date of Accounts	Dec 11	Dec 10	Dec 09
Working Capital	2	19	33
Fixed Assets	N/A	N/A	2
Current Assets	37	67	72

Britannia Health Products Ltd

Forum House 41-51 Brighton Road, Redhill, RH1 6YS
Tel: 01737-773741 **Fax:** 01737-762672
E-mail: admin@britannia-pharm.co.uk
Website: http://www.britannia-pharm.co.uk
Directors: J. Hanlon (Co Sec)
Ultimate Holding Company: STADA ARZNEIMITTEL AG (GERMANY)
Immediate Holding Company: BRITANNIA PHARMACEUTICALS LIMITED
Registration no: 01557088 **Date established:** 1981 **Turnover:** £5m - £10m
No.of Employees: 51 - 100 **Product Groups:** 63

Date of Accounts	Dec 11	Dec 10	Dec 09
Sales Turnover	7m	7m	27m
Pre Tax Profit/Loss	4m	4m	5m
Working Capital	17m	14m	11m
Fixed Assets	3m	4m	4m
Current Assets	19m	15m	12m
Current Liabilities	1m	723	802

British Wax Refining Co. (Office & Works)

62 Holmethorpe Avenue, Redhill, RH1 2NL
Tel: 01737-761242 **Fax:** 01737-761472
E-mail: rob@britishwax.com
Website: http://www.britishwax.com
Bank(s): Lloyds TSB Bank plc
Directors: N. Case-Green (MD)
Immediate Holding Company: BRITISH WAX REFINING COMPANY LIMITED(THE)
Registration no: 00138140 **VAT No.:** GB 209 5600 75
Date established: 2014 **Turnover:** £500,000 - £1m
No.of Employees: 11 - 20 **Product Groups:** 32, 66

Date of Accounts	Apr 11	Apr 10	Apr 09
Working Capital	892	798	688
Fixed Assets	243	231	231
Current Assets	1m	1m	868

Brooklands International Freight Service

Airport House Kings Mill Lane, Redhill, RH1 5JY
Tel: 01737-823575 **Fax:** 01737-823634
E-mail: info@bifs.net
Website: http://www.bifs.net
Bank(s): National Westminster Bank Plc
Managers: N. O'driscoll (Ops Mgr)
Immediate Holding Company: BROOKLANDS INTERNATIONAL FREIGHT SERVICES LIMITED
Registration no: 02470848 **Date established:** 1990 **Turnover:** £2m - £5m
No.of Employees: 11 - 20 **Product Groups:** 72, 74, 76

Date of Accounts	Mar 11	Mar 10	Mar 09
Sales Turnover	N/A	4m	4m
Pre Tax Profit/Loss	N/A	248	181
Working Capital	923	381	179
Fixed Assets	645	647	654
Current Assets	2m	1m	993
Current Liabilities	N/A	549	522

C Brewers & Sons Ltd

27-33 Brighton Road, Redhill, RH1 6PF
Tel: 01737-764242 **Fax:** 01737-765973
E-mail: decorating@brewers.co.uk
Website: http://www.brewers.co.uk
Managers: A. Joyes (District Mgr)
Immediate Holding Company: C.BREWER & SONS LIMITED
Registration no: 00203852 **Date established:** 1925
Turnover: £250,000 - £500,000 **No.of Employees:** 1 - 10
Product Groups: 52, 66

Capex Office Interiors

Robert Denholm House Bletchingley Road, Nutfield, Redhill, RH1 4HW
Tel: 01737-822122 **Fax:** 01737-822112
E-mail: ray.allinson@capexinteriors.com
Website: http://www.capexinteriors.com
Directors: R. Allinson (Dir)
Immediate Holding Company: CAPEX OFFICE INTERIORS LIMITED
Registration no: 05467081 **Date established:** 2005
No.of Employees: 1 - 10 **Product Groups:** 25, 26, 27, 29, 30, 36, 44, 52, 84

Date of Accounts	Nov 11	Nov 10	Nov 09
Working Capital	48	45	72
Fixed Assets	N/A	1	2
Current Assets	259	182	229

City Electrical Factors Ltd

5 Ormside Way Holmethorpe Trading Estate, Redhill, RH1 2LW
Tel: 01737-779880 **Fax:** 01737-779842
E-mail: sales.redhill@cef.co.uk
Website: http://www.cef.co.uk
Directors: R. Kay (Ch), G. Mackie (Grp Chief Exec)
Managers: M. Ansley (District Mgr)
Ultimate Holding Company: CEF HOLDINGS LIMITED
Immediate Holding Company: CITY ELECTRICAL FACTORS LIMITED
Registration no: 00336408 **Date established:** 1938 **Turnover:** £1m - £2m
No.of Employees: 1 - 10 **Product Groups:** 39

Date of Accounts	Apr 11	Apr 10	Apr 09
Sales Turnover	439m	406m	444m
Pre Tax Profit/Loss	22m	26m	34m
Working Capital	53m	172m	164m
Fixed Assets	13m	17m	18m
Current Assets	179m	250m	227m
Current Liabilities	53m	23m	20m

Cliff Electronic Components Ltd

76 Holmethorpe Avenue, Redhill, RH1 2PF
Tel: 01737-771375 **Fax:** 01737-766012
E-mail: sales@cliffuk.co.uk
Website: http://www.cliffuk.co.uk
Directors: C. Jones (Mkt Research)
Managers: J. Hall (Chief Mgr)
Immediate Holding Company: CLIFF ELECTRONIC COMPONENTS LIMITED
Registration no: 01332056 **VAT No.:** GB 219 8454 38
Date established: 1977 **Turnover:** £2m - £5m **No.of Employees:** 21 - 50
Product Groups: 29, 30, 37, 40, 44, 48

Date of Accounts	Sep 11	Sep 10	Sep 09
Working Capital	891	846	1m
Fixed Assets	369	385	402
Current Assets	2m	2m	2m

Coffeetech

9 Holmethorpe Avenue Holmethorpe Industrial Estate, Redhill, RH1 2NB
Tel: 08707-702951 **Fax:** 08707-702954
E-mail: duncan@coffeetech.co.uk
Website: http://www.coffeetech.co.uk
Directors: D. Gaffney (Dir), M. Gaffney (Co Sec)
Immediate Holding Company: COFFEETECH LIMITED
Registration no: 02727128 **Date established:** 1992
No.of Employees: 11 - 20 **Product Groups:** 35, 40, 41, 63, 67

Date of Accounts	Mar 10	Mar 09	Mar 08
Working Capital	164	155	149
Fixed Assets	13	18	23
Current Assets	622	587	536

Cubic Transportation Systems Ltd (Registered As Westinghouse Cubic Ltd)

A F C House Honeycrock Lane, Redhill, RH1 5LA
Tel: 01737-782200 **Fax:** 01737-789759
E-mail: walter.zable@cubic.com
Website: http://www.cubic.com
Bank(s): National Westminster Bank Plc
Directors: S. Hampton (Co Sec), P. Van Campen (Fin), R. Crow (MD), L. Gravett (Pers)
Ultimate Holding Company: CUBIC CORPORATION (USA)
Immediate Holding Company: CUBIC TRANSPORTATION SYSTEMS LIMITED
Registration no: 01381707 **Date established:** 1978
Turnover: £75m - £125m **No.of Employees:** 501 - 1000
Product Groups: 49

Date of Accounts	Sep 11	Sep 10	Sep 09
Sales Turnover	122m	96m	93m
Pre Tax Profit/Loss	28m	25m	24m
Working Capital	69m	54m	34m
Fixed Assets	6m	6m	7m
Current Assets	153m	125m	91m
Current Liabilities	76m	64m	51m

Fit-Out Ltd

Unit 9 Fairlawn Enterprise Park Bonehurst, Salfords, Redhill, RH1 5GH
Tel: 01293-412233 **Fax:** 01293-514675
E-mail: info@fit-out.co.uk
Website: http://www.fit-out.co.uk
Directors: P. Rudkin (Dir), K. George (Co Sec)
Immediate Holding Company: ALPINE CONSTRUCTION SERVICES LIMITED
Registration no: 05480641 **Date established:** 2005 **Turnover:** £1m - £2m
No.of Employees: 1 - 10 **Product Groups:** 35, 52

Flooring Trade Supplies

Oakdene Road, Redhill, RH1 6BT
Tel: 01737-765075
E-mail: sales@flooringtradesuppliesuk.com
Website: http://www.flooringtradesuppliesredhill.co.uk
Directors: S. Gurr (Prop)
Immediate Holding Company: COOLSTREAM LIMITED
Registration no: LP009263 **Date established:** 1983
Turnover: £500,000 - £1m **No.of Employees:** 1 - 10 **Product Groups:** 25, 32, 33, 49, 52, 66

Date of Accounts	May 10	May 09	May 08
Working Capital	-2	-16	847
Current Assets	448	833	882

Forum Products Ltd

Betchworth House 57-65 Station Road, Redhill, RH1 1DL
Tel: 01737-773711 **Fax:** 01737-779382
E-mail: animal.health@forumgroup.co.uk
Website: http://www.forum.co.uk
Ultimate Holding Company: FORUM PRODUCTS HOLDINGS LIMITED
Immediate Holding Company: FORUM BIOSCIENCE HOLDINGS LIMITED
Registration no: 01506034 **Date established:** 1980
Turnover: Up to £250,000 **No.of Employees:** 21 - 50 **Product Groups:** 20

Date of Accounts	Dec 07	Mar 11	Mar 10
Sales Turnover	45m	N/A	80
Pre Tax Profit/Loss	4m	N/A	149
Working Capital	-3m	-0	-0
Fixed Assets	9m	N/A	N/A
Current Assets	16m	N/A	N/A
Current Liabilities	3m	N/A	N/A

Gelpke & Bate Ltd

Camomile House Kings Cross Lane, South Nutfield, Redhill, RH1 5NG
Tel: 01737-822244 **Fax:** 01737-822081
E-mail: sales@gelpkeandbate.co.uk
Website: http://www.gelpkeandbate.co.uk
Bank(s): Bank of Scotland
Directors: K. Sidwell (MD), C. Blackburn (Co Sec), K. Sidwell (MD), K. Gould (Sales)
Managers: A. Blackburn (Tech Serv Mgr)
Immediate Holding Company: GELPKE & BATE LIMITED
Registration no: 03286305 **VAT No.:** GB 219 2831 64
Date established: 1996 **Turnover:** £10m - £20m
No.of Employees: 11 - 20 **Product Groups:** 62, 66

Date of Accounts	Dec 11	Dec 10	Dec 09
Sales Turnover	17m	16m	16m
Pre Tax Profit/Loss	263	273	302
Working Capital	586	486	438
Fixed Assets	334	362	330
Current Assets	4m	4m	3m
Current Liabilities	333	221	339

Hartest Precision Instruments Ltd

2 Gatton Park Business Centre Wells Place, Merstham, Redhill, RH1 3LG
Tel: 01737-649300 **Fax:** 020-8549 3374
E-mail: info@h-pi.co.uk
Website: http://www.h-pi.co.uk
Bank(s): Lloyds TSB Bank plc
Directors: A. Cooper (MD), L. Powell (Sales)
Ultimate Holding Company: ELEKTRON TECHNOLOGY PLC
Immediate Holding Company: HARTEST PRECISION INSTRUMENTS LIMITED
Registration no: 00445493 **VAT No.:** GB 216 2991 60
Date established: 1947 **Turnover:** £5m - £10m
No.of Employees: 51 - 100 **Product Groups:** 38, 67, 85

Date of Accounts	Mar 10	Mar 09	Mar 08
Sales Turnover	9m	8m	9m
Pre Tax Profit/Loss	420	-546	308
Working Capital	10	-409	21
Fixed Assets	989	1m	932
Current Assets	5m	5m	6m
Current Liabilities	884	590	514

H K W Partnership

Robert Denholm House Bletchingley Road, Nutfield, Redhill, RH1 4HW
Tel: 01737-822060 **Fax:** 01737-822830
E-mail: bkw@hkw.co.uk
Managers: P. Brooks (Mgr)
Immediate Holding Company: PARTNERS IN FLOW LIMITED
Registration no: 04299466 **Date established:** 2001
No.of Employees: 1 - 10 **Product Groups:** 35

Date of Accounts	Dec 11	Dec 10	Dec 09
Working Capital	1	3	-3
Fixed Assets	1	1	7
Current Assets	5	12	18

Hockway

6 The Trowers Way Centre Trowers Way, Redhill, RH1 2LP
Tel: 01737-762222 **Fax:** 01737-236100
E-mail: enquiries@hockway.com
Website: http://www.hockway.com
Directors: L. Weight (Fin)
Managers: M. Moffat (Mgr)
Ultimate Holding Company: CARNOT ENERGY ONE LIMITED
Immediate Holding Company: CARNOT ENERGY LIMITED
Registration no: 01198014 **Date established:** 1975 **Turnover:** £2m - £5m
No.of Employees: 11 - 20 **Product Groups:** 23, 27, 29, 30, 31, 32, 33, 34, 35, 36, 37, 38, 39, 40, 42, 48, 51, 52, 67, 76, 84, 85

Date of Accounts	Dec 11	Dec 10	Dec 09
Working Capital	274	787	632
Fixed Assets	N/A	138	193
Current Assets	678	3m	2m

Indespension Ltd

19 Woodhatch Road, Redhill, RH1 5HQ
Tel: 01737-768185 **Fax:** 01737-768610
E-mail: redhill@indespension.co.uk
Website: http://www.indespension.com
Directors: R. Graham (Ch)
Ultimate Holding Company: D.R.A. LTD
Immediate Holding Company: INDESPENSION LTD
Registration no: 02125263 **Date established:** 1987 **Turnover:** £1m - £2m
No.of Employees: 1 - 10 **Product Groups:** 39

Date of Accounts	Jun 11	Jun 10	Jun 09
Sales Turnover	17m	15m	19m
Pre Tax Profit/Loss	550	192	137
Working Capital	2m	1m	2m
Fixed Assets	4m	5m	6m
Current Assets	8m	8m	8m
Current Liabilities	3m	527	783

Inoxpa Ltd

15 Ormside Way Holmethorpe Industrial Estate, Redhill, RH1 2LW
Tel: 01737-378060 **Fax:** 020-8689 0245
E-mail: shutton@inoxpa.com
Website: http://www.inoxpa.com
Managers: S. Hutton (Mgr)
Immediate Holding Company: REALM GROUP LTD
Registration no: 02647623 **Turnover:** £2m - £5m
No.of Employees: 1 - 10 **Product Groups:** 36

J B J Techniques Ltd

28 Ormside Way, Redhill, RH1 2LW
Tel: 01737-767493 **Fax:** 01737-772041
E-mail: info@jbj.co.uk
Website: http://www.jbj.co.uk
Bank(s): Lloyds TSB Bank plc
Directors: J. Evans (Fin), M. Davis (Sales)
Ultimate Holding Company: BELGRAVEBRIDGE LIMITED
Immediate Holding Company: J.B.J. (TECHNIQUES) LIMITED
Registration no: 01185469 **Date established:** 1974 **Turnover:** £2m - £5m
No.of Employees: 11 - 20 **Product Groups:** 29, 34, 35, 36, 38, 39, 40, 42, 43, 48, 67, 84

Date of Accounts	Oct 11	Oct 10	Oct 09
Working Capital	2m	2m	2m
Fixed Assets	315	201	230
Current Assets	2m	2m	2m

Jilks Plastics Ltd

31 Trowers Way, Redhill, RH1 2LH
Tel: 01737-779799 **Fax:** 01737-779800
E-mail: sales@jilksplasticsltd.co.uk
Website: http://www.jilksplasticsltd.co.uk
Directors: S. Jilks (MD)
Immediate Holding Company: JILKS PLASTICS LIMITED
Registration no: 02596324 **Date established:** 1991
Turnover: £500,000 - £1m **No.of Employees:** 11 - 20
Product Groups: 30, 66

Date of Accounts	May 11	May 10	May 09
Sales Turnover	838	872	874
Pre Tax Profit/Loss	27	40	-23
Working Capital	47	62	42
Fixed Assets	29	35	42
Current Assets	195	210	194
Current Liabilities	34	41	32

Kaysafe Engineering Ltd

2nd Floor 12 Linkfield Corner, Redhill, RH1 1BB
Tel: 01737-772210 **Fax:** 01737-771200
E-mail: phil@kaysafe.co.uk
Website: http://www.kaysafe.co.uk
Directors: P. Russell (Dir)
Immediate Holding Company: KAYSAFE ENGINEERING LIMITED
Registration no: 02768247 **VAT No.:** GB 443 1567 59
Date established: 1992 **Turnover:** £1m - £2m **No.of Employees:** 1 - 10
Product Groups: 35, 37, 38, 40, 41, 42, 67

Date of Accounts	Mar 12	Mar 11	Mar 10
Working Capital	391	379	430
Fixed Assets	1	2	3
Current Assets	604	489	665

Kewell Converters Ltd

60 Holmethorpe Avenue, Redhill, RH1 2NL
Tel: 01737-771710 **Fax:** 01737-769732
E-mail: sales@kewell-converters.co.uk
Website: http://www.kewell-converters.co.uk
Bank(s): Barclays
Directors: C. Kewell (MD), N. Kewell (MD)
Managers: M. Kewell (Project Eng), P. Leeves (Accounts)
Immediate Holding Company: KEWELL CONVERTERS LIMITED
Registration no: 01028194 **VAT No.:** GB 218 2786 49
Date established: 1971 **Turnover:** £1m - £2m **No.of Employees:** 11 - 20
Product Groups: 29, 30, 48

Date of Accounts	Jul 09	Jul 08	Jul 07
Working Capital	82	18	-45
Fixed Assets	652	649	682
Current Assets	321	319	344

Korlyns Therapeutics

89 Colman Way, Redhill, RH1 2BB
Tel: 07372-13331 **Fax:** 0737-213331
E-mail: therapeutics@korlynspharm.com
Website: http://www.korlynspharm.com
Directors: C. Iriajen (Dir), E. Iriajen (Fin)
Immediate Holding Company: KORLYNS THERAPEUTICS LIMITED
Registration no: 06215455 **Date established:** 2007 **Turnover:** £1m - £2m
No.of Employees: 1 - 10 **Product Groups:** 63

Date of Accounts	May 11	May 10
Working Capital	-64	-63
Current Assets	30	22

Lombard North Central plc

3 Princess Way, Redhill, RH1 1NP
Tel: 01737-774111 **Fax:** 01737-760031
Website: http://www.lombard.co.uk
Bank(s): Royal Bank Of Scotland
Directors: P. Lynam (MD), L. Cameron (Co Sec), N. Clibbens (Dir), N. Gibbens (Chief Op Offcr)
Managers: J. Murphy (Personnel), N. Edwards (Mktg Serv Mgr)
Immediate Holding Company: LOMBARD NORTH CENTRAL PUBLIC LIMITED COMPANY
Registration no: 00337004 **Date established:** 1938
Turnover: £250m - £500m **No.of Employees:** 1001 - 1500
Product Groups: 82

Date of Accounts	Dec 09	Dec 08	Dec 07
Sales Turnover	357m	484m	408m
Pre Tax Profit/Loss	9m	11m	98m
Working Capital	-3324m	-3545m	-2963m
Fixed Assets	3369m	3664m	3507m
Current Assets	3587m	3694m	3697m
Current Liabilities	57m	35m	51m

Medical Gases Ltd

Aztec House Perrywood Business Park Honeycrock Lane, Redhill, RH1 5DZ
Tel: 01737-378000 **Fax:** 01737-378055
E-mail: sales@medicalgases.uk.com
Website: http://www.medicalgases.uk.com
Directors: R. Smith (Sales), A. Barrett (MD)
Managers: M. Farrell (Chief Acct), M. Sutherland (Tech Serv Mgr)
Ultimate Holding Company: U.K. GAS TECHNOLOGIES LIMITED
Immediate Holding Company: MEDICAL GASES LIMITED
Registration no: 01696776 **Date established:** 1983
Turnover: £500,000 - £1m **No.of Employees:** 21 - 50
Product Groups: 36, 38, 40, 42, 48, 51, 52

Date of Accounts	Mar 11	Mar 10	Mar 09
Working Capital	88	63	287
Current Assets	1m	758	1m

Monotype Imaging Ltd

Unit 2 Perrywood Business Park Honeycrock Lane, Redhill, RH1 5DZ
Tel: 01737-765959 **Fax:** 01737-769243
E-mail: info@fonts.com
Website: http://www.fonts.com
Directors: T. Fraser (Fin)
Managers: S. Quinn (Mgr)
Ultimate Holding Company: MONOTYPE IMAGING HOLDINGS INC (USA)
Immediate Holding Company: MONOTYPE IMAGING LIMITED
Registration no: 02663485 **VAT No.:** GB 602 3722 81
Date established: 1991 **Turnover:** £5m - £10m **No.of Employees:** 21 - 50
Product Groups: 28, 44, 46, 47

Date of Accounts	Dec 11	Dec 10	Dec 09
Sales Turnover	7m	6m	7m
Pre Tax Profit/Loss	478	280	2m
Working Capital	1m	753	901
Fixed Assets	53	20	37
Current Assets	3m	2m	2m
Current Liabilities	1m	687	908

N S S L Ltd

6 Gatton Park Business Centre Wells Place, Merstham, Redhill, RH1 3DR
Tel: 01737-648800 **Fax:** 01737-648888
E-mail: customer.centre@satcom-solutions.com
Website: http://www.satcom-solutions.com
Directors: S. Ray (Sales), S. Gordon (Fin), D. Edwards (Mkt Research), G. Chipping (Pers), R. Chewter (MD)
Managers: J. Dodd (Purch Mgr), P. Diduch (Tech Serv Mgr)
Ultimate Holding Company: WORLD WIDE MOBILE COMMUNICATIONS AS (NORWAY)
Immediate Holding Company: NSSLGLOBAL LIMITED
Registration no: 03879526 **VAT No.:** GB 725 1519 48
Date established: 1999 **Turnover:** £50m - £75m
No.of Employees: 51 - 100 **Product Groups:** 37

Date of Accounts	Dec 11	Dec 10	Dec 09
Sales Turnover	53m	54m	56m
Pre Tax Profit/Loss	6m	5m	4m
Working Capital	591	2m	6m
Fixed Assets	10m	8m	7m
Current Assets	18m	18m	20m
Current Liabilities	10m	9m	7m

N U S Consulting Group

Regent House, Redhill, RH1 1QT
Tel: 01737-781200 **Fax:** 01737-766799
E-mail: service@nusconsulting.co.uk
Website: http://www.nusconsulting.com
Bank(s): Barclays
Directors: G. Pope (Fin)
Managers: L. Williams (Personnel), R. Clare (Chief Mgr), J. Keable (Tech Serv Mgr), I. Mildon (Mktg Serv Mgr)
Immediate Holding Company: NUS CONSULTING GROUP LIMITED
Registration no: 00842122 **Date established:** 1965
Turnover: £10m - £20m **No.of Employees:** 51 - 100 **Product Groups:** 54

Date of Accounts	Dec 11	Dec 10	Dec 09
Sales Turnover	4m	N/A	N/A
Pre Tax Profit/Loss	745	N/A	N/A
Working Capital	5m	5m	4m
Fixed Assets	482	523	1m
Current Assets	6m	5m	4m
Current Liabilities	742	N/A	N/A

Platipus Anchors Ltd

Unit Q Kingsfield Business Centre Philanthropic Road, Redhill, RH1 4DP
Tel: 01737-762300 **Fax:** 01737-773395
E-mail: info@platipus-anchors.com
Website: http://www.platipus-anchors.com
Bank(s): HSBC Bank plc
Directors: C. Agg (MD)
Immediate Holding Company: PLATIPUS ANCHORS LIMITED
Registration no: 01680529 **VAT No.:** GB 644 4078 37
Date established: 1982 **Turnover:** £2m - £5m **No.of Employees:** 11 - 20
Product Groups: 35

Date of Accounts	Feb 12	Feb 11	Feb 10
Working Capital	495	370	291
Fixed Assets	286	228	231
Current Assets	1m	876	972

Prater Ltd

Perrywood Business Park Honeycrock Lane, Redhill, RH1 5JQ
Tel: 01737-772331 **Fax:** 01737-766021
E-mail: mail@prater.co.uk
Website: http://www.prater.co.uk
Bank(s): Barclays
Directors: R. Davies (Co Sec), T. Birkbeck (MD)
Managers: D. Eldridge, D. Cassidy (Tech Serv Mgr), J. Brazier (Personnel), K. Prater (Mktg Serv Mgr)
Ultimate Holding Company: LINDNER GROUP KG (GERMANY)
Immediate Holding Company: PRATER LIMITED
Registration no: 02107097 **Date established:** 1987
Turnover: £50m - £75m **No.of Employees:** 51 - 100 **Product Groups:** 52

Date of Accounts	Dec 11	Dec 10	Dec 09
Sales Turnover	65m	60m	63m
Pre Tax Profit/Loss	3m	3m	7m
Working Capital	7m	5m	5m
Fixed Assets	2m	2m	4m
Current Assets	27m	19m	18m
Current Liabilities	5m	4m	5m

Puretech Process Systems Ltd

Aztec House Perrywood Business Park, Redhill, RH1 5DZ
Tel: 01737-378000 **Fax:** 01737-378055
E-mail: sales@puretech.uk.com
Website: http://www.puretech.uk.com
Bank(s): Barclays
Directors: A. Barrett (MD)
Ultimate Holding Company: U.K. GAS TECHNOLOGIES LIMITED
Immediate Holding Company: PURETECH PROCESS SYSTEMS LIMITED
Registration no: 02267521 **Date established:** 1988
Turnover: £10m - £20m **No.of Employees:** 21 - 50 **Product Groups:** 36, 42, 48, 52, 84

Date of Accounts	Mar 11	Mar 10	Mar 09
Pre Tax Profit/Loss	N/A	N/A	199
Working Capital	77	59	926
Current Assets	1m	796	1m
Current Liabilities	N/A	N/A	63

Richaire Ltd

Unit 40 Holmethorpe Avenue, Redhill, RH1 2NL
Tel: 01737-771131 **Fax:** 01737-773121
E-mail: sales@richaire.co.uk
Website: http://www.richaire.co.uk
Directors: B. Wright (MD)
Immediate Holding Company: RICHAIRE LIMITED
Registration no: 01071934 **VAT No.:** GB 210 1899 89
Date established: 1972 **Turnover:** £2m - £5m **No.of Employees:** 1 - 10
Product Groups: 35, 52

Date of Accounts	Sep 11	Sep 10	Sep 09
Working Capital	516	86	72
Fixed Assets	952	1m	1m
Current Assets	2m	544	403

Risbridger Ltd

25 Trowers Way, Redhill, RH1 2LH
Tel: 08456-442323 **Fax:** 08456-442453
E-mail: annie@risbridger.com
Website: http://www.risbridger.com
Bank(s): National Westminster Bank Plc
Directors: A. Risbridger Hind (MD)
Ultimate Holding Company: RISBRIDGER (UK) LIMITED
Immediate Holding Company: RISBRIDGER LIMITED
Registration no: 00679728 **VAT No.:** GB 210 0796 07
Date established: 1961 **Turnover:** £1m - £2m **No.of Employees:** 11 - 20
Product Groups: 36, 38, 39, 42, 48

Date of Accounts	Dec 11	Dec 10	Dec 09
Working Capital	446	368	401
Fixed Assets	480	523	572
Current Assets	619	591	627

Rivertrace

Unit P Kingsfield Business Centre Philanthropic Road, Redhill, RH1 4DP
Tel: 01737-775500 **Fax:** 08707-702722
E-mail: sales@rivertrace.com
Website: http://www.rivertrace.com
Bank(s): Barclays
Directors: M. Coomber (MD)
Immediate Holding Company: RIVERTRACE ENGINEERING LIMITED
Registration no: 01713924 **VAT No.:** GB 318 5646 42
Date established: 1983 **Turnover:** £1m - £2m **No.of Employees:** 11 - 20
Product Groups: 38, 45

Date of Accounts	Nov 11	Nov 10	Nov 09
Working Capital	2m	2m	1m
Fixed Assets	821	826	830
Current Assets	2m	2m	2m

S E Hydraulics

40d, Holmethorpe Avenue, Redhill, RH1 2NL
Tel: 01737-768011 **Fax:** 01737-773469
E-mail: webmail@seh-ltd.co.uk
Website: http://www.seh-ltd.co.uk
Directors: J. Rumford (Sales)
Registration no: 1185819 **Date established:** 1973 **Turnover:** £2m - £5m
No.of Employees: 21 - 50 **Product Groups:** 38, 40

Samson Controls Ltd

Unit 12 Perrywood Business Park Honeycrock Lane, Redhill, RH1 5JQ
Tel: 01737-766391 **Fax:** 01737-765472
E-mail: sales@samsoncontrols.co.uk
Website: http://www.samsoncontrols.co.uk
Bank(s): HSBC Bank plc
Directors: M. Bruessau (MD)
Ultimate Holding Company: SAMSON INTERNATIONAL HOLDING SA (LUXEMBOURG)
Immediate Holding Company: SAMSON CONTROLS LTD
Registration no: 00598580 **Date established:** 1958 **Turnover:** £2m - £5m
No.of Employees: 11 - 20 **Product Groups:** 36, 38, 40

Date of Accounts	Dec 11	Dec 10	Dec 09
Working Capital	2m	2m	2m
Fixed Assets	946	986	934
Current Assets	3m	3m	3m

South Eastern Hydraulics Ltd

40b Holmethorpe Avenue, Redhill, RH1 2NL
Tel: 01737-768011 **Fax:** 01737-773469
E-mail: jblevins@seh-ltd.co.uk
Website: http://www.seh-ltd.co.uk
Bank(s): Lloyds TSB Bank plc
Directors: C. Blevins (MD), K. Owen (Dir), J. Blevins (Dir)
Immediate Holding Company: SOUTH EASTERN HYDRAULICS LIMITED
Registration no: 01185819 **VAT No.:** GB 211 1228 33
Date established: 1974 **Turnover:** £2m - £5m **No.of Employees:** 11 - 20
Product Groups: 30, 40, 48

Date of Accounts	Sep 11	Sep 10	Sep 09
Sales Turnover	N/A	N/A	2m
Pre Tax Profit/Loss	N/A	N/A	-6
Working Capital	68	149	-0
Fixed Assets	56	82	129
Current Assets	630	551	827
Current Liabilities	N/A	N/A	568

Southern Filter Co

115 Ladbroke Road, Redhill, RH1 1JT
Tel: 01737-766926 **Fax:** 01737-766215
E-mail: sales@southernfilters.co.uk
Website: http://www.southernfilters.co.uk
Directors: D. Sherlock (Prop)
Date established: 1998 **No.of Employees:** 1 - 10 **Product Groups:** 38, 42

Stocksigns Ltd

43 Ormside Way Holmethorpe Industrial Estate, Redhill, RH1 2LG
Tel: 01737-764764 **Fax:** 01737-763763
E-mail: sales@stocksigns.co.uk
Website: http://www.stocksigns.co.uk
Bank(s): The Royal Bank of Scotland
Directors: J. Leathers (MD), B. Harrington (Sales & Mktg)
Managers: F. Burrows (Purch Mgr)
Immediate Holding Company: British & Foreign Wharf Co. Ltd
Registration no: 00556959 **Date established:** 1943 **Turnover:** £5m - £10m
No.of Employees: 51 - 100 **Product Groups:** 30, 37, 39, 40, 45, 49, 68, 84

Date of Accounts	Dec 09	Dec 08	Dec 07
Pre Tax Profit/Loss	-122	29	101
Working Capital	2m	2m	3m
Fixed Assets	3m	3m	2m
Current Assets	3m	3m	3m
Current Liabilities	261	286	348

Swarovski UK Ltd

Unit 10 Perrywood Business Park Honeycrock Lane, Redhill, RH1 5JQ
Tel: 01737-856814 **Fax:** 01737-856856
E-mail: james.dubois@swarovski.com
Website: http://www.swarovski.com
Directors: J. Dubois (Dir)
Ultimate Holding Company: SWAROVSKI INTERNATIONAL HOLDING AG (SWITZERLAND)
Immediate Holding Company: SWAROVSKI UK LIMITED
Registration no: 00835806 **VAT No.:** GB 490 3607 46
Date established: 1965 **Turnover:** £75m - £125m
No.of Employees: 501 - 1000 **Product Groups:** 33, 49, 63, 65

Date of Accounts	Dec 11	Dec 10	Dec 09
Sales Turnover	78m	73m	68m
Pre Tax Profit/Loss	2m	4m	3m
Working Capital	487	5m	4m
Fixed Assets	11m	13m	11m
Current Assets	31m	30m	30m
Current Liabilities	10m	9m	9m

Telegan Protection Ltd

3-5 Holmethorpe Avenue Sealand Centre, Redhill, RH1 2LZ
Tel: 01737-763800 **Fax:** 01737-782727
E-mail: sales@teleganprotection.com
Website: http://www.teleganprotection.com
Directors: T. Egan (MD), A. Chandarana (Dir)
Immediate Holding Company: TELEGAN PRESSED PRODUCTS LTD
Registration no: 01366164 **Date established:** 1978 **Turnover:** £1m - £2m
No.of Employees: 21 - 50 **Product Groups:** 49, 52, 67

Date of Accounts	Sep 11	Sep 10	Sep 08
Sales Turnover	N/A	N/A	1m
Pre Tax Profit/Loss	N/A	N/A	74
Working Capital	311	301	2m
Fixed Assets	49	93	252
Current Assets	451	732	2m
Current Liabilities	N/A	N/A	154

Tiniusolsen Ltd

6 Perrywood Business Park Honeycrock Lane, Redhill, RH1 5DZ
Tel: 01737-765001 **Fax:** 01737-764768
E-mail: info@tiniusolsen.com
Website: http://www.hounsfield.com
Bank(s): National Westminster Bank Plc
Directors: P. Walford (Fin), C. Tait Iii (Pres), M. Wheeler (Sales)
Managers: B. Shackle (Chief Buyer), M. Adams (Tech Serv Mgr)
Ultimate Holding Company: TINIUS OLSEN INTERNATIONAL CO INC (USA)
Immediate Holding Company: TINIUS OLSEN LIMITED
Registration no: 00998521 **VAT No.:** GB 218 1759 57
Date established: 1970 **Turnover:** £2m - £5m **No.of Employees:** 51 - 100
Product Groups: 38

Date of Accounts	Dec 11	Dec 10	Dec 09
Sales Turnover	7m	6m	5m
Pre Tax Profit/Loss	484	500	-380
Working Capital	2m	2m	2m
Fixed Assets	2m	2m	3m
Current Assets	4m	3m	3m
Current Liabilities	806	545	441

Titan Travel Ltd

Hitours House Cross Oak Lane, Redhill, RH1 5EX
Tel: 01293-450460 **Fax:** 01293-450552
E-mail: dwild@titantravel.co.uk
Website: http://www.titantravel.co.uk
Directors: H. Clayson (Mkt Research), D. Wild (Dir)
Managers: E. Farley (Personnel), M. Zaremba (Tech Serv Mgr)
Immediate Holding Company: MHI 1000 LIMITED
Registration no: 01377653 **Date established:** 1978
Turnover: £75m - £125m **No.of Employees:** 251 - 500
Product Groups: 69, 72

Date of Accounts	Aug 06	Aug 05	Sep 08
Sales Turnover	113m	103m	109m
Pre Tax Profit/Loss	-310	-269	234
Working Capital	-7m	-5m	-9m
Fixed Assets	14m	12m	15m
Current Assets	28m	25m	13m
Current Liabilities	360	316	15m

Travelers UK

61-63 London Road, Redhill, RH1 1NA
Tel: 01737-787787 **Fax:** 01737-787172
E-mail: kpurvis@travellers.com
Website: http://www.travelers.co.uk
Directors: M. Gent (Fin), K. Purvis (MD)
Managers: K. Bigwood (Mktg Serv Mgr), A. Rawlinson (Tech Serv Mgr)
Registration no: 03618732 **No.of Employees:** 101 - 250
Product Groups: 82

Date of Accounts	Dec 07
Pre Tax Profit/Loss	76400
Fixed Assets	1156m
Current Assets	104520
Current Liabilities	59890
Total Share Capital	203820
ROCE% (Return on Capital Employed)	6.4

Trevor Blake Ltd

The Fairlawn Business Park Bonehurst Road, Salfords, Redhill, RH1 5GH
Tel: 01293-775509 **Fax:** 01293-776965
E-mail: info@trevorblake.co.uk
Website: http://www.trevorblake.co.uk
Directors: D. Webb (MD)
Managers: C. Woodley (Sales Admin)
Immediate Holding Company: TREVOR BLAKE LTD.
Registration no: 03543848 **Date established:** 1998
No.of Employees: 11 - 20 **Product Groups:** 24, 25, 26, 27, 30, 33, 35, 40, 49, 52, 61, 66, 67

Date of Accounts	Sep 11	Sep 10	Sep 09
Working Capital	192	147	122
Fixed Assets	10	22	48
Current Assets	644	668	522

UK Gas Technologies Ltd

8 Perrywood Business Park Honeycrock Lane, Redhill, RH1 5DZ
Tel: 01737-378000 **Fax:** 01737-378055
E-mail: sales@ukgastech.uk.com
Website: http://www.ukgastech.uk.com
Bank(s): Barclays, Epsom
Directors: A. Barrett (MD)
Ultimate Holding Company: U.K. GAS TECHNOLOGIES LIMITED
Registration no: 02565991 **Date established:** 1990 **Turnover:** £5m - £10m
No.of Employees: 21 - 50 **Product Groups:** 36, 38, 40, 42, 46, 48, 51, 52

Date of Accounts	Mar 11	Mar 10	Mar 09
Sales Turnover	6m	8m	10m
Pre Tax Profit/Loss	683	-2m	475
Working Capital	170	-454	1m
Fixed Assets	658	708	758
Current Assets	2m	2m	3m
Current Liabilities	535	770	798

UK Autotalk Ltd

Perrywood Business Park Honeycrock Lane, Redhill, RH1 5JQ
Tel: 01737-764434
E-mail: peter.warman@ukautotalk.com
Website: http://www.ukautotalk.com
Directors: P. Warman (MD)
Ultimate Holding Company: RAYFIX LIMITED
Immediate Holding Company: RAYFIX LIMITED
Registration no: 01706204 **Date established:** 2007
No.of Employees: 1 - 10 **Product Groups:** 38, 67, 81

Date of Accounts	Dec 11	Dec 10	Dec 09
Sales Turnover	65m	60m	63m
Pre Tax Profit/Loss	3m	4m	7m
Working Capital	6m	4m	5m
Fixed Assets	6m	6m	7m
Current Assets	27m	18m	19m
Current Liabilities	5m	4m	6m

Wika Instruments Ltd
4 Gatton Park Business Centre Wells Place Merstham, Merstham, Redhill, RH1 3LG
Tel: 01737-644008 **Fax:** 01737-644403
E-mail: info@wika.co.uk
Website: http://www.wika.co.uk
Bank(s): Barclays
Directors: D. Phillips (MD)
Managers: L. Evans (Sales Prom Mgr), T. Hays, K. Florence (Fin Mgr), C. McCloughlan (Tech Serv Mgr), A. Avery
Ultimate Holding Company: CELBAR GMBH (GERMANY)
Immediate Holding Company: WIKA INSTRUMENTS LIMITED
Registration no: 01032313 **VAT No.:** GB 218 2729 61
Date established: 1971 **Turnover:** £10m - £20m
No.of Employees: 21 - 50 **Product Groups:** 38

Date of Accounts	Dec 11	Dec 10	Dec 09
Sales Turnover	20m	17m	14m
Pre Tax Profit/Loss	2m	2m	520
Working Capital	6m	11m	10m
Fixed Assets	5m	230	262
Current Assets	9m	14m	13m
Current Liabilities	1m	741	548

Winterbotham Darby & Co. Ltd
Granville House 9 Gatton Park Business Centre Wells Place, Merstham, Redhill, RH1 3AS
Tel: 01737-646646 **Fax:** 01737-646600
E-mail: info@windar.co.uk
Website: http://www.windar.co.uk
Bank(s): HSBC
Directors: G. Wise (Ch), S. Higginson (MD)
Managers: S. Wise (I.T. Exec), L. Rae (Sales Admin)
Ultimate Holding Company: THE COMPLEAT FOOD GROUP LIMITED
Immediate Holding Company: WINTERBOTHAM,DARBY & CO.LIMITED
Registration no: 00736901 **Date established:** 1962
Turnover: £125m - £250m **No.of Employees:** 101 - 250
Product Groups: 20

Date of Accounts	Sep 10	Sep 09	Sep 08
Sales Turnover	129m	109m	95m
Pre Tax Profit/Loss	5m	4m	5m
Working Capital	12m	14m	13m
Fixed Assets	1m	1m	1m
Current Assets	28m	27m	37m
Current Liabilities	7m	1m	4m

Reigate

Affiniti Digital Media Ltd
7 Greystones Drive, Reigate, RH2 0HA
Tel: 0870-165 1474
E-mail: enquiry@affinitimedia.co.uk
Website: http://www.affinitimedia.co.uk
Directors: D. Stafford (MD), D. Silverman (Fin)
Immediate Holding Company: AFFINITI DIGITAL MEDIA LIMITED
Registration no: 05180470 **Date established:** 2004
Turnover: Up to £250,000 **No.of Employees:** 1 - 10 **Product Groups:** 44, 61, 80, 81

Date of Accounts	Oct 11	Oct 10	Oct 09
Working Capital	29	44	86
Fixed Assets	1	1	1
Current Assets	93	106	260

Aquatec
10 Beehive Way, Reigate, RH2 8DY
Tel: 01737-225465 **Fax:** 01737-225465
E-mail: regstubbs@btinternet.com
Managers: R. Stubbs (Mgr)
Date established: 1975 **No.of Employees:** 1 - 10 **Product Groups:** 40

Canon UK Ltd
Cockshot Hill, Reigate, RH2 8BF
Tel: 01737-220000 **Fax:** 01737-220022
E-mail: andy@canon.co.uk
Website: http://www.canon.co.uk
Bank(s): National Westminster Bank Plc
Directors: D. Bateson (Co Sec), A. Vickers (Dir)
Managers: D. Smith (Mktg Serv Mgr), N. Michaelidas (Mktg Serv Mgr)
Ultimate Holding Company: FP002441
Immediate Holding Company: CANON (UK) LIMITED
Registration no: 01264300 **Date established:** 1976
Turnover: £250m - £500m **No.of Employees:** 1501 & over
Product Groups: 44

Date of Accounts	Dec 09	Dec 08	Dec 07
Sales Turnover	275m	307m	310m
Pre Tax Profit/Loss	-2m	13m	17m
Working Capital	130m	132m	123m
Fixed Assets	27m	32m	32m
Current Assets	194m	170m	186m
Current Liabilities	32m	29m	34m

Caparo Testing Technologies Ltd
61 Albert Road North, Reigate, RH2 9RS
Tel: 01737-222211 **Fax:** 01737-224333
E-mail: info@caparotesting.com
Website: http://www.caparotesting.com
Bank(s): Midland
Directors: G. Brown (Dir), S. Bailey (Fin)
Ultimate Holding Company: CAPARO GROUP LIMITED
Immediate Holding Company: MATERIAL MEASUREMENTS LIMITED
Registration no: 00653121 **VAT No.:** GB 216 2162 02
Date established: 1960 **Turnover:** £5m - £10m **No.of Employees:** 21 - 50
Product Groups: 85

Date of Accounts	Dec 11	Dec 10	Dec 09
Sales Turnover	5m	5m	6m
Pre Tax Profit/Loss	447	345	324
Working Capital	2m	3m	3m
Fixed Assets	1m	2m	2m
Current Assets	3m	4m	4m
Current Liabilities	493	662	579

Coversure Insurance Services Ltd (Reigate)
23 Croydon Road, Reigate, RH2 0LY
Tel: 0800-308 1010 **Fax:** 08704-585746
E-mail: markba@coversure.co.uk
Website: http://www.coversure.co.uk
Directors: J. Burgess (Prop)
Immediate Holding Company: COVERSURE INSURANCE SERVICES LIMITED
Registration no: 02381990 **Date established:** 1989
Turnover: £10m - £20m **No.of Employees:** 1 - 10 **Product Groups:** 82

Date of Accounts	Mar 11	Mar 10	Mar 09
Sales Turnover	5m	4m	4m
Pre Tax Profit/Loss	1m	-5	494
Working Capital	935	240	323
Fixed Assets	1m	1m	1m
Current Assets	9m	8m	8m
Current Liabilities	6m	6m	5m

Esure Insurance
The Observatory Castlefield Road, Reigate, RH2 0SG
Tel: 01737-222222 **Fax:** 01737-235000
E-mail: adrian.webb@esure.com
Website: http://www.esure.com
Managers: A. Whitehouse (Fin Mgr), D. Fulton, A. Webb, C. Timms (Personnel), M. Foulsham
Immediate Holding Company: ESURE FINANCE LIMITED
Registration no: 07064319 **Date established:** 2009
Turnover: £75m - £125m **No.of Employees:** 251 - 500
Product Groups: 82

Date of Accounts	Dec 11	Dec 10
Pre Tax Profit/Loss	-8m	210
Working Capital	-31m	4m
Fixed Assets	194m	194m
Current Assets	2m	4m

Fairoak Piling & Foundations Ltd T/A Abbey Pynford
4 West Road, Reigate, RH2 7JT
Tel: 01737-271480 **Fax:** 01737-216163
E-mail: davidpostles@abbeypynford.co.uk
Directors: D. Postles (Dir)
No.of Employees: 1 - 10 **Product Groups:** 51, 52, 66, 84

Date of Accounts	Mar 08	Mar 07	Mar 06
Working Capital	-66	16	73
Fixed Assets	614	391	259
Current Assets	69	57	107
Current Liabilities	135	41	34

Fone-Alarm Installations Ltd
59 Albert Road North, Reigate, RH2 9EL
Tel: 01737-223673 **Fax:** 01737-224349
E-mail: enquiries@fonealarm.co.uk
Website: http://www.fonealarm.co.uk
Directors: J. Hazell (MD), J. Drake (Co Sec), J. Hornor (Mkt Research)
Managers: S. Parkers (Personnel), G. Desborough (I.T. Exec)
Immediate Holding Company: FONE - ALARM INSTALLATIONS LIMITED
Registration no: 01366219 **VAT No.:** GB 220 0097 26
Date established: 1978 **Turnover:** £1m - £2m **No.of Employees:** 21 - 50
Product Groups: 37, 39, 67

Date of Accounts	May 11	May 10	May 09
Working Capital	599	660	735
Fixed Assets	149	165	100
Current Assets	1m	1m	1m

G D C Microscopes
1 Weald Way, Reigate, RH2 7RG
Tel: 01737-240099
E-mail: cliff@gdcmicroscopes.com
Website: http://www.gdcmicroscopes.com
Managers: C. Wayland (Mgr)
Date established: 2008 **No.of Employees:** 1 - 10 **Product Groups:** 38, 49, 65

G E Commercial Finance
Enterprise House Bancroft Road, Reigate, RH2 7RT
Tel: 01737-841200 **Fax:** 01737-841357
E-mail: john.jenkins@ge.com
Website: http://www.businessfinance.co.uk
Bank(s): Barclays
Directors: S. Parker (Ch), S. Boynton (Co Sec), R. Archibald (Fin), K. Todman (I.T. Dir), J. Jenkins (Grp Chief Exec), A. Walker (Serv), J. Bagley (Sales)
Managers: J. Onslow (Sales Prom Mgr)
Ultimate Holding Company: GENERAL ELECTRIC COMPANY (USA)
Immediate Holding Company: GE COMMERCIAL FINANCE LIMITED
Registration no: 01030032 **Date established:** 1971
Turnover: £20m - £50m **No.of Employees:** 101 - 250 **Product Groups:** 82

Date of Accounts	Dec 10	Dec 09	Dec 08
Sales Turnover	31m	34m	54m
Pre Tax Profit/Loss	-2m	-13m	-14m
Working Capital	-4m	256m	-488
Fixed Assets	122m	122m	134m
Current Assets	305m	332m	436m
Current Liabilities	4m	3m	3m

H G H Fire Protection Systems
141 Carlton Road, Reigate, RH2 0JG
Tel: 01737-762428 **Fax:** 01737-762677
Website: http://www.hghigginsons.co.uk
Directors: J. Tofield (Ptnr)
No.of Employees: 1 - 10 **Product Groups:** 36, 37, 40, 52

J D S Catering Equipment
Ridgewood Stud Ironsbottom, Sidlow, Reigate, RH2 8QG
Tel: 01293-825552 **Fax:** 01293-824442
E-mail: sales@jds-catering.co.uk
Website: http://www.jds-catering.co.uk
Directors: J. Spiers (Prop)
Ultimate Holding Company: JDS
Registration no: 03149255 **Turnover:** £500,000 - £1m
No.of Employees: 1 - 10 **Product Groups:** 26, 40, 48, 52, 66, 67, 84

Date of Accounts	Jan 08	Jan 07	Jan 06
Working Capital	47	-2	-15
Fixed Assets	8	9	17
Current Assets	205	170	214
Current Liabilities	158	171	229

Kelstar Fire Engineering
27a Bell Street, Reigate, RH2 7AD
Tel: 01737-222105 **Fax:** 01737-245295
E-mail: info@kelstar.co.uk
Directors: J. Mooney (Dir)
Immediate Holding Company: KELSTAR ENGINEERING LIMITED
Registration no: 02731409 **Date established:** 1992
No.of Employees: 1 - 10 **Product Groups:** 32, 84, 87

Date of Accounts	Jun 11	Jun 10	Jun 09
Working Capital	23	32	26
Fixed Assets	5	7	8
Current Assets	103	104	103

Mr Exhaust
18 London Road, Reigate, RH2 9HY
Tel: 01737-243900 **Fax:** 01737-224705
Website: http://www.mrexhaust.co.uk
Directors: S. Harrison (Prop)
Registration no: 01998311 **VAT No.:** GB 284 7851 14
No.of Employees: 1 - 10 **Product Groups:** 40

Norsan Kemi Ltd
Unit F 61 Albert Road North, Reigate, RH2 9EL
Tel: 01737-221761 **Fax:** 01737-223384
Directors: G. Ayres (MD)
No.of Employees: 1 - 10 **Product Groups:** 36, 40

John Powell
45 Church Street, Reigate, RH2 0AD
Tel: 01737-244111 **Fax:** 01737-247044
Directors: J. Powell (Prop)
Immediate Holding Company: BROOK CONSTRUCTION LIMITED
Registration no: 04562502 **Date established:** 1986
Turnover: Up to £250,000 **No.of Employees:** 1 - 10 **Product Groups:** 36, 39, 40

Date of Accounts	Jul 89	Jul 88	Jul 87
Sales Turnover	1m	10	1
Pre Tax Profit/Loss	4	-1	-1
Fixed Assets	35	N/A	N/A
Current Assets	288	14	19

Promofoam Mark SG Enterprises Limited
The Studio. 7. Margery Hall Reigate Hill, Reigate, RH2 9RL
Tel: 01737-233890 **Fax:** 01737-233600
E-mail: info@promofoam.co.uk
Website: http://www.promofoam.co.uk
No.of Employees: 1 - 10 **Product Groups:** 26, 30, 49, 67

Pyle Consulting Ltd
48 Church Street, Reigate, RH2 0SN
Tel: 01737-245666 **Fax:** 01737-247923
E-mail: admin@pyleconsulting.co.uk
Website: http://www.bv.com
Directors: B. Champion (MD)
Immediate Holding Company: PYLE CAR PARK CONSULTANTS LIMITED
Registration no: 07310744 **Date established:** 2010 **Turnover:** £5m - £10m
No.of Employees: 1 - 10 **Product Groups:** 35

S B E S Ltd
Unit F 47 Blackborough Road, Reigate, RH2 7BU
Tel: 01737-226622 **Fax:** 01737-242442
E-mail: info@sbes.co.uk
Website: http://www.sbes.co.uk
Directors: J. Lanbourne (Dir)
Immediate Holding Company: SBES LIMITED
Registration no: 03440453 **Date established:** 1997
Turnover: £250,000 - £500,000 **No.of Employees:** 1 - 10
Product Groups: 40

Date of Accounts	Sep 11	Sep 10	Sep 09
Sales Turnover	N/A	N/A	382
Pre Tax Profit/Loss	N/A	N/A	44
Working Capital	71	55	53
Fixed Assets	20	8	9
Current Assets	147	129	94
Current Liabilities	N/A	N/A	10

Sharper Image
Castle Court, 41 London Road,, Reigate, RH2 9RJ
Tel: 01737-218767 **Fax:** 01306-743979
E-mail: enquiries@sharper.co.uk
Website: http://www.sharper.co.uk
Directors: J. Terry (Dir)
Immediate Holding Company: The Sharper Image Consulting Ltd
Registration no: 02709769 **Date established:** 2005
Turnover: £500,000 - £1m **No.of Employees:** 1 - 10 **Product Groups:** 81

Star Recruitment Limited
Cobnor House 8 Gatton Road, Reigate, RH2 0EX
Tel: 01737-249211 **Fax:** 01737-240720
E-mail: emailstar@globalnet.co.uk
Website: http://www.engployment.com
Directors: R. Wilson (MD)
Registration no: 01433008 **No.of Employees:** 1 - 10 **Product Groups:** 35

Stentor Music Co. Ltd
44 Albert Road North, Reigate, RH2 9EZ
Tel: 01737-240226 **Fax:** 01737-242748
E-mail: info@stentor-music.com
Website: http://www.stentor-music.com
Bank(s): Barclays, Gatwick Group
Directors: M. Doughty (MD), L. Wilkes (Mkt Research), R. Bogin (Dir), P. Hyman (Fin)
Ultimate Holding Company: MICHAEL C. DOUGHTY LIMITED
Immediate Holding Company: STENTOR MUSIC COMPANY LIMITED
Registration no: 00719958 **VAT No.:** GB 209 5388 47
Date established: 1962 **Turnover:** £5m - £10m **No.of Employees:** 21 - 50
Product Groups: 65

Date of Accounts	May 12	May 11	May 10
Sales Turnover	7m	7m	7m
Pre Tax Profit/Loss	462	617	1m
Working Capital	4m	4m	4m
Fixed Assets	2m	2m	2m
Current Assets	5m	5m	4m
Current Liabilities	450	393	512

thinklaser Ltd

57 Albert Road North, Reigate, RH2 9EL
Tel: 01737-224731 **Fax:** 01737-249124
E-mail: info@thinklaser.com
Website: http://www.thinklaser.com
Registration no: 00004576718 **Turnover:** £1m - £2m
No.of Employees: 1 - 10 **Product Groups:** 28, 33, 37, 40, 42, 44, 45, 46, 47, 48, 81

Date of Accounts	Oct 09	Oct 08	Oct 07
Sales Turnover	695	574	671
Pre Tax Profit/Loss	11	48	14
Working Capital	124	133	108
Fixed Assets	12	16	6
Current Assets	213	375	415
Current Liabilities	64	43	40

V I P Mail Services Ltd

60 Priory Road, Reigate, RH2 8JB
Tel: 01737-242613 **Fax:** 01737-223858
E-mail: louise.martin@vipmail.co.uk
Website: http://www.vipmail.co.uk
Directors: L. Martin (MD)
Immediate Holding Company: V.I.P.MAIL SERVICES & CO.LIMITED
Registration no: 01050429 **Date established:** 1972
Turnover: £500,000 - £1m **No.of Employees:** 1 - 10 **Product Groups:** 80, 81

Date of Accounts	Jan 12	Jan 11	Jan 10
Working Capital	-12	27	64
Fixed Assets	285	296	308
Current Assets	97	130	147

Richmond

Accounts Training

London House 243-253 Lower Mortlake Road, Richmond, TW9 2LL
Tel: 020-8332 7567 **Fax:** 020-8948 8948
E-mail: info@accountstraining.co.uk
Website: http://www.accountstraining.co.uk
Directors: A. Collins (Prop)
Immediate Holding Company: SHEERMANS SS LIMITED
Registration no: 04583361 **Date established:** 1993
Turnover: £500,000 - £1m **No.of Employees:** 1 - 10 **Product Groups:** 86

Date of Accounts	Dec 07	Dec 06	Dec 05
Working Capital	-1	-1	-2
Fixed Assets	2	2	2
Current Assets	11	4	3
Current Liabilities	12	5	5

Achieveglobal

Spencer House 23 Sheen Road, Richmond, TW9 1BN
Tel: 020-8322 4000 **Fax:** 020-8322 4001
E-mail: mark.barrett@achieveglobal.com
Website: http://www.achieveglobal.co.uk
Bank(s): Lloyds TSB Bank plc
Directors: J. Wilson (Co Sec)
Managers: M. Barrett
Ultimate Holding Company: INFORMA PLC (JERSEY)
Immediate Holding Company: ACHIEVE LEARNING (UK) LIMITED
Registration no: 00877923 **Date established:** 1966 **Turnover:** £2m - £5m
No.of Employees: 11 - 20 **Product Groups:** 86

Date of Accounts	Dec 11	Dec 10	Dec 09
Sales Turnover	3m	3m	3m
Pre Tax Profit/Loss	456	206	392
Working Capital	3m	3m	3m
Fixed Assets	6	N/A	1
Current Assets	4m	3m	3m
Current Liabilities	642	332	566

Argentina Autentica Ltd

68 Ennerdale Road, Richmond, TW9 2DL
Tel: 020-7193 6886
E-mail: info@argentinaautentica.com
Website: http://www.argentinaautentica.com
Directors: O. Stone (Dir)
Registration no: 05565767 **Date established:** 2005
No.of Employees: 1 - 10 **Product Groups:** 69

Date of Accounts	Dec 06
Current Assets	12
Current Liabilities	12

Caroline B Designs

58 Marksbury Avenue Kew, Richmond, TW9 4JF
Tel: 020-8255 9783
E-mail: carolinebuck@hotmail.co.uk
Website: http://www.carolinebdesigns.co.uk
Directors: C. Buck (Prop)
No.of Employees: 1 - 10 **Product Groups:** 30, 35, 37

Designer Carpets

2 Ham Street, Richmond, TW10 7HT
Tel: 020-8332 6006 **Fax:** 020-8332 0660
E-mail: info@designercarpets.co.uk
Website: http://www.designercarpets.co.uk
Directors: V. Holdaway (Prop)
Date established: 1986 **No.of Employees:** 1 - 10 **Product Groups:** 23, 24, 29, 39, 63

Fothergill

62 Hill Street, Richmond, TW9 1TW
Tel: 020-8948 4165 **Fax:** 020-8948 5105
E-mail: info@fothergill.uk.com
Website: http://www.fothergill.uk.com
Directors: W. Powell (Dir)
Immediate Holding Company: FOTHERGILL AND COMPANY LIMITED
Registration no: 01418599 **Date established:** 1979
No.of Employees: 1 - 10 **Product Groups:** 35

Date of Accounts	Jan 12	Jan 11	Jan 09
Working Capital	153	150	147
Fixed Assets	9	10	9
Current Assets	269	234	283

Hy-Ten Ltd

12 The Green, Richmond, TW9 1PX
Tel: 020-8332 1266 **Fax:** 020-8332 1757
E-mail: info@hy-ten.co.uk
Website: http://www.bootle.co.uk
Bank(s): National Westminster Bank Plc
Directors: A. Larkins (MD), M. Shattock (Fin)
Managers: J. Morris (Sales Admin), W. Mackay (Sales Prom Mgr)
Immediate Holding Company: HY-TEN LIMITED
Registration no: 00598988 **VAT No.:** GB 318 0520 89
Date established: 1958 **Turnover:** £20m - £50m
No.of Employees: 51 - 100 **Product Groups:** 34

Lambsmead Ltd

PO BOX 543, Richmond, TW9 1FH
Tel: 020-8940 7948 **Fax:** 020-8940 7989
E-mail: lambsmead1@btconnect.com
Website: http://www.lambsmead.co.uk
Directors: I. Deitsch (Dir), L. Deitsch (Dir)
Registration no: 01266863 **VAT No.:** GB 241 8031 93
Date established: 1976 **Turnover:** £1m - £2m **No.of Employees:** 1 - 10
Product Groups: 38

Date of Accounts	Nov 07	Nov 06	Nov 05
Sales Turnover	1476	1638	N/A
Pre Tax Profit/Loss	-11	-59	N/A
Working Capital	54	55	103
Fixed Assets	53	62	74
Current Assets	339	268	275
Current Liabilities	285	212	172
ROCE% (Return on Capital Employed)	-10.5	-50.3	
ROT% (Return on Turnover)	-0.8	-3.6	

Leading Events Ltd

13 Cambridge Cottages, Richmond, TW9 3AY
Tel: 020-8773 1387 **Fax:** 020-8773 1387
E-mail: enquiries@leadingevents.co.uk
Website: http://www.leadingevents.co.uk
Directors: S. Knox Johnston (Co Sec)
Immediate Holding Company: LEADING EVENTS LTD
Registration no: 07382669 **Date established:** 2010
Turnover: Up to £250,000 **No.of Employees:** 1 - 10 **Product Groups:** 89

M Y Works

Suite 161 30 Red Lion Street, Richmond, TW9 1RB
Tel: 020-3394 0454
E-mail: info@my-works.co.uk
Website: http://www.my-works.co.uk
Managers: S. Birchwood (Admin Off)
Immediate Holding Company: MYWORKS LIMITED
Registration no: 07609466 **Date established:** 2011
No.of Employees: 1 - 10 **Product Groups:** 37, 40

Metsa Serla Ltd

13 Parkshot, Richmond, TW9 2RG
Tel: 020-8332 2842 **Fax:** 020-8332 2852
E-mail: sales.uk@metsatissue.com
Website: http://www.catrin.com
Directors: M. Garnett (MD)
Managers: D. Webber (Mgr), S. Amos (Mgr), M. Dewick (Sales Prom Mgr)
Immediate Holding Company: MARCAR HOLDINGS LIMITED
Registration no: 00562474 **Date established:** 1956
No.of Employees: 1 - 10 **Product Groups:** 24, 27

Montien Spice Co. Ltd

214b Sandycombe Road, Richmond, TW9 2EQ
Tel: 020-8332 9888 **Fax:** 020-8287 1010
E-mail: sales@namjai.co.uk
Website: http://www.namjai.co.uk
Directors: T. Wong (Dir)
Immediate Holding Company: MONTIEN SPICE COMPANY LTD.
Registration no: 02884598 **Date established:** 1994
No.of Employees: 1 - 10 **Product Groups:** 20

Date of Accounts	Mar 11	Mar 10	Mar 09
Working Capital	308	307	315
Fixed Assets	N/A	1	1
Current Assets	338	320	335

Penspen Ltd

3 Water Lane, Richmond, TW9 1TJ
Tel: 020-8334 2700 **Fax:** 020-8334 2701
E-mail: info@penspen.com
Website: http://www.penspen.com
Bank(s): Arab Bank
Directors: S. Moore (Fin)
Managers: D. Stanley, G. Raynes (Mktg Serv Mgr), A. Everst (Personnel), P. Trotman (Tech Serv Mgr)
Ultimate Holding Company: DAR AL-HANDASAH CONSULTANTS SHAIR & PARTNERS HLDINGS LT
Immediate Holding Company: PENSPEN LTD
Registration no: 00584446 **Date established:** 1957
Turnover: £50m - £75m **No.of Employees:** 251 - 500
Product Groups: 42, 54, 80, 84

Date of Accounts	Dec 10	Dec 09	Dec 08
Sales Turnover	64m	61m	62m
Pre Tax Profit/Loss	-720	3m	4m
Working Capital	-3m	-2m	1m
Fixed Assets	21m	21m	16m
Current Assets	25m	36m	45m
Current Liabilities	13m	20m	32m

Reed Accountancy Personnel Ltd

21 George Street, Richmond, TW9 1HY
Tel: 020-8940 4483 **Fax:** 020-8332 1837
E-mail: steve.sharpe@reed.co.uk
Website: http://www.reed.co.uk
Managers: J. Phillips (Mgr)
Immediate Holding Company: REED PERSONNEL SERVICES LTD
Registration no: 00973629 **Turnover:** £125m - £250m
No.of Employees: 1 - 10 **Product Groups:** 80

Reed Employment Ltd

George Street, Richmond, TW9 1HY
Tel: 020-8948 2151 **Fax:** 020-8940 1627
E-mail: sandra.hollyhomes@reed.co.uk
Website: http://www.reed.co.uk
Directors: J. Reed (Grp Chief Exec)
Managers: S. Sharpe (Comm), T. Royal (Mgr), S. Hollyhomes (Chief Mgr), T. Royle (Mgr)
Immediate Holding Company: REED EMPLOYMENT LIMITED
Registration no: 00669854 **Date established:** 1960
Turnover: £250m - £500m **No.of Employees:** 1 - 10 **Product Groups:** 80

Reed Exhibition's Ltd

28 The Quadrant, Richmond, TW9 1DN
Tel: 020-8910 7910 **Fax:** 020-8940 2171
E-mail: rxinfo@reedexpo.co.uk
Website: http://www.reedexpo.com
Bank(s): National Westminster Bank Plc
Managers: A. Fowle
Ultimate Holding Company: REED ELSEVIER GROUP PLC
Immediate Holding Company: REED EXHIBITIONS LIMITED
Registration no: 00678540 **VAT No.:** GB 232 4004 20
Date established: 1960 **Turnover:** £50m - £75m
No.of Employees: 251 - 500 **Product Groups:** 81

Date of Accounts	Dec 11	Dec 10	Dec 09
Sales Turnover	74m	72m	60m
Pre Tax Profit/Loss	7m	-19	9m
Working Capital	-32m	-26m	-29m
Fixed Assets	76m	64m	69m
Current Assets	38m	34m	25m
Current Liabilities	36m	29m	27m

Rumsey & Sons

Market House Market Road, Richmond, TW9 4LZ
Tel: 020-8876 1000 **Fax:** 020-8876 9969
E-mail: removals@rumseyandson.com
Website: http://www.rumseyandson.com
Directors: A. Davidson (Ptnr)
Immediate Holding Company: HAMILTON MOTOR FACTORS LIMITED
Registration no: 01294715 **Date established:** 1977
Turnover: £500,000 - £1m **No.of Employees:** 21 - 50
Product Groups: 72, 77

Date of Accounts	Mar 12	Mar 11	Mar 10
Working Capital	-60	-53	-49
Fixed Assets	385	388	392
Current Assets	230	249	267

Securitas Security Services

203-205 Lower Richmond Road, Richmond, TW9 4LN
Tel: 020-8392 6000 **Fax:** 020-8392 2088
E-mail: jenny.campbell@securitas.uk.com
Website: http://www.securitas.com
Managers: J. Norton (Mktg Serv Mgr), A. Dempsey, J. Campbell
Ultimate Holding Company: SECURITAS AB (SWEDEN)
Immediate Holding Company: LOOMIS HOLDING UK LIMITED
Registration no: 02586369 **Date established:** 1991
Turnover: £500,000 - £1m **No.of Employees:** 1501 & over
Product Groups: 81

Date of Accounts	Dec 11	Dec 10	Dec 09
Sales Turnover	656	853	47
Pre Tax Profit/Loss	-943	-1m	-263
Working Capital	2m	3m	4m
Fixed Assets	50m	50m	50m
Current Assets	2m	4m	4m
Current Liabilities	58	47	64

Spaceist Ltd

85 Sheen Road, Richmond, TW9 1YJ
Tel: 020-7247 4340
E-mail: info@spaceist.co.uk
Website: http://www.spaceist.co.uk
Directors: A. Pickles (MD)
Immediate Holding Company: SPACEIST LIMITED
Registration no: 05991444 **Date established:** 2006
No.of Employees: 1 - 10 **Product Groups:** 26, 67

Date of Accounts	Nov 10	Nov 09	Nov 08
Working Capital	39	39	4
Fixed Assets	N/A	N/A	1
Current Assets	110	107	75

Tall Boy Communications Ltd

London House 243-253 Lower Mortlake Road, Richmond, TW9 2LL
Tel: 020-8948 9516 **Fax:** 020-8940 2007
E-mail: info@tallboy.co.uk
Website: http://www.tallboy.co.uk
Directors: S. Banks (MD)
Immediate Holding Company: TALLBOY COMMUNICATIONS LTD
Registration no: 04749194 **Date established:** 2003
Turnover: Up to £250,000 **No.of Employees:** 1 - 10 **Product Groups:** 37, 44, 65, 89

Date of Accounts	Jul 11	Jul 10	Jul 09
Working Capital	56	-6	9
Fixed Assets	26	24	20
Current Assets	141	53	57

Web 4 Marketing UK Ltd

16 The Vineyard, Richmond, TW10 6AN
Tel: 020-8948 1022
E-mail: sales@web4marketing.co.uk
Website: http://www.web4marketing.co.uk
Directors: S. Orr (Grp Chief Exec)
Registration no: 03935735 **Date established:** 2000
Turnover: Up to £250,000 **No.of Employees:** 1 - 10 **Product Groups:** 44, 80, 81

Date of Accounts	Mar 08	Mar 07
Sales Turnover	35	N/A
Working Capital	14	20
Fixed Assets	N/A	1
Current Assets	19	26
Current Liabilities	5	6

William Grant & Sons Distillers Ltd

Independence Road 84 Lower Mortlake Road, Richmond, TW9 2HS
Tel: 020-8332 1188 **Fax:** 020-8332 1695
E-mail: info@glenfiddich.com
Website: http://www.glenfiddich.com
Directors: G. Tait (Fin), S. David (Grp Chief Exec)
Ultimate Holding Company: WILLIAM GRANT & SONS HOLDINGS LIMITED
Immediate Holding Company: WILLIAM GRANT & SONS DISTILLERS LIMITED
Registration no: SC134248 **VAT No.:** 554 6900 29 **Date established:** 1991
No.of Employees: 51 - 100 **Product Groups:** 21

Date of Accounts	Dec 11	Dec 10	Dec 09
Sales Turnover	666m	587m	559m
Pre Tax Profit/Loss	84m	95m	81m
Working Capital	470m	416m	356m
Fixed Assets	198m	129m	125m
Current Assets	1144m	1053m	768m
Current Liabilities	61m	67m	67m

YourParkingSpace.co.uk owned by Parking Enterprises
74 Gainsborough Road, Richmond, TW9 2EA
Tel: 020-8948 6399
E-mail: info@yourparkingspace.co.uk
Website: http://www.yourparkingspace.co.uk
Directors: C. Cridland (Prop)
No.of Employees: 1 - 10 **Product Groups:** 25, 35, 80

South Croydon

A & B Unicorn Kiosk Restorations Ltd
PO Box 866, South Croydon, CR2 7SY
Tel: 020-8651 2436
E-mail: info@unicornkiosks.com
Directors: R. Lewis (MD)
No.of Employees: 1 - 10 **Product Groups:** 35

The Cambria Group PLC
Dove House 113 Brighton Road, South Croydon, CR2 6EE
Tel: 020-8688 3656 **Fax:** 020-8688 7990
Website: http://www.dovesjaguar.co.uk
Directors: J. Mullins (Fin)
Managers: T. Hall, C. Sattar (Sales & Mktg Mg), M. Lavery, R. Jackson (Tech Serv Mgr), N. Boon-caddal (Personnel)
Ultimate Holding Company: CAMBRIA AUTOMOBILES PLC
Immediate Holding Company: DOVE GROUP LIMITED
Registration no: 00229710 **Date established:** 2028
Turnover: Up to £250,000 **No.of Employees:** 21 - 50 **Product Groups:** 68

Date of Accounts	Aug 11	Aug 10	Aug 09
Working Capital	148	148	148
Current Assets	148	148	148

Demountable Partitions Ltd
Unit 4 Twin Bridges Business Park 232 Selsdon Road, South Croydon, CR2 6PL
Tel: 020-8410 3800 **Fax:** 020-8239 0083
E-mail: brian@demountables.co.uk
Website: http://www.demountables.co.uk
Directors: B. Mccauley (Dir)
Immediate Holding Company: DEMOUNTABLE PARTITIONS LIMITED
Registration no: 01141708 **VAT No.:** GB 219 0939 54
Date established: 1973 **Turnover:** £1m - £2m **No.of Employees:** 1 - 10
Product Groups: 26, 30, 33, 35, 52, 66, 84

Date of Accounts	Oct 11	Oct 10	Oct 09
Working Capital	32	4	-2
Fixed Assets	1	1	2
Current Assets	198	146	327

Euro Fire Protection & Maintenance Service
Capital Business Centre Carlton Road, South Croydon, CR2 0BS
Tel: 020-8916 2010 **Fax:** 020-8916 2011
E-mail: enquiries@eurofireprotection.com
Website: http://www.eurofireprotection.com
Directors: C. Linsley (Ptnr)
Immediate Holding Company: DIGITAL EQUIPMENT COMMUNICATION MAINTENANCE LIMITED
Registration no: 04448338 **Date established:** 2002
No.of Employees: 1 - 10 **Product Groups:** 32, 33, 36, 38, 39, 40, 52, 67, 84

Date of Accounts	May 11	May 10	May 09
Working Capital	2	2	2
Current Assets	32	25	32

Francis and Francis Ltd
P.O. Box 3284, South Croydon, CR2 1FU
Tel: 020-8668 9792 **Fax:** 020-8668 9793
E-mail: sales@powertransmissions.co.uk
Website: http://www.powertransmissions.co.uk
Bank(s): National Westminster Bank Plc
Directors: R. Haas (MD)
Registration no: 00479899 **VAT No.:** GB 367 5754 10 100
Date established: 1950 **Turnover:** £250,000 - £500,000
No.of Employees: 11 - 20 **Product Groups:** 29, 30, 35, 37, 38, 40, 44, 46, 47, 66

Date of Accounts	Mar 12	Mar 11	Mar 10
Working Capital	32	37	47
Fixed Assets	3	4	N/A
Current Assets	48	53	68

Gillett & Johnston Croydon Ltd
Unit 9a Twin Bridges Business Park 232 Selsdon Road, South Croydon, CR2 6PL
Tel: 020-8686 2694 **Fax:** 020-8681 4028
E-mail: jenny@gillettjohnston.co.uk
Website: http://www.gillettjohnston.co.uk
Directors: S. Combes (MD), J. Coombes (Fin), J. Coombes (MD)
Managers: P. Alliston (Mgr)
Immediate Holding Company: GILLETT & JOHNSTON(CROYDON)LIMITED
Registration no: 00557325 **VAT No.:** GB 217 9575 33
Date established: 1955 **Turnover:** £250,000 - £500,000
No.of Employees: 1 - 10 **Product Groups:** 49

Date of Accounts	Oct 08	Oct 07	Oct 06
Working Capital	44	29	17
Fixed Assets	14	17	9
Current Assets	117	78	108
Current Liabilities	73	49	91

John Bellman & Associates Ltd
9 Ferns Close Addington Road, South Croydon, CR2 8RG
Tel: 020-8657 1663
E-mail: enq@johnbellman.co.uk
Website: http://www.johnbellman.co.uk
Directors: J. Bellman (Dir)
Immediate Holding Company: JOHN BELLMAN AND ASSOCIATES LIMITED
Registration no: 03445845 **Date established:** 1997
No.of Employees: 1 - 10 **Product Groups:** 35

Date of Accounts	Oct 11	Oct 10	Oct 09
Working Capital	-37	-29	-32
Current Assets	15	20	18

Metax Ltd
Unit 77 Capital Business Centre 22 Carlton Road, South Croydon, CR2 0BS
Tel: 020-8916 2077 **Fax:** 01689-889994
E-mail: info@metax.co.uk
Website: http://www.metax.co.uk
Directors: J. Howard (Dir), I. Roberts (Co Sec)
Ultimate Holding Company: METAX GROUP LIMITED
Immediate Holding Company: METAX LIMITED
Registration no: 00375454 **VAT No.:** GB 460 5981 33
Date established: 1942 **Turnover:** £500,000 - £1m
No.of Employees: 1 - 10 **Product Groups:** 37, 38

Date of Accounts	Mar 11	Mar 10	Mar 09
Working Capital	33	50	8
Fixed Assets	10	12	15
Current Assets	118	166	65
Current Liabilities	N/A	23	N/A

O C S Group Ltd
79 Limpsfield Road Sanderstead, South Croydon, CR2 9LB
Tel: 020-8651 3211 **Fax:** 020-8651 4832
E-mail: enquiries@ocs.co.uk
Website: http://www.ocs.co.uk
Bank(s): Lloyds TSB Bank plc
Directors: C. Cracknell (MD), D. Keepe (Sales), J. Oliver (Chief Op Offcr), N. Haworth (Dir), P. Armitage (Ch), P. Caley (Dir), P. Johnson (Dir), S. Phillips (Dir), R. Salmon (Dir), S. Ward (Dir), S. Bonner (Dir)
Managers: T. Murray (Purch Mgr), J. Clark (Mgr), M. Golden (Mgr), P. Kingham (Mktg Serv Mgr), P. Armitage (Fin Mgr)
Ultimate Holding Company: 01298292
Immediate Holding Company: OCS GROUP UK LIMITED
Registration no: 03056469 **VAT No.:** GB 238 0343 79
Date established: 1995 **Turnover:** £500m - £1,000m
No.of Employees: 21 - 50 **Product Groups:** 23, 52, 69, 81

PR Photographer London
PO Box 555, South Croydon, CR2 7WU
Tel: 07721-398747
E-mail: contact@pr-photographer.com
Website: http://www.pr-photographer.com
Directors: N. Atkinson (Dir)
Date established: 1989 **No.of Employees:** 1 - 10 **Product Groups:** 81

S L E Ltd
Twin Bridges Business Park 232 Selsdon Road, South Croydon, CR2 6PL
Tel: 020-8681 1414 **Fax:** 020-8649 8570
E-mail: sales@sle.co.uk
Website: http://www.sle.co.uk
Bank(s): National Westminster Bank Plc
Directors: B. Nelligan (MD), M. Donovan (Dir), P. Richards (Fin)
Managers: M. Pearcy (Sales & Mktg Mg), S. Jacobs (Tech Serv Mgr), T. Brown
Immediate Holding Company: S.L.E. LIMITED
Registration no: 01649988 **VAT No.:** GB 372 5425 52
Date established: 1982 **Turnover:** £10m - £20m
No.of Employees: 51 - 100 **Product Groups:** 37, 38, 44

Date of Accounts	Jul 11	Jul 10	Jul 09
Sales Turnover	13m	12m	9m
Pre Tax Profit/Loss	736	717	41
Working Capital	4m	3m	3m
Fixed Assets	340	796	718
Current Assets	6m	5m	4m
Current Liabilities	459	1m	258

S P Filtration Services Ltd
170 Selsdon Road, South Croydon, CR2 6PJ
Tel: 020-8649 8820 **Fax:** 020-8649 8820
E-mail: kleggatt@tiscali.co.uk
Directors: K. Leggatt (MD)
Immediate Holding Company: S.P. FILTRATION SERVICES LTD
Registration no: 04252867 **Date established:** 2001
No.of Employees: 1 - 10 **Product Groups:** 38, 42

Date of Accounts	Jul 11	Jul 10	Jul 09
Working Capital	5	11	9
Current Assets	24	31	25

Solitek Ltd
Unit 34 Capital Business Centre 22 Carlton Road, South Croydon, CR2 0BS
Tel: 020-8916 2369 **Fax:** 020-8916 2361
E-mail: sales@solitek.co.uk
Website: http://www.solitek.co.uk
Directors: L. Rose (Dir)
Immediate Holding Company: TIME MANAGEMENT SYSTEMS LIMITED
Registration no: 01036661 **Date established:** 2012
Turnover: £250,000 - £500,000 **No.of Employees:** 1 - 10
Product Groups: 67

Date of Accounts	Jun 11	Jun 10
Sales Turnover	N/A	40
Current Assets	7	8
Current Liabilities	N/A	8

Time Management Systmes
Unit 12 Capital Business Centre 22 Carlton Road, South Croydon, CR2 0BS
Tel: 020-8916 2060 **Fax:** 020-8916 2066
E-mail: info@timemachines.co.uk
Website: http://www.timemanagementsystems.co.uk
Directors: T. Vaudrey (Fin)
Managers: L. Stevens (Mgr)
Immediate Holding Company: TIME MACHINES LIMITED
Registration no: 01029782 **Date established:** 1971
Turnover: £500,000 - £1m **No.of Employees:** 1 - 10 **Product Groups:** 27, 37, 44, 48, 49, 65, 83

Date of Accounts	Jun 11	Jun 10	Jun 09
Working Capital	-16	22	83
Fixed Assets	11	16	19
Current Assets	50	68	120

R Young & Son Printers Ltd
360 Brighton Road, South Croydon, CR2 6AL
Tel: 020-8680 2242 **Fax:** 020-8681 0873
E-mail: info@youngprint.com
Website: http://www.ryoungprint.com
Directors: R. Young (MD)
Immediate Holding Company: R. YOUNG AND SON PRINTERS LIMITED
Registration no: 01768892 **Date established:** 1983
No.of Employees: 11 - 20 **Product Groups:** 28

Date of Accounts	Dec 11	Dec 10	Dec 09
Working Capital	1m	1m	1m
Fixed Assets	661	725	798
Current Assets	2m	2m	2m

Surbiton

Albright International Ltd
125 Red Lion Road, Surbiton, KT6 7QS
Tel: 020-8390 5357 **Fax:** 020-8390 1927
E-mail: nigeledwardlawrence@albright.co.uk
Website: http://www.albright.co.uk
Directors: N. Bedggood (MD), A. Catt (Fin)
Ultimate Holding Company: LEA REDWAY LIMITED
Immediate Holding Company: ALBRIGHT (ENGINEERS) LIMITED
Registration no: 00763629 **VAT No.:** GB 216 0045 16
Date established: 1963 **Turnover:** £20m - £50m **No.of Employees:** 1 - 10
Product Groups: 37

Date of Accounts	Sep 11	Sep 10	Sep 09
Working Capital	5m	5m	5m
Current Assets	5m	5m	5m

Burlodge Ltd
Unit 5 Hook Rise South Industrial Park Hook Rise South, Surbiton, KT6 7LD
Tel: 020-8879 5700 **Fax:** 020-8879 5701
E-mail: frontdesk@burlodge.co.uk
Website: http://www.burlodge.co.uk
Directors: P. Stanfield (MD)
Managers: P. Turner (Comptroller), K. Giles
Ultimate Holding Company: ALI SPA (ITALY)
Immediate Holding Company: BURLODGE LIMITED
Registration no: 02196073 **Date established:** 1987 **Turnover:** £5m - £10m
No.of Employees: 21 - 50 **Product Groups:** 30, 40, 45

Date of Accounts	Aug 11	Aug 10	Aug 09
Sales Turnover	5m	6m	6m
Pre Tax Profit/Loss	302	394	46
Working Capital	1m	2m	3m
Fixed Assets	221	217	158
Current Assets	3m	3m	4m
Current Liabilities	1m	845	687

C Brewer & Sons
Kingston House Estate Portsmouth Road, Long Ditton, Surbiton, KT6 5QG
Tel: 020-8398 7681 **Fax:** 020-8398 7805
E-mail: surbiton@brewers.co.uk
Website: http://www.brewers.co.uk
Directors: S. Carter (I.T. Dir)
Managers: M. Perry (District Mgr), K. Dixon (Sales Prom Mgr), E. Cooper (Chief Acct)
Immediate Holding Company: C.BREWER & SONS LIMITED
Registration no: 00203852 **VAT No.:** GB 192 1565 70
Date established: 1925 **Turnover:** £250m - £500m
No.of Employees: 11 - 20 **Product Groups:** 66

Clover Systems
7 Endsleigh Gardens, Surbiton, KT6 5JL
Tel: 020-8399 1822 **Fax:** 020-8770 0556
E-mail: cloversystems@btconnect.com
Website: http://www.cloversystems.co.uk
Directors: J. Parkes (Dir), J. Parkes (Fin), T. Haskey (Dir)
Immediate Holding Company: CLOVER SYSTEMS LIMITED
Registration no: 01915817 **VAT No.:** GB 391 6199 22
Date established: 1985 **Turnover:** Up to £250,000
No.of Employees: 1 - 10 **Product Groups:** 40, 44

Date of Accounts	Mar 10	Mar 09	Mar 08
Working Capital	N/A	21	35
Current Assets	6	24	40

D S T Global Solutions
D S T House St Marks Hill, Surbiton, KT6 4QD
Tel: 020-8390 5000 **Fax:** 020-8390 7000
E-mail: webmaster@dstintl.com
Website: http://www.dstintl.com
Directors: T. McCann (Dir), K. Holloway (Sales), M. Winn (Grp MD)
Managers: L. Morris (Personnel)
Ultimate Holding Company: D S T SYSTEMS INC (USA)
Immediate Holding Company: DST GLOBAL SOLUTIONS LIMITED
Registration no: 01772349 **Date established:** 1983
Turnover: £20m - £50m **No.of Employees:** 1 - 10 **Product Groups:** 44

Date of Accounts	Dec 11	Dec 10	Dec 09
Sales Turnover	44m	41m	41m
Pre Tax Profit/Loss	4m	-2m	-14m
Working Capital	-7m	-8m	21m
Fixed Assets	28m	32m	17m
Current Assets	44m	39m	61m
Current Liabilities	13m	14m	12m

Dyno Rod Ltd
Zockoll House 143 Maple Road, Surbiton, KT6 4BJ
Tel: 0800-112112 **Fax:** 01256-780417
E-mail: postmaster@dyno.com
Website: http://www.dyno.com
Bank(s): Lloyds TSB Bank plc
Directors: C. Stern (Fin), C. Smith (Dir)
Ultimate Holding Company: Centrica plc
Immediate Holding Company: DYNO-ROD LIMITED
Registration no: 01046906 **Date established:** 1972
Turnover: £10m - £20m **No.of Employees:** 101 - 250 **Product Groups:** 54

Date of Accounts	Dec 07	Dec 06	Dec 05
Sales Turnover	11510	11110	10600
Pre Tax Profit/Loss	4150	5080	5710
Working Capital	19740	14530	10420
Fixed Assets	1450	2240	1330
Current Assets	33460	23480	15380
Current Liabilities	13720	8950	4960
Total Share Capital	150	150	150
ROCE% (Return on Capital Employed)	19.6	30.3	48.6
ROT% (Return on Turnover)	36.1	45.7	53.9

Global Traders & Exporters Ltd
1 Global House Red Lion Business Park Red Lion Road, Surbiton, KT6 7QD
Tel: 020-8974 2780 **Fax:** 020-8974 2781
E-mail: sales@globalpharm.co.uk
Website: http://www.globalpharm.co.uk
Directors: I. Sacranie (Dir), I. Sacranie (Dir)
Ultimate Holding Company: BANNON ENTERPRISES LIMITED
Immediate Holding Company: GLOBAL TRADERS & EXPORTERS LIMITED
Registration no: 03188720 **VAT No.:** GB 674 0351 44
Date established: 1996 **No.of Employees:** 1 - 10 **Product Groups:** 72, 76

see next page

Global Traders & Exporters Ltd - Cont'd

Date of Accounts	Dec 10	Dec 09	Dec 08
Working Capital	64	33	-8
Current Assets	89	71	35

Hartley Engineering Ltd
The Rear of 108-110 Ewell Road, Surbiton, KT6 6HA
Tel: 020-8390 2155 **Fax:** 020-8390 5437
E-mail: sales@hartleyengineering.com
Website: http://www.hartleyengineering.com
Directors: A. Constable (MD)
Immediate Holding Company: HARTLEY ENGINEERING LIMITED
Registration no: 02616131 **VAT No.:** GB 608 9156 22
Date established: 1991 **Turnover:** Up to £250,000
No.of Employees: 1 - 10 **Product Groups:** 48

Date of Accounts	Dec 11	Dec 10	Dec 09
Sales Turnover	N/A	N/A	135
Pre Tax Profit/Loss	N/A	N/A	1
Working Capital	1	-2	-1
Fixed Assets	4	4	5
Current Assets	37	37	41
Current Liabilities	N/A	N/A	6

How Green How Green Ltd
10 Hazel Bank Tolworth, Surbiton, KT5 9RH
Tel: 020-8330 9033
E-mail: tom@howgreen.biz
Website: http://www.howgreen.biz
Directors: T. Palmer (Dir)
Registration no: 06350691 **No.of Employees:** 1 - 10 **Product Groups:** 37, 66, 67

Main Kitchen Supplies
47 Brighton Road, Surbiton, KT6 5LR
Tel: 020-8390 3327 **Fax:** 020-8390 9644
E-mail: info@idineltd.com
Website: http://www.idineltd.com
Directors: A. Bedford (MD)
Immediate Holding Company: MAIN KITCHEN SUPPLIES LTD
Registration no: 03599845 **No.of Employees:** 1 - 10 **Product Groups:** 20, 40, 41

Nuffield Nursing Homes Trust
Nuffield House 1-4 The Crescent, Surbiton, KT6 4BN
Tel: 020-8390 1200 **Fax:** 020-8399 6726
E-mail: info.woking@nuffieldhealth.com
Website: http://www.nuffieldhospitals.org.uk
Directors: D. Mobbs (Grp Chief Exec), J. Jones (Dir)
Managers: A. Lunt (Personnel), J. Anderson (Mktg Serv Mgr)
Immediate Holding Company: Nuffield Health
Registration no: 01279419 **Date established:** 1996
Turnover: £75m - £125m **No.of Employees:** 1 - 10 **Product Groups:** 88

Date of Accounts	Dec 07
Working Capital	1
Current Assets	1
Total Share Capital	1

Pageantry Electronic Systems Ltd
Pageantry House Argent Court, Hook Rise South, Surbiton, KT6 7NL
Tel: 020-8391 8360 **Fax:** 020-8391 2103
E-mail: sales@pageantry.co.uk
Website: http://www.pageantry.co.uk
Bank(s): Lloyds
Directors: E. Leon (Dir), M. Gallione (MD)
Managers: A. Ricca (Chief Mgr), C. Deans (Asst Gen Mgr), G. Hancock (Chief Mgr), P. Elliott (Prod Mgr), R. Head (Chief Mgr)
Immediate Holding Company: Ac Security Solutions Ltd
Registration no: 03101766 **VAT No.:** GB 216 6173 74
Date established: 1993 **Turnover:** £1m - £2m **No.of Employees:** 11 - 20
Product Groups: 37, 40, 52, 85

Date of Accounts	Mar 08	Mar 07	Mar 06
Working Capital	607	453	371
Fixed Assets	23	37	44
Current Assets	799	612	689
Current Liabilities	193	159	318

Stanley Productions Ltd
55 Fleece Road Long Ditton, Surbiton, KT6 5JR
Tel: 020-8398 7843 **Fax:** 020-8339 0350
E-mail: info@stanleyproductions.co.uk
Website: http://www.stanleysonline.com
Directors: S. Arrons (MD)
Immediate Holding Company: STANLEY PRODUCTIONS LIMITED
Registration no: 01368953 **Date established:** 1978
No.of Employees: 1 - 10 **Product Groups:** 37

Date of Accounts	May 11	May 10	May 09
Sales Turnover	N/A	5m	5m
Pre Tax Profit/Loss	N/A	-497	-749
Working Capital	1m	1m	2m
Fixed Assets	233	338	539
Current Assets	2m	2m	3m
Current Liabilities	N/A	159	465

Surrey Microwave
80 Warren Dr South, Surbiton, KT5 9QE
Tel: 07773-921366 **Fax:** 020-8337 0358
Directors: H. Thompson (Prop)
Date established: 1999 **No.of Employees:** 1 - 10 **Product Groups:** 36, 40

Toa Corporation UK Ltd
Unit 2 Hook Rise South Industrial Park, Surbiton, KT6 7LD
Tel: 08707-740987 **Fax:** 08707-770839
E-mail: info@toa.co.uk
Website: http://www.toa.eu
Bank(s): HSBC
Directors: B. Downing (Dir), I. Daisuke (MD)
Ultimate Holding Company: TOA CORPORATION (JAPAN)
Immediate Holding Company: TOA CORPORATION (UK) LIMITED
Registration no: 01694232 **VAT No.:** GB 291 5780 32
Date established: 1983 **Turnover:** £2m - £5m **No.of Employees:** 11 - 20
Product Groups: 37

Date of Accounts	Dec 11	Dec 10	Dec 09
Sales Turnover	5m	4m	3m
Pre Tax Profit/Loss	533	392	57
Working Capital	3m	2m	2m
Fixed Assets	45	60	50
Current Assets	3m	3m	2m
Current Liabilities	656	848	361

Traders Coffee Ltd
274 Ewell Road, Surbiton, KT6 7AG
Tel: 020-8390 0311 **Fax:** 020-8390 8280
E-mail: jag@coffeebay.co.uk
Website: http://www.coffeebay.co.uk
Directors: J. Green (MD)
Immediate Holding Company: TRADERS COFFEE LIMITED
Registration no: 04613848 **Date established:** 2002 **Turnover:** £1m - £2m
No.of Employees: 11 - 20 **Product Groups:** 40, 49, 62, 67, 69

Date of Accounts	Jan 11	Jan 10	Jan 09
Sales Turnover	1m	1m	958
Pre Tax Profit/Loss	82	95	43
Working Capital	219	222	196
Fixed Assets	743	732	711
Current Assets	450	386	348
Current Liabilities	107	79	43

Wilstar Marketing Ltd - The Welding Centre
293 Ewell Road, Surbiton, KT6 7AB
Tel: 020-8399 2449 **Fax:** 020-8390 7710
E-mail: sales@wilstar.co.uk
Website: http://www.wilstar.co.uk
Directors: R. Williams (MD)
Registration no: 00863307 **No.of Employees:** 1 - 10 **Product Groups:** 46

Date of Accounts	Oct 07	Oct 06	Oct 05
Working Capital	15	9	15
Fixed Assets	15	15	13
Current Assets	54	55	55
Current Liabilities	39	46	40
Total Share Capital	1	1	1

Woodfield Welding Services
122 Ewell Road, Surbiton, KT6 6HA
Tel: 020-8390 4062 **Fax:** 020-8399 8025
Directors: D. Cackett (Prop)
Immediate Holding Company: REPTILE KINGDOM LTD
Date established: 2011 **No.of Employees:** 1 - 10 **Product Groups:** 46

The Zockoll Group Ltd
143 Maple Road, Surbiton, KT6 4BJ
Tel: 0800-749927 **Fax:** 020-8481 2288
E-mail: postmaster@dyno.com
Website: http://www.dyno.com
Directors: G. Oatham (Co Sec)
Immediate Holding Company: THE ZOCKOLL GROUP LIMITED
Registration no: 00907055 **VAT No.:** GB 216 1019 12
Date established: 1967 **No.of Employees:** 1 - 10 **Product Groups:** 45, 54

Date of Accounts	Dec 11	Dec 10	Dec 09
Working Capital	1m	1m	1m
Fixed Assets	1m	1m	1m
Current Assets	1m	1m	1m

Sutton

A B C Catering & Party Equipment Hire Ltd
2 Wealdstone Road Kimpton Indus Park, Sutton, SM3 9QN
Tel: 020-8641 6700 **Fax:** 020-8641 9300
E-mail: hire@abchire.co.uk
Website: http://www.abchire.co.uk
Bank(s): National Westminster Bank Plc
Directors: D. Muino (Fin)
Immediate Holding Company: ABC CATERING AND PARTY EQUIPMENT HIRE LIMITED
Registration no: 01426042 **VAT No.:** GB 317 7327 54
Date established: 1979 **No.of Employees:** 11 - 20 **Product Groups:** 67

Date of Accounts	Sep 11	Sep 10	Sep 09
Working Capital	-253	-230	-217
Fixed Assets	757	775	601
Current Assets	112	125	135

Advantage Total Solutions Ltd
487 London Road, Sutton, SM3 8JW
Tel: 020-8337 9933 **Fax:** 020-8288 9403
E-mail: sales@atsgroup.co.uk
Website: http://www.atsgroup.co.uk
Directors: P. Jones (Sales), P. Riley (MD)
Managers: J. Twum (Sales Admin)
Immediate Holding Company: ADVANTAGE TOTAL SOLUTIONS LIMITED
Registration no: 03079212 **Date established:** 1995
No.of Employees: 1 - 10 **Product Groups:** 26

Date of Accounts	Sep 10	Sep 09	Sep 08
Working Capital	50	82	100
Fixed Assets	7	22	33
Current Assets	169	187	269

Angel Plastics Ltd
Angel Plastics Unit 3 Sutton Trade Park 11 Kimpton Road, Sutton, SM3 9DA
Tel: 020-8644 8143 **Fax:** 0845-890 2821
E-mail: sales@angelplastics.co.uk
Website: http://www.angelplastics.co.uk
Directors: S. Cobb (MD)
Immediate Holding Company: ANGEL PLASTICS LIMITED
Registration no: 06317330 **Date established:** 2007
No.of Employees: 1 - 10 **Product Groups:** 30, 52, 66

Date of Accounts	Sep 11	Sep 10	Sep 09
Working Capital	194	88	77
Fixed Assets	169	169	182
Current Assets	485	543	328

Bright Sparks Electrical Wholesalers Ltd
131 Church Hill Road, Sutton, SM3 8LJ
Tel: 020-8644 2228 **Fax:** 020-8644 4533
Directors: S. Davey (MD), J. Davey (Fin)
Managers: S. Davey (Mgr)
Immediate Holding Company: BRIGHT SPARKS ELECTRICAL WHOLESALERS LTD
Registration no: 05031393 **Date established:** 2004
No.of Employees: 1 - 10 **Product Groups:** 36, 40

Date of Accounts	Feb 12	Feb 11	Feb 10
Working Capital	-96	-101	-100
Fixed Assets	2	2	3
Current Assets	53	43	37

C D Sales Recruitment
Century House Station Way, Sutton, SM3 8SW
Tel: 020-8722 8200 **Fax:** 08701-371690
E-mail: simon@cdsr.com
Website: http://www.cdsr.com
Directors: J. Dale (MD), S. Cavey (MD), B. Luton (Sales)
Managers: N. Gawman (Sales Admin)
Immediate Holding Company: CAVEY DALE GROUP LIMITED
Registration no: 03686517 **Date established:** 1990
Turnover: £10m - £20m **No.of Employees:** 21 - 50 **Product Groups:** 80

Date of Accounts	Mar 11	Mar 10	Mar 09
Sales Turnover	N/A	3m	5m
Pre Tax Profit/Loss	N/A	-161	45
Working Capital	6	-18	96
Fixed Assets	36	48	62
Current Assets	923	796	424
Current Liabilities	N/A	603	244

Census3
30 Upper Mulgrave Road, Sutton, SM2 7AZ
Tel: 020-8770 0007 **Fax:** 020-8770 0008
E-mail: info@sensus3.co.uk
Website: http://www.foardcs.co.uk
Directors: S. Jarvis (Dir)
Immediate Holding Company: SENSUS 3 LIMITED
Registration no: 05309558 **Date established:** 2004
No.of Employees: 1 - 10 **Product Groups:** 26, 37, 44

Chappell & Lynn
54 Belmont Rise, Sutton, SM2 6EQ
Tel: 020-8643 7600 **Fax:** 020-8770 0677
E-mail: wdc@chappell-and-lynn.co.uk
Directors: W. Chappell (Prop)
Date established: 2002 **No.of Employees:** 1 - 10 **Product Groups:** 35

Colour-Therm Ltd
92 Burdon Lane, Sutton, SM2 7DA
Tel: 020-8642 6506 **Fax:** 020-8642 4886
E-mail: mdunk@colour-therm.co.uk
Website: http://www.colour-therm.co.uk
Directors: M. Dunk (Fin)
Immediate Holding Company: COLOUR-THERM LIMITED
Registration no: 02708895 **VAT No.:** GB 625 6549 22
Date established: 1992 **Turnover:** £250,000 - £500,000
No.of Employees: 1 - 10 **Product Groups:** 32

Date of Accounts	Feb 11	Feb 10	Feb 09
Working Capital	31	37	42
Fixed Assets	1	1	1
Current Assets	52	71	82

Crown Agents Ltd
St Nicholas House St Nicholas Road, Sutton, SM1 1EL
Tel: 020-8643 3311 **Fax:** 020-8643 9113
E-mail: enquiries@crownagents.co.uk
Website: http://www.crownagents.com
Bank(s): Bank of England
Directors: L. Hale (Co Sec)
Ultimate Holding Company: THE CROWN AGENTS FOUNDATION
Immediate Holding Company: CROWN AGENTS INVESTMENT MANAGEMENT LIMITED
Registration no: 02169973 **VAT No.:** GB 340 6798 41
Date established: 1987 **Turnover:** £2m - £5m
No.of Employees: 251 - 500 **Product Groups:** 61, 76, 80, 82

Date of Accounts	Dec 11	Dec 10	Dec 09
Sales Turnover	3m	3m	2m
Pre Tax Profit/Loss	46	165	114
Working Capital	1m	2m	1m
Fixed Assets	1	18	24
Current Assets	2m	2m	1m
Current Liabilities	177	154	132

Designplan International Ltd
6 Wealdstone Road, Sutton, SM3 9RW
Tel: 020-8254 2020
Website: http://www.designplan.co.uk
Directors: D. Cumper (Dir), M. Cumper (Co Sec)
Ultimate Holding Company: Designplan Management Services Ltd
Immediate Holding Company: DESIGNPLAN INTERNATIONAL LIMITED
Registration no: 02182306 **Date established:** 1987 **Turnover:** £1m - £2m
No.of Employees: 101 - 250 **Product Groups:** 37, 67

Designplan Lighting Ltd
6 Wealdstone Road, Sutton, SM3 9RW
Tel: 020-8254 2000 **Fax:** 020-8644 4253
E-mail: reception@designplan.co.uk
Website: http://www.designplan.co.uk
Bank(s): National Westminster
Directors: M. Cumper (Fin), P. Williamson (MD)
Managers: K. Lowe (Sales Prom Mgr), C. Biancardi (Personnel), N. Dinsdale (Purch Mgr)
Ultimate Holding Company: QUADRANT VENTURES LIMITED
Immediate Holding Company: DESIGNPLAN LIGHTING LIMITED
Registration no: 00784246 **VAT No.:** GB 479 9221 95
Date established: 1963 **Turnover:** £10m - £20m
No.of Employees: 101 - 250 **Product Groups:** 37

Date of Accounts	Dec 11	Dec 10	Dec 09
Sales Turnover	12m	9m	12m
Pre Tax Profit/Loss	965	337	1m
Working Capital	5m	4m	4m
Fixed Assets	366	166	225
Current Assets	7m	7m	6m
Current Liabilities	664	534	796

J Devine Civil Engineering Ltd
133 Church Hill Road, Sutton, SM3 8NE
Tel: 020-8641 0071 **Fax:** 020-8644 5244
E-mail: nigel@jdevine.co.uk
Website: http://www.jdevine.co.uk
Directors: F. Cassem (Fin), N. Jordan (MD)
Managers: P. McCrorie (Buyer)
Ultimate Holding Company: DEVINE HOLDINGS LIMITED
Immediate Holding Company: J DEVINE CIVIL ENGINEERING LTD
Registration no: 01176060 **Date established:** 1974
Turnover: £10m - £20m **No.of Employees:** 11 - 20 **Product Groups:** 51

Date of Accounts	Jul 11	Jul 10	Jul 09
Sales Turnover	14m	18m	19m
Pre Tax Profit/Loss	234	202	321

Working Capital	1m	995	864
Fixed Assets	18	13	15
Current Assets	5m	6m	7m
Current Liabilities	2m	240	272

Elevation Learning Ltd

32 York Road, Sutton, SM2 6HH
Tel: 020-8642 9568 **Fax:** 020-8643 0443
E-mail: info@cst-ltd.co.uk
Website: http://www.cst-ltd.co.uk
Directors: C. Markham (MD)
Immediate Holding Company: ELEVATION LEARNING LIMITED
Registration no: 02439481 **Date established:** 1989
Turnover: £250,000 - £500,000 **No.of Employees:** 1 - 10
Product Groups: 86

Date of Accounts	Dec 11	Dec 10	Dec 09
Sales Turnover	383	370	805
Pre Tax Profit/Loss	N/A	4	18
Working Capital	44	51	61
Fixed Assets	1	1	N/A
Current Assets	71	107	235
Current Liabilities	13	27	105

First Assist Group Ltd (Head Office)

Marshalls Court Marshalls Road, Sutton, SM1 4DU
Tel: 0800-0721197 **Fax:** 020-8661 7604
E-mail: corporate.info@firstassit.co.uk
Website: http://www.firstassist.co.uk
Bank(s): National Westminster
Directors: A. Sutton (Fin), C. Jones (Mkt Research), M. Measures (Serv), P. Smith (Dir), T. Ablett (Grp Chief Exec), T. McAuliffe (Develop)
Managers: B. Morgan (Sales & Mktg Mg), J. Spur (I.T. Exec)
Immediate Holding Company: Firstassist Group Holdings Ltd
Registration no: 04617115 **VAT No.:** GB 165 0008 01
Date established: 2002 **Turnover:** £10m - £20m
No.of Employees: 251 - 500 **Product Groups:** 54, 80, 81, 82, 86

Date of Accounts	Dec 09	Dec 08	Dec 07
Pre Tax Profit/Loss	-6m	-7m	-7m
Working Capital	-9m	-9m	-7m
Fixed Assets	76m	76m	76m
Current Assets	28m	28m	28m
Current Liabilities	28	127	22

G 4 S Cash Solutions

Sutton Park House 15 Carshalton Road, Sutton, SM1 4LD
Tel: 020-8770 7000 **Fax:** 020-8643 1059
Website: http://www.g4s.co.uk
Directors: J. Alston (Fin), N. Buckles (Grp Chief Exec), J. Phillip-Sorensen (Ch), I. Nisbett (MD)
Managers: K. Groenenboom (Mktg Serv Mgr), M. Peacock (Mktg Serv Mgr)
Ultimate Holding Company: G4S PLC
Immediate Holding Company: G4S CASH SOLUTIONS (UK) LIMITED
Registration no: 00354883 **Date established:** 1939
Turnover: £250m - £500m **No.of Employees:** 1 - 10 **Product Groups:** 72, 79

Date of Accounts	Dec 11	Dec 10	Dec 09
Sales Turnover	267m	292m	307m
Pre Tax Profit/Loss	-1m	3m	20m
Working Capital	23m	87m	96m
Fixed Assets	136m	138m	134m
Current Assets	110m	199m	193m
Current Liabilities	25m	48m	50m

Grahams The Plumbers Merchants

Minden Road Kimpton Trade Centre 38 Kimpton Road, Sutton, SM3 9QP
Tel: 020-8644 6083 **Fax:** 020-8644 3389
E-mail: david.godden@sgbd.co.uk
Website: http://www.graham-group.co.uk
Managers: D. Godden (Mgr)
Immediate Holding Company: LAMPS AND TUBES DIRECT LTD
Registration no: 00066738 **Date established:** 2003
Turnover: £250m - £500m **No.of Employees:** 1 - 10 **Product Groups:** 66

Date of Accounts	Jul 11	Jul 10	Jul 09
Working Capital	58	57	53
Current Assets	59	61	61
Current Liabilities	1	N/A	N/A

H J Golding Ltd

Capital House 38 Kimpton Road, Sutton, SM3 9QP
Tel: 020-8641 3300 **Fax:** 020-8641 7260
E-mail: sales@goldingltd.co.uk
Website: http://www.goldingltd.co.uk
Directors: B. Capper (Ptnr)
Immediate Holding Company: H. J. GOLDING & CO. LTD.
Registration no: 04179211 **VAT No.:** GB 235 6045 75
Date established: 2001 **Turnover:** £2m - £5m **No.of Employees:** 11 - 20
Product Groups: 77

Date of Accounts	Jan 12	Jan 11	Jan 10
Working Capital	159	160	178
Current Assets	202	210	249

I C I S

Quadrant House The Quadrant Brighton Road, Sutton, SM2 5AS
Tel: 020-8652 3335 **Fax:** 020-8652 3924
E-mail: firstname.secondname@rbi.co.uk
Website: http://www.icis.com
Bank(s): National Westminster Bank Plc
Directors: K. Jones (Grp Chief Exec)
Ultimate Holding Company: REED ELSEVIER GROUP PLC
Immediate Holding Company: FORMPART (LPR) LIMITED
Registration no: 01957834 **Date established:** 1980
Turnover: £10m - £20m **No.of Employees:** 51 - 100 **Product Groups:** 54, 66, 80, 81, 82

Date of Accounts	Dec 11	Dec 10	Dec 03
Working Capital	408	408	381
Fixed Assets	N/A	N/A	26
Current Assets	408	408	381

I M C D UK Ltd

Times House Throwley Way, Sutton, SM1 4AF
Tel: 020-8770 7090 **Fax:** 020-8770 7295
E-mail: info@imcd.co.uk
Website: http://www.imcdgroup.com
Bank(s): Lloyds TSB Bank plc
Directors: J. Robinson (MD), A. Patel (Fin)
Managers: T. Hoyle (Tech Serv Mgr), D. Dromey (Personnel)
Ultimate Holding Company: IMCD HOLDING BV (NETHERLANDS)
Immediate Holding Company: IMCD UK LIMITED
Registration no: 02297809 **VAT No.:** GB 385 7516 14
Date established: 1988 **Turnover:** £125m - £250m
No.of Employees: 51 - 100 **Product Groups:** 31

Date of Accounts	Dec 11	Dec 10	Dec 09
Sales Turnover	177m	157m	132m
Pre Tax Profit/Loss	7m	7m	5m
Working Capital	26m	21m	16m
Fixed Assets	10m	11m	11m
Current Assets	46m	42m	34m
Current Liabilities	7m	9m	7m

Immersive Media Ltd

56 Frederick Road, Sutton, SM1 2HU
Tel: 020-8401 1278
E-mail: info@immersivemedia.co.uk
Website: http://www.immersivemedia.co.uk
Directors: J. Roberts (Fin), B. Rogan (MD)
Immediate Holding Company: IMMERSIVE MEDIA LTD
Registration no: 05345080 **Date established:** 2005
Turnover: Up to £250,000 **No.of Employees:** 1 - 10 **Product Groups:** 44, 81

Date of Accounts	Jan 11	Jan 10	Jan 09
Sales Turnover	97	79	20
Pre Tax Profit/Loss	3	-6	-2
Working Capital	-14	-16	-10
Current Assets	3	1	2
Current Liabilities	14	4	3

Krauthammer International Ltd

Orion House 19 Cedar Road, Sutton, SM2 5DA
Tel: 020-8770 7200 **Fax:** 020-8770 7748
E-mail: info@krauthammer.com
Website: http://www.krauthammer.com
Directors: B. Saunders (Fin)
Ultimate Holding Company: KRAUTHAMMER INVESTMENTS HOLDING BV (THE NETHERLANDS)
Immediate Holding Company: KRAUTHAMMER INTERNATIONAL LIMITED
Registration no: 02670293 **Date established:** 1991
Turnover: £500,000 - £1m **No.of Employees:** 1 - 10 **Product Groups:** 80, 86

Date of Accounts	Dec 10	Dec 09	Dec 08
Sales Turnover	947	784	800
Pre Tax Profit/Loss	119	55	-335
Working Capital	-554	-772	-825
Fixed Assets	3	5	3
Current Assets	335	199	68
Current Liabilities	137	99	133

Magnetic Separations Ltd

14 Meadowside Road, Sutton, SM2 7PF
Tel: 020-8642 4413 **Fax:** 020-8642 9476
E-mail: info@magneticseparations.com
Website: http://www.magneticseparations.com
Directors: P. Gibbard (Dir)
Immediate Holding Company: MAGNETIC SEPARATIONS LIMITED
Registration no: 01493159 **VAT No.:** GB 317 9763 24
Date established: 1980 **Turnover:** £2m - £5m **No.of Employees:** 1 - 10
Product Groups: 34, 37, 42

Date of Accounts	Apr 11	Apr 10	Apr 09
Working Capital	448	225	204
Fixed Assets	15	19	10
Current Assets	661	352	368

Mardev

Quadrant House The Quadrant Brighton Road, Sutton, SM2 5AS
Tel: 020-8652 3899 **Fax:** 020-8652 4597
E-mail: enquiries@mardevdm2.com
Website: http://www.mardevdm2.com
Directors: Z. Manda (Dir)
Managers: A. Balink (Sales Admin), Z. Taylor
Ultimate Holding Company: REED ELSEVIER GROUP PLC
Immediate Holding Company: FORMPART (CWC) LIMITED
Registration no: 00663674 **Date established:** 2000
No.of Employees: 11 - 20 **Product Groups:** 38, 81

Mekon Ltd

Mekon House 31-35 St Nicholas Way, Sutton, SM1 1JN
Tel: 020-8722 8400 **Fax:** 020-8722 8500
E-mail: info@mekon.com
Website: http://www.mekon.com
Directors: J. Murfitt (MD)
Managers: R. Kalama (Sales Admin)
Immediate Holding Company: MEKON LTD.
Registration no: 02545311 **Date established:** 1990
No.of Employees: 21 - 50 **Product Groups:** 81

Date of Accounts	Sep 11	Sep 10	Sep 09
Working Capital	135	42	150
Fixed Assets	15	90	12
Current Assets	320	323	405

Metalbor Ltd

10 Sandiford Road, Sutton, SM3 9RS
Tel: 020-8641 7788 **Fax:** 020-8641 5511
E-mail: sales@metalbor.com
Website: http://www.metalbor.com
Directors: L. Evans (MD)
Immediate Holding Company: METALBOR LIMITED
Registration no: 00422110 **Date established:** 1946 **Turnover:** £1m - £2m
No.of Employees: 1 - 10 **Product Groups:** 46

Date of Accounts	Apr 11	Apr 10	Apr 09
Working Capital	873	793	765
Fixed Assets	217	230	244
Current Assets	2m	1m	1m

Motor Transport At Reed Business Information (A member of the Reed Elsevier plc group)

Quadrant House The Quadrant, Sutton, SM2 5AS
Tel: 020-8652 3714 **Fax:** 020-8652 3793
E-mail: s.hobson@rbi.co.uk
Website: http://www.roadtransport.com
Directors: D. Feltham (MD), J. Brighouse (MD), J. Muttram (MD), M. Kelsey (Grp Chief Exec), J. Burgess (MD)
Managers: N. Cahill, S. Hobson, C. Pickering (Comptroller)
Immediate Holding Company: REED BUSINESS INFORMATION LIMITED
Registration no: 00151537 **VAT No.:** GB 235 7235 65
Date established: 1918 **Turnover:** £125m - £250m
No.of Employees: 1 - 10 **Product Groups:** 28

Date of Accounts	Dec 09	Dec 08	Dec 07
Sales Turnover	208m	233m	237m
Pre Tax Profit/Loss	-4m	12m	28m
Working Capital	294m	271m	268m
Fixed Assets	158m	181m	167m
Current Assets	417m	405m	423m
Current Liabilities	73m	73m	93m

Ocean Technical Systems Ltd

Oceantech House Station Approach, Cheam, Sutton, SM2 7AU
Tel: 020-8722 6910 **Fax:** 020-8643 6444
E-mail: dmartin@oceantechsys.com
Website: http://www.oceantechsys.co.uk
Directors: T. Helz (Co Sec), D. Martin (MD)
Ultimate Holding Company: COOPER CONTROLS (U.K.) LIMITED
Immediate Holding Company: OCEAN TECHNICAL SYSTEMS LIMITED
Registration no: 01501658 **Date established:** 1980 **Turnover:** £2m - £5m
No.of Employees: 11 - 20 **Product Groups:** 37, 38, 44, 45

Date of Accounts	Dec 11	Dec 10	Dec 09
Sales Turnover	4m	3m	4m
Pre Tax Profit/Loss	929	852	1m
Working Capital	4m	3m	2m
Fixed Assets	22	24	27
Current Assets	5m	4m	3m
Current Liabilities	618	443	539

Pioneer Air Systems Ltd

19 Ewell Road, Sutton, SM3 8DD
Tel: 020-8642 1878 **Fax:** 020-8642 1734
Directors: T. Talib (MD)
Registration no: 02961810 **Date established:** 1994
No.of Employees: 1 - 10 **Product Groups:** 40, 66

Preco Ltd

3 Four Seasons Crescent Kimpton Road, Sutton, SM3 9QR
Tel: 020-8644 4447 **Fax:** 020-8644 0474
E-mail: info@preco.co.uk
Website: http://www.preco.co.uk
Managers: J. Thomas
Immediate Holding Company: PRECO (BROADCAST SYSTEMS) LIMITED
Registration no: 01736815 **VAT No.:** GB 318 5378 41
Date established: 1983 **Turnover:** £5m - £10m **No.of Employees:** 1 - 10
Product Groups: 37

Date of Accounts	Sep 11	Sep 10	Sep 09
Working Capital	35	62	-21
Fixed Assets	2	3	136
Current Assets	189	496	295

Reed Specialist Recruitment

117 High Street, Sutton, SM1 1JF
Tel: 020-8643 6331 **Fax:** 020-8640 8446
E-mail: morden@reed.co.uk
Website: http://www.reed.co.uk
Managers: P. Perry (Mgr)
Ultimate Holding Company: REED GLOBAL LTD (MALTA)
Immediate Holding Company: REED EMPLOYMENT LIMITED
Registration no: 00669854 **Date established:** 1960
Turnover: £75m - £125m **No.of Employees:** 1 - 10 **Product Groups:** 80

Date of Accounts	Jun 11	Jun 10	Dec 07
Sales Turnover	618	450	287m
Pre Tax Profit/Loss	-2m	310	8m
Working Capital	23m	28m	28m
Fixed Assets	31	36	5m
Current Assets	28m	30m	74m
Current Liabilities	37	29	21m

Semi Conductor Supplies International Ltd

128-130 Carshalton Road, Sutton, SM1 4TW
Tel: 020-8643 1126 **Fax:** 020-8643 3937
E-mail: sales@ssi-uk.com
Website: http://www.ssi-uk.com
Bank(s): Coutts
Directors: J. Hawkins (Fin)
Immediate Holding Company: SEMICONDUCTOR STOCKHOLDERS LIMITED
Registration no: 01045192 **VAT No.:** GB 218 2453 76
Date established: 1972 **Turnover:** Up to £250,000
No.of Employees: 11 - 20 **Product Groups:** 44

Date of Accounts	Apr 12	Apr 11	Apr 10
Sales Turnover	26	84	280
Pre Tax Profit/Loss	-2	14	6
Working Capital	245	268	268
Fixed Assets	435	433	436
Current Assets	252	271	300
Current Liabilities	7	4	19

Tomy International

St Nicholas House St Nicholas Road, Sutton, SM1 1EH
Tel: 020-8722 7300
E-mail: robert.mann@tomy.co.uk
Website: http://www.tomy.co.uk
Managers: S. Mills, J. Gray (Mktg Serv Mgr), P. Nicholson (Tech Serv Mgr), G. Hunter
Ultimate Holding Company: TOMY COMPANY LTD (JAPAN)
Immediate Holding Company: TOMY UK LIMITED
Registration no: 01685312 **Date established:** 1982
Turnover: £20m - £50m **No.of Employees:** 21 - 50 **Product Groups:** 65

Date of Accounts	Mar 11	Mar 10	Mar 09
Sales Turnover	48m	49m	43m
Pre Tax Profit/Loss	-1m	925	-996
Working Capital	7m	7m	6m
Fixed Assets	4m	5m	5m
Current Assets	19m	20m	22m
Current Liabilities	2m	5m	3m

Tyco Electronics UK Ltd

Faraday Road, Sutton, SM3 5HH
Tel: 01793-528171 **Fax:** 01793-572629
E-mail: picuk@tycoelectronics.com
Website: http://www.tycoelectronics.com
Bank(s): Barclays, London
Directors: P. Sirs (Sales), T. Gatt (MD), A. Clarke (Dir)
Managers: J. Roberts (Sales Prom Mgr), C. Ockwell (Purch Mgr), J. O'Brian (Purch Mgr)
Ultimate Holding Company: TE CONNECTIVITY LTD (SWITZERLAND)
Immediate Holding Company: TYCO ELECTRONICS UK LTD
Registration no: 00550926 **VAT No.:** GB 681 4714 25
Date established: 1955 **Turnover:** £125m - £250m
No.of Employees: 501 - 1000 **Product Groups:** 35, 36, 37, 38, 39, 40, 41, 42, 44, 45, 46, 47, 48, 63, 67, 68, 85

Date of Accounts	Sep 10	Sep 09	Sep 08
Pre Tax Profit/Loss	15	-3m	-674
Working Capital	-13m	-13m	-13m

see next page

Tyco Electronics UK Ltd - Cont'd

Fixed Assets	71m	71m	74m
Current Assets	15m	15m	15m

Tadworth

D E P

Frith Park Sturts Lane, Walton On The Hill, Tadworth, KT20 7NQ
Tel: 01737-813517 **Fax:** 01737-813442
E-mail: cep@frithpark.com
Website: http://www.frithpark.com
Directors: C. Kahn (Fin)
Managers: J. Knight (Sales Admin)
Immediate Holding Company: D.E.P.
Registration no: 00392866 **Date established:** 1945
Turnover: £250,000 - £500,000 **No.of Employees:** 1 - 10
Product Groups: 27, 30

Doux Poultry Ltd

2nd Floor Office Suite Millfield, Dorking Road, Tadworth, KT20 7TD
Tel: 00-33 298866880 **Fax:** 01737-814008
E-mail: doux.poultry@doux.com
Website: http://www.doux.com
Managers: A. Dolden (Sales Admin), P. Poux
Registration no: 01380609 **Turnover:** £20m - £50m
No.of Employees: 1 - 10 **Product Groups:** 20

Drill Supply Ltd

41 Green Lane Lower Kingswood, Tadworth, KT20 6TJ
Tel: 01737-832820 **Fax:** 01737-833025
E-mail: drillsupply@onetel.com
Directors: J. Eason (MD)
Immediate Holding Company: DRILL SUPPLY LIMITED
Registration no: 01287627 **VAT No.:** GB 293 7216 39
Date established: 1976 **Turnover:** £1m - £2m **No.of Employees:** 1 - 10
Product Groups: 45

Date of Accounts	Sep 11	Sep 10	Sep 09
Working Capital	2	9	15
Fixed Assets	1	1	1
Current Assets	12	19	34

Duval Products Storage Equipment Ltd

80 Brighton Road Lower Kingswood, Tadworth, KT20 6SY
Tel: 08454-707088 **Fax:** 01737-830 323
E-mail: sales@duvalproducts.co.uk
Website: http://www.duvalproducts.co.uk
Directors: S. Kippen (MD)
Immediate Holding Company: DUVAL PRODUCTS STORAGE EQUIPMENT LIMITED
Registration no: 07449435 **VAT No.:** GB 216 0814 92
Date established: 2010 **Turnover:** £500,000 - £1m
No.of Employees: 1 - 10 **Product Groups:** 26

Date of Accounts	Mar 12
Working Capital	16
Fixed Assets	10
Current Assets	389

Kir Consultants

23 Kingswood Grange Babylon, Lower Kingswood, Tadworth, KT20 6UY
Tel: 0845-643 1650
E-mail: kir@kirconsultants.com
Website: http://www.kirconsultants.com
Directors: A. Cook (Fin)
Immediate Holding Company: KIR CONSULTANTS LTD
Registration no: 06169283 **Date established:** 2007
Turnover: Up to £250,000 **No.of Employees:** 1 - 10 **Product Groups:** 80

Merlin Catering Equipment Ltd

17 Vernon Walk, Tadworth, KT20 5QP
Tel: 01737-359415 **Fax:** 01737-371119
Directors: G. Smith (MD), C. Smith (Fin)
Immediate Holding Company: MERLIN CATERING EQUIPMENT LIMITED
Registration no: 04002670 **Date established:** 2000
No.of Employees: 1 - 10 **Product Groups:** 20, 40, 41

Date of Accounts	Mar 09	Mar 08	Mar 07
Working Capital	4	-6	-8
Fixed Assets	1	N/A	N/A
Current Assets	50	38	58

Pobjoy Mint Ltd

Millennia House Kingswood Park, Kingswood, Tadworth, KT20 6AY
Tel: 01737-818181 **Fax:** 01737-818199
E-mail: sales@pobjoy.com
Website: http://www.pobjoy.com
Directors: T. Pobjoy (MD), T. Pobjoy (MD)
Managers: J. Smith, M. Aldridge, T. Warner (Chief Acct)
Ultimate Holding Company: DEREK POBJOY INVESTMENTS LIMITED
Immediate Holding Company: POBJOY MINT LIMITED
Registration no: 00509935 **Date established:** 1952 **Turnover:** £5m - £10m
No.of Employees: 21 - 50 **Product Groups:** 49

Date of Accounts	Dec 11	Dec 10	Dec 09
Working Capital	-2m	-1m	-872
Fixed Assets	215	241	226
Current Assets	1m	659	1m

C F Sparrowhawk Ltd

24 Epsom Lane North, Tadworth, KT20 5EH
Tel: 01737-352889 **Fax:** 01737-371088
E-mail: cfsparrowhawkltd@btconnect.com
Directors: W. Pile (MD)
Immediate Holding Company: C.F.SPARROWHAWK LIMITED
Registration no: 00629391 **Date established:** 1959
Turnover: £500,000 - £1m **No.of Employees:** 1 - 10 **Product Groups:** 66

Date of Accounts	Jun 11	Jun 10	Jun 09
Working Capital	170	243	179
Fixed Assets	382	388	396
Current Assets	432	463	334

Travis Perkins plc

Heathside House Brighton Road, Burgh Heath, Tadworth, KT20 6BE
Tel: 01737-362111 **Fax:** 01737-370476
E-mail: burghheath@travisperkins.co.uk
Website: http://www.travisperkins.co.uk
Managers: M. Pope (Mgr)
Immediate Holding Company: TRAVIS PERKINS PLC
Registration no: 00824821 **VAT No.:** GB 408 5567 37
Date established: 1964 **Turnover:** £75m - £125m
No.of Employees: 1 - 10 **Product Groups:** 66

Date of Accounts	Dec 11	Dec 10	Dec 09
Sales Turnover	4779m	3153m	2931m
Pre Tax Profit/Loss	270m	197m	213m
Working Capital	133m	159m	248m
Fixed Assets	2771m	2749m	2108m
Current Assets	1421m	1329m	1035m
Current Liabilities	473m	412m	109m

Thames Ditton

Expo Technologies Ltd

Unit 1 Hampton Court Estate Summer Road, Thames Ditton, KT7 0RH
Tel: 020-8398 8011 **Fax:** 020-8398 8014
E-mail: sales@expoworldwide.com
Website: http://www.expoworldwide.com
Bank(s): The Royal Bank of Scotland
Directors: A. Nissen (Co Sec), P. Macaulay (MD), S. Wells (Fin)
Managers: C. Murray (Personnel)
Ultimate Holding Company: TELEKTRON (HOLDINGS) LIMITED
Immediate Holding Company: EXPO TECHNOLOGIES LIMITED
Registration no: 02854600 **VAT No.:** GB 674 1149 34
Date established: 1993 **Turnover:** £5m - £10m
No.of Employees: 51 - 100 **Product Groups:** 37, 38, 40, 44

Date of Accounts	Oct 11	Oct 10	Oct 09
Sales Turnover	7m	6m	7m
Pre Tax Profit/Loss	960	857	1m
Working Capital	2m	2m	904
Fixed Assets	70	60	46
Current Assets	3m	3m	2m
Current Liabilities	674	625	715

Pier32 Ltd

32 The Island, Thames Ditton, KT7 0SQ
Tel: 020-8398 2847 **Fax:** 020-8398 2867
E-mail: team@pier32.co.uk
Website: http://www.pier32.co.uk
Directors: V. Hayter (Fin), I. Johnson (Dir)
Immediate Holding Company: PIER 32 LTD
Registration no: 04748676 **Date established:** 2003
No.of Employees: 1 - 10 **Product Groups:** 23, 24, 49

Date of Accounts	Apr 11	Apr 10	Apr 09
Working Capital	26	37	35
Fixed Assets	4	6	10
Current Assets	47	59	72

S H L Group Ltd

The Pavilion 1 Atwell Place, Thames Ditton, KT7 0NE
Tel: 020-8335 8000 **Fax:** 020-8398 9544
E-mail: david.leigh@shl.com
Website: http://www.shl.com
Directors: S. Barrett (Co Sec), S. Barrett (Fin), J. Bateson (Grp Chief Exec), C. Sandham (Ch), D. Leigh (Grp Chief Exec), K. Kerrigan (Reg MD), N. Bain (Ch)
Managers: C. Emms (Mktg Serv Mgr)
Ultimate Holding Company: SHL GROUP HOLDINGS 1 LTD
Immediate Holding Company: SHL GROUP LIMITED
Registration no: 01328744 **Date established:** 1977
Turnover: £20m - £50m **No.of Employees:** 251 - 500
Product Groups: 80, 86

Date of Accounts	Dec 10	Dec 09	Dec 08
Sales Turnover	24m	20m	26m
Pre Tax Profit/Loss	14m	-12m	-2m
Working Capital	5m	-11m	-5m
Fixed Assets	30m	36m	44m
Current Assets	75m	48m	56m
Current Liabilities	15m	5m	8m

Wardray Premise Ltd

3 Hampton Court Estate Summer Road, Thames Ditton, KT7 0SP
Tel: 020-8398 9911 **Fax:** 020-8398 8032
E-mail: sales@wardray-premise.com
Website: http://www.wardray-premise.com
Bank(s): National Westminster
Directors: J. Colquhoun (Co Sec)
Managers: L. Edwards, D. Davies (Tech Serv Mgr), A. Tanner (Publicity)
Immediate Holding Company: WARDRAY PREMISE LIMITED
Registration no: 00347881 **VAT No.:** GB 234 5208 84
Date established: 1938 **Turnover:** £5m - £10m
No.of Employees: 51 - 100 **Product Groups:** 33, 37

Date of Accounts	Dec 11	Dec 10	Dec 09
Sales Turnover	6m	7m	6m
Pre Tax Profit/Loss	18	26	-361
Working Capital	840	790	725
Fixed Assets	994	1m	1m
Current Assets	2m	2m	2m
Current Liabilities	313	304	467

Thornton Heath

Catersales Ltd

119B Penshurst Road, Thornton Heath, CR7 7EF
Tel: 020-8684 6500 **Fax:** 020-8684 6686
E-mail: sales@catersales.co.uk
Website: http://www.catersales.co.uk
Directors: Y. Hasan (MD), G. Hasan (Fin)
Immediate Holding Company: CATERSALES LTD
Registration no: 03490989 **Date established:** 1998
Turnover: £500,000 - £1m **No.of Employees:** 1 - 10 **Product Groups:** 26, 36, 40, 41, 42, 63, 66, 67

Date of Accounts	Dec 11	Dec 10	Dec 09
Sales Turnover	628	522	480
Pre Tax Profit/Loss	-4	14	20
Working Capital	7	17	25
Fixed Assets	174	178	183
Current Assets	290	270	121
Current Liabilities	45	54	28

I C Cool Refrigeration

55 The Drive, Thornton Heath, CR7 8LB
Tel: 020-8771 3836 **Fax:** 020-8771 3836
E-mail: steve@rowlerson.co.uk
Website: http://www.iccool.co.uk
Directors: S. Rowlerson (Prop)
Turnover: Up to £250,000 **No.of Employees:** 1 - 10 **Product Groups:** 40, 52, 63, 67

Kemwall Engineering Co.

52 Bensham Grove, Thornton Heath, CR7 8DA
Tel: 020-8653 7111 **Fax:** 020-8653 9669
E-mail: sales@kemwall.co.uk
Website: http://www.kemwall.co.uk
Directors: N. Wallace (Dir)
Immediate Holding Company: W.J. WALLACE & CO. LTD
Registration no: 00581271 **Date established:** 1966
Turnover: £500,000 - £1m **No.of Employees:** 1 - 10 **Product Groups:** 37, 42, 46

N P D

29 Luna Road, Thornton Heath, CR7 8NZ
Tel: 020-8771 5111 **Fax:** 0845-1260612
E-mail: npd@npdandco.com
Website: http://www.npdandco.com
Directors: J. Smith (Ptnr), M. Smith (Ptnr), S. Metham (Prop)
Immediate Holding Company: NPD & COMPANY (UK) LIMITED
Registration no: 04248340 **Date established:** 2001
Turnover: Up to £250,000 **No.of Employees:** 1 - 10 **Product Groups:** 82

Savannah Estates Ltd

61 Bensham Grove Thornton Heath, Thornton Heath, CR7 8DD
Tel: 020-8771 2050 **Fax:** 020-8771 2051
E-mail: ed_dublin@hotmail.com
Website: http://www.savannahestates.co.uk
Directors: L. Dublin (Fin), E. Dublin (Dir)
Immediate Holding Company: SAVANNAH ESTATES LTD
Registration no: 05593741 **Date established:** 2005
Turnover: Up to £250,000 **No.of Employees:** 1 - 10 **Product Groups:** 44

Date of Accounts	Oct 11	Oct 10	Oct 09
Sales Turnover	16	35	36
Pre Tax Profit/Loss	2	1	-33
Working Capital	-126	-131	-134
Fixed Assets	21	24	26
Current Assets	2	1	N/A
Current Liabilities	2	124	124

Virginia Water

Wentworth Club Ltd

Wentworth Drive, Virginia Water, GU25 4LS
Tel: 01344-842201 **Fax:** 01344-842804
E-mail: reception@wentworthclub.com
Website: http://www.wentworthclub.com
Directors: T. Way (Sales), D. Keaney (Fin)
Managers: K. Dredge (Tech Serv Mgr), J. Pickess (Personnel), J. Maycock, A. Nicholson (Mktg Serv Mgr)
Ultimate Holding Company: WG ACQUISITION LIMITED (JERSEY)
Immediate Holding Company: WENTWORTH CLUB LIMITED
Registration no: 00201357 **VAT No.:** GB 666 2673 07
Date established: 2024 **Turnover:** £10m - £20m
No.of Employees: 101 - 250 **Product Groups:** 89

Date of Accounts	Mar 11	Mar 10	Mar 09
Sales Turnover	17m	14m	19m
Pre Tax Profit/Loss	2m	1m	5m
Working Capital	11m	7m	11m
Fixed Assets	29m	29m	27m
Current Assets	26m	21m	24m
Current Liabilities	10m	9m	8m

Wallington

Ascot International Footwear Ltd

Kingfisher House Restmor Way, Wallington, SM6 7AH
Tel: 020-8773 7800 **Fax:** 020-8773 7815
E-mail: sales@ascot-int.net
Website: http://www.ascot-int.net
Managers: M. Semhi, J. Smith (Sales Prom Mgr), J. Parry (Chief Acct)
Ultimate Holding Company: ASCOT TM LIMITED
Immediate Holding Company: ASCOT INTERNATIONAL FOOTWEAR LIMITED
Registration no: 06765271 **Date established:** 2008 **Turnover:** £5m - £10m
No.of Employees: 1 - 10 **Product Groups:** 22

Date of Accounts	Dec 11	Dec 10	Dec 09
Working Capital	-0	-0	-0

B T S Holdings plc

69-73 Manor Road Manor Road, Wallington, SM6 0DD
Tel: 020-8401 9000 **Fax:** 020-8401 9101
E-mail: info@bts.co.uk
Website: http://www.bts.co.uk
Managers: I. Wright (Comptroller), J. Kendall (Mgr), C. Lawrence (Buyer)
Immediate Holding Company: BTS HOLDINGS PLC
Registration no: 01517630 **Date established:** 1980 **Turnover:** £2m - £5m
No.of Employees: 21 - 50 **Product Groups:** 37, 38, 80

Date of Accounts	Mar 12	Mar 11	Mar 10
Sales Turnover	2m	3m	3m
Pre Tax Profit/Loss	288	388	420
Working Capital	733	746	745
Fixed Assets	886	938	918
Current Assets	2m	2m	2m
Current Liabilities	1m	1m	1m

Bathstore.com Ltd

Unit 2a Felnex Trading Estate, Wallington, SM6 7EL
Tel: 01923-694740 **Fax:** 020-8773 5004
E-mail: enquiries@bathstore.com
Website: http://www.bathstore.com

Directors: D. Riley (Co Sec)
Ultimate Holding Company: WOLSELEY PLC (JERSEY)
Immediate Holding Company: BATHSTORE.COM LIMITED
Registration no: 02240475 **Date established:** 1988
Turnover: £10m - £20m **No.of Employees:** 51 - 100 **Product Groups:** 25, 30, 33, 36

Date of Accounts	Jul 11	Jul 10	Jul 09
Sales Turnover	94m	109m	107m
Pre Tax Profit/Loss	2m	10m	-12m
Working Capital	3m	-3m	-548
Fixed Assets	13m	17m	22m
Current Assets	36m	36m	36m
Current Liabilities	6m	7m	10m

Booth Signs
43-45 Stafford Road, Wallington, SM6 9AP
Tel: 020-8669 1625 **Fax:** 020-8773 3429
E-mail: boothsigns@btinternet.com
Directors: G. Booth (Prop)
Immediate Holding Company: BOOTH SIGNS
VAT No.: GB 218 0181 93 **Date established:** 1959
Turnover: Up to £250,000 **No.of Employees:** 1 - 10 **Product Groups:** 28, 52

Insignia Ltd
5-6 Chalice Close, Wallington, SM6 9RU
Tel: 020-8669 3122 **Fax:** 020-8669 7192
E-mail: sales@insigniauk.com
Website: http://www.insigniauk.com
Directors: C. Appleton (MD), D. Appleton (Fin)
Immediate Holding Company: INSIGNIA LIMITED
Registration no: 01564168 **VAT No.:** GB 344 9079 34
Date established: 1981 **Turnover:** £1m - £2m **No.of Employees:** 1 - 10
Product Groups: 23, 24, 30, 40, 49

Date of Accounts	Dec 11	Dec 10	Dec 09
Working Capital	16	14	33
Fixed Assets	1	2	3
Current Assets	105	114	134

M P S Joinery Ltd
Danbury Mews, Wallington, SM6 0BY
Tel: 020-8773 0451 **Fax:** 020-8773 1942
Directors: M. Smitherman (MD)
Immediate Holding Company: MPS JOINERY LTD
Registration no: 07754303 **VAT No.:** GB 523 6220 78
Date established: 2011 **Turnover:** Up to £250,000
No.of Employees: 1 - 10 **Product Groups:** 52

Mentor Lock & Safe Co.
58 Stafford Road, Wallington, SM6 9AY
Tel: 020-8669 7034
E-mail: lee@mentorlock.co.uk
Website: http://www.mentorlock.co.uk
Directors: L. Macdonald (Prop)
Immediate Holding Company: MENTOR LOCK LTD
Registration no: 07152528 **Date established:** 2010
Turnover: Up to £250,000 **No.of Employees:** 1 - 10 **Product Groups:** 34, 52, 66, 86

Date of Accounts	Feb 12	Feb 11
Sales Turnover	37	40
Pre Tax Profit/Loss	3	13
Working Capital	-4	N/A
Current Assets	1	4
Current Liabilities	5	4

Monument Tools Ltd
Restmor Way, Wallington, SM6 7AH
Tel: 020-8288 1100 **Fax:** 020-8288 1108
E-mail: jonathan@monument-tools.com
Website: http://www.monument-tools.com
Bank(s): HSBC, Brixton Road, SW9 8ER
Directors: J. Collier (MD), J. Collier (MD)
Managers: T. Tedder (Buyer), B. Marsh (Sales Prom Mgr)
Immediate Holding Company: MONUMENT TOOLS LIMITED
Registration no: 00281817 **VAT No.:** GB 217 8102 81
Date established: 1933 **Turnover:** £2m - £5m **No.of Employees:** 21 - 50
Product Groups: 36, 38, 40

Date of Accounts	Mar 11	Mar 10	Mar 09
Working Capital	2m	2m	2m
Fixed Assets	1m	1m	1m
Current Assets	3m	3m	3m

P P M A Ltd
34 Stafford Road, Wallington, SM6 9AA
Tel: 020-8773 8111 **Fax:** 020-8773 0022
E-mail: administration@ppma.co.uk
Website: http://www.ppma.co.uk
Directors: A. Manly (Fin)
Managers: D. Chadd
Immediate Holding Company: P.P.M.A. LIMITED
Registration no: 02116954 **VAT No.:** GB 452 2698 38
Date established: 1987 **Turnover:** £2m - £5m **No.of Employees:** 1 - 10
Product Groups: 81, 84, 85, 87

Date of Accounts	Mar 11	Mar 10	Mar 09
Working Capital	224	69	146
Fixed Assets	712	716	778
Current Assets	1m	664	618

Pool Filtration Ltd
76 Stafford Road, Wallington, SM6 9AY
Tel: 020-8669 0657 **Fax:** 020-8773 0647
E-mail: poolfiltrationltd@tiscali.co.uk
Website: http://www.poolfiltration.com
Directors: I. Smith (MD), S. Smith (Fin)
Immediate Holding Company: POOL FILTRATION LIMITED
Registration no: 01678936 **VAT No.:** GB 372 6687 17
Date established: 1982 **Turnover:** £250,000 - £500,000
No.of Employees: 1 - 10 **Product Groups:** 35, 38, 65

Date of Accounts	Jan 12	Jan 11	Jan 09
Working Capital	88	107	138
Fixed Assets	16	16	27
Current Assets	195	224	194
Current Liabilities	56	N/A	N/A

Porter Foods
270 London Road, Wallington, SM6 7DJ
Tel: 020-8669 3131 **Fax:** 020-8669 7747
E-mail: info@porterfoods.co.uk
Website: http://www.porterfoods.co.uk

Managers: M. Patton (Mgr)
Registration no: 02059565 **No.of Employees:** 11 - 20
Product Groups: 02, 09, 20, 32, 62

Date of Accounts	Mar 07	Mar 06
Working Capital	-14	-71
Fixed Assets	78	86
Current Assets	466	443
Current Liabilities	479	514
Total Share Capital	5	5

Regal Signs & Graphics
2 Restmor Way, Wallington, SM6 7AH
Tel: 020-8835 2332 **Fax:** 020-8835 2326
E-mail: sales@regalsigns.co.uk
Website: http://www.regalsigns.co.uk
Directors: M. Lewis (Prop)
Immediate Holding Company: SCOTT FIRTH LIMITED
Registration no: 04529983 **Date established:** 2007
Turnover: £250,000 - £500,000 **No.of Employees:** 1 - 10
Product Groups: 30, 39, 40

Date of Accounts	Mar 12	Mar 11	Mar 10
Working Capital	-1	7	12
Fixed Assets	7	N/A	N/A
Current Assets	18	20	24

The Sourcing Team Ltd
The Parade Stafford Road, Wallington, SM6 8ND
Tel: 020-8288 8277 **Fax:** 020-8288 8278
E-mail: info@sourcing.co.uk
Website: http://www.sourcing.co.uk
Directors: G. Thorpe (MD)
Immediate Holding Company: THE SOURCING TEAM LIMITED
Registration no: 03199616 **Date established:** 1996
No.of Employees: 1 - 10 **Product Groups:** 22, 24, 25, 27, 28, 29, 30, 32, 49, 65, 77, 80, 81, 87, 89

Date of Accounts	May 12	May 11	May 10
Working Capital	-75	-50	-103
Fixed Assets	248	253	258
Current Assets	254	234	184

Surrey Guns
7 Manor Road, Wallington, SM6 0BW
Tel: 020-8647 7742 **Fax:** 020-8669 9199
E-mail: pfriend@surreyguns.com
Website: http://www.surreyguns.com
Directors: P. Friend (Prop)
Date established: 1953 **No.of Employees:** 1 - 10 **Product Groups:** 36, 39, 40

Target Display Pack Ltd
16 Harcourt Field, Wallington, SM6 8BA
Tel: 020-8395 2401 **Fax:** 020-8647 6800
Directors: B. Smith (MD)
Immediate Holding Company: TARGET DISPLAYPACK LIMITED
Registration no: 02513822 **Date established:** 1990
Turnover: Up to £250,000 **No.of Employees:** 1 - 10 **Product Groups:** 38, 42

Date of Accounts	Jun 05	Jun 04	Jun 03
Sales Turnover	28	26	25
Pre Tax Profit/Loss	-1	2	-1
Working Capital	-0	1	N/A
Current Assets	11	3	6
Current Liabilities	5	N/A	N/A

Wallington Lift Co. Ltd
11 Lakeside, Wallington, SM6 7JY
Tel: 020-8647 7045 **Fax:** 020-8773 4989
E-mail: info@wallingtonlifts.co.uk
Website: http://www.wallingtonlifts.co.uk
Directors: J. O'brien (MD)
Immediate Holding Company: WALLINGTON LIFT MAINTENANCE CO. LIMITED
Registration no: 01116169 **Date established:** 1973
Turnover: Up to £250,000 **No.of Employees:** 1 - 10 **Product Groups:** 35, 39, 45

R A Watts Ltd
36-38 Woodcote Road, Wallington, SM6 0NN
Tel: 020-8647 1074 **Fax:** 020-8773 3595
E-mail: sales@rawatts.fsbusiness.co.uk
Website: http://www.rawatts.co.uk
Directors: T. Partridge (MD)
Immediate Holding Company: R.A.WATTS LIMITED
Registration no: 00525155 **VAT No.:** GB 218 4939 40
Date established: 1953 **Turnover:** £2m - £5m **No.of Employees:** 1 - 10
Product Groups: 61

Date of Accounts	Mar 11	Mar 10	Mar 09
Working Capital	48	28	28
Current Assets	217	224	289

Walton On Thames

A M C Locksmiths
1 Milton Road, Walton On Thames, KT12 3HB
Tel: 01932-242101 **Fax:** 01932-226922
E-mail: amc.locksmiths@virgin.net
Website: http://www.surreylocksmiths.co.uk
Directors: S. Mcmahon (Prop)
No.of Employees: 1 - 10 **Product Groups:** 36, 48, 52, 66

Acuity Solutions Ltd
34 Mosey Road Hersham, Walton On Thames, KT12 4RQ
Tel: 01932-237110 **Fax:** 01932-237111
E-mail: info@acuitysolutions.co.uk
Website: http://www.acuitysolutions.co.uk
Directors: L. Whelan (MD), I. Whelan (Fin)
Immediate Holding Company: ACUITY SOLUTIONS LIMITED
Registration no: 03197329 **Date established:** 1996
No.of Employees: 21 - 50 **Product Groups:** 44

Date of Accounts	Apr 11	Apr 10	Apr 09
Working Capital	20	79	14
Fixed Assets	165	11	34
Current Assets	639	750	601
Current Liabilities	358	N/A	N/A

Akzo Nobel Chemicals Holdings Ltd (Sales Office)
1-5 Queens Road Hersham, Walton On Thames, KT12 5LT
Tel: 01932-247891 **Fax:** 01932-231204
Website: http://www.akzonobel.com
Directors: D. Turner (Dir), K. Van-Neerop (MD)
Immediate Holding Company: AKZO NOBEL CHEMICALS HOLDINGS LIMITED
Registration no: 01004893 **Date established:** 1971
Turnover: £75m - £125m **No.of Employees:** 1 - 10 **Product Groups:** 32

Alexander AC Ltd
Surrey House Pleasant Place Hersham, Walton On Thames, KT12 4HR
Tel: 01932-260609
E-mail: sales@alexanderair.co.uk
Website: http://www.alexanderair.co.uk
Directors: S. Lewis (MD)
Immediate Holding Company: ALEXANDER AC LIMITED
Registration no: 07096425 **Date established:** 2009
Turnover: Up to £250,000 **No.of Employees:** 1 - 10 **Product Groups:** 40, 66

Date of Accounts	Dec 11	Dec 10
Working Capital	-5	8
Current Assets	66	44

Ian Allan Publishing Ltd
Riverdene Business Park Molesey Road Persham, Walton On Thames, KT12 4RG
Tel: 01932-266600
E-mail: sales@ianallanpub.co.uk
Website: http://www.ianallanpub.co.uk
Bank(s): Barclays
Directors: B. Lucas (Publishing), D. Hart (Co Sec), D. Allan (Ch), I. Aitkin (MD), N. Lerwill (Fab)
Managers: N. Passmore (Sales & Mktg Mg)
Immediate Holding Company: Ian Allan Group Ltd
Registration no: 00400981 **Date established:** 1948 **Turnover:** £5m - £10m
No.of Employees: 51 - 100 **Product Groups:** 28, 44

Allegro Microsystems Europe Ltd
Balfour House Churchfield Road, Walton On Thames, KT12 2TD
Tel: 01932-253355 **Fax:** 01932-246622
E-mail: allegroeurope@allegromicro.com
Website: http://www.allegromicro.com
Bank(s): Barclays
Directors: A. Kimball (Dir), B. Pirie (Chief Op Offcr), B. Pirie (Dir), D. Fitzgerald (Dir), F. Windover (Co Sec), L. Fowler (Sales & Mktg), Y. Matsui (Dir)
Managers: S. Lightley (Chief Acct), L. Higgins (I.T. Exec), E. Higgins (Applic Eng)
Ultimate Holding Company: Sanken (Japan)
Immediate Holding Company: Allegro Microsystems Incorporated
Registration no: 02475901 **VAT No.:** GB 792 4278 95
Date established: 1990 **Turnover:** Over £1,000m
No.of Employees: 11 - 20 **Product Groups:** 37, 38, 39, 68

R M Brown
The Forge Rivernook Farm Sunnyside, Walton On Thames, KT12 2ET
Tel: 01932-220980
E-mail: ron@rmbrown.co.uk
Website: http://www.rmbrown.co.uk
Directors: R. Brown (Prop)
Date established: 1981 **No.of Employees:** 1 - 10 **Product Groups:** 26, 35

Cattron Theimeg UK Ltd
Riverdene Business Park Molesey Road, Hersham, Walton On Thames, KT12 4RG
Tel: 01932-247511 **Fax:** 01932-220937
E-mail: imartin@cattronuk.com
Website: http://www.cattron.com
Managers: D. Stagg (Sales Prom Mgr), D. Stagg (Chief Eng), I. Martin (Chief Mgr), S. Roberts (Purch Mgr)
Ultimate Holding Company: LAIRD PLC
Immediate Holding Company: CATTRON-THEIMEG (UK) LIMITED
Registration no: 00998151 **Date established:** 1970 **Turnover:** £1m - £2m
No.of Employees: 1 - 10 **Product Groups:** 37, 39

Date of Accounts	Sep 10	Sep 09	Sep 08
Sales Turnover	771	N/A	N/A
Pre Tax Profit/Loss	-15	N/A	N/A
Working Capital	436	442	505
Fixed Assets	6	15	15
Current Assets	526	487	591
Current Liabilities	82	N/A	N/A

Chase Organics
Molesey Road Hersham, Walton On Thames, KT12 4RG
Tel: 01932-253666 **Fax:** 01932-252707
E-mail: enquiries@chaseorganics.co.uk
Website: http://www.organicgardeningcatalogue.com
Bank(s): Barclays, Shepperton
Directors: D. Hart (Fin)
Ultimate Holding Company: IAN ALLAN GROUP LIMITED
Immediate Holding Company: CHASE ORGANICS (GREAT BRITAIN) LIMITED
Registration no: 00699325 **Date established:** 1961 **Turnover:** £1m - £2m
No.of Employees: 11 - 20 **Product Groups:** 20, 32

Date of Accounts	Nov 11	Nov 10	Nov 09
Sales Turnover	2m	2m	2m
Pre Tax Profit/Loss	205	85	122
Working Capital	861	723	652
Fixed Assets	25	14	16
Current Assets	1m	1m	957
Current Liabilities	75	100	125

Eland Engineering Company
29 Lyon Road, Walton On Thames, KT12 3PU
Tel: 01932-252666 **Fax:** 01932-252583
E-mail: info@elandeng.co.uk
Website: http://www.elandeng.co.uk
Bank(s): Barclays
Directors: G. Marley (Dir), H. Lane (Co Sec), T. Lane (MD)
Managers: M. Benson (Sales Prom Mgr), P. Shine (Sales Prom Mgr)
Immediate Holding Company: Eland Engineering Company Ltd
Registration no: 00371399 **Date established:** 1941 **Turnover:** £1m - £2m
No.of Employees: 21 - 50 **Product Groups:** 38, 67

Date of Accounts	Mar 07	Mar 06
Working Capital	-392	-275
Fixed Assets	659	686

see next page

Eland Engineering Company - *Cont'd*

Current Assets	548	319
Current Liabilities	940	594
Total Share Capital	10	10

Eurobox Ltd
Unit 6 Enterprise House 44-46 Terrace Road, Walton On Thames, KT12 2SD
Tel: 01932-230123 **Fax:** 01932-230111
E-mail: lance@euroboxenclosures.co.uk
Website: http://www.euroboxenclosures.co.uk
Directors: L. Burns (Dir), M. Jones (MD)
Immediate Holding Company: EUROBOX LIMITED
Registration no: 03066146 **Date established:** 1995
No.of Employees: 21 - 50 **Product Groups:** 30

Date of Accounts	Sep 11	Sep 10	Sep 09
Working Capital	-3	-7	56
Fixed Assets	11	12	3
Current Assets	287	232	261

Fimark Ltd
11 Lyon Road, Walton On Thames, KT12 3PU
Tel: 01932-245226 **Fax:** 01932-245873
E-mail: info@fimark.com
Website: http://www.fimark.com
Directors: C. Dean (MD)
Immediate Holding Company: FIMARK LIMITED
Registration no: 03330180 **VAT No.:** GB 707 2459 37
Date established: 1997 **Turnover:** Up to £250,000
No.of Employees: 1 - 10 **Product Groups:** 44, 46, 47, 48, 49, 68, 81, 85

Date of Accounts	Aug 11	Aug 10	Aug 09
Working Capital	41	39	-19
Fixed Assets	24	38	55
Current Assets	110	120	93

Future Reliance Ltd
2 Walton Lodge Bridge Street, Walton On Thames, KT12 1BT
Tel: 08454-503880 **Fax:** 0845-450 6502
E-mail: info@futurereliance.com
Website: http://www.futurereliancegroup.com
Directors: A. Nicklin (MD)
Immediate Holding Company: FUTURE RELIANCE GROUP LIMITED
Registration no: 06793242 **Date established:** 2009
Turnover: Up to £250,000 **No.of Employees:** 11 - 20 **Product Groups:** 44

Date of Accounts	Mar 11	Mar 10
Sales Turnover	242	140
Pre Tax Profit/Loss	37	N/A
Working Capital	58	58
Current Assets	113	64
Current Liabilities	7	6

G S Precision
North Weylands Industrial Estate Molesey Road, Walton On Thames, KT12 3PL
Tel: 01932-246477 **Fax:** 01932-231345
E-mail: s.brewell@gsprecision.co.uk
Website: http://www.bgconnect.com
Directors: S. Brewell (Prop)
VAT No.: GB 384 2140 64 **Turnover:** £500,000 - £1m
No.of Employees: 1 - 10 **Product Groups:** 48

Gargsales (UK) Ltd Garg Inox Ltd.
30 DENTON GROVE, Walton On Thames, KT12 3HE
Tel: 01932-240086 **Fax:** 01932-254424
E-mail: j.juneja@gargwire.com
Website: http://www.gargwire.com
Managers: J. Juneja (Sales Prom)
Registration no: 5422324 **Date established:** 2005 **Turnover:** £1m - £2m
No.of Employees: 1 - 10 **Product Groups:** 35

Jewson Ltd
2 Terrace Road, Walton On Thames, KT12 2ST
Tel: 08456-409538 **Fax:** 01932-245775
Website: http://www.hirepoint.co.uk
Managers: S. Wakeman (Mgr)
Ultimate Holding Company: COMPAGNIE DE SAINT GOBAIN (FRANCE)
Immediate Holding Company: JEWSON LIMITED
Registration no: 00348407 **VAT No.:** GB 394 1212 63
Date established: 1939 **No.of Employees:** 21 - 50 **Product Groups:** 66

Date of Accounts	Dec 11	Dec 10	Dec 09
Sales Turnover	1606m	1547m	1485m
Pre Tax Profit/Loss	18m	100m	45m
Working Capital	-345m	-250m	-349m
Fixed Assets	496m	387m	461m
Current Assets	657m	1005m	1320m
Current Liabilities	66m	120m	64m

K B C Process Technology Ltd
42-50 Hersham Road, Walton On Thames, KT12 1RZ
Tel: 01932-242424 **Fax:** 01932-224214
E-mail: info@kbcat.com
Website: http://www.kbcat.com
Bank(s): HSBC Bank plc
Managers: J. Bower (I.T. Exec), L. Caldwell
Ultimate Holding Company: KBC ADVANCED TECHNOLOGIES PLC
Immediate Holding Company: KBC PROCESS TECHNOLOGY LIMITED
Registration no: 01807381 **VAT No.:** GB 492 9445 04
Date established: 1984 **Turnover:** £20m - £50m
No.of Employees: 101 - 250 **Product Groups:** 44, 51, 54, 80

Date of Accounts	Dec 11	Dec 10	Dec 09
Sales Turnover	26m	21m	25m
Pre Tax Profit/Loss	363	-2m	-17
Working Capital	6m	8m	9m
Fixed Assets	4m	4m	4m
Current Assets	15m	16m	16m
Current Liabilities	3m	2m	3m

M I K O Coffee Ltd
Unit 7 Ember Centre Lyon Road, Walton On Thames, KT12 3PU
Tel: 01932-253787 **Fax:** 01932-253520
E-mail: info@miko.co.uk
Website: http://www.miko.co.uk
Directors: A. Rogers (Co Sec)
Managers: F. Van Tilborg
Ultimate Holding Company: MIKO NV (BELGIUM)
Immediate Holding Company: MIKO COFFEE LIMITED
Registration no: 01677817 **Date established:** 1982 **Turnover:** £5m - £10m
No.of Employees: 21 - 50 **Product Groups:** 20, 27, 32, 40, 42, 49, 62, 67, 69, 86

Date of Accounts	Dec 11	Dec 10	Dec 09
Sales Turnover	8m	6m	6m
Pre Tax Profit/Loss	-78	-137	240
Working Capital	586	1m	2m
Fixed Assets	4m	4m	2m
Current Assets	5m	4m	3m
Current Liabilities	3m	2m	757

Moores Glassworks Ltd
143 Hersham Road, Walton On Thames, KT12 1RR
Tel: 01932-222314 **Fax:** 01932-243330
E-mail: sales@moores-glass.co.uk
Website: http://www.moores-glass.co.uk
Bank(s): Barclays
Directors: A. Ward (MD)
Immediate Holding Company: MAGIC ENTERTAINMENT LIMITED
Registration no: 01317078 **VAT No.:** GB 212 7130 14
Date established: 2012 **Turnover:** Up to £250,000
No.of Employees: 21 - 50 **Product Groups:** 48, 63

Date of Accounts	Apr 11	Apr 10	Apr 09
Working Capital	963	953	889
Fixed Assets	562	565	636
Current Assets	1m	1m	1m

Office Transformation Ltd
Bridge House Bridge Street, Walton On Thames, KT12 1AL
Tel: 01932-254600 **Fax:** 01932-254620
E-mail: info@officetransformation.co.uk
Website: http://www.officetransformation.co.uk
Directors: J. Ratcliffe (Fin)
Immediate Holding Company: OFFICE TRANSFORMATION LIMITED
Registration no: 02011368 **VAT No.:** GB 462 7219 44
Date established: 1986 **No.of Employees:** 1 - 10 **Product Groups:** 26, 32, 48, 67

Date of Accounts	Mar 11	Mar 10	Mar 09
Working Capital	-9	-5	-8
Fixed Assets	5	6	8
Current Assets	39	46	30
Current Liabilities	17	19	12

Pet Mate Ltd
Lyon Road, Walton On Thames, KT12 3PU
Tel: 01932-700000 **Fax:** 01932-700002
E-mail: sales@pet-mate.com
Website: http://www.pet-mate.com
Bank(s): HSBC
Directors: C. Kirk (Prop)
Managers: J. Irving (Sales Prom Mgr), K. Hollister (Comptroller)
Immediate Holding Company: PET MATE LIMITED
Registration no: 01971114 **VAT No.:** GB 438 8852 02
Date established: 1985 **Turnover:** £5m - £10m **No.of Employees:** 11 - 20
Product Groups: 35, 40

Date of Accounts	Jan 12	Jan 11	Jan 10
Working Capital	3m	2m	2m
Fixed Assets	1m	1m	1m
Current Assets	3m	3m	3m

Quality Suppliers Ltd
Unit 13 Lyon Road, Walton On Thames, KT12 3PU
Tel: 01932-248831 **Fax:** 01932-243970
E-mail: sales@quality-suppliers.com
Website: http://www.quality-suppliers.com
Directors: C. Hills (Dir)
Ultimate Holding Company: HILLS & HOWLETT LIMITED
Immediate Holding Company: QUALITY SUPPLIERS LIMITED
Registration no: 01554032 **VAT No.:** GB 358 6878 85
Date established: 1981 **Turnover:** £500,000 - £1m
No.of Employees: 1 - 10 **Product Groups:** 35, 66

Date of Accounts	Jun 12	Jun 11	Jun 10
Sales Turnover	602	541	428
Pre Tax Profit/Loss	35	3	12
Working Capital	197	168	161
Fixed Assets	4	5	9
Current Assets	268	239	235
Current Liabilities	22	18	11

R P Glass Industries Ltd
17 Church Street, Walton On Thames, KT12 2QP
Tel: 01932-224269 **Fax:** 01932-224269
E-mail: enquiries@rp-glass.co.uk
Website: http://www.rp-glass.co.uk
Directors: G. Rushmere (Fin), C. Rushmere (Dir)
Immediate Holding Company: R.P.GLASS INDUSTRIES LIMITED
Registration no: 00439246 **VAT No.:** GB 211 8241 06
Date established: 1947 **Turnover:** Up to £250,000
No.of Employees: 1 - 10 **Product Groups:** 33, 63, 66

Date of Accounts	Aug 11	Aug 10	Aug 07
Sales Turnover	N/A	N/A	119
Pre Tax Profit/Loss	N/A	N/A	3
Working Capital	11	10	15
Fixed Assets	1	1	3
Current Assets	20	20	24
Current Liabilities	N/A	N/A	5

Reed Employment Ltd
20 High Street, Walton On Thames, KT12 1DA
Tel: 01932-231414 **Fax:** 01932-241049
E-mail: helen.anthony@reed.co.uk
Website: http://www.reedglobal.com
Managers: H. Anthony (District Mgr), H. Anthony (Mgr)
Ultimate Holding Company: REED GLOBAL LTD (MALTA)
Immediate Holding Company: REED EMPLOYMENT LIMITED
Registration no: 00669854 **Date established:** 1960
Turnover: £500m - £1,000m **No.of Employees:** 1 - 10
Product Groups: 80

Date of Accounts	Jun 11	Jun 10	Dec 07
Sales Turnover	618	450	287m
Pre Tax Profit/Loss	-2m	310	8m
Working Capital	23m	28m	28m
Fixed Assets	31	36	5m
Current Assets	28m	30m	74m
Current Liabilities	37	29	21m

Rooflight Architectual Ltd
Surrey House The Green, Hersham, Walton On Thames, KT12 4HH
Tel: 01932-230345 **Fax:** 01932-230923
Website: http://www.rooflight.co.uk
Directors: B. Pearce (Sales)
Immediate Holding Company: HENRY LODGE MANAGEMENT CO. LIMITED
Registration no: 01560385 **Date established:** 1982
Turnover: Up to £250,000 **No.of Employees:** 1 - 10 **Product Groups:** 26, 35

Specialist Technologies Ltd
1 Lyon Road, Walton On Thames, KT12 3PU
Tel: 01932-251500 **Fax:** 01932-251510
E-mail: info@spectech.co.uk
Website: http://www.stag-aerospace.com
Bank(s): The Royal Bank of Scotland
Directors: C. Davis (MD)
Immediate Holding Company: SPECIALIST TECHNOLOGIES LTD
Registration no: 02265000 **VAT No.:** GB 493 5907 06
Date established: 1988 **Turnover:** £10m - £20m
No.of Employees: 21 - 50 **Product Groups:** 68

Date of Accounts	Dec 11	Dec 10	Dec 09
Sales Turnover	11m	12m	12m
Pre Tax Profit/Loss	375	833	474
Working Capital	4m	4m	4m
Fixed Assets	217	234	259
Current Assets	8m	8m	8m
Current Liabilities	2m	1m	2m

Thompson Jewellery
41 Beech Close Walton-On-Thames, Hersham, Walton On Thames, KT12 5RQ
Tel: 01932-230488
E-mail: athompson@thompsonjewellery.co.uk
Website: http://www.thompsonjewellery.co.uk
Directors: S. Thompson (Ptnr)
Date established: 2006 **Turnover:** Up to £250,000
No.of Employees: 1 - 10 **Product Groups:** 49

Trojan
3 Lyon Road, Walton On Thames, KT12 3PU
Tel: 01932-232400 **Fax:** 01932-267987
E-mail: bonny@trojansigns.com
Website: http://www.trojansigns.com
Directors: T. Charvetto (Dir)
Managers: P. Kirtland (Mgr), B. Mactherson (Mgr), B. Nersesian (Prod Mgr)
Turnover: £500,000 - £1m **No.of Employees:** 1 - 10 **Product Groups:** 28, 37, 39

W O T Security Group Ltd
17 Bridge Street, Walton On Thames, KT12 1AE
Tel: 01932-250500 **Fax:** 01932-250527
E-mail: enquiries@wotsecurity.com
Website: http://www.wotsecurity.com
Directors: P. Morris (MD)
Immediate Holding Company: WOT SECURITY LIMITED
Registration no: 01768062 **Date established:** 1983 **Turnover:** £2m - £5m
No.of Employees: 1 - 10 **Product Groups:** 36, 40, 52, 66

Date of Accounts	May 09	May 08	Apr 11
Sales Turnover	4m	4m	4m
Pre Tax Profit/Loss	-61	27	71
Working Capital	117	223	541
Fixed Assets	208	245	121
Current Assets	1m	2m	1m
Current Liabilities	145	427	217

Walton Plating Ltd
118 Ashley Road, Walton On Thames, KT12 1HN
Tel: 01932-221206 **Fax:** 01932-246699
E-mail: mike@waltonplating.co.uk
Website: http://www.waltonplating.co.uk
Bank(s): Lloyds TSB Bank plc
Directors: M. Koskela (MD)
Immediate Holding Company: WALTON PLATING LIMITED
Registration no: 01846778 **VAT No.:** GB 413 2703 93
Date established: 1984 **No.of Employees:** 21 - 50 **Product Groups:** 48

Date of Accounts	Nov 11	Nov 10	Nov 09
Working Capital	150	106	58
Fixed Assets	197	217	259
Current Assets	365	303	248

Warlingham

Delta Industrial Ltd
1 Leas Road, Warlingham, CR6 9LN
Tel: 01883-380303 **Fax:** 01883-380304
E-mail: delta.creditcontrol@gmail.com
Website: http://www.deltatools.co.uk
Directors: D. Shaw (Dir)
Immediate Holding Company: DELTA INDUSTRIAL LIMITED
Registration no: 03420177 **Date established:** 1997
Turnover: £250,000 - £500,000 **No.of Employees:** 1 - 10
Product Groups: 37

Date of Accounts	Oct 11	Oct 10	Oct 09
Working Capital	41	43	49
Fixed Assets	11	1	2
Current Assets	146	136	153

Facilities Staff Training
7a Glebe Road, Warlingham, CR6 9NG
Tel: 01883-623839 **Fax:** 01883-626365
E-mail: rlbransby@btconnect.com
Website: http://www.fastrain.co.uk
Directors: R. Bransby (Ptnr)
Turnover: Up to £250,000 **No.of Employees:** 1 - 10 **Product Groups:** 52, 86, 88

June Productions Ltd
The White House 6 Beechwood Lane, Warlingham, CR6 9LT
Tel: 01883-622411 **Fax:** 01883-622081
E-mail: davidmackay99@gmail.com
Website: http://www.mackay99.plus.com
Directors: D. Mackay (Prop)
Immediate Holding Company: JUNE PRODUCTIONS LIMITED
Registration no: 00979683 **Date established:** 1970
Turnover: Up to £250,000 **No.of Employees:** 1 - 10 **Product Groups:** 89

Date of Accounts	Jun 11	Jun 10	Jun 09
Sales Turnover	28	51	46
Pre Tax Profit/Loss	-3	7	4

Working Capital	230	234	223
Fixed Assets	6	6	12
Current Assets	250	257	245
Current Liabilities	N/A	4	4

Llonsson Ltd
49 Court Farm Road, Warlingham, CR6 9BL
Tel: 01883-622068 **Fax:** 01883-623280
E-mail: sales@llonsson.co.uk
Website: http://www.llonsson.co.uk
Directors: H. Mortensson (Sales)
Registration no: 2389444 **Date established:** 1989 **Turnover:**
No.of Employees: 1 - 10 **Product Groups:** 35, 40

Orangutan Sales Promotion Consultants
The Holt Church Lane, Chelsham, Warlingham, CR6 9PG
Tel: 01883-622123 **Fax:** 01883-626242
E-mail: tim@orangutan.co.uk
Website: http://www.orangutan.co.uk
Directors: T. Peniston Third (MD)
Immediate Holding Company: THE HOLT LTD
Registration no: 01725538 **Date established:** 1983
Turnover: £500,000 - £1m **No.of Employees:** 11 - 20
Product Groups: 44, 61, 68, 80, 81, 86, 87

Project Aluminium Ltd
418-420 Limpsfield Road, Warlingham, CR6 9LA
Tel: 01883-624004 **Fax:** 01883-627201
E-mail: lesley@projectali.co.uk
Website: http://www.projectali.co.uk
Directors: L. Watson (Fin)
Immediate Holding Company: PROJECT ALUMINIUM LIMITED
Registration no: 01113810 **Date established:** 1973 **Turnover:** £1m - £2m
No.of Employees: 11 - 20 **Product Groups:** 26, 35

Date of Accounts	Dec 11	Dec 10	Dec 09
Sales Turnover	2m	1m	1m
Pre Tax Profit/Loss	-25	-111	-185
Working Capital	353	371	437
Fixed Assets	46	53	61
Current Assets	542	583	613
Current Liabilities	60	45	51

West Byfleet

Academy Billiard Company
5 Camphill Industrial Estate Camphill Road, West Byfleet, KT14 6EW
Tel: 01932-352067 **Fax:** 01932-353904
E-mail: sales@games-room.com
Website: http://www.games-room.com
Managers: R. Donnachie (Mgr)
Turnover: Up to £250,000 **No.of Employees:** 1 - 10 **Product Groups:** 35, 49, 67

Acord Electronics Ltd
Madeira Road, West Byfleet, KT14 6DN
Tel: 01932-354565 **Fax:** 01932-350140
E-mail: sales@acord.co.uk
Website: http://www.acord.co.uk
Directors: C. Faithful (MD)
Immediate Holding Company: ACORD ELECTRONICS LIMITED
Registration no: 01027335 **VAT No.:** GB 211 5297 91
Date established: 1971 **Turnover:** Up to £250,000
No.of Employees: 1 - 10 **Product Groups:** 37, 44

Date of Accounts	Oct 11	Oct 10	Oct 09
Working Capital	88	90	83
Current Assets	121	128	113
Current Liabilities	34	N/A	N/A

Acoustic Engineering Services UK Ltd
PO Box 322, West Byfleet, KT14 6YN
Tel: 01932-352733 **Fax:** 01932-355265
E-mail: mark.stagg@aesuk.co.uk
Website: http://www.aesuk.co.uk
Directors: M. Stagg (Dir)
Immediate Holding Company: ACOUSTIC ENGINEERING SERVICES (UK) LIMITED
Registration no: 02382818 **Date established:** 1989
Turnover: £500,000 - £1m **No.of Employees:** 1 - 10 **Product Groups:** 54

Date of Accounts	Mar 11	Mar 10	Mar 09
Working Capital	55	72	61
Fixed Assets	3	5	5
Current Assets	86	127	83

Air Parts Ltd
Unit 2 Chertsey Road Byfleet, West Byfleet, KT14 7AX
Tel: 01932-350009 **Fax:** 01932-350116
E-mail: g.ford@air-parts.co.uk
Website: http://www.air-parts.co.uk
Directors: C. Hammond (Sales), G. Ford (MD), C. Ford (Co Sec), C. Ford (Fin)
Managers: S. Mathews (Purch Mgr)
Immediate Holding Company: AIR PARTS LIMITED
Registration no: 02376435 **Date established:** 1989 **Turnover:** £5m - £10m
No.of Employees: 11 - 20 **Product Groups:** 30, 39

Date of Accounts	May 10	May 09	May 08
Working Capital	568	581	835
Fixed Assets	187	173	170
Current Assets	2m	2m	2m

Any Olde Iron Ltd
The Workshop Wintersells Road, Byfleet, West Byfleet, KT14 7LF
Tel: 01483-831070
E-mail: info@anyoldeiron.com
Website: http://www.anyoldeiron.co.uk
Directors: C. Brookes (MD), C. Boss (Fin)
Immediate Holding Company: ANY OLDE IRON LIMITED
Registration no: 04427712 **Date established:** 2002
Turnover: Up to £250,000 **No.of Employees:** 1 - 10 **Product Groups:** 26, 35

Date of Accounts	Apr 11	Apr 10	Apr 07
Sales Turnover	N/A	N/A	83
Pre Tax Profit/Loss	N/A	N/A	41

Working Capital	4	19	N/A
Fixed Assets	N/A	2	N/A
Current Assets	19	35	13
Current Liabilities	N/A	N/A	12

Ashtead Engineering Co. Ltd
Unit 2 3 Camphill Industrial Estate Camphill Road, West Byfleet, KT14 6EW
Tel: 01932-353121 **Fax:** 01932-342968
E-mail: info@ashteadeng.co.uk
Website: http://www.ashteadeng.co.uk
Directors: K. Morrell (Co Sec), M. Harvey (MD)
Immediate Holding Company: ASHTEAD ENGINEERING COMPANY LIMITED
Registration no: 00541377 **VAT No.:** GB 209 5327 67
Date established: 1954 **Turnover:** £1m - £2m **No.of Employees:** 21 - 50
Product Groups: 48

Date of Accounts	Mar 11	Mar 10	Mar 09
Working Capital	112	115	137
Fixed Assets	36	39	46
Current Assets	1m	706	936
Current Liabilities	1m	N/A	N/A

Charles Austen Pumps Ltd
Royston Road Byfleet, West Byfleet, KT14 7NY
Tel: 01932-355277 **Fax:** 01932-351285
E-mail: info@charlesausten.com
Website: http://www.charlesausten.com
Directors: A. Shepherd (MD)
Ultimate Holding Company: CHARLES AUSTEN PUMPS LIMITED
Immediate Holding Company: ROYCOTT LIMITED
Registration no: 00337541 **VAT No.:** GB 211 5081 17
Date established: 1938 **No.of Employees:** 1 - 10 **Product Groups:** 40, 48

Date of Accounts	Jun 11	Jun 10	Jun 09
Working Capital	752	752	752
Current Assets	753	753	769
Current Liabilities	1	1	N/A

B L C Fork Lift Services plc
Cumberland Works Wintersells Road Byfleet, West Byfleet, KT14 7LF
Tel: 01932-344900 **Fax:** 01932-344800
E-mail: david@doainsurance.co.uk
Website: http://www.blcforklifts.com
Directors: T. Daniels (MD)
Immediate Holding Company: ADVANTAGE RENTALS & REPAIRS LIMITED
Registration no: 02760548 **VAT No.:** GB 584 547 **Date established:** 1995
Turnover: £500,000 - £1m **No.of Employees:** 1 - 10 **Product Groups:** 45, 67, 68, 83

Date of Accounts	Mar 12	Mar 11	Mar 10
Sales Turnover	1m	1m	898
Pre Tax Profit/Loss	110	157	131
Working Capital	109	168	125
Fixed Assets	74	44	59
Current Assets	188	309	230
Current Liabilities	36	N/A	N/A

General Hoseclips Ltd
Royston Road Byfleet, West Byfleet, KT14 7NY
Tel: 01932-343515 **Fax:** 01932-351285
E-mail: info@generalhoseclips.com
Directors: W. Shepherd (MD)
Immediate Holding Company: GENERAL HOSECLIPS LIMITED
Registration no: 01500733 **Date established:** 1980
Turnover: £500,000 - £1m **No.of Employees:** 1 - 10 **Product Groups:** 30, 36

Date of Accounts	Jun 11	Jun 10	Jun 08
Working Capital	341	339	345
Current Assets	435	413	364
Current Liabilities	N/A	N/A	8

Harrocell Ltd
15e Wintersells Road Byfleet, West Byfleet, KT14 7LF
Tel: 01932-356347 **Fax:** 01932-356347
E-mail: peter-knox@variabletransformers.co.uk
Website: http://www.variabletransformers.co.uk
Directors: P. Knox (MD)
Managers: R. Calcara (Sales Prom Mgr)
Immediate Holding Company: HARROCELL LIMITED
Registration no: 01296633 **VAT No.:** GB 293 7834 13
Date established: 1977 **Turnover:** £250,000 - £500,000
No.of Employees: 1 - 10 **Product Groups:** 37, 48

Date of Accounts	May 09	May 08	May 07
Working Capital	5	-19	-39
Fixed Assets	N/A	N/A	33
Current Assets	25	31	54

High Tech Tubes Ltd
Unit 15f Wintersells Road, Byfleet, West Byfleet, KT14 7LF
Tel: 01932-355440 **Fax:** 01932-355441
E-mail: sales@hightechtubes.co.uk
Website: http://www.hightechtubes.co.uk
Directors: J. Whiteley (Sales)
Immediate Holding Company: HIGH TECH TUBES LIMITED
Registration no: 02908706 **VAT No.:** GB 644 1918 34
Date established: 1994 **Turnover:** £1m - £2m **No.of Employees:** 1 - 10
Product Groups: 36

Date of Accounts	Jan 11	Jan 10	Jan 09
Working Capital	189	186	154
Fixed Assets	86	88	91
Current Assets	399	365	376

Mclellan & Partners Ltd
Sheer House 7 Station Approach, West Byfleet, KT14 6NL
Tel: 01932-343271 **Fax:** 01932-348037
E-mail: hq@mclellan.co.uk
Website: http://www.mclellan.co.uk
Bank(s): HSBC
Directors: J. Catlow (Dir), T. Inglefield (Co Sec)
Managers: A. Sultan, T. Inglefeild (Comptroller), G. Christensen (Personnel)
Ultimate Holding Company: MORRIS MCLELLAN LIMITED
Immediate Holding Company: MCLELLAN AND PARTNERS LIMITED
Registration no: 01989091 **Date established:** 1986 **Turnover:** £5m - £10m
No.of Employees: 51 - 100 **Product Groups:** 84

Date of Accounts	Jun 08	Jun 09	Jun 10
Sales Turnover	7m	7m	6m
Pre Tax Profit/Loss	418	371	208
Working Capital	3m	3m	3m
Fixed Assets	126	104	325
Current Assets	4m	4m	4m
Current Liabilities	1m	972	1m

Prestige Car Valeting Ltd
8 The Oaks, West Byfleet, KT14 6RL
Tel: 0781-111 1999 **Fax:** 01932-402124
E-mail: a.field@me.com
Managers: A. Field (Mgr)
Immediate Holding Company: PRESTIGE CAR VALETING LIMITED
Registration no: 08024646 **Date established:** 2012
Turnover: Up to £250,000 **No.of Employees:** 1 - 10 **Product Groups:** 32, 39, 68

Sauven Marking Ltd
4 Wintersells Road Byfleet, West Byfleet, KT14 7LF
Tel: 01932-355191 **Fax:** 01932-354511
E-mail: sales@sauven-marking.com
Website: http://www.sauven-marking.com
Directors: D. Sauven (MD), S. Chambers (Sales)
Managers: L. Franklin (Mktg Serv Mgr)
Immediate Holding Company: SAUVEN MARKING LIMITED
Registration no: 01621727 **Date established:** 1982
No.of Employees: 11 - 20 **Product Groups:** 38, 42

Date of Accounts	Sep 11	Sep 10	Sep 09
Working Capital	3m	3m	2m
Fixed Assets	2m	2m	2m
Current Assets	4m	3m	3m

Westweigh Controls Ltd
87 Hollies Avenue, West Byfleet, KT14 6AN
Tel: 01932-344443 **Fax:** 01932-344775
Website: http://www.westweigh.com
Directors: R. Horn (Fin), D. Horn (MD)
Immediate Holding Company: WESTWEIGH CONTROLS LIMITED
Registration no: 04602031 **Date established:** 2002
Turnover: £250,000 - £500,000 **No.of Employees:** 1 - 10
Product Groups: 38, 42

Date of Accounts	Mar 12	Mar 11	Mar 10
Sales Turnover	328	309	136
Pre Tax Profit/Loss	82	71	17
Working Capital	29	28	22
Fixed Assets	11	1	N/A
Current Assets	171	160	98
Current Liabilities	21	19	6

West Molesey

Anglo Nordic Burner Products Ltd
Units 12-14 Island Farm Avenue, West Molesey, KT8 2UZ
Tel: 020-8979 0988 **Fax:** 020-8979 6961
E-mail: sales@anglonordic.co.uk
Website: http://www.anglonordic.co.uk
Directors: B. Lelliott (MD), J. Polley (Fin)
Ultimate Holding Company: FLOWMAX HOLDINGS LIMITED (BVI)
Immediate Holding Company: ANGLO-NORDIC BURNER PRODUCTS LIMITED
Registration no: 01017422 **VAT No.:** GB 318 1525 74
Date established: 1971 **Turnover:** £2m - £5m **No.of Employees:** 1 - 10
Product Groups: 36, 37, 38, 40, 42

Date of Accounts	Apr 12	Apr 11	Apr 10
Working Capital	347	403	430
Fixed Assets	506	498	502
Current Assets	559	645	715
Current Liabilities	114	108	150

Cona Ltd
Unit 3 Island Farm Avenue, West Molesey, KT8 2UZ
Tel: 020-8941 9922 **Fax:** 020-8941 9955
E-mail: info@cona.co.uk
Website: http://www.cona.co.uk
Bank(s): HSBC, Bond St London
Directors: R. Gerrard (MD)
Immediate Holding Company: CONA LIMITED
Registration no: 00195096 **VAT No.:** GB 215 9257 59
Date established: 2024 **Turnover:** £1m - £2m **No.of Employees:** 11 - 20
Product Groups: 27, 36, 40, 67

Date of Accounts	Dec 11	Dec 10	Dec 09
Working Capital	239	261	259
Fixed Assets	486	500	516
Current Assets	259	299	298

Delta Controls Ltd
Island Farm Avenue, West Molesey, KT8 2UZ
Tel: 020-8939 3500 **Fax:** 020-8783 1163
E-mail: sales@delta-controls.com
Website: http://www.delta-controls.com
Bank(s): Lloyds TSB Bank plc
Directors: C. Allen (Sales), J. Clarke (Fin)
Immediate Holding Company: DELTA CONTROLS LIMITED
Registration no: 05369683 **VAT No.:** GB 216 1353 00
Date established: 2005 **Turnover:** £5m - £10m **No.of Employees:** 21 - 50
Product Groups: 37, 38

Date of Accounts	Sep 11	Sep 10	Sep 09
Working Capital	1m	993	852
Fixed Assets	832	771	697
Current Assets	2m	2m	2m

Energy Technique plc
47 Central Avenue, West Molesey, KT8 2QZ
Tel: 020-8941 2199 **Fax:** 020-8783 0140
E-mail: sales@energytechniqueplc.co.uk
Website: http://www.energytechniqueplc.co.uk
Directors: K. Fallon (Dir), L. Stimpson (Jt MD), M. Reid (MD), R. Unsworth (Dir)
Immediate Holding Company: Energy Technique PLC.
Registration no: 00013273 **Date established:** 1979 **Turnover:** £5m - £10m
No.of Employees: 51 - 100 **Product Groups:** 40

Date of Accounts	Mar 08
Sales Turnover	9190
Pre Tax Profit/Loss	580
Working Capital	1820
Fixed Assets	490
Current Assets	3210
Current Liabilities	1390
Total Share Capital	7750
ROCE% (Return on Capital Employed)	25.1

F Bullett & Co.

Island Farm Road, West Molesey, KT8 2UU
Tel: 020-8979 1573 **Fax:** 020-8941 7352
E-mail: nickbullet@fbullet.com
Directors: N. Bullett (Prop)
Immediate Holding Company: F. BULLETT & CO. LIMITED
Registration no: 03184793 **VAT No.:** GB 666 2746 06
Date established: 1996 **Turnover:** £250,000 - £500,000
No.of Employees: 1 - 10 **Product Groups:** 34, 67

Date of Accounts	Apr 12	Apr 11	Apr 10
Working Capital	18	12	30
Fixed Assets	N/A	1	7
Current Assets	133	121	154

Integrated Pharmaceutical Services Ltd

41 Central Avenue, West Molesey, KT8 2QZ
Tel: 020-8481 9720 **Fax:** 020-8481 9729
E-mail: orders@ipslabs.co.uk
Website: http://www.ipslabs.ws
Directors: J. Harris (MD), I. John (Fin)
Managers: B. Patel (Ops Mgr)
Immediate Holding Company: INTEGRATED PHARMACEUTICAL SERVICES (IPS) LIMITED
Registration no: 07112415 **Date established:** 2009 **Turnover:** £5m - £10m
No.of Employees: 21 - 50 **Product Groups:** 31

Date of Accounts	Feb 11
Sales Turnover	7m
Pre Tax Profit/Loss	97
Working Capital	3m
Fixed Assets	26m
Current Assets	7m
Current Liabilities	2m

Molesey Metal Works

22 Island Farm Avenue, West Molesey, KT8 2UA
Tel: 020-8979 1772 **Fax:** 020-8979 7337
E-mail: moleseymetals@yahoo.co.uk
Directors: J. Griffin (Fin), N. Griffin (Dir)
Immediate Holding Company: MOLESEY METAL WORKS LIMITED
Registration no: 00609953 **Date established:** 1958
No.of Employees: 1 - 10 **Product Groups:** 26, 35

Date of Accounts	Aug 11	Aug 10	Aug 09
Working Capital	-30	8	14
Fixed Assets	184	188	192
Current Assets	65	88	81

Pearson Innovation Ltd

34 Cherry Orchard Road, West Molesey, KT8 1QZ
Tel: 020-8547 0470 **Fax:** 020-8547 0123
E-mail: mike.pearson@pearsonmatthews.com
Website: http://www.pmuk.com
Directors: J. Dawton (MD), M. Pearson (MD), M. Pearson (Dir), T. Pearson (Fin)
Managers: D. Billig (Sales & Mktg Mg), P. Dunn (I.T. Exec)
Immediate Holding Company: PEARSON MATTHEWS LIMITED
Registration no: 03524249 **VAT No.:** GB 745 2567 18
Date established: 1998 **Turnover:** £500,000 - £1m
No.of Employees: 1 - 10 **Product Groups:** 48, 81

Date of Accounts	Mar 07	Mar 06
Working Capital	126	148
Fixed Assets	161	194
Current Assets	307	225
Current Liabilities	181	76
Total Share Capital	1	1

R C Brady & Co.

112 Down Street, West Molesey, KT8 2TU
Tel: 020-8783 0760 **Fax:** 020-8783 0811
E-mail: sales@rcbrady.co.uk
Website: http://www.rcbrady.co.uk
Directors: P. Harris (Dir)
Immediate Holding Company: ELK GROUP LTD
Registration no: 03820891 **VAT No.:** GB 734 3901 40
Turnover: £500,000 - £1m **No.of Employees:** 1 - 10 **Product Groups:** 66

S A V UK Ltd

Scandia House Armfield Close, West Molesey, KT8 2JR
Tel: 020-8941 4153 **Fax:** 020-8783 1132
E-mail: j.hansen@savmodules.com
Website: http://www.sav-systems.com
Bank(s): Barclays
Directors: L. Savricius (MD), J. Hansen (Fin), J. Hansen (Dir)
Managers: P. Davies (Chief Buyer), L. Fabricius (Sales & Mktg Mg), J. Hanson (Sec)
Ultimate Holding Company: 03166497
Immediate Holding Company: S.A.V. UNITED KINGDOM LIMITED
Registration no: 00513621 **VAT No.:** 765 3333 24 **Date established:** 1952
Turnover: £2m - £5m **No.of Employees:** 11 - 20 **Product Groups:** 29, 34, 48, 66

Date of Accounts	Sep 06	Sep 05
Working Capital	-30	-31
Fixed Assets	26	28
Current Assets	10	12
Current Liabilities	40	43

Winston Windings Ltd (Head Office)

Glebe House Armfield Close, West Molesey, KT8 2UP
Tel: 020-8941 4889 **Fax:** 020-8941 6919
E-mail: sales@thewinstongroup.co.uk
Website: http://www.winstonwindings.co.uk
Bank(s): Barclays
Directors: A. Moghul (MD)
Immediate Holding Company: WINSTON WINDINGS LIMITED
Registration no: 00906811 **Date established:** 1967
Turnover: £500,000 - £1m **No.of Employees:** 11 - 20 **Product Groups:** 37

Date of Accounts	May 11	May 10	May 09
Working Capital	-3	-3	-5
Fixed Assets	24	28	31
Current Assets	227	220	235

Weybridge

Automotive Export Supplies Ltd

Abbey House, Weybridge, KT13 0TT
Tel: 01932-268550 **Fax:** 01932-268551
E-mail: information@aesltd.co.uk
Website: http://www.aesltd.co.uk
Directors: D. Thomas (MD)
Ultimate Holding Company: FP046999
Immediate Holding Company: AUTOMOTIVE EXPORT SUPPLIES LIMITED
Registration no: 02599593 **VAT No.:** GB 584 3094 24
Date established: 1991 **No.of Employees:** 1 - 10 **Product Groups:** 61

Brooklands College

Heath Road, Weybridge, KT13 8TT
Tel: 01932-797700 **Fax:** 01932-797800
E-mail: info@brooklands.ac.uk
Website: http://www.brooklands.ac.uk
Directors: M. Kilminster (Head)
Managers: D. Smith (Tech Serv Mgr), P. Edwards, G. Hopkins (Personnel), M. Hollywood (Mktg Serv Mgr)
Immediate Holding Company: BROOKLANDS ENTERPRISES LIMITED
Registration no: 02796272 **Date established:** 1993
No.of Employees: 501 - 1000 **Product Groups:** 86

Dytecna

Horizon Business Park Brooklands Road, Weybridge, KT13 0TJ
Tel: 01932-347305 **Fax:** 01932-353063
E-mail: info@dytecna.com
Website: http://www.dytecna.com
Directors: J. Fulford (MD)
Managers: D. Durham (), G. Norman (Develop Mgr)
Ultimate Holding Company: DYTECNA LIMITED
Immediate Holding Company: DYTECNA LIMITED
Registration no: 00865936 **Date established:** 1965 **Turnover:** £5m - £10m
No.of Employees: 1 - 10 **Product Groups:** 37, 84, 85

Date of Accounts	Dec 11	Dec 10	Dec 09
Sales Turnover	25m	42m	40m
Pre Tax Profit/Loss	-2m	2m	1m
Working Capital	-624	304	-810
Fixed Assets	3m	4m	5m
Current Assets	7m	11m	16m
Current Liabilities	2m	6m	8m

Edmundson Electrical Ltd

Unit A301 Brooklands Industrial Park Brooklands Industrial Park, Weybridge, KT13 0YU
Tel: 01932-353011 **Fax:** 01932-347511
E-mail: weybridge.146@eel.co.uk
Website: http://www.edmundson-electrical.co.uk/
Managers: G. Prestwood (District Mgr)
Ultimate Holding Company: BLACKFRIARS CORP (USA)
Immediate Holding Company: EDMUNDSON ELECTRICAL LIMITED
Registration no: 02667012 **Date established:** 1991 **Turnover:** £5m - £10m
No.of Employees: 11 - 20 **Product Groups:** 37

Date of Accounts	Dec 11	Dec 10	Dec 09
Sales Turnover	1023m	852m	788m
Pre Tax Profit/Loss	57m	53m	45m
Working Capital	256m	225m	184m
Fixed Assets	17m	3m	4m
Current Assets	439m	358m	298m
Current Liabilities	59m	38m	37m

Gallaher Overseas Ltd

Members Hill Brookland Road, Weybridge, KT13 0QU
Tel: 01932-859777 **Fax:** 01932-832508
E-mail: eddy.pirard@gallaherltd.com
Website: http://www.gallaher-group.com
Bank(s): The Royal Bank of Scotland
Directors: F. Dugast (Dir), N. Northridge (Grp Chief Exec), J. Gildersleeve (Ch), B. Jenner (MD), A. Bingham (Co Sec), A. Bingham (Dir), E. Pirard (Dir)
Managers: L. Stears (Mktg Serv Mgr)
Ultimate Holding Company: JAPAN TOBACCO INC (JAPAN)
Immediate Holding Company: GALLAHER OVERSEAS LIMITED
Registration no: 02287671 **VAT No.:** GB 174 3331 75
Date established: 1988 **Turnover:** Over £1,000m
No.of Employees: 51 - 100 **Product Groups:** 20

Date of Accounts	Apr 11	Apr 10	Apr 09
Pre Tax Profit/Loss	2m	4m	4m
Working Capital	-3m	-10m	-15m
Fixed Assets	28m	33m	35m
Current Assets	166	9	3m
Current Liabilities	44	N/A	N/A

J T I

Members Hill Brooklands Road, Weybridge, KT13 0QU
Tel: 01932-372000 **Fax:** 01932-832508
E-mail: info@jti.com
Website: http://www.jti.com
Directors: A. Bingham (Fin)
Ultimate Holding Company: JAPAN TOBACCO INC (JAPAN)
Immediate Holding Company: GALLAHER INTERNATIONAL LIMITED
Registration no: 00712565 **Date established:** 1962 **Turnover:** £2m - £5m
No.of Employees: 251 - 500 **Product Groups:** 20, 62

Date of Accounts	Dec 11	Dec 10	Dec 09
Pre Tax Profit/Loss	N/A	N/A	-1
Working Capital	1m	1m	1m
Current Assets	1m	1m	1m

Jedco Product Designers Ltd

Quadrant House 7 Heath Road, Weybridge, KT13 8SX
Tel: 01932-852497 **Fax:** 01932-850186
E-mail: avril.elson@jedco.co.uk
Website: http://www.jedco.co.uk
Directors: A. Elson (MD)
Immediate Holding Company: JEDCO PRODUCT DESIGNERS LTD.
Registration no: 04554085 **VAT No.:** GB 413 2751 82
Date established: 2002 **Turnover:** Up to £250,000
No.of Employees: 1 - 10 **Product Groups:** 85

Date of Accounts	Jan 12	Jan 11	Jan 10
Working Capital	4	-11	-13
Fixed Assets	13	16	17
Current Assets	83	50	65

Lighting & Lamps UK Ltd

Unit 2 Weybridge Business Centre 66 York Road, Weybridge, KT13 9DY
Tel: 01932-851798 **Fax:** 01932-851827
E-mail: info@lighting-lamps.co.uk
Website: http://www.lighting-lamps.co.uk
Product Groups: 30, 33, 36, 37, 38, 39, 40, 44, 49, 51, 52, 67, 83, 84

Date of Accounts	Mar 08	Mar 07
Sales Turnover	206	N/A
Pre Tax Profit/Loss	7	N/A
Working Capital	-4	-11
Fixed Assets	4	5
Current Assets	63	45
Current Liabilities	67	56
Total Share Capital	1	1
ROCE% (Return on Capital Employed)	964.0	
ROT% (Return on Turnover)	3.5	

Noma Lites

Southey House 43 Avro Way Brooklands Business Park, Weybridge, KT13 0XQ
Tel: 01932-411330 **Fax:** 01932-411321
E-mail: sales@noma.co.uk
Website: http://www.noma.co.uk
Directors: J. Mitchison (Co Sec), C. Capel (MD)
Immediate Holding Company: NOMA INTERNATIONAL LIMITED
Registration no: 01512918 **VAT No.:** GB 211 7260 07
Date established: 1980 **Turnover:** £5m - £10m **No.of Employees:** 21 - 50
Product Groups: 33, 49, 65

Date of Accounts	Mar 12	Mar 11	Mar 10
Working Capital	2m	2m	2m
Current Assets	2m	2m	2m

P & G Professional

The Heights Brooklands Industrial Estate, Weybridge, KT13 0XP
Tel: 0800-716854 **Fax:** 01932-896611
Website: http://www.pg.com/en_UK
Product Groups: 32, 40, 44, 52

Paragon Executive Cars Ltd

PO Box 635, Weybridge, KT13 3DT
Tel: 0845-2575777
E-mail: enquiries@paragonec.co.uk
Website: http://www.paragonexecutivecars.co.uk
Directors: T. Joo (Dir), C. Tenniswood (Dir)
Immediate Holding Company: PARAGON EXECUTIVE CARS LIMITED
Registration no: 05152967 **Date established:** 2004
No.of Employees: 1 - 10 **Product Groups:** 72

Date of Accounts	Dec 07
Working Capital	-18
Fixed Assets	14
Current Liabilities	18

Perle Systems Europe Ltd

Abbey House Wellington Way, Brooklands Business Park, Weybridge, KT13 0TT
Tel: 01932-268591 **Fax:** 01932-268592
E-mail: mwebster@perle.com
Website: http://www.perle.com
Directors: A. Oldroyd (Fin), A. Wright (Mkt Research), J. Feeney (MD), J. Mockler (MD), R. Dunlop (Tech Serv), T. Grimstone (Fin), J. McDaniel (Fin)
Managers: A. Whiteman (Chief Mgr), A. Yilmaz (Mktg Serv Mgr), G. Morgan (Sales Prom Mgr), P. Woodhouse (I.T. Exec), S. Vanbelle (Ops Mgr), S. McNichol (Admin Off)
Immediate Holding Company: Joe Perle (Canada)
Registration no: 02058845 **No.of Employees:** 1 - 10 **Product Groups:** 44

Persimmon Homes South East Ltd

11 De Havilland Drive De Havilland Drive Brooklands Business Park, Weybridge, KT13 0YP
Tel: 01932-350555 **Fax:** 01932-350022
E-mail: edward.owens@persimmonhomes.com
Website: http://www.persimmonhomes.com
Directors: A. Richards (Fin), E. Owens (MD), J. Price (Sales & Mktg)
Managers: N. Farrall (Chief Buyer), P. Cook
Ultimate Holding Company: PERSIMMON PUBLIC LIMITED COMPANY
Immediate Holding Company: PERSIMMON HOMES (SOUTH EAST) LIMITED
Registration no: 02044246 **Date established:** 1986
No.of Employees: 21 - 50 **Product Groups:** 80

Pyramid Visuals Ltd

Unit A 303 Vickers Drive North, Brooklands Industrial Park, Weybridge, KT13 0YU
Tel: 01932-338899 **Fax:** 01932-338888
E-mail: info@pyramidvisuals.co.uk
Website: http://www.pyramidvisuals.co.uk
Directors: S. Meader (MD)
Managers: G. Zeila (Mgr)
Immediate Holding Company: PYRAMID INVESTMENT PROPERTIES LIMITED
Registration no: 06312017 **Date established:** 2007 **Turnover:** £1m - £2m
No.of Employees: 21 - 50 **Product Groups:** 28, 49

Date of Accounts	Jul 11	Jul 10	Jul 09
Working Capital	7	9	17
Fixed Assets	145	145	145
Current Assets	9	10	18

Sony Head Office

The Heights Brooklands, Weybridge, KT13 0XW
Tel: 01932-816000 **Fax:** 01932-817000
Website: http://www.eu.sony.com
Directors: S. Dowdle (MD)
Ultimate Holding Company: SONY CORPORATION (JAPAN)
Immediate Holding Company: SONY EUROPE LIMITED
Registration no: 02422874 **Date established:** 1989
Turnover: £500m - £1,000m **No.of Employees:** 1 - 10
Product Groups: 63

Date of Accounts	Mar 11	Mar 10	Mar 09
Sales Turnover	5705m	4543m	6492m
Pre Tax Profit/Loss	-428m	-214m	-261m
Working Capital	-982m	-733m	-548m
Fixed Assets	249m	77m	78m
Current Assets	2923m	1482m	1561m
Current Liabilities	691m	109m	138m

Stuvex Safety Systems Ltd

48 Church Street Cheadle Hulme, Weybridge, KT13 8DP
Tel: 01932-849602 **Fax:** 01932-852171
E-mail: steve.bell@stuvex.com
Website: http://www.stuvex.com

Directors: K. Verluyten (Dir), K. Cooper (Dir), S. Cooper (Prop)
Managers: S. Bell (Mgr), S. Edwards (Sales Admin)
Immediate Holding Company: STUVEX SAFETY SYSTEMS LIMITED
Registration no: 02929560 **Date established:** 1994 **Turnover:** £1m - £2m
No.of Employees: 1 - 10 **Product Groups:** 36, 37, 38, 40, 54, 67, 80, 84

Date of Accounts	Dec 08	Dec 07
Working Capital	124	103
Fixed Assets	28	27
Current Assets	607	377
Current Liabilities	483	274
Total Share Capital	140	140

Thamesway Marine

96 Thames Street, Weybridge, KT13 8NH
Tel: 01932-843072 **Fax:** 01932-843072
E-mail: kevin.o'bryan@thameswaymarineproducts.co.uk
Website: http://www.thameswaymarineproducts.co.uk
Directors: P. Obryan (Fin), K. O'Bryan (Prop)
Registration no: 01117221 **Date established:** 1973
No.of Employees: 1 - 10 **Product Groups:** 35, 36, 39

Date of Accounts	Mar 07	Mar 06	Mar 05
Sales Turnover	N/A	N/A	41
Pre Tax Profit/Loss	N/A	N/A	1
Working Capital	18	13	3
Current Assets	23	22	17
Current Liabilities	5	10	15
Total Share Capital	1	1	1
ROCE% (Return on Capital Employed)			22.8
ROT% (Return on Turnover)			1.6

Thornycroft Engines

96 Thames Street, Weybridge, KT13 8NH
Tel: 01932-843072
Website: http://www.thornycroftengines.co.uk
Product Groups: 39, 40, 68

Yamaha Motor UK Ltd

Sopwith Drive Brooklands Industrial Park, Weybridge, KT13 0UZ
Tel: 01932-358000 **Fax:** 01932-358030
E-mail: andrew.smith@yamaha-motor.co.uk
Website: http://www.yamaha-motor.co.uk
Directors: T. Fujimura (Co Sec), Neesham (Chief Op Offcr), A. Smith (MD)
Managers: A. Kelley (Div Mgr), R. Cross
Ultimate Holding Company: YAMAHA MOTOR COMPANY LTD. (JAPAN)
Immediate Holding Company: YAMAHA MOTOR (UK) LIMITED
Registration no: 01006420 **VAT No.:** GB 710 4988 36
Date established: 1971 **Turnover:** £75m - £125m
No.of Employees: 51 - 100 **Product Groups:** 39, 40, 49, 68

Date of Accounts	Dec 11	Dec 10	Dec 09
Sales Turnover	60m	81m	107m
Pre Tax Profit/Loss	-703	-2m	-4m
Working Capital	-8m	-7m	-5m
Fixed Assets	3m	4m	3m
Current Assets	31m	39m	39m
Current Liabilities	35m	40m	34m

Windlesham

Brighthand Web Design

7 Thorndown Lane, Windlesham, GU20 6DD
Tel: 01276-489004
E-mail: info@brighthand.co.uk
Website: http://www.brighthand.co.uk
Directors: R. Rice (Ptnr)
Immediate Holding Company: BRIGHTHAND IT SOLUTIONS LTD
Registration no: 06945397 **Date established:** 2009
Turnover: Up to £250,000 **No.of Employees:** 1 - 10 **Product Groups:** 44, 67

Foramaflow Ltd

Post House Kennel Lane, Windlesham, GU20 6AA
Tel: 01276-473900 **Fax:** 01276-451446
E-mail: sales@foramaflow.co.uk
Website: http://www.foramaflow.co.uk
Directors: J. Russell Lowe (Co Sec), J. Russell Lowe (Dir)
Immediate Holding Company: FORAMAFLOW LIMITED
Registration no: 00776890 **Date established:** 1963
No.of Employees: 1 - 10 **Product Groups:** 38, 42

Date of Accounts	Dec 11	Dec 10	Dec 09
Working Capital	13	48	35
Fixed Assets	18	7	8
Current Assets	61	98	80

Woking

A B International Ltd

Almac House Church Lane, Bisley, Woking, GU24 9DR
Tel: 01483-488799 **Fax:** 01483-472657
E-mail: sales@ab-international.co.uk
Website: http://www.ab-international.co.uk
Directors: R. Brown (Fin)
Immediate Holding Company: A B INTERNATIONAL LIMITED
Registration no: 02587782 **Date established:** 1991 **Turnover:** £1m - £2m
No.of Employees: 1 - 10 **Product Groups:** 29, 30

Date of Accounts	Nov 11	Nov 10	Nov 09
Working Capital	1m	1m	1m
Fixed Assets	9	6	4
Current Assets	2m	1m	2m

Access Platforms Direct Ltd

5 Quince Drive Bisley, Woking, GU24 9RT
Tel: 01483-475390 **Fax:** 01483-486468
E-mail: info@accessplatformsdirect.co.uk
Website: http://www.accessplatformsdirect.co.uk
Registration no: 06368144 **Product Groups:** 45, 67

Alexander Ramage Associates LLP

Griffin House West Street, Woking, GU21 6BS
Tel: 01483-750701 **Fax:** 01483-740560
E-mail: sandie@ramage.co.uk
Website: http://www.ramage.co.uk
Directors: S. Cox (Co Sec), E. Ramage (Snr Part)
Immediate Holding Company: ALEXANDER RAMAGE ASSOCIATES LLP
Registration no: OC352133 **Date established:** 2010
No.of Employees: 11 - 20 **Product Groups:** 80, 81, 87

Date of Accounts	Apr 11
Working Capital	-126
Fixed Assets	22
Current Assets	331

Armour Home Electronics

Unit B3 Kingswey Business Park Forsyth Road, Woking, GU21 5SA
Tel: 01483-747474 **Fax:** 01483-545600
E-mail: bill.stanley@armourhome.co.uk
Website: http://www.armourhome.co.uk
Bank(s): Nat West
Directors: G. Mcclelland (Jt MD), N. Spence (Fin)
Managers: B. Stanley (Factory Mgr), D. Caswell (I.T. Exec)
Registration no: 01290091 **VAT No.:** GB 224 6234 85
No.of Employees: 11 - 20 **Product Groups:** 37, 44

Badgers

8 St. Johns Road, Woking, GU21 7SE
Tel: 01483-888411 **Fax:** 01483-756627
Website: http://www.chmunday.co.uk
Directors: I. Mundy (Ptnr)
No.of Employees: 1 - 10 **Product Groups:** 24, 49, 65

Michael Bayliss

169 Guildford Road Bisley, Woking, GU24 9EQ
Tel: 01483-472092
Directors: M. Bayliss (Prop)
No.of Employees: 1 - 10 **Product Groups:** 25, 35, 41

Bisley Office Furniture Ltd

Queens Road Bisley, Woking, GU24 9BJ
Tel: 01483-485600 **Fax:** 01483-489962
E-mail: admin@bisley.com
Website: http://www.bisley.com
Directors: J. Atkins (Fin), P. Ashdown (Fin), J. Aitken (Fin)
Immediate Holding Company: BISLEY FURNITURE SYSTEMS LIMITED
Registration no: 01581787 **Date established:** 1981
Turnover: £50m - £75m **No.of Employees:** 101 - 250
Product Groups: 26, 49

Bourne International

Lansbury Estate 102 Lower Guildford Road, Knaphill, Woking, GU21 2EP
Tel: 01483-485789 **Fax:** 01483-475515
E-mail: sales@bourne-intl.co.uk
Website: http://www.bourne-intl.co.uk
Directors: B. Pike (Co Sec)
Immediate Holding Company: BOURNE INTERNATIONAL LIMITED
Registration no: 01915984 **VAT No.:** GB 347 3926 31
Date established: 1985 **Turnover:** £1m - £2m **No.of Employees:** 1 - 10
Product Groups: 22, 23, 24, 25, 27, 28, 30, 32, 33, 35, 36, 37, 38, 44, 49, 63, 64, 65, 81

Date of Accounts	Dec 11	Dec 10	Dec 09
Working Capital	278	449	442
Fixed Assets	6	5	1
Current Assets	673	763	787

Brookwood Community Church

18 Caradon Close, Woking, GU21 3DU
Tel: 01483-825804 **Fax:** 01483-762760
E-mail: martinday@bcc-info.org.uk
Website: http://www.bcc-info.org.uk
Directors: A. Rashbrook (Dir)
Registration no: 04434790 **Date established:** 2005
Turnover: Up to £250,000 **No.of Employees:** 1 - 10 **Product Groups:** 38, 42

Date of Accounts	Dec 06	Dec 05
Sales Turnover	82	91
Pre Tax Profit/Loss	5	12
Working Capital	173	174
Fixed Assets	8	3
Current Assets	174	177
Current Liabilities	1	3
ROCE% (Return on Capital Employed)	2.6	6.7
ROT% (Return on Turnover)	5.7	12.9

Bunny's Bolts

The Depot The Mayford Centre Mayford Green, Woking, GU22 0PP
Tel: 01483-727227 **Fax:** 01483-727995
E-mail: sales@bunnysbolts.com
Website: http://bunnysbolts.com
Directors: W. Smith (Prop)
Immediate Holding Company: BARBER'S FINE ART AUCTIONEERS (CHOBHAM) LIMITED
Registration no: 04086593 **VAT No.:** GB 413 8188 53
Date established: 1978 **Turnover:** £250,000 - £500,000
No.of Employees: 1 - 10 **Product Groups:** 35

Date of Accounts	Apr 11	Apr 10	Apr 09
Working Capital	-26	5	-8
Current Assets	7	20	48

Business Link Surrey

5th Floor Hollywood House Church Street East, Woking, GU21 6HJ
Tel: 08457-494949 **Fax:** 01483-771507
E-mail: sales@businesslinksurrey.co.uk
Website: http://www.businesslinksurrey.co.uk
Directors: R. French (MD)
Managers: A. Bamsoth (Mktg Serv Mgr)
Immediate Holding Company: HATCHFORD MANOR FREEHOLD LIMITED
Registration no: 02908524 **Date established:** 2009 **Turnover:** £5m - £10m
No.of Employees: 51 - 100 **Product Groups:** 80, 81, 86

Date of Accounts	Mar 08	Mar 07	Mar 06
Sales Turnover	5408	5070	5719
Pre Tax Profit/Loss	43	101	-292
Working Capital	1002	960	856
Fixed Assets	49	48	52
Current Assets	1684	1402	1934
Current Liabilities	682	442	1079
ROCE% (Return on Capital Employed)	4.1	10.0	-32.1
ROT% (Return on Turnover)	0.8	2.0	-5.1

Carisbrooke Instruments

Courtenay House Monument Way East, Woking, GU21 5LY
Tel: 01483-722261 **Fax:** 01483-722263
E-mail: info@carisbrookeinstruments.co.uk
Website: http://www.carisbrookeinstruments.co.uk
Directors: R. Tringham (Dir)
Immediate Holding Company: CARISBROOKE INSTRUMENT SERVICES LIMITED
Registration no: 02746026 **Date established:** 1992
No.of Employees: 1 - 10 **Product Groups:** 38

Date of Accounts	Jan 12	Jan 11	Jan 10
Working Capital	18	14	7
Current Assets	30	38	33

Casual Miracles Ltd

14 Orchid Drive Bisley, Woking, GU24 9SB
Tel: 01483-799491 **Fax:** 01483-799491
E-mail: channing.walton@casualmiracles.com
Website: http://www.casualmiracles.com
Directors: C. Walton (Grp Chief Exec), C. Walton (Dir), L. Walton (I.T. Dir)
Immediate Holding Company: CASUAL MIRACLES LIMITED
Registration no: 06051104 **Date established:** 2007
Turnover: £250,000 - £500,000 **No.of Employees:** 1 - 10
Product Groups: 44

Date of Accounts	Dec 08	Dec 07
Working Capital	10	23
Current Assets	13	66
Current Liabilities	2	43

Cookson Electronics Ltd

Forsyth Road, Woking, GU21 5SB
Tel: 01483-758400 **Fax:** 01483-758410
Website: http://www.cooksonelectronics.com
Bank(s): HSBC, Poultry & Princes St
Directors: D. Crimp (MD)
Managers: K. Farrow (Tech Serv Mgr), S. Poole (Comptroller), C. Lopez (Mktg Serv Mgr), M. Robins (Personnel), S. Emery (Buyer)
Ultimate Holding Company: COOKSON GROUP PLC
Immediate Holding Company: ALPHA METALS LIMITED
Registration no: 01804603 **VAT No.:** GB 413 1300 230
Date established: 1962 **Turnover:** £10m - £20m
No.of Employees: 51 - 100 **Product Groups:** 31, 32, 34, 40, 42, 46, 48

Dolphin Mobility Ltd

37 Chertsey Road Chobham, Woking, GU24 8PD
Tel: 01276-856060 **Fax:** 01276-858689
E-mail: sales@dolphinlifts.co.uk
Website: http://www.dolphinlifts.co.uk
Managers: I. Scott (Fin Mgr)
Ultimate Holding Company: DOLPHIN MOBILITY LTD.
Immediate Holding Company: DOLPHIN MOBILITY HOISTS LTD
Registration no: 03747767 **Date established:** 1999 **Turnover:** £2m - £5m
No.of Employees: 11 - 20 **Product Groups:** 45

Date of Accounts	Apr 11	Apr 10	Apr 09
Working Capital	315	329	247
Fixed Assets	22	14	8
Current Assets	530	524	572

Eurograv Ltd

Country Business Centre Lucas Green, West End, Woking, GU24 9LZ
Tel: 01483-474426 **Fax:** 01932-336271
E-mail: sales@eurograv.co.uk
Website: http://www.eurograv.co.uk
Directors: A. Attard (MD)
Immediate Holding Company: EUROGRAV LIMITED
Registration no: 01451117 **Date established:** 1979
No.of Employees: 1 - 10 **Product Groups:** 27, 32, 40, 42, 43, 44, 54, 67

Date of Accounts	Dec 11	Dec 10	Dec 09
Working Capital	91	141	83
Fixed Assets	24	30	19
Current Assets	220	332	240

F C Brown Steel Equipment Ltd

17 Queens Road Bisley, Woking, GU24 9BJ
Tel: 01483-685600 **Fax:** 01483-485610
E-mail: john.irwin@bisley.com
Website: http://www.bisley.com
Bank(s): Nat West, Woking
Directors: J. Irwin (MD)
Managers: V. Voots, P. Westcott (Personnel), R. Hastings (Tech Serv Mgr)
Ultimate Holding Company: BISLEY OFFICE EQUIPMENT LIMITED
Immediate Holding Company: F.C. BROWN (STEEL EQUIPMENT) LIMITED
Registration no: 00693397 **Date established:** 1961
Turnover: £75m - £125m **No.of Employees:** 251 - 500
Product Groups: 26, 36, 38, 49

Date of Accounts	Jul 11	Jul 10	Jul 09
Sales Turnover	62m	58m	64m
Pre Tax Profit/Loss	-2m	-460	-2m
Working Capital	19m	30m	32m
Fixed Assets	34m	35m	37m
Current Assets	28m	38m	41m
Current Liabilities	2m	2m	3m

Fernox

Forsyth Road Sheerwater, Woking, GU21 5RZ
Tel: 01483-793200 **Fax:** 0870-601 5005
E-mail: sales@fernox.com
Website: http://www.fernox.com
Bank(s): Lloyds TSB Bank plc
Directors: F. Wickham (Mkt Research)
Ultimate Holding Company: COOKSON GROUP PLC
Immediate Holding Company: ALPHA METALS LIMITED
Registration no: 00208173 **Date established:** 1962
No.of Employees: 11 - 20 **Product Groups:** 32, 34, 66, 85

Date of Accounts	Dec 11	Dec 10	Dec 09
Pre Tax Profit/Loss	58	27	-5m
Working Capital	16m	15m	16m
Fixed Assets	378	378	378
Current Assets	16m	16m	16m

Format International Ltd

Format House Poole Road, Woking, GU21 6DY
Tel: 01483-726081 **Fax:** 01483-722827
E-mail: just_ask@formatinternational.com
Website: http://www.formatinternational.com
Directors: C. Webster (MD), C. Shrubb (Fin), M. Webster (MD)
Managers: I. Mealey (Accounts), S. Sibbick (Ops Mgr)
Immediate Holding Company: Format Solutions Ltd
Registration no: 01499875 **Date established:** 1980 **Turnover:** £1m - £2m
No.of Employees: 1 - 10 **Product Groups:** 44, 84

Date of Accounts	Dec 07	Dec 06	Dec 05
Working Capital	294	562	420
Fixed Assets	608	632	613

see next page

***Format International Ltd** - Cont'd*

Current Assets	745	1005	756
Current Liabilities	452	443	336

Fox It Ltd
111 Chertsey Road, Woking, GU21 5BW
Tel: 01483-221200 **Fax:** 01483-221500
E-mail: training@foxit.net
Website: http://www.foxit.net
Bank(s): National Westminster Bank Plc
Directors: P. Speers (MD), A. Gray (Co Sec)
Ultimate Holding Company: WPE IT HOLDINGS LIMITED
Immediate Holding Company: FOX IT LIMITED
Registration no: 05234874 **Date established:** 2004 **Turnover:** £5m - £10m
No.of Employees: 11 - 20 **Product Groups:** 44, 80, 86

Date of Accounts	Dec 09	Dec 08	Dec 07
Sales Turnover	6m	6m	6m
Pre Tax Profit/Loss	-1m	452	-755
Working Capital	-450	696	208
Fixed Assets	63	44	80
Current Assets	1m	2m	2m
Current Liabilities	1m	1m	1m

Gemini Ductwork Services
Cherry Street, Woking, GU21 6EE
Tel: 01483-730704 **Fax:** 01483-756766
Directors: L. Rawlings (Ptnr)
Date established: 1997 **No.of Employees:** 1 - 10 **Product Groups:** 37, 40, 48

Harvey Water Softeners Ltd
Hipley Street, Woking, GU22 9LQ
Tel: 01483-753404 **Fax:** 01483-726030
E-mail: info@harvey.co.uk
Website: http://www.harveywatersofteners.co.uk
Directors: H. Bowden (MD)
Managers: G. Halligan (Tech Serv Mgr), C. Narkin (Mktg Serv Mgr), A. Borland (Buyer), D. Parker (Comptroller)
Immediate Holding Company: HARVEY WATER SOFTENERS LIMITED
Registration no: 01362650 **Date established:** 1978
Turnover: £10m - £20m **No.of Employees:** 51 - 100 **Product Groups:** 17, 30, 40

Date of Accounts	Dec 11	Dec 10	Apr 10
Sales Turnover	11m	7m	9m
Pre Tax Profit/Loss	1m	723	1m
Working Capital	6m	5m	5m
Fixed Assets	5m	5m	5m
Current Assets	8m	7m	7m
Current Liabilities	813	547	472

I S S Facilities Services Co GSK
I S S House 1 Genesis Business Park Albert Drive, Woking, GU21 5RW
Tel: 08450-576400 **Fax:** 01483-754999
E-mail: info@uk.issworld.com
Website: http://www.uk.issworld.com
Directors: D. Openshaw (Grp Chief Exec), J. Ahmed (Fin), M. Brown (I.T. Dir), C. Gethin (Fin), A. Price (MD)
Ultimate Holding Company: FS INVEST SARL (LUXEMBOURG)
Immediate Holding Company: ISS FACILITY SERVICES LIMITED
Registration no: 00890885 **Date established:** 1966
Turnover: £500m - £1,000m **No.of Employees:** 1 - 10
Product Groups: 80

Date of Accounts	Dec 11	Dec 10	Dec 09
Sales Turnover	561m	522m	497m
Pre Tax Profit/Loss	24m	23m	21m
Working Capital	56m	44m	32m
Fixed Assets	11m	11m	12m
Current Assets	318m	281m	245m
Current Liabilities	49m	44m	36m

I S S Mediclean Ltd
I S S House 1 Genesis Business Park Albert Drive, Woking, GU21 5RW
Tel: 08450-576300 **Fax:** 0871-429 6300
Website: http://www.uk.issworld.com
Directors: J. Horn (Pers), M. Brabin (Fin)
Managers: H. Andersen
Ultimate Holding Company: FS INVEST SARL (LUXEMBOURG)
Immediate Holding Company: ISS MEDICLEAN LIMITED
Registration no: 01659837 **Date established:** 1982
Turnover: £250m - £500m **No.of Employees:** 101 - 250
Product Groups: 38

Date of Accounts	Dec 11	Dec 10	Dec 09
Sales Turnover	339m	311m	301m
Pre Tax Profit/Loss	22m	18m	18m
Working Capital	62m	59m	52m
Fixed Assets	10m	2m	2m
Current Assets	122m	113m	96m
Current Liabilities	42m	37m	27m

Jewson Ltd
Horsell Moor, Woking, GU21 4NQ
Tel: 01483-715371 **Fax:** 01483-763680
Website: http://www.hirepoint.co.uk
Managers: J. Hood (District Mgr)
Ultimate Holding Company: COMPAGNIE DE SAINT GOBAIN (FRANCE)
Immediate Holding Company: JEWSON LIMITED
Registration no: 00348407 **VAT No.:** GB 497 7184 83
Date established: 1939 **No.of Employees:** 21 - 50 **Product Groups:** 66

Date of Accounts	Dec 11	Dec 10	Dec 09
Sales Turnover	1606m	1547m	1485m
Pre Tax Profit/Loss	18m	100m	45m
Working Capital	-345m	-250m	-349m
Fixed Assets	496m	387m	461m
Current Assets	657m	1005m	1320m
Current Liabilities	66m	120m	64m

K F C Head Office
32 Goldsworth Road, Woking, GU21 6JT
Tel: 01483-717000 **Fax:** 01483-717018
Website: http://www.kfc.co.uk
Directors: T. Ashby (Dir), G. Allan (Dep Pres)
Managers: A. Perren
Ultimate Holding Company: YUM! BRANDS INC (USA)
Immediate Holding Company: K F C ADVERTISING LIMITED
Registration no: 01178568 **VAT No.:** 414 0215 13 **Date established:** 1974
Turnover: £50m - £75m **No.of Employees:** 1 - 10 **Product Groups:** 69

Date of Accounts	Nov 08	Nov 09	Nov 10
Sales Turnover	34m	38m	39m
Pre Tax Profit/Loss	-2m	-44	77
Working Capital	567	536	591
Fixed Assets	5m	6m	6m
Current Liabilities	956	2m	3m

Lab Lateral
Lynton House Station Approach, Woking, GU22 7PY
Tel: 01483-608060 **Fax:** 01483-561100
E-mail: sales@lablateral.com
Website: http://www.lablateral.com
Directors: J. Tooze (Dir)
Immediate Holding Company: LAB LATERAL LTD
Registration no: 04828633 **Date established:** 2003
Turnover: £500,000 - £1m **No.of Employees:** 21 - 50 **Product Groups:** 44

Date of Accounts	Jul 11	Jul 10	Jul 09
Sales Turnover	N/A	N/A	682
Pre Tax Profit/Loss	N/A	N/A	112
Working Capital	-357	45	61
Fixed Assets	142	53	13
Current Assets	134	369	223
Current Liabilities	N/A	N/A	136

M W B Business Exchange
Elizabeth House Duke Street, Woking, GU21 5AS
Tel: 01483-206950 **Fax:** 01329-223223
E-mail: iscott@cecoffices.com
Website: http://www.businesslink.gov.uk
Directors: J. Stevens (Grp Chief Exec)
Managers: G. Harris (Mktg Serv Mgr), S. Webster (I.T. Exec), I. Scott (Mgr), S. Smith (Accounts)
Registration no: 03099070 **Turnover:** £1m - £2m
No.of Employees: 21 - 50 **Product Groups:** 80

Mclaren Racing
Mclaren Technology Centre Chertsey Road, Woking, GU21 4YH
Tel: 01483-261000 **Fax:** 01483-261963
E-mail: webmaster@mclaren.com
Website: http://www.mclaren.com
Directors: M. Ohjeh (Ptnr), M. Whitmarsh (MD)
Managers: B. Illman (Sales Prom Mgr)
Ultimate Holding Company: MCLAREN GROUP LIMITED
Immediate Holding Company: MCLAREN RACING LIMITED
Registration no: 01517478 **VAT No.:** GB 529 0575 35
Date established: 1980 **Turnover:** £125m - £250m
No.of Employees: 251 - 500 **Product Groups:** 39

Date of Accounts	Dec 10	Dec 09	Dec 08
Sales Turnover	149m	175m	139m
Pre Tax Profit/Loss	14m	42m	14m
Working Capital	14m	-3m	-35m
Fixed Assets	25m	26m	25m
Current Assets	109m	119m	75m
Current Liabilities	83m	110m	73m

Magnet Schultz Ltd
3-4 Capital Park High Street, Old Woking, Woking, GU22 9LD
Tel: 01483-794700 **Fax:** 01483-757298
E-mail: sales@magnetschultz.co.uk
Website: http://www.magnetschultz.co.uk
Directors: A. Newton (MD)
Managers: R. Kershaw (Sales Prom Mgr), R. Sam (Tech Serv Mgr)
Ultimate Holding Company: Magnet-Schultz Group
Date established: 1912 **Turnover:** £2m - £5m **No.of Employees:** 11 - 20
Product Groups: 24, 32, 36, 37, 38, 39, 45, 67, 89

Date of Accounts	Jun 10	Jun 09	Jun 08
Working Capital	1m	1m	1m
Fixed Assets	98	106	111
Current Assets	2m	2m	2m

Maingate Ltd
6 Manor Way Old Woking, Woking, GU22 9JX
Tel: 01483-727898 **Fax:** 0845-230 7585
E-mail: ole@maingate.co.uk
Website: http://www.maingate.co.uk
Directors: O. Valentin (MD)
Immediate Holding Company: MAINGATE LIMITED
Registration no: 05753878 **Date established:** 2006
No.of Employees: 1 - 10 **Product Groups:** 41, 45

Date of Accounts	Dec 11	Dec 10	Dec 09
Working Capital	58	-160	-102
Fixed Assets	11	3	3
Current Assets	280	347	265

Management Forum
98-100 Maybury Road, Woking, GU21 5JL
Tel: 01483-730071 **Fax:** 01483-730008
E-mail: info@management-forum.co.uk
Website: http://www.management-forum.co.uk
Bank(s): Barclays Bank
Directors: B. Osborne (Co Sec)
Immediate Holding Company: MANAGEMENT FORUM LIMITED
Registration no: 01470584 **VAT No.:** GB 341 2321 09
Date established: 1980 **No.of Employees:** 11 - 20 **Product Groups:** 81, 86

Date of Accounts	Mar 12	Mar 11	Mar 10
Working Capital	210	115	58
Fixed Assets	3	3	16
Current Assets	826	619	600

Marden Wolfe Ltd
2 High Street Chobham, Woking, GU24 8AA
Tel: 01276-856466 **Fax:** 01276-856709
E-mail: deewalker@mardenwolfe.com
Website: http://www.mardenwolfe.com
Directors: D. Walker (MD)
Immediate Holding Company: MARDEN WOLFE LIMITED
Registration no: 01378596 **Date established:** 1978
No.of Employees: 1 - 10 **Product Groups:** 38, 42

Date of Accounts	Oct 11	Oct 10	Oct 09
Working Capital	115	105	109
Fixed Assets	1	2	3
Current Assets	493	307	240

Martins Printing Group
Old Woking, Woking, GU22 9LH
Tel: 01483-757501 **Fax:** 01483-755168
E-mail: mmilton@mpgltd.co.uk
Website: http://www.mpgltd.co.uk
Directors: M. Croucher (MD), C. Martin (Ch), C. Chandler (Co Sec), M. Andrew (MD), M. Milton (Grp Chief Exec), N. Hussey (Sales)
Managers: V. Andrew (Personnel), M. Price (I.T. Exec)
Ultimate Holding Company: MPG LIMITED
Immediate Holding Company: MARTINS PROPERTIES LIMITED
Registration no: 00558456 **Date established:** 1955
Turnover: Up to £250,000 **No.of Employees:** 1 - 10 **Product Groups:** 28, 64

Date of Accounts	Dec 07	Dec 06	Dec 05
Sales Turnover	66	221	272
Pre Tax Profit/Loss	3m	160	185
Working Capital	-250	-252	-366
Fixed Assets	928	7m	5m
Current Assets	8m	211	21
Current Liabilities	24	N/A	16

Mitchell Horton
1 Bakersgate Courtyard Ash Road Pirbright, Woking, GU24 0NJ
Tel: 01483-233050 **Fax:** 01483-757578
E-mail: engineers@mitchell-horton.co.uk
Website: http://www.mitchell-horton.co.uk
Directors: P. Mitchell (MD)
Immediate Holding Company: MITCHELL-HORTON (HOLDINGS) LIMITED
Registration no: 06335393 **Date established:** 2007
No.of Employees: 1 - 10 **Product Groups:** 35

Date of Accounts	Dec 10	Dec 09	Dec 08
Working Capital	48	-31	-30
Fixed Assets	183	187	191
Current Assets	82	16	14

Mouchel Group
Mouchel Export House, Woking, GU21 6QX
Tel: 01483-731000 **Fax:** 01483-731001
E-mail: info@mouchel.com
Website: http://www.mouchel.com
Bank(s): The Royal Bank of Scotland
Directors: G. Rumbles (Grp Chief Exec), R. Mundy (Pers), D. Tilston (Fin)
Managers: S. Connolly (Mktg Serv Mgr)
Ultimate Holding Company: MOUCHEL GROUP PLC
Immediate Holding Company: MOUCHEL MANAGEMENT CONSULTING LIMITED
Registration no: 02491619 **Date established:** 1990
Turnover: £50m - £75m **No.of Employees:** 251 - 500
Product Groups: 54, 84

Date of Accounts	Jul 11	Jul 10	Jul 09
Sales Turnover	58m	79m	79m
Pre Tax Profit/Loss	-2m	-2m	33
Working Capital	4m	4m	6m
Fixed Assets	1m	5m	4m
Current Assets	14m	16m	21m
Current Liabilities	2m	6m	7m

Multipulse Electronics
Unit 1-3 Goldsworth Park Trading Estate Kestrel Way, Woking, GU21 3BA
Tel: 01483-713600 **Fax:** 01483-729851
E-mail: info@multipulse.com
Website: http://www.multipulse.com
Bank(s): National Westminster
Directors: P. Scott (Fin)
Immediate Holding Company: MULTIPULSE ELECTRONICS LIMITED
Registration no: 01844077 **VAT No.:** GB 417 1533 73
Date established: 1984 **Turnover:** £2m - £5m **No.of Employees:** 21 - 50
Product Groups: 37

Date of Accounts	Mar 11	Mar 09	Mar 08
Working Capital	810	634	736
Fixed Assets	144	41	50
Current Assets	3m	1m	2m

S Murray & Co. Ltd
Holborn House High Street, Old Woking, Woking, GU22 9LB
Tel: 01483-740099 **Fax:** 01483-755111
E-mail: sales@smurray.co.uk
Website: http://www.smurray.co.uk
Bank(s): National Westminster
Directors: P. Murray (MD), D. Pitt (Fin)
Managers: M. Elton (Tech Serv Mgr)
Ultimate Holding Company: MURRAY HOLDINGS LIMITED
Immediate Holding Company: S.MURRAY & COMPANY LIMITED
Registration no: 00145824 **VAT No.:** GB 211 6460 04
Date established: 2017 **Turnover:** £5m - £10m
No.of Employees: 51 - 100 **Product Groups:** 30, 33, 38

Date of Accounts	Dec 11	Dec 10	Dec 09
Sales Turnover	5m	5m	5m
Pre Tax Profit/Loss	-32	-128	35
Working Capital	390	477	593
Fixed Assets	3m	3m	3m
Current Assets	2m	2m	2m
Current Liabilities	213	180	194

Panacea Data Ltd
Unit A Poole Road, Woking, GU21 6DY
Tel: 01483-814040 **Fax:** 01483-814041
Website: http://www.panacea-data.co.uk
Directors: F. Khan (Fin)
Immediate Holding Company: PANACEA DATA LIMITED
Registration no: 02564668 **Date established:** 1990
No.of Employees: 1 - 10 **Product Groups:** 37, 47, 48, 67

Date of Accounts	Dec 10	Dec 08	Dec 07
Working Capital	-27	-29	-28
Fixed Assets	27	29	29
Current Assets	N/A	5	10
Current Liabilities	N/A	7	10

Paragon Fire Protection
Unit 10a Manor Way, Woking, GU22 9JX
Tel: 01483-724484 **Fax:** 01483-724494
E-mail: info@paragonfire.co.uk
Website: http://www.paragonfire.co.uk
Directors: S. White (Ptnr)
Date established: 2004 **No.of Employees:** 1 - 10 **Product Groups:** 38, 42

Pattonair Ltd
Kingsway Business Park Forsyth Road, Sheerwater, Woking, GU21 5SA
Tel: 01483-774600 **Fax:** 01483-774619
E-mail: uksales@pattonair.com
Website: http://www.pattonair.com
Bank(s): Lloyds TSB Bank plc
Directors: G. Puddifoot (Mkt Research), H. Morgan (Comm), N. Robins (MD), S. Bowers (Co Sec)
Ultimate Holding Company: Umeco plc
Immediate Holding Company: Orchard House Ltd
Registration no: 00974964 **Date established:** 1970
Turnover: £20m - £50m **Product Groups:** 39

Date of Accounts	Mar 08	Mar 07	Mar 06
Sales Turnover	35641	30258	33184
Pre Tax Profit/Loss	2669	824	683
Working Capital	9527	10640	9976
Fixed Assets	9142	6849	6330
Current Assets	19226	16984	19847
Current Liabilities	9699	6344	9870
Total Share Capital	78	78	78
ROCE% (Return on Capital Employed)	14.3	4.7	4.2
ROT% (Return on Turnover)	7.5	2.7	2.1

Price & Pierce Softwoods Ltd

Cavendish House 36-40 Goldsworth Road, Woking, GU21 6JT
Tel: 01483-221800 **Fax:** 01483-726203
E-mail: softwood.woking@price-pierce.co.uk
Website: http://www.price-pierce.co.uk
Directors: A. Rhys Davies (Fin)
Immediate Holding Company: PRICE & PIERCE FOREST PRODUCTS LTD
Registration no: 03841742 **VAT No.:** GB 240 1700 20
Date established: 1999 **Turnover:** £10m - £20m **No.of Employees:** 1 - 10
Product Groups: 25, 26

Date of Accounts	Dec 11	Dec 10	Dec 09
Sales Turnover	11m	11m	9m
Pre Tax Profit/Loss	135	278	170
Working Capital	2m	1m	1m
Fixed Assets	3	10	18
Current Assets	6m	5m	5m
Current Liabilities	1m	822	774

Raupack

131 High Street Old Woking, Woking, GU22 9LD
Tel: 01483-736800 **Fax:** 01483-736810
E-mail: info@raupack.co.uk
Website: http://www.raupack.co.uk
Directors: W. Rauch (MD), W. Rauch (MD)
Immediate Holding Company: RAUPACK LIMITED
Registration no: 01583736 **Date established:** 1981 **Turnover:** £5m - £10m
No.of Employees: 11 - 20 **Product Groups:** 38, 42

Date of Accounts	Oct 11	Oct 10	Oct 09
Sales Turnover	7m	8m	7m
Pre Tax Profit/Loss	432	383	403
Working Capital	2m	2m	2m
Fixed Assets	63	73	28
Current Assets	4m	4m	6m
Current Liabilities	505	356	397

Repropoint Ltd

15 Poole Road, Woking, GU21 6BB
Tel: 01483-596281 **Fax:** 01483-596292
E-mail: enquiries@repropoint.com
Website: http://www.repropoint.com
Directors: S. Hallett (MD), A. North (Tech Serv), D. Bennett (Sales)
Managers: B. Jones (Fin Mgr), P. Bailey (Purch Mgr)
Immediate Holding Company: REPROPOINT LIMITED
Registration no: 01228936 **VAT No.:** GB 389 0126 14
Date established: 1975 **Turnover:** £5m - £10m
No.of Employees: 51 - 100 **Product Groups:** 26, 28, 67

Date of Accounts	Oct 11	Oct 10	Oct 09
Sales Turnover	N/A	N/A	6m
Pre Tax Profit/Loss	N/A	N/A	85
Working Capital	-358	-553	-541
Fixed Assets	962	1m	1m
Current Assets	1m	1m	1m
Current Liabilities	N/A	N/A	370

S L D Security & Communications

The Old Forge Ockham Lane, Ockham, Woking, GU23 6PH
Tel: 01483-225633 **Fax:** 01483-225634
E-mail: sales@sld.co.uk
Website: http://www.sld.co.uk
Directors: M. Farkouh (MD)
Date established: 1999 **No.of Employees:** 1 - 10 **Product Groups:** 40, 67

S M P Electronics

Unit 6 Border Farm Station Road, Chobham, Woking, GU24 8AS
Tel: 01276-855166 **Fax:** 01276-855115
E-mail: sales@smpelectronics.com
Website: http://www.samalite.com
Directors: S. Pharro (Ptnr)
Immediate Holding Company: S R NEWMAN LIMITED
Date established: 1998 **No.of Employees:** 1 - 10 **Product Groups:** 37, 39

Date of Accounts	Mar 11	Mar 10	Mar 09
Working Capital	-155	-155	-155
Fixed Assets	751	751	751

S R Designs

1 Hook Hill Park, Woking, GU22 0PX
Tel: 08447-706996 **Fax:** 01483-770919
E-mail: sales@golfprizes.co.uk
Website: http://www.golfprizes.co.uk
Directors: S. Rogers (Dir)
Immediate Holding Company: GRAPEVINE ADVERTISING LIMITED
Registration no: 01629840 **Date established:** 1982
No.of Employees: 1 - 10 **Product Groups:** 22, 24, 49, 65

Date of Accounts	Sep 11	Sep 10	Sep 09
Working Capital	29	25	13
Fixed Assets	N/A	1	1
Current Assets	72	106	68

Shades Photographic

Unit 2 Butts Road, Woking, GU21 6JU
Tel: 01483-740362 **Fax:** 01483-720026
E-mail: shadesphoto@btinternet.com
Website: http://www.shadesphoto.co.uk
Directors: G. Burton (Co Sec)
Registration no: 04449024 **Turnover:** Up to £250,000
No.of Employees: 1 - 10 **Product Groups:** 81

Michael Smith Engineers Ltd (Head Office)

Oaks Road, Woking, GU21 6PH
Tel: 01483-771871 **Fax:** 01483-723110
E-mail: info@michael-smith-engineers.co.uk
Website: http://www.michael-smith-engineers.co.uk
Bank(s): National Westminster Bank Plc
Directors: S. Smith (Dir)
Immediate Holding Company: MICHAEL SMITH ENGINEERS LIMITED
Registration no: 01017871 **Date established:** 1971 **Turnover:** £2m - £5m
No.of Employees: 11 - 20 **Product Groups:** 39, 40, 42

Date of Accounts	Jun 11	Jun 10	Jun 09
Sales Turnover	2m	2m	2m
Pre Tax Profit/Loss	47	-22	-73
Working Capital	279	235	298
Fixed Assets	25	28	51
Current Assets	820	894	620
Current Liabilities	251	234	96

Smithy Crafts

Pankhurst Farm Bagshot Road, West End, Woking, GU24 9QR
Tel: 01276-857198
Directors: P. Smith (Prop)
Date established: 1991 **No.of Employees:** 1 - 10 **Product Groups:** 26, 35

Soma Design

21 Westfield Avenue, Woking, GU22 9PH
Tel: 01483-764491 **Fax:** 01483-764491
E-mail: calvers@soma-design.co.uk
Website: http://www.soma-group.co.uk
Directors: A. Lopez Calvete (Prop)
Turnover: Up to £250,000 **No.of Employees:** 1 - 10 **Product Groups:** 24, 49, 81

Sunley Estates Ltd

Connaught House Portsmouth Road, Send, Woking, GU23 7JY
Tel: 01483-270550 **Fax:** 01483-270551
E-mail: info@sunley.co.uk
Website: http://www.sunley.co.uk
Directors: J. Sunley (Dir)
Registration no: 02266458 **Turnover:** £2m - £5m
No.of Employees: 21 - 50 **Product Groups:** 51

Surrey Fire

Myola Kings Road, West End, Woking, GU24 9LW
Tel: 01483-480567 **Fax:** 01483- 486335
Directors: S. Hill (MD)
Date established: 2004 **No.of Employees:** 1 - 10 **Product Groups:** 38, 42

Tavak Ltd

5 White Cottage Farm Lucas Green Road, West End, Woking, GU24 9LZ
Tel: 08452-235206 **Fax:** 0845-223 5207
E-mail: info@tavak.co.uk
Website: http://www.tavak.co.uk
Bank(s): HSBC Bank plc
Directors: I. Wakeford (Ch)
Ultimate Holding Company: WIAG LIMITED
Immediate Holding Company: TAVAK LIMITED
Registration no: 00615244 **Date established:** 1958
Turnover: £250,000 - £500,000 **No.of Employees:** 11 - 20
Product Groups: 27, 30, 31, 66

Date of Accounts	Mar 11	Mar 10	Mar 09
Sales Turnover	446	484	536
Pre Tax Profit/Loss	-31	41	48
Working Capital	74	111	103
Fixed Assets	18	23	27
Current Assets	149	166	165
Current Liabilities	28	30	29

Tenring Sports Services

Unit G5 The Mayford Centre Mayford Green, Woking, GU22 0PP
Tel: 01483-728958
E-mail: ishirragibb@hotmail.com
Directors: I. Shirra Gibb (Prop)
Immediate Holding Company: THE HOTEL PARTNERSHIP LIMITED
Date established: 2000 **No.of Employees:** 1 - 10 **Product Groups:** 36, 39, 40

Timeplan Ltd

1 Capital Park High Street, Old Woking, Woking, GU22 9LD
Tel: 01483-769766 **Fax:** 01483-730631
E-mail: sales@timeplan.ltd.uk
Website: http://www.timeplan.ltd.uk
Bank(s): Barclays
Directors: D. Thompson (Dir)
Managers: S. Smith (Purch Mgr), B. Bourne
Immediate Holding Company: T3 Group Ltd
Registration no: 01326734 **Date established:** 1977
Turnover: £500,000 - £1m **No.of Employees:** 11 - 20 **Product Groups:** 38

Date of Accounts	Mar 08	Mar 07
Working Capital	184	298
Fixed Assets	348	140
Current Assets	1728	1273
Current Liabilities	1545	975
Total Share Capital	28	28

Tyrrell Services

29 Cavendish Road, Woking, GU22 0EP
Tel: 01483-776684 **Fax:** 01483-776684
Directors: G. Tyrrell (Ptnr)
Immediate Holding Company: TYRRELL SERVICES LIMITED
Registration no: 05734233 **Date established:** 2006
No.of Employees: 1 - 10 **Product Groups:** 20, 40, 41

Date of Accounts	Mar 11	Mar 10
Working Capital	-4	-13
Fixed Assets	16	13
Current Assets	18	16

Vision Engineering Ltd

Monument Way West Monument House, Woking, GU21 5EN
Tel: 01483-248300 **Fax:** 01483-248301
E-mail: mark.curtis@visioneng.co.uk
Website: http://www.visioneng.com
Bank(s): Bank of Scotland, Woking
Directors: M. Curtis (MD), M. Greenslade (Tech Serv), J. Arnold (Fin)
Managers: A. Davison (Purch Mgr), C. Browne (Mktg Serv Mgr), J. Curtis (Personnel)
Immediate Holding Company: VISION ENGINEERING LIMITED
Registration no: 00599506 **VAT No.:** GB 211 3258 14
Date established: 1958 **Turnover:** £10m - £20m
No.of Employees: 101 - 250 **Product Groups:** 38

Date of Accounts	Apr 11	Apr 10	Apr 09
Sales Turnover	16m	10m	13m
Pre Tax Profit/Loss	2m	932	1m
Working Capital	13m	12m	11m
Fixed Assets	4m	4m	4m
Current Assets	16m	14m	13m
Current Liabilities	2m	990	830

Wandsworth Group Ltd

Albert Drive Sheerwater, Woking, GU21 5SE
Tel: 01483-740740 **Fax:** 01483-740384
E-mail: info@wandsworthgroup.com
Website: http://www.wandsworthgroup.com
Bank(s): Lloyds TSB Bank plc
Directors: D. Swinnerton (Fin), G. Stevens (MD)
Managers: J. Woodfield (Mktg Serv Mgr), A. Hardy (Chief Buyer), H. Wynne (Personnel), A. Fowles
Immediate Holding Company: THE WANDSWORTH GROUP LIMITED
Registration no: 00084301 **VAT No.:** GB 211 4947 83
Date established: 2005 **Turnover:** £10m - £20m
No.of Employees: 101 - 250 **Product Groups:** 36, 37, 40

Date of Accounts	Mar 12	Mar 11	Mar 10
Sales Turnover	17m	11m	12m
Pre Tax Profit/Loss	250	-5m	-1m
Working Capital	1m	-1m	73
Fixed Assets	4m	6m	8m
Current Assets	8m	6m	6m
Current Liabilities	940	456	482

Webmaster Intelligent Marketing Ltd

26-28 High Street Chobham, Woking, GU24 8AA
Tel: 01276-855926 **Fax:** 01483-685321
E-mail: info@webintelligentmarketing.com
Website: http://www.webmasterint.com
Directors: W. Blackie (Dir)
Immediate Holding Company: WEB INTELLIGENT MARKETING LTD
Registration no: 07272976 **Date established:** 2010
No.of Employees: 1 - 10 **Product Groups:** 61, 81

Date of Accounts	Jun 11
Fixed Assets	1
Current Assets	20

Wilts Wholesale Electrical

The Hive High Street, Old Woking, Woking, GU22 9LD
Tel: 01483-722422 **Fax:** 01483-769696
Website: http://www.wilts.co.uk
Managers: N. Brown (District Mgr)
Immediate Holding Company: WILTS WHOLESALE ELECTRICAL COMPANY,LIMITED
Registration no: 00679117 **Date established:** 1960
No.of Employees: 1 - 10 **Product Groups:** 36, 40

Woking Funeral Service

119-121 Goldsworth Road, Woking, GU21 6LR
Tel: 01483-772266 **Fax:** 01483-729285
Website: http://www.wokingfunerals.co.uk
Directors: C. Mitchell (Co Sec)
Managers: D. Tresidder (Mgr)
Immediate Holding Company: ALDERWOODS PARTNERSHIP LTD
Registration no: 03461590 **VAT No.:** 571 0617 58 **Date established:** 1973
No.of Employees: 1 - 10 **Product Groups:** 88

Xpress Messenger - Guildford LLP

Unit E Rio Works Polesdon Lane, Ripley, Woking, GU23 6JX
Tel: 08455-191141 **Fax:** 08458-340881
E-mail: scott@xpressmessenger.co.uk
Website: http://www.xpressmessenger.co.uk
Bank(s): Lloyds
Directors: S. White (MD)
Immediate Holding Company: XPRESS MESSENGER-GUILDFORD LLP
Registration no: OC332678 **VAT No.:** 776 6104 11 **Date established:** 2007
Turnover: £250,000 - £500,000 **No.of Employees:** 21 - 50
Product Groups: 79

Date of Accounts	Mar 11	Mar 10	Mar 09
Working Capital	-15	-20	-17
Fixed Assets	47	29	15
Current Assets	289	112	39
Current Liabilities	248	82	28

Young Associates

Heathside Road, Woking, GU22 7HE
Tel: 01483-728225 **Fax:** 01483-714233
Directors: M. Young (Prop)
No.of Employees: 1 - 10 **Product Groups:** 38, 42

Worcester Park

A A Flooring

55 Trent Way, Worcester Park, KT4 8TW
Tel: 020-8330 5419 **Fax:** 020-8330 1180
E-mail: alan.lovell@btinternet.com
Website: http://www.aaflooring.co.uk
Directors: A. Lovell (Prop)
Turnover: Up to £250,000 **No.of Employees:** 1 - 10 **Product Groups:** 25, 30, 31, 52, 63, 66

Cavity Wall & Loft Insulation Grantssolar

57 The Warren, Worcester Park, KT4 7DH
Tel: 020-8330 4711 **Fax:** 020-8330 4711
E-mail: nigel9000@hotmail.com
Directors: N. Campbell (Prop)
Immediate Holding Company: EVERYTHING PROPERTY LIMITED
Registration no: 05252412 **Date established:** 2004
Turnover: Up to £250,000 **No.of Employees:** 1 - 10 **Product Groups:** 18, 37

Date of Accounts	Mar 12	Mar 11
Sales Turnover	N/A	68
Pre Tax Profit/Loss	N/A	-8
Working Capital	3	-9
Fixed Assets	4	1
Current Assets	218	80
Current Liabilities	28	4

Imtech Services

33 The Warren, Worcester Park, KT4 7DH
Tel: 020-8337 6254 **Fax:** 020-8337 6254
E-mail: ian.male@btopenworld.com
Directors: I. Male (Ptnr)
Turnover: Up to £250,000 **No.of Employees:** 1 - 10 **Product Groups:** 36, 38

Mould Growth Consultants Ltd

Mcmillan House Cheam Common Road, Worcester Park, KT4 8RH
Tel: 020-8337 0731 **Fax:** 020-8337 3739
E-mail: info@mgcltd.co.uk
Website: http://www.mgcltd.co.uk
Directors: S. Munnion (Co Sec), P. Munnion (MD)
Ultimate Holding Company: NEWMARKET PROMOTIONS LIMITED
Immediate Holding Company: MOULD GROWTH CONSULTANTS LIMITED
Registration no: 00884771 **Date established:** 1966 **Turnover:** £2m - £5m
No.of Employees: 1 - 10 **Product Groups:** 46, 48

Date of Accounts	Jun 12	Jun 11	Jun 10
Working Capital	106	76	77
Fixed Assets	32	38	51
Current Assets	415	510	650

Quantum Design London Ltd

136b Central Road, Worcester Park, KT4 8HT
Tel: 020-8330 0052 **Fax:** 020-8335 3599
E-mail: tony.hart@quantumdesign.co.uk
Website: http://www.quantumdesign.co.uk
Directors: T. Hart (Dir)
Immediate Holding Company: QUANTUM DESIGN (LONDON) LIMITED
Registration no: 07402175 **Date established:** 2010
Turnover: £500,000 - £1m **No.of Employees:** 1 - 10 **Product Groups:** 20, 40, 41

Date of Accounts	Mar 12
Working Capital	-30
Fixed Assets	31
Current Assets	413

Salute Health Foods

2 Cheam Common Road, Worcester Park, KT4 8RW
Tel: 020-8337 5959 **Fax:** 020-8337 5959
Directors: A. Arcidiacono (Prop)
Date established: 2003 **No.of Employees:** 1 - 10 **Product Groups:** 31, 32

Single Use Instruments Ltd

P.O.Box 52E, Worcester Park, KT4 8LR
Tel: 020-8335 3339 **Fax:** 07092-339335
E-mail: info@single-use-instruments.co.uk
Website: http://www.single-use-instruments.co.uk
Registration no: 06691378 **Turnover:** £500,000 - £1m
No.of Employees: 1 - 10 **Product Groups:** 30, 38

EAST SUSSEX

Battle

Aldershaw Tiles
Parkhold Wood Kent Street, Sedlescombe, Battle, TN33 0SD
Tel: 01424-756777 **Fax:** 01424-756888
E-mail: tiles@aldershaw.co.uk
Website: http://www.aldershaw.co.uk
Directors: A. Kindell (Dir)
Immediate Holding Company: ALDERSHAW HANDMADE TILES LIMITED
Registration no: 03125680 **Date established:** 1995
Turnover: £250m - £500m **No.of Employees:** 1 - 10 **Product Groups:** 33, 35, 66

Date of Accounts	Dec 11	Dec 10	Dec 09
Working Capital	-135	14	-48
Fixed Assets	207	214	208
Current Assets	65	72	40

A R Harley & Sons
Station Road Crowhurst, Battle, TN33 9DB
Tel: 01424-830542 **Fax:** 01424-830532
E-mail: arharley@harleycustom.com
Website: http://www.harleycustom.com
Directors: A. Harley (MD), E. Harley (Fin)
Managers: A. Harley (Chief Mgr)
Immediate Holding Company: A R HARLEY & SONS LIMITED
Registration no: 04907164 **Date established:** 2003
Turnover: £250,000 - £500,000 **No.of Employees:** 1 - 10
Product Groups: 68

Date of Accounts	Dec 08	Dec 07	Dec 06
Working Capital	-48	-48	-25
Fixed Assets	5	5	6
Current Assets	38	19	49
Current Liabilities	86	67	74

Howard Bros Joinery Ltd
Station Approach, Battle, TN33 0DE
Tel: 01424-773272 **Fax:** 01424-773836
E-mail: john@howard-bros-joinery.com
Website: http://www.howardbros.com
Bank(s): National Westminster Bank Plc
Directors: T. Hedges (Fab), A. Royce (Fin), G. Goodwin (Fin), J. Margiotta (Dir), S. Discombe (MD)
Ultimate Holding Company: GREAT WATER PROPERTIES LIMITED
Immediate Holding Company: HOWARD BROS JOINERY LTD.
Registration no: 03178591 **VAT No.:** GB 662 0962 34
Date established: 1996 **Turnover:** £10m - £20m
No.of Employees: 51 - 100 **Product Groups:** 25, 26, 30, 35, 52

Date of Accounts	Dec 11	Dec 10	Dec 09
Sales Turnover	11m	8m	6m
Pre Tax Profit/Loss	61	112	65
Working Capital	349	206	-25
Fixed Assets	653	771	982
Current Assets	2m	2m	1m
Current Liabilities	717	1m	759

Rutherford The Pool People
The Swimshop Rutherfords Business Park, Battle, TN33 0TY
Tel: 01424-775060 **Fax:** 01424-777066
E-mail: info@rutherfordpools.co.uk
Website: http://www.rutherfordpools.co.uk
Directors: G. Rutherford (Prop)
Immediate Holding Company: RUTHERFORD CONSTRUCTION COMPANY LIMITED
VAT No.: 621 6255 63 **Date established:** 1946
Turnover: £250,000 - £500,000 **No.of Employees:** 1 - 10
Product Groups: 30

Date of Accounts	Dec 10	Dec 09	Dec 08
Working Capital	-4	-5	-6
Fixed Assets	2m	2m	2m
Current Assets	28	28	24

Selanex Ltd
Loose Farm Hastings Road, Battle, TN33 0TG
Tel: 01424-773404 **Fax:** 01424-774878
E-mail: sales@selanex.uk.com
Website: http://www.selanex.uk.com
Directors: J. Ringwood (MD), J. Ringwood (Fin)
Immediate Holding Company: SELANEX LIMITED
Registration no: 01052318 **VAT No.:** GB 247 2799 25
Date established: 1972 **Turnover:** £500,000 - £1m
No.of Employees: 1 - 10 **Product Groups:** 30, 36, 40

Date of Accounts	Mar 11	Mar 10	Mar 09
Working Capital	39	21	2
Fixed Assets	9	2	3
Current Assets	303	209	284

Senlac Stone Ltd
Rutherford Business Park Marley Lane, Battle, TN33 0TY
Tel: 01424-772244 **Fax:** 01424-772249
E-mail: senlacstone@aol.com
Website: http://www.senlacstone.co.uk
Directors: G. Rutherford (Sales), M. Rutherford (MD)
Ultimate Holding Company: RUTHERFORD CONSTRUCTION COMPANY LIMITED
Immediate Holding Company: SENLAC STONE LIMITED
Registration no: 00663102 **VAT No.:** GB 583 9670 87
Date established: 1960 **Turnover:** £500,000 - £1m
No.of Employees: 1 - 10 **Product Groups:** 33

Date of Accounts	Dec 11	Dec 10	Dec 09
Working Capital	129	130	73
Fixed Assets	9	5	20
Current Assets	186	177	164

Team Corporation UK Ltd European Division
11 Old Ladies Court High Street, Battle, TN33 0AH
Tel: 01424-777004 **Fax:** 01424-777005
E-mail: sales@teamcorporation.co.uk
Website: http://www.teamcorporation.co.uk
Directors: M. Burt (Fin), B. Huntley (MD)
Immediate Holding Company: TEAM CORPORATION UK LIMITED
Registration no: 04067381 **VAT No.:** GB 771 2186 33
Date established: 2000 **Turnover:** £500,000 - £1m
No.of Employees: 1 - 10 **Product Groups:** 38, 39, 54

Date of Accounts	Sep 11	Sep 10	Sep 09
Working Capital	308	195	96
Fixed Assets	4	5	4
Current Assets	573	664	217

Bexhill On Sea

Alvin Industrial Limited
PO BOX 140, Bexhill On Sea, TN39 3WG
Tel: 01424-846962 **Fax:** 01424-848973
E-mail: info@alvinindustrial.eu
Website: http://www.alvin.net
Directors: M. ROACH (Grp Chief Exec), D. Mackenzie (Fin)
Registration no: 04144109 **Date established:** 2000 **Turnover:** £1m - £2m
No.of Employees: 11 - 20 **Product Groups:** 35

C Brewer & Sons
42 Beeching Road, Bexhill On Sea, TN39 3EW
Tel: 01424-213800 **Fax:** 01424-223511
E-mail: bexhill@brewers.co.uk
Website: http://www.brewers.co.uk
Managers: K. Dobbs (Mgr)
Immediate Holding Company: C.BREWER & SONS LIMITED
Registration no: 00203852 **VAT No.:** GB 195 1565 70
Date established: 1925 **Turnover:** £500,000 - £1m
No.of Employees: 1 - 10 **Product Groups:** 61

Furness Controls Ltd
Beeching Road, Bexhill On Sea, TN39 3LJ
Tel: 01424-730316 **Fax:** 01424-730317
E-mail: info@furness-controls.com
Website: http://www.furness-controls.com
Directors: S. Huntbatch (MD), J. Furness (Dir), S. Huntbatch (Co Sec)
Managers: P. Hale (Buyer), D. Huntbatch (Sales Prom Mgr), D. Huntbach (Export Sales Mg)
Immediate Holding Company: FURNESS CONTROLS LIMITED
Registration no: 00826592 **Date established:** 1964 **Turnover:** £2m - £5m
No.of Employees: 51 - 100 **Product Groups:** 38, 67

Date of Accounts	Dec 11	Dec 10	Dec 09
Working Capital	2m	2m	1m
Fixed Assets	298	203	250
Current Assets	2m	2m	2m

Graham
Beeching Road, Bexhill On Sea, TN39 3LJ
Tel: 01424-215151 **Fax:** 01424-213949
E-mail: gordoncree@graham-group.co.uk
Website: http://www.graham-group.co.uk
Directors: P. Hindle (MD)
Managers: S. Beaumont (District Mgr), M. Allsopp (District Mgr)
Immediate Holding Company: FURNESS CONTROLS LIMITED
Registration no: 00826592 **Date established:** 1964
No.of Employees: 11 - 20 **Product Groups:** 66

Date of Accounts	Dec 10	Dec 09	Dec 08
Working Capital	2m	1m	2m
Fixed Assets	203	250	280
Current Assets	2m	2m	2m

Jewson
2-4 Beeching Road, Bexhill On Sea, TN39 3LG
Tel: 01424-731414 **Fax:** 01424-731887
E-mail: paul.miles@jewson.co.uk
Website: http://www.jewson.co.uk
Managers: P. Miles (District Mgr)
Immediate Holding Company: JEWSON LIMITED
Registration no: 00348407 **Date established:** 1939
Turnover: £500m - £1,000m **No.of Employees:** 11 - 20
Product Groups: 66

Laser Ticketing Systems
96 Cooden Drive, Bexhill On Sea, TN39 3AS
Tel: 01424-225522 **Fax:** 01424-223326
E-mail: info@laserticketing.co.uk
Website: http://www.laserticketing.co.uk
Directors: G. Stovold (Dir), M. Stovold (Fin)
Immediate Holding Company: LASER TICKETING SYSTEMS LIMITED
Registration no: 02261369 **Date established:** 1988 **Turnover:** £1m - £2m
No.of Employees: 1 - 10 **Product Groups:** 44

Date of Accounts	Apr 11	Apr 10	Apr 09
Working Capital	1	30	20
Fixed Assets	23	24	26
Current Assets	35	61	43

London Engineers Pattern Co. Ltd
65 Reginald Road, Bexhill On Sea, TN39 3PQ
Tel: 01424-211049 **Fax:** 01424-734891
E-mail: sales@lepcoltd.co.uk
Bank(s): Lloyds TSB
Managers: M. Marks (Mgr)
Immediate Holding Company: LONDON ENGINEERS PATTERN CO. LTD
Registration no: 00336576 **VAT No.:** GB 217 9468 34
Date established: 1925 **Turnover:** £500,000 - £1m
No.of Employees: 11 - 20 **Product Groups:** 34

Date of Accounts	Apr 08	Apr 07
Sales Turnover	13	20
Pre Tax Profit/Loss	2	7
Working Capital	10	8
Current Assets	10	8
ROT% (Return on Turnover)	12.6	34.3

Mango Electronics
1 Buckhurst Road, Bexhill On Sea, TN40 1QF
Tel: 01424-731500 **Fax:** 01424-731502
E-mail: colin@mango-electronics.co.uk
Website: http://www.mango-electronics.co.uk
Directors: C. Purves (Prop)
Immediate Holding Company: ROTHER VOLUNTARY ACTION
Registration no: 05333784 **VAT No.:** GB 414 1590 79
Date established: 2005 **Turnover:** Up to £250,000
No.of Employees: 1 - 10 **Product Groups:** 14, 25, 26, 33, 37, 38, 39, 40, 66, 67, 84, 85

Date of Accounts	Mar 11	Mar 10	Mar 09
Sales Turnover	215	303	236
Pre Tax Profit/Loss	-9	-8	-22
Working Capital	33	38	45
Fixed Assets	N/A	4	5
Current Assets	89	97	131
Current Liabilities	56	59	86

Model Engineering Supplies Bexhill
Clifford Mews Clifford Road, Bexhill On Sea, TN40 1QA
Tel: 01424-223702 **Fax:** 01424-223702
E-mail: info@model-engineering.co.uk
Website: http://www.model-engineering.co.uk
Directors: R. Neighbour (Prop)
Date established: 1993 **Turnover:** Up to £250,000
No.of Employees: 1 - 10 **Product Groups:** 29, 36, 46, 49, 66

Sonic Windows Ltd
Unit 14-15 Beeching Park Industrial Estate Wainwright Road, Bexhill On Sea, TN39 3UR
Tel: 01424-223864 **Fax:** 01424-215859
E-mail: info@sonicwindows.co.uk
Website: http://www.sonicwindows.co.uk

see next page

***Sonic Windows Ltd** - Cont'd*

Directors: J. Martin (Co Sec), P. Jones (MD)
Immediate Holding Company: SONIC WINDOWS LIMITED
Registration no: 01670615 **Date established:** 1982
Turnover: Up to £250,000 **No.of Employees:** 1 - 10 **Product Groups:** 40, 52

Date of Accounts	Oct 11	Oct 10	Oct 09
Working Capital	112	130	147
Fixed Assets	19	75	81
Current Assets	170	247	297

Brighton

A B C Structures Ltd

1 Hawthorn Way Portslade, Brighton, BN41 2HR
Tel: 01273-891511
E-mail: info@abcmarquees.co.uk
Website: http://www.abcmarquees.co.uk
Directors: D. Coleman (Dir), D. Hunter (MD), D. Hunter (Fin), J. Coleman (Ptnr)
Immediate Holding Company: A.B.C. STRUCTURES LTD
Registration no: 06560511 **Date established:** 2008
No.of Employees: 1 - 10 **Product Groups:** 83

Date of Accounts	Mar 11	Mar 10	Apr 09
Working Capital	-4	-18	-25
Fixed Assets	53	43	56
Current Assets	59	24	29

A Shade Above

Unit 5 Wellington House Camden Street, Portslade, Brighton, BN41 1DU
Tel: 01273-881130 **Fax:** 01273-880600
E-mail: design@ashadeabove.co.uk
Website: http://www.ashadeabove.co.uk
Directors: M. Blake (Prop)
VAT No.: GB 654 3140 56 **Turnover:** £250,000 - £500,000
No.of Employees: 1 - 10 **Product Groups:** 37, 63

A B S Electrical Supplies

Unit A4 Enterprise Industrial Estate Crowhurst Road, Brighton, BN1 8AF
Tel: 01273-541572 **Fax:** 01273-555420
E-mail: sales@abselectrical.co.uk
Website: http://www.abs-electrical.co.uk
Directors: R. Mcbrain (Dir)
Immediate Holding Company: ABS ELECTRICAL SUPPLIES LIMITED
Registration no: 06823419 **Date established:** 2009
No.of Employees: 1 - 10 **Product Groups:** 36, 40

Date of Accounts	Mar 12	Mar 11	Feb 10
Working Capital	111	84	N/A
Fixed Assets	26	6	N/A
Current Assets	377	282	N/A

Aird Company

46 Preston Road, Brighton, BN1 4QF
Tel: 01273-603478 **Fax:** 01273-327191
Website: http://www.aird-tools.co.uk
Directors: R. Warner (Fin), R. Carey (MD)
Immediate Holding Company: AIRD & CO LIMITED
Registration no: 01770779 **Date established:** 1983
No.of Employees: 1 - 10 **Product Groups:** 37

Date of Accounts	Dec 11	Dec 10	Dec 09
Working Capital	41	28	40
Fixed Assets	11	11	13
Current Assets	121	120	129
Current Liabilities	41	7	N/A

Aird & Co. Ltd

14 Bond Street, Brighton, BN1 1RD
Tel: 01273-327191 **Fax:** 01273-327191
E-mail: sales@aird-tools.co.uk
Website: http://www.aird-tools.co.uk
Directors: B. Carey (MD)
Immediate Holding Company: AIRD & CO LIMITED
Registration no: 01770779 **Date established:** 1983
No.of Employees: 1 - 10 **Product Groups:** 37

Date of Accounts	Dec 11	Dec 10	Dec 09
Working Capital	41	28	40
Fixed Assets	11	11	13
Current Assets	121	120	129
Current Liabilities	41	7	N/A

Amplicon Liveline Ltd

Centenary Industrial Estate Hughes Road, Brighton, BN2 4AW
Tel: 01273-608331 **Fax:** 01273-570215
E-mail: sales@amplicon.com
Website: http://www.amplicon.com
Bank(s): Barclays
Directors: D. Saunders (Chief Op Offcr)
Managers: G. Citroni, M. Bernal, R. Amir, K. Kelly (Buyer)
Ultimate Holding Company: AMPLICON GROUP LIMITED
Immediate Holding Company: AMPLICON LIVELINE LIMITED
Registration no: 01091353 **VAT No.:** GB 191 6042 71
Date established: 1973 **Turnover:** £5m - £10m **No.of Employees:** 21 - 50
Product Groups: 37, 38, 44

Date of Accounts	Jun 11	Jun 10	Jun 09
Sales Turnover	9m	8m	8m
Pre Tax Profit/Loss	2m	1m	1m
Working Capital	3m	2m	1m
Fixed Assets	552	554	596
Current Assets	4m	3m	2m
Current Liabilities	746	604	571

Ascent Lift Services Ltd

Unit 4 Hove Enterprise Centre Basin Road North, Portslade, Brighton, BN41 1UY
Tel: 01273-297989
E-mail: richard@liftservices.co.uk
Website: http://liftservices.co.uk
Directors: R. Downs (MD)
Immediate Holding Company: ASCENT LIFT SERVICES LIMITED
Registration no: 03013419 **Date established:** 1995
Turnover: £500,000 - £1m **No.of Employees:** 11 - 20
Product Groups: 35, 39, 45

Date of Accounts	Dec 11	Dec 10	Dec 09
Working Capital	110	109	99
Fixed Assets	5	6	7
Current Assets	161	225	155

Barcoding Solutions Ltd

Maritime House Basin Road North, Portslade, Brighton, BN41 1WR
Tel: 01273-270004 **Fax:** 01273-270005
E-mail: lbrowning@barcoding.org.uk
Website: http://www.barcoding.org.uk
Directors: L. Browning (MD), P. Griffiths (Fin)
Immediate Holding Company: BARCODING SOLUTIONS LIMITED
Registration no: 03259787 **Date established:** 1996
Turnover: £500,000 - £1m **No.of Employees:** 1 - 10 **Product Groups:** 27, 28, 44, 67, 87

Date of Accounts	Feb 11	Feb 10	Feb 09
Working Capital	14	13	38
Current Assets	49	36	110

Be Secure

91b Bernard Road, Brighton, BN2 3ER
Tel: 01273-385183
Directors: D. Millard (Prop)
No.of Employees: 1 - 10 **Product Groups:** 26, 35

Best Solution Consultancy Ltd

Science Park Square Falmer, Brighton, BN1 9SB
Tel: 01273-704473 **Fax:** 01273-704474
E-mail: info@best-solution.co.uk
Website: http://www.best-solution.co.uk
Directors: J. Collyer (Fin), T. Collyer (MD)
Immediate Holding Company: BEST SOLUTION CONSULTANCY LIMITED
Registration no: 03256332 **Date established:** 1996
No.of Employees: 1 - 10 **Product Groups:** 38, 85

Block X

53 Newhaven Street, Brighton, BN2 9NR
Tel: 01273-690002
E-mail: mike.davis@block-x.co.uk
Website: http://www.block-x.co.uk
Directors: M. Davis (Prop)
No.of Employees: 1 - 10 **Product Groups:** 44

Date of Accounts	Mar 08	Mar 07	Mar 06
Working Capital	-4	-3	11
Fixed Assets	4	3	4
Current Assets	12	3	23
Current Liabilities	15	6	12

Brakes

Crowhurst Road, Brighton, BN1 8AF
Tel: 01273-367200
E-mail: leslie.morton@brake.co.uk
Website: http://www.brake.co.uk
Managers: L. Morton (Mgr)
Ultimate Holding Company: BROOKVALE LIMITED
Immediate Holding Company: POTTS & WARD, WOODCOCKS LIMITED
Registration no: 00706764 **Date established:** 1950
Turnover: £10m - £20m **No.of Employees:** 51 - 100 **Product Groups:** 20, 40, 41

Date of Accounts	Jan 11	Jan 10	Jan 09
Working Capital	606	586	655
Fixed Assets	779	783	770
Current Assets	1m	906	989

C & S Nameplate Co. Ltd

37 Vale Road Portslade, Brighton, BN41 1GD
Tel: 01273-419646 **Fax:** 01273-411316
E-mail: sales@candsnameplate.com
Website: http://www.candsnameplate.com
Directors: G. Paterson (MD)
Ultimate Holding Company: C & S NAMEPLATE GROUP LIMITED
Immediate Holding Company: C. & S. NAMEPLATE CO. LIMITED
Registration no: 00957411 **VAT No.:** GB 190 1284 78
Date established: 1969 **Turnover:** Up to £250,000
No.of Employees: 1 - 10 **Product Groups:** 35, 49

Date of Accounts	Jul 11	Jul 10	Jul 09
Working Capital	-13	-19	-24
Fixed Assets	37	39	46
Current Assets	146	118	100

C T S

23-29 Preston Road, Brighton, BN1 4QE
Tel: 01273-670900
E-mail: darrenm@cartersdirect.co.uk
Website: http://www.cartersdirect.co.uk
Managers: D. Mills (Sales Prom Mgr)
Date established: 1985 **No.of Employees:** 11 - 20 **Product Groups:** 36, 40

Catercraft Catering Equipment

Sussex House Fishersgate Terrace, Portslade, Brighton, BN41 1PH
Tel: 01273-411020 **Fax:** 01273-419106
E-mail: info@catercraft.com
Website: http://www.catercraft.com
Directors: M. Keown (Prop), M. McKeown (Prop)
Managers: I. Parnell (Sales Prom Mgr), J. Barry (Tech Serv Mgr)
Ultimate Holding Company: CATERCRAFT (HOLDINGS) LIMITED
Immediate Holding Company: CATERCRAFT (HOLDINGS) LIMITED
Registration no: 03627763 **Date established:** 1998 **Turnover:** £1m - £2m
No.of Employees: 21 - 50 **Product Groups:** 24, 27, 32, 40, 48, 52, 65, 66, 67, 69, 84

Date of Accounts	Jun 11	Jun 10	Jun 09
Working Capital	-69	-69	-69
Fixed Assets	140	140	140
Current Assets	51	54	58

Chlorella Europe UK

82 Crescent Drive South, Brighton, BN2 6RB
Tel: 01273-279408
E-mail: support@chlorella-europe.com
Website: http://www.chlorella-europe.com
Directors: D. Demetris Economou (Prop)
No.of Employees: 1 - 10 **Product Groups:** 20, 31

City Wood Floors

5 Longley Industrial Estate New England Street, Brighton, BN1 4GY
Tel: 01273-680068 **Fax:** 01273-680069
E-mail: simon@citywoodfloors.co.uk
Website: http://www.citywoodfloors.co.uk
Managers: S. Studd (Mgr)
Registration no: 04342300 **Date established:** 2002
No.of Employees: 1 - 10 **Product Groups:** 25, 30, 66

Civil Service Motoring Association

Britannia House 21 Station Street, Brighton, BN1 4DE
Tel: 01273-744721 **Fax:** 01273-744751
E-mail: info@csma.uk.com
Website: http://www.csma.uk.com
Directors: C. Slinn (Co Sec), G. Lockwood (Dir)
Managers: C. Conway (Chief Mgr), M. Branch (I.T. Exec)
Immediate Holding Company: CIVIL SERVICE MOTORING ASSOCIATION,LIMITED(THE)
Registration no: 00252734 **Date established:** 1930
Turnover: £10m - £20m **No.of Employees:** 251 - 500 **Product Groups:** 72

Date of Accounts	Dec 10	Dec 09	Dec 08
Sales Turnover	15m	12m	15m
Pre Tax Profit/Loss	-1m	-3m	-1m
Working Capital	26m	28m	34m
Fixed Assets	17m	17m	15m
Current Assets	30m	34m	37m
Current Liabilities	4m	6m	2m

Clear Thinking Software Ltd

73 Hartington Road, Brighton, BN2 3LS
Tel: 01273-570857 **Fax:** 01273-670730
E-mail: info@clearthinkingsoftware.co.uk
Website: http://www.clearthinkingsoftware.co.uk
Directors: G. Searle (Fin), M. Searle (MD)
Immediate Holding Company: CLEAR THINKING (SOFTWARE) LIMITED
Registration no: 01985278 **VAT No.:** GB 436 0186 65
Date established: 1986 **Turnover:** £500,000 - £1m
No.of Employees: 1 - 10 **Product Groups:** 44

Date of Accounts	Jan 12	Jan 11	Jan 10
Working Capital	210	191	167
Fixed Assets	27	35	36
Current Assets	300	288	271

Compass Components

56 Warren Road, Brighton, BN2 6BA
Tel: 01273-691859 **Fax:** 01273-625777
E-mail: info@compasscomponents.co.uk
Website: http://www.compasscomponents.co.uk
Directors: J. Young (Ptnr)
Date established: 1980 **No.of Employees:** 1 - 10 **Product Groups:** 35

County Hospital & Mortuary Equipment

17 Copse Hill, Brighton, BN1 5GA
Tel: 01273-885441 **Fax:** 01273-240954
E-mail: robin-durant@btconnect.com
Website: http://www.pavilion.co.uk/users/county
Directors: R. Durant (Prop)
Turnover: £250,000 - £500,000 **No.of Employees:** 1 - 10
Product Groups: 26, 36, 40, 67

Custom Pharmaceuticals

Unit 2 Eastergate Road, Brighton, BN2 4QL
Tel: 01273-683444
Website: http://www.custompharm.com
Managers: J. Walton (Mgr)
No.of Employees: 51 - 100 **Product Groups:** 31, 48, 85

Damic Developments & Building Contractors

13 Crescent Drive North, Brighton, BN2 6SP
Tel: 01273-483611 **Fax:** 01273-300034
E-mail: contact@damic.co.uk
Website: http://www.damic.co.uk
Directors: D. Perritt (Ptnr)
Date established: 1983 **No.of Employees:** 1 - 10 **Product Groups:** 52

Datapro Software Ltd

North Street Portslade, Brighton, BN41 1DH
Tel: 01273-886000 **Fax:** 01273-886066
E-mail: info@datapro.co.uk
Website: http://swiftdatapro.com
Directors: N. Dore (Fin), P. Groves (Tech Serv), K. Sieloff (MD)
Managers: F. Grobes (I.T. Exec), G. White (Sales Prom Mgr), J. Postgate (Sales Prom Mgr)
Ultimate Holding Company: SWIFT CORPORATE HOLDINGS LTD
Immediate Holding Company: DATAPRO SOFTWARE LIMITED
Registration no: 07454554 **VAT No.:** GB 620 6389 48
Date established: 2010 **Turnover:** £500,000 - £1m
No.of Employees: 1 - 10 **Product Groups:** 44

Date of Accounts	Apr 08	Jun 07	Jun 06
Sales Turnover	N/A	652	794
Pre Tax Profit/Loss	N/A	5	52
Working Capital	-19	80	91
Fixed Assets	57	54	47
Current Assets	354	171	220
Current Liabilities	374	91	130
ROCE% (Return on Capital Employed)		3.8	37.8
ROT% (Return on Turnover)		0.8	6.6

De Silva Structures

The Brighton Forum 95 Ditchling Road, Brighton, BN1 4ST
Tel: 01273-573802 **Fax:** 01273-689021
E-mail: mail@desilvastructures.co.uk
Website: http://www.desilvastructures.co.uk
Directors: N. De Silva (Dir)
Immediate Holding Company: DE SILVA STRUCTURES LIMITED
Registration no: 06523691 **Date established:** 2008
No.of Employees: 1 - 10 **Product Groups:** 35

Date of Accounts	Mar 11	Mar 10	Mar 09
Working Capital	-0	N/A	-1
Fixed Assets	3	3	2
Current Assets	16	14	15

Diamond Edge Ltd

126 Gloucester Road, Brighton, BN1 4BU
Tel: 01273-605922 **Fax:** 01273-625074
E-mail: diamondedge@btclick.com
Website: http://www.diamondedgeltd.com
Directors: D. Noakes (MD)
Immediate Holding Company: DIAMOND EDGE LIMITED
Registration no: 01054973 **VAT No.:** GB 190 1280 86
Date established: 1972 **Turnover:** £500,000 - £1m
No.of Employees: 1 - 10 **Product Groups:** 32, 36, 40, 63

Date of Accounts	Dec 11	Dec 10	Dec 09
Working Capital	154	196	243
Fixed Assets	5	6	8
Current Assets	240	269	303

E & E Fire Protection
56 The Priory London Road, Patcham, Brighton, BN1 8QT
Tel: 01273-552581
E-mail: contact@eefire.co.uk
Website: http://www.eefire.co.uk
Directors: G. Edmunds (Ptnr)
Date established: 1980 **No.of Employees:** 1 - 10 **Product Groups:** 38, 42

Edo M B M Technology Ltd (Head Office)
Emblem House Home Farm Business Park, Brighton, BN1 9HU
Tel: 01273-810500 **Fax:** 01273-810565
E-mail: info@itt.com
Website: http://www.mbmtech.co.uk
Bank(s): Barclays, Hove
Directors: P. Hills (Dir)
Ultimate Holding Company: ITT CORPORATION (USA)
Immediate Holding Company: EDO MBM TECHNOLOGY LIMITED
Registration no: 00402684 **VAT No.:** GB 620 5182 75
Date established: 1946 **Turnover:** £10m - £20m
No.of Employees: 101 - 250 **Product Groups:** 37, 38, 39, 48

Date of Accounts	Dec 11	Dec 10	Dec 09
Sales Turnover	17m	15m	12m
Pre Tax Profit/Loss	4m	3m	2m
Working Capital	9m	8m	8m
Fixed Assets	1m	1m	1m
Current Assets	13m	11m	9m
Current Liabilities	948	936	925

Escape Hatch Media Recruitment Ltd
5 Orange Row, Brighton, BN1 1UQ
Tel: 01273-710900 **Fax:** 01273-384201
E-mail: info@escapehatchmedia.co.uk
Website: http://www.escapehatchmedia.co.uk
Directors: K. Cowley (Co Sec), D. Grant (MD)
Immediate Holding Company: ESCAPE HATCH MEDIA RECRUITMENT LIMITED
Registration no: 05539454 **Date established:** 2005
Turnover: £250,000 - £500,000 **No.of Employees:** 1 - 10
Product Groups: 80

Date of Accounts	Mar 11	Mar 10	Mar 09
Working Capital	-50	-65	-52
Fixed Assets	61	66	70
Current Assets	1	17	27

Eye Network
125 Queens Road, Brighton, BN1 3WB
Tel: 01273-324422 **Fax:** 08700-565556
E-mail: lisa@eyenetwork.com
Website: http://www.eyenetwork.co.uk
Directors: L. Holnan (Dir)
Ultimate Holding Company: MPG HOLDINGS BV (THE NETHERLANDS)
Immediate Holding Company: PLANON LTD
Registration no: 03752925 **Date established:** 1999
Turnover: £250,000 - £500,000 **No.of Employees:** 11 - 20
Product Groups: 38, 44, 79

Date of Accounts	Dec 11	Dec 10	Dec 09
Working Capital	1m	727	328
Fixed Assets	23	16	11
Current Assets	2m	2m	888

Felton Marine Engineering
The Boatyard Brighton Marina Village, Brighton, BN2 5UG
Tel: 01273-601779 **Fax:** 01273-673258
Website: http://www.feltonmarine.co.uk
Directors: P. Felton (MD)
Managers: L. Russell (Mgr)
Date established: 1983 **No.of Employees:** 1 - 10 **Product Groups:** 35, 36, 39

Harman Plant Hire Ltd
Unit 6 The Hyde Business Park Bevendean, Brighton, BN2 4JE
Tel: 01273-603021 **Fax:** 01273-690647
E-mail: info@harmanhire.co.uk
Website: http://www.harmanhire.co.uk
Directors: M. Court (Fin), V. Harman (MD)
Immediate Holding Company: HARMAN (PLANT HIRE) LIMITED
Registration no: 00624404 **VAT No.:** GB 190 4044 83
Date established: 1959 **Turnover:** £500,000 - £1m
No.of Employees: 1 - 10 **Product Groups:** 83

Date of Accounts	Mar 11	Mar 10	Mar 09
Working Capital	-360	-125	-54
Fixed Assets	691	486	498
Current Assets	312	340	436
Current Liabilities	548	396	424

I C P Search
Jubilee House 1 Jubilee Street, Brighton, BN1 1GE
Tel: 01273-872260
E-mail: info@icpsearch.com
Website: http://www.icpsearch.com
Managers: K. Anderton
Immediate Holding Company: ICP SEARCH LIMITED
Registration no: 05759220 **Date established:** 2006
No.of Employees: 11 - 20 **Product Groups:** 37, 84

Jewson Ltd
77 North Street Portslade, Brighton, BN41 1DZ
Tel: 01273-411843 **Fax:** 01273-430917
Website: http://www.jewson.co.uk
Managers: P. Stillwell (District Mgr)
Ultimate Holding Company: COMPAGNIE DE SAINT GOBAIN (FRANCE)
Immediate Holding Company: JEWSON LIMITED
Registration no: 00348407 **Date established:** 1939
Turnover: £500m - £1,000m **No.of Employees:** 21 - 50
Product Groups: 66

Date of Accounts	Dec 11	Dec 10	Dec 09
Sales Turnover	1606m	1547m	1485m
Pre Tax Profit/Loss	18m	100m	45m
Working Capital	-345m	-250m	-349m
Fixed Assets	496m	387m	461m
Current Assets	657m	1005m	1320m
Current Liabilities	66m	120m	64m

Harvey John Ltd
Lees House 21 Dyke Road, Brighton, BN1 3FE
Tel: 01273-820808 **Fax:** 01273-737127
E-mail: info@harveyjohn.com
Website: http://www.harveyjohn.com
Directors: D. Waddell (Dir)
Immediate Holding Company: HARVEYJOHN LIMITED
Registration no: 05129128 **Date established:** 2004
No.of Employees: 1 - 10 **Product Groups:** 80

Date of Accounts	Jun 11	Jun 10	Jun 09
Working Capital	21	2	4
Fixed Assets	5	6	N/A
Current Assets	89	75	51

Kent Land Yacht Club
140A Warren Road, Brighton, BN2 6DD
Tel: 01273-570507
E-mail: kentlandyachting@hotmail.co.uk
Website: http://www.kentlandyachting.com
Directors: M. Serejko (Ch)
Immediate Holding Company: IWERKS LTD
Date established: 2010 **No.of Employees:** 1 - 10 **Product Groups:** 49, 74

Date of Accounts	Mar 12
Fixed Assets	1
Current Assets	6

Lancing Marine (Prop: Bellamys (M & A) Ltd)
51 Victoria Road Portslade, Brighton, BN41 1XY
Tel: 01273-411765 **Fax:** 01273-430290
E-mail: data@lancingmarine.com
Website: http://www.lancingmarine.com
Directors: M. Dooley (Co Sec), M. Bellamy (MD)
Immediate Holding Company: LANCING MARINE LTD.
Registration no: 01081598 **VAT No.:** GB 192 7321 56
Date established: 1972 **Turnover:** £1m - £2m **No.of Employees:** 1 - 10
Product Groups: 39, 40

The Laptop Shop Ltd
82 Queens Road, Brighton, BN1 3XE
Tel: 01273-220044
E-mail: laptop-station@live.com
Website: http://www.laptopstation.co.uk
Directors: B. West (Prop)
Immediate Holding Company: THE LAPTOP SHOP LIMITED
Registration no: 07649325 **Date established:** 2011
No.of Employees: 1 - 10 **Product Groups:** 36, 37, 44

London & Brighton Plating Company Ltd
100 North Street Portslade, Brighton, BN41 1DG
Tel: 01273-418122 **Fax:** 01273-410316
E-mail: info@lbplating.com
Website: http://www.lbplating.com
Bank(s): Barclays,Portslade
Directors: H. Button (MD), S. Delillis (MD)
Immediate Holding Company: LONDON & BRIGHTON PLATING COMPANY LIMITED(THE)
Registration no: 00407624 **VAT No.:** GB 190 5200 90
Date established: 1946 **Turnover:** £500,000 - £1m
No.of Employees: 21 - 50 **Product Groups:** 48

Date of Accounts	Mar 12	Mar 11	Mar 10
Working Capital	580	575	544
Fixed Assets	493	488	509
Current Assets	768	821	706

London Name Plate Manufacturing Co. Ltd
Zylo Works Sussex St, Brighton, BN2 0HH
Tel: 01273-607025 **Fax:** 01273-571214
E-mail: sales@lnp.co.uk
Website: http://www.lnp.co.uk
Bank(s): National Westminster Bank Plc
Directors: D. Malby (Jt MD)
Managers: K. Tate (Chief Mgr), D. Smith (Sales Prom Mgr)
Registration no: 00155673 **Date established:** 1921 **Turnover:** £2m - £5m
No.of Employees: 51 - 100 **Product Groups:** 27, 28, 30, 35, 49

M S C Gleichmann UK Ltd
Shaftesbury Court Ditchling Road, Brighton, BN1 4ST
Tel: 01273-622446 **Fax:** 01273-622533
E-mail: brighton@msc-ge.com
Website: http://www.msc-ge.com
Bank(s): National Westminster Bank Plc
Directors: G. Young (Dir)
Immediate Holding Company: MSC GLEICHMANN UK LIMITED
Registration no: 03266155 **VAT No.:** DE 143 585 507
Date established: 1996 **Turnover:** £10m - £20m
No.of Employees: 11 - 20 **Product Groups:** 37, 38, 44, 84

Date of Accounts	Dec 11	Dec 10	Dec 09
Working Capital	376	381	308
Fixed Assets	20	21	12
Current Assets	485	431	352

Magic Man Ltd
15 Gordon Road Portslade, Brighton, BN41 1GL
Tel: 08454-581010 **Fax:** 08454-581011
E-mail: info@magicman.co.uk
Website: http://www.magicman.co.uk
Directors: M. Henderson (MD)
Immediate Holding Company: MAGIC MAN LIMITED
Registration no: 04143687 **Date established:** 2001
No.of Employees: 1 - 10 **Product Groups:** 46, 48

Date of Accounts	Mar 11	Mar 10	Mar 09
Working Capital	-369	-203	-220
Fixed Assets	483	600	419
Current Assets	744	552	568

Maple Aggregates UK Ltd
50 Preston Road, Brighton, BN1 4QF
Tel: 01273-699001 **Fax:** 01273-670977
E-mail: enquiries@mapleaggregates.com
Website: http://www.mapleaggregates.com
Directors: C. Bone (Dir)
Immediate Holding Company: MAPLE AGGREGATES (UK) LIMITED
Registration no: 02136304 **Date established:** 1987 **Turnover:** £1m - £2m
No.of Employees: 1 - 10 **Product Groups:** 14, 33

Date of Accounts	Mar 12	Mar 11	Mar 10
Working Capital	64	67	100
Fixed Assets	1	1	1
Current Assets	70	73	302

Maplin Electronics Ltd
65 London Road, Brighton, BN1 4JE
Tel: 08432-277306 **Fax:** 01273-620928
E-mail: customercare@maplin.co.uk
Website: http://www.maplin.co.uk
Managers: R. Body (Mgr)
Ultimate Holding Company: MONTAGU PRIVATE EQUITY LLP
Immediate Holding Company: MAPLIN ELECTRONICS LIMITED
Registration no: 01264385 **Date established:** 1976
Turnover: £125m - £250m **No.of Employees:** 1 - 10 **Product Groups:** 37, 61

Date of Accounts	Dec 11	Dec 08	Dec 09
Sales Turnover	205m	204m	204m
Pre Tax Profit/Loss	25m	32m	35m
Working Capital	118m	49m	75m
Fixed Assets	27m	28m	28m
Current Assets	207m	108m	142m
Current Liabilities	78m	51m	59m

Meadows & Passmore Ltd
1 Ellen Street Portslade, Brighton, BN41 1EU
Tel: 01273-421321 **Fax:** 01273-421322
E-mail: sales@m-p.co.uk
Website: http://www.m-p.co.uk
Directors: P. Meadows (MD)
Immediate Holding Company: MEADOWS & PASSMORE LIMITED
Registration no: 03023507 **Date established:** 1995
Turnover: £500m - £1,000m **No.of Employees:** 1 - 10
Product Groups: 65

Date of Accounts	Mar 11	Mar 10	Mar 09
Working Capital	-96	-122	-103
Fixed Assets	292	298	305
Current Assets	140	133	145
Current Liabilities	212	N/A	N/A

Mersen UK
South Street Portslade, Brighton, BN41 2LX
Tel: 01273-415701 **Fax:** 01273-415673
E-mail: mike.denyer@carbonelorraine.com
Website: http://www.mersen.co.uk
Bank(s): National Westminster Bank Plc
Directors: M. Denyer (MD)
Managers: J. Pittam (Personnel), R. King, C. Pettett (Fin Mgr)
Ultimate Holding Company: LE CARBONE-LORRAINE SA (FRANCE)
Immediate Holding Company: MERSEN UK PORTSLADE LIMITED
Registration no: 00876034 **Date established:** 1966
Turnover: £10m - £20m **No.of Employees:** 51 - 100 **Product Groups:** 17, 33, 34, 35, 36, 37, 39, 40, 42, 45, 48, 84

Date of Accounts	Dec 11	Dec 10	Dec 09
Sales Turnover	14m	15m	12m
Pre Tax Profit/Loss	1m	1m	-98
Working Capital	4m	3m	2m
Fixed Assets	2m	3m	2m
Current Assets	18m	18m	18m
Current Liabilities	717	858	2m

Metway Electrical Industries Ltd
Barrie House 18 North Street, Portslade, Brighton, BN41 1DG
Tel: 01273-439266 **Fax:** 01273-439288
E-mail: sales@metway.co.uk
Website: http://www.metway.co.uk
Bank(s): National Westminster Bank Plc
Directors: S. Chessell (MD)
Managers: L. Turner (Chief Acct), R. Briers
Ultimate Holding Company: METWAY HOLDINGS LIMITED
Immediate Holding Company: METWAY ELECTRICAL INDUSTRIES LIMITED
Registration no: 00378992 **VAT No.:** GB 190 3408 76
Date established: 1943 **Turnover:** £2m - £5m **No.of Employees:** 21 - 50
Product Groups: 37, 40

Date of Accounts	Apr 11	Apr 10	Apr 09
Working Capital	2m	2m	2m
Fixed Assets	101	125	173
Current Assets	3m	3m	3m

Morgan Sindall PLC
72 Dyke Road Drive, Brighton, BN1 6AJ
Tel: 01273-506222 **Fax:** 01273-540424
Website: http://www.bluestone.plc.uk
Directors: J. Jones (Div)
Ultimate Holding Company: MORGAN SINDALL GROUP PLC
Immediate Holding Company: MORGAN SINDALL PLC
Registration no: 04273754 **Date established:** 2001
No.of Employees: 11 - 20 **Product Groups:** 85

Date of Accounts	Dec 11	Dec 10	Dec 09
Sales Turnover	1245m	1233m	732m
Pre Tax Profit/Loss	10m	15m	11m
Working Capital	152m	113m	30m
Fixed Assets	135m	144m	99m
Current Assets	582m	557m	287m
Current Liabilities	324m	364m	184m

Oban Multilingual Ltd
Sussex Innovation Centre The Science Park Square Falmer, Brighton, BN1 9SB
Tel: 01273-704434 **Fax:** 01273-704499
E-mail: greigh@obanmultilingual.com
Website: http://www.obanmultilingual.com
Directors: G. Halbrook (Dir)
Immediate Holding Company: BODYTHERM LIMITED
Date established: 2011 **Turnover:** Up to £250,000
No.of Employees: 11 - 20 **Product Groups:** 80

Date of Accounts	Mar 12	Mar 11	Mar 10
Working Capital	2	51	103
Fixed Assets	2	3	4
Current Assets	147	141	272

Premier Marinas Brighton
Western Concourse Brighton Marina Village, Brighton, BN2 5UP
Tel: 01273-819919 **Fax:** 01273-675082
E-mail: philg@premiermarinas.com
Website: http://www.premiermarinas.com
Managers: P. Godfrey
Ultimate Holding Company: PREMIER MARINAS JERSEY HOLDINGS LTD (JERSEY)

see next page

***Premier Marinas Brighton** - Cont'd*
Immediate Holding Company: PREMIER MARINAS (BRIGHTON) LIMITED
Registration no: 01234892 **VAT No.:** GB 677 4528 90
Date established: 1975 **Turnover:** £2m - £5m **No.of Employees:** 21 - 50
Product Groups: 39, 71, 74

Date of Accounts	Mar 08	Mar 09	Mar 10
Sales Turnover	5m	5m	5m
Pre Tax Profit/Loss	-1m	1m	2m
Working Capital	-11m	-10m	-8m
Fixed Assets	10m	10m	10m
Current Assets	884	520	526
Current Liabilities	2m	2m	2m

Prime Grinding Services
20 St Helens Road, Brighton, BN2 3EE
Tel: 01273-680310
Directors: B. Farmer (Prop)
Date established: 1968 **No.of Employees:** 1 - 10 **Product Groups:** 36

Quality Management Solutions
Tower Point 44 North Road, Brighton, BN1 1YR
Tel: 01273-668896 **Fax:** 01273-668895
E-mail: annabelle@qms-ltd.com
Website: http://www.qms-ltd.com
Directors: C. Park (Dir), A. Ross (MD)
Managers: A. Teale (Accounts), A. Park (Export Sales Mg), M. Blom
Immediate Holding Company: Quality Management Solutions Ltd
Registration no: 04401368 **Date established:** 1998 **Turnover:** £1m - £2m
No.of Employees: 1 - 10 **Product Groups:** 80

R D F Group
2 Bartholomews, Brighton, BN1 1HG
Tel: 01273-200100 **Fax:** 01273-205005
E-mail: info@rdfgroup.com
Website: http://www.rdfgroup.com
Directors: R. Beeforth (Fin), D. Wood (MD)
Managers: A. Fellow (Fin Mgr), J. Scott (Personnel), J. Yeo, I. Wood (Chief Mgr), K. Calimiano
Immediate Holding Company: RDF GROUP PLC
Registration no: 03637683 **Date established:** 1998
Turnover: £20m - £50m **No.of Employees:** 51 - 100 **Product Groups:** 44, 80, 86, 89

Date of Accounts	Mar 12	Mar 11	Mar 10
Sales Turnover	25m	27m	23m
Pre Tax Profit/Loss	728	643	-7
Working Capital	2m	1m	943
Fixed Assets	817	807	808
Current Assets	5m	5m	4m
Current Liabilities	2m	3m	954

R Struthers Ltd
72a Beaconsfield Road, Brighton, BN1 6DD
Tel: 01273-887112 **Fax:** 01273-889666
E-mail: rob@ridstruthers.com
Website: http://www.ridstruthers.com
Directors: R. Struthers (MD)
Date established: 2004 **No.of Employees:** 1 - 10 **Product Groups:** 35

Reed Accountancy Personnel Ltd
132 Queens Road, Brighton, BN1 3WB
Tel: 01273-207710 **Fax:** 01273-728330
E-mail: kate.oconnell@reed.co.uk
Website: http://www.reed.co.uk
Managers: K. O'Connell (Sales Admin)
Immediate Holding Company: REED PERSONNEL SERVICES LTD
Registration no: 00973629 **Turnover:** £125m - £250m
No.of Employees: 101 - 250 **Product Groups:** 80

Reed Employment Ltd
132 Queens Road, Brighton, BN1 3WB
Tel: 01273-207761 **Fax:** 01273-724794
E-mail: kathryn@reed.co.uk
Website: http://www.reed.co.uk
Managers: K. Davies (Mgr)
Ultimate Holding Company: REED GLOBAL LTD (MALTA)
Immediate Holding Company: REED EMPLOYMENT LIMITED
Registration no: 00669854 **Date established:** 1960
Turnover: £75m - £125m **No.of Employees:** 1 - 10 **Product Groups:** 80

Date of Accounts	Jun 11	Jun 10	Dec 07
Sales Turnover	618	450	287m
Pre Tax Profit/Loss	-2m	310	8m
Working Capital	23m	28m	28m
Fixed Assets	31	36	5m
Current Assets	28m	30m	74m
Current Liabilities	37	29	21m

G E Richardson & Sons Ltd
53 New England Street, Brighton, BN1 4GQ
Tel: 01273-570246 **Fax:** 01273-570246
E-mail: metcycle@yahoo.co.uk
Bank(s): National Westminster Bank Plc
Directors: J. Richardson (Dir)
Immediate Holding Company: GEO. E. RICHARDSON & SONS LIMITED
Registration no: 00600056 **VAT No.:** GB 190 8697 18
Date established: 1958 **Turnover:** £2m - £5m **No.of Employees:** 11 - 20
Product Groups: 66

Date of Accounts	Mar 11	Mar 10	Mar 09
Working Capital	2m	1m	1m
Fixed Assets	459	367	415
Current Assets	2m	2m	2m

Rikwoods Presentation
27 Upper Bevendean Avenue, Brighton, BN2 4FG
Tel: 01273-699800 **Fax:** 01273-621133
E-mail: rickwoods.uk@virgin.net
Directors: R. Woods (Prop)
Date established: 1984 **No.of Employees:** 1 - 10 **Product Groups:** 35, 39, 45

Rocc Computers (Branch Office)
Stanford Great South Road, Brighton, BN1 6SB
Tel: 01273-274700 **Fax:** 01273-274707
E-mail: marketing@rocc.co.uk
Website: http://www.rocc.com
Managers: A. Gould (Sales Admin), P. Jones, A. Patel, K. Bristow (Fin Mgr), M. Patel (Sales & Mktg Mg)
Immediate Holding Company: ROCC COMPUTERS LIMITED
Registration no: 02691706 **VAT No.:** GB 209 9698 12
Date established: 1992 **Turnover:** £2m - £5m **No.of Employees:** 21 - 50
Product Groups: 37

Date of Accounts	Mar 11	Mar 10	Mar 09
Sales Turnover	4m	4m	4m
Pre Tax Profit/Loss	198	-66	96
Working Capital	1m	1m	1m
Fixed Assets	1m	1m	1m
Current Assets	3m	3m	3m
Current Liabilities	1m	2m	1m

St Martin Vintners Ltd
Trafalgar Street, Brighton, BN1 4FQ
Tel: 01273-777788 **Fax:** 01273-721403
E-mail: sales@stmartinvintners.co.uk
Website: http://www.stmv.co.uk
Directors: G. Jenner (Fin)
Immediate Holding Company: ST. MARTIN VINTNERS LIMITED
Registration no: 01579313 **Date established:** 1981 **Turnover:** £2m - £5m
No.of Employees: 11 - 20 **Product Groups:** 21, 62

Date of Accounts	Jul 11	Jul 10	Jul 09
Working Capital	471	465	456
Fixed Assets	2	2	5
Current Assets	962	998	1m

Scandinavian Storage Group
Sussex Innovation Centre Science Park Square, Brighton, BN1 9SB
Tel: 01273-704520 **Fax:** 01273-704499
E-mail: danielle@ssg.eu
Website: http://www.ssg-uk.com
Managers: D. Leggatt (Sales Prom Mgr)
Registration no: 06494404 **Date established:** 2008 **Turnover:** £1m - £2m
No.of Employees: 1 - 10 **Product Groups:** 26, 47, 49

Seiki Systems Ltd (a division of Kenard Engineering Group)
Olivier House 18 Marine Parade, Brighton, BN2 1TL
Tel: 01273-666999 **Fax:** 01273-602564
E-mail: sales@seikisystems.co.uk
Website: http://www.seikisystems.co.uk
Directors: J. Davis (MD)
Ultimate Holding Company: KENARD GROUP LIMITED
Immediate Holding Company: SEIKI SYSTEMS LIMITED
Registration no: 04530492 **Date established:** 2002
Turnover: £500,000 - £1m **No.of Employees:** 11 - 20 **Product Groups:** 44

Date of Accounts	Dec 12	Mar 11	Mar 10
Working Capital	-197	-190	-346
Fixed Assets	19	18	10
Current Assets	383	639	303

Selective Asia
72b St Georges Road, Brighton, BN2 1EF
Tel: 01273-670001
E-mail: contact@selectiveasia.com
Website: http://www.selectiveasia.com
Directors: N. Pulley (Prop)
Immediate Holding Company: SELECTIVE ASIA LIMITED
Registration no: 06318621 **Date established:** 2007
Turnover: £250,000 - £500,000 **No.of Employees:** 1 - 10
Product Groups: 69

Date of Accounts	Jul 11	Jul 10	Jul 09
Working Capital	166	36	N/A
Fixed Assets	27	33	N/A
Current Assets	598	454	N/A

Showcase Kitchens
2-2a The Green Southwick, Brighton, BN42 4DA
Tel: 01273-596140 **Fax:** 01273-596140
E-mail: info@showcasekitchens.co.uk
Website: http://www.showcasekitchens.co.uk
Directors: A. Winder (Ptnr)
Immediate Holding Company: SHOWCASE KITCHENS LTD
Registration no: 06788209 **Date established:** 2009
No.of Employees: 1 - 10 **Product Groups:** 32, 63, 66

Date of Accounts	Jan 11	Jan 10
Working Capital	-65	1
Fixed Assets	82	N/A
Current Assets	41	1

Sigta Ltd
26 Abinger Road Portslade, Brighton, BN41 1RZ
Tel: 01273-416989 **Fax:** 01273-423982
E-mail: sales@sigta.co.uk
Website: http://www.sigta.co.uk
Bank(s): National Westminster
Directors: J. Norton (Fin)
Immediate Holding Company: SIGTA LIMITED
Registration no: 01180144 **VAT No.:** GB 423 1318 94
Date established: 1974 **Turnover:** £500,000 - £1m
No.of Employees: 21 - 50 **Product Groups:** 86

Date of Accounts	Aug 11	Aug 10	Aug 09
Sales Turnover	535	618	N/A
Pre Tax Profit/Loss	-10	23	N/A
Working Capital	342	349	312
Fixed Assets	114	117	132
Current Assets	421	400	362
Current Liabilities	57	30	N/A

Smudge Ink
Tallai House Church Lane, Pyecombe, Brighton, BN45 7FE
Tel: 01273-841444 **Fax:** 01273-842442
E-mail: grahamsmudge@talk21.com
Directors: G. Bishop (Ptnr)
Registration no: 02074045 **VAT No.:** GB 350 9635 47
Turnover: £1m - £2m **No.of Employees:** 1 - 10 **Product Groups:** 23

Solo Trading Co.
Flat 1 128 Dyke Road, Brighton, BN1 3TE
Tel: 01273-204490 **Fax:** 01273-727835
E-mail: nisim@solotrading.co.uk
Directors: N. Altabev (Prop)
Immediate Holding Company: MERRYHILL RESIDENTS ASSOCIATION LIMITED
VAT No.: GB 389 9743 66 **Date established:** 1990 **Turnover:** £5m - £10m
No.of Employees: 1 - 10 **Product Groups:** 44, 49, 65, 67

Date of Accounts	Oct 08	Mar 11	Mar 10
Working Capital	-0	-0	-0
Fixed Assets	2	2	2
Current Assets	1	1	1
Current Liabilities	N/A	1	1

Southern Scales & Equipment Co.
15 Chorley Avenue Saltdean, Brighton, BN2 8AQ
Tel: 01273-303692 **Fax:** 01273-279578
E-mail: southernscales@ntlworld.com
Website: http://www.southernscales.co.uk
Directors: M. Bowley (Dir)
No.of Employees: 1 - 10 **Product Groups:** 38, 42

Southern United Ltd
The Old Brewery South Street, Portslade, Brighton, BN41 2LE
Tel: 01273-418636 **Fax:** 01273-423979
E-mail: sales@sunited.co.uk
Website: http://www.sunited.co.uk
Bank(s): National Westminster Bank Plc
Directors: I. Malby (Dir), S. Wood (Sales)
Managers: K. Handy (Quality Control), T. Linsham (Sales Prom Mgr)
Registration no: 00477349 **VAT No.:** GB 192 3470 59
Date established: 1950 **Turnover:** £1m - £2m **No.of Employees:** 51 - 100
Product Groups: 28, 35, 48, 49

Date of Accounts	Dec 09	Dec 08	Dec 07
Working Capital	195	146	132
Fixed Assets	40	44	51
Current Assets	334	286	287

Sovereign Alarms Ltd
142 Saltdean Vale Saltdean, Brighton, BN2 8HF
Tel: 01273-301303 **Fax:** 01273-300937
E-mail: colinchadwick@sovereignalarms.com
Website: http://www.sovereignalarms.com
Directors: C. Chadwick (Comm)
Immediate Holding Company: SOVEREIGN ALARMS LIMITED
Registration no: 02446826 **Date established:** 1989 **Turnover:** £1m - £2m
No.of Employees: 11 - 20 **Product Groups:** 38, 42

Date of Accounts	Mar 11	Mar 10	Mar 09
Sales Turnover	1m	1m	N/A
Pre Tax Profit/Loss	200	294	N/A
Working Capital	24	28	-20
Fixed Assets	148	156	164
Current Assets	312	366	303
Current Liabilities	230	240	N/A

Striking Displays UK Ltd
Display House North Street, Portslade, Brighton, BN41 1DH
Tel: 01273-423623 **Fax:** 01273-420424
E-mail: sales@strikingdisplays.com
Website: http://www.strikingdisplays.com
Bank(s): National Westminster Bank Plc
Directors: J. Bird (Fin), A. Turner (MD)
Immediate Holding Company: STRIKING DISPLAYS (UK) LIMITED
Registration no: 03599934 **VAT No.:** GB 717 6712 24
Date established: 1998 **Turnover:** £500,000 - £1m
No.of Employees: 11 - 20 **Product Groups:** 20, 30, 49, 52

Date of Accounts	Dec 11	Dec 10	Dec 09
Working Capital	-15	-7	-15
Fixed Assets	24	26	28
Current Assets	189	192	166

Sussex Port Forwarding Ltd
Shoreham Port Harbour Office, 84-86 Albion Street, Southwick, Brighton, BN42 4ED
Tel: 01273-598100 **Fax:** 01273-592492
E-mail: info@shoreham-port.co.uk
Website: http://www.shoreham-port.co.uk
Bank(s): Barclays
Directors: R. Alete (Dir), B. Wheeler (Dir), P. Minchin (Dir), B. Tatterton (Dir), T. Waggott (Fin), R. Jumston (Grp Chief Exec)
Managers: V. Stringer (Comm), M. HIll (Personnel)
Ultimate Holding Company: Shoreham Port Authority
Immediate Holding Company: Shoreham Port Development & Investments Ltd
Registration no: 02621885 **VAT No.:** GB 699 2972 55
Turnover: £2m - £5m **No.of Employees:** 51 - 100 **Product Groups:** 71

Date of Accounts	Dec 08	Dec 07	Dec 06
Sales Turnover	3524	3515	2979
Pre Tax Profit/Loss	235	357	192
Working Capital	-526	-210	-291
Fixed Assets	1942	1594	1558
Current Assets	612	1030	760
Current Liabilities	1138	1240	1051
Total Share Capital	100	100	100
ROCE% (Return on Capital Employed)	16.6	25.8	15.2
ROT% (Return on Turnover)	6.7	10.2	6.4

Sussex Sign Co.
Foredown House 2-8 Foredown Drive, Portslade, Brighton, BN41 2BB
Tel: 01273-424900 **Fax:** 01273-424769
E-mail: sales@sussexsigns.com
Website: http://www.sussexsigns.com
Directors: N. Mayhew (MD)
Registration no: 01868344 **Date established:** 1982
Turnover: Up to £250,000 **No.of Employees:** 11 - 20 **Product Groups:** 30, 37, 49, 52, 67, 68, 81

Talbot Tool Co. Ltd
Grip Works Crowhurst Road, Brighton, BN1 8AT
Tel: 01273-508881 **Fax:** 01273-540544
E-mail: info@talbot-tool.co.uk
Website: http://www.talbot-tool.co.uk
Bank(s): National Westminster Bank Plc
Directors: A. Griffiths (Fin)
Immediate Holding Company: TALBOT TOOL COMPANY LIMITED
Registration no: 00362496 **VAT No.:** GB 190 7689 22
Date established: 1940 **Turnover:** £1m - £2m **No.of Employees:** 21 - 50
Product Groups: 46

Date of Accounts	Dec 11	Dec 10	Dec 09
Sales Turnover	N/A	N/A	1m
Pre Tax Profit/Loss	N/A	N/A	-46
Working Capital	640	501	592
Fixed Assets	191	207	188
Current Assets	808	648	699
Current Liabilities	N/A	N/A	101

Teco Ltd
Wellington Road Portslade, Brighton, BN41 1DN
Tel: 01273-410099 **Fax:** 01273-410074
E-mail: info@tecoproducts.co.uk
Website: http://www.tecoproducts.co.uk

Directors: R. Sammons (MD)
Ultimate Holding Company: TECO VENTURES LIMITED
Immediate Holding Company: RON SAMMONS LIMITED
Registration no: 01398336 **Date established:** 1978
Turnover: £250,000 - £500,000 **No.of Employees:** 21 - 50
Product Groups: 35

Date of Accounts	Sep 11	Sep 10	Sep 09
Working Capital	153	136	88
Fixed Assets	137	144	180
Current Assets	624	663	558

The Telemarketing Company Ltd

26-27 Regency Square, Brighton, BN1 2FH
Tel: 01273-765000 **Fax:** 01273-765111
E-mail: info@ttmc.co.uk
Website: http://www.ttmc.co.uk
Directors: N. Habba (MD)
Immediate Holding Company: THE TELE MARKETING CO. LIMITED
Registration no: 02475469 **Date established:** 1990 **Turnover:** £2m - £5m
No.of Employees: 101 - 250 **Product Groups:** 81

Date of Accounts	Aug 11	Aug 10	Aug 09
Working Capital	356	306	515
Fixed Assets	24	31	52
Current Assets	779	625	834

The Argus

Argus House Crowhurst Road, Brighton, BN1 8AR
Tel: 01273-544544 **Fax:** 01273-566114
E-mail: michael.beard@theargus.co.uk
Website: http://www.theargus.co.uk
Bank(s): Barclays
Directors: N. Carpenter (Co Sec)
Managers: M. Beard, L. Elson (Mktg Serv Mgr), S. Mehuex
Ultimate Holding Company: GANNETT CO INC (USA)
Immediate Holding Company: NEWSQUEST (SUSSEX) LIMITED
Registration no: 03223499 **Date established:** 1996 **Turnover:** £5m - £10m
No.of Employees: 51 - 100 **Product Groups:** 28

Date of Accounts	Dec 08	Dec 10	Dec 09
Sales Turnover	20m	10m	11m
Pre Tax Profit/Loss	-24m	436	-92
Working Capital	14m	14m	13m
Fixed Assets	5m	4m	5m
Current Assets	16m	14m	13m
Current Liabilities	2m	133	124

Time Watch plc

Manor Farm Business Centre Poynings Road, Poynings, Brighton, BN45 7AG
Tel: 01273-857771 **Fax:** 01273-857772
E-mail: sales@timewatch.com
Website: http://www.wallchart.com
Directors: G. Wright (MD), A. Wyllie (Tech Serv)
Managers: A. Evans (Admin Off)
Ultimate Holding Company: TIMEWATCH PLC
Immediate Holding Company: WALLCHART INTERNATIONAL LIMITED
Registration no: 03186126 **Date established:** 1996
Turnover: £500,000 - £1m **No.of Employees:** 11 - 20 **Product Groups:** 44

Date of Accounts	Sep 11	Sep 10	Sep 09
Working Capital	418	418	418
Current Assets	418	418	418

University Of Sussex Intellectual Property Ltd

Sussex House University of Sussex Falmer, Falmer, Brighton, BN1 9RH
Tel: 01273-678888 **Fax:** 01273-877456
E-mail: information@sussex.ac.uk
Website: http://www.sussex.ac.uk
Managers: M. Kilpatrick
Ultimate Holding Company: UNIVERSITY OF SUSSEX (ENGLAND)
Immediate Holding Company: UNIVERSITY OF SUSSEX INTELLECTUAL PROPERTY LIMITED
Registration no: 03329002 **Date established:** 1997
Turnover: Up to £250,000 **No.of Employees:** 1 - 10 **Product Groups:** 86

Date of Accounts	Jul 11	Jul 10	Jul 09
Sales Turnover	N/A	N/A	52
Fixed Assets	N/A	100	100
Current Assets	1	2	8
Current Liabilities	N/A	1	1

Vetigraph CAD/CAM Ltd

Unit 4 Level 5 South Wing New England House, New England Street, Brighton, BN1 4GH
Tel: 01273-672400
E-mail: vetigraph_uk@yahoo.co.uk
Website: http://www.vetigraph.com
Directors: H. ANDRIEU (Comm)
Managers: P. JEHAN (Chief Acct)
Registration no: 05540719 **Date established:** 2005 **Turnover:** £1m - £2m
No.of Employees: 11 - 20 **Product Groups:** 43, 44, 67

Date of Accounts	Dec 07	Dec 06
Sales Turnover	93	128
Pre Tax Profit/Loss	-8	1
Working Capital	-8	1
Fixed Assets	1	N/A
Current Assets	18	20
Current Liabilities	26	19
ROCE% (Return on Capital Employed)	118.7	102.3
ROT% (Return on Turnover)	-8.8	1.0

Victory Valve Sales Ltd (Head Office)

Unit 12a Chalex Works, Manorhall Road, Southwick, Brighton, BN42 4NH
Tel: 01273-417398 **Fax:** 01273-430457
E-mail: sales@segl.co.uk
Website: http://www.segl.co.uk
Directors: A. Hughes (Dir)
Managers: A. Tomsett (Sales Admin)
Registration no: 00357557 **VAT No.:** GB 190 3036 87
Turnover: Up to £250,000 **No.of Employees:** 1 - 10 **Product Groups:** 30, 32, 33, 36, 39, 40

Date of Accounts	Mar 12	Mar 11	Mar 10
Working Capital	72	68	48
Fixed Assets	2	3	4
Current Assets	118	126	100

Wemoto Ltd World's End Motorcycles Ltd

Unit 7 Grange Road Industrial Estate - Albion Street, Southwick, Brighton, BN42 4EN
Tel: 08450-292929 **Fax:** 01273-593011
E-mail: info@wemoto.com
Website: http://www.wemoto.com
Directors: C. Coles (Dir)
Ultimate Holding Company: WORLD'S END HOLDINGS LIMITED
Immediate Holding Company: WORLD'S END MOTORCYCLES LIMITED
Registration no: 02592280 **Date established:** 1991 **Turnover:** £1m - £2m
No.of Employees: 21 - 50 **Product Groups:** 68

West Instruments

The Hyde Lower Bevendean, Brighton, BN2 4JU
Tel: 01273-606271 **Fax:** 01273-609990
E-mail: sales@west-cs.com
Website: http://www.west-cs.com
Bank(s): HSBC Bank plc
Directors: T. Bache (MD), N. Macmillan (Fin)
Managers: M. Frisby (Tech Serv Mgr), A. McKenna (Personnel), J. Little (Purch Mgr)
Ultimate Holding Company: DANAHER INC (USA)
Immediate Holding Company: VEEDER-ROOT ENVIRONMENTAL SYSTEMS LTD
Registration no: 00325366 **VAT No.:** GB 654 3401 54
Date established: 1937 **Turnover:** £5m - £10m
No.of Employees: 51 - 100 **Product Groups:** 38, 39, 40

West Marine Services

Marine Trade Centre The Boatyard, Brighton Marina Village, Brighton, BN2 5UG
Tel: 01273-626656 **Fax:** 01273-626656
E-mail: mick@mickwestmarine.com
Website: http://www.mickwestmarine.com
Directors: M. West (MD)
Immediate Holding Company: WEST MARINE SERVICES LIMITED
Registration no: 05597002 **Date established:** 2005
No.of Employees: 1 - 10 **Product Groups:** 35, 36, 39

Date of Accounts	Oct 10	Oct 09	Oct 08
Working Capital	-3	-4	5
Fixed Assets	10	4	2
Current Assets	119	30	63

Williamson Pumps Ltd

Aviation House The Street, Poynings, Brighton, BN45 7AQ
Tel: 01273-857752 **Fax:** 0845-226 3639
E-mail: ah@williamsonpumps.co.uk
Website: http://www.williamsonpumps.co.uk
Directors: H. Hunter (Fin), A. Hunter (MD)
Immediate Holding Company: WILLIAMSON PUMPS LIMITED
Registration no: 01972664 **VAT No.:** GB 407 7124 67
Date established: 1985 **Turnover:** £1m - £2m **No.of Employees:** 1 - 10
Product Groups: 38, 40

Date of Accounts	Dec 11	Dec 10	Dec 09
Working Capital	2m	1m	1m
Fixed Assets	2	2	1
Current Assets	2m	2m	2m
Current Liabilities	N/A	70	49

Crowborough

Alphaglen Laboratories

Unit 12a Millbrook Business Park Sybron Way, Crowborough, TN6 3JZ
Tel: 01892-664224
E-mail: info@alphaglen.co.uk
Website: http://www.alphaglen.co.uk
Directors: A. Lea (Dir), S. Marshall (Sales)
Immediate Holding Company: ALPHAGLEN LABORATORIES LIMITED
Registration no: 02824339 **Date established:** 1993
Turnover: £250,000 - £500,000 **No.of Employees:** 1 - 10
Product Groups: 37

Date of Accounts	Jun 11	Jun 10	Jun 09
Working Capital	37	39	35
Fixed Assets	1	N/A	1
Current Assets	62	47	48
Current Liabilities	N/A	1	2

Apex Electronics Ltd

Brook House Mount Pleasant, Crowborough, TN6 2NE
Tel: 01892-667727 **Fax:** 01892-667742
E-mail: apexmail@netcomuk.co.uk
Website: http://www.apexelectronics.co.uk
Directors: D. Mckay (Dir)
Immediate Holding Company: APEX ELECTRONICS LIMITED
Registration no: 02502622 **Date established:** 1990
Turnover: £500,000 - £1m **No.of Employees:** 1 - 10 **Product Groups:** 37, 39, 67, 68

Date of Accounts	Aug 11	Aug 10	Aug 09
Working Capital	392	309	250
Fixed Assets	63	64	65
Current Assets	493	377	301

Ashdown Control Services Ltd

Unit 10 Millbrook Business Park Sybron Way, Crowborough, TN6 3JZ
Tel: 01892-655538 **Fax:** 01892-667099
E-mail: sales@ashdown-controls.co.uk
Website: http://www.ashdown-controls.co.uk
Bank(s): HSBC
Directors: J. Quinn (Dir), P. Lovering (Dir), S. Lovering (Dir & Co Sec), J. Quinn (Ch), M. Thompson (Sales), P. Lovering (MD)
Managers: H. Wood (Serv Mgr), P. Hamblyn (Sales Prom Mgr), I. Johnson (Eng Serv Mgr), J. Thompson (Chief Acct), D. Barwick (Purch Mgr)
Immediate Holding Company: Evolve Energy Ltd
Registration no: 02351171 **VAT No.:** GB 522 8307 62
Date established: 1983 **Turnover:** £2m - £5m **No.of Employees:** 21 - 50
Product Groups: 38

Baldwin Boxall Communications Ltd

Wealden Industrial Estate Farningham Road, Crowborough, TN6 2JR
Tel: 01892-664422 **Fax:** 01892-663146
E-mail: mail@baldwinboxall.co.uk
Website: http://www.baldwinboxall.co.uk
Bank(s): Barclays, Eastbourne
Directors: B. Shulz (Purch), N. Williams (Fin)
Managers: P. Norris (Tech Serv Mgr)
Immediate Holding Company: BALDWIN BOXALL COMMUNICATIONS LIMITED
Registration no: 01657211 **Date established:** 1982 **Turnover:** £2m - £5m
No.of Employees: 51 - 100 **Product Groups:** 37, 40

Date of Accounts	Sep 11	Sep 10	Sep 09
Working Capital	631	795	792
Fixed Assets	64	102	121
Current Assets	2m	2m	2m

C-Matic Systems

1-3 Warren Court Park Road, Crowborough, TN6 2QX
Tel: 01892-600300 **Fax:** 01892-667515
E-mail: info1@cmatic.co.uk
Website: http://www.cmatic.co.uk
Bank(s): Barclays, Ealing
Managers: M. Stephenson (Chief Mgr)
Immediate Holding Company: C - MATIC SYSTEMS LIMITED
Registration no: 01220986 **VAT No.:** GB 224 3341 02
Date established: 1975 **Turnover:** £2m - £5m **No.of Employees:** 21 - 50
Product Groups: 37, 38, 39, 40, 44, 46, 67, 84

Date of Accounts	Oct 10	Oct 09	Oct 08
Working Capital	2m	3m	2m
Fixed Assets	49	58	70
Current Assets	3m	4m	4m

Conoflex Ltd

9 Sybron Way Millbrook Industrial Estate, Crowborough, TN6 3DZ
Tel: 01892-664388 **Fax:** 01892-664178
E-mail: sales@conoflex.co.uk
Website: http://www.conoflex.co.uk
Directors: A. Mcmanus (MD)
Immediate Holding Company: CONOFLEX LIMITED
Registration no: 03133513 **Date established:** 1995
No.of Employees: 1 - 10 **Product Groups:** 36, 49

Date of Accounts	Mar 11	Mar 09	Mar 08
Working Capital	-190	-126	-99
Current Assets	61	63	108

Coppard Plant Hire Ltd

Wraysbury Crowborough Hill, Crowborough, TN6 2JE
Tel: 01892-662777 **Fax:** 01892-667094
E-mail: sales@coppard.co.uk
Website: http://www.coppard.co.uk
Directors: D. Coppard (MD), C. Coppard (Fin)
Managers: D. Etherington (Tech Serv Mgr), H. Balcombe (Personnel)
Immediate Holding Company: COPPARD PLANT HIRE LIMITED
Registration no: 01056494 **Date established:** 1972 **Turnover:** £5m - £10m
No.of Employees: 21 - 50 **Product Groups:** 07, 23, 24, 25, 29, 30, 33, 35, 36, 37, 38, 40, 41, 42, 45, 46, 47, 48, 51, 52, 63, 66, 67, 68, 72, 83, 84

Date of Accounts	Jun 11	Jun 10	Jun 09
Sales Turnover	8m	7m	7m
Pre Tax Profit/Loss	1m	118	397
Working Capital	2m	1m	696
Fixed Assets	4m	4m	5m
Current Assets	3m	2m	2m
Current Liabilities	634	371	294

Dejay Distribution Ltd

Unit 1 Rocks Farm Business Centre, Stone Cross, Crowborough, TN6 3SJ
Tel: 08453-700266 **Fax:** 0118-978 8123
E-mail: info@dejaydistribution.co.uk
Website: http://www.dejaydistribution.co.uk
Directors: D. Greahead (Sales)
Immediate Holding Company: DEJAY DISTRIBUTION LIMITED
Registration no: 02662054 **Date established:** 1991
No.of Employees: 1 - 10 **Product Groups:** 30, 33, 35, 36, 46, 67

Date of Accounts	Mar 12	Mar 11	Mar 10
Working Capital	45	41	49
Fixed Assets	N/A	N/A	1
Current Assets	97	85	94
Current Liabilities	N/A	N/A	45

Feedback Data Ltd

Park Road, Crowborough, TN6 2QR
Tel: 01892-601400 **Fax:** 01892-601429
E-mail: feedback@fdbk.co.uk
Website: http://www.feedback-data.com
Bank(s): Barclays, Tunbridge Wells
Directors: N. Shepheard (Grp Chief Exec)
Ultimate Holding Company: FEEDBACK PLC
Immediate Holding Company: FEEDBACK DATA PLC
Registration no: 00955977 **VAT No.:** GB 724 6936 13
Date established: 1969 **Turnover:** £1m - £2m **No.of Employees:** 51 - 100
Product Groups: 38, 40, 44, 49

Date of Accounts	May 11	May 10	May 09
Sales Turnover	2m	2m	2m
Pre Tax Profit/Loss	-52	-519	615
Working Capital	395	360	849
Fixed Assets	53	140	170
Current Assets	925	850	1m
Current Liabilities	402	335	326

First Class Print Finish

Unit 4 Wealden Industrial Estate Wealden Industrial Estate Farningham, Crowborough, TN6 2JR
Tel: 01892-610457 **Fax:** 01892-610485
E-mail: info@firstclassprintfinish.co.uk
Directors: R. Hargrave (MD)
Immediate Holding Company: FIRST CLASS PRINT FINISH LTD
Registration no: 07741330 **Date established:** 2011
No.of Employees: 1 - 10 **Product Groups:** 27, 28, 32

Interflow

Medmaw House Farningham Road, Crowborough, TN6 2JP
Tel: 01892-662244
E-mail: customerservices@interflowdispensers.com
Website: http://www.interflowdispensers.com
Directors: M. Stansfield (Ptnr)
No.of Employees: 1 - 10 **Product Groups:** 40, 66

Lamina Keyboards Ltd

32 Southridge Rise, Crowborough, TN6 1LG
Tel: 01892-664633 **Fax:** 01892- 603928
E-mail: sales@lamina-keyboards.com
Website: http://www.lamina-keyboards.com
Directors: R. Holder (Dir)
Managers: N. Morley (Factory Mgr), R. Holder (Tech Serv Mgr)
Turnover: £500,000 - £1m **No.of Employees:** 1 - 10 **Product Groups:** 44

Lo Tek

Friars Gate Farm Estate Mardens Hill, Crowborough, TN6 1XH
Tel: 01892-610010
E-mail: andy@lotek.co.uk
Website: http://www.lo-tekstudios.co.uk

see next page

Lo Tek - Cont'd
Directors: A. Organ (Ptnr)
Registration no: 03771673 **Date established:** 1999
Turnover: Up to £250,000 **No.of Employees:** 1 - 10 **Product Groups:** 89

Longridge Print Ltd (Pimsold Ltd)
10 Sybron Way Millbrook Indl-Est, Crowborough, TN6 3DZ
Tel: 01892-664288 **Fax:** 01892-663681
E-mail: info@longridge.net
Website: http://www.longridge.net
Directors: H. Long (Fin), N. Long (MD)
Managers: M. Penfold (Sales Prom Mgr), R. Merrills (I.T. Exec), N. Long (Mgr)
Immediate Holding Company: PIMSOLD LIMITED
Registration no: 01292634 **Date established:** 1976
No.of Employees: 21 - 50 **Product Groups:** 28

Maxxjet
Southdown Business Centre Western Road, Crowborough, TN6 3EW
Tel: 01892-663074
E-mail: info@maxxjet.co.uk
Website: http://www.maxxjet.co.uk
Directors: B. Braithwaite (Prop)
No.of Employees: 1 - 10 **Product Groups:** 24, 37, 38, 39, 40, 41, 42, 43, 45, 46, 47, 48, 52, 84

Newman Business Solutions
Newman House Farningham Road, Crowborough, TN6 2JR
Tel: 01892-664155 **Fax:** 01892-669591
E-mail: enquiries@newmanbs.co.uk
Website: http://www.newmanbs.co.uk
Bank(s): National Westminster Bank Plc
Directors: A. Deadman (MD), M. Deadman (Co Sec), A. Butcher (Sales)
Managers: J. Page (Personnel), P. Kelly (Purch Mgr), D. Swainsbury (Sales Admin)
Immediate Holding Company: NEWMAN BUSINESS SOLUTIONS LIMITED
Registration no: 01477094 **VAT No.:** GB 339 8807 09
Date established: 1980 **Turnover:** £50m - £75m
No.of Employees: 21 - 50 **Product Groups:** 44

Date of Accounts	Feb 12	Feb 11	Feb 10
Working Capital	50	-73	-125
Fixed Assets	796	805	858
Current Assets	671	671	711

P V L Ltd
9 Lexden Lodge Industrial Estate Crowborough Hill, Crowborough, TN6 2NQ
Tel: 01892-664499 **Fax:** 01892-663690
E-mail: info@pd1.co.uk
Website: http://www.pvl.co.uk
Directors: S. Moorey (Dir), S. Revett (Fin)
Managers: D. Egleton (Sales Prom Mgr)
Immediate Holding Company: PVL Ltd
Registration no: 03711196 **Date established:** 1999 **Turnover:** £1m - £2m
No.of Employees: 1 - 10 **Product Groups:** 37, 38, 40

Pulse Cleaning Services Ltd
Unit 3b Connors Yard Beeches Road, Crowborough, TN6 2AH
Tel: 01892-643585 **Fax:** 01892-653404
E-mail: info@pulse24.co.uk
Website: http://www.pulse24.co.uk
Directors: R. Jackson (Dir), R. Jackson (MD)
Immediate Holding Company: PULSE CLEANING SERVICES LIMITED
Registration no: 04764833 **Date established:** 2003
No.of Employees: 1 - 10 **Product Groups:** 52

Date of Accounts	May 07	May 06
Sales Turnover	N/A	246
Pre Tax Profit/Loss	N/A	35
Working Capital	13	12
Fixed Assets	15	11
Current Assets	69	57
Current Liabilities	56	45
ROCE% (Return on Capital Employed)		152.6
ROT% (Return on Turnover)		14.4

Repolishing.Co.Uk
Unit 6 Connors Yard Crowborough Hill, Crowborough, TN6 2DA
Tel: 01892-668001 **Fax:** 01892-861301
E-mail: gavin@repolishing.co.uk
Website: http://www.repolishing.co.uk
Directors: G. Mason (Prop)
Turnover: Up to £250,000 **No.of Employees:** 1 - 10 **Product Groups:** 26, 31, 32, 48

Safetec Vision Ltd
Unit 7 April Court Sybron Way, Crowborough, TN6 3DZ
Tel: 08455-006060 **Fax:** 01892-724829
E-mail: sales@safetecvision.co.uk
Website: http://www.safetecvision.co.uk
Directors: M. Barnes (MD), A. Barnes (Co Sec), M. Graffin (MD)
Immediate Holding Company: SAFETEC VISION LIMITED
Registration no: 03173724 **Date established:** 1996
Turnover: £250,000 - £500,000 **No.of Employees:** 1 - 10
Product Groups: 40

Date of Accounts	Dec 09	Dec 08	Dec 07
Working Capital	-39	-30	38
Fixed Assets	102	127	157
Current Assets	309	375	411

South East Partitioning Ltd
Sunny Bank Mardens Hill Friars Gate, Crowborough, TN6 1XH
Tel: 01892-667348 **Fax:** 01892-667347
E-mail: chris@partitioning-south.com
Website: http://www.southeastpartitioning.co.uk
Directors: M. Chambers (Dir)
Immediate Holding Company: SOUTH EAST PARTITIONING LIMITED
Registration no: 04478767 **Date established:** 2002 **Turnover:** £1m - £2m
No.of Employees: 1 - 10 **Product Groups:** 25, 33, 35, 52, 66

Date of Accounts	Jul 11	Jul 10	Jul 09
Working Capital	-170	-183	-96
Fixed Assets	219	235	252
Current Assets	220	181	135

Webster Griffin Ltd
Brooklands Park Farningham Road, Crowborough, TN6 2JD
Tel: 01892-664250 **Fax:** 01892-664340
E-mail: info@webstergriffin.com
Website: http://www.webstergriffin.com
Bank(s): HSBC Bank plc
Directors: M. Wilson (MD)
Immediate Holding Company: WEBSTER GRIFFIN LIMITED
Registration no: 01203811 **VAT No.:** GB 204 6081 01
Date established: 1975 **No.of Employees:** 11 - 20 **Product Groups:** 42, 84

Date of Accounts	Mar 12	Mar 11	Mar 10
Working Capital	83	76	74
Fixed Assets	573	581	586
Current Assets	722	605	973

Eastbourne

A R Associates
25 Lushington Road, Eastbourne, BN21 4LG
Tel: 01323-640360 **Fax:** 01323-640321
E-mail: arassocitaes@mistral.co.uk
Website: http://www.mistral.co.uk
Directors: A. Ramezan (Prop)
Date established: 1990 **No.of Employees:** 1 - 10 **Product Groups:** 35

Alfa Laval Eastbourne Ltd
Birch Road, Eastbourne, BN23 6PQ
Tel: 01323-412555 **Fax:** 01323-414515
E-mail: barry.godfrey@alfalaval.com
Website: http://www.alfalaval.com
Bank(s): HSBC Bank plc
Directors: M. Verhoven (Sales), B. Godfrey (MD), B. Westwood (Mkt Research), L. Price (Fin)
Managers: S. Taylor (Personnel), P. Farenden (I.T. Exec), D. Stone (Tech Serv Mgr), J. Baker (Chief Acct)
Immediate Holding Company: ALFA LAVAL EASTBOURNE LIMITED
Registration no: 07427524 **Date established:** 2010
Turnover: £10m - £20m **No.of Employees:** 101 - 250
Product Groups: 40, 41, 42

Date of Accounts	Dec 11
Sales Turnover	19m
Pre Tax Profit/Loss	7m
Working Capital	4m
Fixed Assets	2m
Current Assets	9m
Current Liabilities	1m

Ansvar Insurance
31 St Leonards Road, Eastbourne, BN21 3UR
Tel: 01323-737541 **Fax:** 01323-430977
E-mail: info@ansvar.co.uk
Website: http://www.ansvar.co.uk
Bank(s): National Westminster Bank Plc
Directors: R. Lane (MD), M. Fletcher (Fin)
Managers: S. O'Sullivan (Sales Admin), S. Houghton (Tech Serv Mgr), J. Williams (Sales & Mktg Mg)
Ultimate Holding Company: ALLCHURCHES TRUST LIMITED
Immediate Holding Company: ANSVAR INSURANCE COMPANY LIMITED
Registration no: 00661060 **Date established:** 1960 **Turnover:** £5m - £10m
No.of Employees: 51 - 100 **Product Groups:** 82

Date of Accounts	Dec 10	Dec 09	Dec 08
Pre Tax Profit/Loss	4m	5m	5m
Fixed Assets	46m	39m	46m
Current Assets	16m	16m	14m
Current Liabilities	8m	6m	7m

C Brewers & Sons
Albany House 123-127 Ashford Road, Eastbourne, BN21 3TR
Tel: 01323-411080 **Fax:** 01323-721435
E-mail: enquiries@brewers.co.uk
Website: http://www.brewers.co.uk
Directors: S. Adams (Comm)
Managers: T. Wood, P. Davies (Chief Acct), D. Relf (Tech Serv Mgr), G. Baglin (Personnel)
Immediate Holding Company: C.BREWER & SONS LIMITED
Registration no: 00203852 **Date established:** 2025
Turnover: £75m - £125m **No.of Employees:** 51 - 100
Product Groups: 25, 27, 30, 32, 33

Date of Accounts	Dec 10	Dec 09	Dec 08
Sales Turnover	118m	114m	116m
Pre Tax Profit/Loss	4m	7m	5m
Working Capital	18m	21m	17m
Fixed Assets	22m	21m	21m
Current Assets	38m	34m	31m
Current Liabilities	16m	12m	12m

Caffyns plc
Meads Road, Eastbourne, BN20 7DR
Tel: 01323-730201 **Fax:** 01323-739680
E-mail: info@caffyns.co.uk
Website: http://www.caffyns.co.uk
Bank(s): HSBC Bank plc
Directors: S. Caffyn (Pers), A. Goodburn (Fin), M. Harrison (Fin), S. Caffyn (Grp Chief Exec)
Managers: C. Fullalove (Tech Serv Mgr)
Immediate Holding Company: CAFFYNS PUBLIC LIMITED COMPANY
Registration no: 00105664 **VAT No.:** GB 661 9179 10
Date established: 2009 **Turnover:** £125m - £250m
No.of Employees: 501 - 1000 **Product Groups:** 68

Date of Accounts	Mar 12	Mar 11	Mar 10
Sales Turnover	170m	201m	189m
Pre Tax Profit/Loss	1m	268	970
Working Capital	8m	4m	4m
Fixed Assets	28m	29m	32m
Current Assets	36m	35m	31m
Current Liabilities	15m	15m	13m

Cambridge Polymer Consultants
A 11 South Cliff Tower Bolsover Road, Eastbourne, BN20 7JW
Tel: 01323-729789 **Fax:** 01323-729789
E-mail: tjhenman@lineone.net
Directors: T. Henman (Prop), T. Henman (Head)
VAT No.: GB 370 4506 69 **Date established:** 1997
Turnover: Up to £250,000 **No.of Employees:** 1 - 10 **Product Groups:** 84

Camlock Systems Ltd
Unit 3 Park View Alder Close, Eastbourne, BN23 6QE
Tel: 01323-410996 **Fax:** 01323-411512
E-mail: enquiries@camlock.com
Website: http://www.camlock.com
Bank(s): National Westminster Bank Plc
Directors: R. Carroll (Ch), R. Paterson (Mkt Research), T. Dent (Sales)
Managers: C. Watson (Comptroller)
Immediate Holding Company: CAMLOCK SYSTEMS LIMITED
Registration no: 01323911 **Date established:** 1977
No.of Employees: 21 - 50 **Product Groups:** 35, 36, 37, 39, 40, 46, 66

Date of Accounts	Apr 11	Apr 10	Apr 09
Working Capital	1m	900	818
Fixed Assets	459	503	558
Current Assets	2m	1m	1m

Carfax Catering Equipment
17 Helvellyn Drive, Eastbourne, BN23 8HT
Tel: 01323-460606
E-mail: carfaxes@aol.com
Website: http://www.carfax-catering-equipment.co.uk
Directors: J. Ward (Prop)
Date established: 1995 **No.of Employees:** 1 - 10 **Product Groups:** 20, 40, 41

Cee Vee Engineering Ltd
10 Edison Road, Eastbourne, BN23 6PT
Tel: 01323-504010 **Fax:** 01323-503010
E-mail: sales@ceevee.co.uk
Website: http://www.ceevee.co.uk
Directors: S. Cole (MD)
Immediate Holding Company: CEE VEE ENGINEERING LIMITED
Registration no: 01148710 **Date established:** 1973
No.of Employees: 1 - 10 **Product Groups:** 37, 45, 48, 67

Date of Accounts	Sep 11	Sep 10	Sep 09
Working Capital	-1	-3	-18
Fixed Assets	20	27	36
Current Assets	87	96	112

Co Axel Power Systems
Finmere Road, Eastbourne, BN22 8QL
Tel: 01323-639974 **Fax:** 01323-739654
E-mail: sales@coaxialpower.com
Website: http://www.coaxelpower.com
Directors: S. Roache (Fin)
Immediate Holding Company: COAXIAL POWER SYSTEMS LIMITED
Registration no: 03084502 **VAT No.:** GB 661 7483 17
Date established: 1995 **Turnover:** £250,000 - £500,000
No.of Employees: 1 - 10 **Product Groups:** 37, 47, 84

Date of Accounts	Dec 11	Dec 10	Dec 09
Sales Turnover	621	533	372
Pre Tax Profit/Loss	35	11	-22
Working Capital	-101	-114	-109
Fixed Assets	178	179	182
Current Assets	260	241	152
Current Liabilities	96	247	147

Commsandsound.Com Ltd
Unit 1250 Sstore 51 Brampton Road, Eastbourne, BN22 9AF
Tel: 01273-906696 **Fax:** 01273-906696
E-mail: sales@commsandsound.com
Website: http://www.commsandsound.com
Directors: B. Tugwell (MD)
Immediate Holding Company: ASHKEY PROPERTY INVESTMENT LIMITED
Registration no: 662099323 **Date established:** 2003
No.of Employees: 1 - 10 **Product Groups:** 49, 65, 89

Date of Accounts	Apr 09	Apr 08	Apr 07
Sales Turnover	N/A	N/A	6m
Pre Tax Profit/Loss	N/A	N/A	18
Working Capital	-388	-408	15
Fixed Assets	5	6	6
Current Assets	722	722	1m
Current Liabilities	N/A	N/A	1m

Eastbourne Borough Council
1 Grove Road, Eastbourne, BN21 4TW
Tel: 01323-410000 **Fax:** 01323-410322
E-mail: enquiries@eastbourne.gov.uk
Website: http://www.eastbourne.gov.uk
Directors: R. Cottrill (Dir)
No.of Employees: 1 - 10 **Product Groups:** 54, 69, 72, 80, 81, 84, 87

Eastbourne Motoring Centre
103 Bourne Street, Eastbourne, BN21 3SE
Tel: 01323-745321 **Fax:** 01323-734560
E-mail: enquiries@eastbournevauxhall.co.uk
Website: http://www.emcgroup.org
Bank(s): HSBC Bank plc
Directors: T. Esdaile (Fin), M. Lambird (Sales)
Managers: G. Edwards (Tech Serv Mgr), S. Ullah (Sales Prom Mgr), S. Hadland (Personnel)
Ultimate Holding Company: EMC GROUP HOLDINGS LTD
Immediate Holding Company: EMC TAX FREE LIMITED
Registration no: 03187506 **Date established:** 1996
Turnover: £20m - £50m **No.of Employees:** 21 - 50 **Product Groups:** 68, 80

Date of Accounts	Dec 07	Dec 06	Dec 05
Sales Turnover	N/A	N/A	25464
Pre Tax Profit/Loss	624	604	329
Working Capital	1004	583	518
Fixed Assets	1589	1617	1572
Current Assets	5633	4804	4079
Current Liabilities	4629	4220	3560
Total Share Capital	42	42	42
ROCE% (Return on Capital Employed)	24.1	27.4	15.7
ROT% (Return on Turnover)			1.3

Euroweb S W Ltd
22 Hawthorn Road, Eastbourne, BN23 6QA
Tel: 01323-646925 **Fax:** 01323-728463
E-mail: sales@euroweb.co.uk
Website: http://www.euroweb.uk.com
Bank(s): The Royal Bank of Scotland
Directors: P. Tait (Fin)
Ultimate Holding Company: G.T. FACTORS LIMITED
Immediate Holding Company: EUROWEB (S.W.) LIMITED
Registration no: 02444764 **Date established:** 1989
Turnover: £500,000 - £1m **No.of Employees:** 11 - 20
Product Groups: 23, 35, 39, 40, 45

Date of Accounts	Mar 11	Mar 10	Mar 09
Sales Turnover	779	N/A	N/A
Pre Tax Profit/Loss	136	N/A	N/A

Working Capital	609	500	425
Fixed Assets	N/A	7	1
Current Assets	669	534	463
Current Liabilities	47	N/A	N/A

Fast Heat International UK Ltd

7 Alder Close, Eastbourne, BN23 6QF
Tel: 01323-647375 **Fax:** 01323-410355
E-mail: sales@fastheatuk.com
Website: http://www.fastheatuk.com
Directors: C. Newall (Dir), W. Nugent (Co Sec)
Immediate Holding Company: FAST HEAT INTERNATIONAL (U.K.) LIMITED
Registration no: 02175614 **Date established:** 1987
Turnover: £250,000 - £500,000 **No.of Employees:** 11 - 20
Product Groups: 42

Date of Accounts	Dec 11	Dec 10	Dec 09
Working Capital	640	678	703
Fixed Assets	73	53	56
Current Assets	728	750	792

G T Factors Ltd GTF

22-22a Hawthorn Rd, Eastbourne, BN23 6QA
Tel: 01323-728626 **Fax:** 01323-728890
E-mail: sales@gtf.co.uk
Website: http://www.gtf.co.uk
Bank(s): HSBC
Directors: G. Tait (MD)
Managers: P. Tait (Chief Mgr)
Registration no: 02091081 **VAT No.:** GB 461 7711 46
Date established: 1985 **Turnover:** £2m - £5m **No.of Employees:** 11 - 20
Product Groups: 23, 30, 35, 39, 45, 66, 68

Date of Accounts	Mar 11	Mar 10	Mar 09
Sales Turnover	3m	N/A	N/A
Pre Tax Profit/Loss	384	N/A	N/A
Working Capital	821	620	527
Fixed Assets	613	638	651
Current Assets	2m	1m	1m
Current Liabilities	280	N/A	N/A

Gardners Books Ltd

1 Whittle Drive, Eastbourne, BN23 6QH
Tel: 01323-521777 **Fax:** 01323-521666
E-mail: enquiries@gardners.com
Website: http://www.gardners.com
Bank(s): Lloyds TSB Bank plc
Directors: B. Jackson (Purch), J. Little (MD)
Managers: G. Shepherd (Mktg Serv Mgr), K. Allaway (Tech Serv Mgr), N. Little (Fin Mgr), P. Saunders (Personnel)
Ultimate Holding Company: THE LITTLE GROUP LIMITED
Immediate Holding Company: GARDNERS BOOKS LIMITED
Registration no: 02010127 **VAT No.:** GB 444 9504 37
Date established: 1986 **Turnover:** £125m - £250m
No.of Employees: 501 - 1000 **Product Groups:** 28, 64

Date of Accounts	Feb 08	Feb 11	Feb 10
Sales Turnover	156m	176m	200m
Pre Tax Profit/Loss	7m	6m	8m
Working Capital	25m	31m	27m
Fixed Assets	14m	16m	17m
Current Assets	63m	67m	61m
Current Liabilities	1m	1m	1m

GoPlasticPallets.Com

Unit 6B Alder Close, Eastbourne, BN23 6QF
Tel: 01323-744057 **Fax:** 01323-749662
E-mail: chris@goplasticpallets.com
Website: http://www.goplasticpallets.com
Directors: C. Adam (Dir)
Turnover: £250,000 - £500,000 **No.of Employees:** 1 - 10
Product Groups: 45

Hotchkiss Ltd

7 Marshall Road, Eastbourne, BN22 9AX
Tel: 01323-501234 **Fax:** 01323-508752
E-mail: info@hotchkiss.co.uk
Website: http://www.hotchkiss.co.uk
Bank(s): Barclays Bank Plc
Directors: C. Beadle (Sales), G. Woolley (Grp MD), S. Pottage (Fin)
Managers: J. Peters (Personnel), L. Crunden (Buyer), V. Husband (Tech Serv Mgr)
Ultimate Holding Company: HOTCHKISS GROUP LTD
Immediate Holding Company: HOTCHKISS LTD
Registration no: 00900611 **VAT No.:** GB 190 3076 75
Date established: 1967 **Turnover:** £20m - £50m
No.of Employees: 251 - 500 **Product Groups:** 36, 40, 42, 46, 52, 54

Date of Accounts	Mar 11	Mar 10	Mar 09
Sales Turnover	30m	34m	32m
Pre Tax Profit/Loss	475	209	481
Working Capital	4m	4m	3m
Fixed Assets	558	590	723
Current Assets	17m	19m	17m
Current Liabilities	6m	8m	7m

R S Kain & Co.

1 Windsor Close, Eastbourne, BN23 8JS
Tel: 01342-778580 **Fax:** 01342-327940
E-mail: rodkain@aol.com
Product Groups: 22, 23, 29, 67, 68, 80, 83

L B Lighting Ltd

Unit 6e Southbourne Business Park, Eastbourne, BN22 8UY
Tel: 01323-430047 **Fax:** 01323-732356
E-mail: sales@lblighting.co.uk
Website: http://www.lblighting.co.uk
Managers: D. Murphy
Immediate Holding Company: L.B. LIGHTING LIMITED
Registration no: 00887109 **VAT No.:** GB 389 9089 70
Date established: 1966 **Turnover:** £1m - £2m **No.of Employees:** 1 - 10
Product Groups: 37

Date of Accounts	Nov 09	Nov 08
Working Capital	30	40
Current Assets	30	49

Lister Lutyens Co. Ltd

6 Alder Close, Eastbourne, BN23 6QF
Tel: 01323-431177 **Fax:** 01323-639314
E-mail: sales@listerteak.com
Website: http://www.listerteak.com
Directors: P. Visuttiporn (MD), T. Vayakornvichitr (Prop), T. Vayakornvichitr (Dir)
Managers: A. Maskell (Sales Admin)
Immediate Holding Company: LISTER LUTYENS COMPANY LIMITED
Registration no: 03222200 **Date established:** 1996
Turnover: £500,000 - £1m **No.of Employees:** 1 - 10 **Product Groups:** 26, 49

Date of Accounts	Dec 07	Dec 06	Dec 05
Sales Turnover	1145	1207	1511
Pre Tax Profit/Loss	-53	-574	81
Working Capital	-695	-634	-92
Fixed Assets	12	4	36
Current Assets	823	984	1506
Current Liabilities	1518	1618	1598
Total Share Capital	400	400	400
ROCE% (Return on Capital Employed)	7.8	91.2	-145.5
ROT% (Return on Turnover)	-4.6	-47.6	5.4

Lotus Labels

1 Park View Alder Close, Eastbourne, BN23 6QE
Tel: 01323-737888 **Fax:** 01323-737088
E-mail: sales@lotuslabels.com
Website: http://www.lotuslabels.com
Bank(s): HSBC, Hailsham
Directors: J. Pierce (Dir)
Immediate Holding Company: PIERCE JENKINS LTD
Registration no: 02145720 **VAT No.:** GB 190 5823 54
Turnover: £1m - £2m **No.of Employees:** 11 - 20 **Product Groups:** 22, 23, 27, 28, 29, 30, 35, 36, 43, 44, 49

Date of Accounts	Jan 08	Jan 07	Jan 06
Working Capital	221	173	129
Fixed Assets	90	102	141
Current Assets	513	359	426
Current Liabilities	292	185	296
Total Share Capital	11	10	10

Metalform

Unit 8 Southbourne Business Park Courtlands Road, Eastbourne, BN22 8UY
Tel: 01323-641222 **Fax:** 01323-642122
E-mail: stuart@metalform.biz
Website: http://www.metalform.co.uk
Directors: S. Bennett (Ptnr)
Date established: 1997 **No.of Employees:** 1 - 10 **Product Groups:** 35, 39, 48, 49

New Concept Catering Equipment

Unit 7 Birch Industrial Estate, Eastbourne, BN23 6PH
Tel: 01323-744000
E-mail: sales@concept-cds.co.uk
Website: http://www.newconceptcatering.co.uk
Directors: A. Wright (Prop)
Immediate Holding Company: NEW CONCEPT CATERING EQUIPMENT LIMITED
Registration no: 06365280 **Date established:** 2007
No.of Employees: 11 - 20 **Product Groups:** 20, 40, 41

Date of Accounts	Sep 05
Working Capital	-33
Fixed Assets	52
Current Assets	118
Current Liabilities	151
Total Share Capital	1

RoadtoHealth Ltd

PO Box 2877, Eastbourne, BN22 0WD
Tel: 08451-235320 **Fax:** 0845-123 5321
E-mail: info@roadtohealth.co.uk
Website: http://www.roadtohealth.co.uk
Directors: A. Wickens (MD)
Managers: P. Gaudin, R. Dickinson
Ultimate Holding Company: ROADTOHEALTH GROUP LTD
Immediate Holding Company: ROADTOHEALTH LIMITED
Registration no: 04496145 **Date established:** 2002
No.of Employees: 21 - 50 **Product Groups:** 88

Date of Accounts	Jul 11	Jul 10	Jul 09
Working Capital	-23	-593	-505
Fixed Assets	47	548	282
Current Assets	435	510	640

Rock Build Ltd

Martello House 1A Edward Road, Eastbourne, BN23 8AS
Tel: 01323-514100 **Fax:** 01323-514149
E-mail: rok@rokgroup.com
Website: http://www.rockgroup.com
Managers: A. Collingwood (I.T. Exec)
Registration no: 07204503 **No.of Employees:** 51 - 100
Product Groups: 52

Smith & Ouzman Ltd (Head Office)

45 Brampton Road, Eastbourne, BN23 9AH
Tel: 01323-524000 **Fax:** 01323-524024
E-mail: print@smith-ouzman.com
Website: http://www.smith-ouzman.com
Bank(s): Lloyds TSB Bank plc
Directors: N. Smith (Sales), P. Ellis (Fin)
Managers: J. Filsell (Personnel), P. Leonard (Buyer), S. Hancock (Tech Serv Mgr)
Immediate Holding Company: SMITH & OUZMAN LIMITED
Registration no: 00352738 **VAT No.:** GB 243 1104 18
Date established: 1939 **Turnover:** £10m - £20m
No.of Employees: 51 - 100 **Product Groups:** 28, 32, 44, 80, 81

Date of Accounts	Dec 11	Dec 10	Dec 09
Sales Turnover	9m	13m	8m
Pre Tax Profit/Loss	-104	338	-139
Working Capital	2m	2m	2m
Fixed Assets	3m	3m	3m
Current Assets	4m	4m	3m
Current Liabilities	344	444	191

Stoveshops Woodburning Stoves

21 Hereward Road, Eastbourne, BN23 6TG
Tel: 07779-996916
Directors: P. Holloway (Prop)
Date established: 2000 **No.of Employees:** 1 - 10 **Product Groups:** 40

Sussex Plumbing Supplies Ltd

Unit 3 Hammonds Drive, Eastbourne, BN23 6PW
Tel: 01323-737797 **Fax:** 01323-738739
E-mail: glenn@sussexplumbingsupplies.co.uk
Website: http://www.sussexplumbingsupplies.co.uk
Directors: E. Vinall (Fin), G. Vinall (MD)
Immediate Holding Company: SUSSEX PLUMBING SUPPLIES LIMITED
Registration no: 04023736 **Date established:** 2000
No.of Employees: 11 - 20 **Product Groups:** 66

Date of Accounts	Dec 11	Dec 10	Dec 09
Working Capital	372	375	259
Fixed Assets	145	124	125
Current Assets	1m	1m	1m

T M T Powder Coatings Ltd

62 Hammonds Drive, Eastbourne, BN23 6PW
Tel: 01323-642215 **Fax:** 01323-649963
E-mail: tmt.powder@virgin.net
Directors: S. Weston (Fin), I. Weston (MD)
Immediate Holding Company: T.M.T. POWDER COATING LIMITED
Registration no: 01493513 **VAT No.:** GB 350 8258 56
Date established: 1980 **Turnover:** Up to £250,000
No.of Employees: 1 - 10 **Product Groups:** 48

Date of Accounts	Apr 12	Apr 11	Apr 10
Working Capital	60	79	85
Fixed Assets	9	4	5
Current Assets	105	123	120

Taylor & Goodman Ltd

Faraday Close, Eastbourne, BN22 9AB
Tel: 01323-502151 **Fax:** 01323-520387
E-mail: info@taylorgoodman.co.uk
Website: http://www.taylorgoodman.co.uk
Managers: A. Gundy (District Mgr)
Ultimate Holding Company: ALL AROUND SERVICE LIMITED
Immediate Holding Company: TAYLOR & GOODMAN LIMITED
Registration no: 02783525 **VAT No.:** GB 614 6961 29
Date established: 1993 **Turnover:** £1m - £2m **No.of Employees:** 1 - 10
Product Groups: 37

Date of Accounts	Mar 08	Jun 11	Jun 10
Sales Turnover	N/A	4m	3m
Pre Tax Profit/Loss	274	116	2
Working Capital	-657	-255	-958
Fixed Assets	2m	499	884
Current Assets	3m	1m	974
Current Liabilities	2m	974	2m

Tidmas Townsend Ltd

208-210 Seaside, Eastbourne, BN22 7QS
Tel: 01323-734240 **Fax:** 01323-416894
E-mail: mail@tidmastownsend.co.uk
Website: http://www.tidmastownsend.co.uk
Directors: K. Townsend (MD), P. Townsend (Fin)
Immediate Holding Company: TIDMAS TOWNSEND LIMITED
Registration no: 00603950 **Date established:** 1958
No.of Employees: 1 - 10 **Product Groups:** 38, 42

Date of Accounts	Jan 11	Jan 10	Jan 09
Working Capital	109	106	118
Fixed Assets	13	16	21
Current Assets	171	186	163

Trimseal Ltd

3b Courtlands Road, Eastbourne, BN22 8TR
Tel: 01323-730730 **Fax:** 01424-733666
E-mail: info@trimseal.co.uk
Website: http://www.trimseal.co.uk
Directors: J. Farrell (Dir)
Ultimate Holding Company: TECH-WOOD LIMITED
Immediate Holding Company: TRIMSEAL LIMITED
Registration no: 02272852 **VAT No.:** GB 508 6969 04
Date established: 1988 **Turnover:** £1m - £2m **No.of Employees:** 1 - 10
Product Groups: 26, 30

Date of Accounts	Dec 11	Dec 10	Dec 09
Working Capital	73	64	84
Fixed Assets	6	8	59
Current Assets	204	195	199

Wrightflow Technologies Ltd

Highfield Industrial Estate Edison Road, Eastbourne, BN23 6PT
Tel: 01323-509211 **Fax:** 01323-507306
E-mail: jinfo@idexcorp.com
Website: http://www.johnsonpump.com
Bank(s): Barclays, Eastbourne
Directors: C. Boyd (Dir)
Managers: A. Belk (Cust Serv Mgr), J. Laing (Purch Mgr), M. Taylor (Chief Acct)
Ultimate Holding Company: IDEX CORPORATION (USA)
Immediate Holding Company: WRIGHT FLOW TECHNOLOGIES LIMITED
Registration no: 01342366 **VAT No.:** GB 205 2071 18
Date established: 1977 **Turnover:** £5m - £10m **No.of Employees:** 21 - 50
Product Groups: 38, 40

Date of Accounts	Dec 11	Dec 10	Dec 09
Sales Turnover	8m	7m	5m
Pre Tax Profit/Loss	1m	943	-16
Working Capital	3m	2m	1m
Fixed Assets	169	231	163
Current Assets	4m	3m	2m
Current Liabilities	430	419	244

Etchingham

Individual Fires & Stoves

Chimneys Brookgate Farm, Hurst Green, Etchingham, TN19 7QY
Tel: 01580-860976 **Fax:** 01580-860976
E-mail: sales@cookersandstoves.co.uk
Website: http://www.cookersandstoves.co.uk
Directors: R. Kirk (Prop)
Registration no: 02428692 **Date established:** 1979
No.of Employees: 1 - 10 **Product Groups:** 40

The Main Event Marquee Co.

The White House Fontridge Lane, Etchingham, TN19 7DD
Tel: 01580-819699 **Fax:** 01580-860318
E-mail: mail@themainevent.co.uk
Website: http://www.themainevent.co.uk
Registration no: 04005153 **No.of Employees:** 1 - 10 **Product Groups:** 23, 24, 66, 83

W S H Wireworks Ltd

Riverside Works Church Lane, Etchingham, TN19 7AS
Tel: 01580-819282 **Fax:** 01580-819606
E-mail: roger@wshwireworks.co.uk
Website: http://www.wshwireworks.co.uk

see next page

W S H Wireworks Ltd - *Cont'd*

Directors: R. Hardaway (MD)
Immediate Holding Company: W.S.H. (WIREWORKERS) LIMITED
Registration no: 01034954 **Date established:** 1971
Turnover: £500,000 - £1m **No.of Employees:** 11 - 20
Product Groups: 26, 30, 35, 36, 39, 40, 41, 42, 44, 45, 46, 48, 49, 67

Date of Accounts	Dec 11	Dec 10	Dec 09
Working Capital	91	89	21
Fixed Assets	257	253	258
Current Assets	281	181	156

Forest Row

Air Engineering Systems Ltd

Unit 10 Forest Row Business Park Station Road, Forest Row, RH18 5DW
Tel: 01342-825036 **Fax:** 01342-825040
E-mail: systems@airengineering.co.uk
Website: http://www.airengineering.co.uk
Directors: A. Swan (MD), P. Swan (Co Sec)
Immediate Holding Company: AIR ENGINEERING SYSTEMS LIMITED
Registration no: 02633838 **VAT No.:** GB 528 7457 12
Date established: 1991 **No.of Employees:** 1 - 10 **Product Groups:** 40

Date of Accounts	Aug 11	Aug 10	Aug 09
Working Capital	1	21	18
Fixed Assets	43	34	40
Current Assets	145	161	166

Almit Ltd

7 Forest Row Business Park Station Road, Forest Row, RH18 5DW
Tel: 01342-822844 **Fax:** 01342-824155
E-mail: info@almit.co.uk
Website: http://www.almit.co.uk
Directors: D. Greer (MD)
Immediate Holding Company: ALMIT TECHNOLOGY LIMITED
Registration no: 02942271 **Date established:** 1994
No.of Employees: 1 - 10 **Product Groups:** 32, 34

Date of Accounts	Sep 11	Sep 10	Sep 08
Working Capital	348	457	694
Fixed Assets	255	180	23
Current Assets	386	576	796

The Brambletye Hotel

Lewes Road, Forest Row, RH18 5EZ
Tel: 01342-824144 **Fax:** 01342-824833
E-mail: brambletye.hotel@fullers.co.uk
Website: http://www.gales.co.uk
Directors: P. Sharma (Dir)
Immediate Holding Company: BATHSHIELD (U.K.) LIMITED
Registration no: 02601987 **Date established:** 1991
Turnover: Up to £250,000 **No.of Employees:** 11 - 20 **Product Groups:** 69

Date of Accounts	Jun 11	Jun 10	Jun 09
Working Capital	44	155	75
Fixed Assets	334	232	247
Current Assets	89	155	124

Chequers Inn Hotel (16th Century Posting Inn)

The Square Lewes Road, Forest Row, RH18 5ES
Tel: 01342-823333 **Fax:** 01342-825454
E-mail: enquiries@chequers1452.co.uk
Website: http://www.chequers1452.co.uk
Directors: C. Priori (Prop)
Immediate Holding Company: CHEQUERS INN HOTEL LIMITED
Registration no: 05473576 **Date established:** 2005
No.of Employees: 1 - 10 **Product Groups:** 69

Date of Accounts	Nov 11	Nov 10	Nov 09
Working Capital	-212	10	-252
Fixed Assets	155	177	205
Current Assets	4	10	20

Mid Sussex Timber Co. Ltd

Station Road, Forest Row, RH18 5EL
Tel: 01342-822191 **Fax:** 01342-823052
E-mail: timber@mstc.co.uk
Website: http://www.mstc.co.uk
Directors: L. Bouchard (Fin), L. Bouchard (Fin)
Managers: L. Partridge (Buyer), T. Grantham (Personnel)
Immediate Holding Company: MID-SUSSEX TIMBER CO LIMITED
Registration no: 00434862 **VAT No.:** GB 209 7728 39
Date established: 1947 **Turnover:** £2m - £5m **No.of Employees:** 21 - 50
Product Groups: 25, 26

Date of Accounts	Dec 11	Dec 10	Dec 09
Sales Turnover	5m	5m	5m
Pre Tax Profit/Loss	78	-55	-86
Working Capital	1m	1m	1m
Fixed Assets	1m	1m	1m
Current Assets	2m	2m	2m
Current Liabilities	202	253	205

Quadrachem Ltd

Riverside Forest Row Business Park Station Road, Forest Row, RH18 5DW
Tel: 01342-820820 **Fax:** 01342-820825
E-mail: enquiries@qclscientific.com
Website: http://www.qclscientific.com
Bank(s): Barclays, Crawley
Directors: F. Watts (Cust Serv), F. Watts (Co Sec), C. Peake (Sales & Mktg), C. Peake (Sales), B. Hughes (Fin), F. Watt (Cust Serv), J. Comer (I.T. Dir)
Managers: S. Nicolls (Mktg Serv Mgr), S. Pocock (Ops Mgr), A. Satchwell (I.T. Exec)
Ultimate Holding Company: ADMERICS LIMITED
Immediate Holding Company: QUADRACHEM LABORATORIES LIMITED
Registration no: 01537424 **VAT No.:** GB 350 9764 36
Date established: 1981 **Turnover:** £2m - £5m **No.of Employees:** 21 - 50
Product Groups: 38, 41, 42

Date of Accounts	Apr 11	Apr 10	Apr 09
Working Capital	362	337	330
Fixed Assets	69	70	78
Current Assets	1m	802	810

Sirius Analytical Instruments

Riverside Forest Row Business Park Station Road, Forest Row, RH18 5DW
Tel: 01342-820720 **Fax:** 01342-820725
E-mail: brett.hughes@sirius-analytical.com
Website: http://www.sirius-analytical.com
Directors: J. Comer (I.T. Dir), B. Hughes (Fin), C. Peake (Sales & Mktg)
Ultimate Holding Company: ADMERICS LIMITED
Immediate Holding Company: SIRIUS ANALYTICAL INSTRUMENTS LIMITED
Registration no: 02419461 **Date established:** 1989
No.of Employees: 11 - 20 **Product Groups:** 67, 84

Date of Accounts	Dec 11	Dec 10	Dec 09
Working Capital	1m	1m	635
Fixed Assets	72	91	113
Current Assets	2m	1m	919

Hailsham

Apaseal Ltd

Bowes House 25 Battle Road, Hailsham, BN27 1DX
Tel: 01323-842066 **Fax:** 01323-440450
E-mail: sales@apaseal.co.uk
Website: http://www.apaseal.co.uk
Bank(s): National Westminster
Directors: A. Keith (MD), A. McPeake (Co Sec)
Managers: M. Reeve (Purch Mgr)
Ultimate Holding Company: HALESBURTON HOLDINGS LIMITED
Immediate Holding Company: APASEAL LIMITED
Registration no: 01601877 **Date established:** 1981 **Turnover:** £5m - £10m
No.of Employees: 21 - 50 **Product Groups:** 29, 39

Date of Accounts	Jul 10	Jan 09	Jan 08
Pre Tax Profit/Loss	1m	-344	240
Working Capital	3m	1m	1m
Fixed Assets	416	532	647
Current Assets	4m	5m	6m
Current Liabilities	267	341	595

Britannia Milling Services Ltd

PO Box 1340, Hailsham, BN27 4UE
Tel: 01323-831800 **Fax:** 01323-831970
E-mail: jim@britannia-milling.co.uk
Website: http://www.britannia-milling.co.uk
Directors: P. Burgess (Fin), J. Burgess (MD)
Immediate Holding Company: BRITANNIA MILLING SERVICES LIMITED
Registration no: 01566915 **Date established:** 1981
No.of Employees: 1 - 10 **Product Groups:** 20, 40, 41

Date of Accounts	Mar 11	Mar 10	Mar 09
Working Capital	-2	-7	-9
Fixed Assets	5	7	8
Current Assets	72	73	37
Current Liabilities	32	N/A	1

Club Class

Unit 5 Swan Barn Business Centre Old Swan Lane, Hailsham, BN27 2BY
Tel: 01323-442222 **Fax:** 01323-841443
E-mail: info@clubclassonline.co.uk
Website: http://www.clubclassonline.co.uk
Directors: J. Dow (MD)
Immediate Holding Company: CLUB CLASS INVESTMENTS LTD
Registration no: 04065446 **Date established:** 2008
No.of Employees: 1 - 10 **Product Groups:** 72

Crafty Clare's

4 St Marys Walk, Hailsham, BN27 1AF
Tel: 01323-845300
E-mail: craftyclare@hotmail.com
Website: http://www.craftyclares.co.uk
Directors: C. Cook (Prop)
Turnover: Up to £250,000 **No.of Employees:** 1 - 10 **Product Groups:** 37, 64, 65

Drainage Center Ltd

116 London Road, Hailsham, BN27 3AL
Tel: 01323-442333 **Fax:** 01323-847488
E-mail: sales@drainagecenter.co.uk
Website: http://www.drainagecenter.co.uk
Directors: P. Sheppard (MD), A. Barden (MD)
Managers: S. Prints (District Mgr), S. Irvine (District Mgr), D. Hamblin (Sales Prom Mgr), S. Jackson (Mktg Serv Mgr)
Immediate Holding Company: DRAINAGE CENTER LIMITED
Registration no: 00542977 **VAT No.:** GB 362 0233 93
Date established: 1955 **Turnover:** £1m - £2m **No.of Employees:** 1 - 10
Product Groups: 36, 40

Experience Holidays

1 Town House Garden Market Street, Hailsham, BN27 2AE
Tel: 01323-446550 **Fax:** 01323-446555
E-mail: info@experienceholidays.co.uk
Website: http://www.experienceholidays.co.uk
Directors: J. Appleton (Dir)
Immediate Holding Company: EXPERIENCE HOLIDAYS LTD.
Registration no: 02718826 **Date established:** 1992
No.of Employees: 1 - 10 **Product Groups:** 69

Fristam Pumps UK Ltd

Unit 11 Apex Park Diplocks Way, Hailsham, BN27 3JU
Tel: 01323-849849 **Fax:** 01323-849438
E-mail: sales@fristam.co.uk
Website: http://www.fristam.de
Managers: M. Towsey
Ultimate Holding Company: FRISTAM PUMPEN F STAMP KG GMBH (GERMANY)
Immediate Holding Company: FRISTAM PUMPS (U.K.) LIMITED
Registration no: 01629845 **Date established:** 1982 **Turnover:** £1m - £2m
No.of Employees: 1 - 10 **Product Groups:** 40

Date of Accounts	Sep 11	Sep 10	Sep 09
Working Capital	118	115	111
Fixed Assets	15	15	15
Current Assets	121	118	113

Gearing & Watson Electronics Ltd (Head Office)

South Road, Hailsham, BN27 3JJ
Tel: 01323-846464 **Fax:** 01323-847550
E-mail: sales@dataphysics.com
Website: http://www.dataphysics.com
Bank(s): National Westminster Bank Plc
Directors: S. Potts (MD), G. Murphy (Grp MD), S. Potts (MD)
Managers: D. Robertson (Sales Eng), J. Flannigan (Sales Prom Mgr), K. Robinson (Purch Mgr), C. Leeding (I.T. Exec)
Immediate Holding Company: Gearing & Watson (Holdings) Ltd
Registration no: 01092478 **VAT No.:** GB 191 3159 65
Turnover: £1m - £2m **No.of Employees:** 11 - 20 **Product Groups:** 37, 38

Date of Accounts	Jan 08	Jan 07
Working Capital	114	135
Fixed Assets	142	131
Current Assets	1210	1710
Current Liabilities	1096	1575
Total Share Capital	28	28

H Ripley & Co. Ltd

Apex Way, Hailsham, BN27 3WA
Tel: 01323-440672 **Fax:** 01323-841282
E-mail: jason@hripley.co.uk
Website: http://www.hripley.co.uk
Directors: J. Ripley (Dir)
Ultimate Holding Company: THE PUMP GROUP LIMITED
Immediate Holding Company: H RIPLEY & CO. LIMITED
Registration no: 04868630 **VAT No.:** GB 190 8703 49
Date established: 2003 **Turnover:** £10m - £20m
No.of Employees: 21 - 50 **Product Groups:** 66

Date of Accounts	Mar 11	Mar 10	Mar 09
Sales Turnover	N/A	N/A	4m
Pre Tax Profit/Loss	N/A	N/A	388
Working Capital	2m	1m	945
Fixed Assets	370	432	494
Current Assets	6m	2m	1m
Current Liabilities	N/A	225	171

J M B Catering Equipment

Unit 17 Station Road Indl-Est, Hailsham, BN27 2EY
Tel: 01323-848263 **Fax:** 01323-509932
Website: http://www.jmbcateringequipment.co.uk
Managers: J. Barnes (Mgr), M. Barnes (Mgr)
No.of Employees: 1 - 10 **Product Groups:** 20, 40, 41

Look Designs Ltd

Unit A2-A3 Ropemaker Park Diplocks Way, Hailsham, BN27 3GU
Tel: 01323-841765 **Fax:** 01323-444824
E-mail: lookdesigns@clara.co.uk
Website: http://www.lookdesigns.co.uk
Bank(s): Nat West
Directors: D. Robinson (MD)
Immediate Holding Company: LOOK DESIGNS LIMITED
Registration no: 00840328 **Date established:** 1965 **Turnover:** £1m - £2m
No.of Employees: 11 - 20 **Product Groups:** 65

Date of Accounts	Mar 11	Mar 10	Mar 09
Working Capital	58	59	69
Fixed Assets	413	423	398
Current Assets	406	431	415

Macey Industrial Fixings

The Martlets Diplocks Way, Hailsham, BN27 3JF
Tel: 01323-841916 **Fax:** 01323-849916
E-mail: maceyfixings@tiscali.co.uk
Website: http://www.maceyfixings.co.uk
Directors: K. Macey (Prop)
VAT No.: GB 583 6780 95 **Turnover:** £250,000 - £500,000
No.of Employees: 1 - 10 **Product Groups:** 35, 66

Macro Precision Pumps Ltd

Unit 5 Station Road Industrial Estate, Hailsham, BN27 2EL
Tel: 01323-842331 **Fax:** 01323-842980
E-mail: macropumps@btopenworld.com
Directors: H. Mcallister (MD)
Immediate Holding Company: MACRO PRECISION PUMPS LIMITED
Registration no: 01819577 **VAT No.:** GB 583 6923 02
Date established: 1984 **Turnover:** £500,000 - £1m
No.of Employees: 1 - 10 **Product Groups:** 40, 45

Date of Accounts	Apr 11	Apr 10	Apr 09
Working Capital	14	260	271
Fixed Assets	186	22	28
Current Assets	128	348	340

Marlow Ropes Ltd

Rope Maker Park Dipilocks Way, Hailsham, BN27 3GU
Tel: 01323-444444 **Fax:** 01323-444455
E-mail: sales@marlowropes.com
Website: http://www.marlowropes.com
Bank(s): Bank of Scotland, London
Directors: J. Mitchell (MD)
Ultimate Holding Company: ENGLISH BRAIDS LIMITED
Immediate Holding Company: MARLOW ROPES LIMITED
Registration no: 05648038 **VAT No.:** GB 621 9918 26
Date established: 2005 **No.of Employees:** 21 - 50 **Product Groups:** 23, 30, 35

Date of Accounts	Dec 11	Dec 10	Dec 09
Sales Turnover	7m	5m	6m
Pre Tax Profit/Loss	710	502	321
Working Capital	2m	1m	896
Fixed Assets	152	232	292
Current Assets	3m	3m	2m
Current Liabilities	537	596	301

Maytyne Engineering

Gardner Street Herstmonceux, Hailsham, BN27 4LE
Tel: 01323-833200 **Fax:** 01323-833200
Website: http://www.maytyme.fsbusiness.co.uk
Directors: B. Coomber (Prop)
VAT No.: GB 191 3015 89 **Turnover:** Up to £250,000
No.of Employees: 1 - 10 **Product Groups:** 35

Reigler Aluminium Ltd

Unit 13-15 Station Road Industrial Estate, Hailsham, BN27 2EW
Tel: 01323-841800 **Fax:** 01323-847101
Website: http://www.reigleraluminium.co.uk
Directors: J. Reigler (Dir)
Registration no: 03003219 **Date established:** 1994
No.of Employees: 1 - 10 **Product Groups:** 26, 35

Date of Accounts	Mar 08	Mar 07	Mar 06
Working Capital	68	58	61
Fixed Assets	1	6	8
Current Assets	123	126	92
Current Liabilities	55	68	31
Total Share Capital	7	7	7

S R Tools Ltd
7 Swan Barn Business Centre Old Swan Lane, Hailsham, BN27 2BY
Tel: 01323-845855 **Fax:** 01323-848855
E-mail: raymond.crowley@srtools.co.uk
Website: http://www.srtools.co.uk
Directors: R. Crowley (MD), D. Crowley (Fin)
Immediate Holding Company: S.R. TOOLS LIMITED
Registration no: 01825409 **Date established:** 1984
No.of Employees: 1 - 10 **Product Groups:** 46, 48

Date of Accounts	Jun 09	Jun 08	Jun 07
Working Capital	-78	-61	-43
Fixed Assets	140	141	147
Current Assets	1	6	66

Shep Plastics Ltd (Head Office)
The Old Pottery Lower Dicker, Hailsham, BN27 4AT
Tel: 01323-440088 **Fax:** 01323-841930
E-mail: sales@shep-plastics.co.uk
Website: http://www.shep-plastics.co.uk
Bank(s): Royal Bank of Scotland
Directors: T. Perkin (Comm), L. Quinn (Dir), P. Sheppard (Dir), M. Bradshaw (Fin), M. Bradshaw (Grp Chief Exec), L. Rennie (Tech Serv), L. Rennie (I.T. Dir)
Immediate Holding Company: SHEP PLASTICS LIMITED
Registration no: 01165626 **VAT No.:** GB 191 7423 54
Date established: 1974 **Turnover:** £2m - £5m **No.of Employees:** 51 - 100
Product Groups: 30

Date of Accounts	Dec 07	Dec 06	Dec 05
Sales Turnover	3m	3m	3m
Pre Tax Profit/Loss	2	6	2
Working Capital	-111	-196	-248
Fixed Assets	240	261	310
Current Assets	1m	1m	1m
Current Liabilities	333	391	431

Skinner's Sheds Ltd
World of Water Mulbrooks, Hailsham, BN27 2RH
Tel: 01323-847005
E-mail: info@skinners-sheds.com
Website: http://www.skinners-sheds.com
Managers: A. Ridgers (District Mgr)
Immediate Holding Company: SKINNERS SHEDS LIMITED
Registration no: 03709428 **Date established:** 1999
No.of Employees: 1 - 10 **Product Groups:** 08, 25, 35, 49, 66

Date of Accounts	Feb 12	Feb 11	Feb 10
Working Capital	19	57	46
Fixed Assets	913	156	81
Current Assets	803	774	624

South Coast Catering Equipment Ltd
Unit 4-5 Apex Park Diplocks Way, Hailsham, BN27 3JU
Tel: 01273-444530 **Fax:** 01273- 439136
E-mail: info@sccuk.com
Website: http://www.southcoastcatering.co.uk
Managers: P. Thompson (Sales Prom Mgr)
Immediate Holding Company: SOUTH COAST CATERING EQUIPMENT LIMITED
Registration no: 01877857 **Date established:** 1985 **Turnover:** £2m - £5m
No.of Employees: 1 - 10 **Product Groups:** 20, 40, 41

Date of Accounts	Dec 11	Dec 10	Dec 09
Working Capital	-186	-197	-191
Fixed Assets	9	10	26
Current Assets	208	217	293

Spendor Audio Systems Ltd
Unit G5 Ropemaker Park South Road, Hailsham, BN27 3GY
Tel: 01323-843474 **Fax:** 01323-442254
E-mail: info@spendoraudio.com
Website: http://www.spendoraudio.com
Bank(s): Barclays
Directors: P. Swift (MD)
Immediate Holding Company: SPENDOR AUDIO SYSTEMS LIMITED
Registration no: 03888529 **VAT No.:** GB 210 3212 44
Date established: 1999 **Turnover:** £1m - £2m **No.of Employees:** 11 - 20
Product Groups: 37

Date of Accounts	Dec 11	Dec 10	Dec 09
Working Capital	297	263	467
Fixed Assets	885	889	35
Current Assets	474	456	593

System Hygienics Ltd
8 Industrial Estate Station Road, Hailsham, BN27 2EY
Tel: 01323-481170 **Fax:** 01323-483061
E-mail: onlineenquiry@systemhygienics.co.uk
Website: http://www.systemhygienics.co.uk
Directors: M. Ohly (MD)
Managers: B. Shillinglaw (Mgr), D. Ling (Sales Prom Mgr), P. Verhulpen (I.T. Exec)
Registration no: 01277207 **Turnover:** £2m - £5m
No.of Employees: 1 - 10 **Product Groups:** 52

Date of Accounts	Mar 08	Mar 07	Mar 06
Working Capital	-116	-67	45
Fixed Assets	198	173	171
Current Assets	793	629	635
Current Liabilities	909	696	590

Tobel Sheetmetal Ltd
Diplocks Way, Hailsham, BN27 3JF
Tel: 01323-442244 **Fax:** 01323-440408
E-mail: sales@tobel.co.uk
Website: http://www.tobel.co.uk
Bank(s): HSBC Plc, Hailsham
Directors: T. O'Dell (Dir), P. O'dell (Dir)
Immediate Holding Company: TOBEL SHEET METAL LIMITED
Registration no: 01334227 **VAT No.:** GB 315 5009 90
Date established: 1977 **Turnover:** £1m - £2m **No.of Employees:** 21 - 50
Product Groups: 48

Date of Accounts	Mar 12	Mar 11	Mar 10
Working Capital	233	270	293
Fixed Assets	264	282	274
Current Assets	393	456	485

Viomedex Ltd
Unit 13 Swan Barn Business Centre Old Swan Lane, Hailsham, BN27 2BY
Tel: 01323-446130 **Fax:** 01825-733407
E-mail: vx@viomedex.com
Website: http://www.viomedex.com
Directors: C. Brunsden (MD), C. Leeding (Co Sec)
Ultimate Holding Company: VIO HOLDINGS LIMITED
Immediate Holding Company: VIOMEDEX LIMITED
Registration no: 01310102 **VAT No.:** GB 192 560 454
Date established: 1977 **Turnover:** £1m - £2m **No.of Employees:** 1 - 10
Product Groups: 29, 30, 31, 38, 67

Date of Accounts	Mar 12	Mar 11	Mar 10
Working Capital	474	360	269
Fixed Assets	57	74	50
Current Assets	767	665	538

V-Mech Engineering Ltd
Unit 15 Granary Business Centre North Street, Hellingly, Hailsham, BN27 4DU
Tel: 01323-440048
Directors: A. Groome (Dir)
Immediate Holding Company: V-MECH ENGINEERING LTD
Registration no: 05491168 **Date established:** 2005
Turnover: Up to £250,000 **No.of Employees:** 1 - 10 **Product Groups:** 38, 85

Date of Accounts	Jun 10	Jun 09	Jun 08
Sales Turnover	N/A	25	N/A
Working Capital	1	10	13
Fixed Assets	5	5	5
Current Assets	93	80	91

Wealden Tyres Ltd
23 Granary Business Centre Broadfarm North Street, Hellingly, Hailsham, BN27 4DU
Tel: 01323-845544 **Fax:** 01323-441501
E-mail: sales@wealdentyres.co.uk
Website: http://www.wealdentyres.co.uk
Directors: S. Palmer (Prop)
Immediate Holding Company: WT ADMIN LIMITED
Registration no: 04426972 **Date established:** 2002 **Turnover:** £1m - £2m
No.of Employees: 1 - 10 **Product Groups:** 39

Date of Accounts	Aug 10	Aug 09	Aug 08
Sales Turnover	1m	1m	869
Pre Tax Profit/Loss	-1	43	40
Working Capital	-23	-30	-28
Fixed Assets	37	45	32
Current Assets	392	339	242
Current Liabilities	190	54	53

Wentworth Lifts Ltd
13 Lundy Walk, Hailsham, BN27 3BJ
Tel: 01323-887887 **Fax:** 01323-442538
E-mail: john@wentworthlifts.co.uk
Website: http://www.jackerman.wanadoo.co.uk
Directors: I. Ackerman (Fin), J. Ackerman (MD)
Immediate Holding Company: WENTWORTH LIFTS LIMITED
Registration no: 03157272 **Date established:** 1996
No.of Employees: 1 - 10 **Product Groups:** 35, 39, 45

Date of Accounts	Feb 12	Feb 11	Feb 10
Working Capital	-28	-37	-25
Fixed Assets	10	4	11
Current Assets	32	38	41

Hartfield

Havas Packing & Shipping Ltd
Little Parrock Farm Shepherds Hill, Colemans Hatch, Hartfield, TN7 4HP
Tel: 01342-824388 **Fax:** 01342-825541
E-mail: worldwide@havas.co.uk
Website: http://www.havas.co.uk
Directors: W. De Havas (MD)
Immediate Holding Company: HAVAS PACKING & SHIPPING LIMITED
Registration no: 01346521 **VAT No.:** GB 312 8674 58
Date established: 1978 **Turnover:** Up to £250,000
No.of Employees: 1 - 10 **Product Groups:** 76

Date of Accounts	Dec 11	Dec 10	Dec 08
Working Capital	-34	-23	-21
Fixed Assets	7	8	8
Current Assets	1	4	7

Gordon Herrald Associates
Pear Tree House Cat Street, Upper Hartfield, Hartfield, TN7 4DX
Tel: 01342-822927 **Fax:** 01342-826102
E-mail: info@herrald.co.uk
Website: http://www.herrald.co.uk
Directors: G. Herrald (Snr Part)
Date established: 1985 **Turnover:** £250,000 - £500,000
No.of Employees: 1 - 10 **Product Groups:** 37, 81

Solo Timber Frame Ltd
Hodore Farm Parrock Lane, Upper Hartfield, Hartfield, TN7 4AR
Tel: 01892-771354 **Fax:** 01474-822859
E-mail: info@solotimberframe.co.uk
Website: http://www.12limited.co.uk
Directors: W. Bernardini (Fin), C. Davenport (Dir)
Immediate Holding Company: SOLO TIMBER FRAME LIMITED
Registration no: 04814638 **Date established:** 2003
Turnover: £500,000 - £1m **No.of Employees:** 1 - 10 **Product Groups:** 25

Date of Accounts	Jun 11	Jun 10	Jun 09
Working Capital	-86	-98	14
Fixed Assets	1	N/A	1
Current Assets	159	96	283

Hastings

Advance Engineering Services Ltd
Unit 1 Farley Bank, Hastings, TN35 5QA
Tel: 01424-424720 **Fax:** 01424-442924
E-mail: enquiries@advance-eng.demon.co.uk
Website: http://www.advance-eng.co.uk
Managers: S. Lucent (Mgr)
Immediate Holding Company: ADVANCE ENGINEERING SERVICES LIMITED
Registration no: 05052796 **VAT No.:** GB 347 1770 46
Date established: 2004 **Turnover:** £250,000 - £500,000
No.of Employees: 1 - 10 **Product Groups:** 48, 84, 85

Date of Accounts	Feb 12	Feb 11	Feb 10
Working Capital	81	106	81
Fixed Assets	58	65	57
Current Assets	161	186	141

Air2Air Design Services
Britania Enterprise Centre Waterworks Road, Hastings, TN34 1RT
Tel: 07785-770701
E-mail: info@air2air.co.uk
Website: http://www.air2air.co.uk
Directors: H. Gastall (MD)
Registration no: 05222164 **Date established:** 2005
Turnover: Up to £250,000 **No.of Employees:** 1 - 10 **Product Groups:** 44

Alfa Electric Ltd
14 Burgess Road, Hastings, TN35 4NR
Tel: 01424-424040 **Fax:** 01424-424040
E-mail: sales@alfaelectric.co.uk
Website: http://www.alfaelectric.co.uk
Directors: R. Harrison (MD), A. Harrison (Fin)
Immediate Holding Company: ALFA ELECTRIC LIMITED
Registration no: 04450502 **VAT No.:** GB 332 8527 57
Date established: 2002 **Turnover:** £500,000 - £1m
No.of Employees: 11 - 20 **Product Groups:** 38, 84, 85

Date of Accounts	Oct 11	Oct 10	Oct 09
Working Capital	-21	29	21
Fixed Assets	158	178	187
Current Assets	220	231	277

Art2Craft
Studio 7 Britannia Centre Waterworks Road, Hastings, TN34 1RT
Tel: 01424-715701
E-mail: sales@art2craft.co.uk
Website: http://www.art2craft.co.uk
Managers: L. Jinks (Chief Acct)
Date established: 2000 **No.of Employees:** 1 - 10 **Product Groups:** 23

Carr Taylor Wines Ltd
Wheel Lane Westfield, Hastings, TN35 4SG
Tel: 01424-752501 **Fax:** 01424-751716
E-mail: sales@carr-taylor.co.uk
Website: http://www.carr-taylor.co.uk
Directors: D. Carr Taylor (Fin), L. Carr Taylor (Dir)
Immediate Holding Company: CARR TAYLOR WINES LIMITED
Registration no: 04028905 **VAT No.:** GB 362 1436 74
Date established: 2000 **No.of Employees:** 1 - 10 **Product Groups:** 21, 42

Date of Accounts	Jul 11	Jul 10	Jul 09
Working Capital	-211	-221	-143
Fixed Assets	188	195	7
Current Assets	483	467	369

Clipvalve Ltd
88 Stonefield Road, Hastings, TN34 1QA
Tel: 01424-425682 **Fax:** 01424-438789
E-mail: enquiries@clipvalve.co.uk
Website: http://www.clipvalve.co.uk
Directors: S. Howe (MD), M. Rowse (Fin)
Immediate Holding Company: CLIPVALVE LIMITED
Registration no: 01580586 **Date established:** 1981
Turnover: £500,000 - £1m **No.of Employees:** 1 - 10 **Product Groups:** 52, 66

Date of Accounts	Dec 11	Dec 10	Dec 09
Working Capital	-25	-14	-1
Fixed Assets	60	64	69
Current Assets	100	120	118

D B Fire Consultants Ltd
33 St Helens Park Road, Hastings, TN34 2DN
Tel: 01424-423468 **Fax:** 01424-431727
E-mail: david@amerex.freeserve.co.uk
Website: http://www.amerex.freeserve.co.uk
Directors: D. Brockington (Dir)
Date established: 1996 **No.of Employees:** 21 - 50 **Product Groups:** 38, 42

Forever Living Products
35 St James Road, Hastings, TN34 3LH
Tel: 01424-444851
Directors: M. Crampton (Prop)
No.of Employees: 1 - 10 **Product Groups:** 31, 32

Hartnells Of Hastings
1a Earl Street, Hastings, TN34 1SG
Tel: 01424-425834
Directors: M. Hunt (Prop)
No.of Employees: 1 - 10 **Product Groups:** 35

I Q C International Ltd
Lantern Lodge 146 Martineau Lane, Hastings, TN35 5DR
Tel: 01424-814999 **Fax:** 0845-437 9615
E-mail: info@iqc.co.uk
Website: http://www.iqc.co.uk
Directors: J. Bhabra (MD)
Immediate Holding Company: IQC INTERNATIONAL LIMITED
Registration no: 02048305 **VAT No.:** GB 459 6133 24
Date established: 1986 **Turnover:** £250,000 - £500,000
No.of Employees: 1 - 10 **Product Groups:** 37, 61

Date of Accounts	Aug 11	Aug 10	Aug 09
Working Capital	-93	-106	-99
Fixed Assets	19	23	24
Current Assets	11	27	20

Jaytec Glass Ltd
1 Burgess Road, Hastings, TN35 4NR
Tel: 01424-424181 **Fax:** 01424-721224
E-mail: enquiries@jaytecglass.co.uk
Website: http://www.jaytecglass.co.uk
Bank(s): HSBC Bank plc
Managers: L. Cherry (Admin Off)
Immediate Holding Company: JAYTEC GLASS LIMITED
Registration no: 05116623 **VAT No.:** GB 232 9047 74
Date established: 2004 **Turnover:** £500,000 - £1m
No.of Employees: 11 - 20 **Product Groups:** 33, 63

Date of Accounts	Apr 11	Apr 10	Apr 09
Working Capital	233	665	628
Fixed Assets	2m	661	680
Current Assets	491	746	717

Jewson Ltd
Rock Lane, Hastings, TN35 4JJ
Tel: 01424-426634 **Fax:** 01424-424941
Website: http://www.jewson.co.uk
Managers: B. McKirvy (District Mgr)
Ultimate Holding Company: COMPAGNIE DE SAINT GOBAIN (FRANCE)
Immediate Holding Company: JEWSON LIMITED
Registration no: 00348407 **VAT No.:** GB 497 7184 83
Date established: 1939 **Turnover:** £2m - £5m **No.of Employees:** 1 - 10
Product Groups: 66

Date of Accounts	Dec 11	Dec 10	Dec 09
Sales Turnover	1606m	1547m	1485m
Pre Tax Profit/Loss	18m	100m	45m
Working Capital	-345m	-250m	-349m
Fixed Assets	496m	387m	461m
Current Assets	657m	1005m	1320m
Current Liabilities	66m	120m	64m

Kurt J Lesker Company Ltd (European H.Q.)
15-16 Burgess Road, Hastings, TN35 4NR
Tel: 01424-458100 **Fax:** 01424-421160
E-mail: timp@lesker.com
Website: http://www.lesker.com
Bank(s): National Westminster Bank Plc
Directors: G. Thompson (Fin)
Managers: R. Whitehouse, T. Pearce, J. Ainsley (Personnel), L. Page
Ultimate Holding Company: KURT J LESKER INC.(USA)
Immediate Holding Company: KURT J. LESKER COMPANY LIMITED
Registration no: 02426614 **Date established:** 1989
Turnover: £10m - £20m **No.of Employees:** 101 - 250
Product Groups: 32, 36, 38, 40, 42

Date of Accounts	Dec 11	Dec 10	Dec 09
Sales Turnover	11m	11m	9m
Pre Tax Profit/Loss	358	-111	454
Working Capital	2m	2m	2m
Fixed Assets	275	345	337
Current Assets	4m	4m	4m
Current Liabilities	1m	851	814

Max Appliances Ltd
Unit 16 Wheel Park Farm Industrial Estate Wheel Lane, Westfield, Hastings, TN35 4SE
Tel: 01424-751666 **Fax:** 01424-751444
E-mail: sales@max-appliances.co.uk
Website: http://www.max-appliances.co.uk
Directors: C. Scott (Co Sec)
Immediate Holding Company: MAX APPLIANCES LIMITED
Registration no: 03432279 **VAT No.:** GB 110 6214 33
Date established: 1997 **Turnover:** £500,000 - £1m
No.of Employees: 1 - 10 **Product Groups:** 36, 40, 42, 67

Date of Accounts	Sep 11	Sep 10	Sep 09
Sales Turnover	N/A	N/A	705
Pre Tax Profit/Loss	N/A	N/A	39
Working Capital	206	188	146
Fixed Assets	3	27	51
Current Assets	269	305	223

Meta One Ltd
Creative Media Centre Robertson Street, Hastings, TN34 1HL
Tel: 01424-205420
E-mail: info@metaone.co.uk
Website: http://www.metaone.co.uk
Directors: J. Clements (Dir)
Immediate Holding Company: META ONE LIMITED
Registration no: 03534787 **Date established:** 1998
Turnover: £500,000 - £1m **No.of Employees:** 1 - 10 **Product Groups:** 44

Date of Accounts	Feb 12	Feb 11	Feb 10
Working Capital	118	90	47
Fixed Assets	3	2	3
Current Assets	189	183	123

Nursing & General Supplies
Ivyhouse Industrial Estate Haywood Way, Hastings, TN35 4PL
Tel: 01424-444411 **Fax:** 01424-435009
E-mail: office@nursingandgeneral.co.uk
Directors: P. Bowie (Sales)
Immediate Holding Company: UDIAM CONSTRUCTION LTD
Registration no: 06441374 **Date established:** 2007
No.of Employees: 1 - 10 **Product Groups:** 32, 66

Date of Accounts	Nov 10	Nov 09
Working Capital	-12	-10
Current Assets	636	580

Proficient Fastenings Ltd
Burgess Road, Hastings, TN35 4NR
Tel: 01424-722800 **Fax:** 01424-435278
E-mail: proficientfast@aol.com
Website: http://www.kellysearch.com/partners/proficientfastenings.asp
Directors: A. Coleman (Co Sec)
Immediate Holding Company: PROFICIENT FASTENINGS LIMITED
Registration no: 01958248 **VAT No.:** GB 430 8790 46
Date established: 1985 **Turnover:** £250,000 - £500,000
No.of Employees: 1 - 10 **Product Groups:** 66

Date of Accounts	Dec 11	Dec 10	Dec 09
Sales Turnover	N/A	400	356
Pre Tax Profit/Loss	N/A	54	33
Working Capital	244	231	208
Fixed Assets	26	24	21
Current Assets	318	295	269
Current Liabilities	N/A	24	20

R B Health & Safety Solutions Ltd
Blacklands Business Centre 15 Fearon Road, Hastings, TN34 2EP
Tel: 08452-571489
E-mail: admin@rbhealthandsafety.co.uk
Website: http://www.rbhealthandsafety.co.uk
Managers: M. Collyer (Mktg Serv Mgr), M. Papuha (Mgr)
Immediate Holding Company: RB HEALTH & SAFETY SOLUTIONS LIMITED
Registration no: 04966344 **Date established:** 2003
Turnover: Up to £250,000 **No.of Employees:** 1 - 10 **Product Groups:** 84, 86

Date of Accounts	Mar 11	Mar 10	Mar 09
Working Capital	11	19	8
Fixed Assets	22	10	10
Current Assets	61	70	38

Shirley Leaf & Petal Co. Ltd
58a High Street Old Town, Hastings, TN34 3EN
Tel: 01424-427793 **Fax:** 01424-427793
E-mail: shirleyleafpetalco.hastings@virgin.net
Website: http://www.shirleyleaf.com
Directors: B. Wilson (Prop), B. Wilson (Fin)
Immediate Holding Company: Shirley Leaf & Petal Company Ltd
Registration no: 04562525 **VAT No.:** GB 621 8940 38
Turnover: Up to £250,000 **No.of Employees:** 1 - 10 **Product Groups:** 49

Squires Metal Fabrications Ltd
6 Burgess Road, Hastings, TN35 4NR
Tel: 01424-428794 **Fax:** 01424-431567
E-mail: squiresmetal@tiscali.co.uk
Website: http://www.squiresmetal.co.uk
Bank(s): National Westminster
Directors: H. Pickett (Fin), A. Morton (Dir)
Immediate Holding Company: SQUIRES METAL FABRICATIONS LIMITED
Registration no: 02553757 **VAT No.:** 583 5525 19 **Date established:** 1990
Turnover: £250,000 - £500,000 **No.of Employees:** 11 - 20
Product Groups: 35, 36, 39

Date of Accounts	Dec 11	Dec 10	Dec 09
Sales Turnover	N/A	N/A	466
Pre Tax Profit/Loss	N/A	N/A	-29
Working Capital	262	174	249
Fixed Assets	19	23	29
Current Assets	428	241	316
Current Liabilities	N/A	N/A	12

Tweeny Ltd
Wheel Park Farm Wheel Lane, Westfield, Hastings, TN35 4SE
Tel: 01424-751888 **Fax:** 01424-751444
E-mail: sales@tweeny.co.uk
Website: http://www.tweeny.co.uk
Directors: D. Adderley (MD)
Registration no: 03432279 **VAT No.:** GB 655 9911 92
Turnover: £500,000 - £1m **No.of Employees:** 1 - 10 **Product Groups:** 40

Heathfield

Agmac
Punnetts Town, Heathfield, TN21 9PD
Tel: 01435-830774
Directors: R. Leeves (Prop)
Date established: 1985 **No.of Employees:** 1 - 10 **Product Groups:** 41

Airvert
Ghyll Road Industrial Estate Ghyll Road, Heathfield, TN21 8AW
Tel: 01323-444002 **Fax:** 01435-864838
E-mail: sales@airvert.co.uk
Directors: P. Scott (Dir), A. Mcpeake (Co Sec), A. Lamberton (Fab), M. Thompson (Sales)
Managers: A. Stevens (I.T. Exec)
Ultimate Holding Company: HALESBURTON HOLDINGS LIMITED
Immediate Holding Company: AIRVERT LIMITED
Registration no: 02769542 **VAT No.:** GB 583 6695 86
Date established: 1992 **Turnover:** £5m - £10m **No.of Employees:** 1 - 10
Product Groups: 39, 41

Date of Accounts	Jul 10	Jan 09	Jan 08
Working Capital	82	2m	2m
Fixed Assets	N/A	N/A	4
Current Assets	683	3m	3m

Diamond Shooting Services
Unit 8 Ghyll Industrial Estate, Heathfield, TN21 8AW
Tel: 01435-863295 **Fax:** 01435-863645
Directors: C. Hudson (Prop)
Date established: 1994 **No.of Employees:** 1 - 10 **Product Groups:** 36, 39, 40

C J Dolton
Browning Road, Heathfield, TN21 8DB
Tel: 01435-866350 **Fax:** 01435-866416
E-mail: info@cjdoltonjoinery.co.uk
Website: http://www.cjdoltonjoinery.co.uk
Directors: C. Dolton (MD), C. Dolton (Prop)
VAT No.: 508 7347 33 **Turnover:** Up to £250,000 **No.of Employees:** 1 - 10
Product Groups: 25, 52

Flag Standards
Compass House Waldron, Heathfield, TN21 0RE
Tel: 01435-810080 **Fax:** 01435-810082
E-mail: sales@flagstandards.co.uk
Website: http://www.flagstandards.co.uk
Directors: T. Eustace (Prop)
Turnover: Up to £250,000 **No.of Employees:** 1 - 10 **Product Groups:** 33, 49

Jewson Hirepoint
Isenhurst Saw Mills Cross In Hand, Heathfield, TN21 0UB
Tel: 01435-864411 **Fax:** 01435-865377
E-mail: sarah.durham@jewson.co.uk
Website: http://www.jewson.co.uk
Managers: D. Bates (Asst Gen Mgr)
Ultimate Holding Company: COMPAGNIE DE SAINT GOBAIN (FRANCE)
Immediate Holding Company: JEWSON LIMITED
Registration no: 00348407 **Date established:** 1939
Turnover: £500m - £1,000m **No.of Employees:** 11 - 20
Product Groups: 66

Date of Accounts	Dec 11	Dec 10	Dec 09
Sales Turnover	1606m	1547m	1485m
Pre Tax Profit/Loss	18m	100m	45m
Working Capital	-345m	-250m	-349m
Fixed Assets	496m	387m	461m
Current Assets	657m	1005m	1320m
Current Liabilities	66m	120m	64m

Longlife Stoves
Little London Road Cross in Hand, Heathfield, TN21 0LU
Tel: 01435-863246 **Fax:** 01435-863246
E-mail: info@bernard-davis-stoves.co.uk
Website: http://www.bernard-davis-stoves.co.uk
Directors: K. Leeves (Ptnr)
Immediate Holding Company: GREENFELL SERVICES LTD
Date established: 2012 **No.of Employees:** 1 - 10 **Product Groups:** 40

Saws UK Ltd
Unit 4 Ghyll Industrial Estate, Heathfield, TN21 8AW
Tel: 08448-804511 **Fax:** 01435-862205
E-mail: sales@sawsuk.com
Website: http://www.sawsuk.com
Directors: A. Peatfield (Dir), A. Woodthorpe (Co Sec)
Immediate Holding Company: SAWS (U.K.) LIMITED
Registration no: 02453610 **Date established:** 1989
Turnover: £500,000 - £1m **No.of Employees:** 1 - 10 **Product Groups:** 33, 34, 35, 36, 37, 38, 40, 41, 42, 43, 45, 46, 47, 48, 49, 51, 66, 67, 77, 86

Date of Accounts	Mar 12	Mar 11	Mar 10
Working Capital	210	216	161
Fixed Assets	8	2	2
Current Assets	342	357	317

Southern Rewinds
1 Station Road Industrial Estate Browning Road, Heathfield, TN21 8DB
Tel: 01435-865533 **Fax:** 01435-865533
E-mail: info@southernrewinds.net
Website: http://www.southernrewinds.net
Directors: J. Dyer (Prop)
No.of Employees: 1 - 10 **Product Groups:** 37, 40, 67

T F C Ltd
Hale House Ghyll Industrial Estate, Heathfield, TN21 8AW
Tel: 01435-866011 **Fax:** 01435-866620
E-mail: mclarke@tfc.eu.com
Website: http://www.tfcplc.com
Bank(s): National Westminster Bank Plc
Directors: M. Clarke (MD), G. Smith (Fin)
Managers: T. McGowan (Personnel), K. Kentish, G. Templeman (Sales Prom Mgr)
Ultimate Holding Company: TFC EUROPE LIMITED
Immediate Holding Company: TFC LIMITED
Registration no: 00675195 **Date established:** 1960
Turnover: £10m - £20m **No.of Employees:** 21 - 50 **Product Groups:** 29, 30, 33, 35, 36, 37, 38, 39, 40, 46, 49, 66

Date of Accounts	Mar 11	Mar 10	Mar 09
Sales Turnover	12m	8m	9m
Pre Tax Profit/Loss	1m	1m	82
Working Capital	5m	4m	3m
Fixed Assets	575	624	728
Current Assets	9m	9m	8m
Current Liabilities	1m	2m	3m

Hove

4 Print & Design Ltd
Unit 2 St Josephs Business Park St Josephs Close, Hove, BN3 7ES
Tel: 01273-712520 **Fax:** 01273-731 720
E-mail: sales@4printanddesign.co.uk
Website: http://www.4printanddesign.co.uk
Directors: J. Gibson (Dir)
Immediate Holding Company: 4 PRINT & DESIGN LIMITED
Registration no: 05032740 **Date established:** 2004
Turnover: £500,000 - £1m **No.of Employees:** 1 - 10 **Product Groups:** 28

Date of Accounts	Mar 11	Mar 10	Mar 09
Working Capital	-62	-28	-24
Fixed Assets	41	7	9
Current Assets	180	135	149

Aero Metals International
53 Furze Hill Court Furze Hill, Hove, BN3 1PG
Tel: 01273-383000 **Fax:** 01273-387387
E-mail: sales@aerometals.co.uk
Website: http://www.aerometals.co.uk
Directors: N. Bowley (Ptnr)
VAT No.: GB 466 6533 19 **Date established:** 1987 **Turnover:** £1m - £2m
No.of Employees: 1 - 10 **Product Groups:** 34, 35, 36

Astric Medical
36 Blatchington Road, Hove, BN3 3YN
Tel: 01273-716516 **Fax:** 01273-716516
E-mail: info@astric-medical.co.uk
Website: http://www.astric-medical.co.uk
Directors: S. Spires (Prop)
Immediate Holding Company: ASTRIC MEDICAL LIMITED
Registration no: 07184648 **VAT No.:** GB 190 2439 70
Date established: 2010 **Turnover:** Up to £250,000
No.of Employees: 1 - 10 **Product Groups:** 38

Date of Accounts	Mar 11
Working Capital	1
Fixed Assets	1
Current Assets	15

Automarine Diesel Services
2 St Leonards Road, Hove, BN3 4QR
Tel: 01273-415296 **Fax:** 01273-410603
E-mail: andrews-peter@btconnect.com
Website: http://home.btconnect.com/automarinediesel
Directors: P. Andrews (Prop)
Date established: 1979 **No.of Employees:** 1 - 10 **Product Groups:** 39, 40, 68

Bathglaze.com
30 Brunswick Square, Hove, BN3 1ED
Tel: 01273-711111
E-mail: sales@bathglaze.com
Website: http://www.bathglaze.com
Directors: J. Wordie (Prop)
No.of Employees: 1 - 10 **Product Groups:** 46, 48

Builder Center Ltd
Conway Street, Hove, BN3 3LA
Tel: 01273-778778 **Fax:** 01273-722413
Website: http://www.buildcenter.co.uk

Directors: A. Barden (MD)
Managers: J. Haines (Mgr), M. Simmonds (Mgr), M. Simpson (Mgr)
Ultimate Holding Company: Wolseley plc
Immediate Holding Company: BUILD CENTER LIMITED
Registration no: 00462397 **Date established:** 1948 **Turnover:** £1m - £2m
No.of Employees: 21 - 50 **Product Groups:** 66

C Dugard Ltd Machine Tools

75 Old Shoreham Road, Hove, BN3 7BX
Tel: 01273-732286 **Fax:** 01698-300258
E-mail: sales@dugard.co.uk
Website: http://www.dugard.com
Bank(s): HSBC
Directors: R. Dugard (Ch), E. Dugard (MD)
Managers: N. Gunning (Sales Prom Mgr), R. Starzec (Spares Mgr), E. Vegara (I.T. Exec), S. Campbell (Mktg Serv Mgr)
Immediate Holding Company: EAGLE CNC LIMITED
Registration no: 00355588 **Date established:** 2001 **Turnover:** £5m - £10m
No.of Employees: 21 - 50 **Product Groups:** 46

Date of Accounts	Dec 10	Dec 09	Dec 08
Working Capital	870	388	295
Fixed Assets	450	463	303
Current Assets	903	457	326

C G Tech Ltd

Curtis House 34 Third Avenue, Hove, BN3 2PD
Tel: 01273-773538 **Fax:** 01273-721688
E-mail: info.uk@cgtech.com
Website: http://www.cgtech.com
Directors: J. Reed (MD)
Registration no: 03579362 **Turnover:** £1m - £2m
No.of Employees: 11 - 20 **Product Groups:** 44

Date of Accounts	Dec 09	Dec 08	Dec 07
Sales Turnover	2m	2m	2m
Pre Tax Profit/Loss	90	228	127
Working Capital	835	765	602
Fixed Assets	173	176	175
Current Assets	2m	1m	1m
Current Liabilities	452	378	523

Camberley Auto Factors Ltd

Unit 6-7 196 Old Shoreham Road, Hove, BN3 3TW
Tel: 01273-775488 **Fax:** 01273-822821
E-mail: hove.manager@camberleyautofactors.com
Website: http://www.camberleyautofactors.co.uk
Managers: T. West (District Mgr)
Immediate Holding Company: CAMBERLEY AUTO FACTORS LIMITED
Registration no: 01656353 **VAT No.:** GB 358 6888 82
Date established: 1982 **Turnover:** £1m - £2m **No.of Employees:** 21 - 50
Product Groups: 68

Date of Accounts	Nov 11	Nov 10	Nov 09
Sales Turnover	46m	43m	41m
Pre Tax Profit/Loss	2m	3m	3m
Working Capital	11m	9m	8m
Fixed Assets	2m	2m	2m
Current Assets	18m	18m	16m
Current Liabilities	2m	2m	3m

Canery Cliff Ltd

Maple Works Old Shoreham Road, Hove, BN3 7ED
Tel: 0800-028 6778 **Fax:** 01273-203070
E-mail: jeremy.burbidge@ticketmedia.com
Website: http://www.ticketmedia.com
Bank(s): HSBC Bank plc
Directors: J. Burbidge (MD), E. Castleton (Fin)
Immediate Holding Company: CANARYCLIFF LIMITED
Registration no: 02777670 **VAT No.:** GB 322 0387 94
Date established: 1993 **Turnover:** £1m - £2m **No.of Employees:** 21 - 50
Product Groups: 27, 28

Date of Accounts	May 11	May 10	May 09
Sales Turnover	2m	2m	2m
Pre Tax Profit/Loss	16	155	186
Working Capital	28	21	18
Fixed Assets	1m	1m	726
Current Assets	529	494	471
Current Liabilities	64	121	119

Custom Pharmaceuticals Ltd

Tecore House Conway Street, Hove, BN3 3LW
Tel: 01273-323513 **Fax:** 01273-729483
E-mail: enquiries@custompharm.com
Website: http://www.custompharm.com
Bank(s): Barclays
Directors: N. Baldwin (Co Sec), T. Dawson (Fin)
Managers: S. Haffar (Personnel), D. Kent, D. Lessels (Purch Mgr), M. Brookes (Tech Serv Mgr)
Ultimate Holding Company: CUSTOM HEALTHCARE LIMITED
Immediate Holding Company: CUSTOM PHARMACEUTICALS LIMITED
Registration no: 01431692 **VAT No.:** GB 626 3568 27
Date established: 1979 **Turnover:** £10m - £20m
No.of Employees: 51 - 100 **Product Groups:** 30, 31, 32

Date of Accounts	Dec 11	Dec 10	Dec 09
Sales Turnover	12m	11m	11m
Pre Tax Profit/Loss	-641	22	34
Working Capital	-311	65	-65
Fixed Assets	2m	2m	2m
Current Assets	3m	4m	3m
Current Liabilities	677	694	731

Edf Energy

329 Portland Road, Hove, BN3 5SU
Tel: 01273-422666 **Fax:** 01273-432883
Website: http://www.edfenergy.com
Directors: A. Edgoose (MD), N. Samuels (Sales & Mktg)
Registration no: 02366867 **No.of Employees:** 1 - 10 **Product Groups:** 18

Geos English Academy

55-61 Portland Road, Hove, BN3 5DQ
Tel: 01273-735975 **Fax:** 01273-732884
E-mail: info@ltc-brighton.com
Website: http://www.ltc-brighton.com
Bank(s): HSBC Bank plc
Directors: A. Drury (Head)
Ultimate Holding Company: Geos Corporation
Immediate Holding Company: Amvik UK Ltd
VAT No.: GB 550 1796 47 **No.of Employees:** 21 - 50 **Product Groups:** 86

H T S Optical Group Ltd

Industrial House Conway Street, Hove, BN3 3LU
Tel: 01273-773918 **Fax:** 01273-737246
Directors: J. King (Fin), A. King (MD)
Immediate Holding Company: H.T.S. OPTICAL LTD
Registration no: 00436229 **Date established:** 1947
Turnover: £500,000 - £1m **No.of Employees:** 1 - 10 **Product Groups:** 38

Date of Accounts	Jun 11	Jun 10	Jun 09
Working Capital	-17	-17	-17
Fixed Assets	27	27	27

Robert Harding Computers Ltd

65 Sackville Road, Hove, BN3 3WE
Tel: 01273-728827 **Fax:** 01273-324678
E-mail: info@rh-computers.com
Website: http://www.rh-computers.com
Directors: C. Harding (MD), E. Hunt (Fin)
Immediate Holding Company: ROBERT HARDING (COMPUTERS) LIMITED
Registration no: 01580532 **VAT No.:** GB 351 2210 11
Date established: 1981 **Turnover:** £250,000 - £500,000
No.of Employees: 1 - 10 **Product Groups:** 44

Date of Accounts	Feb 08	Feb 11	Feb 10
Working Capital	-615	-575	-586
Current Assets	7	3	8

Hosiden Besson Ltd

11 St. Josephs Trading Estate St Josephs Close, Hove, BN3 7EZ
Tel: 01273-860000 **Fax:** 01273-777501
E-mail: info@hbl.co.uk
Website: http://www.hbl.co.uk
Bank(s): Mizuho Corporate Bank Limited
Immediate Holding Company: Hosiden Corporation
Registration no: 02444091 **VAT No.:** GB 550 3562 62
Date established: 1953 **Turnover:** £10m - £20m
No.of Employees: 101 - 250 **Product Groups:** 35, 37, 38, 39, 40, 44, 52, 67, 68

Date of Accounts	Mar 12	Mar 11	Mar 10
Sales Turnover	11m	26m	17m
Pre Tax Profit/Loss	121	2m	972
Working Capital	6m	7m	6m
Fixed Assets	565	748	893
Current Assets	9m	14m	13m
Current Liabilities	2m	6m	5m

Indexing Specialists UK Ltd

Indexing House 306a Portland Road, Hove, BN3 5LP
Tel: 01273-424411 **Fax:** 01273-424411
E-mail: george@indexing.co.uk
Website: http://www.indexing.co.uk
Directors: G. Curzon (MD)
Immediate Holding Company: INDEXING SPECIALISTS (UK) LIMITED
Registration no: 03248432 **VAT No.:** GB 449 5297 06
Date established: 1996 **No.of Employees:** 1 - 10 **Product Groups:** 81

Date of Accounts	Mar 12	Mar 11	Mar 10
Working Capital	66	61	48
Fixed Assets	3	2	2
Current Assets	91	84	62

L S Engineering

62 Rutland Road, Hove, BN3 5FE
Tel: 01273-707100 **Fax:** 01273-707101
E-mail: enquiries@lsengineering.co.uk
Website: http://www.lsengineering.co.uk
Directors: L. Sharman (Prop)
Date established: 1996 **No.of Employees:** 1 - 10 **Product Groups:** 36

Logo Sports

Industrial House Conway Street, Hove, BN3 3LW
Tel: 01273-321209 **Fax:** 01273-726769
E-mail: peter@logosports.co.uk
Website: http://www.logosports.co.uk
Directors: P. Small (Prop)
Immediate Holding Company: UNIQUE APPAREL LIMITED
Registration no: 01569064 **Date established:** 1981
No.of Employees: 1 - 10 **Product Groups:** 24, 63

Date of Accounts	Jun 11	Jun 10	Jun 09
Working Capital	-90	-45	-58
Fixed Assets	28	15	19
Current Assets	114	113	109

The Manor Spa

Hove Manor Hove Street, Hove, BN3 2DF
Tel: 01273-748483
E-mail: admin@blakeneymanor.co.uk
Website: http://www.stores.ebay.co.uk
Directors: M. Kelly (Ptnr), E. Marini (Prop), H. Longworth (Prop)
Registration no: 03726871 **Date established:** 1999
Turnover: Up to £250,000 **No.of Employees:** 1 - 10 **Product Groups:** 37, 49, 65

Migrate Media

96 Ethel Street, Hove, BN3 3LL
Tel: 07967-025392
E-mail: info@migratemedia.co.uk
Website: http://www.migratemedia.co.uk
Directors: D. Regan (Prop), D. Regan (Dir)
No.of Employees: 1 - 10 **Product Groups:** 44

Mirlyn

57-59 Coleridge Street, Hove, BN3 5AB
Tel: 01273-733404 **Fax:** 01273-703330
Directors: J. Wilson (Fin), R. Fossella (Prop)
Registration no: 00422737 **Date established:** 1946
No.of Employees: 1 - 10 **Product Groups:** 26, 35

Date of Accounts	Jun 06	Jun 05	Jun 04
Working Capital	4	28	35
Fixed Assets	N/A	13	20
Current Assets	7	45	55
Current Liabilities	3	17	21
Total Share Capital	1	1	1

Namrick Ltd

124 Portland Road, Hove, BN3 5QL
Tel: 01273-736963 **Fax:** 01273-726708
E-mail: sales@namrick.co.uk
Website: http://www.namrick.co.uk
Directors: K. Terry (MD)
Ultimate Holding Company: THE NUT & BOLT STORE LIMITED
Immediate Holding Company: NAMRICK LIMITED
Registration no: 01474740 **VAT No.:** GB 403 2172 08
Date established: 1980 **Turnover:** £250,000 - £500,000
No.of Employees: 1 - 10 **Product Groups:** 35

Date of Accounts	Mar 12	Mar 11	Mar 10
Working Capital	69	46	22
Fixed Assets	4	5	5
Current Assets	172	158	142

Peca Electronics

10 Vallance Road, Hove, BN3 2DA
Tel: 01264-355975 **Fax:** 01264-366536
E-mail: sales@peca-electronics.co.uk
Website: http://www.peca-electronics.co.uk
Directors: J. Dunn (MD), P. Groves (MD)
Immediate Holding Company: FIELDOFFICE LIMITED
Registration no: 02771996 **VAT No.:** GB 631 5046 70
Date established: 1992 **Turnover:** £500,000 - £1m
No.of Employees: 1 - 10 **Product Groups:** 37

Date of Accounts	Mar 11	Mar 10	Mar 09
Working Capital	-189	-189	-195
Current Assets	-2	16	15

C B Powell Ltd

10 St Josephs Close, Hove, BN3 7ES
Tel: 01273-771144 **Fax:** 01273-726966
E-mail: cbpowell@btconnect.com
Website: http://www.cbpowellengineeringsussex.co.uk
Directors: A. Powell (MD)
Immediate Holding Company: C.B. POWELL LIMITED
Registration no: 00410904 **VAT No.:** GB 190 7305 66
Date established: 1946 **Turnover:** £250,000 - £500,000
No.of Employees: 1 - 10 **Product Groups:** 30, 48

Date of Accounts	Apr 12	Apr 11	Apr 10
Sales Turnover	N/A	N/A	277
Pre Tax Profit/Loss	N/A	N/A	8
Working Capital	80	40	47
Fixed Assets	241	252	229
Current Assets	145	135	73
Current Liabilities	N/A	N/A	15

Power Tool Supplies Ltd

379 Kingsway, Hove, BN3 4QD
Tel: 01273-420111 **Fax:** 01273-422313
E-mail: contact@ptshove.co.uk
Website: http://www.bosch-pt.com
Directors: F. Hughes (MD), M. Hollay (MD), M. Hollett (Co Sec)
Managers: K. Dunbar (Chief Mgr), J. Lear (I.T. Exec)
Registration no: 01637795 **Date established:** 1982
No.of Employees: 1 - 10 **Product Groups:** 35, 36

Date of Accounts	Mar 08	Mar 07	Mar 06
Working Capital	395	389	184
Fixed Assets	43	44	62
Current Assets	706	705	620
Current Liabilities	310	316	436
Total Share Capital	50	50	50

The Tile Store UK Ltd

Unit B1 Portland Business Park Portland Road, Hove, BN3 5RY
Tel: 08707-776870
Directors: C. Parkinson (Dir)
No.of Employees: 11 - 20 **Product Groups:** 33, 40, 66

Tisserand Aromatherapy (Tisserand)

4 Clarks Industrial Estate Newtown Road, Hove, BN3 7BA
Tel: 01273-325666 **Fax:** 01273-208444
E-mail: info@tisserand.com
Website: http://www.tisserand.com
Directors: A. Harris (MD), C. Walker (Mkt Research)
Immediate Holding Company: AROMATHERAPY PRODUCTS LIMITED
Registration no: 01814713 **VAT No.:** GB 403 1541 08
Date established: 1984 **No.of Employees:** 21 - 50 **Product Groups:** 31, 32

Zantis & Co.

19 York Road Brighton, Hove, BN3 1DJ
Tel: 01273-208325 **Fax:** 01273-208325
E-mail: zantis@hotmail.co.uk
Website: http://www.accountants-brighton.co.uk
Directors: C. Zantis (Prop)
Date established: 2003 **Turnover:** Up to £250,000
No.of Employees: 1 - 10 **Product Groups:** 80

Lewes

A F M Ltd

Unit 8-10 Parkside Farm Shortgate Lane, Laughton, Lewes, BN8 6DG
Tel: 08454-507500 **Fax:** 0845-450 7501
E-mail: info@afm.ltd.uk
Website: http://www.afm.ltd.uk
Directors: A. Michel (Dir)
Immediate Holding Company: A.F.M LIMITED
Registration no: 03350007 **Date established:** 1997
No.of Employees: 11 - 20 **Product Groups:** 26, 61, 72, 74, 75, 76, 77, 79, 80, 81, 84

Date of Accounts	Mar 11	Mar 10	Mar 09
Working Capital	145	110	121
Fixed Assets	5	7	9
Current Assets	245	262	209

Bulldog Blasting Ltd

4 Caburn Enterprise Park The Broyle, Ringmer, Lewes, BN8 5NP
Tel: 01273-814144 **Fax:** 01273-814148
Directors: S. Long (Co Sec)
Immediate Holding Company: BULLDOG BLASTING LTD
Registration no: 03866701 **Date established:** 1999
No.of Employees: 1 - 10 **Product Groups:** 46, 48

Date of Accounts	Oct 10	Oct 09	Oct 08
Working Capital	-7	-7	-8
Fixed Assets	7	8	9
Current Assets	22	22	22
Current Liabilities	7	6	5

Cleanglass

7 Barn Road, Lewes, BN7 2JH
Tel: 01273-472633
E-mail: cleanglassukltd@yahoo.co.uk
Website: http://www.cleenglass-window-cleaning.co.uk
Directors: N. Tuckey (Prop)
Date established: 2003 **No.of Employees:** 1 - 10 **Product Groups:** 52

Courtin & Warner Ltd
19 Phoenix Place, Lewes, BN7 1JX
Tel: 01273-480611 **Fax:** 01273-472249
E-mail: roy@courtinandwarner.com
Website: http://www.c-and-w.co.uk
Directors: R. Gooch (I.T. Dir), R. Gooch (Tech Serv), M. Johnson (Dir)
Managers: A. Bird (Transport)
Immediate Holding Company: COURTIN AND WARNER LIMITED
Registration no: 00477795 **Date established:** 1950 **Turnover:** £1m - £2m
No.of Employees: 1 - 10 **Product Groups:** 66

Date of Accounts	Jan 11	Jan 10	Jan 09
Working Capital	468	461	406
Fixed Assets	150	138	152
Current Assets	568	672	590

Data Command Ltd
1 Castle Ditch Lane, Lewes, BN7 1YJ
Tel: 01273-483548
E-mail: david.echlin@datacommand.com
Website: http://www.datacommand.com
Directors: D. Echlin (MD), D. Granger (Dir), K. Godwin (Dir)
Immediate Holding Company: DATA COMMAND LIMITED
Registration no: 01621570 **Date established:** 1982
Turnover: £250,000 - £500,000 **No.of Employees:** 1 - 10
Product Groups: 84

Date of Accounts	Mar 11	Mar 10	Mar 09
Working Capital	16	9	1
Fixed Assets	3	3	3
Current Assets	25	22	22

Design Initiative Ltd
The Old Granary The Street, Glynde, Lewes, BN8 6SX
Tel: 01273-858525 **Fax:** 01273-858531
E-mail: info@post.eu.com
Website: http://www.post.eu.com
Directors: S. Smewing (MD)
Immediate Holding Company: DESIGN INITIATIVE LIMITED
Registration no: 01502383 **VAT No.:** GB 423 1098 82
Date established: 1980 **Turnover:** £250,000 - £500,000
No.of Employees: 1 - 10 **Product Groups:** 38, 49

Date of Accounts	Dec 11	Dec 10	Dec 09
Working Capital	65	82	-73
Fixed Assets	796	732	1m
Current Assets	127	202	88

Development Solutions UK Ltd
The Needlemakers West Street, Lewes, BN7 2NZ
Tel: 020-7193 1153 **Fax:** 01273-486974
E-mail: michael@developmentsolutions.co.uk
Website: http://www.developmentsolutions.co.uk
Directors: M. Hartland (MD)
Registration no: 07546732 **Date established:** 1998
Turnover: Up to £250,000 **No.of Employees:** 1 - 10 **Product Groups:** 81

Energy Technology & Control Ltd
25 North Street, Lewes, BN7 2PE
Tel: 01273-480667 **Fax:** 01273-480652
E-mail: sales@energytechnologycontrol.com
Website: http://www.energytechnologycontrol.com
Bank(s): Barclays, Broadgate, London
Directors: C. Snook (Fin)
Immediate Holding Company: ENERGY TECHNOLOGY AND CONTROL LIMITED
Registration no: 02277937 **VAT No.:** GB 654 3402 52
Date established: 1988 **Turnover:** £1m - £2m **No.of Employees:** 11 - 20
Product Groups: 38

Date of Accounts	Mar 11	Mar 10	Mar 09
Working Capital	660	543	538
Fixed Assets	22	32	28
Current Assets	1m	835	1m

Equilibrium Complementary Health Centre
16 Station Street, Lewes, BN7 2DB
Tel: 01273-470955
E-mail: info@equilibrium-clinic.com
Website: http://www.equilibrium-clinic.com
Directors: P. Tucker (Dir)
Immediate Holding Company: SOUTHDOWNS ENVIRONMENTAL CONSULTANTS LIMITED
Registration no: 03150111 **Date established:** 1996
No.of Employees: 1 - 10 **Product Groups:** 26, 29, 38, 49, 65

Date of Accounts	Mar 12	Mar 11	Mar 10
Working Capital	59	53	85
Fixed Assets	70	24	19
Current Assets	359	223	193

The Guild Of Mastercraftsmen G M C Publications Ltd
166 High Street, Lewes, BN7 1XU
Tel: 01273-478449 **Fax:** 01273-478606
E-mail: johnp@thegmcgroup.com
Website: http://www.guildmc.com
Bank(s): National Westminster Bank Plc
Managers: E. Saleh, J. Place (Sales Admin), C. Cranfield (Personnel)
Immediate Holding Company: GUILD OF MASTER CRAFTSMEN (INTERNATIONAL) LIMITED
Registration no: 01535451 **VAT No.:** GB 242 1775 74
Date established: 1980 **Turnover:** £500,000 - £1m
No.of Employees: 101 - 250 **Product Groups:** 87

Date of Accounts	May 10	May 09
Working Capital	8	8
Current Assets	11	11
Current Liabilities	3	3

Hanover Displays Ltd
Unit 24 Cliffe Industrial Estate, Lewes, BN8 6JL
Tel: 01273-477528 **Fax:** 01273-407766
E-mail: sales@hanoverdisplays.com
Website: http://www.hanoverdisplays.com
Bank(s): Barclays, Brighton
Directors: D. Williams (MD)
Immediate Holding Company: HANOVER DISPLAYS LIMITED
Registration no: 01876684 **VAT No.:** GB 412 4946 63
Date established: 1985 **Turnover:** £20m - £50m
No.of Employees: 101 - 250 **Product Groups:** 37, 39, 40

Date of Accounts	Dec 11	Dec 10	Dec 09
Sales Turnover	23m	23m	25m
Pre Tax Profit/Loss	4m	4m	6m
Working Capital	26m	23m	21m
Fixed Assets	1m	926	632
Current Assets	31m	28m	28m
Current Liabilities	3m	3m	4m

In-Pulse Medical Services
Orchard Cottage Brighton Road, Lewes, BN7 3JJ
Tel: 01273-479999 **Fax:** 01273-239999
E-mail: ims@ambulanceservice.gb.com
Website: http://www.ambulanceservice.gb.com
Directors: S. Hilton (Dir)
No.of Employees: 11 - 20 **Product Groups:** 30, 35, 36, 39

Insight Security
Unit 2 Cliffe Industrial Estate, Lewes, BN8 6JL
Tel: 01273-475500 **Fax:** 01273-478800
E-mail: sales@insight-security.com
Website: http://www.insight-security.com
Directors: I. Blatchford (Dir)
No.of Employees: 1 - 10 **Product Groups:** 26, 27, 30, 32, 33, 35, 36, 37, 38, 39, 40, 44, 48, 67, 81

John Gosnell Ltd (Head Office)
20 Phoenix Place, Lewes, BN7 2QJ
Tel: 01273-473772 **Fax:** 01273-472217
E-mail: chris.warner@johngosnell.com
Website: http://www.newscientist.net
Bank(s): National Westminster Bank Plc
Directors: D. Warner (Fin), C. Warner (MD)
Managers: L. Watson (Sales Prom Mgr)
Immediate Holding Company: JOHN GOSNELL & COMPANY,LIMITED
Registration no: 00278523 **VAT No.:** GB 190 1160 96
Date established: 1933 **No.of Employees:** 21 - 50 **Product Groups:** 32

Date of Accounts	Dec 10	Dec 09	Dec 08
Working Capital	3m	3m	3m
Fixed Assets	920	858	864
Current Assets	3m	3m	3m
Current Liabilities	N/A	N/A	10

Mcbean's Orchids
Mcbeans Nursery Resting Oak Hill, Cooksbridge, Lewes, BN8 4PR
Tel: 01273-400228 **Fax:** 01273-401181
E-mail: sales@mcbeansorchids.co.uk
Website: http://www.mcbeansorchids.co.uk
Directors: E. Johnson (Ptnr)
Registration no: 02777331 **No.of Employees:** 1 - 10 **Product Groups:** 02

Neve Engineering
Galleybird Road Barcombe, Lewes, BN8 5TJ
Tel: 01273-400731 **Fax:** 01273-400731
E-mail: neve@neve-engineering.demon.co.uk
Website: http://www.neveengineering.co.uk
Directors: I. Neve (Ptnr)
Registration no: 02657901 **Date established:** 1991
Turnover: Up to £250,000 **No.of Employees:** 1 - 10 **Product Groups:** 35, 45

Oncology Imaging Systems Ltd
7-8 Carriers Way East Hoathly, Lewes, BN8 6AG
Tel: 01825-840633 **Fax:** 01825-841496
E-mail: sales@oncologyimaging.com
Website: http://www.oncologyimaging.com
Directors: S. Imber (MD)
Immediate Holding Company: ONCOLOGY IMAGING SYSTEMS LIMITED
Registration no: 03816098 **Date established:** 1999
No.of Employees: 1 - 10 **Product Groups:** 38, 67

Date of Accounts	Jul 11	Jul 10	Jul 09
Working Capital	793	614	421
Fixed Assets	150	19	22
Current Assets	1m	1m	852

Radio Relay
Old Brighton Road, Lewes, BN7 3JL
Tel: 01273-476456 **Fax:** 01273-483193
E-mail: salesteam@radiorelay.co.uk
Website: http://www.radiorelay.co.uk
Managers: D. Keen (Mgr)
Turnover: £500,000 - £1m **No.of Employees:** 1 - 10 **Product Groups:** 26, 27, 28, 30, 37, 38, 39, 40, 42, 44, 48, 49, 52, 64, 65, 67, 68, 80, 81, 83, 84

Rutherfords
Unit 12 Cliffe Industrial Estate South Street, Lewes, BN8 6JL
Tel: 01273-478860 **Fax:** 01273-479015
E-mail: adrianshorter@rutherfords.info
Website: http://www.jdrutherford.co.uk
Directors: A. Shorter (MD)
Ultimate Holding Company: WBB CAPITA LTD
Immediate Holding Company: PRO CAM CP LTD
Registration no: 01992275 **Turnover:** £2m - £5m
No.of Employees: 1 - 10 **Product Groups:** 30, 35, 37, 40, 41, 42

Date of Accounts	Jun 08
Working Capital	27
Current Assets	27
Total Share Capital	27

Southdowns Environmental Consultants
16 Station Street, Lewes, BN7 2DB
Tel: 01273-488186 **Fax:** 01273-488187
E-mail: general@southdowns.eu.com
Website: http://www.southdowns.eu.com
Directors: R. Methold (Dir)
Immediate Holding Company: SOUTHDOWNS ENVIRONMENTAL CONSULTANTS LIMITED
Registration no: 03150111 **Date established:** 1996
No.of Employees: 11 - 20 **Product Groups:** 54

Date of Accounts	Mar 12	Mar 11	Mar 10
Working Capital	59	53	85
Fixed Assets	70	24	19
Current Assets	359	223	193

Newhaven

Bevan Funnell Ltd
Norton Road, Newhaven, BN9 0BZ
Tel: 01273-616100 **Fax:** 01273-611167
E-mail: sales@bevan-funnell.co.uk
Website: http://www.bevan-funnell.co.uk
Bank(s): National Westminster Bank Plc
Directors: P. Jarvis (Dir), T. Cermeer (MD)
Immediate Holding Company: Swann Furniture Group Ltd
Registration no: 00425363 **VAT No.:** GB 190 2502 89
Date established: 1946 **Turnover:** £250,000 - £500,000
No.of Employees: 101 - 250 **Product Groups:** 26

Date of Accounts	Oct 09	Oct 08	Oct 07
Pre Tax Profit/Loss	N/A	-806	453
Working Capital	3m	3m	4m
Fixed Assets	3m	3m	1m
Current Assets	4m	4m	5m
Current Liabilities	N/A	125	287

Brighton Systems Ltd
Unit K Quarry Road, Newhaven, BN9 9DG
Tel: 01273-515563 **Fax:** 01273-611533
E-mail: sales@brightonsystems.co.uk
Website: http://www.brightonsystems.co.uk
Directors: A. Owen (Fin), G. Bason (Dir)
Immediate Holding Company: BRIGHTON SYSTEMS LIMITED
Registration no: 02622698 **Date established:** 1991
Turnover: £250,000 - £500,000 **No.of Employees:** 1 - 10
Product Groups: 28, 67

Date of Accounts	Jun 11	Jun 10	Jun 09
Working Capital	101	124	117
Fixed Assets	8	2	3
Current Assets	143	157	144

Brightwell Dispenser Ltd
Euro Business Park New Road, Newhaven, BN9 0DQ
Tel: 01273-513566 **Fax:** 01273-516134
E-mail: sales@brightwell.co.uk
Website: http://www.brightwell.co.uk
Bank(s): National Westminster Bank Plc
Directors: N. Pybus (MD), D. Pybus (Pers)
Managers: F. Kinghorn (Buyer), S. Vines (Fin Mgr), H. Brain (Personnel), J. Pybus (Tech Serv Mgr), M. Dwelly (Mktg Serv Mgr)
Immediate Holding Company: BRIGHTWELL DISPENSERS LIMITED
Registration no: 00661996 **Date established:** 1960 **Turnover:** £5m - £10m
No.of Employees: 51 - 100 **Product Groups:** 40

Date of Accounts	Mar 11	Mar 10	Mar 09
Pre Tax Profit/Loss	1m	2m	979
Working Capital	864	2m	2m
Fixed Assets	5m	3m	3m
Current Assets	6m	6m	4m
Current Liabilities	913	1m	577

Cash Bases GB Ltd
Unit 4 The Drove, Newhaven, BN9 0LA
Tel: 01273-616300 **Fax:** 01273-512010
E-mail: sales@cashbases.co.uk
Website: http://www.cashbases.net
Bank(s): Barclays
Directors: P. Stone (MD), S. Roys (Sales & Mktg), P. Hobday (Fin)
Managers: N. Westgate (Tech Serv Mgr), I. Goldsmith (Purch Mgr), E. Davey (Personnel)
Ultimate Holding Company: CASH BASES GROUP LIMITED
Immediate Holding Company: CASH BASES LIMITED
Registration no: 01562459 **VAT No.:** GB 351 0339 90
Date established: 1981 **Turnover:** £10m - £20m
No.of Employees: 21 - 50 **Product Groups:** 36, 44

Date of Accounts	Dec 11	Dec 10	Dec 09
Sales Turnover	14m	13m	12m
Pre Tax Profit/Loss	2m	2m	354
Working Capital	1m	1m	1m
Fixed Assets	1m	834	932
Current Assets	6m	6m	5m
Current Liabilities	781	816	448

Concord Marlin Ltd International Sales Office
Avis Way, Newhaven, BN9 0ED
Tel: 01273-515811 **Fax:** 01273-512688
E-mail: info@concordmarlin.com
Website: http://www.concordmarlin.com
Bank(s): National Westminster Bank Plc
Directors: S. Vouilloz (Co Sec), C. Wheeler (MD)
Managers: C. Wain, F. Bass
Ultimate Holding Company: CML HOLDINGS INTERNATIONAL LLC (USA)
Immediate Holding Company: HAVELLS SYLVANIA UK LIMITED
Registration no: 00484499 **VAT No.:** GB 169 2689 14
Date established: 1987 **Turnover:** £20m - £50m
No.of Employees: 101 - 250 **Product Groups:** 37, 39, 67

E J Group Ltd
Old Cement Works South Heighton, Newhaven, BN9 0HS
Tel: 01273-515103 **Fax:** 01273-516863
Website: http://www.ejgroupltd.co.uk
Directors: C. Hoskins (Dir)
Immediate Holding Company: E J GROUP LIMITED
Registration no: 01265292 **Date established:** 1976 **Turnover:** £1m - £2m
No.of Employees: 11 - 20 **Product Groups:** 26, 30, 35, 36

Date of Accounts	Mar 11	Mar 10	Mar 09
Sales Turnover	2m	2m	2m
Pre Tax Profit/Loss	14	-194	-210
Working Capital	121	69	266
Fixed Assets	70	108	121
Current Assets	511	496	697
Current Liabilities	111	105	105

E Plan Solutions Ltd
Tates Avis Way, Newhaven, BN9 0DH
Tel: 01273-517711 **Fax:** 01273-512889
E-mail: mike@eplansolutions.co.uk
Website: http://www.eplansolutions.co.uk

Directors: M. Townsend (Dir)
Immediate Holding Company: E PLAN SOLUTIONS LIMITED
Registration no: 06238636 **VAT No.:** GB 620 8012 85
Date established: 2007 **Turnover:** £2m - £5m **No.of Employees:** 1 - 10
Product Groups: 26, 39

Date of Accounts	May 11	May 10	May 09
Working Capital	-3	-6	-1
Fixed Assets	3	6	9
Current Assets	16	20	28

Edwards Chemical Management Europe Ltd
Avis Way, Newhaven, BN9 0DP
Tel: 01273-513653 **Fax:** 01273-517449
Directors: C. Bradley (Fin), S. Larkins (Co Sec)
Managers: D. Springall (Chief Mgr)
Immediate Holding Company: EDWARDS CHEMICAL MANAGEMENT EUROPE LIMITED
Registration no: 00903896 **Date established:** 1967 **Turnover:** £5m - £10m
No.of Employees: 11 - 20 **Product Groups:** 36, 37

Excalibur Design Fabrications Ltd
Unit 4 &5 New Road Industrial Estate Avis Way, Newhaven, BN9 0DH
Tel: 01273-612260 **Fax:** 01273-612269
E-mail: sales@excaliburdesign.co.uk
Website: http://www.excaliburdesign.co.uk
Directors: M. Hutchinson (Dir)
Immediate Holding Company: EXCALIBUR DESIGN FABRICATIONS LIMITED
Registration no: 03081487 **Date established:** 1995
No.of Employees: 11 - 20 **Product Groups:** 25, 26, 27

Date of Accounts	Dec 11	Dec 10	Dec 09
Working Capital	-40	-67	-102
Fixed Assets	46	57	72
Current Assets	366	284	293

Felcon Ltd
Euro Business Park New Road, Newhaven, BN9 0DQ
Tel: 01273-513434 **Fax:** 01273-512695
E-mail: ian.mutton@felcon.co.uk
Website: http://www.felcon.co.uk
Bank(s): Lloyds TSB Bank plc
Directors: J. Hollands (Dir), I. Mutton (Dir)
Ultimate Holding Company: HPM PRODUCTS LIMITED
Immediate Holding Company: FELCON LIMITED
Registration no: 03205966 **Date established:** 1996 **Turnover:** £2m - £5m
No.of Employees: 21 - 50 **Product Groups:** 38, 40, 42, 47, 67

Date of Accounts	Jun 11	Jun 10	Jun 09
Working Capital	139	597	671
Fixed Assets	64	67	86
Current Assets	802	1m	1m

Furnace Exchange
56 Wellington Road, Newhaven, BN9 0RH
Tel: 01273-517119 **Fax:** 01273- 517119
E-mail: sales@furnex.net
Website: http://www.furnex.net
Directors: R. Hall (Prop)
Date established: 1994 **No.of Employees:** 1 - 10 **Product Groups:** 40, 42, 46

G W Ironworks
3 Bross Estate New Road, Newhaven, BN9 0EH
Tel: 01273-514448 **Fax:** 01273-611115
E-mail: info@gwironworks.co.uk
Website: http://www.gwironworks.co.uk
Directors: K. Ward (Fin), G. Ward (MD)
Immediate Holding Company: G W IRONWORKS LTD
Registration no: 04748934 **Date established:** 2003
No.of Employees: 1 - 10 **Product Groups:** 26, 35

Date of Accounts	May 11	May 10	May 09
Working Capital	-47	-33	-16
Fixed Assets	7	10	13
Current Assets	58	75	52

Goldsworth Medical Ltd
Unit 11 Euro Business Park New Road, Newhaven, BN9 0DQ
Tel: 01273-516661 **Fax:** 01273-512695
E-mail: alan.pegler@goldsworth.co.uk
Website: http://www.goldsworth.co.uk
Directors: J. Hollands (Dir)
Managers: R. Dolby (Purch Mgr), P. Ireland
Ultimate Holding Company: HPM PRODUCTS LIMITED
Immediate Holding Company: GOLDSWORTH MEDICAL LIMITED
Registration no: 03653156 **Date established:** 1998 **Turnover:** £1m - £2m
No.of Employees: 21 - 50 **Product Groups:** 26, 38, 40, 48, 52, 54, 67, 84, 85

Date of Accounts	Jun 11	Jun 07	Jun 06
Working Capital	N/A	N/A	1
Current Assets	N/A	N/A	6

Interface 2 Ltd
Unit 16 Euro Business Park New Road, Newhaven, BN9 0DQ
Tel: 01273-611008 **Fax:** 01273-512061
E-mail: info@interface2.com
Website: http://www.interface2.com
Directors: A. Stone (MD)
Immediate Holding Company: INTERFACE 2 LIMITED
Registration no: 03165128 **Date established:** 1996 **Turnover:** £1m - £2m
No.of Employees: 21 - 50 **Product Groups:** 30, 37, 48

Date of Accounts	Mar 12	Mar 11	Mar 10
Working Capital	19	42	3
Fixed Assets	85	31	27
Current Assets	607	817	527

Magnum Supplies
181 Hillcrest Road, Newhaven, BN9 9EZ
Tel: 01273-513755 **Fax:** 01273-515325
Directors: M. Elms (Fin)
Date established: 1988 **No.of Employees:** 1 - 10 **Product Groups:** 20, 40, 41

Marco Trailers
Railway Road, Newhaven, BN9 0AP
Tel: 01273-513718 **Fax:** 01273-512132
E-mail: info@marcotrailers.co.uk
Website: http://www.marcotrailers.co.uk
Directors: S. Marsom (Prop)
No.of Employees: 11 - 20 **Product Groups:** 68

Masona Plastics
Avis Way, Newhaven, BN9 0DH
Tel: 01273-612440 **Fax:** 01273-611495
E-mail: info@masona.co.uk
Website: http://www.masona.co.uk
Bank(s): HSBC
Directors: K. Mason (Dir)
Registration no: 00782494 **VAT No.:** GB 217 9531 53
Date established: 1937 **Turnover:** £500,000 - £1m
No.of Employees: 11 - 20 **Product Groups:** 28, 30

Paradise Park Garden Centre
Avis Way, Newhaven, BN9 0DH
Tel: 01273-512123 **Fax:** 01273-616000
E-mail: enquiries@paradisepark.co.uk
Website: http://www.paradisepark.co.uk
Directors: J. Tate (Prop)
Managers: G. Macton
Immediate Holding Company: NATIONAL NUMERACY
Registration no: 00725819 **Date established:** 2011
No.of Employees: 51 - 100 **Product Groups:** 25, 33, 35, 66

Date of Accounts	May 12	May 11	May 10
Working Capital	110	109	84
Fixed Assets	109	126	149
Current Assets	172	177	153

Plastech
Unit 5 North Industrial Estate New Road, Newhaven, BN9 0HE
Tel: 01273-510204 **Fax:** 01444-881244
E-mail: sales@plastch.co.uk
Website: http://www.plastech.com
Directors: D. Richardson (Prop)
Ultimate Holding Company: NORRIS HOLDINGS LIMITED
Immediate Holding Company: FLOTRONIC PUMPS LIMITED
Registration no: 02559708 **Date established:** 1990 **Turnover:** £2m - £5m
No.of Employees: 11 - 20 **Product Groups:** 36

S C A Recycling UK
Lakeside Wharf South Heighton, Newhaven, BN9 0HW
Tel: 01273-513863 **Fax:** 01273-512030
E-mail: john.freshwater@sca.com
Website: http://www.scarecycling.co.uk
Bank(s): National Westminster
Managers: J. Freshwater (District Mgr)
Ultimate Holding Company: SVENSKA CELLULOSA AB (SWEDEN)
Immediate Holding Company: SCA RECYCLING UK LIMITED
Registration no: 00214967 **VAT No.:** GB 205 9140 87
Date established: 1926 **Turnover:** £1m - £2m **No.of Employees:** 11 - 20
Product Groups: 66

Smith Metal Fabrications Ltd
Unit J Rich Industrial Estate Avis Way, Newhaven, BN9 0DU
Tel: 01273-513411 **Fax:** 01273-513086
E-mail: info@smithmetalfabs.co.uk
Website: http://www.smithmetalfabs.co.uk
Directors: M. Smith (Prop)
Immediate Holding Company: SMITH METAL FABRICATIONS LIMITED
Registration no: 01185246 **VAT No.:** GB 192 0568 57
Date established: 1974 **Turnover:** Up to £250,000
No.of Employees: 11 - 20 **Product Groups:** 48

Date of Accounts	Feb 12	Feb 11	Feb 10
Working Capital	428	354	298
Fixed Assets	60	69	83
Current Assets	557	450	354

Peacehaven

Bulldog Engineering Recruitment & Management Services
223a-225 South Coast Road, Peacehaven, BN10 8LB
Tel: 01273-580580
E-mail: recruitment@bulldog.co.uk
Website: http://www.bulldog.co.uk
Directors: T. Lambert (Prop)
Registration no: 06724342 **VAT No.:** GB 508 7630 38
Date established: 2008 **Turnover:** Up to £250,000
No.of Employees: 1 - 10 **Product Groups:** 80, 81

Designs In Aluminium (D I A)
Dayton House Bolney Avenue, Peacehaven, BN10 8HF
Tel: 01273-582241 **Fax:** 01273-580644
E-mail: info@designs-in-aluminium.co.uk
Website: http://www.designs-in-aluminium.co.uk
Directors: G. Friend (Prop)
No.of Employees: 1 - 10 **Product Groups:** 26, 34, 48

E R L Ltd
Iroko House Bolney Avenue, Peacehaven, BN10 8HF
Tel: 01273-581007 **Fax:** 01273-581555
E-mail: info@aquamist.co.uk
Website: http://www.aquamist.co.uk
Directors: R. Lamb (MD)
Immediate Holding Company: E.R.L. LIMITED
Registration no: 01476186 **Date established:** 1980
Turnover: £500,000 - £1m **No.of Employees:** 1 - 10 **Product Groups:** 38

Date of Accounts	Feb 12	Feb 11	Feb 10
Working Capital	-9	1	-26
Fixed Assets	39	47	56
Current Assets	74	60	68

North Brighton Ltd
37 Bramber Avenue, Peacehaven, BN10 8HR
Tel: 01273-584112 **Fax:** 01273-584112
E-mail: info@atlas-menswear.com
Website: http://www.atlas-menswear.com
Directors: T. Sanders (MD)
Date established: 1963 **No.of Employees:** 1 - 10 **Product Groups:** 20, 40, 41

Richypucci Ltd
10 Rosemary Close, Peacehaven, BN10 8BY
Tel: 0845-130 7438
E-mail: info@richypucci.com
Website: http://www.richypucci.com
Directors: M. Rogers (MD), G. Rogers (Fin)
Immediate Holding Company: RICHYPUCCI LIMITED
Registration no: 05385295 **Date established:** 2005
No.of Employees: 1 - 10 **Product Groups:** 24

South Coast Windows Installers Ltd
81-83 South Coast Road, Peacehaven, BN10 8QS
Tel: 01273-585300 **Fax:** 01273-589555
E-mail: info@southcoastwindows.co.uk
Website: http://www.southcoastwindows.co.uk
Directors: H. Hicks (Dir)
Immediate Holding Company: WINDOW WORLD (SOUTHERN) LIMITED
Registration no: 04536433 **Date established:** 2002
No.of Employees: 1 - 10 **Product Groups:** 25, 35, 66

Vinyl Fencing Ltd
16 Downs Walk, Peacehaven, BN10 7RH
Tel: 01273-587260
E-mail: info@vinylfence.co.uk
Website: http://www.vinylfence.co.uk
Directors: M. Dragojevic (Fin), S. Dragojevic (Dir)
Immediate Holding Company: VINYL FENCING LTD
Registration no: 05887860 **Date established:** 2006
Turnover: Up to £250,000 **No.of Employees:** 1 - 10 **Product Groups:** 30, 41, 49, 52

Date of Accounts	Jul 11	Jul 10	Jul 08
Working Capital	-28	-34	-39
Fixed Assets	5	N/A	N/A
Current Assets	76	78	64

Window Workshop
Unit 1 Quay Units 61 Bolney Avenue, Peacehaven, BN10 8HF
Tel: 01273-589066 **Fax:** 01273-586699
Managers: J. Revelle (Mgr)
Immediate Holding Company: JEWEL INTERIORS LIMITED
Registration no: 02613507 **Date established:** 1991
No.of Employees: 1 - 10 **Product Groups:** 46

Date of Accounts	May 10	May 09	May 08
Working Capital	82	78	148
Fixed Assets	4	6	2
Current Assets	100	84	194

Yeomans Brighton
351 South Coast Road Telscombe Cliffs, Peacehaven, BN10 7HH
Tel: 01273-582428 **Fax:** 01273-580838
E-mail: info@yeomanstoyota.co.uk
Website: http://www.yeomans.co.uk
Managers: J. Euesdon, M. Parsons (Sales Prom Mgr)
Ultimate Holding Company: EVANS HALSHAW HOLDINGS P.L.C. GROUP
Registration no: 01593852 **No.of Employees:** 21 - 50 **Product Groups:** 68

Pevensey

Castle Garage Doors
16 High Street Westham, Pevensey, BN24 5LY
Tel: 01323-768379
E-mail: marknoll@btinternet.com
Website: http://www.castle-garage-doors.com
Directors: M. Noll (Ptnr)
No.of Employees: 1 - 10 **Product Groups:** 25, 30, 35, 36

Intercon Scaffolding
Rattle Road Westham, Pevensey, BN24 5DS
Tel: 01323-767777
E-mail: carl@interconscaffolding.co.uk
Website: http://www.interconscaffolding.co.uk
Directors: C. Lynn (Prop), C. Lynn (MD), A. Hudson (Prop)
Turnover: £500,000 - £1m **No.of Employees:** 11 - 20
Product Groups: 36, 49, 52, 83

R D Upton
Unit 2g Hankham Hall Cottages Hankham Hall Road, Hankham, Pevensey, BN24 5AH
Tel: 01323-743006
E-mail: richard@rdupton.co.uk
Website: http://www.rdupton.co.uk
Directors: R. Upton (Prop)
Date established: 2000 **No.of Employees:** 1 - 10 **Product Groups:** 26

Polegate

C D Automation UK Ltd
Unit 10 Mays Estate Selmeston, Polegate, BN26 6TS
Tel: 01323-811100 **Fax:** 01323-879012
E-mail: jez.w@cdautomation.co.uk
Website: http://www.cdautomation.co.uk
Directors: J. Watson (MD)
Immediate Holding Company: CD AUTOMATION UK LTD
Registration no: 06762061 **Date established:** 2008 **Turnover:** £2m - £5m
No.of Employees: 1 - 10 **Product Groups:** 37

Date of Accounts	Dec 10	Dec 09
Working Capital	6	-1
Fixed Assets	2	2
Current Assets	28	15

Continuity-Solutions
23 Gosford Way, Polegate, BN26 6DR
Tel: 07973-731232
E-mail: info@continuity-solutions.co.uk
Website: http://www.continuity-solutions.co.uk
Directors: R. Dunford-Green (Dir), R. Dunford Green (Dir)
No.of Employees: 1 - 10 **Product Groups:** 37, 44, 80, 82

Dakota Print
Mays Farm Selmeston, Polegate, BN26 6TS
Tel: 01323-811445 **Fax:** 01323-811516
E-mail: info@dakotaprint.co.uk
Website: http://www.dakotaprint.co.uk
Directors: S. Gibson (Dir)
Immediate Holding Company: MAYS FARM LIMITED
Registration no: 03106473 **Date established:** 1995
No.of Employees: 1 - 10 **Product Groups:** 28

Date of Accounts	Nov 07	Nov 06	Nov 05
Working Capital	-21	-21	-28
Fixed Assets	20	26	36
Current Assets	42	51	53
Current Liabilities	64	72	81

Fibreglass UK Ltd
Bates Green Farm Tye Hill Road, Arlington, Polegate, BN26 6SH
Tel: 01323-484433 **Fax:** 01323-484436
E-mail: info@fibreglassuk.com
Website: http://www.fibreglassuk.com
Directors: R. Hayward (Dir)
Immediate Holding Company: FIBREGLASS UK LIMITED
Registration no: 05120077 **Date established:** 2004
Turnover: Up to £250,000 **No.of Employees:** 1 - 10 **Product Groups:** 30, 39

Date of Accounts	Apr 11	Apr 10	Apr 09
Working Capital	50	36	32
Fixed Assets	11	14	13
Current Assets	70	63	53

Homecare Exteriors
95 High Street, Polegate, BN26 6AB
Tel: 01323-484040 **Fax:** 01323-487400
E-mail: sales@homecareexteriors.co.uk
Website: http://www.homecareexteriors.co.uk
Directors: D. Tingley (Prop)
No.of Employees: 1 - 10 **Product Groups:** 25, 30, 35, 36, 66

Posturite Ltd
The Mill Berwick, Polegate, BN26 6SZ
Tel: 08453-450010 **Fax:** 08453-450020
E-mail: support@posturite.co.uk
Website: http://www.posturite.co.uk
Directors: J. Jones (Fin)
Managers: K. Pengelly, C. Jones (Tech Serv Mgr), H. Card (Sales Prom Mgr), C. Pratt, T. Riely (Personnel)
Immediate Holding Company: POSTURITE LIMITED
Registration no: 02574809 **Date established:** 1991
Turnover: £10m - £20m **No.of Employees:** 101 - 250
Product Groups: 26, 67

Date of Accounts	Dec 11	Dec 10	Dec 09
Sales Turnover	12m	12m	12m
Pre Tax Profit/Loss	528	183	451
Working Capital	132	163	183
Fixed Assets	1m	1m	1m
Current Assets	3m	3m	2m
Current Liabilities	503	355	456

Robertsbridge

Anvil Tubesmiths Southern Ltd
Sedlescombe Sawmills Hawkhurst Road, Staplecross, Robertsbridge, TN32 5SA
Tel: 01580-830770 **Fax:** 01580-830220
E-mail: barry.luckham@gmail.com
Directors: B. Luckham (MD)
Immediate Holding Company: ANVIL TUBESMITHS (SOUTHERN) LIMITED
Registration no: 01761805 **VAT No.:** GB 390 0400 91
Date established: 1983 **Turnover:** £250,000 - £500,000
No.of Employees: 1 - 10 **Product Groups:** 35, 36, 48, 80

Date of Accounts	Dec 11	Dec 10	Dec 09
Working Capital	154	158	143
Fixed Assets	38	22	27
Current Assets	220	224	187

Blackman Smithy
2 Hoath Hill Mountfield, Robertsbridge, TN32 5LN
Tel: 01580-880133 **Fax:** 01580-880133
Website: http://www.blackmansmithy.co.uk
Directors: S. Blackman (Prop)
Date established: 1986 **No.of Employees:** 1 - 10 **Product Groups:** 26, 35

E O Culverwell Ltd
Station Road, Robertsbridge, TN32 5DG
Tel: 01580-880567 **Fax:** 01580-881022
E-mail: info@culverwells.co.uk
Website: http://www.culverwells.co.uk
Bank(s): Lloyds TSB Bank plc
Directors: R. Cole (Dir)
Immediate Holding Company: E.O. CULVERWELL LIMITED
Registration no: 00261594 **VAT No.:** GB 190 3999 27
Date established: 1932 **Turnover:** £2m - £5m **No.of Employees:** 21 - 50
Product Groups: 27, 30, 33, 41

Date of Accounts	Oct 11	Oct 10	Oct 09
Sales Turnover	4m	5m	5m
Pre Tax Profit/Loss	8	23	-131
Working Capital	874	852	815
Fixed Assets	581	597	615
Current Assets	2m	2m	2m
Current Liabilities	244	431	353

Gray Nicolls
Station Road, Robertsbridge, TN32 5DH
Tel: 01580-880357 **Fax:** 01580-881156
E-mail: info@gray-nicolls.co.uk
Website: http://www.gray-nicolls.co.uk
Bank(s): Yorkshire Bank PLC
Directors: R. Gray (Mkt Research)
Ultimate Holding Company: GRAYS OF CAMBRIDGE (INTERNATIONAL) LIMITED
Immediate Holding Company: GRAY-NICOLLS LIMITED
Registration no: 00043465 **VAT No.:** GB 376 0950 34
Date established: 1995 **Turnover:** £20m - £50m
No.of Employees: 101 - 250 **Product Groups:** 22, 24, 49, 61

Photonic Science Ltd
Millham Mountfield, Robertsbridge, TN32 5JU
Tel: 01580-881199 **Fax:** 01580-880910
E-mail: jacqui@photonic-science.co.uk
Website: http://www.photonic-science.co.uk
Directors: J. Elliott (Fin)
Managers: D. Brau (Mktg Serv Mgr)
Immediate Holding Company: PHOTONIC SCIENCE LIMITED
Registration no: 01966392 **Date established:** 1985
No.of Employees: 21 - 50 **Product Groups:** 44

Date of Accounts	Mar 11	Mar 10	Mar 09
Working Capital	127	317	406
Fixed Assets	567	253	252
Current Assets	2m	2m	1m

Rye

Acorn Garage Doors Ltd
The Garage Door Store Beckley Four Oaks, Beckley, Rye, TN31 6RG
Tel: 01797-260243 **Fax:** 01797-260504
E-mail: contact@acorngaragedoorsltd.co.uk
Website: http://www.acorngaragedoorsltd.co.uk
Managers: L. Paton (Mgr)
Immediate Holding Company: ACORN GARAGE DOORS LTD
Registration no: 05860231 **Date established:** 2006
Turnover: Up to £250,000 **No.of Employees:** 1 - 10 **Product Groups:** 25, 30, 35, 36

Date of Accounts	Jun 11	Jun 10	Jun 09
Working Capital	-3	-3	-2
Fixed Assets	3	3	3
Current Assets	26	37	38

Castle Mouldings
1 Dew Farm Church Lane, Peasmarsh, Rye, TN31 6XD
Tel: 01797-230734
E-mail: info@castlemouldings.co.uk
Website: http://www.castlemouldings.co.uk
Directors: K. Fennell (Prop)
Immediate Holding Company: CASTLE MOULDINGS GRP LIMITED
Registration no: 06546732 **Date established:** 2008
Turnover: Up to £250,000 **No.of Employees:** 1 - 10 **Product Groups:** 30

Chase Protective Coatings Ltd
Harbour Road, Rye, TN31 7TE
Tel: 01797-223561 **Fax:** 01797-224530
E-mail: info@chaseprotectivecoatings.com
Website: http://www.longproducts.co.uk
Bank(s): Barclays P.L.C., London
Directors: R. Walker (MD)
Managers: K. Jeffries (Tech Serv Mgr), S. McArthy
Ultimate Holding Company: CHASE CORPORATION INC (USA)
Immediate Holding Company: LONG PRODUCTS LIMITED
Registration no: 06310842 **VAT No.:** GB 377 9275 920
Date established: 2007 **Turnover:** £1m - £2m **No.of Employees:** 21 - 50
Product Groups: 27, 31, 32, 39

Esi Electrical
Unit 6 Malthouse Business Park The Maltings, Peasmarsh, Rye, TN31 6ST
Tel: 01797-227741 **Fax:** 0870-486 0353
E-mail: jamie@esielectrical.co.uk
Website: http://www.esielectrical.co.uk
Directors: J. Morgan (Dir)
Immediate Holding Company: ESI: ELECTRICAL SAFETY INSPECTIONS LTD
Registration no: 05432757 **Date established:** 2005 **Turnover:** £2m - £5m
No.of Employees: 1 - 10 **Product Groups:** 37, 38, 52, 84

Rycon Shipping & Forwarding Ltd
Rycon Warehouse Rye Harbour Road, Rye, TN31 7TE
Tel: 01797-222747 **Fax:** 01797-224535
E-mail: ryecon@btconnect.com
Directors: S. Williams (MD)
Immediate Holding Company: RYCON SHIPPING & FORWARDING LIMITED
Registration no: 02823951 **VAT No.:** GB 621 6202 84
Date established: 1993 **Turnover:** £250,000 - £500,000
No.of Employees: 1 - 10 **Product Groups:** 76

Date of Accounts	Jul 11	Jul 10	Jul 09
Working Capital	331	395	444
Fixed Assets	153	174	177
Current Assets	373	435	532

Ryepac Packaging
Unit G30 Rye Industrial Park Rye Harbour Road, Rye, TN31 7TE
Tel: 01797-222295 **Fax:** 08717-819208
E-mail: sales@ryepac.co.uk
Website: http://www.ryepac.co.uk
Directors: T. Smith (MD)
Immediate Holding Company: RYE - PAC LTD
Registration no: 07169043 **Date established:** 2010
No.of Employees: 1 - 10 **Product Groups:** 27, 30

S D Traditional Cookers
Stoddards Cottage Stoddards Lane, Beckley, Rye, TN31 6UG
Tel: 01797-260741
Directors: R. Brice (Prop)
No.of Employees: 1 - 10 **Product Groups:** 36, 40

S P Fibreglass
Station Road Northiam, Rye, TN31 6QA
Tel: 01797-252476 **Fax:** 01797-253093
Directors: R. Bathgate (Prop)
Turnover: Up to £250,000 **No.of Employees:** 1 - 10 **Product Groups:** 30

Solar UK
Commonswood Farm Hastings Road, Northiam, Rye, TN31 6HY
Tel: 01797-252747
E-mail: info@solaruk.com
Website: http://www.solaruk.net
Directors: D. Lee (Dir), G. Fox (MD)
Immediate Holding Company: SOLAR UK ENERGY SYSTEMS LTD
Registration no: 07815417 **Date established:** 2011 **Turnover:** £2m - £5m
No.of Employees: 11 - 20 **Product Groups:** 37, 67

Solvent Resource Management Ltd
Rye Harbour Road, Rye, TN31 7TE
Tel: 01797-228200 **Fax:** 01797-226724
E-mail: sales@srm-ltd.com
Website: http://www.srm-ltd.com
Bank(s): SEB, London
Directors: C. Brown (Fin), R. Butcher (Sales)
Managers: K. Bolton (Sales Admin), L. Townsend
Ultimate Holding Company: HEIDELBERG CEMENT AG (GERMANY)
Immediate Holding Company: SOLVENT RESOURCE MANAGEMENT LIMITED
Registration no: 03890526 **VAT No.:** GB 217 9157 51
Date established: 1999 **Turnover:** £20m - £50m
No.of Employees: 51 - 100 **Product Groups:** 31, 32, 42, 66

Date of Accounts	Dec 10	Dec 09	Dec 08
Sales Turnover	35m	32m	40m
Pre Tax Profit/Loss	2m	-1m	4m
Working Capital	7m	6m	6m
Fixed Assets	11m	10m	12m
Current Assets	17m	16m	16m
Current Liabilities	2m	4m	4m

Seaford

Builder Center Ltd
Cradle Hill Industrial Estate Alfriston Road, Seaford, BN25 2AT
Tel: 01323-893243 **Fax:** 01323-891072
Website: http://www.buildercenter.co.uk
Managers: C. Moore (Depot Mgr), C. Moores (Mgr), R. Sorrell (Sales Admin)
Ultimate Holding Company: Wolseley plc
Immediate Holding Company: Wipac Group (Holdings) Ltd
Registration no: 00462397 **Date established:** 1975
No.of Employees: 1 - 10 **Product Groups:** 66

C & P Developments London Ltd
Unit 25 Cradle Hill Industrial Estate, Seaford, BN25 3JE
Tel: 01323-872875 **Fax:** 01323-872874
E-mail: capdevco@aol.com
Directors: W. Morris (Dir)
Immediate Holding Company: C & P DEVELOPMENTS LTD
Registration no: 04436786 **Date established:** 2006
No.of Employees: 1 - 10 **Product Groups:** 35, 45

Kemmel Ltd
Unit 6-7 Cradle Hill Industrial Estate, Seaford, BN25 3JE
Tel: 01323-899010 **Fax:** 01323-893149
E-mail: sales@kemmel.co.uk
Website: http://www.kemmel.co.uk
Bank(s): National Westminster Bank Plc
Directors: J. Frith (Co Sec)
Immediate Holding Company: KEMMEL LIMITED
Registration no: 01602788 **VAT No.:** GB 351 1835 73
Date established: 1981 **Turnover:** £2m - £5m **No.of Employees:** 21 - 50
Product Groups: 67

Date of Accounts	Oct 11	Oct 10	Oct 09
Working Capital	673	502	353
Fixed Assets	281	176	198
Current Assets	915	683	526

St Leonards On Sea

Alpine Components
14-15 Oban Road, St Leonards On Sea, TN37 7DX
Tel: 01424-437000 **Fax:** 01424-722502
E-mail: info@alpine-components.co.uk
Website: http://www.alpine-components.co.uk
Managers: J. Hill (Sales Prom Mgr)
Immediate Holding Company: ALPINE COMPONENTS LTD
Registration no: 05996485 **Date established:** 2006
Turnover: £500,000 - £1m **No.of Employees:** 1 - 10 **Product Groups:** 48

Date of Accounts	Mar 12	Mar 11	Mar 10
Working Capital	690	555	337
Fixed Assets	136	150	161
Current Assets	1m	997	615

Bes Microwaves
52 Bohemia Road, St Leonards On Sea, TN37 6RQ
Tel: 01424-447799 **Fax:** 01424-447070
E-mail: besmicrowaves@btopenworld.com
Website: http://www.microwavesworld.co.uk
Directors: D. Rose (MD)
Managers: P. Hummphreys (Mgr), P. Humphreys (Chief Mgr)
Registration no: 04953853 **No.of Employees:** 1 - 10 **Product Groups:** 40, 67

Biffa Waste Services Ltd
Bexhill Road, St Leonards On Sea, TN38 8AR
Tel: 01424-430788 **Fax:** 01424-713615
E-mail: ian.tridgell@biffa.co.uk
Website: http://www.biffa.co.uk
Managers: I. Tridgell (Mgr)
Immediate Holding Company: BIFFA WASTE SERVICES LIMITED
Registration no: 00946107 **Date established:** 1969
Turnover: Up to £250,000 **No.of Employees:** 1 - 10 **Product Groups:** 32, 54

Date of Accounts	Mar 08	Mar 09	Apr 10
Sales Turnover	555m	574m	492m
Pre Tax Profit/Loss	23m	50m	30m
Working Capital	229m	271m	293m
Fixed Assets	371m	360m	378m
Current Assets	409m	534m	609m
Current Liabilities	50m	100m	115m

Builder Center Ltd
591 Sedlescombe Road North, St Leonards On Sea, TN37 7PY
Tel: 01424-754256 **Fax:** 01424-751481
Website: http://www.buildercenter.co.uk
Managers: L. Matcham (District Mgr), L. Matchem (District Mgr), R. Funnel (Mgr)

Ultimate Holding Company: Wolseley plc
Immediate Holding Company: BUILD CENTER LIMITED
Registration no: 00462397 **Date established:** 1948 **Turnover:** £2m - £5m
No.of Employees: 11 - 20 **Product Groups:** 66

Caterers Choice

170 Old Roar Road, St Leonards On Sea, TN37 7HH
Tel: 01424-850392
Website: http://www.caterers-choice.co.uk
No.of Employees: 1 - 10 **Product Groups:** 20, 40, 41

Charter Controls

6 Hayland Industrial Units Maunsell Road, St Leonards On Sea, TN38 9NN
Tel: 01424-850660 **Fax:** 01424-850990
E-mail: sales@charter-controls.com
Website: http://www.charter-controls.com
Directors: M. Greenhill (MD)
No.of Employees: 1 - 10 **Product Groups:** 37, 38, 49

Collins & Hayes Furniture

Menzies Road Ponswood, St Leonards On Sea, TN38 9XF
Tel: 01424-720027 **Fax:** 01424-720270
E-mail: sales@collinsandhayes.com
Website: http://www.collinsandhayes.com
Bank(s): Barclays
Directors: D. Backler (Co Sec), M. Miller (Dir)
Immediate Holding Company: COLLINS AND HAYES FURNITURE LIMITED
Registration no: 06238369 **VAT No.:** GB 201 0338 38
Date established: 2007 **Turnover:** £5m - £10m
No.of Employees: 101 - 250 **Product Groups:** 26

Date of Accounts	Mar 12	Mar 11	Apr 10
Sales Turnover	9m	10m	10m
Pre Tax Profit/Loss	-226	277	387
Working Capital	313	399	342
Fixed Assets	185	254	282
Current Assets	2m	2m	3m
Current Liabilities	778	745	924

Deutsch UK

4 Stanier Road, St Leonards On Sea, TN38 9RF
Tel: 01424-852721 **Fax:** 01424-851532
E-mail: gcook@deutsch.net
Website: http://www.deutsch.net
Bank(s): HSBC, Crawley
Directors: A. Wake (Fin), G. Cook (MD), S. Hicks (Fin)
Managers: G. Bannister (Mktg Serv Mgr), M. Palmer (Purch Mgr), S. Dadd (Tech Serv Mgr), M. Cimini, J. McInerney (Personnel)
Ultimate Holding Company: WENDEL GROUP (FRANCE)
Immediate Holding Company: DEUTSCH UK
Registration no: 01399905 **VAT No.:** GB 324 6425 70
Date established: 1978 **Turnover:** £20m - £50m
No.of Employees: 251 - 500 **Product Groups:** 33, 37

Date of Accounts	Dec 11	Dec 10	Dec 09
Sales Turnover	28m	24m	22m
Pre Tax Profit/Loss	5m	5m	2m
Working Capital	16m	11m	18m
Fixed Assets	4m	4m	4m
Current Assets	19m	14m	22m
Current Liabilities	2m	1m	2m

FOCUS Sb

Castleham Industrial Estate Napier Road, St Leonards On Sea, TN38 9NY
Tel: 01424-858060 **Fax:** 01424-852001
E-mail: sales@focus-sb.co.uk
Website: http://www.focus-sb.co.uk
Directors: A. Lanworn (Co Sec), R. Kem (MD)
Managers: D. Ray (Buyer), L. Fry (Tech Serv Mgr)
Immediate Holding Company: FOCUS SB LIMITED
Registration no: 04113926 **Date established:** 2000 **Turnover:** £2m - £5m
No.of Employees: 21 - 50 **Product Groups:** 30, 35, 36, 37, 38, 39, 40, 44, 49, 67

Date of Accounts	Dec 11	Dec 10	Dec 09
Working Capital	180	206	96
Fixed Assets	440	458	494
Current Assets	1m	1m	1m
Current Liabilities	548	N/A	421

Fowle & Co. Ltd

Tremlon House Menzies Road, St Leonards On Sea, TN38 9BQ
Tel: 01424-444666 **Fax:** 01424-720442
E-mail: info@fowleco.com
Website: http://www.fowleco.com
Bank(s): Natwest Bank
Directors: A. Fowle (Dir), N. Fowle (MD)
Managers: M. Fowle (Sales Admin)
Immediate Holding Company: FOWLE & CO LIMITED
Registration no: 00973101 **VAT No.:** GB 201 4156 24
Date established: 1970 **Turnover:** £20m - £50m
No.of Employees: 21 - 50 **Product Groups:** 34, 66

Date of Accounts	Mar 11	Mar 10	Mar 09
Sales Turnover	34m	28m	50m
Pre Tax Profit/Loss	377	198	390
Working Capital	2m	2m	2m
Fixed Assets	2m	2m	3m
Current Assets	11m	10m	7m
Current Liabilities	379	392	958

Hastings Paints & Powder Finishers

21 Brunel Road, St Leonards On Sea, TN38 9RT
Tel: 01424-852325 **Fax:** 01424-854109
E-mail: peterboggis@hotmail.co.uk
Directors: P. Boggis (Prop)
Date established: 1985 **No.of Employees:** 1 - 10 **Product Groups:** 46, 48

K T Manufacturing

3 Maunsell Road Castleham Industrial Estate, St Leonards On Sea, TN38 9NL
Tel: 01424-852388
E-mail: sales@ktassemblies.co.uk
Website: http://www.ktassemblies.co.uk
Managers: A. Chambers (Mgr)
Registration no: 04161989 **Date established:** 2001
No.of Employees: 1 - 10 **Product Groups:** 26, 37

L G Optical M F G Ltd

25 Brunel Road, St Leonards On Sea, TN38 9RT
Tel: 01424-851878 **Fax:** 01424-853368
E-mail: info@lgoptical.co.uk
Website: http://www.lgoptical.co.uk
Directors: N. Newby (MD), P. Baggott (Co Sec)
Immediate Holding Company: LG OPTICAL (MFG) LIMITED
Registration no: 03761516 **VAT No.:** GB 322 8731 58
Date established: 1999 **Turnover:** £500,000 - £1m
No.of Employees: 1 - 10 **Product Groups:** 38

Date of Accounts	Dec 11	Dec 10	Dec 09
Working Capital	173	264	225
Fixed Assets	6	3	3
Current Assets	310	419	309

Lumatic Ga Ltd

Theaklen Drive, St Leonards On Sea, TN38 9AZ
Tel: 01424-436343 **Fax:** 01424-429926
E-mail: terry@lumatic.co.uk
Website: http://www.lumatic.co.uk
Directors: T. Brown (MD)
Ultimate Holding Company: MATO HOLDING GMBH (GERMANY)
Immediate Holding Company: LUMATIC (G.A.) LIMITED
Registration no: 00583327 **VAT No.:** GB 444 9588 05
Date established: 1957 **Turnover:** £2m - £5m **No.of Employees:** 1 - 10
Product Groups: 35, 36, 39, 40, 46

Date of Accounts	Sep 11
Fixed Assets	18

Magnus Power (Division of Aker Subsea Ltd)

29-30 Brunel Road Churchfields Industrial Estate, St Leonards On Sea, TN38 9RT
Tel: 01424-853013 **Fax:** 01424-852268
E-mail: magnuspower.sales@akersolutions.com
Website: http://www.magnuspower.co.uk
Bank(s): Barclays
Managers: P. Jenner (Chief Mgr), K. Hammond (Sales Prom Mgr), A. Liddle (Sales Eng), D. Burfoot (Quality Control)
Registration no: SC063277 **VAT No.:** GB 495 4446 09
Turnover: £1m - £2m **No.of Employees:** 11 - 20 **Product Groups:** 37, 39, 68

Nitech Ltd

Unit 4-6 Highfield Business Park Sidney Little Road, St Leonards On Sea, TN38 9UB
Tel: 01424-852788 **Fax:** 01424-851008
E-mail: sales@nitech.co.uk
Website: http://www.nitech.co.uk
Directors: P. Barker (MD)
Immediate Holding Company: NITECH LIMITED
Registration no: 01583244 **VAT No.:** GB 262 2258 67
Date established: 1981 **Turnover:** £1m - £2m **No.of Employees:** 1 - 10
Product Groups: 37, 40

Date of Accounts	Sep 11	Sep 10	Sep 09
Working Capital	32	30	40
Fixed Assets	171	179	190
Current Assets	236	226	237

P C M Tooling UK Ltd

825 The Ridge, St Leonards On Sea, TN37 7PX
Tel: 01424-753174 **Fax:** 01424-753089
E-mail: ukpcmtlg@aol.com
Website: http://www.pcmtooling.co.uk
Directors: L. Baker (Fin)
Immediate Holding Company: PCM TOOLING (UK) LIMITED
Registration no: 03997662 **VAT No.:** GB 201 3868 91
Date established: 2000 **Turnover:** £2m - £5m **No.of Employees:** 1 - 10
Product Groups: 46

Date of Accounts	Dec 11	Dec 10	Dec 09
Working Capital	135	174	170
Fixed Assets	39	41	82
Current Assets	398	283	278

Rand Markings Ltd

39-40 Brunel Road, St Leonards On Sea, TN38 9RT
Tel: 01424-854646 **Fax:** 01424-854645
E-mail: info@randmarkings.co.uk
Website: http://www.randmarkings.co.uk
Directors: S. Smith (MD)
Immediate Holding Company: RAND MARKINGS LIMITED
Registration no: 01020568 **Date established:** 1971
No.of Employees: 1 - 10 **Product Groups:** 30, 49

Date of Accounts	Dec 11	Dec 10	Dec 09
Working Capital	119	108	102
Fixed Assets	119	100	100
Current Assets	157	141	158

Scientific Optical Ltd

Drury Lane Pondswood Industrial Estate, St Leonards On Sea, TN38 9YA
Tel: 01424-430371 **Fax:** 01424-441639
E-mail: sales@scientificoptical.com
Website: http://www.scientificoptical.com
Bank(s): National Westminster Bank Plc
Directors: B. Leach (Fin), J. Griffin (MD)
Immediate Holding Company: SCIENTIFIC OPTICAL LIMITED
Registration no: 03389349 **VAT No.:** GB 347 1605 61
Date established: 1997 **Turnover:** £1m - £2m **No.of Employees:** 11 - 20
Product Groups: 33, 38

Date of Accounts	Dec 11	Dec 10	Dec 09
Working Capital	109	88	121
Fixed Assets	13	14	13
Current Assets	139	144	154

Silverhill Spares Ltd (Silverhill Domestic Appliances Ltd)

Unit 26, The Innovation Centre Highfield Drive, St Leonards On Sea, TN38 9UH
Tel: 01424-858323
E-mail: vacuumbags2u@googlemail.com
Website: http://www.vacuumbags2u.co.uk
Registration no: 07116912 **No.of Employees:** 1 - 10 **Product Groups:** 24, 40, 63

Southern Valve & Fitting Co. Ltd

Units 36 & 37 Innovation Centre Highfield Drive Churchfields, St Leonards On Sea, TN38 9UH
Tel: 01424-858115 **Fax:** 01424-858116
E-mail: sales@southernvalve.co.uk
Website: http://www.southernvalve.co.uk
Directors: N. Poole (MD)
Managers: J. Poole (Comm)
Registration no: 01558132 **VAT No.:** GB 362 1350 84
Date established: 1981 **Turnover:** £500,000 - £1m
No.of Employees: 1 - 10 **Product Groups:** 29, 30, 35, 36, 37, 38, 39, 40, 42, 45, 46, 48, 67

Stevens & Billington

Highfield Drive, St Leonards On Sea, TN38 9UH
Tel: 01424-858260 **Fax:** 01424-858101
E-mail: info@mfaudio.co.uk
Website: http://www.mfaudio.co.uk
Directors: J. Billington (Ptnr)
Immediate Holding Company: COASTAL LAND (SUSSEX) LLP
Registration no: 01379763 **Date established:** 2007
Turnover: Up to £250,000 **No.of Employees:** 1 - 10 **Product Groups:** 37

Date of Accounts	Mar 10	Mar 09
Sales Turnover	199	343
Pre Tax Profit/Loss	-2m	-437
Working Capital	-758	-304
Fixed Assets	5m	N/A
Current Assets	1m	2m
Current Liabilities	1m	2m

Stevens Rowsell & Co. Ltd

6 Wainwright Close, St Leonards On Sea, TN38 9PP
Tel: 01424-852672 **Fax:** 01424-852330
E-mail: admin@stevensrowsell.com
Website: http://www.stevensrowsell.com
Directors: S. Small (MD)
Managers: K. Sweetman (Fin Mgr), J. Thompson (Purch Mgr)
Immediate Holding Company: STEVENS ROWSELL & CO.LIMITED
Registration no: 00864783 **Date established:** 1965 **Turnover:** £2m - £5m
No.of Employees: 21 - 50 **Product Groups:** 48, 67

Date of Accounts	Dec 11	Dec 10	Dec 09
Working Capital	248	221	301
Fixed Assets	1m	1m	1m
Current Assets	1m	1m	981

Swift-Lite Charcoal

Innovation Centre Highfield Drive, St Leonards On Sea, TN38 9UH
Tel: 01424-870333 **Fax:** 01424-870527
E-mail: sales@swift-lite.com
Website: http://www.swift-lite.com
Directors: A. Barnes (MD), S. Barnes (MD)
Managers: D. Price (Sales Admin)
Immediate Holding Company: SWIFT LITE INTERNATIONAL LTD
Registration no: 07555782 **VAT No.:** GB 753 5803 22
Date established: 2011 **Turnover:** £1m - £2m **No.of Employees:** 1 - 10
Product Groups: 31, 66

T M S Vacuum Components

21 Stirling Road, St Leonards On Sea, TN38 9NP
Tel: 01424-853211 **Fax:** 01424-853137
E-mail: tmsvacuum@btconnect.com
Website: http://www.tmsvacuumcomponents.co.uk
Directors: T. Platt (Prop)
No.of Employees: 1 - 10 **Product Groups:** 37, 38

Tunnelling Accessories Ltd

Churchfields Industrial Estate Sidney Little Road, St Leonards On Sea, TN38 9PU
Tel: 01424-854112 **Fax:** 01424-854231
E-mail: info@tunnellingaccessories.co.uk
Website: http://www.tunnellingaccessories.co.uk
Directors: P. Benford (Dir)
Immediate Holding Company: TUNNELLING ACCESSORIES LIMITED
Registration no: 02102715 **Date established:** 1987 **Turnover:** £1m - £2m
No.of Employees: 1 - 10 **Product Groups:** 42, 45

Date of Accounts	Feb 12	Feb 11	Feb 10
Working Capital	2m	2m	937
Fixed Assets	45	43	358
Current Assets	2m	2m	1m

Turner Tools Ltd

15 Armstrong Close, St Leonards On Sea, TN38 9ST
Tel: 01424-853055 **Fax:** 01424-851085
E-mail: turnertools@turnertools.com
Website: http://www.turnertools.com
Directors: P. Turner (MD), M. Hodgson (MD)
Managers: T. Lane (Mgr)
Immediate Holding Company: TELHAM ENTERPRISES LTD
Registration no: 03734935 **Date established:** 1999 **Turnover:** £1m - £2m
No.of Employees: 1 - 10 **Product Groups:** 32, 33, 36, 37, 38, 46, 67

Weforma Dmpfungstechnik GmbH

Innovation Centre Highfield Drive, St Leonards On Sea, TN38 9UH
Tel: 01424-858170 **Fax:** 01424-858172
E-mail: info.uk@weformer.com
Website: http://www.weforma.com/index.php?id=1&L=1
Managers: A. Cummins (Sales Prom Mgr)
Immediate Holding Company: Weforma Gmbh
Registration no: 03610119 **VAT No.:** 712 6913 44 **Date established:** 1989
Turnover: £2m - £5m **No.of Employees:** 1 - 10 **Product Groups:** 29, 35, 38, 39, 40, 45, 46, 67

Date of Accounts	Dec 07	Dec 06	Dec 05
Working Capital	12	20	14
Fixed Assets	6	1	N/A
Current Assets	44	44	54
Current Liabilities	31	23	40
Total Share Capital	19	19	19

Wylie Systems

Drury Lane, St Leonards On Sea, TN38 9BA
Tel: 01424-421235 **Fax:** 01424-433760
E-mail: georges@raycowylie.com
Website: http://www.raycowylie.com
Bank(s): Lloyds TSB Bank plc
Directors: J. Hinse (Fin)
Managers: G. Rodrigue (Ops Mgr)
Ultimate Holding Company: B. & A. ENGINEERING COMPANY LIMITED(THE)
Immediate Holding Company: WYLIE SAFE LOAD INDICATORS LIMITED
Registration no: 00293383 **VAT No.:** GB 201 0595 18
Date established: 1934 **Turnover:** £2m - £5m **No.of Employees:** 11 - 20
Product Groups: 38, 45

Date of Accounts	Dec 11	Dec 10	Dec 09
Working Capital	1	1	1
Current Assets	1	1	1

Uckfield

Addagrip Surface Treatments Ltd
Bell Lane Bellbrook Industrial Estate, Uckfield, TN22 1QL
Tel: 01825-761333 **Fax:** 01825-768566
E-mail: sales@addagrip.co.uk
Website: http://www.addagrip.co.uk
Bank(s): National Westminster Bank Plc
Directors: R. Critchley (MD), D. Goddard (Fin)
Immediate Holding Company: ADDAGRIP SURFACE TREATMENTS U.K. LIMITED
Registration no: 01492055 **VAT No.:** GB 315 9939 25
Date established: 1980 **Turnover:** £2m - £5m **No.of Employees:** 11 - 20
Product Groups: 14, 22, 23, 24, 25, 27, 29, 30, 31, 32, 33, 34, 35, 36, 37, 38, 39, 40, 41, 42, 44, 45, 46, 47, 49, 52, 61, 63, 66, 83, 86

Date of Accounts	Dec 11	Dec 10	Dec 09
Working Capital	784	573	768
Fixed Assets	766	787	797
Current Assets	1m	979	1m

Applications Engineering Ltd
5 Horsted Square Bellbrook Industrial Estate, Uckfield, TN22 1QG
Tel: 01825-764737 **Fax:** 01825-768330
E-mail: info@appeng.co.uk
Website: http://www.appeng.co.uk
Directors: G. Kallmann (Ch), J. Goddard (MD)
Registration no: 01754698 **VAT No.:** GB 403 1410 23
Date established: 1983 **Turnover:** £1m - £2m **No.of Employees:** 1 - 10
Product Groups: 37, 38, 40, 42

Date of Accounts	Jun 11	Jun 10	Jun 09
Working Capital	233	216	203
Fixed Assets	13	25	37
Current Assets	580	502	439
Current Liabilities	222	N/A	N/A

Crowson Fabrics Limited
Crowson House Bellbrook Park, Uckfield, TN22 1QZ
Tel: 01825-761044 **Fax:** 01825-764283
E-mail: sales@crowsonfabrics.com
Website: http://www.crowsonfabrics.com
Bank(s): National Westminster Bank Plc
Directors: D. Crowson (Dir), J. Eden (Co Sec)
Managers: S. Simpson (I.T. Exec), D. Smith (Mktg Serv Mgr)
Immediate Holding Company: Derek Crowson Ltd
Registration no: 01396447 **VAT No.:** GB 583 6477 96
Date established: 1978 **No.of Employees:** 21 - 50 **Product Groups:** 23, 63

Date of Accounts	Sep 09	Sep 08	Sep 07
Sales Turnover	4m	8m	N/A
Pre Tax Profit/Loss	-739	-1m	26
Working Capital	123	841	2m
Fixed Assets	151	171	354
Current Assets	3m	5m	6m
Current Liabilities	337	461	446

Delta Computer Services (Head Office)
4-5 Falmer Court London Road, Uckfield, TN22 1HN
Tel: 01825-768123 **Fax:** 01825-769756
E-mail: sales@deltacomputerservices.co.uk
Website: http://www.deltacomputerservices.co.uk
Bank(s): Barclays
Directors: R. Ballan (Snr Part)
VAT No.: GB 436 0572 60 **Turnover:** £1m - £2m **No.of Employees:** 11 - 20
Product Groups: 44

Design & Display Structures Ltd
The Studio, Amberley Hempstead Road, Uckfield, TN22 1DZ
Tel: 0844-7365995 **Fax:** 0844-7365992
E-mail: sales@design-and-display.co.uk
Website: http://www.design-and-display.co.uk
Bank(s): Royal Bank of Scotland, London
Directors: R. Kiss (Dir)
Managers: A. Curtis
Registration no: 04934691 **VAT No.:** GB 521 9387 39
No.of Employees: 21 - 50 **Product Groups:** 30

Diane Hutt Gallery
95a High Street, Uckfield, TN22 1RJ
Tel: 01825-766440
E-mail: diane@huttgallery.co.uk
Website: http://www.dianehuttgallery.co.uk
Directors: D. Hutt (Prop)
No.of Employees: 1 - 10 **Product Groups:** 25, 26, 36, 49

ECom Media UK Ltd
152 High Street, Uckfield, TN22 1AT
Tel: 01825-765999 **Fax:** 01825-766999
E-mail: info@ecomdda.com
Website: http://www.ecomdda.com
Managers: C. Duchesne (Sales Prom)
Registration no: 04353978 **Date established:** 2002
Turnover: £250,000 - £500,000 **No.of Employees:** 11 - 20
Product Groups: 27, 28, 44

Date of Accounts	Mar 10	Mar 09	Mar 08
Working Capital	-16	5	7
Fixed Assets	19	18	20
Current Assets	104	67	111

Elsan Ltd (Head Office)
15 Brambleside Bellbrook Industrial Estate, Uckfield, TN22 1QF
Tel: 01825-748200 **Fax:** 01825-761212
E-mail: sales@elsan.co.uk
Website: http://www.elsan.co.uk
Bank(s): Barclays
Directors: P. Warwick Smith (MD), T. King (Sales)
Immediate Holding Company: ELSAN LIMITED
Registration no: 00760511 **Date established:** 1963 **Turnover:** £2m - £5m
No.of Employees: 11 - 20 **Product Groups:** 30, 32, 36, 39, 48, 49

Date of Accounts	Dec 11	Dec 10	Dec 09
Working Capital	3m	2m	2m
Fixed Assets	1m	1m	1m
Current Assets	3m	3m	3m

F T Refrigeration Ltd
The Paddock Maresfield, Uckfield, TN22 2HQ
Tel: 01825-761544 **Fax:** 01825-763326
Directors: T. Wallis (Sales)
Immediate Holding Company: F AND T REFRIGERATION LIMITED
Registration no: 01820943 **Date established:** 1984
No.of Employees: 1 - 10 **Product Groups:** 36, 40

Gunnebo Entrance Control Ltd
Bellbrook Business Park Bellbrook Industrial Estate, Uckfield, TN22 1QQ
Tel: 01825-746122 **Fax:** 01825-763835
E-mail: robert.wheeler@csisec.com
Website: http://www.gunneboentrance.com
Directors: M. Matthews (Co Sec), R. Wheeler (Dir)
Managers: S. Pammet (Admin Off)
Ultimate Holding Company: GUNNEBO AB (SWEDEN)
Immediate Holding Company: GUNNEBO ENTRANCE CONTROL LIMITED
Registration no: 02589251 **VAT No.:** GB 583 6335 19
Date established: 1991 **Turnover:** £10m - £20m
No.of Employees: 101 - 250 **Product Groups:** 35, 49

Date of Accounts	Dec 10	Dec 09	Dec 08
Sales Turnover	17m	17m	22m
Pre Tax Profit/Loss	-726	-1m	-4m
Working Capital	2m	2m	3m
Fixed Assets	2m	586	734
Current Assets	6m	8m	9m
Current Liabilities	398	1m	678

H M T Plastics Ltd
Fairway House 31a Framfield Road, Uckfield, TN22 5AH
Tel: 01825-769393 **Fax:** 01825-769494
E-mail: hmtp@aol.com
Website: http://www.bagtagsonline.com
Directors: C. Grundy (Dir), P. Mears (Fin)
Immediate Holding Company: H.M.T. PLASTICS LIMITED
Registration no: 01257992 **Date established:** 1976
Turnover: £250,000 - £500,000 **No.of Employees:** 1 - 10
Product Groups: 49

Date of Accounts	Aug 11	Aug 10	Aug 07
Working Capital	63	177	143
Fixed Assets	219	87	87
Current Assets	95	200	172

Hendry Exhibitions
New Place Pump Lane, Framfield, Uckfield, TN22 5RH
Tel: 01825-890077 **Fax:** 01435-868077
E-mail: hire@hendryexhibitions.co.uk
Website: http://www.hendryexhibitions.co.uk
Directors: I. Hendry (Dir)
No.of Employees: 1 - 10 **Product Groups:** 25, 26, 30, 35, 37, 39, 49, 52, 66, 69, 72, 80, 81, 83, 84

J J Huber Investments Ltd
Heatherdene Farm Buxted Wood Lane, Buxted, Uckfield, TN22 4QE
Tel: 01825-733500 **Fax:** 01825-768274
E-mail: huberuk@aol.com
Directors: C. Huber (MD)
Immediate Holding Company: J.J. HUBER (INVESTMENTS) LIMITED
Registration no: 00453548 **VAT No.:** GB 218 0311 09
Date established: 1948 **Turnover:** £500,000 - £1m
No.of Employees: 1 - 10 **Product Groups:** 44

Date of Accounts	Nov 11	Nov 10	Nov 09
Working Capital	189	193	197
Fixed Assets	176	188	194
Current Assets	243	248	258

Itm Soil Ltd
Bell Lane Bellbrook Industrial Estate, Uckfield, TN22 1QL
Tel: 01825-765044 **Fax:** 01825-761740
E-mail: sales@itmsoil.com
Website: http://www.itmsoil.com
Bank(s): National Westminster Bank Plc
Directors: J. Scott (Dir), J. Cook (Fin)
Managers: J. Allen (Sales & Mktg Mg), J. Gavin (Buyer), J. Nelson (Personnel)
Ultimate Holding Company: ITMSOIL GROUP LTD
Immediate Holding Company: ITMSOIL INSTRUMENTS LTD
Registration no: 00741113 **VAT No.:** GB 228 2526 68
Date established: 1962 **Turnover:** £2m - £5m
No.of Employees: 101 - 250 **Product Groups:** 38, 84, 85

Date of Accounts	Dec 11	Dec 10	Dec 09
Sales Turnover	4m	5m	N/A
Pre Tax Profit/Loss	93	234	N/A
Working Capital	834	706	515
Fixed Assets	81	38	44
Current Assets	2m	2m	2m
Current Liabilities	164	468	N/A

Ixia
New Road Ridgewood, Uckfield, TN22 5SX
Tel: 01825-766800 **Fax:** 01825-766500
E-mail: ixiauk@cs.com
Website: http://www.ixiauk.com
Directors: R. Van-De-Burgh (MD)
No.of Employees: 1 - 10 **Product Groups:** 30, 40, 45, 67

Jemtech UK Ltd
Bell Lane Bellbrook Industrial Estate, Uckfield, TN22 1QL
Tel: 01825-767640 **Fax:** 01825-767635
E-mail: sales@jemtech.co.uk
Website: http://www.jemtech.co.uk
Directors: S. Coull (Fin), S. Coull (MD)
Ultimate Holding Company: SSC HOLDINGS LIMITED
Immediate Holding Company: JEMTECH (UK) LIMITED
Registration no: 03293431 **Date established:** 1996
No.of Employees: 11 - 20 **Product Groups:** 46

Date of Accounts	Sep 11	Sep 10	Sep 09
Working Capital	196	179	175
Fixed Assets	59	31	42
Current Assets	764	578	520

Kennedy Hygiene Products Ltd
Brookside Bellbrook Industrial Estate, Uckfield, TN22 1YA
Tel: 01825-768141 **Fax:** 01825-768143
E-mail: sales@kennedy-hygiene.com
Website: http://www.kennedy-hygiene.com
Bank(s): Barclays
Managers: G. Orme, O. Bizard (Chief Mgr), O. Kovacs (Mktg Serv Mgr)
Ultimate Holding Company: EURAZEO (FRANCE)
Immediate Holding Company: KENNEDY EXPORTS LIMITED
Registration no: 02103231 **Date established:** 1987
Turnover: £250,000 - £500,000 **No.of Employees:** 21 - 50
Product Groups: 30, 32, 36, 40

Date of Accounts	Dec 11	Dec 10	Dec 09
Sales Turnover	300	300	300
Pre Tax Profit/Loss	216	214	206
Working Capital	1m	904	725
Fixed Assets	1m	1m	1m
Current Assets	1m	938	755
Current Liabilities	33	33	30

Lifestyle Shutters & Blinds
8 The Enterprise Centre Bell Lane Industrial Estate, Bellbrook Industrial Estate, Uckfield, TN22 1QL
Tel: 01825-760722 **Fax:** 01825-769305
E-mail: info@lifestyleshutters.co.uk
Website: http://www.lifestyleshutters.co.uk
Directors: N. Clarke (Prop)
Immediate Holding Company: TURNERS REMOVALS LIMITED
Registration no: 05481738 **Date established:** 2000
Turnover: £250,000 - £500,000 **No.of Employees:** 1 - 10
Product Groups: 25, 66

Mitchell & Cooper Ltd (Head Office)
138-140 Framfield Road, Uckfield, TN22 5AU
Tel: 01825-765511 **Fax:** 01825-767173
E-mail: sales@mitchellcooper.co.uk
Website: http://www.mitchellcooper.co.uk
Bank(s): HSBC Bank plc
Directors: G. Cooper (MD), W. Cooper (Ch), A. Cooper (Dir), C. Cooper (Dir)
Managers: D. Jones (Export Sales Mg)
Immediate Holding Company: MITCHELL & COOPER LIMITED
Registration no: 01202604 **Date established:** 1975 **Turnover:** £5m - £10m
No.of Employees: 51 - 100 **Product Groups:** 20, 22, 26, 29, 30, 33, 35, 36, 38, 40, 41, 49, 65, 67

Date of Accounts	Mar 11	Mar 10	Mar 09
Working Capital	205	201	701
Fixed Assets	804	544	322
Current Assets	1m	1m	2m

Neva Consultants LLP
Neva House Piltdown, Uckfield, TN22 3XL
Tel: 01825-720900 **Fax:** 0844-557 5724
E-mail: info@nevaplc.com
Website: http://www.nevaconsultants.com
Directors: N. Collinson (Snr Part)
Immediate Holding Company: NEVA CONSULTANTS LLP
Registration no: OC371013 **Date established:** 2011
No.of Employees: 11 - 20 **Product Groups:** 82

Pure Print Group Beacon Press, East Sussex Press, Ingenious
Beacon House Brambleside, Bellbrook Industrial Estate, Uckfield, TN22 1PL
Tel: 01825-768811 **Fax:** 01825-768062
E-mail: contact@pureprint.com
Website: http://www.pureprint.com
Bank(s): Barclays
Directors: I. Brown (Fin), R. Owers (Sales & Mktg), B. Massey (Fin)
Managers: I. Godden
Ultimate Holding Company: EAST SUSSEX PRESS LIMITED
Immediate Holding Company: PUREPRINT GROUP LIMITED
Registration no: 01493898 **Date established:** 1980
Turnover: £20m - £50m **No.of Employees:** 101 - 250 **Product Groups:** 28

Date of Accounts	Aug 11	Aug 10	Aug 09
Sales Turnover	22m	18m	16m
Pre Tax Profit/Loss	564	278	-681
Working Capital	-320	-648	-426
Fixed Assets	5m	4m	5m
Current Assets	8m	7m	6m
Current Liabilities	4m	3m	3m

Trifast
Trifast House Bolton Close, Bellbrook Industrial Estate, Uckfield, TN22 1QW
Tel: 01825-747200 **Fax:** 01825-767882
E-mail: sales@trfastenings.com
Website: http://www.trfastenings.com
Bank(s): Midland
Directors: S. Murphy (Pers), S. Lawson (Fin)
Managers: C. Coddington (Tech Serv Mgr), D. Baldock (Purch Mgr), S. Wallis (Sales Prom Mgr), A. Eldridge (Mktg Serv Mgr), A. Burnett (Mktg Serv Mgr)
Ultimate Holding Company: TRIFAST PLC
Immediate Holding Company: TRIFAST OVERSEAS HOLDINGS LIMITED
Registration no: 02997039 **Date established:** 1994
Turnover: £75m - £125m **No.of Employees:** 101 - 250
Product Groups: 35, 66

Date of Accounts	Mar 12	Mar 11	Mar 10
Pre Tax Profit/Loss	874	2m	5m
Working Capital	2m	2m	2m
Fixed Assets	15m	10m	10m
Current Assets	2m	2m	3m
Current Liabilities	495	495	595

Triple R Engineering Ltd
Squires Farm Industrial Estate Easons Green, Framfield, Uckfield, TN22 5RB
Tel: 01825-840011 **Fax:** 01825-840953
E-mail: sales@tripler.co.uk
Website: http://www.tripler.co.uk
Directors: J. Wadey (Fin)
Immediate Holding Company: TRIPLE R ENGINEERING LIMITED
Registration no: 02597575 **Date established:** 1991 **Turnover:** £5m - £10m
No.of Employees: 1 - 10 **Product Groups:** 67

Date of Accounts	Mar 11	Mar 10	Mar 09
Working Capital	15	24	19
Fixed Assets	67	50	58
Current Assets	139	151	137
Current Liabilities	N/A	32	38

Tunbridge Wells Fire Protection Ltd
Buckham Hill Works Buckham Hill, Uckfield, TN22 5XY
Tel: 01825-767600 **Fax:** 01825-761693
E-mail: info@twfpltd.co.uk
Website: http://www.twfpltd.co.uk
Directors: K. Francis (Fin)
Managers: P. Mills (Buyer)
Immediate Holding Company: TUNBRIDGE WELLS FIRE PROTECTION LIMITED
Registration no: 01825236 **Date established:** 1984
No.of Employees: 1 - 10 **Product Groups:** 38, 42

Date of Accounts	Dec 11	Dec 10	Dec 09
Working Capital	-53	-6	12
Fixed Assets	48	26	33

Current Assets	86	88	83

MDC Vacuum Products Ltd
3 Horsted Square Bellbrook Industrial Estate, Uckfield, TN22 1QG
Tel: 01825-280450 **Fax:** 01825-280440
E-mail: sales@caburn.co.uk
Website: http://www.mdcvacuum.co.uk
Bank(s): Lloyds TSB Bank plc
Directors: D. Barlow (MD)
Ultimate Holding Company: Ferraris Group Plc
Registration no: 02631363 **Date established:** 1991
Turnover: £10m - £20m **No.of Employees:** 51 - 100 **Product Groups:** 33, 35, 36, 37, 38, 40, 47, 48, 52

Worsell Electrical Contractors Ltd
24a Union Point Eastbourne Road, Ridgewood, Uckfield, TN22 5SR
Tel: 01825-760660 **Fax:** 01825-760880
E-mail: sales@worsell.co.uk
Website: http://www.worsell.co.uk
Bank(s): National Westminster
Directors: J. Worsell (Co Sec)
Immediate Holding Company: WORSELL ELECTRICAL CONTRACTORS LIMITED
Registration no: 02753651 **VAT No.:** GB 621 7323 67
Date established: 1992 **Turnover:** Up to £250,000
No.of Employees: 11 - 20 **Product Groups:** 52

Date of Accounts	Nov 11	Nov 10	Nov 09
Working Capital	69	91	135
Fixed Assets	17	22	30
Current Assets	203	184	315

Zee Associates
Iron Castle Royal Oak Lane, High Hurstwood, Uckfield, TN22 4AN
Tel: 01825-733621 **Fax:** 01825-732350
E-mail: info@zee-associates.co.uk
Website: http://www.zee-associates.co.uk
Directors: D. Whitehorn (Head)
Date established: 1995 **Turnover:** £250,000 - £500,000
No.of Employees: 1 - 10 **Product Groups:** 86

Wadhurst

4Productions Limited
Unit D Durgates Industrial Estate, Wadhurst, TN5 6DF
Tel: 08707-606140 **Fax:** 01892-614811
E-mail: info@4productions.co.uk
Website: http://www.4productions.co.uk
Directors: G. Butler (Dir), L. Henderson (MD)
Registration no: 04136158 **Date established:** 2003
No.of Employees: 1 - 10 **Product Groups:** 79

Atcost Ltd
Spa House Wadhurst Business Park Faircrouch Lane, Wadhurst, TN5 6PT
Tel: 01892-526288 **Fax:** 01892-515348
E-mail: david@faircloth.co.uk
Website: http://www.faircloth.co.uk
Directors: D. Faircloth (MD)
Immediate Holding Company: ATCOST LTD
Registration no: 08107842 **Date established:** 2012
No.of Employees: 1 - 10 **Product Groups:** 52

Date of Accounts	Mar 10	Mar 09	Mar 08
Working Capital	7	3	14
Fixed Assets	12	15	12
Current Assets	74	86	116

Easymatics Ltd
Clock House High Street, Wadhurst, TN5 6AA
Tel: 08702-416275 **Fax:** 0870-458 0387
E-mail: terry@easymatics.net
Website: http://www.easymatics.net
Directors: T. Price (Dir), A. Edwards (Fin), T. Price (Mkt Research)
Immediate Holding Company: EASYMATICS LIMITED
Registration no: 04228025 **Date established:** 2001
Turnover: £250,000 - £500,000 **No.of Employees:** 1 - 10
Product Groups: 44

Date of Accounts	Jun 11	Jun 10	Jun 07
Working Capital	18	15	23
Fixed Assets	2	2	9
Current Assets	20	26	28

Improvia Ltd
The Balaclava Pell Green, Wadhurst, TN5 6EE
Tel: 01892-783383
E-mail: info@improvia.co.uk
Website: http://www.improvia.co.uk
Directors: J. Blackman (Fin), G. Blackman (MD)
Immediate Holding Company: IMPROVIA LIMITED
Registration no: 04015100 **Date established:** 2000
Turnover: Up to £250,000 **No.of Employees:** 1 - 10 **Product Groups:** 81

Date of Accounts	Jun 10	Jun 09	Jun 08
Sales Turnover	127	165	N/A
Working Capital	-43	-88	-80
Fixed Assets	25	33	64
Current Assets	79	34	26
Current Liabilities	111	110	N/A

Nikwax Ltd
Unit F Durgates Industrial Estate Durgates, Wadhurst, TN5 6DF
Tel: 01892-786400 **Fax:** 01892-783748
E-mail: enquiries@nikwax.co.uk
Website: http://www.nikwax.co.uk
Bank(s): National Westminster Bank Plc
Managers: J. McGuire (Sales Prom Mgr), J. Martin (Tech Serv Mgr), D. Christmas (Mktg Serv Mgr), A. Baker (Comptroller), A. Riall (Purch Mgr), C. Gill
Immediate Holding Company: NIKWAX LIMITED
Registration no: 03101664 **VAT No.:** GB 235 3159 75
Date established: 1995 **Turnover:** £5m - £10m
No.of Employees: 101 - 250 **Product Groups:** 32

Date of Accounts	Jul 11	Jul 10	Jul 09
Sales Turnover	9m	9m	6m
Pre Tax Profit/Loss	613	758	483
Working Capital	958	628	320
Fixed Assets	2m	1m	2m
Current Assets	2m	3m	2m
Current Liabilities	344	448	385

Paragon Microfibre Ltd
Cousley Wood Garage, Wadhurst, TN5 6EP
Tel: 01892-784732 **Fax:** 01892-785976
E-mail: sales@paragonmicrofibre.com
Website: http://www.paragonmicrofibre.com
Directors: J. Corke (Co Sec), S. Duffell (MD)
Registration no: 04428125 **Turnover:** £250,000 - £500,000
No.of Employees: 1 - 10 **Product Groups:** 23, 24, 32, 49

Date of Accounts	Mar 08	Mar 07	Mar 06
Sales Turnover	N/A	N/A	324
Pre Tax Profit/Loss	N/A	N/A	31
Working Capital	54	47	30
Fixed Assets	11	83	87
Current Assets	104	98	117
Current Liabilities	50	51	87
ROCE% (Return on Capital Employed)			26.2
ROT% (Return on Turnover)			9.4

Piping Solutions Ltd
Little Orchard - Lokring Southern UK Barndown Road, Stonegate, Wadhurst, TN5 7EJ
Tel: 07802-871688 **Fax:** 01580-200465
E-mail: rlansdowne@lokring.com
Website: http://www.lokringsouthern.com
Product Groups: 30, 34, 35, 36, 38, 39, 40, 42, 45, 46, 47, 48, 51, 66, 67, 71, 83

Date of Accounts	Jun 09	Jun 08	Jun 07
Working Capital	27	24	2
Fixed Assets	12	8	12
Current Assets	171	120	83

Washroom Systems Limited
C S S House The Dens, Wadhurst, TN5 6NJ
Tel: 0800-328 9231 **Fax:** 0870-0523000
E-mail: info@ukcss.com
Website: http://www.ukcss.com
Managers: M. Greenfield (Ops Mgr), P. Phillipson (Export Sales Mg), R. Warren (Develop Mgr), V. Greenfield (Sales Admin)
Registration no: 04258600 **Date established:** 2003
No.of Employees: 1 - 10 **Product Groups:** 30, 35, 54

WEST SUSSEX

Arundel

Arun Fastener Company Ltd
Unit 2-3 Ford Lane, Ford, Arundel, BN18 0DF
Tel: 01243-551484 **Fax:** 01243-551076
E-mail: jbazley1965@aol.com
Directors: J. Bazley (MD)
Immediate Holding Company: ARUN FASTENER COMPANY LIMITED
Registration no: 04157588 **VAT No.:** GB 768 7819 57
Date established: 2001 **Turnover:** Up to £250,000
No.of Employees: 1 - 10 **Product Groups:** 29, 30, 35, 36, 39, 42, 46, 48, 66

Date of Accounts	Mar 12	Mar 11	Mar 10
Working Capital	67	62	39
Fixed Assets	62	60	61
Current Assets	89	94	55

Ashtead Plant Hire Ltd
Ford Airfield Industrial Estate Ford, Arundel, BN18 0HY
Tel: 01903-717431 **Fax:** 01903-732246
E-mail: enquiries@aplant.com
Website: http://www.aplant.com
Bank(s): Lloyds TSB Bank plc
Directors: D. Hudson (Prop)
Immediate Holding Company: ASHTEAD GROUP PLC
Registration no: 00444569 **VAT No.:** GB 214 5687 37
No.of Employees: 11 - 20 **Product Groups:** 72, 83

Blastreat Arundel Ltd
14 Fitzalan Road, Arundel, BN18 9JS
Tel: 01903-883262 **Fax:** 01903-884185
E-mail: enquiries@blastreat.co.uk
Website: http://www.blastreat.co.uk
Directors: R. Robin (Fin)
Immediate Holding Company: BLASTREAT (ARUNDEL) LIMITED
Registration no: 02809866 **Date established:** 1993
Turnover: £250,000 - £500,000 **No.of Employees:** 1 - 10
Product Groups: 32, 34, 48

Date of Accounts	Feb 11	Feb 10	Feb 09
Working Capital	10	-14	-65
Fixed Assets	810	820	822
Current Assets	173	167	189

Chiviott Machine Tools Ltd
Unit C1 Rudford Industrial Estate Ford Road, Ford, Arundel, BN18 0BD
Tel: 01903-721281 **Fax:** 01903-730868
E-mail: sales@chiviott.co.uk
Website: http://www.used-machine-tools-uk.com
Directors: S. Elliott (Dir)
Immediate Holding Company: CHIVIOTT (MACHINE TOOLS) LIMITED
Registration no: 01292861 **Date established:** 1976 **Turnover:** £1m - £2m
No.of Employees: 1 - 10 **Product Groups:** 46

Date of Accounts	Feb 12	Feb 11	Feb 10
Working Capital	-225	-219	-215
Fixed Assets	484	483	488
Current Assets	392	351	302

D & S Services
Unit H2 & H3 Rudford Industrial Estate Ford Road, Ford, Arundel, BN18 0BD
Tel: 01903-732732 **Fax:** 01903-716151
E-mail: sales@dandsservices.co.uk
Website: http://www.dandsservices.co.uk
Directors: S. Chittenden (Prop)
Turnover: £500,000 - £1m **No.of Employees:** 1 - 10 **Product Groups:** 35

I C S Electronics Ltd
Unit V Rudford Industrial Estate Ford Road, Ford, Arundel, BN18 0BF
Tel: 01903-731101 **Fax:** 01903-731105
E-mail: kpage@icselectronics.co.uk
Website: http://www.icselectronics.co.uk
Directors: K. Page (MD), N. Page (Fin)
Immediate Holding Company: I.C.S. ELECTRONICS LIMITED
Registration no: 01615525 **Date established:** 1982 **Turnover:** £1m - £2m
No.of Employees: 1 - 10 **Product Groups:** 49

Date of Accounts	Oct 11	Oct 10	Oct 09
Sales Turnover	N/A	2m	2m
Pre Tax Profit/Loss	N/A	464	285
Working Capital	745	930	689
Fixed Assets	35	54	19
Current Assets	1m	1m	2m
Current Liabilities	N/A	314	857

Orkney Boats Ltd
Unit 1 Ford Lane Business Park, Ford, Arundel, BN18 0UZ
Tel: 01243-551456 **Fax:** 01243-551914
E-mail: r.hay@orkneyboatsltd.co.uk
Website: http://www.orkneyboatsltd.co.uk
Directors: R. Hay (Dir)
Managers: T. Pannell (Sales Prom Mgr)
Ultimate Holding Company: ORKNEY BOATS LIMITED
Immediate Holding Company: PORTLAND REALISATIONS (ORKNEY) LIMITED
Registration no: 02428339 **VAT No.:** GB 737 0267 35
Date established: 1989 **Turnover:** £1m - £2m **No.of Employees:** 1 - 10
Product Groups: 39

Date of Accounts	Dec 09	Dec 08	Dec 07
Working Capital	107	121	223
Fixed Assets	19	25	32
Current Assets	369	321	418

Plastigauge
Unit 2 Gaugemaster Way, Ford, Arundel, BN18 0RX
Tel: 01903-882822 **Fax:** 01903-884962
E-mail: sales@plastigauge.co.uk
Website: http://www.plastigauge.co.uk
Bank(s): Lloyds TSB Bank plc
Directors: A. Bickers (MD)
Managers: L. Harwood (Purch Mgr), S. Harwood (Sales Prom Mgr)
Ultimate Holding Company: Elinvac Ltd
Registration no: 00709383 **VAT No.:** GB 193 6027 55
Date established: 1961 **Turnover:** £250,000 - £500,000
Product Groups: 30, 35, 38, 39

Sprint Electric Ltd
Peregrine House Ford Lane, Ford, Arundel, BN18 0DF
Tel: 01243-558080 **Fax:** 01903-730893
E-mail: info@sprint-electric.com
Website: http://www.sprint-electric.com
Bank(s): Barclays, Chichester
Directors: G. Keen (Sales), D. Van Der Wee (MD), A. Potamianos (Dir), E. Prescott (Ch)
Managers: G. Keen (Sales Prom Mgr), D. Rawlins (Purch Mgr)
Immediate Holding Company: SPRINT ELECTRIC LIMITED
Registration no: 02160651 **VAT No.:** GB 474 2880 23
Date established: 1987 **Turnover:** £2m - £5m **No.of Employees:** 11 - 20
Product Groups: 37, 38, 44

Date of Accounts	Oct 11	Oct 10	Oct 09
Working Capital	1m	1m	905
Fixed Assets	956	124	217
Current Assets	2m	1m	1m
Current Liabilities	N/A	N/A	89

Strap It
4 Queen Street, Arundel, BN18 9JG
Tel: 01903-882699 **Fax:** 01903-660220
E-mail: sales@strap-it.co.uk
Website: http://www.strap-it.co.uk
Directors: R. Gascoigne (Dir)
Registration no: 05019087 **Date established:** 2004
Turnover: Up to £250,000 **No.of Employees:** 1 - 10 **Product Groups:** 35

Styropack UK Ltd
Unit A Rudford Industrial Estate Ford Road, Ford, Arundel, BN18 0BD
Tel: 01903-725282 **Fax:** 01903-731628
E-mail: richard.lee@styropack.co.uk
Website: http://www.styropack.co.uk
Bank(s): National Westminster Bank Plc
Directors: R. Lee (MD)
Ultimate Holding Company: SYNBRA GROUP BV (NETHERLANDS)
Immediate Holding Company: STYROPACK (UK) LIMITED
Registration no: SC041753 **VAT No.:** GB 265 4621 54
Date established: 1965 **Turnover:** £20m - £50m
No.of Employees: 11 - 20 **Product Groups:** 30, 31, 42

Date of Accounts	Dec 11	Dec 10	Dec 09
Sales Turnover	12m	13m	14m
Pre Tax Profit/Loss	-611	-44	-728
Working Capital	-2m	-2m	-2m
Fixed Assets	5m	5m	6m
Current Assets	4m	4m	4m
Current Liabilities	921	1m	1m

Sussex Catering Equipment Services Ltd
E Ford Industrial Estate Ford Lane, Ford, Arundel, BN18 0DF
Tel: 01243-553691 **Fax:** 01243-554449
E-mail: sales@sussexcateringequip.co.uk
Website: http://www.sussexcateringequip.co.uk
Directors: J. Coleman (Fin)
Immediate Holding Company: SUSSEX CATERING EQUIPMENT SERVICES LIMITED
Registration no: 04449299 **Date established:** 2002
Turnover: £500,000 - £1m **No.of Employees:** 1 - 10 **Product Groups:** 67

Date of Accounts	Mar 10	Mar 09	Mar 08
Working Capital	-46	-58	-53
Fixed Assets	70	108	135
Current Assets	231	187	150

Tempcon Instrumentation Ltd
Unit 19 Ford Lane Business Park Ford, Arundel, BN18 0UZ
Tel: 01243-558270 **Fax:** 01243-558288
E-mail: jimcopeland@tempconltd.co.uk
Website: http://www.tempconltd.co.uk
Bank(s): Lloyds TSB
Directors: J. Copeland (MD)
Ultimate Holding Company: SCOLLON LIMITED
Immediate Holding Company: TEMPCON INSTRUMENTATION LIMITED
Registration no: 01535366 **VAT No.:** GB 322 0391 06
Date established: 1980 **Turnover:** £1m - £2m **No.of Employees:** 11 - 20
Product Groups: 30, 37, 38, 40, 67

Date of Accounts	Jul 11	Jul 10	Jul 09
Sales Turnover	1m	1m	1m
Pre Tax Profit/Loss	200	91	30
Working Capital	144	51	126
Fixed Assets	47	65	77
Current Assets	370	321	343
Current Liabilities	99	104	89

Billingshurst

Acalor Contracting
Longcroft The Ride Ifold, Loxwood, Billingshurst, RH14 0TQ
Tel: 01403-752297 **Fax:** 01403-753585
E-mail: acalorcontr@aol.com
Directors: W. Townsend (Prop)
Registration no: 06471107 **Date established:** 2008
No.of Employees: 1 - 10 **Product Groups:** 46, 48

Adaptive Instruments Ltd
Crabtree Farm Estate Skiff Lane Loxwood, Wisborough Green, Billingshurst, RH14 0AG
Tel: 01403-753333 **Fax:** 01403-753386
E-mail: info@adaptive-instruments.com
Website: http://www.adaptive-instruments.com
Managers: C. Jenkins (Chief Mgr), D. Jenkins (Product)
Immediate Holding Company: ADAPTIVE INSTRUMENTS LIMITED
Registration no: 07264999 **Date established:** 2010
Turnover: £10m - £20m **No.of Employees:** 11 - 20 **Product Groups:** 38, 44

Beverley Environmental Ltd (Head Office)
Unit 2 Eagle Estate Brookers Road, Billingshurst, RH14 9RZ
Tel: 01403-782091 **Fax:** 01403-782087
E-mail: info@beverley-environmental.co.uk
Website: http://www.beverley-environmental.co.uk
Directors: A. Dawes (Tech Serv), A. Dawes (Dir), K. Hogg (Dir), W. Smith (Co Sec)
Managers: A. Ratcliffe (Chief Mgr), E. Elliott, J. Elliott, K. Garman (Mktg Serv Mgr)
Ultimate Holding Company: W.T. LAMB HOLDINGS LIMITED
Immediate Holding Company: BEVERLEY ENVIRONMENTAL LIMITED
Registration no: 07572053 **VAT No.:** GB 409 4450 57
Date established: 2011 **Turnover:** £2m - £5m **No.of Employees:** 1 - 10
Product Groups: 34, 36, 39, 40, 42, 48, 66

Date of Accounts	May 09	Sep 08	Sep 07
Sales Turnover	N/A	1m	2m
Pre Tax Profit/Loss	N/A	63	62
Working Capital	768	1m	1m
Fixed Assets	21	277	301
Current Assets	1m	2m	2m
Current Liabilities	N/A	320	325

Billington Export Ltd
1e Gillmans Industrial Estate Natts Lane, Billingshurst, RH14 9EZ
Tel: 01403-784961 **Fax:** 01403-783519
E-mail: sales@bel-tubes.co.uk
Website: http://www.bel-tubes.co.uk
Directors: M. Billington (Dir)
Immediate Holding Company: BILLINGTON EXPORT LIMITED
Registration no: 02728987 **VAT No.:** GB 415 1260 94
Date established: 1992 **Turnover:** £500,000 - £1m
No.of Employees: 1 - 10 **Product Groups:** 33, 37, 61

Date of Accounts	Jun 12	Jun 11	Jun 10
Working Capital	367	346	302
Fixed Assets	76	79	79
Current Assets	478	456	454

Ciretech Ltd
Unit 4 Huffwood Trading Estate, Billingshurst, RH14 9UR
Tel: 01403-784855 **Fax:** 01403-783000
E-mail: david.clark@ciretech.co.uk
Directors: D. Clark (Co Sec)
Immediate Holding Company: CIRETECH LIMITED
Registration no: 02130403 **VAT No.:** GB 461 7915 30
Date established: 1987 **Turnover:** £500,000 - £1m
No.of Employees: 1 - 10 **Product Groups:** 37, 44

Date of Accounts	May 11	May 10	May 09
Working Capital	-6	-5	-9
Fixed Assets	8	8	11
Current Assets	86	123	243

Hayes UK Ltd
Unit 7 Eagle Estate Brookers Road, Billingshurst, RH14 9RZ
Tel: 01403-785857 **Fax:** 08700-711701
E-mail: sales@hayes-uk.com
Website: http://www.hayes-uk.com
Directors: L. Parsons (MD)
Immediate Holding Company: HAYES (UK) LIMITED
Registration no: 03649911 **VAT No.:** GB 620 5639 56
Date established: 1998 **Turnover:** £500,000 - £1m
No.of Employees: 1 - 10 **Product Groups:** 23, 24, 27, 29, 32, 33, 38, 40

Date of Accounts	Dec 11	Nov 10	Nov 09
Working Capital	436	174	100
Fixed Assets	3	3	5
Current Assets	1m	642	264

Hydrachem Ltd (Head Office)
Gilmans Industrial Estate, Billingshurst, RH14 9EZ
Tel: 01403-787700 **Fax:** 01403-785158
E-mail: info@hydrachem.co.uk
Website: http://www.hydrachem.co.uk
Bank(s): National Westminster Bank Plc
Directors: J. Anibarro (Tech Serv), R. Rough (MD)
Managers: D. Soong (Comptroller), P. Pillay (Sales & Mktg Mg), R. Oydle (Buyer)
Ultimate Holding Company: HONEYGLADE LIMITED
Immediate Holding Company: HYDRACHEM LIMITED
Registration no: 01135842 **Date established:** 1973 **Turnover:** £2m - £5m
No.of Employees: 21 - 50 **Product Groups:** 32, 42, 54, 66

Date of Accounts	Oct 08	Oct 09	May 07
Working Capital	307	305	438
Fixed Assets	684	700	404
Current Assets	2m	2m	2m

Interior Concepts Ltd
Unit 1 Russett Place, Kirdford, Billingshurst, RH14 0QQ
Tel: 01403-820000 **Fax:** 05603-132034
E-mail: info@interiorofficeconcepts.co.uk
Website: http://www.interiorofficeconcepts.co.uk
Managers: C. Wells (Sales Prom Mgr)
Immediate Holding Company: INTERIOR CONCEPTS LIMITED
Registration no: 03449543 **Date established:** 1997
Turnover: £250,000 - £500,000 **No.of Employees:** 1 - 10
Product Groups: 23, 25, 26, 27, 33, 40, 52, 62, 66, 84, 86

Date of Accounts	Dec 11	Dec 10	Dec 09
Working Capital	181	178	139
Fixed Assets	3	4	9
Current Assets	212	213	155

Thomas Keating Ltd
Station Mills Daux Road, Billingshurst, RH14 9SH
Tel: 01403-782045 **Fax:** 01403-785464
E-mail: m.bryder@terahertz.co.uk
Website: http://www.terahertz.co.uk
Bank(s): Bank of Scotland
Directors: M. Clack (Works)
Ultimate Holding Company: CHURCHWOOD TRUST LIMITED
Immediate Holding Company: THOMAS KEATING,LIMITED
Registration no: 00203511 **VAT No.:** GB 193 0815 60
Date established: 2025 **Turnover:** £1m - £2m **No.of Employees:** 21 - 50
Product Groups: 42, 46, 48

Date of Accounts	Mar 11	Mar 10	Mar 09
Working Capital	1m	1m	728
Fixed Assets	374	260	249
Current Assets	2m	1m	1m

Lamina Dielectrics Ltd
Daux Road, Billingshurst, RH14 9SJ
Tel: 01403-783131 **Fax:** 01403-782237
E-mail: sales@lamina.uk.com
Website: http://www.lamina.uk.com
Bank(s): Bank of Scotland, Queen Square House, 15 Queen Square, Brighton, BN1 3FD
Directors: P. Hester (Ch)
Immediate Holding Company: LAMINA DIELECTRICS LIMITED
Registration no: 00905145 **VAT No.:** GB 192 9421 42
Date established: 1967 **Turnover:** £2m - £5m **No.of Employees:** 21 - 50
Product Groups: 30, 37

Date of Accounts	Dec 11	Dec 10	Dec 09
Working Capital	2m	2m	2m
Fixed Assets	2m	2m	2m
Current Assets	2m	2m	2m

Liftwell Engineering
Dunsfold Road Plaistow, Billingshurst, RH14 0PW
Tel: 01483-200585 **Fax:** 01483-200585
Directors: C. Patient (Prop)
Date established: 1996 **No.of Employees:** 1 - 10 **Product Groups:** 35, 39, 45

Promocan Ltd
Appletrees Cottage Plaistow Road, Kirdford, Billingshurst, RH14 0JR
Tel: 0845-6120654 **Fax:** 0845-6120655
E-mail: tmursell@promocan.co.uk
Website: http://www.promocan.co.uk
Directors: T. Mursell (MD)
Immediate Holding Company: PROMOCAN LIMITED
Registration no: 04548917 **Date established:** 2002
No.of Employees: 1 - 10 **Product Groups:** 24, 35, 49, 81

R G B Products
Unit 2 Gilmans Industrial Estate, Billingshurst, RH14 9EZ
Tel: 01403-783670 **Fax:** 01403-783670
E-mail: sales@rgbp.co.uk
Website: http://www.rgbproducts.co.uk
Directors: A. Brockman (MD)
Immediate Holding Company: RGB PRODUCTS LIMITED
Registration no: 05842102 **Date established:** 2006
No.of Employees: 1 - 10 **Product Groups:** 35, 45

Date of Accounts	Dec 11	Dec 10	Dec 09
Working Capital	9	-3	3
Fixed Assets	59	75	90
Current Assets	57	72	62

Selvent Pressure Relief Vents
Kingsmead Marringdean Road, Billingshurst, RH14 9HE
Tel: 01403-786254 **Fax:** 01403-782703
E-mail: sales@selvent.co.uk
Website: http://www.selvent.co.uk
Directors: R. Silvester (MD)
Immediate Holding Company: SILVESTER ENGINEERING LIMITED
Date established: 1993 **Turnover:** £250,000 - £500,000
No.of Employees: 1 - 10 **Product Groups:** 35, 40

Date of Accounts	Mar 11	Mar 10	Mar 09
Sales Turnover	290	N/A	508
Pre Tax Profit/Loss	-19	N/A	37
Working Capital	26	32	73
Fixed Assets	47	59	53
Current Assets	99	110	190
Current Liabilities	56	N/A	80

Showerpower
Unit 4 Russett Place Kirdford, Billingshurst, RH14 0QQ
Tel: 08448-841610 **Fax:** 01403-751819
E-mail: info@showerpower.co.uk
Website: http://www.showerpower.co.uk
Directors: J. Gamble (MD)
Date established: 2001 **No.of Employees:** 1 - 10 **Product Groups:** 26, 33

Showmaster Ltd
Taupo House Poundfield Lane, Plaistow, Billingshurst, RH14 0NZ
Tel: 01403-753633 **Fax:** 01403-753520
E-mail: mcardiff@showmaster.co.uk
Website: http://www.showmaster.co.uk
Product Groups: 33

Date of Accounts	Mar 08	Mar 07	Mar 06
Working Capital	432	188	199
Fixed Assets	24	26	28
Current Assets	858	820	882
Current Liabilities	426	633	684
Total Share Capital	20	20	20

Silk Stitch Promotional Textiles Ltd
Unit One Huffwood Trading Estate, Billingshurst, RH14 9UR
Tel: 01403-786678 **Fax:** 01403-786678
E-mail: answers@silkstitch.co.uk
Website: http://www.silkstitch.co.uk
Directors: A. Stubbs (Dir)
Immediate Holding Company: SILK STITCH.... PROMOTIONAL TEXTILES LIMITED
Registration no: 02571145 **Date established:** 1991
Turnover: £500,000 - £1m **No.of Employees:** 1 - 10 **Product Groups:** 22, 23, 24, 25, 30, 35, 44, 49, 63, 65, 66, 67, 75, 77, 80, 81, 83, 84, 85, 86, 87, 89

Date of Accounts	Mar 12	Mar 11	Mar 10
Working Capital	-21	-37	3
Fixed Assets	192	197	205
Current Assets	12	10	27

Silvester Engineering Ltd
Kingsmead Farm Marringdean Road, Billingshurst, RH14 9HE
Tel: 01403-782255 **Fax:** 01403-782703
E-mail: sales@silvesterengineering.co.uk
Website: http://www.silvesterengineering.co.uk
Directors: D. Silvester (Fin)
Immediate Holding Company: SILVESTER ENGINEERING LIMITED
Registration no: 02856405 **Date established:** 1993
Turnover: £250,000 - £500,000 **No.of Employees:** 1 - 10
Product Groups: 30, 32, 46, 48, 84

Date of Accounts	Mar 12	Mar 11	Mar 10
Sales Turnover	313	290	N/A
Pre Tax Profit/Loss	6	-19	N/A
Working Capital	44	26	32
Fixed Assets	35	47	59
Current Assets	102	99	110
Current Liabilities	47	56	N/A

Southern Hydraulic Ram Repairs
Kingsmead Farm Marringdean Road, Billingshurst, RH14 9HE
Tel: 01403-784000 **Fax:** 01403-782703
E-mail: sales@southernhydraulicrams.co.uk
Website: http://www.southernhydraulicrams.co.uk
Immediate Holding Company: SILVESTER ENGINEERING LIMITED
Date established: 1993 **No.of Employees:** 1 - 10 **Product Groups:** 29, 30, 31, 32, 35, 36, 38, 39, 40, 41, 45, 46, 67

Spiring Enterprises Ltd
Unit 8e Gilmans Industrial Estate, Billingshurst, RH14 9EZ
Tel: 01403-784033 **Fax:** 01403-785215
Website: http://www.molymod.com
Directors: P. Spiring (Fin)
Immediate Holding Company: SPIRING ENTERPRISES LIMITED
Registration no: 00904107 **Date established:** 1967
No.of Employees: 1 - 10 **Product Groups:** 64, 65

Date of Accounts	Mar 11	Mar 10	Mar 09
Working Capital	1m	873	1m
Fixed Assets	319	337	360
Current Assets	1m	1m	1m

Stevlite Mouldings Sales Ltd
Unit I Daux Road, Billingshurst, RH14 9SJ
Tel: 01403-784813 **Fax:** 01403-783075
E-mail: info@stevlite.co.uk
Website: http://www.stevlite.co.uk
Directors: K. Stevens (Dir)
Immediate Holding Company: STEVLITE MOULDINGS UK LTD
Registration no: 05574124 **VAT No.:** GB 508 6365 36
Date established: 2005 **Turnover:** Up to £250,000
No.of Employees: 1 - 10 **Product Groups:** 30, 66

Date of Accounts	Nov 06	Nov 05
Working Capital	-290	-209
Fixed Assets	92	124
Current Assets	163	219
Current Liabilities	453	428

Technique Engineering
1 Gilmans Industrial Estate, Billingshurst, RH14 9EZ
Tel: 01403-784678 **Fax:** 01403-784978
E-mail: info@technique-engineering.com
Website: http://www.technique-engineering.com
Directors: M. Divey (Dir)
Immediate Holding Company: TECHNIQUE ENGINEERING LIMITED
Registration no: 02753606 **VAT No.:** GB 620 5713 70
Date established: 1992 **Turnover:** £250,000 - £500,000
No.of Employees: 1 - 10 **Product Groups:** 45, 48, 84

Date of Accounts	Mar 11	Mar 10	Mar 09
Working Capital	31	45	73
Fixed Assets	29	36	44
Current Assets	99	121	142

W T Lamb Holdings Property Services
Nyewood Court Brookers Road, Billingshurst, RH14 9RZ
Tel: 01403-785141 **Fax:** 01403-784663
E-mail: sales@lambsbricks.com
Website: http://www.lambsbricks.com
Managers: L. Frean (Personnel)
Ultimate Holding Company: W.T. LAMB HOLDINGS LIMITED
Immediate Holding Company: W.T. LAMB & SONS LIMITED
Registration no: 01704398 **Date established:** 1983 **Turnover:** £2m - £5m
No.of Employees: 1 - 10 **Product Groups:** 33, 66

Date of Accounts	Dec 11	Dec 10	Dec 09
Sales Turnover	3m	2m	3m
Pre Tax Profit/Loss	-15	-202	110
Working Capital	-102	-103	96
Fixed Assets	395	412	414
Current Assets	743	818	1m
Current Liabilities	589	256	636

Warwick Fraser & Co. Ltd
Spring Gate Guildford Road, Loxwood, Billingshurst, RH14 0QL
Tel: 01403-752469 **Fax:** 01403-752469
E-mail: sales@warwickfraser.co.uk
Website: http://www.warwickfraser.co.uk
Directors: K. Mantell (MD)
Immediate Holding Company: WARWICK FRASER AND COMPANY LIMITED
Registration no: 05498583 **Date established:** 2005
Turnover: Up to £250,000 **No.of Employees:** 1 - 10 **Product Groups:** 22, 26, 30, 32, 33, 35, 36, 37, 40, 44, 45, 52, 66, 67, 80, 84

Date of Accounts	Dec 11	Dec 10	Dec 09
Sales Turnover	N/A	N/A	188
Working Capital	5	10	2
Fixed Assets	44	51	57
Current Assets	22	24	21

Wesbart UK Ltd
Daux Road, Billingshurst, RH14 9YR
Tel: 01403-782738 **Fax:** 01403-784180
E-mail: enquiries@wesbart.co.uk
Website: http://www.wesbart.co.uk
Directors: N. Patey (MD)
Ultimate Holding Company: WESBART LIMITED
Immediate Holding Company: WESBART UK LIMITED
Registration no: 04117105 **VAT No.:** GB 321 8206 90
Date established: 2000 **Turnover:** £500,000 - £1m
No.of Employees: 11 - 20 **Product Groups:** 38, 42, 67

Date of Accounts	Oct 11	Oct 10	Oct 09
Working Capital	921	477	430
Fixed Assets	215	42	56
Current Assets	1m	940	664

Bognor Regis

A P T Glasshouse Services
34 Neville Road, Bognor Regis, PO22 8BJ
Tel: 01243-826737 **Fax:** 01243-826737
Directors: P. Turnill (Prop)
Date established: 1993 **No.of Employees:** 1 - 10 **Product Groups:** 26, 35

Actuated Solutions Ltd
Unit 9 Evans Place, Bognor Regis, PO22 9RY
Tel: 01243-827469 **Fax:** 01243-829418
E-mail: sales@actuated-solutions.co.uk
Website: http://www.actuated-solutions.co.uk
Directors: P. Slaughter (MD)
Immediate Holding Company: ACTUATED SOLUTIONS LIMITED
Registration no: 04649595 **Date established:** 2003
No.of Employees: 1 - 10 **Product Groups:** 38, 39, 40

Date of Accounts	Mar 11	Mar 10	Mar 09
Working Capital	192	132	100
Fixed Assets	5	8	20
Current Assets	644	521	527

Concept Audio Ltd
Unit 20 Elbridge Farm Business Centre Chichester Road, Bognor Regis, PO21 5EF
Tel: 01243-827915 **Fax:** 01243-827195
E-mail: info@conceptaudio.co.uk
Website: http://www.conceptaudio.co.uk
Directors: D. Schurer (Prop)
Immediate Holding Company: CONCEPT AUDIO LIMITED
Registration no: 05653143 **Date established:** 2005
No.of Employees: 1 - 10 **Product Groups:** 37, 52, 67, 83, 84

Date of Accounts	Dec 11	Dec 10	Dec 09
Working Capital	-10	5	-37
Fixed Assets	95	74	58
Current Assets	55	67	51

D A U Components Ltd
70-74 Barnham Road Barnham, Bognor Regis, PO22 0ES
Tel: 01243-553031 **Fax:** 01243-553860
E-mail: admin@dau-components.co.uk
Website: http://www.dau-components.co.uk

see next page

***D A U Components Ltd** - Cont'd*

Directors: P. Harmer (MD)
Immediate Holding Company: DAU COMPONENTS LIMITED
Registration no: 01301508 **Date established:** 1977 **Turnover:** £1m - £2m
No.of Employees: 1 - 10 **Product Groups:** 37, 40

Date of Accounts	Dec 11	Dec 10	Dec 09
Working Capital	366	363	374
Fixed Assets	4	7	7
Current Assets	567	591	531

H & B Sensors Ltd

Odyssey House Durban Road, Bognor Regis, PO22 9RH
Tel: 01243-866866 **Fax:** 01243-869330
E-mail: sales@hbsensors.co.uk
Website: http://www.hbsensors.co.uk
Bank(s): Barclays
Directors: R. Homer (MD), P. Homer (Fin)
Managers: J. Homer (Purch Mgr), A. Homer
Immediate Holding Company: H. & B. SENSORS LIMITED
Registration no: 01448023 **VAT No.:** GB 321 8286 66
Date established: 1979 **Turnover:** £2m - £5m **No.of Employees:** 21 - 50
Product Groups: 38, 40

Date of Accounts	Sep 11	Sep 10	Sep 09
Working Capital	23	-2	42
Fixed Assets	352	399	336
Current Assets	838	867	680

Hilton K E Chartered Structural Engineer

2 Albert Chambers Sudley Road, Bognor Regis, PO21 1EQ
Tel: 01243-865500 **Fax:** 01243-860489
E-mail: k_e_hilton@yahoo.co.uk
Directors: K. Hilton (Prop)
Immediate Holding Company: ALLENBY HOUSE INVESTMENTS LTD
Registration no: 03795646 **Date established:** 1999
No.of Employees: 1 - 10 **Product Groups:** 35

I T L Impex Ltd

Commercial House 19 Station Road, Bognor Regis, PO21 1QD
Tel: 01243-825992 **Fax:** 01243-841734
E-mail: david.mailer1@btinternet.com
Directors: D. Mailer (Develop)
Immediate Holding Company: I T L IMPEX LIMITED
Registration no: 03200603 **VAT No.:** GB 675 5955 54
Date established: 1996 **Turnover:** £2m - £5m **No.of Employees:** 1 - 10
Product Groups: 61

Date of Accounts	Oct 11	Oct 10	Oct 09
Working Capital	-24	10	42
Fixed Assets	N/A	N/A	1
Current Assets	37	71	104

J C Dunn Web Design Solutions

93 Farnhurst Road Barnham, Bognor Regis, PO22 0JW
Tel: 01243-551229
E-mail: enquiries@jcdmedia.co.uk
Website: http://www.jcdunn.co.uk
Directors: C. Dunn (Ptnr), C. Dunn (Prop)
Immediate Holding Company: THE MEDITERRANEAN TOUCH LIMITED
Date established: 2006 **Turnover:** Up to £250,000
No.of Employees: 1 - 10 **Product Groups:** 44, 81

Date of Accounts	Sep 10	Sep 09	Sep 08
Working Capital	-3	-0	-1
Current Liabilities	N/A	1	1

Kedek Ltd

Heath Place, Bognor Regis, PO22 9SL
Tel: 01243-861421 **Fax:** 01243-826108
E-mail: sales@kedek.co.uk
Website: http://www.kedek.co.uk
Directors: K. Tremble (MD), M. Tremble (Fin)
Immediate Holding Company: KEDEK LIMITED
Registration no: 01083461 **VAT No.:** GB 192 8340 47
Date established: 1972 **Turnover:** £500,000 - £1m
No.of Employees: 1 - 10 **Product Groups:** 48, 66

Date of Accounts	Feb 12	Feb 11	Feb 10
Working Capital	816	832	773
Fixed Assets	52	284	301
Current Assets	857	902	824

Lloyd Instruments Ltd

Steyning Way, Bognor Regis, PO22 9ST
Tel: 01243-833370 **Fax:** 01243-833401
E-mail: uk-far.general@ametek.co.uk
Website: http://www.lloyd-instruments.co.uk
Bank(s): Barclays
Directors: K. Sena (Dir), D. Greer (MD)
Managers: T. Rogers (Sales Prom Mgr), A. Jackson (Purch Mgr), J. Hindmarsh (Comptroller)
Immediate Holding Company: Ametek Holdings UK Ltd
Registration no: 02569386 **VAT No.:** GB 568 3389 92
Date established: 1970 **Turnover:** £20m - £50m
No.of Employees: 11 - 20 **Product Groups:** 38, 42, 44, 67

Date of Accounts	Dec 07
Sales Turnover	25101
Pre Tax Profit/Loss	4810
Working Capital	-1511
Fixed Assets	9747
Current Assets	10245
Current Liabilities	11756
Total Share Capital	1100
ROCE% (Return on Capital Employed)	58.4

Orbinox UK Ltd Orbinox Group

Orbinox House 6-7 Clock Park Shripney Road, Bognor Regis, PO22 9NH
Tel: 01243-810240 **Fax:** 08702-407469
E-mail: uk@orbinox.co.uk
Website: http://www.orbinox.co.uk
Directors: S. Penfold (MD)
Immediate Holding Company: ORBINOX (UK) LIMITED
Registration no: 04768955 **Date established:** 2003 **Turnover:** £2m - £5m
No.of Employees: 11 - 20 **Product Groups:** 29, 30, 33, 36, 37, 38, 39, 40, 66, 67

Date of Accounts	Dec 11	Dec 10	Dec 09
Sales Turnover	3m	N/A	N/A
Pre Tax Profit/Loss	190	N/A	N/A
Working Capital	606	447	426
Fixed Assets	103	126	143
Current Assets	2m	1m	987
Current Liabilities	499	N/A	N/A

Osborne Refrigerators Ltd

148 Rose Green Road, Bognor Regis, PO21 3EG
Tel: 01243-267711 **Fax:** 01243-265853
E-mail: sales@osborne-ref.co.uk
Website: http://www.osborne-ref.co.uk
Bank(s): HSBC
Managers: R. Howlett (Sales Prom Mgr)
Immediate Holding Company: OSBORNE REFRIGERATORS LIMITED
Registration no: 00685143 **VAT No.:** 192 9159 25 **Date established:** 1961
Turnover: £1m - £2m **No.of Employees:** 21 - 50 **Product Groups:** 40

Date of Accounts	Oct 11	Oct 10	Oct 09
Sales Turnover	N/A	N/A	2m
Pre Tax Profit/Loss	N/A	N/A	-383
Working Capital	4m	4m	4m
Fixed Assets	2m	2m	2m
Current Assets	4m	4m	5m
Current Liabilities	N/A	N/A	46

Oval Automation Ltd

Pollards Lake Lane, Barnham, Bognor Regis, PO22 0AD
Tel: 01243-555885 **Fax:** 01243-554846
E-mail: paul@oval.org.uk
Website: http://www.oval.org.uk
Directors: P. Wells (Dir), V. Wells (Co Sec)
Immediate Holding Company: OVAL AUTOMATION LIMITED
Registration no: 02897469 **VAT No.:** GB 620 9326 57
Date established: 1994 **Turnover:** Up to £250,000
No.of Employees: 1 - 10 **Product Groups:** 38, 49

Date of Accounts	Mar 12	Mar 11	Mar 10
Working Capital	50	51	49
Fixed Assets	5	5	6
Current Assets	82	76	90

Penfold Metalising Co. Ltd

Barnham Road Barnham, Bognor Regis, PO22 0ES
Tel: 01243-552178 **Fax:** 01243-554472
E-mail: info@penmet.co.uk
Website: http://www.penmet.co.uk
Directors: J. Ruddock (MD)
Immediate Holding Company: PENFOLD METALLISING CO.LIMITED
Registration no: 00536103 **VAT No.:** GB 193 0775 46
Date established: 1954 **Turnover:** £250,000 - £500,000
No.of Employees: 1 - 10 **Product Groups:** 48, 67

Date of Accounts	Dec 11	Dec 10	Dec 09
Working Capital	870	913	1m
Fixed Assets	582	555	553
Current Assets	935	970	1m

Sandhurst Instruments Ltd

30 Sudley Road, Bognor Regis, PO21 1ER
Tel: 01243-820200 **Fax:** 01243-860111
E-mail: info@sandhurstinstruments.co.uk
Website: http://www.sandhurstinstruments.co.uk
Directors: A. Crundwell (Fin), D. Jack (MD)
Immediate Holding Company: SANDHURST INSTRUMENTS LIMITED
Registration no: 03763757 **Date established:** 1999
Turnover: £250,000 - £500,000 **No.of Employees:** 1 - 10
Product Groups: 37, 38

Date of Accounts	Mar 11	Mar 10	Mar 09
Working Capital	35	55	67
Fixed Assets	13	17	23
Current Assets	67	88	95

Schurter Ltd

8 Clock Park Shripney Road, Bognor Regis, PO22 9NH
Tel: 01243-810810 **Fax:** 01243-810800
E-mail: sales@schurter.co.uk
Website: http://www.schurter.co.uk
Managers: T. Mitchell (Mgr)
Immediate Holding Company: SCHURTER LIMITED
Registration no: 00436766 **VAT No.:** GB 651 4444 49 116
Date established: 1947 **Turnover:** £2m - £5m **No.of Employees:** 1 - 10
Product Groups: 37, 38, 44, 67

Date of Accounts	Dec 11	Dec 10	Dec 09
Working Capital	892	926	812
Fixed Assets	13	1	5
Current Assets	1m	2m	2m

Sun X UK Ltd

Unit 5 Durban Road Business Centre Durban Road, Bognor Regis, PO22 9FE
Tel: 01243-826441 **Fax:** 01243-829691
E-mail: sales@sun-x.co.uk
Website: http://www.sun-x.co.uk
Managers: J. Wilson (Sales Prom Mgr)
Immediate Holding Company: SUN X (UK) LIMITED
Registration no: 01382406 **Date established:** 1978
Turnover: £500,000 - £1m **No.of Employees:** 1 - 10 **Product Groups:** 30

Date of Accounts	Apr 11	Apr 10	Apr 09
Working Capital	123	117	129
Fixed Assets	16	20	19
Current Assets	202	188	267

Tam Transformers Ltd

Durban Road, Bognor Regis, PO22 9QT
Tel: 01243-861122 **Fax:** 01243-830870
E-mail: pete@tamtransformers.co.uk
Website: http://www.tamtransformers.co.uk
Directors: J. Martin (Fin)
Managers: P. Martin (Chief Mgr)
Immediate Holding Company: TAM TRANSFORMERS LIMITED
Registration no: 01298062 **VAT No.:** 194 0491 54 **Date established:** 1977
Turnover: £500,000 - £1m **No.of Employees:** 1 - 10 **Product Groups:** 37

Date of Accounts	Feb 12	Feb 11	Feb 10
Working Capital	91	92	78
Fixed Assets	17	17	17
Current Assets	106	105	89

Wessex Metalcraft

Unit 3a Christie Place, Bognor Regis, PO22 9RT
Tel: 01243-829944 **Fax:** 01243-828328
E-mail: info@wessexmetalcraft.co.uk
Website: http://www.wessexmetalcraft.co.uk
Managers: S. Hendry (Mgr)
Date established: 2002 **No.of Employees:** 1 - 10 **Product Groups:** 35

Westside Supplies Ltd

Westside Shripney Road, Bognor Regis, PO22 9NX
Tel: 01243-860626 **Fax:** 01243-866626
E-mail: sales@westside-supplies.co.uk
Website: http://www.westside-supplies.co.uk
Directors: A. Yeates (Ch), G. Yeates (Fin)
Immediate Holding Company: WESTSIDE SUPPLIES LIMITED
Registration no: 02604535 **Date established:** 1991
Turnover: £500,000 - £1m **No.of Employees:** 1 - 10 **Product Groups:** 35, 37, 39, 67, 68

Date of Accounts	Apr 11	Apr 10	Apr 09
Working Capital	655	776	878
Fixed Assets	142	118	121
Current Assets	817	857	907

Burgess Hill

ADA Computer Systems Ltd

Network House Albert Drive, Burgess Hill, RH15 9TN
Tel: 01444-232000 **Fax:** 01444-247754
E-mail: drabson@ada.co.uk
Website: http://www.ada.co.uk
Directors: D. Rabson (Dir), G. Page (Co Sec), L. Ganly (Dir), D. Fordham (Dir)
Ultimate Holding Company: ACORA HOLDINGS LIMITED
Immediate Holding Company: ADA COMPUTER SYSTEMS LIMITED
Registration no: 02348923 **Date established:** 1989
Turnover: £10m - £20m **No.of Employees:** 51 - 100 **Product Groups:** 44, 86

Date of Accounts	Apr 11	Apr 10	Apr 09
Sales Turnover	14m	11m	8m
Pre Tax Profit/Loss	1m	777	523
Working Capital	976	552	170
Fixed Assets	538	377	450
Current Assets	5m	4m	4m
Current Liabilities	3m	2m	2m

Amazing Parties Ltd

277 London Road, Burgess Hill, RH15 9QU
Tel: 01342-712233 **Fax:** 01444-240101
E-mail: steve@amazingpartythemes.com
Website: http://www.amazingpartythemes.com
Directors: S. Hayward (Grp Chief Exec), S. Hayward (MD)
Immediate Holding Company: AMAZING PARTIES LIMITED
Registration no: 04523640 **Date established:** 2002
Turnover: Up to £250,000 **No.of Employees:** 1 - 10 **Product Groups:** 49

Date of Accounts	Sep 10	Sep 09	Sep 08
Working Capital	-10	-9	-12
Fixed Assets	6	9	12
Current Assets	17	12	15

Baty International

Victoria Road, Burgess Hill, RH15 9LR
Tel: 01444-235621 **Fax:** 01444-246985
E-mail: sales@baty.co.uk
Website: http://www.baty.co.uk
Bank(s): HSBC Bank plc
Directors: G. Jackson (MD)
Managers: K. Smith (Sales Prom Mgr), L. Rowland (Comptroller)
Ultimate Holding Company: NEWSHIP PRODUCTS LTD
Immediate Holding Company: NEWSHIP GROUP LTD
Registration no: 00379038 **VAT No.:** GB 190 3712 73
Turnover: £2m - £5m **No.of Employees:** 11 - 20 **Product Groups:** 38, 48

Date of Accounts	Dec 07	Sep 06	Sep 05
Sales Turnover	N/A	N/A	1865
Pre Tax Profit/Loss	N/A	N/A	17
Working Capital	555	480	690
Fixed Assets	56	42	9
Current Assets	1074	968	1125
Current Liabilities	519	488	435
Total Share Capital	1820	1820	1820
ROCE% (Return on Capital Employed)			2.4
ROT% (Return on Turnover)			0.9

Bodle Bros Ltd

Southdown Store Cuckfield Road, Burgess Hill, RH15 8RE
Tel: 01444-247757 **Fax:** 01444-870953
E-mail: shop@bodlebros.co.uk
Website: http://www.bodlebros.co.uk
Directors: M. Sandercock (MD)
Immediate Holding Company: BODLE BROS LIMITED
Registration no: 00430877 **Date established:** 1947 **Turnover:** £5m - £10m
No.of Employees: 11 - 20 **Product Groups:** 02, 07, 20, 23, 30, 41, 62

Date of Accounts	Feb 08	Feb 11	Feb 10
Sales Turnover	6m	7m	6m
Pre Tax Profit/Loss	103	71	22
Working Capital	-53	3	-53
Fixed Assets	509	569	552
Current Assets	759	912	657
Current Liabilities	46	23	24

Custom Technology Ltd

Unit C Kendal House, Victoria Way, Burgess Hill, RH15 9NF
Tel: 01273-358881 **Fax:** 01273-358096
E-mail: sales@customtechnology.co.uk
Website: http://www.customtechnology.co.uk
Directors: G. Geeson (MD), T. Collett (MD)
Managers: H. Cribbes (Sales Prom Mgr)
Registration no: 01615464 **VAT No.:** GB 351 2429 79
Turnover: £500,000 - £1m **No.of Employees:** 1 - 10 **Product Groups:** 37, 38, 44

Date of Accounts	Apr 08	Apr 07	Apr 06
Working Capital	142	54	67
Fixed Assets	23	11	6
Current Assets	370	122	120
Current Liabilities	228	68	53
Total Share Capital	33	33	33

Dansk Technik

Unit 8 Sheddingdean Business Centre Marchants Way, Burgess Hill, RH15 8QY
Tel: 01444-247020 **Fax:** 01444-247121
Website: http://www.heatmat.co.uk
No.of Employees: 11 - 20 **Product Groups:** 37, 40, 48

Dorton Asbestos Removal Services Ltd

2 Albert Drive, Burgess Hill, RH15 9TN
Tel: 01444-253333 **Fax:** 01444-253344
E-mail: info@dortongroup.com
Website: http://www.dortongroup.com
Directors: K. Harvey (MD)
Immediate Holding Company: DORTON ASBESTOS REMOVAL SERVICES LIMITED
Registration no: 04205167 **Date established:** 2001 **Turnover:** £2m - £5m
No.of Employees: 21 - 50 **Product Groups:** 32, 45, 51, 54, 84, 86

Date of Accounts	Apr 11	Apr 10	Apr 09
Working Capital	27	1	60
Fixed Assets	7	8	5
Current Assets	58	115	96

E A O Ltd

Albert Drive, Burgess Hill, RH15 9TN
Tel: 01444-236000 **Fax:** 01444-236641
E-mail: susan.jacques@eao.com
Website: http://www.eao.co.uk
Bank(s): The Royal Bank of Scotland
Directors: S. Jacques (Dir), B. Hills (Fin)
Managers: R. Davies (Mktg Serv Mgr)
Ultimate Holding Company: LOOSLI HOLDING AG (SWITZERLAND)
Immediate Holding Company: EAO LIMITED
Registration no: 00745121 **VAT No.:** GB 268 5905 17
Date established: 1962 **Turnover:** £5m - £10m **No.of Employees:** 21 - 50
Product Groups: 37

Date of Accounts	Dec 11	Dec 10	Dec 09
Sales Turnover	8m	7m	6m
Pre Tax Profit/Loss	327	-48	-261
Working Capital	1m	896	951
Fixed Assets	341	344	307
Current Assets	3m	3m	2m
Current Liabilities	345	309	200

Elite DS Ltd

30 West Street, Burgess Hill, RH15 8NX
Tel: 01444-245145 **Fax:** 01444-245145
Directors: E. Sillett (Dir)
Immediate Holding Company: ELITE DS LIMITED
Registration no: 03787708 **Date established:** 1999
No.of Employees: 21 - 50 **Product Groups:** 38, 67, 88

Date of Accounts	Jun 11	Jun 09	Jun 08
Sales Turnover	1m	N/A	824
Pre Tax Profit/Loss	104	N/A	214
Working Capital	193	57	80
Fixed Assets	133	196	206
Current Assets	277	161	206
Current Liabilities	73	N/A	71

Filter Screen Supply Ltd (Head Office)

2 Paynes Place Farm Cuckfield Road, Burgess Hill, RH15 8RG
Tel: 01444-244406 **Fax:** 01444-230303
E-mail: sales@filterscreensupply.co.uk
Website: http://www.filterscreensupply.co.uk
Directors: R. Sanders (Prop), L. Sanders (Dir)
Immediate Holding Company: FILTER SCREEN SUPPLY LIMITED
Registration no: 02127786 **Date established:** 1987
Turnover: Up to £250,000 **No.of Employees:** 1 - 10 **Product Groups:** 30, 35, 42

Date of Accounts	Apr 12	Apr 11	Apr 10
Sales Turnover	N/A	N/A	239
Pre Tax Profit/Loss	N/A	N/A	20
Working Capital	16	-2	3
Fixed Assets	2	2	N/A
Current Assets	91	58	84
Current Liabilities	N/A	N/A	19

Freeway Tools & Fixings

14 Victoria Way, Burgess Hill, RH15 9NF
Tel: 01444-873000 **Fax:** 01444-873001
E-mail: admin@freewayfixings.com
Website: http://www.freewayfixings.com
Directors: T. Railton (Ptnr)
VAT No.: GB 192 0248 75 **Turnover:** £250,000 - £500,000
No.of Employees: 1 - 10 **Product Groups:** 35, 37

G D Rectifiers Ltd

Victoria Gardens, Burgess Hill, RH15 9NB
Tel: 01444-243452 **Fax:** 01444-870722
E-mail: enquiries@gdrectifiers.co.uk
Website: http://www.gdrectifiers.co.uk
Directors: G. Smith (Dir)
Immediate Holding Company: G.D. RECTIFIERS LIMITED
Registration no: 00828555 **VAT No.:** GB 190 2951 60
Date established: 1964 **Turnover:** £1m - £2m **No.of Employees:** 1 - 10
Product Groups: 37, 40, 46, 67

Date of Accounts	Dec 11	Dec 10	Dec 09
Working Capital	315	181	123
Fixed Assets	27	20	22
Current Assets	761	644	489

H C D Research Ltd

179 Junction Road, Burgess Hill, RH15 0JW
Tel: 01444-232967 **Fax:** 01444-241901
E-mail: info@hcdresearch.co.uk
Website: http://www.hcdresearch.co.uk
Bank(s): Lloyds TSB Bank plc
Directors: P. Davenport (MD)
Immediate Holding Company: H.C.D.RESEARCH LIMITED
Registration no: 00708818 **VAT No.:** GB 190 1166 84
Date established: 1961 **Turnover:** £500,000 - £1m
No.of Employees: 11 - 20 **Product Groups:** 37

Date of Accounts	Mar 11	Mar 10	Mar 09
Working Capital	265	253	240
Fixed Assets	176	188	200
Current Assets	389	351	345

HEIDENHAIN GB LTD

200 London Road, Burgess Hill, RH15 9RD
Tel: 01444-247711 **Fax:** 01444-870024
E-mail: sales@heidenhain.co.uk
Website: http://www.heidenhain.co.uk
Bank(s): National Westminster Bank plc
Directors: M. Laming (Fin), N. Prescott (MD)
Managers: P. Lodge (Sales Prom Mgr), D. Linscer (Serv Mgr)
Immediate Holding Company: HEIDENHAIN(G.B.)LIMITED
Registration no: 00949353 **Date established:** 1969 **Turnover:** £5m - £10m
No.of Employees: 21 - 50 **Product Groups:** 37, 38, 46, 67, 86

Date of Accounts	Dec 11	Dec 10	Dec 09
Sales Turnover	N/A	N/A	5m
Pre Tax Profit/Loss	N/A	N/A	-379
Working Capital	3m	4m	4m
Fixed Assets	621	610	636
Current Assets	5m	6m	4m
Current Liabilities	N/A	N/A	329

Ingenia Solutions Ltd

Braybon Business Park Consort Way, Burgess Hill, RH15 9ND
Tel: 01444-246787 **Fax:** 01444-876929
E-mail: steve@ingeniasolutions.co.uk
Website: http://www.ingeniasolutions.co.uk
Directors: S. Smith (MD)
Immediate Holding Company: INGENIA SOLUTIONS LIMITED
Registration no: 04335740 **Date established:** 2001
Turnover: £500,000 - £1m **No.of Employees:** 11 - 20
Product Groups: 41, 45

Date of Accounts	Jul 11	Jul 10	Jul 09
Working Capital	50	81	-20
Fixed Assets	23	33	23
Current Assets	182	206	114

IT First Ltd

273 London Road, Burgess Hill, RH15 9QU
Tel: 0870-0339506 **Fax:** 01444-247800
E-mail: sales@itfirst.co.uk
Website: http://www.itfirst.co.uk
Managers: S. Gregg (Ops Mgr), J. Dean (Sales Prom)
Registration no: 03222864 **Turnover:** £1m - £2m
No.of Employees: 11 - 20 **Product Groups:** 44

Keymer Tiles Ltd

Nye Road, Burgess Hill, RH15 0LZ
Tel: 01444-232931 **Fax:** 01444-871852
E-mail: info@keymer.co.uk
Website: http://www.keymer.co.uk
Directors: C. Tobin (Dir), G. Norris (Co Sec)
Immediate Holding Company: KEYMER TILES LIMITED
Registration no: 00792690 **Date established:** 1964 **Turnover:** £2m - £5m
No.of Employees: 51 - 100 **Product Groups:** 33

Date of Accounts	Dec 11	Dec 10	Dec 09
Sales Turnover	4m	3m	3m
Pre Tax Profit/Loss	-52	-40	-218
Working Capital	2m	2m	2m
Fixed Assets	3m	3m	3m
Current Assets	3m	3m	2m
Current Liabilities	863	815	867

Knowles Acoustics

York Road, Burgess Hill, RH15 9TT
Tel: 01444-235432 **Fax:** 01444-248724
E-mail: europeinfo@knowles.com
Website: http://www.knowles.com
Managers: Y. O'Brien (Mktg Serv Mgr), N. Harthan (Sales Prom Mgr)
Ultimate Holding Company: Knowles Electronics Inc.
Date established: 1946 **No.of Employees:** 11 - 20 **Product Groups:** 37, 38

Lock Assist

139 Royal George Road, Burgess Hill, RH15 9TD
Tel: 01444-244344 **Fax:** 01444-241324
E-mail: paul@lockassist.co.uk
Website: http://www.lockassist.co.uk
Directors: P. Harper-Smith (Prop)
No.of Employees: 1 - 10 **Product Groups:** 35, 36, 52

M & W Engineering Supplies

Unit 4 Regent Business Centre Jubilee Road, Burgess Hill, RH15 9TL
Tel: 01444-244146 **Fax:** 01444-236041
E-mail: mandweng@tiscali.co.uk
Website: http://www.mweng.co.uk
Directors: R. Payne (Prop)
Date established: 1975 **No.of Employees:** 1 - 10 **Product Groups:** 35

Magnetrol International UK Ltd

1 Regent Business Centre Jubilee Road, Burgess Hill, RH15 9TL
Tel: 01444-871313 **Fax:** 01444-871317
E-mail: sales@magnetrol.co.uk
Website: http://www.magnetrol.co.uk
Directors: M. Saranczak (Fin)
Managers: R. Jeynes
Ultimate Holding Company: MAGNETROL INTERNATIONAL INC (USA)
Immediate Holding Company: MAGNETROL INTERNATIONAL U.K. LIMITED
Registration no: 02385928 **Date established:** 1989 **Turnover:** £2m - £5m
No.of Employees: 1 - 10 **Product Groups:** 38

Date of Accounts	Dec 11	Dec 10	Dec 09
Sales Turnover	2m	2m	3m
Pre Tax Profit/Loss	22	-19	-62
Working Capital	440	406	464
Fixed Assets	136	150	112
Current Assets	1m	785	2m
Current Liabilities	251	135	266

Mail International Ltd

Unit 6 Braybon Business Park Consort Way, Burgess Hill, RH15 9ND
Tel: 01444-871111 **Fax:** 01444-248997
E-mail: gavin@mailint.com
Website: http://www.mailint.com
Bank(s): Lloyds TSB
Directors: R. Owens (Dir)
Immediate Holding Company: MAIL INTERNATIONAL LIMITED
Registration no: 01923564 **VAT No.:** GB 435 9189 20
Date established: 1985 **Turnover:** £5m - £10m **No.of Employees:** 21 - 50
Product Groups: 80, 81

Date of Accounts	Sep 11	Sep 10	Sep 09
Sales Turnover	6m	6m	4m
Pre Tax Profit/Loss	112	127	91
Working Capital	266	137	104
Fixed Assets	349	409	348
Current Assets	1m	1m	981
Current Liabilities	164	293	377

Mexmast Ltd

2 Jubilee Road Victoria Industrial Estate, Burgess Hill, RH15 9TL
Tel: 01444-247197 **Fax:** 01444-246431
E-mail: sales@mexmast.co.uk
Website: http://www.mexmast.co.uk
Directors: D. Baldwin (Chief Op Offcr), B. Kelly (Co Sec)
Immediate Holding Company: MEXMAST LIMITED
Registration no: 02630882 **Date established:** 1991
No.of Employees: 21 - 50 **Product Groups:** 35, 39, 45

Date of Accounts	Dec 11	Dec 10	Dec 09
Working Capital	278	208	136
Fixed Assets	782	640	669
Current Assets	991	658	565

Plasson UK Ltd

Plasson House 27 Albert Drive, Burgess Hill, RH15 9TW
Tel: 01444-244446 **Fax:** 01444-258683
E-mail: sales@plasson.co.uk
Website: http://www.plasson.co.uk
Managers: D. Fisher (Tech Serv Mgr), M. Givon (Mgr), S. Merckel (Sales & Mktg Mg), A. Stafford
Ultimate Holding Company: PLASSON INDUSTRIES LTD (ISRAEL)
Immediate Holding Company: PLASSON U.K. LTD
Registration no: 05835266 **VAT No.:** GB 511 0059 11
Date established: 2006 **Turnover:** £5m - £10m **No.of Employees:** 11 - 20
Product Groups: 30, 36, 37, 38

Date of Accounts	Dec 11	Dec 10	Dec 09
Sales Turnover	2m	N/A	N/A
Pre Tax Profit/Loss	127	-27	-12
Working Capital	124	-2m	-213
Fixed Assets	2m	17m	15m
Current Assets	1m	4m	3m
Current Liabilities	953	6	5

The Print House Group Ltd

8 Albert Drive, Burgess Hill, RH15 9TN
Tel: 01444-871776 **Fax:** 01444-871731
E-mail: info@printhousegroup.com
Website: http://www.printhousegroup.com
Directors: J. Lewis (Dir)
Immediate Holding Company: THE PRINT HOUSE GROUP LIMITED
Registration no: 02934103 **VAT No.:** GB 620 9709 41
Date established: 1994 **Turnover:** £250,000 - £500,000
No.of Employees: 1 - 10 **Product Groups:** 22, 24, 27, 49

Date of Accounts	Jun 11	Jun 10	Jun 09
Sales Turnover	494	N/A	510
Pre Tax Profit/Loss	12	N/A	-44
Working Capital	-25	-53	-62
Fixed Assets	81	97	121
Current Assets	138	148	143
Current Liabilities	39	N/A	32

Quadrant Systems Ltd

Victoria Gardens, Burgess Hill, RH15 9NB
Tel: 01444-246226 **Fax:** 01444-870172
E-mail: info@quadrant-systems.co.uk
Website: http://www.quadrant-systems.co.uk
Bank(s): Barclays
Directors: L. Richards (Co Sec)
Managers: P. Masters (Mktg Serv Mgr), L. Glennie (Personnel)
Ultimate Holding Company: QUADRANT GROUP LIMITED
Immediate Holding Company: QUADRANT SYSTEMS LIMITED
Registration no: 02928987 **Date established:** 1994 **Turnover:** £5m - £10m
No.of Employees: 21 - 50 **Product Groups:** 28, 44, 86

Date of Accounts	May 12	May 11	May 10
Sales Turnover	8m	5m	4m
Pre Tax Profit/Loss	849	-376	-545
Working Capital	-1m	-2m	-2m
Fixed Assets	412	470	363
Current Assets	2m	1m	1m
Current Liabilities	2m	3m	1m

Ringdale UK Ltd

26 Victoria Way, Burgess Hill, RH15 9NF
Tel: 01444-871349 **Fax:** 01444-870228
E-mail: info@ringdale.com
Website: http://www.ringdale.com
Bank(s): Lloyds
Directors: H. Schlieker Bollmann (MD)
Ultimate Holding Company: NETWORK TECHNOLOGY PLC
Immediate Holding Company: RINGDALE UK LIMITED
Registration no: 02877306 **VAT No.:** GB 620 8269 48
Date established: 1993 **Turnover:** £2m - £5m **No.of Employees:** 11 - 20
Product Groups: 44

Date of Accounts	Mar 11	Mar 10	Mar 09
Sales Turnover	2m	2m	1m
Pre Tax Profit/Loss	414	-65	-3
Working Capital	1m	599	556
Fixed Assets	88	141	186
Current Assets	2m	1m	958
Current Liabilities	523	530	310

Roche Diagnostics Ltd

Charles Avenue, Burgess Hill, RH15 9RY
Tel: 01444-256000 **Fax:** 01993-892241
E-mail: burgesshill@roche.com
Website: http://www.roche.com
Bank(s): National Westminster
Directors: R. Daniel (Co Sec), J. Van Den Boer (MD)
Ultimate Holding Company: ROCHE HOLDING AG (SWITZERLAND)
Immediate Holding Company: ROCHE DIAGNOSTICS LIMITED
Registration no: 00571546 **Date established:** 1956
Turnover: £125m - £250m **No.of Employees:** 251 - 500
Product Groups: 37

Date of Accounts	Dec 11	Dec 10	Dec 09
Sales Turnover	245m	226m	203m
Pre Tax Profit/Loss	9m	4m	1m
Working Capital	6m	12m	19m
Fixed Assets	79m	67m	58m
Current Assets	64m	54m	51m
Current Liabilities	24m	38m	20m

Seos Displays Ltd

Unit 1 Maltings Park Edward Way, Burgess Hill, RH15 9UE
Tel: 01444-870888 **Fax:** 01444-870777
E-mail: sales@seos.com
Website: http://www.seos.com
Directors: I. Boyle (Dir), J. Middleton (Co Sec)
Immediate Holding Company: SEOS GROUP LTD
Registration no: 04352543 **VAT No.:** GB 699 1959 52
Date established: 2002 **Turnover:** £20m - £50m **No.of Employees:** 1 - 10
Product Groups: 39, 44, 48

Date of Accounts	Jun 08	Jun 07	Jun 06
Sales Turnover	15111	20024	22865
Pre Tax Profit/Loss	-1676	425	466

see next page

***Seos Displays Ltd** - Cont'd*

Working Capital	-1651	579	1270
Fixed Assets	3412	2444	990
Current Assets	12530	10492	9742
Current Liabilities	14181	9913	8473
Total Share Capital	302	302	302
ROCE% (Return on Capital Employed)	-95.1	14.1	20.6
ROT% (Return on Turnover)	-11.1	2.1	2.0

Technetix Networks

Technetix Communications House, Burgess Hill, RH15 9TZ
Tel: 01444-251200 **Fax:** 01444-258555
E-mail: sales@technetix.com
Website: http://www.technetix.com
Bank(s): TSB, Cambridge
Directors: S. Anderson (Tech Serv)
Managers: J. Murray (Ops Mgr), P. Broadhurst, G. Langford (Mats Contrlr), A. Chater (Comptroller), S. Lloyd (Personnel), A. Unsworth (Mktg Serv Mgr)
Ultimate Holding Company: TECHNETIX GROUP LIMITED
Immediate Holding Company: TECHNETIX GROUP LIMITED
Registration no: 05303822 **VAT No.:** GB 538 4723 25
Date established: 2004 **Turnover:** £50m - £75m
No.of Employees: 51 - 100 **Product Groups:** 37, 67

Date of Accounts	Dec 11	Dec 10	Dec 09
Sales Turnover	65m	60m	60m
Pre Tax Profit/Loss	5m	5m	4m
Working Capital	6m	3m	2m
Fixed Assets	14m	13m	14m
Current Assets	27m	20m	20m
Current Liabilities	4m	8m	10m

Tideland Signal Ltd

Unit B Kendal House Victoria Way, Burgess Hill, RH15 9NF
Tel: 01444-872240 **Fax:** 01444-872241
E-mail: sales@tidelandsignal.ltd.uk
Website: http://www.tidelandsignal.com
Directors: P. Burford (MD)
Ultimate Holding Company: TIDELAND SIGNAL CORP (USA)
Immediate Holding Company: TIDELAND SIGNAL LIMITED
Registration no: 01204143 **Date established:** 1975 **Turnover:** £2m - £5m
No.of Employees: 1 - 10 **Product Groups:** 37, 39, 40, 67

Date of Accounts	Sep 11	Sep 10	Sep 09
Sales Turnover	7m	6m	N/A
Pre Tax Profit/Loss	649	441	N/A
Working Capital	3m	2m	2m
Fixed Assets	532	528	520
Current Assets	6m	5m	4m
Current Liabilities	733	665	N/A

Time 24 Ltd

Robimatic House 19 Victoria Gardens, Burgess Hill, RH15 9NB
Tel: 01444-257655 **Fax:** 01444-259000
E-mail: sales@time24.co.uk
Website: http://www.time24.com
Directors: M. Willifer (Jt MD), D. Shore (Dir)
Managers: K. Taylor (Fin Mgr), T. White (I.T. Exec), N. Osullivan (Chief Buyer), C. Cytowicz (Tech Serv Mgr), C. Young (Sales & Mktg Mg), B. Dumbleton (Mktg Serv Mgr), C. Collins (Personnel), N. O'Sullivan (Purch Mgr)
Immediate Holding Company: TIME 24 HOLDINGS LIMITED
Registration no: 07597284 **Date established:** 2011
No.of Employees: 51 - 100 **Product Groups:** 35

Tricodent Ltd

Unit 8a Teknol House Victoria Road, Burgess Hill, RH15 9LH
Tel: 01444-247752 **Fax:** 01444-239800
E-mail: info@tricodent.com
Website: http://www.tricodent.com
Directors: R. Noakes (MD), C. Noakes (Fin)
Immediate Holding Company: TRICODENT LIMITED
Registration no: 01684089 **VAT No.:** 168 4089 **Date established:** 1982
Turnover: £250,000 - £500,000 **No.of Employees:** 1 - 10
Product Groups: 67

Date of Accounts	Apr 11	Apr 10	Apr 09
Working Capital	91	125	133
Fixed Assets	189	194	198
Current Assets	297	316	315

Vega Controls UK Ltd

Kendal House Victoria Way, Burgess Hill, RH15 9NF
Tel: 01444-870055 **Fax:** 01444-870080
E-mail: info.uk@vega.com
Website: http://www.vegacontrols.co.uk
Bank(s): Lloyds TSB Bank plc
Directors: K. Griffiths (Fin), R. Tregale (MD)
Managers: D. Anderson (Mktg Serv Mgr)
Ultimate Holding Company: GRIESHABER VERWALTUNGS GMBH (GERMANY)
Immediate Holding Company: VEGA CONTROLS LIMITED
Registration no: 01630396 **Date established:** 1982 **Turnover:** £5m - £10m
No.of Employees: 11 - 20 **Product Groups:** 37, 38, 42, 45

Date of Accounts	Dec 11	Dec 10	Dec 09
Sales Turnover	7m	7m	6m
Pre Tax Profit/Loss	68	395	23
Working Capital	3m	3m	3m
Fixed Assets	65	107	139
Current Assets	4m	4m	3m
Current Liabilities	570	620	313

Westcon Group European Operations Ltd

1 Clayton Manor Victoria Gardens, Burgess Hill, RH15 9NB
Tel: 01444-230004 **Fax:** 01444-243889
E-mail: tim.brooks@westcon.com
Website: http://www.westcongroup.com
Bank(s): Bank of Scotland
Managers: I. Macrae (Chief Mgr)
Ultimate Holding Company: DATATEC LTD (BRITISH VIRGIN ISLANDS)
Immediate Holding Company: CRANE TELECOMMUNICATIONS LIMITED
Registration no: 03692313 **Date established:** 1998 **Turnover:** £1m - £2m
No.of Employees: 21 - 50 **Product Groups:** 37, 52

Date of Accounts	Feb 12	Feb 11	Feb 09
Pre Tax Profit/Loss	N/A	N/A	24m

Chichester

Aikona Ltd

Chandler Road Terminus Road Industrial Estate, Chichester, PO19 8UE
Tel: 01243-771790 **Fax:** 01243-532226
E-mail: info@aikona.co.uk
Website: http://www.aikona.co.uk/
Directors: D. Harford (Dir)
Ultimate Holding Company: D.W. PLASTICS LIMITED
Immediate Holding Company: AIKONA LIMITED
Registration no: 04807473 **Date established:** 2003
Turnover: £250,000 - £500,000 **No.of Employees:** 1 - 10
Product Groups: 49

Date of Accounts	Dec 08	Dec 07	Dec 06
Working Capital	38	92	38
Fixed Assets	N/A	1	1
Current Assets	93	131	76

E Allman & Co. Ltd

Allman Business Park Birdham Road, Chichester, PO20 7BT
Tel: 01243-512511 **Fax:** 01243-511171
E-mail: bruce@allman-sprayers.co.uk
Website: http://www.allman-sprayers.co.uk
Bank(s): Barclays
Directors: B. Allman (Dir)
Ultimate Holding Company: BEA HOLDINGS LIMITED
Immediate Holding Company: E ALLMAN & CO. LIMITED
Registration no: 03353571 **VAT No.:** 737 0923 27 **Date established:** 1997
Turnover: £1m - £2m **No.of Employees:** 11 - 20 **Product Groups:** 24, 41

Date of Accounts	Sep 11	Sep 10	Sep 09
Working Capital	180	196	210
Fixed Assets	7	8	14
Current Assets	271	363	369

Arun Sails Ltd

Unit 6 The Sail Centre Southfields Industrial Park Delling Lane, Bosham, Chichester, PO18 8NW
Tel: 01243-573185 **Fax:** 01243-573032
E-mail: info@sailmakers.com
Website: http://www.sailmakers.com
Directors: I. Bole (MD)
Ultimate Holding Company: COASTAL COVERS LIMITED
Immediate Holding Company: ARUN SAILS LIMITED
Registration no: 01160094 **VAT No.:** GB 397 6476 83
Date established: 1974 **Turnover:** Up to £250,000
No.of Employees: 1 - 10 **Product Groups:** 24

Date of Accounts	Dec 11	Dec 10	Dec 07
Working Capital	-53	-18	-6
Fixed Assets	9	14	22
Current Assets	125	160	174

B X Plant Ltd

11 Dukes Court Bognor Road, Chichester, PO19 8FX
Tel: 01243-781970 **Fax:** 01243-533547
E-mail: rhodge@bxplant.com
Website: http://www.bxplant.com
Directors: R. Hodge (Dir)
Immediate Holding Company: BX PLANT LIMITED
Registration no: 03797166 **Date established:** 1999
Turnover: Up to £250,000 **No.of Employees:** 1 - 10 **Product Groups:** 45

Date of Accounts	Aug 11	Aug 10	Aug 09
Sales Turnover	N/A	99	N/A
Pre Tax Profit/Loss	N/A	9	N/A
Working Capital	-3	-6	1
Fixed Assets	1	N/A	1
Current Assets	73	45	18
Current Liabilities	N/A	10	N/A

Bartholomews Specialist Distribution Ltd

Bognor Road, Chichester, PO19 7TT
Tel: 01243-539224 **Fax:** 01243-536341
E-mail: bsd@bartholomews.co.uk
Website: http://www.bsdonline.co.uk
Bank(s): Lloyds TSB Bank plc
Directors: B. Smith (Dir), R. Bartholomew (Dir)
Ultimate Holding Company: BARTHOLOMEWS (HOLDINGS) LIMITED
Immediate Holding Company: BARTHOLOMEWS SPECIALIST DISTRIBUTION LIMITED
Registration no: 01388275 **Date established:** 1978 **Turnover:** £2m - £5m
No.of Employees: 21 - 50 **Product Groups:** 20, 42, 66

Date of Accounts	Dec 11	Dec 10	Dec 09
Sales Turnover	3m	3m	3m
Pre Tax Profit/Loss	32	46	19
Working Capital	157	125	49
Fixed Assets	359	393	460
Current Assets	813	854	579
Current Liabilities	99	167	144

Block Products Ltd

Pals Haven Hook Lane Aldingbourne, Chichester, PO20 3TE
Tel: 01243-545465 **Fax:** 01243-545475
E-mail: millerbrian@btconnect.com
Website: http://www.blockerproducts.co.uk
Directors: B. Miller (Dir)
Registration no: 06645118 **Turnover:** Up to £250,000
No.of Employees: 1 - 10 **Product Groups:** 32, 38, 40, 66, 67

Brewer Metalcraft Ltd

Thicket Lane Halnaker, Chichester, PO18 0QS
Tel: 01243-539639 **Fax:** 01243-533184
E-mail: sales@brewer-cowl.com
Website: http://www.brewercowls.co.uk
Directors: J. Goble (Fin), S. Hodgson (Dir)
Immediate Holding Company: BREWER METALCRAFT LIMITED
Registration no: 02932358 **VAT No.:** GB 615 3285 52
Date established: 1994 **Turnover:** £1m - £2m **No.of Employees:** 1 - 10
Product Groups: 35

Date of Accounts	Mar 11	Mar 10	Mar 09
Sales Turnover	N/A	N/A	1m
Pre Tax Profit/Loss	N/A	N/A	104
Working Capital	140	118	93
Fixed Assets	126	194	250
Current Assets	307	318	292
Current Liabilities	N/A	N/A	136

John Brown Architecture Ltd

The Bricks Manor Farm Barns, Donnington, Chichester, PO20 7PL
Tel: 01243-785342 **Fax:** 01243-789461
E-mail: admin@jbarch.co.uk
Website: http://www.johnbrownarchitecture.com
Directors: J. Brown (Prop)
Immediate Holding Company: JOHN BROWN ARCHITECTURE LIMITED
Registration no: 03836310 **Date established:** 1999
No.of Employees: 1 - 10 **Product Groups:** 84

Date of Accounts	Dec 11	Dec 10	Dec 09
Working Capital	-4	-28	-71
Fixed Assets	8	9	5
Current Assets	41	31	19

C T Products

49 Russell Road West Wittering, Chichester, PO20 8EF
Tel: 01243-673341 **Fax:** 01243-673341
E-mail: jasonspalmer@tiscali.co.uk
Website: http://www.ctpfusiblelinks.co.uk
Directors: J. Palmer (Prop)
No.of Employees: 1 - 10 **Product Groups:** 37

Cambridge Glass House Co. Ltd

27 Manor Road Selsey, Chichester, PO20 0SB
Tel: 01243-607617 **Fax:** 01243-606415
Directors: S. Hinch (Fin)
Ultimate Holding Company: HORNDEAN LTD
Immediate Holding Company: CAMBRIDGE GLASSHOUSE COMPANY LIMITED
Registration no: 04266884 **Date established:** 2001
Turnover: £10m - £20m **No.of Employees:** 21 - 50 **Product Groups:** 26, 35

Date of Accounts	Mar 11	Mar 10	Mar 09
Sales Turnover	12m	8m	N/A
Pre Tax Profit/Loss	411	324	113
Working Capital	1m	1m	1m
Fixed Assets	53	71	79
Current Assets	4m	4m	4m
Current Liabilities	1m	1m	1m

The Carphone Warehouse Ltd

1 North Street, Chichester, PO19 1LB
Tel: 08701-421081 **Fax:** 01243-788792
Website: http://www.carphonewarehouse.com
Managers: R. Oakes (District Mgr)
Ultimate Holding Company: BEST BUY CO INC (USA)
Immediate Holding Company: THE CARPHONE WAREHOUSE LIMITED
Registration no: 02142673 **Date established:** 1987
Turnover: Over £1,000m **No.of Employees:** 1 - 10 **Product Groups:** 37, 48

Date of Accounts	Mar 08	Apr 09	Apr 10
Sales Turnover	1440m	1643m	1583m
Pre Tax Profit/Loss	17m	-43m	62m
Working Capital	201m	260m	501m
Fixed Assets	283m	150m	253m
Current Assets	643m	859m	1041m
Current Liabilities	156m	141m	166m

Cathedral Signs

15 Florence Road, Chichester, PO19 7TB
Tel: 01243-788879
E-mail: info@cathedralsigns.co.uk
Website: http://www.cathedralsigns.co.uk
Directors: G. Jenkins (Fin), S. Batty (Dir)
Immediate Holding Company: CATHEDRAL SIGNS LIMITED
Registration no: 05693899 **Date established:** 2006
Turnover: Up to £250,000 **No.of Employees:** 1 - 10 **Product Groups:** 30, 49, 80

Date of Accounts	Feb 08	Feb 11	Feb 10
Sales Turnover	119	185	147
Pre Tax Profit/Loss	43	72	48
Working Capital	7	3	9
Fixed Assets	24	17	16
Current Assets	24	35	34
Current Liabilities	14	18	15

Cathedral Works Organisation Ltd

Terminus Road, Chichester, PO19 8TX
Tel: 01243-784225 **Fax:** 01243-813700
E-mail: info@cwo.uk.com
Website: http://www.cwo.uk.com
Bank(s): Barclays
Directors: B. Burnes (MD), G. Hooper (Fin), B. Burns (MD)
Managers: G. Raymond, S. Langton, C. Dent (Develop Mgr)
Ultimate Holding Company: CWO HOLDINGS LIMITED
Immediate Holding Company: CATHEDRAL WORKS ORGANISATION (CHICHESTER) LIMITED
Registration no: 01991966 **VAT No.:** GB 193 4435 50
Date established: 1986 **Turnover:** £5m - £10m **No.of Employees:** 21 - 50
Product Groups: 33, 52

Date of Accounts	Mar 11	Mar 10	Mar 09
Sales Turnover	9m	8m	N/A
Pre Tax Profit/Loss	-211	220	896
Working Capital	653	515	540
Fixed Assets	548	516	324
Current Assets	3m	3m	3m
Current Liabilities	496	1m	2m

Cega Group Services Ltd

Cheesemans Lane Hambrook, Chichester, PO18 8UE
Tel: 01243-621001 **Fax:** 01243-773169
E-mail: info@cega-aviation.co.uk
Website: http://www.cegagroup.com
Managers: G. Ponsford
Ultimate Holding Company: CEGA HOLDINGS LIMITED
Immediate Holding Company: CEGA GROUP SERVICES LIMITED
Registration no: 01303318 **Date established:** 1977
Turnover: £20m - £50m **No.of Employees:** 51 - 100 **Product Groups:** 75

Date of Accounts	Dec 11	Dec 10	Dec 09
Sales Turnover	23m	22m	21m
Pre Tax Profit/Loss	449	1m	1m
Working Capital	4m	4m	3m
Fixed Assets	2m	1m	1m
Current Assets	8m	7m	6m
Current Liabilities	3m	2m	2m

Chichester Canvas (a Pridewatch Events Company)

Pridewatch Events Group Chichester Road, Sidlesham Common, Chichester, PO20 7PY
Tel: 01243-641164 **Fax:** 01243-641888
E-mail: info@chicanvas.co.uk
Website: http://www.chicanvas.co.uk
Managers: T. Bottrill (Mgr)
Immediate Holding Company: PRIDEWATCH EVENTS LTD
Registration no: 04126013 **VAT No.:** GB 192 6761 33
Date established: 2000 **Turnover:** £1m - £2m **No.of Employees:** 21 - 50
Product Groups: 24, 83

Date of Accounts	Dec 11	Dec 10	Dec 09
Sales Turnover	N/A	1m	1m
Pre Tax Profit/Loss	N/A	225	157
Working Capital	-102	-103	-81
Fixed Assets	2m	2m	2m
Current Assets	154	209	206
Current Liabilities	15	74	117

City Motor Holdings

Quarry Lane, Chichester, PO19 8NX
Tel: 01243-532424 **Fax:** 01243-531329
E-mail: nick.crabtree@cmgrp.co.uk
Website: http://www.citymotorholdings.com
Bank(s): National Westminster
Managers: G. Simpson
Registration no: 02216072 **VAT No.:** GB 430 5960 62
Turnover: £125m - £250m **No.of Employees:** 21 - 50 **Product Groups:** 68

D & A Plastics

Stubcroft Farm Studios Stubcroft Lane, East Wittering, Chichester, PO20 8PJ
Tel: 01243-671588 **Fax:** 01243-671588
Directors: D. Allen (Prop)
Immediate Holding Company: THE ELECTRIC LOFT LADDER COMPANY LTD
Registration no: 05989982 **Date established:** 2006
Turnover: Up to £250,000 **No.of Employees:** 1 - 10 **Product Groups:** 31

Douglas Press

Gaff House Walton Lane, Bosham, Chichester, PO18 8QF
Tel: 01243-572603 **Fax:** 01243-572603
E-mail: info@douglaspress.co.uk
Website: http://www.douglaspress.co.uk
Directors: M. Tuck (Prop)
Registration no: N/A **Date established:** 1991 **Turnover:** Up to £250,000
No.of Employees: 1 - 10 **Product Groups:** 28

M G Duff International Ltd

Unit 1 Timberlane Industrial Estate Gravel Lane, Chichester, PO19 8PP
Tel: 01243-533336 **Fax:** 01243-533422
E-mail: sales@mgduff.co.uk
Website: http://www.mgduff.co.uk
Bank(s): Barclays, Chichester
Directors: A. Seabrook (MD)
Managers: K. Hood (Tech Serv Mgr), C. Garner (Mktg Serv Mgr)
Immediate Holding Company: M. G. DUFF INTERNATIONAL LIMITED
Registration no: 02621868 **VAT No.:** GB 615 0528 67
Date established: 1991 **Turnover:** £2m - £5m **No.of Employees:** 21 - 50
Product Groups: 35, 37, 52

Date of Accounts	Sep 11	Sep 10	Sep 09
Sales Turnover	5m	5m	4m
Pre Tax Profit/Loss	81	56	-76
Working Capital	691	629	564
Fixed Assets	409	393	437
Current Assets	2m	2m	1m
Current Liabilities	230	196	456

Elite Helicopters & Aviation Services

Goodwood Airfield Goodwood, Chichester, PO18 0PH
Tel: 01243-530165 **Fax:** 01243-539921
E-mail: ops@elitehelicopters.co.uk
Website: http://www.elitehelicopters.co.uk
Directors: G. Curtis (Dir)
Immediate Holding Company: CONCAIR LIMITED
Registration no: 06827346 **Date established:** 2009
Turnover: £500,000 - £1m **No.of Employees:** 1 - 10 **Product Groups:** 68, 75, 86

Date of Accounts	Mar 11	Mar 10
Working Capital	-22	465
Fixed Assets	504	359
Current Assets	79	567

Empire Welding Supplies Ltd

Unit 13 St James Industrial Estate Westhampnett Road, Chichester, PO19 7JU
Tel: 01243-533733
Website: http://www.empirewelding.com
Directors: L. Warner (Fin)
Immediate Holding Company: EMPIRE WELDING SUPPLIES LIMITED
Registration no: 02213580 **Date established:** 1988
No.of Employees: 1 - 10 **Product Groups:** 46

Date of Accounts	Mar 11	Mar 10	Mar 09
Working Capital	24	22	36
Fixed Assets	18	24	6
Current Assets	49	59	75

Mark Francis

The Forge Halnaker, Chichester, PO18 0NQ
Tel: 01243-773431 **Fax:** 01243-773431
E-mail: info@markfrancis.co.uk
Website: http://www.markfrancis.co.uk
Directors: M. Francis (Prop)
Immediate Holding Company: MARK FRANCIS LIMITED
Registration no: 03982723 **Date established:** 2000
No.of Employees: 1 - 10 **Product Groups:** 26, 35

Date of Accounts	Mar 11	Mar 10	Mar 09
Working Capital	-21	-2	-4
Fixed Assets	25	31	23
Current Assets	13	12	36

Fresh Invest Ltd

Unit A Hills Barn Appledram Lane South, Chichester, PO20 7EG
Tel: 01243-527327 **Fax:** 01243-527771
E-mail: info@freshinvest.co.uk
Website: http://www.freshinvest.co.uk
Directors: D. Chamberlain (MD)
Immediate Holding Company: FRESH INVEST LIMITED
Registration no: 05268097 **Date established:** 2004
No.of Employees: 1 - 10 **Product Groups:** 80

Date of Accounts	Oct 11	Oct 10	Oct 09
Working Capital	N/A	N/A	-1
Fixed Assets	1	1	2
Current Assets	25	10	17

Goodwood Hotel

Goodwood, Chichester, PO18 0QB
Tel: 01243-775537 **Fax:** 08704-007325
E-mail: sarah.stacey@goodwood.com
Website: http://www.goodwood.com
Managers: S. Stacey (Mgr)
Ultimate Holding Company: GOODWOOD ESTATE COMPANY LIMITED(THE)
Immediate Holding Company: THE GOODWOOD HOTEL LIMITED
Registration no: 01326672 **VAT No.:** GB 243 2928 64
Date established: 1977 **Turnover:** £5m - £10m
No.of Employees: 101 - 250 **Product Groups:** 69

Date of Accounts	Dec 11	Dec 10	Dec 09
Sales Turnover	6m	6m	6m
Pre Tax Profit/Loss	-533	-441	-191
Working Capital	-3m	-3m	-2m
Fixed Assets	11m	11m	11m
Current Assets	2m	3m	2m
Current Liabilities	699	523	458

Goodwood Metalcraft Ltd

Terminus Industrial Estate, Chichester, PO19 8UH
Tel: 01243-784626 **Fax:** 01243-787643
E-mail: sales@goodwood-metalcraft.co.uk
Website: http://www.goodwood-metalcraft.co.uk
Bank(s): Barclays, Avenue Branch,50/52 London Rd,Southampton
Directors: M. Hughes (MD), B. Dyer (Co Sec)
Ultimate Holding Company: DEXAM INTERNATIONAL (HOLDINGS) LIMITED
Immediate Holding Company: GOODWOOD METALCRAFT LIMITED
Registration no: 00654977 **VAT No.:** GB 192 8572 26
Date established: 1960 **Turnover:** £2m - £5m **No.of Employees:** 21 - 50
Product Groups: 33, 34, 35, 36, 38, 40, 42, 46, 48, 52, 85

Date of Accounts	Dec 10	Dec 09	Dec 08
Sales Turnover	2m	2m	N/A
Pre Tax Profit/Loss	-47	-168	N/A
Working Capital	20	16	-11
Fixed Assets	497	235	273
Current Assets	929	767	679
Current Liabilities	424	392	N/A

Hortiglass Ltd

93 Maplehurst Road, Chichester, PO19 6RP
Tel: 01243-774964 **Fax:** 01243-786601
Directors: A. De Geus (Fin), A. Meager (Fin), H. De Geus (Dir), H. De Geus (MD)
Immediate Holding Company: HORTIGLASS LIMITED
Registration no: 02177853 **Date established:** 1987
Turnover: Up to £250,000 **No.of Employees:** 1 - 10 **Product Groups:** 26, 35

Date of Accounts	Jun 07	Jun 06
Working Capital	-9	-21
Fixed Assets	8	11
Current Assets	15	26
Current Liabilities	24	46
Total Share Capital	5	5

Industrial Computers Ltd

Unit 3 & 4 New Bury Park Marsh Lane Easthampnett, Chichester, PO18 0JW
Tel: 01243-380780 **Fax:** 01243-538035
E-mail: sales@industrial-computers.com
Website: http://www.industrial-computers.com
Managers: S. Massey (Mktg Serv Mgr)
Immediate Holding Company: INDUSTRIAL COMPUTERS LTD
Registration no: 05578804 **Date established:** 2005 **Turnover:** £5m - £10m
No.of Employees: 1 - 10 **Product Groups:** 44

Date of Accounts	Dec 11	Dec 10	Dec 09
Working Capital	604	439	283
Fixed Assets	2	3	6
Current Assets	2m	1m	654

K P Metallurgical Casting Company Ltd

PO Box 559, Chichester, PO19 9DU
Tel: 0845-2606330 **Fax:** 0207-1003785
E-mail: dunndavid@mac.com
Website: http://www.kpmetallurgical.co.uk
Directors: D. Dunn (Dir), J. Bree (MD)
Immediate Holding Company: KP METALLURGICAL CASTING COMPANY LIMITED
Registration no: 05421336 **Date established:** 2005 **Turnover:** £2m - £5m
No.of Employees: 1 - 10 **Product Groups:** 34

Date of Accounts	Apr 08	Apr 07	Apr 06
Working Capital	10	-16	11
Fixed Assets	22	27	N/A
Current Assets	102	87	32
Current Liabilities	92	104	20

Matform Ltd

10 Matform Business Centre Terminus Road, Chichester, PO19 8UL
Tel: 01243-781799 **Fax:** 01243-789029
E-mail: jkelly@matform.net
Website: http://www.matform.co.uk
Bank(s): HSBC Bank plc
Directors: H. Shute (Ch), J. Kelly (MD), P. Down (Sales)
Immediate Holding Company: MATFORM LIMITED
Registration no: 03763381 **VAT No.:** GB 194 0046 75
Date established: 1999 **Turnover:** £2m - £5m **No.of Employees:** 21 - 50
Product Groups: 23, 28, 34, 48, 81

Murray Equipment Co. Ltd

Unit B Charlton Mill Way, Charlton, Chichester, PO18 0HZ
Tel: 01243-811881 **Fax:** 01243-811855
E-mail: john@murrayequipment.co.uk
Website: http://www.murrayequipment.co.uk
Directors: J. Underhill (MD)
Immediate Holding Company: MURRAY EQUIPMENT COMPANY LIMITED
Registration no: 01254272 **Date established:** 1976
Turnover: £250,000 - £500,000 **No.of Employees:** 1 - 10
Product Groups: 38

Date of Accounts	Apr 11	Apr 10	Apr 09
Working Capital	141	134	121
Fixed Assets	69	75	59
Current Assets	213	207	249

Northshore Yachts Ltd

Itchenor, Chichester, PO20 7AY
Tel: 01243-512611 **Fax:** 01243-511473
E-mail: sales@northshore.co.uk
Website: http://www.northshore.co.uk
Bank(s): National Westminster
Directors: J. Warne (MD), L. Legon (Co Sec), D. Hughes (Fin)
Ultimate Holding Company: SUNCHALK LIMITED
Immediate Holding Company: NORTHSHORE YACHTS LIMITED
Registration no: 01021330 **VAT No.:** GB 503 6310 91
Date established: 1971 **Turnover:** £10m - £20m
No.of Employees: 101 - 250 **Product Groups:** 39

Date of Accounts	Dec 11	Dec 10	Dec 09
Sales Turnover	10m	12m	6m
Pre Tax Profit/Loss	67	278	253
Working Capital	641	456	148
Fixed Assets	109	231	263
Current Assets	6m	7m	6m
Current Liabilities	4m	5m	4m

Odin Marine Electronics

Unit 5 Mountbatten Place Ellis Square, Selsey, Chichester, PO20 0AY
Tel: 01243-603129 **Fax:** 01243-607700
E-mail: sales@odinmarine.co.uk
Website: http://www.odinmarine.co.uk
Directors: T. Wood (Prop)
Date established: 1977 **No.of Employees:** 1 - 10 **Product Groups:** 35, 36, 39

Oldham Seals Ltd

Jetpac Works Gravel Lane Quarry Lane Industrial Estate, Chichester, PO19 8PG
Tel: 01243-782296 **Fax:** 01243-781933
E-mail: info@oldhamseals.co.uk
Website: http://www.oldhamseals.co.uk
Directors: A. Oldham (MD), C. Oldham (Sales)
Immediate Holding Company: OLDHAM SEALS LIMITED
Registration no: 00806906 **VAT No.:** GB 192 9278 21
Date established: 1964 **Turnover:** £2m - £5m **No.of Employees:** 51 - 100
Product Groups: 29, 36

Date of Accounts	Apr 11	Apr 10	Apr 09
Working Capital	654	222	544
Fixed Assets	1m	1m	1m
Current Assets	2m	1m	2m

Geoffrey Osborne Ltd

51 Fishbourne Road East, Chichester, PO19 3HZ
Tel: 01243-787811 **Fax:** 01243-531231
E-mail: enquiries@osborne.co.uk
Website: http://www.osborne.co.uk
Bank(s): Barclays
Directors: A. Osborne (Dep Ch), T. Hatton (Co Sec)
Managers: G. Shepherd, P. Andrews, N. Moore (Personnel)
Ultimate Holding Company: GCHO HOLDINGS LIMITED
Immediate Holding Company: GEOFFREY OSBORNE LIMITED
Registration no: 00873093 **Date established:** 1966
Turnover: £250m - £500m **No.of Employees:** 1001 - 1500
Product Groups: 51, 52, 84

Date of Accounts	Mar 12	Mar 11	Mar 10
Sales Turnover	281m	287m	311m
Pre Tax Profit/Loss	1m	4m	3m
Working Capital	18m	21m	18m
Fixed Assets	9m	7m	8m
Current Assets	92m	98m	98m
Current Liabilities	10m	18m	23m

P R Electronics UK Ltd (PR electronics A.S.)

Middle Barn Apuldram, Chichester, PO20 7FD
Tel: 01243-776450 **Fax:** 01243-774065
E-mail: sales@prelectronics.co.uk
Website: http://www.prelectronics.co.uk
Managers: L. Montague (Mgr)
Ultimate Holding Company: PR ELECTRONICS A/S (DENMARK)
Immediate Holding Company: PR ELECTRONICS (UK) LIMITED
Registration no: SC166414 **Date established:** 1996
Turnover: £5m - £10m **No.of Employees:** 1 - 10 **Product Groups:** 37, 38

Date of Accounts	Jun 11	Jun 10	Jun 09
Working Capital	193	33	-99
Fixed Assets	1	2	4
Current Assets	606	501	446

Sealand Aerial Photography Ltd

Pitlands Farm Up Marden, Chichester, PO18 9JP
Tel: 023-9263 1468 **Fax:** 023-9263 1890
E-mail: malcolm@sealandap.co.uk
Website: http://www.sealandap.co.uk
Directors: M. Lamb (Dir)
Immediate Holding Company: SEALAND AERIAL PHOTOGRAPHY LIMITED
Registration no: 05087637 **VAT No.:** GB 193 6300 63
Date established: 2004 **Turnover:** Up to £250,000
No.of Employees: 1 - 10 **Product Groups:** 75, 89

Date of Accounts	Mar 11	Mar 10	Mar 09
Working Capital	31	24	12
Fixed Assets	22	32	39
Current Assets	55	45	43

The Stove Shop Ltd

Phoenix Business Centre Spur Road, Chichester, PO19 8PN
Tel: 01243-536204 **Fax:** 01243-784858
E-mail: info@thestoveshop.co.uk
Directors: K. Nicholls (Dir)
Immediate Holding Company: THE STOVE SHOP LIMITED
Registration no: 04526184 **Date established:** 2002
Turnover: £250,000 - £500,000 **No.of Employees:** 1 - 10
Product Groups: 40

Date of Accounts	Aug 11	Aug 10	Aug 09
Sales Turnover	304	N/A	N/A
Pre Tax Profit/Loss	14	N/A	N/A
Working Capital	2	-7	-8
Fixed Assets	3	4	5
Current Assets	48	38	35
Current Liabilities	14	N/A	N/A

Super Signs Ltd
Unit 3 Spur Road, Chichester, PO19 8PR
Tel: 01243-532045 **Fax:** 01243-532062
E-mail: mail@supersignsltd.co.uk
Website: http://www.supersignsltd.co.uk
Directors: D. Maltby (MD)
Immediate Holding Company: SUPERSIGNS GRAPHICS LIMITED
Registration no: 02502663 **Date established:** 1990
No.of Employees: 1 - 10 **Product Groups:** 30, 39, 40

Date of Accounts	Aug 11	Aug 10	Aug 09
Working Capital	-17	-22	-4
Fixed Assets	49	50	52
Current Assets	56	62	97

System 910 Hydraulics Ltd
7 The Old Granary The Street, Boxgrove, Chichester, PO18 0ES
Tel: 01243-539789 **Fax:** 01243-530307
E-mail: system910@mistral.co.uk
Website: http://www.mistral.co.uk
Directors: R. Allen (MD)
Immediate Holding Company: SYSTEM 910 (HYDRAULICS) LIMITED
Registration no: 02749320 **VAT No.:** GB 615 1257 67
Date established: 1992 **Turnover:** £500,000 - £1m
No.of Employees: 1 - 10 **Product Groups:** 26, 37, 42, 45, 46, 48, 66

Date of Accounts	Nov 11	Nov 09	Nov 08
Working Capital	18	5	28
Fixed Assets	21	11	15
Current Assets	193	123	196

Talking Headsets
The Bridle Lane Hambrook, Chichester, PO18 8UG
Tel: 01243-573226 **Fax:** 01243-574318
E-mail: info@talkingheadsets.co.uk
Website: http://www.talkingheadsets.co.uk
Directors: K. Foote (MD)
Immediate Holding Company: TALKING HEADSETS LIMITED
Registration no: 03957085 **Date established:** 2000
No.of Employees: 1 - 10 **Product Groups:** 24, 37, 40

Date of Accounts	Mar 12	Mar 11	Mar 10
Working Capital	156	158	60
Fixed Assets	54	15	16
Current Assets	523	446	374

Teknoflex
Quarry Lane, Chichester, PO19 8PE
Tel: 01243-832800 **Fax:** 01243-832832
E-mail: sales@teknoflex.com
Website: http://www.teknoflex.co.uk
Bank(s): Bank of Scotland
Directors: P. Taylor (I.T. Dir), B. Shorrock (MD), P. Hawkins (Fin)
Managers: A. Shorrock, A. Neaves (Mats Contrlr)
Ultimate Holding Company: TEKNOFLEX HOLDINGS LIMITED
Immediate Holding Company: TEKNOFLEX LIMITED
Registration no: 02620417 **VAT No.:** GB 684 7206 11
Date established: 1991 **Turnover:** £5m - £10m
No.of Employees: 101 - 250 **Product Groups:** 37, 44, 84

Date of Accounts	Jul 10	Jul 09	Jul 08
Sales Turnover	10m	9m	N/A
Pre Tax Profit/Loss	574	86	2m
Working Capital	1m	1m	961
Fixed Assets	2m	2m	2m
Current Assets	4m	3m	4m
Current Liabilities	811	1m	2m

Total Concept Paints Ltd
3-5 Matform Business Centre Terminus Road, Chichester, PO19 8UL
Tel: 01243-532999 **Fax:** 01243-533438
E-mail: info@totalconceptpaints.co.uk
Website: http://www.totalconceptpaints.co.uk
Directors: T. Gibbons (MD)
Immediate Holding Company: TOTAL CONCEPT PAINTS LIMITED
Registration no: 02378683 **Date established:** 1989
No.of Employees: 1 - 10 **Product Groups:** 32, 49, 68, 84

Date of Accounts	Dec 11	Dec 10	Dec 09
Working Capital	769	762	725
Fixed Assets	32	38	33
Current Assets	1m	962	910

W B Marine
8 Manhood Cottages Almodington Lane, Almodington, Chichester, PO20 7JT
Tel: 01243-512857 **Fax:** 01243-514922
E-mail: warren@wbmarine.co.uk
Directors: W. Butlin (Prop)
Date established: 1984 **No.of Employees:** 1 - 10 **Product Groups:** 35, 36, 39

Weldtech Southern
Unit 3-4 Trident Business Park Chichester Road, Selsey, Chichester, PO20 9DY
Tel: 01243-604633 **Fax:** 01243-605379
E-mail: info@weldtech.org
Website: http://www.weldtech.org
Directors: C. Pulleyblank (MD)
Immediate Holding Company: WELDTECH (SOUTHERN) LIMITED
Registration no: 04683837 **Date established:** 2003
No.of Employees: 11 - 20 **Product Groups:** 35, 84

Date of Accounts	Mar 11	Mar 10	Mar 09
Working Capital	59	125	157
Fixed Assets	47	58	49
Current Assets	311	272	414

John Wiley & Sons Ltd
The Atrium Southern Gate Terminus Road, Chichester, PO19 8SQ
Tel: 01243-779777 **Fax:** 01243-775878
E-mail: sales@wiley.co.uk
Website: http://www.wiley.com
Bank(s): National Westminster Bank Plc
Directors: J. Dicks (MD), S. Joshua (Co Sec)
Managers: D. Alcock (Tech Serv Mgr)
Ultimate Holding Company: JOHN WILEY & SONS INC (USA)
Immediate Holding Company: JOHN WILEY & SONS LIMITED
Registration no: 00641132 **VAT No.:** GB 376 7669 87
Date established: 1959 **Turnover:** £125m - £250m
No.of Employees: 251 - 500 **Product Groups:** 28, 44, 64

Date of Accounts	Apr 11	Apr 10	Apr 09
Sales Turnover	125m	113m	103m
Pre Tax Profit/Loss	20m	12m	5m
Working Capital	6m	-8m	26
Fixed Assets	26m	27m	27m
Current Assets	138m	86m	132m
Current Liabilities	40m	38m	32m

www.opennshut.co.uk
Forum House Stirling Road, Chichester, PO19 7DN
Tel: 08448-584025 **Fax:** 01243-783008
E-mail: info@opennshut.co.uk
Website: http://www.opennshut.co.uk
Directors: S. Dunster (Prop)
Immediate Holding Company: WWW.OPENNSHUT.CO.UK LIMITED
Registration no: 05583069 **Date established:** 2005
No.of Employees: 1 - 10 **Product Groups:** 30

Date of Accounts	Mar 11	Mar 10
Working Capital	-83	N/A
Fixed Assets	135	N/A
Current Assets	108	N/A

Crawley

A S E Co
Parish Lane Pease Pottage, Crawley, RH10 5NY
Tel: 01293-552888 **Fax:** 01293-551644
Directors: M. Anderton (Prop), M. Wilkinson (Prop)
Immediate Holding Company: UNIVERSAL APPLIED COATINGS LIMITED
Registration no: 01810243 **Date established:** 1984
Turnover: £250,000 - £500,000 **No.of Employees:** 1 - 10
Product Groups: 35

Abratech Supplies Ltd
2 Cowdray Close, Crawley, RH10 7BW
Tel: 01293-611110 **Fax:** 01293-611109
Directors: M. Gandy (Fin)
Immediate Holding Company: ABRATECH SUPPLIES LIMITED
Registration no: 02388430 **Date established:** 1989
Turnover: Up to £250,000 **No.of Employees:** 1 - 10 **Product Groups:** 46, 48

Date of Accounts	Mar 12	Mar 11	Mar 10
Sales Turnover	N/A	N/A	33
Pre Tax Profit/Loss	N/A	N/A	4
Working Capital	-1	-0	1
Fixed Assets	2	2	2
Current Assets	2	4	7
Current Liabilities	N/A	N/A	6

Access Garage Doors Ltd
Genesis House Priestley Way, Crawley, RH10 9PR
Tel: 01293-652472 **Fax:** 01293-843417
E-mail: sales@accessgaragedoors.com
Website: http://www.accessgaragedoors.com
Bank(s): National Westminster Bank Plc
Directors: J. Wright (MD)
Immediate Holding Company: ACCESS GARAGE DOORS LIMITED
Registration no: 01255479 **VAT No.:** GB 527 9131 38
Date established: 1976 **No.of Employees:** 21 - 50 **Product Groups:** 25, 30, 35

Date of Accounts	May 11	May 10	May 09
Sales Turnover	7m	6m	7m
Pre Tax Profit/Loss	360	70	-54
Working Capital	957	725	744
Fixed Assets	376	371	395
Current Assets	2m	2m	2m
Current Liabilities	363	268	203

Aeropia Ltd
Aeropia House Newton Road, Crawley, RH10 9TY
Tel: 01293-459500 **Fax:** 01293-459600
E-mail: jkeating@aeropia.co.uk
Website: http://www.aeropia.com
Bank(s): Lloyds TSB Bank plc, Lombard Street, London
Directors: J. Gutknecht (Co Sec), S. Rice (MD), P. Necchi (Fin), P. Lutterloch (Sales), J. Keating (Dir)
Ultimate Holding Company: UMECO PLC
Immediate Holding Company: HAAS GROUP INTERNATIONAL SCM LIMITED
Registration no: 03601549 **VAT No.:** GB 724 9397 02
Date established: 1998 **Turnover:** £20m - £50m
No.of Employees: 51 - 100 **Product Groups:** 30, 31, 32, 85

Date of Accounts	Dec 10	Dec 09	Dec 08
Sales Turnover	31m	20m	14m
Pre Tax Profit/Loss	-77	46	N/A
Working Capital	2m	1m	1m
Fixed Assets	514	1m	1m
Current Assets	23m	11m	9m
Current Liabilities	3m	260	422

Afriso Eurogauge Ltd
Unit 4 Satellite Business Village, Crawley, RH10 9NE
Tel: 01293-658360 **Fax:** 01293-528270
E-mail: sales@eurogauge.co.uk
Website: http://www.eurogauge.co.uk
Bank(s): National Westminster Bank Plc
Directors: W. Lawther (MD)
Ultimate Holding Company: AFRISO-WERK GEORGE FRITZ & CO KG(GERMANY)
Immediate Holding Company: AFRISO EUROGAUGE LIMITED
Registration no: 00738226 **VAT No.:** GB 209 5090 72
Date established: 1962 **Turnover:** £1m - £2m **No.of Employees:** 11 - 20
Product Groups: 38, 45

Date of Accounts	Dec 11	Dec 10	Dec 09
Working Capital	-110	-36	-48
Fixed Assets	N/A	28	58
Current Assets	641	668	719

Allport Ltd
2 The Faraday Centre Faraday Road, Crawley, RH10 9PX
Tel: 01293-510246 **Fax:** 01293-562044
E-mail: info@allport.co.uk
Website: http://www.allport.co.uk
Bank(s): Barclays, Southend
Managers: C. Taylor (Mgr)
Ultimate Holding Company: HUNDRED HONEST LIMITED (HONG KONG)
Immediate Holding Company: ALLPORT LIMITED
Registration no: 00772941 **VAT No.:** GB 226 8344 56
Date established: 1963 **No.of Employees:** 11 - 20 **Product Groups:** 76

Date of Accounts	Dec 11	Dec 10	Dec 09
Sales Turnover	236m	286m	192m
Pre Tax Profit/Loss	2m	-858	6m
Working Capital	5m	5m	3m
Fixed Assets	12m	12m	14m
Current Assets	60m	69m	47m
Current Liabilities	4m	13m	4m

Aseco Container Services Ltd
42/43 The Office Building Gatwick Road, Manor Royal, Crawley, RH10 9RZ
Tel: 01293-459841 **Fax:** 01293-449843
E-mail: aseco@aseco-uk.com
Website: http://www.aseco-uk.com
Product Groups: 72, 76

Date of Accounts	Dec 08	Dec 07	Dec 06
Working Capital	-410	-189	-28
Fixed Assets	N/A	N/A	1
Current Assets	68	39	5
Current Liabilities	477	228	33
Total Share Capital	30	30	30

Ashpool Telecom plc
Worth Corner Turners Hill Road, Pound Hill, Crawley, RH10 7SL
Tel: 01293-885222
Website: http://www.ashpool-telecom.com
Directors: A. Rawlings Lloyd (Co Sec)
Immediate Holding Company: Command Technology Group PLC
Registration no: 02721643 **Date established:** 1992
Turnover: Up to £250,000 **No.of Employees:** 1 - 10 **Product Groups:** 37, 67, 80

Austin Luce & Co. Ltd
Elm Trees Dowlands Lane, Copthorne, Crawley, RH10 3HX
Tel: 01342-713310 **Fax:** 01342-718097
E-mail: sales@austinluce.co.uk
Website: http://www.austinluce.co.uk
Directors: M. Denison (Fin), K. Bull (MD)
Immediate Holding Company: AUSTIN LUCE & CO. LIMITED
Registration no: 01260902 **Date established:** 1976
Turnover: Up to £250,000 **No.of Employees:** 1 - 10 **Product Groups:** 27, 28, 29, 30, 33, 34, 35, 36, 37, 38, 39, 40, 44, 45, 46, 47, 48, 49, 51, 52, 67, 68, 81, 83, 84

Date of Accounts	May 11	May 10	May 09
Sales Turnover	79	77	105
Pre Tax Profit/Loss	11	9	-12
Working Capital	15	5	-14
Fixed Assets	5	6	8
Current Assets	26	18	12
Current Liabilities	8	2	6

B D M Fastenings
10 Royce Road, Crawley, RH10 9NX
Tel: 01293-548186 **Fax:** 01293-553274
E-mail: sales@bdmfastnings.co.uk
Website: http://www.bdm-fastenings.demon.co.uk
Managers: M. Patis (Mgr)
Immediate Holding Company: BIG BOLT LTD
Registration no: 01115833 **VAT No.:** GB 192 3113 83
Turnover: £500,000 - £1m **No.of Employees:** 1 - 10 **Product Groups:** 35, 66

B N Thermic
34 Stephenson Way, Crawley, RH10 1TN
Tel: 01293-547361 **Fax:** 01293-531432
E-mail: sales@bnthermic.co.uk
Website: http://www.bnthermic.co.uk
Directors: L. Westwood (Fin), D. Hillier (MD)
Immediate Holding Company: BN THERMIC LTD
Registration no: 05399744 **VAT No.:** GB 210 1593 16
Date established: 2005 **No.of Employees:** 1 - 10 **Product Groups:** 40

Date of Accounts	Mar 11	Mar 10	Mar 09
Working Capital	95	-12	4
Fixed Assets	16	14	22
Current Assets	762	664	628

B O C Edwards (Head Office)
Crawley Business Quarter Manor Royal, Crawley, RH10 9LW
Tel: 01293-528844 **Fax:** 01293-533453
E-mail: carol.hunt@edwards.boc.com
Website: http://www.edwardsvaccum.com
Bank(s): HSBC, 22 Victoria St, London W1
Directors: C. Bradley (Fin), C. Hunt (Co Sec)
Ultimate Holding Company: EDWARDS HOLDCO LIMITED
Immediate Holding Company: EDWARDS LIMITED
Registration no: 06124750 **VAT No.:** GB 226 5565 55
Date established: 2007 **Turnover:** £250m - £500m
No.of Employees: 501 - 1000 **Product Groups:** 31, 36, 38, 40, 41, 42, 46, 48, 67, 68, 84

Date of Accounts	Dec 11	Dec 10	Dec 09
Sales Turnover	476m	466m	239m
Pre Tax Profit/Loss	20m	20m	20m
Working Capital	4m	65m	18m
Fixed Assets	664m	684m	610m
Current Assets	155m	202m	116m
Current Liabilities	125m	34m	34m

Bard Ltd
Forest House Brighton Road, Crawley, RH11 9BP
Tel: 01293-527888 **Fax:** 01293-552428
E-mail: customer.services@crbard.com
Website: http://www.crbard.com
Bank(s): Barclays
Directors: W. Lovett (Fin), G. Sumpter (Tech Serv), S. Alterio (Co Sec), T. Schermerhorn (Dir)
Managers: S. Croton (Mktg Serv Mgr), C. Samuels (Personnel)
Ultimate Holding Company: CR BARD INC(USA)
Immediate Holding Company: BARD LIMITED
Registration no: 00939600 **VAT No.:** GB 369 0767 14
Date established: 1968 **Turnover:** £50m - £75m
No.of Employees: 101 - 250 **Product Groups:** 24, 29, 30, 33, 38

Date of Accounts	Nov 11	Nov 10	Nov 09
Sales Turnover	57m	56m	54m
Pre Tax Profit/Loss	14m	28m	3m
Working Capital	22m	19m	31m
Fixed Assets	8m	10m	12m
Current Assets	37m	35m	47m
Current Liabilities	5m	5m	5m

Best Electroplating
5 Priestley Way, Crawley, RH10 9NT
Tel: 01293-532843 **Fax:** 01293-523688
E-mail: mark@bestelectroplating.co.uk
Website: http://www.bestelectroplating.co.uk
Directors: M. Eaton (Prop)
Immediate Holding Company: MELLOWS EATON LTD
Registration no: 05898073 **VAT No.:** GB 602 3996 44
Date established: 2006 **Turnover:** £250,000 - £500,000
No.of Employees: 1 - 10 **Product Groups:** 48

Date of Accounts	Oct 11	Oct 10	Oct 08
Working Capital	-16	-12	-7
Fixed Assets	304	305	302
Current Assets	53	57	-3

Boc Gases Ltd
Fleming Way, Crawley, RH10 9NW
Tel: 01293-528733 **Fax:** 01293-611797
E-mail: ron.evans@boc.com
Website: http://www.boc-gases.com
Bank(s): Midland
Managers: R. Evans (Prod Mgr)
Ultimate Holding Company: LINDE AG (GERMANY)
Immediate Holding Company: BOC LIMITED
Registration no: 00337663 **Date established:** 1938 **Turnover:** £5m - £10m
No.of Employees: 101 - 250 **Product Groups:** 31

Date of Accounts	Dec 11	Dec 10	Dec 08
Sales Turnover	726m	691m	721m
Pre Tax Profit/Loss	122m	125m	67m
Working Capital	409m	278m	-219m
Fixed Assets	480m	492m	538m
Current Assets	724m	578m	371m
Current Liabilities	64m	68m	73m

Broadbridge Precision Engineering Ltd
1-5 Marters Avenue Langley Green, Crawley, RH11 7RX
Tel: 01293-525260 **Fax:** 01293-561668
E-mail: broadbridge.eng@pncl.co.uk
Website: http://www.broadbridge-eng.co.uk
Directors: K. Hollamby (MD)
Immediate Holding Company: BROADBRIDGE PRECISION ENGINEERING LIMITED
Registration no: 01313085 **Date established:** 1977 **Turnover:** £1m - £2m
No.of Employees: 1 - 10 **Product Groups:** 39

Date of Accounts	Jul 11	Jul 10	Jul 09
Working Capital	159	180	126
Fixed Assets	93	73	87
Current Assets	272	272	210

Brush Expert Ltd
Unit 2a Kelvin Business Centre Kelvin Way, Crawley, RH10 9SF
Tel: 01293-884111 **Fax:** 01293-884103
E-mail: info@brushexpert.com
Website: http://www.brushexpert.com
Directors: A. Castle (MD)
Immediate Holding Company: BRUSH EXPERT LIMITED
Registration no: 04039035 **Date established:** 2000
No.of Employees: 1 - 10 **Product Groups:** 02, 22, 23, 24, 25, 26, 27, 29, 30, 31, 32, 33, 35, 36, 37, 38, 39, 40, 41, 42, 43, 44, 45, 46, 47, 48, 49, 61, 63, 66, 67, 87

Date of Accounts	Oct 11	Oct 10	Oct 09
Sales Turnover	N/A	N/A	95
Pre Tax Profit/Loss	N/A	N/A	12
Working Capital	-0	1	31
Fixed Assets	1	1	1
Current Assets	27	27	46
Current Liabilities	N/A	N/A	6

Buck & Hickman Ltd
Unit 3 Wallis Court Fleming Way, Crawley, RH10 9NY
Tel: 01293-561651 **Fax:** 01293-561637
E-mail: crawley@buckhickmaninone.com
Website: http://www.buckandhickman.com
Managers: P. Worsley (Mgr)
Ultimate Holding Company: TRAVIS PERKINS PLC
Immediate Holding Company: BOSTON (2011) LIMITED
Registration no: 06028304 **Date established:** 2006
No.of Employees: 11 - 20 **Product Groups:** 33, 36, 37, 41, 46

Date of Accounts	Dec 10	Mar 10	Mar 09
Working Capital	6m	6m	6m
Current Assets	27m	27m	27m

Builders Beams
1 Rutherford Way, Crawley, RH10 9PB
Tel: 01293-561788 **Fax:** 01293-410300
E-mail: sales@buildersbeams.co.uk
Website: http://www.buildersbeams.co.uk
Directors: D. Alexandra (Comm)
Managers: R. Bliss (Mgr), D. May (Purch Mgr)
Ultimate Holding Company: JOHN PARKER & SON LIMITED
Immediate Holding Company: BUILDER'S BEAMS LIMITED
Registration no: 02713024 **Date established:** 1992
No.of Employees: 21 - 50 **Product Groups:** 35

Date of Accounts	Oct 11	Oct 10	Oct 09
Sales Turnover	N/A	N/A	6m
Pre Tax Profit/Loss	N/A	N/A	-328
Working Capital	175	113	33
Fixed Assets	137	175	253
Current Assets	1m	1m	1m
Current Liabilities	N/A	N/A	268

Bunzl Greenhams (Branch)
Tinsley Lane North, Crawley, RH10 9TP
Tel: 01293-525955 **Fax:** 01293-522971
E-mail: crawley.sales@greenham.co.uk
Website: http://www.greenham.com
Bank(s): HSBC Bank plc
Managers: G. Brewster (District Mgr), S. Coventry
Immediate Holding Company: BUNZL PUBLIC LIMITED COMPANY
Registration no: 00358948 **VAT No.:** GB 238 5914 37
Date established: 1940 **Turnover:** £125m - £250m
No.of Employees: 21 - 50 **Product Groups:** 63, 67

C Brewer & Sons
Spindle Way, Crawley, RH10 1DG
Tel: 01293-525356 **Fax:** 01293-611505
Website: http://www.brewers.co.uk
Bank(s): Barclays
Managers: D. Tutton (Mgr)
Immediate Holding Company: C.BREWER & SONS LIMITED
Registration no: 00203852 **Date established:** 1925
No.of Employees: 11 - 20 **Product Groups:** 23, 25, 27, 30, 32, 66

Chemigraphic
Unit A2 Fleming Centre Fleming Way, Crawley, RH10 9NF
Tel: 01293-543517 **Fax:** 01293-552859
E-mail: sales@chemigraphic.co.uk
Website: http://www.chemigraphic.co.uk
Bank(s): National Westminster Bank Plc
Directors: F. Graham (MD), J. Graham (Fin)
Ultimate Holding Company: CHEMIGRAPHIC HOLDINGS LIMITED
Immediate Holding Company: CHEMIGRAPHIC LIMITED
Registration no: 01045772 **Date established:** 1972
Turnover: £20m - £50m **No.of Employees:** 101 - 250
Product Groups: 37, 38, 44, 47, 84

Date of Accounts	Mar 12	Mar 11	Mar 10
Sales Turnover	23m	20m	17m
Pre Tax Profit/Loss	3m	3m	1m
Working Capital	10m	7m	5m
Fixed Assets	1m	895	1m
Current Assets	15m	12m	9m
Current Liabilities	1m	2m	1m

Choice Properties
5-7 Broadwalk, Crawley, RH10 1HJ
Tel: 01293-611002 **Fax:** 01293-565477
E-mail: choices@choices.co.uk
Website: http://www.choices.co.uk
Directors: J. Wells (Sales), S. Black (Fin)
Ultimate Holding Company: INTERLET UK LIMITED
Immediate Holding Company: CHOICES ESTATE AGENTS LIMITED
Registration no: 02374716 **Date established:** 1989 **Turnover:** £2m - £5m
No.of Employees: 1 - 10 **Product Groups:** 80

Date of Accounts	Apr 11	Apr 10	Apr 09
Sales Turnover	4m	4m	4m
Pre Tax Profit/Loss	442	-687	1
Working Capital	-834	-1m	-431
Fixed Assets	360	478	492
Current Assets	1m	2m	2m
Current Liabilities	2m	305	214

Claybrook Computing Holdings Ltd
Sutherland House Russel Way, Crawley, RH10 1UH
Tel: 01293-604028 **Fax:** 01293-604029
E-mail: michael.payten@claybrook.co.uk
Website: http://www.claybrook.co.uk
Directors: R. Burger (Dir), R. Barker (Dir), R. Barker (MD), M. Payten (Dir), S. Atherton (Co Sec)
Managers: C. Stroud (Sales Prom Mgr), R. Whitaker (I.T. Exec)
Ultimate Holding Company: EQUINITI GROUP LIMITED
Immediate Holding Company: CLAYBROOK COMPUTING (HOLDINGS) LIMITED
Registration no: 01080301 **Date established:** 1972
No.of Employees: 51 - 100 **Product Groups:** 44

Date of Accounts	Dec 10	Mar 10	Mar 09
Pre Tax Profit/Loss	N/A	N/A	2m
Working Capital	N/A	N/A	159
Fixed Assets	161	161	1
Current Assets	N/A	N/A	159

Colas Ltd
Wallage Lane Rowfant, Crawley, RH10 4NF
Tel: 01342-711000 **Fax:** 01342-711198
E-mail: info@colas.co.uk
Website: http://www.colas.co.uk
Bank(s): Barclays, Slough
Directors: R. Weddle (Fin)
Ultimate Holding Company: BOUYGUES S.A. (FRANCE)
Immediate Holding Company: COLAS LIMITED
Registration no: 02644726 **VAT No.:** GB 602 3903 77
Date established: 1991 **Turnover:** £250m - £500m
No.of Employees: 501 - 1000 **Product Groups:** 30, 31, 51, 52

Date of Accounts	Dec 11	Dec 10	Dec 09
Sales Turnover	286m	262m	232m
Pre Tax Profit/Loss	3m	5m	8m
Working Capital	9m	3m	26m
Fixed Assets	35m	38m	36m
Current Assets	73m	72m	98m
Current Liabilities	51m	53m	56m

Colour Data UK Ltd (t/a Tollgate Labels)
Unit 7 Hyders Farm Bonnetts Lane, Ifield, Crawley, RH11 0NY
Tel: 01293-551520 **Fax:** 01293-738183
E-mail: sales@tollgatelabels.co.uk
Website: http://www.tollgatelabels.co.uk
Directors: S. Carling (Fin)
Managers: P. Carling (Sales Prom Mgr)
Immediate Holding Company: COLOUR DATA UK LTD
Registration no: 05610309 **Date established:** 2005
No.of Employees: 51 - 100 **Product Groups:** 27, 28

Date of Accounts	Oct 11	Oct 10	Oct 09
Working Capital	73	210	135
Fixed Assets	526	217	218
Current Assets	338	328	287

Consumers Utility Costs Ltd
Longley House International Drive Southgate Avenue, Crawley, RH10 6AQ
Tel: 01293-516521 **Fax:** 01293-512030
E-mail: admin@energyandcarbonmanagement.com
Bank(s): National Westminster Bank Plc
Directors: J. Henderson (Dir)
Ultimate Holding Company: UTILITY MANAGEMENT HOLDINGS LIMITED
Immediate Holding Company: CONSUMERS UTILITY COSTS LIMITED
Registration no: 01041681 **Date established:** 1972
No.of Employees: 11 - 20 **Product Groups:** 54, 80

Date of Accounts	Dec 11	Dec 10	Dec 09
Working Capital	142	88	-6
Fixed Assets	14	5	16
Current Assets	720	479	261

Copy Solutions
Unit 69 Basepoint Business & Innovation Centre Metcalf Way, Crawley, RH11 7XX
Tel: 01293-455035 **Fax:** 01293-813996
E-mail: sales@copysolutions.org.uk
Website: http://www.copysolutions.org.uk
Directors: S. Patrick (Dir)
No.of Employees: 1 - 10 **Product Groups:** 44, 48, 64, 67, 79

Crawley College
College Road, Crawley, RH10 1NR
Tel: 01293-442200 **Fax:** 01293-442399
E-mail: info@centralsussex.ac.uk
Website: http://www.centralsussex.ac.uk
Directors: R. Strutt (Head), S. Radley (Mkt Research), D. Finch (Develop)
Managers: J. Cox, J. Cox ()
VAT No.: GB 602 5878 40 **Date established:** 1958 **Turnover:** £20m - £50m
No.of Employees: 501 - 1000 **Product Groups:** 86

Crawley Mechanical Handling Ltd
Stephenson Way, Crawley, RH10 1TN
Tel: 01293-517911 **Fax:** 01293-616641
E-mail: cmhltd@btconnect.com
Website: http://www.cmhforklifts.co.uk
Directors: N. Thompson (MD)
Immediate Holding Company: CRAWLEY MECHANICAL HANDLING LIMITED
Registration no: 01460904 **Date established:** 1979 **Turnover:** £1m - £2m
No.of Employees: 1 - 10 **Product Groups:** 48, 67, 83

Date of Accounts	Dec 11	Dec 10	Dec 09
Working Capital	35	9	48
Fixed Assets	175	254	344
Current Assets	274	337	349

Cruiseway Packers Ltd
Unit 21 Crompton Way, Crawley, RH10 9QR
Tel: 01293-514576 **Fax:** 01293-518323
E-mail: info@cruiseway.co.uk
Website: http://www.cruiseway.co.uk
Directors: B. Goodwin (MD)
Immediate Holding Company: CRUISEWAY LIMITED
Registration no: 01619533 **Date established:** 1982
Turnover: £500,000 - £1m **No.of Employees:** 1 - 10 **Product Groups:** 07, 20, 23, 25, 27, 28, 30, 31, 32, 33, 34, 35, 36, 37, 38, 39, 40, 41, 42, 43, 44, 45, 48, 54, 66, 67, 72, 76, 80, 83, 84, 85, 86, 87

Date of Accounts	Aug 12	Aug 11	Aug 10
Working Capital	323	227	199
Fixed Assets	263	226	199
Current Assets	668	352	329

D K Technology
1 Adelphi Close Maidenbower, Crawley, RH10 7HA
Tel: 01293-453253 **Fax:** 01293-453253
E-mail: dken428714@aol.com
Directors: D. Kennard (Prop)
Date established: 1998 **No.of Employees:** 1 - 10 **Product Groups:** 46

D S W Technical Services Ltd
9 Little Park Enterprises Charlwood Road, Ifield, Crawley, RH11 0JZ
Tel: 01293-537974 **Fax:** 01293-537974
E-mail: dswdave@tiscali.co.uk
Website: http://www.dswtech.co.uk
Directors: D. Gurr (MD)
Immediate Holding Company: D.S.W. TECHNICAL SERVICES LIMITED
Registration no: 01143546 **Date established:** 1973
No.of Employees: 1 - 10 **Product Groups:** 23, 30, 31, 33, 36, 37, 38, 40, 48, 52, 63, 66, 84

Date of Accounts	Sep 11	Sep 10	Sep 09
Working Capital	25	27	29
Fixed Assets	1	1	1
Current Assets	34	37	41

Davis Industrial Plastics Ltd
1 Dialog Fleming Way, Crawley, RH10 9NQ
Tel: 01293-552836 **Fax:** 01293-553459
E-mail: carol.davis@davis-plastics.co.uk
Website: http://www.davis-plastics.co.uk
Directors: C. Davis (Co Sec)
Immediate Holding Company: DAVIS INDUSTRIAL PLASTICS LIMITED
Registration no: 02065631 **Date established:** 1986 **Turnover:** £2m - £5m
No.of Employees: 1 - 10 **Product Groups:** 30, 31, 36, 40, 48, 49, 52, 54, 66, 84

Date of Accounts	Oct 11	Oct 10	Oct 09
Working Capital	93	108	-5
Fixed Assets	67	54	65
Current Assets	718	745	751

D C L Prints Ltd
9-17 Crompton Way, Crawley, RH10 9QR
Tel: 01293-512688 **Fax:** 01293-552279
E-mail: sales@dclprint.co.uk
Website: http://www.dclprint.com
Bank(s): Barclays
Directors: R. Humphries (Fin), S. Smode (MD)
Immediate Holding Company: DCL PRINT LIMITED
Registration no: 01793064 **VAT No.:** GB 407 6279 43
Date established: 1984 **Turnover:** £2m - £5m **No.of Employees:** 21 - 50
Product Groups: 27

Date of Accounts	May 11	May 10	May 09
Working Capital	862	666	406
Fixed Assets	1m	1m	1m
Current Assets	3m	2m	2m

Defence Fasteners
Brighton Road Pease Pottage, Crawley, RH11 9AF
Tel: 01293-525811 **Fax:** 01293-525814
E-mail: sales@defencefasteners.com
Website: http://www.defencefasteners.com
Managers: G. Doyle (Mgr)
Immediate Holding Company: DEFENCE FASTENERS LIMITED
Registration no: 06373523 **Date established:** 2007 **Turnover:** £2m - £5m
No.of Employees: 1 - 10 **Product Groups:** 35, 36, 37, 39

Doosan Power Systems Ltd
Doosan House Crawley Business Quarter Manor Royal, Crawley, RH10 9AD
Tel: 01293-612888 **Fax:** 01293-584321
E-mail: smoore@doosanbabcock.com
Website: http://www.doosanbabcock.com
Directors: M. Fellows (MD)
Ultimate Holding Company: DOOSAN CORPORATION CO LTD (SOUTH KOREA)
Immediate Holding Company: DOOSAN POWER SYSTEMS LIMITED
Registration no: 00839354 **VAT No.:** GB 516 3040 84
Date established: 1965 **Turnover:** £500m - £1,000m
No.of Employees: 51 - 100 **Product Groups:** 35, 37, 40, 45, 52

Date of Accounts	Dec 11	Dec 10	Dec 09
Sales Turnover	799m	851m	645m
Pre Tax Profit/Loss	74m	130m	72m

see next page

Doosan Power Systems Ltd - Cont'd

Working Capital	36m	68m	95m
Fixed Assets	453m	354m	25m
Current Assets	486m	485m	389m
Current Liabilities	392m	250m	266m

Dualit Ltd
County Oak Way, Crawley, RH11 7ST
Tel: 01293-652500 **Fax:** 01293-652555
E-mail: info@dualit.com
Website: http://www.dualit.com
Bank(s): Barclays
Directors: M. Milton (Fin), L. Gort Barten (Dir)
Managers: L. Sheppard, A. Stone (Fin Mgr), T. Ewing, W. Garrett (Tech Serv Mgr)
Immediate Holding Company: DUALIT LIMITED
Registration no: 00452403 **VAT No.:** GB 235 6789 27
Date established: 1948 **Turnover:** £10m - £20m
No.of Employees: 51 - 100 **Product Groups:** 40

Date of Accounts	Jun 11	Jun 10	Jun 09
Sales Turnover	15m	15m	14m
Pre Tax Profit/Loss	1m	2m	2m
Working Capital	7m	6m	5m
Fixed Assets	388	362	379
Current Assets	8m	8m	7m
Current Liabilities	561	1m	1m

Eco Island Ltd
4 Taunton Close Worth, Crawley, RH10 7XT
Tel: 01293-887107
E-mail: info@ecoisland.co.uk
Website: http://www.ecoisland.co.uk
Directors: S. Fisher (Fin), M. Fisher (MD)
Immediate Holding Company: ECO ISLAND LIMITED
Registration no: 04642228 **Date established:** 2003
Turnover: Up to £250,000 **No.of Employees:** 1 - 10 **Product Groups:** 67

Date of Accounts	Jan 11	Jan 10	Jan 09
Sales Turnover	N/A	2	101
Pre Tax Profit/Loss	N/A	N/A	12
Working Capital	-4	-4	-5
Current Assets	N/A	N/A	6
Current Liabilities	4	N/A	3

Edwards Ltd
Manor Royal, Crawley, RH10 9LW
Tel: 08459-212223
Website: http://www.edwardsvacumm.com
Ultimate Holding Company: EDWARDS HOLDCO LIMITED
Immediate Holding Company: EDWARDS LIMITED
Registration no: 06124750 **Date established:** 2007
No.of Employees: 1 - 10 **Product Groups:** 36, 38, 40, 42, 67

Date of Accounts	Dec 11	Dec 10	Dec 09
Sales Turnover	476m	466m	239m
Pre Tax Profit/Loss	20m	20m	20m
Working Capital	4m	65m	18m
Fixed Assets	664m	684m	610m
Current Assets	155m	202m	116m
Current Liabilities	125m	34m	34m

Eezehaul
Unit 4 Lowfield Heath Industrial Estate Church Road, Lowfield Heath, Crawley, RH11 0PQ
Tel: 01293-434458 **Fax:** 01293-452930
E-mail: mark@eezehaul.co.uk
Website: http://www.eezehaul.co.uk
Directors: M. Duggan (MD), S. Elkins-Green (Dir), M. Avery (Co Sec)
Managers: H. Masih (Comm), M. Brown (Ops Mgr)
Immediate Holding Company: THE SWIMMING POOL WAREHOUSE LIMITED
Registration no: 02557049 **Date established:** 1968
No.of Employees: 21 - 50 **Product Groups:** 79

Elekta Ltd
Linac House Fleming Way, Crawley, RH10 9RR
Tel: 01293-544422 **Fax:** 01293-654321
E-mail: jeff.boyman@elekta.com
Website: http://www.elekta.com
Directors: J. Boyman (Fin)
Ultimate Holding Company: ELEKTA AB (SWEDEN)
Immediate Holding Company: ELEKTA LIMITED
Registration no: 03244454 **Date established:** 1996
Turnover: £250m - £500m **No.of Employees:** 501 - 1000
Product Groups: 37, 38

Date of Accounts	Apr 11	Apr 10	Apr 09
Sales Turnover	305m	267m	218m
Pre Tax Profit/Loss	29m	33m	21m
Working Capital	67m	47m	47m
Fixed Assets	14m	13m	14m
Current Assets	181m	157m	130m
Current Liabilities	53m	47m	23m

Evans Cycles Ltd
Camino Park James Watt Way, Crawley, RH10 9TZ
Tel: 01293-574999
E-mail: info@wizzbike.com
Website: http://www.evanscycles.co.uk
Managers: J. Newman (Mgr), T. Lardent (Personnel), K. Beeley (Tech Serv Mgr), J. Natale, J. Blanchard (Comptroller)
Immediate Holding Company: EVANS CYCLES LIMITED
Registration no: 06649810 **Date established:** 2008
Turnover: £500,000 - £1m **No.of Employees:** 21 - 50 **Product Groups:** 39

Evolution Glass Ltd
Unit 7 Copthorne Business Park Dowlands Lane, Copthorne, Crawley, RH10 3HX
Tel: 01342-718668 **Fax:** 01342-714077
E-mail: danielfoggerson@evolutionglass.co.uk
Website: http://www.evolutionglass.co.uk
Directors: D. Fergurson (Dir)
Immediate Holding Company: EVOLUTION GLASS LIMITED
Registration no: 06596637 **Date established:** 2008
Turnover: £500,000 - £1m **No.of Employees:** 1 - 10 **Product Groups:** 52

Date of Accounts	May 11	May 10	May 09
Working Capital	14	1	6
Fixed Assets	29	36	25
Current Assets	173	129	88

Express 2000 Ltd
Unit 2d Gatwick Gate Industrial Estate, Lowfield Heath, Crawley, RH11 0TG
Tel: 01342-713500 **Fax:** 01342-713520
E-mail: natalie@express2000.co.uk
Website: http://www.express2000.co.uk
Directors: G. Waymark (MD), I. Saunders (MD), N. Waymark (Co Sec)
Immediate Holding Company: EXPRESS 2000 LIMITED
Registration no: 02405810 **Date established:** 1989 **Turnover:** £1m - £2m
No.of Employees: 1 - 10 **Product Groups:** 72, 74, 76, 77, 79

Date of Accounts	Dec 11	Dec 10	Dec 09
Working Capital	46	45	-0
Fixed Assets	N/A	19	13
Current Assets	46	371	301
Current Liabilities	1	N/A	N/A

F M X Ltd
Westfield House Bonnetts Lane, Ifield, Crawley, RH11 0NY
Tel: 01293-560056 **Fax:** 01293-610500
E-mail: admin@cafmexplorer.com
Website: http://www.cafmexplorer.com
Directors: T. Leppard (MD), J. Roberjot (Sales)
Immediate Holding Company: FMX LTD.
Registration no: 03672258 **VAT No.:** GB 515 1513 83
Date established: 1998 **Turnover:** £1m - £2m **No.of Employees:** 21 - 50
Product Groups: 44

Date of Accounts	Mar 11	Mar 10	Mar 09
Working Capital	-2	32	-65
Fixed Assets	454	335	365
Current Assets	1m	967	1m

Fire Prevention Services
Springwell House Crawley Lane, Crawley, RH10 7EG
Tel: 01293-886049 **Fax:** 01293-886049
E-mail: info@fire-preventionservices.co.uk
Website: http://www.preventafire.co.uk
Directors: S. Paul (MD)
Immediate Holding Company: FIRE PREVENTION SERVICES (UK) LTD
Registration no: 06968003 **Date established:** 2009
Turnover: £250,000 - £500,000 **No.of Employees:** 1 - 10
Product Groups: 52, 67, 84

Fixfast
Falcon House Tinsley Lane North, Crawley, RH10 9FF
Tel: 01293-590970 **Fax:** 01293-605929
E-mail: sales@fixfast.co
Website: http://www.fixfast.co
Directors: K. Lynes (Ptnr)
Managers: J. Carron (Sales Prom Mgr), M. Napthine (Mktg Serv Mgr)
Immediate Holding Company: FIXFAST
Registration no: 01488258 **Date established:** 1980
No.of Employees: 21 - 50 **Product Groups:** 32, 35, 66

Date of Accounts	Apr 98	Apr 97	Apr 96
Working Capital	-1	-1	-1

Frontier Pitts Ltd
Crompton House Crompton Way, Crawley, RH10 9QZ
Tel: 01293-548301 **Fax:** 01293-560650
E-mail: sales@frontierpitts.com
Website: http://www.frontierpitts.co.uk
Bank(s): Barclays
Directors: G. Liddle (Dir)
Managers: C. Assleck, S. Osman (Mktg Serv Mgr), K. Zhang (Purch Mgr), J. Patel (Fin Mgr)
Immediate Holding Company: FRONTIER-PITTS LIMITED
Registration no: 02582463 **VAT No.:** GB 528 6523 30
Date established: 1991 **Turnover:** £5m - £10m
No.of Employees: 101 - 250 **Product Groups:** 35, 39, 40, 52

Date of Accounts	Jul 11	Jul 10	Jul 09
Sales Turnover	7m	7m	7m
Pre Tax Profit/Loss	924	570	353
Working Capital	2m	1m	1m
Fixed Assets	184	174	173
Current Assets	3m	3m	3m
Current Liabilities	876	746	805

G 4 S
The Manor Manor Royal, Crawley, RH10 9SU
Tel: 01293-554540 **Fax:** 01293-588680
Website: http://www.g4s.com
Directors: J. Walter (Co Sec), P. Long (Dir)
Managers: C. Johnson (Personnel), T. Dighton (Comptroller)
Immediate Holding Company: G4S PLC
Registration no: 04992207 **Date established:** 2003
Turnover: Over £1,000m **No.of Employees:** 1501 & over
Product Groups: 38, 40, 67, 81

Date of Accounts	Dec 11	Dec 10	Dec 09
Sales Turnover	7522m	7397m	7049m
Pre Tax Profit/Loss	279m	330m	303m
Working Capital	741m	441m	365m
Fixed Assets	3407m	3393m	3317m
Current Assets	2208m	1980m	1847m
Current Liabilities	1113m	1164m	1084m

Gem Stone Graphics Ltd
4 Highdown Court Forestfield, Crawley, RH10 6PR
Tel: 01293-524546
E-mail: info@gsg-ltd.co.uk
Website: http://www.gsg-ltd.co.uk
Directors: G. Cocksedge (Fin), R. Stone (Dir)
Immediate Holding Company: GEM STONE GRAPHICS LIMITED
Registration no: 05204209 **Date established:** 2004
Turnover: Up to £250,000 **No.of Employees:** 1 - 10 **Product Groups:** 44, 80, 81

Date of Accounts	Jul 11	Jul 10	Jul 09
Sales Turnover	24	19	21
Pre Tax Profit/Loss	2	2	-2
Working Capital	-1	-2	-1
Fixed Assets	10	8	9
Current Assets	13	9	10
Current Liabilities	1	1	1

Gingers
63 Tiltwood Drive Crawley Down, Crawley, RH10 4BA
Tel: 07715-171212 **Fax:** 01342-715041
E-mail: charlotte@gingersflowers.co.uk
Website: http://www.gingersflowers.co.uk
Directors: C. Elsey (Prop)
Date established: 2005 **No.of Employees:** 1 - 10 **Product Groups:** 49

Glennfreight Services Ltd
Unit 29 Gatwick International Distribution Centre Cobham Way, Crawley, RH10 9RX
Tel: 01293-437770 **Fax:** 01293-437775
E-mail: info@glennfreight.co.uk
Website: http://www.glennfreight.co.uk
Directors: K. Ingarfield (Co Sec)
Immediate Holding Company: GLENN FREIGHT SERVICES LIMITED
Registration no: 01159629 **VAT No.:** GB 211 0007 54
Date established: 1974 **Turnover:** £2m - £5m **No.of Employees:** 1 - 10
Product Groups: 76, 79

Date of Accounts	Mar 11	Mar 10	Mar 09
Sales Turnover	1m	1m	1m
Pre Tax Profit/Loss	-100	-101	-187
Working Capital	86	181	273
Fixed Assets	16	21	30
Current Assets	344	415	485
Current Liabilities	59	47	46

GLS Foodservice Designs Ltd
14 Cob Close Crawley Down, Crawley, RH10 4EX
Tel: 0845-6349561 **Fax:** 01342-719471
E-mail: info@gls-fsdesigns.co.uk
Website: http://www.gls-fsdesigns.co.uk
Product Groups: 40, 67, 84

Date of Accounts	Aug 08	Aug 07	Aug 06
Sales Turnover	682	252	82
Pre Tax Profit/Loss	226	119	63
Working Capital	224	84	18
Fixed Assets	2	1	1
Current Assets	354	137	65
Current Liabilities	130	53	47
ROCE% (Return on Capital Employed)	100.3	139.8	325.1
ROT% (Return on Turnover)	33.1	47.3	77.2

Hellermanntyton Ltd
Stoner House London Road, Crawley, RH10 8LJ
Tel: 01293-537272
Directors: T. Jones (Fin)
Ultimate Holding Company: HELLERMANNTYTON ALPHA SARL (LUXEMBOURG)
Immediate Holding Company: HELLERMANNTYTON LIMITED
Registration no: 05652018 **Date established:** 2005
Turnover: £20m - £50m **No.of Employees:** 1 - 10 **Product Groups:** 30

Date of Accounts	Dec 11	Dec 10	Dec 09
Sales Turnover	53m	47m	38m
Pre Tax Profit/Loss	-978	-5m	-5m
Working Capital	3m	6m	1m
Fixed Assets	59m	53m	52m
Current Assets	31m	20m	13m
Current Liabilities	4m	5m	4m

Heyland & Whittle
1 Crompton Way, Crawley, RH10 9QR
Tel: 01293-525825 **Fax:** 01293-862580
E-mail: sales@heylandandwhittle.co.uk
Website: http://www.heylandandwhittle.co.uk
Managers: K. Smith (Admin Off), A. Ferguson (Sales Admin)
No.of Employees: 11 - 20 **Product Groups:** 32, 63

Homelife AV
57 Banks Road Pound Hill, Crawley, RH10 7BS
Tel: 07853-220199
E-mail: dale.p1@sky.com
Website: http://www.homelifeav.co.uk
Directors: P. Dale (Prop)
No.of Employees: 1 - 10 **Product Groups:** 37, 84

Hydraquip
2 Raleigh Court Priestley Way, Crawley, RH10 9PD
Tel: 01293-615166 **Fax:** 01293-614965
E-mail: sales@hydraquip.co.uk
Website: http://www.hydraquip.co.uk
Directors: D. Macbain (MD), N. Wray (Fin)
Registration no: 02509057 **Turnover:** £1m - £2m
No.of Employees: 1 - 10 **Product Groups:** 29, 30, 36

I T W Constructions Productions (ITW Construction Products)
Diamond Point Fleming Way, Crawley, RH10 9DP
Tel: 0800-652 9260 **Fax:** 01293-515186
E-mail: jwhite@itwcp.co.uk
Website: http://www.itwcp.co.uk
Managers: J. White (Chief Mgr), R. Forshaw (Comptroller), K. Porter (Personnel), C. Jones (Tech Serv Mgr), A. Marsh (Mktg Serv Mgr), P. Elkings
Ultimate Holding Company: ITW
Immediate Holding Company: I T W HOLDINGS
Registration no: 00559693 **VAT No.:** GB 210 0507 40
Date established: 1955 **No.of Employees:** 21 - 50 **Product Groups:** 35, 37, 42

Imaginit Ltd
Shaw House Pegler Way, Crawley, RH11 7AF
Tel: 08456-027397
E-mail: solutions@imaginit.net
Website: http://www.imaginit.net
Directors: P. Lucas (MD)
Immediate Holding Company: IMAGINIT LIMITED
Registration no: 07515558 **Date established:** 2011
Turnover: £250,000 - £500,000 **No.of Employees:** 1 - 10
Product Groups: 44

Jeppesen UK Ltd
Boeing House Manor Royal, Crawley, RH10 9AD
Tel: 01293-842400
E-mail: sandra.corcoran@jeppesen.com
Website: http://www.jeppesen.com
Bank(s): Barclays, Horley, Surrey
Managers: S. Corcoran
Ultimate Holding Company: BOEING COMPANY (USA)
Immediate Holding Company: JEPPESEN U.K. LIMITED
Registration no: 01321734 **Date established:** 1977
Turnover: £20m - £50m **No.of Employees:** 51 - 100 **Product Groups:** 22, 28, 39, 44, 71

Date of Accounts	Dec 10	Dec 09	Dec 08
Sales Turnover	29m	30m	30m
Pre Tax Profit/Loss	5m	4m	5m

Working Capital	17m	14m	10m
Fixed Assets	552	774	959
Current Assets	20m	18m	15m
Current Liabilities	2m	2m	3m

Jewson Ltd

Stephenson Way, Crawley, RH10 1TN
Tel: 01293-523161 **Fax:** 01293-535824
Website: http://www.jewson.co.uk
Managers: R. Henry (Mgr)
Ultimate Holding Company: COMPAGNIE DE SAINT GOBAIN (FRANCE)
Immediate Holding Company: JEWSON LIMITED
Registration no: 00348407 **VAT No.:** GB 497 7184 83
Date established: 1939 **Turnover:** £500m - £1,000m
No.of Employees: 1 - 10 **Product Groups:** 66

Date of Accounts	Dec 11	Dec 10	Dec 09
Sales Turnover	1606m	1547m	1485m
Pre Tax Profit/Loss	18m	100m	45m
Working Capital	-345m	-250m	-349m
Fixed Assets	496m	387m	461m
Current Assets	657m	1005m	1320m
Current Liabilities	66m	120m	64m

John Humphris Ltd

Unit 10-11 Imperial Centre 41-43 Gatwick Road, Crawley, RH10 9LD
Tel: 01293-539451
E-mail: sales@johnhumphris.com
Website: http://www.johnhumphris.com
Directors: J. Humphris (MD)
Immediate Holding Company: JOHN HUMPHRIS LIMITED
Registration no: 03812922 **Date established:** 1999
No.of Employees: 1 - 10 **Product Groups:** 24, 30, 44

Date of Accounts	Mar 11	Mar 10	Mar 09
Working Capital	55	43	16
Fixed Assets	10	5	6
Current Assets	112	129	122

Just Seychelles Ltd

3-4 The Courtyard East Park, Crawley, RH10 6AG
Tel: 020-8840 0969 **Fax:** 020-7228 5467
E-mail: info@justdestinations.co.uk
Website: http://www.justseychelles.com
Managers: M. Banford (Sales Admin)
Immediate Holding Company: JUST SEYCHELLES LIMITED
Registration no: 04103138 **Date established:** 2000
Turnover: £500,000 - £1m **No.of Employees:** 1 - 10 **Product Groups:** 84

Date of Accounts	Dec 07	Dec 06	Dec 05
Sales Turnover	714	656	591
Pre Tax Profit/Loss	-26	-3	5
Working Capital	-17	9	3
Fixed Assets	N/A	N/A	10
Current Assets	191	172	181
Current Liabilities	209	163	178
Total Share Capital	135	135	135
ROCE% (Return on Capital Employed)	152.6	-34.1	37.6
ROT% (Return on Turnover)	-3.7	-0.5	0.8

Kelgray Products Ltd

Kelgray House Spindle Way, Crawley, RH10 1TH
Tel: 01293-518733 **Fax:** 01293-518803
E-mail: chris@kelgray.co.uk
Website: http://www.kelgray.co.uk
Bank(s): Lloyds TSB Bank plc
Directors: K. Smith (MD), J. Bundock (Sales), C. Hilton Childs (Fin), C. Hilton Childs (Co Sec), W. Smith (Ch), C. Hilton-Childs (Fin)
Managers: A. King (I.T. Exec), T. Smith (Serv Mgr), D. Wildman (Purch Mgr)
Ultimate Holding Company: KELGRAY HOLDINGS LIMITED
Immediate Holding Company: KELGRAY PRODUCTS LTD.
Registration no: 01738123 **VAT No.:** GB 492 5619 17
Date established: 1983 **Turnover:** £2m - £5m **No.of Employees:** 21 - 50
Product Groups: 27, 28, 37, 42, 44, 67

Date of Accounts	Mar 11	Mar 10	Mar 09
Working Capital	767	887	746
Fixed Assets	118	89	99
Current Assets	2m	2m	2m

Komfort Workspace plc

Unit 1-10 Whittle Way, Crawley, RH10 9RT
Tel: 01293-592500 **Fax:** 01293-553271
E-mail: general@komfort.com
Website: http://www.komfort.com
Bank(s): National Westminster Bank Plc
Directors: P. Duckworth (MD), M. Tingey (Cust Serv), G. Davies (Fin), S. Gale (Sales)
Managers: P. Birch (I.T. Exec), J. Terry (Personnel), C. Purdie (Mktg Serv Mgr), C. Rackley (Purch Mgr)
Ultimate Holding Company: SIG PLC
Immediate Holding Company: SIG BLINDS & GRAPHICS LIMITED
Registration no: 02498697 **VAT No.:** GB 602 4642 74
Date established: 1990 **Turnover:** £20m - £50m
No.of Employees: 101 - 250 **Product Groups:** 26, 33, 35

Little Foxes

Charlwood Road Ifield Wood, Crawley, RH11 0JY
Tel: 01293-529206
E-mail: info@littlefoxeshotel.co.uk
Website: http://www.littlefoxeshotel.co.uk
Managers: G. Todd (Mgr)
No.of Employees: 1 - 10 **Product Groups:** 69

Logic Design Interiors Ltd

Unit 2 Orangery Farm Turners Hill Road, Crawley Down, Crawley, RH10 4EY
Tel: 01342-717733 **Fax:** 01342-717733
E-mail: info@ldikitchens.co.uk
Website: http://www.ldikitchens.co.uk
Directors: A. Richardson (Prop)
Immediate Holding Company: LOGIC DESIGN INTERIORS LIMITED
Registration no: 04992695 **Date established:** 2003
No.of Employees: 1 - 10 **Product Groups:** 52, 63

Date of Accounts	Dec 11	Dec 10	Dec 09
Working Capital	7	9	1
Fixed Assets	1	N/A	N/A
Current Assets	38	37	2

Macro 4 Ltd

The Orangery Turners Hill Road, Worth, Crawley, RH10 4SS
Tel: 01293-872000 **Fax:** 01293-872001
E-mail: info@macro4.com
Website: http://www.macro4.com
Bank(s): Lloyds
Directors: C. Hong (Prop)
Ultimate Holding Company: UNICOM SYSTEMS INC (USA)
Immediate Holding Company: MACRO 4 LIMITED
Registration no: 00927588 **VAT No.:** GB 644 6580 20
Date established: 1968 **Turnover:** £20m - £50m
No.of Employees: 51 - 100 **Product Groups:** 44

Date of Accounts	Dec 11	Dec 10	Dec 09
Sales Turnover	23m	21m	43m
Pre Tax Profit/Loss	14m	13m	3m
Working Capital	25m	13m	3m
Fixed Assets	23m	24m	25m
Current Assets	32m	22m	13m
Current Liabilities	7m	8m	10m

Martin Yale International Ltd

Unit C2 Fleming Centre Fleming Way, Crawley, RH10 9NN
Tel: 01293-441900 **Fax:** 01293-611155
E-mail: enquiries@intimus.co.uk
Website: http://www.martinyale.com
Directors: C. Whale (Pers)
Managers: S. Cook (Chief Acct)
Ultimate Holding Company: MARTIN YALE GROUP
Immediate Holding Company: MARTIN YALE INTERNATIONAL LIMITED
Registration no: 01046083 **Date established:** 1972 **Turnover:** £2m - £5m
No.of Employees: 1 - 10 **Product Groups:** 42, 43, 44, 49, 67

Date of Accounts	Dec 11	Dec 10	Dec 09
Sales Turnover	2m	2m	N/A
Pre Tax Profit/Loss	17	33	N/A
Working Capital	275	267	265
Fixed Assets	36	48	N/A
Current Assets	544	522	265
Current Liabilities	252	232	N/A

Medbrook Services Ltd

79 Southgate Drive, Crawley, RH10 6EP
Tel: 01293-420994 **Fax:** 01293-420995
E-mail: david@medbrook.co.uk
Website: http://www.medbrook.co.uk
Directors: G. Roskilly (Dir), D. Roskilly (MD), A. Roskilly (Co Sec)
Immediate Holding Company: MEDBROOK SERVICES LIMITED
Registration no: 04231201 **Date established:** 2001
Turnover: Up to £250,000 **No.of Employees:** 1 - 10 **Product Groups:** 26, 28, 37, 38, 44, 67, 79, 83

Date of Accounts	May 11	May 10	May 09
Sales Turnover	95	78	N/A
Pre Tax Profit/Loss	21	15	N/A
Working Capital	3	-0	3
Fixed Assets	4	5	6
Current Assets	21	15	23
Current Liabilities	9	7	N/A

Menzies Client Solutions

The Enterprise Centre Kelvin Lane, Crawley, RH10 9PT
Tel: 01293-440000 **Fax:** 01293-440006
E-mail: nickie.jackson@menziesaviation.com
Website: http://www.menziesclientsolutions.com
Bank(s): National Westminster Bank Plc
Directors: C. Petterson (Dir)
Managers: N. Jackson (Mgr)
Ultimate Holding Company: JOHN MENZIES PLC
Immediate Holding Company: MENZIES AVIATION UK LTD
Registration no: 02597505 **VAT No.:** GB 270 3484 66
Turnover: £20m - £50m **No.of Employees:** 21 - 50 **Product Groups:** 76

Monier Ltd

Sussex Manor Business Park Gatwick Road, Crawley, RH10 9NZ
Tel: 01293-618418 **Fax:** 01293-614548
E-mail: info@lafarge-roofing.com
Website: http://www.monier.com
Bank(s): Barclays, Gatwick
Directors: R. Zala (Fin), F. Massie (Fin), A. Dennis (Dir), R. Jenkins (Pers)
Managers: S. Orio (Mktg Serv Mgr), S. Reeve (Tech Serv Mgr), G. Palmer (Purch Mgr), A. Forbes
Ultimate Holding Company: MONIER GROUP SARL (LUXEMBOURG)
Immediate Holding Company: MONIER TECHNICAL CENTRE LIMITED
Registration no: 02631240 **VAT No.:** GB 210 4796 84
Date established: 1991 **Turnover:** £5m - £10m
No.of Employees: 51 - 100 **Product Groups:** 66

Date of Accounts	Dec 11	Dec 10	Dec 09
Sales Turnover	7m	7m	6m
Pre Tax Profit/Loss	796	329	29
Working Capital	7m	7m	11m
Fixed Assets	1m	1m	1m
Current Assets	9m	8m	12m
Current Liabilities	1m	1m	1m

Moore Industries Europe Inc (Head Office)

1 Lloyds Court Manor Royal, Crawley, RH10 9QU
Tel: 01293-514488 **Fax:** 01293-536852
E-mail: sales@mooreind.com
Website: http://www.miinet.com
Directors: S. Wood (Fin)
Managers: R. Stockham (Chief Mgr)
Ultimate Holding Company: MOORE INDUSTRIES INTERNATIONAL INC (USA)
Immediate Holding Company: MOORE INDUSTRIES EUROPE INC
Registration no: FC009479 **VAT No.:** GB 315 5039 81
Date established: 1978 **Turnover:** £1m - £2m **No.of Employees:** 1 - 10
Product Groups: 37, 38

Date of Accounts	Dec 11	Dec 10	Dec 09
Sales Turnover	1m	1m	1m
Pre Tax Profit/Loss	62	-18	-6
Working Capital	382	324	336
Fixed Assets	14	11	16
Current Assets	623	521	554
Current Liabilities	20	16	25

N Froy & Son

Focal Point Fleming Way, Crawley, RH10 9DF
Tel: 01293-521764 **Fax:** 01306-712749
E-mail: sales@froy.co.uk
Website: http://www.explorebathrooms.com
Directors: J. Froy (Ptnr), C. Froy (Fin)
Managers: A. Stoneman, J. Johnson (Purch Mgr)
Immediate Holding Company: N. FROY & SONS LIMITED
Registration no: 01325237 **Date established:** 1977
Turnover: £10m - £20m **No.of Employees:** 11 - 20 **Product Groups:** 66

Date of Accounts	Dec 11	Dec 10	Dec 09
Sales Turnover	8m	10m	11m
Pre Tax Profit/Loss	-422	85	206
Working Capital	3m	3m	3m
Fixed Assets	148	243	353
Current Assets	4m	5m	6m
Current Liabilities	201	331	415

Newey & Eyre Ltd

Units 15 16 & 17, Crawley, RH10 9RW
Tel: 01293-517500 **Fax:** 01293-561362
E-mail: neweyandeyre@hagemeyer.co.uk
Website: http://www.neweysonline.co.uk
Bank(s): Lloyds TSB Bank plc & Barclays Bank PLC
Managers: C. Doherty (District Mgr)
Immediate Holding Company: NEWEY & EYRE LIMITED
Registration no: 00216596 **Date established:** 2026 **Turnover:** £5m - £10m
No.of Employees: 21 - 50 **Product Groups:** 77

Date of Accounts	Dec 11	Dec 10	Dec 09
Pre Tax Profit/Loss	N/A	N/A	387
Working Capital	15m	15m	15m
Fixed Assets	265	265	265
Current Assets	15m	15m	15m

P C Paramedics

1 Highdown Court, Crawley, RH10 6PR
Tel: 01293-428882
E-mail: john@hbird.freeserve.co.uk
Turnover: Up to £250,000 **No.of Employees:** 1 - 10 **Product Groups:** 69

PDR BGA/SMT Rework Systems

Unit 3 Stanley Centre Kelvin Way, Crawley, RH10 9SE
Tel: 01293-614 000 **Fax:** 01293-613600
E-mail: sales@pdr.co.uk
Website: http://www.pdr-rework.com
Ultimate Holding Company: Eurotec Industries Ltd
Registration no: 03784857 **Turnover:** £1m - £2m
No.of Employees: 1 - 10 **Product Groups:** 37, 40, 46, 47, 48

Peter Perks Ltd

47 Gatwick Road, Crawley, RH10 9RD
Tel: 01293-427200 **Fax:** 01293-427203
E-mail: info@peterperksltd.com
Website: http://www.peterperksltd.com
Directors: W. Perks (MD)
Immediate Holding Company: PETER PERKS LIMITED
Registration no: 01020580 **Date established:** 1971
Turnover: £500,000 - £1m **No.of Employees:** 11 - 20
Product Groups: 30, 46

Date of Accounts	Oct 11	Oct 10	Oct 09
Working Capital	224	122	175
Fixed Assets	41	62	29
Current Assets	462	418	342

Pie Data UK Ltd

4 Mill Court Spindle Way, Crawley, RH10 1TT
Tel: 01293-510231 **Fax:** 01293-510234
E-mail: sales@pie-data.co.uk
Website: http://www.piedata.com
Directors: H. Patel (Fin)
Immediate Holding Company: PIE-DATA(U.K.) LIMITED
Registration no: 03921414 **Date established:** 2000
Turnover: £250,000 - £500,000 **No.of Employees:** 1 - 10
Product Groups: 31, 37

Date of Accounts	Jun 11	Jun 10	Jun 09
Sales Turnover	456	458	511
Pre Tax Profit/Loss	-2	37	69
Working Capital	96	101	115
Fixed Assets	433	453	434
Current Assets	231	275	406
Current Liabilities	97	127	169

Plating Shop

3 Kelvin Business Centre Kelvin Way, Crawley, RH10 9SF
Tel: 01293-611416 **Fax:** 01293-512362
E-mail: peter.godfrey@blueyonder.co.uk
Website: http://tpsjewellery.co.uk
Directors: G. Pugh (Sales), P. Godfrey (Dir)
Immediate Holding Company: THE PLATING SHOP LIMITED
Registration no: 03138375 **Date established:** 1995
Turnover: Up to £250,000 **No.of Employees:** 1 - 10 **Product Groups:** 46, 48

Date of Accounts	Mar 11	Mar 10	Mar 09
Sales Turnover	229	248	232
Pre Tax Profit/Loss	-0	17	13
Working Capital	131	137	122
Fixed Assets	12	6	8
Current Assets	221	242	220
Current Liabilities	14	15	15

Portakabin

London Road Lowfield Heath, Crawley, RH10 9SN
Tel: 01293-536215 **Fax:** 01293-534802
E-mail: crawley.hire@portakabin.co.uk
Website: http://www.portakabin.co.uk
Managers: P. Spencer (Mgr)
Immediate Holding Company: PORTAKABIN LIMITED
Registration no: 00685303 **Date established:** 1961
Turnover: Up to £250,000 **No.of Employees:** 1 - 10 **Product Groups:** 35, 52

Power Access Systems Ltd

Parish Lane Pease Pottage, Crawley, RH10 5NY
Tel: 01293-561892 **Fax:** 01293-561896
E-mail: mail@poweraccess.co.uk
Website: http://www.poweraccess.co.uk
Directors: A. Porthouse (Dir)
Immediate Holding Company: POWER ACCESS SYSTEMS LIMITED
Registration no: 01707459 **VAT No.:** GB 376 8785 80
Date established: 1983 **Turnover:** £250,000 - £500,000
No.of Employees: 1 - 10 **Product Groups:** 35, 40, 45

Date of Accounts	Jun 11	Jun 10	Jun 09
Sales Turnover	274	345	596
Pre Tax Profit/Loss	-26	24	-22
Working Capital	171	211	189
Fixed Assets	7	9	13
Current Assets	233	256	288
Current Liabilities	29	35	32

Powerlase Photonics Ltd
Imperial House Link 10 Napier Way, Crawley, RH10 9RA
Tel: 01293-456222 **Fax:** 01293-456233
E-mail: sales@powerlase.com
Website: http://www.powerlase.com
Directors: D. Ward (Dir), K. Rearden (Dir), T. King (Grp Chief Exec)
Managers: D. Cooper (Sales Prom Mgr), M. Cook (I.T. Exec)
Immediate Holding Company: POWERLASE LIMITED
Registration no: 03982225 **Date established:** 2000 **Turnover:** £2m - £5m
No.of Employees: 1 - 10 **Product Groups:** 37

Projects Advertising & Marketing Ltd
Grattons Court 74 Grattons Drive, Crawley, RH10 3AG
Tel: 01293-446949 **Fax:** 01293-455071
E-mail: m.richardardson@projects.co.uk
Website: http://www.projectsadv.co.uk
Directors: M. Richardson (MD)
Immediate Holding Company: PROJECTS ADVERTISING & MARKETING LIMITED
Registration no: 03913831 **VAT No.:** GB 725 5540 37
Date established: 2000 **Turnover:** £500,000 - £1m
No.of Employees: 1 - 10 **Product Groups:** 81

Date of Accounts	Jan 11	Jan 10	Jan 09
Working Capital	-2	N/A	13
Fixed Assets	2	3	4
Current Assets	193	235	99

Quality Office Supplies Ltd
Unit 55 Barns Court Turners Hill Road, Crawley Down, Crawley, RH10 4HQ
Tel: 01293-863355 **Fax:** 01293-863329
E-mail: sales@qualityofficesupplies.co.uk
Website: http://www.qualityofficesupplies.co.uk
Managers: B. Millard (Mgr)
Immediate Holding Company: QUALITY OFFICE SUPPLIES LIMITED
Registration no: 03320229 **Date established:** 1997 **Turnover:** £5m - £10m
No.of Employees: 1 - 10 **Product Groups:** 61, 64

Date of Accounts	Mar 11	Mar 10	Mar 09
Sales Turnover	6m	N/A	N/A
Pre Tax Profit/Loss	211	N/A	N/A
Working Capital	247	178	121
Fixed Assets	138	84	93
Current Assets	2m	1m	1m

R S Components Ltd
Unit 2b Old Brighton Road Lowfield Heath, Crawley, RH11 0PW
Tel: 01293-521374 **Fax:** 01293-611400
E-mail: customercare@rscomponents.co.uk
Website: http://www.rswww.com
Managers: C. Martin (Mgr)
Ultimate Holding Company: ELECTROCOMPONENTS PUBLIC LIMITED COMPANY
Immediate Holding Company: RS COMPONENTS LIMITED
Registration no: 01002091 **Date established:** 1971
No.of Employees: 1 - 10 **Product Groups:** 30

Date of Accounts	Mar 11	Mar 10	Mar 09
Sales Turnover	579m	486m	494m
Pre Tax Profit/Loss	41m	26m	55m
Working Capital	19m	-6m	10m
Fixed Assets	89m	77m	83m
Current Assets	229m	177m	145m
Current Liabilities	33m	32m	30m

Radiometer Ltd
Manor Court Manor Royal, Crawley, RH10 9FY
Tel: 01293-517599 **Fax:** 01293-531597
E-mail: roger.wynveldt@radiometer.co.uk
Website: http://www.radiometer.co.uk
Bank(s): Midland
Directors: M. Brink (MD), D. Tunley (Co Sec)
Managers: K. Bage (Sales & Mktg Mg), R. Wynveldt (Mgr), S. Burling (Personnel)
Ultimate Holding Company: DANAHER CORPORATION (DELAWARE U.S.A)
Immediate Holding Company: RADIOMETER LIMITED
Registration no: 02590624 **VAT No.:** GB 479 6583 76
Date established: 1991 **Turnover:** £10m - £20m
No.of Employees: 21 - 50 **Product Groups:** 38

Date of Accounts	Dec 11	Dec 10	Dec 09
Sales Turnover	13m	12m	11m
Pre Tax Profit/Loss	985	-1m	763
Working Capital	8m	7m	8m
Fixed Assets	2m	2m	2m
Current Assets	10m	10m	11m
Current Liabilities	2m	2m	2m

Rawlison Butler
Griffin House 135 High Street, Crawley, RH10 1DQ
Tel: 01293-527744 **Fax:** 01293-520202
E-mail: info@rawlisonbutler.com
Website: http://www.rawlisonbutler.com
Bank(s): Barclays
Directors: D. Armstrong (Snr Part), T. Sadka (Fin)
Managers: D. Belford (Develop Mgr), J. Graver (Personnel), S. Gravett (Fin Mgr), L. Young (Tech Serv Mgr), D. Nightingale (Sales Admin)
Immediate Holding Company: RAWLISON BUTLER LIMITED
Registration no: 05263994 **Date established:** 2004 **Turnover:** £5m - £10m
No.of Employees: 51 - 100 **Product Groups:** 80

Reed Employment Ltd
36 Queens Square, Crawley, RH10 1HA
Tel: 01293-547455 **Fax:** 01293-552691
Website: http://www.reed.co.uk
Managers: J. Davies (District Mgr)
Ultimate Holding Company: REED GLOBAL LTD (MALTA)
Immediate Holding Company: REED EMPLOYMENT LIMITED
Registration no: 00669854 **Date established:** 1960
Turnover: £250m - £500m **No.of Employees:** 1 - 10 **Product Groups:** 80

Date of Accounts	Jun 11	Jun 10	Dec 07
Sales Turnover	618	450	287m
Pre Tax Profit/Loss	-2m	310	8m
Working Capital	23m	28m	28m
Fixed Assets	31	36	5m
Current Assets	28m	30m	74m
Current Liabilities	37	29	21m

Reliance Security Services Ltd
4 Bank Precinct Gatwick Road, Crawley, RH10 9RF
Tel: 01293-402381 **Fax:** 01293-402389
E-mail: annasills@reliancesecurity.co.uk
Website: http://www.reliancesecurity.co.uk
Managers: A. Havers (Chief Mgr), A. Sills (Fin Mgr)
Immediate Holding Company: RELIANCE SECURITY SERVICES LIMITED
Registration no: 01146486 **Date established:** 1973
Turnover: Over £1,000m **No.of Employees:** 11 - 20 **Product Groups:** 81

Rose Auto Supplies
Merlin Centre County Oak Way, Crawley, RH11 7XA
Tel: 01293-536769 **Fax:** 01293-553666
E-mail: roseautos@googlemail.com
Directors: P. Burtenshaw (Prop)
Registration no: 02164943 **VAT No.:** GB 315 7977 27
Turnover: £500,000 - £1m **No.of Employees:** 11 - 20
Product Groups: 35, 66

Rotronic Distribution Services
Unit 1a Crompton Fields Crompton Way, Crawley, RH10 9EE
Tel: 01293-565556 **Fax:** 01293-843710
E-mail: sales@rotronic.co.uk
Website: http://www.rotronic.co.uk
Directors: H. Jones (Dir)
Immediate Holding Company: ROTRONIC AG (CHE)
Registration no: 02408279 **Turnover:** £1m - £2m
No.of Employees: 1 - 10 **Product Groups:** 26, 37, 44, 67

Rotronic Instruments UK Ltd
Unit 1a Crompton Fields Crompton Way, Crawley, RH10 9EE
Tel: 01293-571000 **Fax:** 01293-571008
E-mail: instruments@rotronic.co.uk
Website: http://www.rotronic.co.uk
Bank(s): HSBC
Directors: M. Taraba (Dir), R. Farley (Co Sec)
Ultimate Holding Company: ROTRONIC AG (SWITZERLAND)
Immediate Holding Company: ROTRONIC INSTRUMENTS (UK) LIMITED
Registration no: 02281589 **VAT No.:** GB 523 5389 43
Date established: 1988 **Turnover:** £2m - £5m **No.of Employees:** 11 - 20
Product Groups: 38, 48

Date of Accounts	Jun 12	Jun 11	Jun 10
Sales Turnover	3m	3m	3m
Pre Tax Profit/Loss	81	21	80
Working Capital	734	655	603
Fixed Assets	67	85	130
Current Assets	1m	1m	940
Current Liabilities	139	70	144

Ryebrook Resins Ltd
Unit 4 Kelvin Business Centre, Crawley, RH10 9SF
Tel: 01293-565500 **Fax:** 01293-565472
E-mail: sales@ryebrook.co.uk
Website: http://www.ryebrook.co.uk
Bank(s): Barclays
Directors: A. Hills (MD), A. Hills (Prop), H. Hills (Dir)
Managers: P. Ashley (Property Mgr)
Immediate Holding Company: RYEBROOK RESINS LLP
Registration no: OC362666 **VAT No.:** GB 395 4078 20
Date established: 2011 **Turnover:** £1m - £2m **No.of Employees:** 11 - 20
Product Groups: 52

Date of Accounts	Mar 08	Mar 07	Mar 06
Sales Turnover	1137	1053	783
Pre Tax Profit/Loss	15	3	-17
Working Capital	125	105	112
Fixed Assets	69	90	80
Current Assets	395	367	360
Current Liabilities	270	263	248
ROCE% (Return on Capital Employed)	7.8	1.7	-8.9
ROT% (Return on Turnover)	1.3	0.3	-2.2

S P X Flow Technology
3b Wheatstone Close, Crawley, RH10 9UA
Tel: 01293-553495 **Fax:** 01293-524635
E-mail: peter.robinson@spx.com
Website: http://www.johnson-pump.com
Managers: P. Robinson
Ultimate Holding Company: STORK GROUP NV (HOLLAND)
Immediate Holding Company: STORK HOLDINGS LTD
Registration no: 02188120 **VAT No.:** GB 479 6797 57
Turnover: £2m - £5m **No.of Employees:** 1 - 10 **Product Groups:** 39, 40, 41, 42, 43, 46

Scientific Computers Ltd (Head Office)
Jubliee House Jubilee Walk, Crawley, RH10 1LQ
Tel: 01293-403636 **Fax:** 01293-403641
E-mail: alan@scl.com
Website: http://www.scl.com
Bank(s): Barclays
Directors: A. Hall (MD), M. Rai (Dir), S. Rai (MD)
Immediate Holding Company: SCIENTIFIC COMPUTERS LIMITED
Registration no: 00639839 **VAT No.:** GB 190 3624 70
Date established: 1959 **Turnover:** £1m - £2m **No.of Employees:** 11 - 20
Product Groups: 26, 28, 38, 44, 84

Date of Accounts	Dec 10	Dec 09	Dec 08
Working Capital	-128	-182	-211
Fixed Assets	290	287	294
Current Assets	375	270	227

Sparesmaster
Genesis House Priestley Way, Crawley, RH10 9PR
Tel: 01293-652479 **Fax:** 01293-652485
E-mail: sales@sparesmaster.co.uk
Website: http://www.sparesmaster.co.uk
Directors: D. Hibbert (MD)
Ultimate Holding Company: ACCESS GARAGE DOORS LIMITED
Registration no: 02508631 **Date established:** 1990
No.of Employees: 11 - 20 **Product Groups:** 36, 37, 39

Specialist Engineering Solutions Ltd
Brook House Brookhill Road, Copthorne, Crawley, RH10 3QJ
Tel: 01342-713177 **Fax:** 01342-713177
E-mail: enquiry@ses-ltd.uk.com
Website: http://www.ses-ltd.uk.com
Directors: R. Mears (MD)
Immediate Holding Company: SPECIALIST ENGINEERING SOLUTIONS LIMITED
Registration no: 03933418 **Date established:** 2000
Turnover: Up to £250,000 **No.of Employees:** 11 - 20 **Product Groups:** 84

Date of Accounts	Jun 11	Jun 10	Jun 09
Sales Turnover	N/A	52	131
Working Capital	N/A	9	1
Current Assets	5	9	6

Speedy Lifting
Unit C1 Fleming Centre Fleming Way, Crawley, RH10 9NN
Tel: 01293-615898 **Fax:** 01293-615818
E-mail: 0818.crawley@speedyhire.com
Website: http://www.speedyhire.co.uk
Managers: G. Joyce (Depot Mgr)
Immediate Holding Company: SPEEDY HIRE PLC
Registration no: 04529136 **Turnover:** £20m - £50m
No.of Employees: 1 - 10 **Product Groups:** 35, 37, 38, 39, 45, 48, 83

Spirent plc
Swift House Northwood Park Gatwick Road, Crawley, RH10 9XN
Tel: 01293-767676 **Fax:** 01293-767677
E-mail: info@spirent.com
Website: http://www.spirent.com
Managers: E. Hutchinson, E. Owusu (Tech Serv Mgr)
Ultimate Holding Company: SPIRENT COMMUNICATIONS PLC
Immediate Holding Company: SPIRENT HOLDINGS LIMITED
Registration no: 03451782 **Date established:** 1997 **Turnover:** £2m - £5m
No.of Employees: 21 - 50 **Product Groups:** 38, 67

Date of Accounts	Dec 11	Dec 10	Dec 09
Sales Turnover	3m	N/A	N/A
Pre Tax Profit/Loss	3m	3m	N/A
Working Capital	3m	-213	-3m
Fixed Assets	4m	4m	4m
Current Assets	3m	N/A	N/A

Stakrak Ltd
Unit 19 Pelham Court Pelham Place, Crawley, RH11 9SH
Tel: 01293-538822 **Fax:** 01293-550533
E-mail: sales@stakrak.co.uk
Website: http://www.stakrak.co.uk
Directors: M. Richardson (MD)
Immediate Holding Company: STAKRAK LIMITED
Registration no: 03929361 **Date established:** 2000
Turnover: Up to £250,000 **No.of Employees:** 1 - 10 **Product Groups:** 26, 35, 36, 39, 67, 85

Date of Accounts	Dec 11	Dec 10	Dec 09
Working Capital	78	91	71
Fixed Assets	4	5	5
Current Assets	172	195	164

Steck Depositors Ltd
Heathy Ridge Copthorne Road, Crawley, RH10 3PD
Tel: 01293-873439 **Fax:** 01293-551644
E-mail: admin@steckdepositors.com
Website: http://www.steckdepositors.com
Directors: M. Wilkinson (Prop)
Immediate Holding Company: STECK DEPOSITORS LIMITED
Registration no: 04234790 **Date established:** 2001
No.of Employees: 1 - 10 **Product Groups:** 20, 40, 41

Date of Accounts	Mar 12	Mar 11	Mar 10
Working Capital	141	97	91
Fixed Assets	11	21	19
Current Assets	552	538	567

Stevens Vauxhall & Chevrolet
Fleming Way Manor Royal, Crawley, RH10 9NS
Tel: 01293-540054 **Fax:** 01293-519081
E-mail: info@stevenscrawley.co.uk
Website: http://www.stevensvauxhall.co.uk
Managers: P. Stevens, L. Stevens (Personnel), D. Longhurst
Ultimate Holding Company: EVANS HALSHAW HOLDINGS P.L.C. GROUP
Registration no: 01593852 **No.of Employees:** 51 - 100
Product Groups: 39, 68, 72, 84

T G Steel Fabrications
Parish Lane Pease Pottage, Crawley, RH10 5NY
Tel: 01293-614664 **Fax:** 01293-616066
Directors: T. Guest (Prop)
Immediate Holding Company: UNIVERSAL APPLIED COATINGS LIMITED
Registration no: 01810243 **Date established:** 1984
Turnover: £250,000 - £500,000 **No.of Employees:** 1 - 10
Product Groups: 35

Date of Accounts	Apr 11	Apr 10	Apr 09
Sales Turnover	N/A	394	479
Pre Tax Profit/Loss	N/A	-51	6
Working Capital	35	14	56
Fixed Assets	13	14	22
Current Assets	142	131	122
Current Liabilities	N/A	73	43

Ta Instruments
Fleming Centre Fleming Way, Crawley, RH10 9NB
Tel: 01293-658900 **Fax:** 01293-658901
E-mail: olivia.gibson@taeurope.co.uk
Website: http://www.tainstruments.com
Directors: C. Titschall (Fin)
Managers: K. Yurick (Mktg Serv Mgr), O. Gibson, O. Gibson (), M. Melingo, A. Heritage, C. Titshall (Fin Mgr)
Immediate Holding Company: T A INSTRUMENTS LTD
Registration no: 00879800 **VAT No.:** GB 602 5908 57
Date established: 1966 **Turnover:** £10m - £20m
No.of Employees: 21 - 50 **Product Groups:** 28, 38, 42, 47

Date of Accounts	Dec 07	Dec 06	Dec 05
Sales Turnover	14206	12429	11275
Pre Tax Profit/Loss	5475	4802	4036
Working Capital	6893	3102	2572
Fixed Assets	609	530	520
Current Assets	11433	6896	6432
Current Liabilities	4540	3794	3860
Total Share Capital	105	105	105
ROCE% (Return on Capital Employed)	73.0	132.2	130.5
ROT% (Return on Turnover)	38.5	38.6	35.8

Technical Fabrications
Rowfant Business Centre Wallage Lane, Rowfant, Crawley, RH10 4NQ
Tel: 01342-717523 **Fax:** 01342-715392
E-mail: techfab31@blueyonder.co.uk
Directors: S. Pluckrose (Snr Part)
VAT No.: GB 492 3725 28 **Turnover:** Up to £250,000
No.of Employees: 1 - 10 **Product Groups:** 33, 34, 35, 45, 48

Technical Vacuum Services Ltd
69 Langley Drive Langley Green, Crawley, RH11 7TF
Tel: 01293-400887 **Fax:** 01293-400887
E-mail: sales@technicalvacuumservices.co.uk
Website: http://www.technicalvacuumservices.co.uk

Directors: N. McCulloch (I.T. Dir), L. McCulloch (Fin)
Immediate Holding Company: TECHNICAL VACUUM SERVICES LIMITED
Registration no: 05386448 **Date established:** 2005
Turnover: Up to £250,000 **No.of Employees:** 1 - 10 **Product Groups:** 29, 30, 32, 33, 35, 36, 37, 38, 40, 42, 45, 47, 48, 52, 66, 67, 80, 83, 84, 85

Date of Accounts	Mar 11	Mar 10	Mar 09
Sales Turnover	N/A	N/A	49
Pre Tax Profit/Loss	N/A	N/A	21
Working Capital	-5	-2	-2
Fixed Assets	5	3	3
Current Assets	15	13	8
Current Liabilities	N/A	N/A	5

Telcon Ltd (Head Office)
D1 Old Brighton Road Lowfield Heath, Crawley, RH11 0PR
Tel: 01293-528800 **Fax:** 01293-524466
E-mail: sales@telcon.co.uk
Website: http://www.telcon.co.uk
Directors: P. Brooks (Chief Op Offcr)
Managers: G. Potter, S. Swaine (Prod Eng)
Immediate Holding Company: TELCON LIMITED
Registration no: 01741741 **VAT No.:** GB 528 3170 52
Date established: 1983 **Turnover:** £5m - £10m **No.of Employees:** 21 - 50
Product Groups: 37

Date of Accounts	Jun 11	Jun 10	Jun 09
Sales Turnover	5m	3m	3m
Pre Tax Profit/Loss	637	248	245
Working Capital	1m	1m	886
Fixed Assets	497	355	433
Current Assets	3m	2m	1m
Current Liabilities	478	359	231

Thales Training & Consultancy
Sackville House Northwood Park Gatwick Road, Crawley, RH10 9XN
Tel: 0800-163469 **Fax:** 01293-563301
E-mail: traininginfo@thalesgroup.com
Website: http://www.thales-trainingconsultancy.com
Bank(s): National Westminster
Directors: B. North (Dir)
Managers: S. Davies (Mktg Serv Mgr), M. Smithson
Ultimate Holding Company: SPIRENT COMMUNICATIONS PLC
Immediate Holding Company: SPIRENT FINANCING LIMITED
Registration no: 00426402 **Date established:** 2001
Turnover: £75m - £125m **No.of Employees:** 21 - 50 **Product Groups:** 28, 44, 84

Date of Accounts	Dec 09	Dec 08
Working Capital	250	250
Current Assets	250	250

Thermopol Ltd
Woolborough Lane, Crawley, RH10 2UW
Tel: 01293-543615 **Fax:** 01293-844721
E-mail: info@contitech.de
Website: http://www.thermopolinternational.com/europe.htm
Bank(s): Natiuonal Westminster
Directors: G. Macleod (Ch), P. Khot (Co Sec)
Managers: D. Klemkerk (Mktg Serv Mgr)
Ultimate Holding Company: Thermopol Inc
Immediate Holding Company: Contitech UK Ltd
Registration no: 01076936 **VAT No.:** GB 644 5709 23
Date established: 1995 **Turnover:** £10m - £20m
No.of Employees: 101 - 250 **Product Groups:** 30

Date of Accounts	Dec 07
Sales Turnover	13327
Pre Tax Profit/Loss	-1251
Working Capital	1579
Fixed Assets	1605
Current Assets	6240
Current Liabilities	4661
Total Share Capital	3360
ROCE% (Return on Capital Employed)	-39.3

TheSonicNet
11 Nokes Court Commonwealth Drive, Crawley, RH10 1AL
Tel: 0871-2456699 **Fax:** 0871-2456698
E-mail: kym@thesonicnet.com
Website: http://www.thesonicnet.com
Directors: K. Morris (Grp Chief Exec)
Date established: 2009 **Turnover:** Up to £250,000
No.of Employees: 1 - 10 **Product Groups:** 44, 79, 80

Timberstore Ltd
Rowfant Sawmills Wallage Lane, Rowfant, Crawley, RH10 4NQ
Tel: 01342-717155 **Fax:** 01342-717156
E-mail: info@timberstore.org.uk
Website: http://www.timberstore.org.uk
Managers: S. Briggs
Immediate Holding Company: TIMBERSTORE LIMITED
Registration no: 06158284 **Date established:** 2007
No.of Employees: 1 - 10 **Product Groups:** 23, 25, 26, 33, 35, 39, 66

Date of Accounts	Dec 11	Dec 10	Dec 09
Working Capital	-176	-196	-181
Fixed Assets	265	286	231
Current Assets	432	471	535

Toshiba Medical Systems Ltd (Head Office)
Gatwick Road, Crawley, RH10 9AX
Tel: 01293-653700 **Fax:** 01293-653770
E-mail: mstork@tmse.nl
Website: http://www.toshiba-medical.co.uk
Bank(s): Barclays
Directors: M. Hitchman (MD)
Ultimate Holding Company: TOSHIBA CORPORATION (JAPAN)
Immediate Holding Company: TOSHIBA MEDICAL SYSTEMS LIMITED
Registration no: 00983579 **VAT No.:** GB 218 1388 66
Date established: 1970 **Turnover:** £50m - £75m
No.of Employees: 21 - 50 **Product Groups:** 37, 44

Date of Accounts	Mar 11	Mar 10	Mar 09
Sales Turnover	50m	46m	44m
Pre Tax Profit/Loss	2m	2m	1m
Working Capital	6m	6m	5m
Fixed Assets	3m	3m	3m
Current Assets	19m	25m	20m
Current Liabilities	10m	9m	7m

TSC Music Systems Ltd
T S C House Spindle Way, Crawley, RH10 1TG
Tel: 01293-523441 **Fax:** 01293-553461
Website: http://www.tsc-music.com
Bank(s): Barclays
Directors: A. Abdool (Dir), J. Abdool (MD), N. Abdool (Ch)
Immediate Holding Company: Imagesound plc
Registration no: 01230123 **VAT No.:** GB 602 4098 71
Date established: 1984 **Turnover:** £1m - £2m **No.of Employees:** 11 - 20
Product Groups: 37

UK Platforms
Unit 3 Dialog Fleming Way, Crawley, RH10 9NQ
Tel: 01293-614480 **Fax:** 01293-614478
E-mail: crawley2@ukplatforms.co.uk
Website: http://www.ukplatforms.co.uk
Managers: S. Walters
Registration no: 03925935 **No.of Employees:** 1 - 10 **Product Groups:** 36, 39, 41, 45, 83

Unibind Systems Ltd
3 Oak Court Betts Way, Crawley, RH10 9GG
Tel: 01293-530182 **Fax:** 01293-529272
E-mail: info@unibindsystems.co.uk
Website: http://www.unibindsystems.co.uk
Bank(s): Barclays
Directors: T. Keoshgerian (Dir)
Managers: D. Eastoe (Comptroller), R. Woodward (Nat Sales Mgr), L. Wilson
Ultimate Holding Company: UNIBIND (CYPRUS)
Immediate Holding Company: UNIBIND SYSTEMS LIMITED
Registration no: 02968045 **VAT No.:** GB 644 4358 31
Date established: 1994 **Turnover:** £2m - £5m **No.of Employees:** 21 - 50
Product Groups: 28, 44, 49

Date of Accounts	Dec 11	Dec 10	Dec 09
Sales Turnover	3m	4m	3m
Pre Tax Profit/Loss	211	237	95
Working Capital	2m	1m	1m
Fixed Assets	228	171	124
Current Assets	2m	2m	2m
Current Liabilities	320	410	336

Unique Printing Solutions
8 Spindle Way, Crawley, RH10 1TG
Tel: 01293-553388 **Fax:** 01293-419321
E-mail: salesatunique@aol.com
Directors: G. Hardwick (Prop)
Immediate Holding Company: DEEP SPACE DESIGN LTD
Registration no: 07106534 **Date established:** 2009
Turnover: Up to £250,000 **No.of Employees:** 1 - 10 **Product Groups:** 28, 81

Date of Accounts	Dec 10	Dec 08	Dec 07
Working Capital	11	11	36
Current Assets	14	16	51

Universal Applied Coatings Ltd
Parish Lane Pease Pottage, Crawley, RH10 5NY
Tel: 01293-514943 **Fax:** 01293-552619
Directors: R. Meekins (Dir)
Immediate Holding Company: UNIVERSAL APPLIED COATINGS LIMITED
Registration no: 01810243 **Date established:** 1984
Turnover: £250,000 - £500,000 **No.of Employees:** 1 - 10
Product Groups: 46, 48

Date of Accounts	Apr 11	Apr 10	Apr 09
Sales Turnover	N/A	394	479
Pre Tax Profit/Loss	N/A	-51	6
Working Capital	35	14	56
Fixed Assets	13	14	22
Current Assets	142	131	122
Current Liabilities	N/A	73	43

Vanpoulles Ltd
Telford Place, Crawley, RH10 1SZ
Tel: 01293-590100 **Fax:** 01293-590115
E-mail: sales@vanpoulles.co.uk
Website: http://www.vanpoulles.co.uk
Bank(s): Lloyds TSB Bank plc
Directors: D. Appleton (Fin)
Immediate Holding Company: VANPOULLES LIMITED
Registration no: 00430867 **VAT No.:** GB 239 3365 48
Date established: 1947 **No.of Employees:** 11 - 20 **Product Groups:** 26, 29, 49

Date of Accounts	Jul 11	Jul 10	Jul 09
Working Capital	116	83	137
Fixed Assets	953	970	991
Current Assets	390	406	398

Varian Medical Systems UK Ltd (Registered Office)
Gatwick Road, Crawley, RH10 9RG
Tel: 01293-601200 **Fax:** 01293-510260
Website: http://www.varian.com
Directors: L. Fletcher (Gen Sec)
Managers: D. Flanagan (Prod Mgr), M. Cragg (Serv Mgr)
Ultimate Holding Company: VARIAN MEDICAL SYSTEMS INC (USA)
Immediate Holding Company: VARIAN MEDICAL SYSTEMS UK LIMITED
Registration no: 00558526 **VAT No.:** GB 609 2335 51
Date established: 1955 **Turnover:** £75m - £125m
No.of Employees: 1 - 10 **Product Groups:** 37

Date of Accounts	Sep 11	Sep 08	Oct 09
Sales Turnover	87m	73m	75m
Pre Tax Profit/Loss	11m	9m	17m
Working Capital	40m	24m	32m
Fixed Assets	6m	6m	7m
Current Assets	61m	41m	51m
Current Liabilities	17m	13m	16m

Veritas DGC Ltd
Crompton Way, Crawley, RH10 9QN
Tel: 01293-443000 **Fax:** 01293-443010
Website: http://www.veritasdgc.com
Directors: M. Sayer (Co Sec), N. Bright (MD), R. Thornton (Dir)
Managers: M. Black (Mktg Serv Mgr)
Immediate Holding Company: VERITAS DGC LIMITED
Registration no: 01082778 **VAT No.:** GB 210 4000 54
Date established: 1972 **Turnover:** £75m - £125m
No.of Employees: 501 - 1000 **Product Groups:** 84, 85

Virgin Atlantic Airways Ltd
The Office Manor Royal, Crawley, RH10 9NU
Tel: 08448-110000 **Fax:** 01293-561721
E-mail: sales@virgin-atlantic.com
Website: http://www.virginatlantic.com
Bank(s): Virgin
Directors: B. Pitman (Dir), G. Brady (Pers), T. Livett (Fin)
Managers: S. Godfrey (Sales Admin), M. Billings (Tech Serv Mgr)
Ultimate Holding Company: VIRGIN GROUP HOLDINGS LTD (BVI)
Immediate Holding Company: VIRGIN ATLANTIC AIRWAYS LIMITED
Registration no: 01600117 **VAT No.:** GB 425 2161 84
Date established: 1981 **Turnover:** Over £1,000m
No.of Employees: 1501 & over **Product Groups:** 75

Date of Accounts	Feb 12	Feb 11	Feb 10
Sales Turnover	2402m	2264m	1984m
Pre Tax Profit/Loss	-99m	3m	-159m
Working Capital	-4m	191m	214m
Fixed Assets	409m	344m	357m
Current Assets	991m	1092m	1031m
Current Liabilities	730m	654m	616m

Viscose Closures Ltd
Unit 1 Royce Road, Crawley, RH10 9JY
Tel: 01293-519251 **Fax:** 01293-540005
E-mail: sales@viscose.co.uk
Website: http://www.viscose.co.uk
Bank(s): National Westminster Bank Plc
Directors: W. Cartwright (Dir), D. Gorman (Co Sec), G. Rowlands (MD)
Ultimate Holding Company: VISCOSE SLEEVING LIMITED
Immediate Holding Company: VISCOSE CLOSURES LIMITED
Registration no: 01848065 **VAT No.:** GB 702 3997 34
Date established: 1984 **Turnover:** £5m - £10m **No.of Employees:** 11 - 20
Product Groups: 30, 35, 42

Date of Accounts	Jul 11	Jul 10	Jul 09
Sales Turnover	10m	8m	7m
Pre Tax Profit/Loss	872	491	308
Working Capital	2m	1m	742
Fixed Assets	669	437	446
Current Assets	4m	3m	3m
Current Liabilities	594	626	738

Vulcascot Ltd
Gatwick Gate Industrial Estate Lowfield Heath, Crawley, RH11 0TG
Tel: 01293-560130 **Fax:** 01293-537743
E-mail: sales@vulcascot.co.uk
Website: http://www.vulcascot.com
Bank(s): Bank of Ireland, Croydon
Managers: R. Baker (Nat Sales Mgr), B. Copeman (Sales Prom Mgr)
Immediate Holding Company: VULCASCOT LIMITED
Registration no: 00330088 **VAT No.:** GB 227 3447 65
Date established: 1937 **Turnover:** £5m - £10m **No.of Employees:** 11 - 20
Product Groups: 29, 30

Date of Accounts	Sep 09	Sep 08	Sep 07
Working Capital	-2	142	154
Fixed Assets	23	11	9
Current Assets	1m	1m	2m

Welland Medical Ltd
Unit 7-8 The Brunel Centre Newton Road, Crawley, RH10 9TU
Tel: 01293-615455 **Fax:** 01293-615412
E-mail: info@wellandmedical.com
Website: http://www.wellandmedical.com
Bank(s): Barclays, High Wycombe, Bucks
Directors: A. Brighton (Co Sec), C. Primett (MD)
Managers: H. Gilbert (Personnel), M. Wyn (Fin Mgr), M. Skinner (Purch Mgr), S. Jackson (Product)
Ultimate Holding Company: CLINIMED (HOLDINGS) LIMITED
Immediate Holding Company: WELLAND MEDICAL LIMITED
Registration no: 02170535 **Date established:** 1987
Turnover: £10m - £20m **No.of Employees:** 101 - 250 **Product Groups:** 30

Date of Accounts	Dec 11	Dec 10	Dec 09
Sales Turnover	17m	15m	14m
Pre Tax Profit/Loss	4m	3m	3m
Working Capital	2m	2m	5m
Fixed Assets	4m	2m	2m
Current Assets	6m	6m	7m
Current Liabilities	2m	1m	1m

Whitelegg Machines Ltd
19 Crompton Way Manor Royal, Crawley, RH10 9QR
Tel: 01293-526230 **Fax:** 01293-538910
E-mail: sales@whitelegg.com
Website: http://www.whitelegg.com
Directors: H. Dawson (MD)
Immediate Holding Company: WHITELEGG MACHINES LIMITED
Registration no: 00894034 **VAT No.:** GB 528 5840 23
Date established: 1966 **Turnover:** £2m - £5m **No.of Employees:** 1 - 10
Product Groups: 35, 36, 37, 38, 40, 46, 47

Date of Accounts	Dec 11	Dec 10	Dec 09
Working Capital	131	18	-66
Fixed Assets	100	28	37
Current Assets	929	846	907

Window Mart
Unit 2 Metana House Priestley Way, Crawley, RH10 9NT
Tel: 01293-543513 **Fax:** 01293-543613
Website: http://www.windowmart.co.uk
Directors: M. Barker (Dir)
No.of Employees: 1 - 10 **Product Groups:** 30, 52, 66

Y B Plating Ltd
6 Priestley Way, Crawley, RH10 9NT
Tel: 01293-528974 **Fax:** 01293-552877
Directors: V. Mellows (MD)
Immediate Holding Company: YB PLATING LIMITED
Registration no: 07341908 **Date established:** 2010
No.of Employees: 1 - 10 **Product Groups:** 46, 48

Date of Accounts	Aug 11
Working Capital	9
Fixed Assets	7
Current Assets	53

East Grinstead

ABC Paints
Windsor Court East Grinstead House, East Grinstead, RH19 1XA
Tel: 01342-335869 **Fax:** 01342-335825
E-mail: rodkain@aol.com, **E-mail:** rodkain@aol.comrod.kain@rbi.co.uk
Website: http://gb.kompass.com/profile_GB09045277_en/abc-paints-ltd-ps.html
Product Groups: 32

Advanced Ergonomic Technologies Ltd

201-203 London Road, East Grinstead, RH19 1HA
Tel: 01342-310400 **Fax:** 01342-310401
E-mail: gbt@flexiblespace.com
Website: http://www.flexiblespace.com
Directors: G. Blake Thomas (MD)
Immediate Holding Company: ADVANCED ERGONOMIC TECHNOLOGIES LIMITED
Registration no: 02874101 **Date established:** 1993
No.of Employees: 1 - 10 **Product Groups:** 24, 25, 29, 30, 33, 35, 38, 40, 51, 52, 66

Date of Accounts	Feb 08	Feb 11	Feb 10
Working Capital	1m	543	552
Fixed Assets	322	199	323
Current Assets	2m	828	1m

F A Anderson Country Clothing

47 High Street, East Grinstead, RH19 3AS
Tel: 01342-300906 **Fax:** 01342-302604
Website: http://www.faanderson.co.uk
Directors: P. Wood (Prop)
Date established: 1974 **No.of Employees:** 1 - 10 **Product Groups:** 36, 39, 40

Artisan Websites Ltd

37 Greenstede Avenue, East Grinstead, RH19 3HZ
Tel: 01342-300819 **Fax:** 01342-300819
E-mail: design@artisanwebsites.co.uk
Website: http://www.artisanwebsites.co.uk
Directors: T. Clerkin (Fin), G. Clerkin (MD)
Immediate Holding Company: ARTISAN WEBSITES LTD
Registration no: 04582766 **Date established:** 2002
No.of Employees: 1 - 10 **Product Groups:** 44

Date of Accounts	Nov 11	Nov 10	Nov 09
Working Capital	N/A	5	11
Fixed Assets	N/A	N/A	1
Current Assets	40	37	38

Autarky Automation Ltd

16 Charlwoods Place, East Grinstead, RH19 2HY
Tel: 01342-311388 **Fax:** 01342-323733
E-mail: sales@autarky.com
Website: http://www.autarky.com
Directors: D. North (Dir)
Immediate Holding Company: AUTARKY GROUP LIMITED
Registration no: 03406331 **VAT No.:** GB 210 4967 83
Date established: 1997 **Turnover:** £1m - £2m **No.of Employees:** 21 - 50
Product Groups: 41

Date of Accounts	Jun 11	Jun 10	Jun 09
Working Capital	-609	-627	-635
Fixed Assets	2m	2m	2m
Current Assets	N/A	29	27

The Bankers' Almanac Reed Business Information

Windsor Court East Grinstead House, East Grinstead, RH19 1XA
Tel: 01342-326972 **Fax:** 01342-335612
E-mail: information@reedinfo.co.uk
Website: http://www.bankersalmanac.com
Bank(s): National Westminster Bank Plc
Directors: M. Kelsey (Grp Chief Exec), D. Feltham (MD)
Managers: M. Kelsey
Immediate Holding Company: REED BUSINESS INFORMATION LIMITED
Registration no: 00151537 **VAT No.:** GB 235 7235 65
Date established: 1918 **No.of Employees:** 251 - 500 **Product Groups:** 28, 81, 82

Barong Conservatories South East Ltd

Doves Barn Copthorne Road, Felbridge, East Grinstead, RH19 2PB
Tel: 01342-300903
Website: http://www.barong.co.uk
Directors: J. Wraight (Dir)
Immediate Holding Company: BARONG CONSERVATORIES (SOUTH-EAST) LIMITED
Registration no: 06553764 **Date established:** 2008
Turnover: £250,000 - £500,000 **No.of Employees:** 1 - 10
Product Groups: 30

Date of Accounts	Apr 11	Apr 10	Apr 09
Working Capital	-66	-115	-113
Fixed Assets	98	90	94
Current Assets	7	13	12

Blindmasters UK Ltd

123 Charlwoods Road, East Grinstead, RH19 2JE
Tel: 01342-328534 **Fax:** 07092-885773
E-mail: sales@blindmasters.uk.com
Website: http://www.blindmasters.uk.com
Directors: N. Mockford (Dir)
Immediate Holding Company: BLINDMASTERS UK LIMITED
Registration no: 06055800 **Date established:** 2007
Turnover: Over £1,000m **No.of Employees:** 1 - 10 **Product Groups:** 24

Date of Accounts	Jan 12	Jan 11	Jan 10
Working Capital	-6	-6	-3
Fixed Assets	1	4	7
Current Assets	3	5	10
Current Liabilities	5	N/A	N/A

Clyde Energy Solutions Ltd

13-14 Charlwoods Road, East Grinstead, RH19 2HU
Tel: 01342-305550 **Fax:** 020-8397 4598
E-mail: info@clyde4heat.co.uk
Website: http://www.clyde4heat.co.uk
Bank(s): Clydesdale Bank PLC
Managers: A. Godfrey (Chief Acct)
Ultimate Holding Company: SEMINAL CAPITAL LIMITED (BVI)
Immediate Holding Company: CLYDE ENERGY SOLUTIONS LIMITED
Registration no: SC011520 **Date established:** 2020
No.of Employees: 21 - 50 **Product Groups:** 40

Date of Accounts	Mar 09	Mar 08	Jun 11
Working Capital	301	314	188
Fixed Assets	21	54	17
Current Assets	447	619	557

Co Ordinated Engineering Ltd

2 Cantelupe Mews Cantelupe Road, East Grinstead, RH19 3BG
Tel: 01342-410130 **Fax:** 01342-410125
E-mail: info@cecgroup.org.uk
Website: http://www.cecgroup.fsnet.co.uk
Directors: C. Dawson (MD), A. Dawson (Co Sec), A. Dawson (Fin)
Managers: D. Dawson (Sales Prom Mgr), M. Dawson (Projects)
Immediate Holding Company: CO-ORDINATED ENGINEERING LIMITED
Registration no: 01961143 **VAT No.:** GB 407 3128 79
Date established: 1985 **Turnover:** £1m - £2m **No.of Employees:** 1 - 10
Product Groups: 54, 61, 80, 84

Date of Accounts	Mar 08	Mar 07	Mar 06
Working Capital	69	48	27
Fixed Assets	N/A	1	1
Current Assets	258	277	391
Current Liabilities	190	229	364

Condale Plastics Ltd

Unit 5 Independent Business Park Imberhorne Lane, East Grinstead, RH19 1TU
Tel: 01342-312714 **Fax:** 01342-312615
E-mail: admin@condaleplastics.com
Website: http://www.condale.co.uk
Bank(s): Lloyds TSB Bank plc
Directors: P. Chadwick (MD)
Ultimate Holding Company: MARSDALE PLASTICS
Immediate Holding Company: CONDALE PLASTICS LIMITED
Registration no: 00992692 **Date established:** 1970 **Turnover:** £5m - £10m
No.of Employees: 51 - 100 **Product Groups:** 30, 31, 37, 42, 66

Date of Accounts	May 11	May 10	May 09
Pre Tax Profit/Loss	269	200	535
Working Capital	2m	2m	2m
Fixed Assets	4m	4m	4m
Current Assets	5m	4m	4m
Current Liabilities	2m	996	1m

Eden River Press Ltd

Unit C Charlwoods Business Centre, East Grinstead, RH19 2HH
Tel: 01342-313577 **Fax:** 01342-324125
E-mail: hello@edenriverpress.co.uk
Website: http://www.edenriverpress.co.uk
Directors: P. Winkley (MD)
Immediate Holding Company: EDEN RIVER PRESS LIMITED
Registration no: 02115779 **Date established:** 1987
Turnover: £500,000 - £1m **No.of Employees:** 1 - 10 **Product Groups:** 44, 67

Date of Accounts	Jun 11	Jun 10	Jun 09
Working Capital	-92	-128	-158
Fixed Assets	40	18	56
Current Assets	84	77	60

Electricold Refrigeration

60 Moat Road, East Grinstead, RH19 3LH
Tel: 020-8660 4641 **Fax:** 020-8668 2358
E-mail: info@electricold.co.uk
Website: http://www.electricold.co.uk
Directors: H. Spargo (MD)
Date established: 1950 **Turnover:** Up to £250,000
No.of Employees: 1 - 10 **Product Groups:** 52

Eric Lamprell Blacksmith

1 The Forge Wall Hill Road, Ashurst Wood, East Grinstead, RH19 3TQ
Tel: 01342-822143 **Fax:** 01342-822143
Directors: E. Lamprell (Prop)
Date established: 1986 **No.of Employees:** 1 - 10 **Product Groups:** 26, 35

R A Foster Flooring Services

3 The Belfry West Hill, East Grinstead, RH19 4EP
Tel: 01342-311452
Directors: R. Foster (Prop)
Date established: 1997 **No.of Employees:** 1 - 10 **Product Groups:** 35, 36

G & G Food Supplies

Unit H Queens Walk, East Grinstead, RH19 4DW
Tel: 01342-322795 **Fax:** 01342-315938
Website: http://www.gandgvitamins.com
Managers: L. Du-Bled (Mgr)
Registration no: 02103924 **VAT No.:** GB 702 7593 38
Turnover: £1m - £2m **No.of Employees:** 1 - 10 **Product Groups:** 02, 20

Date of Accounts	Dec 07	Dec 06	Dec 05
Sales Turnover	5099	4446	4634
Pre Tax Profit/Loss	198	-121	114
Working Capital	295	173	250
Fixed Assets	354	370	404
Current Assets	2234	2072	1955
Current Liabilities	1939	1899	1705
Total Share Capital	12	16	16
ROCE% (Return on Capital Employed)	30.6	-22.4	17.4
ROT% (Return on Turnover)	3.9	-2.7	2.5

G & G Food Supplements

Unit 2 Imberhorne Way, East Grinstead, RH19 1RL
Tel: 01342-311401 **Fax:** 01342-315938
E-mail: sales@gandgvitamins.com
Website: http://www.gandgvitamins.com
Directors: M. Mc Entyre (Dir)
Managers: I. Cochran, M. Wood (Buyer)
Immediate Holding Company: G & G FOOD SUPPLIES LIMITED
Registration no: 02103924 **Date established:** 1987 **Turnover:** £2m - £5m
No.of Employees: 21 - 50 **Product Groups:** 88

Date of Accounts	Dec 11	Dec 10	Dec 09
Sales Turnover	4m	3m	4m
Pre Tax Profit/Loss	57	130	204
Working Capital	174	191	48
Fixed Assets	230	218	265
Current Assets	1m	1m	1m
Current Liabilities	408	346	556

Graham

Unit 4b Independent Business Park Imberhorne Lane, East Grinstead, RH19 1TU
Tel: 01342-321481 **Fax:** 01342-327173
E-mail: davidcasey@grahamgroup.co.uk
Website: http://www.graham-group.co.uk
Managers: D. Casey (Mgr)
Ultimate Holding Company: SAINT-GOBAIN PLC
Immediate Holding Company: GRAHAM GROUP LTD
Registration no: 00066738 **No.of Employees:** 1 - 10 **Product Groups:** 66

Insulated Tools

Charlwoods Road, East Grinstead, RH19 2HR
Tel: 01342-324255 **Fax:** 01342-327115
E-mail: john.hallmark@insulatedtools.co.uk
Website: http://www.insulatedtoolsgroup.com
Bank(s): Natwest Bank
Directors: M. Wardle (Prop)
Ultimate Holding Company: INSULATED TOOLS LIMITED
Immediate Holding Company: INSULATED TOOLS LIMITED
Registration no: 00833396 **VAT No.:** GB 209 8274 47
Date established: 1965 **No.of Employees:** 11 - 20 **Product Groups:** 22, 24, 29, 30, 33, 35, 36, 37, 39, 40, 61, 63

Date of Accounts	Mar 12	Mar 11	Mar 10
Working Capital	1m	885	793
Fixed Assets	392	393	411
Current Assets	1m	1m	901

Kogo Ltd

5 Cantelupe Mews Cantelupe Road, East Grinstead, RH19 3BG
Tel: 01342-333000 **Fax:** 01342-333001
E-mail: sales@kogo.co.uk
Website: http://www.kogo.co.uk
Directors: M. Bannister (MD)
Immediate Holding Company: KOGO LIMITED
Registration no: 04185782 **Date established:** 2001
Turnover: £500,000 - £1m **No.of Employees:** 1 - 10 **Product Groups:** 44

Date of Accounts	Mar 12	Mar 11	Mar 10
Sales Turnover	N/A	N/A	538
Pre Tax Profit/Loss	N/A	N/A	40
Working Capital	13	3	-14
Fixed Assets	17	22	29
Current Assets	121	138	94
Current Liabilities	N/A	N/A	37

Kompass (UK)Ltd

St James's House 150 London Road, East Grinstead, RH19 1XA
Tel: 0800-0185882 **Fax:** 01342-327940
E-mail: sales@kompass.co.uk
Website: http://www.kompassinfo.co.uk
Bank(s): Lloyds TSB
Directors: R. Kain (MD)
Managers: T. Cheeseman (Fin Mgr), S. Hoad (Sales Prom Mgr), C. Magner (Sales Prom Mgr)
Immediate Holding Company: Kompass International Neuenschwander S.A.
Registration no: 07819067 **VAT No.:** GB 124 5016 53
Date established: 1959 **Turnover:** £2m - £5m **No.of Employees:** 50
Product Groups: 28, 79, 80, 81

Marco Ltd

The Old Barn Wilderwick Road, East Grinstead, RH19 3NT
Tel: 01342-870103 **Fax:** 01342-870104
E-mail: russel.hilborne@marcoweighing.co.uk
Website: http://www.marco.co.uk
Directors: R. Hilborne (Dir), S. Heads (Co Sec)
Immediate Holding Company: MARCO LIMITED
Registration no: 03495807 **VAT No.:** GB 702 3798 40
Date established: 1998 **Turnover:** £500,000 - £1m
No.of Employees: 1 - 10 **Product Groups:** 48

Date of Accounts	Mar 11	Mar 10	Mar 09
Working Capital	205	567	540
Fixed Assets	99	92	99
Current Assets	2m	2m	2m

Nightfreight (GB) Ltd

Imberhorne Way, East Grinstead, RH19 1RL
Tel: 01342-316221 **Fax:** 01342-316134
E-mail: info@nightfreight.co.uk
Website: http://www.nightfreight.co.uk
Bank(s): HSBC Bank plc
Managers: L. Schifano (Sales & Mktg Mg), M. Wheeler (I.T. Exec), S. Thorp (Chief Mgr)
Ultimate Holding Company: PENGLAIS INVESTMENTS LIMITED
Immediate Holding Company: NIGHTFREIGHT (GB) LIMITED
Registration no: 02402927 **VAT No.:** GB **Date established:** 1989
Turnover: £2m - £5m **No.of Employees:** 51 - 100 **Product Groups:** 45, 72

Date of Accounts	Nov 11	Nov 10	Nov 09
Sales Turnover	121m	118m	122m
Pre Tax Profit/Loss	-4m	-2m	1m
Working Capital	16m	16m	5m
Fixed Assets	11m	15m	17m
Current Assets	47m	47m	52m
Current Liabilities	14m	12m	11m

Omeg Ltd

Imberhorne Industrial Estate, East Grinstead, RH19 1RJ
Tel: 01342-410420 **Fax:** 01342-316253
E-mail: sales@omeg.co.uk
Website: http://www.omeg.co.uk
Bank(s): HSBC Bank plc
Directors: G. Harrison (MD)
Managers: M. Heeley (Tech Serv Mgr), M. Grantham (Sales Prom Mgr)
Ultimate Holding Company: EAST GRINSTEAD PROPERTIES LIMITED
Immediate Holding Company: OMEG LIMITED
Registration no: 00600441 **Date established:** 1958 **Turnover:** £1m - £2m
No.of Employees: 21 - 50 **Product Groups:** 37

Date of Accounts	Jun 12	Jun 11	Jun 10
Working Capital	876	864	822
Fixed Assets	142	167	109
Current Assets	1m	1m	1m

Precision Technology Supplies Ltd

Birches Industrial Estate Imberhornerial Lane, East Grinstead, RH19 1XZ
Tel: 01342-410758 **Fax:** 01342-311464
E-mail: info@pts-uk.com
Website: http://www.pts-uk.com
Directors: J. Collyer (Dir)
Immediate Holding Company: PRECISION TECHNOLOGY SUPPLIES LIMITED
Registration no: 02192324 **Date established:** 1987
Turnover: £500,000 - £1m **No.of Employees:** 11 - 20
Product Groups: 22, 23, 25, 27, 29, 30, 31, 32, 33, 34, 35, 36, 38, 39, 40, 41, 42, 43, 44, 45, 46, 47, 49, 62, 63, 66, 68

Date of Accounts	Mar 11	Mar 10	Mar 09
Working Capital	673	441	369
Fixed Assets	674	678	675
Current Assets	1m	843	689

Provincial Windows Ltd

Unit 3c Birches Industrial Estate, East Grinstead, RH19 1XZ
Tel: 01342-313767 **Fax:** 01342-311407
E-mail: info@provincialwindows.co.uk
Website: http://www.provincialwindows.co.uk

Directors: C. Robinson (Dir)
Ultimate Holding Company: SIBLEY INVESTMENTS LIMITED
Immediate Holding Company: PROVINCIAL WINDOWS LIMITED
Registration no: 01504584 **VAT No.:** GB 395 2876 02
Date established: 1980 **Turnover:** £1m - £2m **No.of Employees:** 1 - 10
Product Groups: 30, 33, 52

Date of Accounts	Dec 11	Mar 11	Mar 10
Sales Turnover	1m	1m	1m
Pre Tax Profit/Loss	72	14	-12
Working Capital	-0	-0	-8
Fixed Assets	N/A	N/A	1
Current Assets	259	243	217
Current Liabilities	89	125	103

Q V S Electrical Wholesale

Unit 4c Birches Industrial Estate, East Grinstead, RH19 1XZ
Tel: 01342-302244 **Fax:** 0800-197 6566
E-mail: sales@qvsdirect.co.uk
Website: http://www.qvsdirect.com
Directors: M. Duggan (Fin)
Managers: M. Harris (Mgr), T. Bruce (Mktg Serv Mgr), L. Brain (Tech Serv Mgr)
Date established: 1994 **No.of Employees:** 21 - 50 **Product Groups:** 40, 66, 67

R O C TekniTronics

33 High Street, East Grinstead, RH19 3AF
Tel: 01342-716907 **Fax:** 01342-716907
E-mail: rocteknitronics.com@compuserve.com
Website: http://www.rocteknitronics.com
Directors: R. Wilson (Snr Part)
Immediate Holding Company: PURLEY GATES MANAGEMENT LIMITED
Registration no: 02784149 **VAT No.:** GB 528 4565 24
Date established: 1987 **Turnover:** Up to £250,000
No.of Employees: 1 - 10 **Product Groups:** 37, 44, 48, 84

Date of Accounts	Mar 12	Mar 11	Mar 10
Sales Turnover	32	31	53
Pre Tax Profit/Loss	N/A	N/A	-1
Working Capital	9	8	8
Current Assets	30	21	10
Current Liabilities	21	13	2

Reddick Forge

Crawley Down Road Felbridge, East Grinstead, RH19 2PS
Tel: 01342-302055 **Fax:** 01342-302055
E-mail: reddickforge@hotmail.com
Website: http://www.reddickforge.co.uk
Directors: J. Jones (Prop)
Turnover: Up to £250,000 **No.of Employees:** 1 - 10 **Product Groups:** 34, 35, 36, 49

Sargents Factors Ltd

Birches Indl-Est, East Grinstead, RH19 1XZ
Tel: 01342-321456 **Fax:** 01342-321598
Directors: J. Sargent (Fin), J. Sargent (Dir)
Managers: C. Waine (Purch Mgr)
Immediate Holding Company: SARGENTS FACTORS LIMITED
Registration no: 01669229 **VAT No.:** 367 4985 93 **Date established:** 1982
Turnover: £500,000 - £1m **No.of Employees:** 1 - 10 **Product Groups:** 68

Date of Accounts	Mar 11	Mar 10	Mar 09
Working Capital	11	36	28
Fixed Assets	11	14	10
Current Assets	198	245	240
Current Liabilities	N/A	52	N/A

Satherley Design Associates

Woodcock Hill Park Farm, Felbridge, East Grinstead, RH19 2RB
Tel: 01342-326060 **Fax:** 01342-302272
E-mail: mr@sathdes.co.uk
Website: http://www.satherley.com
Directors: R. Satherley (Head)
Immediate Holding Company: LINGFIELD PARTNERS LLP
Registration no: OC315406 **Date established:** 2005
Turnover: £250,000 - £500,000 **No.of Employees:** 1 - 10
Product Groups: 37, 44, 85

Date of Accounts	Mar 11	Mar 10	Mar 09
Sales Turnover	N/A	N/A	260
Pre Tax Profit/Loss	N/A	N/A	214
Working Capital	1	-8	-1
Fixed Assets	1	1	2
Current Assets	16	7	12
Current Liabilities	N/A	N/A	13

Secure Access Services Ltd

St Hill Farm St Hill Green, East Grinstead, RH19 4NG
Tel: 01342-311538 **Fax:** 01342-313548
E-mail: info@sasautomation.co.uk
Website: http://www.sasautomation.co.uk
Directors: N. Stocker (Fin), P. Stocker (Dir)
Immediate Holding Company: SECURE ACCESS SERVICES LIMITED
Registration no: 04574890 **Date established:** 2002
No.of Employees: 1 - 10 **Product Groups:** 25, 26, 29, 30, 33, 35, 36, 37, 38, 39, 40, 44, 45, 48, 49, 51, 66, 68, 71, 83, 84, 85, 86

Date of Accounts	Mar 11	Mar 10	Mar 09
Working Capital	97	97	92
Fixed Assets	5	8	10
Current Assets	137	160	140

Southern Testing Laboratories Ltd

Keeble House Stuart Way, East Grinstead, RH19 4QA
Tel: 01342-333100 **Fax:** 01342-410321
E-mail: enquiries@southerntesting.co.uk
Website: http://www.southerntesting.co.uk
Bank(s): Barclays
Directors: M. Stevenson (MD)
Ultimate Holding Company: STL (HOLDINGS) LIMITED
Immediate Holding Company: SOUTHERN TESTING LABORATORIES LIMITED
Registration no: 02183217 **VAT No.:** 367 4740 26 **Date established:** 1987
Turnover: £2m - £5m **No.of Employees:** 21 - 50 **Product Groups:** 84, 85

Date of Accounts	Mar 12	Mar 11	Mar 10
Working Capital	447	391	309
Fixed Assets	457	449	429
Current Assets	1m	1m	895

Squeaky Clean Cleaning

188b London Road, East Grinstead, RH19 1EY
Tel: 01342-312957 **Fax:** 01342-303385
Website: http://www.squeaky-clean.co.uk

Directors: M. Jennings (Prop)
Immediate Holding Company: PROSPER MORTGAGE SERVICES LTD
Registration no: 03859403 **Date established:** 1999
Turnover: Up to £250,000 **No.of Employees:** 1 - 10 **Product Groups:** 23, 40, 52

Date of Accounts	Oct 11	Oct 10	Oct 09
Sales Turnover	48	53	103
Pre Tax Profit/Loss	-6	6	-11
Working Capital	-43	-38	-44
Fixed Assets	245	250	256
Current Liabilities	30	19	32

Wardlock Educational Co. Ltd

1 Christopher Road, East Grinstead, RH19 3BT
Tel: 01342-318980 **Fax:** 01342-410980
E-mail: orders@wleducat.freeserve.co.uk
Website: http://www.lingkee.com
Directors: E. Parsons (Co Sec), K. Au (Dir)
Ultimate Holding Company: LING KEE (U.K.) LIMITED
Immediate Holding Company: WARD LOCK EDUCATIONAL COMPANY LIMITED
Registration no: 00509394 **VAT No.:** GB 362 3850 54
Date established: 1952 **Turnover:** £500,000 - £1m
No.of Employees: 1 - 10 **Product Groups:** 28, 64

Date of Accounts	Jun 11	Jun 09	Jun 08
Working Capital	-2m	-2m	-2m
Current Assets	322	324	381

Gatwick

Chapman Freeborn Air Chartering Ltd

3 City Place Beehive Ring Road, London Gatwick Airport, Gatwick, RH6 0PA
Tel: 01293-572872
E-mail: info@chapman-freeborn.com
Website: http://www.chapman-freeborn.com
Managers: S. Phelps (Personnel), P. Jorder, A. James (Mktg Serv Mgr), B. Bekit
Ultimate Holding Company: CHAPMAN FREEBORN HOLDINGS LIMITED
Immediate Holding Company: CHAPMAN FREEBORN AIRCHARTERING LIMITED
Registration no: 01053714 **Date established:** 1972
Turnover: £125m - £250m **No.of Employees:** 51 - 100
Product Groups: 75

Date of Accounts	Dec 11	Dec 10	Dec 09
Sales Turnover	140m	125m	114m
Pre Tax Profit/Loss	5m	7m	3m
Working Capital	12m	9m	4m
Fixed Assets	1m	621	438
Current Assets	22m	17m	19m
Current Liabilities	5m	4m	4m

Rentokil Initial plc

2 City Place Beehive Ring Road, London Gatwick Airport, Gatwick, RH6 0HA
Tel: 01293-858000 **Fax:** 01342-326229
Website: http://www.rentokil-initial.com
Bank(s): HSBC Bank plc
Directors: P. Griffiths (Co Sec), G. Brown (Dir)
Ultimate Holding Company: RENTOKIL INITIAL PLC
Immediate Holding Company: RENTOKIL OVERSEAS HOLDINGS LIMITED
Registration no: 00630059 **VAT No.:** GB 190 6214 74
Date established: 1959 **Turnover:** Over £1,000m
No.of Employees: 101 - 250 **Product Groups:** 40, 83

Date of Accounts	Dec 11	Dec 10	Dec 09
Working Capital	-218m	-218m	-218m
Fixed Assets	1109m	1109m	1642m
Current Assets	60m	60m	60m

Schlumberger Oilfield UK plc

Schlumberger House Buckingham Gate, London Gatwick Airport, Gatwick, RH6 0NZ
Tel: 01293-556655 **Fax:** 01293-556700
E-mail: pdroy@slb.com
Website: http://www.slb.com
Directors: P. Droy (Dir)
Ultimate Holding Company: SCHLUMBERGER LTD (NETHERLANDS ANTILLES)
Immediate Holding Company: SCHLUMBERGER EVALUATION AND PRODUCTION SERVICES (UK) LIMITED
Registration no: 00548680 **Date established:** 1955
Turnover: £75m - £125m **No.of Employees:** 101 - 250
Product Groups: 51, 84

Date of Accounts	Dec 11	Dec 10	Dec 09
Working Capital	7	7m	7m
Current Assets	7	7m	7m

Hassocks

Acorn Fasteners Ltd (Head Office)

Unit 15-16 Mid Sussex Business Park Folders Lane East, Ditchling, Hassocks, BN6 8SE
Tel: 01342-893500 **Fax:** 01342-892820
E-mail: sales@acornfastenersltd.co.uk
Website: http://www.fasteners.ltd.uk
Bank(s): National Westminster Bank Plc
Directors: C. Till (MD), M. Aitken (Co Sec), M. Aitken (Fin)
Managers: B. McTavish
Immediate Holding Company: ACORN FASTENERS LIMITED
Registration no: 01441238 **VAT No.:** GB 315 8202 81
Date established: 1979 **Turnover:** £1m - £2m **No.of Employees:** 11 - 20
Product Groups: 30, 35, 39, 48, 49

Date of Accounts	Sep 08	Sep 07	Sep 06
Sales Turnover	N/A	N/A	1086
Pre Tax Profit/Loss	N/A	N/A	16
Working Capital	8	53	52
Fixed Assets	133	42	34
Current Assets	313	306	298
Current Liabilities	304	253	246
Total Share Capital	1	1	1
ROCE% (Return on Capital Employed)			18.2
ROT% (Return on Turnover)			1.5

AESpump

Unit 30 Midsussex Business Park
Folders Lane
East Ditchling Common, Hassocks, BN6 8SE
Tel: 01273-891450 **Fax:** 01273-891451
E-mail: sales@absolutevacuum.co.uk
Website: http://www.absolute-vacuum.com
Directors: A. Taylor (MD), S. Davies (Dir)
Registration no: 03878160 **VAT No.:** GB 744 9445 03
Turnover: £250,000 - £500,000 **No.of Employees:** 1 - 10
Product Groups: 29, 30, 32, 33, 36, 37, 38, 39, 40, 41, 42, 45, 46, 47, 48, 52, 66, 67, 68, 83, 84, 87

Aims Engineering

Unit H Ditchling Common Industrial Estate, Ditchling, Hassocks, BN6 8SG
Tel: 01444-870221 **Fax:** 01444-244860
E-mail: mail@aimsengineering.co.uk
Website: http://www.aimsengineering.co.uk
Directors: A. Gaunt (Prop)
Turnover: Up to £250,000 **No.of Employees:** 1 - 10 **Product Groups:** 46, 48

B W Lift Trucks

Unit 9 Firsland Park Estate Henfield Road, Albourne, Hassocks, BN6 9JJ
Tel: 01273-494950 **Fax:** 01273-491481
E-mail: william.bond@bwlifttrucks.co.uk
Website: http://www.bwlifttrucks.co.uk
Directors: A. Bond (Co Sec)
Immediate Holding Company: BW LIFT TRUCKS LIMITED
Registration no: 03434700 **Date established:** 1997
No.of Employees: 1 - 10 **Product Groups:** 35, 39, 45

Date of Accounts	Sep 11	Sep 10	Sep 09
Working Capital	19	3	-29
Fixed Assets	18	20	23
Current Assets	89	69	79

C M L Engineering Services

Southdown Farm Lodge Lane, Hassocks, BN6 8LX
Tel: 01273-845458 **Fax:** 01273- 845458
Directors: C. Maherloughnan (Prop)
Date established: 1998 **No.of Employees:** 1 - 10 **Product Groups:** 41

Jones Cranes Parts

3 Firsland Park Estate Henfield Road, Albourne, Hassocks, BN6 9JJ
Tel: 01273-494020 **Fax:** 01273-494294
E-mail: sales@ironfairycranes.com
Website: http://www.ironfairycranes.com
Directors: S. Prestson (Prop), S. Hodgins (Fin)
Date established: 1998 **Turnover:** £500,000 - £1m
No.of Employees: 1 - 10 **Product Groups:** 35, 39, 45, 48, 51, 52, 67, 68, 83

S B Woodworking Machinery

Henfield Road Firsland Park Estate, Albourne, Hassocks, BN6 9JJ
Tel: 01273-495525 **Fax:** 01273-495279
E-mail: info@sbwoodworkingmachinery.co.uk
Website: http://www.sbwoodworkingmachinery.co.uk
Directors: S. Buckman (Prop)
No.of Employees: 1 - 10 **Product Groups:** 46

Sussex Safetywear

Wearmaster House Malthouse Lane, Hurstpierpoint, Hassocks, BN6 9LA
Tel: 01273-831800 **Fax:** 01273-831880
E-mail: sales@sussexsafety.com
Website: http://www.sussexsafetywear.co.uk
Bank(s): Nat West
Directors: J. Lewis (Prop)
Registration no: 03826908 **VAT No.:** GB 724 7922 19
Date established: 1999 **Turnover:** £1m - £2m **No.of Employees:** 11 - 20
Product Groups: 22, 24, 40

White Eagle Foundry Ltd

199 Cuckfield Road Hurstpierpoint, Hassocks, BN6 9RT
Tel: 01273-832062 **Fax:** 01273-833628
E-mail: sales@wef.co.uk
Website: http://www.wef.co.uk
Bank(s): National Westminster Bank Plc
Directors: R. Sharp (MD), A. Sharp (Fin)
Immediate Holding Company: WHITE EAGLE FOUNDRY LIMITED
Registration no: 01876546 **VAT No.:** GB 423 2009 05
Date established: 1985 **Turnover:** £250,000 - £500,000
No.of Employees: 11 - 20 **Product Groups:** 34, 48

Date of Accounts	May 12	May 11	May 10
Working Capital	137	152	165
Fixed Assets	76	80	82
Current Assets	177	181	204

Haywards Heath

Access Mobility

Unit 31 Bolney Grange Business Park Stairbridge Lane, Bolney, Haywards Heath, RH17 5PA
Tel: 01444-242415
E-mail: mwyatt@accessmobility.co.uk
Website: http://www.accessmobility.co.uk
Directors: M. Wyatt (Fin)
Immediate Holding Company: ACCESS MOBILITY LIMITED
Registration no: 02924906 **Date established:** 1994
No.of Employees: 11 - 20 **Product Groups:** 38, 52

The Adelphi Group Adelphi Group of Companies

Olympus House Mill Green Road, Haywards Heath, RH16 1XQ
Tel: 01444-472300 **Fax:** 01444-472329
E-mail: sales@adelphi.uk.com
Website: http://www.adelphi.uk.com
Bank(s): Barclays, London
Directors: P. Holland (Fin), D. Willis (Sales), S. Holroyd (MD)
Ultimate Holding Company: ADELPHI HOLDINGS LIMITED
Immediate Holding Company: COLDSTREAM (ENGINEERING) LIMITED
Registration no: 02907624 **VAT No.:** GB 233 2902 89
Date established: 1994 **No.of Employees:** 21 - 50 **Product Groups:** 33, 35

see next page

***The Adelphi Group Adelphi Group of Companies** - Cont'd*

Date of Accounts	Sep 11	Sep 10	Sep 09
Working Capital	88	65	48
Fixed Assets	16	5	10
Current Assets	196	193	129

Advanced Desktop Systems Ltd
13 Ledgers Meadow Cuckfield, Haywards Heath, RH17 5EW
Tel: 01444-454487 **Fax:** 01444-448159
E-mail: tony.elphick@advanceddesktop.com
Website: http://www.advanceddesktop.com
Directors: T. Elphick (Prop)
Immediate Holding Company: ADVANCED DESKTOP SYSTEMS LIMITED
Registration no: 05321224 **Date established:** 2004
No.of Employees: 1 - 10 **Product Groups:** 37, 44, 67

Date of Accounts	Dec 06	Dec 05
Working Capital	-0	-0

Archers Specialist Treatments Ltd
Winters Farm North Green Common Road, Wivelsfield Green, Haywards Heath, RH17 7RJ
Tel: 01444-471090 **Fax:** 01444-471095
E-mail: info@archertreatments.com
Website: http://www.archertreatments.com
Registration no: 03237910 **Turnover:** £250,000 - £500,000
No.of Employees: 21 - 50 **Product Groups:** 16, 35, 52, 66

Aventis Behring Ltd
Centeon House Market Place, Haywards Heath, RH16 1DB
Tel: 01444-447400 **Fax:** 01444-447401
Website: http://www.aventisbehring.co.uk
Directors: P. Fellingham (Dir), A. Anderson (Pres)
Managers: N. Pettet (Mktg Serv Mgr)
Ultimate Holding Company: CSL LIMITED (AUSTRALIA)
Immediate Holding Company: ZLB BIOPLASMA UK LIMITED
Registration no: 04385385 **Date established:** 2002
Turnover: £50m - £75m **No.of Employees:** 11 - 20 **Product Groups:** 63

Date of Accounts	Jun 11	Jun 10	Jun 09
Sales Turnover	84m	80m	64m
Pre Tax Profit/Loss	3m	3m	2m
Working Capital	14m	11m	10m
Fixed Assets	132	110	95
Current Assets	28m	28m	27m
Current Liabilities	2m	3m	1m

Bancroft & Co.
Unit 5 Bolney Grange Industrial Park Bolney, Haywards Heath, RH17 5PB
Tel: 01444-248884 **Fax:** 01444-242767
E-mail: sales@bancroft.co.uk
Website: http://www.bancroft.co.uk
Directors: L. Bancroft Hinchey (Fin), L. Bancroft-Hinchey (Fin)
Immediate Holding Company: BANCROFT HINCHEY LIMITED
Registration no: 02496196 **VAT No.:** GB 587 4158 01
Date established: 1990 **Turnover:** £500,000 - £1m
No.of Employees: 1 - 10 **Product Groups:** 35, 37, 38, 39, 40, 48, 67, 68, 85

Date of Accounts	Mar 12	Mar 11	Mar 10
Working Capital	96	100	68
Fixed Assets	322	293	290
Current Assets	244	249	192

C P L Petroleum
Colwood Lane Warninglid, Haywards Heath, RH17 5UE
Tel: 01273-455511 **Fax:** 01273-464813
E-mail: shoreham@cplpetroleum.co.uk
Website: http://www.cplpetroleum.co.uk
Bank(s): National Westminster Bank Plc
Managers: G. Sayers (Depot Mgr), B. Taylor (District Mgr)
Ultimate Holding Company: CPL INDUSTRIES HOLDINGS LIMITED
Immediate Holding Company: CPL PETROLEUM LIMITED
Registration no: 03003860 **VAT No.:** GB 721 5764 39
Date established: 1994 **Turnover:** £75m - £125m
No.of Employees: 21 - 50 **Product Groups:** 66

Date of Accounts	Mar 12	Mar 11	Mar 10
Pre Tax Profit/Loss	N/A	878	904
Working Capital	31	30m	30m
Fixed Assets	26	26m	26m
Current Assets	57	56m	56m
Current Liabilities	26	246	253

Charterhouse Commercial Finance Plc
Oakfield House 35 Perrymount Road, Haywards Heath, RH16 3BW
Tel: 0870-2431836 **Fax:** 0870-2431837
E-mail: sales@charterhousefactoring.com
Website: http://www.charterhousefactoring.com
Directors: K. Brooker (MD), M. Gilbey (Ch)
Immediate Holding Company: Charterhouse Group International Ltd
Registration no: 05106936 **Date established:** 2004
Turnover: Up to £250,000 **No.of Employees:** 51 - 100
Product Groups: 82

Date of Accounts	Sep 08
Sales Turnover	1076
Pre Tax Profit/Loss	997
Working Capital	-164
Fixed Assets	317
Current Assets	6742
Current Liabilities	6905
Total Share Capital	1000
ROCE% (Return on Capital Employed)	648.5

Cullen Scholefield
Maxwelton House 41 Boltro Road, Haywards Heath, RH16 1BJ
Tel: 01444-455052 **Fax:** 01444-459221
E-mail: mscholefield@csgconsult.com
Website: http://www.csgconsult.com
Bank(s): National Westminster Bank Plc
Directors: M. Scholefield (MD)
Immediate Holding Company: CULLEN SCHOLEFIELD LIMITED
Registration no: 03298304 **VAT No.:** GB 451 0721 85
Date established: 1997 **Turnover:** £500,000 - £1m
No.of Employees: 11 - 20 **Product Groups:** 86

Date of Accounts	Dec 11	Dec 10	Dec 09
Working Capital	-1	1	-2
Fixed Assets	16	14	16
Current Assets	60	162	114

Dinnages
22 Wivelsfield Road, Haywards Heath, RH16 4EQ
Tel: 01444-440116 **Fax:** 01444-440141
E-mail: d.broyd@dinnages.co.uk
Website: http://www.dinnages.co.uk
Directors: A. Broyd (Fin), D. Broyd (MD)
Ultimate Holding Company: DINNAGES HOLDINGS LIMITED
Immediate Holding Company: DINNAGES GARAGES LIMITED
Registration no: 00296492 **Date established:** 1935
Turnover: £20m - £50m **No.of Employees:** 51 - 100 **Product Groups:** 82

Date of Accounts	Dec 11	Dec 10	Dec 09
Sales Turnover	36m	38m	37m
Pre Tax Profit/Loss	-51	82	517
Working Capital	-361	-524	-505
Fixed Assets	1m	1m	1m
Current Assets	10m	14m	11m
Current Liabilities	2m	11m	8m

The Ellie Spoon Gift Company
PO Box 650 Lindfield, Haywards Heath, RH16 9AN
Tel: 01444-441800 **Fax:** 01444-441800
E-mail: sales@elliespoon.co.uk
Website: http://www.elliespoon.co.uk
No.of Employees: 1 - 10 **Product Groups:** 24, 49, 65

Europ Assistance Holdings Ltd
Sussex House Perrymount Road, Haywards Heath, RH16 1DN
Tel: 01444-442800 **Fax:** 01444-459292
E-mail: david_crapnell@europ-assistance.co.uk
Website: http://www.europ-assistance.co.uk
Directors: D. Crapnell (Dir), T. Christmas (Fin)
Managers: C. Carroll (Personnel)
Ultimate Holding Company: ASSICURAZIONI GENERALL SPA(ITALY)
Immediate Holding Company: ARIA INSURANCE SERVICES LIMITED
Registration no: 00758979 **Date established:** 1963
Turnover: £10m - £20m **No.of Employees:** 251 - 500
Product Groups: 72, 82

Date of Accounts	Dec 11	Dec 10	Dec 09
Sales Turnover	12m	17m	22m
Pre Tax Profit/Loss	-11m	-3m	-4m
Working Capital	5m	-3m	-1m
Fixed Assets	11m	10m	9m
Current Assets	11m	14m	18m
Current Liabilities	4m	5m	9m

Filton Process Control Engineering
3rd Floor 5a Boltro Road, Haywards Heath, RH16 1BP
Tel: 01444-417880 **Fax:** 01444-417668
E-mail: sales@filton.com
Website: http://www.filton.com
Managers: S. Filmer Cox (District Mgr)
No.of Employees: 1 - 10 **Product Groups:** 38, 40, 44, 67, 85

Flotronic Pumps Ltd (Head Office)
Ricebridge Works Brighton Road, Bolney, Haywards Heath, RH17 5NA
Tel: 01444-881871 **Fax:** 01444-881860
E-mail: sales@flotronicpumps.co.uk
Website: http://www.flotronic.co.uk
Bank(s): HSBC Bank plc
Directors: R. Partlett (Dir), J. Waite (Dir)
Managers: J. Drake (Buyer)
Ultimate Holding Company: NORRIS HOLDINGS LIMITED
Immediate Holding Company: FLOTRONIC PUMPS LIMITED
Registration no: 02559708 **VAT No.:** GB 587 4439 90
Date established: 1990 **Turnover:** £2m - £5m **No.of Employees:** 21 - 50
Product Groups: 40

Date of Accounts	Aug 11	Aug 10	Aug 09
Sales Turnover	3m	3m	2m
Pre Tax Profit/Loss	68	80	-57
Working Capital	274	196	105
Fixed Assets	183	218	211
Current Assets	1m	811	743
Current Liabilities	396	107	89

Flowserve Flow Control GB Ltd
Burrell Road, Haywards Heath, RH16 1TL
Tel: 01444-314560
E-mail: admin@invensys.com
Website: http://www.flowserve.com
Managers: N. Green (Mgr)
Ultimate Holding Company: FLOWSERVE CORP (USA)
Immediate Holding Company: FLOWSERVE GB LIMITED
Registration no: 00316996 **Date established:** 1936
No.of Employees: 101 - 250 **Product Groups:** 36, 37, 38

Freshfield Lane Brickworks Ltd
Danehill, Haywards Heath, RH17 7HH
Tel: 01825-790350 **Fax:** 01825-790779
E-mail: sales@mbhplc.co.uk
Website: http://www.mbhplc.co.uk
Bank(s): National Westminster Bank Plc
Directors: S. Morgan (Fin), F. Hanna (Comm)
Immediate Holding Company: FRESHFIELD LANE BRICKWORKS LIMITED
Registration no: 00804219 **VAT No.:** GB 190 4466 43
Date established: 1964 **Turnover:** £500,000 - £1m
No.of Employees: 51 - 100 **Product Groups:** 66

Date of Accounts	Dec 11	Dec 10	Dec 09
Sales Turnover	N/A	8m	7m
Pre Tax Profit/Loss	319	2m	-683
Working Capital	7m	7m	2m
Fixed Assets	9m	3m	4m
Current Assets	7m	7m	3m
Current Liabilities	N/A	N/A	250

Frontline Automation
Unit 41-42 Bolney Grange Business Park, Bolney, Haywards Heath, RH17 5PB
Tel: 01444-248292 **Fax:** 01444-870936
E-mail: info@frontline-auto.com
Website: http://www.frontline-auto.com
Directors: M. Parsons (Prop)
Date established: 1995 **No.of Employees:** 11 - 20 **Product Groups:** 25, 26, 30, 35, 36, 37, 39, 40, 41, 49, 51, 52, 66, 68

Harbeth Audio Ltd
3 Lindfield Enterprise Park Lewes Road, Lindfield, Haywards Heath, RH16 2LH
Tel: 01444-484371 **Fax:** 01444-487629
E-mail: sound@harbeth.co.uk
Website: http://www.harbeth.com
Directors: A. Shaw (MD), M. Mattison (Co Sec)
Immediate Holding Company: HARBETH AUDIO LTD.
Registration no: 03727963 **Date established:** 1999
Turnover: £500,000 - £1m **No.of Employees:** 1 - 10 **Product Groups:** 37

Date of Accounts	Mar 12	Mar 11	Mar 10
Working Capital	694	430	375
Fixed Assets	178	168	31
Current Assets	864	560	537
Current Liabilities	N/A	N/A	72

Ideal Bean Bags
Unit 3 , Savill Road, Lindfield, Haywards Heath, RH16 2NY
Tel: 01444-482811
E-mail: info@idealbeanbags.co.uk
Website: http://www.idealbeanbags.co.uk
Managers: H. Finlay (District Mgr)
Date established: 2009 **No.of Employees:** 11 - 20 **Product Groups:** 26

Jacobs Young & Westbury
Bridge Road, Haywards Heath, RH16 1UA
Tel: 01444-412411 **Fax:** 01444-457662
E-mail: sales@jyw-uk.com
Website: http://www.jyw-uk.com
Directors: C. Firth (MD)
Immediate Holding Company: JACOBS, YOUNG & WESTBURY LIMITED
Registration no: 00068622 **VAT No.:** GB 190 1863 62
Date established: 2000 **Turnover:** £10m - £20m **No.of Employees:** 1 - 10
Product Groups: 23, 26, 63, 65

Date of Accounts	Mar 11	Mar 10	Mar 09
Working Capital	66	104	146
Fixed Assets	5	6	7
Current Assets	234	192	269

Lloyds T S B Private Banking Ltd
31-33 Perrymount Road, Haywards Heath, RH16 3BN
Tel: 01444-459144 **Fax:** 01444-475057
Website: http://www.lloydstsb.com
Directors: A. Pateman Jones (Prop), A. Pateman-jones (Dir), J. Pain (MD), M. Mitchell (Dist)
Managers: R. Tasker
Ultimate Holding Company: Lloyds Banking Group plc
Immediate Holding Company: LLOYDS TSB PRIVATE BANKING LIMITED
Registration no: 02019697 **Date established:** 1986
No.of Employees: 1 - 10 **Product Groups:** 82

Lowes Fabrication Ltd
Unit 22 Bolney Grange Business Park, Bolney, Haywards Heath, RH17 5PB
Tel: 01444-247895 **Fax:** 01444-247898
Directors: R. Lowes (MD), M. Lowes (Fin)
Immediate Holding Company: LOWES FABRICATION LIMITED
Registration no: 01100269 **Date established:** 1973
Turnover: Up to £250,000 **No.of Employees:** 1 - 10 **Product Groups:** 26, 35

Date of Accounts	Mar 12	Mar 11	Mar 10
Sales Turnover	239	259	271
Pre Tax Profit/Loss	24	-27	-10
Working Capital	134	122	158
Fixed Assets	205	209	214
Current Assets	238	200	249
Current Liabilities	22	14	17

Marlow Industries Europe
Aberdeen House South Road, Haywards Heath, RH16 4NG
Tel: 01444-443404 **Fax:** 01444-443334
E-mail: info@marlow-europe.co.uk
Website: http://www.marlow.com
Directors: T. Jackson (MD)
Managers: P. Marr (Accounts)
Immediate Holding Company: Marlow Industries Inc (U.S.A.)
Registration no: 04317983 **Date established:** 2001
No.of Employees: 1 - 10 **Product Groups:** 38

Date of Accounts	Dec 04
Working Capital	1
Current Assets	1
Total Share Capital	1

Mid Sussex Times & Citizen
7-9 South Road, Haywards Heath, RH16 4LE
Tel: 01444-452201 **Fax:** 01444- 416241
E-mail: john.hammond@sussexnewspapers.co.uk
Website: http://www.midsussextoday.co.uk
Directors: G. Campbell (Dir), J. Hammond (Dir), G. Cambell (Dir)
Managers: E. Hayles (Sec), P. Watson (Publishing), J. Hammond
Immediate Holding Company: SUSSEX NEWSPAPER
Date established: 1987 **No.of Employees:** 11 - 20 **Product Groups:** 28

Nationwide Investigations Ltd
The Priory Syresham Gardens, Haywards Heath, RH16 3LB
Tel: 01444-318325 **Fax:** 01444-455204
E-mail: info@nig.co.uk
Website: http://www.nig.co.uk
Directors: R. Stuart (Dir)
Ultimate Holding Company: NATIONWIDE INVESTIGATIONS (TRADEMARKS) LIMITED
Immediate Holding Company: NATIONWIDE INVESTIGATIONS GROUP (LICENSING) LIMITED
Registration no: 03295717 **Date established:** 1996
No.of Employees: 11 - 20 **Product Groups:** 81

Date of Accounts	Dec 10	Dec 09	Dec 08
Working Capital	3	-5	58
Fixed Assets	5	6	7
Current Assets	30	21	85

Norcon Norris Ltd
8b Brighton Road Bolney, Haywards Heath, RH17 5NA
Tel: 01444-882555 **Fax:** 01444-882666
E-mail: enquiries@norconnorris.com
Website: http://www.norconnorris.com
Directors: J. Wheatley (MD)
Ultimate Holding Company: NORRIS HOLDINGS LIMITED
Immediate Holding Company: NORCON (NORRIS) LIMITED
Registration no: 00860446 **VAT No.:** GB 190 6602 65
Date established: 1965 **Turnover:** Up to £250,000
No.of Employees: 1 - 10 **Product Groups:** 37

Date of Accounts	Aug 11	Aug 10	Aug 09
Working Capital	145	141	175
Fixed Assets	8	15	19
Current Assets	168	166	187

Norris Brothers Ltd

Ricebridge House Brighton Road Bolney, Haywards Heath, RH17 5NA
Tel: 01444-881099 **Fax:** 01444-881631
E-mail: rodpartlett@mac.com
Directors: R. Partlett (Fin)
Ultimate Holding Company: NORRIS HOLDINGS LIMITED
Immediate Holding Company: NORRIS HOLDINGS LIMITED
Registration no: 05149072 **VAT No.:** GB 351 3147 84
Date established: 2004 **Turnover:** £2m - £5m **No.of Employees:** 1 - 10
Product Groups: 80

Date of Accounts	Aug 11	Aug 10	Aug 09
Sales Turnover	N/A	3m	4m
Pre Tax Profit/Loss	N/A	191	-1m
Working Capital	-169	-16	-1m
Fixed Assets	2m	3m	3m
Current Assets	20	1m	1m
Current Liabilities	N/A	340	1m

P S M Instrumentation Ltd

3 Burrell Road, Haywards Heath, RH16 1TW
Tel: 01444-410040 **Fax:** 01444-410121
E-mail: sales@psmmarine.com
Website: http://www.psmmarine.com
Bank(s): HSBC, Crawley
Directors: G. Taylor (MD), M. Jones (Sales)
Managers: S. Ratcliffe (Mktg Serv Mgr)
Immediate Holding Company: PSM INSTRUMENTATION LIMITED
Registration no: 01208673 **VAT No.:** GB 292 0359 58
Date established: 1975 **Turnover:** £1m - £2m **No.of Employees:** 11 - 20
Product Groups: 38, 40

Date of Accounts	Dec 11	Dec 10	Dec 09
Working Capital	93	140	243
Fixed Assets	562	585	516
Current Assets	468	523	702

J F Poynter Ltd (t/a Maxim Lamps Works)

Unit 23 More House Farm Business Centre Ditchling Road, Wivelsfield, Haywards Heath, RH17 7RE
Tel: 01444-471491 **Fax:** 01444-471777
E-mail: sales@maximlamps.co.uk
Website: http://www.maximlamps.co.uk
Directors: P. Slade (Dir)
Immediate Holding Company: J.F.POYNTER LIMITED
Registration no: 00341756 **Date established:** 1938 **Turnover:** £2m - £5m
No.of Employees: 1 - 10 **Product Groups:** 33, 37, 67

Date of Accounts	Mar 11	Mar 10	Mar 09
Working Capital	835	718	855
Fixed Assets	439	435	245
Current Assets	1m	1m	1m

Quadrant Subscription Service

9-17 Perrymount Road, Haywards Heath, RH16 3KK
Tel: 01444-475600 **Fax:** 01444-445531
E-mail: rbi.subscriptions@qss-uk.com
Website: http://www.qss-uk.com
Directors: S. Lacey (MD)
No.of Employees: 251 - 500 **Product Groups:** 44, 64

Rapid Office Solutions

Dales Yard Lewes Road, Scaynes Hill, Haywards Heath, RH17 7PG
Tel: 01444-831385 **Fax:** 08712-427407
E-mail: info@rapid-office-solutions.co.uk
Website: http://www.rapid-office-solutions.co.uk
Managers: P. Tomlinson (Mgr)
Date established: 2004 **Turnover:** £250,000 - £500,000
No.of Employees: 1 - 10 **Product Groups:** 32, 33, 35, 81

Royal Haskoning

Burns House Harlands Road, Haywards Heath, RH16 1PG
Tel: 01444-458551 **Fax:** 01444-440665
E-mail: info@royalhaskoning.com
Website: http://www.royalhaskoning.com
Managers: C. Wickham (Sales Admin)
Ultimate Holding Company: KONINKLIJKE HASKONING GROEP BV (NETHERLANDS)
Immediate Holding Company: HASKONING PROJECT SERVICES LIMITED
Registration no: 05265421 **Date established:** 2004
No.of Employees: 21 - 50 **Product Groups:** 84

Safety Business Services SBS Ltd

6 Rothley Chase, Haywards Heath, RH16 3PE
Tel: 01444-416510
E-mail: adminstration@sbs-associates.co.uk
Website: http://www.sbs-associates.co.uk
Directors: N. Parsons (Fin)
Immediate Holding Company: SAFETY BUSINESS SERVICES (SBS) LTD
Registration no: 05689842 **Date established:** 2006
No.of Employees: 1 - 10 **Product Groups:** 54, 84

Date of Accounts	Jan 09	Jan 08	Jan 07
Working Capital	-1	-0	2
Fixed Assets	8	3	4
Current Assets	1	6	3

Sentinel Laboratories Ltd

Unit 12 Lindfield Enterprise Park Lewes Road, Lindfield, Haywards Heath, RH16 2LH
Tel: 01444-484044 **Fax:** 01444-484045
E-mail: sales@sentinel-laboratories.com
Website: http://www.sentinel-laboratories.com
Directors: K. Browning (Sales)
Immediate Holding Company: SENTINEL LABORATORIES LIMITED
Registration no: 02231670 **VAT No.:** GB 492 4265 31
Date established: 1988 **No.of Employees:** 1 - 10 **Product Groups:** 30, 38

Date of Accounts	Jun 12	Jun 11	Jun 10
Working Capital	273	270	188
Fixed Assets	493	469	482
Current Assets	492	539	451

Sign Solutions

Kingston House The Street, Warninglid, Haywards Heath, RH17 5TR
Tel: 01444-461377 **Fax:** 01444-461819
E-mail: signsolutin@btclick.com
Directors: D. Cherry (Prop)
Immediate Holding Company: SIGN SOLUTIONS (SIGN LANGUAGE INTERPRETING AGENCY) LTD
Registration no: 04802772 **VAT No.:** GB 620 9323 63
Date established: 2003 **Turnover:** Up to £250,000
No.of Employees: 1 - 10 **Product Groups:** 37, 39, 49, 52

Date of Accounts	Jul 10	Jul 09	Jul 08
Working Capital	25	109	92
Fixed Assets	119	129	157
Current Assets	239	259	273

South East Water Holdings Ltd

3 Church Road, Haywards Heath, RH16 3NY
Tel: 01444-448200 **Fax:** 01444-413200
E-mail: mdevlin@southeastwater.co.uk
Website: http://www.southeastwater.co.uk
Directors: G. Maxwell (Dir), N. Truillet (Co Sec)
Ultimate Holding Company: HDF (UK) HOLDINGS LIMITED
Immediate Holding Company: SOUTH EAST WATER (HOLDINGS) LIMITED
Registration no: 04771490 **VAT No.:** GB 583 9570 91
Date established: 2003 **Turnover:** £50m - £75m **No.of Employees:** 1 - 10
Product Groups: 18

Date of Accounts	Mar 12	Mar 11	Mar 10
Pre Tax Profit/Loss	21m	21m	14m
Working Capital	4m	5m	10m
Fixed Assets	361m	361m	361m
Current Assets	4m	5m	10m

Southern Counties Gas

Colwood Lane Warninglid, Haywards Heath, RH17 5UE
Tel: 01444-461674 **Fax:** 01444-461537
E-mail: alan.manning@sef.co.uk
Website: http://www.scf.co.uk
Managers: A. Manning (Mgr)
Ultimate Holding Company: MINELOCK LTD
Registration no: 00903234 **VAT No.:** GB 191 2231 88
Turnover: £20m - £50m **No.of Employees:** 1 - 10 **Product Groups:** 18, 31, 66

Venture Finance Plc

Sheencroft House 10-12 Church Road, Haywards Heath, RH16 3SN
Tel: 01444-441717 **Fax:** 01444-410985
E-mail: info@venture-finance.co.uk
Website: http://www.venture-finance.co.uk
Directors: A. Small (MD)
Ultimate Holding Company: ABN AMRO GROUP NV (THE NETHERLANDS)
Immediate Holding Company: ABN AMRO COMMERCIAL FINANCE PLC
Registration no: 02281768 **Date established:** 1988
Turnover: £20m - £50m **No.of Employees:** 21 - 50 **Product Groups:** 80, 82

Date of Accounts	Dec 11	Dec 10	Dec 09
Sales Turnover	36m	34m	34m
Pre Tax Profit/Loss	17m	10m	6m
Working Capital	37m	24m	16m
Fixed Assets	13m	14m	15m
Current Assets	634m	552m	538m
Current Liabilities	304m	269m	247m

Vulcana Gas Appliances Ltd

30 Bridge Road, Haywards Heath, RH16 1TX
Tel: 01444-415871 **Fax:** 01444-441433
E-mail: vulcanagas@pavilion.co.uk
Website: http://www.vulcanagas.com
Directors: C. Coutts (Co Sec)
Immediate Holding Company: VULCANA GAS APPLIANCES LIMITED
Registration no: 01073726 **Date established:** 1972 **Turnover:** £1m - £2m
No.of Employees: 11 - 20 **Product Groups:** 40

Date of Accounts	Jun 11	Jun 10	Jun 09
Working Capital	-272	-483	-237
Fixed Assets	862	868	871
Current Assets	178	166	202

Wild Industries LLP

Park Farm Hundred Acre Lane, Wivelsfield Green, Haywards Heath, RH17 7RU
Tel: 01273-892930 **Fax:** 01273-891994
E-mail: sales@wild-industries.co.uk
Website: http://www.arccan.co.uk
Directors: C. Bulman (Ptnr)
Immediate Holding Company: WILD INDUSTRIES LLP
Registration no: OC301241 **Date established:** 2002
Turnover: £250,000 - £500,000 **No.of Employees:** 1 - 10
Product Groups: 45, 67

Henfield

A E Adams Ltd

4 Mackley Industrial Estate Henfield Road, Small Dole, Henfield, BN5 9XR
Tel: 01273-493936 **Fax:** 01273-494769
E-mail: sales@aeadams.co.uk
Website: http://www.aeadams.co.uk
Bank(s): Barclays, Horsham
Directors: P. Foster (Pers), A. Milner (MD), D. Fletcher (Dir)
Managers: R. Benfield (Purch Mgr)
Ultimate Holding Company: A.E. ADAMS (HOLDINGS) LIMITED
Immediate Holding Company: A.E.ADAMS(HENFIELD)LIMITED
Registration no: 00840611 **VAT No.:** GB 190 1551 81
Date established: 1965 **Turnover:** £2m - £5m **No.of Employees:** 21 - 50
Product Groups: 31, 32, 48, 84

Date of Accounts	Dec 11	Dec 10	Dec 09
Working Capital	395	320	194
Fixed Assets	248	183	239
Current Assets	1m	962	702

D S A Products Ltd

Henfield Business Park Shoreham Road, Henfield, BN5 9SL
Tel: 01273-495318 **Fax:** 01273-494217
E-mail: sales@dsaproducts.com
Website: http://www.dsaproducts.com
Directors: A. Skilton (Fin), M. Skilton (MD)
Immediate Holding Company: D S A PRODUCTS LIMITED
Registration no: 03787396 **Date established:** 1999
No.of Employees: 1 - 10 **Product Groups:** 33, 36, 46, 47, 48, 49

Date of Accounts	Mar 11	Mar 10	Mar 09
Working Capital	39	31	51
Fixed Assets	135	140	145
Current Assets	100	76	88

Edwards King & Edwards

Backsettown Farm Furners Lane, Henfield, BN5 9HS
Tel: 01273-492488 **Fax:** 01273-493836
E-mail: kingedwards@btconnect.co.uk
Directors: S. King (Prop)
Date established: 1996 **No.of Employees:** 1 - 10 **Product Groups:** 20, 40, 41

Global Parasols Ltd

Abbeylands Farm Wineham Lane, Wineham, Henfield, BN5 9AQ
Tel: 01273-494169 **Fax:** 01273-495972
E-mail: sales@globalparasols.com
Website: http://www.globalparasols.com
Directors: M. Clark (MD)
Immediate Holding Company: GLOBAL PARASOLS LIMITED
Registration no: 04878093 **Date established:** 2003
No.of Employees: 1 - 10 **Product Groups:** 24, 26, 49, 67

Date of Accounts	Dec 11	Dec 10	Dec 09
Working Capital	41	101	81
Fixed Assets	164	174	191
Current Assets	275	367	248

Graphic Art Services

81-82 Mackley Industrial Estate Henfield Road, Small Dole, Henfield, BN5 9XR
Tel: 01273-495793 **Fax:** 01273-494887
E-mail: design@graphicart.co.uk
Website: http://www.graphicart.co.uk
Bank(s): National Westminster Bank Plc
Directors: S. Rowlands (MD)
Registration no: 00572916 **VAT No.:** GB 190 4128 77
Date established: 2000 **Turnover:** £1m - £2m **No.of Employees:** 21 - 50
Product Groups: 23, 28

Grommets Ltd

Unit 2 Hollands Lane Industrial Estate, Henfield, BN5 9QY
Tel: 01273-493355 **Fax:** 01273-493388
E-mail: sales@grommets.co.uk
Website: http://www.grommets.co.uk
Directors: J. Boorsma (Co Sec)
Immediate Holding Company: GROMMETS LIMITED
Registration no: 02842512 **Date established:** 1993
Turnover: £250,000 - £500,000 **No.of Employees:** 1 - 10
Product Groups: 29

Date of Accounts	Aug 11	Aug 10	Aug 09
Working Capital	144	119	134
Fixed Assets	13	13	11
Current Assets	238	185	179

Hayward & Green Aviation Ltd (Head Office Dept K)

Unit 1 & 2 Terrys Cross Farm Horn Lane Woodmancote, Woodmancote, Henfield, BN5 9SA
Tel: 01273-492237 **Fax:** 01273-493898
E-mail: simon.green@haywardandgreen.com
Website: http://www.aviationspares.net
Directors: S. Green (Dir)
Immediate Holding Company: HAYWARD AND GREEN AVIATION LIMITED
Registration no: 02753340 **Date established:** 1992 **Turnover:** £2m - £5m
No.of Employees: 1 - 10 **Product Groups:** 30, 34, 35, 36, 37, 38, 39, 40, 48, 49, 67

Date of Accounts	Aug 11	Aug 10	Aug 09
Working Capital	44	62	118
Fixed Assets	10	8	9
Current Assets	361	604	378

P T Fabrication

Browns Meadow Edburton, Henfield, BN5 9LN
Tel: 01273-857992 **Fax:** 01273-857992
E-mail: ptfabrications@aol.com
Website: http://www.ptfabs.co.uk
Directors: T. Young (Ptnr)
Date established: 2000 **No.of Employees:** 1 - 10 **Product Groups:** 35

Sussex Flat Roofing G R P Ltd

Wheatsheaf Road, Henfield, BN5 9AT
Tel: 01273-493528 **Fax:** 0871-666 0561
E-mail: g.goodridge@atozingrp.co.uk
Website: http://www.atozingrp.co.uk
Directors: G. Goodridge (Prop)
Immediate Holding Company: G.GOODRIDGE LIMITED
Registration no: 05546880 **Date established:** 1960
Turnover: Up to £250,000 **No.of Employees:** 1 - 10 **Product Groups:** 30

Date of Accounts	Jul 11	Jul 10	Jul 09
Sales Turnover	N/A	4	6
Pre Tax Profit/Loss	N/A	2	4
Working Capital	-2	-3	-5
Fixed Assets	5	6	8

Woodwarmth Woodburning Stoves

The Forge Mill End, Henfield, BN5 9UN
Tel: 01273-495511
Directors: G. Jones (Ptnr)
Date established: 1987 **No.of Employees:** 1 - 10 **Product Groups:** 40

Horsham

A X Distribution

Unit 22 Lawson Hunt Industrial Park Guildford Road, Broadbridge Heath, Horsham, RH12 3JR
Tel: 01403-240055 **Fax:** 01403-255657
E-mail: axsales@axdistribution.com
Website: http://www.axdistribution.com
Managers: S. Meyer (Chief Mgr)
Immediate Holding Company: FORM FITTINGS
Registration no: 00461240 **Turnover:** £5m - £10m
No.of Employees: 1 - 10 **Product Groups:** 35, 37

Action Medical Research
31 North Parade, Horsham, RH12 2DP
Tel: 01403-210406 **Fax:** 01403-210541
E-mail: info@action.org.uk
Website: http://www.action.org.uk
Bank(s): National Westminster Bank Plc
Directors: M. Richardson (Fin), J. Buckler (Grp Chief Exec)
Managers: C. Airey (Public Relation)
Ultimate Holding Company: ACTION MEDICAL RESEARCH
Immediate Holding Company: ACTION MEDICAL RESEARCH (TRADING) LTD
Registration no: 00892693 **Date established:** 1966
Turnover: Up to £250,000 **No.of Employees:** 21 - 50 **Product Groups:** 80

Date of Accounts	Dec 11	Dec 10	Dec 09
Sales Turnover	13	8	8
Pre Tax Profit/Loss	-3	1	-0
Working Capital	-3	N/A	-0
Current Assets	13	11	10
Current Liabilities	17	11	3

Active Grounds Maintenance Ltd
Pollingfold Works Rudgwick, Horsham, RH12 3AS
Tel: 01403-823344 **Fax:** 01403-822458
E-mail: active@grasstex-active.com
Website: http://www.activegm.co.uk
Directors: R. Conway (MD)
Immediate Holding Company: ACTIVE GROUNDS MAINTENANCE LTD.
Registration no: 02344511 **Date established:** 1989
Turnover: Up to £250,000 **No.of Employees:** 21 - 50 **Product Groups:** 41, 51, 84

Date of Accounts	Dec 11	Jan 11	Jan 10
Working Capital	303	222	173
Fixed Assets	96	125	140
Current Assets	360	270	215

Advantage Air Systems Ltd
Northlands Business Park Bognor Road, Warnham, Horsham, RH12 3SH
Tel: 01306-628282
Directors: A. Barclay (Fin)
Immediate Holding Company: ADVANTAGE AIR SYSTEMS LIMITED
Registration no: 02945484 **Date established:** 1994
No.of Employees: 1 - 10 **Product Groups:** 40, 66

Date of Accounts	Feb 08	Feb 11	Feb 10
Working Capital	19	-13	-2
Fixed Assets	35	58	50
Current Assets	82	102	96

Aerco Ltd
Unit 16-17 Lawson Hunt Industrial Park, Broadbridge Heath, Horsham, RH12 3JR
Tel: 01403-260206 **Fax:** 01403-259760
E-mail: rlaughton@aerco.co.uk
Website: http://www.aerco.co.uk
Bank(s): National Westminster Bank Plc
Directors: R. Laughton (Dir), R. Laughton (MD)
Ultimate Holding Company: AERCO (HOLDINGS) LIMITED
Immediate Holding Company: AERCO LIMITED
Registration no: 00572109 **VAT No.:** GB 602 4417 81
Date established: 1956 **Turnover:** £10m - £20m
No.of Employees: 21 - 50 **Product Groups:** 37

Date of Accounts	Mar 11	Mar 10	Mar 09
Sales Turnover	12m	10m	N/A
Pre Tax Profit/Loss	206	249	275
Working Capital	3m	3m	3m
Current Assets	7m	6m	5m
Current Liabilities	336	352	202

B & G Machining
The Blacksmiths Shop Worthing Road, West Grinstead, Horsham, RH13 8LW
Tel: 01403-864471 **Fax:** 01403-865365
E-mail: tony@bgmachining.co.uk
Website: http://www.bgmachining.co.uk
Directors: A. Kirkby (Prop)
Immediate Holding Company: KNEPP CASTLE POLO CLUB LIMITED
Registration no: 03223211 **Date established:** 1996
Turnover: Up to £250,000 **No.of Employees:** 1 - 10 **Product Groups:** 07, 30, 34, 35, 36, 39, 46, 48, 49, 51, 52, 84, 85

Baggeridge Brick plc
Lynwick Street Rudgwick, Horsham, RH12 3DH
Tel: 01403-822212 **Fax:** 01403-823357
E-mail: info@baggeridge.co.uk
Website: http://www.baggeridge.co.uk
Bank(s): National Westminster Bank Plc
Directors: A. Baxter (Dir), M. Haines (Fin)
Managers: G. Smith (Mgr), J. Underhill (Prod Mgr), S. O' Dell (Mgr), L. Botting (Sales & Mktg Mg)
Immediate Holding Company: Wienerberger Ltd
Registration no: 00386775 **VAT No.:** GB 210 1586 13
Turnover: £2m - £5m **No.of Employees:** 21 - 50 **Product Groups:** 33

C Brewer & Sons
3 Redkiln Way, Horsham, RH13 5QH
Tel: 01403-252345 **Fax:** 01403-258441
Website: http://www.brewers.co.uk
Bank(s): Barclays
Managers: R. Hutson Pope (Mgr)
Immediate Holding Company: C.BREWER & SONS LIMITED
Registration no: 00203852 **Date established:** 1925 **Turnover:** £1m - £2m
No.of Employees: 11 - 20 **Product Groups:** 66

Central Plant Hire
Holmbush Farm Crawley Road, Faygate, Horsham, RH12 4SE
Tel: 01293-851320 **Fax:** 01293-851009
E-mail: sales@centralplanthire.co.uk
Website: http://www.centralplanthire.co.uk
Directors: M. Fiveash (Fin), T. Fiveash (MD)
Immediate Holding Company: CENTRAL GARAGE (ROFFEY) LIMITED
Registration no: 00538337 **Date established:** 1954
Turnover: £250,000 - £500,000 **No.of Employees:** 1 - 10
Product Groups: 39, 41, 45, 67, 83, 86

Date of Accounts	Sep 11	Sep 10	Sep 09
Working Capital	-47	-68	-61
Fixed Assets	219	221	236
Current Assets	83	74	65

City Electrical Factors Ltd
Foundry Close, Horsham, RH13 5TX
Tel: 01403-262101 **Fax:** 01403-210380
E-mail: sales.horsham@cef.co.uk
Website: http://www.cef.co.uk
Managers: D. Goldsmith (Mgr)
Ultimate Holding Company: CEF HOLDINGS LIMITED
Immediate Holding Company: CITY ELECTRICAL FACTORS LIMITED
Registration no: 00336408 **Date established:** 1938
Turnover: £500,000 - £1m **No.of Employees:** 1 - 10 **Product Groups:** 67

Date of Accounts	Apr 11	Apr 10	Apr 09
Sales Turnover	439m	406m	444m
Pre Tax Profit/Loss	22m	26m	34m
Working Capital	53m	172m	164m
Fixed Assets	13m	17m	18m
Current Assets	179m	250m	227m
Current Liabilities	53m	23m	20m

Complete Business Systems Ltd
Systems House Genesis Business Centre Redkiln Way, Horsham, RH13 5QH
Tel: 01403-217777 **Fax:** 01403-255542
E-mail: sales@c-b-s.co.uk
Website: http://www.c-b-s.co.uk
Directors: K. Gale (MD)
Immediate Holding Company: COMPLETE BUSINESS SYSTEMS LIMITED
Registration no: 02120026 **VAT No.:** GB 461 8700 46
Date established: 1987 **Turnover:** £1m - £2m **No.of Employees:** 1 - 10
Product Groups: 44

Date of Accounts	Dec 11	Dec 10	Dec 09
Working Capital	-127	-124	-133
Fixed Assets	271	265	268
Current Assets	192	205	209

Cordek Ltd (Head Office)
Unit 1-3 Spring Copse Business Park Stane Street, Slinfold, Horsham, RH13 0SZ
Tel: 01403-799600 **Fax:** 01403-791718
E-mail: info@cordek.com
Website: http://www.cordek.com
Bank(s): National Westminster Bank Plc
Directors: P. Fane (Sales), G. Naris (Fin), J. White (MD)
Immediate Holding Company: CORDEK LIMITED
Registration no: 01147946 **VAT No.:** GB 191 6624 49
Date established: 1973 **Turnover:** £10m - £20m
No.of Employees: 51 - 100 **Product Groups:** 30, 31, 33, 66

Date of Accounts	Dec 11	Dec 10	Dec 09
Sales Turnover	14m	13m	11m
Pre Tax Profit/Loss	2m	3m	2m
Working Capital	7m	6m	5m
Fixed Assets	7m	9m	7m
Current Assets	9m	8m	8m
Current Liabilities	1m	1m	1m

Cowfold Precision Engineering Ltd
BMXR Oakendene Industrial Estate Bolney Road, Cowfold, Horsham, RH13 8AZ
Tel: 01403-864945 **Fax:** 01403-864945
E-mail: cowfold.precision@blueyonder.co.uk
Website: http://www.cowfoldprecision.co.uk
Managers: C. Tidd (Mgr)
Immediate Holding Company: COWFOLD PRECISION ENGINEERING LIMITED
Registration no: 06608086 **VAT No.:** GB 475 7748 89
Date established: 2008 **Turnover:** Up to £250,000
No.of Employees: 1 - 10 **Product Groups:** 35, 48

Date of Accounts	Oct 11	Oct 10	Oct 09
Working Capital	-20	-24	-24
Fixed Assets	20	24	27
Current Assets	30	30	15
Current Liabilities	N/A	N/A	9

Denne Metal Finishing Co.
Unit F4 Oakendene Industrial Estate Bolney Road, Cowfold, Horsham, RH13 8AZ
Tel: 01403-864124 **Fax:** 01403-865515
E-mail: bamich6@aol.com
Website: http://www.denne-metal-finishers.co.uk
Directors: M. Ball (Prop)
Immediate Holding Company: DENNE METAL FINISHING LIMITED
Registration no: 05830585 **Date established:** 2006
Turnover: Up to £250,000 **No.of Employees:** 1 - 10 **Product Groups:** 25, 48

Date of Accounts	Mar 11	Mar 10	Mar 09
Working Capital	-2	-2	-3
Fixed Assets	3	3	3
Current Assets	64	63	56

Dixon Hurst Kemp Ltd
Unit 5 Genesis Business Centre Redkiln Way, Horsham, RH13 5QH
Tel: 01403-261999 **Fax:** 01403-261995
E-mail: horsham@dhk.co.uk
Website: http://www.dhk.co.uk
Directors: A. Warburton (Dir)
Immediate Holding Company: DIXON HURST KEMP LIMITED
Registration no: 03438720 **Date established:** 1997
No.of Employees: 1 - 10 **Product Groups:** 35

Date of Accounts	Oct 11	Oct 10	Oct 09
Working Capital	293	302	338
Fixed Assets	90	114	127
Current Assets	481	426	463

Doyle & Tratt
Faygate Lane Faygate, Horsham, RH12 4SJ
Tel: 01293-851584 **Fax:** 01293-851288
E-mail: mail@varilight.co.uk
Website: http://www.varilight.co.uk
Directors: P. Tratt (Dir)
Immediate Holding Company: DOYLE & TRATT PRODUCTS LIMITED
Registration no: 01158034 **Date established:** 1974 **Turnover:** £5m - £10m
No.of Employees: 11 - 20 **Product Groups:** 36, 40

Date of Accounts	Feb 08	Feb 11	Feb 10
Pre Tax Profit/Loss	-307	N/A	N/A
Working Capital	3m	3m	3m
Fixed Assets	30	15	18
Current Assets	3m	4m	3m
Current Liabilities	354	N/A	N/A

The Drain Center (a division of Wolseley)
Unit B Foundry Close, Horsham, RH13 5QD
Tel: 01403-269961 **Fax:** 01403-211517
E-mail: mike.morrissey@wolseley.co.uk
Website: http://www.draincenter.co.uk
Managers: J. Knott (Mgr)
No.of Employees: 1 - 10 **Product Groups:** 30, 36, 39, 40, 42, 48, 66

Dustop Air Filters
2 Clemsfold Farm Guildford Road, Clemsfold, Horsham, RH12 3PW
Tel: 01403-790782 **Fax:** 01403-791079
E-mail: mail@dustop.com
Website: http://www.dustop.com
Directors: A. Bullen (Fin), M. Bullen (MD)
Immediate Holding Company: DUSTOP LIMITED
Registration no: 03066949 **Date established:** 1995
No.of Employees: 1 - 10 **Product Groups:** 38, 42

Date of Accounts	Aug 11	Aug 10	Aug 09
Working Capital	210	176	188
Fixed Assets	3	6	18
Current Assets	329	299	318

E R Edwards & Sons Ltd
Unit 3 Redkiln Close, Horsham, RH13 5QL
Tel: 01403-224400 **Fax:** 01403-224401
E-mail: redwards@eredwards.co.uk
Website: http://www.eredwards.co.uk
Bank(s): National Westminster
Directors: R. Edwards (MD)
Managers: P. Burgess (Buyer), W. Glanfield
Immediate Holding Company: E.R. EDWARDS & SONS LIMITED
Registration no: 01363138 **VAT No.:** GB 321 6143 01
Date established: 1978 **Turnover:** £2m - £5m **No.of Employees:** 11 - 20
Product Groups: 48

Date of Accounts	Apr 11	Apr 10	Apr 09
Working Capital	110	96	91
Fixed Assets	59	69	76
Current Assets	510	478	532

Emcel Filters Ltd
Blatchford Road, Horsham, RH13 5RA
Tel: 01403-253215 **Fax:** 01403-259881
E-mail: filtration@emcelfilters.co.uk
Website: http://www.emcelfilters.co.uk
Bank(s): Barclays
Directors: C. Marshall (MD), C. Marshell (MD), C. Marshall (Ch), E. Marshall (Co Sec), J. Saunders (Works)
Managers: D. Colbourne, D. Spraget (Sales Prom Mgr), J. Allen, P. Cotterill (Buyer), S. Smith (I.T. Exec), P. Cottrell (Purch Mgr), E. Bamfourth (Fin Mgr)
Registration no: 00586725 **Date established:** 1957
No.of Employees: 21 - 50 **Product Groups:** 33, 35, 40, 42

Date of Accounts	Mar 10	Mar 09	Mar 08
Working Capital	739	735	694
Fixed Assets	550	467	508
Current Assets	1m	1m	1m

Eriks UK (Horsham Service Centre)
4 Parsonage Business Park, Horsham, RH12 4AL
Tel: 01403-240000 **Fax:** 01403-217153
E-mail: horsham@eriks.co.uk
Website: http://www.wyko.co.uk
Managers: D. Fleet
Turnover: £250m - £500m **No.of Employees:** 1 - 10 **Product Groups:** 66

F C Lane Electronics Ltd
Slinfold Lodge Stane Street, Slinfold, Horsham, RH13 0RN
Tel: 01403-790661 **Fax:** 01403-790849
E-mail: sales@fclane.com
Website: http://www.fclane.com
Bank(s): Lloyds TSB Bank plc
Directors: P. Jarman (Sales), S. Hammerton (MD)
Managers: B. Clough (Buyer), M. Mitchell, S. Hammerton (Personnel)
Ultimate Holding Company: THE LODGE GROUP LIMITED
Immediate Holding Company: F.C. LANE ELECTRONICS LIMITED
Registration no: 00876597 **VAT No.:** GB 849 7715 69
Date established: 1966 **Turnover:** £5m - £10m **No.of Employees:** 21 - 50
Product Groups: 37, 44

Date of Accounts	May 11	May 10	May 09
Working Capital	4m	4m	4m
Fixed Assets	224	250	222
Current Assets	6m	5m	5m

Flexible Machining Systems Ltd
2-3 Blatchford Road, Horsham, RH13 5QR
Tel: 01403-270466 **Fax:** 01403-270458
E-mail: sales@fmsltd.co.uk
Website: http://www.fmsltd.co.uk
Bank(s): National Westminster Bank Plc
Directors: R. Streeter (MD), A. Streeter (Fin)
Ultimate Holding Company: ASTIME PROPERTIES LIMITED
Immediate Holding Company: FLEXIBLE MACHINING SYSTEMS LIMITED
Registration no: 01671088 **VAT No.:** GB 415 1009 05
Date established: 1982 **Turnover:** £2m - £5m **No.of Employees:** 11 - 20
Product Groups: 46, 48

Date of Accounts	Jun 11	Jun 10	Jun 09
Working Capital	252	491	516
Fixed Assets	635	801	1m
Current Assets	438	654	761

Flomotion Rental Ltd
7 Wilton Close Partridge Green, Horsham, RH13 8RX
Tel: 01403-711170 **Fax:** 01403-711059
E-mail: sales@flomotion.uk.com
Directors: C. Tomlinson (Fin)
Ultimate Holding Company: MARTLET INVESTMENT AND FINANCE LIMITED
Immediate Holding Company: FLOMOTION RENTAL LIMITED
Registration no: 02580293 **VAT No.:** GB 550 4042 83
Date established: 1991 **Turnover:** £250,000 - £500,000
No.of Employees: 1 - 10 **Product Groups:** 20, 35, 45, 76

Date of Accounts	Mar 12	Mar 11	Mar 10
Sales Turnover	372	371	401
Pre Tax Profit/Loss	2	-6	11
Working Capital	31	23	53
Fixed Assets	43	58	53
Current Assets	77	73	94
Current Liabilities	20	19	31

Forgehorns Ironwork
The Forge Crawley Road, Faygate, Horsham, RH12 4SE
Tel: 01293-852400 **Fax:** 01293-852216
E-mail: forgehorns@blueyonder.co.uk
Website: http://www.forgehorns.co.uk
Directors: M. Horn (Prop)
Immediate Holding Company: CENTRAL GARAGE (ROFFEY) LIMITED
Registration no: 00538337 **Date established:** 1954
No.of Employees: 1 - 10 **Product Groups:** 26, 35

G8 Systems
96 Ropeland Way, Horsham, RH12 5NZ
Tel: 01403-262611 **Fax:** 01403-262611
E-mail: info@g8systems.co.uk
Website: http://www.g8systems.co.uk
Directors: C. Manvell (Prop)
No.of Employees: 1 - 10 **Product Groups:** 25, 26, 30, 33, 35, 36, 37, 38, 39, 40, 46, 48, 49, 51, 52, 66, 67, 68, 71, 80, 81, 83

Graham
Unit 2 Horsham Trade Park Foundry Lane, Horsham, RH13 5PX
Tel: 01403-252444 **Fax:** 01403-211374
E-mail: kelvin.rudd@graham-group.co.uk
Website: http://www.graham-group.co.uk
Managers: K. Rudd (Mgr)
Ultimate Holding Company: SAINT GOBAIN (FRANCE)
Immediate Holding Company: JEWSONS
Registration no: SC254141 **Turnover:** £20m - £50m
No.of Employees: 11 - 20 **Product Groups:** 66

Griffin Trading
Griffin House Nightingale Road, Horsham, RH12 2NQ
Tel: 01403-255427 **Fax:** 01403-210238
E-mail: enquiries@griffintrading.co.uk
Website: http://www.griffintrading.co.uk
Directors: J. Mitchell (MD), E. Lloyd (Co Sec)
Immediate Holding Company: GRIFFIN TRADING (U.K.) LIMITED
Registration no: 01445665 **Date established:** 1979
Turnover: £500,000 - £1m **No.of Employees:** 1 - 10 **Product Groups:** 22, 27, 28, 30, 33, 49

Date of Accounts	Dec 11	Dec 10	Dec 09
Working Capital	-83	-29	-24
Fixed Assets	78	80	82
Current Assets	25	108	105

Griffiths & Nielsen Ltd
Stane Street Slinfold, Horsham, RH13 0TW
Tel: 01403-791728 **Fax:** 0845-263 8907
E-mail: giles@gandn.com
Website: http://www.griffithsandnielsen.com
Bank(s): HSBC Bank plc
Directors: G. Griffiths (MD)
Managers: S. Kay (Chief Acct)
Ultimate Holding Company: GRIFFITHS & NIELSEN HOLDINGS LIMITED
Immediate Holding Company: GRIFFITHS & NIELSEN LIMITED
Registration no: 01201146 **VAT No.:** GB 193 7428 32
Date established: 1975 **Turnover:** £2m - £5m **No.of Employees:** 11 - 20
Product Groups: 30, 42, 63, 67, 84

Date of Accounts	Nov 10	Nov 09	Nov 08
Working Capital	128	70	66
Fixed Assets	82	77	79
Current Assets	1m	980	875

Hager & Elsasser UK Ltd
Field Place Estate Broadbridge Heath, Horsham, RH12 3PB
Tel: 01403-272772 **Fax:** 01403-272770
E-mail: sales@he-water.co.uk
Website: http://www.he-water.co.uk
Directors: M. Hutt (MD)
Ultimate Holding Company: RENA GMBH (GERMANY)
Immediate Holding Company: STULZ H + E UK LTD
Registration no: 03734480 **Date established:** 1999
No.of Employees: 1 - 10 **Product Groups:** 30, 32, 39, 41, 42, 46, 52, 54, 66, 67, 84, 85

Date of Accounts	Jun 12	Jun 11	Jun 10
Working Capital	714	843	402
Fixed Assets	39	27	26
Current Assets	2m	2m	2m

Heath Lambert Group
Norfolk House 32-40 North Street, Horsham, RH12 1RZ
Tel: 01403-321000 **Fax:** 01403-321100
E-mail: info@heathlambert.com
Website: http://www.heathlambert.com
Directors: P. Smith (MD), V. Wild (Dir)
Managers: S. Bartlett (Mktg Serv Mgr)
Ultimate Holding Company: HLG HOLDINGS LTD
Immediate Holding Company: HEATH LAMBERT LIMITED
Registration no: 01199129 **Date established:** 1975
Turnover: £125m - £250m **No.of Employees:** 101 - 250
Product Groups: 82

Hub Electronics Ltd
Unit 1 Foundry Lane, Horsham, RH13 5PX
Tel: 01403-255225 **Fax:** 01403-263154
E-mail: sales@protechcc.com
Website: http://www.hubelectronics.com
Directors: P. Latter (Dir)
Immediate Holding Company: HUB ELECTRONICS LIMITED
Registration no: 04168324 **Date established:** 2001 **Turnover:** £1m - £2m
No.of Employees: 1 - 10 **Product Groups:** 37

Date of Accounts	May 12	May 11	May 10
Working Capital	323	273	195
Fixed Assets	4	2	2
Current Assets	489	394	315

Hygienic Valves & Fittings Ltd
Huffwood Trading Estate Partridge Green, Horsham, RH13 8AU
Tel: 01403-710255 **Fax:** 01403-710338
Directors: A. Hicks (MD)
Immediate Holding Company: HYGIENIC VALVES & FITTINGS LIMITED
Registration no: 01716178 **Date established:** 1983
Turnover: £500,000 - £1m **No.of Employees:** 1 - 10 **Product Groups:** 36

Date of Accounts	Jul 11	Jul 10	Jul 09
Sales Turnover	513	470	436
Pre Tax Profit/Loss	82	20	-4
Working Capital	71	12	54
Fixed Assets	14	4	9
Current Assets	234	175	164
Current Liabilities	43	75	46

Identilam plc
John Bostock House Faygate Business Centre Faygate Lane, Faygate, Horsham, RH12 4DN
Tel: 01293-851711 **Fax:** 01293-851742
E-mail: sales@identilam.co.uk
Website: http://www.identilam.co.uk
Directors: D. Stoker (Sales), P. Brealey (Co Sec)
Managers: J. Rutherford (Comptroller), A. Allmey (Prod Mgr)
Immediate Holding Company: IDENTILAM PLC
Registration no: 01958178 **Date established:** 1985 **Turnover:** £1m - £2m
No.of Employees: 21 - 50 **Product Groups:** 30, 36, 37, 40, 44, 81

Date of Accounts	Dec 11	Dec 10	Dec 09
Sales Turnover	2m	2m	2m
Pre Tax Profit/Loss	71	38	57
Working Capital	2m	2m	2m
Fixed Assets	424	462	509
Current Assets	2m	2m	2m
Current Liabilities	267	222	204

John Hall Ltd
9 Piries Place, Horsham, RH12 1EH
Tel: 01403-269430 **Fax:** 01403-269451
E-mail: info@jhal.com
Website: http://www.jha.co.uk
Directors: A. Maguire (Fin), J. Hall (Dir)
Managers: A. Ede (Sales Admin), D. Thorpe (I.T. Exec)
Immediate Holding Company: John Hall Associates Ltd
Registration no: 03407982 **Date established:** 1997
Turnover: £500,000 - £1m **No.of Employees:** 21 - 50 **Product Groups:** 54

Key Source Ltd
North Heath Lane Industrial Estate, Horsham, RH12 5QE
Tel: 01403-243333 **Fax:** 01403-243300
E-mail: info@keysource.co.uk
Website: http://www.keysource.co.uk
Directors: M. West (MD)
Managers: K. McIntyre, C. Harding (Personnel), M. Dyke (Mktg Serv Mgr), M. West
Immediate Holding Company: KEYSOURCE LIMITED
Registration no: 03663128 **VAT No.:** GB 644 5208 45
Date established: 1998 **Turnover:** £10m - £20m
No.of Employees: 51 - 100 **Product Groups:** 37, 44

Date of Accounts	Dec 11	Dec 10	Dec 09
Sales Turnover	13m	13m	14m
Pre Tax Profit/Loss	110	953	556
Working Capital	609	860	731
Fixed Assets	588	467	432
Current Assets	6m	6m	5m
Current Liabilities	5m	4m	4m

Lismore Instruments Ltd
2 Tristar Business Centre Star Road, Partridge Green, Horsham, RH13 8RA
Tel: 01403-713121 **Fax:** 01403-713141
E-mail: sales@lismore.uk.com
Website: http://www.intercall.co.uk
Bank(s): Bank of Scotland
Directors: S. Hardy (Dir)
Immediate Holding Company: LISMORE INSTRUMENTS LIMITED
Registration no: 02085753 **VAT No.:** GB 443 1664 61
Date established: 1986 **Turnover:** £1m - £2m **No.of Employees:** 11 - 20
Product Groups: 37, 40

Date of Accounts	Sep 11	Sep 10	Sep 09
Working Capital	2m	2m	2m
Fixed Assets	570	548	555
Current Assets	4m	3m	3m

M M L Manufacturing E D M Ltd
Foundry Lane, Horsham, RH13 5PX
Tel: 01403-251974 **Fax:** 01403-263083
E-mail: mmlmfg@talktalkbusiness.net
Website: http://www.mmlmfg.talktalkbusiness.net
Directors: G. Fry (Tech Serv)
Immediate Holding Company: MML MANUFACTURING (EDM) LIMITED
Registration no: 01712173 **Date established:** 1983
Turnover: £500,000 - £1m **No.of Employees:** 1 - 10 **Product Groups:** 46, 48, 85

Date of Accounts	May 12	May 11	May 10
Working Capital	161	180	74
Fixed Assets	8	11	15
Current Assets	228	180	141
Current Liabilities	58	N/A	N/A

Macfarlane Group UK Ltd
Oakhurst Business Park Wilberforce Way, Southwater, Horsham, RH13 9RT
Tel: 08447-701419 **Fax:** 08706-086151
E-mail: horsham@macfarlanepackaging.net
Website: http://www.macfarlanegroup.net
Directors: J. Glazier (MD)
Managers: A. Headford (Comm)
Ultimate Holding Company: MACFARLANE GROUP PLC
Immediate Holding Company: MACFARLANE GROUP UK LIMITED
Registration no: 01630389 **Date established:** 1982
No.of Employees: 21 - 50 **Product Groups:** 27, 30, 48

Date of Accounts	Dec 11	Dec 10	Dec 09
Sales Turnover	127m	117m	97m
Pre Tax Profit/Loss	3m	4m	1m
Working Capital	5m	5m	5m
Fixed Assets	17m	15m	11m
Current Assets	43m	41m	34m
Current Liabilities	7m	5m	8m

Maltaward Barriers Ltd
Unit 6 Wellingham Way Holmbush Potteries Crawley Road, Faygate, Horsham, RH12 4SE
Tel: 01293-854930 **Fax:** 01293-854939
E-mail: admin@maltaward.co.uk
Website: http://www.maltaward.co.uk
Directors: J. Treacy (Dir), H. Treacy (Fin), G. Treacy (Prop)
Immediate Holding Company: MALTAWARD (BARRIERS) LIMITED
Registration no: 05016164 **VAT No.:** GB 351 0928 71
Date established: 2004 **Turnover:** £2m - £5m **No.of Employees:** 1 - 10
Product Groups: 51

Date of Accounts	Mar 11	Mar 10	Mar 09
Working Capital	455	376	296
Current Assets	630	547	793

Marstor Systems
PO Box 323, Horsham, RH12 1GP
Tel: 01403-268443
E-mail: sales@marstorsystems.com
Website: http://www.marstorsystems.com
Directors: G. Marsh (Dir)
Immediate Holding Company: MARSTOR SYSTEMS LIMITED
Registration no: 04580602 **Date established:** 2002
Turnover: Up to £250,000 **No.of Employees:** 1 - 10 **Product Groups:** 26

Date of Accounts	Nov 11	Nov 10	Nov 09
Sales Turnover	N/A	N/A	126
Pre Tax Profit/Loss	N/A	N/A	39
Working Capital	14	14	13
Fixed Assets	1	1	1
Current Assets	39	48	38
Current Liabilities	N/A	N/A	11

Mecmesin Ltd
Newton House Spring Copse Business Park, Slinfold, Horsham, RH13 0SZ
Tel: 01403-799979 **Fax:** 01403-799975
E-mail: sales@mecmesin.com
Website: http://www.mecmesin.com
Bank(s): Barclays Bank plc
Directors: D. Wilde (Sales), J. Page (MD)
Managers: D. Dobbs (Purch Mgr), W. Holmes (Personnel), J. Montgomery (Mktg Serv Mgr), A. Rabone (Personnel), J. Montgomery (I.T. Exec)
Registration no: 01302639 **VAT No.:** GB 312 8338 74
Turnover: £2m - £5m **No.of Employees:** 51 - 100 **Product Groups:** 37, 38, 39, 44, 48, 67, 84, 85

Date of Accounts	Mar 11	Mar 10	Mar 09
Working Capital	535	504	540
Fixed Assets	850	362	386
Current Assets	1m	1m	1m
Current Liabilities	N/A	252	399

Mercury Welding Supplies
6-7 Jubilee Estate, Horsham, RH13 5UE
Tel: 01403-260200 **Fax:** 01403-217544
E-mail: sales@mercurywelding.com
Website: http://www.mercurywelding.com
Directors: M. Butler (Prop)
Date established: 1996 **No.of Employees:** 1 - 10 **Product Groups:** 46

Neville & More Ltd
Oakhurst Business Park Wilberforce Way, Southwater, Horsham, RH13 9RT
Tel: 01403-732290 **Fax:** 01403-733507
E-mail: info@nevilleandmore.com
Website: http://www.nevilleandmore.com
Bank(s): HSBC, Fenchurch St, London EC3
Directors: C. Sharpe (Dir)
Ultimate Holding Company: EMPAC LIMITED
Immediate Holding Company: NEVILLE & MORE LIMITED
Registration no: 01419152 **VAT No.:** GB 692 8395 79
Date established: 1979 **Turnover:** £1m - £2m **No.of Employees:** 11 - 20
Product Groups: 30, 33, 66

Date of Accounts	Dec 11	Dec 10	Dec 09
Working Capital	2m	2m	2m
Fixed Assets	98	60	65
Current Assets	3m	3m	3m

Oakes Bros Ltd
Clemsfold Corner Guildford Road, Clemsfold, Horsham, RH12 3PW
Tel: 01403-790777 **Fax:** 01403-790086
E-mail: ccharman@oakesbros.co.uk
Website: http://www.oakesbros.co.uk
Managers: C. Charman (District Mgr)
Ultimate Holding Company: ARMOX TRUST (NEVIS)
Immediate Holding Company: OAKES BROS. LIMITED
Registration no: 00395809 **Date established:** 1945
No.of Employees: 11 - 20 **Product Groups:** 67

Date of Accounts	Dec 11	Dec 10	Dec 09
Sales Turnover	22m	22m	23m
Pre Tax Profit/Loss	381	232	262
Working Capital	2m	3m	3m
Fixed Assets	539	559	600
Current Assets	7m	5m	7m
Current Liabilities	3m	1m	1m

Oetiker UK Ltd (Head Office & Factory)
Unit H Foundry Close, Horsham, RH13 5TX
Tel: 01403-260478 **Fax:** 01403-240690
E-mail: sales@uk.oetiker.com
Website: http://www.oetiker.com
Managers: L. Braham (Chief Mgr)
Ultimate Holding Company: INTER CLAMP HOLDING AG (SWITZERLAND)
Immediate Holding Company: OETIKER UK LIMITED
Registration no: 01372894 **VAT No.:** GB 192 9116 47
Date established: 1978 **Turnover:** £1m - £2m **No.of Employees:** 1 - 10
Product Groups: 35, 36, 37, 40, 45, 46

Date of Accounts	Dec 11	Dec 10	Dec 09
Working Capital	211	128	137
Fixed Assets	175	183	201
Current Assets	566	612	560

Pentagon Plastics Ltd Plastic Injection Moulder
Unit 4 Blatchford Rd, Horsham, RH13 5QR
Tel: 0845-474 4187 **Fax:** 01403-267095
E-mail: websales@pentagonplastics.co.uk
Website: http://www.pentagonplastics.co.uk
Bank(s): Lloyds TSB Bank plc
Directors: J. Edwards (Ch), P. Edwards (MD), D. Whitaker (Fab)
Managers: I. Goddard (Sales Prom Mgr)
Immediate Holding Company: Pentagon Plastics Ltd
Registration no: 01365703 **VAT No.:** GB 193 9901 22 Y
Date established: 1972 **Turnover:** £1m - £2m **No.of Employees:** 21 - 50
Product Groups: 26, 29, 30, 33, 42, 47, 48, 49, 61

Date of Accounts	Jan 10	Jan 09	Jan 08
Working Capital	31	239	296
Fixed Assets	1m	782	695
Current Assets	665	839	859

Phillips Consulting
Hydon High Street, Partridge Green, Horsham, RH13 8HR
Tel: 01403-711129 **Fax:** 01403-711654
E-mail: enquiries@phillipsconsulting.co.uk
Website: http://www.phillipsconsulting.co.uk

see next page

***Phillips Consulting** - Cont'd*

Directors: M. Phillips (Snr Part)
Immediate Holding Company: PHILLIPS MANAGEMENT CONSULTANTS LLP
Registration no: OC300956 **Date established:** 2001
Turnover: £500,000 - £1m **No.of Employees:** 1 - 10 **Product Groups:** 86

Date of Accounts	Apr 12	Apr 11	Apr 10
Working Capital	18	12	15
Fixed Assets	8	10	13
Current Assets	34	24	37

Phoenix Executive Fire Advisory Associates

11 Walmer Close Southwater, Horsham, RH13 9XY
Tel: 01403-732266
E-mail: ray@phoenixexecutive.co.uk
Website: http://www.phoenixexecutive.co.uk
Directors: R. Bosdet (Prop)
No.of Employees: 1 - 10 **Product Groups:** 38, 40, 84, 86

Precision Edge Tools

Unit 5-6 Church Lane Estate Church Lane, Plummers Plain, Horsham, RH13 6LU
Tel: 01403-892510 **Fax:** 01403-891709
E-mail: sales@precisionedge.uk.com
Website: http://www.precisionedge.uk.com
Directors: M. Candfield (Dir)
Immediate Holding Company: PRECISION EDGE LIMITED
Registration no: 04867790 **Date established:** 2003
Turnover: £500,000 - £1m **No.of Employees:** 1 - 10 **Product Groups:** 36, 41, 42, 43, 44, 45, 46, 47, 48

Ringway

Albion House 38 Springfield Road, Horsham, RH12 2RW
Tel: 01403-215800 **Fax:** 01403-215801
E-mail: info@ringway.co.uk
Website: http://www.ringway.co.uk
Bank(s): National Westminster Bank Plc
Directors: D. Binding (Dir), S. Lysionek (Fin)
Managers: T. Elms (Mktg Serv Mgr), K. Pollock (Sales & Mktg Mg)
Ultimate Holding Company: VINCI SA (FRANCE)
Immediate Holding Company: EUROVIA MANAGEMENT LIMITED
Registration no: 01271059 **VAT No.:** GB 321 9318 74
Date established: 1976 **Turnover:** £10m - £20m
No.of Employees: 51 - 100 **Product Groups:** 31

Date of Accounts	Dec 11	Dec 10	Dec 09
Sales Turnover	10m	12m	15m
Pre Tax Profit/Loss	-1m	-3m	312
Working Capital	5m	2m	3m
Fixed Assets	2m	3m	3m
Current Assets	11m	12m	21m
Current Liabilities	4m	3m	2m

Rudgwick Metals Ltd

Church Street Rudgwick, Horsham, RH12 3ED
Tel: 01403-822471 **Fax:** 01403-822311
E-mail: john@rudgwickmetals.co.uk
Website: http://www.rudgwickmetals.co.uk
Directors: J. Bailey (MD), J. Adams (Fin)
Immediate Holding Company: RUDGWICK METALS LIMITED
Registration no: 01483946 **Date established:** 1980 **Turnover:** £1m - £2m
No.of Employees: 11 - 20 **Product Groups:** 34, 35, 66

Date of Accounts	Apr 11	Apr 10	Apr 09
Working Capital	145	140	120
Fixed Assets	133	112	138
Current Assets	461	413	372

S B I Industries

Unit 10a Oakendene Industrial Estate Bolney Road, Cowfold, Horsham, RH13 8AZ
Tel: 01403-864858 **Fax:** 01403-864858
E-mail: info@sbindustries.co.uk
Website: http://www.sbindustries.co.uk
Directors: R. Ball (Ptnr)
Registration no: 05097324 **Date established:** 2004
Turnover: Up to £250,000 **No.of Employees:** 1 - 10 **Product Groups:** 41

Scaffold UK

Oakendene Industrial Estate Bolney Road, Cowfold, Horsham, RH13 8AZ
Tel: 0800-830611 **Fax:** 01403-864019
E-mail: scaffolduk@hotmail.com
Managers: A. Osbourn (Mgr)
Immediate Holding Company: SCAFFOLD UK GROUP LIMITED
Registration no: 05097324 **Date established:** 2004
Turnover: Up to £250,000 **No.of Employees:** 1 - 10 **Product Groups:** 35, 52, 66, 83

Date of Accounts	Apr 05
Sales Turnover	15
Pre Tax Profit/Loss	6
Working Capital	-0
Fixed Assets	1
Current Assets	15
Current Liabilities	8

Scott & Sargeant Woodworking Machinery Ltd

Unit 1 Blatchford Road, Horsham, RH13 5QR
Tel: 01403-273000 **Fax:** 01403-274444
E-mail: sales@scosarg.co.uk
Website: http://www.machines4wood.com
Directors: J. Charnaud (MD)
Ultimate Holding Company: SCOTT & SARGEANT HOLDINGS LIMITED
Immediate Holding Company: SCOTT AND SARGEANT WOOD WORKING MACHINERY LIMITED
Registration no: 02448888 **VAT No.:** 528 3628 31 **Date established:** 1989
Turnover: £1m - £2m **No.of Employees:** 11 - 20 **Product Groups:** 37, 47

Date of Accounts	Dec 11	Dec 10	Dec 09
Working Capital	1m	1m	1m
Fixed Assets	511	513	519
Current Assets	2m	2m	2m
Current Liabilities	N/A	N/A	250

Sea White Of Brighton Ltd

Star Road Trading Estate Partridge Green, Horsham, RH13 8RA
Tel: 01403-711633 **Fax:** 01403-711258
E-mail: info@seawhite.co.uk
Website: http://www.seawhite.co.uk
Directors: S. Tobin (MD)
Managers: P. Jellis
Immediate Holding Company: SEAWHITE OF BRIGHTON LIMITED
Registration no: 01067841 **Date established:** 1972 **Turnover:** £5m - £10m
No.of Employees: 21 - 50 **Product Groups:** 64

Date of Accounts	Dec 11	Dec 10	Dec 09
Sales Turnover	8m	7m	7m
Pre Tax Profit/Loss	670	837	726
Working Capital	4m	4m	3m
Fixed Assets	3m	3m	3m
Current Assets	5m	5m	4m
Current Liabilities	636	693	806

Sicpa

29 Star Road Partridge Green, Horsham, RH13 8RA
Tel: 01403-712700 **Fax:** 01403-712716
E-mail: info@sicpa.com
Website: http://www.sicpa.com
Managers: S. Evans (Mgr)
Immediate Holding Company: SICPA UK LTD
Registration no: 03677783 **Date established:** 1998 **Turnover:** £1m - £2m
No.of Employees: 11 - 20 **Product Groups:** 32, 80, 82

Date of Accounts	Dec 11	Dec 10	Dec 09
Sales Turnover	1m	1m	1m
Pre Tax Profit/Loss	3m	-1m	-496
Working Capital	645	-4m	-2m
Fixed Assets	1m	1m	544
Current Assets	999	629	630
Current Liabilities	291	170	153

Silvertech Safety Consultancy Ltd

Holmwood Broadlands Business Campus, Horsham, RH12 4PN
Tel: 01403-211611 **Fax:** 01403-211058
E-mail: sales@silvertech.co.uk
Website: http://www.silvertech.co.uk
Directors: F. Conway (Co Sec), K. Simpson (Dir)
Immediate Holding Company: SILVERTECH SAFETY CONSULTANCY LTD
Registration no: 06287335 **VAT No.:** GB 423 1140 00
Date established: 2007 **Turnover:** £10m - £20m **No.of Employees:** 1 - 10
Product Groups: 44, 84

Smiths Metal Centres Ltd

Foundry Close, Horsham, RH13 5QB
Tel: 01403-261981 **Fax:** 01403-241820
E-mail: burgessk@smithsmetal.com
Website: http://www.smithmetal.com
Directors: K. Burgess (Dir)
Ultimate Holding Company: HENLEY MANAGEMENT COMPANY (USA)
Immediate Holding Company: SMITHS METAL CENTRES LIMITED
Registration no: 03485838 **Date established:** 1997
Turnover: £20m - £50m **No.of Employees:** 1 - 10 **Product Groups:** 34, 49, 66, 84

Date of Accounts	Dec 11	May 10	May 09
Sales Turnover	45m	46m	49m
Pre Tax Profit/Loss	2m	830	629
Working Capital	7m	12m	13m
Fixed Assets	1m	1m	2m
Current Assets	28m	23m	21m
Current Liabilities	4m	2m	2m

S O R Europe Ltd (European Headquarters)

Farren Court The Street, Cowfold, Horsham, RH13 8BP
Tel: 01403-864000 **Fax:** 01403-864040
E-mail: peter@soreur.co.uk
Website: http://www.soreur.co.uk
Bank(s): Lloyds TSB Bank plc
Directors: P. Waters (MD)
Ultimate Holding Company: SOR CONTROLS GROUP LTD (USA)
Immediate Holding Company: SOR EUROPE LTD.
Registration no: 01810051 **VAT No.:** GB 423 2895 51
Date established: 1984 **Turnover:** £2m - £5m **No.of Employees:** 11 - 20
Product Groups: 37, 38

Date of Accounts	Dec 11	Dec 10	Dec 09
Working Capital	143	181	226
Fixed Assets	12	16	12
Current Assets	286	385	389

Southeast Panels

Unit 8 Oakhurst Business Park Wilberforce Way, Southwater, Horsham, RH13 9RT
Tel: 01403-738666 **Fax:** 01403-738999
Directors: R. Cowley (Prop)
No.of Employees: 1 - 10 **Product Groups:** 26, 35

Steefab Ltd

Unit 11 Huffwood Trading Estate, Partridge Green, Horsham, RH13 8AU
Tel: 01403-711024 **Fax:** 01403-710751
E-mail: steefab@boltblew.com
Website: http://www.boltblue.com
Directors: C. Redford (Fin), B. Redford (MD)
Immediate Holding Company: STEEFAB LIMITED
Registration no: 01687168 **VAT No.:** GB 389 9106 96
Date established: 1982 **Turnover:** Up to £250,000
No.of Employees: 1 - 10 **Product Groups:** 48

Date of Accounts	Jan 12	Jan 11	Jan 10
Working Capital	39	28	26
Fixed Assets	12	14	16
Current Assets	75	53	47

Stevens Vauxhall

78 Billingshurst Road Broadbridge Heath, Horsham, RH12 3LP
Tel: 01403-256464 **Fax:** 01403-255405
E-mail: info@stevenshorsham.co.uk
Website: http://www.stevensvauxhall.co.uk
Managers: J. Reaves (Sales Prom Mgr), P. Stevens
Ultimate Holding Company: EVANS HALSHAW HOLDINGS P.L.C. GROUP
Registration no: 01593852 **Turnover:** £10m - £20m
No.of Employees: 51 - 100 **Product Groups:** 39, 68

Sugg Lighting Ltd

Unit 1 A Foundry Lane, Horsham, RH13 5PX
Tel: 01293-540111 **Fax:** 01293-540114
E-mail: sales@sugglighting.co.uk
Website: http://www.sugglighting.co.uk
Bank(s): Lloyds TSB
Directors: G. White (MD)
Ultimate Holding Company: F.W. THORPE PUBLIC LIMITED COMPANY
Immediate Holding Company: SUGG LIGHTING LIMITED
Registration no: 01099521 **VAT No.:** GB 210 8356 92
Date established: 1973 **Turnover:** £1m - £2m **No.of Employees:** 11 - 20
Product Groups: 36, 37

Date of Accounts	Jun 11	Jun 10	Jun 09
Sales Turnover	2m	1m	1m
Pre Tax Profit/Loss	-6	48	-193
Working Capital	-4m	-4m	-4m
Fixed Assets	48	25	22
Current Assets	693	589	467
Current Liabilities	45	82	41

Synpharma International Ltd

9 Kings Court Harwood Road, Horsham, RH13 5UR
Tel: 01403-217772 **Fax:** 01403-217775
E-mail: pphillips@synpharma.co.uk
Website: http://www.synpharma.co.uk
Directors: P. Phillips (MD)
Ultimate Holding Company: DR GRANDEL GMBH (GERMANY)
Immediate Holding Company: SYNPHARMA INTERNATIONAL LIMITED
Registration no: 02331210 **VAT No.:** GB 550 1517 77
Date established: 1988 **Turnover:** £1m - £2m **No.of Employees:** 1 - 10
Product Groups: 31, 66

Date of Accounts	Dec 11	Dec 10	Dec 09
Sales Turnover	2m	2m	2m
Pre Tax Profit/Loss	34	67	-7
Working Capital	386	484	437
Fixed Assets	204	198	198
Current Assets	592	763	647
Current Liabilities	78	77	71

Tanfield Towbars

Blatchford Road, Horsham, RH13 5QR
Tel: 01403-269100 **Fax:** 01403-251199
E-mail: sales@tanfieldtowing.co.uk
Website: http://www.tanfieldtowing.co.uk
Bank(s): National Westminster
Directors: K. Knapp (MD)
Immediate Holding Company: TANFIELD LIMITED
Registration no: 01246446 **VAT No.:** GB 193 9469 08
Date established: 1976 **Turnover:** £5m - £10m **No.of Employees:** 11 - 20
Product Groups: 35, 39

Date of Accounts	Jan 12	Jan 11	Jan 10
Working Capital	693	2m	809
Fixed Assets	602	585	914
Current Assets	864	2m	989

Thermal Fluid Systems Ltd

The Old Dairy, Theale Farm Lyons Road, Slinfold, Horsham, RH13 0QS
Tel: 01403-791535 **Fax:** 01403-791967
E-mail: tfs@btconnect.com
Website: http://www.thermalfluidsystems.co.uk
Directors: K. Beeney (Dir)
Registration no: 01904870 **Date established:** 2000
Turnover: £500,000 - £1m **No.of Employees:** 1 - 10 **Product Groups:** 40

Date of Accounts	Sep 07	Sep 06	Sep 05
Working Capital	135	135	130
Fixed Assets	11	15	19
Current Assets	255	203	285
Current Liabilities	119	68	155
Total Share Capital	5	5	5

Trend Control Systems Ltd

Albery House Springfield Road, Horsham, RH12 2PQ
Tel: 01403-211888 **Fax:** 01403-241608
E-mail: jon.cooper@trendcontrols.com
Website: http://www.trendcontrols.com
Bank(s): National Westminster
Directors: J. Cooper (Comm)
Managers: S. Gisbourne (Tech Serv Mgr), M. Orbell (Fin Mgr), R. Tunks (Personnel), S. Browning (Sales & Mktg Mg), J. Cooke (Purch Mgr)
Ultimate Holding Company: HONEYWELL INTERNATIONAL INC (USA)
Immediate Holding Company: TREND CONTROL SYSTEMS LIMITED
Registration no: 01664519 **Date established:** 1982
Turnover: £50m - £75m **No.of Employees:** 251 - 500
Product Groups: 37, 38, 40

Date of Accounts	Dec 11	Dec 10	Dec 09
Sales Turnover	59m	54m	57m
Pre Tax Profit/Loss	5m	-18m	1m
Working Capital	51m	53m	107m
Fixed Assets	11m	11m	11m
Current Assets	90m	93m	137m
Current Liabilities	28m	25m	27m

Tugwell Heating Co. Ltd

Bucks Green Rudgwick, Horsham, RH12 3JF
Tel: 01403-823111 **Fax:** 01403-822999
Website: http://www.tugwellheating.co.uk
Managers: K. Hill
Immediate Holding Company: TUGWELL HEATING CO. LIMITED
Registration no: 01178550 **VAT No.:** GB 193 8832 20
Date established: 1974 **Turnover:** £250,000 - £500,000
No.of Employees: 1 - 10 **Product Groups:** 52, 84

Date of Accounts	Apr 12	Apr 11	Apr 10
Working Capital	474	493	454
Fixed Assets	23	26	24
Current Assets	650	669	722

Turbosound Ltd

Unit 1-6 Star Road Industrial Estate Partridge Green, Horsham, RH13 8RY
Tel: 01403-712748 **Fax:** 01403-710155
E-mail: sales@turbosound.com
Website: http://www.turbosound.com
Bank(s): Bank of Scotland
Directors: S. Blackwood (MD)
Immediate Holding Company: TURBOSOUND LTD
Registration no: 05998934 **Date established:** 2006 **Turnover:** £5m - £10m
No.of Employees: 21 - 50 **Product Groups:** 37

Date of Accounts	Dec 11	Dec 10	Dec 09
Sales Turnover	7m	7m	6m
Pre Tax Profit/Loss	348	313	273
Working Capital	859	589	476
Fixed Assets	999	1m	1m
Current Assets	3m	2m	2m
Current Liabilities	284	372	201

Ultimate Freight

Genesis House Field Place, Broadbridge Heath, Horsham, RH12 3PB
Tel: 01403-221858 **Fax:** 01403-276311
E-mail: sales@ultimatefreight.co.uk
Website: http://www.ultimatefreight.co.uk
Directors: D. Weller (Prop)
No.of Employees: 1 - 10 **Product Groups:** 61, 72, 75, 76, 79, 80

Universal Towel Company Ltd

Unit 5 Foundry Court Foundry Lane, Horsham, RH13 5PY
Tel: 01403-242101 **Fax:** 01403-242144
E-mail: info@u-t-c.co.uk
Website: http://www.u-t-c.co.uk
Directors: T. Filer (MD)
Immediate Holding Company: UNIVERSAL TOWEL COMPANY LIMITED
Registration no: 01441242 **VAT No.:** GB 528 3466 31
Date established: 1979 **Turnover:** £2m - £5m **No.of Employees:** 1 - 10
Product Groups: 30, 66, 83

Date of Accounts	May 12	May 11	May 10
Working Capital	924	652	236
Fixed Assets	75	81	349
Current Assets	2m	2m	2m

V R G Air Pollution Control Ltd

Enterprise House Foundry Lane, Horsham, RH13 5PX
Tel: 01403-221000 **Fax:** 01403-271671
E-mail: info@ergapc.co.uk
Website: http://www.ergapc.co.uk
Bank(s): HSBC
Directors: K. Deldefield (Dir)
Ultimate Holding Company: ENTERPRISE SERVICES GROUP LIMITED
Immediate Holding Company: ENTERPRISE CLEANING SERVICES LIMITED
Registration no: 01389099 **Date established:** 1994 **Turnover:** £5m - £10m
No.of Employees: 21 - 50 **Product Groups:** 40, 41, 42, 46, 48, 54, 84

Date of Accounts	Feb 12	Feb 11	Feb 10
Working Capital	187	285	186
Fixed Assets	259	219	186
Current Assets	3m	2m	2m

Vaultland Engineering

Foundry Lane, Horsham, RH13 5PX
Tel: 01403-260271 **Fax:** 01403-263083
E-mail: mmlmfg@talktalkbusiness.net
Managers: D. Smithers (Mgr)
Immediate Holding Company: APPROVED C S LIMITED
Registration no: 02353697 **Date established:** 2007
Turnover: £20m - £50m **No.of Employees:** 1 - 10 **Product Groups:** 38

Date of Accounts	Dec 11	Dec 10	Dec 09
Working Capital	-1m	-1m	-422
Fixed Assets	2m	2m	1m
Current Assets	767	1m	2m
Current Liabilities	N/A	N/A	483

Vistech Cooling Systems

Church Lane Plummers Plain, Horsham, RH13 6LU
Tel: 01403-892622 **Fax:** 01403-892621
E-mail: info@vistechcooling.co.uk
Website: http://www.vistechcooling.co.uk
Directors: M. Crunden (MD)
Immediate Holding Company: VISTECH COOLING SYSTEMS LIMITED
Registration no: 04808079 **Date established:** 2003
No.of Employees: 1 - 10 **Product Groups:** 40, 48, 52, 66, 84

Date of Accounts	Jun 11	Jun 10	Jun 09
Working Capital	204	154	117
Fixed Assets	32	19	24
Current Assets	1m	785	403

W D R

Park Lodge 60 London Road, Horsham, RH12 1AY
Tel: 01403-268251 **Fax:** 01403-210136
E-mail: info@wdr.co.uk
Website: http://www.wdr.co.uk
Directors: J. Dennis (MD)
Ultimate Holding Company: WDR LIMITED
Immediate Holding Company: WDR LIMITED
Registration no: 02625137 **VAT No.:** GB 602 6084 72
Date established: 1991 **Turnover:** £500,000 - £1m
No.of Employees: 21 - 50 **Product Groups:** 44, 80

Date of Accounts	Jun 11	Jun 10	Jun 09
Working Capital	341	-111	-156
Fixed Assets	564	536	565
Current Assets	1m	845	545

A J Walter Ltd

Viscount House Star Road, Partridge Green, Horsham, RH13 8RA
Tel: 01403-711777 **Fax:** 01403-710936
E-mail: enquiries@ajw-aviation.com
Website: http://www.ajw-aviation.com
Bank(s): HSBC Bank plc
Directors: B. Wolstenholme (Grp Chief Exec), P. Bonnichon (Purch), S. Carter (Fin)
Ultimate Holding Company: A J WALTER HOLDINGS LTD (BVI)
Immediate Holding Company: A J WALTER AVIATION LTD
Registration no: 00699050 **VAT No.:** GB 423 2865 60
Date established: 1961 **Turnover:** £125m - £250m
No.of Employees: 101 - 250 **Product Groups:** 39, 68

Date of Accounts	Dec 11	Dec 10	Dec 09
Sales Turnover	185m	143m	119m
Pre Tax Profit/Loss	19m	19m	19m
Working Capital	46m	35m	35m
Fixed Assets	13m	5m	941
Current Assets	108m	75m	67m
Current Liabilities	18m	14m	13m

West Leigh Ltd

Unit 3 Horsham Trading Estate Foundry Lane, Horsham, RH13 5PX
Tel: 01403-242299 **Fax:** 01403-255577
E-mail: info@west-leigh.co.uk
Website: http://www.west-leigh.co.uk
Bank(s): HSBC Bank plc
Directors: M. Partridge (Dir), B. Briggs (MD)
Managers: K. McCaig (Chief Mgr)
Immediate Holding Company: WEST LEIGH LIMITED
Registration no: 00384694 **VAT No.:** GB 662 8441 22
Date established: 1944 **Turnover:** £5m - £10m **No.of Employees:** 11 - 20
Product Groups: 35, 36, 40

West Sussex Gun Co.

Holmbush Farm Crawley Road, Faygate, Horsham, RH12 4SE
Tel: 01293-851808 **Fax:** 01403-864109
E-mail: info@westsussexgunco.com
Website: http://www.westsussexgunco.com
Directors: P. Lamb (Ptnr)
Registration no: 00538337 **Date established:** 1954
No.of Employees: 1 - 10 **Product Groups:** 36, 39, 40

Wilson & Mansfield Ltd

Milestone House 86 Hurst Road, Horsham, RH12 2DT
Tel: 01403-274014 **Fax:** 01403-276946
E-mail: sales@wmjuice.co.uk
Website: http://www.wmjuice.co.uk
Managers: D. Mant (Sales Prom Mgr)
Immediate Holding Company: Woodman (Holdings) Ltd
Registration no: 05582556 **VAT No.:** GB 212 1966 88
Turnover: £10m - £20m **No.of Employees:** 1 - 10 **Product Groups:** 61

Lancing

Ambex Ltd

11 North Road, Lancing, BN15 9AH
Tel: 01903-765123 **Fax:** 01903-765456
Website: http://www.ambex-marine.com
Directors: F. Smith (Sales), W. Smith (Fin)
Immediate Holding Company: AMBEX LIMITED
Registration no: 01160569 **VAT No.:** GB 191 6961 31
Date established: 1974 **Turnover:** £1m - £2m **No.of Employees:** 1 - 10
Product Groups: 84

Date of Accounts	Nov 11	Nov 10	Nov 09
Working Capital	54	19	-27
Fixed Assets	383	364	381
Current Assets	177	161	141

Amerang Group Ltd

Commerce Way, Lancing, BN15 8TA
Tel: 01903-765496 **Fax:** 01903-765178
E-mail: sales@amerang-group.com
Website: http://www.amerang-group.com
Bank(s): National Westminster Bank Plc
Directors: D. Mordecai (Fin), G. Hales (MD), R. Hales (Sales)
Ultimate Holding Company: MODELZONE HOLDINGS LIMITED
Immediate Holding Company: AMERANG LIMITED
Registration no: 00530758 **VAT No.:** GB 192 9784 06
Date established: 1954 **Turnover:** £5m - £10m **No.of Employees:** 21 - 50
Product Groups: 49

Date of Accounts	Dec 09	Dec 08	Jun 11
Sales Turnover	10m	9m	9m
Pre Tax Profit/Loss	300	165	371
Working Capital	2m	2m	3m
Fixed Assets	1m	1m	1m
Current Assets	5m	5m	7m
Current Liabilities	799	1m	567

D W Buckwell Ltd

27 Highview Sompting, Lancing, BN15 0QW
Tel: 01903-763307 **Fax:** 01903-763307
Directors: D. Buckwell (Prop)
Immediate Holding Company: REGENCY IRONWORKS LIMITED
Registration no: 04353594 **Date established:** 2002
Turnover: Up to £250,000 **No.of Employees:** 1 - 10 **Product Groups:** 26, 35

Date of Accounts	Mar 11	Mar 09	Mar 07
Sales Turnover	61	43	53
Working Capital	4	3	1
Fixed Assets	1	2	4
Current Assets	23	19	20
Current Liabilities	N/A	N/A	16

Carlton Beauty & Spa Ltd

Carlton House Commerce Way, Lancing, BN15 8TA
Tel: 01903-761100 **Fax:** 01903-751111
E-mail: charlie@thecarltongroup.co.uk
Website: http://www.dermabrasionmachine.co.uk
Bank(s): HSBC Bank plc
Directors: C. Barbagelata (MD), A. Barbagelata Fabes (Sales)
Ultimate Holding Company: THE CARLTON GROUP (BEAUTY AND SPA) LIMITED
Immediate Holding Company: CARLTON BEAUTY AND SPA LIMITED
Registration no: 00457072 **VAT No.:** GB 232 7567 58
Date established: 1948 **No.of Employees:** 11 - 20 **Product Groups:** 30, 36, 40

Date of Accounts	May 11	May 10	May 09
Working Capital	126	143	166
Fixed Assets	18	9	12
Current Assets	486	516	527

Fine Cut Graphic Imaging Ltd

Marlborough Road Lancing Business Park, Lancing, BN15 8UF
Tel: 01903-751666 **Fax:** 01903-750462
E-mail: info@finecut.co.uk
Website: http://www.finecut.co.uk
Bank(s): HSBC
Directors: P. Tyler (MD)
Registration no: 01871250 **VAT No.:** GB 351 3233 91
Turnover: £500,000 - £1m **No.of Employees:** 21 - 50
Product Groups: 20, 22, 23, 27, 28, 29, 30, 33, 35, 36, 37, 39, 42, 43, 44, 45, 46, 47, 48, 49, 81

Date of Accounts	Sep 11	Sep 10	Sep 09
Sales Turnover	2m	2m	N/A
Pre Tax Profit/Loss	246	129	N/A
Working Capital	-601	-634	-634
Fixed Assets	868	682	725
Current Assets	505	449	431
Current Liabilities	807	797	N/A

Fonant Ltd

31 Greentrees Crescent Sompting, Lancing, BN15 9SY
Tel: 01903-867810
E-mail: ajcartmell@fonant.com
Website: http://www.fonant.com
Directors: A. Cartmell (MD)
Immediate Holding Company: FONANT LIMITED
Registration no: 07006596 **Date established:** 2009
No.of Employees: 1 - 10 **Product Groups:** 44

Date of Accounts	Sep 11	Sep 10
Working Capital	-8	-11
Fixed Assets	10	11
Current Assets	12	11

G T Lifting Solutions Ltd

14 Cokeham Lane Sompting Sompting, Lancing, BN15 9UW
Tel: 08456-037180 **Fax:** 08456-021741
E-mail: sales@gtplant.co.uk
Website: http://www.gtplant.co.uk
Directors: G. Trundell (MD)
Immediate Holding Company: G T LIFTING SOLUTIONS LIMITED
Registration no: 04575148 **Date established:** 2002
No.of Employees: 1 - 10 **Product Groups:** 38, 45, 67, 83

Date of Accounts	Oct 09	Oct 08	Oct 07
Working Capital	-131	-29	-32
Fixed Assets	1m	1m	779
Current Assets	396	447	351

Garden Xtra's

36 Chartwell Road, Lancing, BN15 8TY
Tel: 01903-761222 **Fax:** 01903-761444
Website: http://www.gardenxtras.com
Directors: S. Vincent (MD)
Immediate Holding Company: GARDEN PRIDE MARKETING LIMITED
Registration no: 06766550 **Date established:** 2008
No.of Employees: 1 - 10 **Product Groups:** 26, 35

Date of Accounts	Dec 11	Dec 10	Dec 09
Working Capital	-60	-9	-30
Fixed Assets	20	16	19
Current Assets	270	257	226

Hawksley & Sons Ltd (Head Office)

Marlborough Road, Lancing, BN15 8TN
Tel: 01903-752815 **Fax:** 01903-766050
E-mail: rrobin@hawksley.co.uk
Website: http://www.hawksley.co.uk
Bank(s): HSBC Bank plc
Directors: M. Gale (Fin), R. Robin (Sales)
Ultimate Holding Company: BLASTREAT (ARUNDEL) LIMITED
Immediate Holding Company: HAWKSLEY & SONS LIMITED
Registration no: 01503795 **VAT No.:** GB 321 9771 54
Date established: 1980 **Turnover:** £500,000 - £1m
No.of Employees: 11 - 20 **Product Groups:** 36, 38, 42

Date of Accounts	Feb 11	Feb 10	Feb 09
Working Capital	501	487	459
Fixed Assets	444	446	426
Current Assets	539	577	534

Interlink Fabrications Ltd

Interlink House Commerce Way, Lancing, BN15 8TA
Tel: 01903-763663 **Fax:** 01903-762621
E-mail: interlink@interlink-fabs.co.uk
Website: http://www.kingspanfabrications.com
Bank(s): Lloyds TSB Bank plc
Directors: D. Mulvihill (Fin), K. Walker (Dir), S. Dougall (Sales)
Managers: M. Liddicoate (Fin Mgr), M. Scott (Transport)
Ultimate Holding Company: Kingspan Building Products Ltd
Immediate Holding Company: Kingspan Ltd
Registration no: 01879238 **VAT No.:** GB 415 2132 01
Date established: 1984 **Turnover:** £5m - £10m **No.of Employees:** 21 - 50
Product Groups: 35, 66

Date of Accounts	Dec 07	Dec 06	Dec 05
Sales Turnover	7360	6218	6181
Pre Tax Profit/Loss	495	465	538
Working Capital	276	-84	3079
Fixed Assets	1051	1073	1155
Current Assets	6053	5382	4739
Current Liabilities	5777	5466	1660
ROCE% (Return on Capital Employed)	37.3	47.0	12.7
ROT% (Return on Turnover)	6.7	7.5	8.7

Manhattan Furniture (t/a Manhattan Furniture)

Blenheim Road, Lancing, BN15 8UH
Tel: 01903-524300 **Fax:** 01903-750679
E-mail: jonathanh@manhattan.co.uk
Website: http://www.manhattan.co.uk
Bank(s): Coutts, London
Managers: J. Hind (Develop Mgr)
Immediate Holding Company: MANHATTAN CITY DEVELOPMENTS LIMITED
Registration no: 05559456 **VAT No.:** GB 376 7910 11
Date established: 2005 **Turnover:** £10m - £20m
No.of Employees: 101 - 250 **Product Groups:** 26

Date of Accounts	Jul 11	Jul 10	Jul 09
Working Capital	2	9	15
Current Assets	3	9	130
Current Liabilities	N/A	N/A	16

A W Matthews

Unit B3 Modern Moulds Business Centre Commerce Way, Lancing, BN15 8TA
Tel: 01903-755372 **Fax:** 01273-697265
E-mail: anthony.matthews20@ntlworld.com
Directors: A. Matthews (Prop)
Date established: 1986 **No.of Employees:** 1 - 10 **Product Groups:** 26, 35

Mead Engineering Services Ltd

9 Parkland Business Centre Chartwell Road, Lancing, BN15 8UE
Tel: 01903-854625 **Fax:** 01903-851943
E-mail: wigmore@mead.co.uk
Website: http://www.mead.co.uk
Directors: R. Wigmore (Dir)
Immediate Holding Company: MEAD ENGINEERING SERVICES LIMITED
Registration no: 05200958 **Date established:** 2004
No.of Employees: 1 - 10 **Product Groups:** 39, 40

Date of Accounts	Aug 11	Aug 10	Aug 09
Working Capital	101	79	73
Current Assets	135	126	96

Parafix Tapes & Conversions (Head Office)

Spencer Road Church Hill Industrial Estate, Lancing, BN15 8UA
Tel: 01903-750000 **Fax:** 01903-767728
E-mail: sales@parafix.co.uk
Website: http://www.parafix.com
Bank(s): Royal Bank of Scotland, 62/3 Threadneedle Street, EC2

see next page

Parafix Tapes & Conversions (Head Office) *- Cont'd*

Directors: M. Punter (MD), C. Wills (Mkt Research), E. Cameron (Fin)
Managers: N. Polley (Tech Serv Mgr), S. Barwick (Sales & Mktg Mg), D. Moore, S. Rue (Purch Mgr)
Ultimate Holding Company: PARAFIX HOLDINGS LIMITED
Immediate Holding Company: PARAFIX TAPES AND CONVERSIONS LIMITED
Registration no: 01066993 **VAT No.:** GB 193 0252 78
Date established: 1972 **Turnover:** £5m - £10m
No.of Employees: 51 - 100 **Product Groups:** 27, 30

Date of Accounts	Dec 11	Dec 10	Dec 09
Sales Turnover	5m	6m	5m
Pre Tax Profit/Loss	108	341	22
Working Capital	4m	4m	4m
Fixed Assets	649	664	432
Current Assets	5m	5m	5m
Current Liabilities	824	887	849

Pentagon Instruments Ltd

Suite 1 4 Wayside Commerce Way, Lancing, BN15 8SW
Tel: 01903-765225 **Fax:** 01903-765547
E-mail: sales@pentagoninstruments.com
Website: http://www.pentagoninstruments.com
Directors: T. Cummins (MD), P. Cummins (Co Sec)
Immediate Holding Company: PENTAGON INSTRUMENTS LIMITED
Registration no: 01184254 **VAT No.:** GB 251 2612 96
Date established: 1974 **Turnover:** £250,000 - £500,000
No.of Employees: 1 - 10 **Product Groups:** 37, 38, 44, 67, 84, 85

Date of Accounts	Sep 11	Sep 10	Sep 09
Working Capital	-118	-119	-108
Fixed Assets	3	4	4
Current Assets	34	29	31

Powel Automation Ltd (Head Office)

Powel Buildings Commerce Way, Lancing, BN15 8TA
Tel: 01903-762700 **Fax:** 01903-763652
E-mail: roy@powel.co.uk
Website: http://www.powel.co.uk
Directors: W. Powel (MD)
Immediate Holding Company: POWEL AUTOMATION LIMITED
Registration no: 01001982 **Date established:** 1971 **Turnover:** £1m - £2m
No.of Employees: 1 - 10 **Product Groups:** 45

Date of Accounts	Mar 11	Mar 10	Mar 09
Working Capital	119	210	224
Fixed Assets	N/A	N/A	14
Current Assets	128	221	249
Current Liabilities	1	N/A	18

Safety Wear & Signs Ltd

6 Elm Business Units Chartwell Road, Lancing, BN15 8FD
Tel: 01903-755335 **Fax:** 01903-764951
E-mail: sales@safetywearandsigns.co.uk
Website: http://www.safetywearandsigns.co.uk
Directors: S. Horney (Dir), T. Lyons (Dir), T. Lyons (Prop)
Managers: E. Horney (Chief Acct)
Immediate Holding Company: SAFETY WEAR AND SIGNS LIMITED
Registration no: 01585597 **Date established:** 1981
Turnover: Up to £250,000 **No.of Employees:** 1 - 10 **Product Groups:** 22

Date of Accounts	Sep 10	Sep 09	Sep 08
Sales Turnover	209	133	106
Pre Tax Profit/Loss	-5	7	10
Working Capital	45	38	22
Fixed Assets	4	5	5
Current Assets	80	59	32
Current Liabilities	3	2	2

Seevent Plastics Ltd

Unit 2-7 Peter Road, Lancing, BN15 8TH
Tel: 01903-755877 **Fax:** 01903-753673
E-mail: sales@seevent.co.uk
Website: http://www.seevent.co.uk
Directors: K. Fisher (Dir), K. Fisher (MD)
Managers: M. Melville (Sales Prom Mgr)
Immediate Holding Company: SEEVENT PLASTICS LIMITED
Registration no: 02121368 **VAT No.:** GB 461 8455 33
Date established: 1987 **Turnover:** £2m - £5m **No.of Employees:** 51 - 100
Product Groups: 30

Date of Accounts	Feb 12	Feb 11	Feb 10
Sales Turnover	7m	N/A	N/A
Pre Tax Profit/Loss	461	N/A	N/A
Working Capital	664	418	558
Fixed Assets	816	816	572
Current Assets	2m	2m	1m
Current Liabilities	455	179	N/A

Southern Scientific

Scientific House Rectory Farm Road, Sompting, Lancing, BN15 0DP
Tel: 01903-604000 **Fax:** 01903-604026
E-mail: info@ssl.gb.com
Website: http://www.ssl.gb.com
Bank(s): Lloyds TSB Bank plc
Directors: A. Knight (Dir), K. Frost (Sales & Mktg)
Immediate Holding Company: SOUTHERN SCIENTIFIC LIMITED
Registration no: 01800317 **VAT No.:** GB 397 6460 01
Date established: 1984 **No.of Employees:** 21 - 50 **Product Groups:** 37, 38, 54, 67, 85

Date of Accounts	Jun 10	Jun 09	Jun 08
Working Capital	706	816	642
Fixed Assets	31	15	37
Current Assets	1m	2m	2m

Spa Welding Supplies

Marlborough House Marlborough Road, Lancing, BN15 8UF
Tel: 01903-766909 **Fax:** 01903-756180
E-mail: sales@spawelding.com
Website: http://www.spawelding.com
Directors: S. Aldridge (Prop)
Registration no: 02316990 **Date established:** 1988
Turnover: £250,000 - £500,000 **No.of Employees:** 1 - 10
Product Groups: 46

Date of Accounts	Mar 08	Mar 07	Mar 06
Working Capital	6	-2	-6
Fixed Assets	6	7	3
Current Assets	174	94	94
Current Liabilities	168	96	100

Specialty Electric Motor Sales

23 Winston Business Centre Chartwell Road, Lancing, BN15 8TU
Tel: 01903-765652 **Fax:** 01903-765654
E-mail: derek@sp-t.co.uk
Website: http://www.sp-t.co.uk
Directors: D. Slaughter (Prop), D. Slaughter (MD)
Immediate Holding Company: G.I. MILSIM EUROPE LIMITED
Registration no: 07086017 **Date established:** 2009
No.of Employees: 1 - 10 **Product Groups:** 37, 67

Spray Shop

13-14 Peter Road, Lancing, BN15 8TH
Tel: 01903-851297 **Fax:** 01903-755871
E-mail: info@sprayshop.org
Website: http://www.sprayshop.org
Directors: S. Gregg (MD)
Date established: 2000 **No.of Employees:** 11 - 20 **Product Groups:** 38, 42, 46, 48

Sussex Dishwasher Services

59 Kings Road, Lancing, BN15 8EG
Tel: 01903-762311
Directors: R. Cooper (Prop)
Date established: 1988 **No.of Employees:** 1 - 10 **Product Groups:** 20, 40, 41

Tara Signs Ltd

St Peters Place Western Road, Lancing, BN15 8SB
Tel: 01903-750710 **Fax:** 01903-754008
E-mail: sales@tarasigns.com
Website: http://www.tarasigns.com
Bank(s): HSBC
Directors: L. Finch (Dir)
Immediate Holding Company: TARA SIGNS LIMITED
Registration no: 01032840 **VAT No.:** 193 8393 20 **Date established:** 1971
No.of Employees: 21 - 50 **Product Groups:** 39

Date of Accounts	Jan 12	Jan 11	Jan 10
Working Capital	192	67	175
Fixed Assets	330	313	330
Current Assets	877	856	1m

Triad Timber Components Ltd

Unit A Peter Road, Lancing, BN15 8TH
Tel: 01903-765167 **Fax:** 01903-772236
E-mail: les@triadtimber.co.uk
Website: http://www.kellysearch.com/partners/triadtimbercomponents.asp
Bank(s): National Westminster Bank Plc
Directors: R. Odds (Fin)
Managers: L. Fuller (Mgr)
Ultimate Holding Company: CALLDENE LIMITED
Immediate Holding Company: TRIAD TIMBER COMPONENTS LIMITED
Registration no: 01036744 **VAT No.:** GB 587 5155 02
Date established: 1971 **Turnover:** £2m - £5m **No.of Employees:** 21 - 50
Product Groups: 66

Date of Accounts	Mar 11	Mar 10	Mar 09
Working Capital	-482	-285	223
Fixed Assets	202	112	24
Current Assets	408	329	554

Unipower Europe Ltd

Parkland Business Centre Chartwell Road, Lancing, BN15 8UE
Tel: 01903-768200 **Fax:** 01903-764540
E-mail: info@unipowereurope.com
Website: http://www.unipowereurope.com
Directors: S. Head (MD)
Immediate Holding Company: UNIPOWER EUROPE LIMITED
Registration no: 01079104 **VAT No.:** GB 435 9205 48
Date established: 1972 **Turnover:** £1m - £2m **No.of Employees:** 1 - 10
Product Groups: 37, 38, 44

Date of Accounts	Dec 10	Mar 09	Dec 11
Sales Turnover	N/A	2m	N/A
Pre Tax Profit/Loss	N/A	112	N/A
Working Capital	566	694	896
Fixed Assets	32	37	32
Current Assets	876	964	1m
Current Liabilities	N/A	82	N/A

Whistle Stop Plastics Ltd

Marlborough House Marlborough Road, Lancing, BN15 8UF
Tel: 01903-875888 **Fax:** 01903-875889
E-mail: purchasing@wsplastics.co.uk
Website: http://www.wsplastics.co.uk
Directors: P. Rowe (MD), T. Pumphrey (Co Sec)
Ultimate Holding Company: THE MODERN MOULDS GROUP LIMITED
Immediate Holding Company: WHISTLE-STOP PLASTICS LTD
Registration no: 03153237 **Date established:** 1996
No.of Employees: 51 - 100 **Product Groups:** 29, 30, 31, 38, 42, 43, 48, 49, 80, 84, 85

Date of Accounts	Jan 11	Jan 10	Jan 09
Working Capital	573	511	486
Fixed Assets	124	117	108
Current Assets	1m	956	790
Current Liabilities	N/A	N/A	270

Littlehampton

Air & Water Centre

Artex Avenue Rustington, Littlehampton, BN16 3LN
Tel: 01903-858657 **Fax:** 01903-850345
E-mail: sales@airandwatercentre.com
Website: http://www.airandwatercentre.com
Bank(s): Lloyds TSB Bank plc
Directors: S. Verney (MD)
Immediate Holding Company: J.S. HUMIDIFIERS PLC
Registration no: 07256472 **VAT No.:** GB 373 6118 50
Date established: 1982 **Turnover:** £500,000 - £1m
No.of Employees: 51 - 100 **Product Groups:** 30, 33, 38, 40, 42

Artetch Circuits Ltd

Riverside Industrial Estate Bridge Road, Littlehampton, BN17 5DF
Tel: 01903-725365 **Fax:** 01903-730572
E-mail: sales@artetch.co.uk
Website: http://www.artetch.co.uk
Bank(s): Barclays, Bognor Regis
Directors: J. Elsbury (Fin), M. Morrell (Dir)
Ultimate Holding Company: MEM VENTURES LIMITED
Immediate Holding Company: ARTETCH CIRCUITS LIMITED
Registration no: 01151051 **Date established:** 1973 **Turnover:** £2m - £5m
No.of Employees: 51 - 100 **Product Groups:** 37

Date of Accounts	Dec 09	Dec 08	Dec 07
Sales Turnover	5m	6m	6m
Pre Tax Profit/Loss	-295	116	160
Working Capital	818	1m	794
Fixed Assets	1m	1m	1m
Current Assets	2m	3m	3m
Current Liabilities	424	309	275

Arun District Council

Arun Civic Centre 1 Maltravers Road, Littlehampton, BN17 5LF
Tel: 01903-737500 **Fax:** 01903-730442
E-mail: nigel.lynn@arun.gov.uk
Website: http://www.arun.gov.uk
Directors: N. Lynn (Grp Chief Exec)
Managers: J. Follis (Personnel)
No.of Employees: 251 - 500 **Product Groups:** 87

Arun Pumps Ltd

Unit D7 Dominion Way, Rustington Trading Estate, Rustington, Littlehampton, BN16 3HQ
Tel: 01903-776447 **Fax:** 01903-850709
E-mail: arun.pumps@btconnect.com
Website: http://www.arunpumps.com
Managers: J. Carver (Purch Mgr), P. Turner
Registration no: 01739312 **Turnover:** £250,000 - £500,000
No.of Employees: 1 - 10 **Product Groups:** 40, 42, 48, 54

Date of Accounts	Sep 11	Sep 10	Sep 09
Working Capital	105	105	96
Fixed Assets	4	5	6
Current Assets	221	210	205

Arun Security Centre

8 Beach Road, Littlehampton, BN17 5HT
Tel: 01903-734488 **Fax:** 01903-734488
E-mail: info@arunsecurity.co.uk
Website: http://www.arunsecurity.co.uk
Directors: P. Rambridge (Prop)
Registration no: 04556987 **No.of Employees:** 1 - 10 **Product Groups:** 36, 40, 52, 67

Countplace Ltd

PO Box 52, Littlehampton, BN17 5RZ
Tel: 01903-716802 **Fax:** 01903-715896
E-mail: sales@nukey.co.uk
Website: http://www.newkey.co.uk
Directors: V. Lambert (Dir), V. Porter (Dir)
Ultimate Holding Company: JCM LOCKSMITHS LIMITED
Immediate Holding Company: COUNTPLACE LIMITED
Registration no: 01566884 **Date established:** 1981
No.of Employees: 1 - 10 **Product Groups:** 35, 36

D J B Projects

6 Hobbs Barn Grevatts Lane, Climping, Littlehampton, BN17 5RE
Tel: 01903-723550 **Fax:** 01903-724120
E-mail: info@djbprojects.co.uk
Website: http://www.djbprojects.co.uk
Directors: D. Baldwin (MD)
No.of Employees: 1 - 10 **Product Groups:** 63, 66

Dando Drilling International

Old Customs House Wharf Road, Littlehampton, BN17 5DD
Tel: 01903-731312 **Fax:** 01903-730305
E-mail: info@dando.co.uk
Website: http://www.dando.co.uk
Bank(s): Fortis
Directors: K. Shaw (Fin), M. Fitch Roy (MD)
Ultimate Holding Company: REGENT CORPORATE SERVICES LIMITED
Immediate Holding Company: DANDO DRILLING INTERNATIONAL LIMITED
Registration no: 01770124 **VAT No.:** GB 587 6651 82
Date established: 1983 **Turnover:** £5m - £10m
No.of Employees: 51 - 100 **Product Groups:** 36, 38, 45, 67

Date of Accounts	Dec 11	Jan 11	Jun 10
Sales Turnover	9m	N/A	6m
Pre Tax Profit/Loss	295	N/A	-912
Working Capital	2m	113	666
Fixed Assets	221	214	248
Current Assets	4m	2m	2m
Current Liabilities	1m	N/A	554

Data 2 Patterns & Moulds

Unit 5 The Harwood Centre, Littlehampton, BN17 7AU
Tel: 01903-733380 **Fax:** 01903-734600
E-mail: data2patterns@btconnect.com
Website: http://www.data2patterns.net
Directors: C. Botting (MD)
No.of Employees: 1 - 10 **Product Groups:** 22, 27, 30, 31, 32, 34, 36, 38, 39, 40, 42, 43, 48, 66

Date of Accounts	Mar 08	Mar 07	Mar 06
Working Capital	-45	-60	-43
Fixed Assets	93	62	72
Current Assets	154	98	60
Current Liabilities	199	158	103
Total Share Capital	1	1	1

Educational & Scientific Products Ltd

Unit A2 Dominion Way Rustington, Littlehampton, BN16 3HQ
Tel: 01903-773340 **Fax:** 01903-771108
E-mail: sales@espmodels.co.uk
Website: http://www.espmodels.co.uk
Bank(s): National Westminster Bank Plc
Directors: M. Chaing (Co Sec)
Managers: M. Knowlson (Chief Mgr)
Ultimate Holding Company: CATHAY INVESTMENTS LIMITED
Immediate Holding Company: EDUCATIONAL & SCIENTIFIC PRODUCTS LIMITED
Registration no: 02437468 **VAT No.:** GB 544 0600 78
Date established: 1989 **Turnover:** £500,000 - £1m
No.of Employees: 11 - 20 **Product Groups:** 28, 38, 49, 64

Date of Accounts	Jun 11	Jun 10	Jun 09
Sales Turnover	N/A	N/A	672
Pre Tax Profit/Loss	N/A	N/A	-176

Working Capital	353	319	292
Fixed Assets	11	7	6
Current Assets	401	359	359
Current Liabilities	N/A	N/A	12

Eurofinish Sussex
Unit L3 Riverside Industrial Estate Bridge Road, Littlehampton, BN17 5DF
Tel: 01903-721848 **Fax:** 01903-716139
E-mail: info@eurofinishsussex.com
Website: http://www.eurofinishsussex.com
Managers: C. Griffiths (Tech Consultant)
Date established: 1988 **Turnover:** £250,000 - £500,000
No.of Employees: 1 - 10 **Product Groups:** 46

Fargro
Toddington Lane Wick, Littlehampton, BN17 7QR
Tel: 01903-721591 **Fax:** 01903-730737
E-mail: paul.sopp@fargro.co.uk
Website: http://www.fargro.co.uk
Directors: P. Sopp (Dir), C. Goddard (Co Sec), J. McAlpine (MD)
Managers: J. Blunden-codd (Comm), J. Gulland (Personnel)
Immediate Holding Company: FARGRO LIMITED
Registration no: 06386629 **Date established:** 2007
Turnover: £20m - £50m **No.of Employees:** 21 - 50 **Product Groups:** 82

Date of Accounts	Sep 11	Sep 10	Sep 09
Sales Turnover	21m	18m	15m
Pre Tax Profit/Loss	757	683	269
Working Capital	2m	2m	1m
Fixed Assets	2m	2m	2m
Current Assets	6m	5m	4m
Current Liabilities	984	941	597

Ferrabyrne Ltd (Head Office)
Fort Road Wick, Littlehampton, BN17 7QU
Tel: 01903-721317 **Fax:** 01903-730452
E-mail: sales@ferrabyrne.co.uk
Website: http://www.ferrabyrne.co.uk
Bank(s): National Westminster Bank Plc
Managers: A. Hastings (Sales Prom Mgr), D. Hunt (Tech Serv Mgr), K. Pimm (Purch Mgr), S. Henwood (Fin Mgr), C. Martin (Sales Prom)
Ultimate Holding Company: FLAMEROCK LIMITED
Immediate Holding Company: FERRABYRNE LIMITED
Registration no: 00971894 **VAT No.:** GB 192 8052 52
Date established: 1970 **Turnover:** £2m - £5m **No.of Employees:** 21 - 50
Product Groups: 29, 30, 39, 49

Date of Accounts	Jun 11	Jun 10	Jun 09
Working Capital	2m	2m	2m
Fixed Assets	502	491	584
Current Assets	4m	3m	4m

G P Products (International) LLP
Unit B Harwood Road, Littlehampton, BN17 7AU
Tel: 01903-723428 **Fax:** 01903-733249
E-mail: sales@gpproductsuk.co.uk
Website: http://www.uk-gaskets.co.uk
Bank(s): Nat West
Directors: B. Perry (MD)
Managers: G. Yates (Chief Mgr), J. Clover (Sales Prom Mgr)
Registration no: 02413712 **Turnover:** £1m - £2m
No.of Employees: 11 - 20 **Product Groups:** 22, 23, 24, 25, 27, 29, 30, 32, 33, 36, 37, 39, 40, 42, 43, 44, 45, 47, 48, 49, 66, 68

Date of Accounts	Mar 11	Mar 10	Mar 09
Working Capital	-12	-54	-60
Fixed Assets	547	545	569
Current Assets	311	230	173

HiTek Power Ltd
10 Hawthorn Road, Littlehampton, BN17 7LT
Tel: 01903-712400 **Fax:** 01903-712500
E-mail: sales.uk@hitekpower.com
Website: http://www.hitekpower.com
Bank(s): Lloyds TSB Bank plc
Directors: T. Ballard (Fin)
Managers: J. Coles (Tech Serv Mgr), M. Quiggan (Mktg Serv Mgr), D. Potter, D. Bunce (Mats Contrlr), C. Austin, M. Floyd (Sales Prom Mgr)
Ultimate Holding Company: ASCENT INVESTMENTS LIMITED
Immediate Holding Company: HITEK POWER LIMITED
Registration no: 00908344 **VAT No.:** GB 651 4444 49 004
Date established: 1967 **Turnover:** £10m - £20m
No.of Employees: 101 - 250 **Product Groups:** 37

Date of Accounts	May 11	May 10	May 09
Sales Turnover	14m	7m	6m
Pre Tax Profit/Loss	179	-227	-1m
Working Capital	495	58	-218
Fixed Assets	4m	5m	5m
Current Assets	11m	9m	8m
Current Liabilities	429	526	411

I E C Engineering Ltd
Brookside Avenue Rustington, Littlehampton, BN16 3LF
Tel: 01903-773337 **Fax:** 01903-786619
E-mail: info@iecengineering.com
Website: http://www.iecengineering.com
Bank(s): HSBC Bank plc
Directors: T. Sexton (MD)
Ultimate Holding Company: NASMYTH GROUP LIMITED
Immediate Holding Company: IEC ENGINEERING LIMITED
Registration no: 05476239 **Date established:** 2005 **Turnover:** £5m - £10m
No.of Employees: 51 - 100 **Product Groups:** 34, 35, 39, 48, 85

Date of Accounts	Jan 12	Jan 11	Jan 10
Sales Turnover	8m	7m	6m
Pre Tax Profit/Loss	233	67	-120
Working Capital	288	69	-112
Fixed Assets	393	543	786
Current Assets	3m	2m	2m
Current Liabilities	2m	1m	1m

Inpress Plastics Ltd
1 Harwood Road, Littlehampton, BN17 7AU
Tel: 01903-724128 **Fax:** 01903-730357
E-mail: sales@inpressplastics.co.uk
Website: http://www.inpressplastics.co.uk
Bank(s): Barclays
Directors: R. Parsons (Fin), B. Bull (MD)
Immediate Holding Company: INPRESS PLASTICS LIMITED
Registration no: 03556496 **VAT No.:** GB 717 4037 46
Date established: 1998 **Turnover:** £500,000 - £1m
No.of Employees: 21 - 50 **Product Groups:** 30, 48, 66

Date of Accounts	Dec 11	Dec 10	Dec 09
Working Capital	-42	-39	-30
Fixed Assets	41	8	10
Current Assets	284	236	242

Instrument Solutions
The Laurels The Square, Angmering, Littlehampton, BN16 4EA
Tel: 01903-856846 **Fax:** 01903-856516
E-mail: info@instrumentsolutions.com
Website: http://www.instrumentsolutions.com
Directors: J. Jarvis (Ptnr)
Immediate Holding Company: LOTUS ELECTRICAL SERVICES LIMITED
Registration no: 06676893 **Date established:** 2006
No.of Employees: 1 - 10 **Product Groups:** 38, 48, 67, 84

Intavisual Services Ltd
70 Vermont Drive East Preston, Littlehampton, BN16 1LG
Tel: 01903-770774 **Fax:** 01903-770774
E-mail: info@intavisual.co.uk
Website: http://www.intavisual.co.uk
Directors: M. Johnson (Fin)
Immediate Holding Company: INTAVISUAL SERVICES LIMITED
Registration no: 02213676 **Date established:** 1988
Turnover: £500,000 - £1m **No.of Employees:** 1 - 10 **Product Groups:** 26, 27, 28, 32, 35, 37, 38, 44, 48, 49, 64, 65, 66, 67, 81, 83, 84, 86

Date of Accounts	Jun 11	Jun 10	Jun 07
Working Capital	-4	-0	-2
Fixed Assets	16	20	6
Current Assets	6	6	12

J S Humidifiers plc
Artex Avenue Rustington, Littlehampton, BN16 3LN
Tel: 01903-850200 **Fax:** 01903-850345
E-mail: info@airandwatercentre.com
Website: http://www.airandwatercentre.com
Bank(s): Lloyds TSB Bank plc
Directors: R. Prowen (Chief Op Offcr), S. Verney (Prop), T. Scott (Sales)
Managers: A. Price (Comptroller), D. Buxton (Mktg Serv Mgr), J. Ray, K. Prowen (Personnel)
Immediate Holding Company: J.S. HUMIDIFIERS PLC
Registration no: 01652665 **VAT No.:** GB 358 4968 94
Date established: 1982 **Turnover:** £5m - £10m
No.of Employees: 51 - 100 **Product Groups:** 07, 20, 30, 32, 38, 39, 40, 41, 42, 43, 52, 54, 66, 85

Date of Accounts	Dec 11	Dec 10	Dec 09
Sales Turnover	9m	8m	8m
Pre Tax Profit/Loss	844	49	484
Working Capital	2m	734	559
Fixed Assets	605	809	883
Current Assets	3m	2m	2m
Current Liabilities	1m	514	541

Kittiwake Development Ltd
Unit 3-6 Thorgate Road Wick, Littlehampton, BN17 7LU
Tel: 01903-731470 **Fax:** 01903-731480
E-mail: sales@kittiwake.com
Website: http://www.kittiwake.com
Bank(s): National Westminster Bank Plc
Directors: J. Knight (Co Sec), M. Lucas (MD)
Managers: M. Dines (Sales Prom Mgr), S. Merriot (Tech Serv Mgr), S. Dye (Develop Mgr), W. Bell (Purch Mgr), C. Wright (Personnel)
Immediate Holding Company: KITTIWAKE DEVELOPMENTS LIMITED
Registration no: 02797065 **VAT No.:** GB 620 7446 57
Date established: 1993 **Turnover:** £10m - £20m
No.of Employees: 51 - 100 **Product Groups:** 38, 67, 85

Date of Accounts	Sep 11	Sep 10	Sep 09
Sales Turnover	12m	8m	8m
Pre Tax Profit/Loss	2m	1m	2m
Working Capital	2m	2m	2m
Fixed Assets	997	338	488
Current Assets	5m	4m	3m
Current Liabilities	2m	1m	613

K. Lacey (Engineers) Ltd
Unit 4 Brookside Avenue, Rustington, Littlehampton, BN16 3LF
Tel: 01903-771336 **Fax:** 01903-255411
E-mail: sales@klaceycables.co.uk
Website: http://www.klaceycables.co.uk
Managers: S. Robbins (Sales Prom Mgr)
VAT No.: GB 193 1284 60 **Date established:** 1970
No.of Employees: 1 - 10 **Product Groups:** 30, 35, 37, 39, 67

Date of Accounts	Dec 11	Dec 10	Dec 09
Working Capital	372	318	308
Fixed Assets	404	423	396
Current Assets	604	503	448

Lorlin Electronics Ltd (Halifax Industrial Group)
Harwood Industrial Estate Harwood Road, Littlehampton, BN17 7AT
Tel: 01903-725121 **Fax:** 01903-723919
E-mail: admin@lorlin.co.uk
Website: http://www.lorlinelectronics.com
Bank(s): Royal Bank of Scotland, Edinburgh
Directors: C. Murray (Dir)
Managers: S. Woods (Personnel), D. Murrell (Ops Mgr), G. Stewart (Sales Prom Mgr), R. Peach (Mktg Serv Mgr)
Ultimate Holding Company: SECKLOE 267 LIMITED
Immediate Holding Company: LORLIN ELECTRONICS LIMITED
Registration no: 03204538 **VAT No.:** GB 489 4842 81
Date established: 1996 **Turnover:** £10m - £20m
No.of Employees: 21 - 50 **Product Groups:** 37

Date of Accounts	Sep 11	Sep 10	Sep 09
Working Capital	716	585	458
Fixed Assets	22	25	45
Current Assets	1m	982	651

Lunds
New Factory Brookside Avenue, Rustington, Littlehampton, BN16 3LF
Tel: 01903-784242 **Fax:** 01903-787126
E-mail: sales@lunds.co.uk
Website: http://www.lunds.co.uk
Bank(s): National Westminster Bank Plc
Directors: A. Hobden (Fin), I. Harber (MD)
Ultimate Holding Company: CHATSWORTH FORGE & ENGINEERING LIMITED
Immediate Holding Company: LUND BROS & CO LTD.
Registration no: 01760303 **VAT No.:** GB 216 1798 59
Date established: 1983 **Turnover:** £1m - £2m **No.of Employees:** 21 - 50
Product Groups: 48

Date of Accounts	Sep 11	Sep 10	Sep 09
Working Capital	475	468	487
Fixed Assets	505	569	677
Current Assets	1m	1m	1m

M O G Engineering
Unit 4 Hobbs New Barn Grevatts Lane, Climping, Littlehampton, BN17 5RE
Tel: 01903-733151
Website: http://www.inspiredengineering.co.uk
Directors: M. Ayling (Prop)
Immediate Holding Company: INSPIRED ENGINEERING LTD
Registration no: 05938123 **Date established:** 2006
Turnover: Up to £250,000 **No.of Employees:** 1 - 10 **Product Groups:** 35, 48

Date of Accounts	Dec 09	Dec 08	Dec 07
Sales Turnover	N/A	N/A	106
Pre Tax Profit/Loss	N/A	N/A	44
Working Capital	37	-4	-3
Fixed Assets	6	5	6
Current Assets	37	17	16
Current Liabilities	N/A	N/A	13

Maidment Tankers Ltd
Unit N8 Riverside Industrial Estate Bridge Road, Littlehampton, BN17 5DF
Tel: 01903-717122 **Fax:** 01903-721389
E-mail: sales@maidment-tankers.co.uk
Website: http://www.maidment-tankers.co.uk
Bank(s): Barclays
Directors: A. Hobden (Co Sec), S. Harte (Dir)
Ultimate Holding Company: CHATSWORTH FORGE & ENGINEERING LIMITED
Immediate Holding Company: MAIDMENT TANKER SERVICES LIMITED
Registration no: 01605822 **VAT No.:** GB 322 1667 83
Date established: 1981 **Turnover:** £2m - £5m **No.of Employees:** 21 - 50
Product Groups: 39, 45

Date of Accounts	Sep 10	Sep 09	Sep 08
Working Capital	191	240	178
Fixed Assets	79	95	125
Current Assets	834	754	846

Match Board International Ltd
Unit 24 Eldon Way, Wick, Littlehampton, BN17 7HE
Tel: 01903-716171 **Fax:** 01903-717159
E-mail: sales@matchboard.co.uk
Website: http://www.matchboard.co.uk
Directors: M. Arksey (Dir), I. Arksey (Co Sec)
Immediate Holding Company: MATCH BOARD INTERNATIONAL LIMITED
Registration no: 02709611 **VAT No.:** GB 587 8705 75
Date established: 1992 **Turnover:** £5m - £10m **No.of Employees:** 11 - 20
Product Groups: 25, 26, 49, 63, 66, 67

Date of Accounts	Apr 12	Apr 11	Apr 10
Working Capital	627	467	289
Fixed Assets	293	240	261
Current Assets	884	706	419

Metcraft Ltd
Harwood Road Industrial Estate, Littlehampton, BN17 7BB
Tel: 01903-714226 **Fax:** 01903-723206
E-mail: sales@metcraft.co.uk
Website: http://www.metcraft.co.uk
Bank(s): HSBC Bank plc
Directors: J. Skelton (Co Sec), D. Skelton (Ch), S. Skelton (MD)
Managers: S. Skelton (Eng Serv Mgr), D. Skelton (Trng Mgr), R. Oxley, P. Loe, N. Smith (Accounts)
Registration no: 00606841 **Date established:** 1957 **Turnover:** £1m - £2m
No.of Employees: 21 - 50 **Product Groups:** 35, 36, 38, 39, 48, 52

Date of Accounts	May 12	May 11	May 10
Working Capital	665	681	818
Fixed Assets	564	556	427
Current Assets	1m	925	1m

A K Muller UK Ltd
Unit 4 Brookside Business Park Brookside Avenue, Rustington, Littlehampton, BN16 3LP
Tel: 01903-788888 **Fax:** 01903-785817
E-mail: valves@akmuller.co.uk
Website: http://www.akmuller.co.uk
Managers: T. Barker (Mgr)
Immediate Holding Company: A. K. MULLER (UK) LIMITED
Registration no: 02802161 **Date established:** 1993
No.of Employees: 1 - 10 **Product Groups:** 30, 36

Date of Accounts	Dec 11	Dec 10	Dec 09
Working Capital	276	241	185
Fixed Assets	20	15	22
Current Assets	436	444	430

Naiad Plastics Ltd
16 Thorgate Road Wick, Littlehampton, BN17 7LU
Tel: 01903-724302 **Fax:** 01903-730925
E-mail: michaelsayers@naiadplastics.com
Website: http://www.naiadplastics.com
Bank(s): Barclays Bank P.L.C.
Directors: M. Sayers (MD), L. Sayers (Fin)
Immediate Holding Company: NAIAD PLASTICS LIMITED
Registration no: 01209550 **Date established:** 1975
Turnover: £500,000 - £1m **No.of Employees:** 11 - 20
Product Groups: 30, 42, 48, 66

Date of Accounts	Mar 12	Mar 11	Mar 10
Working Capital	82	64	-1
Fixed Assets	57	54	53
Current Assets	246	269	173

N S Marine Ltd
Rope House Rope Walk, Littlehampton, BN17 5DE
Tel: 01903-724056
E-mail: nsmarine@ntlworld.com
Website: http://www.nsmarine.co.uk
Managers: S. Aragona (Chief Mgr), S. Aragona (Mgr)
Immediate Holding Company: N S MARINE LIMITED
Registration no: 04295362 **Date established:** 2001
No.of Employees: 1 - 10 **Product Groups:** 39

Date of Accounts	Sep 07	Sep 06
Working Capital	-8	-14
Fixed Assets	3	2
Current Assets	36	18
Current Liabilities	44	31

Parker
New Courtwick Lane Wick, Littlehampton, BN17 7PD
Tel: 01903-737000 **Fax:** 01903-737100
E-mail: peter.vos@parker.com
Website: http://www.parker.com

see next page

***Parker** - Cont'd*

Bank(s): HSBC Bank plc, Littlehampton
Managers: G. Shoebridge, R. Jones, M. Kelly (Mgr), G. Hall (Tech Serv Mgr), K. Rogers (Personnel)
Ultimate Holding Company: PARKER HANNIFIN CORP (USA)
Immediate Holding Company: SSD DRIVES LIMITED
Registration no: 01159876 **Date established:** 1974 **Turnover:** £5m - £10m
No.of Employees: 101 - 250 **Product Groups:** 37

Date of Accounts	Jun 11	Jun 10	Jun 09
Pre Tax Profit/Loss	N/A	3m	5m
Working Capital	25m	25m	104m
Current Assets	111m	111m	108m
Current Liabilities	87m	N/A	N/A

Precision Products Brighton Ltd

Brookside Avenue Rustington, Littlehampton, BN16 3LF
Tel: 01903-776171 **Fax:** 01903-774629
E-mail: brian@precisionproducts.co.uk
Website: http://www.precisionproducts.co.uk
Bank(s): National Westminster Bank Plc
Directors: B. Owen (MD), S. Cooke (Chief Op Offcr), S. Thorley (Fin)
Immediate Holding Company: PRECISION PRODUCTS (BRIGHTON) LIMITED
Registration no: 01314364 **VAT No.:** GB 192 5348 46
Date established: 1977 **Turnover:** £2m - £5m **No.of Employees:** 21 - 50
Product Groups: 35, 37

Date of Accounts	Apr 11	Apr 10	Apr 09
Working Capital	391	341	317
Fixed Assets	875	938	1m
Current Assets	1m	769	733

Riverside Precision Ltd

Unit R4 Riverside Industrial Estate Bridge Road, Littlehampton, BN17 5DF
Tel: 01903-732570 **Fax:** 01903-732778
E-mail: jane.riverside@yahoo.co.uk
Website: http://www.riverside-precision.co.uk
Directors: B. Matthews (MD)
Immediate Holding Company: RIVERSIDE PRECISION PRODUCTS LIMITED
Registration no: 02684545 **VAT No.:** GB 587 7387 68
Date established: 1992 **Turnover:** £500,000 - £1m
No.of Employees: 1 - 10 **Product Groups:** 27, 29, 48

Date of Accounts	Feb 12	Feb 11	Feb 10
Working Capital	-60	-43	-26
Fixed Assets	426	374	393
Current Assets	17	21	65

Rudford Property Management

Church Farm Barn Horsemere Green Lane, Climping, Littlehampton, BN17 5QX
Tel: 01903-731177 **Fax:** 01903-726968
E-mail: rudford@pavilion.co.uk
Website: http://www.pavilion.co.uk
Directors: L. Rudd (Prop)
Registration no: 03698444 **Turnover:** £500,000 - £1m
No.of Employees: 1 - 10 **Product Groups:** 80

Date of Accounts	Mar 08	Mar 07	Mar 06
Working Capital	60	39	34
Fixed Assets	1	1	2
Current Assets	192	181	217
Current Liabilities	133	142	183

Securit Ropes & Packaging Ltd

Unit 6 Pheonix Court Dominion Way Rustington, Littlehampton, BN16 3HQ
Tel: 08456-340261 **Fax:** 0845-634 0262
E-mail: sales@securit-ropes-packaging.co.uk
Website: http://www.securit-ropes-packaging.co.uk
Directors: W. Stoner (MD)
Immediate Holding Company: SECURIT ROPES & PACKAGING LTD
Registration no: 02992673 **Date established:** 1994
Turnover: £500,000 - £1m **No.of Employees:** 1 - 10 **Product Groups:** 23, 76

Date of Accounts	Dec 11	Dec 10	Dec 09
Working Capital	138	133	118
Fixed Assets	20	25	17
Current Assets	292	286	301

Silicone Extrusions Ltd

Unit 17 Arndale Road Wick, Littlehampton, BN17 7HD
Tel: 01903-713566 **Fax:** 01903-730883
E-mail: sales@siliconex.com
Website: http://www.siliconex.com
Directors: P. Baker (Dir), S. Baker (Co Sec), N. Coombes (I.T. Dir), N. Coombes (MD)
Managers: B. Little (Sales Prom Mgr)
Immediate Holding Company: SILICONE EXTRUSIONS LIMITED
Registration no: 02062919 **VAT No.:** GB 459 5498 86
Date established: 1986 **Turnover:** £500,000 - £1m
No.of Employees: 1 - 10 **Product Groups:** 29, 30, 49, 63

Date of Accounts	Mar 11	Mar 10	Mar 09
Working Capital	77	143	189
Fixed Assets	112	85	94
Current Assets	397	357	374

Steelex Central Asia Ltd

14 Brendon Way Rustington, Littlehampton, BN16 3PN
Tel: 020-8123 3824 **Fax:** 020-7117 1993
E-mail: admin@steelexcentralasia.com
Website: http://www.steelexcentralasia.com
Directors: C. Perry (Dir)
Immediate Holding Company: STEELEX CENTRAL ASIA LIMITED
Registration no: 06047436 **Date established:** 2007
Turnover: Up to £250,000 **No.of Employees:** 1 - 10 **Product Groups:** 46

Date of Accounts	May 10	May 09	May 08
Sales Turnover	72	N/A	403
Working Capital	11	17	N/A
Fixed Assets	N/A	2	7
Current Assets	12	20	4

Testemp Ltd

Rope Walk, Littlehampton, BN17 5DE
Tel: 01903-714140 **Fax:** 01903-717435
E-mail: sales@testemp.co.uk
Website: http://www.testemp.co.uk
Directors: B. Billingham (Dir)
Immediate Holding Company: TESTEMP LIMITED
Registration no: 00866056 **Date established:** 1965
Turnover: £250,000 - £500,000 **No.of Employees:** 1 - 10
Product Groups: 38

Date of Accounts	Mar 11	Mar 10	Mar 09
Working Capital	269	229	244
Fixed Assets	9	11	13
Current Assets	330	277	300

Transcool Systems Ltd

30 Eldon Way Wick, Littlehampton, BN17 7HE
Tel: 01903-733911 **Fax:** 01903-733188
E-mail: richard.czarnechi@transcoolsystems.co.uk
Website: http://www.transcoolsystems.co.uk
Directors: R. Czarnecki (Dir)
Immediate Holding Company: TRANSCOOL SYSTEMS LIMITED
Registration no: 06006769 **Date established:** 2006
No.of Employees: 11 - 20 **Product Groups:** 40, 66

Date of Accounts	Dec 11	Dec 10	Dec 09
Working Capital	537	121	418
Fixed Assets	26	27	38
Current Assets	926	449	563

Wine Ware Racks & Accessories

PO Box 3135, Littlehampton, BN17 6WJ
Tel: 01903-723557 **Fax:** 01903-723557
E-mail: sales@wineware.co.uk
Website: http://www.wineware.co.uk
Directors: C. Wellman (Dir)
Registration no: 04019913 **Turnover:** £250,000 - £500,000
No.of Employees: 1 - 10 **Product Groups:** 26, 33, 36

Wondertex Ltd

Arndale Road Wick, Littlehampton, BN17 7HD
Tel: 01903-725221 **Fax:** 01903-717508
Website: http://www.wondertex.co.uk
Managers: G. Pierce (Chief Mgr), G. Pearce (Chief Mgr)
Immediate Holding Company: WONDERTEX LIMITED
Registration no: 07055702 **Date established:** 2009 **Turnover:** £2m - £5m
No.of Employees: 1 - 10 **Product Groups:** 33

Date of Accounts	Oct 10
Working Capital	105
Fixed Assets	30
Current Assets	317

Midhurst

Dexam International

Holmbush Industrial Estate, Midhurst, GU29 9HX
Tel: 01730-811864 **Fax:** 01730-815721
E-mail: sales@dexam.co.uk
Website: http://www.dexam.co.uk
Managers: C. Williams (Mgr)
Immediate Holding Company: DEXAM INTERNATIONAL (HOLDINGS) LTD
No.of Employees: 1 - 10 **Product Groups:** 36, 63

Stanley Plastics Ltd

Units 4-7 Holmbush Industrial Estate, Midhurst, GU29 9HX
Tel: 01730-816221 **Fax:** 01730-812877
E-mail: maica@stanleyplastics.co.uk
Website: http://www.stanleyplastics.co.uk
Bank(s): HSBC Bank plc
Directors: M. Simpson (Fin), P. Everley (Sales)
Ultimate Holding Company: THE STANLEY GROUP LIMITED
Immediate Holding Company: STANLEY PLASTICS LIMITED
Registration no: 00722875 **Date established:** 1962 **Turnover:** £1m - £2m
No.of Employees: 11 - 20 **Product Groups:** 30, 31, 49

Date of Accounts	Dec 11	Dec 10	Dec 09
Working Capital	82	77	57
Fixed Assets	25	17	22
Current Assets	410	438	302

Petworth

Fluoro Precision Coatings Cranleigh Ltd

Unit 11 Hampers Common Industrial Estate, Petworth, GU28 9NR
Tel: 01798-343586 **Fax:** 01798-343586
E-mail: sales@fluoroprecision.co.uk
Website: http://www.fluoroprecision.co.uk
Directors: G. Stocking (MD)
Immediate Holding Company: FLUORO PRECISION COATINGS (PETWORTH) LIMITED
Registration no: 06593053 **Date established:** 2008
Turnover: £250,000 - £500,000 **No.of Employees:** 21 - 50
Product Groups: 23, 48

Date of Accounts	May 11	May 10	May 09
Working Capital	1	-1	-11
Fixed Assets	8	10	7
Current Assets	19	20	7

Hot Airlines

Little London Colhook Common, Petworth, GU28 9LF
Tel: 01428-707150
E-mail: rscaife@wsimarketing.com
Website: http://www.hotairlines.co.uk
Directors: G. Scaife (Dir)
Ultimate Holding Company: WILKY GROUP LIMITED(THE)
Immediate Holding Company: WILKY PROPERTY DEVELOPMENTS LIMITED
Registration no: 02666943 **Date established:** 1991 **Turnover:** £2m - £5m
No.of Employees: 1 - 10 **Product Groups:** 39, 75, 86

Date of Accounts	Sep 07	Sep 06	Sep 05
Sales Turnover	N/A	12	N/A
Pre Tax Profit/Loss	N/A	2	N/A
Working Capital	N/A	1	3
Fixed Assets	1	1	1
Current Assets	8	2	7
Current Liabilities	8	1	4
ROCE% (Return on Capital Employed)		98.5	
ROT% (Return on Turnover)		16.1	

J G S Groundwork Services

69b Wyndham Road, Petworth, GU28 0EG
Tel: 01798-342870 **Fax:** 01798-342870
E-mail: jgs.groundworks@tesco.net
Directors: J. Jones (Prop)
Turnover: Up to £250,000 **No.of Employees:** 1 - 10 **Product Groups:** 45, 52, 83, 84

Old Mill Guns

Old Mill Farm Lurgashall, Petworth, GU28 9ER
Tel: 01798-861747 **Fax:** 01798-861747
E-mail: ivor@oldmillguns.com
Website: http://www.oldmillguns.com
Directors: I. Dadswell (Prop)
No.of Employees: 1 - 10 **Product Groups:** 36, 39, 40

Power Blast International

9 Colhook Industrial Park, Petworth, GU28 9LP
Tel: 01428-707895 **Fax:** 01428-707894
E-mail: info@powerblast.co.uk
Website: http://www.powerblast.co.uk
Directors: R. Parkinson (MD)
Immediate Holding Company: POWER BLAST INTERNATIONAL LIMITED
Registration no: 03034261 **VAT No.:** GB 641 5007 73
Date established: 1995 **Turnover:** £1m - £2m **No.of Employees:** 1 - 10
Product Groups: 40, 42, 45, 46, 48

Date of Accounts	Apr 12	Apr 11	Apr 10
Working Capital	29	50	24
Fixed Assets	16	11	14
Current Assets	90	142	173

Printec Ltd

8 Petworth Industrial Estate, Petworth, GU28 9NR
Tel: 01798-343488 **Fax:** 01798-344487
E-mail: sales@printec.co.uk
Website: http://www.printec.co.uk
Bank(s): National Westminster
Directors: I. Kingshott (MD), P. Tarpey (Co Sec)
Immediate Holding Company: PRINTEC LIMITED
Registration no: 02556919 **Date established:** 1990 **Turnover:** £1m - £2m
No.of Employees: 11 - 20 **Product Groups:** 28, 37

Date of Accounts	Mar 08	Mar 07	Mar 06
Sales Turnover	1061	1122	895
Pre Tax Profit/Loss	6	47	25
Working Capital	104	114	93
Fixed Assets	22	67	49
Current Assets	305	338	260
Current Liabilities	200	224	168
ROCE% (Return on Capital Employed)	4.4	25.8	17.7
ROT% (Return on Turnover)	0.5	4.2	2.8

Raker Ltd

1 Colhook Industrial Park, Petworth, GU28 9LP
Tel: 01428-708102 **Fax:** 01428-707030
E-mail: sales@rakers.co.uk
Website: http://www.rakers.co.uk
Directors: A. Kyd (MD), J. Kyd (Fin)
Immediate Holding Company: RAKER LIMITED
Registration no: 03831741 **Date established:** 1999
Turnover: £500,000 - £1m **No.of Employees:** 1 - 10 **Product Groups:** 36, 39, 40

Date of Accounts	Mar 11	Mar 10	Mar 09
Working Capital	229	175	124
Fixed Assets	5	4	9
Current Assets	576	474	417

Wild Grapes

Lurgashall, Petworth, GU28 9EU
Tel: 01428-707862
E-mail: melanie@wild-grapes.co.uk
Website: http://www.wild-grapes.co.uk
Directors: M. Cook (Fin)
Immediate Holding Company: WILD GRAPES LIMITED
Registration no: 05144575 **Date established:** 2004
Turnover: Up to £250,000 **No.of Employees:** 1 - 10 **Product Groups:** 35

Date of Accounts	Mar 11	Mar 10	Mar 08
Sales Turnover	190	168	114
Pre Tax Profit/Loss	-2	24	13
Working Capital	13	21	-30
Fixed Assets	8	2	3
Current Assets	29	52	24
Current Liabilities	3	27	44

Pulborough

All Fire Ltd

Nyetimber Farm Gay Street, Pulborough, RH20 2HH
Tel: 01798-812999 **Fax:** 01273-493131
E-mail: chrisallfire@me.com
Website: http://www.allfireuk.co.uk
Directors: T. Simmonds (MD)
Date established: 1988 **No.of Employees:** 1 - 10 **Product Groups:** 38, 42

American Roundup

P O Box 2008, Pulborough, RH20 1WA
Tel: 01798-865946 **Fax:** 01798-865961
E-mail: sales@americanroundup.com
Website: http://www.americanroundup.com
Directors: N. Selby (Dir)
Managers: K. Friend (Sales Prom Mgr)
Registration no: 01623268 **VAT No.:** GB 370 1498 57
Date established: 1982 **Turnover:** £250,000 - £500,000
No.of Employees: 1 - 10 **Product Groups:** 69

Dan Medica South Ltd

28 Downsview Ave Storrington, Pulborough, RH20 4PS
Tel: 208-1332851 **Fax:** 208-1962364
E-mail: info@danmedicasouth.co.uk
Website: http://www.danmedicasouth.co.uk
Directors: D. Timm (Dir)
Registration no: 437 3372 **Date established:** 2000 **Turnover:**
No.of Employees: 1 - 10 **Product Groups:** 22, 26, 28, 39, 67

Date of Accounts	Feb 10	Feb 09	Feb 07
Sales Turnover	196	249	122
Pre Tax Profit/Loss	-3	55	-12
Working Capital	17	19	-27
Fixed Assets	N/A	N/A	11
Current Assets	30	76	17
Current Liabilities	1	12	8

E C M Electronics Ltd
Penmaen House London Road, Ashington, Pulborough, RH20 3JR
Tel: 01903-892810 **Fax:** 01903-892738
E-mail: colin@ecmelectronics.co.uk
Website: http://www.ecmelectronics.co.uk
Directors: C. Lamberton (MD), K. Lamberton (Fin)
Immediate Holding Company: E C M ELECTRONICS LIMITED
Registration no: 02103897 **Date established:** 1987
No.of Employees: 1 - 10 **Product Groups:** 16, 37, 67

Date of Accounts	Mar 12	Mar 11	Mar 10
Working Capital	191	216	244
Current Assets	222	273	282

Econotech Ltd
Unit 5 Broomers Hill Park Broomers Hill Lane, Pulborough, RH20 2RY
Tel: 01798-875339 **Fax:** 01798-873065
E-mail: enquiries@econotech.co.uk
Website: http://www.econotech.co.uk
Directors: J. Twentyman (Co Sec), R. Twentyman (Dir), A. Thomas (Tech Serv)
Managers: E. Elliott (Fin Mgr)
Immediate Holding Company: ECONOTECH LIMITED
Registration no: 01976186 **VAT No.:** GB 436 0020 02
Date established: 1986 **Turnover:** £1m - £2m **No.of Employees:** 21 - 50
Product Groups: 37, 38, 40, 41, 42, 44, 45

Date of Accounts	Mar 11	Mar 10	Mar 09
Working Capital	378	301	398
Fixed Assets	130	12	33
Current Assets	1m	547	805

Gima Ltd
The Jays Jackets Hill Storrington, Thakeham, Pulborough, RH20 3EF
Tel: 01798-815237 **Fax:** 01798-817231
E-mail: infouk@gima.com
Website: http://www.gima.com
Directors: J. Mitchell (MD)
Registration no: 03910135 **No.of Employees:** 1 - 10 **Product Groups:** 38, 42

Date of Accounts	Dec 07	Dec 06	Dec 05
Working Capital	107	160	232
Fixed Assets	11	22	31
Current Assets	176	196	265
Current Liabilities	69	35	33
Total Share Capital	52	52	52

Hughes Pumps Ltd
Highfield Works Spring Gardens Washington, Pulborough, RH20 3BS
Tel: 01903-892358 **Fax:** 01903-892062
E-mail: pcranford@hughes-pumps.co.uk
Website: http://www.hughes-pumps.co.uk
Bank(s): National Westminster Bank Plc
Directors: R. Hearn (Fin), P. Cranford (MD)
Ultimate Holding Company: GRAMLEY LIMITED
Immediate Holding Company: HUGHES PUMPS LIMITED
Registration no: 01910376 **VAT No.:** GB 620 9127 63
Date established: 1985 **Turnover:** £1m - £2m **No.of Employees:** 21 - 50
Product Groups: 40, 41, 42, 45, 46

Date of Accounts	Mar 12	Mar 11	Mar 10
Working Capital	814	754	956
Fixed Assets	485	416	485
Current Assets	2m	2m	2m

Icam Ltd
Unit 2 Spring Gardens, Washington, Pulborough, RH20 3BS
Tel: 01903-892222 **Fax:** 01903-892277
E-mail: icam@icam.ltd.uk
Website: http://www.icam.ltd.uk
Directors: A. Williamson (MD)
Managers: A. Williams (), A. Williams, D. Daivis (Ops Mgr), D. Davis (Ops Mgr)
Immediate Holding Company: ICAM LIMITED
Registration no: 02133597 **Date established:** 1987
Turnover: £500,000 - £1m **No.of Employees:** 1 - 10 **Product Groups:** 38

Date of Accounts	Jun 07	Jun 06
Working Capital	-400	-247
Fixed Assets	736	634
Current Assets	1323	843
Current Liabilities	1723	1091
Total Share Capital	1	1

Instone Air Services Ltd
Charity Farm Pulborough Road, Cootham, Pulborough, RH20 4HP
Tel: 01903-740101 **Fax:** 01903-740102
E-mail: sales@instoneair.com
Website: http://www.instoneair.com
Directors: J. Instone (MD)
Immediate Holding Company: INSTONE AIR SERVICES LIMITED
Registration no: 01295153 **VAT No.:** GB 242 7183 69
Date established: 1977 **Turnover:** £5m - £10m **No.of Employees:** 1 - 10
Product Groups: 75, 76

Date of Accounts	Nov 11	Nov 10	Nov 09
Working Capital	785	1m	1m
Fixed Assets	493	495	154
Current Assets	2m	2m	2m

Krane Ltd
Unit 9 Broomers Hill Park Broomers Hill Lane, Pulborough, RH20 2RY
Tel: 01798-875958 **Fax:** 01798-872100
E-mail: kraneltd@aol.com
Website: http://www.krane.co.uk
Directors: R. Gardner (Prop)
Immediate Holding Company: KRANE LIMITED
Registration no: 02966683 **Date established:** 1994 **Turnover:** £1m - £2m
No.of Employees: 1 - 10 **Product Groups:** 33, 35, 37, 38, 39, 45, 48, 52, 66, 67, 74

Date of Accounts	Dec 11	Dec 10	Dec 09
Working Capital	20	80	20
Current Assets	70	237	127

Maddison Ltd
Walnut Tree Yard Lower Street, Fittleworth, Pulborough, RH20 1JE
Tel: 01798-865711 **Fax:** 01798-865742
E-mail: info@maddison.co.uk
Website: http://www.maddison.co.uk
Directors: D. Maddison (MD)
Immediate Holding Company: MADDISON LIMITED
Registration no: 02053160 **VAT No.:** GB 449 6883 85
Date established: 1986 **No.of Employees:** 1 - 10 **Product Groups:** 49, 80, 81, 84, 85

Date of Accounts	Sep 11	Sep 10	Sep 09
Working Capital	213	118	149
Fixed Assets	9	14	19
Current Assets	378	340	328

M M H Recycling Systems Ltd
Unit 6 Broomers Hill Park Broomers Hill Lane, Pulborough, RH20 2RY
Tel: 01798-874440 **Fax:** 01798-875613
E-mail: sales@mmhrecsys.com
Website: http://www.mmhrecsys.com
Directors: P. Keatley (Co Sec)
Immediate Holding Company: MMH RECYCLING SYSTEMS LIMITED
Registration no: 03614648 **VAT No.:** GB 396 9028 04
Date established: 1998 **Turnover:** £2m - £5m **No.of Employees:** 1 - 10
Product Groups: 38, 40, 42

Date of Accounts	Dec 11	Dec 10	Dec 09
Working Capital	736	797	778
Fixed Assets	13	20	7
Current Assets	915	969	1m

Paula Rosa Kitchens
Water Lane Storrington, Pulborough, RH20 3DS
Tel: 01903-746666 **Fax:** 01903-742140
E-mail: info@paularosa.com
Website: http://www.paularosa.com
Directors: B. Hammonds (Sales), R. Brew (Co Sec), R. Brew (MD)
Managers: H. Simmons (Personnel), M. Gregory (I.T. Exec)
Ultimate Holding Company: STENA AB (PUBL) (SWEDEN)
Immediate Holding Company: PAULA ROSA LIMITED
Registration no: 03522795 **Date established:** 1998
Turnover: £20m - £50m **No.of Employees:** 101 - 250
Product Groups: 26, 30, 52, 63, 66

Spheric Trafalgar Ltd
Wiston Business Park London Road, Ashington, Pulborough, RH20 3DJ
Tel: 01903-891200 **Fax:** 01903-891220
E-mail: sales@ballbiz.com
Website: http://www.ballbiz.com
Bank(s): HSBC Bank plc
Directors: M. Jennings (Co Sec)
Managers: B. Cane
Immediate Holding Company: SPHERIC-TRAFALGAR LIMITED
Registration no: 01149449 **VAT No.:** GB 219 1842 64
Date established: 1973 **Turnover:** £10m - £20m
No.of Employees: 21 - 50 **Product Groups:** 30, 33, 35, 36, 38, 42, 85

Date of Accounts	Dec 11	Dec 10	Dec 09
Sales Turnover	20m	15m	14m
Pre Tax Profit/Loss	856	675	-454
Working Capital	-2m	-1m	-985
Fixed Assets	13m	7m	6m
Current Assets	9m	9m	7m
Current Liabilities	1m	1m	692

Storrington Auto Repairs Ltd
Old Mill Drive Storrington, Pulborough, RH20 4RH
Tel: 01903-746694 **Fax:** 01903-741101
Website: http://www.basf-c-s.co.uk
Directors: P. Gorringe (Dir)
Immediate Holding Company: STORRINGTON AUTO REPAIRS LIMITED
Registration no: 04533121 **VAT No.:** GB 550 2636 64
Date established: 2002 **Turnover:** Up to £250,000
No.of Employees: 1 - 10 **Product Groups:** 39, 68

Date of Accounts	Dec 10	Dec 09	Dec 08
Working Capital	-5	-2	-13
Fixed Assets	29	35	44
Current Assets	58	62	44

Tesla Engineering Ltd
Water Lane Storrington, Pulborough, RH20 3EA
Tel: 01903-743941 **Fax:** 01903-745548
E-mail: sales@tesla.co.uk
Website: http://www.tesla.co.uk
Bank(s): Barclays, Carfax, Horsham
Directors: M. Begg (MD)
Managers: D. Cracknell (Chief Acct), B. Lelsey (Buyer)
Ultimate Holding Company: STORRINGTON INDUSTRIES LIMITED
Immediate Holding Company: TESLA ENGINEERING LIMITED
Registration no: 02786571 **VAT No.:** GB 665 0452 39
Date established: 1993 **Turnover:** £10m - £20m
No.of Employees: 101 - 250 **Product Groups:** 37, 39, 40, 48

Date of Accounts	Feb 08	Feb 11	Feb 10
Sales Turnover	18m	18m	15m
Pre Tax Profit/Loss	2m	3m	2m
Working Capital	6m	-2m	3m
Fixed Assets	976	10m	715
Current Assets	16m	15m	8m
Current Liabilities	548	3m	2m

Thakeham Tiles Ltd
Rock Road Storrington, Pulborough, RH20 3AD
Tel: 01903-742381 **Fax:** 01903-746341
E-mail: richarddavidge@thakeham.co.uk
Website: http://www.thakeham.co.uk
Directors: R. Davidge (MD), S. Thompson (Sales), E. Taylor (MD)
Immediate Holding Company: THAKEHAM TILES LIMITED
Registration no: 00280073 **Date established:** 1933 **Turnover:** £1m - £2m
No.of Employees: 21 - 50 **Product Groups:** 66

Date of Accounts	Sep 11	Sep 10	Sep 09
Working Capital	538	535	531
Fixed Assets	177	170	188
Current Assets	932	943	796

Shoreham By Sea

3 D I Imagery To Mapping Ltd
1 Ham Business Centre Brighton Road, Shoreham By Sea, BN43 6RE
Tel: 01273-464883 **Fax:** 01273-454238
E-mail: info@towersurveys.co.uk
Website: http://www.3di-international.com
Directors: R. Finch (Dir)
Ultimate Holding Company: 3DI LLC
Immediate Holding Company: 3DI IMAGERY TO MAPPING LIMITED
Registration no: 06367100 **VAT No.:** GB 475 7894 78
Date established: 2007 **Turnover:** £250,000 - £500,000
No.of Employees: 1 - 10 **Product Groups:** 75, 80, 84

Date of Accounts	Dec 11	Dec 10	Dec 09
Working Capital	-0	-7	N/A
Current Assets	14	9	N/A

A M C Security Products Ltd
87 Buckingham Road, Shoreham By Sea, BN43 5UD
Tel: 01273-463344 **Fax:** 01273-463544
E-mail: sales@amcsecurity.com
Website: http://www.amcsecurity.com
Directors: B. Jackson (Dir)
Immediate Holding Company: AMC SECURITY PRODUCTS LIMITED
Registration no: 04422738 **Date established:** 2002
No.of Employees: 1 - 10 **Product Groups:** 25, 33, 35, 36, 37, 38, 39, 40, 44, 49, 51, 52, 66, 80, 81, 82, 84, 87

Date of Accounts	Apr 12	Apr 11	Apr 10
Working Capital	-20	8	4
Fixed Assets	34	24	4
Current Assets	586	309	338

Aardvark Engineering
Shoreham Airport Cecil Pasley Way, Shoreham By Sea, BN43 5FE
Tel: 01273-441694
Website: http://www.aardvarkengineering.co.uk
Directors: P. Filsby (Tech Serv)
Immediate Holding Company: AARDVARK ENGINEERING CONSULTANCY LIMITED
Registration no: 05468199 **Date established:** 2005
Turnover: Up to £250,000 **No.of Employees:** 1 - 10 **Product Groups:** 38, 44, 84

Date of Accounts	May 11	May 10	May 09
Sales Turnover	29	N/A	N/A
Pre Tax Profit/Loss	-10	N/A	N/A
Working Capital	-9	-13	-6
Fixed Assets	13	25	33
Current Assets	20	17	23
Current Liabilities	6	N/A	N/A

At Work Computers Ltd
18 High Street, Shoreham By Sea, BN43 5DA
Tel: 01273-441111
E-mail: gary@atworkcomputers.co.uk
Website: http://www.atworkcomputers.co.uk
Directors: D. Newsom (Jt MD), G. Gwynnde-Smith (Jt MD)
Managers: S. Nickles (Mgr)
Immediate Holding Company: @WORK COMPUTERS LIMITED
Registration no: 04593583 **Date established:** 2002
No.of Employees: 1 - 10 **Product Groups:** 37, 44, 67

Date of Accounts	Nov 10	Nov 09	Nov 08
Working Capital	8	5	10
Fixed Assets	21	23	12
Current Assets	35	41	41

Barnes Daf
44 Dolphin Road, Shoreham By Sea, BN43 6PB
Tel: 01273-454887 **Fax:** 01273-441465
E-mail: info@barnes-group.co.uk
Website: http://www.barnes-group.co.uk
Directors: D. Marshall (Fin)
Managers: A. Matthews (Serv Mgr), A. Haskell
Ultimate Holding Company: EVANS HALSHAW HOLDINGS P.L.C. GROUP
Registration no: 01593852 **Turnover:** £1m - £2m
No.of Employees: 21 - 50 **Product Groups:** 68

Collins & Day Ltd
21-23 Buckingham Road, Shoreham By Sea, BN43 5UA
Tel: 01732-521122 **Fax:** 01732-521133
E-mail: info@collinsandday.co.uk
Website: http://www.collinsandday.co.uk
Bank(s): Coutts
Directors: D. Wetherill (Dir), S. Chapple (Co Sec)
Immediate Holding Company: COLLINS & DAY LIMITED
Registration no: 00606992 **Date established:** 1958 **Turnover:** £1m - £2m
No.of Employees: 11 - 20 **Product Groups:** 52

Date of Accounts	Dec 09	Dec 08	May 10
Working Capital	61	60	110
Fixed Assets	7	2	6
Current Assets	384	433	295

Dorcom Ltd
25 Brunswick Road, Shoreham By Sea, BN43 5WA
Tel: 01273-202851 **Fax:** 01273-220108
E-mail: admin@dorcom.co.uk
Website: http://www.dorcom.co.uk
Managers: M. Fry (Chief Mgr)
Immediate Holding Company: DORCOM LIMITED
Registration no: 01159952 **Date established:** 1974
Turnover: £500,000 - £1m **No.of Employees:** 1 - 10 **Product Groups:** 35, 36, 37, 40, 49, 52

Date of Accounts	Sep 11	Sep 10	Sep 09
Working Capital	322	377	508
Fixed Assets	32	29	29
Current Assets	629	707	781

Dynamic Drawings Ltd (Head Office)
4 Harbour House Harbour Way, Shoreham By Sea, BN43 5HZ
Tel: 01273-464417 **Fax:** 01273-239740
E-mail: ddl@globalnet.co.uk
Website: http://www.hdp.co.uk
Directors: A. Whitehead (MD), S. Robertson (Fin)
Immediate Holding Company: DYNAMIC DRAWINGS LIMITED
Registration no: 03183162 **VAT No.:** GB 760 3092 50
Date established: 1996 **No.of Employees:** 1 - 10 **Product Groups:** 32, 44

Date of Accounts	Mar 11	Mar 10	Mar 09
Working Capital	-27	-16	2
Fixed Assets	64	70	72
Current Assets	49	71	49

E Advantage Solutions
4 Julian Court Wilmot Road, Shoreham By Sea, BN43 6NG
Tel: 01273-358000 **Fax:** 01273-358053
E-mail: pete@eadv.co.uk
Website: http://www.e-advantagesolutions.co.uk
Directors: P. Jenkins (MD)
Immediate Holding Company: E-ADVANTAGE SOLUTIONS LIMITED
Registration no: 03918987 **Date established:** 2000
Turnover: Up to £250,000 **No.of Employees:** 1 - 10 **Product Groups:** 44

see next page

E Advantage Solutions - Cont'd

Date of Accounts	Jun 11	Jun 10	Jun 09
Working Capital	6	3	-3
Fixed Assets	26	27	29
Current Assets	8	7	4

European Metals Recycling Ltd

Kingston Wharf Brighton Road, Shoreham By Sea, BN43 6RN
Tel: 01273-462064 **Fax:** 01273-440666
E-mail: john.edwards@emrltd.com
Website: http://www.elrltd.com
Managers: J. Edwards (Mgr)
Immediate Holding Company: EUROPEAN METAL RECYCLING LIMITED
Registration no: 02954623 **VAT No.:** GB 652 5757 17
Date established: 1994 **Turnover:** £10m - £20m **No.of Employees:** 1 - 10
Product Groups: 42, 66

Date of Accounts	Dec 11	Dec 10	Dec 09
Sales Turnover	3032m	2431m	1843m
Pre Tax Profit/Loss	116m	155m	91m
Working Capital	414m	371m	167m
Fixed Assets	518m	483m	480m
Current Assets	1027m	717m	557m
Current Liabilities	124m	118m	185m

Forac Ltd

Unit 9 Riverbank Business Centre Old Shoreham Road, Shoreham By Sea, BN43 5FL
Tel: 01273-467100 **Fax:** 01273-467101
E-mail: sales@forac.co.uk
Website: http://www.forac.co.uk
Directors: D. Shaw (Co Sec)
Immediate Holding Company: FORAC LIMITED
Registration no: 01769700 **VAT No.:** GB 403 2532 04
Date established: 1983 **Turnover:** £250,000 - £500,000
No.of Employees: 1 - 10 **Product Groups:** 36, 38

Date of Accounts	Mar 11	Mar 10	Mar 09
Working Capital	-7	14	61
Fixed Assets	20	29	41
Current Assets	141	130	218

Headset Services Ltd

7 Cecil Pashley Way Shoreham Airport, Shoreham By Sea, BN43 5FF
Tel: 01273-234181 **Fax:** 01273-234190
E-mail: sales@headsetservices.com
Website: http://www.headsetservices.com
Bank(s): National Westminster Bank Plc
Directors: J. Bedford (Co Sec)
Managers: S. Jefferis (Sales Admin)
Ultimate Holding Company: MEL AVIATION LIMITED
Immediate Holding Company: HEADSET SERVICES LTD.
Registration no: 02962104 **Date established:** 1994 **Turnover:** £1m - £2m
No.of Employees: 21 - 50 **Product Groups:** 24, 29, 36, 37, 39, 40, 67, 84

Date of Accounts	Oct 11	Oct 10	Oct 09
Working Capital	677	605	470
Fixed Assets	13	21	29
Current Assets	1m	1m	936

Horsell Electrics

Unit 1 56 Dolphin Road, Shoreham By Sea, BN43 6PB
Tel: 01273-694124 **Fax:** 01273-603361
E-mail: info@horsellelectrics.co.uk
Website: http://www.horsellelectrics.co.uk
Bank(s): National Westminster Bank Plc
Managers: N. King (Mgr)
Immediate Holding Company: RODHUS PROPERTIES LIMITED
Registration no: 00384200 **VAT No.:** GB 235 5159 65
Date established: 1943 **Turnover:** £500,000 - £1m
No.of Employees: 11 - 20 **Product Groups:** 37

Date of Accounts	Jan 11	Jan 10	Jan 09
Working Capital	-216	88	172
Fixed Assets	217	264	284
Current Assets	172	510	515

MBT (UK)Ltd

Andy Clayton, Suite 19 The Adur Business Centre Little High Street, Shoreham By Sea, BN43 5EG
Tel: 01273-467596 **Fax:** 01273-467600
E-mail: claytonmbtuk@aol.com
Website: http://www.mbbarter.ch
Managers: A. Clayton
Registration no: 04948381 **No.of Employees:** 1 - 10 **Product Groups:** 30, 31

Minelco

Free Wharf Brighton Road, Shoreham By Sea, BN43 6RE
Tel: 01273-452331 **Fax:** 01273-464741
E-mail: bob.bolton@minelco.com
Website: http://www.minelco.com
Bank(s): HSBC Bank plc
Directors: B. Bolton (MD)
Managers: G. Mansfield (Purch Mgr), J. Wheeler (Sales Off Mgr)
Ultimate Holding Company: LKAB (SWEDEN)
Immediate Holding Company: MINELCO LIMITED
Registration no: 04621769 **VAT No.:** GB 192 8614 36
Date established: 2002 **Turnover:** £50m - £75m
No.of Employees: 21 - 50 **Product Groups:** 14, 17, 31, 33

Date of Accounts	Dec 11	Dec 10	Dec 09
Sales Turnover	78m	64m	49m
Pre Tax Profit/Loss	7m	5m	3m
Working Capital	13m	11m	10m
Fixed Assets	26m	27m	29m
Current Assets	39m	32m	30m
Current Liabilities	3m	2m	2m

Pyroban

Endeavour Works 59 Dolphin Road, Shoreham By Sea, BN43 6QG
Tel: 01273-466200 **Fax:** 01629-640247
E-mail: ian.ratcliff@pyroban.com
Website: http://www.pyroban.com
Bank(s): Barclays, Brighton
Directors: I. Ratcliffe (MD)
Ultimate Holding Company: PYROBAN GROUP LIMITED
Immediate Holding Company: PYROBAN LIMITED
Registration no: 01390808 **VAT No.:** GB 587 4165 04
Date established: 1978 **Turnover:** £10m - £20m
No.of Employees: 101 - 250 **Product Groups:** 40

Date of Accounts	Dec 11	Jun 11	Jun 10
Sales Turnover	10m	19m	14m
Pre Tax Profit/Loss	-75	1m	602
Working Capital	7m	6m	5m
Fixed Assets	605	534	545
Current Assets	12m	9m	7m
Current Liabilities	1m	830	1m

Ricardo Consulting Engineers Ltd

Shoreham Technical Centre Old Shoreham Road, Shoreham By Sea, BN43 5FG
Tel: 01273-455611 **Fax:** 01273-464124
E-mail: dave.shemmans@ricardo.com
Website: http://www.ricardo.com
Bank(s): Lloyds
Directors: K. Norwood (Fin)
Managers: T. Hargreaves, D. Shemmans, G. Humphreys, I. Clarke (Tech Serv Mgr), N. Thomas
Ultimate Holding Company: RICARDO PLC
Immediate Holding Company: RICARDO CONSULTING ENGINEERS LIMITED
Registration no: 02251330 **Date established:** 1988
Turnover: £125m - £250m **No.of Employees:** 501 - 1000
Product Groups: 54, 84, 85

Date of Accounts	Jun 11	Jun 10	Jun 09
Pre Tax Profit/Loss	18	-4	-4
Working Capital	-11m	-10m	-10m
Fixed Assets	33m	29m	31m
Current Assets	912	814	814
Current Liabilities	14	10	6

Southern Papers Ltd

Apex House Dolphin Way, Shoreham By Sea, BN43 6NZ
Tel: 01273-440000 **Fax:** 01227-712847
Website: http://www.paperco.co.uk
Directors: K. Davies (Dir), S. Pilkinton (MD), G. Summers (Sales), S. Pilkinson (MD)
Managers: S. Alban (Mgr), J. Quirk (Ops Mgr), B. Ide (Mktg Serv Mgr)
Immediate Holding Company: PAPER LINX
Turnover: £20m - £50m **No.of Employees:** 21 - 50 **Product Groups:** 27

Steyning

Adur Communications Ltd

13 Dawn Crescent Upper Beeding, Steyning, BN44 3WH
Tel: 01903-879526 **Fax:** 01903-879527
E-mail: sales@adurcomms.co.uk
Website: http://www.adurcomms.co.uk
Directors: P. Godbold (MD)
Immediate Holding Company: ADUR COMMUNICATIONS LIMITED
Registration no: 05294028 **Date established:** 2004
Turnover: Up to £250,000 **No.of Employees:** 1 - 10 **Product Groups:** 67

Date of Accounts	Aug 11	Aug 10	Aug 09
Working Capital	3	5	3
Fixed Assets	1	1	N/A
Current Assets	12	12	9

Eurocan Sales & Service Ltd

Unit B1 Newbrook Business Park Pound Lane, Upper Beeding, Steyning, BN44 3JD
Tel: 01903-810110 **Fax:** 01903-810222
E-mail: sales@eurocanltd.com
Website: http://www.eurocanltd.com
Directors: J. Jenner (MD)
Immediate Holding Company: EUROCAN SALES & SERVICE LIMITED
Registration no: 02892394 **Date established:** 1994
No.of Employees: 1 - 10 **Product Groups:** 35, 45

Date of Accounts	Jan 12	Jan 11	Jan 10
Working Capital	45	40	40
Fixed Assets	11	22	29
Current Assets	250	193	161

Nytoy Ltd

4 Manor Road Upper Beeding, Steyning, BN44 3TJ
Tel: 01903-810473 **Fax:** 01903-810163
E-mail: sales@nytoy.co.uk
Website: http://www.nytoy.co.uk
Directors: M. Warburton (MD), C. Goodsman (Fin)
Immediate Holding Company: NYTOY LIMITED
Registration no: 05184278 **Date established:** 2004
Turnover: Up to £250,000 **No.of Employees:** 1 - 10 **Product Groups:** 37

Date of Accounts	Jul 11	Jul 10	Jul 09
Working Capital	2	3	4
Fixed Assets	31	31	31
Current Assets	2	3	4

Rolfe Industries

28 Market Field, Steyning, BN44 3SU
Tel: 08452-303601 **Fax:** 08452-303605
E-mail: brolfe@vac.uk.com
Website: http://www.vacuumschmelze.com
Directors: B. Rolfe (Prop)
Registration no: 01742328 **VAT No.:** GB 397 5931 90
Date established: 1983 **Turnover:** £500,000 - £1m
No.of Employees: 1 - 10 **Product Groups:** 34, 35, 37, 39, 40

S M E Ltd

Mill Road, Steyning, BN44 3GY
Tel: 01903-814321 **Fax:** 01903-814269
E-mail: info@sme.ltd.uk
Website: http://www.sme.ltd.uk
Bank(s): Lloyds
Directors: C. Robertson Aikman (MD), C. Robertson-Aikman (MD)
Managers: L. Daly (Works Gen Mgr), R. Byrne
Immediate Holding Company: S.M.E.LIMITED
Registration no: 00425429 **VAT No.:** GB 190 9269 34
Date established: 1946 **Turnover:** £2m - £5m **No.of Employees:** 51 - 100
Product Groups: 37, 48

Date of Accounts	Aug 11	Aug 10	Aug 09
Sales Turnover	4m	3m	4m
Pre Tax Profit/Loss	196	134	90
Working Capital	3m	3m	3m
Fixed Assets	1m	2m	2m
Current Assets	3m	3m	3m
Current Liabilities	169	181	224

Worthing

A & K Design & Print

4 Victoria Buildings Brighton Road, Worthing, BN11 3EB
Tel: 01903-211441
E-mail: info@fridgemagnet.net
Website: http://www.fridgemagnet.net
Directors: K. Allen (Prop), K. Allens (Prop)
No.of Employees: 1 - 10 **Product Groups:** 28, 40, 49, 65

Advanced Polymers Ltd (t/a Adpol)

Unit 20 Ham Bridge Trading Estate Willowbrook Road, Worthing, BN14 8NA
Tel: 01903-820475 **Fax:** 01903-820969
E-mail: sales@adpol.co.uk
Website: http://www.adpol.co.uk
Bank(s): Abbey plc
Directors: A. White (Fin)
Immediate Holding Company: ADVANCED POLYMERS LIMITED
Registration no: 01164955 **VAT No.:** GB 193 6546 31
Date established: 1974 **Turnover:** £1m - £2m **No.of Employees:** 11 - 20
Product Groups: 29, 30, 31, 32, 37, 39, 40, 42, 48, 66, 68, 85

Date of Accounts	May 12	May 11	May 10
Working Capital	179	176	182
Fixed Assets	23	20	7
Current Assets	525	609	426

Amethyst Mailing Ltd

Amherst House Ferring Street Ferring, Worthing, BN12 5JR
Tel: 01903-700444 **Fax:** 01903-700455
E-mail: jrowling@amethystmailing.co.uk
Website: http://www.amethystmailing.co.uk
Bank(s): Lloyds TSB Bank plc
Directors: J. Rowling (MD)
Immediate Holding Company: AMETHYST MAILING LTD
Registration no: 05417986 **Date established:** 2005
No.of Employees: 11 - 20 **Product Groups:** 80, 81

Date of Accounts	Mar 11	Mar 10	Mar 09
Sales Turnover	702	698	661
Pre Tax Profit/Loss	46	-7	69
Working Capital	-59	-34	-23
Fixed Assets	201	120	128
Current Assets	217	122	92
Current Liabilities	112	118	71

Applied Kilovolts

Woods Way Goring-by-Sea, Worthing, BN12 4QY
Tel: 01903-502744 **Fax:** 01903-708851
E-mail: sales@appliedkilovolts.com
Website: http://www.appliedkilovolts.com
Bank(s): Royal Bank of Scotland
Directors: D. Argent (Fin)
Ultimate Holding Company: APPLIED KILOVOLTS GROUP HOLDINGS LIMITED
Immediate Holding Company: APPLIED KILOVOLTS LIMITED
Registration no: 02101051 **VAT No.:** GB 806 6643 22
Date established: 1987 **Turnover:** £5m - £10m **No.of Employees:** 11 - 20
Product Groups: 37, 38

Date of Accounts	Jun 11	Jun 10	Jun 09
Working Capital	5m	5m	4m
Fixed Assets	882	1m	633
Current Assets	7m	6m	5m

Austen Tapes Ltd

Ivy Arch Road, Worthing, BN14 8BX
Tel: 01892-832141 **Fax:** 01903-205515
E-mail: sarah.gamble@austen-tapes.co.uk
Website: http://www.austen-tapes.co.uk
Directors: N. Howie (MD), S. Howie (Fin)
Ultimate Holding Company: HOWIE HOLDINGS LIMITED
Immediate Holding Company: AUSTEN TAPES LIMITED
Registration no: 00859041 **VAT No.:** GB 202 9777 58
Date established: 1965 **Turnover:** £1m - £2m **No.of Employees:** 1 - 10
Product Groups: 27, 30, 32, 33, 40, 42

Date of Accounts	Dec 11	Dec 10	Dec 09
Working Capital	-108	-67	-69
Fixed Assets	4	6	8
Current Assets	428	390	401

The Brand Surgery

23 Harrow Road, Worthing, BN11 4RB
Tel: 01903-824229 **Fax:** 01903-824230
E-mail: info@thebrandsurgery.co.uk
Website: http://www.thebrandsurgery.co.uk
Directors: V. Vaughn (Dir)
Immediate Holding Company: TALENT WITHIN YOU LIMITED
Registration no: 07049540 **Date established:** 2009
No.of Employees: 1 - 10 **Product Groups:** 81

Date of Accounts	Oct 11	Oct 10
Working Capital	1	1
Current Assets	1	1

Buckhill Ltd

60a Newland Road, Worthing, BN11 1JX
Tel: 01903-238012
E-mail: sales@buckhill.co.uk
Website: http://www.buckhill.co.uk
Managers: S. Buckell
Immediate Holding Company: BUCKHILL LIMITED
Registration no: 05265933 **Date established:** 2004
Turnover: £500,000 - £1m **No.of Employees:** 1 - 10 **Product Groups:** 37, 44

Date of Accounts	Oct 11	Oct 10	Oct 09
Working Capital	14	10	24
Fixed Assets	2	2	3
Current Assets	38	39	46

Business Data Supplies

Dominion Way, Worthing, BN14 8NW
Tel: 01903-206737 **Fax:** 01903-212751
E-mail: sales@nordell.co.uk
Website: http://www.nordell.co.uk

Directors: A. Lamb (MD)
Managers: B. Addison (Admin Off), J. May (Comptroller)
Immediate Holding Company: BUSINESS DATA SUPPLIES LIMITED
Registration no: 01534205 **Date established:** 1980
No.of Employees: 21 - 50 **Product Groups:** 30

Chatsworth Forge Ltd

Woods Way Goring-by-Sea, Worthing, BN12 4RE
Tel: 01903-502221 **Fax:** 01903-700002
E-mail: sales@chatsworthforge.co.uk
Website: http://www.chatsworthforge.co.uk
Bank(s): Barclays, Hove
Directors: A. Hobden (Co Sec), A. Wood (Fab), S. Stephens (MD), S. Stevens (MD), A. Anderson Easey (Chief Est)
Ultimate Holding Company: CHATSWORTH FORGE & ENGINEERING LIMITED
Immediate Holding Company: CHATSWORTH FORGE LIMITED
Registration no: 01499486 **VAT No.:** GB 321 9894 38
Date established: 1980 **Turnover:** £2m - £5m **No.of Employees:** 51 - 100
Product Groups: 35, 40, 66, 81

Date of Accounts	Sep 11	Sep 10	Sep 09
Working Capital	474	482	466
Fixed Assets	85	52	52
Current Assets	1m	1m	2m

Component Moulders (Head Office)

Unit 4-5 Teville Industrials Dominion Way, Worthing, BN14 8NW
Tel: 01903-235765 **Fax:** 01903-212751
E-mail: sales@nordell.co.uk
Website: http://www.nordell.co.uk
Bank(s): HSBC Bank plc
Directors: A. Lamb (Dir)
Ultimate Holding Company: NORDELL LIMITED
Immediate Holding Company: COMPONENT MOULDERS LIMITED
Registration no: 00934586 **Date established:** 1968 **Turnover:** £2m - £5m
No.of Employees: 21 - 50 **Product Groups:** 30, 42, 48, 66

Costal Communications Ltd

11 May Close Goring-by-Sea, Worthing, BN12 6HW
Tel: 01903-705370 **Fax:** 01903-242680
E-mail: james@coastalcomms.co.uk
Website: http://www.coastalcomms.co.uk
Directors: J. Higson (Ptnr), T. Apps (Ptnr), J. Higson (Prop)
Date established: 2004 **No.of Employees:** 1 - 10 **Product Groups:** 67

Date of Accounts	Dec 10	Dec 09	Dec 08
Sales Turnover	213	223	214
Pre Tax Profit/Loss	25	1	38
Working Capital	2	-6	1
Fixed Assets	9	11	8
Current Assets	34	28	46

Cover-Zone

Unit E Easting Close, Worthing, BN14 8HQ
Tel: 01903-201555 **Fax:** 01903-201559
E-mail: info@cover-zone.com
Website: http://www.cover-zone.com
Directors: R. Barton (Ptnr)
Date established: 2000 **Turnover:** £500,000 - £1m
No.of Employees: 1 - 10 **Product Groups:** 39

Engineering Refurbishments

Unit 8 Silverdale Meadow Road, Worthing, BN11 2RZ
Tel: 01903-236186 **Fax:** 01903-217055
E-mail: engineeringrefb@aol.com
Directors: W. James (Prop)
Date established: 2001 **No.of Employees:** 1 - 10 **Product Groups:** 38, 42

Eurogreen Agricultural & Recycling Machinery

North Barn Farm Titnore Lane, Goring-by-Sea, Worthing, BN12 6NZ
Tel: 01903-700678 **Fax:** 01903-247585
E-mail: admin@eurogreenuk.com
Website: http://www.agregister.com/company-30202174.html
Directors: D. Mcintire (Ptnr)
Turnover: £1m - £2m **No.of Employees:** 11 - 20 **Product Groups:** 30, 35, 37, 40, 41, 42

Fire Protection Services

92 St Lawrence Avenue, Worthing, BN14 7JL
Tel: 01903-212646 **Fax:** 01243-553428
E-mail: fire.pro@ntlworld.com
Website: http://www.fireprotection-sussex.co.uk
Directors: M. Peskett (Prop)
Date established: 1994 **No.of Employees:** 1 - 10 **Product Groups:** 38, 42

GB Electronics

Ascoot House Woods Way Goring-By-Sea, Worthing, BN12 4QY
Tel: 01903-244500 **Fax:** 01903-700715
E-mail: sales@gbelectronics.com
Website: http://www.gbelectronics.com
Directors: M. Bullen (Snr Part)
Immediate Holding Company: GB ELECTRONICS (UK) LIMITED
Registration no: 06210991 **VAT No.:** GB 508 6331 53
Date established: 2007 **Turnover:** £1m - £2m **No.of Employees:** 11 - 20
Product Groups: 67

Date of Accounts	Apr 11	Apr 10	Apr 09
Working Capital	-6	-78	-251
Fixed Assets	309	288	308
Current Assets	702	439	420
Current Liabilities	N/A	N/A	671

Hanatek Ltd

10 Sunny Close Goring-By-Sea, Worthing, BN12 4BD
Tel: 01903-246418 **Fax:** 01903-506815
E-mail: info@hanatek.co.uk
Website: http://www.hanatek.co.uk
Directors: R. Hannah (MD), M. Russell (Co Sec)
Registration no: 02694445 **VAT No.:** GB 587 7662 72
Turnover: £250,000 - £500,000 **No.of Employees:** 1 - 10
Product Groups: 38, 85

Homewood Woodworking Machinery

4 King Edward Close, Worthing, BN14 8DJ
Tel: 01903-216113 **Fax:** 01903-213728
E-mail: dave@homewoodltd.co.uk
Website: http://www.homewoodltd.co.uk
Directors: D. Thomas (Ptnr)
Immediate Holding Company: WOODFACTORS LIMITED
Registration no: 05167304 **Date established:** 2001
No.of Employees: 1 - 10 **Product Groups:** 46

Date of Accounts	Oct 10	Oct 09	Oct 08
Sales Turnover	1	12	N/A
Pre Tax Profit/Loss	-0	-3	N/A
Working Capital	1	1	4
Current Assets	77	77	77
Current Liabilities	15	16	N/A

icbaby.com

Unit 20 Oaklands Business Center, Worthing, BN11 5LH
Tel: 0844-8260632
E-mail: enquiries@icbaby.com
Website: http://www.icbaby.com
Directors: J. Wilkinson (Prop)
Product Groups: 24, 29, 30, 61, 63

Instantapes Ltd

5a Ivy Arch Road, Worthing, BN14 8BX
Tel: 01903-232336 **Fax:** 01903-205515
E-mail: enquiries@instantapes.co.uk
Website: http://www.instantapes.co.uk
Directors: N. Howie (MD)
Ultimate Holding Company: HOWIE HOLDINGS LIMITED
Immediate Holding Company: INSTANTAPES LIMITED
Registration no: 00856610 **VAT No.:** GB 192 7065 48
Date established: 1965 **No.of Employees:** 1 - 10 **Product Groups:** 27, 29, 30

Date of Accounts	Dec 11	Dec 10	Dec 09
Working Capital	81	77	72
Fixed Assets	8	11	7
Current Assets	275	275	243

K J Marine Engineering

Unit 1-2 96-98 Dominion Road, Worthing, BN14 8JP
Tel: 01903-230206
E-mail: ken.wilson009@btopenworld.com
Directors: K. Wilson (Prop)
Immediate Holding Company: KD FITNESS LIMITED
Date established: 2006 **No.of Employees:** 1 - 10 **Product Groups:** 35, 36, 39

Kestrel Design

32 Loxwood Avenue, Worthing, BN14 7RA
Tel: 01903-212680 **Fax:** 01903-239001
E-mail: d.elliott@kestrel-design.co.uk
Website: http://www.kestrel-design.co.uk
Directors: D. Elliott (Ptnr)
Date established: 1983 **No.of Employees:** 1 - 10 **Product Groups:** 24, 26, 52, 63, 84

L & S Printing

Unit 10 Hazelwood Trading Estate Hazelwood Close, Worthing, BN14 8NP
Tel: 01903-821005 **Fax:** 01444-242198
E-mail: geoff@ls-printing.com
Website: http://www.ls-printing.com
Bank(s): Barclays
Managers: G. Dagwell
Immediate Holding Company: L & S PRINTING COMPANY LTD
Registration no: 01561973 **VAT No.:** GB 322 1139 11
Turnover: £2m - £5m **No.of Employees:** 51 - 100 **Product Groups:** 28

Date of Accounts	Dec 07	Dec 06	Dec 05
Pre Tax Profit/Loss	-56	218	309
Working Capital	200	178	275
Fixed Assets	2577	2017	1961
Current Assets	1881	2036	2041
Current Liabilities	1682	1858	1766
Total Share Capital	300	300	300
ROCE% (Return on Capital Employed)	-2.0	9.9	13.8

Lemo UK Ltd

12-20 North Street, Worthing, BN11 1DU
Tel: 01903-234543 **Fax:** 01903-206231
E-mail: uksales@lemo.com
Website: http://www.lemo.co.uk
Bank(s): Barclays, Chapel Road
Directors: A. Lurati (Fin), R. Thomas (MD)
Ultimate Holding Company: Interlemo Holding SA (Switzerla
Immediate Holding Company: LEMO (U.K.) LIMITED
Registration no: 01078059 **Date established:** 1972
Turnover: £10m - £20m **No.of Employees:** 21 - 50 **Product Groups:** 37, 38

Date of Accounts	Dec 11	Dec 10	Dec 09
Sales Turnover	10m	9m	7m
Pre Tax Profit/Loss	172	-1m	-139
Working Capital	1m	881	1m
Fixed Assets	9m	10m	5m
Current Assets	3m	5m	3m
Current Liabilities	373	421	300

Lifts Consultancy Services

2 Allington Road, Worthing, BN14 8QD
Tel: 01903-213073 **Fax:** 01903-213073
E-mail: lcs4burchfield@aol.com
Directors: E. Burchfield (Prop)
Date established: 1997 **No.of Employees:** 1 - 10 **Product Groups:** 35, 39, 45

Lintec Antennas

Unit 22 Woods Way Goring-by-Sea, Worthing, BN12 4QY
Tel: 01903-242243 **Fax:** 01903-242588
E-mail: info@lintec-antennas.co.uk
Website: http://www.lintec-antennas.co.uk
Directors: P. Ewens (Dir)
Immediate Holding Company: GB ELECTRONICS (UK) LIMITED
Registration no: 06210991 **Date established:** 2007
Turnover: Up to £250,000 **No.of Employees:** 1 - 10 **Product Groups:** 37

Date of Accounts	Apr 11	Apr 10	Apr 09
Working Capital	-6	-78	-251
Fixed Assets	309	288	308
Current Assets	702	439	420
Current Liabilities	N/A	N/A	671

Littlehampton Book Services Ltd

Faraday Close, Worthing, BN13 3RB
Tel: 01903-828500 **Fax:** 01903-828625
E-mail: peter.roche@lbsltd.co.uk
Website: http://www.lbsltd.co.uk
Bank(s): Barclays, London
Directors: J. Mottram (Fin), P. Roche (Ch), B. May (Co Sec)
Ultimate Holding Company: LAGARDERE SCA (FRANCE)
Immediate Holding Company: LITTLEHAMPTON BOOK SERVICES LIMITED
Registration no: 00250744 **VAT No.:** GB 620 5837 52
Date established: 1930 **Turnover:** £10m - £20m
No.of Employees: 251 - 500 **Product Groups:** 27, 64, 81

Date of Accounts	Dec 11	Dec 10	Dec 09
Sales Turnover	15m	16m	14m
Pre Tax Profit/Loss	948	-672	-170
Working Capital	996	-1m	-1m
Fixed Assets	3m	4m	5m
Current Assets	4m	4m	3m
Current Liabilities	817	937	899

M G M Advantage

M G M House Heene Road, Worthing, BN11 3AT
Tel: 01903-836000 **Fax:** 01903-836001
E-mail: customers@mgmadvantage.com
Website: http://www.mgmadvantage.com
Bank(s): Barclays
Directors: D. Middleton (Fin), G. Shanks (Fin)
Managers: W. Martin (Personnel), A. Banfield (Sales Prom Mgr), A. Gregory, C. Evans, L. Dickinson (Mktg Serv Mgr)
Registration no: 00000006 **VAT No.:** GB 474 3548 26
Turnover: £75m - £125m **No.of Employees:** 251 - 500
Product Groups: 82

George Mah

9 Ivy Arch Road, Worthing, BN14 8BX
Tel: 01903-217721 **Fax:** 01903-217755
Directors: G. Mah (Ptnr)
Immediate Holding Company: SPECIALIST SHOPFITTING AND INSTALLATION LTD
Registration no: 07119343 **Date established:** 2010
No.of Employees: 1 - 10 **Product Groups:** 35

Marine Dental Practice Ltd

36 Marine Parade, Worthing, BN11 3QA
Tel: 01903-234136 **Fax:** 01903-216195
Website: http://www.marinedental.co.uk
Directors: P. Rantzau (Prop)
Immediate Holding Company: MARINE DENTAL PRACTICE LIMITED
Registration no: 07307250 **Date established:** 2010
No.of Employees: 1 - 10 **Product Groups:** 38, 67

Date of Accounts	Dec 11
Working Capital	-328
Fixed Assets	472
Current Assets	12

Moores Domestic Appliances

4-6 South Farm Road, Worthing, BN14 7AA
Tel: 01903-217977 **Fax:** 01903-217977
E-mail: sales@mooresappliances.co.uk
Website: http://www.mooresappliances.co.uk
Directors: R. Moore (Prop)
Immediate Holding Company: MOORES APPLIANCES LIMITED
Registration no: 06729792 **Date established:** 2008
No.of Employees: 1 - 10 **Product Groups:** 36, 40

Natzler Enterprises Entertainments (Magicians)

1 Wakeford Cottages Selden Lane, Worthing, BN11 2LQ
Tel: 01903-211785 **Fax:** 01903-211519
E-mail: info@natzler.com
Website: http://www.natzler.com
Directors: J. Natzler (Ptnr), P. Gordon (Prop)
Turnover: Up to £250,000 **No.of Employees:** 1 - 10 **Product Groups:** 49

Nordell Ltd (inc PB Extrusions and Component Moulders)

4 & 5 Teville Industrials Dominion Way, Worthing, BN14 8NW
Tel: 01903-235765 **Fax:** 01903-212751
E-mail: sales@nordell.co.uk
Website: http://www.nordell.co.uk
Bank(s): HSBC Bank plc
Directors: A. Lamb (MD), P. Mason (Chief Op Offcr)
Registration no: 02971665 **Turnover:** £2m - £5m
No.of Employees: 21 - 50 **Product Groups:** 29, 30, 31, 42, 48, 66

Date of Accounts	Oct 09	Oct 08	Oct 07
Working Capital	623	643	575
Fixed Assets	291	387	474
Current Assets	1m	1m	1m

Opas Southern Limited

Enterprise House St. Lawrence Avenue, Worthing, BN14 7JH
Tel: 01903-239955 **Fax:** 01903-239966
E-mail: sales@opas.co.uk
Website: http://www.opas.co.uk
Directors: D. Ramus (MD)
Registration no: 01838862 **Date established:** 1985
No.of Employees: 1 - 10 **Product Groups:** 22, 23, 30, 35, 36, 43, 47, 63, 66

P B Extrusions Ltd (Nordell)

Unit 3-5 Teville Industrials Dominion Way, Worthing, BN14 8NW
Tel: 01903-211755 **Fax:** 01903-212751
E-mail: sales@nordell.co.uk
Website: http://www.nordell.co.uk
Directors: A. Lamb (MD)
Ultimate Holding Company: NORDELL LIMITED
Immediate Holding Company: P.B. EXTRUSIONS LIMITED
Registration no: 01644644 **Date established:** 1982 **Turnover:** £2m - £5m
No.of Employees: 21 - 50 **Product Groups:** 30, 31, 42, 66

Paineman Waring

Easting Close, Worthing, BN14 8HQ
Tel: 01903-237522 **Fax:** 01903-236511
E-mail: robert@painemanwaring.co.uk
Website: http://www.painemanwaring.co.uk
Bank(s): National Westminster
Directors: F. Woods (Fin), R. Grigson (MD)
Ultimate Holding Company: PAINE MANWARING HEATING LIMITED
Immediate Holding Company: PAINE MANWARING LIMITED
Registration no: 02739418 **VAT No.:** 587 8786 49 **Date established:** 1992
Turnover: £5m - £10m **No.of Employees:** 51 - 100 **Product Groups:** 33, 35, 52

see next page

Paineman Waring - Cont'd

Date of Accounts	Mar 11	Mar 10	Mar 09
Sales Turnover	7m	N/A	N/A
Pre Tax Profit/Loss	49	N/A	N/A
Working Capital	463	453	384
Fixed Assets	39	34	54
Current Assets	2m	1m	1m
Current Liabilities	246	N/A	N/A

Parexel M M S Europe Ltd

Wicker House High Street, Worthing, BN11 1DJ
Tel: 01903-288000 **Fax:** 01903-234862
E-mail: info@parexel-mms.com
Website: http://www.parexel-mms.com
Directors: J. Von Rickenbach (Ch), M. Walshe (Fin)
Ultimate Holding Company: PAREXEL INTERNATIONAL CORP (USA)
Immediate Holding Company: PAREXEL MMS EUROPE LIMITED
Registration no: 01488517 **VAT No.:** GB 587 7276 77
Date established: 1980 **Turnover:** £20m - £50m
No.of Employees: 251 - 500 **Product Groups:** 28, 81

Date of Accounts	Jun 11	Jun 10	Jun 09
Sales Turnover	27m	33m	32m
Pre Tax Profit/Loss	3m	2m	4m
Working Capital	11m	9m	7m
Fixed Assets	596	663	1m
Current Assets	24m	21m	17m
Current Liabilities	6m	10m	8m

Pillar Seals & Gaskets

Willowbrook Road Ham Bridge Trading Estate, Worthing, BN14 8NA
Tel: 01903-207101 **Fax:** 01903-821176
E-mail: pillarseals@aol.com
Website: http://www.pillarseals.com
Bank(s): Barclays
Directors: J. Nighy (Dir)
Immediate Holding Company: Hampson P.L.C.
Registration no: 00717846 **VAT No.:** GB 782 5538 00
Turnover: £2m - £5m **No.of Employees:** 11 - 20 **Product Groups:** 22, 23, 24, 25, 27, 29, 30, 32, 33, 36, 37, 39, 40, 46, 66, 68

Pneutool Power Tools

Springfield Depository Ham Road, Worthing, BN11 2QL
Tel: 01903-823444 **Fax:** 01903- 823444
Directors: D. Woodward (Prop)
Date established: 1995 **No.of Employees:** 1 - 10 **Product Groups:** 37

Polypack Packaging Supplies

48 New Broadway Tarring Road, Worthing, BN11 4HS
Tel: 01903-200984 **Fax:** 01903-200984
E-mail: info@thepolyshop.co.uk
Website: http://www.thepolyshop.co.uk
Directors: L. Laine (Prop)
VAT No.: GB 430 5331 93 **Date established:** 1979
Turnover: £250,000 - £500,000 **No.of Employees:** 1 - 10
Product Groups: 30

Power One

24 Upper High Street, Worthing, BN11 1DL
Tel: 01903-823323 **Fax:** 01903-823324
E-mail: info@power-one.com
Website: http://www.power-one.com
Managers: L. Osborn
Ultimate Holding Company: POWER ONE INC (USA)
Immediate Holding Company: POWER-ONE LIMITED
Registration no: 03103043 **VAT No.:** GB 504 1393 80
Date established: 1995 **Turnover:** £10m - £20m **No.of Employees:** 1 - 10
Product Groups: 37, 44

Date of Accounts	Dec 07	Dec 08	Jan 10
Sales Turnover	17m	20m	20m
Pre Tax Profit/Loss	-835	-785	327
Working Capital	3m	2m	2m
Fixed Assets	35	27	26
Current Assets	9m	8m	6m
Current Liabilities	563	434	427

Powerlink Electronic Ltd

Powerlink House Ivy Arch Road, Worthing, BN14 8BX
Tel: 01903-209550 **Fax:** 01903-215526
E-mail: admin@powerlinkelectronics.co.uk
Website: http://www.powerlinkelectronics.co.uk
Directors: T. Ng (Dir)
Immediate Holding Company: POWERLINK ELECTRONICS LIMITED
Registration no: 02461303 **VAT No.:** GB 544 1310 82
Date established: 1990 **Turnover:** £250,000 - £500,000
No.of Employees: 1 - 10 **Product Groups:** 37, 38, 40

Date of Accounts	Mar 12	Mar 11	Mar 10
Working Capital	1m	1m	984
Fixed Assets	2	3	3
Current Assets	1m	1m	1m

Precision Ball & Gauge Co.

Unit 10-11 Decoy Road, Worthing, BN14 8ND
Tel: 01903-231832 **Fax:** 01903-203111
E-mail: sales@precisionball.co.uk
Website: http://www.precisionball.co.uk
Bank(s): National Westminster Bank Plc
Directors: G. Sayers (MD)
Immediate Holding Company: GMS BALL COMPANY LIMITED
Registration no: 03697171 **VAT No.:** GB 550 3242 80
Date established: 1999 **No.of Employees:** 11 - 20 **Product Groups:** 35, 46

Date of Accounts	Mar 12	Mar 11	Mar 10
Working Capital	25	1	2
Current Assets	84	69	56

Ram Pumps Ltd

Unit C Decoy Road, Worthing, BN14 8ND
Tel: 01903-206622 **Fax:** 01903-205511
E-mail: sales@rampumps.co.uk
Website: http://www.rampumps.co.uk
Bank(s): Lloyds TSB
Managers: D. Attrell (Chief Mgr)
Ultimate Holding Company: DIVERSIFIED DYNAMICS CORPORATION (USA)
Immediate Holding Company: RAM PUMPS LIMITED
Registration no: 01050935 **VAT No.:** GB 806 6162 38
Date established: 1972 **Turnover:** £2m - £5m **No.of Employees:** 11 - 20
Product Groups: 39, 40, 41, 42, 45, 46, 67

Date of Accounts	Nov 11	Nov 10	Nov 09
Working Capital	2m	2m	2m
Fixed Assets	331	263	190
Current Assets	2m	3m	3m

Request Print Ltd

28 Raleigh Crescent Goring-by-Sea, Worthing, BN12 6EE
Tel: 01903-529725 **Fax:** 01903-753914
E-mail: sales@requestprint.co.uk
Website: http://www.requestprint.co.uk
Directors: A. Walker (Fin), B. Walker (Dir)
Immediate Holding Company: REQUEST PRINT LTD
Registration no: 06604656 **Date established:** 2008
No.of Employees: 1 - 10 **Product Groups:** 61, 81

Date of Accounts	May 11	May 10	Mar 09
Working Capital	-7	1	-1
Fixed Assets	7	2	1
Current Assets	15	10	1

Roscomac Ltd

Dominion Way, Worthing, BN14 8NW
Tel: 01903-201701 **Fax:** 01903-201702
E-mail: precision@roscomac.co.uk
Website: http://www.roscomac.co.uk
Directors: N. Rolfe (Fin)
Managers: J. Martello (Mgr), S. Davey (Chief Buyer), L. Cumberland (Personnel)
Immediate Holding Company: ROSCOMAC LIMITED
Registration no: 01254467 **Date established:** 1976
Turnover: £10m - £20m **No.of Employees:** 51 - 100 **Product Groups:** 34, 35, 46, 48, 67

Date of Accounts	Feb 08	Feb 11	Feb 10
Sales Turnover	N/A	14m	9m
Pre Tax Profit/Loss	610	643	14
Working Capital	916	1m	1m
Fixed Assets	3m	5m	3m
Current Assets	4m	5m	4m
Current Liabilities	895	849	852

Rug Doctor Ltd

Unit 29 Decoy Road, Worthing, BN14 8ND
Tel: 01903-235558 **Fax:** 01903-209671
E-mail: customerservices@rugdoctor.co.uk
Website: http://www.rugdoctor.co.uk
Bank(s): Bank of Scotland
Directors: K. Dosanjh (MD)
Managers: M. Muir (Fin Mgr), P. Hansford (Personnel), P. Fildes (Mktg Serv Mgr), C. Atvarnieks (Purch Mgr)
Ultimate Holding Company: AMERICAN CAPITAL STRATEGIES LTD (USA)
Immediate Holding Company: RUG DOCTOR LIMITED
Registration no: 01544366 **VAT No.:** GB 322 0592 93
Date established: 1981 **Turnover:** £5m - £10m **No.of Employees:** 21 - 50
Product Groups: 40

Date of Accounts	Dec 11	Dec 10	Dec 09
Sales Turnover	8m	7m	7m
Pre Tax Profit/Loss	908	700	2m
Working Capital	4m	4m	3m
Fixed Assets	3m	2m	2m
Current Assets	6m	7m	6m
Current Liabilities	1m	597	756

S D B Machinery

39 Maybridge Square Goring By Sea, Goring-by-Sea, Worthing, BN12 6HL
Tel: 01903-501818 **Fax:** 01903-501717
E-mail: sdb.machinery@btconnect.com
Website: http://www.sdbmachinery.co.uk
Managers: S. Brinkley (Mgr)
Turnover: Up to £250,000 **No.of Employees:** 1 - 10 **Product Groups:** 33, 35, 36, 45

S E T S

114 Canterbury Road, Worthing, BN13 1AL
Tel: 07711-674303 **Fax:** 01903-523149
E-mail: info@sets-tms.co.uk
Website: http://www.sets-tms.co.uk
Directors: A. Knowlton (Snr Part)
Immediate Holding Company: COMPLITAS SOLUTIONS LTD
Date established: 2010 **Turnover:** Up to £250,000
No.of Employees: 1 - 10 **Product Groups:** 72, 76, 84

S M E Eurofinance Group plc

Rudham House Rowlands Road, Worthing, BN11 3LD
Tel: 01903-537836 **Fax:** 01903-537936
E-mail: johnr.d@ntlworld.com
Website: http://www.smeeuro.com
Directors: J. Dickinson (Div)
Immediate Holding Company: SME EUROFINANCE GROUP PLC
Registration no: 04472534 **Date established:** 2002 **Turnover:** £1m - £2m
No.of Employees: 1 - 10 **Product Groups:** 82

Date of Accounts	Dec 10	Dec 09	Dec 08
Sales Turnover	3m	2m	3m
Pre Tax Profit/Loss	273	235	215
Working Capital	5m	5m	3m
Fixed Assets	634	748	927
Current Assets	7m	7m	7m
Current Liabilities	2m	2m	2m

Seward Ltd

Dominion House Eastling Close, Worthing, BN14 8HQ
Tel: 01903-823 077 **Fax:** 01903-219 233
E-mail: info@seward.co.uk
Website: http://www.seward.co.uk
Directors: T. Fawcett (MD), B. Minton (Ch), G. Temple (Tech Serv), R. Hockey (Fin)
Managers: S. Ray (Lab Mgr), S. Upson (Purch Mgr), M. Morley (Export Sales Mg)
Registration no: 03211467 **VAT No.:** GB 548 0570 37
Date established: 1880 **Turnover:** £2m - £5m **No.of Employees:** 1 - 10
Product Groups: 30, 38, 41, 42, 67

Date of Accounts	Dec 09	Dec 08	Dec 07
Working Capital	294	139	-170
Fixed Assets	91	86	131
Current Assets	590	616	285

Southern Office Refurbishment Ltd

93 Downside Avenue, Worthing, BN14 0EX
Tel: 01903-877788 **Fax:** 01903-877747
E-mail: sales@sorl.co.uk
Website: http://www.sorl.co.uk
Directors: A. Anderson (MD), T. Anderton (Dir), C. Anderson (Dir)
Immediate Holding Company: TRIPODS HEADS GIMBALS LIMITED
Registration no: 04691878 **VAT No.:** GB 777 3496 74
Date established: 2003 **Turnover:** £250,000 - £500,000
No.of Employees: 1 - 10 **Product Groups:** 52

Date of Accounts	Mar 08	Mar 07	Mar 06
Working Capital	89	57	-1
Fixed Assets	15	17	12
Current Assets	149	157	170
Current Liabilities	60	100	171

Southern Water

Southern House Yeoman Road, Worthing, BN13 3NX
Tel: 08452-720845 **Fax:** 01903-691435
E-mail: joanne.dixon@southernwater.co.uk
Website: http://www.southernwater.co.uk
Directors: K. Hall (Co Sec), K. Hall (Fin)
Managers: J. Dixon
Ultimate Holding Company: GREENSANDS HOLDINGS LIMITED (JERSEY)
Immediate Holding Company: SOUTHERN WATER LIMITED
Registration no: 02366620 **Date established:** 1989
Turnover: £500m - £1,000m **No.of Employees:** 501 - 1000
Product Groups: 54

Date of Accounts	Mar 11	Mar 10	Mar 09
Sales Turnover	600	N/A	N/A
Pre Tax Profit/Loss	600	800	-1m
Working Capital	1120m	1120m	1119m
Fixed Assets	24m	24m	24m
Current Assets	1181m	1181m	1180m

Steeles Of Worthing

Southdownview Way Broadwater Trading Estate, Worthing, BN14 8NL
Tel: 01903-237527 **Fax:** 01903-213961
E-mail: mail@steeles.co.uk
Website: http://www.steeles.co.uk
Directors: A. Steele (Prop)
Registration no: 00886636 **Date established:** 1966
No.of Employees: 21 - 50 **Product Groups:** 29, 39, 68

Sterling Power Tools & Fixings

Unit 11 Northbrook Business Park Northbrook Road, Worthing, BN14 8PQ
Tel: 01903-211543 **Fax:** 01903-523066
Directors: M. Rudd (Dir)
Immediate Holding Company: THERMOSENSING LIMITED
Registration no: 06369989 **Date established:** 1968
No.of Employees: 1 - 10 **Product Groups:** 37

Duncan Stewart Textiles

Aztex House Ivy Arch Road, Worthing, BN14 8BX
Tel: 01903-201251 **Fax:** 01903-520007
E-mail: sales@towelsrus.co.uk
Website: http://www.towelsrus.co.uk
Directors: A. Stewart (Fin)
Immediate Holding Company: DUNCAN STEWART TEXTILES LIMITED
Registration no: 04146234 **Date established:** 2001 **Turnover:** £1m - £2m
No.of Employees: 11 - 20 **Product Groups:** 24, 63

Date of Accounts	Mar 11	Mar 10	Mar 09
Working Capital	37	89	86
Fixed Assets	25	26	68
Current Assets	240	293	288

Stormor Systems Ltd

6 Limbrick Corner Palatine Road, Goring-By-Sea, Worthing, BN12 6JJ
Tel: 01903-244344 **Fax:** 01903-700571
E-mail: info@stormorsystems.co.uk
Website: http://www.stormorsystems.co.uk
Directors: R. Cory (Dir)
Immediate Holding Company: STORMOR SYSTEMS LIMITED
Registration no: 04379562 **Date established:** 2002
Turnover: £250,000 - £500,000 **No.of Employees:** 1 - 10
Product Groups: 35, 85

Date of Accounts	Mar 11	Mar 10	Mar 09
Working Capital	-56	-53	-35
Fixed Assets	27	37	27
Current Assets	54	135	148

Strand Bearings Ltd

2 Aldsworth Avenue Goring-By-Sea, Worthing, BN12 4XQ
Tel: 01903-241621 **Fax:** 01903-241621
E-mail: strandbearings@tiscali.co.uk
Directors: N. Tovey (Prop)
Immediate Holding Company: STRAND BEARINGS LIMITED
Registration no: 02724928 **Date established:** 1992
No.of Employees: 1 - 10 **Product Groups:** 12, 14, 17, 25, 29, 30, 31, 33, 34, 35, 36, 37, 38, 39, 40, 43, 45, 46, 48, 49, 51, 66, 68

Date of Accounts	Jun 11	Jun 10	Jun 09
Working Capital	7	3	1
Fixed Assets	1	1	1
Current Assets	16	14	11

T M Electronics Ltd (Electronic Thermometers and Sensors)

Unit 12 Martlets Way Goring-By-Sea, Worthing, BN12 4HF
Tel: 01903-700651 **Fax:** 01903-244307
E-mail: sales@tmelectronics.co.uk
Website: http://www.tmelectronics.co.uk
Directors: D. Sensier (Sales & Mktg), T. Sensier (Tech Serv)
Managers: R. Fullbrook (Sales Prom Mgr), A. Gerry (Sales Prom Mgr)
Immediate Holding Company: T.M. ELECTRONICS LTD
Registration no: 03977726 **VAT No.:** GB 550 1878 45
Date established: 2000 **Turnover:** Up to £250,000
No.of Employees: 11 - 20 **Product Groups:** 38

Date of Accounts	Apr 11	Apr 10	Apr 09
Sales Turnover	42	48	45
Pre Tax Profit/Loss	-1	N/A	-0
Working Capital	-3	-2	-2
Fixed Assets	1	2	2
Current Assets	5	5	6
Current Liabilities	1	2	3

Talking Design Ltd

5 Liverpool Terrace, Worthing, BN11 1TA
Tel: 01903-218185 **Fax:** 01903-218186
E-mail: enquiries@talkingdesign.net
Website: http://www.talkingdesign.net

Directors: L. Robertson (Fin), S. Richards (MD)
Immediate Holding Company: TALKING DESIGN LIMITED
Registration no: 04695143 **Date established:** 2003
Turnover: Up to £250,000 **No.of Employees:** 1 - 10 **Product Groups:** 79, 81

Date of Accounts	Mar 11	Mar 10	Mar 09
Sales Turnover	107	68	79
Pre Tax Profit/Loss	18	-3	-21
Working Capital	-8	-24	-23
Fixed Assets	3	4	6
Current Assets	40	17	27
Current Liabilities	30	25	25

Thermosensing Ltd

Unit 15 0 Northbrook Business Park, Worthing, BN14 8PQ
Tel: 01903-214466 **Fax:** 01903-214477
Directors: H. Heaver (MD), D. Heaver (Dir)
Managers: J. Cooper (Sales Prom Mgr)
Immediate Holding Company: THERMOSENSING LIMITED
Registration no: 00926685 **VAT No.:** GB 191 0753 68
Date established: 1968 **Turnover:** £500,000 - £1m
No.of Employees: 1 - 10 **Product Groups:** 38

Date of Accounts	Oct 08	Oct 07	Oct 06
Working Capital	485	490	503
Fixed Assets	40	48	57
Current Assets	679	606	583

Tricut Engineering Ltd

Meadow Road, Worthing, BN11 2RT
Tel: 01903-238845 **Fax:** 01903-821529
E-mail: info@tricutengineering.co.uk
Website: http://www.seivad.co.uk
Directors: B. George (MD)
Immediate Holding Company: TRICUT ENGINEERING LIMITED
Registration no: 07075221 **VAT No.:** GB 192 6393 36
Date established: 2009 **Turnover:** £1m - £2m **No.of Employees:** 1 - 10
Product Groups: 48

Date of Accounts	Oct 11	Oct 10
Working Capital	43	26
Fixed Assets	71	40
Current Assets	208	91

Trident Windows & Blinds

193 South Farm Road, Worthing, BN14 7TW
Tel: 01903-202020 **Fax:** 01903-200199
E-mail: trident@ntworld.com
Website: http://www.tridentwindows.biz

Directors: R. Harrow (Ptnr)
Immediate Holding Company: HIGHDOWN MOTOR COMPANY LIMITED
Date established: 2011 **No.of Employees:** 1 - 10 **Product Groups:** 25, 35, 39

UKh2o

Brunswick Road, Worthing, BN11 3NG
Tel: 08451-700500 **Fax:** 01903-531178
E-mail: mark@ukh2o.co.uk
Website: http://www.ukh2o.co.uk
Directors: M. Kennedy (Prop)
Managers: M. Kennedy (Mktg Serv Mgr)
Date established: 2004 **No.of Employees:** 1 - 10 **Product Groups:** 17, 21, 29, 30, 32, 36, 38, 39, 40, 42, 85

Viking Extrusions Ltd

4 Ivy Arch Road, Worthing, BN14 8BX
Tel: 01903-205532 **Fax:** 01903-205534
E-mail: sales@vikext.co.uk
Website: http://www.vikingextrusions.co.uk
Bank(s): National Westminster Bank Plc
Managers: K. Henley (Sales Prom Mgr)
Immediate Holding Company: VIKING EXTRUSIONS LIMITED
Registration no: 02634482 **VAT No.:** GB 587 6513 94
Date established: 1991 **Turnover:** £1m - £2m **No.of Employees:** 11 - 20
Product Groups: 29, 31, 49

Date of Accounts	Aug 12	Aug 11	Aug 10
Sales Turnover	2m	2m	1m
Pre Tax Profit/Loss	176	195	138
Working Capital	67	42	25
Fixed Assets	353	366	355
Current Assets	386	370	343
Current Liabilities	129	205	158

Wenban Smith Ltd

14 Newland Road, Worthing, BN11 1JT
Tel: 01903-230311 **Fax:** 01903-821780
E-mail: sales@wenbans.com
Website: http://www.wenbans.com
Bank(s): Barclays, Worthing
Directors: N. Tooth (Co Sec), J. Kemp-potter (MD), D. Parry (Dir)
Immediate Holding Company: WENBAN-SMITH LIMITED
Registration no: 00233418 **VAT No.:** GB 192 9807 20
Date established: 2028 **Turnover:** £5m - £10m **No.of Employees:** 21 - 50
Product Groups: 08

Date of Accounts	Mar 11	Mar 10	Mar 09
Sales Turnover	7m	6m	7m
Pre Tax Profit/Loss	255	2m	-186
Working Capital	2m	1m	1m
Fixed Assets	880	951	2m
Current Assets	2m	3m	2m
Current Liabilities	339	801	287

Whitecross Engineering Ltd

Columbia House Columbia Drive, Worthing, BN13 3HD
Tel: 01903-690808 **Fax:** 01273-422700
E-mail: sales@whitecross-eng.co.uk
Website: http://www.saqnet.co.uk
Directors: M. Mccullough (MD), H. Guest (Fin)
Immediate Holding Company: WHITECROSS ENGINEERING LIMITED
Registration no: 01587483 **Date established:** 1981
Turnover: £250,000 - £500,000 **No.of Employees:** 1 - 10
Product Groups: 40, 52, 66, 84

Date of Accounts	Dec 11	Dec 10	Dec 09
Working Capital	133	100	101
Fixed Assets	115	115	115
Current Assets	355	245	232

Worthing & Adur Chamber Of Commerce & Industry

17 Liverpool Gardens, Worthing, BN11 1RY
Tel: 01903-203484 **Fax:** 01903-203289
E-mail: info@worthingchamber.co.uk
Website: http://www.worthingchamber.co.uk
Directors: K. Simporis Douglas (Fin), P. Bennett (Dir)
Immediate Holding Company: WORTHING & ADUR CHAMBER OF COMMERCE & INDUSTRY LIMITED
Registration no: 00345261 **Date established:** 1938
Turnover: Up to £250,000 **No.of Employees:** 1 - 10 **Product Groups:** 87

Date of Accounts	Dec 11	Dec 10	Dec 09
Working Capital	-0	6	4
Fixed Assets	36	37	36
Current Assets	16	30	23

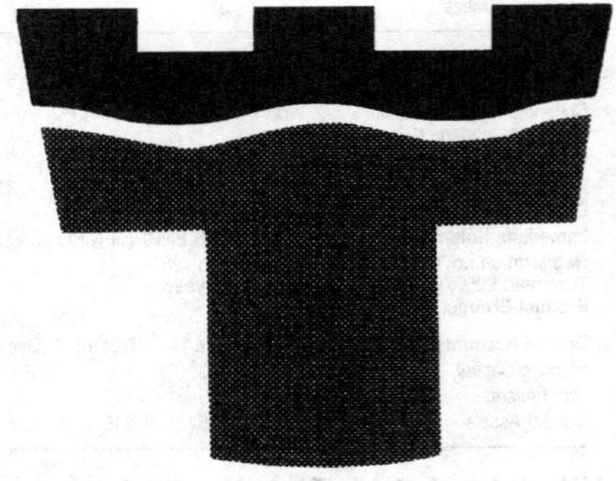

TYNE AND WEAR

Blaydon On Tyne

A M Fabrication
Franklin Park Patterson Street, Blaydon On Tyne, NE21 5TL
Tel: 0191-414 5303
Directors: M. Truman (Ptnr)
Immediate Holding Company: A.M. FABRICATION (NORTHERN) LIMITED
Registration no: 03707882 **Date established:** 1999
No.of Employees: 21 - 50 **Product Groups:** 35

Date of Accounts	Mar 11	Mar 10	Mar 09
Working Capital	196	-14	-126
Fixed Assets	168	154	176
Current Assets	1m	936	654

Architectural Powder Coatings Ltd
Blaydon Industrial Park Chainbridge Road, Blaydon On Tyne, NE21 5AB
Tel: 0191-499 0770 **Fax:** 0191-499 0184
E-mail: robin@architecturalpowdercoatings.co.uk
Website: http://www.architecturalpowdercoatings.co.uk
Bank(s): Barclays, Newcastle
Directors: R. Orchard (MD), R. Sowerby (Co Sec)
Immediate Holding Company: ARCHITECTURAL POWDER COATINGS LIMITED
Registration no: 04384366 **Date established:** 2002 **Turnover:** £1m - £2m
No.of Employees: 21 - 50 **Product Groups:** 48

Date of Accounts	Mar 12	Mar 11	Mar 10
Working Capital	68	50	55
Fixed Assets	835	897	911
Current Assets	365	392	371

Arco Ltd
Chainbridge Industrial Estate Tundry Way, Blaydon On Tyne, NE21 5SJ
Tel: 0191-499 1555 **Fax:** 0191-414 0258
E-mail: sean.churchill@arco.co.uk
Website: http://www.arco.co.uk
Managers: S. Churchill (Reg Sales Mgr), C. Headley (Personnel)
Ultimate Holding Company: ARCO LIMITED
Immediate Holding Company: ARCO LIMITED
Registration no: 00133804 **Date established:** 2014 **Turnover:** £1m - £2m
No.of Employees: 21 - 50 **Product Groups:** 24, 29, 30, 40

Date of Accounts	Jun 11	Jun 10	Jun 09
Sales Turnover	229m	216m	214m
Pre Tax Profit/Loss	8m	6m	260
Working Capital	32m	27m	29m
Fixed Assets	19m	21m	23m
Current Assets	82m	67m	62m
Current Liabilities	12m	13m	8m

Arctic Fabrications Ltd
Unit 5 Derwenthaugh Marina, Blaydon On Tyne, NE21 5LL
Tel: 0191-414 4010 **Fax:** 0191-414 4011
E-mail: a1taskforce@btconnect.com
Website: http://www.a1taskforce.co.uk
Managers: B. Rowlinson (Mgr)
Immediate Holding Company: ARCTIC FABRICATIONS LIMITED
Registration no: 07251437 **Date established:** 2010
No.of Employees: 1 - 10 **Product Groups:** 35

Date of Accounts	Jun 11
Working Capital	-10
Fixed Assets	11
Current Assets	8

Bells Heat Transfer Ltd
Riverside Court Factory Road, Blaydon On Tyne, NE21 5SA
Tel: 0191-414 6789 **Fax:** 0191-414 5890
E-mail: bells.heat.transfer@talk21.com
Bank(s): Lloyds TSB Bank plc
Directors: I. Lockey (MD)
Immediate Holding Company: BELLS HEAT TRANSFER LIMITED
Registration no: 02928922 **Date established:** 1994
Turnover: £500,000 - £1m **No.of Employees:** 11 - 20
Product Groups: 36, 40, 48

Date of Accounts	Sep 07	Sep 06	Sep 05
Working Capital	237	224	186
Fixed Assets	278	308	319
Current Assets	348	375	281
Current Liabilities	111	151	95
Total Share Capital	12	12	12

Blaydon Communications Ltd
Factory Road, Blaydon On Tyne, NE21 5RY
Tel: 0191-414 4241 **Fax:** 0191-414 7978
E-mail: sales@blaydoncomms.co.uk
Website: http://www.blaydoncomms.co.uk
Directors: C. Routledge (Dir)
Immediate Holding Company: BLAYDON COMMUNICATIONS LIMITED
Registration no: 01051050 **VAT No.:** GB 176 1825 48
Date established: 1972 **Turnover:** £500,000 - £1m
No.of Employees: 1 - 10 **Product Groups:** 37

Date of Accounts	Jul 11	Jul 10	Jul 09
Working Capital	49	62	55
Fixed Assets	10	10	10
Current Assets	82	110	89

Diamond Chain Co.
Unit 7-9 Blaydon Industrial Park Chainbridge Road, Blaydon On Tyne, NE21 5AB
Tel: 0191-414 8822 **Fax:** 0191-414 8877
E-mail: sales@diamondchain.co.uk
Website: http://www.diamondchain.co.uk
Managers: C. Wright
Ultimate Holding Company: AMSTED INDUSTRIES INC (USA)
Immediate Holding Company: DIAMOND CHAIN (UK) LIMITED
Registration no: 03705188 **Date established:** 1999 **Turnover:** £5m - £10m
No.of Employees: 1 - 10 **Product Groups:** 35, 45

Date of Accounts	Sep 09	Sep 08
Working Capital	-355	846
Fixed Assets	13	16
Current Assets	2m	2m

Duct Shop Ltd
Unit 4 Banks Court Transbritannia Enterprise Park, Blaydon On Tyne, NE21 5NH
Tel: 0191-414 5522
E-mail: info@ductshop.co.uk
Website: http://www.ductshop.co.uk
Directors: A. High (Dir)
Immediate Holding Company: SUMMERFIELD MUSICAL INSTRUMENTS LIMITED
Registration no: 04581267 **Date established:** 2002
No.of Employees: 1 - 10 **Product Groups:** 37, 40, 48

E M R Ltd
Tynedale Works Factory Road, Blaydon On Tyne, NE21 5RZ
Tel: 0191-414 3618 **Fax:** 0191-414 0751
E-mail: info@emrltd.com
Website: http://www.emr.com
Bank(s): Barclays
Managers: P. Lynes (Mgr), J. Hunt (Admin Off)
Immediate Holding Company: E40 REALISATIONS LIMITED
Registration no: 00941732 **VAT No.:** GB 176 9209 30
Date established: 1968 **No.of Employees:** 11 - 20 **Product Groups:** 66

Forsters Shotblasters
Riverside Factory Factory Road, Blaydon On Tyne, NE21 5SA
Tel: 0191-414 8240 **Fax:** 0191-414 0482
E-mail: kjforster@blastclean.fsnet.co.uk
Website: http://www.abrasive-blastclean.co.uk
Directors: K. Forster (Prop)
Registration no: 04718545 **Date established:** 2003
No.of Employees: 1 - 10 **Product Groups:** 46, 48

Franklin Steel Stockholders plc
Unit 5 Franklin Park Patterson Street, Blaydon On Tyne, NE21 5TL
Tel: 0191-499 0222 **Fax:** 0191-499 0223
E-mail: sales@franklinsteel.co.uk
Website: http://www.franklinsteelplc.co.uk
Bank(s): Bank of Scotland
Directors: M. Wallace (Dir)
Immediate Holding Company: FRANKLIN STEEL STOCKHOLDERS PLC
Registration no: 02050406 **VAT No.:** GB 459 7019 17
Date established: 1986 **Turnover:** £5m - £10m **No.of Employees:** 11 - 20
Product Groups: 66

Date of Accounts	Jan 12	Jan 11	Jan 10
Sales Turnover	7m	7m	6m
Pre Tax Profit/Loss	651	504	416
Working Capital	-668	-648	-171
Fixed Assets	6m	5m	5m
Current Assets	3m	2m	2m
Current Liabilities	413	337	211

GreCon Ltd
3 Willows Business Centre Newburn Bridge Road, Blaydon On Tyne, NE21 4SQ
Tel: 0191-414 7200 **Fax:** 0191-414 7300
E-mail: sales@grecon.org
Website: http://www.grecon.de
Directors: R. Kuhfuss (MD)
Ultimate Holding Company: FAGUS-GRECON GRETEN GMBH & CO KG (GERMANY)
Immediate Holding Company: GRECON LIMITED
Registration no: 02708227 **Date established:** 1992 **Turnover:** £1m - £2m
No.of Employees: 11 - 20 **Product Groups:** 67

Date of Accounts	Dec 11	Dec 10	Dec 09
Working Capital	-11	89	11
Fixed Assets	24	13	30
Current Assets	772	650	450

Hi-Tec Machine Services Ltd
Unit 3 Vance Court Transbritannia Enterprise Park, Blaydon On Tyne, NE21 5NH
Tel: 0191-414 8917 **Fax:** 0191-414 5395
E-mail: info@hitecmachineservices.co.uk
Website: http://www.hitecmachineservices.co.uk
Directors: T. Coupe (MD)
Immediate Holding Company: HI-TEC MACHINE SERVICES LIMITED
Registration no: 03181788 **Date established:** 1996
No.of Employees: 1 - 10 **Product Groups:** 46

Date of Accounts	Jun 11	Jun 10	Jun 09
Working Capital	-1	21	364
Fixed Assets	N/A	N/A	44
Current Assets	33	133	436

Hunter Hields Gearcutting Ltd
Addison Works Haugh Lane, Blaydon On Tyne, NE21 4SB
Tel: 01642-782407 **Fax:** 0191-414 0135
E-mail: kencliffe@gmail.com
Directors: B. Thompson (Co Sec)
Managers: K. Cliffe (Works Gen Mgr)
Ultimate Holding Company: C.A.HIELDS(ENGINEERS)LIMITED
Immediate Holding Company: HUNTER HIELDS GEARCUTTING LIMITED
Registration no: 06850678 **Date established:** 2009
Turnover: £500,000 - £1m **No.of Employees:** 1 - 10 **Product Groups:** 25, 35

Date of Accounts	Sep 11	Sep 10	Sep 09
Working Capital	27	-12	-19
Fixed Assets	36	42	29
Current Assets	195	190	144

Johnson's Chopwell Ltd
Tollbridge Road, Blaydon On Tyne, NE21 5TB
Tel: 0191-414 2455 **Fax:** 0191-414 1640
E-mail: johnsonschopwell@b&k.co.uk
Website: http://www.bandk.co.uk
Bank(s): Lloyds TSB Bank plc
Directors: M. Sheldon (Fin)
Ultimate Holding Company: BOWMER AND KIRKLAND LIMITED
Immediate Holding Company: JOHNSONS (CHOPWELL) LIMITED
Registration no: 00366098 **VAT No.:** GB 176 1988 20
Date established: 1941 **No.of Employees:** 21 - 50 **Product Groups:** 11, 42, 45

Date of Accounts	Aug 11	Aug 10	Aug 09
Working Capital	4m	3m	3m
Fixed Assets	388	78	115
Current Assets	7m	9m	4m

M J Services Ltd
Unit 4 Shibdon Business Park Cowen Road, Blaydon On Tyne, NE21 5TX
Tel: 0191-414 5700 **Fax:** 0191-414 5797
E-mail: info@mjsltd.co.uk
Website: http://www.mjsltd.co.uk
Directors: D. Rainbow (Dir)
Immediate Holding Company: M & J SERVICES LTD
Registration no: 04367120 **Date established:** 2002
No.of Employees: 1 - 10 **Product Groups:** 33, 34, 40, 42, 45, 46, 48, 52, 66, 67

Date of Accounts	Jun 11	Jun 10	Jun 09
Working Capital	155	206	134
Fixed Assets	100	53	69
Current Assets	521	498	460

North East Time Recorders
Factory Road, Blaydon On Tyne, NE21 5RY
Tel: 0191-414 4241 **Fax:** 0191-414 7978
E-mail: sales@netr.co.uk
Website: http://www.uktimesolutions.co.uk

Directors: C. Routledge (Dir)
Immediate Holding Company: NORTH EAST TIME RECORDERS LIMITED
Registration no: 00440431 **Date established:** 1947
Turnover: £500,000 - £1m **No.of Employees:** 11 - 20
Product Groups: 49, 65

Date of Accounts	Jul 11	Jul 10	Jul 09
Working Capital	82	82	67
Fixed Assets	95	90	94
Current Assets	165	167	172

Ornamental Ironworks
Unit 3 Addison Industrial Estate, Blaydon On Tyne, NE21 4TE
Tel: 0191-414 7090 **Fax:** 0191-414 7090
Directors: A. Taylor (Prop)
Date established: 1993 **No.of Employees:** 1 - 10 **Product Groups:** 26, 35

Petersen Stainless Rigging Ltd
Blaydon Business Centre Cowen Road, Blaydon On Tyne, NE21 5TW
Tel: 0191-414 0156 **Fax:** 0191-499 0041
E-mail: sales@petersen-stainless.co.uk
Website: http://www.petersen-stainless.co.uk
Bank(s): Barclays, Gateshead
Directors: N. Bell (Dir)
Immediate Holding Company: PETERSEN STAINLESS RIGGING LIMITED
Registration no: 01372922 **Date established:** 1978 **Turnover:** £1m - £2m
No.of Employees: 21 - 50 **Product Groups:** 35

Date of Accounts	Dec 11	Dec 10	Dec 09
Working Capital	519	375	321
Fixed Assets	1m	1m	1m
Current Assets	1m	800	547

Potts Buckets & Attatchments Ltd
6-9 Longridge Road, Blaydon On Tyne, NE21 6JJ
Tel: 0191-414 4186 **Fax:** 0191-414 2211
E-mail: sales@potts-buckets.com
Website: http://www.potts-buckets.com
Directors: G. Potts (MD)
Immediate Holding Company: POTTS BUCKETS AND ATTACHMENTS LIMITED
Registration no: 07506694 **Date established:** 2011 **Turnover:** £1m - £2m
No.of Employees: 1 - 10 **Product Groups:** 45

Date of Accounts	Jul 09	Jul 08	Jul 07
Working Capital	-176	-211	-187
Fixed Assets	55	47	59
Current Assets	265	205	199

R T Message Services Ltd
Unit 6 Derwenthaugh Marina, Blaydon On Tyne, NE21 5LL
Tel: 0191-414 4506 **Fax:** 0191-414 6559
E-mail: kc@rt-systems.co.uk
Website: http://www.rtms.net
Directors: K. Cornbill (MD), K. Cornvile (MD), J. Cornbill (Fin)
Immediate Holding Company: R.T.MESSAGE SERVICES LIMITED
Registration no: 00965473 **VAT No.:** GB 178 5301 50
Date established: 1969 **No.of Employees:** 1 - 10 **Product Groups:** 37, 38, 79, 80, 84, 86

Date of Accounts	Dec 10	Dec 09	Dec 08
Working Capital	43	41	64
Fixed Assets	81	92	114
Current Assets	118	126	134

Red Rose Engineering
Factory Road, Blaydon On Tyne, NE21 5RU
Tel: 0191-414 5015 **Fax:** 0191-414 1832
E-mail: brian@redrose-eng.fsnet.co.uk
Website: http://www.redrose-eng.fsnet.co.uk
Directors: B. Hindle (Prop)
Registration no: 02125805 **VAT No.:** GB 179 1707 36
Date established: 1977 **Turnover:** £250,000 - £500,000
No.of Employees: 1 - 10 **Product Groups:** 35, 38, 39, 48, 66, 68, 85

Slaters Electricals Ltd
Scotswood Bridge Works, Blaydon On Tyne, NE21 5TE
Tel: 0191-414 2916 **Fax:** 0191-414 1349
E-mail: david@slaters-electricals.com
Website: http://www.slaters-electricals.com
Bank(s): Barclays
Directors: D. Slater (Dir), M. Simblett (Sales), F. Slater (Fin)
Managers: M. Telford, C. Adams, A. Hodgson (Buyer), D. Graham (Chief Acct)
Immediate Holding Company: SLATERS ELECTRICALS LIMITED
Registration no: 00424830 **VAT No.:** GB 177 1169 50
Date established: 1946 **Turnover:** £10m - £20m
No.of Employees: 21 - 50 **Product Groups:** 37, 48, 52, 67

Date of Accounts	Jan 11	Jan 10	Jan 09
Sales Turnover	12m	13m	N/A
Pre Tax Profit/Loss	727	255	721
Working Capital	4m	4m	3m
Fixed Assets	563	656	662
Current Assets	6m	6m	4m
Current Liabilities	933	1m	593

Synergiq
Unit 6 Franklin Park Patterson Street, Blaydon On Tyne, NE21 5TL
Tel: 0191-414 4838 **Fax:** 08707-418837
Directors: K. Taylor (Dir)
Registration no: 05305385 **Date established:** 2004
Turnover: £500,000 - £1m **No.of Employees:** 1 - 10 **Product Groups:** 44, 80, 85, 87

Date of Accounts	Dec 06	Dec 05
Working Capital	-30	33
Fixed Assets	6	13
Current Assets	113	74
Current Liabilities	144	41

Tegrel Ltd
Tundry Way, Blaydon On Tyne, NE21 5TT
Tel: 0191-414 6111 **Fax:** 0191-414 0660
E-mail: richard.leech@tegrel.co.uk
Website: http://www.tegrel.co.uk
Bank(s): Barclays
Directors: R. Leech (MD), R. Leech (Fin)
Managers: S. Scott (Purch Mgr), J. Candlish (Sales Prom Mgr)
Immediate Holding Company: TEGREL LIMITED
Registration no: 01897468 **VAT No.:** GB 569 22011 43
Date established: 1985 **Turnover:** £2m - £5m **No.of Employees:** 51 - 100
Product Groups: 30, 35, 37, 48

Date of Accounts	Mar 11	Mar 10	Mar 09
Working Capital	657	870	588
Fixed Assets	697	840	702
Current Assets	2m	3m	2m

Boldon Colliery

I D S Ltd
Unit 10 Didcot Way Boldon Business Park, Boldon Colliery, NE35 9PD
Tel: 0191-519 0660 **Fax:** 0191-519 0760
E-mail: info.uk@idsplc.com
Website: http://www.idsplc.com
Directors: D. Gamble (Mkt Research), G. Murray (Fin), L. Merrill (Sales & Mktg), P. Hailes (Co Sec), R. Duggan (MD), T. Addison (MD)
Managers: C. Burns (Tech Serv Mgr), T. Kelly (Purch Mgr), J. Knight (Ops Mgr), J. Houston (Personnel)
Immediate Holding Company: I.D.S. LIMITED
Registration no: 03204123 **Date established:** 1996 **Turnover:** £2m - £5m
No.of Employees: 101 - 250 **Product Groups:** 85

Date of Accounts	Sep 11	Sep 10	Sep 09
Working Capital	558	512	474
Current Assets	1m	1m	1m
Current Liabilities	N/A	376	100

Parker Hannisin Ltd
Unit 13 Burford Way, Boldon Business Park, Boldon Colliery, NE35 9PZ
Tel: 0191-519 0066 **Fax:** 0191-519 1400
E-mail: ron.forbister@parker.com
Website: http://www.parker.com
Managers: R. Forbister (Mgr)
Ultimate Holding Company: PARKER HANNIFIN CORP (USA)
Immediate Holding Company: DOMNICK HUNTER FABRICATION LIMITED
Registration no: 02081468 **Date established:** 1986 **Turnover:** £1m - £2m
No.of Employees: 21 - 50 **Product Groups:** 35

Date of Accounts	Jun 11	Jun 10	Jun 09
Pre Tax Profit/Loss	N/A	9	12
Working Capital	18	18	256
Current Assets	263	263	256
Current Liabilities	245	N/A	N/A

East Boldon

Mayflower Glass Ltd
Moor Lane, East Boldon, NE36 0AQ
Tel: 0191-536 0343 **Fax:** 0191-536 8099
E-mail: harry@mayflower-glass.com
Website: http://www.mayflower-glass.com
Directors: G. Thompson (Sales), J. Phipps-Clark (Dir)
Immediate Holding Company: MAYFLOWER GLASS LIMITED
Registration no: 01044730 **VAT No.:** 176 5142 56 **Date established:** 1972
Turnover: Up to £250,000 **No.of Employees:** 1 - 10 **Product Groups:** 33, 63

Date of Accounts	Aug 11	Aug 10	Aug 09
Working Capital	-63	-26	-242
Fixed Assets	1m	1m	1m
Current Assets	343	348	421

Metalcraft
3 Station Approach, East Boldon, NE36 0AB
Tel: 0191-519 1939
Directors: K. Robertson (Prop)
No.of Employees: 1 - 10 **Product Groups:** 21, 36, 40

Gateshead

A M D Specialist Coatings Ltd
6 Derwent Court Earlsway, Team Valley Trading Estate, Gateshead, NE11 0TF
Tel: 0191-487 5758 **Fax:** 0191-487 7727
E-mail: info@amdcoatings.co.uk
Website: http://www.amdspecialistcoatings.co.uk
Directors: S. Davis (MD), L. Cree (Fin)
Ultimate Holding Company: AMD SPECIALIST COATINGS (HOLDINGS) LIMITED
Immediate Holding Company: AMD SPECIALIST COATINGS LIMITED
Registration no: 04100967 **Date established:** 2000
No.of Employees: 11 - 20 **Product Groups:** 46, 48

Date of Accounts	Mar 11	Mar 10	Mar 09
Working Capital	139	69	71
Fixed Assets	105	59	43
Current Assets	580	443	330
Current Liabilities	58	N/A	N/A

Am Graham Fabrication Ltd
Atlas Works West View Terrace, Gateshead, NE11 9EL
Tel: 0191-460 3092 **Fax:** 0191-460 3093
Directors: A. Graham (Prop)
Immediate Holding Company: A.M. GRAHAM FABRICATIONS LIMITED
Registration no: 03404507 **Date established:** 1997
No.of Employees: 1 - 10 **Product Groups:** 35

Date of Accounts	Dec 11	Dec 10	Dec 09
Working Capital	397	321	220
Fixed Assets	255	297	274
Current Assets	604	536	426

A T S Electro Lube UK Ltd
Unit 383l Jedburgh Court, Team Valley Trading Estate, Gateshead, NE11 0BQ
Tel: 0191-491 4212 **Fax:** 0191-491 4224
E-mail: info@atselectrolube.co.uk
Website: http://www.atselectrolube.co.uk
Directors: J. Gray (MD)
Ultimate Holding Company: FAMCO MANAGEMENT INC (CANADA)
Immediate Holding Company: A.T.S. ELECTRO-LUBE (UK) LIMITED
Registration no: 02712637 **Date established:** 1992
Turnover: £500,000 - £1m **No.of Employees:** 1 - 10 **Product Groups:** 36

Date of Accounts	Dec 11	Dec 10	Dec 09
Working Capital	198	197	189
Fixed Assets	2	2	3
Current Assets	346	339	279
Current Liabilities	N/A	N/A	91

Aalco Newcastle
First Avenue Team Valley Trading Estate, Gateshead, NE11 0NU
Tel: 0191-491 1133 **Fax:** 0191-491 1177
E-mail: newcastle@aalco.co.uk
Website: http://www.aalco.co.uk
Bank(s): National Westminster Bank Plc
Directors: A. Dawson (Dir), C. Bush (Sales)
Ultimate Holding Company: UK STEELSTOCK LTD
Immediate Holding Company: AMERI METALS LTD
Registration no: 03551533 **Turnover:** £125m - £250m
No.of Employees: 21 - 50 **Product Groups:** 34, 35, 36, 66

Angus Air Ltd
Staithes Road Dunston, Gateshead, NE11 9DR
Tel: 0191-461 0077 **Fax:** 0191-461 1177
E-mail: angus@angus-air.co.uk
Website: http://www.angus-air.co.uk
Directors: J. Watson (Co Sec), A. Watson (MD)
Immediate Holding Company: ANGUS-AIR LIMITED
Registration no: 02401944 **VAT No.:** GB 569 2023 36
Date established: 1989 **Turnover:** £1m - £2m **No.of Employees:** 1 - 10
Product Groups: 35, 40, 42

Date of Accounts	Feb 12	Feb 11	Feb 10
Working Capital	62	83	72
Fixed Assets	75	42	47
Current Assets	536	581	258

Anixther Fastners
379 Princes Way Team Valley Trading Estate, Gateshead, NE11 0TU
Tel: 0191-497 0200 **Fax:** 0191-497 0226
Website: http://www.anixterfasteners.com
Directors: S. Rutherford (Chief Op Offcr)
Managers: K. Rowell (Ops Mgr)
Registration no: 00248952 **No.of Employees:** 11 - 20
Product Groups: 30, 66

Anson
Seventh Avenue Team Valley Trading Estate, Gateshead, NE11 0JW
Tel: 0191-4820 0220 **Fax:** 0191-487 8835
E-mail: anson-gateshead@anson.co.uk
Website: http://www.anson.co.uk
Directors: R. Anderson (MD), W. Delaney (Works)
Managers: J. Spencer (Chief Acct), I. Robinson (Purch Mgr), C. Henderson (Sales Prom Mgr)
Ultimate Holding Company: THERMON MANUFACTURING INC (USA)
Immediate Holding Company: THERMON (U.K.) LIMITED
Registration no: 01568843 **VAT No.:** GB 353 9523 40
Date established: 1979 **Turnover:** £500,000 - £1m
No.of Employees: 1 - 10 **Product Groups:** 36

Date of Accounts	Dec 10	Dec 09	Sep 07
Sales Turnover	53m	62m	42m
Pre Tax Profit/Loss	26m	13m	7m
Working Capital	50m	29m	13m
Fixed Assets	7m	7m	8m
Current Assets	59m	38m	23m
Current Liabilities	6m	4m	5m

A1 Scales Ltd
Unit 53 Team Valley Business Centre Earlsway, Team Valley Trading Estate, Gateshead, NE11 0QH
Tel: 0191-421 1000 **Fax:** 0191-421 0999
E-mail: sales@a1scales.co.uk
Website: http://www.a1scales.co.uk
Directors: M. Whittle (Dir)
Immediate Holding Company: A1 SCALES LIMITED
Registration no: 05312020 **Date established:** 2004
No.of Employees: 1 - 10 **Product Groups:** 38, 42

Date of Accounts	Dec 11	Dec 10	Dec 09
Working Capital	-11	-18	-25
Fixed Assets	20	27	32
Current Assets	31	29	41

Bell Building Maintenance Ltd
2 Springwell Avenue Wrekenton, Gateshead, NE9 7JL
Tel: 0191-491 5912 **Fax:** 0191-491 5912
E-mail: bellsbuilding2@btconnect.com
Product Groups: 25, 26, 35, 52, 80, 84

Ben Recruitment
William Street, Gateshead, NE10 0JP
Tel: 08452-234493 **Fax:** 0191-495 0141
E-mail: traffic@vanhee.co.uk
Website: http://www.vanhee.co.uk
Managers: H. Farrow (Mgr)
Immediate Holding Company: YOUR DEZREZ LTD
Registration no: 06855190 **Date established:** 2011
No.of Employees: 1 - 10 **Product Groups:** 36, 67, 84

Bizcare Ltd
19 St Vincent Court, Gateshead, NE8 3DZ
Tel: 0191-420 9838 **Fax:** 08712-181954
E-mail: enquiries@bizcare.co.uk
Website: http://www.bizcare.co.uk
Directors: I. Wiles (Fin), R. Wiles (MD)
Immediate Holding Company: BIZCARE LIMITED
Registration no: 04738630 **Date established:** 2003
Turnover: Up to £250,000 **No.of Employees:** 1 - 10 **Product Groups:** 44

Date of Accounts	Dec 11	Dec 10	Oct 09
Working Capital	5	3	-1
Current Assets	9	4	7

Bolton Brady Repair & Service Ltd
Blenheim Place, Gateshead, NE11 9HF
Tel: 0191-460 5201 **Fax:** 0191- 4601877
E-mail: newcastle@boltonbrady.co.uk
Website: http://www.boltonbrady.co.uk
Managers: V. Westall (Chief Mgr), V. Westhall (Mgr)
Ultimate Holding Company: BROOMCO (923) LTD
Immediate Holding Company: KONEMATIC HOLDINGS LTD
Registration no: 03048963 **VAT No.:** GB 588 9719 53
No.of Employees: 1 - 10 **Product Groups:** 35, 36

Carrylift Materials Handling Ltd
Unit 7 Bamburgh Court Off Earlsway, Team Valley Trading Estate, Gateshead, NE11 0TX
Tel: 0191-491 4700 **Fax:** 0191-491 4702
E-mail: info@carryliftgroup.com
Website: http://www.carryliftgroup.com
Managers: R. Berry (Chief Mgr)
Ultimate Holding Company: CORPACQ PLC
Immediate Holding Company: CARRYLIFT MATERIALS HANDLING LIMITED
Registration no: 02221891 **Date established:** 1988
No.of Employees: 11 - 20 **Product Groups:** 45, 67, 83

Date of Accounts	Dec 11	Dec 10	Mar 10
Sales Turnover	17m	14m	18m
Pre Tax Profit/Loss	4m	3m	103
Working Capital	9m	7m	5m
Fixed Assets	3m	3m	3m
Current Assets	15m	14m	15m
Current Liabilities	2m	3m	5m

Certex UK Ltd
Dukesway Court Team Valley Trading Estate, Gateshead, NE11 0BH
Tel: 0191-491 0696 **Fax:** 0191- 4910787
E-mail: sales@certex.co.uk
Website: http://www.certex.co.uk
Managers: D. Ward (Chief Mgr), A. Blacklock (Mgr)
Ultimate Holding Company: AXEL JOHNSON INTERNATIONAL AB (SWEDEN)
Immediate Holding Company: CERTEX (UK) LIMITED
Registration no: 00928803 **Date established:** 1968 **Turnover:** £1m - £2m
No.of Employees: 21 - 50 **Product Groups:** 23, 30, 35

Cintra Payroll Services
Computer House 353 High Street, Gateshead, NE8 1ET
Tel: 0191-478 7000 **Fax:** 0191-478 6060
E-mail: info@centra.co.uk
Website: http://www.cintra.co.uk
Bank(s): National Westminster Bank Plc
Directors: C. Staehr (Grp Chief Exec)
Managers: K. McEvoy, G. Affleck-ward (Purch Mgr), G. Dougal (Fin Mgr)
VAT No.: GB 357 1865 28 **Turnover:** £2m - £5m
No.of Employees: 51 - 100 **Product Groups:** 44

Date of Accounts	Apr 11	Apr 10	Apr 09
Working Capital	304	361	N/A
Fixed Assets	2m	2m	N/A
Current Assets	843	905	N/A

Henry Colbeck Ltd
Seventh Avenue Team Valley Trading Estate, Gateshead, NE11 0HG
Tel: 0191-482 4242 **Fax:** 0191-491 0357
E-mail: accounts@colbeck.co.uk
Website: http://www.colbeck.co.uk
Bank(s): Barclays P.L.C., Gateshead
Directors: G. Colbeck (Dir), D. Colbeck (Dir), A. Naylor (MD), P. Holliday (Fin)
Managers: M. Shone, J. Pearson (Mktg Serv Mgr)
Immediate Holding Company: HENRY COLBECK LIMITED
Registration no: 00822749 **VAT No.:** GB 175 9450 31
Date established: 1964 **Turnover:** £20m - £50m
No.of Employees: 51 - 100 **Product Groups:** 20

Date of Accounts	Mar 11	Mar 10	Mar 09
Sales Turnover	41m	40m	40m
Pre Tax Profit/Loss	411	372	411
Working Capital	2m	2m	1m
Fixed Assets	3m	3m	3m
Current Assets	7m	6m	6m
Current Liabilities	973	831	994

Computer Orbit
400-408 Old Durham Road, Gateshead, NE9 5DQ
Tel: 0191-420 7700 **Fax:** 0191-420 7711
E-mail: info@computerorbit.co.uk
Website: http://www.computerorbit.co.uk
Directors: Q. Malik (MD), F. Malik (Co Sec)
Managers: A. Blackwell (Mktg Serv Mgr), M. Ahmed (Mgr), A. Anwar
Immediate Holding Company: COMPUTER ORBIT LIMITED
Registration no: 01537885 **Date established:** 1981
No.of Employees: 11 - 20 **Product Groups:** 67

Date of Accounts	Dec 11	Dec 10	Dec 09
Working Capital	328	383	398
Fixed Assets	485	496	504
Current Assets	448	525	551

Deminos
8 Bankside The Watermark, Gateshead, NE11 9SY
Tel: 0191-460 0707 **Fax:** 0191-460 0707
E-mail: office@deminos.co.uk
Website: http://www.deminos.co.uk
Directors: N. Atkinson (Fin)
Immediate Holding Company: DEMINOS LTD
Registration no: 06376910 **Date established:** 2007
Turnover: £500,000 - £1m **No.of Employees:** 1 - 10 **Product Groups:** 44, 80

Date of Accounts	Feb 12	Feb 11	Feb 10
Working Capital	-82	-174	-65
Fixed Assets	18	24	18
Current Assets	125	108	37

Paul Dodd & Sons
2 H Nichol Yard South Shore Road, Gateshead, NE8 3AE
Tel: 0191-478 1888 **Fax:** 0191-478 6844
Website: http://www.traditional-wooden-gate.com
Directors: P. Dodd (Prop)
Date established: 2002 **No.of Employees:** 1 - 10 **Product Groups:** 26, 35

D P Supplies (Data Processing Supplies Ltd)
St Andrews House Westfield Terrace, Gateshead, NE8 4LD
Tel: 0191-478 5068 **Fax:** 0191-478 6797
E-mail: sales@dp-supplies.com
Website: http://www.dp-supplies.com
Directors: K. Anderson (MD), J. Gahagan (Fin)
Immediate Holding Company: IT SUPPLIES UK LTD
Registration no: 04699727 **VAT No.:** GB 322 7333 82
Turnover: £2m - £5m **No.of Employees:** 1 - 10 **Product Groups:** 27, 44, 67

Equal & Approved Ltd
Watson House Staithes Road, Dunston, Gateshead, NE11 9DR
Tel: 0191-461 0101 **Fax:** 0191-460 7534
E-mail: info@angus-air.co.uk
Website: http://www.equalandapproved.com
Directors: A. Watson (MD), J. Watson (Fin)
Ultimate Holding Company: HALSTAN HOLDINGS LIMITED
Immediate Holding Company: EQUAL AND APPROVED LIMITED
Registration no: 03868525 **Date established:** 1999
No.of Employees: 1 - 10 **Product Groups:** 30, 34, 35, 37, 38, 39, 40, 42, 47, 48, 65, 66, 67

Date of Accounts	Feb 12	Feb 11	Feb 10
Working Capital	66	63	60
Current Assets	123	100	96
Current Liabilities	4	4	3

Express Engineering Thompson Ltd
Kingsway North Team Valley Trading Estate, Gateshead, NE11 0EG
Tel: 0191-487 2021 **Fax:** 0191-487 3172
E-mail: kevin.scott@express-engineering.co.uk
Website: http://www.express-engineering.co.uk
Directors: K. Scott (Dir), M. Blakey (Fin)
Managers: M. Watson (Personnel), W. Barclay, S. Thompson (Tech Serv Mgr), C. Rowell (Purch Mgr)
Ultimate Holding Company: EXPRESS ENGINEERING (HOLDINGS) LIMITED
Immediate Holding Company: EXPRESS ENGINEERING (THOMPSON) LIMITED
Registration no: 01405214 **VAT No.:** GB 322 7214 90
Date established: 1978 **Turnover:** £10m - £20m
No.of Employees: 101 - 250 **Product Groups:** 48

Date of Accounts	Mar 11	Mar 10	Mar 09
Sales Turnover	11m	12m	15m
Pre Tax Profit/Loss	-77	234	861
Working Capital	2m	2m	2m
Fixed Assets	4m	3m	2m
Current Assets	5m	4m	5m
Current Liabilities	1m	484	827

Extracta Products Ltd
Third Avenue Team Valley Trading Estate, Gateshead, NE11 0PR
Tel: 0191-482 5005 **Fax:** 0191-491 0462
E-mail: sales@extracta.co.uk
Website: http://www.extracta.co.uk
Directors: B. Aldred (Dir), J. Haggath (Dir)
Immediate Holding Company: EXTRACTA PRODUCTS LIMITED
Registration no: 02383010 **VAT No.:** GB 297 9664 75
Date established: 1989 **Turnover:** £250,000 - £500,000
No.of Employees: 1 - 10 **Product Groups:** 40, 66

Date of Accounts	Jul 11	Jul 10	Jul 09
Sales Turnover	365	406	409
Pre Tax Profit/Loss	-54	-18	-57
Working Capital	115	163	177
Fixed Assets	28	35	44
Current Assets	149	194	205
Current Liabilities	14	13	16

Fendor Ltd
Heworth House William Street, Gateshead, NE10 0JP
Tel: 0191-438 3222 **Fax:** 0191-438 1686
E-mail: cd@fendorhansen.co.uk
Website: http://www.fendor.co.uk
Bank(s): Jyske Bank
Directors: M. Blakey (MD), C. Duffy (Dir), G. Statt (Sales & Mktg), C. Duffy (Sales), C. Addy (Co Sec)
Managers: J. Davidson (Sales Prom Mgr), M. Dudley (Personnel), L. Blyth (I.T. Exec), K. Colligan (Accounts), G. Statt (Mktg Serv Mgr)
Ultimate Holding Company: FENDOR HOLDINGS LIMITED
Immediate Holding Company: FENDOR LIMITED
Registration no: 05472268 **VAT No.:** GB 605 4994 25
Date established: 2005 **Turnover:** £5m - £10m **No.of Employees:** 21 - 50
Product Groups: 26, 33, 40

Date of Accounts	Dec 10	Jun 09	Jun 08
Sales Turnover	9m	N/A	N/A
Pre Tax Profit/Loss	308	N/A	N/A
Working Capital	508	464	503
Fixed Assets	360	415	371
Current Assets	3m	2m	2m
Current Liabilities	1m	N/A	2m

G B M Products Ltd
Unit18 E Eleventh Avenue North, Team Valley Trading Estate, Gateshead, NE11 0NJ
Tel: 0191-487 8004 **Fax:** 0191-487 1655
E-mail: info@gbmproducts.co.uk
Website: http://www.gbmproducts.co.uk
Directors: G. Mcilwraith (MD), J. Morgan (Fin)
Immediate Holding Company: G.B.M. PRODUCTS LIMITED
Registration no: 04790843 **Date established:** 2003
Turnover: £500,000 - £1m **No.of Employees:** 1 - 10 **Product Groups:** 35, 36, 39

Date of Accounts	Jun 12	Jun 11	Jun 10
Working Capital	3	-3	-8
Fixed Assets	170	168	175
Current Assets	85	108	86

G O North East Ltd
117 Queen Street, Gateshead, NE8 2UA
Tel: 08456-060260 **Fax:** 0191-420 0225
E-mail: customer_services@gonortheast.co.uk
Website: http://www.simplygo.com
Directors: P. Matthews (MD), P. Matthews (Prop)
Managers: A. Burns (Mktg Serv Mgr), K. Carr (Mgr), C. Mcpherson (Fin Mgr), A. Burns (Sales & Mktg Mg), J. Gifford (I.T. Exec)
Immediate Holding Company: GO NORTH EAST LIMITED
Registration no: 02057284 **Date established:** 1986
No.of Employees: 101 - 250 **Product Groups:** 72

GB Fuels Ltd
Albany Road, Gateshead, NE8 3BP
Tel: 0191-490 4311 **Fax:** 0191-477 9544
Website: http://www.gb-lubricants-fuels.co.uk
Directors: T. Berkeley (Fin), T. Bates (MD)
Ultimate Holding Company: GOODALL BATES & TODD LIMITED
Immediate Holding Company: G.& B.FUELS LIMITED
Registration no: 00891396 **Date established:** 1966
Turnover: £10m - £20m **No.of Employees:** 21 - 50 **Product Groups:** 31

Industrial Finishing Specialists
Unit 23 Fairfield Industrial Park Bill Quay, Gateshead, NE10 0UR
Tel: 0191-495 0698 **Fax:** 0191-495 0698
E-mail: kath@ifspowdercoating.co.uk
Website: http://www.industrial-finishingspecialists.co.uk
Directors: A. Cleghorn (Ptnr), K. Cleghorn (Ptnr), K. Cleghorn (Prop)
Date established: 1992 **No.of Employees:** 1 - 10 **Product Groups:** 48

International Paint Ltd
Stoneygate Lane, Gateshead, NE10 0JY
Tel: 0191-469 6111 **Fax:** 0191-401 2473
E-mail: john.lockhart@akzonobel.com
Website: http://www.akzonobel.com
Managers: J. Lockhart
Ultimate Holding Company: AKZO NOBEL NV (NETHERLANDS)
Immediate Holding Company: INTERNATIONAL PAINT LIMITED
Registration no: 00063604 **Date established:** 1999
No.of Employees: 501 - 1000 **Product Groups:** 32, 66

Date of Accounts	Dec 11	Dec 10	Dec 09
Sales Turnover	188m	177m	193m
Pre Tax Profit/Loss	-40m	-49m	13m
Working Capital	-29m	-3m	42m
Fixed Assets	46m	46m	41m
Current Assets	65m	93m	99m
Current Liabilities	7m	8m	8m

Jewson Ltd
Dunston Sawmills Flour Mill Road, Gateshead, NE11 9JB
Tel: 0191-460 9196 **Fax:** 0191-460 9716
Website: http://jewson.co.uk
Managers: M. Davidson (Mgr)
Ultimate Holding Company: COMPAGNIE DE SAINT GOBAIN (FRANCE)
Immediate Holding Company: JEWSON LIMITED
Registration no: 00348407 **Date established:** 1939
Turnover: £500m - £1,000m **No.of Employees:** 11 - 20
Product Groups: 66

Date of Accounts	Dec 11	Dec 10	Dec 09
Sales Turnover	1606m	1547m	1485m
Pre Tax Profit/Loss	18m	100m	45m
Working Capital	-345m	-250m	-349m
Fixed Assets	496m	387m	461m
Current Assets	657m	1005m	1320m
Current Liabilities	66m	120m	64m

Johnson Cleaners UK Ltd
Kingsway Tvte Team Valley Trading Estate, Gateshead, NE11 0HB
Tel: 0191-482 0088 **Fax:** 0191-482 1750
Website: http://www.johnsoncleaners.co.uk
Bank(s): National Westminster Bank Plc
Managers: C. Evans (Mgr)
Ultimate Holding Company: JOHNSON SERVICE GROUP PLC
Immediate Holding Company: JOHNSON CLEANERS UK LIMITED
Registration no: 02970609 **VAT No.:** GB 618 9265 10
Date established: 1994 **Turnover:** £2m - £5m **No.of Employees:** 51 - 100
Product Groups: 23, 52

Date of Accounts	Dec 11	Dec 10	Dec 09
Sales Turnover	65m	66m	70m
Pre Tax Profit/Loss	1m	-4m	3m
Working Capital	-3m	-2m	472
Fixed Assets	19m	19m	18m
Current Assets	9m	11m	12m
Current Liabilities	10m	11m	9m

Jordan Engineering Ltd
Andaray House Shields Road, Gateshead, NE10 0QE
Tel: 0191-469 7721 **Fax:** 0191-438 6771
E-mail: sales@jordan-engineering.co.uk
Website: http://www.jordan-engineering.co.uk
Directors: P. Jordan (MD)
Managers: D. Taylor (Personnel), E. Kelly (Comptroller), K. Wliiey (Purch Mgr)
Immediate Holding Company: JORDAN ENGINEERING LIMITED
Registration no: 04812739 **VAT No.:** GB 322 6344 82
Date established: 2003 **Turnover:** £2m - £5m **No.of Employees:** 51 - 100
Product Groups: 30

Date of Accounts	Oct 11	Oct 10	Oct 09
Sales Turnover	5m	4m	N/A
Pre Tax Profit/Loss	110	117	N/A
Working Capital	155	84	154
Fixed Assets	361	384	418
Current Assets	2m	2m	2m
Current Liabilities	1m	N/A	N/A

K L B Promotions & Events Ltd
229 Kells Lane Low Fell, Gateshead, NE9 5HT
Tel: 0191-491 5626
E-mail: sales@klbpromotions.freeserve.co.uk
Website: http://www.klb-promotions.co.uk
Directors: C. Sludden (Dir)
Immediate Holding Company: KLB PROMOTIONS AND EVENTS LIMITED
Registration no: 03151865 **Date established:** 1996
No.of Employees: 1 - 10 **Product Groups:** 81

Date of Accounts	Jan 11	Jan 10	Jan 09
Working Capital	-89	-92	-50
Fixed Assets	6	6	6
Current Assets	5	N/A	2

James Latham Ltd
Nest Road Felling Industrial Estate, Gateshead, NE10 0LU
Tel: 0191-469 4211 **Fax:** 0191-469 2615
E-mail: denis@lathams.co.uk
Website: http://www.lathamtimber.co.uk
Managers: G. Hall (Mgr)
Immediate Holding Company: JAMES LATHAM PUBLIC LIMITED COMPANY
Registration no: 00065619 **VAT No.:** GB 175 8264 33
Date established: 2000 **Turnover:** £5m - £10m **No.of Employees:** 11 - 20
Product Groups: 25, 66

Date of Accounts	Mar 12	Mar 11	Mar 10
Sales Turnover	144m	130m	115m
Pre Tax Profit/Loss	7m	8m	6m
Working Capital	40m	39m	36m
Fixed Assets	23m	19m	19m
Current Assets	62m	60m	53m
Current Liabilities	5m	7m	5m

Lifting Gear Hire Ltd
Salt Medows Road, Gateshead, NE8 3EH
Tel: 0191-295 5301 **Fax:** 0191-295 4311
Website: http://www.lgh.co.uk

Directors: D. Lee (MD)
Managers: G. Foster (District Mgr)
Immediate Holding Company: LIFTING GEAR HIRE LIMITED
Registration no: 05566506 **Date established:** 2005
Turnover: £125m - £250m **No.of Employees:** 1 - 10 **Product Groups:** 35, 37, 38, 39, 45, 48, 83

Lindab Ltd

Unit 304a Ninth Avenue East Team Valley Trading Estate, Gateshead, NE11 0EH
Tel: 0191-482 5995 **Fax:** 0191-414 0880
E-mail: elaine.harrison@lindab.co.uk
Website: http://www.lindab.co.uk
Managers: E. Harrison (District Mgr)
Ultimate Holding Company: LINDAB INTERNATIONAL AB (SWEDEN)
Immediate Holding Company: LINDAB LIMITED
Registration no: 01641399 **Date established:** 1982
No.of Employees: 1 - 10 **Product Groups:** 37, 40, 48

Date of Accounts	Dec 11	Dec 10	Dec 09
Sales Turnover	51m	47m	49m
Pre Tax Profit/Loss	1m	-204	354
Working Capital	16m	-3m	-4m
Fixed Assets	16m	20m	22m
Current Assets	22m	20m	23m
Current Liabilities	1m	980	775

Lumsden Grinders Ltd

Hawks Road, Gateshead, NE8 3BT
Tel: 0191-478 3838 **Fax:** 0191-490 0282
E-mail: sales@lumsden-grinders.co.uk
Website: http://www.lumsden-grinders.co.uk
Directors: G. Clark (MD), I. Clark (Fin)
Immediate Holding Company: LUMSDEN GRINDERS LIMITED
Registration no: 04436417 **VAT No.:** GB 605 4947 34
Date established: 2002 **Turnover:** Up to £250,000
No.of Employees: 1 - 10 **Product Groups:** 46

Date of Accounts	Mar 12	Mar 11	Mar 10
Working Capital	23	14	18
Fixed Assets	1	1	1
Current Assets	98	90	23

Maplin Electronics Ltd

Unit 4 Allison Court Beside The Metro Centre, Gateshead, NE11 9YS
Tel: 08432-277308 **Fax:** 0191-488 2830
E-mail: customercare@maplin.co.uk
Website: http://www.maplin.co.uk
Managers: T. Covington (Mgr)
Ultimate Holding Company: MONTAGU PRIVATE EQUITY LLP
Immediate Holding Company: MAPLIN ELECTRONICS LIMITED
Registration no: 01264385 **Date established:** 1976
Turnover: £125m - £250m **No.of Employees:** 1 - 10 **Product Groups:** 37, 61

Date of Accounts	Dec 11	Dec 08	Dec 09
Sales Turnover	205m	204m	204m
Pre Tax Profit/Loss	25m	32m	35m
Working Capital	118m	49m	75m
Fixed Assets	27m	28m	28m
Current Assets	207m	108m	142m
Current Liabilities	78m	51m	59m

Monkhouse & Brown

Teams Street, Gateshead, NE8 2RF
Tel: 0191-460 0220 **Fax:** 0191-460 0334
Website: http://www.hallandpickles.co.uk
Bank(s): Barclays
Managers: J. Mccrudden (Mgr)
Ultimate Holding Company: HALLCO 1812
Immediate Holding Company: HALL & PICKLES
Registration no: 03162309 **VAT No.:** GB 628 7021 41
Turnover: £75m - £125m **No.of Employees:** 11 - 20 **Product Groups:** 34

Myson Radiators

Eastern Avenue Team Valley Trading Estate, Gateshead, NE11 0PG
Tel: 0191-491 4466 **Fax:** 0191-491 7439
E-mail: sales@myson.co.uk
Website: http://www.myson.co.uk
Directors: G. Marshall (Fin), N. Macpherson (MD), M. Wright (Mkt Research), I. Going (I.T. Dir), G. Marshall (Fin)
Managers: L. Currie (Personnel), L. Currie (Personnel), K. Burell, E. Mcbrearty (Nat Sales Mgr), B. Lynch (Mktg Serv Mgr), I. Going (Tech Serv Mgr), K. Mccauley (Purch Mgr)
Ultimate Holding Company: OY RETTIG AB (FINLAND)
Immediate Holding Company: RETTIG (UK) LIMITED
Registration no: 00653648 **Date established:** 1960
Turnover: £50m - £75m **No.of Employees:** 101 - 250 **Product Groups:** 40

Date of Accounts	Dec 11	Dec 10	Dec 09
Sales Turnover	70m	72m	77m
Pre Tax Profit/Loss	-347	2m	1m
Working Capital	11m	13m	11m
Fixed Assets	10m	11m	14m
Current Assets	33m	38m	34m
Current Liabilities	14m	16m	14m

N E S International

2 Kingsway House Kingsway, Team Valley Trading Estate, Gateshead, NE11 0HW
Tel: 0191-487 6888 **Fax:** 0191-487 0777
Website: http://www.nes.co.uk
Managers: L. Miller, D. Pearce (Sales Admin), P. Jones (Mgr)
Date established: 2004 **No.of Employees:** 1 - 10 **Product Groups:** 80

Northern Counties Insurance Brokers

N C I House Lowerys Lane, Gateshead, NE9 5JB
Tel: 0191-482 1219 **Fax:** 0191-420 0097
E-mail: phill@ncicorporate.co.uk
Website: http://www.northerncounties.com
Directors: C. Belgian (Dir), M. Burdett (Mkt Research), P. Belgian (MD), P. Belgian (MD)
Immediate Holding Company: NORTHERN COUNTIES GUARANTEE CORPORATION LIMITED
Registration no: 00235918 **Date established:** 2028 **Turnover:** £1m - £2m
No.of Employees: 21 - 50 **Product Groups:** 82

Date of Accounts	Mar 11	Mar 10	Mar 09
Sales Turnover	N/A	N/A	2m
Pre Tax Profit/Loss	N/A	N/A	4m
Working Capital	-37	-62	3m
Fixed Assets	6m	6m	3m
Current Assets	33	19	4m
Current Liabilities	N/A	N/A	834

Northern Protective Coatings Ltd

16 Fairfield Industrial Park Bill Quay, Gateshead, NE10 0UR
Tel: 0191-438 5555 **Fax:** 0191-438 3082
E-mail: info@npcoatings.co.uk
Website: http://www.npcoatings.co.uk
Bank(s): Barclays
Directors: J. Welsh (MD), V. Goodall (Co Sec)
Immediate Holding Company: NORTHERN PROTECTIVE COATINGS LIMITED
Registration no: 02348204 **Date established:** 1989 **Turnover:** £1m - £2m
No.of Employees: 11 - 20 **Product Groups:** 48

Date of Accounts	Sep 11	Sep 10	Sep 09
Working Capital	-6	-16	-10
Fixed Assets	76	68	80
Current Assets	454	403	358

Northern Signs Engravers Ltd

Green Lane Felling, Gateshead, NE10 0QH
Tel: 0191-469 7311 **Fax:** 0191-438 4996
E-mail: sales@northernsignsltd.com
Website: http://www.northernsignsltd.com
Bank(s): Barclays
Directors: P. Harbottle (Fin), B. Harbottle (Prop)
Immediate Holding Company: NORTHERN SIGNS ENGRAVERS LIMITED
Registration no: 04190389 **VAT No.:** GB 177 5497 13
Date established: 2001 **Turnover:** £500,000 - £1m
No.of Employees: 11 - 20 **Product Groups:** 25, 27, 28, 30, 35, 37, 40, 48, 49

Date of Accounts	Oct 11	Oct 10	Oct 09
Working Capital	94	151	103
Fixed Assets	443	478	456
Current Assets	268	413	354

Northern Switch Gear & Controls Ltd

2 Lloyd Court Dunston, Gateshead, NE11 9EP
Tel: 0191-461 1130 **Fax:** 0191-461 1140
E-mail: sales@northern-switchgear.com
Directors: A. Ord (Dir), M. Burnett (Fin)
Ultimate Holding Company: NORTHERN FUTURES LIMITED
Immediate Holding Company: NORTHERN SWITCHGEAR & CONTROLS LIMITED
Registration no: 02923706 **VAT No.:** GB 605 7251 56
Date established: 1994 **Turnover:** £1m - £2m **No.of Employees:** 1 - 10
Product Groups: 37, 38, 44

Date of Accounts	May 11	May 10	May 09
Working Capital	166	120	74
Fixed Assets	56	30	25
Current Assets	568	401	260

Palintest Ltd Halma Group

Kingsway Team Valley Trading Estate, Gateshead, NE11 0NS
Tel: 0191-491 0808 **Fax:** 0191-482 5372
E-mail: sales@palintest.com
Website: http://www.palintest.com
Bank(s): National Westminster
Directors: C. Welch (Fin)
Managers: L. Noble (Tech Serv Mgr), K. Davies (Buyer), E. Mack (Sales & Mktg Mg)
Ultimate Holding Company: HALMA PUBLIC LIMITED COMPANY
Immediate Holding Company: PALINTEST LIMITED
Registration no: 01204118 **VAT No.:** 178 8236 20 **Date established:** 1975
Turnover: £5m - £10m **No.of Employees:** 51 - 100 **Product Groups:** 31, 32, 38

Date of Accounts	Mar 12	Mar 09	Apr 10
Sales Turnover	11m	7m	8m
Pre Tax Profit/Loss	2m	704	1m
Working Capital	-3m	298	-197
Fixed Assets	5m	2m	3m
Current Assets	4m	3m	3m
Current Liabilities	285	243	253

Parker Dominic Hunter Ltd (Industrial Division)

Dukesway Team Valley Trading Estate, Gateshead, NE11 0PZ
Tel: 0191-402 9000 **Fax:** 0191-482 6296
E-mail: sales@dominichunter.com
Website: http://www.dominichunter.com
Bank(s): Barclays
Managers: D. Clarke (Purch Mgr), D. Cooper (Tech Serv Mgr), D. Turnbell (Chief Mgr), L. Humphrey (Personnel), P. Duncan (Fin Mgr)
Ultimate Holding Company: FERSCHL HOLDINGS LIMITED
Immediate Holding Company: CURECOST LIMITED
Registration no: 02138796 **Date established:** 1987
Turnover: £50m - £75m **No.of Employees:** 101 - 250
Product Groups: 33, 40, 42

Date of Accounts	Mar 12	Feb 11
Working Capital	19	N/A
Fixed Assets	52	N/A
Current Assets	106	N/A

Parmley Graham Ltd

South Shore Road, Gateshead, NE8 3AE
Tel: 0191-478 6222 **Fax:** 0191-478 7109
E-mail: gateshead@parmley-graham.co.uk
Website: http://www.parmley-graham.co.uk
Bank(s): Lloyds
Managers: D. Key (Tech Serv Mgr), W. Whitfield (District Mgr)
Immediate Holding Company: PARMLEY GRAHAM LIMITED
Registration no: 00172842 **Date established:** 2021
Turnover: £20m - £50m **No.of Employees:** 11 - 20 **Product Groups:** 67

Date of Accounts	Dec 11	Dec 10	Dec 09
Sales Turnover	34m	33m	26m
Pre Tax Profit/Loss	1m	910	353
Working Capital	4m	4m	3m
Fixed Assets	1m	1m	1m
Current Assets	10m	9m	7m
Current Liabilities	1m	900	415

Pelaw Presentation Packaging Ltd

Unit 1b Stonehills Shields Road, Gateshead, NE10 0HW
Tel: 0191-495 0204 **Fax:** 0191-495 2998
E-mail: sales@pelawpack.co.uk
Website: http://www.pelawpack.co.uk
Directors: C. Young (Fin), G. Young (MD)
Immediate Holding Company: PELAW PRESENTATION PACKAGING LIMITED
Registration no: 01954884 **Date established:** 1985
No.of Employees: 11 - 20 **Product Groups:** 27, 28

Date of Accounts	Dec 10	Dec 09	Dec 08
Working Capital	5	-51	36
Fixed Assets	34	41	48
Current Assets	246	307	311
Current Liabilities	14	N/A	N/A

Petards Joyce-Loebl Ltd

390 Princesway Team Valley Trading Estate, Gateshead, NE11 0TU
Tel: 0191-420 3000 **Fax:** 0191-420 3030
E-mail: sales@petards.com
Website: http://www.petards.com
Bank(s): Lloyds TSB
Directors: T. Whightman (Ch), A. Wonnacott (Dir), D. Hayes (MD)
Managers: H. Preston (Mktg Serv Mgr), K. Mckie (Serv Mgr)
Ultimate Holding Company: PETARDS GROUP PLC
Immediate Holding Company: PETARDS JOYCE-LOEBL LIMITED
Registration no: 02170100 **VAT No.:** GB 198 1079 31
Date established: 1987 **Turnover:** £10m - £20m
No.of Employees: 51 - 100 **Product Groups:** 44

Date of Accounts	Dec 11	Dec 10	Dec 09
Sales Turnover	12m	11m	13m
Pre Tax Profit/Loss	198	-434	613
Working Capital	3m	2m	3m
Fixed Assets	155	175	240
Current Assets	7m	7m	7m
Current Liabilities	2m	2m	2m

Power Wholesales Ltd

100-104 High West Street, Gateshead, NE8 1NA
Tel: 0191-477 5721 **Fax:** 0191-490 1539
E-mail: neil.cornish@powerwholesale.co.uk
Website: http://www.powerwholesale.co.uk
Directors: N. Cornish (MD)
Immediate Holding Company: POWER WHOLESALE LIMITED
Registration no: 00804586 **Date established:** 1964 **Turnover:** £2m - £5m
No.of Employees: 11 - 20 **Product Groups:** 38, 40

Date of Accounts	Jan 11	Jan 10	Jan 09
Working Capital	231	359	286
Fixed Assets	830	644	523
Current Assets	2m	2m	2m

Premier Equipment Services Ltd

6 Parker Court Dunston, Gateshead, NE11 9EW
Tel: 0191-460 0323 **Fax:** 0191-460 0313
E-mail: general@premierequipment.co.uk
Website: http://www.premierequipment.co.uk
Directors: H. Kinmond (Fin), J. Hughes (MD)
Immediate Holding Company: Samuel Hodge Holdings Ltd
Registration no: 02349979 **Date established:** 1989 **Turnover:** £2m - £5m
No.of Employees: 1 - 10 **Product Groups:** 36, 39, 40, 46, 48, 67, 84, 86

Pressex UK Ltd

Kingsway South Team Valley Trading Estate, Gateshead, NE11 0SH
Tel: 0191-497 3430 **Fax:** 0191-497 3431
E-mail: dennis.henderson@responsive-engineering.com
Website: http://www.responsive-engineering.com
Bank(s): Lloyds
Directors: S. Simpson (Fin), D. Henderson (MD), D. Henderson (MD)
Managers: M. Rogers (Tech Serv Mgr)
Ultimate Holding Company: RESPONSIVE ENGINEERING (HOLDINGS) LIMITED
Immediate Holding Company: PRESSEX UK LIMITED
Registration no: 02593794 **Date established:** 1991
Turnover: £500,000 - £1m **No.of Employees:** 21 - 50 **Product Groups:** 48

Date of Accounts	Mar 11	Mar 10	Mar 09
Sales Turnover	N/A	597	N/A
Pre Tax Profit/Loss	N/A	56	N/A
Working Capital	691	691	583
Fixed Assets	N/A	N/A	92
Current Assets	691	691	1m

Prismtech Ltd

Prismtech House Fifth Avenue, Team Valley Trading Estate, Gateshead, NE11 0NG
Tel: 0191-497 9900 **Fax:** 0191-497 9901
E-mail: phil.wright@prismtechnologies.com
Website: http://www.prismtechnologies.com
Bank(s): National Westminster
Directors: P. Wright (Co Sec), S. Jennis (Mkt Research)
Managers: D. Cox (Personnel), J. Russell, K. Steele
Ultimate Holding Company: PRISMTECH GROUP LIMITED
Immediate Holding Company: PRISMTECH LIMITED
Registration no: 02664365 **VAT No.:** GB 605 3519 60
Date established: 1991 **Turnover:** £2m - £5m **No.of Employees:** 21 - 50
Product Groups: 44, 67, 84

Date of Accounts	Mar 09	Mar 08	Apr 11
Sales Turnover	3m	4m	5m
Pre Tax Profit/Loss	1m	-150	-697
Working Capital	4m	2m	3m
Fixed Assets	760	568	835
Current Assets	9m	8m	10m
Current Liabilities	2m	3m	3m

Protective Coating & Inspection Services Ltd

Unit 3-4 Green Lane Industrial Estate, Pelaw, Gateshead, NE10 0UW
Tel: 0191-418 7773
E-mail: pcisltd@btconnect.com
Website: http://www.pcisltd.com
Directors: D. Back (Admin), D. Chamberlain (Fin), S. Malone (MD)
Immediate Holding Company: PROTECTIVE COATING AND INSPECTION SERVICES LIMITED
Registration no: 04896339 **Date established:** 2003
No.of Employees: 1 - 10 **Product Groups:** 46, 48

Date of Accounts	Oct 08	Oct 07	Oct 06
Working Capital	186	183	-29
Fixed Assets	194	167	191
Current Assets	414	381	198
Current Liabilities	228	198	227

Proten Services (formerly Protim Services Ltd

Mayoral Way Team Valley Trading Estate, Gateshead, NE11 0RT
Tel: 0191-482 3885 **Fax:** 0191-482 3886
E-mail: enquiry@protenservices.co.uk
Website: http://www.protenservices.co.uk
Directors: D. Marshall (Chief Op Offcr)
No.of Employees: 1 - 10 **Product Groups:** 07, 23, 32, 52, 66

Responsive Engineering Group - Weldex

Kingsway South Team Valley Trading Estate, Gateshead, NE11 0SH
Tel: 0191-497 3410 **Fax:** 0191-497 3401
E-mail: sales@responsive-engineering.com
Website: http://www.responsive-engineering.com
Managers: G. Harmer (Mgr), P. Bernard (Mgr)
Ultimate Holding Company: RESPONSIVE ENGINEERING (HOLDINGS) LIMITED
Immediate Holding Company: WELDEX UK LIMITED
Registration no: 02593791 **Date established:** 1991
Turnover: £10m - £20m **No.of Employees:** 21 - 50 **Product Groups:** 22, 23, 25, 27, 29, 30, 32, 33, 34, 35, 36, 37, 38, 39, 40, 42, 43, 45, 46, 47, 48, 49, 51, 52, 61, 66, 67, 68, 83, 84, 85

Date of Accounts	Mar 12	Mar 11	Mar 10
Sales Turnover	13m	11m	10m
Pre Tax Profit/Loss	-1m	783	296
Working Capital	1m	1m	1m
Fixed Assets	4m	3m	2m
Current Assets	6m	5m	3m
Current Liabilities	999	832	531

RS Components Ltd

Dukesway West Team Valley Trading Estate, Gateshead, NE11 0PN
Tel: 0191-491 0900 **Fax:** 0191-491 0490
E-mail: rsint@rs-components.com
Website: http://www.rswww.com
Managers: D. Wilson (District Mgr)
Immediate Holding Company: Electrocomponents plc
Registration no: 01002091 **VAT No.:** GB 243 1640 91
Date established: 1937 **Turnover:** £250m - £500m
No.of Employees: 21 - 50 **Product Groups:** 67

R T R Handelsgesellschaft

8 Kingsway House Kingsway, Team Valley Trading Estate, Gateshead, NE11 0HW
Tel: 0191-491 1292 **Fax:** 0191-491 1246
E-mail: sales@rtr.co.uk
Website: http://www.rtr.co.uk
Directors: P. Ross (Dir)
Turnover: £1m - £2m **No.of Employees:** 1 - 10 **Product Groups:** 36, 48

Rubb Buildings Ltd

Dukesway Team Valley Trading Estate, Gateshead, NE11 0QE
Tel: 0191-482 2211 **Fax:** 0191-482 2516
E-mail: info@rubb.co.uk
Website: http://www.rubb.co.uk
Bank(s): Barclays
Directors: I. Hindmoor (MD)
Managers: A. Knox (Sales Prom Mgr), M. Halpin (Prod Mgr), L. Hindson (Personnel), I. Hindmoor (Mgr)
Immediate Holding Company: RUBB BUILDINGS LIMITED
Registration no: 01309845 **VAT No.:** GB 301 0343 37
Date established: 1977 **Turnover:** £5m - £10m
No.of Employees: 51 - 100 **Product Groups:** 35

Date of Accounts	Dec 11	Dec 10	Dec 09
Sales Turnover	7m	8m	N/A
Pre Tax Profit/Loss	340	1m	N/A
Working Capital	2m	2m	2m
Fixed Assets	315	345	432
Current Assets	3m	4m	4m
Current Liabilities	504	1m	N/A

Saia Burgess (Gateshead) Plc

Dukesway Team Valley Trading Estate, Gateshead, NE11 0UB
Tel: 0191-401 6100 **Fax:** 0191-401 6305
E-mail: office@saia-burgess.com
Website: http://www.saia-burgess.com
Bank(s): HSBC Bank plc
Directors: D. Norman (Dir), D. Norman (MD), S. Adams (Sales)
Ultimate Holding Company: JOHNSON ELECTRIC HOLDINGS LTD (BERMUDA)
Immediate Holding Company: SB ELECTRONICS UK LTD
Registration no: 00911310 **VAT No.:** GB 660 2587 36
Date established: 1993 **Turnover:** £20m - £50m
No.of Employees: 251 - 500 **Product Groups:** 37, 38, 39, 40, 49

Service 2000 Commercial Ltd

4 Park Court Ninth Avenue East, Team Valley Trading Estate, Gateshead, NE11 0EJ
Tel: 0191-420 2899 **Fax:** 0191-420 3885
Website: http://www.service2000.co.uk
Directors: G. Torbitt (MD), G. Torbitt (Fin)
Immediate Holding Company: SERVICE 2000 COMMERCIAL LTD
Registration no: 04305006 **Date established:** 2001
No.of Employees: 1 - 10 **Product Groups:** 20, 40, 41

Date of Accounts	Oct 07	Oct 06	Oct 05
Working Capital	17	36	N/A
Fixed Assets	193	138	99
Current Assets	400	232	146
Current Liabilities	382	197	146
Total Share Capital	1	1	1

Sevcon Ltd

Kingsway South Team Valley Trading Estate, Gateshead, NE11 0QA
Tel: 0191-497 9000 **Fax:** 0191-487 4223
E-mail: info@sevcon.com
Website: http://www.sevcon.com
Bank(s): Barclays
Directors: M. Boyle (Grp Chief Exec), P. Farquhar (Fin)
Managers: D. Errington (Tech Serv Mgr)
Ultimate Holding Company: TECH/OPS SEVCON INC (USA)
Immediate Holding Company: SEVCON LIMITED
Registration no: 00500106 **VAT No.:** 178 5469 12 **Date established:** 1951
Turnover: £10m - £20m **No.of Employees:** 51 - 100 **Product Groups:** 37, 38

Date of Accounts	Sep 11	Sep 10	Sep 09
Sales Turnover	15m	12m	9m
Pre Tax Profit/Loss	607	146	-542
Working Capital	3m	2m	2m
Fixed Assets	2m	4m	4m
Current Assets	7m	6m	4m
Current Liabilities	588	392	476

Shingle Berry Signs

Unit 4 Lloyd Court, Dunston, Gateshead, NE11 9EP
Tel: 0191-461 0084 **Fax:** 0191-460 3929
E-mail: sales@shingleberrysigns.com
Website: http://www.shingleberrysigns.com
Directors: M. Shingler (Ptnr), M. Shingler (Ptnr)
No.of Employees: 1 - 10 **Product Groups:** 30, 37, 40, 49

F Short Ltd

Green Lane, Gateshead, NE10 0EZ
Tel: 0191-469 4627 **Fax:** 0191-438 4680
Website: http://www.integris.co.uk
Bank(s): Royal Bank of Scotland
Directors: J. Anderson (MD), I. Anderson (Co Sec)
Ultimate Holding Company: S.A.H. LIMITED
Immediate Holding Company: F SHORT LIMITED
Registration no: SC259666 **VAT No.:** GB 177 5430 45
Date established: 2003 **Turnover:** £500,000 - £1m
No.of Employees: 21 - 50 **Product Groups:** 39, 72

Date of Accounts	Dec 11	Dec 10	Dec 09
Sales Turnover	1m	1m	1m
Pre Tax Profit/Loss	-39	-83	-22
Working Capital	55	83	118
Current Assets	192	154	176
Current Liabilities	31	16	25

Sloan Electronics Ltd

241 Kells Lane, Gateshead, NE9 5HU
Tel: 0191-491 0191 **Fax:** 0191-482 6762
E-mail: info@sloanelectronics.co.uk
Website: http://www.sloanelectronics.co.uk
Bank(s): National Westminster, Gateshead
Directors: J. Sloan (Fin)
Immediate Holding Company: SLOAN ELECTRONICS LIMITED
Registration no: 03288709 **VAT No.:** GB 686 4122 20
Date established: 1996 **Turnover:** £500,000 - £1m
No.of Employees: 11 - 20 **Product Groups:** 37, 84

Date of Accounts	Mar 11	Mar 10	Mar 09
Working Capital	-29	-25	-21
Fixed Assets	133	138	144
Current Assets	166	193	190

Smiley Fabrications Ltd

Unit 4 Abbotsford Road, Gateshead, NE10 0EX
Tel: 0191-495 0665 **Fax:** 0191-495 0665
E-mail: smileyfabrications@tiscali.co.uk
Website: http://www.smileyfabrications.co.uk
Directors: D. Stirling (MD)
Immediate Holding Company: SMILEY FABRICATIONS LIMITED
Registration no: 07851652 **Date established:** 2011
Turnover: Up to £250,000 **No.of Employees:** 1 - 10 **Product Groups:** 26, 35

Smiths Metal Centres Ltd

Nest Road, Gateshead, NE10 0ES
Tel: 0191-469 5428 **Fax:** 0191-495 0116
E-mail: gatesheadsales@smithmetal.com
Website: http://www.smithmetal.com
Managers: M. Gash (Mgr)
Ultimate Holding Company: HENLEY MANAGEMENT COMPANY (USA)
Immediate Holding Company: SMITHS METAL CENTRES LIMITED
Registration no: 03485838 **Date established:** 1997
No.of Employees: 1 - 10 **Product Groups:** 34, 49, 66

Date of Accounts	Dec 11	May 10	May 09
Sales Turnover	45m	46m	49m
Pre Tax Profit/Loss	2m	830	629
Working Capital	7m	12m	13m
Fixed Assets	1m	1m	2m
Current Assets	28m	23m	21m
Current Liabilities	4m	2m	2m

Snapfast Electrical Products

Unit 1-3 Park Court Ninth Avenue, Team Valley Trading Estate, Gateshead, NE11 0EH
Tel: 0191-482 4075 **Fax:** 0191-491 1799
E-mail: sales@snapfast.co.uk
Directors: A. Richardson (Ptnr)
VAT No.: GB 459 7266 00 **Turnover:** £2m - £5m **No.of Employees:** 1 - 10
Product Groups: 37, 66

Snug Co. Ltd

Stoneygate House Stoneygate Lane, Gateshead, NE10 0HJ
Tel: 0191-495 2322 **Fax:** 0191-495 2321
E-mail: robin.aitken@snug-ltd.com
Website: http://www.snug-ltd.com
Directors: M. Shephard (Sales), R. Aitken (MD)
Managers: B. Powton (Personnel)
Ultimate Holding Company: PORTCHESTER EQUITY LIMITED
Immediate Holding Company: SHO123 LIMITED
Registration no: 01692741 **Date established:** 1983
Turnover: £10m - £20m **No.of Employees:** 51 - 100 **Product Groups:** 23, 24

Date of Accounts	Mar 10	Mar 09	Sep 11
Sales Turnover	12m	13m	13m
Pre Tax Profit/Loss	-243	-2m	-3m
Working Capital	1m	1m	2m
Fixed Assets	3m	3m	2m
Current Assets	5m	5m	6m
Current Liabilities	562	627	2m

Speedy Lifting

Saltmeadows Road, Gateshead, NE8 3AH
Tel: 0191-478 6655 **Fax:** 0191-478 6677
E-mail: ian.moore1@speedyhire.com
Website: http://www.speedyhire.com
Managers: I. Moore (District Mgr)
Ultimate Holding Company: COMPACTYPIST LIMITED
Immediate Holding Company: S.T.C.S. LTD
Registration no: 04529136 **Date established:** 1988
No.of Employees: 1 - 10 **Product Groups:** 35, 39, 45

Date of Accounts	Mar 11	Mar 10	Mar 09
Working Capital	300	315	249
Fixed Assets	1	2	1
Current Assets	370	399	318
Current Liabilities	N/A	N/A	60

Springfields Florist

421 Durham Road, Gateshead, NE9 5AN
Tel: 0191-482 0777 **Fax:** 0191-482 0777
E-mail: info@springfieldsflorists.co.uk
Website: http://www.springfieldsflorists.co.uk
Directors: N. Frazer (Prop)
Immediate Holding Company: SPRINGFIELDS FLORISTS LIMITED
Registration no: 04759255 **Date established:** 2003
Turnover: £500,000 - £1m **No.of Employees:** 1 - 10 **Product Groups:** 62

Date of Accounts	May 11	May 10	May 08
Working Capital	-4	-1	-1
Fixed Assets	10	9	5
Current Assets	19	6	6

Stannah Lift Services Ltd

Wellington Road, Gateshead, NE11 9JL
Tel: 0191-460 0010 **Fax:** 0191-460 1143
Website: http://www.stannah.co.uk
Directors: T. Garner (Dir)
Ultimate Holding Company: STANNAH LIFTS HOLDINGS LIMITED
Immediate Holding Company: STANNAH LIFT SERVICES LIMITED
Registration no: 01189799 **Date established:** 1974
No.of Employees: 21 - 50 **Product Groups:** 35, 39, 45

Date of Accounts	Dec 11	Dec 10	Dec 09
Sales Turnover	84m	82m	87m
Pre Tax Profit/Loss	191	2m	2m
Working Capital	12m	14m	15m
Fixed Assets	4m	4m	3m
Current Assets	21m	24m	24m
Current Liabilities	6m	6m	7m

Sundolitt Ltd

Bath Road, Gateshead, NE10 0JT
Tel: 0191-438 1023 **Fax:** 0191-495 4111
E-mail: paul.brown@sundolitt.com
Website: http://www.sundolitt.com
Managers: P. Brown (Plant)
Immediate Holding Company: SUNDOLITT LIMITED
Registration no: SC211936 **Date established:** 2000
No.of Employees: 1 - 10 **Product Groups:** 38, 42

Date of Accounts	Dec 11	Dec 10	Dec 09
Sales Turnover	10m	8m	7m
Pre Tax Profit/Loss	839	96	-404
Working Capital	856	800	694
Fixed Assets	2m	2m	3m
Current Assets	2m	2m	2m
Current Liabilities	1m	1m	798

Theme Bins International Ltd

Nest Road, Gateshead, NE10 0ES
Tel: 0191-495 0772 **Fax:** 0191-469 4636
E-mail: hq@themebins.co.uk
Website: http://www.themebins.co.uk
Directors: P. Hewitt (Dir)
Immediate Holding Company: THEME BINS (INTERNATIONAL) LTD
Registration no: 02644623 **Date established:** 1991
Turnover: £250,000 - £500,000 **No.of Employees:** 11 - 20
Product Groups: 30, 39

Date of Accounts	Sep 11	Sep 10	Sep 09
Working Capital	64	126	71
Fixed Assets	976	982	1m
Current Assets	396	497	444

Thermon Electrical Heating Equipment

Seventh Avenue Team Valley Trading Estate, Gateshead, NE11 0JW
Tel: 0191-499 4900 **Fax:** 0191-499 4901
E-mail: uk@thermon.com
Website: http://www.thermon.com
Bank(s): ABN AMRO Bank NV
Managers: J. Allison (Chief Mgr)
Ultimate Holding Company: THERMON GROUP HOLDINGS INC(USA)
Immediate Holding Company: THERMON (U.K.) LIMITED
Registration no: 01452401 **VAT No.:** GB 633 6852 26
Date established: 1979 **Turnover:** £500,000 - £1m
No.of Employees: 11 - 20 **Product Groups:** 30, 37, 38, 40

Date of Accounts	Mar 12	Mar 11	Mar 10
Sales Turnover	895	873	858
Pre Tax Profit/Loss	25	42	33
Working Capital	626	614	583
Fixed Assets	20	15	20
Current Assets	888	835	825
Current Liabilities	211	171	205

Tights Tights Tights

5 The Boulevard Metrocentre, Gateshead, NE11 9YN
Tel: 0191-460 9697 **Fax:** 0191-460 9697
E-mail: tights@btconnect.com
Website: http://www.tightstightstights.co.uk
Directors: N. Stocks (Prop)
Date established: 2002 **No.of Employees:** 1 - 10 **Product Groups:** 24

Trade Supplies Ltd

Unit 41 Team Valley Business Centre Earlsway, Team Valley Trading Estate, Gateshead, NE11 0QH
Tel: 0191-487 0311 **Fax:** 0191-487 2423
Website: http://www.tradessupplieslimited.co.uk
Managers: P. Davidson (Mgr)
Immediate Holding Company: TRADE SUPPLIES LIMITED
Registration no: 05223992 **Date established:** 2004
No.of Employees: 1 - 10 **Product Groups:** 37, 40, 48

Date of Accounts	Sep 08	Sep 07	Sep 06
Sales Turnover	6m	5m	7m
Pre Tax Profit/Loss	4m	536	948
Working Capital	3m	232	417
Fixed Assets	2m	186	369
Current Assets	4m	304	508
Current Liabilities	870	N/A	N/A

Tripak Ltd

Europa House Stoneygate Lane, Gateshead, NE10 0LX
Tel: 0191-495 0101 **Fax:** 0191-495 0404
E-mail: william@tripakltd.com
Website: http://www.tripakltd.com
Directors: W. Gluck (MD)
Immediate Holding Company: TRIPAK LTD
Registration no: 01435866 **VAT No.:** GB 353 8639 26
Date established: 1979 **Turnover:** £5m - £10m **No.of Employees:** 11 - 20
Product Groups: 23, 25, 26, 27, 28, 29, 30, 31, 33, 34, 35, 36, 42, 44, 45, 48, 49, 66, 84, 85, 87

Date of Accounts	Jun 11	Jun 10	Jun 09
Sales Turnover	5m	N/A	N/A
Pre Tax Profit/Loss	191	N/A	N/A
Working Capital	539	411	386
Fixed Assets	32	32	42
Current Assets	2m	2m	1m
Current Liabilities	241	N/A	N/A

Tyneside Safety Glass

Kingsway North Team Valley Trading Estate, Gateshead, NE11 0JX
Tel: 0191-487 5064 **Fax:** 0191-487 0358
E-mail: chris@tynesidesafetyglass.co.uk
Website: http://www.safetyglass.co.uk
Bank(s): Lloyds TSB Bank plc

Directors: C. Hannant (MD), G. Mackey (I.T. Dir)
Managers: C. Hills (Personnel)
Ultimate Holding Company: SUNTEX SAFETY GLASS INDUSTRIES LIMITED
Immediate Holding Company: TYNESIDE SAFETY GLASS COMPANY LIMITED
Registration no: 00359744 **Date established:** 1940
Turnover: £10m - £20m **No.of Employees:** 101 - 250
Product Groups: 33, 48

Date of Accounts	Apr 11	Apr 10	Apr 09
Sales Turnover	12m	9m	11m
Pre Tax Profit/Loss	159	-247	27
Working Capital	495	241	241
Fixed Assets	3m	4m	4m
Current Assets	3m	3m	2m
Current Liabilities	679	389	585

UK Ventilation Services

Clock Mill Road, Gateshead, NE8 2QX
Tel: 0191-493 2275 **Fax:** 0191-493 2276
Website: http://www.ukventilation.co.uk
Directors: K. Bone (Prop)
Immediate Holding Company: UK VENTILATION LIMITED
Registration no: 05639366 **Date established:** 2005
No.of Employees: 1 - 10 **Product Groups:** 40, 66

Date of Accounts	Nov 11	Nov 10	Nov 09
Sales Turnover	275	N/A	243
Pre Tax Profit/Loss	38	N/A	-0
Working Capital	46	10	-9
Fixed Assets	36	41	44
Current Assets	82	50	39
Current Liabilities	15	N/A	6

R Vail Ventilation

10 King Street Pelaw, Gateshead, NE10 0RD
Tel: 0191-440 3638 **Fax:** 0191-440 3638
E-mail: rvailventilation@aol.com
Directors: R. Vail (Prop)
Turnover: Up to £250,000 **No.of Employees:** 1 - 10 **Product Groups:** 30, 39, 40, 52

Vanguard 2001 Ltd

Unit 2a Brama Teams Industrial Park Team Street, Gateshead, NE8 2RG
Tel: 0191-460 0500 **Fax:** 0191-460 0333
E-mail: info@vanguard2001.co.uk
Website: http://www.vanguard2001.co.uk
Directors: D. Spence (MD)
Immediate Holding Company: VANGUARD (2001) LTD
Registration no: 04210650 **Date established:** 2001
No.of Employees: 11 - 20 **Product Groups:** 33, 46, 48, 72, 76, 80, 84

Date of Accounts	May 11	May 10	May 09
Working Capital	151	143	129
Fixed Assets	80	83	98
Current Assets	322	252	276

Vendetta Business & Technical Services Ltd

45 West Crescent, Gateshead, NE10 8AY
Tel: 08444-144390
E-mail: wwwsales@vendetta.co.uk
Website: http://www.vendetta.co.uk
Directors: K. Evans (MD), D. Meadows (Fin)
Immediate Holding Company: VENDETTA BUSINESS & TECHNICAL SERVICES LIMITED
Registration no: 03681244 **Date established:** 1998
Turnover: Up to £250,000 **No.of Employees:** 1 - 10 **Product Groups:** 44

Date of Accounts	Dec 11	Dec 10	Dec 09
Sales Turnover	13	10	7
Pre Tax Profit/Loss	-0	2	-8
Working Capital	-25	-25	-27
Fixed Assets	1	1	1
Current Assets	14	12	7
Current Liabilities	39	37	34

Vision Express UK

81-83 Russell Way Metro Centre, Gateshead, NE11 9XX
Tel: 0191-460 0644 **Fax:** 0191-460 0097
Website: http://www.visionexpress.com
Managers: M. Pringle (Mgr)
Ultimate Holding Company: HAL TRUST (BERMUDA)
Immediate Holding Company: VISION EXPRESS (UK) LIMITED
Registration no: 02189907 **Date established:** 1987
No.of Employees: 21 - 50 **Product Groups:** 37, 38, 65

Date of Accounts	Dec 11	Dec 10	Dec 09
Sales Turnover	196m	191m	195m
Pre Tax Profit/Loss	14m	11m	19m
Working Capital	-19m	3m	2m
Fixed Assets	46m	42m	43m
Current Assets	36m	35m	34m
Current Liabilities	15m	14m	16m

Waverley T B S Ltd

Nest Road, Gateshead, NE10 0ES
Tel: 0191-495 5050 **Fax:** 0191-495 2288
E-mail: customer.services@waverleytbs.co.uk
Website: http://www.waverleytbs.co.uk
Bank(s): Royal Bank of Scotland
Managers: M. Wood (Mgr)
Ultimate Holding Company: HUNTINGTOWER INVESTMENT GROUP LIMITED
Immediate Holding Company: WAVERLEYTBS LIMITED
Registration no: 00367326 **VAT No.:** GB 268 6449 12
Date established: 1941 **Turnover:** £125m - £250m
No.of Employees: 251 - 500 **Product Groups:** 62

Date of Accounts	Dec 11	Dec 10	Dec 09
Sales Turnover	309m	350m	504m
Pre Tax Profit/Loss	4m	2m	-9m
Working Capital	12m	18m	2m
Fixed Assets	10m	7m	15m
Current Assets	86m	91m	185m
Current Liabilities	26m	25m	36m

Worthington Armstrong UK Ltd

401 Princesway Team Valley Trading Estate, Gateshead, NE11 0TU
Tel: 0191-487 0606 **Fax:** 0191-491 4085
Website: http://www.armstrong.com
Managers: C. Carr (Comptroller), P. Hamlin (Chief Mgr), P. Gallagher (Personnel)
Ultimate Holding Company: WORTHINGTON ARMSTRONG VENTURE EUROPE (FRANCE)
Immediate Holding Company: WORTHINGTON ARMSTRONG U.K. LIMITED
Registration no: 03316435 **Date established:** 1997
Turnover: £10m - £20m **No.of Employees:** 21 - 50 **Product Groups:** 26, 35

Date of Accounts	Dec 11	Dec 10	Dec 09
Sales Turnover	12m	11m	11m
Pre Tax Profit/Loss	1m	798	666
Working Capital	3m	2m	2m
Fixed Assets	7m	7m	6m
Current Assets	4m	3m	4m
Current Liabilities	373	378	116

Hebburn

A & P Tyne Ltd

Wagonway Road, Hebburn, NE31 1SP
Tel: 0191-430 8600 **Fax:** 0191-428 6228
E-mail: stewart.boak@ap-tyne.co.uk
Website: http://www.ap-group.co.uk
Directors: S. Boak (MD), I. Carey (Fin), N. Jarvis (Comm)
Managers: T. Clements (Tech Serv Mgr), L. McDonald (Personnel), M. Oliver (Purch Mgr)
Ultimate Holding Company: ATLANTIC & PENINSULA MARINE SERVICES LIMITED
Immediate Holding Company: A&P TYNE LIMITED
Registration no: 05127750 **Date established:** 2004
Turnover: £20m - £50m **No.of Employees:** 101 - 250 **Product Groups:** 39

Date of Accounts	Dec 11	Dec 10	Dec 09
Sales Turnover	32m	26m	26m
Pre Tax Profit/Loss	3m	2m	1m
Working Capital	7m	4m	4m
Fixed Assets	7m	8m	6m
Current Assets	13m	14m	8m
Current Liabilities	4m	5m	3m

Clugston Construction (North East Region)

Merchant Court Koppers Way, Monkton Business Park South, Hebburn, NE31 2EX
Tel: 0191-495 0500 **Fax:** 0191-495 0400
E-mail: steve.waggett@clugston.co.uk
Website: http://www.clugston.co.uk
Managers: S. Waggett (Reg Mgr)
Ultimate Holding Company: CLUGSTON GROUP LTD
Immediate Holding Company: CLUGSTON GROUP LTD
Registration no: 00681537 **Date established:** 1946
Turnover: £20m - £50m **No.of Employees:** 11 - 20 **Product Groups:** 51, 52, 81

Crane Express Services Ltd

3 Station Road, Hebburn, NE31 1BD
Tel: 0191-428 6262 **Fax:** 0191-428 6263
E-mail: raywhitelaw@crane-express.com
Website: http://www.crane-express.com
Directors: R. Whitelaw (MD)
Immediate Holding Company: CRANE EXPRESS SERVICES LIMITED
Registration no: 02958647 **Date established:** 1994
No.of Employees: 1 - 10 **Product Groups:** 35, 39, 45

Date of Accounts	Aug 12	Aug 11	Aug 10
Working Capital	21	9	52
Fixed Assets	37	39	9
Current Assets	236	185	208

Ford Component Manufacturing Ltd

Unit 2 Postal Number 3, Hebburn, NE31 2JZ
Tel: 0191-428 6600 **Fax:** 0191-428 6620
E-mail: mark.podmore@ford-aerospace.com
Website: http://www.ford-components.com
Bank(s): Barclays
Directors: R. Ford (Dir), M. Podmore (Chief Op Offcr), J. Shone (MD)
Managers: S. Gribben (Purch Mgr), C. Young (Personnel), P. Batey (Purch Mgr), M. Harrison (I.T. Exec), T. Noble (Sales Prom Mgr), M. Turnbull
Immediate Holding Company: FORD COMPONENT MANUFACTURING LIMITED
Registration no: 06664191 **VAT No.:** GB 176 0986 29
Date established: 2008 **Turnover:** £5m - £10m **No.of Employees:** 11 - 20
Product Groups: 34, 35, 48

Date of Accounts	Sep 10	Mar 10	Mar 09
Sales Turnover	2m	3m	N/A
Pre Tax Profit/Loss	90	-365	N/A
Working Capital	983	783	1m
Fixed Assets	460	452	260
Current Assets	2m	2m	2m
Current Liabilities	291	185	N/A

H M Plant Ltd

Unit 5 Monkton Business Park North, Hebburn, NE31 2JZ
Tel: 0191-430 8400 **Fax:** 0191-430 8500
E-mail: jraine@hmplant.ltd.uk
Website: http://www.hmplant.ltd.uk
Directors: J. Jones (MD), D. Hearne (Sales), A. Baker (Sales)
Managers: T. Ford (Personnel), J. Fenton (Admin Off), J. Raine (Chief Mgr), J. Wales (I.T. Exec), T. Worrell (Chief Mgr)
Ultimate Holding Company: HITACHI LTD (JAPAN)
Immediate Holding Company: HM PLANT LIMITED
Registration no: 01082975 **Date established:** 1972
Turnover: £75m - £125m **No.of Employees:** 21 - 50 **Product Groups:** 45

Date of Accounts	Dec 07	Mar 11	Mar 10
Sales Turnover	139m	83m	84m
Pre Tax Profit/Loss	8m	4m	2m
Working Capital	711	7m	4m
Fixed Assets	4m	4m	4m
Current Assets	47m	36m	38m
Current Liabilities	6m	4m	3m

Northern Cranes & Lifting Equipment Ltd

Unit E Bedewell Industrial Park Adair Way, Hebburn, NE31 2XQ
Tel: 0191-489 5066 **Fax:** 0191-483 9702
E-mail: peter@norcrane.co.uk
Website: http://www.norcrane.co.uk
Directors: P. Smith (MD)
Immediate Holding Company: NORTHERN CRANES AND LIFTING EQUIPMENT LTD
Registration no: 01981031 **Date established:** 1986
No.of Employees: 11 - 20 **Product Groups:** 35, 39, 45

Date of Accounts	Oct 11	Oct 10	Apr 10
Working Capital	-81	16	16
Fixed Assets	18	9	9
Current Assets	217	236	236

Siemens

Off North Farm Road, Hebburn, NE31 1TZ
Tel: 0191-401 7901 **Fax:** 0191-401 5575
E-mail: martin.bell@seamans.com
Website: http://www.siemens.com
Directors: S. Ellis (Fin), G. Weir (Fin), M. Bell (MD)
Managers: C. Wilkes (Sales Prom Mgr), S. Keeble (Tech Serv Mgr), A. Mason (Personnel), L. Doherty (Purch Mgr)
Ultimate Holding Company: SIEMENS AG (GERMANY)
Immediate Holding Company: SIEMENS TRANSMISSION AND DISTRIBUTION LIMITED
Registration no: 00631825 **Date established:** 1959
Turnover: £250,000 - £500,000 **No.of Employees:** 101 - 250
Product Groups: 37, 52, 67

Date of Accounts	Sep 11	Sep 10	Sep 09
Sales Turnover	316m	253m	232m
Pre Tax Profit/Loss	35m	28m	10m
Working Capital	112m	87m	74m
Fixed Assets	15m	18m	21m
Current Assets	242m	204m	167m
Current Liabilities	110m	106m	79m

Thermal Hire Ltd

Unit A Bedewell Industrial Park, Hebburn, NE31 2HQ
Tel: 0191-428 0423 **Fax:** 0191-428 0061
E-mail: enquiries@thermalhire.com
Website: http://www.thermalhire.com
Directors: J. Rielly (MD)
Managers: J. Riley (Mgr), A. Sykes (Mgr)
Immediate Holding Company: THERMAL HIRE LTD
Registration no: 01174472 **Date established:** 1974 **Turnover:** £2m - £5m
No.of Employees: 1 - 10 **Product Groups:** 48

Turbo Engineering Ltd

Unit 14 Prince Consort Industrial Estate, Hebburn, NE31 1EH
Tel: 0191-483 2745 **Fax:** 0191-483 6745
E-mail: dominic.rutherford@btinternet.com
Directors: J. Rutherford (MD)
Immediate Holding Company: TURBO ENG LTD
Registration no: 07065145 **VAT No.:** GB 426 0394 65
Date established: 2009 **Turnover:** £250,000 - £500,000
No.of Employees: 1 - 10 **Product Groups:** 30, 31, 34, 35, 36, 38, 39, 48, 66

Date of Accounts	Oct 10
Working Capital	-27
Fixed Assets	63
Current Assets	85

Houghton Le Spring

Bryan Wilson Services

31 Gillas Lane West, Houghton Le Spring, DH5 8JX
Tel: 0191-584 3408 **Fax:** 0191-584 3408
E-mail: bryan@swmachinery.co.uk
Directors: B. Wilson (Prop)
Date established: 1982 **No.of Employees:** 1 - 10 **Product Groups:** 46

Corus (Steel Stockholders)

Hetton Lyons Industrial Estate Hetton-le-Hole, Houghton le Spring, DH5 0RD
Tel: 0191-526 3288 **Fax:** 0191-517 0138
E-mail: paul.brown@corusgroup.com
Website: http://www.corusgroup.com
Managers: D. White (Sales Prom Mgr), P. Brown (Mgr)
Ultimate Holding Company: Corus (UK) Ltd
Immediate Holding Company: CORUS GROUP LIMITED
Registration no: 03811373 **Date established:** 1999 **Turnover:** £1m - £2m
No.of Employees: 11 - 20 **Product Groups:** 34, 66

CUT 8 Smart repairs

85 Mooresfield, Houghton Le Spring, DH4 5PG
Tel: 0191-580 1888
E-mail: info@cut8.co.uk
Website: http://www.cut8.co.uk
Managers: G. Protheroe (Sales Admin)
Date established: 2009 **Turnover:** **No.of Employees:** Unknown
Product Groups: 39

Elite Bathcare Ltd

Ansty House Waller Terrace, Houghton le Spring, DH5 8LE
Tel: 0191-584 2159 **Fax:** 0191-584 2159
Directors: J. Farrow (MD), A. Lee (Fin)
Immediate Holding Company: ELITE BATHCARE LTD
Registration no: 03890209 **Date established:** 1999
Turnover: Up to £250,000 **No.of Employees:** 1 - 10 **Product Groups:** 46, 48

Date of Accounts	Dec 08	Dec 07	Dec 06
Sales Turnover	39	37	43
Pre Tax Profit/Loss	14	16	21
Working Capital	-2	-2	-2
Fixed Assets	7	8	5
Current Assets	5	5	6
Current Liabilities	7	7	8
ROCE% (Return on Capital Employed)	263.1	303.0	869.0
ROT% (Return on Turnover)	35.2	43.2	49.2

Fletcher UK Ltd

40 Market Street Hetton-Le-Hole, Houghton Le Spring, DH5 9DY
Tel: 0191-526 9195 **Fax:** 0191-526 9195
E-mail: john@fletcheruklimited.com
Website: http://www.fletcheruklimited.com
Directors: J. Fletcher (Co Sec)
Immediate Holding Company: FLETCHER (UK) LIMITED
Registration no: 03724036 **Date established:** 1999
Turnover: £500,000 - £1m **No.of Employees:** 1 - 10 **Product Groups:** 26

Date of Accounts	Mar 11	Mar 10	Mar 09
Working Capital	113	118	-10
Fixed Assets	197	200	210
Current Assets	172	276	137
Current Liabilities	N/A	N/A	52

Identec Ltd
Mercantile Road Rainton Bridge Industrial Estate, Houghton Le Spring, DH4 5PH
Tel: 0191-584 4084 **Fax:** 0191-584 9077
E-mail: info@identec.com
Website: http://www.identec.com
Directors: C. Owen (Sales)
Immediate Holding Company: IDENTEC LIMITED
Registration no: 03043507 **Date established:** 1995
Turnover: £500,000 - £1m **No.of Employees:** 1 - 10 **Product Groups:** 84

Date of Accounts	May 12	May 11	May 10
Working Capital	906	880	828
Fixed Assets	46	43	46
Current Assets	997	1m	982

Ivy House Conservatories
Taylors Farm Stoneygate, Houghton le Spring, DH4 4NL
Tel: 0191-511 0262 **Fax:** 0191-528 1928
Directors: J. Clark (Prop)
No.of Employees: 11 - 20 **Product Groups:** 08, 25, 35

J & N Steelcraft Ltd
Unit 2b Philadelphia Complex Philadelphia, Houghton Le Spring, DH4 4UG
Tel: 0191-512 1570
E-mail: info@jandnsteelcraft.co.uk
Website: http://www.jandnsteelcraft.co.uk
Directors: J. Massingham (MD)
Immediate Holding Company: J & N STEELCRAFT NE LTD
Registration no: 07861512 **Date established:** 2011
No.of Employees: 1 - 10 **Product Groups:** 34, 35, 52

Let Me Find It
30 South Market Street Hetton Le Hole, Hetton-le-hole, Houghton Le Spring, DH5 9DR
Tel: 0191-517 3997
E-mail: letmefinditltd@yahoo.co.uk
Directors: A. Trotter (Fin)
Registration no: 06229502 **Date established:** 2007
Turnover: Up to £250,000 **No.of Employees:** 1 - 10 **Product Groups:** 52

Wessington Cryogenics Ltd
2 Gadwall Road, Houghton le Spring, DH4 5NL
Tel: 0191-512 0677 **Fax:** 0191-512 0745
E-mail: info@wessingtoncryogenics.com
Website: http://www.wessingtoncryogenics.co.uk
Bank(s): The Royal Bank of Scotland
Directors: P. Rowe (MD), G. Southern (Pers)
Managers: J. Graham (Sales Prom Mgr), P. Graham (Purch Mgr), D. Bell (Comptroller)
Immediate Holding Company: WESSINGTON CRYOGENICS LIMITED
Registration no: 01790882 **VAT No.:** GB 407 9581 29
Date established: 1984 **Turnover:** £5m - £10m
No.of Employees: 101 - 250 **Product Groups:** 35, 36, 38, 39, 40, 42, 48, 52, 84, 85

Date of Accounts	Jun 11	Jun 10	Jun 09
Sales Turnover	10m	8m	9m
Pre Tax Profit/Loss	200	245	326
Working Capital	1m	805	738
Fixed Assets	513	559	410
Current Assets	4m	4m	3m
Current Liabilities	1m	1m	908

Jarrow

AHL Pipe Work Ltd
22 Royal Industrial Estate, Jarrow, NE32 3HR
Tel: 0191-428 0282 **Fax:** 0191-483 8893
E-mail: info@ahlpipework.co.uk
Website: http://www.ahlpipework.co.uk
Bank(s): HSBC Bank plc
Directors: M. Hepple (Chief Op Offcr)
Managers: K. Adams (Chief Acct)
Immediate Holding Company: AHL INDUSTRIAL PIPEWORK SPECIALISTS LTD
Registration no: 02354426 **VAT No.:** GB 532 6052 72
Date established: 1989 **Turnover:** £2m - £5m **No.of Employees:** 11 - 20
Product Groups: 35, 48

Date of Accounts	Apr 12	Apr 11	Apr 10
Working Capital	483	414	431
Fixed Assets	11	13	15
Current Assets	734	589	535

Alarm Supplies Scotland
Unit 48a Cuthbert Court Bede Trading Estate, Jarrow, NE32 3EG
Tel: 0191-483 5800 **Fax:** 0191-483 9950
E-mail: maria@alarm-supplies.com
Website: http://www.alarm-supplies.com
Managers: M. Driver (Mgr)
No.of Employees: 1 - 10 **Product Groups:** 37, 38, 44

B B S Rooflight Co. Ltd
Unit 19 Bede Trading Estate, Jarrow, NE32 3HG
Tel: 0191-489 0960 **Fax:** 0191-489 2303
E-mail: david.thompson@bbsrooflights.co.uk
Website: http://www.bbsrooflights.co.uk
Directors: D. Thompson (Dir)
Ultimate Holding Company: FOUR QUARTERS LIMITED
Immediate Holding Company: BBS ROOFLIGHT COMPANY LIMITED
Registration no: 01882454 **Date established:** 1985
No.of Employees: 11 - 20 **Product Groups:** 35

Date of Accounts	Oct 11	Oct 10	Oct 09
Working Capital	-123	-134	-71
Fixed Assets	10	14	19
Current Assets	69	320	83

B D A Enterprises Ltd
109 Leicester Way, Jarrow, NE32 4XT
Tel: 0191-489 2700 **Fax:** 0191-489 2701
E-mail: sales@bdaltd.com
Website: http://www.bda-ltd.com
Directors: S. Little (MD)
Immediate Holding Company: BDA ENTERPRISES LIMITED
Registration no: 04712023 **Date established:** 2003
No.of Employees: 1 - 10 **Product Groups:** 37, 38, 40

Date of Accounts	Mar 11	Mar 10	Mar 09
Working Capital	28	26	28
Current Assets	49	50	45

Diamond Drilling & Cutting Ltd
Unit 13 Bladen Street Industrial Estate, Jarrow, NE32 3HN
Tel: 0191-428 5566 **Fax:** 0191-428 5577
E-mail: enquiries@diamonddriller.co.uk
Website: http://www.diamonddriller.co.uk
Directors: J. McDonnell (Fin), K. Ward (MD)
Immediate Holding Company: DIAMOND DRILLING AND CUTTING LIMITED
Registration no: 03546183 **Date established:** 1998
Turnover: £500,000 - £1m **No.of Employees:** 11 - 20 **Product Groups:** 51

Date of Accounts	Aug 11	Aug 10	Aug 09
Working Capital	4	-1	-21
Fixed Assets	116	139	136
Current Assets	243	231	234

G P Engineering Ltd
21 Royal Industrial Estate, Jarrow, NE32 3HR
Tel: 0191-430 1334 **Fax:** 0191-430 1336
E-mail: petergpeng@aol.com
Directors: P. Bainbridge (MD)
Immediate Holding Company: G P ENGINEERING LTD
Registration no: 04599256 **Date established:** 2002
Turnover: Up to £250,000 **No.of Employees:** 1 - 10 **Product Groups:** 46

Date of Accounts	Dec 11	Dec 10	Dec 09
Sales Turnover	N/A	N/A	215
Pre Tax Profit/Loss	N/A	N/A	33
Working Capital	2	-2	-11
Fixed Assets	12	14	17
Current Assets	36	26	30
Current Liabilities	N/A	N/A	29

H V R International Ltd
Bede Trading Estate, Jarrow, NE32 3EN
Tel: 0191-489 7771 **Fax:** 0191-483 9501
E-mail: sales@hvrint.com
Website: http://www.hvrint.com
Directors: S. Elliott (Sales & Mktg), A. Wilson (MD), J. Ketchin (Fin)
Managers: G. Bullha (Purch Mgr), L. Elves (Personnel), M. Relph (Tech Serv Mgr), M. Relph (I.T. Exec)
Ultimate Holding Company: HVR LIMITED
Immediate Holding Company: HVR LIMITED
Registration no: 06381232 **VAT No.:** GB 569 5215 12
Date established: 2007 **Turnover:** £10m - £20m
No.of Employees: 101 - 250 **Product Groups:** 37

Date of Accounts	May 11	May 10	May 09
Sales Turnover	10m	11m	9m
Pre Tax Profit/Loss	2m	2m	2m
Working Capital	4m	3m	3m
Fixed Assets	2m	2m	2m
Current Assets	5m	5m	4m
Current Liabilities	996	1m	996

Safe-Line Marine After Sales Ltd
24 Royal Industrial Estate, Jarrow, NE32 3HR
Tel: 0191-423 4343 **Fax:** 0191-423 4346
E-mail: sharonhope@safe-line.co.uk
Website: http://www.safe-line.co.uk
Managers: S. Hope (Sales Admin)
Immediate Holding Company: SAFE-LINE MARINE AFTER SALES LTD
Registration no: 04815363 **Date established:** 2003
No.of Employees: 11 - 20 **Product Groups:** 35, 36, 39

Date of Accounts	Jun 11	Jun 10	Jun 09
Working Capital	516	464	422
Fixed Assets	33	28	13
Current Assets	679	678	582

Smartspeed Consulting Limited
Tedco Business Centre Viking Industrial Park, Jarrow, NE32 3DT
Tel: 0191-428 3386 **Fax:** 0844-4435794
E-mail: info@smartspeed.co.uk
Website: http://www.smartspeed.co.uk
Directors: G. Johnston (Dir)
Registration no: 06063450 **Date established:** 2005
Turnover: Up to £250,000 **No.of Employees:** 1 - 10 **Product Groups:** 80

Date of Accounts	Jan 09	Jan 08
Working Capital	8	1
Fixed Assets	9	10
Current Assets	17	9

Newcastle upon Tyne

A R U P
Central Square Forth Street, Newcastle upon Tyne, NE1 3PL
Tel: 0191-261 6080 **Fax:** 0191-261 7879
E-mail: newcastle@arup.com
Website: http://www.arup.com
Directors: A. Balmer (Pers)
Immediate Holding Company: ARUP GROUP LTD
Registration no: SC062237 **No.of Employees:** 101 - 250
Product Groups: 84

Absolute Security
Unit 18 Westerhope Small Business Park Redburn Road, Newcastle upon Tyne, NE5 1NF
Tel: 0191-214 5555
Directors: T. Davison (Prop), T. Davis (Prop)
Immediate Holding Company: CANVAS CITYS LTD
Registration no: OC328938 **Date established:** 2011
Turnover: Up to £250,000 **No.of Employees:** 1 - 10 **Product Groups:** 35, 46, 49

Accommodations UK
Principal House 5 Back Grove Avenue, Gosforth, Newcastle upon Tyne, NE3 1NT
Tel: 0191-213 2131 **Fax:** 0191-213 2211
E-mail: book@accommodationsuk.co.uk
Website: http://www.accommodationsuk.co.uk
Managers: L. Gannie (Mgr)
Immediate Holding Company: TILL SERVICES LIMITED
Registration no: 03314148 **VAT No.:** GB 556 1046 54
Date established: 2006 **Turnover:** £500,000 - £1m
No.of Employees: 1 - 10 **Product Groups:** 69

Date of Accounts	Aug 11	Aug 10	Aug 09
Working Capital	3	13	11
Fixed Assets	4	3	1
Current Assets	25	43	56

Ainsworth Spark Associates
9 Summerhill Terrace, Newcastle upon Tyne, NE4 6EB
Tel: 0191-232 3434 **Fax:** 0191-261 0628
E-mail: architect@ainsworthspark.com
Website: http://www.ainsworthspark.com
Directors: W. Ainsworth (Snr Part)
VAT No.: GB 177 2626 43 **Date established:** 1965 **Turnover:** £2m - £5m
No.of Employees: 1 - 10 **Product Groups:** 84

Airite Designs North East Ltd
97 Front Street Whickham, Newcastle upon Tyne, NE16 4JL
Tel: 0191-488 5955 **Fax:** 0191-488 0049
E-mail: airitedesigns@tiscali.co.uk
Website: http://www.airitebuildingservicesengineers.co.uk
Directors: C. Dixon (Dir)
Ultimate Holding Company: RACERPRESS LIMITED
Immediate Holding Company: AIRITE DESIGNS NORTH EAST LIMITED
Registration no: 00995942 **VAT No.:** GB 177 1529 46
Date established: 1970 **Turnover:** £1m - £2m **No.of Employees:** 1 - 10
Product Groups: 52

Date of Accounts	Dec 11	Dec 10	Dec 09
Working Capital	30	28	44
Fixed Assets	7	9	12
Current Assets	109	110	99

Amecal
Met-Cal House Fisher Street, Newcastle upon Tyne, NE6 4LT
Tel: 0191-262 2266 **Fax:** 0191-262 6622
E-mail: sales@amecal.com
Website: http://www.amecal.com
Managers: D. Heppell (Chief Mgr)
Immediate Holding Company: AEROSPACE METROLOGY & ELECTROMECHANICAL CALIBRATION LIMITED
Registration no: 04612748 **Date established:** 2004
Turnover: £250,000 - £500,000 **No.of Employees:** 1 - 10
Product Groups: 31, 37, 38, 44, 67, 85

Date of Accounts	Apr 12	Apr 11	Apr 10
Working Capital	39	20	-8
Fixed Assets	63	42	50
Current Assets	182	116	68

Antalis Mcnaughton
Wesley Way Benton Square Industrial Estate, Newcastle Upon Tyne, NE12 9TA
Tel: 0191-200 3232 **Fax:** 0191-200 3289
E-mail: jxs@antalis.co.uk
Bank(s): Midland
Managers: T. Dodds (District Mgr)
Immediate Holding Company: DATASTOR (NORTH EAST) LIMITED
Registration no: NF003153 **Date established:** 2002
Turnover: £20m - £50m **No.of Employees:** 21 - 50 **Product Groups:** 66

Date of Accounts	Dec 11	Dec 10	Dec 09
Sales Turnover	451m	393m	256m
Pre Tax Profit/Loss	-1m	-6m	-11m
Working Capital	40m	44m	-21m
Fixed Assets	525	8m	37m
Current Assets	140m	161m	121m
Current Liabilities	14m	11m	43m

Aon Ltd
Fourth Floor Hadrian House Higham Place, Newcastle upon Tyne, NE1 8AF
Tel: 0191-220 3333 **Fax:** 0191-232 8232
E-mail: graeme.cant@aon.co.uk
Website: http://www.aon.com
Bank(s): National Westminster Bank Plc
Managers: G. Carson (District Mgr)
Ultimate Holding Company: AON CORPORATION INC (USA)
Immediate Holding Company: A1 VENTURES LIMITED
Registration no: 04578543 **Date established:** 2002
No.of Employees: 11 - 20 **Product Groups:** 82

Date of Accounts	Dec 11	Dec 10	Dec 09
Sales Turnover	669m	640m	646m
Pre Tax Profit/Loss	140m	100m	28m
Working Capital	537m	591m	540m
Fixed Assets	141m	148m	156m
Current Assets	5145m	5612m	5565m
Current Liabilities	4455m	4790m	4866m

Applaud Web Solutions Ltd
15 Brenkley Way Blezard Business Park, Newcastle upon Tyne, NE13 6DS
Tel: 0845-5042902 **Fax:** 0870-766 8570
E-mail: info@applaud.uk.com
Website: http://www.applaud.uk.com
Managers: C. Tawse (Sales Prom)
Registration no: 04263555 **Date established:** 2001
No.of Employees: 1 - 10 **Product Groups:** 44

Autosounds Ltd
Scotswood Road, Newcastle upon Tyne, NE4 7AP
Tel: 0191-273 6100 **Fax:** 0191-272 3383
E-mail: sales@autosounds.co.uk
Website: http://www.autosounds.co.uk
Directors: S. Coates (Dir)
Managers: K. Robinson (Fin Mgr), I. Hunter (Sales Prom Mgr)
Immediate Holding Company: SUNGOLD AUTOSOUNDS LIMITED
Registration no: 01627920 **Date established:** 1982
No.of Employees: 1 - 10 **Product Groups:** 37

Date of Accounts	Jun 11	Jun 10	Jun 09
Working Capital	-83	-57	-35
Fixed Assets	217	235	254
Current Assets	142	127	201

Baileys Blinds Ltd
Unit 8 Jupiter Court Orion Way, Newcastle Upon Tyne, NE12 9SD
Tel: 0191-258 5956 **Fax:** 0191-266 8993
E-mail: sales@baileys-blinds.co.uk
Website: http://www.baileys-blinds.co.uk
Directors: A. Blainey (MD)
Ultimate Holding Company: CREST PROPERTIES (SCOTLAND) LTD.
Immediate Holding Company: BAILEYS BLINDS LIMITED
Registration no: 02814869 **VAT No.:** GB 621 1236 92
Date established: 1993 **No.of Employees:** 1 - 10 **Product Groups:** 24, 25, 35

Date of Accounts	Aug 11	Aug 10	Aug 09
Working Capital	-314	-293	-228
Fixed Assets	94	53	91

Current Assets	953	915	715

Baker Tilly
1 St James Gate, Newcastle Upon Tyne, NE1 4AD
Tel: 0191-255 7000 **Fax:** 0191-281 6147
E-mail: david.charlton@thecwp.co.uk
Website: http://www.thecwp.co.uk
Directors: D. Charlton (Ptnr)
Ultimate Holding Company: BAKER TILLY UK HOLDINGS LTD
Immediate Holding Company: THE CHARLTON WILLIAMSON PARTNERSHIP LLP
Registration no: OC318549 **VAT No.:** GB 297 771 84
Date established: 2006 **Turnover:** £1m - £2m **No.of Employees:** 51 - 100
Product Groups: 80

Date of Accounts	Mar 10	Mar 09	Mar 08
Working Capital	241	328	476
Fixed Assets	N/A	8	1
Current Assets	435	556	600

Bell Truck Sales Ltd
Bellway Industrial Estate Whitley Road, Longbenton, Newcastle Upon Tyne, NE12 9SW
Tel: 0191-270 0787 **Fax:** 0191-266 4780
E-mail: info@belltruckandvan.co.uk
Website: http://www.belltruckandvan.co.uk
Directors: T. Simmons (MD)
Ultimate Holding Company: BELL TRUCKS (HOLDINGS) LIMITED
Immediate Holding Company: BELL TRUCK SALES LIMITED
Registration no: 01125690 **Date established:** 1973
Turnover: £20m - £50m **No.of Employees:** 51 - 100 **Product Groups:** 39

Date of Accounts	Dec 11	Dec 10	Dec 09
Sales Turnover	47m	44m	35m
Pre Tax Profit/Loss	152	207	-218
Working Capital	526	379	83
Fixed Assets	915	989	1m
Current Assets	18m	18m	10m
Current Liabilities	1m	1m	1m

Bellway PLC
Seaton Burn House Dudley Lane, Seaton Burn, Newcastle upon Tyne, NE13 6BE
Tel: 0191-217 0717 **Fax:** 0191-236 6230
E-mail: peter.johnson@bellway.co.uk
Website: http://www.bellway.co.uk
Bank(s): Barclays, HSBC, Bank of Scotland
Directors: P. Johnson (Dir), G. Wrightson (Co Sec), K. Adey (Fin), K. Wrightson (Co Sec)
Managers: M. Seed (Sales & Mktg Mg), I. Cryer (Purch Mgr)
Ultimate Holding Company: BELLWAY P L C
Immediate Holding Company: BELLWAY P L C
Registration no: 01372603 **VAT No.:** GB 176 6854 16
Date established: 1978 **Turnover:** £500m - £1,000m
No.of Employees: 21 - 50 **Product Groups:** 52

Date of Accounts	Jul 11	Jul 10	Jul 09
Sales Turnover	886m	768m	684m
Pre Tax Profit/Loss	67m	44m	-37m
Working Capital	1143m	1112m	1060m
Fixed Assets	55m	52m	44m
Current Assets	1416m	1340m	1306m
Current Liabilities	178m	161m	194m

Benfield Motor Group
Leopard House Asama Court, Newcastle Business Park, Newcastle Upon Tyne, NE4 7YD
Tel: 0191-298 1400 **Fax:** 0191-272 4855
E-mail: enquiries@benfieldmotorgroup.com
Website: http://www.drivebenfield.com
Bank(s): National Westminster Bank Plc
Directors: N. Mcminn (MD)
Ultimate Holding Company: ADDISON MOTORS LIMITED
Immediate Holding Company: BENFIELD MOTOR GROUP LIMITED
Registration no: 06844413 **Date established:** 2009
Turnover: £250m - £500m **No.of Employees:** 101 - 250
Product Groups: 68

C A Blatchford & Sons Ltd
Freeman Road, Newcastle upon Tyne, NE7 7AF
Tel: 0191-285 8659 **Fax:** 0191-284 3791
E-mail: bposnewcastle@blatchford.co.uk
Website: http://www.blatchford.co.uk
Managers: K. Dowling (Mgr)
No.of Employees: 21 - 50 **Product Groups:** 38, 67

Bob Crosby Agencies Ltd
Crosby House Field Close, Shieldfield, Newcastle Upon Tyne, NE2 1AE
Tel: 0191-209 8000 **Fax:** 0191-209 8001
E-mail: roger@crosbys.co.uk
Website: http://www.crosbys.co.uk
Directors: R. Crosby (MD), J. Crosby (Fin)
Immediate Holding Company: BOB CROSBY AGENCIES LIMITED
Registration no: 04185475 **Date established:** 2001
No.of Employees: 11 - 20 **Product Groups:** 36, 63, 67

Date of Accounts	Mar 12	Mar 11	Mar 10
Working Capital	10	-7	-25
Fixed Assets	177	154	162
Current Assets	709	704	500

Bolton Bros Shoe & Appliance Makers Ltd
Bolton House Penn Street, Newcastle Upon Tyne, NE4 7BG
Tel: 0191-273 2012 **Fax:** 0191-226 0143
E-mail: info@bolton-bros.co.uk
Website: http://www.bolton-bros.co.uk
Directors: R. Sharpe (Co Sec), J. Bolton (MD)
Managers: S. Wilson (Chief Acct)
Immediate Holding Company: BOLTON BROS. (SURGICAL SHOE MAKERS) LIMITED
Registration no: 00510610 **Date established:** 1952
No.of Employees: 21 - 50 **Product Groups:** 38, 67

Date of Accounts	Mar 12	Mar 11	Mar 10
Working Capital	177	163	156
Fixed Assets	190	213	224
Current Assets	378	352	366

British Engines Ltd
St Peters, Newcastle Upon Tyne, NE6 1BS
Tel: 0191-265 9091 **Fax:** 0191-276 3244
E-mail: info@bel.co.uk
Website: http://www.bel.co.uk
Bank(s): Bank of Scotland
Directors: G. Salvesen (Fin), N. Kirkride (MD)
Immediate Holding Company: BRITISH ENGINES LIMITED
Registration no: 07159707 **Date established:** 2010
Turnover: £75m - £125m **No.of Employees:** 501 - 1000
Product Groups: 36

Date of Accounts	Apr 11	Apr 12
Sales Turnover	97m	110m
Pre Tax Profit/Loss	8m	9m
Working Capital	15m	15m
Fixed Assets	37m	38m
Current Assets	39m	41m
Current Liabilities	10m	10m

Ceramic Tile Distributors Ltd
351 Shields Road, Newcastle Upon Tyne, NE6 2UD
Tel: 0191-276 1506 **Fax:** 0191-265 0663
E-mail: sales@ctdtiles.co.uk
Website: http://www.ctdtiles.co.uk
Directors: G. Carter (Fin), N. Holland (MD)
Managers: H. Hardy (Personnel), S. Mason (Purch Mgr)
Ultimate Holding Company: COMPAGNIE DE SAINT GOBAIN (FRANCE)
Immediate Holding Company: MAXON TILE DISTRIBUTORS LIMITED
Registration no: 01141254 **VAT No.:** GB 388 5326 11
Date established: 1973 **No.of Employees:** 101 - 250 **Product Groups:** 33

N H Chapman & Co. Ltd
Siesta House Market Street, Newcastle upon Tyne, NE1 6NA
Tel: 0191-232 7628 **Fax:** 0191-232 7627
E-mail: enquiries@chapmansfurniture.co.uk
Website: http://www.chapmansfurniture.co.uk
Directors: J. Chapman (Dir)
Immediate Holding Company: N.H.CHAPMAN AND COMPANY LIMITED
Registration no: 00252240 **Date established:** 1930 **Turnover:** £2m - £5m
No.of Employees: 21 - 50 **Product Groups:** 61

Date of Accounts	Jan 11	Jan 10	Jan 09
Working Capital	419	614	806
Fixed Assets	24	32	77
Current Assets	1m	1m	2m
Current Liabilities	N/A	N/A	766

Charlton & Co.
14 Roseworth Crescent, Newcastle Upon Tyne, NE3 1NR
Tel: 0191-213 2109 **Fax:** 0191-284 2178
E-mail: mcharlton@charltonco.uk.com
Website: http://www.charltonco.uk.com
Directors: M. Charlton (Prop)
Date established: 1983 **No.of Employees:** 1 - 10 **Product Groups:** 36, 37, 38

Chemplas Ltd
Triskell House Brunswick Industrial Estate, Brunswick Village, Newcastle Upon Tyne, NE13 7BA
Tel: 0191-217 0700 **Fax:** 0191-217 0440
E-mail: mail@chemplas.co.uk
Website: http://www.chemplas.co.uk
Directors: D. Stone (Fin), A. Stone (MD)
Immediate Holding Company: CHEMPLAS LIMITED
Registration no: 00982241 **VAT No.:** GB 176 0970 44
Date established: 1970 **Turnover:** £500,000 - £1m
No.of Employees: 11 - 20 **Product Groups:** 52

Date of Accounts	Jul 11	Jul 10	Jul 09
Working Capital	713	611	575
Fixed Assets	67	73	88
Current Assets	3m	4m	3m

Convergys Customer Management Ltd
Central Square Forth Street, Newcastle Upon Tyne, NE1 3PJ
Tel: 0191-233 3000 **Fax:** 0191-233 3001
Website: http://www.convergys.com
Directors: W. Zimmer Iii (Fin)
Managers: B. Edwards (Mgr), S. Wilson ()
Immediate Holding Company: CONVERGYS CUSTOMER MANAGEMENT INTERNATIONAL INC.
Registration no: FC020515 **Date established:** 1997
Turnover: Over £1,000m **No.of Employees:** 1 - 10 **Product Groups:** 80

Corenso (UK) Ltd
North Tyne Industrial Estate Whitley Road, Longbenton, Newcastle Upon Tyne, NE12 9SZ
Tel: 0191-266 0222 **Fax:** 0191-270 1663
Website: http://www.corenso.com
Directors: J. Reeves (MD), K. Humes (Dir)
Managers: P. Slater (I.T. Exec), R. Malone, W. Hall (Site Co-ord), S. Doyle (Sales Admin)
Ultimate Holding Company: DNR LIMITED
Immediate Holding Company: Stora Enso
Registration no: 02010900 **Date established:** 1993
Turnover: £10m - £20m **No.of Employees:** 21 - 50 **Product Groups:** 27

County House
12 Westmorland Road, Newcastle upon Tyne, NE1 4EG
Tel: 0191-261 6669 **Fax:** 0191-261 9996
Website: http://www.thecountyhouse.co.uk
Directors: P. Crompton (Prop)
Date established: 2000 **No.of Employees:** 1 - 10 **Product Groups:** 36, 39, 40

Crossling
PO Box 5, Newcastle Upon Tyne, NE6 5TP
Tel: 0191-265 4166 **Fax:** 0191-276 4839
E-mail: sales@crossling.co.uk
Website: http://www.crossling.co.uk
Bank(s): Lloyds TSB Bank plc
Directors: C. Errington (Sales), K. Clifford (Fin), R. Errington (MD)
Managers: J. McKey (Tech Serv Mgr), S. Nolan (Grp Purch Mgr), S. Thouret (Mktg Serv Mgr)
Ultimate Holding Company: T. CROSSLING & CO. LIMITED
Immediate Holding Company: CROSSLING LIMITED
Registration no: 00107189 **Date established:** 2010
Turnover: £50m - £75m **No.of Employees:** 101 - 250
Product Groups: 30, 33

Date of Accounts	Dec 11	Dec 10	Dec 09
Sales Turnover	61m	65m	61m
Pre Tax Profit/Loss	2m	1m	645
Working Capital	18m	17m	16m
Fixed Assets	1m	2m	1m
Current Assets	23m	23m	22m
Current Liabilities	1m	1m	874

Crown Speciality Packaging
Edgefield Avenue Fawdon, Newcastle upon Tyne, NE3 3TS
Tel: 0191-285 8168 **Fax:** 0191-284 7570
E-mail: kevin.hall@eur.crowncork.com
Website: http://www.eur.crowncork.com
Managers: D. Hodge (Fin Mgr), K. Hall (Plant)
Ultimate Holding Company: CARNAUD METALBOX S.A.
Immediate Holding Company: CARNAUD METALBOX SPECIALITY PACKAGING EUROPE
Registration no: 02398420 **Turnover:** £10m - £20m
No.of Employees: 51 - 100 **Product Groups:** 34

D P C Screeding Ltd
Brunswick Industrial Estate Brunswick Village, Newcastle Upon Tyne, NE13 7BA
Tel: 0191-236 4226 **Fax:** 0191-236 2242
E-mail: dpcscreeding@btconnect.com
Website: http://www.decorativeplastercompany.com
Directors: B. Hunter (MD)
Immediate Holding Company: D.P.C. (SCREEDING) LIMITED
Registration no: 01852886 **Date established:** 1984
Turnover: £500,000 - £1m **No.of Employees:** 1 - 10 **Product Groups:** 52

Date of Accounts	Dec 11	Dec 10	Dec 09
Working Capital	229	236	256
Fixed Assets	58	73	92
Current Assets	306	357	377

Stan Dawson Ltd
Kirkley Sawmills Kirkley, Newcastle upon Tyne, NE20 0BD
Tel: 01661-860413 **Fax:** 01661-822352
E-mail: anne.dawson@kirkley.org
Directors: G. Dawson (MD)
Immediate Holding Company: STAN DAWSON LIMITED
Registration no: 01581893 **VAT No.:** 297 6702 11 **Date established:** 1981
Turnover: £250,000 - £500,000 **No.of Employees:** 1 - 10
Product Groups: 66

Date of Accounts	Nov 11	Nov 10	Nov 09
Working Capital	104	81	159
Fixed Assets	224	243	161
Current Assets	263	270	345
Current Liabilities	131	N/A	N/A

The Design Group
Mill House Haddricks Mill Road, Newcastle upon Tyne, NE3 1QL
Tel: 0191-284 5334 **Fax:** 0191-284 0772
E-mail: reception@tdgbrand.com
Website: http://www.thedesigngroup.co.uk
Bank(s): Barclays
Directors: J. Halls (Fin), J. Hall (MD), A. Quinn (Sales)
Registration no: 04944810 **VAT No.:** GB 176 1178 55
Date established: 2003 **Turnover:** £2m - £5m **No.of Employees:** 21 - 50
Product Groups: 81

Date of Accounts	Dec 07	Dec 06	Dec 05
Sales Turnover	N/A	4444	5250
Pre Tax Profit/Loss	-262	-279	148
Working Capital	623	1101	1006
Fixed Assets	1318	1384	1402
Current Assets	1565	2138	2600
Current Liabilities	942	1037	1595
Total Share Capital	14	14	14
ROCE% (Return on Capital Employed)	-13.5	-11.2	6.1
ROT% (Return on Turnover)		-6.3	2.8

Elanders
Unit B Merlin Way, New York Industrial Park, Newcastle upon Tyne, NE27 0QG
Tel: 0191-280 0400 **Fax:** 0191-280 0401
E-mail: uk-sales@elanders.com
Website: http://www.elanders.com
Directors: K. Rogers (MD), P. Jacques (Fin)
Ultimate Holding Company: ELANDERS AB (SWEDEN)
Immediate Holding Company: ELANDERS LTD
Registration no: 03788582 **VAT No.:** GB 175 9426 28
Date established: 1999 **Turnover:** £10m - £20m
No.of Employees: 101 - 250 **Product Groups:** 28, 44

Date of Accounts	Dec 11	Dec 10	Dec 09
Sales Turnover	17m	17m	17m
Pre Tax Profit/Loss	375	481	349
Working Capital	4m	3m	2m
Fixed Assets	3m	3m	4m
Current Assets	11m	6m	5m
Current Liabilities	510	520	647

Engineering Support Partnership Ltd
Office Unit 13 Quay Level St Peters Wharf, Newcastle Upon Tyne, NE6 1TZ
Tel: 0191-265 4400 **Fax:** 0191-265 5500
E-mail: enquiries@espprojects.com
Website: http://www.espprojects.com
Directors: D. Lord (Ch)
Managers: K. Nelson (Chief Mgr), D. Short (Sales Prom Mgr)
Immediate Holding Company: ENGINEERING SUPPORT PARTNERSHIP LTD.
Registration no: 02887201 **Date established:** 1994
Turnover: £250,000 - £500,000 **No.of Employees:** 1 - 10
Product Groups: 37, 44, 54, 80, 84

Date of Accounts	Sep 11	Sep 10	Sep 09
Working Capital	62	33	109
Fixed Assets	46	52	60
Current Assets	144	120	289

Enigma Interactive Ltd
Quayside Studios 8-10 Close, Newcastle upon Tyne, NE1 3RE
Tel: 0191-261 2991 **Fax:** 0191-261 2378
E-mail: info@enigma-interactive.co.uk
Website: http://www.enigma-interactive.co.uk
Directors: S. Grainger (MD), J. Grainger (Fin)
Managers: Z. Harthill (Develop Mgr)
Immediate Holding Company: ENIGMA INTERACTIVE LIMITED
Registration no: 03360519 **Date established:** 1997
Turnover: £500,000 - £1m **No.of Employees:** 21 - 50 **Product Groups:** 44

Date of Accounts	Apr 11	Apr 10	Apr 09
Working Capital	399	391	405
Fixed Assets	18	22	24
Current Assets	787	508	878

Entec UK Ltd
Northumbria House Regent Centre, Gosforth, Newcastle upon Tyne, NE3 3PX
Tel: 0191-272 6100 **Fax:** 0191-272 6592
E-mail: reardons@entecuk.co.uk
Website: http://www.entecuk.com
Directors: S. Armes Reardon (Dir), S. Armes-Reardon (MD)
Managers: F. Corsi (Mktg Serv Mgr)
Ultimate Holding Company: 01675285
Immediate Holding Company: AMEC ENVIRONMENT & INFRASTRUCTURE UK LIMITED
Registration no: 02190074 **VAT No.:** GB 652 1693 37
Date established: 1987 **Turnover:** £50m - £75m
No.of Employees: 501 - 1000 **Product Groups:** 54, 84, 85

Date of Accounts	Mar 10	Mar 09	Mar 08
Sales Turnover	56m	64m	61m
Pre Tax Profit/Loss	7m	9m	9m
Working Capital	29m	23m	30m
Fixed Assets	2m	2m	2m
Current Assets	38m	34m	43m
Current Liabilities	6m	8m	9m

Entek International
Mylord Crescent, Newcastle Upon Tyne, NE12 5XG
Tel: 0191-268 5054 **Fax:** 0191-268 8917
E-mail: contact@entek-international.com
Website: http://www.entek-international.com
Bank(s): Lloyds
Directors: M. Lee (MD)
Ultimate Holding Company: MEMBRANE HOLDINGS LLC (UNITED STATES OF AMERICA)
Immediate Holding Company: ENTEK INTERNATIONAL LIMITED
Registration no: 02272415 **VAT No.:** GB 499 7950 56
Date established: 1988 **Turnover:** £20m - £50m
No.of Employees: 101 - 250 **Product Groups:** 30

Date of Accounts	Dec 11	Dec 10	Dec 09
Sales Turnover	44m	46m	31m
Pre Tax Profit/Loss	11m	14m	6m
Working Capital	18m	10m	7m
Fixed Assets	19m	18m	20m
Current Assets	23m	15m	14m
Current Liabilities	2m	3m	2m

Eriks Industrial Services (Newcastle Electro Mechanical)
Mylord Cresent Camperdown Industrial Estate, Newcastle Upon Tyne, NE12 5SN
Tel: 0191-268 2313 **Fax:** 0191-216 0625
E-mail: neilwilkinson@eriks.co.uk
Website: http://www.eriks.co.uk
Managers: N. Wilkinson (District Mgr)
No.of Employees: 21 - 50 **Product Groups:** 35

Eversheds
Central Square South Orchard Street, Newcastle upon Tyne, NE1 3XX
Tel: 08454-979797 **Fax:** 0191-241 6499
E-mail: newcastle@eversheds.com
Website: http://www.eversheds.com
Directors: A. Stanley (Snr Part)
Immediate Holding Company: IS WYNYARD LIMITED LIABILITY PARTNERSHIP
Registration no: OC304065 **Date established:** 2003 **Turnover:** £1m - £2m
No.of Employees: 251 - 500 **Product Groups:** 80

Date of Accounts	Mar 04
Working Capital	-76m
Current Liabilities	76m

Express Reinforcement Ltd
Hannington Works Longrigg, Swalwell, Newcastle Upon Tyne, NE16 3AS
Tel: 0191-495 6060 **Fax:** 0191-495 6078
E-mail: newcastle@expressreinforcements.co.uk
Website: http://www.expressreinforcements.co.uk
Bank(s): Lloyds TSB Bank plc
Managers: M. Ramsey (Chief Mgr)
Immediate Holding Company: Hill & Smith P.L.C.
Registration no: 01808624 **VAT No.:** GB 416 1407 05
Turnover: £2m - £5m **No.of Employees:** 21 - 50 **Product Groups:** 34

Express Sunshades
Unit 1 Georges Road, Newcastle Upon Tyne, NE4 7NQ
Tel: 0191-272 7474 **Fax:** 0191-228 0912
E-mail: info@express-sunshades.com
Website: http://www.express-sunshades.com
Directors: V. Linscott (Prop)
Managers: R. Cornell (Sales Prom Mgr)
No.of Employees: 1 - 10 **Product Groups:** 24, 35, 63

F M Steel Stock Ltd
Newburn Ford House Newburn Bridge Road, Newburn, Newcastle Upon Tyne, NE15 8NR
Tel: 0191-414 0505 **Fax:** 0191-414 0303
E-mail: sales@fmsteelstock.co.uk
Website: http://www.fmsteelstock.com
Directors: B. Maughan (Dir)
Immediate Holding Company: F.M. STEELSTOCK LIMITED
Registration no: 02089006 **VAT No.:** GB 454 9599 90
Date established: 1987 **Turnover:** £2m - £5m **No.of Employees:** 21 - 50
Product Groups: 34

Date of Accounts	Jan 12	Jan 11	Jan 10
Working Capital	640	709	711
Fixed Assets	229	121	140
Current Assets	2m	2m	1m

Fenwick Ltd
39 Northumberland Street, Newcastle Upon Tyne, NE1 7DE
Tel: 0191-232 5100 **Fax:** 0191-261 1164
E-mail: enquiries@fenwick.co.uk
Website: http://www.fenwick.co.uk
Directors: D. Quinn (MD)
Managers: J. Patterson
Immediate Holding Company: FENWICK,LIMITED
Registration no: 00052411 **Date established:** 1997
Turnover: £250m - £500m **No.of Employees:** 1 - 10 **Product Groups:** 61

Date of Accounts	Jan 10	Jan 09	Jan 08
Sales Turnover	290m	290m	283m
Pre Tax Profit/Loss	35m	36m	42m
Working Capital	164m	164m	176m
Fixed Assets	284m	268m	241m
Current Assets	203m	202m	217m
Current Liabilities	22m	19m	24m

Fife Engineering Co. Ltd
Longrigg Swalwell, Newcastle upon Tyne, NE16 3AW
Tel: 0191-496 1133 **Fax:** 0191-496 5502
E-mail: admin@fife-engineering.com
Website: http://www.fife-engineering.com
Bank(s): Barclays, Gateshead
Directors: R. Hogarth (MD), C. Rudd (Fin)
Immediate Holding Company: FIFE ENGINEERING COMPANY LIMITED
Registration no: SC033397 **VAT No.:** GB 176 0968 31
Date established: 1958 **Turnover:** £1m - £2m **No.of Employees:** 21 - 50
Product Groups: 29

Date of Accounts	Mar 11	Mar 10	Mar 09
Working Capital	953	851	898
Fixed Assets	282	298	315
Current Assets	1m	998	1m

Finlays Ltd
Office Suite 1 St Marys Green, Whickham, Newcastle upon Tyne, NE16 4DN
Tel: 0191-488 3144 **Fax:** 01833-638340
E-mail: m.raistick@btconnect.com
Website: http://www.finlays-newsagents.co.uk
Directors: M. Raistrick (Co Sec), W. Gandy (Dir)
Ultimate Holding Company: NEWS 77 LIMITED
Immediate Holding Company: FINLAYS (NORTH EAST) LIMITED
Registration no: 02674165 **VAT No.:** GB 605 3126 79
Date established: 1991 **Turnover:** £10m - £20m
No.of Employees: 101 - 250 **Product Groups:** 26

Date of Accounts	Mar 08	Mar 09	Mar 10
Sales Turnover	N/A	N/A	11m
Pre Tax Profit/Loss	30	58	10
Working Capital	-184	-160	224
Fixed Assets	1m	1m	929
Current Assets	1m	1m	2m
Current Liabilities	288	383	451

Fletcher Electrical Ltd
1 Mylord Crescent Camperdown Industrial Estate, Newcastle Upon Tyne, NE12 5UJ
Tel: 0191-216 0355 **Fax:** 0191-216 0033
E-mail: sfletcher@fletcher.uk.com
Website: http://www.fletcher.uk.com
Directors: S. Fletcher (Dir)
Immediate Holding Company: FLETCHER ECOLECTRICAL LIMITED
Registration no: 08077698 **VAT No.:** GB 176 4436 44
Date established: 2012 **No.of Employees:** 11 - 20 **Product Groups:** 52

Fleur De Lis Furnishing (a division of Fleur Interiors Ltd)
Unit 1 North Tyne Industrial Estate Whitley Road, Benton, Newcastle upon Tyne, NE12 9SZ
Tel: 0191-270 9758 **Fax:** 0191-270 9761
E-mail: garya@fleur-de-lis.co.uk
Website: http://www.fleurdelis.co.uk
Bank(s): HSBC Bank plc
Directors: G. Anderson (Fab), D. Holland (MD)
Managers: K. Bootes (Sales Prom Mgr), M. Southward (Mgr), G. Anderson (Mgr)
Immediate Holding Company: FLEUR-DE-LIS FABRICS LIMITED
Registration no: 07253358 **VAT No.:** GB 177 6724 23
Date established: 2010 **Turnover:** £2m - £5m **No.of Employees:** 21 - 50
Product Groups: 26

Forum Marketing
14 Lansdowne Terrace, Newcastle upon Tyne, NE3 1HN
Tel: 0191-226 8800 **Fax:** 0191-226 8822
E-mail: info@forummarketing.co.uk
Website: http://www.forummarketing.co.uk
Directors: K. Ling (Fin), P. Ling (Dir)
Immediate Holding Company: TYNE & WEAR BUILDING SERVICES LTD
Registration no: 02985910 **Date established:** 2012 **Turnover:** £1m - £2m
No.of Employees: 1 - 10 **Product Groups:** 81

Date of Accounts	Jan 12	Jan 11	Jan 10
Working Capital	73	7	59
Fixed Assets	2	1	1
Current Assets	434	363	321

Fresh Soap Deli
Bartons Building Moor Edge Road, Shiremoor, Newcastle upon Tyne, NE27 0HU
Tel: 0191-252 8300
Directors: S. Dunne (Dir)
Immediate Holding Company: RIDERS (NORTH EAST) LIMITED
Date established: 2003 **No.of Employees:** 1 - 10 **Product Groups:** 32, 63

Date of Accounts	Sep 10	Sep 09	Sep 08
Working Capital	-266	-281	-257
Fixed Assets	340	355	145
Current Assets	137	156	156

Freudenberg Technical Products LP
Unit 3 Merlin Way, New York Industrial Park, Newcastle upon Tyne, NE27 0QG
Tel: 0191-226 9200 **Fax:** 0191-226 9201
E-mail: michael.lawson@fst.com
Website: http://www.sia-abrasives.com
Directors: K. Britain (Mkt Research), M. Lawson (Fin)
Managers: J. Chapple (Mktg Serv Mgr), F. Follows (Purch Mgr), G. Hogarth (Personnel), B. King (Tech Serv Mgr)
Ultimate Holding Company: FREUDENBERG AND CO KG (GERMANY)
Immediate Holding Company: FREUDENBERG TECHNICAL PRODUCTS PENSION TRUST COMPANY LIMITED
Registration no: 02456097 **Date established:** 1989
No.of Employees: 101 - 250 **Product Groups:** 29, 63, 66

G P S Installations
Morgan Business Centre Mylord CR, Camperdown Industrial Estate, Newcastle Upon Tyne, NE12 5UJ
Tel: 0191-216 1200 **Fax:** 0191-216 1200
E-mail: sales@gpsinstallations.co.uk
Website: http://www.gpsinstallations.co.uk
Directors: G. Parks (Dir)
Immediate Holding Company: GPS INSTALLATIONS LTD
Registration no: 06590074 **Date established:** 2008
No.of Employees: 1 - 10 **Product Groups:** 40, 52

Gateland Northeast Ltd
Gradys Yard Ponteland Road, Throckley, Newcastle Upon Tyne, NE15 9EP
Tel: 0191-264 2519
Website: http://www.gateland.co.uk
Directors: K. Thomson (MD)
Immediate Holding Company: GATELAND (NORTH EAST) LIMITED
Registration no: 04657013 **Date established:** 2003
No.of Employees: 1 - 10 **Product Groups:** 35, 49

Date of Accounts	Feb 08	Feb 11	Feb 10
Working Capital	-16	5	-8
Fixed Assets	38	22	21
Current Assets	101	105	89

Geneve International
9a North Tyne Industrial Estate Whitley Road, Benton, Newcastle upon Tyne, NE12 9SZ
Tel: 0191-215 9911 **Fax:** 0191-215 9922
Website: http://www.geneve-international.co.uk
Registration no: 02026988 **No.of Employees:** 21 - 50
Product Groups: 32, 63

Gills Of Byker
33-43 Wilfred Street, Newcastle upon Tyne, NE6 1JQ
Tel: 0191-265 3559 **Fax:** 0191-265 3559
Directors: J. Gill (Ptnr)
Date established: 1956 **No.of Employees:** 1 - 10 **Product Groups:** 26, 35

Go-Ahead Group Pension Plan
41-51 Grey Street, Newcastle Upon Tyne, NE1 6EE
Tel: 0191-222 1444 **Fax:** 0191-221 0315
E-mail: admin@go-ahead.com
Website: http://www.go-ahead.com
Directors: C. Sephton (Co Sec)
Ultimate Holding Company: THE GO-AHEAD GROUP PLC
Immediate Holding Company: THE GO-AHEAD GROUP PLC
Registration no: 02100855 **Date established:** 1987
Turnover: Over £1,000m **No.of Employees:** 21 - 50 **Product Groups:** 71, 72

Date of Accounts	Jun 08	Jun 09	Jul 10
Sales Turnover	2199m	2187m	2202m
Pre Tax Profit/Loss	103m	910m	50m
Working Capital	-60m	-118m	-99m
Fixed Assets	590m	550m	558m
Current Assets	429m	430m	452m
Current Liabilities	281m	338m	282m

Greggs plc
Fernwood House Clayton Road, Newcastle upon Tyne, NE2 1TL
Tel: 0191-281 7721 **Fax:** 0191-281 1444
E-mail: roym@greggs.co.uk
Website: http://www.greggs.co.uk
Bank(s): National Westminster Bank Plc
Directors: J. Holmes (Tech Serv), R. Hutton (Fin), S. Jefferson (Mkt Research), R. Currie (Pers)
Managers: A. Honeyman, R. McDougall (I.T. Exec)
Ultimate Holding Company: GREGGS PLC
Immediate Holding Company: GREGGS PLC
Registration no: 00502851 **Date established:** 1951
Turnover: £500m - £1,000m **No.of Employees:** 51 - 100
Product Groups: 62

Date of Accounts	Dec 11	Dec 08	Jan 10
Sales Turnover	701m	628m	658m
Pre Tax Profit/Loss	61m	49m	49m
Working Capital	-25m	-35m	-14m
Fixed Assets	254m	211m	212m
Current Assets	55m	39m	68m
Current Liabilities	44m	45m	46m

Grosvenor Residential
Grosvenor Road, Newcastle upon Tyne, NE2 2RP
Tel: 0191-281 0543 **Fax:** 0191-240 2656
Website: http://www.grosvenor-residential.co.uk
Bank(s): HSBC Bank plc
Directors: S. Din (Prop)
VAT No.: GB 178 9451 4 **Turnover:** £250,000 - £500,000
No.of Employees: 11 - 20 **Product Groups:** 69

Harper Signs Ltd
12-20 Diana Street, Newcastle upon Tyne, NE4 6DA
Tel: 0191-232 4926 **Fax:** 0191-261 0676
E-mail: sales@harpersigns.co.uk
Website: http://www.harpersigns.co.uk
Bank(s): Barclays, Newcastle
Directors: W. Harper (Dir), K. Makepeace (Dir), W. Harper (MD), G. Harper (Ch & MD)
Managers: V. Frost (Accounts), V. Campion (Admin Off)
Immediate Holding Company: HARPER SIGNS LIMITED
Registration no: 01347995 **VAT No.:** GB 297 5766 87
Date established: 1978 **Turnover:** £1m - £2m **No.of Employees:** 21 - 50
Product Groups: 30, 37

Date of Accounts	Mar 11	Mar 10	Mar 09
Working Capital	397	404	520
Fixed Assets	36	54	65
Current Assets	708	621	733

Hart Door Systems
Redburn Road, Newcastle upon Tyne, NE5 1PJ
Tel: 0191-214 0404 **Fax:** 0191-271 1611
E-mail: doug@speedor.com
Website: http://www.speedor.com
Bank(s): Barclays
Directors: D. Hart (MD), C. Hart (Co Sec)
Immediate Holding Company: HART DOOR SYSTEMS LIMITED
Registration no: 00544631 **Date established:** 1955 **Turnover:** £2m - £5m
No.of Employees: 11 - 20 **Product Groups:** 35, 39, 48

Date of Accounts	Feb 08	Feb 11	Feb 10
Working Capital	2m	2m	2m
Fixed Assets	310	366	415
Current Assets	2m	2m	2m

hedgehog lab
Studio 12 & 13 The Kiln Hoults Yard Hoults Estates Walker Ro, Newcastle Upon Tyne, NE6 1AB
Tel: 0191-265 3101
E-mail: info@hedgehoglab.com
Website: http://www.hedgehoglab.com

Managers: P. Bevis
Immediate Holding Company: HEDGEHOG LAB LIMITED
Registration no: 05993194 **Date established:** 2006
Turnover: £250,000 - £500,000 **No.of Employees:** 11 - 20
Product Groups: 44

Date of Accounts	Apr 11	Apr 10	Apr 09
Working Capital	-18	-1	21
Fixed Assets	2	5	6
Current Assets	23	15	33

Hendersons

Eachwick Lodge Eachwick, Newcastle upon Tyne, NE18 0BL
Tel: 07779-107713 **Fax:** 01661-854155
E-mail: windows2clean@yahoo.co.uk
Directors: M. Henderson (Prop)
Immediate Holding Company: HENDERSON'S INN LIMITED
Registration no: 05190368 **Date established:** 2004
No.of Employees: 1 - 10 **Product Groups:** 25, 32, 52

Date of Accounts	Dec 11	Aug 11	Aug 09
Working Capital	-25	-8	12
Fixed Assets	N/A	44	52
Current Assets	5	34	65

High Integrity Products Group Ltd

Wincomblee Road Low Walker, Newcastle upon Tyne, NE6 3QQ
Tel: 0191-263 8686 **Fax:** 0191-262 6428
E-mail: info@integriti.co.uk
Website: http://www.hipg.co.uk
Directors: T. Townsley (MD)
Managers: A. Pollard (Mktg Serv Mgr), T. Moody (I.T. Exec)
Registration no: 00217605 **VAT No.:** GB 556 0842 35
Turnover: £2m - £5m **No.of Employees:** 21 - 50 **Product Groups:** 34, 48

Holywell Engineering Ltd

Station Road Shiremoor, Newcastle Upon Tyne, NE27 0AE
Tel: 0191-268 4365 **Fax:** 01665-712727
E-mail: eng@holywell.com
Website: http://www.holywel.com
Bank(s): HSBC Bank plc
Directors: A. Little (MD)
Immediate Holding Company: HOLYWELL ENGINEERING GROUP LIMITED
Registration no: 01017094 **Date established:** 1971 **Turnover:** £2m - £5m
No.of Employees: 11 - 20 **Product Groups:** 34, 40, 42, 45, 48

Date of Accounts	Dec 10	Dec 09
Working Capital	685	685
Current Assets	4m	4m

Horncastle Executive Travel Ltd

Hadrian House Higham Place, Newcastle Upon Tyne, NE1 8AF
Tel: 0191-222 1930 **Fax:** 0191-261 6440
E-mail: info@horncastle.co.uk
Website: http://www.horncastle.co.uk
Directors: P. Drummond (MD), C. Drummond (Fin)
Managers: B. Higgott (Tech Serv Mgr), S. Swift (Sales Prom)
Ultimate Holding Company: NORTHERN IKON LIMITED
Immediate Holding Company: HORNCASTLE EXECUTIVE TRAVEL LIMITED
Registration no: 00956609 **Date established:** 1969 **Turnover:** £5m - £10m
No.of Employees: 21 - 50 **Product Groups:** 80, 82

Date of Accounts	Jun 11	Jun 10	Jun 09
Working Capital	446	472	518
Fixed Assets	180	195	159
Current Assets	2m	2m	2m

HSS Hire

Union Road, Newcastle upon Tyne, NE6 1EH
Tel: 0191-224 0442 **Fax:** 0191-224 0185
Website: http://www.hss.com
Managers: G. Walker (Mgr)
Immediate Holding Company: VULCAN SERVICE & SUPPLY COMPANY LIMITED
Registration no: 03080799 **Date established:** 1995
No.of Employees: 1 - 10 **Product Groups:** 35, 67, 83

Date of Accounts	Jul 08	Jul 07	Jul 06
Working Capital	1	464	-4
Fixed Assets	2m	405	179
Current Assets	650	2m	300
Current Liabilities	N/A	219	N/A

Geoff Huntley Plant Ltd

Locomotion Way Camperdown Industrial Estate, Newcastle Upon Tyne, NE12 5US
Tel: 0191-216 0044 **Fax:** 0191-216 0062
E-mail: hire@huntleyplant.co.uk
Website: http://www.huntleyplant.co.uk
Directors: S. Huntley (Fin)
Managers: P. Smith (Ops Mgr)
Immediate Holding Company: GEOFF HUNTLEY PLANT LIMITED
Registration no: 02378955 **Date established:** 1989
No.of Employees: 21 - 50 **Product Groups:** 39, 40, 41, 45, 83

Date of Accounts	Jun 11	Jun 10	Jun 09
Working Capital	-325	-370	-267
Fixed Assets	2m	2m	2m
Current Assets	452	396	314

Integral UK Ltd

Norris House Crawhall Road, Newcastle Upon Tyne, NE1 2BB
Tel: 0191-261 1071 **Fax:** 0191-232 8069
E-mail: paul.dolan@integral.co.uk
Website: http://www.integral.co.uk
Bank(s): National Westminster Bank Plc
Directors: P. Salmons (Fin), P. Dolan (MD), M. Forbes (Pers)
Managers: M. Williams (Tech Serv Mgr)
Ultimate Holding Company: INTEGRAL UK HOLDINGS LIMITED
Immediate Holding Company: INTEGRAL UK LIMITED
Registration no: 05307588 **VAT No.:** GB 239 3550 53
Date established: 2004 **No.of Employees:** 11 - 20 **Product Groups:** 52

Date of Accounts	Dec 11	Dec 10	Dec 09
Sales Turnover	196m	175m	182m
Pre Tax Profit/Loss	9m	16m	9m
Working Capital	19m	14m	17m
Fixed Assets	773	701	N/A
Current Assets	73m	62m	51m
Current Liabilities	30m	26m	20m

iPRT Group Ltd

Iprt House 37 Swanton Close, Newcastle upon Tyne, NE5 4SL
Tel: 0871-9007456 **Fax:** 0871-9007432
E-mail: amer@iprtgroup.com
Website: http://www.iprtgroup.com
Directors: A. Waheed (Ch)
Registration no: 06897300 **Date established:** 1985 **Turnover:** £5m - £10m
No.of Employees: 21 - 50 **Product Groups:** 84

J & J Stanley Ltd

Longrigg Swalwell, Newcastle Upon Tyne, NE16 3AW
Tel: 0191-488 7387 **Fax:** 0191-488 2499
E-mail: gordon@jjstanley.co.uk
Website: http://www.jjstanley.co.uk
Directors: C. Stanley (Fin), G. Stanley (MD), D. Stanley (Fin)
Managers: S. Bartham (Admin Off)
Immediate Holding Company: J & J STANLEY LIMITED
Registration no: 01405928 **Date established:** 1978
Turnover: £10m - £20m **No.of Employees:** 21 - 50 **Product Groups:** 27, 29, 30, 33, 34, 38, 39, 42, 45, 48, 51, 54, 81

Date of Accounts	Mar 11	Mar 10	Mar 09
Sales Turnover	11m	7m	11m
Pre Tax Profit/Loss	311	-279	-113
Working Capital	-160	-164	-91
Fixed Assets	2m	2m	2m
Current Assets	2m	1m	2m
Current Liabilities	836	592	908

J & P Hardware Ltd

8 Invincible Drive Armstrong Industrial Park, Newcastle Upon Tyne, NE4 7HX
Tel: 0191-226 0476 **Fax:** 0191-226 0491
E-mail: info@jphardware.co.uk
Website: http://www.jphardware.co.uk
Directors: J. Boulding (Dir), S. Monaghan (Co Sec)
Ultimate Holding Company: JOHN MONAGHAN (HOLDINGS) LIMITED
Immediate Holding Company: J & P HARDWARE LIMITED
Registration no: 02911859 **Date established:** 1994
Turnover: £500,000 - £1m **No.of Employees:** 1 - 10 **Product Groups:** 30, 33, 35, 36, 66

Date of Accounts	Dec 11	Dec 10	Dec 09
Working Capital	139	171	169
Fixed Assets	15	12	19
Current Assets	191	197	202

J T Dove Ltd

Riversdale Way, Newcastle Upon Tyne, NE15 8SF
Tel: 0191-229 5020 **Fax:** 0191-222 1870
E-mail: steverobinson@jtdove.co.uk
Website: http://www.jtdove.co.uk
Bank(s): HSBC Bank plc
Directors: S. Robinson (MD)
Immediate Holding Company: J.T. DOVE PENSIONS TRUST LIMITED
Registration no: 00528300 **VAT No.:** GB 175 8280 35
Date established: 1954 **Turnover:** £20m - £50m
No.of Employees: 101 - 250 **Product Groups:** 30, 66, 83

Jebb Metals Newcastle Ltd

Station Road Walker, Newcastle Upon Tyne, NE6 3PN
Tel: 0191-262 7099 **Fax:** 0191-262 5458
E-mail: jebbmetals@btconnect.com
Website: http://www.jebbmetals.co.uk
Directors: J. Sheppard (Co Sec), P. Kenney (Dir), S. Kenney (Dir)
Immediate Holding Company: JEBB METALS (NEWCASTLE) LTD
Registration no: 01519167 **Date established:** 1980 **Turnover:** £2m - £5m
No.of Employees: 11 - 20 **Product Groups:** 66

Date of Accounts	Mar 11	Mar 10	Mar 09
Sales Turnover	11m	N/A	N/A
Pre Tax Profit/Loss	212	N/A	248
Working Capital	2m	2m	2m
Fixed Assets	500	518	589
Current Assets	3m	3m	2m
Current Liabilities	470	11	419

Jewson Ltd

Haddricks Mill Road, Newcastle Upon Tyne, NE3 1QL
Tel: 0191-284 6011 **Fax:** 0191-284 0660
Website: http://www.jewson.co.uk
Directors: P. Hindle (MD)
Managers: K. Richardson (District Mgr)
Ultimate Holding Company: COMPAGNIE DE SAINT GOBAIN (FRANCE)
Immediate Holding Company: JEWSON LIMITED
Registration no: 00348407 **VAT No.:** GB 497 7184 83
Date established: 1939 **Turnover:** £1m - £2m **No.of Employees:** 11 - 20
Product Groups: 66

Date of Accounts	Dec 11	Dec 10	Dec 09
Sales Turnover	1606m	1547m	1485m
Pre Tax Profit/Loss	18m	100m	45m
Working Capital	-345m	-250m	-349m
Fixed Assets	496m	387m	461m
Current Assets	657m	1005m	1320m
Current Liabilities	66m	120m	64m

Jobling Purser Ltd

Paradise Works Scotswood Road, Newcastle upon Tyne, NE15 6BZ
Tel: 0191-273 2331 **Fax:** 0191-226 0129
E-mail: info@joblingpurser.com
Website: http://www.joblingpurser.com
Bank(s): Barclays
Directors: J. McCeery (Fin), T. Jobling Purser (Ch)
Immediate Holding Company: JOBLING PURSER LIMITED
Registration no: 02681119 **VAT No.:** GB 556 1853 25
Date established: 1992 **No.of Employees:** 21 - 50 **Product Groups:** 29, 30, 31, 32, 48

Date of Accounts	Dec 11	Dec 10	Dec 09
Working Capital	300	300	300
Current Assets	300	300	300

John Mills & Son Newcastle Ltd

509 Shields Road, Newcastle Upon Tyne, NE6 4PX
Tel: 0191-265 6550 **Fax:** 0191-265 1002
E-mail: noel@johnmui-valves.com
Website: http://www.johnmillsnewcastleltd.co.uk
Bank(s): Barclays
Directors: A. Guest (Co Sec), J. Wall (Dir), K. Daly (Sales), N. Barker (Chief Op Offcr), N. Parker (Chief Op Offcr)
Managers: B. Earl (Sales Prom Mgr)
Immediate Holding Company: JOHN MILLS LIMITED
Registration no: 02021685 **Date established:** 1986
Turnover: £50m - £75m **No.of Employees:** 21 - 50 **Product Groups:** 34, 36

Date of Accounts	Oct 08	Oct 07	Oct 06
Working Capital	363	116	-261
Fixed Assets	111	111	88
Current Assets	657	510	523
Current Liabilities	294	394	784
Total Share Capital	10	10	10

John R Buchan

Unit 3 Station Road, Walker, Newcastle Upon Tyne, NE6 3PN
Tel: 0191-234 4535 **Fax:** 0191-234 4535
E-mail: derek@johnrbuchan.co.uk
Website: http://www.johnrbuchan.co.uk
Directors: D. Reynolds (Prop)
Immediate Holding Company: UNITED FLEXO SUPPLIES LIMITED
Date established: 2009 **No.of Employees:** 1 - 10 **Product Groups:** 26, 29, 30

J R Technical Services UK Ltd

17 Bloomsbury Court Kenton, Newcastle Upon Tyne, NE3 4LW
Tel: 0191-285 5977 **Fax:** 0870-838 1245
E-mail: info@jrts.co.uk
Website: http://www.jrts.co.uk
Directors: J. Sides (Dir)
Immediate Holding Company: J R TECHNICAL SERVICES UK LIMITED
Registration no: 06410355 **Date established:** 2007
Turnover: £250,000 - £500,000 **No.of Employees:** 1 - 10
Product Groups: 35, 38, 41

Date of Accounts	Mar 11	Mar 10	Mar 09
Working Capital	1	1	-1
Fixed Assets	1	2	3
Current Assets	74	75	52
Current Liabilities	4	1	1

KBOS2

Flat 1 65 Rothbury Terrace, Newcastle Upon Tyne, NE6 5XJ
Tel: 07724-165507
E-mail: kbos2hm@yahoo.co.uk
Website: http://www.kbos2.co.uk
Managers: K. Blumer (Mgr)
Date established: 2006 **Turnover:** **No.of Employees:** 1 - 10
Product Groups: 44, 48

Lawsons Fuses Ltd

Meadowfield Ponteland, Newcastle upon Tyne, NE20 9SW
Tel: 01661-823232 **Fax:** 01661-824213
E-mail: info@lawson-fuses.co.uk
Website: http://www.lawson-fuses.co.uk
Bank(s): HSBC Bank plc
Directors: S. Lawson (MD)
Managers: K. Jordan (Comptroller), G. Smith (Mgr), S. Wright (Sales Prom Mgr)
Immediate Holding Company: LAWSON FUSES LIMITED
Registration no: 00342400 **VAT No.:** GB 177 2397 32
Date established: 1938 **Turnover:** £2m - £5m **No.of Employees:** 51 - 100
Product Groups: 37, 67

Date of Accounts	Sep 11	Sep 10	Sep 09
Sales Turnover	3m	3m	3m
Pre Tax Profit/Loss	-334	23	127
Working Capital	1m	2m	2m
Fixed Assets	623	1m	1m
Current Assets	2m	3m	2m
Current Liabilities	134	98	110

Lawsons Timber Ltd

3 Kingsley Terrace, Newcastle upon Tyne, NE4 6PJ
Tel: 0191-273 4387 **Fax:** 0191-272 0899
E-mail: lawtimltd@aol.com
Directors: K. Law (Fin)
Immediate Holding Company: LAWSONS TIMBER LIMITED
Registration no: 02785290 **VAT No.:** GB 621 0461 90
Date established: 1993 **No.of Employees:** 11 - 20 **Product Groups:** 25

Date of Accounts	Mar 12	Mar 11	Mar 10
Working Capital	152	124	163
Fixed Assets	97	87	52
Current Assets	310	312	289

Lowes Financial Management Ltd

Holmwood House Clayton Road, Newcastle upon Tyne, NE2 1TL
Tel: 0191-281 8811 **Fax:** 0191-281 8365
E-mail: postmaster@lowes.co.uk
Website: http://www.lowes.co.uk
Bank(s): HSBC
Directors: I. Lowes (MD), N. McLachlan (Dir)
Managers: A. Baillie (Sales & Mktg Mg), R. King (Tech Serv Mgr), K. Wigham
Ultimate Holding Company: LOWES GROUP PLC
Immediate Holding Company: LOWES FINANCIAL MANAGEMENT LIMITED
Registration no: 01115681 **VAT No.:** GB 500 0665 05
Date established: 1973 **Turnover:** £2m - £5m **No.of Employees:** 21 - 50
Product Groups: 80, 82

Date of Accounts	Dec 11	Dec 10	Dec 09
Sales Turnover	4m	4m	3m
Pre Tax Profit/Loss	341	288	118
Working Capital	617	551	394
Fixed Assets	56	45	41
Current Assets	1m	918	650
Current Liabilities	488	323	217

Michael A Lynn

Toft Hill Belsay, Newcastle upon Tyne, NE20 0HQ
Tel: 01830-530269 **Fax:** 01830-530269
E-mail: malynn@live.co.uk
Directors: M. Lynn (Prop)
Immediate Holding Company: M A LYNN LIMITED
Registration no: 05995587 **Date established:** 2006
No.of Employees: 1 - 10 **Product Groups:** 35

Date of Accounts	Nov 11	Nov 10	Nov 08
Working Capital	9	-3	9
Fixed Assets	55	57	66
Current Assets	88	33	131

Metal Spinners Group Ltd

Newburn Industrial Estate Shelley Road, Newcastle Upon Tyne, NE15 9RT
Tel: 0191-267 1011 **Fax:** 0191-264 7137
E-mail: info@metal-spinners.co.uk
Website: http://www.metal-spinners.co.uk
Bank(s): HSBC Bank plc

see next page

Metal Spinners Group Ltd - Cont'd

Directors: A. Armstrong (MD), M. Shaw (Fin), M. Roberts (Tech Serv), P. Pearce (Sales)
Managers: R. Forsyth (Personnel), L. Lax (Purch Mgr)
Ultimate Holding Company: PRECISION ENGINEERING INTERNATIONAL LIMITED
Immediate Holding Company: METAL SPINNERS GROUP LIMITED
Registration no: 00556473 **VAT No.:** GB 698 4190 81
Date established: 1955 **Turnover:** £2m - £5m
No.of Employees: 101 - 250 **Product Groups:** 35, 36, 39, 40, 48

Date of Accounts	Jun 11	Mar 09	Mar 10
Sales Turnover	4m	14m	10m
Pre Tax Profit/Loss	816	2m	1m
Working Capital	6m	3m	3m
Fixed Assets	724	2m	2m
Current Assets	8m	6m	6m
Current Liabilities	635	675	561

Moore Pay Ltd

Northumbria House Samson Close, Newcastle Upon Tyne, NE12 6DX
Tel: 0191-256 1432 **Fax:** 0191-216 0005
Website: http://www.moorepay.co.uk
Bank(s): Barclays
Managers: S. Mcguire (Mgr)
Ultimate Holding Company: NIS HOLDINGS SARL (LUXEMBOURG)
Immediate Holding Company: MOOREPAY LIMITED
Registration no: 00891686 **VAT No.:** GB 217 3852 63
Date established: 1966 **Turnover:** £2m - £5m **No.of Employees:** 11 - 20
Product Groups: 44, 80, 85

Date of Accounts	Apr 11	Apr 10	Apr 09
Sales Turnover	16m	17m	19m
Pre Tax Profit/Loss	2m	2m	-107
Working Capital	927	-704	-1m
Fixed Assets	18m	19m	18m
Current Assets	6m	19m	16m
Current Liabilities	3m	2m	2m

Newcastle Airport Parking

Newcastle International Airport Woolsington, Newcastle Upon Tyne, NE13 8BZ
Tel: 0191-214 4341 **Fax:** 0191-214 4342
E-mail: efawcett@newcastleinternational.co.uk
Website: http://www.newcastleairport.com
Directors: A. Fisher (Co Sec)
Managers: R. Thompson
Ultimate Holding Company: NEWCASTLE AIRPORT LOCAL AUTHORITY HOLDING COMPANY LIMITED
Immediate Holding Company: NEWCASTLE INTERNATIONAL AIRPORT LIMITED
Registration no: 02077766 **Date established:** 1986
Turnover: £20m - £50m **No.of Employees:** 21 - 50 **Product Groups:** 71

Date of Accounts	Dec 11	Dec 10	Dec 09
Sales Turnover	47m	46m	47m
Pre Tax Profit/Loss	14m	12m	14m
Working Capital	28m	14m	26m
Fixed Assets	238m	242m	249m
Current Assets	49m	32m	38m
Current Liabilities	7m	7m	5m

Newcastle Locksmiths & Safe Co

173 West Road, Newcastle Upon Tyne, NE15 6PQ
Tel: 0191-238 6000 **Fax:** 0191-273 6010
E-mail: info@newcastlelockandsafe.co.uk
Website: http://www.newcastlelockandsafe.co.uk
Directors: P. Wylde (Prop), P. Wid (Ptnr)
Immediate Holding Company: NEWCASTLE LOCKSMITHS & SAFE COMPANY LTD
Registration no: 07738002 **Date established:** 2011
No.of Employees: 1 - 10 **Product Groups:** 35, 36

Nexus

Nexus House St James Boulevard, Newcastle Upon Tyne, NE1 4AX
Tel: 0191-203 3333 **Fax:** 0191-203 3304
E-mail: customerservices@nexus.org.uk
Website: http://www.nexus.org
Managers: J. Souter (Ops Mgr)
Immediate Holding Company: TYNESIDE TRANSPORT SERVICES LIMITED
Date established: 1971 **Turnover:** £5m - £10m
No.of Employees: 101 - 250 **Product Groups:** 72

Date of Accounts	Mar 11	Mar 10	Mar 09
Sales Turnover	505	491	493
Pre Tax Profit/Loss	35	13	13
Working Capital	240	204	167
Fixed Assets	N/A	1	24
Current Assets	349	310	271
Current Liabilities	109	105	103

Nigel Wright Recruitment

78 Grey Street, Newcastle upon Tyne, NE1 6AF
Tel: 0191-222 0770 **Fax:** 0191-222 1786
E-mail: nigel.wright@nigelwright.com
Website: http://www.nigelwright.co.uk
Directors: M. Simpson (Dir)
Managers: I. Scott-bell, J. Higgins
Ultimate Holding Company: NIGEL WRIGHT GROUP HOLDINGS LIMITED
Immediate Holding Company: NIGEL WRIGHT CONSULTANCY LIMITED
Registration no: 03729582 **Date established:** 1999 **Turnover:** £5m - £10m
No.of Employees: 51 - 100 **Product Groups:** 80

Date of Accounts	Apr 12	Apr 11	Apr 10
Sales Turnover	7m	7m	7m
Pre Tax Profit/Loss	-210	-556	700
Working Capital	3m	3m	2m
Fixed Assets	485	244	211
Current Assets	6m	5m	3m
Current Liabilities	574	514	772

Non Linear Dinamics Ltd

Keel House Garth Head, Newcastle upon Tyne, NE1 2JE
Tel: 0191-230 2121 **Fax:** 0191-230 2131
E-mail: info@nonlinear.com
Website: http://www.nonlinear.com
Bank(s): National Westminster
Directors: D. Barrie (Co Sec)
Managers: I. Hargreaves (Tech Serv Mgr), M. Wells (Sales Prom Mgr)
Immediate Holding Company: NONLINEAR DYNAMICS LIMITED
Registration no: 02430277 **Date established:** 1989 **Turnover:** £1m - £2m
No.of Employees: 21 - 50 **Product Groups:** 44

Date of Accounts	Sep 11	Sep 10	Sep 09
Sales Turnover	2m	1m	2m
Pre Tax Profit/Loss	333	205	325
Working Capital	2m	2m	1m
Fixed Assets	905	910	933
Current Assets	3m	3m	2m
Current Liabilities	332	195	372

Norland Burgess Ltd

93-105 St James Boulevard, Newcastle upon Tyne, NE1 4BW
Tel: 0191-232 9722 **Fax:** 0191-232 9722
E-mail: admin@norlandburgess.co.uk
Website: http://www.norlandburgess.co.uk
Directors: W. Burgess (MD)
Immediate Holding Company: NORLAND (WOOLS) LIMITED
Registration no: 00992480 **VAT No.:** GB 177 8470 18
Date established: 1970 **Turnover:** £1m - £2m **No.of Employees:** 1 - 10
Product Groups: 63

Date of Accounts	Dec 11	Dec 10	Dec 09
Working Capital	236	186	185
Current Assets	557	481	309

Norplast Ltd

Adamsez Industrial Estate Scotswood Road, Newcastle Upon Tyne, NE15 6XA
Tel: 0191-274 9777 **Fax:** 0191-228 0146
E-mail: sales@norplast.co.uk
Website: http://www.norplast.co.uk
Directors: C. Downie (MD), L. Downie (Fin)
Ultimate Holding Company: I.C.L. PLASTICS LIMITED
Immediate Holding Company: NORPLAST LIMITED
Registration no: SC059057 **Date established:** 1975
No.of Employees: 1 - 10 **Product Groups:** 30

Date of Accounts	Nov 11	Nov 10	Nov 09
Working Capital	17	16	16
Fixed Assets	1	3	4
Current Assets	89	90	128

Norstead (Division of Metnor P.L.C.)

Metnor House Mylord Crescent, Newcastle upon Tyne, NE12 5YD
Tel: 0191-268 4000 **Fax:** 0191-268 6650
E-mail: engineering@norstead.co.uk
Website: http://www.metnor.co.uk
Bank(s): Lloyds
Directors: K. Atkinson (Fin), B. Thoburn (MD)
Ultimate Holding Company: METNOR GROUP PLC
Immediate Holding Company: AKENSIDE QUAYS II LIMITED
Registration no: 02712072 **VAT No.:** GB 733 8609 17
Date established: 2006 **Turnover:** £2m - £5m **No.of Employees:** 21 - 50
Product Groups: 52, 84

Date of Accounts	Dec 09	Dec 08
Pre Tax Profit/Loss	5	N/A
Working Capital	N/A	1
Current Assets	N/A	6

North British Tapes Ltd

Unit 5 Locomotion Way Camperdown Industrial Estate, Newcastle Upon Tyne, NE12 5US
Tel: 0191-268 6272 **Fax:** 0191-268 7400
E-mail: info@nbtapes.co.uk
Website: http://www.nbtapes.co.uk
Bank(s): HSBC
Directors: P. Bridges (MD), T. Bridges (Sales)
Immediate Holding Company: NORTH BRITISH TAPES LIMITED
Registration no: 00493935 **VAT No.:** GB 175 9647 12
Date established: 1951 **Turnover:** £2m - £5m **No.of Employees:** 11 - 20
Product Groups: 23, 27

Date of Accounts	Dec 11	Dec 10	Dec 09
Working Capital	94	94	88
Fixed Assets	142	122	107
Current Assets	713	448	466

North East Ambulance Service NHS Foundation Trust

The Waterfront Goldcrest Way, Newcastle Upon Tyne, NE15 8NY
Tel: 0191-430 2000 **Fax:** 0191-273 7070
E-mail: simon.featherstone@neas.nhs.uk
Website: http://www.neambulance.nhs.uk
Bank(s): Co-operative
Directors: S. Featherstone (Grp Chief Exec)
Registration no: OC309093 **VAT No.:** GB 654 9344 10
Date established: 2004 **Turnover:** £10m - £20m
No.of Employees: 101 - 250 **Product Groups:** 37, 39, 86

North East Connections Ltd

Unit 43 High Street, Newburn, Newcastle Upon Tyne, NE15 8LN
Tel: 0191-267 7503 **Fax:** 0191-267 7505
E-mail: office@neconnections.co.uk
Website: http://www.neconnections.co.uk
Directors: P. Waggott (Dir)
Immediate Holding Company: NORTH EAST CONNECTIONS LIMITED
Registration no: 05570906 **VAT No.:** GB 722 1908 55
Date established: 2005 **Turnover:** £1m - £2m **No.of Employees:** 1 - 10
Product Groups: 29, 44

Date of Accounts	Dec 07
Working Capital	12
Fixed Assets	15
Current Assets	68
Current Liabilities	56

Northern Recruitment Group

Lloyds Court 56 Grace Street, Newcastle Upon Tyne, NE1 6AH
Tel: 0191-232 1222 **Fax:** 0191-261 8466
E-mail: recruitment@nrgplc.com
Website: http://www.nrgplc.com
Bank(s): Royal Bank of Scotland
Directors: L. Moran (Grp Chief Exec), W. Moran (Co Sec), R. Hutton (Fin), W. Moran (Fin), T. Liddle (MD), T. Liddle (Dir)
Immediate Holding Company: NORTHERN RECRUITMENT GROUP LIMITED
Registration no: 01756216 **Date established:** 1983
Turnover: £10m - £20m **No.of Employees:** 51 - 100 **Product Groups:** 80

Date of Accounts	Dec 10	Dec 09	Jun 08
Sales Turnover	20m	30m	20m
Pre Tax Profit/Loss	680	1m	1m
Working Capital	4m	4m	5m
Fixed Assets	246	250	383
Current Assets	7m	6m	8m
Current Liabilities	2m	2m	2m

Northern Rock plc

Northern Rock House Regent Farm Road, Gosforth, Newcastle Upon Tyne, NE3 4PL
Tel: 0191-285 7191 **Fax:** 0191-279 4703
Website: http://www.northernrock.co.uk
Bank(s): Northern Rock Plc
Directors: A. Leslie (Dir), J. Wilson (Co Sec), M. Ridley (Ch), R. Sandler (Ch), R. Bennett (Fin), G. Hoffman (Grp Chief Exec), D. Baker (Chief Op Offcr), C. Greener (Fin), A. Applegarth (Grp Chief Exec), C. Taylor (Co Sec)
Ultimate Holding Company: UK ASSET RESOLUTION LIMITED
Immediate Holding Company: NORTHERN ROCK (ASSET MANAGEMENT) PLC
Registration no: 03273685 **Date established:** 1996
Turnover: £250m - £500m **No.of Employees:** 1501 & over
Product Groups: 82

Date of Accounts	Dec 11	Dec 10	Dec 09
Sales Turnover	N/A	N/A	1107m
Pre Tax Profit/Loss	941m	401m	-258m
Working Capital	N/A	N/A	811m
Fixed Assets	7144m	9007m	244m
Current Assets	48181m	57269m	87201m
Current Liabilities	52903m	63809m	86390m

Northern Tools & Accessories Ltd

PO Box 5, Newcastle Upon Tyne, NE6 5TP
Tel: 0191-265 2821 **Fax:** 0191-276 2668
E-mail: marketing@crossling.co.uk
Website: http://www.northerntools.co.uk
Bank(s): Lloyds TSB
Managers: I. Crossman (Chief Mgr)
Ultimate Holding Company: T. CROSSLING & CO. LIMITED
Immediate Holding Company: NORTHERN TOOLS & ACCESSORIES LIMITED
Registration no: 00657147 **VAT No.:** GB 176 0964 39
Date established: 1960 **Turnover:** £5m - £10m **No.of Employees:** 21 - 50
Product Groups: 30, 35, 36

Northern Venture Trust P.L.C.

Northumberland House Princess Square, Newcastle Upon Tyne, NE1 8ER
Tel: 0191-244 6000 **Fax:** 0191-244 6001
E-mail: new@nvm.co.uk
Website: http://www.nvm.co.uk
Directors: C. Mellor (Co Sec), T. Levett (Dir)
Immediate Holding Company: Northern Investors Company plc
Registration no: 03090163 **Date established:** 1995 **Turnover:** £1m - £2m
No.of Employees: 1 - 10 **Product Groups:** 82

Nova International

Newcastle House Albany Court Monarch Road, Newcastle Business Park, Newcastle upon Tyne, NE4 7YB
Tel: 0191-272 7033 **Fax:** 0191-272 7036
E-mail: eric.wilkins@nova-international.com
Website: http://www.greatrun.org
Directors: E. Wilkins (Fin)
Immediate Holding Company: NOVA INTERNATIONAL LIMITED
Registration no: 03300783 **VAT No.:** GB 708 7656 04
Date established: 1997 **Turnover:** £1m - £2m **No.of Employees:** 21 - 50
Product Groups: 80

Date of Accounts	Dec 11	Dec 10	Dec 09
Working Capital	5m	3m	1m
Fixed Assets	200	200	200
Current Assets	5m	4m	2m

Office Equipment Selection Ltd

Mylord CR Camperdown Industrial Estate, Newcastle Upon Tyne, NE12 5RF
Tel: 0191-268 3333 **Fax:** 0191-268 0344
E-mail: sales@oesltd.co.uk
Website: http://www.oesltd.co.uk
Bank(s): Lloyds TSB Bank plc
Directors: W. Pitt (MD)
Immediate Holding Company: OFFICE EQUIPMENT SELECTION LIMITED
Registration no: 01450087 **VAT No.:** GB 297 8672 81
Date established: 1979 **Turnover:** £2m - £5m **No.of Employees:** 11 - 20
Product Groups: 64, 67

Date of Accounts	Dec 10	Dec 09	Dec 08
Working Capital	-74	-16	-32
Fixed Assets	297	305	306
Current Assets	207	302	393

One North East

Stella House Goldcrest Way, Newcastle upon Tyne, NE15 8NY
Tel: 0191-229 6200 **Fax:** 0191-229 6201
E-mail: sloyan@ntb.org.uk
Website: http://www.ntb.org.uk
Directors: A. Clarke (Dir)
Immediate Holding Company: HADRIAN'S WALL HERITAGE LIMITED
Registration no: 05820376 **Date established:** 2006 **Turnover:** £1m - £2m
No.of Employees: 1 - 10 **Product Groups:** 80

Date of Accounts	Mar 11	Mar 10	Mar 09
Sales Turnover	4m	5m	5m
Pre Tax Profit/Loss	-123	32	119
Working Capital	-1m	-142	-60
Fixed Assets	N/A	10	12
Current Assets	5m	7m	8m
Current Liabilities	4m	6m	6m

Otterburn Mills Ltd

Otterburn, Newcastle Upon Tyne, NE19 1JT
Tel: 01830-520225 **Fax:** 01830-520032
E-mail: mailorder@otterburnlife.co.uk
Website: http://www.otterburnlife.com
Directors: N. Owen (Dir)
Immediate Holding Company: OTTERBURN MILLS LIMITED
Registration no: SC121260 **Date established:** 1989 **Turnover:** £1m - £2m
No.of Employees: 11 - 20 **Product Groups:** 23

Date of Accounts	Nov 11	Nov 10	Nov 09
Working Capital	-6	15	179
Fixed Assets	200	249	179
Current Assets	554	567	521

Parkdean Holidays

1 Gosforth Business Park Gosforth Park Way Salters Lane, Newcastle upon Tyne, NE12 8ET
Tel: 0191-256 0795 **Fax:** 0191-268 6018
E-mail: john.waterworth@parkdeanholidays.co.uk
Website: http://www.parkdean.com
Directors: J. Waterworth (Grp Chief Exec), M. Norden (Fin)
Managers: J. Tighe (Tech Serv Mgr), A. Ceirns (Mktg Serv Mgr), P. Richardson (Personnel), M. Wilmot (Fin Mgr)

Ultimate Holding Company: PD PARKS HOLDINGS LIMITED
Immediate Holding Company: PARKDEAN HOLIDAYS LIMITED
Registration no: 03864124 **Date established:** 1999
No.of Employees: 101 - 250 **Product Groups:** 69, 80

Date of Accounts	Jan 12	Jan 11	Jan 10
Pre Tax Profit/Loss	609	378	859
Working Capital	-21m	-22m	-22m
Fixed Assets	76m	76m	76m
Current Assets	116m	98m	86m

Parker Hose & Fitting Ltd

Fisher Street, Newcastle Upon Tyne, NE6 4LT
Tel: 0191-262 5321 **Fax:** 0191-263 9799
E-mail: stephenleonard@btconnect.com
Website: http://www.parker-hose.com
Directors: S. Leonard (MD)
Ultimate Holding Company: SERVACE LIMITED
Immediate Holding Company: PARKER HOSE & FITTINGS LIMITED
Registration no: 02608091 **Date established:** 1991
No.of Employees: 11 - 20 **Product Groups:** 22, 23, 24, 27, 29, 30, 32, 33, 35, 36, 37, 38, 39, 40, 46, 48, 49, 51, 52, 63, 67, 83

Date of Accounts	Jun 12	Jun 11	Jun 10
Working Capital	63	18	55
Fixed Assets	230	90	78
Current Assets	2m	978	2m

Parkland Engineering Ltd

Unit 3 North Tyne Industrial Estate Whitley Road Benton, Benton, Newcastle Upon Tyne, NE12 9SZ
Tel: 0191-270 9730 **Fax:** 0191-270 9740
E-mail: sales@parkland-eng.co.uk
Website: http://www.parkland-eng.co.uk
Bank(s): National Westminster Bank Plc
Directors: J. Black (Sales)
Immediate Holding Company: PARKLAND ENGINEERING LIMITED
Registration no: 01363157 **VAT No.:** GB 257 5828 91
Date established: 1978 **Turnover:** £2m - £5m **No.of Employees:** 21 - 50
Product Groups: 22, 23, 29, 30, 35, 36

Date of Accounts	Mar 12	Mar 11	Mar 10
Working Capital	115	55	-24
Fixed Assets	1m	1m	1m
Current Assets	1m	1m	918

Parsons Brinckerhoff

Amber Court William Armstrong Drive, Newcastle Business Park, Newcastle Upon Tyne, NE4 7YQ
Tel: 0191-226 2000 **Fax:** 0191-226 2104
E-mail: pbpower@pbworld.com
Website: http://www.pbworld.com
Bank(s): HSBC Bank plc
Directors: R. Proctor (Co Sec)
Managers: G. Ayres (Chief Acct)
Ultimate Holding Company: BALFOUR BEATTY PLC
Immediate Holding Company: PB POWER LTD
Registration no: 04353230 **VAT No.:** GB 413 855 94
Date established: 2002 **Turnover:** £125m - £250m
No.of Employees: 251 - 500 **Product Groups:** 80, 81, 82, 84, 85

Pearson Engineering

Wincomblee Road, Newcastle Upon Tyne, NE6 3QS
Tel: 0191-234 0001 **Fax:** 0191-234 1000
E-mail: pearson@pearson-eng.com
Website: http://www.pearson-eng.com
Directors: J. Crompton (MD)
Immediate Holding Company: PEARSON ENGINEERING LIMITED
Registration no: 01876136 **Date established:** 1985
Turnover: £125m - £250m **No.of Employees:** 51 - 100
Product Groups: 48

Date of Accounts	Dec 11	Dec 10	Dec 09
Sales Turnover	208m	170m	116m
Pre Tax Profit/Loss	63m	54m	31m
Working Capital	107m	82m	42m
Fixed Assets	3m	4m	4m
Current Assets	139m	118m	90m
Current Liabilities	29m	22m	45m

Permatt Fork Lift Trucks

Unit 7c Mylord CR Camperdown Industrial Estate, Newcastle Upon Tyne, NE12 5UJ
Tel: 0191-216 5320 **Fax:** 08701-451451
E-mail: admin@permatt.com
Website: http://www.permatt.com
Directors: M. Percy (Prop)
Date established: 2003 **No.of Employees:** 11 - 20 **Product Groups:** 35, 39, 45

Pescafish Ltd

50 Wellburn Park, Newcastle Upon Tyne, NE2 2JY
Tel: 07785-262621 **Fax:** 0191-247 5768
E-mail: terry.phillips@pescafish.co.uk
Website: http://www.pescafish.co.uk
Directors: T. Phillips (Prop)
Immediate Holding Company: PESCAFISH LIMITED
Registration no: 05247132 **Date established:** 2004 **Turnover:** £2m - £5m
No.of Employees: 1 - 10 **Product Groups:** 09, 20

Date of Accounts	Sep 11	Sep 10	Sep 09
Sales Turnover	175	119	118
Pre Tax Profit/Loss	54	36	37
Working Capital	2	-9	-6
Fixed Assets	1	1	N/A
Current Assets	88	46	61
Current Liabilities	85	36	66

Plastic Metal & Profiles Ltd

Unit 99 14 North Tyne Industrial Estate Whitley Road, Benton, Newcastle Upon Tyne, NE12 9SZ
Tel: 0191-266 5050 **Fax:** 0191-266 5724
E-mail: sales@pmpnameplates.co.uk
Website: http://www.pmpnameplates.co.uk
Directors: P. Thompson (Dir), R. Hunter (MD)
Ultimate Holding Company: DNR LIMITED
Immediate Holding Company: PLASTIC AND METAL PROFILES LIMITED
Registration no: 02840998 **VAT No.:** GB 621 1529 77
Date established: 1993 **No.of Employees:** 11 - 20 **Product Groups:** 28, 37, 48, 49, 66

Date of Accounts	Feb 12	Feb 11	Feb 10
Working Capital	272	262	248
Fixed Assets	98	141	193
Current Assets	428	457	459

Quick Hydraulics Ltd

North Tyne Industrial Estate Benton, Newcastle upon Tyne, NE12 9SZ
Tel: 0191-257 6548 **Fax:** 0191-296 2683
E-mail: quick@quick-hydraulics.com
Website: http://www.quick-hydraulics.com
Directors: A. Egglestone (Eng Serv), P. Quick (MD)
Registration no: 01289110 **Turnover:** £2m - £5m
No.of Employees: 11 - 20 **Product Groups:** 27, 32, 33, 38, 41, 42, 44, 45, 46, 47, 48, 51, 54, 80, 84, 85

Date of Accounts	Dec 08	Dec 07	Dec 06
Working Capital	411	329	236
Fixed Assets	21	21	21
Current Assets	1028	802	662
Current Liabilities	617	473	426
Total Share Capital	21	21	21

R B Valvetech Ltd

Unit 3 New York Way New York Industrial Park, Newcastle upon Tyne, NE27 0QF
Tel: 01670-736400 **Fax:** 0191-258 8821
E-mail: sales@rbvalvetech.com
Website: http://www.rbvalvetech.com
Directors: M. Ridley (MD), M. Storey (Dir), R. Brown (Co Sec)
Ultimate Holding Company: FEDERAL SIGNAL CORPORATION {USA}
Immediate Holding Company: RB (GB) LIMITED
Registration no: 04176657 **VAT No.:** GB 746 4412 31
Date established: 2001 **No.of Employees:** 1 - 10 **Product Groups:** 36

Date of Accounts	Mar 08	Mar 07	Aug 06
Working Capital	396	363	349
Fixed Assets	22	14	15
Current Assets	1256	1535	905
Current Liabilities	861	1172	556

RB Pipetech

Centurion House New York Way, New York Industrial Estate, Newcastle upon Tyne, NE27 0QF
Tel: 0191-258 8800 **Fax:** 0191-258 8811
E-mail: rbp.sales@fot.com
Website: http://www.rbpipetech.com
Directors: R. Betteridge (MD), R. Brown (Co Sec)
Managers: A. Bain, D. Garrow (Sales Prom Mgr)
Immediate Holding Company: RB (GB) Ltd
Registration no: 03097312 **VAT No.:** GB 801 8183 50
Date established: 1995 **Turnover:** £20m - £50m
No.of Employees: 21 - 50 **Product Groups:** 29, 36

Date of Accounts	Dec 08	Dec 07	Dec 06
Sales Turnover	24m	16m	N/A
Pre Tax Profit/Loss	5m	2m	N/A
Working Capital	6m	4m	2m
Fixed Assets	N/A	47	66
Current Assets	6m	11m	7m
Current Liabilities	N/A	1m	2m

Reed

New England House 10 Ridley Place, Newcastle Upon Tyne, NE1 8JW
Tel: 0191-232 3703 **Fax:** 0191-232 5602
E-mail: megan.blake@reedglobal.com
Website: http://www.reed.co.uk
Managers: M. Blake (Sales Admin)
Registration no: 04598992 **Date established:** 2002
Turnover: £500m - £1,000m **No.of Employees:** 21 - 50
Product Groups: 80

Remploy Ltd

Benton Square Industrial Estate, Newcastle Upon Tyne, NE12 9TA
Tel: 0191-266 3833
E-mail: david.goodings@remploy.co.uk
Website: http://www.remploy.co.uk
Managers: D. Goodings (Factory Mgr)
Immediate Holding Company: REMPLOY LIMITED
Registration no: NF003194 **Date established:** 1995
No.of Employees: 51 - 100 **Product Groups:** 24, 26, 68

Revert Ltd

Brunswick Industrial Estate Brunswick Village, Newcastle Upon Tyne, NE13 7BA
Tel: 0191-236 5999 **Fax:** 0191-236 4466
E-mail: info@revert.ltd.uk
Website: http://www.revert.ltd.uk
Directors: J. Hugill (Fin), K. Knight (MD)
Immediate Holding Company: REVERT LIMITED
Registration no: 04353749 **Date established:** 2002
No.of Employees: 1 - 10 **Product Groups:** 32, 40, 43

Date of Accounts	Mar 11	Mar 10	Mar 09
Working Capital	413	267	192
Fixed Assets	103	118	59
Current Assets	602	484	475

Revol Ltd

Samson Close, Newcastle upon Tyne, NE12 6DZ
Tel: 0191-268 4555 **Fax:** 0191-216 0004
E-mail: sales@revol.co.uk
Website: http://www.revol.co.uk
Directors: R. Wilkes (Dir)
Immediate Holding Company: REVOL LIMITED
Registration no: 00628328 **VAT No.:** GB 177 3776 19
Date established: 1959 **Turnover:** £500,000 - £1m
No.of Employees: 1 - 10 **Product Groups:** 31

Date of Accounts	Jun 11	Jun 10	Jun 09
Sales Turnover	N/A	927	740
Pre Tax Profit/Loss	N/A	45	34
Working Capital	198	209	257
Fixed Assets	104	96	106
Current Assets	372	384	355
Current Liabilities	N/A	32	19

Ringtons Ltd

PO Box 3, Newcastle Upon Tyne, NE6 2YN
Tel: 0191-209 7030 **Fax:** 0191-209 7099
E-mail: info@ringtons.co.uk
Website: http://www.ringtons.co.uk
Bank(s): National Westminster
Directors: C. Moffett (Co Sec), P. Smith (Dir)
Managers: D. Stokoe (Tech Serv Mgr), S. Thompson (Mktg Serv Mgr)
Ultimate Holding Company: RINGTONS HOLDINGS LIMITED
Immediate Holding Company: RINGTONS LIMITED
Registration no: 00572008 **VAT No.:** GB 499 6725 68
Date established: 1956 **Turnover:** £20m - £50m
No.of Employees: 501 - 1000 **Product Groups:** 20, 62

Date of Accounts	Jun 11	Jun 10	Jun 09
Sales Turnover	34m	33m	33m
Pre Tax Profit/Loss	2m	3m	3m
Working Capital	4m	7m	7m
Fixed Assets	7m	7m	7m
Current Assets	10m	12m	12m
Current Liabilities	2m	3m	3m

River I.T Solutions Ltd

44 Greenlee Drive Haydon Grange, Newcastle Upon Tyne, NE7 7GA
Tel: 0191-209 6833 **Fax:** 0191-209 6833
E-mail: michael@river-it.co.uk
Website: http://www.river-it.co.uk
Directors: I. Higginson (Dir)
Immediate Holding Company: RIVER I.T. SOLUTIONS LTD
Registration no: 05236555 **Date established:** 2004
No.of Employees: 1 - 10 **Product Groups:** 44

Date of Accounts	Mar 11	Mar 10	Mar 09
Working Capital	4	4	6
Fixed Assets	43	40	34
Current Assets	17	43	27

A E Robb & Associates Ltd

4 Lambton Road, Newcastle upon Tyne, NE2 4RZ
Tel: 0191-281 3312 **Fax:** 0191-281 4367
E-mail: garry.liddle@aerobb.co.uk
Website: http://www.aerobb.co.uk
Bank(s): National Westminster Bank Plc
Directors: J. Stevenson (MD), G. Liddle (Dir), G. Lidel (Fin), G. Stephenson (Dir)
Managers: C. Wishart (I.T. Exec)
Immediate Holding Company: A.E. ROBB & ASSOCIATES LIMITED
Registration no: 01309169 **VAT No.:** GB 297 5907 95
Date established: 1977 **No.of Employees:** 11 - 20 **Product Groups:** 84

Date of Accounts	Apr 11	Apr 10	Apr 09
Working Capital	106	104	192
Fixed Assets	543	576	283
Current Assets	320	359	472

Robinson & Liddell Ltd

Redburn Road, Newcastle upon Tyne, NE5 1NB
Tel: 0191-286 2049 **Fax:** 0191-214 0564
E-mail: sales@rlfurniture.co.uk
Website: http://www.rlfurniture.co.uk
Bank(s): HSBC Bank plc
Directors: P. Robinson (MD), P. Robinson (Fin), S. Wharmby (I.T. Dir), S. Wharmby (MD), J. Brown (MD)
Immediate Holding Company: ROBINSON & LIDDELL LIMITED
Registration no: 00422746 **VAT No.:** GB 177 3832 35
Date established: 1946 **Turnover:** £1m - £2m **No.of Employees:** 21 - 50
Product Groups: 26, 52

Date of Accounts	Jun 08	Jun 07	Jun 06
Working Capital	-21	12	134
Fixed Assets	76	41	56
Current Assets	391	310	474
Current Liabilities	413	298	340
Total Share Capital	2	2	2

Rotary Power Ltd

11 Glass House Street St Peters, Newcastle Upon Tyne, NE6 1BS
Tel: 0191-276 4444 **Fax:** 0191-276 4462
E-mail: info@rotarypower.com
Website: http://www.rotarypower.com
Bank(s): HSBC Bank plc
Directors: G. Willis (MD), N. Salvesen (Fin)
Managers: L. Hope (Personnel), B. Gibson (I.T. Exec)
Ultimate Holding Company: BRITISH ENGINES LIMITED
Immediate Holding Company: ROTARY POWER LTD.
Registration no: 00931010 **VAT No.:** GB 555 8517 12
Date established: 1968 **Turnover:** £10m - £20m
No.of Employees: 51 - 100 **Product Groups:** 35, 39, 40

Date of Accounts	Apr 11	Apr 12	May 09
Sales Turnover	12m	12m	N/A
Pre Tax Profit/Loss	2m	2m	N/A
Working Capital	2m	2m	964
Fixed Assets	3m	3m	N/A
Current Assets	5m	4m	964
Current Liabilities	992	374	N/A

Royston Ltd

Unit 3 Walker Riverside Wincomblee Road, Newcastle Upon Tyne, NE6 3PF
Tel: 0191-295 8000 **Fax:** 0191-295 8001
E-mail: sales@royston.co.uk
Website: http://www.royston.co.uk
Directors: S. Wade (Comm)
Ultimate Holding Company: ROYSTON POWER GENERATION LIMITED
Immediate Holding Company: ROYSTON ENGINEERING GROUP LIMITED
Registration no: 02908945 **VAT No.:** GB 621 3603 81
Date established: 1994 **Turnover:** Up to £250,000
No.of Employees: 21 - 50 **Product Groups:** 40

Date of Accounts	Feb 08	Feb 11	Feb 10
Sales Turnover	60	6	N/A
Pre Tax Profit/Loss	477	-0	66
Working Capital	819	N/A	924
Fixed Assets	1	N/A	1
Current Assets	1m	2	1m
Current Liabilities	15	N/A	13

S & B Roller Shutters

Unit 16 Mayfair House Redburn Road, Newcastle upon Tyne, NE5 1NB
Tel: 0191-271 3777 **Fax:** 0191-271 4322
E-mail: enquiries@sbrollershutters.co.uk
Website: http://www.sbrollershutters.co.uk
Directors: R. Slack (MD)
Turnover: £250,000 - £500,000 **No.of Employees:** 1 - 10
Product Groups: 35, 48, 52, 66

S C A Packaging Ltd

Planet Place, Newcastle upon Tyne, NE12 6DY
Tel: 0191-268 1142 **Fax:** 0191-268 4252
Website: http://www.sca.com
Managers: A. Smith (Plant), K. Stephenson (Chief Acct)
Ultimate Holding Company: SVENSKA CELLULOSA AB (SWEDEN)
Immediate Holding Company: DS SMITH CORRUGATED PACKAGING LIMITED
Registration no: 00053913 **Date established:** 1997
No.of Employees: 51 - 100 **Product Groups:** 27, 28, 30, 49

see next page

***S C A Packaging Ltd** - Cont'd*

Date of Accounts	Aug 11	Aug 10	Aug 09
Working Capital	-20	-37	-41
Fixed Assets	22	38	44
Current Assets	55	24	33

Sanderson Weatherall Chartered Surveyors

22-24 Grey Street, Newcastle Upon Tyne, NE1 6AD
Tel: 0191-261 2681 **Fax:** 0191-261 4761
E-mail: tim.catterall@sandersonweatherall.com
Website: http://www.sw.co.uk
Directors: M. Archer (Fin), G. Penrice (Ptnr)
Managers: T. Catterall (Mktg Serv Mgr), J. Boulton (Personnel), A. Ridge (Tech Serv Mgr)
Immediate Holding Company: SANDERSON TOWNEND LIMITED
Registration no: 02903380 **VAT No.:** GB 177 0263 63
Date established: 1994 **Turnover:** £5m - £10m **No.of Employees:** 21 - 50
Product Groups: 80

Security Guaranteed UK Ltd

Security House West View Forest Hall, Newcastle upon Tyne, NE12 7JL
Tel: 0191-266 5666 **Fax:** 0191-266 5200
E-mail: securityguaranteedukltd@hotmail.co.uk
Website: http://www.securityguaranteedukltd.co.uk
Directors: P. Mcardle (Dir), S. Patterson (MD)
Immediate Holding Company: SECURITY GUARANTEED (UK) LTD
Registration no: 05881165 **Date established:** 2006
Turnover: £500m - £1,000m **No.of Employees:** 1 - 10
Product Groups: 36, 40, 81, 83

Date of Accounts	Jan 10	Jan 08	Jan 07
Working Capital	N/A	-1	-2
Fixed Assets	N/A	2	3
Current Liabilities	N/A	N/A	2

Service Engines Newcastle Ltd

Great Lime Road, Newcastle Upon Tyne, NE12 6RU
Tel: 0191-268 1000 **Fax:** 0191-216 0838
E-mail: admin@serviceengines.co.uk
Website: http://www.serviceengines.co.uk
Directors: A. Frame (MD), R. Frame (Ch)
Managers: S. Minto (Accounts)
Immediate Holding Company: SERVICE ENGINES (NEWCASTLE) LIMITED
Registration no: 00405832 **VAT No.:** GB 176 3543 48
Date established: 1946 **Turnover:** £2m - £5m **No.of Employees:** 1 - 10
Product Groups: 48

Date of Accounts	Mar 11	Mar 10	Mar 09
Pre Tax Profit/Loss	N/A	N/A	29
Working Capital	359	348	230
Fixed Assets	2m	2m	2m
Current Assets	987	1m	3m
Current Liabilities	N/A	N/A	83

Sicame Electrical Distribution Ltd

2 Industry Road, Newcastle upon Tyne, NE6 5XB
Tel: 0191-275 9977 **Fax:** 01827-65700
E-mail: graham.blackburn@sicame.co.uk
Website: http://www.sicamedistribution.co.uk
Managers: G. Blackburn (Mgr)
Ultimate Holding Company: SICAME SA (FRANCE)
Immediate Holding Company: SICAME ELECTRICAL DISTRIBUTION LIMITED
Registration no: 04476620 **Date established:** 2002
No.of Employees: 1 - 10 **Product Groups:** 36, 40

Date of Accounts	Dec 11	Dec 10	Dec 09
Sales Turnover	2m	2m	1m
Pre Tax Profit/Loss	100	58	19
Working Capital	531	422	462
Fixed Assets	101	123	100
Current Assets	1m	828	662
Current Liabilities	73	59	54

Siemens Energy Service Fossil

C A Parsons Works Shields Road, Newcastle upon Tyne, NE6 2YL
Tel: 0191-276 1188 **Fax:** 0191-276 0276
E-mail: carl.ennis@siemens.com
Website: http://www.siemens.com
Bank(s): National Westminster Bank Plc
Directors: G. Hartley (MD)
Managers: A. Dodd (Buyer), G. Spears (Tech Serv Mgr), M. Jones, P. Warwick (Fin Mgr), T. Boden
Ultimate Holding Company: SIEMENS UK P.L.C.
Immediate Holding Company: SIEMENS POWER GENERATION LTD
Registration no: 03332999 **VAT No.:** GB 479 9852 60
Turnover: £50m - £75m **No.of Employees:** 501 - 1000
Product Groups: 37, 40, 48, 52

Souter Trading Ltd

2 Osborne Road, Newcastle upon Tyne, NE2 2AA
Tel: 0191-212 0500 **Fax:** 0191-212 0600
E-mail: dtimms@souter-trading.com
Website: http://www.souter-trading.com
Directors: D. Timms (MD), E. Souter (Fin)
Immediate Holding Company: SOUTER TRADING INTERNATIONAL LIMITED
Registration no: 03149826 **Date established:** 1996
No.of Employees: 1 - 10 **Product Groups:** 22, 23, 24, 25, 28, 29, 30, 31, 32, 33, 34, 35, 36, 37, 38, 39, 40, 41, 42, 43, 44, 45, 46, 47, 48, 49, 51, 52, 54, 61, 66, 67, 68, 74, 76, 80, 81, 82, 83, 84, 85, 86, 87

Date of Accounts	Mar 12	Mar 11	Mar 10
Working Capital	22	-2	14
Fixed Assets	4	7	10
Current Assets	160	207	139

Springvale E P S Ltd

Coach Lane Hazlerigg, Newcastle Upon Tyne, NE13 7AP
Tel: 0191-217 1144 **Fax:** 0191-217 1212
E-mail: sales@springvale.com
Website: http://www.springvale.com
Directors: T. France (MD)
Ultimate Holding Company: CRH PUBLIC LIMITED COMPANY
Immediate Holding Company: SPRINGVALE EPS LIMITED
Registration no: NI001043 **Date established:** 1936
Turnover: £10m - £20m **No.of Employees:** 21 - 50 **Product Groups:** 30

Date of Accounts	Dec 10	Dec 09	Dec 08
Sales Turnover	17m	14m	16m
Pre Tax Profit/Loss	-1m	289	906
Working Capital	102	8m	7m
Fixed Assets	2m	2m	2m
Current Assets	8m	22m	21m
Current Liabilities	2m	2m	2m

Stanegate Stoves & Cookers

The Old Glass Works Lemington, Newcastle upon Tyne, NE15 8SX
Tel: 0191-267 7100 **Fax:** 0191-267 7811
E-mail: r@worldofstoves.co.uk
Website: http://www.stanegatestoves.com
Directors: R. Mellor (Prop)
Immediate Holding Company: STANEGATE STOVES LIMITED
Registration no: 08119190 **Date established:** 2012
No.of Employees: 1 - 10 **Product Groups:** 40

Sumlock Electronics North East Ltd

Planet House Northumbrian Way, Newcastle Upon Tyne, NE12 6EH
Tel: 0191-216 4868 **Fax:** 0191-222 1540
E-mail: clientsupport@sumlock.co.uk
Website: http://www.sumlock.co.uk
Directors: B. Towers (MD), B. Towart (MD), B. Towert (MD), J. Towart (Co Sec)
Managers: K. Jackson (Purch Mgr), R. Adams (Chief Mgr)
Immediate Holding Company: SUMLOCK ELECTRONICS (NORTH EAST) LIMITED
Registration no: 01292068 **Date established:** 1976 **Turnover:** £2m - £5m
No.of Employees: 21 - 50 **Product Groups:** 44

Date of Accounts	Feb 10	Feb 09	Feb 08
Working Capital	60	295	401
Fixed Assets	42	62	79
Current Assets	594	742	877
Current Liabilities	N/A	N/A	193

Surgo Construction Ltd

Albany Court Newcastle Business Park, Newcastle upon Tyne, NE4 7YB
Tel: 0191-273 3311 **Fax:** 0191-273 6620
E-mail: jameswalker@surgo.co.uk
Website: http://www.surgo.co.uk
Bank(s): Barclays,
Directors: I. Walker (Ch), P. Gregory (Fin), J. Alexander (Mkt Research)
Managers: K. Thompson (Tech Serv Mgr), S. Coombes (Comptroller), S. Alen (I.T. Exec), J. Stephenson (Buyer), J. Alexander (Develop Mgr), C. Wallace (Personnel), B. Adams (Personnel)
Ultimate Holding Company: HAWKPOST LIMITED
Immediate Holding Company: SURGO CONSTRUCTION LIMITED
Registration no: 00235552 **Date established:** 2028
Turnover: £20m - £50m **No.of Employees:** 101 - 250
Product Groups: 51, 52

Date of Accounts	Oct 08	Aug 11	Aug 10
Sales Turnover	55m	25m	36m
Pre Tax Profit/Loss	3m	3m	6m
Working Capital	2m	2m	2m
Fixed Assets	2m	2m	2m
Current Assets	18m	15m	18m
Current Liabilities	13m	8m	11m

Godfrey Syrett Ltd

Planet Place, Newcastle Upon Tyne, NE12 6DY
Tel: 0191-268 1010 **Fax:** 0191-268 3134
E-mail: sales@godfreysyrett.co.uk
Website: http://www.godfreysyrett.co.uk
Bank(s): The Royal Bank of Scotland
Directors: W. Rusga (Ch), N. Tweddle (Dir), G. Nobel (Ch), A. Gardner (Dir)
Managers: N. Tweddle (Ops Mgr), D. Cruise (Sales Prom Mgr), D. Brown (I.T. Exec), C. Scott (Buyer), E. McTaggart (Accounts)
Ultimate Holding Company: GODFREY-SYRETT(HOLDINGS)LIMITED
Immediate Holding Company: GODFREY - SYRETT LIMITED
Registration no: 00751094 **VAT No.:** GB 698 5591 58
Date established: 1963 **Turnover:** £20m - £50m
No.of Employees: 51 - 100 **Product Groups:** 26, 36, 63

Date of Accounts	Jul 10	Jul 09	Jul 08
Sales Turnover	24m	30m	27m
Pre Tax Profit/Loss	913	2m	2m
Working Capital	3m	4m	3m
Fixed Assets	2m	2m	2m
Current Assets	6m	8m	7m
Current Liabilities	2m	2m	2m

Ten Alps Publishing Ltd

Old Brewery Court 156 Sandyford Road, Newcastle Upon Tyne, NE2 1XG
Tel: 0191-499 4200 **Fax:** 0191-499 4205
E-mail: julie.barber@tenalpspublishing.com
Website: http://www.link2portal.com
Directors: D. Morren (Co Sec), J. Barber (MD), J. Barber (Comm)
Immediate Holding Company: CAMERON PUBLISHING LIMITED
Registration no: 02761939 **Date established:** 1992 **Turnover:** £2m - £5m
No.of Employees: 11 - 20 **Product Groups:** 28

Date of Accounts	Dec 10
Working Capital	-272
Fixed Assets	386
Current Assets	314

Tyne Tees Power Tool Co.

96 Heaton Road, Newcastle upon Tyne, NE6 5HL
Tel: 0191-265 9054 **Fax:** 0191-276 5872
Directors: L. Smith (Prop)
Date established: 1969 **No.of Employees:** 1 - 10 **Product Groups:** 35

Tyneside Security Services

325 Benton Road, Newcastle upon Tyne, NE7 7EE
Tel: 0191-270 0808 **Fax:** 0191-266 7485
E-mail: info@tynesidesecurity.co.uk
Website: http://www.tynesidesecurity.co.uk
Directors: R. Pattinson (Prop)
Turnover: £1m - £2m **No.of Employees:** 1 - 10 **Product Groups:** 37, 38, 40, 46, 47

Universal Forwarding

Freight Village Newcastle Int Airport, Woolsington, Newcastle upon Tyne, NE13 8BH
Tel: 0191-214 0800 **Fax:** 0191-214 0811
E-mail: info@universal-forwarding.co.uk
Website: http://www.universal-forwarding.co.uk
Bank(s): National Westminster
Directors: T. Harbottle (Fin)
Managers: D. Henderson
Immediate Holding Company: CAMAIR FREIGHT SOLUTIONS LIMITED
Registration no: 06855411 **VAT No.:** GB 499 9567 45
Date established: 2009 **No.of Employees:** 11 - 20 **Product Groups:** 76

Date of Accounts	May 12	Nov 10	Nov 09
Working Capital	105	71	99
Fixed Assets	100	134	148
Current Assets	553	432	430

Veale Nixon Ltd

Hunter House 17-19 Byron Street, Newcastle upon Tyne, NE2 1XH
Tel: 0191-261 2727 **Fax:** 0191-232 2438
E-mail: admin@veale-nixon.co.uk
Bank(s): Lloyds TSB
Directors: K. Mullen (Dir), V. French (Co Sec)
Ultimate Holding Company: T CLARKE PUBLIC LIMITED COMPANY
Immediate Holding Company: VEALE-NIXON LIMITED
Registration no: 00385769 **VAT No.:** GB 176 8378 12
Date established: 1944 **Turnover:** £10m - £20m
No.of Employees: 51 - 100 **Product Groups:** 52

Date of Accounts	Dec 11	Dec 10	Dec 09
Sales Turnover	8m	10m	14m
Pre Tax Profit/Loss	198	970	1m
Working Capital	1m	1m	2m
Fixed Assets	45	66	36
Current Assets	3m	3m	6m
Current Liabilities	788	421	1m

Victor Products Ltd

New York Way New York Industrial Park, Newcastle upon Tyne, NE27 0QF
Tel: 0191-280 8000 **Fax:** 0191-280 8080
E-mail: sales@victor.co.uk
Website: http://www.victor.co.uk
Bank(s): Bank of Scotland
Directors: B. Wilson (MD), S. Turner (Co Sec)
Managers: A. Morris (Tech Serv Mgr), D. McNalty (Chief Acct), F. Small (Sales Prom Mgr), K. Glynn (Purch Mgr)
Ultimate Holding Company: FEDERAL SIGNAL CORPORATION {USA}
Immediate Holding Company: VICTOR PRODUCTS HOLDINGS LTD
Registration no: 00241316 **Date established:** 2029 **Turnover:** £1m - £2m
No.of Employees: 21 - 50 **Product Groups:** 37

Date of Accounts	Dec 11	Dec 10	Dec 09
Pre Tax Profit/Loss	N/A	N/A	-135
Working Capital	-176	-176	-176
Fixed Assets	4m	4m	4m

Ward Hadaway

102 Quayside, Newcastle Upon Tyne, NE1 3DX
Tel: 0191-204 4000 **Fax:** 0191-204 4001
E-mail: legal@wardhadaway.com
Website: http://www.wardhadaway.com
Bank(s): Barclays
Directors: A. Mearns (Fin), J. Martin (Snr Part), K. Milton (Fin)
Managers: G. Taylor (I.T. Exec), G. Taylor (Tech Serv Mgr), C. Butts (Personnel), C. Butts (Personnel), E. Magnani (Mktg Serv Mgr), E. Magnani
Immediate Holding Company: WARD HADAWAY LLP
Registration no: OC359032 **VAT No.:** GB 176 0808 53
Date established: 2010 **Turnover:** £10m - £20m
No.of Employees: 251 - 500 **Product Groups:** 80

White Bros Newcastle Upon Tyne Ltd

Unit 45 Gosforth Industrial Estate, Newcastle Upon Tyne, NE3 1XD
Tel: 0191-213 0455 **Fax:** 0191-284 1351
E-mail: enquiries@whitebros.co.uk
Website: http://www.whitebros.co.uk
Directors: P. Harding (MD), S. Roberts (Fin)
Managers: G. Wragby (Purch Mgr), P. Banning (Sales Prom Mgr)
Immediate Holding Company: OPTICALFITTERS LIMITED
Registration no: 04680857 **Date established:** 2010 **Turnover:** £2m - £5m
No.of Employees: 51 - 100 **Product Groups:** 36, 48

Your Move

Newcastle House Albany Court, Newcastle Business Park, Newcastle upon Tyne, NE4 7YB
Tel: 0191-233 4600 **Fax:** 0191-273 5005
E-mail: enquiries@your-move.co.uk
Website: http://www.your-move.co.uk
Directors: S. Embley (MD)
Managers: L. Charles-Jones (Personnel)
Ultimate Holding Company: LSL PROPERTY SERVICES PLC
Immediate Holding Company: YOUR MOVE PROPERTIES LIMITED
Registration no: 03776783 **Date established:** 1999
Turnover: £50m - £75m **No.of Employees:** 1 - 10 **Product Groups:** 80

Date of Accounts	May 11	May 10	May 09
Sales Turnover	41	39	43
Pre Tax Profit/Loss	-11	-13	-31
Working Capital	-200	-64	-51
Fixed Assets	868	733	733
Current Assets	2	N/A	28
Current Liabilities	6	56	5

North Shields

A N D Group plc

Tanners Bank, North Shields, NE30 1JH
Tel: 0191-258 1635 **Fax:** 0870-444 9680
E-mail: info@and-group.net
Website: http://www.and-group.net
Directors: I. Robinson (Grp Chief Exec)
Managers: N. Dale (Mktg Serv Mgr), B. Howes (Comptroller), R. Noble (Tech Serv Mgr)
Ultimate Holding Company: AND HOLDINGS LTD
Immediate Holding Company: AND GROUP PLC
Registration no: 02298288 **Date established:** 1988
Turnover: £20m - £50m **No.of Employees:** 21 - 50 **Product Groups:** 39, 52

Date of Accounts	Mar 12	Mar 11	Mar 10
Sales Turnover	12m	13m	25m
Pre Tax Profit/Loss	88	12	162
Working Capital	90	99	557
Fixed Assets	1m	1m	1m
Current Assets	3m	3m	6m
Current Liabilities	1m	148	625

Armadillo Creative

Fish Quay, North Shields, NE30 1JA
Tel: 0191-257 8380 **Fax:** 0191-257 8342
E-mail: berry@armadillo-creative.com
Website: http://www.armadillo-creative.com

Directors: B. Burgess (MD), P. Stewart (Co Sec)
Immediate Holding Company: ARMADILLO CREATIVE LIMITED
Registration no: 05483211 **Date established:** 2005
No.of Employees: 1 - 10 **Product Groups:** 44, 81

Date of Accounts	Nov 10	Nov 09	Nov 08
Working Capital	-8	-6	13
Fixed Assets	12	14	12
Current Assets	93	133	107

Bay Plastics Ltd

1 High Flatworth, North Shields, NE29 7UZ
Tel: 0191-258 0777 **Fax:** 0191-258 1010
E-mail: enquiries@bayplastics.co.uk
Website: http://www.bayplastics.co.uk
Bank(s): HSBC Bank plc
Directors: M. Coral (MD)
Managers: I. Smithson (Sales Prom Mgr), M. Wong (Tech Serv Mgr), D. Schofield (Personnel)
Immediate Holding Company: BAY PLASTICS LIMITED
Registration no: 02325035 **VAT No.:** GB 499 9881 39
Date established: 1988 **Turnover:** £2m - £5m **No.of Employees:** 21 - 50
Product Groups: 30, 48

Date of Accounts	Sep 11	Sep 10	Sep 09
Working Capital	255	168	126
Fixed Assets	216	137	153
Current Assets	2m	1m	1m

David Bilton Engineering Ltd

77 Hudson Street, North Shields, NE30 1DL
Tel: 0191-296 1428 **Fax:** 0191-257 8611
E-mail: info@davidbiltonengineering.co.uk
Website: http://www.davidbiltonengineering.co.uk
Directors: D. Bilton (Prop)
Managers: A. Mowbray (Sales Admin)
Immediate Holding Company: DAVID BILTON ENGINEERING LIMITED
Registration no: 01951852 **VAT No.:** GB 436 1700 72
Date established: 1985 **Turnover:** £1m - £2m **No.of Employees:** 11 - 20
Product Groups: 51, 52, 54

Date of Accounts	Feb 11	Feb 10	Feb 09
Working Capital	249	360	429
Fixed Assets	16	19	23
Current Assets	310	526	527

Brightblue Studio Ltd

9 Cliffords Fort, North Shields, NE30 1JE
Tel: 0191-257 4454 **Fax:** 0191-257 4454
E-mail: solutions@glassarc.com
Website: http://www.brightbluestudio.co.uk
Directors: M. Wilde (Fin), H. Amos (MD)
Immediate Holding Company: BRIGHTBLUE STUDIO LTD
Registration no: 05071982 **Date established:** 2004
No.of Employees: 1 - 10 **Product Groups:** 30

Date of Accounts	Mar 12	Mar 11	Mar 10
Working Capital	98	110	3
Fixed Assets	10	9	10
Current Assets	108	167	10

Buck & Hickman Ltd

Unit 4 Tyne Tunnel Trade Park Narvik Way, Tyne Tunnel Trading Estate, North Shields, NE29 7DE
Tel: 0191-270 4350 **Fax:** 0191-296 0335
E-mail: newcastle@buckandhickman.com
Website: http://www.buckandhickman.com
Managers: T. Ingram (Sales Prom Mgr)
Ultimate Holding Company: TRAVIS PERKINS PLC
Immediate Holding Company: BOSTON (2011) LIMITED
Registration no: 06028304 **Date established:** 2006
No.of Employees: 11 - 20 **Product Groups:** 24, 33, 36, 37, 46

Date of Accounts	Dec 10	Mar 10	Mar 09
Working Capital	6m	6m	6m
Current Assets	27m	27m	27m

Cosalt Kenmore

1 Liddell Street, North Shields, NE30 1HE
Tel: 0191-259 6644 **Fax:** 0191-258 6363
E-mail: sales@cosalt.com
Website: http://www.cosalt.com
Bank(s): National Westminster Bank Plc
Directors: A. Robson (Co Sec), P. Reilly (MD)
Ultimate Holding Company: COSALT P.L.C.
Immediate Holding Company: COSALT INTERNATIONAL LTD
Registration no: 00553893 **VAT No.:** GB 455 4353 44
Turnover: £2m - £5m **No.of Employees:** 11 - 20 **Product Groups:** 23, 24, 35, 39, 40

Diesel Marine International Ltd

Gloucester Road, North Shields, NE29 8RQ
Tel: 0191-257 5577 **Fax:** 0191-258 6398
E-mail: sales@dmiuk.co.uk
Website: http://www.dmiuk.co.uk
Managers: A. Gray, S. Mavin (Tech Serv Mgr)
Immediate Holding Company: DIESEL MARINE INTERNATIONAL LIMITED
Registration no: 04229349 **Date established:** 2001
Turnover: £10m - £20m **No.of Employees:** 251 - 500 **Product Groups:** 48

Date of Accounts	Dec 11	Dec 10	Dec 09
Sales Turnover	13m	15m	17m
Pre Tax Profit/Loss	348	-1m	28
Working Capital	548	940	818
Fixed Assets	6m	6m	7m
Current Assets	4m	5m	6m
Current Liabilities	1m	2m	2m

DMI Young & Cunningham Ltd

West Chirton Industrial Estate Gloucester Road, North Shields, NE29 8RQ
Tel: 0191-270 4690 **Fax:** 0191-270 4691
E-mail: newcastle@yandc.co.uk
Website: http://www.yandc.co.uk
Bank(s): National Westminster
Directors: A. Hennen (MD), M. Stafford (Dir), M. Turnbull (Dir)
Managers: G. Wood (District Mgr), A. Carty (Admin Off)
Ultimate Holding Company: Cunningham & Shearer (Holdings) Ltd
Immediate Holding Company: Young & Cunningham Ltd
Registration no: 05694248 **Date established:** 1924
Turnover: £20m - £50m **No.of Employees:** 21 - 50 **Product Groups:** 35, 36

Date of Accounts	Dec 07	Dec 06
Sales Turnover	1860	1588
Pre Tax Profit/Loss	126	-19
Working Capital	111	-34
Fixed Assets	51	76
Current Assets	568	548
Current Liabilities	457	582
Total Share Capital	50	50
ROCE% (Return on Capital Employed)	78.0	-45.7
ROT% (Return on Turnover)	6.8	-1.2

Dobson & Surrey Ltd

40 Howard Street, North Shields, NE30 1AR
Tel: 0191-258 1086 **Fax:** 0191-258 0574
E-mail: office@dobsonandsurrey.fsbusiness.co.uk
Directors: L. Surrey (Co Sec), M. Surrey (Dir)
Immediate Holding Company: DOBSON & SURREY LIMITED
Registration no: 01246022 **VAT No.:** GB 178 9022 34
Date established: 1976 **Turnover:** £500,000 - £1m
No.of Employees: 1 - 10 **Product Groups:** 52

Date of Accounts	Mar 11	Mar 10	Mar 09
Working Capital	188	196	252
Fixed Assets	19	27	46
Current Assets	363	316	372

Dowse Crane Hire

Dock Road, North Shields, NE29 6EH
Tel: 0191-258 1486 **Fax:** 0191-258 7414
E-mail: dowsecranehire@gmail.com
Website: http://www.dowsecranehire.co.uk
Directors: G. Dowse (Prop), P. Dowse (Fin)
Immediate Holding Company: DOWSE CRANE HIRE LIMITED
Registration no: 04817806 **Date established:** 2003
No.of Employees: 1 - 10 **Product Groups:** 33, 37, 38, 39, 45, 46, 48, 51, 52, 67, 68, 72, 74, 80, 83, 86

Date of Accounts	Jan 12	Jan 11	Jan 10
Working Capital	-44	-32	-8
Fixed Assets	421	586	665
Current Assets	78	98	123

Drain Centre

20 Alder Road West Chirton North Industrial Estate, North Shields, NE29 8SD
Tel: 0191-257 8125 **Fax:** 0191-257 8819
Website: http://www.draincentre.co.uk
Managers: D. Stuart (Mgr)
Immediate Holding Company: SECURICLAD LIMITED
Registration no: 00411732 **Date established:** 2010 **Turnover:** £1m - £2m
No.of Employees: 1 - 10 **Product Groups:** 30, 36, 39, 40, 42, 48

E S R Electronic Components

Station Road Cullercoats, North Shields, NE30 4PQ
Tel: 0191-251 4363 **Fax:** 0191-252 2296
E-mail: sales@esr.co.uk
Website: http://www.esr.co.uk
Directors: A. Graham (Ptnr)
Immediate Holding Company: ESR ELECTRONIC COMPONENTS LTD
Registration no: 06526729 **VAT No.:** GB 393 4192 34
Date established: 2008 **Turnover:** £250,000 - £500,000
No.of Employees: 1 - 10 **Product Groups:** 35, 37, 47, 67

Date of Accounts	Mar 11	Mar 10	Mar 09
Working Capital	68	67	33
Fixed Assets	1	1	1
Current Assets	114	104	90

Elfab Ltd

Alder Road West Chirton North Industrial Estate, North Shields, NE29 8SD
Tel: 0191-293 1234 **Fax:** 0191-293 1200
E-mail: sales@elfab.com
Website: http://www.elfab.com
Bank(s): Barclays, Newcastle
Directors: C. Widdas (Fin), G. Boomer (Dir)
Ultimate Holding Company: HALMA PUBLIC LIMITED COMPANY
Immediate Holding Company: ELFAB LIMITED
Registration no: 00853197 **VAT No.:** GB 476 6293 06
Date established: 1965 **Turnover:** £5m - £10m
No.of Employees: 51 - 100 **Product Groups:** 33, 34, 35, 36, 40, 84

Date of Accounts	Mar 12	Mar 09	Apr 10
Sales Turnover	9m	9m	7m
Pre Tax Profit/Loss	3m	2m	2m
Working Capital	3m	2m	2m
Fixed Assets	3m	3m	3m
Current Assets	4m	5m	4m
Current Liabilities	582	423	565

Encon Insulation Ltd

Unit E2 High Flatworth, North Shields, NE29 7UZ
Tel: 0191-293 1090 **Fax:** 0191-293 1099
E-mail: i.charlton@encon.co.uk
Website: http://www.encon.co.uk
Directors: I. Charlton (Div)
Ultimate Holding Company: LIBERTY2803 LIMITED
Immediate Holding Company: ENCON INSULATION LIMITED
Registration no: 01377342 **Date established:** 1978 **Turnover:** £1m - £2m
No.of Employees: 11 - 20 **Product Groups:** 35, 66

Date of Accounts	Jul 11	Jul 10	Jul 09
Sales Turnover	187m	184m	208m
Pre Tax Profit/Loss	2m	619	-6m
Working Capital	15m	24m	24m
Fixed Assets	8m	11m	12m
Current Assets	82m	98m	99m
Current Liabilities	5m	4m	5m

1st Choice Fabrications

8 Prospect Terrace, North Shields, NE30 1DX
Tel: 0191-257 1133
Directors: T. Crafford (Prop), T. Crawford (Prop)
Date established: 2006 **No.of Employees:** 1 - 10 **Product Groups:** 35

Graham

Narvik Way Tyne Tunnel Trading Estate, North Shields, NE29 7XJ
Tel: 0191-296 1318 **Fax:** 0191-296 1371
E-mail: enquiries@graham.co.uk
Website: http://www.jewson.co.uk
Managers: J. White (District Mgr)
Ultimate Holding Company: SAINT-GOBAIN PLC
Immediate Holding Company: GRAHAM GROUP LTD
Registration no: 00066738 **Turnover:** £500,000 - £1m
No.of Employees: 1 - 10 **Product Groups:** 66

H R P Ltd

Hamar Close Tyne Tunnel Trading Estate, North Shields, NE29 7XB
Tel: 0191-258 0061 **Fax:** 0191-257 3982
E-mail: newcastle@hrpltd.co.uk
Website: http://www.hrponline.co.uk
Managers: D. Murney
Ultimate Holding Company: HRP HOLDINGS LIMITED
Immediate Holding Company: HRP LIMITED
Registration no: 00832237 **Date established:** 1964
Turnover: £50m - £75m **No.of Employees:** 1 - 10 **Product Groups:** 40, 66

Date of Accounts	Dec 11	Dec 10	Dec 09
Sales Turnover	55m	52m	46m
Pre Tax Profit/Loss	1m	1m	651
Working Capital	8m	7m	6m
Fixed Assets	2m	2m	3m
Current Assets	22m	22m	17m
Current Liabilities	3m	4m	3m

James Hogg (Chemical Engineering) Ltd

Collingwood House Lawson Street, North Shields, NE29 6TF
Tel: 0191-257 8247 **Fax:** 0191-296 1445
E-mail: sales@james-hogg.co.uk
Website: http://www.pneumatics.uk.net
Directors: R. Stabler (Prop)
Immediate Holding Company: HOGG ENGINEERING LIMITED
Registration no: 01758365 **VAT No.:** GB 176 1663 48
Date established: 1983 **Turnover:** £2m - £5m **No.of Employees:** 1 - 10
Product Groups: 67

Date of Accounts	Jan 12	Jan 11	Jan 10
Working Capital	182	206	314
Fixed Assets	435	469	435
Current Assets	801	736	678

Honeywell International Inc

Elm Road, North Shields, NE29 8SA
Tel: 0191-258 2821 **Fax:** 0191-258 7040
E-mail: info@holtsauto.com
Website: http://www.honeywell.com
Bank(s): Barclays, Newcastle
Directors: L. Strauchan (MD), O. Thompson (Sales & Mktg), O. Thomssen (Sales & Mktg), T. Murray (I.T. Dir)
Managers: K. Arnold (Buyer), L. Strong (Plant), S. Nixon (Purch Mgr), M. Reece
Ultimate Holding Company: Invensys
Registration no: 00320495 **VAT No.:** GB 242 3380 87
Turnover: £10m - £20m **No.of Employees:** 51 - 100 **Product Groups:** 37, 38

House Of York

Norham Road, North Shields, NE29 7UN
Tel: 0191-257 0101 **Fax:** 0191- 2586649
Bank(s): National Westminster
Directors: W. Deyermond (MD)
Managers: B. Bennett, J. Brannen (Nat Sales Mgr)
Immediate Holding Company: KIRIL MISCHEFF GROUP
Registration no: 01026912 **VAT No.:** GB 235 6543 59
Date established: 1972 **Turnover:** £2m - £5m **No.of Employees:** 11 - 20
Product Groups: 20

Date of Accounts	Sep 07	Sep 06	Sep 05
Sales Turnover	N/A	N/A	169
Working Capital	-1268	-1268	-1268
Current Assets	8	8	41
Current Liabilities	1276	1276	1309
Total Share Capital	55	55	55

Interkool North

28 Tynemouth Road, North Shields, NE30 4AA
Tel: 0191-276 4000
Website: http://www.interkoolnorth.co.uk
Directors: D. Fell (Prop)
Immediate Holding Company: MCGREGOR ASSOCIATES LIMITED
Date established: 2011 **No.of Employees:** 1 - 10 **Product Groups:** 40, 66

Jewson Ltd

Unit S1 Narvik Way Tyne Tunnel Trading Estate, North Shields, NE29 7XJ
Tel: 0191-257 6221 **Fax:** 0191-257 6179
Website: http://www.jewson.co.uk
Bank(s): Barclays
Managers: S. Best (Mgr)
Ultimate Holding Company: COMPAGNIE DE SAINT GOBAIN (FRANCE)
Immediate Holding Company: JEWSON LIMITED
Registration no: 00348407 **VAT No.:** GB 394 1212 63
Date established: 1939 **No.of Employees:** 21 - 50 **Product Groups:** 66

Date of Accounts	Dec 11	Dec 10	Dec 09
Sales Turnover	1606m	1547m	1485m
Pre Tax Profit/Loss	18m	100m	45m
Working Capital	-345m	-250m	-349m
Fixed Assets	496m	387m	461m
Current Assets	657m	1005m	1320m
Current Liabilities	66m	120m	64m

Kwik Kook

16 Selkirk Way, North Shields, NE29 8DD
Tel: 0191-257 1563
Directors: D. Lopez (Prop)
Date established: 1991 **No.of Employees:** 1 - 10 **Product Groups:** 36, 40

John Lilley & Gillie Ltd

Unit 17 Elm Road, North Shields, NE29 8SE
Tel: 0191-257 2217 **Fax:** 0191-257 1521
E-mail: sales@lilleyandgillie.co.uk
Website: http://www.lilleyandgillie.co.uk
Bank(s): Lloyds TSB Bank plc
Directors: D. Addy (Tech Serv), R. Boyer (Fin), G. Heathcote (Dir), M. Boyd (Sales)
Ultimate Holding Company: HARRISON MARITIME (HOLDINGS) LIMITED
Immediate Holding Company: JOHN LILLEY & GILLIE LIMITED
Registration no: 02846087 **VAT No.:** GB 621 2139 85
Date established: 1993 **Turnover:** £5m - £10m **No.of Employees:** 21 - 50
Product Groups: 38, 39, 49

Date of Accounts	Dec 11	Dec 10	Dec 09
Sales Turnover	8m	7m	7m
Pre Tax Profit/Loss	-187	-421	-471
Working Capital	1m	1m	800
Fixed Assets	411	482	490
Current Assets	4m	3m	2m
Current Liabilities	124	194	810

Metro Leisure Developments Ltd
13 Hylton Street, North Shields, NE29 6SQ
Tel: 0191-258 3677 **Fax:** 0191-295 4926
E-mail: johnkelly@metroleisure.co.uk
Website: http://www.metroleisure.co.uk
Directors: J. Kelly (Dir), J. Hudson (Fin)
Immediate Holding Company: METRO LEISURE DEVELOPMENTS (NORTH EAST) LIMITED
Registration no: 07274509 **VAT No.:** GB 436 2114 80
Date established: 2010 **Turnover:** Up to £250,000
No.of Employees: 1 - 10 **Product Groups:** 30

Date of Accounts	Jun 12	Jun 11
Working Capital	-12	-12
Fixed Assets	10	12
Current Assets	N/A	1

Metromold Ltd
Unit 19c Elm Road, North Shields, NE29 8SE
Tel: 0191-296 3303 **Fax:** 0191-296 3303
E-mail: info@metromold.co.uk
Website: http://www.metromold.co.uk
Directors: S. Richards (Co Sec)
Immediate Holding Company: METROMOLD LIMITED
Registration no: 02538303 **VAT No.:** GB 556 0229 51
Date established: 1990 **Turnover:** Up to £250,000
No.of Employees: 1 - 10 **Product Groups:** 30

Date of Accounts	Dec 11	Dec 10	Dec 09
Working Capital	53	38	21
Fixed Assets	14	14	9
Current Assets	127	99	61

Modrec International Holdings Ltd
Bugatti House Norham Road, North Shields, NE29 7HA
Tel: 0191-258 4451 **Fax:** 0191-258 2983
E-mail: sales@modrec.co.uk
Website: http://www.modrecinternational.com
Bank(s): Yorkshire Bank.
Directors: D. Allen (Comm)
Immediate Holding Company: HNM INVESTMENTS LIMITED
Registration no: 00243098 **VAT No.:** GB 141 4362 77
Date established: 2029 **Turnover:** £5m - £10m **No.of Employees:** 11 - 20
Product Groups: 63, 66

Date of Accounts	Dec 11	Dec 10	Dec 09
Working Capital	-261	-304	191
Fixed Assets	4m	4m	4m
Current Assets	459	297	452

Monitor Coatings Ltd
Monitor House 2 Elm Road West Chirton Industrial Estate, North Shields, NE29 8SE
Tel: 0191-293 7040 **Fax:** 0191-293 7041
E-mail: sales@monitorcoatings.co.uk
Website: http://www.monitorcoatings.co.uk
Directors: B. Allcock (MD), M. Findlay (Fin), P. Winstear (Fin)
Managers: M. Thomson, A. Britain
Immediate Holding Company: MONITOR COATINGS LIMITED
Registration no: 04806374 **Date established:** 2003 **Turnover:** £2m - £5m
No.of Employees: 21 - 50 **Product Groups:** 35, 39, 48, 85

Date of Accounts	Oct 11	Oct 10	Oct 09
Working Capital	-241	-220	53
Fixed Assets	2m	2m	2m
Current Assets	1m	1m	913

Norfran Ltd
West Morland Road Wast Chirton Estate, North Shields, NE29 8RF
Tel: 0191-291 6000 **Fax:** 0191-257 1549
E-mail: jb@norfran.co.uk
Website: http://www.norfran.co.uk
Bank(s): Lloyds TSB Bank plc
Managers: M. Smith (Chief Mgr)
Immediate Holding Company: NORFRAN LIMITED
Registration no: SC361880 **VAT No.:** GB 376 4822 23
Date established: 2009 **Turnover:** £5m - £10m
No.of Employees: 51 - 100 **Product Groups:** 34

Date of Accounts	Jun 11	Jun 10
Working Capital	434	169
Fixed Assets	492	145
Current Assets	2m	1m
Current Liabilities	990	N/A

North Shields Grinding
The Old Maltings Tanners Bank, North Shields, NE30 1JH
Tel: 0191-257 2342 **Fax:** 0191-258 5310
E-mail: office@northshieldsgrinding.co.uk
Directors: G. Hurst (Ptnr)
Ultimate Holding Company: AND HOLDINGS LTD
Immediate Holding Company: AND HOLDINGS LTD
Registration no: 03366419 **Date established:** 1999
No.of Employees: 1 - 10 **Product Groups:** 46, 48

Date of Accounts	Oct 11	Oct 10	Oct 09
Working Capital	1m	1m	1m
Fixed Assets	44	73	102
Current Assets	2m	1m	1m

Packaging Solutions
5 Albion House West Percy Street, North Shields, NE29 0DW
Tel: 0191-257 9577 **Fax:** 0191-257 7018
Managers: S. Duffy (Mgr)
Date established: 2001 **No.of Employees:** 1 - 10 **Product Groups:** 38, 42

Recticel Carobel
Norham Road, North Shields, NE29 7UX
Tel: 0191-296 1010 **Fax:** 0191-296 3321
E-mail: bolan.graham@recticel.com
Website: http://www.recticel.com
Managers: G. Bolan (District Mgr), R. Armstrong (Chief Mgr)
Registration no: 00665376 **VAT No.:** GB 175 9286 18
Date established: 2000 **Turnover:** £2m - £5m **No.of Employees:** 51 - 100
Product Groups: 30, 31

G S Robinson & Co. Ltd
Unit 30 West Chirton South Trading Estate, North Shields, NE29 7TY
Tel: 0191-257 5374 **Fax:** 0191-296 1341
E-mail: david@gsrobinson.co.uk
Website: http://www.gsrobinson.co.uk
Bank(s): Barclays
Directors: A. Dougal (Fin), D. Dougal (MD)
Immediate Holding Company: G.S.ROBINSON & CO.LIMITED
Registration no: 00603933 **VAT No.:** GB 176 9733 13
Date established: 1958 **Turnover:** £250,000 - £500,000
No.of Employees: 11 - 20 **Product Groups:** 35, 36, 48

Date of Accounts	Oct 11	Oct 10	Oct 09
Working Capital	53	-12	4
Fixed Assets	23	23	29
Current Assets	269	230	173

Stratton Valves & Engineering Ltd
Unit 2 Prospect Terrace Industrial Estate, North Shields, NE30 1DX
Tel: 0191-296 0050 **Fax:** 0191-296 1637
E-mail: phil@strattonvalves.co.uk
Website: http://www.strattonvalves.co.uk
Directors: P. Martin (MD)
Immediate Holding Company: STRATTON VALVES AND ENGINEERING LIMITED
Registration no: 04314637 **Date established:** 2001
No.of Employees: 1 - 10 **Product Groups:** 36

Date of Accounts	Nov 11	Nov 10	Nov 09
Working Capital	6	16	29
Fixed Assets	12	18	4
Current Assets	134	115	118

Sutton Services International Ltd
Unit 8 Mercury Orion Way, Orion Business Park, North Shields, NE29 7SN
Tel: 0191-296 2999 **Fax:** 0191-296 5296
E-mail: newcastle@sutton.eu
Website: http://www.sutton.eu
Bank(s): Nat West
Directors: P. Kilgour (Dir), S. Crossley (Co Sec)
Managers: T. Ellis (Admin Off)
Ultimate Holding Company: SUTTON GROUP LIMITED
Immediate Holding Company: SUTTON SERVICES INTERNATIONAL LIMITED
Registration no: 02630803 **Date established:** 1991 **Turnover:** £2m - £5m
No.of Employees: 21 - 50 **Product Groups:** 48, 51, 54, 85

Date of Accounts	May 11	May 10	May 09
Sales Turnover	3m	3m	4m
Pre Tax Profit/Loss	-167	-101	271
Working Capital	209	359	547
Fixed Assets	120	141	168
Current Assets	1m	1m	2m
Current Liabilities	186	270	421

Syntema N Eltd
Unit B8 Hamar Close Tyne Tunnel Trading Estate, North Shields, NE29 7XB
Tel: 0191-258 4564 **Fax:** 0191-258 2568
E-mail: mark@syntemaeastmidlands.co.uk
Website: http://www.syntemanortheast.com
Directors: M. Barnes (Dir)
Immediate Holding Company: SYMPHONY COATINGS (NORTH EAST) LIMITED
Registration no: 03212674 **Date established:** 1996
No.of Employees: 1 - 10 **Product Groups:** 46, 48

Tyne Forge
139 Tynemouth Road, North Shields, NE30 1ED
Tel: 0191-258 5060
E-mail: k-hindhaugh@tyneforge.co.uk
Website: http://www.tyneforge.co.uk
Directors: K. Hindhaugh (Prop)
Date established: 1990 **No.of Employees:** 1 - 10 **Product Groups:** 26, 35

Tynemouth Wrought Iron Co
T S T House Cumberland Road, North Shields, NE29 8RD
Tel: 0191-258 4449 **Fax:** 0191-258 4449
Directors: A. Cowie (Prop)
Immediate Holding Company: PERCY ANDERSON LIMITED
Registration no: 06737766 **Date established:** 1978
No.of Employees: 1 - 10 **Product Groups:** 26, 35

Date of Accounts	May 11	May 10	May 09
Working Capital	-379	-441	-135
Fixed Assets	407	425	437
Current Assets	528	449	642

V3 Technologies
Coble Dene Road, North Shields, NE29 6DE
Tel: 0191-259 5544 **Fax:** 0191-259 5544
E-mail: info@v3technologies.com
Website: http://www.v3technologies.com
Directors: C. Qian (Fin), N. Balkhi (Dir)
Immediate Holding Company: INNOVATION INFORMATION TECHNOLOGY LIMITED
Registration no: 05348193 **Date established:** 1999
Turnover: Up to £250,000 **No.of Employees:** 1 - 10 **Product Groups:** 37, 67, 79

Date of Accounts	Dec 05
Pre Tax Profit/Loss	15
Working Capital	12
Fixed Assets	2
Current Assets	18
Current Liabilities	6
ROCE% (Return on Capital Employed)	107.5

Ryton

Datasupplies (Stationery) Ltd
Stargate Industrial Estate, Ryton, NE40 3EX
Tel: 0191-413 5936 **Fax:** 0191-413 4173
E-mail: sales@datasupplies.co.uk
Website: http://www.datasupplies.co.uk
Bank(s): Barclays
Directors: S. Sedlacek (Comm), C. Robson (Sales)
Managers: J. Proud (Mktg Serv Mgr)
Registration no: 01513144 **Turnover:** £2m - £5m
No.of Employees: 11 - 20 **Product Groups:** 22, 23, 24, 25, 26, 27, 28, 29, 30, 32, 35, 37, 40, 42, 44, 48, 49, 63, 64, 65, 67, 77, 81, 83, 89

Date of Accounts	Jul 11	Jul 10	Jul 09
Working Capital	252	248	300
Fixed Assets	388	401	432
Current Assets	1m	1m	1m

Dowding & Mills
Stargate Industrial Estate Bailey House, Ryton, NE40 3DG
Tel: 0191-413 2244 **Fax:** 0191-413 3111
E-mail: paul.snelling@dowdingandmills.com
Website: http://www.dowdingandmills.com
Managers: P. Snelling (Sales Admin), D. Lee (District Mgr), C. Mudd (Chief Mgr), A. Apperley (District Mgr)
Immediate Holding Company: STARGATE PROPERTY COMPANY LIMITED
Registration no: 03378744 **Date established:** 1998
No.of Employees: 1 - 10 **Product Groups:** 35, 37

H Fereday & Sons
11 Holburn Crescent, Ryton, NE40 3DH
Tel: 0191-413 6273
E-mail: david@hfereday.com
Website: http://www.hfereday.com
Directors: D. Fereday (Prop)
Date established: 2001 **No.of Employees:** 1 - 10 **Product Groups:** 38, 42

Jewson Ltd
Stargate Industrial Estate, Ryton, NE40 3DG
Tel: 0191-413 5081 **Fax:** 0191-413 6367
E-mail: mike.elliott@jewson.co.uk
Website: http://www.jewson.co.uk
Managers: M. Elliott (District Mgr)
Ultimate Holding Company: COMPAGNIE DE SAINT GOBAIN (FRANCE)
Immediate Holding Company: JEWSON LIMITED
Registration no: 00348407 **VAT No.:** GB 394 1212 63
Date established: 1939 **Turnover:** £5m - £10m **No.of Employees:** 1 - 10
Product Groups: 66

Date of Accounts	Dec 11	Dec 10	Dec 09
Sales Turnover	1606m	1547m	1485m
Pre Tax Profit/Loss	18m	100m	45m
Working Capital	-345m	-250m	-349m
Fixed Assets	496m	387m	461m
Current Assets	657m	1005m	1320m
Current Liabilities	66m	120m	64m

Material Procurement Asia
10 Holburn Close, Ryton, NE40 3SA
Tel: 0191-422 4569 **Fax:** 0191-422 4569
E-mail: enquiries@materialprocurementasia.com
Website: http://www.materialprocurementasia.com
Managers: M. Astley (Mgr)
Date established: 2008 **Turnover:** Up to £250,000
No.of Employees: 1 - 10 **Product Groups:** 61, 84

South Shields

B C I Stretchers Ltd
386-388 South Eldon Street, South Shields, NE33 5SY
Tel: 0191-455 3984 **Fax:** 0191-456 9653
E-mail: info@bci-stretchers.co.uk
Website: http://www.bci-stretchers.co.uk
Directors: W. Cook (MD)
Immediate Holding Company: B.C.I. (STRETCHERS) LIMITED
Registration no: 04133369 **VAT No.:** 440 9715 48 **Date established:** 2000
Turnover: £250,000 - £500,000 **No.of Employees:** 1 - 10
Product Groups: 30, 38

Date of Accounts	Dec 11	Dec 10	Dec 09
Working Capital	229	214	195
Fixed Assets	3	3	4
Current Assets	248	239	209

J Barbour & Sons Ltd
Simonside, South Shields, NE34 9PD
Tel: 0191-455 4444 **Fax:** 0191-454 2944
E-mail: info@barbour.com
Website: http://www.barbour.com
Bank(s): Barclays, Newcastle Upon Tyne
Directors: I. Beattie (Sales), B. Readman-bell (Fin), S. Buck (Co Sec)
Managers: N. Belby (Personnel), N. Thursby (Tech Serv Mgr)
Immediate Holding Company: J.BARBOUR & SONS,LIMITED
Registration no: 00124201 **VAT No.:** GB 175 9279 15
Date established: 2012 **Turnover:** £75m - £125m
No.of Employees: 501 - 1000 **Product Groups:** 24

Date of Accounts	Dec 11	Dec 10	Dec 09
Sales Turnover	122m	90m	74m
Pre Tax Profit/Loss	17m	11m	10m
Working Capital	38m	36m	36m
Fixed Assets	9m	10m	10m
Current Assets	70m	58m	52m
Current Liabilities	20m	10m	8m

Be Modern Ltd
Western Approach, South Shields, NE33 5QZ
Tel: 0191-455 3571 **Fax:** 0191-456 5556
E-mail: enquiries@bemodern.co.uk
Website: http://www.bemodern.co.uk
Directors: J. Harris (Fin), R. Appleby (MD)
Managers: G. Calderwood (Tech Serv Mgr), M. Hunter, A. Spence (Personnel), K. Gallagher (Purch Mgr), O. Lee (Sales Prom Mgr)
Ultimate Holding Company: BE MODERN HOLDINGS LIMITED
Immediate Holding Company: BE MODERN LIMITED
Registration no: 00829005 **VAT No.:** GB 017 8430 42
Date established: 1964 **Turnover:** £20m - £50m
No.of Employees: 251 - 500 **Product Groups:** 14, 25, 26, 33, 40

Date of Accounts	May 08	May 09	May 10
Sales Turnover	25m	26m	25m
Pre Tax Profit/Loss	2m	2m	1m
Working Capital	8m	9m	8m
Fixed Assets	5m	3m	3m
Current Assets	15m	16m	14m
Current Liabilities	5m	4m	3m

Biffa Waste Services Ltd
Shaftesbury Avenue, South Shields, NE34 9PH
Tel: 0191-454 6500 **Fax:** 0191-454 7548
E-mail: marketing@biffa.co.uk
Website: http://www.biffa.co.uk
Managers: A. Anderson (Mgr)
Immediate Holding Company: BIFFA WASTE SERVICES LIMITED
Registration no: 00946107 **Date established:** 1969
No.of Employees: 21 - 50 **Product Groups:** 32, 54

Date of Accounts	Mar 08	Mar 09	Apr 10
Sales Turnover	555m	574m	492m
Pre Tax Profit/Loss	23m	50m	30m
Working Capital	229m	271m	293m
Fixed Assets	371m	360m	378m
Current Assets	409m	534m	609m
Current Liabilities	50m	100m	115m

Border Leathercrafts Ltd

Shaftsbury Avenue Simonside Industrial Estate, South Shields, NE34 9PH
Tel: 0191-432 4752 **Fax:** 0191-454 7064
E-mail: bob@leathercrafts.com
Website: http://www.leathercrafts.com
Product Groups: 22, 23, 24, 30, 49, 61, 65

Date of Accounts	Sep 09	Sep 08	Sep 07
Working Capital	6	-1	7
Fixed Assets	1	1	N/A
Current Assets	41	47	64

CAL-Logistics Ltd

16 Sea Winnings Way, South Shields, NE33 3NE
Tel: 0191-429 0770 **Fax:** 0191-455 2604
E-mail: info@cal-logistics.com
Website: http://www.cal-logistics.com
Registration no: 3980024 **Date established:** 2006 **Turnover:** £5m - £10m
No.of Employees: 1 - 10 **Product Groups:** 37

Date of Accounts	Apr 08
Working Capital	-40
Fixed Assets	1
Current Liabilities	40

Custom Bags

Unit 2b 102 Throckley Way Middlefields Industrial Estate, South Shields, NE34 0NU
Tel: 0191-427 7766 **Fax:** 0191-427 7755
E-mail: paul@custombags.co.uk
Website: http://www.custombags.co.uk
Bank(s): Barclays
Directors: P. Chaganis (Ptnr), D. Curry (Ptnr)
Managers: A. Curry (Purch Mgr), S. Wilkinson (Sales Admin)
Immediate Holding Company: CUSTOM BAGS LIMITED
Registration no: 07065333 **VAT No.:** 425 9672 24 **Date established:** 2009
Turnover: £500,000 - £1m **No.of Employees:** 21 - 50 **Product Groups:** 30

Denholm Barwil Ltd

Keel House Tyne Dock, South Shields, NE34 9PY
Tel: 0191-454 9829 **Fax:** 0191-454 9844
E-mail: paul.hutchinson@denholm-barwil.com
Website: http://www.denholm-barwil.com
Managers: P. Hutchinson (Mgr)
Immediate Holding Company: DENHOLM BARWIL LIMITED
Registration no: SC032785 **Date established:** 1958
No.of Employees: 1 - 10 **Product Groups:** 72, 74, 76, 84

Date of Accounts	Dec 11	Dec 10	Dec 09
Sales Turnover	7m	8m	9m
Pre Tax Profit/Loss	283	372	406
Working Capital	72	-6	-176
Fixed Assets	312	399	613
Current Assets	6m	7m	5m
Current Liabilities	1m	2m	2m

Elsy & Gibbons

Amos Ayre Place Simonside Industrial Estate, South Shields, NE34 9PE
Tel: 0191-427 0777 **Fax:** 0191-427 0888
E-mail: ian.lock@baxigroup.com
Website: http://www.elsonhotwater.co.uk
Bank(s): Lloyds TSB Bank plc
Directors: M. Mcdonald (MD)
Managers: M. Flowers (I.T. Exec), P. Stevenson (Purch Mgr), P. Dunwoodie (Sales Prom Mgr), K. Higginson (Personnel), M. Webster (Sales Prom Mgr), I. Lock (Chief Mgr)
Ultimate Holding Company: NEWMOND GROUP
Immediate Holding Company: BAXI
VAT No.: GB 439 4758 08 **Turnover:** £5m - £10m
No.of Employees: 51 - 100 **Product Groups:** 35

Europian Metal Recycling Ltd

West Side Tyne Dock, South Shields, NE34 9PL
Tel: 0191-454 1773 **Fax:** 0191-454 3392
E-mail: info@emrltd.com
Website: http://www.emrltd.com
Managers: K. Taylor
Ultimate Holding Company: GRAINCO LIMITED
Immediate Holding Company: GRAINCO SCOTLAND LIMITED
Registration no: 02954623 **Date established:** 2002
Turnover: £10m - £20m **No.of Employees:** 1 - 10 **Product Groups:** 42, 66

Feller UK Ltd

Heddon Way Middlefields Industrial Estate, South Shields, NE34 0NU
Tel: 0191-455 1048 **Fax:** 0191-456 6603
E-mail: trevorevans@feller.co.uk
Website: http://www.feller-at.com
Bank(s): Barclays, Sunderland
Directors: B. Ascher (Fin)
Managers: T. Evans (Mgr), C. Aggas (Sales Prom Mgr)
Ultimate Holding Company: HOCHLAND PRIVATSTIFTUNG (AUSTRIA)
Immediate Holding Company: FELLER (UK) LIMITED
Registration no: 01897323 **Date established:** 1985 **Turnover:** £5m - £10m
No.of Employees: 21 - 50 **Product Groups:** 37

Date of Accounts	Dec 11	Dec 10	Dec 09
Working Capital	1m	895	622
Fixed Assets	170	211	291
Current Assets	1m	1m	898
Current Liabilities	9	N/A	N/A

General Laboratory Services Ltd

Unit 1b Rekendyke Industrial Estate, South Shields, NE33 5BZ
Tel: 0191-427 1060 **Fax:** 0191-456 4787
Website: http://www.freeuk.com
Directors: C. Allan (Dir)
Immediate Holding Company: GENERAL LABORATORY SERVICES LIMITED
Registration no: 02722209 **Date established:** 1992
No.of Employees: 11 - 20 **Product Groups:** 40, 66

Date of Accounts	Jan 11	Jan 10	Jan 09
Working Capital	104	119	110
Fixed Assets	25	34	39
Current Assets	153	189	168

Harlow Printing Ltd

7 Maxwell Street, South Shields, NE33 4PU
Tel: 0191-455 4286 **Fax:** 0191-427 0195
E-mail: sales@harlowprinting.co.uk
Website: http://www.harlowprinting.co.uk
Directors: J. Short (Mkt Research), R. Walker (MD), G. Parfitt (Fin)
Immediate Holding Company: HARLOW PRINTING LIMITED
Registration no: 00435445 **Date established:** 1947 **Turnover:** £5m - £10m
No.of Employees: 51 - 100 **Product Groups:** 27, 44

Date of Accounts	Apr 11	Apr 10	Apr 09
Sales Turnover	8m	8m	7m
Pre Tax Profit/Loss	930	620	392
Working Capital	912	809	489
Fixed Assets	2m	1m	1m
Current Assets	3m	2m	2m
Current Liabilities	1m	746	851

Hedley Engineering Services Ltd

Unit 3 Havelock Street, South Shields, NE33 5DZ
Tel: 0191-456 0250 **Fax:** 0191-455 6040
E-mail: sales@hedley.co.uk
Website: http://www.hedley.co.uk
Directors: P. Dearnaley (Dir)
Immediate Holding Company: HEDLEY (ENGINEERING SERVICES) LIMITED
Registration no: 03904760 **Date established:** 2000
No.of Employees: 1 - 10 **Product Groups:** 30, 38, 39, 40

Date of Accounts	Mar 11	Mar 10	Mar 09
Working Capital	-38	-25	-30
Fixed Assets	80	89	99
Current Assets	166	196	218

Hi Spec Plastics Ltd

Unit 10 Rekendyke Industrial Estate West Walpole Street, South Shields, NE33 5BY
Tel: 0191-456 2146 **Fax:** 0191-427 5553
E-mail: sales@hispecplastics.co.uk
Website: http://www.hispecplastics.co.uk
Managers: C. Hall (Mgr)
Immediate Holding Company: HI-SPEC COMPOSITES LIMITED
Registration no: 04396522 **Date established:** 2002
Turnover: £500,000 - £1m **No.of Employees:** 11 - 20 **Product Groups:** 30

Date of Accounts	Mar 11	Mar 10	Mar 09
Working Capital	144	157	102
Fixed Assets	161	69	93
Current Assets	286	321	317

Lees Cleaning Contractors LLP

43 Maxwell Street, South Shields, NE33 4PU
Tel: 0191-456 8957 **Fax:** 0191-454 2763
E-mail: info@leescleaning.co.uk
Website: http://www.leescleaning.co.uk
Directors: D. West (Dir)
Managers: J. Seely
Immediate Holding Company: LEES CLEANING CONTRACTORS LLP
Registration no: OC350879 **Date established:** 2009
No.of Employees: 11 - 20 **Product Groups:** 41, 42, 52

Date of Accounts	Jan 12	Jan 11
Working Capital	1m	992
Fixed Assets	784	823
Current Assets	2m	1m

Milburn Services Ltd

43 Maxwell Street, South Shields, NE33 4PU
Tel: 0191-455 6197 **Fax:** 0191-454 0874
E-mail: office@milburnservices.co.uk
Website: http://www.milburnservices.co.uk
Bank(s): Lloyds TSB
Directors: D. West (MD), G. Bonnici (Fin)
Ultimate Holding Company: JOSH & TOM LTD
Immediate Holding Company: MILBURN SERVICES LIMITED
Registration no: SC105066 **VAT No.:** GB 459 8555 85
Date established: 1987 **Turnover:** £5m - £10m **No.of Employees:** 11 - 20
Product Groups: 40, 54, 85

Date of Accounts	Mar 08	Apr 09	Apr 10
Sales Turnover	437	658	N/A
Pre Tax Profit/Loss	50	350	N/A
Working Capital	525	782	917
Fixed Assets	34	17	19
Current Assets	2m	1m	1m
Current Liabilities	1m	171	N/A

Port Of Tyne Authority

Maritime House Tyne Dock, South Shields, NE34 9PT
Tel: 0191-455 2671 **Fax:** 0191-455 4687
E-mail: margaret.brooks@portoftyne.co.uk
Website: http://www.portoftyne.co.uk
Bank(s): Barclays
Directors: K. Wilson (MD), M. Davison (Fin), K. Ward (Dir), A. Moffat (Grp Chief Exec), I. Wrigglesworth (Dir)
Managers: J. Dunn (Mktg Serv Mgr), M. Nicholson, J. Gillon (Personnel), I. Blake (I.T. Exec)
Immediate Holding Company: PORT OF TYNE PUBLIC LIMITED COMPANY
Registration no: 03158026 **VAT No.:** GB 176 4425 49
Date established: 1996 **Turnover:** £5m - £10m
No.of Employees: 251 - 500 **Product Groups:** 71, 74, 77, 84

Roundel Manufacturing Ltd

Harton Centre 52 Harton Lane, South Shields, NE34 0EE
Tel: 0191-427 1222 **Fax:** 0191-427 0902
E-mail: info@roundelkitchens.co.uk
Website: http://www.roundelkitchens.co.uk
Directors: L. Oman (Dir)
Immediate Holding Company: ROUNDEL MANUFACTURING LIMITED
Registration no: 01586822 **Date established:** 1981 **Turnover:** £5m - £10m
No.of Employees: 101 - 250 **Product Groups:** 26

Date of Accounts	Jan 12	Jan 11	Jan 10
Sales Turnover	10m	10m	7m
Pre Tax Profit/Loss	1	309	340
Working Capital	884	846	553
Fixed Assets	2m	2m	2m
Current Assets	2m	2m	2m
Current Liabilities	348	266	197

Saft Ltd

River Drive, South Shields, NE33 2TR
Tel: 0191-456 1451 **Fax:** 0191-456 6383
E-mail: sales@saftbatteries.com
Website: http://www.saftbatteries.com
Bank(s): Barclays
Directors: J. Taylor (Sales), T. Collinson (MD)
Managers: D. Stead (Tech Serv Mgr), I. Welsh (Comptroller), P. Knight (Purch Mgr)
Ultimate Holding Company: SAFT GROUPE SA (FRANCE)
Immediate Holding Company: SAFT LIMITED
Registration no: 00328857 **VAT No.:** GB 242 3380 87
Date established: 1937 **Turnover:** £5m - £10m
No.of Employees: 51 - 100 **Product Groups:** 37

Date of Accounts	Dec 11	Dec 10	Dec 09
Sales Turnover	9m	11m	12m
Pre Tax Profit/Loss	1m	1m	1m
Working Capital	4m	3m	2m
Fixed Assets	3m	3m	4m
Current Assets	5m	5m	5m
Current Liabilities	612	652	675

South Tyneside Council

Town Hall Westoe Road, South Shields, NE33 2RL
Tel: 0191-427 7000 **Fax:** 0191-455 0208
E-mail: marketing@southtyneside.gov.uk
Website: http://www.Southtyneside.info
Bank(s): Co-Operative
Directors: M. Swales (Grp Chief Exec)
Immediate Holding Company: SOUTH TYNESIDE HOMES LIMITED
Registration no: 05381705 **Date established:** 2005
Turnover: £75m - £125m **No.of Employees:** 11 - 20 **Product Groups:** 80

Tyne Tubes Ltd

Nile Street, South Shields, NE33 1RH
Tel: 0191-455 1144 **Fax:** 0191-455 4339
E-mail: tynetubes@aol.com
Website: http://www.tynetubes.com
Bank(s): National Westminster Bank Plc
Directors: R. Foster (Ch), D. Armstrong (MD), H. Foster (Dir), J. Foster (Ch), W. McKean (Comm), N. Foster-Hird (Dir), F. Morton (Co Sec)
Managers: I. Lawson (Sales Prom Mgr), J. Kelly (Chief Mgr), C. Jary (Purch Mgr), D. Armstrong (Chief Acct), M. Hendry (Chief Mgr), M. Hickey (Purch Mgr)
Registration no: 05363690 **VAT No.:** GB 605 5074 62
Date established: 1993 **Turnover:** £10m - £20m
No.of Employees: 11 - 20 **Product Groups:** 31, 35, 36, 48

Sunderland

Abfad Ltd

Unit 93 Business & Innovation Centre Silverbriar, Sunderland Enterprise Park, Sunderland, SR5 2TQ
Tel: 0191-516 6223 **Fax:** 0191-516 6224
E-mail: info@abfad.co.uk
Website: http://www.abfad.co.uk
Directors: C. Haritou (Dir)
Immediate Holding Company: ABFAD LIMITED
Registration no: 03165833 **Date established:** 1996
No.of Employees: 11 - 20 **Product Groups:** 46, 48

Date of Accounts	Mar 12	Mar 11	Mar 10
Working Capital	-162	-144	120
Fixed Assets	276	286	310
Current Assets	209	170	161
Current Liabilities	N/A	N/A	20

Acxiom Ltd

Doxford Technology Park, Sunderland, SR9 9XZ
Tel: 0191-525 7000 **Fax:** 0191-525 7100
E-mail: info@2touch.co.uk
Website: http://www.acxiom.com
Bank(s): Barclays
Directors: H. Stein (Co Sec), S. Gray (MD)
Managers: Y. Charlton (Personnel), D. Whiskens, G. Hogg, A. Holte (Fin Mgr), N. Rushden (Tech Serv Mgr)
Ultimate Holding Company: ACXIOM CORP. INC. (USA)
Immediate Holding Company: ACXIOM LIMITED
Registration no: 01182318 **Date established:** 1974 **Turnover:** £5m - £10m
No.of Employees: 11 - 20 **Product Groups:** 44, 80, 81

Advanced Carpentry & Construction

23 Grindon Lane, Sunderland, SR3 4EX
Tel: 0191-528 1494 **Fax:** 0191-523 7722
E-mail: acc.ltd@btconnect.com
Directors: S. Donnigan (Dir), I. Donnigan (Fin)
Immediate Holding Company: ADVANCED CARPENTRY AND CONSTRUCTION LIMITED
Registration no: 06134202 **Date established:** 2007
No.of Employees: 1 - 10 **Product Groups:** 14, 23, 30, 33, 34, 35, 40, 45, 48, 51, 52, 66, 67, 80

Date of Accounts	Oct 07	Oct 06	Oct 05
Working Capital	N/A	1	1
Fixed Assets	6	7	5
Current Assets	8	3	7
Current Liabilities	7	2	5

AMC Ltd

23 Grindon Lane, Sunderland, SR3 4EX
Tel: 0191-528 1494 **Fax:** 0191-523 7722
E-mail: acc.ltd@btconnect.com
Product Groups: 07, 48, 52

Asap Shutters

255 Southwick Road, Sunderland, SR5 2AB
Tel: 0191-516 8833 **Fax:** 0191-516 8833
E-mail: michaellemon@asapshutters.co.uk
Website: http://www.asapshutters.com
Directors: M. Lemon (Prop)
Immediate Holding Company: ASAP SHUTTERS LIMITED
Registration no: 06509763 **Date established:** 2008
No.of Employees: 1 - 10 **Product Groups:** 26, 35

Date of Accounts	Mar 11	Mar 10	Mar 09
Working Capital	17	41	21
Fixed Assets	11	7	8
Current Assets	114	119	95

Azure Graphic & Web Design

Ashmore Villa 1 Ashmore Terrace, Stockton Road, Sunderland, SR2 7DE
Tel: 0191-567 9100 **Fax:** 0191-567 9100
E-mail: info@azure-design.com
Website: http://www.azure-design.com

see next page

Azure Graphic & Web Design - Cont'd

Directors: C. Robinson (MD)
Managers: H. Tilder (Develop Mgr)
Registration no: 05176550 **Date established:** 2006
Turnover: Up to £250,000 **No.of Employees:** 1 - 10 **Product Groups:** 37

Date of Accounts	Mar 08	Mar 07
Working Capital	16	89
Fixed Assets	3	3
Current Assets	30	105
Current Liabilities	14	16

Berghaus Ltd

12 Colima Avenue Sunderland Enterprise Park, Sunderland, SR5 3XB
Tel: 0191-516 5600 **Fax:** 0191-516 5601
E-mail: reception@berghaus.com
Website: http://www.berghaus.com
Directors: R. Leedham (Sales), D. Kennedy (Fin)
Managers: C. Haggan (Sales Admin)
Ultimate Holding Company: PENTLAND GROUP PLC
Immediate Holding Company: BERGHAUS LIMITED
Registration no: 00871405 **Date established:** 1966
Turnover: £50m - £75m **No.of Employees:** 51 - 100 **Product Groups:** 22, 24

Date of Accounts	Dec 11	Dec 10	Dec 09
Sales Turnover	56m	56m	51m
Pre Tax Profit/Loss	-7m	-400	2m
Working Capital	-4m	3m	4m
Fixed Assets	400	500	600
Current Assets	28m	33m	19m
Current Liabilities	4m	5m	4m

Bybell Industrial Services

PO Box 406, Sunderland, SR6 7YB
Tel: 0191-536 5014 **Fax:** 0191-536 5014
E-mail: mail@bybell.co.uk
Website: http://www.bybell.co.uk
Directors: H. Norman (MD)
Product Groups: 40, 80, 83

Cable Jointing Services Ltd

8 Melvyn Gardens, Sunderland, SR6 9LF
Tel: 0191-548 6734 **Fax:** 0191-564 0005
E-mail: mail@cablejointingservices.com
Website: http://www.cablejointingservices.com
Directors: B. Prince (MD)
Immediate Holding Company: CABLE JOINTING SERVICES LIMITED
Registration no: 01575483 **VAT No.:** GB 353 9669 12
Date established: 1981 **Turnover:** Up to £250,000
No.of Employees: 1 - 10 **Product Groups:** 52

Date of Accounts	Jul 09	Apr 12	Apr 11
Working Capital	51	48	41
Fixed Assets	27	5	18
Current Assets	118	86	58

Continental Conveyors Ltd

West Quay Road Sunderland Enterprise Park, Sunderland, SR5 2TD
Tel: 0191-516 5353 **Fax:** 0191-482 1903
E-mail: sales@continental-conveyor.co.uk
Website: http://www.continental-conveyor.co.uk
Bank(s): Barclays, Market Hall, Bradford
Directors: J. Cook (Co Sec)
Managers: P. Burton (Chief Mgr)
Ultimate Holding Company: JOY GLOBAL INC (USA)
Immediate Holding Company: CONTINENTAL CONVEYOR LIMITED
Registration no: 03586316 **VAT No.:** GB 184 4733 43
Date established: 1998 **Turnover:** £20m - £50m
No.of Employees: 101 - 250 **Product Groups:** 45

Date of Accounts	Oct 10	Oct 09	Oct 08
Sales Turnover	27m	28m	26m
Pre Tax Profit/Loss	583	-427	1m
Working Capital	4m	4m	5m
Fixed Assets	831	1m	1m
Current Assets	19m	17m	22m
Current Liabilities	3m	4m	6m

Crossling Plumbers' Merchants

Alexandra Avenue Sunderland Enterprise Park, Sunderland, SR5 2TF
Tel: 0191-516 9966 **Fax:** 0191-516 8655
E-mail: sunderland@crossling.co.uk
Website: http://www.crossling.co.uk
Bank(s): Lloyds TSB Bank plc
Managers: L. Stoddert (Mgr)
Registration no: 00107189 **Turnover:** £50m - £75m
No.of Employees: 11 - 20 **Product Groups:** 30, 33, 35

Haskel Europe Ltd

North Hylton Road, Sunderland, SR5 3JD
Tel: 0191-549 1212 **Fax:** 0191-549 0911
E-mail: sales@haskel.co.uk
Website: http://www.haskel.com
Bank(s): Barclays
Directors: C. Farquhar (Fin)
Managers: P. Harrison (Sales Prom Mgr), D. Price (Purch Mgr), G. Smith (Tech Serv Mgr), N. Miller (Personnel)
Ultimate Holding Company: UNITED TECHNOLOGIES CORP INC (USA)
Immediate Holding Company: HASKEL EUROPE LTD
Registration no: 01278832 **Date established:** 1976
Turnover: £10m - £20m **No.of Employees:** 51 - 100 **Product Groups:** 30, 33, 36, 37, 38, 39, 40, 42, 45, 46, 48, 52, 54, 67, 68, 84, 85

Date of Accounts	Nov 11	Nov 10	Nov 09
Sales Turnover	14m	13m	12m
Pre Tax Profit/Loss	4m	2m	2m
Working Capital	18m	15m	12m
Fixed Assets	2m	2m	1m
Current Assets	20m	16m	15m
Current Liabilities	602	650	838

Hellens Fabrications

3 Henry Street East, Sunderland, SR2 8AU
Tel: 0191-510 8873 **Fax:** 0191-510 8873
E-mail: tomludlow@live.co.uk
Website: http://www.hellensfabrication.co.uk
Directors: T. Hellens (Prop)
Immediate Holding Company: HELLENS FABRICATIONS LIMITED
Registration no: 07996721 **Date established:** 2012
No.of Employees: 1 - 10 **Product Groups:** 26, 35

Herrenknecht International Ltd

Wearfield Sunderland Enterprise Park, Sunderland, SR5 2TZ
Tel: 0191-548 9191 **Fax:** 0191-548 9292
E-mail: enquiries@herrenknecht.com
Website: http://www.herrenknecht.com
Directors: D. Atkinson (Fin)
Ultimate Holding Company: HERRENKNECHT GMBH (GERMANY)
Immediate Holding Company: HERRENKNECHT INTERNATIONAL LIMITED
Registration no: 01796113 **Date established:** 1984 **Turnover:** £5m - £10m
No.of Employees: 1 - 10 **Product Groups:** 42, 45

Date of Accounts	Dec 11	Dec 10	Dec 09
Sales Turnover	6m	2m	3m
Pre Tax Profit/Loss	530	164	943
Working Capital	2m	1m	1m
Fixed Assets	543	787	977
Current Assets	3m	2m	2m
Current Liabilities	870	233	N/A

Hydraulic & Offshore Supplies Ltd

Offshore House Southwick Industrial Estate, Sunderland, SR5 3TX
Tel: 0191-549 7335 **Fax:** 0191-516 0004
E-mail: hos@hos.co.uk
Website: http://www.hos.co.uk
Directors: A. Wills (Prop)
Immediate Holding Company: HYDRAULIC & OFFSHORE SUPPLIES LIMITED
Registration no: 03016257 **Date established:** 1995 **Turnover:** £1m - £2m
No.of Employees: 1 - 10 **Product Groups:** 23, 29, 30, 31, 32, 33, 34, 35, 36, 37, 38, 39, 40, 41, 42, 43, 44, 45, 46, 47, 48, 51, 61, 63, 66, 67, 68, 74, 83, 84, 85

Date of Accounts	Feb 12	Feb 11	Feb 10
Working Capital	367	309	334
Fixed Assets	123	166	113
Current Assets	687	517	641

I Q Management Systems

Business & Innovation Centre Wearfield, Sunderland Enterprise Park, Sunderland, SR5 2TA
Tel: 0191-516 9191 **Fax:** 0191-516 9194
E-mail: enquiries@iqms.co.uk
Website: http://www.iqms.co.uk
Directors: G. Hill (MD)
Immediate Holding Company: IQ MANAGEMENT SYSTEMS LTD
Registration no: 02556339 **Date established:** 1990
Turnover: £250,000 - £500,000 **No.of Employees:** 1 - 10
Product Groups: 86

Date of Accounts	Mar 12	Mar 11	Mar 10
Working Capital	181	131	63
Fixed Assets	51	20	21
Current Assets	318	349	258

J & M Medical

Unit 1 Wheatsheaf Colliery School Yard Southwick Road, Sunderland, SR5 1DD
Tel: 0191-567 4667 **Fax:** 0191-567 4593
E-mail: sales@jmmedical.co.uk
Website: http://www.jmmedical.co.uk
Directors: J. Lissanan (Prop)
No.of Employees: 1 - 10 **Product Groups:** 24

Jennings Winch & Foundry Co. Ltd

Tatham Street, Sunderland, SR1 2AG
Tel: 0191-567 4408 **Fax:** 0191-510 1549
E-mail: info@jenningsfoundry.co.uk
Website: http://www.jenningsfoundry.com
Bank(s): National Westminster
Directors: C. Jennings (Dir)
Immediate Holding Company: JENNINGS WINCH & FOUNDRY COMPANY LIMITED
Registration no: 00245507 **VAT No.:** GB 425 9671 26
Date established: 1930 **Turnover:** £2m - £5m **No.of Employees:** 11 - 20
Product Groups: 34, 35, 36, 48

Date of Accounts	Mar 11	Mar 10	Mar 09
Working Capital	498	482	515
Fixed Assets	256	284	289
Current Assets	1m	992	1m

K & D Installations Ltd

300 Gleneagles Road Grindon, Sunderland, SR4 9QN
Tel: 0191-551 2643 **Fax:** 0191-534 3906
E-mail: burgesskevin@ntlworld.com
Website: http://www.fire-curtains.biz
Product Groups: 35, 36, 39, 52, 66

Date of Accounts	Oct 08
Working Capital	-8
Fixed Assets	2
Current Assets	40
Current Liabilities	48

Leechmere Ices

38g Ellesmere Court Leechmere Industrial Estate, Sunderland, SR2 9UA
Tel: 0191-523 8860
Directors: G. Evans (Ptnr)
Date established: 1987 **No.of Employees:** 1 - 10 **Product Groups:** 20, 40, 41

Leengate Welding Supplies North East Ltd

Unit 35d Pallion Trading Estate, Sunderland, SR4 6SN
Tel: 0191-565 8611 **Fax:** 0191-565 8621
Website: http://www.uk.gases.boc.com
Directors: A. Orcher (Sales), R. Godley (Fin)
Ultimate Holding Company: LINDE AG (GERMANY)
Immediate Holding Company: LEENGATE INDUSTRIAL & WELDING SUPPLIES (NORTH EAST) LTD
Registration no: 03324284 **Date established:** 1997 **Turnover:** £5m - £10m
No.of Employees: 21 - 50 **Product Groups:** 46

Date of Accounts	Dec 11	Dec 10	Dec 09
Sales Turnover	7m	5m	4m
Pre Tax Profit/Loss	313	271	115
Working Capital	2m	1m	1m
Fixed Assets	79	80	58
Current Assets	3m	2m	2m
Current Liabilities	183	97	61

M A J Paints

Unit 2 Simpson Street, Sunderland, SR4 6DR
Tel: 0191-564 0101 **Fax:** 0191-564 0111
Directors: P. Jefferies (Dir)
Immediate Holding Company: MAJ PAINTS 2 LTD
Registration no: 06757203 **Date established:** 2008
No.of Employees: 1 - 10 **Product Groups:** 46, 48

Date of Accounts	Nov 11	Nov 10	Nov 09
Working Capital	-15	-14	-16
Current Assets	69	84	48

Macdonald Martin Fire & Safety Consultants Ltd

Office 1 8 Silksworth Lane, Sunderland, SR3 1LL
Tel: 0191-525 1299 **Fax:** 0191-525 1299
E-mail: andymacmart@aol.com
Website: http://www.macdonald-martin.co.uk
Registration no: 04910537 **Product Groups:** 24, 25, 30, 35, 38, 39, 40, 52, 54, 67, 68, 84, 85, 86, 87

Marcon Engineering Services Ltd

18 Sandmere Road Leechmere Industrial Estate, Sunderland, SR2 9TP
Tel: 0191-521 0200 **Fax:** 0191-523 7722
E-mail: trevor.gillespie@marconengineering.com
Website: http://www.marconengineering.com
Directors: T. Gillespie (MD), I. Donnigan (Fin)
Ultimate Holding Company: MARCON BEHEERMAATSCHAPPIJ NV (NETHERLAND
Immediate Holding Company: MARCON ENGINEERING SERVICES LIMITED
Registration no: 01786386 **Date established:** 1984
No.of Employees: 1 - 10 **Product Groups:** 35, 36, 39

Date of Accounts	Jun 11	Jun 10	Jun 09
Working Capital	228	235	124
Fixed Assets	3	2	2
Current Assets	340	513	276

Megator Ltd

Hendon Street, Sunderland, SR1 2NQ
Tel: 0191-567 5488 **Fax:** 0191-567 8512
E-mail: info@megator.co.uk
Website: http://www.megator.co.uk
Bank(s): National Westminster
Managers: C. Robson
Immediate Holding Company: MEGATOR LIMITED
Registration no: 00404130 **VAT No.:** 176 3324 60 **Date established:** 1946
No.of Employees: 11 - 20 **Product Groups:** 40

Date of Accounts	Mar 12	Mar 11	Mar 10
Working Capital	92	65	94
Fixed Assets	292	304	336
Current Assets	338	292	234

Metal Improvement Co.

37 Pallion Trading Estate, Sunderland, SR4 6SN
Tel: 0191-514 1140 **Fax:** 0191-514 1124
E-mail: steven_meakin@metalimprovement.com
Website: http://www.metalimprovement.com
Managers: S. Meakin (Mgr)
Date established: 1996 **No.of Employees:** 21 - 50 **Product Groups:** 46, 48

Microfilm Bureau North East Ltd

3 North Bridge Street, Sunderland, SR5 1AD
Tel: 0191-567 0104 **Fax:** 0191-510 0166
E-mail: enquiries@microfilmbureau.co.uk
Website: http://www.microfilmandscanning.co.uk
Directors: D. Spoor (Dir)
Immediate Holding Company: MICROFILM BUREAU (NORTH EAST) LIMITED(THE)
Registration no: 00799053 **VAT No.:** GB 176 7378 17
Date established: 1964 **Turnover:** Up to £250,000
No.of Employees: 1 - 10 **Product Groups:** 44, 81

Date of Accounts	Mar 11	Mar 10	Mar 09
Working Capital	145	152	188
Fixed Assets	24	26	26
Current Assets	161	167	207

Neptune Engineering Services Ltd

19 Sandmere Road Leechmere Industrial Estate, Sunderland, SR2 9TP
Tel: 0191-523 6187 **Fax:** 0191-521 0521
E-mail: terry.birtles@neptuneengineering.co.uk
Website: http://www.neptuneengineering.co.uk
Directors: O. Craggs (MD), N. Craggs (MD)
Immediate Holding Company: NEPTUNE ENGINEERING SERVICES LIMITED
Registration no: 04634360 **VAT No.:** GB 176 6583 21
Date established: 2003 **No.of Employees:** 1 - 10 **Product Groups:** 38

Date of Accounts	Dec 09	Dec 08	Dec 07
Working Capital	37	34	46
Fixed Assets	47	60	74
Current Assets	87	87	100

Norloc

11 Ruswarp Drive, Sunderland, SR3 2PH
Tel: 0191-523 8766 **Fax:** 0191-523 8766
E-mail: info@norloc.co.uk
Website: http://www.norloc.co.uk
Directors: G. Ramshaw (Prop)
Date established: 1990 **No.of Employees:** 1 - 10 **Product Groups:** 26, 35

Northeast Press Ltd

Echo House Pennywell Industrial Estate, Sunderland, SR4 9ER
Tel: 0191-501 5800 **Fax:** 0191-534 3807
E-mail: gerry.kenny@northeast-press.co.uk
Website: http://www.sunderlandtoday.co.uk
Bank(s): Barclays
Directors: J. Telfer (Co Sec), S. Birkett (MD)
Ultimate Holding Company: JOHNSTON PRESS PLC
Immediate Holding Company: NORTHEAST PRESS LIMITED
Registration no: 00905215 **Date established:** 1967 **Turnover:** £5m - £10m
No.of Employees: 101 - 250 **Product Groups:** 28

Date of Accounts	Dec 11	Dec 08	Jan 10
Sales Turnover	9m	12m	11m
Working Capital	13m	13m	13m
Current Assets	13m	13m	13m

Oris Ltd

Suite 2e North Sands Business Centre, Sunderland, SR6 0QA
Tel: 0191-565 9755 **Fax:** 0191-567 3613
E-mail: anthony.greaves@oris-uk.com
Website: http://www.oris-uk.com

Directors: A. Greaves (Dir)
Ultimate Holding Company: HESPRI HOLDINGS BV (NETHERLANDS)
Immediate Holding Company: ORIS LIMITED
Registration no: 01424984 **VAT No.:** GB 176 7440 38
Date established: 1979 **Turnover:** £5m - £10m **No.of Employees:** 1 - 10
Product Groups: 20

Date of Accounts	Dec 11	Dec 10	Dec 09
Sales Turnover	9m	9m	9m
Pre Tax Profit/Loss	736	850	1m
Working Capital	991	2m	2m
Fixed Assets	165	173	203
Current Assets	3m	3m	3m
Current Liabilities	243	260	343

Paragon Group UK Ltd

Pallion Trading Estate, Sunderland, SR4 6ST
Tel: 0191-514 0716 **Fax:** 0191-567 1842
E-mail: ukenquiries@paragonuk.com
Website: http://www.paragon-europe.com
Bank(s): Barclays
Directors: L. Salmon (Fin), S. Scott (Sales), G. Stapleton (Fin)
Managers: G. Lees (Tech Serv Mgr), A. Harrington (Chief Mgr), J. Rose (Personnel)
Ultimate Holding Company: PARAGON GROUP LIMITED
Immediate Holding Company: PARAGON GROUP UK LIMITED
Registration no: 00551336 **VAT No.:** GB 708 8765 91
Date established: 1955 **Turnover:** £20m - £50m
No.of Employees: 101 - 250 **Product Groups:** 27, 67

Date of Accounts	Jun 11	Jun 10	Jun 09
Sales Turnover	42m	45m	41m
Pre Tax Profit/Loss	84	-233	1m
Working Capital	668	3m	4m
Fixed Assets	18m	18m	19m
Current Assets	17m	19m	15m
Current Liabilities	2m	3m	3m

Park Lane News Ltd

Unit 5, Sunderland, SR1 3NX
Tel: 0191-567 6925 **Fax:** 0191-567 3714
Managers: S. Pierce (District Mgr)
Immediate Holding Company: PARK LANE NEWS LIMITED
Registration no: 03174947 **VAT No.:** GB 533 6330 64
Date established: 1996 **Turnover:** Up to £250,000
No.of Employees: 1 - 10 **Product Groups:** 49

Date of Accounts	Dec 11	Dec 10	Dec 09
Sales Turnover	N/A	N/A	738
Pre Tax Profit/Loss	N/A	N/A	10
Working Capital	57	51	17
Fixed Assets	4	5	6
Current Assets	79	93	62
Current Liabilities	N/A	N/A	17

Provincial Tyre & Equipment Company (Head Office)

William Street, Sunderland, SR1 1TW
Tel: 0191-565 8141 **Fax:** 0191-565 9296
E-mail: sales@provincialtyres.co.uk
Website: http://www.carpartz.co.uk
Directors: N. Balbach (MD)
Immediate Holding Company: PROVINCIAL TYRE & EQUIPMENT (SUNDERLAND) LIMITED
Registration no: 00188468 **VAT No.:** GB 176 7076 33
Date established: 2023 **Turnover:** £500,000 - £1m
No.of Employees: 1 - 10 **Product Groups:** 32, 68

Date of Accounts	Dec 10	Dec 09	Dec 08
Working Capital	48	43	44
Fixed Assets	129	131	135
Current Assets	145	143	156

Reg Vardy Ltd

Houghton House 3 Emperor Way, Doxford International Business Park, Sunderland, SR3 3XR
Tel: 0191-525 3000 **Fax:** 0191-525 3030
Website: http://www.regvardy.com
Bank(s): Barclays
Directors: G. Murray (Fin), G. Potts (Grp Chief Exec), M. Casha (Fin), P. Vardy (Ch), F. Laughlin (Co Sec), H. Sykes (Co Sec)
Immediate Holding Company: Pendragon plc
Registration no: 00611190 **VAT No.:** GB 389 7000 25
Date established: 1958 **Turnover:** £250m - £500m
No.of Employees: 1501 & over **Product Groups:** 80

Retrofit Rubberroofing

44 Townsend Road, Sunderland, SR3 4LW
Tel: 08450-091975 **Fax:** 08450-092441
E-mail: retrofitrubberroofing@ntlworld.com
Directors: N. Boyd (Prop)
Date established: 2006 **Turnover:** Up to £250,000
No.of Employees: 1 - 10 **Product Groups:** 52

Milton Roy UK Ltd

North Hylton Road, Sunderland, SR5 3JD
Tel: 0191-537 5256 **Fax:** 0118-977 1198
E-mail: contact@miltonroy-europe.com
Website: http://www.dosapro.com
Directors: C. Colgin (Fin), J. Favre Bully (Dir), J. Degremont (Dir), O. Perrin (Dir)
Managers: M. Eagle (Chief Mgr)
Ultimate Holding Company: Sundstrand Corp
Immediate Holding Company: Dosapro Milton Roy SA (France)
Registration no: 01154999 **VAT No.:** GB 240 9131 90
Date established: 2006 **Turnover:** £250,000 - £500,000
No.of Employees: 1 - 10 **Product Groups:** 38, 39, 40, 41

Date of Accounts	Nov 07
Pre Tax Profit/Loss	1
Working Capital	294
Current Assets	680
Current Liabilities	386
Total Share Capital	30
ROCE% (Return on Capital Employed)	0.3

S D C Catering Services Ltd

7 Castellian Road, Sunderland, SR5 3BE
Tel: 0191-549 9578 **Fax:** 0191-549 9578
Directors: J. Stockdale (Fin), D. Stockdale (MD)
Immediate Holding Company: SDC (CATERING) SERVICES LIMITED
Registration no: 04923899 **Date established:** 2003
No.of Employees: 1 - 10 **Product Groups:** 20, 40, 41

Date of Accounts	Dec 11	Dec 10	Dec 09
Working Capital	149	103	94
Fixed Assets	75	35	46
Current Assets	229	183	165

Soho66 PebbleTree Ltd

4 Rowlandson Terrace, Sunderland, SR2 7SU
Tel: 03333-443443
E-mail: support@soho66.co.uk
Website: http://www.soho66.co.uk
Directors: R. Thornton (Dir)
Immediate Holding Company: PEBBLETREE LTD
Date established: 2005 **No.of Employees:** 1 - 10 **Product Groups:** 37, 48, 79

Date of Accounts	Oct 11	Oct 10	Oct 09
Working Capital	1	-1	1
Fixed Assets	7	4	1
Current Assets	55	39	16

Speedings Ltd

48 Carrmere Road Leechmere Industrial Estate, Sunderland, SR2 9TW
Tel: 0191-523 9933 **Fax:** 0191-523 9955
E-mail: mail@speedingsltd.co.uk
Website: http://www.speedingsltd.co.uk
Bank(s): Lloyds
Directors: N. Pemberton (Fin), R. Hammal (MD)
Managers: L. Sandy (Purch Mgr)
Ultimate Holding Company: HAMMAL HOLDINGS LIMITED
Immediate Holding Company: SPEEDING'S LIMITED
Registration no: 00130643 **Date established:** 2013 **Turnover:** £1m - £2m
No.of Employees: 21 - 50 **Product Groups:** 23, 24, 40, 49

Date of Accounts	May 11	May 10	May 09
Sales Turnover	1m	N/A	N/A
Pre Tax Profit/Loss	84	N/A	N/A
Working Capital	47	46	83
Fixed Assets	36	53	58
Current Assets	281	315	255
Current Liabilities	75	N/A	N/A

Stagecoach Ltd

North Bridge Street, Sunderland, SR5 1AQ
Tel: 0191-567 5251 **Fax:** 0191-566 0202
E-mail: john.conroy@stagecoachbus.com
Website: http://www.stagecoachbus.com
Directors: J. Conroy (Reg), C. Brown (Fin)
Managers: R. Knight (Comm), K. Williams (Mktg Serv Mgr), B. Whitehouse (I.T. Exec), M. Pike (Personnel)
Ultimate Holding Company: STAGECOACH GROUP PLC
Immediate Holding Company: STAGECOACH LIMITED
Registration no: 03092390 **Date established:** 1995
No.of Employees: 101 - 250 **Product Groups:** 72

Date of Accounts	Apr 11	Apr 10	Apr 09
Pre Tax Profit/Loss	-251	-240	-531
Working Capital	-13	203	412
Current Assets	2m	2m	2m

Sunderland Diesel Injection Service Centre

East Cross Street, Sunderland, SR1 1XB
Tel: 07808-101391
Directors: K. Fisher (Prop)
Immediate Holding Company: ECLIPSE PERFORMANCE LIMITED
Registration no: 06266817 **Date established:** 2007
No.of Employees: 1 - 10 **Product Groups:** 40

Date of Accounts	Jun 11	Jun 10	Jun 09
Working Capital	-1	39	-24
Fixed Assets	26	30	36
Current Assets	45	39	40

Tiger Filtration Ltd

Unit 4a-4b East Way Rivergreen Industrial Estate, Sunderland, SR4 6AD
Tel: 0191-565 5348 **Fax:** 0191-537 1761
E-mail: sales@tigerfiltration.co.uk
Website: http://www.tigerfiltration.co.uk
Directors: R. Thompson (MD), S. Thompson (Co Sec)
Immediate Holding Company: TIGER FILTRATION LIMITED
Registration no: 05006620 **Date established:** 2004
No.of Employees: 11 - 20 **Product Groups:** 38, 42

Date of Accounts	Jan 12	Jan 11	Jan 10
Working Capital	228	198	209
Fixed Assets	15	19	26
Current Assets	378	379	345

Tradebe Solvent Recycling Ltd

Hendon Dock, Sunderland, SR1 2EW
Tel: 01524-853053 **Fax:** 0191-566 0025
E-mail: smcgown@srm-ltd.com
Website: http://www.tradebe.com
Bank(s): Skadinaviska Enskilda Banken, London
Directors: S. Mcgown (Dir)
Managers: C. Holden (Site Co-ord)
Ultimate Holding Company: GRUPO TRADEBE (SPAIN)
Immediate Holding Company: TRADEBE SOLVENT RECYCLING LIMITED
Registration no: 03890526 **VAT No.:** GB 217 9157 51
Date established: 1999 **Turnover:** £20m - £50m
No.of Employees: 251 - 500 **Product Groups:** 31, 32

Date of Accounts	Dec 11	Dec 10	Dec 09
Sales Turnover	40m	35m	32m
Pre Tax Profit/Loss	2m	2m	-1m
Working Capital	3m	7m	6m
Fixed Assets	11m	11m	10m
Current Assets	16m	17m	16m
Current Liabilities	3m	2m	4m

Unipress UK

Cherry Blossom Way, Sunderland, SR5 3NT
Tel: 0191-418 2000 **Fax:** 0191-418 2131
E-mail: sales@unipres.co.uk
Website: http://www.unipres.co.uk
Bank(s): Bank of Scotland
Directors: G. Baines (Co Sec)
Managers: G. Capstaff (Tech Serv Mgr), N. Prest (Personnel)
Ultimate Holding Company: UNIPRES CORPORATION (JAPAN)
Immediate Holding Company: UNIPRES (UK) LIMITED
Registration no: 02163867 **VAT No.:** GB 495 9324 95
Date established: 1987 **Turnover:** £125m - £250m
No.of Employees: 501 - 1000 **Product Groups:** 34, 39, 48

Date of Accounts	Dec 11	Dec 10	Dec 09
Sales Turnover	174m	146m	119m
Pre Tax Profit/Loss	18m	14m	12m
Working Capital	21m	18m	12m
Fixed Assets	43m	35m	31m
Current Assets	44m	54m	26m
Current Liabilities	6m	21m	6m

Vishay Ltd

Pallion Trading Estate, Sunderland, SR4 6SU
Tel: 0191-514 4155 **Fax:** 0191-567 8662
E-mail: paul.robson@vishay.com
Website: http://www.vishay.com
Bank(s): Barclays, Sunderland
Directors: J. Deller (MD), J. Wheeler (MD), P. Jeffreys (Fin), L. Bell (Admin), L. Cruickshanks (MD)
Managers: A. Moore (Tech Serv Mgr), A. Waites, M. Snook (I.T. Exec), P. Robson (Cust Serv Mgr), M. Neil
Ultimate Holding Company: VISHAY INTERTECHNOLOGY INC (USA)
Immediate Holding Company: E-Sil Components Ltd
Registration no: 00886870 **Date established:** 1966
Turnover: £250,000 - £500,000 **No.of Employees:** 21 - 50
Product Groups: 37, 38

Date of Accounts	Dec 07
Sales Turnover	23191
Pre Tax Profit/Loss	322
Working Capital	23543
Fixed Assets	9977
Current Assets	35920
Current Liabilities	12377
Total Share Capital	10
ROCE% (Return on Capital Employed)	1.0

Wallsend

A Strip Enviromental

Unit 1 Nelson Housedavy Bank, Wallsend, NE28 6UZ
Tel: 0191-262 8944 **Fax:** 0191-567 6487
E-mail: enquiries@a-strip.co.uk
Website: http://www.a-strip.com
Managers: C. Hoggarth (Mgr)
Ultimate Holding Company: OCEANA GROUP (HOLDINGS) LIMITED
Immediate Holding Company: A-STRIP ENVIRONMENTAL LLP
Registration no: OC321848 **Date established:** 2006
No.of Employees: 1 - 10 **Product Groups:** 54

Date of Accounts	Aug 11	Aug 10	Aug 09
Working Capital	-6	14	46
Fixed Assets	51	63	18
Current Assets	142	97	122
Current Liabilities	45	N/A	N/A

Altek UK Ltd

Howdon Lane, Wallsend, NE28 0AL
Tel: 0800-043 3440 **Fax:** 0191-209 6794
E-mail: info@altekuk.co.uk
Website: http://www.altekuk.co.uk
Directors: K. Brown (Dir)
Immediate Holding Company: ALTEK UK LTD
Registration no: 06007722 **Date established:** 2006
Turnover: Up to £250,000 **No.of Employees:** 1 - 10 **Product Groups:** 29, 30, 31

Date of Accounts	Nov 10	Nov 09	Nov 08
Working Capital	-0	-12	-6
Fixed Assets	9	11	15
Current Assets	60	29	50

Aquaseal Rubber Ltd

Unit 13 Point Pleasant Indl-Est, Wallsend, NE28 6HA
Tel: 0191-262 4555 **Fax:** 0191-262 5777
E-mail: eddie@aquasealrubber.co.uk
Website: http://www.aquasealrubber.co.uk
Directors: A. Armstrong (MD), J. Armstrong (MD), J. Armstrong (Dir), E. Armstrong (MD)
Immediate Holding Company: AQUASEAL RUBBER LIMITED
Registration no: 02681117 **VAT No.:** GB 177 9973 84
Date established: 1992 **Turnover:** £500,000 - £1m
No.of Employees: 1 - 10 **Product Groups:** 29, 31, 36, 40, 63

Date of Accounts	Mar 11	Mar 10	Mar 09
Working Capital	-36	-50	-29
Fixed Assets	92	88	87
Current Assets	182	163	117

Askbestus Environmental Ltd Liability Partnership

St Peters House 1 Boyd Road, Wallsend, NE28 7SA
Tel: 0191-567 6488 **Fax:** 0191-567 6487
E-mail: enquiries@a-strip.co.uk
Directors: C. Hoggarth (Dir)
Immediate Holding Company: SAFER PROPERTY LTD
Registration no: OC311939 **Date established:** 2012
Turnover: Up to £250,000 **No.of Employees:** 1 - 10 **Product Groups:** 54

Barrier Ltd

Mipearl Buildings Stephenson Street, Wallsend, NE28 6UE
Tel: 0191-262 0510 **Fax:** 0191-262 8810
E-mail: robert.bowles@barrierltd.co.uk
Website: http://www.barriergroup.com
Bank(s): Lloyds TSB Bank plc
Directors: R. Bowles (MD)
Immediate Holding Company: BARRIER LIMITED
Registration no: 01226016 **VAT No.:** GB 555 9253 15
Date established: 1975 **Turnover:** £10m - £20m
No.of Employees: 51 - 100 **Product Groups:** 48

Date of Accounts	Oct 11	Oct 10	Oct 09
Sales Turnover	11m	16m	26m
Pre Tax Profit/Loss	14	465	5m
Working Capital	4m	4m	4m
Fixed Assets	2m	2m	2m
Current Assets	6m	8m	9m
Current Liabilities	1m	2m	3m

Bridon International Ltd

Willington Quay, Wallsend, NE28 6TT
Tel: 0191-262 5231 **Fax:** 0191-263 4117
E-mail: prattc@bridon.com
Website: http://www.bridon.com
Managers: D. Hyland (Buyer), R. Crawford (Chief Acct), C. Mcdine (Ops Mgr)

see next page

***Bridon International Ltd** - Cont'd*

Ultimate Holding Company: MELROSE PLC
Immediate Holding Company: BRIDON INTERNATIONAL LTD.
Registration no: 00416671 **Date established:** 1946
No.of Employees: 101 - 250 **Product Groups:** 35

Date of Accounts	Dec 11	Dec 10	Dec 09
Sales Turnover	138m	130m	158m
Pre Tax Profit/Loss	5	17m	24m
Working Capital	36m	67m	74m
Fixed Assets	23m	14m	15m
Current Assets	102m	99m	104m
Current Liabilities	42m	9m	13m

Cargotec UK Ltd

Powerhouse Silverlink, Wallsend, NE28 9ND
Tel: 0191-295 2180 **Fax:** 0191-295 2188
E-mail: steven.goodchild@cargotech.com
Website: http://www.cargotec.com
Bank(s): Svenska Handelbanken
Directors: J. Riley (Fin)
Managers: S. Hall (Sales Prom Mgr), S. Goodchild
Ultimate Holding Company: CARGOTEC OYJ (FINLAND)
Immediate Holding Company: MACGREGOR (GBR) LIMITED
Registration no: 01026122 **Date established:** 1971 **Turnover:** £2m - £5m
No.of Employees: 11 - 20 **Product Groups:** 35, 39, 45, 84

Date of Accounts	Dec 10	Dec 09	Dec 08
Sales Turnover	N/A	4m	8m
Pre Tax Profit/Loss	N/A	-609	-952
Working Capital	73	73	3m
Fixed Assets	N/A	N/A	1m
Current Assets	73	73	5m
Current Liabilities	N/A	N/A	835

Chemson Ltd

Hayhole Works Northumberland Dock Road, Wallsend, NE28 0PB
Tel: 0191-259 7000 **Fax:** 0191-259 7001
E-mail: pgoodinson@chemson.com
Website: http://www.chemson.com
Directors: P. Goodinson (MD), A. Hofer (Fin), N. Heaviside (Pers), P. Goodinson (MD)
Managers: D. Greener
Ultimate Holding Company: CHEMSON POLYMER-ADDITIVE AG (AUSTRIA)
Immediate Holding Company: CHEMSON LIMITED
Registration no: 01980314 **Date established:** 1986
Turnover: £20m - £50m **No.of Employees:** 51 - 100 **Product Groups:** 31, 32

Date of Accounts	Dec 10	Dec 09	Dec 08
Sales Turnover	37m	20m	4m
Pre Tax Profit/Loss	-3m	-2m	-2m
Working Capital	-6m	-2m	2m
Fixed Assets	6m	6m	5m
Current Assets	11m	10m	7m
Current Liabilities	1m	983	2m

Hancock Tools Ltd

108 High Street East, Wallsend, NE28 7RH
Tel: 0191-262 6677 **Fax:** 0191-263 1083
E-mail: hancocktools@btconnect.com
Website: http://www.hancocktools.co.uk
Directors: G. Purvis (MD)
Immediate Holding Company: HANCOCK TOOLS LIMITED
Registration no: 00963273 **Date established:** 1969 **Turnover:** £1m - £2m
No.of Employees: 1 - 10 **Product Groups:** 66

Date of Accounts	Sep 11	Sep 10	Sep 09
Working Capital	-7	-1	14
Fixed Assets	53	46	50
Current Assets	183	218	186

International Syalons Newcastle Ltd

Stevenson Street Willington Quay, Wallsend, NE28 6TT
Tel: 0191-295 1010 **Fax:** 0191-263 3847
E-mail: enquiries@syalons.com
Website: http://www.syalons.com
Directors: I. Denton (Chief Op Offcr), N. Fecitt (Tech Serv)
Managers: G. Bradley (Chief Acct)
Immediate Holding Company: INTERNATIONAL SYALONS (NEWCASTLE) LIMITED
Registration no: 02943970 **VAT No.:** GB 621 4409 72
Date established: 1994 **No.of Employees:** 21 - 50 **Product Groups:** 24, 30, 33, 34, 35, 36, 38, 40, 46, 48

Date of Accounts	Dec 11	Dec 10	Dec 09
Working Capital	628	468	345
Fixed Assets	701	570	612
Current Assets	922	726	528

Lift Rite Engineering Services Ltd

Morston House Morston Quays Stephenson Street, Wallsend, NE28 6UE
Tel: 0191-234 3366 **Fax:** 0191-234 2556
E-mail: sales@lift-rite.com
Website: http://www.lift-rite.com
Directors: G. Robson (MD)
Ultimate Holding Company: LIFT-RITE HOLDINGS LIMITED
Immediate Holding Company: LIFT-RITE ENGINEERING SERVICES LIMITED
Registration no: 05081091 **Date established:** 2004
No.of Employees: 11 - 20 **Product Groups:** 29, 30, 35, 36, 37, 38, 39, 40, 41, 42, 43, 45, 48, 52, 67, 83, 84, 85

Date of Accounts	Apr 12	Apr 11	Apr 10
Working Capital	289	467	351
Fixed Assets	276	318	297
Current Assets	852	1m	861

MacGREGOR (GBR) Ltd

1st Floor Power House Silverlink Business Park, Wallsend, NE28 9ND
Tel: 01224-347050 **Fax:** 01224-347051
E-mail: anthony.jamieson@cargotec.com
Website: http://www.macgregor-group.com
Bank(s): Bank of Scotland
Managers: P. Dickinson (Chief Mgr)
Registration no: 01026122 **VAT No.:** GB 415 8829 29
Date established: 1984 **Turnover:** £1m - £2m **No.of Employees:** 21 - 50
Product Groups: 26, 30, 34, 35, 38, 39, 40, 45, 67, 74

Marine Safety Supplies Ltd

Carville Works Hadrian Road, Wallsend, NE28 6HF
Tel: 0191-263 0191 **Fax:** 0191-263 0104
E-mail: john@marinesafetysupplies.com
Website: http://www.marinesafetysupplies.com
Managers: J. Ornsby (Mgr)
Immediate Holding Company: MARINE SAFETY SUPPLIES LIMITED
Registration no: 04779621 **Date established:** 2003
No.of Employees: 1 - 10 **Product Groups:** 23, 25, 35, 39, 41, 52, 63, 74, 80

Date of Accounts	Jul 12	Jul 11	Jul 10
Working Capital	124	54	44
Fixed Assets	2	2	2
Current Assets	235	132	116

Mineral & Chemical Services Ltd

1 Britannia House Britannia Business Park, Wallsend, NE28 6HA
Tel: 0191-262 3311 **Fax:** 0191-262 3344
E-mail: patrickhegarty@minchemical.co.uk
Website: http://www.minchemical.co.uk
Directors: P. Hegarty (Dir)
Immediate Holding Company: MINERAL & CHEMICAL SERVICES LTD
Registration no: 05760588 **Date established:** 2006
No.of Employees: 1 - 10 **Product Groups:** 32, 61

Date of Accounts	Mar 12	Mar 11	Mar 10
Working Capital	579	450	338
Fixed Assets	1	1	1
Current Assets	1m	1m	897

Northern Precision Engineering Ltd

3 Buddle Indl-Est Benton Way, Wallsend, NE28 6DL
Tel: 0191-263 6666 **Fax:** 0191- 2630356
E-mail: chriss@npe.uk.com
Website: http://www.npe.uk.com
Directors: C. Morrison (Dir), I. Oates (MD), D. Graham (Sales), C. Small (Grp Chief Exec), M. Kelly (Fin), C. Small (Dir)
Managers: T. Sanderson (I.T. Exec)
Immediate Holding Company: NORTHERN PRECISION ENGINEERING LIMITED
Registration no: 01212438 **VAT No.:** GB 179 0119 58
Date established: 1975 **No.of Employees:** 51 - 100 **Product Groups:** 46, 48

Date of Accounts	Oct 10	Oct 09	Apr 08
Pre Tax Profit/Loss	N/A	N/A	17
Working Capital	-213	-197	-775
Fixed Assets	2m	2m	2m
Current Assets	2m	1m	1m
Current Liabilities	651	306	1m

Pipe Coil Technology

Hadrian Road, Wallsend, NE28 6HF
Tel: 0191-295 9910 **Fax:** 0191-295 9911
E-mail: gordon@pipecoil.co.uk
Website: http://www.pipecoil.co.uk
Directors: G. Fiddes (Dir), V. Fiddes (Fin)
Immediate Holding Company: PIPE COIL AUTOMATION LTD
Registration no: 02861593 **Date established:** 1993
No.of Employees: 11 - 20 **Product Groups:** 35, 39, 45

Date of Accounts	Dec 11	Dec 10	Dec 09
Sales Turnover	6m	3m	N/A
Pre Tax Profit/Loss	109	-1m	N/A
Working Capital	332	-703	46
Fixed Assets	2m	2m	901
Current Assets	4m	2m	2m
Current Liabilities	2m	667	253

Soil Machine Dynamics Ltd

Davy Bank, Wallsend, NE28 6UZ
Tel: 0191-234 2222 **Fax:** 0191-234 8599
E-mail: michelle.christer@smd.co.uk
Website: http://www.smd.co.uk
Bank(s): The Royal Bank of Scotland
Directors: R. Lowery (Fin)
Managers: V. Bosi (Mktg Serv Mgr), A. Haswell (Tech Serv Mgr), G. Walker (Sales Prom Mgr), M. Wilkinson, S. McAulay (Personnel), M. Christer (Sales Admin)
Ultimate Holding Company: SPECIALIST MACHINE DEVELOPMENTS (SMD) LIMITED
Immediate Holding Company: SOIL MACHINE DYNAMICS LIMITED
Registration no: 01028571 **VAT No.:** GB 553 0031 90
Date established: 1971 **Turnover:** £50m - £75m
No.of Employees: 251 - 500 **Product Groups:** 30, 37, 38, 39, 40, 44, 45, 49, 67, 68

Date of Accounts	Dec 11	Dec 10	Dec 09
Sales Turnover	95m	60m	43m
Pre Tax Profit/Loss	9m	9m	8m
Working Capital	32m	26m	21m
Fixed Assets	5m	3m	3m
Current Assets	77m	46m	29m
Current Liabilities	29m	8m	7m

T S T 2000 Ltd

2 Metnor Business Park Hadrian Road, Wallsend, NE28 6HH
Tel: 0191-234 3500 **Fax:** 0191-234 3600
Directors: G. Brown (Sales), T. Kelso (Fin)
Immediate Holding Company: TYNE SURFACE TREATMENT LIMITED
Registration no: 03911085 **Date established:** 2000
No.of Employees: 1 - 10 **Product Groups:** 46, 48

Date of Accounts	Feb 10	Feb 09	Feb 08
Working Capital	17	-41	-11
Fixed Assets	65	73	86
Current Assets	164	249	314

Tyne Gangway Structures Ltd

Howdon Lane, Wallsend, NE28 0AL
Tel: 0191-262 3657 **Fax:** 0191-262 1498
E-mail: info@tynegangway.co.uk
Website: http://www.tynegangway.co.uk
Bank(s): Barclays
Directors: K. Macdonald (MD)
Immediate Holding Company: TWOBOBS (NORTH EAST) LIMITED
Registration no: 01160021 **VAT No.:** GB 178 3511 49
Date established: 1974 **Turnover:** £1m - £2m **No.of Employees:** 11 - 20
Product Groups: 35, 39

Date of Accounts	Dec 09	Dec 08	Dec 07
Working Capital	224	220	214
Fixed Assets	243	262	278
Current Assets	520	397	406

Tyne Tees Lifting Ltd

1 Metnor Business Park Hadrian Road, Wallsend, NE28 6HH
Tel: 0191-236 9222 **Fax:** 0191-236 9223
E-mail: phil.dixon@tyneteeslifting.co.uk
Website: http://www.tyneteeslifting.co.uk
Directors: P. Dixon (MD), S. Dixon (Fin)
Immediate Holding Company: TYNE TEES LIFTING LTD.
Registration no: 03714005 **Date established:** 1999
Turnover: £250,000 - £500,000 **No.of Employees:** 1 - 10
Product Groups: 26, 29, 35, 36, 37, 38, 39, 40, 41, 42, 43, 45, 48, 52, 67, 83, 84, 85

Date of Accounts	Jul 11	Jul 10	Jul 09
Working Capital	195	57	195
Fixed Assets	127	117	132
Current Assets	489	270	494

Washington

A D C Electrical Ltd

Burtree Works Hertburn Estate, Hertburn, Washington, NE37 2SF
Tel: 0191-416 5222 **Fax:** 0191-416 3996
E-mail: chriscarrick@btconnect.com
Website: http://www.adc-electrical.co.uk
Directors: C. Carrick (MD)
Immediate Holding Company: ADC ELECTRICAL LIMITED
Registration no: 07353942 **VAT No.:** GB 178 5007 50
Date established: 2010 **Turnover:** £250,000 - £500,000
No.of Employees: 1 - 10 **Product Groups:** 37, 46, 48

Date of Accounts	Oct 11
Working Capital	52
Fixed Assets	6
Current Assets	181

A & M Electricals Ltd

Unit 194 Commerce Park Stephenson Road, Washington, NE37 3HR
Tel: 0191-419 1519 **Fax:** 0191-419 2439
E-mail: am_electricals@hotmail.com
Website: http://www.automated-gates.com
Directors: A. Smiles (Dir)
Immediate Holding Company: A&M ELECTRICALS LTD
Registration no: 05718298 **Date established:** 2006 **Turnover:** £1m - £2m
No.of Employees: 11 - 20 **Product Groups:** 26, 35

Date of Accounts	Feb 08	Feb 11	Feb 10
Sales Turnover	1m	1m	865
Pre Tax Profit/Loss	26	66	-12
Working Capital	92	18	-5
Fixed Assets	29	24	25
Current Assets	305	300	152
Current Liabilities	101	234	139

Abacus Design & Fabrication

57 Hutton Close Crowther, Washington, NE38 0AH
Tel: 0191-419 2477 **Fax:** 0191-419 1145
E-mail: keith.purvis@abacusdesignandfab.com
Website: http://www.abacusdesignandfab.com
Directors: K. Purvis (Co Sec)
Immediate Holding Company: ABACUS DESIGN AND FABRICATION LIMITED
Registration no: 04598025 **Date established:** 2002
No.of Employees: 1 - 10 **Product Groups:** 26, 30, 35

Date of Accounts	Nov 11	Nov 10	Nov 09
Working Capital	-10	-9	-8
Fixed Assets	12	15	19
Current Assets	99	80	60

Acorn Industrial Services Ltd

9 Whitworth Road Armstrong, Washington, NE37 1PP
Tel: 0191-417 8899 **Fax:** 0191-419 0001
E-mail: sales@acorn-ind.co.uk
Website: http://www.acorn-ind.co.uk
Managers: S. Gordon (District Mgr)
Ultimate Holding Company: ACORN INDUSTRIAL SERVICES GROUP LTD
Immediate Holding Company: ACORN INDUSTRIAL SERVICES LIMITED
Registration no: 01733820 **Date established:** 1983
No.of Employees: 1 - 10 **Product Groups:** 32, 35, 38

Date of Accounts	Dec 11	Dec 10	Dec 09
Sales Turnover	17m	14m	12m
Pre Tax Profit/Loss	1m	695	897
Working Capital	5m	4m	4m
Fixed Assets	773	409	393
Current Assets	10m	10m	8m
Current Liabilities	2m	427	323

Air Supply North East

Unit 10 Pattinson Industrial Estate Stratford Road, Pattinson Industrial Estate, Washington, NE38 8QP
Tel: 0191-419 2663 **Fax:** 0191-419 2663
E-mail: graham-laidler@airsupplyne.co.uk
Website: http://www.airsupplyne.com
Directors: G. Laidler (Prop)
No.of Employees: 1 - 10 **Product Groups:** 18, 31, 35, 39, 40, 42, 48, 67, 68, 83

Apex Tools (a division of Cooper Great Britain Ltd)

Pennine House, Washington, NE37 1LY
Tel: 0191-419 7700 **Fax:** 0191-417 9421
E-mail: michael.shaw@apextoolgroup.com
Website: http://www.apextoolgroup.com
Directors: M. Shaw (MD)
Ultimate Holding Company: COOPER INDUSTRIES (USA)
Immediate Holding Company: 20:20 CONSULTING LIMITED
Registration no: 05177568 **VAT No.:** GB 193 2018 76
Date established: 2004 **No.of Employees:** 1 - 10 **Product Groups:** 36, 46

Argos Inspection Co. Ltd

Tower Road, Washington, NE37 2SH
Tel: 0191-417 7707 **Fax:** 0191-415 4979
E-mail: peter@argosinspection.com
Website: http://www.argosinspection.com
Directors: E. Reay (Chief Op Offcr), P. Bauckham (MD)
Immediate Holding Company: ARGOS INSPECTION COMPANY LIMITED
Registration no: 01485784 **VAT No.:** GB 334 7766 32
Date established: 1980 **Turnover:** £2m - £5m **No.of Employees:** 21 - 50
Product Groups: 34, 37, 38, 54, 85, 86

Date of Accounts	Nov 11	Nov 10	Nov 09
Working Capital	180	209	241
Fixed Assets	643	541	360
Current Assets	415	407	427

Bastion Glassfibre Ltd
12 Harvey Close Crowther Crowther, Washington, NE38 0AB
Tel: 0191-416 6394 **Fax:** 0191-415 4961
E-mail: sales@bastionwco.denn.co.uk
Website: http://www.bastionwco.denn.co.uk
Directors: J. Redmayne (MD)
Managers: M. Kernohan (Sales & Mktg Mg)
Ultimate Holding Company: BASTION GLASSFIBRE ROD & SECTIONS LIMITED
Immediate Holding Company: BASTION I.T. SERVICES LIMITED
Registration no: 02466905 **VAT No.:** GB 178 5572 19
Date established: 1990 **Turnover:** £1m - £2m **No.of Employees:** 1 - 10
Product Groups: 30, 33

Date of Accounts	Jan 11	Jan 10	Jan 09
Working Capital	-2	-0	21
Fixed Assets	5	9	11
Current Assets	62	65	54

Belt Technologies Europe
Pennine House, Washington, NE37 1LY
Tel: 0191-415 3010 **Fax:** 0191-415 0333
E-mail: sales@bte.co.uk
Website: http://www.belttechnologies.co.uk
Managers: B. Harvison
Immediate Holding Company: 20:20 CONSULTING LIMITED
Registration no: 05177568 **VAT No.:** GB 605 6845 32
Date established: 2004 **No.of Employees:** 1 - 10 **Product Groups:** 35, 45

Canford Audio
Crowther Road, Washington, NE38 0BW
Tel: 0191-418 1000 **Fax:** 0191-416 0392
E-mail: info@canford.co.uk
Website: http://www.canford.co.uk
Bank(s): Lloyds TSB Bank plc
Directors: O. Robson (Fin)
Managers: D. Holloway (Mktg Serv Mgr), D. Brown (Tech Serv Mgr), G. Lyon (Buyer), K. Barron (Personnel)
Ultimate Holding Company: CANFORD GROUP PLC.
Immediate Holding Company: CANFORD GROUP PLC.
Registration no: 03154977 **VAT No.:** GB 660 1163 71
Date established: 1996 **Turnover:** £10m - £20m
No.of Employees: 101 - 250 **Product Groups:** 37

Date of Accounts	Oct 11	Oct 10	Oct 09
Sales Turnover	18m	16m	15m
Pre Tax Profit/Loss	611	504	22
Working Capital	2m	1m	1m
Fixed Assets	2m	2m	2m
Current Assets	6m	5m	6m
Current Liabilities	2m	2m	N/A

Clifford Chapman Metalwork
27 Elswick Road Armstrong, Washington, NE37 1PB
Tel: 0191-417 3135 **Fax:** 0191-417 8519
E-mail: email@cliffordchapman.com
Website: http://www.cliffordchapman.com
Bank(s): Barclays
Directors: C. Chapman (Prop)
Managers: D. Hann (Buyer), S. Bowman (Tech Serv Mgr)
Immediate Holding Company: CLIFFORD CHAPMAN METALWORKS LIMITED
Registration no: 02764508 **VAT No.:** GB 605 4628 50
Date established: 1992 **Turnover:** £1m - £2m **No.of Employees:** 21 - 50
Product Groups: 22, 26, 35, 36, 40

Date of Accounts	Dec 11	Dec 10	Dec 09
Working Capital	-149	-191	-256
Fixed Assets	447	454	470
Current Assets	336	354	190

Cylinder Service Centre Ltd
Sedling Road Wear Industrial Estate, Washington, NE38 9BZ
Tel: 0191-416 6288
E-mail: info@cylinder.co.uk
Website: http://www.cylinder.co.uk
Directors: G. Davidson (MD), G. Davison (MD)
Managers: D. Roberts (Contracts Mgr)
Immediate Holding Company: THE CYLINDER SERVICE CENTRE LIMITED
Registration no: 03166460 **Date established:** 1996
No.of Employees: 21 - 50 **Product Groups:** 40, 48

Date of Accounts	Dec 11	Dec 10	Dec 09
Working Capital	384	283	312
Fixed Assets	2m	2m	2m
Current Assets	887	618	564

D M S Fabrication
24 Stirling Close, Washington, NE38 8QD
Tel: 0191-416 8088 **Fax:** 0191-416 8088
Directors: M. Smith (Prop)
Date established: 1999 **No.of Employees:** 1 - 10 **Product Groups:** 35

D P Fasteners Ltd
14 Donkin Road Armstrong, Washington, NE37 1PF
Tel: 0191-417 7846 **Fax:** 0191-419 4026
E-mail: dpfasteners@btconnect.com
Website: http://www.dpfasteners.co.uk
Bank(s): Yorkshire Bank PLC
Directors: S. Crammond (Dir)
Immediate Holding Company: D.P. FASTENERS LIMITED
Registration no: 02069380 **VAT No.:** GB 459 7322 16
Date established: 1986 **Turnover:** £1m - £2m **No.of Employees:** 11 - 20
Product Groups: 35, 66

Date of Accounts	May 11	May 10	May 09
Working Capital	2m	2m	2m
Fixed Assets	47	72	79
Current Assets	2m	2m	2m

D R Hydraulics & Engineering
Swan Road, Washington, NE38 8JJ
Tel: 0191-415 1115 **Fax:** 0191-415 1116
E-mail: mark@drhydraulics.com
Website: http://www.drhydraulics.co.uk
Directors: M. Dunville (Fin), D. Robson (Dir)
Immediate Holding Company: D R HYDRAULICS & ENGINEERING LIMITED
Registration no: 05332291 **Date established:** 2005
Turnover: £250,000 - £500,000 **No.of Employees:** 1 - 10
Product Groups: 40, 48

Date of Accounts	Mar 11	Mar 10	Mar 09
Working Capital	-1	-13	-14
Fixed Assets	46	54	65

Current Assets	107	93	68

Edu-Sci Ltd
Unit 4 Teal Farm Way, Washington, NE38 8BG
Tel: 0191-417 4173 **Fax:** 0191-497 2920
E-mail: sales@edu-sci.com
Website: http://www.edu-sci.com
Directors: S. Wilson (MD)
Immediate Holding Company: EDU-SCI LTD
Registration no: 05839577 **Date established:** 2006
Turnover: Up to £250,000 **No.of Employees:** 1 - 10 **Product Groups:** 20

Date of Accounts	Jun 11	Jun 10	Jun 09
Working Capital	39	47	41
Fixed Assets	5	3	1
Current Assets	63	67	90
Current Liabilities	N/A	N/A	5

Electric Vehicle Systems Ltd
Unit 11,Glover Industrial Estate Spire Road, Washington, NE37 3HB
Tel: 0191-416 1286 **Fax:** 0191-419 3746
E-mail: info@evsystems.co.uk
Website: http://www.evsystems.co.uk
Directors: G. Holmes (MD)
Managers: M. Jones (Buyer), M. Lumley (Works Gen Mgr), J. Holmes (Sales Prom Mgr)
Registration no: 01488531 **VAT No.:** GB 334 7478 37
Turnover: £500,000 - £1m **No.of Employees:** 1 - 10 **Product Groups:** 37, 39, 45

Date of Accounts	Mar 10	Mar 09	Mar 08
Working Capital	17	32	18
Fixed Assets	42	33	41
Current Assets	206	273	126

Encore Envelopes
Industrial Road Hertburn Industrial Estate, Hertburn, Washington, NE37 2SA
Tel: 0191-417 4327 **Fax:** 0191-419 0834
E-mail: sales@encoreenvelopes.com
Website: http://www.encoreenvelopes.com
Bank(s): National Westminster
Directors: M. Williamson (Fin), R. Croisdale (MD)
Managers: N. Ford (Tech Serv Mgr), J. Carpenter (Purch Mgr), C. Allen (Sales Prom Mgr), J. Corkhill (Mktg Serv Mgr), D. Cooper (Prod Mgr)
Ultimate Holding Company: TYNE & WEAR HOLDINGS LIMITED
Immediate Holding Company: ENCORE ENVELOPES LIMITED
Registration no: 01829336 **Date established:** 1984
Turnover: £20m - £50m **No.of Employees:** 101 - 250
Product Groups: 27, 81

Date of Accounts	Nov 11	Nov 10	Nov 09
Sales Turnover	30m	30m	28m
Pre Tax Profit/Loss	2m	2m	2m
Working Capital	6m	4m	4m
Fixed Assets	9m	10m	11m
Current Assets	16m	16m	16m
Current Liabilities	3m	3m	3m

Express Gates Online
13 Donkin Road Armstrong, Washington, NE37 1PF
Tel: 0191-415 4841 **Fax:** 0191-418 7504
Website: http://www.expressgatesonline.co.uk
Directors: S. French (MD), S. French (Ptnr)
Immediate Holding Company: EXPRESS GATES LIMITED
Registration no: 05098328 **Date established:** 2004
No.of Employees: 1 - 10 **Product Groups:** 26, 35

Date of Accounts	Feb 10	Feb 09	Feb 08
Working Capital	4	-51	-24
Fixed Assets	12	14	17
Current Assets	43	36	48

F K Optical Ltd
14-15 Baird Close, Washington, NE37 3HL
Tel: 0191-415 5135 **Fax:** 0191-415 5128
E-mail: fkoptical@aol.com
Directors: K. Kidman (Grp Chief Exec), R. Froud (Ch), R. Froud (Dir)
Immediate Holding Company: F. K. OPTICAL LIMITED
Registration no: 02328761 **Date established:** 1988
Turnover: £250,000 - £500,000 **No.of Employees:** 1 - 10
Product Groups: 38

Date of Accounts	Mar 11	Mar 10	Mar 09
Working Capital	132	129	131
Fixed Assets	3	4	5
Current Assets	202	252	206

Fairgrieve Mouldings Ltd
15 Sedling Road Wear Industrial Estate, Washington, NE38 9BZ
Tel: 0191-415 9292 **Fax:** 0191-415 9696
E-mail: info@compressionmoulding.co.uk
Website: http://www.compressionmoulding.co.uk
Directors: L. Biggins (Dir)
Immediate Holding Company: FAIRGRIEVE (MOULDINGS) LIMITED
Registration no: 01006284 **VAT No.:** GB 176 9731 17
Date established: 1971 **Turnover:** £250,000 - £500,000
No.of Employees: 1 - 10 **Product Groups:** 30, 39, 66

Date of Accounts	Mar 12	Mar 11	Mar 10
Working Capital	56	14	-41
Fixed Assets	314	447	462
Current Assets	584	576	321
Current Liabilities	N/A	97	N/A

James Gill Ltd
8 Donkin Road Armstrong, Washington, NE37 1PF
Tel: 0191-416 9357 **Fax:** 0191-415 5338
Directors: J. Gill (MD)
Immediate Holding Company: JAMES GILL FASTENINGS LIMITED
Registration no: 01627624 **VAT No.:** GB 368 9734 87
Date established: 1982 **Turnover:** £250,000 - £500,000
No.of Employees: 1 - 10 **Product Groups:** 35, 66

Date of Accounts	Apr 12	Apr 11	Apr 10
Working Capital	149	140	147
Fixed Assets	40	51	32
Current Assets	314	311	265

Hiltrain Ltd
32 Briarfield, Washington, NE38 8RX
Tel: 0191-247 1621
E-mail: enquiries@hiltrain.com
Website: http://www.hiltrain.co.uk
Directors: C. Irvine (Dir), I. Hay (I.T. Dir), S. Lawson (MD), A. Hay (Dir), P. Ivine (Dir)
Registration no: 05790111 **Date established:** 2006
Turnover: Up to £250,000 **No.of Employees:** 1 - 10 **Product Groups:** 86

Date of Accounts	Mar 08
Sales Turnover	92
Working Capital	3
Fixed Assets	2
Current Assets	11
Current Liabilities	9
Total Share Capital	5

Independent Manufacturers Alliance
Bentall Business Park, Washington, NE37 3JD
Tel: 0191-417 8700 **Fax:** 0191-417 8707
Website: http://www.illbruck.com
No.of Employees: 21 - 50 **Product Groups:** 33, 40

Interfit Ltd
29 Wear Industrial Estate, Washington, NE38 9DL
Tel: 0191-416 5791 **Fax:** 0191-415 7076
E-mail: washington@interfit-uk.com
Website: http://www.interfit-uk.com
Managers: J. Collinson (Mgr)
Ultimate Holding Company: TRELLEBORG AB (SWEDEN)
Immediate Holding Company: INTERFIT LIMITED
Registration no: 04340401 **Date established:** 2001
No.of Employees: 1 - 10 **Product Groups:** 29, 68

Date of Accounts	Dec 11	Dec 10	Dec 09
Sales Turnover	9m	10m	12m
Pre Tax Profit/Loss	-444	906	60
Working Capital	69	446	-398
Fixed Assets	657	597	551
Current Assets	3m	4m	5m
Current Liabilities	493	541	565

Isocom Ltd
48 Hutton Close Crowther Industrial Estate, Washington, NE38 0AH
Tel: 0191-416 6546 **Fax:** 0191-415 5055
E-mail: sales@isocom.uk.com
Website: http://www.isocom.uk.com
Directors: T. Bayat (MD)
Managers: M. Bayat (Sales Prom Mgr)
Registration no: 02981651 **Date established:** 1994
Turnover: £500,000 - £1m **No.of Employees:** 11 - 20 **Product Groups:** 67

Mchugh Engineering Ltd
25 Elswick Road Armstrong, Washington, NE37 1LH
Tel: 0191-416 2224 **Fax:** 0191-415 4957
E-mail: mchugheng@hotmail.com
Website: http://www.mchughchains.co.uk
Directors: A. Bell (MD)
Immediate Holding Company: MCHUGH ENGINEERING LTD.
Registration no: 01882847 **Date established:** 1985
No.of Employees: 1 - 10 **Product Groups:** 35, 39, 45

Date of Accounts	Mar 12	Mar 11	Mar 10
Working Capital	38	33	39
Fixed Assets	7	10	9
Current Assets	97	104	101

Mayfield Engineering Ltd
Unit 44 Hutton Close Crowther, Washington, NE38 0AH
Tel: 0191-497 2988 **Fax:** 0191-497 2989
E-mail: mayfield@mayfieldengineeringltd.co.uk
Website: http://www.mayfieldengineeringltd.co.uk
Directors: A. Hetherington (Co Sec)
Immediate Holding Company: MAYFIELD ENGINEERING LIMITED
Registration no: 03612196 **Date established:** 1998
No.of Employees: 11 - 20 **Product Groups:** 35

Date of Accounts	Oct 11	Oct 10	Oct 09
Working Capital	143	137	122
Fixed Assets	111	120	125
Current Assets	530	659	353

Nevesco Ltd
3 Lee Close, Washington, NE38 8QF
Tel: 0191-415 0037 **Fax:** 0191-415 3532
E-mail: tim@nevesco.co.uk
Website: http://www.nevesco.co.uk
Directors: A. Gordon (Fin), T. Gordon (MD)
Immediate Holding Company: NEVESCO LIMITED
Registration no: 02401942 **VAT No.:** GB 441 0496 73
Date established: 1989 **Turnover:** £250,000 - £500,000
No.of Employees: 1 - 10 **Product Groups:** 66

Date of Accounts	Sep 11	Sep 10	Sep 09
Working Capital	99	36	31
Fixed Assets	8	11	18
Current Assets	593	499	584

North East Observation Ltd
34 Pembridge, Washington, NE38 0LQ
Tel: 07931-999123
E-mail: enquiries@pattestingnortheast.co.uk
Website: http://www.pattestingnortheast.co.uk
Directors: M. Emmett (Dir)
Immediate Holding Company: NORTH EAST OBSERVATION LTD
Registration no: 06042435 **Date established:** 2007
No.of Employees: 1 - 10 **Product Groups:** 85

Date of Accounts	Jan 11	Jan 10	Jan 09
Working Capital	-4	-4	2
Fixed Assets	5	5	2
Current Assets	4	10	7

Nulite Ltd
51 Hutton Close Crowther, Washington, NE38 0AH
Tel: 0191-419 1111
E-mail: sales@nulite-ltd.co.uk
Website: http://www.nulite-ltd.co.uk
Directors: W. Harris (Prop)
Immediate Holding Company: NULITE LTD
Registration no: 03490017 **Date established:** 1998
No.of Employees: 1 - 10 **Product Groups:** 26, 35

Date of Accounts	Jun 11	Jun 10	Jun 09
Working Capital	-137	104	146
Fixed Assets	140	155	178
Current Assets	75	346	329

Orwin Automation Ltd
1-3 Brockwell Road Crowther, Washington, NE38 0AF
Tel: 0191-417 7092 **Fax:** 0191-416 7277
E-mail: sales@orwin.co.uk
Website: http://www.orwin.co.uk
Bank(s): Lloyds TSB Bank plc

see next page

Orwin Automation Ltd - Cont'd

Directors: B. Gleave (Develop), C. Whiteley (MD), M. Cooke (Fin)
Managers: J. Crawford (Buyer), J. Crawford (Buyer), J. Howard (Sales Admin)
Ultimate Holding Company: WHITELEY MURPHY LIMITED
Immediate Holding Company: ORWIN LIMITED
Registration no: 04628123 **VAT No.:** GB 389 5787 66
Date established: 2003 **Turnover:** £2m - £5m **No.of Employees:** 51 - 100
Product Groups: 48, 84, 85

Date of Accounts	Oct 11	Oct 10	Oct 09
Working Capital	239	254	196
Fixed Assets	443	254	302
Current Assets	2m	2m	1m

Pegasus Material Handling

1 Bridgewater Road, Washington, NE37 2SG
Tel: 0191-419 0003 **Fax:** 0191-419 2050
E-mail: enquiries@pegasusmh.co.uk
Website: http://www.pegasusmh.co.uk
Directors: R. Wilson (MD)
Immediate Holding Company: PEGASUS MATERIAL HANDLING LTD
Registration no: 04755094 **Date established:** 2003
No.of Employees: 1 - 10 **Product Groups:** 35, 39, 45

Date of Accounts	Mar 11	Mar 10	Mar 09
Working Capital	101	62	38
Fixed Assets	104	133	167
Current Assets	296	191	240

Penn Elcom

9-10 Parsons Road Parsons Industrial Estate, Washington, NE37 1HB
Tel: 0191-416 1717 **Fax:** 0191-419 3715
E-mail: info@penn-elcom.com
Website: http://www.penn-elcom.com
Bank(s): HSBC Bank plc
Managers: G. Mcgrath (Sales Prom Mgr)
Registration no: 00961889 **VAT No.:** GB 209 1005 12
Date established: 1974 **Turnover:** £5m - £10m
No.of Employees: 51 - 100 **Product Groups:** 22, 26, 30, 35, 36, 37, 44, 45

Date of Accounts	Nov 11	Nov 10	Nov 09
Working Capital	420	-304	171
Fixed Assets	6m	6m	5m
Current Assets	736	140	374

Pentair Thermal Management UK Limited

3 Rutherford Road Stephenson Industrial Estate, Washington, NE37 3HX
Tel: 0191-419 8200 **Fax:** 0191-419 8201
E-mail: salesuk@tycothermal.com
Website: http://www.tycothermal.com
Managers: K. Summerton
Ultimate Holding Company: TYCO INTERNATIONAL LIMITED (SWITZERLAND)
Immediate Holding Company: TYCO THERMAL CONTROLS UK LIMITED
Registration no: 03710607 **Date established:** 1999
Turnover: £20m - £50m **No.of Employees:** 21 - 50 **Product Groups:** 37, 38, 49

Date of Accounts	Sep 11	Sep 08	Sep 09
Sales Turnover	19m	23m	18m
Pre Tax Profit/Loss	2m	4m	1m
Working Capital	11m	11m	12m
Fixed Assets	156	405	383
Current Assets	18m	22m	21m
Current Liabilities	991	3m	3m

Posi-Thread UK Ltd

4 Bridgewater Road, Washington, NE37 2SG
Tel: 0191-417 8178 **Fax:** 0191-415 3120
E-mail: info@posithread.co.uk
Website: http://www.posithread.co.uk
Bank(s): Lloyds TSB
Managers: M. Allen (Fin Mgr), N. Gillon (Purch Mgr), D. Evans (Cust Serv Mgr), A. Dunn (Plant)
Immediate Holding Company: POSI-THREAD (U.K.) LTD.
Registration no: 01924756 **VAT No.:** 440 9001 87 **Date established:** 1985
Turnover: £2m - £5m **No.of Employees:** 21 - 50 **Product Groups:** 33, 36, 37, 47

Date of Accounts	Dec 11	Sep 10	Sep 09
Sales Turnover	2m	N/A	N/A
Pre Tax Profit/Loss	-2	N/A	N/A
Working Capital	429	417	504
Fixed Assets	310	386	457
Current Assets	1m	1m	1m
Current Liabilities	141	107	160

Rayovac Europe Ltd

Unit 2 A Stephenson Industrial Estate, Washington, NE37 3HW
Tel: 0845-6431 675 **Fax:** 01784-411412
Website: http://www.rayovac.eu
Directors: K. Shepard (MD)
Managers: C. Clark (I.T. Exec), J. Nisbet (Sales Prom Mgr), R. Roof, C. Gough (Mktg Serv Mgr)
Ultimate Holding Company: ROV Industries Inc. (USA)
Immediate Holding Company: Raoyovac Corporation (USA)
Registration no: 00316436 **VAT No.:** GB 532 7834 37
Turnover: £20m - £50m **No.of Employees:** 21 - 50 **Product Groups:** 32, 66

Date of Accounts	Sep 09	Sep 08	Sep 07
Sales Turnover	55m	55m	63m
Pre Tax Profit/Loss	11m	18m	8m
Working Capital	36m	58m	45m
Fixed Assets	48m	50m	51m
Current Assets	51m	75m	66m
Current Liabilities	5m	7m	N/A

Rocket Medical plc

2-4 Sedling Road Wear Industrial Estate, Washington, NE38 9BZ
Tel: 0191-419 4488 **Fax:** 0191-416 5693
E-mail: les@rocketmedical.com
Website: http://www.rocketmedical.com
Directors: L. Todd (Chief Op Offcr), L. Todd (Dir), J. Leech (Dir)
Managers: A. Robson, E. Lovett (Comm)
Immediate Holding Company: ROCKET MEDICAL PLC
Registration no: 03276608 **Date established:** 1996
No.of Employees: 101 - 250 **Product Groups:** 38, 67

Date of Accounts	Mar 11	Mar 10	Mar 09
Sales Turnover	12m	11m	11m
Pre Tax Profit/Loss	2m	646	1m
Working Capital	5m	4m	4m
Fixed Assets	933	1m	1m
Current Assets	6m	5m	5m
Current Liabilities	941	938	932

S I E Industrial Ltd

Faraday House Station Road, Washington, NE38 7LW
Tel: 0191-416 5127 **Fax:** 0191-415 3876
E-mail: info@sieindustrial.co.uk
Website: http://www.sieindustrial.co.uk
Bank(s): H.S.B.C.
Directors: P. Bowen (MD)
Immediate Holding Company: S.I.E. INDUSTRIAL LIMITED
Registration no: 01627236 **VAT No.:** GB 369 0231 55
Date established: 1982 **Turnover:** £2m - £5m **No.of Employees:** 11 - 20
Product Groups: 46

Date of Accounts	Dec 07	Jun 11	Jun 10
Working Capital	269	377	345
Fixed Assets	219	110	146
Current Assets	810	815	806

Sitelink Communications Ltd

18 Bridgewater Road, Washington, NE37 2SG
Tel: 0191-417 4084
E-mail: sales@sitelink.co.uk
Website: http://www.sitelink.co.uk
Managers: I. Richie (District Mgr), S. Bernip (Mgr)
Immediate Holding Company: SITELINK COMMUNICATIONS LIMITED
Registration no: 01018478 **Date established:** 1971
No.of Employees: 1 - 10 **Product Groups:** 37, 67

Date of Accounts	Sep 11	Sep 10	Sep 09
Working Capital	641	414	658
Fixed Assets	497	738	1m
Current Assets	1m	1m	1m

Smithers Oasis

Crowther Road, Washington, NE38 0AQ
Tel: 0191-417 5595 **Fax:** 0191-417 8516
E-mail: ukmarketing@oasisfloral.com
Website: http://www.oasisfloral.com
Bank(s): Barclays
Directors: S. Short (MD)
Managers: L. Proudfoot (Personnel), S. Fuller (Purch Mgr), P. Rising (Tech Serv Mgr), S. Garrett (Comptroller)
Ultimate Holding Company: SMITHERS-OASIS COMPANY (USA)
Immediate Holding Company: SMITHERS-OASIS U.K. LIMITED
Registration no: 01542218 **VAT No.:** GB 353 9063 48
Date established: 1981 **Turnover:** £10m - £20m
No.of Employees: 101 - 250 **Product Groups:** 49, 62

Date of Accounts	Mar 11	Mar 10	Mar 09
Sales Turnover	17m	18m	N/A
Pre Tax Profit/Loss	1m	2m	1m
Working Capital	9m	5m	4m
Fixed Assets	4m	4m	4m
Current Assets	11m	7m	6m
Current Liabilities	955	1m	2m

Speedarc Welding Supplies

Unit 2a Glover Industrial Estate Spire Road, Washington, NE37 3ES
Tel: 0191-419 4115
E-mail: info@speedarc.com
Website: http://www.speedarc.com
Managers: M. Wharton (Mgr)
Immediate Holding Company: SPEEDARC WELDING SUPPLIES LIMITED
Registration no: 04131389 **Date established:** 2000
No.of Employees: 1 - 10 **Product Groups:** 46

Date of Accounts	Oct 11	Oct 10	Oct 09
Working Capital	43	41	41
Fixed Assets	19	12	15
Current Assets	160	178	123

Statebourne Cryogenics Ltd

19 Parsons Road, Washington, NE37 1EZ
Tel: 0191-416 4104 **Fax:** 0191-415 0369
E-mail: johns@statebourne.com
Website: http://www.statebourne.com
Bank(s): National Westminster
Directors: J. Short (Fin)
Immediate Holding Company: STATEBOURNE (CRYOGENIC) LIMITED
Registration no: 00952351 **VAT No.:** GB 176 6400 55
Date established: 1969 **Turnover:** £5m - £10m **No.of Employees:** 21 - 50
Product Groups: 39, 40

Date of Accounts	Mar 11	Mar 10	Mar 09
Sales Turnover	7m	4m	N/A
Pre Tax Profit/Loss	115	-132	192
Working Capital	1m	804	984
Fixed Assets	1m	1m	1m
Current Assets	3m	2m	3m
Current Liabilities	133	202	198

Sundwel Solar Ltd

Unit 1 Tower Road, Washington, NE37 2SH
Tel: 0800-980 8939 **Fax:** 0191-415 4297
E-mail: solar@sundwel.com
Website: http://www.sundwel.com
Directors: L. Woods (MD), S. Woods (Dir), A. Levene (MD)
Managers: K. Wilkinson (Chief Mgr)
Ultimate Holding Company: SUNUSER LIMITED
Immediate Holding Company: SUNDWEL SOLAR LIMITED
Registration no: 01554609 **VAT No.:** GB 353 9232 51
Date established: 1981 **Turnover:** £500,000 - £1m
No.of Employees: 1 - 10 **Product Groups:** 37

Date of Accounts	Feb 08	Feb 10	Feb 09
Working Capital	68	76	70
Fixed Assets	N/A	4	N/A
Current Assets	138	106	122

Tanfield Group plc

Vigo Centre Birtley Road, Washington, NE38 9DA
Tel: 0191-417 2170 **Fax:** 01207-523318
E-mail: roy.stanley@tanfieldgroup.com
Website: http://www.tanfieldgroup.com
Directors: C. Brooks (Co Sec), R. Stanley (Dir)
Immediate Holding Company: TANFIELD GROUP PLC
Registration no: 04061965 **Date established:** 2000
Turnover: £20m - £50m **No.of Employees:** 1001 - 1500
Product Groups: 28

Date of Accounts	Dec 11	Dec 10	Dec 09
Sales Turnover	48m	44m	58m
Pre Tax Profit/Loss	-16m	-17m	-22m
Working Capital	23m	35m	42m
Fixed Assets	8m	10m	22m
Current Assets	37m	53m	62m
Current Liabilities	6m	13m	11m

Teams Roofing Ltd

Wylam Close Stephenson Industrial Estate East, Washington, NE37 3BE
Tel: 0191-419 2233 **Fax:** 0191-416 2210
E-mail: enquiries@teamsroofing.com
Website: http://www.teamsroofing.com
Directors: S. Willis (Dir), A. Willis (MD)
Immediate Holding Company: TEAMS ROOFING LIMITED
Registration no: 01307648 **Date established:** 1977 **Turnover:** £2m - £5m
No.of Employees: 21 - 50 **Product Groups:** 35, 52

Date of Accounts	Mar 12	Mar 11	Mar 10
Working Capital	329	376	434
Fixed Assets	412	411	394
Current Assets	712	618	629

Universal Sealents UK Ltd

Kingston House 3 Walton Road Pattinson North, Washington, NE38 8QA
Tel: 0191-416 1530 **Fax:** 0191-415 5966
E-mail: info@ufluk.com
Website: http://www.ufluk.com
Bank(s): National Westminster P.L.C.
Directors: N. Simpson (Fin), N. Bennett (MD), N. Simpson (Fin), R. Forsyth (Div)
Managers: C. Bell (Mktg Serv Mgr), D. Wandless (Purch Mgr), R. Carty (Mktg Serv Mgr), K. Hewitson (Personnel), K. Hewitson (Personnel)
Ultimate Holding Company: UNIVERSAL SEALANTS (U.K.) LIMITED
Immediate Holding Company: NUFINS LIMITED
Registration no: 00877754 **VAT No.:** GB 353 8952 22
Date established: 1966 **Turnover:** £10m - £20m
No.of Employees: 101 - 250 **Product Groups:** 36

Date of Accounts	May 11	May 10	Mar 09
Sales Turnover	17m	21m	20m
Pre Tax Profit/Loss	3m	-306	5m
Working Capital	1m	22	1m
Fixed Assets	7m	7m	7m
Current Assets	10m	8m	7m
Current Liabilities	2m	912	2m

Visage Ltd

Parsons Industrial Estate Parsons Road, Washington, NE37 1EZ
Tel: 0191-415 1133 **Fax:** 0191-427 1580
E-mail: sanjeev.mehan@visage-group.com
Website: http://www.visage.ltd.uk
Directors: R. Bacon (Co Sec), S. Mehan (Dir)
Ultimate Holding Company: LI & FUNG LIMITED (BERMUDA)
Immediate Holding Company: VISAGE LIMITED
Registration no: 01568110 **Date established:** 1981
Turnover: £125m - £250m **No.of Employees:** 501 - 1000
Product Groups: 24

Date of Accounts	Dec 11	Dec 10	Jan 10
Sales Turnover	194m	190m	198m
Pre Tax Profit/Loss	3m	3m	10m
Working Capital	46m	43m	38m
Fixed Assets	5m	7m	7m
Current Assets	86m	134m	117m
Current Liabilities	16m	26m	70m

Walker Filtration Ltd

Birtley Road, Washington, NE38 9DA
Tel: 0191-417 7816 **Fax:** 0191-415 3748
E-mail: reception@walkerfiltration.co.uk
Website: http://www.walkerfiltration.com
Bank(s): Lloyds TSB Bank plc
Directors: D. Barnes (Fin)
Managers: M. Welsh (Fin Mgr), J. King (Purch Mgr), A. Wright (Sales Prom Mgr), J. Macewen (Personnel), S. Palmer (Tech Serv Mgr)
Immediate Holding Company: WALKER FILTRATION LIMITED
Registration no: 01726079 **Date established:** 1983
Turnover: £10m - £20m **No.of Employees:** 101 - 250
Product Groups: 23, 29, 30, 33, 34, 35, 36, 38, 39, 40, 42, 68

Date of Accounts	Aug 11	Aug 10	Aug 09
Sales Turnover	19m	17m	14m
Pre Tax Profit/Loss	1m	2m	937
Working Capital	7m	6m	5m
Fixed Assets	7m	3m	2m
Current Assets	10m	9m	8m
Current Liabilities	1m	889	1m

WaterTite Roofing

25 Finchdale Biddick, Washington, NE38 7HE
Tel: 0191-416 1688 **Fax:** 0191-417 6735
E-mail: sharon@srobson4.wanadoo.co.uk
Product Groups: 30, 33, 35, 39, 45, 48, 52

Westray Recruitment Consultants

13-14 Concord House Speculation Place, Washington, NE37 2AS
Tel: 0191-415 1100 **Fax:** 0191-415 5148
E-mail: shodgson@westray.co.uk
Website: http://www.westrayrecruitment.co.uk
Directors: S. Hodgson (Fin)
Ultimate Holding Company: WESTRAY HOLDINGS LIMITED
Immediate Holding Company: WESTRAY RECRUITMENT CONSULTANTS LIMITED
Registration no: 02464679 **Date established:** 1990
No.of Employees: 11 - 20 **Product Groups:** 80

Date of Accounts	Mar 11	Mar 10	Mar 09
Working Capital	91	14	4
Fixed Assets	210	127	157
Current Assets	824	650	670

Whitley Bay

F & R Belbin Ltd

Back of 165-169 Whitley Road, Whitley Bay, NE26 2DN
Tel: 0191-252 2875 **Fax:** 0191-297 0812
E-mail: sales@frbelbin.co.uk
Website: http://www.frbelbin.co.uk
Bank(s): Barclays
Directors: E. Gowdy (Co Sec), R. Belbin (Ch), D. Belbin (MD), P. Belbin (Dir)
Immediate Holding Company: F.& R.BELBIN LIMITED
Registration no: 00696284 **VAT No.:** GB 176 0820 63
Date established: 1961 **Turnover:** £250,000 - £500,000
No.of Employees: 11 - 20 **Product Groups:** 36, 46, 48

Date of Accounts	Mar 08	Mar 07	Mar 06
Working Capital	124	88	79
Fixed Assets	104	105	116

Current Assets	262	230	178
Current Liabilities	137	142	98
Total Share Capital	4	4	4

Duncan Stephen Associates
37 Davison Avenue, Whitley Bay, NE26 1SQ
Tel: 0191-252 0715 **Fax:** 0191-251 9891
E-mail: ddstephen@dsas.freeserve.co.uk
Directors: D. Stephen (Prop)
Turnover: Up to £250,000 **No.of Employees:** 1 - 10 **Product Groups:** 86

A L Graham
8 The Crest Seaton Sluice, Whitley Bay, NE26 4BG
Tel: 0191-237 1733 **Fax:** 0191-237 1733
Directors: A. Graham (Prop)
Date established: 1983 **No.of Employees:** 1 - 10 **Product Groups:** 20, 40, 41

Invetel Ltd
10 Marden Road, Whitley Bay, NE26 2JH
Tel: 0191-252 9129 **Fax:** 0191-252 9129
E-mail: sales@invetel.com
Website: http://www.invetel.com
Directors: A. Gasparyan (Fin), J. Higgins (MD)
Immediate Holding Company: INVETEL LIMITED
Registration no: 04194514 **Date established:** 2001
Turnover: £500,000 - £1m **No.of Employees:** 1 - 10 **Product Groups:** 38

Date of Accounts	Mar 11	Mar 10	Mar 09
Working Capital	7	15	38
Fixed Assets	2	2	3
Current Assets	37	26	44

Kingfisher Services
13 Ashkirk Way Seaton Delaval, Whitley Bay, NE25 0JT
Tel: 0191-237 7032 **Fax:** 0800-756 5643
E-mail: lesbowman@kfservices.com
Website: http://www.kfservices.com
Managers: L. Bowman (Mgr)
Date established: 1990 **Turnover:** £10m - £20m **No.of Employees:** 1 - 10
Product Groups: 67, 69, 84

M Kelley Ltd (t/a First Impressions)
12 Rockcliffe Avenue, Whitley Bay, NE26 2NN
Tel: 0191-251 4000
E-mail: mike@cvs.demon.co.uk
Website: http://www.cv-service.org
Managers: M. Kelley (Consultant)
Registration no: 05101963 **Date established:** 1990
No.of Employees: 1 - 10 **Product Groups:** 80

Date of Accounts	Apr 08	Apr 07
Working Capital	11	-3
Fixed Assets	18	18
Current Assets	16	3
Current Liabilities	6	6

Pavex Co.
11 Maple Avenue, Whitley Bay, NE25 8JR
Tel: 0191-252 4729
Directors: A. Rutherford (Ptnr)
Date established: 1954 **No.of Employees:** 1 - 10 **Product Groups:** 42, 45

Pipetawse Ltd
New Hartley Industrial Estate Double Row, Seaton Delaval, Whitley Bay, NE25 0QT
Tel: 0191-237 6237 **Fax:** 0191-237 7184
E-mail: reception@pipetawse.com
Website: http://www.pipetawselimited.co.uk
Directors: R. Murray (Sales), T. Armstrong (MD)
Managers: B. Hope (Purch Mgr), L. Edgar (Sales Admin)
Immediate Holding Company: PIPETAWSE LIMITED
Registration no: 01587668 **Date established:** 1981 **Turnover:** £2m - £5m
No.of Employees: 51 - 100 **Product Groups:** 51, 52, 54, 84

Date of Accounts	Dec 11	Dec 10	Dec 09
Working Capital	647	697	821
Fixed Assets	948	1m	1m
Current Assets	2m	1m	1m

WARWICKSHIRE

Alcester

Autolamps Ltd
Adams Way Springfield Business Park, Alcester, B49 6PU
Tel: 01789-765996 **Fax:** 01789-400321
E-mail: sales@autolamps.co.uk
Website: http://www.autolamps.co.uk
Bank(s): Lloyds TSB Bank plc
Directors: R. Wilding (MD), T. Preston (Sales)
Immediate Holding Company: AUTOLAMPS LIMITED
Registration no: 03134980 **VAT No.:** GB 698 8511 82
Date established: 1995 **No.of Employees:** 21 - 50 **Product Groups:** 39

Date of Accounts	Apr 11	Apr 10	Apr 09
Working Capital	751	671	657
Fixed Assets	38	56	41
Current Assets	1m	1m	1m

Avon Bridge Conservatories
Unit 10 Smallbrook Business Centre, Bidford-On-Avon, Alcester, B50 4JE
Tel: 01789-778592 **Fax:** 01789-490939
E-mail: info@avonbridgeconservatories.co.uk
Website: http://www.avonbridgeconservatories.co.uk
Directors: L. Spragg (Dir)
Immediate Holding Company: AVONBRIDGE CONSERVATORIES & WINDOWS LTD
Registration no: 04194927 **Date established:** 2001
Turnover: Up to £250,000 **No.of Employees:** 1 - 10 **Product Groups:** 08, 25, 35

Date of Accounts	Mar 11	Mar 10	Mar 09
Working Capital	-15	9	N/A
Fixed Assets	20	6	N/A
Current Assets	45	49	N/A

Bromford Industries Ltd
Unit 9 Kinwarton Farm Road, Kinwarton, Alcester, B49 6EH
Tel: 01789-400340 **Fax:** 01789-400690
E-mail: sales@wb2000.co.uk
Website: http://www.bromfordindustries.co.uk
Bank(s): Barclays
Directors: H. Kimberley (Co Sec)
Managers: M. Tew (Ops Mgr), R. Stanyer (Purch Mgr), R. Roe (Comptroller)
Ultimate Holding Company: BROMFORD HOLDINGS LIMITED
Immediate Holding Company: BROMFORD INDUSTRIES LIMITED
Registration no: 00474681 **VAT No.:** GB 473 8128 29
Date established: 1949 **Turnover:** £500,000 - £1m
No.of Employees: 21 - 50 **Product Groups:** 48

Date of Accounts	Mar 09	Mar 08	Sep 11
Sales Turnover	28m	30m	24m
Pre Tax Profit/Loss	2m	2m	-332
Working Capital	14m	17m	11m
Fixed Assets	20m	21m	11m
Current Assets	22m	23m	19m
Current Liabilities	2m	2m	4m

Cal Gavin Ltd Process Intensification Engineering
Station Road, Alcester, B49 5ET
Tel: 01789-400401 **Fax:** 01789-400411
E-mail: info@calgavin.com
Website: http://www.calgavin.com
Directors: M. Gough (MD), M. Gough (Fin)
Immediate Holding Company: CAL GAVIN LIMITED
Registration no: 01505148 **VAT No.:** GB 352 2959 44
Date established: 1980 **Turnover:** £1m - £2m **No.of Employees:** 21 - 50
Product Groups: 35, 42, 48, 66, 84, 85

Date of Accounts	Dec 11	Dec 10	Dec 09
Working Capital	1m	1m	918
Fixed Assets	521	477	424
Current Assets	2m	2m	1m

Carpenter Technology UK Ltd
3 Adams Way Springfield Business Park, Alcester, B49 6PU
Tel: 01789-767340 **Fax:** 01789-767341
E-mail: pbugler@cartech.com
Website: http://www.cartech.com
Directors: P. Bugler (Comm)
Ultimate Holding Company: CARPENTER TECHNOLOGY CORP (USA)
Immediate Holding Company: CARPENTER TECHNOLOGY (UK) LIMITED
Registration no: 01741625 **Date established:** 1983
Turnover: £20m - £50m **No.of Employees:** 1 - 10 **Product Groups:** 34

Date of Accounts	Jun 11	Jun 10	Jun 09
Sales Turnover	20m	18m	21m
Pre Tax Profit/Loss	731	1m	-5m
Working Capital	6m	5m	5m
Fixed Assets	N/A	N/A	9
Current Assets	13m	8m	9m
Current Liabilities	157	53	626

Claymore
1b Waterloo Industrial Estate Waterloo Road, Bidford-on-Avon, Alcester, B50 4JH
Tel: 01789-490177 **Fax:** 01789-490170
E-mail: sales@claymoregrass.co.uk
Website: http://www.fgmclaymore.co.uk
Directors: K. Christian (MD), P. Butterley (MD)
Managers: H. Finfield (Admin Off)
Immediate Holding Company: PARKS AND GROUNDS MACHINERY LIMITED
Registration no: 00120044 **Date established:** 1989 **Turnover:** £2m - £5m
No.of Employees: 21 - 50 **Product Groups:** 41, 67

Date of Accounts	Dec 10	Dec 09	Dec 08
Working Capital	634	583	447
Fixed Assets	835	766	833
Current Assets	3m	4m	4m

Collins Extrusions Ltd
Bidavon Industrial Estate Waterloo Road, Bidford-On-Avon, Alcester, B50 4JW
Tel: 01789-773536 **Fax:** 01789-490225
E-mail: coltec1@yahoo.com
Website: http://www.collins-extrusions.co.uk
Bank(s): Lloyds TSB Bank plc
Directors: R. Collins (MD)
Immediate Holding Company: COLLINS (EXTRUSIONS) LIMITED
Registration no: 01004790 **VAT No.:** GB 274 1219 71
Date established: 1971 **Turnover:** £500,000 - £1m
No.of Employees: 11 - 20 **Product Groups:** 30, 40

Date of Accounts	Mar 12	Mar 11	Mar 10
Working Capital	275	325	300
Fixed Assets	29	34	29
Current Assets	374	402	361

Famous Little Lamp Shop
12 Arden Business Centre Arden Road, Alcester, B49 6HW
Tel: 01789-766007 **Fax:** 01789-766007
E-mail: julie@thefamouslittlelampshop.co.uk
Website: http://www.thefamouslittlelampshop.com
Directors: J. Gwilliam (Prop)
Date established: 2000 **No.of Employees:** 1 - 10 **Product Groups:** 33, 37

Fletcher Fabrications
Arden Road, Alcester, B49 6HN
Tel: 01789-762481 **Fax:** 01789-762481
Directors: B. Fletcher (Prop)
Ultimate Holding Company: MELROSE PLC
Immediate Holding Company: PHOENIX (MCKECHNIE) TRAVEL LIMITED
Registration no: 04559480 **Date established:** 1993
Turnover: £20m - £50m **No.of Employees:** 1 - 10 **Product Groups:** 35, 48, 66

Date of Accounts	Dec 11	Dec 10	Dec 09
Pre Tax Profit/Loss	93	99	-56
Working Capital	9m	9m	8m
Fixed Assets	3m	3m	3m
Current Assets	9m	9m	8m

H P F Energy Services
Unit 3 Kinwarton Farm Road Kinwarton, Alcester, B49 6EH
Tel: 01789-761212 **Fax:** 01789-761222
E-mail: alcester@hpf-energy.com
Website: http://www.hpf-energy.co.uk
Directors: S. Faulkner (MD), S. Cooper (Sales), S. Cooper (Jt MD), C. Barnett (Jt MD)
Managers: T. Smith (Chief Acct), C. McCormack (Personnel), S. Crook
Ultimate Holding Company: MARLA TUBE FITTINGS LIMITED
Immediate Holding Company: REDDITCH FITTINGS & FLANGES LIMITED
Registration no: 00572373 **Date established:** 1973
Turnover: £20m - £50m **No.of Employees:** 51 - 100 **Product Groups:** 36

Date of Accounts	Oct 10	Oct 09	Oct 08
Sales Turnover	50m	65m	62m
Pre Tax Profit/Loss	3m	7m	6m
Working Capital	38m	39m	36m
Fixed Assets	8m	7m	6m
Current Assets	44m	46m	44m
Current Liabilities	1m	2m	1m

Joe Turner Equipment Ltd
Mill Ford Cottage Coughton Fields Lane, Coughton, Alcester, B49 6BS
Tel: 01789-763958 **Fax:** 01789-400330
E-mail: sales@joturnerequipment.co.uk
Website: http://www.joeturnerequipment.co.uk
Directors: B. Turner (Fin)
Immediate Holding Company: JOE TURNER (EQUIPMENT) LIMITED
Registration no: 02100797 **Date established:** 1987
Turnover: £250,000 - £500,000 **No.of Employees:** 1 - 10
Product Groups: 41, 48

Date of Accounts	Jul 11	Jul 10	Jul 09
Working Capital	-15	4	1
Fixed Assets	18	9	11
Current Assets	192	228	222

Marla Tube Fittings Ltd
Unit 1-2 Kinwarton Farm Road Kinwarton, Alcester, B49 6EH
Tel: 01789-761234 **Fax:** 01789-761205
E-mail: sales@marla.co.uk
Website: http://www.hpf-energy.com
Bank(s): Barclays Bank P.L.C.
Directors: L. Barnes (Fin), S. Preedy (MD), J. Preedy (Fin)
Managers: D. Edwards (Sales Prom Mgr), C. McCormack (Personnel), S. Crook (Tech Serv Mgr)
Immediate Holding Company: MARLA TUBE FITTINGS LIMITED
Registration no: 00572373 **Date established:** 1956
Turnover: £50m - £75m **No.of Employees:** 51 - 100 **Product Groups:** 36

Date of Accounts	Oct 11	Oct 10	Oct 09
Sales Turnover	69m	50m	65m
Pre Tax Profit/Loss	6m	3m	7m
Working Capital	42m	38m	39m
Fixed Assets	8m	8m	7m
Current Assets	53m	44m	46m
Current Liabilities	4m	1m	2m

Malcolm Nicholls Ltd
Waterloo Industrial Estate Waterloo Road, Bidford-On-Avon, Alcester, B50 4JH
Tel: 01789-490382 **Fax:** 01789-490130
E-mail: virginia@mnl.co.uk
Website: http://www.mnl.co.uk
Bank(s): HSBC, Stratford-upon-Avon
Directors: V. Nicholls (Fin)
Managers: R. Nicholls (Chief Mgr), T. Nicholls (Sales Prom Mgr)
Immediate Holding Company: MALCOLM NICHOLLS LIMITED
Registration no: 01364746 **VAT No.:** GB 349 2614 43
Date established: 1978 **Turnover:** £500,000 - £1m
No.of Employees: 11 - 20 **Product Groups:** 44, 48

Date of Accounts	Mar 11	Mar 10	Mar 09
Working Capital	33	-95	-83
Fixed Assets	390	377	404
Current Assets	223	172	183

Peak Trailers Ltd
Unit 2a Waterloo Industrial Estate Waterloo Road, Bidford-On-Avon, Alcester, B50 4JH
Tel: 01789-778041 **Fax:** 01789-490331
E-mail: sales@peaktrailers.com
Website: http://www.peaktrailers.com
Bank(s): Barclays
Directors: A. Muller (Dir), S. Sayer (Fin)
Managers: L. Matthews (Personnel), P. Prosser, V. Vardy-smith (Personnel)
Ultimate Holding Company: PEAK TRAILERS (HOLDINGS) LIMITED
Immediate Holding Company: PEAK TRAILERS LIMITED
Registration no: 01000461 **Date established:** 1971 **Turnover:** £2m - £5m
No.of Employees: 21 - 50 **Product Groups:** 39

Date of Accounts	Dec 11	Dec 10	Dec 09
Working Capital	2m	2m	2m
Fixed Assets	382	500	492
Current Assets	2m	2m	2m

Piltec Rubber & Plastics Ltd
Unit 17 Waterloo Park, Bidford-On-Avon, Alcester, B50 4JG
Tel: 01789-778271 **Fax:** 01789-772886
E-mail: antonio@piltec.com
Website: http://www.piltec.com
Directors: A. Pileci (Dir)
Immediate Holding Company: PILTEC RUBBER & PLASTICS LIMITED
Registration no: 03020345 **Date established:** 1995
Turnover: £500,000 - £1m **No.of Employees:** 1 - 10 **Product Groups:** 29, 32, 49

Date of Accounts	Jul 11	Jul 10	Jul 09
Working Capital	125	-144	-176
Fixed Assets	325	351	378
Current Assets	374	392	319

Propak Midlands Ltd

Tything Road Kinwarton, Alcester, B49 6EP
Tel: 01789-765111 **Fax:** 01789-765720
E-mail: iwhite@propakbox.com
Website: http://www.propakbox.com
Bank(s): HSBC, Birmingham
Directors: I. White (MD)
Immediate Holding Company: PROPAK (MIDLANDS) LIMITED
Registration no: 05125794 **VAT No.:** GB 294 5641 28
Date established: 2004 **Turnover:** £1m - £2m **No.of Employees:** 11 - 20
Product Groups: 27

Q Lawns In The Midlands a division of David P. Fisher Landscapes

41 Grafton Lane Bidford-on-Avon, Alcester, B50 4DX
Tel: 01789-772626 **Fax:** 01789-772963
E-mail: davidpfisher@btconnect.com
Website: http://www.qlawnsinthemidlands.co.uk
Directors: D. Fisher (Prop)
No.of Employees: 1 - 10 **Product Groups:** 02, 25, 51, 52, 66, 84

Roba Metals Ltd

Kinwarton Farm Road Arden Forest Industrial Estate, Kinwarton, Alcester, B49 6EH
Tel: 01789-763232 **Fax:** 01789-400660
E-mail: info@robametals.co.uk
Website: http://www.robametals.co.uk
Bank(s): Barclays
Directors: T. Sandford (MD)
Managers: J. Sweetman (Comptroller)
Ultimate Holding Company: ROBA HOLDINGS BV (NETHERLANDS)
Immediate Holding Company: ROBA METALS LIMITED
Registration no: 02090606 **VAT No.:** GB 454 8315 38
Date established: 1987 **Turnover:** £20m - £50m
No.of Employees: 11 - 20 **Product Groups:** 34, 61, 66

Date of Accounts	Dec 11	Dec 10	Dec 09
Sales Turnover	23m	22m	9m
Pre Tax Profit/Loss	-179	597	432
Working Capital	244	1m	938
Fixed Assets	3m	1m	1m
Current Assets	7m	7m	5m
Current Liabilities	175	2m	153

S J G International Ltd

Unit 6 Tything Road East Kinwarton, Alcester, B49 6ES
Tel: 01789-763721 **Fax:** 01789-765922
E-mail: sales@sjginternational.com
Website: http://www.sjginternational.com
Directors: M. James (MD)
Immediate Holding Company: SJG INTERNATIONAL LIMITED
Registration no: 00974659 **VAT No.:** GB 110 6415 23
Date established: 1970 **Turnover:** £5m - £10m **No.of Employees:** 21 - 50
Product Groups: 25, 30, 48

Date of Accounts	Sep 11	Sep 10	Sep 09
Sales Turnover	5m	5m	5m
Pre Tax Profit/Loss	118	59	4
Working Capital	-14	-195	-182
Fixed Assets	2m	3m	3m
Current Assets	2m	2m	2m
Current Liabilities	596	608	722

S J G International

Unit 24 Tything Road East, Kinwarton, Alcester, B49 6EX
Tel: 01789-764547 **Fax:** 01789-764070
E-mail: sales@sjginternational.com
Website: http://www.THESJGROUP.COM
Directors: J. Suggitt (Dir), M. James (Dir), R. Jacks (MD)
Immediate Holding Company: SJG INTERNATIONAL LIMITED
Registration no: 00974659 **Date established:** 1970 **Turnover:** £2m - £5m
No.of Employees: 1 - 10 **Product Groups:** 35, 36, 39, 41

Date of Accounts	Sep 09	Sep 08	Sep 07
Sales Turnover	5m	6m	5m
Pre Tax Profit/Loss	4	-146	253
Working Capital	-182	-238	151
Fixed Assets	3m	3m	3m
Current Assets	2m	2m	2m
Current Liabilities	722	523	479

Salfab Steel Fabricators

Kinwarton Farm Road Kinwarton, Alcester, B49 6EH
Tel: 01789-400671 **Fax:** 01789-400571
E-mail: salfabwelding@aol.com
Directors: B. Sallis (Ptnr)
Immediate Holding Company: MARLA TUBE FITTINGS LIMITED
Registration no: 02634596 **Date established:** 1991
No.of Employees: 1 - 10 **Product Groups:** 35

Seco Tools UK Ltd

4 Kinwarton Farm Road Kinwarton, Alcester, B49 6EL
Tel: 01789-764341 **Fax:** 01789-761170
E-mail: uk.sales@secotools.com
Website: http://www.secotools.com
Bank(s): Svenska Handels Banken
Directors: C. Gillespie (Co Sec), R. Jelfs (MD)
Managers: K. Manning (Purch Mgr), V. Stuart-Smith, P. Dhir (Tech Serv Mgr), M. Fleming (Sales & Mktg Mg)
Ultimate Holding Company: SANDVIK AB (SWEDEN)
Immediate Holding Company: SECO TOOLS (U.K.) LIMITED
Registration no: 01151087 **VAT No.:** GB 276 2071 60
Date established: 1973 **Turnover:** £20m - £50m
No.of Employees: 51 - 100 **Product Groups:** 33, 35, 36, 37, 46

Date of Accounts	Dec 11	Dec 10	Dec 09
Sales Turnover	25m	21m	19m
Pre Tax Profit/Loss	3m	1m	124
Working Capital	7m	5m	4m
Fixed Assets	2m	3m	2m
Current Assets	12m	9m	7m
Current Liabilities	2m	1m	718

Select Engineering (Redditch) Ltd

Station House Sambourne Lane, Coughton, Alcester, B49 5HT
Tel: 01789-766008 **Fax:** 01789-766206
E-mail: sales@sea-tech-construction.com
Website: http://www.select-asiaco.com
Directors: S. Spencer (Dir)
Registration no: 02148118 **Date established:** 1984
No.of Employees: 1 - 10 **Product Groups:** 34, 35, 36, 37, 45, 61

Date of Accounts	Jul 10	Jul 09	Jul 08
Working Capital	289	312	365
Fixed Assets	219	212	212

Current Assets	307	319	372

Severn Lamb UK Ltd

Tything Road East Kinwarton, Alcester, B49 6ET
Tel: 01789-400140 **Fax:** 01789-400240
E-mail: sales@severn-lamb.com
Website: http://www.severn-lamb.com
Directors: P. Lamb (Dir)
Immediate Holding Company: SEVERN-LAMB UK LIMITED
Registration no: 05308055 **Date established:** 2004 **Turnover:** £2m - £5m
No.of Employees: 11 - 20 **Product Groups:** 49, 84

Date of Accounts	Dec 11	Dec 10	Dec 09
Working Capital	-256	-223	-16
Fixed Assets	18	16	17
Current Assets	443	402	616

Malcolm W Shaw

Church Farm Coughton Fields Lane, Coughton, Alcester, B49 6BS
Tel: 01789-763453 **Fax:** 01789-400451
E-mail: malcomshaw@mwshaw.com
Website: http://www.mwshaw.com
Directors: M. Shaw (Prop)
Immediate Holding Company: FRENCH FISHING HOLIDAYS LIMITED
Registration no: 03653825 **Date established:** 1998
No.of Employees: 1 - 10 **Product Groups:** 41

Smith Bros & Webb Ltd

22 Tything Road East Kinwarton, Alcester, B49 6EX
Tel: 01789-400096 **Fax:** 01789-400231
E-mail: sales@vehicle-washing-systems.co.uk
Website: http://www.vehicle-washing-systems.co.uk
Bank(s): HSBC Bank plc
Directors: J. Bennett (Fin)
Immediate Holding Company: SMITH BROS. & WEBB LIMITED
Registration no: 00314689 **VAT No.:** GB 111 0538 31
Date established: 1936 **Turnover:** £2m - £5m **No.of Employees:** 51 - 100
Product Groups: 37, 39, 40, 68

Date of Accounts	Dec 10	Dec 09	Jun 09
Sales Turnover	N/A	3m	N/A
Pre Tax Profit/Loss	N/A	340	N/A
Working Capital	316	533	-39
Fixed Assets	142	57	65
Current Assets	3m	3m	2m
Current Liabilities	N/A	492	N/A

Special Metal Welding Products

Waterloo Road Bidford-on-Avon, Alcester, B50 4JN
Tel: 01789-491780 **Fax:** 01789-491781
E-mail: dwebster@smwpc.com
Website: http://www.specialmetals.com
Managers: D. Webster (Mgr)
Registration no: 01053632 **Date established:** 1972
Turnover: Up to £250,000 **No.of Employees:** 21 - 50 **Product Groups:** 46

Superline A P Ltd

Unit 12 Smallbrook Business Centre, Bidford-On-Avon, Alcester, B50 4JE
Tel: 01789-490555
Directors: R. Day (MD)
No.of Employees: 1 - 10 **Product Groups:** 35

T J Mutton Press Tool

Waterloo Industrial Estate Waterloo Road, Bidford-On-Avon, Alcester, B50 4JH
Tel: 01789-772950 **Fax:** 01789-772950
Directors: T. Mutton (Prop)
Date established: 2000 **No.of Employees:** 1 - 10 **Product Groups:** 36

Techsil Ltd

34 Bidavon Industrial Estate Waterloo Road, Bidford-On-Avon, Alcester, B50 4JN
Tel: 01789-773232 **Fax:** 01789-774239
E-mail: sales@techsil.co.uk
Website: http://www.techsil.co.uk
Bank(s): Barclays
Directors: A. Briars (Dir)
Ultimate Holding Company: TECHSIL HOLDINGS LIMITED
Immediate Holding Company: TECHSIL LIMITED
Registration no: 02447014 **VAT No.:** GB 927 4584 91
Date established: 1989 **Turnover:** £1m - £2m **No.of Employees:** 11 - 20
Product Groups: 29, 31, 32, 35

Date of Accounts	Jul 12	Jul 11	Jul 10
Working Capital	3m	3m	3m
Fixed Assets	68	80	88
Current Assets	4m	4m	4m

Tornado Wire Ltd

4b Waterloo Road Bidford-on-Avon, Alcester, B50 4JH
Tel: 08450-710890 **Fax:** 01789-490508
E-mail: sales@tornadowire.co.uk
Website: http://www.tornadowire.co.uk
Bank(s): The Royal Bank of Scotland
Managers: A. Wellman (Mktg Serv Mgr), C. Barbour (Purch Mgr), M. Blackford (Mgr), M. Blackford (Mgr), P. Osbourne (Tech Serv Mgr), L. Hall
Ultimate Holding Company: TORNADO GROUP LIMITED
Immediate Holding Company: TORNADO WIRE LIMITED
Registration no: SC064920 **VAT No.:** GB 300 7810 03
Date established: 1978 **Turnover:** £5m - £10m **No.of Employees:** 11 - 20
Product Groups: 25, 30, 35

Date of Accounts	Dec 11	Dec 10	Dec 09
Sales Turnover	15m	14m	11m
Pre Tax Profit/Loss	1m	1m	755
Working Capital	3m	2m	3m
Fixed Assets	994	1m	1m
Current Assets	4m	4m	4m
Current Liabilities	588	622	517

Turner Machine Tools

23 Waterloo Park Bidford-on-Avon, Alcester, B50 4JG
Tel: 01789-772921 **Fax:** 01789-778614
E-mail: info@turner-riveters.co.uk
Website: http://www.turner-riviters.co.uk
Directors: P. Knowles (Dir)
Registration no: 00306266 **VAT No.:** GB 110 5557 08
Date established: 2003 **Turnover:** £500,000 - £1m
No.of Employees: 1 - 10 **Product Groups:** 46, 84

Date of Accounts	Sep 08	Sep 07	Sep 06
Working Capital	350	379	382
Fixed Assets	90	93	94

Current Assets	378	466	421
Current Liabilities	29	87	39
Total Share Capital	18	18	18

Warwick Design Consultants Ltd

Unit 12 Waterloo Park, Bidford-On-Avon, Alcester, B50 4JG
Tel: 01789-490591 **Fax:** 01789-490592
E-mail: wdc@warwickdesign.com
Website: http://www.warwickdesign.com
Managers: A. Gibbs (Design Mgr)
Immediate Holding Company: WARWICK DESIGN CONSULTANTS LIMITED
Registration no: 02366945 **Date established:** 1989
Turnover: £500,000 - £1m **No.of Employees:** 1 - 10 **Product Groups:** 30, 37, 84

Date of Accounts	Mar 11	Mar 10	Mar 09
Working Capital	100	100	111
Fixed Assets	15	19	24
Current Assets	133	136	147

Welding Supply Ltd

2 Cheapside Bickmarsh, Bidford-On-Avon, Alcester, B50 4PB
Tel: 01789-773168 **Fax:** 01789-772153
Website: http://www.weldingsupplyltd.co.uk
Directors: J. Curry (Dir), C. Curry (Fin)
Immediate Holding Company: WELDING SUPPLY LIMITED
Registration no: 02018998 **Date established:** 1986
No.of Employees: 1 - 10 **Product Groups:** 46

Date of Accounts	Dec 11	Dec 10	Dec 06
Working Capital	-1	1	-0
Fixed Assets	4	5	18
Current Assets	39	33	57

Westmore Business Systems Ltd

2 Arrow Court Adams Way Springfield Business Park, Alcester, B49 6PU
Tel: 08452-306500 **Fax:** 0845-230 6511
E-mail: sales@westmore.co.uk
Website: http://www.westmore.co.uk
Managers: J. Williams (Sales Admin)
Ultimate Holding Company: FIELD HOLDINGS LIMITED
Immediate Holding Company: WESTMORE BUSINESS SYSTEMS LIMITED
Registration no: 02741960 **Date established:** 1992
Turnover: £500,000 - £1m **No.of Employees:** 11 - 20
Product Groups: 27, 28, 32, 38, 44, 48, 49, 64, 66, 67, 80

Date of Accounts	Nov 11	Nov 10	Nov 09
Working Capital	-194	-118	-116
Fixed Assets	195	136	132
Current Assets	728	630	505

Atherstone

Andrews Automation

14 Main Street Orton-on-the-Hill, Atherstone, CV9 3NN
Tel: 08452-010626 **Fax:** 01827-881160
Website: http://www.andrewsautomation.com
Directors: H. Davenport (Fin), A. Forman (MD)
Immediate Holding Company: ANDREWS AUTOMATION LIMITED
Registration no: 04777815 **Date established:** 2003
No.of Employees: 1 - 10 **Product Groups:** 35, 39, 45

Date of Accounts	Jul 08	Jul 07	Jul 06
Working Capital	9	-7	-2
Fixed Assets	1	2	4
Current Assets	270	209	36
Current Liabilities	261	217	38

Anker Towbars Ltd

Appleby Hill Austrey, Atherstone, CV9 3ER
Tel: 01827-830039 **Fax:** 01827-830862
E-mail: sales@ankertowbars.co.uk
Website: http://www.ankertowbars.com
Directors: W. Barton (MD)
Registration no: 01692976 **VAT No.:** GB 113 0288 16
Date established: 1983 **Turnover:** £500,000 - £1m
No.of Employees: 1 - 10 **Product Groups:** 39

Date of Accounts	Oct 09	Oct 08	Oct 07
Working Capital	116	50	421
Fixed Assets	159	165	173
Current Assets	288	263	526

B & G Cleaning Systems Ltd

Abeles Way Holly Lane Industrial Estate, Atherstone, CV9 2QZ
Tel: 01827-717028 **Fax:** 01827-714041
E-mail: martin@bgclean.co.uk
Website: http://www.bgclean.co.uk
Bank(s): Barclays
Directors: M. Reece (Fin)
Immediate Holding Company: B & G CLEANING SYSTEMS LIMITED
Registration no: 02492527 **VAT No.:** GB 372 2005 89
Date established: 1990 **Turnover:** £2m - £5m **No.of Employees:** 21 - 50
Product Groups: 29, 30, 31, 32, 36, 37, 39, 40, 41, 42, 45, 46, 47, 48, 49, 66, 67, 68

Date of Accounts	Apr 11	Apr 10	Apr 09
Working Capital	182	195	258
Fixed Assets	272	270	274
Current Assets	805	642	696

Coler Supply Solutions

Manor Road Industrial Estate, Atherstone, CV9 1QY
Tel: 01827-712910 **Fax:** 01827-62776
E-mail: info@coler.co.uk
Website: http://www.coler.co.uk
Directors: K. Barker (MD)
Immediate Holding Company: CLAIMS AID LTD
Registration no: 6787189 **Date established:** 2005 **Turnover:** £2m - £5m
No.of Employees: 1 - 10 **Product Groups:** 40

Easiclean Wipers

Unit 1 Hurley Hall Industrial Estate Atherstone Lane, Hurley, Atherstone, CV9 2HT
Tel: 01827-874787 **Fax:** 01827-874745
E-mail: info@easicleanwipers.com
Website: http://www.easicleanwipers.com

see next page

Easiclean Wipers - Cont'd
Directors: M. Collins (MD), L. Sears (Dir)
Immediate Holding Company: EASICLEAN WIPERS LIMITED
Registration no: 06543521 **VAT No.:** GB 346 1880 45
Date established: 2008 **Turnover:** £1m - £2m **No.of Employees:** 1 - 10
Product Groups: 23, 24, 27, 30, 32, 36, 40, 44, 49, 63, 66

Electricars Ltd (Manufacturing Division)
Carlyon Road, Atherstone, CV9 1LQ
Tel: 01827-716888 **Fax:** 01827-717841
Website: http://www.electricars-group.com
Directors: I. Mason (Dir)
Immediate Holding Company: ELECTRICARS LIMITED
Registration no: 00320542 **VAT No.:** GB 410 0954 96
Date established: 1936 **Turnover:** £5m - £10m **No.of Employees:** 1 - 10
Product Groups: 39, 45

Date of Accounts	Jun 09	Jun 08	Jun 07
Working Capital	N/A	N/A	-675
Fixed Assets	N/A	N/A	40
Current Assets	N/A	N/A	208

GB Marine Transmission Specialists
36 Fourways, Atherstone, CV9 1LG
Tel: 01827-718350 **Fax:** 01827-718350
E-mail: g.knight@gb-marine.co.uk
Website: http://www.gb-marine.co.uk
Directors: G. Knights (Prop)
Date established: 1983 **No.of Employees:** 1 - 10 **Product Groups:** 35, 36, 39

Krampe Trailers
Warton Lane Grendon, Atherstone, CV9 3DT
Tel: 01827-892295 **Fax:** 01827-892432
E-mail: lee@krampe.co.uk
Website: http://www.krampe.co.uk
Directors: A. Krampe (MD), L. Sutton (Ptnr)
Managers: J. Kocks (Prod Mgr)
No.of Employees: 51 - 100 **Product Groups:** 41

Lunn Engineering Co. Ltd
Manor Road Industrial Estate, Atherstone, CV9 1RB
Tel: 01827-713228 **Fax:** 01827-717624
E-mail: info@lunnengineering.co.uk
Website: http://www.lunnengineering.co.uk
Bank(s): Yorkshire Bank PLC
Directors: F. Lunn (Dir)
Ultimate Holding Company: LUNN HOLDINGS LIMITED
Immediate Holding Company: LUNN ENGINEERING CO.LIMITED
Registration no: 00508446 **VAT No.:** GB 114 2673 94
Date established: 1952 **Turnover:** £250,000 - £500,000
No.of Employees: 11 - 20 **Product Groups:** 45, 46, 48, 67, 84

Date of Accounts	Mar 11	Mar 10	Mar 09
Working Capital	200	179	482
Fixed Assets	457	396	452
Current Assets	522	503	795

M C Systems PHONE POINTS CCTV ACCESS CONTROL SYSTEMS
8 Jean Street Baddesley Ensor, Atherstone, CV9 2EA
Tel: 01827-720209 **Fax:** 08000-665970
E-mail: mcsystems@btinternet.com
Website: http://www.aerialupgrades.org
Directors: M. Couzens (Prop)
No.of Employees: 1 - 10 **Product Groups:** 37

M J C A
Baddefley Colliery Offices Baxterley, Atherstone, CV9 2LE
Tel: 01827-717891 **Fax:** 01827-718507
E-mail: leslieheasman@mjca.co.uk
Website: http://www.mjca.co.uk
Directors: L. Heasman (MD)
Immediate Holding Company: MJCA TRUSTEES LIMITED
Registration no: 05947107 **VAT No.:** GB 372 2674 46
Date established: 2006 **Turnover:** £2m - £5m **No.of Employees:** 21 - 50
Product Groups: 54, 84, 85

Date of Accounts	May 11	May 10	May 09
Working Capital	-30	-30	-30
Fixed Assets	30	30	30
Current Liabilities	30	30	30

M J Sheetmetal
Unit 12 Innage Park Off Abeles Way, Holly Lane Industrial Estate, Atherstone, CV9 2QX
Tel: 01827-722622 **Fax:** 01827-722622
E-mail: sales@mjsheetmetal.co.uk
Website: http://www.mjsheetmetal.co.uk
Directors: M. Jordan (Prop)
No.of Employees: 1 - 10 **Product Groups:** 34, 35, 36, 48, 49

M & M Group Handling Ltd
Unit 15 Carlyon Road Industrial Estate Carlyon Road, Atherstone, CV9 1LQ
Tel: 01827-711111 **Fax:** 01827-717841
Website: http://www.mmgrouphandling.co.uk
Directors: R. Mason (MD), I. Mason (MD)
Ultimate Holding Company: PRESSMARK PRESSINGS LIMITED
Immediate Holding Company: ELECTRICARS LIMITED
Registration no: 00320542 **Date established:** 1936
No.of Employees: 1 - 10 **Product Groups:** 35, 39, 45

M R Tools Atherstone Ltd
Netherwood Industrial Estate Ratcliffe Road, Atherstone, CV9 1HY
Tel: 01827-713097 **Fax:** 01827-718518
E-mail: mrtoolsales@btconnect.com
Website: http://www.mr-tools.co.uk
Bank(s): Royal Bank of Scotland, 17 Church St, Rugby, Warwickshire, CV21 3PP
Directors: D. Pugh (Fab), M. Hughes (Dir), M. Fawcett (Fin)
Immediate Holding Company: M.R. TOOL (ATHERSTONE) LIMITED
Registration no: 02614859 **VAT No.:** GB 545 2384 42
Date established: 1991 **Turnover:** £500,000 - £1m
No.of Employees: 21 - 50 **Product Groups:** 46

Date of Accounts	May 11	May 10	May 09
Working Capital	268	266	309
Fixed Assets	643	666	734
Current Assets	641	598	702

Merlin Plastics
Charity Farm Baxterley, Atherstone, CV9 2LN
Tel: 01827-874572 **Fax:** 01827-874898
E-mail: merlin.plastics@btconnect.com
Directors: K. Broomfield (Prop)
Date established: 1970 **Turnover:** Up to £250,000
No.of Employees: 1 - 10 **Product Groups:** 30, 42

On The Dot Typing Ltd
The Arcade 71 Long Street, Atherstone, CV9 1AZ
Tel: 08450-171580 **Fax:** 01827-713113
E-mail: admin@onthedottyping.co.uk
Website: http://www.onthedottyping.co.uk
Directors: P. Caldicott (Dir), S. Caldicott (Fin)
Immediate Holding Company: ON THE DOT TYPING LIMITED
Registration no: 05863507 **Date established:** 2006
No.of Employees: 1 - 10 **Product Groups:** 44, 79, 80

Date of Accounts	Jun 11	Jun 10	Jun 08
Working Capital	-1	-4	-6
Fixed Assets	N/A	4	12
Current Assets	11	8	5

P N Tools
Unit 33 34 Fourways, Carlyon Road Industrial Estate, Atherstone, CV9 1LH
Tel: 01827-720013 **Fax:** 01827-720039
E-mail: info@pntools.co.uk
Website: http://www.pntools.co.uk
Directors: P. Newham (Ptnr)
No.of Employees: 1 - 10 **Product Groups:** 36

Panelcraft Access Panels
Unit H The Pavilons, Abeles Way, Holly Lane Industrial Estate, Atherstone, CV9 2QZ
Tel: 01827-720830 **Fax:** 01827-720860
E-mail: sales@panelcraftaccesspanels.com
Website: http://www.panelcraftaccesspanels.com
Product Groups: 30, 35, 66

Parex Ltd
Abeles Way Holly Lane Industrial Estate, Atherstone, CV9 2QZ
Tel: 01827-711755 **Fax:** 01827-711330
E-mail: enquiries@parex.co.uk
Website: http://www.parex.co.uk
Bank(s): National Westminster
Directors: M. Shorrock (MD), A. Cogbill (Fin)
Ultimate Holding Company: MATERIS PARENT SARL (LUXEMBOURG)
Immediate Holding Company: PAREX LTD
Registration no: 02450579 **VAT No.:** GB 661 5419 36
Date established: 1989 **Turnover:** £10m - £20m
No.of Employees: 21 - 50 **Product Groups:** 30, 32

Date of Accounts	Dec 11	Dec 10	Dec 09
Sales Turnover	11m	7m	7m
Pre Tax Profit/Loss	1m	-81	770
Working Capital	3m	3m	2m
Fixed Assets	3m	4m	5m
Current Assets	5m	4m	3m
Current Liabilities	914	527	522

Pressmark Pressings Ltd
18 Carlyon Road, Atherstone, CV9 1LQ
Tel: 01827-716381 **Fax:** 01827-716162
E-mail: general@pressmark.co.uk
Website: http://www.pressmark.co.uk
Bank(s): Nat West
Directors: M. Carter (Fin)
Managers: A. Robinson (Sales Prom Mgr), Y. Smith (Prod Mgr)
Immediate Holding Company: PRESSMARK PRESSINGS LIMITED
Registration no: 02540509 **Date established:** 1990
No.of Employees: 51 - 100 **Product Groups:** 48

Date of Accounts	Dec 11	Dec 10	Dec 09
Working Capital	832	997	834
Fixed Assets	303	307	291
Current Assets	2m	2m	2m

Rare
Manor Park Twycross, Atherstone, CV9 3QN
Tel: 01827-883400 **Fax:** 01827-883410
Website: http://www.rareware.com
Directors: K. Dolliver (MD)
Managers: S. Betts
Ultimate Holding Company: MICRO-SOFT CORPORATION (USA)
Immediate Holding Company: RARE LIMITED
Registration no: 01905690 **Date established:** 1985
Turnover: £10m - £20m **No.of Employees:** 101 - 250
Product Groups: 44, 49

Date of Accounts	Jun 11	Jun 08	Jul 09
Sales Turnover	21m	15m	15m
Pre Tax Profit/Loss	2m	4m	3m
Working Capital	15m	22m	17m
Fixed Assets	3m	3m	3m
Current Assets	18m	23m	18m
Current Liabilities	2m	907	1m

Rekord Sales
Manor Road Mancetter, Atherstone, CV9 1RJ
Tel: 01827-712424 **Fax:** 01827-715133
E-mail: terry@universal.co.uk
Website: http://www.rekord.com
Directors: M. White (MD)
Immediate Holding Company: REKORD SALES (GREAT BRITAIN) LIMITED
Registration no: 00564684 **Date established:** 1956
No.of Employees: 1 - 10 **Product Groups:** 41

Date of Accounts	Dec 11	Dec 10	Dec 09
Working Capital	69	51	15
Fixed Assets	45	47	49
Current Assets	107	87	93

Smart-Space.co.uk
Manor House Farm Dordon Hall Lane, Grendon, Atherstone, CV9 2EX
Tel: 01827-330000 **Fax:** 01827-898600
E-mail: jennie@smart-space.co.uk
Website: http://www.smart-space.co.uk
Product Groups: 35, 52, 77, 83

Universal Heat Transfer Ltd
Well Spring Close Carlyon Road Industrial Estate, Atherstone, CV9 1HU
Tel: 01827-722171 **Fax:** 01827-722174
E-mail: enquiries@uhtltd.com
Website: http://www.universalheattransfer.co.uk
Directors: N. Salter (Co Sec), K. Salter (MD)
Managers: J. Salter, D. Alexander, J. Stone (Purch Mgr)
Immediate Holding Company: UNIVERSAL HEAT TRANSFER LIMITED
Registration no: 03526041 **Date established:** 1998
No.of Employees: 21 - 50 **Product Groups:** 39, 40, 48

Date of Accounts	Apr 11	Apr 10	Apr 09
Working Capital	644	537	456
Fixed Assets	324	273	241
Current Assets	1m	1m	1m

Whitehall Box Co. Ltd
Racemeadow Road Carlyon Road Industrial Estate, Atherstone, CV9 1LJ
Tel: 01827-715709 **Fax:** 08453-300203
E-mail: sales@whitehall-box.co.uk
Website: http://www.whitehall-box.co.uk
Directors: M. Wall (Dir), P. Bates (Comm)
Ultimate Holding Company: PICKAPACK LIMITED
Immediate Holding Company: WHITEHALL BOX COMPANY LIMITED
Registration no: 03477758 **Date established:** 1997
No.of Employees: 21 - 50 **Product Groups:** 27, 48

Date of Accounts	Mar 11	Mar 10	Mar 09
Working Capital	2m	2m	2m
Fixed Assets	291	335	391
Current Assets	3m	3m	3m

Bedworth

A & T Doors Ltd
112 Leicester Road, Bedworth, CV12 8AG
Tel: 024-7649 0514 **Fax:** 024-7649 0514
E-mail: atlamley@aol.com
Website: http://hometown.aol.co.uk/atlamley/myhomepage/business.html
Directors: T. Lamley (Dir)
Immediate Holding Company: A & T DOORS LIMITED
Registration no: 03709659 **Date established:** 1999
Turnover: Up to £250,000 **No.of Employees:** 1 - 10 **Product Groups:** 33, 35, 40

Date of Accounts	Mar 11	Mar 10	Mar 08
Sales Turnover	N/A	148	278
Pre Tax Profit/Loss	N/A	-3	1
Working Capital	7	1	4
Fixed Assets	7	N/A	N/A
Current Assets	47	21	48

All Saints C Of E Infant School
Priory Road Off Mitchell Road, Bedworth, CV12 9HP
Tel: 024-7631 3387 **Fax:** 024-7631 4081
E-mail: admin@allsaintsnurserybedworth.co.uk
Website: http://www.3301.wgsl.net
Managers: T. Keeling
Date established: 1996 **No.of Employees:** 21 - 50 **Product Groups:** 86

Cadel Packaging Supplies
10 Florence Close, Bedworth, CV12 0BY
Tel: 024-7636 4776
Directors: D. Leighton (Ptnr)
Date established: 1988 **No.of Employees:** 1 - 10 **Product Groups:** 38, 42

Forklift & Access Sales
137 Dark Lane, Bedworth, CV12 0JQ
Tel: 024-7636 7366 **Fax:** 07976-737312
E-mail: mike@fltsales.co.uk
Website: http://www.fltsales.co.uk
Directors: M. Jones (Prop)
Turnover: Up to £250,000 **Product Groups:** 35, 45, 48, 67

Knight Catering Equipment
288 Newtown Road, Bedworth, CV12 0AL
Tel: 024-7635 2727 **Fax:** 024-7635 2727
E-mail: john@mongan1.fsnet.co.uk
Directors: J. Mongan (Prop)
Date established: 1989 **No.of Employees:** 1 - 10 **Product Groups:** 20, 40, 41

Parkes' Office & Event Solutions Ltd
3 The Priors, Bedworth, CV12 9NZ
Tel: 024-7631 7007 **Fax:** 024-7675 8822
E-mail: info@parkesoes.com
Website: http://www.parkesoes.com
Directors: M. Parkes (MD)
Immediate Holding Company: PARKES' OFFICE & EVENT SOLUTIONS LIMITED
Registration no: 05176202 **Date established:** 2004
Turnover: Up to £250,000 **No.of Employees:** 1 - 10 **Product Groups:** 44, 80

Date of Accounts	Sep 11	Sep 10	Sep 09
Working Capital	N/A	-2	-5
Fixed Assets	6	4	5
Current Assets	11	3	3

Toye Kenning & Spencer Ltd
Regalia House Newtown Road, Bedworth, CV12 8QR
Tel: 024-7684 8800 **Fax:** 024-7664 3018
E-mail: sales@toye.com
Website: http://www.toye.com
Bank(s): Barclays, London
Directors: B. Toye (Ch), F. Toye (Grp Chief Exec), N. Haynes (Fin)
Managers: P. Burgess (Personnel), T. Harvey (Tech Serv Mgr), T. Harvey (I.T. Exec), C. Cushing, A. Wright (Grp Mktg Mgr)
Ultimate Holding Company: TOYE & COMPANY PUBLIC LIMITED COMPANY
Immediate Holding Company: TOYE, KENNING & SPENCER LIMITED
Registration no: 01121668 **VAT No.:** GB 232 5841 74
Date established: 1973 **Turnover:** £5m - £10m
No.of Employees: 101 - 250 **Product Groups:** 23, 24, 30, 49

Date of Accounts	Dec 11	Dec 10	Dec 09
Sales Turnover	8m	8m	8m
Pre Tax Profit/Loss	-371	128	-178

Working Capital	811	1m	1m
Fixed Assets	258	276	285
Current Assets	3m	3m	3m
Current Liabilities	261	421	329

Kenilworth

Agco International Ltd
Abbey Park Stareton, Kenilworth, CV8 2TQ
Tel: 024-7669 4400 **Fax:** 024-7685 2495
E-mail: info@masseyferguson.com
Website: http://www.masseyferguson.com
Bank(s): Bank of America NA
Directors: R. Batkin (Dir), K. Randall (Fin), A. Deeley (Sales & Mktg), R. Markwell (MD)
Managers: C. Hefford (Chief Acct), M. Ward (Mgr)
Ultimate Holding Company: AGCO CORP (USA)
Immediate Holding Company: AGCO INTERNATIONAL LIMITED
Registration no: 02388894 **VAT No.:** GB 646 8198 92
Date established: 1989 **Turnover:** Over £1,000m
No.of Employees: 1501 & over **Product Groups:** 39, 41, 45, 49, 67, 83

Date of Accounts	Dec 11	Dec 10	Dec 09
Pre Tax Profit/Loss	6m	136m	81m
Working Capital	-201m	-209m	68m
Fixed Assets	502m	506m	506m
Current Assets	222m	219m	280m
Current Liabilities	785	817	700

Agriculture & Horticulture Development Board
Board National Agricultural Centre, Stoneleigh Park, Kenilworth, CV8 2TL
Tel: 024-7669 2051 **Fax:** 01908-609221
E-mail: info@ahdb.org.uk
Website: http://www.ahdb.org.uk
Directors: T. Taylor (MD), C. Goodwin (Fin), J. Dubery (Pers)
Managers: A. Churchill, M. Brown (Tech Serv Mgr)
Immediate Holding Company: CROP EVALUATION LIMITED
Date established: 2000 **Turnover:** £50m - £75m
No.of Employees: 251 - 500 **Product Groups:** 85

Date of Accounts	Mar 10	Mar 09	Mar 08
Sales Turnover	1m	1m	903
Current Assets	199	226	208
Current Liabilities	199	226	208

British Association Of Landscape Industries
Landscape House 10th Street, Stoneleigh Park, Kenilworth, CV8 2LG
Tel: 024-7669 0333 **Fax:** 024-7669 0077
E-mail: admin@barli.co.uk
Website: http://www.bali.org.uk
Directors: D. Billing (Co Sec)
Managers: W. Grills
Immediate Holding Company: BRITISH ASSOCIATION OF LANDSCAPE INDUSTRIES(THE)
Registration no: 01254410 **Date established:** 1976
Turnover: £250,000 - £500,000 **No.of Employees:** 1 - 10
Product Groups: 87

Date of Accounts	Mar 12	Mar 11	Mar 10
Working Capital	106	116	67
Fixed Assets	24	8	10
Current Assets	452	341	204

Buckingham Swimming Pools Ltd
Dalehouse Lane, Kenilworth, CV8 2EB
Tel: 01926-852351 **Fax:** 01926-512387
E-mail: info@buckinghampools.com
Website: http://www.buckinghampools.com
Bank(s): The Royal Bank of Scotland, Birmingham
Directors: D. Ledbrooke (MD), I. Goodwin (Fin), P. Mason (Dir)
Managers: M. Roberts (Tech Serv Mgr)
Ultimate Holding Company: BUCKINGHAM SWIMMING POOLS HOLDINGS LIMITED
Immediate Holding Company: BUCKINGHAM SWIMMING POOLS LIMITED
Registration no: 02452107 **VAT No.:** GB 545 2880 30
Date established: 1989 **Turnover:** £5m - £10m **No.of Employees:** 21 - 50
Product Groups: 30, 52

Date of Accounts	Dec 11	Dec 10	Dec 09
Sales Turnover	6m	5m	6m
Pre Tax Profit/Loss	748	515	504
Working Capital	1m	2m	3m
Fixed Assets	368	340	332
Current Assets	4m	4m	5m
Current Liabilities	974	973	874

C A K Tanks
Aqua House Princes Drive Industrial Estate, Kenilworth, CV8 2FD
Tel: 08444-142324
E-mail: sales@caktanks.com
Website: http://www.caktanks.com
Directors: J. Frost (MD)
Ultimate Holding Company: CARAVAN ACCESSORIES (KENILWORTH) LIMITED
Immediate Holding Company: C.A.K. TANKS LIMITED
Registration no: 03722518 **Date established:** 1999
No.of Employees: 1 - 10 **Product Groups:** 30, 37, 39

Caldaro
42 Warwick Road, Kenilworth, CV8 1HE
Tel: 0800-169 7950 **Fax:** 0800-169 7960
E-mail: info@caldaro.co.uk
Website: http://www.caldaro.co.uk
Directors: S. Aase (MD)
Managers: P. Lofgren (Sales Prom Mgr)
Immediate Holding Company: KEYWORKS LIMITED
Registration no: 04385906 **Date established:** 1999
No.of Employees: 1 - 10 **Product Groups:** 37, 44

Date of Accounts	May 11	May 10	May 09
Working Capital	-13	-14	-28
Fixed Assets	1	1	1
Current Assets	N/A	N/A	3

C C L Midlands
St Michaels Stud Farm Meer End Road, Kenilworth, CV8 1PU
Tel: 01676-535340 **Fax:** 01404-540333
E-mail: dean@computercomponents.com
Website: http://www.computercomponents.com
Managers: D. Semple (Mgr)
Immediate Holding Company: HERITAGE FUEL PRODUCTS LIMITED
Registration no: OC330635 **Date established:** 2009
Turnover: £5m - £10m **No.of Employees:** 1 - 10 **Product Groups:** 33, 61, 67, 84

City Electrical Factors Ltd
141 Farmer Ward Road, Kenilworth, CV8 2SU
Tel: 01926-514355 **Fax:** 01926-514340
E-mail: headoffice@cef.co.uk
Website: http://www.cef.co.uk
Bank(s): HSBC Bank plc
Managers: A. Meads
Ultimate Holding Company: CEF HOLDINGS LIMITED
Immediate Holding Company: CITY ELECTRICAL FACTORS LIMITED
Registration no: 00336408 **Date established:** 1938
Turnover: £250m - £500m **No.of Employees:** 51 - 100
Product Groups: 67

Date of Accounts	Apr 11	Apr 10	Apr 09
Sales Turnover	439m	406m	444m
Pre Tax Profit/Loss	22m	26m	34m
Working Capital	53m	172m	164m
Fixed Assets	13m	17m	18m
Current Assets	179m	250m	227m
Current Liabilities	53m	23m	20m

Clear Managed Service
Unit D2 Holly Farm Business Park Honiley, Kenilworth, CV8 1NP
Tel: 08456-019949 **Fax:** 01926-485248
Directors: C. Potter (Dir)
No.of Employees: 1 - 10 **Product Groups:** 40, 66

Cooper Specialised Handling Ltd
Holly Farm Business Park Honiley, Kenilworth, CV8 1NP
Tel: 01926-484633 **Fax:** 01926-484310
E-mail: david@coopersh.com
Website: http://www.coopersh.com
Directors: D. Cooper (MD)
Ultimate Holding Company: COOPER SPECIALISED HANDLING LIMITED
Immediate Holding Company: BAUMANN SIDELOADERS LIMITED
Registration no: 03908886 **Date established:** 2000
No.of Employees: 1 - 10 **Product Groups:** 35, 39, 45

Date of Accounts	Mar 11	Mar 10	Mar 07
Working Capital	3	3	1
Current Assets	3	3	1m

Corporate Business Finance Ltd
29 Garlick Drive, Kenilworth, CV8 2TT
Tel: 01926-863550 **Fax:** 01926-850977
E-mail: jeffery.tyrer@ukcontracthire.co.uk
Website: http://www.ukcontracthire.co.uk
Directors: J. Tyrer (MD), D. Tyrer (Fin)
Immediate Holding Company: CORPORATE BUSINESS FINANCE LIMITED
Registration no: 03677805 **Date established:** 1998
Turnover: Up to £250,000 **No.of Employees:** 1 - 10 **Product Groups:** 82

Date of Accounts	Mar 11	Mar 10	Mar 09
Working Capital	N/A	N/A	6
Fixed Assets	1	1	2
Current Assets	21	19	28

Robert E Cotterrell
Table Oak Farm Table Oak Lane, Kenilworth, CV8 1PX
Tel: 01676-534598 **Fax:** 01676-534598
Directors: R. Cotterrell (Prop)
Date established: 1997 **No.of Employees:** 1 - 10 **Product Groups:** 41

Cromac Smith Ltd
34-40 Warwick Road, Kenilworth, CV8 1HE
Tel: 01926-865800 **Fax:** 01926-865808
E-mail: albatros@cromacsmith.com
Website: http://www.cromacsmith.com
Directors: C. Sullivan (Dir)
Immediate Holding Company: CROMAC SMITH LIMITED
Registration no: 02416452 **Date established:** 1989
No.of Employees: 1 - 10 **Product Groups:** 76

Date of Accounts	Apr 12	Apr 11	Apr 10
Working Capital	29	86	120
Fixed Assets	5	9	12
Current Assets	104	132	171

Dayton Progress Ltd
Unit C12 Holly Farm Business Park Honiley, Kenilworth, CV8 1NP
Tel: 01926-484192 **Fax:** 01926-484172
E-mail: info@daytonprogress.co.uk
Website: http://www.daytonprogress.co.uk
Directors: P. Hughes (Dir)
Ultimate Holding Company: FEDERAL SIGNAL CORPORATION (USA)
Immediate Holding Company: DAYTON PROGRESS LIMITED
Registration no: 00856663 **Date established:** 1965 **Turnover:** £1m - £2m
No.of Employees: 1 - 10 **Product Groups:** 36, 37, 46, 47

Date of Accounts	Dec 11	Dec 10	Dec 09
Working Capital	205	160	199
Fixed Assets	13	15	18
Current Assets	349	338	297

F E C Services Ltd
Stoneleigh Park, Kenilworth, CV8 2LS
Tel: 024-7669 6512 **Fax:** 024-7669 6360
E-mail: info@fecservices.co.uk
Website: http://www.fecservices.co.uk
Directors: C. Plackett (Dir)
Immediate Holding Company: F E C SERVICES LIMITED
Registration no: 04056474 **Date established:** 2000
Turnover: £500,000 - £1m **No.of Employees:** 11 - 20
Product Groups: 37, 38, 54, 80, 84, 85

Date of Accounts	Mar 12	Mar 11	Mar 10
Working Capital	296	305	197
Fixed Assets	43	45	44
Current Assets	419	464	284

Farming & Wildlife Advisory Group Ltd
National Agricultural Centre Stoneleigh Park, Kenilworth, CV8 2RX
Tel: 024-7669 6699 **Fax:** 024-7669 6760
E-mail: ceo@fwag.org.uk
Website: http://www.fwag.org.uk
Directors: M. Woodhouse (Dir), A. Orniston (MD), A. Ormiston (Grp Chief Exec)
Managers: E. Darlinson (Sales Admin)
Immediate Holding Company: FARMING AND WILDLIFE ADVISORY GROUP LTD
Registration no: 01705669 **Date established:** 1983 **Turnover:** £2m - £5m
No.of Employees: 101 - 250 **Product Groups:** 80

Date of Accounts	Mar 10	Mar 09	Mar 08
Sales Turnover	4m	4m	5m
Pre Tax Profit/Loss	45	-167	-310
Working Capital	218	172	307
Fixed Assets	271	272	304
Current Assets	1m	1m	1m
Current Liabilities	791	778	708

Ice Productions Ltd
Warwick Corner 42 Warwick Road, Kenilworth, CV8 1HE
Tel: 01926-864800
E-mail: admin@ice-productions.com
Website: http://www.ice-productions.com
Directors: S. Griffiths (MD), C. Henson (Fin)
Immediate Holding Company: ICE PRODUCTIONS LIMITED
Registration no: 03764234 **Date established:** 1999
Turnover: £500,000 - £1m **No.of Employees:** 1 - 10 **Product Groups:** 80, 89

Date of Accounts	Aug 11	Aug 10	Aug 09
Working Capital	24	57	36
Fixed Assets	48	34	52
Current Assets	33	98	74

M C S Corporate
10 Station Road, Kenilworth, CV8 1JJ
Tel: 01926-512475 **Fax:** 01926-512477
E-mail: info@mcs-net.com
Website: http://www.mcs-corporate.com
Directors: G. Warwick (Dir)
Immediate Holding Company: MCS CORPORATE LIMITED
Registration no: 04444704 **VAT No.:** GB 487 7086 90
Date established: 2002 **Turnover:** £1m - £2m **No.of Employees:** 1 - 10
Product Groups: 80, 82

Marketing Direct
10 Avon Road, Kenilworth, CV8 1DH
Tel: 01926-855920 **Fax:** 01926-779833
E-mail: tony@marketing-direct.co.uk
Website: http://www.marketing-direct.co.uk
Directors: T. Dalton (Ptnr)
Immediate Holding Company: IN TOUCH SYSTEM LTD
Registration no: 06909088 **Date established:** 2009
Turnover: Up to £250,000 **No.of Employees:** 1 - 10 **Product Groups:** 79

Media & Marketing Services
230 Warwick Road, Kenilworth, CV8 1FD
Tel: 01926-864834 **Fax:** 01926-851061
E-mail: info@m-ms.co.uk
Website: http://www.m-ms.co.uk
Directors: M. Heath (Prop)
Immediate Holding Company: PR MEDIA & MARKETING SERVICES LTD
Registration no: 07687914 **Date established:** 2011
Turnover: Up to £250,000 **No.of Employees:** 1 - 10 **Product Groups:** 44, 79, 81

Multishifter & Ancilliary Systems
9 Kineton Road, Kenilworth, CV8 2AW
Tel: 01926-851619 **Fax:** 01926-850478
E-mail: parts@mash-b.co.uk
Website: http://www.mash-b.co.uk
Directors: D. Parry (MD), M. Parry (Fin)
Immediate Holding Company: M.A.S.H.-B. (MULTISHIFTER & ANCILLIARY SYSTEMS HANDLING-BATTERIES) LIM
Registration no: 02004209 **Date established:** 1986
No.of Employees: 1 - 10 **Product Groups:** 35, 39, 45

Date of Accounts	May 11	May 10	May 09
Working Capital	96	102	105
Fixed Assets	1	1	2
Current Assets	111	127	145

Passion For Chocolate
25 Lulworth Park, Kenilworth, CV8 2XG
Tel: 01926-512422 **Fax:** 01926-512422
E-mail: info@passionforchocolate.co.uk
Website: http://www.passionforchocolate.co.uk
Directors: C. Tabor (Prop)
No.of Employees: 1 - 10 **Product Groups:** 20, 21

Premier Design & Engineering Ltd
25d Clinton Lane, Kenilworth, CV8 1AS
Tel: 01926-513115 **Fax:** 01926-513027
Directors: P. Leach (MD)
No.of Employees: 1 - 10 **Product Groups:** 20, 40, 41

Richard Keenan UK Ltd
6th Street National Agricultural Centre, Stoneleigh Park, Kenilworth, CV8 2RL
Tel: 024-7669 8288 **Fax:** 024-7669 8273
E-mail: info@keenansystem.com
Website: http://www.keenansystem.com
Managers: C. Metcalfe (Ops Mgr)
Ultimate Holding Company: RICHARD KEENAN HOLDINGS LTD (EIRE)
Immediate Holding Company: RICHARD KEENAN (UK) LIMITED
Registration no: 02339739 **Date established:** 1989 **Turnover:** £5m - £10m
No.of Employees: 1 - 10 **Product Groups:** 41, 42

Date of Accounts	Dec 11	Dec 10	Dec 09
Sales Turnover	12m	9m	10m
Pre Tax Profit/Loss	698	-99	-911
Working Capital	-5m	-5m	-5m
Fixed Assets	158	169	154
Current Assets	42m	35m	31m
Current Liabilities	784	299	440

Saldon Products Ltd
Warwick House Station Road, Kenilworth, CV8 1JF
Tel: 01926-858126 **Fax:** 01926-850448
E-mail: john@saldonproducts.co.uk
Website: http://www.tamlite.co.uk
Directors: A. Swift (Fin), J. Allden (MD)
Ultimate Holding Company: SALDON LIMITED (JERSEY)
Immediate Holding Company: SALDON PRODUCTS LIMITED
Registration no: 00494829 **Date established:** 1951
Turnover: £20m - £50m **No.of Employees:** 251 - 500
Product Groups: 37, 67

Date of Accounts	Apr 11	Apr 10	Apr 09
Sales Turnover	N/A	N/A	28m
Pre Tax Profit/Loss	4m	991	868
Working Capital	11m	7m	8m
Fixed Assets	715	810	636
Current Assets	16m	13m	14m
Current Liabilities	2m	2m	5m

Slater Tangent Ltd
12 Station Road, Kenilworth, CV8 1JJ
Tel: 01926-863444 **Fax:** 01926-654321
E-mail: slatertangent@yahoo.co.uk
Directors: K. Leedham (Fin), P. Grimmer (MD)
Immediate Holding Company: SLATER TANGENT LIMITED
Registration no: 02860212 **VAT No.:** GB 643 0271 69
Date established: 1993 **Turnover:** Up to £250,000
No.of Employees: 1 - 10 **Product Groups:** 35

Date of Accounts	Oct 11	Oct 10	Oct 09
Working Capital	6	-0	3
Fixed Assets	1	N/A	1
Current Assets	59	45	42

Supports U
31 Hermitage Way, Kenilworth, CV8 2DW
Tel: 01926-777169
E-mail: tina.watkins@ntlworld.com
Website: http://www.supports-u.co.uk
Directors: T. Watkins (Prop)
No.of Employees: 1 - 10 **Product Groups:** 80

Syscomm Ltd
Syscomm House 2 Park Road, Kenilworth, CV8 2GF
Tel: 01926-856000 **Fax:** 01926-851158
E-mail: info@syscomm.co.uk
Website: http://www.syscomm.co.uk
Directors: M. Tyler (Fin), R. Tyler (MD)
Immediate Holding Company: SYSCOMM LTD.
Registration no: 01826787 **Date established:** 1984
No.of Employees: 1 - 10 **Product Groups:** 37, 38, 44, 52, 79, 80, 84

Date of Accounts	Aug 11	Aug 10	Aug 09
Working Capital	163	136	92
Fixed Assets	2	4	7
Current Assets	229	220	152
Current Liabilities	4	N/A	N/A

Threadmaster Gauges Ltd (Screw Gauge & Plain Gauge Manufacturers)
Princes Drive Industrial Estate Coventry Road, Kenilworth, CV8 2FD
Tel: 01926-852428 **Fax:** 01926-850047
E-mail: sales@threadmastergauges.co.uk
Website: http://www.threadmastergauges.co.uk
Bank(s): National Westminster Bank Plc
Directors: G. Ratcliffe (MD), A. Ratcliffe (Fin)
Immediate Holding Company: THREADMASTER GAUGES LIMITED
Registration no: 01311276 **VAT No.:** GB 274 0430 80
Date established: 1977 **Turnover:** £500,000 - £1m
No.of Employees: 21 - 50 **Product Groups:** 38, 46, 85

Date of Accounts	May 11	May 10	May 09
Working Capital	-171	-20	34
Fixed Assets	743	572	541
Current Assets	397	341	327
Current Liabilities	N/A	N/A	48

Trinity Protection Systems
Unit B12a Holly Farm Business Park Honiley, Kenilworth, CV8 1NP
Tel: 01926-485080 **Fax:** 01926-485090
E-mail: sales@trinityprotection.co.uk
Website: http://www.trinityprotection.co.uk
Directors: P. Bartlett (Reg)
Immediate Holding Company: FURNESS VENTURE LIMITED
Date established: 2009 **No.of Employees:** 21 - 50 **Product Groups:** 37, 40, 67

Walter Machines UK Ltd Represented by K--rber Schleifring UK
Unit B13 Holly Farm Business Park Honiley, Kenilworth, CV8 1NP
Tel: 01926-485047 **Fax:** 01926-485049
E-mail: info@walter-machines.com
Website: http://www.walter-machines.com
Managers: N. Whittingham (Chief Mgr)
Immediate Holding Company: WALTER MACHINES UK LIMITED
Registration no: 05251605 **Date established:** 2004
No.of Employees: 1 - 10 **Product Groups:** 37, 46

Date of Accounts	Dec 11	Dec 10	Dec 09
Sales Turnover	628	535	580
Pre Tax Profit/Loss	34	-12	10
Working Capital	115	91	109
Fixed Assets	17	16	9
Current Assets	188	127	140
Current Liabilities	44	35	30

Warwick Test Supplies
93a Warwick Road, Kenilworth, CV8 1HP
Tel: 01926-851007 **Fax:** 01926-851588
E-mail: steve@warwickts.com
Website: http://www.warwickts.com
Directors: S. Trammer (Fin), C. Vaufrouard (Dir), S. Trammer (MD), S. Tranner (Dir)
Immediate Holding Company: WARWICK TEST SUPPLIES LIMITED
Registration no: 02983405 **Date established:** 1994
No.of Employees: 1 - 10 **Product Groups:** 35, 36, 37, 38, 44

Date of Accounts	Mar 08	Mar 07	Mar 06
Working Capital	26	29	37
Fixed Assets	1	1	1
Current Assets	68	69	85
Current Liabilities	42	40	48

Whitehouse Machine Tools Ltd
7 Princes Drive Industrial Estate Coventry Road, Kenilworth, CV8 2FD
Tel: 01926-852725 **Fax:** 01926-850620
E-mail: tomh@wmtcnc.com
Website: http://www.wmtcnc.com
Directors: T. Hughes (Sales)
Immediate Holding Company: WHITEHOUSE MACHINE TOOLS LIMITED
Registration no: 02117070 **Date established:** 1987 **Turnover:** £2m - £5m
No.of Employees: 11 - 20 **Product Groups:** 46

Date of Accounts	Apr 12	Apr 11	Apr 10
Working Capital	349	194	166
Fixed Assets	479	481	476
Current Assets	1m	1m	862

Leamington Spa

A C Lloyd Holdings Ltd
1 Chapel Street, Leamington Spa, CV31 1EJ
Tel: 01926-421326 **Fax:** 01926-451731
E-mail: gnicholls@aclloyd.com
Website: http://www.aclloyd.com
Directors: G. Nicholls (MD), M. Reading (Fin), P. Mayman (Co Sec)
Ultimate Holding Company: A.C. LLOYD (ASSET MANAGEMENT) LIMITED
Immediate Holding Company: A.C. LLOYD HOLDINGS LIMITED
Registration no: 00459351 **Date established:** 1948
Turnover: Up to £250,000 **No.of Employees:** 1 - 10 **Product Groups:** 51, 52

Date of Accounts	Sep 11	Sep 10	Sep 09
Sales Turnover	148	N/A	450
Pre Tax Profit/Loss	659	573	727
Working Capital	2m	2m	2m
Fixed Assets	4m	4m	4m
Current Assets	12m	10m	9m
Current Liabilities	336	339	296

AGA Rangemaster (Glynwed Consumer Products Ltd)
Clarence Street, Leamington Spa, CV31 2AD
Tel: 01926-457400 **Fax:** 01926-450526
E-mail: mbufton@rangemaster.co.uk
Website: http://www.rangemaster.co.uk
Bank(s): Lloyds TSB Bank plc
Directors: R. Fozard (Mkt Research), R. Hird (Sales), P. Tonks (Pers), M. Bufton (MD), G. Killer (Fin)
Managers: I. Hassan (Tech Serv Mgr), C. Chamberlain
Immediate Holding Company: RESULTS SEARCH & SELECTION LIMITED
Registration no: 03872754 **Date established:** 2001 **Turnover:** £1m - £2m
No.of Employees: 251 - 500 **Product Groups:** 40

Date of Accounts	Apr 12	Apr 11	Apr 10
Working Capital	153	116	105
Current Assets	192	143	113

Angel Tuning Ltd
3 Church Terrace Harbury, Leamington Spa, CV33 9HL
Tel: 01926-614027
E-mail: info@angeltuning.co.uk
Website: http://www.angeltuning.co.uk
Directors: N. Bennett (Chief Op Offcr)
Immediate Holding Company: NUOVA 500 SHOP LIMITED
Registration no: 06068626 **Date established:** 2007
Turnover: Up to £250,000 **No.of Employees:** 1 - 10 **Product Groups:** 39

Automotive Technology Ltd
3 Morton Street, Leamington Spa, CV32 5SY
Tel: 01926-882201 **Fax:** 01926-420934
E-mail: admin@atl-uk.com
Website: http://www.atl-uk.com
Directors: P. Purdom (Ch)
Immediate Holding Company: AUTOMOTIVE TECHNOLOGY LIMITED
Registration no: 02546067 **Date established:** 1990 **Turnover:** £1m - £2m
No.of Employees: 1 - 10 **Product Groups:** 39, 40, 42, 45

Date of Accounts	Dec 11	Dec 10	Dec 09
Working Capital	212	204	179
Fixed Assets	1	1	2
Current Assets	260	256	227

Backgammon & Board Games Co.
10 Coppice Road Whitnash, Leamington Spa, CV31 2JE
Tel: 01926-881613 **Fax:** 01926-881613
E-mail: ct@bgshop.com
Website: http://www.bgshop.com
Directors: C. Ternel (Prop)
Immediate Holding Company: THE BACKGAMMON AND BOARD GAMES COMPANY LIMITED
Registration no: 05233314 **Date established:** 2004
Turnover: Up to £250,000 **No.of Employees:** 1 - 10 **Product Groups:** 49

Date of Accounts	Sep 11	Sep 10	Sep 09
Working Capital	-3	-1	-0
Current Assets	58	47	57

Bob Becks Diesels
Unit 19 Victoria Business Centre Neilston Street, Leamington Spa, CV31 2AZ
Tel: 01926-888110
Directors: R. Beck (Prop)
Date established: 1991 **No.of Employees:** 1 - 10 **Product Groups:** 40

Biffa Waste Services Ltd
Southam Road Ufton, Leamington Spa, CV33 9PP
Tel: 01926-614248 **Fax:** 01926-613471
E-mail: marketing@biffa.co.uk
Website: http://www.biffa.co.uk
Managers: A. Ives (Mgr)
Immediate Holding Company: BIFFA WASTE SERVICES LIMITED
Registration no: 00946107 **Date established:** 1969
No.of Employees: 1 - 10 **Product Groups:** 32, 54

Date of Accounts	Mar 08	Mar 09	Apr 10
Sales Turnover	555m	574m	492m
Pre Tax Profit/Loss	23m	50m	30m
Working Capital	229m	271m	293m
Fixed Assets	371m	360m	378m
Current Assets	409m	534m	609m
Current Liabilities	50m	100m	115m

Box Factory Ltd
2 Caswell Road, Leamington Spa, CV31 1QD
Tel: 01926-430510 **Fax:** 01926-430505
E-mail: sales@boxfactory.co.uk
Website: http://www.boxfactory.co.uk
Directors: N. Price (Dir)
Managers: J. Evans, K. Cooper (Buyer)
Immediate Holding Company: THE BOX FACTORY LIMITED
Registration no: 02664682 **Date established:** 1991 **Turnover:** £5m - £10m
No.of Employees: 51 - 100 **Product Groups:** 27

Date of Accounts	Dec 11	Dec 10	Dec 09
Sales Turnover	7m	7m	5m
Pre Tax Profit/Loss	302	139	163
Working Capital	-172	-296	-18
Fixed Assets	3m	3m	3m
Current Assets	2m	1m	1m
Current Liabilities	257	197	190

Britannia Kitchen Ventilation
10 Highdown Road, Leamington Spa, CV31 1XT
Tel: 01926-463540 **Fax:** 01926-463541
E-mail: sales@kitchen-ventilation.co.uk
Website: http://www.kitchen-ventilation.co.uk
Directors: I. Levin (Dir), P. Taylor (Sales & Mktg)
Managers: R. Lazell
Immediate Holding Company: LINCAT GROUP PLC
Registration no: 03062962 **Date established:** 1995
Turnover: Up to £250,000 **No.of Employees:** 21 - 50 **Product Groups:** 26, 37, 40, 42, 52, 67

Alan Browne Gauges Ltd
Blackdown Mill Blackdown, Leamington Spa, CV32 6QT
Tel: 01926-424278 **Fax:** 01926-451865
E-mail: info@alanbrowne.co.uk
Website: http://www.alanbrowne.co.uk
Bank(s): Yorkshire Bank PLC
Directors: B. Castelino (MD)
Immediate Holding Company: ALAN BROWNE GAUGES LIMITED
Registration no: 00713694 **VAT No.:** GB 272 5143 70
Date established: 1962 **Turnover:** £500,000 - £1m
No.of Employees: 11 - 20 **Product Groups:** 46, 85

Date of Accounts	Apr 11	Apr 10	Apr 09
Working Capital	23	31	28
Fixed Assets	23	25	28
Current Assets	127	132	125

C J R Welding & Fabrication
Oakdene Coventry Road Cubbington, Leamington Spa, CV32 7UJ
Tel: 07944-742440 **Fax:** 01926-883128
E-mail: cjrwelding@yahoo.co.uk
Website: http://www.cjrwelding.co.uk
Directors: C. Richardson (Prop)
Immediate Holding Company: OAKDENE NURSERY LIMITED
Registration no: 04806666 **Date established:** 2003
No.of Employees: 1 - 10 **Product Groups:** 35

Date of Accounts	Aug 10	Aug 09	Aug 08
Working Capital	-48	-43	-49
Fixed Assets	52	48	55
Current Assets	1	12	5

Cologne & Cotton
74 Regent Street, Leamington Spa, CV32 4NS
Tel: 01926-339880 **Fax:** 01926-332575
E-mail: info@cologneandcotton.com
Website: http://www.cologneandcotton.com
Directors: R. Dew (Dir), R. Dew (Dir), V. Shepherd (Dir)
Managers: S. Van Rensberg
Immediate Holding Company: COLOGNE & COTTON LIMITED
Registration no: 02356848 **Date established:** 1989
No.of Employees: 1 - 10 **Product Groups:** 24

Date of Accounts	Sep 11	Sep 10	Sep 09
Working Capital	515	506	493
Fixed Assets	351	353	376
Current Assets	865	863	780

Comtec Translations
62 Brandon Parade Holly Walk, Leamington Spa, CV32 4JE
Tel: 01926-335681 **Fax:** 01926-834619
E-mail: info@comtectranslations.com
Website: http://www.comtectranslations.com
Directors: S. Howe (Dir)
Immediate Holding Company: COMTEC TRANSLATIONS LIMITED
Registration no: 04534240 **Date established:** 2002
No.of Employees: 1 - 10 **Product Groups:** 80

Date of Accounts	Sep 11	Sep 10	Sep 09
Working Capital	84	15	-87
Fixed Assets	88	106	122
Current Assets	327	286	179

Cook Shop
112 Regent Street, Leamington Spa, CV32 4NR
Tel: 01926-888588 **Fax:** 01926-888155
E-mail: info@cookshop.net
Website: http://www.cookshop.net
Directors: T. Mclellan (Prop)
Immediate Holding Company: CATERER'S HIRE AND SALES LIMITED
Registration no: 02971453 **Date established:** 1994
No.of Employees: 1 - 10 **Product Groups:** 20, 40, 41

Date of Accounts	Dec 11	Dec 08
Working Capital	101	89
Fixed Assets	7	4
Current Assets	185	172

Drain Center Ltd
The Wolseley Center Harrison Way, Leamington Spa, CV31 3HH
Tel: 0845-2710500 **Fax:** 01494-444923
Website: http://www.draincenter.co.uk
Managers: A. Miller (District Mgr)
Ultimate Holding Company: Wolseley plc
Immediate Holding Company: Wipac Group (Holdings) Ltd
Registration no: 00424702 **Date established:** 2005
No.of Employees: 1 - 10 **Product Groups:** 30, 31, 36, 39, 40, 42, 48, 66

Elisabeth The Chef Ltd
4 Berrington Road, Leamington Spa, CV31 1NB
Tel: 01926-311531 **Fax:** 01926-426888
E-mail: enquiries@elisabeth-the-chef.co.uk
Website: http://www.elisabeth-the-chef.co.uk

Directors: E. Valdher (Fin), S. Richards (Sales & Mktg)
Managers: F. Maidment (Personnel), J. Powell (Admin Off)
Ultimate Holding Company: SENOBLE SAS (FRANCE)
Immediate Holding Company: SENOBLE UK LIMITED
Registration no: 01561100 **Date established:** 1981
Turnover: £75m - £125m **No.of Employees:** 21 - 50 **Product Groups:** 20, 62

Date of Accounts	Dec 11	Dec 08	Dec 09
Sales Turnover	73m	73m	89m
Pre Tax Profit/Loss	-10m	-761	-6m
Working Capital	-43m	-3m	-17m
Fixed Assets	30m	9m	17m
Current Assets	14m	14m	13m
Current Liabilities	6m	6m	11m

Gauge Service & Supply Co Leamington Ltd

3 Park Street, Leamington Spa, CV32 4QN
Tel: 01926-336137 **Fax:** 01926-450636
E-mail: sales@gssuk.co.uk
Website: http://www.gssuk.co.uk
Directors: M. Smith (Dir)
Ultimate Holding Company: GSS HOLDINGS LIMITED
Immediate Holding Company: GAUGE SERVICE AND SUPPLY COMPANY (LEAMINGTON) LIMITED
Registration no: 00995750 **VAT No.:** GB 272 3518 63
Date established: 1970 **Turnover:** £1m - £2m **No.of Employees:** 1 - 10
Product Groups: 38, 46, 48

Date of Accounts	Dec 11	Dec 10	Dec 09
Working Capital	60	67	65
Current Assets	123	122	113

Heritage Iron

Quarry Farm Blackdown, Leamington Spa, CV32 6RW
Tel: 01926-420420
Directors: J. Eales (Prop)
Registration no: 03488838 **Date established:** 1998
No.of Employees: 1 - 10 **Product Groups:** 26, 35

I C Fabrication

46 Heathcote Road Whitnash, Leamington Spa, CV31 2NF
Tel: 01926-430525 **Fax:** 01926-430525
Directors: I. Cooper (Prop)
Date established: 1991 **No.of Employees:** 1 - 10 **Product Groups:** 35

Ingersoll Security Technologies Ltd

Berrington Road Sydenham Industrial Estate, Leamington Spa, CV31 1NB
Tel: 01926-437000 **Fax:** 01926-437005
E-mail: doromatic_sales@irco.com
Website: http://www.ingerrand.com
Bank(s): Royal Bank of Scotland
Managers: J. Stanley (Chief Mgr)
Ultimate Holding Company: INGERSOLL RAND GROUP
Registration no: 01262027 **Turnover:** £5m - £10m
No.of Employees: 51 - 100 **Product Groups:** 35

Jewson Ltd

The Sawmills Rugby Road, Leamington Spa, CV32 6AR
Tel: 01926-831351 **Fax:** 01926-450247
Website: http://www.jewson.co.uk
Managers: G. Boot (Mgr)
Ultimate Holding Company: COMPAGNIE DE SAINT GOBAIN (FRANCE)
Immediate Holding Company: JEWSON LIMITED
Registration no: 00348407 **Date established:** 1939
Turnover: £500m - £1,000m **No.of Employees:** 11 - 20
Product Groups: 66

Date of Accounts	Dec 11	Dec 10	Dec 09
Sales Turnover	1606m	1547m	1485m
Pre Tax Profit/Loss	18m	100m	45m
Working Capital	-345m	-250m	-349m
Fixed Assets	496m	387m	461m
Current Assets	657m	1005m	1320m
Current Liabilities	66m	120m	64m

Lawnet

93-95 Bedford Street, Leamington Spa, CV32 5BB
Tel: 01926-886990 **Fax:** 01926-886553
E-mail: admin@lawnet.co.uk
Website: http://www.lawnet.co.uk
Managers: J. Thomas
Immediate Holding Company: LAWNET LIMITED
Registration no: 02538900 **VAT No.:** GB 559 0751 20
Date established: 1990 **Turnover:** £1m - £2m **No.of Employees:** 1 - 10
Product Groups: 80, 87

Date of Accounts	May 12	May 11	May 10
Sales Turnover	1m	1m	1m
Pre Tax Profit/Loss	50	-0	32
Working Capital	161	120	116
Fixed Assets	10	12	17
Current Assets	372	293	279
Current Liabilities	41	31	32

Leamington Spa Courier

32 Hamilton Terrace Holly Walk, Leamington Spa, CV32 4LY
Tel: 01926-457777 **Fax:** 01926-451690
E-mail: editorial@leamingtoncourier.co.uk
Website: http://www.leamingtoncourier.co.uk
Bank(s): Barclays
Managers: C. Lillington
Immediate Holding Company: JOHNSTON PRESS PLC
Registration no: 00025139 **Date established:** 1976
Turnover: Up to £250,000 **No.of Employees:** 21 - 50 **Product Groups:** 28

Machine Vision Technology Ltd

Blackdown Mill Kenilworth Road, Leamington Spa, CV32 6QT
Tel: 01926-422043 **Fax:** 01926-339538
E-mail: sales@machine-vision-technology.co.uk
Website: http://www.machine-vision-technology.co.uk
Directors: R. Marshall (Sales & Mktg), B. Castelino (MD)
Managers: J. Hoggarth (I.T. Exec)
Registration no: 03927054 **Date established:** 1998
No.of Employees: 1 - 10 **Product Groups:** 38, 44

Date of Accounts	Mar 10	Mar 09	Mar 08
Working Capital	-83	-63	-174
Fixed Assets	744	744	745
Current Assets	62	14	33

Main Choice

Unit 6 Churchlands Farm Industrial Estate Bascote Road, Ufton, Leamington Spa, CV33 9PL
Tel: 01926-613906 **Fax:** 01926-614215
Directors: D. Vincent (Dir)
No.of Employees: 1 - 10 **Product Groups:** 40, 66

Mercia Metals Ltd

19-21 Wise Street, Leamington Spa, CV31 3AP
Tel: 01926-421508 **Fax:** 01926-314399
Website: http://www.merciametals.co.uk
Directors: R. Mcgee (MD)
Immediate Holding Company: MERCIA METALS LIMITED
Registration no: 03212025 **VAT No.:** GB 376 0823 41
Date established: 1996 **Turnover:** £1m - £2m **No.of Employees:** 1 - 10
Product Groups: 66, 83

Date of Accounts	Jun 12	Jun 11	Jun 10
Working Capital	97	185	94
Fixed Assets	242	284	257
Current Assets	243	426	315

O T C Welding Products

10 Avonlea Rise, Leamington Spa, CV32 6HT
Tel: 01926-882222 **Fax:** 01926-888802
E-mail: info@otc-daihen.co.uk
Website: http://www.otc-daihen.co.uk
Directors: G. Hanson (Prop)
Immediate Holding Company: SPRITE LIMITED
Registration no: 02987956 **Date established:** 1994
No.of Employees: 1 - 10 **Product Groups:** 46

Date of Accounts	Nov 11	Nov 10	Nov 09
Working Capital	N/A	8	5
Fixed Assets	3	N/A	1
Current Assets	11	22	15

R G I S Inventory Specialists (Head Office)

Imperial Court Holly Walk, Leamington Spa, CV32 4YB
Tel: 01926-888882 **Fax:** 01926-888883
E-mail: sales@rgis.com
Website: http://www.rgis.com
Bank(s): Barclays
Directors: P. Street (Dir), A. Simmonds (Pers), M. Roberts (Fin), E. Cordier (Co Sec)
Managers: J. Passmore (Tech Serv Mgr)
Immediate Holding Company: RGIS INVENTORY SPECIALISTS LIMITED
Registration no: 03859648 **VAT No.:** GB 747 8104 16
Date established: 1999 **Turnover:** £10m - £20m
No.of Employees: 1001 - 1500 **Product Groups:** 80

Date of Accounts	Dec 11	Dec 10	Dec 09
Sales Turnover	17m	15m	13m
Pre Tax Profit/Loss	2m	743	638
Working Capital	3m	3m	4m
Fixed Assets	627	597	794
Current Assets	5m	4m	5m
Current Liabilities	2m	1m	703

Roger Morris Machine Tool Services LLP

14 The Gardens Radford Semele, Leamington Spa, CV31 1TH
Tel: 01926-882212 **Fax:** 01926-882212
E-mail: rogermorris@rmmts.co.uk
Website: http://www.rmmts.co.uk
Directors: R. Morris (Prop)
Immediate Holding Company: ROGER MORRIS MACHINE TOOL SERVICES LLP
Registration no: OC303788 **Date established:** 2003
No.of Employees: 1 - 10 **Product Groups:** 46

Date of Accounts	Jan 11	Jan 10	Jan 09
Working Capital	9	5	20
Fixed Assets	26	27	31
Current Assets	14	16	31

SRCS Creative

8-9 South Terrace Whitnash, Leamington Spa, CV31 2HY
Tel: 01926-337440
E-mail: enquiries@srcscreative.com
Website: http://www.srcscreative.com
Directors: S. Lijnzaad (Dir)
Registration no: 551013 **Date established:** 2010 **Turnover:**
No.of Employees: 1 - 10 **Product Groups:** 80, 81

Thwaites Ltd

Welsh Road Works, Leamington Spa, CV32 7NQ
Tel: 01926-422471 **Fax:** 01926-337155
E-mail: sales@thwaitesdumpers.co.uk
Website: http://www.thwaitesdumpers.co.uk
Bank(s): HSBC Bank plc
Directors: A. Earles (MD), I. Brown (Sales), S. Trotman (Co Sec)
Managers: K. Phelan (Purch Mgr), M. Beard (Tech Serv Mgr), S. Hill (Comptroller)
Immediate Holding Company: THWAITES LIMITED
Registration no: 00387579 **Date established:** 1944
Turnover: £20m - £50m **No.of Employees:** 101 - 250 **Product Groups:** 45

Date of Accounts	Aug 11	Aug 10	Aug 09
Sales Turnover	33m	19m	12m
Pre Tax Profit/Loss	4m	1m	-2m
Working Capital	15m	14m	13m
Fixed Assets	2m	2m	3m
Current Assets	22m	18m	14m
Current Liabilities	4m	2m	591

Trelawny S P T Ltd

13 Highdown Road, Leamington Spa, CV31 1XT
Tel: 01926-883781 **Fax:** 01926-450352
E-mail: steve.williams@trelawny.co.uk
Website: http://www.trelawnyspt.co.uk
Bank(s): HSBC
Managers: S. Williams (Chief Mgr)
Immediate Holding Company: TRELAWNY SPT LIMITED
Registration no: 04943839 **VAT No.:** GB 163 3143 89
Date established: 2003 **Turnover:** £2m - £5m **No.of Employees:** 21 - 50
Product Groups: 37, 40

Date of Accounts	Dec 11	Dec 10	Dec 09
Working Capital	849	673	553
Fixed Assets	806	805	825
Current Assets	1m	1m	948

Unbounded

PO Box 1041, Leamington Spa, CV32 5TQ
Tel: 01926-424337 **Fax:** 01926-424337
E-mail: enquiries@unbounded.co.uk
Website: http://www.unbounded.co.uk
Directors: S. Smith (Dir)
No.of Employees: 1 - 10 **Product Groups:** 80, 81

V A T Vacuum Products Ltd

Edmund House Rugby Road, Leamington Spa, CV32 6EL
Tel: 01926-452753 **Fax:** 01926-452758
E-mail: uk@vatvalve.com
Website: http://www.vatvalve.com
Directors: S. Manbridge (MD)
Ultimate Holding Company: VAT HOLDING AG (SWITZERLAND)
Immediate Holding Company: VAT VACUUM PRODUCTS LIMITED
Registration no: 02451377 **Date established:** 1989
Turnover: Up to £250,000 **No.of Employees:** 1 - 10 **Product Groups:** 36, 37, 40

Date of Accounts	Dec 11	Dec 10	Dec 09
Working Capital	1m	978	681
Fixed Assets	49	34	37
Current Assets	2m	4m	2m

Woodhouse UK plc

Harrison Way, Leamington Spa, CV31 3HL
Tel: 01926-314313 **Fax:** 01926-883778
E-mail: enquire@woodhouse.co.uk
Website: http://www.woodhouse.co.uk
Bank(s): National Westminster Bank Plc
Directors: C. Baxandall (Co Sec)
Managers: C. Hirst (Mktg Serv Mgr), R. Rawlings, D. Mayrick, A. Bridgeman, J. Haynes
Ultimate Holding Company: MARSHALLS PLC
Immediate Holding Company: WOODHOUSE UK LIMITED
Registration no: 02090464 **VAT No.:** GB 705 3207 71
Date established: 1987 **No.of Employees:** 21 - 50 **Product Groups:** 26, 37

Nuneaton

A-Plant Ltd (Ashtead Plant Hire Co. Ltd)

Eastboro Way, Nuneaton, CV11 6SQ
Tel: 024-7634 1916 **Fax:** 024-7635 0510
E-mail: johnbrooks@aplant.com
Website: http://www.aplant.com
Managers: J. Brookes (District Mgr), J. Brookes (Mgr)
Ultimate Holding Company: DEMARK HOLDINGS LTD.
Immediate Holding Company: A.PLANT LIMITED
Registration no: 05407712 **VAT No.:** GB 209 5687 37
Date established: 2005 **No.of Employees:** 1 - 10 **Product Groups:** 83

Arleigh International Ltd

Unit 1-5 Century Park Ballin Road, Nuneaton, CV10 9GA
Tel: 024-7639 0100 **Fax:** 024-7639 0810
E-mail: info@arleigh.co.uk
Website: http://www.arleigh.co.uk
Bank(s): HBOS
Directors: A. Thomas (MD), J. Ayres (Fin), A. Thomas (MD), D. Randle (Chief Op Offcr)
Managers: K. Reay
Ultimate Holding Company: ARLEIGH GROUP LIMITED
Immediate Holding Company: ARLEIGH INTERNATIONAL LIMITED
Registration no: 01559541 **VAT No.:** GB 844 2929 14
Date established: 1981 **Turnover:** £10m - £20m
No.of Employees: 21 - 50 **Product Groups:** 26, 30, 35, 36, 37, 39, 40, 49, 68, 69

Date of Accounts	Dec 11	Dec 10	Dec 09
Sales Turnover	15m	13m	10m
Pre Tax Profit/Loss	1m	786	670
Working Capital	912	944	2m
Fixed Assets	1m	649	606
Current Assets	6m	3m	4m
Current Liabilities	2m	862	995

ARRK Europe

Unit 2 Centrovell Buildings, Nuneaton, CV11 4NG
Tel: 024-7658 0700 **Fax:** 024-7658 0727
E-mail: info@arrkeurope.com
Website: http://www.arrkeurope.com
Directors: K. Clarke (Fin), J. Argyle (Sales), N. Baker (MD)
Managers: S. White (Maint), C. Smith (Transport)
Ultimate Holding Company: ARRK CORPORATION (JAPAN)
Immediate Holding Company: ARRK EUROPE LIMITED
Registration no: 03418673 **Date established:** 1997
Turnover: £10m - £20m **No.of Employees:** 51 - 100 **Product Groups:** 48, 67

Date of Accounts	Dec 11	Dec 10	Dec 09
Sales Turnover	36m	19m	11m
Pre Tax Profit/Loss	-503	50	399
Working Capital	-666	-34	-399
Fixed Assets	4m	2m	2m
Current Assets	13m	5m	2m
Current Liabilities	3m	2m	568

Art Fabrication

Lodge Farm Fenny Drayton, Nuneaton, CV13 6BH
Tel: 01827-714535 **Fax:** 01827-714535
Website: http://www.artfabs.co.uk
Directors: A. Langley (Prop)
Date established: 1997 **No.of Employees:** 1 - 10 **Product Groups:** 35

Automation Experts

4 Barling Way, Nuneaton, CV10 7RH
Tel: 024-7679 6666 **Fax:** 024-7679 6667
E-mail: info@automationexperts.co.uk
Website: http://www.automationexperts.co.uk
Directors: S. Hill (MD)
Immediate Holding Company: AUTOMATION EXPERTS LIMITED
Registration no: 04211196 **Date established:** 2001
No.of Employees: 11 - 20 **Product Groups:** 80

Date of Accounts	Mar 12	Mar 11	Mar 10
Working Capital	238	133	96
Fixed Assets	61	69	42
Current Assets	382	259	204

B J Tooling Services Ltd
87 Lutterworth Road, Nuneaton, CV11 6QA
Tel: 024-7632 0986 **Fax:** 024-7632 9269
Directors: D. Jones (Fin), B. Jones (MD)
Immediate Holding Company: B.J.TOOLING SERVICES LIMITED
Registration no: 04413153 **Date established:** 2002
No.of Employees: 1 - 10 **Product Groups:** 46

Date of Accounts	Jun 12	Jun 11	Jun 10
Working Capital	22	12	24
Fixed Assets	1	1	1
Current Assets	55	51	40

Biddle Air Systems Ltd
St Marys Road, Nuneaton, CV11 5AU
Tel: 024-7638 4233 **Fax:** 024-7637 3621
E-mail: sales@biddle-air.co.uk
Website: http://www.biddle-air.co.uk
Bank(s): Barclays, High St, Hitchin
Directors: M. Cook (Fin), S. Rees (MD)
Managers: M. Goadby (Personnel), A. Saxon (I.T. Exec), S. Harrison (Purch Mgr)
Ultimate Holding Company: CARVER GROUP LIMITED
Immediate Holding Company: BIDDLE AIR SYSTEMS LIMITED
Registration no: 00388866 **VAT No.:** GB 113 7487 72
Date established: 1944 **Turnover:** £2m - £5m **No.of Employees:** 51 - 100
Product Groups: 39, 40, 52

Date of Accounts	Jul 11	Jul 10	Jul 09
Sales Turnover	5m	5m	5m
Pre Tax Profit/Loss	924	861	799
Working Capital	4m	5m	4m
Fixed Assets	297	218	712
Current Assets	6m	6m	5m
Current Liabilities	460	349	285

Bito Storage Systems Ltd
Eastboro Fields Hemdale Business Park, Nuneaton, CV11 6GL
Tel: 024-7638 8850 **Fax:** 024-7638 8860
E-mail: info@bito.co.uk
Website: http://www.bito.co.uk
Directors: R. Schillinger (Co Sec)
Immediate Holding Company: BITO STORAGE SYSTEMS LIMITED
Registration no: 03712760 **Date established:** 1999
No.of Employees: 1 - 10 **Product Groups:** 35, 42, 45

Date of Accounts	Dec 11	Dec 10	Dec 09
Working Capital	199	61	-172
Fixed Assets	168	202	214
Current Assets	3m	2m	1m

Bonomi UK Ltd
Thomas Industrial Park, Nuneaton, CV11 6BQ
Tel: 024-7632 0768 **Fax:** 024-7635 4143
E-mail: sales@bonomi.co.uk
Website: http://www.bonomi.co.uk
Bank(s): National Westminster Bank Plc
Directors: P. Wozniak (Fin)
Managers: L. Hargrave (Sales & Mktg Mg), J. Bryson (Sales Admin)
Immediate Holding Company: BONOMI (UK) LIMITED
Registration no: 04586514 **Date established:** 2002 **Turnover:** £2m - £5m
No.of Employees: 21 - 50 **Product Groups:** 36, 40

Date of Accounts	Dec 11	Dec 10	Dec 09
Working Capital	418	338	276
Fixed Assets	49	76	40
Current Assets	941	880	698

Browick Engineering
278 Gadsby Street, Nuneaton, CV11 4PF
Tel: 024-7638 3156 **Fax:** 024-7635 0427
Directors: L. Brown (Prop)
Immediate Holding Company: BROWICK ENGINEERING LIMITED
Registration no: 04675213 **Date established:** 2003
No.of Employees: 1 - 10 **Product Groups:** 46

Date of Accounts	Dec 07	Mar 11	Mar 10
Working Capital	-5	-6	-8
Current Assets	5	7	3

Bucher Hydraulics Ltd
9 Eastboro Fields Hemdale Business Park, Nuneaton, CV11 6GL
Tel: 024-7635 3561 **Fax:** 024-7635 3572
E-mail: info@bucherhydraulics.com
Website: http://www.bucherhydraulics.com
Directors: S. Tipton (Fin)
Ultimate Holding Company: BUCHER INDUSTRIES AG (SWITZERLAND)
Immediate Holding Company: BUCHER HYDRAULICS LIMITED
Registration no: 02453191 **VAT No.:** GB 549 4985 79
Date established: 1989 **Turnover:** £1m - £2m **No.of Employees:** 1 - 10
Product Groups: 36, 38, 40, 45, 46, 84

Date of Accounts	Dec 11	Dec 10	Dec 09
Sales Turnover	N/A	2m	N/A
Pre Tax Profit/Loss	N/A	288	N/A
Working Capital	925	416	346
Fixed Assets	25	25	38
Current Assets	1m	670	472
Current Liabilities	N/A	138	N/A

Camozzi Pneumatics Ltd
The Fluid Power Centre Watling Street, Nuneaton, CV11 6BQ
Tel: 024-7637 4114 **Fax:** 024-7634 7520
E-mail: sales@camozzi.co.uk
Website: http://www.camozzi.com/uk
Directors: N. Chappell (Fin), D. Snow (Sales), D. Snow (Sales)
Managers: J. Cane (I.T. Exec), M. Ludbrook (Purch Mgr), L. Hargrave (Mktg Serv Mgr), L. Hargrave (Mktg Serv Mgr), J. Cane (Tech Serv Mgr)
Immediate Holding Company: CAMOZZI PNEUMATICS LIMITED
Registration no: 04586521 **VAT No.:** GB 585 0436 31
Date established: 2002 **Turnover:** £5m - £10m **No.of Employees:** 21 - 50
Product Groups: 36, 37, 38, 40, 46, 84

Date of Accounts	Dec 11	Dec 10	Dec 09
Working Capital	789	658	721
Fixed Assets	250	322	232
Current Assets	2m	2m	2m

Caterers Supplies Ltd
Unit 6 Centrovell Buildings Centrovell Industrial Estate Caldwell Road, Nuneaton, CV11 4NG
Tel: 024-7632 7108 **Fax:** 024-7664 5014
E-mail: sales@catererssupplies.co.uk
Website: http://www.catererssupplies.co.uk
Directors: P. Mayling (Prop), P. Mayling (MD)
Immediate Holding Company: CATERERS SUPPLIES LIMITED
Registration no: 04597924 **Date established:** 2002
No.of Employees: 11 - 20 **Product Groups:** 38, 40, 67

Central Lifting Services UK Ltd
8 B Trident Business Park Attleborough Road, Nuneaton, CV11 4NS
Tel: 024-7664 1684 **Fax:** 024-7664 1713
E-mail: enquiries@centrallifting.com
Website: http://www.centrallifting.com
Directors: C. Stringer (MD)
Immediate Holding Company: CENTRAL LIFTING SERVICES UK LIMITED
Registration no: 02546571 **Date established:** 1990
No.of Employees: 1 - 10 **Product Groups:** 35, 39, 45

Date of Accounts	Sep 11	Sep 10	Sep 09
Working Capital	11	-39	5
Fixed Assets	11	14	6
Current Assets	179	189	214

Chillaire Ltd
Unit 1 Veasey Close Attleborough Fields Ind Estate, Nuneaton, CV11 6RT
Tel: 024-7632 0300 **Fax:** 024-7632 0400
E-mail: info@chillaire.co.uk
Website: http://www.chillaire.co.uk
Directors: N. Thandi (Co Sec), G. Fowler (Sales)
Immediate Holding Company: CHILLAIRE LIMITED
Registration no: 02686557 **Date established:** 1992
No.of Employees: 1 - 10 **Product Groups:** 30, 38, 39, 40, 66, 83, 84, 87

Date of Accounts	Feb 12	Feb 11	Feb 10
Working Capital	-61	-95	-99
Fixed Assets	42	54	42
Current Assets	278	188	292
Current Liabilities	60	8	130

J J Churchill Ltd
Station Road Market Bosworth, Nuneaton, CV13 0PF
Tel: 01455-299600 **Fax:** 01455-292330
E-mail: kevin.mccormik@jjchurchill.com
Website: http://www.jjchurchill.com
Bank(s): Barclays, Coventry
Directors: K. McCormik (Sales & Mktg), M. Wallace (Fin)
Managers: D. Sidwell (Personnel)
Immediate Holding Company: J.J.CHURCHILL LIMITED
Registration no: 00335195 **Date established:** 1937
Turnover: £20m - £50m **No.of Employees:** 101 - 250
Product Groups: 36, 39, 40, 46, 48, 66, 67, 85

Date of Accounts	Mar 12	Mar 11	Mar 10
Sales Turnover	23m	19m	13m
Pre Tax Profit/Loss	1m	2m	269
Working Capital	4m	3m	3m
Fixed Assets	5m	4m	4m
Current Assets	10m	9m	6m
Current Liabilities	2m	2m	1m

Classic Coils Ltd
Anker Street, Nuneaton, CV11 4JL
Tel: 024-7634 5833 **Fax:** 024-7634 5844
E-mail: classiccoils@aol.com
Website: http://www.classiccoils.co.uk
Directors: M. Pritchards (MD)
Immediate Holding Company: CLASSIC COILS LIMITED
Registration no: 03171501 **VAT No.:** GB 670 1276 51
Date established: 1996 **Turnover:** £500,000 - £1m
No.of Employees: 1 - 10 **Product Groups:** 36, 39, 40

Date of Accounts	Feb 11	Feb 10	Feb 09
Working Capital	-27	-34	16
Fixed Assets	9	14	14
Current Assets	125	133	180

Classic Gates
57 Fitton Street, Nuneaton, CV11 5RZ
Tel: 024-7637 1427
E-mail: stevenedge1@hotmail.com
Website: http://www.classicgates.net
Directors: S. Edge (Prop)
Date established: 1993 **No.of Employees:** 1 - 10 **Product Groups:** 26, 35

Cogsdill Nuneaton Ltd
Tenlons Road, Nuneaton, CV10 7HR
Tel: 024-7638 3792 **Fax:** 024-7634 4433
E-mail: sales@cogsdill.co.uk
Website: http://www.cogsdill.com
Bank(s): Lloyds TSB Bank plc
Directors: P. Bird (Fin), K. Johnson (MD)
Managers: D. Allen, B. Johnson (Sales Prom Mgr), A. Kumar (Tech Serv Mgr), A. Quinn (Works Gen Mgr), C. Bates
Ultimate Holding Company: COGSDILL TOOL PRODUCTS INC (USA)
Immediate Holding Company: COGSDILL-NUNEATON, LIMITED
Registration no: 00701333 **VAT No.:** GB 399 7898 40
Date established: 1961 **Turnover:** £2m - £5m **No.of Employees:** 21 - 50
Product Groups: 48

Date of Accounts	Dec 11	Dec 10	Dec 09
Sales Turnover	4m	4m	2m
Pre Tax Profit/Loss	429	40	-97
Working Capital	1m	1m	1m
Fixed Assets	1m	692	704
Current Assets	2m	2m	2m
Current Liabilities	268	175	58

R A Cooper Machine Tools Ltd
51 Webb Street, Nuneaton, CV10 8JG
Tel: 024-7634 4698 **Fax:** 024-7634 4698
Directors: J. Cooper (MD)
Immediate Holding Company: R.A.COOPER (MACHINE TOOLS) LIMITED
Registration no: 01015677 **Date established:** 1971
Turnover: Up to £250,000 **No.of Employees:** 1 - 10 **Product Groups:** 46

Date of Accounts	Mar 12	Mar 11	Mar 09
Sales Turnover	N/A	N/A	30
Working Capital	-26	-17	-21
Fixed Assets	34	34	33
Current Assets	9	18	15
Current Liabilities	33	28	N/A

Custom Chrome Ltd
Lomond House Weddington Terrace, Nuneaton, CV10 0AG
Tel: 024-7638 7808 **Fax:** 024-7634 1660
E-mail: nigel@custom-chrome.co.uk
Website: http://www.customchromeracing.co.uk
Directors: M. Wing (Co Sec), N. Swift (MD)
Immediate Holding Company: CUSTOM CHROME LIMITED
Registration no: 01440870 **Date established:** 1979
Turnover: £500,000 - £1m **No.of Employees:** 1 - 10 **Product Groups:** 39, 40

Date of Accounts	Aug 11	Aug 10	Aug 09
Working Capital	-33	-19	-1
Fixed Assets	60	70	60
Current Assets	164	133	160

Datum Engineering Co. Ltd
Whitacre Road Industrial Estate, Nuneaton, CV11 6BP
Tel: 024-7638 3032 **Fax:** 024-7634 5130
E-mail: sales@datumuk.com
Website: http://www.datumuk.com
Bank(s): Barclays
Directors: D. Twigger (MD)
Ultimate Holding Company: DATUM HOLDINGS LIMITED
Immediate Holding Company: DATUM ENGINEERING COMPANY LIMITED
Registration no: 02486254 **VAT No.:** GB 114 0686 95
Date established: 1990 **Turnover:** £2m - £5m **No.of Employees:** 21 - 50
Product Groups: 30, 33, 34, 35, 39, 46, 48, 67

Date of Accounts	Oct 11	Oct 10	Oct 09
Working Capital	2m	2m	482
Fixed Assets	89	90	1m
Current Assets	2m	3m	1m

E N A Trading Ltd T/A Phoenix Forklifts (t/a Phoenix Forklifts)
Basin Bridge Lane Stoke Golding, Nuneaton, CV13 6JJ
Tel: 01455-213401 **Fax:** 01455- 213867
E-mail: marks@phoenixforklifts.co.uk
Website: http://www.phoenixforklifts.net
Directors: M. Edwards (Dir), A. Edward (Dir), A. Edwards (Dir)
Date established: 2003 **No.of Employees:** 1 - 10 **Product Groups:** 35, 39, 45

Date of Accounts	Mar 08	Mar 07	Mar 06
Sales Turnover	N/A	N/A	252
Pre Tax Profit/Loss	N/A	N/A	24
Working Capital	-78	-44	-96
Fixed Assets	184	164	205
Current Assets	62	75	47
Current Liabilities	140	119	142
Total Share Capital	10	10	N/A
ROCE% (Return on Capital Employed)			22.0
ROT% (Return on Turnover)			9.6

Electro Cables Ltd
Unit 2 Alliance Close Attleborough Fields Ind Estate, Nuneaton, CV11 6SD
Tel: 024-7632 0066 **Fax:** 024-7632 0122
E-mail: sales@electrocables.co.uk
Website: http://www.electrocables.co.uk
Directors: G. Sears (Fin), J. Hayes (MD)
Immediate Holding Company: ELECTRO CABLES LIMITED
Registration no: 02108516 **Date established:** 1987 **Turnover:** £1m - £2m
No.of Employees: 1 - 10 **Product Groups:** 37

Date of Accounts	Dec 11	Dec 10	Dec 09
Working Capital	282	262	207
Fixed Assets	5	6	7
Current Assets	458	402	321

Eram UK Ltd
110 Malvern Avenue, Nuneaton, CV10 8NB
Tel: 024-7632 7184 **Fax:** 024-7634 2607
E-mail: eramuk@ntlworld.com
Website: http://www.eram.ch
Directors: T. Sutton (Sales)
Immediate Holding Company: ERAM (U.K.) LIMITED
Registration no: 01223342 **VAT No.:** 478 4375 02 **Date established:** 1975
Turnover: £10m - £20m **No.of Employees:** 1 - 10 **Product Groups:** 35, 48

FactoryMaster Ltd
The Old Grain Store 14 The Green, Hartshill, Nuneaton, CV10 0SW
Tel: 024-7699 8661 **Fax:** 024-7639 9466
E-mail: sales@factorymaster.co.uk
Website: http://www.factorymaster.co.uk
Directors: D. Neary (MD)
Immediate Holding Company: FACTORYMASTER LIMITED
Registration no: 03231323 **Date established:** 1996
No.of Employees: 11 - 20 **Product Groups:** 44, 45, 80

Date of Accounts	Aug 11	Aug 10	Aug 09
Working Capital	71	62	44
Fixed Assets	20	24	20
Current Assets	349	288	218

Freeman & Procter Ltd
PO Box 22, Nuneaton, CV11 4NG
Tel: 024-7638 2032 **Fax:** 024-7637 4353
E-mail: info@freemanandproctor.co.uk
Website: http://www.freemanandproctor.co.uk
Bank(s): The Royal Bank of Scotland
Managers: G. Long (Buyer), N. Torpey (Chief Mgr), O. Beesley (Personnel)
Immediate Holding Company: FREEMAN AND PROCTOR LIMITED
Registration no: 06820161 **Date established:** 2009 **Turnover:** £5m - £10m
No.of Employees: 51 - 100 **Product Groups:** 33, 34, 36, 39, 48, 85, 87

Date of Accounts	Mar 11	Mar 10
Working Capital	40	1m
Fixed Assets	36	36
Current Assets	3m	2m

Mick Furniss Agricultural Engineering
Higham Fields Farm Basin Bridge Lane, Higham-on-the-Hill, Nuneaton, CV13 6ET
Tel: 01455-213124
Directors: M. Furniss (Prop)
Date established: 1985 **No.of Employees:** 1 - 10 **Product Groups:** 41

G P D Developments Ltd
Kelsey Close Attleborough Fields Industrial Estate, Attleborough Fields Ind Estate, Nuneaton, CV11 6RS
Tel: 024-7635 1227 **Fax:** 024-7638 1033
E-mail: sales@gpd-developments.co.uk
Website: http://www.gpd-developments.co.uk
Bank(s): National Westminster Bank Plc
Directors: S. Davis (MD), S. Davis (MD), H. Davis (Co Sec)
Immediate Holding Company: GPD DEVELOPMENTS LIMITED
Registration no: 04621092 **Date established:** 2002 **Turnover:** £1m - £2m
No.of Employees: 21 - 50 **Product Groups:** 34

Date of Accounts	Dec 11	Dec 10	Dec 09
Working Capital	5	-3	-3
Fixed Assets	27	16	20
Current Assets	238	225	119

G R S Roadstone Ltd

10 Goldsmith Way Eliot Business Park, Nuneaton, CV10 7RJ
Tel: 024-7658 0800 **Fax:** 024-7658 0888
E-mail: martinhill@grs.com
Website: http://www.grsroadstone.co.uk
Bank(s): Lloyds TSB Bank plc
Directors: M. Hill (MD)
Ultimate Holding Company: GRS ROADSTONE HOLDINGS LIMITED
Immediate Holding Company: GRS ROADSTONE HOLDINGS LIMITED
Registration no: 05089357 **VAT No.:** GB 272 4175 62
Date established: 2004 **Turnover:** £50m - £75m
No.of Employees: 51 - 100 **Product Groups:** 14

Date of Accounts	Dec 11	Dec 10	Dec 09
Sales Turnover	53m	50m	41m
Pre Tax Profit/Loss	918	518	505
Working Capital	3m	2m	2m
Fixed Assets	1m	1m	1m
Current Assets	14m	15m	12m
Current Liabilities	2m	1m	1m

Genus Group The Microfilm Shop

15 Hammond Close, Nuneaton, CV11 6RY
Tel: 024-7625 4955 **Fax:** 024-7638 2319
E-mail: info@genusit.com
Website: http://www.genusit.com
Bank(s): National Westminster Bank Plc
Directors: P. Negus (MD)
Managers: C. Sellick (Accounts), C. Elwell (Chief Mgr), I. Case (Sales Prom Mgr), K. Stout
Ultimate Holding Company: J and J Negus Ltd
Registration no: 01168979 **VAT No.:** GB 273 5431 59
Date established: 1974 **Turnover:** £2m - £5m **No.of Employees:** 21 - 50
Product Groups: 38, 44, 65, 67, 80, 81, 83, 89

Date of Accounts	Mar 12	Mar 11
Working Capital	1	3
Current Assets	5	8

Graphic Press

15 Hammond Close Attleborough Fields Ind Estate, Nuneaton, CV11 6RY
Tel: 024-7625 4941 **Fax:** 024-7638 2319
E-mail: sales@graphicpress.co.uk
Website: http://www.graphicpress.co.uk
Managers: A. Stain (Chief Mgr)
Registration no: 02504762 **Date established:** 1998
No.of Employees: 1 - 10 **Product Groups:** 27, 28, 44, 61, 64, 80, 81

Herbert & Criddan Ltd

Unit 5 Anker Court Alliance Close, Attleborough Fields Ind Estate, Nuneaton, CV11 6SD
Tel: 024-7638 3400 **Fax:** 024-7638 5999
E-mail: ken@herbertandcridan.com
Website: http://www.herbertandcridan.com
Directors: K. Powell (MD)
Immediate Holding Company: ANCOT SERVICES LTD
Registration no: 02007049 **Date established:** 1995
No.of Employees: 1 - 10 **Product Groups:** 46

Holland & Barrett Ltd

Samuel Ryder House Townsend Drive, Attleborough Fields Ind Estate, Nuneaton, CV11 6XW
Tel: 01455-251900 **Fax:** 024-7632 0094
E-mail: rcraddock@hollandandbarrett.co.uk
Website: http://www.hollandandbarrett.com
Directors: R. Craddock (Fin), R. Craddock (Co Sec), G. Day (Fin), B. Vickers (Grp Chief Exec), P. Aldis (Comm), G. Warhurst (Tech Serv)
Managers: K. Krauth (Personnel), P. Geary (Mktg Serv Mgr)
Ultimate Holding Company: NBTY INC (USA)
Immediate Holding Company: HOLLAND & BARRETT LIMITED
Registration no: 00390308 **Date established:** 1944
Turnover: £50m - £75m **No.of Employees:** 21 - 50 **Product Groups:** 02, 20, 62

Date of Accounts	Sep 10	Sep 09	Sep 08
Working Capital	6m	6m	6m
Current Assets	6m	6m	6m

Knights Design & Manufacturer

Trident Business Park Holman Way, Nuneaton, CV11 4PN
Tel: 024-7634 4822 **Fax:** 024- 76344822
Directors: D. Knights (Prop)
VAT No.: GB 399 7546 71 **Turnover:** £250,000 - £500,000
No.of Employees: 1 - 10 **Product Groups:** 48

Kumi Solutions Ltd

Unit 6 Innovation Centre St Davids Way, Bermuda Park, Nuneaton, CV10 7SG
Tel: 024-7635 0360 **Fax:** 05601-277115
E-mail: simon@kumi-solutions.com
Website: http://www.kumi-solutions.com
Directors: S. Graham (MD)
Immediate Holding Company: KUMI SOLUTIONS LIMITED
Registration no: 04400660 **Date established:** 2002
Turnover: Up to £250,000 **No.of Employees:** 1 - 10 **Product Groups:** 46

Date of Accounts	Mar 11	Mar 10	Mar 09
Working Capital	24	6	18
Fixed Assets	23	2	4
Current Assets	58	45	65

Lanemark International Ltd

Whitacre Road Industrial Estate Whitacre Road, Nuneaton, CV11 6BW
Tel: 024-7635 2000 **Fax:** 024-7634 1166
E-mail: info@lanemark.com
Website: http://www.lanemark.com
Bank(s): HSBC Bank plc
Directors: J. Foster (Dir), P. Collier (MD), A. Thompson (Dir)
Managers: R. Lee (Fin Mgr)
Ultimate Holding Company: MIDCO EUROPE LIMITED
Immediate Holding Company: LANEMARK INTERNATIONAL LIMITED
Registration no: 01561585 **VAT No.:** GB 307 5790 48
Date established: 1981 **Turnover:** £2m - £5m **No.of Employees:** 11 - 20
Product Groups: 40, 67

Date of Accounts	Oct 11	Oct 10	Oct 09
Working Capital	20	9	-33
Fixed Assets	478	584	612
Current Assets	884	1m	779

Laserplas Ltd

58 Thornhill Drive, Nuneaton, CV11 6XG
Tel: 024-7637 4210 **Fax:** 024-7638 3847
E-mail: sales@laserplas.co.uk
Website: http://www.laserplas.co.uk
Directors: R. Eales (Dir)
Immediate Holding Company: LASERPLAS LIMITED
Registration no: 05699602 **Date established:** 2006
Turnover: £250,000 - £500,000 **No.of Employees:** 1 - 10
Product Groups: 67

Date of Accounts	Dec 11	Dec 10	Dec 09
Working Capital	127	47	33
Fixed Assets	10	13	17
Current Assets	441	410	227

Leader C N C Technologies

Unit 7 Eastboro Fields Hemdale Business Park, Nuneaton, CV11 6GL
Tel: 024-7635 3874 **Fax:** 024-7635 2874
E-mail: service@leadercnc.co.uk
Website: http://www.leadercnc.co.uk
Directors: R. Prosser (Dir)
Immediate Holding Company: LEADER CNC TECHNOLOGIES LIMITED
Registration no: 03500786 **Date established:** 1998
No.of Employees: 1 - 10 **Product Groups:** 42, 46

Date of Accounts	Jan 11	Jan 10	Jan 09
Working Capital	-18	10	43
Fixed Assets	73	102	144
Current Assets	2m	2m	742

Leniks Motor Panels Ltd

Unit 14 Slingsby Close, Attleborough Fields Ind Estate, Nuneaton, CV11 6RP
Tel: 024-7638 4728 **Fax:** 024-7638 4728
Directors: N. Hamnell (Dir)
Immediate Holding Company: LENIKS MOTOR PANELS LIMITED
Registration no: 04290503 **Date established:** 2001
Turnover: Up to £250,000 **No.of Employees:** 1 - 10 **Product Groups:** 39, 48

Date of Accounts	Jul 11	Jul 10	Jul 09
Working Capital	21	15	14
Fixed Assets	2	2	3
Current Assets	29	24	23

M A C Manufacturing Ltd

Eagle House Slingsby Close, Attleborough Fields Industrial Estate, Nuneaton, CV11 6RP
Tel: 024-7632 9849 **Fax:** 024-7632 9630
E-mail: jan@macmanufacturing.co.uk
Website: http://www.macmanufacturing.co.uk
Directors: J. Mokrzycki (MD)
Immediate Holding Company: M.A.C. Manufacturing Ltd
Registration no: 06028971 **Date established:** 2006
No.of Employees: 1 - 10 **Product Groups:** 33, 35, 48, 81, 85

Date of Accounts	Dec 07
Working Capital	-15
Fixed Assets	1
Current Assets	6
Current Liabilities	21

Medical Ltd

1 Hazell Way Off Bermuda Road, Nuneaton, CV10 7HP
Tel: 024-7634 0933 **Fax:** 024-7634 5307
E-mail: sales@presstigeplastics.co.uk
Website: http://www.prestigeplastics.co.uk
Directors: S. Gill (Co Sec), S. Gill (Fin), K. Gill (Ptnr), K. Gill (Prop)
Immediate Holding Company: PRESTIGE PLASTICS MEDICAL LIMITED
Registration no: 05321851 **Date established:** 2004
Turnover: £250,000 - £500,000 **No.of Employees:** 1 - 10
Product Groups: 30, 48, 66

Microbore Tooling Systems

Whitacre Road Industrial Estate Whitacre Road, Nuneaton, CV11 6BX
Tel: 024-7637 3355 **Fax:** 024-7637 3322
E-mail: sales@microbore.com
Website: http://www.microbore.com
Bank(s): Barclays
Directors: W. Atkinson (Fin)
Ultimate Holding Company: SYMMETRY MEDICAL INC (USA)
Immediate Holding Company: MICROBORE TOOLING SYSTEMS LIMITED
Registration no: 02587290 **VAT No.:** 565 8064 16 **Date established:** 1991
Turnover: £1m - £2m **No.of Employees:** 11 - 20 **Product Groups:** 45, 46

Date of Accounts	Dec 11	Dec 10	Dec 09
Working Capital	184	82	105
Fixed Assets	117	109	97
Current Assets	372	281	239

Microfilm Shop

Hammond Close Attleborough Fields Ind Estate, Nuneaton, CV11 6RY
Tel: 024-7638 3998 **Fax:** 024-7638 2319
E-mail: paulnegus@microfilm.com
Website: http://www.genusit.com
Bank(s): National Westminster Bank Plc
Directors: P. Negus (MD), S. Elwell (Mkt Research)
Managers: I. Case (Sales Prom Mgr)
Ultimate Holding Company: J. AND J. NEGUS LIMITED
Immediate Holding Company: THE MICROFILM FACTORY LIMITED
Registration no: 02200742 **Date established:** 1987 **Turnover:** £2m - £5m
No.of Employees: 21 - 50 **Product Groups:** 27, 35, 38, 44, 81

Date of Accounts	May 12	May 11	May 10
Working Capital	21	21	21
Current Assets	21	21	21

Mira Ltd

Watling Street, Nuneaton, CV10 0TU
Tel: 024-7635 5000 **Fax:** 024-7635 8000
E-mail: graham.townsend@mire.co.uk
Website: http://www.mira.co.uk
Bank(s): National Westminster Bank Plc
Directors: G. Davies (Dir), D. Allen (Chief Op Offcr)
Managers: D. Hill (Tech Serv Mgr), L. Rowles, D. Williams, S. Lone
Immediate Holding Company: MIRA LIMITED
Registration no: 00402570 **VAT No.:** GB 114 5409 96
Date established: 1946 **Turnover:** £20m - £50m
No.of Employees: 251 - 500 **Product Groups:** 38, 40, 42, 44, 54, 80

Date of Accounts	Dec 11	Dec 10	Dec 09
Sales Turnover	42m	37m	33m
Pre Tax Profit/Loss	2m	1m	492

Working Capital	3m	5m	6m
Fixed Assets	20m	16m	16m
Current Assets	13m	13m	12m
Current Liabilities	7m	5m	5m

Mount & More Disability Equipment Ltd

Willow Park Industrial Estate Upton Lane, Stoke Golding, Nuneaton, CV13 6EU
Tel: 01455-212777 **Fax:** 01455-212677
E-mail: sales@aac.com
Website: http://www.aacmounts.com
Directors: I. Bulluck (Dir)
Immediate Holding Company: MOUNTS & MORE LTD
Registration no: 05194042 **Date established:** 2004
No.of Employees: 1 - 10 **Product Groups:** 38

Date of Accounts	Aug 11	Aug 10	Aug 09
Working Capital	21	14	37
Fixed Assets	5	11	13
Current Assets	107	107	98

N S I Group Ltd

Whitacre Road Industrial Estate, Nuneaton, CV11 6BY
Tel: 024-7637 5656 **Fax:** 024-7664 1191
E-mail: sales@nsigroupltd.com
Website: http://www.nsigroup.co.uk
Directors: S. Owen (Fin), L. Bates (MD)
Managers: A. Merryman (Tech Serv Mgr), L. Striger (Sales Prom Mgr)
Ultimate Holding Company: PROJECT FABRICATIONS LIMITED
Immediate Holding Company: NSI GROUP LIMITED
Registration no: 01136352 **Date established:** 1973 **Turnover:** £2m - £5m
No.of Employees: 51 - 100 **Product Groups:** 46, 48

Date of Accounts	Apr 11	Apr 10	Apr 09
Sales Turnover	N/A	N/A	4m
Pre Tax Profit/Loss	N/A	N/A	-244
Working Capital	1m	1m	1m
Fixed Assets	2m	2m	2m
Current Assets	3m	2m	2m
Current Liabilities	N/A	N/A	427

Norbert Dentressangle Logistics UK

Townsend Drive Attleborough Fields Ind Estate, Nuneaton, CV11 6TJ
Tel: 024-7632 4000 **Fax:** 024-7635 0935
E-mail: sarah.banshaw@norbert-dentressangle.com
Website: http://www.salvesen.com
Managers: R. Shroff (Fin Mgr), S. Banshaw (Mgr)
Registration no: SC007173 **Turnover:** £2m - £5m
No.of Employees: 51 - 100 **Product Groups:** 39, 72, 84

Nuneaton Precisions Ltd

Veasey Close Attleborough Fields Ind Estate, Nuneaton, CV11 6RT
Tel: 024-7634 3116 **Fax:** 024-7664 2355
E-mail: kaye.wale@nuneaton-precisions.com
Website: http://www.nuneaton-precisions.com
Bank(s): Lloyds TSB Bank plc
Directors: K. Wale (Fin), P. Bailey (MD)
Immediate Holding Company: NUNEATON PRECISIONS LIMITED
Registration no: 01922724 **VAT No.:** GB 418 8382 27
Date established: 1985 **Turnover:** £1m - £2m **No.of Employees:** 21 - 50
Product Groups: 38, 46, 48

Date of Accounts	Dec 11	Dec 10	Dec 09
Working Capital	367	242	616
Fixed Assets	245	286	345
Current Assets	721	507	881

Nuneaton Signs

3 Kelsey Close Attleborough Fields Ind Estate, Nuneaton, CV11 6RS
Tel: 024-7634 1922 **Fax:** 024-7664 1305
E-mail: sales@nuneatonsigns.co.uk
Website: http://www.nuneatonsigns.co.uk
Bank(s): HSBC Bank plc
Directors: R. Munday (Dir)
Managers: G. Phipps, G. Crane, A. Ellis, K. Munday (Buyer)
Immediate Holding Company: NUNEATON SIGNS LIMITED
Registration no: 07207123 **VAT No.:** GB 355 3812 51
Date established: 2010 **Turnover:** £2m - £5m **No.of Employees:** 21 - 50
Product Groups: 28, 30, 37, 49, 84

Date of Accounts	Mar 12	Mar 11
Working Capital	501	465
Fixed Assets	91	133
Current Assets	989	838

Nuneaton Welding Supply

Whitacre Road, Nuneaton, CV11 6BY
Tel: 024-7632 5909 **Fax:** 024-7638 8048
Directors: J. Tew (Ptnr)
Immediate Holding Company: NWS GASES LIMITED
Registration no: 05245573 **Date established:** 2004
No.of Employees: 1 - 10 **Product Groups:** 46

Date of Accounts	Apr 11	Apr 10	Apr 09
Working Capital	61	56	50
Fixed Assets	12	N/A	N/A
Current Assets	85	69	65

Nutripack UK Ltd

Unit 5 Kingfisher Court, Hemdale Business Park, Nuneaton, CV11 6GY
Tel: 024-7635 1300 **Fax:** 024-7634 9250
E-mail: py.berthe@proplast-group.com
Website: http://www.nutripack.co.uk
Directors: P. Berthe (MD)
Ultimate Holding Company: NUTRIPACK SA (FRANCE)
Immediate Holding Company: NUTRIPACK UK LIMITED
Registration no: 02220919 **Date established:** 1988
No.of Employees: 1 - 10 **Product Groups:** 30, 42

Date of Accounts	Dec 11	Dec 10	Dec 09
Working Capital	314	240	193
Fixed Assets	84	99	77
Current Assets	509	412	449

Optimum Supplies

33 Walsingham Drive, Nuneaton, CV10 7RW
Tel: 08443-573985 **Fax:** 0845-116 1892
E-mail: info@optimumsupplies.co.uk
Website: http://www.optimumsupplies.co.uk
Managers: M. Oliver (Sales Prom Mgr)
Immediate Holding Company: BERMUDA PARK LIMITED
Registration no: 06843446 **Date established:** 2008
No.of Employees: 1 - 10 **Product Groups:** 26

Painting & Decorating Association
32 Coton Road, Nuneaton, CV11 5TW
Tel: 024-7635 3776 **Fax:** 024-7635 4513
E-mail: info@paintingdecoratingassociation.co.uk
Website: http://www.paintingdecoratingassociation.co.uk
Directors: N. Ogildie (Grp Chief Exec)
No.of Employees: 1 - 10 **Product Groups:** 39, 48, 52

Phillips Tuftex Ltd
Albion Buildings Attleborough Road, Nuneaton, CV11 4JJ
Tel: 024-7638 2100 **Fax:** 024-7634 2449
E-mail: info@phillipstuftex.co.uk
Website: http://www.tuftexsports.co.uk
Directors: S. Robinson (MD), J. Robinson (Fin)
Ultimate Holding Company: TUFTEX PROPERTIES LIMITED
Immediate Holding Company: PHILLIPS-TUFTEX LIMITED
Registration no: 01943550 **Date established:** 1985 **Turnover:** £1m - £2m
No.of Employees: 11 - 20 **Product Groups:** 49, 65

Date of Accounts	Dec 11	Dec 10	Dec 09
Working Capital	471	489	510
Fixed Assets	47	53	36
Current Assets	909	962	857

Phoenix Windows
Alliance Close Unit 8, Attleborough Fields Ind Estate, Nuneaton, CV11 6SD
Tel: 024-7635 0330 **Fax:** 024-7635 1133
E-mail: suemccord@yahoo.co.uk
Website: http://www.phoenix-windows-nuneaton.co.uk
Directors: S. Mccord (Co Sec)
No.of Employees: 1 - 10 **Product Groups:** 33, 35, 36, 40

Polyform Ltd
Eliot Park Innovation Centre Barling Way, Nuneaton, CV10 7RH
Tel: 0870-7551016 **Fax:** 0870-75510107
E-mail: sales@polyformedge.co.uk
Website: http://www.polyformedge.co.uk
Directors: D. Johnston (Dir)
Registration no: 02784869 **Date established:** 1994
No.of Employees: 1 - 10 **Product Groups:** 46

Powerkut Engineering Services Ltd
79 Vale View Stockingford, Nuneaton, CV10 8AP
Tel: 07816-054461 **Fax:** 07967-200159
E-mail: sales@powerkut.co.uk
Website: http://www.powerkut.co.uk
Directors: R. Everitt (Fin)
Immediate Holding Company: POWERKUT LIMITED
Registration no: 04523675 **Date established:** 2002 **Turnover:** £1m - £2m
No.of Employees: 1 - 10 **Product Groups:** 46

Q C R Coatings Ltd QCR Motors Ltd
Whitacre Road Industrial Estate, Nuneaton, CV11 6BX
Tel: 024-7638 5296 **Fax:** 024-7664 1211
E-mail: johnyhook@tiscali.co.uk
Website: http://www.qcrcoatings.co.uk
Directors: D. Whitmore (MD)
Managers: B. Ashley
Immediate Holding Company: QCR COATINGS LTD
Registration no: 06210930 **Date established:** 2007
No.of Employees: 21 - 50 **Product Groups:** 32, 48

Date of Accounts	Sep 11	Sep 10	Sep 08
Working Capital	199	-8	N/A
Fixed Assets	17	14	N/A
Current Assets	551	195	N/A

Howard Roberts Automotive
8 Eastboro Fields Hemdale Business Park, Nuneaton, CV11 6GL
Tel: 024-7664 2484 **Fax:** 024-7632 9020
E-mail: sales@howardroberts.com
Website: http://www.howardroberts.com
Bank(s): Royal Bank of Scotland
Directors: R. Taylor (Sales)
VAT No.: GB 418 6482 33 **Date established:** 1987 **Turnover:** £1m - £2m
No.of Employees: 11 - 20 **Product Groups:** 29, 39, 40

Samco Silicone Products
4 Veasey Close Attleborough Fields Ind Estate, Nuneaton, CV11 6RT
Tel: 024-7664 1270 **Fax:** 024-7634 4992
E-mail: sales@samco.co.uk
Website: http://www.samco.co.uk
Managers: G. Gordon (Chief Mgr)
Ultimate Holding Company: CURRIE & WARNER (HOLDINGS) LTD
Immediate Holding Company: GLENSON (HOLDINGS) LTD
Registration no: 02307356 **VAT No.:** GB 538 3711 37
Date established: 1988 **No.of Employees:** 11 - 20 **Product Groups:** 23, 27, 29, 30, 31, 32, 39, 48, 49, 61, 63, 66

Peter Savage Ltd
Liberty House Liberty Way, Attleborough Fields Ind Estate, Nuneaton, CV11 6RZ
Tel: 024-7664 1777 **Fax:** 024-7637 5250
E-mail: sales@peter-savage.co.uk
Website: http://www.peter-savage.co.uk
Directors: A. Moore (Sales), S. Cooke (Fin), S. Hodgeson (Fin)
Managers: B. Brown
Ultimate Holding Company: EUROPEAN DRAINAGE SYSTEMS HOLDINGS LIMITED
Immediate Holding Company: PETER SAVAGE LIMITED
Registration no: 01271357 **Date established:** 1976
Turnover: £10m - £20m **No.of Employees:** 51 - 100 **Product Groups:** 33, 34, 35

Date of Accounts	Dec 11	Dec 10	Dec 09
Sales Turnover	16m	15m	15m
Pre Tax Profit/Loss	353	837	702
Working Capital	5m	5m	5m
Fixed Assets	615	679	433
Current Assets	10m	9m	9m
Current Liabilities	382	700	682

Simplicity Health Ltd
41 Centenary Business Centre Hammond Close, Nuneaton, CV11 6RY
Tel: 024-76377 210 **Fax:** 024-7637 5151
E-mail: info@simplicityhealth.co.uk
Website: http://www.simplicityhealth.co.uk
Registration no: 05230889 **Product Groups:** 31, 38, 67

Stayclean Contract Cleaning Services Ltd
Unit 14 Centenary Business Centre Hammond Close, Attleborough Fields Ind Estate, Nuneaton, CV11 6RY
Tel: 024-7638 5830 **Fax:** 024-7638 5830
E-mail: info@staycleanltd.co.uk
Directors: R. Tenchio (Dir)
Immediate Holding Company: STAYCLEAN CONTRACT CLEANING SERVICES LIMITED
Registration no: 02898263 **Date established:** 1994
Turnover: Up to £250,000 **No.of Employees:** 1 - 10 **Product Groups:** 52

Date of Accounts	Aug 11	Aug 10	Aug 09
Working Capital	23	18	15
Fixed Assets	6	8	10
Current Assets	58	49	41

Suhner UK Ltd
Unit 1 Pool Road Business Centre Pool Road, Nuneaton, CV10 9AQ
Tel: 024-7638 4333 **Fax:** 024-7638 4777
E-mail: info.uk@suhner.com
Website: http://www.suhner.com
Managers: A. Mumford (Mgr)
Ultimate Holding Company: SUHNER HOLDING AG (SWITZERLAND)
Immediate Holding Company: SUHNER (UK) LIMITED
Registration no: 03671997 **Date established:** 1998
Turnover: Up to £250,000 **No.of Employees:** 1 - 10 **Product Groups:** 37

Date of Accounts	Dec 11	Dec 10	Dec 09
Sales Turnover	251	177	152
Pre Tax Profit/Loss	23	-8	-1
Working Capital	87	66	71
Fixed Assets	6	5	8
Current Assets	134	132	86
Current Liabilities	23	15	6

Techniforce Ltd
24 Coton Road, Nuneaton, CV11 5TW
Tel: 024-7635 1414 **Fax:** 024-7635 0870
E-mail: sales@eureka-software.com
Website: http://www.eureka-software.com
Directors: A. Carmichael (Dir), I. Carmichael (Dir)
Immediate Holding Company: TECHNIFORCE LIMITED
Registration no: 01775047 **Date established:** 1983
Turnover: £500,000 - £1m **No.of Employees:** 11 - 20 **Product Groups:** 44

Thermoscreens Ltd
St Marys Road, Nuneaton, CV11 5AU
Tel: 024-7638 4646 **Fax:** 024-7638 8578
E-mail: sales@thermoscreens.com
Website: http://www.thermoscreens.com
Bank(s): Barclays
Directors: M. Cooke (Fin), M. Francis (MD)
Managers: S. Harrison (Purch Mgr), J. Lewis (Personnel), N. Lafayette (Sales Off Mgr), S. Holmes (Tech Serv Mgr)
Ultimate Holding Company: CARVER GROUP LIMITED
Immediate Holding Company: THERMOSCREENS LIMITED
Registration no: 00691333 **VAT No.:** GB 188 1120 67
Date established: 1961 **Turnover:** £2m - £5m **No.of Employees:** 51 - 100
Product Groups: 40

Date of Accounts	Jul 11	Jul 10	Jul 09
Sales Turnover	6m	5m	5m
Pre Tax Profit/Loss	1m	736	908
Working Capital	906	1m	1m
Fixed Assets	169	187	208
Current Assets	2m	2m	2m
Current Liabilities	548	403	495

Thompson Strategy Works
18 Arnold Road Stoke Golding, Nuneaton, CV13 6JG
Tel: 0116-332 2157 **Fax:** 07971-091513
E-mail: info@thompsonsw.co.uk
Website: http://www.thompsonsw.co.uk
Directors: N. Thompson (Prop)
Date established: 2001 **Turnover:** Up to £250,000
No.of Employees: 1 - 10 **Product Groups:** 80, 81, 86

Triton Showers
Triton Road Shepperton Business Park, Nuneaton, CV11 4NR
Tel: 024-7634 4441 **Fax:** 024-7634 9828
E-mail: lornafellowes@tritonshowers.co.uk
Website: http://www.tritonshowers.co.uk
Bank(s): Lloyds TSB Bank plc
Directors: C. Whitell (Fin), T. Applegate (Sales), L. Fellowes (MD), T. Simpson (Mkt Research)
Managers: S. Ridgway (Personnel), K. Patricks (Purch Mgr), M. Harris (Tech Serv Mgr)
Ultimate Holding Company: NORCROS PLC
Immediate Holding Company: TRITON PLC
Registration no: 01211050 **VAT No.:** GB 278 4006 49
Date established: 1975 **Turnover:** £50m - £75m
No.of Employees: 251 - 500 **Product Groups:** 33, 40

Date of Accounts	Mar 10	Mar 09
Working Capital	3m	3m
Current Assets	3m	3m

Twistlink Ltd
Unit 14 Alliance Close Attleborough Fields Industrial Estate, Attleborough Fields Ind Estate, Nuneaton, CV11 6SD
Tel: 08458-690626 **Fax:** 0800-066 4420
E-mail: sales@twistlink.co.uk
Website: http://www.twistlink.co.uk
Directors: L. Mcnicholl (MD)
Immediate Holding Company: TWISTLINK LIMITED
Registration no: 03222398 **VAT No.:** 459 9069 89 **Date established:** 1996
Turnover: Up to £250,000 **No.of Employees:** 1 - 10 **Product Groups:** 23

Date of Accounts	Jul 11	Jul 10	Jul 09
Working Capital	85	64	41
Fixed Assets	2	3	4
Current Assets	105	97	109

Rugby

A F P Medical Ltd
15 Arches Business Centre Mill Road, Rugby, CV21 1QW
Tel: 01788-579408 **Fax:** 01788-540199
E-mail: info@afpmedical.com
Website: http://www.afpmedical.com
Directors: G. Pavis (MD)
Immediate Holding Company: AFP MEDICAL LIMITED
Registration no: 01384123 **VAT No.:** GB 307 3429 73
Date established: 1978 **Turnover:** £500,000 - £1m
No.of Employees: 1 - 10 **Product Groups:** 38

Date of Accounts	Aug 11	Aug 10	Aug 09
Working Capital	97	95	99
Fixed Assets	19	22	24
Current Assets	104	98	145

Air America Rugby Ltd
Midland Trading Estate Consul Road, Rugby, CV21 1PB
Tel: 01788-574555 **Fax:** 01788-547997
E-mail: air.america@wyko.co.uk
Website: http://www.wyko.co.uk
Managers: C. Markham (Chief Mgr)
Immediate Holding Company: WILLOW WREN CRUISING HOLIDAYS LTD
Registration no: 04570978 **Date established:** 2002
Turnover: £250,000 - £500,000 **No.of Employees:** 1 - 10
Product Groups: 66

Date of Accounts	Apr 06	Apr 05
Working Capital	68	68
Current Assets	68	68
Total Share Capital	1	1

A P Fork Lift Services Ltd
The Midlands Fork Lift Centre Market Street, Rugby, CV21 3HG
Tel: 01788-339200 **Fax:** 01788-339201
E-mail: info@apforkliftservices.co.uk
Website: http://www.apforkliftservices.co.uk
Managers: A. Peck (Mgr)
Immediate Holding Company: AP FORKLIFT SERVICES LIMITED
Registration no: 03822923 **Date established:** 1999
No.of Employees: 1 - 10 **Product Groups:** 35, 39, 45

Date of Accounts	Aug 11	Aug 10	Aug 09
Working Capital	-1	-0	4
Fixed Assets	7	9	12
Current Assets	5	3	5

Arrow Engineering Supply Co. Ltd
Unit 6 Hunters Lane Industrial Estate, Rugby, CV21 1EA
Tel: 01788-574107 **Fax:** 01788-542179
E-mail: sales@arrowrugby.com
Website: http://www.arrowrugby.com
Directors: B. Holt (Fin), F. Holt (MD)
Immediate Holding Company: ARROW ENGINEERING SUPPLY COMPANY LIMITED
Registration no: 02057550 **VAT No.:** GB 418 5168 44
Date established: 1986 **No.of Employees:** 1 - 10 **Product Groups:** 30, 33, 34, 35

Date of Accounts	Jan 12	Jan 11	Jan 10
Working Capital	27	10	22
Fixed Assets	5	7	9
Current Assets	130	132	142

Auto Dark Helmet Ltd
43 Long Hassocks, Rugby, CV23 0JS
Tel: 01788-573056 **Fax:** 01788-573057
E-mail: sales@autodarkhelmet.co.uk
Website: http://www.autodarkhelmet.co.uk
Directors: J. Devonport (Dir)
Immediate Holding Company: JADE PRODUCTS RUGBY LIMITED
Registration no: 05688913 **Date established:** 2006
No.of Employees: 1 - 10 **Product Groups:** 24, 36, 40, 63

Date of Accounts	Mar 11	Mar 10	Mar 09
Working Capital	24	14	-1
Fixed Assets	1	10	20
Current Assets	28	60	49

Bourton Group Ltd (Head Office)
Bourton Hall Bourton, Rugby, CV23 9SD
Tel: 01926-633333 **Fax:** 01926-633450
E-mail: info@bourton.co.uk
Website: http://www.bourton.co.uk
Bank(s): Barclays
Directors: J. Cresswell (Co Sec)
Immediate Holding Company: BOURTON GROUP LIMITED
Registration no: 02187570 **VAT No.:** GB 307 4571 65
Date established: 1987 **Turnover:** £2m - £5m **No.of Employees:** 11 - 20
Product Groups: 80, 81, 84

Date of Accounts	Dec 11	Dec 10	Dec 09
Working Capital	267	410	489
Fixed Assets	19	28	24
Current Assets	493	686	712
Current Liabilities	1	N/A	N/A

Brain Power International Ltd
Prospect Way, Rugby, CV21 3UU
Tel: 01788-568686 **Fax:** 01788-579917
E-mail: paul@callbpi.com
Website: http://www.callbpi.com
Managers: J. Brill
Immediate Holding Company: BRAIN POWER INTERNATIONAL LIMITED
Registration no: 01842016 **VAT No.:** GB 398 4782 80
Date established: 1984 **Turnover:** £500,000 - £1m
No.of Employees: 1 - 10 **Product Groups:** 32

Date of Accounts	Dec 11	Dec 10	Dec 09
Working Capital	-603	-340	-197
Fixed Assets	707	727	747
Current Assets	762	911	1m

W.G. Challenor
54 Coventry Road Pailton, Rugby, CV23 0QB
Tel: 01788-833301 **Fax:** 01788-833481
E-mail: mcjepp@mcjepp.co.uk
Website: http://www.wgchallenor.co.uk

Directors: W. Challenor (MD)
No.of Employees: 1 - 10 **Product Groups:** 39, 40, 43, 45, 46, 48, 67

Contitech

Chestnut Field House Chestnut Field, Rugby, CV21 2PA
Tel: 01788-571482 **Fax:** 01788-542245
Website: http://www.contitech.co.uk
Directors: M. Griffin (MD)
Immediate Holding Company: CONTITECH (GERMANY)
Registration no: 01076936 **Turnover:** £10m - £20m
No.of Employees: 1 - 10 **Product Groups:** 29

Converteam UK Ltd

Boughton Road, Rugby, CV21 1BU
Tel: 01788-563563 **Fax:** 01788-560767
E-mail: sales@converteam.com
Website: http://www.converteam.com
Bank(s): Lloyds TSB
Directors: A. Adkins (Pers), M. Studdart (Fin)
Managers: D. Prescott (Tech Serv Mgr), S. Raynor
Ultimate Holding Company: CVT HOLDINGS SAS (FRANCE)
Immediate Holding Company: GE ENERGY POWER CONVERSION UK LIMITED
Registration no: 05571739 **Date established:** 2005
Turnover: £250m - £500m **No.of Employees:** 501 - 1000
Product Groups: 37, 38, 44

Date of Accounts	Dec 10	Dec 09	Dec 08
Sales Turnover	319m	311m	277m
Pre Tax Profit/Loss	29m	31m	38m
Working Capital	59m	36m	33m
Fixed Assets	14m	12m	14m
Current Assets	189m	167m	164m
Current Liabilities	69m	93m	99m

Dana Spicer Europe Ltd

Unit 16 Davy Court, Rugby, CV23 0UZ
Tel: 01788-545370 **Fax:** 01788-545398
E-mail: michael.maidment@dana.com
Website: http://www.dana.com
Directors: M. Maidman (MD)
Managers: M. Maidment (Chief Acct), P. Wood (Purch Mgr)
Immediate Holding Company: DANA SPICER EUROPE LIMITED
Registration no: 00467474 **Date established:** 1949
Turnover: £75m - £125m **No.of Employees:** 1 - 10 **Product Groups:** 39

Draka UK

Unit C Swift Park Old Leicester Road, Rugby, CV21 1DZ
Tel: 01788-551944 **Fax:** 01788-536018
E-mail: keith.may@draka.com
Website: http://www.draka.com
Managers: K. May (Transport)
Ultimate Holding Company: DELTA P.L.C.
Registration no: 00002307 **Turnover:** £2m - £5m
No.of Employees: 11 - 20 **Product Groups:** 77

G S I Group Ltd

Cosford Lane Swift Valley Indl-Est, Rugby, CV21 1QN
Tel: 01788-570321 **Fax:** 01788-579824
E-mail: sales@jklasers.com
Website: http://www.gsiglasers.com
Bank(s): National Westminster Bank Plc
Directors: T. Miah (Fin), S. Kew (Co Sec), S. Kew (MD), R. Tomassoni (Mkt Research), M. Greenwood (MD)
Managers: H. Snape (Purch Mgr), T. Barsby (Comptroller), D. Rice (I.T. Exec), R. Jessett (Applic Mgr)
Ultimate Holding Company: GSI GROUP INC (CANADA)
Immediate Holding Company: GSI GROUP LIMITED
Registration no: 01041317 **Date established:** 1972
Turnover: £10m - £20m **No.of Employees:** 51 - 100 **Product Groups:** 37, 38, 46, 47

Date of Accounts	Dec 09	Dec 08	Dec 07
Sales Turnover	16m	33m	44m
Pre Tax Profit/Loss	-2m	-5m	3m
Working Capital	28m	27m	26m
Fixed Assets	5m	8m	15m
Current Assets	31m	31m	30m
Current Liabilities	942	1m	860

Gun Shop

62a Lawford Road, Rugby, CV21 2ED
Tel: 01788-575198 **Fax:** 01788-546360
E-mail: sales@gunshoprugby.com
Website: http://www.gunshoprugby.com
Directors: R. Coates (Ptnr)
Date established: 1979 **No.of Employees:** 1 - 10 **Product Groups:** 36, 39, 40

H K Technologies Ltd

Unit 7 Hadrians Way Glebe Farm Industrial Estate, Rugby, CV21 1ST
Tel: 01788-577288 **Fax:** 01788-562808
E-mail: smitht@hktechnology.com
Website: http://www.hktechnologies.com
Bank(s): Lloyds TSB Bank plc
Directors: T. Smith (Dir)
Ultimate Holding Company: H K (HOLDINGS) LIMITED
Immediate Holding Company: H K TECHNOLOGIES LIMITED
Registration no: 04658229 **Date established:** 2003 **Turnover:** £2m - £5m
No.of Employees: 11 - 20 **Product Groups:** 44, 46, 47

Date of Accounts	Mar 12	Mar 11	Mar 10
Working Capital	51	6	-49
Fixed Assets	41	49	45
Current Assets	819	533	746

Hafele UK Ltd

Brownsover Road, Rugby, CV21 1RD
Tel: 01788-542020 **Fax:** 01788-544440
E-mail: info@hafele.co.uk
Website: http://www.hafele.co.uk
Bank(s): HSBC Bank plc
Directors: G. Marlowe (MD)
Ultimate Holding Company: HAFELE HOLDING GMBH (GERMANY)
Immediate Holding Company: HAFELE U.K. LIMITED
Registration no: 01486136 **VAT No.:** GB 307 3713 76
Date established: 1980 **Turnover:** £75m - £125m
No.of Employees: 251 - 500 **Product Groups:** 25, 30, 35, 36

Date of Accounts	Dec 11	Dec 10	Dec 09
Sales Turnover	77m	79m	73m
Pre Tax Profit/Loss	8m	10m	9m
Working Capital	24m	23m	20m
Fixed Assets	20m	20m	21m
Current Assets	33m	34m	29m
Current Liabilities	5m	4m	3m

Innolas UK Ltd

67 Somers Road, Rugby, CV22 7DG
Tel: 01788-550777 **Fax:** 01788-550888
E-mail: sales@innolas.co.uk
Website: http://www.innolas.co.uk
Directors: J. Hull (Fin), I. Duckett (I.T. Dir)
Immediate Holding Company: INNOLAS (UK) LIMITED
Registration no: 03451423 **Date established:** 1997
Turnover: £500,000 - £1m **No.of Employees:** 1 - 10 **Product Groups:** 37, 48

Date of Accounts	Nov 11	Nov 10	Nov 09
Sales Turnover	905	602	660
Pre Tax Profit/Loss	72	25	2
Working Capital	301	278	266
Fixed Assets	60	8	13
Current Assets	492	349	378
Current Liabilities	84	49	23

Inspirational Labels

25 Noble Drive Cawston, Rugby, CV22 7FL
Tel: 01788-817047 **Fax:** 01788-817047
E-mail: rdore@inspirationallabels.com
Website: http://www.inspirationallabels.com
Directors: R. Dore (Prop)
Date established: 2006 **No.of Employees:** 1 - 10 **Product Groups:** 27

Intec Business College

Old School Pennington Court, Rugby, CV21 2BB
Tel: 01788-575090 **Fax:** 01788-575411
E-mail: nikki.allman@getoncourse.net
Website: http://www.getoncourse.net
Bank(s): Lloyds TSB Bank plc
Managers: T. Ivens (Fin Mgr), J. Webster, S. Wright, N. Allman (Mktg Serv Mgr), D. Ludlow (Tech Serv Mgr)
Immediate Holding Company: INTEC BUSINESS COLLEGES PLC
Registration no: 02494959 **Date established:** 1990 **Turnover:** £2m - £5m
No.of Employees: 11 - 20 **Product Groups:** 86

Date of Accounts	Sep 11	Sep 10	Sep 09
Sales Turnover	4m	5m	5m
Pre Tax Profit/Loss	-27	214	339
Working Capital	968	978	883
Fixed Assets	67	85	94
Current Assets	1m	1m	1m
Current Liabilities	142	283	328

J P Lennard Ltd

Swift Point, Rugby, CV21 1PX
Tel: 01788-542777 **Fax:** 01788- 541851
E-mail: nigel@jpl.co.uk
Website: http://www.jplennard.com
Bank(s): National Westminster Bank Plc
Directors: N. Lennard (Dir)
Immediate Holding Company: J.P. LENNARD LIMITED
Registration no: 00750393 **VAT No.:** GB 272 7438 41
Date established: 1963 **Turnover:** £5m - £10m **No.of Employees:** 21 - 50
Product Groups: 29, 49

Date of Accounts	Dec 11	Dec 10	Dec 09
Sales Turnover	10m	10m	10m
Pre Tax Profit/Loss	1m	1m	2m
Working Capital	2m	2m	3m
Fixed Assets	2m	2m	2m
Current Assets	3m	3m	4m
Current Liabilities	637	547	703

K & C Machinery Ltd

Midland Trading Estate Sparta Close, Rugby, CV21 1PS
Tel: 01788-576381 **Fax:** 01788-570182
E-mail: sales@kc-machinery.com
Website: http://www.kc-machinery.com
Directors: M. Gee (Dir)
Immediate Holding Company: K.& C.MACHINERY LIMITED
Registration no: 00649484 **VAT No.:** GB 272 5070 71
Date established: 1960 **Turnover:** £2m - £5m **No.of Employees:** 21 - 50
Product Groups: 67

Date of Accounts	Feb 12	Feb 11	Feb 10
Working Capital	1m	1m	992
Fixed Assets	92	71	95
Current Assets	2m	1m	2m

Lenoch Engineering Ltd

55 Somers Road, Rugby, CV22 7DG
Tel: 01788-576434 **Fax:** 01788-541398
E-mail: lenocheng@aol.com
Website: http://www.lenochengineering.com
Bank(s): National Westminster Bank Plc
Directors: J. Rushbrooke (MD)
Ultimate Holding Company: P & D ENGINEERING (COVENTRY) LTD.
Immediate Holding Company: LENOCH ENGINEERING LIMITED
Registration no: 04878090 **VAT No.:** GB 272 5765 36
Date established: 2003 **Turnover:** £250,000 - £500,000
No.of Employees: 21 - 50 **Product Groups:** 48

Date of Accounts	Dec 11	Dec 10	Dec 09
Working Capital	558	311	327
Fixed Assets	700	747	277
Current Assets	1m	1m	972

Mapal Ltd

Swift Park Old Leicester Road, Rugby, CV21 1DZ
Tel: 01788-574700 **Fax:** 01788-569551
E-mail: sales@uk.mapal.com
Website: http://www.mapal.com
Directors: P. Frey (Fin)
Managers: G. Lowe (Sales Admin), W. Whitehouse (Chief Mgr)
Immediate Holding Company: MAPAL LIMITED
Registration no: 02787157 **Date established:** 1993 **Turnover:** £5m - £10m
No.of Employees: 21 - 50 **Product Groups:** 36, 46, 66

Date of Accounts	Dec 11	Dec 10	Dec 09
Sales Turnover	10m	6m	5m
Pre Tax Profit/Loss	1m	685	290
Working Capital	2m	2m	2m
Fixed Assets	1m	2m	2m
Current Assets	4m	3m	3m
Current Liabilities	995	641	515

Metso Minerals UK Ltd

Parkfield Road, Rugby, CV21 1QJ
Tel: 01788-532100 **Fax:** 01788-560442
E-mail: sami.tackaluma@metso.com
Website: http://www.metso.com
Directors: T. Slator (MD)
Managers: S. Barnes (Personnel), M. Jarvis (Sales & Mktg Mg), R. Panchal (Tech Serv Mgr), S. Tackaluma
Ultimate Holding Company: METSO CORP (FINLAND)
Immediate Holding Company: METSO MINERALS (UK) LIMITED
Registration no: 01142030 **VAT No.:** GB 706 1528 55
Date established: 1973 **Turnover:** £10m - £20m
No.of Employees: 21 - 50 **Product Groups:** 29, 30, 40, 42, 45, 46, 67

Date of Accounts	Dec 11	Dec 10	Dec 09
Sales Turnover	12m	16m	22m
Pre Tax Profit/Loss	236	-2m	-5m
Working Capital	2m	-481	8m
Fixed Assets	12	658	102
Current Assets	7m	9m	14m
Current Liabilities	2m	2m	3m

Morgan Advanced Ceramics Ltd

4 Central Park Drive, Rugby, CV23 0WE
Tel: 01788-542166 **Fax:** 01788-541941
E-mail: theresa.linton@morganplc.com
Website: http://www.morganadvancedceramics.com
Bank(s): Lloyds TSB, Stourport-on-Severn
Directors: C. Cobb (MD)
Managers: D. Wykes (Accounts), K. Parker (Chief Mgr), B. Lambert (I.T. Exec), T. Linton (Personnel), T. Linton
Ultimate Holding Company: MORGAN CRUCIBLE CO. P.L.C.
Immediate Holding Company: MORGAN CRUCIBLE COMPANY PLC(THE)
Registration no: 00262938 **Turnover:** £20m - £50m
No.of Employees: 51 - 100 **Product Groups:** 48

Peter Moulton

25 The Horsepool Lilbourne, Rugby, CV23 0SU
Tel: 01788-860575
E-mail: info@petermoulton.com
Website: http://www.petermoulton.com
Directors: P. Moulton (Prop)
No.of Employees: 1 - 10 **Product Groups:** 33, 34

Niagara Ltd

Central Warehouse Paynes Lane, Rugby, CV21 2UW
Tel: 01788-542191 **Fax:** 01788-535352
E-mail: growson@niag.com
Website: http://www.macreadys.co.uk
Bank(s): HSBC Bank plc
Directors: J. Withers (Fin), G. Rowson (MD)
Managers: J. Timhill (Sales & Mktg Mg)
Ultimate Holding Company: KNIA HOLDINGS INC (USA)
Immediate Holding Company: NIAGARA-LASALLE (UK) LTD
Registration no: 03725308 **Date established:** 1999
Turnover: £75m - £125m **No.of Employees:** 21 - 50 **Product Groups:** 34, 35, 36

Parcels To Ireland

Lawford Road, Rugby, CV21 2UY
Tel: 01788-542500 **Fax:** 01788-550896
E-mail: christopher.putt@parcelstoireland.co.uk
Website: http://www.parcelstoireland.co.uk
Directors: C. Putt (Dir), N. Putt (Dir), N. Putt (Co Sec)
Immediate Holding Company: PARCELS TO IRELAND LIMITED
Registration no: 02389345 **Date established:** 1989
Turnover: £500,000 - £1m **No.of Employees:** 1 - 10 **Product Groups:** 72

Date of Accounts	Dec 09	Dec 08	Dec 07
Working Capital	467	370	368
Fixed Assets	377	408	432
Current Assets	1m	941	1m

Pro Enviro Ltd

8 Davy Court Central Park, Rugby, CV23 0UZ
Tel: 01788-538150 **Fax:** 01788-538151
E-mail: nersisalehi@proenviro.com
Website: http://www.proenviro.com
Directors: S. Stones (Chief Op Offcr)
Immediate Holding Company: PRO ENVIRO LIMITED
Registration no: 02973663 **Date established:** 1994
Turnover: £500,000 - £1m **No.of Employees:** 11 - 20 **Product Groups:** 80

Date of Accounts	Sep 11	Sep 10	Sep 09
Working Capital	7	9	-5
Fixed Assets	72	72	88
Current Assets	229	190	314

Profit Growth Unlimited

21 Ruskin Close, Rugby, CV22 5RU
Tel: 01788-812050
E-mail: info@profit-growth.co.uk
Website: http://www.profit-growth.co.uk
Directors: J. Holder (Prop)
Turnover: Up to £250,000 **No.of Employees:** 1 - 10 **Product Groups:** 44

Reco Floors

28 Faraday Road, Rugby, CV22 5ND
Tel: 01788-569980 **Fax:** 01788-569978
E-mail: info@recoflooring.co.uk
Website: http://recoflooring.co.uk
Directors: C. Pugh (Prop)
Immediate Holding Company: RECO FLOORING LTD
Registration no: 03654190 **Date established:** 1998
Turnover: Up to £250,000 **No.of Employees:** 1 - 10 **Product Groups:** 52

Rugby Electronics

57 Somers Road, Rugby, CV22 7DG
Tel: 01788-572492 **Fax:** 01788-540005
E-mail: mel@rugbyelectronics.com
Website: http://www.rugbyelectronics.com
Directors: M. Hoskin (Prop)
VAT No.: GB 272 7072 57 **No.of Employees:** 1 - 10 **Product Groups:** 35, 37, 38, 44, 49, 84

Rugby Fabrications

9 Upton Road, Rugby, CV22 7DL
Tel: 01788-543090 **Fax:** 01788-537623
E-mail: info@rugbyfabs.fsnet.co.uk
Website: http://www.rugbyfabrications.co.uk

see next page

***Rugby Fabrications** - Cont'd*
Directors: J. Cressey (Prop)
No.of Employees: 1 - 10 **Product Groups:** 35

Rugby Paper Sacks Ltd
70 Vernon Avenue, Rugby, CV22 5HP
Tel: 01788-844171 **Fax:** 01788-844172
Website: http://www.rugbypapersacks.co.uk
Directors: A. Wilson (Fin), J. Wilson (MD)
Immediate Holding Company: RUGBY PAPER SACKS LIMITED
Registration no: 04837630 **Date established:** 2003
No.of Employees: 1 - 10 **Product Groups:** 35, 42

Date of Accounts	Dec 11	Dec 10	Dec 08
Working Capital	1	N/A	4
Fixed Assets	N/A	N/A	1
Current Assets	30	31	30

Rugby Recruitment Services Ltd
26 Regent Place, Rugby, CV21 2PN
Tel: 01788-541601 **Fax:** 01788-543590
E-mail: jobs@rugbyrecruitment.co.uk
Website: http://www.rugbyrecruitment.co.uk
Directors: C. Bend (MD)
Immediate Holding Company: RUGBY RECRUITMENT SERVICES LIMITED
Registration no: 02251793 **Date established:** 1988 **Turnover:** £2m - £5m
No.of Employees: 1 - 10 **Product Groups:** 80

Date of Accounts	Oct 11	Oct 10	Oct 09
Working Capital	522	440	384
Fixed Assets	27	10	11
Current Assets	866	723	595

S D I Group UK Ltd
20 Somers Road Somers Road Industrial Estate, Rugby, CV22 7DH
Tel: 01788-574666 **Fax:** 01788-574696
E-mail: sales@sdigroupuk.com
Website: http://www.sdigroupuk.com
Directors: H. Smith (Prop)
Immediate Holding Company: SDI GROUP PLC
Registration no: 03298541 **Date established:** 1998
No.of Employees: 11 - 20 **Product Groups:** 35, 39, 45

Shaw Sheet Metal
2-6 Upton Road, Rugby, CV22 7DL
Tel: 01788-536033 **Fax:** 01788-536922
E-mail: sales@shawsheetmetal.co.uk
Website: http://www.shawsheetmetal.co.uk
Bank(s): Lloyds TSB
Directors: P. Shaw (MD), V. Shaw (Fin)
Immediate Holding Company: SHAW SHEET METAL (RUGBY) LIMITED
Registration no: 02589661 **VAT No.:** 536 1982 28 **Date established:** 1991
Turnover: £250,000 - £500,000 **No.of Employees:** 21 - 50
Product Groups: 48

Date of Accounts	Jul 11	Jul 10	Jul 09
Working Capital	135	104	179
Fixed Assets	1m	2m	1m
Current Assets	1m	981	1m

Stagecoach Ltd
Railway Terrace, Rugby, CV21 3HS
Tel: 01788-535555 **Fax:** 01788-572221
E-mail: wark.enquiries@stagecoachbus.com
Website: http://www.stagecoachbus.com
Directors: S. Burd (MD)
Managers: A. Rideout (Sales & Mktg Mg), A. Rideout (Mktg Serv Mgr)
Ultimate Holding Company: STAGECOACH GROUP PLC
Immediate Holding Company: STAGECOACH LIMITED
Registration no: 03092390 **Date established:** 1995
Turnover: £10m - £20m **No.of Employees:** 101 - 250 **Product Groups:** 72

Date of Accounts	Apr 11	Apr 10	Apr 09
Pre Tax Profit/Loss	-251	-240	-531
Working Capital	-13	203	412
Current Assets	2m	2m	2m

T D T Technology Ltd
Unit 20 Woodside Park, Rugby, CV21 2NP
Tel: 01788-570411 **Fax:** 01788-567632
E-mail: sales@tdt-technology.co.uk
Website: http://www.tdt-technology.co.uk
Directors: S. Hewson (Dir)
Immediate Holding Company: T.D.T. (TECHNOLOGY) LIMITED
Registration no: 02807286 **VAT No.:** GB 623 5637 42
Date established: 1993 **Turnover:** £1m - £2m **No.of Employees:** 1 - 10
Product Groups: 67

Date of Accounts	Dec 11	Dec 10	Dec 09
Working Capital	80	58	58
Fixed Assets	5	2	4
Current Assets	324	196	184

Technoset
Unit 3a Roman Way, Glebe Farm Industrial Estate, Rugby, CV21 1DB
Tel: 01788-560522 **Fax:** 01788-541196
E-mail: sales@technoset.com
Website: http://www.technoset.com
Bank(s): Lloyds TSB
Directors: M. Ronayne (Fin), K. Kane (MD)
Ultimate Holding Company: TECHNO GROUP LIMITED
Immediate Holding Company: TECHNOSET LIMITED
Registration no: 03061083 **VAT No.:** GB 661 3053 62
Date established: 1995 **No.of Employees:** 11 - 20 **Product Groups:** 35

Date of Accounts	Dec 11	Dec 10	Dec 09
Working Capital	212	56	-14
Fixed Assets	39	39	47
Current Assets	581	437	307

21st Century Lighting 21st Century Lighting
Ronaldsay Main Street, Willey, Rugby, CV23 0SH
Tel: 01455-203027 **Fax:** 01455-203028
E-mail: sales@21stcenturylighting.com
Website: http://www.21stcenturylighting.com
Directors: M. Conner (Prop)
Immediate Holding Company: 21ST CENTURY LIGHTING & SECURITY LTD
Registration no: 06846411 **Date established:** 2009
No.of Employees: 1 - 10 **Product Groups:** 37, 38, 40, 48, 67

WAGO Ltd
Triton Park Swift Valley Industrial Estate, Rugby, CV21 1SG
Tel: 01788-568008 **Fax:** 01788-568050
E-mail: uksales@wago.com
Website: http://www.wago.com
Bank(s): HSBC Bank plc
Directors: D. Tarlton (Co Sec), G. Smith (MD)
Managers: A. Wyatt, L. Gillis, N. Tarlton, P. Witherington (Mktg Serv Mgr), J. Bourne
Ultimate Holding Company: WAGO KONTAKTTECHNICK GMBH & CO KG (GERMANY)
Immediate Holding Company: WAGO LIMITED
Registration no: 02495884 **VAT No.:** GB 528 5203 55
Date established: 1990 **Turnover:** £10m - £20m
No.of Employees: 21 - 50 **Product Groups:** 30, 37, 52

Date of Accounts	Dec 11	Dec 10	Dec 09
Sales Turnover	11m	11m	10m
Pre Tax Profit/Loss	381	N/A	-29
Working Capital	3m	2m	2m
Fixed Assets	60	69	39
Current Assets	3m	3m	3m
Current Liabilities	563	656	396

Whitehouse Plastics Ltd
Unit 4 Tiber Way Glebe Farm Industrial Estate, Rugby, CV21 1ED
Tel: 01788-541042 **Fax:** 01788-552314
E-mail: sales@whitehouseplastics.co.uk
Website: http://www.whitehouseplastics.co.uk
Directors: M. Whitehouse (MD)
Immediate Holding Company: WHITEHOUSE PLASTICS LIMITED
Registration no: 02254125 **VAT No.:** GB 531 9812 43
Date established: 1988 **Turnover:** £500,000 - £1m
No.of Employees: 1 - 10 **Product Groups:** 30

Date of Accounts	Mar 12	Mar 11	Mar 10
Working Capital	233	222	168
Fixed Assets	76	79	88
Current Assets	313	343	332

Zeiss
Unit 2 Hadrians Way Glebe Farm Industrial Estate, Rugby, CV21 1ST
Tel: 01788-821770 **Fax:** 01788-821755
E-mail: a.thompson@zeiss.co.uk
Website: http://www.zeiss.co.uk
Managers: A. Thompson (Mgr)
No.of Employees: 21 - 50 **Product Groups:** 46

Shipston On Stour

Mathew C Blythe & Son Ltd
The Green Tredington, Shipston On Stour, CV36 4NJ
Tel: 01608-662295 **Fax:** 01608-662006
E-mail: sales@matthewcblythe.co.uk
Website: http://www.mcblythe.co.uk
Directors: C. Blythe (Co Sec)
Immediate Holding Company: MATTHEW C.BLYTHE & SON LIMITED
Registration no: 00900189 **Date established:** 1967 **Turnover:** £1m - £2m
No.of Employees: 1 - 10 **Product Groups:** 33, 37, 38

Date of Accounts	Mar 12	Mar 11	Mar 10
Sales Turnover	2m	N/A	2m
Pre Tax Profit/Loss	140	N/A	122
Working Capital	1m	1m	1m
Fixed Assets	4	6	10
Current Assets	2m	2m	2m
Current Liabilities	175	91	138

Holdsworth Windows Ltd
Shipston Industrial Estate Darlingscote Road, Shipston On Stour, CV36 4PR
Tel: 01608-661883 **Fax:** 01608-661008
E-mail: info@holdsworthwindows.co.uk
Website: http://www.holdsworthwindows.co.uk
Directors: M. Glover (MD)
Immediate Holding Company: HOLDSWORTH WINDOWS LIMITED
Registration no: 00924242 **Date established:** 1967
No.of Employees: 11 - 20 **Product Groups:** 26, 35

Date of Accounts	Nov 11	Nov 10	Nov 09
Working Capital	494	450	406
Fixed Assets	45	53	69
Current Assets	635	587	563

Lightmaster Direct
Unit 17 Blackwell Business Park Blackwell, Shipston On Stour, CV36 4PE
Tel: 01608-682115 **Fax:** 01608-682114
E-mail: info@lightmaster-direct.co.uk
Website: http://www.lightmaster-direct.co.uk
Directors: R. Nock (MD)
Immediate Holding Company: LIGHTMASTER (DIRECT) LTD
Registration no: 03611133 **Date established:** 1998
No.of Employees: 1 - 10 **Product Groups:** 37, 67

Date of Accounts	Sep 11	Sep 10	Sep 09
Working Capital	2	-19	-39
Fixed Assets	44	52	49
Current Assets	248	196	187

Mandalay Venue Finding
East Wing Stourton, Shipston On Stour, CV36 5HJ
Tel: 0870-0201610 **Fax:** 0870-0201611
E-mail: look@mandalaypartners.co.uk
Website: http://www.mandalaypartners.co.uk
Directors: L. Fairbrother (MD)
Date established: 2001 **No.of Employees:** 1 - 10 **Product Groups:** 89

Mattei Compressors Ltd
Admington Lane Admington, Shipston On Stour, CV36 4JJ
Tel: 01789-450577 **Fax:** 01789-450698
E-mail: andy.jones@mattei.co.uk
Website: http://www.mattei.co.uk
Directors: A. Jones (Fin)
Ultimate Holding Company: ABBEY HOLDINGS SA (LUXEMBOURG)
Immediate Holding Company: MATTEI COMPRESSORS LIMITED
Registration no: 02100638 **Date established:** 1987 **Turnover:** £1m - £2m
No.of Employees: 1 - 10 **Product Groups:** 40, 48, 67, 83

Date of Accounts	Dec 11	Dec 10	Dec 09
Working Capital	584	576	636
Fixed Assets	38	32	29
Current Assets	1m	1m	992

Midland Slurry Systems Ltd
Shepherds Close Whichford, Shipston On Stour, CV36 5PG
Tel: 01608-684415 **Fax:** 01608-684723
E-mail: peter@midlandslurrysystems.co.uk
Website: http://www.midlandslurrysystems.co.uk
Directors: D. Russell (Co Sec)
Immediate Holding Company: MIDLAND SLURRY SYSTEMS LIMITED
Registration no: 02847114 **Date established:** 1993
No.of Employees: 1 - 10 **Product Groups:** 41

Date of Accounts	Nov 11	Nov 10	Nov 09
Working Capital	-37	-55	-46
Fixed Assets	197	146	135
Current Assets	225	188	199

Morris Conferencing
The Old School New Street, Shipston On Stour, CV36 4EN
Tel: 08701-624909 **Fax:** 01608-682862
E-mail: info@corporateconferences.co.uk
Website: http://www.uk-conference-venues.co.uk
Directors: M. Morris (MD)
Immediate Holding Company: MORRIS CONFERENCING ETC LIMITED
Registration no: 03976769 **Date established:** 2000
Turnover: Up to £250,000 **No.of Employees:** 1 - 10 **Product Groups:** 69, 81, 83, 89

Date of Accounts	Apr 11	Apr 10	Apr 09
Sales Turnover	N/A	164	231
Pre Tax Profit/Loss	N/A	11	36
Working Capital	2	7	-4
Fixed Assets	5	7	10
Current Assets	24	27	27
Current Liabilities	N/A	15	25

Process Link Ltd
Tilemans Lane, Shipston On Stour, CV36 4QZ
Tel: 01608-662878 **Fax:** 01608-662968
E-mail: info@processlink.co.uk
Website: http://www.processlink.co.uk
Directors: C. Snape (Co Sec)
Managers: B. Bosworth (Sales Prom Mgr)
Immediate Holding Company: PROCESS LINK LIMITED
Registration no: 02272506 **Date established:** 1988
Turnover: £500,000 - £1m **No.of Employees:** 21 - 50 **Product Groups:** 54

Date of Accounts	Mar 12	Mar 11	Mar 10
Working Capital	575	701	575
Fixed Assets	851	848	861
Current Assets	631	876	669

Wright Wrought Iron
Unit 5 Blackwell Business Park Blackwell, Shipston On Stour, CV36 4PE
Tel: 01608-682600 **Fax:** 0121-707 1003
Website: http://www.wrightwroughtiron.co.uk
Directors: J. Wright (Prop)
Date established: 1999 **No.of Employees:** 1 - 10 **Product Groups:** 26, 35

Southam

AL-KO Kober Ltd
South Warwickshire Business Park Kineton Rd, Southam, CV47 0AL
Tel: 01926-818500 **Fax:** 01926-818562
E-mail: marketing@al-ko.co.uk
Website: http://www.al-ko.co.uk
Bank(s): Barclays, The Parade
Directors: P. Eustace (MD)
Managers: P. Jones (Mktg Serv Mgr), H. Kober, H. Hiller, A. Sparkes (Accounts), G. Hudson (Purch Mgr)
Ultimate Holding Company: AL-KO Kober AG (Germany)
Immediate Holding Company: AL-KO Kober (Holdings) Ltd
Registration no: 00492005 **VAT No.:** GB 272 3073 75
Date established: 1937 **Turnover:** £20m - £50m
No.of Employees: 51 - 100 **Product Groups:** 36, 39, 40, 41, 45, 67, 68

Date of Accounts	Dec 11	Dec 10	Dec 09
Sales Turnover	29m	28m	23m
Pre Tax Profit/Loss	1m	2m	694
Working Capital	8m	7m	7m
Fixed Assets	4m	4m	4m
Current Assets	10m	12m	9m
Current Liabilities	1m	2m	926

B K Marine Systems Ltd
Wigrams Tomlow Road, Stockton, Southam, CV47 8HX
Tel: 01926-810310 **Fax:** 01926-810310
Website: http://www.boatcentralheating.co.uk
Directors: B. Kaye (MD), J. Kaye (MD), A. Kaye (Fin)
Immediate Holding Company: B K MARINE SYSTEMS LIMITED
Registration no: 06568067 **Date established:** 2008
Turnover: £500,000 - £1m **No.of Employees:** 1 - 10 **Product Groups:** 35, 36, 39

Date of Accounts	Jun 09
Working Capital	-15
Fixed Assets	16
Current Assets	37

W E Bates Ltd
Bath Meadow Gaydon Road, Bishops Itchington, Southam, CV47 2QZ
Tel: 01926-613222 **Fax:** 01926-614222
E-mail: sales@w-e-bates.com
Website: http://www.w-e-bates.com
Bank(s): Barclays
Directors: J. Baynham (Sales), W. Romney (MD)
Immediate Holding Company: W E BATES LIMITED
Registration no: 05332144 **Date established:** 2005 **Turnover:** £2m - £5m
No.of Employees: 11 - 20 **Product Groups:** 36, 48, 66

Date of Accounts	Dec 11	Dec 10	Dec 09
Working Capital	401	184	111
Fixed Assets	187	216	236
Current Assets	906	901	571

Central Surveys
Ladbroke Farm Ladbroke, Southam, CV47 2BY
Tel: 01926-812380
Website: http://www.centralsurveys.co.uk
Directors: D. Allcott (Prop)
Date established: 2003 **No.of Employees:** 1 - 10 **Product Groups:** 35

Date of Accounts	Apr 11
Working Capital	-3
Fixed Assets	49

Current Assets	6

Clearwater Group
Welsh Road East, Southam, CV47 1NA
Tel: 01926-818283 **Fax:** 01926-818284
E-mail: sales@clearwatergroup.co.uk
Website: http://www.clearwatergroup.co.uk
Directors: J. Dalby (Dir), S. Hogarth (Co Sec), R. Allen (MD)
Ultimate Holding Company: CLEARWATER GROUP INTERNATIONAL LIMITED
Immediate Holding Company: CLEARWATER SYSTEMS LTD
Registration no: 04525993 **Date established:** 2002
No.of Employees: 11 - 20 **Product Groups:** 38, 42

Date of Accounts	Mar 11	Mar 10	Mar 09
Working Capital	-177	-154	-121
Fixed Assets	961	935	935
Current Assets	28	51	38

Compton Buildings
Station Works Fenny Compton, Southam, CV47 2XB
Tel: 01295-770111 **Fax:** 01295-770748
E-mail: richard.curtis@compton-buildings.co.uk
Website: http://www.comptonbuildings.co.uk
Bank(s): National Westminster Bank Plc
Directors: R. Curtis (MD)
Ultimate Holding Company: MARSHALLS PLC
Immediate Holding Company: MARSHALLS MONO LTD
Registration no: 03325457 **VAT No.:** GB 687 8943 51
Date established: 1958 **Turnover:** £10m - £20m
No.of Employees: 21 - 50 **Product Groups:** 25, 33

Date of Accounts	Dec 06	Dec 05
Pre Tax Profit/Loss	N/A	1543
Working Capital	1106	1106
Current Assets	1106	1106
Total Share Capital	240	240

Dywidag Systems International Ltd
Northfield Road Kineton Road Industrial Estate, Southam, CV47 0FG
Tel: 01926-813980 **Fax:** 01926-813817
E-mail: sales@dywidag.co.uk
Website: http://www.dywidag-systems.com/uk
Bank(s): HSBC Bank plc
Directors: C. Irvin (Tech Sales), I. Jarvis (Comm)
Managers: T. Coton (Comptroller)
Immediate Holding Company: DYWIDAG SYSTEMS INTERNATIONAL LIMITED
Registration no: 02049781 **Date established:** 1986 **Turnover:** £5m - £10m
No.of Employees: 21 - 50 **Product Groups:** 34, 35, 45, 51, 84

Date of Accounts	Dec 11	Dec 10	Dec 09
Sales Turnover	9m	7m	8m
Pre Tax Profit/Loss	568	-635	359
Working Capital	2m	1m	2m
Fixed Assets	1m	2m	2m
Current Assets	3m	3m	4m
Current Liabilities	543	449	717

Elite Spiral Stairs
Unit 7 Elite House Blue Lias Industrial Estate Rugby Road, Stockton, Southam, CV47 8HN
Tel: 01926-812060 **Fax:** 01926-812825
E-mail: contact@elitespiralstairs.co.uk
Website: http://www.elitespiralstairs.co.uk
Directors: S. Scott (Prop)
Immediate Holding Company: ELITE SPIRAL STAIRS LTD
Registration no: 06982445 **Date established:** 2009
No.of Employees: 1 - 10 **Product Groups:** 25, 35, 40

Date of Accounts	Sep 11	Sep 10
Working Capital	11	11
Fixed Assets	4	5
Current Assets	72	69

Metallic Protectives Ltd
Unit 1 The Cobalt Centre Kineton Road, Southam, CV47 0FD
Tel: 01926-811851 **Fax:** 01926-815801
E-mail: garryn@pmdgroup.co.uk
Website: http://www.pmdgroup.co.uk
Bank(s): National Westminster Bank Plc
Directors: G. Newman (MD)
Ultimate Holding Company: P.M.D. GROUP LIMITED
Immediate Holding Company: METALLIC PROTECTIVES LIMITED
Registration no: 00422735 **VAT No.:** GB 272 6078 50
Date established: 1946 **No.of Employees:** 21 - 50 **Product Groups:** 48

Date of Accounts	Dec 11	Dec 10	Dec 09
Working Capital	73	52	11
Fixed Assets	214	255	302
Current Assets	881	844	797
Current Liabilities	N/A	N/A	233

Power Deck Ltd
Unit 1a Canalside Industrial Estate Wharf Road Fenny Compton, Southam, CV47 2XD
Tel: 01295-771135 **Fax:** 01295-770838
E-mail: sales@powerdeck.co.uk
Website: http://www.powerdeck.co.uk
Directors: E. Bromage (MD), S. Leather (Fin)
Immediate Holding Company: POWERDECK LIMITED
Registration no: 04365378 **Date established:** 2002 **Turnover:** £1m - £2m
No.of Employees: 1 - 10 **Product Groups:** 26

Date of Accounts	Mar 11	Mar 10	Mar 09
Working Capital	-126	-107	-90
Fixed Assets	8	49	93
Current Assets	105	114	132

Praxair Surface Technologies Ltd
Westfield Road Kineton Road Industrial Estate, Southam, CV47 0JH
Tel: 01926-812348 **Fax:** 01926-817775
E-mail: paul_kent@praxair.com
Website: http://www.praxair.com
Bank(s): Bank of America
Managers: P. Kent (Mgr)
Ultimate Holding Company: PRAXAIR INC (USA)
Immediate Holding Company: PRAXAIR SURFACE TECHNOLOGIES LIMITED
Registration no: 02416734 **VAT No.:** GB 535 6150 54
Date established: 1989 **No.of Employees:** 21 - 50 **Product Groups:** 48

Date of Accounts	Dec 11	Dec 10	Dec 09
Sales Turnover	36m	33m	24m
Pre Tax Profit/Loss	2m	-710	2m
Working Capital	4m	148	2m
Fixed Assets	12m	15m	10m
Current Assets	10m	8m	5m
Current Liabilities	2m	2m	2m

Prima Lingua UK
Brewsters Corner Pendicke Street, Southam, CV47 1PN
Tel: 01926-817972 **Fax:** 01926-812873
E-mail: info@primalingua.com
Website: http://primalingua.com
Directors: A. Ashton (MD)
Immediate Holding Company: PRIMA LINGUA (UK) LIMITED
Registration no: 04466449 **VAT No.:** GB 753 7624 12
Date established: 2002 **Turnover:** £1m - £2m **No.of Employees:** 1 - 10
Product Groups: 44, 80

Date of Accounts	Jun 11	Jun 10	Jun 07
Working Capital	388	142	37
Fixed Assets	7	9	12
Current Assets	605	242	224

Scholastic School Book Fairs
Unit 6 Westfield Road, Southam, CV47 0RA
Tel: 0800-212281 **Fax:** 0845-603 9092
E-mail: enquiries@scholastic.co.uk
Website: http://www.scholastics.co.uk
Managers: J. Goodchild (Mgr)
Ultimate Holding Company: SCHOLASTIC CORP (USA)
Immediate Holding Company: SCHOLASTIC BOOK FAIRS LTD
Registration no: 01186606 **VAT No.:** GB 241 3593 76
Date established: 1974 **Turnover:** £5m - £10m **No.of Employees:** 1 - 10
Product Groups: 28

Date of Accounts	May 11	May 10	May 08
Working Capital	N/A	N/A	1m
Current Assets	N/A	N/A	1m

Southam Tyres
Southam Drive Kineton Road Industrial Estate, Southam, CV47 0RB
Tel: 01926-813510 **Fax:** 01926-817724
E-mail: sales@southamtyres.co.uk
Website: http://www.protyre.co.uk
Bank(s): Barclays
Managers: S. Archer, F. Tate (Sales & Mktg Mg)
Immediate Holding Company: JUST TYRES HOLDINGS LTD
Registration no: 02263290 **Date established:** 1986
Turnover: £500,000 - £1m **No.of Employees:** 21 - 50 **Product Groups:** 29

Wandfluh UK Ltd
Northfield Road Kineton Road Industrial Estate, Southam, CV47 0FG
Tel: 01926-810081 **Fax:** 01926-810066
E-mail: sales@wandfluh.co.uk
Website: http://www.wandfluh.co.uk
Bank(s): Barclays
Directors: T. Allen (MD)
Ultimate Holding Company: WANDFLUH HOLDINGS AG (SWITZERLAND)
Immediate Holding Company: WANDFLUH UK LIMITED
Registration no: 02635311 **Date established:** 1991 **Turnover:** £2m - £5m
No.of Employees: 11 - 20 **Product Groups:** 37, 38, 40, 67

Date of Accounts	Dec 11	Dec 10	Dec 09
Working Capital	1m	559	534
Fixed Assets	554	481	484
Current Assets	2m	2m	986

Stratford Upon Avon

A G D Equipment Ltd
Avonbrook House 198 Masons Road, Stratford Upon Avon, CV37 9LQ
Tel: 01789-292227 **Fax:** 01789-268350
E-mail: info@agd-equipment.co.uk
Website: http://www.agd-equipment.co.uk
Directors: W. Law (Ch), R. Law (MD), L. Law (Gen Sec)
Managers: E. Law (Commun Mgr), T. Owen (Comptroller)
Ultimate Holding Company: AGD HOLDINGS PLC
Immediate Holding Company: AGD EQUIPMENT LIMITED
Registration no: 01275753 **Date established:** 1976
Turnover: £10m - £20m **No.of Employees:** 51 - 100 **Product Groups:** 34, 35, 38, 45, 51, 66, 67, 80

Date of Accounts	Jun 11	Jun 10	Jun 09
Sales Turnover	10m	14m	15m
Pre Tax Profit/Loss	483	2m	2m
Working Capital	1m	648	-807
Fixed Assets	13m	12m	16m
Current Assets	4m	3m	4m
Current Liabilities	263	925	319

Arden Garages Ltd
Masons Road, Stratford Upon Avon, CV37 9NF
Tel: 01789-267446 **Fax:** 01789-414446
E-mail: dt@ardengarages.co.uk
Website: http://www.ardengarages.co.uk
Bank(s): HSBC Bank plc
Directors: D. Titchmarsh (Dir)
Managers: R. Ingram (Sales Prom Mgr)
Immediate Holding Company: ARDEN GARAGES LIMITED
Registration no: 00458326 **VAT No.:** GB 272 3502 78
Date established: 1948 **No.of Employees:** 11 - 20 **Product Groups:** 39

Date of Accounts	Dec 09	Dec 08	Dec 07
Working Capital	407	421	415
Fixed Assets	1m	1m	1m
Current Assets	727	682	721

Arringold Steel Fabricators
Whitehill Building Alderminster, Stratford Upon Avon, CV37 8BW
Tel: 01789-450716 **Fax:** 01789-450826
E-mail: arringold@btconnect.com
Directors: E. Arnold (MD)
Managers: D. Arnold (Mgr)
Immediate Holding Company: YOUNG PLANTS LIMITED
Registration no: 01473363 **Date established:** 1941
No.of Employees: 1 - 10 **Product Groups:** 35

Date of Accounts	Jul 10	Jul 09	Jul 08
Working Capital	333	357	255
Fixed Assets	837	845	842
Current Assets	2m	2m	2m

Astromezz Ltd
Unit B1 Beecham Buildings Rough Farm Industrial Estate, Atherstone On Stour, Stratford Upon Avon, CV37 8DX
Tel: 01789-450041 **Fax:** 01789-450081
E-mail: sales@astromezz.co.uk
Website: http://www.astromezz.co.uk
Directors: B. Chadwick (Fin), S. Kennedy (MD)
Immediate Holding Company: ASTROMEZZ LIMITED
Registration no: 03415576 **Date established:** 1997
No.of Employees: 1 - 10 **Product Groups:** 26, 35

Date of Accounts	Aug 11	Aug 10	Aug 09
Working Capital	-20	-15	-15
Fixed Assets	35	31	36
Current Assets	86	104	47

Bio Clinique
The Exchange Mill Lane, Newbold on Stour, Stratford Upon Avon, CV37 8DR
Tel: 01789-450304 **Fax:** 01789-450892
Website: http://www.bioclinique.co.uk
Directors: M. Robertson-Smith (MD), C. Robertson-Smith (Sales)
Ultimate Holding Company: Scientific & Industrial Technology Ltd
Registration no: 04929818 **VAT No.:** GB 687 8948 41
Turnover: £250,000 - £500,000 **No.of Employees:** 1 - 10
Product Groups: 38

Date of Accounts	Oct 06	Oct 05	Oct 04
Working Capital	9	8	9
Fixed Assets	N/A	N/A	1
Current Assets	14	14	17
Current Liabilities	5	6	8
Total Share Capital	5	5	5

Bridgetown Developments Ltd
13 John Street, Stratford Upon Avon, CV37 6UB
Tel: 01789-414646 **Fax:** 01789-414475
E-mail: iancartwright@bridgetowndevelopments.co.uk
Website: http://www.bridgetowndevelopments.co.uk
Directors: J. Cartwright (Fin), I. Cartwright (MD)
Immediate Holding Company: BRIDGETOWN DEVELOPMENTS LIMITED
Registration no: 01889730 **Date established:** 1985
No.of Employees: 1 - 10 **Product Groups:** 26, 35

Date of Accounts	May 12	May 11	May 10
Working Capital	325	383	368
Fixed Assets	5	4	5
Current Assets	488	515	412

Building Profiles Ltd
Timothys Bridge Road Stratford Enterprise Park, Stratford Upon Avon, CV37 9NQ
Tel: 01789-414044 **Fax:** 01789-415273
E-mail: info@buildingprofiles.co.uk
Website: http://www.buildingprofiles.co.uk
Bank(s): Lloyds TSB Bank plc
Directors: J. Cheriton (MD)
Immediate Holding Company: BUILDING PROFILES LIMITED
Registration no: 01309274 **VAT No.:** GB 307 0091 02
Date established: 1977 **Turnover:** £1m - £2m **No.of Employees:** 11 - 20
Product Groups: 25, 29, 30, 36, 40

Date of Accounts	Mar 11	Mar 10	Mar 09
Working Capital	383	365	368
Fixed Assets	256	276	298
Current Assets	746	688	755

Bulte Plastics Ltd
13 John Street, Stratford Upon Avon, CV37 6UB
Tel: 01789-263753 **Fax:** 01789-264015
E-mail: sales@bulteplastics.co.uk
Website: http://www.bulte.com
Directors: S. Haner (Sales)
Immediate Holding Company: BULTE PLASTICS (UK) LIMITED
Registration no: 03787175 **Date established:** 1999
No.of Employees: 1 - 10 **Product Groups:** 30, 35

Date of Accounts	Dec 10	Dec 09	Dec 07
Working Capital	42	25	15
Fixed Assets	1	1	2
Current Assets	67	82	65

Crescent Industrial
170 Masons Road, Stratford Upon Avon, CV37 9NF
Tel: 08453-377695 **Fax:** 08453-378695
E-mail: info@c-ind.co.uk
Website: http://www.crescentindustrial.co.uk
Managers: S. Stacy (Mgr)
No.of Employees: 1 - 10 **Product Groups:** 37, 40, 45, 49, 52, 63, 83

D G Protective Coatings
12 Banbury Road Ettington, Stratford Upon Avon, CV37 7TB
Tel: 01789-740286 **Fax:** 01789-740599
E-mail: sales@dgprotective.co.uk
Website: http://www.dgprotective.co.uk
Directors: D. Gee (Prop)
Date established: 1977 **Turnover:** Up to £250,000
No.of Employees: 1 - 10 **Product Groups:** 32

Bruce Davis Associates
Meadow House Ingon Lane, Stratford Upon Avon, CV37 0QF
Tel: 01789-731007 **Fax:** 01789-731003
E-mail: info@bda.co.uk
Website: http://www.bda.co.uk
Directors: M. Davis (Ptnr)
Immediate Holding Company: BDA BUSINESS INTELLIGENCE LIMITED
Registration no: 04380631 **Date established:** 2002
Turnover: £10m - £20m **No.of Employees:** 1 - 10 **Product Groups:** 81

Date of Accounts	Dec 06	Dec 05	Dec 04
Working Capital	28	29	29
Fixed Assets	16	18	19
Current Assets	90	79	94
Current Liabilities	62	50	65

C T Farr
Timothys Bridge Road Stratford Enterprise Park, Stratford Upon Avon, CV37 9NQ
Tel: 01789-267161 **Fax:** 01789-415719
Directors: E. Farr (Prop)
Immediate Holding Company: STRATFORD FINANCIAL SERVICES LIMITED
Registration no: 04127176 **Date established:** 2003
No.of Employees: 1 - 10 **Product Groups:** 26, 35, 36, 41, 45, 48

Grange Tool & Industrial
Ingon Lane, Stratford Upon Avon, CV37 0QF
Tel: 01789-731741
E-mail: sales@grangetool.co.uk
Website: http://www.grangetool.co.uk
Directors: S. Gardner (Snr Part)
Date established: 1994 **No.of Employees:** 1 - 10 **Product Groups:** 46

Grove Industries Ltd
Unit 5 The Courtyard Timothys Bridge Road, Stratford Enterprise Park, Stratford Upon Avon, CV37 9NP
Tel: 01789-415566 **Fax:** 01789-415501
E-mail: info@groveind.co.uk
Website: http://www.gilinvestments.com
Directors: L. Litwinowicz (Grp Chief Exec)
Managers: T. Middleton
Immediate Holding Company: GROVE INDUSTRIES LIMITED
Registration no: 02566311 **Date established:** 1990
Turnover: £20m - £50m **No.of Employees:** 1 - 10 **Product Groups:** 80, 82

Date of Accounts	Dec 07	Mar 11	Mar 10
Sales Turnover	N/A	35m	29m
Pre Tax Profit/Loss	3m	2m	2m
Working Capital	9m	7m	6m
Fixed Assets	5m	12m	12m
Current Assets	9m	19m	15m
Current Liabilities	541	4m	5m

Guns & Sports
26 Henley Street, Stratford Upon Avon, CV37 6QW
Tel: 01789-267100 **Fax:** 01789-267100
Directors: J. Cooper (Ptnr)
Date established: 1975 **No.of Employees:** 1 - 10 **Product Groups:** 36, 39, 40

Guy Salmon Land Rover
Avenue Farm Industrial Estate Birmingham Road, Stratford Upon Avon, CV37 0HR
Tel: 01789-205990 **Fax:** 01789-268932
E-mail: nealdelo@sytner.co.uk
Website: http://www.sytner.co.uk/guy-salmon-land-rover
Directors: M. Morris (Co Sec), G. Nieuwenhuys (Dir), R. Dunn (MD)
Managers: N. Delo, G. Sim
Immediate Holding Company: GUY SALMON LIMITED
Registration no: 03574418 **Date established:** 1998
No.of Employees: 21 - 50 **Product Groups:** 39

Holdsworth Personnel Ltd
27 Rother Street, Stratford Upon Avon, CV37 6NE
Tel: 01926-316866 **Fax:** 01926-453852
E-mail: recruit@holdsworthpersonnel.com
Website: http://www.holdsworthpersonnel.com
Directors: C. Sheen (Mkt Research), P. Muir (Dir)
Immediate Holding Company: HOLDSWORTH PERSONNEL LIMITED
Registration no: 03817013 **VAT No.:** GB 436 8088 25
Date established: 1999 **Turnover:** £1m - £2m **No.of Employees:** 1 - 10
Product Groups: 80, 86

Date of Accounts	Apr 12	Apr 11	Apr 10
Working Capital	-25	-35	-34
Fixed Assets	96	108	123
Current Assets	39	27	31

Thomas Jacks Ltd
Unit B2 The Bridge Business Centre, Stratford Enterprise Park, Stratford Upon Avon, CV37 9HW
Tel: 01789-264100 **Fax:** 01789-264200
E-mail: sales@thomasjacks.co.uk
Website: http://www.thomasjacks.co.uk
Directors: M. Gosbell (Dir)
Immediate Holding Company: THOMAS JACKS LIMITED
Registration no: 02911691 **Date established:** 1994 **Turnover:** £1m - £2m
No.of Employees: 1 - 10 **Product Groups:** 38, 67

Date of Accounts	Aug 11	Aug 10	Aug 09
Working Capital	1m	1m	1m
Fixed Assets	424	394	396
Current Assets	2m	1m	2m

Listgrove Ltd
16 The Courtyard Timothys Bridge Road, Stratford Enterprise Park, Stratford Upon Avon, CV37 9NP
Tel: 01789-207070 **Fax:** 01789-207096
E-mail: contact@listgrove.com
Website: http://www.listgrove.com
Directors: R. Kirby (Chief Op Offcr)
Ultimate Holding Company: SURFCALL LIMITED
Immediate Holding Company: LISTGROVE LIMITED
Registration no: 01197713 **Date established:** 1975 **Turnover:** £1m - £2m
No.of Employees: 1 - 10 **Product Groups:** 20, 27, 28, 30, 31, 32, 34, 38, 42, 44, 48, 67, 80, 85, 86

Date of Accounts	Dec 11	Dec 10	Dec 09
Working Capital	36	22	8
Fixed Assets	12	13	15
Current Assets	165	128	112

Pageant Graphics Ltd
Mulbury House 201 Banbury Road, Stratford Upon Avon, CV37 7HT
Tel: 01789-292829 **Fax:** 01789-298270
E-mail: jim@pageantgraphics.co.uk
Website: http://www.pageantgraphics.co.uk
Directors: S. Page (MD)
Immediate Holding Company: PAGEANT GRAPHICS LIMITED
Registration no: 01747572 **Date established:** 1983
No.of Employees: 1 - 10 **Product Groups:** 29, 32, 44, 67

Date of Accounts	Apr 12	Apr 11	Apr 10
Working Capital	2m	2m	2m
Fixed Assets	289	315	100
Current Assets	2m	2m	2m

Pashley Cycles Ltd
Masons Road, Stratford Upon Avon, CV37 9NL
Tel: 01789-292263 **Fax:** 01789-414201
E-mail: hello@pashley.co.uk
Website: http://www.pashley.co.uk
Bank(s): Natwest
Directors: A. Williams (Dir)
Managers: L. Pillinger (Mktg Serv Mgr), K. White (Fin Mgr)
Immediate Holding Company: PASHLEY HOLDINGS LIMITED
Registration no: 02974132 **VAT No.:** GB 661 5514 42
Date established: 1994 **Turnover:** £2m - £5m **No.of Employees:** 21 - 50
Product Groups: 39

Date of Accounts	Dec 11	Dec 10	Dec 09
Working Capital	2m	1m	1m
Fixed Assets	470	482	483
Current Assets	2m	2m	2m

Pressavon Ltd
Masons Road Stratford Enterprise Park, Stratford Upon Avon, CV37 9NP
Tel: 01789-206610 **Fax:** 01789-415735
E-mail: sales@pressavon.co.uk
Website: http://www.pressavon.co.uk
Directors: T. Barnsdale (MD)
Ultimate Holding Company: TAPPEX THREAD INSERTS LIMITED
Immediate Holding Company: PRESSAVON LIMITED
Registration no: 00491242 **Date established:** 1951
Turnover: £250,000 - £500,000 **No.of Employees:** 1 - 10
Product Groups: 39, 46, 48

Date of Accounts	Dec 11	Dec 10	Dec 09
Sales Turnover	585	487	472
Pre Tax Profit/Loss	-7	-107	-44
Working Capital	1m	1m	1m
Fixed Assets	337	377	408
Current Assets	1m	1m	1m
Current Liabilities	40	39	14

Radarlux Radar Systems UK Ltd
1a Grove Business Park Atherstone On Stour, Stratford Upon Avon, CV37 8DX
Tel: 01789-459199 **Fax:** 01789-459143
E-mail: salesassist@radarlux.co.uk
Website: http://www.radarlux.co.uk
Directors: K. French (Dir)
Immediate Holding Company: RADARLUX RADAR SYSTEMS (U.K) LIMITED
Registration no: 04780703 **Date established:** 2003
No.of Employees: 1 - 10 **Product Groups:** 38, 39, 46

Date of Accounts	May 11	May 10	May 09
Working Capital	84	82	83
Fixed Assets	1	2	1
Current Assets	116	138	169

Sims Garden Machinery Ltd
20-21 The Waterways, Stratford Upon Avon, CV37 0AW
Tel: 01789-205671 **Fax:** 01789-299006
E-mail: admin@simsgardenmachinery.co.uk
Website: http://www.simsgardenmachinery.co.uk
Directors: B. Sims (MD), C. Sims (Fin)
Immediate Holding Company: SIMS GARDEN MACHINERY LIMITED
Registration no: 00308487 **VAT No.:** GB 109 9733 44
Date established: 1935 **Turnover:** £1m - £2m **No.of Employees:** 1 - 10
Product Groups: 41

Date of Accounts	Sep 11	Sep 10	Sep 09
Working Capital	100	153	193
Fixed Assets	980	1m	1m
Current Assets	399	382	504

Sims Group U K Ltd (Sims Group)
Long Marston, Stratford Upon Avon, CV37 8AQ
Tel: 01789-720 431 **Fax:** 01789-720 940
Website: http://www.sims-group.co.uk
Directors: J. Price (Dir)
Managers: T. Howe (Reg Mgr), D. Shelbourne (Sales Admin)
Registration no: 03242331 **Date established:** 1968 **Turnover:** £2m - £5m
No.of Employees: 21 - 50 **Product Groups:** 54

Sims Recycling Solutions
Long Marston, Stratford Upon Avon, CV37 8AQ
Tel: 01789-720431 **Fax:** 01789-720940
E-mail: infouk@mirec.com
Website: http://eu.simsrecycling.com
Managers: P. Miller
Ultimate Holding Company: SITA
Immediate Holding Company: MIREC BV
Registration no: SC141132 **No.of Employees:** 101 - 250
Product Groups: 44, 48, 66, 67

Si-Plan Electronics Research Ltd
8-9 Avenue Farm Industrial Estate Birmingham Road, Stratford Upon Avon, CV37 0HR
Tel: 01789-205849 **Fax:** 01789-415550
E-mail: enquiries@si-plan.com
Website: http://www.si-plan.com
Bank(s): Barclays
Directors: M. Bollons (MD), T. Stanberry Flynn (Dir), A. Bollons (Dir)
Immediate Holding Company: SI PLAN ELECTRONICS (RESEARCH) LIMITED
Registration no: 01362444 **VAT No.:** 307 0347 90 **Date established:** 1978
Turnover: £500,000 - £1m **No.of Employees:** 11 - 20
Product Groups: 37, 38, 44, 45

Date of Accounts	Mar 11	Mar 10	Mar 09
Working Capital	1m	1m	872
Fixed Assets	779	754	575
Current Assets	2m	2m	1m

Sitel UK Ltd
Sitel House Timothys Bridge Road, Stratford Enterprise Park, Stratford Upon Avon, CV37 9HY
Tel: 01789-299622 **Fax:** 01789-292341
E-mail: karl.brough@sitel.co.uk
Website: http://www.sitel.com
Bank(s): Royal Bank of Scotland
Directors: N. Russell-smith (Mkt Research), K. Brough (Dir), J. Hayward (Fin)
Managers: B. Butterworth (Personnel), J. Wilkins (Purch Mgr)
Ultimate Holding Company: ONEX CORPORATION (CANADA)
Immediate Holding Company: SITEL UK LIMITED
Registration no: 03450786 **VAT No.:** GB 551 4553 52
Date established: 1997 **Turnover:** £50m - £75m
No.of Employees: 251 - 500 **Product Groups:** 81

Date of Accounts	Dec 11	Dec 10	Dec 09
Sales Turnover	60m	46m	48m
Pre Tax Profit/Loss	-503	-1m	5m
Working Capital	6m	456	1m
Fixed Assets	3m	3m	3m
Current Assets	50m	24m	20m
Current Liabilities	4m	3m	3m

Space Electronics
Unit 12 Avenue Fields Industrial Estate Farm Avenue, Stratford Upon Avon, CV37 0HT
Tel: 01789-269179 **Fax:** 01789-295757
E-mail: sales@space-electronics.co.uk
Website: http://www.space-electronics.co.uk
Directors: D. Crossley (Dir)
Immediate Holding Company: SPACE ELECTRONICS LTD.
Registration no: 03330558 **Date established:** 1997 **Turnover:** £1m - £2m
No.of Employees: 1 - 10 **Product Groups:** 37, 38, 44

Date of Accounts	Mar 12	Mar 11	Mar 10
Working Capital	424	405	407
Fixed Assets	3	1	1
Current Assets	567	535	478

Spring & Presstech
111 Aston Cantlow Road Wilmcote, Stratford Upon Avon, CV37 9XW
Tel: 01789-204531 **Fax:** 01789-264064
E-mail: cnjleedfl@aol.com
Website: http://www.springandpresstech.com
Directors: N. Lee (MD)
No.of Employees: 1 - 10 **Product Groups:** 35

Stebul Furniture Tubes Ltd
35 Timothys Bridge Road Stratford Enterprise Park, Stratford Upon Avon, CV37 9NQ
Tel: 01789-207479 **Fax:** 01789-207478
E-mail: sales@stebul.co.uk
Website: http://www.stebul.co.uk
Directors: S. Murphy (MD), S. Murphy (Dir), R. Poole (MD), S. Fellows (Fin)
Ultimate Holding Company: COLOR ESTATES LIMITED
Immediate Holding Company: STEBUL FURNITURE LIMITED
Registration no: 03484305 **Date established:** 1997
No.of Employees: 1 - 10 **Product Groups:** 26, 36, 67

Date of Accounts	Dec 10	Dec 09	Dec 08
Working Capital	20	33	36
Current Assets	171	83	67

Structured Training Ltd
Prospero Barn The Green, Snitterfield, Stratford Upon Avon, CV37 0TR
Tel: 01789-734300 **Fax:** 01789-730791
E-mail: info@structuredtraining.com
Website: http://www.structuredtraining.com
Bank(s): Lloyds TSB Bank plc
Directors: A. Brown (Dir)
Immediate Holding Company: STRUCTURED TRAINING LIMITED
Registration no: 02776864 **Date established:** 1993 **Turnover:** £1m - £2m
No.of Employees: 11 - 20 **Product Groups:** 80, 81, 85, 86

Date of Accounts	Dec 11	Dec 10	Dec 09
Working Capital	234	226	223
Fixed Assets	520	524	528
Current Assets	334	302	292

Sweet Knowle Aquatics
Sweet Knowle Farm Sweet Knowle, Preston on Stour, Stratford Upon Avon, CV37 8NR
Tel: 01789-450036 **Fax:** 01789-450036
E-mail: sweetknowleaquatics@hotmail.com
Website: http://www.sweetknowleaquatics.co.uk
Directors: D. Harding (Prop)
No.of Employees: 1 - 10 **Product Groups:** 32, 37, 42, 67

T U V Product Service
Snitterfield Road Bearley, Stratford Upon Avon, CV37 0EX
Tel: 01789-731155 **Fax:** 01789-731264
E-mail: admin@tuvps.co.uk
Website: http://www.tuvps.co.uk
Managers: D. West (Mgr)
Date established: 1992 **Turnover:** Over £1,000m **No.of Employees:** 1 - 10
Product Groups: 37, 44, 67, 85

Tappex Thread Inserts Ltd
Masons Road, Stratford Upon Avon, CV37 9NT
Tel: 01789-206600 **Fax:** 01789-414194
E-mail: sales@tappex.co.uk
Website: http://www.tappex.co.uk
Bank(s): HSBC Bank plc
Directors: T. Barnsdale (MD), J. Bebbington (Fin)
Managers: D. Fielding (Admin Off), R. Hunt (Chief Acct), T. Warner (Tech Serv Mgr), A. Fitzpatrick (Mktg Serv Mgr)
Immediate Holding Company: TAPPEX THREAD INSERTS LIMITED
Registration no: 00575166 **VAT No.:** GB 273 1109 84
Date established: 1956 **Turnover:** £5m - £10m **No.of Employees:** 21 - 50
Product Groups: 30, 35, 39, 42, 66

Date of Accounts	Dec 11	Dec 10	Dec 09
Sales Turnover	7m	6m	4m
Pre Tax Profit/Loss	809	467	-622
Working Capital	6m	5m	5m
Fixed Assets	1m	1m	1m
Current Assets	7m	6m	5m
Current Liabilities	670	383	248

The Berdant Group
Avenue Farm Industrial Estate Birmingham Road, Stratford Upon Avon, CV37 0HR
Tel: 01789-293722 **Fax:** 01789-295397
E-mail: marketing@biffa.co.uk
Website: http://www.biffa.co.uk
Managers: N. Smith (District Mgr), J. Hughes (Comm)
Immediate Holding Company: UNIVERSAL TESTING LABORATORIES LIMITED
Registration no: 00946107 **Date established:** 1997
Turnover: Up to £250,000 **No.of Employees:** 51 - 100
Product Groups: 32, 54

Date of Accounts	Mar 99	Mar 02	Mar 01
Working Capital	1	1	3
Fixed Assets	2	N/A	1
Current Assets	8	7	9

Watling & Hope
1 Goldicote Business Park Banbury Road, Goldicote, Stratford Upon Avon, CV37 7NB
Tel: 01789-740757 **Fax:** 01789-740404
E-mail: enquiries@watlinghopedirect.co.uk
Website: http://www.watling-hope.co.uk
Directors: M. Palin (Fin), M. Palin (Ch), D. Sexton (Fin)
Managers: A. Newman (Reg Sales Mgr)
Immediate Holding Company: WATLING HOPE (INSTALLATIONS) LIMITED

Registration no: 02837332 **Date established:** 1993 **Turnover:** £5m - £10m
No.of Employees: 11 - 20 **Product Groups:** 42

Date of Accounts	Jul 11	Jul 10	Jul 09
Sales Turnover	5m	5m	4m
Pre Tax Profit/Loss	240	311	216
Working Capital	31	48	25
Fixed Assets	60	64	102
Current Assets	1m	1m	874
Current Liabilities	226	302	227

WinterfieldSafes.co.uk (Styles Creative Ltd)

Midland House Wharf Road, Stratford Upon Avon, CV37 0AD
Tel: 0845-0048328 **Fax:** 01677-450774
E-mail: info@winterfieldsafes.co.uk
Website: http://www.winterfieldsafes.co.uk
Directors: A. Willis (Fin), H. Bell (Dir)
Immediate Holding Company: Winterfield Safes Ltd
Registration no: 05379420 **Date established:** 2005
Turnover: £250,000 - £500,000 **No.of Employees:** 1 - 10
Product Groups: 35, 36

Date of Accounts	Mar 07	Mar 06
Working Capital	43	20
Fixed Assets	1	N/A
Current Assets	68	23
Current Liabilities	25	3

Wright Manufacturing Services Ltd

9 Avenue Farm Industrial Estate Birmingham Road, Stratford Upon Avon, CV37 0HR
Tel: 01789-299859 **Fax:** 01789-414346
E-mail: sales@wrightmfg.co.uk
Website: http://www.wrightmfg.co.uk
Directors: K. Joyce (MD), P. White (Fin)
Immediate Holding Company: WRIGHT MANUFACTURING SERVICES LIMITED
Registration no: 01731086 **Date established:** 1983
Turnover: Up to £250,000 **No.of Employees:** 11 - 20 **Product Groups:** 35

Date of Accounts	Aug 11	Aug 10	Aug 09
Working Capital	724	683	587
Fixed Assets	264	298	334
Current Assets	1m	970	814

Studley

Dispense Technology Services Ltd

19a Watts Road, Studley, B80 7PT
Tel: 01527-853014 **Fax:** 01527-853014
E-mail: j_pickering@btconnect.com
Website: http://www.beer-coolers.co.uk
Directors: T. Pickering (Fin)
Immediate Holding Company: DISPENSE TECHNOLOGY SERVICES LIMITED
Registration no: 02782281 **Date established:** 1993
Turnover: Up to £250,000 **No.of Employees:** 1 - 10 **Product Groups:** 40

Date of Accounts	Jan 11	Jan 10	Jan 09
Working Capital	11	7	9
Fixed Assets	1	1	1
Current Assets	33	31	36

High Road Records Ltd

The Granary Manor Farm Morton Bagot, Studley, B80 7ED
Tel: 01527-857013
E-mail: info@highroadballoons.co.uk
Website: http://www.highroadballoons.co.uk
Directors: R. Collins (MD), K. Collins (Fin)
Immediate Holding Company: HIGH ROAD VENTURES LTD
Registration no: 04399427 **Date established:** 2002
Turnover: Up to £250,000 **No.of Employees:** 1 - 10 **Product Groups:** 39, 75

Date of Accounts	Mar 12	Mar 11	Mar 10
Working Capital	-12	-15	-12
Fixed Assets	9	11	17
Current Assets	15	17	16

M S M Environmental Services Ltd

Liberal House Bell Lane, Studley, B80 7LR
Tel: 01527-852344 **Fax:** 01527-853115
E-mail: admin@msmenvironmental.co.uk
Website: http://www.msmenvironmental.co.uk
Directors: A. Mcdonald (MD), W. Smith (Fin)
Immediate Holding Company: M.S.M. ENVIRONMENTAL SERVICES LIMITED
Registration no: 03051722 **Date established:** 1995
No.of Employees: 1 - 10 **Product Groups:** 54

Date of Accounts	Jun 11	Jun 10	Jun 09
Working Capital	59	35	74
Fixed Assets	57	46	15
Current Assets	230	237	224

Namco Tooling Ltd

New Road, Studley, B80 7LZ
Tel: 01527-853667 **Fax:** 01527-852668
E-mail: gsc@namco-tooling.com
Website: http://www.namco-tooling.com
Bank(s): HSBC Bank plc
Directors: G. Cooke (Dir)
Immediate Holding Company: NAMCO TOOLING LIMITED
Registration no: 01863234 **VAT No.:** GB 416 9022 60
Date established: 1984 **Turnover:** £500,000 - £1m
No.of Employees: 21 - 50 **Product Groups:** 36, 46, 48

Date of Accounts	Mar 11	Mar 10	Mar 09
Working Capital	286	318	340
Fixed Assets	577	577	608
Current Assets	492	512	548

Standard Industry Ltd

34 High Street, Studley, B80 7HJ
Tel: 01527-850020 **Fax:** 01527-850021
E-mail: info@standard-industry.com
Website: http://www.standard-industry.com
Directors: H. Simoens (Dir), P. Cholle (Fin)
Immediate Holding Company: STANDARD INDUSTRY LIMITED
Registration no: 02209604 **Date established:** 1988
No.of Employees: 1 - 10 **Product Groups:** 45

Date of Accounts	Dec 11	Dec 10	Dec 09
Working Capital	-20	-25	-36
Fixed Assets	1	4	10
Current Assets	269	73	37

Techni Measure

Alexandra Buildings 59 Alcester Road, Studley, B80 7NJ
Tel: 01527-854103 **Fax:** 01527-853267
E-mail: sales@techni-measure.co.uk
Website: http://www.techni-measure.co.uk
Directors: P. Ramage (Ptnr)
Managers: I. Ramage (Sales Prom Mgr)
Immediate Holding Company: TECHNIMEASURE LIMITED
Registration no: 01824810 **VAT No.:** GB 208 2692 65
Date established: 1971 **Turnover:** £1m - £2m **No.of Employees:** 1 - 10
Product Groups: 37, 38, 39, 40, 45, 85

Wexco Ltd

Unit 6 Poplars Industrial Estate Redditch Road, Studley, B80 7AY
Tel: 01527-852919
E-mail: sales@wexco.com
Website: http://www.wexco.com
Directors: A. Rose (MD)
Immediate Holding Company: WEXCO LIMITED
Registration no: 01946148 **Date established:** 1985
Turnover: £250,000 - £500,000 **No.of Employees:** 11 - 20
Product Groups: 30, 40

Date of Accounts	Sep 11	Sep 10	Sep 09
Working Capital	-26	-60	-36
Fixed Assets	112	111	110
Current Assets	83	54	63

Warwick

Alchemie Ltd

Warwick Road Kineton, Warwick, CV35 0HU
Tel: 01926-641600 **Fax:** 01926-641698
E-mail: sales@alchemie.com
Website: http://www.alchemie.com
Directors: M. Haggett (Dir)
Immediate Holding Company: ALCHEMIE LIMITED
Registration no: 02185916 **Date established:** 1987 **Turnover:** £2m - £5m
No.of Employees: 11 - 20 **Product Groups:** 30, 31, 32

Date of Accounts	Mar 11	Mar 10	Mar 09
Working Capital	2m	2m	1m
Fixed Assets	8	14	30
Current Assets	2m	2m	2m

Aluminium Service Co Warwick Ltd

Millers Road, Warwick, CV34 5AE
Tel: 01926-491824 **Fax:** 01926-410072
E-mail: info@aluminiumservice.co.uk
Website: http://www.aluminiumservice.co.uk
Directors: P. Brown (Fin), A. Brown (MD)
Immediate Holding Company: ALUMINIUM SERVICE COMPANY (WARWICK) LIMITED
Registration no: 00390061 **Date established:** 1944
Turnover: £500,000 - £1m **No.of Employees:** 11 - 20
Product Groups: 34, 39

Date of Accounts	Dec 11	Dec 10	Dec 09
Working Capital	247	271	453
Fixed Assets	505	562	630
Current Assets	613	637	688

Baxi Group UK Ltd

Brooks House Coventry Road, Warwick, CV34 4LL
Tel: 08706-096096 **Fax:** 01926-410006
E-mail: lee.robinson@baxi.co.uk
Website: http://www.baxigroup.com
Managers: L. Robinson
Ultimate Holding Company: BDR THERMEA GROUP BV (NETHERLANDS)
Immediate Holding Company: BAXI GROUP LIMITED
Registration no: 04061959 **Date established:** 2000
Turnover: £125m - £250m **No.of Employees:** 251 - 500
Product Groups: 40

Date of Accounts	Dec 11	Dec 10	Dec 09
Pre Tax Profit/Loss	25m	3m	49m
Working Capital	-44m	-71m	-74m
Fixed Assets	154m	160m	160m
Current Assets	940m	911m	888m
Current Liabilities	2m	4m	5m

Bespoke Wheels Ltd

Unit 2 Block B Harriott Drive, Heathcote Industrial Estate, Warwick, CV34 6TJ
Tel: 01926-887722
E-mail: sales@bespokewheels.co.uk
Website: http://www.bespoketyres.co.uk
Managers: M. Mannion (Mgr)
Immediate Holding Company: BESPOKE WHEELS LIMITED
Registration no: 04694018 **Date established:** 2003
Turnover: Up to £250,000 **No.of Employees:** 1 - 10 **Product Groups:** 29

Date of Accounts	Mar 11	Mar 10	Mar 09
Working Capital	24	-1	-1
Fixed Assets	5	6	10
Current Assets	57	27	31

Bridgestone UK Ltd

Athena Drive Tachbrook Park, Warwick, CV34 6UX
Tel: 01926-488500 **Fax:** 01926-488600
E-mail: john.mcnaught@bridgestone-eu.com
Website: http://www.bridgestone.eu
Directors: F. Iijima (Sales & Mktg), J. Folliss (Co Sec), J. Mcnaught (MD), P. Curran (Fin), P. Lorrie (Pers)
Managers: J. Bushell (Tech Serv Mgr)
Ultimate Holding Company: BRIDGESTONE CORPORATION
Immediate Holding Company: BRIDGESTONE UK LIMITED
Registration no: 01040790 **Date established:** 1972
Turnover: £250m - £500m **No.of Employees:** 251 - 500
Product Groups: 29

Date of Accounts	Dec 11	Dec 10	Dec 09
Sales Turnover	270m	251m	256m
Pre Tax Profit/Loss	4m	3m	4m
Working Capital	22m	20m	20m
Fixed Assets	9m	9m	6m
Current Assets	79m	89m	93m
Current Liabilities	5m	4m	5m

Bubbles Translation Services

Unit 2 Olympus Court, Tachbrook Park, Warwick, CV34 6RZ
Tel: 08707-777750 **Fax:** 08707-777751
E-mail: info@bubblestrans.com
Website: http://www.bubblestrans.com
Directors: N. Jeewa (Dir)
No.of Employees: 1 - 10 **Product Groups:** 80

Date of Accounts	Jan 09	Jan 08	Jan 07
Working Capital	189	102	369
Fixed Assets	599	601	1
Current Assets	333	328	480
Current Liabilities	144	225	111

Calor Gas Ltd

Athena Drive Tachbrook Park, Warwick, CV34 6RL
Tel: 01926-330088 **Fax:** 01926-420609
E-mail: srennie@calor.co.uk
Website: http://www.calor.co.uk
Bank(s): Lloyds TSB
Directors: J. Wakkerman (Fin), S. Rennie (MD)
Ultimate Holding Company: SHV HOLDINGS NV (NETHERLANDS)
Immediate Holding Company: CALOR GAS LIMITED
Registration no: 00303703 **VAT No.:** GB 207 6109 84
Date established: 1935 **Turnover:** £250m - £500m
No.of Employees: 251 - 500 **Product Groups:** 18, 31, 36, 40

Date of Accounts	Dec 11	Dec 08	Dec 09
Sales Turnover	479m	446m	390m
Pre Tax Profit/Loss	54m	41m	36m
Working Capital	69m	76m	76m
Fixed Assets	180m	167m	169m
Current Assets	162m	155m	149m
Current Liabilities	21m	16m	13m

Cranequip Ltd

Cattell Road Cape Industrial Estate, Warwick, CV34 4JN
Tel: 01926-406900 **Fax:** 01926-406910
E-mail: cranequip@uk.gantry.com
Website: http://www.cranequip.com
Directors: R. Shearsby (Co Sec)
Ultimate Holding Company: DPM HOLDINGS SA (BELGUIM)
Immediate Holding Company: CRANEQUIP LIMITED
Registration no: 02025458 **VAT No.:** GB 443 9986 96
Date established: 1986 **Turnover:** £2m - £5m **No.of Employees:** 1 - 10
Product Groups: 37, 39, 45

Date of Accounts	Dec 11	Dec 10	Dec 09
Working Capital	347	929	99
Fixed Assets	7	7	6
Current Assets	612	5m	1m

C S C Forecourt Services Ltd (Petrol Retail)

6 Timon View Heathcote, Warwick, CV34 6ES
Tel: 01926-882377 **Fax:** 01926-882377
E-mail: info@cscspec.com
Website: http://www.cscspec.com
Directors: L. Binnie (Fin)
Immediate Holding Company: CSC FORECOURT SERVICES LIMITED
Registration no: 05188651 **Date established:** 2004
Turnover: Up to £250,000 **No.of Employees:** 1 - 10 **Product Groups:** 35, 39, 48, 52, 67

Date of Accounts	Jul 11	Jul 10	Jul 09
Working Capital	-9	-11	-8
Fixed Assets	18	19	24
Current Assets	65	40	31

Dca Design International Ltd

19 Church Street, Warwick, CV34 4AB
Tel: 01926-499461 **Fax:** 01926-401134
E-mail: sales@dca-design.com
Website: http://www.dca-design.com
Bank(s): National Westminster Bank Plc
Managers: D. Barraud
Ultimate Holding Company: DCA DESIGN INTERNATIONAL LIMITED
Immediate Holding Company: DCA DESIGN INTERNATIONAL LIMITED
Registration no: 01995159 **VAT No.:** GB 307 1291 86
Date established: 1986 **Turnover:** £10m - £20m
No.of Employees: 101 - 250 **Product Groups:** 28, 30, 38, 44, 48, 49, 66, 67, 80, 81, 84, 85

Date of Accounts	May 11	May 10	May 09
Sales Turnover	12m	10m	9m
Pre Tax Profit/Loss	3m	2m	2m
Working Capital	3m	2m	1m
Fixed Assets	1m	1m	1000
Current Assets	8m	5m	5m
Current Liabilities	4m	3m	3m

Delphi Lockheed Automotive Ltd

PO Box 1743, Warwick, CV34 6ZQ
Tel: 01926-470000 **Fax:** 01926-472000
E-mail: info@aplockheed.com
Website: http://www.delphi.com
Directors: J. Parsons (MD)
Ultimate Holding Company: DELPHI AUTOMOTIVE LLP
Immediate Holding Company: DELPHI LOCKHEED AUTOMOTIVE LIMITED
Registration no: 03796206 **VAT No.:** GB 487 7667 70
Date established: 1999 **Turnover:** £75m - £125m
No.of Employees: 251 - 500 **Product Groups:** 35, 39, 43, 84

Date of Accounts	Dec 11	Dec 10	Dec 09
Sales Turnover	97m	86m	72m
Pre Tax Profit/Loss	7m	6m	4m
Working Capital	11m	4m	261
Fixed Assets	3m	2m	962
Current Assets	41m	41m	35m
Current Liabilities	10m	9m	7m

Delta A G Ltd

10 The Butts, Warwick, CV34 4SS
Tel: 01926-493017 **Fax:** 01926-403711
E-mail: davidj@delta-ag.co.uk
Website: http://www.delta-ag.co.uk

see next page

Delta A G Ltd - *Cont'd*

Directors: D. Francis (Dir)
Immediate Holding Company: DELTA (A.G.) LIMITED
Registration no: 03045501 **Date established:** 1995
Turnover: £250,000 - £500,000 **No.of Employees:** 1 - 10
Product Groups: 32, 52

Date of Accounts	Jul 11	Jul 10	Jul 09
Working Capital	-66	-45	-19
Fixed Assets	2	1	2
Current Assets	35	41	53

Durr Ltd

Broxell Close, Warwick, CV34 5QF
Tel: 01926-418800 **Fax:** 01926-400679
E-mail: bsiddorn@durr.co.uk
Website: http://www.durr.com
Directors: B. Siddorn (Co Sec)
Managers: B. Dovey (Sales Prom Mgr), S. Curzons (Personnel), S. Edwards (Tech Serv Mgr), H. Matcham (Fin Mgr)
Ultimate Holding Company: DURR AG (GERMANY)
Immediate Holding Company: DURR LIMITED
Registration no: 01002684 **Date established:** 1971
Turnover: £20m - £50m **No.of Employees:** 51 - 100 **Product Groups:** 45, 46, 47, 48, 80

Date of Accounts	Dec 11	Dec 10	Dec 09
Sales Turnover	24m	32m	48m
Pre Tax Profit/Loss	2m	829	700
Working Capital	6m	5m	5m
Fixed Assets	1m	1m	1m
Current Assets	15m	10m	31m
Current Liabilities	3m	3m	12m

Eagleburgmann Industries UK Llp

Welton Road, Warwick, CV34 5PZ
Tel: 01926-417600 **Fax:** 01926-417617
E-mail: warwick@uk.eagleburgmann.co.uk
Website: http://www.burgmann.com
Directors: B. Finlayson (MD)
Ultimate Holding Company: FEODOR BURGMANN DICHTUNGSWERKE GMBH & CO. KG (DEU)
Registration no: 02393188 **VAT No.:** GB 544 8371 27
Date established: 1994 **Turnover:** £10m - £20m
No.of Employees: 21 - 50 **Product Groups:** 25, 29, 30, 32, 33

Fairhurst

19-20 Wellesbourne House Walton Road, Wellesbourne, Warwick, CV35 9JB
Tel: 01789-470512 **Fax:** 01789-470619
E-mail: gary.speller@fairhurst.co.uk
Website: http://www.fairhurst.co.uk
Directors: G. Speller (Tech Serv)
Ultimate Holding Company: WARWICK ENERGY HOLDINGS LIMITED
Immediate Holding Company: DUDGEON OFFSHORE WIND LIMITED
Registration no: SC159839 **Date established:** 2002
Turnover: £10m - £20m **No.of Employees:** 1 - 10 **Product Groups:** 54, 80, 81, 84, 85

Date of Accounts	Sep 11	Sep 10	Sep 09
Pre Tax Profit/Loss	N/A	N/A	236
Working Capital	392	390	408
Fixed Assets	100	97	79
Current Assets	392	390	408

Farm Services Ltd

Chesterton Estate Yard Banbury Road, Lighthorne, Warwick, CV35 0AF
Tel: 01926-651540 **Fax:** 01926-651540
E-mail: info@farmservicesltd.co.uk
Website: http://www.farmservicesltd.co.uk
Managers: L. Clarkson (Sales Admin)
Ultimate Holding Company: CHESTERTON UTILITIES LIMITED
Immediate Holding Company: FARM SERVICES LIMITED
Registration no: 00373857 **Date established:** 1942
Turnover: £500,000 - £1m **No.of Employees:** 11 - 20
Product Groups: 51, 84

Date of Accounts	Mar 12	Mar 11	Mar 10
Working Capital	-72	-59	-51
Fixed Assets	208	238	279
Current Assets	202	191	172

Fozmula Ltd

Hermes Close Tachbrook Park, Warwick, CV34 6UF
Tel: 01926-466700 **Fax:** 01926-450473
E-mail: sales@fozmula.com
Website: http://www.fozmula.com
Bank(s): Royal Bank of Scotland
Directors: P. Holtby (Sales), R. Smythe (Fin), S. Jackson (MD)
Managers: L. Leahy (Admin Off), D. Knowles (Purch Mgr), P. Fisher (Mktg Serv Mgr)
Ultimate Holding Company: FOZMULA (HOLDINGS) LIMITED
Immediate Holding Company: FOZMULA LIMITED
Registration no: 01342163 **VAT No.:** GB 307 3451 80
Date established: 1977 **Turnover:** £2m - £5m **No.of Employees:** 51 - 100
Product Groups: 36, 38, 39, 40, 67

Date of Accounts	Mar 11	Mar 10	Mar 09
Working Capital	3m	2m	2m
Fixed Assets	175	50	57
Current Assets	4m	3m	2m

Gem Integrated Solutions Ltd G E M Group Ltd

4 Welton Road Wedgnock Industrial Estate, Warwick, CV34 5PZ
Tel: 01926-497778 **Fax:** 01926-410128
E-mail: sales@gem-group.co.uk
Website: http://www.gem-group.co.uk
Bank(s): HSBC Bank Plc
Directors: P. Barratt (Fin), G. Manning (MD)
Managers: M. Swan (Chief Mgr), G. Hall
Ultimate Holding Company: G.E.M. GROUP LIMITED
Immediate Holding Company: G.E.M. INTEGRATED SOLUTIONS LIMITED
Registration no: 01620057 **VAT No.:** GB 307 6827 46
Date established: 1982 **Turnover:** £2m - £5m **No.of Employees:** 21 - 50
Product Groups: 48, 52

Date of Accounts	May 11	May 10	May 09
Working Capital	313	306	447
Fixed Assets	19	24	731
Current Assets	789	691	682

George Worrell Engineering Ltd

8 Collins Road Heathcote Industrial Estate, Warwick, CV34 6TF
Tel: 01926-422733 **Fax:** 01926-832396
E-mail: management@gwe-ltd.co.uk
Website: http://www.gwe-ltd.co.uk
Directors: R. Ferguson (MD)
Ultimate Holding Company: CROMALT LIMITED
Immediate Holding Company: GEORGE WORRALL ENGINEERING LIMITED
Registration no: 01577699 **VAT No.:** GB 272 9436 35
Date established: 1981 **Turnover:** £500,000 - £1m
No.of Employees: 1 - 10 **Product Groups:** 35, 36, 48, 49, 66, 84

Date of Accounts	Dec 11	Dec 10	Dec 09
Working Capital	232	209	205
Fixed Assets	9	11	20
Current Assets	358	292	284

Gerflor Ltd

Wedgnock House Wedgnock Lane, Warwick, CV34 5AP
Tel: 01926-622600 **Fax:** 01926-401647
E-mail: pbuchon@gerflor.com
Website: http://www.gerflor.co.uk
Directors: P. Buchon (MD)
Managers: J. Bannister (Develop Mgr), M. Valle (Fin Mgr), M. Redgrave (Buyer), N. Dhillon (Sales & Mktg Mg)
Ultimate Holding Company: GERFIN SA (FRANCE)
Immediate Holding Company: GERFLOR LIMITED
Registration no: 00613508 **Date established:** 1958 **Turnover:** £2m - £5m
No.of Employees: 21 - 50 **Product Groups:** 30

Date of Accounts	Dec 11	Dec 10	Dec 09
Sales Turnover	4m	4m	4m
Pre Tax Profit/Loss	-10	-193	354
Working Capital	829	1m	1m
Fixed Assets	26	32	39
Current Assets	1m	2m	2m
Current Liabilities	479	384	301

Godiva Ltd

Charles Street, Warwick, CV34 5LR
Tel: 01926-623600 **Fax:** 01926-623666
E-mail: godiva@idexcorp.com
Website: http://www.godiva.co.uk
Bank(s): Lloyds TSB Bank plc
Directors: M. Noel (Chief Op Offcr), R. Reynolds (Pers)
Managers: L. Purcell (Tech Serv Mgr), D. Burton (Sales & Mktg Mg), R. Yarnall (Fin Mgr)
Ultimate Holding Company: IDEX CORPORATION (USA)
Immediate Holding Company: GODIVA LIMITED
Registration no: 00011943 **VAT No.:** GB 200 4622 27
Date established: 1978 **Turnover:** £10m - £20m
No.of Employees: 51 - 100 **Product Groups:** 40

Date of Accounts	Dec 11	Dec 10	Dec 09
Sales Turnover	15m	15m	15m
Pre Tax Profit/Loss	2m	567	2m
Working Capital	6m	6m	5m
Fixed Assets	2m	2m	2m
Current Assets	14m	13m	13m
Current Liabilities	771	844	643

Gravograph Ltd

Unit 3 Trojan Business Centre Touch Brooke Park Drive, Warwick, CV34 6RH
Tel: 01926-884433 **Fax:** 01926-883879
E-mail: info@gravograph.co.uk
Website: http://www.gravograph.co.uk
Bank(s): National Westminster Bank Plc
Directors: Z. Vawda (Fin)
Managers: M. Tissut
Ultimate Holding Company: LBO FRANCE
Immediate Holding Company: GRAVOGRAPH LIMITED
Registration no: 00419338 **Date established:** 1946 **Turnover:** £2m - £5m
No.of Employees: 21 - 50 **Product Groups:** 28, 33, 37, 44, 45

Date of Accounts	Dec 10	Dec 09	Dec 08
Sales Turnover	4m	4m	4m
Pre Tax Profit/Loss	364	81	102
Working Capital	568	267	155
Fixed Assets	48	39	70
Current Assets	1m	964	1m
Current Liabilities	350	198	405

Guthrie Douglas Ltd

Unit 1 Titan Business Centre Spartan Close, Warwick, CV34 6RR
Tel: 01926-452452 **Fax:** 01926-336417
E-mail: receptionist@guthriedouglas.com
Website: http://www.guthriedouglas.com
Bank(s): Lloyds TSB Bank plc
Directors: A. Collett (Sales & Mktg), A. Kitching (Fin), R. Guthrie (Dir), G. Guthrie (Fin)
Managers: M. Snell, T. Lange (Tech Serv Mgr), S. Steele (Personnel)
Ultimate Holding Company: GUTHRIE DOUGLAS GROUP LIMITED
Immediate Holding Company: GUTHRIE DOUGLAS LIMITED
Registration no: 01489927 **VAT No.:** GB 307 3656 62
Date established: 1980 **Turnover:** £5m - £10m **No.of Employees:** 21 - 50
Product Groups: 37, 52

Date of Accounts	Sep 11	Sep 10	Sep 09
Sales Turnover	6m	6m	6m
Pre Tax Profit/Loss	163	121	1m
Working Capital	799	1m	1m
Fixed Assets	145	200	267
Current Assets	2m	3m	3m
Current Liabilities	377	281	600

I M Properties Finance Ltd

Saxon House Haseley Business Centre, Haseley, Warwick, CV35 7LS
Tel: 024-7653 7100 **Fax:** 024-7653 7101
Website: http://www.improperties.co.uk
Directors: M. Jones (Dir), N. Jones (Comm), P. O'gorman (Co Sec), M. Adams (Dir), G. Hutton (Grp Chief Exec)
Managers: P. Foster
Ultimate Holding Company: I.M. GROUP LIMITED
Immediate Holding Company: I.M. PROPERTIES INVESTMENT LIMITED
Registration no: 02937496 **Date established:** 1994 **Turnover:** £1m - £2m
No.of Employees: 11 - 20 **Product Groups:** 80

Date of Accounts	Dec 11	Dec 10	Dec 09
Sales Turnover	638	1m	843
Pre Tax Profit/Loss	4m	-2m	1m
Working Capital	39m	343	39m
Fixed Assets	93m	128m	91m
Current Assets	39m	22m	39m
Current Liabilities	1	22m	8

Infogenerics Ltd

Unit 4 Innovation Centre Warwick Technology Park Gallows Hill, Warwick, CV34 6UW
Tel: 01926-422911
E-mail: info@infogenerics.net
Website: http://www.infogenerics.net
Directors: F. Galal (Dir)
Immediate Holding Company: INFOGENERICS LIMITED
Registration no: 05877914 **Date established:** 2006
Turnover: £500,000 - £1m **No.of Employees:** 1 - 10 **Product Groups:** 44

Insight Presentation Systems Ltd

Spartan Close Tachbrook Park, Warwick, CV34 6RS
Tel: 01926-888298 **Fax:** 01926-888299
E-mail: office@insightps.com
Website: http://www.insightps.com
Directors: I. Verge (MD), D. Verge (Co Sec)
Immediate Holding Company: INSIGHT PRESENTATION SYSTEMS LIMITED
Registration no: 02783744 **Date established:** 1993
No.of Employees: 1 - 10 **Product Groups:** 38, 49

Date of Accounts	Mar 12	Mar 11	Mar 10
Working Capital	-167	-147	104
Fixed Assets	575	585	610
Current Assets	264	265	326

J C Merralls & Sons LLP

20 Wake Grove, Warwick, CV34 6PN
Tel: 01926-400018 **Fax:** 01926-403764
E-mail: jcmerralls@btconnect.com
Directors: S. Merralls (Ptnr)
Immediate Holding Company: J C MERRALLS & SONS LLP
Registration no: OC328958 **Date established:** 2007
No.of Employees: 1 - 10 **Product Groups:** 26, 35

Date of Accounts	Mar 12	Mar 11	Mar 10
Working Capital	12	12	35
Fixed Assets	5	7	8
Current Assets	25	24	46

K A D Roofing Ltd

14 Dongan Road, Warwick, CV34 4JW
Tel: 01926-400044 **Fax:** 01926-494775
E-mail: nick@kadroofing.co.uk
Website: http://www.kadroofing.co.uk
Directors: N. Day (MD)
Registration no: 00789224 **Turnover:** £500,000 - £1m
No.of Employees: 11 - 20 **Product Groups:** 14, 31, 33, 35, 52, 66

Kigass Aero Components Ltd

Montague Road, Warwick, CV34 5LW
Tel: 01926-493833 **Fax:** 01926-401456
E-mail: accounts.dept@kigassaero.co.uk
Website: http://www.kigassaero.co.uk
Bank(s): HSBC, Leamington Spa
Directors: P. Platt (Fin)
Managers: N. Hall (Tech Serv Mgr), A. Puga (Purch Mgr), R. Knee
Ultimate Holding Company: KIGASS MANUFACTURING LIMITED
Immediate Holding Company: KIGASS AERO COMPONENTS LIMITED
Registration no: 01080068 **VAT No.:** GB 272 8944 21
Date established: 1972 **Turnover:** £5m - £10m
No.of Employees: 51 - 100 **Product Groups:** 39, 48

Date of Accounts	Jun 11	Jun 10	Jun 09
Sales Turnover	5m	5m	7m
Pre Tax Profit/Loss	-43	42	172
Working Capital	349	387	244
Fixed Assets	1m	1m	2m
Current Assets	2m	2m	2m
Current Liabilities	876	799	508

L Pickering & Sons

Pickering Building Ladbroke Park, Warwick, CV34 5AN
Tel: 01926-418700 **Fax:** 01926-418701
E-mail: info@system-standex.co.uk
Website: http://www.system-standex.co.uk
Directors: D. Pickering (Co Sec), T. Pickering (Sales & Mktg), J. Baker (Plant), R. Pickering (Tech Serv)
Immediate Holding Company: L. PICKERING & SONS LIMITED
Registration no: 00479118 **VAT No.:** GB 487 7005 19
Date established: 1950 **Turnover:** £2m - £5m **No.of Employees:** 1 - 10
Product Groups: 29, 34, 35, 36, 48

Date of Accounts	Mar 11	Mar 10	Mar 09
Working Capital	509	405	255
Fixed Assets	1m	1m	1m
Current Assets	807	695	488

Lead In Research Ltd

Unit 5a Charles Court Budbrooke Industrial Estate, Warwick, CV34 5LZ
Tel: 01926-403720 **Fax:** 01789-471550
E-mail: info@leadinresearch.co.uk
Website: http://www.leadinresearch.co.uk
Directors: M. Hurley (MD)
Immediate Holding Company: LEAD-IN RESEARCH LIMITED
Registration no: 03997380 **Date established:** 2000
Turnover: £250,000 - £500,000 **No.of Employees:** 1 - 10
Product Groups: 80

Date of Accounts	Dec 10	Mar 10	Mar 09
Sales Turnover	387	N/A	N/A
Pre Tax Profit/Loss	48	N/A	N/A
Working Capital	-98	-582	-151
Fixed Assets	N/A	112	279
Current Assets	N/A	392	412

Load Match

28 Kineton Road Wellesbourne, Warwick, CV35 9LQ
Tel: 01789-471541 **Fax:** 01789-881105
E-mail: bob@loadmatch.co.uk
Website: http://www.loadmatch.co.uk
Directors: R. Lawley (Prop)
Date established: 2005 **Turnover:** Up to £250,000
No.of Employees: 1 - 10 **Product Groups:** 76

M D Electronics

9 Quarry Fields Leek Wootton, Warwick, CV35 7RS
Tel: 01926-850315 **Fax:** 01926-850315
E-mail: info@mdelectronics.co.uk
Website: http://www.mdelectronics.co.uk
Directors: M. Darby (Prop)
Date established: 1987 **No.of Employees:** 1 - 10 **Product Groups:** 37, 38, 44

Midland Bar Supplies
2 Hill Wootton Road Leek Wootton, Warwick, CV35 7QL
Tel: 01926-513160 **Fax:** 07092-170204
E-mail: caterquiper@yahoo.co.uk
Website: http://www.midlandbarsupplies.webs.com
Directors: A. Bajaj (Snr Part)
No.of Employees: 1 - 10 **Product Groups:** 26, 36, 40, 52, 62

Mills C N C
Unit 2-3 Tachbrook Link Tachbrook Park Drive, Warwick, CV34 6SN
Tel: 01926-736736 **Fax:** 01926-736737
E-mail: sales@millscnc.co.uk
Website: http://www.millscnc.co.uk
Directors: N. Ahluwalia (Fin), N. Frampton (MD), P. Hooper-keeley (Fin)
Managers: G. Goldstein
Ultimate Holding Company: ENSCO 881 LIMITED
Immediate Holding Company: MILLS CNC LIMITED
Registration no: 01156673 **Date established:** 1974
Turnover: £20m - £50m **No.of Employees:** 51 - 100 **Product Groups:** 67

Date of Accounts	Dec 11	Dec 10	Dec 09
Sales Turnover	47m	27m	27m
Pre Tax Profit/Loss	3m	2m	2m
Working Capital	11m	8m	8m
Fixed Assets	276	259	294
Current Assets	27m	22m	17m
Current Liabilities	5m	4m	2m

Millward Brown
Olympus Avenue Tachbrook Park, Warwick, CV34 6RJ
Tel: 01926-452233 **Fax:** 01926-833600
E-mail: info@uk.millwardbrown.com
Website: http://www.millwardbrown.com
Directors: S. Bowron (Fin), K. White (Pers), S. Potter (Fin)
Managers: D. Chantry
Ultimate Holding Company: WPP PLC (JERSEY)
Immediate Holding Company: MILLWARD BROWN UK LIMITED
Registration no: 01915514 **VAT No.:** GB 418 7062 50
Date established: 1985 **Turnover:** £75m - £125m
No.of Employees: 501 - 1000 **Product Groups:** 81

Date of Accounts	Dec 11	Dec 10	Dec 09
Sales Turnover	123m	122m	107m
Pre Tax Profit/Loss	10m	13m	11m
Working Capital	16m	23m	41m
Fixed Assets	5m	4m	3m
Current Assets	54m	62m	67m
Current Liabilities	23m	26m	18m

Motion Drives & Controls Ltd
1a Budbrooke Road Budbrooke Industrial Estate, Warwick, CV34 5XH
Tel: 01926-411544 **Fax:** 01926-411541
E-mail: sales@motion.uk.com
Website: http://www.motiondrivesandcontrols.co.uk
Directors: K. Hanson (Fin)
Immediate Holding Company: MOTION DRIVES AND CONTROLS LIMITED
Registration no: 02741407 **Date established:** 1992
Turnover: £500,000 - £1m **No.of Employees:** 1 - 10 **Product Groups:** 35, 37, 38, 40, 43, 44, 45, 46

Date of Accounts	Mar 12	Mar 11	Mar 10
Working Capital	160	165	142
Fixed Assets	66	50	41
Current Assets	658	511	453

Murley Agricultural Supplies Ltd
Nelson Lane, Warwick, CV34 5JB
Tel: 01926-494336 **Fax:** 01926-401510
E-mail: sales@murley-agri.co.uk
Website: http://www.murley.co.uk
Managers: D. Forty (Chief Mgr)
Ultimate Holding Company: MURLEY LIMITED
Immediate Holding Company: MURLEY AGRICULTURAL SUPPLIES LIMITED
Registration no: 00625731 **Date established:** 1959
Turnover: £10m - £20m **No.of Employees:** 11 - 20 **Product Groups:** 67

Date of Accounts	Dec 10	Dec 09	Dec 08
Sales Turnover	15m	14m	14m
Pre Tax Profit/Loss	181	180	179
Working Capital	668	515	359
Fixed Assets	3m	3m	3m
Current Assets	5m	5m	4m
Current Liabilities	141	222	453

National Electric & Engineering Ltd
Cattell Road Cape Indl-Est, Warwick, CV34 4JQ
Tel: 01926-492132 **Fax:** 01926-494891
E-mail: steve.kennedy@nationalelectric.co.uk
Website: http://www.nationalelectric.co.uk
Directors: S. Kennedy (MD), S. Kennedy (Dir), M. Tilt (Co Sec)
Ultimate Holding Company: MORGAN BENNETT HOLDINGS LIMITED
Immediate Holding Company: NATIONAL ELECTRIC & ENGINEERING COMPANY(BIRMINGHAM)LIMITED(THE)
Registration no: 00418988 **VAT No.:** GB 110 3232 46
Date established: 1946 **Turnover:** £2m - £5m **No.of Employees:** 1 - 10
Product Groups: 84

Date of Accounts	Dec 09	Dec 08	Dec 07
Working Capital	22	8	-266
Fixed Assets	146	187	133
Current Assets	784	923	1m

National Grid
National Grid House Warwick Technology Park Gallows Hill, Warwick, CV34 6DA
Tel: 01926-653000 **Fax:** 01926-654378
E-mail: marketinguk@ngridwireless.com
Website: http://www.nationalgrid.com
Directors: S. Holiday (MD)
Ultimate Holding Company: THE MIDCOUNTIES CO-OPERATIVE LIMITED
Immediate Holding Company: CODSALL TRAVEL CENTRE LIMITED
Date established: 1992 **No.of Employees:** 1501 & over
Product Groups: 37, 40, 44, 49, 67, 79, 84, 89

Date of Accounts	Sep 02	Sep 01	Jan 12
Working Capital	-23	-23	-23
Current Liabilities	N/A	N/A	23

Norman Hyde Ltd
Rigby Close Heathcote, Warwick, CV34 6TL
Tel: 01926-430562 **Fax:** 01926-832352
E-mail: sales@normanhyde.co.uk
Website: http://www.normanhyde.co.uk
Directors: N. Hyde (Dir)
Immediate Holding Company: NORMAN HYDE LIMITED
Registration no: 04763591 **Date established:** 2003
Turnover: £250,000 - £500,000 **No.of Employees:** 1 - 10
Product Groups: 68

Date of Accounts	Oct 11	Oct 10	Oct 09
Working Capital	30	-8	-27
Fixed Assets	21	27	30
Current Assets	246	213	160

P H I Lighting Ltd
Unit 8 Brookhampton Lane Dene Valley Business Centre Kineton, Warwick, CV35 0JD
Tel: 01926-640366
E-mail: mail@phi-lighting.com
Website: http://www.phi-lighting.com
Directors: J. Dale (Dir)
Immediate Holding Company: PHI LIGHTING LIMITED
Registration no: 04656474 **Date established:** 2003
No.of Employees: 1 - 10 **Product Groups:** 37, 67

Date of Accounts	Mar 12	Mar 11	Mar 10
Working Capital	236	278	125
Fixed Assets	77	8	9
Current Assets	322	477	233

P J Tooling Ltd
33 Millers Road, Warwick, CV34 5AE
Tel: 01926-492693 **Fax:** 01926-410057
Website: http://www.pjtooling.co.uk
Directors: M. Webb (MD)
Managers: L. Hewitt (Comptroller)
Immediate Holding Company: P.J.TOOLING LIMITED
Registration no: 01006083 **Date established:** 1971
No.of Employees: 21 - 50 **Product Groups:** 46

Date of Accounts	Apr 12	Apr 11	Apr 10
Working Capital	20	-23	4
Fixed Assets	359	202	237
Current Assets	227	183	161

Parker Hannifin
Tachbrook Park Drive, Warwick, CV34 6TU
Tel: 01926-317878 **Fax:** 01926-889 172
E-mail: nigel_judd@parker.com
Website: http://www.parker.com
Bank(s): Barclays
Directors: C. Gill (Co Sec), G. Crame (MD), G. Creame (Ch), G. Ellinor (Co Sec), I. Molyneux (Dir)
Managers: N. Judd (Mgr)
Ultimate Holding Company: PARKER HANNIFIN (HOLDINGS) LTD
Immediate Holding Company: PARKER HANNIFIN LTD
Registration no: 04806503 **VAT No.:** GB 580 3805 41
Date established: 1991 **Turnover:** £250m - £500m
No.of Employees: 251 - 500 **Product Groups:** 33, 34, 35, 36, 38, 40, 42

Date of Accounts	Jun 07	Dec 05
Sales Turnover	4346	2116
Pre Tax Profit/Loss	154	139
Working Capital	664	552
Fixed Assets	12	25
Current Assets	1492	1000
Current Liabilities	828	448
Total Share Capital	420	420
ROCE% (Return on Capital Employed)	22.8	24.1
ROT% (Return on Turnover)	3.5	6.6

Princess International Sales & Service Ltd
Athena Drive Tachbrook Park, Warwick, CV34 6RT
Tel: 01926-359977 **Fax:** 01926-461591
E-mail: sales@princess.co.uk
Website: http://www.princess.co.uk
Bank(s): Barclays
Directors: C. Cleverly (Sales & Mktg), C. Rubython (MD), J. Rubython (MD)
Managers: S. Hill (Mktg Serv Mgr), N. Johnson (Chief Acct)
Immediate Holding Company: Princess Motor Yacht Sales Holdings Ltd
Registration no: 00829659 **Date established:** 1964
Turnover: £50m - £75m **No.of Employees:** 51 - 100 **Product Groups:** 39

Date of Accounts	Dec 07
Sales Turnover	80450
Pre Tax Profit/Loss	1610
Working Capital	5490
Fixed Assets	1410
Current Assets	25080
Current Liabilities	19590
Total Share Capital	100
ROCE% (Return on Capital Employed)	23.3

PromoLingua
22 Bromhurst Way, Warwick, CV34 6NS
Tel: 01926-402934
E-mail: enquiries@promolingua.com
Website: http://www.promolingua.com
Directors: S. Clarke (Prop)
Date established: 2008 **Turnover:** Up to £250,000
No.of Employees: 1 - 10 **Product Groups:** 80, 86

Quantum Manufacturing Ltd
1 Heathcote Way Heathcote Industrial Estate, Warwick, CV34 6TE
Tel: 01926-885564 **Fax:** 01926-450387
E-mail: info@quantumprecisiontoolmakers.co.uk
Website: http://www.quantumprecisiontoolmakers.co.uk
Bank(s): Royal Bank of Scotland
Directors: C. Corton (MD), D. Yeomans (Fin)
Immediate Holding Company: QUANTUM MANUFACTURING LIMITED
Registration no: 02796301 **VAT No.:** GB 585 2412 35
Date established: 1993 **Turnover:** £500,000 - £1m
No.of Employees: 11 - 20 **Product Groups:** 46

Date of Accounts	Mar 11	Mar 10	Mar 09
Working Capital	168	256	119
Fixed Assets	167	219	216
Current Assets	509	582	702

Schenck Ltd
Broxell Close, Warwick, CV34 5QF
Tel: 01926-474090 **Fax:** 01926-474034
E-mail: sales@schenck.co.uk
Website: http://www.schenck.co.uk
No.of Employees: 21 - 50 **Product Groups:** 37, 38, 39, 48, 85

Date of Accounts	Dec 09	Dec 08	Dec 07
Sales Turnover	3m	4m	5m
Pre Tax Profit/Loss	309	519	493
Working Capital	4m	4m	3m
Fixed Assets	59	50	71
Current Assets	5m	6m	5m
Current Liabilities	502	1m	995

Selux UK Ltd
Titan Business Centre Spartan Close, Warwick, CV34 6RR
Tel: 01926-833455 **Fax:** 01926-339844
E-mail: enquire@selux.co.uk
Website: http://www.selux.co.uk
Managers: A. Burdett (Sales Admin), A. Burdett (Sales Admin)
Ultimate Holding Company: SEMPERLUX AKTRENGESELLSCHAFT (GERMANY)
Immediate Holding Company: SE LUX U.K. LIMITED
Registration no: 02440744 **Date established:** 1989 **Turnover:** £1m - £2m
No.of Employees: 1 - 10 **Product Groups:** 33, 36, 37

Date of Accounts	Dec 11	Dec 10	Dec 09
Working Capital	387	401	286
Fixed Assets	79	35	41
Current Assets	1m	1m	1m

Silbury Marketing Ltd
2 Trinity Mews Priory Road, Warwick, CV34 4NA
Tel: 01926-410022 **Fax:** 01926-476200
E-mail: adrian@silbury.co.uk
Website: http://www.silbury.co.uk
Directors: A. Hall (Fin)
Managers: L. Redfern (Personnel)
Immediate Holding Company: SILBURY MARKETING LIMITED
Registration no: 01944922 **Date established:** 1985
Turnover: £20m - £50m **No.of Employees:** 11 - 20 **Product Groups:** 62

Date of Accounts	Oct 11	Oct 10	Oct 09
Sales Turnover	26m	30m	30m
Pre Tax Profit/Loss	507	811	899
Working Capital	2m	2m	2m
Fixed Assets	276	209	243
Current Assets	5m	6m	5m
Current Liabilities	168	283	358

Silverline International Ltd
Unit 4 Nelson Lane, Warwick, CV34 5JB
Tel: 01926-490002 **Fax:** 01926-490003
E-mail: info@silverlinewheels-tyres.com
Website: http://www.silverlinewheels-tyres.com
Directors: T. Wilkinson (Fin)
Immediate Holding Company: SILVERLINE INTERNATIONAL LIMITED
Registration no: 02567452 **Date established:** 1990
No.of Employees: 1 - 10 **Product Groups:** 29, 68

Date of Accounts	Mar 12	Mar 11	Mar 10
Working Capital	190	198	150
Fixed Assets	40	60	85
Current Assets	862	870	884

Spa Fasteners Ltd
26 Hurlbutt Road Heathcote Industrial Estate, Warwick, CV34 6TD
Tel: 01926-883671 **Fax:** 01926-430953
E-mail: postmaster@spafasteners.co.uk
Website: http://www.spafasteners.co.uk
Directors: B. Hammond (MD), D. Turrall (Co Sec)
Registration no: 01279007 **VAT No.:** 398 4563 92 **Date established:** 1978
Turnover: £250,000 - £500,000 **No.of Employees:** 1 - 10
Product Groups: 35, 66

Stewart Gill Conveyors Ltd (a division of Air-Log Ltd)
1 Brook Business Park Brookhampton Lane, Kineton, Warwick, CV35 0JA
Tel: 01926-641424 **Fax:** 01926-641426
E-mail: info@stewart-gill.co.uk
Website: http://www.stewart-gill.co.uk
Bank(s): Lloyds, Guildford
Managers: P. Walker (Mgr)
Immediate Holding Company: STEWART GILL CONVEYORS LIMITED
Registration no: 04064423 **VAT No.:** GB 757 3296 96
Date established: 2000 **Turnover:** £2m - £5m **No.of Employees:** 11 - 20
Product Groups: 35, 41, 45

Date of Accounts	Dec 11	Dec 10	Dec 09
Working Capital	-2	36	80
Fixed Assets	22	25	59
Current Assets	523	576	382

Stratford Blinds
Redhill Wellesbourne, Warwick, CV35 9SP
Tel: 01789-551922 **Fax:** 01789-555936
E-mail: joy.hodge@ntlworld.com
Website: http://www.stratford-blinds.co.uk
Directors: J. Hodge (Prop), J. Hodges (Prop)
Immediate Holding Company: STRATFORD BLINDS LTD
Registration no: 06515578 **Turnover:** Up to £250,000
No.of Employees: 1 - 10 **Product Groups:** 24, 25, 63, 66

Support Communications Ltd
13c Collins Road Heathcote Industrial Estate, Warwick, CV34 6TF
Tel: 03333-213720 **Fax:** 0121-766 3086
E-mail: sales@supportcomms.co.uk
Website: http://www.supportcomms.co.uk
Directors: S. Foley (Fin)
Managers: A. Foley (Sales Prom Mgr), A. Foley (Sales Prom Mgr)
Immediate Holding Company: SUPPORT COMMS LIMITED
Registration no: 04301407 **Date established:** 2001
No.of Employees: 1 - 10 **Product Groups:** 30, 37, 67

Date of Accounts	Dec 11	Dec 10	Dec 09
Working Capital	7	4	-3
Fixed Assets	3	5	10
Current Assets	158	169	126

Sweeney First Aid Supplies Ltd
13 Scar Bank, Warwick, CV34 5DB
Tel: 01926-497108 **Fax:** 01926-497109
E-mail: sales@sweeneyfirstaid.co.uk
Website: http://www.sweeneyfirstaid.co.uk
Directors: P. Sweeney (MD)
Immediate Holding Company: SWEENEY FIRST AID SUPPLIES LIMITED
Registration no: 03167774 **Date established:** 1996
No.of Employees: 1 - 10 **Product Groups:** 24, 29, 38

Date of Accounts	Aug 11	Aug 10	Aug 07
Working Capital	16	24	39
Fixed Assets	1	1	1
Current Assets	38	44	63

Sword Scientific Ltd

Athena Court Athena Drive, Tachbrook Park, Warwick, CV34 6RT
Tel: 01926-336663 **Fax:** 01926-336663
E-mail: sales@sword-scientific.com
Website: http://www.sword-scientific.com
Directors: T. Schofield (Dir)
Managers: J. Perry (Admin Off), J. Parker (Admin Off)
Immediate Holding Company: SWORD SCIENTIFIC LIMITED
Registration no: 05960696 **Date established:** 2006
Turnover: £250,000 - £500,000 **No.of Employees:** 1 - 10
Product Groups: 85

Date of Accounts	Oct 08	Oct 07
Working Capital	-30	-60
Fixed Assets	34	61
Current Assets	87	110
Current Liabilities	117	170
Total Share Capital	2	2

Technical Support

39a Millers Road, Warwick, CV34 5AE
Tel: 01926-402261 **Fax:** 01926-490978
E-mail: sales@tsupport.co.uk
Website: http://www.tsupport.co.uk
Directors: J. Bennett (Ptnr)
Immediate Holding Company: T. SUPPORT LTD
Date established: 2003 **Turnover:** £1m - £2m **No.of Employees:** 1 - 10
Product Groups: 37

Technifor

Tachbrook Park Drive, Warwick, CV34 6RH
Tel: 01926-884422 **Fax:** 01926-883105
E-mail: sales@ltd.technifor.com
Website: http://www.technifor.com
Bank(s): Bank of Scotland
Managers: M. Tissut (Mgr), Z. Vawda (Fin Mgr)
Immediate Holding Company: TECHNIFOR LTD
Registration no: 03161058 **VAT No.:** GB 663 5515 28
Date established: 1996 **Turnover:** £1m - £2m **No.of Employees:** 21 - 50
Product Groups: 28, 29, 30, 33, 34, 35, 36, 37, 38, 39, 40, 42, 44, 46, 47, 48, 49, 66, 67, 80, 81, 83, 85

Date of Accounts	Dec 07	Dec 06	Dec 05
Sales Turnover	1m	1m	1m
Pre Tax Profit/Loss	-212	-112	169
Working Capital	51	271	348
Fixed Assets	55	56	57
Current Assets	803	763	1m
Current Liabilities	752	491	673
Total Share Capital	65	65	65

Tomax

3 Lammas Centre Budbrooke Road, Budbrooke Industrial Estate, Warwick, CV34 5WQ
Tel: 01926-497752 **Fax:** 01926-410175
Website: http://www.eriks.co.uk
Managers: P. Howe (Mgr)
Immediate Holding Company: WYKO GROUP LTD
Registration no: 01576053 **No.of Employees:** 1 - 10 **Product Groups:** 35, 39, 45

Date of Accounts	Dec 07	Dec 06	Apr 06
Working Capital	N/A	N/A	214
Current Assets	214	214	214
Current Liabilities	214	214	N/A

Trident Design & Fabrication

Unit 3 Block T Harriott Drive, Heathcote Industrial Estate, Warwick, CV34 6TJ
Tel: 01926-886444 **Fax:** 01926-885666
E-mail: trident123@ukonline.co.uk
Website: http://www.tridentfabrications.co.uk
Directors: P. Bullock (Dir)
Immediate Holding Company: TRIDENT DESIGN AND FABRICATION LLP
Registration no: OC302563 **Date established:** 2002
No.of Employees: 1 - 10 **Product Groups:** 35

Date of Accounts	Jul 04	Jul 03	Mar 05
Working Capital	22	50	8
Fixed Assets	19	16	16
Current Assets	58	63	46

Volvo Group UK Ltd

Wedgnock Lane, Warwick, CV34 5YA
Tel: 01926-401777 **Fax:** 01869-345016
E-mail: marketinguk@volvo.com
Website: http://www.volvotrucks.co.uk
Directors: G. Nyberg (MD), M. Olkinuora (Dir)
Ultimate Holding Company: AB VOLVO (SWEDEN)
Immediate Holding Company: VOLVO GROUP UK LIMITED
Registration no: 02190944 **VAT No.:** GB 293 6582 19
Date established: 1987 **No.of Employees:** 101 - 250 **Product Groups:** 39, 68

Date of Accounts	Dec 11	Dec 10	Dec 09
Sales Turnover	1471m	923m	357m
Pre Tax Profit/Loss	14m	14m	9m
Working Capital	66m	58m	62m
Fixed Assets	95m	113m	114m
Current Assets	289m	299m	186m
Current Liabilities	87m	111m	60m

Volvo Penta UK (c/o Volvo Group UK Ltd)

Wedgnock Lane, Warwick, CV34 5YA
Tel: 01926-622500
E-mail: info.vpuk@volvo.com
Website: http://www.volvopenta.co.uk
Bank(s): SEB, 2 Cannon St, London EC4M 6XX
Managers: G. Corbett
Immediate Holding Company: A.B. Volvo (publ), S-405 08, Gothenburg, Sweden
Date established: 1976 **Turnover:** £20m - £50m
No.of Employees: 21 - 50 **Product Groups:** 39, 40, 41, 42, 68

Warwick Machinery Ltd

Unit 6 Budbrooke Road Budbrooke Industrial Estate, Warwick, CV34 5XH
Tel: 01926-497806 **Fax:** 01926-401039
E-mail: imcdonald@ywmuk.com
Website: http://www.warwickmachinery.co.uk
Directors: G. Navarini (Co Sec)
Managers: I. Mcdonald (Chief Mgr)
Ultimate Holding Company: YUASA TRADING CO LTD (JAPAN)
Immediate Holding Company: WARWICK MACHINERY LIMITED
Registration no: 01323273 **Date established:** 1977 **Turnover:** £5m - £10m
No.of Employees: 1 - 10 **Product Groups:** 46

Date of Accounts	Dec 11	Dec 10	Dec 09
Working Capital	297	-43	-146
Fixed Assets	29	1	2
Current Assets	623	854	161

Watapot Ltd

24 Priory Road, Warwick, CV34 4NA
Tel: 01926-411400
E-mail: stephen.banholzer@watapot.com
Website: http://www.watapot.com
Directors: S. Banholzer (Prop)
Immediate Holding Company: BANHAUS LTD
Registration no: 05654481 **Date established:** 2005
No.of Employees: 1 - 10 **Product Groups:** 30, 33

Date of Accounts	Dec 10	Dec 09	Dec 08
Working Capital	-11	-11	-12
Fixed Assets	2	2	2
Current Assets	5	5	15

Zenzero Solutions Ltd

Innovation Centre Warwick Technology Park Gallows Hill, Warwick, CV34 6UW
Tel: 08449-670706 **Fax:** 0870-134 1010
E-mail: info@zenzero.co.uk
Website: http://www.zenzero.co.uk
Directors: A. Tasker (MD)
Immediate Holding Company: ZENZERO SOLUTIONS LIMITED
Registration no: 03313680 **Date established:** 1997
No.of Employees: 1 - 10 **Product Groups:** 44

Date of Accounts	Mar 11	Mar 10	Mar 09
Working Capital	53	23	-1
Fixed Assets	47	46	39
Current Assets	189	114	71

WILTSHIRE

Bradford On Avon

Anthony Best Dynamics Ltd
Holt Road, Bradford On Avon, BA15 1AJ
Tel: 01225-860200 **Fax:** 01225-860201
E-mail: sales@abd.uk.com
Website: http://www.abd.uk.com
Bank(s): Bank of Scotland
Directors: A. Best (Dir)
Immediate Holding Company: ANTHONY BEST DYNAMICS LIMITED
Registration no: 01658222 **VAT No.:** GB 378 7397 82
Date established: 1982 **Turnover:** £5m - £10m **No.of Employees:** 21 - 50
Product Groups: 29, 38, 44, 54, 84, 85

Date of Accounts	Aug 11	Aug 10	Aug 09
Working Capital	3m	3m	3m
Fixed Assets	304	340	415
Current Assets	5m	3m	4m
Current Liabilities	N/A	559	N/A

Ashley Industrial Ltd
South Wraxall, Bradford On Avon, BA15 2RL
Tel: 01225-868083 **Fax:** 01225-868089
E-mail: japapps@aol.com
Website: http://www.ashley-group.co.uk
Directors: C. Papps (MD), J. Papps (Fin)
Immediate Holding Company: ASHLEY INDUSTRIAL LIMITED
Registration no: 04345902 **VAT No.:** GB 318 7954 21
Date established: 2001 **Turnover:** £250,000 - £500,000
No.of Employees: 1 - 10 **Product Groups:** 35, 49

Date of Accounts	Dec 11	Dec 10	Dec 09
Working Capital	-2	3	6
Current Assets	8	12	19
Current Liabilities	10	N/A	N/A

The Moulton Bicycle Co. Ltd
Holt Road, Bradford On Avon, BA15 1AH
Tel: 01225-865895 **Fax:** 01225-864742
E-mail: office@moultonbicycles.co.uk
Website: http://www.moultonbicycles.co.uk
Bank(s): Lloyds TSB Bank plc
Managers: S. Moulton (Chief Mgr)
Immediate Holding Company: MOULTON DEVELOPMENTS LIMITED
Registration no: 01204181 **VAT No.:** GB 639 6919 81
Date established: 1975 **Turnover:** £1m - £2m **No.of Employees:** 11 - 20
Product Groups: 39

Date of Accounts	Dec 09	Dec 08	Dec 07
Working Capital	-412	-387	-325
Fixed Assets	41	26	42
Current Assets	25	55	208

Calne

Baz Roll International Ltd
Portemarsh Road, Calne, SN11 9BW
Tel: 01249-822222 **Fax:** 01249-822300
E-mail: mark@bazroll.co.uk
Website: http://www.bazroll.co.uk
Bank(s): Lloyds TSB Bank plc
Directors: M. Farrell (MD), P. Edmondson (Fin), T. Walker (Sales)
Immediate Holding Company: BAZ-ROLL INTERNATIONAL LIMITED
Registration no: 02603821 **VAT No.:** GB 200 1652 33
Date established: 1991 **Turnover:** £1m - £2m **No.of Employees:** 21 - 50
Product Groups: 29, 39

Date of Accounts	May 12	May 11	May 10
Working Capital	1m	995	934
Fixed Assets	765	784	686
Current Assets	2m	2m	2m
Current Liabilities	N/A	482	539

Calne Engineering Ltd
Stanier Road Porte Marsh Industrial Estate, Calne, SN11 9PX
Tel: 01249-813288 **Fax:** 01249-821266
E-mail: sales@calne-engineering.co.uk
Website: http://www.calne-engineering.co.uk
Bank(s): Lloyds TSB Bank plc
Directors: M. Board (MD), P. Andrews (Dir), P. Woolford (Sales)
Immediate Holding Company: CALNE ENGINEERING LIMITED
Registration no: 01405035 **VAT No.:** GB 318 7339 41
Date established: 1978 **Turnover:** £2m - £5m **No.of Employees:** 21 - 50
Product Groups: 48

Date of Accounts	Dec 11	Dec 10	Dec 09
Working Capital	69	142	179
Fixed Assets	1m	1m	2m
Current Assets	834	697	836

D P Scaffolding Ltd
25 The Rise Rookery Park, Calne, SN11 0LG
Tel: 01249-822018 **Fax:** 01793-721310
E-mail: miapaull7@hotmail.com
Managers: D. Paull (Mgr)
Immediate Holding Company: D & P SCAFFOLDING LIMITED
Registration no: 03881100 **Date established:** 1999
No.of Employees: 1 - 10 **Product Groups:** 35, 52, 66, 83

Date of Accounts	Mar 09	Feb 12	Feb 11
Working Capital	112	62	80
Fixed Assets	238	109	147
Current Assets	339	225	277

Deceuninck Ltd
2 Stanier Road, Calne, SN11 9PX
Tel: 01249-816969 **Fax:** 01249-815234
E-mail: jon.skinner@deceuninck.com
Website: http://www.deceuninck.co.uk
Bank(s): Lloyds TSB Bank plc
Directors: J. Skinner (Comm)
Managers: D. Keevan, V. Gees-thorneton (Tech Serv Mgr)
Ultimate Holding Company: DECEUNINCK NV (BELGIUM)
Immediate Holding Company: DECEUNINCK LIMITED
Registration no: 01565521 **VAT No.:** GB 348 4720 40
Date established: 1981 **Turnover:** £20m - £50m
No.of Employees: 51 - 100 **Product Groups:** 30

Date of Accounts	Dec 11	Dec 10	Dec 09
Sales Turnover	15m	18m	29m
Pre Tax Profit/Loss	-2m	-3m	-5m
Working Capital	-24m	-21m	-12m
Fixed Assets	543	617	944
Current Assets	5m	9m	11m
Current Liabilities	507	384	804

Exception E M S
32 Harris Road, Calne, SN11 9PT
Tel: 01249-814081 **Fax:** 01249-821035
E-mail: kay.bartlett@exceptionems.com
Website: http://www.exceptiongroup.com
Bank(s): HSBC Bank plc
Directors: P. Fowler (Co Sec), N. Murphy (Co Sec)
Managers: K. Bartlett, J. Goward (Personnel), S. Bennett, D. Parker, K. Barlett
Ultimate Holding Company: EXCEPTION GROUP LIMITED
Immediate Holding Company: EXCEPTION EMS LIMITED
Registration no: 01336602 **Date established:** 1977
Turnover: £10m - £20m **No.of Employees:** 101 - 250
Product Groups: 35, 37, 38, 48, 84

Date of Accounts	Dec 08	Dec 07	Jun 11
Sales Turnover	20m	18m	15m
Pre Tax Profit/Loss	597	-1m	-366
Working Capital	392	-445	-520
Fixed Assets	2m	2m	1m
Current Assets	7m	7m	6m
Current Liabilities	3m	3m	2m

Exception V A R
Pacific House Redman Road, Calne, SN11 9PR
Tel: 01249-815815 **Fax:** 01249-810710
E-mail: ann.harwood@exceptionvar.com
Website: http://www.exceptiongroup.com
Managers: M. O'connor
Ultimate Holding Company: EXCEPTION GROUP LIMITED
Immediate Holding Company: EXCEPTION VAR LIMITED
Date established: 1981 **Turnover:** Over £1,000m
No.of Employees: 101 - 250 **Product Groups:** 30

Date of Accounts	Dec 08	Dec 07	Jun 11
Sales Turnover	23m	20m	14m
Pre Tax Profit/Loss	36	-63	3m
Working Capital	174	95	4m
Fixed Assets	173	221	47
Current Assets	9m	7m	11m
Current Liabilities	5m	3m	3m

Healthmatic Ltd
Redman Road Porte Marsh Industrial Estate, Calne, SN11 9PR
Tel: 01249-822063 **Fax:** 01249-823140
E-mail: ops@healthmatic.com
Website: http://www.healthmatic.com
Bank(s): National Westminster Bank Plc
Directors: R. Berry (MD)
Immediate Holding Company: HEALTHMATIC LIMITED
Registration no: 02065014 **VAT No.:** GB 442 5581 51
Date established: 1986 **Turnover:** £1m - £2m **No.of Employees:** 51 - 100
Product Groups: 36

Date of Accounts	Apr 11	Apr 10	Apr 09
Working Capital	-268	-152	26
Fixed Assets	1m	1m	646
Current Assets	2m	1m	2m

L M L Products Ltd
13 Porte Marsh Road, Calne, SN11 9BN
Tel: 01249-814271 **Fax:** 01249-812182
E-mail: sales@lmlproducts.co.uk
Website: http://www.lmlproducts.co.uk
Bank(s): Lloyds TSB Bank plc
Directors: C. Langridge (Prop)
Managers: C. Wilson (Sales Prom Mgr), K. Goodman, M. Wolfe, C. Firenzio (Fin Mgr)
Ultimate Holding Company: CHOULDEN HOLDINGS LIMITED
Immediate Holding Company: L.M.L. PRODUCTS LIMITED
Registration no: 00942029 **VAT No.:** GB 138 3760 56
Date established: 1968 **Turnover:** £2m - £5m **No.of Employees:** 21 - 50
Product Groups: 35, 37

Date of Accounts	Dec 11	Dec 10	Dec 09
Sales Turnover	3m	3m	3m
Pre Tax Profit/Loss	5	92	-525
Working Capital	459	455	151
Fixed Assets	84	121	156
Current Assets	1m	1m	1m
Current Liabilities	681	167	586

P P Injection Moulds & Moulding Ltd
Beversbrook Indl-Est Redman Road, Calne, SN11 9PL
Tel: 01249-823100 **Fax:** 01249-823103
E-mail: enquiries@ppmoulds.co.uk
Website: http://www.ppmoulds.co.uk
Bank(s): Nat West
Directors: J. Few (MD), K. Evans (Dir), M. Rushin (Dir)
Ultimate Holding Company: AVON GROUP MANUFACTURING (HOLDINGS) LIMITED
Immediate Holding Company: P.P. INJECTION MOULDS & MOULDINGS LIMITED
Registration no: 02058367 **VAT No.:** 302 6183 94 **Date established:** 1986
Turnover: £1m - £2m **No.of Employees:** 21 - 50 **Product Groups:** 30, 48

Date of Accounts	Mar 11	Mar 10	Mar 09
Sales Turnover	2m	3m	N/A
Pre Tax Profit/Loss	7	17	46
Working Capital	2m	2m	2m
Fixed Assets	2m	1m	1m
Current Assets	3m	3m	3m
Current Liabilities	365	574	575

Romarsh Ltd
Clarke Avenue, Calne, SN11 9BS
Tel: 01249-812624 **Fax:** 01249-816134
E-mail: stewart@romarsh.co.uk
Website: http://www.romarsh.co.uk
Bank(s): Barclays
Directors: P. Ling (Sales & Mktg), D. Zirger (I.T. Dir), P. Haigh (Fin), S. Cursley (MD)
Managers: N. Waddicor (Chief Acct)
Ultimate Holding Company: TAMURA CORP (JAPAN)
Immediate Holding Company: ROMARSH LIMITED
Registration no: 02554232 **VAT No.:** GB 543 4721 52
Date established: 1990 **Turnover:** £5m - £10m
No.of Employees: 101 - 250 **Product Groups:** 37

Date of Accounts	Dec 10	Dec 09	Dec 08
Sales Turnover	9m	9m	9m
Pre Tax Profit/Loss	717	565	307
Working Capital	1m	1m	772
Fixed Assets	2m	771	724
Current Assets	4m	3m	3m
Current Liabilities	2m	2m	1m

Sebakmt UK Ltd
Unit C Beversbrook Centre Redman Road, Calne, SN11 9PR
Tel: 01249-816181 **Fax:** 01249-816186
E-mail: sales@sebakmtuk.com
Website: http://www.sebakmtuk.com

see next page

***Sebakmt UK Ltd** - Cont'd*

Directors: M. Napper (MD)
Ultimate Holding Company: SEBAKMT HOLDING GMBH (GERMANY)
Immediate Holding Company: SEBA KMT UK LIMITED
Registration no: 04593899 **Date established:** 2002 **Turnover:** £2m - £5m
No.of Employees: 1 - 10 **Product Groups:** 37, 38, 39, 48, 54, 83, 85, 86

Date of Accounts	Dec 11	Dec 10	Dec 09
Sales Turnover	3m	2m	2m
Pre Tax Profit/Loss	99	39	-180
Working Capital	-699	-801	-855
Fixed Assets	10	13	29
Current Assets	986	1m	917
Current Liabilities	98	100	68

H C Starck Ltd

Unit 1 Harris Road, Calne, SN11 9PT
Tel: 01249-822122 **Fax:** 01249-823800
E-mail: info@hcstarck.com
Website: http://www.hcstarck.com
Bank(s): Lloyds TSB Bank plc
Directors: P. Smith (Co Sec), S. Goode (MD)
Managers: D. Milner (Tech Serv Mgr), D. King (Contrlr), C. Brewer (Fin Mgr)
Ultimate Holding Company: THE CARLYLE GROUP LLC (USA)
Immediate Holding Company: H.C. STARCK LIMITED
Registration no: 02829540 **VAT No.:** GB 601 2706 90
Date established: 1993 **Turnover:** £10m - £20m
No.of Employees: 51 - 100 **Product Groups:** 32, 34, 35, 36, 37, 39, 40, 42, 46, 48, 84

Date of Accounts	Dec 11	Dec 10	Dec 09
Sales Turnover	10m	11m	14m
Pre Tax Profit/Loss	1m	18	-409
Working Capital	7m	6m	6m
Fixed Assets	1m	1m	2m
Current Assets	8m	8m	8m
Current Liabilities	383	1m	764

T W International Ltd

247 Oxford Road, Calne, SN11 8RS
Tel: 01249-822100 **Fax:** 01249-821919
E-mail: sales@twinternational.com
Website: http://www.twinternational.com
Directors: R. Wheeler (MD)
Immediate Holding Company: T W INTERNATIONAL LTD
Registration no: 02600896 **Date established:** 1991 **Turnover:** £2m - £5m
No.of Employees: 1 - 10 **Product Groups:** 35, 44

Date of Accounts	Mar 11	Mar 10	Mar 09
Working Capital	176	315	360
Fixed Assets	104	28	11
Current Assets	284	313	547

Tamura Europe Ltd

Clarke Avenue, Calne, SN11 9BS
Tel: 01380-731700 **Fax:** 01380-731702
E-mail: info-uk@tamura-europe.co.uk
Website: http://www.tamura-europe.co.uk
Directors: S. Cursley (Fin), S. Cursley (Fin)
Managers: B. Ingleson (Personnel), J. Parker, P. Randle
Ultimate Holding Company: TAMURA CORP (JAPAN)
Immediate Holding Company: TAMURA-EUROPE LIMITED
Registration no: 00463530 **VAT No.:** GB 501 9766 45
Date established: 1949 **Turnover:** £50m - £75m
No.of Employees: 11 - 20 **Product Groups:** 33, 37, 44

Date of Accounts	Dec 10	Dec 09	Dec 08
Sales Turnover	47m	39m	52m
Pre Tax Profit/Loss	-324	32	2m
Working Capital	3m	4m	5m
Fixed Assets	9m	863	586
Current Assets	21m	11m	16m
Current Liabilities	3m	2m	2m

Thornbury Surfacing Chippenham Ltd

3 Harris Road, Calne, SN11 9PT
Tel: 01249-813435 **Fax:** 01249-813233
E-mail: iainsaunders@thornburysurfacing.co.uk
Website: http://www.thornburysurfacing.co.uk
Directors: N. Blackmore (MD)
Immediate Holding Company: THORNBURY SURFACING CHIPPENHAM LIMITED
Registration no: 04089532 **Date established:** 2000
No.of Employees: 1 - 10 **Product Groups:** 14, 17, 31, 33, 51, 52, 84

Date of Accounts	Jun 12	Jun 11	Jun 10
Working Capital	1m	938	956
Fixed Assets	639	597	477
Current Assets	2m	2m	2m

Westcode UK Ltd

Unit 1 Porte Marsh Industrial Estate Carnegie Road, Calne, SN11 9PS
Tel: 01249-822283
E-mail: tonypark@westcodeuk.com
Website: http://www.westcodeus.com
Directors: T. Park (MD), S. Hendon (Fin)
Immediate Holding Company: WESTCODE (U.K.) LIMITED
Registration no: 03390528 **Date established:** 1997 **Turnover:** £1m - £2m
No.of Employees: 11 - 20 **Product Groups:** 35, 39, 66

Date of Accounts	Dec 11	Dec 10	Dec 09
Sales Turnover	N/A	2m	2m
Pre Tax Profit/Loss	N/A	96	133
Working Capital	830	544	508
Fixed Assets	136	118	112
Current Assets	1m	934	970
Current Liabilities	N/A	167	246

Chippenham

W & S Allely Ltd

Bumpers Way Bumpers Farm, Chippenham, SN14 6LH
Tel: 01249-443033 **Fax:** 01249-443826
E-mail: chippenham@allely.co.uk
Website: http://www.allely.co.uk
Managers: I. Neil (Mgr)
Ultimate Holding Company: ALLELY EDEN HOLDINGS LIMITED
Immediate Holding Company: W. & S. ALLELY LIMITED
Registration no: 00292572 **VAT No.:** GB 547 6741 12
Date established: 1934 **Turnover:** Up to £250,000
No.of Employees: 1 - 10 **Product Groups:** 34, 37, 49, 66

Date of Accounts	Dec 11	Dec 10	Dec 09
Working Capital	465	401	371
Fixed Assets	22	25	43
Current Assets	3m	2m	2m
Current Liabilities	N/A	N/A	166

B T Rolatruc

4a Lansdowne Court Bumpers Way, Bumpers Farm, Chippenham, SN14 6RZ
Tel: 01249-447633 **Fax:** 01249- 447679
Website: http://www.bt-rolatruc.com
Managers: P. Shephard (Sales Prom Mgr)
Ultimate Holding Company: SANDPIPER CORPORATION LIMITED
Immediate Holding Company: MOBILE COMPUTER STORE LIMITED
Registration no: 05859480 **Date established:** 2002
No.of Employees: 21 - 50 **Product Groups:** 35, 39, 45

Brim

26 Fitzwarren Close, Chippenham, SN15 3UF
Tel: 01249-447706
E-mail: adam@thebrim.co.uk
Website: http://www.thebrim.co.uk
Directors: A. Freeman (Prop), A. Freeman (Head)
No.of Employees: 1 - 10 **Product Groups:** 81

Brunel Microscopes Ltd

2 Vincients Road Bumpers Farm, Chippenham, SN14 6NQ
Tel: 01249-462655 **Fax:** 01249-445156
E-mail: brunelmicro@compuserve.com
Website: http://www.brunelmicroscopes.co.uk
Directors: A. Potter (Fin)
Immediate Holding Company: BRUNEL MICROSCOPES LIMITED
Registration no: 02060047 **Date established:** 1986
No.of Employees: 1 - 10 **Product Groups:** 38, 65

Date of Accounts	Oct 11	Oct 10	Oct 09
Working Capital	324	316	329
Fixed Assets	14	13	21
Current Assets	453	427	398

Capita Secure Information Solutions

Unit 7-8 Prospect West Bumpers Way Bumpers Farm, Chippenham, SN14 6FH
Tel: 08456-041999 **Fax:** 07002-929999
E-mail: info@vivista.sungard.co.uk
Website: http://www.capitasecureinformationsolutions.co.uk
Directors: C. Rodgerson (Grp Chief Exec), H. Wallis (Co Sec), D. Hatton (Pers), A. Burge (Fin)
Managers: D. White (Mktg Serv Mgr), J. Rowland (Purch Mgr), K. Day (Tech Serv Mgr)
Ultimate Holding Company: CAPITA PLC
Immediate Holding Company: CAPITA SECURE INFORMATION SOLUTIONS LIMITED
Registration no: 01593831 **Date established:** 1981
Turnover: £125m - £250m **No.of Employees:** 51 - 100
Product Groups: 44, 80, 84

Date of Accounts	Dec 11	Dec 09	Dec 08
Sales Turnover	140m	111m	103m
Pre Tax Profit/Loss	-1m	10m	7m
Working Capital	14m	33m	37m
Fixed Assets	9m	8m	8m
Current Assets	49m	70m	67m
Current Liabilities	17m	27m	20m

Colston Engineering Services Ltd

Brunel Park Vincients Road, Bumpers Farm, Chippenham, SN14 6NQ
Tel: 01249-652652 **Fax:** 01249-444684
E-mail: sales@colstonltd.co.uk
Website: http://www.colstonltd.co.uk
Bank(s): Barclays
Directors: B. Goad (Eng Serv)
Managers: S. Billingham (Sales Prom Mgr), G. Mears (Fin Mgr)
Ultimate Holding Company: COLSTON ENGINEERING SERVICES LIMITED
Immediate Holding Company: THE COLSTON MANUFACTURING (ENGINEERING) COMPANY LIMITED
Registration no: 00216350 **VAT No.:** GB 137 4128 77
Date established: 2026 **Turnover:** £2m - £5m **No.of Employees:** 51 - 100
Product Groups: 40, 48

Date of Accounts	Jul 11	Jul 10	Jul 09
Working Capital	154	154	154
Current Assets	154	154	154

De Marchi Engineering

Bumpers Farm Industrial Estate Vincients Road, Chippenham, SN14 6NQ
Tel: 01249-448860 **Fax:** 01249-445496
E-mail: sales@demarchi.co.uk
Website: http://www.demarchi.co.uk
Directors: R. Collins (MD)
Immediate Holding Company: EXECUTIVE JET SUPPORT LIMITED
Registration no: 02871026 **Date established:** 1994
Turnover: £500,000 - £1m **No.of Employees:** 11 - 20 **Product Groups:** 48

Date of Accounts	Dec 11	Jun 10	Jun 09
Working Capital	3m	2m	2m
Fixed Assets	264	186	190
Current Assets	3m	3m	3m

F C G Software Solutions Ltd

Whitelands Cottage Kington Langley, Chippenham, SN15 5PD
Tel: 01522-722232 **Fax:** 01249-750151
E-mail: software@fcgagric.com
Website: http://www.fcgagric.com
Directors: M. Sealy (Fin)
Immediate Holding Company: FCG SOFTWARE SOLUTIONS LIMITED
Registration no: 03631093 **Date established:** 1998
Turnover: Up to £250,000 **No.of Employees:** 1 - 10 **Product Groups:** 44

Date of Accounts	Nov 10	Nov 09	Nov 08
Sales Turnover	16	17	18
Pre Tax Profit/Loss	-1	3	3
Working Capital	-8	-7	-10
Current Assets	15	16	13
Current Liabilities	13	13	13

Gewiss UK Ltd

Bumpers Farm Industrial Estate Bumpers Farm, Chippenham, SN14 6LH
Tel: 01249-444734 **Fax:** 01249-444514
E-mail: michael.kingsbury@gewiss.co.uk
Website: http://www.gewiss.com
Bank(s): HSBC Bank plc
Directors: M. Kingsbury (Co Sec), N. Owen (MD)
Managers: M. Kingsbury (Comptroller), R. Thomas (Sales Prom Mgr), S. Goodman (Tech Ad), E. Davis (Personnel)
Ultimate Holding Company: POLIFIN SA (LUXEMBOURG)
Immediate Holding Company: GEWISS-UK-LIMITED
Registration no: 01844418 **Date established:** 1984 **Turnover:** £2m - £5m
No.of Employees: 11 - 20 **Product Groups:** 30, 37

Date of Accounts	Dec 07	Dec 06	Dec 05
Sales Turnover	4686	4394	4499
Pre Tax Profit/Loss	86	70	40
Working Capital	855	753	654
Fixed Assets	671	690	721
Current Assets	1765	1684	1731
Current Liabilities	910	931	1077
Total Share Capital	1000	1000	1000
ROCE% (Return on Capital Employed)	5.7	4.8	2.9
ROT% (Return on Turnover)	1.8	1.6	0.9

Great Western Ambulance Sevice N H S Trust

Dorman House Malmesbury Road, Chippenham, SN15 5LN
Tel: 01249-443939 **Fax:** 01249-443217
E-mail: exec.office@wiltsambs.nhs.uk
Website: http://www.wiltsamb.nhs.uk
Bank(s): Lloyds
Directors: T. Skelton (Grp Chief Exec)
Date established: 1991 **No.of Employees:** 21 - 50 **Product Groups:** 39

Integrated Water Services

Vincients Road Bumpers Farm Industrial Estate, Bumpers Farm, Chippenham, SN14 6NQ
Tel: 08702-402689 **Fax:** 01249-461766
E-mail: contact@integrated-water.co.uk
Website: http://www.integrated-water.co.uk
Managers: D. Abbott (Develop Mgr)
Ultimate Holding Company: HYDRIADES V LTD
Immediate Holding Company: BROCOL CONSULTANTS LIMITED
Registration no: 02434172 **Date established:** 1989 **Turnover:** £5m - £10m
No.of Employees: 11 - 20 **Product Groups:** 84, 85

Jepway Associates Ltd

Euridge Works Thickwood Lane, Chippenham, SN14 8BG
Tel: 01225-742301 **Fax:** 01225-743457
E-mail: info@jetway.co.uk
Website: http://www.jetway.co.uk
Bank(s): National Westminster Bank Plc
Directors: R. Read (Sales), P. Bambrough (MD)
Registration no: 02766912 **VAT No.:** GB 601 1446 95
Date established: 1993 **Turnover:** £500,000 - £1m
No.of Employees: 21 - 50 **Product Groups:** 26, 35, 39, 40, 46, 67

Jewson Ltd

Bath Road, Chippenham, SN14 0AB
Tel: 01249-653351 **Fax:** 01249-650412
Website: http://jewson.co.uk
Managers: S. Atkin (District Mgr)
Ultimate Holding Company: COMPAGNIE DE SAINT GOBAIN (FRANCE)
Immediate Holding Company: JEWSON LIMITED
Registration no: 00348407 **Date established:** 1939 **Turnover:** £2m - £5m
No.of Employees: 1 - 10 **Product Groups:** 66

Date of Accounts	Dec 11	Dec 10	Dec 09
Sales Turnover	1606m	1547m	1485m
Pre Tax Profit/Loss	18m	100m	45m
Working Capital	-345m	-250m	-349m
Fixed Assets	496m	387m	461m
Current Assets	657m	1005m	1320m
Current Liabilities	66m	120m	64m

Kerrie's Krazy Faces

21 Fitzwarren Close Pewsham, chippenham, SN15 3UF
Tel: 01249-446686
E-mail: kerrie@kerrieskrazyfaces.co.uk
Website: http://www.kerrieskrazyfaces.co.uk
Directors: K. Naylor (Prop), K. Naylor (MD), K. Laylor (Prop)
Date established: 2008 **No.of Employees:** 1 - 10 **Product Groups:** 89

Leadline Services Ltd

Brinkworth House Brinkworth, Chippenham, SN15 5DF
Tel: 01905-724000 **Fax:** 01905- 726888
E-mail: info@leadline.co.uk
Website: http://www.leadline.co.uk
Directors: C. Brewerton (MD)
Ultimate Holding Company: THE VIRTUAL BUSINESS CENTRE LIMITED
Immediate Holding Company: LEADLINE SERVICES LIMITED
Registration no: 03260056 **Date established:** 1996
No.of Employees: 1 - 10 **Product Groups:** 79, 80, 81

Date of Accounts	Oct 11	Oct 10	Jan 10
Working Capital	-35	-11	13
Fixed Assets	1	3	6
Current Assets	21	30	36

Deborah Mather

Woodseaves Upper North Wraxall, Chippenham, SN14 7AG
Tel: 01225-891379 **Fax:** 08700-516263
E-mail: debbie@matherwood.co.uk
Website: http://www.matherwood.co.uk
Directors: D. Mather (Prop)
No.of Employees: 1 - 10 **Product Groups:** 24, 63

Guy Morgan Design

Woodbury Hill House, 4 Gibb Road Upper Castle Combe, Chippenham, SN14 7NQ
Tel: 01249-783859
E-mail: guy@gmdesign.co.uk
Website: http://www.gmdesign.co.uk
Directors: G. Morgan (Prop)
VAT No.: GB 332 6780 55 **Date established:** 1964
Turnover: Up to £250,000 **No.of Employees:** 1 - 10 **Product Groups:** 26, 30, 35, 39, 49, 52, 81, 83, 84

Multiquip Supplies Ltd

Unit 1 Glenmore Business Park Vincients Road, Bumpers Farm, Chippenham, SN14 6BB
Tel: 01249-654945 **Fax:** 01249-654255
E-mail: sales@multiquipsupplies.co.uk
Website: http://www.multiquip.co.uk
Directors: J. Phillips (Prop)
Immediate Holding Company: MULTIQUIP SUPPLIES LIMITED
Registration no: 04603329 **VAT No.:** GB 452 7150 61
Date established: 2002 **Turnover:** £250,000 - £500,000
No.of Employees: 1 - 10 **Product Groups:** 66, 67

Date of Accounts	Dec 11	Dec 10	Dec 09
Working Capital	435	324	358
Fixed Assets	315	302	177
Current Assets	546	440	446

Openda Ltd
Unit 6 Callow Park Callow Hill, Brinkworth, Chippenham, SN15 5FD
Tel: 01666-510022
E-mail: enquiries@openda.com
Website: http://www.openda.com
Directors: N. Bell (Ch)
Managers: L. Hopkinson ()
Registration no: 03301305 **Date established:** 1990
No.of Employees: 1 - 10 **Product Groups:** 44

Date of Accounts	Mar 08	Mar 07	Mar 06
Working Capital	119	111	92
Fixed Assets	6	7	13
Current Assets	207	175	151
Current Liabilities	89	63	59

Pangea Ltd
185 Oxford Road Calne, Chippenham, SN15 1EN
Tel: 01249-462677 **Fax:** 01249-463841
E-mail: sales@pangeauk.com
Website: http://www.pangeauk.com
Directors: D. Simpson (MD), R. Simpson (Fin)
Immediate Holding Company: PANGEA LIMITED
Registration no: 03316560 **Date established:** 1997
Turnover: Up to £250,000 **No.of Employees:** 1 - 10 **Product Groups:** 32

Date of Accounts	Apr 11	Apr 10
Working Capital	5	1
Current Assets	31	35

P D T Ltd
Langley Building Kington Park, Kington Langley, Chippenham, SN15 5PZ
Tel: 01249-758425 **Fax:** 01249-758421
E-mail: support@pdtlimited.co.uk
Website: http://www.pdtlimited.co.uk
Directors: T. Myers (Dir)
Immediate Holding Company: PDT LIMITED
Registration no: 04211478 **Date established:** 2001
Turnover: £250,000 - £500,000 **No.of Employees:** 1 - 10
Product Groups: 81

Date of Accounts	May 11	May 10	May 09
Working Capital	128	125	160
Current Assets	375	449	166

Platinum Vauxhall
16-17 The Causeway, Chippenham, SN15 3DA
Tel: 01249-654321 **Fax:** 01249-462683
E-mail: glen.gilliam@renrodmg.co.uk
Website: http://www.platinumvauxhall.co.uk
Managers: G. Gilliam
Registration no: 06897092 **Date established:** 2009
No.of Employees: 21 - 50 **Product Groups:** 29, 39

Preactor International
Cornbrash Park Bumpers Farm, Chippenham, SN14 6RA
Tel: 01249-650316 **Fax:** 01249-443413
E-mail: graham.hackwell@preactor.com
Website: http://www.preactor.com
Directors: G. Hackwell (Dir), M. Novels (MD), Z. Wren (Fin)
Ultimate Holding Company: THE PREACTOR GROUP LIMITED
Immediate Holding Company: PREACTOR INTERNATIONAL LIMITED
Registration no: 01275683 **Date established:** 1976 **Turnover:** £1m - £2m
No.of Employees: 21 - 50 **Product Groups:** 44

Date of Accounts	Dec 11	Dec 10	Dec 09
Working Capital	819	876	558
Fixed Assets	165	155	104
Current Assets	2m	2m	1m

R T L Enterprises
Windrush Tormarton Road, Marshfield, Chippenham, SN14 8NN
Tel: 01225-891899 **Fax:** 01225-891890
E-mail: sales@rtlenterprises.co.uk
Directors: J. Traynor (Prop)
Date established: 1981 **No.of Employees:** 1 - 10 **Product Groups:** 20, 40, 41

Rawlings & White
Oaks Farm Rode Hill, Colerne, Chippenham, SN14 8AR
Tel: 01225-859536 **Fax:** 01225-859536
Directors: P. Rawlings (Ptnr)
Date established: 1990 **No.of Employees:** 1 - 10 **Product Groups:** 41

Rexel Senate Electrical Wholesalers Ltd
K Bumpers Farm Industrial Estate Bristol Road, Bumpers Farm, Chippenham, SN14 6LH
Tel: 01249-656127 **Fax:** 01249-654122
E-mail: chippenham@rexelsenate.co.uk
Website: http://www.rexelsenate.co.uk
Managers: J. Morse (Mgr)
Immediate Holding Company: TRIC LIMITED
Registration no: 05324053 **VAT No.:** GB 587 2692 88
Date established: 2005 **No.of Employees:** 1 - 10 **Product Groups:** 67

Date of Accounts	Jan 09
Sales Turnover	10
Pre Tax Profit/Loss	-4
Working Capital	-4

R H D First Aid Training
6 Wyndham Close, Chippenham, SN15 3SE
Tel: 01249-658378
E-mail: roydel76@hotmail.co.uk
Website: http://www.rhdtraining.co.uk
Directors: R. Delahaye (Prop)
Date established: 2005 **No.of Employees:** 1 - 10 **Product Groups:** 86

Rohmann UK Ltd
Unit 6 Glenmore Centre Vincients Road, Bumpers Farm, Chippenham, SN14 6BB
Tel: 01249-659346 **Fax:** 01249-443097
E-mail: info@rohmann.co.uk
Website: http://www.rohmann.co.uk
Directors: S. Barnes (MD)
Immediate Holding Company: ROHMANN (UK) LIMITED
Registration no: 01883996 **Date established:** 1985
Turnover: £250,000 - £500,000 **No.of Employees:** 1 - 10
Product Groups: 37, 38

Date of Accounts	Dec 11	Dec 10	Dec 09
Working Capital	215	189	125
Fixed Assets	9	5	3
Current Assets	315	413	337

Rota Val Ltd
Bumpers Way Bumpers Farm Industrial Estate, Bumpers Farm, Chippenham, SN14 6LH
Tel: 01249-651138
E-mail: steve.parkin@rotaval.co.uk
Website: http://www.rotaval.co.uk
Directors: B. Ford (Fin)
Managers: S. Winton (Sales Prom Mgr), S. Parkin (Ops Mgr), J. Cuthbertson (Tech Serv Mgr)
Ultimate Holding Company: GERICKE HOLDING AG (SWITZERLAND)
Immediate Holding Company: ROTA VAL HOLDINGS LIMITED
Registration no: 01785228 **Date established:** 1984
No.of Employees: 21 - 50 **Product Groups:** 36, 37, 38

Date of Accounts	Dec 11	Dec 10	Dec 09
Fixed Assets	115	115	115

Small Engine Services Ltd
5 & 6 Barrow End Centre Chippenham Road, Lyneham, Chippenham, SN15 4NY
Tel: 01249-892906 **Fax:** 01249-892911
E-mail: info@small-engine-services.co.uk
Website: http://www.small-engine-services.co.uk
Directors: S. Ewers (Dir)
Registration no: 03771642 **VAT No.:** 736 7913 01 **Date established:** 1990
Turnover: Up to £250,000 **No.of Employees:** 1 - 10 **Product Groups:** 29, 33, 35, 36, 37, 39, 40, 41, 46, 47, 48, 67, 68, 83

Date of Accounts	Jul 08	Jul 07	Jul 06
Working Capital	24	16	14
Fixed Assets	N/A	2	2
Current Assets	98	85	68
Current Liabilities	73	69	54

Softcaw Ltd
7 Wetherby Close Cepan Park South, Chippenham, SN14 0SU
Tel: 01249-444496 **Fax:** 07043-326267
E-mail: c.wilson@softcaw.com
Website: http://www.softcaw.com
Directors: C. Wilson (MD)
Immediate Holding Company: SOFTCAW LIMITED
Registration no: 04851056 **Date established:** 2003
No.of Employees: 1 - 10 **Product Groups:** 44

Date of Accounts	Jul 12	Jul 11	Jul 10
Working Capital	-6	N/A	-4
Current Assets	12	19	13

Surecast Alloys Ltd
Unit R11 Langley Park Foundry Lane, Chippenham, SN15 1JB
Tel: 01249-446017
E-mail: elliot@surecast.co.uk
Website: http://www.surecastalloys.co.uk
Directors: E. Eaton (Dir)
Managers: E. Eaton (Mgr)
Immediate Holding Company: SURECAST ALLOYS LIMITED
Registration no: 00888549 **Date established:** 1966
No.of Employees: 51 - 100 **Product Groups:** 40, 48

Date of Accounts	Mar 10	Mar 09	Mar 08
Working Capital	-44	-36	-213
Fixed Assets	740	675	679
Current Assets	2m	2m	1m

Tri-State
Unit 2 Glenmore Business Park Vincients Road, Bumpers Farm, Chippenham, SN14 6BB
Tel: 01249-464650 **Fax:** 01249-445414
E-mail: mikenickless@msn.com
Directors: M. Nicolas (Prop)
Immediate Holding Company: WINDHAGER UK LIMITED
Registration no: 04705307 **VAT No.:** GB 139 2748 45
Date established: 2007 **Turnover:** Up to £250,000
No.of Employees: 1 - 10 **Product Groups:** 30, 37, 38, 44, 68

Date of Accounts	Nov 09	Nov 08	Sep 11
Working Capital	N/A	N/A	69
Fixed Assets	N/A	N/A	17
Current Assets	N/A	N/A	574

Vysal Ltd
Unit 3 Lovett Farm Little Somerford, Chippenham, SN15 5BP
Tel: 01666-822059 **Fax:** 01666-822422
E-mail: sales@vysal.com
Website: http://www.vysal.com
Directors: R. Luthwyche (Comm)
Immediate Holding Company: VYSAL LIMITED
Registration no: 03136604 **Date established:** 1995
No.of Employees: 1 - 10 **Product Groups:** 37, 67

Date of Accounts	Mar 11	Mar 10	Mar 09
Working Capital	79	75	63
Fixed Assets	40	35	42
Current Assets	311	280	273

Watson Petroleum Ltd
Causeway End Brinkworth, Chippenham, SN15 5DN
Tel: 01666-510345 **Fax:** 01666-510684
E-mail: enquiries@watsonfuels.co.uk
Website: http://www.watsonfuels.co.uk
Directors: T. Watson (MD), G. Rutherford (Fin)
Managers: R. Street (Tech Serv Mgr)
Immediate Holding Company: WATSON PETROLEUM LIMITED
Registration no: 00594001 **VAT No.:** GB 195 0460 59
Date established: 1957 **Turnover:** £500m - £1,000m
No.of Employees: 21 - 50 **Product Groups:** 13

Date of Accounts	Apr 11	Apr 10	Apr 09
Sales Turnover	834m	585m	500m
Pre Tax Profit/Loss	8m	4m	9m
Working Capital	-2m	-6m	-3m
Fixed Assets	49m	45m	40m
Current Assets	91m	73m	43m
Current Liabilities	11m	10m	4m

Wavin Ltd
Parsonage Way, Chippenham, SN15 5PN
Tel: 01249-766600 **Fax:** 01249-443286
E-mail: andrew.taylor@wavin.co.uk
Website: http://www.wavin.co.uk
Bank(s): Lloyds TSB
Directors: K. Barker (Comm), J. Sage (Pers), P. Taylor (Fin), A. Taylor (Dir)
Managers: D. Merrell (Tech Serv Mgr), A. England
Ultimate Holding Company: WAVIN NV (NETHERLANDS)
Immediate Holding Company: WAVIN LIMITED
Registration no: 00405836 **VAT No.:** GB 222 7070 96
Date established: 1946 **Turnover:** £125m - £250m
No.of Employees: 501 - 1000 **Product Groups:** 30

Date of Accounts	Dec 10	Dec 09	Dec 08
Sales Turnover	176m	99m	119m
Pre Tax Profit/Loss	10m	4m	2m
Working Capital	-14m	-18m	-6m
Fixed Assets	56m	54m	34m
Current Assets	173m	163m	52m
Current Liabilities	63m	57m	29m

Westcode Semiconductors Ltd
Langley Park Way Langley Park, Chippenham, SN15 1GE
Tel: 01249-444524 **Fax:** 01249-659448
E-mail: m.hobbs@ixys.net
Website: http://www.westcode.com
Bank(s): Lloyds
Directors: M. Hobbs (Dir)
Ultimate Holding Company: IXYS CORPORATION (USA)
Immediate Holding Company: IXYS UK WESTCODE LTD.
Registration no: 03426095 **VAT No.:** GB 692 3716 13
Date established: 1997 **Turnover:** £20m - £50m
No.of Employees: 101 - 250 **Product Groups:** 37

Date of Accounts	Mar 11	Mar 10	Mar 09
Sales Turnover	34m	26m	29m
Pre Tax Profit/Loss	2m	211	1m
Working Capital	11m	9m	8m
Fixed Assets	1m	1m	2m
Current Assets	17m	16m	15m
Current Liabilities	924	942	941

Corsham

Chadwick Materials Handling Ltd
Unit 18 Edinburgh Way, Corsham, SN13 9XZ
Tel: 01225-810081 **Fax:** 01225-812234
E-mail: chadwicks@chadmh.co.uk
Website: http://www.chadmh.co.uk
Directors: P. Simmonds (Co Sec), T. Chadwick (MD)
Immediate Holding Company: CHADWICK MATERIALS HANDLING LIMITED
Registration no: 03671427 **Date established:** 1998
No.of Employees: 11 - 20 **Product Groups:** 35, 39, 45

Date of Accounts	Dec 11	Dec 10	Dec 09
Working Capital	652	605	564
Fixed Assets	456	484	511
Current Assets	740	804	632

F P F Packaging & Tubes
Unit 8-8b Leafield Industrial Estate Leafield Way, Corsham, SN13 9SW
Tel: 01225-810103 **Fax:** 01225-810663
E-mail: barbara@fpfpackaging.com
Bank(s): The Royal Bank of Scotland
Directors: B. Short (Dir)
VAT No.: GB 452 7673 29 **Turnover:** £500,000 - £1m
No.of Employees: 11 - 20 **Product Groups:** 27, 30

Fairyglass
28 Brunel Way Box, Corsham, SN13 8LR
Tel: 01225-743104
E-mail: info@fairyglass.co.uk
Website: http://www.fairyglass.co.uk
Directors: B. Biscoe (Prop)
Registration no: 07421797 **Turnover:** Up to £250,000
No.of Employees: 1 - 10 **Product Groups:** 65

J Price Bath Ltd
Quarry Hill Works Box, Corsham, SN13 8LH
Tel: 01225-742141 **Fax:** 01225-743237
E-mail: derek@jpricebath.co.uk
Website: http://www.jpricebath.co.uk
Directors: D. Price (MD)
Immediate Holding Company: J.PRICE(BATH)LIMITED
Registration no: 00438794 **VAT No.:** GB 137 8269 39
Turnover: £500,000 - £1m **No.of Employees:** 1 - 10 **Product Groups:** 29, 30, 31

Linguarama Ltd
Cheney Court Ditteridge, Box, Corsham, SN13 8QF
Tel: 01225-743557 **Fax:** 01225-743916
E-mail: cheneycourt@linguarama.com
Website: http://www.linguarama.com
Bank(s): Lloyds TSB Bank plc
Directors: J. Birkett (MD), L. Chandler (Fin)
Ultimate Holding Company: MARCUS EVANS INVESTMENTS LTD (BERMUDA)
Immediate Holding Company: LINGUARAMA LIMITED
Registration no: 00846378 **VAT No.:** GB 522 4808 60
Date established: 1965 **Turnover:** £10m - £20m
No.of Employees: 21 - 50 **Product Groups:** 86

Date of Accounts	Sep 11	Sep 10	Sep 09
Sales Turnover	6m	5m	6m
Pre Tax Profit/Loss	744	608	1m
Working Capital	7m	6m	6m
Fixed Assets	226	255	308
Current Assets	9m	8m	7m
Current Liabilities	1m	980	797

David Nightingale
20 Gastard Lane Gastard, Corsham, SN13 9QN
Tel: 01249-701271 **Fax:** 01249-701271
E-mail: david.nightingale@coachtrimming.co.uk
Website: http://www.coachtrimming.co.uk
Directors: D. Nightingale (Prop)
Date established: 1991 **Turnover:** Up to £250,000
No.of Employees: 1 - 10 **Product Groups:** 22, 29, 39

P & B Weir Electrical

Unit 1 Leafield Industrial Estate Leafield Way, Corsham, SN13 9SW
Tel: 01225-811449 **Fax:** 01225-810909
E-mail: sales@pbsigroup.com
Website: http://www.pbsigroup.com
Bank(s): National Westminster Bank Plc
Directors: G. Evans (MD)
Immediate Holding Company: PBSI LTD
Registration no: 02030212 **VAT No.:** GB 519 5499 07
Date established: 1927 **Turnover:** £1m - £2m **No.of Employees:** 21 - 50
Product Groups: 28, 37, 38

P & D Manufacturing Ltd

Unit A11 Fiveways Trading Estate Westwells Road, Hawthorn, Corsham, SN13 9RG
Tel: 01225-812900 **Fax:** 01225-812600
E-mail: mark.rushin@panddmanufacturing.co.uk
Website: http://www.pdmanufacturing.co.uk
Directors: A. Penton (Chief Op Offcr), M. Rushin (MD)
Managers: J. Evans (Sales Admin)
Ultimate Holding Company: AVON GROUP MANUFACTURING (HOLDINGS) LIMITED
Immediate Holding Company: P & D MANUFACTURING LIMITED
Registration no: 03035814 **VAT No.:** GB 399 0160 31
Date established: 1995 **Turnover:** £2m - £5m **No.of Employees:** 21 - 50
Product Groups: 30, 44, 46, 47, 48

Date of Accounts	Mar 12	Mar 11	Mar 10
Sales Turnover	4m	3m	2m
Pre Tax Profit/Loss	58	58	27
Working Capital	524	444	570
Fixed Assets	411	452	175
Current Assets	2m	2m	1m
Current Liabilities	520	730	242

Slatebond Ltd

Unit 27 Leafield Industrial Estate Leafield Way Neston, Corsham, SN13 9RS
Tel: 01225-810099 **Fax:** 01225-811413
E-mail: sales@slatebond.com
Website: http://www.slatebond.com
Bank(s): National Westminster Bank
Directors: J. Higson (Dir)
Managers: K. Ireland (Chief Mgr), A. Butts (Buyer)
Immediate Holding Company: SLATEBOND LIMITED
Registration no: 01614615 **VAT No.:** 357 5877 01 **Date established:** 1982
Turnover: £2m - £5m **No.of Employees:** 21 - 50 **Product Groups:** 30

Date of Accounts	Apr 12	Apr 11	Apr 10
Working Capital	273	289	257
Fixed Assets	474	507	518
Current Assets	512	558	514

Stephens Plastics Ltd (Plastics)

Hawthorn Works, Corsham, SN13 9RD
Tel: 01225-810324 **Fax:** 01225-811390
E-mail: info@stephens.co.uk
Website: http://www.stephens-plastics.co.uk
Bank(s): HSBC
Directors: A. Marshall (MD), L. Marshall (Fin)
Ultimate Holding Company: LANDMARC PRODUCTS LIMITED
Immediate Holding Company: STEPHENS (PLASTICS) LIMITED
Registration no: 00572598 **VAT No.:** GB 137 8925 31
Date established: 1956 **Turnover:** £2m - £5m **No.of Employees:** 21 - 50
Product Groups: 24, 29, 30, 48

Date of Accounts	Dec 11	Dec 10	Dec 09
Working Capital	736	760	750
Fixed Assets	47	65	60
Current Assets	1m	1m	1m

Teague Precision Chokes

Edinburgh Way, Corsham, SN13 9XZ
Tel: 01225-811614 **Fax:** 01225-811555
E-mail: sales@teaguechokes.co.uk
Website: http://www.teaguechokes.co.uk
Directors: K. Hiscock (Dir)
Ultimate Holding Company: GEWEFA JOSEPH C PFISTER GmbH (GERMANY)
Immediate Holding Company: GEWEFA U.K. LIMITED
Registration no: 02573632 **Date established:** 1991 **Turnover:** £1m - £2m
No.of Employees: 1 - 10 **Product Groups:** 36, 39, 40

Wansdyke Security Ltd

PO Box 179, Corsham, SN13 9TL
Tel: 01225-810225 **Fax:** 01225-810625
E-mail: sales@wansdyke.co.uk
Website: http://www.clarity-integration.com
Bank(s): Bank of Scotland
Directors: L. Ford (Co Sec), E. Marshall (Dir)
Managers: M. Read (Purch Mgr)
Ultimate Holding Company: GERALDTON SERVICES INC (USA)
Immediate Holding Company: WANSDYKE SECURITY LIMITED
Registration no: 04087743 **VAT No.:** GB 771 1770 29
Date established: 2000 **Turnover:** £5m - £10m
No.of Employees: 51 - 100 **Product Groups:** 77

Date of Accounts	Dec 11	Dec 10	Dec 09
Sales Turnover	5m	5m	5m
Pre Tax Profit/Loss	2m	2m	1m
Working Capital	10m	2m	-274
Fixed Assets	4m	8m	7m
Current Assets	11m	4m	2m
Current Liabilities	963	687	843

Weatherform Ltd

Unit 16 Leafield Industrial Estate Leafield Way, Corsham, SN13 9SW
Tel: 01225-812757 **Fax:** 01225-812758
E-mail: martyn@weatherform.co.uk
Website: http://www.weatherform.co.uk
Directors: M. Young (Dir)
Immediate Holding Company: WEATHERFORM LIMITED
Registration no: 02435438 **VAT No.:** GB 543 3785 32
Date established: 1989 **Turnover:** £500,000 - £1m
No.of Employees: 11 - 20 **Product Groups:** 30, 40

Date of Accounts	Oct 11	Oct 10	Oct 09
Sales Turnover	727	704	566
Pre Tax Profit/Loss	138	79	18
Working Capital	166	146	160
Fixed Assets	19	13	24
Current Assets	297	218	206
Current Liabilities	68	19	21

Devizes

Analytical Technology & Control Ltd

Broadway Market Lavington, Devizes, SN10 5RQ
Tel: 01380-818411 **Fax:** 01380-812733
E-mail: alistair.crawford@atacgroup.com
Website: http://www.atacgroup.com
Bank(s): Barclays
Directors: A. Crawford (MD)
Immediate Holding Company: ANALYTICAL TECHNOLOGY AND CONTROL LIMITED
Registration no: 02828636 **VAT No.:** GB 139 8703 37
Date established: 1993 **Turnover:** £2m - £5m **No.of Employees:** 21 - 50
Product Groups: 38, 84

Date of Accounts	Dec 11	Dec 10	Aug 09
Working Capital	2m	2m	2m
Fixed Assets	116	84	143
Current Assets	2m	3m	3m

Ball Aerocan UK Ltd

Folly Road Roundway, Devizes, SN10 2HT
Tel: 01380-732400 **Fax:** 01380-732440
E-mail: jason.galley@aerocan.eu
Website: http://www.aerocan.eu
Directors: J. Galley (Dir), I. Rumbold (Co Sec)
Managers: J. Blottiere (Sales Prom Mgr), M. Freegard (Tech Serv Mgr), M. Wilkins (Personnel), D. Livingson-alder (Purch Mgr), T. White (Comptroller)
Ultimate Holding Company: BALL CORPORATION (USA)
Immediate Holding Company: BALL AEROCAN UK LIMITED
Registration no: 01813312 **VAT No.:** GB 422 9049 61
Date established: 1984 **Turnover:** £20m - £50m
No.of Employees: 101 - 250 **Product Groups:** 30, 33, 35, 36

Date of Accounts	Dec 11	Dec 10	Dec 09
Sales Turnover	27m	23m	20m
Pre Tax Profit/Loss	6m	5m	4m
Working Capital	12m	11m	9m
Fixed Assets	2m	2m	2m
Current Assets	17m	16m	12m
Current Liabilities	2m	1m	2m

Canburg

Hopton Indl-Est, Devizes, SN10 2EU
Tel: 01380-729090 **Fax:** 01380-727771
Website: http://www.smallbone.co.uk
Bank(s): Barclays
Directors: S. Wilkinson (MD), C. Smallbone (Ch), M. Warbrick (MD), N. Johnson (Dir)
Managers: M. Eagland (I.T. Exec)
Immediate Holding Company: CANBURG LIMITED
Registration no: 06841786 **VAT No.:** GB 790 2025 49
Date established: 2009 **Turnover:** £20m - £50m
No.of Employees: 101 - 250 **Product Groups:** 26, 63, 67

Date of Accounts	Dec 09
Sales Turnover	27m
Pre Tax Profit/Loss	-4m
Working Capital	-10m
Fixed Assets	8m
Current Assets	5m
Current Liabilities	14m

Carter Pumps Ltd

Beechfield Road Hopton Industrial Estate, Devizes, SN10 2DX
Tel: 01380-734900 **Fax:** 01380-734901
E-mail: sales@carterpumps.co.uk
Website: http://www.carterpumps.co.uk
Directors: M. Sowden (MD)
Immediate Holding Company: CARTER PUMPS LIMITED
Registration no: 04078313 **VAT No.:** GB 398 9839 52
Date established: 2000 **No.of Employees:** 11 - 20 **Product Groups:** 40, 51, 67

Date of Accounts	Nov 11	Nov 10	Nov 09
Working Capital	-112	34	159
Fixed Assets	236	154	51
Current Assets	212	221	462

Crypton Ltd

Hopton Road Hopton Park Industrial Estate, Devizes, SN10 2EU
Tel: 01278-436205 **Fax:** 01278-450567
E-mail: sales@cryptontechnology.com
Website: http://www.cryptontechnology.com
Bank(s): Lloyds TSB Bank plc
Directors: P. Houlden (Dir), J. Coward (Co Sec)
Ultimate Holding Company: TIDEWAY HOLDINGS LIMITED (JERSEY)
Immediate Holding Company: CRYPTON LIMITED
Registration no: 03451389 **Date established:** 1997 **Turnover:** £2m - £5m
No.of Employees: 21 - 50 **Product Groups:** 38, 39

Date of Accounts	Mar 12	Mar 11	Mar 10
Sales Turnover	5m	4m	4m
Pre Tax Profit/Loss	58	51	359
Working Capital	584	839	972
Fixed Assets	268	80	24
Current Assets	2m	2m	3m
Current Liabilities	292	369	400

Hallmark Flooring Ltd

24 Market Place, Devizes, SN10 1JQ
Tel: 01380-723102 **Fax:** 01380-723102
E-mail: info@hallmarkflooring.co.uk
Website: http://www.hallmarkflooring.co.uk
Directors: N. Fautley (Dir)
Immediate Holding Company: HALLMARK FLOORING COMPANY LIMITED
Registration no: 04464142 **Date established:** 2002
Turnover: £250,000 - £500,000 **No.of Employees:** 1 - 10
Product Groups: 23, 25, 29

Date of Accounts	Jun 11	Jun 10	Jun 09
Working Capital	-69	-58	-31
Fixed Assets	1	2	7
Current Assets	3	10	15

Jewson Ltd

Garden Trading Estate London Road, Devizes, SN10 2HL
Tel: 01380-725441 **Fax:** 01380-729306
E-mail: terry.bushell@jewson.co.uk
Website: http://www.jewson.co.uk
Managers: A. Morgan (Mgr)
Ultimate Holding Company: COMPAGNIE DE SAINT GOBAIN (FRANCE)
Immediate Holding Company: JEWSON LIMITED
Registration no: 00348407 **Date established:** 1939 **Turnover:** £2m - £5m
No.of Employees: 21 - 50 **Product Groups:** 66

Date of Accounts	Dec 11	Dec 10	Dec 09
Sales Turnover	1606m	1547m	1485m
Pre Tax Profit/Loss	18m	100m	45m
Working Capital	-345m	-250m	-349m
Fixed Assets	496m	387m	461m
Current Assets	657m	1005m	1320m
Current Liabilities	66m	120m	64m

Latchways plc

Waller Road, Devizes, SN10 2JP
Tel: 01380-732700 **Fax:** 01380-732701
E-mail: info@latchways.com
Website: http://www.latchways.com
Bank(s): The Royal Bank of Scotland, London
Directors: A. Hogg (Sales)
Managers: P. Applegate (Mktg Serv Mgr)
Immediate Holding Company: LATCHWAYS PLC
Registration no: 01189060 **Date established:** 1974
Turnover: £20m - £50m **No.of Employees:** 101 - 250
Product Groups: 35, 67

Date of Accounts	Mar 12	Mar 11	Mar 10
Sales Turnover	41m	40m	34m
Pre Tax Profit/Loss	10m	9m	8m
Working Capital	20m	20m	16m
Fixed Assets	10m	10m	10m
Current Assets	26m	26m	21m
Current Liabilities	3m	4m	3m

Mosses & Mitchell Ltd

18 The Street All Cannings, Devizes, SN10 3PA
Tel: 01380-722993 **Fax:** 01380-728422
E-mail: sales@mosses-mitchel.com
Website: http://www.mosses-mitchell.com
Directors: A. Wilson (Fin), P. Wilson (MD)
Immediate Holding Company: MOSSES & MITCHELL LIMITED
Registration no: 03855575 **VAT No.:** GB 188 4711 29
Date established: 1999 **Turnover:** £500,000 - £1m
No.of Employees: 1 - 10 **Product Groups:** 37

Protect Fire Equipment Ltd

Unit 3A The Pound Coate, Devizes, SN10 3LG
Tel: 01380-860011 **Fax:** 01380-860022
E-mail: mail@protect-fire.co.uk
Website: http://www.protect-fire.co.uk
Directors: V. Davis (Dir), A. Davis (Fin)
Immediate Holding Company: PROTECT FIRE EQUIPMENT LIMITED
Registration no: 05549345 **Date established:** 2005
No.of Employees: 1 - 10 **Product Groups:** 38, 42

Date of Accounts	Sep 11	Sep 10	Sep 09
Working Capital	-17	-16	-16
Fixed Assets	17	19	21
Current Assets	40	46	46
Current Liabilities	50	N/A	N/A

Relcross

Hambleton Avenue, Devizes, SN10 2RT
Tel: 01380-729600 **Fax:** 01380-729888
E-mail: info@relcross.co.uk
Website: http://www.relcross.co.uk
Directors: M. Dallaway (MD), R. White (Co Sec)
Immediate Holding Company: RELCROSS LIMITED
Registration no: 04137277 **Date established:** 2001 **Turnover:** £2m - £5m
No.of Employees: 11 - 20 **Product Groups:** 30, 33, 35, 36, 40, 66

Date of Accounts	Mar 11	Mar 10	Mar 09
Working Capital	954	780	760
Fixed Assets	462	480	383
Current Assets	1m	1m	1m

Ryder plc

Unit 1-3 Prince Maurice Court Hambleton Avenue, Devizes, SN10 2RT
Tel: 01380-731500 **Fax:** 01380-720785
E-mail: pat_obrien@ryder.com
Website: http://www.ryder.com
Bank(s): Barclays
Directors: T. Dillon (Chief Op Offcr), C. Deevey (Purch), M. Parker (Tech Serv), S. Mulley (Chief Op Offcr)
Managers: B. Howard (Sales Prom Mgr), R. White (Mktg Serv Mgr)
Ultimate Holding Company: RYDER SYSTEM INC (USA)
Immediate Holding Company: RYDER LIMITED
Registration no: 01019474 **VAT No.:** GB 222 6757 65
Date established: 1971 **Turnover:** £125m - £250m
No.of Employees: 51 - 100 **Product Groups:** 80, 84

Date of Accounts	Dec 11	Dec 10	Dec 09
Sales Turnover	205m	147m	158m
Pre Tax Profit/Loss	19m	12m	12m
Working Capital	57m	-21m	-23m
Fixed Assets	309m	151m	148m
Current Assets	108m	76m	68m
Current Liabilities	19m	18m	28m

T H White Holdings Limited Company

Nursteed Road, Devizes, SN10 3EA
Tel: 07702-724308 **Fax:** 01242-820108
Website: http://www.thwhite.co.uk
Managers: G. Norman (Mgr)
Immediate Holding Company: T. H. White Holdings Ltd
Registration no: 00133886 **Date established:** 2003
No.of Employees: 1 - 10 **Product Groups:** 41

T Y M Seals & Gaskets Ltd

Unit A Beacon Business Centre Hopton Park, Devizes, SN10 2EY
Tel: 01380-734510 **Fax:** 01380-734511
E-mail: sales@tym.co.uk
Website: http://www.tym.co.uk
Directors: L. Phillips (Dir)
Immediate Holding Company: T.Y.M. SEALS AND GASKETS LIMITED
Registration no: 02806321 **Date established:** 1993 **Turnover:** £1m - £2m
No.of Employees: 11 - 20 **Product Groups:** 23, 25, 27, 29, 30, 31, 36, 38, 40, 41, 44, 65

Date of Accounts	Apr 11	Apr 10	Apr 09
Working Capital	327	265	298
Fixed Assets	69	70	61
Current Assets	521	425	431

Thermal Designs UK Ltd
Broadway Market Lavington, Devizes, SN10 5RQ
Tel: 01380-816079 **Fax:** 01380-813394
E-mail: sales@tdiuk.com
Website: http://www.tdiuk.com
Managers: A. Bragg (Chief Mgr)
Ultimate Holding Company: THERMAL DESIGNS INC (USA)
Immediate Holding Company: THERMAL DESIGNS U.K. LIMITED
Registration no: 03240260 **Date established:** 1996
Turnover: Up to £250,000 **No.of Employees:** 1 - 10 **Product Groups:** 33

Date of Accounts	Dec 11	Dec 10	Dec 09
Working Capital	26	15	-83
Fixed Assets	134	122	101
Current Assets	372	406	227

Wadworth & Co. Ltd
41-45 Northgate Street, Devizes, SN10 1JW
Tel: 01380-723361 **Fax:** 01380-724342
E-mail: sales@wadworth.co.uk
Website: http://www.wadworth.co.uk
Bank(s): Lloyds TSB Bank plc
Directors: A. West (Sales), G. Percy (Fin), P. Sullivan (Mkt Research), R. Gordon Finlayson (Fin)
Managers: P. Eustice (Buyer), D. Youngman (Personnel)
Immediate Holding Company: WADWORTH AND COMPANY LIMITED
Registration no: 00030177 **VAT No.:** GB 137 4872 46
Date established: 1989 **Turnover:** £50m - £75m
No.of Employees: 501 - 1000 **Product Groups:** 21

Date of Accounts	Sep 11	Sep 10	Sep 09
Sales Turnover	55m	52m	53m
Pre Tax Profit/Loss	4m	5m	5m
Working Capital	-620	213	-16m
Fixed Assets	113m	113m	112m
Current Assets	8m	9m	7m
Current Liabilities	5m	4m	3m

T H White Ltd
Nursteed Road, Devizes, SN10 3EA
Tel: 01380-722381 **Fax:** 01380-729147
E-mail: enquiries@thwhite.co.uk
Website: http://www.phwhite.co.uk
Bank(s): LLoyds
Directors: D. Scott (MD)
Managers: D. Ernist (I.T. Exec), P. Barker (Sec), S. Meadows (Sales & Mktg Mg)
Immediate Holding Company: T. H. WHITE HOLDINGS LIMITED
Registration no: 00133886 **VAT No.:** GB 137 5670 53
Date established: 2014 **Turnover:** £75m - £125m
No.of Employees: 11 - 20 **Product Groups:** 67

Date of Accounts	Dec 07	Dec 06	Dec 05
Sales Turnover	84395	79638	75806
Pre Tax Profit/Loss	2518	1523	1447
Working Capital	8195	7955	7475
Fixed Assets	1752	1722	1906
Current Assets	24134	22882	21420
Current Liabilities	15939	14927	13946
Total Share Capital	403	403	403
ROCE% (Return on Capital Employed)	25.3	15.7	15.4
ROT% (Return on Turnover)	3.0	1.9	1.9

T H White Installation Ltd
Unit 3 Nursteed Road Trading Estate William Road, Devizes, SN10 3EW
Tel: 01380-726656 **Fax:** 01380-725707
E-mail: gcv@thwhite.co.uk
Website: http://www.thwhitesecurityandfire.co.uk
Bank(s): Lloyds TSB Bank plc
Directors: C. McGowan (Fin), P. Barker (Co Sec), J. Higgs (Pers)
Managers: D. Ernest, G. Venning (Div Mgr)
Ultimate Holding Company: T. H. WHITE HOLDINGS LIMITED
Immediate Holding Company: T.H. WHITE, INSTALLATION, LIMITED
Registration no: 01406798 **VAT No.:** GB 137 5670 53
Date established: 1978 **Turnover:** £10m - £20m
No.of Employees: 21 - 50 **Product Groups:** 38, 67

Date of Accounts	Dec 11	Dec 10	Dec 09
Sales Turnover	14m	11m	18m
Pre Tax Profit/Loss	512	534	925
Working Capital	2m	2m	1m
Fixed Assets	307	234	193
Current Assets	4m	3m	3m
Current Liabilities	2m	810	1m

Wyvern Partnership
10 Long Street, Devizes, SN10 1NJ
Tel: 01380-723532 **Fax:** 01380-726304
E-mail: wyvernexperts@btconnect.com
Bank(s): Lloyds TSB
Directors: M. Valentine (Ptnr)
Immediate Holding Company: WYVERN ARCHITECTS-DEVIZES LTD
Registration no: 04867306 **VAT No.:** 543 3522 63 **Date established:** 1974
Turnover: Up to £250,000 **No.of Employees:** 11 - 20 **Product Groups:** 84

Malmesbury

Alvan Blanch Development Co. Ltd
Chelworth Manor Crudwell, Malmesbury, SN16 9SG
Tel: 01666-577333 **Fax:** 01666-577339
E-mail: info@alvanblanch.co.uk
Website: http://www.alvanblanch.co.uk
Bank(s): National Westminster Bank Plc
Directors: H. Blanch (Fin), A. Blanch (MD)
Immediate Holding Company: ALVAN BLANCH DEVELOPMENT COMPANY LIMITED
Registration no: 00507937 **VAT No.:** GB 137 4224 81
Date established: 1952 **Turnover:** £10m - £20m
No.of Employees: 51 - 100 **Product Groups:** 35, 38, 40, 41, 42, 43, 44, 45, 46, 47, 48, 67, 84

Date of Accounts	Dec 11	Dec 10	Dec 09
Sales Turnover	9m	11m	6m
Pre Tax Profit/Loss	601	645	228
Working Capital	677	1m	576
Fixed Assets	2m	2m	1m
Current Assets	4m	4m	2m
Current Liabilities	1m	2m	298

Custom Transformers Ltd
Unit 23 Whitewalls, Easton Grey, Malmesbury, SN16 0RD
Tel: 01666-824411 **Fax:** 01666-824413 /823931
E-mail: kevin.baldwin@custom-transformers.co.uk
Website: http://www.custom-transformers.co.uk
Bank(s): HSBC Bank plc
Directors: K. Baldwin (MD)
Managers: V. Easterling (Accounts), J. Pike (Trng Mgr), C. Picter (Purch Mgr)
Registration no: 01068311 **VAT No.:** GB 137 5898 23
Date established: 1972 **Turnover:** £1m - £2m **No.of Employees:** 21 - 50
Product Groups: 37

Date of Accounts	Dec 11	Dec 10	Dec 09
Working Capital	247	167	131
Fixed Assets	91	85	97
Current Assets	508	461	286

Leading Resolutions Ltd
Riverside Business Village Swindon Road, Malmesbury, SN16 9RS
Tel: 08450-600601 **Fax:** 0845-060 0602
E-mail: info@leadingresolutions.com
Website: http://www.leadingresolutions.com
Managers: L. Motto (Sales Admin)
Immediate Holding Company: LEADING RESOLUTIONS LIMITED
Registration no: 04307011 **Date established:** 2001
No.of Employees: 1 - 10 **Product Groups:** 44

Date of Accounts	Dec 11	Dec 10	Dec 09
Working Capital	788	530	355
Fixed Assets	384	208	106
Current Assets	2m	2m	1m

Nor-Cal UK Ltd
Units 5 & 6 Home Farm Business Centre, Minety, Malmesbury, SN16 9PL
Tel: 01666-861221 **Fax:** 01666-861223
E-mail: jjudson1@aol.com
Website: http://www.norcaluk.com
Directors: J. Judson (MD)
Immediate Holding Company: NOR-CAL UK LIMITED
Registration no: 03501061 **Date established:** 1998
No.of Employees: 1 - 10 **Product Groups:** 33, 35, 36, 37, 40, 42, 46, 67

Date of Accounts	Dec 11	Dec 10	Dec 09
Working Capital	449	292	229
Fixed Assets	1	1	2
Current Assets	741	520	275

People Orientated Solutions In I T Ltd
6 Wychurch Road Reeds Farm, Malmesbury, SN16 9XT
Tel: 01666-825476
E-mail: info@pos-itive.biz
Website: http://www.pos-itive.biz
Directors: M. Brown (MD)
Immediate Holding Company: PEOPLE ORIENTATED SOLUTIONS IN I T LIMITED
Registration no: 04701334 **Date established:** 2003
No.of Employees: 1 - 10 **Product Groups:** 37, 44, 67, 80

Date of Accounts	Mar 11	Mar 10	Mar 05
Working Capital	N/A	1	-1
Fixed Assets	1	1	1
Current Assets	6	11	1

Stretch Line UK Ltd
Old Silk Mill Sherston, Malmesbury, SN16 0NG
Tel: 01666-842100 **Fax:** 01666-840903
E-mail: philip.allen@stretchline.com
Website: http://www.stretchline.com
Directors: P. Allen (Sales), C. Tubbs (Fin)
Managers: N. Saunders (Prod Mgr), C. Somers (I.T. Exec)
Immediate Holding Company: STRETCHLINE (UK) LIMITED
Registration no: 04207389 **Date established:** 2001
No.of Employees: 21 - 50 **Product Groups:** 23, 24, 29, 30, 63

Date of Accounts	Dec 11	Dec 10	Dec 09
Sales Turnover	6m	5m	5m
Pre Tax Profit/Loss	797	538	-133
Working Capital	1m	524	895
Fixed Assets	6m	6m	5m
Current Assets	4m	3m	3m
Current Liabilities	2m	3m	2m

Supply Lines
Gloucester Road Industrial Estate, Malmesbury, SN16 9JT
Tel: 0800-587 0415
Website: http://www.hilditchauctions.co.uk
Directors: M. Hilditch (Prop)
No.of Employees: 1 - 10 **Product Groups:** 38, 61, 67

Tinplate Products
The Old Granary Pinkney Park Pinkney, Malmesbury, SN16 0NX
Tel: 01666-841600 **Fax:** 0117-958 6777
E-mail: info@tinplate-products.com
Website: http://www.tinplate-products.com
Bank(s): Natwest
Directors: R. Christmas (Ptnr)
Immediate Holding Company: TINPLATE PRODUCTS LIMITED
Registration no: 04542636 **VAT No.:** GB 800 4348 70
Date established: 2002 **Turnover:** £500,000 - £1m
No.of Employees: 11 - 20 **Product Groups:** 20, 22, 31, 34, 35, 36, 46, 48

Date of Accounts	Sep 11	Sep 10	Sep 09
Working Capital	427	373	352
Fixed Assets	1	N/A	N/A
Current Assets	664	500	473

Marlborough

Advanced Battery Care Ltd
Unit 5 Whittonditch Works, Ramsbury, Marlborough, SN8 2XB
Tel: 01672-520572 **Fax:** 01672-520717
E-mail: david.fremlin@batterycare.co.uk
Website: http://www.batterycare.co.uk
Directors: D. Fremlin (MD)
Immediate Holding Company: ADVANCED BATTERY CARE LIMITED
Registration no: 02949484 **Date established:** 1994
Turnover: £250,000 - £500,000 **No.of Employees:** 1 - 10
Product Groups: 37, 38, 44

Date of Accounts	Dec 11	Dec 10	Dec 09
Working Capital	14	32	105
Fixed Assets	88	105	78
Current Assets	281	172	261

C O Vehicle Services
Marlborough Road Aldbourne, Marlborough, SN8 2DD
Tel: 01672-520362 **Fax:** 01672-541676
E-mail: suencol@btinternet.com
Directors: C. Ockwell (Prop)
Immediate Holding Company: ERFOLG LIMITED
Date established: 1995 **No.of Employees:** 1 - 10 **Product Groups:** 39, 40, 48, 85

Trevor Cook
8 Garlands Cadley, Collingbourne Ducis, Marlborough, SN8 3EB
Tel: 01264-850024 **Fax:** 01264-850025
Directors: T. Cook (Prop)
Date established: 1998 **No.of Employees:** 1 - 10 **Product Groups:** 35

Force Technologies Ltd
2 Ashley Court Henley, Marlborough, SN8 3RH
Tel: 01264-731200 **Fax:** 01264-731444
E-mail: ann.salmon@forcetechnologies.co.uk
Website: http://www.forcetechnologies.co.uk
Directors: A. Salmon (Fin)
Immediate Holding Company: FORCE TECHNOLOGIES LIMITED
Registration no: 02028735 **Date established:** 1986 **Turnover:** £5m - £10m
No.of Employees: 1 - 10 **Product Groups:** 37, 44

Date of Accounts	Sep 11	Sep 10	Sep 09
Working Capital	456	587	613
Fixed Assets	149	121	196
Current Assets	1m	1m	2m

K D Tank Supplies Ltd
2 Westfields Farm Ogbourne St George, Marlborough, SN8 1SX
Tel: 0800-622866
E-mail: info@kdtanksupplies.co.uk
Website: http://www.kdtanksupplies.co.uk
Directors: E. Smith (Fin)
Immediate Holding Company: K D TANK SUPPLIES LIMITED
Registration no: 04397183 **Date established:** 2002
No.of Employees: 11 - 20 **Product Groups:** 35, 42, 45

Date of Accounts	Mar 12	Mar 11	Mar 10
Working Capital	106	117	109
Fixed Assets	78	105	144
Current Assets	207	256	208

Kennet Optical
3 New Road, Marlborough, SN8 1AH
Tel: 01672-512568
Website: http://www.haineandsmith.co.uk
Managers: E. Noyes (Mgr)
No.of Employees: 11 - 20 **Product Groups:** 37, 38, 65

London Facilities Ltd
Lloran House 42a High Street, Marlborough, SN8 1HQ
Tel: 01672-511112 **Fax:** 01672-511113
E-mail: info@londonfacilities.co.uk
Website: http://www.londonfacilities.co.uk
Directors: E. Baliszewski (MD), I. Rowley (Fin)
Managers: C. Knowles (Purch Mgr)
Registration no: 01493026 **Date established:** 1980
No.of Employees: 1 - 10 **Product Groups:** 54

Date of Accounts	Oct 08	Oct 07	Oct 06
Working Capital	-24	-18	-13
Fixed Assets	1	1	2
Current Assets	11	12	13
Current Liabilities	35	29	26

Marlborough Tiles
Elcot Lane, Marlborough, SN8 2AY
Tel: 01672-512422 **Fax:** 01672-515791
E-mail: sales@marlboroughtiles.com
Website: http://www.marlboroughtiles.com
Bank(s): National Westminster
Directors: C. Whately (Fin), T. Putt (Sales), J. Robb (MD)
Ultimate Holding Company: MARLBOROUGH TILES HOLDINGS LIMITED
Immediate Holding Company: PACKARD AND ORD LIMITED
Registration no: 01619266 **VAT No.:** 194 7573 17 **Date established:** 1982
Turnover: £2m - £5m **No.of Employees:** 11 - 20 **Product Groups:** 30, 33

Mill Engineers Pewsey Ltd
Unit 3 Hatfield Farm Oare, Marlborough, SN8 4JE
Tel: 01672-569900 **Fax:** 01672-569910
Website: http://www.westernharvesters.co.uk
Managers: R. Hayward
No.of Employees: 1 - 10 **Product Groups:** 41

Parker Young
5 Kennet Rise Axford, Marlborough, SN8 2EZ
Tel: 0845-1080185
E-mail: jeremy@parkeryoung.co.uk
Website: http://www.parkeryoung.co.uk
Product Groups: 32, 52

Sir William Bentley Billiards
Marten, Marlborough, SN8 3SJ
Tel: 01264-731210 **Fax:** 01264-731480
E-mail: sales@billiards.co.uk
Website: http://www.billiards.co.uk
Directors: T. Nettleton (Prop)
Managers: N. Le Bon (Tech Serv Mgr)
VAT No.: GB 501 6879 47 **Date established:** 1938
Turnover: £500,000 - £1m **No.of Employees:** 11 - 20 **Product Groups:** 33

Tenable Screw Co. Ltd
Stonebridge Close, Marlborough, SN8 2AE
Tel: 01672-512900 **Fax:** 01672-513915
E-mail: sales@tenable.co.uk
Website: http://www.tenable.co.uk
Managers: C. Holden (Chief Mgr), C. Halden (Chief Mgr)
Immediate Holding Company: STUBBINGS GROUP LIMITED
Registration no: 01180177 **VAT No.:** GB 216 3175 85
Date established: 1974 **Turnover:** £5m - £10m **No.of Employees:** 21 - 50
Product Groups: 35, 48

Melksham

Arrow Radiators Melksham Ltd
Unit 6a Bowerhill Industrial Estate Bowerhill, Melksham, SN12 6TS
Tel: 01225-707996 **Fax:** 01225-704767
E-mail: admin@arrowrad.co.uk
Website: http://www.arrowrad.co.uk
Directors: T. Mckenzie (MD)
Immediate Holding Company: ARROW RADIATORS (MELKSHAM) LIMITED
Registration no: 05202806 **VAT No.:** GB 357 5767 08
Date established: 2004 **Turnover:** £250,000 - £500,000
No.of Employees: 1 - 10 **Product Groups:** 40, 84

Date of Accounts	Apr 11	Apr 10	Apr 09
Sales Turnover	316	4	N/A
Working Capital	6	-12	28
Fixed Assets	43	48	20
Current Assets	76	61	70

ATI Stellram
Bowerhill, Melksham, SN12 6YH
Tel: 01225-897100 **Fax:** 01225-897111
E-mail: stellram.sales@atimetals.com
Website: http://www.stellram.co.uk
Bank(s): Nat West
Directors: D. Hogan (Dir), E. Davis (Co Sec)
Managers: S. Trust (Comptroller)
Ultimate Holding Company: ALLEGHENY TECHNOLOGIES INC (USA)
Immediate Holding Company: ATI STELLRAM LTD
Registration no: 01506705 **Date established:** 1980 **Turnover:** £5m - £10m
No.of Employees: 51 - 100 **Product Groups:** 12, 20, 31, 34

Date of Accounts	Dec 11	Dec 10	Dec 09
Sales Turnover	8m	7m	7m
Pre Tax Profit/Loss	168	-60	-727
Working Capital	5m	5m	5m
Fixed Assets	9m	9m	10m
Current Assets	7m	7m	6m
Current Liabilities	221	178	158

Avon Impact Management
Hampton Park West Semington Rd, Melksham, SN12 6NB
Tel: 01225-896421 **Fax:** 01225-896301
E-mail: sales@avon-impact.com
Website: http://www.avon-impact.com
Managers: K. Jeffery (Sales Prom Mgr)
Registration no: LP005341 **Date established:** 0120 **Turnover:**
No.of Employees: 1001 - 1500 **Product Groups:** 39

Bearings Plus
17 Pegasus Way Bowerhill, Melksham, SN12 6TR
Tel: 01225-702777 **Fax:** 01225-700031
E-mail: sales@bearings-plus.co.uk
Website: http://www.bearings-plus.co.uk
Directors: J. Perry (Dir)
Immediate Holding Company: ORTAC LIMITED
Registration no: 06754846 **Date established:** 2008
No.of Employees: 1 - 10 **Product Groups:** 25, 29, 30, 31, 33, 34, 35, 36, 37, 38, 39, 40, 43, 47, 48, 49, 66, 67, 68, 84

Date of Accounts	Dec 11	Nov 10	Nov 09
Working Capital	1	N/A	N/A
Current Assets	1	N/A	N/A

Bluemay Multicap a Division of the Bluemay Group
Bidmead Park Sells Green, Seend, Melksham, SN12 6RS
Tel: 01380-821800 **Fax:** 01380-821898
E-mail: multicap@bluemay.co.uk
Website: http://www.bluemaymulticap.co.uk
Managers: A. Robson (Sales Prom Mgr)
Registration no: 01115531 **Date established:** 2002 **Turnover:** £2m - £5m
No.of Employees: 21 - 50 **Product Groups:** 30, 35

Cooper Tire & Rubber Company Europe Ltd
Bath Road, Melksham, SN12 8AA
Tel: 01225-703101 **Fax:** 01225-707880
E-mail: jstride@coopertire.com
Website: http://www.coopertire.com
Bank(s): Barclays
Directors: J. Schumaker (Sales & Mktg), J. Stride (Fin)
Managers: A. Watts, G. Champion (Personnel), S. Slade (Purch Mgr)
Ultimate Holding Company: COOPER TIRE & RUBBER CO (USA)
Immediate Holding Company: COOPER TIRE & RUBBER COMPANY INTERNATIONAL DEVELOPMENT LIMITED
Registration no: 00894744 **VAT No.:** GB 682 5804 13
Date established: 1966 **Turnover:** £2m - £5m
No.of Employees: 501 - 1000 **Product Groups:** 68

Date of Accounts	Dec 11	Dec 10	Dec 09
Working Capital	-734	-829	-212
Fixed Assets	697	792	176

D H F Engineering Ltd
Unit 1 Harrier Court Merlin Way, Bowerhill, Melksham, SN12 6TJ
Tel: 01225-790225 **Fax:** 01225-703570
E-mail: sales@dhfengineering.co.uk
Website: http://www.dhfengineering.co.uk
Directors: D. Houghton (MD)
Immediate Holding Company: DHF ENGINEERING LIMITED
Registration no: 03828297 **Date established:** 1999
No.of Employees: 1 - 10 **Product Groups:** 26, 34, 35, 40, 46, 48, 51, 52

Date of Accounts	Feb 12	Feb 11	Feb 10
Working Capital	-33	-62	-20
Fixed Assets	40	44	39
Current Assets	129	222	165

Dispak Ltd
Lysander House Bowerhill, Melksham, SN12 6SP
Tel: 01225-705252 **Fax:** 01225-706915
E-mail: sales@dispak.co.uk
Website: http://www.dispak.co.uk
Directors: S. Brown (Dir)
Managers: C. Roper (Sales Prom Mgr)
Ultimate Holding Company: DISPAK LIMITED
Immediate Holding Company: DISPAK LIMITED
Registration no: 02050242 **Date established:** 1986 **Turnover:** £5m - £10m
No.of Employees: 1 - 10 **Product Groups:** 27, 66

Date of Accounts	Mar 11	Mar 10	Mar 09
Sales Turnover	N/A	N/A	9m
Pre Tax Profit/Loss	N/A	N/A	188
Working Capital	389	360	265
Fixed Assets	129	116	129
Current Assets	2m	2m	2m
Current Liabilities	N/A	N/A	204

G Plan Upholstery Ltd
Hampton Park West, Melksham, SN12 6GU
Tel: 01225-700880 **Fax:** 01225-792397
E-mail: info@gplan.co.uk
Website: http://www.gplan.co.uk
Bank(s): Barclays
Directors: G. Brown (Fin), M. Daly (Sales)
Managers: D. Rhodes (Personnel), A. Walker (Buyer), F. Oxley (Tech Serv Mgr), P. Andeky
Immediate Holding Company: G PLAN UPHOLSTERY LIMITED
Registration no: 00149073 **VAT No.:** GB 133 4836 74
Date established: 2017 **Turnover:** £20m - £50m
No.of Employees: 101 - 250 **Product Groups:** 26

Date of Accounts	Dec 07	Jun 11	Jun 10
Sales Turnover	25m	36m	29m
Pre Tax Profit/Loss	3m	4m	4m
Working Capital	8m	10m	10m
Fixed Assets	279	453	215
Current Assets	12m	18m	18m
Current Liabilities	2m	3m	3m

Ian Berg Plastics Ltd
Unit 4 Avro Business Centre Avro Way, Bowerhill, Melksham, SN12 6TP
Tel: 01225-700877 **Fax:** 01225-700860
E-mail: info@ianberg-plastics.co.uk
Website: http://www.ibpl.freeserve.co.uk
Directors: B. Hanks (MD)
Ultimate Holding Company: BOMARK PLASTICS LIMITED
Immediate Holding Company: IAN BERG PLASTICS LIMITED
Registration no: 02043837 **VAT No.:** GB 357 5939 05
Date established: 1986 **Turnover:** £500,000 - £1m
No.of Employees: 11 - 20 **Product Groups:** 30, 42, 43, 48, 84

Date of Accounts	Jun 11	Jun 10	Jun 09
Working Capital	60	88	62
Fixed Assets	122	125	141
Current Assets	189	196	193

J D A Fixings
Unit 7 & 8 Indus Acre Avro Way, Bowerhill, Melksham, SN12 6TP
Tel: 01225-709970 **Fax:** 01225-709995
E-mail: sales@jdafixings.com
Website: http://www.jdafixings.com
Directors: C. Atkinson (Ptnr)
VAT No.: GB 436 9848 00 **Turnover:** £250,000 - £500,000
No.of Employees: 1 - 10 **Product Groups:** 30, 35, 66

N B A Refrigeration Company Ltd
Unit 2 Indus Acre Avro Way, Bowerhill, Melksham, SN12 6TP
Tel: 01225-709506 **Fax:** 01225-709666
E-mail: sales@retardersprovers.co.uk
Website: http://www.nbarefrigeration.co.uk
Directors: A. Mould (Fin)
Immediate Holding Company: N.B.A. REFRIGERATION COMPANY LIMITED
Registration no: 02024940 **VAT No.:** GB 437 0606 63
Date established: 1986 **Turnover:** £250,000 - £500,000
No.of Employees: 1 - 10 **Product Groups:** 40, 48

Date of Accounts	Mar 11	Mar 10	Mar 09
Sales Turnover	N/A	N/A	449
Pre Tax Profit/Loss	N/A	N/A	168
Working Capital	34	41	54
Fixed Assets	6	6	7
Current Assets	125	92	132
Current Liabilities	N/A	N/A	42

Rembrook Development
Unit 4 Merlin Way Bowerhill, Melksham, SN12 6TJ
Tel: 01225-791184 **Fax:** 01225-700477
Website: http://www.genesisindustriesinc.com
Directors: M. Anderson (Dir)
Ultimate Holding Company: GENESIS MANUFACTURING LTD.
Immediate Holding Company: REMBROOK DEVELOPMENTS LIMITED
Registration no: 02217722 **Date established:** 1988
No.of Employees: 1 - 10 **Product Groups:** 30, 38

Date of Accounts	Mar 11	Mar 10	Mar 09
Working Capital	85	72	71
Current Assets	88	72	79

Robatech UK Ltd
The Street Broughton Gifford, Melksham, SN12 8PH
Tel: 01225-783456 **Fax:** 01225-783400
E-mail: general@robatech.co.uk
Website: http://www.robatech.co.uk
Directors: K. Baldy (MD), N. Woodrow (Sales)
Managers: D. Parker (Comptroller)
Immediate Holding Company: ROBATECH (U.K.) LIMITED
Registration no: 01849686 **Date established:** 1984
No.of Employees: 11 - 20 **Product Groups:** 38, 42

Date of Accounts	Dec 11	Dec 10	Nov 09
Working Capital	872	884	1m
Fixed Assets	177	161	161
Current Assets	1m	2m	2m

Smithpack Ltd
1 Pegasus Way Bowerhill, Melksham, SN12 6TR
Tel: 01225-709628 **Fax:** 01225-709884
E-mail: kna@smithpack.co.uk
Website: http://www.smithpack.co.uk
Directors: K. Allwood (MD), T. Coverdale (Fin), A. Brigstock (Sales)
Ultimate Holding Company: WSPH LIMITED
Immediate Holding Company: SMITHPACK LIMITED
Registration no: 01850712 **Date established:** 1984 **Turnover:** £5m - £10m
No.of Employees: 51 - 100 **Product Groups:** 38, 42

Date of Accounts	Apr 11	Apr 10	Apr 09
Sales Turnover	7m	7m	7m
Pre Tax Profit/Loss	105	73	-400
Working Capital	226	66	-187
Fixed Assets	431	528	752
Current Assets	2m	2m	2m
Current Liabilities	872	1m	1m

V B Leisure
17 Lime Avenue, Melksham, SN12 6UY
Tel: 01225-708865
E-mail: enquiries@vbleisure.co.uk
Website: http://www.vbleisure.co.uk
Directors: I. Hobbs (Prop)
No.of Employees: 1 - 10 **Product Groups:** 29, 49, 69

Valldata Services
2a Halifax Road, Melksham, SN12 6UB
Tel: 01225-354201 **Fax:** 01225-709689
E-mail: sales@valldata.co.uk
Website: http://www.valldata.co.uk
Directors: H. Horton (Grp Chief Exec)
Ultimate Holding Company: VALLDATA GROUP LIMITED
Immediate Holding Company: VALLDATA SERVICES LIMITED
Registration no: 01671518 **VAT No.:** GB 378 8650 91
Date established: 1982 **Turnover:** £5m - £10m
No.of Employees: 101 - 250 **Product Groups:** 44, 81

Date of Accounts	Mar 12	Mar 11	Mar 10
Sales Turnover	7m	6m	5m
Pre Tax Profit/Loss	710	793	737
Working Capital	390	270	55
Fixed Assets	466	364	448
Current Assets	2m	2m	2m
Current Liabilities	667	665	630

Veterinary Concept
4 Merlin Way Bowerhill, Melksham, SN12 6TJ
Tel: 01225-700476 **Fax:** 01225-700477
Website: http://www.genesisindustriesinc.com
Managers: L. Smith (Mgr)
Ultimate Holding Company: GENESIS MANUFACTURING LTD.
Immediate Holding Company: VETERINARY CONCEPTS EUROPE LIMITED
Registration no: 02496265 **Date established:** 1990
No.of Employees: 1 - 10 **Product Groups:** 30

Date of Accounts	Mar 11	Mar 10	Mar 09
Working Capital	22	21	22
Current Assets	30	29	71

Pewsey

Loheat
Fordbrook Estate Marlborough Road, Pewsey, SN9 5NT
Tel: 01672-564601 **Fax:** 01672-564602
E-mail: sales@loheat.com
Website: http://www.loheat.com
Directors: M. Daly (Tech Serv)
Immediate Holding Company: LOHEAT LIMITED
Registration no: 02970950 **VAT No.:** GB 641 6863 26
Date established: 1994 **Turnover:** £500,000 - £1m
No.of Employees: 1 - 10 **Product Groups:** 37, 41

Date of Accounts	Feb 12	Feb 11	Feb 10
Working Capital	214	176	142
Fixed Assets	22	N/A	N/A
Current Assets	369	325	330

Shredhouse Gift Packaging
Salisbury Road Business Park Salisbury Road, Pewsey, SN9 5PZ
Tel: 01672-564333 **Fax:** 01672-564301
E-mail: sales@shredhouse.co.uk
Website: http://www.shredhouse.co.uk
Directors: J. Stephens (Dir)
Registration no: 05289338 **Date established:** 2004
No.of Employees: 1 - 10 **Product Groups:** 38, 42

Signal Business Systems Ltd
Swan Corner, Pewsey, SN9 5HL
Tel: 01672-563333 **Fax:** 01672-562391
E-mail: post@signalbusinesssystems.co.uk
Website: http://www.gopher-systems.co.uk
Directors: C. Spencer (MD)
Immediate Holding Company: SIGNAL BUSINESS SYSTEMS LIMITED
Registration no: 00818723 **VAT No.:** GB 199 3652 11
Date established: 1964 **Turnover:** Up to £250,000
No.of Employees: 1 - 10 **Product Groups:** 49

Date of Accounts	Dec 10	Dec 09	Dec 08
Working Capital	126	47	98
Fixed Assets	N/A	126	51
Current Assets	133	61	127

Tye Engineering
Ayrshire Farm Sharcott, Pewsey, SN9 5PA
Tel: 01672-563791
Directors: N. Tye (Dir), T. Tye (Fin)
Immediate Holding Company: TYE ENGINEERING LIMITED
Registration no: 05855939 **Date established:** 2006
Turnover: Up to £250,000 **No.of Employees:** 1 - 10 **Product Groups:** 26, 35, 52

Date of Accounts	Mar 11	Mar 10	Mar 09
Sales Turnover	N/A	N/A	174
Pre Tax Profit/Loss	N/A	N/A	29
Working Capital	-47	-43	-43
Fixed Assets	64	57	62
Current Assets	36	44	32
Current Liabilities	N/A	N/A	20

Salisbury

Aim Flooring
14 Fairview Road, Salisbury, SP1 1JX
Tel: 01722-339766 **Fax:** 01722-339766
E-mail: info@aim-flooring.com
Website: http://www.aim-flooring.com
Directors: G. Mcenhill (Prop)
Date established: 1985 **No.of Employees:** 1 - 10 **Product Groups:** 52

Aquaflex Ltd
1 Edison Road Churchfields, Salisbury, SP2 7NU
Tel: 01722-328873 **Fax:** 01722-413068
E-mail: info@aquaflex.co.uk
Website: http://www.aquaflex.co.uk
Bank(s): Lloyds TSB Bank plc
Directors: M. Crossman (Co Sec), N. Dalziel (Dir)
Managers: P. Johns (Tech Serv Mgr)
Immediate Holding Company: AQUAFLEX LIMITED
Registration no: 02838628 **VAT No.:** GB 631 6853 36
Date established: 1993 **Turnover:** £1m - £2m **No.of Employees:** 21 - 50
Product Groups: 29, 30

Date of Accounts	Dec 11	Dec 10	Dec 09
Working Capital	228	242	237
Fixed Assets	654	672	705
Current Assets	635	672	665

Avago Karting & Laster Clay Pigeon Shooting
1 Windrush Cottages West Dean, Salisbury, SP5 1HR
Tel: 01794-884693
E-mail: tntrwbrdg@aol.com
Website: http://www.avago.co.uk
Directors: T. Throwbridge (Prop)
Date established: 1995 **Turnover:** Up to £250,000
No.of Employees: 1 - 10 **Product Groups:** 49, 83, 89

R D Avery
New Road Landford, Salisbury, SP5 2AZ
Tel: 01794-323296 **Fax:** 01794-323480
E-mail: hello@rdavery.com
Website: http://www.rdavery.com
Directors: R. Avery (Prop)
Date established: 1983 **No.of Employees:** 11 - 20 **Product Groups:** 39

J Battle
Pipers Drier Studio Clarendon Park, Salisbury, SP5 3ES
Tel: 01722-711770 **Fax:** 01722-506707
E-mail: jay.battle@ntlworld.com
Directors: J. Battle (Prop)
No.of Employees: 1 - 10 **Product Groups:** 25, 33, 35, 49, 52, 66

Beyond Design
South Newton Industrial Estate Warminster Road, South Newton, Salisbury, SP2 0QW
Tel: 01722-743822 **Fax:** 01722- 743822
E-mail: sales@beyond-design.co.uk
Website: http://www.beyonddesign.co.uk
Directors: P. Spiller (Dir)
Immediate Holding Company: BEYOND DESIGN (SALISBURY) LIMITED
Registration no: 06226682 **Date established:** 2007
No.of Employees: 1 - 10 **Product Groups:** 35

Brilliant Embroidery Ltd
Unit 5b Landford Common Farm, Landford, Salisbury, SP5 2AZ
Tel: 01794-322332 **Fax:** 01794-323444
E-mail: jenny@brilliantembroidery.co.uk
Website: http://www.brilliantembroidery.co.uk
Directors: J. Cree (Ptnr)
Managers: C. Cree (Mgr)
Immediate Holding Company: BRILLIANT EMBROIDERY LIMITED
Registration no: 05072260 **Date established:** 2004
No.of Employees: 1 - 10 **Product Groups:** 23, 24

Burlen Fuel Systems Ltd
Spitfire Hous Castle Road, Salisbury, SP1 3SA
Tel: 01722-412500 **Fax:** 01722-334221
E-mail: info@burlen.co.uk
Website: http://www.burlen.co.uk
Bank(s): Lloyds TSB Bank plc
Directors: J. Cridge (MD), M. Burnett (MD), L. Burnett (Co Sec)
Managers: D. Williams (Buyer)
Immediate Holding Company: BURLEN FUEL SYSTEMS LIMITED
Registration no: 02005550 **Date established:** 1986 **Turnover:** £2m - £5m
No.of Employees: 51 - 100 **Product Groups:** 40

Date of Accounts	Dec 11	Dec 10	Dec 09
Working Capital	1m	1m	1m
Fixed Assets	635	526	453
Current Assets	2m	2m	2m

C B Skips Ltd
St Thomas Farm, Salisbury, SP1 3YU
Tel: 01722-320544 **Fax:** 01722-410329
E-mail: info@cbskiphire.co.uk
Website: http://www.cbskiphire.co.uk
Managers: P. Forrest (Transport)
Immediate Holding Company: C.BIALEK LIMITED
Registration no: 00725936 **Date established:** 1962
No.of Employees: 21 - 50 **Product Groups:** 14, 39, 45, 54, 83

Date of Accounts	May 11	May 10	May 09
Working Capital	190	288	733
Fixed Assets	573	560	672
Current Assets	711	679	934

C I Precision
2 Brunel Road, Salisbury, SP2 7PX
Tel: 01722-424100 **Fax:** 01722-323222
E-mail: adrian.roberts@cielec.com
Website: http://www.cielec.com
Bank(s): National Westminster
Directors: E. Roberts (Mkt Research), J. Roberts (Tech Serv), A. Roberts (Dir)
Managers: W. Eaden (Sales Prom Mgr), J. Cox (Fin Mgr), R. Snook (Buyer)
Immediate Holding Company: C.I.ELECTRONICS LIMITED
Registration no: 00850159 **VAT No.:** GB 188 2226 46
Date established: 1965 **Turnover:** £1m - £2m **No.of Employees:** 21 - 50
Product Groups: 37, 38

Date of Accounts	May 11	May 10	May 09
Working Capital	158	5	-10
Fixed Assets	393	394	414
Current Assets	526	367	481

C & O Tractors Ltd
West Street Wilton, Salisbury, SP2 0DG
Tel: 01722-742141 **Fax:** 01722-744497
E-mail: enquiries@candotractors.co.uk
Website: http://www.candotractors.com
Managers: P. Shutler (District Mgr)
Ultimate Holding Company: C & O HOLDINGS LIMITED
Immediate Holding Company: C & O TRACTORS LIMITED
Registration no: 03431352 **Date established:** 1997 **Turnover:** £2m - £5m
No.of Employees: 11 - 20 **Product Groups:** 07

Date of Accounts	Mar 11	Mar 10	Mar 09
Sales Turnover	31m	33m	N/A
Pre Tax Profit/Loss	301	369	230
Working Capital	2m	751	561
Fixed Assets	240	1m	1m
Current Assets	14m	14m	17m
Current Liabilities	1m	2m	1m

Certis Europe
1b Boscombe Down Business Park Mills Way, Amesbury, Salisbury, SP4 7RX
Tel: 01980-676500 **Fax:** 01980-626555
E-mail: info@certiseurope.co.uk
Website: http://www.certiseurope.co.uk
Bank(s): Lloyds TSB Bank plc
Managers: J. Clovis (Mgr)
Ultimate Holding Company: MITSUI & CO. LTD (JAPAN)
Registration no: 01201539 **Turnover:** £1m - £2m
No.of Employees: 11 - 20 **Product Groups:** 32

Champion Materials Handling Ltd
Glendale Farm Southampton Road, Whiteparish, Salisbury, SP5 2QW
Tel: 01202-430323 **Fax:** 01794-884413
E-mail: sales@champion-forklifts.co.uk
Website: http://www.champion-forklifts.co.uk
Directors: D. Martin (MD)
Immediate Holding Company: CHAMPION MATERIALS HANDLING LIMITED
Registration no: 03011424 **Date established:** 1995
No.of Employees: 1 - 10 **Product Groups:** 35, 39, 45

Date of Accounts	Jun 11	Jun 10	Jun 09
Working Capital	17	-8	-33
Fixed Assets	96	56	49
Current Assets	252	229	241

Chemring Countermeasures
High Post, Salisbury, SP4 6AS
Tel: 01722-411611 **Fax:** 01722-428798
E-mail: info@chemringcm.com
Website: http://www.chemringcm.com
Directors: D. Corbin (Fin), P. Goddard (Mkt Research), S. Darling (MD), P. Walker (Pers), S. Ellard (Co Sec)
Managers: A. Carr (Chief Buyer), S. Morley (Tech Serv Mgr)
Ultimate Holding Company: CHEMRING GROUP PLC
Immediate Holding Company: CHEMRING COUNTERMEASURES LIMITED
Registration no: 00218229 **Date established:** 2026
Turnover: £20m - £50m **No.of Employees:** 251 - 500
Product Groups: 37, 39, 40

Date of Accounts	Oct 11	Oct 10	Oct 09
Sales Turnover	43m	54m	52m
Pre Tax Profit/Loss	7m	14m	14m
Working Capital	3m	-63	3m
Fixed Assets	42m	32m	22m
Current Assets	31m	20m	19m
Current Liabilities	7m	5m	7m

Clarke Instruments Ltd (Head Office and Works)
Distloc House Old Sarum Airfield, Old Sarum, Salisbury, SP4 6DZ
Tel: 01722-323451 **Fax:** 01722-335154
E-mail: chris@clarke-inst.com
Website: http://www.clarke-inst.com
Bank(s): Lloyds TSB Bank plc
Directors: A. White (Sales), T. Clarke (MD), B. Cross (Dir), C. Graham (Sales), C. Graham (Dir), W. Clarke (Ch), M. Clarke (MD)
Managers: E. Scovell (Purch Mgr)
Immediate Holding Company: CLARKE INSTRUMENTS LIMITED
Registration no: 00953610 **VAT No.:** GB 211 3233 30
Date established: 1969 **Turnover:** £1m - £2m **No.of Employees:** 21 - 50
Product Groups: 35, 36, 40

Date of Accounts	Sep 10	Sep 09	Sep 08
Working Capital	687	648	512
Fixed Assets	165	178	214
Current Assets	927	990	958

Custom Accessories Europe Ltd
Unit 10 Minton Distribution Park London Road, Amesbury, Salisbury, SP4 7RT
Tel: 01980-676400 **Fax:** 01980-676401
E-mail: sales@caeurope.co.uk
Website: http://www.caeurope.co.uk
Directors: S. King (MD), S. Morgan (Co Sec)
Managers: D. Barnhard (I.T. Exec), M. Greves (Mktg Serv Mgr), M. Wright (Comptroller)
Immediate Holding Company: CUSTOM ACCESSORIES,EUROPE, LIMITED
Registration no: 02642811 **VAT No.:** GB 570 0402 85
Date established: 1991 **Turnover:** £2m - £5m **No.of Employees:** 21 - 50
Product Groups: 68

Date of Accounts	Dec 09	Dec 08	Dec 07
Sales Turnover	4m	6m	6m
Pre Tax Profit/Loss	16	74	32
Working Capital	626	585	802
Fixed Assets	279	267	337
Current Assets	2m	2m	3m
Current Liabilities	1m	1m	2m

D O Systems
Unit 4 Woodford Centre Old Sarum Park Lysander Way, Old Sarum, Salisbury, SP4 6BU
Tel: 01722-333394 **Fax:** 01722-333395
E-mail: accounts@dosystems.co.uk
Website: http://www.dosystems.co.uk
Managers: G. Orne (Fin Mgr)
Immediate Holding Company: DO SYSTEMS LTD
Registration no: 06203306 **Date established:** 2007
No.of Employees: 11 - 20 **Product Groups:** 38, 39, 84

Date of Accounts	Sep 11	Sep 10	Sep 09
Working Capital	-1m	-532	916
Fixed Assets	786	965	1m
Current Assets	2m	2m	2m

Design Group Ltd
Unit 2 Avon Terrace, Salisbury, SP2 7BX
Tel: 01722-335112 **Fax:** 01722-412521
E-mail: engineering@listgroup.co.uk
Website: http://www.listgroup.co.uk
Bank(s): Barclays
Directors: D. List (MD), C. List (Fin)
Managers: C. Long (Mgr), C. Long (Asst Gen Mgr), E. Perkins (Chief Mgr)
Immediate Holding Company: DESIGN GROUP LIMITED
Registration no: 06661437 **Date established:** 2008
Turnover: Up to £250,000 **No.of Employees:** 11 - 20 **Product Groups:** 44, 81, 84

Downton Diggers Ground Works
Tanglewood Salisbury Road, Shrewton, Salisbury, SP3 4EE
Tel: 01980-621865
E-mail: downtondiggers@btinternet.com
Directors: B. Musselwhite (Prop)
No.of Employees: 1 - 10 **Product Groups:** 45, 83

Downton Signs
1 Vale Road Woodfalls, Salisbury, SP5 2LT
Tel: 01725-511218 **Fax:** 01725-511218
E-mail: downton-signs@hotmail.co.uk
Website: http://www.downton-signs.co.uk
Directors: B. Jackson (Prop)
Date established: 1980 **Turnover:** Up to £250,000
No.of Employees: 1 - 10 **Product Groups:** 28

Equinox International
Castlegate Business Park Old Sarum, Salisbury, SP4 6QX
Tel: 01722-424000 **Fax:** 01722-424001
E-mail: sales@eqx.com
Website: http://www.equinox.com
Bank(s): Bank of Scotland
Directors: K. Winterton (Ch), C. Fairman (Co Sec)
Managers: J. Lee (Sales Prom Mgr), P. Sharp (Accounts), B. King (Chief Acct), C. Elder, S. Kirk (Works Gen Mgr), C. Ford (Chief Mgr)
Immediate Holding Company: AMARI METALS LTD
Registration no: 02565339 **VAT No.:** GB 608 8799 82
Turnover: £20m - £50m **No.of Employees:** 21 - 50 **Product Groups:** 34, 35, 66

Date of Accounts	Dec 07
Sales Turnover	25130
Pre Tax Profit/Loss	-1820
Working Capital	-1320
Fixed Assets	450
Current Assets	11290
Current Liabilities	12610
Total Share Capital	890
ROCE% (Return on Capital Employed)	209.2

Esco GB Ltd
Unit 20 Parkers Close, Downton Industrial Estate, Salisbury, SP5 3RB
Tel: 01725-514555 **Fax:** 01725-514551
E-mail: info@escogb.com
Website: http://www.escogb.com
Directors: G. Barrett (MD)
Immediate Holding Company: ESCO GB LIMITED
Registration no: 05823830 **Date established:** 2006
No.of Employees: 1 - 10 **Product Groups:** 40, 66

Date of Accounts	Dec 11	Dec 10	Dec 09
Working Capital	375	413	349
Fixed Assets	14	15	18
Current Assets	520	610	482

Flowplant Group Ltd (Harben Neolith)
Gemini House 3 Brunel Road, Salisbury, SP2 7PU
Tel: 01722-325424 **Fax:** 01722-411329
E-mail: info@flowplant.com
Website: http://www.flowplant.co.uk
Bank(s): Barclays
Directors: A. Hiscock (Mkt Research), A. Drew (Co Sec), M. Bastable (Dir)
Managers: M. Wakeman (Tech Serv Mgr), B. Bennett (Purch Mgr)
Ultimate Holding Company: FLOWPLANT HOLDINGS LIMITED
Immediate Holding Company: FLOWPLANT GROUP LIMITED
Registration no: 03612438 **VAT No.:** GB 715 5370 43
Date established: 1998 **Turnover:** £10m - £20m
No.of Employees: 21 - 50 **Product Groups:** 39, 40, 41, 45, 46

Date of Accounts	Sep 11	Sep 10	Sep 09
Sales Turnover	6m	5m	5m
Pre Tax Profit/Loss	330	240	154
Working Capital	2m	1m	994
Fixed Assets	244	198	203
Current Assets	3m	3m	2m
Current Liabilities	665	241	159

Francis Frith Collection
Oakley Wylye Road, Dinton, Salisbury, SP3 5EU
Tel: 01722-716376 **Fax:** 01722-716881
E-mail: john_buck@francisfrith.co.uk
Website: http://www.francisfrith.com
Directors: J. Buck (Dir)
Immediate Holding Company: Meyrick Marketing Ltd
Registration no: 05918837 **VAT No.:** GB 619 8856 83
Date established: 2006 **No.of Employees:** 11 - 20 **Product Groups:** 87, 89

Hassett Industries
Stonehenge Road Durrington, Salisbury, SP4 8BN
Tel: 01980-654333 **Fax:** 01980-654326
E-mail: info@hassettindustries.com
Website: http://www.hassettindustries.com

see next page

Hassett Industries - Cont'd

Directors: L. Hassett (MD), J. Andrews (Fin)
Immediate Holding Company: HASSETT INDUSTRIES LIMITED
Registration no: 02995317 **VAT No.:** GB 329 9757 00
Date established: 1994 **Turnover:** £500,000 - £1m
No.of Employees: 1 - 10 **Product Groups:** 29, 37, 40, 41, 46

Date of Accounts	Jun 11	Jun 10	Jun 09
Working Capital	65	42	6
Fixed Assets	4	5	11
Current Assets	242	236	201

The Health Protection Agency

Porton Down, Salisbury, SP4 0JG
Tel: 01980-612100 **Fax:** 01980-611096
E-mail: roger.gilmour@hpa.org.uk
Website: http://www.hpa.org.uk
Bank(s): RBS
Directors: R. Gilmour (Dir)
Immediate Holding Company: SIMPLY RIGHT SOLUTIONS LTD
Registration no: 07000025 **VAT No.:** GB 654 9630 09
Date established: 2009 **Turnover:** £125m - £250m
No.of Employees: 1501 & over **Product Groups:** 85

Date of Accounts	Mar 05	Mar 04
Sales Turnover	203m	177
Pre Tax Profit/Loss	-950	-3m
Working Capital	978	1
Fixed Assets	115m	116
Current Assets	51m	43
Current Liabilities	36m	29

Hydor Ltd

8 Parkers Close Downton Business Centre Downton Industrial Estate, Salisbury, SP5 3RB
Tel: 01725-511422 **Fax:** 01725-512637
E-mail: info@hydor.co.uk
Website: http://www.hydor.co.uk
Directors: D. Burl (MD)
Ultimate Holding Company: ELTA GROUP LIMITED
Immediate Holding Company: HYDOR LIMITED
Registration no: 04776217 **Date established:** 2003 **Turnover:** £1m - £2m
No.of Employees: 11 - 20 **Product Groups:** 37, 40, 67

Date of Accounts	Mar 11	Mar 10	Mar 09
Sales Turnover	3m	2m	2m
Pre Tax Profit/Loss	115	72	-320
Working Capital	606	541	-111
Fixed Assets	67	68	76
Current Assets	1m	1m	1m
Current Liabilities	75	68	46

Images At Work Ltd

Unit 1-3 Whaddon Business Park Whaddon, Salisbury, SP5 3HF
Tel: 01722-711117 **Fax:** 01722-711019
E-mail: sales@iaw.co.uk
Website: http://www.iaw.co.uk
Bank(s): Lloyds TSB Bank plc
Directors: E. Greene (MD)
Managers: M. O'Kane (Tech Serv Mgr), R. Condell (Fin Mgr)
Immediate Holding Company: IMAGES AT WORK LIMITED
Registration no: 03683670 **VAT No.:** GB 541 7274 48
Date established: 1998 **Turnover:** £2m - £5m **No.of Employees:** 11 - 20
Product Groups: 24

Date of Accounts	Sep 09	Sep 08	Nov 10
Working Capital	50	231	-117
Fixed Assets	125	420	105
Current Assets	832	995	739

Innotec Supplies

Unit 25 Glenmore Business Park Telford Road, Salisbury, SP2 7GL
Tel: 01722-411744 **Fax:** 01722-411788
E-mail: emma@innotecworld.com
Website: http://www.innotecworld.com
Bank(s): HSBC Bank plc
Directors: M. Murrell (MD)
Managers: E. Thomson Murrell (Mgr), E. Thomson-Murrell (Mgr), E. Thompson-Murrell (Mgr)
Immediate Holding Company: INNOTEC SUPPLIES (UK) LIMITED
Registration no: 03454402 **VAT No.:** GB 712 0617 78
Date established: 1997 **Turnover:** £500,000 - £1m
No.of Employees: 21 - 50 **Product Groups:** 27, 30, 31, 32, 34, 36, 37, 39, 48, 66, 68

Date of Accounts	Dec 10	Dec 09	Dec 08
Working Capital	167	143	130
Fixed Assets	40	47	66
Current Assets	333	275	311

Janspeed Technologies Ltd

Castle Works Castle Road, Salisbury, SP1 3RX
Tel: 01722-321833 **Fax:** 01722-412308
E-mail: sales@janspeed.com
Website: http://www.janspeed.com
Bank(s): Lloyds TSB Bank plc
Directors: M. Vaughan (MD)
Immediate Holding Company: JANSPEED TECHNOLOGIES LIMITED
Registration no: 05636296 **VAT No.:** GB 188 2708 28
Date established: 2005 **Turnover:** £2m - £5m **No.of Employees:** 21 - 50
Product Groups: 39, 68

Date of Accounts	Dec 11	Dec 10	Dec 09
Working Capital	-90	-82	-3
Fixed Assets	142	185	197
Current Assets	626	467	410

Jay Engineering

Three Arches Bridge Station Road, Tisbury, Salisbury, SP3 6RA
Tel: 01747-871010 **Fax:** 01747-871079
E-mail: info@postpuncher.co.uk
Website: http://www.postpuncher.org
Directors: K. Meade (Sales), K. Meade (MD)
Immediate Holding Company: JAY ENGINEERING LTD
Registration no: 06533251 **Date established:** 2008
No.of Employees: 1 - 10 **Product Groups:** 41

Date of Accounts	Mar 10	Mar 09
Working Capital	-103	-29
Fixed Assets	18	20
Current Assets	24	26

Jewson Ltd

Southampton Road Whiteparish, Salisbury, SP5 2QW
Tel: 01794-884246 **Fax:** 01794-884047
E-mail: jon.east@jewson.co.uk
Website: http://www.jewson.co.uk
Managers: J. East (Mgr)
Ultimate Holding Company: COMPAGNIE DE SAINT GOBAIN (FRANCE)
Immediate Holding Company: JEWSON LIMITED
Registration no: 00348407 **Date established:** 1939 **Turnover:** £2m - £5m
No.of Employees: 1 - 10 **Product Groups:** 66

Date of Accounts	Dec 11	Dec 10	Dec 09
Sales Turnover	1606m	1547m	1485m
Pre Tax Profit/Loss	18m	100m	45m
Working Capital	-345m	-250m	-349m
Fixed Assets	496m	387m	461m
Current Assets	657m	1005m	1320m
Current Liabilities	66m	120m	64m

John H Mitchell

The Old School House West Street, Wilton, Salisbury, SP2 0DG
Tel: 01722-742777 **Fax:** 01722-742777
E-mail: office@jhm-electrical.co.uk
Website: http://www.jhm-electrical.co.uk
Directors: R. Churchill (Ptnr)
Turnover: Up to £250,000 **No.of Employees:** 1 - 10 **Product Groups:** 37, 52, 84

Kitagawa Europe Ltd

Unit 1 The Headlands Salisbury Road, Downton, Salisbury, SP5 3JJ
Tel: 01725-514000 **Fax:** 01725-514001
E-mail: rthreipland@kitagawaeurope.com
Website: http://www.kitagawaeurope.com
Bank(s): Lloyds
Directors: M. Jones (Fin)
Managers: R. Threipland (Export Sales Mg), C. Peebles (Sales Prom Mgr)
Immediate Holding Company: KITAGAWA EUROPE LIMITED
Registration no: 01662295 **VAT No.:** GB 370 0994 50
Date established: 1982 **Turnover:** £10m - £20m
No.of Employees: 21 - 50 **Product Groups:** 46

Date of Accounts	Dec 11	Dec 10	Dec 09
Sales Turnover	13m	10m	6m
Pre Tax Profit/Loss	-177	-392	-601
Working Capital	-643	-385	-150
Fixed Assets	995	973	954
Current Assets	9m	6m	5m
Current Liabilities	170	680	887

L W S

Bratch Lane Dinton, Salisbury, SP3 5EB
Tel: 01722-716969 **Fax:** 01722-716949
E-mail: enquiries@lws.uk.com
Website: http://www.lws.uk.com
Managers: N. Chippett (Product), S. Edginton (Chief Mgr)
Ultimate Holding Company: M.J. ABBOTT LIMITED
Immediate Holding Company: LANDSCAPE WATERING SYSTEMS LIMITED
Registration no: 03480689 **Date established:** 1997
No.of Employees: 1 - 10 **Product Groups:** 41

Date of Accounts	Mar 11	Mar 10	Mar 09
Working Capital	135	108	141
Fixed Assets	1	1	2
Current Assets	453	364	287

Lascar Electronics Ltd

Module House Whiteparish, Salisbury, SP5 2SJ
Tel: 01794-884567 **Fax:** 01794-884616
E-mail: sales@lascar.co.uk
Website: http://www.lascarelectronics.com
Bank(s): National Westminster Bank Plc
Directors: A. Darcy (Dir), G. Allen (Dir), R. Piwowarski (MD)
Ultimate Holding Company: LARASIAN LIMITED
Immediate Holding Company: LASCAR ELECTRONICS LIMITED
Registration no: 05472682 **Date established:** 2005 **Turnover:** £5m - £10m
No.of Employees: 21 - 50 **Product Groups:** 38

Date of Accounts	Dec 11	Dec 10	Dec 09
Sales Turnover	N/A	6m	5m
Pre Tax Profit/Loss	N/A	853	518
Working Capital	4m	3m	3m
Fixed Assets	127	144	130
Current Assets	6m	5m	3m
Current Liabilities	N/A	421	259

Lime Green Ltd

Unit 2 Centre One Old Sarum Park Lysander Way Old Sarum, Salisbury, SP4 6BU
Tel: 08454-508855 **Fax:** 01722- 330606
E-mail: info@limegreen.tv
Website: http://www.limegreen.tv
Directors: L. Painter (Prop), L. Painter (MD)
Immediate Holding Company: LIME GREEN LIMITED
Registration no: 06378053 **Date established:** 2007
No.of Employees: 1 - 10 **Product Groups:** 37, 48, 67, 81

Date of Accounts	Sep 11	Sep 10	Sep 09
Working Capital	-2	-2	1
Fixed Assets	1	1	1
Current Assets	N/A	1	2

Liquid Web Design &Marketing

5 Forders Close Woodfalls, Salisbury, Salisbury, SP5 2QB
Tel: 01725-512138
E-mail: info@liquid-webdesign.co.uk
Website: http://www.liquid-webdesign.co.uk
Managers: L. Kingshott (Chief Acct)
Date established: 2006 **Turnover:** Up to £250,000
No.of Employees: 1 - 10 **Product Groups:** 44

Lovell

Jacks Bush Lopcombe, Salisbury, SP5 1BZ
Tel: 01264-783438 **Fax:** 01264-783438
E-mail: malovell22@aol.com
Directors: M. Lovell (Prop)
Date established: 2001 **No.of Employees:** 1 - 10 **Product Groups:** 41

Douglas Mcleod Incorporating Lacewing Framing

44 Trinity Street, Salisbury, SP1 2BD
Tel: 01722-337565 **Fax:** 01722-337565
E-mail: douglascrmcleod@yahoo.co.uk
Directors: S. Mcleod (Fin)
Immediate Holding Company: DOUGLAS MCLEOD - PERIOD FRAMES LTD
Registration no: 01660474 **Date established:** 1982
No.of Employees: 1 - 10 **Product Groups:** 25, 26, 36

Date of Accounts	Dec 10	Dec 09	Dec 08
Working Capital	47	47	48
Fixed Assets	1	1	1
Current Assets	122	107	97

Mahle Filter Systems Ltd

High Post, Salisbury, SP4 6AT
Tel: 01722-782611 **Fax:** 01722-783539
E-mail: sales@mahle.com
Website: http://www.mahle.com
Directors: P. Knitting (MD), P. Everett (Fin), P. Everitt (Fin), P. Metzger (Dir)
Managers: A. Carter (Sales & Mktg Mg), I. Greene (I.T. Exec)
Ultimate Holding Company: MAHLE VENTILTRIEB GMBH (GERMANY)
Immediate Holding Company: Tennex (Japan)
Registration no: 07143653 **Date established:** 1981
Turnover: £75m - £125m **No.of Employees:** 251 - 500
Product Groups: 39, 42

Mineral Engineering Processes Ltd

6 Wilton Business Centre Kingsway Wilton, Salisbury, SP2 0AH
Tel: 01722-744799 **Fax:** 0870-705 2951
E-mail: enquiries@ukmep.com
Website: http://www.ukmep.com
Directors: S. Hyde (Dir)
Immediate Holding Company: MINERAL ENGINEERING PROCESSES LIMITED
Registration no: 01920647 **VAT No.:** GB 754 7299 88
Date established: 1985 **Turnover:** £1m - £2m **No.of Employees:** 1 - 10
Product Groups: 42

Date of Accounts	Aug 11	Aug 10	Aug 09
Working Capital	70	60	47
Fixed Assets	18	23	24
Current Assets	310	773	282

Moleroda Finishing Systems Ltd

March Farm Lucewood Lane Farley, Salisbury, SP5 1AX
Tel: 01722-712610 **Fax:** 01722-712434
E-mail: moleroda@btinternet.com
Website: http://www.moleroda.com
Immediate Holding Company: MOLERODA FINISHING SYSTEMS LIMITED
Registration no: 01749485 **Date established:** 1983
No.of Employees: 1 - 10 **Product Groups:** 23, 32, 36, 46, 47, 48

Date of Accounts	Oct 09	Oct 08	Oct 07
Working Capital	307	319	325
Fixed Assets	45	57	70
Current Assets	440	497	496

Moore Bros Surgical Ltd

Unit 8 The Headlands, Downton, Salisbury, SP5 3JJ
Tel: 01725-512551 **Fax:** 01725-512699
E-mail: moore.bros@virgin.net
Website: http://www.moorebros.co.uk
Directors: J. Mcaleese (MD)
Immediate Holding Company: MOORE BROS (ORTHOPAEDIC FOOTWEAR) LIMITED
Registration no: 01678280 **VAT No.:** GB 382 5190 46
Date established: 1982 **Turnover:** £500,000 - £1m
No.of Employees: 1 - 10 **Product Groups:** 22

Multitex G R P

Unit 5 Dolphin Industrial Estate, Salisbury, SP1 2NB
Tel: 01722-332139 **Fax:** 01722-338458
E-mail: kevin@multitex.co.uk
Website: http://www.multitex.co.uk
Directors: K. Roycroft (Dir), K. Roycroft (Ptnr), P. Webber (Ptnr), J. Conlin (Ptnr)
Immediate Holding Company: MULTITEX GRP LLP
Registration no: OC311991 **VAT No.:** 382 6442 40 **Date established:** 2005
Turnover: £2m - £5m **No.of Employees:** 21 - 50 **Product Groups:** 30

Naim Audio Ltd

Southampton Road, Salisbury, SP1 2LN
Tel: 01722-426600 **Fax:** 01722-412034
E-mail: info@naimaudio.com
Website: http://www.naimaudio.com
Bank(s): National Westminster
Directors: P. Stephenson (Sales)
Immediate Holding Company: NAIM AUDIO LIMITED
Registration no: 01116428 **VAT No.:** GB 189 3922 15
Date established: 1973 **Turnover:** £10m - £20m
No.of Employees: 101 - 250 **Product Groups:** 37

Date of Accounts	Dec 11	Mar 11	Mar 10
Sales Turnover	11m	16m	14m
Pre Tax Profit/Loss	475	839	689
Working Capital	4m	4m	3m
Fixed Assets	2m	2m	2m
Current Assets	6m	6m	5m
Current Liabilities	271	770	819

Naish Felts Ltd

Crow Lane Wilton, Salisbury, SP2 0HD
Tel: 01722-743505 **Fax:** 01722-743910
E-mail: sales@naishfelts.co.uk
Website: http://www.naishfelts.co.uk
Directors: D. Legatti (MD), D. Streeter (Co Sec), G. Naish (Comm)
Ultimate Holding Company: E.V. NAISH LIMITED
Immediate Holding Company: NAISH FELTS LIMITED
Registration no: 02816943 **VAT No.:** GB 631 7158 49
Date established: 1993 **Turnover:** £2m - £5m **No.of Employees:** 21 - 50
Product Groups: 22, 23, 24, 25, 26, 27, 29, 30, 31, 32, 33, 34, 36, 37, 38, 39, 40, 42, 43, 44, 45, 47, 48, 49, 52, 61, 63, 66, 67, 76

Date of Accounts	Dec 08	Sep 11	Sep 10
Working Capital	-55	838	682
Fixed Assets	367	259	320
Current Assets	1m	2m	1m

Noble Metal Works

6 Landford Common Farm New Road, Landford, Salisbury, SP5 2AZ
Tel: 01794-324252 **Fax:** 01794-324252
E-mail: rod@noblemetalworks.co.uk
Website: http://www.noblemetalworks.co.uk
Directors: R. Noble (Prop)
Date established: 1992 **No.of Employees:** 11 - 20 **Product Groups:** 35

Package Control UK Ltd
Unit 5 Bunas Business Park Hollom Down Road, Lopcombe, Salisbury, SP5 1BP
Tel: 01264-782143 **Fax:** 0844-880 0384
E-mail: sales@package-control.co.uk
Website: http://www.package-control.co.uk
Directors: W. Judd (Dir)
Ultimate Holding Company: L STOUTE BEHEER BV (NETHERLANDS)
Immediate Holding Company: PACKAGE CONTROL (U.K.) LIMITED
Registration no: 02612326 **Date established:** 1991 **Turnover:** £1m - £2m
No.of Employees: 1 - 10 **Product Groups:** 45

Date of Accounts	Dec 11	Dec 10	Dec 09
Working Capital	27	11	27
Fixed Assets	13	16	15
Current Assets	169	207	224

Pains Fireworks Ltd
The Old Chalkpit Romsey Road, Whiteparish, Salisbury, SP5 2SD
Tel: 01794-884040 **Fax:** 01794-884015
E-mail: sales@painsfireworks.com
Website: http://www.painsfireworks.com
Bank(s): HSBC
Directors: S. Lind (Dir), D. Alvis (Dir)
Managers: G. Deeker (Admin Off)
Immediate Holding Company: PAINS FIREWORKS LIMITED
Registration no: 01467177 **VAT No.:** GB 304 1220 30
Date established: 1979 **Turnover:** £2m - £5m **No.of Employees:** 21 - 50
Product Groups: 32, 89

Date of Accounts	Mar 11	Mar 10	Mar 09
Working Capital	836	775	739
Fixed Assets	118	104	110
Current Assets	1m	946	1m
Current Liabilities	N/A	N/A	281

Quality Lift Products Ltd
Unit 6 Whaddon Business Park Whaddon, Salisbury, SP5 3HF
Tel: 01722-711122 **Fax:** 01722-711041
E-mail: ingo@qualitylifts.co.uk
Website: http://www.orona.co.uk
Bank(s): National Westminster
Directors: A. Orueta Jannone (Co Sec), F. Mateo (MD), J. Saenz De Buruaga Gabilondo (Dir), L. Lete Fernandez De Matauco (Dir)
Managers: A. Richardson (Sales Prom Mgr), A. Webster (Purch Mgr), S. Cox (Sales Prom Mgr)
Immediate Holding Company: Electra Vitoria SCL (Spain)
Registration no: 01761628 **VAT No.:** GB 619 8825 94
Turnover: £10m - £20m **No.of Employees:** 21 - 50 **Product Groups:** 45

Date of Accounts	Dec 07
Sales Turnover	17370
Pre Tax Profit/Loss	80
Working Capital	-590
Fixed Assets	1400
Current Assets	4830
Current Liabilities	5420
Total Share Capital	10
ROCE% (Return on Capital Employed)	9.9

Reliance Engineering
Giles Lane Landford, Salisbury, SP5 2BG
Tel: 01794-322904 **Fax:** 01794-323620
E-mail: info@relianceengineering.co.uk
Website: http://www.relianceengineering.co.uk
Managers: M. Millar
Ultimate Holding Company: BROOKS & WEBB ENGINEERING LTD
Registration no: 01352536 **Turnover:** £250,000 - £500,000
No.of Employees: 1 - 10 **Product Groups:** 48

Rolamat Ltd
Hollom Down Lopcombe, Salisbury, SP5 1BP
Tel: 01264-782143 **Fax:** 01264-782580
E-mail: info@rolamat.co.uk
Website: http://www.rolamat.co.uk
Directors: W. Judd (Dir)
Immediate Holding Company: ROLAMAT LIMITED
Registration no: 02623379 **Date established:** 1991
Turnover: £250,000 - £500,000 **No.of Employees:** 1 - 10
Product Groups: 35, 45, 47

Date of Accounts	Dec 11	Dec 10	Dec 09
Working Capital	45	38	36
Current Assets	171	150	170

Sarum Hydraulics Ltd
7 Centre One Old Sarum Park Lysander Way, Old Sarum, Salisbury, SP4 6BU
Tel: 01722-328388 **Fax:** 01722-414307
E-mail: pumpsales@sarum-hydraulics.co.uk
Website: http://www.sarum-hydraulics.co.uk
Directors: M. Foster (Fin)
Immediate Holding Company: SARUM HYDRAULICS LIMITED
Registration no: 03037960 **VAT No.:** GB 619 9922 91
Date established: 1995 **Turnover:** £1m - £2m **No.of Employees:** 1 - 10
Product Groups: 38, 39, 40, 45, 84

Date of Accounts	Mar 11	Mar 10	Mar 09
Working Capital	467	657	489
Fixed Assets	5	5	6
Current Assets	767	855	748

Satcom Global (a division of Sat Com Group)
Unit 3, The Woodford Centre Lysander Way, Old Sarum, Salisbury, SP4 6BU
Tel: 01722-410800 **Fax:** 01722-410777
E-mail: emea@satcomglobal.com
Website: http://www.satcomdistribution.com
Directors: M. Ward (Co Sec), S. Johnson (MD)
Managers: G. Leitch (Sales Prom Mgr), M. Jarman (Stores Mgr)
Immediate Holding Company: Satcom Group Holdings plc
Registration no: 05208041 **Date established:** 2001 **Turnover:** £5m - £10m
No.of Employees: 21 - 50 **Product Groups:** 37

Date of Accounts	Jun 08	Jun 07	Jun 06
Sales Turnover	14m	17m	29m
Pre Tax Profit/Loss	-160	51	2m
Working Capital	433	793	652
Fixed Assets	709	680	545
Current Assets	12m	19m	15m
Current Liabilities	12m	18m	14m
Total Share Capital	461	461	461

Solair Group Architectural Products
Smeaton Road, Salisbury, SP2 7NQ
Tel: 01722-323036 **Fax:** 01722-337546
E-mail: bill.whitston@solair.co.uk
Website: http://www.solair.co.uk
Directors: S. Hollihan (MD)
Managers: B. Whitston (Chief Mgr), D. King (Tech Serv Mgr)
Immediate Holding Company: J B S Industries
Registration no: 02826982 **VAT No.:** GB 643 1077 60
Turnover: £1m - £2m **No.of Employees:** 21 - 50 **Product Groups:** 30

Stagecraft Technical Services Ltd
Unit E Porton Business Centre Porton, Salisbury, SP4 0ND
Tel: 08458-382015 **Fax:** 0845-838 2016
E-mail: lisat@stagecraft.co.uk
Website: http://www.stagecraft.co.uk
Bank(s): Barclays
Directors: L. Tapper (Dir), K. Flynn (Dir), D. Goodrich (Dir)
Managers: M. Newton (Sales Admin), I. Hibberd (Accounts), S. Millard, M. Guliami (Sales Prom Mgr), D. Witt (Sales Prom Mgr), M. Palmer (Projects)
Immediate Holding Company: STAGECRAFT TECHNICAL SERVICES LIMITED
Registration no: 06738339 **VAT No.:** GB 329 8484 14
Date established: 2008 **Turnover:** £1m - £2m **No.of Employees:** 11 - 20
Product Groups: 26, 32, 37, 81, 83

The Sterilization & Disinfection Unit
Salisbury District Hospital Odstock Road, Salisbury, SP2 8BJ
Tel: 01722-429213
Managers: P. Wells (Mgr)
Immediate Holding Company: ODSTOCK MEDICAL LIMITED
Date established: 2005 **No.of Employees:** 21 - 50 **Product Groups:** 38, 67

Date of Accounts	Mar 11	Mar 10	Mar 09
Sales Turnover	1m	1m	1m
Pre Tax Profit/Loss	26	118	139
Working Capital	148	102	19
Fixed Assets	39	58	48
Current Assets	406	489	542
Current Liabilities	39	81	68

Paul Stevens Architecture
108a Fisherton Street, Salisbury, SP2 7QY
Tel: 01722-349384 **Fax:** 01722-331578
E-mail: admin@paulstevensarchitecture.co.uk
Website: http://www.paulstevensarchitecture.co.uk
Directors: P. Stevens (Prop)
Immediate Holding Company: PAUL STEVENS ARCHITECTURE LIMITED
Registration no: 07149194 **Date established:** 2010
No.of Employees: 1 - 10 **Product Groups:** 84

Date of Accounts	Jan 12	Jan 11
Sales Turnover	127	159
Pre Tax Profit/Loss	10	18
Working Capital	-3	3
Fixed Assets	18	23
Current Assets	25	25
Current Liabilities	13	13

Stock Electronics Ltd
10 Edison Road, Salisbury, SP2 7NU
Tel: 01722-321758 **Fax:** 01722-413079
E-mail: enquiries@stockelectronics.co.uk
Website: http://www.stockelectronics.org.uk
Directors: T. Bronsdon (MD)
Immediate Holding Company: STOCK ELECTRONICS LIMITED
Registration no: 01009690 **VAT No.:** GB 187 4683 14
Date established: 1971 **Turnover:** £250,000 - £500,000
No.of Employees: 1 - 10 **Product Groups:** 37, 38

Date of Accounts	Mar 11	Mar 10	Mar 09
Sales Turnover	401	384	524
Pre Tax Profit/Loss	9	-40	-51
Working Capital	105	42	77
Fixed Assets	15	18	23
Current Assets	172	170	197
Current Liabilities	19	25	35

Target Fluid Services
Whitehouse Farm Pound Hill, Landford, Salisbury, SP5 2AA
Tel: 01794-390001 **Fax:** 023-8066 6882
E-mail: bjack@btinternet.com
Website: http://www.targetfluid.co.uk
Directors: B. Jackson (MD)
Immediate Holding Company: TARGET FLUID SERVICES LIMITED
Registration no: 03357452 **Date established:** 1997
Turnover: Up to £250,000 **No.of Employees:** 1 - 10 **Product Groups:** 36, 38, 40

Date of Accounts	Mar 11	Mar 10	Mar 09
Working Capital	-1	-6	-6
Fixed Assets	5	6	6
Current Assets	35	32	16

Trethowans Solicitors
1 London Road Office Park London Road, Salisbury, SP1 3HP
Tel: 01722-412512 **Fax:** 01722-411300
E-mail: info@trethowans.com
Website: http://www.trethowans.com
Bank(s): Royal Bank of Scotland
Directors: A. Duckworth (Fin), S. Rhodes (Snr Part), C. Macrae (Co Sec)
Managers: J. Cummings (Sales Admin), B. Hughes (Sales & Mktg Mg), T. Wilkinson (I.T. Exec)
Immediate Holding Company: TRETHOWANS LLP
Registration no: OC342356 **VAT No.:** GB 188 0928 24
Date established: 2008 **Turnover:** £5m - £10m
No.of Employees: 51 - 100 **Product Groups:** 80

Date of Accounts	Mar 11	Mar 10
Sales Turnover	9m	8m
Pre Tax Profit/Loss	3m	3m
Working Capital	5m	4m
Fixed Assets	702	689
Current Assets	6m	5m
Current Liabilities	523	540

Trinity Photography
22-24 Trinity Street, Salisbury, SP1 2BD
Tel: 07786-376777
E-mail: info@trinity-photography.co.uk
Website: http://www.trinity-photography.co.uk
Managers: F. McWilliam (Mgr)
Date established: 2002 **No.of Employees:** 1 - 10 **Product Groups:** 81

Valley Forge
The Garage The Street, East Knoyle, Salisbury, SP3 6AJ
Tel: 07870-155775 **Fax:** 01985-841204
Directors: I. Hamilton (Prop)
Date established: 2002 **No.of Employees:** 1 - 10 **Product Groups:** 26, 35

W Shipsey & Sons Ltd
Unit 8 Castlegate Business Park Old Sarum, Salisbury, SP4 6QX
Tel: 01722-322645 **Fax:** 01722-410722
E-mail: sales@shipseys.co.uk
Website: http://www.shipseys.co.uk
Directors: R. Shipsey (Prop)
Immediate Holding Company: W. SHIPSEY & SONS LIMITED
Registration no: 02122973 **Date established:** 1987
Turnover: £500,000 - £1m **No.of Employees:** 1 - 10 **Product Groups:** 24, 69, 83

Date of Accounts	Jan 12	Jan 11	Jan 10
Working Capital	-137	-157	-121
Fixed Assets	379	406	394
Current Assets	26	46	46

Wallgate
Crow Lane Wilton, Salisbury, SP2 0HB
Tel: 01722-744594 **Fax:** 01722-742096
E-mail: sales@wallgate.com
Website: http://www.wallgate.com
Bank(s): Lloyds TSB Bank plc
Directors: T. Powell (MD), L. Runnacles (Co Sec)
Managers: J. Donovan (Mktg Serv Mgr), J. Wells
Ultimate Holding Company: E.V. NAISH LIMITED
Immediate Holding Company: WALLGATE LIMITED
Registration no: 00156022 **VAT No.:** GB 188 2039 45
Date established: 2019 **Turnover:** £5m - £10m **No.of Employees:** 21 - 50
Product Groups: 40, 66

Date of Accounts	Sep 11	Sep 10	Sep 09
Sales Turnover	7m	6m	7m
Pre Tax Profit/Loss	732	754	1m
Working Capital	1m	2m	2m
Fixed Assets	1m	924	855
Current Assets	3m	4m	3m
Current Liabilities	1m	1m	1m

Whitehead Vizard
Close Gate Chambers 60 High Street, Salisbury, SP1 2PQ
Tel: 01722-412141 **Fax:** 01722-411177
E-mail: enq@whitehead-vizard.co.uk
Website: http://www.whitehead-vizard.co.uk
Bank(s): Lloyds
Directors: C. Parsons (Ptnr), A. Hodder (Ptnr)
Immediate Holding Company: ARMSTRONG HOUSE RTM COMPANY LIMITED
VAT No.: GB 188 5702 25 **Date established:** 2011
No.of Employees: 11 - 20 **Product Groups:** 80

Swindon

A S T Distribution Ltd
Unit 16 Berkshire House, Swindon, SN1 2NR
Tel: 01793-541890 **Fax:** 01793-541891
E-mail: info@catsdistribution.co.uk
Website: http://www.astcables.co.uk
Directors: V. Hulbert (Dir), G. Hulbert (Co Sec)
Managers: J. Fouch (Sales Eng)
Immediate Holding Company: A.S.T. Manufacturing Ltd
Registration no: 02934739 **Date established:** 1994 **Turnover:** £1m - £2m
No.of Employees: 21 - 50 **Product Groups:** 37

Date of Accounts	Sep 07	Sep 06	Sep 05
Working Capital	-223	-14	-50
Fixed Assets	30	47	53
Current Assets	188	379	366
Current Liabilities	412	394	416
Total Share Capital	10	N/A	N/A

Access Displays Ltd
Take Notice Westmead Industrial Estate, Westlea, Swindon, SN5 7UH
Tel: 01793-613088 **Fax:** 01793-541495
E-mail: sales@accessdisplays.co.uk
Website: http://www.accessdisplays.co.uk
Immediate Holding Company: ACCESS DISPLAYS LIMITED
Registration no: 02528447 **Date established:** 1990
No.of Employees: 21 - 50 **Product Groups:** 26, 28, 30, 35, 37, 38, 49, 52, 67, 81, 84, 86

Date of Accounts	Jul 11	Jul 10	Jul 09
Working Capital	-49	-104	-104
Fixed Assets	127	134	147
Current Assets	710	766	496

AccessPlus Marketing Services Ltd
Dorcan 300 Murdock Road, Swindon, SN3 5HY
Tel: 0844-800 1066 **Fax:** 0844-800 9220
E-mail: healthcheck@accessplus.co.uk
Website: http://www.accessplus.co.uk
Bank(s): HSBC Bank plc
Ultimate Holding Company: Triple Arc PLC
Registration no: 01594411 **VAT No.:** GB 357 8426 19
Turnover: £50m - £75m **No.of Employees:** 251 - 500
Product Groups: 27, 28, 44, 64, 80, 81

Accord Office Supplies Ltd
Unit 22 Bridge Mead Westmead Industrial Estate, Westlea, Swindon, SN5 7TL
Tel: 01793-541500 **Fax:** 0845-602 4522
E-mail: sales@accordoffice.co.uk
Website: http://www.accordoffice.co.uk
Bank(s): HSBC Bank plc
Managers: K. Child (Mktg Serv Mgr)
Ultimate Holding Company: OFFICE2OFFICE PLC
Immediate Holding Company: ACCORD OFFICE SUPPLIES LIMITED
Registration no: 02405637 **Date established:** 1989 **Turnover:** £5m - £10m
No.of Employees: 21 - 50 **Product Groups:** 23, 26, 32, 49

Date of Accounts	Dec 11	Dec 10	Dec 09
Sales Turnover	5m	9m	9m
Pre Tax Profit/Loss	259	650	-139

see next page

Accord Office Supplies Ltd - Cont'd

Working Capital	-2m	-2m	-2m
Fixed Assets	2m	3m	2m
Current Assets	1m	2m	2m
Current Liabilities	2m	2m	2m

Adcutech Ltd
P A C M House Blackworth Estate, Highworth, Swindon, SN6 7NA
Tel: 01793-765405 **Fax:** 01793-766060
E-mail: sales@adcutech.co.uk
Website: http://www.adcutech.com
Directors: G. Colman (Dir)
Ultimate Holding Company: SG CNC LIMITED
Immediate Holding Company: ADCUTECH LIMITED
Registration no: 04771031 **Date established:** 2003
Turnover: Up to £250,000 **No.of Employees:** 1 - 10 **Product Groups:** 35, 46, 48, 66, 67, 68, 84, 85

Date of Accounts	Jun 12	Jun 11	Jun 10
Working Capital	253	245	212
Fixed Assets	228	120	74
Current Assets	369	345	309

Agralan Ltd
The Old Brickyard Ashton Keynes, Swindon, SN6 6QR
Tel: 01285-860015 **Fax:** 01285-860056
E-mail: sales@agralan.co.uk
Website: http://www.agralan.co.uk
Directors: A. Frost (Dir)
Immediate Holding Company: AGRALAN LIMITED
Registration no: 02039849 **Date established:** 1986
No.of Employees: 1 - 10 **Product Groups:** 32

Date of Accounts	Sep 11	Sep 10	Sep 09
Working Capital	204	183	146
Fixed Assets	26	34	40
Current Assets	414	423	396

Alpunch Tooling Ltd
Unit 24 Ganton Way, Techno Trading Estate, Swindon, SN2 8EZ
Tel: 01793-613185 **Fax:** 01793-642628
E-mail: info@alpunch.co.uk
Website: http://www.alpunchtooling.co.uk
Bank(s): Barclays
Directors: G. Harvey (MD)
Immediate Holding Company: ALPUNCH TOOLING LIMITED
Registration no: 02288475 **VAT No.:** GB 348 5764 15
Date established: 1988 **Turnover:** £500,000 - £1m
No.of Employees: 11 - 20 **Product Groups:** 46

Date of Accounts	Dec 11	Dec 10	Dec 09
Sales Turnover	N/A	N/A	713
Pre Tax Profit/Loss	N/A	N/A	1
Working Capital	256	272	113
Fixed Assets	144	168	200
Current Assets	376	428	400
Current Liabilities	N/A	N/A	31

Anstee Ware Ltd
Unit 59a Thornhill Industrial Estate South Marston, Swindon, SN3 4TA
Tel: 01793-832828 **Fax:** 01793-831955
E-mail: jon.hill@ansteeware.co.uk
Website: http://www.ansteeware.co.uk
Managers: J. Hill (Mgr)
Ultimate Holding Company: A W HOLDING COMPANY LIMITED
Immediate Holding Company: ANSTEE & WARE LIMITED
Registration no: 00477097 **Date established:** 1950
No.of Employees: 11 - 20 **Product Groups:** 37, 52

Date of Accounts	Dec 11	Dec 10	Dec 09
Sales Turnover	19m	16m	15m
Pre Tax Profit/Loss	842	713	183
Working Capital	2m	1m	911
Fixed Assets	1m	1m	1m
Current Assets	8m	6m	6m
Current Liabilities	4m	3m	4m

Aquatic Management Services Ltd
8 Churchway Blunsdon, Swindon, SN26 7DG
Tel: 01793-700241 **Fax:** 01793-700241
E-mail: info@aquaticmanagement.co.uk
Website: http://www.aquaticmanagement.co.uk
Directors: J. Usherwood (Fin)
Immediate Holding Company: AQUATIC MANAGEMENT SERVICES LIMITED
Registration no: 05616737 **Date established:** 2005
No.of Employees: 1 - 10 **Product Groups:** 29, 42, 67

Date of Accounts	Mar 11	Mar 10	Mar 09
Working Capital	-8	-11	-12
Fixed Assets	18	22	28
Current Assets	8	5	4

Arval UK Ltd
Arval Centre Windmill Hill Business Park Whitehill Way, Swindon, SN5 6PE
Tel: 01793-887000 **Fax:** 0870-419 6688
Website: http://www.arval.co.uk
Bank(s): National Westminster
Directors: B. Beckers (MD)
Managers: A. Firth (Personnel), T. Roddy (Tech Serv Mgr), E. Movray (Fin Mgr), M. Kershaw, B. Flood (Purch Mgr), M. Curtis
Ultimate Holding Company: BNP PARIBAS S.A. (FRANCE)
Immediate Holding Company: ARVAL LIMITED
Registration no: 03171162 **VAT No.:** 224 2359 85 **Date established:** 1996
Turnover: £125m - £250m **No.of Employees:** 501 - 1000
Product Groups: 82

Date of Accounts	Dec 11	Dec 10	Dec 09
Sales Turnover	144m	173m	179m
Pre Tax Profit/Loss	14m	21m	8m
Working Capital	36m	-430m	-360m
Fixed Assets	N/A	465m	372m
Current Assets	36m	34m	23m
Current Liabilities	N/A	50m	46m

Austin Leisure
153-154 Victoria Road, Swindon, SN1 3BU
Tel: 01793-528505 **Fax:** 01793-613469
E-mail: office@austingroup.co.uk
Website: http://www.austingroup.co.uk
Directors: D. Austin (Prop)
Immediate Holding Company: AUSTIN LEISURE LIMITED
Registration no: 07947086 **VAT No.:** GB 535 7611 39
Date established: 2012 **Turnover:** £500,000 - £1m
No.of Employees: 1 - 10 **Product Groups:** 52

B M Magnetics UK Ltd
Pennyfields Malmesbury Road, Leigh, Swindon, SN6 6RA
Tel: 01793-752394 **Fax:** 01793-759238
E-mail: sales@bmmagnetics.co.uk
Website: http://www.bmmagnetics.co.uk
Directors: M. Armstrong (MD)
Ultimate Holding Company: BAKKER MAGNETICS BV (NETHERLANDS)
Immediate Holding Company: B.M. MAGNETICS (UK) LIMITED
Registration no: 02328648 **VAT No.:** GB 484 9310 22
Date established: 1988 **Turnover:** Up to £250,000
No.of Employees: 1 - 10 **Product Groups:** 29, 30, 34, 37, 42, 45, 46, 49, 67

Date of Accounts	Dec 11	Dec 10	Dec 09
Working Capital	172	137	105
Fixed Assets	3	6	8
Current Assets	221	186	146

Barlow World Handling
Bridge End Road, Swindon, SN3 4PE
Tel: 01793-423887 **Fax:** 01843-296254
Directors: G. Fan (Prop)
No.of Employees: 1 - 10 **Product Groups:** 35, 39, 45

The Battery Shop UK LTD
Unit 20 Orbit Centre Ashworth Road, Bridgemead, Swindon, SN5 7YG
Tel: 01793-421509 **Fax:** 01793-432010
E-mail: info@thebatteryshop.co.uk
Website: http://www.thebatteryshop.co.uk
Managers: S. Dyer (Mgr)
Immediate Holding Company: THE BATTERY SHOP (U.K.) LIMITED
Registration no: 04689852 **Date established:** 2003
No.of Employees: 1 - 10 **Product Groups:** 37

Date of Accounts	Mar 11	Mar 10	Mar 09
Working Capital	-57	-46	-32
Fixed Assets	24	32	29
Current Assets	44	37	52

Baumer Electric Ltd
33-36 Majors Road Watchfield, Swindon, SN6 8TZ
Tel: 01793-783839 **Fax:** 01793-783814
E-mail: sales.uk@baumer.com
Website: http://www.baumer.com
Bank(s): Barclays
Directors: G. Smith (Fin)
Ultimate Holding Company: BAUMER HOLDING AG (SWITZERLAND)
Immediate Holding Company: BAUMER LIMITED
Registration no: 00645201 **VAT No.:** GB 238 5370 51
Date established: 1959 **Turnover:** £2m - £5m **No.of Employees:** 11 - 20
Product Groups: 28, 37, 38, 39, 44, 45

Date of Accounts	Sep 11	Sep 10	Sep 09
Working Capital	-259	-484	-233
Fixed Assets	248	262	273
Current Assets	841	1m	935

British Computer Society
1st Block D North Star House North Star Avenue, Swindon, SN2 1FA
Tel: 01793-417417 **Fax:** 01793-480270
E-mail: bcshq@hq.bcs.org.uk
Website: http://www.bcs.org.uk
Bank(s): Lloyds TSB Bank plc
Directors: D. Clarke (Grp Chief Exec)
Ultimate Holding Company: BRITISH COMPUTER SOCIETY (RC000724)
Immediate Holding Company: BCS LEARNING & DEVELOPMENT LIMITED
Registration no: 01005485 **Date established:** 1971
Turnover: £500,000 - £1m **No.of Employees:** 101 - 250
Product Groups: 87

Date of Accounts	Aug 11	Aug 10	Aug 09
Sales Turnover	N/A	N/A	897
Pre Tax Profit/Loss	N/A	N/A	461
Working Capital	8	8	8
Current Assets	8	8	8

Bunce Ashbury Ltd
Ashbury, Swindon, SN6 8LW
Tel: 01793-710212 **Fax:** 01793-710437
E-mail: philip.bunce@bunce.co.uk
Website: http://www.bunce.co.uk
Bank(s): Lloyds TSB Bank plc
Directors: P. Bunce (Dir), P. Bunce (Fin), S. Bunce (Dir), A. Bunce (Dir)
Managers: P. Newman (Purch Mgr)
Immediate Holding Company: BUNCE (ASHBURY) LIMITED
Registration no: 01008283 **VAT No.:** GB 435 3258 57
Date established: 1971 **Turnover:** £2m - £5m **No.of Employees:** 21 - 50
Product Groups: 29, 30, 41, 44, 45, 49

Date of Accounts	Mar 11	Mar 10	Mar 09
Working Capital	1m	968	752
Fixed Assets	122	66	68
Current Assets	2m	1m	1m

Butler Toll
Unit 62 Shrivenham Hundred Business Park Majors Road, Watchfield, Swindon, SN6 8TY
Tel: 01793-786300 **Fax:** 01793-786349
E-mail: info@butlertoll.co.uk
Website: http://www.butlertoll.co.uk
Managers: A. Westall
Ultimate Holding Company: BUTLER TOLL HOLDINGS LIMITED
Immediate Holding Company: BUTLER TOLL LIMITED
Registration no: 05460739 **Date established:** 2005
Turnover: £500,000 - £1m **No.of Employees:** 1 - 10 **Product Groups:** 80, 82

Date of Accounts	Sep 11	Sep 10	Sep 09
Working Capital	267	227	85
Fixed Assets	4	13	21
Current Assets	504	523	479

C I Automation Ltd
Shaftesbury Centre Percy Street, Swindon, SN2 2AZ
Tel: 01793-530063 **Fax:** 01793-530064
Directors: G. Williams (MD)
Immediate Holding Company: C. I. AUTOMATION LIMITED
Registration no: 02029280 **Date established:** 1986
Turnover: Up to £250,000 **No.of Employees:** 1 - 10 **Product Groups:** 38, 39

Date of Accounts	Mar 11	Mar 10	Mar 09
Working Capital	10	12	12
Current Assets	22	19	22

Cadillac Plastic Ltd
Rivermead Industrial Estate Rivermead Drive, Westlea, Swindon, SN5 7EX
Tel: 01793-648500 **Fax:** 01793-648505
E-mail: info@cadillacplastic.co.uk
Website: http://www.cadillacplastic.co.uk
Bank(s): National Westminster
Directors: J. Jones (Fin), A. Kennedy (MD)
Ultimate Holding Company: RIVERMEAD PLASTIC LIMITED
Immediate Holding Company: CADILLAC PLASTIC LIMITED
Registration no: 01649342 **VAT No.:** GB 348 6758 05
Date established: 1982 **Turnover:** £5m - £10m **No.of Employees:** 11 - 20
Product Groups: 27, 30

Date of Accounts	Dec 11	Dec 10	Dec 09
Working Capital	4m	4m	4m
Fixed Assets	106	77	53
Current Assets	5m	5m	5m
Current Liabilities	627	671	N/A

Cal-Bay Systems Europe Ltd
Suite 4 Shrivenham Hundred Business Park Majors Road Watchfield, Swindon, SN6 8TZ
Tel: 01793-784386 **Fax:** 01793-784386
E-mail: ian@calbay.com
Website: http://www.calbay.com
Directors: I. Crighton (MD)
Immediate Holding Company: CAL-BAY SYSTEMS EUROPE LIMITED
Registration no: 06009749 **Date established:** 2006
No.of Employees: 1 - 10 **Product Groups:** 38, 44, 84

Date of Accounts	Dec 07
Working Capital	-10
Fixed Assets	1
Current Assets	70
Current Liabilities	80

Capture C C T V Solutions Ltd
Suite 64 Pure Offices Kembrey Park, Swindon, SN2 8BW
Tel: 08451-566818
E-mail: info@capturecctv.co.uk
Website: http://www.capturecctv.co.uk
Directors: K. Davey (MD)
Immediate Holding Company: CAPTURE CCTV SOLUTIONS LIMITED
Registration no: 06659152 **Date established:** 2008
No.of Employees: 1 - 10 **Product Groups:** 37, 38, 40, 83

Date of Accounts	Jul 12	Jul 11	Jul 10
Working Capital	-0	-103	-15
Fixed Assets	37	123	31
Current Assets	51	14	20

Castrol UK Ltd
Wakefield House Pipers Way, Swindon, SN3 1RE
Tel: 0151-355 3737 **Fax:** 01793-513506
Website: http://www.castrol.com
Bank(s): Barclays
Directors: R. Hewins (Fin)
Managers: C. Sedgwick (Mktg Serv Mgr), M. Johnson, C. Stephens (Personnel)
Ultimate Holding Company: BP P.L.C.
Immediate Holding Company: CASTROL LIMITED
Registration no: 00149435 **VAT No.:** GB 233 2517 92
Date established: 2018 **Turnover:** £125m - £250m
No.of Employees: 251 - 500 **Product Groups:** 31, 32

Date of Accounts	Dec 11	Dec 10	Dec 09
Sales Turnover	179m	164m	142m
Pre Tax Profit/Loss	228m	99m	77m
Working Capital	447m	22m	-64m
Fixed Assets	227m	435m	431m
Current Assets	679m	158m	47m
Current Liabilities	2m	647	341

Ceiling Pro UK Southwest Ltd
30 Whittingham Drive Wroughton, Swindon, SN4 0TE
Tel: 0800-005 1096 **Fax:** 0871-714 2015
E-mail: info@cpuksouthwest.co.uk
Website: http://www.cpuksouthwest.co.uk
Directors: N. Maidment (Dir)
Registration no: 06289288 **Date established:** 2007
Turnover: Up to £250,000 **No.of Employees:** 1 - 10 **Product Groups:** 52

Charles Lucas & Marshall
Eastcott House 4 High Street, Swindon, SN1 3EP
Tel: 01793-511055 **Fax:** 01793-610518
E-mail: reception@clmlaw.co.uk
Website: http://www.clmlaw.co.uk
Bank(s): Lloyds TSB Bank plc
Directors: B. Chandler (Ptnr)
Immediate Holding Company: CHARLES LUCAS & MARSHALL LLP
Registration no: OC355683 **VAT No.:** GB 199 0673 18
Date established: 2010 **Turnover:** £2m - £5m **No.of Employees:** 11 - 20
Product Groups: 80

Childs Play International Ltd
Ashworth Road Bridgemead, Swindon, SN5 7YD
Tel: 01793-616286 **Fax:** 01793-512795
E-mail: office@childs-play.com
Website: http://www.childs-play.com
Directors: A. Twinn (MD), N. Burden (Fin)
Immediate Holding Company: CHILDS PLAY (INTERNATIONAL) LIMITED
Registration no: 01076760 **VAT No.:** GB 194 4604 47
Date established: 1972 **Turnover:** £2m - £5m **No.of Employees:** 1 - 10
Product Groups: 28, 49

Date of Accounts	Mar 11	Mar 10	Mar 09
Working Capital	1m	1m	1m
Fixed Assets	726	736	744
Current Assets	2m	2m	2m

Complete Welding Supplies
4 Central Trading Estate Signal Way, Swindon, SN3 1PD
Tel: 01793-525444
Website: http://www.allenwelding.co.uk
Directors: K. Allen (Prop), K. Hemmings (Prop)
Registration no: 01933766 **Date established:** 1985 **Turnover:** £5m - £10m
No.of Employees: 1 - 10 **Product Groups:** 46

Constructor Group UK
Murdock Road Dorcan, Swindon, SN3 5HY
Tel: 01793-694071 **Fax:** 01793-610516
E-mail: sales@planned-storage.co.uk
Website: http://www.constructor-group.co.uk
Bank(s): Lloyds TSB Bank plc

Directors: A. Leese (Co Sec), K. Paine (Fin), R. Moss (Dir)
Ultimate Holding Company: CONSTRUCTOR GROUP AS (NORWAY)
Immediate Holding Company: PLANNED STORAGE SYSTEMS LIMITED
Registration no: 01028915 **VAT No.:** GB 443 6828 32
Date established: 1971 **Turnover:** £5m - £10m
No.of Employees: 51 - 100 **Product Groups:** 26

Date of Accounts	Dec 11	Dec 10	Dec 09
Sales Turnover	5m	9m	8m
Pre Tax Profit/Loss	-116	-635	-2m
Working Capital	-5m	-3m	2m
Fixed Assets	288	304	207
Current Assets	2m	6m	11m
Current Liabilities	7m	9m	8m

Critical Environment Solutions Ltd (CES)
Unit 2276 Dunbeath Road, Elgin Industrial Estate, Swindon, SN2 8EA
Tel: 01793-512505 **Fax:** 01793-541884
E-mail: a.holbrook@cesltd.uk.com
Website: http://www.cleanroomdirect.com
Directors: A. Holbrook (MD)
Immediate Holding Company: CRITICAL ENVIRONMENT SOLUTIONS LTD
Registration no: 06516748 **Date established:** 2008 **Turnover:** £2m - £5m
No.of Employees: 1 - 10 **Product Groups:** 30

Date of Accounts	May 12	May 11	May 10
Working Capital	514	478	397
Fixed Assets	14	5	10
Current Assets	869	810	646
Current Liabilities	N/A	N/A	12

Crown Lift Trucks Ltd
Stirling Road South Marston Industrial Estate, Swindon, SN3 4TS
Tel: 08458-509270 **Fax:** 01925-425656
Website: http://www.crown.com
Bank(s): Lloyds TSB Bank plc
Directors: R. Baxter (Cust Serv)
Managers: R. Cox
Ultimate Holding Company: CROWN EQUIPMENT CORPORATION (USA)
Immediate Holding Company: CROWN LIFT TRUCKS LIMITED
Registration no: 02319386 **Date established:** 1988
No.of Employees: 11 - 20 **Product Groups:** 45, 67

Date of Accounts	Mar 09	Mar 08	Mar 06
Working Capital	-820	-820	-820
Fixed Assets	5m	5m	5m

Deloro Stellite Ltd
Unit 3 Kembrey Street, Elgin Industrial Estate, Swindon, SN2 8UY
Tel: 01793-498500 **Fax:** 01793-498501
E-mail: sales@delorostellite.co.uk
Website: http://www.stellite.com
Bank(s): National Westminster Bank Plc
Managers: M. Gilbert
Ultimate Holding Company: DUKE STREET CAPITAL HOLDINGS LTD (GUERNSEY)
Immediate Holding Company: DELORO STELLITE UK (DIRECTOR) LIMITED
Registration no: 05289105 **VAT No.:** GB 332 7904 58
Date established: 2004 **Turnover:** £10m - £20m
No.of Employees: 11 - 20 **Product Groups:** 34

Destec Systems Ltd
21 Grovelands Avenue, Swindon, SN1 4ET
Tel: 01793-496217 **Fax:** 01793-610739
E-mail: info@destecsystems.co.uk
Website: http://www.destec.sagehost.co.uk
Directors: G. Fenton (MD), G. Fenton (Prop)
Immediate Holding Company: DESTEC SYSTEMS LIMITED
Registration no: 05761460 **Date established:** 2006
Turnover: £250,000 - £500,000 **No.of Employees:** 1 - 10
Product Groups: 81

Date of Accounts	Mar 10	Mar 09	Mar 08
Working Capital	28	9	34
Fixed Assets	1	15	3
Current Assets	144	96	128

Dexion
Murdock Road Dorcan, Swindon, SN3 5HY
Tel: 08702-240220 **Fax:** 0870-224 0221
E-mail: enquiries@dexion.co.uk
Website: http://www.dexion.co.uk
Directors: M. Grierson (MD)
Ultimate Holding Company: CONSTRUCTOR GROUP AS (NORWAY)
Immediate Holding Company: CONSTRUCTOR GROUP UK LIMITED
Registration no: 04695697 **Date established:** 2003
Turnover: £10m - £20m **No.of Employees:** 21 - 50 **Product Groups:** 26, 67

Date of Accounts	Dec 11	Dec 10	Dec 09
Sales Turnover	15m	15m	13m
Pre Tax Profit/Loss	-83	-52	244
Working Capital	2m	2m	2m
Fixed Assets	876	838	848
Current Assets	6m	6m	3m
Current Liabilities	966	1m	653

Dick Lovett BMW Swindon Ltd
Wootton Bassett Road, Swindon, SN5 8WG
Tel: 01793-615999 **Fax:** 01793-439650
E-mail: enquiries@dicklovett.co.uk
Website: http://www.dicklovett.co.uk
Bank(s): National Westminster Bank Plc
Directors: J. Moulton (Co Sec)
Managers: M. Moore (Tech Serv Mgr)
Ultimate Holding Company: DICK LOVETT COMPANIES LIMITED
Immediate Holding Company: DICK LOVETT (SPECIALIST CARS) LIMITED
Registration no: 02567241 **VAT No.:** GB 576 1316 37
Date established: 1990 **Turnover:** £50m - £75m
No.of Employees: 101 - 250 **Product Groups:** 68

Date of Accounts	Dec 11	Dec 10	Dec 09
Sales Turnover	55m	51m	48m
Pre Tax Profit/Loss	808	1000	883
Working Capital	2m	3m	3m
Fixed Assets	721	364	213
Current Assets	10m	11m	9m
Current Liabilities	2m	5m	3m

Dusty Sweeps Chimney Services
3 Bridge End Road, Swindon, SN3 4PD
Tel: 01793-326188
E-mail: info@dustysweeps.co.uk
Website: http://www.dustysweeps.co.uk
Turnover: Up to £250,000 **Product Groups:** 40, 49, 52

E S P Colour
Elgin Drive, Swindon, SN2 8XU
Tel: 01793-438400 **Fax:** 01793-530403
E-mail: info@espcolour.co.uk
Website: http://www.espcolour.co.uk
Bank(s): Barclays
Directors: S. O'connell (Co Sec), A. Thirlby (MD), S. O'Connell (Fin)
Immediate Holding Company: ESP COLOUR LIMITED
Registration no: 03513763 **VAT No.:** GB 195 6399 06
Date established: 1998 **Turnover:** £10m - £20m
No.of Employees: 51 - 100 **Product Groups:** 28, 44, 81

Date of Accounts	Dec 11	Dec 10	Dec 09
Sales Turnover	11m	11m	11m
Pre Tax Profit/Loss	302	322	446
Working Capital	-394	-620	-943
Fixed Assets	4m	3m	3m
Current Assets	3m	3m	3m
Current Liabilities	839	1m	1m

Eastbrook Farm Organic Meat Ltd
The Calf House Cues Lane, Bishopstone, Swindon, SN6 8PL
Tel: 01793-790460 **Fax:** 01793-791239
E-mail: info@helenbrowningorganics.co.uk
Website: http://www.helenbrowningorganics.co.uk
Directors: R. Cloke (Fin), T. Finney (MD)
Immediate Holding Company: EASTBROOK FARM ORGANIC PIGS LIMITED
Registration no: 03894618 **Date established:** 1999 **Turnover:** £2m - £5m
No.of Employees: 1 - 10 **Product Groups:** 20

Date of Accounts	Mar 06
Working Capital	-760
Current Liabilities	760
Total Share Capital	50

Edmundson Electrical Ltd
Unit 31c Ganton Way Techno Trading Estate, Swindon, SN2 8ES
Tel: 01793-522241 **Fax:** 01793-524504
E-mail: swindon.274@eel.co.uk
Website: http://www.edmundson-electrical.co.uk/
Managers: C. Livesley (District Mgr)
Ultimate Holding Company: BLACKFRIARS CORP (USA)
Immediate Holding Company: EDMUNDSON ELECTRICAL LIMITED
Registration no: 02667012 **Date established:** 1991 **Turnover:** £1m - £2m
No.of Employees: 1 - 10 **Product Groups:** 38

Date of Accounts	Dec 11	Dec 10	Dec 09
Sales Turnover	1023m	852m	788m
Pre Tax Profit/Loss	57m	53m	45m
Working Capital	256m	225m	184m
Fixed Assets	17m	3m	4m
Current Assets	439m	358m	298m
Current Liabilities	59m	38m	37m

Elbmar Ltd
5 Oppenheimer Centre Greenbridge Road, Greenbridge Industrial Estate, Swindon, SN3 3JD
Tel: 01793-644155 **Fax:** 01793-513170
E-mail: kevin@elbmar.co.uk
Website: http://www.elbmar.co.uk
Bank(s): Barclays
Directors: K. Rich (MD), S. Jones (Co Sec)
Managers: P. Baker (Fin Mgr)
Immediate Holding Company: ELBMAR LIMITED
Registration no: 01148931 **VAT No.:** GB 195 5435 33
Date established: 1973 **Turnover:** £1m - £2m **No.of Employees:** 21 - 50
Product Groups: 30, 39, 42, 48, 66

Date of Accounts	Dec 11	Dec 10	Dec 09
Working Capital	57	27	90
Fixed Assets	560	522	529
Current Assets	579	470	539

Enterprise Works Swindon
Units 1 A & 1 B Gipsy Lane Business Park, Swindon, SN2 8DT
Tel: 01793-616288 **Fax:** 01793-542235
E-mail: enterpriseworks@swindon.gov.uk
Website: http://www.swindon.gov.uk
Managers: D. Rowlands (Mgr)
Immediate Holding Company: SWINDON BOROUGH COUNCIL
No.of Employees: 21 - 50 **Product Groups:** 25, 28, 45, 48, 49

Excelerate Software
32 Tower Road Peatmoor, Swindon, SN5 5BG
Tel: 07919-316713
E-mail: info@exceleratesoftware.co.uk
Website: http://www.exceleratesoftware.co.uk
Directors: P. Goodchild (Prop)
Date established: 2005 **Turnover:** Up to £250,000
No.of Employees: 1 - 10 **Product Groups:** 44

Farepak plc
Farepack House Westmead Indl-Est, Westlea, Swindon, SN5 7YZ
Tel: 01793-486441 **Fax:** 01793- 606200
Website: http://www.farepak.co.uk
Bank(s): National Westminster Bank Plc
Directors: G. Pollock (Dir), N. Gilodi-johnson (MD), N. Gilodi Johnson (MD), S. Hicks (Fin), C. Hulland (Dir)
Immediate Holding Company: CLEANEASY
Registration no: 04740401 **Date established:** 2006
Turnover: £50m - £75m **No.of Employees:** 101 - 250 **Product Groups:** 85

Fastlink Data Cables
Unit 2 Enterprise House Cheney Manor Industrial Estate, Swindon, SN2 2YZ
Tel: 01793-512251 **Fax:** 01793-512252
E-mail: sales@fastlink.co.uk
Website: http://www.fastlink.co.uk
Directors: C. Jell (Dir), A. Oakes (Dir)
Immediate Holding Company: FASTLINK DATA CABLES LIMITED
Registration no: 02846270 **Date established:** 1993
No.of Employees: 21 - 50 **Product Groups:** 35, 37, 39, 44, 47, 66, 67, 68

Date of Accounts	Aug 11	Aug 10	Aug 09
Working Capital	125	103	167
Fixed Assets	145	134	10
Current Assets	384	316	332

Finishrink
Unit 8 Hillmead Industrial Estate Marshall Road, Hillmead, Swindon, SN5 5FZ
Tel: 01793-758721 **Fax:** 01793-876059
E-mail: sales@finishrink.com
Website: http://www.finishrink.com
Directors: B. Wragg (MD)
Registration no: 02781247 **Turnover:** Up to £250,000
No.of Employees: 1 - 10 **Product Groups:** 30, 36

Fires & Fireplaces
Unit 22 Whitehill Industrial Estate Whitehill Lane, Wootton Bassett, Swindon, SN4 7DB
Tel: 01793-854100 **Fax:** 01793-849777
E-mail: kevin@fires-fireplaces.co.uk
Website: http://www.fires-fireplaces.co.uk
Directors: K. Law (Prop)
No.of Employees: 1 - 10 **Product Groups:** 25, 33

First Great Western
Milford House 1 Milord Street, Swindon, SN1 1HL
Tel: 01793-499400 **Fax:** 01793-499516
E-mail: mark.hopwood@firstgroup.com
Website: http://www.firstgreatwestern.co.uk
Directors: B. Caswell (Fin), M. Hopwood (MD)
Managers: R. Noyle (Tech Serv Mgr), S. Johnson (Personnel), K. Bartlett
Ultimate Holding Company: FIRSTGROUP PLC
Immediate Holding Company: FIRST GREATER WESTERN LIMITED
Registration no: 05113733 **Date established:** 2004
Turnover: £500m - £1,000m **No.of Employees:** 101 - 250
Product Groups: 71

Date of Accounts	Mar 11	Mar 10	Mar 09
Sales Turnover	903m	845m	767m
Pre Tax Profit/Loss	-54m	7m	-13m
Working Capital	-17m	-28m	-35m
Fixed Assets	83m	101m	116m
Current Assets	180m	186m	172m
Current Liabilities	141m	117m	92m

Fish Brothers Honda
Ashworth Road, Swindon, SN5 7UZ
Tel: 01793-535455 **Fax:** 01793-422922
E-mail: mri@fish-bros.co.uk
Website: http://www.fish-bros.co.uk
Bank(s): National Westminster Bank Plc
Managers: M. Vellender (Comm), R. Archer, M. Riddiford, C. Pearcey (Personnel)
Ultimate Holding Company: FISH BROTHERS (HOLDINGS) LIMITED
Immediate Holding Company: FISH BROTHERS (SWINDON) LIMITED
Registration no: 02583215 **Date established:** 1991
Turnover: £75m - £125m **No.of Employees:** 21 - 50 **Product Groups:** 68

Date of Accounts	Dec 11	Dec 10	Dec 09
Sales Turnover	86m	78m	72m
Pre Tax Profit/Loss	1m	1m	967
Working Capital	9m	8m	8m
Fixed Assets	728	1m	1m
Current Assets	15m	16m	14m
Current Liabilities	2m	2m	1m

Flowforms Wiltshire Ltd
PO Box 2460, Swindon, SN4 0ZR
Tel: 01793-740111 **Fax:** 01793-741634
E-mail: sales@flowforms.co.uk
Website: http://www.flowforms.co.uk
Directors: N. Keen (Fin), P. Hayman (Dir)
Immediate Holding Company: FLOWFORMS (WILTSHIRE) LIMITED
Registration no: 02124764 **VAT No.:** GB 466 8188 00
Date established: 1987 **Turnover:** £1m - £2m **No.of Employees:** 1 - 10
Product Groups: 27, 28

Date of Accounts	Jul 11	Jul 10	Jul 09
Working Capital	-68	-75	-68
Fixed Assets	3	4	4
Current Assets	26	24	43

Fotek School Portraits
1b Bramble Road Techno Trading Estate, Swindon, SN2 8HZ
Tel: 01793-615681 **Fax:** 01793-512826
E-mail: roberts@fotekportraits.co.uk
Website: http://www.fotekportraits.co.uk
Bank(s): National Westminster Bank Plc
Directors: V. Robinson (Fin), S. Roberts (Dir), P. Ellis (Sales & Mktg), S. Roberts (MD), S. Woods (Dir & Buyer)
Managers: A. Salvage (Sales Admin), S. Lang (Personnel), C. Spencer (), P. Ellis (Sales Prom Mgr), O. Paxton (I.T. Exec)
Ultimate Holding Company: GROUND AREA LIMITED
Immediate Holding Company: FOTEK PORTRAITS LIMITED
Registration no: 02041548 **VAT No.:** GB 448 4119 41
Date established: 1986 **Turnover:** £5m - £10m **No.of Employees:** 11 - 20
Product Groups: 86

Date of Accounts	Dec 10	Dec 09	Dec 08
Sales Turnover	N/A	3m	N/A
Pre Tax Profit/Loss	N/A	-88	N/A
Working Capital	-548	-432	-390
Fixed Assets	N/A	2	49
Current Assets	113	144	302
Current Liabilities	N/A	351	N/A

G P Burners C I B Ltd
2d Hargreaves Road Groundwell Industrial Estate, Swindon, SN25 5AZ
Tel: 01793-709050 **Fax:** 01793-709060
E-mail: info@gpburners.co.uk
Website: http://www.gpburners.co.uk
Directors: J. Spearing (Dir)
Ultimate Holding Company: INMED VENTURES LIMITED (GIBRALTAR)
Immediate Holding Company: WELLMAN THERMAL ENGINEERING LIMITED
Registration no: 02535201 **VAT No.:** GB 239 9422 32
Date established: 1990 **Turnover:** £1m - £2m **No.of Employees:** 1 - 10
Product Groups: 40

Date of Accounts	Dec 10	Dec 09	Dec 08
Sales Turnover	1m	982	1m
Pre Tax Profit/Loss	-256	32	100
Working Capital	123	388	365
Fixed Assets	2	3	2
Current Assets	864	696	672
Current Liabilities	25	48	36

G & P Cases
Richmond Works
Station Road
Wootton Bassett, Swindon, SN4 7EA
Tel: 01793-852156 **Fax:** 01793-848641
E-mail: chris.phillips@gpcases.co.uk
Website: http://www.gpcases.co.uk
Directors: D. Waldron (MD), J. Waldron (Co Sec)
Immediate Holding Company: G.AND P.CASES LIMITED
Registration no: 00950197 **Date established:** 1969
No.of Employees: 11 - 20 **Product Groups:** 25, 66, 76

Date of Accounts	Dec 11	Dec 10	Dec 09
Working Capital	794	633	571
Fixed Assets	53	58	62
Current Assets	1m	875	819

G W P Packaging
Unit 20 Chelworth Industrial Estate Chelworth Road, Cricklade, Swindon, SN6 6HE
Tel: 01793-754444 **Fax:** 01793-754445
E-mail: sales@gwp.co.uk
Website: http://www.gwp.co.uk
Directors: D. Pedley (Ch)
Immediate Holding Company: PENSIONS AND ANNUITIES LIMITED
Registration no: 02455095 **VAT No.:** GB 535 8760 17
Date established: 2008 **Turnover:** £5m - £10m **No.of Employees:** 21 - 50
Product Groups: 27, 28, 45

Date of Accounts	Mar 08	Mar 07	Mar 06
Sales Turnover	8028	7126	N/A
Pre Tax Profit/Loss	662	538	342
Working Capital	155	-223	-92
Fixed Assets	1465	1595	1138
Current Assets	2830	2195	1862
Current Liabilities	2674	2417	1954
Total Share Capital	10	10	10
ROCE% (Return on Capital Employed)	40.9	39.2	32.7
ROT% (Return on Turnover)	8.2	7.6	

Glen-Pac Southern Ltd
Unit 23 Poplar Business Park, Castle Eaton, Swindon, SN6 6JX
Tel: 08454-750070 **Fax:** 08454-750080
E-mail: info@glenpac.com
Website: http://www.glenpac.com
Directors: J. Stapleton (MD)
Immediate Holding Company: GLEN-PAC (SOUTHERN) LIMITED
Registration no: 03044158 **VAT No.:** GB 348 5442 37
Date established: 1995 **Turnover:** £1m - £2m **No.of Employees:** 1 - 10
Product Groups: 25, 27, 30, 42, 45, 48, 66, 76

Date of Accounts	Mar 11	Mar 10	Mar 09
Working Capital	112	73	47
Fixed Assets	13	15	18
Current Assets	231	189	160

Globec UK
Unit 15 Shrivenham Hundred Business Park Majors Road, Watchfield, Swindon, SN6 8TZ
Tel: 01793-780790 **Fax:** 01793-780776
E-mail: info@globec.co.uk
Website: http://www.globec.co.uk
Directors: I. Hopgood (Dir)
Ultimate Holding Company: GLOBEC PROPERTIES LIMITED
Immediate Holding Company: GLOBEC (UK) LIMITED
Registration no: 02713264 **VAT No.:** Gb 596 2911 04
Date established: 1992 **Turnover:** £500,000 - £1m
No.of Employees: 1 - 10 **Product Groups:** 37, 38, 84

Date of Accounts	Jul 11	Jul 10	Jul 09
Working Capital	14	7	-6
Fixed Assets	18	19	21
Current Assets	293	301	216

Hi Reach Equipment TD
Blackworth Industrial Estate Highworth, Swindon, SN6 7NA
Tel: 01793-766744 **Fax:** 01793-763503
E-mail: prichards@hi-reach.co.uk
Website: http://www.hi-reach.co.uk
Directors: P. Richards (Dir)
Immediate Holding Company: HI-REACH LIMITED
Registration no: 02532933 **Date established:** 1990
Turnover: £250,000 - £500,000 **No.of Employees:** 1 - 10
Product Groups: 39, 45, 83

Date of Accounts	Jan 12	Jan 11	Jan 10
Working Capital	3	3	3
Current Assets	3	3	3

Hochtief Construction Ltd
Epsilon Windmill Hill Business Park Whitehill Way, Swindon, SN5 6NX
Tel: 01793-755555 **Fax:** 01793-755556
E-mail: enquiries@hochtief.co.uk
Website: http://www.hochtief.co.uk
Directors: J. Jackson (MD)
Managers: T. Lloyd
Ultimate Holding Company: HOCHTIEF AKTIENGESELLSCHAFT
Immediate Holding Company: HOCHTIEF (UK) CONSTRUCTION LIMITED
Registration no: 02489026 **Date established:** 1990
Turnover: £20m - £50m **No.of Employees:** 21 - 50 **Product Groups:** 51, 52

Date of Accounts	Dec 11	Dec 10	Dec 09
Sales Turnover	41m	48m	43m
Pre Tax Profit/Loss	599	650	481
Working Capital	9m	8m	8m
Fixed Assets	312	489	413
Current Assets	19m	26m	26m
Current Liabilities	1m	5m	1m

Honda Connectors Ltd (Honda Tsushin Kogyo Co. Ltd)
B1 Marston Gate South Marston Park, South Marston Industrial Estate, Swindon, SN3 4DE
Tel: 01793-836250 **Fax:** 01793-836255
E-mail: info@hondaconnectors.co.uk
Website: http://www.hondaconnectors.co.uk
Directors: S. Murawicki (Fin)
Managers: J. Bamford (Buyer)
Ultimate Holding Company: HONDA TSUSHIN KOGYO CO LTD (JAPAN)
Immediate Holding Company: HONDA CONNECTORS LIMITED
Registration no: 02924320 **Date established:** 1994 **Turnover:** £5m - £10m
No.of Employees: 21 - 50 **Product Groups:** 37

Date of Accounts	Dec 11	Dec 10	Dec 09
Sales Turnover	4m	4m	4m
Pre Tax Profit/Loss	70	71	-3
Working Capital	821	763	714
Fixed Assets	74	83	106
Current Assets	1m	1m	1m
Current Liabilities	84	74	90

Honda Of The UK Manufacturer Ltd
Highworth Road South Marston, Swindon, SN3 4TZ
Tel: 01793-831183 **Fax:** 01793-831177
Website: http://www.honda-eu.com
Directors: A. Takano (MD)
Ultimate Holding Company: HONDA MOTOR CO LTD (JAPAN)
Immediate Holding Company: HONDA OF THE U.K. MANUFACTURING LIMITED
Registration no: 01887872 **VAT No.:** GB 422 4433 85
Date established: 1985 **Turnover:** Over £1,000m
No.of Employees: 1501 & over **Product Groups:** 39

Date of Accounts	Mar 12	Mar 11	Mar 10
Sales Turnover	1653m	1981m	1411m
Pre Tax Profit/Loss	4m	7m	20m
Working Capital	67m	144m	202m
Fixed Assets	393m	303m	247m
Current Assets	484m	476m	523m
Current Liabilities	98m	105m	122m

Hunger Hydraulic UK Ltd
Redwood House Templars Way Industrial Estate, Wootton Bassett, Swindon, SN4 7SR
Tel: 01793-859615 **Fax:** 01793-849004
E-mail: info@hunger-hydraulic.co.uk
Website: http://www.hunger-hydraulic.co.uk
Managers: J. Jarrett (Mgr)
Immediate Holding Company: HUNGER HYDRAULIC U.K. LIMITED
Registration no: 01120845 **Date established:** 1973
Turnover: £500,000 - £1m **No.of Employees:** 1 - 10 **Product Groups:** 29, 30, 35, 36, 38, 40, 44, 48

Date of Accounts	Dec 10	Dec 09	Dec 08
Working Capital	49	22	20
Fixed Assets	18	29	10
Current Assets	877	75	131

Hydra Electric International Ltd
Shrivenham Hundred Business Park 13-14 Majors Road, Watchfield, Swindon, SN6 8TZ
Tel: 01793-783920 **Fax:** 01793-783532
E-mail: ww@ccsdualsnap.co.uk
Website: http://www.hydroelectric.com
Directors: W. Wainwright (Fin)
Ultimate Holding Company: DAVIS INDUSTRIES INC (UNITED STATES OF AMERICA)
Immediate Holding Company: HYDRA-ELECTRIC INTERNATIONAL LIMITED
Registration no: 02297428 **Date established:** 1988
Turnover: Up to £250,000 **No.of Employees:** 1 - 10 **Product Groups:** 37, 40

Date of Accounts	Apr 11	Apr 10	Apr 09
Pre Tax Profit/Loss	29	14	-184
Working Capital	-36	47	39
Current Assets	96	193	190
Current Liabilities	130	10	11

Hydraulogic Hydraulic Engineers
Unit 2270b Dunbeath Road, Elgin Industrial Estate, Swindon, SN2 8EA
Tel: 01793-435587 **Fax:** 01793-527051
E-mail: ivor.hydraulogic@btinternet.com
Directors: E. Sheppard (Fin), I. Cheater (MD)
Immediate Holding Company: HYDRAULOGIC LIMITED
Registration no: 04605117 **Date established:** 2002
No.of Employees: 1 - 10 **Product Groups:** 29, 36, 40, 45, 46

Date of Accounts	Nov 11	Nov 10	Nov 09
Working Capital	45	54	75
Fixed Assets	57	57	73
Current Assets	122	112	165

I S Rayfast Ltd
2 Lydiard Fields, Swindon, SN5 8UB
Tel: 01793-616700 **Fax:** 01793-644304
E-mail: sales@israyfast.com
Website: http://www.israyfast.com
Bank(s): Bank of Scotland
Directors: K. French (Dir)
Ultimate Holding Company: DIPLOMA PLC
Immediate Holding Company: IS-RAYFAST LIMITED
Registration no: 01408491 **VAT No.:** GB 650 9912 23
Date established: 1979 **Turnover:** £20m - £50m
No.of Employees: 21 - 50 **Product Groups:** 30, 37

Date of Accounts	Sep 11	Sep 10	Sep 09
Sales Turnover	33m	28m	23m
Pre Tax Profit/Loss	7m	6m	5m
Working Capital	11m	9m	4m
Fixed Assets	5m	6m	6m
Current Assets	17m	15m	12m
Current Liabilities	2m	2m	2m

I S Y S Ltd
Churchward House Fire Fly Avenue, Swindon, SN2 2EY
Tel: 08448-802919 **Fax:** 01793-715470
E-mail: info@isys-group.co.uk
Website: http://www.isys-group.co.uk
Directors: M. Nutter (MD)
Ultimate Holding Company: NATIONAL TRUST
Immediate Holding Company: ISYS GROUP LIMITED
Registration no: 03699640 **Date established:** 1999 **Turnover:** £2m - £5m
No.of Employees: 21 - 50 **Product Groups:** 44, 49, 83

Date of Accounts	Apr 11	Apr 10	Apr 09
Working Capital	485	406	348
Fixed Assets	164	206	215
Current Assets	2m	2m	2m

Icomplete Ltd
Providence House 12a South Street South Street, Swindon, SN1 3LA
Tel: 01793-250000 **Fax:** 01793-250009
E-mail: myles@icomplet.com
Website: http://www.icomplete.com
Managers: M. Hantler
Immediate Holding Company: ICOMPLETE LIMITED
Registration no: 06225352 **Date established:** 2007
No.of Employees: 1 - 10 **Product Groups:** 44

Date of Accounts	Mar 11	Mar 10	Mar 09
Working Capital	-582	-570	-430
Fixed Assets	236	275	214
Current Assets	42	9	9

Industrial Electronic Wiring
Unit 10 Birch, Kembrey Park, Swindon, SN2 8UU
Tel: 01793-694033 **Fax:** 01793-496295
E-mail: info@iew.co.uk
Website: http://www.iew.co.uk
Bank(s): National Westminster Bank Plc
Directors: L. Wheeler (Ch)
Immediate Holding Company: INDUSTRIAL ELECTRONIC WIRING LIMITED
Registration no: 03256680 **Date established:** 1996
No.of Employees: 21 - 50 **Product Groups:** 37

Date of Accounts	Jan 12	Jan 11	Jan 10
Working Capital	473	370	221
Fixed Assets	512	424	416
Current Assets	1m	1m	1m

Intel Investments UK Ltd
Pipers Way, Swindon, SN3 1RJ
Tel: 01793-403000 **Fax:** 01793-641440
E-mail: gary.jones@intel.com
Website: http://www.intel.co.uk
Directors: G. Jones (Dir)
Ultimate Holding Company: INTEL CORP (USA)
Immediate Holding Company: INTEL CORPORATION (UK) LIMITED
Registration no: 01134945 **Date established:** 1973
Turnover: Over £1,000m **No.of Employees:** 1501 & over
Product Groups: 44

Date of Accounts	Dec 11	Dec 08	Dec 09
Sales Turnover	4070m	3709m	3298m
Pre Tax Profit/Loss	111m	97m	70m
Working Capital	382m	51m	498m
Fixed Assets	247m	121m	121m
Current Assets	966m	1346m	929m
Current Liabilities	44m	38m	33m

Interconnect Products Ltd
Marlborough Road Wootton Bassett, Swindon, SN4 7SA
Tel: 01793-849811 **Fax:** 01793-849809
E-mail: michael.m@interconnect.demon.co.uk
Website: http://www.InterconnectProducts.co.uk
Directors: M. Mills (Dir)
Ultimate Holding Company: REFLEX ELECTRONICS LIMITED
Immediate Holding Company: INTERCONNECT PRODUCTS LIMITED
Registration no: 02455502 **Date established:** 1989
Turnover: £20m - £50m **No.of Employees:** 11 - 20 **Product Groups:** 37

Date of Accounts	Mar 12	Mar 11	Mar 10
Sales Turnover	39m	32m	24m
Pre Tax Profit/Loss	6m	5m	4m
Working Capital	5m	4m	3m
Fixed Assets	467	395	353
Current Assets	13m	11m	9m
Current Liabilities	966	821	721

Intergraph UK Ltd
Delta Business Park Great Western Way, Swindon, SN5 7XP
Tel: 01793-619999 **Fax:** 01793-618508
E-mail: info-uk@intergraph.com
Website: http://www.intergraph.com/uk
Bank(s): National Westminster Bank Plc
Directors: A. Jones (MD)
Ultimate Holding Company: INTERGRAPH CORPORATION (USA)
Immediate Holding Company: INTERGRAPH (UK) LIMITED
Registration no: 01457814 **VAT No.:** GB 576 3974 86
Date established: 1979 **Turnover:** £20m - £50m
No.of Employees: 51 - 100 **Product Groups:** 44

Date of Accounts	Dec 11	Dec 10	Dec 09
Sales Turnover	17m	23m	18m
Pre Tax Profit/Loss	3m	923	2m
Working Capital	3m	312	-614
Fixed Assets	14m	14m	14m
Current Assets	12m	9m	8m
Current Liabilities	6m	4m	6m

International Decorative Surfaces
Unit 9 Euro Way Euro Way, Blagrove, Swindon, SN5 8YW
Tel: 01793-513181 **Fax:** 01793-513995
E-mail: swindonsales@idsurfaces.co.uk
Website: http://www.idsurfaces.co.uk
Managers: D. Flack (Mgr)
Immediate Holding Company: MEYER FOREST PRODUCTS
Registration no: 00070341 **VAT No.:** GB 394 1212 63
Turnover: £2m - £5m **No.of Employees:** 21 - 50 **Product Groups:** 30

Isotron Ltd
Moray Road Elgin Industrial Estate, Swindon, SN2 8XS
Tel: 01793-601000 **Fax:** 01793-601010
E-mail: johnbarker@isotemp.co.uk
Website: http://www.isotron.com
Bank(s): National Westminster Bank Plc
Directors: J. Barker (Prop)
Ultimate Holding Company: SYNERGY HEALTH PLC
Immediate Holding Company: ISOTRON LIMITED
Registration no: 04828896 **Date established:** 2003
Turnover: £10m - £20m **No.of Employees:** 21 - 50 **Product Groups:** 37, 84, 85

Isotron
Thornhill Road South Marston, Swindon, SN3 4TA
Tel: 01793-823451 **Fax:** 01793-827320
E-mail: smarston@isotron.co.uk
Website: http://www.isotron.co.uk
Managers: S. Sugden (Ops Mgr), D. Lyall, A. Dabal (Plant)
Registration no: 01771333 **Turnover:** £10m - £20m
No.of Employees: 11 - 20 **Product Groups:** 20, 84

Jewson Ltd
3 Larch Close, Swindon, SN2 8YR
Tel: 01793-528251 **Fax:** 01793-431625
Website: http://www.hirepoint.co.uk
Directors: M. Boyce (MD)
Ultimate Holding Company: COMPAGNIE DE SAINT GOBAIN (FRANCE)
Immediate Holding Company: JEWSON LIMITED
Registration no: 00348407 **Date established:** 1939
Turnover: £500m - £1,000m **No.of Employees:** 11 - 20
Product Groups: 66

Date of Accounts	Dec 11	Dec 10	Dec 09
Sales Turnover	1606m	1547m	1485m
Pre Tax Profit/Loss	18m	100m	45m

Working Capital	-345m	-250m	-349m
Fixed Assets	496m	387m	461m
Current Assets	657m	1005m	1320m
Current Liabilities	66m	120m	64m

K D Training Solutions
18 New Road Wootton Bassett, Swindon, SN4 7DG
Tel: 01793-853222 **Fax:** 01793-853889
E-mail: garydennis@ntlworld.com
Website: http://www.kdtraining.co.uk
Directors: G. Dennis (Prop)
No.of Employees: 1 - 10 **Product Groups:** 86

Keepable Hearing & Mobilty
7 Clive Parade Cricklade Road, Swindon, SN2 1AJ
Tel: 01793-701313 **Fax:** 01793-701303
E-mail: teresa.kelly-nurse@keepable.co.uk
Website: http://www.hearingandmobility.com
Managers: T. Kelly Nurse (District Mgr), G. Williams (Mgr)
No.of Employees: 1 - 10 **Product Groups:** 37, 38, 39

Kembrey Wiring Systems Ltd
1 Garrards Way, Swindon, SN3 3HY
Tel: 01793-693361 **Fax:** 01793-614298
E-mail: enquiries@kembrey.co.uk
Website: http://www.kembrey.co.uk
Directors: A. Mckerrow (Fin), J. Ginson (MD)
Managers: J. Toussaint (Tech Serv Mgr), C. Heath (Sales Prom Mgr)
Ultimate Holding Company: KEMBREY AEROSPACE LIMITED
Immediate Holding Company: KEMBREY WIRING SYSTEMS LIMITED
Registration no: 01356836 **Date established:** 1978
Turnover: £10m - £20m **No.of Employees:** 101 - 250 **Product Groups:** 37

Date of Accounts	Mar 10	Mar 09	Mar 08
Sales Turnover	16m	17m	15m
Pre Tax Profit/Loss	-20	142	323
Working Capital	3m	3m	3m
Fixed Assets	96	104	85
Current Assets	7m	9m	12m
Current Liabilities	538	573	411

Kemdent
Kemdent Works Cricklade Road, Purton, Swindon, SN5 4HT
Tel: 01793-770256 **Fax:** 01793-772256
E-mail: sales@kemdent.co.uk
Website: http://www.kemdent.co.uk
Bank(s): Lloyds TSB Bank plc
Directors: G. Squires (Fin), G. Mayoh (MD)
Managers: C. Mayoh (Chief Mgr), J. Horsell (Purch Mgr), L. Stone
Immediate Holding Company: ASSOCIATED DENTAL PRODUCTS LIMITED
Registration no: 00327337 **VAT No.:** GB 194 2213 72
Date established: 1937 **Turnover:** £1m - £2m **No.of Employees:** 21 - 50
Product Groups: 31, 32

Date of Accounts	Mar 11	Mar 10	Mar 09
Working Capital	596	464	424
Fixed Assets	91	68	86
Current Assets	918	743	674

Kingfisher Windows & Conservatories
7 Barnfield Road, Swindon, SN2 2DJ
Tel: 01793-610190 **Fax:** 01793-495195
E-mail: kingfisher_windows@btconnect.com
Website: http://www.kingfisherwindows.org.uk
Directors: M. Cole (Dir), J. Reason (Co Sec)
No.of Employees: 1 - 10 **Product Groups:** 25, 30, 33, 36

Klaw Services Group
Unit 10 Athena Avenue Elgin Industrial Estate, Swindon, SN2 8EJ
Tel: 01793-520555 **Fax:** 01793-433430
E-mail: info@klawsvs.orangehome.co.uk
Directors: P. Walker (Ptnr)
Date established: 1979 **No.of Employees:** 11 - 20 **Product Groups:** 36, 45, 72

Lake Interconnection Systems
Unit 4 Bagbury Park Lydiard Millicent, Swindon, SN5 3LW
Tel: 01793-771111 **Fax:** 01793-778100
E-mail: sales@lakeics.com
Website: http://www.lakeics.com
Bank(s): National Westminster
VAT No.: GB 535 8523 31 **Date established:** 1990
Turnover: £500,000 - £1m **No.of Employees:** 11 - 20
Product Groups: 37, 39, 47, 68

Date of Accounts	Mar 11
Working Capital	-465
Fixed Assets	527
Current Assets	223

Lighting Bug Swindon Ltd
Unit 16-17 Westmead Industrial Estate Westmead, Swindon, SN5 7YT
Tel: 01793-616018
Website: http://www.lightingbug.co.uk
Directors: B. Savill (Dir)
Immediate Holding Company: LIGHTING BUG (MK) LIMITED
Registration no: 07057199 **Date established:** 2009
No.of Employees: 1 - 10 **Product Groups:** 37, 67

Loadpoint Ltd
Unit K Chelworth Industrial Estate Chelworth Road, Cricklade, Swindon, SN6 6HE
Tel: 01793-751160 **Fax:** 01793-750155
E-mail: sales@loadpoint.co.uk
Website: http://www.loadpoint.co.uk
Bank(s): Lloyds TSB Bank plc
Directors: D. Pedley (Dir), M. Green (Tech Serv)
Managers: C. Paish (Fin Mgr)
Immediate Holding Company: LOADPOINT LIMITED
Registration no: 07206519 **VAT No.:** GB 348 2149 50
Date established: 2010 **Turnover:** £2m - £5m **No.of Employees:** 11 - 20
Product Groups: 35, 36, 37, 38, 42, 46, 47, 48, 84

Date of Accounts	Mar 12	Mar 11
Working Capital	13	3
Fixed Assets	58	57
Current Assets	361	317

M C S Technical Products Ltd
Building 2 Westmead Industrial Estate Westmead, Swindon, SN5 7YT
Tel: 01793-538308 **Fax:** 01793-522324
E-mail: sales@mcstechproducts.co.uk
Website: http://www.mcstechproducts.co.uk
Directors: S. Snow (MD)
Immediate Holding Company: M.C.S. TECHNICAL PRODUCTS LIMITED
Registration no: 02998039 **Date established:** 1994 **Turnover:** £5m - £10m
No.of Employees: 1 - 10 **Product Groups:** 38, 40, 41, 67

Date of Accounts	Dec 11	Dec 10	Dec 09
Working Capital	214	170	174
Fixed Assets	27	34	23
Current Assets	879	692	475

Magnaflux (a division of I T W Ltd)
Faraday Road Dorcan, Swindon, SN3 5HE
Tel: 01793-524566 **Fax:** 01793-619498
E-mail: sales@magnaflux.co.uk
Website: http://www.eu.magnaflux.com
Bank(s): HSBC
Managers: T. Lewis (Chief Mgr)
Ultimate Holding Company: I T W CORPORATION
Immediate Holding Company: I T W LTD
Registration no: 01536272 **VAT No.:** GB 531 8325 59
Date established: 1974 **Turnover:** £2m - £5m **No.of Employees:** 21 - 50
Product Groups: 32, 37, 38

Date of Accounts	Nov 01
Working Capital	1456
Current Assets	1456
Total Share Capital	218

Magnet Sales & Service
Unit 31 Blackworth Industrial Estate Highworth, Swindon, SN6 7NA
Tel: 01793-862100 **Fax:** 01793-862101
E-mail: sales@magnetsales.co.uk
Website: http://www.magnetsales.co.uk
Bank(s): Lloyds TSB Bank plc
Directors: A. Lobb (MD)
Immediate Holding Company: MAGNET SALES AND SERVICE LIMITED
Registration no: 02858057 **VAT No.:** GB 618 2810 46
Date established: 1993 **Turnover:** £1m - £2m **No.of Employees:** 11 - 20
Product Groups: 34, 35, 37, 38, 40, 42, 45, 85

Date of Accounts	Jul 11	Jul 10	Jul 09
Working Capital	334	560	335
Fixed Assets	2m	1m	1m
Current Assets	635	780	521

Mason Price Fluid Solutions Ltd
The Workshops 13 Bath Road, Wootton Bassett, Swindon, SN4 7DF
Tel: 01793-321020 **Fax:** 01793-321019
E-mail: enquiries@masonprice.co.uk
Website: http://www.masonprice.co.uk
Directors: S. Price (MD)
Immediate Holding Company: MASON-PRICE FLUID SOLUTIONS LTD
Registration no: 06039347 **Date established:** 2007
Turnover: £250,000 - £500,000 **No.of Employees:** 1 - 10
Product Groups: 18, 29, 40, 42, 45, 51, 52, 54, 67, 84

Date of Accounts	Jan 12	Jan 11	Jan 10
Working Capital	5	-23	8
Fixed Assets	10	9	4
Current Assets	88	42	24

Media Plant Ltd
3a Lancaster House Edison Park Hindle Way, Swindon, SN3 3RT
Tel: 01793-498040 **Fax:** 01793-498041
E-mail: sales@mediaplant.co.uk
Website: http://www.mediaplant.co.uk
Directors: S. Gough (Sales)
Immediate Holding Company: MEDIA PLANT LTD
Registration no: 05751376 **Date established:** 2006 **Turnover:** £1m - £2m
No.of Employees: 11 - 20 **Product Groups:** 27, 30, 44, 48, 89

Date of Accounts	May 11	May 10	May 09
Working Capital	120	43	44
Fixed Assets	119	133	70
Current Assets	896	644	729

Medion
Unit 120 Faraday Park Faraday Road, Dorcan, Swindon, SN3 5JF
Tel: 08713-761020 **Fax:** 01793-715716
E-mail: info@medion.co.uk
Website: http://www.medion.com
Directors: K. Perrett (Fin), N. Shenton (MD)
Managers: R. Munday (Mktg Serv Mgr)
Ultimate Holding Company: LENOVO GROUP LIMITED (HONG KONG)
Immediate Holding Company: MEDION ELECTRONICS LIMITED
Registration no: 03678084 **Date established:** 1998 **Turnover:** £2m - £5m
No.of Employees: 21 - 50 **Product Groups:** 36, 40

Date of Accounts	Dec 11	Dec 10	Dec 09
Sales Turnover	3m	4m	4m
Pre Tax Profit/Loss	-328	251	221
Working Capital	154	375	168
Fixed Assets	10	50	96
Current Assets	909	890	772
Current Liabilities	370	341	385

Medisco Medical Systems Ltd
Unit 13 Isis Trading Estate, Swindon, SN1 2PG
Tel: 01793-692781 **Fax:** 01793-491688
E-mail: admin@redman-sheet-metal.co.uk
Website: http://www.redman-sheet-metal.co.uk
Bank(s): Barclays, Swindon
Directors: J. Hyland (Dir), P. Tanner (Dir), J. Hyland (MD)
Immediate Holding Company: REDMAN SHEET METAL LIMITED
Registration no: 02173515 **Date established:** 1987
No.of Employees: 21 - 50 **Product Groups:** 48

Date of Accounts	May 11	May 10	May 09
Working Capital	225	159	-32
Fixed Assets	329	375	357
Current Assets	847	548	634

Metalfast - A Division Of Thyssenkrupp UK (a division of Thyssen Crupp Materials UK Ltd)
Blackworth Industrial Estate Highworth, Swindon, SN6 7RF
Tel: 01793-767676 **Fax:** 01793-767654
E-mail: sales@thyssenkrupp.com
Website: http://www.metalfast.co.uk
Bank(s): National Westminster Bank Plc
Managers: A. Hitchman (Sales Prom Mgr)
VAT No.: GB 392 0833 48 **Turnover:** £2m - £5m **No.of Employees:** 21 - 50
Product Groups: 34

Date of Accounts	Sep 07	Sep 06	Dec 05
Sales Turnover	N/A	5356	13220
Pre Tax Profit/Loss	N/A	343	778
Working Capital	12	12	1880
Fixed Assets	N/A	N/A	2045
Current Assets	12	12	6989
Current Liabilities	N/A	N/A	5109
Total Share Capital	12	12	12
ROCE% (Return on Capital Employed)			19.8
ROT% (Return on Turnover)		6.4	5.9

Mirotec UK
89 Groundwell Road, Swindon, SN1 2NA
Tel: 01793-433500 **Fax:** 01793-433500
E-mail: info@mirotec.co.uk
Website: http://www.mirotec.co.uk
Directors: A. Robinson (MD)
Immediate Holding Company: MIROTEC UK LIMITED
Registration no: 05461717 **Date established:** 2005
No.of Employees: 1 - 10 **Product Groups:** 38, 41, 49, 67, 83

Date of Accounts	May 07	May 06
Working Capital	14	21
Fixed Assets	1	1
Current Assets	64	89

MMG MagDev Limited (a subidiary of TT electronics plc)
Unit 105 Faraday Park Faraday Road, Dorcan, Swindon, SN3 5JF
Tel: 01793-425600 **Fax:** 01793-524357
E-mail: info@magdev.co.uk
Website: http://www.magdev.co.uk
Directors: F. Crisell (Develop), N. Walker (Dir), P. Wharmby (MD), W. Sharp (Co Sec)
Ultimate Holding Company: TT Electronics plc
Immediate Holding Company: Magnetic Materials Holdings Ltd
Registration no: 00383732 **VAT No.:** GB 196 2441 47
Date established: 1943 **Turnover:** £1m - £2m **No.of Employees:** 21 - 50
Product Groups: 29, 30, 34, 35, 37, 38, 39, 45, 46, 48, 49, 67

Date of Accounts	Dec 09	Dec 08	Dec 07
Sales Turnover	2m	2m	3m
Pre Tax Profit/Loss	452	86	171
Working Capital	712	208	146
Fixed Assets	69	95	113
Current Assets	2m	1m	2m
Current Liabilities	78	95	109

Motorola GTSS
North Swindon District Centre Thamesdown Drive, Swindon, SN25 4XY
Tel: 01793-541541 **Fax:** 01793-541227
Website: http://www.motorola.co.uk
Bank(s): Barclays
Managers: B. Sharples (Mgr)
Immediate Holding Company: Motorola Inc
Registration no: 00912182 **Date established:** 1967
No.of Employees: 501 - 1000 **Product Groups:** 37, 52, 86

Multisets Ltd
Stephenson Road, Swindon, SN25 5AE
Tel: 01793-729500 **Fax:** 01793-729177
E-mail: robertfellows@multisets.co.uk
Website: http://www.multisets.co.uk
Bank(s): Barclays
Directors: I. Cox (Sales), M. Pulley (Fin), R. Fellows (MD)
Managers: A. Holcombe (Est)
Ultimate Holding Company: MULTISETS (UK) LIMITED
Immediate Holding Company: MULTISETS LIMITED
Registration no: 00735944 **VAT No.:** GB 232 8910 66
Date established: 1962 **Turnover:** £2m - £5m **No.of Employees:** 51 - 100
Product Groups: 28

Date of Accounts	Jun 11	Jun 10	Jun 09
Sales Turnover	5m	4m	N/A
Pre Tax Profit/Loss	178	185	N/A
Working Capital	127	65	87
Fixed Assets	879	990	1m
Current Assets	2m	2m	2m
Current Liabilities	804	N/A	204

Multivac UK Ltd
Multivac House Rivermead Drive, Swindon, SN5 7UY
Tel: 01793-425800 **Fax:** 01793-616219
E-mail: sales@multivac.co.uk
Website: http://www.multivac.co.uk
Bank(s): National Westminster
Directors: J. Miners (Fin), J. Campbell (MD)
Managers: S. Watson (Personnel), A. Stark (Mktg Serv Mgr), I. Cutler (Tech Serv Mgr)
Ultimate Holding Company: MULTIVAC EXPORT AG (SWITZERLAND)
Immediate Holding Company: MULTIVAC U.K. LIMITED
Registration no: 01865375 **Date established:** 1984
Turnover: £20m - £50m **No.of Employees:** 51 - 100 **Product Groups:** 42

Date of Accounts	Dec 11	Dec 10	Dec 09
Sales Turnover	33m	26m	19m
Pre Tax Profit/Loss	3m	2m	1m
Working Capital	8m	7m	6m
Fixed Assets	1m	1m	1m
Current Assets	13m	13m	10m
Current Liabilities	3m	3m	2m

N P Automotive Coatings Europe Ltd
Britannia Trade Park Radway Road, Swindon, SN3 4ND
Tel: 01793-823361 **Fax:** 01793-823127
E-mail: iwamura_np4012@npc.nipponpaint.co.jp
Website: http://www.npae.co.uk
Directors: M. Iwamura (MD)
Managers: C. Bleathman (Fin Mgr)
Ultimate Holding Company: NIPPON PAINT CO. LTD (JAPAN)
Immediate Holding Company: N P AUTOMOTIVE COATINGS (EUROPE) LIMITED
Registration no: 02651443 **Date established:** 1991
Turnover: £10m - £20m **No.of Employees:** 51 - 100 **Product Groups:** 32

Date of Accounts	Dec 11	Dec 10	Dec 09
Sales Turnover	14m	13m	10m
Pre Tax Profit/Loss	-425	-1m	-1m
Working Capital	3m	2m	2m
Fixed Assets	3m	4m	3m
Current Assets	7m	8m	6m
Current Liabilities	472	569	441

Natural Environment Research Council

Polaris House North Star Avenue, Swindon, SN2 1EU
Tel: 01793-411500 **Fax:** 01793-411501
E-mail: requests@nerc.ac.uk
Website: http://www.nerc.ac.uk
Bank(s): Bank of England
Directors: D. Wingham (Grp Chief Exec), M. Wilson-Jarvis (Dir), A. Thorpe (Grp Chief Exec), D. Bullard (Fin)
Managers: C. Lowther (I.T. Exec)
Registration no: 06106043 **Date established:** 2007
Turnover: £125m - £250m **No.of Employees:** 101 - 250
Product Groups: 82, 85

Newman Enterprises Sales Ltd

The Gables Ballards Ash, Wootton Bassett, Swindon, SN4 8DT
Tel: 01793-853807 **Fax:** 01793-851510
E-mail: newman-enterprises@supanet.com
Website: http://www.newman-enterprises.com
Directors: H. Newman (MD)
Immediate Holding Company: NEWMAN ENTERPRISES (SALES) LIMITED
Registration no: 03627193 **Date established:** 1998
No.of Employees: 1 - 10 **Product Groups:** 41

Date of Accounts	Jun 11	Jun 10	Jun 09
Working Capital	85	97	102
Fixed Assets	3	N/A	N/A
Current Assets	171	147	197

Office Clearance & Wholesale Ltd

Bay 1 Evolution House Westmead Industrial Estate, Westmead, Swindon, SN5 7YT
Tel: 01793-619744 **Fax:** 01793-619497
E-mail: sales@officecw.co.uk
Website: http://www.officecw.co.uk
Directors: P. Smith (MD)
Ultimate Holding Company: CELVEY LIMITED
Immediate Holding Company: OFFICE CLEARANCE AND WHOLESALE LIMITED
Registration no: 05508156 **Date established:** 2005
No.of Employees: 11 - 20 **Product Groups:** 23, 25, 26, 49, 52, 61, 67, 83

Date of Accounts	Mar 12	Mar 11	Mar 10
Working Capital	284	239	25
Fixed Assets	63	43	33
Current Assets	783	557	364

P M G

Whitehill Industrial Estate Whitehill Lane, Wootton Bassett, Swindon, SN4 7DB
Tel: 01793-840840 **Fax:** 01793-840740
E-mail: sales@pmgcompany.co.uk
Website: http://www.pmgcompany.co.uk
Directors: T. Ackery (MD)
Registration no: 03580148 **No.of Employees:** 1 - 10 **Product Groups:** 27, 30, 35, 37, 39

Date of Accounts	Dec 07	Dec 06	Dec 05
Working Capital	148	120	55
Fixed Assets	26	19	24
Current Assets	365	254	165
Current Liabilities	216	135	110

Pestcatcher

27 Iffley Road, Swindon, SN2 1DL
Tel: 01793-324982
E-mail: markb@pestcatcher.co.uk
Website: http://www.pestcatcher.co.uk
Directors: M. Burnett (Prop)
Date established: 2005 **Turnover:** £250,000 - £500,000
No.of Employees: 1 - 10 **Product Groups:** 07, 41, 52

Petzetakis GB

Unit 5 Ravenseft Park Cheney Manor Industrial Estate, Swindon, SN2 2QJ
Tel: 01793-480300 **Fax:** 01488-674675
Website: http://www.eurohose.co.uk
Directors: A. Norris Hill (Fin), G. Petzetakis (Grp Chief Exec)
Immediate Holding Company: EUROHOSE LIMITED
Registration no: 04267571 **Date established:** 2001
No.of Employees: 1 - 10 **Product Groups:** 30, 66

P H S Treadsmart

Unit L Hawksworth Trading Estate Newcombe Drive, Hawksworth Trading Estate, Swindon, SN2 1DZ
Tel: 01793-420088 **Fax:** 01793-431113
E-mail: iandavies@phs.co.uk
Website: http://www.phs.co.uk
Managers: I. Davies (Ops Mgr)
Ultimate Holding Company: PHS GROUP HOLDINGS LIMITED
Immediate Holding Company: CLEAN STEP LIMITED
Registration no: 02088599 **Date established:** 1987
No.of Employees: 21 - 50 **Product Groups:** 23, 24, 83

Date of Accounts	Mar 11	Mar 10	Mar 05
Pre Tax Profit/Loss	N/A	N/A	4m
Working Capital	20	20	20
Current Assets	20	20	20

Plantronics Ltd

Interface Business Park Binknoll Lane, Wootton Bassett, Swindon, SN4 8QQ
Tel: 01793-848999 **Fax:** 01793-848853
E-mail: barbara.scherer@plantronics.com
Website: http://www.plantronics.com
Bank(s): HSBC Bank plc
Directors: G. Tyrrell (Dir), P. Vanhoutte (MD), T. Williams (Tech Serv), N. Pierce (Pers)
Managers: L. Woodruff (Sales & Mktg Mg), L. Duffy (Purch Mgr)
Ultimate Holding Company: PLANTRONICS INC (USA)
Immediate Holding Company: PLANTRONICS LIMITED
Registration no: 01773891 **VAT No.:** GB 421 2996 57
Date established: 1983 **Turnover:** £10m - £20m
No.of Employees: 101 - 250 **Product Groups:** 37

Date of Accounts	Mar 08	Mar 09	Apr 10
Sales Turnover	15m	15m	12m
Pre Tax Profit/Loss	-969	34	979
Working Capital	1m	2m	2m
Fixed Assets	3m	3m	3m
Current Assets	5m	8m	5m
Current Liabilities	2m	1m	2m

Powervar

Unit 5 Birch Kembrey Park, Swindon, SN2 8UU
Tel: 01793-553980 **Fax:** 01793-535350
E-mail: sales@powervar.co.uk
Website: http://www.powervar.co.uk
Managers: R. Morris (Mgr)
Ultimate Holding Company: PFINGSTEN PARTNERS LLC (USA)
Immediate Holding Company: POWERVAR LIMITED
Registration no: 03407619 **Date established:** 1997
No.of Employees: 1 - 10 **Product Groups:** 28, 37, 44, 67

Date of Accounts	Dec 11	Dec 10	Dec 09
Working Capital	2m	1m	1m
Fixed Assets	30	36	28
Current Assets	2m	2m	1m

Praxair Surface Technologies Ltd

Drakes Way, Swindon, SN3 3HX
Tel: 01793-512555 **Fax:** 01793-611608
E-mail: info@praxair.com
Website: http://www.praxair.com
Bank(s): Bank of America
Directors: J. Winterburn (Fin), J. Philpott (Pers)
Managers: M. Burton
Ultimate Holding Company: PRAXAIR INC (USA)
Immediate Holding Company: PRAXAIR SURFACE TECHNOLOGIES LIMITED
Registration no: 02416734 **VAT No.:** GB 535 6150 54
Date established: 1989 **Turnover:** £20m - £50m
No.of Employees: 51 - 100 **Product Groups:** 32, 40, 48

Date of Accounts	Dec 11	Dec 10	Dec 09
Sales Turnover	36m	33m	24m
Pre Tax Profit/Loss	2m	-710	2m
Working Capital	4m	148	2m
Fixed Assets	12m	15m	10m
Current Assets	10m	8m	5m
Current Liabilities	2m	2m	2m

Premdor Crosby Ltd

Gemini House Hargreaves Road, Groundwell Indl-Est, Swindon, SN25 5AJ
Tel: 01793-708200 **Fax:** 01793- 708254
Website: http://www.premdor.co.uk
Bank(s): National Westminster
Directors: K. McKenzie (MD)
Managers: M. Faren (I.T. Exec), P. Cotton (), W. Alexander (Mgr)
Ultimate Holding Company: MASONITE INTERNATIONAL CORPORATION (CANADA)
Immediate Holding Company: PREMDOR CROSBY LIMITED
Registration no: 03227274 **Date established:** 1996
No.of Employees: 21 - 50 **Product Groups:** 25

Date of Accounts	Dec 07	Dec 08	Jan 10
Sales Turnover	108m	83m	54m
Pre Tax Profit/Loss	328	-9m	-13m
Working Capital	36m	-5m	-16m
Fixed Assets	23m	20m	19m
Current Assets	57m	41m	25m
Current Liabilities	4m	3m	2m

R C M Catering

32 The Knoll, Swindon, SN1 4DQ
Tel: 01793-521119 **Fax:** 01793-521119
Website: http://www.rcmcateringequipment.co.uk
Directors: A. Ratcliffe (MD)
Immediate Holding Company: RCM CATERING EQUIPMENT LIMITED
Registration no: 05567806 **Date established:** 2005
No.of Employees: 1 - 10 **Product Groups:** 20, 40, 41

Date of Accounts	Nov 11	Nov 10	Nov 09
Working Capital	-15	-0	-2
Fixed Assets	15	N/A	3
Current Assets	38	39	46

R W E Npower (Headquarters)

Windmill Hill Business Park Whitehill Way, Swindon, SN5 6PB
Tel: 01793-877777 **Fax:** 01905-727100
E-mail: info@npower.com
Website: http://www.rwenpower.com
Bank(s): HSBC Bank plc
Managers: J. Hagan
Ultimate Holding Company: RWE AG (GERMANY)
Immediate Holding Company: RWE NPOWER HOLDINGS PLC
Registration no: 03987817 **Date established:** 2000
Turnover: £500m - £1,000m **No.of Employees:** 101 - 250
Product Groups: 18, 52, 84

Date of Accounts	Dec 11	Dec 10	Dec 09
Pre Tax Profit/Loss	4m	3m	64m
Working Capital	243m	365m	483m
Fixed Assets	1162m	1162m	1162m
Current Assets	244m	366m	487m
Current Liabilities	1m	1m	4m

Reed

43 Bridge Street, Swindon, SN1 1BL
Tel: 01793-532230 **Fax:** 01793-514355
Website: http://www.reed.co.uk
Managers: J. King (Comm)
Immediate Holding Company: REED EMPLOYMENT LIMITED
Registration no: 00669854 **Date established:** 1960
No.of Employees: 11 - 20 **Product Groups:** 80

Robnor Resins Ltd

Hunts Rise South Marston, Swindon, SN3 4TE
Tel: 01793-823741 **Fax:** 01793-827033
E-mail: drew@robnor.co.uk
Website: http://www.robnor.co.uk
Bank(s): Bank of Scotland
Directors: D. Warren (MD)
Managers: V. Pusey (Fin Mgr), M. Rose (Sales Prom Mgr), M. Roger (Chief Mgr)
Ultimate Holding Company: HALIFAX INDUSTRIAL LIMITED
Immediate Holding Company: ROBNOR RESINS LIMITED
Registration no: 00664718 **VAT No.:** GB 194 4985 09
Date established: 1960 **Turnover:** £2m - £5m **No.of Employees:** 21 - 50
Product Groups: 31, 32, 37

Date of Accounts	Sep 11	Sep 10	Sep 09
Working Capital	1m	847	611
Fixed Assets	66	96	118
Current Assets	3m	2m	2m

Sauer-Danfoss Ltd

130 Faraday Park Faraday Road, Swindon, SN3 5JF
Tel: 01793-716 000 **Fax:** 01793-716 015
Website: http://www.sauer-danfoss.com
Bank(s): Natwest
Directors: W. Cochrane (Co Sec)
Managers: J. Langrick (Chief Acct), A. Whiteford (Sales Prom Mgr), R. Lawton (Plant), J. Manfield (I.T. Exec), G. Best, D. Yandell (Personnel)
Ultimate Holding Company: Sauer Inc. (USA)
Immediate Holding Company: Sauer-Sundstrand GmbH (Germany)
Registration no: 02179360 **VAT No.:** GB 455 5850 25
Date established: 1960 **Turnover:** £20m - £50m
No.of Employees: 21 - 50 **Product Groups:** 40, 45, 67

Select Solar Ltd

Unit 5 Blakehill Business Park Chelworth Road, Cricklade, Swindon, SN6 6JD
Tel: 01793-752032 **Fax:** 0870-4584936
E-mail: enquiries@selectsolar.co.uk
Website: http://www.selectsolar.co.uk
Directors: F. Tattersall (Dir), F. Tattersael (Dir)
Managers: J. Bird (Mktg Serv Mgr)
Immediate Holding Company: SELECT SOLAR LTD
Registration no: 04303044 **Date established:** 2001
No.of Employees: 1 - 10 **Product Groups:** 37, 49, 65

Shawcity Ltd

Unit 91-92 Shrivenham Hundred Business Park Majors Road, Watchfield, Swindon, SN6 8TY
Tel: 01367-241675 **Fax:** 01367-242491
E-mail: info@shawcity.co.uk
Website: http://www.shawcity.co.uk
Bank(s): Lloyds
Directors: N. O'regan (MD)
Ultimate Holding Company: ION SCIENCE LIMITED
Immediate Holding Company: SHAWCITY LIMITED
Registration no: 01273269 **VAT No.:** GB 200 8689 72
Date established: 1976 **Turnover:** £1m - £2m **No.of Employees:** 11 - 20
Product Groups: 37, 38, 40, 45, 85

Date of Accounts	Dec 11	Dec 10	Dec 09
Working Capital	244	372	396
Fixed Assets	381	70	79
Current Assets	735	563	730

Shrink 1st Ltd

Bridgewater Close Hawkesworth Trading Estate, Hawksworth Trading Estate, Swindon, SN2 1ED
Tel: 01793-612072 **Fax:** 01793-534649
E-mail: sales@shrinkfast.co.uk
Website: http://www.shrinkfast.co.uk
Bank(s): Barclays, Victoria Square, Droitwich
Directors: R. Summerfield (Dir)
Ultimate Holding Company: SHFT PACKAGING LIMITED
Immediate Holding Company: SHRINK 1ST LIMITED
Registration no: 01589536 **VAT No.:** GB 589 5907 66
Date established: 1981 **Turnover:** £1m - £2m **No.of Employees:** 11 - 20
Product Groups: 30, 31, 42, 67

Date of Accounts	Dec 11	Dec 10	Dec 09
Sales Turnover	N/A	N/A	2m
Pre Tax Profit/Loss	N/A	N/A	-692
Working Capital	584	502	464
Fixed Assets	42	61	39
Current Assets	1m	1m	802
Current Liabilities	N/A	N/A	54

Spooner Brothers Ltd

Unit 10 Central Trading Estate Signal Way, Swindon, SN3 1PD
Tel: 01793-336333 **Fax:** 01793-336333
E-mail: sales@spoonerbrothers.co.uk
Website: http://www.spoonerbrothers.co.uk
Directors: P. Spooner (Prop)
Immediate Holding Company: SPOONER BROTHERS LTD
Registration no: 05741244 **Date established:** 2006
No.of Employees: 1 - 10 **Product Groups:** 25, 30, 35

Date of Accounts	Mar 11	Mar 10	Mar 09
Working Capital	-41	-41	-40
Fixed Assets	63	68	73
Current Assets	15	74	70

Stainless Design Services Ltd

C The Old Bakery Kiln Lane, Swindon, SN2 2NP
Tel: 01793-692666 **Fax:** 01793-487242
E-mail: barry.nugent@stainlessdesign.co.uk
Website: http://www.stainlessdesign.co.uk
Bank(s): Lloyds
Directors: B. Nugent (MD), A. Macpherson (Fin)
Immediate Holding Company: STAINLESS DESIGN SERVICES LIMITED
Registration no: 01751976 **VAT No.:** GB 392 0894 28
Date established: 1983 **Turnover:** £1m - £2m **No.of Employees:** 21 - 50
Product Groups: 30, 33, 36

Date of Accounts	Nov 11	Nov 10	Nov 09
Working Capital	15	31	38
Fixed Assets	120	106	119
Current Assets	271	309	312

Stanley Security Solutions Ltd

Stanley House Bramble Road, Techno Trading Estate, Swindon, SN2 8ER
Tel: 01793-692401 **Fax:** 01793-615848
E-mail: bginnever@stanleyworks.com
Website: http://www.stanleysecuritysolutions.co.uk
Directors: M. Page (Sales)
Managers: A. Prior (Personnel), M. Rose (Mktg Serv Mgr), J. Klimkowski (Tech Serv Mgr)
Ultimate Holding Company: STANLEY WORKS INC (USA)
Immediate Holding Company: BLICK TELEFUSION COMMUNICATIONS LIMITED
Registration no: 01476705 **Date established:** 1980
Turnover: £500,000 - £1m **No.of Employees:** 1 - 10 **Product Groups:** 37

Date of Accounts	Dec 11	Dec 10	Dec 09
Sales Turnover	484	540	636
Pre Tax Profit/Loss	291	324	382
Working Capital	9m	9m	9m
Fixed Assets	14m	14m	14m
Current Assets	11m	11m	10m

Strategic Maintenance Planning Ltd (SMP)

Unit 4 Stanton Court Stirling Road, South Marston Industrial Estate, Swindon, SN3 4YH
Tel: 01793-823013 **Fax:** 01793-823014
E-mail: info@smpltd.co.uk
Website: http://www.smpltd.co.uk
Directors: J. Grant (Dir)
Immediate Holding Company: STRATEGIC MAINTENANCE PLANNING LIMITED

Registration no: 03265332 **Date established:** 1996 **Turnover:** £1m - £2m
No.of Employees: 11 - 20 **Product Groups:** 44

Date of Accounts	Oct 11	Oct 10	Oct 09
Sales Turnover	N/A	1m	648
Pre Tax Profit/Loss	N/A	337	81
Working Capital	155	220	52
Fixed Assets	251	268	257
Current Assets	501	431	141
Current Liabilities	N/A	170	48

Swindon Aerial Services

31 Newport Street Old Town, Swindon, SN1 3DP
Tel: 01793-531400 **Fax:** 01793-431831
E-mail: swindonaerialservices@yahoo.co.uk
Website: http://www.swindonarials.com
Directors: R. Symthe (Prop)
VAT No.: GB 195 1212 73 **Date established:** 1973
No.of Employees: 1 - 10 **Product Groups:** 37

Swindon Engineering Metalworkers

Unit 10 Bramble Close, Swindon, SN2 8DW
Tel: 01793-641808 **Fax:** 01793-513029
E-mail: sgawluk@swindoneng.com
Website: http://www.swindoneng.com
Bank(s): National Westminster Bank Plc
Directors: S. Gawluk (Prop)
Registration no: 02347056 **VAT No.:** GB 576 0904 25
Turnover: £250,000 - £500,000 **No.of Employees:** 11 - 20
Product Groups: 33, 35, 38, 46, 48

Swindon Lifting Gear Ltd

Unit 9a-11a Workshop A Station Industrial Estate, Swindon, SN1 5DE
Tel: 01793-542051 **Fax:** 01793-497187
E-mail: info@swindonlifting.com
Website: http://www.swindonlifting.com
Directors: G. Woodsford (MD), G. Woodsford (Fin)
Immediate Holding Company: SWINDON LIFTING GEAR LTD.
Registration no: 03634280 **Date established:** 1998
No.of Employees: 1 - 10 **Product Groups:** 35, 39, 45

Date of Accounts	Oct 11	Oct 09	Oct 08
Working Capital	110	150	177
Fixed Assets	9	8	4
Current Assets	210	248	268

Swindon Silicon Systems Ltd

Radnor Street, Swindon, SN1 3PR
Tel: 01793-649400 **Fax:** 01793-616215
E-mail: sales@swindonsilicon.co.uk
Website: http://www.swindonsilicon.co.uk
Directors: D. Burton (Co Sec), L. Robbins (Fin), G. Hall (Dir)
Managers: P. Seal (Tech Serv Mgr), R. Mount (Sales & Mktg Mg), B. Hall (Personnel)
Ultimate Holding Company: PINAFORE COOPERATIEF U.A. (NETHERLANDS)
Immediate Holding Company: SWINDON SILICON SYSTEMS LIMITED
Registration no: 01378199 **Date established:** 1978
Turnover: £10m - £20m **No.of Employees:** 51 - 100 **Product Groups:** 37, 84

Date of Accounts	Dec 11	Dec 10	Jan 09
Sales Turnover	19m	18m	12m
Pre Tax Profit/Loss	3m	3m	2m
Working Capital	5m	8m	5m
Fixed Assets	2m	1m	976
Current Assets	8m	10m	7m
Current Liabilities	1m	1m	1m

Swindon Soft Water Centre

260 Ferndale Road, Swindon, SN2 1HB
Tel: 01793-616699 **Fax:** 01793-616699
Directors: M. Siville (Prop)
Immediate Holding Company: BETTAGLAZE LIMITED
Registration no: 06730256 **Date established:** 2008
No.of Employees: 1 - 10 **Product Groups:** 38, 42

T S S I Sytems

Rutland House Hargreaves Road Groundwell Industrial Estate, Swindon, SN25 5AZ
Tel: 01793-747700 **Fax:** 01793-747701
E-mail: sales@tssi.co.uk
Website: http://www.tssi.co.uk
Directors: D. Chapchal (Ch), J. Coad (Co Sec)
Managers: N. Stokes (Tech Serv Mgr)
Immediate Holding Company: TSSI SYSTEMS LIMITED
Registration no: 05433732 **Date established:** 2005 **Turnover:** £2m - £5m
No.of Employees: 11 - 20 **Product Groups:** 30, 40, 52

Date of Accounts	May 09	May 08	Nov 11
Working Capital	-813	N/A	-2m
Fixed Assets	1m	1	705
Current Assets	570	1	367

Tate Engineering

Tate Estate Kingsdown Road, Swindon, SN25 6SF
Tel: 01793-820503 **Fax:** 01793-820504
E-mail: tate.engineering@virgin.net
Directors: P. Tate (Prop)
VAT No.: GB 391 9818 05 **Date established:** 1992
Turnover: £250,000 - £500,000 **No.of Employees:** 1 - 10
Product Groups: 48

Techno Transformers Ltd

Whitehill Industrial Estate Whitehill Lane, Wootton Bassett, Swindon, SN4 7DB
Tel: 01793-853898 **Fax:** 01793-855025
E-mail: sales@technotransformers.co.uk
Website: http://www.technotransformers.co.uk
Bank(s): Barclays Bank PLC
Directors: N. Higginbottom (Dir)
Immediate Holding Company: TECHNO TRANSFORMERS LIMITED
Registration no: 02822781 **VAT No.:** GB 650 8245 41
Date established: 1993 **Turnover:** £1m - £2m **No.of Employees:** 11 - 20
Product Groups: 37, 38, 67

Date of Accounts	Apr 11	Apr 10	Apr 09
Working Capital	25	12	-4
Fixed Assets	362	399	411
Current Assets	350	352	267

Teeone Ltd

18 Aspen Close, Swindon, SN2 8AJ
Tel: 01793-610555 **Fax:** 01993-774746
E-mail: info@teeone.co.uk
Website: http://www.teeone.co.uk
Directors: M. Henderson (MD)
Immediate Holding Company: TEEONE LIMITED
Registration no: 05328374 **Date established:** 2005
No.of Employees: 1 - 10 **Product Groups:** 24, 49, 52

Date of Accounts	Jan 12	Jan 11	Jan 10
Sales Turnover	N/A	269	305
Pre Tax Profit/Loss	N/A	43	24
Working Capital	8	-13	-16
Fixed Assets	16	17	24
Current Assets	44	36	37
Current Liabilities	N/A	17	8

Terrapart International Ltd

Blacksmith's Yard Broad Hinton, Swindon, SN4 9PB
Tel: 01793-731990 **Fax:** 01793-731791
E-mail: sales@terrapart.com
Website: http://www.terrapart.com
Directors: C. Drewett (MD)
Immediate Holding Company: TERRAPART INTERNATIONAL LIMITED
Registration no: 02446271 **VAT No.:** GB 535 7289 18
Date established: 1989 **Turnover:** £1m - £2m **No.of Employees:** 1 - 10
Product Groups: 67

Date of Accounts	Mar 12	Mar 11	Mar 10
Working Capital	264	39	6
Fixed Assets	16	20	23
Current Assets	839	635	707

Thread Grinding Services Ltd

Unit 3 Napier Close Hawksworth Trading Estate, Swindon, SN2 1TY
Tel: 01793-641700 **Fax:** 01793-513268
Directors: A. Janicki (Co Sec)
Immediate Holding Company: THREAD GRINDING SERVICES LIMITED
Registration no: 01869253 **Date established:** 1984
Turnover: £250,000 - £500,000 **No.of Employees:** 1 - 10
Product Groups: 35, 36, 38, 46, 48

Date of Accounts	Jul 12	Jul 11	Jul 10
Working Capital	73	48	43
Fixed Assets	77	80	84
Current Assets	111	83	89

Toolcraft Plastics Swindon Ltd

Unit 1-5 Argyle Commercial Centre Argyle Street, Swindon, SN2 8AR
Tel: 01793-641040 **Fax:** 01793-615483
E-mail: help@toolcraft.co.uk
Website: http://www.toolcraft.co.uk
Bank(s): HSBC
Managers: N. Sturney (Sales Admin)
Immediate Holding Company: TOOLCRAFT PLASTICS (SWINDON) LIMITED
Registration no: 01661446 **Date established:** 1982
Turnover: £250,000 - £500,000 **No.of Employees:** 11 - 20
Product Groups: 30

Date of Accounts	Mar 11	Mar 10	Mar 09
Sales Turnover	N/A	387	500
Pre Tax Profit/Loss	N/A	11	65
Working Capital	345	332	311
Fixed Assets	303	322	337
Current Assets	410	402	401
Current Liabilities	N/A	31	41

Tops Security Solutions

Unit 17 Star West Westmead Drive Westlea, Swindon, SN5 7SW
Tel: 01793-616626
E-mail: sales@tops-security.co.uk
Website: http://www.tops-security.co.uk
Directors: S. Rushton (Dir)
Immediate Holding Company: TOPS SECURITY SOLUTIONS LTD
Registration no: 05771238 **Date established:** 2004
Turnover: £500,000 - £1m **No.of Employees:** 1 - 10 **Product Groups:** 35, 40

Trans XL International

Thornhill South Marston, Swindon, SN3 4TA
Tel: 01793-832766 **Fax:** 01793-823826
E-mail: sales@transxl.co.uk
Website: http://www.transxl.co.uk
Directors: C. Wood (Fin), J. Napper (MD), J. Napper (Dir)
Managers: B. Hayllar (Ops Mgr), S. Hobbs (Buyer), T. Wrighton (Sales Prom Mgr), J. Smith (Sales Prom Mgr), J. Smith (Mktg Serv Mgr)
Immediate Holding Company: TRANS XL INTERNATIONAL LIMITED
Registration no: 01168886 **VAT No.:** GB 195 6600 39
Date established: 1974 **Turnover:** £2m - £5m **No.of Employees:** 1 - 10
Product Groups: 38, 40, 42, 44, 67

Date of Accounts	Apr 11	Apr 10	Apr 09
Working Capital	449	451	446
Fixed Assets	51	77	75
Current Assets	882	927	819

Treadways

12 Browning Close Stratton, Swindon, SN3 4XS
Tel: 01793-823888
Directors: J. Smith (Ptnr)
Date established: 1994 **No.of Employees:** 1 - 10 **Product Groups:** 35, 36

Triumph International Ltd

Arkwright Road Groundwell Industrial Estate, Swindon, SN25 5BE
Tel: 01793-722200 **Fax:** 01793-728341
E-mail: noreen.gallagher@triumph.com
Website: http://www.triumph.com
Bank(s): Barclays Swindon
Directors: S. Hawkins (Co Sec)
Managers: L. St George (Personnel), N. Gallagher (Chief Mgr), G. Harvey (Fin Mgr), G. Arthur (Sales & Mktg Mg)
Ultimate Holding Company: TRIUMPH UNIVERSA AG (SWITZERLAND)
Immediate Holding Company: TRIUMPH INTERNATIONAL LIMITED
Registration no: 00536483 **VAT No.:** GB 535 7869 00
Date established: 1954 **Turnover:** £20m - £50m
No.of Employees: 51 - 100 **Product Groups:** 24

Date of Accounts	Dec 11	Dec 10	Dec 09
Sales Turnover	45m	42m	46m
Pre Tax Profit/Loss	-3m	-6m	-5m
Working Capital	3m	7m	14m
Fixed Assets	2m	2m	1m
Current Assets	10m	15m	19m
Current Liabilities	1m	2m	2m

Troax UK Ltd

Enterprise House Murdock Road, Dorcan, Swindon, SN3 5HY
Tel: 01793-542000 **Fax:** 01793-618784
E-mail: sales@troax.co.uk
Website: http://www.gunnebotroax.sa
Bank(s): National Westminster Bank Plc
Directors: D. Teulon (MD), K. Cooper (Fin)
Managers: D. Chapman (Purch Mgr)
Ultimate Holding Company: GUNNEBO AB (SWEDEN)
Immediate Holding Company: TROAX (U.K.) LIMITED
Registration no: 01707609 **VAT No.:** GB 385 5923 11
Date established: 1983 **Turnover:** £5m - £10m **No.of Employees:** 21 - 50
Product Groups: 26, 35, 36, 41

Date of Accounts	Dec 11	Dec 10	Dec 09
Sales Turnover	6m	6m	5m
Pre Tax Profit/Loss	735	545	519
Working Capital	456	418	-45
Fixed Assets	402	424	432
Current Assets	2m	2m	2m
Current Liabilities	562	501	264

Trolley Maintenance Services Ltd

Unit 1 Chelworth Lodge Cricklade, Swindon, SN6 6HP
Tel: 01793-759184 **Fax:** 01793-759469
E-mail: info@trolleymaintenance.co.uk
Website: http://www.trolleymaintenance.co.uk
Managers: A. Dickson
Immediate Holding Company: TROLLEY MAINTENANCE SERVICES LIMITED
Registration no: 04462167 **Date established:** 2002
Turnover: £500,000 - £1m **No.of Employees:** 11 - 20
Product Groups: 45, 48

Date of Accounts	Jun 11	Jun 10	Jun 09
Working Capital	210	235	205
Fixed Assets	121	103	96
Current Assets	390	382	349

UK Process Valves Ltd

Unit 6 Cheney Manor Industrial Estate, Swindon, SN2 2QJ
Tel: 01793-613003 **Fax:** 01793-613004
E-mail: sales@ukprocessvalves.com
Website: http://www.ukprocessvalves.com
Managers: D. Angell (Sales Prom Mgr)
Immediate Holding Company: UK PROCESS VALVES (HOLDINGS) LIMITED
Registration no: 07071311 **Date established:** 2009 **Turnover:** £2m - £5m
No.of Employees: 1 - 10 **Product Groups:** 30, 36, 38, 40, 45

Date of Accounts	Apr 11	Apr 10
Fixed Assets	2m	2m

UK Office Direct

Unit 5 Blackworth Court Blackworth Industrial Estate, Highworth, Swindon, SN6 7NS
Tel: 0800-652 6060 **Fax:** 01793-762777
E-mail: info@ukofficedirect.co.uk
Website: http://www.ukofficedirect.co.uk
Managers: R. Ward (I.T. Exec)
Immediate Holding Company: UK OFFICE DIRECT LIMITED
Registration no: 04490044 **VAT No.:** GB 758 1556 03
Date established: 2002 **No.of Employees:** 11 - 20 **Product Groups:** 22, 25, 26, 27, 28, 29, 30, 32, 35, 40, 44, 49, 52, 61, 64, 66, 67

Date of Accounts	Aug 10	Aug 09	Mar 12
Sales Turnover	N/A	N/A	5m
Pre Tax Profit/Loss	N/A	N/A	513
Working Capital	41	-29	671
Fixed Assets	68	93	N/A
Current Assets	764	654	2m
Current Liabilities	N/A	N/A	321

Vastern Timber Co. Ltd

Saw Mills Wootton Bassett, Swindon, SN4 7PD
Tel: 01793-853281 **Fax:** 01793-855336
E-mail: enquiries@vastern.co.uk
Website: http://www.vastern.co.uk
Directors: J. Barnes (MD), J. Barns (Dir)
Ultimate Holding Company: BARNES,BRANCH & CO.LIMITED
Immediate Holding Company: VASTERN TIMBER COMPANY LIMITED
Registration no: 00308754 **Date established:** 1935 **Turnover:** £2m - £5m
No.of Employees: 11 - 20 **Product Groups:** 08, 25, 39, 66

Date of Accounts	Dec 11	Dec 10	Dec 09
Sales Turnover	3m	3m	3m
Pre Tax Profit/Loss	65	95	-171
Working Capital	1m	1m	1m
Fixed Assets	1m	974	932
Current Assets	3m	2m	3m
Current Liabilities	279	294	241

Vikan UK Ltd

1-3 Avro Gate South Marston Park, South Marston Industrial Estate, Swindon, SN3 4AG
Tel: 01793-716760 **Fax:** 01793-716761
E-mail: sales@vikan.co.uk
Website: http://www.vikan.co.uk
Bank(s): Danske Bank, London Ec4
Managers: L. Julich (Mgr)
Ultimate Holding Company: VISSING HOLDING A/S (DENMARK)
Immediate Holding Company: VIKAN (UK) LIMITED
Registration no: 02790284 **VAT No.:** GB 601 1919 78
Date established: 1993 **Turnover:** £2m - £5m **No.of Employees:** 11 - 20
Product Groups: 29, 30, 32

Date of Accounts	Dec 11	Dec 10	Dec 09
Working Capital	677	645	767
Fixed Assets	63	80	101
Current Assets	2m	2m	2m

W P S UK Ltd

Suite 16 Cherry Orchard West Kembrey Park, Swindon, SN2 8UP
Tel: 01793-541080 **Fax:** 01793-495595
E-mail: info@wps-uk.com
Website: http://www.wps-uk.com
Bank(s): National Westminster Bank Plc
Directors: K. Willaims (MD)
Managers: C. Gannon, D. Smith, A. Jones, A. Airey
Ultimate Holding Company: IMTECH NV (NETHERLANDS)
Immediate Holding Company: WPS UNITED KINGDOM LIMITED
Registration no: 04211140 **VAT No.:** GB 650 9314 43
Date established: 2001 **Turnover:** £2m - £5m **No.of Employees:** 21 - 50
Product Groups: 80, 81

see next page

W P S UK Ltd - *Cont'd*

Date of Accounts	Dec 10	Dec 09	Dec 08
Sales Turnover	4m	4m	4m
Pre Tax Profit/Loss	19	-37	-106
Working Capital	251	634	565
Fixed Assets	583	648	754
Current Assets	1m	2m	3m
Current Liabilities	1m	1m	1m

W R C plc

Frankland Road Blagrove, Swindon, SN5 8YF
Tel: 01793-865000 **Fax:** 01793-865001
E-mail: solutions@wrcplc.co.uk
Website: http://www.wrcplc.co.uk
Bank(s): HSBC Bank plc
Directors: K. McLintock (Co Sec), R. Chapman (Ch)
Managers: M. Hing, L. Porter (I.T. Exec), F. Smith (Personnel), F. Smith (Personnel), G. Jones (Mktg Serv Mgr), D. Russell (Tech Serv Mgr), D. Peters (Sales Prom Mgr), T. Griffiths
Immediate Holding Company: WRC P.L.C.
Registration no: 02262098 **VAT No.:** GB 527 1804 53
Date established: 1988 **Turnover:** £5m - £10m
No.of Employees: 51 - 100 **Product Groups:** 54, 80, 81, 84, 85

Date of Accounts	Mar 12	Mar 11	Mar 10
Sales Turnover	8m	7m	10m
Pre Tax Profit/Loss	-444	-930	-247
Working Capital	1m	1m	3m
Fixed Assets	5m	5m	5m
Current Assets	4m	4m	5m
Current Liabilities	2m	3m	2m

Westwire Harnessing Ltd

Unit 10 Headlands Trading Estate, Swindon, SN2 7JQ
Tel: 01793-537217 **Fax:** 01793-421039
E-mail: geoff.kenington@fiinfo.com
Website: http://www.westwireharnessing.co.uk
Bank(s): Lloyds TSB Bank plc
Directors: G. Kennington (Dir)
Immediate Holding Company: WESTWIRE HARNESSING LIMITED
Registration no: 02142617 **Date established:** 1987 **Turnover:** £2m - £5m
No.of Employees: 21 - 50 **Product Groups:** 37, 39, 67

Date of Accounts	Jun 11	Jun 10	Jun 09
Working Capital	892	804	610
Fixed Assets	71	82	94
Current Assets	1m	1m	1m

WH Smith Retail Ltd

Greenbridge Road, Swindon, SN3 3LD
Tel: 08456-046543 **Fax:** 01793-562616
E-mail: customer.relations@whsmith.co.uk
Website: http://www.whsmith.co.uk
Directors: R. Moorhead (Fin), R. Walker (Ch), K. Swan (Grp Chief Exec)
Ultimate Holding Company: WH SMITH PLC
Immediate Holding Company: WH SMITH TRAVEL HOLDINGS LIMITED
Registration no: 05681969 **Date established:** 2006
Turnover: Over £1,000m **No.of Employees:** 1 - 10 **Product Groups:** 61, 64

Date of Accounts	Aug 11	Aug 10	Aug 09
Pre Tax Profit/Loss	33m	52m	492m
Working Capital	158m	292m	242m
Fixed Assets	308m	308m	308m
Current Assets	367m	367m	370m
Current Liabilities	N/A	N/A	1m

Wilson Tool International Ltd

Stirling Road South Marston Industrial Estate, Swindon, SN3 4TQ
Tel: 01793-831818 **Fax:** 01793-831945
E-mail: colin.blackwell@wilsontool.eu.com
Website: http://www.wilsontool.com
Bank(s): Barclays
Directors: C. Blackwell (MD)
Managers: I. McCartney (Comm), T. Davies (Personnel), G. Beveridge (Comptroller), M. Bailey, S. Holley
Immediate Holding Company: WILSON TOOL INTERNATIONAL [EUROPE] LIMITED
Registration no: 05882186 **Date established:** 2006
Turnover: £10m - £20m **No.of Employees:** 101 - 250
Product Groups: 37, 45, 46, 67

Date of Accounts	Dec 11	Dec 10	Dec 09
Sales Turnover	19m	17m	17m
Pre Tax Profit/Loss	2m	736	139
Working Capital	8m	7m	8m
Fixed Assets	8m	8m	8m
Current Assets	11m	9m	9m
Current Liabilities	858	578	564

Wiltshire Rod & Gun Ltd

135 Victoria Road, Swindon, SN1 3BU
Tel: 01793-497455 **Fax:** 01793-525666
E-mail: sales@wiltsrodguns.com
Website: http://www.wiltsrodguns.com
Directors: T. Manvell (Dir)
Immediate Holding Company: WILTSHIRE ROD & GUN LTD
Registration no: 06087313 **Date established:** 2007
No.of Employees: 1 - 10 **Product Groups:** 36, 39, 40

Date of Accounts	Mar 12	Mar 11	Mar 10
Working Capital	-7	-8	-9
Fixed Assets	10	9	31
Current Assets	209	184	160

Wroughton Developments

14 Barcelona Cresent Wroughton, Swindon, SN4 9EE
Tel: 01793-812292 **Fax:** 01793-812292
Directors: W. Polwarth (Prop)
Date established: 1978 **Turnover:** Up to £250,000
No.of Employees: 1 - 10 **Product Groups:** 48

Young Black I S Ltd

Radway Road, Swindon, SN3 4ND
Tel: 01793-838400 **Fax:** 01793-838401
E-mail: sales@youngblack.co.uk
Website: http://www.youngblack.co.uk
Bank(s): National Westminster
Directors: L. Young (MD)
Ultimate Holding Company: NIPPON PAINT CO. LTD (JAPAN)
Immediate Holding Company: N P AUTOMOTIVE COATINGS (EUROPE) LIMITED
Registration no: SC075801 **VAT No.:** GB 334 2483 69
Date established: 1991 **Turnover:** £10m - £20m
No.of Employees: 11 - 20 **Product Groups:** 35, 37, 42, 43, 47, 49

Date of Accounts	Mar 11	Mar 10	Mar 09
Working Capital	44	76	117
Fixed Assets	39	30	19
Current Assets	96	137	168

Trowbridge

A C Bedrooms

Carders Corner White Horse Business Park, Trowbridge, BA14 7DT
Tel: 01225-340388
E-mail: acbedrooms@yahoo.co.uk
Website: http://www.acbedrooms.co.uk
Directors: D. Farmer (Dir)
Date established: 2006 **Turnover:** £500,000 - £1m
No.of Employees: 1 - 10 **Product Groups:** 26, 63

Air Control Systems

Andil House Court Street, Trowbridge, BA14 8BR
Tel: 01225-752494 **Fax:** 01225-763486
E-mail: sales@aircontrol-systems.co.uk
Website: http://www.aircontrol-systems.co.uk
Directors: R. Coombe (Prop)
Immediate Holding Company: KINGSMILL REVERSION PARTNERSHIP LLP
Registration no: 03126300 **Date established:** 2007
Turnover: Up to £250,000 **No.of Employees:** 1 - 10 **Product Groups:** 38, 40, 45, 66

Date of Accounts	Mar 12	Mar 11	Mar 10
Sales Turnover	84	71	60
Pre Tax Profit/Loss	6	-14	-21
Working Capital	35	28	42
Fixed Assets	1	1	1
Current Assets	37	30	46
Current Liabilities	2	1	N/A

Airofreem Ltd

Canal Road Industrial Estate, Trowbridge, BA14 8RQ
Tel: 01225-779150 **Fax:** 01225-777029
E-mail: sales@airofreem.co.uk
Website: http://www.airofreem.co.uk
Directors: A. Pocock (Fab), T. Lisanti (MD), J. Lewis (Fin)
Ultimate Holding Company: AIRSPRUNG GROUP PLC
Immediate Holding Company: AIROFREEM LIMITED
Registration no: 01668524 **VAT No.:** GB 137 6009 75
Date established: 1982 **No.of Employees:** 21 - 50 **Product Groups:** 30, 48

Airsprung Furniture Group plc

Canal Road Industrial Estate Canal Road, Trowbridge, BA14 8RQ
Tel: 01225-754411 **Fax:** 01225-763256
E-mail: info@airsprung-group.co.uk
Website: http://www.airsprungbeds.co.uk
Bank(s): Fortis
Directors: A. Lisanti (Grp Chief Exec), T. Dallaway (Co Sec)
Immediate Holding Company: AIRSPRUNG GROUP PLC
Registration no: 01277785 **VAT No.:** GB 137 6009 75
Date established: 1976 **Turnover:** £20m - £50m
No.of Employees: 251 - 500 **Product Groups:** 24, 26, 63

Date of Accounts	Mar 12	Mar 11	Mar 10
Sales Turnover	48m	45m	47m
Pre Tax Profit/Loss	877	484	978
Working Capital	7m	6m	5m
Fixed Assets	10m	10m	8m
Current Assets	17m	15m	13m
Current Liabilities	5m	3m	4m

Apetito Ltd

Canal Road, Trowbridge, BA14 8RJ
Tel: 01225-753636 **Fax:** 01225-777084
E-mail: info@apetito.co.uk
Website: http://www.apetito.co.uk
Bank(s): HSBC Bank plc
Directors: C. Morris (Pers), P. Freeston (Grp Chief Exec), R. Ring (Fin)
Managers: G. Juniper (Tech Serv Mgr), E. Pender (Mktg Serv Mgr), C. Harris (Purch Mgr)
Ultimate Holding Company: APETITO AG (GERMANY)
Immediate Holding Company: APETITO LIMITED
Registration no: 00233851 **Date established:** 2028
Turnover: £75m - £125m **No.of Employees:** 501 - 1000
Product Groups: 20, 62

Date of Accounts	Dec 11	Dec 10	Dec 09
Sales Turnover	102m	98m	93m
Pre Tax Profit/Loss	15m	14m	14m
Working Capital	14m	12m	9m
Fixed Assets	16m	14m	13m
Current Assets	31m	27m	23m
Current Liabilities	8m	8m	6m

Applegate & Associates

2b Kenton Drive, Trowbridge, BA14 7JR
Tel: 01225-752135 **Fax:** 01225-777115
E-mail: george-applegate@hotmail.co.uk
Website: http://www.george-applegate.co.uk
Directors: G. Applegate (Prop)
Registration no: 01330870 **Turnover:** £250,000 - £500,000
No.of Employees: 1 - 10 **Product Groups:** 84

Care Plus Mobility Bath Ltd

64 Shails Lane, Trowbridge, BA14 8LN
Tel: 01225-774433
E-mail: info@cpm2009.co.uk
Website: http://www.careplusmobility.co.uk
Directors: S. Showering (Dir)
No.of Employees: 1 - 10 **Product Groups:** 39, 45, 67

Gage Technique International Ltd

PO Box 30, Trowbridge, BA14 8YD
Tel: 01761-431777 **Fax:** 01761-431888
E-mail: info@gage-technique.demon.co.uk
Website: http://www.gage-technique.com
Directors: M. Pratt (Dir), G. Trafford (Co Sec)
Immediate Holding Company: GAGE TECHNIQUE INTERNATIONAL LIMITED
Registration no: 03650488 **VAT No.:** GB 713 7136 53
Date established: 1998 **Turnover:** £250,000 - £500,000
No.of Employees: 1 - 10 **Product Groups:** 84

Date of Accounts	Dec 11	Dec 10	Dec 09
Sales Turnover	368	334	663
Pre Tax Profit/Loss	-49	6	10
Working Capital	286	-201	-206
Current Assets	312	364	732
Current Liabilities	3	4	34

Gainsborough Ltd

Canal Road, Trowbridge, BA14 8RQ
Tel: 01225-779132 **Fax:** 01225-779129
E-mail: sales@gainsborough-beds.co.uk
Website: http://www.gainsborough-beds.co.uk
Bank(s): Funtis Bank
Directors: G. Allen (Sales & Mktg), J. Francis (Fin), T. Dallaway (Co Sec)
Ultimate Holding Company: AIRSPRUNG GROUP PLC
Immediate Holding Company: GAINSBOROUGH LIMITED
Registration no: 00287299 **VAT No.:** GB 137 6009 75
Date established: 1934 **Turnover:** £2m - £5m **No.of Employees:** 51 - 100
Product Groups: 26, 35

Date of Accounts	Mar 10
Working Capital	300
Current Assets	2m
Current Liabilities	2m

Harford Control Ltd

35 Harford Street, Trowbridge, BA14 7HL
Tel: 01225-764461 **Fax:** 01225-769733
E-mail: clive@harfordcontrol.com
Website: http://www.harfordcontrol.com
Directors: C. Green (Chief Op Offcr)
Immediate Holding Company: HARFORD CONTROL LIMITED
Registration no: 01207483 **Date established:** 1975
No.of Employees: 11 - 20 **Product Groups:** 38, 85

Date of Accounts	Nov 11	Nov 10	Nov 09
Working Capital	142	83	-41
Fixed Assets	101	67	68
Current Assets	1m	851	407

Haven Fire Security Consultants Ltd

Unit 1-6 The Epsom Centre White Horse Business Park, Trowbridge, BA14 0XG
Tel: 01225-762667 **Fax:** 01392-410436
E-mail: mailbox@haven-fire.co.uk
Website: http://www.haven-fire.co.uk
Bank(s): Lloyds TSB (heavitree - essex)
Directors: B. Yates (Dir)
Immediate Holding Company: HAVEN FIRE SECURITY CONSULTANTS LTD.
Registration no: 01624086 **VAT No.:** GB 409 0769 44
Date established: 1982 **Turnover:** £2m - £5m **No.of Employees:** 21 - 50
Product Groups: 52

Date of Accounts	May 12	May 11	May 10
Working Capital	388	395	272
Fixed Assets	22	25	26
Current Assets	679	755	705

Hiscock Engineers

28 Union Street, Trowbridge, BA14 8RY
Tel: 01225-752106 **Fax:** 01225-751326
E-mail: hiscockengineers@btconnect.com
Directors: E. Hiscock (Prop)
Immediate Holding Company: HISCOCK ENGINEERS (TROWBRIDGE) LIMITED
Registration no: 00440014 **VAT No.:** GB 137 9241 56
Date established: 1947 **Turnover:** £250,000 - £500,000
No.of Employees: 1 - 10 **Product Groups:** 48

Date of Accounts	Feb 12	Feb 11	Feb 10
Working Capital	-29	-27	-13
Fixed Assets	103	106	109
Current Assets	92	90	98

L F Beauty UK Ltd

Aintree Avenue White Horse Business Park, Trowbridge, BA14 0XB
Tel: 01225-768491 **Fax:** 01225-716100
E-mail: gary.armstrong@pbbeauty.com
Website: http://www.lfbeauty-uk.com
Directors: J. Pearce (Tech Serv), H. Trueman (Pers), B. Sharpe (Fin), G. Armstrong (MD)
Managers: C. Swordy (Comptroller)
Ultimate Holding Company: PETER BLACK HOLDINGS LIMITED
Immediate Holding Company: LF BEAUTY (UK) LIMITED
Registration no: 00483352 **VAT No.:** GB 303 3834 88
Date established: 1950 **Turnover:** £75m - £125m
No.of Employees: 501 - 1000 **Product Groups:** 32

Date of Accounts	Dec 11	Dec 10	Dec 09
Sales Turnover	104m	92m	81m
Pre Tax Profit/Loss	8m	7m	4m
Working Capital	8m	12m	8m
Fixed Assets	28m	4m	3m
Current Assets	39m	34m	25m
Current Liabilities	8m	6m	5m

Mini-Organic

Clarence Road, Trowbridge, BA14 7BX
Tel: 01225-767003
E-mail: chris@mini-organic.co.uk
Website: http://www.mini-organic.co.uk
Directors: C. Watts (Prop)
No.of Employees: 1 - 10 **Product Groups:** 24, 63, 65

Platinum Vauxhall

2 Meridian Business Park North Bradley, Trowbridge, BA14 0BJ
Tel: 01225-759585 **Fax:** 01225-759576
Website: http://www.platinumvauxhall.co.uk
Directors: R. Cuff (MD), J. Cuff (MD)
Managers: S. Pillinger (Sales Admin), J. Gray (Sales Prom Mgr)
No.of Employees: 51 - 100 **Product Groups:** 29, 39

Pork Farm Bowyers

55 Stallard Street, Trowbridge, BA14 8HH
Tel: 01225-777367 **Fax:** 01225-777367
E-mail: mike.godley@pork-farms.co.uk
Website: http://www.pork-farms-bowyers.co.uk
Bank(s): HSBC
Managers: M. Godley (Chief Mgr), R. Head (Sales Prom Mgr), W. Barrett (Purch Mgr)
Immediate Holding Company: Northern Foods (Hull)
VAT No.: GB 168 7433 30 **Date established:** 1850
Turnover: £75m - £125m **No.of Employees:** 501 - 1000
Product Groups: 20

Premier Training International Ltd (Premier Fitness Jobs)

Unit 2 Willowside Park Canal Road, Trowbridge, BA14 8RH
Tel: 08451-909090 **Fax:** 01225-353556
Website: http://www.premierglobal.co.uk
Directors: F. Cook (Fin), P. Rogers (Fin), P. Rogers (Co Sec), N. Higginbottom (Dir)
Ultimate Holding Company: PREMIER GLOBAL LIMITED
Immediate Holding Company: PREMIER TRAINING INTERNATIONAL LIMITED
Registration no: 02720312 **Date established:** 1992 **Turnover:** £5m - £10m
No.of Employees: 101 - 250 **Product Groups:** 86

Date of Accounts	Aug 11	Aug 10	Aug 09
Sales Turnover	8m	8m	8m
Pre Tax Profit/Loss	911	-497	311
Working Capital	347	-303	367
Fixed Assets	112	152	166
Current Assets	3m	3m	3m
Current Liabilities	2m	2m	2m

R D Food Machinery

Unit 16 Marsh Farm Marsh Road, Hilperton Marsh, Trowbridge, BA14 7PJ
Tel: 01225-769955 **Fax:** 01225-751538
E-mail: jan.doel@sky.com
Directors: R. Doel (Ptnr)
Date established: 1998 **No.of Employees:** 1 - 10 **Product Groups:** 20, 40, 41

S D System Solutions Ltd

129 Devizes Road Hilperton, Trowbridge, BA14 7QJ
Tel: 01225-751822 **Fax:** 01225-764863
E-mail: info@sdss.co.uk
Website: http://www.sdss.co.uk
Directors: P. Shepard (Dir)
Immediate Holding Company: SD SYSTEM SOLUTIONS LTD.
Registration no: 05798383 **Date established:** 2006
Turnover: £500,000 - £1m **No.of Employees:** 1 - 10 **Product Groups:** 37, 38, 44, 67, 80, 84

Date of Accounts	Apr 11	Apr 10	Apr 09
Sales Turnover	N/A	469	422
Working Capital	373	284	262
Fixed Assets	7	5	6
Current Assets	440	350	326
Current Liabilities	64	66	N/A

Trojan Engineering

Whaddon Lane Whaddon, Trowbridge, BA14 6NR
Tel: 01225-765859 **Fax:** 01225-775475
E-mail: trrojanengineering@aol.com
Website: http://www.trojanengineering.com
Directors: R. Bealing (Prop)
Turnover: Up to £250,000 **No.of Employees:** 1 - 10 **Product Groups:** 35, 48

West Of England Water Softeners

258 The Common Holt, Trowbridge, BA14 6QL
Tel: 01225-782216
E-mail: enquiries@balloonsdirect.co.uk
Website: http://www.bathsoftwater.co.uk
Directors: L. Hodges (Ptnr)
Immediate Holding Company: BALLOONS DIRECT LIMITED
Registration no: 02278570 **Date established:** 1988
No.of Employees: 1 - 10 **Product Groups:** 38, 42

Wilts Wholesale Electrical

Kennet Way Canal Road Industrial Estate, Trowbridge, BA14 8BL
Tel: 01225-777300 **Fax:** 01225-777001
E-mail: trowbridge@wilts.co.uk
Website: http://www.wilts.co.uk
Bank(s): HSBC Bank plc
Directors: R. Ovens (Pers), R. Yates (Sales), P. Wheatcroft (Fin), I. Webb (Fin)
Managers: S. Barnes, J. Hart (Mktg Serv Mgr), R. Pryor (Personnel), G. Roberts (District Mgr), K. Burns
Ultimate Holding Company: WW HOLDINGS LIMITED (GUERNSEY)
Immediate Holding Company: FERNTURN HOLDINGS LIMITED
Registration no: 00679117 **VAT No.:** GB 422 9006 79
Date established: 1960 **Turnover:** £75m - £125m
No.of Employees: 11 - 20 **Product Groups:** 77

Date of Accounts	Mar 10	Mar 09	Mar 08
Sales Turnover	83m	115m	114m
Pre Tax Profit/Loss	-7m	2m	5m
Working Capital	4m	14m	15m
Fixed Assets	18m	14m	14m
Current Assets	28m	36m	40m
Current Liabilities	3m	6m	7m

Warminster

Andrich International Ltd

10 Sambourne Road, Warminster, BA12 8LJ
Tel: 01985-846181 **Fax:** 01985-846163
E-mail: info@andrich.com
Website: http://www.andrich.com
Directors: R. Curtis (MD)
Immediate Holding Company: ANDRICH INTERNATIONAL LIMITED
Registration no: 02111077 **Date established:** 1987
Turnover: £250,000 - £500,000 **No.of Employees:** 1 - 10
Product Groups: 28, 54, 81

Date of Accounts	Sep 11	Sep 10	Sep 09
Working Capital	-10	-6	-18
Fixed Assets	1	1	N/A
Current Assets	29	15	17
Current Liabilities	24	2	N/A

Anti Vibration Methods Rubber Co. Ltd

Unit 5 Woodcock Industrial Estate Woodcock Road, Warminster, BA12 9DX
Tel: 01985-219032 **Fax:** 01985-219849
E-mail: joy.dunn@antivibrationmethods.co.uk
Website: http://www.antivibrationmethods.com
Directors: J. Dunn (Ptnr)
Immediate Holding Company: ANTI-VIBRATION METHODS (RUBBER) CO. LIMITED
Registration no: 02277135 **VAT No.:** GB 422 9997 14
Date established: 1988 **Turnover:** £500,000 - £1m
No.of Employees: 1 - 10 **Product Groups:** 29

Date of Accounts	Jun 12	Jun 11	Jun 10
Working Capital	302	274	251
Fixed Assets	259	26	31
Current Assets	389	374	325

C M G Ltd Exclusive Distributors of No Skidding Products inc

Unit 30 Deverill Road Trading Estate Deverill Road, Sutton Veny, Warminster, BA12 7BZ
Tel: 01985-840400 **Fax:** 01985-841088
E-mail: cm.group@btinternet.com
Website: http://www.contractmaintenacegroup.co.uk
Directors: M. Stoneman (Prop)
Ultimate Holding Company: LOGICA LIMITED
Immediate Holding Company: CMG LIMITED
Registration no: 00930965 **Date established:** 1968
No.of Employees: 1 - 10 **Product Groups:** 32, 66, 88

Date of Accounts	Dec 11	Dec 10	Dec 09
Pre Tax Profit/Loss	4m	4m	6m
Working Capital	230m	228m	226m
Fixed Assets	250m	250m	250m
Current Assets	230m	228m	226m

C M S Profab Ltd

Unit 15c Deverill Road Trading Estate Deverill Road, Sutton Veny, Warminster, BA12 7BZ
Tel: 01985-840447 **Fax:** 01985-840447
Directors: R. Farrow (Ptnr)
Immediate Holding Company: CMS PROFAB LIMITED
Registration no: 06416347 **Date established:** 2007
No.of Employees: 1 - 10 **Product Groups:** 35

Date of Accounts	Oct 11	Oct 10	Oct 09
Working Capital	-7	-45	-54
Fixed Assets	49	46	54
Current Assets	201	92	88

Dents (a division of Dewhurst Dent P.L.C.)

Warminster Business Park Furnax Lane, Warminster, BA12 8PE
Tel: 01985-217367 **Fax:** 01985-216435
E-mail: customerservice@dents.co.uk
Website: http://www.dents.co.uk
Bank(s): HSBC Bank plc
Directors: S. Lee (Co Sec), R. Yentob (MD)
Managers: H. Randall (Chief Acct), J. Evans (Tech Serv Mgr)
Immediate Holding Company: DEWHURST DENT P.L.C.
Registration no: 00161147 **VAT No.:** GB 146 0051 08
Turnover: £2m - £5m **No.of Employees:** 51 - 100 **Product Groups:** 24, 63

Date of Accounts	Jan 08	Jan 07	Jan 06
Working Capital	855	855	855
Fixed Assets	197	197	197
Current Assets	855	855	855
Total Share Capital	500	500	500

Elms Cross Packaging Company Ltd

Unit 1 Northlands Industrial Estate Copheap Lane, Warminster, BA12 0BG
Tel: 01985-848480 **Fax:** 01985-848481
E-mail: sales@elmscrosspackaging.co.uk
Website: http://www.elmscrosspackaging.co.uk
Directors: J. Lewis (Fin), M. Lewis (Dir)
Immediate Holding Company: ELMS CROSS PACKAGING COMPANY LIMITED
Registration no: 03784022 **Date established:** 1999
No.of Employees: 1 - 10 **Product Groups:** 38, 42

Date of Accounts	Aug 11	Aug 10	Aug 09
Working Capital	227	168	116
Fixed Assets	13	17	7
Current Assets	503	398	328
Current Liabilities	3	N/A	N/A

Ethos Candles Ltd

Quarryfield Industrial Estate Mere, Warminster, BA12 6LA
Tel: 01747-860960 **Fax:** 01747-860934
E-mail: sales@charlesfarris.co.uk
Website: http://www.charlesfarris.co.uk
Managers: S. Gale
Immediate Holding Company: ETHOS CANDLES LIMITED
Registration no: 00979942 **Date established:** 1970 **Turnover:** £1m - £2m
No.of Employees: 1 - 10 **Product Groups:** 32

Date of Accounts	Mar 12	Mar 11	Mar 10
Working Capital	36	36	36
Current Assets	36	36	36

R Hamilton & Co. Ltd (Hamilton Litestat Group)

Quarry Industrial Estate Mere, Warminster, BA12 6LA
Tel: 01747-860088 **Fax:** 01747-861032
E-mail: info@hamilton-litestat.com
Website: http://www.hamilton-litestat.com
Bank(s): Barclays, Pall Mall, London
Directors: R. Haines (Fin), A. Hamilton (Dir)
Managers: B. Hewitt (Personnel), R. Middleton (Tech Serv Mgr), I. Driver (Purch Mgr), R. Thomas (Nat Sales Mgr)
Immediate Holding Company: R.HAMILTON & CO. LIMITED
Registration no: 00941624 **VAT No.:** GB 222 6607 84
Date established: 1968 **Turnover:** £5m - £10m
No.of Employees: 101 - 250 **Product Groups:** 37

Date of Accounts	Jun 11	Jun 10	Jun 09
Sales Turnover	9m	9m	10m
Pre Tax Profit/Loss	461	392	467
Working Capital	4m	4m	3m
Fixed Assets	874	745	814
Current Assets	6m	6m	6m
Current Liabilities	1m	1m	2m

The Hill Brush Company Ltd

Woodlands Road Mere, Warminster, BA12 6BS
Tel: 01747-860494 **Fax:** 01747-860137
E-mail: info@hillbrush.com
Website: http://www.hillbrush.com
Bank(s): Lloyds TSB Bank plc
Directors: M. Coward (Fin)
Managers: C. Coward, P. Norris, S. Hawkes (Tech Serv Mgr)
Immediate Holding Company: THE HILL BRUSH COMPANY LTD
Registration no: 03464746 **VAT No.:** GB 188 0464 40
Date established: 1997 **Turnover:** £5m - £10m
No.of Employees: 51 - 100 **Product Groups:** 25, 30, 33, 35, 38

Date of Accounts	Dec 11	Dec 10	Dec 09
Sales Turnover	8m	7m	7m
Pre Tax Profit/Loss	572	86	64
Working Capital	3m	3m	3m
Fixed Assets	6m	6m	6m
Current Assets	5m	4m	4m
Current Liabilities	1m	569	479

Hussey Seatway

3 Centurion Way Crusader Park, Warminster, BA12 8BT
Tel: 01985-847200 **Fax:** 01985-847200
E-mail: info@husseyseatway.com
Website: http://www.husseyseatway.com
Directors: D. Black (Dir)
Immediate Holding Company: INVENIAM BLUE LIMITED
Registration no: 04166039 **Date established:** 2011 **Turnover:** £1m - £2m
No.of Employees: 11 - 20 **Product Groups:** 26, 52

Date of Accounts	Mar 11	Mar 10	Mar 09
Sales Turnover	N/A	N/A	749
Pre Tax Profit/Loss	N/A	N/A	77
Working Capital	-23	-343	-349
Fixed Assets	390	348	349
Current Assets	296	247	220
Current Liabilities	N/A	N/A	495

Lyons Seafoods Ltd

3 Fairfield Road, Warminster, BA12 9DA
Tel: 01985-224300 **Fax:** 01985-847117
E-mail: sales@lyons-seafoods.com
Website: http://www.lyons-seafoods.com
Directors: P. Vita (Mkt Research), J. Hodgson (Sales), J. Hall (Tech Serv)
Managers: T. Watkinson (Grp Purch Mgr), A. Nday (Personnel), B. Thorley (Fin Mgr), S. Ashman (Mgr)
Ultimate Holding Company: ALFESCA HF (ICELAND)
Immediate Holding Company: LYONS SEAFOODS LIMITED
Registration no: 02987743 **VAT No.:** GB 639 5710 15
Date established: 1994 **Turnover:** £75m - £125m
No.of Employees: 101 - 250 **Product Groups:** 09, 20, 62

Date of Accounts	Jun 08	Jun 09	Jun 10
Sales Turnover	97m	95m	103m
Pre Tax Profit/Loss	11m	11m	11m
Working Capital	14m	18m	19m
Fixed Assets	15m	15m	15m
Current Assets	27m	28m	36m
Current Liabilities	8m	4m	10m

Menu Shop

38 High Street, Warminster, BA12 9AF
Tel: 01985-217000 **Fax:** 01985-218000
E-mail: info@menushop.co.uk
Website: http://www.menushop.co.uk
Directors: I. Meaden (Prop)
Date established: 1999 **No.of Employees:** 11 - 20 **Product Groups:** 20, 40, 41

Mere Fabricating & Welding Services

Unit 1e Quarryfields Industrial Estate Mere, Warminster, BA12 6LA
Tel: 01747-860317 **Fax:** 01747-860317
Directors: J. Davies (Prop)
Ultimate Holding Company: SENEX CAPITAL LIMITED
Immediate Holding Company: CHARLES FARRIS LIMITED
Registration no: 02252575 **Date established:** 1988
No.of Employees: 1 - 10 **Product Groups:** 35

Date of Accounts	Mar 10	Mar 09	Mar 08
Sales Turnover	3m	N/A	N/A
Pre Tax Profit/Loss	69	87	97
Working Capital	747	692	615
Fixed Assets	80	78	88
Current Assets	2m	2m	1m
Current Liabilities	127	116	158

O J Electronics Ltd

Crusader House Roman Way Crusader Park, Warminster, BA12 8SJ
Tel: 01985-213003 **Fax:** 01985-213310
Website: http://www.oj.dk
Directors: J. Olsen (Fin), E. Damsgaard (MD), P. Murphy (MD)
Immediate Holding Company: Oj Electronics Ltd
Registration no: 04682784 **Turnover:** Up to £250,000
No.of Employees: 1 - 10 **Product Groups:** 37, 38, 40, 49

Date of Accounts	Apr 12	Apr 11	Apr 10
Working Capital	336	310	292
Fixed Assets	32	46	20
Current Assets	395	521	345

Sureset Permeable Resin Bound Paving

Unit 32 Deverill Road Trading Estate Deverill Road, Sutton Veny, Warminster, BA12 7BZ
Tel: 01985-841180 **Fax:** 01985-841260
E-mail: mail@sureset.co.uk
Website: http://www.sureset.co.uk
Directors: K. Weston (MD), P. Watts (Fin), D. Crowther (Co Sec)
Managers: J. Carpenter
Immediate Holding Company: SURESET UK LIMITED
Registration no: 03334410 **Date established:** 1997 **Turnover:** £1m - £2m
No.of Employees: 21 - 50 **Product Groups:** 31, 51, 66

Date of Accounts	Jul 11	Jul 10	Jul 09
Working Capital	488	500	286
Fixed Assets	61	55	75
Current Assets	920	1m	800

Yapp Brothers Ltd

The Old Brewery Water Street, Mere, Warminster, BA12 6DY
Tel: 01747-860423 **Fax:** 01747-860929
E-mail: sales@yapp.co.uk
Website: http://www.yapp.co.uk
Directors: J. Yapp (Sales), T. Ashworth (Fin)
Immediate Holding Company: YAPP BROTHERS LIMITED
Registration no: 01888369 **VAT No.:** 329 6336 39 **Date established:** 1985
Turnover: £1m - £2m **No.of Employees:** 1 - 10 **Product Groups:** 21

Date of Accounts	Jan 12	Jan 11	Jan 10
Working Capital	553	575	559
Fixed Assets	46	62	57
Current Assets	1m	1m	1m

Westbury

A L H Systems Ltd
1 Kingdom Avenue Northacre Industrial Park, Westbury, BA13 4WE
Tel: 01373-858234 **Fax:** 01373-858235
E-mail: sales@alh-systems.co.uk
Website: http://www.alh-systems.co.uk
Directors: A. Lucas (MD), A. Cousins (Dir)
Managers: C. Dicks, K. Duerden (Sales Off Mgr)
Ultimate Holding Company: ALH POLYMERS LIMITED
Immediate Holding Company: A L H SYSTEMS LIMITED
Registration no: 01255492 **Date established:** 1976 **Turnover:** £2m - £5m
No.of Employees: 21 - 50 **Product Groups:** 30, 32, 35

Date of Accounts	Sep 11	Sep 10	Sep 09
Working Capital	2m	2m	1m
Fixed Assets	78	86	90
Current Assets	3m	3m	2m
Current Liabilities	N/A	480	56

A V M Air Spring Ltd
Unit 2a Brook Lane Industrial Estate, Westbury, BA13 4EP
Tel: 01373-858223 **Fax:** 01373-858224
E-mail: info@avmspring.com
Website: http://www.avmspring.com
Managers: W. Seager (Mgr)
Immediate Holding Company: A.V.M. AIR SPRING LIMITED
Registration no: 01901079 **VAT No.:** 018 1423 03 **Date established:** 1985
Turnover: £500,000 - £1m **No.of Employees:** 1 - 10 **Product Groups:** 29

Date of Accounts	Dec 11	Dec 10	Dec 09
Working Capital	261	316	321
Fixed Assets	117	107	21
Current Assets	604	564	471

Atkinson Equipment
Moat Road West Wilts Trading Estate West Wilts Trading Estate, Westbury, BA13 4JF
Tel: 01373-822220 **Fax:** 01373-826996
E-mail: sales@atkinsonequipment.com
Website: http://www.atkinsonequipment.com
Bank(s): HSBC, Bristol
Directors: S. Pearce (Fin), C. Atkinson (Prop)
Managers: P. Carter (Sales Prom Mgr)
Immediate Holding Company: ATKINSON EQUIPMENT LIMITED
Registration no: 01050233 **VAT No.:** GB 639 5858 80
Date established: 1972 **Turnover:** £10m - £20m
No.of Employees: 21 - 50 **Product Groups:** 36, 38, 46

Date of Accounts	Mar 11	Mar 10	Mar 09
Sales Turnover	17m	15m	14m
Pre Tax Profit/Loss	1m	1m	530
Working Capital	2m	1m	2m
Fixed Assets	2m	2m	2m
Current Assets	6m	5m	4m
Current Liabilities	2m	2m	906

Audience Systems Ltd
19b Washington Road West Wilts Trading Estate, Westbury, BA13 4JP
Tel: 01373-865050 **Fax:** 01373-827545
E-mail: sales@audiencesystems.com
Website: http://www.audiencesystems.com
Directors: M. Cowley (MD), M. Rich (Sales), K. Vooght (Fin)
Managers: A. Lewis (Tech Serv Mgr), K. Anderson-hill (Purch Mgr), J. Tucker (Fin Mgr), J. Wylam (Personnel), N. Parmenter (Mktg Serv Mgr)
Ultimate Holding Company: KOTOBUKI HOLDINGS K K (JAPAN)
Immediate Holding Company: AUDIENCE SYSTEMS LIMITED
Registration no: 01043134 **Date established:** 1972
Turnover: £10m - £20m **No.of Employees:** 51 - 100 **Product Groups:** 26, 52

Date of Accounts	Mar 12	Mar 11	Mar 10
Sales Turnover	11m	10m	9m
Pre Tax Profit/Loss	494	544	638
Working Capital	4m	3m	3m
Fixed Assets	1m	1m	1m
Current Assets	5m	5m	5m
Current Liabilities	1m	1m	914

Roger Bullivant Ltd
Innovation House 7 Kingdom Avenue, Northacre Industrial Park, Westbury, BA13 4FG
Tel: 01373-865012 **Fax:** 01278-433694
Website: http://www.roger-bullivant.co.uk
Managers: P. Merry (Sales Prom Mgr)
Immediate Holding Company: ROGER BULLIVANT LIMITED
Registration no: 07681731 **VAT No.:** GB 354 5361 54
Date established: 2011 **Turnover:** £20m - £50m
No.of Employees: 21 - 50 **Product Groups:** 51

Date of Accounts	Dec 11
Sales Turnover	27m
Pre Tax Profit/Loss	-614
Working Capital	3m
Fixed Assets	4m
Current Assets	20m
Current Liabilities	898

Cifer Data Systems Ltd
1 Main Street West Wilts Trading Estate, Westbury, BA13 4JU
Tel: 01373-824128 **Fax:** 01373-824127
E-mail: enquiries@cifer.co.uk
Website: http://www.cifer.co.uk
Bank(s): HSBC Bank plc
Directors: M. Rice (Sales), P. Tait (Co Sec)
Immediate Holding Company: CIFER DATA SYSTEMS LIMITED
Registration no: 02739905 **VAT No.:** GB 601 0857 79
Date established: 1992 **Turnover:** £500,000 - £1m
No.of Employees: 11 - 20 **Product Groups:** 44

Date of Accounts	Dec 11	Dec 10	Dec 09
Working Capital	-17	-2	-5
Fixed Assets	18	20	23
Current Assets	203	170	205

Complete Fire Security
PO Box 4263, Westbury, BA13 3WB
Tel: 01373-823131 **Fax:** 01373-864423
E-mail: info@completefiresecurity.co.uk
Website: http://www.completefiresecurity.co.uk
Directors: D. Stannard (Prop)
Immediate Holding Company: COMPLETE FIRE SECURITY LIMITED
Registration no: 06542849 **Date established:** 2008
Turnover: Up to £250,000 **No.of Employees:** 1 - 10 **Product Groups:** 35, 38, 40, 52, 67, 84

Date of Accounts	Mar 12	Mar 11	Mar 10
Sales Turnover	N/A	N/A	131
Working Capital	-9	-10	-12
Fixed Assets	18	12	15
Current Assets	28	31	41

Daco Packaging UK Ltd
Clivey House Tollhouse, Dilton Marsh, Westbury, BA13 4BB
Tel: 01373-823450
E-mail: annie@dacouk.com
Website: http://www.dacouk.com
Directors: B. Harris (Fin), D. Harris (MD)
Immediate Holding Company: DACO PACKAGING (UK) LIMITED
Registration no: 03495171 **Date established:** 1998
No.of Employees: 1 - 10 **Product Groups:** 35, 38, 42

Date of Accounts	Mar 12	Mar 11	Mar 10
Working Capital	250	270	283
Fixed Assets	65	62	66
Current Assets	256	323	331

Dreamworks Beds
7 Brook Lane Industrial Estate, Westbury, BA13 4EP
Tel: 01373-859913 **Fax:** 01373-859917
E-mail: johnbolt@dreamworksbeds.com
Website: http://www.dreamworksbeds.com
Directors: P. Ziemniak (Fin)
Managers: S. Edwards (Personnel), J. Bolt, R. Bartlett
Immediate Holding Company: DREAMWORKS BEDS LIMITED
Registration no: 04773416 **Date established:** 2003
No.of Employees: 21 - 50 **Product Groups:** 26

Date of Accounts	May 12	May 11	May 10
Working Capital	467	-675	-703
Current Assets	1m	1m	2m

Future Bags
Units 8 & 9 Oakfield Business Centre Northacre Industrial Estate Stephenson Road, Westbury, BA13 4WF
Tel: 01373-825837 **Fax:** 01373-865984
E-mail: sales@futurebags.co.uk
Website: http://www.futurebags.co.uk
Managers: F. Fizailne (Admin Off)
Registration no: 05278131 **Date established:** 2008
No.of Employees: 1 - 10 **Product Groups:** 22, 24

Date of Accounts	Jan 10
Working Capital	89
Current Assets	272

Insight Global Ltd
4 Ray Down Offices Edington, Westbury, BA13 4NW
Tel: 01373-858691
E-mail: sales@insightglobal.ws
Website: http://www.insightglobal.co.uk
Directors: S. Brown (Fin), G. Brown (MD)
Immediate Holding Company: INSIGHT GLOBAL LIMITED
Registration no: 04136394 **Date established:** 2001
No.of Employees: 1 - 10 **Product Groups:** 28, 44, 49, 79, 80, 81, 84, 86, 89

Date of Accounts	Jan 11	Jan 10	Jan 09
Working Capital	-4	-4	-9
Fixed Assets	4	4	N/A
Current Assets	15	14	25

Jaymart Roberts & Plastics Ltd
Woodland Trading Estate Eden Fell Road, Westbury, BA13 3QS
Tel: 01373-864926 **Fax:** 01373-858454
E-mail: sales@jaymart.net
Website: http://www.jaymart.net
Bank(s): Lloyds TSB Bank plc
Directors: M. Bunyard (Dir), F. Byron (MD)
Managers: J. Chapman (Personnel)
Immediate Holding Company: JAYMART RUBBER & PLASTICS LIMITED
Registration no: 00914626 **Date established:** 1967 **Turnover:** £2m - £5m
No.of Employees: 21 - 50 **Product Groups:** 23, 29, 30, 35, 49

L M C Hadrian Ltd
Quartermaster Road West Wilts Trading Estate, Westbury, BA13 4JT
Tel: 01373-865088 **Fax:** 01373-865464
E-mail: ken@lmchadrian.com
Website: http://www.hadriancarpanels.com
Directors: D. Bowman (Fin), D. Bowman (Dir)
Immediate Holding Company: LMC HADRIAN LIMITED
Registration no: 02786909 **Date established:** 1993
Turnover: Up to £250,000 **No.of Employees:** 21 - 50 **Product Groups:** 31, 32, 33, 35, 36, 37, 39, 40, 46, 68

Date of Accounts	Mar 10	Mar 09	Mar 08
Working Capital	247	158	168
Fixed Assets	178	194	152
Current Assets	2m	2m	2m

M P D Hook & Loop Ltd
19-24 White Hays North Quartermaster Road, West Wilts Trading Estate, Westbury, BA13 4JT
Tel: 01373-827111 **Fax:** 01373-827222
E-mail: info@mpdhookandloop.com
Website: http://www.mpdhookandloop.com
Directors: C. Gibbons (MD)
Immediate Holding Company: MPD HOOK AND LOOP LIMITED
Registration no: 06391674 **VAT No.:** GB 609 3653 32
Date established: 2007 **Turnover:** £250,000 - £500,000
No.of Employees: 1 - 10 **Product Groups:** 26, 30, 35, 37, 49, 52, 67, 81, 83, 84

Macfarlane Packaging UK Ltd
1 Quartermaster Road West Wilts Trading Estate, Westbury, BA13 4JT
Tel: 08447-701435 **Fax:** 01373-858999
E-mail: binglis@macfarlanepackaging.com
Website: http://www.macfarlanegroup.net
Directors: B. Inglis (Chief Op Offcr)
Immediate Holding Company: MACFARLANE GROUP UK LIMITED
Registration no: 01630389 **Date established:** 1982
No.of Employees: 51 - 100 **Product Groups:** 25, 27, 30

Piling Equipment Ltd
1 Camargue Road, Westbury, BA13 3GG
Tel: 07885-379866
E-mail: info@piling-equipmnet-ltd.com
Website: http://www.piling-equipment-ltd.com
Managers: R. Simpson (Mktg Serv Mgr)
Registration no: 06377344 **Date established:** 1997
Turnover: £500,000 - £1m **No.of Employees:** 1 - 10 **Product Groups:** 34, 45, 51, 66

Prosec Consultancy Ltd
Unit 10 Oakfield Business Centre Northacre Industrial Park, Westbury, BA13 4WF
Tel: 01373-228055 **Fax:** 01373-228313
E-mail: info@prosec-ltd.com
Website: http://www.prosec-ltd.com
Directors: A. Lister (Dir)
Immediate Holding Company: PROSEC CONSULTANCY LIMITED
Registration no: 05927953 **Date established:** 2006
Turnover: Up to £250,000 **No.of Employees:** 1 - 10 **Product Groups:** 81

Date of Accounts	Sep 11	Sep 10	Sep 09
Working Capital	2	-9	-1
Fixed Assets	20	18	9
Current Assets	62	56	46

South West Doors
112 Eden Vale Road, Westbury, BA13 3QE
Tel: 01373-865067 **Fax:** 01373-301811
E-mail: ianmap@yahoo.co.uk
Website: http://www.southwestdoors.co.uk
Directors: I. Mapperson (Prop)
No.of Employees: 1 - 10 **Product Groups:** 26, 35

Spectra Specialist Engineering Ltd
31b Link Road West Wilts Trading Estate, Westbury, BA13 4JB
Tel: 01373-865548 **Fax:** 01373-858172
E-mail: sales@spectra.uk.net
Website: http://www.spectra.uk.net
Bank(s): Lloyds TSB Bank plc
Managers: N. Brown (Comptroller), Y. Kirkham (Personnel), R. Kirkham (Purch Mgr), R. Hayes (Sales Prom Mgr)
Immediate Holding Company: SPECTRA SPECIALIST ENGINEERING LIMITED
Registration no: 02121500 **VAT No.:** GB 357 4538 28
Date established: 1987 **Turnover:** £2m - £5m **No.of Employees:** 21 - 50
Product Groups: 84

Date of Accounts	May 11	May 10	May 09
Working Capital	9	-202	-220
Fixed Assets	266	264	326
Current Assets	995	862	1m

T Shirt & Sons
11 Washington Road West Wilts Trading Estate, Westbury, BA13 4JP
Tel: 01373-301645 **Fax:** 01373-301646
E-mail: sales@tshirtandsons.co.uk
Website: http://www.tshirtandsons.co.uk
Directors: J. Lunt (MD)
Immediate Holding Company: T SHIRT & SONS LIMITED
Registration no: 04745669 **Date established:** 2003
No.of Employees: 11 - 20 **Product Groups:** 23, 24, 28, 63

Date of Accounts	Apr 11	Apr 10	Apr 09
Working Capital	-183	-215	-238
Fixed Assets	277	222	240
Current Assets	278	211	87

Taylor Davis Ltd
Moat Road West Wilts Trading Estate, Westbury, BA13 4JF
Tel: 01373-858021 **Fax:** 01373-858021
E-mail: sales@taylor-davis.co.uk
Website: http://www.taylor-davis.co.uk
Bank(s): HSBC
Directors: B. James (Dir), S. Pearce (Fin)
Managers: J. Byrne (Sales Admin)
Ultimate Holding Company: ATKINSON EQUIPMENT LIMITED
Immediate Holding Company: TAYLOR-DAVIS LIMITED
Registration no: 00978584 **VAT No.:** GB 639 5858 80
Date established: 1970 **Turnover:** £10m - £20m
No.of Employees: 21 - 50 **Product Groups:** 30, 35

Date of Accounts	Mar 11	Mar 10	Mar 09
Sales Turnover	13m	12m	11m
Pre Tax Profit/Loss	1m	996	661
Working Capital	2m	2m	817
Fixed Assets	820	715	685
Current Assets	5m	4m	3m
Current Liabilities	705	670	588

Tes Transmissions Ltd
Unit 50 Link Road West Wilts Trading Estate, Westbury, BA13 4JB
Tel: 01373-822041 **Fax:** 01373-858790
E-mail: mark@testransmissions.co.uk
Website: http://www.testransmissions.co.uk
Directors: G. Peers (Co Sec), M. Jones (MD)
Immediate Holding Company: TES TRANSMISSIONS LIMITED
Registration no: 01185286 **Date established:** 1974 **Turnover:** £1m - £2m
No.of Employees: 11 - 20 **Product Groups:** 48

Date of Accounts	Mar 12	Mar 11	Mar 10
Working Capital	332	307	217
Fixed Assets	91	104	95
Current Assets	465	463	332

Thermal Technology Sales Ltd
Bridge House Station Road, Westbury, BA13 4HR
Tel: 01373-865454 **Fax:** 01373-864425
E-mail: sales@thermaltechnology.co.uk
Website: http://www.thermaltechnology.co.uk
Directors: D. Applegate (MD)
Immediate Holding Company: THERMAL TECHNOLOGY (SALES) LTD.
Registration no: 02882538 **Date established:** 1993 **Turnover:** £1m - £2m
No.of Employees: 1 - 10 **Product Groups:** 38, 40

Date of Accounts	Jan 12	Jan 11	Jan 10
Working Capital	-20	-21	-31
Fixed Assets	19	22	40
Current Assets	414	289	244

Top Gun & Rod

31 Warminster Road, Westbury, BA13 3PD
Tel: 01373-822866 **Fax:** 01373-822890
E-mail: markwestall@topgunandrod.co.uk
Website: http://www.topgunandrod.co.uk
Directors: M. Westall (Prop)
Date established: 2005 **No.of Employees:** 1 - 10 **Product Groups:** 36, 39, 40

Westbury Packaging Ltd

Unit 1a & 1b Woodland Industrial Estate Eden Vale Road, Westbury, BA13 3QS
Tel: 01373-826329 **Fax:** 01373-858342
E-mail: sales@westbury-pkg.co.uk
Website: http://www.westbury-pkg.co.uk
Directors: S. Scott (Fin), B. Tupman (MD)
Managers: J. Mead (Personnel)
Immediate Holding Company: WESTBURY PACKAGING LIMITED
Registration no: 01865360 **VAT No.:** GB 398 8318 85
Date established: 1984 **Turnover:** £2m - £5m **No.of Employees:** 21 - 50
Product Groups: 27, 35, 44, 49, 66

Date of Accounts	Nov 08	Sep 11	Sep 10
Working Capital	-282	-55	-198
Fixed Assets	616	558	634
Current Assets	1m	2m	2m

WORCESTERSHIRE

Bewdley

Advantage Controls (Europe) Ltd
Bridge House Riverside North, Bewdley, DY12 1AB
Tel: 01299-406380 **Fax:** 01299-400986
E-mail: sales@advantagecontrols.co.uk
Website: http://www.advantagecontrols.co.uk
Product Groups: 38, 40

Aegis Advanced Materials Ltd
Crundalls Farmhouse Crundalls Lane, Bewdley, DY12 1NB
Tel: 01299-404153 **Fax:** 01299-401468
E-mail: jk@aegis-ceramics.co.uk
Website: http://www.aegis-ceramics.co.uk
Directors: M. Kingsley (MD)
Immediate Holding Company: AEGIS ADVANCED MATERIALS LIMITED
Registration no: 02604099 **Date established:** 1991
Turnover: £250,000 - £500,000 **No.of Employees:** 1 - 10
Product Groups: 33, 34, 35, 36, 40, 43, 44, 45, 46, 48

Date of Accounts	Apr 11	Apr 10	Apr 09
Sales Turnover	N/A	N/A	291
Pre Tax Profit/Loss	N/A	N/A	75
Working Capital	586	508	535
Current Assets	757	557	602
Current Liabilities	N/A	N/A	36

Bondloc UK Ltd
Unit 2 Bewdley Business Park Long Bank, Bewdley, DY12 2TB
Tel: 01299-269269 **Fax:** 01299-269210
E-mail: enquiries@bondloc.co.uk
Website: http://www.bondloc.co.uk
Directors: M. Adams (Dir), W. Wilkinson (Dir)
Immediate Holding Company: BONDLOC (UK) LIMITED
Registration no: 03018597 **Date established:** 1995
No.of Employees: 11 - 20 **Product Groups:** 23, 27, 30, 31, 32, 35, 37, 42, 66, 68

Date of Accounts	Jan 12	Jan 11	Jan 10
Working Capital	34	49	9
Fixed Assets	16	31	67
Current Assets	535	514	436

EMSAS Ltd
Bridge House Riverside North, Bewdley, DY12 1AB
Tel: 0845-0940485 **Fax:** 0845-0940486
E-mail: info@emsas.biz
Website: http://www.emsas.biz
Product Groups: 54, 84, 85, 86

Furnace Engineering & Equipment Ltd
2 The Orchard, Bewdley, DY12 2LZ
Tel: 01299-404631 **Fax:** 01299-404664
E-mail: furnaceeng@aol.com
Website: http://www.furnaceengineering.co.uk
Directors: C. Colclough (Fin)
Immediate Holding Company: FURNACE ENGINEERING & EQUIPMENT LIMITED
Registration no: 02774892 **Date established:** 1992
Turnover: £250,000 - £500,000 **No.of Employees:** 1 - 10
Product Groups: 33, 46

Date of Accounts	Mar 11	Mar 10	Mar 09
Working Capital	471	519	553
Fixed Assets	1	1	1
Current Assets	541	606	579

Lanway Ltd
PO Box 3568, Bewdley, DY12 1ZU
Tel: 01299-861733 **Fax:** 08717-333899
E-mail: enquiries@lanway.ltd.uk
Website: http://www.lanway.ltd.uk
Bank(s): HSBC Bank plc
Directors: M. MacMaster (MD), E. MacMaster (Co Sec), E. Macmaster (Fin)
Immediate Holding Company: LANWAY LIMITED
Registration no: 04055658 **Date established:** 2000
Turnover: £500,000 - £1m **No.of Employees:** 21 - 50
Product Groups: 36, 40, 42, 45

Date of Accounts	Sep 10	Sep 09	Sep 08
Working Capital	-28	-19	-24
Fixed Assets	3	3	4
Current Assets	64	73	60

Lynden Way Nuts & Bolts Ltd
7 Button Bridge Paddock Cottage, Kinlet, Bewdley, DY12 3AN
Tel: 01299-841144 **Fax:** 01384-393933
E-mail: info@comfast.co.uk
Website: http://www.comfast.co.uk
Directors: G. Hemming (MD)
Immediate Holding Company: FOAM WIZARDS LIMITED
Registration no: 04746685 **Date established:** 2002
No.of Employees: 11 - 20 **Product Groups:** 35

M P B Garden Buildings Ltd
Lye Head, Bewdley, DY12 2UX
Tel: 01299-266000 **Fax:** 01299-266644
E-mail: sales@themalverncollection.co.uk
Website: http://www.themalverncollection.co.uk
Bank(s): Lloyds TSB Bank plc
Directors: L. Irwin (Comm), P. Kerr (Fin)
Managers: P. Beddoes (Personnel), D. Tolley (Tech Serv Mgr)
Ultimate Holding Company: PALMER TIMBER LIMITED
Immediate Holding Company: MPB GARDEN BUILDINGS LTD
Registration no: 01084328 **Date established:** 1972
Turnover: £10m - £20m **No.of Employees:** 101 - 250
Product Groups: 25, 49, 52, 83

Date of Accounts	Sep 11	Sep 10	Sep 09
Sales Turnover	14m	13m	12m
Pre Tax Profit/Loss	405	585	119
Working Capital	3m	3m	3m
Fixed Assets	827	861	900
Current Assets	7m	6m	5m
Current Liabilities	2m	1m	994

Midland Portable Buildings Ltd
Coppice Gate Farm Lye Head, Bewdley, DY12 2UX
Tel: 01299-266666 **Fax:** 01299-266644
Website: http://www.malverncollection.co.uk
Bank(s): Lloyds TSB Bank plc
Directors: J. Anson (MD), K. Whitehouse (Ch), L. Irwin (Mkt Research), L. Irwin (Dir), P. Kerr (Fin), S. Griffiths (Dir), S. Horan (Dir), T. Jones (Dir)
Managers: S. Russ (Sales Admin)
Immediate Holding Company: Palmer Timber Ltd
Registration no: 01084328 **Turnover:** £10m - £20m
No.of Employees: 51 - 100 **Product Groups:** 25, 26, 33, 49, 52, 83

Original Metal Craft & Fabrication
26 Park Lane, Bewdley, DY12 2EU
Tel: 07779-766048
Directors: M. Childe (Prop)
No.of Employees: 1 - 10 **Product Groups:** 26, 35

Parweld Ltd
Bewdley Business Park Long Bank, Bewdley, DY12 2TZ
Tel: 01299-266800 **Fax:** 01299-266900
E-mail: reception@parweld.co.uk
Website: http://www.parweld.com
Directors: G. Perry (Chief Op Offcr), C. Parker (MD)
Managers: S. Williams (Comptroller), M. McGarragh (Purch Mgr), E. Saunders (Mktg Serv Mgr), J. Websdell (Tech Serv Mgr)
Ultimate Holding Company: PARWELD INTERNATIONAL LIMITED
Immediate Holding Company: PARWELD LIMITED
Registration no: 01088134 **Date established:** 1972 **Turnover:** £5m - £10m
No.of Employees: 51 - 100 **Product Groups:** 46

Date of Accounts	Mar 08	Sep 11	Sep 10
Sales Turnover	N/A	9m	7m
Pre Tax Profit/Loss	171	310	165
Working Capital	2m	1m	1m
Fixed Assets	215	103	126
Current Assets	4m	4m	3m
Current Liabilities	933	690	706

Renderplas Ltd
Number 2 70 - 72 High Street, Bewdley, DY12 2DJ
Tel: 01299-888333 **Fax:** 01299-888234
E-mail: enquiry@renderplas.co.uk
Website: http://www.renderplas.co.uk
Directors: K. Leedham-Green (Ch), J. Leedham-Green (Dir), D. Leedham-Green (MD)
Registration no: 02459865 **VAT No.:** GB 547 3467 21
Date established: 1990 **Turnover:** £1m - £2m **No.of Employees:** 1 - 10
Product Groups: 33, 35

Date of Accounts	Jun 11	Jun 10	Jun 09
Working Capital	139	257	363
Fixed Assets	461	326	199
Current Assets	712	826	826

Wyre Forest Guns
Bower Hill Pound Green, Arley, Bewdley, DY12 3LJ
Tel: 01299-403730 **Fax:** 01299-403730
E-mail: barrywfg@talktalk.net
Directors: B. Cheadle (Prop)
Date established: 1990 **No.of Employees:** 1 - 10 **Product Groups:** 36, 39, 40

Broadway

Auto Sleepers Ltd
Orchard Works Industrial Estate Willersey, Broadway, WR12 7QF
Tel: 01386-853338 **Fax:** 01386-858343
E-mail: info@auto-sleepers.co.uk
Website: http://www.auto-sleepers.co.uk
Bank(s): Lloyds TSB Bank plc
Directors: A. Brand (Mkt Research)
Managers: G. Scott, T. Henley (Tech Serv Mgr), D. Clarkson (Sales Prom Mgr), D. Troth (Purch Mgr)
Ultimate Holding Company: AUTO-SLEEPERS INVESTMENTS LIMITED
Immediate Holding Company: AUTO-SLEEPERS GROUP LIMITED
Registration no: 03978237 **VAT No.:** GB 274 1339 61
Date established: 2000 **Turnover:** £50m - £75m
No.of Employees: 101 - 250 **Product Groups:** 39

Date of Accounts	Aug 11	Aug 10	Aug 09
Sales Turnover	72m	65m	55m
Pre Tax Profit/Loss	2m	1m	-3m
Working Capital	8m	7m	6m
Fixed Assets	6m	5m	5m
Current Assets	23m	21m	16m
Current Liabilities	2m	3m	2m

Heming Services Ltd
Collin Lane Willersey, Broadway, WR12 7PE
Tel: 01386-853295 **Fax:** 01386-858074
E-mail: office@heming-services.co.uk
Website: http://www.heming-services.co.uk
Directors: P. Heming (Dir)
Ultimate Holding Company: HSL COMPANIES LIMITED
Immediate Holding Company: HEMING SERVICES LIMITED
Registration no: 04972682 **Date established:** 2003
No.of Employees: 11 - 20 **Product Groups:** 41

Date of Accounts	Dec 11	Dec 10	Dec 09
Working Capital	223	121	160
Fixed Assets	187	173	154
Current Assets	761	484	303

Systematic Servicing Equipment Ltd
Field Works Broadway Road, Willersey, Broadway, WR12 7PH
Tel: 01386-852342 **Fax:** 01386-858556
E-mail: sales@systematic-servicing.co.uk
Website: http://www.systematic-servicing.co.uk
Bank(s): Midland
Directors: E. Westwood (MD), R. Plumb (MD), R. Hall (Dir), N. Harrison (Dir)
Immediate Holding Company: SYSTEMATIC SERVICING (EQUIPMENT) LIMITED
Registration no: 01192724 **VAT No.:** GB 276 7073 31
Date established: 1974 **Turnover:** £1m - £2m **No.of Employees:** 21 - 50
Product Groups: 54

Date of Accounts	Apr 11	Apr 10	Apr 09
Sales Turnover	1m	2m	2m
Pre Tax Profit/Loss	35	56	91
Working Capital	47	19	16
Fixed Assets	429	537	457
Current Assets	552	602	595
Current Liabilities	204	310	266

Waste Equipment Hire Broadway Ltd
Field House Willersey, Broadway, WR12 7PH
Tel: 01386-858461 **Fax:** 01386-858556
E-mail: sales@systematic-servicing.co.uk
Website: http://wasteequipmentinworcestershire.com
Directors: G. Thompson (Dir)
Immediate Holding Company: Systematic Servicing (Equipment) Ltd
Registration no: 01609086 **Date established:** 1974 **Turnover:** £1m - £2m
No.of Employees: 11 - 20 **Product Groups:** 38, 42

Bromsgrove

Air Technology Systems Ltd
8 Aston Court Bromsgrove Technology Park, Bromsgrove, B60 3AL
Tel: 01527-833383 **Fax:** 01562-731811
E-mail: sales@atsclimate.com
Website: http://www.atsclimate.com
Managers: L. Parker, D. Castle (Sales Prom Mgr)
Immediate Holding Company: AIR TECHNOLOGY SYSTEMS LIMITED
Registration no: 02753492 **Date established:** 1992 **Turnover:** £1m - £2m
No.of Employees: 11 - 20 **Product Groups:** 40, 52

Date of Accounts	Oct 11	Oct 10	Oct 09
Working Capital	829	679	361
Fixed Assets	297	129	65
Current Assets	2m	2m	952

Airfil Ltd
Unit E Saxon Business Park Hanbury Road, Stoke Prior, Bromsgrove, B60 4AD
Tel: 01527-576714 **Fax:** 01527-836202
E-mail: airfil@dial.pipex.com
Website: http://www.alvechurch5.freeserve.co.uk
Directors: H. Jones (MD)
Immediate Holding Company: AIRFIL LIMITED
Registration no: 01832655 **Date established:** 1984
No.of Employees: 1 - 10 **Product Groups:** 38, 42

Date of Accounts	Mar 11	Mar 10	Mar 07
Working Capital	30	41	15
Current Assets	41	41	55

Airware International Ltd
Smithsway Saxon Business Park Stoke Prior, Bromsgrove, B60 4AD
Tel: 01527-870110 **Fax:** 01527-872388
E-mail: andrew@awi.co.uk
Website: http://www.awi.co.uk
Directors: A. Ward (Ptnr)
Immediate Holding Company: AIRWARE INTERNATIONAL LIMITED
Registration no: 02822965 **Date established:** 1993
Turnover: £500,000 - £1m **No.of Employees:** 1 - 10 **Product Groups:** 23, 29, 30, 35, 38, 39, 40, 42, 48, 67, 68, 83

Date of Accounts	Dec 11	Dec 10	Dec 09
Sales Turnover	702	687	663
Pre Tax Profit/Loss	35	34	33
Working Capital	100	85	75
Fixed Assets	25	34	46
Current Assets	184	184	203
Current Liabilities	56	33	44

Albion Packaging Services Ltd
Unit 9 Aston Fields Trading Estate Aston Road, Bromsgrove, B60 3EX
Tel: 01527-881901 **Fax:** 01527-881915
E-mail: sales@albionpackaging.co.uk
Website: http://www.albionpackaging.co.uk
Directors: S. Busfield (Dir)
Immediate Holding Company: ALBION PACKAGING SERVICES LIMITED
Registration no: 04210058 **Date established:** 2001
No.of Employees: 1 - 10 **Product Groups:** 38, 42

Date of Accounts	Feb 12	Feb 11	Feb 10
Working Capital	301	288	273
Fixed Assets	20	23	28
Current Assets	516	497	484

Arkinstall Ltd
Unit 10a Buntsford Park Road, Bromsgrove, B60 3DX
Tel: 01527-872962 **Fax:** 01527-837127
E-mail: info@arkinstall.co.uk
Website: http://www.arkinstall.co.uk
Bank(s): Barclays, Birmingham
Directors: T. Straker (Dir), M. Straker (Fin)
Immediate Holding Company: ARKINSTALL LIMITED
Registration no: 06584066 **VAT No.:** GB 109 4427 76
Date established: 2008 **Turnover:** £1m - £2m **No.of Employees:** 11 - 20
Product Groups: 26, 35

Date of Accounts	Aug 10	Jul 11	Sep 09
Working Capital	N/A	1	N/A
Current Assets	N/A	66	N/A

Barton Firtop Engineering
Stoke Heath Works Hanbury Road, Stoke Heath, Bromsgrove, B60 4LT
Tel: 01527-831664 **Fax:** 01527-832638
E-mail: sales@bartonfirtop.co.uk
Website: http://www.bartonfirtop.co.uk
Bank(s): HSBC, Birmingham
Directors: F. Stephen (MD)
Managers: N. Key (I.T. Exec)
Immediate Holding Company: BARTON FIRTOP ENGINEERING CO LIMITED
Registration no: 01117835 **VAT No.:** GB 112 6949 71
Date established: 1973 **Turnover:** £5m - £10m **No.of Employees:** 21 - 50
Product Groups: 35, 40, 42

Date of Accounts	Oct 11	Oct 10	Oct 09
Sales Turnover	9m	7m	7m
Pre Tax Profit/Loss	1m	751	1m
Working Capital	3m	2m	2m
Fixed Assets	425	438	347
Current Assets	5m	4m	4m
Current Liabilities	420	242	395

C D M Shop Fitting Ltd
Unit 60 Sugarbrook Road, Bromsgrove, B60 3DN
Tel: 01527-575671 **Fax:** 01527-578102
E-mail: sales@shop-fitting.org.uk
Website: http://www.cdmshopfitting.com
Directors: C. Dowling (Dir), C. Dowling (MD)
Ultimate Holding Company: ESTRELLA GROUP LIMITED
Immediate Holding Company: CDM SHOPFITTING LIMITED
Registration no: 03045911 **Date established:** 1995
No.of Employees: 1 - 10 **Product Groups:** 52

Date of Accounts	May 10	May 09	May 08
Sales Turnover	3m	3m	4m
Pre Tax Profit/Loss	17	-109	289
Working Capital	461	333	524
Fixed Assets	11	139	26
Current Assets	2m	1m	2m
Current Liabilities	482	247	525

C J Plant Ltd
27d Harris Business Park Hanbury Road, Stoke Prior, Bromsgrove, B60 4DJ
Tel: 01527-870793 **Fax:** 01527-831310
E-mail: info@cjplant.com
Website: http://www.cjplantmaintenance.com
Directors: J. Jones (Dir)
Immediate Holding Company: C.J.PLANT LIMITED
Registration no: 05769983 **Date established:** 2006
No.of Employees: 1 - 10 **Product Groups:** 35, 38, 40, 48, 85

Date of Accounts	Mar 11	Mar 10	Mar 08
Working Capital	-16	-11	-0
Fixed Assets	16	11	N/A
Current Assets	67	34	7

Caldo Engineering Ltd
1 Worcester Court Smiths Way Saxon Business Park, Stoke Prior, Bromsgrove, B60 4FH
Tel: 01527-579000 **Fax:** 01527-579036
E-mail: chris@caldo.com
Website: http://www.caldo.com
Directors: C. Withers (MD)
Immediate Holding Company: CALDO ENGINEERING LIMITED
Registration no: 02605889 **VAT No.:** GB 594 4023 35
Date established: 1991 **No.of Employees:** 1 - 10 **Product Groups:** 34, 40, 42, 46

Date of Accounts	Jan 12	Jan 11	Jan 10
Working Capital	-39	-59	-54
Fixed Assets	2	3	3
Current Assets	88	33	40

Chichester Caravans
Worcester Road Upton Warren, Bromsgrove, B61 7EX
Tel: 01527-836888 **Fax:** 01527-870315
E-mail: bromsgrove@chichester-caravans.co.uk
Website: http://www.chichester-caravans.co.uk
Bank(s): HSBC Bank plc
Directors: J. Bolton (Prop)
Managers: G. Porter (Admin Off)
VAT No.: GB 661 4491 33 **No.of Employees:** 11 - 20 **Product Groups:** 39

Crosscheck Systems Ltd
Office 29 Greenbox Weston Hall Road, Stoke Prior, Bromsgrove, B60 4AL
Tel: 01527-839010 **Fax:** 01527-839011
E-mail: sales@x-check.co.uk
Website: http://www.x-check.co.uk
Directors: P. Mason (Prop)
Immediate Holding Company: CROSS-CHECK SYSTEMS LIMITED
Registration no: 07159446 **Date established:** 2010 **Turnover:** £1m - £2m
No.of Employees: 1 - 10 **Product Groups:** 44, 67

Date of Accounts	Dec 11	Dec 10
Working Capital	8	9
Fixed Assets	3	6
Current Assets	94	91

Deeley Precision Engineering Ltd
Unit 1 Aston Fields Industrial Estate Aston Road, Bromsgrove, B60 3EX
Tel: 01527-870001 **Fax:** 01527-579101
E-mail: deeleypricisioneng@yahoo.co.uk
Directors: S. Wearing (Fin), I. Deeley (MD)
Immediate Holding Company: DEELEY PRECISION ENGINEERING LIMITED
Registration no: 03859672 **VAT No.:** GB 695 4233 10
Date established: 1999 **Turnover:** £250,000 - £500,000
No.of Employees: 1 - 10 **Product Groups:** 46

Date of Accounts	Oct 11	Oct 10	Oct 09
Sales Turnover	N/A	253	N/A
Pre Tax Profit/Loss	N/A	9	16
Working Capital	-177	-237	-170
Fixed Assets	270	270	194
Current Assets	120	98	61
Current Liabilities	N/A	12	18

Electro Technik Ltd
Unit 10-12 Shaw Lane Industrial Estate 152 Shaw Lane, Stoke Prior, Bromsgrove, B60 4ED
Tel: 01527-831794 **Fax:** 01527-574470
E-mail: trevor@electro-technick.com
Website: http://www.electro-technik.com
Bank(s): Barclays
Directors: T. Atkins (MD), D. Atkins (Fin)
Immediate Holding Company: ELECTRO-TECHNIK LIMITED
Registration no: 01846417 **VAT No.:** GB 389 4400 24
Date established: 1984 **Turnover:** £2m - £5m **No.of Employees:** 11 - 20
Product Groups: 37

Date of Accounts	Sep 11	Sep 10	Sep 09
Working Capital	315	436	690
Fixed Assets	5	10	4
Current Assets	718	677	935

Elevated Lifts Ltd
Banham Court 138 Hanbury Road, Stoke Prior, Bromsgrove, B60 4JZ
Tel: 0121-440 4040 **Fax:** 0121-440 5676
E-mail: john_walmsley@libeone.net
Website: http://www.elevated.co.uk
Directors: J. Walmsley (Dir)
Immediate Holding Company: ELEVATED LIFTS LIMITED
Registration no: 03056715 **Date established:** 1995
No.of Employees: 1 - 10 **Product Groups:** 35, 39, 45

Date of Accounts	May 11	May 10	May 09
Working Capital	16	24	24
Fixed Assets	4	6	7
Current Assets	46	49	57

Elster Kromschroder UK
9 The Croft Buntsford Drive Stoke Heath, Bromsgrove, B60 4JE
Tel: 01527-888820 **Fax:** 01562-744129
E-mail: info@kromschroder.co.uk
Website: http://www.kromschroder.co.uk
Bank(s): Barclays
Directors: A. Brown (Sales), K. Vollmer (Co Sec), P. Morris (MD)
Immediate Holding Company: MARSHALLSAY MUMFORD LIMITED
Registration no: 01185374 **VAT No.:** GB 281 3573 54
Date established: 1996 **Turnover:** £2m - £5m **No.of Employees:** 11 - 20
Product Groups: 38, 40

Date of Accounts	Dec 06	Dec 05
Sales Turnover	4416	4045
Pre Tax Profit/Loss	522	435

Working Capital	1272	885
Fixed Assets	343	373
Current Assets	1998	2065
Current Liabilities	726	1180
ROCE% (Return on Capital Employed)	32.3	34.6
ROT% (Return on Turnover)	11.8	10.8

Fast Fit Nationwide Ltd
Unit 3 Buntsford Park Road, Bromsgrove, B60 3DX
Tel: 01527-575729 **Fax:** 01527-576175
E-mail: davefowler@fastfitnationwide.co.uk
Website: http://www.fastfitnationwide.co.uk
Directors: D. Fowler (Dir)
Immediate Holding Company: FASTFIT NATIONWIDE LIMITED
Registration no: 03413923 **Date established:** 1997
No.of Employees: 21 - 50 **Product Groups:** 23, 35, 36, 37, 39, 40, 66, 67, 68

Date of Accounts	Jan 11	Jan 10	Jan 09
Working Capital	24	-2	67
Fixed Assets	71	84	95
Current Assets	427	346	392
Current Liabilities	362	N/A	N/A

Foster Welding & Fabrication Ltd
Woodside Farm Woodland Road, Dodford, Bromsgrove, B61 9BT
Tel: 0781-215 8009 **Fax:** 01527-836444
E-mail: fosterwelding@hotmail.co.uk
Directors: P. Foster (Dir)
Immediate Holding Company: FOSTER WELDING & FABRICATIONS LTD
Registration no: 06805746 **Date established:** 2009
No.of Employees: 1 - 10 **Product Groups:** 30, 35, 36, 48, 49, 66

Date of Accounts	Mar 11	Mar 10
Working Capital	-31	-22
Fixed Assets	36	40
Current Assets	51	57

Fuel Parts UK Ltd
Buntsford Park Road, Bromsgrove, B60 3DX
Tel: 01527-835555 **Fax:** 01527-831111
E-mail: sales@fuel-parts.co.uk
Website: http://www.fuel-parts.co.uk
Directors: K. Sears (Co Sec), A. West (MD), N. Morgan (Dir)
Managers: R. Guhman (Sales Prom Mgr), E. Lee-smith, K. Talyor, N. McCann (Personnel)
Immediate Holding Company: FUEL PARTS UK LIMITED
Registration no: 06263577 **Date established:** 2007
Turnover: £10m - £20m **No.of Employees:** 51 - 100 **Product Groups:** 68

Date of Accounts	Sep 11	Sep 10	Sep 09
Sales Turnover	12m	13m	12m
Pre Tax Profit/Loss	-28	536	392
Working Capital	-414	-549	-979
Fixed Assets	1m	1m	1m
Current Assets	4m	4m	4m
Current Liabilities	2m	2m	3m

Harris Cleaning Services
Hanbury Road Hanbury, Bromsgrove, B60 4BU
Tel: 01527-575441 **Fax:** 01953-455905
E-mail: sales@lgharris.co.uk
Directors: J. McGrath (MD)
Managers: I. Cook (Chief Mgr)
Immediate Holding Company: HARRIS CLEANING SERVICES LIMITED
Registration no: 03584120 **VAT No.:** GB 107 5333 92
Date established: 1998 **Turnover:** £5m - £10m **No.of Employees:** 1 - 10
Product Groups: 25, 30, 33, 35, 36, 37, 38, 39, 40, 41, 43, 49, 63, 64, 66

L G Harris & Co. Ltd
Hanbury Road Stoke Prior, Bromsgrove, B60 4AE
Tel: 01527-575441 **Fax:** 01527-575366
E-mail: garyj@lgharris.co.uk
Website: http://www.lgharris.co.uk
Bank(s): Lloyds TSB Bank plc
Directors: S. Hobbs (Sales), G. Jordan (MD), D. Cooper (Fin)
Managers: H. Lett (Mgr), S. Mallaby (Mktg Serv Mgr)
Ultimate Holding Company: MORFIS NINETY FIVE LIMITED
Immediate Holding Company: L.G.HARRIS & CO.LIMITED
Registration no: 00249316 **Date established:** 1930
Turnover: £20m - £50m **No.of Employees:** 251 - 500
Product Groups: 02, 24, 27, 32, 33, 35, 36, 38, 40, 49, 63, 66, 67

Date of Accounts	Jun 11	Jun 10	Jun 09
Sales Turnover	50m	45m	36m
Pre Tax Profit/Loss	620	507	1m
Working Capital	14m	12m	11m
Fixed Assets	12m	7m	7m
Current Assets	32m	27m	21m
Current Liabilities	10m	9m	6m

I P P E C Systems Ltd
21 Buntsford Drive, Bromsgrove, B60 3AJ
Tel: 01527-579705 **Fax:** 01527-574109
E-mail: info@ippec.co.uk
Website: http://www.ippec.co.uk
Directors: M. Namih (Dir)
Immediate Holding Company: IPPEC SYSTEMS LIMITED
Registration no: 03468652 **VAT No.:** GB 695 6578 03
Date established: 1997 **No.of Employees:** 1 - 10 **Product Groups:** 38, 40

Date of Accounts	Dec 11	Dec 10	Dec 09
Working Capital	-79	-82	-67
Fixed Assets	22	20	19
Current Assets	68	73	68

Inwido UK Ltd
Delta House Harris Business Park Stoke Prior, Bromsgrove, B60 4DJ
Tel: 01527-881060 **Fax:** 01527-881061
E-mail: mail@inwido.co.uk
Website: http://www.inwido.co.uk
Directors: B. Auskerin (MD), C. Thawley (MD), R. Bushell (MD)
Registration no: 01110137 **VAT No.:** GB 244 4169 66
Date established: 2008 **Turnover:** £500,000 - £1m
No.of Employees: 1 - 10 **Product Groups:** 52

Date of Accounts	Dec 07	Dec 06	Dec 05
Pre Tax Profit/Loss	-993	N/A	N/A
Working Capital	-73	-100	-658
Fixed Assets	691	119	39
Current Assets	2891	1672	383
Current Liabilities	2964	1771	1041
Total Share Capital	560	250	250
ROCE% (Return on Capital Employed)	-160.5		

Kingfisher Rubber & Plastics

1 Woden Court Saxon Business Park Hanbury Road, Stoke Prior, Bromsgrove, B60 4AD
Tel: 01527-570570 **Fax:** 01527-575200
E-mail: sales@kingfisherrubber.co.uk
Website: http://www.kingfisherrubber.co.uk
Directors: M. Lewis (Prop)
VAT No.: GB 478 5182 08 **Turnover:** £500,000 - £1m
No.of Employees: 1 - 10 **Product Groups:** 29, 30

The Logistics Business Ltd

Old Court House The Crescent, Bromsgrove, B60 2DF
Tel: 01527-889060 **Fax:** 01527-559192
E-mail: info@logistics.co.uk
Website: http://www.logistics.co.uk
Directors: R. Ballard (Dir)
Immediate Holding Company: THE LOGISTICS BUSINESS LIMITED
Registration no: 02619692 **Date established:** 1991 **Turnover:** £1m - £2m
No.of Employees: 1 - 10 **Product Groups:** 80, 84

Date of Accounts	Oct 11	Oct 10	Oct 09
Working Capital	109	114	70
Fixed Assets	10	4	4
Current Assets	233	327	182

Mason & Jones

Unit 6 Buntsford Park Road, Bromsgrove, B60 3DX
Tel: 01527-577123 **Fax:** 01527-577248
E-mail: hughmason@masonandjones.com
Website: http://www.masonandjones.com
Directors: H. Mason (Grp Chief Exec)
VAT No.: GB 589 5572 71 **Turnover:** £500,000 - £1m
No.of Employees: 1 - 10 **Product Groups:** 23, 24, 30

Miles Partitioning Industries Ltd

Miles House Sherwood Road, Bromsgrove, B60 3DR
Tel: 01527-877226 **Fax:** 01527-879033
E-mail: dave@milesindustries.com
Website: http://www.milesindustries.com
Bank(s): National Westminster
Directors: M. Lee (Contracts), M. Lee (Fin), J. Lee (Ch), D. Norris (MD), K. Kowalewski (Contracts)
Managers: J. Elmer, S. Watts (Accounts), D. Norris
Ultimate Holding Company: MILES INDUSTRIES PROPERTY HOLDINGS LIMITED
Immediate Holding Company: MILES PARTITIONING INDUSTRIES LIMITED
Registration no: 01697817 **VAT No.:** GB 488 0717 13
Date established: 1983 **Turnover:** Up to £250,000
No.of Employees: 21 - 50 **Product Groups:** 30, 33, 35, 52

Date of Accounts	Mar 10	Mar 09	Mar 08
Working Capital	202	207	182
Fixed Assets	117	130	149
Current Assets	1m	2m	1m

MWP Advanced Manufacturing

Ascent B2B, Unit 2 Sugar Brook Court Aston Road, Bromsgrove, B60 3EX
Tel: 020-7970 4420 **Fax:** 020-7970 4494
E-mail: mike.excell@centaur.co.uk
Website: http://www.advancedmanufacturing.co.uk
Directors: D. Rodgers (MD)
Managers: D. Rogers (Mgr)
No.of Employees: 11 - 20 **Product Groups:** 28

Omega Training Services

188 Worcester Road, Bromsgrove, B61 7AZ
Tel: 01527-558917 **Fax:** 0121-476 4985
E-mail: alb.bates@gmail.com
Directors: A. Bates (Prop)
Immediate Holding Company: OMEGA TRAINING SERVICES LIMITED
Registration no: 03184824 **Date established:** 1996
No.of Employees: 1 - 10 **Product Groups:** 35, 39, 45

Date of Accounts	Jul 12	Jul 11	Jul 10
Working Capital	255	279	276
Fixed Assets	59	43	41
Current Assets	292	336	328

Ortlinghaus UK Ltd

Unit 19 Sugarbrook Road, Bromsgrove, B60 3DN
Tel: 01527-579123 **Fax:** 01527-579077
E-mail: sales@ortlinghaus.co.uk
Website: http://www.ortlinghaus.co.uk
Directors: W. Wright (MD)
Ultimate Holding Company: ORTLINGHAUS AG (SWITZERLAND)
Immediate Holding Company: ORTLINGHAUS UK LIMITED
Registration no: 01404506 **Date established:** 1978 **Turnover:** £1m - £2m
No.of Employees: 1 - 10 **Product Groups:** 35, 44

Date of Accounts	Dec 11	Dec 10	Dec 09
Working Capital	1m	1m	1m
Fixed Assets	25	32	28
Current Assets	2m	1m	1m

P N R UK Ltd

Unit 13 Sugarbrook Road, Bromsgrove, B60 3DW
Tel: 01527-579066 **Fax:** 01527-579067
E-mail: spraynozzles@pnr.co.uk
Website: http://www.pnr.co.uk
Directors: R. Faulkner (MD), L. Faulkner (Fin)
Immediate Holding Company: PNR UK LIMITED
Registration no: 02306776 **VAT No.:** GB 488 0643 16
Date established: 1988 **Turnover:** £250,000 - £500,000
No.of Employees: 1 - 10 **Product Groups:** 36, 40

Date of Accounts	Dec 11	Dec 10	Dec 09
Working Capital	69	191	118
Fixed Assets	22	27	24
Current Assets	283	362	320

ProfilGruppen Ltd

Unit 26 Basepoint Business Centre Bromsgrove Technology Park, Isidore Road, Bromsgrove, B60 3ET
Tel: 01527-834640 **Fax:** 01527-471683
E-mail: martin.eyles@profilgruppen.se
Website: http://www.profilgruppen.com
No.of Employees: 1 - 10 **Product Groups:** 31, 34

Date of Accounts	Dec 08	Dec 07	Dec 06
Sales Turnover	182	N/A	N/A
Pre Tax Profit/Loss	20	21	5
Working Capital	25	13	-11
Fixed Assets	30	26	33
Current Assets	37	26	15
Current Liabilities	12	13	12

Quicklift Ltd

636 Birmingham Road Lydiate Ash, Bromsgrove, B61 0QB
Tel: 0121-457 8995 **Fax:** 0121-457 8935
E-mail: sales@quicklift.co.uk
Website: http://www.quicklift.co.uk
Directors: J. Grady (MD)
Immediate Holding Company: QUICKLIFT LIMITED
Registration no: 02255329 **Date established:** 1988
No.of Employees: 1 - 10 **Product Groups:** 35, 39, 45

Date of Accounts	Feb 11	Feb 10	Feb 09
Working Capital	14	16	18
Fixed Assets	12	15	19
Current Assets	89	87	78
Current Liabilities	16	12	10

Reddi Roll Ltd

Unit 14 Harris Business Park Hanbury Road Stoke Prior, Bromsgrove, B60 4AA
Tel: 01527-881993 **Fax:** 01527-881994
E-mail: mark@reddiroll.co.uk
Website: http://www.reddiroll.co.uk
Directors: M. Norton (Dir)
Immediate Holding Company: REDDIROLL LIMITED
Registration no: 01543598 **VAT No.:** GB 338 1707 54
Date established: 1981 **Turnover:** £250,000 - £500,000
No.of Employees: 1 - 10 **Product Groups:** 48

Date of Accounts	Apr 11	Apr 10	Apr 09
Working Capital	-20	-20	-35
Fixed Assets	102	117	138
Current Assets	74	35	40

S E W Eurodrive Ltd

5 Sugarbrook Court Aston Road, Bromsgrove, B60 3EX
Tel: 01527-877319 **Fax:** 01527-575245
E-mail: sales@sew-eurodrive.co.uk
Website: http://www.sew-eurodrive.co.uk
Managers: L. Rafferty (Mgr)
Ultimate Holding Company: BV BETEILGUNG GMBH & CO KG
Immediate Holding Company: SEW-EURODRIVE LIMITED
Registration no: 00947360 **Date established:** 1969
Turnover: £250,000 - £500,000 **No.of Employees:** 1 - 10
Product Groups: 35, 37

Date of Accounts	Feb 08	Feb 11	Feb 10
Sales Turnover	25m	27m	22m
Pre Tax Profit/Loss	5m	5m	2m
Working Capital	11m	11m	9m
Fixed Assets	2m	8m	6m
Current Assets	14m	16m	14m
Current Liabilities	1m	2m	367

S T Grinding Ltd

Saxon Business Park Hanbury Road, Stoke Prior, Bromsgrove, B60 4AD
Tel: 01527-878137 **Fax:** 01527-878990
E-mail: paul@spring-tooling.co.uk
Website: http://www.spring-tooling.co.uk
Directors: A. Wright (MD)
Ultimate Holding Company: BOBBY'S FOODS PLC
Immediate Holding Company: THERAPY2000 T/A WWW.I TREATMENTCOUCH.COM LIMITED
Registration no: 03818408 **Date established:** 2003 **Turnover:** £2m - £5m
No.of Employees: 1 - 10 **Product Groups:** 46

Date of Accounts	Sep 11	Sep 10	Sep 09
Sales Turnover	2m	2m	2m
Pre Tax Profit/Loss	122	-72	1
Working Capital	247	218	304
Fixed Assets	109	98	59
Current Assets	509	391	547
Current Liabilities	89	59	88

Schofield Fabrications Bromsgrove Ltd

Sugarbrook Road Aston Fields Industrial Estate, Bromsgrove, B60 3DN
Tel: 01527-870220 **Fax:** 01527-575409
E-mail: kevin.schofield@schofab.co.uk
Website: http://www.schofab.co.uk
Bank(s): National Westminster Bank Plc
Directors: K. Schofield (MD)
Ultimate Holding Company: SCHOFIELD FABRICATIONS HOLDINGS LIMITED
Immediate Holding Company: SCHOFIELD FABRICATIONS (BROMSGROVE) LIMITED
Registration no: 01447047 **VAT No.:** GB 338 0109 79
Date established: 1979 **Turnover:** £500,000 - £1m
No.of Employees: 11 - 20 **Product Groups:** 48

Date of Accounts	Sep 11	Sep 10	Sep 09
Working Capital	465	425	431
Fixed Assets	177	182	188
Current Assets	693	574	541

Second City Customs

5 Sherwood Road Aston Fields Industrial Estate, Bromsgrove, B60 3DR
Tel: 01527-576996
E-mail: info@secondcitycustoms.co.uk
Website: http://www.secondcitycustoms.co.uk
Directors: I. Cushing (Prop)
Immediate Holding Company: SECOND CITY CUSTOMS LTD
Registration no: 06487918 **Date established:** 2008
No.of Employees: 1 - 10 **Product Groups:** 24, 39

Date of Accounts	Jan 12	Jan 11	Jan 10
Working Capital	N/A	5	-26
Fixed Assets	21	25	11
Current Assets	73	85	38
Current Liabilities	N/A	12	1

Sifco Applied Surface Concepts UK Ltd

Unit 12-14 Aston Fields Trading Estate Aston Road, Bromsgrove, B60 3EX
Tel: 01527-557740 **Fax:** 01527-832856
E-mail: m.smith@sifco.co.uk
Website: http://www.sifcoasc.com
Bank(s): Barclays
Directors: M. Smith (MD)
Ultimate Holding Company: SIFCO INDUSTRIES INC [USA]
Immediate Holding Company: SIFCO APPLIED SURFACE CONCEPTS (UK) LIMITED
Registration no: 02312115 **VAT No.:** GB 488 0981 93
Date established: 1988 **Turnover:** £2m - £5m **No.of Employees:** 11 - 20
Product Groups: 46, 48

Date of Accounts	Sep 11	Sep 10	Sep 09
Working Capital	148	-8	32
Fixed Assets	458	407	396
Current Assets	437	293	329

Spring Tooling Ltd

Alfred Court Saxon Business Park Hanbury Road, Stoke Prior, Bromsgrove, B60 4AD
Tel: 01527-876412 **Fax:** 01527-878990
E-mail: enquire@spring-tooling.co.uk
Website: http://www.spring-tooling.co.uk
Bank(s): Lloyds TSB
Directors: D. Darby (Dir), A. Wright (Dir)
Immediate Holding Company: SPRING TOOLING LIMITED
Registration no: 01178868 **Date established:** 1974 **Turnover:** £2m - £5m
No.of Employees: 21 - 50 **Product Groups:** 36, 46

Date of Accounts	Jul 12	Jul 11	Jul 10
Working Capital	523	408	278
Fixed Assets	1m	1m	992
Current Assets	829	865	509

Synventive Holding Ltd

Unit 1/2 Silver Birches Business Park Aston Road, Bromsgrove, B60 3EU
Tel: 01527-577417
E-mail: sales@synventive.com
Website: http://www.synventive.com
Registration no: 04834434 **Date established:** 2003
No.of Employees: 11 - 20 **Product Groups:** 36, 38, 42, 48

Tis 2000 Ltd

9 Hewell Lane Tardebigge, Bromsgrove, B60 1LP
Tel: 01527-880688 **Fax:** 01527-880691
E-mail: info@tis2000.ltd.uk
Website: http://www.tis2000.com
Directors: E. Welters (MD), E. Ingram (MD), T. Ingram (Dir)
Registration no: 00517438 **Turnover:** £250,000 - £500,000
No.of Employees: 1 - 10 **Product Groups:** 48, 49, 52

Date of Accounts	May 08	May 07	May 06
Working Capital	-14	4	-2
Fixed Assets	8	7	7
Current Assets	49	47	39
Current Liabilities	63	43	40

U K F Stainless Ltd

12 Buntsford Park Road, Bromsgrove, B60 3DX
Tel: 01527-578686 **Fax:** 01527-837792
E-mail: info@ukfstainless.co.uk
Website: http://www.ukfstainless.co.uk
Bank(s): National Westminster Bank Plc
Directors: I. Humphries (Comm), P. Morris (Fin)
Managers: J. Pointer, W. Bagnall (Sales Prom Mgr), J. Finch
Ultimate Holding Company: UKF STAINLESS HOLDINGS LIMITED
Immediate Holding Company: U.K.F. STAINLESS LIMITED
Registration no: 02834163 **VAT No.:** GB 589 4224 02
Date established: 1993 **Turnover:** £10m - £20m
No.of Employees: 21 - 50 **Product Groups:** 36, 66

Date of Accounts	Sep 11	Sep 10	Sep 09
Sales Turnover	11m	10m	8m
Pre Tax Profit/Loss	309	324	102
Working Capital	553	675	617
Fixed Assets	575	357	281
Current Assets	4m	4m	4m
Current Liabilities	2m	1m	1m

Uroglas

Unit 2 Buntsford Hill Business Park Buntsford Park Road, Bromsgrove, B60 3DX
Tel: 01527-577477 **Fax:** 01527-576577
E-mail: mm@uroglas.com
Website: http://www.uroglas.com
Directors: S. McCreedy (Prop)
No.of Employees: 1 - 10 **Product Groups:** 39, 68

V K F Renzel Ltd

20e Harris Business Park Hanbury Road, Stoke Prior, Bromsgrove, B60 4BD
Tel: 01527-878311 **Fax:** 01527-878411
E-mail: sales@vkf-renzel.co.uk
Website: http://www.vkf-renzel.co.uk
Directors: J. Bishop (MD)
Ultimate Holding Company: HEINZ RENZEL HOLDING GMBH (GERMANY)
Immediate Holding Company: VKF RENZEL (UK) LIMITED
Registration no: 02978351 **Date established:** 1994
Turnover: £500,000 - £1m **No.of Employees:** 1 - 10 **Product Groups:** 25

Date of Accounts	Dec 11	Dec 10	Dec 09
Working Capital	-193	-134	-163
Fixed Assets	309	316	316
Current Assets	369	293	291

Vinci Construction

86-92 Worcester Road, Bromsgrove, B61 7AQ
Tel: 01527-575588 **Fax:** 01527-575258
E-mail: info@vinciconstruction.co.uk
Website: http://www.vinciconstruction.co.uk
Bank(s): Lloyds TSB
Directors: N. McGinnity (Grp Chief Exec)
Immediate Holding Company: VINCI CONSTRUCTION UK LTD
Registration no: 02295904 **VAT No.:** GB 551 5442 56
Date established: 1865 **Turnover:** £20m - £50m
No.of Employees: 21 - 50 **Product Groups:** 52

Walter GB Ltd

Unit 1 The Courtyard Buntsford Drive, Bromsgrove, B60 3DJ
Tel: 01527-839450 **Fax:** 01527-839499
E-mail: service.uk@walter-tools.com
Website: http://www.walter-tools.com
Bank(s): Barclays
Managers: G. O'hagan (Chief Mgr)
Ultimate Holding Company: SANDVIK AB (SWEDEN)
Immediate Holding Company: WALTER GB LIMITED
Registration no: 01070170 **VAT No.:** GB 277 8026 29
Date established: 1972 **Turnover:** Up to £250,000
No.of Employees: 21 - 50 **Product Groups:** 36, 46

Date of Accounts	Dec 11	Dec 10	Dec 09
Sales Turnover	15	14m	11m
Pre Tax Profit/Loss	1	61	245
Working Capital	1	528	524
Fixed Assets	N/A	101	72
Current Assets	4	4m	3m
Current Liabilities	1	697	591

Widney Leisure Ltd
5 Alfred Court Saxon Business Park Hanbury Road, Stoke Prior, Bromsgrove, B60 4AD
Tel: 01527-577800 **Fax:** 01527-577900
E-mail: david.jones@imperial-fires.co.uk
Website: http://www.widney-leisure.co.uk
Bank(s): Barclays
Directors: K. Cowie (Dir), N. Beardsley (Dir), D. Jones (Co Sec)
Ultimate Holding Company: CARVER GROUP LIMITED
Immediate Holding Company: WIDNEY LEISURE LIMITED
Registration no: 02558737 **Date established:** 1990 **Turnover:** £2m - £5m
No.of Employees: 21 - 50 **Product Groups:** 38, 40, 63

Date of Accounts	Jul 11	Jul 10	Jul 09
Sales Turnover	3m	4m	3m
Pre Tax Profit/Loss	7	402	78
Working Capital	943	936	641
Fixed Assets	72	83	93
Current Assets	1m	2m	1m
Current Liabilities	137	301	156

Worlifts Ltd
Guilds House Sandy Lane, Wildmoor, Bromsgrove, B61 0QU
Tel: 0121-460 1113 **Fax:** 0121-525 1022
E-mail: info@worlifts.co.uk
Website: http://www.worlifts.co.uk
Bank(s): HSBC. Birmingham
Directors: J. Worley (MD), P. Smith (Sales)
Immediate Holding Company: WORLIFTS LIMITED
Registration no: 01282246 **VAT No.:** GB 300 0964 11
Date established: 1976 **Turnover:** £250,000 - £500,000
No.of Employees: 21 - 50 **Product Groups:** 39, 40, 45, 67

Date of Accounts	Oct 11	Oct 10	Oct 09
Working Capital	93	35	40
Fixed Assets	92	102	74
Current Assets	876	565	615

Droitwich

A W S Turner Fain
Roman Acre House West Bank Ten Acres, Berry Hill Industrial Estate, Droitwich, WR9 9AE
Tel: 01905-774267 **Fax:** 01905-775565
E-mail: info@turnerfainltd.co.uk
Directors: D. Nebett (Dir)
Ultimate Holding Company: AWS GROUP PLC
Immediate Holding Company: A W S GROUP P.L.C.
Registration no: 01679056 **VAT No.:** GB 641 0667 56
Turnover: £2m - £5m **No.of Employees:** 1 - 10 **Product Groups:** 26, 52

Date of Accounts	May 08	May 07	May 06
Sales Turnover	4286	4491	3733
Pre Tax Profit/Loss	217	278	210
Working Capital	108	120	121
Fixed Assets	39	20	25
Current Assets	953	1301	1188
Current Liabilities	845	1181	1066
Total Share Capital	100	100	100
ROCE% (Return on Capital Employed)	147.7	199.3	143.3
ROT% (Return on Turnover)	5.1	6.2	5.6

Advance Weighing Systems
15 Pridzor Road, Droitwich, WR9 8LQ
Tel: 01905-799205
Directors: M. O'connell (Prop)
Date established: 2006 **No.of Employees:** 1 - 10 **Product Groups:** 38, 42

Bettridge Turner & Partners
Orchard House 2 Victoria Square, Droitwich, WR9 8DS
Tel: 01905-794784 **Fax:** 01905-774425
Website: http://www.bt-p.co.uk
Managers: R. Wellands (Mgr)
Immediate Holding Company: DROITWICH MRI LIMITED
Registration no: 04028383 **Date established:** 1995
No.of Employees: 1 - 10 **Product Groups:** 35

Date of Accounts	Dec 11	Dec 09	Dec 08
Working Capital	-14	11	12
Fixed Assets	15	220	220
Current Assets	3	12	13

Cherox Precision Engineering
Unit 25d North Bank, Berry Hill Industrial Estate, Droitwich, WR9 9AU
Tel: 01905-826235 **Fax:** 01905-826236
Website: http://www.cherox.co.uk
Directors: J. Wild (Prop)
Immediate Holding Company: CHEROX (JW) PRECISION ENGINEERING COMPANY LIMITED
Registration no: 05941097 **Date established:** 2006
Turnover: £500,000 - £1m **No.of Employees:** 1 - 10 **Product Groups:** 35, 48, 84, 85

Date of Accounts	Dec 08	Dec 11	Dec 10
Sales Turnover	707	N/A	N/A
Pre Tax Profit/Loss	103	N/A	N/A
Working Capital	-7	33	11
Fixed Assets	154	102	96
Current Assets	109	61	73

Chess Plastics Ltd
2 George Baylis Road Berry Hill Industrial Estate, Droitwich, WR9 9RB
Tel: 01905-794405 **Fax:** 01905-794495
E-mail: gareth@chessplastics.co.uk
Website: http://www.chessplastics.co.uk
Bank(s): Lloyds TSB Bank plc
Directors: G. Olden (MD), G. Olden (Fin)
Managers: T. Olden (Purch Mgr)
Immediate Holding Company: CHESS PLASTICS LIMITED
Registration no: 00931102 **VAT No.:** GB 207 7441 71
Date established: 1968 **Turnover:** £5m - £10m
No.of Employees: 51 - 100 **Product Groups:** 30

Date of Accounts	Mar 11	Mar 10	Mar 09
Working Capital	232	263	53
Fixed Assets	1m	814	938
Current Assets	2m	1m	975
Current Liabilities	N/A	166	N/A

Doidge Fastenings
Unit 1-2 Berry Hill Industrial Estate George Baylis Road, Berry Hill Industrial Estate, Droitwich, WR9 9RB
Tel: 01905-779448 **Fax:** 0845-078 0334
E-mail: info@doidge.com
Website: http://www.doidge.com
Managers: P. Heim (Chief Mgr)
Ultimate Holding Company: RYV INVESTMENTS
Registration no: 00573452 **VAT No.:** GB 248 1624 59
Turnover: £1m - £2m **No.of Employees:** 11 - 20 **Product Groups:** 35

Dopag UK Ltd
Rylands Business Centre Rylands Lane, Elmley Lovett, Droitwich, WR9 0PT
Tel: 01299-250740 **Fax:** 01299-250860
E-mail: uksales@dopag.co.uk
Website: http://www.dopag.co.uk
Managers: D. Holyhead (Chief Mgr)
Immediate Holding Company: DOPAG (U.K.) LIMITED
Registration no: 04296994 **Date established:** 2001
No.of Employees: 1 - 10 **Product Groups:** 36, 38, 40, 42, 84

Date of Accounts	Dec 11	Dec 10	Dec 09
Working Capital	254	230	192
Fixed Assets	11	15	9
Current Assets	428	438	372

Droitwich Plastics Ltd
Unit 14 Wassage Way, Hampton Lovett, Droitwich, WR9 0NX
Tel: 01905-7969709 **Fax:** 01905-796067
Directors: P. Jordan (Fin), B. Jordan (MD)
Immediate Holding Company: DROITWICH PLASTICS LIMITED
Registration no: 03044920 **Date established:** 1995
Turnover: Up to £250,000 **No.of Employees:** 1 - 10 **Product Groups:** 30

Date of Accounts	Mar 12	Mar 11	Mar 10
Working Capital	N/A	-3	-0
Fixed Assets	2	2	1
Current Assets	18	9	9
Current Liabilities	10	9	7

Droitwich Roofing & Building Specialist
George Baylis Road Berry Hill Industrial Estate, Droitwich, WR9 9RB
Tel: 01905-778120 **Fax:** 01905-774900
E-mail: droitwichroofing@lineone.net
Website: http://www.lineone.net
Managers: K. Dobbs (Mgr)
Immediate Holding Company: DROITWICH ROOFING AND BUILDING SPECIALISTS LIMITED
Registration no: 03142789 **Date established:** 1996
No.of Employees: 1 - 10 **Product Groups:** 23, 30, 52, 66

Date of Accounts	Jan 11	Jan 10	Jan 09
Working Capital	61	71	-7
Fixed Assets	193	178	158
Current Assets	217	149	156

Exova
Unit 6-7 Furlong Business Centre The Furlong, Berry Hill Industrial Estate, Droitwich, WR9 9AH
Tel: 01905-774861 **Fax:** 01905-776598
E-mail: droitwich@exova.com
Website: http://www.exova.com
Managers: S. Smith (Ops Mgr)
Ultimate Holding Company: ROWAN TECHNOLOGIES INC (USA)
Immediate Holding Company: INDUCTOTHERM EUROPE LIMITED
Registration no: 00519057 **VAT No.:** GB 553 5266 38
Date established: 1936 **Turnover:** £2m - £5m **No.of Employees:** 11 - 20
Product Groups: 39, 51, 54, 84, 85

Date of Accounts	Dec 11	Dec 10	Dec 09
Sales Turnover	18m	15m	21m
Pre Tax Profit/Loss	4m	4m	2m
Working Capital	6m	6m	6m
Fixed Assets	2m	2m	2m
Current Assets	11m	11m	10m
Current Liabilities	5m	5m	3m

1st Call Stairways
4 De Wyche Road Wychbold, Droitwich, WR9 7PL
Tel: 01527-861733 **Fax:** 01527-861733
Website: http://www.1stcallstairways.co.uk
Directors: D. Eveson (Prop)
No.of Employees: 1 - 10 **Product Groups:** 26, 35

Fisher Alvin Ltd
Unit 102 Pointon Way, Stonebridge Cross Business Park, Droitwich, WR9 0LW
Tel: 01905-779944 **Fax:** 01905-779133
E-mail: info@fisheralvin.com
Website: http://www.fisheralvin.com
Bank(s): Lloyds TSB Bank plc
Directors: A. Blackwell (MD)
Managers: D. Blackwell (Mgr)
Registration no: 00133584 **VAT No.:** GB 109 8539 45
Turnover: £1m - £2m **No.of Employees:** 21 - 50 **Product Groups:** 35, 36

Date of Accounts	Mar 10	Mar 09	Mar 08
Working Capital	-849	-837	-827
Fixed Assets	876	876	876

Goodrick Gear Co. Ltd
Lazygraze Hadzor, Droitwich, WR9 7DR
Tel: 01905-826076 **Fax:** 01905-826076
E-mail: sales@goodrickgear.co.uk
Website: http://www.goodrickgear.co.uk
Directors: L. Pickerill (Dir), D. Pickerill (Co Sec)
Immediate Holding Company: GOODRICK GEAR COMPANY LIMITED
Registration no: 00521861 **VAT No.:** GB 276 9632 11
Date established: 1953 **Turnover:** Up to £250,000
No.of Employees: 1 - 10 **Product Groups:** 25, 30, 35, 40, 66

Date of Accounts	Mar 11	Mar 10	Mar 09
Working Capital	78	77	84
Fixed Assets	9	10	13
Current Assets	109	98	98

Hydrair Ltd
Berry Hill Berry Hill Industrial Estate, Droitwich, WR9 9AB
Tel: 01905-772302 **Fax:** 01905-770309
E-mail: sales@hydrair-systems.com
Website: http://www.hydrair-systems.com
Bank(s): Midland Bank, Sheffield
Directors: J. Fletcher (Dir)
Managers: J. Tubes (Fin Mgr)
Ultimate Holding Company: LINTER HOLDINGS LIMITED
Immediate Holding Company: HYDRAIR LIMITED
Registration no: 06078286 **Date established:** 2007 **Turnover:** £2m - £5m
No.of Employees: 11 - 20 **Product Groups:** 40

Date of Accounts	Dec 11	Dec 10	Dec 09
Sales Turnover	821	1m	1m
Pre Tax Profit/Loss	-90	35	93
Working Capital	-400	-344	-391
Fixed Assets	7	10	20
Current Assets	562	708	614
Current Liabilities	81	102	70

Inductotherm Europe Ltd
The Furlong Berry Hill Industrial Estate, Droitwich, WR9 9AH
Tel: 01905-795100 **Fax:** 01905-795138
E-mail: sales@inductotherm.co.uk
Website: http://www.inductotherm.co.uk
Bank(s): HSBC, Droitwich
Directors: D. Heavey (Sales), J. Fletcher (Fin), S. Hill (MD)
Managers: D. Hitchiner, S. Lewis (Buyer)
Ultimate Holding Company: ROWAN TECHNOLOGIES INC (USA)
Immediate Holding Company: INDUCTOTHERM EUROPE LIMITED
Registration no: 00316229 **VAT No.:** GB 274 3062 68
Date established: 1936 **Turnover:** £10m - £20m
No.of Employees: 51 - 100 **Product Groups:** 40, 46

Date of Accounts	Dec 11	Dec 10	Dec 09
Sales Turnover	18m	15m	21m
Pre Tax Profit/Loss	4m	4m	2m
Working Capital	6m	6m	6m
Fixed Assets	2m	2m	2m
Current Assets	11m	11m	10m
Current Liabilities	5m	5m	3m

Koito
Hampton Lovett Industrial Estate Kingswood Road, Hampton Lovett, Droitwich, WR9 0QH
Tel: 01905-790800 **Fax:** 01905-798432
E-mail: david.bevan@koito-europe.co.uk
Website: http://www.koito-europe.co.uk
Bank(s): The Royal Bank of Scotland
Directors: D. Bevan (Co Sec)
Managers: J. Donnelly (Personnel), D. Slater (Sales Prom Mgr), D. Ologhlin, M. Winnall (Purch Mgr)
Ultimate Holding Company: KOITO MANUFACTURING CO LIMITED (JAPAN)
Immediate Holding Company: KOITO EUROPE LIMITED
Registration no: 00945580 **VAT No.:** GB 274 9286 16
Date established: 1969 **Turnover:** £20m - £50m
No.of Employees: 251 - 500 **Product Groups:** 39, 68

Date of Accounts	Dec 11	Dec 10	Dec 09
Sales Turnover	35m	37m	37m
Pre Tax Profit/Loss	-5m	-7m	-5m
Working Capital	8m	-8m	-33m
Fixed Assets	7m	8m	10m
Current Assets	19m	13m	12m
Current Liabilities	894	14m	740

Macleod Engineering
23 North Street Industrial Estate, Droitwich, WR9 8JB
Tel: 01905-794578 **Fax:** 01905-794965
Directors: N. Macleod (Prop)
VAT No.: GB 488 1372 16 **Date established:** 1988
No.of Employees: 1 - 10 **Product Groups:** 46

Merit Badge & Regalia Company Ltd
Unit 4 George Baylis Road, Berry Hill Industrial Estate, Droitwich, WR9 9RB
Tel: 01905-791350 **Fax:** 0121-440 1037
E-mail: sales@meritbadge.co.uk
Website: http://www.meritbadge.co.uk
Directors: P. Fabel (MD), P. Sabel (Fin)
Immediate Holding Company: THE MERIT BADGE & REGALIA COMPANY LIMITED
Registration no: 02644046 **Date established:** 1991
No.of Employees: 11 - 20 **Product Groups:** 34, 49, 65

Date of Accounts	Aug 11	Aug 10	Aug 09
Working Capital	62	70	77
Fixed Assets	42	70	79
Current Assets	228	472	383
Current Liabilities	N/A	N/A	119

Meta System UPS Ltd
Oakmoore Court Kingswood Road, Hampton Lovett, Droitwich, WR9 0QH
Tel: 01905-791700 **Fax:** 01905-791701
E-mail: ruggieroannunziata@metasystemups.co.uk
Website: http://www.metasystem.co.uk
Immediate Holding Company: META SYSTEM UPS LIMITED
Registration no: 05175047 **Date established:** 2004
Turnover: £75m - £125m **No.of Employees:** 1 - 10 **Product Groups:** 37, 44, 67

Date of Accounts	Dec 07	Dec 06	Dec 05
Working Capital	29	-2	-2
Fixed Assets	1	1	2
Current Assets	69	29	19
Current Liabilities	40	31	21

Motovario Ltd
Rushock Trading Estate Rushock, Droitwich, WR9 0NR
Tel: 01299-250859 **Fax:** 01299-251493
E-mail: sales@motovario.co.uk
Website: http://www.motovario.co.uk
Bank(s): National Westminster Bank Plc
Directors: I. Partridge (Dir)
Ultimate Holding Company: MOTOVARIO SPA (ITALY)
Immediate Holding Company: MOTOVARIO LIMITED
Registration no: 02523314 **VAT No.:** GB 551 5595 31
Date established: 1990 **Turnover:** £2m - £5m **No.of Employees:** 11 - 20
Product Groups: 35, 37, 40, 43, 45

Date of Accounts	Dec 11	Dec 10	Dec 09
Working Capital	-445	-557	-761
Fixed Assets	311	353	343
Current Assets	2m	2m	2m

Mountfield C N C Ltd
Unit 2 Berry Hill Industrial Estate West Stone, Berry Hill Industrial Estate, Droitwich, WR9 9AS
Tel: 01905-776637
E-mail: phil.dix@btconnect.com

see next page

Mountfield C N C Ltd - Cont'd

Managers: M. Williams (Mgr)
Immediate Holding Company: MOUNTFIELD CNC LTD
Registration no: 05410020 **Date established:** 2005 **Turnover:** £2m - £5m
No.of Employees: 1 - 10 **Product Groups:** 35

Date of Accounts	Mar 12	Mar 11	Mar 10
Working Capital	-166	-147	-138
Fixed Assets	272	256	285
Current Assets	133	144	162

Nu Way

PO Box 1, Droitwich, WR9 8NA
Tel: 01905-794331 **Fax:** 01905-794017
E-mail: info@nu-way.co.uk
Website: http://www.nu-way.co.uk
Bank(s): Lloyds
Managers: C. Rees (Comptroller), L. Snape (Personnel), R. Hancox, N. Cooney (Purch Mgr), C. Allen (Tech Serv Mgr), M. Baker
Ultimate Holding Company: INTER RESTED LIMITED
Immediate Holding Company: ENERTECH LIMITED
Registration no: 00299044 **VAT No.:** GB 765 3297 02
Date established: 1935 **Turnover:** £10m - £20m
No.of Employees: 51 - 100 **Product Groups:** 40

Date of Accounts	Dec 11	Dec 10	Dec 09
Sales Turnover	11m	10m	10m
Pre Tax Profit/Loss	447	47	-7
Working Capital	119	-190	-268
Fixed Assets	122	110	155
Current Assets	5m	4m	4m
Current Liabilities	595	889	659

P F C Group Ltd

Roman Way Business Centre Berry Hill Industrial Estate, Droitwich, WR9 9AJ
Tel: 01905-797000 **Fax:** 01905-797274
E-mail: alistair.t@pfcgroup.co.uk
Website: http://www.pfcgroup.co.uk
Directors: A. Trow (MD), C. Trow (Co Sec)
Ultimate Holding Company: DURMAST GROUP LIMITED
Immediate Holding Company: PFC GROUP LIMITED
Registration no: 00870592 **Date established:** 1966
No.of Employees: 1 - 10 **Product Groups:** 27, 28

Date of Accounts	Dec 11	Dec 10	Dec 09
Working Capital	1m	1m	1m
Fixed Assets	130	145	164
Current Assets	3m	3m	3m

Pallisers Of Hereford Ltd

Mere Green Hanbury, Droitwich, WR9 7DZ
Tel: 01527-821194 **Fax:** 01527-821195
Website: http://www.pallisers.co.uk
Directors: D. Palliser (MD)
Immediate Holding Company: PALLISERS OF HEREFORD LTD.
Registration no: 02850220 **Date established:** 1993
No.of Employees: 1 - 10 **Product Groups:** 41

Date of Accounts	Dec 11	Dec 10	Dec 09
Working Capital	397	426	489
Fixed Assets	151	160	155
Current Assets	2m	2m	2m

Pipe Supports Ltd

Unit 22 West Stone Berry Hill Industrial Estate, Droitwich, WR9 9AS
Tel: 01905-795500 **Fax:** 01905-794126
E-mail: sjb@pipesupports.com
Website: http://www.pipesupports.com
Directors: S. Barry (Tech Serv)
Managers: D. Cox (Purch Mgr), D. Abbott (Fin Mgr)
Ultimate Holding Company: HILL & SMITH HOLDINGS PLC
Immediate Holding Company: PIPE SUPPORTS LIMITED
Registration no: 00926644 **Date established:** 1968
Turnover: £10m - £20m **No.of Employees:** 51 - 100 **Product Groups:** 35

Date of Accounts	Dec 11	Dec 10	Dec 09
Sales Turnover	19m	8m	16m
Pre Tax Profit/Loss	634	-386	2m
Working Capital	2m	2m	2m
Fixed Assets	2m	2m	2m
Current Assets	10m	4m	5m
Current Liabilities	1m	458	1m

Plex Display Ltd

The Furlong Berry Hill Industrial Estate, Droitwich, WR9 9BG
Tel: 01905-795432 **Fax:** 01905-791888
E-mail: enquiries@plexdisplay.com
Website: http://www.plexdisplay.com
Bank(s): National Westminster Bank Plc
Directors: O. Boylan (MD), S. Ryman (Fin), M. Senatore (Pers)
Managers: T. Burbury (Tech Serv Mgr), M. Wheatley
Ultimate Holding Company: REDDIPLEX 2011 LTD
Immediate Holding Company: PLEX DISPLAY LIMITED
Registration no: 05104548 **VAT No.:** GB 488 0557 09
Date established: 2004 **Turnover:** £5m - £10m **No.of Employees:** 11 - 20
Product Groups: 26, 30, 35, 37, 49, 52, 67, 81, 83, 84

Date of Accounts	Apr 11	Apr 10	Apr 09
Working Capital	482	630	678
Current Assets	1m	2m	2m

Potter Group Logistics

Site 7 Kidderminster Road Cutnall Green, Rushock, Droitwich, WR9 0NS
Tel: 01299-851441 **Fax:** 01299-851390
E-mail: droitwich@pottergroup.co.uk
Website: http://www.pottergroup.co.uk
Directors: J. Thomson (MD)
Managers: P. Reed (I.T. Exec), P. Reed (Tech Serv Mgr), S. Conrad (Cust Serv Mgr)
Ultimate Holding Company: THE POTTER GROUP (HOLDINGS) PLC
Immediate Holding Company: ADVANCED GLASS PRODUCTS (WORCESTER) LIMITED
Registration no: 01392251 **Date established:** 2010
No.of Employees: 51 - 100 **Product Groups:** 07, 45, 72, 77, 80, 84

Q Com Outsourcing Ltd

3 Hampton Park Wassage Way, Hampton Lovett, Droitwich, WR9 0NX
Tel: 01905-827650 **Fax:** 01905-827626
E-mail: sales@qcom.co.uk
Website: http://www.qcom.co.uk
Bank(s): Barclays
Directors: N. Anderson (MD)
Immediate Holding Company: QCOM OUTSOURCING LTD
Registration no: 01372621 **VAT No.:** GB 294 6893 93
Date established: 1978 **No.of Employees:** 11 - 20 **Product Groups:** 44

Date of Accounts	Oct 10	Apr 12	Apr 11
Working Capital	-66	61	11
Fixed Assets	223	132	180
Current Assets	731	661	800

R S Hydro Ltd

Churchfield House Salwarpe, Droitwich, WR9 0AH
Tel: 01905-774002 **Fax:** 01905-778443
E-mail: info@rshydro.co.uk
Website: http://www.rshydro.co.uk
Directors: R. Stevens (MD)
Immediate Holding Company: RS HYDRO LIMITED
Registration no: 03452628 **Date established:** 1997
No.of Employees: 1 - 10 **Product Groups:** 38, 85

Date of Accounts	Mar 12	Mar 11	Mar 10
Working Capital	997	925	678
Fixed Assets	206	214	175
Current Assets	1m	1m	968

Recaf Equipment Ltd

Stone Cross Business Park Pointon Way, Hampton Lovett, Droitwich, WR9 0LW
Tel: 01905-823456 **Fax:** 01905-797564
E-mail: brian.merriman@recaf.co.uk
Website: http://www.recaf.co.uk
Bank(s): Barclays, Worcester
Directors: B. Merriman (Prop)
Immediate Holding Company: RECAF EQUIPMENT LIMITED
Registration no: 01187727 **VAT No.:** GB 299 0075 30
Date established: 1974 **Turnover:** £5m - £10m
No.of Employees: 51 - 100 **Product Groups:** 49, 65

Date of Accounts	Apr 12	Apr 11	Apr 10
Sales Turnover	N/A	N/A	6m
Pre Tax Profit/Loss	N/A	N/A	255
Working Capital	-106	-151	-702
Fixed Assets	2m	2m	2m
Current Assets	1m	1m	1m
Current Liabilities	N/A	N/A	487

Reddiplex Ltd

The Furlong Berry Hill Industrial Estate, Droitwich, WR9 9BG
Tel: 01905-795432 **Fax:** 01905-795757
E-mail: reception@reddiplex.com
Website: http://www.reddiplex.com
Bank(s): National Westminster Bank Plc
Directors: S. Ryman (Fin), M. Senatore (Pers), T. Young (Fin), O. Boylan (MD), F. Lancina (Mkt Research)
Managers: K. Long (Mktg Serv Mgr), T. Burbury (Tech Serv Mgr)
Ultimate Holding Company: REDDIPLEX 2011 LTD
Immediate Holding Company: REDDIGLAZE LIMITED
Registration no: 01387347 **Date established:** 1978 **Turnover:** £5m - £10m
No.of Employees: 101 - 250 **Product Groups:** 29, 30

Date of Accounts	Apr 11	Apr 10	Apr 01
Working Capital	9	9	9
Current Assets	9	9	9

Severn Business Interiors Ltd

Unit 4 Kidderminster Road, Ombersley, Droitwich, WR9 0JH
Tel: 01905-621691 **Fax:** 01905-621345
E-mail: sales@shirebusinessinteriors.co.uk
Website: http://www.shirebusinessinteriors.co.uk
Directors: N. Mooney (MD)
Immediate Holding Company: SEVERN BUSINESS INTERIORS LIMITED
Registration no: 06919349 **VAT No.:** GB 614 4951 42
Date established: 2009 **Turnover:** Up to £250,000
No.of Employees: 1 - 10 **Product Groups:** 26, 38, 49, 52, 67, 80, 84

Date of Accounts	May 11	May 10
Sales Turnover	79	65
Pre Tax Profit/Loss	-3	2
Working Capital	-9	-4
Fixed Assets	21	6
Current Assets	6	7
Current Liabilities	2	N/A

Stour Precision Tools Ltd

George Baylis Road Berry Hill Industrial Estate, Droitwich, WR9 9RB
Tel: 01905-773932 **Fax:** 01905-776434
E-mail: sales@sptwww.co.uk
Website: http://www.spt.uk.com
Bank(s): Lloyds Bank, Birmingham
Directors: C. Chaplin (MD), R. Chaplin (Fin)
Managers: S. Dalton (Chief Mgr)
Immediate Holding Company: STOUR PRECISION TOOLS LIMITED
Registration no: 00876483 **VAT No.:** 488 0637 11 **Date established:** 1966
Turnover: £2m - £5m **No.of Employees:** 21 - 50 **Product Groups:** 38, 46, 48

Date of Accounts	Feb 12	Feb 11	Feb 10
Working Capital	-182	54	81
Fixed Assets	545	292	276
Current Assets	3m	438	247

Swedish Steel

De Salis Court De Salis Drive, Hampton Lovett, Droitwich, WR9 0QE
Tel: 01905-795794 **Fax:** 01905-794736
E-mail: ssabuk@ssab.com
Website: http://www.swedishsteel.co.uk
Directors: A. Lagerqvist (MD), H. Hedman (Dir), S. Rost (Co Sec)
Managers: G. Glace (Mgr), J. Gregory (Sales Prom Mgr), J. Smale (Chief Mgr), C. Nash (Chief Acct), P. Cartwright (Mgr)
Ultimate Holding Company: SSAB SVENSKT STAL AB (SWEDEN)
Immediate Holding Company: KITHEAD LIMITED
Registration no: 01071388 **Date established:** 1985 **Turnover:** £1m - £2m
No.of Employees: 1 - 10 **Product Groups:** 34, 42, 46

Egbert H Taylor & Co. Ltd

Oak Park Rylands Lane, Elmley Lovett, Droitwich, WR9 0QZ
Tel: 01299-251333 **Fax:** 01299-254142
E-mail: david.williams@taylorbins.co.uk
Website: http://www.taylorbins.co.uk
Directors: D. Williams (MD)
Managers: J. Lacey (Personnel), T. Biddulph (Mktg Serv Mgr), C. Lewis, R. Davies (Buyer), R. Norgrove (Tech Serv Mgr)
Ultimate Holding Company: TAYLOR CONTINENTAL GROUP LTD
Immediate Holding Company: EGBERT H. TAYLOR & COMPANY LIMITED
Registration no: 00718441 **Date established:** 1962
Turnover: £20m - £50m **No.of Employees:** 101 - 250 **Product Groups:** 42

Date of Accounts	Jun 11	Jun 10	Jun 09
Sales Turnover	22m	20m	23m
Pre Tax Profit/Loss	2m	2m	3m
Working Capital	13m	11m	9m
Fixed Assets	1m	1m	1m
Current Assets	19m	16m	16m
Current Liabilities	1m	977	808

Teer Coatings

West Stone House West Stone Berry Hill Industrial Estate, Droitwich, WR9 9AS
Tel: 01905-827550 **Fax:** 0870-220 3911
E-mail: enquiries@teercoatings.co.uk
Website: http://www.teercoatings.co.uk
Directors: P. Teer (Fin)
Managers: D. Griffin (Purch Mgr), B. Parker, A. Byrne (Personnel), G. Dyson (Mktg Serv Mgr), M. Gattinger (Site Co-ord)
Immediate Holding Company: TEER COATINGS LIMITED
Registration no: 01643376 **VAT No.:** GB 376 1455 39
Date established: 1982 **Turnover:** £2m - £5m **No.of Employees:** 51 - 100
Product Groups: 29, 30, 31, 32, 33, 48

Date of Accounts	Jul 10	Jul 09	Jan 12
Sales Turnover	3m	4m	3m
Pre Tax Profit/Loss	94	-361	-132
Working Capital	2m	2m	1m
Fixed Assets	2m	1m	2m
Current Assets	2m	3m	2m
Current Liabilities	265	798	351

Vax Ltd

Kingswood Road Hampton Lovett, Droitwich, WR9 0QH
Tel: 01905-795959 **Fax:** 01905-794804
E-mail: slawson@vax.oxford.co.uk
Website: http://www.vax.co.uk
Directors: K. Daines (Pers), S. Lawson (MD), M. Raybould (Fin)
Managers: N. Martin, A. Plimmer, R. Dale
Ultimate Holding Company: TECHTRONIC INDUSTRIES CO LTD (HONG KONG)
Immediate Holding Company: VAX LIMITED
Registration no: 01341840 **Date established:** 1977
Turnover: £50m - £75m **No.of Employees:** 101 - 250
Product Groups: 32, 40, 63, 66

Date of Accounts	Dec 11	Dec 10	Dec 09
Sales Turnover	84m	68m	61m
Pre Tax Profit/Loss	118	7m	4m
Working Capital	18m	15m	9m
Fixed Assets	5m	7m	3m
Current Assets	45m	39m	33m
Current Liabilities	3m	2m	2m

Wych Display

1 Old Market Court High Street, Droitwich, WR9 8ES
Tel: 01905-795165 **Fax:** 01905-795155
E-mail: robin@wychdisplay.co.uk
Website: http://www.wychdisplay.co.uk
Directors: R. Jones (Prop)
Date established: 1999 **No.of Employees:** 1 - 10 **Product Groups:** 26, 49, 83

Evesham

Abssac Ltd

Unit E1a Enterprise Way Vale Park, Evesham, WR11 1GS
Tel: 01386-421005 **Fax:** 01386-831500
E-mail: sales@abssac.co.uk
Website: http://www.abssac.co.uk
Directors: K. Easton (Fin), S. Cattle (MD)
Immediate Holding Company: ABSSAC LIMITED
Registration no: 01677177 **Date established:** 1982
Turnover: £500,000 - £1m **No.of Employees:** 1 - 10 **Product Groups:** 35, 38, 46

Date of Accounts	Mar 12	Mar 11	Mar 10
Working Capital	246	213	178
Fixed Assets	38	35	28
Current Assets	446	406	338

Active Learning & Development

Horizons House Vine Street, Evesham, WR11 4RE
Tel: 01386-422244 **Fax:** 01386-423324
E-mail: gill_green@aldltd.co.uk
Website: http://www.aldltd.co.uk
Directors: G. Green (Dir)
Ultimate Holding Company: AL & D LIMITED
Immediate Holding Company: ACTIVE LEARNING & DEVELOPMENT LIMITED
Registration no: 02539519 **Date established:** 1990
No.of Employees: 1 - 10 **Product Groups:** 86

Date of Accounts	May 11	May 10	May 08
Working Capital	312	304	188
Fixed Assets	145	148	155
Current Assets	527	510	364

Alesco Fabrications Ltd

162 Pershore Road, Evesham, WR11 2PJ
Tel: 01386-48357 **Fax:** 01386-44357
Directors: L. James (MD)
Date established: 1978 **No.of Employees:** 1 - 10 **Product Groups:** 46, 48

Allen Fabrications Ltd

Davies Road Four Pools Industrial Estate, Evesham, WR11 1DR
Tel: 01386-47277 **Fax:** 01386- 765450
E-mail: info@allenfabs.co.uk
Website: http://www.allenfabs.co.uk
Bank(s): HSBC Bank plc
Directors: B. Sharp (Ch), A. Berryman (MD)
Managers: A. Onions
Immediate Holding Company: ALLEN FABRICATIONS LIMITED
Registration no: 00750465 **VAT No.:** GB 551 1200 03
Date established: 1963 **No.of Employees:** 21 - 50 **Product Groups:** 35

Date of Accounts	Mar 11	Mar 10	Mar 09
Working Capital	-776	-1m	-487
Fixed Assets	14m	15m	17m
Current Assets	836	1m	566

Associated Spring

Unit 4 Grosvenor Business Centre Vale Park, Evesham, WR11 1GS
Tel: 01386-443366 **Fax:** 01386-446669
E-mail: sales@assocspring.co.uk
Website: http://www.assocspring.co.uk

Bank(s): Lloyds, 29 High Street, Chippenham
Managers: A. Jacobs (Chief Mgr)
Immediate Holding Company: Barnes Group Inc (USA)
Registration no: 02042504 **Turnover:** £1m - £2m
No.of Employees: 11 - 20 **Product Groups:** 29, 34, 35, 36, 38, 39, 40, 43, 45, 48, 49, 66, 68, 85

Business Resources Development Ltd
Suite 7 Haddons Acre Station Road, Offenham, Evesham, WR11 8JJ
Tel: 01386-833535
E-mail: office@brdee.com
Website: http://www.brdee.com
Directors: K. Lewis (MD)
Ultimate Holding Company: EFI HOLDINGS LIMITED
Immediate Holding Company: BUSINESS RESOURCE DEVELOPMENT LTD
Registration no: 03788516 **Date established:** 1999 **Turnover:** £5m - £10m
No.of Employees: 1 - 10 **Product Groups:** 44

Date of Accounts	Jun 11	Jun 10	Jun 09
Working Capital	48	30	16
Fixed Assets	117	72	76
Current Assets	69	58	29
Current Liabilities	18	17	9

E M Coating Services
Enterprise Way Vale Park, Evesham, WR11 1GX
Tel: 01386-421444 **Fax:** 01386-765410
E-mail: emukenquiries@metalimprovement.com
Website: http://www.emcoatingsuk.com
Bank(s): HSBC
Managers: J. Cooke (Sales Prom Mgr), J. Masterson (Mgr), K. Adsett (Mats Contrlr), A. Stephens
Ultimate Holding Company: CURTISS WRIGHT
Immediate Holding Company: EVESHAM DIVISION OF METAL IMPROVEMENT CO. LLC
Date established: 2000 **Turnover:** £2m - £5m **No.of Employees:** 21 - 50
Product Groups: 29, 30, 31, 32, 48, 84

Euro Stock Springs Ltd
PO Box 133, Evesham, WR11 1ZJ
Tel: 01527-540600 **Fax:** 01527-540700
E-mail: rr@eurostock.co.uk
Website: http://www.eurostock.co.uk
Directors: A. Jacobs (MD)
Registration no: 00959034 **Turnover:** £250,000 - £500,000
No.of Employees: 1 - 10 **Product Groups:** 23, 25, 26, 27, 29, 30, 31, 33, 34, 35, 36, 38, 39, 40, 42, 43, 45, 46, 47, 48, 49, 66, 68, 85

Evenproducts Ltd
A46 Evesham Bypass, Evesham, WR11 4TU
Tel: 01386-760950 **Fax:** 01386-765404
E-mail: sales@evenproducts.com
Website: http://www.evenproducts.com
Bank(s): Lloyds
Directors: S. Jones (Sales)
Managers: K. Harrison (Tech Serv Mgr), R. Hughes
Ultimate Holding Company: POWERSHARE LIMITED
Immediate Holding Company: EVENPRODUCTS LIMITED
Registration no: 00836010 **VAT No.:** GB 274 1035 81
Date established: 1965 **Turnover:** £2m - £5m **No.of Employees:** 11 - 20
Product Groups: 29, 30, 35, 41, 67, 84

Date of Accounts	Oct 11	Oct 10	Oct 09
Working Capital	699	462	540
Fixed Assets	385	422	441
Current Assets	2m	2m	1m
Current Liabilities	298	N/A	N/A

Fibreknight Ltd
PO Box 245, Evesham, WR11 9AF
Tel: 01386-576148 **Fax:** 01386-442836
E-mail: john@fibreknight.co.uk
Website: http://www.fibreknight.co.uk
Directors: J. Cotterill (Tech Serv)
Immediate Holding Company: FIBREKNIGHT LIMITED
Registration no: 06699683 **Date established:** 2008
Turnover: Up to £250,000 **No.of Employees:** 1 - 10 **Product Groups:** 33, 37, 48

Indenco
Unit 35 St Richards Road Four Pools Industrial Estate, Evesham, WR11 1XJ
Tel: 01386-443946 **Fax:** 01386-45279
E-mail: enquiries@indenco.co.uk
Website: http://www.indenco.co.uk
Bank(s): National Westminster Bank Plc
Managers: M. Perri (Chief Mgr)
Ultimate Holding Company: UNIVERSAL COMPONENTS LTD
Immediate Holding Company: UNIVERSAL COMPONANTS LTD
Registration no: 01532208 **VAT No.:** GB 303 2425 13
Date established: 1971 **Turnover:** £500,000 - £1m
No.of Employees: 11 - 20 **Product Groups:** 46

K L Evesham Ltd
Weston Industrial Estate Honeybourne, Evesham, WR11 7QB
Tel: 01386-840566 **Fax:** 01386-841041
E-mail: paulh@klevesham.com
Website: http://www.klevesham.com
Directors: S. McConville (Fin)
Immediate Holding Company: K.L. (EVESHAM) LIMITED
Registration no: 02485021 **Date established:** 1990
No.of Employees: 1 - 10 **Product Groups:** 46, 48

Date of Accounts	Mar 11	Mar 10	Mar 09
Working Capital	98	96	14
Fixed Assets	71	78	71
Current Assets	307	314	206
Current Liabilities	55	N/A	N/A

LawsonJohnston
May Tree Cottage 32 Badsey Lane, Evesham, WR11 3EZ
Tel: 01386-424283 **Fax:** 01386-421292
E-mail: sales@lawson-johnston.co.uk
Website: http://www.lawson-johnston.co.uk
Directors: A. Davies (Dir)
Date established: 1999 **No.of Employees:** 1 - 10 **Product Groups:** 30, 36, 40, 63

Mifa Aluminium BV
67 Lavender Walk, Evesham, WR11 2LN
Tel: 07785-256537 **Fax:** 01386-421270
E-mail: info@mifa.nl
Website: http://www.mifa.nl
Directors: H. Zipman (MD), J. Zitman (Dir)
Managers: C. Stanley (Sales Prom Mgr)
Ultimate Holding Company: Aalberts Industries (Holland)
Immediate Holding Company: Mifa Aluminium BV (Netherlands)
Registration no: FC025206 **Turnover:** £20m - £50m
No.of Employees: 1 - 10 **Product Groups:** 30, 32, 34, 48

Millvale Ltd
Briar Close, Evesham, WR11 4JT
Tel: 01386-446661 **Fax:** 01386-442931
E-mail: sales@millvaleltd.co.uk
Website: http://www.millvaleltd.co.uk
Bank(s): Natwest
Directors: C. Millward (MD)
Immediate Holding Company: MILLVALE LIMITED
Registration no: 00590002 **VAT No.:** 274 3445 52 **Date established:** 1957
Turnover: £250,000 - £500,000 **No.of Employees:** 11 - 20
Product Groups: 27

Date of Accounts	Oct 11	Oct 10	Oct 09
Working Capital	127	145	200
Fixed Assets	526	320	331
Current Assets	332	269	335

Potter & Walker
Pershore Road, Evesham, WR11 2NB
Tel: 01386-47241 **Fax:** 01386-47241
E-mail: potterandwalker@yahoo.co.uk
Directors: L. Potter (Prop), D. Walker (Prop)
Date established: 1986 **No.of Employees:** 1 - 10 **Product Groups:** 36, 39, 40

Reliance Water Controls Ltd
Worcester Road, Evesham, WR11 4RA
Tel: 01386-712400 **Fax:** 01386-47028
E-mail: reception@rwc.co.uk
Website: http://www.rwc.co.uk
Bank(s): Lloyds
Managers: S. Pearson (Tech Serv Mgr), O. Johnson (Mktg Serv Mgr), W. Burman, G. Hay (Chief Mgr), I. Barker
Ultimate Holding Company: NATESKA PTY (AUSTRALIA)
Immediate Holding Company: RELIANCE WATER CONTROLS LIMITED
Registration no: 01223637 **Date established:** 1975
Turnover: £10m - £20m **No.of Employees:** 21 - 50 **Product Groups:** 36, 40

Date of Accounts	Jun 11	Jun 10	Jun 09
Sales Turnover	18m	16m	16m
Pre Tax Profit/Loss	2m	1m	1m
Working Capital	9m	9m	8m
Fixed Assets	518	520	435
Current Assets	12m	11m	10m
Current Liabilities	1m	703	539

Seed Marketing Communications Ltd
The Old School The Green, Rous Lench, Evesham, WR11 4UN
Tel: 01386-792700
E-mail: martin@seed-communications.com
Website: http://www.seed-communications.com
Directors: M. Thurley (MD)
Immediate Holding Company: SEED MARKETING COMMUNICATIONS LIMITED
Registration no: 05454455 **Date established:** 2005
Turnover: £250,000 - £500,000 **No.of Employees:** 11 - 20
Product Groups: 81

Date of Accounts	May 11	May 10	May 09
Working Capital	14	23	1
Fixed Assets	22	5	4
Current Assets	64	43	42
Current Liabilities	50	N/A	N/A

Spearhead Machinery
Station Road Salford Priors, Evesham, WR11 8SW
Tel: 01789-491860 **Fax:** 01789-778683
E-mail: gjones@spearhead.uk.com
Website: http://www.spearhead.uk.com
Directors: E. Madden (Fin)
Managers: G. Jones (Sales Admin), O. Needles (Personnel), M. Dyson (Tech Serv Mgr)
Ultimate Holding Company: ALAMO GROUP INC (USA)
Immediate Holding Company: SPEARHEAD MACHINERY LIMITED
Registration no: 02312982 **VAT No.:** GB 488 1878 81
Date established: 1988 **Turnover:** £5m - £10m **No.of Employees:** 1 - 10
Product Groups: 41, 67

Date of Accounts	Dec 11	Dec 10	Dec 09
Sales Turnover	8m	8m	6m
Pre Tax Profit/Loss	784	795	809
Working Capital	4m	4m	3m
Fixed Assets	29	20	37
Current Assets	5m	4m	4m
Current Liabilities	290	294	280

Transcend Group Ltd
Crab Apple Way Vale Park, Evesham, WR11 1GP
Tel: 01386-764900 **Fax:** 0870-705 2886
E-mail: info@transcend-group.com
Website: http://www.transcend-group.com
Directors: R. Edmonds (MD)
Immediate Holding Company: TRANSCEND GROUP LIMITED
Registration no: 04314346 **Date established:** 2001
Turnover: £500,000 - £1m **No.of Employees:** 11 - 20
Product Groups: 80, 86

Date of Accounts	Mar 11	Mar 10	Mar 09
Working Capital	14	8	-29
Fixed Assets	28	34	40
Current Assets	60	50	35

Watts Industries UK Ltd
Grosvenor Business Centre Enterprise Way, Vale Park, Evesham, WR11 1GA
Tel: 01386-446997 **Fax:** 01386-41923
E-mail: adams@wattsindustries.co.uk
Website: http://www.wattsindustries.com
Bank(s): Barclays
Directors: P. McEntee (Sales), S. Adams (Dir)
Managers: T. Hampton (Buyer), V. Harvey (Comptroller)
Ultimate Holding Company: WATTS WATER TECHNOLOGIES INC (USA)
Immediate Holding Company: WATTS INDUSTRIES UK LIMITED
Registration no: 02642521 **VAT No.:** GB 590 7580 12
Date established: 1991 **Turnover:** £5m - £10m **No.of Employees:** 11 - 20
Product Groups: 30, 36, 38, 40

Date of Accounts	Dec 11	Dec 10	Dec 09
Sales Turnover	6m	6m	6m
Pre Tax Profit/Loss	436	278	2m
Working Capital	830	1m	2m
Fixed Assets	5m	5m	5m
Current Assets	3m	3m	3m
Current Liabilities	437	382	282

Woodlands Generators
Crab Apple Way Vale Park, Evesham, WR11 1GP
Tel: 01386-442622 **Fax:** 01386-442740
E-mail: j.preece@woodlands-generators.com
Website: http://www.woodlands-generators.com
Directors: J. Preece (Dir)
Managers: J. Williams (Chief Mgr), S. Stayt (Cr Control)
Immediate Holding Company: WOODLANDS GENERATORS LIMITED
Registration no: 03812175 **Date established:** 1999 **Turnover:** £1m - £2m
No.of Employees: 11 - 20 **Product Groups:** 37, 40, 83

Date of Accounts	Mar 11	Mar 10	Mar 09
Working Capital	-2	-2	-2
Current Assets	34	34	34

Worcester Electrical Distributors Ltd
Unit 16 St Richards Road Four Pools Industrial Estate, Evesham, WR11 1XJ
Tel: 01386-422199 **Fax:** 01386-423477
E-mail: evesham@worcesterelectrical.co.uk
Website: http://www.swansons.co.uk
Managers: M. Rushton (Mgr)
Immediate Holding Company: WORCESTER ELECTRICAL DISTRIBUTORS LIMITED
Registration no: 02203536 **Date established:** 1987
No.of Employees: 1 - 10 **Product Groups:** 37, 38, 67

Date of Accounts	Mar 12	Mar 11	Mar 10
Sales Turnover	13m	11m	8m
Pre Tax Profit/Loss	583	252	-153
Working Capital	436	76	-192
Fixed Assets	249	231	307
Current Assets	5m	4m	3m
Current Liabilities	1m	192	1m

Wychavon Packaging
Honeybrook Shinehill Lane, South Littleton, Evesham, WR11 8TP
Tel: 01386-831349 **Fax:** 01386-834030
Directors: M. Woodford (Ptnr)
Date established: 1983 **No.of Employees:** 1 - 10 **Product Groups:** 38, 42

Kidderminster

A I S Sheet Metal Ltd
Hoo Farm Industrial Estate Worcester Road, Kidderminster, DY11 7RA
Tel: 01562-820700 **Fax:** 01562-829401
E-mail: enquiries@aissheetmetal.co.uk
Website: http://www.aissheetmetal.co.uk
Directors: P. Brannon (MD)
Ultimate Holding Company: A.I.S. (HOLDINGS) LIMITED
Immediate Holding Company: A.I.S.SHEET METAL LIMITED
Registration no: 01023962 **Date established:** 1971
Turnover: £500,000 - £1m **No.of Employees:** 11 - 20 **Product Groups:** 48

Date of Accounts	Sep 11	Sep 10	Sep 09
Working Capital	52	57	248
Fixed Assets	44	52	68
Current Assets	345	203	333

A P B Trading Ltd
Unit 38 Hartlebury Trading Estate Hartlebury, Kidderminster, DY10 4JB
Tel: 01299-250174 **Fax:** 01299-251752
E-mail: enquiries@apbtrading.co.uk
Website: http://www.apbtrading.co.uk
Directors: P. Bond (MD)
Immediate Holding Company: A.P.B. TRADING LIMITED
Registration no: 02081999 **Date established:** 1986
No.of Employees: 1 - 10 **Product Groups:** 39

Date of Accounts	Mar 12	Mar 11	Mar 10
Working Capital	109	123	163
Fixed Assets	77	77	81
Current Assets	221	278	317

Abzorboil Ltd
Robtec House High Street Cleobury Mortimer, Kidderminster, DY14 8DP
Tel: 01299-270179 **Fax:** 01299-271015
E-mail: ann.walker@abzorboil.com
Website: http://www.abzorboil.com
Directors: A. Walker (Fin)
Immediate Holding Company: ABZORBOIL LIMITED
Registration no: 06514143 **Date established:** 2008
No.of Employees: 1 - 10 **Product Groups:** 32, 40, 45, 54, 86

Date of Accounts	Mar 10	Mar 09
Working Capital	187	285
Fixed Assets	23	31
Current Assets	304	522

Adam Carpets Ltd
Birmingham Road, Kidderminster, DY10 2SH
Tel: 01562-822247 **Fax:** 01562-751471
E-mail: info@adamcarpets.com
Website: http://www.adamcarpets.com
Bank(s): Lloyds TSB Bank plc
Directors: A. Hardwick (Sales), C. Adam (MD), E. Prescott (Sales), P. Chell (Fin)
Managers: T. Ward
Immediate Holding Company: ADAM CARPETS LIMITED
Registration no: 01641463 **VAT No.:** GB 454 8810 28
Date established: 1982 **Turnover:** £5m - £10m
No.of Employees: 51 - 100 **Product Groups:** 23

Date of Accounts	Mar 11	Mar 10	Mar 09
Sales Turnover	9m	10m	11m
Pre Tax Profit/Loss	-350	-201	-995
Working Capital	3m	3m	3m
Fixed Assets	3m	4m	4m
Current Assets	4m	4m	4m
Current Liabilities	454	538	415

Agricultural Composites
171 Sutton Park Road, Kidderminster, DY11 6LF
Tel: 01562-630616
E-mail: agricultural-composites@hotmail.co.uk
Website: http://www.agricultural-composites.co.uk
Directors: J. Bogunicki (Prop)
Date established: 2006 **No.of Employees:** 1 - 10 **Product Groups:** 30

Air Tube Technologies Ltd
5 Hartlebury Trading Estate Hartlebury, Kidderminster, DY10 4JB
Tel: 01299-254254 **Fax:** 01299-254299
E-mail: sales@airtubegroup.co.uk
Website: http://www.airtubegroup.co.uk
Bank(s): National Westminster Bank Plc
Directors: G. Siddle (Dir)
Managers: M. Hussey
Immediate Holding Company: AIRTUBE TECHNOLOGIES LIMITED
Registration no: 06550607 **VAT No.:** GB 655 2819 18
Date established: 2008 **Turnover:** £5m - £10m **No.of Employees:** 21 - 50
Product Groups: 33, 36, 37, 45, 49, 67

Date of Accounts	Mar 09	Sep 11	Sep 10
Working Capital	1	560	75
Fixed Assets	1	8	5
Current Assets	1	1m	1m
Current Liabilities	N/A	N/A	292

Alatas Ltd
Arthur Drive Hoo Farm Industrial Estate, Kidderminster, DY11 7RA
Tel: 01562-747050 **Fax:** 01562-747053
E-mail: uk@alatas.com
Website: http://www.alatas.com
Directors: M. Dodwell (MD)
Managers: T. Monahan (Tech Serv Mgr), L. Broomhall, D. Barnaby (Parts Mgr)
Immediate Holding Company: ALATAS LIMITED
Registration no: 06236876 **Date established:** 2007 **Turnover:** £2m - £5m
No.of Employees: 21 - 50 **Product Groups:** 39, 45, 48, 51, 74, 80, 83

Amada UK Ltd
Spennells Valley Road, Kidderminster, DY10 1XS
Tel: 01562-749500 **Fax:** 01562-749510
E-mail: info@amada.co.uk
Website: http://www.amada.co.uk
Bank(s): Dai-Ichi Kangyo, Moorgate, London; National Westminster, Castle Street, Dudley, West Midlands.
Directors: G. Stainforth (Co Sec)
Managers: R. Cross (Fin Mgr), J. Jones (I.T. Exec), A. Crones (Sales & Mktg Mg), C. Driscoll
Ultimate Holding Company: AMADA CO LTD (JAPAN)
Immediate Holding Company: AMADA ESSEX LIMITED
Registration no: 03345205 **Date established:** 1997
Turnover: £20m - £50m **No.of Employees:** 51 - 100 **Product Groups:** 67

Date of Accounts	Dec 10	Dec 09	Dec 05
Working Capital	37	37	37
Current Assets	37	37	37

Amodil Supplies
Forest Park Cleobury Mortimer, Kidderminster, DY14 9BD
Tel: 01299-270771 **Fax:** 01299-270080
E-mail: sales@amodil.co.uk
Website: http://www.amodil.co.uk
Directors: C. Selly (Sales), S. Hector (Fin), W. Slingsby (MD)
Immediate Holding Company: AMODIL HOLDINGS LIMITED
Registration no: 01242469 **VAT No.:** GB 276 2737 27
Date established: 1976 **Turnover:** £20m - £50m
No.of Employees: 21 - 50 **Product Groups:** 34

Date of Accounts	May 12	May 11	May 10
Pre Tax Profit/Loss	118	279	64
Working Capital	2m	2m	1m
Fixed Assets	2m	2m	2m
Current Assets	3m	3m	1m
Current Liabilities	1m	1m	164

Ashland Specialties UK Ltd
Vale Industrial Estate, Kidderminster, DY11 7QU
Tel: 01562-821300 **Fax:** 01562-740785
E-mail: jgadd@ashland.com
Website: http://www.ashland.com
Bank(s): National Westminster Bank Plc
Managers: D. Lawson (Plant), B. Meddows (Personnel)
Ultimate Holding Company: ASHLAND INC (USA)
Immediate Holding Company: ASHLAND UK LIMITED
Registration no: 00830143 **VAT No.:** GB 551 2838 46
Date established: 1964 **Turnover:** £20m - £50m
No.of Employees: 21 - 50 **Product Groups:** 31

Date of Accounts	Sep 11	Sep 10	Sep 09
Sales Turnover	50m	70m	63m
Pre Tax Profit/Loss	9m	4m	-220
Working Capital	23m	15m	15m
Fixed Assets	7m	9m	10m
Current Assets	26m	25m	26m
Current Liabilities	1m	3m	2m

Babyjacks
Daguerre House Hoo Farm Industrial Estate Worcester Road, Kidderminster, DY11 7RA
Tel: 01562-741717
Website: http://www.babyjacks.co.uk
Directors: A. Ulyatt (Prop)
No.of Employees: 1 - 10 **Product Groups:** 24, 26, 61

Beakbane Ltd
Stourport Road, Kidderminster, DY11 7QT
Tel: 01562-820561 **Fax:** 01562-820560
E-mail: info@beakbane.co.uk
Website: http://www.beakbane.co.uk
Bank(s): Barclays, 66 Oxford Street, Kidderminster
Directors: M. Southwell (MD), B. Reeves (MD)
Managers: T. Daniels (Sales Prom Mgr), D. Bragg (Purch Mgr), C. Sheldon (Tech Serv Mgr)
Immediate Holding Company: BEAKBANE LIMITED
Registration no: 00534430 **Date established:** 1954 **Turnover:** £5m - £10m
No.of Employees: 101 - 250 **Product Groups:** 29, 36, 38, 39

Date of Accounts	Apr 11	Apr 10	Apr 09
Sales Turnover	5m	3m	6m
Pre Tax Profit/Loss	104	147	364
Working Capital	2m	2m	3m
Fixed Assets	1m	1m	2m
Current Assets	3m	3m	3m
Current Liabilities	414	334	455

Bentley Chemicals Ltd
Hoo Farm Industrial Estate Frederick Road, Kidderminster, DY11 7RA
Tel: 01562-515121 **Fax:** 01562-515847
E-mail: info@bentleychemicals.co.uk
Website: http://www.bentleychemicals.co.uk
Directors: C. Edwards (MD)
Ultimate Holding Company: BENTLEY CHEMICALS HOLDINGS LIMITED
Immediate Holding Company: BENTLEY CHEMICALS LIMITED
Registration no: 01351166 **VAT No.:** GB 299 1431 29
Date established: 1978 **Turnover:** £1m - £2m **No.of Employees:** 1 - 10
Product Groups: 24, 29, 30, 31, 32, 33, 38, 48, 89

Date of Accounts	Apr 12	Apr 11	Apr 10
Working Capital	120	94	17
Fixed Assets	159	218	187
Current Assets	1m	1m	958

Birmingham Barbed Tape Ltd
Unit 11 Hartlebury Trading Estate Hartlebury, Kidderminster, DY10 4JB
Tel: 01299-251770 **Fax:** 01299-251776
E-mail: rsmith@bbtltd.com
Website: http://www.birminghambarbedtape.co.uk
Directors: R. Smith (MD)
Ultimate Holding Company: GREENOCK HOLDINGS LIMITED
Immediate Holding Company: BIRMINGHAM BARBED TAPE LIMITED
Registration no: 02291462 **VAT No.:** GB 486 8936 70
Date established: 1988 **Turnover:** £2m - £5m **No.of Employees:** 1 - 10
Product Groups: 45, 66

Date of Accounts	Jun 11	Jun 10	Jun 09
Working Capital	853	421	1m
Fixed Assets	11	5	6
Current Assets	4m	3m	2m

Bond Worth
Townshend Works Puxton Lane, Kidderminster, DY11 5DF
Tel: 01562-745000 **Fax:** 01562-732827
E-mail: enquiries@bondworth.co.uk
Website: http://www.bondworth.co.uk
Directors: M. Oakes (MD)
Ultimate Holding Company: BOND WORTH HOLDINGS LTD (ANGUILLA)
Immediate Holding Company: BOND WORTH LIMITED
Registration no: 05028461 **Date established:** 2004 **Turnover:** £2m - £5m
No.of Employees: 1 - 10 **Product Groups:** 23

Date of Accounts	Aug 11	Aug 10	Aug 09
Working Capital	-133	-173	208
Fixed Assets	270	310	351
Current Assets	406	435	976

Boremasters
High Street Cleobury Mortimer, Kidderminster, DY14 8DS
Tel: 01299-270942 **Fax:** 01299-270212
E-mail: alanrobins@boremasters.co.uk
Website: http://www.boremasters.co.uk
Directors: A. Robins (Dir), J. Skitt (Fin)
Managers: K. Rooke (Sales Prom Mgr)
Immediate Holding Company: BOREMASTERS LIMITED
Registration no: 00747434 **Date established:** 1963
Turnover: Up to £250,000 **No.of Employees:** 1 - 10 **Product Groups:** 36, 46, 47, 48, 66

Date of Accounts	Mar 07	Mar 06	Mar 98
Working Capital	7	7	7
Current Assets	7	7	7

Brintons Carpets Ltd
PO Box 16, Kidderminster, DY10 1AG
Tel: 01562-820000 **Fax:** 01562-634737
E-mail: pjohansen@brintons.co.uk
Website: http://www.brintons.co.uk
Bank(s): Lloyds TSB Bank plc
Directors: A. Edwards (Fin), P. Johansen (Dir)
Managers: J. Stone, S. Hall-evans (Personnel), N. Hewitt, J. Bywater (Tech Serv Mgr), A. Todd
Ultimate Holding Company: LYTHAM HOLDCO LIMITED
Immediate Holding Company: WOODWARD GROSVENOR EXPORT LIMITED
Registration no: 02029747 **VAT No.:** GB 274 1843 50
Date established: 1986 **Turnover:** £500,000 - £1m
No.of Employees: 21 - 50 **Product Groups:** 23

Brockway Carpets Ltd
Hoobrook, Kidderminster, DY10 1XW
Tel: 01562-824737 **Fax:** 01562-863598
E-mail: sales@brockway.co.uk
Website: http://www.brockway.co.uk
Directors: F. Vaccaro (Fin), R. Annable (Ch)
Managers: N. Lane (Tech Serv Mgr), S. Glover (Mktg Serv Mgr)
Ultimate Holding Company: BROCKWAY CARPETS (HOLDINGS) LIMITED
Immediate Holding Company: BROCKWAY CARPETS LIMITED
Registration no: 00298275 **Date established:** 1935
Turnover: £10m - £20m **No.of Employees:** 101 - 250 **Product Groups:** 23

Date of Accounts	Mar 11	Mar 10	Mar 09
Sales Turnover	13m	15m	N/A
Pre Tax Profit/Loss	-496	310	181
Working Capital	4m	4m	4m
Fixed Assets	2m	2m	2m
Current Assets	6m	7m	7m
Current Liabilities	461	502	467

Carpet Foundation
60 New Road, Kidderminster, DY10 1AQ
Tel: 01562-755568 **Fax:** 01562-865405
E-mail: info@carpetfoundation.com
Website: http://www.carpetfoundation.com
Directors: A. Stanbridge (Grp Chief Exec), D. Whitefoot (I.T. Dir)
Immediate Holding Company: THE CARPET FOUNDATION
Registration no: 03833797 **VAT No.:** GB 241 4417 91
Date established: 1999 **Turnover:** £250,000 - £500,000
No.of Employees: 1 - 10 **Product Groups:** 87

Date of Accounts	Jul 11	Jul 10	Jul 09
Working Capital	59	49	96
Fixed Assets	6	7	2
Current Assets	93	86	138

Central Weighing Ltd
Unit 142 Hartlebury Trading Estate Hartlebury, Kidderminster, DY10 4JB
Tel: 01299-251242 **Fax:** 01299-250002
E-mail: sales@centralweighing.co.uk
Website: http://www.central-weighing.co.uk
Bank(s): Barclays
Directors: I. Ball (Co Sec), R. Stokes (MD)
Managers: C. Smith (Sales Prom Mgr), M. Wilcox (Chief Mgr)
Immediate Holding Company: CENTRAL WEIGHING LTD
Registration no: 01869891 **Date established:** 1984 **Turnover:** £1m - £2m
No.of Employees: 21 - 50 **Product Groups:** 38

Date of Accounts	Jun 11	Jun 10	Jun 09
Working Capital	155	172	118
Fixed Assets	238	221	229
Current Assets	879	707	665

Cheshire Colour Mail Ltd
Coventry Street, Kidderminster, DY10 2BW
Tel: 01562-820491 **Fax:** 01562- 828366
Website: http://www.cheshires.co.uk
Bank(s): Whiteaway Laidlaw Bank Ltd, Manchester
Directors: R. Bignall (Co Sec)
Ultimate Holding Company: GREAT UNIVERSAL STORES PLC
Immediate Holding Company: G.U.S. PRINTERS LTD
Registration no: 00218145 **VAT No.:** GB 274 1357 59
Turnover: £5m - £10m **No.of Employees:** 101 - 250 **Product Groups:** 27, 44

Chips Away International
Chips Away House Hoo Farm Industrial Estate Worcester Road, Kidderminster, DY11 7RA
Tel: 0800-028 7878 **Fax:** 01482-864969
E-mail: info@chipsaway.co.uk
Website: http://www.chipsaway.co.uk
Directors: A. Ball (Tech Serv), T. Harris (Sales), R. Auld (Mkt Research), J. Ball (Fin)
Managers: R. Leonard
Ultimate Holding Company: FRANCHISE BRANDS WORLDWIDE LIMITED
Immediate Holding Company: CHIPSAWAY INTERNATIONAL LTD.
Registration no: 02962763 **Date established:** 1994 **Turnover:** £2m - £5m
No.of Employees: 1 - 10 **Product Groups:** 39

Date of Accounts	Dec 11	Dec 10	Dec 09
Sales Turnover	5m	5m	5m
Pre Tax Profit/Loss	87	35	218
Working Capital	3m	3m	3m
Fixed Assets	440	232	253
Current Assets	4m	4m	4m
Current Liabilities	408	687	502

Christian Day Ltd
The Old Dye House Puxton Lane, Kidderminster, DY11 5DF
Tel: 01562-515579 **Fax:** 01299-250335
E-mail: christiandayltd@aol.com
Website: http://www.potsofplanters.co.uk
Directors: D. Garrington (MD)
Immediate Holding Company: CHRISTIAN DAY LIMITED
Registration no: 02490708 **Date established:** 1990
Turnover: £500,000 - £1m **No.of Employees:** 1 - 10 **Product Groups:** 25, 30, 49

Date of Accounts	Apr 11	Apr 10	Apr 09
Working Capital	85	89	79
Fixed Assets	7	11	16
Current Assets	280	239	301

Colart Fine Art & Graphics Ltd (t/a Winsor & Newton)
Goldthorn Road, Kidderminster, DY11 7JN
Tel: 020-8427 4343 **Fax:** 020-8863 7177
E-mail: l.pepall@colart.co.uk
Website: http://www.windsornewton.co.uk
Bank(s): Merita, London
Directors: L. Pepall (Fin), S. Chamberlain (Sales & Mktg), H. Beagley (Pers), J. Rickard (Purch)
Managers: A. Clark (Mgr), N. Robson (Comptroller)
Ultimate Holding Company: LINDEN GRUPPEN AB (SWEDEN)
Immediate Holding Company: COLART FINE ART & GRAPHICS LIMITED
Registration no: 00016193 **VAT No.:** GB 541 3941 55
Date established: 1981 **Turnover:** £20m - £50m
No.of Employees: 51 - 100 **Product Groups:** 64

Date of Accounts	Dec 11	Dec 10	Dec 09
Sales Turnover	30m	41m	36m
Pre Tax Profit/Loss	3m	5m	5m
Working Capital	10m	15m	8m
Fixed Assets	10m	12m	14m
Current Assets	16m	27m	16m
Current Liabilities	2m	7m	3m

D M S Chromium
Unit 1 Firs Industrial Estate, Kidderminster, DY11 7QN
Tel: 01562-744711 **Fax:** 01562-863332
E-mail: info@dmschromium.co.uk
Website: http://www.dmschromium.co.uk
Managers: N. Mills (Ops Mgr)
Immediate Holding Company: SMARTIC TRUCKWASH LTD
Date established: 1998 **No.of Employees:** 21 - 50 **Product Groups:** 46, 48

Date of Accounts	Dec 11	Dec 10	Dec 09
Working Capital	-314	113	-383
Fixed Assets	1m	657	999
Current Assets	485	907	462
Current Liabilities	253	N/A	N/A

D Tech Recruitment
32 M C F Complex 60 New Road, Kidderminster, DY10 1AQ
Tel: 01562-510444 **Fax:** 01562-510555
E-mail: enquiries@dtechrecruitment.co.uk
Website: http://www.dtechrecruitment.co.uk
Directors: J. Desogus (Prop)
Immediate Holding Company: D TECH RECRUITMENT LIMITED
Registration no: 05428033 **Date established:** 2005
Turnover: Up to £250,000 **No.of Employees:** 1 - 10 **Product Groups:** 80

Date of Accounts	Mar 12	Mar 11	Mar 10
Working Capital	2	6	-26
Fixed Assets	1	1	N/A
Current Assets	44	61	25

Daymark Ltd
Unit 70 Hartlebury Trading Estate Hartlebury, Kidderminster, DY10 4JB
Tel: 01299-251365 **Fax:** 01299-251386
E-mail: enquiries@labelsandtags.com
Website: http://www.labelsandtags.com
Bank(s): Barclays

Directors: J. Bird (MD)
Immediate Holding Company: DAYMARK LIMITED
Registration no: 01158843 **VAT No.:** GB 281 3081 75
Date established: 1974 **Turnover:** £500,000 - £1m
No.of Employees: 21 - 50 **Product Groups:** 22, 49

Date of Accounts	Dec 11	Dec 10	Dec 09
Working Capital	-2	-49	-25
Fixed Assets	316	397	425
Current Assets	360	346	358

Denvic Ltd
Unit C2 Greenhill Industrial Estate, Kidderminster, DY10 2RN
Tel: 01562-755274 **Fax:** 01562-755274
E-mail: denvic1985@yahoo.co.uk
Bank(s): HSBC Bank plc
Directors: D. Wills (MD), S. Wills (Fin)
Immediate Holding Company: DENVIC LIMITED
Registration no: 01886002 **VAT No.:** GB 276 3253 49
Date established: 1985 **Turnover:** £250,000 - £500,000
No.of Employees: 11 - 20 **Product Groups:** 48

Date of Accounts	Mar 12	Mar 11	Mar 10
Working Capital	30	17	30
Fixed Assets	44	49	35
Current Assets	210	195	186
Current Liabilities	180	N/A	N/A

E V O Instrumentation Ltd
31a Coppice Trading Estate, Kidderminster, DY11 7QY
Tel: 01562-741212 **Fax:** 01562-741666
E-mail: sales@evoinstrumentation.co.uk
Website: http://www.evoinstrumentation.co.uk
Directors: N. Savage (Fin)
Immediate Holding Company: E.V.O. INSTRUMENTATION LIMITED
Registration no: 01916635 **VAT No.:** GB 419 2942 39
Date established: 1985 **Turnover:** £500,000 - £1m
No.of Employees: 1 - 10 **Product Groups:** 38, 85

Date of Accounts	Dec 11	Dec 10	Dec 09
Working Capital	162	153	152
Fixed Assets	5	7	1
Current Assets	336	303	254

Emp Building Services
Arthur Drive Hoo Farm Industrial Estate Worcester Road, Kidderminster, DY11 7RA
Tel: 01562-755555 **Fax:** 01562-755555
E-mail: empbodyguarding@hotmail.com
Website: http://www.exmilitary-personnel.co.uk
Directors: M. White (MD)
No.of Employees: 1 - 10 **Product Groups:** 40, 81, 86

Fencewell
Bower Court Farm Rock, Kidderminster, DY14 9SB
Tel: 07966-519636
E-mail: fencewell@ic24.net
Directors: A. Greenhalgh (Prop)
No.of Employees: 1 - 10 **Product Groups:** 35, 36, 66

Filtration Service Engineering Ltd
Unit 15 Oldington Trading Estate, Kidderminster, DY11 7QP
Tel: 01562-60233 **Fax:** 01562- 748387
E-mail: j.roche@fse.co.uk
Website: http://www.fse.co.uk
Bank(s): HSBC, Droitwich
Directors: J. Roche (MD), K. Cinnamond (Sales)
Managers: D. Bloore (Fin Mgr), K. Pattinson (Purch Mgr)
Immediate Holding Company: FILTRATION SERVICE ENGINEERING LIMITED
Registration no: 00633635 **VAT No.:** GB 110 2832 8
Date established: 1959 **Turnover:** £2m - £5m **No.of Employees:** 21 - 50
Product Groups: 36, 42, 45

Date of Accounts	Apr 11	Apr 10	Apr 09
Working Capital	106	132	99
Fixed Assets	41	51	85
Current Assets	2m	1m	1m
Current Liabilities	307	N/A	N/A

Flooring Services UK Ltd
3a Ricketts Close Firs Industrial Estate, Kidderminster, DY11 7QN
Tel: 01562-751816
E-mail: phil@monarch-flooring.co.uk
Website: http://www.monarch-flooring.co.uk
Managers: P. Brook (Mgr)
Immediate Holding Company: FLOORING SERVICES (UK) LIMITED
Registration no: 07939583 **Date established:** 2012
No.of Employees: 1 - 10 **Product Groups:** 30, 32, 35, 36, 54

Forest Garden plc
Unit 291 296 Hartlebury Trading Estate, Hartlebury, Kidderminster, DY10 4JB
Tel: 08701-919800 **Fax:** 08701-919898
E-mail: jhalford@forestgarden.co.uk
Website: http://www.forestgarden.co.uk
Bank(s): HSBC Bank plc
Directors: J. Halford (Fin), J. Halford (MD)
Managers: J. Mayo, J. Gomersall (Sales Prom Mgr), V. Barker (Mktg Serv Mgr)
Ultimate Holding Company: FOREST GARDEN GROUP LIMITED
Immediate Holding Company: FOREST GARDEN LIMITED
Registration no: 01771349 **VAT No.:** GB 439 4758 08
Date established: 1983 **Turnover:** £20m - £50m
No.of Employees: 251 - 500 **Product Groups:** 25

Date of Accounts	Dec 10	Dec 09	Dec 08
Sales Turnover	40m	43m	47m
Pre Tax Profit/Loss	2m	451	-517
Working Capital	4m	-2m	-3m
Current Assets	13m	14m	12m
Current Liabilities	3m	4m	3m

Formet Sheet Metal Ltd
Unit F Hoo Farm Industrial Estate Worcester Road, Kidderminster, DY11 7RA
Tel: 01562-744440 **Fax:** 01562-829976
E-mail: formetsheetmetal@hotmail.com
Website: http://www.wemico.com
Directors: A. Taylor (MD)
Immediate Holding Company: FORMET SHEET METAL LIMITED
Registration no: 01923174 **VAT No.:** GB 419 2641 53
Date established: 1985 **Turnover:** Up to £250,000
No.of Employees: 1 - 10 **Product Groups:** 48

Date of Accounts	Jul 11	Jul 09	Jul 08
Working Capital	132	116	145
Fixed Assets	30	31	1
Current Assets	166	144	179

Foster Crane & Equipment Ltd
Unit 248 Ikon Industrial Estate Droitwich Road, Hartlebury, Kidderminster, DY10 4EU
Tel: 01299-253610 **Fax:** 01299-250913
E-mail: andrewfoster@fostercranes.co.uk
Website: http://www.fostercranes.co.uk
Directors: A. Foster (MD)
Immediate Holding Company: FOSTER CRANE AND EQUIPMENT LIMITED
Registration no: 04328070 **Date established:** 2001 **Turnover:** £2m - £5m
No.of Employees: 1 - 10 **Product Groups:** 48, 67, 83

Date of Accounts	Dec 11	Dec 10	Dec 09
Working Capital	425	384	150
Fixed Assets	65	159	573
Current Assets	2m	1m	973

Gilberts
King Charles Square Swan Centre, Kidderminster, DY10 2BA
Tel: 01562-755255
E-mail: chrissarjeant@tiscali.co.uk
Website: http://www.gilbertsinteriors.co.uk
Directors: C. Sarjeant (Prop)
Immediate Holding Company: LOOKAROUND LIMITED
Date established: 1999 **No.of Employees:** 1 - 10 **Product Groups:** 24, 27, 63, 66

Date of Accounts	Jun 11	Jun 10	Jun 09
Working Capital	-100	-19	-26
Fixed Assets	15	18	9
Current Assets	27	46	15

D J Hinton & Co. Ltd
Road 2 Hoobrook Industrial Estate Worcester Road, Kidderminster, DY10 1HY
Tel: 01299-402455 **Fax:** 01299-405714
E-mail: admin@djhintons.co.uk
Website: http://www.dj-hinton.co.uk
Directors: J. Hinton (MD), W. Hinton (Co Sec)
Immediate Holding Company: D J HINTON & CO LIMITED
Registration no: 04397152 **Date established:** 2002
No.of Employees: 11 - 20 **Product Groups:** 54

Date of Accounts	Mar 11	Mar 10	Mar 09
Working Capital	228	324	331
Fixed Assets	81	80	95
Current Assets	391	436	503

Ikon A V S Ltd
238 Ikon Indl-Est Hartlebury, Kidderminster, DY10 4EU
Tel: 01299-250991 **Fax:** 01299-250983
E-mail: sales@Ikonavs.com
Website: http://www.ikonavs.com
Directors: D. Tyas (MD)
Immediate Holding Company: IKON AVS LTD.
Registration no: 03489165 **Date established:** 1998 **Turnover:** £1m - £2m
No.of Employees: 1 - 10 **Product Groups:** 67

Date of Accounts	Sep 10	Sep 09	Sep 08
Working Capital	8	19	24
Fixed Assets	1	1	1
Current Assets	115	111	113

Kidderminster Fencing
94 Beauchamp Avenue, Kidderminster, DY11 7AQ
Tel: 01562-745427
E-mail: kidderminsterfencing@yahoo.co.uk
Website: http://www.kidderminsterfencing.co.uk
Directors: S. Sanders (Prop)
Date established: 1998 **No.of Employees:** 1 - 10 **Product Groups:** 25, 33, 35, 52

Kla
38 Meadow Mill Industrial Estate Dixon Street, Kidderminster, DY10 1HH
Tel: 01562-863003
E-mail: info@klaonline.co.uk
Website: http://www.klaonline.co.uk
Directors: D. Andrews (Ptnr)
Date established: 1998 **No.of Employees:** 1 - 10 **Product Groups:** 43

Lost Wax Development
Ricketts Close Firs Industrial Estate, Kidderminster, DY11 7QN
Tel: 01562-827575 **Fax:** 01299-877352
E-mail: sales@lwd.co.uk
Website: http://www.lwd.co.uk
Bank(s): HSBC Bank plc
Directors: B. Bird (Fin), B. Grundy (Co Sec)
Managers: W. Bennett
Immediate Holding Company: LOST WAX DEVELOPMENT LIMITED
Registration no: 01312448 **VAT No.:** GB 299 1108 36
Date established: 1977 **Turnover:** £1m - £2m **No.of Employees:** 21 - 50
Product Groups: 34

Date of Accounts	Dec 11	Dec 10	Dec 09
Working Capital	25	50	57
Fixed Assets	1m	1m	1m
Current Assets	877	771	744

Lowland Sheet Metal Ltd
Unit 2 Coppice Trading Estate, Kidderminster, DY11 7QY
Tel: 01562-743215 **Fax:** 01562-863436
E-mail: sales@lowlandsheetmetal.co.uk
Website: http://www.lowlandsheetmetal.co.uk
Directors: R. Evans (Prop)
Immediate Holding Company: LOWLAND SHEET METAL LIMITED
Registration no: 02031665 **Date established:** 1986
Turnover: Up to £250,000 **No.of Employees:** 1 - 10 **Product Groups:** 48

Date of Accounts	Dec 11	Dec 10	Dec 09
Working Capital	129	116	99
Fixed Assets	2	N/A	N/A
Current Assets	176	161	139

M R W Holdings Ltd
Unit 30 Rowland Way, Kidderminster, DY11 7RA
Tel: 01562-745042 **Fax:** 01562-746472
E-mail: julian@mrwe.co.uk
Website: http://www.mrwe.co.uk
Directors: A. Wesson (Fin), J. Wesson (MD), M. Wesson (Dir)
Immediate Holding Company: MRW HOLDINGS LIMITED
Registration no: 04429977 **VAT No.:** GB 100 4125 49
Date established: 2002 **Turnover:** £250,000 - £500,000
No.of Employees: 1 - 10 **Product Groups:** 22, 23, 24, 35

Date of Accounts	Dec 09	Dec 08	Aug 07
Working Capital	-60	-9	2
Fixed Assets	102	21	N/A
Current Assets	50	50	49
Current Liabilities	N/A	N/A	14

Mac Machining Ltd
Unit 26 Hoobrook Enterprise Centre Worcester Road, Kidderminster, DY10 1HY
Tel: 01562-67619 **Fax:** 01562- 861243
E-mail: info@macmachining.com
Website: http://www.macmachining.com
Directors: C. Jordan (Fin)
Immediate Holding Company: MAC MACHINING LIMITED
Registration no: 02934853 **VAT No.:** GB 650 2467 53
Date established: 1994 **Turnover:** Up to £250,000
No.of Employees: 1 - 10 **Product Groups:** 48

Date of Accounts	Aug 11	Aug 10	Aug 09
Working Capital	14	-4	-5
Fixed Assets	20	25	29
Current Assets	77	68	56

Monosol A F Ltd
Unit 313 Hartlebury Trading Estate, Hartlebury, Kidderminster, DY10 4JB
Tel: 01299-251335 **Fax:** 01299-251601
E-mail: sales@aquafilmuk.com
Website: http://www.monsol.com
Managers: J. Fleming (Ops Mgr)
Ultimate Holding Company: MONOSOL HOLDCO LLC (USA)
Immediate Holding Company: MONOSOL AF, LTD.
Registration no: 04108419 **Date established:** 2000
Turnover: £10m - £20m **No.of Employees:** 21 - 50 **Product Groups:** 23, 27, 30, 48, 63

Date of Accounts	Dec 11	Dec 10	Dec 09
Sales Turnover	10m	8m	8m
Pre Tax Profit/Loss	1m	1m	1m
Working Capital	2m	1m	1m
Fixed Assets	972	910	1m
Current Assets	3m	2m	2m
Current Liabilities	368	426	432

Muller England Ltd
High Street Cleobury Mortimer, Kidderminster, DY14 8DT
Tel: 01299-270271 **Fax:** 01299-270877
E-mail: sales@muller-england.co.uk
Website: http://www.muller-england.co.uk
Bank(s): Barclays
Directors: G. Farr (Dir), P. Bethell (MD)
Ultimate Holding Company: MULLER HOLDINGS LIMITED
Immediate Holding Company: MULLER ENGLAND LIMITED
Registration no: 01687555 **Date established:** 1982
Turnover: £10m - £20m **No.of Employees:** 21 - 50 **Product Groups:** 48

Date of Accounts	Dec 11	Dec 10	Dec 09
Sales Turnover	13m	10m	7m
Pre Tax Profit/Loss	288	-648	454
Working Capital	2m	1m	2m
Fixed Assets	4m	4m	2m
Current Assets	5m	5m	4m
Current Liabilities	460	315	724

Music Room Research UK Ltd
Klark Teknik Building Coppice Trading Estate, Kidderminster, DY11 7HJ
Tel: 01562-741515 **Fax:** 01562-745371
E-mail: jonathan.chitty@music-group.com
Website: http://www.midasconsoles.com
Bank(s): National Westminster Bank Plc
Directors: D. Cooper (Sales & Mktg)
Managers: A. Hunt, C. Rogers (I.T. Exec), C. Green (Personnel), J. Godbehaer (Mktg Serv Mgr), J. Biggs (Tech Serv Mgr), J. Chitty (Sales Prom Mgr), L. Cork (Personnel), Z. Johnson
Ultimate Holding Company: ROBERT BOSCH GMBH (GERMANY)
Immediate Holding Company: MUSIC GROUP RESEARCH UK LIMITED
Registration no: 07070987 **VAT No.:** GB 589 2040 22
Date established: 2009 **Turnover:** £5m - £10m
No.of Employees: 51 - 100 **Product Groups:** 37, 38, 52

Date of Accounts	Dec 10
Sales Turnover	9m
Pre Tax Profit/Loss	-3m
Working Capital	4m
Fixed Assets	2m
Current Assets	6m
Current Liabilities	519

Oasis Art & Craft Products Ltd
Goldthorn Road, Kidderminster, DY11 7JN
Tel: 01562-744522 **Fax:** 01562-823181
E-mail: penny.waldron@colart.co.uk
Website: http://www.windsornewton.com
Bank(s): HSBC Bank plc
Directors: P. Woodwood (MD)
Managers: P. Waldron (), P. Woodward (Site Co-ord), J. Yeomans (Sales Prom Mgr), A. Wothos (Mktg Serv Mgr), P. Waldron
Immediate Holding Company: OASIS ART & CRAFT PRODUCTS LIMITED
Registration no: 02196366 **VAT No.:** GB 333 1135 06
Date established: 1987 **Turnover:** £10m - £20m
No.of Employees: 51 - 100 **Product Groups:** 49

Date of Accounts	Dec 10	Dec 09	Dec 08
Sales Turnover	14m	13m	11m
Pre Tax Profit/Loss	1m	54	-196
Working Capital	3m	2m	2m
Fixed Assets	346	664	864
Current Assets	5m	4m	5m
Current Liabilities	876	678	435

Omegaslate Superseal Systems Ltd
2 Chirk Close Forest Gate, Kidderminster, DY10 1YG
Tel: 01562-751095
Directors: J. Griffiths (MD)
Immediate Holding Company: OMEGASLATE SUPERSEAL SYSTEMS LIMITED
Registration no: 03376711 **Date established:** 1997
No.of Employees: 1 - 10 **Product Groups:** 40, 42

Pembar Ltd (t/a Hatt Kitchens)
Unit 111 Hartlebury Trading Estate, Hartlebury, Kidderminster, DY10 4JB
Tel: 01299-251320 **Fax:** 01299-251579
E-mail: sales@hatt.co.uk
Website: http://www.half.co.uk
Bank(s): Lloyds TSB

see next page

Pembar Ltd (t/a Hatt Kitchens) - Cont'd

Directors: D. Powle (Asst MD)
Ultimate Holding Company: HATT KITCHENS LIMITED
Immediate Holding Company: PEMBAR LIMITED
Registration no: 04089902 **VAT No.:** GB 478 5966 71
Date established: 2000 **No.of Employees:** 51 - 100 **Product Groups:** 26

Date of Accounts	Apr 11	Apr 10	Apr 09
Working Capital	-257	-185	-369
Fixed Assets	874	876	895
Current Assets	1m	1m	1m

PLM Illumination Ltd

6 Hoo Farm Industrial Estate Arthur Drive, Kidderminster, DY11 7RA
Tel: 01562-66441 **Fax:** 01562-829992
E-mail: kelly@plmgroup.co.uk
Website: http://www.plmgroup.co.uk
Directors: C. Dredge (Co Sec), J. Ding (Dir), P. Martin (MD)
Managers: C. Brown (Admin Off)
Immediate Holding Company: PLM Group Holdings Ltd
Registration no: 03302416 **Date established:** 1997 **Turnover:** £2m - £5m
No.of Employees: 1 - 10 **Product Groups:** 37, 39, 40, 49, 52, 67, 84

Date of Accounts	Jan 10	Jan 09	Jan 08
Working Capital	142	49	-5
Fixed Assets	36	8	13
Current Assets	236	305	260

Powertest UK

Comberton Hall Bungalow Comberton Road, Kidderminster, DY10 3DU
Tel: 01562-746762
E-mail: darren.smith@powertestuk.co.uk
Website: http://www.powertestuk.co.uk
Directors: A. Hughes (Fin)
Immediate Holding Company: POWERTEST UK LIMITED
Registration no: 06223031 **Date established:** 2007
No.of Employees: 1 - 10 **Product Groups:** 38, 85

Prinsuk.com

Unit 140 Hartlebury Trading Estate, Kidderminster, DY10 4JB
Tel: 01299-251400 **Fax:** 01299-251800
E-mail: sales@prinsuk.com
Website: http://www.prinsuk.com
Directors: R. Prins (Dir), H. Vondrak (Fin)
Date established: 1987 **No.of Employees:** 21 - 50 **Product Groups:** 38, 42

Date of Accounts	Sep 06	Sep 05
Working Capital	-17	-34
Current Assets	N/A	454
Current Liabilities	17	488

Protekor UK Ltd

Powerforce House Hoo Farm Industrial Estate Worcester Road, Kidderminster, DY11 7RA
Tel: 01562-515200 **Fax:** 01562-864063
E-mail: info@protektor.co.uk
Website: http://www.protektor.co.uk
Bank(s): HSBC Bank plc
Directors: C. Mossey (Sales), P. Broadfield (MD), C. Mossey (Sales & Mktg), J. Whitehouse (Co Sec)
Managers: J. Simpson (Personnel), G. Norton (Factory Mgr)
Ultimate Holding Company: PROTEKTORWERK FLORENZ MAISCH GMBH & CO KG (GERMANY)
Immediate Holding Company: CORNERCARE REALISATIONS LIMITED
Registration no: 01356486 **VAT No.:** GB 299 1396 05
Date established: 1978 **Turnover:** £2m - £5m **No.of Employees:** 21 - 50
Product Groups: 17, 30, 33, 34, 35, 40, 45, 52, 66

Date of Accounts	Dec 08	Dec 07	Dec 06
Working Capital	335	386	373
Fixed Assets	445	399	432
Current Assets	2m	2m	2m

Rea Plasrack Ltd

Unit 18e Hartlebury Trading Estate Hartlebury, Kidderminster, DY10 4JB
Tel: 01299-251960 **Fax:** 01299-253670
E-mail: info@plasgroup.co.uk
Website: http://www.plasgroup.co.uk
Directors: C. Salter (MD), B. Bentley (Co Sec)
Immediate Holding Company: REA PLASRACK LTD.
Registration no: 02723716 **Date established:** 1992
No.of Employees: 1 - 10 **Product Groups:** 26, 30, 40, 65, 67, 84

Date of Accounts	Aug 11	Aug 10	Aug 09
Working Capital	18	21	19
Fixed Assets	1	3	4
Current Assets	86	64	82

Redspeed International Ltd

Unit 21 26 Coppice Trading Estate, Kidderminster, DY11 7QY
Tel: 01562-747137 **Fax:** 01562-747165
E-mail: sales@monitron.com
Website: http://www.redspeed-int.com
Directors: D. Zaydman (MD)
Immediate Holding Company: REDSPEED INTERNATIONAL LIMITED
Registration no: 05152563 **Date established:** 2004 **Turnover:** £5m - £10m
No.of Employees: 21 - 50 **Product Groups:** 37, 39

Date of Accounts	Dec 11	Dec 10	Dec 09
Sales Turnover	8m	10m	15m
Pre Tax Profit/Loss	604	414	480
Working Capital	-3m	-1m	-5m
Fixed Assets	6m	7m	7m
Current Assets	3m	3m	3m
Current Liabilities	3m	2m	1m

Rigging Services

Road 3 Hoobrook Indl-Est Worcester Road, Kidderminster, DY10 1HY
Tel: 01562-822922 **Fax:** 01562-862648
E-mail: julie@riggingservicesltd.com
Website: http://www.riggingservicesltd.com
Directors: N. Watts (MD), J. Watts (Co Sec), J. Watts (Fin)
Immediate Holding Company: RIGGING SERVICES LIMITED
Registration no: 04148830 **Date established:** 2001 **Turnover:** £1m - £2m
No.of Employees: 1 - 10 **Product Groups:** 67

Date of Accounts	Mar 11	Mar 10	Mar 09
Working Capital	288	353	1m
Fixed Assets	44	68	83
Current Assets	707	469	1m

Rivco Ltd

Unit 10 Finepoint Finepoint Way, Kidderminster, DY11 7FB
Tel: 01562-513910 **Fax:** 01562-69666
E-mail: sales@rivco.co.uk
Website: http://www.rivco.co.uk
Directors: M. Roden (Fin)
Immediate Holding Company: RIVCO LIMITED
Registration no: 02929026 **Date established:** 1994
Turnover: £500,000 - £1m **No.of Employees:** 11 - 20 **Product Groups:** 35

Date of Accounts	Jun 11	Jun 10	Jun 09
Working Capital	277	306	221
Fixed Assets	68	70	28
Current Assets	952	807	732

Rowan Steels Ltd

2 Park Street Works Park Street, Kidderminster, DY11 6TN
Tel: 01562-67476 **Fax:** 01562- 515412
E-mail: sales@rowansteels.co.uk
Website: http://www.rowansteels.co.uk
Directors: I. Trow (MD)
Immediate Holding Company: ROWAN STEELS LIMITED
Registration no: 01352116 **Date established:** 1978 **Turnover:** £1m - £2m
No.of Employees: 1 - 10 **Product Groups:** 48, 66

Date of Accounts	Jan 12	Jan 11	Jan 10
Working Capital	157	140	115
Fixed Assets	27	32	37
Current Assets	958	999	671
Current Liabilities	12	N/A	N/A

Roxel Ltd

Summerfield Lane Summerfield, Kidderminster, DY11 7RZ
Tel: 01562-824061 **Fax:** 01562-828119
E-mail: tim.roberts@roxelgroup.com
Website: http://www.roxelgroup.com
Managers: G. Irving (Purch Mgr), I. White, J. Harding (Sales & Mktg Mg), K. Harris (Fin Mgr), P. Adams (Personnel), P. Mock (Tech Serv Mgr)
Immediate Holding Company: ROXEL (UK ROCKET MOTORS) LIMITED
Registration no: 04543318 **Date established:** 2002
Turnover: £20m - £50m **No.of Employees:** 251 - 500 **Product Groups:** 39

Date of Accounts	Dec 11	Dec 10	Dec 09
Sales Turnover	27m	20m	25m
Pre Tax Profit/Loss	8m	4m	3m
Working Capital	3m	-6m	-4m
Fixed Assets	18m	20m	21m
Current Assets	26m	18m	17m
Current Liabilities	17m	21m	19m

Sealine International Ltd

Whitehouse Road, Kidderminster, DY10 1HT
Tel: 01562-740900 **Fax:** 01562-747709
E-mail: chris.oconnor@sealine.com
Website: http://www.sealine.com
Bank(s): Midlands
Directors: M. Turner (Procurement), N. Turner (Sales & Mktg), C. O'Connor (MD), R. Bonham (MD)
Managers: W. Bailey-allen (Systems Mgr)
Ultimate Holding Company: BRUNSWICK CORPORATION (USA)
Immediate Holding Company: SEALINE INTERNATIONAL LIMITED
Registration no: 01113881 **VAT No.:** GB 101 2800 41
Date established: 1973 **Turnover:** £20m - £50m
No.of Employees: 501 - 1000 **Product Groups:** 39, 68

Date of Accounts	Dec 11	Dec 10	Dec 09
Sales Turnover	33m	37m	33m
Pre Tax Profit/Loss	-4m	-756	-3m
Working Capital	7m	5m	7m
Fixed Assets	10m	9m	8m
Current Assets	21m	35m	29m
Current Liabilities	9m	7m	6m

Seton Engineering

Meadow Mill Industrial Estate Dixon Street, Kidderminster, DY10 1HH
Tel: 01562-820820 **Fax:** 01562-820820
E-mail: setonprecision@tiscali.co.uk
Managers: R. Stone (Mgr)
Immediate Holding Company: THE ORIGINAL PWH ASSISTANCE LTD
Date established: 2010 **No.of Employees:** 1 - 10 **Product Groups:** 35, 42, 46, 48

Sony Centre

Unit 4 Weavers Wharf, Kidderminster, DY10 1AA
Tel: 01562-827100 **Fax:** 01562-820808
E-mail: deepak@victoruk.com
Website: http://www.victoruk.com
Managers: D. Dave (Mgr)
Ultimate Holding Company: SEAMAP LTD
Immediate Holding Company: ALERTBIND LTD
Registration no: 00377588 **No.of Employees:** 1 - 10 **Product Groups:** 36, 40

T W Packaging

23 Lisle Avenue Unit 1, Kidderminster, DY11 7DE
Tel: 01562-69510 **Fax:** 01562- 827024
E-mail: enquiries@twpackaging.co.uk
Website: http://www.twpackaging.co.uk
Managers: A. Todd Wood (Mgr)
Registration no: 05162953 **VAT No.:** GB 110 1894 10
Date established: 1961 **No.of Employees:** 11 - 20 **Product Groups:** 27

Date of Accounts	Jun 08	Jun 07	Aug 06
Working Capital	-111	-72	-2
Fixed Assets	7	9	5
Current Assets	83	89	140
Current Liabilities	194	161	142

Tailored Software Solutions

11 Osborne Close, Kidderminster, DY10 3YY
Tel: 01562-823036 **Fax:** 07092-224019
E-mail: bje@tailoredsoftwaresolutions.co.uk
Website: http://www.tailoredsoftwaresolutions.co.uk
Directors: B. Ecclesdon (Prop)
Date established: 1995 **No.of Employees:** 1 - 10 **Product Groups:** 44

John Tainton (a division of Hawlco (1812) Ltd)

Hoo Farm Industrial Estate Worcester Road, Kidderminster, DY11 7RA
Tel: 01562-740477 **Fax:** 01562-68765
E-mail: roy.harwood@johntainton.co.uk
Website: http://www.johntainton.co.uk
Directors: R. Harwood (Comm)
Ultimate Holding Company: HALL & PICKLES 1812 LIMITED
Immediate Holding Company: JOHN TAINTON LIMITED
Registration no: 03162315 **VAT No.:** GB 275 0670 54
Date established: 1996 **Turnover:** £500,000 - £1m
No.of Employees: 51 - 100 **Product Groups:** 34

Trueline Expanded Products

Parker Place Firs Industrial Estate, Kidderminster, DY11 7QN
Tel: 01562-823267 **Fax:** 01562-823867
E-mail: enquiries@truelineproducts.co.uk
Website: http://www.truelineproducts.co.uk
Directors: S. Mares (Dir)
Managers: L. Wellings (Purch Mgr), A. Davies (Chief Mgr), J. Silcock (Fin Mgr)
Immediate Holding Company: SMARTIC TRUCKWASH LTD
Registration no: 04413306 **Date established:** 1998
No.of Employees: 21 - 50 **Product Groups:** 35

Date of Accounts	Dec 11	Dec 10	Dec 09
Working Capital	-314	113	-383
Fixed Assets	1m	657	999
Current Assets	485	907	462
Current Liabilities	253	N/A	N/A

UK Blinds

1 Highfield Road, Kidderminster, DY10 2TL
Tel: 01562-634467 **Fax:** 01562-634467
E-mail: jacqui.penn@blueyonder.co.uk
Website: http://www.amixbuilding.co.uk
Directors: M. Penn (Prop)
Immediate Holding Company: UK BLINDS (MANUFACTURING) LTD
Registration no: 02488368 **Turnover:** Up to £250,000
No.of Employees: 1 - 10 **Product Groups:** 24, 63, 66

Versaduct Sheet Metal Ltd

Hoo Farm Industrial Estate Worcester Road, Kidderminster, DY11 7RA
Tel: 01562-824913 **Fax:** 01562-823809
E-mail: enquiries@versaduct.co.uk
Website: http://www.versaduct.co.uk
Directors: S. Haines (MD)
Immediate Holding Company: VERSADUCT SHEET METAL LIMITED
Registration no: 02031647 **VAT No.:** 436 8654 18 **Date established:** 1986
Turnover: £250,000 - £500,000 **No.of Employees:** 1 - 10
Product Groups: 23, 40

Date of Accounts	Mar 12	Mar 11	Mar 10
Working Capital	-74	-39	3
Fixed Assets	7	9	10
Current Assets	56	48	59

Victoria Carpets Ltd

Worcester Road, Kidderminster, DY10 1JR
Tel: 01562-749300 **Fax:** 01562-749349
E-mail: sales@victoriacarpets.com
Website: http://www.victoriacarpets.com
Bank(s): Barclays, Oxford Street, Kidderminster
Directors: T. Danks (Fin), A. Bullock (MD)
Managers: K. Millinchip, M. Hagan (Personnel), S. Lewis (Sales & Mktg Mg), S. Leighton
Ultimate Holding Company: VICTORIA P.L.C.
Immediate Holding Company: VICTORIA CARPETS LIMITED
Registration no: 01178145 **VAT No.:** GB 377 1040 62
Date established: 1974 **Turnover:** £20m - £50m
No.of Employees: 101 - 250 **Product Groups:** 23

Date of Accounts	Mar 08	Apr 09	Apr 10
Sales Turnover	28m	25m	22m
Pre Tax Profit/Loss	663	-383	-440
Working Capital	3m	3m	2m
Fixed Assets	4m	4m	3m
Current Assets	12m	11m	12m
Current Liabilities	1m	849	813

West Design Products Ltd

Stoney Lane Industrial Estate 5-7 Red Sands Road, Kidderminster, DY10 2LG
Tel: 01303-297888 **Fax:** 01730-815714
E-mail: sales@westdesignproducts.co.uk
Website: http://www.westdesignproducts.co.uk
Bank(s): Girobank & Lloyds TSB
Directors: M. Bray (MD)
Managers: S. White, P. Crayford (Comptroller), V. Chambers (Tech Serv Mgr), M. Robinson (Buyer)
Ultimate Holding Company: WHINCROFT LIMITED
Immediate Holding Company: WEST DESIGN PRODUCTS LIMITED
Registration no: 02723202 **VAT No.:** 611 8773 38 **Date established:** 1992
Turnover: £5m - £10m **No.of Employees:** 21 - 50 **Product Groups:** 27, 30, 38, 64

Date of Accounts	Jan 11	Jan 10	Jan 09
Sales Turnover	10m	7m	7m
Pre Tax Profit/Loss	516	3m	119
Working Capital	2m	2m	2m
Fixed Assets	1m	904	1m
Current Assets	7m	4m	4m
Current Liabilities	961	398	268

Wrekin Frame & Truss (Gang-Nail Systems Ltd)

Unit 24 Churchfields Business Park Clensmore Street, Kidderminster, DY10 2JY
Tel: 01562-747555 **Fax:** 01562-748555
Directors: F. Morris (Dir)
Immediate Holding Company: H & S DIRECT LTD
Registration no: 03332161 **No.of Employees:** 11 - 20
Product Groups: 35, 66

XPR Systems

P O Box 4698, Kidderminster, DY11 7WX
Tel: 0870-8030977 **Fax:** 0870-8030877
E-mail: info@xprsystems.co.uk
Website: http://www.xprsystems.co.uk
Product Groups: 25, 28, 33, 35, 40, 45, 52, 66, 85

Malvern

Alloy Die & Cast

14a Hanley Road, Malvern, WR14 4PQ
Tel: 01684-576622 **Fax:** 01684-576622
Directors: A. Owens (Dir)
Date established: 2001 **No.of Employees:** 1 - 10 **Product Groups:** 46

John Banner
Lydes Road, Malvern, WR14 2BY
Tel: 01684-569285 **Fax:** 01684-568946
E-mail: jbworcs@hotmail.com
Directors: J. Banner (Prop)
Immediate Holding Company: GREAT MALVERN ACADEMY LIMITED
Date established: 2011 **Turnover:** Up to £250,000
No.of Employees: 1 - 10 **Product Groups:** 83

Bauromat UK
Beauchamp Business Centre Sparrowhawk Close, Malvern, WR14 1GL
Tel: 01684-575757 **Fax:** 01684-569887
E-mail: admin@bauromat.co.uk
Website: http://www.bauromat.co.uk
Directors: J. D'angelillo (MD)
Immediate Holding Company: BAUROMAT (UK) LTD
Registration no: 03328668 **Date established:** 1997
No.of Employees: 11 - 20 **Product Groups:** 46

Date of Accounts	Mar 12	Mar 11	Mar 10
Working Capital	355	301	315
Fixed Assets	274	308	337
Current Assets	1m	2m	1m

Biffa Waste Services Ltd
Guinness Park Farm Leigh Sinton, Malvern, WR13 5EQ
Tel: 01299-828838 **Fax:** 01886-833812
E-mail: greg.fuller@biffa.co.uk
Website: http://www.biffa.co.uk
Managers: G. Fuller (Mgr)
Immediate Holding Company: BIFFA WASTE SERVICES LIMITED
Registration no: 00946107 **Date established:** 1969
No.of Employees: 11 - 20 **Product Groups:** 54, 72, 83

Date of Accounts	Mar 08	Mar 09	Apr 10
Sales Turnover	555m	574m	492m
Pre Tax Profit/Loss	23m	50m	30m
Working Capital	229m	271m	293m
Fixed Assets	371m	360m	378m
Current Assets	409m	534m	609m
Current Liabilities	50m	100m	115m

C Churchfield Engineering
Unit 7 Howsell Road Industrial Estate, Malvern, WR14 1UJ
Tel: 01684-892150 **Fax:** 01684-892150
Directors: C. Churchfield (Prop)
Turnover: Up to £250,000 **No.of Employees:** 1 - 10 **Product Groups:** 45, 46

C P Engineering Ltd
Sandys Road, Malvern, WR14 1JJ
Tel: 01684-584850 **Fax:** 01684-573088
E-mail: sales@cpengineering.com
Website: http://www.cpengineering.com
Bank(s): Lloyds TSB Bank plc
Directors: M. Hird (MD)
Managers: G. Robertson (Comptroller)
Immediate Holding Company: CP ENGINEERING SYSTEMS LIMITED
Registration no: 02827565 **VAT No.:** GB 640 9013 64
Date established: 1993 **Turnover:** £2m - £5m **No.of Employees:** 21 - 50
Product Groups: 37, 38, 39

Date of Accounts	Sep 11	Sep 10	Sep 09
Working Capital	1m	445	549
Fixed Assets	277	303	347
Current Assets	3m	3m	2m

Camtek Ltd (Jetcam International)
Camtek House 117 Church Street, Malvern, WR14 2AJ
Tel: 01684-892290 **Fax:** 01684-892269
E-mail: sales@camtek.co.uk
Website: http://www.camtek.co.uk
Bank(s): National Westminster Bank Plc
Directors: B. Warner (MD), D. Babbs (Dir)
Managers: C. Hart (Mktg Serv Mgr), M. Brookes (Chief Acct), T. Antrobus (Sales Prom Mgr)
Immediate Holding Company: Vero Software plc
Registration no: 01725620 **VAT No.:** GB 396 1406 38
Turnover: £1m - £2m **No.of Employees:** 21 - 50 **Product Groups:** 44

Chance Glass Ltd
Pickersleigh Avenue, Malvern, WR14 2LP
Tel: 01684-892353 **Fax:** 01684-892647
E-mail: sales@chanceglass.co.uk
Website: http://www.chanceglass.co.uk
Directors: T. Charles (Co Sec)
Managers: G. Davis (Chief Mgr)
Immediate Holding Company: CHANCE GLASS LIMITED
Registration no: 02692155 **Date established:** 1992
No.of Employees: 21 - 50 **Product Groups:** 33, 38

Date of Accounts	Mar 12	Mar 11	Mar 10
Working Capital	544	502	409
Fixed Assets	184	169	174
Current Assets	701	645	518

The Coaster Company
Coasters House Spring Lane South, Malvern, WR14 1AT
Tel: 01684-577177 **Fax:** 01684-577188
E-mail: info@coaster.co.uk
Website: http://www.coaster.co.uk
Directors: K. Beecroft (Dir)
No.of Employees: 11 - 20 **Product Groups:** 49, 67

Coldtraila
Danemoor Farm Welland, Malvern, WR13 6NL
Tel: 01684-311811 **Fax:** 08707-059776
E-mail: mail@coldtraila.co.uk
Website: http://www.coldtraila.co.uk
Managers: R. Pushman (Mktg Serv Mgr)
Product Groups: 40, 63, 72

Colwall Sheet Metal & Engineering Services
Spring Lane, Malvern, WR14 1BY
Tel: 01684-567900 **Fax:** 01684-573700
E-mail: sales@colwallsheetmetal.com
Website: http://www.colwallsheetmetal.co.uk
Directors: S. Chorley (Fin)
Managers: L. Wood (Chief Mgr)
Immediate Holding Company: COLWALL SHEET METAL & ENGINEERING SERVICES LIMITED
Registration no: 03047581 **Date established:** 1995
No.of Employees: 11 - 20 **Product Groups:** 48

Date of Accounts	Aug 11	Aug 10	Aug 09
Working Capital	74	70	70
Fixed Assets	32	36	31
Current Assets	154	173	215

Elaces
120 Clevelode Clevelode, Malvern, WR13 6PD
Tel: 07516-749463
E-mail: info@elaces.co.uk
Website: http://www.elaces.co.uk
Directors: M. Bond (MD)
Immediate Holding Company: ELACES LIMITED
Registration no: 06808327 **Date established:** 2009
No.of Employees: 1 - 10 **Product Groups:** 22, 24, 49, 65

English Braids Ltd
Spring Lane, Malvern, WR14 1AL
Tel: 01684-892222 **Fax:** 01684-892111
E-mail: info@englishbraids.com
Website: http://www.englishbraids.com
Bank(s): Barclays, Bromsgrove
Directors: P. Earp (MD), M. Earp (Fin)
Immediate Holding Company: ENGLISH BRAIDS LIMITED
Registration no: 00932500 **VAT No.:** GB 377 1091 45
Date established: 1968 **Turnover:** £5m - £10m
No.of Employees: 51 - 100 **Product Groups:** 23, 30, 35, 39

Date of Accounts	Dec 11	Dec 10	Dec 09
Sales Turnover	9m	7m	7m
Pre Tax Profit/Loss	2m	1m	484
Working Capital	9m	8m	7m
Fixed Assets	5m	5m	5m
Current Assets	13m	11m	9m
Current Liabilities	4m	2m	2m

Fleet Line Markers Ltd
Spring Lane South, Malvern, WR14 1AT
Tel: 01684-573535 **Fax:** 01684-892784
E-mail: sales@fleetlinemarkers.com
Website: http://www.fleetlinemarkers.com
Bank(s): Barclays, Malvern Link
Directors: I. Mcguffie (MD), H. Tolley (Fin)
Managers: I. Courage (Sales Prom Mgr), E. Short (Mktg Serv Mgr), M. Phillips
Ultimate Holding Company: LOCH SPORT LIMITED
Immediate Holding Company: FLEET(LINE MARKERS)LIMITED
Registration no: 00588668 **Date established:** 1957 **Turnover:** £1m - £2m
No.of Employees: 21 - 50 **Product Groups:** 29, 30, 45

Date of Accounts	Dec 11	Dec 10	Dec 09
Working Capital	1m	607	766
Fixed Assets	764	1m	964
Current Assets	2m	2m	2m

G & B Projects Co.
Barnards Green Road, Malvern, WR14 3LY
Tel: 01684-574367 **Fax:** 01684-560225
E-mail: info@gandbprojects.co.uk
Website: http://www.gandbprojects.co.uk
Directors: R. Ellis (Ptnr)
Registration no: 06748895 **VAT No.:** GB 275 2883 27
Date established: 2008 **Turnover:** £2m - £5m **No.of Employees:** 11 - 20
Product Groups: 30

G Webb Automation Ltd
Howsell Road, Malvern, WR14 1TF
Tel: 01684-892929 **Fax:** 01684-892880
E-mail: salesadmin@webbautomation.co.uk
Website: http://www.webbautomation.co.uk
Bank(s): Lloyds TSB Bank plc
Directors: G. Webb (Fin), P. Webb (MD)
Managers: C. Lancett, C. Head (Sales Prom Mgr), M. Robinson (Buyer), S. Baker (Tech Serv Mgr)
Immediate Holding Company: G. WEBB AUTOMATION LIMITED
Registration no: 01172548 **VAT No.:** GB 349 2160 56
Date established: 1974 **Turnover:** £2m - £5m **No.of Employees:** 21 - 50
Product Groups: 38, 41, 42, 45, 67, 83

Date of Accounts	Aug 11	Aug 10	Aug 09
Sales Turnover	3m	2m	2m
Pre Tax Profit/Loss	130	67	-130
Working Capital	573	466	413
Fixed Assets	30	26	36
Current Assets	2m	1m	1m
Current Liabilities	576	422	241

Integrated Telemarketing
17 Graham Road, Malvern, WR14 2HR
Tel: 01684-567500 **Fax:** 01684-891182
E-mail: info@integrated-telemarketing.co.uk
Website: http://www.integrated-telemarketing.co.uk
Directors: S. Webb (Fin)
Immediate Holding Company: INTEGRATED TELEMARKETING LIMITED
Registration no: 03237935 **Date established:** 1996
No.of Employees: 1 - 10 **Product Groups:** 80, 81, 86

Date of Accounts	Aug 11	Aug 10	Aug 09
Working Capital	-117	-92	-80
Fixed Assets	1	1	2
Current Assets	19	13	13

Malvern Fencing
38 Meadway, Malvern, WR14 1SB
Tel: 01886-830232
E-mail: stevenmlv4@aol.com
Directors: S. Jordan (Prop)
Date established: 2001 **No.of Employees:** 1 - 10 **Product Groups:** 25, 35, 52

Malvern Glass Fibre
4 Merebrook Industrial Estate Hanley Road, Welland, Malvern, WR13 6NP
Tel: 01684-311099 **Fax:** 01684-311399
E-mail: william.allen1956@yahoo.com
Website: http://www.malvernglassfibre.co.uk
Directors: R. Jenkins (Ptnr)
VAT No.: GB 589 3925 74 **Turnover:** Up to £250,000
No.of Employees: 1 - 10 **Product Groups:** 30

Malvern Instruments Ltd
Grovewood Road, Malvern, WR14 1XZ
Tel: 01684-892456 **Fax:** 01684-892789
E-mail: helpdesk@malvern.com
Website: http://www.malvern.com
Bank(s): Lloyds TSB Bank plc
Directors: J. Bishop (Mkt Research), P. Walker (MD), D. Roberts (Mkt Research), R. Prestidge (Fin)
Managers: M. Senemore (Tech Serv Mgr), R. Flaxnam, W. Milne-bennett (Personnel)
Ultimate Holding Company: SPECTRIS PLC
Immediate Holding Company: MALVERN INSTRUMENTS LIMITED
Registration no: 01020602 **Date established:** 1971
Turnover: £75m - £125m **No.of Employees:** 101 - 250
Product Groups: 38, 41

Date of Accounts	Dec 11	Dec 10	Dec 09
Sales Turnover	81m	67m	57m
Pre Tax Profit/Loss	19m	14m	14m
Working Capital	34m	19m	8m
Fixed Assets	10m	10m	10m
Current Assets	53m	36m	24m
Current Liabilities	9m	9m	10m

Malvern Lapidary
39 Broadlands Drive, Malvern, WR14 1PW
Tel: 01684-561537 **Fax:** 01684-891611
Website: http://www.malvernlapidary.co.uk
Managers: R. Jones (Mgr)
Date established: 1970 **No.of Employees:** 1 - 10 **Product Groups:** 36

M D M Pumps Ltd
Spring Lane, Malvern, WR14 1BP
Tel: 01684-892678 **Fax:** 01684-892841
E-mail: info@mdmpumps.co.uk
Website: http://www.mdmpumps.co.uk
Bank(s): National Westminster Bank Plc
Directors: D. Petersen (MD)
Immediate Holding Company: MDM PUMPS LTD.
Registration no: 00184815 **VAT No.:** GB 274 3090 63
Date established: 2022 **Turnover:** £1m - £2m **No.of Employees:** 11 - 20
Product Groups: 40, 41, 42

Date of Accounts	Dec 11	Dec 10	Dec 09
Working Capital	67	62	72
Fixed Assets	189	205	221
Current Assets	185	169	152

Metal Finishing Services
Unit 9 Spring Court Spring Lane South, Malvern, WR14 1AT
Tel: 01684-565713 **Fax:** 01684-565713
Website: http://www.metalfinishingservices.co.uk
Directors: R. Haynes (Prop)
Date established: 1982 **No.of Employees:** 1 - 10 **Product Groups:** 46, 48

Microbial Developments Ltd
Spring Lane North, Malvern, WR14 1BU
Tel: 01684-891055 **Fax:** 01684-891060
E-mail: info@micdev.com
Website: http://www.microbialdevelopments.com
Directors: G. Swan (Fin), T. Nelson (MD)
Ultimate Holding Company: NCORE LIMITED
Immediate Holding Company: MICROBIAL DEVELOPMENTS LIMITED
Registration no: 01607787 **Date established:** 1982 **Turnover:** £1m - £2m
No.of Employees: 11 - 20 **Product Groups:** 20

Date of Accounts	Dec 11	Dec 10	Dec 09
Working Capital	706	589	524
Fixed Assets	826	758	781
Current Assets	921	731	677

Morgan Motor Co. Ltd
Pickersleigh Road, Malvern, WR14 2LL
Tel: 01684-573104 **Fax:** 01684-892295
E-mail: contacts@morgan-motor.co.uk
Website: http://www.morgan-motor.co.uk
Bank(s): Lloyds TSB
Directors: C. Morgan (Grp Chief Exec), M. Parkin (Sales), T. Whitworth (Fin)
Managers: G. Chapman, S. Morris, S. Baldwin (Personnel)
Ultimate Holding Company: MORGAN TECHNOLOGIES LIMITED
Immediate Holding Company: MORGAN MOTOR COMPANY LIMITED
Registration no: 00971255 **VAT No.:** 274 1253 71 **Date established:** 1970
Turnover: £20m - £50m **No.of Employees:** 101 - 250 **Product Groups:** 39

Date of Accounts	Dec 11	Dec 10	Dec 09
Sales Turnover	25m	29m	27m
Pre Tax Profit/Loss	14m	2m	661
Working Capital	4m	6m	4m
Fixed Assets	2m	2m	2m
Current Assets	9m	13m	11m
Current Liabilities	3m	4m	3m

Neoperl UK Ltd
Nimrod Works Enigma Park, Malvern, WR14 1GH
Tel: 01684-564869 **Fax:** 01684-584847
E-mail: info@neoperl.net
Website: http://www.neoperl.net
Bank(s): National Westminster Bank Plc
Directors: O. Denzler (Dir)
Managers: N. Neath, A. Andrews
Ultimate Holding Company: NEOPERL HOLDING AG (SWITZERLAND)
Immediate Holding Company: NEOPERL U.K. LIMITED
Registration no: 02535431 **VAT No.:** GB 551 4526 55
Date established: 1990 **Turnover:** £5m - £10m
No.of Employees: 51 - 100 **Product Groups:** 30, 46

Date of Accounts	Dec 08	Dec 07	Dec 06
Pre Tax Profit/Loss	2m	2m	3m
Working Capital	2m	1m	3m
Fixed Assets	3m	3m	3m
Current Assets	4m	3m	5m
Current Liabilities	1m	2m	2m

Nicholson & Co. Ltd
Interfields Lower Interfields, Malvern, WR14 1UU
Tel: 01886-833338 **Fax:** 01886-833339
E-mail: adm@nicholsonorgans.co.uk
Website: http://www.nicholsonorgans.co.uk
Bank(s): Lloyds TSB Bank plc
Directors: A. Moyes (MD)
Immediate Holding Company: NICHOLSON & CO.(WORCESTER)LIMITED

see next page

Nicholson & Co. Ltd - Cont'd
Registration no: 00176514 **VAT No.:** GB 274 8055 40
Date established: 2021 **Turnover:** £500,000 - £1m
No.of Employees: 11 - 20 **Product Groups:** 49

Date of Accounts	Apr 11	Apr 10	Apr 09
Working Capital	141	154	70
Fixed Assets	483	476	481
Current Assets	392	410	480

Particle Measuring Systems Inc
Grovewood Road, Malvern, WR14 1XZ
Tel: 01684-581000 **Fax:** 01684-560337
E-mail: dhall@pmeasuring.co.uk
Website: http://www.pmeasuring.com
Managers: D. Hall
Immediate Holding Company: PARTICLE MEASURING SYSTEMS INC
Registration no: FC022943 **Date established:** 2001 **Turnover:** £1m - £2m
No.of Employees: 1 - 10 **Product Groups:** 38

Pendragon Presentation Packaging Ltd
The Haysfield, Malvern, WR14 1GF
Tel: 01684-560699 **Fax:** 01684-892562
E-mail: phil@pendragonpack.co.uk
Website: http://www.pendragonpack.co.uk
Bank(s): HSBC Bank plc
Directors: G. Alford (Co Sec), P. Humphreys (Dir), G. Henderson (Co Sec)
Managers: B. Williams, A. Henderson (Sales Prom Mgr)
Immediate Holding Company: PENDRAGON PRESENTATION PACKAGING LIMITED
Registration no: 02814560 **VAT No.:** GB 589 5644 72
Date established: 1993 **Turnover:** £1m - £2m **No.of Employees:** 21 - 50
Product Groups: 27

Date of Accounts	Dec 11	Dec 10	Dec 09
Working Capital	603	544	538
Fixed Assets	61	58	70
Current Assets	934	844	728

Peter Dorrell & Co.
Madresfield Road Sherrards Green, Malvern, WR13 5AS
Tel: 01684-567504 **Fax:** 01684-563101
E-mail: sales@peterdorrell.freeserve.co.uk
Website: http://www.peterdorrell.co.uk
Directors: P. Dorrell (Prop)
VAT No.: GB 377 2735 22 **Turnover:** £250,000 - £500,000
No.of Employees: 1 - 10 **Product Groups:** 52

N A Priday
3 Marlbank Road Welland, Malvern, WR13 6ND
Tel: 01684-311240
Directors: N. Priday (Prop)
No.of Employees: 1 - 10 **Product Groups:** 41

Quickfix Midlands
Unit B1 The Haysfield Business Centre, Malvern, WR14 1GF
Tel: 01684-560700 **Fax:** 01684-560020
E-mail: sales@quick-fix.demon.co.uk
Website: http://www.quickfixmidlands.co.uk
Directors: R. Brant (Prop)
Immediate Holding Company: QUICKFIX (MIDLANDS) LIMITED
Registration no: 04538850 **VAT No.:** GB 539 4212 09
Date established: 2002 **Turnover:** Up to £250,000
No.of Employees: 1 - 10 **Product Groups:** 35, 66

Reflow
Unit 2 Spring Lane North, Malvern, WR14 1BU
Tel: 01684-578849
E-mail: info@reflow.co.uk
Website: http://www.reflow.co.uk
Directors: L. Mason (MD)
Immediate Holding Company: M. & A. PACKAGING SERVICES LIMITED
Date established: 1985 **Turnover:** Up to £250,000
No.of Employees: 1 - 10 **Product Groups:** 37, 44, 48

Date of Accounts	Apr 11	Apr 10	Apr 09
Working Capital	84	81	80
Fixed Assets	5	6	11
Current Assets	459	376	321

S T P Motor Services
The Chase Works Spring Lane South, Malvern, WR14 1AT
Tel: 01684-563307 **Fax:** 01684-563307
Directors: T. Carpenter (Prop)
Ultimate Holding Company: ADVANTAGE CHEMICALS HOLDINGS LIMITED
Immediate Holding Company: ADVANTAGE CHEMICALS HOLDINGS LIMITED
Registration no: 00588668 **Date established:** 1991
No.of Employees: 1 - 10 **Product Groups:** 46, 48

Date of Accounts	Mar 11	Mar 10	Mar 09
Working Capital	-40	-159	44
Fixed Assets	1m	1m	1m
Current Assets	462	324	546

Stone Technology Limited
Link House Sandys Road, Malvern, WR14 1JJ
Tel: 0844-3578045 **Fax:** 0844-3576945
E-mail: sales@redantsoftware.co.uk
Website: http://www.redantsoftware.co.uk
Directors: M. Coleman (Dir)
Registration no: 05151869 **Date established:** 2003
Turnover: £500,000 - £1m **No.of Employees:** 1 - 10 **Product Groups:** 44

Date of Accounts	Sep 07	Sep 06	Sep 05
Working Capital	-12	-13	-10
Current Assets	28	26	2
Current Liabilities	39	39	12

Synthotec Ltd
Sandys Road, Malvern, WR14 1JJ
Tel: 01684-571900 **Fax:** 01684-571909
E-mail: sales@synthotec.com
Directors: A. Barker (Dir)
Ultimate Holding Company: PEMBERSTONE VENTURES LIMITED
Immediate Holding Company: SYNTHOTEC LIMITED
Registration no: 02498447 **VAT No.:** GB 572 2569 27
Date established: 1990 **Turnover:** £1m - £2m **No.of Employees:** 11 - 20
Product Groups: 30

Date of Accounts	Dec 11	Dec 10	Jan 10
Working Capital	1m	1m	1m
Fixed Assets	569	699	649
Current Assets	2m	1m	1m

Thermaco Ltd
Sandys Road, Malvern, WR14 1JJ
Tel: 01684-566163 **Fax:** 01684-892356
E-mail: info@thermaco.co.uk
Website: http://www.thermaco.co.uk
Bank(s): National Westminster Bank Plc
Directors: H. Bucktin (Co Sec), A. Walker (MD)
Ultimate Holding Company: SUNGAS HOLDINGS LIMITED
Immediate Holding Company: THERMACO LIMITED
Registration no: 01414038 **Date established:** 1979
No.of Employees: 11 - 20 **Product Groups:** 36, 38, 40, 49

Date of Accounts	Dec 07	Mar 11	Mar 10
Working Capital	1m	2m	2m
Fixed Assets	12	8	10
Current Assets	2m	2m	2m
Current Liabilities	13	N/A	N/A

Threshold Consulting Ltd
11 Ebrington Road West Malvern, Malvern, WR14 4NL
Tel: 01684-891566 **Fax:** 01684-891566
E-mail: eoinm@threshold.uk.com
Website: http://www.threshold.uk.com
Directors: P. Kingston (Fin), E. McCarthy (MD)
Immediate Holding Company: THRESHOLD CONSULTING LIMITED
Registration no: 03687839 **Date established:** 1998
No.of Employees: 1 - 10 **Product Groups:** 80

Date of Accounts	Dec 11	Dec 10	Dec 09
Working Capital	5	4	-3
Fixed Assets	1	1	1
Current Assets	5	4	4

Pershore

Bikers Clearance World Ltd
Worcester Road Drakes Broughton, Pershore, WR10 2AG
Tel: 01905-841842
Website: http://www.bikersworldshops.co.uk
Directors: W. Harding (MD), R. Barnwell (Dir)
Immediate Holding Company: BIKERS CLEARANCE WORLD LIMITED
Registration no: 03536562 **Date established:** 1998
No.of Employees: 1 - 10 **Product Groups:** 24, 39, 40, 63

Direct Design Management Services Ltd
Unit 7 Cobham Road, Pershore, WR10 2DL
Tel: 01386-561500 **Fax:** 01386-561502
E-mail: spencer.da@btconnect.com
Website: http://www.ddinsulation.co.uk
Directors: P. Spencer (Fin), D. Spencer (MD)
Managers: M. Green (Mgr)
Immediate Holding Company: DIRECT DESIGN MANAGEMENT SERVICES LIMITED
Registration no: 03631319 **Date established:** 1998
No.of Employees: 1 - 10 **Product Groups:** 40, 48

Date of Accounts	Sep 07	Sep 06	Sep 05
Working Capital	-3	1	26
Fixed Assets	15	20	18
Current Assets	192	283	293
Current Liabilities	195	282	267

Freddy Products Ltd
Unit 19 Kempton Road, Pershore, WR10 2TA
Tel: 01386-561113 **Fax:** 01386-556401
E-mail: lisashaw@freddy-products.co.uk
Website: http://www.freddy-products.co.uk
Directors: L. Shaw (Fin)
Managers: G. Ward (Sales Prom Mgr)
Ultimate Holding Company: PAUL DE LA PENA LIMITED
Immediate Holding Company: FREDDY PRODUCTS LIMITED
Registration no: 02907462 **Date established:** 1994 **Turnover:** £1m - £2m
No.of Employees: 1 - 10 **Product Groups:** 36, 40, 42

Date of Accounts	Mar 12	Mar 11	Mar 10
Working Capital	375	238	97
Fixed Assets	78	30	54
Current Assets	626	507	466

Ics Systems UK Ltd
27 Aintree Road Keytec 7 Business Park, Pershore, WR10 2JN
Tel: 01386-552032 **Fax:** 01386-661135
E-mail: ian.stevenson@keronite.com
Website: http://www.icssystems.co.uk
Directors: I. Stevenson (Dir)
Immediate Holding Company: I C S SYSTEMS UK LIMITED
Registration no: 06865029 **VAT No.:** GB 641 0650 73
Date established: 2009 **Turnover:** £250,000 - £500,000
No.of Employees: 1 - 10 **Product Groups:** 37, 46

Date of Accounts	Mar 11	Mar 10
Working Capital	2	-1
Fixed Assets	2	2
Current Assets	29	27
Current Liabilities	25	20

Mechanical & Pipework Fabrications Ltd
Racecourse Road, Pershore, WR10 2EY
Tel: 01386-554048 **Fax:** 01386-556695
E-mail: sales@mpf-ltd.co.uk
Website: http://www.mpf-ltd.co.uk
Bank(s): Lloyds TSB
Directors: S. Ellis (MD), C. Ellis (Fin)
Managers: K. Goodman, I. Parker (Sales Prom Mgr), R. Faizey (Chief Mgr)
Ultimate Holding Company: MECHANICAL & PIPEWORK HOLDINGS LIMITED
Immediate Holding Company: MECHANICAL & PIPEWORK FABRICATIONS LIMITED
Registration no: 01298017 **Date established:** 1977 **Turnover:** £2m - £5m
No.of Employees: 21 - 50 **Product Groups:** 48

Date of Accounts	Dec 11	Dec 10	Dec 09
Sales Turnover	5m	5m	5m
Pre Tax Profit/Loss	130	157	195
Working Capital	798	648	548
Fixed Assets	535	579	554
Current Assets	2m	2m	2m
Current Liabilities	246	261	474

Mercia Interiors Ltd
Unit 31 Pershore Trading Estate, Pershore, WR10 2DD
Tel: 01386-556565 **Fax:** 01386-556525
E-mail: diane.thorner@lineone.net
Bank(s): Lloyds TSB
Directors: D. Thorner (Fin), L. Thorner (Prop)
Immediate Holding Company: MERCIA INTERIORS LIMITED
Registration no: 02044120 **VAT No.:** GB 454 7497 11
Date established: 1986 **Turnover:** £500,000 - £1m
No.of Employees: 11 - 20 **Product Groups:** 35, 52

Date of Accounts	Sep 08	Sep 07	Sep 06
Working Capital	1	5	-4
Fixed Assets	2	3	15
Current Assets	196	225	119

Metal Mesh UK Ltd
Unit 15-17 Kempton Road, Pershore, WR10 2TA
Tel: 01386-555500 **Fax:** 01386-555 200
E-mail: sales@metal-mesh.co.uk
Website: http://www.metal-mesh.co.uk
Directors: D. Renolds (Dir)
Ultimate Holding Company: LOCUSRITE HOLDINGS LIMITED
Immediate Holding Company: METAL MESH UK LIMITED
Registration no: 06582396 **Date established:** 2008
No.of Employees: 1 - 10 **Product Groups:** 34

Date of Accounts	Dec 11	Dec 10	Dec 09
Working Capital	66	40	44
Fixed Assets	232	207	6
Current Assets	661	475	519

Mico Europe Ltd
15 Goodwood Road, Pershore, WR10 2RY
Tel: 01386-555562
E-mail: sales@offhighwaybrakes.co.uk
Website: http://www.mico.com
Directors: D. Mcgrath (Dir), B. Ellis (Co Sec)
Managers: C. Reynolds (Chief Mgr)
Immediate Holding Company: OFF HIGHWAY BRAKES & CONTROLS LTD.
Registration no: 02328874 **Date established:** 1988
No.of Employees: 11 - 20 **Product Groups:** 37, 38, 40

Date of Accounts	Dec 10	Dec 09	Dec 08
Working Capital	1m	1m	1m
Fixed Assets	338	336	362
Current Assets	1m	1m	2m

N W Flooring
Unit 9 Lyttleton Road, Pershore, WR10 2DF
Tel: 0781-369 6618
E-mail: nickwinnall@aol.com
Website: http://www.nwflooring.co.uk
Directors: N. Winnall (Prop)
No.of Employees: 1 - 10 **Product Groups:** 25, 30, 33, 35, 40, 52, 66

Northwick Associates
27 Aintree Road Keytec 7 Business Park, Pershore, WR10 2JN
Tel: 01386-555630 **Fax:** 01386-556283
E-mail: info@northwickassociates.co.uk
Website: http://www.northwickassociates.co.uk
Directors: J. Isaacs (MD)
Immediate Holding Company: NORTHWICK ASSOCIATES LTD
Registration no: 04714313 **VAT No.:** GB 729 5682 90
Date established: 2003 **Turnover:** Up to £250,000
No.of Employees: 1 - 10 **Product Groups:** 39, 40, 43, 46, 48, 67

Date of Accounts	Mar 12	Mar 11	Mar 10
Working Capital	7	14	-10
Fixed Assets	46	20	27
Current Assets	60	125	62

Peco Controls-Europe Ltd
4 Kempton Road, Pershore, WR10 2TA
Tel: 01386-556622 **Fax:** 01386-552252
E-mail: office@peco-europe.com
Website: http://www.peco-europe.com
Directors: K. Allcock (Fin)
Immediate Holding Company: PECO CONTROLS - EUROPE LIMITED
Registration no: 02435145 **VAT No.:** GB 552 6705 39
Date established: 1989 **Turnover:** £500,000 - £1m
No.of Employees: 1 - 10 **Product Groups:** 37, 42

Date of Accounts	Dec 11	Dec 10	Dec 09
Working Capital	170	198	147
Fixed Assets	93	29	38
Current Assets	404	351	387

Pershore Plating Ltd
17a Pershore Trading Estate, Pershore, WR10 2DD
Tel: 01386-561756 **Fax:** 01386-561756
Directors: K. Walters (Fin), M. Walters (MD)
Immediate Holding Company: PERSHORE PLATING LTD
Registration no: 04464981 **Date established:** 2002
No.of Employees: 1 - 10 **Product Groups:** 46, 48

Date of Accounts	Jun 11	Jun 10	Jun 09
Working Capital	-23	-33	-48
Fixed Assets	25	29	33
Current Assets	21	23	39

Sailes Marketing Ltd
15 Aintree Road Keytec 7 Business Park, Pershore, WR10 2JN
Tel: 01386-554210 **Fax:** 01386-552461
E-mail: sales@sailesmarketing.com
Website: http://www.sailesmarketing.com
Directors: M. Sailes (MD)
Immediate Holding Company: SAILES MARKETING LIMITED
Registration no: 03941062 **VAT No.:** GB 305 7705 67
Date established: 2000 **Turnover:** £500,000 - £1m
No.of Employees: 1 - 10 **Product Groups:** 38, 39

Date of Accounts	Mar 12	Mar 11	Mar 10
Working Capital	341	328	340
Fixed Assets	87	99	111
Current Assets	404	375	393

Schloetter Co. Ltd
Abbey Works New Road, Pershore, WR10 1BY
Tel: 01386-552331 **Fax:** 01386-556864
E-mail: info@schloetter.co.uk
Website: http://www.schloetter.co.uk
Bank(s): Barclays, Birmingham

Directors: P. Griffiths (Dir), R. Whatcott (Dir)
Managers: D. Haslam (Tech Serv Mgr), D. Grundy (Purch Mgr)
Ultimate Holding Company: SCHLOETTER (IRELAND) LIMITED
Immediate Holding Company: SCHLOETTER COMPANY LIMITED
Registration no: 00947371 **VAT No.:** GB 274 7177 31
Date established: 1969 **Turnover:** £5m - £10m **No.of Employees:** 21 - 50
Product Groups: 31, 32, 42, 46

Date of Accounts	Dec 11	Dec 10	Dec 09
Sales Turnover	9m	9m	7m
Pre Tax Profit/Loss	79	322	-146
Working Capital	5m	5m	4m
Fixed Assets	2m	2m	2m
Current Assets	5m	5m	5m
Current Liabilities	254	279	191

Simply Yoga YOGA.EU LTD
Florence Cottages 5 Manor Road, Lower Moor, Pershore, WR10 2NZ
Tel: 0845-3951945
E-mail: shop@simply-yoga.co.uk
Website: http://www.simply-yoga.co.uk
Turnover: Up to £250,000 **No.of Employees:** 1 - 10 **Product Groups:** 29, 49, 65

Sprint Refrigeration & Catering Equipment
1 Cobham Road, Pershore, WR10 2DL
Tel: 01386-555922 **Fax:** 01386-555207
E-mail: sales@sprint-group.co.uk
Website: http://www.sprint-group.co.uk
Directors: A. Day (Fin), D. Ryan (MD)
Immediate Holding Company: SPRINT REFRIGERATION & CATERING EQUIPMENT LTD.
Registration no: 03000134 **Date established:** 1994
No.of Employees: 1 - 10 **Product Groups:** 20, 40, 41

Date of Accounts	Apr 11	Apr 10	Apr 09
Working Capital	437	391	347
Fixed Assets	183	91	83
Current Assets	1m	1m	801

Vale Stove Spares & Repair
Lower Hill Evesham Road, Wick, Pershore, WR10 3JR
Tel: 01386-555456 **Fax:** 01386-555456
Directors: R. Gowing (Prop)
Date established: 2000 **No.of Employees:** 1 - 10 **Product Groups:** 40

Worcester Powder Coating Ltd
Unit 7 Pershore Trading Estate, Pershore, WR10 2DD
Tel: 01386-556613
E-mail: nigelwager@googlemail.com
Directors: N. Wager (Prop)
Immediate Holding Company: WORCESTER POWDER COATING LTD
Registration no: 06143755 **Date established:** 2007
Turnover: Up to £250,000 **No.of Employees:** 1 - 10 **Product Groups:** 46

Date of Accounts	Mar 11	Mar 10	Mar 09
Working Capital	21	-28	5
Fixed Assets	51	61	27
Current Assets	120	91	63

Redditch

A & M Fasteners & Engineering Supplies Ltd
Unit 77 The Washford Industrial Estate Heming Road, Redditch, B98 0EA
Tel: 01527-520770 **Fax:** 01527-520670
Website: http://www.thetoolcentre.co.uk
Directors: M. Rossall (Dir), M. Rossall (Dir)
Immediate Holding Company: A & M FASTENER & ENGINEERING SUPPLIES LIMITED
Registration no: 06435633 **Date established:** 2007
Turnover: £500,000 - £1m **No.of Employees:** 1 - 10 **Product Groups:** 22, 29, 30, 31, 32, 33, 35, 36, 37, 39, 40, 45, 46, 47, 63, 66, 67

Date of Accounts	Apr 11	Apr 10	Apr 09
Working Capital	-10	-33	-37
Fixed Assets	22	25	28
Current Assets	82	46	41

A1 Plating
36 Padgets Lane, Redditch, B98 0RB
Tel: 01527-528852 **Fax:** 01527-528852
E-mail: office@a1-plating.co.uk
Website: http://www.a1plating.co.uk
Directors: A. Griffin (Prop)
VAT No.: GB 113 5000 39 **Turnover:** Up to £250,000
No.of Employees: 1 - 10 **Product Groups:** 48

A T & T
Highfield House Headless Cross Drive, Redditch, B97 5EQ
Tel: 01527-518181 **Fax:** 01527-402408
E-mail: paul.brazier@att.com
Website: http://www.att.com
Directors: D. Hawkes (Pers), K. Harvey (MD), A. Gunninghum (I.T. Dir)
Managers: G. Pugh (Fin Mgr), B. Stanton
Immediate Holding Company: AT & T PENSION SCHEME TRUSTEE LIMITED
Registration no: 03899827 **Date established:** 1999
Turnover: £125m - £250m **No.of Employees:** 1001 - 1500
Product Groups: 44, 80

A W G Pipework & Plumbing Services
51 The Slough Crabbs Cross, Redditch, B97 5JR
Tel: 01527-547965 **Fax:** 01527-547965
E-mail: info@airwatergas.com
Website: http://www.airwatergas.com
Directors: K. Ricketts (Prop)
Immediate Holding Company: MODERNFORCE LIMITED
Date established: 1985 **Turnover:** Up to £250,000
No.of Employees: 1 - 10 **Product Groups:** 52

Date of Accounts	Sep 11	Sep 10	Sep 09
Working Capital	-1	-1	-1
Fixed Assets	N/A	1	1
Current Assets	1	1	1

Accurate Cutting Services Ltd
Units 44-45 Crossgate Rd, Park Farm Industrial Estate, Redditch, B98 7SN
Tel: 01527-527058 **Fax:** 01527-527541
E-mail: sales@accurate-cutting.co.uk
Website: http://www.accurate-cutting.co.uk
Bank(s): HSBC Bank plc
Directors: M. Fleeming (Ch), G. Fleeming (Fin), M. Pomeroy (MD)
Managers: M. Arnold (Sales Prom Mgr), C. Dempsey, K. Clayton, D. Vedmore (Mgr)
Registration no: 00948502 **VAT No.:** GB 111 6495 90
Date established: 1969 **Turnover:** £2m - £5m **No.of Employees:** 51 - 100
Product Groups: 36, 46, 47, 48, 66, 67

Date of Accounts	Mar 11	Mar 10	Mar 09
Pre Tax Profit/Loss	N/A	N/A	25
Working Capital	1m	1m	1m
Fixed Assets	774	922	992
Current Assets	2m	2m	2m
Current Liabilities	N/A	N/A	186

Aerial Supplies Redditch Ltd
6 Widney House Broomsgrove Road, Redditch, B97 4SP
Tel: 01527-66884 **Fax:** 01527-595766
Directors: J. Wharrad (Co Sec), K. Wharrad (MD)
Immediate Holding Company: JDR PRODUCTS LIMITED
Registration no: 01481617 **Date established:** 1980
Turnover: Up to £250,000 **No.of Employees:** 1 - 10 **Product Groups:** 34, 35, 36, 40, 46, 48, 52

Alcester Broach & Tool Co. Ltd
Pipers Road Park Farm Industrial Estate, Redditch, B98 0HU
Tel: 01527-523107 **Fax:** 01527-526137
E-mail: sales@alcesterbroach.com
Website: http://www.alcesterbroach.com
Directors: C. Gerrard (MD), D. Gerrard (Fin)
Immediate Holding Company: ALCESTER BROACH & TOOL CO.LIMITED
Registration no: 01038785 **Date established:** 1972
Turnover: £500,000 - £1m **No.of Employees:** 1 - 10 **Product Groups:** 46

Date of Accounts	Apr 12	Apr 11	Apr 10
Working Capital	379	367	364
Fixed Assets	96	104	110
Current Assets	473	438	410

Alliance Seals Ltd
Unit 27 Enfield Industrial Estate, Redditch, B97 6BG
Tel: 01527-584000 **Fax:** 01527-584005
E-mail: sales@allianceseals.co.uk
Website: http://www.allianceseals.co.uk
Bank(s): Barclays, Alcester St, Redditch
Directors: D. Zdanko (Fin), J. Zdanko (Dir)
Immediate Holding Company: ALLIANCE SEALS LIMITED
Registration no: 02379893 **VAT No.:** GB 640 9072 48
Date established: 1989 **Turnover:** £500,000 - £1m
No.of Employees: 11 - 20 **Product Groups:** 29, 33, 36, 37, 38, 40, 43, 49, 63, 66

Date of Accounts	Mar 12	Mar 11	Mar 10
Working Capital	19	-7	N/A
Fixed Assets	373	378	381
Current Assets	147	140	126

Alpha Of Redditch Powder Coating
Unit 10 Enfield Industrial Estate, Redditch, B97 6BG
Tel: 01527-596750 **Fax:** 01527-596750
E-mail: morley@tiscali.co.uk
Directors: M. Morley (Prop)
Date established: 2001 **No.of Employees:** 1 - 10 **Product Groups:** 46, 48

Alto Tower Systems
24 Walkers Road North Moons, Moons Moat North Industrial Estate, Redditch, B98 9HE
Tel: 01527-62946 **Fax:** 01527-597444
E-mail: sales@alto-towers.co.uk
Website: http://www.alto-group.co.uk
Directors: C. Mansell (Tech Serv), J. Hodgetts (Ch), J. Moreby (Co Sec), N. Hardacre (Dir), P. Pritchard (Sales)
Managers: A. Edwards (Sales Prom), K. Baker (Sales Prom Mgr), K. Law (Mgr), M. Parker (Accounts)
Ultimate Holding Company: Alto Systems Holdings Ltd
Immediate Holding Company: ALTO TOWER SYSTEMS LIMITED
Registration no: 04051262 **VAT No.:** GB 614 0450 84
Date established: 2000 **Turnover:** £2m - £5m **No.of Employees:** 1 - 10
Product Groups: 35, 39, 81

Date of Accounts	Dec 09	Dec 08	Dec 07
Working Capital	2m	2m	2m
Fixed Assets	7	14	22
Current Assets	3m	2m	2m
Current Liabilities	N/A	45	N/A

Amari Copper Alloys
Unit 47
Eagle Road
North Moons Moat, Redditch, B98 9HF
Tel: 01527-405600 **Fax:** 01527-405605
E-mail: sales@amaricopperalloys.co.uk
Website: http://www.amaricopperalloys.com
Product Groups: 27, 34, 35, 36, 37, 66, 67

Arrowvale Electronics
Arrow Business Park Shawbank Road, Redditch, B98 8YN
Tel: 01527-514151 **Fax:** 01527-514321
E-mail: info@arrowvale.co.uk
Website: http://www.arrowvale.co.uk
Directors: G. Sutherland (Fin)
Managers: M. Cooper (Personnel), G. Jhutty (Tech Serv Mgr), S. Beard (Sales & Mktg Mg), E. Beard (Chief Buyer)
Immediate Holding Company: GRINSTY RAIL LIMITED
Registration no: 01751418 **Date established:** 2011 **Turnover:** £2m - £5m
No.of Employees: 51 - 100 **Product Groups:** 35, 37

Date of Accounts	Jun 11	Jun 10	Jun 09
Working Capital	1m	1m	1m
Fixed Assets	18	26	21
Current Assets	2m	2m	2m

Ateq UK Ltd
Unit 71 The Washford Industrial Estate Heming Road, Redditch, B98 0EA
Tel: 01527-520011 **Fax:** 01527-520022
E-mail: janice.cooper@ateq.co.uk
Website: http://www.ateq.co.uk
Managers: J. Cooper (Sales Admin)
Immediate Holding Company: ATEQ UK LIMITED
Registration no: 02896068 **VAT No.:** GB 613 4581 55
Date established: 1994 **Turnover:** £500,000 - £1m
No.of Employees: 1 - 10 **Product Groups:** 38

Date of Accounts	Dec 11	Dec 10	Dec 09
Working Capital	9	-3	-34
Fixed Assets	1	6	9
Current Assets	213	260	172

Autonational Ltd
The Old Hymatic Works Unit 1 Glover Street, Small Wood, Redditch, B98 7BG
Tel: 01527-62940 **Fax:** 01527-62951
E-mail: sales@autonationalltd.co.uk
Website: http://www.autonational.ltd.uk
Bank(s): Barclays
Directors: J. Shannon (MD), D. Ghanon (MD), D. Shannon (MD)
Managers: V. Clarke (Sales Prom Mgr), C. Maynard (I.T. Exec), D. Anistasis (Sales Prom Mgr)
Registration no: 06270524 **VAT No.:** GB 111 3128 35
Turnover: £2m - £5m **No.of Employees:** 11 - 20 **Product Groups:** 68

Date of Accounts	Dec 05	Dec 04	Dec 03
Working Capital	502	228	230
Fixed Assets	3	39	27
Current Assets	768	426	459
Current Liabilities	266	198	229
Total Share Capital	7	7	7

Axis Lighting Ltd
Merse Road, Redditch, B98 9HH
Tel: 01527-583200
E-mail: admin@sugglighting.co.uk
Immediate Holding Company: F.W. Thorpe PLC
Registration no: 01555514 **Date established:** 1981
No.of Employees: 1 - 10 **Product Groups:** 37, 67

Aztech Components Ltd
78 Atcham Close Winyates East, Redditch, B98 0NZ
Tel: 01527-500151 **Fax:** 01527-500151
E-mail: sales@aztech.uk.net
Website: http://www.aztech.uk.net
Directors: C. Ricketts (MD)
Immediate Holding Company: AZTECH COMPONENTS LIMITED
Registration no: 03656688 **Date established:** 1998
Turnover: Up to £250,000 **No.of Employees:** 1 - 10 **Product Groups:** 29, 30, 32, 35, 36, 37, 38, 40, 46, 48, 66, 67, 84

Date of Accounts	Oct 11	Oct 10	Oct 09
Sales Turnover	8	8	N/A
Pre Tax Profit/Loss	-1	-6	N/A
Working Capital	-2	-6	-10
Current Assets	3	4	6

B Hepworth Ltd
Unit 4 Merse Road Moons Moat North Industrial Estate, Redditch, B98 9HL
Tel: 01527-61243 **Fax:** 01527-66836
E-mail: j-eddy@b-hepworth.com
Website: http://www.b-hepworth.com
Bank(s): Barclays
Directors: N. Dalton (Fin)
Managers: J. Prender Gast
Ultimate Holding Company: B. HEPWORTH AND COMPANY LIMITED
Immediate Holding Company: WYNSTRUMENTS LIMITED
Registration no: 00489244 **Date established:** 1950
No.of Employees: 101 - 250 **Product Groups:** 39

Date of Accounts	Mar 10	Mar 09	Mar 08
Sales Turnover	2m	6m	N/A
Pre Tax Profit/Loss	-1m	191	N/A
Working Capital	N/A	2m	1m
Fixed Assets	N/A	16	35
Current Assets	6	3m	3m
Current Liabilities	6	739	999

Baylis & Harding
Nash Road, Redditch, B98 7AS
Tel: 01527-505000 **Fax:** 01527-505001
E-mail: reception@bayhar.com
Website: http://www.bayhar.com
Bank(s): Barclays
Directors: C. Fallon (Sales), D. Patten (Co Sec)
Immediate Holding Company: BAYLIS & HARDING PUBLIC LIMITED COMPANY
Registration no: 01389887 **Date established:** 1978
Turnover: £20m - £50m **No.of Employees:** 51 - 100 **Product Groups:** 63, 84

Date of Accounts	May 11	May 10	May 09
Sales Turnover	24m	19m	23m
Pre Tax Profit/Loss	2m	89	300
Working Capital	3m	3m	3m
Fixed Assets	1m	1m	1m
Current Assets	6m	5m	5m
Current Liabilities	1m	474	1m

Belleville Springs Ltd
Arthur Street, Redditch, B98 8JY
Tel: 01527-500500 **Fax:** 01527-517039
E-mail: info@bellevillesprings.com
Website: http://www.bellevillesprings.com
Bank(s): HSBC Bank plc
Directors: C. Roberts (Fin), B. Grange (Sales & Mktg), M. Evans (Fin)
Managers: A. Martin (Chief Mgr)
Ultimate Holding Company: SPRINGMASTERS LIMITED
Immediate Holding Company: BELLEVILLE SPRINGS LIMITED
Registration no: 01337456 **Date established:** 1977
Turnover: £500,000 - £1m **No.of Employees:** 101 - 250
Product Groups: 35, 36, 39, 66

Date of Accounts	May 11	May 10	May 09
Working Capital	2m	1m	1m
Fixed Assets	11	15	11
Current Assets	2m	1m	1m

Bendi Driver Training
55 Padgets Lane, Redditch, B98 0RD
Tel: 01527-523500 **Fax:** 01527-523277
E-mail: sales@benditraining.co.uk
Website: http://www.bendi-flt.co.uk
Directors: J. Handley (MD)
Date established: 2003 **No.of Employees:** 1 - 10 **Product Groups:** 35, 39, 45

Bennett Mahler
2 Merse Road Moons Moat North Industrial Estate, Redditch, B98 9HL
Tel: 01527-64444 **Fax:** 01527-591668
E-mail: bennettmahler@msn.com
Website: http://www.bennettmahler.com
Bank(s): Bank of Scotland
Directors: J. Mahler (MD)
Immediate Holding Company: BENNETT-MAHLER LIMITED
Registration no: 01702973 **VAT No.:** GB 378 2299 10
Date established: 1983 **Turnover:** £1m - £2m **No.of Employees:** 11 - 20
Product Groups: 46

Date of Accounts	Feb 08	Feb 11	Feb 10
Sales Turnover	N/A	1m	680
Pre Tax Profit/Loss	N/A	50	-120
Working Capital	356	172	62
Fixed Assets	556	523	533
Current Assets	679	482	475
Current Liabilities	N/A	274	259

Brayman Springs & Production Engineering
7 28 Heming Road, Redditch, B98 0DH
Tel: 01527-510004 **Fax:** 01527-510004
Directors: D. Price (Prop)
Immediate Holding Company: BRAYMAN SPRINGS & PRODUCTION ENGINEERING LIMITED
Registration no: 04780708 **VAT No.:** GB 478 5028 18
Date established: 2003 **Turnover:** Up to £250,000
No.of Employees: 1 - 10 **Product Groups:** 35, 48

Date of Accounts	Jul 11	Jul 10	Jul 09
Working Capital	14	10	8
Current Assets	29	37	36

Brocock Ltd
Unit 32u The Washford Industrial Estate Heming Road, Redditch, B98 0DH
Tel: 01527-527800 **Fax:** 01527-527850
E-mail: sales@brocock.co.uk
Website: http://www.brocock.co.uk
Directors: C. Lewis (Fin)
Immediate Holding Company: BROCOCK LIMITED
Registration no: 02391463 **Date established:** 1989
No.of Employees: 1 - 10 **Product Groups:** 36, 39, 40

Date of Accounts	Aug 11	Aug 10	Aug 09
Working Capital	-112	-98	12
Fixed Assets	556	568	545
Current Assets	461	477	651

Butchers Printed Products Ltd
Unit 8 Upper Crossgate Road Park Farm Industrial Estate, Redditch, B98 7SR
Tel: 0121-440 2612 **Fax:** 01527-524360
E-mail: sales@bppdigital.co.uk
Website: http://www.bppdigital.co.uk
Bank(s): HSBC, Balsall Heath
Directors: M. Elmes (MD)
Ultimate Holding Company: ELMES GROUP LIMITED
Immediate Holding Company: BUTCHERS PRINTED PRODUCTS LIMITED
Registration no: 02503552 **VAT No.:** GB 558 9305 04
Date established: 1990 **Turnover:** £1m - £2m **No.of Employees:** 11 - 20
Product Groups: 28

Date of Accounts	Sep 11	Sep 10	Sep 09
Working Capital	925	874	880
Fixed Assets	16	22	27
Current Assets	1m	968	972

Bywell Springs & Pressings Ltd
Units 4b-4b1 Millsborough House Ipsley Street, Redditch, B98 7AL
Tel: 01527-66551 **Fax:** 01527-66024
E-mail: sales@bywell.co.uk
Website: http://www.bywell.co.uk
Directors: B. Faulkner (Dir), D. Lawley (Co Sec)
Immediate Holding Company: BYWELL SPRINGS AND PRESSINGS LIMITED
Registration no: 02632149 **VAT No.:** GB 478 5241 18
Date established: 1991 **No.of Employees:** 1 - 10 **Product Groups:** 30, 35

Date of Accounts	Mar 12	Mar 11	Mar 10
Working Capital	55	-1	-4
Fixed Assets	5	7	9
Current Assets	181	242	121

Centaur Cable Management Systems
Pipers Road Park Farm Industrial Estate, Redditch, B98 0HU
Tel: 01527-501183 **Fax:** 01527-500882
E-mail: admin@centaurmfg.co.uk
Website: http://www.centaurmfg.co.uk
Managers: G. Hobday (Chief Mgr), I. Upright (Mgr), I. Upwright (Mgr)
Immediate Holding Company: ADVANCED CASTING COMPANY LIMITED
Registration no: 07100358 **Date established:** 2010 **Turnover:** £5m - £10m
No.of Employees: 51 - 100 **Product Groups:** 36, 37

Central Springs & Pressings Ltd
Springside Works Howard Road, Redditch, B98 7SE
Tel: 01527-514300 **Fax:** 01527-514301
E-mail: centralsprings@btclick.com
Website: http://www.centralsprings.com
Directors: B. Clark (Dir), M. Fleming (Dir)
Registration no: 02530310 **Turnover:** £1m - £2m
No.of Employees: 21 - 50 **Product Groups:** 34, 35, 36, 39, 48, 66

Date of Accounts	Sep 11	Sep 10	Sep 09
Working Capital	-33	-61	-124
Fixed Assets	120	132	151
Current Assets	185	226	153

C F S Carpets (Part of Landsdon Group)
Arrow Valley Claybrook Drive, Redditch, B98 0FY
Tel: 01527-511860 **Fax:** 01527-511861
E-mail: redditch@carpetandflooring.co.uk
Website: http://www.cfscarpets.co.uk
Bank(s): HSBC Bank plc
Directors: P. Gordon (MD)
Managers: J. Stringer (Mktg Serv Mgr), S. Fox (Comm), A. Davies
Registration no: 02678036 **VAT No.:** GB 705 3168 55
Turnover: £50m - £75m **No.of Employees:** 21 - 50 **Product Groups:** 23, 63

Date of Accounts	Feb 08
Sales Turnover	40560
Pre Tax Profit/Loss	21630
Working Capital	3520
Current Assets	3520
Total Share Capital	1620

Customer Champions
Charity Barn Astwood Lane, Astwood Bank, Redditch, B96 6PS
Tel: 01527-894521
E-mail: c@customerchampions.co.uk
Website: http://www.customerchampions.co.uk
Directors: C. Bates (MD), C. Bates (Dir), J. Miller (Fin)
Immediate Holding Company: CUSTOMER CHAMPIONS LIMITED
Registration no: 03787888 **Date established:** 1999
Turnover: Up to £250,000 **No.of Employees:** 1 - 10 **Product Groups:** 81

Date of Accounts	Jun 10	Jun 09	Jun 08
Sales Turnover	190	174	215
Pre Tax Profit/Loss	126	114	147
Working Capital	43	56	38
Fixed Assets	4	2	2
Current Assets	121	142	131
Current Liabilities	76	86	87

D & K Europe Ltd
Unit 38-39 Crossgate Road, Park Farm Industrial Estate, Redditch, B98 7SN
Tel: 01527-520073 **Fax:** 01527-524056
E-mail: robin@dkeurope.co.uk
Website: http://www.dkeurope.co.uk
Bank(s): Barclays
Directors: R. French (MD)
Managers: S. Baggott, K. Turner (Comm)
Ultimate Holding Company: D & K GROUP INC (USA)
Immediate Holding Company: D & K EUROPE LIMITED
Registration no: 02110183 **VAT No.:** GB 454 8897 87
Date established: 1987 **Turnover:** £5m - £10m **No.of Employees:** 21 - 50
Product Groups: 30, 44

Date of Accounts	Jun 11	Jun 10	Jun 09
Working Capital	-256	-530	16
Fixed Assets	530	540	549
Current Assets	4m	4m	3m

Dacoma Ltd
1 Dunlop Road, Redditch, B97 5XP
Tel: 01527-402200 **Fax:** 01527-402171
E-mail: rghinn@lubetech.co.uk
Website: http://www.spillexcel.com
Directors: R. Ghinn (Dir)
Immediate Holding Company: WELO UK LIMITED
Registration no: 03264152 **Date established:** 2000 **Turnover:** £1m - £2m
No.of Employees: 21 - 50 **Product Groups:** 38, 40

Date of Accounts	Dec 11	Dec 10	Dec 09
Working Capital	-218	-200	-187
Fixed Assets	10	10	11
Current Assets	92	99	92

David Hart Alcester Ltd
Berrowhill Lane Feckenham, Redditch, B96 6QS
Tel: 01527-821197 **Fax:** 01527-821503
E-mail: fran@dhart.co.uk
Website: http://www.dhartgraphite.co.uk
Managers: F. Cowie (Comm)
Immediate Holding Company: DAVID HART (ALCESTER) LIMITED
Registration no: 00652212 **VAT No.:** GB 110 1169 37
Date established: 1960 **Turnover:** £1m - £2m **No.of Employees:** 1 - 10
Product Groups: 31, 33, 42

Date of Accounts	Dec 11	Dec 10	Dec 09
Working Capital	565	986	1m
Fixed Assets	3m	2m	2m
Current Assets	806	1m	1m

Domic Welding Services
Unit 8 Victor Business Centre, Redditch, B98 8JY
Tel: 01527-510041 **Fax:** 01527-510403
E-mail: doug@domic-pjwelding.fsnet.co.uk
Directors: D. Bevan (Prop), P. Jones (Dir), D. Bevan (Dir)
Managers: D. Bevan
Immediate Holding Company: DOMIC WELDING AND SHEET METAL SERVICES LIMITED
Registration no: 04315676 **VAT No.:** GB 436 7947 08
Date established: 2001 **Turnover:** £250,000 - £500,000
No.of Employees: 1 - 10 **Product Groups:** 48

Date of Accounts	Apr 09	Apr 08	Apr 07
Working Capital	-80	-44	-32
Fixed Assets	43	52	60
Current Assets	64	124	157

Dormer Plant Hire Ltd
87 Evesham Road, Redditch, B97 4JX
Tel: 01527-542724 **Fax:** 01527-542725
E-mail: accounts@dormerplanthire.co.uk
Website: http://www.dormerplanthire.co.uk
Directors: M. Dormer (MD)
Ultimate Holding Company: DORMER HIRE CENTRE LIMITED
Immediate Holding Company: DORMER PLANT HIRE LIMITED
Registration no: 04224211 **Date established:** 2001
No.of Employees: 1 - 10 **Product Groups:** 41, 45, 83

Date of Accounts	Mar 12	Mar 11	Mar 10
Working Capital	-11	-108	-265
Fixed Assets	476	454	479
Current Assets	86	137	146

Eaton Aerospace
2 Broad Ground Road, Redditch, B98 8YS
Tel: 01527-517555 **Fax:** 01527-517556
E-mail: leohayes@eaton.com
Website: http://www.eaton.com
Bank(s): National Westminster, Portsmouth
Managers: E. Trevaskis (Personnel), J. Evans, L. Hayes (Plant), T. Owen (Comptroller)
Immediate Holding Company: EATON CORPORATION
Registration no: 00155621 **VAT No.:** 227 2876 47 **Turnover:** £10m - £20m
No.of Employees: 101 - 250 **Product Groups:** 30, 36

Economy Saw Services Ltd
Unit 18 Charles Martin Business Park Arrow Road North, Redditch, B98 8NT
Tel: 01527-67441 **Fax:** 01527- 510548
E-mail: sales@jordansaws.co.uk
Website: http://www.jordansaws.co.uk
Directors: J. Masters (Dir)
Immediate Holding Company: ECONOMY SAW SERVICES LIMITED
Registration no: 02218697 **Date established:** 1988
No.of Employees: 1 - 10 **Product Groups:** 46, 48

Date of Accounts	Feb 11	Feb 10	Feb 09
Working Capital	-10	-10	-5
Fixed Assets	2	3	3
Current Assets	15	13	14

Esko-Graphics
D S M House Paper Mill Drive, Redditch, B98 8QJ
Tel: 01527-585805 **Fax:** 01527-584395
E-mail: nathan.chapman@esko.com
Website: http://www.esko.com
Directors: C. Knudsen (Grp Chief Exec)
Managers: N. Chapman (Sales Admin), P. Bates (Sales Prom Mgr)
Immediate Holding Company: BARCO GRAPHICS GHENT BELGIUM
Registration no: 02753446 **Turnover:** £5m - £10m
No.of Employees: 21 - 50 **Product Groups:** 44

Date of Accounts	Mar 11	Mar 10	Mar 09
Sales Turnover	10m	11m	9m
Pre Tax Profit/Loss	701	732	522
Working Capital	3m	2m	2m
Fixed Assets	2m	2m	2m
Current Assets	5m	4m	4m
Current Liabilities	662	653	528

The Events Company Co. UK
Unit 16 Thornhill Road, Moons Moat North, Redditch, B98 9ND
Tel: 0800-068 5707 **Fax:** 01527-62368
E-mail: info@theeventscompany.co.uk
Website: http://www.theeventscompany.co.uk
Registration no: 05983752 **No.of Employees:** 1 - 10 **Product Groups:** 24, 69, 81, 89

Experior Technical Services Ltd
35 Walkers Road Moons Moat North Industrial Estate, Redditch, B98 9HD
Tel: 01527-592560 **Fax:** 01527-68141
E-mail: info@experiortech.co.uk
Website: http://www.experiortech.co.uk
Directors: C. Howse (Dir)
Immediate Holding Company: EXPERIOR TECHNICAL SERVICES LIMITED
Registration no: 05659781 **Date established:** 2005
No.of Employees: 1 - 10 **Product Groups:** 38

Date of Accounts	Dec 11	Dec 10	Dec 09
Working Capital	6	4	1
Fixed Assets	14	18	18
Current Assets	119	108	87

Expresso (a division of Parrs)
Merse Road, Redditch, B98 9PL
Tel: 01527-68384 **Fax:** 01527-66430
E-mail: expresso@parrs.co.uk
Website: http://www.parrs.co.uk
Bank(s): Lloyds TSB Bank plc
Directors: J. Scholes (Dir), R. Scholes (MD)
Managers: J. Hollier (Purch Mgr), S. Donlon (Mktg Serv Mgr)
Ultimate Holding Company: MERSE HOLDINGS LIMITED
Immediate Holding Company: F. PARR LIMITED
Registration no: 04038748 **Date established:** 2000
Turnover: £250,000 - £500,000 **No.of Employees:** 11 - 20
Product Groups: 61, 84

Felspar Finishings Ltd
Unit 5 Phoenix Works Windsor Road, Redditch, B97 6DJ
Tel: 01527-585878 **Fax:** 01527-63167
E-mail: felsparfinish@aol.com
Directors: J. Danks (Fin)
Ultimate Holding Company: FELSPAR HOLDINGS LTD
Immediate Holding Company: FELSPAR FINISHING LIMITED
Registration no: 02150322 **Date established:** 1987
Turnover: £500,000 - £1m **No.of Employees:** 1 - 10 **Product Groups:** 48

Date of Accounts	Mar 12	Jan 11	Jan 08
Working Capital	259	223	20
Fixed Assets	10	11	14
Current Assets	340	321	84

First Floors UK Ltd
Westall Centre Holberrow Green, Redditch, B96 6JY
Tel: 01386-793305 **Fax:** 01527-550306
E-mail: roger@firstfloors.co.uk
Website: http://www.firstfloors.co.uk
Directors: R. Prior (Dir)
Immediate Holding Company: FIRST FLOORS (UK) LIMITED
Registration no: 03433385 **Date established:** 1997
No.of Employees: 1 - 10 **Product Groups:** 35, 52

Date of Accounts	Feb 11	Feb 10	Feb 09
Working Capital	-3	-27	-7
Fixed Assets	2	4	7
Current Assets	84	50	91

Foursome Vehicle Heaters Ltd
Brockhill Works Windsor Road, Redditch, B97 6DJ
Tel: 01527-64126 **Fax:** 01527-584611
E-mail: info@vehicleheaters.co.uk
Website: http://www.vehicleheaters.co.uk
Directors: M. Hemming (MD)
Immediate Holding Company: FOURSOME VEHICLE HEATERS LIMITED
Registration no: 01242877 **VAT No.:** GB 112 9980 62
Date established: 1976 **Turnover:** £500,000 - £1m
No.of Employees: 1 - 10 **Product Groups:** 39

Date of Accounts	May 11	May 10	May 09
Working Capital	31	34	13
Fixed Assets	28	23	26
Current Assets	191	182	150

Gardner Denver Ltd
Claybrook Drive Washford Industrial Estate, Redditch, B98 0DS
Tel: 01527-525522 **Fax:** 01457-838630
E-mail: sales@compair.com
Website: http://www.gardnerdenver.com
Bank(s): National Westminster Bank Plc
Directors: S. Kendrick (Fin), C. Barker (MD)
Managers: C. Mander, H. Clark (Personnel), D. Evans, I. Watson (Tech Serv Mgr)
Ultimate Holding Company: GARDNER DENVER INC (USA)
Immediate Holding Company: GARDNER DENVER LTD
Registration no: 03047245 **VAT No.:** GB 504 2409 86
Date established: 1995 **Turnover:** £20m - £50m
No.of Employees: 101 - 250 **Product Groups:** 40, 48

Date of Accounts	Dec 11	Dec 10	Dec 09
Sales Turnover	136m	136m	67m
Pre Tax Profit/Loss	8m	2m	-668

Working Capital	-11m	-23m	26m
Fixed Assets	86m	92m	101m
Current Assets	45m	44m	63m
Current Liabilities	11m	6m	10m

Gast Group Ltd (incorporating Jun-Air UK Ltd & Gast Manufacturing)

Unit 11 The I O Centre Nash Road, Redditch, B98 7AS
Tel: 01527-504040 **Fax:** 01527-525262
E-mail: alee@idexcorp.com
Website: http://www.gastmfg.com
Bank(s): Unibank
Directors: A. Lee (MD)
Ultimate Holding Company: IDEX CORPORATION (USA)
Immediate Holding Company: GAST GROUP LIMITED
Registration no: 00919355 **VAT No.:** GB 650 6429 41
Date established: 1967 **Turnover:** £1m - £2m **No.of Employees:** 11 - 20
Product Groups: 38, 39, 40, 42, 48, 83

Date of Accounts	Dec 11	Dec 10	Dec 09
Sales Turnover	15m	10m	6m
Pre Tax Profit/Loss	761	836	541
Working Capital	-208	-288	1m
Fixed Assets	3m	3m	290
Current Assets	5m	4m	3m
Current Liabilities	380	225	2m

R Gogerly

1 Winyates Centre, Redditch, B98 0NR
Tel: 01527-502266
E-mail: rg@rachelgogerly.co.uk
Website: http://www.rachelgogerly.co.uk
Directors: R. Gogerly (Prop)
Date established: 2002 **No.of Employees:** 1 - 10 **Product Groups:** 46, 48

Goodturn Engineering Ltd

Unit 2 Brook Street, Redditch, B98 8NG
Tel: 01527-596325 **Fax:** 01527-597325
E-mail: mail@goodturn-engineering.co.uk
Website: http://www.goodturn-engineering.co.uk
Directors: L. Mcilravey (Co Sec)
Ultimate Holding Company: GOODTURN ENGINEERING HOLDINGS LIMITED
Immediate Holding Company: GOODTURN ENGINEERING LIMITED
Registration no: 04095566 **VAT No.:** GB 436 8128 39
Date established: 2000 **Turnover:** £250,000 - £500,000
No.of Employees: 1 - 10 **Product Groups:** 48

Date of Accounts	Apr 12	Apr 11	Apr 10
Working Capital	-99	-125	-152
Fixed Assets	272	301	333
Current Assets	374	353	309

Greville Hardfacing & Engineering Co. Ltd

4 Palmers Road, Redditch, B98 0RF
Tel: 01527-525395 **Fax:** 01527-510949
E-mail: ghf@btconnect.com
Website: http://www.grevillehardfacing.com
Directors: C. Springer (MD), J. Springer (Co Sec)
Ultimate Holding Company: SPRINGER HOLDINGS LIMITED
Immediate Holding Company: GREVILLE HARDFACING & ENGINEERING CO. LIMITED
Registration no: 00980011 **VAT No.:** GB 109 9389 33
Date established: 1970 **Turnover:** £2m - £5m **No.of Employees:** 1 - 10
Product Groups: 34, 48

Date of Accounts	Jun 12	Jun 11	Jun 10
Working Capital	585	586	574
Fixed Assets	88	84	96
Current Assets	931	914	863

Gunnebo Industries Ltd

Woolaston Road Park Farm North, Redditch, B98 7SG
Tel: 01527-522560 **Fax:** 01527-510185
E-mail: sales@gunneboindustries.co.uk
Website: http://www.gunneboindustries.co.uk
Bank(s): S.E.B.
Managers: F. Caren (Chief Acct)
Ultimate Holding Company: SEGULAH STELLATA HOLDING AB (SWEDEN)
Immediate Holding Company: GUNNEBO INDUSTRIES LIMITED
Registration no: 01169996 **VAT No.:** GB 492 8706 96
Date established: 1974 **Turnover:** £2m - £5m **No.of Employees:** 11 - 20
Product Groups: 23, 29, 35, 36, 39, 41, 45, 48

Date of Accounts	Dec 11	Dec 10	Dec 09
Sales Turnover	N/A	5m	5m
Pre Tax Profit/Loss	N/A	-108	-64
Working Capital	77	359	422
Fixed Assets	84	289	296
Current Assets	2m	3m	3m
Current Liabilities	N/A	131	184

Halfords Autocenter

Icknield Street Drive, Redditch, B98 0DE
Tel: 01527-513600 **Fax:** 01527-513201
E-mail: reception@halfordsautocentres.co.uk
Website: http://www.halfordsautocentres.co.uk
Bank(s): Barclays, Colmore Row
Directors: B. Duffy (Grp Chief Exec), A. Stevens (Fin), P. Mcclenaghan (Comm)
Managers: I. Bailey (Personnel), R. Carling, K. Cooke (Tech Serv Mgr)
Ultimate Holding Company: HALFORDS GROUP PLC
Immediate Holding Company: HALFORDS AUTOCENTRES LIMITED
Registration no: 04050548 **Date established:** 2000
Turnover: £75m - £125m **No.of Employees:** 501 - 1000
Product Groups: 32, 36, 39, 46, 48

Date of Accounts	Dec 08	Mar 12	Apr 10
Sales Turnover	93m	111m	122m
Pre Tax Profit/Loss	7m	4m	8m
Working Capital	7m	14m	15m
Fixed Assets	12m	19m	12m
Current Assets	35m	52m	44m
Current Liabilities	11m	13m	12m

Hamgreen Farm Services

Ham Green Farm Brookhouse Lane, Ham Green, Redditch, B97 5PR
Tel: 01527-544291
Directors: M. Jones (Prop)
Date established: 1977 **No.of Employees:** 1 - 10 **Product Groups:** 41

Hands & Bayley Ltd

145-147 Evesham Road, Redditch, B97 4JX
Tel: 01527-403600
E-mail: info@handsbayley.com
Website: http://www.handsbayley.com
Managers: J. Hands (Mgr)
Immediate Holding Company: HANDS & BAYLEY LIMITED
Registration no: 06774531 **Date established:** 2008
No.of Employees: 1 - 10 **Product Groups:** 80

Date of Accounts	Dec 09	Mar 11
Working Capital	-16	-12
Fixed Assets	2	1
Current Assets	1	2

Harper & Simmons Ltd

19 Howard Road, Redditch, B98 7SE
Tel: 01527-518121 **Fax:** 01527-518123
E-mail: robertsimmons@harperandsimmons.co.uk
Website: http://www.harperandsimmons.co.uk
Directors: R. Simmons (MD)
Managers: G. Hill (Chief Mgr)
Registration no: 04418684 **Turnover:** £1m - £2m
No.of Employees: 11 - 20 **Product Groups:** 37, 46

Heartbeat Manufacturing Ltd

Arthur Street, Redditch, B98 8JY
Tel: 01527-522020 **Fax:** 01527-524919
E-mail: james.pritchard@heartbeatuk.com
Website: http://www.heartbeatuk.com
Bank(s): HSBC Bank plc
Directors: P. Pritchard (Dir), C. Stubbings (Dir), J. Pritchard (MD)
Managers: J. McDiarmid (Purch Mgr)
Immediate Holding Company: HEARTBEAT HOLDINGS LIMITED
Registration no: 01288620 **Date established:** 1976 **Turnover:** £5m - £10m
No.of Employees: 51 - 100 **Product Groups:** 26

Date of Accounts	Dec 11	Dec 10	Dec 09
Sales Turnover	12m	9m	6m
Pre Tax Profit/Loss	1m	1m	266
Working Capital	3m	3m	3m
Fixed Assets	2m	1m	1m
Current Assets	5m	5m	4m
Current Liabilities	1m	1m	462

Heller Machine Tools

1 Acanthus Road, Redditch, B98 9EX
Tel: 0121-275 3300 **Fax:** 0121-275 3380
E-mail: info@heller.co.uk
Website: http://www.heller.co.uk
Bank(s): National Westminster Bank Plc
Directors: J. Dyer (Fin), G. Lloyd (MD)
Managers: J. Potter (Purch Mgr), N. Harris (Personnel), J. Killingsworth (Tech Serv Mgr), E. Pollard (Sales & Mktg Mg)
Ultimate Holding Company: HELLER GMBH (GERMANY)
Immediate Holding Company: HELLER MACHINE TOOLS LIMITED
Registration no: 01414150 **Date established:** 1979
Turnover: £20m - £50m **No.of Employees:** 101 - 250
Product Groups: 46, 47, 67

Date of Accounts	Dec 11	Dec 10	Dec 09
Sales Turnover	39m	25m	21m
Pre Tax Profit/Loss	1m	324	-3m
Working Capital	2m	962	72
Fixed Assets	7m	7m	7m
Current Assets	12m	8m	5m
Current Liabilities	1m	820	661

Hendrick Industrial Equipment Ltd

Unit 32d The Washford Industrial Estate Heming Road, Redditch, B98 0DH
Tel: 01527-523712 **Fax:** 01527-514545
E-mail: sales@hendrick.co.uk
Website: http://www.hendrick.co.uk
Directors: R. Hendrick (MD)
Registration no: 00998445 **Date established:** 1970
Turnover: £250,000 - £500,000 **No.of Employees:** 1 - 10
Product Groups: 40, 46

Date of Accounts	Mar 08	Mar 07	Mar 06
Working Capital	58	53	18
Fixed Assets	7	8	7
Current Assets	88	114	52
Current Liabilities	30	61	34
Total Share Capital	1	1	1

Hycontrol Ltd

Larchwood House Orchard Street, Redditch, B98 7DP
Tel: 01527-406800 **Fax:** 01527-60046
E-mail: ballen@hycontrol.com
Website: http://www.hycontrol.com
Bank(s): HSBC, 130 New Street, Birmingham
Directors: B. Allen (MD), S. Tillirides (Fin)
Ultimate Holding Company: HYCONTROL LIMITED
Immediate Holding Company: HYCONTROL TECHNOLOGY LIMITED
Registration no: 02147358 **VAT No.:** GB 389 1933 04
Date established: 1987 **Turnover:** Up to £250,000
No.of Employees: 21 - 50 **Product Groups:** 36, 37, 38, 40

Indecs Group

Unit 8 Colemeadow Road, Moons Moat North Industrial Estate, Redditch, B98 9PB
Tel: 01527-406622 **Fax:** 01527-406644
E-mail: info@indecsgroup.co.uk
Website: http://www.indecsgroup.co.uk
Directors: N. Jones (Dir)
Registration no: 02897943 **Date established:** 1994 **Turnover:** £2m - £5m
No.of Employees: 51 - 100 **Product Groups:** 44

Date of Accounts	Jun 09	Jun 08	Jun 07
Working Capital	329	586	544
Fixed Assets	38	90	160
Current Assets	874	777	948

Industrial Batteries UK Ltd

Unit 32 Greenlands Business Centre Studley Road, Redditch, B98 7HD
Tel: 01527-520052 **Fax:** 01527-520053
E-mail: sales@ibluk.co.uk
Website: http://www.ibluk.co.uk
Directors: J. Hall (MD)
Immediate Holding Company: INDUSTRIAL BATTERIES (UK) LIMITED
Registration no: 03421179 **Date established:** 1997
No.of Employees: 1 - 10 **Product Groups:** 36, 37, 39, 54, 67

Date of Accounts	Aug 11	Aug 10	Aug 09
Working Capital	136	162	209
Fixed Assets	73	79	67
Current Assets	315	318	454

Invent Heat Transfer

103 Redstone Close, Redditch, B98 9AF
Tel: 01527-598793 **Fax:** 01527-585224
E-mail: info@inventheattransfer.co.uk
Website: http://www.inventheattransfer.co.uk
Directors: R. Dunn (Prop)
Date established: 2000 **No.of Employees:** 1 - 10 **Product Groups:** 37, 40, 48

Jewson Ltd

Clive Road, Redditch, B97 4DH
Tel: 01527-63721 **Fax:** 01527-66456
Website: http://www.jewson.co.uk
Managers: N. Mcmanus (District Mgr)
Ultimate Holding Company: COMPAGNIE DE SAINT GOBAIN (FRANCE)
Immediate Holding Company: JEWSON LIMITED
Registration no: 00348407 **VAT No.:** GB 497 7184 83
Date established: 1939 **Turnover:** £2m - £5m **No.of Employees:** 1 - 10
Product Groups: 66

Date of Accounts	Dec 11	Dec 10	Dec 09
Sales Turnover	1606m	1547m	1485m
Pre Tax Profit/Loss	18m	100m	45m
Working Capital	-345m	-250m	-349m
Fixed Assets	496m	387m	461m
Current Assets	657m	1005m	1320m
Current Liabilities	66m	120m	64m

K N Products Ltd

Unit 49 Enfield Industrial Estate, Redditch, B97 6DE
Tel: 01527-67602 **Fax:** 01527-60183
E-mail: sales@kn-products.co.uk
Website: http://www.kn-products.co.uk
Bank(s): HSBC Bank plc
Directors: M. Tracey (I.T. Dir), L. Hadley (Fin)
Immediate Holding Company: K. N. PRODUCTS LIMITED
Registration no: 01700011 **VAT No.:** GB 378 226 37
Date established: 1983 **Turnover:** £500,000 - £1m
No.of Employees: 11 - 20 **Product Groups:** 30, 35

Date of Accounts	Dec 11	Dec 10	Dec 09
Working Capital	357	341	292
Fixed Assets	80	85	95
Current Assets	496	497	404

Kac Alarm Co. Ltd

Kac House Thorn Hill Road, Moons Moat North Industrial Estate, Redditch, B98 9ND
Tel: 01527-406655 **Fax:** 01527-406677
E-mail: dwilson@kac.co.uk
Website: http://www.kac.co.uk
Bank(s): Barclays, High St, Whitchurch, Salop
Directors: D. Wilson (MD)
Managers: J. Prendergast (Purch Mgr), M. Thompson (Mktg Serv Mgr), A. Richie (Personnel), E. Voss (Fin Mgr)
Ultimate Holding Company: HONEYWELL INTERNATIONAL INC (USA)
Immediate Holding Company: KAC ALARM COMPANY LIMITED
Registration no: 01205354 **VAT No.:** GB 276 4904 29
Date established: 1975 **Turnover:** £10m - £20m
No.of Employees: 101 - 250 **Product Groups:** 40

Date of Accounts	Dec 11	Dec 10	Dec 09
Sales Turnover	19m	19m	18m
Pre Tax Profit/Loss	4m	6m	3m
Working Capital	10m	5m	20m
Fixed Assets	1m	1m	1m
Current Assets	25m	8m	22m
Current Liabilities	574	790	882

Kalamazoo Secure Solutions Ltd

Unit 1 Arrow Valley Claybrook Drive, Redditch, B98 0FY
Tel: 01527-838820 **Fax:** 0844-576 6886
E-mail: julian_coghlan@ksp.co.uk
Website: http://www.kalamazoosecure.co.uk
Bank(s): Lloyds TSB Bank plc
Directors: J. Coghlan (MD), P. Slocombe (Fin)
Managers: M. Berry (Tech Serv Mgr), C. Golding (Personnel), P. Muller (Sales Prom Mgr), M. Ganderton (Mktg Serv Mgr)
Ultimate Holding Company: MAVISBANK LIMITED
Immediate Holding Company: KALAMAZOO SECURE SOLUTIONS LIMITED
Registration no: 03365087 **VAT No.:** GB 559 0369 17
Date established: 1997 **Turnover:** £10m - £20m
No.of Employees: 51 - 100 **Product Groups:** 27, 28

Date of Accounts	Oct 11	Oct 10	Oct 09
Sales Turnover	16m	15m	16m
Pre Tax Profit/Loss	2m	1m	652
Working Capital	9m	8m	7m
Fixed Assets	3m	3m	3m
Current Assets	12m	16m	10m
Current Liabilities	2m	4m	2m

Kettler GB Ltd

Merse Road Moons Moat North Industrial Estate, Redditch, B98 9HL
Tel: 01527-591901 **Fax:** 01527-62423
E-mail: sales@kettler.co.uk
Website: http://www.kettler.co.uk
Bank(s): HSBC Bank plc
Directors: P. Bevington (MD)
Immediate Holding Company: KETTLER (GB) LTD
Registration no: 01937415 **VAT No.:** GB 488 0092 27
Date established: 1985 **Turnover:** £5m - £10m **No.of Employees:** 21 - 50
Product Groups: 26, 49, 63, 65

Date of Accounts	Dec 11	Dec 10	Dec 09
Sales Turnover	8m	N/A	N/A
Pre Tax Profit/Loss	35	N/A	N/A
Working Capital	-2m	-2m	-977
Fixed Assets	2m	2m	2m
Current Assets	5m	4m	4m
Current Liabilities	567	N/A	N/A

Linco Engineering

88 Heming Road, Redditch, B98 0EA
Tel: 01527-518333 **Fax:** 01527-518666
E-mail: linco@btconnect.com
Directors: C. Poole (Prop)
No.of Employees: 11 - 20 **Product Groups:** 30, 40, 66

Linread Northbridge
Crossgate Road, Redditch, B98 7TD
Tel: 01527-525719 **Fax:** 01527-526881
E-mail: graham.swan@linreadnorthbridge.co.uk
Website: http://www.linreadnorthbridge.com
Bank(s): National Westminster Bank Plc
Directors: G. Swan (Co Sec), P. Brown (MD)
Managers: C. Tamburro (Tech Serv Mgr), J. Princer (Personnel), J. Harvey (Purch Mgr)
Ultimate Holding Company: MELROSE PLC
Immediate Holding Company: LINREAD LIMITED
Registration no: 00207655 **VAT No.:** GB 152 9211 81
Date established: 2025 **Turnover:** £20m - £50m
No.of Employees: 101 - 250 **Product Groups:** 35, 39, 48

Date of Accounts	Dec 11	Dec 10	Dec 09
Sales Turnover	29m	26m	35m
Pre Tax Profit/Loss	3m	5m	7m
Working Capital	10m	30m	25m
Fixed Assets	2m	3m	3m
Current Assets	14m	34m	28m
Current Liabilities	2m	1m	1m

Lucid Computer Solutions
Office 2 Midland Glass Works Charles Street, Redditch, B97 5AA
Tel: 01527-908646 **Fax:** 0808-280 0526
E-mail: support@lucidcomputersolutions.co.uk
Website: http://www.lucidcomputersolutions.co.uk
Directors: G. Moorhouse (Dir)
Immediate Holding Company: LUCID COMPUTER SOLUTIONS LTD
Registration no: 06551419 **Date established:** 2008
Turnover: Up to £250,000 **No.of Employees:** 1 - 10 **Product Groups:** 44

Date of Accounts	Apr 11	Apr 10	Apr 09
Working Capital	16	14	-1
Current Assets	20	27	8

M B C Precision Castints
Shaw Bank Road Lakeside, Redditch, B98 8YN
Tel: 01527-527501 **Fax:** 01527-502533
Directors: J. Welsh (Sales), D. Millward (MD)
Immediate Holding Company: GRINSTY RAIL LIMITED
Registration no: 01751418 **Date established:** 2011
Turnover: £250,000 - £500,000 **No.of Employees:** 1 - 10
Product Groups: 34

Date of Accounts	Jun 11	Jun 10	Jun 09
Working Capital	1m	1m	1m
Fixed Assets	18	26	21
Current Assets	2m	2m	2m

M P J Services
271 Bromsgrove Road, Redditch, B97 4SH
Tel: 01527-66262 **Fax:** 01527-453052
Website: http://www.firstaid.co.uk
Directors: M. Wilkes (Prop), M. Wilks (Prop), J. James (Prop)
Date established: 1987 **No.of Employees:** 1 - 10 **Product Groups:** 38, 42

Marubeni Komatsu Ltd (Head Office)
Padgets Lane, Redditch, B98 0RT
Tel: 01527-512512 **Fax:** 01527-502310
E-mail: info@mkl.co.uk
Website: http://www.mkl.co.uk
Bank(s): Natwest & Barclays
Directors: M. Carrington (Sales)
Managers: E. Porsser (Mktg Serv Mgr), E. Prosser (Mktg Serv Mgr)
Ultimate Holding Company: MARUBENI CORPORATION (JAPAN)
Immediate Holding Company: MARUBENI - KOMATSU LIMITED
Registration no: 01040079 **Date established:** 1972
Turnover: £125m - £250m **No.of Employees:** 51 - 100
Product Groups: 45

Date of Accounts	Mar 12	Mar 11	Mar 10
Sales Turnover	138m	81m	71m
Pre Tax Profit/Loss	3m	1m	-644
Working Capital	-3m	-12m	-7m
Fixed Assets	39m	53m	58m
Current Assets	35m	24m	21m
Current Liabilities	22m	25m	21m

Master Magnets Ltd (Incorporating Metal Detection Ltd)
Burnt Meadow Road Moons Moat North Industrial Estate, Redditch, B98 9PA
Tel: 01527-65858 **Fax:** 01527-65868
E-mail: info@mastermagnets.co.uk
Website: http://www.mastermagnets.com
Bank(s): Barclays, Kings Heath, Birmingham B14 7LA
Directors: A. Coleman (MD)
Managers: J. Millington, P. Tree (Sales Eng), A. Rea (Sales Eng), S. Buckley (Comptroller)
Immediate Holding Company: MASTER MAGNETS LIMITED
Registration no: 01303706 **Date established:** 1977 **Turnover:** £2m - £5m
No.of Employees: 11 - 20 **Product Groups:** 29, 34, 37, 38, 42, 45, 46

Date of Accounts	Jul 11	Jul 10	Jul 09
Working Capital	887	606	383
Fixed Assets	802	843	873
Current Assets	2m	1m	954

Mateline Engineering Ltd
42 Walkers Road Moons Moat North Industrial Estate, Redditch, B98 9HD
Tel: 01527-63213 **Fax:** 01527- 584530
E-mail: matelineengineering@tiscali.co.uk
Website: http://www.mateline.com
Directors: M. Griffiths (MD)
Immediate Holding Company: MATELINE ENGINEERING LIMITED
Registration no: 00986219 **Date established:** 1970
Turnover: £250,000 - £500,000 **No.of Employees:** 1 - 10
Product Groups: 41

Date of Accounts	Mar 12	Mar 11	Mar 10
Working Capital	198	223	278
Fixed Assets	10	13	5
Current Assets	370	384	428

Maxwell Jones Studios
58k Arthur Street, Redditch, B98 8JY
Tel: 01527-502900 **Fax:** 01527-510265
E-mail: roger@maxwelljones.com
Directors: R. Baker (Dir), C. Amess (Dir), S. Baker (Co Sec)
Immediate Holding Company: MAXWELL JONES STUDIOS LIMITED
Registration no: 01208145 **VAT No.:** GB 112 7175 95
Date established: 1975 **Turnover:** £1m - £2m **No.of Employees:** 21 - 50
Product Groups: 26, 30, 37, 49, 52

Date of Accounts	Dec 11	Dec 10	Dec 09
Working Capital	353	322	235
Fixed Assets	700	644	645
Current Assets	675	586	454

Merricom Services Ltd (t/a Galleyslave)
161 Hither Green Lane Abbey Park, Redditch, B98 9AZ
Tel: 01527-592089
E-mail: info@galleyslaves.co.uk
Website: http://www.galleyslave.co.uk
Directors: B. Morris (MD), J. Morris (Co Sec)
Registration no: 04010750 **Turnover:** Up to £250,000
No.of Employees: 1 - 10 **Product Groups:** 30

Date of Accounts	Oct 07	Oct 06	Oct 03
Working Capital	8	11	3
Fixed Assets	7	10	8
Current Assets	26	25	11

Mettis Aerospace Ltd
Windsor Road, Redditch, B97 6EF
Tel: 01527-406400 **Fax:** 01527-406401
E-mail: info@mettis-aerospace.com
Website: http://www.mettis-aerospace.com
Bank(s): Barclays
Directors: P. Hughes (Sales & Mktg), S. Andrews (Pers), D. Stark (Fin), A. Macpherson (Dir), N. White (Co Sec)
Managers: S. Wilson, D. Green (Tech Serv Mgr)
Ultimate Holding Company: SAINTS CAPITAL CHAMONIX LP (USA)
Immediate Holding Company: METTIS AEROSPACE LIMITED
Registration no: 03292360 **Date established:** 1996
Turnover: £20m - £50m **No.of Employees:** 251 - 500
Product Groups: 39, 48

Date of Accounts	Dec 11	Mar 11	Mar 10
Sales Turnover	39m	48m	51m
Pre Tax Profit/Loss	533	439	2m
Working Capital	22m	22m	22m
Fixed Assets	14m	14m	17m
Current Assets	44m	41m	41m
Current Liabilities	2m	2m	3m

Midland Valves
42 Crossgate Road Park Farm Industrial Estate, Redditch, B98 7SN
Tel: 01527-517542 **Fax:** 01527-518087
E-mail: mike@midlandvalves.fsnet.co.uk
Website: http://www.midlandvalves.com
Directors: M. Latham (Prop)
No.of Employees: 11 - 20 **Product Groups:** 36, 37, 38

Moparmatic Co.
Rivet Works 1154 Evesham Rd, Astwood Bank, Redditch, B96 6DT
Tel: 01527-892413 **Fax:** 01527-892413
E-mail: mows@mopar.freeserve.co.uk
Website: http://www.kellysearch.com/partners/moparmatic.asp
Turnover: Up to £250,000 **No.of Employees:** 1 - 10 **Product Groups:** 35, 46, 66

Morgan Am & T
Unit 13 Madeley Road, Moons Moat North Industrial Estate, Redditch, B98 9NB
Tel: 01527-69205 **Fax:** 01299-827187
E-mail: mormetalloys@mormet.co.uk
Website: http://www.morganamandt.com
Bank(s): Barclays, Stourport
Managers: G. Hill (Site Co-ord), I. Cutts (Sales Prom Mgr)
Immediate Holding Company: Morgan Crucible Company Plc(The)
Registration no: 00286773 **Date established:** 1946
Turnover: £20m - £50m **No.of Employees:** 21 - 50 **Product Groups:** 84, 85

Mount Pleasant Windows
13 Bartleet Road, Redditch, B98 0DQ
Tel: 01527-510400 **Fax:** 01527-526700
Website: http://mountpleasantwindows.co.uk
Directors: J. Dennis (Co Sec)
Managers: K. Newman (Chief Mgr)
Registration no: 03356560 **Date established:** 1997
No.of Employees: 1 - 10 **Product Groups:** 25, 30, 35, 39

Opus Fabrication
Unit 3 Phoenix Works Windsor Road, Redditch, B97 6DJ
Tel: 01527-68533 **Fax:** 01527-68534
E-mail: info@opus-fab.co.uk
Website: http://www.opus-fab.co.uk
Managers: A. Danks (Mgr)
Registration no: 01102488 **VAT No.:** GB 111 8640 00
Turnover: £250,000 - £500,000 **No.of Employees:** 1 - 10
Product Groups: 26, 35, 40, 43, 49, 81

A E Oscroft & Sons
49d Pipers Road Park Farm Industrial Estate, Redditch, B98 0HU
Tel: 01527-502203 **Fax:** 01527-510378
E-mail: info@aeoscroft.co.uk
Website: http://www.aeoscroft.co.uk
Bank(s): HSBC
Directors: C. Oscroft (Dir), C. Oscroft (MD), G. Oscroft (Fin)
Managers: P. Dawson, D. Churcher (Fin Mgr)
Immediate Holding Company: A E OSCROFT & SONS LIMITED
Registration no: 04496910 **VAT No.:** GB 109 8832 47
Date established: 2002 **Turnover:** £2m - £5m **No.of Employees:** 21 - 50
Product Groups: 29, 48

Date of Accounts	Mar 12	Mar 11	Mar 10
Working Capital	232	209	180
Fixed Assets	29	40	25
Current Assets	2m	1m	960

P M Services
Unit 10-11 Enterprise Works 28 Heming Road, Redditch, B98 0DH
Tel: 01527-524194 **Fax:** 01527-525571
Directors: M. Sallows (Snr Part)
Ultimate Holding Company: ROCKLINE INDUSTRIES INC (USA)
Immediate Holding Company: ROCKLINE INDUSTRIES LIMITED
Registration no: 03025769 **Date established:** 1995
Turnover: £20m - £50m **No.of Employees:** 1 - 10 **Product Groups:** 35, 36, 39, 45

P S R Sheetmetal Services Ltd
5 Bartleet Road, Redditch, B98 0DQ
Tel: 01527-502565 **Fax:** 01527-502568
E-mail: admin@psrsheetmetal.co.uk
Directors: P. Rigby (MD)
Immediate Holding Company: PSR SHEET METAL SERVICES LIMITED
Registration no: 03994282 **Date established:** 2000
No.of Employees: 1 - 10 **Product Groups:** 46, 48

Date of Accounts	Jul 11	Jul 10	Jul 09
Working Capital	29	27	28
Fixed Assets	213	217	102
Current Assets	121	113	79

Parrs Ltd
Merse Road, Redditch, B98 9PL
Tel: 01527-585777 **Fax:** 0800-074 7434
E-mail: sales@parrs.co.uk
Website: http://www.parrs.co.uk
Bank(s): Lloyds TSB Bank plc
Directors: R. Scholes (MD), J. Scholes (Ch)
Managers: S. Craddock (Purch Mgr), N. Brookes (Mktg Serv Mgr), P. Clark (Chief Mgr)
Ultimate Holding Company: F. PARR HOLDINGS LIMITED
Immediate Holding Company: F. PARR LIMITED
Registration no: 00273462 **VAT No.:** GB 487 9409 82
Date established: 1933 **Turnover:** £2m - £5m **No.of Employees:** 11 - 20
Product Groups: 35, 45

Date of Accounts	Dec 10	Dec 09	Dec 08
Working Capital	418	352	388
Fixed Assets	15	21	31
Current Assets	912	735	1m
Current Liabilities	26	N/A	N/A

Paul Savage
Unit 17 Enterprise Workshops 28 Heming Road Washford Industrial Estate, Redditch, B98 0DH
Tel: 01527-521666 **Fax:** 01527-521666
Directors: P. Savage (Prop)
Ultimate Holding Company: ROCKLINE INDUSTRIES INC (USA)
Immediate Holding Company: ROCKLINE INDUSTRIES LIMITED
Registration no: 03025769 **Date established:** 1995
Turnover: £20m - £50m **No.of Employees:** 1 - 10 **Product Groups:** 35, 66

Date of Accounts	Jun 12	Jun 11	Jun 10
Sales Turnover	46m	38m	32m
Pre Tax Profit/Loss	-1m	-2m	-4m
Working Capital	11m	9m	7m
Fixed Assets	7m	8m	8m
Current Assets	16m	17m	11m
Current Liabilities	2m	1m	1m

Peco Studios Ltd
Unit 5 Arrow Road North Lakeside, Redditch, B98 8NT
Tel: 01527-595364 **Fax:** 01527-595366
E-mail: info@pecostudios.com
Website: http://www.pecostudios.com
Directors: T. May (MD)
Immediate Holding Company: PECO STUDIOS LIMITED
Registration no: 04793266 **Date established:** 2003
Turnover: Up to £250,000 **No.of Employees:** 1 - 10 **Product Groups:** 37, 49

Date of Accounts	Jun 11	Jun 10	Jun 09
Working Capital	57	38	35
Fixed Assets	6	13	24
Current Assets	157	151	147

Pertemps plc
6 Church Green West, Redditch, B97 4DY
Tel: 01527-591091 **Fax:** 01527-60795
E-mail: info@pertemps.co.uk
Website: http://www.pertemps.co.uk
Managers: H. Hibbet (Mgr)
Immediate Holding Company: PERTEMPS RECRUITMENT PARTNERSHIP LIMITED
Registration no: 01644241 **Date established:** 1982
Turnover: £250m - £500m **No.of Employees:** 1 - 10 **Product Groups:** 80

Date of Accounts	Dec 11	Dec 10	Dec 09
Sales Turnover	310m	286m	232m
Pre Tax Profit/Loss	5m	9m	3m
Working Capital	9m	20m	13m
Fixed Assets	28m	16m	10m
Current Assets	70m	56m	41m
Current Liabilities	41m	33m	24m

Peterson Spring Europe Ltd Heath Plant
Unit 21 Trescott Road, Redditch, B98 7AH
Tel: 01527-585657 **Fax:** 01527-58837
E-mail: sales@pspring.eu.com
Website: http://pspring.com
Directors: G. Tarbuck (Ch & MD), D. Strain (Fin), J. Iliffe (Tech Serv), E. Roberts (Grp Chief Exec), A. Peterson Jnr (Dir)
Managers: C. Taylor (Personnel), R. Bray (Comm), J. Heath (I.T. Exec)
Immediate Holding Company: PETERSON SPRING EUROPE LIMITED
Registration no: 01363153 **Date established:** 1978
No.of Employees: 1 - 10 **Product Groups:** 23, 35, 48

Date of Accounts	Dec 07	Dec 06
Sales Turnover	5341	5460
Pre Tax Profit/Loss	-93	-132
Working Capital	817	867
Fixed Assets	3125	3168
Current Assets	2182	2146
Current Liabilities	1365	1279
Total Share Capital	3194	3194
ROCE% (Return on Capital Employed)	-2.4	-3.3
ROT% (Return on Turnover)	-1.7	-2.4

Pinstructure Ltd
Unit 50 Enfield Industrial Estate, Redditch, B97 6DE
Tel: 01527-67999 **Fax:** 01527-66557
E-mail: sales@pinstructure.com
Website: http://www.pinstructure.com
Bank(s): HSBC Bank plc
Directors: M. Tracey (MD)
Immediate Holding Company: PINSTRUCTURE LIMITED
Registration no: 01580637 **VAT No.:** GB 416 9199 25
Date established: 1981 **No.of Employees:** 11 - 20 **Product Groups:** 25, 29, 30, 35, 36, 37, 38, 39, 40, 42, 66

Date of Accounts	Jan 12	Jan 11	Jan 10
Working Capital	960	934	859
Fixed Assets	453	367	375
Current Assets	1m	1m	1m

Precia-Molen
Unit 30 Walkers Road Moons Moat North Industrial Estate, Redditch, B98 9HE
Tel: 01527-590300 **Fax:** 01527-590301
E-mail: john.swinburne@preciamolen.co.uk
Website: http://www.preciamolen.com
Directors: J. Swinburne (MD), J. Swinburne (Co Sec)
Managers: B. Sallows (Sec), M. Gray (I.T. Exec), L. White (Sales Prom Mgr)
Ultimate Holding Company: LA GROUPE PRECIA SA (FRANCE)
Immediate Holding Company: PRECIA-MOLEN UK LIMITED
Registration no: 02174040 **VAT No.:** GB 436 7411 49
Date established: 1987 **Turnover:** £2m - £5m **No.of Employees:** 1 - 10
Product Groups: 38

Date of Accounts	Dec 11	Dec 10	Dec 09
Working Capital	403	351	229
Fixed Assets	451	506	457
Current Assets	2m	1m	2m

Protaform Springs & Pressings Ltd
Orchard Works 76 Arthur Street, Redditch, B98 8LJ
Tel: 01527-517500 **Fax:** 01527-502373
E-mail: sales@protaform.com
Website: http://www.protaform.com
Directors: D. Buggins (Dir), G. Fagg (MD), P. Taylor (Fin)
Ultimate Holding Company: Protoform Holdings Ltd
Immediate Holding Company: Protaform Holdings Ltd
Registration no: 01759238 **VAT No.:** GB 661 5478 20
Date established: 1983 **Turnover:** £2m - £5m **No.of Employees:** 1 - 10
Product Groups: 35, 48

Protaform Springs And Pressings Ltd
Orchard Works 76 Arthur Street, Lakeside, Redditch, B98 8LJ
Tel: 01527-527777 **Fax:** 01527-527785
E-mail: sales@protaform.com
Website: http://www.protaform.com
Bank(s): HSBC Bank plc
Directors: D. Fagg (MD)
Managers: C. Derson (Mgr), W. Simmons (Chief Mgr)
Immediate Holding Company: Protaform Holdings Ltd
Registration no: 01759238 **Date established:** 2002 **Turnover:** £1m - £2m
No.of Employees: 21 - 50 **Product Groups:** 35, 48

Protective Finishing Group
33 Crossgate Road Park Farm Industrial Estate, Redditch, B98 7SN
Tel: 01527-524126 **Fax:** 01527-510361
E-mail: sales@profingroup.co.uk
Website: http://www.profingroup.co.uk
Directors: K. Clarke (MD)
Immediate Holding Company: PROTECTIVE FINISHING GROUP LIMITED
Registration no: 00763586 **Date established:** 1963 **Turnover:** £1m - £2m
No.of Employees: 21 - 50 **Product Groups:** 26, 30, 31, 32, 34, 46, 48, 49, 52

Protex Fasteners Ltd
Arrow Road, Redditch, B98 8PA
Tel: 01527-63231 **Fax:** 01527-66770
E-mail: sales@protex-fasteners.com
Website: http://www.protex.com
Directors: H. Cooke (Dir), J. Ashley (Fin)
Ultimate Holding Company: HOWARD S. COOKE & CO. (HOLDINGS) LIMITED
Immediate Holding Company: PROTEX FASTENERS LIMITED
Registration no: 00534440 **VAT No.:** GB 110 6342 24
Date established: 1954 **Turnover:** £2m - £5m **No.of Employees:** 1 - 10
Product Groups: 35, 36, 39, 48

Date of Accounts	Mar 12	Mar 11	Mar 10
Sales Turnover	5m	5m	4m
Pre Tax Profit/Loss	374	374	265
Working Capital	1m	1m	834
Fixed Assets	14	14	14
Current Assets	2m	2m	2m
Current Liabilities	114	120	192

Raldon Precision Engineering Ltd
Unit 32 U and V Hemming Road, Washford Industrial Estate, Redditch, B98 0DH
Tel: 01527-527 800 **Fax:** 01527-527 850
E-mail: sales@raldonengineering.com
Website: http://www.raldonengineering.co.uk
Directors: N. Silcock (MD), C. Lewis (Fin)
Immediate Holding Company: Budget Properties Ltd
Registration no: 01769869 **Date established:** 2006 **Turnover:** £5m - £10m
No.of Employees: 1 - 10 **Product Groups:** 48

Red Forge Ltd
9 Palmers Road, Redditch, B98 0RF
Tel: 01527-526112 **Fax:** 01527-523862
E-mail: sales@redforge.co.uk
Website: http://www.redforge.co.uk
Bank(s): Lloyds
Directors: A. Freeman (Dir)
Managers: P. Bridge (Sales Off Mgr)
Immediate Holding Company: RED FORGE LIMITED
Registration no: 01265166 **VAT No.:** GB 113 1934 06
Date established: 1976 **Turnover:** £500,000 - £1m
No.of Employees: 11 - 20 **Product Groups:** 39

Date of Accounts	Jun 12	Jun 11	Jun 10
Working Capital	100	118	168
Fixed Assets	1m	1m	1m
Current Assets	439	498	525

Redditch Anodising
37 Heming Road, Redditch, B98 0DP
Tel: 01527-526855 **Fax:** 01527-502856
E-mail: marysalter@redditchanodising.wanadoo.co.uk
Website: http://www.redditchanodising.wanadoo.co.uk
Bank(s): Lloyds TSB Bank plc
Directors: P. Birdsall (MD)
Managers: K. Fisher (Chief Mgr)
Registration no: 05639665 **VAT No.:** GB 224 5097 44
Date established: 2005 **Turnover:** £250,000 - £500,000
No.of Employees: 21 - 50 **Product Groups:** 48

Redditch Electro Plating Co. Ltd
Argent Works Arrow Road North, Redditch, B98 8NT
Tel: 01527-63858 **Fax:** 01527- 591504
E-mail: mark@redditch-ep.co.uk
Website: http://www.redditch-ep.co.uk
Directors: M. Harris (MD), T. Harris (Co Sec)
Immediate Holding Company: REDDITCH ELECTRO PLATING COMPANY LIMITED(THE)
Registration no: 00103467 **Date established:** 2009
Turnover: £500,000 - £1m **No.of Employees:** 1 - 10 **Product Groups:** 48

Date of Accounts	Apr 12	Apr 11	Apr 10
Working Capital	727	698	638
Fixed Assets	162	191	201
Current Assets	759	739	665

Redditch Gears & Engineering Ltd
24 Lakeside Industrial Estate New Meadow Road, Redditch, B98 8YW
Tel: 01527-514160 **Fax:** 01527-514161
E-mail: redditchgears@btconnect.com
Website: http://www.redditchgears.co.uk
Directors: J. Ward (Dir), C. Colebrook (Fin)
Immediate Holding Company: REDDITCH GEARS & ENGINEERING LIMITED
Registration no: 03359164 **Date established:** 1997
No.of Employees: 11 - 20 **Product Groups:** 35, 45

Date of Accounts	Dec 11	Dec 10	Dec 09
Working Capital	133	87	48
Fixed Assets	21	14	4
Current Assets	379	353	272

Redditch Shotblasting Co. Ltd
6 Bartleet Road, Redditch, B98 0DQ
Tel: 01527-529659 **Fax:** 01527-516946
E-mail: sales@redditchshotblasting.co.uk
Website: http://www.redditchshotblasting.co.uk
Directors: L. Farron (Fin)
Immediate Holding Company: REDDITCH SHOTBLASTING CO. LIMITED
Registration no: 01360972 **VAT No.:** GB 338 1877 29
Date established: 1978 **No.of Employees:** 1 - 10 **Product Groups:** 48

Date of Accounts	Mar 11	Mar 10	Mar 09
Working Capital	24	7	3
Fixed Assets	19	22	27
Current Assets	51	41	42

Redhill Manufacturing
Unit 6 Padgets Lane, Redditch, B98 0RA
Tel: 01527-529002 **Fax:** 01527-523950
E-mail: sales@redhillmanufacturing.co.uk
Website: http://www.tradercatalogue.co.uk
Bank(s): Barclays
Directors: K. Colley (MD)
Managers: A. Colley (Sales Prom Mgr), K. Balcombe (Works Gen Mgr)
Immediate Holding Company: REDHILL MANUFACTURING LTD
Registration no: 01346744 **VAT No.:** GB 113 6981 69
Turnover: £2m - £5m **No.of Employees:** 21 - 50 **Product Groups:** 26, 39, 40, 41, 45

Rexnord NV UK
Office 32 Imex Business Centre Oxleasow Road, Redditch, B98 0RE
Tel: 01527-830473 **Fax:** 01527-830501
E-mail: robert.sillis@rexnord.com
Website: http://www.rexnord.co.uk
Directors: D. Mack (Sales)
Managers: R. Sillis (Sales Prom Mgr)
Ultimate Holding Company: WESTCO LIMITED
Immediate Holding Company: B. A. THORNE (MACHINERY) LIMITED
Registration no: 07065358 **VAT No.:** GB 242 3380 873 394
Date established: 1974 **Turnover:** £5m - £10m **No.of Employees:** 1 - 10
Product Groups: 35

Date of Accounts	Feb 08	Feb 11	Feb 10
Working Capital	11	65	34
Fixed Assets	8	26	20
Current Assets	164	160	132

Rossano Bennett Graphics
Unit 19 The Rubicon Centre Broad Ground Road, Redditch, B98 8YP
Tel: 01527-524708 **Fax:** 01527-526069
E-mail: b.rossano@exhibitiongraphics.uk.com
Website: http://www.exhibitiongraphics.uk.com
Directors: B. Rossano (Fin)
Immediate Holding Company: ROSSANO BENNETT GRAPHICS LIMITED
Registration no: 02805281 **Date established:** 1993
No.of Employees: 1 - 10 **Product Groups:** 28, 39

Date of Accounts	Mar 11	Mar 10	Mar 09
Working Capital	8	23	15
Fixed Assets	5	6	8
Current Assets	27	58	44

RSF Commercial Services Ltd
Unit 24 Walkers Road Moons Moat North Industrial Estate, Redditch, B98 9HE
Tel: 01527-598777 **Fax:** 01527-598538
E-mail: office@rsfonline.co.uk
Website: http://www.rsfonline.co.uk
Directors: J. Smart (Sales), P. Farrugia (Dir)
Managers: P. Knowles (Chief Mgr)
Registration no: 06404052 **Date established:** 2007 **Turnover:** £1m - £2m
No.of Employees: 1 - 10 **Product Groups:** 61, 76

Sallu Plastics
21 Ferney Hill Avenue, Redditch, B97 4RU
Tel: 01527-404305 **Fax:** 01527-908863
E-mail: sales@sallu.co.uk
Website: http://www.sallu.co.uk
Directors: M. Vale (Dir)
Registration no: 06294418 **Date established:** 1980
No.of Employees: 1 - 10 **Product Groups:** 30, 31, 66

Sangre Engineering Ltd
Unit 32c The Washford Industrial Estate Heming Road, Redditch, B98 0DH
Tel: 01527-524782 **Fax:** 01527-510323
E-mail: sales@sangre.co.uk
Website: http://www.sangre.co.uk
Directors: N. Ratheram (MD)
Immediate Holding Company: SANGRE ENGINEERING LIMITED
Registration no: 01099221 **Date established:** 1973
Turnover: £250,000 - £500,000 **No.of Employees:** 1 - 10
Product Groups: 40, 42, 45, 52, 54

Date of Accounts	May 11	May 10	May 09
Working Capital	10	34	62
Fixed Assets	4	5	5
Current Assets	68	86	116

Servicom High Tech Ltd
Unit 8 The I O Centre Nash Road, Redditch, B98 7AS
Tel: 01527-510800 **Fax:** 01527-510975
E-mail: sales@servicom.co.uk
Website: http://www.servicom.co.uk
Directors: I. Gudger (Dir)
Immediate Holding Company: SERVICOM (HIGH TECH) LIMITED
Registration no: 02353848 **Date established:** 1989 **Turnover:** £1m - £2m
No.of Employees: 1 - 10 **Product Groups:** 30, 37, 38, 52, 67, 79, 83

Date of Accounts	Jun 11	Jun 10	Jun 09
Working Capital	236	234	220
Fixed Assets	634	585	651
Current Assets	691	937	728

Frank Shaw Bayonet Ltd
Merse Road Moons Moat North Industrial Estate, Redditch, B98 9HL
Tel: 01527-66241 **Fax:** 01527-584455
E-mail: jeremy@frankshaw.co.uk
Website: http://www.frankshaw.co.uk
Bank(s): Lloyds TSB Bank plc
Directors: J. Scholes (MD), J. Scholes (Ch)
Immediate Holding Company: FRANK SHAW (BAYONET) LIMITED
Registration no: 01195363 **VAT No.:** GB 487 9409 82
Date established: 1975 **Turnover:** £1m - £2m **No.of Employees:** 11 - 20
Product Groups: 23, 35, 36, 66

Sigma Industries Ltd
Unit 25 Dunlop Road Hunt End Industrial Estate, Redditch, B97 5XP
Tel: 01527-547771 **Fax:** 01527-547772
E-mail: sales.sigmaind@btopenworld.com
Website: http://www.sigmaind.f9.co.uk
Directors: J. Anson (Fin), J. Anson (MD)
Immediate Holding Company: SIGMA INDUSTRIES LIMITED
Registration no: 01537159 **VAT No.:** GB 551 4566 43
Date established: 1981 **Turnover:** £2m - £5m **No.of Employees:** 11 - 20
Product Groups: 30, 31, 35, 45, 48, 66

Date of Accounts	Mar 11	Mar 10	Mar 09
Working Capital	-24	-79	-81
Fixed Assets	36	52	64
Current Assets	318	292	275
Current Liabilities	N/A	81	N/A

Sign Specialists Ltd
19 Oxleasow Road, Redditch, B98 0RE
Tel: 01527-504250 **Fax:** 01527-504251
E-mail: enquiry@sign-specialists.co.uk
Website: http://www.sign-specialists.co.uk
Directors: R. Tisdale (MD), B. Hilson (Fin)
Immediate Holding Company: SIGN SPECIALISTS LIMITED
Registration no: 00688806 **VAT No.:** GB 110 0827 50
Date established: 1961 **Turnover:** £5m - £10m
No.of Employees: 51 - 100 **Product Groups:** 49

Date of Accounts	Mar 11	Mar 10	Mar 09
Sales Turnover	8m	7m	7m
Pre Tax Profit/Loss	-134	141	116
Working Capital	655	1m	1m
Fixed Assets	2m	2m	2m
Current Assets	3m	2m	2m
Current Liabilities	357	319	462

Spherical Components Ltd
Unit 6 Alders Drive, Redditch, B98 0RF
Tel: 01527-510144 **Fax:** 01527-518102
E-mail: info@sphericalcomponents.co.uk
Website: http://www.sphericalcomponents.co.uk
Bank(s): National Westminster Bank Plc
Directors: I. Richardson (MD), R. Mansfield (Fin)
Immediate Holding Company: SPHERICAL COMPONENTS LIMITED
Registration no: 02219240 **Date established:** 1988
Turnover: £500,000 - £1m **No.of Employees:** 11 - 20
Product Groups: 36, 40

Date of Accounts	Sep 11	Sep 10	Sep 09
Working Capital	317	241	226
Fixed Assets	102	86	101
Current Assets	546	385	378

Springmasters Ltd
55 Arthur Street, Redditch, B98 8LF
Tel: 01527-521000 **Fax:** 01527-528866
E-mail: sales@springmasters.com
Website: http://www.springmasters.com
Bank(s): HSBC, Redditch
Directors: D. Clarke (Sales), I. Whitehead (MD), M. Evans (Fin)
Managers: C. Roberts (Personnel)
Immediate Holding Company: SPRINGMASTERS LIMITED
Registration no: 00897155 **VAT No.:** GB 112 2629 12
Date established: 1967 **Turnover:** £5m - £10m
No.of Employees: 51 - 100 **Product Groups:** 35, 36, 39, 66

Date of Accounts	May 11	May 10	May 09
Sales Turnover	7m	6m	6m
Pre Tax Profit/Loss	736	531	549
Working Capital	3m	3m	4m
Fixed Assets	3m	3m	3m
Current Assets	6m	5m	5m
Current Liabilities	1m	2m	628

Steatite Batteries
Acanthus Road Ravensbank Business Park, Redditch, B98 9EX
Tel: 01527-512400 **Fax:** 01527-512419
E-mail: sales@steatite-batteries.co.uk
Website: http://www.steatite-batteries.co.uk
Directors: J. Lavery (MD)
Registration no: 4403746 **Date established:** 1930 **Turnover:**
No.of Employees: 51 - 100 **Product Groups:**

Sterimedix Ltd
Unit 1 Madeley Road Moons Moat North Industrial Estate, Redditch, B98 9NB
Tel: 01527-501480 **Fax:** 01527-501491
E-mail: sales@sterimedix.co.uk
Website: http://www.sterimedix.com
Bank(s): Barclays
Directors: R. Mcfarlane (MD)
Immediate Holding Company: STERIMEDIX LIMITED
Registration no: 02453871 **VAT No.:** GB 551 4723 53
Date established: 1989 **Turnover:** £1m - £2m **No.of Employees:** 11 - 20
Product Groups: 67

see next page

Sterimedix Ltd - Cont'd

Date of Accounts	Dec 11	Dec 10	Dec 09
Working Capital	660	596	577
Fixed Assets	1m	945	234
Current Assets	1m	1m	974

Surgicraft Ltd

16 The Oaks Clews Road, Redditch, B98 7ST
Tel: 01527-555888 **Fax:** 01527-551166
E-mail: customerservice@surgicraft.co.uk
Website: http://www.surgicraft.co.uk
Directors: R. Turner (Co Sec)
Managers: A. Hull
Ultimate Holding Company: CENTINEL SPINE INC (USA)
Immediate Holding Company: SURGICRAFT LIMITED
Registration no: 00392541 **VAT No.:** GB 589 5218 89
Date established: 1945 **Turnover:** £2m - £5m **No.of Employees:** 1 - 10
Product Groups: 30, 37, 38

Date of Accounts	Dec 10	Dec 09	Dec 08
Working Capital	-11m	-11m	-183
Fixed Assets	N/A	N/A	160
Current Assets	13	793	1m

Swisslog Healthcare UK Ltd

2 Brooklands, Redditch, B98 9DW
Tel: 01527-551600 **Fax:** 01527-551664
E-mail: emma.rawlinson@swisslog.com
Website: http://www.swisslog.com
Bank(s): National Westminster Bank Plc & Svenska Handelsbanken AB
Directors: A. Manchip (MD), J. Adams (Fin)
Managers: P. Akujobi (Purch Mgr), E. Rawlinson (Sales & Mktg Mg), H. Dumbombe (Personnel)
Ultimate Holding Company: SWISSLOG HOLDING AG (SWITZERLAND)
Immediate Holding Company: SWISSLOG HOLDINGS (UK) LTD.
Registration no: 03471372 **VAT No.:** GB 669 4866 65
Date established: 1997 **Turnover:** £20m - £50m
No.of Employees: 51 - 100 **Product Groups:** 38, 45, 80, 84

Date of Accounts	Dec 11	Dec 10	Dec 09
Pre Tax Profit/Loss	95	-292	-4m
Working Capital	5m	4m	4m
Fixed Assets	N/A	N/A	377
Current Assets	6m	5m	5m
Current Liabilities	15	13	101

Takisawa UK Ltd

Meir Road, Redditch, B98 7SY
Tel: 01527-522211 Fax: 01527-510728
E-mail: takisawa@btconnect.com
Website: http://www.takisawa.com
Directors: S. Hamada (MD), D. Evans (Dir & Gen Mgr)
Ultimate Holding Company: TAKISAWA MACHINE TOOL COMPANY LTD (JAPAN)
Immediate Holding Company: ROCKWELL MACHINE TOOLS LIMITED
Registration no: 00522310 **VAT No.:** GB 579 4181 01
Date established: 1953 **No.of Employees:** 1 - 10 **Product Groups:** 46, 67

Date of Accounts	Dec 10	Dec 09	Dec 08
Working Capital	461	563	691
Fixed Assets	29	4	5
Current Assets	1m	1m	2m

Tamlite

Rear of 48b Pipers Road Park Farm Industrial Estate, Redditch, B98 0HU
Tel: 01527-528556 Fax: 01527-526671
Website: http://www.tamlite.co.uk
No.of Employees: 1 - 10 **Product Groups:** 37, 67

Samuel Taylor Ltd

Arthur Street Central Lakeside, Redditch, B98 8JY
Tel: 01527-504 910 Fax: 01527-500869
E-mail: info@samueltaylor.co.uk
Website: http://www.samueltaylor.co.uk
Bank(s): Lloyds TSB
Directors: A. Gordon (MD), J. Gordon (MD), R. Gordon (Dir), R. Pick (Co Sec)
Immediate Holding Company: Samuel Taylor,Limited
Registration no: 00063351 **VAT No.:** GB 109 6799 29
Date established: 1999 **Turnover:** £2m - £5m **No.of Employees:** 51 - 100
Product Groups: 33, 34, 46

Date of Accounts	Dec 07	Dec 06	Dec 05
Pre Tax Profit/Loss	166	216	67
Working Capital	-119	-399	-498
Fixed Assets	2891	3068	3063
Current Assets	3509	2845	2158
Current Liabilities	3627	3244	2656
Total Share Capital	10	10	10
ROCE% (Return on Capital Employed)	6.0	8.1	2.6

Thermex Ltd

Merse Road Moons Moat North Industrial Estate, Redditch, B98 9HL
Tel: 01527-62210 Fax: 01527-60138
E-mail: sales@thermex.co.uk
Website: http://www.thermex.co.uk
Bank(s): Bank of Scotland
Directors: M. Jordan (Fin), B. Wilson (Comm)
Ultimate Holding Company: DIAMOND RAIN LIMITED
Immediate Holding Company: THERMEX LIMITED
Registration no: 01420384 **VAT No.:** GB 294 6653 16
Date established: 1979 **Turnover:** £2m - £5m **No.of Employees:** 21 - 50
Product Groups: 35, 40, 42

Date of Accounts	Sep 11	Sep 10	Sep 09
Working Capital	908	900	883
Fixed Assets	841	831	811
Current Assets	2m	2m	2m

Thorlux Lighting

Merse Road, Redditch, B98 9HH
Tel: 01527-583200
E-mail: michael.alcock@thorlux.co.uk
Website: http://www.thorlux.com
Directors: C. Muncaster (Fin), M. Alcock (MD)
Managers: S. Lewis
Ultimate Holding Company: F.W. THORPE PUBLIC LIMITED COMPANY
Immediate Holding Company: COMPACT LIGHTING LIMITED
Registration no: 02649528 **Date established:** 1991
No.of Employees: 251 - 500 **Product Groups:** 37, 67

Date of Accounts	Jun 11	Jun 10	Jun 09
Sales Turnover	5m	4m	4m
Pre Tax Profit/Loss	88	74	-102
Working Capital	939	1m	1m
Fixed Assets	476	228	247
Current Assets	3m	2m	2m
Current Liabilities	116	92	97

Tmi

The Holos Beoley, Redditch, B98 9ET
Tel: 01527-851741 **Fax:** 01527-851777
E-mail: jon_penrose@tmi.co.uk
Website: http://www.tmi.co.uk
Bank(s): Lloyds TSB, Henley-in-Arden
Directors: J. Penrose (Fin), S. Mitterer (Sales)
Managers: A. Brey (Mktg Serv Mgr)
Ultimate Holding Company: CELLO GROUP PLC
Immediate Holding Company: LABINAH MANAGEMENT TRAINING LIMITED
Registration no: 04061940 **Date established:** 1977 **Turnover:** £5m - £10m
No.of Employees: 11 - 20 **Product Groups:** 80, 86

A C Tonks Orthopaedics Ltd

5 Riverside Industrial Estate Meir Road, Redditch, B98 7SY
Tel: 01527-518611 Fax: 01527-518612
E-mail: office@actonks.co.uk
Website: http://www.comfortshoesuk.com
Directors: A. Tonks (MD)
Managers: N. Tonks (Mgr)
Immediate Holding Company: A.C. TONKS (ORTHOPAEDICS) LIMITED
Registration no: 01194840 **Date established:** 1974 **Turnover:** £1m - £2m
No.of Employees: 11 - 20 **Product Groups:** 38

Date of Accounts	Dec 11	Dec 10	Dec 09
Sales Turnover	N/A	N/A	1m
Working Capital	234	183	160
Fixed Assets	189	198	213
Current Assets	383	349	330
Current Liabilities	N/A	N/A	33

Top Service

Unit 93a The Washford Industrial Estate Heming Road, Redditch, B98 0EA
Tel: 01527-518800 Fax: 01527-518801
E-mail: helpdesk@top-service.co.uk
Website: http://www.top-service.co.uk
Directors: L. Cardus (Dir), M. Ricketts (Dir), E. Bridges (Dir)
Ultimate Holding Company: TOP SERVICE (HOLDINGS) LIMITED
Immediate Holding Company: TOP SERVICE LIMITED
Registration no: 03662973 **Date established:** 1998
Turnover: £10m - £20m **No.of Employees:** 11 - 20 **Product Groups:** 81, 82

Date of Accounts	Sep 11	Sep 10	Sep 09
Working Capital	19	10	8
Fixed Assets	4	7	12
Current Assets	307	221	216

Translift Bendi Ltd

Unit 22 Padgets Lane, Redditch, B98 0RB
Tel: 01527-527411 Fax: 01527-510177
E-mail: info@bendi.co.uk
Website: http://www.bendi.co.uk
Bank(s): Barclays
Directors: S. Brown (MD), J. Kirby (Fin)
Managers: A. Nicholson (Purch Mgr), J. Kirby (Fin Mgr)
Ultimate Holding Company: ARTICULATED LIFT TRUCKS LIMITED
Immediate Holding Company: TRANSLIFT BENDI LIMITED
Registration no: 00833384 **Date established:** 1965
Turnover: £10m - £20m **No.of Employees:** 51 - 100 **Product Groups:** 45

Date of Accounts	Mar 11	Mar 10	Mar 09
Sales Turnover	13m	12m	18m
Pre Tax Profit/Loss	252	674	894
Working Capital	4m	4m	4m
Fixed Assets	916	951	802
Current Assets	7m	6m	6m
Current Liabilities	1m	904	786

Treble R Fabrications

Unit 42 Crossgate Road, Park Farm Industrial Estate, Redditch, B98 7SN
Tel: 01527-510401 **Fax:** 01527-503325
E-mail: nigel@treblerfabrications.co.uk
Website: http://www.treblerfabrications.co.uk
Directors: N. Trigger (MD)
No.of Employees: 11 - 20 **Product Groups:** 35

Trenton Engineering Ltd

Trenton Works Hewell Road, Redditch, B97 6AR
Tel: 01527-64200 Fax: 01527-66187
E-mail: info@trentonelectroplating.co.uk
Website: http://www.trentonelectroplating.co.uk
Bank(s): HSBC
Directors: J. Perry (Co Sec)
Immediate Holding Company: TRENTON ENGINEERING CO.(REDDITCH)LIMITED
Registration no: 00714082 **Date established:** 1962 **Turnover:** £1m - £2m
No.of Employees: 21 - 50 **Product Groups:** 48

Date of Accounts	Dec 11	Dec 10	Dec 09
Working Capital	40	41	32
Fixed Assets	722	731	740
Current Assets	186	147	126

Vernier Spring Co. Ltd

Fox House Edward Street, Redditch, B97 6HA
Tel: 01527-582950 **Fax:** 01527-584614
E-mail: info@verniersprings.com
Website: http://www.verniersprings.com
Directors: W. Hawkins (MD)
Managers: C. Davies (Chief Acct)
Ultimate Holding Company: WORCESTERSHIRE METAL HOLDINGS LIMITED
Immediate Holding Company: VERNIER SPRINGS AND PRESSINGS LIMITED
Registration no: 00596653 **VAT No.:** GB 110 5770 08
Date established: 1958 **No.of Employees:** 21 - 50 **Product Groups:** 35, 48

Date of Accounts	Nov 11	Jun 10	Jun 09
Sales Turnover	N/A	N/A	3m
Pre Tax Profit/Loss	N/A	N/A	-335
Working Capital	66	685	325
Fixed Assets	646	939	1m
Current Assets	2m	3m	2m
Current Liabilities	N/A	844	723

Vulco Spring & Presswork Co. Ltd

Evesham Road Astwood Bank, Redditch, B96 6DU
Tel: 01527-892447 **Fax:** 01527-892196
E-mail: sales@vulcosprings.com
Website: http://www.vulcosprings.com
Bank(s): Lloyds TSB Bank plc
Directors: D. Draper (Dir), P. Draper (MD)
Immediate Holding Company: VULCO SPRING & PRESSWORK COMPANY LIMITED
Registration no: 00262414 **VAT No.:** GB 109 4959 43
Date established: 1932 **Turnover:** £500,000 - £1m
No.of Employees: 21 - 50 **Product Groups:** 34, 35, 36, 37, 38, 39, 43, 44, 46, 48, 85

Date of Accounts	Jan 11	Jan 10	Jan 09
Working Capital	159	33	282
Fixed Assets	740	775	223
Current Assets	707	531	758

Weg Electric Motors UK Ltd

Unit 28 29 Walkers Road, Moons Moat North Industrial Estate, Redditch, B98 9HE
Tel: 01527-596748 **Fax:** 01527-591133
E-mail: sales@wegelectricmotors.co.uk
Website: http://www.wegelectricmotors.co.uk
Directors: P. O'neil (MD), P. O'Neill (Co Sec)
Ultimate Holding Company: WEG SA (BRAZIL)
Immediate Holding Company: WEG ELECTRIC MOTORS (UK) LIMITED
Registration no: 03283255 **VAT No.:** GB 695 2136 18
Date established: 1996 **Turnover:** £20m - £50m
No.of Employees: 21 - 50 **Product Groups:** 37, 40, 67

Date of Accounts	Dec 11	Dec 10	Dec 09
Sales Turnover	24m	19m	19m
Pre Tax Profit/Loss	691	274	367
Working Capital	3m	2m	2m
Fixed Assets	40	32	43
Current Assets	15m	9m	8m
Current Liabilities	1m	597	428

White & Street International Ltd

Unit 18 Enfield Industrial Estate, Redditch, B97 6BN
Tel: 01527-67881 Fax: 01527-69966
E-mail: stephenstreet@btconnect.com
Website: http://www.whiteandstreet.com
Directors: S. Street (MD)
Immediate Holding Company: WHITE & STREET INTERNATIONAL LIMITED
Registration no: 00676977 **Date established:** 1960
No.of Employees: 1 - 10 **Product Groups:** 42, 44, 46

Date of Accounts	Mar 11	Mar 10	Mar 09
Working Capital	296	354	366
Fixed Assets	164	166	168
Current Assets	432	448	456

Wiseman Treading Tools Ltd

Unit 11 Padgets Lane, Redditch, B98 0RA
Tel: 01527-520580 **Fax:** 0121-764 6499
E-mail: info@threadtools.co.uk
Website: http://www.threadtools.co.uk
Managers: M. Veglianti (Mgr)
Immediate Holding Company: WISEMAN THREADING TOOLS LIMITED
Registration no: 02703287 **Date established:** 1992
Turnover: £500,000 - £1m **No.of Employees:** 11 - 20
Product Groups: 36, 46

Date of Accounts	Jul 11	Jul 10	Jul 09
Working Capital	209	75	45
Fixed Assets	3	20	28
Current Assets	826	811	723

Worcestershire Steels Co.

Unit 61 Enfield Industrial Estate, Redditch, B97 6DE
Tel: 01527-67777 Fax: 01527-64225
E-mail: worcestershire.steels@virgin.net
Website: http://www.tamworthsteel.co.uk
Managers: T. Chambers (Chief Mgr)
Immediate Holding Company: TAMWORTH STEEL STOCKHOLDERS LTD
Registration no: 01109834 **VAT No.:** GB 111 7047 15
Date established: 1993 **Turnover:** £1m - £2m **No.of Employees:** 1 - 10
Product Groups: 34, 66

Stourport On Severn

Access Management Systems

Bewdley Road, Stourport On Severn, DY13 8QR
Tel: 020-7078 4394 **Fax:** 01299-872909
E-mail: j.scharff@amsgroup.uk.com
Website: http://www.amsgroup.uk.com
Directors: J. Scharff (Mkt Research), J. Scharff (MD)
Managers: E. Cope (Sales Admin)
Ultimate Holding Company: MORGAN CRUCIBLE COMPANY PLC(THE)
Immediate Holding Company: MORGAN TECHNICAL CERAMICS LIMITED
Registration no: 06669565 **VAT No.:** GB 841 7915 12
Date established: 1932 **Turnover:** £20m - £50m **No.of Employees:** 1 - 10
Product Groups: 22, 27, 36, 37, 39, 40, 44, 49, 65, 67, 81, 83

Date of Accounts	Jan 09	Jan 08	Jan 10
Sales Turnover	20m	19m	18m
Pre Tax Profit/Loss	-2m	-2m	-243
Working Capital	-632	-2m	6m
Fixed Assets	14m	15m	13m
Current Assets	6m	6m	10m
Current Liabilities	2m	2m	993

Allum Fabrications

Wilden Industrial Estate, Stourport On Severn, DY13 9JY
Tel: 01299-821388 **Fax:** 01299-821389
E-mail: sales@dallumfabrications.co.uk
Website: http://www.dallumfabrications.co.uk
Managers: D. Allum (Mgr)
Immediate Holding Company: D ALLUM FABRICATIONS LIMITED
Registration no: 04961484 **Date established:** 2003
Turnover: Up to £250,000 **No.of Employees:** 1 - 10 **Product Groups:** 34, 35, 36, 45, 49, 66

Date of Accounts	Dec 11	Dec 10	Dec 09
Working Capital	-7	-6	-18
Fixed Assets	14	6	9

Current Assets	68	46	26

B M B Mould Tools Stourport Ltd
81 Barracks Road, Stourport On Severn, DY13 9QB
Tel: 01299-877784 **Fax:** 01299-827590
E-mail: bmbmouldtools@aol.com
Directors: A. Garbett (MD)
Immediate Holding Company: B.M.B. MOULD TOOLS (STOURPORT) LIMITED
Registration no: 01905000 **VAT No.:** GB 419 1933 45
Date established: 1985 **No.of Employees:** 1 - 10 **Product Groups:** 30, 42

Date of Accounts	Mar 11	Mar 10	Mar 09
Working Capital	-7	-13	-36
Fixed Assets	13	17	18
Current Assets	76	73	63

Birch Bros Ltd
89-90 Barracks Road Sandy Lane Industrial Estate, Stourport On Severn, DY13 9QB
Tel: 01299-826227 **Fax:** 01299-826229
E-mail: richard.cumming@birch-brothers.co.uk
Website: http://www.birch-brothers.co.uk
Directors: J. Birch (Co Sec), R. Cumming (MD)
Immediate Holding Company: BIRCH BROTHERS (KIDDERMINSTER) LIMITED
Registration no: 01480871 **Date established:** 1980 **Turnover:** £1m - £2m
No.of Employees: 11 - 20 **Product Groups:** 51, 84

Date of Accounts	Sep 11	Sep 10	Sep 09
Working Capital	472	531	602
Fixed Assets	204	220	240
Current Assets	800	665	770

C R Engineering
Bridge Works Worcester Road, Stourport On Severn, DY13 9AS
Tel: 01299-824584 **Fax:** 01299-824584
Directors: E. Roberts (Prop), C. Roberts (Prop)
Ultimate Holding Company: LYN OAKES LIMITED
Immediate Holding Company: BROOK YORK (MENSWEAR) LIMITED
Registration no: 03257239 **Date established:** 1996
No.of Employees: 1 - 10 **Product Groups:** 35

Date of Accounts	Dec 10	Dec 09	Dec 08
Working Capital	132	136	138
Fixed Assets	109	104	119
Current Assets	772	640	533

Conveyor Units Ltd
Sandy Lane Titton, Stourport On Severn, DY13 9PT
Tel: 01299-877541 **Fax:** 01299- 877921
E-mail: conveyorsales@conveyor-units.co.uk
Website: http://www.conveyor-units.co.uk
Bank(s): Barclays
Directors: E. Toye (MD), M. Toye (MD), A. Meek (Dir), I. Bytheway (Fin)
Managers: C. Nock (Sales Off Mgr)
Ultimate Holding Company: NEW CONVEYOR LIMITED
Immediate Holding Company: CONVEYOR UNITS LIMITED
Registration no: 00771623 **Date established:** 1963 **Turnover:** £5m - £10m
No.of Employees: 11 - 20 **Product Groups:** 45

Date of Accounts	Dec 11	Dec 10	Dec 09
Sales Turnover	10m	8m	6m
Pre Tax Profit/Loss	2m	349	520
Working Capital	5m	4m	3m
Fixed Assets	982	717	2m
Current Assets	7m	6m	4m
Current Liabilities	687	436	383

Dortrend International Ltd
Riverside Business Centre Worcester Road, Stourport On Severn, DY13 9BZ
Tel: 01299-827837 **Fax:** 01299-827094
E-mail: sales@dortrend.co.uk
Website: http://www.dortrend.co.uk
Bank(s): National Westminster, London
Directors: S. Midlane (Fin), P. Dean (MD)
Immediate Holding Company: DORTREND INTERNATIONAL LIMITED
Registration no: 01079790 **VAT No.:** GB 275 8162 33
Date established: 1972 **Turnover:** £1m - £2m **No.of Employees:** 11 - 20
Product Groups: 36, 39, 66

Date of Accounts	Dec 11	Dec 10	Dec 09
Working Capital	643	625	725
Fixed Assets	45	62	59
Current Assets	2m	2m	2m

Form-Fab Worcs Ltd
Sandy Lane Industrial Estate, Stourport On Severn, DY13 9QB
Tel: 01299-879271 **Fax:** 01299-877339
E-mail: sales@form-fab.com
Website: http://www.form-fab.com
Directors: J. Wood (MD)
Immediate Holding Company: FORM-FAB (WORCS) LIMITED
Registration no: 01841377 **Date established:** 1984
Turnover: £500,000 - £1m **No.of Employees:** 1 - 10 **Product Groups:** 45

Date of Accounts	Aug 11	Aug 10	Aug 09
Working Capital	37	67	93
Fixed Assets	13	22	32
Current Assets	302	301	288

A Hawkes Associates
3 Hafren Way, Stourport On Severn, DY13 8SJ
Tel: 01299-823689 **Fax:** 01299-824210
E-mail: andrewhawkes7@aol.com
Directors: A. Hawkes (Prop), D. Hawkes (Co Sec)
Ultimate Holding Company: A. HAWKES HOLDINGS LTD
Immediate Holding Company: A.HAWKES ASSOCIATES LTD
Registration no: 03831088 **Date established:** 1999
No.of Employees: 1 - 10 **Product Groups:** 35, 39, 45

Date of Accounts	Jun 11	Jun 10	Jun 09
Working Capital	17	2	2
Fixed Assets	N/A	1	1
Current Assets	31	10	19

Hawkley Timotex Ltd
Lodge Road, Stourport On Severn, DY13 9HE
Tel: 01299-823850 **Fax:** 01420-479090
E-mail: info@hawkleygroup.com
Website: http://www.hawkleygroup.com
Directors: B. Millar (MD)
Immediate Holding Company: HAWKLEY TIMOTEX LIMITED
Registration no: 01918695 **Date established:** 1985
No.of Employees: 1 - 10 **Product Groups:** 36, 38, 39, 45, 46, 48, 67, 83, 85

Date of Accounts	Mar 11	Mar 10	Mar 09
Working Capital	110	115	152
Fixed Assets	71	63	62
Current Assets	348	265	414
Current Liabilities	101	79	113

Richard Hoare Plant & Machinery Ltd
Mill Road, Stourport On Severn, DY13 9BL
Tel: 01299-879263 **Fax:** 01299-877319
E-mail: sales@hoaremachines.com
Website: http://www.hoaremachines.com
Directors: R. Hoare (MD)
Ultimate Holding Company: ISTOBAL SA (SPAIN)
Immediate Holding Company: RICHARD HOARE (PLANT AND MACHINERY) LIMITED
Registration no: 01317665 **Date established:** 1977
Turnover: £500,000 - £1m **No.of Employees:** 1 - 10 **Product Groups:** 46

Date of Accounts	Dec 10	Dec 09	Dec 07
Working Capital	-21	-37	-34
Fixed Assets	35	42	39
Current Assets	147	126	156

Pearl Dental Ceramics
Grinnall Business Centre Sandy Lane Industrial Estate, Stourport On Severn, DY13 9QB
Tel: 01299-823000
E-mail: koisser@btinternet.com
Directors: D. Koisser (Ptnr)
Immediate Holding Company: EQUIMIX (FEEDS) LIMITED
Date established: 1975 **No.of Employees:** 1 - 10 **Product Groups:** 38, 67

Date of Accounts	May 11	May 10	May 09
Working Capital	-85	-91	-100
Fixed Assets	101	108	113
Current Assets	234	253	234

Polyplas Extrusions Ltd
Unit 1 Wilden Industrial Estate Wilden Lane, Stourport On Severn, DY13 9JY
Tel: 01299-827344 **Fax:** 01299-827016
E-mail: info@polyplas.co.uk
Website: http://polyplas.co.uk
Directors: G. Tidman (Dir), C. Tidman (Dir)
Immediate Holding Company: POLYPLAS EXTRUSIONS LIMITED
Registration no: 02362849 **Date established:** 1989 **Turnover:** £1m - £2m
No.of Employees: 21 - 50 **Product Groups:** 30, 31, 42

Date of Accounts	Dec 11	Dec 10	Dec 09
Working Capital	447	223	419
Fixed Assets	204	258	307
Current Assets	1m	810	668

Frank Salt & Co. Ltd
Barracks Road Sandy Lane Industrial Estate, Stourport On Severn, DY13 9QG
Tel: 01299-827006 **Fax:** 01299-877901
E-mail: website@franksalt.co.uk
Website: http://www.franksalt.co.uk
Directors: W. Ward (Dir)
Immediate Holding Company: FRANK SALT & COMPANY LIMITED
Registration no: 00462319 **VAT No.:** GB 275 3131 69
Date established: 1948 **Turnover:** £500,000 - £1m
No.of Employees: 1 - 10 **Product Groups:** 46, 48

Date of Accounts	Dec 10	Dec 09	Dec 08
Working Capital	-60	-67	-188
Fixed Assets	1m	1m	868
Current Assets	28	25	35

Sandfield Engineering Co. Ltd
Sandy Lane Industrial Estate, Stourport On Severn, DY13 9QB
Tel: 01299-823158 **Fax:** 01299-827011
E-mail: sales@sandfieldengineering.com
Website: http://www.sandfieldengineering.com
Bank(s): HSBC Bank plc
Directors: E. Tebbett (MD)
Immediate Holding Company: SANDFIELD ENGINEERING COMPANY LIMITED
Registration no: 00847205 **VAT No.:** GB 275 4128 53
Date established: 1965 **Turnover:** £2m - £5m **No.of Employees:** 21 - 50
Product Groups: 36, 40

Date of Accounts	Jul 11	Jul 10	Jul 09
Working Capital	-22	1	-7
Fixed Assets	234	240	244
Current Assets	630	439	475

Severn Fast Food Services Ltd
5 Burlish Close, Stourport On Severn, DY13 8XN
Tel: 01299-827735 **Fax:** 01299-827735
Directors: J. Price (Fin), J. Price (MD)
Immediate Holding Company: SEVERN FAST FOOD SERVICES LIMITED
Registration no: 04596722 **Date established:** 2002
No.of Employees: 1 - 10 **Product Groups:** 20, 40, 41

Date of Accounts	Dec 09	Dec 08	Dec 07
Working Capital	-6	-8	-7
Fixed Assets	7	8	12
Current Assets	16	15	12

Severn Metalworking Machinery
53 Lickhill Road, Stourport On Severn, DY13 8SL
Tel: 01299-824005 **Fax:** 01299-822274
Website: http://www.smm.co.uk
Directors: K. Cherrington (Ptnr)
Registration no: 06598208 **Date established:** 2008
No.of Employees: 1 - 10 **Product Groups:** 38, 46

Sharmic Engineering Ltd
Baldwin Road, Stourport On Severn, DY13 9AX
Tel: 01299-822135 **Fax:** 01299-879409
E-mail: info@sharmic.co.uk
Website: http://www.sharmic.co.uk
Managers: S. Edwards (Sales Admin)
Immediate Holding Company: SHARMIC ENGINEERING LIMITED
Registration no: 01252591 **VAT No.:** GB 276 7658 03
Date established: 1976 **Turnover:** £1m - £2m **No.of Employees:** 1 - 10
Product Groups: 32, 33, 42, 46, 47

Date of Accounts	Mar 12	Mar 11	Mar 10
Working Capital	6	13	2
Fixed Assets	232	202	195
Current Assets	228	246	158

Signtech (Midlands) Limited
18-19 Bell Row Lion Hill, Stourport On Severn, DY13 9HG
Tel: 01299-827309 **Fax:** 01299-877086
E-mail: info@signtech.co.uk
Website: http://www.signtech.co.uk
Directors: S. Purvin (Dir), D. Dixon (Dir)
Registration no: 04662789 **Turnover:** £250,000 - £500,000
No.of Employees: 1 - 10 **Product Groups:** 30, 37

Date of Accounts	Feb 10	Feb 09	Feb 08
Working Capital	12	-13	13
Fixed Assets	31	34	48
Current Assets	55	35	54

Specialist Machine Parts
Baldwin Road, Stourport On Severn, DY13 9AX
Tel: 01299-878965 **Fax:** 01562-748300
E-mail: info@specialistmachineparts.co.uk
Website: http://www.specialistmachineparts.co.uk
Directors: T. Ball (MD), J. Ball (Co Sec)
Immediate Holding Company: SPECIALIST MACHINE PARTS LIMITED
Registration no: 03708053 **Date established:** 1999
No.of Employees: 1 - 10 **Product Groups:** 46

Date of Accounts	Feb 08	Feb 11	Feb 10
Working Capital	66	37	21
Fixed Assets	11	258	258
Current Assets	96	88	59

UK Fuel Ltd
18 Lombard Street, Stourport On Severn, DY13 8DT
Tel: 01299-871717
E-mail: peter.bridgland@fuellingservices.co.uk
Website: http://www.fuellingservices.com
Directors: P. Bridgland (MD)
Managers: W. HERBERT (Sales Prom Mgr)
Immediate Holding Company: FUELLING SERVICES LIMITED
Registration no: 04316957 **Date established:** 2001 **Turnover:** £5m - £10m
No.of Employees: 1 - 10 **Product Groups:** 66

Date of Accounts	Mar 11	Mar 10	Mar 09
Sales Turnover	N/A	9m	9m
Pre Tax Profit/Loss	N/A	72	114
Working Capital	114	89	92
Fixed Assets	N/A	1	1
Current Assets	1m	1m	850
Current Liabilities	N/A	63	66

Wyvern Handling & Storage Equipment Ltd
PO Box 5483, Stourport On Severn, DY13 3BG
Tel: 01299-829300 **Fax:** 01299-825799
E-mail: sales@wyvernhandling.co.uk
Website: http://www.wyvernhandling.co.uk
Directors: J. Disturnal (Co Sec)
Immediate Holding Company: WYVERN HANDLING & STORAGE EQUIPMENT LIMITED
Registration no: 01872237 **Date established:** 1984
No.of Employees: 1 - 10 **Product Groups:** 35, 39, 45

Date of Accounts	Mar 12	Mar 11	Mar 10
Working Capital	24	24	5
Fixed Assets	N/A	1	1
Current Assets	62	88	30

Tenbury Wells

Bedford Dials Ltd
Corn Exchange Teme Street, Tenbury Wells, WR15 8BB
Tel: 01584-810345 **Fax:** 01584-810683
E-mail: info@bedforddials.co.uk
Website: http://www.bedforddials.co.uk
Bank(s): Lloyds TSB Bank plc
Directors: J. Rickett (MD)
Ultimate Holding Company: A H BEDFORD & SON LIMITED
Immediate Holding Company: BEDFORD DIALS LIMITED
Registration no: 01548978 **Date established:** 1981
Turnover: £500,000 - £1m **No.of Employees:** 11 - 20
Product Groups: 30, 38, 39, 48, 49

Date of Accounts	Mar 12	Mar 11	Mar 10
Working Capital	173	186	187
Fixed Assets	172	183	135
Current Assets	220	246	249

Botanix
Eardiston, Tenbury Wells, WR15 8JJ
Tel: 01584-881361 **Fax:** 01584-881498
E-mail: sales@botanix.co.uk
Website: http://www.botanix.co.uk
Bank(s): National Westminster Bank Plc
Managers: R. Smith (Mgr)
Ultimate Holding Company: JOH BARTH & SOHN GMBH & CO KG (GERMANY)
Immediate Holding Company: THE WIGAN HOP COMPANY LIMITED
Registration no: 00945110 **Date established:** 1969 **Turnover:** £5m - £10m
No.of Employees: 11 - 20 **Product Groups:** 02, 20, 31, 62, 66

Corporate Finance Associates
The Coach House Rochford, Tenbury Wells, WR15 8SP
Tel: 01584-781601 **Fax:** 08700-336935
E-mail: info@corporatefinanceassociates.co.uk
Website: http://www.corporatefinanceassociates.co.uk
Directors: D. Winter (Prop)
Date established: 1990 **No.of Employees:** 1 - 10 **Product Groups:** 82

Don Evans Deisel Engines
Bell Lane Broadheath, Tenbury Wells, WR15 8QX
Tel: 01886-853279 **Fax:** 01886-853279
Directors: D. Evans (Prop)
Date established: 1970 **No.of Employees:** 1 - 10 **Product Groups:** 35, 36, 39

Simply Stoves
Six Acres Barn Sutton, Tenbury Wells, WR15 8RN
Tel: 01885-410556
E-mail: simplystoves@btconnect.com
Website: http://www.simplystoves.co.uk
Directors: P. Robinson (Prop)
Immediate Holding Company: J.G.BANFIELD & SONS,LIMITED
Date established: 1914 **No.of Employees:** 1 - 10 **Product Groups:** 40

Worcester

A A Global Language Services Ltd
Global House, Worcester, WR1 2BU
Tel: 01905-616262 **Fax:** 0870-199 2499
E-mail: info@aaglobal.co.uk
Website: http://www.aaglobal.co.uk
Directors: K. Akdemir (MD)
Immediate Holding Company: AA GLOBAL LANGUAGE SERVICES LIMITED
Registration no: 04299764 **Date established:** 2001
No.of Employees: 1 - 10 **Product Groups:** 80

Date of Accounts	Mar 11	Mar 10	Mar 09
Working Capital	53	50	29
Fixed Assets	10	10	6
Current Assets	116	138	85

A B Tech
43 Larkspur Road, Worcester, WR5 3RU
Tel: 01905-355134
E-mail: helpdesk@abtech.info
Website: http://www.abtech.info
Registration no: 05842845 **Product Groups:** 38, 48, 52, 84

Abbey Spares & Supplies
Unit 17 Top Barn Business Centre Worcester Road, Holt Heath, Worcester, WR6 6NH
Tel: 01905-621666 **Fax:** 01905-621866
E-mail: sales@abbeyspares.co.uk
Website: http://www.abbeyspares.co.uk
Directors: P. Mckenzie (MD)
Immediate Holding Company: ABBEY SPARES AND SUPPLIES LIMITED
Registration no: 05031994 **VAT No.:** GB 487 4426 10
Date established: 2004 **Turnover:** £500,000 - £1m
No.of Employees: 1 - 10 **Product Groups:** 38, 45

Date of Accounts	Mar 11	Mar 10	Mar 09
Sales Turnover	N/A	N/A	324
Working Capital	29	28	31
Fixed Assets	3	3	3
Current Assets	61	64	51

Adroit Modular Buildings plc
Trow Way, Worcester, WR5 3BX
Tel: 01905-356018 **Fax:** 01905-351868
E-mail: mail@adroitgroup.co.uk
Website: http://www.adroitmodular.com
Bank(s): Barclays
Directors: D. Broome (MD), P. Baister (Sales & Mktg), D. Broom (MD)
Managers: A. Bacon (Purch Mgr)
Ultimate Holding Company: 00527081
Immediate Holding Company: ADROIT MODULAR BUILDINGS PLC
Registration no: 00668542 **VAT No.:** GB 277 8845 90
Date established: 1960 **Turnover:** £2m - £5m **No.of Employees:** 11 - 20
Product Groups: 25, 35, 36, 39, 83

Advanced N D T Ltd
Orchard House Orchard Close, Severn Stoke, Worcester, WR8 9JJ
Tel: 01905-371460 **Fax:** 01905-371477
E-mail: sales@advanced-ndt.co.uk
Website: http://www.advanced-ndt.co.uk
Directors: T. Mullins (Fin)
Immediate Holding Company: ADVANCED NDT LIMITED
Registration no: 05957975 **VAT No.:** GB 589 5903 74
Date established: 2006 **No.of Employees:** 1 - 10 **Product Groups:** 37, 38, 44, 45, 67, 85

Date of Accounts	Oct 11	Oct 10	Oct 09
Working Capital	79	75	100
Fixed Assets	44	43	48
Current Assets	169	189	171

Albion Ltd
Suite 12 Malvern Gate, Bromwich Road, Worcester, WR2 4BN
Tel: 01905-427555 **Fax:** 0845-2801716
E-mail: info@albionltd.co.uk
Website: http://www.albionltd.co.uk
Directors: J. Walters (MD)
Managers: R. Kirby, S. Hardacre (Sales Prom Mgr)
Registration no: 06300240 **VAT No.:** GB 133 5764 68
Date established: 1980 **Turnover:** Up to £250,000
No.of Employees: 21 - 50 **Product Groups:** 24, 63

Date of Accounts	Apr 08	Apr 07
Sales Turnover	7329	10392
Pre Tax Profit/Loss	-340	-2041
Working Capital	-2344	-2008
Fixed Assets	52	57
Current Assets	1848	4393
Current Liabilities	4192	6402
Total Share Capital	157	157
ROCE% (Return on Capital Employed)	14.8	104.6
ROT% (Return on Turnover)	-4.6	-19.6

Applied Thoughts Ltd
The Cottage Bevere Green, Bevere, Worcester, WR3 7RG
Tel: 01905-756061 **Fax:** 01905-756061
E-mail: laura@washingnet.org.uk
Website: http://www.washingnet.org.uk
Directors: L. Thomas (Fin), L. Thomas (MD)
Immediate Holding Company: APPLIED THOUGHTS LTD.
Registration no: 03701653 **Date established:** 1999
No.of Employees: 1 - 10 **Product Groups:** 43

Date of Accounts	Mar 11	Mar 10	Mar 09
Working Capital	1	1	2
Current Assets	64	48	58

Ashem Crafts
2 Oakleigh Avenue Hallow, Worcester, WR2 6NG
Tel: 01905-640070
E-mail: enquiries@ashemcrafts.com
Website: http://www.ashemcrafts.com
Directors: P. Hindle (Prop)
Date established: 1993 **No.of Employees:** 1 - 10 **Product Groups:** 36

Atwell International Ltd
1 Ball Mill Top Business Park Hallow, Worcester, WR2 6PD
Tel: 01905-641881 **Fax:** 01905-641298
Website: http://www.atwellinternational.com
Directors: W. Burtenshaw (Fin)
Immediate Holding Company: ATWELL INTERNATIONAL LIMITED
Registration no: 03167927 **Date established:** 1996
No.of Employees: 1 - 10 **Product Groups:** 35, 39, 45

Date of Accounts	Feb 12	Feb 11	Feb 10
Working Capital	127	112	-20
Fixed Assets	35	40	50
Current Assets	838	882	737

Auto Proud UK Ltd Fluid Technology International Ltd
Unit 3 Pope Iron Road, Worcester, WR1 3HB
Tel: 0845-8738869 **Fax:** 01905-734973
E-mail: info@autoproud.co.uk
Website: http://www.autoproud.co.uk
Registration no: 05352721 **Product Groups:** 32, 48, 52

Axis Engineering Ltd
Shrub Hill, Worcester, WR4 9EL
Tel: 01905-20640 **Fax:** 01905-20641
Website: http://www.access-engineering.co.uk
Directors: N. Bishop (Dir)
Registration no: 03216149 **Date established:** 1996
No.of Employees: 1 - 10 **Product Groups:** 35, 48

Aztec Tooling & Moulding Company Ltd
Buckholt Drive, Worcester, WR4 9ND
Tel: 01905-754466 **Fax:** 01905-754475
E-mail: aztectmltd@aol.com
Website: http://www.aztecmouldings.co.uk
Directors: K. Mulcock (MD), P. Shearsmith (Fin)
Immediate Holding Company: AZTEC TOOLING & MOULDING CO. LIMITED
Registration no: 01645002 **VAT No.:** GB 377 1830 33
Date established: 1982 **Turnover:** £500,000 - £1m
No.of Employees: 1 - 10 **Product Groups:** 30, 42

Date of Accounts	Jun 12	Jun 11	Jun 10
Working Capital	224	227	216
Fixed Assets	159	174	187
Current Assets	272	264	262

Boston Munchy Ltd
Navigation Road, Worcester, WR5 3DE
Tel: 01905-763100 **Fax:** 01905-763101
E-mail: sales@bostonmatthews.co.uk
Website: http://www.bostonmatthews.co.uk
Bank(s): The Royal Bank of Scotland
Directors: C. Brookes (MD)
Managers: S. Brookes (Sales Prom Mgr), R. Brookes (Mktg Serv Mgr), K. Harris (Buyer)
Immediate Holding Company: BOSTON MATTHEWS MACHINERY LIMITED
Registration no: 01815679 **VAT No.:** GB 589 5262 86
Date established: 1984 **Turnover:** £2m - £5m **No.of Employees:** 21 - 50
Product Groups: 38, 42, 67

Date of Accounts	Sep 11	Sep 10	Sep 09
Working Capital	200	113	59
Fixed Assets	224	233	254
Current Assets	229	123	64

Britax P S V Wypers Ltd
Navigation Road, Worcester, WR5 3DE
Tel: 01905-350500 **Fax:** 01905-763928
E-mail: paul.curry@psvwypers.com
Website: http://www.psvwypers.com
Bank(s): Barclays, Birmingham
Directors: P. Curry (Works)
Managers: L. Foxall (Sales Prom Mgr)
Ultimate Holding Company: PSE NEWCO LIMITED
Immediate Holding Company: BRITAX PSV WYPERS LIMITED
Registration no: 01472333 **VAT No.:** GB 379 2273 43
Date established: 1980 **Turnover:** £1m - £2m **No.of Employees:** 21 - 50
Product Groups: 39, 40

Date of Accounts	Dec 11	Dec 10	Jun 10
Sales Turnover	1m	538	1m
Pre Tax Profit/Loss	-117	272	-170
Working Capital	168	278	-12
Fixed Assets	47	12	14
Current Assets	757	550	589
Current Liabilities	38	36	38

British Security Industry Association
Kirkham House John Comyn Drive, Worcester, WR3 7NS
Tel: 08453-893889
E-mail: info@bsia.co.uk
Website: http://www.bsia.co.uk
Directors: J. Kelly (Grp Chief Exec)
Managers: P. Turner (Consultant), A. Beesley
Immediate Holding Company: BRITISH SECURITY INDUSTRY ASSOCIATION LIMITED(THE)
Registration no: 00896431 **Date established:** 1967 **Turnover:** £1m - £2m
No.of Employees: 21 - 50 **Product Groups:** 87

Date of Accounts	Dec 11	Dec 10	Dec 09
Working Capital	-19	119	136
Fixed Assets	1m	1m	1m
Current Assets	559	725	1m

Brockhouse Modernfold Ltd
Kay One 23 The Tything, Worcester, WR1 1HD
Tel: 01905-330055 **Fax:** 01905-330234
E-mail: markdavis@brockhouse.net
Website: http://www.brockhouse.net
Directors: N. O'halleran (Dir)
Ultimate Holding Company: LIONFORCE LIMITED
Immediate Holding Company: BROCKHOUSE MODERNFOLD LIMITED
Registration no: 03169374 **VAT No.:** GB 676 0233 38
Date established: 1996 **Turnover:** £2m - £5m **No.of Employees:** 1 - 10
Product Groups: 25, 35, 40

Date of Accounts	Dec 11	Dec 10	Dec 09
Working Capital	221	119	58
Fixed Assets	84	94	100
Current Assets	1m	1m	939

Calder Ltd
Gregorys Bank, Worcester, WR3 8AB
Tel: 01905-723255 **Fax:** 01905-723904
E-mail: peter.elton@calder.co.uk
Website: http://www.calder.co.uk
Bank(s): HSBC, Worcester
Directors: I. Calder-Potts (MD), S. Davies (Co Sec), S. Davis (Co Sec), P. Elliot-Moore (Eng Serv), P. Elton (MD), S. Sharp (Sales)
Immediate Holding Company: CALDER LIMITED
Registration no: 01524351 **VAT No.:** GB 342 9568 31
Date established: 1980 **Turnover:** £5m - £10m **No.of Employees:** 21 - 50
Product Groups: 39, 40, 42, 45, 46, 48, 67

Date of Accounts	Mar 11	Mar 10	Mar 09
Sales Turnover	12m	10m	N/A
Pre Tax Profit/Loss	1m	772	959
Working Capital	2m	2m	1m
Fixed Assets	257	268	350
Current Assets	5m	4m	4m
Current Liabilities	1m	1m	568

Carmichael Support Services
Weir Lane, Worcester, WR2 4AY
Tel: 01905-420044 **Fax:** 01905-420120
E-mail: brianw@amdac-carmichael.com
Website: http://www.carmichael-int.co.uk
Bank(s): HSBC Bank plc
Directors: B. Wiggins (Sales & Mktg), P. Morton (Co Sec), R. Yahaya (Comm)
Managers: S. Breakwell (Tech Serv Mgr)
Immediate Holding Company: MCGEE & O'CONNELL LLP
Registration no: OC334142 **VAT No.:** GB 589 3446 86
Date established: 2010 **Turnover:** £2m - £5m **No.of Employees:** 51 - 100
Product Groups: 40

Date of Accounts	Jul 11	Jul 10	Jul 09
Working Capital	322	312	4
Current Assets	323	313	4

Chamer Of Commerce
Severn House Prescott Drive, Worcester, WR4 9NE
Tel: 08456-411641 **Fax:** 0845-641 4641
E-mail: helenk@hwchamber.co.uk
Website: http://www.hwchamber.co.uk/
Managers: H. King (Mgr)
Ultimate Holding Company: HEREFORDSHIRE AND WORCESTERSHIRE CHAMBER OF COMMERCE
Immediate Holding Company: CHAMBER OF COMMERCE TRAINING COMPANY LIMITED
Registration no: 01936795 **Date established:** 1985
No.of Employees: 1 - 10 **Product Groups:** 80, 81, 86

Cleaning & Packaging Supplies Worcester
Unit A Perrywood Trading Park Wylds Lane, Worcester, WR5 1DZ
Tel: 01905-763500 **Fax:** 01905-763363
E-mail: sales@cpsw.co.uk
Website: http://www.heronsupplies.co.uk
Bank(s): The Royal Bank Of Scotland
Directors: M. Smith (MD)
Immediate Holding Company: THOMPSONS ONLINE LIMITED
Registration no: 06686726 **VAT No.:** GB 715 5656 25
Date established: 2008 **Turnover:** £250,000 - £500,000
No.of Employees: 11 - 20 **Product Groups:** 27, 30, 63

John C Collins
Honeysuckle Cottage Worcester Road, Inkberrow, Worcester, WR7 4JP
Tel: 01386-792591 **Fax:** 01386-792591
Directors: J. Collins (Prop)
Registration no: 02816337 **VAT No.:** GB 109 6711 69
Date established: 1863 **Turnover:** Up to £250,000
No.of Employees: 1 - 10 **Product Groups:** 41

County Enterprises
St Pauls Street, Worcester, WR1 2BA
Tel: 01905-23819 **Fax:** 01905-27832
E-mail: aosborne@worcestershire.gov.uk
Website: http://www.countyenterprises.co.uk
Bank(s): HSBC Bank plc
Managers: R. Davies (Mgr)
Immediate Holding Company: WORCESTERSHIRE COUNTY COUNCIL
Turnover: £500,000 - £1m **No.of Employees:** 21 - 50
Product Groups: 36, 48

Cryoservice Ltd
Prescott Drive, Worcester, WR4 9RH
Tel: 01905-758200 **Fax:** 01905-754060
E-mail: info@cryoservice.co.uk
Website: http://www.cryoservice.co.uk
Bank(s): Lloyds TSB Bank plc
Directors: N. Grimshaw (Fin), N. Grimshore (Fin), M. Davey (Fin), C. Kinnear (Ch)
Managers: D. Desouza, J. Carver, N. Ali (Sales & Mktg Mg)
Ultimate Holding Company: AIR PRODUCTS & CHEMICALS INC (USA)
Immediate Holding Company: CRYOSERVICE LIMITED
Registration no: 00976552 **VAT No.:** GB 436 8067 33
Date established: 1970 **Turnover:** £20m - £50m
No.of Employees: 251 - 500 **Product Groups:** 31, 42, 48, 52, 85

Date of Accounts	Aug 08	Sep 11	Sep 10
Sales Turnover	33m	39m	37m
Pre Tax Profit/Loss	6m	11m	9m
Working Capital	68	14m	8m
Fixed Assets	32m	30m	31m
Current Assets	7m	21m	14m
Current Liabilities	2m	4m	3m

Cytoplan Ltd
Unit 8 Hanley Workshops Hanley Swan, Worcester, WR8 0DX
Tel: 01684-310099 **Fax:** 01684-312000
E-mail: ian@cytoplan.co.uk
Website: http://www.cytoplan.co.uk
Bank(s): Lloyds TSB Bank plc
Directors: A. Williams (MD)
Managers: J. Turner, C. Smith (Fin Mgr)
Immediate Holding Company: CYTOPLAN LIMITED
Registration no: 02401115 **VAT No.:** GB 540 5101 95
Date established: 1989 **No.of Employees:** 21 - 50 **Product Groups:** 31

Date of Accounts	Aug 11	Aug 10	Aug 09
Working Capital	331	264	249
Fixed Assets	N/A	1	1
Current Assets	444	381	344

Dero Fabrication Ltd
Unit 67 Blackpole Trading Estate West, Worcester, WR3 8TJ
Tel: 01905-455199 **Fax:** 01905-754152
E-mail: sales@dero.co.uk
Website: http://www.dero.co.uk

Directors: J. Taylor (MD), J. Taylor (Fin)
Immediate Holding Company: DERO FABRICATION LIMITED
Registration no: 04040729 **VAT No.:** GB 299 0795 93
Date established: 2000 **Turnover:** £5m - £10m **No.of Employees:** 11 - 20
Product Groups: 35, 48

Date of Accounts	Dec 11	Dec 10	Dec 09
Working Capital	17	-10	-37
Fixed Assets	334	10	32
Current Assets	248	169	122
Current Liabilities	9	26	31

Diemac Ltd

14b Backfields Upton-upon-Severn, Worcester, WR8 0JH
Tel: 01684-594995 **Fax:** 01684- 594995
Directors: M. Heath (Fin)
No.of Employees: 1 - 10 **Product Groups:** 20, 40, 41

Diverco Ltd

4 Bank Street, Worcester, WR1 2EW
Tel: 01905-23383 **Fax:** 01905- 613523
Website: http://www.diverco.co.uk
Directors: D. Dodgson (Dir)
Immediate Holding Company: DIVERCO LIMITED
Registration no: 01220421 **Date established:** 1975
Turnover: £500,000 - £1m **No.of Employees:** 1 - 10 **Product Groups:** 61

Date of Accounts	Jan 12	Jan 11	Jan 10
Working Capital	262	276	168
Fixed Assets	14	17	19
Current Assets	285	302	188

DLServe

Kemerton Lodge Crowle, Worcester, WR7 4AY
Tel: 01905-381824 **Fax:** 01905-381824
E-mail: sales@dlserve.com
Website: http://www.dlserve.com
Managers: D. Bungay (Sales Prom Mgr)
Date established: 2008 **No.of Employees:** 1 - 10 **Product Groups:** 33, 37

Door Panels Ltd

Rectory Road Upton-upon-Severn, Worcester, WR8 0LX
Tel: 01684-594561 **Fax:** 01684-593431
E-mail: sales@doorpanels.co.uk
Website: http://www.doorpanels.co.uk
Directors: D. Ronaldi (Sales), S. Hlywiak (Dir), J. Murray-Brown (Fin), J. Murray Brown (Fin)
Managers: G. Allen (Mktg Serv Mgr), A. Bullock (Tech Serv Mgr)
Immediate Holding Company: DOOR PANELS LIMITED
Registration no: 07214018 **VAT No.:** GB 119 7195 49
Date established: 2010 **Turnover:** £10m - £20m
No.of Employees: 21 - 50 **Product Groups:** 30

Date of Accounts	Dec 10
Working Capital	-324
Fixed Assets	941
Current Assets	1m

Double-Take Software

Elgar House Shrub Hill Road, Worcester, WR4 9EE
Tel: 01905-22948 **Fax:** 01905- 745722
E-mail: sales@doubletake.com
Website: http://www.doubletake.com
Managers: L. Master (District Mgr)
Ultimate Holding Company: ZIMUR SRL (ITALY)
Immediate Holding Company: DOUBLE-TAKE SOFTWARE UK LIMITED
Registration no: 04984118 **Date established:** 2003 **Turnover:** £5m - £10m
No.of Employees: 1 - 10 **Product Groups:** 44

Date of Accounts	Dec 11	Dec 10	Dec 09
Sales Turnover	5m	6m	7m
Pre Tax Profit/Loss	289	249	301
Working Capital	497	274	102
Fixed Assets	109	106	109
Current Assets	3m	3m	3m
Current Liabilities	3m	2m	3m

F Durrant & Son

3 Mealcheapen Street, Worcester, WR1 2DH
Tel: 01905-25247
E-mail: sales@fdurrantandson.com
Website: http://www.fdurrantandson.com
Directors: T. Smith (Prop)
Date established: 1912 **No.of Employees:** 1 - 10 **Product Groups:** 36, 39, 40

Dynamometer Services Group Ltd

Stock End Station Road, Bransford, Worcester, WR6 5JH
Tel: 01886-834860 **Fax:** 01886-834879
E-mail: sales@dsgroup.uk.com
Website: http://www.dsgroup.uk.com
Directors: D. Derrett (Fin), G. Atkins (Sales), J. Derrett (Chief Op Offcr)
Immediate Holding Company: DYNAMOMETER SERVICES GROUP LIMITED
Registration no: 03901838 **Date established:** 2000
Turnover: £250,000 - £500,000 **No.of Employees:** 21 - 50
Product Groups: 35, 38, 44, 68

Date of Accounts	Mar 11	Mar 10	Mar 09
Working Capital	244	204	253
Fixed Assets	155	131	175
Current Assets	682	408	754

E & E Engineering Ltd

Unit 74 Blackpole Trading Estate West, Worcester, WR3 8TJ
Tel: 01905-453527 **Fax:** 01905-457395
E-mail: julia.wild@univar.co.uk
Website: http://www.e-and-e.co.uk
Directors: J. Wild (Fin), P. Wild (MD)
Registration no: 02998000 **Date established:** 1994
Turnover: £250,000 - £500,000 **No.of Employees:** 1 - 10
Product Groups: 48

Date of Accounts	Mar 08	Mar 07	Mar 06
Working Capital	67	60	72
Fixed Assets	31	38	44
Current Assets	123	102	146
Current Liabilities	56	42	74

E M C Component Handling

Priors Mead Alcester Road, Inkberrow, Worcester, WR7 4HN
Tel: 01386-793471 **Fax:** 01386-793471
E-mail: efox2011@hotmail.co.uk
Website: http://www.componenthandling.co.uk
Directors: E. Fox (Prop)
No.of Employees: 1 - 10 **Product Groups:** 45, 67

Exmac

Gregorys Bank, Worcester, WR3 8AB
Tel: 01905-721500 **Fax:** 01905-613024
E-mail: gjs@exmac.co.uk
Website: http://www.exmacautomation.co.uk
Bank(s): Bank of Scotland
Directors: G. Sweeney (MD), H. Chana (Sales & Mktg), M. Hunter (Dir)
Managers: B. Knightley (Chief Acct)
Immediate Holding Company: EXCEL AUTOMATION LIMITED
Registration no: 02675250 **VAT No.:** GB 661 5381 35
Date established: 1992 **Turnover:** £5m - £10m **No.of Employees:** 21 - 50
Product Groups: 45

Date of Accounts	Dec 08	Dec 07	Dec 06
Sales Turnover	8m	7m	6m
Pre Tax Profit/Loss	79	249	146
Working Capital	438	471	553
Fixed Assets	451	287	128
Current Assets	3m	2m	2m
Current Liabilities	2m	1m	2m
Total Share Capital	45	45	60

Fairway Hydraulics Ltd

Unit 96a Blackpole Trading Estate West, Worcester, WR3 8TJ
Tel: 01905-457519 **Fax:** 01905-456054
E-mail: enquiries@fairwayhydraulics.co.uk
Website: http://www.fairwayhydraulics.co.uk
Bank(s): Barclays, Droitwich
Directors: C. Chang (Fin), R. Dowdeswell (MD)
Immediate Holding Company: FAIRWAY HYDRAULICS LIMITED
Registration no: 04613317 **VAT No.:** GB 276 5104 56
Date established: 2002 **Turnover:** £500,000 - £1m
No.of Employees: 11 - 20 **Product Groups:** 23, 29, 30, 33, 34, 35, 36, 37, 38, 39, 40, 41, 42, 46, 67, 84

Date of Accounts	Dec 11	Dec 10	Dec 09
Working Capital	287	114	76
Fixed Assets	21	28	21
Current Assets	588	402	354

Fata Automation Ltd

Elgar House Shrub Hill Road, Worcester, WR4 9EE
Tel: 01905-613931 **Fax:** 01905-613913
E-mail: nicola.cipolletta@madacaserta.com
Website: http://www.fataautomation.co.uk
Directors: N. Cipolletta (Dir)
Immediate Holding Company: FATA AUTOMATION LIMITED
Registration no: 01230401 **Date established:** 1975
Turnover: £500,000 - £1m **No.of Employees:** 1 - 10 **Product Groups:** 45, 84

Date of Accounts	Dec 11	Dec 10	Dec 09
Sales Turnover	N/A	792	2m
Pre Tax Profit/Loss	N/A	4	43
Working Capital	245	295	288
Fixed Assets	N/A	2	5
Current Assets	539	417	490
Current Liabilities	N/A	99	130

First Solution Technologies Ltd

County House St Mary's Street, Worcester, WR1 1HB
Tel: 0845-8382998 **Fax:** 0870-0523897
E-mail: sales@firstsolution.co.uk
Website: http://www.firstsolution.co.uk
Directors: T. Blake (MD)
Registration no: 04491556 **Date established:** 2002
Turnover: £250,000 - £500,000 **No.of Employees:** 1 - 10
Product Groups: 44

Date of Accounts	Jul 07	Jul 06
Working Capital	-1	21
Fixed Assets	5	6
Current Assets	58	70
Current Liabilities	59	49

Froude Hofmann Ltd (part of the F K I Group of Companies)

Blackpole Road, Worcester, WR3 8YB
Tel: 01905-856800 **Fax:** 01905-856881
E-mail: bhemstock@froudehofmann.com
Website: http://www.froudehofmann.com
Bank(s): Barclays Bank, Bradford
Directors: R. Guest (MD), J. Harris (Dir), B. Hemstock (MD), G. Deakin (Sales), P. Smith (Fin)
Managers: T. Salter, S. Sharpe (Chief Mgr), S. Ruffley (Develop Mgr)
Ultimate Holding Company: HWH INVESTMENTS LIMITED
Immediate Holding Company: FROUDE HOFMANN LIMITED
Registration no: 06298578 **VAT No.:** GB 184 4733 43
Date established: 2007 **Turnover:** £10m - £20m
No.of Employees: 101 - 250 **Product Groups:** 38, 39, 67

Date of Accounts	Mar 11	Mar 10	Mar 09
Sales Turnover	19m	17m	9m
Pre Tax Profit/Loss	-2m	-1m	-2m
Working Capital	-2m	-722	-795
Fixed Assets	1m	914	792
Current Assets	9m	8m	7m
Current Liabilities	4m	2m	2m

G D K Engineering Co. Ltd

Unit 65 Blackpole Trading Estate West, Worcester, WR3 8TJ
Tel: 01905-454261 **Fax:** 01905-454231
E-mail: sales@gdk-engineering.co.uk
Website: http://www.gdk-engineering.co.uk
Directors: S. Easthope (Dir)
Ultimate Holding Company: ACCESSORIES COMPONENTS AND EQUIPMENT LIMITED
Immediate Holding Company: G.D.K. ENGINEERING COMPANY LIMITED
Registration no: 01165344 **VAT No.:** GB 276 3281 44
Date established: 1974 **Turnover:** £500,000 - £1m
No.of Employees: 1 - 10 **Product Groups:** 35, 36, 39, 45, 48

Date of Accounts	Mar 11	Mar 10	Mar 09
Sales Turnover	728	528	716
Pre Tax Profit/Loss	1	-6	-49
Working Capital	833	838	890
Fixed Assets	339	362	387
Current Assets	1m	1m	1m
Current Liabilities	65	N/A	119

Griffin Enamellers Ltd

Unit 4 Navigation Road, Worcester, WR5 3DF
Tel: 01905-350511 **Fax:** 01905-354500
E-mail: griffin@intrac.co.uk
Website: http://www.wtlwww.co.uk
Managers: S. Powell (Works Gen Mgr)
Immediate Holding Company: GRIFFIN ENAMELLERS LTD.
Registration no: 02081837 **Date established:** 1986
Turnover: £250,000 - £500,000 **No.of Employees:** 1 - 10
Product Groups: 32, 48

Date of Accounts	Jan 12	Jan 11	Jan 10
Working Capital	35	22	-1
Fixed Assets	3	8	12
Current Assets	90	43	24

A J Griffiths Engineering

Greenacre Suckley, Worcester, WR6 5EH
Tel: 01886-884294 **Fax:** 01886-884294
Directors: A. Griffiths (Fin), A. Griffiths (MD)
Immediate Holding Company: A J GRIFFITHS ENGINEERING LIMITED
Registration no: 04517623 **Date established:** 2002
No.of Employees: 1 - 10 **Product Groups:** 35

Date of Accounts	Sep 11	Sep 10	Sep 09
Working Capital	-4	-0	-4
Fixed Assets	19	27	29
Current Assets	79	64	83

Harrison Clark

5 Deansway, Worcester, WR1 2JG
Tel: 01905-612001 **Fax:** 01905-20433
E-mail: jbrew@harrison-clark.co.uk
Website: http://www.harrison-clark.co.uk
Bank(s): Barclays
Directors: J. Brew (Snr Part), J. Brew (Ptnr), R. Thomas (MD)
Managers: N. Powell (Sales Admin)
Immediate Holding Company: HARRISON CLARK LLP
Registration no: OC315067 **VAT No.:** GB 274 4866 23
Date established: 2005 **Turnover:** £5m - £10m
No.of Employees: 101 - 250 **Product Groups:** 80

Heasman Water Softeners

5 Morton Avenue Fernhill Heath, Worcester, WR3 7UE
Tel: 01905-759886
Directors: E. Heasman (Prop)
Date established: 1998 **No.of Employees:** 1 - 10 **Product Groups:** 38, 42

Highfields International Exhibition Services Ltd

Unit 98b Blackpole Trading Estate West Hindlip Lane, Worcester, WR3 8TJ
Tel: 01905-754158 **Fax:** 01905-456218
E-mail: sales@highfields.co.uk
Website: http://www.highfields.co.uk
Directors: J. Rammell (Fin), G. Jones (Sales)
Immediate Holding Company: HIGHFIELDS INTERNATIONAL EXHIBITION SERVICES LIMITED
Registration no: 01942888 **Date established:** 1985 **Turnover:** £1m - £2m
No.of Employees: 11 - 20 **Product Groups:** 81

Date of Accounts	Aug 12	Aug 11	Aug 10
Sales Turnover	2m	1m	1m
Pre Tax Profit/Loss	63	-56	58
Working Capital	696	731	804
Fixed Assets	82	32	44
Current Assets	860	884	916
Current Liabilities	106	93	50

Highway Drainage Services Ltd

Unit 67e Blackpole Trading Estate West, Worcester, WR3 8TJ
Tel: 08456-431117 **Fax:** 0845-643 1118
E-mail: danny.martin@hdsenvironmental.com
Website: http://www.hdsenvironmental.com
Bank(s): Lloyds TSB Bank plc
Directors: J. Turford (Fin), R. Dodge (Dir), P. Howells (MD)
Managers: R. Lister (Mgr), J. Turnford (Purch Mgr), D. Martin (Sales Prom Mgr), B. Nelson (Mgr), E. Howells (Mgr)
Immediate Holding Company: THE LITTLE PUB REFURBISHMENT COMPANY LIMITED
Registration no: 04807664 **VAT No.:** GB 816 3815 27
Date established: 2007 **Turnover:** £2m - £5m **No.of Employees:** 21 - 50
Product Groups: 45, 51, 52, 54

Date of Accounts	Nov 10	Nov 09	Nov 08
Working Capital	78	58	40
Fixed Assets	31	37	48
Current Assets	119	93	70

Industrial Trading Co. Ltd

PO Box 51, Worcester, WR1 1QE
Tel: 01905-20373 **Fax:** 01905-27158
Directors: S. Atkinson (Dir)
Immediate Holding Company: INDUSTRIAL TRADING COMPANY LIMITED
Registration no: 00612995 **VAT No.:** GB 274 3553 49
Date established: 1958 **Turnover:** £250,000 - £500,000
No.of Employees: 1 - 10 **Product Groups:** 35, 66

Date of Accounts	Mar 12	Mar 11	Mar 10
Working Capital	157	167	184
Fixed Assets	62	61	56
Current Assets	173	182	201

Isla Components Ltd

Bishops Frome Technology Park Bishops Frome, Worcester, WR6 5AY
Tel: 01885-485950 **Fax:** 01885-490472
E-mail: islasales@lineone.net
Website: http://www.islacomponents.co.uk
Directors: J. Parkes (MD)
Ultimate Holding Company: BITSTORE LIMITED
Immediate Holding Company: ISLA COMPONENTS LIMITED
Registration no: 02859781 **VAT No.:** GB 661 0109 90
Date established: 1993 **No.of Employees:** 1 - 10 **Product Groups:** 30, 39, 45, 67, 68

Date of Accounts	Dec 11	Dec 10	Dec 09
Working Capital	28	59	80
Fixed Assets	36	40	45
Current Assets	240	231	257

Jewson Ltd

Navigation Road, Worcester, WR5 3EF
Tel: 01905-350000 **Fax:** 01905-350145
Website: http://www.jewson.co.uk

see next page

Jewson Ltd - Cont'd

Managers: J. Willows (Mgr)
Ultimate Holding Company: COMPAGNIE DE SAINT GOBAIN (FRANCE)
Immediate Holding Company: JEWSON LIMITED
Registration no: 00348407 **Date established:** 1939
Turnover: £500m - £1,000m **No.of Employees:** 11 - 20
Product Groups: 66

Date of Accounts	Dec 11	Dec 10	Dec 09
Sales Turnover	1606m	1547m	1485m
Pre Tax Profit/Loss	18m	100m	45m
Working Capital	-345m	-250m	-349m
Fixed Assets	496m	387m	461m
Current Assets	657m	1005m	1320m
Current Liabilities	66m	120m	64m

Joy Mining Machinery Ltd

Bromyard Road, Worcester, WR2 5EG
Tel: 08702-521000 **Fax:** 0870-252 1888
E-mail: mmannion@joy.co.uk
Website: http://www.joy.com
Bank(s): National Westminster Bank Plc
Directors: M. Mannion (MD)
Managers: V. Willis (Fin Mgr), M. Walker (Buyer), S. Outwin (Personnel)
Ultimate Holding Company: JOY GLOBAL INC (USA)
Immediate Holding Company: JOY MINING MACHINERY LIMITED
Registration no: 02546087 **VAT No.:** GB 535 5644 34
Date established: 1990 **Turnover:** £250m - £500m
No.of Employees: 251 - 500 **Product Groups:** 45, 67, 83

Date of Accounts	Oct 08	Oct 09	Oct 10
Sales Turnover	319m	332m	290m
Pre Tax Profit/Loss	56m	43m	88m
Working Capital	27m	57m	76m
Fixed Assets	203m	202m	201m
Current Assets	169m	159m	201m
Current Liabilities	33m	33m	38m

K M E

Severn House Prescott Drive, Worcester, WR4 9NE
Tel: 01905-751800 **Fax:** 01905-751801
E-mail: info-uk@kme.com
Website: http://www.kme.com
Bank(s): Barclays, Birmingham
Directors: P. Stewart (Co Sec), R. Mclean (MD)
Managers: R. Clowes
Ultimate Holding Company: OAKLAND PROPERTY SERVICES LTD.
Immediate Holding Company: OAKLAND CONTRACTS LIMITED
Registration no: 02347847 **Date established:** 2007
Turnover: £50m - £75m **No.of Employees:** 11 - 20 **Product Groups:** 34, 35, 36

Date of Accounts	Mar 12	Mar 11	Mar 10
Sales Turnover	2m	2m	2m
Pre Tax Profit/Loss	-24	181	93
Working Capital	-247	-125	-275
Fixed Assets	1m	1m	1m
Current Assets	498	571	732
Current Liabilities	530	379	389

Kinnersley Engineering Ltd

Kerswell Green, Worcester, WR5 3PF
Tel: 01905-371200 **Fax:** 01905-371049
Website: http://www.kinnersleyengineering.co.uk
Directors: D. Whittal Williams (Dir), J. Whittal Williams (Co Sec)
Immediate Holding Company: KINNERSLEY ENGINEERING LIMITED
Registration no: 01414398 **Date established:** 1979
Turnover: Up to £250,000 **No.of Employees:** 1 - 10 **Product Groups:** 84

Date of Accounts	Apr 11	Apr 10	Apr 09
Working Capital	4	-4	-7
Fixed Assets	76	78	80
Current Assets	59	50	50
Current Liabilities	18	11	21

Lesk Engineers

9-11 Carden Street, Worcester, WR1 2AX
Tel: 01905-23187 **Fax:** 01905- 612536
E-mail: company@leskengineers.co.uk
Website: http://www.leskengineers.co.uk
Directors: P. Brown (MD)
Ultimate Holding Company: LESK ENGINEERING GROUP LIMITED
Immediate Holding Company: LESK ENGINEERS (WORCESTER) LIMITED
Registration no: 00836447 **VAT No.:** GB 274 5081 54
Date established: 1965 **Turnover:** £500,000 - £1m
No.of Employees: 11 - 20 **Product Groups:** 48

Date of Accounts	Feb 12	Feb 11	Feb 10
Working Capital	1m	1m	1m
Fixed Assets	426	357	962
Current Assets	2m	2m	2m

Lohmann GB Ltd

Shire Business Park Wainwright Road, Worcester, WR4 9FA
Tel: 01905-459460 **Fax:** 01526-352022
E-mail: j.adams@lohmanngb.co.uk
Website: http://www.lohmanngb.co.uk
Directors: D. Scott (MD)
Managers: J. Adams (Comptroller)
Immediate Holding Company: LOHMANN GB LIMITED
Registration no: 04087186 **Date established:** 2000
Turnover: £10m - £20m **No.of Employees:** 1 - 10 **Product Groups:** 01

Date of Accounts	Jun 11	Jun 10	Jun 09
Sales Turnover	12m	13m	11m
Pre Tax Profit/Loss	1m	1m	545
Working Capital	2m	2m	1m
Fixed Assets	1m	1m	1m
Current Assets	4m	5m	4m
Current Liabilities	392	819	302

M A P Group

12-14 Maylite Trading Estate Berrow Green Road, Martley, Worcester, WR6 6PQ
Tel: 01886-888713 **Fax:** 01886-888364
E-mail: sales@themapgroup.co.uk
Website: http://www.themapgroup.co.uk
Bank(s): Lloyds TSB Bank plc
Directors: S. Whitehead (MD)
Immediate Holding Company: MALVERN ART PRODUCTS LIMITED
Registration no: 01934214 **Date established:** 1985 **Turnover:** £1m - £2m
No.of Employees: 11 - 20 **Product Groups:** 23, 27, 28, 49

Date of Accounts	Sep 11	Sep 10	Sep 09
Working Capital	51	49	53
Fixed Assets	82	74	95
Current Assets	203	185	249

Mapa Spontex

Berkeley Business Park Wainwright Road, Worcester, WR4 9ZS
Tel: 01905-450300 **Fax:** 01905-450350
E-mail: robert.gibbons@spontex.co.uk
Website: http://www.spontex.co.uk
Directors: P. Sagot (Co Sec), K. Blake (Sales), J. Butterworth (Fin)
Managers: J. Evans (Mktg Serv Mgr), A. Mughal (Tech Serv Mgr), L. Willetts (Personnel), R. Gibbons
Ultimate Holding Company: JARDEN CORPORATION LTD (NEW ZEALAND)
Immediate Holding Company: MAPA SPONTEX UK LIMITED
Registration no: 01372811 **Date established:** 1978
Turnover: £10m - £20m **No.of Employees:** 21 - 50 **Product Groups:** 24, 29, 30, 40

Date of Accounts	Dec 11	Dec 10	Dec 09
Sales Turnover	19m	18m	19m
Pre Tax Profit/Loss	1m	3m	358
Working Capital	4m	3m	2m
Fixed Assets	31	59	89
Current Assets	8m	9m	9m
Current Liabilities	1m	1m	2m

Marine Performance Parts & Service

Upton Marina Upton-upon-Severn, Worcester, WR8 0PB
Tel: 01684-594540 **Fax:** 01684-594935
Website: http://www.marineperformanace.co.uk
Directors: W. Mitchell (Prop)
Date established: 1988 **No.of Employees:** 1 - 10 **Product Groups:** 35, 36, 39

Marl Bank Sheet Metal Co. Ltd

Newtown Road, Worcester, WR5 1HA
Tel: 01905-22801 **Fax:** 01905- 726235
E-mail: frederick@zoom.co.uk
Bank(s): Barclays
Directors: F. Raw (MD)
Immediate Holding Company: MARL BANK SHEET METAL CO. (1977) LIMITED
Registration no: 01104802 **VAT No.:** GB 299 0728 11
Date established: 1973 **Turnover:** £250,000 - £500,000
No.of Employees: 11 - 20 **Product Groups:** 48

Date of Accounts	Mar 11	Mar 10	Mar 09
Working Capital	-72	-42	-22
Fixed Assets	207	95	96
Current Assets	141	126	115

Mercia Fine Foods

Bromyard Road A44 Crown East, Worcester, WR2 5TR
Tel: 01905-422245 **Fax:** 01905-337186
E-mail: sales@merciafinefoods.com
Directors: H. Roberts (Ptnr)
Registration no: 02644222 **No.of Employees:** 11 - 20
Product Groups: 20, 62, 69

Midland Communications Co. Ltd

Orchard Works Backfields, Upton-upon-Severn, Worcester, WR8 0JH
Tel: 08447-881000 **Fax:** 01684-594189
E-mail: enq@midlandcomms.co.uk
Website: http://www.midlandcomms.co.uk
Directors: D. Webster (Dir), L. Mico (Fin), P. Stubbs-thomas (Tech Serv), S. Mico (Dir)
Managers: G. Birchal (Mktg Serv Mgr)
Ultimate Holding Company: DWSM LIMITED
Immediate Holding Company: MIDLAND COMMUNICATIONS COMPANY LIMITED
Registration no: 01273257 **Date established:** 1976
No.of Employees: 11 - 20 **Product Groups:** 37

Date of Accounts	Jun 11	Jun 10	Jun 09
Working Capital	547	502	379
Fixed Assets	57	96	81
Current Assets	1m	1m	1m

Midland Power Machinery Distributors

Reed House Orchard Street, Worcester, WR5 3DW
Tel: 01905-763027 **Fax:** 01905-354241
E-mail: mpmd@midlandpower.co.uk
Website: http://www.midlanpower.co.uk
Directors: A. Gunn (Ptnr)
Managers: C. Graham, S. Drinkwater (Sales Prom Mgr)
Immediate Holding Company: MIDLAND POWER MACHINERY DISTRIBUTORS LIMITED
Registration no: 01128556 **Date established:** 1973 **Turnover:** £5m - £10m
No.of Employees: 21 - 50 **Product Groups:** 41, 67

Date of Accounts	Sep 11	Sep 10	Sep 09
Working Capital	-44	-83	23
Fixed Assets	459	461	480
Current Assets	16	N/A	451
Current Liabilities	N/A	N/A	21

Molten Metal Products Ltd

Unit 7 Crucible Business Park Woodbury Lane, Norton, Worcester, WR5 2PU
Tel: 01905-728200 **Fax:** 01905-767877
E-mail: marketing@morganitecrucible.com
Website: http://www.morganitecrucible.com
Bank(s): National Westminster Bank Plc
Directors: D. Finck (Sales & Mktg)
Managers: B. Martin, J. Mackintosh (I.T. Exec), M. Harthill (Chief Buyer), S. Cooper (Personnel), T. Venables (Mktg Serv Mgr)
Ultimate Holding Company: The Morgan Crucible Co. P.L.C.
Registration no: 02133533 **VAT No.:** GB 589 4378 72
Turnover: £20m - £50m **No.of Employees:** 101 - 250
Product Groups: 33, 40, 42, 46

Date of Accounts	Jan 10	Jan 09	Jan 08
Sales Turnover	2m	7m	11m
Pre Tax Profit/Loss	-2m	-3m	-60
Working Capital	-425	-242	-2m
Fixed Assets	3m	4m	7m
Current Assets	5m	6m	8m
Current Liabilities	497	878	3m

Morelli Central Ltd

24 Cumberland Street, Worcester, WR1 1QE
Tel: 01905-20474 **Fax:** 01905- 723736
E-mail: sales@morelli-worcesterfsbusiness.co.uk
Website: http://www.morelli.co.uk
Managers: C. Fletcher (District Mgr), C. Fletcher (Mgr), R. Horton ()
Ultimate Holding Company: MORELLI GROUP LIMITED
Immediate Holding Company: MORELLI GROUP LIMITED
Registration no: 02711932 **Date established:** 1992
No.of Employees: 1 - 10 **Product Groups:** 39, 68

Date of Accounts	May 10	May 09	May 06
Working Capital	-63	-63	-63
Current Liabilities	63	63	N/A

N A L

Weir Lane, Worcester, WR2 4AY
Tel: 01905-769713 **Fax:** 01905-427 030
E-mail: sales@nal.ltd.uk
Website: http://www.nal.ltd.uk
Managers: F. O'Connell (Mgr), M. McGee (Mgr)
Immediate Holding Company: NAL LIMITED
Registration no: 03289863 **Date established:** 1996
No.of Employees: 1 - 10 **Product Groups:** 26, 35

Date of Accounts	Jul 08	Jul 07	Jan 06
Working Capital	-140	-109	41
Fixed Assets	215	174	5
Current Assets	2131	1450	601
Current Liabilities	2272	1559	560

Natures Own Ltd

Hanley Workshops Hanley Swan, Worcester, WR8 0DX
Tel: 01684-310022 **Fax:** 01684-312022
E-mail: jim@natures-own.co.uk
Website: http://www.natures-own.co.uk
Bank(s): HSBC Malvern
Directors: J. Turner (MD), A. Williams (Dir)
Managers: C. Smith (Fin Mgr)
Immediate Holding Company: NATURE'S OWN LIMITED
Registration no: 01493205 **VAT No.:** GB 589 5698 49
Date established: 1980 **Turnover:** £2m - £5m **No.of Employees:** 21 - 50
Product Groups: 20, 31

Date of Accounts	Aug 11	Aug 10	Aug 09
Working Capital	682	703	583
Fixed Assets	355	331	314
Current Assets	1m	1m	1m

Open G I

Buckholt Drive, Worcester, WR4 9SR
Tel: 01905-754455 **Fax:** 01905-754441
E-mail: stacy.prosser@opengi.co.uk
Website: http://www.opengi.co.uk
Directors: C. Guillaume (Grp Chief Exec), D. Bailey (Fin), S. Hughes (Sales & Mktg)
Managers: S. Benge (Personnel), A. Clarkson (Mktg Serv Mgr), V. Maycroft, B. Clarke
Ultimate Holding Company: BROOMCO (4099) LIMITED
Immediate Holding Company: OPEN G I LIMITED
Registration no: 01519547 **VAT No.:** 438 0035 39 **Date established:** 1980
Turnover: £20m - £50m **No.of Employees:** 251 - 500
Product Groups: 44, 84

Date of Accounts	May 11	May 10	May 09
Sales Turnover	37m	33m	30m
Pre Tax Profit/Loss	19m	24m	18m
Working Capital	38m	17m	-2m
Fixed Assets	6m	13m	13m
Current Assets	88m	64m	39m
Current Liabilities	9m	8m	7m

Polymer Coating Solutions Ltd

Unit 7 Strensham Business Park Strensham, Worcester, WR8 9JZ
Tel: 01684-850440 **Fax:** 01684-296699
E-mail: polysol@btconnect.com
Website: http://www.polymercoating.co.uk
Directors: S. Fenton (Dir)
Immediate Holding Company: POLYMER COATING SOLUTIONS LTD
Registration no: 04393119 **Date established:** 2002
No.of Employees: 1 - 10 **Product Groups:** 46, 48

Date of Accounts	Mar 11	Mar 10	Mar 08
Working Capital	19	10	-9
Fixed Assets	5	5	8
Current Assets	102	66	46

Powell Machinery

The Bungalow Bank Farm Collins Green, Knightwick, Worcester, WR6 5PS
Tel: 01886-821089 **Fax:** 01886-821089
Directors: M. Powell (Prop)
Date established: 1984 **No.of Employees:** 1 - 10 **Product Groups:** 41

Proline Rainwater Systems Ltd

59 Sycamore Road, Worcester, WR4 9RU
Tel: 0800-756 6560
E-mail: jason@prolinerainwatersystemsltd.co.uk
Website: http://www.prolinerainwatersystemsltd.co.uk
Directors: L. James (Fin)
Registration no: 06586143 **Date established:** 2008
Turnover: £250,000 - £500,000 **No.of Employees:** 1 - 10
Product Groups: 30, 33, 35, 52

Pulse Power Limited

James House East Waterside, Upton Upon Severn, Worcester, WR8 0PB
Tel: 01684-592344 **Fax:** 01684-594941
E-mail: info@pulse-piv.co.uk
Website: http://www.pulse-piv.co.uk
Directors: D. Moreland (MD), J. Moreland (Dir)
Immediate Holding Company: James Holdings Ltd
Registration no: 04014309 **VAT No.:** GB 551 5236 59
Turnover: Up to £250,000 **No.of Employees:** 1 - 10 **Product Groups:** 40

Date of Accounts	Dec 06	Dec 05
Working Capital	31	26
Fixed Assets	2	2
Current Assets	100	98
Current Liabilities	70	72

Raque Food Systems Sales Ltd

9 Ball Mill Top Business Park Hallow, Worcester, WR2 6PD
Tel: 01905-642820 **Fax:** 01905-641379
Website: http://www.raque.com
Directors: J. Rose (MD), J. Rose (Fin)
Immediate Holding Company: RAQUE FOOD SYSTEMS SALES, LIMITED
Registration no: 03006508 **Date established:** 1994
Turnover: £500,000 - £1m **No.of Employees:** 1 - 10 **Product Groups:** 20, 40, 41

Date of Accounts	Dec 09	Dec 08	Dec 07
Working Capital	121	-626	-519
Fixed Assets	N/A	N/A	1

Current Assets	136	105	216

Regency Mouldings Worcester Ltd
Hylton Road, Worcester, WR2 5JS
Tel: 01905-424909 **Fax:** 01905-748310
E-mail: timco@btclick.com
Website: http://www.rmwl.co.uk
Directors: D. Hardiman (Dir)
Immediate Holding Company: REGENCY MOULDINGS (WORCESTER) LIMITED
Registration no: 01419773 **Date established:** 1979
Turnover: £500,000 - £1m **No.of Employees:** 1 - 10 **Product Groups:** 30

Date of Accounts	Feb 08	Feb 10	Feb 09
Working Capital	-111	-179	-206
Fixed Assets	190	149	167
Current Assets	234	128	154

Rigidal Systems Ltd
Unit 62 Blackpole Trading Estate West, Worcester, WR3 8ZJ
Tel: 01905-750500 **Fax:** 01905-750555
E-mail: sales@rigidal.co.uk
Website: http://www.rigidal.co.uk
Bank(s): The Bank of Scotland plc
Directors: G. Rankin (Sales), P. Taylor (MD), S. Neale (Fin), V. Burman (Fin), W. Burman (Fin), L. Taylor (Pers)
Managers: N. Knowles (Purch Mgr)
Ultimate Holding Company: BALNEAVES INVESTMENTS LTD (GIBRALTER)
Immediate Holding Company: RIGISYSTEMS LTD
Registration no: 04137351 **VAT No.:** GB 632 1961 52
Date established: 2001 **Turnover:** £10m - £20m
No.of Employees: 21 - 50 **Product Groups:** 34, 35, 39, 48, 66

Date of Accounts	Apr 11	Apr 10	Apr 09
Sales Turnover	19m	16m	18m
Pre Tax Profit/Loss	851	702	899
Working Capital	6m	6m	5m
Fixed Assets	530	500	595
Current Assets	16m	14m	13m
Current Liabilities	5m	3m	4m

M J & H M Roberts
The Smithy Bungalow Bromyard Road, Bringsty, Worcester, WR6 5TA
Tel: 01885-482775
Directors: M. Roberts (Prop)
No.of Employees: 1 - 10 **Product Groups:** 41

Rocon Foam Products Ltd
Unit 14 Shrub Hill Industrial Estate, Worcester, WR4 9EL
Tel: 01905-26616 **Fax:** 01905-612319
E-mail: sales@roconfoam.co.uk
Website: http://www.roconfoam.co.uk
Directors: R. Pinfield (MD), I. Pinfield (Fin)
Immediate Holding Company: ROCON FOAM PRODUCTS LIMITED
Registration no: 03016977 **VAT No.:** GB 670 4837 22
Date established: 1995 **No.of Employees:** 1 - 10 **Product Groups:** 30, 40

Date of Accounts	Jul 11	Jul 10	Jul 09
Working Capital	-40	-40	-40
Fixed Assets	23	10	10
Current Assets	126	126	79
Current Liabilities	N/A	164	N/A

S C R Associates Ltd
2 Trefoil Close, Worcester, WR5 3QR
Tel: 01905-352882
E-mail: info@scrassociates.com
Website: http://www.scrassociates.com
Directors: S. Rooke (MD)
Immediate Holding Company: SCR ASSOCIATES LIMITED
Registration no: 05337247 **Date established:** 2005
No.of Employees: 1 - 10 **Product Groups:** 86

Date of Accounts	Mar 11	Mar 10	Mar 09
Working Capital	-5	-5	N/A
Fixed Assets	N/A	2	3
Current Assets	4	15	15

S P X Cooling Technologies UK Ltd
Knightsbridge Park Wainwright Road, Worcester, WR4 9FA
Tel: 01905-750270 **Fax:** 01905-750299
E-mail: info@spx.com
Website: http://www.spx.com
Bank(s): Lloyds TSB Bank plc
Directors: D. Townley (Fin)
Managers: R. Underwood, B. Giles, G. Munroe (Chief Mgr), M. Hamill
Ultimate Holding Company: SPX CORPORATION INC (USA)
Immediate Holding Company: SPX COOLING TECHNOLOGIES UK LIMITED
Registration no: 03076564 **VAT No.:** GB 651 8970 08
Date established: 1995 **Turnover:** £20m - £50m
No.of Employees: 21 - 50 **Product Groups:** 31, 40, 42, 44, 48, 52, 54, 67, 84

Date of Accounts	Dec 10	Dec 09	Dec 08
Sales Turnover	29m	24m	9m
Pre Tax Profit/Loss	2m	-415	-1m
Working Capital	535	-788	-17
Fixed Assets	1m	1m	862
Current Assets	9m	10m	8m
Current Liabilities	815	7m	6m

Scherdel GB Ltd
Alexander House High Street, Inkberrow, Worcester, WR7 4DT
Tel: 01386-793443 **Fax:** 01386-792282
E-mail: sales@scherdel.de
Website: http://www.scherdel.de
Managers: J. Gould (Sales Prom Mgr), S. Delahaye
Ultimate Holding Company: S SCHERDEL & CO KG (GERMANY)
Immediate Holding Company: C E P SCHERDEL (GB) LIMITED
Registration no: 02327160 **VAT No.:** GB 488 1038 28
Date established: 1988 **Turnover:** Up to £250,000
No.of Employees: 1 - 10 **Product Groups:** 35, 36, 39, 48

Date of Accounts	Dec 11	Dec 10	Dec 09
Sales Turnover	176	N/A	N/A
Working Capital	2	-3	-8
Fixed Assets	12	15	19
Current Assets	32	27	26

Severn Instruments
4 Court Street Upton-upon-Severn, Worcester, WR8 0JT
Tel: 01684-594164 **Fax:** 01684-593364
E-mail: severninstrument@aol.com
Directors: J. Roberts (Prop)
Date established: 1997 **No.of Employees:** 1 - 10 **Product Groups:** 20, 40, 41

Sleepy Weasel Ltd
125 Newtown Road, Worcester, WR5 1HL
Tel: 07951-294087 **Fax:** 01905-764260
E-mail: swltd@hotmail.co.uk
Website: http://www.sleepyweasel.info
Directors: T. Underwood (Dir)
Registration no: 6699742 **Date established:** 2008
Turnover: Up to £250,000 **No.of Employees:** 1 - 10 **Product Groups:** 44

Smith & Deakin Plastics
75 Blackpole Trading Estate West, Worcester, WR3 8TJ
Tel: 01905-458886 **Fax:** 01905-458889
E-mail: info@smithanddeakin.co.uk
Website: http://www.smithanddeakin.co.uk
Directors: M. Smith (Prop)
VAT No.: GB 275 4379 28 **Date established:** 1965
Turnover: Up to £250,000 **No.of Employees:** 1 - 10 **Product Groups:** 30

Southco Manufacturing Co.
Shire Business Park Wainright Road, Worcester, WR4 9FA
Tel: 01905-751000 **Fax:** 01905-751090
E-mail: info@southco.com
Website: http://www.southco.com
Bank(s): National Westminster Bank Plc
Directors: S. Austin (Pers)
Managers: D. Kelly (Sales Prom Mgr), P. Reichle (Mktg Serv Mgr), S. Hunt (Tech Serv Mgr), R. Kitchen (Purch Mgr), I. Gillott, M. Griffiths (Ops Mgr)
Ultimate Holding Company: SOUTH CHESTER TUBE COMPANY (USA)
Immediate Holding Company: SOUTHCO MANUFACTURING LIMITED
Registration no: 04328069 **VAT No.:** GB 396 1210 55
Date established: 2001 **Turnover:** £50m - £75m
No.of Employees: 251 - 500 **Product Groups:** 35, 36, 66

Date of Accounts	Dec 11	Dec 10	Dec 09
Sales Turnover	72m	65m	54m
Pre Tax Profit/Loss	7m	5m	4m
Working Capital	14m	8m	635
Fixed Assets	25m	27m	29m
Current Assets	23m	25m	21m
Current Liabilities	4m	4m	4m

Stevens Saws
Moat End Farm Hindlip Lane, Hindlip, Worcester, WR3 8SA
Tel: 01905-455470 **Fax:** 01905-455470
E-mail: info@stevens-saws.co.uk
Website: http://www.stevens-saws.co.uk
Directors: M. Stevens (Ptnr)
No.of Employees: 1 - 10 **Product Groups:** 36, 46, 47, 48

Superform UK
Cosgrove Close, Worcester, WR3 8UA
Tel: 01905-874300 **Fax:** 01905-874301
E-mail: reception@superform-aluminium.com
Website: http://www.superform-aluminium.com
Bank(s): Royal Bank of Scotland, London
Directors: N. Preston (Fin), S. Tarmey (MD)
Managers: S. Hughes (Tech Serv Mgr), A. Lowerson, S. Tandy-gray (Personnel)
Immediate Holding Company: BRITISH ALUMINIUM LIMITED
Registration no: 03376625 **VAT No.:** GB 668 2142 26
Turnover: £5m - £10m **No.of Employees:** 51 - 100 **Product Groups:** 34, 35, 48

Total Interiors Direct Ltd
Cadbury House Blackpole East, Blackpole Road, Worcester, WR3 8SG
Tel: 01905-757506 **Fax:** 01905-757526
E-mail: sales@totalinteriorsdirect.co.uk
Website: http://www.totalinteriorsdirect.co.uk
Directors: H. Ruane (Mkt Research), G. Ruane (Co Sec), J. Ruane (Sales), J. Ruane (Dir)
Immediate Holding Company: TOTAL INTERIORS DIRECT LIMITED
Registration no: 03156899 **Date established:** 1996
No.of Employees: 1 - 10 **Product Groups:** 35, 42, 45

Date of Accounts	Dec 10	Dec 09	Dec 08
Working Capital	434	399	283
Fixed Assets	47	21	24
Current Assets	1m	925	887

Truckstop-Mobiles
Unit 87a Blackpole Trading Estate West, Worcester, WR3 8TJ
Tel: 01905-758600 **Fax:** 01905-758620
E-mail: sales@truckstophawkes.co.uk
Website: http://www.truckstophawkes.co.uk
Bank(s): H S B C/ Lloyds T S B
Directors: M. Stiley (MD)
Immediate Holding Company: TRUCK STOP HAWKES LTD
VAT No.: GB 416 9066 44 **Date established:** 1980 **Turnover:** £2m - £5m
No.of Employees: 11 - 20 **Product Groups:** 39

Tyden Brooks
Unit 3 Berrow Green Road Martley, Worcester, WR6 6PQ
Tel: 01886-887820 **Fax:** 01886-812243
E-mail: sales@tydenbrooks.eu
Website: http://www.tydenbrooks.eu
Directors: N. Dancey (Dir), W. Robbins (Co Sec), M. Ash (Chief Op Offcr)
Managers: N. Vanes (Tech Serv Mgr)
Ultimate Holding Company: E.J. BROOKS U.K., LIMITED
Immediate Holding Company: E J BROOKS (EUROPE) LIMITED
Registration no: 01677695 **Date established:** 1982
Turnover: Up to £250,000 **No.of Employees:** 21 - 50 **Product Groups:** 23, 27, 28, 29, 30, 35, 36, 44, 49, 67

Date of Accounts	Dec 11	Dec 10	Dec 09
Working Capital	286	408	614
Fixed Assets	139	128	61
Current Assets	2m	2m	1m

Verminater Pest & Vermin Control
298 Astwood Road, Worcester, WR3 8HD
Tel: 01905-619939
E-mail: nigel@verminaterpestcontrol.co.uk
Website: http://www.verminaterpestcontrol.co.uk
Directors: N. Probert (Prop)
No.of Employees: 1 - 10 **Product Groups:** 07, 32, 52

Vibratory Stress Relieving Company
Shrub Hill Industrial Estate Unit 13a, Worcester, WR4 9EL
Tel: 01905-731810 **Fax:** 01905-731811
E-mail: enquiries@v-s-r.co.uk
Website: http://www.v-s-r.co.uk
Directors: A. Bentley (Ptnr)
VAT No.: GB 748 0281 28 **Turnover:** £500,000 - £1m
No.of Employees: 1 - 10 **Product Groups:** 38, 48

W T Services
24 Hill View Defford, Worcester, WR8 9BH
Tel: 01386-751118 **Fax:** 01386-751152
E-mail: wtsair@gmail.com
Website: http://www.wtsair.co.uk/
Managers: L. Smith (Mgr)
No.of Employees: 1 - 10 **Product Groups:** 38, 40, 42, 48

Waste Spectrum Environmental Ltd
Spectrum House Checketts Lane Industrial Estate Checketts Lane, Worcester, WR3 7JW
Tel: 01905-362100 **Fax:** 01905-362101
E-mail: sales@wastespectrum.com
Website: http://www.spectrumenvironmental.com
Directors: S. Hunt (MD), E. Hunt (Fin)
Managers: M. Thomas (Chief Mgr)
Ultimate Holding Company: SPECTRUM ENVIRONMENTAL LIMITED
Immediate Holding Company: SPECTRUM ENVIRONMENTAL LIMITED
Registration no: 03074285 **Date established:** 1995
Turnover: £500,000 - £1m **No.of Employees:** 21 - 50 **Product Groups:** 54

Date of Accounts	Aug 11	Aug 10	Aug 09
Working Capital	-37	-87	-79
Fixed Assets	795	800	805
Current Assets	136	117	114

Waterchem Ltd
Unit 2c Derwent Close, Worcester, WR4 9TY
Tel: 01905-23669 **Fax:** 01905- 729959
E-mail: john.dobson@waterchem.co.uk
Website: http://www.waterchem.co.uk
Bank(s): National Westminster, St. John's
Directors: J. Dobson (Fin), C. Butler (Sales)
Ultimate Holding Company: GREEN COMPLIANCE PLC
Immediate Holding Company: GREEN COMPLIANCE WATER DIVISION LIMITED
Registration no: 03572340 **Date established:** 1998 **Turnover:** £5m - £10m
No.of Employees: 11 - 20 **Product Groups:** 32

Date of Accounts	Dec 09	Dec 08	Dec 07
Sales Turnover	8m	5m	N/A
Pre Tax Profit/Loss	1m	245	N/A
Working Capital	1m	-48	-213
Fixed Assets	180	436	494
Current Assets	3m	2m	1m
Current Liabilities	1m	883	N/A

Watts Truck & Van
Bath Road Broomhall, Worcester, WR5 3HR
Tel: 01905-829800 **Fax:** 01905-829808
E-mail: grahamcarpenter@wattstvc.co.uk
Website: http://www.wattstruckandvan.co.uk
Directors: E. Jones (MD), G. Carpenter (Snr Part), J. Thurston (Ch)
Managers: R. Tilley (Sales Prom Mgr)
Immediate Holding Company: LITTLE HOOTS NURSERY LIMITED
Registration no: 01293756 **VAT No.:** GB 274 9312 41
Date established: 2002 **Turnover:** £10m - £20m
No.of Employees: 11 - 20 **Product Groups:** 68

Date of Accounts	Aug 11	Aug 10	Aug 09
Working Capital	-34	-46	-52
Fixed Assets	16	23	28
Current Assets	7	8	13

Wickens Engineering Ltd
1 Shire Business Park Wainwright Road, Worcester, WR4 9FA
Tel: 01905-456780 **Fax:** 01905-456073
E-mail: sales@wickens.co.uk
Website: http://www.wickens.co.uk
Bank(s): Barkleys
Directors: K. Wickens (Fin), A. Cross (Sales), S. Knowles (I.T. Dir), S. Wickens (Dir), S. Wickens (MD)
Immediate Holding Company: WICKENS ENGINEERING LIMITED
Registration no: 01371393 **VAT No.:** 454 7375 25 **Date established:** 1978
Turnover: £2m - £5m **No.of Employees:** 21 - 50 **Product Groups:** 26

Date of Accounts	Mar 12	Mar 11	Mar 10
Working Capital	569	520	454
Fixed Assets	255	302	353
Current Assets	2m	2m	1m
Current Liabilities	N/A	37	149

Worcester Bosch Group Ltd (t/a The Bosch Group)
Cotsworld Way, Worcester, WR4 9SW
Tel: 08448-929900 **Fax:** 01905-754863
E-mail: carl.arntzen@uk.bosch.com
Website: http://www.worcester-bosch.co.uk
Bank(s): Barclays
Directors: S. Lister (Sales), B. Malige (Fin), U. Sannwald (Purch), C. Wilson (Pers), M. Bridges (Mkt Research), C. Arntzen (MD), I. Smith (Tech Serv)
Ultimate Holding Company: ROBERT BOSCH GMBH (GERMANY)
Immediate Holding Company: WORCESTER HEAT SYSTEMS LIMITED
Registration no: 05213115 **Date established:** 2004
Turnover: £250m - £500m **No.of Employees:** 1501 & over
Product Groups: 40

Date of Accounts	Dec 11	Dec 10	Dec 09
Pre Tax Profit/Loss	28m	47m	126
Working Capital	24m	24m	26m
Fixed Assets	100	100	100
Current Assets	24m	24m	26m
Current Liabilities	10	10	10

Worcester Diesel Services
1 Derwent Close, Worcester, WR4 9TY
Tel: 01905-27030
Directors: D. Jones (Dir)
Date established: 2002 **No.of Employees:** 1 - 10 **Product Groups:** 40

Wulstan Design & Controls Ltd

8 Tennyson Close, Worcester, WR3 8DF
Tel: 01905-458555 **Fax:** 01905-454325
E-mail: mgw@talktalk.net
Website: http://www.wulstandesigns.fsbusiness.co.uk
Directors: M. Woodward (Fin)
Immediate Holding Company: WULSTAN DESIGNS & CONTROLS LIMITED
Registration no: 01218534 **VAT No.:** GB 276 5656 17
Date established: 1975 **Turnover:** Up to £250,000
No.of Employees: 1 - 10 **Product Groups:** 37, 38, 44, 84

Date of Accounts	Jul 12	Jul 11	Jul 10
Sales Turnover	55	37	32
Pre Tax Profit/Loss	23	17	14
Working Capital	28	25	27
Current Assets	57	63	55
Current Liabilities	27	28	20

Yamazaki Machinery UK Ltd

Badgeworth Drive Warndon, Worcester, WR4 9NF
Tel: 01905-755755 **Fax:** 01905-755001
E-mail: dcleugh@mazak.co.uk
Website: http://www.mazak.eu
Bank(s): National Westminster Bank Plc
Directors: K. Gilbert (Fin), A. Saunders (Sales)
Managers: R. Pratt (Mktg Serv Mgr), A. Bailey (Admin Off), P. Gane (I.T. Exec), D. Cleugh (Mktg Serv Mgr), M. Lawrence (Personnel)
Ultimate Holding Company: YAMAZAKI MAZAK TRADING CORP (JAPAN)
Immediate Holding Company: YAMAZAKI MAZAK U.K. LIMITED
Registration no: 01508951 **VAT No.:** GB 488 0174 25
Date established: 1980 **Turnover:** £250m - £500m
No.of Employees: 501 - 1000 **Product Groups:** 44, 46, 47, 67, 84

Date of Accounts	Mar 12	Mar 11	Mar 10
Sales Turnover	293m	197m	128m
Pre Tax Profit/Loss	4m	-4m	-3m
Working Capital	84m	82m	84m
Fixed Assets	22m	23m	25m
Current Assets	170m	152m	131m
Current Liabilities	9m	11m	5m

Z E D Systems

63 Tetbury Drive, Worcester, WR4 9LS
Tel: 01905-456282 **Fax:** 01905-456282
Website: http://www.zedsystems.co.uk
Directors: K. Cattell (Prop)
Date established: 2001 **No.of Employees:** 1 - 10 **Product Groups:** 35, 39, 45

NORTH YORKSHIRE

Filey

Cirrus Research plc
Unit 2 Hunmanby Industrial Estate Hunmanby, Filey, YO14 0PH
Tel: 01723-891655 **Fax:** 01723-891742
E-mail: sales@cirrusresearch.co.uk
Website: http://www.cirrusresearch.co.uk
Bank(s): National Westminster Bank Plc
Directors: D. Wallis (MD)
Managers: L. White (Comptroller)
Ultimate Holding Company: SCIENTIFIC MEASUREMENTS INC (USA)
Immediate Holding Company: CIRRUS RESEARCH PLC
Registration no: 00987160 **VAT No.:** GB 316 8777 24
Date established: 1970 **Turnover:** £2m - £5m **No.of Employees:** 21 - 50
Product Groups: 37, 38, 52, 54, 85

Date of Accounts	Jun 11	Jun 10	Jun 09
Sales Turnover	3m	2m	2m
Pre Tax Profit/Loss	14	60	-346
Working Capital	778	780	597
Fixed Assets	103	29	5
Current Assets	2m	1m	1m
Current Liabilities	126	173	143

Scaife Fabrications
Clarence Drive, Filey, YO14 0AA
Tel: 01723-515086 **Fax:** 01723-514330
Directors: C. Scaife (Prop)
Immediate Holding Company: SCAIFE FABRICATIONS LIMITED
Registration no: 07791929 **Date established:** 2011 **Turnover:** £1m - £2m
No.of Employees: 1 - 10 **Product Groups:** 35

Harrogate

A D V Lighting Ltd
22 Electric Avenue, Harrogate, HG1 2BB
Tel: 01423-545493 **Fax:** 0845-280 1640
E-mail: advlighting@advlighting.co.uk
Website: http://www.advlighting.co.uk
Directors: A. Davy (MD), S. Davy (Fin)
Immediate Holding Company: ADV LIGHTING LIMITED
Registration no: 04459619 **Date established:** 2002
No.of Employees: 1 - 10 **Product Groups:** 37, 67

Date of Accounts	Jun 11	Jun 10	Jun 09
Working Capital	13	4	8
Fixed Assets	3	2	2
Current Assets	36	24	37

Absolute Search Ltd
Hamilton House 39 Hookstone Road, Harrogate, HG2 8BT
Tel: 01423-544785
E-mail: info@absolutesearch.co.uk
Website: http://www.absolutesearch.co.uk
Directors: M. Beckett (Dir)
Registration no: 06521930 **Date established:** 2002
No.of Employees: 1 - 10 **Product Groups:** 80

Adtec Software Ltd
5 Cardale Park Greengate, Harrogate, HG3 1GY
Tel: 01423-700250 **Fax:** 0113-250 5217
E-mail: sales@adtecsoftware.com
Website: http://www.adtecsoftware.com
Directors: G. Adkin (MD)
Immediate Holding Company: ADTEC SOFTWARE LIMITED
Registration no: 03834409 **Date established:** 1999
Turnover: £250,000 - £500,000 **No.of Employees:** 1 - 10
Product Groups: 44

Date of Accounts	Sep 11	Sep 10	Sep 09
Working Capital	67	-0	173
Fixed Assets	69	112	87
Current Assets	119	73	223

Aetna UK Ltd
20 Gordon Avenue, Harrogate, HG1 3DH
Tel: 01423-562348 **Fax:** 01423-562348
E-mail: info@aetna.co.uk
Website: http://www.aetna.co.uk
Managers: D. Walkingshaw (Mgr)
Immediate Holding Company: AETNA (UK) LIMITED
Registration no: 02522111 **Date established:** 1990
No.of Employees: 1 - 10 **Product Groups:** 38, 42

Date of Accounts	Dec 11	Dec 10	Dec 09
Sales Turnover	N/A	4m	3m
Pre Tax Profit/Loss	N/A	138	-98
Working Capital	368	292	131
Fixed Assets	28	36	74
Current Assets	2m	1m	1m
Current Liabilities	N/A	378	336

Architectural Plastics Ltd
1 St Roberts Mews, Harrogate, HG1 1HR
Tel: 01423-561852 **Fax:** 01423-520728
E-mail: architecturalplastics@hotmail.co.uk
Website: http://www.architecturalplastics.co.uk
Directors: P. Herington (MD), V. Herington (Fin)
Immediate Holding Company: ARCHITECTURAL PLASTICS (HANDRAIL) LIMITED
Registration no: 00978979 **VAT No.:** GB 698 1901 89
Date established: 1970 **Turnover:** Up to £250,000
No.of Employees: 1 - 10 **Product Groups:** 29, 30, 35, 36, 48

Date of Accounts	Sep 11	Sep 10	Sep 09
Working Capital	25	23	32
Fixed Assets	15	7	10
Current Assets	67	54	59

B C L Distribution (Bradford Consultants Ltd)
Hornbeam Park Hookstone Road, Harrogate, HG2 8QT
Tel: 01423-879787 **Fax:** 01423-879030
E-mail: sales@bcldistribution.com
Website: http://www.bcldistribution.com
Directors: P. Turtun (MD)
Ultimate Holding Company: THE FAIRCHILD CORPORATION (USA)
Immediate Holding Company: HEIN GERICKE (U.K.) LIMITED
Registration no: 02256744 **VAT No.:** GB 171 9396 35
Date established: 1990 **Turnover:** £1m - £2m **No.of Employees:** 1 - 10
Product Groups: 67

Date of Accounts	Sep 11	Sep 10	Sep 09
Sales Turnover	19m	19m	22m
Pre Tax Profit/Loss	-1m	-2m	-1m
Working Capital	-1m	696	471
Fixed Assets	2m	3m	3m
Current Assets	6m	6m	7m
Current Liabilities	1m	942	2m

Bathstore.com Ltd
87 Leeds Road, Harrogate, HG2 8BE
Tel: 01423-874200 **Fax:** 01423-874400
E-mail: harrogate@bathstore.com
Website: http://www.bathstore.com
Managers: M. Gill
Ultimate Holding Company: WOLSELEY PLC (JERSEY)
Immediate Holding Company: BATHSTORE.COM LIMITED
Registration no: 02240475 **Date established:** 1988 **Turnover:** £1m - £2m
No.of Employees: 1 - 10 **Product Groups:** 26, 30, 66

Date of Accounts	Jul 11	Jul 10	Jul 09
Sales Turnover	94m	109m	107m
Pre Tax Profit/Loss	2m	10m	-12m
Working Capital	3m	-3m	-548
Fixed Assets	13m	17m	22m
Current Assets	36m	36m	36m
Current Liabilities	6m	7m	10m

Belzona International Ltd
Claro Road, Harrogate, HG1 4DS
Tel: 01423-567641 **Fax:** 01423-505967
E-mail: com@belzona.co.uk
Website: http://www.belzona.com
Bank(s): Lloyds TSB Bank plc
Directors: J. Svendsen (Dir)
Ultimate Holding Company: ORBEX LTD (BERMUDA)
Immediate Holding Company: BELZONA INTERNATIONAL LIMITED
Registration no: 00532158 **VAT No.:** GB 168 9633 12
Date established: 1954 **Turnover:** £20m - £50m
No.of Employees: 101 - 250 **Product Groups:** 32, 34

Date of Accounts	Dec 11	Dec 10	Dec 09
Sales Turnover	22m	20m	19m
Pre Tax Profit/Loss	2m	2m	1m
Working Capital	8m	6m	5m
Fixed Assets	9m	10m	9m
Current Assets	10m	8m	7m
Current Liabilities	1m	1m	873

Billie & Gruff
32 Montpellier Parade, Harrogate, HG1 2TG
Tel: 01423-817396
E-mail: info@do3.co.uk
Website: http://www.billieandgruff.co.uk
Managers: G. Ambler (Mgr)
Immediate Holding Company: ROCCABYEBABY LTD
Date established: 2009 **No.of Employees:** 1 - 10 **Product Groups:** 23, 24, 66

Binns-Tomlinson Safety Training Services Ltd
Garth House Grayston Plain Lane, Hampsthwaite, Harrogate, HG3 2HS
Tel: 01423-551818
E-mail: admin@safetytrainingservicesltd.co.uk
Website: http://www.safetytrainingservicesltd.co.uk
Directors: C. Tomlinson (Jt MD)
Registration no: 5939593 **Date established:** 2006
Turnover: Up to £250,000 **No.of Employees:** 1 - 10 **Product Groups:** 84, 86

Date of Accounts	Nov 07	Nov 06
Working Capital	1	1
Fixed Assets	2	N/A
Current Assets	8	1
Current Liabilities	6	N/A
Total Share Capital	1	1

Centrex Police
Yew Tree Lane, Harrogate, HG2 9JZ
Tel: 01423-871201 **Fax:** 01423-859132
Website: http://www.centrex.pnn.police.uk
Directors: J. Walker (Head), E. McGowan (Pers)
Managers: A. McGowan (Personnel), H. Atkinson (Sales Admin), S. Lambert (I.T. Exec), S. Rogers (Mgr)
No.of Employees: 101 - 250 **Product Groups:** 80, 85, 86

Chemical Release Co. Ltd
5 Cheltenham Mount, Harrogate, HG1 1DW
Tel: 01423-569715 **Fax:** 01423-563384
E-mail: crc@releaseagents.co.uk
Website: http://www.releaseagents.co.uk
Directors: K. Godber (MD)
Immediate Holding Company: CHEMICAL RELEASE COMPANY LIMITED
Registration no: 02603652 **VAT No.:** GB 545 6913 21
Date established: 1991 **Turnover:** £1m - £2m **No.of Employees:** 1 - 10
Product Groups: 31, 32, 66

Date of Accounts	Apr 12	Apr 11	Apr 10
Working Capital	96	85	-6
Fixed Assets	6	7	7
Current Assets	475	547	441

Choice Building Supplies Ltd
PO Box 422, Harrogate, HG1 4WU
Tel: 01423-888678 **Fax:** 01423-888661
E-mail: sales@choicebuildingsupplies.co.uk
Website: http://www.choicebuildingsupplies.co.uk
Directors: A. Maccormack (Dir)
Immediate Holding Company: CHOICE BUILDING SUPPLIES LTD
Registration no: 04705624 **Date established:** 2003
Turnover: £500,000 - £1m **No.of Employees:** 1 - 10 **Product Groups:** 25, 30, 33, 66

Date of Accounts	Mar 11	Mar 10	Mar 09
Working Capital	4	30	47
Fixed Assets	10	2	2
Current Assets	74	88	128

Co Star
Jubilee Mills Copgrove, Harrogate, HG3 3TB
Tel: 01423-340066 **Fax:** 01423-340077
E-mail: sales@co-star.co.uk
Website: http://www.co-star.co.uk
Directors: M. Cosgrove (Snr Part)
Immediate Holding Company: BDL MARKETING LIMITED
Date established: 2006 **No.of Employees:** 11 - 20 **Product Groups:** 37, 67

Date of Accounts	Dec 11	Dec 10	Dec 09
Sales Turnover	N/A	N/A	41
Pre Tax Profit/Loss	N/A	N/A	20
Working Capital	-28	-98	-108
Fixed Assets	N/A	N/A	3
Current Assets	1	16	17
Current Liabilities	N/A	N/A	1

Covance Laboratories Ltd
Otley Road, Harrogate, HG3 1PY
Tel: 01423-500011 **Fax:** 01423-569595
Website: http://www.covancelaboratory.com
Directors: K. Masters (Co Sec)
Ultimate Holding Company: COVANCE INC (USA)
Immediate Holding Company: COVANCE LABORATORIES LIMITED
Registration no: 01171833 **Date established:** 1974
Turnover: £75m - £125m **No.of Employees:** 1001 - 1500
Product Groups: 85

Date of Accounts	Dec 11	Dec 10	Dec 09
Sales Turnover	100m	91m	81m
Pre Tax Profit/Loss	-5m	8m	5m
Working Capital	28m	24m	23m
Fixed Assets	72m	82m	76m
Current Assets	55m	52m	45m
Current Liabilities	25m	25m	19m

D J Circuits Ltd
Jubilee Works Anchor Road, Harrogate, HG1 4TA
Tel: 01423-889055 **Fax:** 01423-884912
E-mail: enquiries@djcircuits.com
Website: http://www.djcircuits.com
Directors: D. Lupton (Dir), J. Lupton (Dir)
Managers: S. Hurdle (Sales Prom Mgr)
Immediate Holding Company: D.J.CIRCUITS LIMITED
Registration no: 00938445 **Date established:** 1968 **Turnover:** £2m - £5m
No.of Employees: 21 - 50 **Product Groups:** 37, 44, 48, 84

Date of Accounts	Sep 11	Sep 10	Sep 09
Working Capital	669	746	842
Fixed Assets	344	272	299
Current Assets	944	1m	988

D L B Partnership
The Old School House Darley, Harrogate, HG3 2PZ
Tel: 01423-781576 **Fax:** 01423-781831
Managers: G. Downing (Mgr)
Immediate Holding Company: K.C.H. BUILDING & JOINERY CONTRACTORS LIMITED
Date established: 2002 **No.of Employees:** 1 - 10 **Product Groups:** 35

Date of Accounts	Mar 12	Mar 11	Mar 10
Working Capital	-14	-13	-6
Fixed Assets	44	76	106
Current Assets	3	24	26

The Epos Store
3 Mill Cottages Pateley Bridge, Harrogate, HG3 5BA
Tel: 08456-447809 **Fax:** 0871-714 5609
E-mail: sales@epos-store.co.uk
Website: http://www.epos-store.co.uk
Directors: A. Carnall (Prop)
No.of Employees: 1 - 10 **Product Groups:** 44, 67

F T A V Ltd
Unit 4-5 Grove Park View, Harrogate, HG1 4BT
Tel: 01423-857830 **Fax:** 01423-857831
E-mail: info@ftav.co.uk
Website: http://www.ftav.co.uk
Directors: R. Lawson (MD)
Immediate Holding Company: J. HEWSON (BUILDERS) LIMITED
Registration no: 06819410 **Date established:** 1978
No.of Employees: 1 - 10 **Product Groups:** 83

Date of Accounts	Sep 11	Apr 10
Working Capital	-171	-144
Fixed Assets	72	89
Current Assets	12	5

First 4 It Ltd
Sceptre House 1 Hornbeam Square North, Harrogate, HG2 8PB
Tel: 01423-859370 **Fax:** 01423-859371
E-mail: markg@putpeoplefirst.com
Website: http://www.first4it.co.uk
Directors: M. Granger (Dir)
Ultimate Holding Company: PEOPLE FIRST GROUP LIMITED
Immediate Holding Company: FIRST 4 IT LIMITED
Registration no: 04716196 **Date established:** 2003
No.of Employees: 1 - 10 **Product Groups:** 26, 37, 38, 44, 80

Date of Accounts	Mar 11	Mar 10	Mar 09
Working Capital	-20	-9	-27
Fixed Assets	21	24	28
Current Assets	172	103	145

Flow-Mon Ltd
Chatsworth House 15 Chatsworth Terrace, Harrogate, HG1 5HT
Tel: 01423-561972 **Fax:** 01423-502063
E-mail: nathan@flow-mon.com
Website: http://www.flow-mon.com
Bank(s): Lloyds TSB
Directors: N. Smith (MD)
Ultimate Holding Company: THE EVERETT SMITH GROUP LIMITED
Immediate Holding Company: FLOW-MON LIMITED
Registration no: 01007511 **VAT No.:** GB 168 9656 00
Date established: 1971 **Turnover:** £500,000 - £1m
No.of Employees: 11 - 20 **Product Groups:** 38, 40, 44, 85

Date of Accounts	Dec 11	Dec 10	Dec 09
Working Capital	149	141	227
Fixed Assets	85	92	78
Current Assets	489	346	402

Geoplan Spatial Intelligence Ltd
Bilton Court Wetherby Road, Harrogate, HG3 1GP
Tel: 01423-569538 **Fax:** 01423-819494
E-mail: sales@geoplan.com
Website: http://www.geoplan.com
Bank(s): Barclays
Directors: E. Wilson (Co Sec), J. Taylor (MD)
Immediate Holding Company: GEOPLAN SPATIAL INTELLIGENCE LIMITED
Registration no: 02039116 **VAT No.:** GB 482 1477 38
Date established: 1986 **Turnover:** £2m - £5m **No.of Employees:** 11 - 20
Product Groups: 44

Date of Accounts	Jan 12	Jan 11	Jan 10
Working Capital	122	119	-127
Fixed Assets	2m	2m	2m
Current Assets	738	858	730

Groundforce
Beckwith Knowle Otley Road, Beckwithshaw, Harrogate, HG3 1UD
Tel: 01423-852295 **Fax:** 01423-536731
E-mail: groundforce.northern@vibroplant.co.uk
Website: http://www.groundforce.uk.com
Directors: D. Williams (MD), A. Bainbridge (Fin)
Ultimate Holding Company: ACKERS P INVESTMENT COMPANY LIMITED
Immediate Holding Company: VIBROPLANT TRUSTEES LIMITED
Registration no: 03634680 **VAT No.:** GB 169 4064 44
Date established: 1998 **No.of Employees:** 251 - 500 **Product Groups:** 40, 51

Date of Accounts	Mar 11	Mar 10	Mar 04
Working Capital	112	112	112
Current Assets	112	112	112

Hall Accountancy Services Ltd
Sunnycroft Glasshouses, Harrogate, HG3 5QY
Tel: 01423-712367 **Fax:** 01423-712367
E-mail: gaynor@hall-accountancy.co.uk
Website: http://www.hall-accountancy.co.uk
Directors: G. Hall (MD)
Immediate Holding Company: HALL ACCOUNTANCY SERVICES LIMITED
Registration no: 04507385 **Date established:** 2002
Turnover: £250,000 - £500,000 **No.of Employees:** 1 - 10
Product Groups: 80

Date of Accounts	Jul 11	Jul 10	Jul 09
Working Capital	9	6	11
Current Assets	15	15	17

Hamilton Data Imaging Ltd
22 Leeds Road, Harrogate, HG2 8AA
Tel: 01423-565223 **Fax:** 01423-526223
E-mail: info@hdi-online.co.uk
Website: http://www.hdi-online.co.uk
Directors: S. Haines (MD)
No.of Employees: 1 - 10 **Product Groups:** 28, 44, 81

Harrogate Catering Services
23 Grasmere Crescent, Harrogate, HG2 0ED
Tel: 01423-529949 **Fax:** 01423-529979
Directors: M. Turnock (Prop)
Date established: 2006 **No.of Employees:** 1 - 10 **Product Groups:** 20, 40, 41

Harrogate Gates & Railings
The Coach House, Harrogate, HG1 5EE
Tel: 01423-701780
Directors: S. Kerwin (Ptnr)
Date established: 2002 **No.of Employees:** 1 - 10 **Product Groups:** 26, 35

Hijack Systems
Mews Cottage 9 Otley Road, Harrogate, HG2 0DJ
Tel: 01423-563879 **Fax:** 01423-520344
E-mail: enquiries@hijacksystems.com
Website: http://www.hijacksystems.com
Directors: K. Skelton (Prop)
Turnover: Up to £250,000 **No.of Employees:** 1 - 10 **Product Groups:** 26, 40, 41, 45

I X P Ltd
40 Otley Road, Harrogate, HG2 0DP
Tel: 01423-564800 **Fax:** 01423-505690
E-mail: enquiries@ixpltd.co.uk
Website: http://www.ixpsecurity.co.uk
Directors: M. Wayman (MD)
Immediate Holding Company: I.X.P. LIMITED
Registration no: 00970427 **VAT No.:** GB 179 5001 56
Date established: 1970 **No.of Employees:** 1 - 10 **Product Groups:** 37, 38, 46, 47

Date of Accounts	Mar 11	Mar 10	Mar 09
Working Capital	-37	-39	-35
Fixed Assets	367	371	377
Current Assets	63	43	78

In Technology plc
Central House Beckwith Knowle Otley Road, Harrogate, HG3 1UG
Tel: 01423-850000 **Fax:** 01423-858866
E-mail: sales@intechnology.co.uk
Website: http://www.intechnology.co.uk
Directors: N. Duffield (Sales), P. Handley (Mkt Research), B. Sage (Sales), A. Kaberry (Fin), P. Hambly (Mkt Research)
Managers: A. Kolazinski (Tech Serv Mgr), R. Dixon (Personnel), C. Loizou
Immediate Holding Company: INTECHNOLOGY PLC
Registration no: 03916586 **Date established:** 2000
Turnover: £20m - £50m **No.of Employees:** 101 - 250
Product Groups: 36, 44, 61, 67, 81

Date of Accounts	Mar 12	Mar 11	Mar 10
Sales Turnover	41m	40m	39m
Pre Tax Profit/Loss	2m	632	-765
Working Capital	18m	17m	17m
Fixed Assets	53m	48m	50m
Current Assets	26m	25m	23m
Current Liabilities	5m	5m	4m

J A P S Engineering
Clint Bank Burnt Yates, Harrogate, HG3 3DW
Tel: 01423-771584
Directors: J. Shaw (Prop)
Immediate Holding Company: P & R CONSTRUCTION & BUILDING MATERIALS LIMITED
Date established: 2010 **No.of Employees:** 1 - 10 **Product Groups:** 35

Date of Accounts	Nov 11
Working Capital	27
Fixed Assets	83
Current Assets	162

J M Church Supplies
Unit 2b Follifoot Ridge Farm Business Park Pannal Road, Follifoot, Harrogate, HG3 1DP
Tel: 01423-816968 **Fax:** 01423-816969
E-mail: sales@jmchurchsupplies.co.uk
Website: http://www.jmchurchsupplies.com
Directors: J. Mitchell (MD)
Registration no: 04845325 **Date established:** 2003
Turnover: £250,000 - £500,000 **No.of Employees:** 1 - 10
Product Groups: 25, 26, 35, 65

Jewson Ltd
1 Freemans Way, Harrogate, HG3 1RW
Tel: 01423-885944 **Fax:** 01423-881019
Website: http://www.jewson.co.uk
Managers: M. Freer (Mgr)
Ultimate Holding Company: COMPAGNIE DE SAINT GOBAIN (FRANCE)
Immediate Holding Company: JEWSON LIMITED
Registration no: 00348407 **VAT No.:** GB 497 7184 83
Date established: 1939 **No.of Employees:** 1 - 10 **Product Groups:** 66

Date of Accounts	Dec 11	Dec 10	Dec 09
Sales Turnover	1606m	1547m	1485m
Pre Tax Profit/Loss	18m	100m	45m
Working Capital	-345m	-250m	-349m
Fixed Assets	496m	387m	461m
Current Assets	657m	1005m	1320m
Current Liabilities	66m	120m	64m

Kitz Corporation
Windsor House Cornwall Road, Harrogate, HG1 2PW
Tel: 01423-875225 **Fax:** 01423-875226
E-mail: office@kitzcorporation.com
Website: http://www.kitzcorporation.com
Directors: H. Fujihara (Dir), K. Kobayashi (Grp Chief Exec), Y. Shimizu (Ch)
Managers: R. Oldfield (Sales Prom Mgr), A. Shiomitsu (Ops Mgr), S. Eguchi (Sales Prom Mgr), S. Terry (Chief Mgr)
Immediate Holding Company: KITZ CORPORATION
Registration no: FC025195 **Date established:** 2004
No.of Employees: 1 - 10 **Product Groups:** 33, 36, 40, 66

L T T Leathercare
Langdale House 105b Wetherby Road, Harrogate, HG2 7SH
Tel: 01423-881027 **Fax:** 01423-887324
E-mail: enquiries@lttsolutions.net
Website: http://www.lttsolutions.net
Directors: J. Bass (Dir)
Immediate Holding Company: LTT LEATHERCARE LTD
Registration no: 07281788 **Date established:** 2010
Turnover: Up to £250,000 **No.of Employees:** 1 - 10 **Product Groups:** 32

Date of Accounts	Jun 11
Working Capital	-10
Fixed Assets	5
Current Assets	30

Lancashire Fittings Ltd
The Science Village Claro Road, Harrogate, HG1 4AF
Tel: 01423-522355 **Fax:** 01423-506111
E-mail: sales@lancashirefittings.com
Website: http://www.lancashirefittings.com
Directors: K. Idle (MD)
Immediate Holding Company: LANCASHIRE FITTINGS LIMITED
Registration no: 00981150 **VAT No.:** GB 170 9945 34
Date established: 1970 **Turnover:** £1m - £2m **No.of Employees:** 1 - 10
Product Groups: 36, 40, 48

Date of Accounts	Sep 11	Sep 10	Sep 09
Working Capital	429	495	557
Fixed Assets	17	33	62
Current Assets	473	552	624

Make 96
Unit 8 Thompsons Yard, Harrogate, HG1 5BA
Tel: 01423-527820 **Fax:** 01423-527820
Directors: G. Wallace (Prop)
Date established: 1995 **No.of Employees:** 1 - 10 **Product Groups:** 26, 35

Marlyn Metal Craft Wrought Iron Workers
2 Provincial Works The Avenue, Harrogate, HG1 4QE
Tel: 01423-888080 **Fax:** 01423-881087
Directors: J. Walker (Ptnr)
Immediate Holding Company: MARLYN METALCRAFT LIMITED
Registration no: 05810275 **Date established:** 2006
No.of Employees: 1 - 10 **Product Groups:** 26, 35

Date of Accounts	Jun 12	Jun 11	Jun 10
Working Capital	-7	-4	-0
Fixed Assets	12	14	17
Current Assets	81	105	105

N Minikin & Sons Ltd
Spa House Hookstone Park, Harrogate, HG2 7DB
Tel: 01423-889845 **Fax:** 01423-880724
E-mail: tony.minikin@minikins.co.uk
Website: http://www.minikins.co.uk
Directors: J. Minikin (Fin), A. Minikin (MD)
Immediate Holding Company: N. MINIKIN & SONS LIMITED
Registration no: 01387785 **VAT No.:** GB 313 5368 74
Date established: 1978 **Turnover:** £1m - £2m **No.of Employees:** 1 - 10
Product Groups: 29, 36, 42

Date of Accounts	Dec 11	Dec 10	Dec 09
Working Capital	108	151	141
Fixed Assets	276	267	276
Current Assets	236	254	263

Montpellier Engineers Ltd
Claro Road, Harrogate, HG1 4AT
Tel: 01423-530123 **Fax:** 01423- 508479
E-mail: wbirch@montpelliereng.co.uk
Website: http://www.montpelliereng.co.uk
Directors: W. Birch (Ch), J. Horner (Co Sec), D. Bailey (Fin), G. Williams (MD)
Ultimate Holding Company: MONTPELLIER HOLDINGS LIMITED
Immediate Holding Company: MONTPELLIER ENGINEERS LIMITED
Registration no: 00992268 **VAT No.:** GB 444 3119 70
Date established: 1970 **No.of Employees:** 21 - 50 **Product Groups:** 35

Date of Accounts	Mar 10	Mar 09	Mar 08
Working Capital	733	864	836
Fixed Assets	67	104	141
Current Assets	1m	2m	2m

N I P S UK
Hornbeam Park Hookstone Road, Harrogate, HG2 8QU
Tel: 01423-871794 **Fax:** 01423-879015
E-mail: enquiries@nipsuk.com
Website: http://www.nipsuk.com
Directors: D. Mackinnon (MD)
Managers: B. Taylor (Consultant)
Ultimate Holding Company: IMPOSED CONDITION LIMITED
Immediate Holding Company: NORTHERN INSULATION AND PIPELINE STOCKISTS LIMITED
Registration no: 01487761 **Date established:** 1980
Turnover: £500,000 - £1m **No.of Employees:** 1 - 10 **Product Groups:** 31, 40

Date of Accounts	Sep 11	Sep 10	Sep 09
Working Capital	241	233	254
Fixed Assets	15	11	14
Current Assets	335	340	364

Nidd Vale Group Ltd

Nidd Vale Corner 91 Leeds Road, Harrogate, HG2 8EY
Tel: 01423-500005 **Fax:** 01423-500404
E-mail: sales@niddvale.co.uk
Website: http://www.niddvale.co.uk
Bank(s): HSBC Bank plc
Directors: N. Crossley (MD)
Ultimate Holding Company: NIDD VALE GROUP LIMITED
Immediate Holding Company: NIDD VALE MOTORS HOLDINGS LIMITED
Registration no: 04823947 **VAT No.:** GB 168 9993 79
Date established: 2003 **Turnover:** £50m - £75m
No.of Employees: 21 - 50 **Product Groups:** 68

Date of Accounts	Dec 10	Dec 09	Dec 08
Pre Tax Profit/Loss	-65	84	316
Working Capital	-8m	-4m	-3m
Fixed Assets	9m	9m	9m
Current Liabilities	N/A	16	34

Nidd Valley Medical Ltd

Nidd Valley House Unit 22 Claro Court Business Centre Claro Road, Harrogate, HG1 4BA
Tel: 01423-817920 **Fax:** 01423-817933
E-mail: sales@niddvalley.co.uk
Website: http://www.niddvalley.co.uk
Managers: J. Siekierkowski (Sales Prom Mgr)
Immediate Holding Company: NIDD VALLEY MEDICAL LIMITED
Registration no: 01854745 **Date established:** 1984
Turnover: Up to £250,000 **No.of Employees:** 1 - 10 **Product Groups:** 67

Date of Accounts	Jan 12	Jan 11	Jan 10
Working Capital	74	72	68
Fixed Assets	1	4	6
Current Assets	118	109	106

O S M

Woodside Back Road, High Birstwith, Harrogate, HG3 2JH
Tel: 01423-772222 **Fax:** 01423-770284
E-mail: sarah.austin@osm.ltd.uk
Website: http://www.osm.ltd.uk
Directors: S. Austin (Dir)
No.of Employees: 1 - 10 **Product Groups:** 80

Date of Accounts	Jun 08	Jun 07	Jun 06
Working Capital	46	4	3
Fixed Assets	2	N/A	1
Current Assets	81	38	19
Current Liabilities	35	34	16

Process Conbustion Ltd

Harbeam Park Hookstone Road, Harrogate, HG2 8PB
Tel: 01423-879944 **Fax:** 01423-879946
E-mail: mail@process-combustion.co.uk
Website: http://www.process-combustion.co.uk
Directors: D. Bishon (MD), C. Asquith (Fin)
Managers: G. Van-bellen (Sales Prom Mgr)
Immediate Holding Company: GOELST UK LIMITED
Registration no: 04741327 **Date established:** 1991 **Turnover:** £5m - £10m
No.of Employees: 51 - 100 **Product Groups:** 40, 42

Date of Accounts	Dec 11	Dec 10	Dec 09
Working Capital	452	463	477
Fixed Assets	19	18	21
Current Assets	718	746	628

Pullman Instruments

Chatsworth House Chatsworth Terrace, Harrogate, HG1 5HT
Tel: 01423-720360 **Fax:** 01423-720361
E-mail: sales@pullman.co.uk
Website: http://www.pullman.co.uk
Bank(s): Lloyds
Directors: M. Kendall (Dir)
Managers: N. Smith (Mgr)
Registration no: 03681420 **VAT No.:** GB 545 6749 08
Turnover: £500,000 - £1m **No.of Employees:** 21 - 50 **Product Groups:** 85

R & B Group

17-18 Claro Court Business Centre Claro Road, Harrogate, HG1 4BA
Tel: 01423-567188
E-mail: info@rbgroup.co.uk
Website: http://www.rbgroup.co.uk
Managers: G. Frost (District Mgr)
Immediate Holding Company: UGS (HARROGATE) LIMITED
Registration no: 06595292 **Date established:** 2008
No.of Employees: 1 - 10 **Product Groups:** 81

Rousselet Robatel UK Ltd

Parkside House 17 East Parade, Harrogate, HG1 5LF
Tel: 01423-530093 **Fax:** 01423-530120
E-mail: sales@rousselet-robatel.co.uk
Website: http://www.rousselet.com
Directors: C. Evans (Sales), M. L'kherba (Fin)
Immediate Holding Company: ROUSSELET/ROBATEL UK LIMITED
Registration no: 04922092 **Date established:** 2003
No.of Employees: 1 - 10 **Product Groups:** 38, 42

Date of Accounts	Dec 11	Dec 10	Dec 09
Working Capital	75	73	72
Fixed Assets	1	1	1
Current Assets	82	79	77

Safilo UK Ltd

Lambert House 108 Station Parade, Harrogate, HG1 1HQ
Tel: 01423-520303 **Fax:** 01423-565889
E-mail: info@safilo.com
Website: http://www.saflio.com
Bank(s): Lloyds TSB
Directors: K. Gardner (Co Sec)
Managers: R. Merrywick (Mgr), R. Meyrick
Ultimate Holding Company: SAFILO GROUP SPA (ITALY)
Immediate Holding Company: SAFILO UK LIMITED
Registration no: 02773194 **VAT No.:** GB 229 7069 39
Date established: 1992 **Turnover:** £10m - £20m
No.of Employees: 11 - 20 **Product Groups:** 38, 65

Date of Accounts	Dec 11	Dec 10	Dec 09
Sales Turnover	16m	16m	18m
Pre Tax Profit/Loss	-2m	399	521
Working Capital	2m	3m	3m
Fixed Assets	29	29	65
Current Assets	7m	7m	7m
Current Liabilities	2m	2m	1m

Salzgitter Mannesmann UK Ltd

Windsor House Cornwall Road, Harrogate, HG1 2PW
Tel: 01423-566660 **Fax:** 01423-505777
E-mail: chris.bagnall@szuk.co.uk
Website: http://www.szuk.co.uk
Directors: C. Bagnall (MD)
Ultimate Holding Company: SALZGITTER AG (GERMANY)
Immediate Holding Company: SALZGITTER MANNESMANN (UK) LIMITED
Registration no: 02442586 **Date established:** 1989
Turnover: £500,000 - £1m **No.of Employees:** 11 - 20 **Product Groups:** 66

Date of Accounts	Dec 11	Dec 10	Dec 09
Sales Turnover	33m	23m	15m
Pre Tax Profit/Loss	818	551	-3m
Working Capital	931	110	-505
Fixed Assets	1	8	21
Current Assets	20m	17m	9m
Current Liabilities	286	435	310

Serenity of Harrogate

PO Box 579, Harrogate, HG1 9DP
Tel: 01423-528262
E-mail: info@serenityofharrogate.co.uk
Website: http://www.serenityofharrogate.co.uk
Registration no: 01715981 **Turnover:** Up to £250,000
No.of Employees: 1 - 10 **Product Groups:** 31, 32, 63

Shakespeare Engineering Supplies

20 Freemans Way Harrogate Business Park, Harrogate, HG3 1DH
Tel: 01423-881600 **Fax:** 01423-881617
E-mail: sales@shakespearehydraulics.co.uk
Website: http://www.shakespearehydraulics.co.uk
Directors: M. Shakespeare (Dir)
Immediate Holding Company: SHAKESPEARE HYDRAULICS LIMITED
Registration no: 02736246 **Date established:** 1992
Turnover: £250,000 - £500,000 **No.of Employees:** 1 - 10
Product Groups: 29

Date of Accounts	Jul 12	Jul 11	Jul 10
Sales Turnover	440	435	300
Pre Tax Profit/Loss	76	27	15
Working Capital	1	-29	-46
Fixed Assets	44	47	50
Current Assets	132	107	98
Current Liabilities	32	18	13

Swiss Travel Products UK

14 Crown House Hornbeam Square North, Harrogate, HG2 8PB
Tel: 01423-853190 **Fax:** 01423-853190
E-mail: sales@swisstravelproducts.co.uk
Website: http://www.swisstravelproducts.co.uk
Directors: S. Winstanley (Dir), K. Winstanley (Fin)
Immediate Holding Company: SWISS TRAVEL PRODUCTS UK LTD
Registration no: 05660840 **Date established:** 2005
No.of Employees: 11 - 20 **Product Groups:** 22, 37, 49, 67

Switched Reluctance Drives Ltd

East Park House Otley Road, Beckwithshaw, Harrogate, HG3 1PR
Tel: 01423-845200 **Fax:** 01423-845201
E-mail: roy.blake@srdrives.co.uk
Website: http://www.srdrives.co.uk
Directors: R. Blake (MD), G. Haines (Non Exec)
Managers: D. Sugden (Develop Mgr), P. Hutchinson (Buyer)
Ultimate Holding Company: Digital Appliance Controls UK Ltd
Immediate Holding Company: SWITCHED RELUCTANCE DRIVES LIMITED
Registration no: 01517273 **VAT No.:** GB 343 1397 66
Date established: 1980 **Turnover:** £2m - £5m **No.of Employees:** 21 - 50
Product Groups: 37, 39, 40, 47, 84, 85

Date of Accounts	Sep 09	Sep 08	Sep 07
Sales Turnover	3m	3m	3m
Pre Tax Profit/Loss	301	612	490
Working Capital	10m	9m	9m
Fixed Assets	1m	1m	2m
Current Assets	10m	10m	9m
Current Liabilities	135	223	208

Town Or Country

79 Hookstone Avenue, Harrogate, HG2 8EP
Tel: 07949-904652
E-mail: dh@harrogatehouseclearance.com
Website: http://www.harrogatehouseclearance.com
Directors: D. Halls (Ptnr)
Registration no: 05603175 **Date established:** 2005
No.of Employees: 1 - 10 **Product Groups:** 54

Tushingham Sails Ltd

PO Box 1, Harrogate, HG3 5BN
Tel: 01423-712424 **Fax:** 01423-712273
E-mail: windsurfing@tushingham.com
Website: http://www.tushingham.com
Directors: D. Hackford (Mkt Research), R. Tushingham (Prop)
Immediate Holding Company: TUSHINGHAM SAILS LIMITED
Registration no: 01371094 **Date established:** 1978 **Turnover:** £1m - £2m
No.of Employees: 1 - 10 **Product Groups:** 49

Date of Accounts	Feb 12	Feb 11	Feb 10
Working Capital	815	735	810
Fixed Assets	38	70	97
Current Assets	1m	1m	1m

Unit 4 Business Software Ltd (a division of Science Systems P.L.C.)

2 Cardale Park Beckwith Head Road, Harrogate, HG3 1RY
Tel: 01423-509999 **Fax:** 01423-530525
E-mail: info@coda.com
Website: http://www.unit4.com
Directors: A. Robinson (Dir), A. Marlow (Fin)
Ultimate Holding Company: UNIT 4 AGRESSO NV (NETHERLANDS)
Immediate Holding Company: UNIT4 BUSINESS SOFTWARE LIMITED
Registration no: 01737985 **Date established:** 1983
Turnover: £20m - £50m **No.of Employees:** 101 - 250 **Product Groups:** 44

Date of Accounts	Dec 11	Dec 10	Dec 09
Sales Turnover	63m	31m	34m
Pre Tax Profit/Loss	16m	-193	25m
Working Capital	3m	-4m	25m
Fixed Assets	166m	170m	162m
Current Assets	77m	68m	42m
Current Liabilities	22m	24m	10m

V P plc

Central House Beckwith Knowle Otley Road, Beckwithshaw, Harrogate, HG3 1UD
Tel: 01423-533400 **Fax:** 01423-565657
E-mail: enquiries@vpplc.com
Website: http://www.vpplc.com
Bank(s): National Westminster
Directors: A. Bainbridge (Fin), J. Pilkington (Ch)
Managers: D. Stonard (Personnel), T. Wilson (Tech Serv Mgr)
Ultimate Holding Company: ACKERS P INVESTMENT COMPANY LIMITED
Immediate Holding Company: VP PLC
Registration no: 00481833 **VAT No.:** GB 169 4064 44
Date established: 1950 **Turnover:** £125m - £250m
No.of Employees: 101 - 250 **Product Groups:** 83

Date of Accounts	Mar 12	Mar 11	Mar 10
Sales Turnover	164m	141m	134m
Pre Tax Profit/Loss	15m	12m	14m
Working Capital	-4m	-14m	-43m
Fixed Assets	150m	141m	138m
Current Assets	45m	44m	33m
Current Liabilities	31m	19m	14m

Ventrolla Ltd

Crimple Court Ventrolla House Hornbeam Square North, Harrogate, HG2 8PB
Tel: 01423-859323 **Fax:** 01423-859321
E-mail: info@ventrolla.co.uk
Website: http://www.ventrolla.co.uk
Bank(s): Midland
Directors: D. Greaves (MD)
Ultimate Holding Company: LUPUS CAPITAL PLC
Immediate Holding Company: VENTROLLA LIMITED
Registration no: 01687922 **VAT No.:** GB 387 9576 71
Date established: 1982 **Turnover:** £5m - £10m **No.of Employees:** 11 - 20
Product Groups: 25

Date of Accounts	Dec 08
Working Capital	308
Current Assets	308

Wrought Iron Solutions Ltd

The Old Forge Otley Road, Killinghall, Harrogate, HG3 2DW
Tel: 01423-568396
E-mail: info@wroughtironsolutions.co.uk
Website: http://www.wroughtironsolutions.co.uk
Directors: R. Snuggs (Dir)
Immediate Holding Company: WROUGHT IRON SOLUTIONS LIMITED
Registration no: 07157185 **Date established:** 2010
No.of Employees: 1 - 10 **Product Groups:** 26, 35

Date of Accounts	Mar 11
Working Capital	-1
Fixed Assets	1
Current Assets	8

Yorkshire Gun Room

Bishop Thornton, Harrogate, HG3 3JN
Tel: 01765-620602 **Fax:** 01765-620656
Directors: J. Lupton (MD)
Date established: 1972 **No.of Employees:** 1 - 10 **Product Groups:** 36, 39, 40

Yorkshire Metal Roofing

Unit 2 The Old Station Nidd, Harrogate, HG3 3BN
Tel: 01423-779555 **Fax:** 01423-779666
E-mail: enquiries@bradclad.com
Website: http://www.bradclad.com
Directors: K. Bradley (MD)
Immediate Holding Company: YORKSHIRE METAL ROOFING LIMITED
Registration no: 05333194 **Date established:** 2005
Turnover: £10m - £20m **No.of Employees:** 1 - 10 **Product Groups:** 34, 48

Knaresborough

A1 Garage Doors & Openings Ltd

Field View 12 Orchard Close, Knaresborough, HG5 0NH
Tel: 01423-869374 **Fax:** 01423-869374
E-mail: graham@keithburham.wanadoo.co.uk
Website: http://www.a1-doors.co.uk
Directors: G. Burnham (Prop)
Immediate Holding Company: A1 GARAGE DOORS & OPENINGS LIMITED
Registration no: 05258362 **Date established:** 2004
No.of Employees: 1 - 10 **Product Groups:** 25, 30, 35, 37

Date of Accounts	Oct 11	Oct 10	Oct 07
Working Capital	-9	-6	7
Fixed Assets	22	28	48
Current Assets	18	50	67

Claro Precision Engineering Ltd

Unit 4 & 5 Manse Lane Industrial Estate, Knaresborough, HG5 8LF
Tel: 01423-867413 **Fax:** 01423-861959
E-mail: engineering@claro.co.uk
Website: http://www.claro.co.uk
Bank(s): National Westminster Bank Plc
Directors: M. Lewis (Sales), M. Doxey (MD)
Managers: D. Booth (Personnel)
Ultimate Holding Company: CLARO LIMITED
Immediate Holding Company: CLARO PRECISION ENGINEERING LIMITED
Registration no: 01374225 **VAT No.:** GB 301 3575 94
Date established: 1978 **Turnover:** £2m - £5m **No.of Employees:** 51 - 100
Product Groups: 30, 34, 35, 36, 42, 46, 48

Date of Accounts	Dec 11	Dec 10	Dec 09
Working Capital	2m	2m	2m
Fixed Assets	519	566	650
Current Assets	2m	2m	2m

Craven & Co. Ltd
Manse Lane, Knaresborough, HG5 8ET
Tel: 01423-796200 **Fax:** 01423-869189
E-mail: sales@craven-solutions.com
Website: http://www.craven-solutions.com
Bank(s): National Westminster Bank Plc
Directors: J. Milnes (Dir)
Managers: C. Goodchild (Nat Sales Mgr), M. Walsh (Buyer)
Ultimate Holding Company: CRAVEN & CO. LIMITED
Immediate Holding Company: RICHARD CRAVEN & CO.LIMITED
Registration no: 00597982 **VAT No.:** GB 747 1774 06
Date established: 1958 **Turnover:** £2m - £5m **No.of Employees:** 21 - 50
Product Groups: 26, 35, 40, 41, 45, 67

Flying Colours Flag Makers
The Flag Rooms 1 -4 Orchard Court Iles Lane, Knaresborough, HG5 8PP
Tel: 01423-860007 **Fax:** 01423-861858
E-mail: admin@flyingcolours.org
Website: http://www.flyingcolours.org
Directors: A. Ormrod (Prop)
Immediate Holding Company: FLYING COLOURS FLAGMAKERS LIMITED
Registration no: 04672024 **Date established:** 2003
Turnover: £250,000 - £500,000 **No.of Employees:** 11 - 20
Product Groups: 49, 83

Date of Accounts	Mar 11	Mar 10	Mar 09
Working Capital	-28	10	10
Fixed Assets	57	34	33
Current Assets	63	73	60

The Fuel Cards Company UK Ltd (UK Fuel Cards)
Unit 3 Grimbald Crag Court, Knaresborough, HG5 8QB
Tel: 08454-561400 **Fax:** 0845-456 1700
E-mail: customerservice@fuelcards.co.uk
Website: http://www.thefuelcardcompany.co.uk
Directors: P. Draycott (MD)
Managers: C. Snales (Fin Mgr)
Ultimate Holding Company: FLEETCOR TECHNOLOGIES INC (USA)
Immediate Holding Company: THE FUELCARD COMPANY UK LIMITED
Registration no: 05939102 **VAT No.:** GB 387 4549 02
Date established: 2006 **Turnover:** £250m - £500m
No.of Employees: 51 - 100 **Product Groups:** 38, 39

Date of Accounts	Dec 11	Dec 10	Dec 09
Sales Turnover	447m	485m	355m
Pre Tax Profit/Loss	5m	10m	6m
Working Capital	-6m	2m	-6m
Fixed Assets	38m	43m	44m
Current Assets	42m	66m	57m
Current Liabilities	12m	25m	11m

Haredata Electronics
Unit 6 Stoneacres Grimbald Crag Close, Knaresborough, HG5 8PJ
Tel: 01423-853180 **Fax:** 01423-853199
E-mail: sales@haredata.co.uk
Website: http://www.haredata.co.uk
Directors: K. Winstanley (Fin)
Managers: R. Barnes (Sales Prom Mgr)
Ultimate Holding Company: KASTRONIX LIMITED
Immediate Holding Company: HAREDATA ELECTRONICS LIMITED
Registration no: 02893647 **Date established:** 1994
No.of Employees: 11 - 20 **Product Groups:** 37

Interprint Ltd
Lingerfield Business Park Market Flat Lane, Scotton, Knaresborough, HG5 9JA
Tel: 0800-975 7514 **Fax:** 01423-798470
E-mail: sbruce@interprint-ltd.co.uk
Website: http://www.interprint.co.uk
Directors: R. Reeve (MD), S. Bruce (MD)
Managers: A. Clark (I.T. Exec), L. Dobby (Mktg Serv Mgr)
Immediate Holding Company: INTERPRINT LIMITED
Registration no: 06368591 **Date established:** 2007 **Turnover:** £2m - £5m
No.of Employees: 21 - 50 **Product Groups:** 28

Date of Accounts	Aug 08	Jun 11	Jun 10
Working Capital	31	225	99
Fixed Assets	710	358	424
Current Assets	1m	1m	1m
Current Liabilities	N/A	237	N/A

Manse Masterdor Ltd
Halfpenny Lane, Knaresborough, HG5 0SL
Tel: 01423-866868 **Fax:** 01423-866368
E-mail: sales@masterdor.co.uk
Website: http://www.masterdor.co.uk
Bank(s): Barclays
Managers: J. Tapscott
Ultimate Holding Company: L. B. PLASTICS LIMITED
Immediate Holding Company: MANSE MASTERDOR LIMITED
Registration no: 03530099 **VAT No.:** GB 509 3067 53
Date established: 1998 **Turnover:** £10m - £20m
No.of Employees: 51 - 100 **Product Groups:** 25

Date of Accounts	Dec 11	Dec 10	Dec 09
Sales Turnover	9m	11m	15m
Pre Tax Profit/Loss	-1m	-871	-816
Working Capital	3m	4m	5m
Fixed Assets	2m	2m	2m
Current Assets	4m	5m	6m
Current Liabilities	325	376	503

Niddal Windows Ltd
13 Iles Lane, Knaresborough, HG5 8DY
Tel: 01423-866588 **Fax:** 01423-869358
E-mail: sales@niddal.co.uk
Website: http://www.niddal.co.uk
Directors: J. Woodford (Fin), R. McCabe (MD)
Managers: K. Wadsworth (Sales Prom Mgr)
Immediate Holding Company: NIDDAL WINDOWS LIMITED
Registration no: 01324113 **Date established:** 1977
No.of Employees: 11 - 20 **Product Groups:** 26, 35

Date of Accounts	Jul 11	Jul 10	Jul 09
Working Capital	70	123	120
Fixed Assets	178	181	179
Current Assets	323	333	292

Resimac Ltd
Knaresborough Technology Park Manse Lane, Knaresborough, HG5 8LF
Tel: 01765-677757 **Fax:** 01765-677757
E-mail: info@resimac.co.uk
Website: http://www.resimac.co.uk
Directors: M. McDonnell (Tech Serv)
Registration no: 07029948 **Date established:** 2009
Turnover: £250,000 - £500,000 **No.of Employees:** 1 - 10
Product Groups: 32

Sarah Nuttall
11 Hambleton Terrace, Knaresborough, HG5 0DD
Tel: 020-3239 6789
E-mail: sarah@sarahnuttallcopywriter.co.uk
Website: http://www.sarahnuttall.com
Directors: S. Nuttall (Prop)
Date established: 2001 **Turnover:** Up to £250,000
No.of Employees: 1 - 10 **Product Groups:** 81

Tarmac Northern Ltd
Lingerfield Scotton, Knaresborough, HG5 9JN
Tel: 01423-796800 **Fax:** 01423-796808
E-mail: johnibbotson@tarmac.co.uk
Website: http://www.tarmac.co.uk
Directors: J. Ibbotson (Dir)
Ultimate Holding Company: ANGLO AMERICAN PLC
Immediate Holding Company: TARMAC NORTHERN LIMITED
Registration no: 03140596 **Date established:** 1995
No.of Employees: 21 - 50 **Product Groups:** 33

Date of Accounts	Dec 11	Dec 10	Dec 09
Pre Tax Profit/Loss	5m	4m	3m
Working Capital	84m	80m	77m
Current Assets	103m	98m	94m
Current Liabilities	19m	18m	17m

Tomrods Ltd
Manse Lane, Knaresborough, HG5 8LF
Tel: 01423-867333 **Fax:** 01423-867834
E-mail: j.thompson@tomrods.co.uk
Website: http://www.tomrods.co.uk
Bank(s): Lloyds TSB
Directors: J. Thompson (MD), K. McKee (Comm), S. Lockwood (Dir), M. Bruce (Co Sec)
Managers: B. Hoyle (Sales Prom Mgr), M. Cowgill (Works Gen Mgr)
Ultimate Holding Company: Rossett Group Ltd
Immediate Holding Company: TOMRODS LIMITED
Registration no: 01137143 **VAT No.:** GB 171 4456 68
Date established: 1973 **Turnover:** £10m - £20m
No.of Employees: 21 - 50 **Product Groups:** 34, 36, 66

Date of Accounts	Dec 09	Dec 08	Dec 07
Sales Turnover	16m	21m	30m
Pre Tax Profit/Loss	16	571	534
Working Capital	1m	1m	2m
Fixed Assets	1m	1m	551
Current Assets	7m	7m	12m
Current Liabilities	920	2m	1m

Travis Perkins plc
Manse Lane, Knaresborough, HG5 8LF
Tel: 01423-862277 **Fax:** 01423-862251
E-mail: meliss.evans@travisperkins.co.uk
Website: http://www.travisperkins.co.uk
Managers: G. Bingham (Mgr)
Immediate Holding Company: TRAVIS PERKINS PLC
Registration no: 00824821 **Date established:** 1964 **Turnover:** £2m - £5m
No.of Employees: 11 - 20 **Product Groups:** 52, 66

Date of Accounts	Dec 11	Dec 10	Dec 09
Sales Turnover	4779m	3153m	2931m
Pre Tax Profit/Loss	270m	197m	213m
Working Capital	133m	159m	248m
Fixed Assets	2771m	2749m	2108m
Current Assets	1421m	1329m	1035m
Current Liabilities	473m	412m	109m

Trelleborg Applied Technology
Halfpenny Lane, Knaresborough, HG5 0PP
Tel: 01423-862677 **Fax:** 01423-868340
E-mail: paul.habberfield@trelleborg.com
Website: http://www.trelleborg.com/appliedtechnology
Directors: J. Wilson (MD), I. Elcock (Co Sec)
Managers: P. Habberfield (Sales Prom Mgr)
Ultimate Holding Company: TRELLEBORG AB (SWEDEN)
Immediate Holding Company: UNITEX LIMITED
Registration no: 01004676 **Date established:** 1971
No.of Employees: 21 - 50 **Product Groups:** 29, 30, 31, 32, 39, 41, 44, 48, 52, 66

Date of Accounts	Dec 10
Working Capital	13
Current Assets	13

Leyburn

Barber Health Care
Unit 3 Beckside Court, Harmby Road, Leyburn, DL8 5QA
Tel: 01969-625995 **Fax:** 01969-623961
E-mail: info@barberhealthcare.com
Website: http://www.barberhealthcare.com
Directors: E. Barber (Dir)
Ultimate Holding Company: Glovo Holding SDN BHD
Immediate Holding Company: Barber Health Care Ltd
Registration no: 06234602 **VAT No.:** GB 698 2517 85
Date established: 2007 **Turnover:** £500,000 - £1m
No.of Employees: 1 - 10 **Product Groups:** 29, 85

Date of Accounts	Mar 10	Mar 09	Mar 08
Working Capital	-5	-4	-16
Fixed Assets	6	11	10
Current Assets	203	168	193

Copley Decor Ltd
1 Leyburn Business Park Harmby Road, Leyburn, DL8 5QA
Tel: 01969-623410 **Fax:** 01969-624398
E-mail: info@copleydecor.co.uk
Website: http://www.copleydecor.co.uk
Directors: B. Storr (MD), W. Horton (Co Sec)
Immediate Holding Company: SANDCO 1233 LIMITED
Registration no: 02393861 **VAT No.:** GB 292 7898 90
Date established: 1989 **Turnover:** £500,000 - £1m
No.of Employees: 1 - 10 **Product Groups:** 30

Date of Accounts	Dec 11	Dec 10	Dec 09
Working Capital	138	137	127
Fixed Assets	N/A	9	23
Current Assets	138	220	296

Weatherald Wood Components Ltd
Abbey Works Askrigg, Leyburn, DL8 3JT
Tel: 01969-650160 **Fax:** 01969-650661
E-mail: sales@weatheraldwood.com
Website: http://www.weatheraldwood.com
Directors: J. Bianco (Fin), R. Fishwick (MD)
Managers: D. Glancy
Ultimate Holding Company: HAMBLETON HOLDINGS LIMITED
Immediate Holding Company: WEATHERALD WOOD COMPONENTS LIMITED
Registration no: 03938497 **Date established:** 2000
No.of Employees: 21 - 50 **Product Groups:** 25, 26, 47, 48, 63, 66, 67, 84

Date of Accounts	Dec 11	Mar 11	Mar 10
Working Capital	731	520	482
Fixed Assets	324	325	314
Current Assets	1m	1m	1m
Current Liabilities	N/A	519	N/A

Wensleydale Longwool Sheep Shop
Cross Lanes Farm Garriston, Leyburn, DL8 5JU
Tel: 01969-623840 **Fax:** 01969-623840
E-mail: sheepshop@lineone.net
Website: http://www.wensleydalelongwoolsheepshop.co.uk
Directors: A. Bowlam (Prop)
Turnover: Up to £250,000 **No.of Employees:** 1 - 10 **Product Groups:** 23

Malton

J Anderson & Son
4 Saville Street, Malton, YO17 7LL
Tel: 01653-692367 **Fax:** 01653-691149
Directors: S. Fletcher (Prop)
Date established: 1979 **No.of Employees:** 1 - 10 **Product Groups:** 36, 39, 40

A Basnett
The Forge Espersykes, Old Malton, Malton, YO17 6RE
Tel: 01653-694001 **Fax:** 01653-694001
E-mail: andybasnett@hotmail.com
Directors: A. Basnett (Prop)
Registration no: 04745949 **Date established:** 2003
No.of Employees: 1 - 10 **Product Groups:** 26, 35

Boortmalt Group
Maltings West Knapton, Malton, YO17 6RN
Tel: 01944-753000 **Fax:** 01944-758682
E-mail: charles.halliwell@paulsmalt.co.uk
Website: http://www.ukmalt.com
Managers: K. Drillot (Mgr)
Date established: 1958 **No.of Employees:** 21 - 50 **Product Groups:** 20, 40, 41

Bright Steels Ltd
Norton Works, Malton, YO17 9BD
Tel: 01653-694961 **Fax:** 01653-695856
E-mail: sales@bright-steels.com
Website: http://www.bright-steels.com
Bank(s): National Westminster Bank Plc
Directors: A. Chouler (Dir), P. Jackson (Comm)
Managers: D. Paterson (Buyer), R. Rawson, S. Morris (Tech Serv Mgr)
Immediate Holding Company: BRIGHT STEELS LIMITED
Registration no: 00159061 **VAT No.:** GB 166 8255 35
Date established: 2019 **Turnover:** £10m - £20m
No.of Employees: 51 - 100 **Product Groups:** 34

Date of Accounts	Dec 11	Dec 10	Dec 09
Sales Turnover	16m	12m	8m
Pre Tax Profit/Loss	2m	883	-544
Working Capital	8m	7m	7m
Fixed Assets	2m	2m	2m
Current Assets	11m	10m	8m
Current Liabilities	936	810	348

Ellis Patents Ltd
High Street Rillington, Malton, YO17 8LA
Tel: 01944-758395 **Fax:** 01944-758808
E-mail: sales@ellispatents.co.uk
Website: http://www.ellispatents.co.uk
Bank(s): Barclays, Malton
Directors: P. Sargent (Fin)
Ultimate Holding Company: ELLIS PATENTS HOLDINGS LIMITED
Immediate Holding Company: ELLIS PATENTS LIMITED
Registration no: 01293983 **VAT No.:** GB 335 2146 81
Date established: 1977 **Turnover:** £5m - £10m
No.of Employees: 51 - 100 **Product Groups:** 30, 36, 37

Date of Accounts	Feb 12	Feb 11	Feb 10
Sales Turnover	5m	5m	5m
Pre Tax Profit/Loss	610	631	807
Working Capital	2m	2m	2m
Fixed Assets	3m	3m	3m
Current Assets	3m	2m	2m
Current Liabilities	429	318	436

Escada Systems Ltd
Swinton Grange, Malton, YO17 6QR
Tel: 01653-697378 **Fax:** 01653-697595
E-mail: sandra.hinds@escadasystems.co.uk
Website: http://www.escadasystems.co.uk
Directors: G. Bushby (Ch), M. Reed (Dir)
Registration no: 01939461 **VAT No.:** GB 433 5348 58
Turnover: £2m - £5m **No.of Employees:** 21 - 50 **Product Groups:** 37, 44

Date of Accounts	Aug 10	Aug 09	Aug 08
Working Capital	-258	-125	-182
Fixed Assets	884	875	882
Current Assets	31	167	79

Grand Age Engineering Ltd
Elm Tree Farm Kirby Misperton, Malton, YO17 6XT
Tel: 01653-668288 **Fax:** 01653-668289
E-mail: sales@grandsweep.com
Website: http://www.grandsweep.com

Directors: C. Lund (Fin), J. Lund (MD)
Immediate Holding Company: GRANDAGE ENGINEERING LIMITED
Registration no: 03819545 **Date established:** 1999
Turnover: £250,000 - £500,000 **No.of Employees:** 1 - 10
Product Groups: 67

Date of Accounts	May 11	May 10	May 09
Working Capital	63	55	40
Fixed Assets	16	14	16
Current Assets	86	85	55

The Gun Room

Barthorpe Grange Barthorpe, Malton, YO17 9RW
Tel: 01759-369980 **Fax:** 01759-369968
E-mail: info@thegun-room.co.uk
Website: http://www.thegun-room.co.uk
Directors: R. Hall (Prop)
Date established: 2006 **No.of Employees:** 1 - 10 **Product Groups:** 36, 39, 40

Hydramotion Ltd

1 Seven Street York Road Business Park, Malton, YO17 6YA
Tel: 01653-600294 **Fax:** 01653-693446
E-mail: sales@hydramotion.com
Website: http://www.hydramotion.com
Directors: J. Gallagher (MD)
Managers: O. Brown (Tech Serv Mgr), R. Simpson (Mktg Serv Mgr), D. Morbey (Sales Prom Mgr)
Immediate Holding Company: HYDRAMOTION LIMITED
Registration no: 02074338 **Date established:** 1986
No.of Employees: 11 - 20 **Product Groups:** 38, 67

Date of Accounts	Nov 11	Nov 10	Nov 09
Working Capital	893	605	929
Fixed Assets	424	450	470
Current Assets	1m	1m	1m

Jewson Ltd

Showfield Lane, Malton, YO17 6BT
Tel: 01653-600073 **Fax:** 01653-600239
Website: http://www.jewson.co.uk
Managers: D. Usherwood (Mgr)
Ultimate Holding Company: COMPAGNIE DE SAINT GOBAIN (FRANCE)
Immediate Holding Company: JEWSON LIMITED
Registration no: 00348407 **VAT No.:** GB 497 7184 83
Date established: 1939 **No.of Employees:** 11 - 20 **Product Groups:** 66

Date of Accounts	Dec 11	Dec 10	Dec 09
Sales Turnover	1606m	1547m	1485m
Pre Tax Profit/Loss	18m	100m	45m
Working Capital	-345m	-250m	-349m
Fixed Assets	496m	387m	461m
Current Assets	657m	1005m	1320m
Current Liabilities	66m	120m	64m

Malton Motors Ltd

York Road, Malton, YO17 6TB
Tel: 0845-128 6402 **Fax:** 01653-693010
Website: http://www.maltonbmw.co.uk
Directors: C. Mccormack (Dir)
Managers: M. Whiteley (Chief Mgr)
Ultimate Holding Company: Inchcape plc
Immediate Holding Company: European Motor Holdings Ltd
Registration no: 00554231 **Turnover:** £125m - £250m
No.of Employees: 251 - 500 **Product Groups:** 68

Neaco Ltd

Norton Grove Industrial Estate Scarborough Road, Norton, Malton, YO17 9HQ
Tel: 01653-695721 **Fax:** 01653-600418
E-mail: sales@neaco.co.uk
Website: http://www.neaco.co.uk
Directors: A. Green (Sales), D. North (I.T. Dir), P. Sparks (Fin)
Managers: P. Buridge (Ops Mgr), R. Richardson-derry (Nat Sales Mgr)
Immediate Holding Company: NEACO LIMITED
Registration no: 03056577 **VAT No.:** GB 168 2239 51
Date established: 1995 **Turnover:** £2m - £5m **No.of Employees:** 21 - 50
Product Groups: 35

Date of Accounts	Mar 11	Mar 10	Mar 09
Pre Tax Profit/Loss	N/A	N/A	250
Working Capital	-188	-38	-189
Fixed Assets	919	919	919
Current Assets	N/A	137	N/A

Paleys Bros

1 Castle Howard Drive, Malton, YO17 7BA
Tel: 07790-547676
E-mail: lloydwilliam1982@yahoo.co.uk
Website: http://www.paley-bros.co.uk
Directors: L. Paley (Prop)
No.of Employees: 1 - 10 **Product Groups:** 45, 51, 83

Remote Marine Systems

Derwent Road York Road Business Park, Malton, YO17 6YB
Tel: 01653-690001 **Fax:** 01653-690002
E-mail: sales@rmsltd.com
Website: http://www.rmsltd.com
Bank(s): HSBC
Directors: D. Wardie (Tech Serv), G. Robertson (Jt MD), J. Vick (Co Sec), S. Everett (Sales)
Ultimate Holding Company: James Fisher & Sons plc
Immediate Holding Company: James Fisher Nuclear Ltd
Registration no: 01745584 **Date established:** 1926 **Turnover:** £2m - £5m
No.of Employees: 21 - 50 **Product Groups:** 45

Date of Accounts	Dec 06	Dec 05
Sales Turnover	3188	4649
Pre Tax Profit/Loss	869	993
Working Capital	3260	3133
Fixed Assets	466	461
Current Assets	4102	4338
Current Liabilities	842	1205
Total Share Capital	41	41
ROCE% (Return on Capital Employed)	23.3	27.6
ROT% (Return on Turnover)	27.3	21.4

Rimco Services (t/a Rimco Services)

20 Orchard Road, Malton, YO17 7BH
Tel: 01653-600707 **Fax:** 01653-696888
E-mail: sales@rimco.co.uk
Website: http://www.rimco.co.uk
Directors: A. Cuthbertson (Prop)
Immediate Holding Company: RIMCO SERVICES LIMITED
Registration no: 02729159 **Date established:** 1992
Turnover: £250,000 - £500,000 **No.of Employees:** 1 - 10
Product Groups: 30, 31

Date of Accounts	Jun 11	Jun 10	Jun 09
Working Capital	-35	-43	-33
Fixed Assets	3	4	6
Current Assets	25	15	19

Robinson & Co.

Norton Road Norton, Malton, YO17 9RU
Tel: 01653-697442 **Fax:** 01653-696555
E-mail: sales@robinsonsequestrian.co.uk
Website: http://www.robinsonsequestrian.co.uk
Managers: S. Hancock (District Mgr)
No.of Employees: 1 - 10 **Product Groups:** 20, 22, 24, 49, 63

Stained & Leaded Glass

3 Rectory Close West Heslerton, Malton, YO17 8RZ
Tel: 01944-728469 **Fax:** 07050-656779
E-mail: chris@stainedandleadedglass.co.uk
Website: http://www.stainedandleadedglass.co.uk
Directors: C. Dixon (Prop)
Turnover: Up to £250,000 **No.of Employees:** 1 - 10 **Product Groups:** 33, 40, 45

T G Precision Engineering Ltd

Derwent Road York Road Business Park, Malton, YO17 6YB
Tel: 01653-600378 **Fax:** 01653-695317
E-mail: kevin@tgprecisionengineeringltd.co.uk
Website: http://www.tgprecisionengineeringltd.co.uk
Directors: K. Gray (Dir)
Immediate Holding Company: T.G. PRECISION ENGINEERING LIMITED
Registration no: 02448880 **VAT No.:** GB 501 0707 09
Date established: 1989 **Turnover:** Up to £250,000
No.of Employees: 1 - 10 **Product Groups:** 48

Date of Accounts	Dec 11	Dec 10	Dec 09
Working Capital	10	9	5
Fixed Assets	18	19	25
Current Assets	65	48	39

Tate Smith Ltd

Sundella House Castlegate, Malton, YO17 7EE
Tel: 01653-693196 **Fax:** 01653-600376
E-mail: info@tatesmith.com
Website: http://www.tatesmith.com
Bank(s): National Westminster
Directors: C. Tate Smith (Co Sec), P. Tate Smith (MD)
Managers: L. Reed (Mktg Serv Mgr), M. Sellers (Buyer)
Immediate Holding Company: TATE-SMITH LIMITED
Registration no: 00653307 **Date established:** 1960
No.of Employees: 21 - 50 **Product Groups:** 62

Date of Accounts	Jan 12	Jan 11	Jan 10
Working Capital	601	589	442
Fixed Assets	623	610	682
Current Assets	2m	2m	2m

Travis Perkins plc

7 Seph Way York Road Industrial Estate, Malton, YO17 6YF
Tel: 01653-692444 **Fax:** 01653-600453
E-mail: david.harcourt@travisperkins.co.uk
Website: http://www.travisperkins.co.uk
Managers: D. Harcourt (Mgr)
Immediate Holding Company: TRAVIS PERKINS PLC
Registration no: 00824821 **Date established:** 1964
Turnover: Over £1,000m **No.of Employees:** 1 - 10 **Product Groups:** 66

Date of Accounts	Dec 11	Dec 10	Dec 09
Sales Turnover	4779m	3153m	2931m
Pre Tax Profit/Loss	270m	197m	213m
Working Capital	133m	159m	248m
Fixed Assets	2771m	2749m	2108m
Current Assets	1421m	1329m	1035m
Current Liabilities	473m	412m	109m

Ward Insulated Panels Ltd

Sherburn, Malton, YO17 8PQ
Tel: 01944-710591 **Fax:** 01944-710777
E-mail: wbc@wards.co.uk
Website: http://www.wards.co.uk
Bank(s): Barclays
Directors: T. Clark (Sales)
Managers: A. Tolley (Chief Buyer)
Ultimate Holding Company: Kingspan Group P.L.C
Registration no: 03263720 **Turnover:** £75m - £125m
No.of Employees: 251 - 500 **Product Groups:** 35

Date of Accounts	Dec 07	Dec 06	Dec 05
Sales Turnover	47745	44275	44233
Pre Tax Profit/Loss	2954	3210	2564
Working Capital	5234	7099	5067
Current Assets	14911	12651	14921
Current Liabilities	9677	5552	9854
Total Share Capital	50	50	50
ROCE% (Return on Capital Employed)	56.5	45.2	50.6
ROT% (Return on Turnover)	6.2	7.3	5.8

World Wide Shopping Mall Ltd

Chancery Lane, Malton, YO17 7HW
Tel: 01653-602880
E-mail: sales@worldwideshoppingmall.co.uk
Website: http://www.worldwideshoppingmall.co.uk
Directors: M. Chalk (MD), S. Chalk (Fin)
Immediate Holding Company: WORLD WIDE SHOPPING MALL LIMITED
Registration no: 03307834 **Date established:** 1997
No.of Employees: 11 - 20 **Product Groups:** 25, 30, 33, 36, 63

Date of Accounts	Dec 11	Dec 10	Dec 09
Working Capital	127	139	136
Fixed Assets	3	6	9
Current Assets	324	342	315
Current Liabilities	74	67	88

Northallerton

Allerton Steel Ltd

Allerton House Thurston Road, Northallerton, DL6 2NA
Tel: 01609-774471 **Fax:** 01609-780364
E-mail: reception@allertonsteel.co.uk
Website: http://www.allertonsteel.co.uk
Directors: G. Penn (Dir), P. Denning (Sales)
Managers: E. Tracey (Buyer), A. Blackwell (Personnel)
Ultimate Holding Company: ALLERTON GROUP LIMITED
Immediate Holding Company: AE 2009 LIMITED
Registration no: 01451804 **Date established:** 1979 **Turnover:** £5m - £10m
No.of Employees: 51 - 100 **Product Groups:** 35, 45

Date of Accounts	Dec 07	Dec 06	Dec 05
Sales Turnover	6m	5m	5m
Pre Tax Profit/Loss	919	723	855
Working Capital	-5	-4	2m
Fixed Assets	615	242	334
Current Assets	4m	3m	3m
Current Liabilities	1m	572	640

Lewis & Cooper Ltd

92 High Street, Northallerton, DL7 8PT
Tel: 01609-772880 **Fax:** 01609-777933
E-mail: sales@lewis-and-cooper.co.uk
Website: http://www.lewisandcooper.co.uk
Managers: B. Bell
Immediate Holding Company: LEWIS & COOPER LIMITED
Registration no: 00076221 **Date established:** 2003
Turnover: £500,000 - £1m **No.of Employees:** 1 - 10 **Product Groups:** 20, 33, 49, 65, 81

Date of Accounts	Mar 11	Mar 10	Mar 09
Working Capital	-149	-30	29
Fixed Assets	883	904	924
Current Assets	477	497	390

North Yorkshire Fire Protection Co.

280 High Street, Northallerton, DL7 8DW
Tel: 01609-779746 **Fax:** 01609-779746
Directors: J. Logan (Prop)
Date established: 2003 **No.of Employees:** 1 - 10 **Product Groups:** 38, 42

Northallerton Shooting Supplies

1 The Fairway, Northallerton, DL7 8AY
Tel: 01609-774922 **Fax:** 01609-774922
Website: http://www.nsac.co.uk
Managers: T. Pickersgill (Mgr)
Date established: 1994 **No.of Employees:** 1 - 10 **Product Groups:** 36, 39, 40

Prest Engineering

Springhouse Farm Northallerton Road, Scruton, Northallerton, DL7 9LG
Tel: 01677-423386 **Fax:** 01677-423387
E-mail: info@prestengineering.co.uk
Website: http://www.prestengineering.co.uk
Directors: P. Prest (Prop)
Date established: 1999 **No.of Employees:** 1 - 10 **Product Groups:** 35

Tanfield Engineering Services

Tutin Road Leeming Bar Industrial Estate, Northallerton, DL7 9UJ
Tel: 01677-423370 **Fax:** 01677-423370
E-mail: tanfieldengineer@aol.com
Website: http://www.tanfieldengineering.co.uk
Managers: K. Bosworth (Mgr)
Immediate Holding Company: TANFIELD ENGINEERING SERVICES LIMITED
Registration no: 07263240 **Date established:** 2010
No.of Employees: 1 - 10 **Product Groups:** 35

Date of Accounts	Mar 11
Working Capital	25
Fixed Assets	4
Current Assets	154

Walter Thompson Contractors Ltd (a division of the FT Construction Group)

17 High Street North End, Northallerton, DL7 8ED
Tel: 01609-780700 **Fax:** 01609-777236
E-mail: wtcl@ftcg.co.uk
Website: http://www.stcg.co.uk
Bank(s): Lloyds TSB Bank plc
Directors: N. Fordy (MD), P. Blade (Dir)
Managers: R. Chaimberline (Sales Admin), P. Blade (Ops Mgr), M. Teesdale (Buyer), M. Sharp (I.T. Exec), K. Caygill (Personnel)
Ultimate Holding Company: F.T. CONSTRUCTION GROUP (HOLDINGS) LTD.
Immediate Holding Company: WALTER THOMPSON (CONTRACTORS) LIMITED
Registration no: 00402706 **VAT No.:** GB 258 1699 21
Date established: 1946 **Turnover:** £20m - £50m
No.of Employees: 21 - 50 **Product Groups:** 51, 52

Date of Accounts	Dec 10	Dec 09	Dec 08
Sales Turnover	20m	23m	27m
Pre Tax Profit/Loss	425	1m	814
Working Capital	2m	2m	138
Fixed Assets	541	649	3m
Current Assets	6m	5m	5m
Current Liabilities	590	751	1m

Wallace Wrought Iron

Archers Yard Springwell Lane, Northallerton, DL7 8QJ
Tel: 01609-779092 **Fax:** 01609-779092
Directors: D. Wallace (Prop)
Date established: 2006 **No.of Employees:** 1 - 10 **Product Groups:** 26, 35

Pickering

Andrew R Cornforth
Westfield Grange Cropton Lane, Pickering, YO18 8HQ
Tel: 01751-417416
Website: http://www.arcaggric.co.uk
Directors: A. Cornforth (Prop)
Date established: 1984 **No.of Employees:** 1 - 10 **Product Groups:** 41

Interpower International
PO Box 70, Pickering, YO18 7XU
Tel: 01751-474034 **Fax:** 01751-476103
E-mail: info@interpower.co.uk
Website: http://www.interpower.co.uk
Directors: J. Hudson (MD), E. Hudson (Co Sec)
Immediate Holding Company: INTERPOWER INTERNATIONAL LIMITED
Registration no: 01982614 **VAT No.:** GB 601 8661 56
Date established: 1986 **Turnover:** £5m - £10m **No.of Employees:** 11 - 20
Product Groups: 37, 67

Date of Accounts	May 11	May 10	May 09
Sales Turnover	N/A	3m	N/A
Pre Tax Profit/Loss	N/A	295	N/A
Working Capital	343	256	28
Fixed Assets	60	53	45
Current Assets	975	843	1m
Current Liabilities	N/A	259	N/A

Invicta Bakeware Ltd
Westgate Business Park Westgate Carr Road, Pickering, YO18 8LX
Tel: 01751-473483 **Fax:** 01751-476522
E-mail: john@invictabakeware.co.uk
Website: http://www.invictabakeware.co.uk
Bank(s): HSBC Bank plc
Directors: G. Gregory (Co Sec), J. Waddington (MD)
Ultimate Holding Company: INVICTA BAKEWARE HOLDINGS LIMITED
Immediate Holding Company: INVICTA BAKEWARE LIMITED
Registration no: 00204587 **VAT No.:** GB 169 6723 20
Date established: 2025 **Turnover:** £1m - £2m **No.of Employees:** 21 - 50
Product Groups: 41

Date of Accounts	Dec 11	Dec 10	Dec 09
Working Capital	912	783	767
Fixed Assets	483	504	531
Current Assets	1m	1m	1m

Jewson Ltd
Vivis Lane, Pickering, YO18 8DL
Tel: 01751-476565 **Fax:** 01751-476703
Website: http://www.jewson.co.uk
Managers: P. Marson (District Mgr)
Ultimate Holding Company: COMPAGNIE DE SAINT GOBAIN (FRANCE)
Immediate Holding Company: JEWSON LIMITED
Registration no: 00348407 **VAT No.:** GB 394 1212 63
Date established: 1939 **Turnover:** £2m - £5m **No.of Employees:** 1 - 10
Product Groups: 66

Date of Accounts	Dec 11	Dec 10	Dec 09
Sales Turnover	1606m	1547m	1485m
Pre Tax Profit/Loss	18m	100m	45m
Working Capital	-345m	-250m	-349m
Fixed Assets	496m	387m	461m
Current Assets	657m	1005m	1320m
Current Liabilities	66m	120m	64m

Mckechnie Plastic Components
Westgate Carr Road, Pickering, YO18 8LX
Tel: 01751-471100 **Fax:** 01751-476408
E-mail: john.woodhead@mpcpick.com
Website: http://www.mpcpick.com
Bank(s): National Westminster
Directors: M. Sturgess (Fin), M. Murphy (Sales), J. Woodhead (Dir)
Managers: V. Lovman (Personnel), M. Brearey (Comm), P. Aconley (Tech Serv Mgr)
Immediate Holding Company: INVICTA BAKEWARE HOLDINGS LIMITED
Registration no: 00204587 **VAT No.:** 152 9211 81 **Date established:** 2010
Turnover: £20m - £50m **No.of Employees:** 251 - 500
Product Groups: 48, 84

Date of Accounts	Dec 11	Dec 10
Working Capital	-17	-17
Fixed Assets	1m	1m

Malton Plastics UK Ltd
29 Enterprise Way Thornton Road Indl-Est, Pickering, YO18 7NA
Tel: 01751-477720 **Fax:** 01751-477760
E-mail: sales@maltonplastics.com
Website: http://www.maltonplastics.com
Directors: G. Smith (MD)
Managers: R. Smith (Works Gen Mgr)
Immediate Holding Company: MALTON PLASTICS (UK) LIMITED
Registration no: 04019121 **VAT No.:** GB 747 1067 31
Date established: 2000 **Turnover:** £250,000 - £500,000
No.of Employees: 1 - 10 **Product Groups:** 30, 66

Date of Accounts	Dec 10	Dec 09	Dec 08
Working Capital	40	52	91
Fixed Assets	205	174	184
Current Assets	214	209	207

Pickering Airguns
8 Birdgate, Pickering, YO18 7AL
Tel: 01751-476904 **Fax:** 01751-477773
E-mail: info@pickeringairguns.co.uk
Website: http://www.pickeringairguns.co.uk
Directors: R. Foster (Ptnr)
Date established: 2001 **No.of Employees:** 1 - 10 **Product Groups:** 36, 39, 40

Rosedale Lighting
Red House Rosedale Abbey, Pickering, YO18 8SE
Tel: 01751-417616
Immediate Holding Company: ROSEDALE LIGHTING LTD.
Registration no: 04496329 **Date established:** 2002
No.of Employees: 1 - 10 **Product Groups:** 37, 67

Date of Accounts	Mar 11	Mar 10	Sep 07
Working Capital	-95	-73	27
Fixed Assets	486	487	6
Current Assets	27	50	51

Richmond

Borough House Business Centre
Borough House 5 Borough Road, Gallowfields Trading Estate, Richmond, DL10 4SX
Tel: 01748-822713 **Fax:** 0870-838 6562
E-mail: enquiries@borough-house.co.uk
Website: http://www.borough-house.co.uk
Directors: J. Brown (Prop)
Immediate Holding Company: FORCES HOMES LIMITED
Registration no: 06969886 **Date established:** 2006
No.of Employees: 1 - 10 **Product Groups:** 26, 69, 80, 83

Date of Accounts	Mar 11	Mar 10	Mar 09
Working Capital	9	-12	-15
Fixed Assets	37	44	47
Current Assets	41	11	2

Easby Electronics Ltd
Mercury Road Gallowfields Trading Estate, Richmond, DL10 4TQ
Tel: 01748-850555 **Fax:** 01748-850556
E-mail: ian@easby.co.uk
Website: http://www.easby.com
Bank(s): Lloyds TSB Bank plc
Directors: J. Hodgetts (Sales), T. Morris (MD)
Ultimate Holding Company: EASBY HOLDINGS LIMITED
Immediate Holding Company: EASBY ELECTRONICS LIMITED
Registration no: 01537952 **VAT No.:** GB 324 3146 46
Date established: 1981 **Turnover:** £5m - £10m **No.of Employees:** 21 - 50
Product Groups: 37

Date of Accounts	Feb 08	Feb 11	Feb 10
Sales Turnover	N/A	10m	6m
Pre Tax Profit/Loss	27	441	-21
Working Capital	3m	3m	3m
Fixed Assets	455	956	407
Current Assets	4m	4m	4m
Current Liabilities	102	275	94

Electrical Appliance Testing (E-A-T)
PO Box 120, Richmond, DL10 7XW
Tel: 0800-033 7317 **Fax:** 0871-871 0096
E-mail: sales@e-a-t.co.uk
Website: http://www.e-a-t.co.uk
Directors: T. Edwards (Prop)
No.of Employees: 1 - 10 **Product Groups:** 38, 85

Just Marble Ltd
60 Ravensworth Ravensworth, Richmond, DL11 7ES
Tel: 0191-452 7066 **Fax:** 01325-718433
E-mail: mail@justmarble.co.uk
Website: http://www.justmarble.co.uk
Directors: M. Makin (Dir)
Registration no: 05172361 **Date established:** 2004
No.of Employees: 1 - 10 **Product Groups:** 14, 33, 66

Date of Accounts	Mar 08	Mar 07	Mar 06
Working Capital	-1	2	1
Fixed Assets	2	2	1
Current Assets	28	41	34
Current Liabilities	29	38	33

Merlin Control System Ltd
Station Road Brompton on Swale, Richmond, DL10 7SE
Tel: 01748-810811 **Fax:** 01748-810881
E-mail: info@merlin-controls.com
Website: http://www.merlin-controls.com
Directors: L. Lamont (Fin), D. Lamont (MD)
Immediate Holding Company: MERLIN CONTROL SYSTEMS LIMITED
Registration no: 03799143 **VAT No.:** GB 734 0291 56
Date established: 1999 **No.of Employees:** 1 - 10 **Product Groups:** 37, 38, 45, 46, 48

Date of Accounts	Jun 11	Jun 10	Jun 09
Working Capital	16	-3	6
Fixed Assets	156	163	170
Current Assets	97	65	77

Pipeline Engineering & Supply Company Ltd
Gatherley Road Industrial Estate Brompton On Swale, Richmond, DL10 7JG
Tel: 01748-813000 **Fax:** 01748-818039
E-mail: sales@pipelineengineering.com
Website: http://www.pipelineengineering.com
Directors: J. Benn (Fin), A. Marwood (Dir), D. Bacon (I.T. Dir), N. Bowerman (Fin)
Managers: C. Marshall (Projects), K. Rolf (Tech Serv Mgr)
Ultimate Holding Company: CIRCOR INTERNATIONAL INC (USA)
Immediate Holding Company: PIPELINE ENGINEERING & SUPPLY CO. LIMITED
Registration no: 03341992 **VAT No.:** GB 258 0307 69
Date established: 1997 **Turnover:** £20m - £50m
No.of Employees: 101 - 250 **Product Groups:** 30, 31, 34, 35, 36, 38, 42, 45, 48, 51, 54, 85

Date of Accounts	Dec 11	Dec 10	Dec 09
Sales Turnover	22m	20m	11m
Pre Tax Profit/Loss	2m	-147	-54
Working Capital	4m	2m	2m
Fixed Assets	4m	5m	4m
Current Assets	12m	9m	7m
Current Liabilities	3m	2m	1m

Reeth Garage Ltd
Arkengarthdale Road Reeth, Richmond, DL11 6QT
Tel: 01748-84243 **Fax:** 01748-884691
E-mail: reeth.garage@virgin.net
Directors: H. Smith (Co Sec), J. Robinson (MD)
Immediate Holding Company: REETH GARAGE LIMITED
Registration no: 01351540 **Date established:** 1978
Turnover: £500,000 - £1m **No.of Employees:** 11 - 20 **Product Groups:** 41

Date of Accounts	Apr 10	Apr 09	Apr 08
Working Capital	191	180	151
Fixed Assets	244	249	257
Current Assets	291	280	303

Viking Heating
119 Brompton Park Brompton on Swale, Richmond, DL10 7JR
Tel: 01748-818622
E-mail: enquiries@vikingheating.co.uk
Website: http://www.vikingheating.co.uk
Directors: A. Beswick (Prop)
No.of Employees: 1 - 10 **Product Groups:** 40, 52

Ripon

Agri Motors Of Dallowgill
Greystone Edge Kirkby Moor Road, Kirkby Malzeard, Ripon, HG4 3QR
Tel: 01765-658558
Directors: E. Sidgwick (Prop)
Date established: 1945 **No.of Employees:** 1 - 10 **Product Groups:** 41

Allton Contractors Ltd
Ure Bank Top, Ripon, HG4 1JE
Tel: 01765-604351 **Fax:** 01765-600669
E-mail: alton@eborconcrete.co.uk
Website: http://www.eborconcrete.co.uk
Directors: A. Riley Smith (Co Sec), A. Riley-Smith (Co Sec), I. Riley (MD), M. Hutchinson (Ch)
Managers: A. Carr (Admin Off)
Ultimate Holding Company: MEADS TRUST.LIMITED
Immediate Holding Company: ALLTON CONTRACTORS LIMITED
Registration no: 00331349 **VAT No.:** GB 169 1788 17
Date established: 1937 **Turnover:** £2m - £5m **No.of Employees:** 1 - 10
Product Groups: 52

Date of Accounts	Mar 11	Mar 10	Mar 09
Working Capital	-85	118	344
Fixed Assets	55	77	83
Current Assets	265	521	576

Black Sheep Brewery plc
Wellgarth Crosshills, Masham, Ripon, HG4 4EN
Tel: 01765-689227 **Fax:** 01765-689746
E-mail: reception@blacksheep.co.uk
Website: http://www.blacksheepbrewery.com
Directors: S. Constable (Co Sec), B. Smith (Sales)
Managers: H. Allison
Immediate Holding Company: THE BLACK SHEEP BREWERY PLC
Registration no: 02686985 **Date established:** 1992
Turnover: £10m - £20m **No.of Employees:** 101 - 250 **Product Groups:** 21

Date of Accounts	Mar 12	Mar 11	Mar 10
Sales Turnover	20m	18m	19m
Pre Tax Profit/Loss	504	465	614
Working Capital	-11	101	429
Fixed Assets	10m	10m	9m
Current Assets	4m	4m	4m
Current Liabilities	1m	2m	1m

C P L Petroleum
Dallamires Lane, Ripon, HG4 1TT
Tel: 01765-607606 **Fax:** 01765-606715
E-mail: ripon@cplpetroleum.co.uk
Website: http://www.cplpetroleum.co.uk
Managers: A. Storey (Mgr)
Ultimate Holding Company: CPL INDUSTRIES HOLDINGS LIMITED
Immediate Holding Company: CPL PETROLEUM LIMITED
Registration no: 03003860 **VAT No.:** GB 721 5764 39
Date established: 1994 **Turnover:** £50m - £75m **No.of Employees:** 1 - 10
Product Groups: 66

Date of Accounts	Mar 12	Mar 11	Mar 10
Pre Tax Profit/Loss	N/A	878	904
Working Capital	31	30m	30m
Fixed Assets	26	26m	26m
Current Assets	57	56m	56m
Current Liabilities	26	246	253

Ebor Concrete Ltd
PO Box 4, Ripon, HG4 1JE
Tel: 01765-604351 **Fax:** 01765-690065
E-mail: paul.whitham@eborconcrete.co.uk
Website: http://www.eborconcrete.co.uk
Directors: P. Whitham (MD)
Ultimate Holding Company: MEADS TRUST.LIMITED
Immediate Holding Company: EBOR CONCRETES LIMITED
Registration no: 00375753 **Date established:** 1942 **Turnover:** £1m - £2m
No.of Employees: 1 - 10 **Product Groups:** 33

Date of Accounts	Mar 11	Mar 10	Mar 09
Working Capital	240	319	567
Fixed Assets	778	841	821
Current Assets	674	759	1m

Econ Engineering Ltd
Boroughbridge Road, Ripon, HG4 1UE
Tel: 01765-605321 **Fax:** 01765-607487
E-mail: sales@econ.uk.com
Website: http://www.econ.uk.com
Directors: A. Lupton (Sales)
Managers: D. Dench (Sales Admin), K. Price (Purch Mgr)
Immediate Holding Company: ECON ENGINEERING LIMITED
Registration no: 00644062 **VAT No.:** GB 500 5794 66
Date established: 1959 **Turnover:** £20m - £50m
No.of Employees: 51 - 100 **Product Groups:** 45

Date of Accounts	Mar 11	Mar 10	Mar 09
Sales Turnover	23m	20m	N/A
Pre Tax Profit/Loss	2m	562	2m
Working Capital	7m	8m	9m
Fixed Assets	12m	9m	8m
Current Assets	19m	16m	13m
Current Liabilities	8m	6m	3m

Hemingways Marketing Services
Metcalfe House 23h Kirkgate, Ripon, HG4 1PB
Tel: 01765-607070 **Fax:** 01765-690218
E-mail: andrewjohnson@dial.pipex.com
Website: http://www.voucherexpress.co.uk
Directors: C. Bentley (Co Sec), M. Johnson (MD)
Managers: D. Naylor (Tech Serv Mgr), D. Solan (Sales & Mktg Mg), J. Baker-hood (Personnel)
Ultimate Holding Company: HEMINGWAYS (FURNISHERS) LIMITED
Immediate Holding Company: HEMINGWAYS MARKETING SERVICES LIMITED
Registration no: 00453174 **Date established:** 1948
Turnover: £20m - £50m **No.of Employees:** 21 - 50 **Product Groups:** 20, 49, 62, 81, 82

Date of Accounts	Apr 11	Apr 10	Apr 09
Sales Turnover	39m	35m	37m
Pre Tax Profit/Loss	929	1m	839

Working Capital	7m	6m	6m
Fixed Assets	171	147	160
Current Assets	10m	10m	10m
Current Liabilities	135	61	78

Jewson Ltd

Bondgate Green, Ripon, HG4 1QW
Tel: 01765-601666 **Fax:** 01765-604359
Website: http://www.jewson.co.uk
Managers: B. Parkin (Mgr)
Ultimate Holding Company: COMPAGNIE DE SAINT GOBAIN (FRANCE)
Immediate Holding Company: JEWSON LIMITED
Registration no: 00348407 **Date established:** 1939
Turnover: £500m - £1,000m **No.of Employees:** 1 - 10
Product Groups: 66

Date of Accounts	Dec 11	Dec 10	Dec 09
Sales Turnover	1606m	1547m	1485m
Pre Tax Profit/Loss	18m	100m	45m
Working Capital	-345m	-250m	-349m
Fixed Assets	496m	387m	461m
Current Assets	657m	1005m	1320m
Current Liabilities	66m	120m	64m

Nidd Transport Ltd

Barker Business Park Melmerby Green Lane, Melmerby, Ripon, HG4 5NB
Tel: 01765-641510 **Fax:** 01765-641550
E-mail: jane@nidd-transport.com
Website: http://www.nidd-transport.com
Directors: T. White (MD), S. Curtis (Dir), H. Glegg (Fin)
Immediate Holding Company: NIDD TRANSPORT LIMITED
Registration no: 01841325 **Date established:** 1984 **Turnover:** £5m - £10m
No.of Employees: 21 - 50 **Product Groups:** 77

Date of Accounts	Apr 11	Apr 10	Apr 09
Sales Turnover	7m	7m	7m
Pre Tax Profit/Loss	228	306	169
Working Capital	292	776	647
Fixed Assets	2m	166	201
Current Assets	2m	2m	2m
Current Liabilities	187	187	143

Potter Group Ltd

Melmerby Indl-Est Melmerby Green Lane, Melmerby, Ripon, HG4 5HP
Tel: 01765-640495 **Fax:** 01765-640588
E-mail: enquiries@pottergroup.co.uk
Website: http://www.pottergroup.co.uk
Directors: M. Steele (Fin)
Managers: P. Reed (I.T. Exec), J. Ganley (Mgr), C. Watts (Mgr), C. Watt (Chief Mgr), D. Hick (Develop Mgr)
Ultimate Holding Company: THE POTTER GROUP (HOLDINGS) PLC
Immediate Holding Company: THE POTTER GROUP LIMITED
Registration no: 01392251 **Date established:** 1978
Turnover: £10m - £20m **No.of Employees:** 21 - 50 **Product Groups:** 07, 39, 45, 72, 77, 80, 84

Date of Accounts	Apr 11	Apr 10	Apr 09
Sales Turnover	15m	15m	16m
Pre Tax Profit/Loss	447	355	28
Working Capital	7m	7m	6m
Fixed Assets	4m	3m	4m
Current Assets	11m	10m	11m
Current Liabilities	2m	1m	3m

Quasar Automation

Unit Q Old Sleningford Farm North Stainley, Ripon, HG4 3JB
Tel: 01765-635508 **Fax:** 01765-635588
E-mail: admin@quasar.gb.com
Website: http://www.quasar.gb.com
Directors: R. Hinchcliffe (MD), S. Hinchcliffe (Fin)
Immediate Holding Company: QUASAR AUTOMATION LIMITED
Registration no: 07452457 **Date established:** 2010
Turnover: £500,000 - £1m **No.of Employees:** 11 - 20
Product Groups: 20, 40, 41

Date of Accounts	Jan 12
Working Capital	28
Fixed Assets	32
Current Assets	64

Ripon Select Foods Ltd

Dallamires Way North, Ripon, HG4 1TL
Tel: 01765-601711 **Fax:** 01765-607481
E-mail: thomas@rsf.co.uk
Website: http://www.rsf.co.uk
Bank(s): Barclays
Directors: A. Gordon (Co Sec), T. Wood (MD)
Immediate Holding Company: RIPON SELECT FOODS LIMITED
Registration no: 01161649 **VAT No.:** 171 5790 51 **Date established:** 1974
Turnover: £10m - £20m **No.of Employees:** 51 - 100 **Product Groups:** 20

Date of Accounts	Mar 11	Mar 10	Mar 09
Sales Turnover	20m	19m	N/A
Pre Tax Profit/Loss	476	322	-110
Working Capital	2m	1m	2m
Fixed Assets	6m	6m	5m
Current Assets	5m	4m	5m
Current Liabilities	922	1m	1m

Ritchey Ltd

Fearby Road Masham, Ripon, HG4 4ES
Tel: 01765-689541 **Fax:** 01765-689851
E-mail: info@ritchey.co.uk
Website: http://www.ritchey.co.uk
Bank(s): Barclays
Managers: N. Hale (Personnel), K. Parker (Comptroller), N. Myers (Ops Mgr), P. Alderson (Tech Serv Mgr), S. Nowaczek (Mktg Serv Mgr)
Ultimate Holding Company: ANIMALCARE GROUP PLC
Immediate Holding Company: ANIMALCARE LTD
Registration no: 01500876 **VAT No.:** GB 997 3108 79
Date established: 1980 **Turnover:** £10m - £20m
No.of Employees: 51 - 100 **Product Groups:** 30

Date of Accounts	Jun 11	Jun 10	Jun 09
Sales Turnover	12m	11m	10m
Pre Tax Profit/Loss	3m	3m	2m
Working Capital	1m	3m	2m
Fixed Assets	922	988	818
Current Assets	4m	5m	4m
Current Liabilities	1m	1m	649

UK Site Painters Ltd

Markenfield Hall, Ripon, HG4 3AD
Tel: 01765-609147
E-mail: uksitepainters@aol.com
Website: http://www.uksitepainters.co.uk
Directors: A. Foster (MD)
Immediate Holding Company: UK SITE PAINTERS LIMITED
Registration no: 04870402 **Date established:** 2003
No.of Employees: 1 - 10 **Product Groups:** 52

Date of Accounts	Aug 11	Aug 10	Aug 09
Working Capital	217	128	294
Fixed Assets	469	477	267
Current Assets	290	216	415

T & R Williamson Ltd

36 Stonebridgegate, Ripon, HG4 1TP
Tel: 01765-607711 **Fax:** 01765-607908
E-mail: info@trwilliamson.co.uk
Website: http://www.trwilliamson.co.uk
Directors: A. Sheibani (Dir)
Immediate Holding Company: T.& R.WILLIAMSON LIMITED
Registration no: 00040651 **VAT No.:** 170 2400 14 **Date established:** 1994
Turnover: £1m - £2m **No.of Employees:** 1 - 10 **Product Groups:** 32, 48

Date of Accounts	Sep 11	Sep 10	Sep 09
Working Capital	379	383	349
Fixed Assets	384	378	389
Current Assets	2m	629	747

Wolseley UK

PO Box 21 Boroughbridge Road, Ripon, HG4 1SL
Tel: 01765-690690 **Fax:** 01224-637598
Website: http://www.draincenter.co.uk
Bank(s): Lloyds TSB
Directors: A. Barden (MD)
Managers: W. Smith (Mgr)
Ultimate Holding Company: WOLSELEY LIMITED
Immediate Holding Company: DAHLL LIMITED
Registration no: 00424702 **Date established:** 2000
Turnover: Over £1,000m **No.of Employees:** 251 - 500
Product Groups: 66

Date of Accounts	Jul 07
Sales Turnover	2206m
Pre Tax Profit/Loss	72080
Working Capital	198310
Fixed Assets	2013m
Current Assets	966350
Current Liabilities	768040
Total Share Capital	20040
ROCE% (Return on Capital Employed)	3.3

Scarborough

1st Dental

Salter Road Eastfield, Scarborough, YO11 3UZ
Tel: 01723-584034 **Fax:** 01723-581345
E-mail: paulfowler@1stdental.co.uk
Website: http://www.1stdental.co.uk
Managers: P. Fowler (Mgr)
Ultimate Holding Company: 1ST DENTAL LABORATORIES PLC
Immediate Holding Company: ENVIROMETRICS LIMITED
Registration no: 01319234 **Date established:** 1982
No.of Employees: 11 - 20 **Product Groups:** 38, 67

Date of Accounts	Jun 11	Jun 10	Jun 09
Working Capital	10	33	33
Fixed Assets	507	507	507
Current Assets	18	60	55

Able Engineering

Dunslow Road Eastfield, Scarborough, YO11 3UT
Tel: 01723-585639 **Fax:** 01723-581605
E-mail: admin@nswinches.co.uk
Website: http://www.nswinches.co.uk
Directors: J. Gretten (MD)
Immediate Holding Company: PANDIONIDAE LIMITED
Registration no: 06577158 **Date established:** 2008
No.of Employees: 11 - 20 **Product Groups:** 39, 40, 45

Date of Accounts	May 11	May 10	May 09
Fixed Assets	1m	1m	1m

Andy Whitelaw Joinery

Lakeside House Hopper Hill Road, Eastfield, Scarborough, YO11 3YS
Tel: 01723-581040 **Fax:** 01723-586030
Website: http://www.andywhitelawjoinery.co.uk
Directors: A. Whitelaw (Dir)
Ultimate Holding Company: LAKESIDE HOLDINGS LIMITED
Immediate Holding Company: ANDY WHITELAW JOINERY LIMITED
Registration no: 05123556 **Date established:** 2004 **Turnover:** £1m - £2m
No.of Employees: 11 - 20 **Product Groups:** 25, 26, 30

Date of Accounts	Nov 09	Nov 08	Nov 07
Sales Turnover	N/A	1m	N/A
Working Capital	-179	-135	-58
Fixed Assets	86	106	57
Current Assets	157	288	303
Current Liabilities	N/A	271	N/A

Anti Ltd

6 Albermarle Crescent, Scarborough, YO11 1XT
Tel: 01723-368700
E-mail: info@antiknowsbest.com
Website: http://www.antiknowsbest.com
Directors: J. Bastiman (MD)
Date established: 2005 **No.of Employees:** 1 - 10 **Product Groups:** 44

Aquamonde Lifestyle Ltd

Farfield Business Park Main Road, Wykeham, Scarborough, YO13 9QB
Tel: 01723-865777 **Fax:** 01723-865778
E-mail: aquamonde@btconnect.com
Website: http://www.aquamonde.co.uk
Directors: P. Harrison (MD)
Registration no: 05384426 **No.of Employees:** 1 - 10 **Product Groups:** 61

Date of Accounts	Aug 07	Aug 06
Working Capital	57	69
Fixed Assets	47	59
Current Assets	127	118
Current Liabilities	70	49

Bed Warehouse

Wrea Lane, Scarborough, YO12 7PN
Tel: 01723-351313 **Fax:** 01723-353971
E-mail: info@bedwarehouse.com
Website: http://www.bedwarehouse.com
Directors: S. Hardy (Prop)
Date established: 1983 **No.of Employees:** 1 - 10 **Product Groups:** 24, 26, 29, 63, 66

Castle Group Ltd

Salter Road Eastfield, Scarborough, YO11 3UZ
Tel: 01723-584250 **Fax:** 01723-583728
E-mail: enquiries@castlegroup.co.uk
Website: http://www.castlegroup.co.uk
Bank(s): Barclays
Directors: P. Hudson (Fin), S. Bull (Sales)
Ultimate Holding Company: ENVIROMETRICS LIMITED
Immediate Holding Company: CASTLE GROUP LIMITED
Registration no: 02388128 **VAT No.:** GB 167 0593 49
Date established: 1989 **Turnover:** £1m - £2m **No.of Employees:** 11 - 20
Product Groups: 30, 38, 40, 44, 45, 49, 54, 84

Date of Accounts	Jun 11	Jun 10	Jun 09
Working Capital	320	319	-60
Fixed Assets	101	77	74
Current Assets	595	562	533

Clanalvex Ltd

Ings Lane Brompton-by-Sawdon, Scarborough, YO13 9DR
Tel: 01723-859463 **Fax:** 01723-859190
E-mail: kevinw@clanalvex.co.uk
Website: http://www.clanalvex.co.uk
Bank(s): Royal Bank of Scotland
Directors: J. Scott (Dir), K. Wallace (Dir), K. Wallis (Dir), R. Trowsdale (Admin), S. Scott (Sales), M. Hill (Fin)
Immediate Holding Company: CLANALVEX LIMITED
Registration no: 00737964 **VAT No.:** 167 0302 86 **Date established:** 1962
Turnover: £1m - £2m **No.of Employees:** 11 - 20 **Product Groups:** 48

Date of Accounts	Sep 09	Sep 08	Sep 07
Working Capital	-125	-61	-100
Fixed Assets	334	403	398
Current Assets	150	227	227

Duraweld Ltd

Salter Road Eastfield, Scarborough, YO11 3UP
Tel: 01723-584091 **Fax:** 01723-581509
E-mail: sales@duraweld.co.uk
Website: http://www.duraweld.co.uk
Directors: M. Yeung (Dir), M. Young (Ptnr)
Managers: B. Snowdon (Tech Serv Mgr), T. Cooke (Sales Prom Mgr), J. Harper (Mktg Serv Mgr), J. Bulmer (Personnel)
Immediate Holding Company: TWENTY TEN PROPERTIES LIMITED
Registration no: 01647624 **VAT No.:** GB 282 3352 64
Date established: 1982 **Turnover:** £2m - £5m **No.of Employees:** 51 - 100
Product Groups: 30

Date of Accounts	Jun 11	Jun 10	Jun 09
Working Capital	872	955	914
Fixed Assets	1m	1m	474
Current Assets	894	1m	1m

Graham

Queen Margarets Road, Scarborough, YO11 2YH
Tel: 01723-363656 **Fax:** 01723-367082
E-mail: joehakings@graham-group.co.uk
Website: http://www.graham-group.co.uk
Managers: J. Hakings (Mgr)
Immediate Holding Company: A.S. ROOFING SPECIALISTS LTD
Registration no: 00066738 **VAT No.:** GB 497 7184 33
Date established: 2012 **Turnover:** £2m - £5m **No.of Employees:** 1 - 10
Product Groups: 66

High Reaching Solutions

52 West Bank, Scarborough, YO12 4DX
Tel: 07963-933644
E-mail: sales@highreachingsolutions.co.uk
Website: http://www.highreachingsolutions.co.uk
Directors: S. Wakeford (Prop)
Turnover: Up to £250,000 **No.of Employees:** 1 - 10 **Product Groups:** 45, 67, 83, 86

Jewson Ltd

Brook Street, Scarborough, YO12 7AB
Tel: 01723-363441 **Fax:** 01723-373625
E-mail: joe.hakings@jewson.co.uk
Website: http://www.jewson.co.uk
Managers: J. Hakings (District Mgr)
Ultimate Holding Company: COMPAGNIE DE SAINT GOBAIN (FRANCE)
Immediate Holding Company: JEWSON LIMITED
Registration no: 00348407 **VAT No.:** GB 497 7184 83
Date established: 1939 **No.of Employees:** 11 - 20 **Product Groups:** 66

Date of Accounts	Dec 11	Dec 10	Dec 09
Sales Turnover	1606m	1547m	1485m
Pre Tax Profit/Loss	18m	100m	45m
Working Capital	-345m	-250m	-349m
Fixed Assets	496m	387m	461m
Current Assets	657m	1005m	1320m
Current Liabilities	66m	120m	64m

Mustang Communications Ltd

Dunslow Road Eastfield, Scarborough, YO11 3UT
Tel: 01723-582555 **Fax:** 01723-581673
E-mail: info@mustang.com
Website: http://www.mustang.co.uk
Directors: M. Tetley (MD)
Immediate Holding Company: MUSTANG COMMUNICATIONS LIMITED
Registration no: 02389242 **VAT No.:** 546 7819 02 **Date established:** 1989
Turnover: £500,000 - £1m **No.of Employees:** 1 - 10 **Product Groups:** 37, 40

Date of Accounts	Feb 08	Feb 11	Feb 10
Working Capital	31	30	7
Fixed Assets	11	2	3
Current Assets	127	77	82

Chris Naylor Research Ltd

14 Castle Gardens, Scarborough, YO11 1QU
Tel: 01723-354590
E-mail: chrisnaylor@chrisnaylor.co.uk
Website: http://www.chrisnaylor.co.uk
Directors: C. Naylor (MD)
Immediate Holding Company: CHRIS NAYLOR RESEARCH LIMITED
Registration no: 03249624 **VAT No.:** GB 664 9048 07
Date established: 1996 **Turnover:** Up to £250,000
No.of Employees: 1 - 10 **Product Groups:** 44

see next page

Chris Naylor Research Ltd - Cont'd

Date of Accounts	Aug 11	Aug 10	Aug 08
Working Capital	-4	-3	-1
Fixed Assets	2	3	1
Current Liabilities	4	3	N/A

North East Security Shutters
Ness House Knox Lane, Scarborough, YO11 2BD
Tel: 01723-351133 **Fax:** 01723-361644
E-mail: nessdoorsinfo@aol.com
Website: http://www.nessdoors.co.uk
Directors: K. Jennison (Prop), T. Jennison (Prop)
Date established: 1968 **No.of Employees:** 1 - 10 **Product Groups:** 35

North Sea Winches Ltd
Dunslow Road Eastfield, Scarborough, YO11 3UT
Tel: 01723-584080 **Fax:** 01723-581605
E-mail: rob@nswinches.co.uk
Website: http://www.nswinches.co.uk
Bank(s): HSBC, Westgate, Bridlington
Directors: R. Gretton (MD)
Immediate Holding Company: NORTH SEA WINCHES LIMITED
Registration no: 00992188 **VAT No.:** GB 167 3676 30
Date established: 1970 **Turnover:** £1m - £2m **No.of Employees:** 11 - 20
Product Groups: 39, 45

Date of Accounts	Sep 11	Sep 10	Sep 09
Working Capital	295	319	330
Fixed Assets	112	128	129
Current Assets	461	474	474

Osprey Ltd
Dunslow Road Eastfield, Scarborough, YO11 3UT
Tel: 01723-585333 **Fax:** 01723-585226
E-mail: md@osprey-plastics.co.uk
Website: http://www.osprey-plastics.co.uk
Bank(s): Lloyds TSB Bank plc
Directors: J. Smith (Dir)
Ultimate Holding Company: PANDIONIDAE LIMITED
Immediate Holding Company: OSPREY LIMITED
Registration no: 00628763 **VAT No.:** GB 167 1201 87
Date established: 1959 **Turnover:** £2m - £5m **No.of Employees:** 51 - 100
Product Groups: 30

Date of Accounts	May 11	May 10	May 09
Pre Tax Profit/Loss	212	365	326
Working Capital	3m	3m	3m
Fixed Assets	909	761	579
Current Assets	4m	3m	3m
Current Liabilities	249	273	224

Pindar plc
Thornborough Road Eastfield, Scarborough, YO11 3UY
Tel: 01723-581581 **Fax:** 01723-583086
E-mail: enquiries@pindar.com
Website: http://www.pindar.co.uk
Directors: A. Dalton (Grp Chief Exec), D. Noakes (Co Sec), P. Duggleby (MD), J. Piercy (Sales)
Managers: A. Bosomworth (Fin Mgr), H. Kent (Mktg Serv Mgr), T. Fletcher (Mktg Serv Mgr)
Immediate Holding Company: PINDAR PLC
Registration no: 02428709 **Date established:** 1989
Turnover: £50m - £75m **No.of Employees:** 501 - 1000
Product Groups: 28

Raflatac Ltd
Wareham Road Eastfield, Scarborough, YO11 3DX
Tel: 01723-583661 **Fax:** 01723-584896
E-mail: info@upmraflatac.com
Website: http://www.upmraflatac.com
Bank(s): National Westminster Bank Plc
Directors: D. Chalmers (Dir)
Ultimate Holding Company: UPM-KYMMENE CORPORATION (FINLAND)
Immediate Holding Company: UPM RAFLATAC LIMITED
Registration no: 00774341 **VAT No.:** GB 209 1444 83
Date established: 1963 **Turnover:** £125m - £250m
No.of Employees: 101 - 250 **Product Groups:** 27

Date of Accounts	Dec 11	Dec 10	Dec 09
Sales Turnover	140m	155m	153m
Pre Tax Profit/Loss	13m	19m	9m
Working Capital	108m	101m	86m
Fixed Assets	5m	6m	7m
Current Assets	129m	130m	116m
Current Liabilities	10m	10m	6m

S & P Darwell Ltd
Scarborough Business Park Hopper Hill Road, Eastfield, Scarborough, YO11 3YS
Tel: 01723-582000 **Fax:** 01723-582828
E-mail: cad@darwells.fsnet.co.uk
Website: http://www.darwells.fsnet.co.uk
Bank(s): Barclays
Directors: S. Darwell (MD), S. Darwell (Dir)
Managers: C. Thomson (Works Gen Mgr)
Immediate Holding Company: S & P DARWELL LIMITED
Registration no: 02500280 **VAT No.:** 347 6047 44 **Date established:** 1990
Turnover: £500,000 - £1m **No.of Employees:** 11 - 20 **Product Groups:** 48

Date of Accounts	May 08	May 07	May 06
Working Capital	38	28	8
Fixed Assets	98	111	129
Current Assets	622	407	482
Current Liabilities	584	379	474

Schneider Electric Ltd
Cayton Low Road Eastfield, Scarborough, YO11 3DA
Tel: 01723-502800 **Fax:** 01723-502860
E-mail: tom.mennell@schneider-electric.com
Website: http://www.schneider-electric.co.uk
Bank(s): National Westminster
Directors: T. Mennell (MD)
Managers: D. Henderson (Comptroller), N. Roberts (Sales Prom Mgr)
Ultimate Holding Company: SCHNEIDER ELECTRIC SA (FRANCE)
Immediate Holding Company: SCHNEIDER ELECTRIC LIMITED
Registration no: 01407228 **VAT No.:** GB 301 4285 05
Date established: 1978 **Turnover:** £10m - £20m
No.of Employees: 101 - 250 **Product Groups:** 37, 67

Date of Accounts	Dec 11	Dec 10	Dec 09
Sales Turnover	444m	407m	357m
Pre Tax Profit/Loss	28m	37m	38m
Working Capital	188m	164m	124m
Fixed Assets	35m	32m	20m
Current Assets	314m	263m	219m
Current Liabilities	48m	39m	34m

Sulzer Bootham Engineering
Premises Cayton Low Road Eastfield, Scarborough, YO11 3BZ
Tel: 01723-582621 **Fax:** 01723-583455
E-mail: scarborough@boothamengineers.com
Website: http://www.dowdingandmills.com
Managers: P. Atkinson (District Mgr)
Ultimate Holding Company: DOWDING & MILLS PLC, BIRMINGHAM
Registration no: 00270442 **VAT No.:** GB 109 5683 53
No.of Employees: 51 - 100 **Product Groups:** 48

Tri Met
Barrys Lane, Scarborough, YO12 4HA
Tel: 01723-376883 **Fax:** 01723-354921
E-mail: trimetbkg@aol.com
Directors: D. Grout (MD), J. Barnfather (MD)
Managers: K. Wrona (Admin Off)
Immediate Holding Company: PREMIER ENGINEERING CO (SCARBOROUGH) LIMITED
Registration no: 07047170 **VAT No.:** GB 602 1202 20
Date established: 1986 **Turnover:** £1m - £2m **No.of Employees:** 1 - 10
Product Groups: 26, 35, 49

Unison
Unit 1-2 Olympian Trading Estate Cayton Low Road, Eastfield, Scarborough, YO11 3BT
Tel: 01723-582868 **Fax:** 01723-582379
E-mail: alanp@unisonltd.com
Website: http://www.unisonltd.com
Bank(s): HSBC Bank plc
Directors: J. Kitcher (Fin), A. Pickering (MD)
Managers: J. Saynor (Sales & Mktg Mg), M. Gerrard (Software Eng), A. Wheeler (Ops Mgr), C. Helm (Buyer)
Immediate Holding Company: UNISON LIMITED
Registration no: 01105991 **VAT No.:** GB 168 4964 14
Date established: 1973 **Turnover:** £2m - £5m **No.of Employees:** 21 - 50
Product Groups: 46

Date of Accounts	Sep 11	Apr 10	Apr 09
Working Capital	-72	-31	-140
Fixed Assets	478	430	358
Current Assets	938	998	686

Yorkshire Regional Newspapers Ltd
17-23 Aberdeen Walk, Scarborough, YO11 1BB
Tel: 01723-363636 **Fax:** 01723-383825
E-mail: editorial@scarborougheveningnews.co.uk
Website: http://www.scarboroughtoday.co.uk
Directors: C. Green (Dir), R. Davies (Tech Serv)
Ultimate Holding Company: JOHNSTON PRESS PLC
Immediate Holding Company: YORKSHIRE REGIONAL NEWSPAPERS LIMITED
Registration no: 00237165 **Date established:** 2029 **Turnover:** £2m - £5m
No.of Employees: 101 - 250 **Product Groups:** 28

Date of Accounts	Dec 11	Dec 08	Jan 10
Sales Turnover	2m	3m	3m
Working Capital	-1m	-1m	-1m
Current Assets	469	469	469

Selby

Bolton Priestley
27 Ousegate Business Centre Ousegate, Selby, YO8 4NN
Tel: 01757-212122 **Fax:** 01757-213509
E-mail: selby@boltonpriestley.co.uk
Website: http://www.boltonpriestley.co.uk
Directors: G. Othick (Dir)
Immediate Holding Company: BOLTON PRIESTLEY LTD
Registration no: 03002711 **No.of Employees:** 11 - 20 **Product Groups:** 35

Computer Repairs 4 U
4 Moorfields Wistow, Selby, YO8 3YN
Tel: 07887-735853
E-mail: geoffwright@uk2.net
Website: http://www.computerrepairs4u.net
Directors: G. Wright (Prop)
Date established: 1998 **No.of Employees:** 1 - 10 **Product Groups:** 44

GB UK Healthcare Ltd
Unit 4 Blackwood Hall Business Park North Duffield, Selby, YO8 5DD
Tel: 01757-288587 **Fax:** 020-8688 8557
E-mail: info@gbukhealthcare.com
Website: http://www.gbukhealthcare.com
Bank(s): Lloyds TSB Bank plc
Directors: M. Thompson (MD)
Immediate Holding Company: YPSOMED LIMITED
Registration no: 01081549 **VAT No.:** GB 611 8876 28
Date established: 2010 **Turnover:** £1m - £2m **No.of Employees:** 11 - 20
Product Groups: 67

Date of Accounts	Jul 11	Jul 10	Jul 09
Working Capital	20	-133	508
Fixed Assets	3m	2m	869
Current Assets	169	83	534

House Warming Stoves & Fireplaces
56 Flaxley Road, Selby, YO8 4BW
Tel: 01757-212992 **Fax:** 01757-212993
E-mail: info@housewarmingselby.co.uk
Website: http://www.housewarmingselby.co.uk
Directors: R. Taylor (Ptnr)
Date established: 1999 **No.of Employees:** 1 - 10 **Product Groups:** 40

Jewson Ltd
Unit 3 Bawtry Road, Selby, YO8 8NB
Tel: 01757-703668 **Fax:** 01757-701933
Website: http://www.jewson.co.uk
Managers: G. Stoud (District Mgr)
Ultimate Holding Company: COMPAGNIE DE SAINT GOBAIN (FRANCE)
Immediate Holding Company: JEWSON LIMITED
Registration no: 00348407 **VAT No.:** GB 497 7184 33
Date established: 1939 **Turnover:** £2m - £5m **No.of Employees:** 11 - 20
Product Groups: 66

Date of Accounts	Dec 11	Dec 10	Dec 09
Sales Turnover	1606m	1547m	1485m
Pre Tax Profit/Loss	18m	100m	45m
Working Capital	-345m	-250m	-349m
Fixed Assets	496m	387m	461m
Current Assets	657m	1005m	1320m
Current Liabilities	66m	120m	64m

Nationwide Catering Services Ltd
Unit 4-6 21 Bondgate Business Centre Bondgate, Selby, YO8 3LX
Tel: 01757-210887 **Fax:** 01757-213914
E-mail: enquiries@nationwidecateringservices.co.uk
Website: http://www.nationwidecateringservices.co.uk
Directors: S. Atkinson (Dir)
Immediate Holding Company: NATIONWIDE CATERING SERVICES LIMITED
Registration no: 00522751 **Date established:** 1953
No.of Employees: 1 - 10 **Product Groups:** 20, 40, 41

Date of Accounts	Dec 11	Dec 10	Dec 09
Working Capital	159	161	179
Fixed Assets	67	63	68
Current Assets	256	242	314
Current Liabilities	61	54	N/A

P Oates Forklift Trucks
East View Hirst Road, Chapel Haddlesey, Selby, YO8 8QQ
Tel: 01757-270207 **Fax:** 01757-270438
Directors: G. Oates (Prop)
Date established: 1963 **No.of Employees:** 1 - 10 **Product Groups:** 35, 39, 45

Potter Group Ltd
Barlby Road, Selby, YO8 5DZ
Tel: 01757-702303 **Fax:** 01757-210834
E-mail: potterselby@easynet.co.uk
Website: http://www.pottergroup.co.uk
Managers: N. Brightey (Mgr)
Ultimate Holding Company: THE POTTER GROUP (HOLDINGS) PLC
Immediate Holding Company: THE POTTER GROUP LIMITED
Registration no: 01392251 **Date established:** 1978
No.of Employees: 21 - 50 **Product Groups:** 07, 39, 45, 72, 77, 80, 84

Date of Accounts	Apr 11	Apr 10	Apr 09
Sales Turnover	15m	15m	16m
Pre Tax Profit/Loss	447	355	28
Working Capital	7m	7m	6m
Fixed Assets	4m	3m	4m
Current Assets	11m	10m	11m
Current Liabilities	2m	1m	3m

Selby Metalcraft
Mayo House Hagg Lane, South Duffield, Selby, YO8 6TF
Tel: 01757-638569 **Fax:** 01757-638569
E-mail: rchrd_wilton@yahoo.co.uk
Website: http://www.selbymetalcraft.co.uk
Directors: R. Wilton (Ptnr)
Date established: 1982 **No.of Employees:** 1 - 10 **Product Groups:** 35

UK Hire Jobs
The Old Brickworks Hull Road, Hemingbrough, Selby, YO8 6QG
Tel: 08451-631202 **Fax:** 01904-211020
E-mail: info@ukhirejobs.com
Website: http://www.ukhirejobs.com
Directors: G. Hewitt (Dir)
Registration no: 06883044 **Date established:** 2008
Turnover: Up to £250,000 **No.of Employees:** 1 - 10 **Product Groups:** 80

Upton Refreshment Systems
Vending House Vivars Way Canal Road, Selby, YO8 8BE
Tel: 01757-629112 **Fax:** 01757-294600
E-mail: sales@theuptongroup.co.uk
Website: http://www.uptonvending.co.uk
Directors: R. Macdonald (MD)
Immediate Holding Company: UPTON VENDING LIMITED
Registration no: 01071192 **Date established:** 1972 **Turnover:** £1m - £2m
No.of Employees: 21 - 50 **Product Groups:** 48, 49, 61

Date of Accounts	Oct 11	Oct 10	Oct 09
Working Capital	-95	-21	-33
Fixed Assets	1m	1m	1m
Current Assets	38	94	28

Viking Shipping Services Ltd
The Goods Yard Ousegate, Selby, YO8 8BL
Tel: 01757-702688 **Fax:** 01757-701601
E-mail: sales2@vikingshipping.co.uk
Website: http://www.vikingshipping.co.uk
Directors: G. Pickering (MD)
Managers: R. Edgell (Chief Acct)
Ultimate Holding Company: STAR CARGO PLC
Immediate Holding Company: VIKING SHIPPING SERVICES LIMITED
Registration no: 02452183 **VAT No.:** GB 540 1080 00
Date established: 1989 **Turnover:** £1m - £2m **No.of Employees:** 1 - 10
Product Groups: 76

Date of Accounts	Sep 11	Sep 10	Sep 09
Sales Turnover	2m	1m	1m
Pre Tax Profit/Loss	133	81	74
Working Capital	214	112	75
Fixed Assets	192	197	162
Current Assets	525	452	293
Current Liabilities	96	89	32

A S Walls & Sons
Elm Tree House Hull Road, Cliffe, Selby, YO8 6NH
Tel: 01757-638245 **Fax:** 01757-638245
Directors: K. Walls (Prop)
Date established: 1982 **No.of Employees:** 1 - 10 **Product Groups:** 41

Waste Tech Environmental Ltd
Foggathorpe, Selby, YO8 6PX
Tel: 01757-288022
E-mail: info@wte-ltd.co.uk
Website: http://www.wte-ltd.co.uk
Directors: M. Webb (Dir)
Immediate Holding Company: WASTE TECH ENVIRONMENTAL LIMITED
Registration no: 02278782 **Date established:** 1988 **Turnover:** £1m - £2m
No.of Employees: 1 - 10 **Product Groups:** 42

Date of Accounts	Apr 12	Apr 11	Apr 10
Working Capital	-7	153	-5
Fixed Assets	8	5	5
Current Assets	42	153	132

Westdale Filters
Larabridge Farm Cliffe Common, Selby, YO8 6EF
Tel: 01757-288355 **Fax:** 01757-288444
E-mail: info@westdalefilters.co.uk
Website: http://www.westdalefilters.co.uk
Directors: D. Watton (Fin), J. Binks (MD), R. Jewitt (Dir)
Immediate Holding Company: WESTDALE FILTERS LIMITED
Registration no: 01674366 **VAT No.:** GB 361 6423 64
Date established: 1982 **Turnover:** £250,000 - £500,000
No.of Employees: 1 - 10 **Product Groups:** 42

Date of Accounts	Oct 09	Oct 08	Oct 07
Working Capital	44	28	27
Fixed Assets	75	2	3
Current Assets	85	75	71
Current Liabilities	19	25	23

Wetherells Contracts Ltd
9 The Crescent, Selby, YO8 4PD
Tel: 01757-702161 **Fax:** 01757-704026
Directors: M. Wetherell (Dir)
Immediate Holding Company: WETHERELLS CONTRACTS LIMITED
Registration no: 00183668 **VAT No.:** GB 181 7052 70
Date established: 2022 **Turnover:** £500,000 - £1m
No.of Employees: 1 - 10 **Product Groups:** 26, 30, 66

Date of Accounts	Jan 12	Jan 11	Jan 10
Working Capital	875	779	740
Fixed Assets	4m	4m	4m
Current Assets	2m	2m	2m

Settle

Fire Hosetech
New Road Sowarth Industrial Estate, Settle, BD24 9AG
Tel: 01729-825999 **Fax:** 01729-825777
E-mail: info@firehosetech.co.uk
Website: http://www.firehosetech.co.uk
Directors: B. Coultherd (Ptnr)
Immediate Holding Company: FIRE HOSETECH LIMITED
Registration no: 06761911 **Date established:** 2008
No.of Employees: 1 - 10 **Product Groups:** 38, 42

Date of Accounts	Dec 11	Dec 10	Dec 09
Working Capital	-143	-166	-355
Fixed Assets	526	387	374
Current Assets	305	314	232

S & M Fire Protection Services
Ribble View Studfold, Horton-in-Ribblesdale, Settle, BD24 0ER
Tel: 01729-860275
Directors: M. Ogden (Ptnr)
Date established: 1964 **No.of Employees:** 1 - 10 **Product Groups:** 38, 42

Skipton

A C W A Services Ltd
Acwa House Acorn Business Park Keighley Road, Skipton, BD23 2UE
Tel: 01756-794794 **Fax:** 01756-790898
E-mail: pripley@acwa.co.uk
Website: http://www.acwa.co.uk
Bank(s): National Westminster Bank Plc
Directors: D. Clegg (Fin), P. Ripley (MD)
Ultimate Holding Company: S & K HOLDING SAL (LEBANON)
Immediate Holding Company: ACWA SERVICES LIMITED
Registration no: 02024837 **Date established:** 1986 **Turnover:** £2m - £5m
No.of Employees: 21 - 50 **Product Groups:** 42

Date of Accounts	Dec 11	Dec 10	Dec 09
Sales Turnover	6m	4m	7m
Pre Tax Profit/Loss	-517	-130	-956
Working Capital	-957	-479	-3m
Fixed Assets	371	385	442
Current Assets	6m	6m	19m
Current Liabilities	429	703	14m

Brooksbank Holdings
Station Yard Elslack, Skipton, BD23 3AS
Tel: 01282-444610 **Fax:** 01282-444611
E-mail: sales@brooksbank.com
Website: http://www.brooksbank.com
Directors: J. Haunch (Co Sec), J. Brooksbank (Dir)
Immediate Holding Company: BROOKSBANK HOLDINGS LIMITED
Registration no: 06145119 **Date established:** 2007 **Turnover:** £1m - £2m
No.of Employees: 1 - 10 **Product Groups:** 22, 29, 43

Date of Accounts	Jul 11	Jul 10	Jul 09
Working Capital	-276	-276	-276
Fixed Assets	960	960	960
Current Liabilities	N/A	276	276

Brooksbank Valves Ltd
Sackville Street, Skipton, BD23 2PS
Tel: 01756-792346 **Fax:** 01756-792347
E-mail: sales@brooksbank.co.uk
Website: http://www.brooksbank.co.uk
Bank(s): HSBC Bank plc
Directors: J. Brooksbank (MD), J. Davis (Sales), J. Haunch (Co Sec)
Managers: J. Berry, H. Brownfather (Tech Serv Mgr), L. Brown (Purch Mgr)
Ultimate Holding Company: ALUMINIUM BRONZE VALVES LIMITED
Immediate Holding Company: BROOKSBANK VALVES LIMITED
Registration no: 01004518 **VAT No.:** GB 179 4213 46
Date established: 1971 **Turnover:** £1m - £2m **No.of Employees:** 21 - 50
Product Groups: 36, 39

Date of Accounts	Mar 11	Mar 10	Mar 09
Working Capital	912	1m	1m
Fixed Assets	1m	1m	1m
Current Assets	2m	2m	2m

Daikin UK East Ltd
Broughton Hall Broughton, Skipton, BD23 3AE
Tel: 01756-799899 **Fax:** 01756-693779
Managers: D. Petty (Mgr)
Immediate Holding Company: CLOVER COURT (SKIPTON) MANAGEMENT COMPANY LIMITED
Date established: 1988 **No.of Employees:** 1 - 10 **Product Groups:** 40, 66

Date of Accounts	Jul 11	Jul 10
Working Capital	69	71
Fixed Assets	2	2
Current Assets	125	90

Dalesway Print Technology
Victoria House Gisburn Road, West Marton, Skipton, BD23 3UA
Tel: 08452-241204 **Fax:** 0845-224 1205
E-mail: info@dalesway.co.uk
Website: http://www.dalesway.co.uk
Directors: A. Stocking (Ptnr)
Date established: 1995 **Turnover:** Over £1,000m **No.of Employees:** 1 - 10
Product Groups: 44

Dickinson Philips & Co.
Snaygill Industrial Estate Keighley Road, Skipton, BD23 2QR
Tel: 01756-700359 **Fax:** 01756-700360
E-mail: simon@dickinsonphilips.com
Website: http://www.dickinsonphilips.com
Directors: S. Harris (Ptnr)
Immediate Holding Company: SDV ESCALATORS (MEDIA) LIMITED
Registration no: 03561520 **VAT No.:** GB 343 5782 43
Date established: 2009 **No.of Employees:** 11 - 20 **Product Groups:** 30

Date of Accounts	Jun 11	Jun 10	Jun 09
Working Capital	36	44	55
Fixed Assets	63	64	65
Current Assets	41	50	57

Fibrelite Composites Ltd
Unit 2 Snaygill Industrial Estate, Skipton, BD23 2QR
Tel: 01756-799773 **Fax:** 01756-799539
E-mail: ian@fibrelite.com
Website: http://www.fibrelite.com
Directors: I. Thompson (MD), J. Stott (Mkt Research), A. Preston (Co Sec), J. Preston (Fin), J. Westwood (Dir)
Managers: J. Hickson, S. Beverstock (Tech Serv Mgr)
Ultimate Holding Company: FIBRESEC LIMITED
Immediate Holding Company: FIBRESEC LIMITED
Registration no: 05562073 **VAT No.:** GB 607 0571 61
Date established: 2005 **Turnover:** £10m - £20m
No.of Employees: 21 - 50 **Product Groups:** 33, 35

Date of Accounts	Dec 11	Dec 10	Dec 09
Sales Turnover	11m	10m	9m
Pre Tax Profit/Loss	815	925	883
Working Capital	673	280	-169
Fixed Assets	2m	2m	2m
Current Assets	4m	4m	3m
Current Liabilities	551	643	704

Fibresec Holdings Ltd
Unit 2 Snaygill Indl-Est, Skipton, BD23 2QR
Tel: 01756-799822
Website: http://www.fibrelite.com
Directors: I. Thompson (Dir), A. Preston (Co Sec), J. Westwood (Dir)
Immediate Holding Company: FIBRESEC LIMITED
Registration no: 05562073 **Date established:** 2005
Turnover: £10m - £20m **No.of Employees:** 51 - 100 **Product Groups:** 33, 34, 35

Date of Accounts	Dec 10	Dec 09	Dec 08
Sales Turnover	10m	9m	11m
Pre Tax Profit/Loss	925	883	1m
Working Capital	280	-169	-627
Fixed Assets	2m	2m	2m
Current Assets	4m	3m	4m
Current Liabilities	643	704	934

Fray Design Ltd
Ghyll Way Airedale Business Centre Keighley Road, Skipton, BD23 2TZ
Tel: 01756-704040 **Fax:** 01756-704041
E-mail: sales@fraydesign.co.uk
Website: http://www.fraydesign.co.uk
Bank(s): Barclays
Directors: B. Fray (Dir), E. Fray (Co Sec)
Ultimate Holding Company: PRINCIPLE HEALTHCARE HOLDINGS LIMITED
Immediate Holding Company: AIRE VALLEY PLASTICS LIMITED
Registration no: 01310599 **VAT No.:** GB 362 0858 53
Date established: 1977 **Turnover:** £2m - £5m **No.of Employees:** 21 - 50
Product Groups: 26

Date of Accounts	Dec 10	Dec 09	Dec 08
Working Capital	-325	66	-18
Fixed Assets	420	453	501
Current Assets	244	383	704

Guy Machinery Ltd
Unit 21 Auction Mart Gargrave Road, Skipton, BD23 1UD
Tel: 01756-799184 **Fax:** 01756-793335
E-mail: sales@guymachinery.co.uk
Website: http://www.guymachinery.co.uk
Directors: G. Guy (MD)
Immediate Holding Company: GUY MACHINERY LIMITED
Registration no: 05548235 **Date established:** 2005
No.of Employees: 1 - 10 **Product Groups:** 41, 45, 67, 83

Date of Accounts	Dec 11	Dec 10	Dec 09
Working Capital	-71	-0	119
Fixed Assets	217	273	114
Current Assets	1m	1m	531

Guyson International Ltd
Snaygill Industrial Estate Keighley Road, Skipton, BD23 2QR
Tel: 01756-799911 **Fax:** 01756-790213
E-mail: info@guyson.co.uk
Website: http://www.guyson.co.uk
Bank(s): National Westminster Bank Plc
Managers: S. Bridge (Mktg Serv Mgr)
Immediate Holding Company: GUYSON INTERNATIONAL LIMITED
Registration no: 01549447 **VAT No.:** GB 197 6215 30
Date established: 1981 **Turnover:** £5m - £10m
No.of Employees: 101 - 250 **Product Groups:** 37, 42, 46

Date of Accounts	May 11	May 10	May 09
Sales Turnover	17m	14m	14m
Pre Tax Profit/Loss	938	-138	-286
Working Capital	7m	6m	5m
Fixed Assets	2m	2m	2m
Current Assets	10m	9m	8m
Current Liabilities	2m	1m	1m

L J Hydleman & Co. Ltd
Marton Street, Skipton, BD23 1TF
Tel: 01756-706700 **Fax:** 01756-798083
E-mail: info@hydleman.co.uk
Website: http://www.hydleman.co.uk
Bank(s): National Westminster Bank Plc
Directors: A. Thompson (Fin), M. Hydleman (MD)
Ultimate Holding Company: Gedore Werkzeugfabrik Otto Dowidat (Germany)
Immediate Holding Company: Gedore U.K. Ltd
Registration no: 01703068 **Date established:** 1983 **Turnover:** £2m - £5m
No.of Employees: 21 - 50 **Product Groups:** 35, 36, 37, 45, 66

Date of Accounts	Dec 07	Dec 06	Dec 05
Pre Tax Profit/Loss	N/A	N/A	433
Working Capital	1647	1533	1494
Fixed Assets	849	582	574
Current Assets	2551	2339	2310
Current Liabilities	904	806	817
Total Share Capital	3	3	3
ROCE% (Return on Capital Employed)			21.0

Precision Instruments
PO Box 127, Skipton, BD23 4WZ
Tel: 01756-748929 **Fax:** 01756-748929
E-mail: alanjonespi@btconnect.com
Website: http://www.pimedical.co.uk
Directors: A. Jones (Prop)
No.of Employees: 1 - 10 **Product Groups:** 38, 67, 85

Reward Manufacturing Co. Ltd
Sackville Mills Sackville Street, Skipton, BD23 2PR
Tel: 01756-797755 **Fax:** 01756-796644
E-mail: jonathan.hooper@rewardtrolleys.com
Website: http://www.rewardtrolleys.com
Directors: S. Hooper (Fin), J. Hooper (MD)
Immediate Holding Company: REWARD MANUFACTURING COMPANY LIMITED
Registration no: 00644293 **VAT No.:** GB 461 4329 58
Date established: 1959 **No.of Employees:** 11 - 20 **Product Groups:** 26, 39, 40, 41, 45, 67

Date of Accounts	Apr 11	Apr 10	Apr 09
Working Capital	138	135	223
Fixed Assets	467	510	491
Current Assets	311	403	555

Skipton Building Society plc
PO Box 7, Skipton, BD23 1AP
Tel: 01756-705030 **Fax:** 01756-705700
Website: http://www.skipton.co.uk
Managers: D. Stott (Buyer)
Immediate Holding Company: SKIPTON BUILDING SOCIETY CHARITABLE FOUNDATION
Registration no: 03937073 **Date established:** 2000
Turnover: Up to £250,000 **No.of Employees:** 11 - 20 **Product Groups:** 82

Date of Accounts	Feb 12	Feb 11	Feb 10
Sales Turnover	121	121	121
Pre Tax Profit/Loss	10	-34	-18
Working Capital	64	54	88
Current Assets	64	54	88

Tadcaster

Blucher UK Ltd
Station Road Industrial Estate, Tadcaster, LS24 9SG
Tel: 01937-838000 **Fax:** 01937-832454
E-mail: mail@blucher.co.uk
Website: http://www.blucher.co.uk
Directors: T. Guyler (Fin), P. Hardiman (MD)
Managers: F. Netherwood (Tech Serv Mgr), T. McDermott (Mktg Serv Mgr)
Ultimate Holding Company: WATTS WATER TECHNOLOGIES INC (USA)
Immediate Holding Company: BLUCHER UK LIMITED
Registration no: 01395057 **Date established:** 1978 **Turnover:** £2m - £5m
No.of Employees: 11 - 20 **Product Groups:** 35, 36

Date of Accounts	Dec 11	Dec 10	Dec 09
Sales Turnover	4m	5m	5m
Pre Tax Profit/Loss	628	879	864
Working Capital	1m	1m	1m
Fixed Assets	281	315	347
Current Assets	2m	2m	2m
Current Liabilities	317	326	287

Dynamite Pictures
8 Wilkinson Terrace Stutton, Tadcaster, LS24 9BP
Tel: 07816-319195
E-mail: contact@dynamitepictures.co.uk
Website: http://www.dynamitepictures.co.uk
Directors: R. Ball (MD)
No.of Employees: 1 - 10 **Product Groups:** 37, 44, 79, 89

Industrial Services York Ltd
Station Estate Station Road, Tadcaster, LS24 9SG
Tel: 01937-832761 **Fax:** 01937-833012
E-mail: info@suremark.ltd.uk
Website: http://www.suremark.ltd.uk
Directors: M. King (Fin), R. King (MD)
Immediate Holding Company: INDUSTRIAL SERVICES (YORK) LIMITED
Registration no: 00903228 **Date established:** 1967
Turnover: £500,000 - £1m **No.of Employees:** 11 - 20 **Product Groups:** 49

Date of Accounts	Dec 11	Dec 10	Dec 09
Sales Turnover	573	567	490
Pre Tax Profit/Loss	-11	N/A	-27
Working Capital	199	179	172
Fixed Assets	133	166	172
Current Assets	273	303	265
Current Liabilities	30	20	32

Lambert Engineering Ltd
Station Estate, Tadcaster, LS24 9SG
Tel: 01937-832921 **Fax:** 01937-835604
E-mail: sales@lamberteng.com
Website: http://www.lamberteng.com
Bank(s): Barclays
Directors: I. Hampton (Dir), M. Williams (Ch), S. Stanley (Pers), M. Cox (Sales)

see next page

Lambert Engineering Ltd - Cont'd

Managers: S. Sissons (Purch Mgr), J. Carr (Tech Serv Mgr)
Ultimate Holding Company: LAMBERT AUTOMATION LIMITED
Immediate Holding Company: LAMBERT ENGINEERING LIMITED
Registration no: 01089426 **VAT No.:** GB 171 0029 10
Date established: 1973 **Turnover:** £10m - £20m
No.of Employees: 101 - 250 **Product Groups:** 32, 37, 38, 40, 41

Date of Accounts	Dec 11	Dec 10	Dec 09
Sales Turnover	19m	11m	9m
Pre Tax Profit/Loss	2m	1m	799
Working Capital	6m	5m	5m
Fixed Assets	1m	977	1m
Current Assets	12m	9m	8m
Current Liabilities	4m	2m	2m

Wighill Park Guns

Wighill Park Nurseries Wighill Park, Tadcaster, LS24 8BW
Tel: 01937-833757 **Fax:** 01937-530563
E-mail: info@wighillparkguns.co.uk
Website: http://www.wighillparkguns.co.uk
Directors: N. Lambert (Prop)
No.of Employees: 1 - 10 **Product Groups:** 36, 38, 40, 49

Thirsk

A One Feed Supplements Ltd

North Hill Dishforth Airfield, Thirsk, YO7 3DH
Tel: 01423-322706 **Fax:** 01423-323260
E-mail: norman.gordon@a-one.co.uk
Website: http://www.a-one.co.uk
Bank(s): Barclays
Directors: D. Day (Sales & Mktg), N. Gordon (MD)
Managers: A. Blund (Personnel), P. Ingham (Chief Buyer), C. Waites (Personnel)
Ultimate Holding Company: RAINHEATH LIMITED
Immediate Holding Company: A.ONE FEED SUPPLEMENTS LIMITED
Registration no: 01207930 **VAT No.:** GB 171 8557 42
Date established: 1975 **Turnover:** £10m - £20m
No.of Employees: 21 - 50 **Product Groups:** 20, 41, 62

Date of Accounts	Nov 11	Nov 10	Nov 09
Sales Turnover	18m	16m	13m
Pre Tax Profit/Loss	164	137	396
Working Capital	3m	3m	3m
Fixed Assets	884	953	989
Current Assets	4m	4m	4m
Current Liabilities	265	321	169

Austin Reed Ltd

Station Road, Thirsk, YO7 1QH
Tel: 01845-573000 **Fax:** 01845-525536
E-mail: sales@austinreed.co.uk
Website: http://www.austinreed.co.uk
Directors: R. Tewson (Tech Serv), D. Hollis (Pers), A. Charlton (Fin)
Ultimate Holding Company: GAJAN HOLDINGS LIMITED
Immediate Holding Company: AUSTIN REED LIMITED
Registration no: 00399575 **Date established:** 1945
Turnover: £75m - £125m **No.of Employees:** 1001 - 1500
Product Groups: 61

Date of Accounts	Jan 11	Jan 10	Jan 09
Sales Turnover	50m	50m	56m
Pre Tax Profit/Loss	-5m	-4m	-685
Working Capital	9m	10m	12m
Fixed Assets	8m	9m	9m
Current Assets	24m	21m	20m
Current Liabilities	9m	7m	3m

Firmenich UK Ltd

Dalton Airfield Dalton, Thirsk, YO7 3HE
Tel: 01845-576400 **Fax:** 01845-576404
E-mail: sales@firmenich.com
Website: http://www.firmenich.com
Bank(s): HSBC Bank plc
Directors: A. Mailler (Co Sec)
Managers: J. Croft (Mgr), K. Singleton (Mktg Serv Mgr)
Ultimate Holding Company: FIRMENICH INTERNATIONAL SA (SWITZERLAND)
Immediate Holding Company: FIRMENICH UK LIMITED
Registration no: 02503296 **VAT No.:** GB 452 9769 06
Date established: 1990 **Turnover:** £2m - £5m **No.of Employees:** 21 - 50
Product Groups: 20, 62

Date of Accounts	Jun 12	Jun 11	Jun 10
Sales Turnover	33m	36m	39m
Pre Tax Profit/Loss	6m	-599	6m
Working Capital	12m	10m	8m
Fixed Assets	16m	12m	15m
Current Assets	18m	16m	15m
Current Liabilities	4m	2m	2m

G S M Graphic Art

Castlegarth Works Masonic Lane, Thirsk, YO7 1PS
Tel: 01845-522184 **Fax:** 01845-522206
E-mail: barrydodd@gsmprimographic.co.uk
Website: http://www.gsmgraphicarts.co.uk
Bank(s): Lloyds, Thirsk
Directors: A. Perry (Fin), B. Dodd (MD)
Managers: J. Butler (Personnel), P. Young
Ultimate Holding Company: G S M GROUP LIMITED
Immediate Holding Company: G.S.M. GRAPHIC ARTS LIMITED
Registration no: 01165307 **VAT No.:** GB 259 2035 60
Date established: 1974 **Turnover:** £250,000 - £500,000
No.of Employees: 101 - 250 **Product Groups:** 49

Date of Accounts	May 11	May 10	May 09
Working Capital	904	823	747
Fixed Assets	365	389	453
Current Assets	2m	2m	2m
Current Liabilities	1	N/A	N/A

Hawkesworth Appliance Testing

Guidance House York Road, Thirsk, YO7 3BT
Tel: 01845-524498 **Fax:** 01845-526884
E-mail: t.crowley@hawketest.co.uk
Website: http://www.hawktest.co.uk
Directors: R. Maddock (Chief Op Offcr)
Managers: S. Hardcastle (Fin Mgr), R. Cowton, D. Tonge (Sales & Mktg Mg), C. Haslam (Tech Serv Mgr)
Immediate Holding Company: HAWKESWORTH APPLIANCE TESTING LIMITED
Registration no: 05374162 **Date established:** 2005
No.of Employees: 21 - 50 **Product Groups:** 38

Date of Accounts	Jun 11	Jun 10	Jun 09
Working Capital	606	125	199
Fixed Assets	1m	1m	1m
Current Assets	1m	768	731

Jewson Ltd

Unit 2 Thirsk Industrial Park York Road, Thirsk, YO7 3BX
Tel: 01845-525572 **Fax:** 01845-524772
E-mail: trevor.arnott@jewson.co.uk
Website: http://www.jewson.co.uk
Managers: T. Arnott (Mgr)
Ultimate Holding Company: COMPAGNIE DE SAINT GOBAIN (FRANCE)
Immediate Holding Company: JEWSON LIMITED
Registration no: 00348407 **VAT No.:** GB 497 7184 83
Date established: 1939 **Turnover:** £500m - £1,000m
No.of Employees: 1 - 10 **Product Groups:** 66

Date of Accounts	Dec 11	Dec 10	Dec 09
Sales Turnover	1606m	1547m	1485m
Pre Tax Profit/Loss	18m	100m	45m
Working Capital	-345m	-250m	-349m
Fixed Assets	496m	387m	461m
Current Assets	657m	1005m	1320m
Current Liabilities	66m	120m	64m

Pickhill Engineers Ltd

Pickhill, Thirsk, YO7 4JU
Tel: 01845-567234 **Fax:** 01845-567690
E-mail: enquiries@pickhill-engineers.co.uk
Website: http://www.pickhill-engineers.co.uk
Directors: A. Cunningham (Dir)
Immediate Holding Company: PICKHILL ENGINEERS LIMITED
Registration no: 00633918 **VAT No.:** GB 613 3323 82
Date established: 1959 **Turnover:** £500,000 - £1m
No.of Employees: 1 - 10 **Product Groups:** 46

Date of Accounts	Mar 11	Mar 10	Mar 09
Working Capital	1m	970	2m
Fixed Assets	2m	2m	1m
Current Assets	1m	1m	2m

Power Plastics

Station Road, Thirsk, YO7 1PZ
Tel: 01845-525503 **Fax:** 01845-525485
E-mail: info@powerplastics.co.uk
Website: http://www.powerplastics.co.uk
Bank(s): Barclays
Directors: S. Price (Dir), K. Stead (Co Sec), A. Beetles (Dir)
Immediate Holding Company: POWER PLASTICS LIMITED
Registration no: 04328236 **Date established:** 2001 **Turnover:** £1m - £2m
No.of Employees: 11 - 20 **Product Groups:** 23, 24, 29, 30, 52

Date of Accounts	Mar 11	Mar 10	Mar 09
Working Capital	530	438	490
Fixed Assets	278	324	387
Current Assets	1m	829	986

R S Hall Engineering Ltd

16 Chapel Street, Thirsk, YO7 1LU
Tel: 01845-522990 **Fax:** 01845-522256
E-mail: chaps@hallwebs.co.uk
Website: http://www.hallwebs.co.uk
Directors: R. Hall (MD), S. Hall (Fin)
Immediate Holding Company: R.S. HALL ENGINEERING LIMITED
Registration no: 01376703 **Date established:** 1978
No.of Employees: 11 - 20 **Product Groups:** 41

Date of Accounts	Jan 12	Jan 11	Jan 10
Working Capital	185	330	206
Fixed Assets	834	855	894
Current Assets	546	663	569
Current Liabilities	N/A	N/A	185

Trac Lighting Controls Ltd

Euro Park Station Road, Thirsk, YO7 1QH
Tel: 01845-526006 **Fax:** 01845-526010
E-mail: sales@trac.co.uk
Website: http://www.trac.co.uk
Bank(s): HSBC
Directors: F. Morales (Sales), I. Appleyard (MD)
Managers: C. Chapman (Buyer), S. Horsfield (Tech Eng)
Immediate Holding Company: TRAC LIGHTING CO. LIMITED
Registration no: 02520263 **VAT No.:** GB 332 2012 23
Date established: 1990 **Turnover:** £5m - £10m **No.of Employees:** 21 - 50
Product Groups: 37, 49

Viresco UK Ltd

50a Market Place, Thirsk, YO7 1LH
Tel: 01845-525585 **Fax:** 01845-523133
E-mail: sales@viresco-uk.com
Website: http://www.viresco-uk.com
Directors: F. Mclauchlan (Dir), M. McLauchlan (Fin)
Immediate Holding Company: VIRESCO (UK) LIMITED
Registration no: 05079726 **Date established:** 2004 **Turnover:** £1m - £2m
No.of Employees: 1 - 10 **Product Groups:** 31, 32

Date of Accounts	Apr 11	Apr 10	Apr 09
Working Capital	30	-30	-24
Fixed Assets	150	162	174
Current Assets	82	21	33

Whitby

Dockend Engineering

Green Lane, Whitby, YO22 4EH
Tel: 01947-820484 **Fax:** 01947-820484
Directors: P. Mcque (Ptnr)
Immediate Holding Company: SITENSOUND LIMITED
Registration no: 06826928 **Date established:** 2009
No.of Employees: 1 - 10 **Product Groups:** 35

Gibbon Brother Engineer Ltd

21 Rigg View Stainsacre, Whitby, YO22 4NR
Tel: 01947-602250 **Fax:** 01947-602250
E-mail: gibbonbrothers@hotmail.co.uk
Directors: I. Gibbon (Dir)
Immediate Holding Company: GIBBON BROTHERS ENGINEERING LIMITED
Registration no: 05414863 **Date established:** 2005
No.of Employees: 1 - 10 **Product Groups:** 35

Date of Accounts	Apr 11	Apr 10	Apr 09
Working Capital	49	43	56
Fixed Assets	11	14	16
Current Assets	67	75	109

Jewson Ltd

Stainsacre Lane Industrial Estate Fairfield Way, Whitby, YO22 4PU
Tel: 01947-603381 **Fax:** 01947-600415
E-mail: peter.graham@jewson.co.uk
Website: http://www.jewson.co.uk
Managers: P. Graham (District Mgr)
Ultimate Holding Company: COMPAGNIE DE SAINT GOBAIN (FRANCE)
Immediate Holding Company: JEWSON LIMITED
Registration no: 00348407 **VAT No.:** GB 497 7184 83
Date established: 1939 **No.of Employees:** 1 - 10 **Product Groups:** 66

Date of Accounts	Dec 11	Dec 10	Dec 09
Sales Turnover	1606m	1547m	1485m
Pre Tax Profit/Loss	18m	100m	45m
Working Capital	-345m	-250m	-349m
Fixed Assets	496m	387m	461m
Current Assets	657m	1005m	1320m
Current Liabilities	66m	120m	64m

John R. HOGGARTH

Thorneywaite House Glaisdale, Whitby, YO21 2QU
Tel: 01947-897338
E-mail: john@johnrhoggarth.co.uk
Website: http://www.johnrhoggarth.co.uk
Product Groups: 28, 30, 35, 49

Royal Hotel Whitby

West Cliff, Whitby, YO21 3HA
Tel: 01947-602234 **Fax:** 01947-820355
Website: http://www.shearings.com
Managers: V. Glenn (Chief Mgr), K. Billington (District Mgr)
Immediate Holding Company: SHEARINGS
Registration no: 00024759 **VAT No.:** GB 643 6546 26
Date established: 1994 **Turnover:** £2m - £5m **No.of Employees:** 21 - 50
Product Groups: 69

Whitby Tanks Ltd

Custom House 1 Old Market Place, Whitby, YO21 3BT
Tel: 01947-606237 **Fax:** 01947-602876
E-mail: sales@whitbytanks.co.uk
Website: http://www.whitbytanks.co.uk
Directors: J. Taylor (Fin)
Immediate Holding Company: WHITBY TANKS LIMITED
Registration no: 02747039 **Date established:** 1992
No.of Employees: 1 - 10 **Product Groups:** 38, 42

Date of Accounts	Sep 11	Sep 10	Sep 09
Working Capital	43	18	-2
Fixed Assets	2	3	4
Current Assets	212	188	152

York

Acousticabs Industrial Noise Control Ltd

Unit 52 Pocklington Industrial Estate Pocklington, York, YO42 1NR
Tel: 01759-305266 **Fax:** 01759-305268
E-mail: info@acousticabs.com
Website: http://www.acousticabs.com
Directors: D. Lewin (Dir)
Immediate Holding Company: ACOUSTICABS INDUSTRIAL NOISE CONTROL LIMITED
Registration no: 01667774 **VAT No.:** GB 392 1403 68
Date established: 1982 **Turnover:** £250,000 - £500,000
No.of Employees: 1 - 10 **Product Groups:** 44

Date of Accounts	Jun 11	Jun 10	Jun 09
Working Capital	108	84	114
Fixed Assets	6	7	7
Current Assets	149	145	192

Adm Services UK Ltd

Unit 422 Clifford House 7-9 Clifford Street, York, YO1 9RA
Tel: 01904-349400 **Fax:** 01904-337770
E-mail: info@admfire.co.uk
Website: http://www.admfire.co.uk
Managers: M. Henderson (Mgr)
Immediate Holding Company: ADM SERVICES (UK) LTD
Registration no: 05517767 **Date established:** 2005
No.of Employees: 1 - 10 **Product Groups:** 40

Date of Accounts	Dec 11	Dec 10	Dec 09
Working Capital	-1	-4	-4
Fixed Assets	1	2	3
Current Assets	14	12	12

Adva Optical Networking Ltd

Advantage House Tribune Way, York, YO30 4RY
Tel: 01904-692700 **Fax:** 01904-692097
E-mail: info@advaoptical.com
Website: http://www.advaoptical.com
Managers: S. Ahmed, J. Morse (Purch Mgr), J. Steel (Sales Admin), K. Langham (Personnel)
Ultimate Holding Company: ADVA AG OPTICAL NETWORKING (GERMANY)
Immediate Holding Company: ADVA OPTICAL NETWORKING LIMITED
Registration no: 03593238 **VAT No.:** GB 598 8106 84
Date established: 1998 **Turnover:** £50m - £75m
No.of Employees: 51 - 100 **Product Groups:** 67

Date of Accounts	Dec 11	Dec 10	Dec 09
Sales Turnover	51m	59	54
Pre Tax Profit/Loss	-622	1	-0
Working Capital	4m	4	3
Fixed Assets	1m	2	2
Current Assets	20m	22	18
Current Liabilities	3m	10	3

Alarm Monitoring Company Ltd

School House Raskelf, York, YO61 3LG
Tel: 01347-822111 **Fax:** 01347-824507
E-mail: lesquigley@afid.co.uk
Website: http://www.afid.co.uk

Directors: L. Quigley (Fin)
Immediate Holding Company: THE ALARM MONITORING COMPANY LIMITED
Registration no: 03133703 **Date established:** 1995
No.of Employees: 1 - 10 **Product Groups:** 36, 40, 67

Date of Accounts	Oct 11	Oct 10	Oct 09
Working Capital	78	35	35
Fixed Assets	23	23	18
Current Assets	188	150	111

Alarming Fire Safety
2 Dee Close, York, YO24 2XP
Tel: 01904-704654
Directors: M. Harrison (Prop)
Immediate Holding Company: YORK FIRE SAFETY LTD
Registration no: 07735489 **Date established:** 2011
No.of Employees: 1 - 10 **Product Groups:** 38, 42

Alstoe Ltd
16-20 Dale Road Sheriff Hutton, York, YO60 6RZ
Tel: 01347-878606 **Fax:** 01347-878333
E-mail: info@alstoe.co.uk
Website: http://www.alstoe.co.uk
Directors: J. Nellis (Dir)
Immediate Holding Company: ALSTOE LIMITED
Registration no: 02937525 **Date established:** 1994
No.of Employees: 11 - 20 **Product Groups:** 63

Date of Accounts	Dec 11	Dec 10	Dec 09
Pre Tax Profit/Loss	1m	N/A	N/A
Working Capital	3m	2m	2m
Fixed Assets	620	662	606
Current Assets	5m	4m	4m
Current Liabilities	780	N/A	N/A

Apollo
Pond House Bulmer Lane, Holme-on-Spalding-Moor, York, YO43 4HE
Tel: 01430-860049 **Fax:** 01430-861550
E-mail: sales@apolloultrasonics.co.uk
Website: http://www.apolloultrasonics.co.uk
Directors: L. Wood (Prop)
Immediate Holding Company: APOLLO INDUSTRIAL DOORS LTD
Registration no: 06513230 **VAT No.:** GB 642 6393 31
Date established: 1988 **No.of Employees:** 1 - 10 **Product Groups:** 32, 37, 38, 42, 46, 47, 48

Edwin Ashworth Marine Ltd
10 Dove Way Kirkby Mills Industrial Estate, Kirkbymoorside, York, YO62 6QR
Tel: 01751-433039 **Fax:** 01751-433039
E-mail: info@bisontrawldoors.com
Website: http://www.bisontrawldoors.com
Directors: J. Ashworth (MD)
Immediate Holding Company: EDWIN ASHWORTH MARINE LIMITED
Registration no: 00384277 **Date established:** 1943
Turnover: £250,000 - £500,000 **No.of Employees:** 1 - 10
Product Groups: 39

Date of Accounts	Mar 11	Mar 10	Mar 09
Working Capital	-42	-19	-16
Fixed Assets	57	18	21
Current Assets	69	44	38

Associated Knowledge Systems Ltd
The Old Smithy Heaton House, Boroughbridge, York, YO51 9HE
Tel: 01423-321450 **Fax:** 01423-321451
E-mail: roy.slater@aksbedale.co.uk
Website: http://www.aksbedale.co.uk
Directors: R. Slater (Dir)
Managers: K. Bell (Chief Acct)
Immediate Holding Company: ASSOCIATED KNOWLEDGE SYSTEMS LIMITED
Registration no: 02062760 **VAT No.:** GB 500 6213 10
Date established: 1986 **No.of Employees:** 1 - 10 **Product Groups:** 44

Date of Accounts	Jul 11	Jul 10	Jul 09
Working Capital	49	48	46
Fixed Assets	1	2	1
Current Assets	75	68	69

Aurora Conservatories
The Old Station Naburn, York, YO19 4RW
Tel: 01904-653380 **Fax:** 01904-610318
E-mail: info@btconnect.com
Directors: R. Kent (Dir)
Turnover: £500,000 - £1m **No.of Employees:** 21 - 50 **Product Groups:** 25

Date of Accounts	Apr 06
Working Capital	12
Fixed Assets	94
Current Assets	215
Current Liabilities	203
Total Share Capital	3

Aviation & Marine Engineering Ltd
Dove Way Kirkby Mills Industrial Estate, Kirkbymoorside, York, YO62 6QR
Tel: 01751-432472 **Fax:** 01751-432667
E-mail: karen.ward@swiftaircraft.co.uk
Website: http://www.a-mel.co.uk
Directors: T. Stanbridge (Fin)
Managers: K. Ward (Sales Admin)
Ultimate Holding Company: SWIFT TECHNOLOGY GROUP LIMITED
Immediate Holding Company: AVIATION AND MARINE ENGINEERING LIMITED
Registration no: 01646529 **Date established:** 1982
Turnover: Up to £250,000 **No.of Employees:** 1 - 10 **Product Groups:** 30, 39

Date of Accounts	Mar 12	Mar 11	Mar 10
Sales Turnover	64	N/A	N/A
Pre Tax Profit/Loss	-32	N/A	N/A
Working Capital	-12	-14	-10
Fixed Assets	2	2	3
Current Assets	N/A	5	9
Current Liabilities	6	N/A	N/A

Barker
Arden Grange Main Street, Bilbrough, York, YO23 3PH
Tel: 01937-833259 **Fax:** 01937-833259
E-mail: suzanne@ardengrange.plus.com
Directors: A. Barker (Ptnr), S. Barker (Ptnr)
Immediate Holding Company: THE THREE HARES AT BILBROUGH LIMITED
Registration no: 03416783 **Date established:** 2009
No.of Employees: 1 - 10 **Product Groups:** 41

Best Western International Ltd
Consort House Aimee Johnson Way, York, YO30 4GP
Tel: 01904-695400 **Fax:** 020-8541 5562
E-mail: enquiries@bestwestern.co.uk
Website: http://www.bestwestern.co.uk
Directors: D. Clarke (Grp Chief Exec), D. Kong (Pres), R. Borges (Fin)
Managers: K. Packham, H. Parker (Sales Prom Mgr), Heathfield (Software Mgr)
Ultimate Holding Company: BEST WESTERN INTERNATIONAL INC (USA)
Immediate Holding Company: BEST WESTERN INTERNATIONAL LIMITED
Registration no: 01939154 **Date established:** 1985
No.of Employees: 101 - 250 **Product Groups:** 69

William Birch & Sons Ltd
Link Road Court Osbaldwick, York, YO10 3JQ
Tel: 01904-411411 **Fax:** 01904-428428
E-mail: chris.birch@williambirch.co.uk
Website: http://www.williambirch.co.uk
Bank(s): Barclays
Directors: A. Birch (Fin), C. Birch (MD), C. Birch (MD)
Managers: A. Marshall (Buyer), K. Shooter
Immediate Holding Company: WILLIAM BIRCH & SONS LIMITED
Registration no: 00129834 **VAT No.:** GB 168 8745 06
Date established: 2013 **Turnover:** £10m - £20m
No.of Employees: 21 - 50 **Product Groups:** 52

Date of Accounts	Dec 11	Dec 10	Dec 09
Sales Turnover	18m	20m	21m
Pre Tax Profit/Loss	61	78	-1m
Working Capital	3m	4m	3m
Fixed Assets	9m	9m	10m
Current Assets	7m	7m	14m
Current Liabilities	540	532	655

Brockwell Fabrications
Pocklington Industrial Estate Pocklington, York, YO42 1NP
Tel: 01759-304742 **Fax:** 01759-304742
E-mail: enquiries@brockwellfabrications.co.uk
Website: http://www.brockwellfabrications.co.uk
Directors: P. Brockwell (Prop)
Ultimate Holding Company: MISAUN AKTIENGESELLSCHAFT AG (LIECHTENSTEIN)
Immediate Holding Company: ELVINGTON LEISURE LIMITED
Registration no: 03968371 **VAT No.:** GB 390 4978 14
Date established: 2000 **Turnover:** Up to £250,000
No.of Employees: 1 - 10 **Product Groups:** 26, 35, 48

Peter Brown Agricultural Engineers
Holly Cottage Seaton Ross, York, YO42 4NH
Tel: 01759-318793 **Fax:** 01759-318793
Directors: P. Brown (Prop)
Date established: 1989 **No.of Employees:** 1 - 10 **Product Groups:** 41

Buckles
97 Micklegate, York, YO1 6LE
Tel: 01904-623080 **Fax:** 01904- 623080
Directors: P. Buckle (Prop)
Date established: 1999 **No.of Employees:** 1 - 10 **Product Groups:** 20, 40, 41

Builder Center Ltd
1 Hazel Court James Street, York, YO10 3DS
Tel: 01904-430044 **Fax:** 01904-430306
E-mail: york@buildercentre.co.uk
Website: http://www.buildercenter.co.uk
Directors: A. Bykhovsky (Ch)
Managers: A. Timson (Mgr), A. Tinson (Mgr), G. Dunnington (Sales Prom Mgr), P. Reed (Asst Gen Mgr)
Ultimate Holding Company: Wolseley plc
Immediate Holding Company: BUILD CENTER LIMITED
Registration no: 00462397 **VAT No.:** GB 362 0233 93
Date established: 1948 **Turnover:** £500,000 - £1m
No.of Employees: 21 - 50 **Product Groups:** 25, 66

C F Engineering
29 Viking Drive Riccall, York, YO19 6PS
Tel: 07803-866355
E-mail: chris.frankish@sky.com
Website: http://www.fbsnet.co.uk
Directors: C. Frankish (Prop)
Date established: 2001 **No.of Employees:** 1 - 10 **Product Groups:** 41

P J Capstick
East House School Lane, Nawton, York, YO62 7SF
Tel: 01439-771249 **Fax:** 01439-771481
E-mail: pj.capstick@dsl.pipex.com
Directors: P. Capstick (Prop)
Date established: 1987 **No.of Employees:** 1 - 10 **Product Groups:** 41

Castle Pest Control
41 Cherry Drive Holme-on-Spalding-Moor, York, YO43 4HT
Tel: 01430-861123 **Fax:** 01430-861152
E-mail: info@castlepestcontrol.co.uk
Website: http://www.genie.co.uk
Directors: D. Wells (Co Sec), K. Smith (Prop)
Immediate Holding Company: Castle Pest Control Ltd
Registration no: 04581549 **No.of Employees:** 1 - 10 **Product Groups:** 32

Cellhire plc
Park House Clifton Park Avenue, York, YO30 5PB
Tel: 0800-610610 **Fax:** 01904- 611028
E-mail: info@fonefix.com
Website: http://www.cellhire.co.uk
Directors: T. Taylor (Fin), H. Williams (Co Sec), M. Stevens (MD)
Managers: P. Walerton (Tech Serv Mgr), M. Arnell (Sales Prom Mgr), J. Potter (Personnel)
Ultimate Holding Company: CELLHIRE GROUP LIMITED
Immediate Holding Company: CELLHIRE PLC
Registration no: 02159836 **Date established:** 1987
Turnover: £10m - £20m **No.of Employees:** 51 - 100 **Product Groups:** 37, 79, 83

Date of Accounts	Apr 12	Apr 11	Apr 10
Sales Turnover	20m	19m	16m
Pre Tax Profit/Loss	1m	1m	476
Working Capital	1m	156	-1m
Fixed Assets	5m	5m	5m
Current Assets	6m	6m	4m
Current Liabilities	2m	2m	2m

Claudius Consulting
5 Whin Road, York, YO24 1JU
Tel: 0845-658 5755 **Fax:** 0870-127 2471
E-mail: mail@claudius-consulting.co.uk
Website: http://www.claudius-consulting.co.uk
Directors: B. Claudius Cole (Fin), C. Claudius Cole (Dir)
Immediate Holding Company: CLAUDIUS CONSULTING LIMITED
Registration no: 06107243 **Date established:** 2007
No.of Employees: 1 - 10 **Product Groups:** 54, 80, 81, 84, 85, 86, 87

Date of Accounts	Feb 08	Feb 11	Feb 10
Working Capital	-247	1	-125
Fixed Assets	360	245	284
Current Assets	116	330	183

The Cleaner Company
107 Danebury Drive, York, YO26 5HA
Tel: 01904-787485 **Fax:** 01904-789424
E-mail: chris@hsyork.co.uk
Website: http://www.hsyork.co.uk
Directors: C. Barrett (Prop)
Immediate Holding Company: PLANNING ANGELS LTD
Registration no: 07130141 **Date established:** 2010
Turnover: £250,000 - £500,000 **No.of Employees:** 1 - 10
Product Groups: 23, 40, 52

Computercare.Co.Uk
22 Back Lane Holme-On-Spalding-Moor, York, YO43 4AW
Tel: 01757-705622 **Fax:** 08717-146853
E-mail: info@computer-care.co.uk
Website: http://www.computercare.co.uk
Directors: R. Lobsiger (Prop)
No.of Employees: 1 - 10 **Product Groups:** 37, 44, 79

Crucible Technologies Ltd
11 Glaisdale Road Northminster Business Park, York, YO26 6QT
Tel: 01904-792211 **Fax:** 01904-352400
E-mail: sales@crucible-technologies.co.uk
Website: http://www.crucible-technologies.co.uk
Directors: S. Segaran (MD), J. Segaran (Fin)
Immediate Holding Company: Crucible Technologies Ltd
Registration no: 02965308 **Date established:** 1988
No.of Employees: 1 - 10 **Product Groups:** 37

Cyclops Electronics Ltd
Link Business Park Osbaldwick Link Road, York, YO10 3JB
Tel: 01904-415415 **Fax:** 01904-424424
E-mail: sales@cyclops-electronics.com
Website: http://www.cyclops-electronics.com
Directors: L. Yodaiken (Fin)
Managers: B. Scott (Mktg Serv Mgr), T. Dowling (Tech Serv Mgr), S. Mellor (Fin Mgr), M. Sinclair (Sales Admin), S. Singer (Sales Prom Mgr)
Immediate Holding Company: CYCLOPS ELECTRONICS LIMITED
Registration no: SC128862 **Date established:** 1990
Turnover: £10m - £20m **No.of Employees:** 51 - 100 **Product Groups:** 33, 35, 37, 38, 39, 44, 67, 80, 84

Date of Accounts	Mar 11	Mar 10	Mar 09
Sales Turnover	12m	8m	N/A
Pre Tax Profit/Loss	55	52	778
Working Capital	3m	2m	2m
Fixed Assets	515	403	128
Current Assets	6m	5m	4m
Current Liabilities	2m	908	800

Dayward Services Ltd
Unit A-C Lancaster Road Pocklington Industrial Estate, Pocklington, York, YO42 1NP
Tel: 01759-305900 **Fax:** 01759-305900
Website: http://www.industrial-filters.co.uk
Directors: J. Ward (Fin), D. Ward (MD)
Immediate Holding Company: DAYWARD SERVICES LIMITED
Registration no: 04499827 **Date established:** 2002
No.of Employees: 1 - 10 **Product Groups:** 38, 42

Date of Accounts	Aug 11	Aug 10	Aug 08
Working Capital	-5	-12	-18
Fixed Assets	12	13	16
Current Assets	37	35	21

Detectamet Ltd
Unit 55, Halifax Way Pocklington Industrial Estate, Pocklington, York, YO42 1NR
Tel: 01759-304200 **Fax:** 01759-305236
E-mail: angela.musson@detectamet.com
Website: http://www.detectamet.com
Directors: S. Smith (MD)
Managers: A. Musson-Smith (Sales Prom Mgr)
Registration no: 05103699 **Turnover:** £250,000 - £500,000
No.of Employees: 1 - 10 **Product Groups:** 45, 67

Direct Stone Importers
3 Kettlestring Lane, York, YO30 4XF
Tel: 01904-692903 **Fax:** 01904-693783
E-mail: info@directtiles.co.uk
Website: http://www.directtiles.co.uk
Managers: S. Humphries (Mktg Serv Mgr)
Immediate Holding Company: DIRECT STONE IMPORTERS
Registration no: 05378440 **Date established:** 2005
No.of Employees: 1 - 10 **Product Groups:** 32, 33

P D Earnshaw Artistic Iron Work
9 Midway Avenue Nether Poppleton, York, YO26 6NT
Tel: 01904-798852 **Fax:** 01904-798852
Website: http://www.yorkironworks.co.uk
Directors: P. Earnshaw (Prop)
No.of Employees: 1 - 10 **Product Groups:** 26, 35

Eborcraft Ltd
11-12 Chessingham Park Common Road Dunnington, York, YO19 5SE
Tel: 01904-481020 **Fax:** 01904-481022
E-mail: sales@eborcraft.co.uk
Website: http://www.eborcraft.co.uk
Bank(s): HSBC Bank plc
Managers: J. Miles (Sales Admin)
Immediate Holding Company: EBORCRAFT LIMITED
Registration no: 00247508 **VAT No.:** GB 168 9494 00
Date established: 1930 **Turnover:** £1m - £2m **No.of Employees:** 21 - 50
Product Groups: 26

see next page

Eborcraft Ltd - Cont'd

Date of Accounts	Dec 11	Dec 10	Dec 09
Working Capital	447	456	353
Fixed Assets	2m	2m	2m
Current Assets	728	781	571

Elcock's Ltd
Hospital Fields Road Fulford Industrial Estate, York, YO10 4FT
Tel: 01904-611100 **Fax:** 01904-628453
E-mail: andrew@elcocks.co.uk
Website: http://www.elcocks.co.uk
Directors: A. Elcock (MD), I. Elcock (Tech Serv)
Managers: J. Holdsworth (Mktg Serv Mgr), E. Atkinson, E. Atkinson
Immediate Holding Company: ELCOCKS LIMITED
Registration no: 01294435 **Date established:** 1977 **Turnover:** £2m - £5m
No.of Employees: 11 - 20 **Product Groups:** 37

Date of Accounts	Mar 11	Mar 10	Mar 09
Working Capital	6	188	253
Fixed Assets	225	227	229
Current Assets	840	786	1m

Electronics Direct Ltd
Headway House Dale Road, Sheriff Hutton, York, YO60 6RZ
Tel: 01347-878210 **Fax:** 08702-202291
E-mail: sales@electronics-direct.com
Website: http://www.electronics-direct.com
Managers: S. Jackson
Immediate Holding Company: ELECTRONICS DIRECT LIMITED
Registration no: 03884011 **Date established:** 1999
No.of Employees: 11 - 20 **Product Groups:** 34, 37, 67

Date of Accounts	Apr 11	Apr 10	Apr 09
Working Capital	277	117	166
Fixed Assets	31	17	14
Current Assets	644	332	358

Equity Shoes Ltd
Catherine House Upper Poppleton, York, YO26 6QU
Tel: 0844-8440203 **Fax:** 01904-528 791
E-mail: helpdesk@pavers.co.uk
Website: http://www.equityshoes.com
Bank(s): Co-Operative
Managers: P. Crumbie (Sales Prom Mgr), R. Jones (Buyer), R. Spencer (Chief Mgr), J. Davis
Immediate Holding Company: EQUITY SHOES LIMITED
Registration no: IP02572R **VAT No.:** GB 113 8457 76
Date established: 1967 **Turnover:** £5m - £10m
No.of Employees: 251 - 500 **Product Groups:** 22

Date of Accounts	Dec 06	Nov 05
Sales Turnover	7m	7m
Pre Tax Profit/Loss	19	-340
Working Capital	3m	3m
Fixed Assets	1m	1m
Current Assets	4m	4m
Current Liabilities	839	690
Total Share Capital	8	8

Eurocell Building Plastics Ltd
1 Sterling Park, York, YO30 4WU
Tel: 01904-479201 **Fax:** 01904-475440
Website: http://www.eurocell.co.uk
Managers: H. Scaise (Mgr)
Ultimate Holding Company: TESSENDERLO CHEMIE NV (BELGIUM)
Immediate Holding Company: EUROCELL BUILDING PLASTICS LIMITED
Registration no: 03071407 **Date established:** 1995
No.of Employees: 1 - 10 **Product Groups:** 31, 32, 61

Date of Accounts	Dec 11	Dec 10	Dec 09
Sales Turnover	82m	80m	68m
Pre Tax Profit/Loss	4m	5m	4m
Working Capital	15m	12m	7m
Fixed Assets	3m	3m	5m
Current Assets	29m	29m	20m
Current Liabilities	4m	4m	3m

Eye for Marketing
34 Queen Anne's Road Bootham, YORK, YO30 7AA
Tel: 01904-625182
E-mail: support@eyeformarketing.com
Website: http://www.eyeformarketing.com
Directors: K. Mason (Prop)
Date established: 2010 **Turnover:** **No.of Employees:** 1 - 10
Product Groups: 44, 81

Fabric Gallery & Interiors
13 York Street Dunnington, York, YO19 5PN
Tel: 01904-481101 **Fax:** 01904-481101
E-mail: steve@fabricgallery.co.uk
Website: http://www.fabricgallery.co.uk
Directors: S. Whitt (Dir)
No.of Employees: 1 - 10 **Product Groups:** 23, 25, 63, 66

Flatford
York Road Elvington, York, YO41 4DY
Tel: 01904-608383 **Fax:** 01904-608483
E-mail: sales@flatford.co.uk
Directors: J. Barry (MD)
Immediate Holding Company: FLATFORD LIMITED
Registration no: 01082375 **VAT No.:** GB 170 6988 31
Date established: 1972 **Turnover:** £500,000 - £1m
No.of Employees: 11 - 20 **Product Groups:** 39, 48, 84

Date of Accounts	Aug 11	Aug 10	Aug 09
Sales Turnover	915	668	597
Pre Tax Profit/Loss	1	-10	-97
Working Capital	186	181	185
Fixed Assets	169	173	179
Current Assets	420	344	360
Current Liabilities	5	4	6

Focus 4 Print Ltd
1 James Street, York, YO10 3WW
Tel: 01904-673030 **Fax:** 01904-541027
E-mail: office@focus4print.co.uk
Website: http://www.focus4print.co.uk
Directors: G. Hastings (Dir)
Immediate Holding Company: FOCUS 4 PRINT LIMITED
Registration no: 06613271 **Date established:** 2008
No.of Employees: 1 - 10 **Product Groups:** 28, 44

Date of Accounts	May 11	May 10	May 09
Working Capital	17	6	1
Fixed Assets	11	11	14
Current Assets	73	58	41

Foss Controls
11 Glen Road, York, YO31 0XQ
Tel: 01904-415253
E-mail: sales@fosscontrols.co.uk
Website: http://www.fosscontrols.co.uk
Directors: M. Gilkes (Prop)
Date established: 2001 **No.of Employees:** 1 - 10 **Product Groups:** 20, 40, 41

Hambaker Adams Ltd
PO Box 15, York, YO30 4XE
Tel: 01904-695695 **Fax:** 01904-695600
E-mail: enquiries@hambakeradams.co.uk
Website: http://www.hambakeradams.co.uk
Bank(s): National Westminster Bank Plc
Directors: J. Milner (Pers), R. Hammerton (Fin)
Managers: G. Brereton (Comptroller), S. Smith (Tech Serv Mgr)
Ultimate Holding Company: WTB HOLDINGS LIMITED
Immediate Holding Company: ADAMS-HYDRAULICS,LIMITED
Registration no: 00076236 **VAT No.:** GB 551 7838 21
Date established: 2003 **Turnover:** £2m - £5m
No.of Employees: 101 - 250 **Product Groups:** 36, 42

Date of Accounts	Dec 11	Dec 10	Dec 09
Sales Turnover	615	4m	8m
Pre Tax Profit/Loss	-233	-3m	-712
Working Capital	N/A	-1m	2m
Fixed Assets	N/A	75	146
Current Assets	N/A	1m	5m
Current Liabilities	N/A	549	810

Harsh Ltd
The Industrial Estate Full Sutton, York, YO41 1HS
Tel: 01759-372100 **Fax:** 01759-371414
E-mail: grant.faulkner@harshuk.com
Website: http://www.harshuk.com
Directors: R. Faulkner (MD)
Immediate Holding Company: HARSH LIMITED
Registration no: 02168135 **Date established:** 1987 **Turnover:** £2m - £5m
No.of Employees: 11 - 20 **Product Groups:** 40

Date of Accounts	Feb 12	Feb 11	Feb 10
Working Capital	1m	1m	1m
Fixed Assets	572	494	518
Current Assets	2m	2m	2m

J E Hartley Ltd
Rothill Lane Thorganby, York, YO19 6DJ
Tel: 01904-448556 **Fax:** 01904-448479
E-mail: info@jehartleyfrozenveg.co.uk
Website: http://www.jehartleyfrozenveg.co.uk
Managers: T. Verity (Mgr)
Immediate Holding Company: J.E.HARTLEY LIMITED
Registration no: 00531889 **Date established:** 1954
Turnover: £10m - £20m **No.of Employees:** 51 - 100 **Product Groups:** 20, 40, 41

Date of Accounts	Dec 10	Dec 09	Dec 08
Sales Turnover	11m	9m	8m
Pre Tax Profit/Loss	428	110	435
Working Capital	2m	2m	2m
Fixed Assets	276	12m	11m
Current Assets	4m	4m	4m
Current Liabilities	882	1m	1m

Ashley Hastings
20 Manor Heath Copmanthorpe, York, YO23 3SL
Tel: 01904-700847
E-mail: info@ashleyhastings.co.uk
Website: http://www.ashleyhastings.co.uk
Directors: A. Hastings (Prop)
Turnover: Up to £250,000 **No.of Employees:** 1 - 10 **Product Groups:** 81

Hawthorn Printmaker Supplies
Hawthorn Houseappleton Roebuck, Appleton Roebuck, York, YO23 7DA
Tel: 01904-744649 **Fax:** 01904-744649
E-mail: hpsupplies@tiscali.co.uk
Website: http://www.hawthornprintmaker.co.uk
Directors: B. Rushton (Prop)
Date established: 2003 **Turnover:** Up to £250,000
No.of Employees: 1 - 10 **Product Groups:** 32

Herbert Todd & Son
Percys Lane, York, YO1 9TP
Tel: 01904-628676 **Fax:** 01904-653328
E-mail: enquiries@htodd.co.uk
Website: http://www.htodd.co.uk
Bank(s): Lloyds TSB Bank plc
Directors: G. Todd (Prop), M. Todd (Ptnr)
VAT No.: GB 169 9441 15 **Turnover:** £1m - £2m **No.of Employees:** 21 - 50
Product Groups: 52, 63

Heymark Metals Ltd
Unit 4 Becklands Close Bar Lane, Roecliffe, York, YO51 9NR
Tel: 01423-323388 **Fax:** 01423-326888
E-mail: info@heymark.co.uk
Website: http://www.heymark.co.uk
Directors: A. Heyes (MD)
Immediate Holding Company: HEYMARK METALS LIMITED
Registration no: 01527056 **Date established:** 1980 **Turnover:** £2m - £5m
No.of Employees: 1 - 10 **Product Groups:** 34, 66

Date of Accounts	Jul 11	Jul 10	Jul 09
Sales Turnover	N/A	4m	4m
Pre Tax Profit/Loss	N/A	384	376
Working Capital	491	402	251
Fixed Assets	154	180	216
Current Assets	865	1m	2m
Current Liabilities	256	478	585

Holmes Catering Equipment Ltd
The Industrial Estate Full Sutton, York, YO41 1HS
Tel: 01759-375500 **Fax:** 01759-375509
E-mail: alawson@hce.co.uk
Website: http://www.hce.co.uk
Directors: A. Lawson (Fin), I. Free (Comm)
Managers: J. Holmes (Personnel)
Ultimate Holding Company: HOLMES CATERING GROUP LTD
Immediate Holding Company: HOLMES CATERING EQUIPMENT LTD.
Registration no: 01649809 **Date established:** 1982
No.of Employees: 21 - 50 **Product Groups:** 26, 40, 48, 66, 67, 84

Date of Accounts	Dec 11	Dec 10	Dec 09
Working Capital	933	519	-26
Fixed Assets	N/A	N/A	15
Current Assets	3m	3m	2m

Holztechnik Machinery Services Ltd
Unit 21a Evans Business Centre Marston Moor Business Park, Tockwith, York, YO26 7QF
Tel: 01423-359234 **Fax:** 01423-359234
E-mail: holzmachineryuk@btconnect.com
Website: http://www.holztechnik-machinery.co.uk
Directors: P. Treen (MD)
Immediate Holding Company: HOLZTECHNIK MACHINERY SERVICES LIMITED
Registration no: 02098968 **Date established:** 1987
Turnover: Up to £250,000 **No.of Employees:** 1 - 10 **Product Groups:** 46

Date of Accounts	Mar 11	Mar 10	Mar 09
Sales Turnover	99	104	149
Pre Tax Profit/Loss	13	-9	12
Working Capital	-17	-18	-13
Fixed Assets	21	12	15
Current Assets	46	44	24
Current Liabilities	10	6	8

Hydrographics
Brockett Industrial Estate The Airfield, Acaster Malbis, York, YO23 2PT
Tel: 01904-778188 **Fax:** 01904-778188
Website: http://www.hydro-graphics.co.uk
Directors: M. Sykes (Co Sec), J. Sykes (Dir)
Immediate Holding Company: HYDRO GRAPHICS LTD
Registration no: 04774187 **Date established:** 2003
No.of Employees: 1 - 10 **Product Groups:** 46, 48

I-Comm
70 Bondgate Helmsley, York, YO62 5EZ
Tel: 08449-024880 **Fax:** 0870-777 4881
E-mail: info@i-ccom.com
Website: http://www.i-ccom.com
Managers: F. Brunton (Sales Admin)
Immediate Holding Company: ICCOM LIMITED
Registration no: 03746088 **Date established:** 1999 **Turnover:** £2m - £5m
No.of Employees: 1 - 10 **Product Groups:** 37

Date of Accounts	Apr 11	Apr 10	Apr 09
Working Capital	-170	42	-1
Fixed Assets	14	16	23
Current Assets	115	223	151

IMPACT JOINERS
20 Ryedale view kirkbymoorside, york, YO62 6EH
Tel: 01751-431436
E-mail: impactjoiners@btinternet.com
Website: http://www.impactjoiners.co.uk
Managers: D. EILSON (Chief Acct)
Registration no: SC328508 **Date established:** 1985
No.of Employees: 1 - 10 **Product Groups:** 25

Industrial Textiles & Plastics Ltd
Easingwold Business Park Oaklands Way, Easingwold, York, YO61 3FA
Tel: 01347-825200 **Fax:** 01347-825222
E-mail: mv@itpltd.com
Website: http://www.indtex.co.uk
Directors: M. Van Der Voort (MD), A. Menage (Co Sec)
Immediate Holding Company: INDUSTRIAL TEXTILES & PLASTICS LTD
Registration no: 02382352 **VAT No.:** GB 551 8501 51
Date established: 1989 **Turnover:** £10m - £20m
No.of Employees: 11 - 20 **Product Groups:** 23, 24, 30, 31, 35, 36, 39, 66

Date of Accounts	Mar 11	Mar 10	Mar 09
Working Capital	510	362	203
Fixed Assets	350	345	404
Current Assets	1m	2m	1m

J H P Training Ltd
Merchant Chambers 44-46 Fossgate, York, YO1 9TF
Tel: 01904-641721 **Fax:** 01904-610348
E-mail: york.business.centre@jhp-group.com
Website: http://www.jhptraining.com
Managers: K. Thompson (Mgr)
Immediate Holding Company: JHP TRAINING LIMITED
Registration no: 03247918 **Date established:** 1996 **Turnover:** £1m - £2m
No.of Employees: 1 - 10 **Product Groups:** 86

Jewson Ltd
Kettlestring Lane, York, YO30 4WF
Tel: 01904-690441 **Fax:** 01904-690552
Website: http://www.jewson.co.uk
Bank(s): Barclays
Directors: T. Newman (Sales), P. Hindle (MD)
Managers: R. Jarvis (District Mgr)
Ultimate Holding Company: COMPAGNIE DE SAINT GOBAIN (FRANCE)
Immediate Holding Company: JEWSON LIMITED
Registration no: 00348407 **Date established:** 1939
Turnover: £500m - £1,000m **No.of Employees:** 21 - 50
Product Groups: 66

Date of Accounts	Dec 11	Dec 10	Dec 09
Sales Turnover	1606m	1547m	1485m
Pre Tax Profit/Loss	18m	100m	45m
Working Capital	-345m	-250m	-349m
Fixed Assets	496m	387m	461m
Current Assets	657m	1005m	1320m
Current Liabilities	66m	120m	64m

Kubernesis Partnership LLP
36 Acomb Wood Drive, York, YO24 2XN
Tel: 01904-788885 **Fax:** 01904-339117
E-mail: info@kubernesis.co.uk
Website: http://www.kubernesis.co.uk
Directors: G. Morgan (Snr Part)
Immediate Holding Company: THE KUBERNESIS PARTNERSHIP LLP
Registration no: OC340834 **VAT No.:** GB 698 4883 50
Date established: 2008 **Turnover:** Up to £250,000
No.of Employees: 1 - 10 **Product Groups:** 80

Date of Accounts	Oct 11	Oct 10	Oct 09
Working Capital	11	8	12
Fixed Assets	N/A	1	1
Current Assets	15	15	19

Langdale International Ltd
52 Langdale Road Market Weighton, York, YO43 3DG
Tel: 01430-874157 **Fax:** 01430-871033
E-mail: sales@langint.co.uk
Website: http://www.langtel.co.uk
Directors: C. Hemmerman (Dir), P. Hemmerman (MD), P. Hemmerman (Dir)
Managers: S. Cox (Sales Admin)
Immediate Holding Company: LANGDALE INTERNATIONAL LIMITED
Registration no: 03072806 **Date established:** 1995
No.of Employees: 1 - 10 **Product Groups:** 27, 39

Date of Accounts	May 11	May 10	May 09
Working Capital	-1	-2	-1
Fixed Assets	3	4	4
Current Assets	25	21	28

Langthorpe Plating Ltd
Brickyard Road Roecliffe, York, YO51 9NS
Tel: 01423-325099 **Fax:** 01423-325117
Directors: P. Outhwaite (Dir)
Immediate Holding Company: LANGTHORPE PLATING LIMITED
Registration no: 06086146 **Date established:** 2007
No.of Employees: 1 - 10 **Product Groups:** 46, 48

Date of Accounts	Mar 11	Mar 10	Mar 09
Working Capital	220	68	61
Fixed Assets	56	57	73
Current Assets	341	118	131

Leerco Engineering
Full Sutton Industrial Estate Stamford Bridge, York, YO41 1HS
Tel: 01759-371128 **Fax:** 01759-371034
E-mail: sales@leerco.com
Website: http://www.leerco.com
Directors: M. Thornton (Dir), S. Blayze (MD), S. Blazye (MD)
Ultimate Holding Company: R.M. ENGLISH & SON LIMITED
Registration no: 03452150 **VAT No.:** GB 324 7879 26
Date established: 1954 **Turnover:** £2m - £5m **No.of Employees:** 1 - 10
Product Groups: 37, 40, 45, 46

Linmech Technical Solutions Ltd
York Eco Business Centre Amy Johnson Way, Clifton Moor, York, YO30 4AG
Tel: 01904-479701 **Fax:** 01347-811138
E-mail: enquiries@linmech.co.uk
Website: http://www.linmech.co.uk
Registration no: 05265038 **Product Groups:** 38, 44, 48, 67, 80, 81, 83, 84, 85, 86

Date of Accounts	Oct 07	Oct 06	Oct 05
Working Capital	-1	N/A	3
Fixed Assets	6	6	8
Current Assets	17	8	10
Current Liabilities	18	7	6

M S S Clean Technology
Castle House 14 Dale Road, Sheriff Hutton, York, YO60 6RZ
Tel: 01347-878877 **Fax:** 01347-878878
E-mail: postbox@mss-ct.co.uk
Website: http://www.mss-ct.co.uk
Bank(s): HSBC Bank plc
Directors: N. Squires (Fin), P. Walters (MD)
Managers: R. Pollard (Tech Serv Mgr)
Ultimate Holding Company: MSS GROUP (UK) LIMITED
Immediate Holding Company: MSS CLEAN TECHNOLOGY LIMITED
Registration no: 01652830 **Date established:** 1982
Turnover: £10m - £20m **No.of Employees:** 21 - 50 **Product Groups:** 40, 66

Date of Accounts	Jun 11	Jun 10	Jun 09
Working Capital	457	552	474
Fixed Assets	18	25	36
Current Assets	1m	1m	2m

Machines Automation Robotic Systems Ltd
Stamford Bridge Road Dunnington, York, YO19 5LJ
Tel: 01904-489888
E-mail: sales@mars.gb.net
Website: http://www.mars.gb.net
Directors: M. Askhan (Dir)
Immediate Holding Company: MACHINES AUTOMATION ROBOTIC SYSTEMS LTD
Registration no: 01814364 **Date established:** 1984
No.of Employees: 1 - 10 **Product Groups:** 45, 84

Date of Accounts	Dec 11	Dec 10	Dec 09
Working Capital	-30	62	-17
Fixed Assets	19	20	22
Current Assets	22	140	43

Marshall Arts
Unit 7 Elvington Industrial Estate York Road, Elvington, York, YO41 4AR
Tel: 01904-607055 **Fax:** 01904-608188
E-mail: paul@marshall-art.net
Website: http://www.marshallarts.co.uk
Directors: P. Marshall (MD)
Registration no: 04182992 **Date established:** 1977
Turnover: £500,000 - £1m **No.of Employees:** 1 - 10 **Product Groups:** 25

K B & J D Medley
Ball Hall Farm Storwood, York, YO42 4TD
Tel: 01759-318752 **Fax:** 01759-318509
Directors: K. Medley (Ptnr)
Date established: 2001 **No.of Employees:** 1 - 10 **Product Groups:** 35

Michael Lupton Associates Ltd
Halifax House Seaton Ross, York, YO42 4LU
Tel: 01759-318557 **Fax:** 01759-318947
E-mail: sales@mlaltd.co.uk
Website: http://www.mlaltd.co.uk
Directors: J. Lupton (Fin), M. Lupton (MD)
Immediate Holding Company: MICHAEL LUPTON ASSOCIATES LIMITED
Registration no: 03127622 **VAT No.:** GB 317 2846 55
Date established: 1995 **No.of Employees:** 1 - 10 **Product Groups:** 24, 63

Date of Accounts	Mar 12	Mar 11	Mar 10
Working Capital	264	240	193
Fixed Assets	68	61	32
Current Assets	1m	785	714

Micro Metalsmiths Ltd
Kirkdale Road Kirkbymoorside, York, YO62 6PX
Tel: 01751-432355 **Fax:** 01751-432061
E-mail: c.shaw@micrometalsmiths.co.uk
Website: http://www.micrometalsmiths.com
Bank(s): Barclays
Directors: C. Shaw (Dir)
Managers: S. Hodgeson, D. Cumming, J. Pashley
Immediate Holding Company: MICRO-METALSMITHS LIMITED
Registration no: 00786649 **VAT No.:** GB 167 0017 85
Date established: 1964 **Turnover:** £5m - £10m
No.of Employees: 101 - 250 **Product Groups:** 34, 37, 38, 39, 40, 42, 46, 48, 66, 67, 84, 85

Date of Accounts	Mar 11	Mar 10	Mar 09
Sales Turnover	6m	6m	6m
Pre Tax Profit/Loss	138	96	302
Working Capital	1m	2m	1m
Fixed Assets	3m	2m	3m
Current Assets	2m	3m	3m
Current Liabilities	280	464	538

Milestone Metal Works
The Old Gas Works Kirbymills Kirkbymoorside, York, YO62 6DN
Tel: 01751-433213 **Fax:** 01751-431799
Directors: R. Milestone (Prop)
Date established: 1983 **No.of Employees:** 1 - 10 **Product Groups:** 35

Minster Engineering Co. Ltd
Ebor Industrial Estate 74 Hallfield Road, York, YO31 7XD
Tel: 01904-717220 **Fax:** 01904-717222
E-mail: christine@minstereng.freeserve.co.uk
Website: http://www.minsterengineering.co.uk
Bank(s): Barclays
Directors: G. Allison (Dir)
Managers: C. Vardy (Chief Mgr)
Immediate Holding Company: TAGA HOMES LIMITED
Registration no: 03375919 **VAT No.:** GB 721 3484 55
Date established: 1997 **No.of Employees:** 11 - 20 **Product Groups:** 48

Date of Accounts	May 11	May 10	May 09
Working Capital	932	875	880
Fixed Assets	16	1	N/A
Current Assets	1m	1m	1m

Newitt & Co.
Claxton Hall Flaxton, York, YO60 7RE
Tel: 01904-468551 **Fax:** 01904-468386
E-mail: nnewitt@newitts.com
Website: http://www.newitts.com
Bank(s): The Royal Bank of Scotland
Directors: N. Newitt (Dir), N. Newitt (Prop)
Managers: F. Newitt (Purch Mgr)
Immediate Holding Company: NEWITT & CO LIMITED
Registration no: 04561672 **VAT No.:** GB 169 8326 20
Date established: 2002 **Turnover:** £5m - £10m **No.of Employees:** 21 - 50
Product Groups: 28, 49, 65

Normanton Laminating Services Ltd
Lincoln Road Airfield Industrial Estate, Pocklington, York, YO42 1NR
Tel: 01759-322160 **Fax:** 01759-322170
E-mail: enquiries@normanton.co.uk
Website: http://www.normanton.co.uk
Directors: G. Heathcote (Dir)
Managers: K. Bird (Accounts)
Registration no: 01392189 **Date established:** 1978 **Turnover:** £5m - £10m
No.of Employees: 21 - 50 **Product Groups:** 25

Date of Accounts	Mar 10	Mar 09	Mar 08
Working Capital	1m	1m	1m
Fixed Assets	726	745	866
Current Assets	2m	2m	3m

Northern Crop Driers Ltd
Melrose Farm Melbourne, York, YO42 4SS
Tel: 01759-318396 **Fax:** 01759-318948
E-mail: info@northerncropdriers.co.uk
Website: http://www.northerncropdriers.co.uk
Directors: P. Rowbottom (Dir)
Immediate Holding Company: NORTHERN CROP DRIERS LIMITED
Registration no: 01343050 **Date established:** 1977 **Turnover:** £1m - £2m
No.of Employees: 1 - 10 **Product Groups:** 20

Date of Accounts	Mar 12	Mar 11	Mar 10
Sales Turnover	N/A	N/A	1m
Pre Tax Profit/Loss	N/A	N/A	169
Working Capital	490	1m	961
Fixed Assets	1m	902	844
Current Assets	751	2m	1m
Current Liabilities	N/A	N/A	210

Northmoor Engineering Ltd
Unit 2 Tholthorpe Business Park, Tholthorpe, York, YO61 1SS
Tel: 01347-833377
Immediate Holding Company: NORTH MOOR ENGINEERING LIMITED
Registration no: 04129888 **Date established:** 2000
Turnover: Up to £250,000 **No.of Employees:** 1 - 10 **Product Groups:** 39, 40, 44

Date of Accounts	Jan 11	Jan 10	Jan 09
Sales Turnover	106	145	122
Working Capital	23	21	22
Fixed Assets	33	35	40
Current Assets	29	25	29
Current Liabilities	N/A	1	1

O S D I M T Marine Consultants Ltd
Escrick Grange Stillingfleet Road, Escrick, York, YO19 6EB
Tel: 01904-728904 **Fax:** 01904-728910
E-mail: info@imtmarine.com
Website: http://www.offshoreshipdesigners.com
Managers: S. Reasbeck (Chief Mgr)
Immediate Holding Company: I M T MARINE CONSULTANTS LTD
Registration no: SC298023 **No.of Employees:** 1 - 10 **Product Groups:** 37, 84

P M S York Ltd
34 Buckingham Street, York, YO1 6DW
Tel: 01904-636969 **Fax:** 01904-647724
E-mail: training@pmsyork.co.uk
Website: http://www.pmsyork.co.uk
Managers: D. Helstrip (Sales Admin)
Immediate Holding Company: PMS (YORK) LIMITED
Registration no: 03693528 **VAT No.:** GB 392 1323 66
Date established: 1999 **Turnover:** Up to £250,000
No.of Employees: 1 - 10 **Product Groups:** 86

Date of Accounts	Feb 12	Feb 11	Feb 10
Sales Turnover	N/A	N/A	227
Pre Tax Profit/Loss	N/A	N/A	17
Working Capital	172	158	165
Fixed Assets	22	12	15
Current Assets	252	219	226
Current Liabilities	N/A	N/A	37

P R Elsworth & Co.
The Joiners Shop North End, Raskelf, York, YO61 3LF
Tel: 01347-822654 **Fax:** 01347-821375
Directors: C. Elsworth (Ptnr)
Date established: 1955 **No.of Employees:** 1 - 10 **Product Groups:** 35

P Silk
18 Bridge Street Helmsley, York, YO62 5DX
Tel: 01439-770051
Directors: E. Walters (Prop)
No.of Employees: 1 - 10 **Product Groups:** 24, 26, 61

P T G Treatments Ltd
A7 Riccall Business Park Selby Road, Riccall, York, YO19 6QR
Tel: 01757-249908 **Fax:** 01757-248808
E-mail: info@ptgtreatments.co.uk
Website: http://www.ptgtreatments.co.uk
Directors: S. Adams (Dir)
Ultimate Holding Company: UNION MUTUAL PENSION FUND (L) LTD (MALAYSIA)
Immediate Holding Company: PTG TREATMENTS LIMITED
Registration no: 00549613 **Date established:** 1955 **Turnover:** £2m - £5m
No.of Employees: 1 - 10 **Product Groups:** 25, 32

Date of Accounts	Mar 11	Mar 10	Mar 09
Working Capital	996	746	439
Fixed Assets	577	447	638
Current Assets	2m	2m	1m

Partners In Training Ltd
8 Marsden Park, York, YO30 4GX
Tel: 01904-691777 **Fax:** 01904-691102
E-mail: info@pint.co.uk
Website: http://www.pint.co.uk
Bank(s): natwest
Directors: P. Ogden (Fin), R. Hawker (Sales & Mktg), K. Peckitt (MD), B. Stainthorp (Mkt Research)
Managers: M. Fenton (Fin Mgr)
Immediate Holding Company: PARTNERS IN TRAINING LIMITED
Registration no: 01499497 **VAT No.:** GB 349 4733 25
Date established: 1980 **Turnover:** £1m - £2m **No.of Employees:** 21 - 50
Product Groups: 86

Date of Accounts	Dec 11	Dec 10	Dec 09
Working Capital	552	572	569
Fixed Assets	131	154	149
Current Assets	692	786	929

Perry Slingsby Systems Ltd
Ings Lane Kirkbymoorside, York, YO62 6EZ
Tel: 01751-431751 **Fax:** 01751-431388
E-mail: info@perrymail.com
Website: http://www.perryslingsbysystems.com
Bank(s): Barclays, Slough
Directors: J. Marsden (Fin), J. Marsden (Co Sec)
Managers: K. Taylor
Immediate Holding Company: PERRY SLINGSBY SYSTEMS LIMITED
Registration no: 01401160 **VAT No.:** GB 500 7609 77
Date established: 1978 **Turnover:** £20m - £50m
No.of Employees: 101 - 250 **Product Groups:** 39

Date of Accounts	Dec 10	Dec 09	Dec 08
Sales Turnover	48m	21m	29m
Pre Tax Profit/Loss	9m	3m	2m
Working Capital	13m	7m	7m
Fixed Assets	1m	754	2m
Current Assets	32m	18m	16m
Current Liabilities	5m	6m	3m

Persimmon Homes Ltd
Persimmon House Fulford, York, YO19 4FE
Tel: 01904-642199 **Fax:** 01904-610014
E-mail: human.resources@persimmonhomes.com
Website: http://www.persimmonhomes.com
Directors: D. Thornton (Dir), R. Wright (Dir), M. Killoran (Fin), M. Killoran (Dir), K. Saunders (Dir), S. Feneley (MD), J. White (Grp Chief Exec), D. Bryant (Ch), D. Bryant (Reg MD), D. Broadbent (Dir), C. Johnson (Dir), A. Hadman (Dir), J. Davies (Dir)
Ultimate Holding Company: PERSIMMON PUBLIC LIMITED COMPANY
Immediate Holding Company: PERSIMMON HOMES DEVELOPMENTS LIMITED
Registration no: 02572895 **Date established:** 1991
Turnover: Over £1,000m **No.of Employees:** 51 - 100 **Product Groups:** 52

Date of Accounts	Dec 10	Dec 09	Dec 08
Working Capital	N/A	28	N/A
Current Assets	N/A	22m	N/A

Polar Ford York
Jockey Lane Huntington, York, YO32 9GY
Tel: 01904-625371 **Fax:** 01904-622238
E-mail: sales@polarmotor.co.uk
Website: http://www.polarmotor.co.uk
Bank(s): HSBC, 26 North Station Rd, Colchester
Directors: A. Beattie (MD), M. Brown (Sales & Mktg)
Managers: P. Blythe (Comptroller), R. Ford (Sales Prom Mgr)
Ultimate Holding Company: JARDINE MOTOR GROUP
Immediate Holding Company: LANCASTER MANAGEMENT
VAT No.: GB 406 9746 29 **No.of Employees:** 101 - 250
Product Groups: 68

Portakabin Ltd
New Lane Huntington, York, YO32 9PT
Tel: 01904-611655 **Fax:** 01233-661557
E-mail: sales@portakabin.com
Website: http://www.portakabin.com
Directors: S. Price (Ch), C. Brown (Fin), D. Shaw (Mkt Research), S. Price (Dir)
Immediate Holding Company: PORTAKABIN LIMITED
Registration no: 00685303 **VAT No.:** GB 551 8552 34
Date established: 1961 **Turnover:** £125m - £250m
No.of Employees: 1 - 10 **Product Groups:** 35, 52, 66, 83

Date of Accounts	Jun 11	Jun 10	Jun 09
Sales Turnover	171m	174m	202m
Pre Tax Profit/Loss	27m	26m	30m
Working Capital	35m	25m	8m
Fixed Assets	104m	103m	113m
Current Assets	79m	76m	67m
Current Liabilities	27m	35m	29m

Portasilo Ltd
New Lane Huntington, York, YO32 9PR
Tel: 01904-624872 **Fax:** 01904-611760
E-mail: bulk@portasilo.co.uk
Website: http://www.portasilo.co.uk
Directors: K. Swallow (Fin), P. Clarke (Co Sec)
Managers: G. Lawrence (Purch Mgr), C. Bonello (Tech Serv Mgr), M. Vest (Chief Acct)
Immediate Holding Company: PORTASILO LIMITED
Registration no: 00525808 **Date established:** 1953
Turnover: £10m - £20m **No.of Employees:** 101 - 250
Product Groups: 35, 45, 67

Date of Accounts	Jun 11	Jun 10	Jun 09
Sales Turnover	11m	24m	36m
Pre Tax Profit/Loss	3m	345	2m
Working Capital	5m	10m	3m
Fixed Assets	412	1m	8m
Current Assets	8m	15m	12m
Current Liabilities	871	2m	6m

Portastor Ltd
New Lane Huntington, York, YO32 9PR
Tel: 01904-656869 **Fax:** 01904-687257
E-mail: action@portastor.com
Website: http://www.portastor.com
Managers: P. Overton (Personnel), D. Faddy (Tech Serv Mgr), J. Frazer, J. Frazier (Chief Mgr), K. Swallow (Comptroller), M. Tempest-mitchell (Sales Prom Mgr), P. Overton (Personnel), C. Macdonald (Chief Buyer)
Ultimate Holding Company: SHEPHERD BUILDING GROUP LIMITED
Immediate Holding Company: PORTASTOR LIMITED
Registration no: 06956110 **VAT No.:** GB 169 6911 19
Date established: 2009 **No.of Employees:** 101 - 250 **Product Groups:** 35, 37

Date of Accounts	Jun 11	Jun 10
Sales Turnover	14m	N/A
Pre Tax Profit/Loss	880	N/A
Working Capital	5m	N/A
Fixed Assets	325	N/A
Current Assets	8m	N/A
Current Liabilities	781	N/A

W Richards Liverpool Ltd
10 Pavement Pocklington, York, YO42 2AX
Tel: 01759-305088 **Fax:** 01759-305088
E-mail: chris@wrichardsguns.co.uk
Website: http://www.wrichardsguns.co.uk
Directors: L. Caine (Fin), C. Caine (MD)
Immediate Holding Company: W. RICHARDS (LIVERPOOL) LIMITED
Registration no: 03900332 **Date established:** 1999
Turnover: £250,000 - £500,000 **No.of Employees:** 1 - 10
Product Groups: 36, 39, 40

Date of Accounts	Dec 11	Dec 10	Dec 09
Working Capital	87	111	119
Current Assets	134	126	143

Rolawn Ltd
at Rolawn Head Office Elvington, York, YO41 4XR
Tel: 08456-046075 **Fax:** 01904-608272
E-mail: info@rolawn.co.uk
Website: http://www.rolawn.co.uk
Directors: P. Bray (Fin), P. Oakshott (Co Sec), D. Mumby (Fin), T. Ryan (Sales & Mktg)
Managers: D. Turner (Personnel), L. Willis (Mktg Serv Mgr), C. McMillian (Sales Prom Mgr), P. Brooks (Tech Serv Mgr)
Immediate Holding Company: ROLAWN LIMITED
Registration no: 04373077 **Date established:** 2002
Turnover: £10m - £20m **No.of Employees:** 21 - 50 **Product Groups:** 02

Date of Accounts	Feb 08	Feb 11	Feb 10
Sales Turnover	N/A	12m	12m
Pre Tax Profit/Loss	280	127	-916
Working Capital	2m	2m	2m
Fixed Assets	4m	2m	2m
Current Assets	5m	5m	4m
Current Liabilities	1m	666	713

Rollits Solicitors
Rowntree Wharf Navigation Road, York, YO1 9WE
Tel: 01904-688500 **Fax:** 01904-625807
E-mail: info@rollits.com
Website: http://www.rollits.com
Bank(s): Barclays
Directors: D. Robertson (Fin), M. Wasling (Tech Serv), R. Field (Snr Part)
Managers: P. Coyle, S. Wilson (Purch Mgr)
Immediate Holding Company: ROLLITS COMPANY SECRETARIES YORK LIMITED
Registration no: 03934287 **Date established:** 2000
Turnover: £500,000 - £1m **No.of Employees:** 51 - 100
Product Groups: 80

Rosti Mckechnie Ltd
Bridge Works Stamford Bridge, York, YO41 1AL
Tel: 01759-371551 **Fax:** 01759-371517
E-mail: sgreenwood@mpc-sbridge.co.uk
Website: http://www.mckechnie-plastics.co.uk
Bank(s): Lloyds TSB Bank plc
Directors: B. Mann (MD), M. Murphy (Sales & Mktg), M. Sturgess (Fin)
Managers: P. Aconley (Tech Serv Mgr), T. Goldsmith (Personnel), P. Cox
Ultimate Holding Company: MELROSE PLC
Immediate Holding Company: ROSTI MCKECHNIE LTD
Registration no: 03984537 **VAT No.:** GB 152 9211 81
Date established: 2000 **Turnover:** £50m - £75m
No.of Employees: 101 - 250 **Product Groups:** 30, 66

Date of Accounts	Dec 11	Dec 10	Dec 09
Sales Turnover	71m	46m	34m
Pre Tax Profit/Loss	2m	-922	-3m
Working Capital	12m	16m	19m
Fixed Assets	17m	11m	9m
Current Assets	29m	29m	25m
Current Liabilities	6m	8m	1m

S C A Packaging Ltd
95a James Street, York, YO10 3WW
Tel: 01904-430915 **Fax:** 01904-430921
Website: http://www.sca.com
Managers: H. Laurence, D. Bushnall (Plant), S. Coverdale (Prod Mgr), D. Bushnall (Mgr)
Immediate Holding Company: Sca Holding Ltd
Registration no: 00053913 **No.of Employees:** 21 - 50
Product Groups: 27, 28, 30, 49

Sandalwood Gates & Timber Products
Unit G7 Elvington Industrial Estate York Road, Elvington, York, YO41 4AR
Tel: 01904-608542
E-mail: enquiries@sandalwoodgates.co.uk
Website: http://www.sandalwoodgates.co.uk
Directors: S. Barnard (Prop)
Date established: 1986 **No.of Employees:** 1 - 10 **Product Groups:** 26, 35

Sasco
York Eco Business Centre Amy Johnson Way, York, YO30 4AG
Tel: 01904-785700 **Fax:** 01904-785500
E-mail: r.parkin@diyor.co.uk
Website: http://www.diyor.co.uk
Managers: R. Parkin (Mgr)
Immediate Holding Company: DIGITAL STAGE & MEDIA LTD
VAT No.: GB 647 5120 41 **Date established:** 2011
No.of Employees: 1 - 10 **Product Groups:** 26, 76

Date of Accounts	Mar 11	Mar 10
Sales Turnover	N/A	7
Pre Tax Profit/Loss	N/A	-31
Working Capital	-2	1
Fixed Assets	31	35
Current Assets	N/A	5
Current Liabilities	N/A	4

Sessions Of York
Huntington Road, York, YO31 9HS
Tel: 01904-659224 **Fax:** 01904- 644888
E-mail: nick.barnes@ppandp.co.uk
Website: http://www.sessionsofyork.co.uk
Bank(s): National Westminster Bank Plc
Directors: N. Barnes (Dir), D. Greenwood (Dir), D. Greenwood (Chief Op Offcr), J. Nooman (Dir), D. Embleton (Mkt Research), D. Mottram (Fin), W. Sessions (Ch)
Managers: D. Embleton (Sales Prom Mgr), B. Kale (Buyer)
Immediate Holding Company: JACKSON MORLEY AND SESSIONS LIMITED
Registration no: 01919758 **Date established:** 1985 **Turnover:** £5m - £10m
No.of Employees: 21 - 50 **Product Groups:** 27, 28, 44

Shepherd Construction Ltd
Frederick House Fulford Road, York, YO10 4EA
Tel: 01904-634431 **Fax:** 01904-610256
E-mail: ggaillatt@shepherd-construction.co.uk
Website: http://www.shepherd-construction.co.uk
Bank(s): Midland, Parliament Street
Directors: M. Porter (Fin)
Managers: P. Smith (Personnel), P. Eastwood (Purch Mgr), S. Slater (Tech Serv Mgr), G. Gillatt (Mktg Serv Mgr), G. Gillett (Mktg Serv Mgr)
Ultimate Holding Company: SHEPHERD BUILDING GROUP LIMITED
Immediate Holding Company: SHEPHERD CONSTRUCTION LIMITED
Registration no: 00201860 **Date established:** 2024
Turnover: £250m - £500m **No.of Employees:** 51 - 100
Product Groups: 51, 52, 84

Date of Accounts	Jun 11	Jun 10	Jun 09
Sales Turnover	251m	185m	327m
Pre Tax Profit/Loss	5m	-2m	-15m
Working Capital	18m	14m	13m
Fixed Assets	6m	6m	8m
Current Assets	102m	85m	111m
Current Liabilities	33m	24m	98m

Shepherd Engineering Services Ltd
Mill Mount, York, YO24 1GH
Tel: 01904-629151 **Fax:** 01904-610175
E-mail: info@ses-ltd.co.uk
Website: http://www.ses-ltd.co.uk
Bank(s): HSBC
Directors: C. Symeonides (Comm), D. Mason (Dir), P. Nichol (Fin), P. Clarke (Co Sec), L. Stevenson (Pers)
Immediate Holding Company: SHEPHERD ENGINEERING SERVICES LIMITED
Registration no: 00690190 **VAT No.:** GB 170 7793 41
Date established: 1961 **Turnover:** £125m - £250m
No.of Employees: 501 - 1000 **Product Groups:** 52

Date of Accounts	Jun 11	Jun 10	Jun 09
Sales Turnover	147m	117m	136m
Pre Tax Profit/Loss	3m	3m	3m
Working Capital	7m	5m	3m
Fixed Assets	3m	3m	4m
Current Assets	45m	41m	32m
Current Liabilities	10m	10m	9m

Sheppee International Ltd
Airfield Business Park York Road, Elvington, York, YO41 4AU
Tel: 01904-608999 **Fax:** 01904-608777
E-mail: sales@sheppee.com
Website: http://www.sheppee.com
Bank(s): Lloyds TSB Bank plc
Directors: J. Wilson (Fin), R. Moore (Sales)
Managers: I. Timlin (Purch Mgr)
Ultimate Holding Company: SHEPPEE HOLDINGS LTD
Immediate Holding Company: SHEPPEE INTERNATIONAL LIMITED
Registration no: 02792576 **VAT No.:** GB 599 0499 73
Date established: 1993 **Turnover:** £2m - £5m **No.of Employees:** 21 - 50
Product Groups: 45

Date of Accounts	Jun 12	Jun 11	Jun 10
Working Capital	5m	4m	3m
Fixed Assets	184	148	173
Current Assets	7m	7m	4m

W J Shields & Sons
Hall Farm Main Street, Shipton by Beningbrough, York, YO30 1AA
Tel: 01904-470263 **Fax:** 01904-471872
Directors: D. Shields (Ptnr)
Date established: 1939 **No.of Employees:** 1 - 10 **Product Groups:** 41

Signs Express York
Unit 2 Osbaldwick Industrial Estate Outgang Lane, Osbaldwick, York, YO19 5UX
Tel: 01904-431343 **Fax:** 01904-431344
E-mail: york@signsexpress.co.uk
Website: http://www.signsexpress.co.uk
Directors: I. Dawson (Dir)
Registration no: 02375913 **Date established:** 1993
No.of Employees: 1 - 10 **Product Groups:** 30, 39, 40, 80, 81, 84

Silesia Grill Systems
9 Richmond Close Market Weighton, York, YO43 3EX
Tel: 01430-879967 **Fax:** 01482-671768
E-mail: sales@silesiagrill.co.uk
Website: http://www.silesiagrill.co.uk
Directors: M. Scott (Prop)
Immediate Holding Company: SGS (MARKET WEIGHTON) LIMITED
Registration no: 04701707 **Date established:** 2009
No.of Employees: 1 - 10 **Product Groups:** 20, 40, 41

Date of Accounts	Apr 11	Apr 10
Working Capital	4	8
Fixed Assets	2	1
Current Assets	17	40

Simons Construction Ltd
Outgang Lane Osbaldwick, HESLINGTON, York, YO19 5GP
Tel: 01904-430200 **Fax:** 01904-430210
E-mail: yorkhelpdesk@simonsgroup.com
Website: http://www.simonsgroup.com
Bank(s): National Westminster Bank Plc
Directors: P. Bewers (Dir), P. Hodgkinson (Ch)
Managers: M. Bewers (Purch Mgr)
Ultimate Holding Company: Simons Group Ltd
Immediate Holding Company: Simons Group Ltd
Registration no: 00961095 **Date established:** 2001
Turnover: £250m - £500m **No.of Employees:** 21 - 50
Product Groups: 35, 48, 51, 52, 84

Smith Brothers York
Osbaldwick Link Road, York, YO10 3WA
Tel: 01904-415222 **Fax:** 01904-413219
E-mail: admin@smithbrothersyork.com
Website: http://www.smithbrothersyork.co.uk
Directors: M. Bishop (Co Sec)
Managers: G. Mcgowan (Chief Mgr)
Ultimate Holding Company: GRAFTON GROUP PUBLIC LIMITED COMPANY
Immediate Holding Company: SMITH BROTHERS (YORK) LIMITED
Registration no: 01376354 **Date established:** 1978 **Turnover:** £2m - £5m
No.of Employees: 21 - 50 **Product Groups:** 35, 45, 61

Date of Accounts	Dec 10	Dec 09	Dec 08
Sales Turnover	N/A	4m	6m
Pre Tax Profit/Loss	N/A	-371	185
Working Capital	2m	-393	-63
Fixed Assets	N/A	2m	2m
Current Assets	2m	897	917
Current Liabilities	N/A	397	13

Spruce & Hawe Ltd
Blind Lane Tockwith, York, YO26 7QJ
Tel: 01423-358601 **Fax:** 01423-358325
E-mail: sprucehawe@btconnect.com
Directors: M. Hawe (Dir)
Immediate Holding Company: SPRUCE & HAWE LIMITED
Registration no: 05662091 **Date established:** 2005
No.of Employees: 1 - 10 **Product Groups:** 41

Date of Accounts	Jan 12	Jan 11	Jan 10
Working Capital	82	31	28
Fixed Assets	70	79	90
Current Assets	250	227	202

Sundora Foods Ltd
Burnby Lane Pocklington, York, YO42 2QB
Tel: 01759-302365 **Fax:** 01759-304707
E-mail: info@sundora.co.uk
Website: http://www.sundora.co.uk
Directors: B. Young (Grp Chief Exec)
Managers: R. Gilderdale (Comptroller)
Ultimate Holding Company: AMERICAN CAPITAL STRATEGIES LTD (USA)
Immediate Holding Company: SUNDORA FOODS LIMITED
Registration no: 05413782 **Date established:** 2005
No.of Employees: 101 - 250 **Product Groups:** 20, 62

Date of Accounts	Apr 10	Apr 09	Apr 08
Working Capital	-277	-277	-277

Techviz
33A Fossgate, York, YO1 9TA
Tel: 01904-630721
E-mail: martin@techviz.co.uk
Website: http://www.techviz.co.uk
Directors: M. Hargreaves (Prop)
Date established: 1999 **Turnover:** Up to £250,000
No.of Employees: 1 - 10 **Product Groups:** 81

Tele-Products Ltd
11 Glaisdale Road Northminster Business Park Upper Poppleton, York, YO26 6QT
Tel: 01904-794200 **Fax:** 01904-780054
E-mail: sales@firststopsafety.co.uk
Website: http://www.tele-products.com
Directors: T. Segaran (Fin), S. Segaran (Dir)
Immediate Holding Company: TELE-PRODUCTS LIMITED
Registration no: 02295985 **VAT No.:** 500 8077 79 **Date established:** 1988
Turnover: £500,000 - £1m **No.of Employees:** 1 - 10 **Product Groups:** 67

Date of Accounts	Oct 11	Oct 10	Oct 09
Working Capital	92	76	85
Fixed Assets	34	40	48
Current Assets	215	207	185

Thorpe Trees
Thorpe Green Lane Thorpe Underwood, York, YO26 9TA
Tel: 01423-330977 **Fax:** 01423-331348
E-mail: sales@thorpetrees.com
Website: http://www.thorpetrees.com
Directors: C. Taylor (Prop)
Immediate Holding Company: THORPE TREES LIMITED
Registration no: 05320280 **Date established:** 2004
Turnover: £500,000 - £1m **No.of Employees:** 11 - 20
Product Groups: 02, 62

Date of Accounts	Jun 11	Jun 10	Jun 09
Working Capital	301	251	180
Fixed Assets	107	91	81
Current Assets	522	476	379

Tsys
Fulford Moor House Fulford Road, York, YO10 4EY
Tel: 01904-562000 **Fax:** 020-7244 7233
E-mail: sales@tsys.com
Website: http://www.tsys.com

Managers: V. Winn
Ultimate Holding Company: CARD TECHNOLOGY LTD (CAYMAN ISLANDS)
Immediate Holding Company: TSYS CARD TECH LIMITED
Registration no: 05843091 **VAT No.:** GB 503 4278 71
Date established: 2006 **No.of Employees:** 251 - 500 **Product Groups:** 84

Date of Accounts	Dec 11	Dec 10	Dec 09
Sales Turnover	29m	26m	30m
Pre Tax Profit/Loss	-405	685	-8m
Working Capital	3m	-637	-4m
Fixed Assets	21m	20m	8m
Current Assets	14m	15m	18m
Current Liabilities	10m	13m	13m

Tukans Ltd

3 Bramleys Barn The Menagerie Skipwith Road, Escrick, York, YO19 6ET
Tel: 01904-720617 **Fax:** 01904-720974
E-mail: sales@tukans.com
Website: http://www.tukans.com
Directors: A. Popely (MD)
Immediate Holding Company: TUKANS LIMITED
Registration no: 04139671 **Date established:** 2001 **Turnover:** £1m - £2m
No.of Employees: 1 - 10 **Product Groups:** 37, 67

Date of Accounts	Mar 11	Mar 10	Mar 09
Working Capital	-25	4	99
Fixed Assets	1	2	4
Current Assets	313	423	452

V6marketing

Glebe Farm Londesborough, York, YO43 3LQ
Tel: 01430-874031
E-mail: debbie@v6marketing.co.uk
Website: http://www.v6marketing.co.uk
Directors: D. Potter (Prop)
Managers: D. Potter (Chief Acct)
Date established: 2007 **Turnover:** Up to £250,000
No.of Employees: 1 - 10 **Product Groups:** 44

J J Westaby & Partners

Cape Farm Sheriff Hutton, York, YO60 6RT
Tel: 01347-878703 **Fax:** 01347-878771
E-mail: jjwestaby@btconnect.com
Directors: A. Westaby (Prop)
No.of Employees: 1 - 10 **Product Groups:** 07

Wolds Engineering Services Ltd

Unit 1 The Wolds Building Pocklington Industrial Estate, Pocklington, York, YO42 1NR
Tel: 01759-303877 **Fax:** 01759-306952
E-mail: john@woldsengineering.co.uk
Website: http://www.woldsengineering.co.uk
Directors: J. Hairsine (Fin), J. Oxley (MD)
Immediate Holding Company: WOLDS ENGINEERING SERVICES LIMITED
Registration no: 03832351 **Date established:** 1999
Turnover: Up to £250,000 **No.of Employees:** 11 - 20 **Product Groups:** 22, 23, 24, 26, 29, 30, 31, 33, 34, 35, 36, 37, 38, 39, 40, 44, 45, 46, 47, 48, 63, 66, 67, 68

Date of Accounts	Oct 11	Oct 10	Oct 09
Working Capital	779	662	590
Fixed Assets	785	715	710
Current Assets	1m	1m	1m

J Wood & Son Bilsdale Ploughs Ltd

Kirby Mills Industrial Estate Kirkbymoorside, York, YO62 6QR
Tel: 01751-433434 **Fax:** 01751-433094
E-mail: info@johnwoods.co.uk
Website: http://www.johnwoods.co.uk
Directors: M. Bentley (MD)
Immediate Holding Company: J.WOOD & SON(BILSDALE PLOUGHS)LIMITED
Registration no: 00602231 **VAT No.:** GB 166 8532 35
Date established: 1958 **Turnover:** £2m - £5m **No.of Employees:** 1 - 10
Product Groups: 07

Date of Accounts	Dec 11	Dec 10	Dec 09
Working Capital	683	652	645
Fixed Assets	252	237	240
Current Assets	864	843	792

X Y Z Printers

1 Londesborough Road Market Weighton, York, YO43 3AZ
Tel: 01430-872315 **Fax:** 01430-874046
Website: http://www.xyztypesetters.demon.co.uk
Managers: M. Brown (Mgr)
Date established: 1998 **No.of Employees:** 1 - 10 **Product Groups:** 28

York Archaeological Trust For Excavation & Research Ltd

Cuthbert Morrell House 47 Aldwark, York, YO1 7BX
Tel: 01904-663000 **Fax:** 01904-663024
E-mail: pnicholson@yorkarchaeology.co.uk
Website: http://www.yorkarchaeoligy.co.uk
Bank(s): Barclays
Directors: P. Nicholson (Fin)
Managers: K. Bettsworth (Personnel), D. Scott, M. Rains
Immediate Holding Company: YORK ARCHAEOLOGICAL TRUST FOR EXCAVATION AND RESEARCH LIMITED
Registration no: 01430801 **VAT No.:** GB 433 5246 66
Date established: 1979 **Turnover:** £5m - £10m
No.of Employees: 101 - 250 **Product Groups:** 80, 84

Date of Accounts	Mar 11	Mar 10	Mar 09
Sales Turnover	5m	5m	7m
Pre Tax Profit/Loss	-300	-687	2m
Working Capital	2m	2m	3m
Fixed Assets	1m	2m	2m
Current Assets	3m	3m	4m
Current Liabilities	798	797	688

York Brewery Co. Ltd

12 Toft Green, York, YO1 6JT
Tel: 01904-621162 **Fax:** 01904-621216
E-mail: sales@york-brewery.co.uk
Website: http://www.york-brewery.co.uk
Directors: J. Wilkinson (Co Sec), A. Barker (MD)
Ultimate Holding Company: MITCHELL'S BREWERY LIMITED
Immediate Holding Company: THE YORK BREWERY CO. LTD.
Registration no: 03117802 **Date established:** 1995 **Turnover:** £2m - £5m
No.of Employees: 11 - 20 **Product Groups:** 21

Date of Accounts	Jul 08	Feb 11	Feb 10
Sales Turnover	N/A	3m	3m
Pre Tax Profit/Loss	N/A	185	103
Working Capital	-113	41	-197
Fixed Assets	914	773	832
Current Assets	349	1m	800
Current Liabilities	N/A	335	250

York Coffee Systems York Tea and Coffee Co.

Unit 1 Acaster Estates Cowper Lane, Acaster Malbis, York, YO23 2TX
Tel: 01904-702016 **Fax:** 01904-702016
E-mail: info@yorkcoffeesystems.com
Website: http://www.yorkcoffeesystems.com
Directors: V. Whittall (Ptnr)
No.of Employees: 1 - 10 **Product Groups:** 40, 67

York Distribution Ltd

23-24 Auster Road, York, YO30 4XA
Tel: 01904-693969 **Fax:** 01904-693255
E-mail: normanmcneil@ydl.co.uk
Website: http://www.ydl.co.uk
Directors: J. Mcneil (Dir)
Immediate Holding Company: YORK DISTRIBUTION LIMITED
Registration no: 02632426 **Date established:** 1991
Turnover: £500,000 - £1m **No.of Employees:** 1 - 10 **Product Groups:** 37, 44, 46

Date of Accounts	Jun 11	Jun 10	Jun 09
Working Capital	71	90	101
Fixed Assets	13	14	15
Current Assets	116	134	138

York Elevator Services

The Reverie The Village, Stockton on the Forest, York, YO32 9UW
Tel: 01904-400888 **Fax:** 01904-400888
Directors: M. Watson (Dir), D. Watson (Fin)
Immediate Holding Company: YORK ELEVATOR SERVICES LIMITED
Registration no: 06990439 **Date established:** 2009
No.of Employees: 1 - 10 **Product Groups:** 35, 39, 45

Date of Accounts	Aug 11	Aug 10
Working Capital	15	10
Fixed Assets	2	2
Current Assets	179	136

York Lift Trucks Ltd

147 Hull Road, York, YO10 3JX
Tel: 01904-422115 **Fax:** 01904-422115
Website: http://www.yorklifttrucks.co.uk
Directors: M. Ovenden (Dir), J. Ovenden (Dir)
Immediate Holding Company: YORK LIFT TRUCKS LIMITED
Registration no: 03526163 **Date established:** 1998
No.of Employees: 1 - 10 **Product Groups:** 35, 39, 45

Date of Accounts	Mar 11	Mar 10	Mar 09
Working Capital	127	87	33
Fixed Assets	70	85	35
Current Assets	164	143	65

York Medical Technologies

Unit 12 Brookfield Business Park Clay Lane York Road, Shiptonthorpe, York, YO43 3PU
Tel: 01430-803113 **Fax:** 01757-702744
E-mail: sales@yorkmedicaltechnologies.com
Website: http://www.yorkmedicaltechnologies.com
Directors: S. Blight (Dir)
Immediate Holding Company: YORK MEDICAL TECHNOLOGIES LIMITED
Registration no: 05014156 **Date established:** 2004
No.of Employees: 1 - 10 **Product Groups:** 38, 67

Date of Accounts	Mar 11	Mar 10	Mar 09
Working Capital	114	12	-8
Fixed Assets	7	13	22
Current Assets	292	270	361

York Transmission Supplies Ltd

Newton Grange Shipton by Beningbrough, York, YO30 1BA
Tel: 01347-848999 **Fax:** 01347-848555
Directors: G. Shaw (I.T. Dir), S. Crowder (Fin)
Immediate Holding Company: YORK TRANSMISSION SUPPLIES LIMITED
Registration no: 01733781 **Date established:** 1983
Turnover: Up to £250,000 **No.of Employees:** 1 - 10 **Product Groups:** 35, 45

Date of Accounts	Jun 11	Jun 10	Jun 09
Sales Turnover	203	195	190
Pre Tax Profit/Loss	19	26	21
Working Capital	79	78	58
Fixed Assets	20	2	2
Current Assets	152	114	96
Current Liabilities	9	13	10

Yorkon Ltd

New Lane Huntington, York, YO32 9PT
Tel: 01904-610990 **Fax:** 01904-610880
E-mail: contact@yorkon.com
Website: http://www.yorkon.co.uk
Bank(s): HSBC
Directors: C. Brown (Fin), D. Shaw (Mkt Research), S. Ambler (Sales), A. Stainton (Pers)
Managers: C. Bonello (Tech Serv Mgr), M. Cotton (Purch Mgr)
Ultimate Holding Company: SHEPHERD BUILDING GROUP LIMITED
Immediate Holding Company: YORKON LIMITED
Registration no: 01552549 **Date established:** 1981
Turnover: £10m - £20m **No.of Employees:** 501 - 1000
Product Groups: 35

Date of Accounts	Jun 11	Jun 10	Jun 09
Sales Turnover	16m	21m	39m
Pre Tax Profit/Loss	610	2m	3m
Working Capital	5m	5m	5m
Fixed Assets	N/A	3	7
Current Assets	8m	12m	14m
Current Liabilities	2m	4m	5m

SOUTH YORKSHIRE

Barnsley

A B I Electronics Ltd
Unit 2 Dodworth Business Park, Dodworth, Barnsley, S75 3SP
Tel: 01226-207420 **Fax:** 01226-207620
E-mail: sales@abielectronics.co.uk
Website: http://www.abielectronics.co.uk
Bank(s): Barclays
Directors: I. Fletcher (MD), A. Fletcher (Dir)
Managers: S. Hayes (Sales Prom Mgr)
Immediate Holding Company: A.B.I. ELECTRONICS LIMITED
Registration no: 01824588 **VAT No.:** GB 381 4898 13
Date established: 1984 **Turnover:** £1m - £2m **No.of Employees:** 21 - 50
Product Groups: 38

Date of Accounts	Jun 11	Jun 10	Jun 09
Working Capital	527	547	481
Fixed Assets	76	46	58
Current Assets	742	686	596

Albion Valves Ltd
Unit 9a Fall Bank Industrial Estate Dodworth, Barnsley, S75 3LS
Tel: 01226-729900 **Fax:** 01226-288011
E-mail: sales@albionvalvesuk.com
Website: http://www.albionvalvesuk.com
Directors: D. Keys (MD), L. Littlewood (Sales), P. Guppy (Fin)
Immediate Holding Company: ALBION VALVES (UK) LIMITED
Registration no: 03081412 **Date established:** 1995 **Turnover:** £2m - £5m
No.of Employees: 11 - 20 **Product Groups:** 30, 36, 66

Date of Accounts	Mar 12	Mar 11	Mar 10
Working Capital	1m	885	893
Fixed Assets	80	25	21
Current Assets	2m	2m	2m

Alwyn Richards Ltd
Barnsley Business & Innovation Centre Snydale Road, Cudworth, Barnsley, S72 8RP
Tel: 01226-718428 **Fax:** 01226-711353
E-mail: general@alwynrichards.com
Website: http://www.alwynrichards.com
Directors: A. Richards (Prop)
Immediate Holding Company: ALWYN RICHARDS LIMITED
Registration no: 07054994 **Date established:** 2009
No.of Employees: 1 - 10 **Product Groups:** 35, 48, 66, 86

Date of Accounts	Apr 11
Working Capital	-212
Fixed Assets	226
Current Assets	90

Amocura Ltd
Roshni Keresforth Hill Road, Barnsley, S70 6RF
Tel: 01226-779100 **Fax:** 01226-731466
E-mail: mfrench@amocura.co.uk
Website: http://www.amocura.co.uk
Directors: M. French (MD), P. Robinson (Fin)
Ultimate Holding Company: AMOCURA INVESTMENTS LIMITED
Immediate Holding Company: AMOCURA LTD.
Registration no: 03022243 **Date established:** 1995 **Turnover:** £5m - £10m
No.of Employees: 1 - 10 **Product Groups:** 88

Date of Accounts	Aug 11	Aug 10	Aug 09
Sales Turnover	N/A	6m	7m
Pre Tax Profit/Loss	N/A	283	137
Working Capital	1m	934	740
Fixed Assets	2	N/A	1
Current Assets	2m	2m	1m
Current Liabilities	N/A	471	478

Ardagh Group Ltd
Burton Road Monk Bretton, Barnsley, S71 2QG
Tel: 01226-710211 **Fax:** 01226-716808
E-mail: info@ardaghglass.com
Website: http://www.ardaghglass.com
Directors: N. Pritchard (Co Sec), I. Steadman (Dir)
Managers: P. Woodward (Personnel)
Ultimate Holding Company: ARDAGH GLASS GROUP SA (LUXEMBOURG)
Immediate Holding Company: ARDAGH GLASS LIMITED
Registration no: 00567801 **Date established:** 1956
Turnover: £250m - £500m **No.of Employees:** 251 - 500
Product Groups: 33, 66

Date of Accounts	Dec 10	Dec 09	Dec 08
Sales Turnover	288m	283m	274m
Pre Tax Profit/Loss	46m	24m	5m
Working Capital	313m	153m	131m
Fixed Assets	124m	132m	145m
Current Assets	378m	224m	221m
Current Liabilities	27m	9m	12m

D H Armitage
Fairfield Sheffield Road, Hoyland, Barnsley, S74 0DP
Tel: 01226-747940 **Fax:** 01226-350313
Directors: D. Armitage (Prop)
Immediate Holding Company: D.H. ARMITAGE TRANSPORT LIMITED
Registration no: 01077882 **Date established:** 1972
Turnover: Up to £250,000 **No.of Employees:** 11 - 20 **Product Groups:** 72

Date of Accounts	Dec 11	Dec 10	Dec 09
Working Capital	45	50	-45
Fixed Assets	300	366	372
Current Assets	227	302	169

Ashton Seals Ltd
Ashton Building Cortonwood Drive, Brampton, Barnsley, S73 0UF
Tel: 01226-273700 **Fax:** 01226-756774
E-mail: sales@ashton-group.co.uk
Website: http://www.ashtongroup.co.uk
Directors: J. Burley (Fin), B. Austin (Sales)
Managers: D. Robinson (Tech Serv Mgr), J. Gratehead (Mktg Serv Mgr), A. Marsh (Purch Mgr), E. Dean (Personnel)
Ultimate Holding Company: THOMAS A. ASHTON LIMITED
Immediate Holding Company: ASHTON SEALS LIMITED
Registration no: 00748676 **VAT No.:** GB 728 0557 27
Date established: 1963 **Turnover:** £1m - £2m **No.of Employees:** 21 - 50
Product Groups: 22, 24, 27, 28, 30, 44, 48, 49, 84

Date of Accounts	Dec 11	Dec 10	Dec 09
Working Capital	102	70	39
Fixed Assets	1m	1m	1m
Current Assets	2m	1m	998

B R C Manufacturing
Whaley Road South Yorkshire Industrial Estate, Barnsley, S75 1HT
Tel: 01226-283438 **Fax:** 01226-248738
E-mail: sales@weldgrip.co.uk
Website: http://www.brc-uk.co.uk
Managers: J. Collins (Mgr)
Ultimate Holding Company: COMPASS HOLDINGS LIMITED
Immediate Holding Company: REACTIVE METAL ENGINEERING LIMITED
Registration no: 01408395 **Date established:** 1979
No.of Employees: 51 - 100 **Product Groups:** 35

Booker Ltd
Twibell Street, Barnsley, S71 1DN
Tel: 01226-243556 **Fax:** 01226-202227
E-mail: stevenwurr@booker.co.uk
Website: http://www.booker.co.uk
Managers: S. Wurr (Mgr)
Ultimate Holding Company: BOOKER GROUP PLC
Immediate Holding Company: BOOKER LIMITED
Registration no: 00197380 **VAT No.:** GB 222 3640 04
Date established: 2024 **No.of Employees:** 21 - 50 **Product Groups:** 61

Date of Accounts	Mar 12	Mar 09	Mar 10
Sales Turnover	3736m	3094m	3285m
Pre Tax Profit/Loss	65m	34m	53m
Working Capital	404m	212m	248m
Fixed Assets	154m	398m	387m
Current Assets	1043m	638m	746m
Current Liabilities	59m	48m	56m

Business Link Ltd
1 Capitol Court Capitol Business Park, Dodworth, Barnsley, S75 3TZ
Tel: 0845-6048048 **Fax:** 01904-686020
E-mail: info@businesslinkyorkshire.co.uk
Website: http://www.businesslink.gov.uk/yorkshire.html
Bank(s): Barclays
Directors: H. West (Grp Chief Exec)
Managers: K. Marsden (Mgr)
Immediate Holding Company: Yny Ltd
Registration no: 03591108 **Turnover:** £250,000 - £500,000
No.of Employees: 51 - 100 **Product Groups:** 80, 81

Cameron Forecourt Ltd
Platts Common Industrial Estate Hoyland, Barnsley, S74 9SE
Tel: 01226-742441 **Fax:** 01226-747441
E-mail: barryjenner@cameron-forecourt.co.uk
Website: http://www.cameron-forecourt.co.uk
Bank(s): National Westminster Bank Plc
Directors: B. Jenner (MD), K. Jenner (Fin)
Managers: M. Gent (Mktg Serv Mgr), D. Lound (Tech Serv Mgr), G. Webb (Chief Mgr)
Ultimate Holding Company: F E GROUP LIMITED
Immediate Holding Company: CAMERON FORECOURT LIMITED
Registration no: 03522200 **VAT No.:** GB 716 4367 31
Date established: 1998 **Turnover:** £2m - £5m **No.of Employees:** 21 - 50
Product Groups: 39, 42, 48

Date of Accounts	Oct 11	Oct 10	Oct 09
Working Capital	471	490	487
Fixed Assets	22	28	47
Current Assets	2m	2m	1m

Carlton Main Brickworks Ltd
Clayburn Road Grimethorpe, Barnsley, S72 7BE
Tel: 01226-711521 **Fax:** 01226-780417
E-mail: oliver.stephenson@dial.pipex.co.uk
Website: http://www.carltonbrick.com
Bank(s): Yorkshire Bank PLC
Directors: O. Stephenson (Dir), M. Fogg (Co Sec)
Immediate Holding Company: CARLTON MAIN BRICKWORKS LIMITED
Registration no: 00479716 **VAT No.:** GB 181 3290 74
Date established: 1950 **Turnover:** £5m - £10m
No.of Employees: 51 - 100 **Product Groups:** 33

Date of Accounts	Mar 11	Mar 10	Mar 09
Sales Turnover	8m	7m	N/A
Pre Tax Profit/Loss	1m	904	424
Working Capital	5m	4m	5m
Fixed Assets	5m	5m	4m
Current Assets	6m	5m	6m
Current Liabilities	989	811	655

Ceag Ltd
Unit K Zenith Park Whaley Road, Barnsley, S75 1HT
Tel: 01226-206842 **Fax:** 01226-731645
E-mail: sales@ceag.co.uk
Website: http://www.ceag.co.uk
Bank(s): HSBC Bank plc
Directors: M. Caldcleugh (I.T. Dir)
Immediate Holding Company: CEAG LIMITED
Registration no: 01597911 **VAT No.:** GB 404 8613 65
Date established: 1981 **Turnover:** £1m - £2m **No.of Employees:** 21 - 50
Product Groups: 37, 39

Date of Accounts	Mar 12	Mar 11	Mar 10
Working Capital	553	514	459
Fixed Assets	616	635	655
Current Assets	659	613	583

Cidon Construction Ltd
Mason Way Hoyland, Barnsley, S74 9TG
Tel: 01226-360622 **Fax:** 01226-360633
E-mail: enquiries@cidon.co.uk
Website: http://www.cidon.co.uk
Directors: C. Donnelly (MD), C. Donnelly (Fin)
Immediate Holding Company: CIDON CONSTRUCTION LIMITED
Registration no: 04066292 **Date established:** 2000
No.of Employees: 1 - 10 **Product Groups:** 33

Date of Accounts	Feb 12	Feb 11	Feb 10
Working Capital	757	630	588
Fixed Assets	223	129	145
Current Assets	2m	2m	2m

Compass Engineering Ltd
Whaley Road, Barnsley, S75 1HT
Tel: 01226-298388 **Fax:** 01226-283215
E-mail: andrew.hibbins@compass-eng.co.uk
Website: http://www.compass-eng.co.uk
Bank(s): HSBC Bank plc
Directors: A. Hibbins (Prop), T. Broadbent (Dir), E. Raynor (Dir)
Ultimate Holding Company: COMPASS HOLDINGS LIMITED
Immediate Holding Company: COMPASS ENGINEERING LIMITED
Registration no: 02447366 **Date established:** 1989 **Turnover:** £5m - £10m
No.of Employees: 51 - 100 **Product Groups:** 51

Date of Accounts	Dec 11	Dec 10	Dec 09
Sales Turnover	9m	7m	7m
Pre Tax Profit/Loss	594	32	356
Working Capital	3m	3m	3m
Fixed Assets	346	434	542
Current Assets	5m	4m	4m
Current Liabilities	579	169	283

Crosby Europe UK Ltd
Units 12 & 13 Barnsley Business & Innovation Centre Innovation Way, Barnsley, S75 1JL
Tel: 01226-290516 **Fax:** 01226-240118
E-mail: sales@crosbyeurope.co.uk
Website: http://www.thecrosbygroup.com

Directors: A. Charlesworth (MD)
Ultimate Holding Company: MELROSE PLC
Immediate Holding Company: CROSBY EUROPE (UK) LIMITED
Registration no: 02455933 **VAT No.:** GB 184 4733 43
Date established: 1989 **No.of Employees:** 1 - 10 **Product Groups:** 35, 45

Date of Accounts	Dec 11	Dec 10	Dec 09
Pre Tax Profit/Loss	4	2	2
Working Capital	1m	1m	1m
Current Assets	1m	1m	1m

Dale Products Plastics Ltd
Barnsley Road Hoyland, Barnsley, S74 0QW
Tel: 01226-742511 **Fax:** 01226-350496
E-mail: dale.products@fsbdial.co.uk
Website: http://www.daleproducts.co.uk
Bank(s): HSBC Bank plc
Directors: J. Crawshaw (Co Sec), R. Crawshaw (MD)
Managers: L. Nutt (Accounts)
Immediate Holding Company: DALE PRODUCTS (PLASTICS) LIMITED
Registration no: 00629660 **VAT No.:** GB 172 5073 73
Date established: 1959 **Turnover:** £500,000 - £1m
No.of Employees: 21 - 50 **Product Groups:** 30

Date of Accounts	Jun 08	Jun 07	Jun 06
Working Capital	489	497	487
Fixed Assets	185	203	225
Current Assets	591	568	544
Current Liabilities	102	70	57
Total Share Capital	2	2	2

Darfield Branch Library
Church Street Darfield, Barnsley, S73 9LG
Tel: 01226-752548
Website: http://www.darfield.co.uk
Managers: S. Manterfield (Mgr)
Immediate Holding Company: FORKTRUCKS UK LIMITED
Date established: 1992 **No.of Employees:** 1 - 10 **Product Groups:** 22, 25, 29, 30, 33, 36

Denby Dale Clothing Ltd
Unit J Zenith Park Industrial Estate, Barnsley, S75 1HT
Tel: 01226-738390 **Fax:** 01226-289140
E-mail: enquiries@denbydaleshirt.co.uk
Bank(s): The Royal Bank of Scotland
Directors: C. Mallinson (Dir)
Immediate Holding Company: DENBY DALE SHIRT CO.,LIMITED
Registration no: 00862857 **VAT No.:** GB 518 4942 27
Date established: 1965 **Turnover:** £500,000 - £1m
No.of Employees: 21 - 50 **Product Groups:** 24, 63

Date of Accounts	Nov 11	Nov 10	Nov 09
Working Capital	386	237	352
Fixed Assets	702	726	756
Current Assets	1m	959	758

Dimensions Training Solutions
Archway House Langdale Road, Barnsley, S71 1AQ
Tel: 01226-730112 **Fax:** 01226-786555
E-mail: 2bill@billshaw.co.uk
Website: http://www.dimensions-training-solutions.com
Bank(s): Barclays
Directors: B. Shaw (Ch)
Immediate Holding Company: INCORPORATED GUILD OF HAIRDRESSERS,WIGMAKERS AND PERFUMERS(THE)
Registration no: 02577945 **VAT No.:** GB 716 6453 28
Date established: 2000 **No.of Employees:** 21 - 50 **Product Groups:** 86

Date of Accounts	Dec 11	Dec 10	Dec 09
Sales Turnover	3	7	6
Pre Tax Profit/Loss	1	1	-8
Working Capital	8	7	6
Fixed Assets	12	12	12
Current Assets	9	9	12
Current Liabilities	1	2	3

Elsecar Antiques Centre
Building 18 Elsecar Heritage Centre Wath Road, Elsecar, Barnsley, S74 8HJ
Tel: 01226-744425
E-mail: iwilson@elsecarantiques.co.uk
Website: http://www.elsecarantiques.co.uk
Directors: I. Wilson (Ptnr)
Immediate Holding Company: GROUNDHOG COURIERS LIMITED
Registration no: 02461769 **Date established:** 2010 **Turnover:** £5m - £10m
No.of Employees: 1 - 10 **Product Groups:** 65

Date of Accounts	Aug 11	Aug 10	Aug 09
Sales Turnover	6m	6m	7m
Pre Tax Profit/Loss	-426	-1m	-2m
Working Capital	324	2m	2m
Fixed Assets	349	397	391
Current Assets	3m	3m	3m
Current Liabilities	693	556	665

Elsecar Railway Preservation Group Ltd
Elsecar Heritage Railway Wath Road, Elsecar, Barnsley, S74 8HJ
Tel: 01226-746746
E-mail: david.pannett@elsecarantiques.co.uk
Website: http://www.elsecarrailway.co.uk
Directors: M. Cooper (Dir), M. Royston (Prop), D. Pannett (Fin)
Managers: M. Cooper
Immediate Holding Company: ELSECAR HERITAGE RAILWAY LTD
Registration no: 04457467 **Date established:** 2002
Turnover: Up to £250,000 **No.of Employees:** 51 - 100
Product Groups: 26, 35

Date of Accounts	Dec 07	Jun 11	Jun 09
Sales Turnover	75	4	N/A
Pre Tax Profit/Loss	-4	-11	N/A
Working Capital	18	12	15
Fixed Assets	1	1	1
Current Assets	21	13	16
Current Liabilities	1	N/A	N/A

European Tank Installations Ltd
52 Hemingfield Road Hemingfield, Barnsley, S73 0QA
Tel: 01226-758834 **Fax:** 01226-759185
Directors: T. March (Co Sec)
Immediate Holding Company: EVE666 LTD
Registration no: 03406139 **Date established:** 2010
No.of Employees: 1 - 10 **Product Groups:** 35, 42, 45

Date of Accounts	Sep 11
Working Capital	10
Current Assets	10

Euroweld Technologies
Unit 8 Maple Estate Stocks Lane, Barnsley, S75 2BL
Tel: 01226-770300 **Fax:** 01226-770400
E-mail: sales@eurowelduk.com
Website: http://www.eurowelduk.com
Directors: M. Webb (MD)
Date established: 1991 **Turnover:** £1m - £2m **No.of Employees:** 11 - 20
Product Groups: 33, 46, 48

FireworkGuy.Co.Uk
Rear of 92 Grange Lane, Barnsley, S71 5QQ
Tel: 07940-074044 **Fax:** 01226-246101
E-mail: info@fireworkguy.co.uk
Website: http://www.fireworkguy.co.uk
Directors: J. Hebdon (Prop)
Immediate Holding Company: FIREWORKGUY LTD
Registration no: 05968039 **Date established:** 2006
Turnover: Up to £250,000 **No.of Employees:** 1 - 10 **Product Groups:** 32, 89

Date of Accounts	Oct 11	Oct 10	Oct 09
Working Capital	-7	-5	-4
Fixed Assets	2	N/A	N/A
Current Assets	20	4	7

Flex Seal Couplings Ltd
Endeavour Works Newlands Way Valley Park Industrial Estate, Wombwell, Barnsley, S73 0UW
Tel: 01226-340222 **Fax:** 01226-340400
E-mail: sales@flexseal.co.uk
Website: http://www.flexseal.co.uk
Bank(s): The Royal Bank of Scotland
Directors: S. Riding (Comm), A. Williams (Fin), J. Crean (Sales & Mktg)
Managers: D. Robinson (Tech Serv Mgr), E. Fairfield (Mktg Serv Mgr), C. Elliott (Sales & Mktg Mg)
Ultimate Holding Company: FERNCO INC (USA)
Immediate Holding Company: FLEX-SEAL COUPLINGS LIMITED
Registration no: 02450903 **VAT No.:** GB 471 1485 52
Date established: 1989 **Turnover:** £10m - £20m
No.of Employees: 51 - 100 **Product Groups:** 29, 30, 36

Date of Accounts	Dec 11	Dec 10	Dec 09
Sales Turnover	12m	11m	11m
Pre Tax Profit/Loss	1m	1m	2m
Working Capital	3m	3m	3m
Fixed Assets	3m	3m	3m
Current Assets	5m	5m	6m
Current Liabilities	1m	1m	1m

G A Fixings Ltd
Cannon Way Claycliffe Business Park Claycliffe Road, Barugh Green, Barnsley, S75 1JU
Tel: 01226-380779 **Fax:** 01226-385558
E-mail: info@gafixings.com
Website: http://www.gafixings.com
Directors: G. Hensby (MD)
Immediate Holding Company: G.A. FIXINGS LIMITED
Registration no: 03798526 **Date established:** 1999
Turnover: £500,000 - £1m **No.of Employees:** 1 - 10 **Product Groups:** 34, 35, 37, 66, 67

Date of Accounts	Jul 12	Jul 11	Jul 10
Sales Turnover	N/A	N/A	917
Pre Tax Profit/Loss	N/A	N/A	68
Working Capital	148	157	116
Fixed Assets	305	260	222
Current Assets	405	542	362
Current Liabilities	N/A	N/A	47

Goldcrest Chemicals Ltd
Dodworth Business Park Dodworth, Barnsley, S75 3SP
Tel: 0370-780 0100 **Fax:** 01506-630087
E-mail: customerservices@goldcrestchemicals.co.uk
Website: http://www.goldcrestchemicals.co.uk
Bank(s): Barclays Bank Huddersfield
Directors: A. Morris (Co Sec), A. Smalley (Dir)
Immediate Holding Company: GOLDCREST CHEMICALS LIMITED
Registration no: 01364179 **VAT No.:** GB 333 4396 60
Date established: 1978 **Turnover:** £2m - £5m **No.of Employees:** 11 - 20
Product Groups: 23, 32

Date of Accounts	Jul 11	Jul 10	Jul 09
Working Capital	214	263	-20
Fixed Assets	402	392	387
Current Assets	1m	1m	1m

Hand Pallet Truck Services
7 Millside Shafton, Barnsley, S72 8NX
Tel: 01226-781332 **Fax:** 01226-781332
Website: http://www.handpallettruckservices.co.uk
Directors: S. Cox (Fin)
Immediate Holding Company: HAND PALLET TRUCK SERVICES LIMITED
Registration no: 04785043 **Date established:** 2003
No.of Employees: 1 - 10 **Product Groups:** 35, 39, 45

Date of Accounts	Jun 11	Jun 10	Jun 08
Working Capital	2	5	5
Fixed Assets	9	12	7
Current Assets	11	15	18

Hawk Lifting
Unit 3 Spring Park
Clayburn Road
Grimethorpe, Barnsley, S72 7FD
Tel: 01226-718830
E-mail: info@hawklifting.co.uk
Website: http://www.hawklifting.co.uk
Directors: D. Nixon (MD), B. Johnson (MD)
Registration no: 06643817 **Date established:** 2008
Turnover: £500,000 - £1m **Product Groups:** 35, 36, 39, 45, 48, 84

Date of Accounts	Mar 10	Mar 09
Working Capital	21	-29
Fixed Assets	53	64
Current Assets	216	172
Current Liabilities	108	N/A

H J C Design Ltd
Barnsley Business & Innovation Centre Innovation Way, Barnsley, S75 1JL
Tel: 01226-771505 **Fax:** 01226-786295
E-mail: info@hjcdesign.co.uk
Website: http://www.hjcdesign.co.uk
Directors: M. Conley (MD)
Immediate Holding Company: H J C DESIGN LTD
Registration no: 05213430 **Date established:** 2004
Turnover: Up to £250,000 **No.of Employees:** 1 - 10 **Product Groups:** 30, 84

Date of Accounts	Sep 11	Sep 10	Sep 09
Working Capital	53	31	13
Fixed Assets	25	29	22
Current Assets	129	160	85

J G P Engineering
Mitchells Industrial Park Bradberry Balk Lane, Wombwell, Barnsley, S73 8HR
Tel: 01226-755140 **Fax:** 01226-757594
E-mail: sales@jgpfixings.co.uk
Website: http://www.autoelectricgates.co.uk
Directors: G. Phillis (MD)
Immediate Holding Company: JGP UK LIMITED
Registration no: 05897357 **Date established:** 2006
No.of Employees: 11 - 20 **Product Groups:** 33, 36, 66

Jacquet UK Ltd
Rockingham House Wentworth Way, Tankersley, Barnsley, S75 3DH
Tel: 01226-745000 **Fax:** 01226-746000
E-mail: k.bonnington@myjacquet.com
Website: http://www.myjacquet.com
Directors: K. Bonnington (MD)
Ultimate Holding Company: JACQUET INDUSTRIES SA (FRANCE)
Immediate Holding Company: JACQUET (UK) LIMITED
Registration no: 03275210 **Date established:** 1996 **Turnover:** £5m - £10m
No.of Employees: 11 - 20 **Product Groups:** 34, 66

Date of Accounts	Dec 11	Dec 10	Dec 09
Sales Turnover	7m	6m	5m
Pre Tax Profit/Loss	736	897	534
Working Capital	2m	2m	2m
Fixed Assets	1m	723	770
Current Assets	4m	4m	4m
Current Liabilities	486	417	415

Keeler Ltd
Unit 12 Carlton Industrial Estate Albion Road, Carlton, Barnsley, S71 3HW
Tel: 01226-728769 **Fax:** 01226-728779
E-mail: kathriner@keeler.co.uk
Website: http://www.keeler.co.uk
Managers: K. Rossey (Mgr)
Ultimate Holding Company: HALMA PUBLIC LIMITED COMPANY
Immediate Holding Company: KEELER LIMITED
Registration no: 00408759 **Date established:** 1946
No.of Employees: 1 - 10 **Product Groups:** 38, 67

Date of Accounts	Mar 12	Mar 09	Apr 10
Sales Turnover	17m	16m	15m
Pre Tax Profit/Loss	4m	3m	3m
Working Capital	9m	9m	9m
Fixed Assets	3m	2m	3m
Current Assets	11m	11m	11m
Current Liabilities	734	531	498

L N S Turbo UK Ltd
Waterside Park Valley Way, Wombwell, Barnsley, S73 0BB
Tel: 01226-270033 **Fax:** 01226-270044
E-mail: sales@lnsturbouk.com
Website: http://www.lns-world.com
Directors: L. Bott (Sales)
Managers: M. Dorma (Fin Mgr), S. Parfitt (District Mgr)
Ultimate Holding Company: LNS SA (SWITZERLAND)
Immediate Holding Company: LNS TURBO UK LTD
Registration no: 03503010 **Date established:** 1998 **Turnover:** £5m - £10m
No.of Employees: 21 - 50 **Product Groups:** 46

Date of Accounts	Dec 11	Dec 10	Dec 09
Sales Turnover	7m	4m	2m
Pre Tax Profit/Loss	179	24	-857
Working Capital	1m	872	1m
Fixed Assets	2m	2m	2m
Current Assets	3m	2m	1m
Current Liabilities	280	189	155

Lynx Machinery ltd
P.O Box 201, Barnsley, S75 1YN
Tel: 01226-732137 **Fax:** 01226-730865
E-mail: sales@lynxmachinery.co.uk
Website: http://www.lynxmachinery.co.uk
Directors: M. Manley (MD)
Product Groups: 42, 43, 44

Date of Accounts	Jan 11	Jan 10	Jan 07
Working Capital	10	22	1
Fixed Assets	3	3	4
Current Assets	23	49	25

Mccallum Manufacturing Ltd
Redbrook Business Park Wilthorpe Road, Barnsley, S75 1JF
Tel: 01226-248348
Directors: I. Mccallum (MD), I. McCallum (MD)
Immediate Holding Company: MCCALLUM MANUFACTURING LIMITED
Registration no: 02204399 **Date established:** 1987
No.of Employees: 1 - 10 **Product Groups:** 32, 63

Date of Accounts	Dec 11	Dec 10	Dec 09
Working Capital	159	123	81
Fixed Assets	129	128	117
Current Assets	291	284	257

Machineco Ltd
181a Burton Road Monk Bretton Barnsley, Barnsley, S71 2HG
Tel: 01226-321919 **Fax:** 01226-249328
E-mail: sales@machineco.co.uk
Website: http://www.machineco.co.uk
Directors: J. Brears (Fin), P. Brears (MD)
Immediate Holding Company: MACHINECO LIMITED
Registration no: 05271383 **VAT No.:** GB 852 3196 25
Date established: 2004 **Turnover:** Up to £250,000
No.of Employees: 1 - 10 **Product Groups:** 35, 36, 38, 41, 43, 44, 45, 46, 66, 77

Date of Accounts	Oct 11	Oct 10	Oct 09
Sales Turnover	N/A	86	50
Pre Tax Profit/Loss	N/A	3	-4
Working Capital	-10	-6	-9
Fixed Assets	5	6	7
Current Assets	87	29	20
Current Liabilities	N/A	2	4

Magna Colours Ltd

3 Dodworth Business Park Upper Cliffe Road, Dodworth, Barnsley, S75 3SP
Tel: 01226-731751 **Fax:** 01226-731752
E-mail: enquiries@magnacolours.com
Website: http://www.magnacolours.com
Bank(s): HSBC
Directors: T. Abbey (MD)
Ultimate Holding Company: MAGNA COLOURS HOLDINGS LIMITED
Immediate Holding Company: MAGNA COLOURS LIMITED
Registration no: 01378495 **VAT No.:** GB 185 1644 51
Date established: 1978 **Turnover:** £2m - £5m **No.of Employees:** 11 - 20
Product Groups: 31, 32

Date of Accounts	Apr 11	Apr 10	Apr 09
Working Capital	2m	1m	1m
Fixed Assets	215	1m	1m
Current Assets	3m	3m	2m

Manor Bakeries

Fish Dam Lane, Barnsley, S71 3HQ
Tel: 01226-286191 **Fax:** 01226-291003
Website: http://www.manor-bakeries.co.uk
Directors: A. Allner (Fin)
Managers: K. Simpkin (Fin Mgr), M. Cornick (Personnel), G. Cluer, J. Colbourne (Buyer)
Ultimate Holding Company: PREMIER FOODS PLC
Immediate Holding Company: MANOR BAKERIES LIMITED
Registration no: 00285602 **VAT No.:** GB 665 2356 25
Date established: 1934 **No.of Employees:** 1001 - 1500
Product Groups: 20

Date of Accounts	Dec 10	Dec 09	Dec 08
Working Capital	N/A	N/A	50m
Fixed Assets	N/A	N/A	5
Current Assets	N/A	N/A	50m

Metalliform Holdings

Chambers Road Hoyland, Barnsley, S74 0EZ
Tel: 01226-350555 **Fax:** 01226-350112
E-mail: sales@metalliform.co.uk
Website: http://www.metalliform.co.uk
Directors: L. Fisher (Co Sec), L. Benstead (Sales)
Managers: C. Knight (Purch Mgr)
Ultimate Holding Company: METALLIFORM HOLDINGS LIMITED
Immediate Holding Company: METALLIFORM PRODUCTS LIMITED
Registration no: 05247165 **VAT No.:** GB 600 0609 07
Date established: 2004 **Turnover:** £5m - £10m
No.of Employees: 51 - 100 **Product Groups:** 26

Midas 1 Ltd

Towngate Mapplewell, Barnsley, S75 6AT
Tel: 01226-380777 **Fax:** 01226-380588
E-mail: greg@midas1.com
Website: http://www.midas1.com
Managers: G. Bennett (Sales Prom Mgr)
Immediate Holding Company: MIDAS 1 LTD
Registration no: 04680438 **Date established:** 2003
No.of Employees: 1 - 10 **Product Groups:** 28, 48, 81, 83, 86

Date of Accounts	Feb 08	Feb 07
Working Capital	12	85
Fixed Assets	246	32
Current Assets	498	335
Current Liabilities	487	250

Minova Weldgrip Ltd

Unit 19 Redbrook Business Park Wilthorpe Road, Barnsley, S75 1JN
Tel: 01226-280567 **Fax:** 01226-731563
E-mail: steve.jackson@minovaint.com
Website: http://www.weldgrip.com
Directors: S. Jackson (MD)
Ultimate Holding Company: ORICA LIMITED (AUSTRALIA)
Immediate Holding Company: MINOVA WELDGRIP LIMITED
Registration no: 05557873 **VAT No.:** GB 666 8046 04
Date established: 2005 **Turnover:** £5m - £10m **No.of Employees:** 11 - 20
Product Groups: 35, 36, 40, 45

Date of Accounts	Sep 11	Sep 10	Sep 09
Sales Turnover	18m	16m	12m
Pre Tax Profit/Loss	542	1m	2m
Working Capital	6m	5m	2m
Fixed Assets	4m	5m	864
Current Assets	11m	10m	6m
Current Liabilities	3m	3m	2m

Monckton Coke & Chemical Co.

PO Box 25, Barnsley, S71 4BE
Tel: 01226-722601 **Fax:** 01226-700307
E-mail: iarchibold@hargreavesservices.co.uk
Website: http://www.moncktoncoke.com
Bank(s): LLoyds TSB
Directors: I. Archibald (Dir)
Ultimate Holding Company: HARGREAVES SERVICES PLC
Immediate Holding Company: MONCKTON COKE & CHEMICAL COMPANY LIMITED(THE)
Registration no: 00070960 **VAT No.:** GB 580 9685 92
Date established: 2001 **Turnover:** £50m - £75m
No.of Employees: 101 - 250 **Product Groups:** 31

Date of Accounts	May 11	May 10	May 09
Sales Turnover	51m	47m	40m
Pre Tax Profit/Loss	2m	3m	2m
Working Capital	2m	1m	2m
Fixed Assets	7m	7m	5m
Current Assets	79m	38m	15m
Current Liabilities	3m	2m	2m

Moorland Plastics Barnsley

Moorland Avenue, Barnsley, S70 6PQ
Tel: 01226-242753 **Fax:** 01226-293401
E-mail: moorlandplastics@barnsley.gov.uk
Website: http://www.moorlandplastics.co.uk
Managers: P. Farmer (Chief Mgr), A. Bateman (Sales Prom Mgr), R. Leadbeater (Tech Serv Mgr)
Date established: 1966 **No.of Employees:** 21 - 50 **Product Groups:** 30, 48

Naylor Drainage Ltd

Clough Green Cawthorne, Barnsley, S75 4AD
Tel: 01226-790591 **Fax:** 01226-790531
E-mail: sales@naylor.co.uk
Website: http://www.naylor.co.uk
Bank(s): Bank of Scotland, Leeds
Directors: A. Trippitt (Co Sec), E. Naylor (Dir)
Managers: E. Kilner (Sales Prom Mgr), H. Waller (Personnel), J. Wilby (Fin Mgr), L. Hudson (Mktg Serv Mgr), M. Harris (Tech Serv Mgr)
Ultimate Holding Company: NAYLOR INDUSTRIES PLC
Immediate Holding Company: NAYLOR CONCRETE PRODUCTS LTD
Registration no: 00379438 **VAT No.:** GB 183 8089 30
Date established: 1943 **Turnover:** £2m - £5m
No.of Employees: 101 - 250 **Product Groups:** 33

Date of Accounts	Feb 12	Feb 11	Feb 10
Sales Turnover	4m	4m	4m
Pre Tax Profit/Loss	807	275	538
Working Capital	370	-227	1m
Fixed Assets	513	639	729
Current Assets	2m	1m	2m
Current Liabilities	966	947	905

Northern Cullet Ltd

Pontefract Road, Barnsley, S71 1HJ
Tel: 01226-246541 **Fax:** 01226-704529
E-mail: sales@northerncullet.co.uk
Website: http://www.potterseurope.com
Bank(s): HSBC Bank plc
Directors: W. Mayall (MD)
Ultimate Holding Company: PQ CORPORATION (USA)
Immediate Holding Company: NORTHERN CULLET LIMITED
Registration no: 01447140 **VAT No.:** GB 183 2775 43
Date established: 1979 **No.of Employees:** 11 - 20 **Product Groups:** 33, 48

Date of Accounts	Dec 05
Working Capital	499
Current Assets	499

Northern Forecourts

Unit 11 Grange Lane Indl-Est Carrwood Road, Barnsley, S71 5AS
Tel: 01226-241818
Directors: G. Mcmarham (Dir)
Date established: 2001 **No.of Employees:** 1 - 10 **Product Groups:** 40

Padgett Bros A To Z Ltd

Darton Business Park Barnsley Road, Darton, Barnsley, S75 5QX
Tel: 01226-381188 **Fax:** 01226-388855
E-mail: info@padgettatoz.co.uk
Website: http://www.padgettatoz.co.uk
Directors: T. Padgett (MD), A. Padgett (MD)
Managers: L. Craven (Comptroller), M. Bagg (Chief Acct), S. Winder (Quality Control)
Immediate Holding Company: PADGETT BROTHERS (A TO Z) LIMITED
Registration no: 01968315 **Date established:** 1985 **Turnover:** £5m - £10m
No.of Employees: 21 - 50 **Product Groups:** 49

Date of Accounts	Mar 11	Mar 10	Mar 09
Pre Tax Profit/Loss	N/A	N/A	557
Working Capital	1m	2m	2m
Fixed Assets	164	125	119
Current Assets	4m	4m	4m
Current Liabilities	N/A	N/A	823

Pelectro Ltd

Unit 2 Zenith Park Whaley Road, Barnsley, S75 1HT
Tel: 01226-240330
E-mail: pete@pelectro.com
Website: http://www.pelectro.com
Directors: P. Williams (MD), L. Williams (Fin)
Immediate Holding Company: PELECTRO LIMITED
Registration no: 03311406 **Date established:** 1997
Turnover: Up to £250,000 **No.of Employees:** 1 - 10 **Product Groups:** 37, 48, 84

Date of Accounts	Feb 11	Feb 10	Feb 09
Working Capital	-4	-6	-4
Fixed Assets	5	6	8
Current Assets	5	3	8

Potters Europe Ltd

Pontefract Road, Barnsley, S71 1HJ
Tel: 01226-704500 **Fax:** 01226-207615
E-mail: wmayall@pottersgroup.com
Website: http://www.potterseurope.com
Directors: W. Mayall (MD)
Managers: D. Mendes (I.T. Exec), D. Mendes (Tech Serv Mgr), P. Curdy (Sales Prom Mgr), G. Law (Fin Mgr), J. Curdy (Sales Prom Mgr)
Ultimate Holding Company: PQ CORPORATION (USA)
Immediate Holding Company: POTTERS-BALLOTINI LIMITED
Registration no: 00591872 **Date established:** 1957 **Turnover:** £5m - £10m
No.of Employees: 21 - 50 **Product Groups:** 33, 38

Date of Accounts	Dec 11	Dec 10	Dec 09
Sales Turnover	11m	8m	6m
Pre Tax Profit/Loss	-569	-550	-512
Working Capital	-1m	-132	764
Fixed Assets	3m	3m	3m
Current Assets	6m	5m	4m
Current Liabilities	483	371	447

Premdor Crosby Ltd (Export Sales Department)

Huddersfield Road Darton, Barnsley, S75 5JS
Tel: 01226-383434 **Fax:** 01226-388808
E-mail: ukmarketing@premdor.com
Website: http://www.premdor.co.uk
Bank(s): National Westminster
Directors: R. Baker (Sales & Mktg), M. Armstrong (Fin)
Managers: M. Farrant (Tech Serv Mgr), B. Broughton (Personnel), M. Armstrong (Purch Mgr), J. Walker
Ultimate Holding Company: MASONITE INTERNATIONAL CORPORATION (CANADA)
Immediate Holding Company: PREMDOR CROSBY LIMITED
Registration no: 03227274 **Date established:** 1996
Turnover: £50m - £75m **No.of Employees:** 251 - 500
Product Groups: 25, 30, 35

Date of Accounts	Dec 11	Dec 08	Jan 10
Sales Turnover	55m	83m	54m
Pre Tax Profit/Loss	-2m	-9m	-13m
Working Capital	-24m	-5m	-16m
Fixed Assets	19m	20m	19m
Current Assets	27m	41m	25m
Current Liabilities	2m	3m	2m

Prism

Bbic Innovation Way, Barnsley, S75 1JL
Tel: 01226-321202 **Fax:** 01226-294797
E-mail: info@sespauk.com
Website: http://www.prismuk.org
Directors: P. Kiddell (MD)
Managers: M. Whaley (Admin Off), M. Whalley (Admin Off)
Immediate Holding Company: CREATE LEARN INSPIRE LTD
Registration no: 00475170 **Date established:** 2011
Turnover: Up to £250,000 **No.of Employees:** 1 - 10 **Product Groups:** 28, 87

Pro Display T M Ltd

Unit 5 Shortwood Court Shortwood Business Park, Hoyland, Barnsley, S74 9LH
Tel: 08707-668438 **Fax:** 0870-766 8437
E-mail: sales@prodisplay.co.uk
Website: http://www.prodisplay.com
Directors: P. Beswick (MD)
Immediate Holding Company: PRO DISPLAY TM LIMITED
Registration no: 05008682 **Date established:** 2004
No.of Employees: 11 - 20 **Product Groups:** 38

Date of Accounts	May 11	May 10	May 09
Working Capital	659	389	234
Fixed Assets	227	175	169
Current Assets	995	568	454

Qualter Hall & Co. Ltd

16 Johnson Street, Barnsley, S75 2BY
Tel: 01226-205761 **Fax:** 01226-286269
E-mail: admin@qualterhall.co.uk
Website: http://www.qualterhall.co.uk
Bank(s): HSBC Bank plc
Directors: G. Orton (MD)
Managers: C. Smith (Sales & Mktg Mg), D. Kenyon (Purch Mgr), G. Wild (Personnel), C. Middleton (Chief Acct)
Ultimate Holding Company: WAAGNER-BIRO AG (AUSTRIA)
Immediate Holding Company: QUALTER,HALL & CO.,LIMITED
Registration no: 00112626 **VAT No.:** GB 656 2190 34
Date established: 2010 **Turnover:** £10m - £20m
No.of Employees: 101 - 250 **Product Groups:** 35, 36, 45, 48

Date of Accounts	Dec 11	Dec 10	Dec 09
Sales Turnover	16m	14m	18m
Pre Tax Profit/Loss	2m	2m	1m
Working Capital	3m	3m	3m
Fixed Assets	4m	4m	4m
Current Assets	7m	7m	8m
Current Liabilities	2m	2m	3m

R J Wood Products

Unit 2 Metro Trading Centre Barugh Green Road, Barugh Green, Barnsley, S75 1JT
Tel: 01226-391852 **Fax:** 01226-391852
E-mail: jjaques@blueyonder.co.uk
Website: http://www.woodengatessouthyorkshire.co.uk
Directors: R. Jaques (Prop)
Date established: 2004 **No.of Employees:** 1 - 10 **Product Groups:** 26, 35

Rag Group

Centenary Works Wakefield Road, Barnsley, S71 1UG
Tel: 01226-215959 **Fax:** 01226- 244283
Website: http://www.theraggroup.com
Managers: T. Richardson (Mgr)
No.of Employees: 1 - 10 **Product Groups:** 35

Remora Electrical

Unit 8a Shortwood Court Shortwood Business Park, Hoyland, Barnsley, S74 9LH
Tel: 01226-352000 **Fax:** 0114-242 6830
E-mail: sales@remora.net
Website: http://www.remora.net
Directors: T. Demain (Co Sec)
Managers: A. Young (Chief Acct)
Immediate Holding Company: REMORA ELECTRICAL LIMITED
Registration no: 01115519 **Date established:** 1973
Turnover: £500,000 - £1m **No.of Employees:** 1 - 10 **Product Groups:** 30, 37, 67

Date of Accounts	Sep 11	Sep 10	Sep 09
Working Capital	353	288	245
Fixed Assets	45	53	58
Current Assets	714	615	674

Risk Assessment Products

11 Kingsway Wombwell, Barnsley, S73 0EB
Tel: 07974-970905
E-mail: sales@risk-assessment-products.co.uk
Website: http://risk-assessment-products.co.uk
Directors: C. Maltby (Prop)
Date established: 2006 **No.of Employees:** 1 - 10 **Product Groups:** 61

Rockley Dene Nursing Home

Park Road Worsbrough, Barnsley, S70 5AD
Tel: 01226-207916 **Fax:** 01226-280187
Bank(s): National Westminster
Directors: S. Ruparelia (MD)
Managers: L. Slyvester (Mgr), W. Lawson (Mgr)
Immediate Holding Company: Angel Care P.L.C.
Turnover: £500,000 - £1m **No.of Employees:** 21 - 50 **Product Groups:** 88

Rollem Ltd

3A wentworth Industrial Estate
Wentworth Way
Tankersley, Barnsley, ST5 3DH
Tel: 01226-745476 **Fax:** 0114-246 5487
E-mail: info@rollem.com
Website: http://www.rollem.co.uk
Bank(s): Royal Bank of Scotland,The Common,Ecclesfield
Directors: S. Murphy (Dir), R. Hamstead (Fin), C. Pears (Dir), C. Pears (Works)
Managers: D. Reckless (Purch Mgr)
Ultimate Holding Company: ROLLEM LIMITED
Immediate Holding Company: ROLLEM PATENT PRODUCTS LIMITED
Registration no: 00374392 **VAT No.:** GB 172 7781 36
Date established: 1942 **Turnover:** £2m - £5m **No.of Employees:** 21 - 50
Product Groups: 44

Date of Accounts	Mar 11	Mar 10	Mar 09
Working Capital	2m	2m	2m
Fixed Assets	381	398	421
Current Assets	2m	2m	2m
Current Liabilities	54	54	54

Royston Lead Ltd
Pogmoor Works Stocks Lane, Barnsley, S75 2DS
Tel: 01226-770110 **Fax:** 01226-730359
E-mail: info@roystonlead.co.uk
Website: http://www.roystonlead.co.uk
Bank(s): HSBC Bank plc
Managers: G. Farnell (Mgr)
Ultimate Holding Company: SIMMENTAL LTD (ISLE OF MAN)
Immediate Holding Company: ROYSTON LEAD LIMITED
Registration no: 00411322 **Date established:** 1946
Turnover: £10m - £20m **No.of Employees:** 21 - 50 **Product Groups:** 30, 33, 34, 35, 36

Date of Accounts	Dec 11	Dec 10	Dec 09
Sales Turnover	15m	16m	14m
Pre Tax Profit/Loss	837	334	132
Working Capital	2m	1m	1m
Fixed Assets	1m	925	774
Current Assets	5m	6m	8m
Current Liabilities	2m	3m	3m

Rubber Recovery
Engine Lane Shafton, Barnsley, S72 8SP
Tel: 01226-717091 **Fax:** 01226-714219
E-mail: ciaran@rp-recovery.com
Website: http://www.rubber-recovery.com
Managers: C. Brady (Mgr)
Immediate Holding Company: SHERLING STEEL (UK) LTD
Registration no: 03670817 **Date established:** 1998
Turnover: Up to £250,000 **No.of Employees:** 11 - 20 **Product Groups:** 29

Date of Accounts	Feb 08	Feb 11	Feb 10
Sales Turnover	N/A	8m	9m
Pre Tax Profit/Loss	N/A	-2m	-2m
Working Capital	2m	2m	3m
Fixed Assets	2m	2m	2m
Current Assets	9m	8m	9m
Current Liabilities	N/A	483	346

Seals Packing & Gasket Ltd
Mount Osbourne Industrial Park, Barnsley, S71 1HH
Tel: 01226-299401 **Fax:** 01226-204558
E-mail: sales@spg-gaskets.co.uk
Website: http://www.spg-gaskets.co.uk
Bank(s): Barclays, Fitzalan Branch, Sheffield
Directors: J. Morris (Fin)
Managers: G. Wakelin (Ops Mgr), M. Hyland (Prod Mgr)
Ultimate Holding Company: SHV HOLDINGS NV (NETHERLANDS)
Immediate Holding Company: SEALS PACKINGS & GASKETS LIMITED
Registration no: 01025728 **Date established:** 1971 **Turnover:** £5m - £10m
No.of Employees: 51 - 100 **Product Groups:** 29, 33, 40

Date of Accounts	Dec 10	Dec 09	Dec 08
Sales Turnover	9m	8m	10m
Pre Tax Profit/Loss	2m	1m	269
Working Capital	2m	1m	444
Fixed Assets	1m	1m	1m
Current Assets	4m	4m	4m
Current Liabilities	808	530	334

Sematic UK Ltd
Meadow Gate Valley Park Industrial Estate, Wombwell, Barnsley, S73 0UN
Tel: 01226-344800 **Fax:** 01226-344811
E-mail: info@sematic.com
Website: http://www.sematic.com
Directors: S. Brunton (MD), P. Zappa (Co Sec)
Managers: S. Robinson, P. Hullock, C. Shodiya, C. Price (Personnel), D. Duker
Ultimate Holding Company: SAPA SRL (ITALY)
Immediate Holding Company: SEMATIC U.K. LIMITED
Registration no: 02205395 **Date established:** 1987
Turnover: £10m - £20m **No.of Employees:** 51 - 100 **Product Groups:** 35, 39, 45

Date of Accounts	Dec 11	Dec 10	Dec 09
Sales Turnover	10m	9m	9m
Pre Tax Profit/Loss	2m	913	2m
Working Capital	4m	3m	8m
Fixed Assets	2m	2m	2m
Current Assets	6m	5m	10m
Current Liabilities	511	93	429

South Yorkshire Shooting Supplies Ltd
178 Everill Gate Lane Wombwell, Barnsley, S73 0YQ
Tel: 01226-756332 **Fax:** 01226-751321
E-mail: enquiries@rimfiremagic.co.uk
Website: http://www.rimfiremagic.co.uk
Directors: S. Francis (Fin), R. Francis (MD)
Immediate Holding Company: SOUTH YORKSHIRE SHOOTING SUPPLIES LIMITED
Registration no: 04826728 **Date established:** 2003
No.of Employees: 1 - 10 **Product Groups:** 36, 39, 40

Date of Accounts	Mar 11	Mar 10	Mar 09
Working Capital	248	274	293
Fixed Assets	73	76	77
Current Assets	504	544	541

Sterling Mechanical Services Ltd
Unit 12 Wilthorpe Road, Barnsley, S75 1JN
Tel: 01226-247054 **Fax:** 01226-296640
E-mail: info@sterlingmechanical.co.uk
Website: http://www.sterlingmechanical.co.uk
Directors: A. Jones (Fin), M. Jones (Dir)
Ultimate Holding Company: STERLING POWER GROUP HOLDINGS LIMITED
Immediate Holding Company: STERLING MECHANICAL SERVICES LIMITED
Registration no: 05617350 **Date established:** 2005
Turnover: £500m - £1,000m **No.of Employees:** 21 - 50
Product Groups: 35

Date of Accounts	Mar 11	Mar 10	Mar 09
Working Capital	-408	-129	6
Fixed Assets	29	13	11
Current Assets	527	337	229

The Barnsley Chronicle Ltd
47 Church Street, Barnsley, S70 2AS
Tel: 01226-734734 **Fax:** 01226-734444
E-mail: enquiries@barnsley-chronicle.co.uk
Website: http://www.barnsley-chronicle.co.uk
Bank(s): Barclays
Directors: M. Hewitt (Sales), E. West (Purch)
Managers: J. Barton (Mktg Serv Mgr), Y. West (Buyer), K. Bassinder (Comptroller), J. Barton (Mktg Serv Mgr), A. Crossland (Tech Serv Mgr), K. Bassinder (Comptroller)
Ultimate Holding Company: ACREDULA GROUP LIMITED
Immediate Holding Company: THE BARNSLEY CHRONICLE LIMITED
Registration no: 00029043 **VAT No.:** GB 565 6362 18
Date established: 1989 **Turnover:** £5m - £10m
No.of Employees: 101 - 250 **Product Groups:** 28

Date of Accounts	Dec 11	Dec 10	Dec 09
Sales Turnover	7m	7m	8m
Pre Tax Profit/Loss	-77	-146	-241
Working Capital	3m	3m	2m
Fixed Assets	2m	2m	3m
Current Assets	3m	3m	3m
Current Liabilities	491	409	467

Thomas C Henry Chartered Engineer
Digital Multimedia Centre County Way, Barnsley, S70 2JW
Tel: 01226-201951 **Fax:** 01226-201951
E-mail: enquiries@tomhenry.co.uk
Website: http://www.structuralreports.com
Directors: T. Henry (Prop)
Immediate Holding Company: AFFILISEARCH LTD
Date established: 2011 **No.of Employees:** 1 - 10 **Product Groups:** 35

Thornhill Heat Exchangers Ltd
Long Royd Grimethorpe, Barnsley, S72 7PT
Tel: 01226-710000
E-mail: info@thornhill-ltd.co.uk
Website: http://www.thornhillheatexchangers.co.uk
Managers: M. Ingram (Works Gen Mgr)
Immediate Holding Company: THORNHILL HEAT EXCHANGERS LIMITED
Registration no: 02370591 **Date established:** 1989 **Turnover:** £5m - £10m
No.of Employees: 51 - 100 **Product Groups:** 38, 42

Date of Accounts	Dec 11	Dec 10	Dec 09
Sales Turnover	8m	7m	6m
Pre Tax Profit/Loss	457	677	214
Working Capital	1m	1m	525
Fixed Assets	1m	1m	1m
Current Assets	3m	2m	2m
Current Liabilities	1m	557	1m

Tray-Tech UK Ltd
Unit 19-27 Sandybridge Lane Indl-Est, Shafton, Barnsley, S72 8PH
Tel: 01226-710200
E-mail: vicki@traytech.co.uk
Website: http://www.traytech.co.uk
Directors: V. Shirtliff (Dir)
Immediate Holding Company: TRAY-TECH (UK) LIMITED
Registration no: 02896587 **Date established:** 1994
No.of Employees: 11 - 20 **Product Groups:** 36, 63, 66

Date of Accounts	Mar 11	Mar 10	Mar 09
Working Capital	290	210	220
Fixed Assets	119	119	124
Current Assets	786	742	784

Trist Draper Hydraulics
Unit 6f Redbrook Business Park Wilthorpe Road, Barnsley, S75 1JN
Tel: 01226-281140 **Fax:** 01226-243223
E-mail: sales@tristdraper.co.uk
Website: http://www.tristdraper.co.uk
Managers: S. Johnson (Mgr)
Immediate Holding Company: REGENT HOSE & HYDRAULICS LTD
Registration no: 01599363 **Date established:** 1990 **Turnover:** £1m - £2m
No.of Employees: 1 - 10 **Product Groups:** 29, 30, 36, 66

Triten International Ltd
Shawfield Road, Barnsley, S71 3HS
Tel: 01226-702300 **Fax:** 01226-702311
E-mail: sales@triten.co.uk
Website: http://www.tritenapg.com
Bank(s): National Westminster
Directors: N. Bush (Fin), P. Leonard (MD), P. Leonard (MD)
Managers: A. Smith
Ultimate Holding Company: TRITEN CORP (USA)
Immediate Holding Company: TRITEN INTERNATIONAL LIMITED
Registration no: 02385191 **VAT No.:** 174 0651 72 **Date established:** 1989
Turnover: £5m - £10m **No.of Employees:** 51 - 100 **Product Groups:** 34, 35, 48

Date of Accounts	Apr 12	Apr 11	Apr 10
Sales Turnover	6m	4m	4m
Pre Tax Profit/Loss	304	137	-66
Working Capital	1m	2m	2m
Fixed Assets	2m	2m	2m
Current Assets	4m	3m	3m
Current Liabilities	490	348	400

Vesseltech UK Ltd
Unit 9 Maple Estate Stocks Lane, Barnsley, S75 2BL
Tel: 01226-732170 **Fax:** 01226-732170
Directors: I. Smith (MD), V. Smith (Fin)
Immediate Holding Company: VESSELTEC UK LIMITED
Registration no: 03806325 **Date established:** 1999
No.of Employees: 1 - 10 **Product Groups:** 35

Date of Accounts	Mar 11	Mar 10	Mar 09
Working Capital	116	154	182
Fixed Assets	56	25	28
Current Assets	250	185	215

Warwick Ward Machinery Ltd
Blacker Hill Sidings Blacker Hill, Barnsley, S74 0RE
Tel: 01226-747260 **Fax:** 01226-350129
E-mail: info@warwick-ward.co.uk
Website: http://www.warwick-ward.co.uk
Directors: A. Ward (Dir)
Managers: M. Ward (Mgr)
Immediate Holding Company: WARWICK WARD (MACHINERY) LIMITED
Registration no: 00988708 **VAT No.:** GB 172 9505 50
Date established: 1970 **Turnover:** £10m - £20m
No.of Employees: 21 - 50 **Product Groups:** 42, 45

Date of Accounts	Sep 11	Sep 10	Sep 09
Sales Turnover	15m	12m	11m
Pre Tax Profit/Loss	750	635	12
Working Capital	2m	2m	2m
Fixed Assets	743	690	428
Current Assets	6m	5m	4m
Current Liabilities	824	1m	875

Watsons Anodising
3 Platts Common Industrial Estate Chambers Road, Hoyland, Barnsley, S74 9SA
Tel: 01226-748524 **Fax:** 01226-747881
E-mail: sales@watsonsanodising.co.uk
Website: http://www.watsonsanodising.co.uk
Bank(s): Royal Bank of Scotland
Directors: D. Watson (Co Sec), R. Jackson (Chief Op Offcr)
Ultimate Holding Company: HIGHFIELD ELECTRONICS LIMITED
Immediate Holding Company: WATSON'S ANODISING LIMITED
Registration no: 00591057 **VAT No.:** GB 308 4180 74
Date established: 1957 **Turnover:** £500,000 - £1m
No.of Employees: 11 - 20 **Product Groups:** 23, 27, 28, 29, 30, 32, 33, 34, 36, 37, 40, 42, 44, 45, 48, 49, 68

Date of Accounts	Sep 11	Sep 10	Sep 09
Sales Turnover	624	551	530
Pre Tax Profit/Loss	35	6	-5
Working Capital	121	90	75
Fixed Assets	30	36	52
Current Assets	270	255	235
Current Liabilities	46	33	17

Wybone Ltd
Mason Way Hoyland, Barnsley, S74 9TF
Tel: 01226-744010 **Fax:** 01226-350105
E-mail: sales@wybone.co.uk
Website: http://www.wybone.co.uk
Bank(s): Yorkshire
Directors: C. Wyatt (Ch), D. Tucker (Pers)
Managers: J. Sagar (Fin Mgr), M. Scholey (Purch Mgr)
Immediate Holding Company: WYBONE LIMITED
Registration no: 00952455 **VAT No.:** GB 182 0886 50
Date established: 1969 **Turnover:** £2m - £5m **No.of Employees:** 51 - 100
Product Groups: 26, 29, 30, 33, 35, 36, 45, 67

Date of Accounts	Apr 11	Apr 10	Apr 09
Working Capital	470	-10	77
Fixed Assets	2m	2m	2m
Current Assets	1m	1m	2m

Doncaster

A & J Geo Technical Services
Carcroft Enterprise Park Station Road, Carcroft, Doncaster, DN6 8DD
Tel: 01302-339345 **Fax:** 01302-339456
E-mail: accounts@aj-geotechnical.co.uk
Website: http://www.aj-geotechnical.co.uk
Directors: D. Evans (MD)
Immediate Holding Company: CADDY CONSULTANCY LIMITED
Date established: 2008 **Turnover:** £250m - £500m
No.of Employees: 1 - 10 **Product Groups:** 33, 34, 35, 45, 51, 66, 84

Date of Accounts	Mar 11	Mar 10	Mar 09
Working Capital	70	85	73
Fixed Assets	162	176	290
Current Assets	303	234	210

A P C O UK
L K H Estate Tickhill Road, Doncaster, DN4 8QG
Tel: 01302-311121 **Fax:** 01302-311852
E-mail: rachel.blackburn@norking.com
Website: http://www.apcosigns.co.uk
Managers: R. Blackburn
Ultimate Holding Company: CLAYFIELD 2008 LIMITED
Immediate Holding Company: CLAYFIELD CONSTRUCTION LIMITED
Registration no: 01432812 **Date established:** 1966
No.of Employees: 51 - 100 **Product Groups:** 30, 39, 40

Date of Accounts	Apr 11	Apr 10	Apr 09
Working Capital	389	226	159
Fixed Assets	551	719	811
Current Assets	692	555	488

Accelerating Development Consultancy Ltd
45 St Marys Road Dunsville, Doncaster, DN7 4DL
Tel: 01302-882304
Website: http://www.acceleratingdc.co.uk
Directors: P. Auton (Fin), R. Auton (MD)
Immediate Holding Company: ACCELERATING DEVELOPMENT CONSULTANCY LIMITED
Registration no: 04988676 **VAT No.:** GB 828 8636 80
Date established: 2003 **Turnover:** Up to £250,000
No.of Employees: 1 - 10 **Product Groups:** 80, 84, 86

Date of Accounts	Dec 11	Dec 10	Dec 09
Working Capital	-13	-19	-16
Current Assets	3	2	2

Airflo Envirorental
Kelham Street, Doncaster, DN1 3TA
Tel: 01302-730000 **Fax:** 01302-321222
E-mail: admin@airflo.org
Website: http://www.airflo.org
Directors: P. Smith (Ptnr)
VAT No.: GB 182 1464 71 **Date established:** 1972 **Turnover:** £1m - £2m
No.of Employees: 1 - 10 **Product Groups:** 39, 40, 42, 66

AJ Hurst Foundation Engineering Ltd
Imex, Unit 9G2 Carcroft Enterprise Park, Station Road, Carcroft, Doncaster, DN6 8DD
Tel: 01302-339345 **Fax:** 01302-339600
E-mail: alan.hurst@ajhpiling.co.uk
Website: http://www.ajhpiling.co.uk
Product Groups: 33, 34, 35, 41, 45, 51, 66, 84

Date of Accounts	Mar 08	Mar 07	Mar 06
Working Capital	7	24	-4
Fixed Assets	64	11	13
Current Assets	413	78	4
Current Liabilities	407	54	8

Ardagh Glass Ltd
Barnby Dun Road, Doncaster, DN2 4RH
Tel: 01302-563200 **Fax:** 01302-563450
E-mail: wayne.rodgers@ardaghgroup.com
Website: http://www.ardaghglass.com

see next page

***Ardagh Glass Ltd** - Cont'd*

Directors: W. Rodgers (Plant)
Managers: C. Phillip (Personnel), M. Pyle (Personnel), R. Simmonds (Sales Prom Mgr)
Ultimate Holding Company: ARDAGH GLASS GROUP SA (LUXEMBOURG)
Immediate Holding Company: ARDAGH GLASS LIMITED
Registration no: 00567801 **Date established:** 1956
Turnover: £50m - £75m **No.of Employees:** 251 - 500 **Product Groups:** 33

Date of Accounts	Dec 11	Dec 10	Dec 09
Sales Turnover	297m	288m	283m
Pre Tax Profit/Loss	29m	46m	24m
Working Capital	326m	313m	153m
Fixed Assets	114m	124m	132m
Current Assets	406m	378m	224m
Current Liabilities	27m	27m	9m

B K Safety

20 Pembroke Rise, Doncaster, DN5 8PP
Tel: 01302-785063 **Fax:** 01302-785063
E-mail: kevin-irwin@bksafety.co.uk
Website: http://www.bksafety.co.uk
Directors: K. Irwin (Ptnr)
Date established: 1997 **Turnover:** Up to £250,000
No.of Employees: 1 - 10 **Product Groups:** 33, 38, 40, 42, 45, 54

Bridon International Ltd

Ground Floor Icon Building First Point Balby Carr Bank, Doncaster, DN4 8JQ
Tel: 01302-565100 **Fax:** 01302-382263
E-mail: sales@bridonstocksbridge.com
Website: http://www.bridon.com
Bank(s): National Westminster Bank Plc
Directors: A. Parker (Sales), A. Snowdon (Tech Serv), G. Hardcastle (Fin), M. Porter (Fin), A. Hurst (Pers)
Managers: S. Merrills (Personnel), J. Templeman, J. Ferguson (Mktg Serv Mgr)
Ultimate Holding Company: MELROSE PLC
Immediate Holding Company: BRIDON INTERNATIONAL LTD.
Registration no: 00416671 **VAT No.:** GB 524 1839 45
Date established: 1946 **Turnover:** £10m - £20m
No.of Employees: 1001 - 1500 **Product Groups:** 34, 35

Date of Accounts	Dec 11	Dec 10	Dec 09
Sales Turnover	138m	130m	158m
Pre Tax Profit/Loss	5	17m	24m
Working Capital	36m	67m	74m
Fixed Assets	23m	14m	15m
Current Assets	102m	99m	104m
Current Liabilities	42m	9m	13m

Robin Brown & Associates

Croft View Brookfield Mews, Arksey, Doncaster, DN5 0UB
Tel: 01302-875519 **Fax:** 01302-875530
E-mail: robinbrownuk@aol.com
Website: http://www.robinianbrown.com
Directors: R. Brown (Prop)
Immediate Holding Company: DONCASTER PROPERTY LIMITED
Registration no: 04026697 **Date established:** 2000
No.of Employees: 1 - 10 **Product Groups:** 35

BST Products

Unit 7 Delta Court Sky Business Park, Robin Hood Airport, Doncaster, DN9 3GN
Tel: 0845-643 0950 **Fax:** 0845-643 0960
E-mail: info@detectable-products.co.uk
Website: http://www.detectable-products.co.uk
Directors: J. Teasdale (MD)
Managers: S. Ball (Mgr), I. Bond (Sales Prom Mgr)
Registration no: 03600536 **VAT No.:** GB 715 9845 02
Date established: 1985 **Turnover:** £500,000 - £1m
No.of Employees: 1 - 10 **Product Groups:** 23, 24, 27, 29, 30, 32, 33, 36, 38, 39, 40, 49

C B I Fleetwood Ltd

Plumtree Farm Industrial Estate Plumtree Road, Bircotes, Doncaster, DN11 8EW
Tel: 01302-711056 **Fax:** 01302-710802
E-mail: lee.pinder@fgwa.com
Website: http://www.centralbottling.com
Bank(s): Yorkshire
Directors: L. Pinder (Dir)
Managers: N. Birkin (Sales Prom Mgr), S. Bailey (Tech Serv Mgr)
Ultimate Holding Company: BARRY WEHMILLER INC (USA)
Immediate Holding Company: CENTRAL BOTTLING INTERNATIONAL FLEETWOOD LIMITED
Registration no: 05197694 **VAT No.:** GB 295 297 214
Date established: 2004 **Turnover:** £10m - £20m
No.of Employees: 51 - 100 **Product Groups:** 41

Date of Accounts	Sep 11	Sep 10	Sep 09
Sales Turnover	16m	17m	14m
Pre Tax Profit/Loss	1m	325	-2m
Working Capital	3m	2m	187
Fixed Assets	3m	3m	1m
Current Assets	9m	6m	6m
Current Liabilities	3m	2m	2m

Cartonplast UK Ltd

Unit 21-22 Shaw Lane Industrial Estate Ogden Road, Doncaster, DN2 4SQ
Tel: 01302-323054
E-mail: clive.spink@cartonplast.co.uk
Website: http://www.cartonplast.com
Directors: M. Dewan (Dir), P. Picton (MD)
Immediate Holding Company: CARTONPLAST (UK) LIMITED
Registration no: 04092100 **Date established:** 2000
No.of Employees: 21 - 50 **Product Groups:** 30, 35, 48

Date of Accounts	Dec 11	Dec 10	Dec 09
Working Capital	359	-444	-242
Fixed Assets	3m	669	132
Current Assets	2m	2m	2m

Caswick Ltd

Sandtoft Road Belton, Doncaster, DN9 1PN
Tel: 01427-872017 **Fax:** 01427-873541
E-mail: info@caswick.com
Website: http://www.caswick.com
Bank(s): Yorkshire, Doncaster
Directors: G. Cawte (Dir)
Immediate Holding Company: CASWICK LIMITED
Registration no: 01955577 **Date established:** 1985 **Turnover:** £1m - £2m
No.of Employees: 11 - 20 **Product Groups:** 30, 66

Date of Accounts	Dec 11	Dec 10	Dec 09
Working Capital	391	355	451
Fixed Assets	443	447	535
Current Assets	994	1m	876

Cementation Skanska

Bentley House Jossey Lane, Doncaster, DN5 9ED
Tel: 01302-821100 **Fax:** 01302-821111
E-mail: lynne.brown@skanska.co.uk
Website: http://www.skanska.co.uk
Managers: L. Brown, I. Phillips
Immediate Holding Company: SKANSKA GROUP
Registration no: 00937574 **Date established:** 2001
Turnover: £50m - £75m **No.of Employees:** 51 - 100 **Product Groups:** 51, 86

Certex UK Ltd

Unit C1blyth Road Harworth, Doncaster, DN11 8NE
Tel: 01302-756779 **Fax:** 029-2068 3659
E-mail: ksmith@certex.co.uk
Website: http://www.certex.co.uk
Directors: T. Stringer (MD)
Ultimate Holding Company: AXEL JOHNSON INTERNATIONAL AB (SWEDEN)
Immediate Holding Company: CERTEX (UK) LIMITED
Registration no: 00928803 **Date established:** 1968
No.of Employees: 21 - 50 **Product Groups:** 23, 30, 35

Challenge Supply Co.

Unit 14 Durham Lane, Armthorpe, Doncaster, DN3 3FE
Tel: 01302-836777 **Fax:** 01302-836788
E-mail: sales@challengesupply.com
Website: http://www.challengesupply.com
Directors: M. Layton (Ptnr)
No.of Employees: 1 - 10 **Product Groups:** 22, 30

Clyde Bergemann Materials Handling Ltd

Lakeside Boulevard, Doncaster, DN4 5PL
Tel: 01302-552200 **Fax:** 01302-369055
E-mail: jhudson@cbmh.co.uk
Website: http://www.cbmh.co.uk
Directors: J. Hudson (MD), M. Radcliffe (Fin), M. Ratcliffe (Fin)
Managers: P. Williamson (Purch Mgr), R. Turner (Tech Serv Mgr)
Ultimate Holding Company: CLYDE BERGEMANN POWER GROUP INC (USA)
Immediate Holding Company: CLYDE BERGEMANN MATERIALS HANDLING LIMITED
Registration no: 02919367 **Date established:** 1994
Turnover: £20m - £50m **No.of Employees:** 51 - 100 **Product Groups:** 40, 45, 48

Date of Accounts	Feb 12	Feb 11	Feb 10
Sales Turnover	13m	20m	N/A
Pre Tax Profit/Loss	-3m	2m	N/A
Working Capital	8m	9m	7m
Fixed Assets	2m	2m	3m
Current Assets	19m	16m	17m
Current Liabilities	5m	728	945

Clyde Process Ltd

Carolina Court Lakeside, Doncaster, DN4 5RA
Tel: 01302-321313 **Fax:** 01302-554400
E-mail: solutions@clydematerials.co.uk
Website: http://www.clydematerials.co.uk
Bank(s): The Royal Bank of Scotland
Directors: J. Hall (Fin), N. Jones (MD), R. Sims (MD)
Managers: M. Patchett (Purch Mgr), R. Turner (Tech Serv Mgr), J. Lunley (Personnel)
Ultimate Holding Company: SCHENCK PROCESS HOLDING GMBH (GERMANY)
Immediate Holding Company: CLYDE PROCESS SOLUTIONS LIMITED
Registration no: 05341832 **VAT No.:** GB 801 8627 40
Date established: 2005 **Turnover:** £50m - £75m
No.of Employees: 51 - 100 **Product Groups:** 36, 40, 45, 84

Date of Accounts	Dec 11	Feb 10	Feb 09
Sales Turnover	N/A	73m	82m
Pre Tax Profit/Loss	468	5m	6m
Working Capital	843	3m	1m
Fixed Assets	39m	73m	77m
Current Assets	2m	26m	33m
Current Liabilities	55	13m	21m

Colbear Advertising Ltd

Unit 8 Durham Lane, Armthorpe, Doncaster, DN3 3FE
Tel: 01302-836170 **Fax:** 01302-836171
E-mail: scott@colbear.co.uk
Website: http://www.colbear.co.uk
Directors: M. Colbear (Ch), S. Colbear (MD), J. Cooper (Dir), S. Colbear (Prop)
Managers: G. Ellis (I.T. Exec)
Immediate Holding Company: COLBEAR ADVERTISING LIMITED
Registration no: 00793944 **VAT No.:** GB 181 3184 73
Date established: 1964 **Turnover:** £2m - £5m **No.of Employees:** 1 - 10
Product Groups: 81

Date of Accounts	Feb 08	Feb 11	Feb 10
Working Capital	125	-42	20
Fixed Assets	739	294	688
Current Assets	353	75	124

Cooplands (Doncaster) Ltd (Head Office)

Victoria Mill Business Park Wharf Road, Doncaster, DN1 2SX
Tel: 01302-818000 **Fax:** 01302-329776
E-mail: customer.service@cooplands.co.uk
Website: http://www.cooplands.co.uk
Directors: D. Jenkinson (MD), W. Mcllroy (Co Sec), A. Wagstaff (Dir), M. Mcllroy (Ch)
Managers: A. Jaques (Purch Mgr), R. Mcllroy (Mktg Serv Mgr)
Immediate Holding Company: Cooplands (Edlington) Ltd
Registration no: 00279007 **Date established:** 1962
Turnover: £10m - £20m **No.of Employees:** 1 - 10 **Product Groups:** 20

Date of Accounts	Jun 09	Jun 08	Jun 07
Sales Turnover	19m	18m	17m
Pre Tax Profit/Loss	-55	262	290
Working Capital	-2m	-2m	-2m
Fixed Assets	10m	10m	8m
Current Assets	2m	2m	1m
Current Liabilities	1m	1m	1m

Coulstock & Place Engineering Co. Ltd

1-6 Bankwood Lane New Rossington, Doncaster, DN11 0PS
Tel: 01302-865400 **Fax:** 01302-865009
E-mail: info@coulstockandplace.co.uk
Website: http://www.coulstockandplace.co.uk
Bank(s): Barclays
Directors: I. Creasey (Co Sec)
Managers: E. Hanley (Sales Admin), G. Chamberlain (Fin Mgr)
Ultimate Holding Company: DAIKIN INDUSTRIES LTD (JAPAN)
Immediate Holding Company: COULSTOCK & PLACE ENGINEERING CO LIMITED
Registration no: 02040654 **VAT No.:** GB 436 6994 04
Date established: 1986 **Turnover:** £2m - £5m **No.of Employees:** 21 - 50
Product Groups: 48

Date of Accounts	Dec 11	Dec 10	Dec 09
Sales Turnover	4m	3m	2m
Pre Tax Profit/Loss	267	21	-1
Working Capital	1m	981	957
Fixed Assets	143	158	170
Current Assets	2m	2m	1m
Current Liabilities	115	36	85

D B Controls Ltd

9 Station Road Adwick-Le-Street, Doncaster, DN6 7BB
Tel: 01302-330837 **Fax:** 01302-724731
E-mail: david.brown@dbcontrols.co.uk
Website: http://www.dbcontrols.co.uk
Bank(s): National Westminster Bank Plc
Directors: D. Brown (Dir), D. Trueman (Sales), D. Brown (MD), G. Brown (Fin)
Managers: G. Allmendinger (I.T. Exec), J. Stokeon (Contracts Mgr)
Immediate Holding Company: EURO CONTROL SYSTEMS LIMITED
Registration no: 01636127 **VAT No.:** GB 590 9605 12
Date established: 1982 **Turnover:** £1m - £2m **No.of Employees:** 11 - 20
Product Groups: 37, 38, 39, 40, 44, 52, 66

Darfen Durafencing Ltd

Herons Way Balby, Doncaster, DN4 8WA
Tel: 01302-360242 **Fax:** 01302-364359
E-mail: northern@darfen.co.uk
Website: http://www.darfen.co.uk
Directors: T. Pitts (Chief Op Offcr)
Ultimate Holding Company: CRH PUBLIC LIMITED COMPANY
Immediate Holding Company: TANGORAIL LIMITED
Registration no: 07860336 **Date established:** 1992 **Turnover:** £5m - £10m
No.of Employees: 1 - 10 **Product Groups:** 33, 35, 40, 49, 52

Date of Accounts	Dec 11	Dec 10	Dec 09
Sales Turnover	2m	2m	2m
Pre Tax Profit/Loss	321	330	431
Working Capital	3m	3m	3m
Fixed Assets	N/A	1	10
Current Assets	3m	3m	3m
Current Liabilities	10	N/A	369

Darfen Steelhoard (Part CRH Group Ltd)

Herons Way Balby, Doncaster, DN4 8WA
Tel: 08457-023878 **Fax:** 01302-327135
E-mail: sales@steelhoard.co.uk
Website: http://www.steelhoard.co.uk
Directors: P. Chadwick (Fin), S. Towers (MD)
Managers: A. Street (Purch Mgr), G. Wild (Product), G. Wilde (Mgr), S. Nicholson (Projects), S. Buckley (Mktg Serv Mgr)
Ultimate Holding Company: CRH PUBLIC LIMITED COMPANY
Immediate Holding Company: TANGORAIL LIMITED
Registration no: 03863428 **Date established:** 1992 **Turnover:** £2m - £5m
No.of Employees: 11 - 20 **Product Groups:** 35, 52, 83

Disano UK

Unit 2 Railway Court, Doncaster, DN4 5FB
Tel: 01302-762160
Website: http://www.disano.it
Directors: B. Jubb (MD)
Immediate Holding Company: DISANO ILLUMINAZIONE UK LIMITED
Registration no: 04947891 **Date established:** 2003
No.of Employees: 1 - 10 **Product Groups:** 37, 67

Date of Accounts	Dec 11	Dec 10	Dec 09
Working Capital	-24	-366	797
Fixed Assets	31	31	47
Current Assets	807	983	1m

Dmat Systems Ltd

70 Balby Road, Doncaster, DN4 0JL
Tel: 01302-711822
E-mail: sales@dmat.co.uk
Website: http://www.dmat.co.uk
Directors: D. Matthews (MD), A. Blackburn (Fin)
Immediate Holding Company: DMAT SYSTEMS LIMITED
Registration no: 03377144 **Date established:** 1997
No.of Employees: 11 - 20 **Product Groups:** 27, 30, 66

Date of Accounts	May 11	May 10	May 09
Working Capital	2m	1m	2m
Fixed Assets	3m	3m	2m
Current Assets	2m	3m	3m

Don Valley Engineering Co. Ltd

Sandall Stones Road Kirk Sandall Industrial Estate, Doncaster, DN3 1QR
Tel: 01302-881188
E-mail: info@donvalleyeng.com
Website: http://www.donvalleyeng.com
Bank(s): Royal Bank of Scotland
Directors: E. Allen (Ch)
Managers: A. Bullass (Sales & Mktg Mg), B. Smith (Chief Mgr)
Immediate Holding Company: DON VALLEY ENGINEERING HOLDINGS LIMITED
Registration no: 07210081 **VAT No.:** GB 181 4937 45
Date established: 2010 **Turnover:** £5m - £10m **No.of Employees:** 21 - 50
Product Groups: 33

Date of Accounts	Jul 11	Jul 10
Sales Turnover	5m	890
Pre Tax Profit/Loss	-455	-120
Working Capital	2m	2m
Fixed Assets	3m	3m
Current Assets	4m	3m
Current Liabilities	295	232

Doncaster Vehicle Spares Ltd

Scope House Station Road, Barnby Dun, Doncaster, DN3 1HQ
Tel: 01302-885464 **Fax:** 01302-880401
E-mail: sales@doncastervehiclespares.co.uk
Bank(s): HSBC Bank plc

Directors: S. Towle (Dir)
Registration no: 01833064 **VAT No.:** GB 404 8615 61
Date established: 1984 **Turnover:** £500,000 - £1m
No.of Employees: 11 - 20 **Product Groups:** 35, 39, 40, 68

Date of Accounts	Jul 08	Jul 07	Jul 06
Working Capital	232	209	204
Fixed Assets	206	203	192
Current Assets	521	468	463
Current Liabilities	289	259	260

Eastfield Process Equipment

Eastfield Farm Doncaster Road, Tickhill, Doncaster, DN11 9JD
Tel: 01302-751444 **Fax:** 01302-751444
Website: http://www.eastfieldprocessequipment.co.uk
Directors: J. Brittain (Prop)
Date established: 1997 **No.of Employees:** 1 - 10 **Product Groups:** 20, 40, 41

Electrofix Of Doncaster Ltd

162 St Sepulchre Gate West, Doncaster, DN1 3AQ
Tel: 01302-341177 **Fax:** 01302-341480
Website: http://www.electrofix-doncaster.co.uk
Directors: S. Toplis (Fin), S. Sharma (MD)
Immediate Holding Company: ELECTROFIX OF DONCASTER LIMITED
Registration no: 04356926 **VAT No.:** GB 182 0279 71
Date established: 2002 **Turnover:** £500,000 - £1m
No.of Employees: 1 - 10 **Product Groups:** 48

Date of Accounts	Mar 11	Mar 10	Mar 09
Working Capital	11	25	34
Fixed Assets	23	29	37
Current Assets	37	42	155

G. Elliot Engineering Services Ltd

P.O. Box 935 Bircotes, Doncaster, DN11 8WR
Tel: 0844-8002989 **Fax:** 01302-745071
E-mail: sales@elliotteng.co.uk
Website: http://www.elliotteng.co.uk
Bank(s): The Royal Bank of Scotland
Directors: G. Elliot (Dir), C. Grainger (MD)
Managers: P. Gillbert (Chief Mgr), P. Gilbert (Sales & Mktg Mg)
Registration no: 02797492 **Turnover:** £500,000 - £1m
No.of Employees: 11 - 20 **Product Groups:** 48, 87

Eriks UK (Doncaster Service Centre)

Shaw Lane Industrial Estate Ogden Road, Doncaster, DN2 4SE
Tel: 01302-344422 **Fax:** 01302-349594
E-mail: doncaster@eriks.co.uk
Website: http://www.eriks.co.uk
Managers: G. Reaney
No.of Employees: 1 - 10 **Product Groups:** 66

Euroguns

Mill Race Farm Wroot Road, Finningley, Doncaster, DN9 3DY
Tel: 01302-773301 **Fax:** 01302-773305
Website: http://www.euroguns.co.uk
Directors: S. Drage (Prop)
Immediate Holding Company: EUROGUNS LTD
Registration no: 05181954 **Date established:** 2004
No.of Employees: 1 - 10 **Product Groups:** 36, 39, 40

Date of Accounts	Feb 11	Feb 10	Feb 09
Working Capital	-72	-30	-58
Fixed Assets	278	323	371
Current Assets	312	363	289

Eyre Fabrication

51 Askern Industrial Estate Moss Road, Askern, Doncaster, DN6 0DD
Tel: 01302-701190 **Fax:** 01302-701190
Directors: J. Hedley (Dir)
Immediate Holding Company: EYRE FABRICATIONS LIMITED
Registration no: 06356956 **Date established:** 2007
No.of Employees: 1 - 10 **Product Groups:** 35

Date of Accounts	Jul 12	Jul 11	Jul 10
Working Capital	84	48	52
Fixed Assets	37	41	43
Current Assets	141	118	125

Fairclough & Wood Ltd

Unit 10b Carcroft Enterprise Park Carcroft, Doncaster, DN6 8DD
Tel: 01302-726027 **Fax:** 01302-330221
E-mail: sales@faircloughwood.co.uk
Website: http://www.faircloughwood.co.uk
Directors: G. Wood (D-G), D. Wood (MD), R. Wood (Sales)
Managers: R. Wood (Admin Off)
Immediate Holding Company: CADDY CONSULTANCY LIMITED
Registration no: 02064331 **VAT No.:** GB 447 6046 38
Date established: 2008 **No.of Employees:** 1 - 10 **Product Groups:** 37, 66

Date of Accounts	Oct 08	Oct 07	Oct 06
Working Capital	76	82	66
Fixed Assets	36	48	34
Current Assets	253	323	280
Current Liabilities	176	241	214

Fern Dale Supplies

2 Brooklands Road Carcroft Industrial Estate, Adwick-Le-Street, Doncaster, DN6 7BA
Tel: 01302-330110 **Fax:** 01302-724427
Directors: A. Spencer (Ptnr)
Date established: 1982 **No.of Employees:** 1 - 10 **Product Groups:** 38, 42

Finish Line Products

Unit 16 Clayfield Industrial Estate Tickhill Road, Doncaster, DN4 8QG
Tel: 01302-856666 **Fax:** 01302-571572
E-mail: sales@finishlineproducts.co.uk
Website: http://www.finishlineproducts.co.uk
Managers: C. Hoare (Mgr)
Immediate Holding Company: SYSTCO - UNILAP LIMITED
Date established: 1983 **Turnover:** £1m - £2m **No.of Employees:** 1 - 10
Product Groups: 32, 35, 36, 37, 46, 49, 68

Date of Accounts	Apr 11	Apr 10	Apr 09
Working Capital	389	226	159
Fixed Assets	551	719	811
Current Assets	692	555	488

Flowtek H D D Ltd

Unit B Sandall Stones Road Kirk Sandall Industrial Estate, Doncaster, DN3 1QR
Tel: 01302-880582 **Fax:** 01302-884590
E-mail: flowtekuk@btconnect.com
Website: http://www.flowtekhdduk.co.uk
Directors: C. Preston (MD)
Immediate Holding Company: FLOWTEK HDD (UK) LIMITED
Registration no: 06530736 **VAT No.:** GB 930 2327 59
Date established: 2008 **Turnover:** £250,000 - £500,000
No.of Employees: 1 - 10 **Product Groups:** 38, 39, 45, 46, 48, 51, 52, 54, 67, 84

Date of Accounts	Mar 11	Mar 10	Mar 09
Working Capital	-41	18	-3
Fixed Assets	122	139	3
Current Assets	503	274	163

Geist Manufacturing Co. Ltd

Askern Industrial Estate Moss Road, Askern, Doncaster, DN6 0DD
Tel: 01302-700367 **Fax:** 01302-709988
E-mail: geistmanltd@aol.com
Directors: I. Smith (MD)
Immediate Holding Company: GEIST MANUFACTURING CO.LIMITED
Registration no: 00772785 **VAT No.:** GB 181 4091 75
Date established: 1963 **Turnover:** Up to £250,000
No.of Employees: 1 - 10 **Product Groups:** 35, 36, 37, 40

Date of Accounts	Nov 11	Nov 10	Nov 09
Working Capital	-20	-23	-25
Fixed Assets	23	28	35
Current Assets	68	110	101

General Catering Ltd

Unit 1 Churchill Business Park Churchill Road, Doncaster, DN1 2TF
Tel: 01302-340742 **Fax:** 01302-343385
E-mail: info@generalcatering.co.uk
Website: http://www.generalcatering.co.uk
Directors: G. Coward (Chief Op Offcr)
Immediate Holding Company: GENERAL CATERING LTD
Registration no: 06238959 **Date established:** 2007
No.of Employees: 1 - 10 **Product Groups:** 20, 21, 23, 25, 26, 27, 29, 30, 32, 33, 34, 35, 36, 37, 38, 40, 41, 45, 48, 49, 63, 66, 67, 80, 83

Date of Accounts	May 11	May 10	May 09
Working Capital	12	8	-1
Fixed Assets	8	8	N/A
Current Assets	64	106	N/A

Global- M S I PLC

Carr Hill Balby, Doncaster, DN4 8DH
Tel: 01302-361558 **Fax:** 01302-730198
E-mail: info@global-msi.com
Website: http://www.global-msi.com
Bank(s): Yorkshire
Directors: T. Fernley (Fin), M. Bell (Ch)
Managers: M. Allen, B. Shepherd, C. Sellers, M. Allen (I.T. Exec), A. Smith (Comm)
Ultimate Holding Company: MS INTERNATIONAL PLC
Immediate Holding Company: GLOBAL - MSI PUBLIC LIMITED COMPANY
Registration no: 02849288 **VAT No.:** GB 591 0849 23
Date established: 1993 **Turnover:** £5m - £10m
No.of Employees: 51 - 100 **Product Groups:** 52

Date of Accounts	Apr 11	May 08	May 09
Sales Turnover	7m	17m	14m
Pre Tax Profit/Loss	90	2m	401
Working Capital	1m	2m	2m
Fixed Assets	N/A	1m	898
Current Assets	1m	6m	4m
Current Liabilities	N/A	2m	929

H J M Fabrication Ltd

7 Waggons Way Stainforth, Doncaster, DN7 5TZ
Tel: 01302-846671
Website: http://www.hjmfabs.wanadoo.co.uk
Directors: D. Humphries (MD)
Immediate Holding Company: HJM FABRICATIONS LTD
Registration no: 06475937 **Date established:** 2008
No.of Employees: 1 - 10 **Product Groups:** 35

Date of Accounts	Jan 11	Jan 10	Jan 09
Working Capital	65	23	1
Fixed Assets	27	31	N/A
Current Assets	159	109	1

Haith Tickhill Group Ltd

Cow House Lane Armthorpe, Doncaster, DN3 3EE
Tel: 01302-831911 **Fax:** 01302-300173
E-mail: sales@haith.co.uk
Website: http://www.haith.co.uk
Bank(s): Barclays
Directors: J. Brindley (Fin), G. Haith (MD)
Ultimate Holding Company: Tickhill Engineering Co Ltd
Immediate Holding Company: A.J.HARRIS AND SON(FARMERS)LIMITED
Registration no: 00505344 **VAT No.:** GB 181 7026 71
Date established: 1952 **Turnover:** £5m - £10m
No.of Employees: 51 - 100 **Product Groups:** 41, 45

Date of Accounts	Dec 10	Dec 09
Working Capital	5	N/A
Current Assets	8	N/A

Herose Ltd

3 Lindley Road Finningley, Doncaster, DN9 3DQ
Tel: 01302-773114 **Fax:** 01302-770763
E-mail: sales@herose.co.uk
Website: http://www.herose.co.uk
Directors: A. Stewart (Fin), J. Stewart (MD)
Immediate Holding Company: HEROSE LIMITED
Registration no: 03679575 **Date established:** 1998
No.of Employees: 1 - 10 **Product Groups:** 30, 36, 38, 40, 46, 68

Date of Accounts	Dec 11	Dec 10	Dec 09
Working Capital	639	348	225
Fixed Assets	59	56	30
Current Assets	2m	906	804

Humber Merchants Ltd

Unit 2 & 3 Network Centre Doncaster Road, Kirk Sandall, Doncaster, DN3 1HP
Tel: 01302-858583
Website: http://www.humbermerchants.co.uk
Registration no: 01045179 **Date established:** 1972
No.of Employees: 1 - 10 **Product Groups:** 36, 37, 40

Impact Handling

Unit 1 Derbyshire Court Armthorpe, Doncaster, DN3 3FD
Tel: 01302-834924 **Fax:** 01302-834823
Website: http://www.impact-handling.com
Managers: S. Kent (Depot Mgr)
Date established: 2001 **No.of Employees:** 1 - 10 **Product Groups:** 35, 39, 45

Industrial Power Generation Ltd

38 Carcroft Enterprise Park, Station Road Carcroft, Doncaster, DN6 8DD
Tel: 0845-1665537 **Fax:** 01302-721202
E-mail: sales@ipguk.co.uk
Website: http://www.generator.co.uk
Directors: J. Watkinson (MD), R. Whaley (Sales)
Registration no: 7279561 **Date established:** 2010
Turnover: £500,000 - £1m **Product Groups:** 37, 38, 39, 40, 42, 52, 67, 83

Isotron plc

Alpha Court Thorne, Doncaster, DN8 5TZ
Tel: 01405-741170 **Fax:** 01405-741171
E-mail: michael.turner@isotron.com
Website: http://www.isotron.com
Managers: M. Turner (Chief Mgr), S. Wheatman (Chief Mgr)
No.of Employees: 11 - 20 **Product Groups:** 31, 48, 85, 88

Jenkinson Electrical Engineering

Jenkinson House White Rose Way, Doncaster, DN4 5GJ
Tel: 01302-321042 **Fax:** 01302-327514
E-mail: info@sjenkinson.co.uk
Website: http://www.sjenkinson.co.uk
Directors: M. Jenkinson (MD)
Immediate Holding Company: S. JENKINSON & SONS LTD
Registration no: 01693919 **VAT No.:** GB 181 5845 45
Date established: 1983 **Turnover:** £1m - £2m **No.of Employees:** 21 - 50
Product Groups: 52

John Leach Spares & Equipment

Rowan Cott Everton, Doncaster, DN10 5AU
Tel: 01777-817708 **Fax:** 01777-817708
Directors: J. Leach (Prop)
Registration no: 02412549 **Date established:** 1993
Turnover: £250,000 - £500,000 **No.of Employees:** 1 - 10
Product Groups: 67

Kiremko Food Processing Equipment UK Ltd

Armstrong House First Avenue, Doncaster Finningley Airport, Doncaster, DN9 3GA
Tel: 01302-772929 **Fax:** 01302-770548
E-mail: sales.uk@kiremko.com
Website: http://www.kiremko.com
Directors: A. Gowing (MD), F. Fisher (Fin)
Immediate Holding Company: KIREMKO FOOD PROCESSING EQUIPMENT (U.K.) LIMITED
Registration no: 01694467 **VAT No.:** GB 381 3973 30
Date established: 1983 **Turnover:** Up to £250,000
No.of Employees: 1 - 10 **Product Groups:** 40, 41

Date of Accounts	Dec 11	Dec 10	Dec 09
Sales Turnover	N/A	215	115
Pre Tax Profit/Loss	N/A	-3	-51
Working Capital	261	217	212
Fixed Assets	N/A	8	15
Current Assets	287	230	254
Current Liabilities	N/A	6	38

Lamphouse Ltd

Fitzgerald House 9 Avenue Road, Doncaster, DN2 4AH
Tel: 08456-440100 **Fax:** 01302-563855
E-mail: mike@lamphouse.co.uk
Website: http://www.lamphouse.co.uk
Directors: M. Brennon (MD)
Immediate Holding Company: LAMPHOUSE LIMITED
Registration no: 05849023 **Date established:** 2006
No.of Employees: 1 - 10 **Product Groups:** 28, 33, 37, 38, 40, 44, 48, 49, 61, 65, 67, 81, 83, 86

Lite-Tec

Unit 5 Hutton Business Park Hangthwaite Road, Adwick-le-Street, Doncaster, DN6 7BD
Tel: 01302-338210 **Fax:** 05601-138409
E-mail: info@litetec.co.uk
Website: http://www.litetec.co.uk
Managers: G. Miles (Chief Mgr)
Immediate Holding Company: COPARTFINDER LIMITED
Registration no: 07045469 **Date established:** 2009
Turnover: £250m - £500m **No.of Employees:** 1 - 10 **Product Groups:** 67

M S I Forks

Carr Hill, Doncaster, DN4 8DH
Tel: 01302-366961 **Fax:** 01302-340663
E-mail: info@msi-forks.com
Website: http://www.msi-mechforge.com
Directors: M. Bell (Ch)
Ultimate Holding Company: MS INTERNATIONAL PLC
Immediate Holding Company: MSI-FORKS LIMITED
Registration no: 01843622 **Date established:** 1984
No.of Employees: 101 - 250 **Product Groups:** 35, 39, 45

Date of Accounts	Apr 11	May 09	May 10
Working Capital	200	N/A	N/A
Current Assets	200	200	200

M S I Quality Forgings Ltd

Carr Hill, Doncaster, DN4 8DH
Tel: 01302-325906 **Fax:** 01302-760511
E-mail: info@msi-forge.com
Website: http://www.msi-forge.com
Bank(s): HSBC Bank plc
Directors: M. Bell (Ch), D. Pyle (Co Sec)
Managers: L. Miree (Works Gen Mgr), J. Atherly (Tech Serv Mgr), R. Forrestall
Ultimate Holding Company: MS INTERNATIONAL PLC
Immediate Holding Company: MSI - QUALITY FORGINGS LIMITED
Registration no: 02197909 **Date established:** 1987 **Turnover:** £2m - £5m
No.of Employees: 21 - 50 **Product Groups:** 34, 46, 48, 66

Date of Accounts	Apr 11
Working Capital	-41
Current Liabilities	41

Mccormick Tractors
Wheatley Hall Road, Doncaster, DN2 4PE
Tel: 01302-733487 **Fax:** 01392-733491
E-mail: victoria.morley@cnh.com
Website: http://www.mccormick-intl.com
Directors: A. Negri (MD)
Managers: G. Milnes (Mgr), I. Shaw (I.T. Exec), S. Ditch (Purch Mgr)
Ultimate Holding Company: ARGO SpA (ITALY)
Registration no: 04126642 **VAT No.:** GB 763 8750 92
Date established: 2000 **Turnover:** £75m - £125m
No.of Employees: 251 - 500 **Product Groups:** 67

Maplin Electronics Ltd
29 Kingsgate, Doncaster, DN1 3JU
Tel: 01302-360950 **Fax:** 01302-326789
Website: http://www.maplin.co.uk
Ultimate Holding Company: MONTAGU PRIVATE EQUITY LLP
Immediate Holding Company: MAPLIN ELECTRONICS LIMITED
Registration no: 01264385 **Date established:** 1976
Turnover: £125m - £250m **No.of Employees:** 1 - 10 **Product Groups:** 37, 61

Date of Accounts	Dec 07	Dec 08	Dec 09
Sales Turnover	180m	204m	204m
Pre Tax Profit/Loss	24m	32m	35m
Working Capital	28m	49m	75m
Fixed Assets	26m	28m	28m
Current Assets	78m	108m	142m
Current Liabilities	44m	51m	59m

Marcrist International Ltd
Marcrist House Sandall Stones Road, Kirk Sandall Industrial Estate, Doncaster, DN3 1QR
Tel: 01302-890888 **Fax:** 01302-883864
E-mail: info@marcrist.com
Website: http://www.marcrist.com
Bank(s): Royal Bank Scotland
Directors: M. Willis (Fin)
Immediate Holding Company: MARCRIST INTERNATIONAL LIMITED
Registration no: 03799367 **VAT No.:** GB 404 8127 74
Date established: 1999 **Turnover:** £5m - £10m **No.of Employees:** 21 - 50
Product Groups: 33, 48, 49, 66

Date of Accounts	Feb 08	Feb 11	Feb 10
Sales Turnover	10m	9m	8m
Pre Tax Profit/Loss	559	-122	-124
Working Capital	390	2m	1m
Fixed Assets	8m	6m	6m
Current Assets	5m	5m	3m
Current Liabilities	745	2m	2m

Maus Mould Services
Milethorn Lane, Doncaster, DN1 2SU
Tel: 01302-327999 **Fax:** 01302-327999
E-mail: info@mausmouldservices.co.uk
Website: http://www.mausmouldservices.co.uk
Managers: A. Marsh (Mgr)
Immediate Holding Company: MAUS MOULD SERVICES LIMITED
Registration no: 04448633 **Date established:** 2002
No.of Employees: 1 - 10 **Product Groups:** 46, 48

Date of Accounts	Jan 12	Jan 11	Jan 10
Working Capital	-9	-22	-36
Fixed Assets	9	9	12
Current Assets	115	109	76

Mechtronic Industries Ltd
Innovation Centre Kirton Lane, Stainforth, Doncaster, DN7 5DA
Tel: 01302-845000 **Fax:** 01302-844440
E-mail: sales@mechtronic.co.uk
Website: http://www.mechtronic.co.uk
Directors: J. Maulson (MD)
Immediate Holding Company: MECHTRONIC INDUSTRIES LIMITED
Registration no: 02554721 **Date established:** 1990 **Turnover:** £1m - £2m
No.of Employees: 1 - 10 **Product Groups:** 37, 46, 47

Date of Accounts	Jun 12	Jun 11	Jun 10
Working Capital	-129	-87	-132
Fixed Assets	249	203	133
Current Assets	50	136	5

Mecmar Driers 2000 Ltd
Council Farm Gunthorpe, Doncaster, DN9 1BQ
Tel: 01427-728186
E-mail: info@mecmar.co.uk
Website: http://www.mecmar.co.uk
Directors: W. Mcarthur (Dir)
Immediate Holding Company: MECMAR DRIERS 2000 LIMITED
Registration no: 03877827 **Date established:** 1999
Turnover: £500,000 - £1m **No.of Employees:** 1 - 10 **Product Groups:** 41, 62

Date of Accounts	Dec 09	Dec 08	Mar 12
Working Capital	86	14	129
Fixed Assets	35	12	124
Current Assets	197	523	1m

Nine Hundred Communications Ltd
White Rose Way, Doncaster, DN4 5JH
Tel: 01302-368866 **Fax:** 01302-340363
E-mail: info@ninehundred.co.uk
Website: http://www.ninehundred.co.uk
Managers: S. Robinson (Sales & Mktg Mg), S. Cuff (Tech Serv Mgr), J. Hall, D. Schofield
Immediate Holding Company: NINE HUNDRED COMMUNICATIONS LIMITED
Registration no: 01741966 **Date established:** 1983
No.of Employees: 51 - 100 **Product Groups:** 37

Date of Accounts	Sep 11	Sep 10	Sep 09
Working Capital	505	686	780
Fixed Assets	1m	904	860
Current Assets	1m	1m	1m

Noel Village Steel Founder Ltd
Balby Carr Bank, Doncaster, DN4 8DE
Tel: 01302-768000 **Fax:** 01302-360665
E-mail: anv@noelvillage.com
Website: http://www.noelvillage.com
Bank(s): Yorkshire Bank PLC
Directors: A. Village (Ch), C. Village (Co Sec)
Immediate Holding Company: NOEL VILLAGE (STEEL FOUNDER) LIMITED
Registration no: 01527500 **Date established:** 1980
Turnover: £10m - £20m **No.of Employees:** 101 - 250
Product Groups: 34, 39

Date of Accounts	Nov 08	Nov 11	Nov 10
Sales Turnover	10m	10m	7m
Pre Tax Profit/Loss	33	71	-191
Working Capital	1m	411	545
Fixed Assets	1m	1m	950
Current Assets	4m	4m	3m
Current Liabilities	708	3m	2m

Norking Aluminium Ltd
Tickhill Road, Doncaster, DN4 8QG
Tel: 01302-855907 **Fax:** 01302-310204
E-mail: sales@norking.com
Website: http://www.norking.com
Bank(s): National Westminster, Doncaster
Directors: S. Whiting (Sales), G. Gibson (MD), J. Driver (Fin)
Managers: K. Vernon (Purch Mgr)
Immediate Holding Company: NORKING ALUMINIUM LIMITED
Registration no: 01089451 **VAT No.:** GB 182 2615 71
Date established: 1973 **Turnover:** £10m - £20m
No.of Employees: 101 - 250 **Product Groups:** 26

Date of Accounts	Mar 11	Mar 10	Mar 09
Sales Turnover	16m	13m	22m
Pre Tax Profit/Loss	231	-536	253
Working Capital	1m	847	1m
Fixed Assets	1m	2m	2m
Current Assets	5m	5m	5m
Current Liabilities	422	N/A	577

Chris Oakley
56 Woodhouse Road, Doncaster, DN2 4DF
Tel: 01302-328879
Website: http://www.cjoakley.co.uk
Directors: C. Oakley (Prop)
Date established: 1991 **No.of Employees:** 1 - 10 **Product Groups:** 46, 48

Oilcheck Laboratory Services Ltd
Denison House Hexthorpe Road, Doncaster, DN4 0BF
Tel: 01302-329609 **Fax:** 0560-153 8047
E-mail: mvolante@oilcheck.co.uk
Website: http://www.oil-check.com
Managers: M. Volante (Mgr)
Immediate Holding Company: OIL CHECK LABORATORY SERVICES LIMITED
Registration no: 06393078 **Date established:** 2007
Turnover: Up to £250,000 **No.of Employees:** 1 - 10 **Product Groups:** 38, 85

Date of Accounts	Dec 11	Dec 10	Dec 09
Working Capital	-19	-15	-20
Fixed Assets	43	75	108
Current Assets	44	48	37

P Clay Fabrications
Whitehouse Farm Haxey Road, Misterton, Doncaster, DN10 4BA
Tel: 01427-890482 **Fax:** 01427-890482
E-mail: whitehousefarm@aol.com
Website: http://www.pclayfabrications.co.uk
Directors: P. Clay (Prop)
Date established: 2000 **No.of Employees:** 1 - 10 **Product Groups:** 26, 35

Page Systems
2 Corn Hill Conisbrough, Doncaster, DN12 2BG
Tel: 01709-863384
E-mail: pagesystems@btinternet.com
Website: http://page-systems.co.uk
Directors: G. Kelsall (Prop)
Immediate Holding Company: PAGE SERVICES YORKSHIRE LIMITED
Registration no: 06478513 **Date established:** 2008
Turnover: Up to £250,000 **No.of Employees:** 1 - 10 **Product Groups:** 40

Date of Accounts	Dec 11	Dec 10	Dec 09
Working Capital	-1	-1	-4
Fixed Assets	6	8	1
Current Assets	11	10	7
Current Liabilities	10	10	8

Palram Europe Ltd
Unit 2 Doncaster Carr Industrial Estate White Rose Way, Doncaster, DN4 5JH
Tel: 01302-344121 **Fax:** 01302-344121
E-mail: steve.shore@palram.com
Website: http://www.palram.com
Directors: S. Store (Sales)
Ultimate Holding Company: Palram Industries (1990) Ltd (Israel)
Immediate Holding Company: Palram Europe Limited
Registration no: 03013725 **Date established:** 1940
Turnover: £250m - £500m **No.of Employees:** 100 **Product Groups:** 30, 31

Date of Accounts	Dec 11	Dec 10	Dec 09
Sales Turnover	3m	2m	2m
Pre Tax Profit/Loss	367	90	79
Working Capital	923	500	519
Fixed Assets	118	200	109
Current Assets	13m	18m	14m
Current Liabilities	455	513	434

Parkinson Plastics Ltd
Bankwood Lane New Rossington, Doncaster, DN11 0PS
Tel: 01302-864959 **Fax:** 01302-864954
E-mail: mail@parkinsonplastics.co.uk
Website: http://www.parkinsonplastics.co.uk
Directors: C. Parkinson (Dir)
Immediate Holding Company: PARKINSON PLASTICS LIMITED
Registration no: 02441149 **Date established:** 1989 **Turnover:** £5m - £10m
No.of Employees: 1 - 10 **Product Groups:** 46, 48

Date of Accounts	Mar 12	Mar 11	Mar 10
Working Capital	-80	-70	-62
Fixed Assets	164	171	175
Current Assets	69	64	73

Phoenix Accident Recovery Services
Stephen Toddunit 12 Bentlymore Lane Wellsyke Industrial Estate, Doncaster, DN6 7DB
Tel: 01302-618377 **Fax:** 01302-728547
E-mail: phoenixrecovery@hotmail.co.uk
Website: http://www.dial-a-recovery.co.uk
Managers: S. Todd (Chief Acct)
Registration no: 07218238 **Date established:** 1997
Turnover: Up to £250,000 **No.of Employees:** 1 - 10 **Product Groups:** 39

Plasmatech (UK) Limited
5 Heather Court Shaw Wood Way, Doncaster, DN2 5YL
Tel: 01302-556051 **Fax:** 01302-556052
E-mail: info@plasmatech.co.uk
Website: http://www.plasmatech.co.uk
Directors: W. Ross (Prop)
Immediate Holding Company: PLASMATECH (UK) LIMITED
Registration no: 03693923 **VAT No.:** GB 737 9470 90
Date established: 1999 **No.of Employees:** 1 - 10 **Product Groups:** 46, 48, 84

Date of Accounts	Dec 11	Dec 10	Dec 09
Working Capital	604	540	541
Fixed Assets	7	5	6
Current Assets	841	768	765

Polydon Industries Ltd
Polydon Park Milethorn Lane, Doncaster, DN1 2SU
Tel: 01302-327172 **Fax:** 01302-341483
E-mail: sales@polydon.co.uk
Website: http://www.polydon.co.uk
Directors: H. Howard (Dir)
Managers: C. Howard (Comm), R. Price (Works Gen Mgr), M. Smith (Chief Acct), C. Bain (Sales Prom Mgr), J. Howard (Tech Serv Mgr)
Immediate Holding Company: POLYDON INDUSTRIES LIMITED
Registration no: 01944818 **Date established:** 1985
No.of Employees: 21 - 50 **Product Groups:** 07, 35, 44, 45, 46, 47, 48, 67, 84

Date of Accounts	Oct 11	Oct 10	Oct 09
Working Capital	410	425	814
Fixed Assets	451	437	481
Current Assets	657	586	997

Polypipe Building Products
Broomhouse Lane Edlington, Doncaster, DN12 1ES
Tel: 01302-792244 **Fax:** 01709-770001
E-mail: john.fairhurst@polypipe.com
Website: http://www.polypipe.co.uk
Directors: R. Balcam (Fin), B. Watson (Dir), A. Smith (Fin), J. Fairhurst (MD)
Managers: J. Becker (Personnel)
Ultimate Holding Company: IMI PLC
Immediate Holding Company: POLYPIPE BUILDING PRODUCTS LIMITED
Registration no: 02729243 **Date established:** 1992
Turnover: £125m - £250m **No.of Employees:** 251 - 500
Product Groups: 25, 30, 36

Date of Accounts	Dec 10	Dec 09	Dec 08
Sales Turnover	201m	187m	180m
Pre Tax Profit/Loss	-7m	-5m	-31m
Working Capital	9m	41m	18m
Fixed Assets	113m	121m	146m
Current Assets	41m	73m	65m
Current Liabilities	14m	8m	31m

Polypipe Ventilation Ltd
Sandall Stones Road Kirk Sandall Industrial Estate, Doncaster, DN3 1QR
Tel: 01799-541175 **Fax:** 01799-541143
E-mail: sales@polypipe.com
Website: http://www.polypipe.com/ventilation
Directors: P. Shepherd (Fin)
Ultimate Holding Company: Pipe Holdings 2 Ltd
Immediate Holding Company: POLYPIPE VENTILATION LIMITED
Registration no: 01977055 **Date established:** 1986
Turnover: Up to £250,000 **No.of Employees:** 21 - 50 **Product Groups:** 40, 66

Powell Engineering UK Ltd
Belton Road Sandtoft, Doncaster, DN8 5SX
Tel: 01724-712904
Directors: B. Powell (Dir), D. Powell (MD)
Managers: H. Barrass (Sales Admin)
Immediate Holding Company: POWELL ENGINEERING UK LIMITED
Registration no: 03854782 **Date established:** 1999 **Turnover:** £2m - £5m
No.of Employees: 51 - 100 **Product Groups:** 37, 48, 52

Date of Accounts	Oct 11	Oct 10	Oct 09
Sales Turnover	N/A	N/A	5m
Pre Tax Profit/Loss	N/A	N/A	491
Working Capital	2m	2m	1m
Fixed Assets	273	317	270
Current Assets	3m	3m	3m
Current Liabilities	N/A	N/A	2m

Premier Storage & Office Solutions Ltd
Unit 4 Delta Court Sky Business Park, Auckley, Doncaster, DN9 3GN
Tel: 01302-300200 **Fax:** 01302-601436
E-mail: hello@premier-storage.co.uk
Website: http://www.premier-storage.co.uk
Managers: S. Jepson (Mgr)
Immediate Holding Company: PREMIER STORAGE & OFFICE SOLUTIONS LIMITED
Registration no: 06338841 **Date established:** 2007
Turnover: £500,000 - £1m **No.of Employees:** 1 - 10 **Product Groups:** 26, 35, 45, 85

Date of Accounts	Aug 11	Aug 10	Aug 09
Working Capital	-2	-20	22
Fixed Assets	43	27	6
Current Assets	139	46	94

Proweld Welding Supplies Ltd
James Road Adwick-le-Street, Doncaster, DN6 7HH
Tel: 01302-728999 **Fax:** 01302-729100
Directors: C. Walton (Fin), R. Walton (MD)
Immediate Holding Company: PROWELD WELDING SUPPLIES LIMITED
Registration no: 03964062 **Date established:** 2000
No.of Employees: 11 - 20 **Product Groups:** 46

Date of Accounts	May 12	May 11	May 10
Working Capital	4	-20	-6
Fixed Assets	38	45	31
Current Assets	265	250	247

Purple Penguin Media
1a The Hutton Business Centre Bentley Road, Doncaster, DN5 9QP
Tel: 01302-247010 **Fax:** 01302-822237
E-mail: chris@purplepenguinmedia.co.uk
Website: http://www.purplepenguinmedia.co.uk
Directors: C. Potter (Tech Serv)
Immediate Holding Company: PURPLE PENGUIN MEDIA LIMITED
Registration no: 06675646 **Date established:** 2008
Turnover: Up to £250,000 **No.of Employees:** 1 - 10 **Product Groups:** 44, 61

Date of Accounts	Jul 11	Jul 10	Jul 09
Working Capital	N/A	-8	-6
Fixed Assets	5	9	13
Current Assets	35	13	19

R Bance & Co. Ltd Powamate Division

3i Sandall Stones Road Kirk Sandall Industrial Estate, Doncaster, DN3 1QR
Tel: 01302-887821 **Fax:** 01302-887823
E-mail: admin@bance.com
Website: http://www.powamate.co.uk
Managers: P. Oakley
Registration no: 01052713 **Turnover:** Up to £250,000
No.of Employees: 11 - 20 **Product Groups:** 30, 37, 38, 39, 45, 48, 67, 85

Date of Accounts	Dec 07	Dec 06	Dec 05
Working Capital	248	551	438
Fixed Assets	209	121	39
Current Assets	1148	945	656
Current Liabilities	900	394	218
Total Share Capital	94	94	94

R M H Security

Unit 19 Riverdale Business Park Wheatley Hall Road, Doncaster, DN2 4PF
Tel: 01302-322116 **Fax:** 01302-322116
E-mail: rmhs50@hotmail.com
Directors: R. Hart (Prop)
Immediate Holding Company: DENTON & NICKELS LIMITED
Date established: 2006 **No.of Employees:** 1 - 10 **Product Groups:** 35

R O Arnold Ltd

Station Road Barnby Dun, Doncaster, DN3 1HQ
Tel: 01302-349231 **Fax:** 01302-881101
E-mail: info@roarnold.co.uk
Website: http://www.roarnold.co.uk
Directors: C. Gaylor (Co Sec), D. Gaylor (MD), G. Baker (Fin), L. Walters (Chief Op Offcr)
Ultimate Holding Company: NUTLEY-GORING HOLDINGS LIMITED
Immediate Holding Company: R.O.ARNOLD,LIMITED
Registration no: 00191363 **VAT No.:** 419 3763 34 **Date established:** 2023
Turnover: £5m - £10m **No.of Employees:** 51 - 100 **Product Groups:** 30, 33, 35

Date of Accounts	Dec 11	Dec 10	Dec 09
Sales Turnover	9m	8m	8m
Pre Tax Profit/Loss	271	305	272
Working Capital	892	822	793
Fixed Assets	2m	2m	2m
Current Assets	4m	4m	4m
Current Liabilities	2m	2m	2m

R S Displays Ltd

3-5 Fourth Avenue Doncaster Finningley Business Park Finningley Airport, Doncaster, DN9 3GE
Tel: 01302-802080 **Fax:** 01302-802081
E-mail: enquiries@rsdisplays.co.uk
Website: http://www.rsdisplays.co.uk
Directors: J. Hancox (Fin)
Immediate Holding Company: R.S. DISPLAYS & EXHIBITIONS LTD.
Registration no: 03204136 **Date established:** 1996
Turnover: Over £1,000m **No.of Employees:** 11 - 20 **Product Groups:** 81

Date of Accounts	May 11	May 10	May 09
Working Capital	227	224	326
Fixed Assets	48	63	67
Current Assets	614	432	540

Rendit Ltd

One Acre Thorpe In Balne, Doncaster, DN6 0DZ
Tel: 01302-884385 **Fax:** 01302-885498
E-mail: support@rendit.co.uk
Website: http://www.rendit.co.uk
Directors: M. Kitching (MD)
Immediate Holding Company: RENDIT LIMITED
Registration no: 02960488 **VAT No.:** GB 642 7778 06
Date established: 1994 **Turnover:** £5m - £10m **No.of Employees:** 1 - 10
Product Groups: 33

Date of Accounts	Aug 11	Aug 10	Aug 09
Working Capital	58	72	60
Fixed Assets	42	39	26
Current Assets	130	136	143

Resin Bonded Surfacing

51 Ansten Crescent, Doncaster, DN4 6EZ
Tel: 01302-533562 **Fax:** 01302-533562
E-mail: resinsurfacing@aol.com
Website: http://www.resinbondedsurfacing.co.uk
Directors: D. Tweedy (Prop)
Date established: 2003 **Turnover:** £500,000 - £1m
No.of Employees: 1 - 10 **Product Groups:** 29, 30, 33, 35, 49, 52

Resin Building Products Ltd

Resbuild House Unit 2, Durham Lane, Doncaster, DN3 3FE
Tel: 01302-300822 **Fax:** 01302-300833
E-mail: carl@resbuild.co.uk
Website: http://www.resbuild.co.uk
Directors: C. Taylor (Sales), R. Ayrton (Tech Serv)
Managers: R. Ayrton (Purch Mgr), C. Taylor (Sales Prom)
Registration no: 03047467 **VAT No.:** GB 656 3145 34
Date established: 1995 **Turnover:** £1m - £2m **No.of Employees:** 1 - 10
Product Groups: 29, 30, 31, 32, 33, 48, 49, 52

Date of Accounts	Dec 11	Dec 10	Dec 09
Working Capital	159	140	124
Fixed Assets	231	237	256
Current Assets	435	404	389

Rota Services Ltd

Churchill Road, Doncaster, DN1 2TF
Tel: 01302-328253 **Fax:** 01302-321405
E-mail: charles@gpservicesuk.co.uk
Website: http://www.weldingsuppliesdoncaster.co.uk
Directors: M. Thompson (Fin), C. Thompson (MD)
Immediate Holding Company: ROTA SERVICES LIMITED
Registration no: 04082790 **Date established:** 2000
No.of Employees: 1 - 10 **Product Groups:** 46

Date of Accounts	Nov 11	Nov 10	Nov 09
Working Capital	133	142	142
Fixed Assets	44	44	50
Current Assets	173	193	189

S3i - Stainless Steel Solutions

The Old Cafe Hudsons Yard, Doncaster Road, Bawtry, Doncaster, DN10 6NX
Tel: 01302-714513 **Fax:** 01302-714532
E-mail: info@s3i.co.uk
Website: http://www.stainlesssteelbalustrade.com
Directors: J. Arrowsmith (MD), N. Arrowsmith (Dir)
Registration no: 04876280 **VAT No.:** GB 746 1483 23
Date established: 2000 **Turnover:** £20m - £50m **No.of Employees:** 1 - 10
Product Groups: 23, 26, 33, 34, 35, 36, 37, 39, 40, 41, 46, 48, 49, 66

Date of Accounts	Dec 11	Dec 10	Dec 09
Working Capital	79	33	15
Fixed Assets	39	49	49
Current Assets	325	157	145

Sandtoft Holdings Ltd

Sandtoft, Doncaster, DN8 5SY
Tel: 01427-872696 **Fax:** 01427-871222
E-mail: info@sandtoft.co.uk
Website: http://www.sandtoft.co.uk
Bank(s): National Westminster
Directors: N. Oldridge (Mkt Research), S. Oldridge (Ch)
Managers: I. Barlthrop (I.T. Exec), M. Pears (Purch Mgr)
Immediate Holding Company: Sandtoft Holdings Ltd
Registration no: 01094518 **VAT No.:** GB 555 4285 27
Date established: 1904 **Turnover:** £20m - £50m
No.of Employees: 251 - 500 **Product Groups:** 33, 66

Date of Accounts	Dec 07
Sales Turnover	40020
Pre Tax Profit/Loss	2130
Working Capital	1400
Fixed Assets	26830
Current Assets	14240
Current Liabilities	12840
Total Share Capital	10
ROCE% (Return on Capital Employed)	7.5

Scotts Co (U K) Ltd

British Moss Peat Works The Levels, Thorne, Doncaster, DN8 5TE
Tel: 01405-813231
Website: http://www.lovethegarden.com
No.of Employees: 21 - 50 **Product Groups:** 02, 32

Senior Architectural Systems

Eland Road Denaby Main, Doncaster, DN12 4HA
Tel: 01709-772600 **Fax:** 01709-772601
E-mail: enquiries@seniorarchitectural.co.uk
Website: http://www.seniorarchitectural.co.uk
Directors: M. Wadsworth (Dir), J. Hopkins (Co Sec)
Ultimate Holding Company: CLYTHA HOLDINGS LIMITED
Immediate Holding Company: SENIOR ARCHITECTURAL SYSTEMS LIMITED
Registration no: 03909137 **Date established:** 2000
Turnover: £20m - £50m **No.of Employees:** 101 - 250 **Product Groups:** 35

Date of Accounts	Jun 11	Jun 10	Jun 09
Sales Turnover	21m	19m	20m
Pre Tax Profit/Loss	627	-226	-88
Working Capital	-508	-1m	-2m
Fixed Assets	2m	2m	3m
Current Assets	12m	10m	8m
Current Liabilities	5m	6m	5m

Sercal Electronics Ltd

33 Arksey Lane Bentley, Doncaster, DN5 0RX
Tel: 01302-739998 **Fax:** 01302-739739
E-mail: sales@sercalelectronics.co.uk
Website: http://www.sercal-testequipmentsales.co.uk
Directors: J. Cawkwell (Dir)
Immediate Holding Company: SERCAL ELECTRONICS LIMITED
Registration no: 04827376 **VAT No.:** GB 829 4194 03
Date established: 2003 **No.of Employees:** 1 - 10 **Product Groups:** 37, 38, 39, 48, 67, 85

Date of Accounts	Feb 08	Feb 11	Feb 10
Working Capital	9	-1	4
Fixed Assets	17	13	14
Current Assets	68	63	53

Smith Bros Caer Conan Wholesale Ltd

Greyfriars House Sidings Court Whiterose Way, Doncaster, DN4 5NU
Tel: 01302-366922 **Fax:** 01302-329025
E-mail: info@smithbrosuk.com
Website: http://www.smithbros.uk.com
Directors: M. Jervis (Dir)
Immediate Holding Company: SMITH BROS.(CAERCONAN)WHOLESALE LIMITED
Registration no: 00267023 **VAT No.:** GB 181 3212 94
Date established: 1932 **Turnover:** £20m - £50m
No.of Employees: 51 - 100 **Product Groups:** 77

Date of Accounts	Dec 11	Dec 10	Dec 09
Sales Turnover	31m	29m	20m
Pre Tax Profit/Loss	657	674	1m
Working Capital	11m	10m	12m
Fixed Assets	602	709	2m
Current Assets	13m	12m	15m
Current Liabilities	675	565	155

South Yorkshire Newspapers Ltd

10 Sunny Bar, Doncaster, DN1 1NB
Tel: 01302-819111 **Fax:** 01302-814396
E-mail: editorial@dearnetoday.co.uk
Website: http://www.doncasterfreepress.co.uk
Bank(s): Barclays
Directors: D. Astinall (Fin)
Managers: S. Brandom, G. Huston, M. Incson (I.T. Exec), S. Jarvis (Tech Serv Mgr), E. Hanson
Ultimate Holding Company: JOHNSTON PRESS PLC
Immediate Holding Company: SOUTH YORKSHIRE NEWSPAPERS LIMITED
Registration no: 03103977 **VAT No.:** GB 551 0827 61
Date established: 1995 **Turnover:** £2m - £5m **No.of Employees:** 21 - 50
Product Groups: 28

Date of Accounts	Dec 11	Dec 08	Jan 10
Sales Turnover	2m	4m	4m
Pre Tax Profit/Loss	-1m	-886	-773
Fixed Assets	6m	8m	7m

Stanwood Engineering Ltd

21 Church Street Bawtry, Doncaster, DN10 6HR
Tel: 01302-710661 **Fax:** 01302-711663
E-mail: sales@stanwoodengineering.com
Directors: C. Weston Taylor (Co Sec), J. Weston Taylor (Dir), P. Berry (MD)
Immediate Holding Company: STANWOOD ENGINEERING LIMITED
Registration no: 01209481 **Date established:** 1975
No.of Employees: 11 - 20 **Product Groups:** 35, 36, 39

Date of Accounts	Mar 08	Mar 07	Mar 06
Working Capital	83	77	78
Fixed Assets	41	46	67
Current Assets	269	283	283
Current Liabilities	185	206	205
Total Share Capital	24	24	24

Stay Sharp Engineering

Unit 6 Sandall Stones Road, Kirk Sandall Industrial Estate, Doncaster, DN3 1QR
Tel: 01302-890610 **Fax:** 01302-890610
Directors: C. Harrod (Prop)
Date established: 1989 **No.of Employees:** 1 - 10 **Product Groups:** 36

Steel Supplies Ltd

Arksey Lane Bentley, Doncaster, DN5 0ST
Tel: 01302-874321 **Fax:** 01302-876287
E-mail: steel@steelsupplies.co.uk
Website: http://www.steelsupplies.co.uk
Bank(s): National Westminster
Directors: S. Todd (Dir), H. Todd (Dir)
Immediate Holding Company: STEEL SUPPLIES LIMITED
Registration no: 03773451 **Date established:** 1999 **Turnover:** £5m - £10m
No.of Employees: 21 - 50 **Product Groups:** 34, 35

Date of Accounts	Oct 11	Oct 10	Oct 09
Sales Turnover	N/A	N/A	5m
Pre Tax Profit/Loss	N/A	N/A	-112
Working Capital	-242	-187	-106
Fixed Assets	801	782	808
Current Assets	2m	2m	2m
Current Liabilities	N/A	N/A	978

Stokplas Ltd

Sandall Park Barnby Dun Road, Long Sandall, Doncaster, DN2 4QL
Tel: 01302-342121 **Fax:** 01302-556950
E-mail: stokplas@crossling.co.uk
Website: http://www.stokplas.co.uk
Directors: B. Pinder (MD)
Managers: D. Snell, P. Norton (Chief Mgr)
Ultimate Holding Company: T. Crossling & Co. Ltd
Immediate Holding Company: Crossling Ltd
Registration no: 04943851 **VAT No.:** GB 183 4426 58
Date established: 1980 **Turnover:** £1m - £2m **No.of Employees:** 1 - 10
Product Groups: 30

T P Trailer Parts

Askern Road Garage Askern Road, Bentley, Doncaster, DN5 0EP
Tel: 01302-872333 **Fax:** 01302-872333
E-mail: k.postle@btconnect.com
Website: http://www.tptrailerparts.co.uk
Directors: K. Postle (Prop)
Immediate Holding Company: JOHN MASSARELLA LIMITED
Registration no: 00951046 **Date established:** 1969
No.of Employees: 1 - 10 **Product Groups:** 36, 37, 39

Date of Accounts	Mar 12	Mar 11	Mar 10
Working Capital	106	98	96
Fixed Assets	433	436	438
Current Assets	120	112	109

Tanks & Vessels Industries

Bankwood Lane Industrial Estate Bankwood Lane, New Rossington, Doncaster, DN11 0PS
Tel: 01302-867328 **Fax:** 01302-864990
E-mail: sales@tanksandvessels.com
Website: http://www.tanksandvessels.com
Managers: A. Henstock (Sales Prom Mgr)
Immediate Holding Company: TANKS AND VESSELS INDUSTRIES LIMITED
Registration no: 01307388 **VAT No.:** GB 295 2972 14
Date established: 1977 **No.of Employees:** 11 - 20 **Product Groups:** 35, 41

Date of Accounts	Apr 11	Apr 10	Apr 09
Working Capital	1m	1m	1m
Fixed Assets	7m	8m	8m
Current Assets	5m	4m	4m

Thermofuse Pipelines Ltd

Unit 4 Brunel Park Industrial Estate, Harworth, Doncaster, DN11 8RW
Tel: 01302-759400 **Fax:** 01302-759400
E-mail: info@tpl.uk.com
Website: http://www.tpl.uk.com
Bank(s): Lloyds T.S.B
Directors: K. Hurst (MD)
Immediate Holding Company: THERMOFUSE PIPELINES LIMITED
Registration no: 03325359 **Date established:** 1997 **Turnover:** £1m - £2m
No.of Employees: 11 - 20 **Product Groups:** 18, 30, 36, 37, 38, 39, 40, 41, 42, 45, 48, 51, 52, 54, 66, 84

Date of Accounts	Mar 11	Mar 10	Mar 09
Working Capital	200	225	145
Fixed Assets	670	658	643
Current Assets	429	390	254
Current Liabilities	33	N/A	N/A

Thorite Ltd

Whittingtons Court Wheatley Hall Road, Doncaster, DN2 4PE
Tel: 01302-325491 **Fax:** 01302-341007
E-mail: doncaster@thorite.co.uk
Website: http://www.thorite.co.uk
Managers: D. Lindsay
Ultimate Holding Company: THOMAS WRIGHT/THORITE GROUP LIMITED
Immediate Holding Company: THORITE LIMITED
Registration no: 00648628 **VAT No.:** GB 169 0303 72
Date established: 1960 **Turnover:** £75m - £125m
No.of Employees: 1 - 10 **Product Groups:** 35, 36, 38, 40

Date of Accounts	Mar 12	Mar 11	Mar 10
Working Capital	70	70	70
Current Assets	70	70	70

Tickhill Engineering Co. Ltd

Cow House Lane Armthorpe, Doncaster, DN3 3ED
Tel: 01302-831911 **Fax:** 01302-300173
E-mail: sales@haith.co.uk
Website: http://www.haith.co.uk
Bank(s): Barclays

see next page

Tickhill Engineering Co. Ltd - *Cont'd*
Directors: N. Haith (Dir), G. Haith (MD)
Managers: R. Marriot, N. Haith, J. Brindley (Sales Admin)
Immediate Holding Company: TICKHILL ENGINEERING COMPANY LIMITED
Registration no: 00809228 **VAT No.:** GB 181 7026 71
Date established: 1964 **Turnover:** £5m - £10m
No.of Employees: 51 - 100 **Product Groups:** 41, 67

Date of Accounts	Dec 11	Dec 10	Dec 09
Sales Turnover	12m	10m	8m
Pre Tax Profit/Loss	2m	545	210
Working Capital	3m	1m	1m
Fixed Assets	2m	2m	2m
Current Assets	6m	5m	4m
Current Liabilities	882	712	906

Trimesh Guarding Ltd
Unit 3p Lake Enterprise Park Sandall Stones Road, Kirk Sandall Industrial Estate, Doncaster, DN3 1QR
Tel: 01302-888808 **Fax:** 01302-888606
E-mail: admin@trimesh-guarding.com
Website: http://www.trimesh-guarding.com
Directors: S. Stockdale (Fin)
Immediate Holding Company: TRIMESH GUARDING LIMITED
Registration no: 02872993 **Date established:** 1993
No.of Employees: 1 - 10 **Product Groups:** 26, 35

Date of Accounts	Dec 11	Dec 10	Dec 09
Working Capital	8	1	26
Fixed Assets	7	8	6
Current Assets	33	19	66

Truepart Ltd
Decoy Bank, Doncaster, DN4 5JD
Tel: 01302-342211 **Fax:** 01302-327191
E-mail: ib@trupart.co.uk
Website: http://www.truepart.co.uk
Bank(s): Barclays
Directors: I. Biddle (MD), D. Learoyd (Sales)
Managers: G. Williams (Purch Mgr), K. Bramhall (Personnel)
Ultimate Holding Company: INHOCO 2082 LIMITED
Immediate Holding Company: TRUPART LIMITED
Registration no: 01966822 **VAT No.:** GB 228 0054 93
Date established: 1985 **Turnover:** £5m - £10m **No.of Employees:** 21 - 50
Product Groups: 68

Date of Accounts	Dec 11	Dec 10	Dec 09
Sales Turnover	9m	9m	9m
Pre Tax Profit/Loss	569	599	813
Working Capital	1m	2m	2m
Fixed Assets	1m	1m	100
Current Assets	3m	4m	4m
Current Liabilities	773	774	816

Twelco Fabrications Ltd
Old Airfield Belton Road, Sandtoft, Doncaster, DN8 5SX
Tel: 01724-710844 **Fax:** 01724-710188
E-mail: enquiries@twelcofabrications.com
Website: http://www.twelcofabrications.com
Directors: J. Twell (Dir)
Managers: A. Clarke (Purch Mgr), K. Twell (Personnel)
Immediate Holding Company: TWELCO FABRICATIONS LIMITED
Registration no: 02846746 **VAT No.:** GB 591 0825 35
Date established: 1993 **Turnover:** £2m - £5m **No.of Employees:** 21 - 50
Product Groups: 48

Date of Accounts	Sep 11	Sep 10	Sep 09
Working Capital	202	135	161
Fixed Assets	41	22	27
Current Assets	1m	546	498
Current Liabilities	N/A	N/A	149

UK Grants Ltd Patrick H Heywood Consultancy
39 Airedale Avenue Tickhill, Doncaster, DN11 9UH
Tel: 08701-121871 **Fax:** 0870-112 1872
E-mail: hey@uk-grants.co.uk
Website: http://www.uk-grants.co.uk
Directors: I. Heywood (Dir), P. Heywood (MD)
Immediate Holding Company: UK GRANTS LIMITED
Registration no: 04340714 **VAT No.:** GB 590 8860 01
Date established: 2001 **Turnover:** Up to £250,000
No.of Employees: 1 - 10 **Product Groups:** 80, 81

Date of Accounts	Mar 11	Mar 10	Mar 09
Working Capital	-1	-1	-1
Fixed Assets	1	1	1
Current Assets	32	35	25

UK Coal Mining
Harworth Park Blyth Road, Harworth, Doncaster, DN11 8DB
Tel: 01302-751751 **Fax:** 01302-752420
E-mail: enquire@ukcoal.com
Website: http://www.ukcoal.com
Directors: C. Reed (Pers), D. Brockson (Fin), J. Cox (Ch), S. Byway (Comm)
Managers: D. Woods
Ultimate Holding Company: UK COAL PLC
Immediate Holding Company: UK COAL MINING LTD
Registration no: 02997374 **VAT No.:** GB 580 9685 92
Date established: 1994 **Turnover:** £250m - £500m
No.of Employees: 101 - 250 **Product Groups:** 67

Date of Accounts	Dec 11	Dec 08	Dec 09
Sales Turnover	482m	371m	308m
Pre Tax Profit/Loss	61m	-7m	-105m
Working Capital	142m	152m	38m
Fixed Assets	258m	372m	399m
Current Assets	306m	275m	165m
Current Liabilities	57m	81m	67m

Urban Hygiene Ltd
Unit 9 Delta Court Sky Business Park, Auckley, Doncaster, DN9 3GN
Tel: 01302-623193 **Fax:** 01302-623167
E-mail: enquiries@urbanhygiene.com
Website: http://www.urbanhygiene.com
Directors: M. Johnson (Dir)
Immediate Holding Company: URBAN HYGIENE LIMITED
Registration no: 04953332 **Date established:** 2003
Turnover: £250,000 - £500,000 **No.of Employees:** 1 - 10
Product Groups: 32

Date of Accounts	Mar 12	Mar 11	Mar 10
Working Capital	-19	-17	-19
Fixed Assets	24	31	40
Current Assets	65	42	58

Visions in Plastics
Unit 3 Delta Court Sky Business Park, Auckley, Doncaster, DN9 3GN
Tel: 01302-775920 **Fax:** 01302-773482
E-mail: sales@visionsinplastics.co.uk
Website: http://www.visionsinplastics.co.uk
Directors: C. Lees (Dir)
Registration no: 01917928 **Turnover:** Up to £250,000
No.of Employees: 1 - 10 **Product Groups:** 23, 26, 27, 28, 30, 31, 32, 33, 37, 38, 39, 40, 49, 63, 66, 67, 68

Webasto Products UK Ltd
Webasto House White Rose Way, Doncaster, DN4 5JH
Tel: 01302-322232 **Fax:** 01302-322231
E-mail: p.hankin@webastouk.com
Website: http://www.webasto.co.uk
Directors: E. Cooper (Co Sec), E. Errington (Co Sec), P. Hankin (MD)
Managers: R. Stoakes (Purch Mgr), S. Powell (Sales & Mktg Mg)
Ultimate Holding Company: WEBASTO AG FAHRZEUGTECHNIK (GERMANY)
Immediate Holding Company: WEBASTO THERMO & COMFORT UK LTD
Registration no: 02191825 **Date established:** 1987 **Turnover:** £5m - £10m
No.of Employees: 21 - 50 **Product Groups:** 39

Date of Accounts	Dec 11	Dec 10	Dec 09
Sales Turnover	6m	7m	7m
Pre Tax Profit/Loss	103	503	363
Working Capital	1m	1m	2m
Fixed Assets	646	468	486
Current Assets	2m	2m	3m
Current Liabilities	358	463	392

B P Wren
104 High Street Epworth, Doncaster, DN9 1JS
Tel: 01427-873122
Directors: B. Wren (Prop)
Date established: 1994 **No.of Employees:** 1 - 10 **Product Groups:** 41

Yorkshire Metalcraft
Unit 8 Gunhills Lane Armthorpe, Doncaster, DN3 3EB
Tel: 01302-835296
E-mail: info@yorkshiremetalcrafts.co.uk
Website: http://www.yorkshiremetalcrafts.co.uk
Directors: W. Adams (Prop)
Date established: 1983 **No.of Employees:** 1 - 10 **Product Groups:** 26, 35

Yorkshire Precision Gauges Ltd
Cuckoo Lane Hatfield, Doncaster, DN7 6QF
Tel: 01302-840303 **Fax:** 01302-843570
E-mail: gauges@ypg.co.uk
Website: http://www.ypg.co.uk
Directors: P. Edwards (Ch)
Immediate Holding Company: YORKSHIRE PRECISION GAUGES LIMITED
Registration no: 00498827 **VAT No.:** GB 181 3774 52
Date established: 1951 **Turnover:** £5m - £10m **No.of Employees:** 1 - 10
Product Groups: 38, 46, 85

Date of Accounts	Dec 11	Dec 10	Dec 09
Working Capital	675	635	617
Fixed Assets	97	66	78
Current Assets	1m	1m	1m

Mexborough

Bolt & Nut Manufacturing
White Lee Road Swinton, Mexborough, S64 8BH
Tel: 01709-570212 **Fax:** 01709-584125
E-mail: sales@tachart.com
Website: http://www.tachart.com
Bank(s): Barclays, Fitzalan Sq, Sheffield
Directors: D. Lancashire (MD), E. Lancashire (Ch), M. Flute (Co Sec)
Managers: K. West (Sales & Mktg Mg), P. Hinder (Develop Mgr), R. Bullivant (Mats Contrlr)
Immediate Holding Company: BNM (BOLT & NUT MANUFACTURING) LIMITED
Registration no: 06679940 **VAT No.:** GB 308 4287 56
Date established: 2008 **Turnover:** £1m - £2m **No.of Employees:** 21 - 50
Product Groups: 30, 35, 36, 37, 66

Constant Security Services
Constant House Cliff Street, Mexborough, S64 9HU
Tel: 08453-304400 **Fax:** 01709-586183
E-mail: contact@constant-services.com
Website: http://www.constant-services.com
Directors: C. Lee (Co Sec), A. Lee (Grp Chief Exec)
Managers: M. Booth (Personnel), A. Lee (Mktg Serv Mgr)
Immediate Holding Company: CONSTANT SECURITY SERVICES LIMITED
Registration no: 01933481 **Date established:** 1985 **Turnover:** £5m - £10m
No.of Employees: 251 - 500 **Product Groups:** 37, 80, 81

Date of Accounts	Jul 11	Jul 10	Jul 09
Sales Turnover	10m	9m	9m
Pre Tax Profit/Loss	173	117	197
Working Capital	846	810	740
Fixed Assets	323	220	284
Current Assets	2m	2m	2m
Current Liabilities	1m	1m	1m

D Y N Ltd
Swinton Meadows Industrial Estate Meadow Way, Swinton, Mexborough, S64 8AB
Tel: 01709-578222 **Fax:** 01709-579764
E-mail: info@dyneleven.co.uk
Website: http://www.dyneleven.co.uk
Directors: I. Edley (Dir)
Immediate Holding Company: DYNELEVEN LIMITED
Registration no: 03569469 **Date established:** 1998
No.of Employees: 11 - 20 **Product Groups:** 38, 40, 47

Date of Accounts	Jun 11	Jun 10	Jun 09
Working Capital	-36	-75	-53
Fixed Assets	23	14	20
Current Assets	287	211	149

Fireguard Ltd
Swinton Bridge Workshops Rowms Lane, Swinton, Mexborough, S64 8AE
Tel: 01709-571421 **Fax:** 01709-579991
E-mail: sales@fireguardlimited.co.uk
Website: http://www.fireguardltd.com
Directors: J. Wall (Sales), M. Wall (Dir)
Immediate Holding Company: FIREGUARD LIMITED
Registration no: 06081193 **Date established:** 2007
No.of Employees: 1 - 10 **Product Groups:** 84, 86, 87

Date of Accounts	Feb 12	Feb 11	Feb 10
Working Capital	3	-20	-23
Fixed Assets	6	6	5
Current Assets	65	34	44

Hattersleys Solicitors
1 Hope Street, Mexborough, S64 9HR
Tel: 01709-582434 **Fax:** 01709-584129
E-mail: tcseal@hattersleys.co.uk
Website: http://www.hattersleys.co.uk
Directors: T. Seal (Snr Part)
Date established: 1895 **Turnover:** £1m - £2m **No.of Employees:** 1 - 10
Product Groups: 80

High Design Gates & Railings
William Street Swinton, Mexborough, S64 8BP
Tel: 07790-206702 **Fax:** 01709-570800
E-mail: terry.reed1957@btinternet.com
Website: http://www.highdesigngatesandrailings.co.uk
Directors: T. Reed (Prop)
Immediate Holding Company: MICRON ENTERPRISES LIMITED
Registration no: 03242132 **Date established:** 1997
No.of Employees: 1 - 10 **Product Groups:** 26, 35

Lyndhurst Cooling & Heating Services Ltd
Unit 3e Swinton Meadows Industrial Estate Meadow Way, Swinton, Mexborough, S64 8AB
Tel: 01709-590526 **Fax:** 01709-512729
E-mail: info@lyndhurstservices.co.uk
Website: http://www.lyndhurstservices.co.uk
Directors: G. Oliver (MD)
Immediate Holding Company: LYNDHURST COOLING & HEATING SERVICES LIMITED
Registration no: 05530913 **Date established:** 2005
No.of Employees: 11 - 20 **Product Groups:** 38, 52

Date of Accounts	Aug 11	Aug 10	Aug 09
Working Capital	213	131	94
Fixed Assets	64	47	13
Current Assets	446	321	227

Morphy Richards Ltd
Talbot Road Swinton, Mexborough, S64 8AJ
Tel: 01709-582402 **Fax:** 01709-587510
E-mail: info@glendimplex.com
Website: http://www.morphyrichards.co.uk
Directors: S. O'Driscoll (Dir)
Ultimate Holding Company: GLEN DIMPLEX (ROI)
Immediate Holding Company: MORPHY RICHARDS APPLIANCES LIMITED
Registration no: 01610139 **Date established:** 1982
Turnover: £50m - £75m **No.of Employees:** 1 - 10 **Product Groups:** 40, 77

Date of Accounts	Mar 11	Mar 10	Mar 09
Working Capital	3m	3m	3m
Fixed Assets	2m	2m	2m
Current Assets	3m	3m	3m

Pladrest Ltd
Cliff Street, Mexborough, S64 9HU
Tel: 01709-584296 **Fax:** 01709-581493
E-mail: sales@pladrest.co.uk
Website: http://www.pladrest.co.uk
Bank(s): Yorkshire
Directors: M. Davis (Fin), A. Dye (MD)
Immediate Holding Company: PLADREST LIMITED
Registration no: 06984138 **VAT No.:** GB 978 7160 65
Date established: 2009 **Turnover:** £1m - £2m **No.of Employees:** 11 - 20
Product Groups: 40, 46, 48

Date of Accounts	Jul 11	Jul 10
Working Capital	-26	-30
Fixed Assets	42	39
Current Assets	65	59

Redirack Ltd
Wharf Road Kilnhurst, Mexborough, S64 5SU
Tel: 01709-584711 **Fax:** 01709-589821
E-mail: rob.dargue@redirack.co.uk
Website: http://www.redirack.co.uk
Bank(s): National Westminster
Directors: R. Dargue (Fin), A. Forsythe (MD), R. Phelan (Sales)
Managers: D. Howard (Tech Serv Mgr), K. McVicar (Personnel)
Immediate Holding Company: REDIRACK LIMITED
Registration no: 04930523 **VAT No.:** 660 5822 37 **Date established:** 2003
Turnover: £10m - £20m **No.of Employees:** 51 - 100 **Product Groups:** 26, 35

Date of Accounts	Dec 11	Dec 10	Dec 09
Sales Turnover	11m	8m	7m
Pre Tax Profit/Loss	28	-211	-358
Working Capital	-375	-388	-60
Fixed Assets	1m	1m	1m
Current Assets	3m	2m	1m
Current Liabilities	636	973	402

Roberts Radio Ltd
PO Box 130, Mexborough, S64 8AJ
Tel: 01709-571722 **Fax:** 01709-571255
E-mail: information@robertsradio.co.uk
Website: http://www.robertsradio.co.uk
Bank(s): Allied Irish
Managers: N. Holmes
Ultimate Holding Company: GLEN DIMPLEX (ROI)
Immediate Holding Company: ROBERTS RADIO LIMITED
Registration no: 02978869 **VAT No.:** GB 287 1315 50
Date established: 1994 **Turnover:** £20m - £50m
No.of Employees: 11 - 20 **Product Groups:** 37

Date of Accounts	Mar 11	Mar 10	Mar 09
Sales Turnover	23m	22m	17m
Pre Tax Profit/Loss	2m	2m	748
Working Capital	6m	4m	3m
Fixed Assets	722	901	724
Current Assets	9m	8m	6m
Current Liabilities	1m	2m	647

Stelrad Group Ltd
Stelrad House Marriott Road, Swinton, Mexborough, S64 8BN
Tel: 01709-578950 **Fax:** 0870-498058
E-mail: info@stelrad.com
Website: http://www.stelrad.com

Directors: M. Conlon (MD)
Ultimate Holding Company: Isg Holdings Ltd
Immediate Holding Company: STELRAD LIMITED
Registration no: 04049017 **Date established:** 1988
Turnover: £50m - £75m **No.of Employees:** 251 - 500
Product Groups: 35, 40, 66

Date of Accounts	Dec 07	Dec 06	Dec 05
Sales Turnover	71400	73090	71660
Pre Tax Profit/Loss	3860	4960	2900
Working Capital	53890	49360	34860
Fixed Assets	7840	8440	9100
Current Assets	72870	68830	64620
Current Liabilities	18980	19470	29760
Total Share Capital	5000	5000	5000
ROCE% (Return on Capital Employed)	6.3	8.6	6.6
ROT% (Return on Turnover)	5.4	6.8	4.0

Rotherham

1st Choice Roller Shutters
Unit 3 Pennyhill Lane, Thurcroft, Rotherham, S66 9BQ
Tel: 01909-551195 **Fax:** 01909-551196
Website: http://www.1stchoice-rollershutters.co.uk
Managers: L. Robinson (Sales Admin)
Immediate Holding Company: 1ST CHOICE ROLLER SHUTTERS LTD
Registration no: 04255348 **Date established:** 2001
No.of Employees: 1 - 10 **Product Groups:** 26, 35

Date of Accounts	Jul 11	Jul 10	Jul 09
Working Capital	-118	-43	4
Fixed Assets	23	17	16
Current Assets	169	191	159

A & A Stainless Fabrications Ltd
Unit 10 Aspen Court Centurion Business Park, Rotherham, S60 1FB
Tel: 01709-365532 **Fax:** 0560-310 0246
E-mail: andyfortune@aandastainlessfabrications.co.uk
Website: http://www.aandastainlessfabrications.co.uk
Directors: A. Fortune (Prop)
Immediate Holding Company: A&A STAINLESS FABRICATIONS LTD
Registration no: 06571124 **Date established:** 1941
No.of Employees: 1 - 10 **Product Groups:** 35, 36, 40, 48, 67

A P Tyres Specialists
Broad Street Parkgate, Rotherham, S62 6ER
Tel: 01709-523817 **Fax:** 01709-528242
Website: http://www.ap-tyres.co.uk
Directors: P. Hutchingson (Prop), P. Hutchinson (Prop)
No.of Employees: 11 - 20 **Product Groups:** 29, 40

A S D Lighting plc
Mangham Road Greasbrough, Rotherham, S61 4RJ
Tel: 01709-374898 **Fax:** 01709-830533
E-mail: sales@asdlighting.com
Website: http://www.asdlighting.com
Bank(s): Barclays
Directors: K. Thomas (Co Sec), A. Stewart (MD), J. Finelli (Sales), J. Finelli (Sales & Mktg)
Managers: M. Oakley (Mktg Serv Mgr), R. Stewart (Export Sales Mg)
Ultimate Holding Company: ASD LIGHTING HOLDINGS LIMITED
Immediate Holding Company: ASD LIGHTING PLC
Registration no: 01677887 **VAT No.:** GB 308 9179 34
Date established: 1982 **Turnover:** £10m - £20m
No.of Employees: 101 - 250 **Product Groups:** 37, 38, 67, 84

Date of Accounts	Dec 11	Dec 10	Dec 09
Sales Turnover	21m	18m	17m
Pre Tax Profit/Loss	4m	2m	3m
Working Capital	8m	5m	4m
Fixed Assets	5m	6m	5m
Current Assets	13m	10m	9m
Current Liabilities	2m	2m	2m

Aardvark Display Lighting
Unit 9 Century Business Centre Century Park, Manvers, Rotherham, S63 5DA
Tel: 01709-300050 **Fax:** 0114-266 5856
Website: http://www.transformlighting.co.uk
Directors: T. Binns (MD)
Immediate Holding Company: TIMBER SOLUTIONS YORKSHIRE LIMITED
Registration no: 03764916 **Date established:** 2012
No.of Employees: 1 - 10 **Product Groups:** 37, 67

Acorn Industrial Services Ltd
Midland Road, Rotherham, S61 1TE
Tel: 01709-789999 **Fax:** 01709-789988
E-mail: sales@acorn-ind.co.uk
Website: http://www.acorn-ind.co.uk
Directors: P. Spillings (Sales), M. Povey (Dir), J. Chapman (Pers)
Managers: A. Biggs (Buyer)
Ultimate Holding Company: ACORN INDUSTRIAL SERVICES GROUP LTD
Immediate Holding Company: ACORN INDUSTRIAL SERVICES LIMITED
Registration no: 01733820 **Date established:** 1983
Turnover: £10m - £20m **No.of Employees:** 51 - 100 **Product Groups:** 35, 38, 40, 66

Date of Accounts	Dec 11	Dec 10	Dec 09
Sales Turnover	17m	14m	12m
Pre Tax Profit/Loss	1m	695	897
Working Capital	5m	4m	4m
Fixed Assets	773	409	393
Current Assets	10m	8m	8m
Current Liabilities	2m	427	323

Aizlewoods Buildbase
Crinoline Commercial Area 163 Rawmarsh Road, Rotherham, S60 1SA
Tel: 01709-375850 **Fax:** 01709-362365
E-mail: ian.wild@buildbase.co.uk
Website: http://www.aizlewoods.co.uk
Managers: M. Dauris (Reg Mgr)
Immediate Holding Company: GRAFTON MERCHANTING GB LIMITED
Registration no: 04725313 **Date established:** 2003
No.of Employees: 1 - 10 **Product Groups:** 66

All Fabs
10 Cambridge Street, Rotherham, S65 2TD
Tel: 01709-720724

Directors: K. Baldwin (Prop)
Registration no: 06875654 **Date established:** 2009
No.of Employees: 1 - 10 **Product Groups:** 35

D. A'mours
7 Flintway Wath Upon Dearne, Rotherham, S63 7TS
Tel: 01709-873094 **Fax:** 01709-873094
E-mail: enquries@damours.co.uk
Website: http://www.damours.co.uk
Turnover: Up to £250,000 **No.of Employees:** 1 - 10 **Product Groups:** 23, 24, 63

Asquith G M Fabrications Ltd
13 Angel Street Bolton-Upon-Dearne, Rotherham, S63 8NA
Tel: 01709-888098 **Fax:** 01709-888098
E-mail: dawn.asquith@btconnect.com
Website: http://www.gmasquithfabrications.co.uk
Directors: D. Asquith (Fin)
Immediate Holding Company: THE ANGEL BOLTON UPON DEARNE LTD
Registration no: 04362705 **Date established:** 2008
No.of Employees: 1 - 10 **Product Groups:** 35

B & B Press Parkgate Ltd
Lloyd Street Parkgate, Rotherham, S62 6DY
Tel: 01709-710000 **Fax:** 01709-710111
E-mail: sales@bbpress.co.uk
Website: http://www.bbpress.co.uk
Directors: B. Liversidge (MD), N. Tolley (Fab)
Managers: S. Sylvester (Tech Serv Mgr), D. Dean (Develop Mgr)
Immediate Holding Company: B. AND B.PRESS (PARKGATE) LIMITED
Registration no: 00767737 **Date established:** 1963 **Turnover:** £2m - £5m
No.of Employees: 21 - 50 **Product Groups:** 28

Date of Accounts	Jun 12	Jun 11	Jun 10
Working Capital	809	751	722
Fixed Assets	1m	1m	1m
Current Assets	1m	1m	1m

Backer Electric Co. Ltd
Fitzwilliam Road Eastwood Trading Estate, Rotherham, S65 1TE
Tel: 01709-828292 **Fax:** 01709-828388
E-mail: finance@backer.co.uk
Website: http://www.backerelectric.com
Bank(s): HSBC
Directors: S. Patten (Co Sec), P. Daffin (MD)
Managers: P. Leng (Sales Prom Mgr)
Ultimate Holding Company: TEMPLETRUST LIMITED (BRITISH VIRGIN ISLA
Immediate Holding Company: BACKER ELECTRIC COMPANY LIMITED
Registration no: 00432388 **Date established:** 1947 **Turnover:** £2m - £5m
No.of Employees: 21 - 50 **Product Groups:** 33, 37

Date of Accounts	Dec 11	Dec 10	Dec 09
Working Capital	3m	3m	3m
Fixed Assets	875	921	950
Current Assets	4m	5m	5m

Beatson Clark Ltd
The Glass Works Greasbrough Road, Rotherham, S60 1TZ
Tel: 01709-828141 **Fax:** 01709-835388
E-mail: sales@beatsonclark.co.uk
Website: http://www.beatsonclark.co.uk
Bank(s): HSBC Bank plc
Directors: T. Mcloughlin (MD), S. Fletcher (I.T. Dir), L. Fidebottom (Sales & Mktg), L. Sidebottom (Sales), A. Jones (MD), S. Owens (Co Sec)
Managers: P. Moran (Sales Prom Mgr), J. McQuillin (Personnel), C. Saysell (Purch Mgr), S. Baxendale (Export Sales Mg)
Ultimate Holding Company: NEWSHIP LIMITED
Immediate Holding Company: BEATSON CLARK LIMITED
Registration no: 00110186 **Date established:** 2010
Turnover: £20m - £50m **No.of Employees:** 251 - 500 **Product Groups:** 33

Date of Accounts	Dec 10	Dec 09	Dec 08
Sales Turnover	44m	41m	39m
Pre Tax Profit/Loss	2m	2m	1m
Working Capital	-4m	-2m	-2m
Fixed Assets	24m	26m	25m
Current Assets	17m	20m	21m
Current Liabilities	2m	3m	2m

Beecroft & Partners Ltd
Northfield Road, Rotherham, S60 1RR
Tel: 01709-377881 **Fax:** 01709-369264
E-mail: sales@beecroft-science.co.uk
Website: http://www.beecroft-science.co.uk
Directors: R. Scott (MD)
Immediate Holding Company: BEECROFT & PARTNERS LIMITED
Registration no: 02057053 **Date established:** 1986 **Turnover:** £2m - £5m
No.of Employees: 11 - 20 **Product Groups:** 66

Date of Accounts	Sep 11	Sep 10	Sep 09
Working Capital	99	90	80
Fixed Assets	22	10	13
Current Assets	510	469	455

Ben Bennett JR Ltd
Lisle Road, Rotherham, S60 2RL
Tel: 01709-382251 **Fax:** 01709-369206
E-mail: pudell@benbennettjr.co.uk
Website: http://www.benbennettjr.co.uk
Directors: B. Bennett (MD), P. Udell (Co Sec)
Managers: B. Rippon
Immediate Holding Company: BEN BENNETT JR LIMITED
Registration no: 00210739 **VAT No.:** GB 172 3507 76
Date established: 2025 **Turnover:** £5m - £10m **No.of Employees:** 1 - 10
Product Groups: 14, 31, 32, 33, 34

Date of Accounts	Dec 11	Dec 10	Dec 09
Sales Turnover	8m	8m	6m
Pre Tax Profit/Loss	607	407	290
Working Capital	3m	3m	3m
Fixed Assets	3m	3m	3m
Current Assets	5m	4m	4m
Current Liabilities	710	651	532

Ben Bennett Junior Ltd
Eastwood Rolling Mills Fitzwilliam Road, Rotherham, S65 1SH
Tel: 01709-382006 **Fax:** 01709-829890
E-mail: benbennettjr@btconnect.com
Website: http://www.benbennettjr.co.uk
Bank(s): HSBC Bank plc
Directors: J. Bennett (Dir)
Registration no: 00210739 **VAT No.:** GB 172 3507 76
Turnover: £2m - £5m **No.of Employees:** 11 - 20 **Product Groups:** 34

Boc Tradequip
Bawtry Road Brinsworth, Rotherham, S60 5NT
Tel: 01709-842216 **Fax:** 01709-828919
E-mail: tim.surr@boc.com
Website: http://www.boc.com
Directors: A. Brackfield (Co Sec), J. Masters Jr (Dir)
Managers: J. Whiting (Mgr), T. Surr (Mgr)
Ultimate Holding Company: Linde UK Holdings Ltd
Immediate Holding Company: Boc Netherlands Holdings Ltd
Registration no: 00337663 **Turnover:** £500m - £1,000m
No.of Employees: 1 - 10 **Product Groups:** 31

Boreflex Ltd
Unit 9 Gateway Court Parkgate, Rotherham, S62 6LH
Tel: 01709-522333 **Fax:** 01709-522663
E-mail: sales@boreflex.co.uk
Website: http://www.boreflex.co.uk
Directors: R. Fox (MD)
Immediate Holding Company: BOREFLEX LIMITED
Registration no: 03201075 **VAT No.:** GB 678 9368 55
Date established: 1996 **Turnover:** £500,000 - £1m
No.of Employees: 1 - 10 **Product Groups:** 29, 30, 31, 32, 40, 48

Date of Accounts	Mar 12	Mar 11	Mar 10
Working Capital	23	-6	-18
Fixed Assets	145	125	146
Current Assets	175	129	116

Bramall Construction
3 Callflex Business Park Golden Smithies Lane, Wath-upon-Dearne, Rotherham, S63 7ER
Tel: 01709-766000 **Fax:** 01709-766001
E-mail: info@keepmoat.com
Website: http://www.bramall.com
Bank(s): HSBC
Directors: J. Wilcox (Mkt Research), N. Baxter (MD)
Managers: P. Atherton (Personnel), G. Gastmitt (Buyer)
Ultimate Holding Company: LAKESIDE 1 LIMITED
Immediate Holding Company: BRAMALL CONSTRUCTION LIMITED
Registration no: 01467161 **Date established:** 1979
Turnover: £20m - £50m **No.of Employees:** 101 - 250 **Product Groups:** 52

Date of Accounts	Mar 11	Mar 10	Mar 09
Sales Turnover	225m	242m	246m
Pre Tax Profit/Loss	20m	29m	27m
Working Capital	43m	38m	36m
Fixed Assets	1m	815	844
Current Assets	103m	104m	96m
Current Liabilities	17m	21m	20m

Brimset Ltd
2 Stocks Lane Rawmarsh, Rotherham, S62 6NL
Tel: 01709-522270 **Fax:** 01709-527240
E-mail: contracts@brimset.f9.co.uk
Website: http://www.brimset.f9.co.uk
Directors: R. Jennings (Ch), R. Jennings (Sales), C. Thompson (Dir), I. Jennings (Fin)
Managers: M. Stainrod (Mgr)
Immediate Holding Company: BRIMSET LIMITED
Registration no: 01540974 **Date established:** 1981 **Turnover:** £1m - £2m
No.of Employees: 1 - 10 **Product Groups:** 84

Date of Accounts	Mar 09	Mar 08	Mar 07
Working Capital	477	379	385
Fixed Assets	144	163	34
Current Assets	694	690	743

Builder Center Ltd
Mangham Road Parkgate, Rotherham, S62 6EF
Tel: 01709-820333 **Fax:** 01709-820624
Website: http://www.build-center.co.uk
Bank(s): National Westminster Bank Plc
Directors: A. Bykhovsky (Ch)
Managers: C. Lucock (Mgr), S. Day (Mgr), T. Meadows (Mgr)
Ultimate Holding Company: Wolseley plc
Immediate Holding Company: BUILD CENTER LIMITED
Registration no: 00462397 **VAT No.:** GB 222 8284 72
Date established: 1948 **Turnover:** £50m - £75m
No.of Employees: 11 - 20 **Product Groups:** 25, 66

C F Booth Ltd
Clarence Metal Works Armer Street, Rotherham, S60 1AF
Tel: 01709-559198 **Fax:** 01709-561859
E-mail: info@cfbooth.com
Website: http://www.cfbooth.com
Bank(s): National Westminster
Directors: J. Booth (MD)
Ultimate Holding Company: C.F.BOOTH LIMITED
Immediate Holding Company: C.F. BOOTH (ENGINEERING) LIMITED
Registration no: 01470572 **VAT No.:** GB 172 3243 84
Date established: 1980 **Turnover:** £2m - £5m
No.of Employees: 101 - 250 **Product Groups:** 34, 66

Date of Accounts	Mar 11	Mar 10	Mar 09
Sales Turnover	4m	3m	3m
Pre Tax Profit/Loss	518	456	368
Working Capital	880	841	891
Fixed Assets	1m	845	902
Current Assets	2m	1m	1m
Current Liabilities	324	259	107

Carillion Energy Services
Unit G02 Magna 34, Temple Close, Rotherham, S60 1FH
Tel: 01522-563550 **Fax:** 01522-563551
E-mail: j.cox@millfoldgroup.com
Website: http://www.millfoldgroup.com
Directors: J. Cox (Prop)
Date established: 1982 **Turnover:** £20m - £50m
No.of Employees: 11 - 20 **Product Groups:** 30, 33, 45, 52, 66, 84

Carl Stahl Evita Ltd
Carl Stahl House Farfield Park Manvers, Rotherham, S63 5DB
Tel: 08451-302299 **Fax:** 08451-304499
E-mail: roy@carlstahlevita.co.uk
Website: http://www.carlstahlevita.com
Managers: S. Bates
Immediate Holding Company: LIFTING SYSTEMS SOLUTIONS LIMITED
Registration no: 03651319 **Date established:** 1998
No.of Employees: 1 - 10 **Product Groups:** 23, 25, 29, 30, 31, 34, 35, 36, 37, 38, 39, 40, 41, 45, 46, 48, 66, 67, 68, 86

Date of Accounts	Dec 11	Dec 10	Dec 09
Working Capital	-2m	N/A	N/A

Carlton Catering Equipment
Grange Farm Braithwell Road, Ravenfield, Rotherham, S65 4LP
Tel: 01709-540004
Website: http://www.chippersandpeelers.com
Directors: P. Ward (Prop)
Date established: 1997 **No.of Employees:** 1 - 10 **Product Groups:** 20, 40, 41

Carter Controls UK Ltd
4 The Gateway Place The Gateway Industrial Estate, Parkgate, Rotherham, S62 6LL
Tel: 01709-525800 **Fax:** 01709-710717
E-mail: sales@cartercontrols.fsnet.co.uk
Directors: L. Morley (Fin), G. Morley (MD)
Immediate Holding Company: CARTER CONTROLS (UK) LIMITED
Registration no: 03031689 **Date established:** 1995
No.of Employees: 1 - 10 **Product Groups:** 40

Date of Accounts	Dec 11	Dec 10	Dec 09
Working Capital	-41	-37	-30
Fixed Assets	43	43	44
Current Assets	174	173	147

Castings Technology International Ltd
Advanced Manufacturing Park Brunel Way, Catcliffe, Rotherham, S60 5WG
Tel: 0114-254 1144 **Fax:** 0114-273 0852
E-mail: m.ashton@castingstechnology.com
Website: http://www.castingstechnology.com
Bank(s): National Westminster Bank Plc
Directors: M. Ashton (MD), A. Village (Fin)
Immediate Holding Company: CASTINGS TECHNOLOGY INTERNATIONAL
Registration no: 03157646 **Date established:** 1996 **Turnover:** £5m - £10m
No.of Employees: 51 - 100 **Product Groups:** 80, 87

Date of Accounts	Mar 11	Mar 10	Mar 09
Sales Turnover	7m	8m	10m
Pre Tax Profit/Loss	-859	-2m	-466
Working Capital	-731	-4m	-1m
Fixed Assets	13m	14m	15m
Current Assets	3m	2m	5m
Current Liabilities	3m	4m	4m

Cavendish Tea Coffee Ltd
Toad Lane Brampton-En-Le-Morthen, Rotherham, S66 9BG
Tel: 01709-703417 **Fax:** 01709-703517
Directors: R. Briddon (Dir)
Immediate Holding Company: CAVENDISH TEA & COFFEE LIMITED
Registration no: 04556473 **Date established:** 2002
Turnover: Up to £250,000 **No.of Employees:** 1 - 10 **Product Groups:** 62

Date of Accounts	Oct 11	Oct 10	Oct 05
Working Capital	18	13	-29
Fixed Assets	40	48	68
Current Assets	40	34	26

Cetix Ltd
Sycamore Road Eastwood Trading Estate, Rotherham, S65 1EN
Tel: 01709-538200 **Fax:** 01709-376903
E-mail: info@salemautomation.net
Website: http://www.cetix-group.com
Bank(s): Nat West
Directors: L. Franklin (MD), J. Turner (Fin)
Managers: A. Grant (Sales & Mktg Mg)
Ultimate Holding Company: HITEC INDUSTRIES AS (NORWAY)
Immediate Holding Company: CETIX LIMITED
Registration no: 02184213 **VAT No.:** GB 690 1821 38
Date established: 1987 **Turnover:** £2m - £5m **No.of Employees:** 21 - 50
Product Groups: 37, 38, 44

Date of Accounts	Dec 11	Dec 10	Dec 09
Sales Turnover	2m	2m	2m
Pre Tax Profit/Loss	-189	73	-257
Working Capital	623	780	927
Fixed Assets	70	102	79
Current Assets	1m	2m	1m
Current Liabilities	508	531	262

Corus Engineering Steels
PO Box 50, Rotherham, S60 1DW
Tel: 01709-371234 **Fax:** 01709-826233
E-mail: christianname.surname@corusgroup.com
Website: http://www.corus.com
Directors: C. Jackson (Fab), D. Tuner (MD), G. Toye (Dir), I. Davies (Tech Serv), K. Stolwijk (MD), M. Howell (Comm), V. Naik (Fin)
Managers: M. Edwards (Buyer), D. Stansfield (Shipping Mgr), G. Carter (Personnel), I. Cooper (Comptroller), P. Hogg (Mgr), P. Hogg (Chief Mgr)
Immediate Holding Company: Corus Management Ltd
Registration no: 04892733 **Date established:** 2003
Turnover: £500m - £1,000m **No.of Employees:** 501 - 1000
Product Groups: 34, 66

Cutting & Wear Resistant Development Ltd
Greasbrough Road, Rotherham, S60 1RW
Tel: 01709-361041 **Fax:** 01709-374211
E-mail: tony.mettam@cwuk.com
Website: http://www.cwuk.com
Directors: A. Mettam (Fin), J. Barnett (Chief Op Offcr), M. Russell (MD), T. Mettam (Fin), G. McDonald (Dir)
Managers: S. Jones (Sales & Mktg Mg), B. Russell (), J. Hardy (Sales Prom)
Immediate Holding Company: CUTTING & WEAR RESISTANT DEVELOPMENTS LIMITED
Registration no: 00942427 **VAT No.:** GB 172 3148 78
Date established: 1968 **Turnover:** £2m - £5m **No.of Employees:** 21 - 50
Product Groups: 34, 45

Date of Accounts	Sep 11	Sep 10	Sep 09
Sales Turnover	8m	N/A	N/A
Pre Tax Profit/Loss	877	584	271
Working Capital	2m	2m	2m
Fixed Assets	3m	578	460
Current Assets	4m	4m	3m
Current Liabilities	701	612	579

D P W
43 Armstrong Walk Maltby, Rotherham, S66 8QQ
Tel: 01709-815900 **Fax:** 01709-815900
Managers: R. Ward (Mgr)
Date established: 2000 **No.of Employees:** 1 - 10 **Product Groups:** 46

De-signage
Briarwood House 32 Briarwood Gardens, Sunnyside, Rotherham, S66 3XR
Tel: 01709-700309 **Fax:** 01709-700309
E-mail: sales@de-signage.com
Website: http://www.de-signage.com
Directors: M. Harris (Prop)
No.of Employees: 1 - 10 **Product Groups:** 30, 49, 67

Dormer Tools Ltd
Unit 8 Morse Way, Catcliffe, Rotherham, S60 5BJ
Tel: 0114-293 3800 **Fax:** 01909-534701
E-mail: john.odonoghue@dormertools.com
Website: http://www.dormertools.com
Directors: J. Odonoghue (MD), S. Brabham (Fin)
Managers: S. Flood (Fin Mgr), R. Bloomfield (Personnel), S. Teds (Tech Serv Mgr), S. Winstanley (Mktg Serv Mgr)
Ultimate Holding Company: SANDVIK AB (SWEDEN)
Immediate Holding Company: DORMER TOOLS LIMITED
Registration no: 00440053 **Date established:** 1947
Turnover: £10m - £20m **No.of Employees:** 51 - 100 **Product Groups:** 36, 45, 46, 47, 48

Date of Accounts	Dec 11	Dec 10	Dec 09
Sales Turnover	18m	18m	15m
Pre Tax Profit/Loss	204	260	-745
Working Capital	-445	-1m	-3m
Fixed Assets	824	1m	3m
Current Assets	3m	3m	3m
Current Liabilities	1m	4m	888

Drawmer Electronics Ltd
Coleman Street Parkgate, Rotherham, S62 6EL
Tel: 01709-527574 **Fax:** 01709-526871
E-mail: tech@drawmer.com
Website: http://www.drawmer.com
Bank(s): National Westminster Bank Plc
Directors: S. Middleton (Fin)
Immediate Holding Company: DRAWMER ELECTRONICS LIMITED
Registration no: 01716420 **Date established:** 1983
Turnover: £500,000 - £1m **No.of Employees:** 11 - 20 **Product Groups:** 37

Date of Accounts	Mar 11	Mar 10	Mar 09
Working Capital	841	863	875
Fixed Assets	328	328	328
Current Assets	915	926	925

E S P Laser Cutting Ltd
Unit 3 Centurion Business Park Bessemer Way, Rotherham, S60 1FB
Tel: 01709-720480 **Fax:** 01709-821500
E-mail: sales@esplaser.com
Website: http://www.esplaser.com
Bank(s): National Westminster Bank Plc
Directors: P. Short (Fab)
Immediate Holding Company: E.S.P. LASER CUTTING LIMITED
Registration no: 02966436 **VAT No.:** GB 646 4841 16
Date established: 1994 **Turnover:** £500,000 - £1m
No.of Employees: 11 - 20 **Product Groups:** 23, 24, 25, 27, 28, 33, 45, 46, 47, 48, 49, 61, 77, 84

Date of Accounts	Oct 11	Oct 10	Oct 09
Working Capital	969	797	582
Fixed Assets	777	651	854
Current Assets	2m	2m	1m

Eldon Electric Ltd
Rother Way Hellaby, Rotherham, S66 8QN
Tel: 01709-701234 **Fax:** 01709-701209
E-mail: martin.roberts@eldon.com
Website: http://www.eldon.com/uk
Bank(s): Svenska Handelsbanken
Directors: P. Hird (Sales & Mktg), M. Roberts (Fin)
Managers: H. Rogerson
Ultimate Holding Company: ELDON HOLDING AB (SWEDEN)
Immediate Holding Company: ELDON ELECTRIC LIMITED
Registration no: 00924071 **VAT No.:** GB 207 7079 62
Date established: 1967 **Turnover:** £10m - £20m
No.of Employees: 51 - 100 **Product Groups:** 26, 30, 35, 37, 38, 40, 46

Date of Accounts	Dec 11	Dec 10	Dec 09
Sales Turnover	12m	11m	10m
Pre Tax Profit/Loss	-488	455	30
Working Capital	2m	3m	2m
Fixed Assets	406	152	183
Current Assets	4m	4m	4m
Current Liabilities	509	347	257

Electronic & Engraving Services Ltd
Unit 16 Braithwell Way, Hellaby, Rotherham, S66 8QY
Tel: 01709-701715 **Fax:** 01709-701619
E-mail: ees.sales@dial.pipex.com
Website: http://www.e-es.co.uk
Bank(s): National Westminster Bank Plc
Directors: G. Spratt (Co Sec), N. Spratt (MD), R. Rider (Dir)
Managers: Kelly (Prod Mgr), T. Didlock (I.T. Exec)
Immediate Holding Company: ELECTRONIC AND ENGRAVING SERVICES PROJECTS LIMITED
Registration no: 03494568 **Date established:** 1998 **Turnover:** £2m - £5m
No.of Employees: 51 - 100 **Product Groups:** 38

Date of Accounts	Mar 12	Mar 11	Mar 10
Working Capital	33	14	14
Fixed Assets	4	6	7
Current Assets	86	97	85

Empire Tapes
Houndhill Park Bolton Road, Rotherham, S63 7LG
Tel: 01709-768300 **Fax:** 01709-768333
E-mail: sales@empiretapes.com
Website: http://www.empiretapes.com
Directors: D. Sherriff (MD)
Managers: N. Law (Mgr), M. Putwain (Fin Mgr)
Registration no: 02797901 **Date established:** 1993 **Turnover:** £5m - £10m
No.of Employees: 50 **Product Groups:** 27

Emuge UK
2 Claire Court Rawmarsh Road, Rotherham, S60 1RU
Tel: 01709-364494 **Fax:** 01709-364540
E-mail: sales@emuge-uk.co.uk
Website: http://emuge-uk.co.uk
Directors: P. Ellis (Co Sec), H. Glimpel (Dir)
Ultimate Holding Company: EMUGE FRANKEN BETEILIGUNGEN GMBH (GERMANY)
Immediate Holding Company: EMUGE UK LIMITED
Registration no: 02239015 **Date established:** 1988 **Turnover:** £1m - £2m
No.of Employees: 1 - 10 **Product Groups:** 35, 36, 46, 48

Date of Accounts	Dec 11	Dec 10	Dec 09
Working Capital	406	329	251
Fixed Assets	48	27	46
Current Assets	838	678	496

Energy Alloys UK Ltd
Advantage House Poplar Way, Catcliffe, Rotherham, S60 5TR
Tel: 01709-788000 **Fax:** 01709-788030
E-mail: mwilliams@ealloys.com
Website: http://www.energyalloys.com
Directors: J. Murray (MD), P. Morris (MD), M. Colbourne (Fin)
Managers: J. Spencer (Personnel)
Immediate Holding Company: ENERGY ALLOYS UK LIMITED
Registration no: 05044016 **Date established:** 2004
Turnover: £20m - £50m **No.of Employees:** 21 - 50 **Product Groups:** 34, 36, 48

Date of Accounts	Dec 11	Dec 10	Dec 09
Sales Turnover	46m	36m	37m
Pre Tax Profit/Loss	4m	2m	-4m
Working Capital	16m	18m	19m
Fixed Assets	5m	6m	7m
Current Assets	31m	26m	28m
Current Liabilities	1m	836	911

Eplan Divison Of Rittal Ltd (Rittal Ltd)
Braithwell Way Hellaby, Rotherham, S66 8QY
Tel: 01709-704100 **Fax:** 01709-730283
E-mail: info@eplan.co.uk
Website: http://www.eplan.co.uk
Directors: K. Christie (MD)
Managers: H. Lewis
Ultimate Holding Company: FRIEDHELM LOH STIFTUNG & CO KG (GERMANY)
Immediate Holding Company: RITTAL LIMITED
Registration no: 01389120 **Date established:** 1978
Turnover: £20m - £50m **No.of Employees:** 1 - 10 **Product Groups:** 44, 47, 84

Date of Accounts	Dec 11	Dec 10	Dec 09
Sales Turnover	40m	33m	64m
Pre Tax Profit/Loss	-268	-1m	-7m
Working Capital	7m	8m	16m
Fixed Assets	3m	3m	3m
Current Assets	12m	15m	20m
Current Liabilities	1m	987	923

Eskro Hydra Mining Divison
Rotheham Works Wortley Road, Rotherham, S61 1LZ
Tel: 01709-857500 **Fax:** 01709- 857501
E-mail: john@hydramining.com
Website: http://www.hydramining.com
Bank(s): Barclays
Directors: J. Warren (MD), G. McShannon (Grp Chief Exec), J. Mcshannon (Fin)
Managers: T. Sutton (I.T. Exec), S. Clappam (Sales & Mktg Mg)
Immediate Holding Company: ESCO HYDRA (UK) LIMITED
Registration no: 03966405 **VAT No.:** GB 533 8225 51
Date established: 2000 **Turnover:** £10m - £20m
No.of Employees: 51 - 100 **Product Groups:** 45

Date of Accounts	Jun 11	Jun 10	Jun 09
Sales Turnover	18m	12m	12m
Pre Tax Profit/Loss	4m	2m	2m
Working Capital	8m	5m	4m
Fixed Assets	665	759	542
Current Assets	11m	7m	6m
Current Liabilities	2m	1m	954

Europa Engineering Ltd
Holmes Lock Works Steel Street, Rotherham, S61 1DF
Tel: 01709-364115 **Fax:** 01709-364696
E-mail: paul.cheetham@europaengineering.com
Website: http://www.europaengineering.com
Directors: P. Cheetham (MD), J. Cheetham (Fin)
Managers: D. Marshall (Tech Serv Mgr), N. Newton (Buyer)
Immediate Holding Company: EUROPA ENGINEERING LTD.
Registration no: 02465896 **Date established:** 1990 **Turnover:** £5m - £10m
No.of Employees: 21 - 50 **Product Groups:** 35, 39, 45

Date of Accounts	Mar 11	Mar 10	Mar 09
Sales Turnover	9m	7m	N/A
Pre Tax Profit/Loss	245	293	702
Working Capital	1m	1m	1m
Fixed Assets	N/A	N/A	10
Current Assets	3m	3m	3m
Current Liabilities	566	457	330

Fabricated Products
Unit 2 Sheffield Road, Rotherham, S60 1BN
Tel: 01709-720842 **Fax:** 01709-720846
E-mail: info@fabricatedproducts.co.uk
Website: http://www.fabricatedproducts.co.uk
Directors: D. Brown (Grp Chief Exec)
Immediate Holding Company: FABRICATED PRODUCTS (UK) LIMITED
Registration no: 05004247 **Date established:** 2003
Turnover: £250,000 - £500,000 **No.of Employees:** 1 - 10
Product Groups: 35, 38, 42, 48

Date of Accounts	Dec 11	Dec 10	Dec 09
Working Capital	536	637	559
Fixed Assets	964	20	26
Current Assets	860	807	723

First South Yorkshire
Midland Road, Rotherham, S61 1TF
Tel: 01709-566000 **Fax:** 01709-566063
E-mail: info@firstmainline.co.uk
Website: http://www.firstgroup.com
Managers: W. Simpson (Personnel), L. Turner, D. Farrar (Purch Mgr)
Ultimate Holding Company: FIRSTGROUP PLC
Immediate Holding Company: FIRST SOUTH YORKSHIRE LIMITED
Registration no: 02332529 **Date established:** 1989
Turnover: £50m - £75m **No.of Employees:** 1501 & over
Product Groups: 72

Date of Accounts	Mar 08	Mar 09	Mar 10
Sales Turnover	69m	72m	70m
Pre Tax Profit/Loss	3m	1m	2m
Working Capital	-5m	-3m	2m
Fixed Assets	33m	38m	33m
Current Assets	35m	27m	31m
Current Liabilities	11m	7m	4m

Flowplant Group Ltd
15 Stadium Court Parkgate, Rotherham, S62 6EW
Tel: 01709-838308 **Fax:** 01709-838028
E-mail: info@flowplant.com
Website: http://www.flowplant.com

Managers: M. Preston (Sales Prom Mgr)
Ultimate Holding Company: FLOWPLANT HOLDINGS LIMITED
Immediate Holding Company: FLOWPLANT GROUP LIMITED
Registration no: 03612438 **Date established:** 1998 **Turnover:** £5m - £10m
No.of Employees: 1 - 10 **Product Groups:** 40, 45, 46

Date of Accounts	Sep 11	Sep 10	Sep 09
Sales Turnover	6m	5m	5m
Pre Tax Profit/Loss	330	240	154
Working Capital	2m	1m	994
Fixed Assets	244	198	203
Current Assets	3m	3m	2m
Current Liabilities	665	241	159

Focus N D T Ltd

Unit 21 Aspen Court Centurion Business Park Bessemer Way, Rotherham, S60 1FB
Tel: 01709-377443 **Fax:** 01709-377449
E-mail: sales@focusndt.co.uk
Website: http://www.focusndt.co.uk
Directors: D. Ackernley (Fin), D. Ackernley (MD)
Immediate Holding Company: FOCUS NDT LIMITED
Registration no: 03808306 **Date established:** 1991 **Turnover:** £1m - £2m
No.of Employees: 11 - 20 **Product Groups:** 37, 38, 72, 85

Date of Accounts	Jul 11	Jul 10	Jul 09
Working Capital	-3	-113	-29
Fixed Assets	62	56	87
Current Assets	338	148	166

Gates & Railing

3 Hillside Court, Rotherham, S61 4RP
Tel: 01709-363325 **Fax:** 01709-363325
Directors: M. O'brian (Prop)
Date established: 2001 **No.of Employees:** 1 - 10 **Product Groups:** 26, 35

Gefco UK Ltd

Fields End Business Park Thurnscoe, Rotherham, S63 0JF
Tel: 01709-886000 **Fax:** 01709-886006
E-mail: sales.uk@gefco.co.uk
Website: http://www.gefco.net
Managers: G. Lippett (Chief Mgr)
Ultimate Holding Company: PEUGEOT SA (FRANCE)
Immediate Holding Company: GEFCO U.K. LIMITED
Registration no: 01544410 **Date established:** 1981
Turnover: £20m - £50m **No.of Employees:** 11 - 20 **Product Groups:** 72, 76

Date of Accounts	Dec 10	Dec 09	Dec 08
Sales Turnover	115m	106m	138m
Pre Tax Profit/Loss	-3m	-11m	3m
Working Capital	5m	6m	13m
Fixed Assets	7m	7m	9m
Current Assets	32m	40m	35m
Current Liabilities	2m	6m	1m

Generic Engineering Ltd

Unit 4 Henley Grove Industrial Henley Grove Road, Rotherham, S61 1RS
Tel: 01709-558230 **Fax:** 01709-554887
Website: http://www.genericengineeringltd.com
Directors: T. Scarafile (MD), T. Scarafile (Dir)
Immediate Holding Company: GENERIC ENGINEERING LIMITED
Registration no: 05387147 **Date established:** 2005
No.of Employees: 1 - 10 **Product Groups:** 30, 48, 85

Date of Accounts	Mar 11	Mar 10	Mar 09
Working Capital	31	16	16
Fixed Assets	47	58	70
Current Assets	141	100	101

Globus Surgical Ltd

6 Blackburn Road Sheffield, Rotherham, S61 2DR
Tel: 01709-557711 **Fax:** 01709-557700
E-mail: shafqat@globussurgical.co.uk
Website: http://www.globussurgical.co.uk
Managers: S. Saharan (Mgr), C. Zhao
Immediate Holding Company: GLOBUS SURGICAL LIMITED
Registration no: 02552486 **Date established:** 1990
No.of Employees: 1 - 10 **Product Groups:** 38, 48, 67

Heaps, Arnold & Heaps Ltd

Unit D1 Quintec Court, Barbot Hall Industrial Estate, Rotherham, S61 4RN
Tel: 01709-837669 **Fax:** 01709-837671
E-mail: heaps@heapsarnold.com
Website: http://www.heapsarnold.com
Bank(s): Nat West
Directors: A. Steel (Fab), D. Briscoe (Fin), S. Eades (Tech Serv)
Registration no: 02798893 **Date established:** 1770 **Turnover:** £2m - £5m
No.of Employees: 11 - 20 **Product Groups:** 34, 35, 36, 66

Date of Accounts	Mar 11	Mar 10	Mar 09
Working Capital	635	478	561
Fixed Assets	270	266	217
Current Assets	979	777	900

Hempel Wire Ltd

Primrose Park Greasbrough Road, Rotherham, S60 1RH
Tel: 01709-376625 **Fax:** 01709-537099
E-mail: info@watson-wire.co.uk
Website: http://www.hempel-metals.com
Directors: J. Roper (MD)
Managers: T. Morton (Chief Acct)
Ultimate Holding Company: F W HEMPEL & CO ERZE UND METALLE (GMBH & CO) (GER)
Immediate Holding Company: HEMPEL WIRE LIMITED
Registration no: 01026114 **VAT No.:** GB 163 4643 64
Date established: 1971 **Turnover:** £10m - £20m
No.of Employees: 11 - 20 **Product Groups:** 34

Date of Accounts	Dec 11	Dec 10	Dec 09
Sales Turnover	15m	11m	13m
Pre Tax Profit/Loss	970	514	455
Working Capital	3m	3m	3m
Fixed Assets	2m	1m	1m
Current Assets	6m	5m	4m
Current Liabilities	506	363	212

Huthwaite International

Hoober House Hoober, Rotherham, S62 7SA
Tel: 01709-710081 **Fax:** 01709-710065
E-mail: info@huthwaite.co.uk
Website: http://www.huthwaite.co.uk
Bank(s): Lloyds TSB Bank plc
Directors: K. Watson (Co Sec), D. Freedman (Sales), A. Hughes (Dir)
Managers: P. Wilson (Fin Mgr), H. Hague (Personnel), J. Goodwin, C. Hanwell (Mktg Serv Mgr)
Ultimate Holding Company: HUTHWAITE INTERNATIONAL LIMITED
Immediate Holding Company: HUTHWAITE INTERNATIONAL (2001) LIMITED
Registration no: 04118305 **Date established:** 2000 **Turnover:** £5m - £10m
No.of Employees: 21 - 50 **Product Groups:** 44, 67, 80, 81, 86

Date of Accounts	Mar 12	Mar 11	Mar 10
Pre Tax Profit/Loss	-50	729	875
Working Capital	3m	-2m	-2m
Fixed Assets	N/A	4m	4m
Current Assets	4m	4m	6
Current Liabilities	55	55	199

Hydraulic Pumps UK Ltd

2 The Summit Barbot Hall Industrial Estate Mangham Road, Greasbrough, Rotherham, S61 4RJ
Tel: 01709-360370 **Fax:** 01709-372913
E-mail: sales@hydraulicpumps.co.uk
Website: http://www.hydraulicpumps.co.uk
Directors: D. Sangster (Dir), N. Marshall (Co Sec)
Immediate Holding Company: HYDRAULIC PUMPS (UK) LIMITED
Registration no: 02206972 **Date established:** 1987 **Turnover:** £2m - £5m
No.of Employees: 1 - 10 **Product Groups:** 39, 40

Date of Accounts	Mar 11	Mar 10	Mar 09
Working Capital	66	59	45
Fixed Assets	129	116	111
Current Assets	563	474	443

I.F.S. Rotherham Nuts Bolts Adhesives Tools

Masbrough Street, Rotherham, S60 1ER
Tel: 01895-818181 **Fax:** 01709-362825
Website: http://www.anixterindustrial.com
Managers: D. Lynch (District Mgr)
Ultimate Holding Company: Industrial Fastener Supplies (Sheffield) Ltd
No.of Employees: 1 - 10 **Product Groups:** 67, 68

Inditherm

Houndhill Park Bolton Road, Wath-upon-Dearne, Rotherham, S63 7LG
Tel: 01709-761000 **Fax:** 01709-761066
E-mail: info@indithermplc.com
Website: http://www.inditherm.com
Directors: I. Smith (Fin), N. Bettles (MD)
Ultimate Holding Company: INDITHERM PLC
Immediate Holding Company: INDITHERM PLC
Registration no: 03587944 **Date established:** 1998 **Turnover:** £1m - £2m
No.of Employees: 11 - 20 **Product Groups:** 33, 37, 40, 42, 52, 83

Date of Accounts	Dec 11	Dec 10	Dec 09
Sales Turnover	2m	1m	1m
Pre Tax Profit/Loss	-121	-409	-1m
Working Capital	2m	2m	2m
Fixed Assets	76	120	147
Current Assets	2m	2m	3m
Current Liabilities	137	138	166

Industrial Software Ltd

Assured House 8 The Point, Rotherham, S60 1BP
Tel: 01709-388110 **Fax:** 01709-388 119
E-mail: info@industrialsoftwareltd.co.uk
Website: http://www.industrialsoftwareltd.co.uk
Directors: Z. Cooper (Dir)
Immediate Holding Company: INDUSTRIAL SOFTWARE LIMITED
Registration no: 04146453 **Date established:** 2001
No.of Employees: 1 - 10 **Product Groups:** 37, 38, 39, 42, 44, 45, 48, 80, 85

Date of Accounts	Mar 11	Mar 10	Mar 09
Working Capital	42	30	34
Fixed Assets	4	5	3
Current Assets	84	72	145

Kast Fabrications Ltd

Unit 3 Riverside Development Chesterton Road, Eastwood Trading Estate, Rotherham, S65 1SU
Tel: 01709-835566 **Fax:** 01709-835566
E-mail: suescothern@hotmail.com
Directors: A. Scothern (MD), S. Scothern (Fin)
Immediate Holding Company: KAST FABRICATIONS LTD
Registration no: 06277400 **Date established:** 2007
No.of Employees: 1 - 10 **Product Groups:** 35

Date of Accounts	Jun 11	Jun 10
Working Capital	1	1
Current Assets	1	1

KDS Civil Engineering

B2 Broad Street Parkgate, Rotherham, S62 6ES
Tel: 01709-529972 **Fax:** 01709-527274
E-mail: stephen.jeffs@btconnect.com
Website: http://www.kdsconstruction.co.uk
Product Groups: 29, 33, 51, 52, 66, 68, 80, 84

Kelvin Steels England Ltd

Sheffield Road, Rotherham, S60 1DX
Tel: 01709-362820 **Fax:** 01709-362830
E-mail: info@kelvinsteels.com
Website: http://www.kelvinsteels.com
Directors: H. Nugent (MD), W. Nugent (Co Sec)
Ultimate Holding Company: WESTSTRAND LIMITED
Immediate Holding Company: KELVIN STEELS (ENGLAND) LIMITED
Registration no: 03960782 **Date established:** 2000
No.of Employees: 11 - 20 **Product Groups:** 34, 66

Date of Accounts	Nov 11	Nov 10	Nov 09
Working Capital	1m	1m	1m
Fixed Assets	130	73	92
Current Assets	3m	2m	2m

Keyspline Engineering Ltd

Station Works Masbrough Street, Rotherham, S60 1HT
Tel: 01709-559933 **Fax:** 01709-513011
E-mail: sales@keyspline.com
Website: http://www.keyspline.com
Directors: C. Dodd (MD)
Immediate Holding Company: KEYSPLINE ENGINEERING LIMITED
Registration no: 02521006 **Date established:** 1990
No.of Employees: 11 - 20 **Product Groups:** 35, 45

Date of Accounts	May 12	May 11	May 10
Working Capital	662	362	339
Fixed Assets	633	682	554
Current Assets	934	567	482

Lantern Engineering Ltd

Hamilton Road Maltby, Rotherham, S66 7NE
Tel: 01709-813636 **Fax:** 01709-817130
E-mail: info@lantern.co.uk
Website: http://www.lantern.co.uk
Bank(s): Bank of Scotland
Directors: R. Green (MD)
Managers: M. Warren, J. Thompson
Ultimate Holding Company: KINDMARKET LIMITED
Immediate Holding Company: LANTERN ENGINEERING LIMITED
Registration no: 01985790 **VAT No.:** GB 600 2287 90
Date established: 1986 **No.of Employees:** 21 - 50 **Product Groups:** 36, 48

Date of Accounts	Jun 11	Jun 10	Jun 09
Working Capital	-622	-635	-682
Fixed Assets	563	577	607
Current Assets	1m	1m	2m

Lighting Bug Ltd

Bawtry Road Bramley, Rotherham, S66 2TW
Tel: 01709-530731 **Fax:** 01709-530657
Website: http://www.directlight.co.uk
Directors: M. Hayes (Dir)
Immediate Holding Company: LIGHTING BUG LIMITED
Registration no: 02799524 **Date established:** 1993
No.of Employees: 1 - 10 **Product Groups:** 37, 67

Date of Accounts	Apr 11	Apr 10	Apr 09
Working Capital	77	114	127
Fixed Assets	31	10	12
Current Assets	212	185	194

Lilleker Bros Ltd

30 Moorgate Road, Rotherham, S60 2AG
Tel: 01709-374073 **Fax:** 01709-364517
E-mail: info@lillekerbros.com
Website: http://www.lillekerbros.com
Bank(s): Midland Bank, 35 College St, Rotherham
Directors: M. Ralton (MD), D. Atkin (Fin), D. Ede (Fin)
Ultimate Holding Company: LILLEKER BROS. LTD.
Immediate Holding Company: LILLEKER BROS. LTD.
Registration no: 02815786 **VAT No.:** GB 716 1077 55
Date established: 1993 **Turnover:** £2m - £5m **No.of Employees:** 21 - 50
Product Groups: 52

Date of Accounts	May 11	May 10	May 09
Working Capital	409	466	595
Fixed Assets	183	210	261
Current Assets	1m	818	2m

Lilleker Engineering Co. Ltd

Unit 3b Lincoln Street, Rotherham, S60 1RP
Tel: 01709-829541 **Fax:** 01709-829542
E-mail: sales@lilleker.co.uk
Website: http://www.lilleker.co.uk
Bank(s): Nat West
Directors: P. Wilson (MD)
Immediate Holding Company: LILLEKER ENGINEERING CO. LIMITED
Registration no: 01747393 **VAT No.:** GB 391 0020 95
Date established: 1983 **Turnover:** £1m - £2m **No.of Employees:** 11 - 20
Product Groups: 48

Date of Accounts	Mar 11	Mar 10	Mar 09
Working Capital	339	380	349
Fixed Assets	157	15	21
Current Assets	718	584	556

London & Scandinavian Metallurgical Co. Ltd (Analytical Services)

Fullerton Road, Rotherham, S60 1DL
Tel: 01709-828500 **Fax:** 01709-833772
E-mail: iresende@lsm.co.uk
Website: http://www.lsm.co.uk
Bank(s): Barclays
Directors: D. Beare (Co Sec), I. Resende (MD), J. Hamer (Fin)
Managers: C. Ions (Personnel), K. Jaques (Tech Serv Mgr), M. Giovanardi (Purch Mgr), L. Thompson (Mktg Serv Mgr)
Ultimate Holding Company: AMG ADVANCED METALLURGICAL GROUP (NETHERLANDS)
Immediate Holding Company: LONDON & SCANDINAVIAN METALLURGICAL CO LIMITED
Registration no: 00345279 **Date established:** 1938
Turnover: £125m - £250m **No.of Employees:** 251 - 500
Product Groups: 85

Lureflash International

Chesterton Road Eastwood Trading Estate, Rotherham, S65 1SU
Tel: 01709-724700 **Fax:** 01709-724701
E-mail: sales@lureflash.co.uk
Website: http://www.lureflash.co.uk
Bank(s): Bank of Scotland
Directors: S. Gross (MD)
Managers: P. Hegarty
Immediate Holding Company: LUREFLASH INTERNATIONAL LIMITED
Registration no: 02641312 **VAT No.:** GB 436 5871 25
Date established: 1991 **Turnover:** £2m - £5m **No.of Employees:** 21 - 50
Product Groups: 23, 35, 49, 65

Date of Accounts	Dec 11	Dec 10	Dec 09
Working Capital	348	46	79
Fixed Assets	180	262	362
Current Assets	2m	2m	1m

MAN Hydraulics & Engineering Ltd

Unit 9 Thurnscoe Business Centre Princess Drive, Thurnscoe, Rotherham, S63 0BL
Tel: 01709-880520 **Fax:** 05601-165945
E-mail: manhydeng@yahoo.co.uk
Website: http://www.man-hydraulics.co.uk
Directors: S. Malkin (Dir)
Immediate Holding Company: MAN HYDRAULICS & ENGINEERING LIMITED
Registration no: 05315204 **Date established:** 2004
Turnover: Up to £250,000 **No.of Employees:** 1 - 10 **Product Groups:** 40

Date of Accounts	Mar 11	Mar 10	Mar 09
Working Capital	22	39	31
Fixed Assets	2	2	3
Current Assets	40	50	36
Current Liabilities	15	N/A	N/A

Marsden Weighing Machine Group Ltd
Unit 7 Centurion Business Park Bessemer Way, Rotherham, S60 1FB
Tel: 01709-364296 **Fax:** 01709-364293
E-mail: service@marsdengroup.co.uk
Website: http://www.marsden-weighing.co.uk
Directors: M. Coates (Fab), K. Williamson (Sales)
Ultimate Holding Company: MARSDEN GROUP HOLDINGS LIMITED
Immediate Holding Company: MARSDEN WEIGHING MACHINE GROUP LIMITED
Registration no: 01014815 **Date established:** 1971
No.of Employees: 21 - 50 **Product Groups:** 38, 67

Date of Accounts	Dec 11	Dec 10	Dec 09
Working Capital	2m	1m	1m
Fixed Assets	230	154	105
Current Assets	2m	2m	2m

Newburgh Engineering Co. Ltd (T/A Newgurgh Pelleting Solutions)
Centurion Business Park Bessemer Way, Rotherham, S60 1FB
Tel: 01709-724260 **Fax:** 01709-839312
E-mail: vincent.middleton@newburgh.co.uk
Website: http://www.newburgh.co.uk
Bank(s): Barclays
Directors: C. Gibson (Co Sec), V. Middleton (MD)
Managers: A. Wood (Purch Mgr), D. Crookes, M. Jewitt (Comm)
Immediate Holding Company: NEWBURGH ENGINEERING CO LIMITED
Registration no: 00371040 **VAT No.:** GB 308 4518 63
Date established: 1941 **Turnover:** £10m - £20m
No.of Employees: 101 - 250 **Product Groups:** 45

Date of Accounts	Mar 11	Mar 10	Mar 09
Sales Turnover	11m	9m	N/A
Pre Tax Profit/Loss	642	-8	662
Working Capital	278	353	946
Fixed Assets	7m	7m	8m
Current Assets	4m	4m	3m
Current Liabilities	707	391	611

Nicotra-Gebhardt Ltd
Unit D Parkgate Business Park Rail Mill Way, Parkgate, Rotherham, S62 6JQ
Tel: 01709-780760 **Fax:** 01732-866370
E-mail: info@kiloheat.co.uk
Website: http://www.nicotra-gebhardt.com
Managers: M. Bowley (Chief Mgr)
Ultimate Holding Company: NICOTRA SPA (ITALY)
Immediate Holding Company: NICOTRA GEBHARDT LTD.
Registration no: 00611342 **VAT No.:** GB 205 7122 02
Date established: 1958 **Turnover:** £2m - £5m **No.of Employees:** 1 - 10
Product Groups: 40, 48

Date of Accounts	Dec 11	Dec 10	Dec 09
Sales Turnover	3m	N/A	N/A
Pre Tax Profit/Loss	-54	N/A	N/A
Working Capital	763	-168	-121
Fixed Assets	300	N/A	N/A
Current Assets	1m	197	182
Current Liabilities	51	88	44

Nikken UK Ltd
Precision House Mangham Way, Rotherham, S61 4RL
Tel: 01709-366306 **Fax:** 01709-376683
E-mail: info@nikken-world.com
Website: http://www.nikken-world.com
Bank(s): National Westminster Bank Plc
Directors: A. Bowkett (Dir)
Managers: R. Allison (Chief Acct), T. Moore (Purch Mgr), S. Eckersall (Mktg Serv Mgr), R. Allison (Chief Acct), J. Healey (Tech Serv Mgr), J. Healey (I.T. Exec), R. Prior (Mktg Serv Mgr)
Immediate Holding Company: NIKKEN KOSAKUSHO EUROPE LIMITED
Registration no: 02312143 **VAT No.:** GB 509 3064 59
Date established: 1988 **Turnover:** £10m - £20m
No.of Employees: 21 - 50 **Product Groups:** 36, 46

Date of Accounts	Dec 10	Dec 09	Dec 08
Sales Turnover	13m	9m	18m
Pre Tax Profit/Loss	-157	-982	-95
Working Capital	4m	4m	4m
Fixed Assets	2m	2m	2m
Current Assets	11m	7m	15m
Current Liabilities	5m	2m	8m

Northern Protection
Unit S 7Palmers Yard Old Doncaster Road, Wath-upon-Dearne, Rotherham, S63 7EU
Tel: 0844-3511 257 **Fax:** 0844-3576656
E-mail: admin@northernprotection.me.uk
Website: http://www.northernprotection.co.uk
Directors: D. Cort (MD)
Managers: D. Court (Mgr)
Date established: 1996 **No.of Employees:** 1 - 10 **Product Groups:** 40, 67, 81

P J O Industrial Ltd
Commercial Road Goldthorpe Industrial Estate, Goldthorpe, Rotherham, S63 9BL
Tel: 01709-890102 **Fax:** 01709-894505
E-mail: sales@pjoindustrial.co.uk
Website: http://www.pjoindustrial.co.uk
Directors: J. O'grady (MD), J. O'grady (MD)
Ultimate Holding Company: MECHAN CONTROLS PLC
Immediate Holding Company: PJO INDUSTRIAL LIMITED
Registration no: 04720375 **VAT No.:** GB 590 9244 18
Date established: 2003 **Turnover:** £1m - £2m **No.of Employees:** 11 - 20
Product Groups: 51, 52, 54

Date of Accounts	Dec 11	Dec 10	Dec 09
Sales Turnover	N/A	1m	1m
Pre Tax Profit/Loss	N/A	93	141
Working Capital	308	151	130
Fixed Assets	169	184	146
Current Assets	553	448	455
Current Liabilities	55	91	135

P R Services
Unit 5 Sycamore Centre Sycamore Road, Eastwood Trading Estate, Rotherham, S65 1EN
Tel: 01709-360099 **Fax:** 01709-360089
E-mail: info@prservicesonline.co.uk
Website: http://www.prservicesonline.co.uk
Directors: N. Redfern (Ptnr)
Registration no: 06446851 **Date established:** 2007
No.of Employees: 1 - 10 **Product Groups:** 39, 45

Parkway Sheet Metal Works Ltd
Rawmarsh Road, Rotherham, S60 1RZ
Tel: 01709-374726 **Fax:** 01709-829739
Directors: B. Buckley (Fin), P. Buckley (MD)
Immediate Holding Company: PARKWAY SHEET METAL WORKS LIMITED
Registration no: 01775514 **VAT No.:** 173 7119 59 **Date established:** 1983
Turnover: £500,000 - £1m **No.of Employees:** 1 - 10 **Product Groups:** 48

Date of Accounts	Sep 11	Sep 10	Sep 09
Working Capital	5	-9	12
Fixed Assets	22	34	45
Current Assets	178	126	114

Pelican School Of Motoring
7 West Hall Fold Wentworth, Rotherham, S62 7TJ
Tel: 01226-742950 **Fax:** 01226-749205
E-mail: info@pelicandriving.com
Website: http://www.pelicandriving.com
Directors: C. Bailey (Prop), M. Bailey (Prop)
Date established: 1994 **Turnover:** Up to £250,000
No.of Employees: 11 - 20 **Product Groups:** 86

Plasflow Ltd Pipework Systems Stockists
Canklow Meadows Industrial Estate West Bawtry Road, Rotherham, S60 2XL
Tel: 01709-786970 **Fax:** 01709-378970
E-mail: info@plasflow.co.uk
Website: http://www.plasflow.com
Directors: A. Smith (MD)
Ultimate Holding Company: BERNDORF AKTIENGESELLSCHAFT (AUSTRIA)
Immediate Holding Company: PALOGISTICS LIMITED
Registration no: 04934332 **Date established:** 2003
Turnover: £500,000 - £1m **No.of Employees:** 11 - 20
Product Groups: 30, 35, 36, 41, 42, 48, 66

PLB Industrial Doors
8 Stamford Road, Rotherham, S66 3YY
Tel: 01709-700234 **Fax:** 0560-209 4812
E-mail: info@plb-doors.co.uk
Website: http://www.plb-doors.co.uk
Directors: P. Betcher (Prop), P. Wodger (Prop)
Registration no: 05965462 **Date established:** 2006
No.of Employees: 1 - 10 **Product Groups:** 26, 35

Pointer Pet Products
Unit E Chesterton Business Centre Chesterton Court, Eastwood Trading Estate, Rotherham, S65 1SJ
Tel: 01709-820569 **Fax:** 01709-837415
E-mail: office@pointerpetfoods.co.uk
Website: http://www.pointerpetfoods.co.uk
Bank(s): Royal Bank of Scotland
Directors: N. Whitley (MD)
Managers: M. Jones (Comptroller), A. Child (Sales & Mktg Mg), T. Haigh (Buyer), V. Hall
Immediate Holding Company: POINTER PET FOODS LIMITED
Registration no: 00622298 **VAT No.:** GB 172 5532 67
Date established: 1959 **Turnover:** £2m - £5m **No.of Employees:** 21 - 50
Product Groups: 20

Date of Accounts	Dec 07	Dec 06	Dec 05
Working Capital	-962	-403	-98
Fixed Assets	1m	1m	1m
Current Assets	2m	1m	1m

Pressure Design Hydraulics Ltd
Commercial Road Goldthorpe, Rotherham, S63 9BL
Tel: 01709-897121 **Fax:** 01709-895305
E-mail: sales@pressuredesign.co.uk
Website: http://www.pressuredesign.co.uk
Bank(s): National Westminster Bank Plc
Directors: A. Grundy (MD)
Ultimate Holding Company: PRESSURE DESIGN & ENGINEERING LIMITED
Immediate Holding Company: PRESSURE DESIGN HYDRAULICS LIMITED
Registration no: 02939483 **VAT No.:** GB 656 2199 16
Date established: 1994 **Turnover:** £2m - £5m **No.of Employees:** 21 - 50
Product Groups: 36, 38, 39, 40, 41, 42, 43, 44, 45, 46, 47, 48, 67, 84

Date of Accounts	Aug 11	Aug 10	Aug 09
Working Capital	634	555	512
Current Assets	2m	1m	992

Prospec International Ltd
Cranklow Meadows Industrial Estate, Rotherham, S60 2XL
Tel: 01709-377147 **Fax:** 01709-375239
E-mail: mailbox@prospec.co.uk
Website: http://www.prospec.co.uk
Bank(s): HSBC Bank plc
Directors: R. Mitchell (Dir)
Managers: J. Watkin (Fin Mgr), J. Pearson (Sales & Mktg Mg), I. Holsworth (Purch Mgr), C. Senton (Tech Serv Mgr)
Ultimate Holding Company: PROSPEC LTD.
Immediate Holding Company: PROSPEC LTD.
Registration no: 01311949 **VAT No.:** GB 646 4162 36
Date established: 1977 **Turnover:** £5m - £10m
No.of Employees: 51 - 100 **Product Groups:** 26

Date of Accounts	Dec 11	Dec 10	Dec 09
Sales Turnover	9m	7m	9m
Pre Tax Profit/Loss	469	239	604
Working Capital	2m	2m	2m
Fixed Assets	142	154	138
Current Assets	4m	4m	4m
Current Liabilities	643	563	584

Purex International Ltd
Purex House Farfield Park, Manvers, Rotherham, S63 5DB
Tel: 01709-763000 **Fax:** 01709-763001
E-mail: philip-mullins@purexltd.co.uk
Website: http://www.purex.co.uk
Directors: J. Hodgson (Comm), J. Mullins (Fin)
Managers: A. Easey (Chief Mgr), J. Young (Mktg Serv Mgr), J. Young (Sales & Mktg Mg)
Ultimate Holding Company: DOMINO PRINTING SCIENCES PUBLIC LIMITED COMPANY
Immediate Holding Company: PUREX INTERNATIONAL LIMITED
Registration no: 05136616 **VAT No.:** GB 395 4675 02
Date established: 2004 **Turnover:** £5m - £10m **No.of Employees:** 21 - 50
Product Groups: 40, 52, 54

Date of Accounts	Oct 11	Oct 10	Oct 09
Sales Turnover	6m	6m	6m
Pre Tax Profit/Loss	-510	30	614

Working Capital	2m	1m	1m
Fixed Assets	3m	4m	4m
Current Assets	4m	3m	2m
Current Liabilities	240	211	233

Qualconvey Ltd
76 Station Road Bolton Upon Dearne, Bolton-Upon-Dearne, Rotherham, S63 8AD
Tel: 01709-881490
Website: http://www.qualconvey.com
Directors: D. Dooley (Fin), G. Dooley (MD)
Immediate Holding Company: QUALCONVEY LIMITED
Registration no: 03206655 **Date established:** 1996
No.of Employees: 1 - 10 **Product Groups:** 45, 83

Quality Heat Treatments Ltd
Chesterton Way Eastwood Trading Estate, Rotherham, S65 1ST
Tel: 01709-379188 **Fax:** 01709-829849
E-mail: j.mcconaghy@qhtltd.com
Website: http://www.qhtltd.com
Managers: L. Moss
Immediate Holding Company: QUALITY HEAT TREATMENTS LIMITED
Registration no: 00828842 **Date established:** 1964
No.of Employees: 11 - 20 **Product Groups:** 46, 48

Date of Accounts	Sep 11	Sep 10	Sep 09
Working Capital	455	364	271
Fixed Assets	1m	1m	1m
Current Assets	1m	743	684

R J D Engineering Co. (t/a R J D Engineering Co)
Hellaby Industrial Estate Hellaby Lane, Hellaby, Rotherham, S66 8HN
Tel: 01709-531951 **Fax:** 01709-700252
E-mail: info@rjd-eng.com
Website: http://www.rjd-eng.com
Bank(s): National Westminster Bank Plc
Directors: M. Howard (MD)
Ultimate Holding Company: GEO. ROBSON & CO. (CONVEYORS) LIMITED
Immediate Holding Company: R.J.D.FABRICATIONS LIMITED
Registration no: 00946783 **VAT No.:** GB 125 4889 48
Date established: 1969 **Turnover:** £5m - £10m **No.of Employees:** 21 - 50
Product Groups: 26, 35, 36, 39, 40, 45, 46, 48

Date of Accounts	Jun 11	Jun 10	Jun 09
Sales Turnover	7m	7m	7m
Pre Tax Profit/Loss	-220	916	283
Working Capital	4m	4m	4m
Fixed Assets	387	308	292
Current Assets	5m	6m	5m
Current Liabilities	488	521	415

Richard Fletcher Associates
Common Lane Wath-Upon-Dearne, Rotherham, S63 7DX
Tel: 01709-877271 **Fax:** 01709-871304
E-mail: richard@qty-surveyor.com
Website: http://www.qty-surveyor.com
Directors: R. Fletcher (Tech Serv)
Immediate Holding Company: RICHARD FLETCHER ASSOCIATES LIMITED
Registration no: 06007705 **Date established:** 2006
No.of Employees: 1 - 10 **Product Groups:** 84

Date of Accounts	Apr 10	Apr 09	Apr 08
Working Capital	-1	3	9
Fixed Assets	9	10	1
Current Assets	49	49	42

C Roberts Steel Services Ltd (Part of Barrett Steel Group)
Eastwood Trading Estate, Rotherham, S65 1SU
Tel: 01709-789200 **Fax:** 01709-828429
E-mail: sales@c-roberts-steel.co.uk
Website: http://www.steelweb.co.uk
Bank(s): HSBC Bank plc
Directors: J. Childs (Dir), R. Watson (Sales)
Managers: T. Barrett
Ultimate Holding Company: BARRETT STEEL LIMITED
Immediate Holding Company: C. ROBERTS STEEL SERVICES LIMITED
Registration no: 03027501 **VAT No.:** GB 616 9866 93
Date established: 1995 **Turnover:** £10m - £20m
No.of Employees: 51 - 100 **Product Groups:** 34, 35

Date of Accounts	Sep 08
Working Capital	1
Current Assets	1

Rosebys
Rosedale House Bramley Way, Hellaby, Rotherham, S66 8QB
Tel: 01709-800800 **Fax:** 01709-532273
Website: http://www.rosebys.com
Directors: J. Daral (Co Sec), R. Jalan (Dir)
Immediate Holding Company: The Furnishings Place Ltd
Registration no: 00984968 **VAT No.:** GB 599 9544 49
Date established: 2004 **Turnover:** £1m - £2m
No.of Employees: 1501 & over **Product Groups:** 61

Rotherham Stainless & Nickel Alloys Ltd
Northfield Road, Rotherham, S60 1RR
Tel: 01709-828055 **Fax:** 01709-829716
Bank(s): National Westminster, Rotherham
Directors: K. Booth (Co Sec), K. Booth (Ch), C. Booth (MD)
Managers: D. Pearce (Chief Mgr)
Immediate Holding Company: ROTHERHAM STAINLESS & NICKEL ALLOYS LIMITED
Registration no: 00928334 **Date established:** 1968 **Turnover:** £1m - £2m
No.of Employees: 11 - 20 **Product Groups:** 34

Date of Accounts	Mar 08	Mar 07	Mar 06
Sales Turnover	2329	1834	2154
Pre Tax Profit/Loss	171	146	145
Working Capital	1463	1793	1690
Fixed Assets	121	65	66
Current Assets	2258	2574	2173
Current Liabilities	796	781	483
Total Share Capital	100	100	100
ROCE% (Return on Capital Employed)	10.8	7.9	8.3
ROT% (Return on Turnover)	7.3	8.0	6.7

R S Y Air Conditioning Ltd

Cross Street Parkgate, Rotherham, S62 6FT
Tel: 01709-553355 **Fax:** 01709-740814
E-mail: info@rsyairconditioning.co.uk
Website: http://www.rsyairconditioning.co.uk
Bank(s): Midland
Directors: P. Daley (Fin)
Managers: L. Saville (Tech Sales Mgr)
Ultimate Holding Company: GASPER HOLDINGS LIMITED
Immediate Holding Company: RSY (AIR CONDITIONING) LIMITED
Registration no: 01853482 **VAT No.:** GB 501 0226 25
Date established: 1984 **Turnover:** £1m - £2m **No.of Employees:** 11 - 20
Product Groups: 40, 52

Date of Accounts	Apr 12	Apr 11	Apr 10
Working Capital	1m	1m	1m
Fixed Assets	123	65	98
Current Assets	2m	2m	1m

E Russum & Sons Ltd

Edward House Tenter Street, Rotherham, S60 1LB
Tel: 01709-365005 **Fax:** 01709-829982
E-mail: info@russums.co.uk
Website: http://www.russum.co.uk
Bank(s): The Royal Bank of Scotland
Directors: P. Russum (Prop)
Managers: J. Marsden (Mktg Serv Mgr), R. Russum (Comm)
Immediate Holding Company: E.RUSSUM & SONS,LIMITED
Registration no: 00091335 **VAT No.:** GB 172 3311 93
Date established: 2006 **Turnover:** £1m - £2m **No.of Employees:** 21 - 50
Product Groups: 24, 36, 67

Date of Accounts	Dec 11	Dec 10	Dec 09
Working Capital	1m	993	764
Fixed Assets	939	992	1m
Current Assets	2m	2m	2m

Russums

Edward House Tenter Street, Rotherham, S60 1LB
Tel: 01709-372345 **Fax:** 01709-829982
E-mail: info@russums.co.uk
Website: http://www.russums.co.uk
Directors: R. Russum (MD)
Managers: J. Marsden (Sales Prom Mgr), C. Coyne (Buyer)
Ultimate Holding Company: E.RUSSUM & SONS,LIMITED
Immediate Holding Company: E.RUSSUM & SONS,LIMITED
Registration no: 00091335 **Date established:** 2006 **Turnover:** £1m - £2m
No.of Employees: 21 - 50 **Product Groups:** 22, 23, 24, 26, 27, 30, 32, 33, 34, 35, 36, 37, 38, 39, 40, 41, 42, 45, 48, 49, 63, 64, 66, 67, 69, 83

Date of Accounts	Dec 11	Dec 10	Dec 09
Working Capital	1m	993	764
Fixed Assets	939	992	1m
Current Assets	2m	2m	2m

S H S Freight Services Ltd

Unit 20 Riverside Development Chesterton Road, Eastwood Trading Estate, Rotherham, S65 1SU
Tel: 01709-377071 **Fax:** 01709-820959
E-mail: lucy.barber@shsfreight.co.uk
Website: http://www.shsfreight.co.uk
Directors: L. Barber (Fin)
Ultimate Holding Company: HS (552) LIMITED
Immediate Holding Company: S.H.S. FREIGHT SERVICES LIMITED
Registration no: 02496507 **VAT No.:** GB 534 0060 91
Date established: 1990 **Turnover:** £500,000 - £1m
No.of Employees: 1 - 10 **Product Groups:** 72, 74, 77

Date of Accounts	Dec 11	Dec 10	Dec 09
Working Capital	1m	1m	997
Fixed Assets	2m	2m	2m
Current Assets	1m	1m	1m

S P I Developments Ltd

Unit 8a Braithwell Way Hellaby Industrial Estate, Hellaby, Rotherham, S66 8QY
Tel: 01709-541143
E-mail: enquiries@spidevelopments.com
Website: http://www.spidevelopments.com
Directors: P. Leverick (Ch)
Immediate Holding Company: S.P.I. DEVELOPMENTS LIMITED
Registration no: 04532216 **Date established:** 2002
No.of Employees: 11 - 20 **Product Groups:** 37, 41, 42

Date of Accounts	Mar 11	Mar 10	Mar 09
Working Capital	224	139	73
Fixed Assets	60	67	71
Current Assets	532	352	428
Current Liabilities	N/A	32	N/A

S W P Welded Products Ltd

Old Doncaster Road Wath-upon-Dearne, Rotherham, S63 7EU
Tel: 01709-761200 **Fax:** 01709-761201
E-mail: bobbeaumont.swp@dsl.pipex.com
Directors: R. Beaumont (MD)
Turnover: £250,000 - £500,000 **No.of Employees:** 1 - 10
Product Groups: 34, 35, 36, 39, 46, 48, 49, 52, 65, 84, 85

Sanderson Group Plc

Sanderson House Poplar Way, Catcliffe, Rotherham, S60 5TR
Tel: 01709-787 787 **Fax:** 01709-787788
E-mail: info@sanderson.com
Website: http://www.sanderson.com
Bank(s): The Royal Bank of Scotland
Directors: C. Winn (Ch), D. O'Byrne (Dir)
Managers: P. Weir (Mgr), H. Billingham (Mktg Serv Mgr), J. Plant (Purch Mgr), S. Rutherford (Sec)
Ultimate Holding Company: Sandsenor Limited
Immediate Holding Company: Sanderson Group Limited
Registration no: 04968444 **Turnover:** £50m - £75m
No.of Employees: 51 - 100 **Product Groups:** 44, 80, 84

Sheffield Bolt & Nut Co. Ltd

Unit G Meadow Bank Industrial Estate Harrison Street, Rotherham, S61 1EE
Tel: 01709-550101 **Fax:** 01709-550176
E-mail: sales.sbn@btconnect.com
Directors: A. Sylvester (MD)
Ultimate Holding Company: JOHN SYLVESTER ENGINEERING COMPANY LIMITED
Immediate Holding Company: SHEFFIELD BOLT & NUT CO. LIMITED
Registration no: 01547040 **VAT No.:** GB 179 9987 61
Date established: 1981 **Turnover:** £1m - £2m **No.of Employees:** 1 - 10
Product Groups: 66

Date of Accounts	Mar 12	Mar 11	Mar 10
Working Capital	164	162	227
Fixed Assets	40	40	17
Current Assets	408	424	421

Special Alloys Northern Ltd

PO Box 1, Rotherham, S60 1RW
Tel: 01709-828333 **Fax:** 01709-829915
E-mail: nickeightyatspecialalloys@fsmail.net
Website: http://www.specialalloys.co.uk
Directors: N. Ackroyd (MD)
Ultimate Holding Company: SPECIAL ALLOYS HOLDINGS LIMITED
Immediate Holding Company: SPECIAL ALLOYS (NORTHERN) LIMITED
Registration no: 01025830 **Date established:** 1971 **Turnover:** £2m - £5m
No.of Employees: 1 - 10 **Product Groups:** 34, 66

Date of Accounts	Dec 11	Dec 10	Dec 09
Sales Turnover	4m	3m	3m
Pre Tax Profit/Loss	177	113	97
Working Capital	309	239	356
Fixed Assets	35	45	37
Current Assets	2m	1m	1m
Current Liabilities	89	59	30

Special Metals Supplies

Unit C3 The Poplars Business Park Poplar Way Catcliffe, Rotherham, S60 5PZ
Tel: 01709-363633 **Fax:** 01709-374341
Website: http://www.specialmetalssupplies.co.uk
Managers: A. Booth (Mgr)
Registration no: 04889711 **Date established:** 2004
No.of Employees: 1 - 10 **Product Groups:** 35

Stafforce

Reginald Arthur House 2-8 Percy Street, Rotherham, S65 1ED
Tel: 01709-370000 **Fax:** 01709-370037
E-mail: info@stafforce.co.uk
Website: http://www.stafforce.co.uk
Bank(s): HSBC
Directors: N. Cragg (Ch), B. Allen (Fin)
Managers: J. Kemp, C. Myres (Commun Mgr), S. Holbrook, I. Anderson
Ultimate Holding Company: NICHOLAS ASSOCIATES LIMITED
Immediate Holding Company: CRA-CRO TECHNICAL SERVICES LIMITED
Registration no: 01336278 **VAT No.:** GB 646 3511 42
Date established: 1977 **Turnover:** £20m - £50m
No.of Employees: 101 - 250 **Product Groups:** 80

Date of Accounts	Dec 11	Dec 10	Dec 09
Working Capital	125	125	125
Current Assets	125	125	125

Staniforth H K B

Chesterton Road Eastwood Trading Estate, Rotherham, S65 1SU
Tel: 01709-789229 **Fax:** 01709-789228
E-mail: sales@staniforth-hkb-steel.co.uk
Website: http://www.staniforth-hkb-steel.co.uk
Directors: A. Warcup (Fin), J. Barrett (Sales), J. Childs (MD)
Ultimate Holding Company: BARRETT STEEL LIMITED
Immediate Holding Company: HKB STEEL SERVICES LIMITED
Registration no: 04028042 **Date established:** 2000
Turnover: £10m - £20m **No.of Employees:** 21 - 50 **Product Groups:** 34, 36, 48, 66

Date of Accounts	Sep 08	Sep 07
Sales Turnover	15m	15m
Working Capital	1	1
Current Assets	1	1

Struers Ltd

Unit 11 Whittle Way, Catcliffe, Rotherham, S60 5BL
Tel: 08456-046664 **Fax:** 0845-604 6651
E-mail: info@struers.co.uk
Website: http://www.struers.com
Directors: L. Cobb (MD)
Ultimate Holding Company: ROPER INDUSTRIES INC (USA)
Immediate Holding Company: STRUERS LIMITED
Registration no: 01895693 **Date established:** 1985 **Turnover:** £2m - £5m
No.of Employees: 11 - 20 **Product Groups:** 38, 86

Date of Accounts	Dec 11	Dec 10	Dec 09
Sales Turnover	3m	3m	2m
Pre Tax Profit/Loss	195	83	35
Working Capital	236	123	139
Fixed Assets	390	375	291
Current Assets	1m	2m	1m
Current Liabilities	320	220	129

Sumo IT

35 Brunswick Street Thurnscoe, Rotherham, S63 0HU
Tel: 07507-445855
E-mail: info@sumoit.co.uk
Website: http://www.sumoit.co.uk
Directors: S. Thompson (Prop)
Date established: 2010 **Turnover:** **No.of Employees:** 1 - 10
Product Groups: 44, 48, 79, 80, 86

Tarmac Ltd

Blyth Road Maltby, Rotherham, S66 8HX
Tel: 01709-817665 **Fax:** 01709-818867
E-mail: geoffvarney@tarmac.co.uk
Website: http://www.tarmac.co.uk
Directors: P. Fleetham (MD)
Managers: G. Varney (Chief Mgr), I. Olleremshaw (Chief Acct)
Ultimate Holding Company: Anglo American plc
Immediate Holding Company: TARMAC LIMITED
Registration no: 00453791 **Date established:** 1948
No.of Employees: 51 - 100 **Product Groups:** 31

Tech Spray-Limited

Unit 2B Waddington Way Aldwarke Wharf Business Park, Rotherham, S65 3SH
Tel: 01709-915040 **Fax:** 01709-541594
E-mail: adam@tech-spray.com
Website: http://www.tech-spray.com
Turnover: Up to £250,000 **Product Groups:** 22, 23, 25, 26, 30, 32, 33, 35, 37, 38, 39, 40, 42, 46, 48, 49, 52, 66

Date of Accounts	Mar 09
Working Capital	-79
Fixed Assets	50
Current Assets	257

Technical Cranes Ltd

Holmes Lock Works Steel Street, Rotherham, S61 1DF
Tel: 01709-561861 **Fax:** 01709-556516
E-mail: info@technicalcranes.co.uk
Website: http://www.technicalcranes.co.uk
Directors: K. Simpson (Fin), J. Simpson (Dir)
Immediate Holding Company: TECHNICAL CRANES LIMITED
Registration no: 01552256 **VAT No.:** GB 308 5931 50
Date established: 1981 **Turnover:** £1m - £2m **No.of Employees:** 21 - 50
Product Groups: 48

Date of Accounts	Mar 12	Mar 11	Mar 10
Working Capital	-64	-124	-67
Fixed Assets	2m	2m	1m
Current Assets	981	651	587

Tek Machinery Ltd

9 Stadium Court Barbot Hall Industrial Estate, Parkgate, Rotherham, S62 6EW
Tel: 01709-820820 **Fax:** 01709-382504
E-mail: sales@tekmachinery.co.uk
Website: http://www.tekmachinery.co.uk
Directors: I. Claridge (Fin), J. Baxter (Tech Serv), J. Baxter (Dir), M. Claridge (MD), H. Claridge (Fin)
Immediate Holding Company: TEK MACHINERY LIMITED
Registration no: 01612924 **VAT No.:** GB 308 7719 38
Date established: 1982 **Turnover:** £1m - £2m **No.of Employees:** 1 - 10
Product Groups: 30, 40, 42

Date of Accounts	Dec 07	Dec 06	Dec 05
Working Capital	67	101	70
Fixed Assets	30	17	25
Current Assets	231	539	286
Current Liabilities	164	438	216

Thornhill Electrical & Mechanical Service

41-43 Holm Flatt Street Parkgate, Rotherham, S62 6HJ
Tel: 01709-528033 **Fax:** 01709-528034
E-mail: kkbroadhead@tiscali.co.uk
Directors: K. Broadhead (Ptnr)
Immediate Holding Company: THORNHILL SALES LTD
Registration no: 03557759 **VAT No.:** GB 391 0088 61
Turnover: £500,000 - £1m **No.of Employees:** 1 - 10 **Product Groups:** 48, 52

Traffic Systems Co-Operative Ltd

Unit 10 Stadium Court, Parkgate, Rotherham, S62 6EW
Tel: 01709-362855 **Fax:** 01709-360007
E-mail: jilliankelly@trafficsystems.co.uk
Website: http://www.trafficsystems.co.uk
Directors: H. Wright (Co Sec), A. Winkley (Ch)
Managers: G. Kelly (Comptroller), G. Kelly (Chief Mgr), A. Beedham (Mgr), A. Webster
Registration no: 00023633 **VAT No.:** GB 308 7892 24
Date established: 1982 **Turnover:** £2m - £5m **No.of Employees:** 51 - 100
Product Groups: 39

Transform Leather Interior Specialists Ltd

Unit 1 Wortley Road, Rotherham, S61 1LZ
Tel: 01709-857160
E-mail: craig.simnett@transformleather.co.uk
Website: http://www.transformleather.com
Directors: C. Simnett (MD)
Immediate Holding Company: TRANSFORM (LEATHER INTERIOR SPECIALISTS) LIMITED
Registration no: 04068292 **Date established:** 2000
No.of Employees: 11 - 20 **Product Groups:** 22, 23, 24

Date of Accounts	Dec 11	Dec 10	Dec 09
Working Capital	307	365	345
Fixed Assets	31	24	38
Current Assets	407	544	530

Trelleborg Sealing Solutions

Dodds Close, Rotherham, S60 1BX
Tel: 01709-789800 **Fax:** 01709-374819
E-mail: barry.davies@trelleborg.com
Website: http://www.trelleborg.com
Managers: B. Davies (Chief Mgr), M. Naylor (Comptroller), P. Benford (Sales Prom Mgr), P. Wright (Tech Serv Mgr)
Registration no: 00446036 **No.of Employees:** 101 - 250
Product Groups: 30, 35, 66

Wath Rubber & Plastics Ltd

Pump House Station Road, Wath-upon-Dearne, Rotherham, S63 7DQ
Tel: 01709-876900 **Fax:** 01709-877998
E-mail: info@wath.co.uk
Website: http://www.wath.co.uk
Bank(s): Barclays
Directors: L. Bedford (Dir), J. Bedford (Dir)
Immediate Holding Company: WATH RUBBER & PLASTICS LIMITED
Registration no: 01499568 **VAT No.:** GB 334 4865 45
Date established: 1980 **Turnover:** £2m - £5m **No.of Employees:** 21 - 50
Product Groups: 29, 37, 45

Date of Accounts	Jun 11	Jun 10	Jun 09
Working Capital	331	348	374
Fixed Assets	292	289	293
Current Assets	1m	999	1m

Welding Plant Repair Ltd

Old Hague Works Westfield Road, Parkgate, Rotherham, S62 6HD
Tel: 01709-710470
E-mail: wpr@oldhaguewks.fsnet.co.uk
Website: http://www.oldhaguewks.fsnet.co.uk
Directors: J. McHale (MD), C. Rowe (Fin)
Immediate Holding Company: WELDING PLANT REPAIRS LIMITED
Registration no: 01725999 **Date established:** 1983
Turnover: £500,000 - £1m **No.of Employees:** 11 - 20 **Product Groups:** 46

Date of Accounts	Jul 09	Jul 08	Jul 07
Sales Turnover	661	820	730
Pre Tax Profit/Loss	8	23	22
Working Capital	14	20	30
Fixed Assets	20	29	21
Current Assets	189	307	246
Current Liabilities	21	37	21

Wilfab UK Repair Services

Unit 2 Holmes Lane, Rotherham, S61 1AZ
Tel: 01709-553132 **Fax:** 01709-553132
Directors: M. Willey (Prop)
Date established: 1979 **No.of Employees:** 1 - 10 **Product Groups:** 35

Xiang Trading Ltd

18a Kilnhurst Road Rawmarsh, Rotherham, S62 5NE
Tel: 01709-523797 **Fax:** 01709-523906
E-mail: brett@xiangtrading.com
Website: http://www.xiangtrading.com

see next page

Xiang Trading Ltd - Cont'd
Directors: B. Ainsbury (Tech Serv), B. Ainsworth (MD), B. Ainsworth (Prop), A. Greaves (Tech Serv)
Managers: C. Ainsworth (I.T. Exec)
Immediate Holding Company: XIANG TRADING LIMITED
Registration no: 04360892 **Date established:** 2002
Turnover: £500,000 - £1m **No.of Employees:** 1 - 10 **Product Groups:** 14, 37, 40, 42, 46

Date of Accounts	Jun 08	Jun 07	Jun 06
Working Capital	155	138	155
Fixed Assets	10	7	4
Current Assets	201	152	195
Current Liabilities	46	13	40

Xiang Trading
Midland Road, Rotherham, S61 1SZ
Tel: 01709-557722
Directors: C. Anifworth (Prop)
No.of Employees: 1 - 10 **Product Groups:** 35, 45, 81

Yorkshire Spin Galvanising Ltd
Unit 5 Cornish Way Parkgate, Rotherham, S62 6EG
Tel: 01709-373403 **Fax:** 01709-373404
Managers: P. Wagstaff (Chief Mgr)
Immediate Holding Company: YORKSHIRE SPIN GALVANISING LIMITED
Registration no: 02729310 **Date established:** 1992
No.of Employees: 11 - 20 **Product Groups:** 46, 48

Date of Accounts	Feb 08	Aug 11	Aug 10
Working Capital	259	148	48
Fixed Assets	434	1m	1m
Current Assets	633	760	624

Yorkshire Window Co. Ltd
Hellaby Lane Hellaby, Rotherham, S66 8HN
Tel: 01709-540982 **Fax:** 01302-366684
E-mail: info@ywcgroup.co.uk
Website: http://www.ywcgroup.co.uk
Bank(s): The Royal Bank of Scotland
Directors: S. Cousins (MD)
Ultimate Holding Company: YWC GROUP LIMITED
Immediate Holding Company: YORKSHIRE WINDOW CO. LIMITED
Registration no: 01458752 **VAT No.:** GB 308 4610 75
Date established: 1979 **Turnover:** £5m - £10m
No.of Employees: 101 - 250 **Product Groups:** 30

Date of Accounts	Mar 09	Mar 08
Working Capital	12	12
Current Assets	12	12

J Youle & Co. Ltd
Chesterton Road Eastwood Trading Estate, Rotherham, S65 1SU
Tel: 01709-375349 **Fax:** 01709-363872
E-mail: chris@youleandco.co.uk
Website: http://www.youleandco.com
Bank(s): HSBC Bank plc
Directors: C. Roberts (Dir)
Immediate Holding Company: J.YOULE AND COMPANY LIMITED
Registration no: 00121288 **VAT No.:** GB 172 5886 32
Date established: 2012 **Turnover:** £250,000 - £500,000
No.of Employees: 11 - 20 **Product Groups:** 26

Date of Accounts	Dec 11	Dec 10	Dec 09
Working Capital	30	24	23
Fixed Assets	135	143	154
Current Assets	110	113	96

Sheffield

1st Dental Sheffield
51 Wisewood Road, Sheffield, S6 4TB
Tel: 0114-233 3244 **Fax:** 0114-233 3254
Website: http://www.artdental.co.uk
Managers: G. Jenkinson (Mgr)
No.of Employees: 11 - 20 **Product Groups:** 38, 67

ADT Fire & Security plc
President Buildings Savile St East, Sheffield, S4 7UQ
Tel: 0114-253 6999 **Fax:** 0114-270 6444
Website: http://www.adt.co.uk
Managers: B. Flinn (Chief Mgr), P. Laverick (Mgr)
Immediate Holding Company: Tyco Holdings (U.K.) Ltd
Registration no: 01161045 **Date established:** 2008
No.of Employees: 21 - 50 **Product Groups:** 37, 38

A I Materials
Otter Street, Sheffield, S9 3WL
Tel: 0114-243 1206 **Fax:** 0114-261 1419
E-mail: sales@ai-materials.co.uk
Website: http://www.ai-materials.co.uk
Directors: M. Burton (MD), M. Andrews (Dir)
Immediate Holding Company: AI MATERIALS LIMITED
Registration no: 02859881 **Date established:** 1993 **Turnover:** £2m - £5m
No.of Employees: 21 - 50 **Product Groups:** 34

Date of Accounts	Dec 09	Dec 08	Jan 12
Working Capital	569	487	199
Fixed Assets	59	73	N/A
Current Assets	2m	2m	1m

A K S Heat Transfer Ltd
25b Orgreave Crescent, Sheffield, S13 9NQ
Tel: 0114-269 4002 **Fax:** 0114-293 9164
E-mail: tech@aksheattransfer.com
Website: http://www.aksheattransfer.com
Directors: A. Stuart (Ptnr)
Ultimate Holding Company: JELD-WEN HOLDINGS INC (USA)
Immediate Holding Company: AKS HEAT TRANSFER LIMITED
Registration no: 07956683 **Date established:** 2012
No.of Employees: 1 - 10 **Product Groups:** 40, 48

A M K Fence-In Ltd
Wallace Road, Sheffield, S3 9SR
Tel: 0114-273 9372 **Fax:** 0114-273 9373
E-mail: amkfencing@aol.com
Website: http://www.amkfence-in.co.uk
Directors: W. Kynoch (MD)
Managers: A. Kynoch (Sales & Mktg Mg)
Immediate Holding Company: A M K FENCE-IN LIMITED
Registration no: 01548148 **Date established:** 1981
No.of Employees: 11 - 20 **Product Groups:** 35

Date of Accounts	Mar 11	Mar 10	Mar 09
Working Capital	96	89	134
Fixed Assets	135	159	199
Current Assets	435	442	463

A M Time Services
8 Ivyside Close Killamarsh, Sheffield, S21 1JT
Tel: 0114-248 5855 **Fax:** 0114-248 5855
E-mail: sales@amtime.co.uk
Website: http://www.amtime.co.uk
Directors: M. Thompson (Ptnr)
Turnover: Up to £250,000 **No.of Employees:** 1 - 10 **Product Groups:** 38, 44, 48, 49, 65, 67

A R Wentworth Sheffield Ltd
Monarch Works Catley Road, Sheffield, S9 5JF
Tel: 0114-244 7693 **Fax:** 0114-242 3159
E-mail: sales@wentworth-pewter.com
Website: http://www.wentworth-pewter.com
Directors: R. Abdy (Dir), M. Abdy (MD)
Managers: P. Simons (Prod Mgr)
Immediate Holding Company: A.R. WENTWORTH (SHEFFIELD) LIMITED
Registration no: 01687942 **VAT No.:** GB 172 8056 58
Date established: 1982 **No.of Employees:** 21 - 50 **Product Groups:** 49, 65

Date of Accounts	Dec 11	Dec 10	Dec 09
Working Capital	66	21	-21
Fixed Assets	331	361	372
Current Assets	502	409	322

A V A Cooling Systems Ltd
Unit 26 Bookers Way, Dinnington, Sheffield, S25 3SH
Tel: 01909-550944 **Fax:** 01909-568403
E-mail: stewart@ava-cooling.co.uk
Website: http://www.ava.eu
Directors: S. Inglis (Prop)
No.of Employees: 1 - 10 **Product Groups:** 36, 39, 40, 41, 68

AA Electrical Wholesalers Ltd
Unit 5 Riverside Park Sheaf Gardens, Sheffield, S2 4 BB
Tel: 0114-272 7707 **Fax:** 0114-272 7670
E-mail: aaelectrical@hotmail.com
Directors: R. Ibbotson (MD)
Immediate Holding Company: AA ELECTRICAL WHOLESALERS LIMITED
Registration no: 04158693 **Date established:** 2001 **Turnover:** £1m - £2m
No.of Employees: 1 - 10 **Product Groups:** 67

Date of Accounts	Mar 11	Mar 10	Mar 09
Sales Turnover	N/A	1m	1m
Pre Tax Profit/Loss	N/A	211	189
Working Capital	139	146	116
Fixed Assets	9	17	22
Current Assets	479	305	338
Current Liabilities	N/A	47	42

Abacon Ltd
2 Atlas Way, Sheffield, S4 7QQ
Tel: 0114-256 2266 **Fax:** 0114-256 2268
E-mail: eric@abacon.co.uk
Website: http://www.abacon.co.uk
Bank(s): Yorkshire Bank PLC
Directors: E. Goodall (Fin), J. Goodall (Sales)
Ultimate Holding Company: 02406680
Immediate Holding Company: ABACON LIMITED
Registration no: 02022555 **VAT No.:** GB 439 0446 47
Date established: 1986 **Turnover:** £1m - £2m **No.of Employees:** 11 - 20
Product Groups: 33, 36, 40

Date of Accounts	Mar 08	Mar 07	Aug 06
Working Capital	105	-44	-78
Fixed Assets	27	438	450
Current Assets	246	186	208
Current Liabilities	141	229	287

Abbey Forged Products Ltd
Beeley Wood Works Beeley Wood Lane, Sheffield, S6 1ND
Tel: 0114-231 2271 **Fax:** 0114-232 4983
E-mail: lee.thomas@abbeyfp.co.uk
Website: http://www.abbeyforgedproducts.co.uk
Bank(s): National Westminster Bank Plc
Directors: J. Neal (Prop), J. Neal (MD)
Managers: L. Thomas (Develop Mgr), M. Flounders (Mgr), H. Rowbottom (Mgr), A. Forster (I.T. Exec), J. Wildsmith (Prod Mgr), G. Watson (Tech Serv Mgr)
Immediate Holding Company: ABBEY FORGED PRODUCTS LIMITED
Registration no: 01644542 **VAT No.:** GB 172 7824 44
Date established: 1982 **Turnover:** £20m - £50m
No.of Employees: 101 - 250 **Product Groups:** 34, 36, 46, 48

Date of Accounts	Oct 11	Oct 10	Oct 09
Sales Turnover	27m	17m	16m
Pre Tax Profit/Loss	9m	2m	3m
Working Capital	9m	4m	5m
Fixed Assets	N/A	7m	6m
Current Assets	16m	10m	9m
Current Liabilities	2m	4m	2m

Abbeydale Storage
51 Springfield Road, Sheffield, S7 2GE
Tel: 0114-281 9299 **Fax:** 0114-281 9399
E-mail: sales@abbeydalestorage.co.uk
Website: http://www.abbeydalestorage.co.uk
Directors: S. Stringer (Ptnr)
Date established: 1991 **Turnover:** £500,000 - £1m
No.of Employees: 1 - 10 **Product Groups:** 26

Abel Magnets Ltd
Balaclava Road, Sheffield, S6 3BG
Tel: 0114-249 5949 **Fax:** 0114-249 5950
E-mail: info@magnetic-paper.com
Website: http://www.magnetic-paper.com
Directors: M. Brooks (MD)
Ultimate Holding Company: NUMILL ENGINEERING LIMITED
Immediate Holding Company: ABEL MAGNETS LIMITED
Registration no: 03671776 **VAT No.:** GB 716 7536 19
Date established: 1998 **No.of Employees:** 1 - 10 **Product Groups:** 22, 27, 29, 30, 34, 35, 37, 38, 47, 49, 65

Date of Accounts	Mar 11	Mar 10	Mar 09
Working Capital	969	1m	947
Fixed Assets	128	118	110
Current Assets	1m	1m	1m

Access Credit Management Limited
Suite A2 Sheffield Business Centre, Europa Link, Sheffield, S9 1XZ
Tel: 0114-249 9970 **Fax:** 0114-249 9972
E-mail: enquiry@accesscm.co.uk
Website: http://www.accesscm.co.uk
Directors: J. Cardwell (Comm), J. Flaherty (MD), S. Flaherty (Admin)
Immediate Holding Company: Access Credit Management Ltd
Registration no: 03937357 **Date established:** 2000
Turnover: £250,000 - £500,000 **No.of Employees:** 1 - 10
Product Groups: 80, 82

Date of Accounts	Mar 10	Mar 09	Mar 08
Working Capital	27	180	148
Fixed Assets	4	4	5
Current Assets	48	218	192

Acme United Europe
Estate Office Thorncliffe Park Estate Newton Chambers Road, Chapeltown, Sheffield, S35 2PH
Tel: 0114-220 3709 **Fax:** 0114-220 3706
E-mail: sales@acmeunited.co.uk
Website: http://www.acmeunitedeurope.co.uk
Directors: A. Poole (MD), P. Smeralbi (I.T. Dir)
Managers: V. Swift (Mgr), C. Hoppe (Mktg Serv Mgr)
Ultimate Holding Company: OGILVIE GROUP LIMITED
Immediate Holding Company: OGILVIE FLEET PCH LIMITED
Registration no: 03422307 **VAT No.:** GB 706 3544 47
Date established: 1989 **Turnover:** £2m - £5m **No.of Employees:** 1 - 10
Product Groups: 36

Date of Accounts	Mar 11
Working Capital	2
Current Assets	23

Active Metals
Unit F Holbrook Green Holbrook Industrial Estate, Holbrook, Sheffield, S20 3FE
Tel: 0114-247 3662 **Fax:** 0114-247 8372
E-mail: sales@activemetals.co.uk
Website: http://www.activemetals.co.uk
Directors: M. Lee (MD), R. Lee (Co Sec)
Ultimate Holding Company: M & T METALS LIMITED
Immediate Holding Company: ACTIVE METALS LIMITED
Registration no: 01810084 **VAT No.:** GB 401 6880 70
Date established: 1984 **Turnover:** £2m - £5m **No.of Employees:** 1 - 10
Product Groups: 34, 66

Date of Accounts	Jun 12	Jun 11	Jun 10
Working Capital	534	516	501
Fixed Assets	19	26	35
Current Assets	1m	1m	1m

J Adams Ltd
124 Scotland Street, Sheffield, S3 7DE
Tel: 0114-272 3612 **Fax:** 0114-275 0290
E-mail: info@sheffieldknives.co.uk
Website: http://www.sheffieldknives.co.uk
Bank(s): T.S.B.
Directors: J. Adams (MD)
Immediate Holding Company: J. ADAMS LIMITED
Registration no: 02310912 **VAT No.:** GB 172 9441 50
Date established: 1988 **Turnover:** £250,000 - £500,000
No.of Employees: 11 - 20 **Product Groups:** 36

Date of Accounts	Dec 11	Dec 10	Dec 09
Working Capital	174	214	304
Fixed Assets	182	195	156
Current Assets	297	295	348

Adelphi Translations Ltd
15 Paternoster Row The Workstation, Sheffield, S1 2BX
Tel: 0114-272 3772 **Fax:** 0114-221 0401
E-mail: info@adelphitranslations.com
Website: http://www.adelphitranslations.com
Directors: N. Sutcliffe (MD)
Immediate Holding Company: ADELPHI TRANSLATIONS LIMITED
Registration no: 06989736 **Date established:** 2009
No.of Employees: 1 - 10 **Product Groups:** 80

Date of Accounts	Nov 11	Nov 10
Working Capital	-6	-8
Fixed Assets	36	36
Current Assets	58	64

Advanced Fluid Technologies Ltd
35 Finchwell Road, Sheffield, S13 9AS
Tel: 0114-244 8560 **Fax:** 0114-248 6997
E-mail: info@advancedfluid.co.uk
Website: http://www.advancedfluid.co.uk
Managers: Y. Davis (Mgr)
Immediate Holding Company: ADVANCED FLUID TECHNOLOGIES LTD
Registration no: 04701270 **Date established:** 2003
Turnover: Up to £250,000 **No.of Employees:** 1 - 10 **Product Groups:** 36

Date of Accounts	Mar 11	Mar 09	Mar 08
Working Capital	50	49	37
Fixed Assets	4	1	2
Current Assets	85	49	83

Advanced Titanium Materials Ltd
Unit 1 Bruce Works Mowbray Street, Sheffield, S3 8EN
Tel: 0114-239 5771 **Fax:** 0114-264 4251
E-mail: sales@advancedtitaniummaterials.com
Website: http://www.advancedtitaniummaterials.com
Product Groups: 12, 31, 32, 34, 35, 36, 37, 38, 39, 40, 42, 46, 48, 66

Allpumps Ltd
448 Brightside Lane, Sheffield, S9 2SP
Tel: 0114-244 2203 **Fax:** 0114-242 5885
E-mail: sales@torrespumps.co.uk
Website: http://www.allpumps.co.uk
Directors: K. Torres (Dir)
Immediate Holding Company: ALLPUMPS LIMITED
Registration no: 02024099 **Date established:** 1986
Turnover: £250,000 - £500,000 **No.of Employees:** 1 - 10
Product Groups: 67

Date of Accounts	Mar 11	Mar 10	Mar 09
Working Capital	322	253	212
Fixed Assets	2	3	4
Current Assets	594	497	448

Allsportsawards
Unit 1 Princess Works Princess Street, Sheffield, S4 7UU
Tel: 0845-6018370 **Fax:** 0845-6018369
E-mail: sales@allsportsawards.com
Website: http://www.allsportsawards.co.uk
Managers: E. Sommerville (Chief Mgr)
Registration no: 07527052 **Date established:** 1977
Turnover: £250,000 - £500,000 **No.of Employees:** 1 - 10
Product Groups: 33, 49, 65

Amefa
15 Orgreave Drive, Sheffield, S13 9NR
Tel: 0114-254 2530 **Fax:** 0844-555 3435
E-mail: sales@amefa.co.uk
Website: http://www.amefa.co.uk
Bank(s): Fortis Bank
Managers: J. Horton (Mktg Serv Mgr), S. Barker (Buyer), V. Houghton (Personnel), N. Davies (Fin Mgr), A. Peskov (Tech Serv Mgr)
Ultimate Holding Company: AMEFA HOLDING BV (NETHERLANDS)
Immediate Holding Company: RICHARDSON SHEFFIELD LIMITED
Registration no: 06552927 **VAT No.:** GB 599 9153 64
Date established: 2008 **Turnover:** £2m - £5m **No.of Employees:** 21 - 50
Product Groups: 36

Anchor Magnets Ltd
Bankside Works Darnall Road, Sheffield, S9 5AH
Tel: 0114-244 1171 **Fax:** 0114-242 6612
E-mail: sales@anchormagnets.com
Website: http://www.anchormagnets.co.uk
Directors: M. Burton (Sales), P. Holmes (MD), W. Turner (Fin)
Ultimate Holding Company: ANCHOR MAGNETS LIMITED
Immediate Holding Company: ANCHOR MAGNETS (UK) LIMITED
Registration no: 03521196 **Date established:** 1998
No.of Employees: 21 - 50 **Product Groups:** 27, 35, 37, 38, 49, 65, 66, 67, 81

Date of Accounts	Dec 10	Dec 09	Dec 08
Working Capital	N/A	N/A	950
Current Assets	N/A	N/A	950

Anchor Manufacturing Ltd
70 Broad Oaks, Sheffield, S9 3HJ
Tel: 0114-242 0444 **Fax:** 0114-242 0777
E-mail: info@anchormanufacturing.co.uk
Website: http://www.anchormanufacturing.co.uk
Directors: K. Linaker (Co Sec), S. Linaker (MD)
Immediate Holding Company: ANCHOR MANUFACTURING LIMITED
Registration no: 03887898 **Date established:** 1999
No.of Employees: 1 - 10 **Product Groups:** 35, 48

Date of Accounts	Mar 11	Mar 10	Mar 09
Working Capital	1	12	N/A
Current Assets	23	38	N/A

Anchor Seals Ltd
73 Everard Avenue, Sheffield, S17 4LY
Tel: 0114-235 6388 **Fax:** 0114-236 3836
E-mail: bill_muro@fsmail.net
Directors: L. Munro (Fin), W. Munro (MD)
Immediate Holding Company: ANCHOR SEALS LIMITED
Registration no: 03620955 **Date established:** 1998
No.of Employees: 1 - 10 **Product Groups:** 38, 42

Date of Accounts	Nov 11	Nov 10	Nov 09
Working Capital	7	11	11
Fixed Assets	N/A	N/A	1
Current Assets	7	15	15

Ancient Wisdom
Block B Parkwood Business Park 75 Parkwood Road, Sheffield, S3 8AL
Tel: 0114-272 9165 **Fax:** 0114-255 8352
E-mail: info@ancientwisdom.biz
Website: http://www.ancientwisdom.biz
Directors: D. Hardy (MD)
Managers: T. Balan (Mktg Serv Mgr), S. Hardy (Chief Mgr)
Immediate Holding Company: ANCIENT WISDOM MARKETING LIMITED
Registration no: 04108870 **Date established:** 2000 **Turnover:** £2m - £5m
No.of Employees: 21 - 50 **Product Groups:** 14, 31, 32, 33, 35, 36, 49, 63, 65

Date of Accounts	Mar 11	Mar 10	Mar 09
Working Capital	1m	835	644
Fixed Assets	73	60	68
Current Assets	1m	1m	1m

Ancon Building Products
9 President Way President Park, Sheffield, S4 7UR
Tel: 0114-275 5224 **Fax:** 0114-276 8543
E-mail: info@ancon.co.uk
Website: http://www.ancon.co.uk
Directors: S. Maxwell (MD), J. Welburn (Fin)
Ultimate Holding Company: CRH PUBLIC LIMITED COMPANY
Immediate Holding Company: ANCON LIMITED
Registration no: 00210138 **Date established:** 2025
Turnover: £20m - £50m **No.of Employees:** 101 - 250
Product Groups: 33, 34, 35

Date of Accounts	Dec 11	Dec 10	Dec 09
Sales Turnover	38m	32m	31m
Pre Tax Profit/Loss	6m	5m	5m
Working Capital	19m	15m	11m
Fixed Assets	6m	5m	5m
Current Assets	30m	24m	20m
Current Liabilities	7m	6m	6m

Anglo Abrasives Ltd
Unit 5 218 Newhall Road, Sheffield, S9 2QL
Tel: 0114-244 9126 **Fax:** 0114-243 5116
E-mail: sheffield@angloabrasives.com
Website: http://www.angloabrasives.com
Directors: P. Firth (Fin), B. Sneezby (MD)
Managers: G. Roberts (Chief Mgr), J. Partridge (Sales Prom Mgr)
Immediate Holding Company: ABRASIVE BLADES LIMITED
Registration no: 00478958 **Date established:** 1950 **Turnover:** £2m - £5m
No.of Employees: 1 - 10 **Product Groups:** 33, 47

Date of Accounts	Mar 11	Mar 10	Mar 09
Working Capital	405	67	73
Fixed Assets	573	582	593
Current Assets	732	503	616

Anixter Industrial Ltd
Fastener House 3 Edmund Road, Sheffield, S2 4EB
Tel: 0114-273 8961 **Fax:** 0114-269 7171
Website: http://www.anixterindustrial.com
Directors: C. Tyrall (MD)
Managers: K. Wilkes (Personnel), J. McCandless (Chief Mgr), M. Dunsden, M. Dunsten (Sales Prom Mgr)
Ultimate Holding Company: ANIXTER INTERNATIONAL INC (USA)
Immediate Holding Company: ANIXTER(U.K.)LIMITED
Registration no: 01017023 **VAT No.:** GB 308 7039 60
Date established: 1971 **Turnover:** £5m - £10m **No.of Employees:** 11 - 20
Product Groups: 27, 32

Date of Accounts	Dec 07	Jan 11	Jan 09
Pre Tax Profit/Loss	478	-239	662
Working Capital	16m	1m	1m
Fixed Assets	10m	10m	10m
Current Assets	21m	4m	4m
Current Liabilities	132	99	321

Arce Lormittal
Birley Vale Close, Sheffield, S12 2DB
Tel: 0114-239 2601 **Fax:** 0114-264 2514
E-mail: fencingsales@arcelormittal.com
Website: http://www.arcelormittal.com
Directors: D. Hawkes (Co Sec), E. Glodt (Sales)
Ultimate Holding Company: ARCELORMITTAL SA (LUXEMBOURG)
Immediate Holding Company: ARCELORMITTAL SHEFFIELD LIMITED
Registration no: 02314470 **Date established:** 1988
Turnover: £10m - £20m **No.of Employees:** 21 - 50 **Product Groups:** 35

Date of Accounts	Dec 11	Dec 10	Dec 09
Sales Turnover	14m	12m	12m
Pre Tax Profit/Loss	48	-69	421
Working Capital	1m	1m	652
Fixed Assets	2m	2m	2m
Current Assets	4m	4m	4m
Current Liabilities	283	324	325

Arup Ltd
New Oxford House 30 Barkers Pool, Sheffield, S1 2HB
Tel: 0114-272 8247 **Fax:** 0114-275 9553
E-mail: justin.evans@arup.com
Website: http://www.arup.com
Directors: J. Evans (MD)
Immediate Holding Company: ARUP LIMITED
Registration no: 02461313 **Date established:** 1990
No.of Employees: 101 - 250 **Product Groups:** 80

Date of Accounts	Mar 11	Mar 10	Mar 09
Sales Turnover	3m	2m	N/A
Pre Tax Profit/Loss	582	416	N/A
Working Capital	819	-153	73
Fixed Assets	15m	16m	N/A
Current Assets	3m	497	73
Current Liabilities	538	610	N/A

Asmet
Jubilee House 61C Sheffield Road, Sheffield, S18 2HU
Tel: 01246-290300 **Fax:** 01246-291855
E-mail: contact@asmet.com
Website: http://www.asmet.com
Directors: P. McCarthy (Sales), J. Furness (Export), M. Parker (Fab), R. Parker (Purch), D. Tittensor (Tech Serv), A. Parker (Chief Op Offcr)
Date established: 1993 **Turnover:** £20m - £50m **No.of Employees:** 10
Product Groups: 31, 33, 34, 35, 42, 66

Date of Accounts	Sep 11	Sep 10	Sep 09
Sales Turnover	27m	18m	19m
Pre Tax Profit/Loss	2m	3m	2m
Working Capital	7m	6m	8m
Fixed Assets	391	210	230
Current Assets	18m	15m	11m
Current Liabilities	3m	2m	2m

Asterix Catering Equipment Ltd
Unit 2 Brookdale Court, Chapeltown, Sheffield, S35 2PT
Tel: 0114-232 9922 **Fax:** 0114-240 3605
E-mail: andrea@asterixcatering.co.uk
Website: http://www.asterixuk.co.uk
Directors: N. Senior (Prop)
Managers: A. Matkin (Chief Mgr)
Immediate Holding Company: ASTERIX CATERING EQUIPMENT LIMITED
Registration no: 04219364 **Date established:** 2001
Turnover: £250,000 - £500,000 **No.of Employees:** 11 - 20
Product Groups: 48, 84

Date of Accounts	Aug 07	Aug 06
Working Capital	43	64
Fixed Assets	71	89
Current Assets	1286	1165
Current Liabilities	1243	1101

Atkinson-Walker Saws Ltd
1 Cotton Mill Row, Sheffield, S3 8RU
Tel: 0114-275 2121 **Fax:** 0114-272 5065
E-mail: sales@atkinson-walker-saws.co.uk
Website: http://www.atkinson-walker-saws.co.uk
Bank(s): Barclays
Directors: C. Walker (Dir)
Ultimate Holding Company: ATKINSON WALKER SAWS (HOLDINGS) LIMITED
Immediate Holding Company: ATKINSON-WALKER (SAWS) LIMITED
Registration no: 00229203 **VAT No.:** GB 172 3222 92
Date established: 2028 **Turnover:** £1m - £2m **No.of Employees:** 11 - 20
Product Groups: 36, 37

Date of Accounts	Dec 11	Dec 10	Dec 09
Working Capital	163	148	128
Fixed Assets	142	159	168
Current Assets	322	320	269

B Braun Medical Ltd
Unit 8 Brookdale Road Thorncliffe Park Estate, Chapeltown, Sheffield, S35 2PY
Tel: 0114-225 9000 **Fax:** 0114-225 9111
E-mail: deborah.darling@bbraun.com
Website: http://www.bbraun.com
Directors: D. Thorp (Fin), P. Skelton (Sales), D. Darling (MD)
Ultimate Holding Company: B BRAUN MELSUNGEN AG (GERMANY)
Immediate Holding Company: B. BRAUN MEDICAL LIMITED
Registration no: 02296559 **VAT No.:** GB 471 2842 49
Date established: 1988 **Turnover:** £75m - £125m
No.of Employees: 101 - 250 **Product Groups:** 24, 29, 30, 31

Date of Accounts	Dec 11	Dec 10	Dec 09
Sales Turnover	86m	84m	91m
Pre Tax Profit/Loss	5m	-6m	3m
Working Capital	4m	4m	11m
Fixed Assets	13m	12m	15m
Current Assets	55m	55m	67m
Current Liabilities	8m	6m	7m

B N P Paribas Real Estae (Sheffield Office)
Belgrave House Bank Street, Sheffield, S1 2DR
Tel: 0114-241 2200 **Fax:** 0114-275 2565
Website: http://www.atisreal.com
Directors: L. Thomas (Dir), M. Coles (MD)
Managers: P. Danks, T. Lamb (Char Surv)
Date established: 1987 **No.of Employees:** 11 - 20 **Product Groups:** 80, 82

Baldwin & Francis Ltd
President Way, Sheffield, S4 7UR
Tel: 0114-286 6000 **Fax:** 0114-286 6059
E-mail: ewalton@baldwinandfrancis.com
Website: http://www.baldwinandfrancis.com
Bank(s): Lloyds TSB Bank plc
Directors: E. Walton (Fin), S. Middleton (Fin), M. Ramsden (Dir), P. Easter (Chief Op Offcr)
Managers: J. Brooks
Ultimate Holding Company: BALDWIN & FRANCIS (HOLDINGS) LIMITED
Immediate Holding Company: BALDWIN & FRANCIS (HOLDINGS) LIMITED
Registration no: 05230143 **VAT No.:** GB 646 3436 30
Date established: 2004 **Turnover:** £5m - £10m
No.of Employees: 51 - 100 **Product Groups:** 37

Date of Accounts	Mar 11	Mar 10	Mar 09
Sales Turnover	10m	12m	13m
Pre Tax Profit/Loss	-401	-51	-2
Working Capital	815	1m	1m
Fixed Assets	228	290	336
Current Assets	6m	5m	6m
Current Liabilities	980	235	388

Balfour Beatty Rail
PO Box 42, Sheffield, S9 1QW
Tel: 0114-244 6621 **Fax:** 0114-284 1601
E-mail: tony.holmes@bbrail.com
Website: http://www.bbrail.com
Bank(s): Barclays, Fitzallen Sq.
Directors: D. Eyre (Chief Op Offcr), R. Laird (MD)
Managers: A. Dalziel (), D. Day (Sales Prom Mgr), T. Holmes (Mgr)
Registration no: 01982627 **VAT No.:** GB 173 8330 58
Date established: 1900 **Turnover:** £10m - £20m
No.of Employees: 21 - 50 **Product Groups:** 39

Date of Accounts	Dec 07	Dec 06	Dec 05
Working Capital	1	1	1
Current Assets	1	1	1
Total Share Capital	1	1	1

Balfour Beatty Utility Solutions Ltd
Park Square Newton Chambers Road Thorncliffe Park Chapeltown, Chapeltown, Sheffield, S35 2PH
Tel: 0114-232 9700 **Fax:** 0114-232 9701
E-mail: jane.shepherd@bbusl.com
Website: http://www.bbusl.com
Bank(s): Royal Bank of Scotland, Manchester
Directors: M. Duncan (Fin), P. Joyce (Pers)
Managers: J. Cowley, R. Jagger, J. Shepherd (Mktg Serv Mgr)
Ultimate Holding Company: BALFOUR BEATTY PLC
Immediate Holding Company: BALFOUR BEATTY UTILITY SOLUTIONS LIMITED
Registration no: 01062438 **Date established:** 1972
Turnover: £20m - £50m **No.of Employees:** 101 - 250
Product Groups: 45, 48, 51, 52

Date of Accounts	Dec 11	Dec 10	Dec 09
Working Capital	15m	15m	15m
Current Assets	15m	15m	15m

Ballast Tools UK Ltd
Unit 5 Longacre Way Holbrook, Sheffield, S20 3FS
Tel: 0114-247 8290 **Fax:** 0114-248 6365
E-mail: gkennedy@btukltd.com
Website: http://www.btukltd.com
Managers: G. Kennedy (Mgr)
Immediate Holding Company: BALLAST TOOLS (UK) LIMITED
Registration no: 02554775 **Date established:** 1990
No.of Employees: 1 - 10 **Product Groups:** 37, 39

Barmond International
Kiveton Park Station, Sheffield, S26 6NQ
Tel: 01909-775500 **Fax:** 01909-775544
E-mail: steel@barmond.com
Website: http://www.barmond.com
Directors: A. Collington (MD), P. Harris (Co Sec)
Ultimate Holding Company: KIVETON PARK (HOLDINGS) LIMITED
Immediate Holding Company: BARMOND INTERNATIONAL LIMITED
Registration no: 00873974 **VAT No.:** GB 384 2401 62
Date established: 1966 **Turnover:** £5m - £10m **No.of Employees:** 1 - 10
Product Groups: 34

Date of Accounts	Jun 11	Jun 10	Jun 09
Working Capital	334	350	122
Fixed Assets	8	8	227
Current Assets	363	979	1m

Batchglow Ltd
Units 3-4 Bookers Way Dinnington, Sheffield, S25 3SH
Tel: 01909-550966 **Fax:** 01909-550955
E-mail: info@batchglow.co.uk
Website: http://www.batchglow.co.uk
Bank(s): Barclays
Directors: C. Smart (MD)
Immediate Holding Company: BATCHGLOW LIMITED
Registration no: 01595539 **VAT No.:** GB 308 7875 24
Date established: 1981 **Turnover:** £2m - £5m **No.of Employees:** 21 - 50
Product Groups: 48

Date of Accounts	Apr 12	Apr 11	Apr 10
Working Capital	-25	-136	-269
Fixed Assets	257	223	269
Current Assets	496	482	444

Beatson Fans & Motors Ltd
16 Newhall Road, Sheffield, S9 2QL
Tel: 0114-244 9955 **Fax:** 0114-244 9956
E-mail: enquiries@beatson.co.uk
Website: http://www.beatson.co.uk

see next page

***Beatson Fans & Motors Ltd** - Cont'd*

Directors: T. Beatson (MD)
Immediate Holding Company: BEATSON FANS & MOTORS LIMITED
Registration no: 00720861 **VAT No.:** GB 172 3564 64
Date established: 1962 **Turnover:** £500,000 - £1m
No.of Employees: 1 - 10 **Product Groups:** 29, 35, 37, 38, 39, 40, 46, 48, 66, 67, 83

Date of Accounts	Mar 12	Mar 11	Mar 10
Working Capital	188	172	150
Fixed Assets	19	24	31
Current Assets	397	399	324

William Beckett Plastics Ltd

Unit 5-6a Shepcote Way, Tinsley Industrial Estate, Sheffield, S9 1TH
Tel: 0114-243 4399 **Fax:** 0114-256 0196
E-mail: william.beckett@beckettplastics.co.uk
Website: http://www.beckettplastics.com
Bank(s): The Royal Bank of Scotland
Directors: W. Beckett (MD), K. Goodison (Fin)
Managers: A. Atkin (Personnel)
Immediate Holding Company: WILLIAM BECKETT PLASTICS LIMITED
Registration no: 01304215 **VAT No.:** GB 646 4450 31
Date established: 1977 **Turnover:** £250,000 - £500,000
No.of Employees: 21 - 50 **Product Groups:** 30

Date of Accounts	Dec 11	Dec 10	Dec 09
Working Capital	263	270	224
Fixed Assets	717	562	556
Current Assets	1m	903	852

Bedford Steels

Effingham Road, Sheffield, S4 7YS
Tel: 0114-276 9643 **Fax:** 0114-276 0689
E-mail: sales@bedfordsteels.co.uk
Website: http://www.bedfordsteels.co.uk
Bank(s): National Westminster Bank Plc
Managers: K. Allsbrook (Comm), K. Allsebrook (Comm)
Immediate Holding Company: EFFINGHAM TYRES AND EXHAUSTS LIMITED
Registration no: 02778086 **Date established:** 2010
No.of Employees: 51 - 100 **Product Groups:** 34

Bell Gearbox Refurbishment

Frestan Works Carwood Road, Sheffield, S4 7SE
Tel: 0114-243 5067 **Fax:** 0114-243 2428
E-mail: sales@bell-gears.co.uk
Website: http://www.bell-gears.co.uk
Bank(s): Midland
Directors: J. Bell (Dir), G. Bell (MD), T. Sykes (Fin)
Managers: G. Holman (Mgr), C. Bell (I.T. Exec)
Immediate Holding Company: BELL GEARS LIMITED
Registration no: 00536737 **Date established:** 1954 **Turnover:** £1m - £2m
No.of Employees: 21 - 50 **Product Groups:** 25, 35, 39

Date of Accounts	Oct 12	Oct 10	Oct 09
Working Capital	202	127	157
Fixed Assets	147	161	162
Current Assets	529	483	358

Belmont Safety Services

55 Hollybank Drive Intake, Sheffield, S12 2BS
Tel: 0114-221 9811
E-mail: info@belmontsafetyservices.co.uk
Website: http://www.belmontsafetyservices.co.uk
Managers: R. Addenbrooke (Consultant)
Date established: 2006 **No.of Employees:** 1 - 10 **Product Groups:** 84

Birley Manufacturing Ltd

11 Birley Vale Avenue, Sheffield, S12 2AX
Tel: 0114-280 3200 **Fax:** 0114-280 3201
E-mail: info@birleyml.com
Website: http://www.birleyml.com
Directors: S. English (MD)
Ultimate Holding Company: BIRLEY MANUFACTURING HOLDINGS LIMITED
Immediate Holding Company: BIRLEY MANUFACTURING HOLDINGS LIMITED
Registration no: 05852116 **Date established:** 2006
Turnover: Up to £250,000 **No.of Employees:** 51 - 100
Product Groups: 36

Date of Accounts	Dec 11	Dec 10	Dec 09
Sales Turnover	49	8m	7m
Pre Tax Profit/Loss	49	323	274
Working Capital	N/A	2m	1m
Fixed Assets	26	132	132
Current Assets	N/A	3m	3m
Current Liabilities	N/A	535	324

Blake UK Ltd

177-187 Rutland Road, Sheffield, S3 9PT
Tel: 0114-275 9729 **Fax:** 0114-275 6061
E-mail: sales@blake-uk.com
Website: http://www.blake-uk.com
Bank(s): HSBC, Fargate
Directors: P. Blake (MD)
Immediate Holding Company: BLAKE U.K. LIMITED
Registration no: 01007506 **VAT No.:** GB 172 4943 51
Date established: 1971 **No.of Employees:** 21 - 50 **Product Groups:** 35, 37

Date of Accounts	Mar 11	Mar 10	Mar 09
Working Capital	224	198	138
Fixed Assets	2m	2m	2m
Current Assets	1m	1m	2m

Chas A Blatchfords

11 Atlas Way, Sheffield, S4 7QQ
Tel: 01256-483600 **Fax:** 0114-263 7901
E-mail: adrians@blatchford.co.uk
Website: http://www.blatchford.co.uk
Managers: A. Stenson (Mgr)
No.of Employees: 51 - 100 **Product Groups:** 38, 67

Edwin Blyde & Co. Ltd

Little London Road, Sheffield, S8 0UH
Tel: 0114-249 1930 **Fax:** 0114-249 1950
E-mail: derek.stones@edwinblyde.co.uk
Website: http://www.edwinblyde.co.uk
Directors: D. Stones (Dir), J. Trower (Dir), J. Trickett (Ch)
Immediate Holding Company: EDWIN BLYDE & CO,LIMITED
Registration no: 00231877 **Date established:** 2028
Turnover: £500,000 - £1m **No.of Employees:** 11 - 20
Product Groups: 34, 49

Date of Accounts	Dec 10	Dec 09	Dec 08
Working Capital	12	6	14
Fixed Assets	37	42	46
Current Assets	155	158	198

Brass Founders Europa Engineering Ltd

Carlisle Street, Sheffield, S4 7LJ
Tel: 0114-272 7557 **Fax:** 0114-272 7811
E-mail: sales@brassfounders.com
Website: http://www.brassfounders.com
Directors: J. Hutton (MD)
Managers: P. Earl (Sales Prom Mgr)
No.of Employees: 11 - 20 **Product Groups:** 34, 35, 48, 66

Brfrangi UK Ltd

PO Box 129, Sheffield, S9 1HR
Tel: 01709-857800 **Fax:** 01709-857888
Website: http://www.bifrangi.co.uk
Bank(s): The Royal Bank of Scotland
Directors: R. Biasion (Dir)
Managers: A. Howard (Fin Mgr), P. Chilton (Plant)
Ultimate Holding Company: BIFRANGI SPA (ITALY)
Immediate Holding Company: BIFRANGI UK LIMITED
Registration no: 04279501 **VAT No.:** GB 438 9587 87
Date established: 2001 **Turnover:** £20m - £50m
No.of Employees: 101 - 250 **Product Groups:** 40, 48

Date of Accounts	Dec 09	Dec 08	Dec 07
Sales Turnover	32m	56m	41m
Pre Tax Profit/Loss	-3m	2m	-43
Working Capital	1m	3m	3m
Fixed Assets	13m	13m	12m
Current Assets	12m	19m	16m
Current Liabilities	1m	2m	1m

Bridewell UK Ltd

25 Carbrook Hall Road, Sheffield, S9 2EJ
Tel: 0114-249 0333 **Fax:** 0114-249 3856
E-mail: info@bridewelluk.co.uk
Website: http://www.bridewelluk.co.uk
Directors: C. Dyson (Sales & Mktg), S. Grocott (Dir)
Immediate Holding Company: BRIDEWELL U.K. LIMITED
Registration no: 02896961 **VAT No.:** GB 390 9863 06
Date established: 1994 **Turnover:** £20m - £50m
No.of Employees: 11 - 20 **Product Groups:** 87

Date of Accounts	Dec 11	Dec 10	Dec 09
Sales Turnover	32m	33m	33m
Pre Tax Profit/Loss	314	427	327
Working Capital	2m	1m	1m
Fixed Assets	807	842	818
Current Assets	6m	6m	6m
Current Liabilities	1m	1m	1m

British Silverware Ltd

Windsor Street, Sheffield, S4 7WB
Tel: 0114-286 0500 **Fax:** 0114-286 0501
E-mail: office@britishsilverware.co.uk
Website: http://www.britishsilverware.co.uk
Bank(s): Barclays
Directors: J. Tear (Dir)
Immediate Holding Company: BRITISH SILVERWARE LIMITED
Registration no: 05409533 **Date established:** 2005 **Turnover:** £5m - £10m
No.of Employees: 21 - 50 **Product Groups:** 36, 49

Date of Accounts	Aug 11	Aug 10	Aug 09
Working Capital	45	-58	37
Fixed Assets	100	117	157
Current Assets	522	669	2m

Broder Metals Group ltd

2 Starnhill Close Ecclesfield, Sheffield, S35 9TG
Tel: 0114-232 9241 **Fax:** 0114-2611519
E-mail: mike.andrews@broder-metals-group.com
Website: http://www.broder-metals-group.com
Directors: M. Burton (MD), M. Andrews (Prop)
Date established: 2006 **Turnover:** £5m - £10m **No.of Employees:** 11 - 20
Product Groups: 32, 34, 35, 36, 37, 46, 48, 66

Brooke Concrete Products Ltd

Monksbridge Road Dinnington, Sheffield, S25 3QS
Tel: 01909-550455 **Fax:** 01909-568780
E-mail: claz.smyth@brooke.concrete.co.uk
Website: http://www.brookeconcrete.co.uk
Bank(s): Barclays
Directors: C. Symth (MD), D. Brooke (Dir), G. Bolsover (Dir), M. Ford (Co Sec)
Managers: P. Kirk (Works Gen Mgr), L. Dowson (Sales Prom Mgr)
Immediate Holding Company: BROOKE CONCRETE PRODUCTS LIMITED
Registration no: 01579123 **VAT No.:** GB 457 8597 81
Date established: 1981 **Turnover:** £2m - £5m **No.of Employees:** 21 - 50
Product Groups: 33

Date of Accounts	Dec 07	Dec 06	Dec 05
Sales Turnover	4702	4146	3964
Pre Tax Profit/Loss	877	529	771
Working Capital	2952	2299	1783
Fixed Assets	749	789	949
Current Assets	4370	3651	2600
Current Liabilities	1418	1352	816
Total Share Capital	119	119	119
ROCE% (Return on Capital Employed)	23.7	17.1	28.2
ROT% (Return on Turnover)	18.6	12.8	19.5

Browill Rewind Co. (Incorporating Alpha)

50a Effingham Road, Sheffield, S4 7YS
Tel: 0114-275 4570 **Fax:** 0114-272 4353
E-mail: sales@browillalpha.co.uk
Website: http://www.browillalpha.co.uk
Managers: J. Taylor (Mgr)
No.of Employees: 1 - 10 **Product Groups:** 37, 40, 48, 52, 67

Bruce R I D Recycling Ltd

March Street, Sheffield, S9 5DQ
Tel: 0114-243 3637 **Fax:** 0114-244 8521
E-mail: info@weee-recycler.co.uk
Website: http://www.weee-recycler.co.uk
Managers: S. Doherty (Mgr)
Immediate Holding Company: BRUCE METALS REFINING LIMITED
Registration no: 06740800 **VAT No.:** GB 391 2457 46
Date established: 2008 **Turnover:** £1m - £2m **No.of Employees:** 21 - 50
Product Groups: 34, 46, 54, 66

Date of Accounts	Aug 11	Aug 10	Aug 09
Working Capital	529	495	486
Fixed Assets	13	54	64
Current Assets	546	509	495

Buck & Hickman Ltd

Unit 12 Riverside Court, Sheffield, S9 2TJ
Tel: 0114-244 1012 **Fax:** 0114-244 5372
E-mail: sheffield@buckhickman.co.uk
Website: http://www.buckhickman.co.uk
Directors: H. Lust (MD)
Managers: A. Thorpe (District Mgr)
Ultimate Holding Company: TRAVIS PERKINS PLC
Immediate Holding Company: BOSTON (2011) LIMITED
Registration no: 06028304 **Date established:** 2006
No.of Employees: 1 - 10 **Product Groups:** 24, 29, 30, 33, 36, 37, 41, 46

Date of Accounts	Dec 10	Mar 10	Mar 09
Working Capital	6m	6m	6m
Current Assets	27m	27m	27m

Builder Center Ltd

Nunnery Drive, Sheffield, S2 1TA
Tel: 0114-272 4001 **Fax:** 0114-241 2840
E-mail: enquiries@buildercentre.co.uk
Website: http://www.thebuilderscentre.com
Managers: K. Judson (Mgr)
Ultimate Holding Company: Wolseley plc
Immediate Holding Company: Wipac Group (Holdings) Ltd
Registration no: 00262608 **Date established:** 2007 **Turnover:** £1m - £2m
No.of Employees: 1 - 10 **Product Groups:** 25, 33, 35, 66

Builders Centre Sheffield Ltd

Nunnery Drive, Sheffield, S2 1TA
Tel: 0114-272 4001 **Fax:** 0114-241 2840
E-mail: info@builderscentre.co.uk
Website: http://www.thebuilderscentre.co.uk
Bank(s): HSBC Bank plc
Directors: J. Allen (Fin), P. Eyre (MD), T. O'Brien (Ch)
Managers: J. Allen (Accounts), M. Letch (Sales & Mktg Mg)
Immediate Holding Company: BUILDERS CENTRE (SHEFFIELD) LIMITED(THE)
Registration no: 00624494 **VAT No.:** GB 172 8147 55
Date established: 1959 **Turnover:** £5m - £10m **No.of Employees:** 11 - 20
Product Groups: 66

Date of Accounts	Mar 07	Mar 06
Sales Turnover	5986	6627
Pre Tax Profit/Loss	1114	776
Working Capital	834	1748
Fixed Assets	1227	1231
Current Assets	2073	3065
Current Liabilities	1239	1317
Total Share Capital	1	1
ROCE% (Return on Capital Employed)	54.0	26.0
ROT% (Return on Turnover)	18.6	11.7

Burgon & Ball Ltd

La Plata Works Holme Lane, Sheffield, S6 4JY
Tel: 0114-233 8262 **Fax:** 0114-285 2518
E-mail: enquiries@burgonandball.com
Website: http://www.burgonandball.com
Directors: T. Vine (Co Sec), P. Jackson (Dir)
Immediate Holding Company: BURGON & BALL LIMITED
Registration no: 02074260 **VAT No.:** GB 690 4654 16
Date established: 1986 **Turnover:** £2m - £5m **No.of Employees:** 21 - 50
Product Groups: 36, 41, 67

Date of Accounts	Dec 11	Dec 10	Dec 09
Working Capital	631	661	461
Fixed Assets	278	276	279
Current Assets	2m	1m	1m

Burkett Quicksign

Unit 19 Carbrook Business Park Dunlop Street, Sheffield, S9 2HR
Tel: 0114-256 0720 **Fax:** 0114-256 0192
E-mail: c.burkett@burkettquicksign.co.uk
Website: http://www.burkettquicksign.co.uk
Directors: C. Burkett (Prop)
Date established: 1984 **Turnover:** Up to £250,000
No.of Employees: 1 - 10 **Product Groups:** 28, 37, 49, 52

Burley Fabrications Ltd

Unit 10 35 Catley Road, Sheffield, S9 5JF
Tel: 0114-244 8462 **Fax:** 0114-242 3304
E-mail: johnburkinshaw@btconnect.com
Directors: J. Burkinshaw (MD)
Immediate Holding Company: BURLEY FABRICATIONS LIMITED
Registration no: 01566607 **VAT No.:** GB 308 6123 76
Date established: 1981 **Turnover:** £500,000 - £1m
No.of Employees: 1 - 10 **Product Groups:** 48

Date of Accounts	May 12	May 11	May 10
Working Capital	94	63	148
Fixed Assets	50	53	61
Current Assets	409	328	416

Burn Tree Vehicle Hire

1 Lawrence Street, Sheffield, S9 3RG
Tel: 0114-244 1741 **Fax:** 0114-243 5993
E-mail: david.hewson@burnt-tree.co.uk
Website: http://www.burnt-tree.co.uk
Bank(s): HSBC Bank plc
Managers: D. Hewson (Mgr)
Immediate Holding Company: BURNT TREE LIMITED
Registration no: 05298684 **VAT No.:** GB 489 3533 02
Date established: 2004 **Turnover:** £2m - £5m **No.of Employees:** 11 - 20
Product Groups: 72

C A Grant Ltd

Orgreave Crescent, Sheffield, S13 9NQ
Tel: 0114-269 5498 **Fax:** 0114-269 5412
E-mail: sales@cagrant.co.uk
Website: http://www.grantmarking.com
Bank(s): Bank of Scotland
Directors: C. Grant (Dir), S. Grant (MD), M. Bedford (Dir), M. Grant (Dir)
Ultimate Holding Company: 07026654
Immediate Holding Company: C A GRANT LIMITED
Registration no: 05307766 **VAT No.:** GB 534 1491 59
Date established: 2004 **Turnover:** £500,000 - £1m
No.of Employees: 11 - 20 **Product Groups:** 28, 36, 44, 46, 47, 48, 49

Date of Accounts	Jul 08	Jul 07	Sep 06
Sales Turnover	443	252	N/A
Pre Tax Profit/Loss	70	-8	N/A

Working Capital	20	-30	26
Fixed Assets	121	130	54
Current Assets	147	97	108
Current Liabilities	128	127	83
ROCE% (Return on Capital Employed)	50.1	-7.7	
ROT% (Return on Turnover)	15.9	-3.0	

C A Martin & Son

Upper Belle Clive Farm Hartcliff Road, Penistone, Sheffield, S36 9FE
Tel: 01226-764444 **Fax:** 01226-762336
E-mail: info@camartinandson.co.uk
Directors: J. Martin (Prop)
VAT No.: GB 173 2820 71 **Turnover:** Up to £250,000
No.of Employees: 1 - 10 **Product Groups:** 40

C P D Distribution

Hillsborough Works Langsett Road, Sheffield, S6 2LW
Tel: 0114-285 6300 **Fax:** 0114-231 8031
E-mail: marketing@cpdplc.co.uk
Website: http://www.sigplc.co.uk
Directors: J. Hetworth (Fin), T. Mann (Sales & Mktg), C. Perry (Sales), R. Barkley (MD), R. Monro (Fin)
Ultimate Holding Company: SIG PLC
Immediate Holding Company: CPD DISTRIBUTION PLC
Registration no: 01540271 **Date established:** 1981
Turnover: £50m - £75m **No.of Employees:** 251 - 500
Product Groups: 23, 25, 30, 33, 35, 37, 40, 66

Date of Accounts	**Dec 08**
Working Capital	1m
Current Assets	1m

C P L Petroleum

Parkway Avenue, Sheffield, S9 3BJ
Tel: 0114-244 0537 **Fax:** 0114-243 7282
E-mail: sheffield@cplpetroleum.co.uk
Website: http://www.cplpetroleum.co.uk
Managers: I. Hatcher (District Mgr), B. Blake (Mktg Serv Mgr)
Ultimate Holding Company: CPL INDUSTRIES HOLDINGS LIMITED
Immediate Holding Company: CPL PETROLEUM LIMITED
Registration no: 03003860 **VAT No.:** GB 275 0972 38
Date established: 1994 **Turnover:** £250m - £500m
No.of Employees: 1 - 10 **Product Groups:** 66

Date of Accounts	**Mar 12**	**Mar 11**	**Mar 10**
Pre Tax Profit/Loss	N/A	878	904
Working Capital	31	30m	30m
Fixed Assets	26	26m	26m
Current Assets	57	56m	56m
Current Liabilities	26	246	253

C & S Fabrications Ltd

Club Mill Road, Sheffield, S6 2FH
Tel: 0114-234 7567 **Fax:** 0114-231 4513
E-mail: info@csfabs.co.uk
Website: http://www.csfabs.co.uk
Bank(s): HSBC, Sheffield
Directors: S. Siddall (MD), A. Siddall (Fin)
Immediate Holding Company: C. & S. FABRICATIONS LIMITED
Registration no: 01717000 **VAT No.:** GB 308 6963 32
Date established: 1983 **Turnover:** £500,000 - £1m
No.of Employees: 11 - 20 **Product Groups:** 48

Date of Accounts	**May 11**	**May 10**	**May 09**
Working Capital	47	61	70
Fixed Assets	212	74	82
Current Assets	371	348	365

C T W Hardfacing Ltd

Quality Works Mowbray Street, Sheffield, S3 8EN
Tel: 0114-275 4786 **Fax:** 0114-275 0004
E-mail: janetcooke@aol.com
Website: http://www.ctwhardfacing.co.uk
Directors: K. Cooke (MD), P. Brearley (Dir)
Managers: M. Hill (Works Gen Mgr), M. Vaughan (Chief Acct), J. Cooke (Mgr)
Ultimate Holding Company: C.T.W. (HOLDINGS) LIMITED
Immediate Holding Company: C.T.W. HARDFACING LIMITED
Registration no: 01082919 **Date established:** 1972 **Turnover:** £5m - £10m
No.of Employees: 21 - 50 **Product Groups:** 48

Date of Accounts	**Dec 11**	**Dec 10**	**Dec 09**
Working Capital	595	363	884
Fixed Assets	558	492	433
Current Assets	2m	2m	2m

Caledonian Plastics Ltd

Holbrook Rise Holbrook Industrial Estate, Holbrook, Sheffield, S20 3FG
Tel: 0114-247 8248 **Fax:** 0114-251 0147
E-mail: sales@caledonianplastics.co.uk
Website: http://www.caledonianplastics.co.uk
Bank(s): HSBC Bank plc
Directors: J. Laing (MD)
Managers: R. Lees (Prod Mgr)
Ultimate Holding Company: LYDGATE LANE HOLDINGS LIMITED
Immediate Holding Company: CALEDONIAN PLASTICS LIMITED
Registration no: 00931307 **Date established:** 1968 **Turnover:** £1m - £2m
No.of Employees: 21 - 50 **Product Groups:** 30, 48, 66

Date of Accounts	**Jun 11**	**Jun 10**	**Jun 09**
Working Capital	219	168	101
Fixed Assets	715	644	709
Current Assets	711	616	521

Cam Fork Lift Trucks

20 Carlisle Street, Sheffield, S4 7LJ
Tel: 0114-272 9115 **Fax:** 0114-249 3959
E-mail: mac@camforklifts.co.uk
Website: http://www.camforklifts.co.uk
Directors: A. Mason (MD)
Immediate Holding Company: Cam Fork Lift Trucks Ltd
Registration no: 04660063 **VAT No.:** GB 598 5628 69
Date established: 2003 **No.of Employees:** 1 - 10 **Product Groups:** 45, 48, 67, 71, 83

Date of Accounts	**Mar 08**	**Mar 07**	**Mar 06**
Working Capital	36	30	18
Fixed Assets	95	62	54
Current Assets	363	288	221
Current Liabilities	328	258	203

Camelot Silverware Ltd

173 Gibraltar Street, Sheffield, S3 8UA
Tel: 0114-272 4935 **Fax:** 0114-273 7149
E-mail: enquiries@camelotsilverware.co.uk
Website: http://www.camelotsilverware.co.uk
Directors: G. Nicols (Dir)
Immediate Holding Company: CAMELOT PROPERTIES LIMITED
Registration no: 01132157 **VAT No.:** GB 173 6004 81
Date established: 1973 **Turnover:** £500,000 - £1m
No.of Employees: 1 - 10 **Product Groups:** 49

Date of Accounts	**Dec 11**	**Dec 09**	**Dec 08**
Working Capital	43	111	129
Fixed Assets	60	70	79
Current Assets	45	273	274

Carl Spaeter GmbH

8 Broadlands Croft, Sheffield, S20 6SZ
Tel: 07852-337376
E-mail: c.nutt@spaeter.de
Website: http://www.spaeter.de
Directors: H. Schurmann (MD)
Managers: K. Dohemesen (), C. Nutt (Sales Prom Mgr)
VAT No.: GB 845 8352 01 **Date established:** 1890 **Turnover:** £20m - £50m
Product Groups: 31, 32, 33, 38, 61, 66

Carrs E L G Stainless Steel Ltd

Wadsley Bridge Penistone Road North, Sheffield, S6 1LL
Tel: 0114-285 5866 **Fax:** 0114-285 5734
E-mail: info@elgcarrs.co.uk
Website: http://www.elgcars.co.uk
Bank(s): Barclays
Directors: J. Baker (MD)
Managers: N. Buxton (Comm), L. Baker (Purch Mgr)
Ultimate Holding Company: FRANZ HANIEL CIE GMBH
Immediate Holding Company: ELG HANIEL METALS LTD
Registration no: 01517971 **VAT No.:** GB 438 9246 16
Turnover: £10m - £20m **No.of Employees:** 51 - 100 **Product Groups:** 34

Castle Brook Tools Ltd

Unit 7 Shepcote Way, Tinsley Industrial Estate, Sheffield, S9 1TH
Tel: 0114-261 7200 **Fax:** 0114-261 7370
E-mail: info@castlebrooke.co.uk
Website: http://www.castlebrooke.co.uk
Bank(s): Barclays, London, NW10 7JA
Directors: J. Ellison (Fin)
Ultimate Holding Company: WESTCROWN LIMITED
Immediate Holding Company: CASTLE BROOKE TOOLS (UK) LIMITED
Registration no: 01490504 **VAT No.:** GB 600 2295 91
Date established: 1980 **Turnover:** £1m - £2m **No.of Employees:** 11 - 20
Product Groups: 35, 36, 38, 46, 47

Date of Accounts	**Dec 11**	**Dec 10**	**Dec 09**
Working Capital	425	106	164
Fixed Assets	49	47	59
Current Assets	2m	2m	1m

Celcoat Ltd

3 Crown Works Rotherham Road, Beighton, Sheffield, S20 1AH
Tel: 0114-269 0771 **Fax:** 0114-254 0495
E-mail: celcoatltd@tiscali.co.uk
Directors: K. Cook (Dir)
Ultimate Holding Company: C.T.W. (HOLDINGS) LIMITED
Immediate Holding Company: CELCOAT LIMITED
Registration no: 02526521 **VAT No.:** GB 534 0670 64
Date established: 1990 **Turnover:** £500,000 - £1m
No.of Employees: 1 - 10 **Product Groups:** 48

Date of Accounts	**Dec 11**	**Dec 10**	**Dec 09**
Working Capital	2	2	2
Current Assets	2	2	2

Central Metallurgical Laboratory

53 Sussex Street, Sheffield, S4 7YY
Tel: 0114-272 1735 **Fax:** 0114-275 6797
E-mail: neilellis@centralmet.co.uk
Website: http://www.centralmet.co.uk
Directors: N. Ellis (Prop)
VAT No.: GB 174 0578 56 **Turnover:** Up to £250,000
No.of Employees: 1 - 10 **Product Groups:** 85

Century Plastics Ltd

Unit G, Vector 31
Waleswood Way
Wales Bar, Sheffield, S26 5NU
Tel: 01909-773037
E-mail: sales@centuryplastics.co.uk
Website: http://www.centuryplastics.co.uk
Managers: A. Taylor (District Mgr)
Ultimate Holding Company: PALRAM INDUSTRIES (1990) LTD (ISRAEL)
Immediate Holding Company: CENTURY PLASTICS LIMITED
Registration no: 02558642 **Date established:** 1992 **Turnover:** £2m - £5m
No.of Employees: 11 - 20 **Product Groups:** 30, 33, 48

Date of Accounts	**Dec 11**	**Dec 10**	**Dec 09**
Sales Turnover	3m	3m	3m
Pre Tax Profit/Loss	14	-66	-116
Working Capital	-200	-267	-721
Fixed Assets	133	189	205
Current Assets	1m	1m	939
Current Liabilities	51	51	44

Ceratizit UK Ltd

Sheffield Airport Business Park Europa Link, Sheffield, S9 1XU
Tel: 01925-261161 **Fax:** 01925-267933
E-mail: info.uk@ceratizit.com
Website: http://www.ceratizit.com
Bank(s): Barclays
Directors: T. Pennington (MD)
Managers: L. Ross (Ops Mgr), J. Mann
Ultimate Holding Company: CERATIZIT SA (LUXEMBOURG)
Immediate Holding Company: CERATIZIT UK LIMITED
Registration no: 01795331 **Date established:** 1984 **Turnover:** £5m - £10m
No.of Employees: 21 - 50 **Product Groups:** 36, 46

Date of Accounts	**Feb 12**	**Feb 11**	**Feb 10**
Sales Turnover	10m	8m	6m
Pre Tax Profit/Loss	313	232	-499
Working Capital	2m	2m	1m
Fixed Assets	79	245	247
Current Assets	4m	4m	3m
Current Liabilities	619	575	374

Cermag Ltd

94 Holywell Road, Sheffield, S4 8AS
Tel: 0114-244 6136 **Fax:** 0114-256 1769
E-mail: sales@cermag.co.uk
Website: http://www.cermag.co.uk
Bank(s): National Westminster Bank Plc
Directors: R. Marshall (MD)
Immediate Holding Company: CERMAG LIMITED
Registration no: 01385250 **VAT No.:** GB 308 1884 53
Date established: 1978 **Turnover:** £2m - £5m **No.of Employees:** 11 - 20
Product Groups: 34, 37, 38, 45, 67

Date of Accounts	**Jun 11**	**Jun 10**	**Jun 09**
Working Capital	99	36	-243
Fixed Assets	155	133	506
Current Assets	583	360	336

Chamber Recruitment Services

Albion House Savile Street, Sheffield, S4 7UD
Tel: 0114-249 1283 **Fax:** 0114-201 8946
E-mail: stephen.hinchliffe@scci.org.uk
Website: http://www.scci.org.uk
Managers: S. Hinchliffe
Immediate Holding Company: CHAMBER TRAINING SERVICES LIMITED
Registration no: 04469081 **Date established:** 2002 **Turnover:** £5m - £10m
No.of Employees: 1 - 10 **Product Groups:** 87

Champion Hire Ltd

323 Abbeydale Road, Sheffield, S7 1FS
Tel: 08453-456902 **Fax:** 0114-249 4202
E-mail: info@championhire.com
Website: http://www.championhire.com
Directors: K. White (MD), T. Hale (Ch)
Managers: H. Price (Mgr), J. Cross (Mgr)
Immediate Holding Company: CHAMPION HIRE LIMITED
Registration no: 00950396 **Date established:** 1969
No.of Employees: 1 - 10 **Product Groups:** 83

Date of Accounts	**Mar 08**	**Mar 07**
Sales Turnover	7302	6296
Pre Tax Profit/Loss	264	89
Working Capital	-1922	-1594
Fixed Assets	8107	6226
Current Assets	1986	1734
Current Liabilities	3908	3328
Total Share Capital	1	1
ROCE% (Return on Capital Employed)	4.3	1.9
ROT% (Return on Turnover)	3.6	1.4

Citisigns Ltd

2a Church Lane Dinnington, Sheffield, S25 2LY
Tel: 01909-567474 **Fax:** 01909-564141
E-mail: j.hearnshaw@citisigns.co.uk
Website: http://www.citisigns.co.uk
Bank(s): National Westminster Bank Plc
Directors: P. Carroll (MD), J. Hearnshaw (Fin)
Managers: N. Spooner (I.T. Exec), J. Hernshaw (Accounts)
Immediate Holding Company: CITISIGNS LIMITED
Registration no: 01362899 **VAT No.:** GB 308 1112 09
Date established: 1978 **Turnover:** £500,000 - £1m
No.of Employees: 11 - 20 **Product Groups:** 37, 39, 49

Date of Accounts	**Mar 10**	**Mar 09**	**Mar 08**
Working Capital	547	733	682
Fixed Assets	466	479	486
Current Assets	563	826	787

City Steel Lighting Ltd

Valley Road, Sheffield, S8 9FX
Tel: 0114-258 0248
Website: http://www.liteworksonline.co.uk
No.of Employees: 1 - 10 **Product Groups:** 37, 67

Clarkson-Osborn International

108 The Innovation Centre 217 Portobello, Sheffield, S1 4DP
Tel: 0114-276 8622 **Fax:** 0114-275 4400
E-mail: sales@clarkson-osborn.co.uk
Website: http://www.clarksonosborn.co.uk
Managers: M. Poole (Chief Acct)
Immediate Holding Company: CLARKSON OSBORN INTERNATIONAL LIMITED
Registration no: 04142918 **Date established:** 2001 **Turnover:** £2m - £5m
No.of Employees: 1 - 10 **Product Groups:** 46

Date of Accounts	**Dec 11**	**Dec 10**	**Dec 09**
Sales Turnover	N/A	N/A	2m
Pre Tax Profit/Loss	N/A	N/A	-23
Working Capital	2m	2m	1m
Fixed Assets	8	12	20
Current Assets	5m	5m	6m
Current Liabilities	N/A	N/A	2m

Clear View Secondary Glazing

Omnia One Queen Street, Sheffield, S1 2DU
Tel: 0114-279 2875
E-mail: a.saunby@clearviewsg.co.uk
Website: http://www.clearviewsg.co.uk
Directors: A. Saunby (Dir)
Immediate Holding Company: HOCAPITO LIMITED
Registration no: 06457167 **Date established:** 2005
No.of Employees: 1 - 10 **Product Groups:** 66

Date of Accounts	**Jan 11**	**Jan 10**	**Jan 08**
Working Capital	2	-3	41
Current Assets	5	6	62

Clico Sheffield Tooling Ltd

7 Fell Road, Sheffield, S9 2AL
Tel: 0114-243 3007 **Fax:** 0114-243 4158
E-mail: info@clico.co.uk
Website: http://www.clico.co.uk
Bank(s): National Westminster Bank Plc
Directors: A. Reid (MD)
Immediate Holding Company: CLICO (SHEFFIELD) TOOLING LIMITED
Registration no: 01727929 **VAT No.:** GB 390 9280 30
Date established: 1983 **Turnover:** £1m - £2m **No.of Employees:** 21 - 50
Product Groups: 31, 36, 46

Date of Accounts	**Jul 11**	**Jul 10**	**Jul 09**
Working Capital	144	163	155
Fixed Assets	146	159	187
Current Assets	685	648	691

Coates Signs

84 Holme Lane, Sheffield, S6 4JW
Tel: 0114-234 4834 **Fax:** 0114-234 4834
E-mail: coatesigns@talk21.com
Website: http://www.coatesigns.co.uk
Directors: S. Coates (Prop)
No.of Employees: 1 - 10 **Product Groups:** 49, 67

Coffilta Coffee & Spring Water Services

340 Abbey Lane, Sheffield, S8 0BY
Tel: 0114-221 4642 **Fax:** 0114-221 4642
E-mail: kdmurray@hotmail.com
Directors: C. Murray (Ptnr), K. Murray (Prop)
Immediate Holding Company: JAMES AIMER
No.of Employees: 1 - 10 **Product Groups:** 62

Cogne UK Ltd (division of Cogne UK Ltd)

19 Don Road, Sheffield, S9 2UD
Tel: 0114-221 2020 **Fax:** 0114-221 3030
E-mail: peter@cogne.co.uk
Website: http://www.cogne.co.uk
Bank(s): Lloyds TSB
Directors: P. Ford (Dir)
Ultimate Holding Company: MEG SA (LUXEMBOURG)
Immediate Holding Company: COGNE U.K. LIMITED
Registration no: 03298004 **VAT No.:** GB 172 3025 94
Date established: 1996 **Turnover:** £20m - £50m
No.of Employees: 51 - 100 **Product Groups:** 34

Date of Accounts	Dec 11	Dec 10	Dec 09
Sales Turnover	38m	36m	33m
Pre Tax Profit/Loss	640	573	-2m
Working Capital	1m	638	4m
Fixed Assets	3m	3m	3m
Current Assets	24m	22m	23m
Current Liabilities	8m	7m	7m

Colour Kote Ltd

Unit 12-14 Evans Business Centre Nobel Way, Dinnington, Sheffield, S25 3QB
Tel: 01909-569003 **Fax:** 01909-569220
E-mail: colourkote@btconnect.com
Website: http://www.colourkote.co.uk
Directors: N. Rodgers (MD)
Immediate Holding Company: COLOUR KOTE LIMITED
Registration no: 03573937 **Date established:** 1998
No.of Employees: 1 - 10 **Product Groups:** 46, 48

Date of Accounts	Mar 11	Mar 10	Mar 09
Working Capital	1	-0	-2
Fixed Assets	5	6	7
Current Assets	44	53	61

Colourcraft C & A Ltd

Unit 5 555 Carlisle Street East, Sheffield, S4 8DT
Tel: 0114-242 1431 **Fax:** 0114-243 4844
E-mail: sales@colourcraft-ltd.com
Website: http://www.colourcraftltd.com
Directors: M. Burkinshaw (Comm)
Immediate Holding Company: COLOURCRAFT (COLOURS & ADHESIVES) LIMITED
Registration no: 01406270 **VAT No.:** GB 308 3901 69
Date established: 1978 **No.of Employees:** 1 - 10 **Product Groups:** 64

Date of Accounts	Mar 11	Mar 10	Mar 09
Working Capital	-9	-29	-25
Fixed Assets	48	52	55
Current Assets	88	69	68

Combass Ltd

Rotherham Close Norwood Industrial Estate, Killamarsh, Sheffield, S21 2JU
Tel: 0114-248 0616 **Fax:** 0114-248 2684
E-mail: irmackie@aol.com
Bank(s): National Westminster Bank Plc
Directors: I. Mackie (Dir)
Immediate Holding Company: COMBASS LIMITED
Registration no: 01390891 **Date established:** 1978
No.of Employees: 11 - 20 **Product Groups:** 28, 30, 33, 34, 41, 42, 43, 47, 48, 76

Date of Accounts	Sep 11	Sep 10	Sep 09
Working Capital	158	170	152
Fixed Assets	166	170	172
Current Assets	320	286	292

Compactor Wheel Technology Ltd

Quality Works Mowbray Street, Sheffield, S3 8EN
Tel: 0114-275 0992 **Fax:** 0114-275 0004
Website: http://www.ctwhardfacing.co.uk
Directors: K. Cooke (MD)
Ultimate Holding Company: C.T.W. (HOLDINGS) LIMITED
Immediate Holding Company: COMPACTOR WHEEL TECHNOLOGY LIMITED
Registration no: 02214048 **Date established:** 1988
No.of Employees: 21 - 50 **Product Groups:** 35, 39, 45

Date of Accounts	Dec 11	Dec 10	Dec 09
Working Capital	10	10	10
Current Assets	10	10	10

Contract Kitchens Ltd

Unit 7 Portland Business Park 130 Richmond Park Road, Sheffield, S13 8HS
Tel: 0114-275 0018 **Fax:** 0114-279 8787
E-mail: info@contractkitchensltd.com
Website: http://www.contractkitchensltd.com
Directors: M. Watson (Dir)
Immediate Holding Company: CONTRACT KITCHENS LIMITED
Registration no: 03890193 **Date established:** 1999 **Turnover:** £1m - £2m
No.of Employees: 1 - 10 **Product Groups:** 63

Date of Accounts	Apr 11	Apr 10	Apr 09
Working Capital	29	177	163
Fixed Assets	7	10	15
Current Assets	125	249	270

Contract Lighting Ltd

842 Ecclesall Road, Sheffield, S11 8TD
Tel: 0114-267 8281
Directors: T. Beinns (Prop)
No.of Employees: 1 - 10 **Product Groups:** 37, 67

Cooper & Turner

Templeborough Works Sheffield Road, Sheffield, S9 1RS
Tel: 0114-256 0057 **Fax:** 0114-244 5529
E-mail: davide@cooperandturner.co.uk
Website: http://www.cooperandturner.co.uk
Directors: Z. Khan (Dir), G. Sanderson (Fin), D. Edwards (Sales)
Managers: E. Parfitt (Personnel), N. Preece (Tech Serv Mgr), C. Butler (Purch Mgr)
Ultimate Holding Company: NORTHERN ENDEAVOUR LIMITED
Immediate Holding Company: COOPER & TURNER LIMITED
Registration no: 04021697 **Date established:** 2000
Turnover: £10m - £20m **No.of Employees:** 251 - 500
Product Groups: 35, 39

Date of Accounts	Feb 08	Feb 11	Feb 10
Sales Turnover	N/A	18m	24m
Pre Tax Profit/Loss	1m	752	3m
Working Capital	2m	7m	6m
Fixed Assets	4m	7m	7m
Current Assets	8m	12m	9m
Current Liabilities	3m	2m	858

Corton Sheet Metal Work Ltd

Parkway Avenue, Sheffield, S9 4WB
Tel: 0114-276 6559 **Fax:** 0114-272 2223
E-mail: cortonsmfabs@aol.com
Website: http://www.steelfabricationssheffield.co.uk
Directors: A. Corton (MD)
Immediate Holding Company: CORTON SHEET METAL FABRICATIONS LIMITED
Registration no: 03970258 **Date established:** 2000
No.of Employees: 11 - 20 **Product Groups:** 33, 34, 35, 40, 48, 52

Date of Accounts	Sep 11	Sep 10	Sep 09
Working Capital	153	78	58
Fixed Assets	12	14	17
Current Assets	638	586	442

Crawford UK Ltd

7 Churchill Way 35a Business Park, Chapeltown, Sheffield, S35 2PY
Tel: 0114-257 4330 **Fax:** 0114-257 4399
E-mail: sales.uk@crawfordsolutions.com
Website: http://www.crawfordsolutions.com
Directors: A. Broadbent (Pers)
Managers: A. Stockdale, A. Collins, N. Chapman
Ultimate Holding Company: CARDO AB (SWEDEN)
Immediate Holding Company: CRAWFORD UK LIMITED
Registration no: 00937594 **Date established:** 1968
Turnover: £10m - £20m **No.of Employees:** 101 - 250
Product Groups: 26, 35

Date of Accounts	Dec 11	Dec 10	Dec 09
Sales Turnover	12m	10m	11m
Pre Tax Profit/Loss	3	659	407
Working Capital	2m	2m	1m
Fixed Assets	481	513	532
Current Assets	5m	4m	3m
Current Liabilities	971	715	795

Crawshaw Silversmiths

26 Trinity Street, Sheffield, S3 7AJ
Tel: 0114-273 9799 **Fax:** 0114-270 0229
Directors: D. Caley (Ptnr)
Turnover: Up to £250,000 **No.of Employees:** 1 - 10 **Product Groups:** 49

Criterion Packaging Ltd

Unit 3c Nunnery Drive, Sheffield, S2 1TA
Tel: 0114-276 7755 **Fax:** 0114-276 9898
E-mail: info@criterion-packaging.co.uk
Website: http://www.criterion-packaging.co.uk
Directors: J. Morton (Sales)
Immediate Holding Company: CRITERION PACKAGING LIMITED
Registration no: 02861038 **Date established:** 1993
Turnover: £250,000 - £500,000 **No.of Employees:** 11 - 20
Product Groups: 48

Date of Accounts	Dec 11	Dec 10	Dec 09
Working Capital	528	416	303
Fixed Assets	466	545	631
Current Assets	748	692	531

Crossfield Engineering Co

Barrow Road, Sheffield, S9 1JZ
Tel: 0114-243 8441 **Fax:** 0114-243 9266
E-mail: sales@crossfielduk.com
Website: http://www.hbinghamgroup.com
Directors: A. Justice (MD), R. Wheatley (Dir), S. Watson (Dir), L. Smith (Co Sec)
Immediate Holding Company: BINGHAM MANUFACTURING LIMITED
Registration no: 02764733 **VAT No.:** GB 172 5140 84
Date established: 1992 **Turnover:** £1m - £2m **No.of Employees:** 21 - 50
Product Groups: 38, 42, 44, 45, 84

Custom Brakes & Hydraulics Ltd

Prospect House City Road, Sheffield, S2 5HH
Tel: 0114-276 7971 **Fax:** 0114-272 3538
E-mail: sales@custombrakes.co.uk
Website: http://www.custombrakes.co.uk
Directors: J. Hepworth (Fin), S. Hepworth (MD)
Immediate Holding Company: CUSTOM BRAKES & HYDRAULICS LIMITED
Registration no: 01511441 **Date established:** 1980
Turnover: £500,000 - £1m **No.of Employees:** 1 - 10 **Product Groups:** 29, 32, 33, 34, 35, 38, 39, 40, 41, 45, 46, 47, 66, 67, 68

Date of Accounts	Feb 08	Feb 11	Feb 10
Working Capital	26	60	29
Fixed Assets	9	10	16
Current Assets	53	128	96

D C Precision Taps

6 233 Handsworth Road, Sheffield, S13 9BL
Tel: 0114-244 0442 **Fax:** 0114-242 0666
E-mail: salesdctaps@tiscali.co.uk
Website: http://www.dcpt.co.uk
Directors: I. Mclean (Prop)
Date established: 1996 **No.of Employees:** 1 - 10 **Product Groups:** 46

D E M Machines UK Ltd

Unit 4 50 Rother Valley Way Holbrook, Sheffield, S20 3RW
Tel: 0114-248 1165 **Fax:** 0114-248 8415
E-mail: info@demmachines.com
Website: http://www.demmachines.com
Directors: O. Hayden (Fin), D. Mcclean (MD)
Ultimate Holding Company: D.E.M. MACHINES LIMITED
Immediate Holding Company: DEM MACHINES UK LIMITED
Registration no: 04671749 **Date established:** 2003
No.of Employees: 1 - 10 **Product Groups:** 38, 42

Date of Accounts	Dec 11	Dec 10	Feb 10
Pre Tax Profit/Loss	N/A	N/A	-84
Working Capital	204	221	140
Fixed Assets	27	36	48
Current Assets	290	298	235

D L A Piper

1 St Pauls Place 121 Norfolk Street, Sheffield, S1 2JX
Tel: 0114-283 3250 **Fax:** 0114-270 0568
E-mail: enquiries@dlapiper.com
Website: http://www.dlapiper.com
Directors: R. May (Ptnr)
Managers: L. Parker (Personnel), M. Fenoughty (Fin Mgr), S. Johnson, P. Nundy
Ultimate Holding Company: DLA PIPER INTERNATIONAL LLP
Immediate Holding Company: DLA PIPER LIMITED
Registration no: 05048236 **Date established:** 2004
No.of Employees: 251 - 500 **Product Groups:** 80

D M R Seals Ltd

Units 22-26 Julian Road, Sheffield, S9 1FZ
Tel: 0114-243 2777 **Fax:** 0114-242 2300
E-mail: sales@dmrseals.co.uk
Website: http://www.dmrseals.co.uk
Directors: R. O'connor (MD)
Immediate Holding Company: D M R SEALS LIMITED
Registration no: 04851586 **VAT No.:** GB 827 5194 10
Date established: 2003 **Turnover:** £1m - £2m **No.of Employees:** 11 - 20
Product Groups: 22, 29, 30, 33, 34, 35, 36, 37, 39, 40, 42

Date of Accounts	Apr 11	Apr 10	Apr 09
Working Capital	352	210	160
Fixed Assets	276	222	252
Current Assets	711	537	471

D P Doors & Shutters

23b Orgreave Crescent, Sheffield, S13 9NQ
Tel: 0114-269 7554 **Fax:** 0114-293 9193
E-mail: sales@dpdoorsandshutters.co.uk
Website: http://www.dpdoorsandshutters.co.uk
Directors: A. Bolsover (MD)
Immediate Holding Company: D.P. DOORS AND SHUTTERS LIMITED
Registration no: 03428508 **Date established:** 1997
Turnover: £250,000 - £500,000 **No.of Employees:** 1 - 10
Product Groups: 25, 30, 34, 35, 36, 39, 48, 66

Date of Accounts	Aug 11	Aug 10	Aug 09
Working Capital	-74	-62	-36
Fixed Assets	99	113	113
Current Assets	728	553	313

D & S Grinding Co.

Unit 11 Rotherham Close Norwood Industrial Estate, Killamarsh, Sheffield, S21 2JU
Tel: 0114-247 7159 **Fax:** 0114-247 7159
Directors: S. Bright (Ptnr)
Date established: 1986 **No.of Employees:** 1 - 10 **Product Groups:** 46

Datech Scientific Ltd

2 Wortley Road Deepcar, Sheffield, S36 2UZ
Tel: 08707-469810 **Fax:** 08707-469811
E-mail: sales@datech-scientific.co.uk
Website: http://www.datech-scientific.co.uk
Directors: L. Matthews (Dir)
Immediate Holding Company: DATECH SCIENTIFIC LIMITED
Registration no: 03726722 **Date established:** 1999
Turnover: £250,000 - £500,000 **No.of Employees:** 1 - 10
Product Groups: 38, 42

Date of Accounts	Mar 12	Mar 11	Mar 10
Working Capital	24	55	61
Fixed Assets	7	18	22
Current Assets	272	126	121

Davy Markham Ltd

Darnall Works Prince of Wales Road, Sheffield, S9 4EX
Tel: 0114-244 9971 **Fax:** 0114-244 9641
E-mail: sales@davymarkham.com
Website: http://www.davymarkham.com
Bank(s): Barclays Bank Plc, 2 Arena Court, Sheffield, South Yorkshire, S9 2LF
Directors: J. Watson (Fab)
Ultimate Holding Company: CHARIOT (DM) LLP
Immediate Holding Company: DAVYMARKHAM LIMITED
Registration no: 06218755 **VAT No.:** GB 911 3944 38
Date established: 2006 **Turnover:** £20m - £50m
No.of Employees: 101 - 250 **Product Groups:** 34, 35, 37, 45, 48, 51, 80, 81, 84, 85

Date of Accounts	Dec 09	Dec 08	Dec 07
Sales Turnover	21m	21m	22m
Pre Tax Profit/Loss	1m	746	-4m
Working Capital	2m	635	-478
Fixed Assets	1m	1m	1m
Current Assets	5m	7m	5m
Current Liabilities	2m	4m	4m

Charles Day Steels Ltd

Downgate Drive, Sheffield, S4 8BT
Tel: 0114-244 5544 **Fax:** 0114-244 5588
E-mail: philip.wooffinden@daysteel.co.uk
Website: http://www.daysteel.co.uk
Bank(s): The Royal Bank of Scotland
Directors: P. Wooffinden (MD), P. Woofingdon (MD)
Managers: C. Reed (Chief Acct), P. Law (Purch Mgr)
Immediate Holding Company: CHARLES DAY (STEELS) LIMITED
Registration no: 01289020 **Date established:** 1976 **Turnover:** £2m - £5m
No.of Employees: 21 - 50 **Product Groups:** 34, 35, 48

Date of Accounts	Oct 11	Oct 10	Oct 09
Working Capital	-221	189	-161
Fixed Assets	817	893	1m
Current Assets	3m	2m	2m

B P Dempsey Ltd

8 March Street, Sheffield, S9 5DQ
Tel: 0114-242 1900 **Fax:** 0114-243 2232
E-mail: info@bpdempsey.com
Website: http://www.bpdempsey.com
Managers: S. Cowen (Mgr)
Immediate Holding Company: B.P. DEMPSEY LIMITED
Registration no: 00582895 **VAT No.:** GB 241 6082 86
Date established: 1957 **Turnover:** £500,000 - £1m
No.of Employees: 1 - 10 **Product Groups:** 52

Date of Accounts	Dec 11	Dec 10	Dec 09
Working Capital	562	443	356
Fixed Assets	24	3	6
Current Assets	697	544	432

Derwent Tool Co. Ltd
1 Wallace Road, Sheffield, S3 9SR
Tel: 0114-275 4829 **Fax:** 0114-272 5665
E-mail: sales@derwent-tools.co.uk
Website: http://www.derwent-tools.co.uk
Directors: J. Hoyle (MD)
Immediate Holding Company: DERWENT TOOL COMPANY LIMITED
Registration no: 01595237 **Date established:** 1981
No.of Employees: 1 - 10 **Product Groups:** 46

Date of Accounts	Dec 11	Dec 10	Dec 09
Working Capital	50	64	13
Fixed Assets	39	44	47
Current Assets	105	114	115

Distinctive Doors Ltd
14-15 Chambers Ways Newton Chambers Road, Chapeltown, Sheffield, S35 2PH
Tel: 0114-220 2250 **Fax:** 0114-220 2254
E-mail: sales@distinctivedoors.co.uk
Website: http://www.distinctivedoors.co.uk
Directors: R. Staniforte (Dir)
Immediate Holding Company: DISTINCTIVE DOORS LIMITED
Registration no: 05125435 **Date established:** 2004
No.of Employees: 11 - 20 **Product Groups:** 25, 26, 30, 33, 35, 36, 39, 47, 66, 68

Date of Accounts	Nov 11	Nov 10	Nov 09
Working Capital	168	89	-28
Fixed Assets	289	288	309
Current Assets	789	827	584

Don Springs Sheffield Ltd
340 Coleford Road, Sheffield, S9 5PH
Tel: 0114-244 1545 **Fax:** 0114-243 5291
E-mail: tony@donsprings.co.uk
Website: http://www.donsprings.co.uk
Directors: A. Cope (MD)
Immediate Holding Company: DON SPRINGS (SHEFFIELD) LIMITED
Registration no: 00859935 **Date established:** 1965
Turnover: £250,000 - £500,000 **No.of Employees:** 1 - 10
Product Groups: 35, 36, 39

Date of Accounts	Oct 11	Oct 10	Oct 09
Working Capital	95	68	55
Fixed Assets	6	15	27
Current Assets	213	159	137

Doncasters F B C Ltd
PO Box 160, Sheffield, S4 7QY
Tel: 0114-243 1041 **Fax:** 0114-243 1358
E-mail: pthompson@doncasters.com
Website: http://www.doncasters.com
Bank(s): HSBC Bank plc
Managers: I. Jones (Sales Prom Mgr), P. Thompson (Ops Mgr)
Immediate Holding Company: DONCASTERS P.L.C.
Registration no: 01669815 **VAT No.:** GB 547 3690 18
Date established: 1982 **No.of Employees:** 21 - 50 **Product Groups:** 34, 36, 48

Doncasters Structures Ltd (Bramah Division)
Holbrook Works Station Road, Halfway, Sheffield, S20 3GB
Tel: 0114-248 3981 **Fax:** 0114-247 4105
E-mail: n.middleton@doncasters.com
Website: http://www.doncasters.com
Bank(s): National Westminster Bank Plc
Directors: S. Rice (I.T. Dir), H. Jackson (Co Sec), C. Harrex (Pers)
Managers: N. Middleton (Sales Prom Mgr), G. Chapman (Chief Acct)
Ultimate Holding Company: DUBAI INTERNATIONAL CAPITAL LLC (DUBAI)
Immediate Holding Company: DONCASTERS STRUCTURES LIMITED
Registration no: 00266421 **VAT No.:** GB 389 1553 14
Date established: 1932 **Turnover:** £10m - £20m
No.of Employees: 101 - 250 **Product Groups:** 48

Door Maintenance 2003 Ltd
10 Titterton Close, Sheffield, S9 3TQ
Tel: 0114-242 1833
E-mail: info@dm2003.co.uk
Website: http://www.dm2003.co.uk
Directors: L. Hobson (Dir)
Immediate Holding Company: DOOR MAINTENANCE (2003) LIMITED
Registration no: 04108880 **Date established:** 2000
No.of Employees: 1 - 10 **Product Groups:** 35, 48

Date of Accounts	Jun 11	Jun 09	Jun 08
Working Capital	63	52	73
Fixed Assets	38	31	32
Current Assets	169	219	254

Dorvic Engineering Ltd
New Street Holbrook Industrial Estate, Holbrook, Sheffield, S20 3GH
Tel: 0114-248 5633 **Fax:** 0114-251 0654
E-mail: sales@dorvic.com
Website: http://www.dorvic.com
Directors: J. Hill (Fin)
Ultimate Holding Company: HILLMAN INC (USA)
Immediate Holding Company: DORVIC ENGINEERING CO. LIMITED
Registration no: 01160712 **VAT No.:** GB 173 7055 59
Date established: 1974 **Turnover:** £500,000 - £1m
No.of Employees: 1 - 10 **Product Groups:** 35, 36, 45, 48, 84

Date of Accounts	Dec 11	Dec 10	Dec 09
Working Capital	691	795	801
Fixed Assets	117	124	128
Current Assets	837	885	889

D P M Electronics Ltd
53 West Bank Drive Anston South Anston, Sheffield, S25 5JG
Tel: 01909-567105
E-mail: dave@dpm.org.uk
Website: http://www.dpm.org.uk
Directors: J. Marriott (Fin), D. Marriott (MD)
Immediate Holding Company: D.P.M. ELECTRONICS LIMITED
Registration no: 04652183 **Date established:** 2003
Turnover: Up to £250,000 **No.of Employees:** 1 - 10 **Product Groups:** 44

Date of Accounts	Jan 12	Jan 11	Jan 10
Sales Turnover	N/A	N/A	11
Working Capital	-2	-4	-5
Fixed Assets	1	1	1
Current Assets	7	4	3

Drain Centre Wolseley UK Ltd
386-392 Coleridge Road, Sheffield, S9 5DD
Tel: 0114-244 0926 **Fax:** 0114-243 5990
E-mail: p24.sheffield@wolseley.co.uk
Website: http://www.wolseley.co.uk
Managers: S. Walker (District Mgr)
Immediate Holding Company: GLYNWED INTERNATIONAL P.L.C.
Registration no: 00424702 **Turnover:** £2m - £5m
No.of Employees: 1 - 10 **Product Groups:** 30, 36, 39, 40, 48, 66

Drayton Tank & Accessories Ltd
3 Crown House
Market Street
Penistone, Sheffield, S36 6BZ
Tel: 0871-2884213 **Fax:** 0871-2884214
E-mail: info@draytontank.co.uk
Website: http://www.draytontank.co.uk
Directors: S. Lockley (MD)
Registration no: 03251904 **Turnover:** £1m - £2m
No.of Employees: 1 - 10 **Product Groups:** 30, 33, 35, 36, 37, 38, 39, 40, 41, 42, 44, 48, 51, 52, 54, 66

Date of Accounts	Mar 12	Mar 11	Mar 10
Sales Turnover	487	423	338
Working Capital	-77	-47	-59
Fixed Assets	2	2	2
Current Assets	123	115	66

Durham Duplex
312 Petre Street, Sheffield, S4 8LT
Tel: 0114-243 2313 **Fax:** 0114-244 4329
E-mail: sales@durham-duplex.co.uk
Website: http://www.durham-duplex.co.uk
Bank(s): H.S.B.C.
Directors: P. Lindley (Fin), P. Bottomley (Sales), J. Hudson (MD)
Managers: D. Bagshaw (Sales Admin)
Ultimate Holding Company: EDWARD TURNER & SON LIMITED
Immediate Holding Company: DURHAM DUPLEX LIMITED
Registration no: 00109587 **VAT No.:** GB 391 1950 45
Date established: 2010 **Turnover:** £2m - £5m **No.of Employees:** 21 - 50
Product Groups: 36, 38, 40, 41, 42, 43, 44, 46, 47, 48, 66

James Durrans & Sons Ltd
Phoenix Works Thurlstone, Sheffield, S36 9QU
Tel: 01226-370000 **Fax:** 01226-370336
E-mail: info@durrans.co.uk
Website: http://www.durrans.co.uk
Bank(s): Lloyds TSB
Directors: M. Toole (Fin), B. Broomhead (Fin), C. Durrans (MD)
Managers: S. Dekort (Purch Mgr), C. Smith
Immediate Holding Company: JAMES DURRANS & SONS,LIMITED
Registration no: 00172023 **VAT No.:** GB 172 4452 70
Date established: 2020 **Turnover:** £50m - £75m
No.of Employees: 51 - 100 **Product Groups:** 33

Date of Accounts	Dec 11	Dec 10	Dec 09
Sales Turnover	69m	56m	37m
Pre Tax Profit/Loss	5m	3m	3m
Working Capital	13m	10m	8m
Fixed Assets	6m	6m	5m
Current Assets	25m	20m	16m
Current Liabilities	2m	1m	2m

Dyson Thermal Technologies
Griff Works Stopes Road, Stannington, Sheffield, S6 6BW
Tel: 0114-234 8663 **Fax:** 0114-232 2519
E-mail: enquiries@dysontt.com
Website: http://www.dysontt.com
Directors: A. Parker (Fin), J. Lomas (Dir), N. Beard (Ch)
Managers: D. Bartells (I.T. Exec)
Immediate Holding Company: J & J DYSON P.L.C.
Registration no: 01187031 **Turnover:** £50m - £75m
No.of Employees: 1 - 10 **Product Groups:** 17, 33

Dyson Thermal Technologies
Baslow Road Totley, Sheffield, S17 3BL
Tel: 0114-235 5300 **Fax:** 0114-235 6010
E-mail: enq@dysontt.com
Website: http://www.dysontt.com
Bank(s): HSBC Bank plc
Directors: G. Rosson (Fin), R. Taylor (MD)
Ultimate Holding Company: DYSON GROUP PLC
Immediate Holding Company: SANDYGATE MOTOR SERVICES LIMITED
Registration no: 01137031 **VAT No.:** GB 308 5483 51
Date established: 1965 **No.of Employees:** 11 - 20 **Product Groups:** 33, 52

Date of Accounts	Mar 99	Mar 98	Mar 97
Sales Turnover	3m	3m	3m
Pre Tax Profit/Loss	5	28	62
Working Capital	357	337	287
Fixed Assets	158	165	178
Current Assets	795	760	755
Current Liabilities	60	71	51

E C U S
Endcliffe Holt 343 Fulwood Road, Sheffield, S10 3BQ
Tel: 0114-266 9292 **Fax:** 0114-266 7707
E-mail: contactus@ecusltd.co.uk
Website: http://www.ecusltd.co.uk
Directors: C. Routh (MD), C. Ralph (Dir), P. Pattison (Co Sec), R. Parker (Fin)
Managers: C. Routh (Mgr)
Ultimate Holding Company: University of Sheffield
Immediate Holding Company: ECUS (HOLDINGS) LIMITED
Registration no: 05159614 **Date established:** 2004
Turnover: £500,000 - £1m **No.of Employees:** 11 - 20
Product Groups: 07, 08, 32, 54, 86, 87

Date of Accounts	Dec 09	Dec 08	Dec 07
Working Capital	29	159	183
Fixed Assets	29	27	7
Current Assets	231	446	433

E E Ingleton Engineering Ltd
Adelaide Works 55 Mowbray Street, Sheffield, S3 8EZ
Tel: 0114-275 7834 **Fax:** 0114-272 9672
E-mail: sales@eeingleton.co.uk
Website: http://www.eeingleton.co.uk
Directors: T. Hodges (MD)
Ultimate Holding Company: R & G (SHEFFIELD) LIMITED
Immediate Holding Company: E.E. INGLETON ENGINEERING LIMITED
Registration no: 01292113 **Date established:** 1976
No.of Employees: 21 - 50 **Product Groups:** 30, 34, 35, 41, 48

Date of Accounts	Dec 11	Dec 10	Dec 09
Working Capital	750	778	794
Fixed Assets	121	132	139
Current Assets	1m	1m	1m

E F Westawaway
Jessell Street, Sheffield, S9 3HY
Tel: 0114-244 9857 **Fax:** 0114-243 0682
E-mail: info@efwestaway.co.uk
Website: http://www.efwestaway.co.uk
Bank(s): National Westminster Bank Plc
Directors: H. Westaway (Fin), D. Westaway (Prop)
Immediate Holding Company: E.F.WESTAWAY LIMITED
Registration no: 00363081 **Date established:** 1940 **Turnover:** £1m - £2m
No.of Employees: 11 - 20 **Product Groups:** 48, 54

Date of Accounts	Sep 11	Sep 10	Sep 09
Working Capital	1m	569	390
Fixed Assets	154	348	351
Current Assets	2m	736	779

E L G Haniel Metals Ltd (Head Office)
Templeborough Works Sheffield Road, Tinsley, Sheffield, S9 1RT
Tel: 0114-244 3333 **Fax:** 0114-256 1742
E-mail: enquiries@elg.co.uk
Website: http://www.elg.co.uk
Bank(s): Barclays
Directors: J. Greenwood (Fin), M. Vaughan (MD), M. Wright (Ch)
Managers: I. Grace (Tech Serv Mgr), S. Perks (Personnel)
Ultimate Holding Company: FRANZ HANIEL & CIE GMBH (GERMANY)
Immediate Holding Company: E.L.G. HANIEL METALS LIMITED
Registration no: 01517971 **VAT No.:** GB 438 9246 16
Date established: 1980 **Turnover:** £250m - £500m
No.of Employees: 51 - 100 **Product Groups:** 54, 66

Date of Accounts	Dec 11	Dec 10	Dec 09
Sales Turnover	333m	309m	182m
Pre Tax Profit/Loss	8m	10m	9m
Working Capital	-7m	-4m	268
Fixed Assets	28m	26m	26m
Current Assets	63m	92m	58m
Current Liabilities	3m	3m	2m

E Magnets UK Ltd (A divison of Sterlings Tools Ltd)
Samson Works, Sheffield, S2 5QT
Tel: 0114-276 2264 **Fax:** 0114-275 2759
E-mail: sales@e-magnetsuk.com
Website: http://www.e-magnetsuk.com
Directors: A. Richardson (Dir), A. Richardson (Fin), I. Asquith (Dir)
Managers: D. Whitham (Comm), E. Marrison (Admin Off)
Immediate Holding Company: E-MAGNETS UK LIMITED
Registration no: 06515204 **Date established:** 2008
No.of Employees: 1 - 10 **Product Groups:** 37

Date of Accounts	Mar 12	Mar 11	Mar 10
Working Capital	201	115	140
Fixed Assets	165	184	168
Current Assets	509	327	289

East End Fabrications
28 Princess Street, Sheffield, S4 7UW
Tel: 0114-272 7495 **Fax:** 0114-272 7495
Directors: G. Hartland (Prop)
Date established: 1968 **No.of Employees:** 1 - 10 **Product Groups:** 35

Eastgate Metalwork
5 Precision Works Garter Street, Sheffield, S4 7QX
Tel: 0114-261 1557 **Fax:** 0114- 2611557
Directors: S. Hinchliffe (Prop), S. Hinchcliffe (Prop)
Date established: 1995 **No.of Employees:** 1 - 10 **Product Groups:** 26, 35

Ecclesfield Engineering Ltd
68 Yew Lane, Sheffield, S5 9AN
Tel: 0114-246 2087 **Fax:** 0114-245 0384
E-mail: lhartley@tiscali.co.uk
Directors: L. Hartley (Dir)
Immediate Holding Company: ECCLESFIELD ENGINEERING LIMITED
Registration no: 02884533 **Date established:** 1994
No.of Employees: 1 - 10 **Product Groups:** 35, 36, 39

Date of Accounts	Mar 11	Mar 10	Mar 09
Working Capital	-5	-1	-1
Fixed Assets	5	5	5
Current Assets	35	41	30

Eclipse Magnetics Ltd
Atlas Way, Sheffield, S4 7QQ
Tel: 0114-225 0600 **Fax:** 0114-225 0610
E-mail: sales@eclipse-magnetics.co.uk
Website: http://www.eclipse-magnetics.co.uk
Directors: J. Dargavel (Sales)
Managers: D. Higgins (Tech Serv Mgr), N. Fowler (Mktg Serv Mgr)
Ultimate Holding Company: NEILL TOOLS LIMITED
Immediate Holding Company: ECLIPSE MAGNETICS LIMITED
Registration no: 00531327 **Date established:** 1954 **Turnover:** £5m - £10m
No.of Employees: 51 - 100 **Product Groups:** 35, 36, 37, 38, 39, 40, 42, 44, 45, 46, 49, 67, 84, 85

Date of Accounts	Sep 11	Sep 10	Sep 09
Sales Turnover	9m	8m	8m
Pre Tax Profit/Loss	1m	592	993
Working Capital	6m	5m	5m
Fixed Assets	130	130	130
Current Assets	11m	10m	9m
Current Liabilities	220	162	128

Edmundson Electrical Ltd
38-40 Catley Road, Sheffield, S9 5JF
Tel: 0114-244 4641 **Fax:** 0114-242 2035
E-mail: sheffield.070@eel.co.uk
Website: http://www.edmundson-electrical.co.uk/
Managers: D. Budd (District Mgr)
Ultimate Holding Company: BLACKFRIARS CORP (USA)
Immediate Holding Company: EDMUNDSON ELECTRICAL LIMITED
Registration no: 02667012 **VAT No.:** GB 172 9454 41
Date established: 1991 **Turnover:** £2m - £5m **No.of Employees:** 1 - 10
Product Groups: 77

Date of Accounts	Dec 11	Dec 10	Dec 09
Sales Turnover	1023m	852m	788m
Pre Tax Profit/Loss	57m	53m	45m

see next page

Edmundson Electrical Ltd - Cont'd

Working Capital	256m	225m	184m
Fixed Assets	17m	3m	4m
Current Assets	439m	358m	298m
Current Liabilities	59m	38m	37m

Edward Pryor & Son Ltd
Egerton Street, Sheffield, S1 4JX
Tel: 0114-276 6044 **Fax:** 0114-276 6890
E-mail: n.andrew@pryormarking.com
Website: http://www.pryormarking.com
Directors: N. Andrew (Dir)
Immediate Holding Company: EDWARD PRYOR & SON LIMITED
Registration no: 00313230 **Date established:** 1936 **Turnover:** £5m - £10m
No.of Employees: 101 - 250 **Product Groups:** 36, 47, 48

Egginton Bros Ltd
25-31 Allen Street, Sheffield, S3 7AW
Tel: 0114-276 6123 **Fax:** 0114-273 8465
E-mail: steve@eggintongroup.co.uk
Website: http://www.eggintongroup.co.uk
Bank(s): The Royal Bank of Scotland
Directors: S. Brooks (MD)
Managers: J. Goodwin (Sales & Mktg Mg), J. Goodwin (Sales & Mktg Mg)
Immediate Holding Company: RODGERS WOSTENHOLM LIMITED
Registration no: 01973187 **VAT No.:** GB 172 4702 73
Date established: 1985 **Turnover:** £1m - £2m **No.of Employees:** 21 - 50
Product Groups: 36, 40, 41, 49, 65, 67, 68

The Electric Gate Shop Ltd
Stoneycroft Cottage Midhopestones, Sheffield, S36 4GP
Tel: 01226-370549 **Fax:** 01405-785300
E-mail: info@theelectricgateshop.co.uk
Website: http://www.theelectricgateshop.co.uk
Directors: G. Pearson (Dir)
Immediate Holding Company: THE ELECTRIC GATE SHOP LTD
Registration no: 05923481 **Date established:** 2006
No.of Employees: 1 - 10 **Product Groups:** 35, 36, 66

Date of Accounts	Dec 11	Dec 10	Dec 09
Working Capital	191	140	90
Fixed Assets	79	42	49
Current Assets	316	222	162

Electro Group Ltd
Unit 9 Meadowbrook Park Halfway, Sheffield, S20 3PJ
Tel: 0114-276 4300 **Fax:** 0114-248 6654
E-mail: sales@electro-group.co.uk
Website: http://www.electro-group.co.uk
Directors: I. Scruby (Co Sec), T. Bannister (I.T. Dir), R. Surfleet (MD), S. Ward (Sales)
Immediate Holding Company: ELECTRO GROUP LIMITED
Registration no: 02557527 **VAT No.:** GB 534 1113 88
Date established: 1990 **Turnover:** £1m - £2m **No.of Employees:** 1 - 10
Product Groups: 35

Date of Accounts	Dec 11	Dec 10	Dec 09
Working Capital	405	390	412
Fixed Assets	1m	1m	1m
Current Assets	911	848	783

Electronic Data Processing plc
Beauchief Hall Beauchief, Sheffield, S8 7BA
Tel: 0114-262 1621 **Fax:** 0114-262 1126
Website: http://www.edp.co.uk
Directors: M. Heller (Ch), J. Wassell (Fin), P. Davey (Sales), R. Jowitt (MD), J. Waffell (Grp Chief Exec)
Managers: C. Sticer (I.T. Exec)
Immediate Holding Company: ELECTRONIC DATA PROCESSING PUBLIC LIMITED COMPANY
Registration no: 00853560 **Date established:** 1965 **Turnover:** £5m - £10m
No.of Employees: 1 - 10 **Product Groups:** 44

Elkem Ltd
305 Glossop Road, Sheffield, S10 2HL
Tel: 0114-270 0334 **Fax:** 0114-275 3103
E-mail: david.wilkinson@elkem.no
Website: http://www.elkem.com
Directors: D. Wilkinson (Dir)
Ultimate Holding Company: ORKLA ASA (NORWAY)
Immediate Holding Company: ELKEM LIMITED
Registration no: 01940808 **VAT No.:** GB 305 9805 53
Date established: 1985 **Turnover:** £1m - £2m **No.of Employees:** 11 - 20
Product Groups: 32, 34

Date of Accounts	Dec 11	Dec 10	Dec 09
Sales Turnover	2m	1m	2m
Pre Tax Profit/Loss	177	47	-62
Working Capital	474	464	540
Fixed Assets	2m	2m	2m
Current Assets	1m	1m	1m
Current Liabilities	74	80	77

Emergency Power Systems
Carley Drive Business Area Westfield, Sheffield, S20 8NQ
Tel: 0114-247 8369 **Fax:** 0114-247 8367
E-mail: sales@emergencypowersystems.co.uk
Website: http://www.emergencypowersystems.com
Bank(s): Barclays
Directors: P. Stamper (Tech Serv), R. Thomson (Sales), A. Howgate (Dir)
Ultimate Holding Company: EMERSON ELECTRIC CO INC (USA)
Immediate Holding Company: EMERGENCY POWER SYSTEMS LIMITED
Registration no: 02752248 **VAT No.:** GB 593 4067 21
Date established: 1992 **Turnover:** £5m - £10m
No.of Employees: 51 - 100 **Product Groups:** 37

Date of Accounts	Aug 09	Mar 10	Sep 11
Sales Turnover	7m	5m	10m
Pre Tax Profit/Loss	320	-439	272
Working Capital	824	370	739
Fixed Assets	1m	198	N/A
Current Assets	4m	4m	739
Current Liabilities	2m	485	N/A

Encomech Engineering Developments Ltd
Sheffield Airport Business Park Europa Link, Sheffield, S9 1XU
Tel: 01709-726500 **Fax:** 0141-261 1719
Website: http://www.siemens-vai.com
Directors: J. Laws (Co Sec), W. Laws (MD)
Immediate Holding Company: GOLDWING DEVELOPMENTS (HOLDINGS) LIMITED
Registration no: 07356613 **Date established:** 2010
Turnover: Up to £250,000 **No.of Employees:** 1 - 10 **Product Groups:** 85

Engel Europa International Ltd
Unit 19c Orgreave Close Doorhouse Idustrial Estate, Sheffield, S13 9NP
Tel: 0114-269 4556 **Fax:** 0114-278 6797
E-mail: sales@engeleuropa.com
Website: http://www.engeleuropa.com
Directors: D. Summerhayes (Dir)
Immediate Holding Company: ENGEL EUROPA INTERNATIONAL LIMITED
Registration no: 01704714 **Date established:** 1983
No.of Employees: 1 - 10 **Product Groups:** 46

Date of Accounts	Mar 12	Mar 11	Mar 10
Working Capital	141	156	182
Fixed Assets	361	167	179
Current Assets	612	569	751

Engineering & Lift Services
4 Bay Court Killamarsh, Sheffield, S21 1HL
Tel: 0114-251 0707 **Fax:** 0114-251 0707
E-mail: liftengineer@btconnect.com
Directors: R. Priestley (Prop)
Date established: 2003 **No.of Employees:** 1 - 10 **Product Groups:** 35, 39, 45

English Pewter Company
1 Blackmore Street, Sheffield, S4 7TZ
Tel: 0114-272 3920 **Fax:** 0114-276 1416
E-mail: a@englishpewter.co.uk
Website: http://www.englishpewter.co.uk
Directors: A. Sharp (Dir)
Immediate Holding Company: A.J. SHARP LIMITED
Registration no: 03754576 **Date established:** 1999 **Turnover:** £1m - £2m
No.of Employees: 21 - 50 **Product Groups:** 34, 49, 65

Environmental Fabrications
Unit 1 Rex Works Harvest Lane, Sheffield, S3 8EA
Tel: 0114-278 8777 **Fax:** 0114-254 4974
E-mail: m.brightmore@watertankrefurbishment.com
Website: http://www.watertankrefurbishment.com
Directors: M. Brightmoore (Prop)
Registration no: 04333637 **Date established:** 2001
Turnover: £250,000 - £500,000 **No.of Employees:** 1 - 10
Product Groups: 40, 54

Ergix Data Communications Ltd
15 Sanders Way Dinnington, Sheffield, S25 3QF
Tel: 07970-264144
E-mail: scott@cawthorne962.fsnet.co.uk
Managers: S. Cawthorne (Mgr)
Immediate Holding Company: ERGIX DATA COMMUNICATIONS LTD
Registration no: 05905228 **Date established:** 2006
No.of Employees: 1 - 10 **Product Groups:** 37, 48, 52, 67, 84

Date of Accounts	Aug 11	Aug 10	Aug 09
Working Capital	-1	4	-3
Fixed Assets	1	1	1
Current Assets	7	10	7

Erodatools Ltd
Unit 4 Laurence Works Sheffield Road, Penistone, Sheffield, S36 6HF
Tel: 01226-763725 **Fax:** 01226-767139
E-mail: info@erodatoolsltd.co.uk
Website: http://www.erodatoolsltd.co.uk
Directors: K. Rolfe (Dir)
Registration no: 01040150 **VAT No.:** GB 172 8149 51
Turnover: £500,000 - £1m **No.of Employees:** 1 - 10 **Product Groups:** 33, 35, 37, 46, 48

Euchner UK Ltd
Unit 2 Petre Drive, Sheffield, S4 7PZ
Tel: 0114-256 0123 **Fax:** 0114-242 5333
E-mail: sales@euchner.co.uk
Website: http://www.euchner.com
Managers: M. Clarke (Mgr)
Ultimate Holding Company: EUCHNER INDUSTIRE BETEILIGUNGEN GMBH (GERMANY)
Immediate Holding Company: EUCHNER (U.K.) LIMITED
Registration no: 01665576 **Date established:** 1982
Turnover: Up to £250,000 **No.of Employees:** 1 - 10 **Product Groups:** 67

Date of Accounts	Dec 11	Dec 10	Dec 09
Working Capital	326	248	181
Fixed Assets	46	13	30
Current Assets	622	567	413

Eurocoms Ltd
12 Cardwell Avenue, Sheffield, S13 7XA
Tel: 0845-2570 753
E-mail: dford@eurocoms.co.uk
Website: http://www.eurocoms.co.uk
Directors: B. Ford (Fin), D. Ford (Dir)
Immediate Holding Company: EUROCOMS LTD
Registration no: 05712823 **Date established:** 2006
Turnover: Up to £250,000 **No.of Employees:** 1 - 10 **Product Groups:** 37

Date of Accounts	Mar 11	Mar 10	Mar 09
Sales Turnover	N/A	N/A	136
Pre Tax Profit/Loss	N/A	N/A	8
Working Capital	N/A	-0	-1
Fixed Assets	5	5	6
Current Assets	47	36	39
Current Liabilities	N/A	N/A	29

Evo Engineering
130 Chippingham Street, Sheffield, S9 3SE
Tel: 0114-243 1267 **Fax:** 0114-256 2936
Directors: E. Oakley (Prop)
Immediate Holding Company: E.V.O. (ENGINEERING) LIMITED
Registration no: 01044127 **VAT No.:** GB 172 7885 24
Date established: 1972 **Turnover:** Up to £250,000
No.of Employees: 1 - 10 **Product Groups:** 35, 46, 48

Date of Accounts	Mar 12	Mar 11	Mar 10
Working Capital	37	35	30
Fixed Assets	27	27	28
Current Assets	77	80	43
Current Liabilities	24	39	N/A

Ewen Engineering
Roscoe Road, Sheffield, S3 7DZ
Tel: 0114-273 0327 **Fax:** 0114-275 1955
E-mail: sales@ewenengineering.co.uk
Website: http://www.ewenengineering.co.uk
Bank(s): Bank of Scotland
Directors: R. Clack (MD), M. Unwin (Co Sec)
Ultimate Holding Company: HEATHERMOOR LIMITED
Immediate Holding Company: EWEN ENGINEERING LIMITED
Registration no: 04096350 **VAT No.:** GB 306 4063 90
Date established: 2000 **Turnover:** £2m - £5m **No.of Employees:** 21 - 50
Product Groups: 35, 36, 39, 40, 45, 46, 47, 48, 66, 67, 68, 84

Express Grinding Services
Unit 1 Bardwell Road, Sheffield, S3 8AS
Tel: 0114-275 9349 **Fax:** 0114-275 9349
Directors: D. Parkyn (Prop), D. Park (Prop)
Immediate Holding Company: OSBORNE FLATS (FILEY) LIMITED
Registration no: 00865586 **Date established:** 1965
No.of Employees: 1 - 10 **Product Groups:** 46

F E M Ltd
Unit 7 Kiveton Park Industrial Estate Manor Road, Kiveton Park Station, Sheffield, S26 6PB
Tel: 01909-774836 **Fax:** 01909-772391
E-mail: femltd1@hotmail.co.uk
Website: http://www.femltd.com
Directors: B. Morley (MD), A. Morley (Fin)
Immediate Holding Company: FEM LIMITED
Registration no: 03824118 **VAT No.:** GB 308 8072 57
Date established: 1999 **Turnover:** £250,000 - £500,000
No.of Employees: 1 - 10 **Product Groups:** 48

Date of Accounts	Aug 11	Aug 10	Aug 09
Working Capital	3	2	2
Current Assets	3	3	2

F F Franklin & Co. Ltd
Platt Street, Sheffield, S3 8BQ
Tel: 0114-272 1429 **Fax:** 0114-272 7030
E-mail: sales@franklin-tools.co.uk
Website: http://www.franklin-tools.co.uk
Bank(s): Barclays
Directors: R. Wilkinson (Dir)
Immediate Holding Company: F.F.FRANKLIN & CO.,LIMITED
Registration no: 00298140 **VAT No.:** GB 172 4865 45
Date established: 1935 **Turnover:** £2m - £5m **No.of Employees:** 11 - 20
Product Groups: 38, 39

Date of Accounts	Mar 11	Mar 10	Mar 09
Working Capital	466	457	416
Fixed Assets	62	63	93
Current Assets	1m	996	948

Facom UK Ltd
4 Europa View, Sheffield, S9 1XH
Tel: 0114-291 7212 **Fax:** 0114-291 7131
E-mail: customerservices@facom.com
Website: http://www.britool.co.uk
Directors: G. Collins (MD), A. Cash (Sales), T. Harris (Fin), D. Johnson (Sales)
Managers: D. Burchnall (Mgr), M. Jarvis (I.T. Exec), A. Warner (Mktg Serv Mgr)
Ultimate Holding Company: STANLEY WORKS INC (USA)
Immediate Holding Company: FACOM UK LIMITED
Registration no: 04140357 **VAT No.:** GB 213 1834 02
Date established: 2001 **Turnover:** £2m - £5m **No.of Employees:** 1 - 10
Product Groups: 35, 36, 37, 39, 44

Date of Accounts	Dec 10	Dec 09	Dec 07
Pre Tax Profit/Loss	N/A	N/A	604
Working Capital	-692	-692	-692
Current Assets	5m	5m	5m
Current Liabilities	N/A	11	11

Fernite Of Sheffield Ltd
Fernite Works Coleford Road, Sheffield, S9 5NJ
Tel: 0114-244 0527 **Fax:** 0114-244 5922
E-mail: sales@fernite.co.uk
Website: http://www.fernite.co.uk
Bank(s): National Westminster Bank Plc
Directors: N. Bowie (Dir), G. Bowie (Fin), D. Sayles (Dir)
Immediate Holding Company: FERNITE OF SHEFFIELD LIMITED
Registration no: 03133576 **VAT No.:** GB 658 1096 19
Date established: 1995 **Turnover:** £2m - £5m **No.of Employees:** 21 - 50
Product Groups: 36, 42, 47

Date of Accounts	Sep 11	Sep 10	Sep 09
Working Capital	447	321	175
Fixed Assets	538	589	640
Current Assets	759	585	593

Fine Sign
Oldcotes Road Dinnington, Sheffield, S25 2QX
Tel: 01909-518886 **Fax:** 01909-518662
E-mail: sales@fine-sign.co.uk
Website: http://www.fine-sign.co.uk
Directors: B. Williams (Ptnr)
Turnover: Up to £250,000 **No.of Employees:** 1 - 10 **Product Groups:** 30, 39, 40

Fire Safety Specialists
10 Martin Rise Eckington Eckington, Sheffield, S21 4HH
Tel: 01246-434314 **Fax:** 01246-434 314
E-mail: chrismaher@fire-safety-specialists.co.uk
Website: http://www.fire-safety-specialists.co.uk
Directors: V. Maher (Prop)
Immediate Holding Company: FIRE SAFETY SPECIALISTS LTD
Registration no: 05285984 **Date established:** 2004
Turnover: Up to £250,000 **No.of Employees:** 1 - 10 **Product Groups:** 84, 86

Date of Accounts	Nov 11	Nov 10	Nov 09
Working Capital	1	N/A	N/A
Current Assets	47	50	43

Firma Chrome Ltd
Soho Works Saxon Road, Sheffield, S8 0XZ
Tel: 0114-255 4343 **Fax:** 0114-258 7375
E-mail: enquiries@firmachrome.co.uk
Website: http://www.firmachrome.co.uk
Managers: L. Chambers (Fin Mgr)
Ultimate Holding Company: BROOK BROS. LIMITED
Immediate Holding Company: FIRMA-CHROME LIMITED
Registration no: 02115619 **VAT No.:** GB 457 8382 05
Date established: 1987 **Turnover:** £500,000 - £1m
No.of Employees: 1 - 10 **Product Groups:** 48

Date of Accounts	Jun 11	Jun 10	Jun 09
Working Capital	18	68	68
Fixed Assets	63	13	41
Current Assets	158	123	142

1st Call

51 Staniforth Avenue Eckington, Sheffield, S21 4GQ
Tel: 01246-430941 **Fax:** 01246-430941
Directors: M. Kirk (Prop)
Date established: 2001 **No.of Employees:** 1 - 10 **Product Groups:** 26, 35

First Link Industrial Ltd

Unit 6 Amberley Court, Sheffield, S9 2LQ
Tel: 0114-243 8100 **Fax:** 0114-243 8101
E-mail: admin@firstlinkindustrial.co.uk
Website: http://www.firstlinkindustrial.co.uk
Directors: J. Shen (MD)
Immediate Holding Company: FIRSTLINK INDUSTRIAL LIMITED
Registration no: 04337596 **Date established:** 2001
No.of Employees: 1 - 10 **Product Groups:** 39, 68

Date of Accounts	Mar 11	Mar 10	Mar 09
Working Capital	271	322	299
Fixed Assets	28	23	18
Current Assets	642	654	649

Firth Rixson Ltd

Firth House Meadowhall Road, Sheffield, S9 1JD
Tel: 0114-219 3000 **Fax:** 01709-388889
E-mail: info@firthrixson.com
Website: http://www.firthrixson.com
Bank(s): The Royal Bank of Scotland
Managers: R. Humphries (Mktg Serv Mgr)
Ultimate Holding Company: FIRTH RIXSON (CYPRUS) LIMITED (CYPRUS).
Immediate Holding Company: FIRTH RIXSON LIMITED
Registration no: 00230737 **VAT No.:** GB 308 8766 24
Date established: 2028 **Turnover:** £2m - £5m **No.of Employees:** 21 - 50
Product Groups: 34, 48

Date of Accounts	Sep 11	Sep 10	Sep 09
Pre Tax Profit/Loss	-3m	N/A	-155
Working Capital	947	-2m	-2m
Fixed Assets	36m	42m	42m
Current Assets	947	69	69

Firwood Paint & Varnish Co. Ltd

54 Broadfield Road, Sheffield, S8 0XJ
Tel: 0114-255 5355 **Fax:** 0114-258 5872
Website: http://www.firwood.co.uk
Directors: M. Warren (MD)
Managers: I. Willin (Mktg Serv Mgr), M. Sullivan (Sales Prom Mgr), S. Stratford (Asst Gen Mgr)
Registration no: 00207861 **No.of Employees:** 1 - 10 **Product Groups:** 32

Flame Hardeners Ltd

Shorter Works Bailey Lane, Sheffield, S1 3BL
Tel: 0114-276 8167 **Fax:** 0114-273 8657
E-mail: mail@flamehardeners.co.uk
Website: http://www.flamehardeners.co.uk
Directors: R. Haw (MD)
Immediate Holding Company: FLAME-HARDENERS LIMITED
Registration no: 00399098 **Date established:** 1945
No.of Employees: 1 - 10 **Product Groups:** 48

Date of Accounts	Sep 11	Sep 10	Sep 09
Working Capital	-26	1	41
Fixed Assets	51	55	67
Current Assets	141	175	200

C W Fletcher & Sons Ltd

Sterling Works Mansfield Road, Wales Bar, Sheffield, S26 5PQ
Tel: 0114-294 2200 **Fax:** 0114-294 2211
E-mail: pl@cwfletcher.co.uk
Website: http://www.cwfletcher.co.uk
Bank(s): Royal Bank of Scotland, Church Street
Directors: D. Fletcher (Tech Serv), P. Llewellyn (Fin)
Managers: J. Needham (Buyer), J. Martin (Sales & Mktg Mg), H. Jenkinson (Personnel)
Immediate Holding Company: C.W.FLETCHER & SONS,LIMITED
Registration no: 00097913 **VAT No.:** GB 172 5190 69
Date established: 2008 **Turnover:** £20m - £50m
No.of Employees: 101 - 250 **Product Groups:** 30, 33, 34, 37, 39

Date of Accounts	Dec 11	Dec 10	Dec 09
Sales Turnover	21m	18m	18m
Pre Tax Profit/Loss	806	610	625
Working Capital	4m	4m	4m
Fixed Assets	6m	6m	6m
Current Assets	10m	8m	7m
Current Liabilities	1m	605	431

Flowgroup Ltd Bestobell Valves & Conflow

President Way, Sheffield, S4 7UR
Tel: 0114-224 0200 **Fax:** 0114-278 4974
E-mail: lyndab@flowgroup.co.uk
Website: http://www.flowgroup.co.uk
Directors: A. Guest (Co Sec), A. Guest (Fin), J. Wall (MD), M. Ansell (Grp Chief Exec)
Managers: S. Montgomery, F. Crosland (Projects)
Immediate Holding Company: WILLOUGHBY (301) LIMITED
Registration no: 04100778 **VAT No.:** GB 581 5570 26
Date established: 2000 **Turnover:** £5m - £10m
No.of Employees: 51 - 100 **Product Groups:** 36

Forticrete Ltd

Anstone Works Kiveton Park Station, Sheffield, S26 6NP
Tel: 01909-775000 **Fax:** 01909-773549
E-mail: dseekings@forticrete.com
Website: http://www.forticrete.co.uk
Managers: D. Seekings (Factory Mgr)
Ultimate Holding Company: CRH PUBLIC LIMITED COMPANY
Immediate Holding Company: FORTICRETE LIMITED
Registration no: 00221210 **Date established:** 2027
Turnover: Over £1,000m **No.of Employees:** 51 - 100 **Product Groups:** 14, 33

Date of Accounts	Dec 11	Dec 10	Dec 09
Sales Turnover	21m	19m	12m
Pre Tax Profit/Loss	104	-980	-3m
Working Capital	4m	5m	-4m
Fixed Assets	19m	20m	7m
Current Assets	8m	8m	6m
Current Liabilities	1m	1m	829

Fretwell-Downing Hospitality Ltd

1 Hawke Street, Sheffield, S9 2SU
Tel: 0114-281 6060 **Fax:** 0114-281 6061
E-mail: info@fdhospitality.com
Website: http://www.fdhospitality.com
Directors: B. Hogan (Fin), N. Prime (MD)
Managers: A. Pond (Mktg Serv Mgr), C. Cox (Tech Serv Mgr)
Ultimate Holding Company: FDHG LIMITED
Immediate Holding Company: FRETWELL-DOWNING HOSPITALITY LIMITED
Registration no: 03152100 **VAT No.:** GB 600 2098 93
Date established: 1996 **Turnover:** £2m - £5m **No.of Employees:** 21 - 50
Product Groups: 44

Date of Accounts	May 11	May 10	May 09
Working Capital	648	756	690
Fixed Assets	266	93	56
Current Assets	2m	2m	2m

Furniss & White Foundries Ltd

Unit 17 Abbey Way North Anston Trading Estate, North Anston, Sheffield, S25 4JL
Tel: 01909-568831 **Fax:** 01909-569322
E-mail: es@f-w-f.co.uk
Website: http://www.f-w-f.co.uk
Bank(s): National Westminster Bank Plc
Directors: J. Scholes (Sales), E. Scholes (Dir)
Managers: M. Barnes (Chief Acct)
Immediate Holding Company: FURNISS AND WHITE (FOUNDRIES) LIMITED
Registration no: 01486701 **VAT No.:** GB 308 4392 59
Date established: 1980 **Turnover:** £10m - £20m
No.of Employees: 51 - 100 **Product Groups:** 46, 48

Date of Accounts	Mar 11	Mar 10	Mar 09
Sales Turnover	10m	9m	N/A
Pre Tax Profit/Loss	431	60	500
Working Capital	178	781	333
Fixed Assets	2m	2m	2m
Current Assets	3m	3m	3m
Current Liabilities	799	554	1m

Furniture For Less

381 Chesterfield Road, Sheffield, S8 0RW
Tel: 0114-258 6217 **Fax:** 0114-258 6283
E-mail: info@furnitureforhome.co.uk
Website: http://www.furnitureforless.co.uk
Managers: S. Fordshan
No.of Employees: 11 - 20 **Product Groups:** 26

G B H Exhibition Forwarding Ltd

10 Orgreave Drive, Sheffield, S13 9NR
Tel: 0114-269 0641 **Fax:** 0114-269 3624
E-mail: info@gbhforwarding.com
Website: http://www.gbhforwarding.com
Directors: M. Hunter (MD)
Immediate Holding Company: GBH EXHIBITION FORWARDING LIMITED
Registration no: 01251491 **VAT No.:** GB 174 0635 70
Date established: 1976 **Turnover:** £500,000 - £1m
No.of Employees: 1 - 10 **Product Groups:** 72

Date of Accounts	Dec 11	Dec 10	Dec 09
Working Capital	2	2	-7
Fixed Assets	44	45	59
Current Assets	245	283	207

G M E Springs

9 Orgreave Place, Sheffield, S13 9LU
Tel: 0114-254 8600 **Fax:** 0114-254 8700
E-mail: accountants@gmesprings.co.uk
Website: http://www.gmesprings.co.uk
Directors: J. Boyes (Dir)
Immediate Holding Company: G.M.E. MOTOR ENGINEERS (COVENTRY) LIMITED
Registration no: 04481043 **Date established:** 1971
Turnover: £250,000 - £500,000 **No.of Employees:** 1 - 10
Product Groups: 35, 39, 66

Date of Accounts	Dec 09	Dec 08	Dec 07
Working Capital	-108	-81	-65
Fixed Assets	1m	1m	1m
Current Assets	8	10	21

Phil Geesin Machinery Ltd

101 Carlisle Street East, Sheffield, S4 7QN
Tel: 0114-279 7619 **Fax:** 0114-279 7620
E-mail: phil@philgeesinmachinery.co.uk
Website: http://www.philgeesinmachinery.co.uk
Directors: L. Geesin (Fin), J. Geesin (MD)
Immediate Holding Company: PHIL GEESIN MACHINERY LIMITED
Registration no: 03607961 **VAT No.:** GB 439 0737 36
Date established: 1998 **Turnover:** £500,000 - £1m
No.of Employees: 1 - 10 **Product Groups:** 37, 45, 46, 48, 67

Date of Accounts	Sep 11	Sep 10	Sep 09
Working Capital	176	106	195
Fixed Assets	116	79	91
Current Assets	311	220	263

Geo Robson & Co Conveyors Ltd

Coleford Road, Sheffield, S9 5PA
Tel: 0114-244 4221 **Fax:** 0114-243 3066
E-mail: info@robson.co.uk
Website: http://www.robson.co.uk
Bank(s): National Westminster Bank Plc
Directors: D. Billington (Co Sec), J. Robson (Prop)
Managers: I. Atkinson (Develop Mgr), J. Sharland (Drawing Office), J. Davies, P. Deakin (Tech Serv Mgr)
Immediate Holding Company: GEO. ROBSON & CO. (CONVEYORS) LIMITED
Registration no: 00379606 **VAT No.:** GB 172 9271 49
Date established: 1943 **Turnover:** £20m - £50m
No.of Employees: 101 - 250 **Product Groups:** 42, 44, 45, 46, 81, 84

Date of Accounts	Jun 11	Jun 10	Jun 09
Sales Turnover	23m	18m	21m
Pre Tax Profit/Loss	272	1m	14
Working Capital	9m	9m	9m
Fixed Assets	5m	5m	5m
Current Assets	14m	13m	16m
Current Liabilities	1m	1m	3m

George H Greensmith & Co.

Hallcar Street, Sheffield, S4 7JY
Tel: 0114-272 2808 **Fax:** 0114-272 7956
E-mail: sales@ghgreensmith.co.uk
Directors: D. Greensmith (Prop)
VAT No.: GB 173 9637 27 **Date established:** 1965
Turnover: £500,000 - £1m **No.of Employees:** 1 - 10 **Product Groups:** 48

Glass Technology Services Ltd

Unit 9 Churchill Way Chapeltown, Sheffield, S35 2PY
Tel: 0114-290 1801 **Fax:** 0114-290 1851
E-mail: info@glass-ts.com
Website: http://www.glass-ts.com
Bank(s): National Westminster Bank Plc
Managers: L. Mackrell (Fin Mgr), J. Chisholm (Mgr), R. Edgar (Commun Mgr)
Ultimate Holding Company: THE BRITISH GLASS MANUFACTURERS CONFEDERATION
Immediate Holding Company: GLASS TECHNOLOGY SERVICES LTD
Registration no: 02832216 **VAT No.:** GB 646 3416 36
Date established: 1993 **Turnover:** £1m - £2m **No.of Employees:** 21 - 50
Product Groups: 33, 85

Date of Accounts	Jun 12	Jun 11	Jun 10
Sales Turnover	1m	1m	1m
Pre Tax Profit/Loss	160	48	-26
Working Capital	462	302	254
Current Assets	462	302	254

M J Gleeson Group plc

Broadfield Court, Sheffield, S8 0XF
Tel: 0114-250 0600 **Fax:** 0114-250 0121
E-mail: sheffieldoffice@gleesonbuilding.co.uk
Website: http://www.mjgleeson.com
Directors: D. Couch (Sales & Mktg), E. Lawrie (Co Sec), C. Mclellan (Dir), A. Couch (Sales & Mktg), M. Smart (MD)
Managers: D. Woodruffe (Personnel)
Immediate Holding Company: M J GLEESON GROUP PUBLIC LIMITED COMPANY
Registration no: 00479529 **VAT No.:** GB 216 2716 82
Date established: 1950 **Turnover:** Up to £250,000
No.of Employees: 1 - 10 **Product Groups:** 51, 52

Date of Accounts	Jun 11	Jun 10	Jun 09
Sales Turnover	41m	47m	55m
Pre Tax Profit/Loss	2m	447	-54m
Working Capital	87m	84m	85m
Fixed Assets	13m	17m	22m
Current Assets	108m	115m	119m
Current Liabilities	8m	12m	17m

Gooding Group Ltd

Unit 1-3 Holbrook Avenue Holbrook Industrial Estate, Holbrook, Sheffield, S20 3FF
Tel: 0114-263 3600 **Fax:** 0114-251 1808
E-mail: sales@goodinggroup.co.uk
Directors: L. Gooding (Dir)
Immediate Holding Company: GOODING GROUP LIMITED
Registration no: 03219205 **VAT No.:** GB 678 8538 61
Date established: 1996 **No.of Employees:** 1 - 10 **Product Groups:** 26

Date of Accounts	Dec 11	Dec 10	Dec 09
Working Capital	-104	-160	-123
Fixed Assets	537	506	317
Current Assets	1m	1m	801

Granton Medical Ltd (t/a The Granton Knife Co.)

Parkway Close, Sheffield, S9 4WJ
Tel: 0114-275 7290 **Fax:** 0114-263 4833
E-mail: info@granton.co.uk
Website: http://www.granton.co.uk
Bank(s): Royal Bank of Scotland, Sheffield
Directors: N. Mcgovern (Comm)
Ultimate Holding Company: GRANTON RAGG LIMITED
Immediate Holding Company: GRANTON MEDICAL LIMITED
Registration no: 03025366 **Date established:** 1995 **Turnover:** £2m - £5m
No.of Employees: 21 - 50 **Product Groups:** 29, 30, 36, 38, 49, 67

Date of Accounts	Dec 11	Dec 10	Dec 09
Working Capital	185	413	509
Fixed Assets	1m	1m	1m
Current Assets	920	980	1m

Gray Associates

Unit 10 Meadowcourt Amos Road, Sheffield, S9 1BX
Tel: 0114-244 4110 **Fax:** 0114-244 4141
E-mail: enquiries@gray-associates.co.uk
Website: http://www.gray-associates.co.uk
Directors: A. Gray (Prop)
Immediate Holding Company: GRAYS ASSOCIATES LIMITED
Registration no: 02929779 **Date established:** 1994
Turnover: Up to £250,000 **No.of Employees:** 1 - 10 **Product Groups:** 81

Date of Accounts	Mar 11	Mar 09	Mar 08
Sales Turnover	N/A	72	65
Pre Tax Profit/Loss	N/A	29	12
Working Capital	110	35	16
Fixed Assets	525	N/A	N/A
Current Assets	420	48	28
Current Liabilities	N/A	11	6

Greaves Powder Coating

16 Hicks Street, Sheffield, S3 8BL
Tel: 0114-276 3383 **Fax:** 0114-276 3383
E-mail: mgxjs@yahoo.co.uk
Directors: M. Greaves (Prop)
Immediate Holding Company: GREAVES POWDER COATING LIMITED
Registration no: 07998387 **Date established:** 2012
No.of Employees: 1 - 10 **Product Groups:** 46, 48

Grybrook Ltd T/A Ronald Gill Associates (t/a Ronald Gill Associates)

4 Chapel Road Burncross, Sheffield, S35 1ZG
Tel: 0114-246 0711 **Fax:** 0114-246 0711
E-mail: ronaldgill@msn.com
Website: http://www.trommel.co.uk
Directors: S. Gill (Fin), R. Gill (MD)
Immediate Holding Company: GRYBROOK LIMITED
Registration no: 04472976 **Date established:** 2002
Turnover: £250,000 - £500,000 **No.of Employees:** 1 - 10
Product Groups: 40, 42

Date of Accounts	Jul 11	Jul 10	Jul 09
Working Capital	39	-1	4
Fixed Assets	5	1	1
Current Assets	96	52	33

H A F Powertools Ltd

Unit 8 Fell Road, Sheffield, S9 2AL
Tel: 0114-261 1633 **Fax:** 0114-244 1688

see next page

H A F Powertools Ltd - Cont'd

Directors: J. Robinson (MD)
Immediate Holding Company: HAF POWERTOOLS LIMITED
Registration no: 02895923 **Date established:** 1994
No.of Employees: 1 - 10 **Product Groups:** 37

Date of Accounts	May 11	May 10	May 09
Working Capital	1m	923	874
Fixed Assets	53	56	69
Current Assets	2m	1m	1m

H D Sports Ltd

Rutland Way, Sheffield, S3 8DG
Tel: 0114-272 5190 **Fax:** 0114-272 9330
E-mail: customerservice@hdsports.co.uk
Website: http://www.theworldsbestblades.com
Bank(s): HSBC Bank plc
Directors: P. Ineson (Co Sec), R. Margereson (MD), G. Brumpton (Dir)
Managers: A. Pearce (Prod Mgr)
Immediate Holding Company: HD SPORTS LTD
Registration no: 03152095 **VAT No.:** GB 660 5533 44
Date established: 1996 **Turnover:** £2m - £5m **No.of Employees:** 21 - 50
Product Groups: 49

Date of Accounts	May 11	May 10	May 09
Sales Turnover	2m	2m	3m
Pre Tax Profit/Loss	-160	400	656
Working Capital	761	560	155
Fixed Assets	617	703	768
Current Assets	1m	976	1m
Current Liabilities	112	174	666

Hadfield Cawkwell Davidson Ltd

17 Broomgrove Road, Sheffield, S10 2LZ
Tel: 0114-266 8181 **Fax:** 0114-266 6246
E-mail: email@hcd.co.uk
Website: http://www.hcd.co.uk
Bank(s): National Westminster Bank Plc
Directors: D. Peel (MD)
Managers: A. Travis, P. Adcock (Tech Serv Mgr), T. Winslow
Immediate Holding Company: HADFIELD CAWKWELL DAVIDSON LIMITED
Registration no: 06428199 **VAT No.:** GB 172 5200 92
Date established: 2007 **Turnover:** £5m - £10m
No.of Employees: 51 - 100 **Product Groups:** 54, 84

Date of Accounts	Mar 12	Mar 11	Mar 10
Sales Turnover	6m	6m	5m
Pre Tax Profit/Loss	634	943	469
Working Capital	843	834	686
Fixed Assets	2m	2m	2m
Current Assets	2m	3m	2m
Current Liabilities	960	1m	739

G & J Hall Ltd

Burgess Road, Sheffield, S9 3WD
Tel: 0114-244 0562 **Fax:** 0114-244 9256
E-mail: info@gjhall.co.uk
Website: http://www.gjhall.co.uk
Bank(s): Royal Bank of Scotland, Sheffield
Directors: W. Towning (Co Sec), P. Edwards (MD)
Managers: J. Cox (Mktg Serv Mgr), J. Ede (Nat Sales Mgr)
Ultimate Holding Company: RH TRADING LIMITED
Immediate Holding Company: G & J HALL LIMITED
Registration no: 00240401 **VAT No.:** GB 172 6507 61
Date established: 2029 **Turnover:** £2m - £5m **No.of Employees:** 51 - 100
Product Groups: 36, 46

Date of Accounts	Sep 11	Sep 10	Sep 09
Sales Turnover	4m	4m	4m
Pre Tax Profit/Loss	-160	-494	-508
Working Capital	1m	758	1m
Fixed Assets	1m	1m	1m
Current Assets	2m	2m	2m
Current Liabilities	138	117	129

Hallamshire Hardmetal Products Ltd

315 Coleford Road, Sheffield, S9 5NF
Tel: 0114-244 1483 **Fax:** 0114-244 2712
E-mail: sales@halhard.co.uk
Website: http://www.halhard.co.uk
Bank(s): The Royal Bank of Scotland
Directors: A. Armstrong (Dir), T. Stevenson (Jt MD), T. Hattersley (Jt MD), A. Armstrong (Non Exec), I. Wilkins (Dir), R. Stopforth (Fin)
Ultimate Holding Company: HARDMETAL PRODUCTS LIMITED
Immediate Holding Company: HALLAMSHIRE HARDMETAL PRODUCTS LIMITED
Registration no: 03289670 **VAT No.:** GB 172 5327 68
Date established: 1996 **Turnover:** £1m - £2m **No.of Employees:** 21 - 50
Product Groups: 31, 34, 35, 36, 38, 45, 46

Date of Accounts	Mar 11	Mar 10	Mar 09
Working Capital	834	816	769
Fixed Assets	552	583	659
Current Assets	1m	1m	1m

Andy Hanselman Consulting

Sheffield Technology Park 60 Shirland Lane, Sheffield, S9 3SP
Tel: 0114-243 4666 **Fax:** 0114-221 1701
E-mail: info@competeorgetbeat.com
Website: http://www.competeorgetbeat.com
Directors: A. Hanselman (Ptnr)
Immediate Holding Company: VIN MAGNIFIQUE LIMITED
Registration no: 04993387 **Date established:** 2011
Turnover: Up to £250,000 **No.of Employees:** 1 - 10 **Product Groups:** 84

Date of Accounts	Jan 11	Jan 10	Jan 09
Working Capital	86	80	73
Fixed Assets	1	2	2
Current Assets	107	102	103

Hardy's Gunsmiths

367 Ecclesall Road, Sheffield, S11 8PF
Tel: 0114-266 8403 **Fax:** 0114-266 8403
E-mail: john889guns@o2email.co.uk
Managers: J. Hutchinson (Mgr)
Immediate Holding Company: HARDY'S GUNSMITHS LIMITED
Registration no: 04027714 **Date established:** 2000
No.of Employees: 1 - 10 **Product Groups:** 36, 39, 40

Date of Accounts	Jul 11	Jul 10	Jul 09
Working Capital	54	50	43
Current Assets	84	84	70

Haritsol Consulting

Provincial House Solly Street, Sheffield, S1 4BB
Tel: 0114-263 4534
E-mail: info@haritsol.com
Website: http://www.haritsol.com
Directors: S. Oberoi (Dir)
Immediate Holding Company: HARITSOL CONSULTING LTD.
Registration no: 06221231 **Date established:** 2007
No.of Employees: 1 - 10 **Product Groups:** 44

Date of Accounts	Apr 12	Apr 11	Apr 09
Working Capital	6	3	-12
Fixed Assets	1	1	1
Current Assets	18	21	3

K Hartwall Ltd

4 Park Square Thorncliffe Park Estate Newton Chambers Road, Chapeltown, Sheffield, S35 2PH
Tel: 0114-257 3631 **Fax:** 0114-257 3630
E-mail: chris.sampson@k-hartwall.com
Website: http://www.k-hartwall.com
Managers: C. Sampson (Comm)
Ultimate Holding Company: K HARTWALL OY AB (FINLAND)
Immediate Holding Company: K.HARTWALL LIMITED
Registration no: 01934771 **VAT No.:** GB 258 2765 29
Date established: 1985 **Turnover:** £5m - £10m **No.of Employees:** 1 - 10
Product Groups: 26, 27, 28, 30, 35, 36, 41, 43, 45, 48, 49, 66, 84

Date of Accounts	Dec 11	Dec 10	Dec 09
Sales Turnover	6m	7m	12m
Pre Tax Profit/Loss	591	151	-3m
Working Capital	-287	263	377
Fixed Assets	1m	299	1m
Current Assets	226	5m	4m
Current Liabilities	86	555	863

Heath Lambert Ltd

Enterprise House 1 Broad Field Court, Sheffield, S8 0XF
Tel: 0114-267 2000 **Fax:** 0114-267 8585
Website: http://www.heathlambert.com
Directors: D. Colegate (MD)
Ultimate Holding Company: HLG HOLDINGS LIMITED
Immediate Holding Company: HEATH LAMBERT LIMITED
Registration no: 01199129 **Date established:** 1975
Turnover: £125m - £250m **No.of Employees:** 11 - 20 **Product Groups:** 82

Date of Accounts	Dec 10	Dec 09	Dec 08
Sales Turnover	91m	93m	107m
Pre Tax Profit/Loss	11m	9m	18m
Working Capital	101m	92m	87m
Fixed Assets	10m	12m	14m
Current Assets	262m	258m	304m
Current Liabilities	162m	12m	16m

Henry Boot

Banner Cross Hall, Sheffield, S11 9PD
Tel: 0114-255 5444 **Fax:** 0114-258 5548
E-mail: pr@henryboot.co.uk
Website: http://www.henryboot.co.uk
Bank(s): Barclays, Nat West, The Royal Bank of Scotland & L
Directors: E. Boot (MD)
Ultimate Holding Company: HENRY BOOT PLC
Immediate Holding Company: FIRST NATIONAL HOUSING TRUST LIMITED
Registration no: 00276288 **VAT No.:** GB 308 6726 46
Date established: 1933 **Turnover:** £250,000 - £500,000
No.of Employees: 51 - 100 **Product Groups:** 52, 80

Date of Accounts	Dec 11	Dec 10	Dec 09
Sales Turnover	489	228	244
Pre Tax Profit/Loss	566	519	600
Working Capital	10m	9m	13m
Fixed Assets	2m	2m	2m
Current Assets	10m	9m	13m

Heron Cabinets Ltd

Unit B Staniforth Works, Sheffield, S12 4LB
Tel: 0114-248 5894
E-mail: info@glass-display-cabinets.co.uk
Website: http://www.glass-display-cabinets.co.uk
Managers: M. Heron (Mgr)
Immediate Holding Company: HERON CABINETS LTD
Registration no: 06497838 **Date established:** 2008
No.of Employees: 1 - 10 **Product Groups:** 26, 40, 67

Date of Accounts	Mar 11	Mar 10
Working Capital	18	18
Fixed Assets	2	2
Current Assets	51	50

Walter Heselwood Ltd

Stevenson Road, Sheffield, S9 2SG
Tel: 0114-244 2042 **Fax:** 0114-243 2806
E-mail: admin@heselwood.com
Website: http://www.heselwood.com
Bank(s): HSBC
Directors: R. Turner (Fin), G. Turner (MD)
Immediate Holding Company: WALTER HESELWOOD LIMITED
Registration no: 00598338 **VAT No.:** GB 172 6337 60
Date established: 1958 **Turnover:** £10m - £20m
No.of Employees: 11 - 20 **Product Groups:** 42

Date of Accounts	Jan 12	Jan 11	Jan 10
Sales Turnover	10m	N/A	N/A
Pre Tax Profit/Loss	175	N/A	N/A
Working Capital	2m	1m	2m
Fixed Assets	1m	1m	1m
Current Assets	3m	3m	2m
Current Liabilities	235	N/A	N/A

Hi Tech Special Steels Ltd

Rotherham Road Dinnington, Sheffield, S25 3RF
Tel: 01909-564545 **Fax:** 01909-550682
E-mail: harrypriest@hitechspecialsteels.co.uk
Website: http://www.hi-techspecialsteelsltd.co.uk
Directors: H. Priest (MD), T. Johnston (Fin)
Ultimate Holding Company: ROTATION PATTERN LIMITED
Immediate Holding Company: HI-TECH SPECIAL STEELS LIMITED.
Registration no: 01921116 **Date established:** 1985
No.of Employees: 21 - 50 **Product Groups:** 34

Date of Accounts	Dec 11	Dec 10	Dec 09
Working Capital	110	114	102
Fixed Assets	152	124	138
Current Assets	3m	2m	2m

High Access Solutions Ltd

Access House 41 Clun Street, Sheffield, S4 7JS
Tel: 0114-242 4811 **Fax:** 0114-242 4822
E-mail: info@1hasl.co.uk
Website: http://www.highaccesssolutions.co.uk
Directors: G. Forster (Fin), P. Forester (Chief Op Offcr)
Immediate Holding Company: HIGH ACCESS SOLUTIONS LIMITED
Registration no: 04825531 **Date established:** 2003
No.of Employees: 1 - 10 **Product Groups:** 35, 51

Date of Accounts	Mar 12	Mar 11	Mar 10
Working Capital	401	414	90
Fixed Assets	169	119	114
Current Assets	704	683	270

Hill Cliffe Garage

48 Catley Road, Sheffield, S9 5JF
Tel: 0114-261 9965 **Fax:** 0114-242 3319
E-mail: info@hillcliffe.co.uk
Website: http://www.hillcliffegarage.co.uk
Directors: F. Riaz (Prop)
Immediate Holding Company: HILLCLIFFE GARAGE LIMITED
Registration no: 07532971 **VAT No.:** GB 172 4802 69
Date established: 2011 **Turnover:** £1m - £2m **No.of Employees:** 1 - 10
Product Groups: 35, 36, 46

Date of Accounts	Apr 10	Apr 09	Apr 08
Working Capital	6	4	16
Fixed Assets	5	7	9
Current Assets	99	93	196

Ernest H Hill Ltd

Unit 10-12 Meadowbrook Park, Halfway, Sheffield, S20 3PJ
Tel: 0114-248 4882 **Fax:** 0114-248 9142
E-mail: info@hillpumps.com
Website: http://www.hillpumps.com
Bank(s): The Royal Bank of Scotland
Directors: C. Dale (Fin)
Managers: B. Fox
Ultimate Holding Company: TOWNGATE HOLDINGS LIMITED
Immediate Holding Company: ERNEST H.HILL,LIMITED
Registration no: 00091553 **VAT No.:** GB 172 4470 68
Date established: 2007 **Turnover:** £2m - £5m **No.of Employees:** 21 - 50
Product Groups: 36, 39, 40

Date of Accounts	Sep 11	Sep 10	Sep 09
Sales Turnover	2m	2m	2m
Pre Tax Profit/Loss	109	5	-9
Working Capital	426	330	306
Fixed Assets	100	121	163
Current Assets	721	777	636
Current Liabilities	134	83	71

T Hill

Prospect Road Heeley, Sheffield, S2 3EN
Tel: 0114-262 1714 **Fax:** 0114-296 2384
Website: http://www.tht.co.uk
Directors: T. Hill (Prop)
Immediate Holding Company: FREEWAY SPORTS SOLUTIONS LTD
Registration no: 00185544 **Date established:** 2011
No.of Employees: 1 - 10 **Product Groups:** 46

Date of Accounts	Aug 11
Working Capital	98
Fixed Assets	36
Current Assets	100

Hillfoot Multi Metals Head Office

Herries Road, Sheffield, S6 1HP
Tel: 0114-233 1133 **Fax:** 0114-233 9931
E-mail: douglas.jackson@hillfoot.com
Website: http://www.hillfootmultimetals.com
Directors: D. Jackson (MD)
Ultimate Holding Company: SPECIAL STEEL CO.,LIMITED
Immediate Holding Company: SPECIAL FORGED PRODUCTS LIMITED
Registration no: 00663388 **Date established:** 1960 **Turnover:** £2m - £5m
No.of Employees: 101 - 250 **Product Groups:** 34, 35, 36, 48, 66

Date of Accounts	Dec 07	May 11	May 10
Sales Turnover	44m	N/A	4m
Pre Tax Profit/Loss	7m	N/A	-193
Working Capital	7m	2m	2m
Fixed Assets	3m	229	682
Current Assets	28m	3m	4m
Current Liabilities	2m	N/A	399

Hillfoot Multi Metals

Herries Road, Sheffield, S6 1 HP
Tel: 0114-233 1133 **Fax:** 0114-285 2802
E-mail: craig.james@hillfootmultimetals.com
Website: http://www.hillfootmultimetals.com
Bank(s): National Westminster Bank Plc
Directors: C. James (Comm), C. Hausley (Dir), S. Collard (Dir)
Managers: S. Taylor (Purch Mgr)
Ultimate Holding Company: Murray International Holdings Ltd
Registration no: 00663388 **Date established:** 1923 **Turnover:** £2m - £5m
No.of Employees: 101 - 250 **Product Groups:** 34, 35, 36, 48, 66

Hillsborough Steelstock Ltd

Scapa Works 2 Penistone Road North, Sheffield, S6 1LE
Tel: 0114-285 5525 **Fax:** 0114-232 0972
E-mail: sales@hillsboroughsteelstock.co.uk
Website: http://www.hillsboroughsteelstock.co.uk
Directors: J. Wigglesworth (MD), M. Daniel (Fin), I. Coe (Sales)
Immediate Holding Company: HILLSBOROUGH STEELSTOCK LIMITED
Registration no: 02409345 **VAT No.:** GB 600 1671 94
Date established: 1989 **Turnover:** £10m - £20m
No.of Employees: 21 - 50 **Product Groups:** 66

Date of Accounts	Dec 11	Dec 10	Dec 09
Sales Turnover	12m	11m	8m
Pre Tax Profit/Loss	-155	295	-72
Working Capital	29	-70	43
Fixed Assets	1m	1m	1m
Current Assets	4m	4m	3m
Current Liabilities	160	290	357

Hodge Clemco Ltd

Orgreave Drive, Sheffield, S13 9NR
Tel: 0114-254 0600 **Fax:** 0114-254 0250
E-mail: sales@hodgeclemco.co.uk
Website: http://www.hodgeclemco.co.uk
Bank(s): National Westminster Bank Plc

Directors: P. Grattan (Comm)
Ultimate Holding Company: SAMUEL HODGE HOLDINGS LIMITED
Immediate Holding Company: HODGE CLEMCO LIMITED
Registration no: 00626216 **VAT No.:** GB 172 5288 52
Date established: 1959 **Turnover:** £10m - £20m
No.of Employees: 51 - 100 **Product Groups:** 24, 32, 33, 37, 39, 40, 42, 43, 45, 46, 47, 48, 52, 63, 66, 67, 68, 83, 84

Date of Accounts	Mar 12	Mar 11	Mar 10
Sales Turnover	11m	10m	11m
Pre Tax Profit/Loss	2m	-112	503
Working Capital	1m	1m	431
Fixed Assets	929	2m	2m
Current Assets	6m	5m	5m
Current Liabilities	541	373	520

Hogg Diesel Injection Ltd
386 Cricket Inn Road, Sheffield, S2 5AX
Tel: 0114-272 5692 **Fax:** 0114-278 0898
E-mail: hoggdieselltd@yahoo.co.uk
Website: http://www.johnhogg.co.uk
Directors: C. Hogg (Dir)
Immediate Holding Company: HOGG DIESEL INJECTION LIMITED
Registration no: 06541833 **Date established:** 2008
No.of Employees: 1 - 10 **Product Groups:** 40

Date of Accounts	Mar 11	Mar 10	Mar 09
Working Capital	-54	-97	-139
Fixed Assets	134	155	176
Current Assets	76	86	66

F E & J R Hopkinson Ltd
124 Scotland Street, Sheffield, S3 7DE
Tel: 0114-272 7486 **Fax:** 0114-275 0290
E-mail: info@sheffieldknives.co.uk
Website: http://www.sheffieldknives.co.uk
Bank(s): Lloyds TSB Bank plc
Directors: J. Turton (Fin)
Ultimate Holding Company: J. ADAMS LIMITED
Immediate Holding Company: F.E. & J.R.HOPKINSON LIMITED
Registration no: 00388186 **VAT No.:** GB 172 6539 48
Date established: 1944 **Turnover:** Up to £250,000
No.of Employees: 11 - 20 **Product Groups:** 36, 37, 39, 49

Date of Accounts	Dec 11	Dec 10	Dec 09
Working Capital	179	179	179
Fixed Assets	90	91	91
Current Assets	266	268	267

Hose Components Supplies
2 Hunsley Street, Sheffield, S4 8DY
Tel: 0114-261 9766 **Fax:** 0114-272 2401
E-mail: sales@rshgroup.co.uk
Directors: C. Hodgskin (Fin), R. Hand (MD)
Immediate Holding Company: RUBBER SAFETY & HYGIENE LIMITED
Registration no: 00869367 **VAT No.:** GB 534 0275 70
Date established: 1990 **Turnover:** £1m - £2m **No.of Employees:** 11 - 20
Product Groups: 29, 63

Date of Accounts	Dec 09	Dec 08	Mar 12
Working Capital	-58	231	203
Fixed Assets	1m	1m	41
Current Assets	1m	2m	2m

Hostombe Group Ltd
Minalloy House 10-16 Regent Street, Sheffield, S1 3NJ
Tel: 0114-272 4324 **Fax:** 0114-272 9550
E-mail: roger.hostombe@hostombe.co.uk
Website: http://www.hostombe.co.uk
Directors: P. Righton (Fin), R. Hostombe (Ch)
Ultimate Holding Company: HOSTOMBE GROUP LIMITED
Immediate Holding Company: R. HOSTOMBE LIMITED
Registration no: 02348124 **Date established:** 1989
Turnover: £20m - £50m **No.of Employees:** 1 - 10 **Product Groups:** 12, 14, 17, 31, 32, 33, 34, 35, 66

Date of Accounts	Mar 11	Mar 10	Mar 09

House Of Logos
714 Attercliffe Road, Sheffield, S9 3RP
Tel: 0114-243 4595 **Fax:** 0114-242 6636
E-mail: sales@houseoflogos.co.uk
Website: http://www.houseoflogos.co.uk
Directors: M. Elliott (Fin)
Immediate Holding Company: HOUSE OF LOGOS LIMITED
Registration no: 05096076 **Date established:** 2004
Turnover: Up to £250,000 **No.of Employees:** 1 - 10 **Product Groups:** 49

Date of Accounts	Mar 12	Mar 11	Mar 10
Sales Turnover	N/A	N/A	139
Pre Tax Profit/Loss	N/A	N/A	48
Working Capital	135	131	129
Fixed Assets	46	46	47
Current Assets	204	164	147
Current Liabilities	N/A	N/A	11

W H Hulley
26 Ebenezer Street, Sheffield, S3 8SR
Tel: 0114-272 1205 **Fax:** 0114-276 5621
E-mail: m-hulley@hulley-ladders.co.uk
Website: http://www.hulley-ladders.co.uk
Directors: M. Hulley (Prop)
Turnover: Up to £250,000 **No.of Employees:** 1 - 10 **Product Groups:** 25, 35, 66

Hydrainer Pumps Ltd
Rotherham Close Norwood Industrial Estate, Killamarsh, Sheffield, S21 2JU
Tel: 0114-248 4868 **Fax:** 0114-247 2060
E-mail: davestock@hydrainer.co.uk
Website: http://www.hydrainer.com
Bank(s): Bank of Scotland
Directors: D. Stock (MD)
Managers: L. Barden (Tech Serv Mgr), R. Allan (Comptroller)
Ultimate Holding Company: ORRMAC (NO 50) LIMITED
Immediate Holding Company: HYDRAINER PUMPS LIMITED
Registration no: 01197269 **Date established:** 1975 **Turnover:** £2m - £5m
No.of Employees: 11 - 20 **Product Groups:** 40

Date of Accounts	Sep 11	Sep 10	Sep 09
Working Capital	2m	2m	2m
Fixed Assets	41	47	47
Current Assets	2m	2m	2m

Hytemp Ltd
Herries Road, Sheffield, S6 1RP
Tel: 0114-233 8163 **Fax:** 0114-233 8211
E-mail: sales@hytemp.com
Website: http://www.hytemp.com
Bank(s): National Westminster Bank Plc
Directors: C. Fell (Fin), S. Hepplewhite (MD), M. Elsworth (Dir & Gen Mgr), M. Elsworth (MD), I. Kirkham (Ch), G. Bell (MD), D. Jackson (Sales & Mktg), G. Bell (Prop)
Managers: J. Cotterill (Ops Mgr)
Ultimate Holding Company: MURRAY INTERNATIONAL HOLDINGS LIMITED
Immediate Holding Company: HYTEMP LTD
Registration no: 07096937 **VAT No.:** GB 438 9377 01
Date established: 2009 **No.of Employees:** 11 - 20 **Product Groups:** 34, 35, 36

I M L Labels & Systems Ltd
441 Brightside Lane, Sheffield, S9 2RS
Tel: 0114-242 2111 **Fax:** 0114-240 3410
E-mail: shiggins@iml-labels.co.uk
Website: http://www.iml-labels.co.uk
Directors: S. Cook (Dir), K. Cook (Fin)
Managers: H. Higgins (Mktg Serv Mgr)
Immediate Holding Company: IML LABELS & SYSTEMS LIMITED
Registration no: 03396128 **VAT No.:** GB 694 9149 77
Date established: 1997 **Turnover:** £2m - £5m **No.of Employees:** 21 - 50
Product Groups: 27, 28, 30, 49

Date of Accounts	Jan 12	Jan 11	Jan 09
Working Capital	-327	-183	-498
Fixed Assets	1m	913	1m
Current Assets	1m	1m	789

I P S L Proclad Ltd
2 Sanderson Street, Sheffield, S9 2TW
Tel: 0114-279 9188 **Fax:** 0114-279 9175
E-mail: sales@ipsluk.co.uk
Website: http://www.ipsluk.co.uk
Bank(s): Yorkshire Bank PLC
Directors: A. Matchett (MD)
Registration no: 03084525 **Turnover:** £500,000 - £1m
No.of Employees: 11 - 20 **Product Groups:** 30, 31

George Ibbotson Steels Ltd
16 Atlas Way, Sheffield, S4 7QQ
Tel: 0114-244 7400 **Fax:** 0114-244 7412
E-mail: sales@ibbotsonsteels.co.uk
Website: http://www.kellysearch.com/partners/80099923/8009992d.005005.htm
Directors: J. Church (Dir), V. Church (Fin)
Immediate Holding Company: GEORGE IBBOTSON (STEELS) LIMITED
Registration no: 02772547 **Date established:** 1992
Turnover: £250,000 - £500,000 **No.of Employees:** 1 - 10
Product Groups: 34, 66

Date of Accounts	Dec 11	Dec 10	Dec 09
Working Capital	499	468	444
Fixed Assets	143	153	164
Current Assets	571	512	490

Ideasbynet Promotional Items
Kings Croft Savage Lane, Sheffield, S17 3GW
Tel: 08448-117566 **Fax:** 0114-262 1201
E-mail: sales@ideasbynet.com
Website: http://www.ideasbynet.com
Bank(s): The Royal Bank of Scotland plc
Directors: S. Roberts (Sales), P. Howarth (Grp Chief Exec)
Managers: S. Morgan
Immediate Holding Company: IDEASBYNET LIMITED
Registration no: 03810054 **VAT No.:** GB 391 2769 27
Date established: 1999 **Turnover:** £1m - £2m **No.of Employees:** 21 - 50
Product Groups: 22, 24, 25, 27, 28, 29, 30, 44, 49, 65, 81

iM3 Sheffield
Electric Works 3 Concourse Way, Sheffield, S1 2BJ
Tel: 07730-518185
E-mail: info@seoclock.co.uk
Website: http://www.im3.co.uk
Managers: N. Palmer (Mktg Serv Mgr)
Registration no: 06331170 **Date established:** 2005
Turnover: Up to £250,000 **No.of Employees:** 1 - 10 **Product Groups:** 44

Images Labels Ltd
12 Aintree Avenue Eckington, Sheffield, S21 4JA
Tel: 01246-436876 **Fax:** 01246-435987
E-mail: info@imageslabels.com
Website: http://www.imageslabels.com
Directors: S. Metcalfe (Fin)
Immediate Holding Company: IMAGES LABELS LIMITED
Registration no: 02518335 **Date established:** 1990
Turnover: Up to £250,000 **No.of Employees:** 1 - 10 **Product Groups:** 23, 27, 28, 30, 49

Date of Accounts	Jun 12	Jun 11	Jun 10
Working Capital	54	56	57
Fixed Assets	N/A	1	1
Current Assets	110	114	94

Impact Carbides Ltd
36 East Bank Road, Sheffield, S2 3PS
Tel: 0114-272 7216 **Fax:** 0114-272 4854
E-mail: sales@impactcarbides.co.uk
Website: http://www.impactcarbides.co.uk
Bank(s): Barclays
Directors: S. Briggs (Ptnr), P. Bell (MD)
Ultimate Holding Company: IMPACT CARBIDES HOLDINGS LIMITED
Immediate Holding Company: IMPACT CARBIDES LIMITED
Registration no: 01672893 **Date established:** 1982
Turnover: £500,000 - £1m **No.of Employees:** 21 - 50
Product Groups: 36, 46

Date of Accounts	Mar 11	Mar 10	Mar 09
Working Capital	431	354	359
Fixed Assets	555	591	621
Current Assets	937	838	709

Inductelec Ltd
137 Carlisle Street, Sheffield, S4 7LJ
Tel: 0114-272 3369 **Fax:** 0114-276 1499
E-mail: info@inductelec.co.uk
Website: http://www.inductelec.co.uk
Directors: G. Wade (Fin), T. Wade (MD)
Immediate Holding Company: INDUCTELEC LIMITED
Registration no: 00928358 **Date established:** 1968
No.of Employees: 11 - 20 **Product Groups:** 47

Date of Accounts	Mar 11	Mar 10	Mar 09
Working Capital	353	354	260
Fixed Assets	430	510	505
Current Assets	813	829	693

Induction Heating Services
18 Dalewood Road, Sheffield, S8 0EB
Tel: 07730-200098 **Fax:** 0114-236 4441
Website: http://www.inductionheatingservices.co.uk
Directors: R. Burton (Prop), J. Burton (Co Sec)
Immediate Holding Company: ALLUM AUTOMATION LTD
Registration no: 04503873 **Date established:** 2011
No.of Employees: 1 - 10 **Product Groups:** 46, 48

Industrial Battery & Charger Services Ltd
46 Catley Road, Sheffield, S9 5JF
Tel: 0114-243 3993 **Fax:** 0114-242 4845
E-mail: sales@ibcs.co.uk
Website: http://www.forklift-batteries.co.uk
Bank(s): HSBC Bank plc
Directors: P. Hewson (Sales), G. Woon (Co Sec), J. Jones (MD)
Managers: P. Hewson (Sales Prom Mgr), P. Garratt (Sales Prom Mgr)
Immediate Holding Company: INDUSTRIAL BATTERY AND CHARGER SERVICES LIMITED
Registration no: 04125570 **Date established:** 2000
No.of Employees: 11 - 20 **Product Groups:** 30, 31, 37, 39

Date of Accounts	Jun 11	Jun 10	Jun 09
Working Capital	446	361	310
Fixed Assets	455	464	470
Current Assets	1m	777	528

Infraglo Sheffield Ltd
Dannemora Drive, Sheffield, S9 5DF
Tel: 0114-249 5445 **Fax:** 0114-249 5066
E-mail: ken.crane@infraglo.co.uk
Website: http://www.infraglo.co.uk
Bank(s): National Westminster Bank Plc
Directors: K. Crane (Dir)
Immediate Holding Company: INFRAGLO (SHEFFIELD) LIMITED
Registration no: 02460631 **VAT No.:** GB 534 0038 84
Date established: 1990 **Turnover:** £500,000 - £1m
No.of Employees: 11 - 20 **Product Groups:** 40, 41, 42, 46, 83

Date of Accounts	Jun 12	Jun 11	Jun 10
Working Capital	280	263	251
Fixed Assets	218	223	228
Current Assets	387	436	362

Inman & Co Electrical Ltd
2-4 Orgreave Place, Sheffield, S13 9LU
Tel: 0114-254 2400 **Fax:** 0114-254 2410
E-mail: mlobar@inmanselectrical.co.uk
Website: http://www.inmanswebstore.co.uk
Bank(s): National Westminster Bank Plc
Directors: R. Lobar (Sales), M. Lobar (Sales), M. Mchale (Grp Chief Exec), S. Hollingshead (Chief Op Offcr), C. Wright (Ch), B. Brown (Co Sec)
Managers: J. Savage (Mktg Serv Mgr), M. Mould (Comptroller), M. Parkinson (Purch Mgr), M. Stancey (I.T. Exec), M. Lobar (Sales Prom Mgr), C. Simpson (I.T. Exec)
Ultimate Holding Company: WHITE ROSE HOLDINGS LIMITED
Immediate Holding Company: INMAN & CO. (ELECTRICAL) LIMITED
Registration no: 03902678 **VAT No.:** GB 172 8570 44
Date established: 2000 **Turnover:** £10m - £20m
No.of Employees: 51 - 100 **Product Groups:** 77

Date of Accounts	Mar 11	Mar 10	Mar 09
Sales Turnover	20m	25m	24m
Pre Tax Profit/Loss	-1m	57	-480
Working Capital	2m	3m	3m
Fixed Assets	290	336	361
Current Assets	7m	6m	8m
Current Liabilities	881	842	810

Inman Sheffield Ltd
Britannia Steelworks Furnival Road, Sheffield, S4 7YA
Tel: 0114-272 1153 **Fax:** 0114-272 0560
E-mail: vickyevola@live.co.uk
Directors: V. Evola (MD)
Immediate Holding Company: INMAN SHEFFIELD LTD
Registration no: 06717042 **Date established:** 2008
No.of Employees: 1 - 10 **Product Groups:** 30, 34, 48

Date of Accounts	Oct 11	Oct 10	Oct 09
Working Capital	-38	36	46
Fixed Assets	3	3	4
Current Assets	74	76	68
Current Liabilities	N/A	40	22

Inman Sheffield ltd
Britannia Steel Works Furnival Road, Sheffield, S4 7 YA
Tel: 0114-2721153 **Fax:** 0114-2720560
E-mail: vickyevola@live.co.uk
Date established: 2008 **Turnover:** Up to £250,000 **Product Groups:** 34, 66

Insight Direct (UK) Limited
The Technology Building Insight Campus, Sheffield, KT12 2TZ
Tel: 0871-669 933 **Fax:** 01932-244590
E-mail: insight@insight.co.uk
Website: http://www.insight.co.uk
Bank(s): HSBC Bank plc
Directors: I. Glover (Dir)
Managers: A. Pearson (Personnel), I. Price (Mktg Serv Mgr), J. Morton (Consultant)
Immediate Holding Company: Siemens
VAT No.: GB 564 2872 21 **Turnover:** £5m - £10m
No.of Employees: 51 - 100 **Product Groups:** 80

Institute Of Spring Technology
Henry Street, Sheffield, S3 7EQ
Tel: 0114-276 0771 **Fax:** 0114-272 6344
E-mail: l.peel@ist.org.uk
Website: http://www.ist.org.uk
Managers: L. Peel (Mgr)
Immediate Holding Company: THE INSTITUTE OF SPRING TECHNOLOGY LTD.

see next page

***Institute Of Spring Technology** - Cont'd*

Registration no: 03305326 **VAT No.:** GB 690 0145 57
Date established: 1997 **Turnover:** £500,000 - £1m
No.of Employees: 1 - 10 **Product Groups:** 29, 35, 36, 38, 39, 40, 44, 46, 49, 66, 67, 68, 84, 85, 86, 87

Date of Accounts	Dec 11	Dec 10	Dec 09
Working Capital	-310	530	-306
Fixed Assets	501	465	472
Current Assets	414	530	-306

Intelesis Ltd

Unit 7 First Floor Offices Aizlewood's Mill Business Centre, Nursery Street, Sheffield, S3 8GG
Tel: 0844-8444555 **Fax:** 0844-8444567
E-mail: info@intelesis.co.uk
Website: http://www.intelesis.co.uk
Directors: N. Liverton (Dir)
Registration no: 05189456 **Date established:** 2000
Turnover: £250,000 - £500,000 **No.of Employees:** 1 - 10
Product Groups: 67, 80

Date of Accounts	Dec 07	Dec 06	Dec 05
Sales Turnover	N/A	N/A	76
Pre Tax Profit/Loss	N/A	N/A	46
Working Capital	28	18	4
Fixed Assets	2	2	3
Current Assets	60	46	28
Current Liabilities	32	28	24
ROCE% (Return on Capital Employed)			640.7
ROT% (Return on Turnover)			60.1

Interfit Industrial Tyres Ltd

4 Roman Ridge Road, Sheffield, S9 1GB
Tel: 0114-244 0176 **Fax:** 0114-242 4110
E-mail: industrial@watts-tyres.co.uk
Website: http://www.wattstyres.com
Directors: I. Bland (MD)
Managers: D. Baldwin (Depot Mgr), D. Baldwin (Mgr)
Immediate Holding Company: TASKERS UK LIMITED
Registration no: 01434811 **Date established:** 1985
Turnover: £10m - £20m **No.of Employees:** 1 - 10 **Product Groups:** 29, 68

Date of Accounts	Sep 11	Sep 10	Sep 09
Working Capital	27	-31	-48
Fixed Assets	52	34	48
Current Assets	282	323	241

Intermet Refractory Products Ltd

Platts Lane Oughtibridge, Sheffield, S35 0HP
Tel: 0114-286 3761 **Fax:** 0114-286 3766
E-mail: sales@intermet.co.uk
Website: http://www.intermet.co.uk
Bank(s): Yorkshire Bank PLC
Directors: T. Staton (Dir), T. Statham (MD)
Managers: J. Boat (Fin Mgr)
Immediate Holding Company: INTERMET REFRACTORY PRODUCTS LIMITED
Registration no: 06473835 **VAT No.:** GB 457 7666 93
Date established: 2008 **Turnover:** £2m - £5m **No.of Employees:** 21 - 50
Product Groups: 33

Date of Accounts	Mar 11	Mar 10	Mar 09
Working Capital	-43	-171	-208
Fixed Assets	929	949	955
Current Assets	2m	1m	1m

Intertruck

100 Rutland Road, Sheffield, S3 9PJ
Tel: 0114-276 5050 **Fax:** 0114-273 9616
Website: http://www.intertruck.co.uk
Managers: P. Buckle (Mgr)
Date established: 1999 **No.of Employees:** 1 - 10 **Product Groups:** 35, 45

Iris Refactory Services Ltd

8 Causeway Gardens, Sheffield, S17 3EY
Tel: 0114-236 3303 **Fax:** 0114-236 3303
Directors: C. Hook (MD)
Immediate Holding Company: IRIS REFRACTORY SERVICES LIMITED
Registration no: 03775308 **Date established:** 1999
Turnover: Up to £250,000 **No.of Employees:** 1 - 10 **Product Groups:** 40, 42, 46

Date of Accounts	May 11	May 10	May 09
Sales Turnover	N/A	134	N/A
Pre Tax Profit/Loss	N/A	23	N/A
Working Capital	-251	16	-2
Fixed Assets	287	1	1
Current Assets	32	312	311
Current Liabilities	N/A	6	115

J B Hats & Things

18 Ellesmere Road, Sheffield, S4 7JB
Tel: 0114-278 6660
E-mail: jbahatsnthing@aol.com
Directors: P. Biki (Prop)
Turnover: Up to £250,000 **No.of Employees:** 1 - 10 **Product Groups:** 22, 24, 63

J B Stainless Ltd

61 Washford Road, Sheffield, S9 3XW
Tel: 0114-242 0042 **Fax:** 0114-243 0043
E-mail: sales@jbstainlessandalloys.com
Website: http://www.jbstainlessandalloys.com
Directors: J. Bamforth (Sales), A. Bamforth West (Co Sec)
Immediate Holding Company: J B STAINLESS & ALLOYS LIMITED
Registration no: 02213422 **Date established:** 1988 **Turnover:** £2m - £5m
No.of Employees: 1 - 10 **Product Groups:** 34, 39, 48, 66

Date of Accounts	Mar 12	Mar 11	Mar 10
Working Capital	332	228	183
Fixed Assets	64	60	71
Current Assets	2m	1m	1m

J P S Fire Protection

51 Clarkegrove Road, Sheffield, S10 2NH
Tel: 0114-288 1980 **Fax:** 0114-288 1002
E-mail: info@jpsfire.co.uk
Directors: J. Portman (Prop)
Immediate Holding Company: JPS FIRE PROTECTION LIMITED
Registration no: 04532928 **Date established:** 2002
No.of Employees: 1 - 10 **Product Groups:** 38, 42

Date of Accounts	Aug 11	Aug 10	Sep 09
Working Capital	3	2	N/A
Fixed Assets	2	2	2
Current Assets	17	12	8

J R I Ltd

Unit 18 Churchill Way, Chapeltown, Sheffield, S35 2PY
Tel: 0114-345 3200 **Fax:** 0114-257 3204
E-mail: keith.jackson@jri-ltd.co.uk
Website: http://www.jri-ltd.co.uk
Directors: C. Fifield (Fin), K. Jackson (MD)
Managers: D. Chung, P. Probets (Mktg Serv Mgr), E. Morley, M. Brooks (Comptroller)
Immediate Holding Company: J.R.I. LTD
Registration no: 05905154 **Turnover:** £10m - £20m
No.of Employees: 51 - 100 **Product Groups:** 38

J & T Fabrications

Old Globe Steelworks Alma Street, Sheffield, S3 8SA
Tel: 0114-249 1788 **Fax:** 0114-249 1788
Directors: A. Dunwell (Prop)
Immediate Holding Company: A W TOOLS (EUROPE) LIMITED
Registration no: 05982085 **Date established:** 2006
No.of Employees: 1 - 10 **Product Groups:** 26, 35

Date of Accounts	Dec 11	Dec 10	Dec 09
Working Capital	401	403	417
Fixed Assets	331	356	383
Current Assets	516	451	486

W Jackson

2 Quarry Road Handsworth, Sheffield, S13 9AZ
Tel: 0114-242 6263 **Fax:** 0114- 2435915
E-mail: jacksonmetal@hotmail.com
Directors: W. Jackson (Prop)
Date established: 1994 **No.of Employees:** 1 - 10 **Product Groups:** 46, 48

Jeld Wen UK Ltd

Retford Road Woodhouse Mill, Sheffield, S13 9WH
Tel: 0114-254 2000 **Fax:** 0114-254 2860
E-mail: martin.crowther@jeld-wen.co.uk
Website: http://www.jeld-wen.co.uk
Directors: M. Miles (Fin), M. Ward (Dir), V. Freemantle (Fin)
Managers: G. Campbell (Mktg Serv Mgr), J. Pitchard (Tech Serv Mgr), S. Pinder (Purch Mgr), K. Ryland (Sales Prom Mgr), L. Abbotts (Personnel)
Ultimate Holding Company: JELD-WEN HOLDINGS INC (USA)
Immediate Holding Company: JELD-WEN UK LIMITED
Registration no: 00499622 **Date established:** 1951
Turnover: £75m - £125m **No.of Employees:** 251 - 500
Product Groups: 52

Date of Accounts	Dec 11	Dec 10	Dec 09
Sales Turnover	108m	108m	99m
Pre Tax Profit/Loss	-13m	-16m	-14m
Working Capital	328	-22m	-5m
Fixed Assets	12m	14m	14m
Current Assets	55m	45m	45m
Current Liabilities	11m	8m	10m

Jepson & Co. Ltd

44 East Bank Road, Sheffield, S2 3QN
Tel: 0114-273 1151 **Fax:** 0114-273 1156
E-mail: sales@jepsonandco.com
Website: http://www.jepsonandco.com
Directors: J. Hartley (Dir), P. McGuire (Fin)
Managers: R. Corbett (Works Gen Mgr)
Ultimate Holding Company: JEPSON HOLDINGS LIMITED
Immediate Holding Company: JEPSON & CO LIMITED
Registration no: 00112990 **VAT No.:** GB 172 6169 55
Date established: 2010 **Turnover:** £5m - £10m **No.of Employees:** 21 - 50
Product Groups: 39

Date of Accounts	Jun 11	Jun 10	Jun 09
Sales Turnover	7m	6m	6m
Pre Tax Profit/Loss	272	77	136
Working Capital	4m	4m	4m
Fixed Assets	3m	3m	2m
Current Assets	7m	7m	9m
Current Liabilities	341	181	87

The Jewel Blade Ltd

442 Penistone Road, Sheffield, S6 2FU
Tel: 0114-221 7000 **Fax:** 0114-285 2473
E-mail: jtaylor@jewelblade.co.uk
Website: http://www.jewelblade.com
Bank(s): HSBC Bank plc
Managers: J. Marshall (Chief Mgr)
Ultimate Holding Company: W.R.SWANN & CO.LIMITED
Immediate Holding Company: JEWEL BLADE LIMITED
Registration no: 04798723 **VAT No.:** GB 172 3705 72
Date established: 2003 **Turnover:** £2m - £5m **No.of Employees:** 51 - 100
Product Groups: 36, 38, 41, 42, 43, 44

Date of Accounts	Oct 11	Oct 10	Oct 09
Working Capital	2m	39	648
Fixed Assets	3m	2m	2m
Current Assets	2m	2m	1m

Jewson

Caledonia Works 100 Harvest Lane, Sheffield, S3 8EQ
Tel: 0114-270 0744 **Fax:** 0114-276 6109
Website: http://www.jewson.co.uk
Bank(s): Barclays
Managers: W. Ashmoore (Mgr)
Ultimate Holding Company: SAINT-GOBAIN LTD
Immediate Holding Company: JEWSON LIMITED
Registration no: 00348407 **Date established:** 1939
Turnover: £500m - £1,000m **No.of Employees:** 11 - 20
Product Groups: 66

Jewson Hirepoint

425-453 Queens Road, Sheffield, S2 4DR
Tel: 0114-275 5285 **Fax:** 0114-272 6108
E-mail: stewart.watts@jewson.co.uk
Website: http://www.jewson.co.uk
Managers: S. Watts (Mgr)
Ultimate Holding Company: COMPAGNIE DE SAINT GOBAIN (FRANCE)
Immediate Holding Company: JEWSON LIMITED
Registration no: 00348407 **VAT No.:** GB 497 7184 33
Date established: 1939 **Turnover:** £2m - £5m **No.of Employees:** 11 - 20
Product Groups: 66

Date of Accounts	Dec 11	Dec 10	Dec 09
Sales Turnover	1606m	1547m	1485m
Pre Tax Profit/Loss	18m	100m	45m
Working Capital	-345m	-250m	-349m
Fixed Assets	496m	387m	461m
Current Assets	657m	1005m	1320m
Current Liabilities	66m	120m	64m

John Wilson Skates and MK Blades

2 Bells Square, Sheffield, S1 2FY
Tel: 0114-272 5190 **Fax:** 0114-324 0189
E-mail: customerservice@hdsports.co.uk
Website: http://www.mkblades.com
Managers: D. Mallinder (Mgr)
Ultimate Holding Company: SLM International Inc. (Canada)
Registration no: 01467459 **VAT No.:** 660 5533 44 **Date established:** 1984
Turnover: £2m - £5m **No.of Employees:** 21 - 50 **Product Groups:** 49

King Kitchen Appliances

3 Concourse Way, Sheffield, S1 2BJ
Tel: 0114-275 6479
E-mail: kingappliances@live.co.uk
Website: http://www.kingkitchenappliances.co.uk
Product Groups: 40, 63, 67

Kiveton Park Holdings Ltd

Kiveton Park Kiveton Park Station, Sheffield, S26 6NQ
Tel: 01909-770252 **Fax:** 01909-772949
E-mail: sales@kpsteel.co.uk
Website: http://www.kpsteel.co.uk
Bank(s): Yorkshire
Directors: M. Lacey (Tech Serv), K. Harris (Pers), S. Whiteley (Fin)
Managers: J. Webster, M. Jones
Immediate Holding Company: KIVETON PARK (HOLDINGS) LIMITED
Registration no: 01552539 **VAT No.:** GB 471 2230 80
Date established: 1981 **Turnover:** £20m - £50m
No.of Employees: 101 - 250 **Product Groups:** 82

Date of Accounts	Jun 11	Jun 10	Jun 09
Sales Turnover	32m	22m	21m
Pre Tax Profit/Loss	664	522	101
Working Capital	6m	7m	6m
Fixed Assets	2m	2m	2m
Current Assets	14m	12m	9m
Current Liabilities	919	782	610

Knowledge Now Limited

The Innovation Centre 217 Portobello Sheffield, Sheffield, S1 4DP
Tel: 0114-224 2420
E-mail: info@k-now.co.uk
Website: http://www.k-now.co.uk/
Directors: S. Chapman (Dir)
Registration no: 06428241 **Date established:** 2008
Turnover: Up to £250,000 **No.of Employees:** 1 - 10 **Product Groups:** 44, 80

Date of Accounts	Jul 10	Jul 09	Jul 08
Sales Turnover	142	38	N/A
Pre Tax Profit/Loss	18	2	N/A
Working Capital	23	8	9
Fixed Assets	5	3	N/A
Current Assets	201	18	9
Current Liabilities	173	6	N/A

Kutrite Of Sheffield Ltd

72 Russell Street, Sheffield, S3 8RW
Tel: 0114-273 9977 **Fax:** 0114-276 8876
E-mail: sales@kutrite-of-sheffield.co.uk
Website: http://www.kutrite-of-sheffield.co.uk
Directors: P. Wright (Fin)
Immediate Holding Company: KUTRITE OF SHEFFIELD LIMITED
Registration no: 02912795 **VAT No.:** GB 471 3266 48
Date established: 1994 **Turnover:** £250,000 - £500,000
No.of Employees: 1 - 10 **Product Groups:** 36, 49

Date of Accounts	Apr 10	Apr 09	Apr 08
Working Capital	-41	-30	9
Fixed Assets	2	3	3
Current Assets	116	121	175

L A W Universal Grinding

1 Princess Street, Sheffield, S4 7UU
Tel: 0114-279 9777 **Fax:** 0114-279 9777
Directors: L. Wyzyloewicz (Prop)
Date established: 2001 **No.of Employees:** 1 - 10 **Product Groups:** 46

L U K Ltd

Waleswood Road Wales Bar, Sheffield, S26 5PN
Tel: 01909-510500 **Fax:** 01909-515151
E-mail: frank.jurgens@luk.co.uk
Website: http://www.luk.co.uk
Directors: H. Hoch (MD), P. Evans (Fin)
Managers: J. Walker, U. Sorter (Tech Serv Mgr), K. Brookbank (Personnel)
Ultimate Holding Company: INA HOLDING SCHAEFFLER KG (GERMANY)
Immediate Holding Company: LUK (UK) LIMITED
Registration no: 02158744 **Date established:** 1987
Turnover: £75m - £125m **No.of Employees:** 251 - 500
Product Groups: 39

Date of Accounts	Dec 11	Dec 10	Dec 09
Sales Turnover	122m	109m	97m
Pre Tax Profit/Loss	7m	1m	4m
Working Capital	14m	7m	7m
Fixed Assets	10m	12m	13m
Current Assets	50m	51m	56m
Current Liabilities	3m	40m	48m

Lablogic Systems Ltd

Paradigm House 3 Melbourne Avenue Broomhill, Sheffield, S10 2QJ
Tel: 0114-266 7267 **Fax:** 0114-266 3944
E-mail: solutions@lablogic.com
Website: http://www.lablogic.com
Bank(s): Yorkshire
Directors: R. Brown (MD), M. Brown (Co Sec), H. Loaring (Dir), R. Kenningham (Fin)
Managers: R. Woodcock (Mktg Serv Mgr)
Immediate Holding Company: LABLOGIC SYSTEMS LIMITED
Registration no: 02062398 **VAT No.:** GB 457 7173 19
Date established: 1986 **Turnover:** £2m - £5m **No.of Employees:** 21 - 50
Product Groups: 44

Date of Accounts	Jun 11	Jun 10	Jun 09
Working Capital	3m	2m	1m
Fixed Assets	1m	1m	1m
Current Assets	6m	4m	3m

Latrobe Specialty Steel Company

Newhall Road, Sheffield, S9 2QL
Tel: 0114-242 0500 **Fax:** 0114-244 3055
E-mail: sales@latrobesteel.com
Website: http://www.latrobesteel.com
Managers: P. Ballin (Ops Mgr)
Immediate Holding Company: JOHN GREEN (MACHINE TOOLS) LIMITED
Registration no: 00782320 **Date established:** 1963
No.of Employees: 1 - 10 **Product Groups:** 34

Arnold Laver Call Collect (Gang-Nail Systems Ltd)

Oxclose Park Road North Halfway, Sheffield, S20 8GN
Tel: 0114-276 4800 **Fax:** 0114-276 4801
E-mail: sales@sheffield.timberworld.co.uk
Website: http://www.arnoldlavertimberworld.co.uk
Managers: D. Bree (Mgr)
Ultimate Holding Company: ARNOLD LAVER HOLDINGS LIMITED
Immediate Holding Company: ARNOLD LAVER & COMPANY LIMITED
Registration no: 00267843 **Date established:** 1932
No.of Employees: 21 - 50 **Product Groups:** 08, 35, 66

Date of Accounts	Jun 11	Jun 10	Jun 09
Sales Turnover	99m	89m	88m
Pre Tax Profit/Loss	3m	1m	-829
Working Capital	17m	20m	21m
Fixed Assets	92m	104m	109m
Current Assets	47m	45m	41m
Current Liabilities	5m	4m	3m

Lechler Ltd

1 Fell Street, Sheffield, S9 2TP
Tel: 0114-249 2020 **Fax:** 0114-249 3600
E-mail: sarahecclest@lechler.com
Website: http://www.lechler.co.uk
Bank(s): National Westminster Bank Plc
Directors: D. Lloyd (MD)
Managers: D. Columbine (Mgr), M. Ledger (Mgr), C. Roberts (Mgr), A. Hewitt (Mgr), J. O'Connor (Ops Mgr), C. Burgess (Eng Serv Mgr)
Ultimate Holding Company: LECHLER INTERNATIONAL GMBH (GERMANY)
Registration no: 01044217 **Date established:** 1979 **Turnover:** £5m - £10m
No.of Employees: 21 - 50 **Product Groups:** 20, 25, 30, 31, 32, 33, 36, 38, 39, 40, 41, 42, 44, 45, 46, 47, 48, 54, 66, 67, 74

Date of Accounts	Dec 11	Dec 10	Dec 09
Sales Turnover	5m	4m	3m
Pre Tax Profit/Loss	190	361	-812
Working Capital	95	73	-828
Fixed Assets	2m	2m	2m
Current Assets	3m	2m	1m
Current Liabilities	669	638	547

Libra Weighing Machines Ltd

The Haven Pipworth Lane, Eckington, Sheffield, S21 4EY
Tel: 01246-433400
E-mail: sales@libraweighing.co.uk
Website: http://www.libraweighing.co.uk
Directors: S. Seaton (Dir)
Immediate Holding Company: LIBRA WEIGHING MACHINES LIMITED
Registration no: 02974856 **Date established:** 1994
No.of Employees: 1 - 10 **Product Groups:** 38, 45, 52

Date of Accounts	Dec 11	Dec 10	Dec 09
Working Capital	71	105	146
Fixed Assets	14	18	22
Current Assets	278	359	437

Lift Doctor Ltd

Globe Ii Business Centre 128 Maltravers Road, Sheffield, S2 5AZ
Tel: 0114-221 0710 **Fax:** 0114-221 0701
Website: http://www.lift-docter.com
Directors: S. Jeffery (Fin), K. Jeffery (MD)
Immediate Holding Company: LIFT DOCTOR LIMITED
Registration no: 04365469 **Date established:** 2002
No.of Employees: 1 - 10 **Product Groups:** 35, 39, 45

Date of Accounts	Jun 09	Jun 08	Jun 07
Working Capital	6	11	2
Fixed Assets	9	10	14
Current Assets	156	157	101

Lifting Gear Products (Europa Engineering Ltd)

Goliath Works 395 Petre Street, Sheffield, S4 8LN
Tel: 0114-244 3456 **Fax:** 0114-243 3373
E-mail: lgp@liftinggearprod.co.uk
Website: http://www.liftinggearprod.co.uk
Bank(s): National Westminster
Directors: C. Christie (Dir)
Ultimate Holding Company: Europa Engineering Ltd
Registration no: 02465896 **Date established:** 1953 **Turnover:** £5m - £10m
No.of Employees: 11 - 20 **Product Groups:** 35, 37, 39, 45, 83

Lincol Ltd

Well Meadow Works Upper Allen Street, Sheffield, S3 7GW
Tel: 0114-276 2662 **Fax:** 0114-276 2710
E-mail: sales@lincol.co.uk
Website: http://www.lincol.co.uk
Directors: J. Earle (Fin), G. Earle (MD)
Immediate Holding Company: LINCOL LIMITED
Registration no: 04339472 **Date established:** 2001
No.of Employees: 1 - 10 **Product Groups:** 38, 42

Date of Accounts	Dec 11	Dec 10	Dec 09
Working Capital	6	11	10
Fixed Assets	6	8	10
Current Assets	56	54	59

Lincoln Electric UK Ltd

Mansfield Road Aston, Sheffield, S26 2BS
Tel: 0114-287 2401 **Fax:** 0114-287 2582
E-mail: salesuk@lincolnelectric.eu
Website: http://www.lincolnelectric.eu
Directors: M. Chalmers (Comm)
Managers: D. Kirkwood (Sales Prom Mgr), P. Davison (Comptroller), S. Walsh (Personnel)
Ultimate Holding Company: LINCOLN ELECTRIC HOLDINGS INC (USA)
Immediate Holding Company: LINCOLN ELECTRIC (U.K.) LIMITED
Registration no: 01982670 **VAT No.:** GB 308 6562 50
Date established: 1986 **Turnover:** £20m - £50m
No.of Employees: 51 - 100 **Product Groups:** 24, 30, 32, 33, 34, 35, 37, 38, 40, 45, 46

Date of Accounts	Dec 10	Dec 09	Dec 08
Sales Turnover	27m	22m	29m
Pre Tax Profit/Loss	2m	633	2m
Working Capital	12m	10m	10m
Fixed Assets	3m	3m	3m
Current Assets	17m	14m	14m
Current Liabilities	1m	484	817

Linmar Site Services Ltd

Baltic Works Effingham Road, Sheffield, S9 3QA
Tel: 0114-244 8400 **Fax:** 0114-243 7124
E-mail: sales@linmarsiteservices.co.uk
Website: http://www.linmarsiteservices.co.uk
Directors: M. Lindley (Dir), A. Lindley (Fin)
Immediate Holding Company: LINMAR SITE SERVICES LIMITED
Registration no: 05988539 **Date established:** 2006
No.of Employees: 1 - 10 **Product Groups:** 37, 40, 48

Date of Accounts	Mar 11	Mar 10	Mar 09
Working Capital	-33	-36	-36
Fixed Assets	33	33	37
Current Assets	73	119	119

Llanrad Distribution plc

Unit 26 Bookers Way Dinnington, Sheffield, S25 3SH
Tel: 01909-550944 **Fax:** 01909-568403
E-mail: albert.haugg@llanrad.co.uk
Website: http://www.llanrad.co.uk
Bank(s): Lloyds
Directors: A. Haugg (Dir)
Managers: S. English (Chief Mgr)
Immediate Holding Company: LLANRAD DISTRIBUTION PLC
Registration no: 02689612 **Date established:** 1992 **Turnover:** £2m - £5m
No.of Employees: 11 - 20 **Product Groups:** 39

Date of Accounts	Dec 11	Dec 10	Dec 09
Sales Turnover	N/A	N/A	4m
Pre Tax Profit/Loss	N/A	N/A	371
Working Capital	2m	2m	1m
Fixed Assets	40	54	47
Current Assets	2m	2m	2m
Current Liabilities	N/A	N/A	106

Lloyd Catering Equipment

4 Foremost Industrial Estate Grange Mill Lane, Sheffield, S9 1HW
Tel: 01709-555594 **Fax:** 01709-561822
Managers: A. Gee (Mgr)
Date established: 1997 **No.of Employees:** 11 - 20 **Product Groups:** 20, 40, 41

Loxleys Print Ltd

Kiln Street, Sheffield, S8 0YS
Tel: 0114-250 1150 **Fax:** 0114-250 1034
E-mail: enquiries@loxleys.co.uk
Website: http://www.loxleys.co.uk
Bank(s): Yorkshire, Sheffield
Directors: R. Bacon (MD)
Managers: H. Roberts (Tech Serv Mgr), R. Field (Comptroller)
Ultimate Holding Company: LOXLEYS HOLDINGS LIMITED
Immediate Holding Company: LOXLEYS PRINT LIMITED
Registration no: 02998178 **VAT No.:** GB 646 5606 21
Date established: 1994 **Turnover:** £5m - £10m
No.of Employees: 51 - 100 **Product Groups:** 27, 44

Date of Accounts	Mar 12	Mar 11	Mar 10
Pre Tax Profit/Loss	217	233	114
Working Capital	2m	2m	2m
Fixed Assets	752	840	923
Current Assets	4m	4m	4m
Current Liabilities	717	739	685

M B S

6 Carley Drive Westfield, Sheffield, S20 8NQ
Tel: 0114-246 4787 **Fax:** 0114-240 1737
E-mail: info@mbsimaging.co.uk
Website: http://www.mbsimaging.co.uk
Directors: J. Rose (Dir), H. Rose (Fin)
Immediate Holding Company: MICROFILM BUSINESS SYSTEMS LIMITED
Registration no: 02560816 **VAT No.:** GB 534 1787 38
Date established: 1990 **Turnover:** £250,000 - £500,000
No.of Employees: 1 - 10 **Product Groups:** 38

Date of Accounts	Mar 12	Mar 11	Mar 10
Working Capital	56	42	63
Fixed Assets	72	91	99
Current Assets	175	95	172

M S Hire

38 East Bank Road, Sheffield, S2 3PS
Tel: 0114-275 0431 **Fax:** 0114-272 9813
E-mail: esh@mfhgroup.co.uk
Website: http://www.mfhgroup.co.uk
Bank(s): National Westminster Bank Plc
Managers: M. Hopkins
Ultimate Holding Company: M.F.H. ENGINEERING (HOLDINGS) LIMITED
Immediate Holding Company: M.F. HIRE LIMITED
Registration no: 01362202 **Date established:** 1978
No.of Employees: 11 - 20 **Product Groups:** 83

Date of Accounts	Mar 11	Mar 10	Mar 09
Working Capital	349	328	359
Fixed Assets	166	210	264
Current Assets	532	480	528

Mac 1 Motor Sport

Richmond Business Park Unit 14 Stradbroke Place, Sheffield, S13 8SH
Tel: 0114-261 9633 **Fax:** 0114-261 9633
E-mail: m.hinchcliffe@mac1motorsports.co.uk
Website: http://www.mac1motorsports.co.uk
Directors: M. Hinchcliffe (Prop), S. Hinchcliffe (Mkt Research)
Registration no: 03948230 **Date established:** 2000
No.of Employees: 1 - 10 **Product Groups:** 68

Mac'Ants Abrasives

Todwick Road Dinnington, Sheffield, S25 3SE
Tel: 01909-552500 **Fax:** 01909-568726
E-mail: group@macants.co.uk
Website: http://www.macants.co.uk
Bank(s): The Royal Bank of Scotland
Directors: E. Lutkin (MD)
Ultimate Holding Company: MAC'ANTS HOLDING COMPANY LIMITED
Immediate Holding Company: MAC-ANTS ABRASIVES LIMITED
Registration no: 01303998 **VAT No.:** GB 174 2002 02
Date established: 1977 **Turnover:** £5m - £10m **No.of Employees:** 11 - 20
Product Groups: 14, 31, 33, 34, 36, 40, 42, 45, 46, 48, 66

Date of Accounts	Mar 11	Mar 10	Mar 09
Working Capital	2m	1m	1m
Fixed Assets	2m	2m	2m
Current Assets	2m	2m	2m

Mach One International Ltd

Unit S Norfolk Bridge Business Park Foley Street, Sheffield, S4 7YW
Tel: 0114-270 0545 **Fax:** 0114-276 7438
E-mail: sales@mach-int.com
Website: http://www.mach-int.com
Directors: M. Fitzgerald (MD)
Ultimate Holding Company: MACH ONE (HOLDINGS) LIMITED
Immediate Holding Company: MACH ONE (HOLDINGS) LIMITED
Registration no: 03628229 **Date established:** 1998
Turnover: £10m - £20m **No.of Employees:** 1 - 10 **Product Groups:** 33, 35

Date of Accounts	Dec 11	Dec 10	Dec 09
Working Capital	-38	-49	-54
Fixed Assets	65	65	65
Current Assets	N/A	N/A	3

Machinagraph Ltd

Unit 2 Bailey Drive Killamarsh, Sheffield, S21 2JF
Tel: 0114-228 0006 **Fax:** 0114-228 0440
E-mail: machinagraph@msn.com
Website: http://www.machinagraph.co.uk
Managers: A. Wood (Mgr)
Immediate Holding Company: MACHINAGRAPH LIMITED
Registration no: 00877044 **Date established:** 1966
Turnover: Up to £250,000 **No.of Employees:** 1 - 10 **Product Groups:** 28, 30, 35, 49

Date of Accounts	Apr 11	Apr 10	Apr 09
Working Capital	-19	-18	-16
Fixed Assets	4	4	4
Current Assets	16	13	16

Magnetic Rubber Direct Ltd

64 Salisbury Road, Sheffield, S10 1WB
Tel: 0114-231 9840 **Fax:** 0114-242 0081
E-mail: info@mrd-magnets.com
Website: http://www.mrd-magnets.com
Managers: J. Bower (Chief Acct)
Registration no: 06245291 **Date established:** 2004 **Turnover:** £1m - £2m
No.of Employees: 1 - 10 **Product Groups:** 29

Magnetic Systems Technology Ltd

222-226 Newhall Road, Sheffield, S9 2QL
Tel: 0114-244 8416 **Fax:** 0114-244 8417
E-mail: info@magtec.co.uk
Website: http://www.magtec.co.uk
Bank(s): The Royal Bank of Scotland
Directors: M. Jenkins (MD)
Immediate Holding Company: MAGNETIC SYSTEMS TECHNOLOGY LIMITED
Registration no: 02763007 **Date established:** 1992 **Turnover:** £1m - £2m
No.of Employees: 21 - 50 **Product Groups:** 37, 39, 84

Date of Accounts	Dec 10	Dec 09	Dec 08
Working Capital	303	106	242
Fixed Assets	54	31	40
Current Assets	846	480	625

Magnify B

205 Woodseats Road, Sheffield, S8 0PL
Tel: 0114-258 0088
E-mail: info@magnifyb.co.uk
Website: http://www.magnifyb.co.uk
Directors: K. Murphy Kaytan (Prop)
Date established: 2010 **Turnover:** **No.of Employees:** 1 - 10
Product Groups: 44, 61

Maher Ltd

2 Brightside Way, Sheffield, S9 2RQ
Tel: 0114-290 9200 **Fax:** 0114-290 9290
E-mail: info@maher.com
Website: http://www.maher.com
Bank(s): HSBC, Church Street
Directors: I. Plant (Fin), D. Saul (Sales), G. Clark (Develop), J. Foreman (Fin)
Managers: M. Elliott (Personnel)
Immediate Holding Company: MAHER LIMITED
Registration no: 00508859 **Date established:** 1952
Turnover: £20m - £50m **No.of Employees:** 51 - 100 **Product Groups:** 34, 39, 48

Date of Accounts	Jun 11	Jun 10	Jun 09
Sales Turnover	24m	24m	29m
Pre Tax Profit/Loss	290	2m	3m
Working Capital	14m	13m	11m
Fixed Assets	1m	1m	2m
Current Assets	19m	19m	17m
Current Liabilities	2m	1m	2m

Maplin Electronics Ltd

413 Langsett Road, Sheffield, S6 2LL
Tel: 08432-277307 **Fax:** 0114-285 4389
E-mail: customercare@maplin.co.uk
Website: http://www.maplin.co.uk
Managers: J. Hendley (Mgr)
Ultimate Holding Company: MONTAGU PRIVATE EQUITY LLP
Immediate Holding Company: MAPLIN ELECTRONICS LIMITED
Registration no: 01264385 **Date established:** 1976
Turnover: £125m - £250m **No.of Employees:** 1 - 10 **Product Groups:** 37, 61

Date of Accounts	Dec 11	Dec 08	Dec 09
Sales Turnover	205m	204m	204m
Pre Tax Profit/Loss	25m	32m	35m
Working Capital	118m	49m	75m
Fixed Assets	27m	28m	28m
Current Assets	207m	108m	142m
Current Liabilities	78m	51m	59m

Maplin Electronics Ltd

38-40 Pinstone Street, Sheffield, S1 2HN
Tel: 08432-277344 **Fax:** 0114-275 9574
E-mail: customercare@maplin.co.uk
Website: http://www.maplin.co.uk
Ultimate Holding Company: MONTAGU PRIVATE EQUITY LLP
Immediate Holding Company: MAPLIN ELECTRONICS LIMITED
Registration no: 01264385 **Date established:** 1976
Turnover: £125m - £250m **No.of Employees:** 21 - 50
Product Groups: 37, 61

see next page

Maplin Electronics Ltd - Cont'd

Date of Accounts	Dec 11	Dec 08	Dec 09
Sales Turnover	205m	204m	204m
Pre Tax Profit/Loss	25m	32m	35m
Working Capital	118m	49m	75m
Fixed Assets	27m	28m	28m
Current Assets	207m	108m	142m
Current Liabilities	78m	51m	59m

George Marshall Power Tools Ltd

18 Johnson Street, Sheffield, S3 8GT
Tel: 0114-276 7071 **Fax:** 0114-273 8084
E-mail: john@geomarshall.co.uk
Website: http://www.geomarshall.co.uk
Directors: K. Marshall (Fin), J. Marshall (MD)
Immediate Holding Company: GEORGE MARSHALL (POWER TOOLS) LIMITED
Registration no: 01019232 **Date established:** 1971
Turnover: £250,000 - £500,000 **No.of Employees:** 1 - 10
Product Groups: 37, 83

Date of Accounts	Jul 11	Jul 10	Jul 09
Working Capital	104	127	176
Fixed Assets	311	314	311
Current Assets	138	146	185

Marshalls Hard Metals Ltd

Windsor Street, Sheffield, S4 7WB
Tel: 0114-275 2282 **Fax:** 0114-273 8499
E-mail: sales@hardmet.com
Website: http://www.hardmet.com
Bank(s): HSBC P.L.C., Bradford
Directors: M. Denton (Fin)
Managers: C. Phillips (Sales Off Mgr), L. Burrows (Sales & Mktg Mg), N. Thomas (Tech Serv Mgr), J. Moylan
Ultimate Holding Company: MHM HOLDINGS LIMITED
Immediate Holding Company: MARSHALLS HARD METALS LIMITED
Registration no: 03187983 **VAT No.:** GB 640 8425 46
Date established: 1996 **Turnover:** £5m - £10m
No.of Employees: 51 - 100 **Product Groups:** 34, 36, 45, 46

Date of Accounts	Mar 11	Mar 10	Mar 09
Sales Turnover	6m	5m	N/A
Pre Tax Profit/Loss	397	47	179
Working Capital	2m	2m	2m
Fixed Assets	3m	3m	3m
Current Assets	3m	3m	3m
Current Liabilities	652	419	355

Massey Truck Engineering Ltd

Station Road Halfway, Sheffield, S20 3GX
Tel: 0114-248 3751 **Fax:** 0114-247 8246
E-mail: mail@masseytruckengineering.co.uk
Website: http://www.masseytruckengineering.co.uk
Directors: D. Brooks (Dir), S. Willis (Co Sec)
Managers: S. Shaw (Buyer)
Immediate Holding Company: MASSEY TRUCK ENGINEERING LIMITED
Registration no: 02602321 **VAT No.:** GB 599 8023 82
Date established: 1991 **Turnover:** £10m - £20m
No.of Employees: 101 - 250 **Product Groups:** 39, 45

Date of Accounts	Sep 11	Sep 08	Oct 09
Sales Turnover	13m	N/A	8m
Pre Tax Profit/Loss	294	505	250
Working Capital	3m	3m	3m
Fixed Assets	1m	2m	1m
Current Assets	7m	5m	4m
Current Liabilities	1m	624	471

Mattec Ltd

Units 23-24 Dinnington Business Centre Outgang Lane, Dinnington, Sheffield, S25 3QX
Tel: 01909-561544 **Fax:** 01909-560675
E-mail: info@mattec.com
Website: http://www.mattec.com
Directors: N. Kaiser (Fin)
Managers: H. Hurdadoyal (Admin Off)
Immediate Holding Company: MATTEC LIMITED
Registration no: 02541261 **Date established:** 1990
Turnover: £20m - £50m **No.of Employees:** 1 - 10 **Product Groups:** 38, 44, 67, 80, 85

Date of Accounts	Mar 12	Mar 11	Mar 10
Working Capital	386	304	200
Fixed Assets	2	1	4
Current Assets	460	678	402

Matthew Hebden

54 Blackamoor Road, Sheffield, S17 3GJ
Tel: 0114-236 8122 **Fax:** 0114-236 8127
E-mail: sales@matthewhebden.co.uk
Website: http://www.matthewhebden.co.uk
Directors: R. Smith (Dir)
Registration no: 01622974 **No.of Employees:** 1 - 10 **Product Groups:** 14, 23, 30, 31, 33, 35, 66

Meadowhall Centre Ltd

The Management Suite 1 The Oasis, Sheffield, S9 1EP
Tel: 0114-256 8800 **Fax:** 0114-256 8666
E-mail: colleen.carter@meadowhall.co.uk
Website: http://www.meadowhall.co.uk
Bank(s): HSBC
Managers: C. Breeze (Tech Serv Mgr), D. Pearce, J. Lynch, R. Pinfold (Mktg Serv Mgr), S. Batty (Sales Admin), C. Carter (Commun Mgr)
Ultimate Holding Company: BRITISH LAND COMPANY PUBLIC LIMITED COMPANY(THE)
Immediate Holding Company: MEADOWHALL CENTRE LIMITED
Registration no: 03918066 **Date established:** 2000
Turnover: £20m - £50m **No.of Employees:** 21 - 50 **Product Groups:** 89

Date of Accounts	Mar 11	Mar 10	Mar 09
Sales Turnover	N/A	N/A	498
Pre Tax Profit/Loss	8m	-2m	69
Working Capital	3m	4m	3m
Fixed Assets	31m	24m	26m
Current Assets	4m	5m	4m
Current Liabilities	N/A	N/A	43

Mechan Ltd

Sir John Brown Building Prince of Wales Road, Sheffield, S9 4EX
Tel: 0114-257 0563 **Fax:** 0114-245 1124
E-mail: info@mechan.co.uk
Website: http://www.mechan.co.uk
Directors: A. Bradshaw (Fin), R. Carr (MD), Z. Altaf (Fin)
Ultimate Holding Company: MECHAN GROUP LIMITED
Immediate Holding Company: MECHAN LIMITED
Registration no: 00947728 **Date established:** 1969 **Turnover:** £1m - £2m
No.of Employees: 21 - 50 **Product Groups:** 39, 45

Date of Accounts	Mar 12	Mar 11	Mar 10
Sales Turnover	3m	2m	N/A
Pre Tax Profit/Loss	255	106	N/A
Working Capital	244	304	345
Fixed Assets	67	105	62
Current Assets	1m	717	861
Current Liabilities	425	101	N/A

Thomas Meldrum Ltd

Freedom Works John Street, Sheffield, S2 4QT
Tel: 0114-272 5156 **Fax:** 0114-272 6409
E-mail: sales@melco-tools.co.uk
Website: http://www.thomasmeldrumltd.co.uk
Bank(s): HSBC
Directors: R. Meldrum (MD)
Immediate Holding Company: THOMAS MELDRUM LIMITED
Registration no: 00409438 **VAT No.:** GB 172 7057 61
Date established: 1946 **Turnover:** £1m - £2m **No.of Employees:** 11 - 20
Product Groups: 36, 39

Date of Accounts	Mar 12	Mar 11	Mar 10
Working Capital	248	247	299
Fixed Assets	78	81	85
Current Assets	326	327	367

Merlin 360 International Ltd

Redwall Close Dinnington, Sheffield, S25 3QA
Tel: 01909-567111 **Fax:** 01909-566770
E-mail: gberry@merlin360.com
Website: http://www.merlin360.com
Directors: G. Berry (Dir), S. Berry (Fin)
Immediate Holding Company: MERLIN 360 INTERNATIONAL LIMITED
Registration no: 04437038 **Date established:** 2002
No.of Employees: 1 - 10 **Product Groups:** 37

Date of Accounts	May 08	May 07	May 06
Working Capital	-140	-118	-143
Fixed Assets	32	14	6
Current Assets	59	87	30
Current Liabilities	199	205	173
Total Share Capital	1	1	1

Moeschle UK Ltd

99 Parkway Avenue, Sheffield, S9 4WG
Tel: 0114-227 0536 **Fax:** 0114-227 0539
E-mail: sales@moeschle.co.uk
Website: http://www.moeschle.com
Directors: A. Wall (Dir)
Immediate Holding Company: MOESCHLE (UK) LIMITED
Registration no: 04511756 **Date established:** 2002 **Turnover:** £1m - £2m
No.of Employees: 1 - 10 **Product Groups:** 35, 41, 42

Date of Accounts	Dec 11	Dec 10	Dec 09
Working Capital	77	31	-23
Fixed Assets	5	5	3
Current Assets	536	597	308

Monks & Crane Industrial Group Ltd

4a Stevenson Way, Sheffield, S9 3WZ
Tel: 0114-256 0250 **Fax:** 0114-243 7262
E-mail: sheffield@monks-crane.com
Website: http://www.monks-crane.com
Managers: L. Phillips
Ultimate Holding Company: ADOLF WURTH GMBH & CO KG (GERMANY)
Immediate Holding Company: MONKS & CRANE INDUSTRIAL GROUP LIMITED
Registration no: 00342072 **Date established:** 1938
Turnover: Up to £250,000 **No.of Employees:** 11 - 20 **Product Groups:** 36, 37, 46, 66, 83

Date of Accounts	Dec 11	Dec 10	Dec 09
Sales Turnover	45m	43m	48m
Pre Tax Profit/Loss	-2m	-1m	-2m
Working Capital	2m	3m	3m
Fixed Assets	553	701	556
Current Assets	16m	15m	17m
Current Liabilities	1m	1m	2m

Harold Moore Ltd

Bailey Works Bailey Street, Sheffield, S1 4EH
Tel: 0114-270 0513 **Fax:** 0114-275 5828
E-mail: accounts@haroldmoore.co.uk
Website: http://www.haroldmoore.co.uk
Bank(s): HSBC Bank plc
Directors: D. Moore (MD), S. Moore (Fin)
Immediate Holding Company: HAROLD MOORE LIMITED
Registration no: 01406609 **VAT No.:** GB 438 9878 76
Date established: 1978 **Turnover:** £1m - £2m **No.of Employees:** 11 - 20
Product Groups: 30, 36, 40, 41, 45, 66

Date of Accounts	Dec 11	Dec 10	Dec 09
Working Capital	1m	1m	933
Fixed Assets	111	122	120
Current Assets	2m	2m	1m

Moorland Woodcliffe

39 Hutcliffe Wood Road, Sheffield, S8 0EY
Tel: 0114-236 1766 **Fax:** 0114-262 0262
E-mail: b.gall262@btinternet.com
Website: http://www.machinery-plant.com
Directors: B. Gall (Prop)
Date established: 2000 **No.of Employees:** 1 - 10 **Product Groups:** 29, 30, 42, 46, 47

J E Morrison & Sons Ltd

Burton Weir Works Warren Street, Sheffield, S4 7WT
Tel: 0114-270 1525 **Fax:** 0114-243 4158
Bank(s): National Westminster Bank Plc
Directors: E. Reid (Co Sec), A. Reid (Dir)
Managers: N. Mycroft (Works Gen Mgr)
Immediate Holding Company: J.E. MORRISON & SONS LTD
Registration no: 02030505 **VAT No.:** GB 457 7260 24
Date established: 1986 **Turnover:** £250,000 - £500,000
No.of Employees: 21 - 50 **Product Groups:** 36

Date of Accounts	Jul 07	Jul 06
Working Capital	-15	52
Fixed Assets	10	13
Current Assets	277	315
Current Liabilities	291	263
Total Share Capital	98	63

Moss Express

Unit 2a Shepcote Way, Tinsley Industrial Estate, Sheffield, S9 1TH
Tel: 0114-244 6614 **Fax:** 0114-244 6615
E-mail: sales@mossexpress.co.uk
Website: http://www.mossexpress.co.uk
Directors: P. Hussey (Fin)
Managers: G. Hopkinson (Chief Mgr)
Ultimate Holding Company: FILTRONA PLC
Immediate Holding Company: MOSS PLASTIC PARTS LTD
Registration no: 07306524 **VAT No.:** GB 457 7482 06
Turnover: £2m - £5m **No.of Employees:** 1 - 10 **Product Groups:** 30

Mott Macdonald Ltd

Mott Macdonald House 111 St Marys Road, Sheffield, S2 4AP
Tel: 0114-276 1242 **Fax:** 0114-272 4699
E-mail: sheffield@mottmac.com
Website: http://www.mottmac.com
Directors: C. Trinder (MD), R. Trinder (MD)
Managers: E. Nutland (I.T. Exec)
Ultimate Holding Company: MOTT MACDONALD GROUP LIMITED
Immediate Holding Company: MOTT MACDONALD LIMITED
Registration no: 01243967 **Date established:** 1976
No.of Employees: 101 - 250 **Product Groups:** 42, 54, 84

Date of Accounts	Dec 11	Dec 10	Dec 09
Sales Turnover	531m	573m	610m
Pre Tax Profit/Loss	13m	25m	21m
Working Capital	288m	302m	299m
Fixed Assets	19m	19m	19m
Current Assets	498m	505m	502m
Current Liabilities	124m	120m	131m

MP Plastic Building Supplies

Unit 1 Rex Works Harvest Lane, Sheffield, S3 8EA
Tel: 0845-505 1840
E-mail: sales@plasticbuildingsupplies.com
Website: http://www.plasticbuildingsupplies.com
Product Groups: 25, 27, 30, 33, 35, 42, 54, 85

Mudfords Ltd

400 Petre Street, Sheffield, S4 8LU
Tel: 0114-243 3033 **Fax:** 0114-244 4536
E-mail: sales@mudfords.co.uk
Website: http://www.mudfords.co.uk
Bank(s): National Westminster, High Street, Sheffield
Directors: G. Dove (MD), M. Murphy (Co Sec)
Managers: V. Boyse (Purch Mgr)
Immediate Holding Company: MUDFORDS LIMITED
Registration no: 02632883 **VAT No.:** 599 9598 26 **Date established:** 1991
Turnover: £2m - £5m **No.of Employees:** 21 - 50 **Product Groups:** 23, 24

Date of Accounts	Mar 12	Mar 11	Mar 10
Working Capital	747	805	757
Fixed Assets	111	67	76
Current Assets	1m	1m	1m

Multijet Hardening Ltd

8 West Don Street, Sheffield, S6 3BH
Tel: 0114-234 5592 **Fax:** 0114-231 4772
E-mail: multijet@aol.com
Website: http://www.multijet-hardening.com
Directors: M. Bramhill (Fin), D. Bramhill (MD)
Immediate Holding Company: MULTIJET HARDENING LIMITED
Registration no: 01340401 **Date established:** 1977
No.of Employees: 1 - 10 **Product Groups:** 46, 48

Date of Accounts	Nov 11	Nov 10	Nov 09
Working Capital	-5	-18	-14
Fixed Assets	34	39	45
Current Assets	42	36	47

J Murphy & Sons Ltd

Rotherham Road Dinnington, Sheffield, S25 3RD
Tel: 01909-564911 **Fax:** 01909-565170
E-mail: jimodonnell@murphygroup.co.uk
Website: http://www.murphygroup.co.uk
Managers: J. O'donnell (Mgr)
Ultimate Holding Company: MARYLAND LIMITED (ISLE OF MAN)
Immediate Holding Company: J. MURPHY & SONS LIMITED
Registration no: 00492042 **Date established:** 1951
Turnover: £75m - £125m **No.of Employees:** 51 - 100 **Product Groups:** 51

Date of Accounts	Dec 11	Dec 10	Dec 09
Sales Turnover	485m	401m	408m
Pre Tax Profit/Loss	26m	23m	25m
Working Capital	94m	142m	125m
Fixed Assets	94m	36m	37m
Current Assets	205m	210m	192m
Current Liabilities	65m	31m	30m

N D T Ltd

Maltravers Road, Sheffield, S2 5AD
Tel: 0114-272 7317 **Fax:** 0114-272 7319
E-mail: sales@ndt.ltd.uk
Website: http://www.ndt.ltd.uk
Directors: P. Firth (MD)
Immediate Holding Company: N.D.T. LIMITED
Registration no: 01992209 **Date established:** 1986 **Turnover:** £2m - £5m
No.of Employees: 21 - 50 **Product Groups:** 34, 38, 54, 85, 86

Date of Accounts	Mar 11	Mar 10	Mar 09
Working Capital	426	275	441
Fixed Assets	680	622	495
Current Assets	731	508	707

N E Electrical

Unit 14b Shepcote Way, Tinsley Industrial Estate, Sheffield, S9 1TH
Tel: 0114-256 0640 **Fax:** 0114-256 0807
Website: http://www.ne-electrical.co.uk
Managers: S. Brailsford (Mgr)
Immediate Holding Company: N E ELECTRICAL WHOLESALERS LIMITED
Registration no: 04220545 **Date established:** 2001
No.of Employees: 11 - 20 **Product Groups:** 36, 40

Date of Accounts	Dec 11	Dec 10	Dec 09
Working Capital	329	181	249
Fixed Assets	111	106	83
Current Assets	2m	1m	2m

Nationwide Stainless Ltd
Bacon Lane, Sheffield, S9 3NH
Tel: 0114-275 5199 **Fax:** 0114-272 6351
E-mail: daveb@nationwidestainless.co.uk
Website: http://www.nationwidestainless.co.uk
Bank(s): Bank of Scotland
Directors: D. Nicoll (Sales), D. Nicoll (Fin), D. Burns (MD), D. Burns (Dir)
Managers: D. Nicoll (Mgr)
Immediate Holding Company: NATIONWIDE STAINLESS LIMITED
Registration no: 03905629 **VAT No.:** GB 427 8048 17
Date established: 2000 **Turnover:** £5m - £10m **No.of Employees:** 11 - 20
Product Groups: 66

Date of Accounts	May 11	May 10	May 09
Sales Turnover	N/A	N/A	5m
Pre Tax Profit/Loss	N/A	N/A	195
Working Capital	361	109	69
Fixed Assets	836	877	925
Current Assets	2m	2m	1m
Current Liabilities	N/A	N/A	405

Nederman Service Division
Unit 4 Shepcote Office Village 333 Shepcote Lane, Sheffield, S9 1TG
Tel: 0845-2743434 **Fax:** 0845-2743433
E-mail: info@nederman.co.uk
Website: http://www.nederman.co.uk
Directors: P. Sheerin (Mkt Research), P. Grayson (MD), C. Marsden (MD)
Managers: A. Mason (Accounts)
Registration no: 05224923 **VAT No.:** GB 728 6845 89
Date established: 1999 **Turnover:** £1m - £2m **No.of Employees:** 1 - 10
Product Groups: 54

Date of Accounts	Dec 08	Dec 07	Dec 06
Working Capital	23	53	57
Fixed Assets	22	21	N/A
Current Assets	163	188	136
Current Liabilities	140	135	79

Nickel Blanks Co Ltd
6 Smithfield, Sheffield, S3 7AR
Tel: 0114-272 5792 **Fax:** 0114-276 8519
E-mail: shefcutler@aol.com
Website: http://www.901.com
Bank(s): National Westminster Bank Plc
Directors: J. Whitehead (Co Sec), D. Kynman (Dir), P. Brownhill (Ch & MD), P. Coleclough (Fin)
Immediate Holding Company: N.B. Realisations Ltd
Registration no: 00271291 **Date established:** 2005 **Turnover:** £1m - £2m
No.of Employees: 51 - 100 **Product Groups:** 36, 48

Date of Accounts	Dec 07
Sales Turnover	1648
Pre Tax Profit/Loss	172
Working Capital	2503
Fixed Assets	2354
Current Assets	4394
Current Liabilities	1891
Total Share Capital	3
ROCE% (Return on Capital Employed)	3.5

Nimbus Products Sheffield Ltd
Julian Way Tyler Street Industrial Estate, Sheffield, S9 1GD
Tel: 0114-243 2362 **Fax:** 0114-243 5046
E-mail: sales@nimbusproducts.co.uk
Website: http://www.nimbusproducts.co.uk
Bank(s): Barclays
Directors: S. Beck (Dir)
Immediate Holding Company: NIMBUS PRODUCTS (SHEFFIELD) LIMITED
Registration no: 01017941 **VAT No.:** GB 727 8491 94
Date established: 1971 **Turnover:** £1m - £2m **No.of Employees:** 11 - 20
Product Groups: 39

Date of Accounts	Mar 12	Mar 11	Mar 10
Working Capital	590	483	385
Fixed Assets	151	144	145
Current Assets	1m	739	635

Northend Ltd
Clyde Road, Sheffield, S8 0TZ
Tel: 0114-250 0331 **Fax:** 0114-250 0676
E-mail: info@northend.co.uk
Website: http://www.northend.co.uk
Bank(s): HSBC Bank plc
Directors: N. Stubley (Dir), B. Marsden (Fin)
Managers: S. Taylor (Sales Prom Mgr), D. Betts (Personnel), P. Wright
Immediate Holding Company: J.W. NORTHEND LIMITED
Registration no: 02914773 **VAT No.:** GB 172 9494 29
Date established: 1994 **Turnover:** Up to £250,000
No.of Employees: 21 - 50 **Product Groups:** 28

Date of Accounts	Mar 12	Mar 11	Mar 10
Working Capital	-457	-557	-581
Fixed Assets	1m	1m	2m
Current Assets	975	819	735

Northern Blacking Ltd
47 Catley Road, Sheffield, S9 5JF
Tel: 0114-244 5333 **Fax:** 0114-261 8891
Directors: J. Aistrop (Fin), R. Aistrop (MD)
Immediate Holding Company: NORTHERN BLACKING LIMITED
Registration no: 01919641 **VAT No.:** GB 295 7775 88
Date established: 1985 **Turnover:** £250,000 - £500,000
No.of Employees: 1 - 10 **Product Groups:** 48

Date of Accounts	Apr 11	Apr 10	Apr 09
Working Capital	41	29	27
Fixed Assets	6	6	12
Current Assets	116	73	69

Northern Special Metals Ltd
Unit 5 Waleswood Road, Wales Bar, Sheffield, S26 5PY
Tel: 01909-770799 **Fax:** 01909-515032
E-mail: sales@nsmfabs.co.uk
Website: http://www.nsmfabs.co.uk
Directors: B. Mason (MD)
Immediate Holding Company: NORTHERN SPECIAL METAL (FABRICATORS) LIMITED
Registration no: 02339576 **Date established:** 1989
No.of Employees: 11 - 20 **Product Groups:** 48

Date of Accounts	Dec 11	Dec 10	Mar 10
Working Capital	41	129	52
Fixed Assets	70	92	89
Current Assets	697	748	790

Northern Woodworking Machinery
150 Worksop Road, Sheffield, S9 3TN
Tel: 0114-261 1101 **Fax:** 0114-261 1102
E-mail: paul@northernwoodworking.co.uk
Website: http://www.northernwoodworking.co.uk
Directors: P. Hood (Prop)
Immediate Holding Company: DIO-MET FABRICATIONS LIMITED
Registration no: 02571825 **Date established:** 1991
Turnover: £500,000 - £1m **No.of Employees:** 1 - 10 **Product Groups:** 46

Date of Accounts	May 11	May 10	May 09
Sales Turnover	635	619	883
Pre Tax Profit/Loss	36	46	157
Working Capital	448	466	491
Fixed Assets	157	154	131
Current Assets	533	535	613
Current Liabilities	18	17	52

Norton Cast Products Ltd
Capital Steel Works Tinsley Park Road, Sheffield, S9 5DL
Tel: 0114-244 8722 **Fax:** 0114-242 5523
E-mail: pauli@nortoncast.com
Website: http://www.nortoncast.co.uk
Bank(s): Yorkshire Bank PLC
Directors: P. Ingall (Dir)
Ultimate Holding Company: J.B. INGALL LIMITED
Immediate Holding Company: NORTON CAST PRODUCTS LIMITED
Registration no: 01376835 **VAT No.:** GB 308 1473 74
Date established: 1978 **Turnover:** £5m - £10m
No.of Employees: 51 - 100 **Product Groups:** 34, 66

Date of Accounts	Jan 12	Jan 11	Jan 10
Sales Turnover	10m	8m	6m
Pre Tax Profit/Loss	130	40	30
Working Capital	1m	1m	2m
Fixed Assets	354	335	379
Current Assets	5m	4m	3m
Current Liabilities	401	262	228

Numill Ltd
Balaclava Road, Sheffield, S6 3BG
Tel: 0114-285 5450 **Fax:** 0114-234 4363
E-mail: sales@numill.co.uk
Website: http://www.numill.co.uk
Directors: S. Wilson (Co Sec), A. Wilson (Fin)
Ultimate Holding Company: NUMILL ENGINEERING LIMITED
Immediate Holding Company: NUMILL LIMITED
Registration no: 04846115 **Date established:** 2003
No.of Employees: 11 - 20 **Product Groups:** 48, 84

Date of Accounts	Aug 11	Aug 10	Aug 09
Working Capital	10	-67	-94
Fixed Assets	152	181	222
Current Assets	333	229	188

Ormac Coatings Ltd
Thorncliffe Park Estate Newton Chambers Road, Chapeltown, Sheffield, S35 2PH
Tel: 0114-246 1237 **Fax:** 0114-257 0151
E-mail: orrmac@aol.com
Website: http://www.ormac.co.uk
Directors: G. Haslam (MD)
Managers: M. Prince
Immediate Holding Company: MWL CONSULTANTS LIMITED
Registration no: 04603315 **Date established:** 2002
No.of Employees: 21 - 50 **Product Groups:** 48

Date of Accounts	Nov 11	Nov 10	Nov 09
Working Capital	105	143	192
Fixed Assets	1	1	N/A
Current Assets	205	303	308

Outokumpu Ltd
Stevenson Road, Sheffield, S9 3XG
Tel: 0114-242 1124 **Fax:** 0114-242 2152
Website: http://www.outokumpu.com
Managers: J. Hulse (Mgr), M. O'Brien (Purch Mgr), A. Watson (Fin Mgr)
Registration no: 04670716 **Date established:** 2003
Turnover: Up to £250,000 **No.of Employees:** 51 - 100
Product Groups: 66

Outokumpu Stainless
PO Box 3541, Sheffield, S9 1ZT
Tel: 01694-771858 **Fax:** 0114-244 8280
E-mail: alison.kinna@outokumpu.com
Website: http://www.outokumpu.com
Directors: A. Kinna (MD)
Ultimate Holding Company: OUTOKUMPU (FINLAND)
Immediate Holding Company: OUTOKUMPU STAINLESS LIMITED
Registration no: 02794127 **Date established:** 1993
Turnover: £500m - £1,000m **No.of Employees:** 1 - 10
Product Groups: 34, 66

Date of Accounts	Dec 11	Dec 10	Dec 09
Sales Turnover	788m	617m	409m
Pre Tax Profit/Loss	21m	8m	-8m
Working Capital	134m	57m	40m
Fixed Assets	60m	70m	63m
Current Assets	203m	215m	143m
Current Liabilities	9m	5m	8m

Oval Industries Ltd
379 Penistone Road, Sheffield, S6 2FL
Tel: 0114-232 3188 **Fax:** 0114-233 8958
E-mail: sales@oval.co.uk
Website: http://www.oval.co.uk
Directors: I. Arthur (MD)
Immediate Holding Company: OVAL INDUSTRIES LIMITED
Registration no: 02166210 **Date established:** 1987
No.of Employees: 1 - 10 **Product Groups:** 31, 32

Date of Accounts	Dec 10	Dec 09	Dec 08
Working Capital	107	144	177
Fixed Assets	6	9	11
Current Assets	217	224	223

Overdale Of Sheffield
6 381 Penistone Road, Sheffield, S6 2FL
Tel: 0114-233 1266 **Fax:** 0114-233 1266
E-mail: dflack@stay-cool.net
Website: http://www.stay-cool.net
Directors: B. Flack (MD)
Turnover: Up to £250,000 **No.of Employees:** 1 - 10 **Product Groups:** 20, 40, 41

P G S Supplies Ltd
Worthing Road, Sheffield, S9 3JB
Tel: 0114-276 5566 **Fax:** 0114-276 5265
E-mail: sales@pgs-supplies.co.uk
Website: http://www.pgs-supplies.co.uk
Directors: C. Snape (Fin)
Immediate Holding Company: P.G.S. SUPPLIES LIMITED
Registration no: 02643624 **VAT No.:** GB 600 0121 37
Date established: 1991 **Turnover:** £500,000 - £1m
No.of Employees: 1 - 10 **Product Groups:** 30

Date of Accounts	Nov 11	Nov 10	Nov 09
Working Capital	-56	-41	-16
Fixed Assets	13	23	34
Current Assets	104	88	104

P S Mesh & Engineering
2c Cadman Street Mosborough, Sheffield, S20 5BU
Tel: 0114-248 4372 **Fax:** 0114-248 4372
E-mail: petersouth@talktalk.net
Directors: P. South (MD)
No.of Employees: 1 - 10 **Product Groups:** 35

Panache Lingerie
7 Drake House Crescent Waterthorpe, Sheffield, S20 7HT
Tel: 0114-241 8888 **Fax:** 0114-241 8889
E-mail: info@panache-lingerie.com
Website: http://www.panache-lingerie.com
Bank(s): HSBC Services (Midland)
Directors: P. Cronin (Sales), J. Cower (MD)
Managers: J. Gayle (Fin Mgr), S. Hazelhurst (Mktg Serv Mgr), S. Knight (Tech Serv Mgr), C. Christopher (Personnel)
Immediate Holding Company: PANACHE LINGERIE LIMITED
Registration no: 01524006 **VAT No.:** GB 308 5800 65
Date established: 1980 **Turnover:** £20m - £50m
No.of Employees: 51 - 100 **Product Groups:** 24

Date of Accounts	Jun 11	Jun 10	Jun 09
Sales Turnover	23m	24m	24m
Pre Tax Profit/Loss	710	2m	3m
Working Capital	5m	4m	3m
Fixed Assets	4m	5m	5m
Current Assets	10m	10m	8m
Current Liabilities	2m	2m	2m

Panel Systems Ltd
Unit 3-9 Welland Close, Sheffield, S3 9QY
Tel: 0114-275 2881 **Fax:** 0114-276 8807
E-mail: sales@panelsystems.co.uk
Website: http://www.panelsystems.co.uk
Bank(s): Royal Bank of Scotland, Sheffield
Directors: C. Ibbotson (MD), C. Fairburn (Fin)
Managers: D. Phelan (Sales Prom Mgr), S. Ballard (Mats Contrlr)
Ultimate Holding Company: PANEL SYSTEMS (HOLDINGS) LIMITED
Immediate Holding Company: PANEL SYSTEMS LIMITED
Registration no: 01179701 **VAT No.:** GB 599 8107 76
Date established: 1974 **Turnover:** £5m - £10m **No.of Employees:** 21 - 50
Product Groups: 30, 35

Date of Accounts	Dec 11	Dec 10	Dec 09
Sales Turnover	9m	8m	7m
Pre Tax Profit/Loss	455	344	273
Working Capital	1m	921	807
Fixed Assets	234	228	222
Current Assets	2m	2m	2m
Current Liabilities	269	203	240

Parkway Packaging Ltd
Unit 5e Parkway Drive, Sheffield, S9 4WN
Tel: 0114-244 2190
E-mail: sales@parkwaypackaging.com
Website: http://www.parkwaypackaging.com
Directors: T. Chapman (MD)
Immediate Holding Company: PARKWAY PACKAGING LIMITED
Registration no: 01208414 **Date established:** 1975
Turnover: £250,000 - £500,000 **No.of Employees:** 1 - 10
Product Groups: 38, 42

Date of Accounts	Jun 11	Jun 10	Jun 09
Sales Turnover	336	320	347
Pre Tax Profit/Loss	7	9	14
Working Capital	32	22	14
Fixed Assets	2	3	3
Current Assets	66	66	66
Current Liabilities	3	4	13

Peak Dean Interactive
Unit 9 The South West Centre Troutbeck Road, Sheffield, S7 2QA
Tel: 0114-262 9230 **Fax:** 0114-255 2431
E-mail: alison.riggott@peakdean.co.uk
Website: http://www.peakdean.co.uk
Directors: M. Johnston-Smith (MD), P. Ross (Co Sec), A. Riggott (Dir)
Managers: L. Leary (Accounts)
Immediate Holding Company: PEAKDEAN INTERACTIVE LIMITED
Registration no: 02503924 **Date established:** 1990
Turnover: £250,000 - £500,000 **No.of Employees:** 1 - 10
Product Groups: 44, 86

Date of Accounts	Mar 10	Mar 09	Mar 08
Working Capital	71	120	153
Fixed Assets	3	7	10
Current Assets	93	157	197

Pennine Instrument Services Ltd
82-86 Upper Allen Street, Sheffield, S3 7GW
Tel: 0114-273 0534 **Fax:** 0114-275 1818
E-mail: info@pennineinstruments.co.uk
Website: http://www.pennineinstruments.co.uk
Directors: G. Bell (MD)
Immediate Holding Company: PENNINE INSTRUMENT SERVICES LIMITED
Registration no: 01452244 **Date established:** 1979 **Turnover:** £5m - £10m
No.of Employees: 11 - 20 **Product Groups:** 31, 37, 38

Date of Accounts	Mar 11	Mar 10	Mar 09
Working Capital	99	79	65
Fixed Assets	389	375	383
Current Assets	217	188	152

Pennine Lubricants
Unit 35 Limestone Cottage Lane, Sheffield, S6 1NJ
Tel: 0114-285 2987 **Fax:** 0114-285 2988
E-mail: info@penninelubricants.co.uk
Website: http://www.penninelubricants.co.uk

see next page

***Pennine Lubricants** - Cont'd*
Directors: A. McClean (MD)
Managers: J. Grierson (Sales Prom Mgr)
Immediate Holding Company: PENNINE LUBRICANTS LIMITED
Registration no: 03510091 **Date established:** 1989 **Turnover:** £2m - £5m
No.of Employees: 11 - 20 **Product Groups:** 31, 32, 46, 66, 68

Date of Accounts	Dec 11	Dec 10	Dec 09
Working Capital	547	333	125
Fixed Assets	440	437	435
Current Assets	979	718	548

Pentag Gears & Oil Field Equipment Ltd
PO Box 24, Sheffield, S2 4QR
Tel: 0114-258 3473 **Fax:** 0114-258 4264
E-mail: a.larkin@pentag-gears.com
Website: http://www.pentag-gears.com
Directors: R. Bridger (Sales & Tech), A. Sheldon (Sales), A. Larkin (MD)
Managers: A. Sheldon (Sales Prom Mgr)
Immediate Holding Company: PENTAG GEARS & OILFIELD EQUIPMENT LTD
Registration no: 05194362 **Date established:** 2004 **Turnover:** £2m - £5m
No.of Employees: 1 - 10 **Product Groups:** 25, 35, 45

Date of Accounts	Sep 11	Sep 10	Sep 09
Working Capital	633	582	512
Fixed Assets	39	35	46
Current Assets	804	707	684

Pentone Ltd
203 Abbeyfield Road, Sheffield, S4 7AW
Tel: 0114-244 0303 **Fax:** 0114-244 9916
E-mail: robert.lock@jamboree-shop.co.uk
Website: http://www.pentone.co.uk
Directors: R. Lock (Fin)
Immediate Holding Company: PENTONE LIMITED
Registration no: 02789064 **VAT No.:** GB 600 1684 85
Date established: 1993 **Turnover:** Up to £250,000
No.of Employees: 1 - 10 **Product Groups:** 37, 67, 72, 79

Date of Accounts	Feb 08	Feb 11	Feb 10
Working Capital	3	-16	-6
Fixed Assets	4	1	2
Current Assets	14	3	6

Peterman Fork Lift Trucks
Bailey Drive Norwood Industrial Estate, Killamarsh, Sheffield, S21 2JF
Tel: 0114-248 8180 **Fax:** 0114-251 0624
E-mail: johnarmitage@petermanforklifts.com
Website: http://www.petermanforklifts.com
Directors: A. Hessey (Fin), J. Armitage (Dir)
Immediate Holding Company: PETERMAN ENGINEERING SERVICES LIMITED
Registration no: 01220733 **Date established:** 1975
No.of Employees: 11 - 20 **Product Groups:** 39, 45

Date of Accounts	Jul 11	Jul 10	Jul 09
Working Capital	66	33	42
Fixed Assets	48	59	73
Current Assets	545	506	461

Phoenix Catering Equipment
Woodside Lane, Sheffield, S3 9PB
Tel: 0114-272 7600 **Fax:** 0114-275 2684
Directors: S. Shelley (Prop)
Immediate Holding Company: PRO-TECH SYSTEMS (NORTHERN) LIMITED
Registration no: 06103510 **Date established:** 1996
Turnover: Up to £250,000 **No.of Employees:** 1 - 10 **Product Groups:** 20, 40, 41

Date of Accounts	Jun 11	Jun 10	Jun 09
Sales Turnover	113	161	93
Pre Tax Profit/Loss	-12	4	-15
Working Capital	-29	-18	-25
Fixed Assets	8	9	13
Current Assets	21	58	20
Current Liabilities	11	6	2

Phoenix Mechanical Services Ltd
44 Wilson Street, Sheffield, S3 8DD
Tel: 0114-273 0737 **Fax:** 0114-272 4904
E-mail: admin@pms-sheffield.co.uk
Website: http://www.pms-sheffield.co.uk
Bank(s): National Westminster Bank Plc
Directors: J. Mettam (Fin), J. Sykes (MD)
Immediate Holding Company: PHOENIX MECHANICAL SERVICES LIMITED
Registration no: 01672849 **VAT No.:** GB 308 9650 38
Date established: 1982 **Turnover:** £1m - £2m **No.of Employees:** 11 - 20
Product Groups: 30, 36, 37, 39, 40, 41, 46, 48, 51, 52, 54, 80, 84

Date of Accounts	Oct 11	Oct 10	Oct 09
Working Capital	2m	2m	2m
Fixed Assets	375	317	348
Current Assets	2m	2m	2m

Pickard Communication
Unit 11 Riverside Park Sheaf Gardens, Sheffield, S2 4BB
Tel: 0114-275 7222 **Fax:** 0114-275 8866
E-mail: info@pickards.org.uk
Website: http://www.pickards.org.uk
Directors: C. Pickard (Ptnr)
Date established: 1997 **No.of Employees:** 1 - 10 **Product Groups:** 81

S Pickersgill & Sons
63 Jenkin Road, Sheffield, S9 1AT
Tel: 0114-256 2251 **Fax:** 0114-256 2251
E-mail: sandtpickersgill@tiscali.co.uk
Directors: S. Pickersgill (Ptnr)
Immediate Holding Company: THE HOLLTECK COMPANY LIMITED
Registration no: 04288234 **Date established:** 2001 **Turnover:** £1m - £2m
No.of Employees: 1 - 10 **Product Groups:** 26, 35

Date of Accounts	Sep 11	Sep 10	Sep 09
Working Capital	491	476	517
Fixed Assets	52	68	71
Current Assets	894	978	1m
Current Liabilities	N/A	N/A	55

A Pinder Ltd
16 Moore Street, Sheffield, S3 7US
Tel: 0114-272 7574 **Fax:** 0114-275 1071
E-mail: sales@pindersofsheffield.co.uk
Website: http://www.pindersofsheffield.co.uk
Directors: M. Whiteway (Mkt Research), D. Whiteway (MD)
Managers: A. Billard (Buyer), J. Hoyland (Fin Mgr), J. Oxley (Tech Serv Mgr)
Immediate Holding Company: A.PINDER LIMITED
Registration no: 00346067 **VAT No.:** GB 172 5704 64
Date established: 1938 **Turnover:** £500,000 - £1m
No.of Employees: 21 - 50 **Product Groups:** 64, 80

Date of Accounts	Dec 11	Dec 10	Dec 09
Working Capital	1m	1m	1m
Fixed Assets	858	604	612
Current Assets	1m	1m	2m

Pipe Ten Hosting
Office 4 The Cube 1 Brittain Street, Sheffield, S1 4RJ
Tel: 0114-303 0040
E-mail: support@pipeten.co.uk
Website: http://www.pipeten.com
Directors: G. Kimpton (Dir)
Immediate Holding Company: PIPE TEN HOSTING LTD
Registration no: 05823310 **Date established:** 2006
No.of Employees: 1 - 10 **Product Groups:** 44, 79

Date of Accounts	Aug 11	Aug 10	Aug 09
Working Capital	53	45	33
Fixed Assets	45	38	40
Current Assets	194	134	127

Pitchmastic P M B
Royds Works Attercliffe Road, Sheffield, S4 7WZ
Tel: 0114-270 0100 **Fax:** 0114-276 8782
E-mail: info@pitchmasticpmb.co.uk
Website: http://www.pitchmasticpmb.co.uk
Bank(s): Lloyds TSB Bank plc
Directors: D. Hall (Comm)
Ultimate Holding Company: RPM INTERNATIONAL INC (USA)
Immediate Holding Company: PITCHMASTIC PMB LIMITED
Registration no: 05825725 **Date established:** 2006
Turnover: £125m - £250m **No.of Employees:** 11 - 20
Product Groups: 25, 30, 31, 33, 35

Date of Accounts	May 11	May 10	Mar 09
Sales Turnover	11m	16m	9m
Pre Tax Profit/Loss	2m	3m	1m
Working Capital	6m	4m	2m
Fixed Assets	875	913	827
Current Assets	7m	7m	5m
Current Liabilities	942	635	705

Portabello Fabrications
3 Long Acre Close Holbrook Industrial Estate, Holbrook, Sheffield, S20 3FR
Tel: 0114-251 3092 **Fax:** 0114-248 7936
E-mail: sales@pfl-rmf.co.uk
Website: http://www.portobello-fab.co.uk
Bank(s): HSBC, Barnsley
Directors: G. Avill (MD), R. Walker (Fin)
Managers: D. Churm (Mktg Serv Mgr)
Ultimate Holding Company: COMPASS HOLDINGS LTD
Immediate Holding Company: COMPASS HOLDINGS LTD
Registration no: 04042438 **Date established:** 1933 **Turnover:** £2m - £5m
No.of Employees: 21 - 50 **Product Groups:** 35, 36, 37, 40, 42, 48

Date of Accounts	Dec 07	Dec 06	Dec 05
Working Capital	410	-518	-285
Fixed Assets	212	1526	1461
Current Assets	1257	1034	1649
Current Liabilities	848	1553	1934

Portakabin Ltd
Barleywood Road, Sheffield, S9 5FJ
Tel: 0114-244 3211 **Fax:** 0114-244 4332
E-mail: sheffield.hire@portakabin.com
Website: http://www.portakabin.co.uk
Managers: G. Robinson (Mgr)
Immediate Holding Company: PORTAKABIN LIMITED
Registration no: 00685303 **Date established:** 1961
No.of Employees: 1 - 10 **Product Groups:** 35

Date of Accounts	Jun 11	Jun 10	Jun 09
Sales Turnover	171m	174m	202m
Pre Tax Profit/Loss	27m	26m	30m
Working Capital	35m	25m	8m
Fixed Assets	104m	103m	113m
Current Assets	79m	76m	67m
Current Liabilities	27m	35m	29m

Portec Rail Ltd
Stamford Street, Sheffield, S9 2TX
Tel: 0114-256 2225 **Fax:** 0114-261 7826
E-mail: uksales@portecrail.co.uk
Website: http://www.portecrail.co.uk
Bank(s): HSBC Bank plc
Directors: P. Jones (Fin), S. Roberts (Fin)
Managers: P. Broadhead (Purch Mgr)
Ultimate Holding Company: PORTEC RAIL PRODUCTS INC (USA)
Immediate Holding Company: CORONET RAIL LIMITED
Registration no: 04616486 **VAT No.:** GB 715 8123 45
Date established: 2002 **Turnover:** £2m - £5m **No.of Employees:** 21 - 50
Product Groups: 39, 48

Date of Accounts	Dec 11	Dec 10	Dec 09
Sales Turnover	3m	3m	3m
Pre Tax Profit/Loss	375	180	202
Working Capital	2m	2m	1m
Fixed Assets	119	106	163
Current Assets	2m	2m	2m
Current Liabilities	154	231	138

Powerbor(by G + J Hall)
Burgess Road, Sheffield, S9 3WD
Tel: 0114-244 0562 **Fax:** 0114-244 9256
E-mail: info@gjhall.co.uk
Website: http://www.powerbor.co.uk
Directors: P. Edwards (MD)
Date established: 1864 **Turnover:** £2m - £5m **No.of Employees:** 100
Product Groups: 36, 37, 45, 46, 67

Powertech Industrial Ltd
Unit 2c Ellisons Road Norwood Industrial Estate, Killamarsh, Sheffield, S21 2JG
Tel: 0114-247 4080 **Fax:** 0114-247 4860
E-mail: sales@powertech-industrial.co.uk
Website: http://www.powertech-industrial.co.uk
Directors: M. Robinson (MD)
Immediate Holding Company: POWERTECH INDUSTRIAL LIMITED
Registration no: 03931843 **Date established:** 2000
No.of Employees: 11 - 20 **Product Groups:** 35, 37, 39, 45

Date of Accounts	Apr 12	Apr 11	Apr 10
Working Capital	349	264	277
Fixed Assets	15	18	12
Current Assets	983	837	777

Practical Control Ltd
448 Brightside Lane, Sheffield, S9 2SP
Tel: 0114-256 1888 **Fax:** 0114-261 7052
E-mail: dennis.holdsworth@practicalcontrol.co.uk
Website: http://www.practicalcontrol.co.uk
Directors: S. Milner (Fin), D. Holdsworth (MD), E. Holdsworth (MD)
Immediate Holding Company: PRACTICAL CONTROL LIMITED
Registration no: 04117809 **Date established:** 2000
Turnover: £500,000 - £1m **No.of Employees:** 11 - 20 **Product Groups:** 44

Date of Accounts	Nov 09	Nov 08	Nov 07
Working Capital	-19	-52	30
Fixed Assets	34	47	28
Current Assets	130	124	113

Pre Formed Windings Ltd
Farm View Sheffield Road, Hackenthorpe, Sheffield, S12 4LT
Tel: 0114-248 4391 **Fax:** 0114-247 7663
E-mail: vfletcher@preformed.co.uk
Website: http://www.preformed.co.uk
Bank(s): Barclays
Managers: V. Fletcher (Mgr)
Ultimate Holding Company: DERITEND INDUSTRIES LIMITED
Immediate Holding Company: PREFORMED WINDINGS LIMITED
Registration no: 07462547 **VAT No.:** 785 4020 26 **Date established:** 2010
Turnover: £1m - £2m **No.of Employees:** 21 - 50 **Product Groups:** 37

Date of Accounts	Dec 11
Sales Turnover	2m
Pre Tax Profit/Loss	158
Working Capital	508
Fixed Assets	5m
Current Assets	1m
Current Liabilities	162

Premark Cutlery Mnfrs
17 Copper Street, Sheffield, S3 7AG
Tel: 0114-278 6731
Directors: T. Lakin (Prop)
Date established: 1990 **No.of Employees:** 1 - 10 **Product Groups:** 36, 40

Presto International UK Ltd
Newton Chambers Road
Thorncliffe Park Estate
Chapeltown, Sheffield, S35 2PH
Tel: 0114-257 8932 **Fax:** 0114-234 7446
E-mail: kevin.blackwell@presto-tools.com
Website: http://www.presto-tools.com
Bank(s): Barclays Bank Plc
Directors: K. Blackwell (Sales), S. Chen (MD), J. McDonald (Dir)
Ultimate Holding Company: Suncraft Corporation
Registration no: 06550550 **VAT No.:** GB 930 3761 38
Date established: 1843 **Turnover:** £10m - £20m
No.of Employees: 11 - 20 **Product Groups:** 34, 35, 36, 37, 40, 42, 45, 46, 47, 48, 66, 67

Date of Accounts	Apr 11	Apr 10	Apr 09
Working Capital	786	768	776
Fixed Assets	49	53	71
Current Assets	3m	2m	2m

Printaply
Highfield Lane, Sheffield, S13 9NA
Tel: 0114-269 3322 **Fax:** 08450-850077
E-mail: sales@printaply.co.uk
Website: http://www.printaply-direct.co.uk
Directors: S. Smith (Ptnr)
VAT No.: 308 8510 59 **Date established:** 1982 **Turnover:** Up to £250,000
No.of Employees: 1 - 10 **Product Groups:** 23, 27, 30

Pro Dek Design & Storage Systems Ltd
3 Atlas Way, Sheffield, S4 7QQ
Tel: 0114-244 0100 **Fax:** 0114-244 4721
E-mail: mail@pro-dek.co.uk
Website: http://www.pro-dek.co.uk
Directors: C. Ellis (Fin)
Managers: B. Ellis (Mgr)
Immediate Holding Company: PRO-DEK DESIGN & STORAGE SYSTEMS LIMITED
Registration no: 02776819 **Date established:** 1993
No.of Employees: 1 - 10 **Product Groups:** 35, 42, 45

Date of Accounts	Dec 11	Dec 10	Dec 09
Working Capital	272	229	172
Fixed Assets	4	5	159
Current Assets	637	559	355

Pro-Mech Fork-Lift Service
Unit 31 Enterprise Park Worthing Road, Sheffield, S9 3JL
Tel: 0114-244 9730 **Fax:** 0114-244 9730
E-mail: info@pro-mechforkliftservices.co.uk
Website: http://www.pro-mechforkliftservices.co.uk
Directors: P. Taylor (MD)
No.of Employees: 1 - 10 **Product Groups:** 35, 39, 45

Pro Roll Ltd
Little Matlock Rolling Mill Low Matlock Lane, Loxley, Sheffield, S6 6RN
Tel: 0114-232 4242 **Fax:** 0114-233 4848
E-mail: gillian.havenhand@rolling-mills.co.uk
Website: http://www.rolling-mills.co.uk
Directors: S. Havenhand (MD), G. Havenhand (Fin)
Immediate Holding Company: PRO-ROLL LIMITED
Registration no: 04133477 **Date established:** 2000
No.of Employees: 11 - 20 **Product Groups:** 35, 39, 45

Date of Accounts	Dec 11	Dec 10	Dec 09
Working Capital	24	-41	-56
Fixed Assets	620	575	569
Current Assets	201	157	114

Professional Lifting Services Ltd
Unit 7 870 Penistone Road, Sheffield, S6 2DL
Tel: 0114-285 5488 **Fax:** 0114-285 4553
E-mail: geraldspencer@plsltd.co.uk
Website: http://www.plsltd.co.uk
Bank(s): HSBC
Directors: G. Spencer (MD), M. Padgett (Fin)
Managers: C. Harrison (Sales Prom Mgr)
Immediate Holding Company: PROFESSIONAL LIFTING SERVICES LIMITED

Registration no: 01906401 **VAT No.:** GB 391 2998 12
Date established: 1985 **Turnover:** £1m - £2m **No.of Employees:** 21 - 50
Product Groups: 39, 45, 48, 84

Date of Accounts	Sep 11	Sep 10	Sep 09
Working Capital	90	64	58
Fixed Assets	164	136	153
Current Assets	813	616	686

Pro-Finish Services Ltd

Carwood Road, Sheffield, S4 7SD
Tel: 07931-803289 **Fax:** 0114-249 5223
Directors: T. Butler (Co Sec)
Immediate Holding Company: PRO-FINISH SERVICES LIMITED
Registration no: 04537661 **Date established:** 2002
No.of Employees: 1 - 10 **Product Groups:** 46, 48

Date of Accounts	Feb 08	Feb 11	Feb 10
Working Capital	-9	-19	-16
Fixed Assets	20	20	20
Current Assets	12	1	3

Progressive Systems

Unit 3 Station Road, Ecclesfield, Sheffield, S35 9YR
Tel: 0114-257 7160 **Fax:** 0114-257 7161
E-mail: geoff@progressivesystems.co.uk
Website: http://www.progressivesystems.co.uk
Directors: G. Capewell (Fin)
Immediate Holding Company: PROGRESSIVE CATERING EQUIPMENT LIMITED
Registration no: 06113940 **Date established:** 2007
Turnover: Up to £250,000 **No.of Employees:** 1 - 10 **Product Groups:** 20, 40, 41

Pryor Marking Technology Ltd

Egerton Street, Sheffield, S1 4JX
Tel: 0114-276 6044 **Fax:** 0114-276 6890
E-mail: j.tiffiman@pryormarking.com
Website: http://www.pryormarking.com
Bank(s): National Westminster Bank Plc
Directors: R. Hearn (Purch), A. Davies (Fin), J. Tiffiman (Ch)
Managers: A. Theaker, J. Fletcher (Personnel), R. Allen (Tech Serv Mgr)
Ultimate Holding Company: EDWARD PRYOR & SON LIMITED
Immediate Holding Company: PRYOR MARKING TECHNOLOGY LIMITED
Registration no: 00701896 **VAT No.:** GB 390 9398 07
Date established: 1961 **Turnover:** £5m - £10m
No.of Employees: 51 - 100 **Product Groups:** 28, 29, 30, 33, 34, 35, 36, 37, 38, 39, 40, 42, 44, 46, 47, 48, 49, 66, 67, 80, 81, 83, 85

Purple Wave AV Ltd

7 Wicker Arches Walker Street, Sheffield, S3 8GZ
Tel: 0845-8380546 **Fax:** 0845-8380547
E-mail: pete@purplewaveav.com
Website: http://www.purplewaveav.com
Registration no: 05484476 **No.of Employees:** 1 - 10 **Product Groups:** 37, 63, 69, 89

Pyramid Diamond Products Ltd

397a Petre Street, Sheffield, S3 8LL
Tel: 0114-256 2522 **Fax:** 0114-256 2533
E-mail: mark@pyramid-diamonds.co.uk
Website: http://www.pyramid-diamonds.co.uk
Directors: D. Watkinson (Dir), M. Massam (Dir), R. Swift (Fin)
Immediate Holding Company: DAVID WATKINSON ABRASIVES LIMITED
Registration no: 03475990 **Date established:** 1997
No.of Employees: 1 - 10 **Product Groups:** 37

Date of Accounts	Dec 10	Dec 09	Dec 08
Working Capital	N/A	-11	-6
Fixed Assets	N/A	8	7
Current Assets	8	76	105

Pyramid Fire Protection Ltd

132 Rutland Road, Sheffield, S3 9PP
Tel: 0114-272 8921 **Fax:** 0114-272 7631
E-mail: sales@pyramid-fire.co.uk
Website: http://www.pyramid-fire.co.uk
Bank(s): The Royal Bank of Scotland
Directors: V. Hawley (Fin)
Immediate Holding Company: PYRAMID FIRE PROTECTION LIMITED
Registration no: 00927954 **VAT No.:** GB 172 9247 46
Date established: 1968 **Turnover:** £500,000 - £1m
No.of Employees: 11 - 20 **Product Groups:** 37, 38, 39, 40, 52, 67

Date of Accounts	Sep 11	Sep 10	Sep 09
Working Capital	318	226	135
Fixed Assets	222	204	208
Current Assets	532	468	338

Qualimach Ltd

Hawke Street, Sheffield, S9 2SU
Tel: 0114-249 5400 **Fax:** 0114-249 5409
E-mail: info@qualimach.co.uk
Website: http://www.qualimach.co.uk
Bank(s): National Westminster Bank Plc
Directors: J. Sommerton (Dir)
Immediate Holding Company: QUALIMACH LIMITED
Registration no: 01516994 **VAT No.:** GB 353 5470 55
Date established: 1980 **Turnover:** £2m - £5m **No.of Employees:** 11 - 20
Product Groups: 46

Date of Accounts	Mar 12	Mar 11	Mar 10
Working Capital	-234	-263	-182
Fixed Assets	341	358	372
Current Assets	683	751	600

R J Stokes Company Ltd

Little London Road, Sheffield, S8 0UH
Tel: 0114-258 9595 **Fax:** 0114-250 9836
E-mail: sales@rjstokes.co.uk
Website: http://www.rjstokes.co.uk
Bank(s): National Westminster Bank Plc
Directors: J. Stokes (MD)
Managers: A. Yates (Purch Mgr), C. Seller (Tech Serv Mgr), K. Shaw (Sales Prom Mgr)
Immediate Holding Company: EDWIN BLYDE & CO,LIMITED
Registration no: 00190422 **VAT No.:** GB 172 6774 38
Date established: 2028 **No.of Employees:** 21 - 50 **Product Groups:** 32, 33, 61

Date of Accounts	Dec 07	Dec 06	Dec 05
Pre Tax Profit/Loss	816	1030	587
Working Capital	3443	3905	3937
Fixed Assets	5659	4535	3810
Current Assets	5985	5717	5804
Current Liabilities	2542	1812	1867
Total Share Capital	45	45	45
ROCE% (Return on Capital Employed)	9.0	12.2	7.6

R & R Polishing Ltd

Jerico Works Holme Lane, Sheffield, S6 4JR
Tel: 0114-231 4093 **Fax:** 0114-287 8271
Website: http://www.randrsheffieldcutlery.com
Managers: R. Idell (Mgr)
Immediate Holding Company: R. & R. POLISHING LIMITED
Registration no: 01407366 **Date established:** 1979
No.of Employees: 1 - 10 **Product Groups:** 36, 40

Date of Accounts	Mar 11	Mar 10	Mar 08
Working Capital	44	46	59
Fixed Assets	14	15	16
Current Assets	70	64	82

Recut Ltd

6 Petre Drive, Sheffield, S4 7PZ
Tel: 0114-261 9868 **Fax:** 0114-261 9874
E-mail: sales@recutltd.com
Website: http://www.recutltd.com
Product Groups: 33, 34, 36, 37, 39, 40, 41, 42, 43, 44, 45, 46, 47, 48, 66

Date of Accounts	Feb 08	Feb 11	Feb 10
Working Capital	-27	-18	-17
Fixed Assets	67	44	54
Current Assets	125	96	88

Refmet Ceramics Ltd

Unit 3 Thorncliffe Park Estate Newton Chambers Road, Chapeltown, Sheffield, S35 2PH
Tel: 0114-257 7277 **Fax:** 0114-257 7288
E-mail: sales@diamond-like-carbon.com
Website: http://www.diamond-like-carbon.com
Directors: L. Lawrence (Fin)
Immediate Holding Company: REFMET CERAMICS LIMITED
Registration no: 02405658 **Date established:** 1989
No.of Employees: 1 - 10 **Product Groups:** 46, 48

Date of Accounts	Mar 11	Mar 10	Mar 09
Working Capital	553	556	573
Fixed Assets	87	92	93
Current Assets	659	610	776

Remploy Ltd

445 Brightside Lane, Sheffield, S9 2RR
Tel: 0114-254 3900 **Fax:** 0114-254 3932
E-mail: stephenowen@remploy.co.uk
Website: http://www.remploy.co.uk
Managers: S. Allen, S. Owen (Mgr)
Immediate Holding Company: REMPLOY LIMITED
Registration no: NF003194 **VAT No.:** GB 226 5029 76
Date established: 1995 **Turnover:** £2m - £5m **No.of Employees:** 51 - 100
Product Groups: 77

Roebuck & Clarke Galvanizing Ltd

Quantim House Campbell Way, Dinnington, Sheffield, S25 3QD
Tel: 01709-560888 **Fax:** 01709-554277
E-mail: enquiries@roebuckandclarke.co.uk
Website: http://www.roebuckandclarke.co.uk
Bank(s): Midland, Rotherham
Directors: A. Mitchell (MD), G. Eyre (Fin)
Managers: E. Stewart, L. Trimebaeth, L. Blackett
Immediate Holding Company: R & C REALISATIONS LIMITED
Registration no: 02522083 **VAT No.:** GB 599 9130 76
Date established: 1990 **Turnover:** £2m - £5m **No.of Employees:** 51 - 100
Product Groups: 48

Date of Accounts	Dec 09	Dec 08	Dec 07
Working Capital	1m	998	1m
Fixed Assets	486	474	469
Current Assets	3m	2m	2m

Ronseal Ltd

Thorncliffe Park Chapeltown, Sheffield, S35 2YP
Tel: 0114-246 7171 **Fax:** 0114-245 5629
E-mail: enquiries@ronseal.co.uk
Website: http://www.ronseal.co.uk
Directors: H. Hargreaves (Fin), J. Smith (Mkt Research)
Managers: D. Poulson (Personnel), L. Brammer (Tech Serv Mgr), A. Greeves (Buyer)
Immediate Holding Company: RONSEAL LIMITED
Registration no: 02968830 **VAT No.:** GB 646 4785 00
Date established: 1994 **Turnover:** £50m - £75m
No.of Employees: 251 - 500 **Product Groups:** 32

Date of Accounts	Dec 11	Dec 10	Dec 09
Sales Turnover	61m	56m	54m
Pre Tax Profit/Loss	1m	1m	1m
Working Capital	4m	2m	3m
Fixed Assets	21m	23m	23m
Current Assets	20m	20m	17m
Current Liabilities	8m	12m	7m

Room Search Ltd

Bartle House 28 Bartle Road, Sheffield, S12 2QQ
Tel: 0114-265 1654 **Fax:** 0114-265 1653
E-mail: joanne@room-search.co.uk
Website: http://www.room-search.co.uk
Directors: J. Rollitt (Dir)
Immediate Holding Company: ROOMSEARCH LIMITED
Registration no: 05611744 **Date established:** 2005
Turnover: Up to £250,000 **No.of Employees:** 1 - 10 **Product Groups:** 69

Date of Accounts	Nov 11	Nov 10	Nov 09
Working Capital	2	1	18
Fixed Assets	6	8	10
Current Assets	23	26	113

Ross & Catherall Ltd

Forge Lane Killamarsh, Sheffield, S21 1BA
Tel: 0114-248 6404 **Fax:** 0114-247 5999
E-mail: bhunt@doncasters.com
Website: http://www.doncasters.com
Bank(s): Lloyds TSB, National Westminster
Managers: B. Hunt (Sales Prom Mgr)
Ultimate Holding Company: DUBAI HOLDING LLC (DUBAI)
Immediate Holding Company: ROSS & CATHERALL LIMITED
Registration no: 04110786 **VAT No.:** GB 125 8260 76
Date established: 2000 **No.of Employees:** 101 - 250 **Product Groups:** 31, 34, 66

Date of Accounts	Dec 11	Dec 10	Dec 09
Sales Turnover	91m	72m	62m
Pre Tax Profit/Loss	12m	10m	8m
Working Capital	84m	71m	60m
Fixed Assets	9m	10m	10m
Current Assets	97m	80m	67m
Current Liabilities	631	812	660

Rotamag

41 Capley Road Darnall, Sheffield, S9 5JF
Tel: 0114-291 1020 **Fax:** 0114-261 8186
E-mail: sales@bryar.co.uk
Website: http://www.rotamag.co.uk
Bank(s): Bank of Scotland
Directors: V. Archer (MD)
Managers: M. Kaye (Design Mgr), S. Shaw (Purch Mgr)
Immediate Holding Company: Bryar Group
Registration no: 04370770 **VAT No.:** GB 651 6312 56
Turnover: £2m - £5m **No.of Employees:** 21 - 50 **Product Groups:** 46

Rotary Engineering UK Ltd

Old Lane Halfway, Sheffield, S20 3GZ
Tel: 0114-251 3134 **Fax:** 0114-258 6066
E-mail: sales@rotary.co.uk
Website: http://www.rotary.co.uk
Bank(s): National Westminster Bank Plc
Directors: J. Rooker (Dir), R. Fennell (MD)
Immediate Holding Company: ROTARY ENGINEERING UK LIMITED
Registration no: 04648787 **Date established:** 2003 **Turnover:** £1m - £2m
No.of Employees: 11 - 20 **Product Groups:** 36

Rotor Clip Ltd

Meadowbrook Park Halfway, Sheffield, S20 3PJ
Tel: 0114-247 3399 **Fax:** 0114-247 4499
E-mail: geoff.haigh@rotorclip.com
Website: http://www.rotorclip.com
Directors: G. Haigh (Dir)
Immediate Holding Company: ROTOR CLIP LIMITED
Registration no: 03839280 **Date established:** 1999
Turnover: £20m - £50m **No.of Employees:** 11 - 20 **Product Groups:** 35, 36

Date of Accounts	Dec 11	Dec 10	Dec 09
Sales Turnover	10m	N/A	N/A
Pre Tax Profit/Loss	383	N/A	N/A
Working Capital	-121	464	1m
Fixed Assets	1m	38	37
Current Assets	7m	4m	3m
Current Liabilities	7m	N/A	N/A

William Rowland Ltd

9-13 Meadow Street, Sheffield, S3 7BL
Tel: 0114-276 9421 **Fax:** 0114-275 9429
E-mail: geoff.morley@william-rowland.co.uk
Website: http://www.william-rowland.com
Bank(s): Barclays, Fitzalan Square
Directors: G. Morley (Co Sec)
Ultimate Holding Company: AMCO INVESTMENTS LIMITED
Immediate Holding Company: WILLIAM ROWLAND LIMITED
Registration no: 00853661 **VAT No.:** GB 173 1205 96
Date established: 1965 **Turnover:** £50m - £75m
No.of Employees: 11 - 20 **Product Groups:** 12, 17, 30, 31, 33, 34, 35, 37, 66

Date of Accounts	Dec 11	Dec 10	Dec 09
Sales Turnover	74m	63m	28m
Pre Tax Profit/Loss	2m	1m	599
Working Capital	11m	11m	6m
Fixed Assets	998	978	961
Current Assets	19m	19m	10m
Current Liabilities	623	425	1m

Roxspur Measurement & Control Ltd

2 Downgate Drive, Sheffield, S4 8BT
Tel: 0114-224 9200 **Fax:** 0114-243 4838
E-mail: gswindell@roxspur.com
Website: http://www.roxspur.com
Bank(s): Barclays
Directors: A. Roberts (Sales), G. Swindell (Dir), M. Graham (Fin)
Managers: D. Smith
Ultimate Holding Company: CONTROLS DIRECT LIMITED
Immediate Holding Company: ROXSPUR MEASUREMENT & CONTROL LIMITED
Registration no: 00881547 **Date established:** 1966 **Turnover:** £5m - £10m
No.of Employees: 101 - 250 **Product Groups:** 38, 67

Date of Accounts	Jun 11	Jun 10	Jun 09
Sales Turnover	9m	8m	9m
Pre Tax Profit/Loss	983	-67	165
Working Capital	10m	9m	9m
Fixed Assets	3m	3m	4m
Current Assets	12m	10m	10m
Current Liabilities	798	863	793

Royal Tool Control Ltd

Unit 1 Amberley Court, Sheffield, S9 2LQ
Tel: 0114-244 1411 **Fax:** 0114-243 2247
E-mail: royal@royaltool.co.uk
Website: http://www.royaltool.co.uk
Directors: P. Crump (MD)
Ultimate Holding Company: J H P INC (USA)
Immediate Holding Company: ROYAL TOOL CONTROL LIMITED
Registration no: 00944111 **Date established:** 1968 **Turnover:** £1m - £2m
No.of Employees: 11 - 20 **Product Groups:** 67

Date of Accounts	Aug 11	Aug 10	Aug 09
Working Capital	951	925	838
Fixed Assets	49	54	55
Current Assets	1m	1m	1m

S K M

111 Charles Street, Sheffield, S1 2ND
Tel: 0114-275 8998 **Fax:** 0114-273 8968
Website: http://www.skmconsulting.com
Directors: A. Bernau (Dir)
Managers: E. Duffey (Mgr)
Turnover: £20m - £50m **No.of Employees:** 11 - 20 **Product Groups:** 35

S Murray & Company Ltd

President Way, Sheffield, S4 7UR
Tel: 0114-279 4900
E-mail: rodney.nowlin@smurray.co.uk
Website: http://www.smurray.co.uk

see next page

S Murray & Company Ltd - Cont'd

Managers: R. Nowlin (District Mgr)
Ultimate Holding Company: MURRAY HOLDINGS LIMITED
Immediate Holding Company: S.MURRAY & COMPANY LIMITED
Registration no: 00145824 **Date established:** 2017
No.of Employees: 11 - 20 **Product Groups:** 38, 67

Date of Accounts	Dec 11	Dec 10	Dec 09
Sales Turnover	5m	5m	5m
Pre Tax Profit/Loss	-32	-128	35
Working Capital	390	477	593
Fixed Assets	3m	3m	3m
Current Assets	2m	2m	2m
Current Liabilities	213	180	194

S P C Patterns Ltd

191 Vincent Road, Sheffield, S7 1BZ
Tel: 0114-255 0040 **Fax:** 0114-255 8023
E-mail: office@spcpatterns.co.uk
Directors: K. Harrison (Fin), R. Hern (MD)
Immediate Holding Company: S.P.C. PATTERNS LIMITED
Registration no: 01107865 **VAT No.:** GB 173 6719 40
Date established: 1973 **Turnover:** £250,000 - £500,000
No.of Employees: 1 - 10 **Product Groups:** 25, 30, 33, 34, 48

Date of Accounts	Dec 11	Dec 10	Dec 09
Working Capital	134	90	89
Fixed Assets	5	7	8
Current Assets	204	173	132

S R L Countertech Ltd

Leigh Street, Sheffield, S9 2PR
Tel: 0114-256 0020 **Fax:** 0114-256 0070
E-mail: paul@srl-countertech.co.uk
Website: http://www.srl-countertech.co.uk
Directors: P. Wells (Fin)
Ultimate Holding Company: SHEFFIELD REFRIGERATION LIMITED
Immediate Holding Company: SRL COUNTERTECH LIMITED
Registration no: 02716480 **Date established:** 1992
Turnover: £250,000 - £500,000 **No.of Employees:** 21 - 50
Product Groups: 67

Date of Accounts	Aug 11	Aug 10	Aug 09
Working Capital	32	32	32
Current Assets	32	32	32

Salomon Engineering Ltd

High Hazel Works Catley Road, Sheffield, S9 5JF
Tel: 0114-261 0690 **Fax:** 0114-261 0691
E-mail: jreid@salomoneng.co.uk
Website: http://www.salomoneng.co.uk
Directors: K. Saloman (Prop)
Immediate Holding Company: SALOMON ENGINEERING LIMITED
Registration no: 04471951 **Date established:** 2002
Turnover: £250,000 - £500,000 **No.of Employees:** 1 - 10
Product Groups: 40

Date of Accounts	Jun 12	Jun 11	Jun 10
Working Capital	30	5	26
Fixed Assets	170	188	209
Current Assets	154	131	160

T W Sampson Ltd

2 Birley Moor Road, Sheffield, S12 4WD
Tel: 0114-253 0520 **Fax:** 0114- 2530550
Website: http://www.twsampson.co.uk
Bank(s): Midland, Sheffield
Directors: P. Glover (Dir), S. Risley (Co Sec)
Ultimate Holding Company: T.W. SAMPSON (HOLDINGS) LIMITED
Immediate Holding Company: T.W.SAMPSON & CO.,LIMITED
Registration no: 00394298 **Date established:** 1945 **Turnover:** £5m - £10m
No.of Employees: 21 - 50 **Product Groups:** 52

Date of Accounts	Mar 07	Mar 06	Mar 05
Pre Tax Profit/Loss	-445	129	-281
Working Capital	129	560	406
Fixed Assets	150	165	189
Current Assets	2m	4m	2m
Current Liabilities	527	815	622

Samuel Staniforth Ltd

Smithfield Works Alma Street, Sheffield, S3 8SA
Tel: 0114-272 3191
E-mail: sales@s-staniforth.co.uk
Website: http://www.s-staniforth.co.uk
Directors: L. Hopkinson (MD), S. Hopkinson (Fin)
Immediate Holding Company: SAMUEL STANIFORTH LIMITED
Registration no: 04006548 **Date established:** 2000
No.of Employees: 1 - 10 **Product Groups:** 36, 40

Date of Accounts	Oct 11	Oct 10	Oct 09
Working Capital	165	199	206
Fixed Assets	59	68	65
Current Assets	611	605	206

Sandvik Bioline

Longacre Way Holbrook Industrial Estate, Holbrook, Sheffield, S20 3FS
Tel: 0114-263 3100 **Fax:** 0114-263 3111
E-mail: stephencowan@sandvik.com
Website: http://www.sandvik.com
Bank(s): Barclays
Directors: S. Coward (MD)
Managers: C. Hague (Export Sales Mg), L. LaBraca (Sales Prom Mgr), R. Taylor (I.T. Exec), S. Cowen (Chief Mgr)
Ultimate Holding Company: C N HOLDINGS LIMITED
Immediate Holding Company: HALLAM STEELSTOCK LIMITED
Registration no: 01648874 **VAT No.:** GB 281 4525 60
Date established: 1982 **Turnover:** £2m - £5m **No.of Employees:** 11 - 20
Product Groups: 34, 35, 36, 38, 48, 66

Saturn Machine Knives

Unit 6 Neepsend Industrial Estate 80 Parkwood Road, Sheffield, S3 8AG
Tel: 0114-278 9090
E-mail: sales@saturnmachineknives.co.uk
Website: http://www.saturnmachineknives.co.uk
Managers: S. Jackson (Mgr)
Immediate Holding Company: SATURN MACHINE KNIVES LIMITED
Registration no: 04498316 **Date established:** 2002
No.of Employees: 1 - 10 **Product Groups:** 46

Date of Accounts	Dec 11	Dec 10	Dec 09
Working Capital	-10	-15	11
Fixed Assets	66	61	48
Current Assets	99	77	70

School Of East Asian Studies University Of Sheffield

6-8 Shearwood Road, Sheffield, S10 2TD
Tel: 0114-222 8400 **Fax:** 0114-222 8432
E-mail: postmaster@shef.ac.uk
Website: http://www.seas.ac.uk
Managers: X. Zang
Ultimate Holding Company: UNIVERSITY OF SHEFFIELD
Registration no: 05667109 **VAT No.:** GB 648 2388 08
Date established: 2006 **Turnover:** £10m - £20m
No.of Employees: 21 - 50 **Product Groups:** 86

Search Sheffield

191 Woodbourn Road, Sheffield, S9 3LQ
Tel: 0114-244 6521 **Fax:** 0114-256 2093
E-mail: info@wgsearch.co.uk
Website: http://www.wgsearch.co.uk
Managers: A. Collings
Immediate Holding Company: DIRECT HEATING SUPPLIES LTD
Registration no: 04227571 **VAT No.:** GB 477 0776 10
Date established: 2001 **No.of Employees:** 1 - 10 **Product Groups:** 45, 48, 72, 83, 84

The Section Bending Company Ltd

Houghton Road North Anston Trading Estate, North Anston, Sheffield, S25 4JJ
Tel: 01909-550080 **Fax:** 01909-550114
E-mail: sales@thebending.co.uk
Website: http://www.thebending.co.uk
Bank(s): Royal bank of scotland
Directors: C. Skelton (MD), J. Bleasdale (Co Sec)
Managers: C. Havenhand (Buyer), R. Newman (Prod Mgr)
Immediate Holding Company: T.H.E. SECTION BENDING COMPANY LIMITED
Registration no: 03184442 **VAT No.:** 678 9008 85 **Date established:** 1996
Turnover: £1m - £2m **No.of Employees:** 21 - 50 **Product Groups:** 48

Date of Accounts	Apr 12	Apr 11	Apr 10
Working Capital	-220	-247	-199
Fixed Assets	598	637	684
Current Assets	784	1m	857

Servalift Ltd

Unit 2a Dannemora Drive, Sheffield, S9 5DF
Tel: 0114-247 4449 **Fax:** 0114-247 4201
E-mail: info@servalift.com
Website: http://www.servalift.co.uk
Directors: B. Carnall (Dir)
Immediate Holding Company: SERVALIFT LIMITED
Registration no: 03494906 **Date established:** 1998
No.of Employees: 1 - 10 **Product Groups:** 35, 39, 45

Date of Accounts	Jan 12	Jan 11	Jan 10
Working Capital	-5	-7	-9
Fixed Assets	6	9	12
Current Assets	43	28	39

John S Shackleton Sheffield Ltd

4 Downgate Drive, Sheffield, S4 8BU
Tel: 0114-244 4767 **Fax:** 0114-242 5965
E-mail: chris@john-s-shackleton.co.uk
Bank(s): Yorkshire Bank PLC
Directors: C. Lilleyman (MD), C. Lilleyman (MD)
Immediate Holding Company: JOHN S. SHACKLETON (SHEFFIELD) LIMITED
Registration no: 01141245 **VAT No.:** GB 174 1482 64
Date established: 1973 **Turnover:** £2m - £5m **No.of Employees:** 11 - 20
Product Groups: 66

Date of Accounts	Mar 11	Mar 10	Mar 09
Working Capital	3m	3m	3m
Fixed Assets	683	713	709
Current Assets	4m	4m	4m

Sheaf Engineering Services Ltd

Bankside Works Lumley Street, Sheffield, S4 7ZJ
Tel: 0114-275 6851 **Fax:** 0114-275 6851
Directors: M. Griffiths (Fin)
Immediate Holding Company: SHEAF ENGINEERING SERVICES LIMITED
Registration no: 03989782 **Date established:** 2000
Turnover: Up to £250,000 **No.of Employees:** 1 - 10 **Product Groups:** 46

Date of Accounts	May 11	May 10	May 09
Sales Turnover	N/A	148	114
Pre Tax Profit/Loss	N/A	73	44
Working Capital	56	54	32
Fixed Assets	5	8	6
Current Assets	90	86	59
Current Liabilities	N/A	28	22

Sheafpower Ltd

Wardpower Works Wicker Lane, Sheffield, S3 8HQ
Tel: 0114-273 8855 **Fax:** 0114-273 9780
E-mail: sales@wardpower.co.uk
Website: http://www.wardpower.co.uk
Bank(s): Midland, Chesterfield
Directors: K. Marshall (Ch)
Immediate Holding Company: SHEAF POWER LIMITED
Registration no: 02107580 **VAT No.:** 457 7674 94 **Date established:** 1987
Turnover: £2m - £5m **No.of Employees:** 21 - 50 **Product Groups:** 37

Date of Accounts	Jul 10	Jul 09	Jul 08
Working Capital	189	162	93
Fixed Assets	217	217	228
Current Assets	2m	2m	2m

Sheffield Assay Office

Beulah Road, Sheffield, S6 2AN
Tel: 0114-231 2121
E-mail: reception@assayoffice.co.uk
Website: http://www.assayoffice.co.uk
Bank(s): Royal Bank of Scotland Plc
Directors: A. Carson (MD), H. Seeker (Fin)
Managers: N. Guest (Personnel)
Turnover: £2m - £5m **No.of Employees:** 51 - 100 **Product Groups:** 38, 85

Sheffield Electrical Co. Ltd

330 Petre Street, Sheffield, S4 8LU
Tel: 0114-243 0236 **Fax:** 0114-243 9849
E-mail: enquiries@sheffieldelectric.co.uk
Website: http://www.sheffieldelectric.co.uk
Bank(s): Yorkshire
Directors: A. Hancock (Fin)
Immediate Holding Company: SHEFFIELD ELECTRICAL CO. (CONTRACTORS) LIMITED
Registration no: 00654127 **VAT No.:** GB 172 8735 38
Date established: 1960 **Turnover:** £1m - £2m **No.of Employees:** 11 - 20
Product Groups: 84

Date of Accounts	Mar 12	Mar 11	Mar 10
Sales Turnover	N/A	N/A	2m
Pre Tax Profit/Loss	N/A	N/A	36
Working Capital	52	33	14
Fixed Assets	23	26	29
Current Assets	572	382	475
Current Liabilities	N/A	N/A	110

Sheffield Insulations Ltd

Hillsborough Works Langsett Road, Sheffield, S6 2LW
Tel: 0114-285 6300 **Fax:** 0114-285 6375
E-mail: info@sigplc.co.uk
Website: http://www.sheffins.co.uk
Bank(s): National Westminster Bank Plc
Directors: A. Mander (Pers), D. Picking (Tech Serv), D. Robertson (Fin), R. Monro (Co Sec), R. Barclay (MD)
Ultimate Holding Company: SIG PLC
Immediate Holding Company: SHEFFIELD INSULATIONS LIMITED
Registration no: 00577389 **VAT No.:** GB 172 4820 67
Date established: 1957 **Turnover:** £500m - £1,000m
No.of Employees: 101 - 250 **Product Groups:** 33, 67

Date of Accounts	Dec 11	Dec 10	Dec 09
Working Capital	5m	5m	5m
Fixed Assets	386	386	386
Current Assets	5m	5m	5m

Sheffield Precision Engineering Co. Ltd

346 Brightside Lane, Sheffield, S9 2SP
Tel: 0114-221 1777 **Fax:** 0114-221 1778
Directors: J. Roberts (Fin), J. Roberts (MD)
Managers: J. Roberts (Sales Prom Mgr)
Immediate Holding Company: SHEFFIELD PRECISION ENGINEERING CO LIMITED
Registration no: 01343507 **Date established:** 1977
Turnover: £500,000 - £1m **No.of Employees:** 1 - 10 **Product Groups:** 35, 48

Sheffield Refractories

113 Laughton Road Dinnington, Sheffield, S25 2PP
Tel: 01909-568444 **Fax:** 01909-568525
E-mail: enquiries@sheffieldrefractories.com
Website: http://www.sheffield-refractories.co.uk
Directors: T. Staton (MD)
Managers: L. Taylor (Purch Mgr), J. Staton (Tech Serv Mgr), J. Gray
Ultimate Holding Company: TJS HOLDINGS LIMITED
Immediate Holding Company: SHEFFIELD REFRACTORIES LIMITED
Registration no: 01279115 **VAT No.:** GB 646 5101 51
Date established: 1976 **Turnover:** £5m - £10m **No.of Employees:** 1 - 10
Product Groups: 33, 66

Date of Accounts	Sep 11	Sep 10	Sep 09
Sales Turnover	7m	6m	6m
Pre Tax Profit/Loss	53	7	147
Working Capital	2m	2m	2m
Fixed Assets	632	673	713
Current Assets	4m	3m	3m
Current Liabilities	76	110	140

Sheffield Superturn Ltd

Unit 17 18 Limestone Cottage Lane, Sheffield, S6 1NJ
Tel: 0114-243 2898 **Fax:** 0114-232 2879
Website: http://www.superturn.com
Bank(s): National Westminster Bank Plc
Directors: A. Taylor (MD), A. Taylor (Fin)
Immediate Holding Company: X-CEL SUPERTURN (GB) LIMITED
Registration no: 01710788 **VAT No.:** GB 173 9236 45
Date established: 1983 **Turnover:** £10m - £20m
No.of Employees: 11 - 20 **Product Groups:** 48

Date of Accounts	Mar 11	Mar 10	Mar 09
Sales Turnover	12m	11m	N/A
Pre Tax Profit/Loss	1m	2m	3m
Working Capital	1m	1m	1m
Fixed Assets	5m	5m	5m
Current Assets	5m	5m	5m
Current Liabilities	778	800	976

Sheffield Testing Laboratories Ltd

Nursery Street, Sheffield, S3 8GP
Tel: 0114-272 6581 **Fax:** 0114-272 3248
E-mail: drt@sheffieldtesting.com
Website: http://www.sheffieldtesting.com
Bank(s): Barclays
Directors: H. Hooge Venterink (Fin)
Managers: D. Tame (Chief Mgr), R. Martin
Ultimate Holding Company: ELEMENT MATERIALS TECHNOLOGY HOLDING UK LTD
Immediate Holding Company: ELEMENT MATERIALS TECHNOLOGY SHEFFIELD LTD
Registration no: 00076383 **VAT No.:** 172 8037 62 **Date established:** 2003
Turnover: £1m - £2m **No.of Employees:** 21 - 50 **Product Groups:** 38, 80, 85

Date of Accounts	Dec 11	Dec 10	Dec 09
Sales Turnover	2m	N/A	N/A
Pre Tax Profit/Loss	405	N/A	N/A
Working Capital	517	777	600
Fixed Assets	239	201	138
Current Assets	762	1m	738
Current Liabilities	187	N/A	N/A

Sheffield United Football Club Ticket Office

Bramhall Lane, Sheffield, S2 4SU
Tel: 08719-951889 **Fax:** 0870-442 8813
E-mail: boxoffice@sufc.co.uk
Website: http://www.sufc.co.uk
Managers: C. Payne (Cust Serv Mgr)
Ultimate Holding Company: SCARBOROUGH GROUP INTERNATIONAL LIMITED
Immediate Holding Company: SHEFFIELD UNITED PLC
Registration no: 00396956 **Date established:** 1945
Turnover: £500,000 - £1m **No.of Employees:** 1 - 10 **Product Groups:** 87

Date of Accounts	Jun 11	Jun 10	Jun 09
Sales Turnover	16m	21m	32m
Pre Tax Profit/Loss	-14m	-19m	6m

Working Capital	-3m	-25m	-9m
Fixed Assets	27m	45m	53m
Current Assets	24m	31m	37m
Current Liabilities	21m	35m	27m

Sheffield Waterjet Cutting Company
Unit 2 Well Meadow Works Well Meadow Street, Sheffield, S3 7GS
Tel: 0114-272 0077 **Fax:** 0114-279 9277
E-mail: sheffieldwaterjetcutting@yahoo.co.uk
Website: http://www.sheffieldwaterjetcutting.com
Directors: C. Rooney (Prop)
Registration no: 07566638 **Date established:** 2006
Turnover: Up to £250,000 **No.of Employees:** 1 - 10 **Product Groups:** 48

Shotblast Solutions
7 Twentywell View Bradway, Sheffield, S17 4PX
Tel: 0114-236 2012 **Fax:** 0114-236 2012
E-mail: sales@shotblastsolutions.co.uk
Directors: J. Ramsden (Fin), A. Ramsden (Dir)
Immediate Holding Company: SHOTBLAST SOLUTIONS LTD
Registration no: 06300225 **Date established:** 2007
Turnover: Up to £250,000 **No.of Employees:** 1 - 10 **Product Groups:** 46, 67

Date of Accounts	Jul 11	Jul 10	Jul 09
Working Capital	-4	-6	-5
Fixed Assets	6	8	10
Current Assets	49	40	38

Simm Engineering Group
Gilbertson Works Jessell Street, Sheffield, S9 3HY
Tel: 0114-244 0764 **Fax:** 0114-244 2725
E-mail: tony.lewis@simmengineeringgroup.co.uk
Website: http://www.simmengineeringgroup.co.uk
Bank(s): Barclays
Directors: T. Lewis (MD)
Immediate Holding Company: COMPRESSOR MAINTENANCE LIMITED
Registration no: 00814814 **VAT No.:** GB 172 9310 65
Date established: 1964 **No.of Employees:** 11 - 20 **Product Groups:** 45, 67

Simonds Industries Ltd
Unit 3 Motorway Industrial Estate Tyler Street, Sheffield, S9 1DH
Tel: 0114-243 3701 **Fax:** 0114-243 3879
Website: http://www.simondsind.com
Directors: S. Carr (MD)
Ultimate Holding Company: SIMONDS INDUSTRIES INC (USA)
Immediate Holding Company: SIMONDS INDUSTRIES LIMITED
Registration no: 02232753 **Date established:** 1988 **Turnover:** £2m - £5m
No.of Employees: 1 - 10 **Product Groups:** 34, 36, 37, 44

Date of Accounts	Dec 10	Dec 09	Dec 08
Sales Turnover	3m	2m	3m
Pre Tax Profit/Loss	-225	-456	-419
Working Capital	1m	2m	2m
Fixed Assets	63	90	94
Current Assets	2m	3m	3m
Current Liabilities	40	43	23

A L Simpkin Co. Ltd
3 Hunter Road, Sheffield, S6 4LD
Tel: 0114-234 8736 **Fax:** 0114-232 5635
E-mail: karen.simpkin@alsimpkin.com
Website: http://www.alsimpkin.com
Bank(s): Barclays
Directors: K. Simpkin (Dir)
Managers: L. Wilkinson (Fin Mgr), D. Sinclair (Sales & Mktg Mg)
Ultimate Holding Company: HLW 106 LIMITED
Immediate Holding Company: A.L.SIMPKIN & CO.LIMITED
Registration no: 00244390 **VAT No.:** GB 172 3753 61
Date established: 2029 **Turnover:** £2m - £5m **No.of Employees:** 51 - 100
Product Groups: 20, 31, 63

Date of Accounts	Dec 11	Dec 10	Dec 09
Working Capital	863	951	998
Fixed Assets	99	99	110
Current Assets	2m	2m	2m

Simpson Electrical Ltd
Rotherham Close Killamarsh, Sheffield, S21 2JU
Tel: 0114-247 1483 **Fax:** 0114- 2472377
Website: http://www.letsweldit.com
Directors: M. Simpson (MD)
Immediate Holding Company: SIMPSON ELECTRICAL LIMITED
Registration no: 07726431 **Date established:** 2011
No.of Employees: 1 - 10 **Product Groups:** 46

Date of Accounts	Dec 08	Dec 06	Dec 05
Working Capital	-33	-35	-42
Fixed Assets	N/A	36	43
Current Assets	N/A	29	39
Current Liabilities	33	65	81

Sims F E Mottram Ltd
Oakes Green, Sheffield, S9 3WS
Tel: 0114-261 1453 **Fax:** 0114-242 5344
E-mail: dnix@femottram.com
Website: http://www.femottram.co.uk
Bank(s): Lloyds TSB Bank plc
Directors: D. Nix (MD)
Managers: J. Birks (Chief Acct)
Immediate Holding Company: F.E. MOTTRAM LIMITED
Registration no: 01110500 **VAT No.:** GB 158 4422 57
Date established: 1973 **Turnover:** £5m - £10m **No.of Employees:** 21 - 50
Product Groups: 34

Date of Accounts	Dec 09	Dec 08	Dec 07
Sales Turnover	7m	55m	59m
Pre Tax Profit/Loss	-736	-655	276
Working Capital	513	2m	1m
Fixed Assets	2m	3m	4m
Current Assets	2m	10m	13m
Current Liabilities	406	5m	3m

Ski Optical Ltd
902 Ecclesall Road, Sheffield, S11 8TR
Tel: 0114-267 1123 **Fax:** 0114-266 4740
E-mail: enquiries@skioptical.co.uk
Website: http://www.skioptical.com
Directors: M. Kemp (Dir)
Immediate Holding Company: SKI OPTICAL WORKS LIMITED
Registration no: 01474417 **Date established:** 1980
No.of Employees: 1 - 10 **Product Groups:** 37, 38, 65

Date of Accounts	Sep 11	Sep 10	Sep 09
Working Capital	53	-25	-53
Fixed Assets	85	94	75

Current Assets	148	124	141
Current Liabilities	64	N/A	N/A

Herbert M Slater Ltd
332 Coleford Road, Sheffield, S9 5PH
Tel: 0114-261 2308 **Fax:** 0114-261 2305
E-mail: info@slaterknives.co.uk
Website: http://www.slaterknives.co.uk
Directors: B. Gandy (MD), L. Gandy (Co Sec)
Immediate Holding Company: HERBERT M. SLATER (1853) LIMITED
Registration no: 02568724 **VAT No.:** GB 534 1532 71
Date established: 1990 **Turnover:** £500,000 - £1m
No.of Employees: 1 - 10 **Product Groups:** 36

Date of Accounts	Dec 11	Dec 10	Dec 09
Working Capital	25	11	-4
Current Assets	122	128	119

Smithery Wrought Iron Ltd
Unit 27 Rotherwood Business Park Rotherham Close, Killamarsh, Sheffield, S21 2JU
Tel: 0114-251 3355 **Fax:** 0114-251 3355
E-mail: davesmith@smitherywroughtiron.co.uk
Website: http://www.smitherywroughtiron.co.uk
Directors: D. Smith (Prop), P. Smith (Fin)
Immediate Holding Company: SMITHERY WROUGHT IRON LIMITED
Registration no: 04806396 **Date established:** 2003
No.of Employees: 1 - 10 **Product Groups:** 26, 35

Date of Accounts	Jun 09	Jun 08	Jun 07
Working Capital	-11	-4	-11
Fixed Assets	4	5	6
Current Assets	12	20	12

Robert Sorby
Athol Road, Sheffield, S8 0PA
Tel: 0114-225 0700 **Fax:** 0114-225 0710
E-mail: sales@robert-sorby.co.uk
Website: http://www.robert-sorby.co.uk
Bank(s): HSBC
Directors: P. Proctor (Dir)
Managers: R. Walton (Mktg Serv Mgr)
Immediate Holding Company: TOOLS LTD
Registration no: 00609353 **VAT No.:** GB 172 4019 84
Date established: 1985 **Turnover:** £2m - £5m **No.of Employees:** 21 - 50
Product Groups: 36, 48

South Yorkshire Printers Ltd & Educational Planners Ltd
Harvest Lane, Sheffield, S3 8EG
Tel: 0114-272 1105 **Fax:** 0114-276 0633
E-mail: design@southyorkshireprinters.co.uk
Website: http://www.SouthYorkshirePrinters.co.uk
Directors: C. Gray (Sales)
Immediate Holding Company: SOUTH YORKSHIRE PRINTERS LIMITED
Registration no: 01622717 **Date established:** 1982
No.of Employees: 21 - 50 **Product Groups:** 28

South Yorkshire Welding Supplies
Venture One Business Park 19 Long Acre Close Holbrook Industrial Estate, Holbrook, Sheffield, S20 3FR
Tel: 0114-247 6166 **Fax:** 0114-247 7575
E-mail: alan@southyorkshirewelding.co.uk
Website: http://www.southyorkshirewelding.co.uk
Directors: I. Shepherd (MD)
Ultimate Holding Company: PCT HOLDINGS LIMITED
Registration no: 01758284 **Date established:** 1983
No.of Employees: 1 - 10 **Product Groups:** 46

Spear & Jackson plc (Neill Tools Ltd)
Atlas Way, Sheffield, S4 7QQ
Tel: 0114-281 4242 **Fax:** 0114-225 0810
E-mail: sales@spear-and-jackson.com
Website: http://www.spear-and-jackson.com
Bank(s): HSBC Bank plc
Directors: I. Archer (Sales & Mktg)
Ultimate Holding Company: UNITED PACIFIC INDUSTRIES LIMITED (BERMUDA)
Immediate Holding Company: SPEAR & JACKSON LIMITED
Registration no: 02422675 **VAT No.:** GB 172 4019 84
Date established: 1989 **Turnover:** Up to £250,000
No.of Employees: 101 - 250 **Product Groups:** 30, 35, 36, 37, 38, 41, 43, 46, 47

Date of Accounts	Sep 11	Sep 10	Sep 09
Sales Turnover	204	236	355
Pre Tax Profit/Loss	232	2m	5m
Working Capital	15m	N/A	N/A
Fixed Assets	3m	3m	3m
Current Assets	15m	15m	13m
Current Liabilities	33	62	109

Springcoil Ltd
2 Woodbourn Hill, Sheffield, S9 3NE
Tel: 0114-273 1111 **Fax:** 0114-273 0222
E-mail: enquiries@springcoil.co.uk
Website: http://www.springcoil.co.uk
Bank(s): Bank of Scotland
Directors: C. Martin (Sales), K. Grimshaw (MD)
Immediate Holding Company: SPRINGCOIL LIMITED
Registration no: 05401138 **VAT No.:** GB 379 2819 04
Date established: 2005 **Turnover:** £250,000 - £500,000
No.of Employees: 11 - 20 **Product Groups:** 35, 36, 39, 40, 66, 68

Date of Accounts	Mar 11	Mar 10	Mar 09
Working Capital	-50	-76	-143
Fixed Assets	107	136	172
Current Assets	239	196	135

Stainless Finishing Services Ltd
Unit 4 Norfolk Bridge Business Park Foley Street, Sheffield, S4 7YW
Tel: 0114-273 8216 **Fax:** 0114-273 9771
E-mail: smpgroup@btconnect.com
Website: http://www.stainlessfinishing.co.uk
Directors: N. Williams (MD), S. Williams (Fin)
Immediate Holding Company: STAINLESS FINISHING SERVICES LIMITED
Registration no: 04015848 **Date established:** 2000
No.of Employees: 1 - 10 **Product Groups:** 46, 48

Date of Accounts	Jan 11	Jan 10	Jan 09
Working Capital	2	2	2
Current Assets	4	4	4
Current Liabilities	2	1	1

Stainless Plating Ltd
24 Don Road, Sheffield, S9 2UB
Tel: 0114-242 2000 **Fax:** 0114-242 2003
E-mail: brenda@stainlessplating.co.uk
Website: http://www.stainlessplating.co.uk
Bank(s): Midland, Church St
Managers: E. Stalyarover (Fin Mgr)
Immediate Holding Company: STAINLESS PLATING LIMITED
Registration no: 00216037 **VAT No.:** GB 173 1248 78
Date established: 2026 **Turnover:** £500,000 - £1m
No.of Employees: 11 - 20 **Product Groups:** 48

Date of Accounts	Dec 11	Dec 10	Dec 09
Working Capital	238	178	266
Fixed Assets	226	222	256
Current Assets	441	316	341
Current Liabilities	N/A	41	N/A

Staniforth Motor Cycles Wholesale Ltd
182 Church Street Ecclesfield, Sheffield, S35 9WG
Tel: 0114-246 2027 **Fax:** 0114-245 4232
E-mail: peterstaniforth@staniforths.co.uk
Website: http://www.staniforth.co.uk
Bank(s): Nat West
Directors: P. Staniforth (MD), H. Staniforth (Fin)
Immediate Holding Company: STANIFORTHS MOTOR CYCLES (WHOLESALE) LIMITED
Registration no: 01144891 **VAT No.:** GB 173 6366 47
Date established: 1973 **No.of Employees:** 11 - 20 **Product Groups:** 68

Date of Accounts	Dec 11	Dec 10	Dec 09
Working Capital	664	648	666
Fixed Assets	41	58	69
Current Assets	720	719	811

H C Starck (UK Liaison Office)
UK Liaison Office Aizlewoods Mill Nursery Street, Sheffield, S3 8GG
Tel: 0114-282 3156 **Fax:** 0114-282 3244
E-mail: malcolm.greaves.mg@bayer.co.uk
Website: http://www.hcstarck.com
Managers: M. Greaves (Chief Mgr)
Ultimate Holding Company: SHEFFIELD CO-OPERATIVE DEVELOPMENT GROUP
Immediate Holding Company: JUNGLESALE LTD.
Registration no: 03022323 **VAT No.:** GB 646 3138 38
Date established: 2000 **Turnover:** £500,000 - £1m
No.of Employees: 1 - 10 **Product Groups:** 12, 17, 31, 33, 34, 36, 40, 42

Date of Accounts	Sep 11	Sep 10	Sep 09
Working Capital	1	12	4
Current Assets	15	29	15

Steel City Marketing Ltd
Allen Street, Sheffield, S3 7AW
Tel: 0114-275 4150 **Fax:** 0114-275 0010
E-mail: sales@steel-city.co.uk
Website: http://www.steel-city.co.uk
Directors: J. Biggin (MD)
Immediate Holding Company: STEEL CITY MARKETING LIMITED
Registration no: 01511741 **VAT No.:** GB 308 5430 72
Date established: 1980 **No.of Employees:** 1 - 10 **Product Groups:** 20, 22, 23, 24, 28, 30, 33, 35, 36, 37, 38, 41, 44, 49, 63, 65, 80, 81

Date of Accounts	Mar 12	Mar 11	Mar 10
Working Capital	10	56	46
Fixed Assets	7	8	10
Current Assets	321	372	441

Style Workwear Ltd
International House Nunnery Drive, Sheffield, S2 1TA
Tel: 0114-279 8136 **Fax:** 0114-279 8138
E-mail: sales@styleww.co.uk
Website: http://www.styleww.co.uk
Directors: D. Dugdale (MD)
Managers: L. Brown (Comptroller)
Immediate Holding Company: STYLE WORKWEAR LTD.
Registration no: 02802905 **Date established:** 1993
No.of Employees: 21 - 50 **Product Groups:** 24, 63

Date of Accounts	Mar 11	Mar 10	Mar 09
Working Capital	204	349	355
Fixed Assets	27	290	304
Current Assets	287	440	429

Summit Glow Ltd
Windsor Street, Sheffield, S4 7WB
Tel: 0114-276 1563 **Fax:** 0114-279 7402
E-mail: gregatter@sumitglow.co.uk
Directors: P. Watkinson (MD)
Managers: G. Atter (Mgr)
Ultimate Holding Company: DATA SOLUTIONS (HOLDINGS) LIMITED
Immediate Holding Company: SUMMITGLOW LIMITED
Registration no: 01711912 **Date established:** 1983
No.of Employees: 11 - 20 **Product Groups:** 46, 48

Date of Accounts	Oct 11	Oct 10	Oct 09
Working Capital	247	190	193
Fixed Assets	449	463	464
Current Assets	397	298	304

Summitglow Ltd
45 Harleston Street, Sheffield, S4 7QB
Tel: 0114-270 1866 **Fax:** 0114-272 3247
E-mail: enquiries@summitglow.co.uk
Website: http://www.summitglow.co.uk
Bank(s): Yorkshire Bank plc
Directors: B. Watkinson (Fin), P. Watkinson (MD)
Immediate Holding Company: SUMMITGLOW LIMITED
Registration no: 01711912 **Date established:** 1983
Turnover: £500,000 - £1m **No.of Employees:** 21 - 50 **Product Groups:** 48

Date of Accounts	Oct 11	Oct 10	Oct 09
Working Capital	247	190	193
Fixed Assets	449	463	464
Current Assets	397	298	304

Symmetry Medical European Headquarters
Beulah Road, Sheffield, S6 2AN
Tel: 0114-285 5881 **Fax:** 0114-233 6978
E-mail: liam.fox@symmetrymedical.com
Website: http://www.symmetrymedical.com

see next page

Symmetry Medical European Headquarters - *Cont'd*

Managers: L. Fox (Purch Mgr)
Ultimate Holding Company: SYMMETRY MEDICAL INC (USA)
Immediate Holding Company: SYMMETRY MEDICAL SHEFFIELD LTD.
Registration no: 00293190 **VAT No.:** GB 471 2108 77
Date established: 1934 **Turnover:** £20m - £50m
No.of Employees: 251 - 500 **Product Groups:** 38, 39, 48

Date of Accounts	Dec 11	Dec 10	Dec 09
Sales Turnover	21m	24m	26m
Pre Tax Profit/Loss	-950	576	-737
Working Capital	-6m	-6m	-32m
Fixed Assets	20m	21m	23m
Current Assets	9m	9m	9m
Current Liabilities	555	1m	2m

T & A Precision Grinding Ltd

101 Carlisle Street East, Sheffield, S4 7QN
Tel: 0114-273 1582 **Fax:** 0114-273 9658
Website: http://www.silver-steel.co.uk
Directors: A. Oates (MD), C. Oates (Co Sec)
Immediate Holding Company: T & A PRECISION GRINDING CO. LIMITED
Registration no: 01918382 **Date established:** 1985
No.of Employees: 1 - 10 **Product Groups:** 46

Date of Accounts	Apr 12	Apr 11	Apr 10
Working Capital	469	305	363
Fixed Assets	100	67	67
Current Assets	777	682	511

T D R Transmissions

5 Hunsley Street, Sheffield, S4 8DY
Tel: 0114-262 6050 **Fax:** 0114-243 1826
E-mail: sales@tdrtrans.co.uk
Website: http://www.tdrtransmission.co.uk
Bank(s): National Westminster
Directors: K. Walkland (MD)
Managers: J. Siddall (Mktg Serv Mgr)
Ultimate Holding Company: TDR HOLDINGS LIMITED
Immediate Holding Company: TDR HOLDINGS LIMITED
Registration no: 03799057 **VAT No.:** GB 308 7344 55
Date established: 1999 **No.of Employees:** 21 - 50 **Product Groups:** 48

Date of Accounts	Aug 08	Nov 11	Nov 10
Working Capital	-181	-255	-159
Fixed Assets	1m	1m	1m
Current Assets	12	3	5

T E K Personnel Consultants

Unit 8 Sheffield Airport Business Park Europa Link, Sheffield, S9 1XU
Tel: 0114-252 5730 **Fax:** 0114-252 5731
E-mail: admin@tekpersonnel.co.uk
Website: http://www.tekpersonnel.co.uk
Managers: G. Chandler (Ops Mgr)
Immediate Holding Company: SHEFFIELD CARERS CENTRE
Registration no: 01825462 **Date established:** 1994 **Turnover:** £5m - £10m
No.of Employees: 1 - 10 **Product Groups:** 80

Date of Accounts	Mar 10	Mar 09	Mar 08
Working Capital	279	526	604
Fixed Assets	25	46	51
Current Assets	823	1m	2m

Henry Taylor Tools Ltd

Unit 5-8 Peacock Trading Estate Livesey Street, Sheffield, S6 2BL
Tel: 0114-234 0282 **Fax:** 0114-285 2015
E-mail: sales@henrytaylortools.co.uk
Website: http://www.henrytaylortools.co.uk
Bank(s): HSBC Bank plc
Directors: B. Surplice (MD)
Immediate Holding Company: HENRY TAYLOR (TOOLS) LIMITED
Registration no: 01094293 **VAT No.:** GB 727 8552 03
Date established: 1973 **Turnover:** £500,000 - £1m
No.of Employees: 11 - 20 **Product Groups:** 66

Date of Accounts	Dec 11	Dec 10	Dec 09
Working Capital	327	316	286
Fixed Assets	77	69	92
Current Assets	514	559	518

Techscribe

52 Stanwood Crescent, Sheffield, S6 5JB
Tel: 0114-232 6776
E-mail: mike@techscribe.co.uk
Website: http://www.techscribe.co.uk
Directors: M. Unwalla (Prop), H. Glearing (Fin)
Immediate Holding Company: TECHSCRIBE LIMITED
Registration no: 03865454 **Date established:** 1999
Turnover: Up to £250,000 **No.of Employees:** 1 - 10 **Product Groups:** 80, 81

Date of Accounts	Mar 08	Mar 07	Mar 06
Sales Turnover	52	88	64
Pre Tax Profit/Loss	27	34	30
Working Capital	1	3	1
Current Assets	8	16	14
Current Liabilities	6	12	9

The Barlow Group

1 Keetons Hill, Sheffield, S2 4NW
Tel: 0114-280 3000 **Fax:** 0114-280 3001
E-mail: info@barlowgroup.co.uk
Website: http://www.barlowgroup.co.uk
Bank(s): HSBC Bank plc
Directors: L. Walker (MD)
Ultimate Holding Company: BARLOW GROUP HOLDINGS LIMITED
Immediate Holding Company: BARLOW METAL FABRICATIONS LIMITED
Registration no: 02419183 **VAT No.:** 533 8673 24 **Date established:** 1989
Turnover: £10m - £20m **No.of Employees:** 51 - 100 **Product Groups:** 80

Date of Accounts	Dec 11	Dec 10	Dec 09
Working Capital	168	168	168
Current Assets	168	168	168

Therco Ltd

1 Long Acre Close Holbrook Industrial Estate, Holbrook, Sheffield, S20 3FR
Tel: 0114-251 0339
E-mail: rsawtell@thercoheatexchangers.com
Directors: J. Brooks (Comm), R. Sawtell (MD)
Managers: G. Hand (Purch Mgr)
Ultimate Holding Company: THERCO HOLDINGS LIMITED
Immediate Holding Company: THERCO LIMITED
Registration no: 04970481 **Date established:** 2003 **Turnover:** £5m - £10m
No.of Employees: 51 - 100 **Product Groups:** 32, 40, 84

Date of Accounts	Dec 11	Dec 10	Dec 09
Sales Turnover	8m	7m	7m
Pre Tax Profit/Loss	122	-154	67
Working Capital	233	179	198
Fixed Assets	525	645	762
Current Assets	3m	3m	3m
Current Liabilities	1m	777	1m

Thessco Ltd

Royds Mill Windsor Street, Sheffield, S4 7WB
Tel: 0114-272 0966 **Fax:** 0114-275 2655
E-mail: sales@thessco.co.uk
Website: http://www.thessco.co.uk
Bank(s): Barclays, Commercial Street
Directors: P. Tear (Grp Chief Exec), M. Rathbone (Dir), P. Wrench (Mkt Research), M. Rathbone (Fin)
Managers: B. Lees (Personnel), P. Heminsley (Purch Mgr), P. Hemmingsley (Purch Mgr), G. Brough (Sales Prom Mgr)
Ultimate Holding Company: SOLPRO MANUFACTURING LIMITED
Immediate Holding Company: THESSCO LIMITED
Registration no: 01819860 **VAT No.:** GB 391 0685 43
Date established: 1984 **Turnover:** £20m - £50m
No.of Employees: 51 - 100 **Product Groups:** 32, 33, 34, 35, 37, 48, 66

Date of Accounts	Dec 09	Dec 08	Dec 07
Sales Turnover	22m	33m	29m
Pre Tax Profit/Loss	-2m	-3m	2m
Working Capital	262	11m	14m
Fixed Assets	6m	6m	8m
Current Assets	7m	17m	24m
Current Liabilities	2m	2m	833

Thomas Flinn & Co.

114 Harvest Lane, Sheffield, S3 8EG
Tel: 0114-272 5387 **Fax:** 0114-272 5389
E-mail: info@flinn-garlick-saws.co.uk
Website: http://www.flinn-garlick-saws.co.uk
Directors: P. Ellis (Prop)
Turnover: Up to £250,000 **No.of Employees:** 1 - 10 **Product Groups:** 36, 41

Timberwise UK Ltd

Suite 103 Devonshire House 49 Eldon Street, Sheffield, S1 4NR
Tel: 0114-256 1411 **Fax:** 0114-256 1422
E-mail: sheffield@timberwise.co.uk
Website: http://www.timberwise.co.uk
Managers: N. Hartley (District Mgr)
Ultimate Holding Company: TIMBERWISE HOLDINGS LIMITED
Immediate Holding Company: TIMBERWISE (UK) LIMITED
Registration no: 03230356 **Date established:** 1996
No.of Employees: 11 - 20 **Product Groups:** 07, 32, 52

Date of Accounts	Dec 11	Dec 10	Dec 09
Sales Turnover	N/A	N/A	5m
Pre Tax Profit/Loss	N/A	N/A	214
Working Capital	397	343	326
Fixed Assets	265	291	301
Current Assets	1m	1m	1m
Current Liabilities	N/A	N/A	585

Tomah Engineers Ltd

16 Cossey Road, Sheffield, S4 7PY
Tel: 0114-272 1199 **Fax:** 0114-276 8675
E-mail: tomaheng@aol.com
Directors: D. Oxley (Prop)
Immediate Holding Company: TOMAH ENGINEERS LIMITED
Registration no: 00987409 **VAT No.:** 173 7004 76 **Date established:** 1970
No.of Employees: 1 - 10 **Product Groups:** 46, 48

Date of Accounts	Aug 11	Aug 10	Aug 09
Working Capital	317	234	202
Fixed Assets	49	58	60
Current Assets	524	393	389

Tool & Die Heat Treatment Ltd

Tinsley Park Road, Sheffield, S9 5DL
Tel: 0114-244 2024 **Fax:** 0114-242 1180
Directors: J. Thompson (Co Sec), G. Cooke (Dir)
Ultimate Holding Company: J.B. INGALL LIMITED
Immediate Holding Company: TOOL & DIE HEAT TREATMENT COMPANY LIMITED
Registration no: 00402148 **Date established:** 1945 **Turnover:** £5m - £10m
No.of Employees: 1 - 10 **Product Groups:** 48

Date of Accounts	May 11	Mar 10	Mar 09
Working Capital	3	-8	-23
Fixed Assets	73	87	100
Current Assets	203	204	167

Toolroom Engineering Ltd

141-143 Carlisle Street, Sheffield, S4 7LJ
Tel: 0114-275 8800 **Fax:** 0114-275 8855
E-mail: craig.singleton@sky.com
Directors: C. Singleton (MD)
Immediate Holding Company: TOOLROOM ENGINEERING LIMITED
Registration no: 04942357 **Date established:** 2003
No.of Employees: 1 - 10 **Product Groups:** 36, 46

Date of Accounts	Oct 11	Oct 10	Oct 09
Working Capital	-17	-39	-39
Fixed Assets	114	79	91
Current Assets	74	43	29

Torque Solutions Ltd

Unit 5 Abbey Way North Anston, Sheffield, S25 4JL
Tel: 01909-550767 **Fax:** 01909-550825
E-mail: sales@torque-solutions.co.uk
Website: http://www.torque-solutions.co.uk
Directors: P. Allsopp (Dir)
Immediate Holding Company: TORQUE SOLUTIONS LIMITED
Registration no: 04593835 **Date established:** 2002
No.of Employees: 1 - 10 **Product Groups:** 35, 36, 37, 38, 39, 40, 45, 46, 47, 48, 66, 67, 83, 84, 85

Date of Accounts	Nov 11	Nov 10	Nov 09
Working Capital	-96	-85	-38
Fixed Assets	123	114	69
Current Assets	183	163	125

Torres Engineering & Pumps Ltd

448 Brightside Lane, Sheffield, S9 2SP
Tel: 0114-249 3377 **Fax:** 0114-242 5885
E-mail: ken_torres@torrespumps.co.uk
Website: http://www.torrespumps.co.uk
Bank(s): Lloyds
Directors: D. Torres (Asst MD), Torres (MD), K. Torres (MD)
Managers: D. Torres (Sales & Mktg Mg)
Immediate Holding Company: TORRES ENGINEERING AND PUMPS LIMITED
Registration no: 01547962 **VAT No.:** GB 308 5788 29
Date established: 1981 **Turnover:** £2m - £5m **No.of Employees:** 11 - 20
Product Groups: 39, 40

Total Warehouse Solutions Co M Ltd

21 Leebrook Place Owlthorpe, Sheffield, S20 6QL
Tel: 0800-032 4770 **Fax:** 0870-850 1614
E-mail: sales@totalwarehousesolutions.com
Website: http://www.totalwarehousesolutions.com
Directors: I. Humphries (Ptnr)
Managers: I. Humphries (Comm)
Immediate Holding Company: TOTAL WAREHOUSE SOLUTIONS.COM LIMITED
Registration no: 05421416 **Date established:** 2005
Turnover: £250,000 - £500,000 **No.of Employees:** 1 - 10
Product Groups: 26

Date of Accounts	Jul 08	Apr 07	Apr 06
Working Capital	-16	9	10
Fixed Assets	12	13	16
Current Assets	334	264	92

Tractel UK Ltd

Holbrook Industrial Estate Old Lane, Halfway, Sheffield, S20 3GA
Tel: 0114-248 2266 **Fax:** 0114-247 3350
E-mail: martyn.reed@tractel.co.uk
Website: http://www.tractel.com
Bank(s): Barclays, Sheffield Moor
Managers: L. Peake (Works Gen Mgr), I. Hitchings, M. Reed (Eng Serv Mgr), L. Peake (Works Gen Mgr), S. Woodhead (Sales Prom Mgr)
Ultimate Holding Company: TRACTEL INTERNATIONAL SAS (FRANCE)
Immediate Holding Company: TRACTEL (UK) LIMITED
Registration no: 00533669 **Date established:** 1954 **Turnover:** £5m - £10m
No.of Employees: 21 - 50 **Product Groups:** 35, 36, 39, 42, 45, 67, 84

Date of Accounts	Dec 11	Dec 10	Dec 09
Sales Turnover	5m	5m	7m
Pre Tax Profit/Loss	491	252	220
Working Capital	1m	698	1m
Fixed Assets	77	126	151
Current Assets	2m	2m	2m
Current Liabilities	384	243	369

The Training Foundry

City Campus Pond Street, Sheffield, S1 1WB
Tel: 0114-225 5888 **Fax:** 0114-225 5889
E-mail: itfoundry@shu.ac.uk
Website: http://www.thetrainingfoundry.co.uk
Managers: D. Rotherham
Ultimate Holding Company: SHEFFIELD HALLAM UNIVERSITY
Immediate Holding Company: COLLEGIATE PROPERTIES (2) LIMITED
Registration no: 04994922 **Date established:** 1993
Turnover: £250,000 - £500,000 **No.of Employees:** 1 - 10
Product Groups: 86

Date of Accounts	Jul 11	Jul 10	Jul 09
Sales Turnover	6m	5m	4m
Working Capital	-16	-22	-28
Fixed Assets	17	24	30
Current Assets	994	1m	932
Current Liabilities	744	624	480

Transition International Ltd

480 Penistone Road, Sheffield, S6 2FU
Tel: 0114-285 5222 **Fax:** 0114-233 3071
E-mail: david@transition-international.com
Bank(s): National Westminster
Directors: D. Ingel (MD)
Immediate Holding Company: TRANSITION INTERNATIONAL LIMITED
Registration no: 04787596 **VAT No.:** GB 646 4591 13
Date established: 2003 **Turnover:** £2m - £5m **No.of Employees:** 21 - 50
Product Groups: 34, 49, 66

Date of Accounts	Dec 10	Dec 09	Dec 08
Sales Turnover	N/A	5m	N/A
Pre Tax Profit/Loss	N/A	224	-563
Working Capital	2m	2m	925
Fixed Assets	45	24	251
Current Assets	3m	3m	3m
Current Liabilities	N/A	244	837

Travis Perkins plc

Greenland Work Coleford Road, Sheffield, S9 5NN
Tel: 0114-244 1081 **Fax:** 0114-243 5276
E-mail: sheffield@travisperkins.co.uk
Website: http://www.travisperkins.co.uk
Managers: P. Ridley (District Mgr)
Immediate Holding Company: TRAVIS PERKINS PLC
Registration no: 00824821 **Date established:** 1964
Turnover: £75m - £125m **No.of Employees:** 11 - 20 **Product Groups:** 66

Date of Accounts	Dec 11	Dec 10	Dec 09
Sales Turnover	4779m	3153m	2931m
Pre Tax Profit/Loss	270m	197m	213m
Working Capital	133m	159m	248m
Fixed Assets	2771m	2749m	2108m
Current Assets	1421m	1329m	1035m
Current Liabilities	473m	412m	109m

Traxys UK Ltd

Suite 8 - 99 Parkway Avenue, Sheffield, S9 4WG
Tel: 0114-244 7991 **Fax:** 0114-242 1548
E-mail: paul.clayton@traxys.com
Website: http://www.traxys.com
Directors: P. Clayton (Dir)
Immediate Holding Company: TRAXYS (UK) LIMITED
Registration no: 02212312 **Date established:** 1988
Turnover: £10m - £20m **No.of Employees:** 1 - 10 **Product Groups:** 66

Date of Accounts	Nov 11	Nov 10	Nov 09
Sales Turnover	12m	8m	4m
Pre Tax Profit/Loss	-226	-4	164
Working Capital	1m	1m	4m
Fixed Assets	3	4	3
Current Assets	4m	3m	5m
Current Liabilities	276	246	117

Trianco Heating Products Ltd

Thorncliffe Chapeltown, Sheffield, S35 2PH
Tel: 0114-257 2349 **Fax:** 0114-257 1419
E-mail: info@trianco.co.uk
Website: http://www.trianco.co.uk
Directors: P. Ferguson (MD)
Managers: J. Bennett (Purch Mgr), M. Armstrong (I.T. Exec), L. Simons (Mktg Serv Mgr)

Ultimate Holding Company: Bullough P.L.C.
Immediate Holding Company: TRIANCO HEATING PRODUCTS LIMITED
Registration no: 05757277 **VAT No.:** GB 211 4455 07
Date established: 2006 **Turnover:** £10m - £20m **No.of Employees:** 1 - 10
Product Groups: 40

Date of Accounts	Mar 08	Mar 07
Working Capital	313	565
Fixed Assets	42	N/A
Current Assets	2m	2m
Current Liabilities	2m	1m

Tron
80-82 Holywell Road, Sheffield, S4 8AS
Tel: 0114-242 5244 **Fax:** 0114-244 4991
Managers: D. Smith (Mgr)
Registration no: SC214968 **Date established:** 2001
Turnover: Up to £250,000 **No.of Employees:** 1 - 10 **Product Groups:** 84

Date of Accounts	Dec 95	Dec 94
Sales Turnover	43	47
Pre Tax Profit/Loss	-16	-17
Working Capital	-45	-41
Fixed Assets	30	24
Current Assets	15	23
Current Liabilities	60	64

Tuffnelln Parcels Express
Shepcote House Shepcote Lane, Sheffield, S9 1UW
Tel: 0114-256 1111 **Fax:** 0114-256 0459
E-mail: info@tuffnells.co.uk
Website: http://www.expressvalves.co.uk
Bank(s): Bank of Scotland, Leeds
Directors: I. Brewer (Fin), L. Dunn (Sales)
Ultimate Holding Company: THE BIG GREEN PARCEL HOLDING COMPANY LIMITED
Immediate Holding Company: THE BIG GREEN PARCEL MACHINE LIMITED
Registration no: 03125293 **VAT No.:** GB 173 3178 63
Date established: 1995 **Turnover:** £75m - £125m
No.of Employees: 21 - 50 **Product Groups:** 72

Date of Accounts	Dec 11	Dec 10	Dec 09
Pre Tax Profit/Loss	7m	7m	6m
Working Capital	7m	25m	18m
Fixed Assets	28m	28m	28m
Current Assets	7m	25m	18m

Turret Brazing Products Ltd
Unit 3 Meadowbrook Park Halfway, Sheffield, S20 3PJ
Tel: 0114-228 0324 **Fax:** 0114-251 3077
Website: http://www.turret-brazing.com
Directors: D. Haynes (Fin)
Immediate Holding Company: TURRET BRAZING PRODUCTS LIMITED
Registration no: 02582754 **Date established:** 1991
No.of Employees: 1 - 10 **Product Groups:** 46

Date of Accounts	Mar 08	Mar 07	Mar 06
Working Capital	-17	-9	-34
Fixed Assets	56	37	23
Current Assets	760	617	491

Unigraph UK Ltd
287 Pitsmoor Road, Sheffield, S3 9AS
Tel: 0114-275 2801 **Fax:** 0114-275 9769
E-mail: sales@unigraph.co.uk
Website: http://www.unigraph.co.uk
Bank(s): Barclays
Directors: S. Hunter (MD)
Immediate Holding Company: UNIGRAPH (UK) LIMITED
Registration no: 01484878 **VAT No.:** GB 172 8769 21
Date established: 1980 **Turnover:** £2m - £5m **No.of Employees:** 11 - 20
Product Groups: 27, 28, 44, 64, 67

Date of Accounts	Jul 11	Jul 10	Jul 09
Working Capital	320	409	424
Fixed Assets	264	243	228
Current Assets	589	708	701

United Crane Services Ltd
Niagara Forge Claywheels Lane, Sheffield, S6 1LZ
Tel: 0114-285 2801 **Fax:** 0114-232 5626
E-mail: unitedcranes@aol.com
Website: http://www.unitedcranes.co.uk
Directors: S. Lister (Fin)
Immediate Holding Company: UNITED CRANE SERVICES LIMITED
Registration no: 02056025 **VAT No.:** GB 391 0196 58
Date established: 1986 **Turnover:** £1m - £2m **No.of Employees:** 1 - 10
Product Groups: 45

Date of Accounts	Apr 12	Apr 11	Apr 10
Working Capital	-15	-50	8
Fixed Assets	56	56	51
Current Assets	309	249	246

V H S Hydraulic Components Ltd
Unit 2 Carley Drive Westfield, Sheffield, S20 8NQ
Tel: 0114-276 4430 **Fax:** 0114-247 2526
E-mail: info@hydraulic-components.net
Website: http://www.hydraulic-components.net
Directors: D. Whitehead (MD)
Immediate Holding Company: VHS HYDRAULIC COMPONENTS LIMITED
Registration no: 04510681 **Date established:** 2002
No.of Employees: 11 - 20 **Product Groups:** 30, 31, 32, 33, 34, 35, 36, 37, 38, 39, 40, 41, 42, 43, 44, 45, 46, 47, 48, 51, 61, 67, 68, 83, 84, 85, 86

Date of Accounts	Dec 11	Dec 10	Dec 09
Working Capital	169	109	54
Fixed Assets	432	436	445
Current Assets	990	878	712

Valbruna UK Ltd
Unit 4 Brookdale Road Thorncliffe Distribution Centre, Chapeltown, Sheffield, S35 2PW
Tel: 0114-257 7676 **Fax:** 0114-257 7589
E-mail: sales@valbruna.co.uk
Website: http://www.valbruna.co.uk
Bank(s): Barclays
Directors: M. Ormiston (Asst MD)
Ultimate Holding Company: AMENDUNI ACCIAIO SPA (ITALY)
Immediate Holding Company: VALBRUNA UK LIMITED
Registration no: 02015096 **Date established:** 1986 **Turnover:** £2m - £5m
No.of Employees: 11 - 20 **Product Groups:** 66

Date of Accounts	Dec 11	Dec 10	Dec 09
Sales Turnover	31m	24m	20m
Pre Tax Profit/Loss	1m	632	35
Working Capital	10m	7m	4m
Fixed Assets	4m	4m	4m
Current Assets	24m	20m	18m
Current Liabilities	1m	904	311

Van Leeuwen Wheeler Ltd
Unit 1a Rotunda Business Centre Thorncliffe Road, Chapeltown, Sheffield, S35 2PG
Tel: 0114-257 3800 **Fax:** 0114-257 0639
E-mail: iwaller@vlwheeler.co.uk
Website: http://www.vanleeuwenwheeler.co.uk
Managers: I. Waller (District Mgr)
Ultimate Holding Company: VAN LEEUWEN PIPE & TUBE GROUP BV (NETHER
Immediate Holding Company: VAN LEEUWEN LIMITED
Registration no: 01991207 **VAT No.:** GB 439 5911 21
Date established: 1986 **No.of Employees:** 1 - 10 **Product Groups:** 36

Date of Accounts	Dec 11	Dec 10	Dec 09
Sales Turnover	41m	32m	28m
Pre Tax Profit/Loss	1m	1m	-130
Working Capital	10m	9m	7m
Fixed Assets	1m	1m	1m
Current Assets	19m	16m	13m
Current Liabilities	2m	1m	324

Vanasyl 2000
32 Cavendish Road, Sheffield, S11 9BH
Tel: 0114-258 7229 **Fax:** 0114-250 0239
E-mail: db4ram@vanasyl.com
Website: http://www.vanasyl.com
Managers: D. Baram (Mgr)
Turnover: Up to £250,000 **No.of Employees:** 1 - 10 **Product Groups:** 36, 42

Viking Pump Ltd
Viking House Dannemore Drive, Sheffield, S9 5DF
Tel: 0114-244 7701 **Fax:** 0114-243 2614
E-mail: sales@viking-pumps.co.uk
Managers: P. Cumberland (Ops Mgr)
Ultimate Holding Company: CEMA LIMITED
Immediate Holding Company: VIKING PUMPS LIMITED
Registration no: 01689336 **Date established:** 1982 **Turnover:** £1m - £2m
No.of Employees: 21 - 50 **Product Groups:** 40, 83

Date of Accounts	Dec 11	Dec 10	Dec 09
Working Capital	1m	1m	1m
Fixed Assets	205	78	95
Current Assets	2m	2m	2m

Viscount Catering Ltd Enodis UK Food Service
Provincial Park Nether Lane, Ecclesfield, Sheffield, S35 9ZX
Tel: 0114-257 0100 **Fax:** 0114-257 0251
E-mail: ccommile@viscount-catering.co.uk
Website: http://www.viscount-catering.com
Directors: C. Cammoile (Dir), J. Rolt (Fin), K. Blades (Fin), S. Loughton (MD)
Managers: D. Johnson (Mktg Serv Mgr), H. Hutson (Cust Serv Mgr)
Ultimate Holding Company: THE MANITOWOC CO INC(USA)
Immediate Holding Company: MANITOWOC FOODSERVICE UK LIMITED
Registration no: 02656967 **Date established:** 1991 **Turnover:** £5m - £10m
No.of Employees: 101 - 250 **Product Groups:** 67

Date of Accounts	Dec 10	Dec 09	Dec 08
Sales Turnover	15m	17m	20m
Pre Tax Profit/Loss	-2m	-1m	-3m
Working Capital	-5m	-3m	-2m
Fixed Assets	N/A	346	463
Current Assets	N/A	10m	10m
Current Liabilities	N/A	2m	2m

W N T UK Ltd
Sheffield Airport Business Park Europa Link, Sheffield, S9 1XU
Tel: 0114-249 6249 **Fax:** 0114-249 6250
E-mail: tony.pennington@wntuk.com
Website: http://www.wntuk.com
Directors: T. Wolter (MD), T. Pennington (MD)
Managers: C. Carey (I.T. Exec), G. Stanton (Sales Prom Mgr)
Immediate Holding Company: WNT (UK) LIMITED
Registration no: 03772242 **Date established:** 1999
Turnover: £10m - £20m **No.of Employees:** 21 - 50 **Product Groups:** 46

Date of Accounts	Feb 10	Feb 09	Feb 08
Sales Turnover	11m	13m	13m
Pre Tax Profit/Loss	-840	-149	1m
Working Capital	232	935	1m
Fixed Assets	194	262	231
Current Assets	4m	4m	4m
Current Liabilities	689	580	1m

Ward Hi-Tech Ltd
1 Atlas Way, Sheffield, S4 7QQ
Tel: 0114-256 0333 **Fax:** 0114-256 1629
E-mail: sales@wardhitech.co.uk
Website: http://www.wardhitech.co.uk
Directors: P. Scott (Co Sec)
Immediate Holding Company: WARD HI-TECH LIMITED
Registration no: 01778217 **VAT No.:** GB 390 9737 11
Date established: 1983 **Turnover:** £2m - £5m **No.of Employees:** 21 - 50
Product Groups: 67

Date of Accounts	Mar 11	Mar 10	Mar 09
Sales Turnover	N/A	5m	N/A
Pre Tax Profit/Loss	N/A	178	343
Working Capital	2m	3m	3m
Fixed Assets	25	14	28
Current Assets	5m	5m	5m
Current Liabilities	N/A	590	376

Peter Ward Engineering
Sheaf Bank, Sheffield, S2 3DA
Tel: 0114-255 0633 **Fax:** 0114-255 5371
E-mail: peter@pwards.co.uk
Website: http://www.peterwardengineering.net
Directors: P. Ward (Prop)
Registration no: 04771482 **VAT No.:** GB 173 3042 88
Date established: 2003 **Turnover:** £1m - £2m **No.of Employees:** 1 - 10
Product Groups: 48

T W Ward CNC Machinery Ltd
Savile Street, Sheffield, S4 7UD
Tel: 0114-276 5411 **Fax:** 0114-270 0786
E-mail: sales@wardcnc.com
Website: http://www.wardcnc.com
Directors: A. Elliott (Sales)
Immediate Holding Company: T.W. WARD C.N.C. MACHINERY LIMITED
Registration no: 01762383 **Date established:** 1983 **Turnover:** £5m - £10m
No.of Employees: 21 - 50 **Product Groups:** 38, 46, 48

Date of Accounts	Mar 11	Mar 10	Mar 09
Sales Turnover	9m	10m	N/A
Pre Tax Profit/Loss	236	276	225
Working Capital	2m	2m	2m
Fixed Assets	2m	2m	2m
Current Assets	8m	6m	8m
Current Liabilities	3m	2m	3m

T W Ward Industrial Boilers Ltd
Albion Works Saile Street, Sheffield, S4 7UL
Tel: 0114-275 6755 **Fax:** 0114-273 7091
E-mail: m.webster@twward.co.uk
Website: http://www.twward.co.uk
Directors: M. Webster (Dir)
Immediate Holding Company: T W WARD INDUSTRIAL BOILERS LIMITED
Registration no: 03077243 **VAT No.:** GB 650 7723 36
Date established: 1995 **Turnover:** £1m - £2m **No.of Employees:** 1 - 10
Product Groups: 38, 40, 48

Date of Accounts	Apr 12	Apr 11	Apr 10
Working Capital	88	-2	36
Fixed Assets	48	29	47
Current Assets	292	224	215

Wavin UK
Hazlehead Docksbridge, Sheffield, S30 5HG
Tel: 01226-768262 **Fax:** 01226-764827
E-mail: tim.thompson@wavin.co.uk
Website: http://www.wavinuk.co.uk
Bank(s): Ulster Bank
Directors: P. Taylor (Fin)
Managers: R. Stokes (Purch Mgr), D. Atkinson (Personnel), T. Thompson (Site Co-ord), P. Wydell (Mktg Serv Mgr), I. Jessop
Ultimate Holding Company: WAVIN NV (NETHERLANDS)
Immediate Holding Company: HEPWORTH BUILDING PRODUCTS (HOLDINGS) LIMITED
Registration no: 00180603 **VAT No.:** GB 255 0445 75
Date established: 2022 **Turnover:** £2m - £5m
No.of Employees: 101 - 250 **Product Groups:** 66

Date of Accounts	Dec 10	Dec 09	Dec 08
Working Capital	12m	12m	12m
Fixed Assets	54m	54m	54m
Current Assets	12m	12m	12m

Wear Resistance Ltd
Beeley Wood Works Claywheels Lane, Sheffield, S6 1ND
Tel: 0114-285 2090 **Fax:** 0114-231 2176
E-mail: info@wearresistance.com
Website: http://www.wearresistance.com
Directors: C. Jowle (MD)
Immediate Holding Company: WEAR RESISTANCE LIMITED
Registration no: 00968264 **VAT No.:** GB 173 0429 79
Date established: 1969 **No.of Employees:** 11 - 20 **Product Groups:** 34, 35, 45, 48

Date of Accounts	Dec 11	Dec 10	Dec 09
Working Capital	552	516	551
Fixed Assets	30	30	23
Current Assets	770	749	754

Webster Technologies
8 Bishopdale Rise Mosborough, Sheffield, S20 5PE
Tel: 0114-247 2580
Directors: I. Webster (Grp Chief Exec)
Immediate Holding Company: WEBSTER TECHNOLOGIES LIMITED
Registration no: 03931532 **Date established:** 2000
No.of Employees: 1 - 10 **Product Groups:** 45

Date of Accounts	Mar 11	Mar 10	Mar 09
Working Capital	174	124	67
Fixed Assets	11	12	11
Current Assets	606	353	276

Weighwell Engineering Ltd
23 Orgreave Place, Sheffield, S13 9LU
Tel: 0114-269 9955 **Fax:** 0114-269 9256
E-mail: sales@weighwell.co.uk
Website: http://www.weighwell.co.uk
Directors: P. Horsfall (MD)
Immediate Holding Company: WEIGH WELL ENGINEERING LIMITED
Registration no: 02261763 **Date established:** 1988
Turnover: £500,000 - £1m **No.of Employees:** 1 - 10 **Product Groups:** 38

Date of Accounts	Jun 12	Jun 11	Jun 10
Working Capital	898	745	731
Fixed Assets	458	473	471
Current Assets	996	863	1m

Welding Equipment Service & Sales
Percy Street, Sheffield, S3 8BT
Tel: 0114-270 1217 **Fax:** 0114-270 1217
Directors: T. Doncaster (Snr Part)
Date established: 2003 **No.of Employees:** 1 - 10 **Product Groups:** 46

Weldtool Ltd
2 Bessemer Place, Sheffield, S9 3XR
Tel: 0114-261 0079 **Fax:** 0114-243 8416
Directors: A. Gavins (Dir)
Immediate Holding Company: WELDTOOL LIMITED
Registration no: 07935956 **Date established:** 2012
No.of Employees: 1 - 10 **Product Groups:** 46

Date of Accounts	May 09	May 08	May 07
Working Capital	790	712	598
Fixed Assets	19	25	34
Current Assets	1m	989	881

Thomas C Wild
Vulcan Works Tinsley Park Road, Sheffield, S9 5DP
Tel: 0114-244 2471 **Fax:** 0114-244 2052
E-mail: jhancock@tc-wild.co.uk
Website: http://www.tc-wild.co.uk
Bank(s): Lloyds TSB
Directors: G. Lewis (Fin), J. Hancocks (MD), M. Justice (Chief Op Offcr), M. Howson (Develop)

see next page

Thomas C Wild - Cont'd

Managers: G. Lewis (Chief Acct), S. Walkinshaw (Works Eng)
Immediate Holding Company: THOS. C. WILD LIMITED
Registration no: 05516830 **VAT No.:** GB 172 3439 67
Date established: 2005 **Turnover:** £5m - £10m **No.of Employees:** 21 - 50
Product Groups: 48

Date of Accounts	Aug 11	Aug 10	Aug 09
Sales Turnover	9m	7m	10m
Pre Tax Profit/Loss	634	348	1m
Working Capital	-85	-23	298
Fixed Assets	9m	4m	3m
Current Assets	4m	3m	3m
Current Liabilities	1m	500	1m

William Whiteley & Sons Sheffield Ltd

Unit 1 Lakeside Rother Valley Wa Holbrook Industrial Estate, Holbrook, Sheffield, S20 3RW
Tel: 0114-251 4999 **Fax:** 0114-251 2919
E-mail: sales@whiteley.co.uk
Website: http://www.whiteley.co.uk
Directors: S. Ward (Dir)
Managers: S. Thompson
Immediate Holding Company: WILLIAM WHITELEY & SONS (SHEFFIELD) LIMITED
Registration no: 03312910 **Date established:** 1997
No.of Employees: 11 - 20 **Product Groups:** 36, 40

Date of Accounts	Jun 11	Jun 10	Jun 09
Working Capital	132	122	121
Fixed Assets	69	72	64
Current Assets	328	348	330

Williams Fasteners

Unit 4a Shepcote Way, Tinsley Industrial Estate, Sheffield, S9 1TH
Tel: 0114-256 5200 **Fax:** 0114-256 5210
E-mail: sales@williamsfasteners.com
Website: http://www.williamsfasteners.com
Bank(s): Midland
Directors: S. Battersby (MD), B. Ward (Sales), P. Ward (Purch)
Managers: R. Todd (Personnel)
Ultimate Holding Company: WILLIAMS (FASTENERS) LIMITED
Immediate Holding Company: WILLIAMS BROTHERS (SHEFFIELD) LIMITED
Registration no: 02238887 **Date established:** 1988 **Turnover:** £5m - £10m
No.of Employees: 51 - 100 **Product Groups:** 35, 49

Date of Accounts	Mar 11	Mar 10	Mar 09
Sales Turnover	7m	6m	8m
Pre Tax Profit/Loss	-23	-281	-82
Working Capital	1m	1m	1m
Fixed Assets	172	232	299
Current Assets	3m	3m	3m
Current Liabilities	1m	1m	1m

Wilson Company Sharrow Ltd

PO Box 32, Sheffield, S11 8PL
Tel: 0114-266 2677 **Fax:** 0114-267 0504
E-mail: info@sharrowmills.com
Website: http://www.sharrowmills.com
Bank(s): National Westminster Bank Plc
Directors: D. Young (MD)
Immediate Holding Company: WILSONS & CO. (SHARROW) LIMITED
Registration no: 02805993 **VAT No.:** GB 600 1985 71
Date established: 1993 **Turnover:** £2m - £5m **No.of Employees:** 11 - 20
Product Groups: 20, 49

Date of Accounts	Mar 12	Mar 11	Mar 10
Working Capital	1m	997	925
Fixed Assets	74	84	87
Current Assets	1m	1m	1m

Wincro Metal Industries Ltd

3 Fife Street, Sheffield, S9 1NJ
Tel: 0114-242 2171 **Fax:** 0114-243 4306
E-mail: accounts@wincro.com
Website: http://www.wincro.com
Bank(s): Royal Bank of Scotland
Directors: M. Swann (Fin), P. Butler (Dir)
Immediate Holding Company: WINCRO METAL INDUSTRIES LIMITED
Registration no: 02484337 **VAT No.:** GB 308 9603 47
Date established: 1990 **Turnover:** £2m - £5m **No.of Employees:** 21 - 50
Product Groups: 34, 35

Date of Accounts	Mar 11	Mar 10	Mar 09
Working Capital	4m	3m	2m
Fixed Assets	496	518	559
Current Assets	4m	4m	3m

Winterthur Technology UK Ltd

Unit 2 Oakham Drive, Sheffield, S3 9QX
Tel: 0114-275 4211 **Fax:** 0114-275 4132
E-mail: ralf.egger@wgmbh.wendtgroup.com
Website: http://www.wendtgroup.com
Bank(s): Barclays, Maidstone
Directors: P. Cox (Dir & Co Sec), N. Lamers (Dir), C. Harford (MD)
Managers: M. Smith
Ultimate Holding Company: 3M COMPANY (USA)
Immediate Holding Company: WINTERTHUR TECHNOLOGY UK LIMITED
Registration no: 03477016 **VAT No.:** GB 680 1789 15
Date established: 1997 **Turnover:** £2m - £5m **No.of Employees:** 11 - 20
Product Groups: 33, 36, 45, 46, 47, 48

Date of Accounts	Dec 11	Dec 10	Dec 09
Working Capital	660	168	-95
Fixed Assets	14	230	232
Current Assets	2m	1m	1m

Wolf Safety Lamp Company Ltd

Saxon Road, Sheffield, S8 0YA
Tel: 0114-255 1051 **Fax:** 0114-255 7988
E-mail: info@wolf-safety.co.uk
Website: http://www.wolf-safety.co.uk
Bank(s): National Westminster Bank Plc
Directors: M. Jackson (Mkt Research), I. Tinker (MD)
Managers: S. Pendlebury (Ops Mgr)
Immediate Holding Company: WOLF SAFETY LAMP COMPANY LIMITED(THE)
Registration no: 00145428 **VAT No.:** GB 172 7221 74
Date established: 2016 **Turnover:** £5m - £10m **No.of Employees:** 21 - 50
Product Groups: 37, 40

Date of Accounts	Jun 12	Jun 11	Jun 10
Sales Turnover	9m	8m	7m
Pre Tax Profit/Loss	1m	1m	1m
Working Capital	4m	3m	4m
Fixed Assets	3m	3m	2m
Current Assets	6m	5m	5m
Current Liabilities	1m	1m	837

Wolstenholme Machine Knifes Ltd

1 Downgate Drive, Sheffield, S4 8BT
Tel: 0114-244 5600 **Fax:** 0114-244 6556
E-mail: sales@wolstenholme.co.uk
Website: http://www.wolstenholme.co.uk
Bank(s): Royal Bank of Scotland
Directors: A. Hodgkinson (Fin), A. Hodkinson (Fin), N. Wilkinson (Mkt Research), N. Harrison (MD), R. Wolstenholme (Prop), H. Firth (Co Sec)
Ultimate Holding Company: TGW (HOLDINGS) LIMITED
Immediate Holding Company: WOLSTENHOLME MACHINE KNIVES LIMITED
Registration no: 02532135 **VAT No.:** 534 1011 02 **Date established:** 1990
Turnover: £2m - £5m **No.of Employees:** 51 - 100 **Product Groups:** 44

Date of Accounts	Mar 11	Mar 10	Mar 09
Sales Turnover	7m	6m	N/A
Pre Tax Profit/Loss	1m	164	55
Working Capital	5m	4m	3m
Fixed Assets	2m	2m	2m
Current Assets	6m	6m	6m
Current Liabilities	559	327	348

A Wright & Son Ltd

158 Charles Street, Sheffield, S1 2NE
Tel: 0114-272 2677 **Fax:** 0114-278 7157
E-mail: john.maleham@mgtools.co.uk
Website: http://www.penknives-and-scissors.co.uk
Directors: J. Maleham (MD), J. Maleham (Fin)
Immediate Holding Company: A. WRIGHT & SON LIMITED
Registration no: 00429584 **Date established:** 1947
Turnover: Up to £250,000 **No.of Employees:** 1 - 10 **Product Groups:** 30, 41

Date of Accounts	Dec 11	Dec 10	Dec 07
Working Capital	35	39	43
Fixed Assets	1	1	1
Current Assets	88	72	80

Wright Bros Partnership Ltd

Waverley Road, Sheffield, S9 4PL
Tel: 0114-244 1807 **Fax:** 0114-243 9277
E-mail: steve.foster@wright-brothers.co.uk
Bank(s): National Westminster Bank Plc
Directors: S. Foster (Fin)
Immediate Holding Company: WRIGHT BROTHERS PARTNERSHIP LIMITED
Registration no: 00525329 **VAT No.:** GB 172 8855 28
Date established: 1953 **Turnover:** £250,000 - £500,000
No.of Employees: 11 - 20 **Product Groups:** 52

Date of Accounts	Mar 12	Mar 11	Mar 10
Working Capital	133	130	130
Fixed Assets	28	35	34
Current Assets	353	365	327

Yokota UK

Low Common Road Dinnington, Sheffield, S25 2RJ
Tel: 01909-552471 **Fax:** 01909-552472
E-mail: info@duro-diamonds.co.uk
Website: http://www.yokota.co.uk
Managers: S. Hunt (District Mgr)
Immediate Holding Company: BRM HI-TECH LIMITED
Registration no: 03633151 **Date established:** 1998 **Turnover:** £1m - £2m
No.of Employees: 11 - 20 **Product Groups:** 29, 30, 33, 36, 40, 45, 46, 47, 48, 66, 67, 84

Date of Accounts	Mar 12	Mar 11	Mar 10
Working Capital	N/A	-166	-181
Fixed Assets	N/A	496	509
Current Assets	N/A	442	246

Zook Europe Ltd

Navigation House Bridge Street, Killamarsh, Sheffield, S21 1AL
Tel: 01909-560999 **Fax:** 01909-560860
E-mail: zookeurope@zook.cc
Website: http://www.zook.cc
Directors: D. Harrington (Dir), R. Varos (Fin)
Immediate Holding Company: ZOOK EUROPE LIMITED
Registration no: 03629472 **Date established:** 1998
Turnover: £500,000 - £1m **No.of Employees:** 1 - 10 **Product Groups:** 33, 36

Date of Accounts	Dec 11	Dec 10	Dec 09
Working Capital	216	334	381
Fixed Assets	366	375	18
Current Assets	1m	902	959

WEST YORKSHIRE

Batley

A1 Catering Disposable Products
Providence Works Henry Street, Batley, WF17 6JJ
Tel: 01924-456786 **Fax:** 01924-456786
E-mail: admin@a1cdp.com
Website: http://www.a1cdp.com
Directors: M. Kika (Prop)
Date established: 1994 **Turnover:** £500,000 - £1m
No.of Employees: 1 - 10 **Product Groups:** 30

A S K Tools Ltd
Unit 18a Carr Mills Bradford Road, Birstall, Batley, WF17 9JX
Tel: 01924-440610 **Fax:** 01924-444445
E-mail: sales@asktools.co.uk
Website: http://www.asktools.co.uk
Directors: S. Kebble (Fin), R. Kebble (MD)
Immediate Holding Company: ASK TOOLS LIMITED
Registration no: 04433835 **Date established:** 2002
No.of Employees: 1 - 10 **Product Groups:** 37

Date of Accounts	Jul 11	Jul 10	Jul 09
Working Capital	9	9	1
Fixed Assets	3	4	5
Current Assets	38	38	37

Adwebtiser
300 Bradford Road, Batley, WF17 5PW
Tel: 01924-420712
E-mail: info@adwebtiser.com
Website: http://www.adwebtiser.com
Managers: H. Shirzad
No.of Employees: 1 - 10 **Product Groups:** 44

Allied Textile Companies Ltd
Allied House Centre 27 Business Park Bankwood Way, Birstall, Batley, WF17 9TB
Tel: 01924-443366 **Fax:** 01924-442525
Website: http://www.jbbroadley.co.uk
Directors: J. Grace (Co Sec), D. Wilkinson (Dir), G. Willshaw (Dir), J. Corrin (Grp Chief Exec), M. Derbyshire (Dir)
Immediate Holding Company: ALLIED TEXTILE COMPANIES LIMITED
Registration no: 00081338 **VAT No.:** GB 746 6221 28
Date established: 2004 **Turnover:** £50m - £75m **No.of Employees:** 1 - 10
Product Groups: 23

Date of Accounts	Dec 07	Sep 06	Sep 05
Pre Tax Profit/Loss	4m	4m	3m
Working Capital	61m	62m	59m
Fixed Assets	3m	5m	9m
Current Assets	88m	90m	91m
Current Liabilities	27m	27m	33m
Total Share Capital	18m	18m	18m

Angloco Ltd
Upper Station Road, Batley, WF17 5TA
Tel: 01924-441212 **Fax:** 01924-471918
E-mail: sales@angloco.co.uk
Website: http://www.angloco.co.uk
Bank(s): Barclays, Bradford
Directors: W. Brown (MD), J. Brown (Fin)
Immediate Holding Company: ANGLOCO LIMITED
Registration no: 01958909 **VAT No.:** GB 427 5452 46
Date established: 1985 **Turnover:** £10m - £20m
No.of Employees: 51 - 100 **Product Groups:** 40

Date of Accounts	Dec 11	Dec 10	Dec 09
Sales Turnover	16m	12m	15m
Pre Tax Profit/Loss	1m	917	832
Working Capital	3m	3m	2m
Fixed Assets	552	506	439
Current Assets	9m	9m	8m
Current Liabilities	4m	4m	3m

Ark Site Fabrications
Unit 5 Grange Road, Batley, WF17 6LH
Tel: 01924-420874 **Fax:** 01924-359744
E-mail: brian@arksite.co.uk
Directors: B. Mahoney (Prop)
Immediate Holding Company: GREENHILL TEXTILE COMPANY LIMITED
Registration no: 05131305 **Date established:** 2004
No.of Employees: 1 - 10 **Product Groups:** 35, 48

Date of Accounts	May 11	May 10	May 09
Working Capital	103	150	176
Fixed Assets	31	71	90
Current Assets	336	346	412

B & D Bolts Ltd
Central Warehouse Bradford Road, Batley, WF17 5LW
Tel: 01924-470331 **Fax:** 01924-473749
Website: http://www.bdbolts.co.uk
Directors: W. Bradley (MD), E. Bradley (Fin)
Immediate Holding Company: B AND D BOLTS LIMITED
Registration no: 01396675 **VAT No.:** GB 185 1956 32
Date established: 1978 **Turnover:** £250,000 - £500,000
No.of Employees: 1 - 10 **Product Groups:** 35, 66

Date of Accounts	Mar 11	Mar 10	Mar 09
Working Capital	25	34	43
Fixed Assets	3	5	6
Current Assets	98	77	85

Bedfords Ltd
Pheasant Drive Birstall, Batley, WF17 9LT
Tel: 01924-422456 **Fax:** 01924-422437
E-mail: info@bedfordstransport.co.uk
Website: http://www.bedfordstransport.co.uk
Directors: S. Pfadenhauer (MD), P. Smith (Fin)
Managers: B. Rowe (Tech Serv Mgr), L. Slack, N. Taylor (Sales Prom Mgr), P. Himple (Personnel)
Ultimate Holding Company: BEDFORDS HOLDINGS LIMITED
Immediate Holding Company: BEDFORDS LIMITED
Registration no: 02613524 **Date established:** 1991
Turnover: £20m - £50m **No.of Employees:** 101 - 250 **Product Groups:** 77

Date of Accounts	Sep 09	Sep 08	Sep 10
Sales Turnover	12m	14m	22m
Pre Tax Profit/Loss	-145	822	988
Working Capital	4m	5m	4m
Fixed Assets	3m	3m	3m
Current Assets	7m	8m	9m
Current Liabilities	900	805	1m

C B Collections Ltd
11 Grosvenor Road, Batley, WF17 0LX
Tel: 01924-478315 **Fax:** 01924-478315
E-mail: tiedesign@o2.co.uk
Website: http://www.cbcollections.co.uk
Directors: C. Buckle (MD), J. Buckle (Dir)
Immediate Holding Company: C.B. Collections Ltd
Registration no: 02135736 **Date established:** 1987
Turnover: £250,000 - £500,000 **No.of Employees:** 1 - 10
Product Groups: 24, 49, 81

Date of Accounts	Jun 08	Jun 07
Working Capital	117	-89
Fixed Assets	90	241
Current Assets	129	97
Current Liabilities	12	186

Cattles Ltd
Kingston House Centre 27 Business Park Woodhead Road, Birstall, Batley, WF17 9TD
Tel: 01924-444466 **Fax:** 01924-442255
E-mail: info@cattles.co.uk
Website: http://www.cattles.co.uk
Bank(s): First National Bank of Chicago, HSBC, Royal Bank o
Directors: J. Brigg (Fin), R. Todd (Co Sec)
Managers: R. Parr (Mktg Serv Mgr), S. Walker, J. Cotton (Personnel)
Immediate Holding Company: CATTLES LIMITED
Registration no: 00543610 **Date established:** 1955
Turnover: £250m - £500m **No.of Employees:** 51 - 100
Product Groups: 80, 81, 82

Date of Accounts	Dec 11	Dec 10	Dec 09
Sales Turnover	N/A	285m	512m
Pre Tax Profit/Loss	2224m	-247m	-685m
Working Capital	54m	-1824m	-1836m
Fixed Assets	N/A	507m	830m
Current Assets	55m	534m	625m
Current Liabilities	1m	1167m	1045m

Crossroads Truck & Bus Ltd
Pheasant Drive Birstall, Batley, WF17 9LR
Tel: 01924-425000 **Fax:** 01924-441111
E-mail: martin.cronin@crossroads.co.uk
Website: http://www.crossroad.co.uk
Bank(s): HSBC Bank plc
Directors: M. Cronin (Dir)
Ultimate Holding Company: MAPK HOLDINGS LIMITED (JERSEY)
Immediate Holding Company: CROSSROADS COMMERCIALS GROUP LIMITED
Registration no: 02112644 **VAT No.:** GB 183 4612 61
Date established: 1987 **Turnover:** £50m - £75m
No.of Employees: 251 - 500 **Product Groups:** 68

Date of Accounts	Dec 11	Dec 10	Dec 09
Pre Tax Profit/Loss	N/A	3m	4m
Working Capital	1	1	-496
Fixed Assets	N/A	N/A	3m
Current Assets	1	1	17m
Current Liabilities	N/A	N/A	20

Fox's Biscuits
1 Wellington Street, Batley, WF17 5JE
Tel: 01924-444333 **Fax:** 01924-470200
E-mail: info@foxs-biscuits.co.uk
Website: http://www.foxs-biscuits.co.uk
Directors: M. Carey (Dir), M. Richards (Fin)
Immediate Holding Company: NORTHERN FOODS P L C
Registration no: 02327356 **VAT No.:** GB 168 7433 30
Turnover: £75m - £125m **No.of Employees:** 251 - 500
Product Groups: 20

Peter Hope Metals Ltd
2 Grange Road Business Park Grange Road, Batley, WF17 6LL
Tel: 01924-440055 **Fax:** 01924-442200
E-mail: peterhope.metalsltd@virgin.net
Website: http://www.peterhope-metals.co.uk
Directors: S. Rawlinson (MD)
Immediate Holding Company: PETER HOPE (METALS) LIMITED
Registration no: 01219552 **VAT No.:** GB 185 2445 52
Date established: 1975 **Turnover:** £500,000 - £1m
No.of Employees: 1 - 10 **Product Groups:** 48, 66

Date of Accounts	Aug 11	Aug 10	Aug 09
Working Capital	233	215	242
Fixed Assets	17	18	29
Current Assets	660	659	883
Current Liabilities	169	N/A	N/A

IID Solutions Ltd
Suite 7 - 10 Wesley House Huddersfield Road, Birstall, Batley, WF17 9EJ
Tel: 01924-424600 **Fax:** 01924-424601
E-mail: sales@iidsolutions.co.uk
Website: http://www.iidsolutions.co.uk
Directors: S. Carrington (MD)
Managers: R. Moore (Projects)
Turnover: £5m - £10m **No.of Employees:** 1 - 10 **Product Groups:** 37

Javah Ltd
Warwick Mills Howard Street, Batley, WF17 6JH
Tel: 01924-452156 **Fax:** 01924-455015
E-mail: sales@javah.com
Website: http://www.javah.com
Bank(s): Barclays
Directors: M. Frizzell (Jt MD), T. Hughes (Jt MD), K. Yeo (Co Sec)
Immediate Holding Company: Transport Packaging Solutions Ltd
Registration no: 06479774 **Date established:** 2008 **Turnover:** £1m - £2m
No.of Employees: 11 - 20 **Product Groups:** 30, 34, 35, 42

Date of Accounts	Oct 07	Oct 06	Oct 05
Working Capital	160	180	193
Fixed Assets	287	301	117
Current Assets	613	457	481
Current Liabilities	453	277	287

Joshua Ellis & Co.
Grange Valley Road, Batley, WF17 6GH
Tel: 01924-350070 **Fax:** 01924-350071
E-mail: genoffice@joshuaellis.co.uk
Website: http://www.joshuaellis.co.uk
Bank(s): HSBC, Bradford
Directors: R. Riley (MD)
Ultimate Holding Company: STONECROFT HOLDINGS PLC
Immediate Holding Company: JOSHUA ELLIS AND COMPANY,LIMITED
Registration no: 00067442 **VAT No.:** GB 168 8279 09
Date established: 2000 **Turnover:** £2m - £5m **No.of Employees:** 21 - 50
Product Groups: 23, 24

Date of Accounts	Dec 11	Dec 10	Dec 09
Sales Turnover	4m	3m	3m
Pre Tax Profit/Loss	238	63	-252
Working Capital	2m	1m	1m
Fixed Assets	63	90	108
Current Assets	4m	4m	3m
Current Liabilities	2m	2m	1m

Kings Computers
300 Bradford Road, Batley, WF17 5PW
Tel: 01924-420712
E-mail: info@kingscomputers.co.uk
Website: http://www.kingscomputers.co.uk

see next page

Kings Computers - Cont'd
Directors: H. Shirzad (Prop)
Date established: 2001 **Turnover:** Up to £250,000
No.of Employees: 1 - 10 **Product Groups:** 44

D Middleton
Unit 5 Lady Ann Mills Lady Ann Road, Batley, WF17 0PS
Tel: 01924-470807 **Fax:** 01924-470764
E-mail: richardmid1@aol.com
Website: http://www.stainlessmiddleton.co.uk
Directors: D. Middleton (Prop)
Date established: 1989 **No.of Employees:** 1 - 10 **Product Groups:** 35

Nelsons Birstall Ltd
Gelderd Road Birstall, Batley, WF17 9PX
Tel: 01924-474981 **Fax:** 01924-440871
E-mail: enquiries@nelsoneng.co.uk
Website: http://www.nelsoneng.co.uk
Directors: C. Hartley (MD)
Ultimate Holding Company: CROSS RIGG (HOLDINGS) LIMITED
Immediate Holding Company: NELSONS (BIRSTALL) LIMITED
Registration no: 00428122 **VAT No.:** GB 170 2371 92
Date established: 1947 **Turnover:** £500,000 - £1m
No.of Employees: 1 - 10 **Product Groups:** 51

Date of Accounts	Dec 11	Dec 10	Dec 09
Working Capital	300	295	273
Fixed Assets	38	43	50
Current Assets	434	406	349

Oil Pollution Environmental Control Ltd
Martin Street Birstall, Batley, WF17 9PJ
Tel: 01924-442701 **Fax:** 01924-471925
E-mail: info@opec.co.uk
Website: http://www.opec.co.uk
Directors: J. Ilsley (Dir)
Immediate Holding Company: OIL POLLUTION, ENVIRONMENTAL CONTROL LIMITED
Registration no: 01476775 **VAT No.:** GB 330 9016 89
Date established: 1980 **Turnover:** £500,000 - £1m
No.of Employees: 1 - 10 **Product Groups:** 39

Date of Accounts	Mar 11	Mar 10	Mar 09
Working Capital	186	48	77
Fixed Assets	8	8	9
Current Assets	1m	145	221

P P Profiles West Yorkshire Ltd
Springfield Works Stocks Lane, Batley, WF17 8PA
Tel: 01924-441381 **Fax:** 01924-472681
E-mail: info@pp-profiles.co.uk
Website: http://www.pp-profiles.co.uk
Directors: M. Broadbent (Dir)
Immediate Holding Company: P.P. PROFILES (WEST YORKSHIRE) LIMITED
Registration no: 01371189 **VAT No.:** GB 185 1457 50
Date established: 1978 **Turnover:** £1m - £2m **No.of Employees:** 21 - 50
Product Groups: 46, 48

Date of Accounts	Jul 11	Jul 10	Jul 09
Working Capital	2m	1m	1m
Fixed Assets	708	871	628
Current Assets	3m	2m	2m

Pallet Truck Services
Britannia Mills Gelderd Road, Birstall, Batley, WF17 9QD
Tel: 01924-444355 **Fax:** 01924-444355
Directors: P. Robinson (Ptnr)
Date established: 1994 **No.of Employees:** 1 - 10 **Product Groups:** 35, 39, 45

Planet Dance UK
2nd Floor Middle Mill, Batley, WF17 8LL
Tel: 01924-471340 **Fax:** 0113-226 9295
E-mail: sales@planetdance.com
Website: http://www.planetdance.com
Directors: P. Wintersgill (Fin), J. Buckle (Dir)
Immediate Holding Company: PLANET DANCE (UK) LTD
Registration no: 06361555 **Date established:** 2007
Turnover: Up to £250,000 **No.of Employees:** 1 - 10 **Product Groups:** 22, 24, 63

Date of Accounts	Sep 11	Sep 10	Sep 09
Working Capital	-19	-26	-23
Fixed Assets	41	45	49
Current Assets	114	83	86

Pound World Ltd
Unit 27 Oakwell Way Birstall, Batley, WF17 9LU
Tel: 01924-220511 **Fax:** 01924-220512
E-mail: info@poundworld.net
Website: http://www.inthepink.fsnet.co.uk
Directors: A. Ahmed (Fin), C. Edwards (Dir)
Managers: C. Edwards (Mgr)
Immediate Holding Company: POUND WORLD LTD
Registration no: 07392089 **Date established:** 2010
Turnover: Up to £250,000 **No.of Employees:** 21 - 50 **Product Groups:** 61, 63

Date of Accounts	Mar 11	Mar 10	Mar 09
Sales Turnover	133m	94m	67m
Pre Tax Profit/Loss	5m	1m	1m
Working Capital	-7m	-4m	-2m
Fixed Assets	14m	8m	6m
Current Assets	28m	15m	11m
Current Liabilities	12m	4m	2m

Reliance Security Services Ltd
Unit 7 Centre 27 Business Park Bankwood Way, Birstall, Batley, WF17 9TB
Tel: 01924-355000 **Fax:** 01924-473791
E-mail: s.thomas@reliancesecurity.co.uk
Website: http://www.reliancesecurity.co.uk
Directors: K. Allison (Ch), R. Ban (Fin)
Managers: S. Thomas (Chief Mgr)
Immediate Holding Company: RELIANCE SECURITY SERVICES LIMITED
Registration no: 01146486 **Date established:** 1973
Turnover: Over £1,000m **No.of Employees:** 11 - 20 **Product Groups:** 81

Rest Assured Ltd
Mill Forest Way, Batley, WF17 6RA
Tel: 01924-474477 **Fax:** 01924- 472736
E-mail: nealm@rest-assured.co.uk
Website: http://www.rest-assured.co.uk
Bank(s): National Westminster, Leeds
Directors: R. Noise (Sales & Mktg), P. Mckoen (Fin), N. Mernock (Dir), M. Mcllroy (MD), M. McKilroy (MD)
Ultimate Holding Company: FAMCO HOLDINGS LIMITED
Immediate Holding Company: RAL REALISATIONS 2011 LIMITED
Registration no: 03474127 **Date established:** 1997
Turnover: £10m - £20m **No.of Employees:** 101 - 250
Product Groups: 26, 35

Richardson Engineering
Unit 8f Lady Ann Mills Lady Ann Road, Batley, WF17 0PS
Tel: 01924-479002 **Fax:** 01924- 479002
Directors: A. Richardson (Prop)
Date established: 1999 **No.of Employees:** 1 - 10 **Product Groups:** 26, 35

S K Packaging
37 Warwick Road, Batley, WF17 6BU
Tel: 01924-455088 **Fax:** 01924-455088
E-mail: sales@skpackaging.co.uk
Website: http://www.skpackaging.co.uk
Directors: S. Raja (Prop)
Date established: 1996 **No.of Employees:** 1 - 10 **Product Groups:** 38, 42

S P Carpentry & Joinery
Skipton Street, Batley, WF17 6AE
Tel: 07988-693188
E-mail: soybercafe03@hotmail.com
Managers: S. PANDOR (Mgr)
Date established: 2004 **No.of Employees:** 1 - 10 **Product Groups:** 36

Scobie & Mcintosh Ltd
Oakwell Business Centre Dark Lane, Birstall, Batley, WF17 9LW
Tel: 01924-432940 **Fax:** 01924-432942
E-mail: sales@scobie-equipment.co.uk
Website: http://www.scobie-equipment.co.uk
Managers: S. Curran
Immediate Holding Company: SCOBIE & MCINTOSH LIMITED
Registration no: SC012259 **Date established:** 2022
No.of Employees: 21 - 50 **Product Groups:** 20, 40, 41

Date of Accounts	Dec 11	Dec 10	Dec 09
Sales Turnover	12m	9m	9m
Pre Tax Profit/Loss	971	705	639
Working Capital	2m	1m	1m
Fixed Assets	502	526	508
Current Assets	4m	3m	3m
Current Liabilities	1m	1m	1m

Shape Engineering
3 Lady Ann Mills Lady Ann Road, Batley, WF17 0PS
Tel: 01924-420066 **Fax:** 01924-422568
Directors: T. Pearson (Prop)
Date established: 1988 **No.of Employees:** 1 - 10 **Product Groups:** 35

Shopacheck Financial Services
Kingston House Centre 27 Business Park Woodhead Road, Birstall, Batley, WF17 9TD
Tel: 0800-280 0690 **Fax:** 01924-442255
E-mail: shaun.mann@cattles.co.uk
Website: http://www.shopacheck.co.uk
Directors: P. Kirby (MD), S. Mahon (Grp Chief Exec)
Ultimate Holding Company: BOVESS HOLDING LIMITED
Immediate Holding Company: SHOPACHECK FINANCIAL SERVICES LIMITED
Registration no: 07067456 **Date established:** 2009
Turnover: £125m - £250m **No.of Employees:** 1 - 10 **Product Groups:** 82

Date of Accounts	Dec 10
Pre Tax Profit/Loss	-0

R Spivey & Son Ltd (a division of R. Spivey & Son Ltd)
30 Pheasant Drive Birstall, Batley, WF17 9LT
Tel: 01924-422552 **Fax:** 01924-420006
E-mail: d.garsed@spiveydrums.co.uk
Website: http://www.spiveydrums.co.uk
Bank(s): Barclays, Drewsbury
Directors: D. Garsed (Sales)
Managers: L. Foulds (Personnel)
Immediate Holding Company: R. SPIVEY AND SON LIMITED
Registration no: 01508468 **VAT No.:** GB 169 7823 11
Date established: 1980 **No.of Employees:** 21 - 50 **Product Groups:** 30, 35, 48

Date of Accounts	Jul 11	Jul 10	Jul 09
Working Capital	1m	1m	2m
Fixed Assets	214	136	142
Current Assets	2m	2m	2m

Spraytec West Yorkshire Ltd
Foxhall Farm Owler Lane, Birstall, Batley, WF17 9BW
Tel: 01924-445665 **Fax:** 01924-445665
Directors: S. Thorton (Dir)
Ultimate Holding Company: C.I.S. INDUSTRIAL GROUP LIMITED
Immediate Holding Company: SPRAYTEC (WEST YORKSHIRE) LIMITED
Registration no: 06619107 **Date established:** 2008
No.of Employees: 1 - 10 **Product Groups:** 46, 48

Date of Accounts	Jun 11	Jun 10
Working Capital	20	15
Fixed Assets	6	8
Current Assets	77	88
Current Liabilities	44	57

Stelbound Ltd
Warwick Mills Howard Street, Batley, WF17 6JH
Tel: 01924-452156 **Fax:** 01924-455015
E-mail: general@javah.com
Website: http://www.stelbound.com
Directors: M. Frizell (Dir), T. Hughes (MD), K. Yeo (Fin)
Registration no: 01525504 **VAT No.:** GB 698 7738 44
Date established: 1980 **No.of Employees:** 1 - 10 **Product Groups:** 29, 34

Date of Accounts	Oct 07	Oct 06	Oct 05
Working Capital	26	133	65
Fixed Assets	N/A	1	1
Current Assets	197	280	229

Tennants Distribution
Gelderd Road Birstall, Batley, WF17 9LY
Tel: 01924-474447 **Fax:** 01924-477842
E-mail: steve.kilburn@tennantsdistribution.com
Website: http://www.tennantsdistribution.com
Directors: A. Mitchell (Dir)
Managers: S. Kilburn, A. Taylor (Tech Serv Mgr)
Ultimate Holding Company: TENNANTS CONSOLIDATED LTD
Immediate Holding Company: TENNANTS LANCASHIRE LTD
Registration no: 00246637 **Date established:** 1989 **Turnover:** £5m - £10m
No.of Employees: 11 - 20 **Product Groups:** 31, 32

Tom W Beaumont Ltd
Spafield Mills Upper Road, Batley, WF17 7LR
Tel: 01924-461401 **Fax:** 01924-461378
Website: http://www.yorkshirewiper.co.uk
Directors: S. Jackson (MD), H. Males (Sales & Mktg), H. May (Dir)
Managers: C. Ross
Immediate Holding Company: TOM W. BEAUMONT LIMITED
Registration no: 05180444 **Date established:** 2004
No.of Employees: 11 - 20 **Product Groups:** 54

Date of Accounts	Sep 11	Sep 10	Sep 09
Working Capital	-54	-67	-88
Fixed Assets	123	81	31
Current Assets	207	206	109

Wabco Automotive UK Ltd
Grange Valley Road, Batley, WF17 6GH
Tel: 01924-595400 **Fax:** 0113-252 6162
E-mail: dave.rickell@wabco-auto.com
Website: http://www.wabco-auto.com
Bank(s): Lloyds TSB Bank plc
Directors: D. Colquhoun (Fin)
Managers: A. Sykes (Mktg Serv Mgr), D. Rickell, M. Harris (Buyer), S. Cage (Sales Prom Mgr)
Ultimate Holding Company: WABCO HOLDINGS INC (USA)
Immediate Holding Company: WABCO AUTOMOTIVE U.K. LIMITED
Registration no: 00709827 **Date established:** 1961
Turnover: £20m - £50m **No.of Employees:** 21 - 50 **Product Groups:** 39

Date of Accounts	Dec 11	Dec 10	Dec 09
Sales Turnover	41m	48m	45m
Pre Tax Profit/Loss	2m	-1m	2m
Working Capital	-772	-1m	-2m
Fixed Assets	7m	352	3m
Current Assets	9m	8m	9m
Current Liabilities	3m	3m	1m

Y C E Catering Ltd
Brookroyd Mills Bradford Road, Batley, WF17 8ND
Tel: 01924-470757 **Fax:** 01924-475608
E-mail: info@yce.co.uk
Website: http://www.yce.co.uk
Directors: L. Moorby (Dir), S. Trobridge (Fin)
Immediate Holding Company: YCE CATERING EQUIPMENT LIMITED
Registration no: 02041598 **Date established:** 1986
No.of Employees: 21 - 50 **Product Groups:** 20, 40, 41

Date of Accounts	Jun 11	Jun 10	Jun 09
Working Capital	-619	-765	N/A
Fixed Assets	859	816	N/A
Current Assets	2m	800	N/A
Current Liabilities	N/A	504	N/A

Y P Electronics Ltd
Centre 27 Business Park Bankwood Way, Birstall, Batley, WF17 9TB
Tel: 01924-350600 **Fax:** 01924-479800
E-mail: sales@ypelectronics.co.uk
Website: http://www.ypelectronics.co.uk
Directors: A. Mckelvie (Co Sec), C. Adams (Dir), I. Harris (MD), P. Smith (Co Sec)
Managers: J. Shipstone (Sales Prom Mgr)
Ultimate Holding Company: P&H (2008) Ltd
Immediate Holding Company: Y.P. ELECTRONICS LIMITED
Registration no: 02272818 **Date established:** 1988 **Turnover:** £2m - £5m
No.of Employees: 21 - 50 **Product Groups:** 44

Date of Accounts	Apr 08
Sales Turnover	2435
Pre Tax Profit/Loss	-696
Working Capital	-196
Fixed Assets	80
Current Assets	877
Current Liabilities	1072
Total Share Capital	1
ROCE% (Return on Capital Employed)	603.4

Bingley

A Shade Blind
Falcon Road, Bingley, BD16 4DW
Tel: 01274-510742 **Fax:** 01274-510742
E-mail: sales@ashadeblind.co.uk
Website: http://www.ashadeblind.co.uk
Directors: D. Hodgson (Prop)
Turnover: Up to £250,000 **No.of Employees:** 1 - 10 **Product Groups:** 24, 35, 63, 66

Norman Bailey Engineers Ltd
Britannia Works Britannia Street, Bingley, BD16 2NS
Tel: 01274-562194 **Fax:** 01274-562121
E-mail: norman-bailey@lycos.co.uk
Directors: C. Sheard (MD)
Immediate Holding Company: NORMAN BAILEY (ENGINEERS) LIMITED
Registration no: 00356858 **VAT No.:** GB 179 3130 55
Date established: 1939 **Turnover:** Up to £250,000
No.of Employees: 1 - 10 **Product Groups:** 52

Date of Accounts	Oct 10	Oct 09	Oct 08
Working Capital	-8	4	21
Fixed Assets	24	27	31
Current Assets	40	33	50

Damart Thermal Wear Ltd
Bowling Green Mills Lime Street, Bingley, BD97 1AD
Tel: 01274-568211 **Fax:** 01274-551024
E-mail: andrew.hill@damart.com
Website: http://www.damart.co.uk
Directors: J. Bottomley (Mkt Research), A. Hill (MD), D. Whittle (Dir), A. Hill (Dir)
Managers: A. Caines (Mgr)
Ultimate Holding Company: DAMARTEX SA (FRANCE)
Immediate Holding Company: DAMARTEX UK LIMITED
Registration no: 00852773 **Date established:** 1965
Turnover: £75m - £125m **No.of Employees:** 501 - 1000
Product Groups: 24

Date of Accounts	Jun 11	Jun 10	Jun 09
Working Capital	N/A	N/A	105
Current Assets	N/A	N/A	105
Current Liabilities	N/A	N/A	1

Dotcom Infoway UK
Croft Road Crossflatts, Bingley, BD22 9UA
Tel: 01274-256785 **Fax:** 01274-554422
E-mail: dcico.uk@gmail.com
Website: http://www.dotcominfoway.co.uk
Date established: 1990 **No.of Employees:** 251 - 500 **Product Groups:** 80

Electrical Power Ltd
PO Box 115, Bingley, BD16 1WQ
Tel: 01274-510970 **Fax:** 01274-511109
E-mail: epsrec@hotmail.com
Directors: S. Robertshaw (Dir), C. Robertshaw (Co Sec)
Registration no: 02354056 **VAT No.:** GB 520 7332 80
Date established: 1989 **Turnover:** £2m - £5m **No.of Employees:** 1 - 10
Product Groups: 37

Date of Accounts	Mar 08	Mar 07	Mar 06
Working Capital	-29	-19	-7
Fixed Assets	1	1	1
Current Assets	75	82	84
Current Liabilities	105	101	91
Total Share Capital	1	1	1

J R Services
35 Woodside Cresent, Bingley, BD16 1RE
Tel: 01274-568920 **Fax:** 01274-568920
Directors: R. Davis (Prop)
Date established: 1999 **No.of Employees:** 1 - 10 **Product Groups:** 38, 42

Penico Systems Ltd
Albion Works Keighley Road, Bingley, BD16 2RD
Tel: 01274-511044 **Fax:** 01274-510770
E-mail: sales@penico.com
Website: http://www.penico.com
Directors: A. Bridge (Dir)
Immediate Holding Company: PENICO SYSTEMS LIMITED
Registration no: 03531758 **Date established:** 1998
Turnover: £250,000 - £500,000 **No.of Employees:** 1 - 10
Product Groups: 46

Date of Accounts	Feb 08	Feb 11	Feb 10
Working Capital	52	49	16
Fixed Assets	115	87	95
Current Assets	260	163	196
Current Liabilities	145	85	77

Phoenix Fixings Ltd
21 Park Road, Bingley, BD16 4BQ
Tel: 01274-779001 **Fax:** 01274-771277
E-mail: info@phoenixfixings.co.uk
Website: http://www.phoenixfixings.co.uk
Directors: J. Hurst (MD), H. Hurst (Co Sec)
Immediate Holding Company: PHOENIX FIXINGS LIMITED
Registration no: 02046921 **VAT No.:** GB 447 5876 02
Date established: 1986 **No.of Employees:** 11 - 20 **Product Groups:** 35, 66

Date of Accounts	Aug 11	Aug 10	Aug 09
Working Capital	7	-19	-29
Fixed Assets	44	37	40
Current Assets	303	321	233
Current Liabilities	296	N/A	N/A

Stentorgate Ltd
Beech Grove Eldwick, Bingley, BD16 3EG
Tel: 01274-560600
E-mail: bern-leech@stentorgate.co.uk
Website: http://www.stentorgate.co.uk
Directors: R. Leech (Fin), B. Leech (Dir)
Immediate Holding Company: STENTORGATE LIMITED
Registration no: 02354293 **Date established:** 1989
No.of Employees: 1 - 10 **Product Groups:** 35, 39, 45

Date of Accounts	Aug 11	Aug 10	Aug 09
Working Capital	235	234	231
Fixed Assets	13	13	14
Current Assets	678	472	598

Trico V E Ltd
Castlefields Mill Castlefields Lane, Bingley, BD16 2AB
Tel: 01274-510101 **Fax:** 01274-510105
E-mail: info@trico-ve.co.uk
Website: http://www.trico-ve.co.uk
Directors: K. Dunk (Fin)
Ultimate Holding Company: MARINER HOLDINGS PLC
Immediate Holding Company: TRICO V.E. LIMITED
Registration no: 03613138 **Date established:** 1998 **Turnover:** £1m - £2m
No.of Employees: 21 - 50 **Product Groups:** 32

Date of Accounts	Mar 11	Mar 10	Mar 09
Sales Turnover	2m	2m	2m
Pre Tax Profit/Loss	93	58	86
Working Capital	266	155	317
Fixed Assets	214	262	318
Current Assets	536	474	1m
Current Liabilities	200	154	790

James Walker Moorflex Ltd
John Escritt Road, Bingley, BD16 2BS
Tel: 01274-562211 **Fax:** 01274-566623
E-mail: sales.moorflex.uk@jameswalker.biz
Website: http://www.jameswalker.biz
Directors: D. Kirwin (MD)
Managers: J. Simms (Mktg Serv Mgr)
Ultimate Holding Company: JAMES WALKER GROUP LIMITED
Immediate Holding Company: JAMES WALKER MOORFLEX LIMITED
Registration no: 00575005 **Date established:** 1956 **Turnover:** £5m - £10m
No.of Employees: 51 - 100 **Product Groups:** 27, 29, 30, 33, 36, 40, 48

Date of Accounts	Mar 12	Mar 11	Mar 10
Sales Turnover	11m	9m	8m
Pre Tax Profit/Loss	-270	6	16
Working Capital	4m	4m	4m
Fixed Assets	1m	1m	1m
Current Assets	6m	5m	5m
Current Liabilities	454	185	169

Bradford

A D T Flexibles UK Ltd
Cockersdale Works Whitehall Road, Drighlington, Bradford, BD11 1NQ
Tel: 0113-285 3009 **Fax:** 0113-285 3709
E-mail: office@adtflex.co.uk
Website: http://www.adtflex.co.uk
Directors: A. Taffinder (Dir)
Immediate Holding Company: A.D.T FLEXIBLES (UK) LTD
Registration no: 01670585 **Date established:** 1982
No.of Employees: 11 - 20 **Product Groups:** 30, 36

Date of Accounts	Aug 11	Aug 10	Aug 09
Working Capital	235	151	111
Fixed Assets	156	107	127
Current Assets	835	693	503

A E S Seal plc
Unit 2-3 Venlo Industrial Estate Knowles Street, Bradford, BD4 6HA
Tel: 01274-688870 **Fax:** 01274-688890
E-mail: rob.weaver@aesseal.com
Website: http://www.aesseal.co.uk
Managers: R. Weaver (District Mgr)
Ultimate Holding Company: A.E.S. ENGINEERING LIMITED
Immediate Holding Company: AESSEAL PLC
Registration no: 02101607 **Date established:** 1987
No.of Employees: 21 - 50 **Product Groups:** 29, 63, 66

Date of Accounts	Dec 11	Dec 10	Dec 09
Sales Turnover	42m	37m	30m
Pre Tax Profit/Loss	7m	5m	2m
Working Capital	10m	10m	10m
Fixed Assets	9m	9m	8m
Current Assets	18m	15m	15m
Current Liabilities	3m	2m	1m

A K Pumps
39-45 Hammerton Street, Bradford, BD3 9QN
Tel: 01274-740200 **Fax:** 01274-740300
E-mail: akpumps@msn.com
Directors: A. Khan (Prop)
Registration no: 05991398 **Turnover:** £250,000 - £500,000
No.of Employees: 1 - 10 **Product Groups:** 40, 48

A T C Dyers
Royds Hall Lane Buttershaw, Bradford, BD6 2NE
Tel: 01274-691169 **Fax:** 01274-690016
E-mail: atcdyers@legend.co.uk
Website: http://www.bulmerandlumb.com
Directors: M. Whitehead (Fin)
Managers: M. Catterall (Mgr), S. Robertshaw (Tech Serv Mgr), N. Dixon
Immediate Holding Company: TAYLOR & LODGE (HUDDERSFIELD) LIMITED
Registration no: 04229894 **Date established:** 1982
Turnover: £10m - £20m **No.of Employees:** 21 - 50 **Product Groups:** 23

Able Manufacturing
900 Thornton Road Fairweather Green, Bradford, BD8 0JG
Tel: 01274-771856 **Fax:** 01274-771811
E-mail: jan@kf-man.co.uk
Website: http://www.kf-man.co.uk
Directors: M. Jefferson (Fin), B. Jefferson (Dir)
Immediate Holding Company: ABLE MANUFACTURING LTD.
Registration no: 03559246 **Date established:** 1998
No.of Employees: 1 - 10 **Product Groups:** 25, 26, 34, 35

Date of Accounts	May 11	May 10	May 09
Working Capital	13	6	-20
Fixed Assets	N/A	N/A	1
Current Assets	100	106	102

Adams Sheet Metal Ltd
Mill Street Wibsey, Bradford, BD6 3BQ
Tel: 01274-693630 **Fax:** 01274-693631
E-mail: adam@a-s-m.co.uk
Website: http://www.a-s-m.co.uk
Directors: S. Watson (Co Sec), A. Watson (MD)
Immediate Holding Company: ADAMS SHEET METAL LIMITED
Registration no: 02752007 **Date established:** 1992
Turnover: £250,000 - £500,000 **No.of Employees:** 1 - 10
Product Groups: 36

Date of Accounts	Jan 12	Jan 11	Jan 10
Working Capital	-51	-57	-41
Fixed Assets	137	181	197
Current Assets	424	387	319

Advanced Dynamics Ltd
250 Thornton Road, Bradford, BD1 2LB
Tel: 01274-220300 **Fax:** 01274-308953
E-mail: malcolm@advanceddynamics.co.uk
Website: http://www.advanceddynamics.co.uk
Directors: M. Essler (Dir), W. Birkinhead (Jt MD), M. Little (Dir), W. Birkinhead (MD)
Managers: P. Collins (Eng Serv Mgr)
Ultimate Holding Company: WRAPID GROUP LIMITED
Immediate Holding Company: ADVANCED DYNAMICS LIMITED
Registration no: 05277581 **Date established:** 2004 **Turnover:** £1m - £2m
No.of Employees: 1 - 10 **Product Groups:** 22, 23, 29, 30, 32, 37, 38, 42, 43, 44

Date of Accounts	Dec 09	Dec 08	Dec 07
Working Capital	117	148	4
Fixed Assets	32	30	35
Current Assets	529	602	360

Airedale Technical Services Ltd
Coldseal Works Victoria Road, Eccleshill, Bradford, BD2 2BN
Tel: 01274-626970 **Fax:** 01274-626972
E-mail: paul.connolly@airedale-group.co.uk
Website: http://www.airedale-group.co.uk
Directors: J. Rhodes (Dir), P. Connolly (MD)
Immediate Holding Company: AIREDALE TECHNICAL SERVICES LIMITED
Registration no: 02884539 **Date established:** 1994
No.of Employees: 1 - 10 **Product Groups:** 20, 40, 41

Date of Accounts	Sep 09	Sep 08	Sep 07
Working Capital	159	118	86
Fixed Assets	76	57	57
Current Assets	459	349	305

Albany Standard Pumps (a division of Albany Engineering Co. Ltd)
Richter Works Garnett Street, Bradford, BD3 9HB
Tel: 01274-725351 **Fax:** 01274-742467
E-mail: john.bramley@albany-pumps.co.uk
Website: http://www.albany-pumps.co.uk
Managers: J. Bramley (Mgr)
Ultimate Holding Company: ALBANY ENGINEERING COMPANY LIMITED(THE)
Immediate Holding Company: STANHOPE ENGINEERS (BRADFORD) LIMITED
Registration no: 00479775 **Date established:** 1950
Turnover: Up to £250,000 **No.of Employees:** 1 - 10 **Product Groups:** 39, 40, 46

Date of Accounts	Mar 98	Mar 11	Mar 10

Albion Dyestuffs Ltd
Rook Lane Mills Law Street, Bradford, BD4 9NF
Tel: 01274-652907 **Fax:** 01274-689359
E-mail: albiondyestuffs@aol.com
Directors: W. Nash (Fin)
Immediate Holding Company: ALBION DYESTUFFS LIMITED
Registration no: 02065987 **VAT No.:** GB 447 6545 20
Date established: 1986 **Turnover:** £1m - £2m **No.of Employees:** 1 - 10
Product Groups: 32

Date of Accounts	Apr 11	Apr 10	Apr 09
Working Capital	69	66	60
Fixed Assets	39	45	50
Current Assets	352	247	262

Allan Industrial Products Ltd
Barrett House Cutler Heights Lane, Dudley Hill, Bradford, BD4 9HU
Tel: 01462-454021 **Fax:** 01462-421312
E-mail: sales@allanindustrial.co.uk
Website: http://www.allan-industrial.co.uk
Directors: J. Peett (Dir)
Immediate Holding Company: Barrett Steel Ltd
Registration no: 03012240 **VAT No.:** GB 301 7355 92
Date established: 1995 **Turnover:** £5m - £10m **No.of Employees:** 1 - 10
Product Groups: 66

Alpha Moisture Systems
Alpha House 96 City Road, Bradford, BD8 8ES
Tel: 01274-733100 **Fax:** 01274-733200
E-mail: info@amsystems.co.uk
Website: http://www.amsystems.co.uk
Bank(s): Barclays Bank PLC, Bradford
Directors: B. Mcdonald (Fin)
Immediate Holding Company: ALPHA MOISTURE SYSTEMS LIMITED
Registration no: 03902302 **VAT No.:** GB 607 2075 63
Date established: 2000 **No.of Employees:** 11 - 20 **Product Groups:** 38, 42, 67, 85

Date of Accounts	Dec 11	Dec 10	Dec 09
Working Capital	2m	2m	1m
Fixed Assets	135	136	160
Current Assets	2m	2m	2m

Alpine Glass Ltd
900 Thornton Road, Bradford, BD8 0JG
Tel: 01274-494940 **Fax:** 01274-484850
E-mail: matt@alpineroofs.co.uk
Website: http://www.alpineroofs.co.uk
Directors: M. Thomson (Ptnr)
Immediate Holding Company: ALPINE GLASS LTD
Registration no: 08006668 **Date established:** 2012
Turnover: Up to £250,000 **No.of Employees:** 1 - 10 **Product Groups:** 30, 33, 35, 36

Amini Textile International
Amini House 5 Rees Way, Bradford, BD3 0DZ
Tel: 01274-725950 **Fax:** 01274-309675
E-mail: sales@amini-international.com
Website: http://www.amini-international.com
Directors: N. Amini (Prop)
Registration no: 13488341 **Turnover:** £1m - £2m
No.of Employees: 1 - 10 **Product Groups:** 61, 63

Angel Windows
9 Vale Grove Queensbury, Bradford, BD13 2QR
Tel: 01274-884049
E-mail: info@angelwindows.com
Website: http://www.angelwindows.com
Directors: S. Robertson (Prop)
No.of Employees: 1 - 10 **Product Groups:** 30, 52

Arco Bradford Ltd
Unit 1 Bow Beck, Bradford, BD4 8SL
Tel: 01274-732211 **Fax:** 01274-732244
E-mail: dave.pearson@arco.co.uk
Website: http://www.arco.co.uk
Managers: D. Pearson (Mgr)
No.of Employees: 1 - 10 **Product Groups:** 24, 29, 30, 40

Arthur Walton Ltd
Arthur Walton House Merrydale Road Euroway Industrial Estate, Bradford, BD4 6SD
Tel: 01274-686186 **Fax:** 01274-686189
E-mail: sales@arthurwalton.co.uk
Website: http://www.arthurwalton.co.uk
Directors: C. Walton (MD)
Immediate Holding Company: ARTHUR WALTON LIMITED
Registration no: 00512652 **Date established:** 1952
No.of Employees: 11 - 20 **Product Groups:** 20, 40, 41

Date of Accounts	Feb 08	Feb 11	Feb 10
Working Capital	562	237	375
Fixed Assets	480	479	495
Current Assets	1m	1m	1m

Ashtree Glass Ltd
Ashtree Works Brownroyd Street, Bradford, BD8 9AF
Tel: 01274-546732 **Fax:** 01274-548525
E-mail: sales@ashtreeglass.co.uk
Website: http://www.ashtreeglass.co.uk
Bank(s): Bank of Scotland

see next page

Ashtree Glass Ltd - Cont'd

Directors: J. Roper (Dir), A. Roper (MD)
Immediate Holding Company: ASHTREE GLASS LIMITED
Registration no: 01660674 **VAT No.:** GB 303 3413 15
Date established: 1982 **Turnover:** £2m - £5m **No.of Employees:** 21 - 50
Product Groups: 33, 39, 68

Date of Accounts	Nov 11	Nov 10	Nov 09
Working Capital	2m	2m	1m
Fixed Assets	94	117	155
Current Assets	2m	2m	2m

Astracast P.L.C.

Woodlands Roydsdale Way, Euroway Trading Estate, Bradford, BD4 6SE
Tel: 01274-475179 **Fax:** 01274-654176
E-mail: sales@astracast.co.uk
Website: http://www.astracast.co.uk
Managers: D. Attia (Export Sales Mg)
Immediate Holding Company: US Industries
Registration no: 02744335 **Turnover:** £20m - £50m
No.of Employees: 11 - 20 **Product Groups:** 33, 36, 39, 66

Date of Accounts	Sep 08	Sep 07	Sep 06
Working Capital	500	500	500
Current Assets	500	500	500
Total Share Capital	500	500	500

Terex Atlas UK

Wharfedale Road Euroway Industrial Estate, Bradford, BD4 6SL
Tel: 08444-996688 **Fax:** 01274-653785
Website: http://www.terex.com
Directors: J. Kilcoyne (Fin)
Managers: C. Watson (Mgr)
Registration no: SC038800 **No.of Employees:** 21 - 50
Product Groups: 35, 39, 45

Auker Rhodes Chartered Accountants

Royd House Manningham Lane, Bradford, BD8 7BP
Tel: 01274-548000 **Fax:** 01274- 548888
E-mail: sales@aukerrhodes.co.uk
Website: http://www.auker-rhodes.co.uk
Directors: G. Rudloff (Dir), R. Kenyon (Co Sec)
Immediate Holding Company: AUKER RHODES TAX & FINANCIAL PLANNING LTD
Registration no: 04471138 **Date established:** 2002 **Turnover:** £1m - £2m
No.of Employees: 21 - 50 **Product Groups:** 80

Date of Accounts	Mar 10	Mar 09	Mar 08
Working Capital	785	693	564
Fixed Assets	968	1m	1m
Current Assets	863	758	720

B A S F

Cleckheaton Road Low Moor, Bradford, BD12 0JZ
Tel: 01274-417000 **Fax:** 01274-606499
E-mail: info@cibasc.com
Website: http://www.basf.com
Directors: R. Wilkinson (Co Sec), W. Huemmer (Dir)
Managers: J. Ell (Fin Mgr), K. Bain (Personnel), M. Solfrank
Ultimate Holding Company: BASF SOCIETAS EUROPAEA (GERMANY)
Immediate Holding Company: CIBA SPECIALTY CHEMICALS WATER TREATMENTS LIMITED
Registration no: 00722043 **Date established:** 1962 **Turnover:** £5m - £10m
No.of Employees: 501 - 1000 **Product Groups:** 32

Date of Accounts	Dec 11	Dec 10	Dec 09
Pre Tax Profit/Loss	N/A	N/A	2
Working Capital	371m	371m	371m
Fixed Assets	275m	275m	275m
Current Assets	371m	371m	371m

J W Baker & Sons Bradford Ltd

Factory Lane Dudley Hill, Bradford, BD4 9NT
Tel: 01274-651650 **Fax:** 01274-681984
E-mail: bakerfabrication@btconnect.com
Website: http://www.bakerfabrications.com
Directors: N. Baker (MD)
Immediate Holding Company: J.W.BAKER & SONS (BRADFORD) LIMITED
Registration no: 00598007 **VAT No.:** GB 179 3677 09
Date established: 1958 **Turnover:** £500,000 - £1m
No.of Employees: 1 - 10 **Product Groups:** 48

Date of Accounts	Jan 11	Jan 10	Jan 09
Working Capital	20	38	77
Fixed Assets	19	23	28
Current Assets	197	146	210

Ballachree Ltd

Canal Road Frizinghall, Bradford, BD2 1AU
Tel: 01274-593131 **Fax:** 01274-596752
E-mail: paul@ballachree.co.uk
Website: http://www.ballachree.co.uk
Bank(s): National Westminster Bank Plc
Directors: P. Leadbeater (MD)
Immediate Holding Company: BALLACHREE LIMITED
Registration no: 01360489 **VAT No.:** GB 303 4629 84
Date established: 1978 **Turnover:** £2m - £5m **No.of Employees:** 11 - 20
Product Groups: 34, 66

Date of Accounts	Mar 12	Mar 11	Mar 10
Working Capital	592	463	291
Fixed Assets	366	323	333
Current Assets	3m	3m	2m

The Banner People

21 Commondale Way Euroway Industrial Estate, Bradford, BD4 6SF
Tel: 08702-409983 **Fax:** 01274-686464
E-mail: contact@thebannerpeople.com
Website: http://www.thebannerpeople.com
Directors: J. Stuart (Dir)
Ultimate Holding Company: M1 ENGINEERING HOLDINGS LIMITED
Immediate Holding Company: M 1 ENGINEERING LIMITED
Registration no: 01455554 **Date established:** 1972
No.of Employees: 1 - 10 **Product Groups:** 30, 39, 40, 49

Bar Graphic Machinery Ltd

Rhodes House 71 Shetcliffe Lane, Bradford, BD4 6QJ
Tel: 01274-680020 **Fax:** 01274-688890
E-mail: bargraphic@hotmail.com
Website: http://www.bargraphic.com
Directors: B. Rhodes (Ptnr)
Immediate Holding Company: BAR GRAPHIC MACHINERY LIMITED
Registration no: 05247574 **Date established:** 2004
No.of Employees: 1 - 10 **Product Groups:** 44

Date of Accounts	Oct 11	Oct 10	Oct 09
Working Capital	145	108	142
Fixed Assets	114	107	122
Current Assets	304	212	313

Barair Systems Ltd

8 John Street Thornton, Bradford, BD13 3JS
Tel: 01274-426770 **Fax:** 01274-426771
E-mail: sales@barair.co.uk
Website: http://www.barair.co.uk
Directors: B. Lowes (Fin), A. Lowes (MD)
Immediate Holding Company: BARAIR SYSTEMS LIMITED
Registration no: 04883464 **Date established:** 2003
Turnover: Up to £250,000 **No.of Employees:** 1 - 10 **Product Groups:** 80, 84

Date of Accounts	Sep 11	Sep 10	Sep 09
Working Capital	-3	-25	-42
Fixed Assets	4	5	7
Current Assets	34	13	13

Barrett Steel Buildings Ltd

Barrett House Cutler Heights Lane, Bradford, BD4 9HZ
Tel: 01274-266800 **Fax:** 01274-266859
E-mail: bsb@barrettonline.co.uk
Website: http://www.barrettonline.co.uk
Bank(s): HSBC Bank plc
Directors: J. Barrett (Grp Chief Exec), A. Hirst (Sales), J. Barrett (Grp Chief Exec), J. Wood (Works), P. Chasney (Fin), R. Butcher (Ch), R. Barrett (Dir), S. Sharples (Co Sec)
Managers: C. Lamb (Comm), R. Simpson (Sales Prom), T. Bakes (Sales Prom Mgr)
Ultimate Holding Company: Barrett Structures Ltd
Immediate Holding Company: Barrett Steel Ltd
Registration no: 02739854 **VAT No.:** GB 651 7770 21
Date established: 1992 **Turnover:** £125m - £250m
No.of Employees: 101 - 250 **Product Groups:** 66

Date of Accounts	Sep 10	Sep 09	Sep 08
Sales Turnover	197m	201m	306m
Pre Tax Profit/Loss	8m	-6m	23m
Working Capital	43m	30m	58m
Fixed Assets	37m	37m	36m
Current Assets	104m	80m	144m
Current Liabilities	22m	17m	30m

Edmund Bell & Co. Ltd

Euroway Industrial Estate, Bradford, BD4 6SU
Tel: 01274-680000 **Fax:** 01274-680699
E-mail: sales@edmundbell.co.uk
Website: http://www.edmundbell.co.uk
Directors: G. Henderson (MD)
Managers: D. Stanley
Immediate Holding Company: EDMUND BELL & CO., LIMITED
Registration no: 06582047 **VAT No.:** GB 179 3070 47
Date established: 2008 **Turnover:** £10m - £20m **No.of Employees:** 1 - 10
Product Groups: 23

Date of Accounts	Nov 07	Nov 06	Nov 05
Sales Turnover	17342	17050	13593
Pre Tax Profit/Loss	292	669	451
Working Capital	910	602	4715
Fixed Assets	116	174	100
Current Assets	8509	7716	8026
Current Liabilities	7599	7114	3311
Total Share Capital	18	18	18
ROCE% (Return on Capital Employed)	28.5	86.2	9.4
ROT% (Return on Turnover)	1.7	3.9	3.3

Benson Industries Ltd

Valley Mills Valley Road, Bradford, BD1 4RU
Tel: 01274-722204 **Fax:** 01274-306319
Directors: G. Holmes (Prop)
Immediate Holding Company: BENSON INDUSTRIES LIMITED
Registration no: 00407006 **VAT No.:** GB 179 3206 48
Date established: 1946 **Turnover:** £500,000 - £1m
No.of Employees: 1 - 10 **Product Groups:** 36

Date of Accounts	Mar 12	Mar 11	Mar 10
Working Capital	186	174	196
Fixed Assets	N/A	1	24
Current Assets	196	187	210

Benthan & Holroyd Ltd

Prospect Works Allerton, Bradford, BD15 7AF
Tel: 01274-541327 **Fax:** 01274-547396
E-mail: info@benthams.com
Website: http://www.benthams.com
Bank(s): National Westminster Bank Plc
Directors: I. Christie (MD)
Immediate Holding Company: BENTHAM & HOLROYD LIMITED
Registration no: 00185672 **VAT No.:** GB 179 4279 16
Date established: 2022 **Turnover:** £500,000 - £1m
No.of Employees: 21 - 50 **Product Groups:** 48, 51, 84

Date of Accounts	Sep 11	Sep 10	Sep 09
Working Capital	255	228	276
Fixed Assets	689	769	631
Current Assets	852	636	615

Biscor Ltd

Kingsmark Freeway Oakenshaw, Bradford, BD12 7HW
Tel: 01274-694684 **Fax:** 01274-694685
E-mail: info@biscor.com
Website: http://www.biscor.com
Directors: G. Bowler (MD)
Ultimate Holding Company: GAMMA HOLDING NV (NETHERLANDS)
Immediate Holding Company: BISCOR LIMITED
Registration no: 01262669 **VAT No.:** GB 181 2811 77
Date established: 1976 **Turnover:** £2m - £5m **No.of Employees:** 1 - 10
Product Groups: 23

Date of Accounts	Dec 10	Dec 09	Dec 08
Sales Turnover	3m	3m	3m
Pre Tax Profit/Loss	-1m	-2m	-760
Working Capital	-4m	-3m	-2m
Fixed Assets	107	340	636
Current Assets	1m	2m	2m
Current Liabilities	208	60	86

Bower Green Ltd

Dryden Street, Bradford, BD1 5ND
Tel: 01274-733537 **Fax:** 01274-393511
E-mail: info@bowergreen.co.uk
Website: http://www.bowergreen.co.uk
Bank(s): Barclays
Directors: A. Gregory (Fin), A. Pattison (MD)
Managers: P. Smtih (Sales Admin)
Immediate Holding Company: BOWER GREEN LIMITED
Registration no: 03368517 **VAT No.:** GB 179 5903 16
Date established: 1997 **Turnover:** £5m - £10m
No.of Employees: 51 - 100 **Product Groups:** 72, 76, 77

Date of Accounts	Jul 11	Jul 10	Jul 09
Sales Turnover	7m	7m	6m
Pre Tax Profit/Loss	10	36	-63
Working Capital	35	56	30
Fixed Assets	3m	3m	3m
Current Assets	2m	1m	1m
Current Liabilities	603	570	440

Bradford Armature Winding Company Ltd

429 Bowling Old Lane, Bradford, BD5 8HN
Tel: 01274-728379 **Fax:** 01274-731518
E-mail: clawn@bawco.com
Website: http://www.bawco.com
Directors: C. Grogan (Sales), C. Lawn (Ch), K. Harrison (Works), K. Lawn (Co Sec)
Managers: C. Lawn (Sales Prom Mgr)
Immediate Holding Company: BRADFORD ARMATURE WINDING COMPANY LIMITED(THE)
Registration no: 00367472 **VAT No.:** GB 179 4325 35
Date established: 1941 **Turnover:** £1m - £2m **No.of Employees:** 1 - 10
Product Groups: 48

Date of Accounts	Jun 08	Jun 07	Jun 06
Working Capital	127	85	100
Fixed Assets	77	59	53
Current Assets	488	402	404
Current Liabilities	361	316	304
Total Share Capital	18	18	18

Bradford Chamber Of Commerce

Devere House Vicar Lane, Bradford, BD1 5AH
Tel: 01274-772777 **Fax:** 01274-230081
E-mail: info@bradfordchamber.co.uk
Website: http://www.bradfordchamber.co.uk
Directors: S. Meedham (Grp Chief Exec)
Managers: J. Wright (Personnel), C. Main, J. Snook
Immediate Holding Company: BRADFORD CHAMBER OF COMMERCE & INDUSTRY
Registration no: 00054940 **Date established:** 1997 **Turnover:** £2m - £5m
No.of Employees: 21 - 50 **Product Groups:** 80, 81

Date of Accounts	Mar 11	Mar 10	Mar 09
Sales Turnover	4m	5m	5m
Pre Tax Profit/Loss	24	38	9
Working Capital	3m	3m	2m
Fixed Assets	3m	3m	2m
Current Assets	4m	5m	5m
Current Liabilities	1m	2m	2m

Bradford & District Association For Mental Health

37 Wilmer Drive, Bradford, BD9 4AS
Tel: 01274-545098 **Fax:** 01274-723634
E-mail: queensgrange@yahoo.co.uk
Website: http://www.thetelegraphandargus.co.uk
Bank(s): HSBC
Managers: E. Lawrence (Mgr)
Ultimate Holding Company: NEWSQUEST LTD
Registration no: 05723898 **VAT No.:** GB 180 4263 78
Date established: 2006 **Turnover:** Up to £250,000
No.of Employees: 11 - 20 **Product Groups:** 28

Bradford Door & Gate Co

130 Thornton Road, Bradford, BD1 2DX
Tel: 01274-370000 **Fax:** 01274-370022
E-mail: dssbdg@hotmail.co.uk
Website: http://www.bradforddoorandgate.com
Turnover: £500,000 - £1m **No.of Employees:** 1 - 10 **Product Groups:** 25, 33, 52

Bradford Grinders UK Ltd

Mount Street, Bradford, BD3 9SN
Tel: 01274-733141 **Fax:** 01274-734610
E-mail: sales@bguk.co.uk
Website: http://www.bguk.co.uk
Bank(s): Lloyds TSB Bank plc
Directors: R. Chera (MD)
Immediate Holding Company: BRADFORD GRINDERS (U.K.) LIMITED
Registration no: 01095836 **VAT No.:** GB 180 6081 74
Date established: 1973 **Turnover:** £1m - £2m **No.of Employees:** 21 - 50
Product Groups: 39, 48

Date of Accounts	Feb 11	Feb 10	Feb 09
Working Capital	668	662	674
Fixed Assets	39	40	43
Current Assets	1m	1m	1m

Bradford Laser Cutting Ltd

Planetrees Road Laisterdyke, Bradford, BD4 8AE
Tel: 01274-200 112 **Fax:** 01274-400400
E-mail: sales@bradfordlaser.com
Website: http://www.bradfordlaser.com
Directors: G. Wilson (Dir), R. Simmonite (Dir)
Registration no: 05107880 **Date established:** 2004
Turnover: £250,000 - £500,000 **No.of Employees:** 1 - 10
Product Groups: 24, 33, 45, 48, 84

Date of Accounts	Mar 10	Mar 09	Mar 08
Working Capital	131	66	110
Fixed Assets	120	148	173
Current Assets	303	212	255

Bradford Rubber Services

Unit 1c Bowling Park Close, Bradford, BD4 7HG
Tel: 01274-307030 **Fax:** 01274-305699
E-mail: sales@bradfordrubber.co.uk
Website: http://www.bradfordrubber.co.uk
Directors: D. Fernie (Dir)
Immediate Holding Company: BRADFORD RUBBER SERVICES LIMITED
Registration no: 00646003 **VAT No.:** GB 179 3570 27
Date established: 1959 **Turnover:** Up to £250,000
No.of Employees: 1 - 10 **Product Groups:** 25, 29, 30, 40

Date of Accounts	Mar 12	Mar 11	Mar 10
Working Capital	452	387	289
Fixed Assets	134	159	188
Current Assets	584	500	446

Bradford Tool Group
Beta Works 1 Tong Street, Bradford, BD4 9PW
Tel: 01274-683902 **Fax:** 01274-651168
Website: http://www.bradtool.co.uk
Directors: S. Sheldon (MD), W. Mcgrath (Prop), A. McGrath (Fin)
Immediate Holding Company: BLAKEPOINT LIMITED
Registration no: 04572685 **VAT No.:** GB 179 6678 89
Date established: 2002 **Turnover:** £2m - £5m **No.of Employees:** 21 - 50
Product Groups: 46

Date of Accounts	Dec 11	Dec 10	Dec 09
Working Capital	650	595	106
Fixed Assets	891	904	919
Current Assets	2m	2m	1m

C A Brown
5 Young Street Industrial Estate Young Street, Bradford, BD8 9RE
Tel: 01274-488099 **Fax:** 01274-498868
E-mail: sales@castortruckladder.co.uk
Directors: H. Buttery (Dir)
Immediate Holding Company: CASTOR TRUCK & LADDER CO. LTD
Registration no: 00958534 **VAT No.:** GB 179 7360 18
Turnover: Up to £250,000 **No.of Employees:** 1 - 10 **Product Groups:** 25, 26, 32, 35, 63

Brumfitt Factory Equipment Ltd
Gibson Street, Bradford, BD3 9TB
Tel: 01274-666760 **Fax:** 01274-666760
Directors: J. Drake (MD)
Immediate Holding Company: UNIQUE CARS CENTRE LTD
Registration no: 06754354 **Date established:** 2010
Turnover: Up to £250,000 **No.of Employees:** 1 - 10 **Product Groups:** 39, 45

Date of Accounts	May 11
Working Capital	-7
Fixed Assets	8
Current Assets	3

Bulmer & Lumb Group Ltd
Royds Hall Lane Buttershaw, Bradford, BD6 2NE
Tel: 01274-690965 **Fax:** 01274-691239
E-mail: sales@bulmerandlumb.com
Website: http://www.bulmerandlumb.com
Bank(s): Lloyds TSB Bank plc & National Westminster Bank Plc
Directors: D. Midgley (MD), M. Whitehead (Fin)
Managers: S. Robertshaw (Tech Serv Mgr)
Immediate Holding Company: SIR JAMES HILL & SONS TOPMAKERS LIMITED
Registration no: 04229539 **Date established:** 2001
Turnover: £10m - £20m **No.of Employees:** 101 - 250
Product Groups: 23, 49

Butterfield Signs Ltd
174 Sunbridge Road, Bradford, BD1 2RZ
Tel: 01274-722244 **Fax:** 01274-848998
E-mail: enquiries@butterfieldsigns.co.uk
Website: http://www.butterfieldsigns.co.uk
Directors: E. Butterfield (Prop)
Immediate Holding Company: BUTTERFIELD SIGNS LIMITED
Registration no: 00409815 **Date established:** 1946
Turnover: £10m - £20m **No.of Employees:** 1 - 10 **Product Groups:** 30, 37, 40, 49

Date of Accounts	Dec 11	Dec 10	Dec 09
Sales Turnover	15m	13m	11m
Pre Tax Profit/Loss	100	374	169
Working Capital	1m	1m	905
Fixed Assets	1m	1m	1m
Current Assets	4m	4m	5m
Current Liabilities	904	733	2m

C A S Coatings
Old Mill Victoria Road, Bradford, BD2 2BH
Tel: 01274-634493 **Fax:** 01274-634493
E-mail: info@cascoatings.com
Website: http://www.cascoatings.com
Directors: P. Stephenson (Prop)
VAT No.: GB 287 3299 12 **Turnover:** Up to £250,000
No.of Employees: 1 - 10 **Product Groups:** 48

Car Care Plan Ltd
5 Jubilee House Thornbury, Bradford, BD3 7AG
Tel: 08445-738000 **Fax:** 08707-527100
E-mail: info@carcareplan.co.uk
Website: http://www.carcareplan.com
Directors: G. Whiley (Co Sec)
Managers: S. Wright, T. Heavisides, L. Fuller, P. Stead (Tech Serv Mgr), A. Jackson (Mktg Serv Mgr), P. Morrison (Sales Prom Mgr)
Ultimate Holding Company: ALLY FINANCIAL INC (USA)
Immediate Holding Company: CAR CARE PLAN LIMITED
Registration no: 00850195 **Date established:** 1965
Turnover: £10m - £20m **No.of Employees:** 101 - 250 **Product Groups:** 82

Date of Accounts	Dec 11	Dec 10	Dec 09
Sales Turnover	17m	19m	16m
Pre Tax Profit/Loss	-647	-1m	283
Working Capital	4m	4m	5m
Fixed Assets	2m	2m	2m
Current Assets	48m	39m	32m
Current Liabilities	37m	32m	22m

Chesapeake Branded Packaging
Hollingwood Lane Lidget Green, Bradford, BD7 2RQ
Tel: 01274-420420 **Fax:** 01274-423431
E-mail: marketing@chesapeakecorp.com
Website: http://www.chesapeakecorp.com
Directors: C. Mudd (Sales), T. Whitfield (Dir)
Managers: J. McCallion (Chief Mgr), M. O'Connell (Mgr), M. O'Connell (Chief Mgr)
Immediate Holding Company: Field Group P.L.C.
Registration no: 01502024 **Date established:** 1980
No.of Employees: 251 - 500 **Product Groups:** 27, 28

Christeyns UK Ltd
Rutland Street, Bradford, BD4 7EA
Tel: 01274-393286 **Fax:** 01274-309143
E-mail: headoffice@christeyns.co.uk
Website: http://www.christeyns.co.uk
Bank(s): Barclays
Directors: N. Garthwaite (MD), P. O'connor (Chief Op Offcr)
Managers: J. Ingham (Personnel), D. Brent (Purch Mgr), J. Gledhill (Tech Serv Mgr)
Ultimate Holding Company: ALGIMO NV (BELGIUM)
Immediate Holding Company: CHRISTEYNS UK LTD
Registration no: 00847863 **VAT No.:** GB 708 3639 24
Date established: 1965 **Turnover:** £20m - £50m
No.of Employees: 101 - 250 **Product Groups:** 32, 63, 66

Date of Accounts	Dec 11	Dec 10	Dec 09
Sales Turnover	21m	21m	21m
Pre Tax Profit/Loss	2m	2m	2m
Working Capital	4m	3m	2m
Fixed Assets	4m	5m	5m
Current Assets	8m	7m	8m
Current Liabilities	1m	1m	1m

J H Clissold & Son Ltd
Old Gate Mill North Wing, Bradford, BD3 0DH
Tel: 01274-721455 **Fax:** 01274-370694
E-mail: sales@clissold.co.uk
Website: http://www.clissold.co.uk
Bank(s): HSBC Bank plc
Directors: F. O'Reilly (Co Sec), L. Cooper (Fin)
Ultimate Holding Company: TOM JAMES COMPANY INC (USA)
Immediate Holding Company: J.H. CLISSOLD & SON LTD.
Registration no: 01232206 **Date established:** 1975 **Turnover:** £5m - £10m
No.of Employees: 21 - 50 **Product Groups:** 38

Date of Accounts	Dec 11	Dec 10	Dec 09
Sales Turnover	6m	6m	8m
Pre Tax Profit/Loss	401	43	133
Working Capital	2m	1m	1m
Fixed Assets	39	116	152
Current Assets	4m	4m	4m
Current Liabilities	271	105	158

D & M Connell
Shay Dene Shaw Lane, Queensbury, Bradford, BD13 2LD
Tel: 01274-881099 **Fax:** 01274-881099
Directors: M. Connell (Ptnr)
Date established: 1987 **Turnover:** Up to £250,000
No.of Employees: 1 - 10 **Product Groups:** 14, 23, 49

Crompton Lamps Ltd
Unit 2 Marr Tree Business Park Bowling Back Lane, Bradford, BD4 8QE
Tel: 01274-657080
E-mail: sales@cromptonlamps.com
Website: http://www.cromptonlamps.com
Directors: R. Lumb (Fin), A. Hiscoe (Chief Op Offcr), K. Gorlay (Sales), M. Lewandowski (Purch)
Managers: M. Crosely (Mgr)
Immediate Holding Company: CROMPTON LAMPS LIMITED
Registration no: 05590551 **Date established:** 2005
Turnover: £10m - £20m **No.of Employees:** 21 - 50 **Product Groups:** 37, 67

Date of Accounts	Dec 11	Dec 10	Dec 09
Sales Turnover	16m	14m	14m
Pre Tax Profit/Loss	3m	1m	522
Working Capital	4m	2m	562
Fixed Assets	55	78	112
Current Assets	9m	6m	5m
Current Liabilities	4m	3m	3m

D L S J
83 Harbour Road, Bradford, BD6 3RG
Tel: 01274-604289
Directors: D. Richardson (Prop)
Date established: 1989 **No.of Employees:** 1 - 10 **Product Groups:** 26, 35

D P M Fabrications Ltd
Challenge Way Cutler Heights Lane, Dudley Hill, Bradford, BD4 8NW
Tel: 01274-660020 **Fax:** 01274-660029
No.of Employees: 11 - 20 **Product Groups:** 30, 33, 34, 35, 36, 46, 48, 51, 52, 84

Date of Accounts	Jun 08	Jun 07	Jun 06
Working Capital	74	122	177
Fixed Assets	35	45	49
Current Assets	411	481	344
Current Liabilities	338	358	166

Dantex Graphics Ltd
Danon House 5 Kings Road, Bradford, BD2 1EY
Tel: 01274-777777 **Fax:** 01274-777755
E-mail: newells@dantex.co.uk
Website: http://www.dantex.com
Bank(s): National Westminster Bank Plc
Directors: T. Steffen (Dir), A. Abbott (Dir), R. Danon (MD)
Immediate Holding Company: Dantex Group Ltd
Registration no: 00899688 **VAT No.:** GB 179 5081 32
Date established: 1967 **Turnover:** £10m - £20m
No.of Employees: 11 - 20 **Product Groups:** 28, 44, 85

Date of Accounts	Dec 11	Dec 10	Dec 09
Sales Turnover	17m	15m	14m
Pre Tax Profit/Loss	1m	53	1m
Working Capital	8m	7m	7m
Fixed Assets	1m	1m	1m
Current Assets	14m	14m	12m
Current Liabilities	946	1m	1m

Davy Textiles Ltd
Prince Street, Bradford, BD4 6HQ
Tel: 01274-651751 **Fax:** 01274-347 1237
E-mail: info@davytextiles.co.uk
Bank(s): National Westminster
Directors: M. Davy (MD)
Immediate Holding Company: DAVY TEXTILES LIMITED
Registration no: 06544194 **Date established:** 2008 **Turnover:** £2m - £5m
No.of Employees: 21 - 50 **Product Groups:** 23, 33, 66

Date of Accounts	Jun 11	Jun 10	Jun 09
Working Capital	872	763	865
Fixed Assets	297	337	391
Current Assets	2m	2m	2m

Dempson Crooke Ltd
Premier Works 134-140 Idle Road, Bradford, BD2 4NE
Tel: 01274-632911 **Fax:** 01274-626126
E-mail: sales@dempson.co.uk
Website: http://www.dempson.co.uk
Bank(s): National Westminster
Directors: N. Perkins (Fin)
Managers: P. Laskey (Mktg Serv Mgr), M. Rea
Ultimate Holding Company: MEESDEN PROPERTIES LTD (ISLE OF MAN)
Immediate Holding Company: R.S.CROOKE & CO.(PAPER SALES)LIMITED
Registration no: 00473449 **VAT No.:** GB 179 3078 31
Date established: 1949 **Turnover:** £2m - £5m **No.of Employees:** 21 - 50
Product Groups: 27

Date of Accounts	Jun 11	Jun 10	Jun 09
Working Capital	4m	4m	4m
Fixed Assets	279	279	279
Current Assets	4m	4m	4m

Denholme Velvets Ltd
Halifax Road Denholme, Bradford, BD13 4EZ
Tel: 01274-832185 **Fax:** 01274-832646
E-mail: sales@denholme-velvets.co.uk
Website: http://www.denholmevelvetsltd.co.uk
Directors: S. Boardman (MD)
Immediate Holding Company: DENHOLME VELVETS LIMITED
Registration no: 00327694 **VAT No.:** GB 179 5460 24
Date established: 1937 **Turnover:** £5m - £10m **No.of Employees:** 1 - 10
Product Groups: 22, 23, 24, 26

Date of Accounts	Dec 11	Dec 10	Dec 09
Working Capital	807	788	785
Fixed Assets	318	346	362
Current Assets	947	898	888

Dennis Price Woodworking Machinery Ltd
Unit 6 Low Moor Business Park Common Road Low Moor, Bradford, BD12 0NB
Tel: 01274-604616 **Fax:** 01274-604617
Website: http://www.dpwltd.com
Directors: D. Price (MD), J. Price (Fin)
Immediate Holding Company: DENNIS PRICE WOODWORKING MACHINERY LIMITED
Registration no: 03297046 **Date established:** 1996
No.of Employees: 1 - 10 **Product Groups:** 46

Date of Accounts	Dec 11	Dec 10	Dec 09
Working Capital	239	249	254
Fixed Assets	116	120	124
Current Assets	272	268	282

Dent Steel Services Yorkshire Ltd
New Works Road Low Moor, Bradford, BD12 0QN
Tel: 01274-607070 **Fax:** 01274-672979
E-mail: enquiries@dentsteel.co.uk
Website: http://www.dentsteel.co.uk
Bank(s): Barclays
Directors: J. Dent (Sales), J. Dent (Sales & Mktg), M. Rogers (Fin)
Managers: G. Smith (Personnel), S. Spencer (Purch Mgr)
Ultimate Holding Company: DENT STEEL HOLDINGS LIMITED
Immediate Holding Company: DENT STEEL SERVICES (YORKSHIRE) LIMITED
Registration no: 01291878 **VAT No.:** GB 184 8888 91
Date established: 1976 **Turnover:** £20m - £50m
No.of Employees: 21 - 50 **Product Groups:** 34, 61, 66

Date of Accounts	Dec 11	Dec 10	Dec 09
Sales Turnover	31m	30m	27m
Pre Tax Profit/Loss	2m	3m	2m
Working Capital	6m	6m	5m
Fixed Assets	1m	1m	1m
Current Assets	12m	12m	10m
Current Liabilities	1m	2m	1m

Drake Extrusion Ltd
Old Mills Moor Top, Drighlington, Bradford, BD11 1BY
Tel: 0113-285 2202 **Fax:** 0113-285 3328
E-mail: cporteous@drakeuk.com
Website: http://www.drakeuk.com
Bank(s): Barclays
Directors: A. Weatherstone (Co Sec), C. Porteous (MD)
Ultimate Holding Company: INTERNATIONAL FIBRES GROUP (HOLDINGS) LIMITED
Immediate Holding Company: DRAKE EXTRUSION LIMITED
Registration no: 00395431 **VAT No.:** GB 184 3385 45
Date established: 1945 **Turnover:** £20m - £50m
No.of Employees: 51 - 100 **Product Groups:** 23, 66

Date of Accounts	Mar 10	Mar 09	Mar 08
Sales Turnover	26m	25m	25m
Pre Tax Profit/Loss	1m	23	90
Working Capital	5m	5m	443
Fixed Assets	2m	2m	2m
Current Assets	11m	9m	11m
Current Liabilities	904	507	564

E. & L. (Erhardt & Leimer) Limited
9 Wool Gate, Fairfax House Cottingley Business Park, Bingley, Bradford, BD16 IPE
Tel: 0870-7559 773 **Fax:** 0870-7559774
E-mail: info-uk@erhardt-leimer.com
Website: http://www.erhardt-leimer.com
Directors: C. Harper (Co Sec), J. Brau (Dir), N. Thornton (Co Sec)
Immediate Holding Company: Erhardt & Leimer GmbH
Registration no: 01326451 **Date established:** 1977
Turnover: £125m - £250m **No.of Employees:** 1 - 10 **Product Groups:** 30, 37, 38, 44

Eclipse Colours
Unit 3f Hillam Road, Bradford, BD2 1QN
Tel: 01274-731552 **Fax:** 01274-738118
E-mail: sales@eclipsecolours.co.uk
Website: http://www.eclipsecolours.co.uk
Directors: J. Ruddy (Dir)
Immediate Holding Company: ECLIPSE COLOURS LIMITED
Registration no: 03715432 **Date established:** 1999
Turnover: £500,000 - £1m **No.of Employees:** 11 - 20 **Product Groups:** 32

Date of Accounts	Aug 11	Aug 10	Aug 09
Working Capital	492	499	388
Fixed Assets	644	681	661
Current Assets	831	800	697

Electric Actuator Co. Ltd
Bolling Road, Bradford, BD4 7BZ
Tel: 01274-732931 **Fax:** 01274-393674
Bank(s): HSBC Bank plc
Directors: D. Sharp (MD)
Immediate Holding Company: ELECTRIC ACTUATOR CO.LIMITED(THE)
Registration no: 00591396 **Date established:** 1957 **Turnover:** £1m - £2m
No.of Employees: 11 - 20 **Product Groups:** 38

Date of Accounts	Dec 11	Dec 10	Dec 09
Working Capital	904	890	904
Fixed Assets	214	218	205
Current Assets	996	939	927

Electric Design Company
Little Moorland Mill Moorland Road, Drighlington, Bradford, BD11 1JY
Tel: 0113-287 9900 **Fax:** 0113-287 9901
E-mail: contact@electric-design.co.uk
Website: http://www.electric-design.co.uk
Directors: B. Kennedy (MD)
Immediate Holding Company: THE ELECTRIC DESIGN COMPANY LIMITED
Registration no: 02613425 **Date established:** 1991
Turnover: £500,000 - £1m **No.of Employees:** 1 - 10 **Product Groups:** 44, 49, 81

Date of Accounts	Jul 12	Jul 11	Jul 10
Sales Turnover	N/A	N/A	524
Pre Tax Profit/Loss	N/A	N/A	7
Working Capital	-29	-29	-20
Fixed Assets	457	470	482
Current Assets	88	103	83
Current Liabilities	N/A	N/A	43

Elliot Musgraves
Jackson Street Off Hammerton Street Bradford, Bradford, BD3 9SJ
Tel: 01274-731115 **Fax:** 01274-722691
E-mail: info@elliott-musgrave.co.uk
Website: http://www.elliott-musgrave.co.uk
Directors: J. Hodgkinson (MD)
Ultimate Holding Company: ELLIOTT MUSGRAVE LIMITED
Immediate Holding Company: PNEUMATIC CONVEYORS TEXTILE MACHINERY LIMITED
Registration no: 05078270 **VAT No.:** GB 179 9093 05
Date established: 2004 **Turnover:** £500,000 - £1m
No.of Employees: 1 - 10 **Product Groups:** 84

Ellison Construction Ltd
3 Old Mill Yard Wilsden, Bradford, BD15 0DR
Tel: 08708-509023 **Fax:** 0870-850 9024
E-mail: info@ellisonconstruction.co.uk
Website: http://www.ellisonconstruction.co.uk
Directors: C. Ellison (Co Sec), M. Ellison (MD)
Managers: L. McMannus (Personnel), D. Drake (Est)
Immediate Holding Company: ELLISON CONSTRUCTION LIMITED
Registration no: 05401372 **Date established:** 2005
No.of Employees: 11 - 20 **Product Groups:** 35, 51, 52, 84

Date of Accounts	May 11	May 10	May 09
Working Capital	224	226	288
Fixed Assets	118	89	102
Current Assets	465	464	567

Emballator Packaging
City Link Industrial Park Unit 1 Phoenix Way, Tyersal, Bradford, BD4 8JP
Tel: 01274-668855 **Fax:** 01274-668833
E-mail: admin@emballator.co.uk
Website: http://www.emballator.co.uk
Directors: G. Dibb (Dir), P. Troop (Fin)
Managers: S. Mousegray (Sales Prom Mgr), S. Simpson (Personnel), S. Mousegray (Sales & Mktg Mg), P. Mann (Buyer)
Ultimate Holding Company: HERENCO AB (SWEDEN)
Immediate Holding Company: EMBALLATOR PACKAGING LIMITED
Registration no: 03648259 **Date established:** 1998
No.of Employees: 21 - 50 **Product Groups:** 35, 36, 45

Eurocell Building Plastics Ltd
15 Great Russell Court Fieldhead Business Centre, Bradford, BD7 1JZ
Tel: 01274-732101 **Fax:** 01274-732555
Website: http://www.eurocell.co.uk
Managers: R. Bolter (District Mgr)
Ultimate Holding Company: TESSENDERLO CHEMIE NV (BELGIUM)
Immediate Holding Company: EUROCELL BUILDING PLASTICS LIMITED
Registration no: 03071407 **Date established:** 1995
Turnover: £50m - £75m **No.of Employees:** 1 - 10 **Product Groups:** 30

Date of Accounts	Dec 11	Dec 10	Dec 09
Sales Turnover	82m	80m	68m
Pre Tax Profit/Loss	4m	5m	4m
Working Capital	15m	12m	7m
Fixed Assets	3m	3m	5m
Current Assets	29m	29m	20m
Current Liabilities	4m	4m	3m

European Lamp Group
Knowles Lane, Bradford, BD4 9AB
Tel: 08449-914400 **Fax:** 0870-445 0001
E-mail: sales@europeanlampgroup.com
Website: http://www.edmundson-electrical.co.uk/
Bank(s): National Westminster Bank Plc
Managers: A. Sykes (District Mgr)
Ultimate Holding Company: DENMANS ELECTRICAL P.L.C.
Registration no: 01144233 **Turnover:** £5m - £10m
No.of Employees: 21 - 50 **Product Groups:** 37

European Metals Recycling Ltd
Planetrees Road, Bradford, BD4 8AE
Tel: 01274-663681 **Fax:** 01274-656133
E-mail: mark.jones@emrltd.com
Website: http://www.emrltd.com
Directors: M. Hughes (Pers), C. Sheperd (I.T. Dir)
Managers: M. Jones
Immediate Holding Company: EUROPEAN METAL RECYCLING LIMITED
Registration no: 02954623 **Date established:** 1994
No.of Employees: 21 - 50 **Product Groups:** 42, 66

Date of Accounts	Dec 11	Dec 10	Dec 09
Sales Turnover	3032m	2431m	1843m
Pre Tax Profit/Loss	116m	155m	91m
Working Capital	414m	371m	167m
Fixed Assets	518m	483m	480m
Current Assets	1027m	717m	557m
Current Liabilities	124m	118m	185m

EvolutionDB Ltd
43-47 High Street Queensbury, Bradford, BD13 2PE
Tel: 01274-460008 **Fax:** 0871-9895742
E-mail: info@evolutiondb.co.uk
Website: http://www.evolutiondb.co.uk
Directors: J. Wetherill (I.T. Dir), G. Holt (MD)
Managers: C. Monkman (Sales Prom Mgr)
Immediate Holding Company: Evolutiondb Ltd
Registration no: 04335746 **Turnover:** Up to £250,000
No.of Employees: 1 - 10 **Product Groups:** 79

Date of Accounts	Dec 07	Dec 06	Dec 05
Working Capital	1	9	29
Fixed Assets	84	53	7
Current Assets	57	51	44
Current Liabilities	56	42	16
Total Share Capital	2	2	2

F D W Packaging
Allerton Mills Allerton Road, Allerton, Bradford, BD15 7QX
Tel: 01274-491013 **Fax:** 01274-481752
Directors: F. Wensworth (MD)
Immediate Holding Company: ALLERTON MILLS LIMITED
Registration no: 02205585 **VAT No.:** GB 363 8275 33
Date established: 1987 **Turnover:** £250,000 - £500,000
No.of Employees: 1 - 10 **Product Groups:** 27, 30, 35

Date of Accounts	Dec 11	Aug 10	Aug 09
Sales Turnover	11m	10m	8m
Pre Tax Profit/Loss	188	329	-119
Working Capital	971	1m	857
Fixed Assets	2m	2m	2m
Current Assets	3m	4m	4m
Current Liabilities	480	508	263

Fabricate UK
Farnham Road, Bradford, BD7 3JE
Tel: 01274-575126 **Fax:** 01274-575127
E-mail: info@fabricateuk.com
Website: http://www.fabricateuk.com
Directors: R. Shackleton (Prop)
Immediate Holding Company: FABRICATE (UK) LIMITED
Registration no: 03837418 **VAT No.:** GB 343 4962 46
Date established: 1999 **Turnover:** £500,000 - £1m
No.of Employees: 1 - 10 **Product Groups:** 48

Date of Accounts	Feb 11	Feb 10	Feb 09
Working Capital	N/A	-3	4
Fixed Assets	15	10	12
Current Assets	61	59	49

Falcon Sportswear Ltd
Falcon House Hutson Street, Bradford, BD5 7LZ
Tel: 01274-306440 **Fax:** 01274-390937
E-mail: email@falconsports.co.uk
Website: http://www.falconsports.co.uk
Bank(s): Barclays
Directors: G. Brumfitt (Dir)
Immediate Holding Company: FALCON SPORTSWEAR LIMITED
Registration no: 01188220 **VAT No.:** GB 181 0185 86
Date established: 1974 **No.of Employees:** 11 - 20 **Product Groups:** 24, 63

Date of Accounts	Dec 11	Dec 10	Dec 09
Working Capital	523	518	511
Fixed Assets	459	411	444
Current Assets	1m	929	850

Fantas-Tak Ltd
Hillside House Stewart Close, Bradford, BD2 2EE
Tel: 01274-466666 **Fax:** 01274-466664
E-mail: richardturner@fantastak.com
Website: http://www.fantastak.com
Directors: R. Turner (MD)
Managers: J. Merry (Sales Prom Mgr), S. Handforth, M. Boyd (Tech Serv Mgr)
Immediate Holding Company: FANTAS-TAK LIMITED
Registration no: 03885856 **Date established:** 1999 **Turnover:** £1m - £2m
No.of Employees: 21 - 50 **Product Groups:** 66

Date of Accounts	Oct 11	Oct 10	Oct 09
Working Capital	255	145	74
Fixed Assets	208	246	295
Current Assets	963	830	754

Farmers Boy Ltd (Part of Morrisons Chain)
Greenside Park, Bradford, BD8 9RU
Tel: 01274-549222 **Fax:** 01274-367124
Website: http://www.morrisonsplc.co.uk
Directors: G. McMahon (Co Sec), S. Clayborough (Chief Op Offcr)
Managers: J. Collett (Fin Mgr), R. Clayton (Personnel)
Ultimate Holding Company: WM MORRISON SUPERMARKETS P L C
Immediate Holding Company: FARMERS BOY LIMITED
Registration no: 01053837 **Date established:** 1972
Turnover: £250m - £500m **No.of Employees:** 1001 - 1500
Product Groups: 20, 62

Date of Accounts	Jan 10	Jan 11	Feb 08
Sales Turnover	353m	369m	275m
Pre Tax Profit/Loss	50m	55m	26m
Working Capital	111m	142m	78m
Fixed Assets	31m	41m	4m
Current Assets	142m	176m	100m
Current Liabilities	19m	24m	10m

Federal Mogul Bradford Ltd
Neville Road, Bradford, BD4 8TU
Tel: 01274-764000 **Fax:** 01274-723727
E-mail: martin.fincham@federalmogul.com
Website: http://www.federal-mogul.com
Directors: E. Swift (Co Sec)
Managers: L. Alderson (Personnel), A. Moon (Tech Serv Mgr), G. Vickers (Plant), M. Fincham (Mktg Serv Mgr)
Ultimate Holding Company: FEDERAL MOGUL CORPORATION (USA)
Immediate Holding Company: FEDERAL-MOGUL BRADFORD LIMITED
Registration no: 00106848 **Date established:** 2010
Turnover: £10m - £20m **No.of Employees:** 101 - 250 **Product Groups:** 40

Date of Accounts	Dec 11	Dec 10	Dec 09
Fixed Assets	4m	4m	4m

Five Star Windows
385 Tong Street, Bradford, BD4 9RU
Tel: 01274-680476 **Fax:** 01274-680476
Directors: N. Muffitt (Prop)
Date established: 2001 **Turnover:** Up to £250,000
No.of Employees: 1 - 10 **Product Groups:** 25, 30, 35, 39

Fleet Autobodies Ltd
Hydromech House Hillam Road, Bradford, BD2 1QN
Tel: 01274-306411 **Fax:** 01274-305546
E-mail: sales@fleettip.co.uk
Website: http://www.fleettip.co.uk
Directors: Z. Millan (MD)
Immediate Holding Company: FLEET AUTO BODIES LIMITED
Registration no: 07376811 **VAT No.:** GB 287 3880 09
Date established: 2010 **Turnover:** £2m - £5m **No.of Employees:** 11 - 20
Product Groups: 35, 45

Date of Accounts	Sep 11
Working Capital	-68
Current Assets	279

Flexiform Business Furniture Ltd (Head Office, Factory and Northern Showroom)
The Office Furniture Centre 1392 Leeds Road, Bradford, BD3 7AE
Tel: 01274-656013 **Fax:** 01274-665760
E-mail: info@flexiform.co.uk
Website: http://www.flexiform.co.uk
Bank(s): Lloyds TSB Bank plc
Directors: J. Downs (Fin), N. Saunders (Sales & Mktg)
Managers: T. Alam
Ultimate Holding Company: INFO SUPPLIER LIMITED
Immediate Holding Company: FLEXIFORM BUSINESS FURNITURE LIMITED
Registration no: 02542123 **Date established:** 1990
Turnover: £10m - £20m **No.of Employees:** 21 - 50 **Product Groups:** 20, 26, 38, 49

Date of Accounts	Aug 11	Aug 10	Aug 09
Sales Turnover	11m	11m	16m
Pre Tax Profit/Loss	25	-297	-223
Working Capital	-127	-147	229
Fixed Assets	519	654	754
Current Assets	3m	2m	3m
Current Liabilities	2m	927	2m

Folding Sliding Doors
FSD Works Hopbine Avenue West Bowling, Bradford, BD5 8ER
Tel: 01274-715880 **Fax:** 0845-6446631
E-mail: tracey.shearman@foldingslidingdoors.com
Website: http://www.foldingslidingdoors.com
Directors: P. Shearman (Prop), K. Wormald (MD), T. Shearman (Co Sec), P. Shearman (Dir)
Managers: C. Garside
Immediate Holding Company: FOLDING SLIDING DOORS LIMITED
Registration no: 04267386 **Date established:** 2001 **Turnover:** £2m - £5m
No.of Employees: 51 - 100 **Product Groups:** 25, 66

Date of Accounts	Dec 09	Dec 08	Dec 07
Working Capital	-34	-309	-120
Fixed Assets	2m	2m	392
Current Assets	793	706	1m

Formflow (Equipment) Ltd
Unit 37, Royds Enterprise Park Future Fields, Bradford, BD6 3EW
Tel: 01274-600515 **Fax:** 01274-677007
E-mail: info@formflow.co.uk
Website: http://www.formflow.co.uk
Directors: D. Bucknall (MD), D. Bucknell (MD), K. Matthews (Dir)
Immediate Holding Company: Formflow (Equipment) Ltd
Registration no: 01518624 **Turnover:** £500,000 - £1m
No.of Employees: 1 - 10 **Product Groups:** 42, 44, 49, 67

Date of Accounts	Sep 07	Sep 06	Sep 05
Working Capital	27	30	40
Fixed Assets	54	61	64
Current Assets	72	76	103
Current Liabilities	45	45	63
Total Share Capital	4	4	4

G P Elm
Unit 14 Peel Park View, Bradford, BD3 0JY
Tel: 01274-632463
Directors: G. Jovicic (Ptnr)
Date established: 2006 **No.of Employees:** 1 - 10 **Product Groups:** 35

Gamma Beta Holdings Ltd
Briggella Mills, Bradford, BD5 0QA
Tel: 01274-525508 **Fax:** 01274-521157
E-mail: furnishing@hield.co.uk
Website: http://www.hield.co.uk
Bank(s): Barclays, Keighley
Directors: J. Johnson (Co Sec), S. Chamsi Pasha (Dir)
Immediate Holding Company: GAMMA BETA HOLDINGS LIMITED
Registration no: 00185665 **Date established:** 2022 **Turnover:** £5m - £10m
No.of Employees: 51 - 100 **Product Groups:** 23, 63

Date of Accounts	Apr 11	Apr 10	Apr 09
Sales Turnover	N/A	7m	8m
Pre Tax Profit/Loss	208	-46	-185
Working Capital	224	-933	-964
Fixed Assets	N/A	1m	1m
Current Assets	750	6m	6m
Current Liabilities	N/A	299	302

Gatek
37 Kenstone Crescent, Bradford, BD10 8RY
Tel: 01274-616269 **Fax:** 01274-616269
E-mail: gatek@blueyonder.co.uk
Website: http://www.gatek.co.uk
Directors: D. Tyne (Prop)
Date established: 2006 **No.of Employees:** 1 - 10 **Product Groups:** 26, 35

George Barkers (A Member Of The Epta Group)
Highfield Road Highfield Works, Idle, Bradford, BD10 8RF
Tel: 01274-703200 **Fax:** 01274-615916
E-mail: info@georgebarker.co.uk
Website: http://www.georgebarker.co.uk
Bank(s): Barclays, Leeds
Directors: J. Gray (Sales), T. Callaghan (Chief Op Offcr), G. McKinney (Sales), S. Taylor (Fin)
Managers: N. Patel (Personnel), D. Wormald (Tech Serv Mgr), M. Fluin (Purch Mgr)
Ultimate Holding Company: EPTA SPA (ITALY)
Immediate Holding Company: GEORGE BARKER & COMPANY (LEEDS) LIMITED
Registration no: 00229443 **VAT No.:** GB 427 8624 28
Date established: 2028 **Turnover:** £50m - £75m
No.of Employees: 251 - 500 **Product Groups:** 26, 40, 52, 84

Date of Accounts	Dec 11	Dec 10	Dec 09
Sales Turnover	49m	52m	54m
Pre Tax Profit/Loss	-2m	1m	4m
Working Capital	23m	25m	23m
Fixed Assets	7m	7m	7m
Current Assets	38m	40m	34m
Current Liabilities	3m	3m	3m

Graham
Hillam Road, Bradford, BD2 1QN
Tel: 01274-735831 **Fax:** 01274-720395
E-mail: markcorbally@graham-group.co.uk
Website: http://www.graham-group.co.uk

Managers: M. Corbally (Mgr)
Immediate Holding Company: SALOU PRODUCTS LIMITED
Registration no: 03715432 **Date established:** 1988 **Turnover:** £5m - £10m
No.of Employees: 1 - 10 **Product Groups:** 40, 52

Date of Accounts	Dec 11	Dec 10	Dec 09
Working Capital	680	610	662
Fixed Assets	2	5	8
Current Assets	794	842	906

Graham Hart Process Technology Ltd
Friars Industrial Estate Bradford Road Idle, Bradford, BD10 8SW
Tel: 01274-617021 **Fax:** 01274-618614
E-mail: post@graham-hart.com
Website: http://www.graham-hart.com
Bank(s): Yorkshire Bank PLC
Directors: S. Hart (Dir)
Immediate Holding Company: GRAHAM HART (PROCESS TECHNOLOGY) LIMITED
Registration no: 01110538 **VAT No.:** GB 180 7906 47
Date established: 1973 **Turnover:** £1m - £2m **No.of Employees:** 21 - 50
Product Groups: 40

Date of Accounts	Dec 11	Dec 10	Dec 09
Working Capital	-44	-80	48
Fixed Assets	1m	1m	1m
Current Assets	1m	872	1m

Grattan plc
Anchor House Ingleby Road, Bradford, BD99 2XG
Tel: 01274-575511 **Fax:** 01274-625591
E-mail: sales@grattan.co.uk
Website: http://www.grattan.co.uk
Directors: N. Moore (Dir), W. Zimmermann (Dir), P. Anderson (I.T. Dir), M. Hancox (MD), C. West (Fin), A. Lord (Fin)
Managers: A. Thorne
Ultimate Holding Company: OTTO AKTIENGESELLSCHAFT FUER BETEILIGUNGEN (GERMANY)
Immediate Holding Company: GRATTAN PUBLIC LIMITED COMPANY
Registration no: 00249001 **VAT No.:** GB 557 1452 37
Date established: 1930 **Turnover:** £75m - £125m
No.of Employees: 1001 - 1500 **Product Groups:** 61

Date of Accounts	Feb 09	Feb 08	Feb 10
Sales Turnover	362m	385m	85m
Pre Tax Profit/Loss	-44m	27m	-76m
Working Capital	39m	63m	-117m
Fixed Assets	43m	47m	169m
Current Assets	198m	241m	100m
Current Liabilities	99m	45m	22m

Greenwood Menswear
2nd Floor Bradford Business Park Kings Gate, Bradford, BD1 4SJ
Tel: 01274-659650 **Fax:** 01274-659691
E-mail: sales@gwmw.com
Website: http://www.1860.com
Bank(s): HSBC Bank plc
Directors: R. Davies (Co Sec), T. Flint (Pers), P. Smith (Purch), N. Roberts (MD), M. Muffitt (Fin)
Managers: F. Simpson (Mktg Serv Mgr), P. Moffatt
Ultimate Holding Company: HANSON PARTNERS LIMITED
Immediate Holding Company: GM REALISATIONS LIMITED
Registration no: 04658217 **Date established:** 2003
Turnover: £20m - £50m **No.of Employees:** 21 - 50 **Product Groups:** 24

Date of Accounts	Feb 04	Feb 05	Mar 07
Sales Turnover	19m	23m	25m
Pre Tax Profit/Loss	378	113	22
Working Capital	366	-295	130
Fixed Assets	2m	3m	3m
Current Assets	5m	5m	6m
Current Liabilities	2m	2m	2m

Greenwood Personal Credit
Colonnade Sunbridge Road, Bradford, BD1 2LQ
Tel: 01274-304044 **Fax:** 01274-722715
E-mail: enquiries@providentfinancial.com
Website: http://www.greenwoodpersonalcredit.co.uk
Directors: F. Forfar (Dir), P. Crook (MD), P. Kettle (MD), E. Versluys (Co Sec), E. Versluys (Fin)
Managers: Y. Muir (Mktg Serv Mgr)
Ultimate Holding Company: Provident Financial plc
Immediate Holding Company: GREENWOOD PERSONAL CREDIT LIMITED
Registration no: 00125150 **Date established:** 1912
Turnover: £75m - £125m **No.of Employees:** 251 - 500
Product Groups: 82

Date of Accounts	Dec 08	Dec 07	Dec 06
Sales Turnover	78m	70m	67m
Pre Tax Profit/Loss	8m	11m	1m
Working Capital	15m	9m	337
Fixed Assets	453	720	1m
Current Assets	99m	85m	73m
Current Liabilities	83m	76m	73m
Total Share Capital	17	17	17

H D C Media Group (H D C 115)
Bracken House 53 Broad Lane, Bradford, BD4 8PA
Tel: 01274-656565 **Fax:** 01274-656574
E-mail: info@hdc.uk.com
Website: http://www.hdc.uk.com
Directors: D. Underwood (Dir)
Immediate Holding Company: OPTICAL MEDIA GROUP LIMITED
Registration no: 05396855 **Date established:** 2005
No.of Employees: 11 - 20 **Product Groups:** 28, 48, 61

Date of Accounts	Aug 08	Aug 07	Aug 06
Working Capital	-75	-86	-24
Fixed Assets	133	136	150
Current Assets	610	497	391
Current Liabilities	685	583	414
Total Share Capital	10	10	10

H Dawson Sons & Co Wool Ltd
Mercury House Essex Street, Bradford, BD4 7PG
Tel: 01274-727464 **Fax:** 01274-723326
E-mail: marketing@hdawson.co.uk
Website: http://www.hdawson.co.uk
Directors: S. Greenwood (Fin), J. Dawson (MD)
Managers: P. Pickles, E. Harper, N. Gunicen (Tech Serv Mgr)
Immediate Holding Company: H. DAWSON SONS AND COMPANY (WOOL) LIMITED
Registration no: 00274345 **VAT No.:** GB 698 1221 14
Date established: 1933 **Turnover:** £20m - £50m
No.of Employees: 21 - 50 **Product Groups:** 23, 66

Date of Accounts	Aug 11	Aug 10	Aug 09
Sales Turnover	34m	29m	27m
Pre Tax Profit/Loss	1m	507	103
Working Capital	5m	5m	4m
Fixed Assets	582	496	583
Current Assets	14m	11m	12m
Current Liabilities	1m	579	974

H S G Packing Cases Ltd
New Works Road Low Moor, Bradford, BD12 0QN
Tel: 01274-601137 **Fax:** 01274-678597
E-mail: richardwalton@hsg-packing-cases.co.uk
Website: http://www.hsg-packing-cases.co.uk
Directors: H. Ginesi (MD)
Immediate Holding Company: H.S.G. (PACKING CASES) LIMITED
Registration no: 01360065 **VAT No.:** GB 185 1336 62
Date established: 1978 **Turnover:** £2m - £5m **No.of Employees:** 21 - 50
Product Groups: 27

Date of Accounts	Aug 12	Aug 11	Aug 10
Working Capital	696	446	432
Fixed Assets	2m	2m	2m
Current Assets	1m	1m	985

Hallmark Cards
Bingley Road, Bradford, BD9 6SD
Tel: 01274-252000
E-mail: steven.wright@hallmark.co.uk
Website: http://www.hallmarkuk.com
Directors: B. Sullivan (Tech Serv), A. Parker (Fin), A. Shields (Pers), S. Wright (MD)
Managers: L. Hutson, E. Barnes, C. Parker
Ultimate Holding Company: HALLMARK CARDS INC (USA)
Immediate Holding Company: HALLMARK CARDS (HOLDINGS) LIMITED
Registration no: 02087658 **Date established:** 1987
Turnover: £125m - £250m **No.of Employees:** 1501 & over
Product Groups: 27

Date of Accounts	Dec 11	Dec 10	Dec 09
Pre Tax Profit/Loss	-35m	-157	-439
Working Capital	-182m	-182m	-180m
Fixed Assets	201m	236m	236m
Current Assets	86m	86m	86m

Hallmark Cards
Dawson Lane, Bradford, BD4 6HN
Tel: 01274-784200 **Fax:** 01274-687386
Website: http://www.hallmark-uk.com
Directors: M. McDavid (MD), P. Gardiner (Co Sec)
Immediate Holding Company: HM Acquisitions Company Ltd
Registration no: 01213043 **VAT No.:** GB 673 6931 02
Turnover: £125m - £250m **No.of Employees:** 1 - 10 **Product Groups:** 27, 28

Heaton Valves Ltd
Heaton House Riverside Drive, Huntsworth Lane, Bradford, BD4 6RX
Tel: 01274-700000 **Fax:** 01274-700111
E-mail: info@heaton-valves.co.uk
Website: http://www.heaton-valves.co.uk
Bank(s): HSBC
Directors: N. Wagstaff (MD), S. Heaton (Ch)
Managers: J. Hill (Sales Prom Mgr)
Registration no: 01505555 **VAT No.:** GB 343 4783 46
Date established: 1980 **Turnover:** £10m - £20m
No.of Employees: 51 - 100 **Product Groups:** 36

Henry Schein
Unit 14 Commondale Court, Euroway Industrial Estate, Bradford, BD4 6SF
Tel: 01274-474450 **Fax:** 08700-102089
E-mail: kai.turck@henryschein.co.uk
Website: http://www.henryschein.co.uk
Managers: K. Turck (Chief Mgr), K. Turck (Mgr)
Ultimate Holding Company: M1 ENGINEERING HOLDINGS LIMITED
Immediate Holding Company: M 1 ENGINEERING LIMITED
Registration no: 01059299 **Date established:** 1972 **Turnover:** £5m - £10m
No.of Employees: 1 - 10 **Product Groups:** 26, 31, 38, 40, 67

Hewitson Fabrications Ltd
900 Thornton Road, Bradford, BD8 0JG
Tel: 01274-544067
E-mail: andrew@hewitson-fabrications.co.uk
Website: http://www.hewitson-fabrications.co.uk
Directors: A. Hewitson (Dir)
Immediate Holding Company: A T HEWITSON FABRICATION LIMITED
Registration no: 04941708 **Date established:** 2003
No.of Employees: 1 - 10 **Product Groups:** 35, 48

Date of Accounts	Dec 11	Dec 10	Dec 09
Working Capital	93	124	102
Fixed Assets	18	19	21
Current Assets	182	214	167

Higgins Fabrications
1 Haigh Hall, Bradford, BD10 9BB
Tel: 01274-620186
Directors: M. Higgins (Prop)
Date established: 1985 **No.of Employees:** 1 - 10 **Product Groups:** 26, 35

A B Hobley Ltd
Victoria Road, Bradford, BD2 2DD
Tel: 01274-639619 **Fax:** 01274-641877
E-mail: paulhobley@abhobley.co.uk
Website: http://www.abhobley.co.uk
Directors: P. Hobley (MD)
Immediate Holding Company: A.B.HOBLEY LIMITED
Registration no: 00604101 **VAT No.:** GB 179 3888 93
Date established: 1958 **Turnover:** £250,000 - £500,000
No.of Employees: 1 - 10 **Product Groups:** 84

Date of Accounts	Sep 11	Sep 10	Sep 09
Working Capital	160	47	123
Fixed Assets	23	25	30
Current Assets	509	123	240

Hoerbiger Rings & Packings Ltd
Edderthorpe Street, Bradford, BD3 9RB
Tel: 01274-733801 **Fax:** 01274-736887
E-mail: mark.woodward@hoerbiger.com
Website: http://www.hoerbiger.com
Bank(s): Barclays
Directors: M. Woodward (Chief Op Offcr)
Managers: B. Martin (Fin Mgr)
Ultimate Holding Company: HOERBIGER HOLDING AG (SWITZERLAND)
Immediate Holding Company: HOERBIGER UK LIMITED
Registration no: 02072970 **VAT No.:** GB 651 7091 41
Date established: 1986 **Turnover:** £5m - £10m
No.of Employees: 51 - 100 **Product Groups:** 30, 33, 34, 36, 40

Date of Accounts	Dec 11	Dec 10	Dec 09
Sales Turnover	8m	8m	9m
Pre Tax Profit/Loss	373	-814	-18
Working Capital	2m	1m	2m
Fixed Assets	1m	3m	3m
Current Assets	3m	3m	3m
Current Liabilities	385	557	332

Holmes Mann & Co. Ltd
Holman House Harris Street, Bradford, BD1 5HZ
Tel: 01274-735881 **Fax:** 01274-306324
E-mail: info@holman.co.uk
Website: http://www.holman.co.uk
Directors: S. Rains (Fin), P. Holmes (MD)
Managers: A. Jenner (Admin Off), P. Emmery (Sales Prom Mgr)
Immediate Holding Company: HOLMES MANN & CO LTD
Registration no: 00481315 **Date established:** 1950 **Turnover:** £2m - £5m
No.of Employees: 21 - 50 **Product Groups:** 25, 26, 27, 30, 42, 45

Date of Accounts	Mar 12	Mar 11	Mar 10
Working Capital	183	138	103
Fixed Assets	408	462	485
Current Assets	1m	1m	1m

Thomas Hopkinson & Son Ltd
Victor Works Bolton Hall Road, Bradford, BD2 1BQ
Tel: 01274-582056 **Fax:** 01274-531328
E-mail: ian@triple-king.co.uk
Website: http://www.triple-king.co.uk
Bank(s): Midland
Directors: I. Peers (MD), A. Peers (Fin)
Managers: D. Peers (Purch Mgr)
Immediate Holding Company: THOMAS HOPKINSON & SON LIMITED
Registration no: 00637168 **VAT No.:** GB 179 5536 17
Date established: 1959 **Turnover:** £1m - £2m **No.of Employees:** 21 - 50
Product Groups: 26

Date of Accounts	Sep 08	Sep 07	Sep 06
Working Capital	66	36	82
Fixed Assets	380	303	194
Current Assets	286	342	309
Current Liabilities	220	306	226
Total Share Capital	15	15	15

M Howgate Ltd
1 Listerhills Road, Bradford, BD7 1HX
Tel: 01274-731660 **Fax:** 01274-394755
Directors: S. Hall (Fin)
Ultimate Holding Company: ROUND MOVE LIMITED
Immediate Holding Company: M. HOWGATE LIMITED
Registration no: 01252411 **VAT No.:** GB 181 2527 74
Date established: 1976 **Turnover:** Up to £250,000
No.of Employees: 1 - 10 **Product Groups:** 23

Date of Accounts	Mar 11	Mar 10	Mar 09
Working Capital	992	968	965
Fixed Assets	5	6	8
Current Assets	1m	1m	1m

I E Bolt & Nut Ltd
Unit 14 Alma Works Alma Street Cutler Heights, Bradford, BD4 9JE
Tel: 01274-686805 **Fax:** 01274-680361
E-mail: sales@iebolt.co.uk
Website: http://www.iebolt.co.uk
Directors: P. Kenny (Dir)
Immediate Holding Company: I.E. BOLT & NUT LTD
Registration no: 01084448 **VAT No.:** GB 179 6343 23
Date established: 1972 **Turnover:** £1m - £2m **No.of Employees:** 1 - 10
Product Groups: 35

Date of Accounts	Mar 10	Mar 09	Mar 08
Working Capital	-11	68	53
Fixed Assets	39	51	54
Current Assets	319	501	550

International Scientific Supplies Ltd
Richmond House, Bradford, BD2 1AL
Tel: 01274-720070 **Fax:** 01274-728295
E-mail: info@intscientific.com
Website: http://www.intscientific.com
Bank(s): HSBC plc
Managers: M. Bright (Chief Acct), K. Petty (Purch Mgr), A. Littlewood (Chief Mgr)
Immediate Holding Company: INTERNATIONAL SCIENTIFIC SUPPLIES LIMITED
Registration no: 04373041 **VAT No.:** GB 790 1469 18
Date established: 2002 **No.of Employees:** 21 - 50 **Product Groups:** 24, 29, 30, 33, 38, 42

Date of Accounts	Apr 11	Apr 10	Apr 09
Working Capital	222	182	132
Fixed Assets	253	236	214
Current Assets	676	711	581

Isotron Ltd
Roydsdale Way Euroway Trading Estate, Euroway Industrial Estate, Bradford, BD4 6SE
Tel: 01274-686011 **Fax:** 01274-686061
E-mail: kevin.lines@isotron.com
Website: http://www.isotron.com
Managers: K. Lines (Site Co-ord)
Ultimate Holding Company: SYNERGY HEALTH PLC
Immediate Holding Company: ISOTRON LIMITED
Registration no: 01771333 **Date established:** 1983
Turnover: £10m - £20m **No.of Employees:** 21 - 50 **Product Groups:** 84

J & K Stainless
Unit 3 D P M Industrial Estate Challenge Way, Bradford, BD4 8NW
Tel: 01274-666555 **Fax:** 0113-256 0099
E-mail: info@jandkstainless.co.uk
Website: http://www.jandkstainless.co.uk
Directors: K. Probert (MD)
Immediate Holding Company: J & K STAINLESS LIMITED
Registration no: 05609642 **Date established:** 2005
No.of Employees: 1 - 10 **Product Groups:** 35, 48

Date of Accounts	Nov 10	Nov 09	Nov 08
Working Capital	128	39	90
Fixed Assets	23	30	39

see next page

J & K Stainless - Cont'd

Current Assets	217	74	155

Jacomb Hoare (Bradford)Ltd

Standard House Trevor Foster Way, Bradford, BD5 8HB
Tel: 01274-495511 **Fax:** 01274-493310
E-mail: woolinfo@jacombhoare.com
Website: http://www.standard-wool.com
Directors: D. Bell (Dir), P. Hughes (Dir)
Registration no: 00790083 **Turnover:** £500,000 - £1m
No.of Employees: 1 - 10 **Product Groups:** 23, 66

Date of Accounts	Mar 96	Mar 95	Mar 94
Working Capital	50	50	50
Current Assets	50	50	50

Jespro 2000 Ltd

Central Mills Raymond Street, Bradford, BD5 8DT
Tel: 01274-735446 **Fax:** 01274- 394909
E-mail: sales@jespro.com
Website: http://www.jespro.com
Directors: N. Sharp (Fin), E. Sharp (MD)
Immediate Holding Company: JESPRO (2000) LIMITED
Registration no: 03698259 **Date established:** 1999 **Turnover:** £1m - £2m
No.of Employees: 1 - 10 **Product Groups:** 39, 40

Date of Accounts	Dec 08	Dec 07	Dec 06
Working Capital	22	21	23
Fixed Assets	27	33	40
Current Assets	154	153	148

John Foster Ltd

Black Dyke Mills Brighouse Road, Queensbury, Bradford, BD13 1QA
Tel: 01274-885800 **Fax:** 01274-885810
E-mail: sales@john-foster.co.uk
Website: http://www.john-foster.co.uk
Bank(s): National Westminster Bank Plc
Directors: C. Antich (Ch), D. Gallimore (MD), S. Oxley (Co Sec)
Immediate Holding Company: John Foster Of England Ltd
Registration no: 04315348 **VAT No.:** GB 779 8077 57
Date established: 2001 **Turnover:** £2m - £5m **No.of Employees:** 11 - 20
Product Groups: 23

Date of Accounts	Dec 07	Dec 06	Dec 05
Working Capital	116	116	116
Current Assets	116	116	116
Total Share Capital	116	116	116

Johnson & Akam Ltd

Old Park Court Harris Street, Bradford, BD1 5HW
Tel: 01274-726375 **Fax:** 01274-307946
E-mail: general@johnsonandakam.co.uk
Website: http://www.johnsonandakam.co.uk
Bank(s): HSBC Bank plc
Directors: A. Sadler (MD), J. Akam (MD)
Immediate Holding Company: JOHNSON & AKAM,LIMITED
Registration no: 00044985 **VAT No.:** GB 179 6680 05
Date established: 1995 **Turnover:** £2m - £5m **No.of Employees:** 11 - 20
Product Groups: 25, 27

Date of Accounts	Apr 11	Apr 10	Apr 09
Working Capital	368	342	396
Fixed Assets	303	319	337
Current Assets	603	541	575

Robert Jowitt & Sons Ltd

153 Sunbridge Road, Bradford, BD1 2PA
Tel: 01274-724664 **Fax:** 01274-740910
Bank(s): Barclays
Directors: N. Matthews (MD), R. Heaton (Dir), W. Jowitt (Dir)
Immediate Holding Company: PRO AUDIO SYSTEMS LIMITED
Registration no: 00159454 **VAT No.:** GB 665 4222 36
Date established: 1988 **Turnover:** £500,000 - £1m
No.of Employees: 21 - 50 **Product Groups:** 23

Date of Accounts	Aug 10	Aug 09	Aug 08
Working Capital	-131	-184	-272
Fixed Assets	312	345	370
Current Assets	372	380	287
Current Liabilities	N/A	N/A	111

K M K Compensators Ltd

7 Whitehall Properties Town Gate, Wyke, Bradford, BD12 9JQ
Tel: 01274-600991 **Fax:** 01274-691044
E-mail: accounts@kmkcompensators.co.uk
Website: http://www.kmkcompensators.com
Bank(s): Lloyds TSB Bank plc
Directors: I. Turner (MD), M. Cooney (Dir)
Immediate Holding Company: KMK COMPENSATORS LIMITED
Registration no: 03714968 **Date established:** 1999 **Turnover:** £1m - £2m
No.of Employees: 11 - 20 **Product Groups:** 22, 23, 29, 30, 35, 36, 39, 40, 45

Date of Accounts	Mar 11	Mar 10	Mar 09
Working Capital	328	382	367
Fixed Assets	12	16	12
Current Assets	458	540	551

K & N Packing Services Ltd

Unit 32 Fireclay Business Park Thornton Road, Thornton, Bradford, BD13 3QG
Tel: 01274-830277 **Fax:** 01274-830277
E-mail: kblackburn2512@yahoo.co.uk
Directors: K. Blackburn (MD)
Immediate Holding Company: K & N PACKING SERVICES LIMITED
Registration no: 05301218 **Date established:** 2004
No.of Employees: 1 - 10 **Product Groups:** 38, 42

Date of Accounts	Nov 11	Nov 10	Nov 09
Working Capital	28	41	25
Fixed Assets	6	6	5
Current Assets	47	66	45
Current Liabilities	15	22	16

Kashmir Crown Bakeries & Sweets

Worthington Street, Bradford, BD8 8ET
Tel: 08450-943030 **Fax:** 01274-740405
E-mail: info@kcb-uk.com
Website: http://www.kcb-uk.com
Directors: A. Saleem (Snr Part)
Managers: H. Arshad (Personnel), K. Hanif (Transport), S. Hussain (Fin Mgr)
Immediate Holding Company: KASHMIR CROWN BAKERIES LIMITED
Registration no: 02825141 **Date established:** 1993
No.of Employees: 101 - 250 **Product Groups:** 20

Kelda Group

Western House Western Way, Buttershaw, Bradford, BD6 2SZ
Tel: 01274-600111 **Fax:** 01274-608608
E-mail: kevin.whiteman@keldagroup.com
Website: http://www.keldagroup.com
Bank(s): National Westminster Bank Plc
Directors: J. Hurbert (Mkt Research), J. Napier (Ch & MD), K. Whiteman (Dir), P. Wyin (Reg Sales), S. Mcfarlane (Co Sec)
Managers: A. Harrison (I.T. Exec)
Immediate Holding Company: KELDA GROUP LIMITED
Registration no: 02366627 **VAT No.:** GB 500 5557 80
Date established: 1989 **Turnover:** £2m - £5m
No.of Employees: 1501 & over **Product Groups:** 18

Date of Accounts	Mar 10	Mar 09	Mar 08
Sales Turnover	4m	4m	878m
Pre Tax Profit/Loss	208m	84m	224m
Working Capital	-230m	-237m	-313m
Fixed Assets	1081m	1093m	4217m
Current Assets	31m	31m	183m
Current Liabilities	5m	3m	436m

Kendrion Binder Magnete UK Ltd

171 Huddersfield Road Low Moor, Bradford, BD12 0TQ
Tel: 01274-601111 **Fax:** 01274-691093
E-mail: uk@kendrion.com
Website: http://www.binder-magnete.com
Directors: H. Freitag (Dir), J. Smithies (Co Sec)
Ultimate Holding Company: KENDRION NV (NETHERLANDS)
Immediate Holding Company: KENDRION (UK) LIMITED
Registration no: 01124810 **VAT No.:** GB 180 8277 47
Date established: 1973 **Turnover:** £2m - £5m **No.of Employees:** 1 - 10
Product Groups: 35, 37, 38, 45, 67

Date of Accounts	Dec 11	Dec 10	Dec 09
Sales Turnover	3m	3m	3m
Pre Tax Profit/Loss	670	530	451
Working Capital	684	571	659
Fixed Assets	169	175	187
Current Assets	1m	977	913
Current Liabilities	202	175	130

Klinger Ltd

Klinger Building Wharfedale Road, Euroway Industrial Estate, Bradford, BD4 6SG
Tel: 01274-688222 **Fax:** 01274-688962
E-mail: info@klingeruk.co.uk
Website: http://www.klingeruk.co.uk
Directors: G. Beaumont (Fin), A. Bates (MD)
Ultimate Holding Company: BETAL NETHERLAND HOLDING BV (NETHERLANDS)
Immediate Holding Company: KLINGER LIMITED
Registration no: 01021936 **Date established:** 1971
Turnover: £20m - £50m **No.of Employees:** 101 - 250
Product Groups: 25, 29, 30, 32, 33, 34, 35, 36, 39, 40, 46, 66, 68

Date of Accounts	Dec 11	Dec 10	Dec 09
Sales Turnover	27m	23m	24m
Pre Tax Profit/Loss	5m	4m	3m
Working Capital	8m	8m	9m
Fixed Assets	2m	1m	2m
Current Assets	11m	11m	12m
Current Liabilities	1m	1m	844

Knightsbridge Ltd

191 Thornton Road, Bradford, BD1 2JT
Tel: 01274-731442 **Fax:** 01274-736641
E-mail: mmiller@knightsbridge-furniture.co.uk
Website: http://www.knightsbridge-furniture.co.uk
Bank(s): National Westminster Bank Plc
Directors: C. Addyman (Sales & Mktg), M. Miller (Prop), A. Moore (Ch)
Managers: D. Neilan (I.T. Exec), K. Weeks (Personnel)
Immediate Holding Company: KNIGHTSBRIDGE FURNITURE PRODUCTIONS LIMITED
Registration no: 00597265 **VAT No.:** GB 179 6456 10
Date established: 1958 **Turnover:** £5m - £10m
No.of Employees: 51 - 100 **Product Groups:** 26, 67

Date of Accounts	Mar 06
Total Share Capital	13

L H Plastics Ltd

Allenby House Rees Way, Bradford, BD3 0DZ
Tel: 01274-736330 **Fax:** 01274- 736332
E-mail: ian@lhplastics.co.uk
Website: http://www.lhplastics.co.uk
Bank(s): National Westminster Bank Plc
Directors: I. Thornton (MD), L. Hurvatu (Co Sec)
Managers: C. Hodgson (Personnel), K. Locock, J. Smith (Sales Prom Mgr)
Immediate Holding Company: L H PLASTICS LIMITED
Registration no: 03512451 **VAT No.:** GB 708 1014 74
Date established: 1998 **No.of Employees:** 51 - 100 **Product Groups:** 28, 30

Date of Accounts	Dec 09	Dec 08	Dec 07
Pre Tax Profit/Loss	N/A	-8	242
Working Capital	2m	2m	2m
Fixed Assets	256	294	343
Current Assets	3m	2m	3m
Current Liabilities	N/A	35	163

The Label Makers Ltd

Labmak House Prince Street, Bradford, BD4 6HQ
Tel: 01274-681151 **Fax:** 01274-651090
E-mail: info@labmak.co.uk
Website: http://www.labmak.co.uk
Bank(s): Barclays, Bradford
Directors: Z. Parfaniuk (Dir), K. Lyons (Sales)
Managers: S. Low (Fin Mgr)
Immediate Holding Company: THE LABEL MAKERS LIMITED
Registration no: 00778850 **Date established:** 1963 **Turnover:** £5m - £10m
No.of Employees: 51 - 100 **Product Groups:** 27, 30

Date of Accounts	Oct 11	Oct 10	Oct 09
Sales Turnover	6m	6m	6m
Pre Tax Profit/Loss	46	85	31
Working Capital	3m	3m	3m
Fixed Assets	3m	3m	3m
Current Assets	4m	4m	4m
Current Liabilities	722	713	540

Lancaster & Winter Ltd

Brownroyd Street, Bradford, BD8 9AE
Tel: 01274-546303 **Fax:** 01274-481143
E-mail: contact@lancasterwinter.co.uk
Website: http://www.lancasterandwinterltd.co.uk
Directors: J. Aydon (MD), W. Emmerson (Fin)
Immediate Holding Company: LANCASTER & WINTER LIMITED
Registration no: 01958906 **VAT No.:** GB 447 5448 23
Date established: 1985 **Turnover:** £1m - £2m **No.of Employees:** 1 - 10
Product Groups: 66

Date of Accounts	Mar 12	Mar 11	Mar 10
Working Capital	241	255	269
Fixed Assets	130	126	126
Current Assets	605	681	556

Last Cawthra Feather Solicitors

128 Sunbridge Road, Bradford, BD1 2AT
Tel: 01274-848800 **Fax:** 01274-390644
E-mail: jwright@lcf.co.uk
Website: http://www.lcf.co.uk
Directors: J. Wright (Snr Part), C. Holmes (Fin), S. Styles (Snr Part)
Managers: H. Hall (I.T. Exec), C. Holmes (Chief Acct), A. Littlesome (Personnel), S. Stell (), S. Stell (Mgr), Homes (Mgr)
Immediate Holding Company: LAST CAWTHRA FEATHER LLP
Registration no: OC307436 **VAT No.:** GB 180 1663 77
Date established: 2004 **Turnover:** £5m - £10m
No.of Employees: 101 - 250 **Product Groups:** 80

Date of Accounts	Mar 11	Mar 10	Mar 09
Working Capital	932	1m	850
Fixed Assets	134	94	148
Current Assets	3m	3m	2m

Lectra UK Ltd

Albion Road Greengates, Bradford, BD10 9TQ
Tel: 01274-623080 **Fax:** 01274-623099
E-mail: j.murphy@lectra.com
Website: http://www.lectra.com
Bank(s): National Westminster Bank Plc
Managers: J. Murphy (Mktg Serv Mgr)
Ultimate Holding Company: LECTRA SYSTEMES S A (FRANCE)
Immediate Holding Company: LECTRA UK LIMITED
Registration no: 01596644 **VAT No.:** GB 363 8503 44
Date established: 1981 **Turnover:** £2m - £5m **No.of Employees:** 21 - 50
Product Groups: 42, 43, 44

Date of Accounts	Dec 11	Dec 10	Dec 09
Sales Turnover	5m	5m	4m
Pre Tax Profit/Loss	438	234	33
Working Capital	398	54	-154
Fixed Assets	87	124	172
Current Assets	3m	3m	2m
Current Liabilities	2m	3m	3m

Leman Ltd

120 Dealburn Road Low Moor, Bradford, BD12 0RG
Tel: 01274-693231 **Fax:** 01274-693190
E-mail: bradford@leman.co.uk
Website: http://www.leman.co.uk
Managers: L. Marshall
Ultimate Holding Company: BALSPEED AG (SWITZERLAND)
Immediate Holding Company: LEMAN LIMITED
Registration no: 01032653 **VAT No.:** GB 127 8896 19
Date established: 1971 **Turnover:** £2m - £5m **No.of Employees:** 1 - 10
Product Groups: 72, 76

Date of Accounts	Dec 11	Dec 10	Dec 09
Sales Turnover	2m	4m	8m
Pre Tax Profit/Loss	-453	-314	274
Working Capital	2m	2m	2m
Fixed Assets	135	341	462
Current Assets	2m	2m	3m
Current Liabilities	226	123	552

Lift Truck Training Services

Spartan Road Low Moor, Bradford, BD12 0RY
Tel: 01274-608777 **Fax:** 01274-608555
E-mail: training@lifttruck.f9.co.uk
Website: http://reachup.co.uk
Managers: S. Ingham (Trng Mgr)
Immediate Holding Company: SOS RECOVERY LIMITED
Registration no: 06523079 **Date established:** 2000
No.of Employees: 1 - 10 **Product Groups:** 35, 39, 45

Date of Accounts	Mar 11	Mar 10	Mar 09
Working Capital	123	219	299
Fixed Assets	197	228	287
Current Assets	195	339	461

M Linkogel & Co. Ltd

PO Box 137, Bradford, BD4 9TF
Tel: 01274-651444 **Fax:** 01274-651668
E-mail: ian@linkogel.com
Directors: I. Crease (Sales), R. Linkogel (MD)
Ultimate Holding Company: ARKOSE LIMITED
Immediate Holding Company: M.LINKOGEL & CO.LIMITED
Registration no: 00847044 **VAT No.:** GB 179 8589 78
Date established: 1965 **Turnover:** £2m - £5m **No.of Employees:** 1 - 10
Product Groups: 23, 63, 66

Date of Accounts	Dec 11	Dec 10	Dec 09
Working Capital	1m	933	526
Current Assets	2m	2m	1m

Lindapter International

Brackenbeck Road, Bradford, BD7 2NF
Tel: 01274-521444 **Fax:** 01274-521130
E-mail: enquiries@lindapter.com
Website: http://www.lindapter.com
Bank(s): Midland
Directors: G. Browning (MD)
Managers: A. Taylor (Purch Mgr), A. Anstice (Comptroller), W. Golden (Mktg Serv Mgr), H. Liddle (Personnel)
Immediate Holding Company: TYCO EUROPEAN METAL FRAMING LTD
Registration no: 03704354 **Date established:** 1934
No.of Employees: 21 - 50 **Product Groups:** 35

Line Markings Ltd

New Works Road Low Moor, Bradford, BD12 0RU
Tel: 01274-606770 **Fax:** 01274-602802
E-mail: johnrainey@rommco-uk-ltd.com
Website: http://www.linemarkingsltd.com
Directors: J. Rainey (MD)
Ultimate Holding Company: AB GEVEKO (SWEDEN)
Immediate Holding Company: MARIEHOLM CONTRACTING LIMITED
Registration no: 01400059 **VAT No.:** GB 461 4273 59
Date established: 1978 **Turnover:** £2m - £5m **No.of Employees:** 1 - 10
Product Groups: 51

Date of Accounts	Dec 10	Dec 09	Dec 08
Sales Turnover	5m	7m	8m
Pre Tax Profit/Loss	-761	-54	91

Working Capital	1m	2m	2m
Fixed Assets	1m	1m	1m
Current Assets	2m	3m	4m
Current Liabilities	282	525	615

Lister Engineering Ltd
164 Harris Street, Bradford, BD1 5JA
Tel: 01274-721855 **Fax:** 01274-721251
E-mail: j.lister@listerengineering.co.uk
Website: http://www.listerengineering.co.uk
Directors: V. Lister (Fin), J. Lister (MD)
Immediate Holding Company: LISTER ENGINEERING LIMITED
Registration no: 03735965 **VAT No.:** GB 179 9423 10
Date established: 1999 **Turnover:** Up to £250,000
No.of Employees: 1 - 10 **Product Groups:** 27, 29, 48

Date of Accounts	Apr 12	Apr 11	Apr 10
Working Capital	117	115	120
Fixed Assets	45	52	45
Current Assets	198	210	222

Lithgow Saekaphen Ltd
Birksland Street, Bradford, BD3 9SU
Tel: 01274-721188 **Fax:** 01274-720088
E-mail: gary@qgroup.com
Website: http://www.qgroup.com
Bank(s): Barclay, Bradford
Managers: G. Kerr (Sales Prom Mgr)
Ultimate Holding Company: KUE GROUP LTD
Immediate Holding Company: LITHGOW SAEKAPHEN LIMITED
Registration no: 00468613 **Date established:** 1949
Turnover: £500,000 - £1m **No.of Employees:** 51 - 100
Product Groups: 30, 33, 48, 51, 52

Date of Accounts	Dec 11	Dec 10	Dec 09
Sales Turnover	505	271	237
Pre Tax Profit/Loss	72	87	4
Working Capital	-692	-759	-339
Fixed Assets	2m	2m	2m
Current Assets	233	110	53
Current Liabilities	55	47	10

M 1 Engineering Ltd
Commondale Way Euroway Industrial Estate, Bradford, BD4 6SQ
Tel: 01274-416000 **Fax:** 01274-420307
E-mail: sales@m1engineering.com
Website: http://www.m1engineering.com
Directors: P. Fox (MD), M. Procter (Chief Op Offcr), J. Gill (Sales)
Managers: B. Parkinson (Comptroller), N. Dixon (Prod Mgr), I. Probyn (Purch Mgr)
Ultimate Holding Company: M1 ENGINEERING HOLDINGS LIMITED
Immediate Holding Company: M 1 ENGINEERING LIMITED
Registration no: 01059299 **Date established:** 1972
No.of Employees: 51 - 100 **Product Groups:** 35, 42, 45

Date of Accounts	Sep 11	Sep 10	Sep 09
Sales Turnover	8m	8m	9m
Pre Tax Profit/Loss	303	263	469
Working Capital	1m	1m	1m
Fixed Assets	367	377	346
Current Assets	4m	5m	5m
Current Liabilities	2m	2m	2m

M & M
65 Nesfield Street, Bradford, BD1 3ET
Tel: 01274-392911
Website: http://www.metalfabs.co.uk
Managers: A. Khan (Mgr)
No.of Employees: 1 - 10 **Product Groups:** 36, 40, 48

Macart Textiles Machinery Ltd
The Grange Industrial Park Macart House Farnham Road, Bradford, BD7 3JG
Tel: 01274-525900 **Fax:** 01274-525901
E-mail: sales@macart.com
Website: http://www.macart.com
Bank(s): HSBC Bank plc
Managers: S. Turner (Chief Acct)
Immediate Holding Company: MACART TEXTILES(MACHINERY)LIMITED
Registration no: 00571194 **VAT No.:** GB 180 4332 85
Date established: 1956 **Turnover:** £5m - £10m **No.of Employees:** 11 - 20
Product Groups: 22, 27, 30, 35, 38, 42, 43, 46, 49

Date of Accounts	Sep 11	Sep 10	Sep 09
Working Capital	306	275	265
Fixed Assets	134	161	183
Current Assets	525	572	532

Mailway Packaging Group
Unit 12-16 Pitcliffe Way, Bradford, BD5 7SG
Tel: 01274-720019 **Fax:** 01274-370132
E-mail: reception@mailway.co.uk
Website: http://www.mailway.co.uk
Bank(s): HSBC
Directors: R. Bramma (MD), J. Lister (Co Sec)
Immediate Holding Company: BCLW GROUP LIMITED
Registration no: 03719252 **Date established:** 1999
No.of Employees: 101 - 250 **Product Groups:** 48

Date of Accounts	Jun 08	Jun 07	Jun 06
Pre Tax Profit/Loss	-153	7	-31
Working Capital	-213	-249	-297
Fixed Assets	4m	4m	4m
Current Assets	139	111	63
Current Liabilities	156	160	47

Manningham Concrete Ltd
Greenside Works Cemetery Road, Bradford, BD8 9RY
Tel: 01274-493311 **Fax:** 01274-548913
E-mail: info@manninghamconcrete.co.uk
Website: http://www.manninghamconcrete.co.uk
Directors: A. Tomlinson (Ch), A. Tomlinson (MD)
Managers: M. Lees (Sales Admin)
Immediate Holding Company: MANNINGHAM CONCRETE LIMITED
Registration no: 00747932 **Date established:** 1963 **Turnover:** £5m - £10m
No.of Employees: 51 - 100 **Product Groups:** 14, 25, 26, 27, 29, 30, 31, 32, 33, 34, 35, 36, 37, 38, 40, 41, 45, 46, 49, 63, 66, 67

Date of Accounts	Dec 11	Dec 10	Dec 09
Sales Turnover	6m	5m	5m
Pre Tax Profit/Loss	50	40	50
Working Capital	-41	-46	-55
Fixed Assets	3m	3m	3m
Current Assets	1m	1m	1m
Current Liabilities	233	204	235

Marble Furniture Company
Peel Park Works Peel Park View, Bradford, BD3 0JY
Tel: 01274-638811
E-mail: contracts@marblefurnitureco.com
Website: http://www.marblefurnitureco.com
Directors: M. alam (Grp Chief Exec)
Registration no: 2267422 **Date established:** 2002
No.of Employees: 1 - 10 **Product Groups:** 26, 30, 31, 33, 35, 63, 66

Martsmiths Bradford
114 Caledonia Street, Bradford, BD4 7BJ
Tel: 01274-721721
E-mail: info@martsmiths.co.uk
Website: http://www.martsmiths.co.uk
Directors: S. Ali (Prop)
No.of Employees: 1 - 10 **Product Groups:** 28, 36, 48

Matchmakers International Ltd
Park View Mills Wibsey Park Avenue, Wibsey, Bradford, BD6 3SR
Tel: 01274-711011 **Fax:** 01274-711030
E-mail: david.brook@matchmakers.co.uk
Website: http://www.harryhall.co.uk
Bank(s): Barclays
Directors: D. Brook (Fin), N. Ziff (Purch), R. Lawrence (Sales & Mktg)
Managers: D. Brawn (Tech Serv Mgr)
Ultimate Holding Company: ANDREW MERCER LIMITED
Immediate Holding Company: MATCHMAKERS INTERNATIONAL LIMITED
Registration no: 01362323 **VAT No.:** 758 9593 54 **Date established:** 1978
Turnover: £5m - £10m **No.of Employees:** 21 - 50 **Product Groups:** 24, 49

Date of Accounts	Jan 12	Jan 11	Jan 10
Sales Turnover	9m	10m	10m
Pre Tax Profit/Loss	187	115	-182
Working Capital	4m	4m	4m
Fixed Assets	183	213	239
Current Assets	5m	5m	5m
Current Liabilities	325	354	275

Meller Flowtrans Ltd
12 Millersdale Close Euroway Industrial Estate, Bradford, BD4 6RX
Tel: 01274-687687 **Fax:** 01274-687744
E-mail: info@mellerflowtrans.co.uk
Website: http://www.mellerflowtrans.co.uk
Bank(s): National Westminster Bank Plc
Directors: R. Van Beers (Co Sec)
Managers: M. Mullane (Fin Mgr), M. Alcock (Chief Mgr), M. Allcock (Chief Mgr)
Ultimate Holding Company: VADO BEHEER BV (HOLLAND)
Immediate Holding Company: MELLER FLOW TRANS LIMITED
Registration no: 04085371 **Date established:** 2000 **Turnover:** £2m - £5m
No.of Employees: 11 - 20 **Product Groups:** 37, 38, 39, 40, 44

Date of Accounts	Dec 11	Dec 10	Dec 09
Working Capital	973	673	424
Fixed Assets	38	190	282
Current Assets	2m	2m	2m

Melrose Textile Co. Ltd
Allerton Mills Allerton Road, Allerton, Bradford, BD15 7QX
Tel: 01274-491277 **Fax:** 01274-547231
E-mail: bill@melrose-textile.co.uk
Website: http://www.melrose-textile.co.uk
Directors: K. Malone (Pers), W. Edgley (MD), T. Sormus (Fin)
Managers: H. Jackson
Immediate Holding Company: MELROSE TEXTILE CO.,LIMITED
Registration no: 00932195 **Date established:** 1968
Turnover: £10m - £20m **No.of Employees:** 51 - 100 **Product Groups:** 23

Date of Accounts	Dec 11	Aug 10	Aug 09
Sales Turnover	11m	10m	8m
Pre Tax Profit/Loss	188	329	-119
Working Capital	971	1m	857
Fixed Assets	2m	2m	2m
Current Assets	3m	4m	4m
Current Liabilities	480	508	263

Meridian Colour UK Ltd
Black Dyke Mills Brighouse Road, Queensbury, Bradford, BD13 1QA
Tel: 01274-884900 **Fax:** 08712-216425
Directors: G. Riach (Dir), M. D'lorio (Fin)
Immediate Holding Company: MERIDIAN COLOUR (UK) LIMITED
Registration no: 06197691 **Date established:** 2007
Turnover: Up to £250,000 **No.of Employees:** 1 - 10 **Product Groups:** 32

Date of Accounts	Mar 11	Mar 10	Mar 09
Working Capital	-17	-20	-17
Fixed Assets	19	22	26
Current Assets	7	13	15

Metaltreat Ltd
359 Canal Road, Bradford, BD2 1AN
Tel: 01274-211555 **Fax:** 01274-221520
E-mail: metaltreat@wedge-galv.co.uk
Website: http://www.wedge-galv.co.uk
Bank(s): National Westminster Bank Plc
Directors: D. Lynam (Dir)
Ultimate Holding Company: B.E. WEDGE HOLDINGS LIMITED
Immediate Holding Company: METALTREAT LIMITED
Registration no: 00799625 **Date established:** 1964 **Turnover:** £2m - £5m
No.of Employees: 11 - 20 **Product Groups:** 48

Date of Accounts	Mar 11	Mar 10	Mar 09
Pre Tax Profit/Loss	12	12	12
Working Capital	84	84	84
Current Assets	87	87	86
Current Liabilities	3	3	2

Micron Hydraulics Ltd
Wharfedale Road Euroway Industrial Estate, Bradford, BD4 6SG
Tel: 01274-653400 **Fax:** 01274-653350
E-mail: info@micron.org.uk
Website: http://www.micron-hydraulics.co.uk
Bank(s): Lloyds TSB Bank plc
Directors: L. Plowman (Dir)
Managers: S. Doherty
Ultimate Holding Company: MICRON HYDRAULICS HOLDINGS LIMITED
Immediate Holding Company: MICRON HYDRAULICS LIMITED
Registration no: 01863010 **VAT No.:** GB 406 0779 59
Date established: 1984 **Turnover:** £2m - £5m **No.of Employees:** 21 - 50
Product Groups: 39, 40, 48, 54

Date of Accounts	Dec 11	Dec 10	Dec 09
Working Capital	1m	1m	956
Fixed Assets	105	96	84
Current Assets	2m	2m	2m

Midland Rubber Company Ltd
Unit 8 Commerce Court Challenge Way, Bradford, BD4 8NW
Tel: 01274-820268 **Fax:** 01274-820271
Directors: D. Jones (Prop)
Immediate Holding Company: MIDLAND RUBBER CO. LIMITED(THE)
Registration no: 00290475 **VAT No.:** 179 8075 12 **Date established:** 1934
Turnover: £250,000 - £500,000 **No.of Employees:** 1 - 10
Product Groups: 29

Date of Accounts	Jul 11	Jul 10	Jul 08
Working Capital	-52	-63	-65
Fixed Assets	6	8	13
Current Assets	29	22	19

Modern Health Systems
Glydegate, Bradford, BD5 0BQ
Tel: 01274-590235 **Fax:** 01274-590235
E-mail: sales@modernhealthsystems.com
Website: http://www.modernhealthsystems.com
Directors: E. Vasey (Fin), L. Vasey (MD)
Immediate Holding Company: MODERN HEALTH SYSTEMS LTD
Registration no: 04189918 **Date established:** 2001
Turnover: £500,000 - £1m **No.of Employees:** 1 - 10 **Product Groups:** 84, 88

Date of Accounts	Mar 12	Mar 11	Mar 10
Working Capital	18	6	2
Fixed Assets	23	25	1
Current Assets	33	32	28

Moore & Wright (Sheffield) Limited
32 Leeds Old Road, Bradford, BD3 8HU
Tel: 01274-223456 **Fax:** 01274-223444
E-mail: sales@moore-and-wright.com
Website: http://www.moore-and-wright.com
Directors: S. White (MD)
Managers: C. Neilan (Sales Prom Mgr), T. Redding, J. Nuttall (Mktg Serv Mgr)
Immediate Holding Company: Spear & Jackson plc
Registration no: 03465986 **Date established:** 1957 **Turnover:** £2m - £5m
No.of Employees: 1 - 10 **Product Groups:** 28, 30, 33, 34, 36, 37, 38, 39, 41, 44, 45, 46, 47, 48, 49, 68, 83, 85

Multiple Fabric Co. Ltd Arville Holdings
Vulcan Mills William Street, Tong, Bradford, BD4 9QX
Tel: 01274-682323 **Fax:** 01274-651341
E-mail: info@multiplefabric.co.uk
Website: http://www.multiplefabric.co.uk
Directors: R. Wight (MD), G. Ford (Co Sec)
Managers: Z. Desai (Chief Mgr)
Ultimate Holding Company: ARVILLE HOLDINGS LIMITED
Immediate Holding Company: MULTIPLE FABRIC COMPANY LIMITED
Registration no: 00056871 **VAT No.:** 179 8376 95 **Date established:** 1998
Turnover: £500,000 - £1m **No.of Employees:** 1 - 10 **Product Groups:** 23

Date of Accounts	May 08	May 09	May 10
Working Capital	949	1m	1m
Fixed Assets	135	117	99
Current Assets	1m	1m	1m

The Music Company
Hillam Road, Bradford, BD2 1QN
Tel: 01274-370966 **Fax:** 01274-308706
E-mail: chris.smith@tmc.ltd.uk
Website: http://tmc.ltd.uk
Directors: P. Smith (Dir)
Managers: C. Smith (Mgr)
Immediate Holding Company: T.M.C. LTD
Registration no: 02146296 **Date established:** 1987
No.of Employees: 21 - 50 **Product Groups:** 37, 61, 83

Date of Accounts	Feb 08	Feb 11	Feb 10
Working Capital	436	342	426
Fixed Assets	61	80	78
Current Assets	1m	1m	1m
Current Liabilities	N/A	693	N/A

National Flexible Ltd
Battlefield View Birkenshaw, Bradford, BD11 2PT
Tel: 01274-685566 **Fax:** 0113-252 2786
E-mail: sales@nationalflexible.co.uk
Website: http://www.nationalflexible.co.uk
Directors: J. Fletcher (Fin), G. Slack (MD), M. Thompson (Dir)
Ultimate Holding Company: NAT FLEX GROUP LIMITED
Immediate Holding Company: NATIONAL FLEXIBLE LIMITED
Registration no: 03486101 **Date established:** 1997 **Turnover:** £5m - £10m
No.of Employees: 21 - 50 **Product Groups:** 30, 31, 44

Date of Accounts	Dec 11	Dec 10	Dec 09
Sales Turnover	10m	8m	7m
Pre Tax Profit/Loss	387	-84	308
Working Capital	1m	1m	1m
Fixed Assets	334	368	435
Current Assets	5m	5m	4m
Current Liabilities	983	653	694

Niko Coatings Ltd
Unit D Springmill Street, Bradford, BD5 7HF
Tel: 01274-734122 **Fax:** 01274-309255
E-mail: info@nikocoatings.com
Website: http://www.nikocoatings.com
Directors: P. Kelly (Mkt Research), R. Davidson (Fab), M. Davidson (Dir)
Managers: S. Jordan (Factory Mgr)
Immediate Holding Company: NIKO EXTRUSIONS LIMITED
Registration no: 01543402 **Date established:** 1981
No.of Employees: 21 - 50 **Product Groups:** 46, 48

Date of Accounts	Mar 11	Mar 10	Mar 09
Working Capital	-220	-352	-332
Fixed Assets	2m	2m	2m
Current Assets	158	68	101

Norpak Ltd
Unit 3 Mitre Court, Bradford, BD4 9JY
Tel: 01274-681022 **Fax:** 01274-680318
E-mail: info@norpakltd.com
Website: http://www.norpakltd.com
Directors: A. Parry (Fin), C. Parry (MD)
Immediate Holding Company: NORPAK LIMITED
Registration no: 01550919 **VAT No.:** GB 557 0379 26
Date established: 1981 **Turnover:** £1m - £2m **No.of Employees:** 1 - 10
Product Groups: 42

Date of Accounts	Mar 12	Mar 11	Mar 10
Working Capital	-74	-75	-71
Fixed Assets	211	224	227

see next page

***Norpak Ltd** - Cont'd*

Current Assets	208	224	238

Northern Design Ltd

228 Bolton Road, Bradford, BD3 0QW
Tel: 01274-729533 **Fax:** 01274-750024
E-mail: admin@ndmeter.co.uk
Website: http://www.ndmeter.co.uk
Bank(s): Barclays
Directors: C. Adams (Fin), K. Szajdzicki (MD)
Immediate Holding Company: NORTHERN DESIGN (ELECTRONICS) LIMITED
Registration no: 02237837 **VAT No.:** 171 3000 10 **Date established:** 1988
Turnover: £2m - £5m **No.of Employees:** 21 - 50 **Product Groups:** 37, 38

Date of Accounts	Jun 11	Jun 10	Jun 09
Sales Turnover	4m	3m	3m
Pre Tax Profit/Loss	247	396	228
Working Capital	617	600	434
Fixed Assets	326	228	97
Current Assets	1m	2m	1m
Current Liabilities	122	251	205

O H S Ltd

Unit 11-17 Campus Road Listerhills Science Park, Bradford, BD7 1HR
Tel: 01274-735848 **Fax:** 0121-414 1137
E-mail: info@ohs.co.uk
Website: http://www.ohs.co.uk
Bank(s): Yorkshire Bank PLC
Directors: J. Ray (Fin)
Managers: M. Thair (Tech Serv Mgr), T. Bailey (Admin Off)
Ultimate Holding Company: OHS GROUP (UK) LIMITED
Immediate Holding Company: OHS LIMITED
Registration no: 01790018 **VAT No.:** GB 363 7686 15
Date established: 1984 **Turnover:** £2m - £5m **No.of Employees:** 21 - 50
Product Groups: 80, 85, 86, 88

Date of Accounts	Mar 11	Mar 10	Mar 09
Working Capital	934	873	712
Fixed Assets	771	398	120
Current Assets	4m	2m	1m

On The Dot Ltd

Ripley Road, Bradford, BD4 7EX
Tel: 01274-723626 **Fax:** 01274-723626
Directors: S. Whitaker (Dir)
Immediate Holding Company: ON THE DOT LIMITED
Registration no: 01181465 **Date established:** 1974
Turnover: Up to £250,000 **No.of Employees:** 1 - 10 **Product Groups:** 42, 66

Date of Accounts	Oct 11	Oct 10	Oct 09
Working Capital	-4	4	8
Fixed Assets	36	38	33
Current Assets	77	89	96
Current Liabilities	N/A	72	N/A

Optical Test & Calibration Ltd

21-23 Campus Road Listerhills Science Park, Bradford, BD7 1HR
Tel: 01274-393857 **Fax:** 01274-393336
E-mail: sales@otc.co.uk
Website: http://www.otc.co.uk
Directors: K. Dove (Dir), J. Bateson (Co Sec)
Ultimate Holding Company: OPTICAL TEST & CALIBRATION (UK) LIMITED
Immediate Holding Company: OPTICAL TEST AND CALIBRATION LIMITED
Registration no: 02638435 **Date established:** 1991 **Turnover:** £2m - £5m
No.of Employees: 21 - 50 **Product Groups:** 37, 38

Date of Accounts	Sep 11	Sep 10	Sep 09
Working Capital	652	602	574
Fixed Assets	203	174	189
Current Assets	900	899	790
Current Liabilities	N/A	45	29

Ormandy Rycroft (a division of BAXI Heating UK Ltd)

Duncombe Road, Bradford, BD8 9TB
Tel: 01274-490911 **Fax:** 01274- 498580
E-mail: sales@rycroft.com
Website: http://www.rycroft.com
Bank(s): National Westminster Bank Plc
Directors: P. Cooper (MD), K. Roberts (Co Sec)
Managers: R. Slater (Purch Mgr), C. Stocks (Sales Prom Mgr), C. Woodhouse (Sales Prom Mgr), M. Carter (Sales Prom Mgr), N. Marlow (Mktg Serv Mgr)
Ultimate Holding Company: BAXI HOLDINGS LIMITED
Immediate Holding Company: NEWMOND (NUMBER 3) LIMITED
Registration no: 00704542 **VAT No.:** GB 670 3234 57
Date established: 1961 **Turnover:** £10m - £20m
No.of Employees: 101 - 250 **Product Groups:** 40, 42

Osborn Steel Extrusions Ltd

Brighouse Road Low Moor, Bradford, BD12 0QL
Tel: 01274-677331 **Fax:** 01274-607858
E-mail: igale@osbornmetals.com
Website: http://www.osbornmetals.com
Directors: R. Taylor (Fin), I. Gale (MD)
Managers: M. Horsfield (Admin Off), M. Rhodes (Buyer), B. Bendall, R. Towers (Sales & Mktg Mg)
Ultimate Holding Company: OSBORN METALS LIMITED
Immediate Holding Company: OSBORN STEEL EXTRUSIONS LIMITED
Registration no: 04179181 **Date established:** 2001
Turnover: £10m - £20m **No.of Employees:** 51 - 100 **Product Groups:** 34

Date of Accounts	Mar 12	Mar 11	Mar 10
Sales Turnover	16m	14m	13m
Pre Tax Profit/Loss	2m	2m	2m
Working Capital	7m	6m	5m
Fixed Assets	1m	1m	1m
Current Assets	11m	10m	7m
Current Liabilities	1m	856	802

Pamma Rugs

25-29 Northgate, Bradford, BD1 3JR
Tel: 01274-739505 **Fax:** 01274-739505
E-mail: sales@pammarugs.com
Website: http://www.pammarugs.com
Directors: S. Pamma (Prop)
Immediate Holding Company: PAMMA RUGS LTD
Registration no: 07262098 **Date established:** 2010 **Turnover:**
No.of Employees: 1 - 10 **Product Groups:** 23

Paramount Learning Ltd

478 Halifax Road, Bradford, BD6 2LH
Tel: 01274-675014
E-mail: info@paramountlearning.co.uk
Website: http://www.paramountlearning.co.uk
Directors: P. Ramsden (MD)
Immediate Holding Company: PARAMOUNT LEARNING LIMITED
Registration no: 05392250 **Date established:** 2005
Turnover: £250,000 - £500,000 **No.of Employees:** 1 - 10
Product Groups: 86

Date of Accounts	Mar 11	Mar 10	Mar 09
Working Capital	-0	-0	N/A
Fixed Assets	N/A	1	1
Current Assets	15	5	8

Patchett Engineering Ltd

Ryefield Works Highgate Road, Queensbury, Bradford, BD13 1DS
Tel: 01274-882333 **Fax:** 01274-816362
E-mail: paul@patchett.co.uk
Website: http://www.patchett.co.uk
Directors: L. Patchett (Fin), P. Patchett (MD)
Immediate Holding Company: PATCHETT (ENGINEERING) LIMITED
Registration no: 03202700 **VAT No.:** GB 647 5862 94
Date established: 1996 **Turnover:** £500,000 - £1m
No.of Employees: 1 - 10 **Product Groups:** 30, 41

Date of Accounts	Dec 11	Dec 10	Dec 09
Working Capital	25	38	40
Fixed Assets	1	1	2
Current Assets	32	64	47

Pennine Cycles Whitaker & Mapplebeck Ltd

1019 Thornton Road, Bradford, BD8 0PA
Tel: 01274-881030 **Fax:** 01274-881030
E-mail: penninecycles@yahoo.com
Website: http://www.penninecycles.com
Directors: P. Corcoran (MD)
Immediate Holding Company: WHITAKER & MAPPLEBECK (CYCLES) LIMITED
Registration no: 00497166 **VAT No.:** GB 303 3474 92
Date established: 1951 **Turnover:** Up to £250,000
No.of Employees: 1 - 10 **Product Groups:** 39

Date of Accounts	Dec 10	Dec 09	Dec 07
Working Capital	49	46	50
Fixed Assets	1	1	1
Current Assets	62	62	76

Pink Pineapple

Rossefield Hall Rossefield Road, Bradford, BD9 4DD
Tel: 01274-546001 **Fax:** 01274-546001
E-mail: sales@pinkpineapple.co.uk
Website: http://www.pinkpineapple.co.uk
Directors: P. Clark Evans (Ptnr)
VAT No.: 516 4981 29 **Turnover:** £500,000 - £1m **No.of Employees:** 1 - 10
Product Groups: 27

Pitts Wilson Electrical Ltd

Cutler House Wakefield Road, Bradford, BD4 7LU
Tel: 01274-771100 **Fax:** 01274-771188
E-mail: enquiries@pwe-elec.com
Website: http://www.pittswilson.com
Bank(s): National Westminster
Directors: D. Hooley (Sales & Mktg), M. Flude (MD)
Managers: T. Oman (Purch Mgr), B. Hardy (Comptroller), R. Cadman (Personnel)
Ultimate Holding Company: PITTS WILSON HOLDINGS LIMITED
Immediate Holding Company: PITTS WILSON ELECTRICAL LIMITED
Registration no: 03312519 **VAT No.:** GB 179 7297 96
Date established: 1997 **Turnover:** £10m - £20m
No.of Employees: 21 - 50 **Product Groups:** 38, 52

Date of Accounts	Jun 11	Jun 10	Jun 09
Sales Turnover	15m	15m	22m
Pre Tax Profit/Loss	2m	2m	2m
Working Capital	3m	2m	2m
Fixed Assets	448	514	582
Current Assets	6m	5m	6m
Current Liabilities	1m	1m	2m

Premier Guillotine Systems Ltd

Fairweather Green Works Rear of 900 Thornton Road, Bradford, BD8 0JG
Tel: 01274-499832 **Fax:** 01274-547818
E-mail: enquiries@pgsystems.co.uk
Website: http://www.pgsystems.co.uk
Directors: J. Barraclough (Dir), A. Borsos (Co Sec)
Immediate Holding Company: PREMIER GUILLOTINE SYSTEMS LIMITED
Registration no: 00521530 **VAT No.:** GB 447 7124 39
Date established: 1953 **Turnover:** £1m - £2m **No.of Employees:** 1 - 10
Product Groups: 48

Date of Accounts	Sep 11	Sep 10	Sep 09
Working Capital	44	44	39
Fixed Assets	48	45	48
Current Assets	196	211	187

Press Brake Tool Company Ltd

1 Hanworth Road Low Moor, Bradford, BD12 0SG
Tel: 01274-698978 **Fax:** 01535-647013
E-mail: mark@pressbraketool.com
Website: http://www.pressbraketool.com
Directors: D. Hanson (MD), S. Hollis (MD)
Immediate Holding Company: PRESS BRAKE TOOL COMPANY LIMITED
Registration no: 06676107 **Date established:** 2008
No.of Employees: 11 - 20 **Product Groups:** 36, 46

Prestige Fibres Ltd

Ccl House Inmoor Road, Tong, Bradford, BD11 2PS
Tel: 0113-815 1125 **Fax:** 01274-542634
E-mail: info@prestigefibres.com
Website: http://www.prestigefibres.com
Directors: A. Robinson (Co Sec)
Registration no: 02939828 **Date established:** 1994
No.of Employees: 1 - 10 **Product Groups:** 23

Date of Accounts	Sep 07	Sep 06	Sep 05
Working Capital	40	8	13
Fixed Assets	1	2	2
Current Assets	76	80	261
Current Liabilities	36	71	247
Total Share Capital	90	90	100

Prima Yorkshire

31 Mortimer Street, Bradford, BD8 9RL
Tel: 01274-481222 **Fax:** 01274-482111
E-mail: mail@primayorks.co.uk
Website: http://www.primayorks.co.uk
Directors: R. Cragg (Dir), A. Birkinshaw (Fin), A. Berkinshaw (Dir), M. Bouchier (Sales)
Registration no: 04104917 **No.of Employees:** 1 - 10 **Product Groups:** 27, 28, 30

Date of Accounts	Nov 11	Nov 10	Nov 09
Working Capital	82	44	34
Fixed Assets	94	104	116
Current Assets	273	214	242

Princes Soft Drinks

Swaledale House Weaverthorpe Road, Bradford, BD4 6SX
Tel: 01274-651777 **Fax:** 01274-651088
E-mail: enquiries@princes.co.uk
Website: http://www.princes.co.uk
Bank(s): Lloyds TSB
Directors: K. Ito (Fin)
Managers: P. Jackson (Chief Mgr)
Ultimate Holding Company: MITSUBISHI CORPORATION
Immediate Holding Company: PRINCES LTD
Registration no: 02295092 **Date established:** 1988
Turnover: £125m - £250m **No.of Employees:** 251 - 500
Product Groups: 21, 62

Date of Accounts	Mar 08	Mar 07
Working Capital	13730	13730
Current Assets	13730	13730

Printing Roller Services Ltd

16 Bolling Road, Bradford, BD4 7BG
Tel: 01274-741321 **Fax:** 01274-741334
E-mail: sales@printingrollerservices.co.uk
Website: http://www.printingrollerservices.co.uk
Directors: L. Patterson (MD), S. Patterson (Fin)
Immediate Holding Company: PRINTING ROLLER SERVICES LTD
Registration no: 05162503 **Date established:** 2004
No.of Employees: 1 - 10 **Product Groups:** 23, 29, 35, 36, 41, 43, 44, 45

Date of Accounts	Jul 11	Jul 10	Jul 09
Working Capital	57	54	50
Fixed Assets	142	122	66
Current Assets	212	224	146

Pro Plus Plastics Ltd

82 Richmond Road, Bradford, BD7 1DL
Tel: 01274-744388
Website: http://www.proplusplastics.co.uk
Directors: J. Wood (Dir)
No.of Employees: 1 - 10 **Product Groups:** 30, 33, 36

Provident Financial

Colonnade Sunbridge Road, Bradford, BD1 2LQ
Tel: 01274-351135 **Fax:** 01274-727300
E-mail: info@provident.co.uk
Website: http://www.providentpersonalcredit.com
Bank(s): Barclays
Directors: A. Fisher (Fin), P. Cook (Grp Chief Exec), J. Graham (Pers)
Managers: L. Orme (Mktg Serv Mgr), R. Atkinson, L. Ashman
Immediate Holding Company: Provident Financial plc
Registration no: 00328933 **VAT No.:** GB 180 5559 52
Date established: 1937 **Turnover:** £75m - £125m
No.of Employees: 501 - 1000 **Product Groups:** 82

Date of Accounts	Dec 07	Dec 06	Dec 05
Pre Tax Profit/Loss	-74	-534	-60m
Working Capital	-7m	-8m	-8m
Current Assets	20	252	349
Current Liabilities	7m	8m	8m
Total Share Capital	52m	52m	52m

Quick Stitch

11 Clayton Road, Bradford, BD7 2LT
Tel: 01274-504790 **Fax:** 01274-504790
E-mail: enquiries@quick-stitch.co.uk
Directors: S. Ingleson (Prop)
Immediate Holding Company: BISCAYNEXPRESS LIMITED
Date established: 2011 **Turnover:** Up to £250,000
No.of Employees: 1 - 10 **Product Groups:** 43

R E W Engineering

1 Peel Park Works Peel Park View, Bradford, BD3 0JY
Tel: 01274-639133 **Fax:** 01274-639133
Directors: I. Rhodes (Ptnr)
Date established: 1994 **No.of Employees:** 1 - 10 **Product Groups:** 35

R H Plastics Technology

Unit 1a Bowling Park Close, Bradford, BD4 7HG
Tel: 01274-306060 **Fax:** 01274-589745
E-mail: sales@rhplastics.com
Website: http://www.rhplastics.com
Directors: R. Haxby (Prop)
No.of Employees: 1 - 10 **Product Groups:** 20, 27, 30, 31, 33, 38, 40, 41, 42, 46, 48, 67, 83, 84

Rapide Lift Truck Services Ltd

61 Bradford Road Drighlington, Bradford, BD11 1AE
Tel: 0113-287 9141 **Fax:** 0113-287 9141
Website: http://www.rapideliftruckservices.co.uk
Directors: P. Balaam (Dir), M. Balaam (Fin)
Immediate Holding Company: RAPIDE LIFT TRUCK SERVICES LIMITED
Registration no: 02705973 **Date established:** 1992
No.of Employees: 1 - 10 **Product Groups:** 35, 39, 45

Date of Accounts	Mar 08	Mar 07	Mar 06
Working Capital	10	10	8
Fixed Assets	10	9	12
Current Assets	20	32	17
Current Liabilities	10	22	9

Redcats UK

2 Holdsworth Street, Bradford, BD1 4AH
Tel: 01274-729544 **Fax:** 01274-729544
E-mail: sales@empirestores.co.uk
Website: http://www.redcats.com
Bank(s): Barclays
Directors: M. Truluck (Fin)
Managers: A. Roberts (Comptroller), M. Roberts, B. Naylor
Ultimate Holding Company: PINAULT-PRINTEMPS-REDOUTE SA (FRANCE)

Immediate Holding Company: REDCATS (UK) PLC
Registration no: 00106691 **Date established:** 2009
Turnover: £250m - £500m **No.of Employees:** 51 - 100
Product Groups: 61

Date of Accounts	Dec 11	Dec 10	Dec 08
Pre Tax Profit/Loss	14	136m	-1m
Working Capital	-49m	-49m	N/A
Fixed Assets	502m	503m	510m
Current Assets	6m	7m	2m
Current Liabilities	16	53	71

Redhead International

Dealburn Road Low Moor, Bradford, BD12 0RG
Tel: 01274-464646 **Fax:** 01274-464244
E-mail: mjd@redhead-int.com
Website: http://www.redhead-int.com
Directors: R. Thacker (Sales), T. Suggitt (MD)
Managers: A. Duffy (Mktg Serv Mgr), M. Wheeler (Tech Serv Mgr), K. Lawford (Personnel)
Ultimate Holding Company: REDHEAD HOLDINGS LIMITED
Immediate Holding Company: REDHEAD FREIGHT LIMITED
Registration no: 01355753 **Date established:** 1978
Turnover: £20m - £50m **No.of Employees:** 101 - 250 **Product Groups:** 77

Date of Accounts	Mar 12	Mar 11	Mar 10
Sales Turnover	31m	29m	25m
Pre Tax Profit/Loss	1m	1m	1m
Working Capital	3m	2m	2m
Fixed Assets	3m	3m	2m
Current Assets	12m	11m	11m
Current Liabilities	773	1m	1m

James Robinson Fibres Ltd

Wharfedale Road Euroway Industrial Estate, Bradford, BD4 6SG
Tel: 01274-689400 **Fax:** 01274-685986
E-mail: info@jrfibres.co.uk
Website: http://www.jrfibres.co.uk
Bank(s): HSBC Bank plc
Directors: S. Walker (Fin), K. Taylor Cole (Co Sec), J. Taylor (Dir), C. Taylor (MD), M. Longley (Sales)
Immediate Holding Company: JAMES ROBINSON FIBRES LIMITED
Registration no: 00388999 **VAT No.:** GB 183 5923 39
Date established: 1944 **Turnover:** £10m - £20m
No.of Employees: 21 - 50 **Product Groups:** 23, 66

Date of Accounts	Jun 11	Jun 10	Jun 09
Sales Turnover	16m	13m	11m
Pre Tax Profit/Loss	514	330	236
Working Capital	6m	5m	3m
Fixed Assets	4m	4m	4m
Current Assets	9m	7m	5m
Current Liabilities	897	709	533

S P I Ltd

Morley Carr House Morley Carr Road, Low Moor, Bradford, BD12 0RA
Tel: 01274-691777 **Fax:** 01274-693832
E-mail: info@styrene.biz
Website: http://www.styrene.biz
Bank(s): National Westminster Bank Plc
Directors: L. Lea (Dir), M. Edge (MD)
Immediate Holding Company: STYRENE PACKAGING & INSULATION LIMITED
Registration no: 01800539 **VAT No.:** GB 408 7639 28
Date established: 1984 **Turnover:** £5m - £10m
No.of Employees: 51 - 100 **Product Groups:** 30, 31

Date of Accounts	May 12	May 11	May 10
Sales Turnover	10m	9m	8m
Pre Tax Profit/Loss	268	394	169
Working Capital	-2m	-2m	-2m
Fixed Assets	8m	9m	8m
Current Assets	855	1m	1m
Current Liabilities	290	222	182

Servaclean Bar Systems Ltd

Gower Street, Bradford, BD5 7JF
Tel: 01274-390038 **Fax:** 01274-394840
E-mail: info@servaclean.co.uk
Website: http://www.servaclean.co.uk
Directors: C. Royston (MD), D. Roberts (Fin)
Ultimate Holding Company: BARPLAN LIMITED
Immediate Holding Company: SERVACLEAN LIMITED
Registration no: 02160311 **Date established:** 1987 **Turnover:** £1m - £2m
No.of Employees: 11 - 20 **Product Groups:** 67, 69

Date of Accounts	Feb 12	Feb 11	Feb 10
Working Capital	469	318	345
Fixed Assets	308	309	323
Current Assets	681	576	578

Shackleton Mortimer & Sons Ltd

25 Pitcliffe Way, Bradford, BD5 7SG
Tel: 01274-726890 **Fax:** 01274-390384
E-mail: sales@shackletonmortimer.co.uk
Website: http://www.shackletonmortimer.co.uk
Directors: R. Mortimer (Dir), L. Mortimer (Fin)
Immediate Holding Company: SHACKLETON, MORTIMER AND SONS LIMITED
Registration no: 01318817 **Date established:** 1977
No.of Employees: 1 - 10 **Product Groups:** 26, 35

Date of Accounts	Jul 11	Jul 10	Jul 09
Working Capital	89	106	139
Fixed Assets	9	12	4
Current Assets	226	234	306

Shaw Moisture Meters

Len Shaw Building Bolton Lane, Bradford, BD2 1AF
Tel: 01274-733582 **Fax:** 01274-370151
E-mail: mail@shawmeters.com
Website: http://www.shawmeters.com
Bank(s): Yorkshire Bank PLC
Directors: T. Peters (MD)
Ultimate Holding Company: RENFIELD LTD (BVI)
Immediate Holding Company: SHAW MOISTURE METERS (U.K.) LIMITED
Registration no: 02730480 **VAT No.:** GB 606 9779 95
Date established: 1992 **No.of Employees:** 11 - 20 **Product Groups:** 38, 85

Date of Accounts	Dec 11	Dec 10	Dec 09
Working Capital	1m	993	836
Fixed Assets	407	360	268
Current Assets	2m	1m	1m

Sherborne Upholstery Ltd

Pasture Lane Clayton, Bradford, BD14 6LT
Tel: 01274-882633 **Fax:** 01274-815129
E-mail: sales@sherborne-uph.co.uk
Website: http://www.sherborneupholstery.co.uk
Bank(s): HSBC
Directors: C. Fort (Ch), C. Walker (Sales & Mktg), A. Sparkes (Fin)
Managers: H. Haig (Tech Serv Mgr), N. Bournes (Purch Mgr)
Immediate Holding Company: SHERBORNE UPHOLSTERY LIMITED
Registration no: 00520353 **VAT No.:** GB 179 3335 37
Date established: 1953 **Turnover:** £20m - £50m
No.of Employees: 101 - 250 **Product Groups:** 26

Date of Accounts	Jun 11	Jun 10	Jun 09
Sales Turnover	21m	23m	24m
Pre Tax Profit/Loss	-267	718	185
Working Capital	7m	7m	6m
Fixed Assets	2m	3m	3m
Current Assets	9m	9m	9m
Current Liabilities	1m	1m	1m

E L Sibbles Ltd

Woolbloch House Bolling Road, Bradford, BD4 7BT
Tel: 01274-729433 **Fax:** 01274-370611
E-mail: angela@elsibbles.com
Website: http://www.elsibbles.com
Directors: A. Sibbles (Dir)
Immediate Holding Company: E L SIBBLES LIMITED
Registration no: 00482948 **VAT No.:** GB 179 6695 89
Date established: 1950 **Turnover:** £2m - £5m **No.of Employees:** 1 - 10
Product Groups: 76

Date of Accounts	May 12	May 11	May 10
Working Capital	-37	-49	-55
Fixed Assets	106	94	98
Current Assets	306	223	205

Smith Harrison Shade Cards Ltd

Unit 2 Factory Street, Bradford, BD4 9NW
Tel: 01274-683579 **Fax:** 01274-688936
E-mail: info@smithharrison.co.uk
Website: http://www.smithharrison.co.uk
Bank(s): Lloyds TSB
Directors: I. Gardner (Dir), M. Sykes (Sales & Mktg), J. Gardner (MD)
Ultimate Holding Company: GBI LIMITED
Immediate Holding Company: SMITH HARRISON(SHADE CARDS)LIMITED
Registration no: 00682290 **VAT No.:** GB 651 7929 10
Date established: 1961 **Turnover:** £250,000 - £500,000
No.of Employees: 21 - 50 **Product Groups:** 23

Date of Accounts	Jan 12	Jan 11	Jan 10
Working Capital	107	57	116
Fixed Assets	53	64	49
Current Assets	485	573	511

Richard Smith Cash Registers

866 Manchester Road, Bradford, BD5 8DJ
Tel: 01274-722473 **Fax:** 01274-732747
E-mail: richard.smith@richardsmithsales.co.uk
Website: http://www.richardsmithsales.co.uk
Directors: R. Smith (Prop)
Turnover: Up to £250,000 **No.of Employees:** 1 - 10 **Product Groups:** 44

Southern & Redfern Building Services Ltd

Forward House Mount Street, Bradford, BD3 9SR
Tel: 01274-733333 **Fax:** 01274-731300
E-mail: bernard.davies@southern-redfern.co.uk
Website: http://www.southern-redfern.co.uk
Directors: L. Horton (MD), G. Mudd (Elec), B. Davies (MD), B. Davies (Dir)
Ultimate Holding Company: 06410221
Immediate Holding Company: SOUTHERN & REDFERN BUILDING SERVICES LIMITED
Registration no: 00198113 **Date established:** 1924 **Turnover:** £5m - £10m
No.of Employees: 51 - 100 **Product Groups:** 35, 37, 52

Spectrum Computer Supplies Ltd

PO Box 199, Bradford, BD1 5RJ
Tel: 01274-308188 **Fax:** 01274-307264
E-mail: admin@spectrumltd.co.uk
Website: http://www.spectrumltd.co.uk
Bank(s): Lloyds TSB Bank plc
Directors: R. Thaxter (Sales)
Managers: M. Dawson (Purch Mgr), D. Buckley (Comptroller), S. Peale, N. Mistry
Immediate Holding Company: SPECTRUM COMPUTER SERVICES LIMITED
Registration no: 00959182 **VAT No.:** GB 179 6582 05
Date established: 1969 **Turnover:** £20m - £50m
No.of Employees: 51 - 100 **Product Groups:** 44

Date of Accounts	Oct 11	Oct 10	Oct 09
Sales Turnover	50m	48m	44m
Pre Tax Profit/Loss	3m	3m	3m
Working Capital	10m	9m	8m
Fixed Assets	1m	107	32
Current Assets	20m	20m	17m
Current Liabilities	1m	2m	1m

Spruce Work & Leisure Wear

Unit 3 Ground Floor Kyme Mill Johnson Street, Bradford, BD3 8HW
Tel: 01274-667788 **Fax:** 01274-656090
E-mail: sales@spruceworkwear.com
Website: http://www.spruceworkwear.com
Directors: M. Mehmi (Dir)
Immediate Holding Company: ARENA FASHIONS LIMITED
Registration no: 06612984 **Date established:** 2008
No.of Employees: 1 - 10 **Product Groups:** 24, 63

Stephenson Group Ltd

P.O. Box 305 Listerhills Road, Bradford, BD7 1HY
Tel: 01274-723811 **Fax:** 01274-370108
E-mail: newsmakers@stephensongroup.com
Website: http://www.stephensongroup.com
Bank(s): HSBC Bank plc
Directors: A. Barker (Chief Op Offcr), J. Bentley (Dir), M. Gardner (Co Sec), T. Bentley (Dir)
Immediate Holding Company: Thos. Bentley & Son Ltd
Registration no: 00068499 **VAT No.:** GB 500 4431 10
Date established: 1841 **Turnover:** Over £1,000m
No.of Employees: 51 - 100 **Product Groups:** 29, 32

Sun Branding Solutions

Albion Mills Greengates, Bradford, BD10 9TQ
Tel: 01274-200700 **Fax:** 01274-202425
E-mail: info@gilchrist.co.uk
Website: http://www.sunbrandingsolutions.com
Bank(s): National Westminster
Managers: D. Roberts (Tech Serv Mgr), I. Schofield (Sales Prom Mgr), J. Whiteleg, M. Kinnier (Personnel), S. Wilfred (Mktg Serv Mgr)
Ultimate Holding Company: DAINIPPON INK & CHEMICALS INC (JAPAN)
Immediate Holding Company: SUN BRANDING SOLUTIONS LTD
Registration no: 00873405 **Date established:** 1966
Turnover: £20m - £50m **No.of Employees:** 101 - 250
Product Groups: 28, 80, 81

Date of Accounts	Dec 11	Dec 10	Dec 09
Sales Turnover	22m	24m	16m
Pre Tax Profit/Loss	667	3m	263
Working Capital	8m	7m	5m
Fixed Assets	851	1m	1m
Current Assets	12m	13m	8m
Current Liabilities	2m	3m	2m

Sunbridge Electrical Wholesalers Ltd

Duncan Street, Bradford, BD5 0EQ
Tel: 01274-735329 **Fax:** 01274-737539
E-mail: sunbrd@rexelsenate.co.uk
Website: http://www.rexelsenate.co.uk
Directors: P. Massard (Fin)
Managers: T. Bairestow (District Mgr)
Ultimate Holding Company: RAY INVESTMENT SARL (LUXEMBOURG)
Immediate Holding Company: SUNBRIDGE ELECTRICAL WHOLESALERS LIMITED
Registration no: 01036666 **VAT No.:** GB 587 2692 88
Date established: 1971 **Turnover:** £5m - £10m **No.of Employees:** 1 - 10
Product Groups: 77

Date of Accounts	Dec 10	Dec 09
Working Capital	-411	-411
Fixed Assets	469	469
Current Assets	638	638

Switch2 Energy Solutions

High Mill Mill Street, Cullingworth, Bradford, BD13 5HA
Tel: 0871-4234242 **Fax:** 0871-4236161
E-mail: sales@switch2.com
Website: http://www.switch2.com
Bank(s): Lloyds
Directors: J. Clare (MD)
Managers: I. Allan (I.T. Exec), M. Thomson (Sales Prom), M. Thompson (Mktg Serv Mgr)
Immediate Holding Company: Switch2 Metering Ltd
Registration no: 02409803 **VAT No.:** GB 405 9010 84
Date established: 2003 **Turnover:** £2m - £5m **No.of Employees:** 21 - 50
Product Groups: 37, 38

Date of Accounts	Mar 08	Dec 06	Dec 05
Sales Turnover	9220	N/A	3966
Pre Tax Profit/Loss	544	N/A	99
Working Capital	1154	787	976
Fixed Assets	480	478	306
Current Assets	2466	1527	2046
Current Liabilities	1313	740	1070
Total Share Capital	300	300	300
ROCE% (Return on Capital Employed)	33.3		7.7
ROT% (Return on Turnover)	5.9		2.5

John Sylvester Fasteners & Plastics Ltd

Vulcan Street, Bradford, BD4 9QU
Tel: 01274-684040 **Fax:** 01274-684240
E-mail: sales@jsylvester.co.uk
Website: http://www.jsylvester.co.uk
Bank(s): Barclays, 10 Market Street
Directors: A. Sylvester (Fin)
Ultimate Holding Company: JOHN SYLVESTER ENGINEERING COMPANY LIMITED
Immediate Holding Company: JOHN SYLVESTER (FASTENERS & PLASTICS) LIMITED
Registration no: 00893725 **VAT No.:** GB 179 9987 61
Date established: 1966 **Turnover:** £2m - £5m **No.of Employees:** 21 - 50
Product Groups: 30, 35, 36, 66

Date of Accounts	Mar 12	Mar 11	Mar 10
Working Capital	611	613	617
Fixed Assets	36	33	30
Current Assets	801	741	741

T W P For Packaging Ltd

Shelby House Westgate Hill Street, Bradford, BD4 0SJ
Tel: 01274-680333 **Fax:** 01274-653500
E-mail: clive.thompson@twpforpackaging.co.uk
Website: http://www.twpforpackaging.co.uk
Directors: C. Thompson (MD)
Immediate Holding Company: TWP PACKAGING SOLUTIONS LTD
Registration no: 05821908 **Date established:** 2011
No.of Employees: 1 - 10 **Product Groups:** 27, 28, 30, 48, 76

Date of Accounts	Feb 08	Feb 09	Feb 07
Working Capital	-216	-258	N/A
Fixed Assets	254	363	N/A
Current Assets	399	585	N/A

Technology Media

PO Box 802, Bradford, BD10 9WX
Tel: 08432-899254
E-mail: sales@tekno-media.com
Website: http://www.tekno-media.com
Managers: G. Blackmore (Sales Prom Mgr), S. Wood (Sales & Mktg Mg)
Turnover: Up to £250,000 **No.of Employees:** 1 - 10 **Product Groups:** 44, 79

Thermocable Ltd

Pasture Lane Clayton, Bradford, BD14 6LU
Tel: 01274-882359 **Fax:** 01274-882229
E-mail: info@thermocable.com
Website: http://www.thermocable.com
Bank(s): Yorkshire Bank
Directors: A. Rayner (MD), H. Rayner (Co Sec)
Immediate Holding Company: THERMOCARE LIMITED
Registration no: 03654218 **Date established:** 1998
Turnover: £250,000 - £500,000 **No.of Employees:** 21 - 50
Product Groups: 29, 30

Thermocrete
Mortimer Street, Bradford, BD8 9RL
Tel: 01274-544442 **Fax:** 01274-484448
E-mail: info@thermocrete.com
Website: http://www.thermocrete.com
Directors: A. Barnes (Ch)
Immediate Holding Company: THERMOCRETE LIMITED
Registration no: 02039670 **Date established:** 1986 **Turnover:** £1m - £2m
No.of Employees: 1 - 10 **Product Groups:** 32

Date of Accounts	Mar 99	Mar 98	Mar 11
Working Capital	-0	-0	N/A

Thermsave Welding Ltd
9 Wavertree Park Gardens Low Moor, Bradford, BD12 0UY
Tel: 01274-424478 **Fax:** 01274-424479
E-mail: robert@thermsavewelding.co.uk
Website: http://www.thermsavewelding.co.uk
Directors: R. Carter (Dir), R. Carter (Prop)
Immediate Holding Company: THERMSAVE WELDING LIMITED
Registration no: 05983585 **Date established:** 2006
Turnover: Up to £250,000 **No.of Employees:** 1 - 10 **Product Groups:** 48

Date of Accounts	Dec 10	Dec 09	Dec 08
Working Capital	10	13	15
Fixed Assets	15	18	14
Current Assets	38	64	61

A G Thomas Bradford Ltd
Tompion House Heaton Road, Bradford, BD8 8RB
Tel: 01274-497171 **Fax:** 01274-547407
E-mail: info@agthomas.co.uk
Website: http://www.agthomas.co.uk
Directors: S. Thomas (Dir)
Immediate Holding Company: A G THOMAS (BRADFORD) LIMITED
Registration no: 00414605 **VAT No.:** GB 179 3633 29
Date established: 1946 **Turnover:** £1m - £2m **No.of Employees:** 11 - 20
Product Groups: 49, 65

Date of Accounts	Dec 11	Dec 10	Dec 09
Working Capital	105	108	113
Fixed Assets	5	6	8
Current Assets	353	370	380

Thomas Wright-Thorite
Thorite House Laisterdyke, Bradford, BD4 8BZ
Tel: 01274-663471 **Fax:** 01274-668296
E-mail: info@thorite.co.uk
Website: http://www.thorite.co.uk
Bank(s): National Westminster
Directors: I. Gurmin (Fin), S. Wright (MD), R. Gowler (Sales), S. Ryan (MD)
Managers: G. Stephenson (Buyer)
Ultimate Holding Company: 00177707
Immediate Holding Company: THOMAS WRIGHT AIR CENTRES LIMITED
Registration no: 01009759 **VAT No.:** GB 179 3058 37
Date established: 1971 **Turnover:** £10m - £20m
No.of Employees: 51 - 100 **Product Groups:** 35, 36, 38, 40

Date of Accounts	Mar 10	Mar 09	Mar 08
Working Capital	70	70	70
Current Assets	70	70	70

Ties n Tags
6 Penrose Drive Great Horton, Bradford, BD7 4RW
Tel: 01274-504284 **Fax:** 01274-521523
E-mail: sales@tiesntags.co.uk
Website: http://www.tiesntags.co.uk
Directors: S. Robertshaw (Prop)
Date established: 2006 **Turnover:** Up to £250,000
No.of Employees: 1 - 10 **Product Groups:** 23, 24, 30, 49, 63

Tong Glass & Windows Ltd
Highfield Tong Street, Bradford, BD4 9PP
Tel: 01274-681600 **Fax:** 01274-681009
Directors: J. O' Malley (Prop)
Immediate Holding Company: TONG GLASS & WINDOWS LIMITED
Registration no: 05018483 **Date established:** 2004
No.of Employees: 1 - 10 **Product Groups:** 25, 35, 36

Date of Accounts	Jan 12	Jan 11	Jan 10
Working Capital	21	64	27
Fixed Assets	27	25	11
Current Assets	125	196	103

Topside Group
17 Carrbottom Road, Bradford, BD5 9AG
Tel: 01274-736970 **Fax:** 01274- 736978
E-mail: info@topside.co.uk
Website: http://www.topside.co.uk
Directors: I. Hutchison (MD)
No.of Employees: 1 - 10 **Product Groups:** 30, 33, 35, 52

Travis Perkins plc
Fairfield Street, Bradford, BD4 9QP
Tel: 01274-681065 **Fax:** 01274-688843
E-mail: bradford@travisperkins.co.uk
Website: http://www.travisperkins.co.uk
Managers: M. Bedford (District Mgr)
Immediate Holding Company: TRAVIS PERKINS PLC
Registration no: 00824821 **VAT No.:** GB 408 5567 37
Date established: 1964 **No.of Employees:** 1 - 10 **Product Groups:** 66

Date of Accounts	Dec 11	Dec 10	Dec 09
Sales Turnover	4779m	3153m	2931m
Pre Tax Profit/Loss	270m	197m	213m
Working Capital	133m	179m	248m
Fixed Assets	2771m	2749m	2108m
Current Assets	1421m	1329m	1035m
Current Liabilities	473m	412m	109m

United Steel Services Leeds Ltd
282 Cutler Heights Lane, Bradford, BD4 9HU
Tel: 01274-654254 **Fax:** 01274-688208
E-mail: united@steels.co.uk
Website: http://www.united-steel-leeds.co.uk
Directors: J. Barrett (MD), J. Barrett (Dir), P. Chasney (Ch)
Managers: P. Chasney (Chief Acct), A. Heeley (Personnel), D. Redgewick (Sales Prom Mgr)
Ultimate Holding Company: 02755663
Immediate Holding Company: UNITED STEEL SERVICES (LEEDS) LIMITED
Registration no: 02878515 **VAT No.:** GB 601 1489 41
Date established: 1993 **Turnover:** £10m - £20m **No.of Employees:** 1 - 10
Product Groups: 66

Date of Accounts	Sep 08	Sep 07	Sep 06
Sales Turnover	N/A	10m	8m
Pre Tax Profit/Loss	N/A	507	474
Working Capital	1	1	1
Current Assets	1	1	1

Univer Manufacturing Company
Univer House 6 Station Road, Bradford, BD1 4SF
Tel: 01274-725777 **Fax:** 01274-725111
E-mail: cpix@univer.co.uk
Website: http://www.univer.co.uk
Directors: D. Pix (Co Sec), C. Pix (Dir), C. Pix (Sales)
Managers: E. Phillip, A. Pinto (Personnel), C. Thurman (Tech Serv Mgr), S. Littlewood (Purch Mgr)
Immediate Holding Company: UNIVER MANUFACTURING COMPANY LTD
Registration no: 02208794 **Date established:** 1987 **Turnover:** £5m - £10m
No.of Employees: 21 - 50 **Product Groups:** 35, 37, 38, 40, 46, 84

Date of Accounts	Dec 11	Dec 10	Dec 09
Working Capital	1m	2m	1m
Fixed Assets	1m	867	913
Current Assets	2m	2m	2m

Universal Carbon Fibres Ltd
Station Mills Station Road, Wyke, Bradford, BD12 8LA
Tel: 01274-600600 **Fax:** 01274-711666
E-mail: info@ucfltd.co.uk
Website: http://www.ucfltd.co.uk
Directors: J. Parkinson (Fin)
Managers: V. Bowen
Ultimate Holding Company: UNIVERSAL CARBON FIBRES (HOLDINGS) LIMITED
Immediate Holding Company: UNIVERSAL CARBON FIBRES LIMITED
Registration no: 05447389 **VAT No.:** GB 588 8960 53
Date established: 2005 **Turnover:** £2m - £5m **No.of Employees:** 21 - 50
Product Groups: 23, 40

Date of Accounts	Jun 11	Jun 10	Jun 09
Working Capital	470	314	252
Fixed Assets	93	62	81
Current Assets	1m	974	639

USB Extra Limited
Carlisle Business Centre 60 Carlisle Road, Bradford, BD8 8BD
Tel: 01274-404594 **Fax:** 0800-0322703
E-mail: info@usb-extra.co.uk
Website: http://www.usb-extra.co.uk
Directors: A. Hammond (Sales)
Registration no: 05726066 **Date established:** 2006
No.of Employees: 1 - 10 **Product Groups:** 49

Victor Manufacturing Ltd
Lonsdale Works Gibson Street, Bradford, BD3 9TF
Tel: 01274-722125 **Fax:** 01274-307082
E-mail: email@victormanufacturing.co.uk
Website: http://www.victoronline.co.uk
Bank(s): Barclays
Directors: A. Gibson (Sales), P. Crossley (I.T. Dir), C. Foster (Fin), M. Shaddock (MD)
Managers: P. Brewin (Mktg Serv Mgr), J. Hopkinson (Admin Off)
Immediate Holding Company: VICTOR MANUFACTURING LIMITED
Registration no: 00390738 **Date established:** 1944 **Turnover:** £5m - £10m
No.of Employees: 51 - 100 **Product Groups:** 40, 67

Date of Accounts	Mar 12	Mar 09	Mar 10
Sales Turnover	7m	N/A	5m
Pre Tax Profit/Loss	427	252	-332
Working Capital	4m	4m	4m
Fixed Assets	525	640	388
Current Assets	6m	5m	5m
Current Liabilities	706	405	324

Vishay PM Onboard Ltd
Airedale House Canal Road, Bradford, BD2 1AG
Tel: 01274-771177 **Fax:** 01274-781178
E-mail: matthew.burridge@pmonboard.com
Website: http://www.pmonboard.com
Directors: A. Tearne (Fin), A. Kapil (Sales), M. Burridge (Dir)
Managers: R. Simons (Tech Serv Mgr), L. Bell (Personnel)
Ultimate Holding Company: VISHAY INTERTECHNOLOGY INC (USA)
Immediate Holding Company: VISHAY PM ONBOARD LIMITED
Registration no: 03001454 **Date established:** 1994 **Turnover:** £5m - £10m
No.of Employees: 21 - 50 **Product Groups:** 38, 42

Date of Accounts	Dec 11	Dec 10	Dec 09
Sales Turnover	8m	7m	7m
Pre Tax Profit/Loss	474	-163	-703
Working Capital	4m	3m	3m
Fixed Assets	3m	3m	3m
Current Assets	5m	5m	5m
Current Liabilities	492	392	343

W M Spence Ltd
PO Box 344 Laurel Works Laurel Street, Bradford, BD3 9TH
Tel: 01274-661824 **Fax:** 01274-656032
E-mail: enquiries@wmspence.co.uk
Website: http://www.wmspence.co.uk
Directors: T. Davis (Works), S. Jackson (Dir)
Managers: R. Hunter (Chief Acct)
VAT No.: GB 181 0018 08 **Turnover:** £1m - £2m **No.of Employees:** 11 - 20
Product Groups: 48

Walker & Holmes Ltd
Linton Street, Bradford, BD4 7EZ
Tel: 01274-728655 **Fax:** 01274-723678
E-mail: walkerholmesltd@aol.com
Website: http://www.walkerhomes.co.uk
Directors: M. Lee (Fin), P. Lee (MD)
Immediate Holding Company: WALKER AND HOLMES LIMITED
Registration no: 00692306 **VAT No.:** GB 180 1213 11
Date established: 1961 **Turnover:** £250,000 - £500,000
No.of Employees: 1 - 10 **Product Groups:** 52, 54, 84

Date of Accounts	Mar 12	Mar 11	Mar 10
Working Capital	-42	-33	-34
Fixed Assets	50	51	52
Current Assets	90	76	37

Francis Ward Ltd
219-221 Bowling Back Lane, Bradford, BD4 8SJ
Tel: 01274-707030 **Fax:** 01274-724704
E-mail: info@francisward.com
Website: http://www.francisward.com
Bank(s): HSBC Bank plc
Directors: V. Kliene (Dir)
Managers: W. Birtwistle
Immediate Holding Company: FRANCIS WARD LIMITED
Registration no: 01860646 **Date established:** 1984 **Turnover:** £2m - £5m
No.of Employees: 11 - 20 **Product Groups:** 30

Date of Accounts	Jan 12	Jan 11	Jan 10
Working Capital	-106	103	58
Fixed Assets	1m	1m	1m
Current Assets	597	600	450

Web M & E Products Ltd
Unit 5 Bingley Street, Bradford, BD8 9BU
Tel: 01274-547260 **Fax:** 01274-481345
E-mail: david@web-ltd.co.uk
Website: http://www.web-ltd.co.uk
Bank(s): Barclays
Directors: D. Thompson (Dir)
Ultimate Holding Company: BHJT (HOLDINGS) LIMITED
Immediate Holding Company: WEB (M&E) PRODUCTS LIMITED
Registration no: 03681884 **VAT No.:** GB 179 3282 32
Date established: 1998 **Turnover:** £1m - £2m **No.of Employees:** 11 - 20
Product Groups: 67

Date of Accounts	Apr 11	Apr 10	Apr 09
Working Capital	67	68	72
Fixed Assets	299	322	356
Current Assets	1m	1m	786

Wetherby Engineering Co. Ltd
Britannia Mills Portland Street, Bradford, BD5 0DW
Tel: 01274-783434 **Fax:** 01274-390527
E-mail: charles@wetherby-engineering.co.uk
Website: http://www.wetherby-engineering.co.uk
Bank(s): HSBC Bank plc
Directors: C. Wyatt (MD)
Immediate Holding Company: WETHERBY ENGINEERING COMPANY LIMITED
Registration no: 00825128 **Date established:** 1964 **Turnover:** £1m - £2m
No.of Employees: 21 - 50 **Product Groups:** 48

Date of Accounts	Oct 11	Oct 10	Oct 09
Working Capital	592	545	570
Fixed Assets	137	153	168
Current Assets	794	750	729

Whitaker & Co Denholme Ltd
Denholme Gate, Bradford, BD13 4EW
Tel: 01274-833611 **Fax:** 01274-833782
E-mail: carol.whitaker@whitakerandco.co.uk
Website: http://www.whitakerandco.co.uk
Directors: A. Cam (I.T. Dir), B. Jennings (Co Sec), G. Winnard (Pers), C. Whitaker (MD)
Managers: G. Winnard
Immediate Holding Company: WHITAKER & CO. (DENHOLME) LIMITED
Registration no: 00531197 **Date established:** 1954 **Turnover:** £2m - £5m
No.of Employees: 51 - 100 **Product Groups:** 26, 35

Date of Accounts	Dec 07
Sales Turnover	3116
Pre Tax Profit/Loss	-308
Working Capital	27
Fixed Assets	1039
Current Assets	1222
Current Liabilities	1194
Total Share Capital	30
ROCE% (Return on Capital Employed)	-28.9

M Widdup & Sons Ltd
Tunwell Mills Tunwell Lane, Bradford, BD2 2HG
Tel: 01274-638838 **Fax:** 01274-626185
E-mail: enquiries@widdup.co.uk
Website: http://www.widdup.co.uk
Bank(s): National Westminster Bank Plc
Directors: G. Widdup (Dir)
Immediate Holding Company: M WIDDUP & SONS LIMITED
Registration no: 00490809 **Date established:** 1951 **Turnover:** £1m - £2m
No.of Employees: 11 - 20 **Product Groups:** 28

Date of Accounts	Mar 12	Mar 11	Mar 10
Working Capital	568	575	598
Fixed Assets	113	142	150
Current Assets	862	774	805
Current Liabilities	36	27	19

Windsor Engineering
Wharfedale Road Euroway Industrial Estate, Bradford, BD4 6SG
Tel: 01274-473220
E-mail: pbenton@windsor-mh.co.uk
Website: http://www.windsorkomatsu.co.uk
Managers: P. Benton (Mgr)
No.of Employees: 1 - 10 **Product Groups:** 35, 39, 45

Date of Accounts	Jun 11	Jun 10	Jun 09
Working Capital	-277	-165	-176
Fixed Assets	457	348	348
Current Assets	11	16	N/A

World Textile Publications Ltd
Perkins House 1 Longlands Street, Bradford, BD1 2TP
Tel: 01274-378800 **Fax:** 01274-378811
E-mail: mjarvis@world-textile.net
Website: http://www.ingeletex.com
Directors: M. Jarvis (MD), T. Hempenstall (Dir), P. Vincent (Dir), M. Andresco (Sales), K. Higginbottom (MD), G. Moss (Co Sec)
Managers: G. Welsh (Mktg Serv Mgr), M. Keighley (Publishing), A. Wilson (Publishing), A. Thornton (Publishing), P. Owen (Publishing)
Ultimate Holding Company: WORLD TEXTILE INFORMATION NETWORK LIMITED
Immediate Holding Company: LONGLANDS MEDIA LIMITED
Registration no: 02426502 **VAT No.:** GB 556 9452 03
Date established: 1989 **No.of Employees:** 11 - 20 **Product Groups:** 28

Date of Accounts	Dec 10	Dec 09	Dec 08
Working Capital	-243	-275	-267
Fixed Assets	241	272	295
Current Assets	212	388	468

Wrapid Manufacturing Ltd
250 Thornton Road, Bradford, BD1 2LB
Tel: 01274-220220 **Fax:** 01274-736195
E-mail: sales@wrapid.co.uk
Website: http://www.wrapid.co.uk
Bank(s): Barclays

Directors: N. Birkinhead (Co Sec), W. Birkinhead (Dir)
Managers: V. Seed, T. Fletcher (Tech Serv Mgr), S. York (Fin Mgr)
Ultimate Holding Company: WRAPID GROUP LIMITED
Immediate Holding Company: WRAPID HOLDINGS LIMITED
Registration no: 02067210 Date established: 1986
Turnover: £10m - £20m No.of Employees: 101 - 250
Product Groups: 30, 42, 44

Date of Accounts	Dec 11	Dec 10	Dec 09
Pre Tax Profit/Loss	639	504	301
Working Capital	16	16	16
Current Assets	16	27	27

Xtex Polythene

Spring Mills Main Street, Wilsden, Bradford, BD15 0DX
Tel: 01535-272871 Fax: 01535-275702
E-mail: sales@xtex.co.uk
Website: http://www.xtex.co.uk
Directors: R. Bentley (MD), J. Clarkson (Co Sec)
Immediate Holding Company: XTEX POLYTHENE LIMITED
Registration no: 01519288 VAT No.: 343 5161 75 Date established: 1980
No.of Employees: 1 - 10 Product Groups: 30

Date of Accounts	Jul 11	Jul 10	Jul 09
Working Capital	313	303	295
Fixed Assets	95	88	95
Current Assets	598	648	502

Yorkshire Braiders

Old Mill Victoria Road, Bradford, BD2 2BH
Tel: 01274-626528 Fax: 01274-626528
Directors: J. Spurden (Prop)
Date established: 1990 No.of Employees: 1 - 10 Product Groups: 36, 40

Yorkshire Building Society

Yorkshire House Yorkshire Drive, Bradford, BD5 8LJ
Tel: 01274-740740 Fax: 01274-652134
E-mail: atgosling@ybs.co.uk
Website: http://www.ybs.co.uk
Directors: I. Cornish (Grp Chief Exec), J. Daves (Dir), R. Jackson (Chief Op Offcr), A. Gosling (Fin)
Ultimate Holding Company: YORKSHIRE BUILDING SOCIETY
Immediate Holding Company: YORKSHIRE BUILDING SOCIETY CHARITABLE FOUNDATION
Registration no: 09000090 Date established: 1998
Turnover: Up to £250,000 No.of Employees: 501 - 1000
Product Groups: 82

Date of Accounts	Dec 10	Dec 09	Dec 08
Sales Turnover	30	31	41
Pre Tax Profit/Loss	-9	-10	-18
Working Capital	-156	-112	-143
Fixed Assets	107	139	107
Current Assets	5	N/A	50
Current Liabilities	50	1	82

Yorkshire Water

Western House Halifax, Buttershaw, Bradford, BD6 2SZ
Tel: 01274-691111 Fax: 01274-608608
E-mail: kevin.whiteman@yorkshirewater.com
Website: http://www.yorkshirewater.com
Directors: K. Whiteman (Ch), S. McFarlane (Co Sec), P. Rogerson (Pers)
Managers: J. Herdman, M. Kettlewell, L. Barber, S. Barwick (Buyer)
Ultimate Holding Company: KELDA HOLDINGS LIMITED (JERSEY)
Immediate Holding Company: KELDA GROUP LIMITED
Registration no: 02366627 Date established: 1989 Turnover: £5m - £10m
No.of Employees: 1501 & over Product Groups: 51

Date of Accounts	Mar 12	Mar 11	Mar 10
Sales Turnover	6m	6m	4m
Pre Tax Profit/Loss	61m	45m	208m
Working Capital	-247m	-245m	-230m
Fixed Assets	1068m	1084m	1081m
Current Assets	13m	14m	31m
Current Liabilities	3m	2m	5m

Brighouse

A One Tools & Fixings Brighouse Ltd

370 Bradford Road, Brighouse, HD6 4DJ
Tel: 01484-710282 Fax: 01484-400550
E-mail: sales@aonetools.co.uk
Website: http://www.aonetools.co.uk
Directors: D. Stephenson (MD)
Immediate Holding Company: A-ONE TOOLS & FIXINGS (BRIGHOUSE) LIMITED
Registration no: 01580714 Date established: 1981
No.of Employees: 11 - 20 Product Groups: 37

Date of Accounts	Aug 12	Aug 11	Aug 10
Working Capital	642	217	59
Fixed Assets	641	640	634
Current Assets	2m	1m	1m

Alco Valves

Mission Works Birds Royd Lane, Brighouse, HD6 1LQ
Tel: 01484-710511 Fax: 01484-713009
E-mail: uk@alco-valves.com
Website: http://www.alco-valves.com
Bank(s): Lloyds TSB Bank plc
Directors: A. Mitchell (Fin), B. Watson (Purch), P. Delaney (Sales), S. Lomax (Dir)
Managers: M. Cunningham (Tech Serv Mgr)
Ultimate Holding Company: XAMOL LIMITED
Immediate Holding Company: ALCO VALVES LIMITED
Registration no: 01330693 VAT No.: GB 640 6261 60
Date established: 1977 Turnover: £5m - £10m
No.of Employees: 51 - 100 Product Groups: 36, 39, 40

Date of Accounts	Oct 11	Oct 10	Oct 09
Working Capital	563	267	215
Fixed Assets	206	178	192
Current Assets	3m	2m	2m

Asquith Butler

Spring Vale Industrial Estate Brookfoot Lane, Brighouse, HD6 2RA
Tel: 01484-726620 Fax: 01484-718708
E-mail: info@asquithbutler.com
Website: http://www.asquithbutler.com
Directors: P. Hinchcliffe (MD), P. Hinchliffe (MD)
Immediate Holding Company: ONAN HOLDINGS LIMITED
Registration no: 01133008 Date established: 1973 Turnover: £1m - £2m
No.of Employees: 21 - 50 Product Groups: 67

Date of Accounts	Jun 08	Jun 07	Jun 06
Working Capital	384	137	66
Fixed Assets	229	220	197
Current Assets	1700	1772	1334
Current Liabilities	1316	1635	1268
Total Share Capital	1	1	1

Avercet Hardware Ltd

Brookfoot Mills Elland Road, Brookfoot, Brighouse, HD6 2RW
Tel: 01484-711700 Fax: 01484-720124
E-mail: post@avocet-hardware.co.uk
Website: http://www.avercet-hardware.co.uk
Bank(s): HSBC Bank plc
Managers: J. Heaton
Ultimate Holding Company: MASCO INC (USA)
Immediate Holding Company: WMS PVCU HARDWARE LIMITED
Registration no: 01303372 Date established: 1977 Turnover: £5m - £10m
No.of Employees: 101 - 250 Product Groups: 30, 32, 35, 36, 40

Date of Accounts	Jul 11	Jul 10	Jul 09
Working Capital	-1	-1	N/A
Current Assets	8	22	N/A

Biffa Waste Services Ltd

Huntingdon Road, Brighouse, HD6 1PZ
Tel: 01484-720175 Fax: 01484-711359
E-mail: marketing@biffa.co.uk
Website: http://www.biffa.co.uk
Managers: A. Oates (Depot Mgr)
Immediate Holding Company: BIFFA WASTE SERVICES LIMITED
Registration no: 00946107 Date established: 1969
No.of Employees: 21 - 50 Product Groups: 32, 54

Date of Accounts	Mar 08	Mar 09	Apr 10
Sales Turnover	555m	574m	492m
Pre Tax Profit/Loss	23m	50m	30m
Working Capital	229m	271m	293m
Fixed Assets	371m	360m	378m
Current Assets	409m	534m	609m
Current Liabilities	50m	100m	115m

Blackhall Engineering Ltd

Cedar House 362 Bradford Road, Brighouse, HD6 4DJ
Tel: 01484-407080 Fax: 01484-400155
E-mail: sales@blackhall.co.uk
Website: http://www.blackhall.co.uk
Directors: A. Blackhall (MD)
Immediate Holding Company: BLACKHALL ENGINEERING LIMITED
Registration no: 00846484 Date established: 1965 Turnover: £2m - £5m
No.of Employees: 21 - 50 Product Groups: 36, 39, 40, 42, 48, 52, 54

Date of Accounts	Mar 11	Mar 10	Mar 09
Working Capital	230	208	153
Fixed Assets	1m	963	681
Current Assets	3m	2m	2m

Boge Compressors Ltd

Rastrick Common, Brighouse, HD6 3DR
Tel: 01484-719921 Fax: 01484-712516
E-mail: info@boge.co.uk
Website: http://www.boge.co.uk
Directors: I. Svenson (Fin)
Managers: B. Taylor (Mktg Serv Mgr), M. Whitmore (Chief Mgr)
Ultimate Holding Company: BOGE KOMPRESSOREN OTTO BOGE GMBH & CO KG (GERMANY)
Immediate Holding Company: BOGE COMPRESSORS LIMITED
Registration no: 03009782 Date established: 1995 Turnover: £5m - £10m
No.of Employees: 21 - 50 Product Groups: 36, 40, 48, 52

Date of Accounts	Dec 11	Dec 10	Dec 09
Sales Turnover	6m	N/A	N/A
Pre Tax Profit/Loss	192	407	149
Working Capital	648	1m	1m
Fixed Assets	300	305	270
Current Assets	2m	3m	3m
Current Liabilities	752	607	741

Brighouse Domestics

14 Anvil Street, Brighouse, HD6 1TP
Tel: 01484-716130
E-mail: brighouse.domestics@blueyonder.co.uk
Directors: D. Rayner (MD)
Immediate Holding Company: BRIGHOUSE DOMESTICS LIMITED
Registration no: 04728157 Date established: 2003
No.of Employees: 1 - 10 Product Groups: 43

Date of Accounts	Mar 12	Mar 11	Mar 10
Working Capital	N/A	2	2
Fixed Assets	1	1	N/A
Current Assets	4	6	4

Brunswick Tooling Ltd

3 The Sidings Industrial Park Birds Royd Lane, Brighouse, HD6 1LQ
Tel: 01484-719900 Fax: 01484-404727
E-mail: pbriggs@brunswicktooling.co.uk
Website: http://www.brunswicktooling.co.uk
Bank(s): Lloyds TSB Bank plc
Directors: T. Beaumont (Co Sec), P. Briggs (MD)
Managers: A. Briggs (Tech Serv Mgr), B. Kitson (Sales Prom Mgr), M. Sharp (Buyer)
Ultimate Holding Company: BRUNSWICK TOOLING LIMITED
Immediate Holding Company: G R BOOTH LIMITED
Registration no: 01575786 VAT No.: GB 183 4552 53
Date established: 1981 Turnover: £1m - £2m No.of Employees: 21 - 50
Product Groups: 33, 36, 37, 45, 46, 48

Date of Accounts	Mar 11	Mar 10	Mar 07
Working Capital	35	35	35
Current Assets	35	35	35

Ceramic Prints Ltd

George Street, Brighouse, HD6 1PU
Tel: 01484-712522 Fax: 01484-719540
E-mail: info@ceramicprints.com
Website: http://www.ceramicprints.com
Bank(s): Barclays
Directors: A. Taylor (Ch), D. Shaw (Dir), J. Lamb (Fin), J. Taylor (Ch)
Managers: J. Clarkson
Immediate Holding Company: CERAMIC PRINTS LIMITED
Registration no: 01717473 VAT No.: GB 401 5150 15
Date established: 1983 Turnover: £20m - £50m
No.of Employees: 101 - 250 Product Groups: 33

Date of Accounts	Sep 09	Sep 08	Sep 07
Sales Turnover	27m	38m	35m
Pre Tax Profit/Loss	1m	205	318
Working Capital	7m	6m	6m
Fixed Assets	1m	946	925
Current Assets	20m	22m	20m
Current Liabilities	7m	9m	7m

Denford Ltd

Armytage House Armytage Road, Brighouse, HD6 1QF
Tel: 01484-728000 Fax: 01484-722160
E-mail: info@denford.co.uk
Website: http://www.denford.co.uk
Bank(s): HSBC Bank plc
Directors: S. Moorhouse (MD), S. Oddy (Tech Serv), M. Stirk (Fin)
Managers: K. Darbyson (Sales Prom Mgr), K. Hullock, N. Denford (Admin Off)
Immediate Holding Company: DENFORD LIMITED
Registration no: 00386161 VAT No.: GB 183 4383 50
Date established: 1944 Turnover: £2m - £5m No.of Employees: 11 - 20
Product Groups: 44, 46

Date of Accounts	Sep 11	Sep 10	Sep 09
Working Capital	826	1m	1m
Fixed Assets	507	148	146
Current Assets	1m	2m	2m

John Drury & Co. Ltd

River Street, Brighouse, HD6 1NJ
Tel: 01484-714461 Fax: 01484-716794
E-mail: sales@john-drury.co.uk
Website: http://www.john-drury.co.uk
Bank(s): National Westminster
Directors: M. Drury (Dir)
Managers: S. Entwhistle, E. Drury (Chief Mgr)
Ultimate Holding Company: JOHN DRURY HOLDINGS LIMITED
Immediate Holding Company: JOHN DRURY & CO. LIMITED
Registration no: 00813618 VAT No.: GB 183 5165 55
Date established: 1964 Turnover: £2m - £5m No.of Employees: 21 - 50
Product Groups: 32, 63

Date of Accounts	Dec 11	Dec 10	Dec 09
Working Capital	771	892	520
Fixed Assets	73	90	97
Current Assets	1m	1m	1m

Dust Collector Tube & Webbing Strap Co.

97 Lightcliffe Road, Brighouse, HD6 2HJ
Tel: 01484-712552 Fax: 01484-712552
Directors: P. Court (MD), J. Court (Fin)
Immediate Holding Company: DUST COLLECTOR TUBE & WEBBING STRAP CO. LIMITED(THE)
Registration no: 01377154 Date established: 1978
No.of Employees: 1 - 10 Product Groups: 38, 42

Date of Accounts	Jul 11	Jul 10	Jul 09
Working Capital	1	N/A	N/A
Fixed Assets	1	1	1
Current Assets	12	12	11

Dyson Insulation Ltd

Dyson House Armytage Road, Brighouse, HD6 1PT
Tel: 01484-406060 Fax: 01484-406061
E-mail: anthonyhardiman@dysoninsulations.co.uk
Website: http://www.dysoninsulations.co.uk
Bank(s): Yorkshire Bank PLC
Directors: N. Brown (Dir), A. Allsop (Fin), A. Hardiman (MD)
Managers: C. Scott (Personnel), C. Taberner (Sales & Mktg Mg), H. Brawn
Ultimate Holding Company: SAND CLOCK LIMITED
Immediate Holding Company: DYSON INSULATIONS LIMITED
Registration no: 01956726 Date established: 1985
Turnover: £20m - £50m No.of Employees: 21 - 50 Product Groups: 52

Date of Accounts	Dec 11	Dec 10	Dec 09
Sales Turnover	25m	22m	25m
Pre Tax Profit/Loss	902	-1m	136
Working Capital	1m	491	1m
Fixed Assets	1m	1m	2m
Current Assets	6m	6m	6m
Current Liabilities	2m	648	690

Firth Steels Ltd

Calderbank River Street, Brighouse, HD6 1LU
Tel: 01484-405940
E-mail: sales@firth-steels.co.uk
Website: http://www.firth-steels.co.uk
Directors: R. Firth (Ptnr)
Immediate Holding Company: FIRTH STEELS LIMITED
Registration no: 01715793 Date established: 1983
Turnover: £10m - £20m No.of Employees: 11 - 20 Product Groups: 35, 61

Date of Accounts	Jul 11	Jul 10	Jul 09
Sales Turnover	11m	8m	14m
Pre Tax Profit/Loss	456	-118	686
Working Capital	4m	3m	3m
Fixed Assets	6m	6m	6m
Current Assets	8m	9m	8m
Current Liabilities	1m	770	2m

Flemings Seals Ltd (Flemings Seals Ltd)

Atlas Mills Atlas Mill Road, Brighouse, HD6 1ES
Tel: 01484-718391 Fax: 01484-711585
E-mail: sales@flemings-seals.co.uk
Website: http://www.flemings-seals.co.uk
Directors: D. Galloway (Fin)
Ultimate Holding Company: JAMES WALKER GROUP LIMITED
Immediate Holding Company: FLEMINGS SEALS LIMITED
Registration no: 00137356 Date established: 2014
No.of Employees: 11 - 20 Product Groups: 30, 48, 66

Date of Accounts	Mar 12	Mar 11	Mar 10
Working Capital	232	141	74
Fixed Assets	19	25	28
Current Assets	346	254	210

G A Valves Sales Ltd

PO Box 5, Brighouse, HD6 1LQ
Tel: 01484-711983 Fax: 01484-719848
E-mail: sales@gavalves.co.uk
Website: http://www.gavalves.co.uk
Directors: K. Baker (Co Sec)
Ultimate Holding Company: GOLDEN ANDERSON UK LIMITED
Immediate Holding Company: G.A. VALVES SALES LIMITED
Registration no: 02535998 VAT No.: GB 516 2359 56
Date established: 1990 Turnover: £1m - £2m No.of Employees: 11 - 20
Product Groups: 36, 39, 40, 66

see next page

G A Valves Sales Ltd - Cont'd

Date of Accounts	Apr 12	Apr 11	Apr 10
Working Capital	555	605	630
Fixed Assets	37	37	44
Current Assets	2m	2m	2m

G E Mitchell

Springvale Works Brookfoot, Brighouse, HD6 2RW
Tel: 01484-717607 **Fax:** 01484-720484
E-mail: sales@gemitchell.co.uk
Website: http://www.gemitchell.co.uk
Directors: J. Lowe (MD)
Immediate Holding Company: G.E. MITCHELL (ELECTRICAL) LIMITED
Registration no: 01127026 **VAT No.:** GB 184 3298 40
Date established: 1973 **Turnover:** £250,000 - £500,000
No.of Employees: 11 - 20 **Product Groups:** 38

Date of Accounts	Aug 11	Aug 10	Aug 09
Working Capital	231	196	220
Fixed Assets	13	19	9
Current Assets	796	801	547

Halifax Fan Ltd

Mistral Works Unit 11 Brookfoot Business Park, Brookfoot, Brighouse, HD6 2SD
Tel: 01484-475123 **Fax:** 01484-475122
E-mail: sales@halifax-fan.com
Website: http://www.halifax-fan.co.uk
Directors: A. Fisher (Co Sec), A. Khan (Fin), I. Mcevoy (Dir), M. Staff (Grp Chief Exec)
Managers: K. Garvutt
Ultimate Holding Company: HALIFAX FAN GROUP LIMITED
Immediate Holding Company: HALIFAX FAN LIMITED
Registration no: 02960571 **VAT No.:** GB 686 5636 81
Date established: 1994 **No.of Employees:** 51 - 100 **Product Groups:** 40

Date of Accounts	Dec 11	Dec 10	Dec 09
Working Capital	691	725	546
Fixed Assets	171	146	227
Current Assets	2m	2m	1m

Halifax Rack & Screw Cutting Co. Ltd

Coronation Works Armytage Road, Brighouse, HD6 1QA
Tel: 01484-714667 **Fax:** 01484-712532
E-mail: info@hrs-ccl.co.uk
Website: http://www.halifaxrs.com
Bank(s): The Royal Bank of Scotland
Directors: M. Robinson (Fab), C. Jones (Fin)
Managers: M. Mitchell (Prod Mgr), D. Norman (Sales Prom Mgr), M. Mitchell (I.T. Exec)
Immediate Holding Company: HALIFAX RACK & SCREW CUTTING CO. LIMITED
Registration no: 05202733 **VAT No.:** GB 538 6867 88 019
Date established: 2004 **Turnover:** £2m - £5m **No.of Employees:** 21 - 50
Product Groups: 35, 46, 48

Date of Accounts	Sep 11	Sep 10	Sep 09
Working Capital	670	392	387
Fixed Assets	646	587	583
Current Assets	2m	2m	2m

Hamelin Stationery Ltd

River Street, Brighouse, HD6 1LU
Tel: 01484-385600 **Fax:** 01484-385602
E-mail: francis.werner@hamelinstationery.com
Website: http://www.hamelinstationery.com
Directors: S. Hamelin (Fin), F. Werner (MD)
Managers: S. Cunliffe (Prod Mgr), J. Grant, A. Fletcher (Fin Mgr), P. Hislop (Chief Mgr), D. Heeley (Purch Mgr)
Immediate Holding Company: SCREENPRINT PRODUCTIONS LIMITED
Registration no: 04511067 **VAT No.:** GB 803 9716 24
Date established: 1983 **Turnover:** £5m - £10m
No.of Employees: 51 - 100 **Product Groups:** 27

Date of Accounts	Aug 10	Aug 09	Aug 08
Pre Tax Profit/Loss	N/A	N/A	-111
Working Capital	335	304	357
Fixed Assets	161	435	757
Current Assets	562	606	970
Current Liabilities	N/A	N/A	248

I M I Cornelius UK Ltd

Russell Way, Brighouse, HD6 4LX
Tel: 01484-714584 **Fax:** 01789-761469
E-mail: jeremyf@corneliusuk.com
Website: http://www.corneliusuk.com
Bank(s): Barclays, Colmore Row , Birmingham
Directors: N. Wells (Procurement), A. Caldwell (Fin), I. Davies (Fin), A. Hume (MD)
Managers: S. Walker-lee (Personnel), K. Booth (Purch Mgr), D. Plant (Tech Serv Mgr)
Ultimate Holding Company: IMI PLC
Immediate Holding Company: IMI CORNELIUS (UK) LIMITED
Registration no: 00440427 **Date established:** 1947
Turnover: £20m - £50m **No.of Employees:** 101 - 250
Product Groups: 36, 37, 40, 41

Date of Accounts	Dec 11	Dec 10	Dec 09
Sales Turnover	37m	38m	40m
Pre Tax Profit/Loss	-645	-1m	-3m
Working Capital	11m	11m	11m
Fixed Assets	875	881	1m
Current Assets	37m	37m	38m
Current Liabilities	1m	1m	767

Arthur Jackson & Co. Ltd

Rastrick Common, Brighouse, HD6 3DR
Tel: 01484-713345 **Fax:** 01484-718150
E-mail: sarah@ajack.demon.co.uk
Directors: A. Jackson (MD)
Immediate Holding Company: ARTHUR JACKSON & CO.,LIMITED
Registration no: 00556299 **VAT No.:** GB 183 9306 43
Date established: 1955 **No.of Employees:** 11 - 20 **Product Groups:** 48

Date of Accounts	Oct 11	Oct 10	Oct 09
Working Capital	331	361	171
Fixed Assets	380	343	793
Current Assets	527	487	442

John Walton Machine Tools Ltd

The Smithy Smithy Carr Lane, Brighouse, HD6 2HL
Tel: 01484-712507 **Fax:** 01484-710549
E-mail: c-young@chucks.co.uk
Website: http://www.chucks.co.uk
Directors: C. Young (MD)
Immediate Holding Company: JOHN WALTON (MACHINE TOOLS) LIMITED
Registration no: 01157196 **VAT No.:** GB 184 3854 36
Date established: 1974 **Turnover:** £500,000 - £1m
No.of Employees: 1 - 10 **Product Groups:** 35, 36, 46

Date of Accounts	Jul 11	Jul 10	Jul 09
Working Capital	-96	-135	-93
Fixed Assets	201	201	206
Current Assets	489	387	331

Lords Photodigital Ltd

78 Commercial Street, Brighouse, HD6 1AQ
Tel: 01484-713869
E-mail: info@lordsphotodigital.co.uk
Website: http://www.lordsphotodigital.co.uk
Directors: J. Lord (Dir)
Immediate Holding Company: W.B.H. LORD & SONS LIMITED
Registration no: 01148497 **VAT No.:** GB 184 3781 37
Date established: 1973 **Turnover:** £250,000 - £500,000
No.of Employees: 1 - 10 **Product Groups:** 81

Date of Accounts	Dec 11	Dec 10	Dec 09
Working Capital	74	87	90
Fixed Assets	2	3	2
Current Assets	180	209	188

Metallicus Ltd

Slade Lane Works, Brighouse, HD6 3PP
Tel: 01484-716651
Directors: A. Thomas (MD), M. Thomas (MD)
Immediate Holding Company: METALLICUS LIMITED
Registration no: 04867491 **Date established:** 2003
No.of Employees: 1 - 10 **Product Groups:** 35, 36

Date of Accounts	Dec 11	Dec 10	Dec 09
Working Capital	3	3	3
Current Assets	4	4	4

Millers Oils Ltd

Hillside Oil Works Rastrick, Brighouse, HD6 3DP
Tel: 01484-713201 **Fax:** 01484-721263
E-mail: martyn.mann@millersoils.co.uk
Website: http://www.millersoils.co.uk
Bank(s): National Westminster Bank Plc
Directors: S. Woollven (Sales), S. Miller (Dir), M. Mann (Dir), R. Miller (MD), N. Hall (Co Sec)
Managers: P. Woodward (I.T. Exec), B. Weale, N. Richardson (Mktg Serv Mgr)
Immediate Holding Company: MILLERS OILS LIMITED
Registration no: 00137671 **VAT No.:** GB 183 5337 52
Date established: 2014 **Turnover:** £10m - £20m
No.of Employees: 101 - 250 **Product Groups:** 31, 66

Date of Accounts	Mar 11	Mar 10	Jan 09
Working Capital	10	10	-11
Fixed Assets	N/A	N/A	477
Current Assets	10	10	609

N M A Agencies Ltd

Birds Royd Lane, Brighouse, HD6 1LQ
Tel: 01484-400488 **Fax:** 01484-711012
E-mail: info@nmauk.com
Website: http://www.nmauk.com
Directors: M. Wright (Fin)
Ultimate Holding Company: XAMOL LIMITED
Immediate Holding Company: N M A (AGENCIES) LIMITED
Registration no: 03962261 **Date established:** 2000
Turnover: Up to £250,000 **No.of Employees:** 1 - 10 **Product Groups:** 46

Date of Accounts	Dec 11	Dec 10	Dec 09
Working Capital	136	167	202
Fixed Assets	136	144	160
Current Assets	1m	1m	1m
Current Liabilities	718	652	N/A

Powersaver Electrical Distributors

The Industrial Estate Armytage Road, Brighouse, HD6 1PT
Tel: 01484-718888 **Fax:** 01484-401888
E-mail: brighouse@powersaver.co.uk
Website: http://www.powersaver.co.uk
Managers: S. Taylor (Sales Prom Mgr)
Immediate Holding Company: POWER SAVER LTD
Registration no: 03484214 **Date established:** 2004
No.of Employees: 1 - 10 **Product Groups:** 36, 40

Rapid Fire Extinguishers Ltd

2 Atlas Mill Road, Brighouse, HD6 1ES
Tel: 01484-400040 **Fax:** 01484-421499
Directors: D. Hunter (MD), L. Hunter (Fin)
Immediate Holding Company: RAPID FIRE EXTINGUISHERS LIMITED
Registration no: 02803464 **Date established:** 1993
No.of Employees: 1 - 10 **Product Groups:** 38, 42

Date of Accounts	Apr 12	Apr 11	Apr 10
Working Capital	22	36	41
Fixed Assets	11	5	8
Current Assets	55	64	69

Rolla Ltd

Atlas Mill Road, Brighouse, HD6 1ES
Tel: 01484-710226 **Fax:** 01484-718608
E-mail: sales@rolla.co.uk
Website: http://www.rolla.co.uk
Bank(s): Barclays
Directors: R. Greenwood (I.T. Dir), H. Booth (Co Sec)
Immediate Holding Company: ROLLA LIMITED
Registration no: 00480927 **VAT No.:** GB 183 3184 61
Date established: 1950 **No.of Employees:** 21 - 50 **Product Groups:** 37

Date of Accounts	Jun 12	Jun 11	Jun 10
Working Capital	138	-16	67
Fixed Assets	934	1m	1m
Current Assets	656	860	368

S F Fire Protection

Raths Ryg Shepherds Thorn Lane, Brighouse, HD6 3TT
Tel: 01484-714076 **Fax:** 01484-712967
E-mail: amanda@ssffireprotection.co.uk
Website: http://www.sffireprotection.co.uk
Directors: K. Stock (Prop)
Date established: 1987 **No.of Employees:** 11 - 20 **Product Groups:** 38, 42

Sherwood Coatings Ltd

Sherwood Road, Brighouse, HD6 1QG
Tel: 01484-710137 **Fax:** 01484-710345
E-mail: info@sherwoodcoatings.co.uk
Website: http://www.sherwoodcoatings.co.uk
Directors: D. Illingworth (Dir)
Immediate Holding Company: SHERWOOD COATINGS LIMITED
Registration no: 02350699 **Date established:** 1989
Turnover: £250,000 - £500,000 **No.of Employees:** 1 - 10
Product Groups: 46, 48

Date of Accounts	Jun 11	Jun 10	Jun 09
Sales Turnover	N/A	N/A	398
Working Capital	-5	-121	-95
Fixed Assets	209	222	215
Current Assets	120	109	91
Current Liabilities	N/A	144	116

Sillaford Ltd

Martin House 2 Martin Street, Brighouse, HD6 1DA
Tel: 01484-710231 **Fax:** 01484-714607
E-mail: john@sillaford.com
Directors: C. Haigh (Co Sec)
Managers: J. Haigh (Sales Eng)
Immediate Holding Company: SILLAFORD LIMITED
Registration no: 01040507 **VAT No.:** GB 180 7022 85
Date established: 1972 **Turnover:** £2m - £5m **No.of Employees:** 1 - 10
Product Groups: 23, 34, 35

Date of Accounts	Dec 11	Dec 10	Dec 09
Working Capital	393	356	299
Fixed Assets	32	18	2
Current Assets	635	599	599

Spring Vale Engineering Ltd

Unit 5 Brookfoot Business Park, Brookfoot, Brighouse, HD6 2SD
Tel: 01484-720205 **Fax:** 01484-400056
E-mail: john@springvalegroup.com
Website: http://www.springvalegroup.com
Directors: J. Auckland (Dir)
Immediate Holding Company: SPRING VALE ENGINEERING LTD
Registration no: 07218813 **VAT No.:** GB 361 6003 86
Date established: 2010 **Turnover:** £1m - £2m **No.of Employees:** 1 - 10
Product Groups: 45

Date of Accounts	Apr 11
Working Capital	-33
Fixed Assets	36
Current Assets	35

Tev Ltd

Armytage Road, Brighouse, HD6 1QF
Tel: 01484-405600 **Fax:** 01484-403620
E-mail: sales@tevlimited.com
Website: http://www.tevlimited.com
Bank(s): Barclays, Colmore Row, Birmingham
Directors: R. Dossett (Grp Chief Exec)
Ultimate Holding Company: THERMAL ENERGY VENTURES LIMITED
Immediate Holding Company: TEV LIMITED
Registration no: 04865581 **Date established:** 2003 **Turnover:** £5m - £10m
No.of Employees: 21 - 50 **Product Groups:** 52

Date of Accounts	Dec 11	Dec 10	Dec 09
Sales Turnover	6m	6m	7m
Pre Tax Profit/Loss	-244	-76	-10
Working Capital	3m	3m	3m
Fixed Assets	104	126	173
Current Assets	5m	5m	5m
Current Liabilities	1m	467	587

Wyke Plastics Plastic Moulders

Bradford Road, Brighouse, HD6 4BW
Tel: 01484-710414 **Fax:** 01484-711649
E-mail: david@wyke-plastics.co.uk
Website: http://www.wyke-plastics.co.uk
Directors: D. Snowball (Ptnr)
Immediate Holding Company: QUICKSLIDE WINDOWS DIRECT LTD
Registration no: 00114839 **VAT No.:** GB 287 3962 07
Date established: 2012 **No.of Employees:** 11 - 20 **Product Groups:** 30

Yorkshire Glass & Dishwashers

Unit 1 Wood Street, Brighouse, HD6 1PW
Tel: 01484-712270 **Fax:** 01484-712369
E-mail: paul@yorkshireglassanddish.com
Website: http://www.yorkshireglassanddish.com
Directors: P. Wormald (Snr Part)
Date established: 1991 **No.of Employees:** 1 - 10 **Product Groups:** 20, 40, 41

Castleford

A J Glass Fibre Ltd

Carr Wood Industrial Estate Carr Wood Road, Castleford, WF10 4SB
Tel: 01977-603651 **Fax:** 01977-603650
E-mail: info@ajglassfibre.co.uk
Website: http://www.ajglassfibre.co.uk
Directors: A. Mallinson (MD)
Managers: L. Kenney (Sales Admin)
Immediate Holding Company: A.J.GLASSFIBRE LIMITED
Registration no: 03755671 **Date established:** 1999 **Turnover:** £2m - £5m
No.of Employees: 21 - 50 **Product Groups:** 30, 33, 45

Date of Accounts	Jun 11	Jun 10	Jun 09
Working Capital	11	-7	21
Fixed Assets	536	524	529
Current Assets	728	579	552

Bapp Industrial Supplies Castleford Ltd

Methley Road, Castleford, WF10 1PA
Tel: 01977-510640 **Fax:** 01977-516514
E-mail: sales@bappcastleford.co.uk
Website: http://www.bapp.co.uk
Directors: C. Garwood (Dir), C. Garwood (Fin), D. Cook (MD)
Managers: C. Baker (Sales Prom Mgr)
Immediate Holding Company: BAPP INDUSTRIAL SUPPLIES (CASTLEFORD) LIMITED
Registration no: 01403572 **VAT No.:** GB 183 1568 53
Date established: 1978 **Turnover:** £250,000 - £500,000
No.of Employees: 1 - 10 **Product Groups:** 24, 35, 66

Date of Accounts	Dec 07	Dec 06	Dec 05
Working Capital	-1	7	-12
Fixed Assets	58	24	41
Current Assets	228	145	133
Current Liabilities	229	138	145
Total Share Capital	24	24	24

C & J Metal Craft
Crowther Place, Castleford, WF10 5BZ
Tel: 01977-514157 **Fax:** 01977-514157
Directors: E. Jones (MD)
Immediate Holding Company: C & J METALCRAFTS LIMITED
Registration no: 04634159 **Date established:** 2003
No.of Employees: 1 - 10 **Product Groups:** 26, 35

Date of Accounts	Mar 11	Mar 10	Mar 06
Working Capital	15	46	25
Fixed Assets	2	3	1
Current Assets	55	84	50

Castleford Transport Documentation Ltd
24 Granville Street, Castleford, WF10 5HF
Tel: 01977-556055 **Fax:** 01977-551030
E-mail: sales@ctdocumentation.co.uk
Website: http://www.ctdocumentation.co.uk
Directors: P. North (MD)
Immediate Holding Company: CASTLEFORD TRANSPORT DOCUMENTATION LIMITED
Registration no: 03953245 **Date established:** 2000
No.of Employees: 1 - 10 **Product Groups:** 27

Date of Accounts	Aug 11	Aug 10	Aug 08
Working Capital	5	-1	7
Fixed Assets	1	1	1
Current Assets	22	22	32

C C L Labels Decorative Sleeves
Unit 6 Pioneer Way, Castleford, WF10 5QU
Tel: 01977-510030 **Fax:** 01977-521240
E-mail: mrayner@cclind.com
Website: http://www.ccllabel.co.uk
Bank(s): HSBC Bank plc
Managers: M. Rayner (Mgr), W. Firth (Sales Prom Mgr), M. Beckram (Comptroller)
Ultimate Holding Company: CCL INDUSTRIES INC (CANADA)
Immediate Holding Company: CCL LABEL LIMITED
Registration no: 04310986 **Date established:** 2001
Turnover: £20m - £50m **No.of Employees:** 21 - 50 **Product Groups:** 27

Date of Accounts	Dec 11	Dec 10	Dec 09
Sales Turnover	40m	39m	40m
Pre Tax Profit/Loss	5m	4m	3m
Working Capital	18m	15m	10m
Fixed Assets	34m	32m	33m
Current Assets	24m	21m	17m
Current Liabilities	715	997	2m

Crendon Timber Engineering Ltd (Gang-Nail Systems Ltd)
Carr Wood Road, Castleford, WF10 4PS
Tel: 01977-554220 **Fax:** 01977-513017
E-mail: sales@crendon.co.uk
Website: http://www.crendon.co.uk
Managers: T. Burrow (Mgr)
Ultimate Holding Company: BRADFORD & SONS LTD
Immediate Holding Company: HY. ARNOLD (CASTLEFORD) LIMITED
Registration no: 01425125 **Date established:** 1979 **Turnover:** £2m - £5m
No.of Employees: 21 - 50 **Product Groups:** 35, 66

Thomas Fawcett & Sons Ltd
8 Eastfield Lane, Castleford, WF10 4LE
Tel: 01977-552490 **Fax:** 01977-519076
E-mail: enquiries@fawcett-maltsters.co.uk
Website: http://www.fawcett-maltsters.co.uk
Bank(s): Barclays
Directors: B. Fawcett (Prop)
Immediate Holding Company: THOMAS FAWCETT & SONS,LIMITED
Registration no: 00153755 **VAT No.:** GB 181 4820 66
Date established: 2019 **Turnover:** £5m - £10m **No.of Employees:** 21 - 50
Product Groups: 41, 84

Date of Accounts	Sep 11	Sep 10	Sep 09
Sales Turnover	10m	9m	10m
Pre Tax Profit/Loss	839	521	599
Working Capital	3m	2m	2m
Fixed Assets	3m	3m	4m
Current Assets	5m	4m	4m
Current Liabilities	917	687	1m

John Frost Designer Bridalwear
44 Smawthorne Lane, Castleford, WF10 4EW
Tel: 01977-552913 **Fax:** 01977-604646
E-mail: designerbridalwear@btconnect.com
Directors: J. Frost (Prop)
No.of Employees: 1 - 10 **Product Groups:** 23, 24, 63

Interserve Project Services Ltd
1 Thunderhead Ridge, Castleford, WF10 4UA
Tel: 01977-522300 **Fax:** 01977-522301
E-mail: kevin.frain@interserve.com
Website: http://www.interserve.com
Bank(s): HSBC Bank plc
Directors: K. Frain (Dir)
Ultimate Holding Company: INTERSERVE PLC
Immediate Holding Company: INTERSERVE PROJECT SERVICES LIMITED
Registration no: 03299588 **Date established:** 1997
Turnover: £250m - £500m **No.of Employees:** 21 - 50
Product Groups: 51, 52

Jewson Ltd
Carr Wood Road, Castleford, WF10 4SP
Tel: 01977-558866 **Fax:** 01977-551060
Website: http://www.jewson.co.uk
Directors: P. Hindle (MD)
Managers: D. Schofield (District Mgr)
Ultimate Holding Company: COMPAGNIE DE SAINT GOBAIN (FRANCE)
Immediate Holding Company: JEWSON LIMITED
Registration no: 00348407 **VAT No.:** GB 497 7184 33
Date established: 1939 **Turnover:** £2m - £5m **No.of Employees:** 1 - 10
Product Groups: 66

Date of Accounts	Dec 11	Dec 10	Dec 09
Sales Turnover	1606m	1547m	1485m
Pre Tax Profit/Loss	18m	100m	45m
Working Capital	-345m	-250m	-349m
Fixed Assets	496m	387m	461m
Current Assets	657m	1005m	1320m
Current Liabilities	66m	120m	64m

John Rhodes & Son Ltd
Hightown Foundry Rhodes Street, Castleford, WF10 5LN
Tel: 01977-552324 **Fax:** 01977-668011
E-mail: info@johnrhodes.co.uk
Website: http://www.johnrhodes.co.uk
Directors: R. Shaw (MD)
Immediate Holding Company: John Rhodes & Son (Ironfounders) Ltd
Registration no: 04293893 **VAT No.:** GB 660 1057 70
Date established: 2001 **Turnover:** £500,000 - £1m
No.of Employees: 1 - 10 **Product Groups:** 34

Lambson Fine Chemicals Ltd
Cinder Lane, Castleford, WF10 1LU
Tel: 01977-510511 **Fax:** 01977-603049
E-mail: sales@lambson.com
Website: http://www.lambson.com
Bank(s): HSBC Bank plc
Directors: I. Hall (Ch), P. Calvert (Co Sec)
Immediate Holding Company: LAMBSON LIMITED
Registration no: 02838052 **VAT No.:** GB 591 0392 42
Date established: 1993 **Turnover:** £2m - £5m **No.of Employees:** 21 - 50
Product Groups: 31, 32

Date of Accounts	Dec 11	Dec 10	Dec 09
Working Capital	2m	2m	1m
Fixed Assets	254	234	246
Current Assets	4m	3m	3m

Linpac Plastics Recycling
Newton Lane Allerton Bywater, Castleford, WF10 2AL
Tel: 01977-604080 **Fax:** 01977-603355
E-mail: ian.porter@linpac.com
Website: http://www.linpac.com
Managers: I. Porter (Chief Mgr), C. Ellis (Ops Mgr)
Immediate Holding Company: REGAIN POLYMERS LIMITED
Registration no: 00949597 **VAT No.:** GB 482 0964 32
Date established: 2010 **Turnover:** £5m - £10m
No.of Employees: 51 - 100 **Product Groups:** 30, 31, 42

Memflex Advanced Memory Foam
Calder House Saville Road, Castleford, WF10 1BJ
Tel: 0845-8339223 **Fax:** 01977-669693
E-mail: sales@bedworld.net
Website: http://www.memflex.co.uk
Registration no: 04915967 **Product Groups:** 26, 35, 63, 66

Microsense Systems Ltd
Whitwood Enterprise Park Whitwood Lane, Whitwood, Castleford, WF10 5PX
Tel: 01977-603026
Website: http://www.microsense.co.uk
Ultimate Holding Company: Pension Corporation Llp
Immediate Holding Company: Tseu Group Ltd
Registration no: 01585953 **Date established:** 1981
Turnover: £500,000 - £1m **No.of Employees:** 11 - 20
Product Groups: 37, 38, 39

N G F
Unit 11 Allerton Bywater, Castleford, WF10 2DB
Tel: 08456-444566 **Fax:** 08456-445123
E-mail: info@ngfindustrialdoors.co.uk
Website: http://www.ngfindustrialdoors.co.uk
Directors: N. Furby (Prop)
Immediate Holding Company: N.G.F. INDUSTRIAL DOORS LIMITED
Registration no: 03679823 **VAT No.:** GB 686 6625 81
Date established: 1998 **No.of Employees:** 1 - 10 **Product Groups:** 25, 26, 30, 35, 36, 37, 39, 40, 48, 52, 66

Date of Accounts	Nov 11	Nov 10	Nov 09
Working Capital	-35	-36	-31
Fixed Assets	125	130	119
Current Assets	393	406	433

Oxbow Handling & Transport Services Ltd
Savile Road Garage Savile Road, Castleford, WF10 1PD
Tel: 01977-519613 **Fax:** 01977-604565
E-mail: info@oxbowlifttrucks.co.uk
Directors: E. Wilkinson (MD)
Immediate Holding Company: OXBOW HANDLING & TRANSPORT SERVICES LIMITED
Registration no: 01682696 **Date established:** 1982
No.of Employees: 1 - 10 **Product Groups:** 35, 39, 45

Date of Accounts	Oct 11	Oct 10	Oct 09
Working Capital	51	53	55
Fixed Assets	83	81	84
Current Assets	266	280	277

Peek Traffic
Unit 3 Letchmire Road Allerton Bywater, Castleford, WF10 2DB
Tel: 01977-628130 **Fax:** 01977-558379
Website: http://www.peek-traffic.co.uk
Managers: C. Bosworth (Reg Mgr)
No.of Employees: 21 - 50 **Product Groups:** 37, 39, 40

Poskitt Painters Ltd
Empire Works Holywell Lane, Castleford, WF10 3HJ
Tel: 01977-553089 **Fax:** 01977-555765
E-mail: sales@poskitts.com
Website: http://www.poskitts.co.uk
Directors: J. Hindle (MD)
Immediate Holding Company: POSKITT PAINTERS LIMITED
Registration no: 01217985 **VAT No.:** GB 181 7057 06
Date established: 1975 **Turnover:** £500,000 - £1m
No.of Employees: 1 - 10 **Product Groups:** 25, 45

Date of Accounts	Sep 11	Sep 10	Sep 09
Working Capital	9	39	28
Fixed Assets	3	4	5
Current Assets	28	68	53

Sporting Arms & Ammunition
67 Bridge Street, Castleford, WF10 1HH
Tel: 01977-552912 **Fax:** 01977-552912
E-mail: i.longfield257@btinternet.com
Directors: I. Longfield (Ptnr)
Date established: 1942 **No.of Employees:** 1 - 10 **Product Groups:** 36, 39, 40

Toyota Material Handling UK Ltd
Unit 2 Pioneer Business Park, Castleford, WF10 5QG
Tel: 08708-501400 **Fax:** 01977-712001
E-mail: we.deliver@uk.toyota-industries.eu
Website: http://www.toyota-forklifts.co.uk
Directors: M. Mathias (MD), D. Newton (Co Sec)
Immediate Holding Company: TOYOTA INDUSTRIAL EQUIPMENT (UK) LTD.
Registration no: 00898399 **Date established:** 1967
Turnover: £10m - £20m **No.of Employees:** 11 - 20 **Product Groups:** 35, 39, 45

Vehicle Window Centre (VWC Ltd)
Methley Road, Castleford, WF10 1NJ
Tel: 01977-604977 **Fax:** 01977-603466
E-mail: info@vehiclewindows.co.uk
Website: http://www.vehiclewindows.co.uk
Directors: S. Stromberg (Fin)
Immediate Holding Company: VWC LIMITED
Registration no: 03533614 **Date established:** 1998
Turnover: £500,000 - £1m **No.of Employees:** 1 - 10 **Product Groups:** 39

Date of Accounts	Jan 08	Jan 07	Jan 06
Working Capital	61	10	-36
Fixed Assets	84	94	125
Current Assets	199	206	146
Current Liabilities	138	196	182
Total Share Capital	1	1	1

Woods Packaging Ltd
Unit D4 & D5 Whitwood Enterprise Park Whitwood Lane, Whitwood, Castleford, WF10 5PX
Tel: 01977-604050 **Fax:** 01977-604400
E-mail: sales@woods-packaging.co.uk
Website: http://www.woods-packaging.co.uk
Directors: T. Woods (MD)
Ultimate Holding Company: ENSOR HOLDINGS P L C
Immediate Holding Company: WOOD'S PACKAGING LIMITED
Registration no: 05374724 **Date established:** 2005
No.of Employees: 1 - 10 **Product Groups:** 38, 42

Date of Accounts	Mar 12	Mar 11	Mar 10
Sales Turnover	2m	2m	2m
Pre Tax Profit/Loss	90	62	230
Working Capital	384	114	288
Fixed Assets	534	588	580
Current Assets	762	679	636
Current Liabilities	75	58	45

Cleckheaton

Alice Collins
Middleton Business Park Cartwright Street, Cleckheaton, BD19 5LY
Tel: 01274-870600 **Fax:** 01274-870222
E-mail: info@alicecollins.com
Website: http://www.alicecollins.com
Bank(s): HSBC Bank plc
Directors: M. Barber (MD), L. Collins (MD)
Immediate Holding Company: Glenhusky Group Ltd
Registration no: 00463045 **VAT No.:** GB 399 3990 72
Turnover: £5m - £10m **No.of Employees:** 11 - 20 **Product Groups:** 24

Automatic Components Stanningley Ltd
Unit E1 Stubs Beck Lane West 26 Industrial Estate, Cleckheaton, BD19 4TT
Tel: 01274-851751 **Fax:** 01274-851771
E-mail: lorraine@acle1.co.uk
Website: http://www.acle1.co.uk
Directors: R. Berry (Dir), R. Berry (MD), M. Berry (Fin)
Managers: P. Ratcliffe (Works Gen Mgr), C. Prior, D. Wilkinson (Sec)
Ultimate Holding Company: VTL (HOLDINGS) LIMITED
Immediate Holding Company: ACL PRECISION LIMITED
Registration no: 00636834 **Date established:** 1959 **Turnover:** £5m - £10m
No.of Employees: 51 - 100 **Product Groups:** 84

Date of Accounts	Dec 10	Jan 10	Jan 09
Sales Turnover	13m	7m	N/A
Pre Tax Profit/Loss	681	-159	-109
Working Capital	-47	2m	2m
Fixed Assets	3m	3m	3m
Current Assets	4m	3m	3m
Current Liabilities	693	198	91

Benson Beltings Ltd
Spenvale Works Balme Road, Cleckheaton, BD19 4EW
Tel: 01274-851600 **Fax:** 01274-851620
E-mail: info@overmap.co.uk
Website: http://www.benson-beltings.co.uk
Directors: C. Schofield (Fin), B. Schofield (MD)
Ultimate Holding Company: CONVEY PLUS LIMITED
Immediate Holding Company: BENSON BELTINGS LIMITED
Registration no: 00305308 **VAT No.:** GB 183 5938 26
Date established: 1935 **Turnover:** £1m - £2m **No.of Employees:** 1 - 10
Product Groups: 23, 29, 35, 45

Date of Accounts	Sep 11	Sep 10	Sep 09
Working Capital	1m	1m	959
Fixed Assets	47	54	37
Current Assets	1m	1m	1m

Birkett Cutmaster Ltd
Cartwright Street, Cleckheaton, BD19 5LY
Tel: 01274-870311 **Fax:** 01274-862754
E-mail: bryn.pritchard@carclo-plc.com
Website: http://www.birkett-cutmaster.co.uk
Directors: B. Pritchard (MD), E. Cook (Fin)
Ultimate Holding Company: CARCLO PLC
Immediate Holding Company: BIRKETT CUTMASTER LIMITED
Registration no: 00931252 **Date established:** 1968 **Turnover:** £1m - £2m
No.of Employees: 1 - 10 **Product Groups:** 33, 34, 35, 36, 37, 46

Date of Accounts	Mar 11	Mar 10	Mar 09
Sales Turnover	2m	1m	2m
Pre Tax Profit/Loss	37	-22	-12
Working Capital	525	488	489
Fixed Assets	38	57	77
Current Assets	995	884	1m
Current Liabilities	108	67	49

Francis W Birkett & Sons Ltd
PO Box 16, Cleckheaton, BD19 5JT
Tel: 01274-873366 **Fax:** 01274-851615
E-mail: info@fwbirkett.com
Website: http://www.fwbirkett.com
Bank(s): Lloyds TSB Bank plc

see next page

Francis W Birkett & Sons Ltd - Cont'd
Directors: J. Salisbury (Dir), M. Richards (Fin)
Managers: A. Sugden, S. Carrington-ward (Sales Prom Mgr)
Ultimate Holding Company: MUSGRAVE HOLDINGS LIMITED
Immediate Holding Company: FRANCIS W BIRKETT & SONS LIMITED
Registration no: 00115131 **VAT No.:** GB 183 3648 45
Date established: 2011 **Turnover:** £2m - £5m **No.of Employees:** 51 - 100
Product Groups: 34, 35, 39, 48

Date of Accounts	Aug 11	Aug 10	Aug 09
Sales Turnover	5m	4m	4m
Pre Tax Profit/Loss	125	-197	-566
Working Capital	2m	2m	2m
Fixed Assets	1m	1m	1m
Current Assets	3m	4m	3m
Current Liabilities	215	269	250

Border Technologies Ltd
Whitechapel Road, Cleckheaton, BD19 6HY
Tel: 01274-866200 **Fax:** 01274-866220
E-mail: george.wilson@bordertextiles.co.uk
Website: http://www.bordertextiles.co.uk
Bank(s): Royal Bank of Scotland, Galashiels
Directors: Y. Wilson (Co Sec), G. Wilson (MD), P. Hextall (Sales)
Immediate Holding Company: BORDER TECHNOLOGIES LIMITED
Registration no: 01228328 **Date established:** 1975 **Turnover:** £2m - £5m
No.of Employees: 11 - 20 **Product Groups:** 22, 29, 37, 38, 42, 43

Date of Accounts	Feb 12	Feb 11	Feb 10
Working Capital	223	170	129
Fixed Assets	66	78	77
Current Assets	729	666	542

Bradford Business Machines
155 Bradford Road, Cleckheaton, BD19 3SX
Tel: 01274-879608 **Fax:** 01274-879608
E-mail: alanhudson7@btinternet.com
Website: http://www.bradfordbusinessmachines.co.uk
Directors: A. Hudson (Ptnr)
Date established: 1987 **Turnover:** Up to £250,000
No.of Employees: 1 - 10 **Product Groups:** 42, 44, 48, 67, 79, 80

Brupaks Brewing Equipment
Unit B Middleton Business Park Cartwright Street, Cleckheaton, BD19 5LY
Tel: 01274-865544 **Fax:** 01484-663359
E-mail: brupaks@brupaks.com
Website: http://www.brupaks.com
Directors: C. Donald (Prop), C. Donnald (Prop)
Immediate Holding Company: BRUPAKS (UK) LIMITED
Registration no: 06999973 **Date established:** 2009
No.of Employees: 1 - 10 **Product Groups:** 20, 40, 41

Date of Accounts	Aug 11	Aug 10
Working Capital	-16	-24
Fixed Assets	42	47
Current Assets	172	108

Burnhill Services Ltd
Middleton Business Park Cartwright Street, Cleckheaton, BD19 5LY
Tel: 01274-872423 **Fax:** 01274-861499
E-mail: info@burnhillequestrian.com
Website: http://www.burnhillequestrian.com
Directors: J. Burnhill (Fin), B. Burnhill (Dir)
Immediate Holding Company: BURNHILL SERVICES LIMITED
Registration no: 04499108 **Date established:** 2002
No.of Employees: 1 - 10 **Product Groups:** 62

Date of Accounts	Jul 11	Jul 10	Jul 09
Working Capital	125	120	112
Fixed Assets	73	65	64
Current Assets	247	217	200

Clemo
PO Box 24, Cleckheaton, BD19 3TT
Tel: 01274-863700 **Fax:** 01274-863725
E-mail: info@clemo.co.uk
Website: http://www.clemo.co.uk
Bank(s): HSBC Bank plc
Directors: R. Smith (Grp Chief Exec)
Immediate Holding Company: CROSSLEY DRYLINING LIMITED
Registration no: 03984487 **VAT No.:** GB 183 4955 31
Date established: 2007 **No.of Employees:** 51 - 100 **Product Groups:** 68

Date of Accounts	Mar 08	Mar 07	Mar 06
Working Capital	-14	-5	-43
Fixed Assets	43	50	53
Current Assets	182	182	41

Firetec Ltd
Westend Drive, Cleckheaton, BD19 6JD
Tel: 01274-855226 **Fax:** 07092-358471
E-mail: sales@firetec.co.uk
Website: http://www.firetec.co.uk
Directors: C. Coley (MD)
Immediate Holding Company: Firetec (North) Ltd
Registration no: 02582133 **No.of Employees:** 1 - 10 **Product Groups:** 38, 42

Flexitallic Ltd
Scandinavia Mills Hunsworth Lane, Cleckheaton, BD19 4LN
Tel: 01274-851273 **Fax:** 01274-851386
E-mail: dmitchell@flexitallic.com
Website: http://www.flexitallic.eu
Bank(s): National Westminster Bank Plc
Directors: P. Kelshaw (MD), S. Harper (Fin)
Managers: S. Tywang (Personnel), R. Singh (Buyer), K. Brooks (Sales & Mktg Mg), J. Senior (Tech Serv Mgr)
Ultimate Holding Company: OFI PRIVATE EQUITY CAPITAL (FRANCE)
Immediate Holding Company: FLEXITALLIC LTD.
Registration no: 03308289 **VAT No.:** GB 145 2609 76
Date established: 1997 **Turnover:** £10m - £20m
No.of Employees: 101 - 250 **Product Groups:** 23, 25, 29, 33, 36, 66, 67

Date of Accounts	Dec 11	Dec 10	Dec 09
Sales Turnover	17m	18m	15m
Pre Tax Profit/Loss	2m	2m	3m
Working Capital	17m	15m	13m
Fixed Assets	4m	4m	4m
Current Assets	21m	23m	21m
Current Liabilities	1m	1m	817

Garnett Wire Ltd
Woodroyd Mills South Parade, Cleckheaton, BD19 3AF
Tel: 01274-875741 **Fax:** 01274-851675
E-mail: sales@garnettwire.com
Website: http://www.garnettwire.com
Bank(s): National Westminster Bank Plc
Directors: M. Carline (Dir)
Immediate Holding Company: GARNETT WIRE LIMITED
Registration no: 02624315 **Date established:** 1991
No.of Employees: 11 - 20 **Product Groups:** 37, 43, 46

Date of Accounts	Mar 12	Mar 11	Mar 10
Working Capital	349	302	302
Fixed Assets	347	373	367
Current Assets	632	576	561

Goldpress
1 Lower Green Avenue Scholes, Cleckheaton, BD19 6PB
Tel: 01274-878488 **Fax:** 01274-878488
E-mail: badges@goldpress.co.uk
Website: http://www.goldpress.co.uk
Directors: D. Broadbent (Prop)
Registration no: 05359160 **No.of Employees:** 1 - 10 **Product Groups:** 38, 44, 49, 65

Goliath Footwear Ltd
Chain Bar Road, Cleckheaton, BD19 3QF
Tel: 08453-306430 **Fax:** 0845-330 6431
E-mail: enquiries@goliath.co.uk
Website: http://www.goliath.co.uk
Directors: S. Hall (MD)
Immediate Holding Company: GOLIATH FOOTWEAR LIMITED
Registration no: 04910073 **VAT No.:** GB 145 1242 02
Date established: 2003 **No.of Employees:** 1 - 10 **Product Groups:** 22

Date of Accounts	Dec 11	Dec 10	Dec 09
Working Capital	2m	2m	2m
Fixed Assets	332	226	100
Current Assets	3m	3m	2m

J Roberts Ltd
St Peg Lane, Cleckheaton, BD19 3SL
Tel: 01274-874631 **Fax:** 01274-851084
E-mail: bok@jroberts.co.uk
Website: http://www.jroberts.co.uk
Bank(s): Lloyds TSB plc
Directors: C. Bok (Fin), M. Roberts (Dir)
Managers: J. Travers (Tech Serv Mgr)
Immediate Holding Company: J. ROBERTS BRONZE COMPONENTS LIMITED
Registration no: 00351587 **VAT No.:** GB 183 6587 24
Date established: 1939 **Turnover:** £1m - £2m **No.of Employees:** 11 - 20
Product Groups: 30, 33, 34, 35, 36, 39, 48, 66, 68

Date of Accounts	Mar 11	Mar 10	Mar 09
Working Capital	1m	1m	1m
Fixed Assets	90	99	115
Current Assets	1m	1m	2m

Jay Be Ltd
Spen Lane Gomersal, Cleckheaton, BD19 4PN
Tel: 01924-517820 **Fax:** 01924-517910
E-mail: sales@jaybe.co.uk
Website: http://www.jay-be.co.uk
Bank(s): Yorkshire Bank PLC
Directors: M. Burrows (Jt MD), W. Burrows (MD)
Managers: R. Gullans (Sales & Mktg Mg), C. Wilson
Ultimate Holding Company: JAY-BE HOLDINGS LIMITED
Immediate Holding Company: JAY-BE LIMITED
Registration no: 00977944 **VAT No.:** GB 168 9069 15
Date established: 1970 **Turnover:** £2m - £5m
No.of Employees: 101 - 250 **Product Groups:** 26

Date of Accounts	Apr 07	Apr 06	Apr 05
Sales Turnover	10m	11m	13m
Pre Tax Profit/Loss	-1m	-1m	-708
Working Capital	1m	16	3m
Fixed Assets	4m	2m	2m
Current Assets	4m	4m	7m
Current Liabilities	468	579	527

Leuco Service Centre Ltd
Quarry Road Westgate, Cleckheaton, BD19 5HP
Tel: 01274-851827 **Fax:** 01274-852686
E-mail: sales@leucogb.com
Website: http://www.leucogb.co.uk
Directors: T. Harvey (Dir)
Registration no: 04167778 **Date established:** 2001
No.of Employees: 1 - 10 **Product Groups:** 46, 48

Major Recruitment Ltd
Premier House Bradford Road, Cleckheaton, BD19 3TT
Tel: 01924-298969 **Fax:** 01274-875688
E-mail: info@major-recruitment.com
Website: http://www.major-recruitment.com
Managers: J. King (Mgr)
Immediate Holding Company: MAJOR RECRUITMENT LIMITED
Registration no: 06570143 **Date established:** 2008
No.of Employees: 21 - 50 **Product Groups:** 80

Date of Accounts	Dec 08	Mar 11	Jun 10
Sales Turnover	N/A	10m	17m
Pre Tax Profit/Loss	N/A	242	-300
Working Capital	N/A	-237	-383
Fixed Assets	N/A	240	168
Current Assets	N/A	2m	2m
Current Liabilities	N/A	2m	2m

Novus Sealing
Hunsworth Lane, Cleckheaton, BD19 4EJ
Tel: 01274-878787 **Fax:** 01274-862588
E-mail: mailbox@novussealing.com
Website: http://www.novussealing.com
Bank(s): Barclays
Directors: S. Lewis (Dir)
Managers: G. Duffin (Tech Serv Mgr)
Ultimate Holding Company: OFI PRIVATE EQUITY CAPITAL (FRANCE)
Immediate Holding Company: NOVUS SEALING LIMITED
Registration no: 01334747 **VAT No.:** GB 708 3109 53
Date established: 1977 **Turnover:** £10m - £20m
No.of Employees: 51 - 100 **Product Groups:** 25, 29, 32, 33, 36, 40

Date of Accounts	Dec 11	Dec 10	Dec 09
Sales Turnover	13m	11m	8m
Pre Tax Profit/Loss	796	360	110
Working Capital	2m	2m	2m
Fixed Assets	2m	1m	1m
Current Assets	7m	5m	4m
Current Liabilities	718	390	288

Oxford Holt & Company Ltd
7 Brier Hill Close, Cleckheaton, BD19 6ND
Tel: 01274-879232 **Fax:** 01274-879232
E-mail: jkh@oxfordholt.co.uk
Website: http://www.oxfordholt.co.uk
Directors: J. Holt (MD)
Immediate Holding Company: OXFORD HOLT & COMPANY LIMITED
Registration no: 02373318 **Date established:** 1989
No.of Employees: 1 - 10 **Product Groups:** 80

Date of Accounts	Apr 12	Apr 11	Apr 10
Working Capital	-9	-0	4
Fixed Assets	N/A	1	1
Current Assets	N/A	9	7

Printgraphica
Unit 2 Netherfield Works Bradford Road, Cleckheaton, BD19 3JP
Tel: 01274-877740 **Fax:** 01274-877750
Website: http://www.printgraphica.co.uk
Directors: N. Abrahams (Prop)
No.of Employees: 1 - 10 **Product Groups:** 27, 42, 44, 49

Shaped Wires Ltd
Scholes Lane Scholes, Cleckheaton, BD19 6NH
Tel: 01274-876891 **Fax:** 01274-851116
E-mail: sales@shapedwires.com
Website: http://www.shapedwires.com
Bank(s): HSBC Bank plc
Directors: P. Priestley (Dir)
Immediate Holding Company: SHAPED WIRES LIMITED
Registration no: 01050564 **Date established:** 1972
No.of Employees: 11 - 20 **Product Groups:** 35

Date of Accounts	Mar 11	Mar 10	Mar 09
Working Capital	218	175	183
Fixed Assets	131	136	138
Current Assets	383	365	354

Slingtak Hoists Ltd
Quarry Road Westgate, Cleckheaton, BD19 5HP
Tel: 01274-851724 **Fax:** 01274-851724
E-mail: info@slingtak.co.uk
Website: http://www.slingtak.co.uk
Directors: A. Walker (Dir), A. Duce (Co Sec)
Immediate Holding Company: SLINGTAK HOISTS LIMITED
Registration no: 02133998 **Date established:** 1987
No.of Employees: 1 - 10 **Product Groups:** 35, 39, 45

Date of Accounts	Mar 11	Mar 10	Mar 09
Working Capital	37	26	24
Fixed Assets	3	3	6
Current Assets	166	97	76

Sontex Machinery Ltd
Unit B1 Cartwright Street, Cleckheaton, BD19 5LY
Tel: 01274-872299 **Fax:** 01274-862829
E-mail: info@sontex.co.uk
Website: http://www.sontex.co.uk
Directors: Y. Evans (Fin), D. Rawson (MD)
Immediate Holding Company: SONTEX (MACHINERY) LIMITED
Registration no: 00684985 **VAT No.:** GB 183 7422 51
Date established: 1961 **No.of Employees:** 1 - 10 **Product Groups:** 30, 42

Date of Accounts	Mar 12	Mar 11	Mar 10
Working Capital	488	453	353
Fixed Assets	281	274	277
Current Assets	818	828	619

Spen Bearings
129 Westgate, Cleckheaton, BD19 5EJ
Tel: 01274-851700 **Fax:** 01274-869736
E-mail: admin@spen-bearings.co.uk
Website: http://www.spen-bearings.co.uk
Bank(s): Lloyds TSB Bank plc
Managers: J. Haley (District Mgr)
Turnover: £2m - £5m **No.of Employees:** 11 - 20 **Product Groups:** 22, 23, 29, 30, 32, 34, 35, 36, 38, 39, 45, 48

Talon Lifting
Unit 2 Brook Forge Hightown Road, Cleckheaton, BD19 5JS
Tel: 01274-871242 **Fax:** 01274-869716
Directors: A. Knox (Prop)
Date established: 1985 **No.of Employees:** 1 - 10 **Product Groups:** 35, 39, 45

Dewsbury

Amir Power Transmission Ltd
2 Victory Court Flagship Square, Shaw Cross Business Park, Dewsbury, WF12 7TH
Tel: 01924-465500 **Fax:** 01924-469335
Website: http://www.amirpower.co.uk
Managers: M. Laher (Mgr)
Immediate Holding Company: AMIR POWER TRANSMISSION LIMITED
Registration no: 01741522 **Date established:** 1983 **Turnover:** £2m - £5m
No.of Employees: 1 - 10 **Product Groups:** 35, 37, 38, 39

Ash Mouldings UK Ltd
Brett Court Bretton Street, Dewsbury, WF12 9BB
Tel: 01924-485978 **Fax:** 01924-485978
E-mail: admin@ashmouldings.co.uk
Website: http://www.ashmouldings.co.uk
Directors: R. Spurgeon (MD), C. Spurgeon (Fin)
Immediate Holding Company: ASH MOULDINGS UK LTD
Registration no: 03687200 **Date established:** 1998
Turnover: £500,000 - £1m **No.of Employees:** 1 - 10 **Product Groups:** 29, 30, 31, 32, 33, 39, 43, 48, 67

Date of Accounts	Dec 11	Dec 10	Dec 09
Working Capital	75	68	32
Fixed Assets	33	7	10
Current Assets	145	152	76

Bibby Transmissions Ltd
Cannon Way, Dewsbury, WF13 1EH
Tel: 01924-460801 **Fax:** 01924-457668
E-mail: sales@bibbytransmissions.co.uk
Website: http://www.bibbytransmissions.co.uk
Bank(s): Barclays, London

Directors: C. Christenson (MD), G. Barga (Fin), S. Broomhead (Sales)
Managers: F. Thompson (Purch Mgr), J. Norton
Ultimate Holding Company: ALTRA HOLDINGS INC (USA)
Immediate Holding Company: BIBBY TRANSMISSIONS LIMITED
Registration no: 00158829 **Date established:** 2019
Turnover: £10m - £20m **No.of Employees:** 101 - 250
Product Groups: 29, 30, 35

Date of Accounts	Dec 11	Dec 10	Dec 09
Sales Turnover	13m	12m	11m
Pre Tax Profit/Loss	3m	4m	2m
Working Capital	12m	10m	3m
Fixed Assets	2m	2m	5m
Current Assets	15m	12m	5m
Current Liabilities	803	1m	1m

Branova Cleaning Services

Meadow Mills Carlton Road, Dewsbury, WF13 2BA
Tel: 01924-486000 **Fax:** 01924-486010
E-mail: sales@branova.com
Website: http://www.branova.com
Bank(s): Barclays
Directors: D. Barnes (Grp Mktg), K. Barnes (Ch), S. Brewer (Dir)
Ultimate Holding Company: Branta Group Ltd
Immediate Holding Company: BRANOVA LIMITED
Registration no: 04080795 **VAT No.:** GB 439 9832 94
Date established: 2000 **Turnover:** £500,000 - £1m
No.of Employees: 11 - 20 **Product Groups:** 23, 24, 27, 32, 33, 39, 40, 46, 61, 63, 68

Date of Accounts	Mar 10	Mar 09	Mar 08
Working Capital	-264	-266	-364
Fixed Assets	39	29	32
Current Assets	221	705	594

Calderdale Carpets Ltd

Dewsbury Mills Thornhill Road, Dewsbury, WF12 9QE
Tel: 01924-487800 **Fax:** 01924-487801
E-mail: sales@calderdalecarpets.com
Website: http://www.calderdalecarpets.com
Bank(s): Barclays
Directors: G. Bedford (MD)
Ultimate Holding Company: CALDER GROUP (DEWSBURY) LIMITED
Immediate Holding Company: CALDERDALE CARPETS LIMITED
Registration no: 02151352 **Date established:** 1987
No.of Employees: 51 - 100 **Product Groups:** 23

Date of Accounts	Jun 11	Jun 10	Jun 09
Working Capital	568	486	438
Fixed Assets	225	248	262
Current Assets	1m	1m	1m

Chauvin Arnoux

Unit 1 Nelson Court
Flagship Square
Shaw Cross Business Park, Dewsbury, WF12 7TH
Tel: 01924-460494 **Fax:** 01924-455328
E-mail: info@chauvin-arnoux.co.uk
Website: http://www.chauvin-arnoux.com
Directors: A. Arnoux (Pres), W. Smith (Grp Chief Exec)
Managers: N. Shell (Chief Mgr)
Date established: 1986 **Turnover:** £1m - £2m **No.of Employees:** 10
Product Groups: 28, 37, 38, 40, 46, 48, 67

Chauvin Arnoux UK Ltd

Nelson Court 1 Flagship Square, Shaw Cross Business Park, Dewsbury, WF12 7TH
Tel: 01924-460494 **Fax:** 01628-628099
E-mail: info@chauvin-arnoux.co.uk
Website: http://www.chauvin-arnoux.co.uk
Directors: D. Arnoux (Dir), W. Smith (Co Sec)
Managers: N. Shell (Chief Mgr)
Immediate Holding Company: CHAUVIN ARNOUX U.K. LIMITED
Registration no: 02001521 **VAT No.:** GB 448 5717 16
Date established: 1986 **Turnover:** £1m - £2m **No.of Employees:** 1 - 10
Product Groups: 37, 38, 44, 67

Date of Accounts	Dec 11	Dec 10	Dec 09
Working Capital	170	175	169
Fixed Assets	65	55	43
Current Assets	399	734	451

Classic Door Panels Ltd

Bretfield Court Bretton Street Industrial Estate, Dewsbury, WF12 9BG
Tel: 01924-462191 **Fax:** 01924-430530
E-mail: p.carr@classicdoorpanels.co.uk
Website: http://www.classicdoorpanels.co.uk
Directors: C. Tobin (MD), P. Carr (Fin)
Managers: N. Wood (Factory Mgr)
Ultimate Holding Company: STORK NV (NETHERLANDS)
Immediate Holding Company: CLASSIC DOOR PANELS LIMITED
Registration no: 02317792 **Date established:** 1988 **Turnover:** £5m - £10m
No.of Employees: 21 - 50 **Product Groups:** 30

Date of Accounts	Feb 12	Feb 11	Feb 10
Working Capital	124	124	118
Fixed Assets	101	136	183
Current Assets	528	463	611

Cleanaway Ltd

Ravensthorpe Road, Dewsbury, WF12 9EG
Tel: 01924-462171 **Fax:** 01924-459242
Website: http://www.cleanaway.com
Managers: M. Booth (Site Co-ord), P. Hasnip (Mgr)
Immediate Holding Company: CLEANAWAY LIMITED
Registration no: NF002533 **VAT No.:** GB 352 1129 90
Date established: 1981 **No.of Employees:** 21 - 50 **Product Groups:** 54

Connectomatic

Unit E Bretfield Court, Dewsbury, WF12 9BG
Tel: 01924-452444 **Fax:** 01924-430607
E-mail: sales@connectomatic.co.uk
Website: http://www.connectomatic.co.uk
Directors: R. Cheetham (MD)
Immediate Holding Company: CONNECTOMATIC LIMITED
Registration no: 01468140 **VAT No.:** GB 333 5104 94
Date established: 1979 **Turnover:** £500,000 - £1m
No.of Employees: 1 - 10 **Product Groups:** 36, 40, 41

Date of Accounts	Sep 11	Sep 10	Sep 09
Working Capital	40	213	134
Fixed Assets	4	2	2
Current Assets	334	370	286

Cubicle Centre

Caldervale Mills 33 Huddersfield Road, Dewsbury, WF13 3JL
Tel: 08451-701240 **Fax:** 01924-437600
E-mail: sales@plumbware.co.uk
Website: http://www.plumbware.co.uk
Managers: A. Thorpe (Mgr)
Immediate Holding Company: PLUMBWARE.CO.UK LTD
Registration no: 06851971 **Date established:** 2009 **Turnover:** £2m - £5m
No.of Employees: 11 - 20 **Product Groups:** 25, 66

Cutwel Ltd

Central Offices Central Street, Dewsbury, WF13 2LZ
Tel: 01924-869610 **Fax:** 01924-869611
E-mail: sales@cutwel.net
Website: http://www.cutweltools.co.uk
Managers: A. Gillard (Chief Mgr), K. Barker (Purch Mgr)
Immediate Holding Company: CUTWEL LIMITED
Registration no: 03202912 **Date established:** 1996 **Turnover:** £2m - £5m
No.of Employees: 11 - 20 **Product Groups:** 36

Date of Accounts	Apr 12	Apr 11	Apr 10
Working Capital	592	298	158
Fixed Assets	196	218	116
Current Assets	2m	2m	1m

Dewsbury Dyeing Co. Ltd

Oaklands Mill Netherfield Road, Dewsbury, WF13 3JY
Tel: 01924-463321 **Fax:** 01924-460899
E-mail: dews.dyeing@btclick.com
Bank(s): National Westminster Bank Plc
Directors: J. Smith (Fin)
Managers: R. Smith (Mgr)
Immediate Holding Company: DEWSBURY DYEING COMPANY LIMITED
Registration no: 01233278 **VAT No.:** GB 184 7417 38
Date established: 1975 **Turnover:** £1m - £2m **No.of Employees:** 11 - 20
Product Groups: 23

Date of Accounts	Jan 12	Jan 11	Jan 10
Working Capital	291	125	92
Fixed Assets	91	67	88
Current Assets	291	324	349

Dust Control Systems Ltd

Churwell Vale Shaw Cross Business Park, Dewsbury, WF12 7RD
Tel: 01924-482500 **Fax:** 01924-482530
E-mail: sales@dcslimited.co.uk
Website: http://www.dcslimited.co.uk
Directors: P. Oldfield (Fin), C. Oldfield (Dir)
Managers: G. Tempest (Mgr)
Ultimate Holding Company: DUST CONTROL SYSTEMS LIMITED
Immediate Holding Company: DUST CONTROL SYSTEMS HOLDINGS LIMITED
Registration no: 03239342 **Date established:** 1996 **Turnover:** £2m - £5m
No.of Employees: 21 - 50 **Product Groups:** 40, 41

F C P Mechanical Handling

4 Hoyle Head Mills New Street, Earlsheaton, Dewsbury, WF12 8JJ
Tel: 01924-466258 **Fax:** 01924-466258
E-mail: andy@fcpmechanicalhandling.fsnet.co.uk
Website: http://www.fcpmechanicalhandling.fsnet.co.uk
Directors: A. Whiteley (Dir)
Immediate Holding Company: FCP MECHANICAL HANDLING LIMITED
Registration no: 03763675 **Date established:** 1999
No.of Employees: 1 - 10 **Product Groups:** 35, 39, 45

Date of Accounts	May 10	May 09	May 08
Working Capital	-12	-17	-12
Fixed Assets	25	30	18
Current Assets	29	36	42

Forkway Ltd

Unit 1a Horace Waller V C Parade Shaw Cross Business Park, Dewsbury, WF12 7RF
Tel: 01924-465999 **Fax:** 01924-465888
E-mail: dewsbury@forkway.co.uk
Website: http://www.forkway.co.uk
Directors: T. Hunter (Dir)
Ultimate Holding Company: FORKWAY GROUP LIMITED
Immediate Holding Company: FORKWAY LIMITED
Registration no: 00788654 **Date established:** 1964 **Turnover:** £1m - £2m
No.of Employees: 21 - 50 **Product Groups:** 45, 67

Date of Accounts	Jan 12	Jan 11	Jan 10
Sales Turnover	9m	8m	7m
Pre Tax Profit/Loss	173	199	-1m
Working Capital	-46	-79	-343
Fixed Assets	2m	3m	3m
Current Assets	2m	2m	2m
Current Liabilities	766	810	667

Gamma Illuminations

Conway House Tenter Fields, Dewsbury, WF12 9QT
Tel: 01924-464343 **Fax:** 01924-438388
E-mail: sales@gamma-uk.co.uk
Website: http://www.gamma-uk.com
Directors: C. Marney (MD), M. Coult (Chief Op Offcr), A. Smith (Sales)
Managers: S. Whittington, J. Senior (Purch Mgr), A. Fowler
Immediate Holding Company: GAMMA ILLUMINATION (UK) LIMITED
Registration no: 02689289 **Date established:** 1992
No.of Employees: 51 - 100 **Product Groups:** 37

Gee Graphite Ltd

Ravensthorpe Industrial Estate Havelock Street, Dewsbury, WF13 3LU
Tel: 01924-480011 **Fax:** 01924-480017
E-mail: sales@geegraphite.com
Website: http://www.geegraphite.com
Bank(s): Lloyds TSB Bank plc
Directors: A. Whitehead (Fin), C. Richmond (MD)
Immediate Holding Company: GEE GRAPHITE LIMITED
Registration no: 02306442 **Date established:** 1988 **Turnover:** £2m - £5m
No.of Employees: 21 - 50 **Product Groups:** 25, 29, 30, 33, 36

Date of Accounts	Jan 12	Jan 11	Jan 10
Working Capital	360	274	265
Fixed Assets	395	473	448
Current Assets	2m	1m	1m

William S Graham & Sons Dewsbury Ltd

Ravens Ing Mills Huddersfield Road, Dewsbury, WF13 3JF
Tel: 01924-462456 **Fax:** 01924- 457985
E-mail: info@wsgraham.co.uk
Website: http://www.wsgraham.co.uk
Bank(s): HSBC
Directors: J. Graham (MD), N. Graham (Dir), N. Graham (MD), P. Sutton (Co Sec)
Immediate Holding Company: WILLIAM S. GRAHAM & SONS (DEWSBURY) LIMITED
Registration no: 00852497 **VAT No.:** GB 169 5625 25
Date established: 1965 **Turnover:** £20m - £50m
No.of Employees: 251 - 500 **Product Groups:** 23

Date of Accounts	Dec 10	Dec 09	Dec 08
Sales Turnover	41m	33m	39m
Pre Tax Profit/Loss	-714	-193	116
Working Capital	2m	3m	4m
Fixed Assets	10m	12m	10m
Current Assets	10m	10m	10m
Current Liabilities	3m	2m	2m

Hardy & Hanson Ltd

Longlands Road, Dewsbury, WF13 4AB
Tel: 01924-462353 **Fax:** 01924-457883
E-mail: info@hardy-hanson.co.uk
Website: http://www.hardy-hanson.co.uk
Directors: G. Howorth (MD)
Ultimate Holding Company: ABCO SEALS HOLDINGS LIMITED
Immediate Holding Company: HARDY AND HANSON LIMITED
Registration no: 00474421 **VAT No.:** GB 169 4885 04
Date established: 1949 **Turnover:** £2m - £5m **No.of Employees:** 1 - 10
Product Groups: 23, 26, 63, 64

Date of Accounts	Jun 11	Jun 10	Jun 09
Working Capital	1m	1m	1m
Fixed Assets	46	52	58
Current Assets	2m	1m	1m

Holstan Pipework Fabrication Ltd

Low Mill Lane, Dewsbury, WF13 3LX
Tel: 01924-499588 **Fax:** 01924-499599
Directors: S. Bentley (Dir)
Ultimate Holding Company: KOZEE SLEEP BEDS LIMITED
Immediate Holding Company: HOLSTAN (PIPEWORK FABRICATIONS) LIMITED
Registration no: 01549280 **Date established:** 1981 **Turnover:** £2m - £5m
No.of Employees: 11 - 20 **Product Groups:** 37, 40, 48

Date of Accounts	Mar 12	Mar 11	Mar 10
Working Capital	289	307	254
Fixed Assets	206	208	53
Current Assets	427	550	331

Hotwork Combustion Technology

Bretton Street Savile Town, Dewsbury, WF12 9DB
Tel: 01924-465272 **Fax:** 01924-506311
E-mail: info@hotworkct.com
Website: http://www.hotworkct.com
Directors: D. Robinson (MD), B. Crowther (Fin)
Managers: L. Ellis (Personnel), P. Rooney (I.T. Exec), D. Hunzinger (Mktg Serv Mgr), C. Jessop (Purch Mgr)
Immediate Holding Company: HOTWORK COMBUSTION TECHNOLOGY LIMITED
Registration no: 04386957 **Date established:** 2002 **Turnover:** £2m - £5m
No.of Employees: 1 - 10 **Product Groups:** 38, 40, 46, 48

Date of Accounts	Mar 11	Mar 10	Mar 09
Working Capital	309	286	173
Fixed Assets	133	156	192
Current Assets	1m	1m	2m

Luke Howgate & Son Ltd

PO Box 10, Dewsbury, WF13 1LL
Tel: 01924-465361 **Fax:** 01924-465361
Website: http://www.lukehowgate.co.uk
Bank(s): National Westminster
Directors: D. Goldthorpe (Sales), J. Howgate (MD)
Immediate Holding Company: LUKE HOWGATE & SON.LIMITED
Registration no: 00163590 **VAT No.:** GB 169 0498 31
Date established: 2020 **Turnover:** £1m - £2m **No.of Employees:** 21 - 50
Product Groups: 49

Date of Accounts	Jun 12	Jun 11	Jun 10
Working Capital	551	554	549
Fixed Assets	117	104	106
Current Assets	770	741	751

J & G Profiles Ltd

Netherfield Road, Dewsbury, WF13 3JY
Tel: 01924-485228 **Fax:** 01924-485228
Directors: J. Gledhill (MD), M. Morton (Fin)
Immediate Holding Company: DEWSBURY DYEING COMPANY LIMITED
Registration no: 04369031 **Date established:** 1975
No.of Employees: 1 - 10 **Product Groups:** 37, 67

Date of Accounts	Apr 11	Apr 10	Apr 09
Working Capital	-85	-61	-16
Fixed Assets	504	529	548
Current Assets	532	369	404

C R Longley & Co. Ltd

Ravensthorpe Road, Dewsbury, WF12 9EF
Tel: 01924-464283 **Fax:** 01924-459183
E-mail: sales@longley.uk.com
Website: http://www.longley.uk.com
Bank(s): Barclays
Directors: J. Longley (Fin), M. Longley (Dir)
Managers: V. Dunkley (Mktg Serv Mgr)
Immediate Holding Company: LONGLEY HOLDINGS LIMITED
Registration no: 02027916 **VAT No.:** GB 525 7408 43
Date established: 1986 **Turnover:** £10m - £20m
No.of Employees: 51 - 100 **Product Groups:** 33

Date of Accounts	Jul 11	Jul 10	Jul 09
Sales Turnover	14m	11m	9m
Pre Tax Profit/Loss	751	723	-159
Working Capital	2m	1m	1m
Fixed Assets	3m	3m	3m
Current Assets	5m	4m	3m
Current Liabilities	522	462	324

Machine Engineering Services

Forge Lane, Dewsbury, WF12 9EL
Tel: 01924-466406 **Fax:** 01924-466906
E-mail: machineengserr@aol.com
Website: http://www.machine-engser.com
Directors: S. Goldthorpe (Dir), P. Goldthorpe (Fin)
Immediate Holding Company: MACHINE ENGINEERING SERVICES LIMITED
Registration no: 04345798 **Date established:** 2001
No.of Employees: 1 - 10 **Product Groups:** 46, 48

Date of Accounts	Jan 11	Jan 10	Jan 09
Working Capital	-50	-60	51
Fixed Assets	157	170	70

see next page

Machine Engineering Services - Cont'd

Current Assets	138	119	146

Martech UK Ltd

Conway House Thornhill Road Business Park Tenter Fields, Dewsbury, WF12 9QT
Tel: 01924-482700 **Fax:** 01924-438388
E-mail: sales@martech-uk.com
Website: http://www.martech-uk.com
Directors: M. Choult (Chief Op Offcr), C. Marney (Dir), A. Smith (Sales)
Managers: L. Fox (Comptroller), S. Taylor (Mktg Serv Mgr), S. Whitington (Personnel), J. Senior (Purch Mgr)
Immediate Holding Company: MARTECH (UK) LTD
Registration no: 03045150 **Date established:** 1995
No.of Employees: 51 - 100 **Product Groups:** 33, 37

Date of Accounts	Apr 12	Apr 11	Apr 10
Sales Turnover	7m	N/A	N/A
Pre Tax Profit/Loss	806	N/A	N/A
Working Capital	1m	915	1m
Fixed Assets	1m	1m	1m
Current Assets	2m	2m	2m
Current Liabilities	491	N/A	N/A

Northern Creative Metal Arts

Lock Street, Dewsbury, WF12 9BZ
Tel: 01924-466770 **Fax:** 01924-469944
Website: http://www.dewsburygates.com
Directors: M. Beecher (Ptnr)
Date established: 1981 **No.of Employees:** 1 - 10 **Product Groups:** 26, 35

C Perkin Ltd

Shaw Cross Court Horace Waller V C Parade, Shaw Cross Business Park, Dewsbury, WF12 7RF
Tel: 01924-439449 **Fax:** 01924-438908
E-mail: info@cperkin.com
Website: http://www.cperkin.com
Directors: C. Perkin (MD), J. Whitaker (Dir)
Ultimate Holding Company: PERKIN HOLDINGS LIMITED
Immediate Holding Company: C PERKIN LIMITED
Registration no: 03773374 **Date established:** 1999 **Turnover:** £2m - £5m
No.of Employees: 11 - 20 **Product Groups:** 27, 44

Date of Accounts	May 11	May 10	May 09
Working Capital	136	76	120
Fixed Assets	87	74	27
Current Assets	838	580	431

PM Display

Unit 2.3 &4 Central Business Park, Central Street, Dewsbury, WF13 2NN
Tel: 01924-455877 **Fax:** 01924-455879
E-mail: info@pm-display.co.uk
Website: http://www.pm-display.co.uk
Directors: C. Stokes (Dir), K. Haigh (MD)
Managers: S. Wydell (Mktg Serv Mgr)
Registration no: 05214115 **Date established:** 2005
No.of Employees: 1 - 10 **Product Groups:** 28, 49, 81

Date of Accounts	Oct 07	Oct 06	Oct 05
Working Capital	-32	-35	-22
Fixed Assets	30	23	22
Current Assets	56	21	9
Current Liabilities	88	57	32

Pumps & Gear Boxes Ltd

Churwell Vale Shaw Cross Business Park, Dewsbury, WF12 7RD
Tel: 01924-468683 **Fax:** 01924-469247
E-mail: info@pumpsandgearboxes.co.uk
Website: http://www.pumpsANDgearboxes.co.uk
Directors: S. Gill (Dir)
Ultimate Holding Company: PUMPS & GEARBOXES HOLDINGS (UK) LIMITED
Immediate Holding Company: PUMPS & GEARBOXES HOLDINGS (UK) LIMITED
Registration no: 06262277 **VAT No.:** GB 169 2832 35
Date established: 2007 **Turnover:** £1m - £2m **No.of Employees:** 1 - 10
Product Groups: 66

Date of Accounts	Apr 12	Apr 11	Apr 10
Fixed Assets	1	1	1

Pure Spice Global Ltd

201 Bretton Street Enterprise Centre Bretton Street, Dewsbury, WF12 9DB
Tel: 01924-454454 **Fax:** 01924-454454
E-mail: purespice@btconnect.com
Directors: S. Potgieter (MD)
Managers: S. Potgieter (Sales Prom Mgr)
Immediate Holding Company: IQBALTI LIMITED
Registration no: 04463261 **Date established:** 2011
Turnover: Up to £250,000 **No.of Employees:** 1 - 10 **Product Groups:** 02, 20, 31

Richard Alan Engineering Company Ltd

Richard Alan House Churwell Vale, Shaw Cross Business Park, Dewsbury, WF12 7RD
Tel: 01924-467040 **Fax:** 01924-454377
E-mail: robertjohnson@richardalan.co.uk
Website: http://www.richard-allen.co.uk
Directors: S. Deakes (Co Sec), R. Johnson (MD)
Managers: A. Jackson (Tech Serv Mgr), L. Phillips (Personnel), G. Lyles (Mktg Serv Mgr)
Ultimate Holding Company: RICHARD ALAN GROUP LIMITED
Immediate Holding Company: RICHARD ALAN ENGINEERING COMPANY LIMITED
Registration no: 00973280 **Date established:** 1970
Turnover: £10m - £20m **No.of Employees:** 101 - 250
Product Groups: 46, 48

Date of Accounts	Apr 12	Apr 11	Apr 10
Sales Turnover	11m	8m	8m
Pre Tax Profit/Loss	204	118	107
Working Capital	1m	1m	1m
Fixed Assets	3m	3m	2m
Current Assets	4m	4m	4m
Current Liabilities	753	538	515

R S Richardson Belting Co. Ltd

Crown Works Staincliffe Road, Dewsbury, WF13 4SB
Tel: 01924-468191 **Fax:** 01924-458065
E-mail: mail@diepress-richardson.co.uk
Website: http://www.diepress-richardson.co.uk
Directors: C. Atkinson (Dir)
Immediate Holding Company: R.S. RICHARDSON BELTING COMPANY LIMITED
Registration no: 01268656 **Date established:** 1976
Turnover: £250,000 - £500,000 **No.of Employees:** 1 - 10
Product Groups: 22, 23, 29, 30, 32, 33, 35, 45, 66, 67

Date of Accounts	Jun 11	Jun 10	Jun 09
Working Capital	106	76	61
Fixed Assets	3	4	4
Current Assets	129	98	99

Rotajet Systems

Richard Alan House Shaw Cross Business Park, Dewsbury, WF12 7RD
Tel: 01924-468769 **Fax:** 01924-485376
E-mail: info@rotajet.co.uk
Website: http://www.rotajet.co.uk
Directors: B. Trafford (MD), C. Steward (Co Sec)
Ultimate Holding Company: DUST CONTROL SYSTEMS LIMITED
Immediate Holding Company: ROTAJET SYSTEMS LIMITED
Registration no: 06086220 **Date established:** 2007 **Turnover:** £1m - £2m
No.of Employees: 1 - 10 **Product Groups:** 39, 42, 46

Date of Accounts	Apr 10	Apr 09	Apr 08
Sales Turnover	1m	N/A	N/A
Working Capital	30	13	-11
Fixed Assets	15	21	39
Current Assets	423	218	213
Current Liabilities	64	N/A	N/A

Rushlift Ltd

Low Mill Lane Ravensthorpe Industrial Estate, Dewsbury, WF13 3LN
Tel: 01924-497805 **Fax:** 01924-490024
E-mail: sales@rushlift.co.uk
Website: http://www.rushlift.co.uk
Directors: G. Holyland (Grp Chief Exec), W. Cheesebrough (Fin)
Ultimate Holding Company: THE SPECIALIST HIRE GROUP LIMITED
Immediate Holding Company: RUSHLIFT LIMITED
Registration no: 05493140 **Date established:** 2005
No.of Employees: 21 - 50 **Product Groups:** 35, 39, 45

Date of Accounts	Aug 11	Aug 10	Aug 09
Sales Turnover	18m	15m	16m
Pre Tax Profit/Loss	1m	757	1m
Working Capital	-3m	928	316
Fixed Assets	28m	11m	12m
Current Assets	6m	6m	6m
Current Liabilities	2m	2m	2m

Saville Heaton Ltd

Heaton House Bradford Road, Dewsbury, WF13 2EE
Tel: 01924-466333 **Fax:** 01924-456654
E-mail: sales@saville-heaton.co.uk
Website: http://www.saville-heaton.co.uk
Directors: C. Davis (Co Sec), J. Heaton (Dir)
Immediate Holding Company: SAVILLE HEATON & CO. LIMITED
Registration no: 00514945 **Date established:** 1953 **Turnover:** £2m - £5m
No.of Employees: 21 - 50 **Product Groups:** 24

Date of Accounts	Dec 11	Dec 10	Dec 09
Sales Turnover	4m	5m	4m
Pre Tax Profit/Loss	129	314	318
Working Capital	2m	2m	2m
Fixed Assets	300	364	371
Current Assets	2m	2m	3m
Current Liabilities	221	364	203

Scales Spares & Services Ltd

Thornhill Road Business Park Tenter Fields, Dewsbury, WF12 9QT
Tel: 01924-464967 **Fax:** 01924-465208
E-mail: sales@scalessparesservices.co.uk
Website: http://www.scalessparesservices.co.uk
Directors: A. Saville (MD)
Immediate Holding Company: SCALES, SPARES & SERVICES LIMITED
Registration no: 01461221 **Date established:** 1979
No.of Employees: 1 - 10 **Product Groups:** 38, 42

Date of Accounts	Aug 11	Aug 10	Aug 09
Working Capital	77	83	109
Fixed Assets	400	418	398
Current Assets	167	143	193

Sewtec Automation Ltd

3 Riverside Way, Dewsbury, WF13 3LG
Tel: 01924-494047 **Fax:** 01924-480949
E-mail: sales@sewtec.co.uk
Website: http://www.sewtec.co.uk
Bank(s): National Westminster
Directors: H. Meehan (Fin), B. Meehan (MD)
Ultimate Holding Company: SEWTEC HOLDINGS LIMITED
Immediate Holding Company: SEWTEC AUTOMATION LIMITED
Registration no: 01699297 **VAT No.:** GB 361 6940 44
Date established: 1983 **Turnover:** £500,000 - £1m
No.of Employees: 51 - 100 **Product Groups:** 48, 84

Date of Accounts	Aug 11	Feb 11	Feb 10
Working Capital	2m	2m	1m
Fixed Assets	631	634	406
Current Assets	20m	12m	6m

Simpson Packaging

Unit 1 Shaw Cross Court Horace Waller V C Parade, Shaw Cross Business Park, Dewsbury, WF12 7RF
Tel: 01924-869010 **Fax:** 01924-437666
E-mail: sales@simpson-packaging.co.uk
Website: http://www.simpson-packaging.co.uk
Directors: J. Simpson (Snr Part), T. Dawes (Ptnr)
Managers: A. Simpson (Sales Prom Mgr)
Immediate Holding Company: IN INC LIMITED
Registration no: 06349698 **VAT No.:** GB 461 3581 53
Date established: 2007 **Turnover:** £2m - £5m **No.of Employees:** 21 - 50
Product Groups: 30

Date of Accounts	Aug 11	Aug 10	Aug 09
Working Capital	-9	-6	-5
Fixed Assets	6	7	8
Current Assets	40	28	30

Skopos Design Ltd

Providence Mill Syke Lane, Dewsbury, WF12 8HT
Tel: 01924-465191 **Fax:** 01924-454575
E-mail: a.webb@skopos.co.uk
Website: http://www.skoposdesignltd.com
Directors: S. Spurgeon (MD), J. Duncan Lee (Dir)
Managers: P. Perry (Mgr), R. Talbot (Personnel), G. Meakin (Tech Serv Mgr), L. Young (Mgr)
Ultimate Holding Company: WEB CIRCLE LIMITED
Immediate Holding Company: SKOPOS DESIGN LIMITED
Registration no: 01157536 **Date established:** 1974 **Turnover:** £5m - £10m
No.of Employees: 51 - 100 **Product Groups:** 23

Date of Accounts	Dec 11	Dec 10	Dec 09
Sales Turnover	7m	7m	9m
Pre Tax Profit/Loss	-27	-286	-320
Working Capital	1m	1m	544
Fixed Assets	853	918	825
Current Assets	3m	3m	3m
Current Liabilities	429	437	457

Sonic Solutions

21 Riverside Way, Dewsbury, WF13 3LG
Tel: 01924-495975 **Fax:** 01924-495976
E-mail: admin@sonicsolutionsltd.com
Website: http://www.sonicsolutionsltd.com
Directors: A. Taylor (MD)
Immediate Holding Company: SONIC SOLUTIONS LIMITED
Registration no: 05240314 **Date established:** 2004
Turnover: £250,000 - £500,000 **No.of Employees:** 1 - 10
Product Groups: 32, 37, 38, 48

Date of Accounts	Jun 11	Jun 10	Jun 09
Working Capital	-25	16	-3
Fixed Assets	71	88	110
Current Assets	56	41	50

Swift Windows

Unit 7 Staincliffe Mill Yard Halifax Road, Staincliffe, Dewsbury, WF13 4AR
Tel: 01924-406333 **Fax:** 01924-406777
Website: http://www.swiftwindowsconservatories.co.uk
Directors: H. Stead (Prop)
Immediate Holding Company: HORIZON PRINT & EMBROIDERY LTD
Date established: 2011 **No.of Employees:** 1 - 10 **Product Groups:** 33, 35, 36

Taylor Studwelding Systems Ltd

Commercial Road, Dewsbury, WF13 2BD
Tel: 01924-452123 **Fax:** 01924-430059
E-mail: davet@taylor-studwelding.com
Website: http://www.taylor-studwelding.com
Bank(s): Yorkshire Bank PLC
Directors: D. Taylor (Dir)
Immediate Holding Company: TAYLOR STUDWELDING SYSTEMS LIMITED
Registration no: 01839530 **VAT No.:** GB 461 2380 68
Date established: 1984 **Turnover:** £1m - £2m **No.of Employees:** 11 - 20
Product Groups: 35, 46, 49

Date of Accounts	Mar 11	Mar 10	Mar 09
Working Capital	581	537	502
Fixed Assets	199	186	168
Current Assets	1m	1m	868

Elland

ACS - Health Safety & Environment Ltd

41 Elizabeth Street, Elland, HX5 0JH
Tel: 01422-370588 **Fax:** 01422-377739
E-mail: info@acs-hse.co.uk
Website: http://www.asbestosconsultancyservices.co.uk
Directors: R. Tiffany (Dir)
Immediate Holding Company: ACS HEALTH,SAFETY & ENVIRONMENT LIMITED
Registration no: 06756394 **Date established:** 2008
No.of Employees: 1 - 10 **Product Groups:** 38, 40, 54, 84, 85

Date of Accounts	Feb 12	Feb 11	Feb 10
Sales Turnover	N/A	N/A	334
Working Capital	-3	-11	-13
Fixed Assets	28	32	27
Current Assets	94	102	70
Current Liabilities	N/A	33	N/A

Alzin Engineering Ltd

Century Works, Elland, HX5 9HG
Tel: 01422-373456 **Fax:** 01422-373813
E-mail: info@alzin.co.uk
Website: http://www.alzin.co.uk
Directors: G. Wormald (MD)
Immediate Holding Company: ALZIN ENGINEERING LIMITED
Registration no: 01131977 **VAT No.:** GB 184 8402 46
Date established: 1973 **Turnover:** £500,000 - £1m
No.of Employees: 11 - 20 **Product Groups:** 34

Date of Accounts	Apr 12	Apr 11	Apr 10
Working Capital	319	238	268
Fixed Assets	255	231	135
Current Assets	529	404	381

Archway Engineering UK Ltd

Ainley Industrial Estate, Elland, HX5 9JP
Tel: 01422-373101 **Fax:** 01422-374847
E-mail: info@archway-engineering.com
Website: http://www.archway-engineering.com
Bank(s): Barclays
Directors: R. Arak (Ch)
Immediate Holding Company: ARCHWAY ENGINEERING (U.K.) LIMITED
Registration no: 02600814 **VAT No.:** GB 525 9092 34
Date established: 1991 **No.of Employees:** 21 - 50 **Product Groups:** 36, 40, 45, 46, 47, 67, 83

Date of Accounts	Apr 12	Apr 11	Apr 10
Working Capital	752	684	576
Fixed Assets	436	390	436
Current Assets	1m	1m	923

Combserve Ltd

Unit 2 Brookfield Works Wood Street, Elland, HX5 9AP
Tel: 01422-370051 **Fax:** 01422-377374
E-mail: combserve@hotmail.co.uk
Website: http://www.combserve.co.uk
Directors: B. Mitchell (Dir)
Immediate Holding Company: COMBSERVE LIMITED
Registration no: 02783974 **VAT No.:** GB 361 5410 78
Date established: 1993 **Turnover:** £500,000 - £1m
No.of Employees: 1 - 10 **Product Groups:** 38, 65

Date of Accounts	Dec 07	Apr 11	Apr 10
Working Capital	67	57	14
Fixed Assets	6	61	89
Current Assets	237	503	490

Decorative Panels Ltd
Factory Building Premier Way, Lowfields Business Park, Elland, HX5 9HF
Tel: 01484-658341 **Fax:** 10484-658812
E-mail: s.gaunt@decorativepanels.co.uk
Website: http://www.decorativepanels.co.uk
Directors: G. Metcalffe (MD), T. Jones (Co Sec), T. Jones (Fin)
Managers: A. Wortley (Personnel), R. Cadwell (Sales & Mktg Mg)
Ultimate Holding Company: DECORATIVE PANELS HOLDINGS LIMITED
Immediate Holding Company: DECORATIVE PANELS HOLDINGS LIMITED
Registration no: 00792998 **Date established:** 1964
Turnover: £50m - £75m **No.of Employees:** 101 - 250 **Product Groups:** 25

Date of Accounts	Mar 11	Mar 10	Mar 09
Sales Turnover	71m	58m	37m
Pre Tax Profit/Loss	6m	4m	2m
Working Capital	4m	2m	3m
Fixed Assets	19m	15m	13m
Current Assets	23m	17m	13m
Current Liabilities	7m	4m	2m

Direct Visual Ltd
The Gateway Lowfields Close, Lowfields Business Park, Elland, HX5 9DX
Tel: 08453-575757 **Fax:** 01422-313473
E-mail: marketing@direct-visual.com
Website: http://www.direct-visual.com
Managers: A. Cowley (Comm), M. Stoves, S. Shaw (Sales Prom Mgr), A. Thorneton (Mktg Serv Mgr), G. Sykes (Tech Serv Mgr), L. Chaple (Personnel)
Ultimate Holding Company: DATATEC LTD (BRITISH VIRGIN ISLANDS)
Immediate Holding Company: DIRECT VISUAL LIMITED
Registration no: 03018453 **Date established:** 1995 **Turnover:** £5m - £10m
No.of Employees: 51 - 100 **Product Groups:** 67

Date of Accounts	Mar 11	Mar 10	Mar 09
Sales Turnover	6m	8m	8m
Pre Tax Profit/Loss	-247	183	180
Working Capital	-502	156	96
Fixed Assets	217	339	340
Current Assets	3m	2m	3m
Current Liabilities	3m	520	839

Feather Diesel Services
Unit G12 Lock View, Lowfields Business Park, Elland, HX5 9HD
Tel: 01422-387800 **Fax:** 01422-378787
E-mail: enquiries@feather-diesel.co.uk
Website: http://www.feather-diesel.co.uk
Directors: S. Smith (MD)
Managers: S. Westaway (Fin Mgr)
Ultimate Holding Company: FEATHER DIESEL HOLDINGS LIMITED
Immediate Holding Company: FEATHER DIESEL SERVICES LIMITED
Registration no: 00957030 **Date established:** 1969 **Turnover:** £1m - £2m
No.of Employees: 21 - 50 **Product Groups:** 39, 40, 68

Date of Accounts	Sep 11	Sep 10	Sep 09
Working Capital	433	506	449
Fixed Assets	637	688	724
Current Assets	1m	1m	1m

Fuel Tanks Direct
Norman Street, Elland, HX5 9BS
Tel: 01422-310111 **Fax:** 01422-370786
E-mail: neville@fueltanksdirect.co.uk
Website: http://www.fueltanksdirect.co.uk
Product Groups: 29, 35, 39

G F A Premier
Wistons Lane, Elland, HX5 9DT
Tel: 01422-314375 **Fax:** 01422-377521
E-mail: customer.services@gfapremier.co.uk
Website: http://www.gfapremier.com
Directors: B. Gibbons (MD)
Ultimate Holding Company: EOI FIRE SARL (LUXEMBOURG)
Immediate Holding Company: GFA PREMIER LIMITED
Registration no: 02020406 **Date established:** 1986 **Turnover:** £1m - £2m
No.of Employees: 51 - 100 **Product Groups:** 40

Date of Accounts	Dec 11	Dec 10	Dec 09
Sales Turnover	1m	1m	1m
Pre Tax Profit/Loss	332	331	375
Working Capital	582	283	3m
Fixed Assets	214	272	347
Current Assets	2m	2m	5m
Current Liabilities	221	244	317

Garlock GB Ltd
Premier Way Lowfields Business Park, Elland, HX5 9HF
Tel: 01422-313600 **Fax:** 01924-422244
E-mail: sales-uk@garlock.co.uk
Website: http://www.garlock.co.uk
Bank(s): HSBC Bank plc
Directors: D. Mortiboy (MD), I. Whitley (Fin)
Managers: J. Spangles, P. Stroud (Personnel), L. Murphy
Ultimate Holding Company: ENPRO INDUSTRIES INC (USA)
Immediate Holding Company: GARLOCK (GREAT BRITAIN) LIMITED
Registration no: 01014770 **VAT No.:** GB 614 5767 30
Date established: 1971 **Turnover:** £2m - £5m **No.of Employees:** 21 - 50
Product Groups: 23, 29, 30

Date of Accounts	Dec 11	Dec 10	Dec 09
Sales Turnover	10m	9m	9m
Pre Tax Profit/Loss	-585	-2m	-1m
Working Capital	3m	3m	3m
Fixed Assets	5m	4m	4m
Current Assets	6m	5m	4m
Current Liabilities	2m	1m	372

W T Knowles & Sons Ltd
Ash Grove Sanitary Pipe Works Elland Road, Elland, HX5 9JA
Tel: 01422-372833 **Fax:** 01422-370900
E-mail: sales@wtknowles.co.uk
Website: http://www.wtknowles.co.uk
Bank(s): Barclays
Directors: M. Knowles (MD), H. Flockton (Co Sec)
Immediate Holding Company: W.T. KNOWLES & SONS LIMITED
Registration no: 00215100 **VAT No.:** GB 183 4342 64
Date established: 2026 **Turnover:** £2m - £5m **No.of Employees:** 21 - 50
Product Groups: 33

Date of Accounts	Mar 12	Mar 11	Mar 10
Working Capital	1m	1m	1m
Fixed Assets	426	392	301
Current Assets	2m	2m	2m

Newsome Ltd
Calderbank Saddleworth Road, Elland, HX5 0RY
Tel: 01422-371711 **Fax:** 01422-377372
E-mail: robert.siwerski@newsome.ltd.uk
Website: http://www.newsome.ltd.uk
Bank(s): Yorkshire Bank
Directors: D. Harker (Dir), D. Harker (MD), G. Speight (Contracts), G. Walker (Contracts), J. Fielding (Tech Serv)
Managers: P. Waddington, R. Siwerski (Projects)
Immediate Holding Company: NEWSOME HOLDINGS LIMITED
Registration no: 01161739 **VAT No.:** GB 525 6344 48
Date established: 1974 **Turnover:** £1m - £2m **No.of Employees:** 11 - 20
Product Groups: 40, 41, 52, 66, 84

Date of Accounts	Mar 10	Mar 09	Mar 08
Working Capital	356	121	-28
Fixed Assets	128	127	105
Current Assets	1m	492	892

Nu Swift International Ltd
PO Box 10, Elland, HX5 9DS
Tel: 01422-372852 **Fax:** 01422-379569
E-mail: rpollard@nuswift.co.uk
Website: http://www.nuswift.co.uk
Bank(s): Lloyds TSB Bank plc
Directors: R. Pollard (Fin)
Ultimate Holding Company: EOI FIRE SARL (LUXEMBOURG)
Immediate Holding Company: NU-SWIFT INTERNATIONAL LIMITED
Registration no: 00276465 **VAT No.:** GB 183 6152 59
Date established: 1933 **Turnover:** £2m - £5m **No.of Employees:** 51 - 100
Product Groups: 27, 29, 30, 33, 35, 37, 38, 39, 40, 49, 52, 67, 84, 86

Date of Accounts	Dec 11	Dec 10	Dec 09
Sales Turnover	3m	3m	3m
Pre Tax Profit/Loss	674	4m	829
Working Capital	13m	12m	9m
Fixed Assets	987	1m	1m
Current Assets	16m	16m	15m
Current Liabilities	1m	1m	2m

P T G Heavy Industries
Units 5-6 Rosemount Works Huddersfield Road, Elland, HX5 0EE
Tel: 01422-379222 **Fax:** 01422-379122
E-mail: sales@ymtools.com
Website: http://www.ptgheavyindustries.com
Managers: A. Mccampbell (Ops Mgr)
Immediate Holding Company: NORTHERN FLATTENING LIMITED
Registration no: 03390129 **Date established:** 2004
No.of Employees: 21 - 50 **Product Groups:** 46, 47, 66

Date of Accounts	Mar 11	Mar 10	Mar 09
Working Capital	-10	-14	-25
Fixed Assets	7	10	15
Current Assets	18	33	36

P T M Shot Blasting
Bridgefield Mills, Elland, HX5 0SQ
Tel: 01422-327275 **Fax:** 01422-327275
Directors: P. Kemp (Ptnr)
Date established: 2004 **No.of Employees:** 1 - 10 **Product Groups:** 46, 48

Promec Cutting Tools
Lowfields Way Lowfields Business Park, Elland, HX5 9DA
Tel: 01422-311121 **Fax:** 01422-311171
E-mail: sales@promeccuttingtools.co.uk
Website: http://www.promeccuttingtools.co.uk
Managers: V. Jagger (Mgr)
Ultimate Holding Company: TERBERG BEHEER BV (NETHERLANDS)
Immediate Holding Company: R.L. DISTRIBUTION LIMITED
Date established: 1998 **No.of Employees:** 1 - 10 **Product Groups:** 36, 37, 46

Date of Accounts	Dec 09	Dec 08
Working Capital	30	30
Current Assets	30	30

Prosep Filter Systems
Unit G19 River Bank Way Lowfields Business Park, Elland, HX5 9DN
Tel: 01422-377367 **Fax:** 01422-377369
E-mail: sales@prosep.co.uk
Website: http://www.prosep.co.uk
Directors: S. Parker (Dir)
Immediate Holding Company: PROSEP FILTER SYSTEMS LIMITED
Registration no: 02345525 **Date established:** 1989
Turnover: £500,000 - £1m **No.of Employees:** 1 - 10 **Product Groups:** 14, 20, 23, 24, 25, 27, 29, 30, 31, 32, 33, 34, 35, 36, 37, 38, 39, 40, 41, 42, 44, 45, 49, 66, 67, 68

Date of Accounts	Apr 11	Apr 10	Apr 09
Working Capital	52	21	30
Fixed Assets	257	249	252
Current Assets	306	267	250

Quality Conveyors Ltd
10-13 Elland Lane, Elland, HX5 9DU
Tel: 01422-377166 **Fax:** 01422-377238
E-mail: qconveyor@aol.com
Directors: T. Hogan (MD), S. Hogan (Fin)
Immediate Holding Company: QUALITY CONVEYORS LIMITED
Registration no: 04128852 **Date established:** 2000
No.of Employees: 11 - 20 **Product Groups:** 30, 41, 45

Date of Accounts	Dec 11	Dec 10	Dec 09
Working Capital	219	208	297
Fixed Assets	26	28	31
Current Assets	597	670	439

Rol Trac Automatic Doors Ltd
Unit 1 Brookfield Works Quebec Street, Elland, HX5 9AP
Tel: 08450-042502 **Fax:** 01422-379076
E-mail: info@roltrac.com
Website: http://www.roltrac.com
Directors: A. Benson (Dir)
Immediate Holding Company: ROL-TRAC (AUTOMATIC DOORS) LIMITED
Registration no: 02735480 **Date established:** 1992
Turnover: £500,000 - £1m **No.of Employees:** 11 - 20
Product Groups: 30, 37, 40

Date of Accounts	Jun 11	Jun 10	Jun 09
Working Capital	21	25	20
Fixed Assets	19	16	9
Current Assets	253	201	178

Spata Wrought Iron Work
Woodside Mills Halifax Road, Elland, HX5 0SH
Tel: 01422-379929 **Fax:** 01422-379929
Directors: G. Green (MD), K. Green (Fin)
Immediate Holding Company: SPATA WROUGHT IRON WORK LTD
Registration no: 04437041 **Date established:** 2002
No.of Employees: 1 - 10 **Product Groups:** 26, 35

Date of Accounts	Mar 11	Mar 10	Mar 07
Working Capital	-12	-12	-1
Fixed Assets	17	17	17
Current Assets	5	3	6
Current Liabilities	17	13	N/A

Ultrasyntec Ltd
Unit 3 Ashday Works Business Park Elland Road, Elland, HX5 9JD
Tel: 01422-377708 **Fax:** 01422-377857
E-mail: info@ultrasynteclt d.co.uk
Website: http://www.ultrasynteclt d.co.uk
Directors: V. Hoyle (Fin)
Immediate Holding Company: ULTRASYNTEC LIMITED
Registration no: 03251121 **Date established:** 1996
Turnover: £500,000 - £1m **No.of Employees:** 1 - 10 **Product Groups:** 52

Date of Accounts	Sep 11	Sep 10	Sep 09
Working Capital	85	81	75
Fixed Assets	9	11	18
Current Assets	182	236	121

Vilene Interlinings
Unit B9 Lowfields Close, Lowfields Business Park, Elland, HX5 9DX
Tel: 01422-327900 **Fax:** 01422-327999
E-mail: per.henriksen@freudenberg-nw.com
Website: http://www.freudenberg-nw.com
Managers: P. Henriksen (Chief Mgr)
Ultimate Holding Company: CARL FREUDENBERG (GERMANY)
Immediate Holding Company: FREUDENBERG NONWOVENS LP.
VAT No.: GB 477 9938 62 **Turnover:** £20m - £50m
No.of Employees: 1 - 10 **Product Groups:** 23

Walker Brothers Elland Ltd
Ainley Industrial Estate, Elland, HX5 9JP
Tel: 01422-310767 **Fax:** 01422-377837
E-mail: sales@wbelland.com
Website: http://www.wbelland.com
Directors: A. Hunter (MD), L. Hunter (Fin)
Managers: C. Parkinson (Purch Mgr)
Ultimate Holding Company: THE H GROUP LIMITED
Immediate Holding Company: WALKER BROS (ELLAND) LIMITED
Registration no: 03294347 **VAT No.:** GB 148 5684 25
Date established: 1996 **Turnover:** £1m - £2m **No.of Employees:** 21 - 50
Product Groups: 48

Date of Accounts	Dec 11	Dec 10	Dec 09
Working Capital	242	265	247
Fixed Assets	149	108	88
Current Assets	493	572	599

Weir Valves & Controls
Markets Britannia House, Elland, HX5 9JR
Tel: 01422-282000 **Fax:** 01422-282100
E-mail: info@weirgroup.com
Website: http://www.weirgroup.com
Managers: P. Myers (I.T. Exec)
Ultimate Holding Company: WEIR GROUP PLC(THE)
Immediate Holding Company: WEIR VALVES & CONTROLS UK LIMITED
Registration no: 00869208 **Date established:** 1966
Turnover: £20m - £50m **No.of Employees:** 101 - 250 **Product Groups:** 36

Date of Accounts	Dec 10	Dec 11	Dec 08
Sales Turnover	33m	35m	35m
Pre Tax Profit/Loss	2m	2m	1m
Working Capital	13m	15m	11m
Fixed Assets	2m	2m	2m
Current Assets	23m	22m	26m
Current Liabilities	3m	3m	2m

Halifax

A B C Fire Protection Halifax Ltd
Gate Farm Scar Bottom Lane, Greetland, Halifax, HX4 8NW
Tel: 01422-373636 **Fax:** 01422-375155
E-mail: enquiries@abcfireprotection.co.uk
Website: http://www.abcfireprotection.co.uk
Directors: C. Mcfadzean (MD)
Immediate Holding Company: ABC FIRE PROTECTION (HALIFAX) LIMITED
Registration no: 05369134 **Date established:** 2005
No.of Employees: 1 - 10 **Product Groups:** 38, 39, 40, 52, 67

Date of Accounts	Mar 12	Mar 11	Mar 10
Working Capital	-2	-15	-24
Fixed Assets	33	45	57
Current Assets	44	35	44

A M T Shotblast Engineers
New Bond Street, Halifax, HX1 5EZ
Tel: 01422-347722 **Fax:** 01422-347733
E-mail: enquiries@shotblastuk.com
Website: http://www.shotblastuk.com
Directors: P. Connell (MD)
Registration no: 04891913 **Turnover:** Up to £250,000
No.of Employees: 1 - 10 **Product Groups:** 33, 40, 42, 45, 46, 48, 52, 72

Date of Accounts	Sep 11	Sep 10	Sep 09
Working Capital	22	20	-3
Fixed Assets	7	9	12
Current Assets	59	77	47

Acorn Woodworking Machinery
Unit 5 The Market Business Centre Hanson Lane, Halifax, HX1 5PF
Tel: 01422-369900
Directors: M. Coral (Dir)
Date established: 1995 **No.of Employees:** 1 - 10 **Product Groups:** 46

Aquaspersions Ltd
Beacon Hill Road, Halifax, HX3 6AQ
Tel: 01422-386200 **Fax:** 01422-386239
E-mail: info@aquaspersions.co.uk
Website: http://www.aquaspersions.co.uk
Bank(s): National Westminster Bank Plc

see next page

***Aquaspersions Ltd** - Cont'd*

Directors: M. Richardson (Dir)
Immediate Holding Company: AQUASPERSIONS LIMITED
Registration no: 01167065 **Date established:** 1974
Turnover: £10m - £20m **No.of Employees:** 11 - 20 **Product Groups:** 30, 32

Date of Accounts	Jul 11	Jul 10	Jul 09
Sales Turnover	11m	9m	7m
Pre Tax Profit/Loss	625	574	420
Working Capital	2m	2m	1m
Fixed Assets	2m	2m	2m
Current Assets	5m	4m	3m
Current Liabilities	1m	1m	821

Architectural Fabrications
Leeds Road, Halifax, HX3 8SX
Tel: 01422-206608
Directors: P. Whelan (Prop)
Date established: 2002 **No.of Employees:** 1 - 10 **Product Groups:** 26, 35

Avena Carpets Ltd
Bankfield Mills Haley Hill, Halifax, HX3 6ED
Tel: 01422-330261 **Fax:** 01422- 348399
E-mail: avena@btconnect.com
Website: http://www.avena-carpets.com
Bank(s): Yorkshire Bank PLC
Directors: N. Crossley (Dir), J. Crossley (Dir), J. Tighe (MD), J. Tighe (Dir)
Managers: R. Tighe (I.T. Exec)
Immediate Holding Company: AVENA CARPETS LIMITED
Registration no: 04962240 **VAT No.:** GB 184 2070 93
Date established: 2003 **Turnover:** £1m - £2m **No.of Employees:** 11 - 20
Product Groups: 23

Banson Tool Hire Ltd
East Mount 125 Pellon Lane, Halifax, HX1 5QN
Tel: 01422-254999 **Fax:** 01422-254778
E-mail: sales@banson.uk.com
Website: http://www.banson.uk.com
Directors: R. Davies (MD)
Ultimate Holding Company: C. BANCROFT LIMITED
Immediate Holding Company: BANSON TOOL HIRE LIMITED
Registration no: 00927963 **Date established:** 1968 **Turnover:** £2m - £5m
No.of Employees: 1 - 10 **Product Groups:** 83

Date of Accounts	Jan 12	Jan 11	Jan 10
Working Capital	689	684	660
Fixed Assets	87	149	222
Current Assets	911	952	934

Bead & Shotblasting Ltd
Unit 2 Lee Bridge Industrial Estate Dean Clough Industrial Park, Halifax, HX3 5AT
Tel: 01422-368758 **Fax:** 01422-363795
E-mail: m.rushworth@beadshot.co.uk
Website: http://www.beadshot.co.uk
Directors: M. Rushworth (Dir)
Immediate Holding Company: BEAD & SHOTBLASTING LIMITED
Registration no: 03091849 **VAT No.:** GB 184 9277 18
Date established: 1995 **Turnover:** £250,000 - £500,000
No.of Employees: 1 - 10 **Product Groups:** 48

Date of Accounts	Dec 11	Dec 10	Dec 09
Working Capital	-16	-14	24
Fixed Assets	49	52	43
Current Assets	111	80	75

Blueprint Innovation Ltd
Holroyd Mill Dean Clough Office Park, old lane, Halifax, HX3 5AX
Tel: 01422-385000 **Fax:** 01422-384218
E-mail: innovation@blueprintdev.com
Website: http://www.blueprintdev.com
Directors: M. Karol (MD), D. Lee (Dir)
Immediate Holding Company: Holroyd Intellectual Property Ltd
Registration no: 03935524 **Date established:** 1997
No.of Employees: 21 - 50 **Product Groups:** 85

Bower Green Ltd (a division of Bower Green Ltd.)
Station Road Norwood Green, Halifax, HX3 8QD
Tel: 01274-672450 **Fax:** 01274-693136
E-mail: rpatterson@bowergreen.co.uk
Website: http://www.bowergreen.co.uk
Directors: R. Patterson (Dir)
Immediate Holding Company: BOWER GREEN LIMITED
Registration no: 03368517 **Date established:** 1997 **Turnover:** £1m - £2m
No.of Employees: 1 - 10 **Product Groups:** 76, 77

Date of Accounts	Jul 11	Jul 10	Jul 09
Sales Turnover	7m	7m	6m
Pre Tax Profit/Loss	10	36	-63
Working Capital	35	56	30
Fixed Assets	3m	3m	3m
Current Assets	2m	1m	1m
Current Liabilities	603	570	440

Boxford Ltd
Wheatley, Halifax, HX3 5AF
Tel: 01422-358311 **Fax:** 01422-355924
E-mail: sales@boxford.co.uk
Website: http://www.boxford.co.uk
Bank(s): Lloyds
Directors: G. Barrett (MD), P. Barraclough (MD)
Ultimate Holding Company: Boxford Holdings
Registration no: 01699916 **VAT No.:** GB 361 7295 42
Turnover: £2m - £5m **No.of Employees:** 21 - 50 **Product Groups:** 46

Date of Accounts	Apr 10	Apr 09	Apr 08
Working Capital	2m	1m	1m
Fixed Assets	147	180	83
Current Assets	3m	3m	4m

Boxtrees Precision Engineering Ltd
Boxtrees Mill Boy Lane, Wheatley, Halifax, HX3 5AF
Tel: 01422-358311 **Fax:** 01422-355924
E-mail: sales@boxford.co.uk
Website: http://www.boxford.co.uk
Bank(s): Lloyds TSB Bank plc
Directors: R. Wright (Fin), R. Greenway (MD)
Managers: S. Randerson (Chief Mgr), P. Naylor (Quality Control), M. Harris (Accounts)
Immediate Holding Company: Boxford Holdings Ltd
Registration no: 02004928 **Turnover:** £1m - £2m
No.of Employees: 11 - 20 **Product Groups:** 48

Date of Accounts	Apr 08	Apr 07	Apr 06
Working Capital	126	131	187
Fixed Assets	135	113	23
Current Assets	135	141	207

Brenntag Colours Ltd
High Level Way, Halifax, HX1 4PN
Tel: 01422-358431 **Fax:** 01422-330867
E-mail: colours.sales@albionchemicals.co.uk
Website: http://www.brenntag-colours.com
Directors: A. Stamataris (MD)
Ultimate Holding Company: BRENNTAG AG (GERMANY)
Immediate Holding Company: BRENNTAG COLOURS LIMITED
Registration no: 04227005 **Date established:** 2001
No.of Employees: 21 - 50 **Product Groups:** 32

Date of Accounts	Dec 11	Dec 10	Dec 09
Sales Turnover	18m	18m	15m
Pre Tax Profit/Loss	1m	1m	845
Working Capital	13m	12m	10m
Fixed Assets	5m	5m	5m
Current Assets	16m	14m	12m
Current Liabilities	438	411	172

A H Buckley & Sons
Little Brow Jagger Green Dean, Holywell Green, Halifax, HX4 9DQ
Tel: 01422-378210
Directors: M. Buckley (Prop)
Date established: 1979 **No.of Employees:** 1 - 10 **Product Groups:** 26, 35

Cengar Ltd
70 Lister Lane, Halifax, HX1 5DN
Tel: 01422-354626 **Fax:** 01422-349024
E-mail: enquiries@cengar.com
Website: http://www.cengar.com
Managers: R. Fletcher (Chief Mgr)
Ultimate Holding Company: CENGAR (HOLDINGS) LIMITED
Immediate Holding Company: CENGAR LIMITED
Registration no: 00399541 **Date established:** 1945
Turnover: £500,000 - £1m **No.of Employees:** 1 - 10 **Product Groups:** 36, 40, 46

Date of Accounts	Dec 11	Dec 10	Dec 09
Working Capital	706	604	589
Fixed Assets	220	203	158
Current Assets	838	656	619

Columbia Metals Ltd
Union Street South, Halifax, HX1 2LA
Tel: 01422-343026 **Fax:** 01422-346587
E-mail: export@columbiametals.co.uk
Website: http://www.columbiametals.co.uk
Managers: S. Margison (Mgr)
Immediate Holding Company: COLUMBIA METALS LIMITED
Registration no: 00700585 **Date established:** 1961 **Turnover:** £2m - £5m
No.of Employees: 1 - 10 **Product Groups:** 34

Date of Accounts	Oct 11	Oct 10	Oct 09
Working Capital	4m	4m	4m
Fixed Assets	396	416	452
Current Assets	5m	4m	4m

Complete Packaging Services Ltd
Unit 5 Brunswick Works Brassey Street, Halifax, HX1 2EA
Tel: 01422-368634 **Fax:** 01422-383087
E-mail: mark@completepackagingservices.co.uk
Website: http://www.completepackagingservices.co.uk
Directors: M. Barnett (MD)
Immediate Holding Company: COMPLETE PACKAGING SERVICES LIMITED
Registration no: 02819500 **Date established:** 1993
No.of Employees: 1 - 10 **Product Groups:** 38, 42

Date of Accounts	Nov 11	Nov 10	Nov 09
Working Capital	-0	-12	5
Fixed Assets	3	4	5
Current Assets	154	92	106

Cristel Paint Finishers Ltd
Dunkirk Mills Dunkirk Street, Halifax, HX1 3TB
Tel: 01422-300580 **Fax:** 01422-349686
E-mail: admin@cristelgraphics.co.uk
Website: http://www.cristelpaintfinishers.co.uk
Bank(s): Barclays
Directors: J. Wormald (Dir), T. Broadbend (MD)
Immediate Holding Company: Cristel Group Ltd
Registration no: 02394242 **VAT No.:** GB 721 2736 59
Date established: 1991 **Turnover:** £1m - £2m **No.of Employees:** 11 - 20
Product Groups: 49

Date of Accounts	Jun 08	Jun 07	Jun 06
Working Capital	-20	-30	-77
Fixed Assets	176	211	234
Current Assets	284	298	285
Current Liabilities	303	327	362
Total Share Capital	10	10	10

Crosslee plc
Lightcliffe Factory Hipperholme, Halifax, HX3 8DE
Tel: 01422-203555 **Fax:** 01422-206304
E-mail: general@crosslee.co.uk
Website: http://www.crosslee.co.uk
Directors: S. Hothersall (Sales), D. Boyle (MD), G. Chedwick (Fin)
Managers: A. Delaney, J. Jukes (Personnel)
Ultimate Holding Company: CROSSLEE HOLDINGS LIMITED
Immediate Holding Company: CROSSLEE PLC
Registration no: 02007937 **Date established:** 1986
Turnover: £20m - £50m **No.of Employees:** 251 - 500
Product Groups: 26, 40

Date of Accounts	Jul 11	Jul 10	Jul 09
Sales Turnover	42m	43m	36m
Pre Tax Profit/Loss	3m	3m	-378
Working Capital	7m	6m	5m
Fixed Assets	15m	15m	11m
Current Assets	12m	13m	8m
Current Liabilities	3m	2m	1m

R E Dickie Ltd
West End Works Parkinson Lane, Halifax, HX1 3UW
Tel: 01422-341516 **Fax:** 01422-357891
E-mail: sales@dickie.co.uk
Website: http://britishwool.com
Directors: J. Dickie (Fin)
Immediate Holding Company: R.E. DICKIE LIMITED
Registration no: 00486931 **VAT No.:** GB 183 5415 58
Date established: 1950 **Turnover:** £5m - £10m **No.of Employees:** 1 - 10
Product Groups: 23, 66

Date of Accounts	Jun 11	Jun 10	Jun 09
Working Capital	1m	1m	1m
Fixed Assets	960	973	960
Current Assets	2m	2m	2m

Dorlux Beds
Elizabeth Industrial Estate Shroggs Road, Halifax, HX3 5HA
Tel: 01422-399250 **Fax:** 01422-399251
E-mail: denise.morgan@dorlux.co.uk
Website: http://www.dorlux.co.uk
Bank(s): HSBC Bank plc
Directors: A. Afzal (MD), D. Morgan (Prop)
Managers: T. Pazir (Sales Prom Mgr), M. Zafar (Mktg Serv Mgr), P. Keane (Tech Serv Mgr), J. Smith (Fin Mgr), K. Parker (Purch Mgr)
Immediate Holding Company: SOHA LIMITED
Registration no: 00803368 **VAT No.:** GB 183 5459 38
Date established: 2011 **Turnover:** £10m - £20m
No.of Employees: 101 - 250 **Product Groups:** 26

Date of Accounts	Feb 12
Working Capital	824
Fixed Assets	139
Current Assets	2m

Electro Power Engineering
Brian Royd Mills Saddleworth Road, Greetland, Halifax, HX4 8NF
Tel: 01422-379570 **Fax:** 01422-370612
E-mail: enquiries@electropower.co.uk
Website: http://www.electropower.co.uk
Directors: P. Rhodes (MD)
Immediate Holding Company: ELECTRO POWER ENGINEERING LIMITED
Registration no: 02963903 **Date established:** 1994
Turnover: Up to £250,000 **No.of Employees:** 1 - 10 **Product Groups:** 37, 48

Date of Accounts	Oct 11	Oct 10	Oct 09
Working Capital	1	1	1
Current Assets	1	1	1

Exhaust Ejector Co. Ltd
11 Wade House Road Shelf, Halifax, HX3 7PE
Tel: 01274-679524 **Fax:** 01274-607344
E-mail: simon.conway@eeco-ltd.co.uk
Website: http://www.eeco-ltd.co.uk
Directors: S. Conway (Dir)
Immediate Holding Company: EXHAUST EJECTOR CO.LIMITED(THE)
Registration no: 00539526 **VAT No.:** GB 183 5576 34
Date established: 1954 **Turnover:** £1m - £2m **No.of Employees:** 1 - 10
Product Groups: 30, 33, 39

Date of Accounts	Sep 10	Sep 09	Sep 08
Working Capital	-32	9	37
Fixed Assets	119	125	132
Current Assets	92	244	192

F P D Medical Ltd
Brian Royd Mills Saddleworth Road, Greetland, Halifax, HX4 8NF
Tel: 01422-378569 **Fax:** 01422-376064
E-mail: craig.barson@clean-air-healthcare.co.uk
Website: http://www.fpdmedical.co.uk
Directors: C. Barson (MD), C. Barsen (MD), C. Barson (Dir)
Managers: D. Turner (Sales Prom Mgr), N. Martin (Mktg Serv Mgr), K. Ormand (Prod Mgr)
Ultimate Holding Company: FOCUS PRODUCT DEVELOPMENTS LIMITED
Immediate Holding Company: FPD MEDICAL LIMITED
Registration no: 01395741 **Date established:** 1978 **Turnover:** £1m - £2m
No.of Employees: 1 - 10 **Product Groups:** 26

Date of Accounts	Feb 11	Feb 10	Feb 09
Working Capital	139	113	77
Current Assets	187	179	131

F S C Halifax Ltd
Grantham House Grantham Road, Halifax, HX3 6PL
Tel: 01422-347872 **Fax:** 01422-321758
E-mail: kw@fscooper.com
Website: http://www.fscooper.com
Directors: K. Walker (MD)
Immediate Holding Company: FSC (HALIFAX) LIMITED
Registration no: 05217660 **VAT No.:** GB 157 1026 86
Date established: 2004 **Turnover:** £250,000 - £500,000
No.of Employees: 1 - 10 **Product Groups:** 45

Date of Accounts	Aug 11	Aug 10	Aug 06
Working Capital	30	24	16
Fixed Assets	3	3	2
Current Assets	63	53	109

Fan Systems Group Ltd
Brookwoods Industrial Estate Burrwood Way Holywell Green, Halifax, HX4 9BH
Tel: 01422-378131 **Fax:** 01422-378672
E-mail: martin.booth@fansystems.co.uk
Website: http://www.fansystems.co.uk
Bank(s): Lloyds Bank
Directors: M. Booth (MD)
Managers: M. Downs (Sales Prom Mgr), K. Booth (Purch Mgr), H. Kennedy (Personnel), S. Ashworth (Comptroller)
Ultimate Holding Company: WITT & SON UK HOLDINGS LIMITED
Immediate Holding Company: FAN SYSTEMS GROUP LIMITED
Registration no: 00479576 **VAT No.:** GB 145 6674 45
Date established: 1950 **No.of Employees:** 21 - 50 **Product Groups:** 29, 35, 40, 48

Date of Accounts	Dec 11	Dec 10	Dec 09
Working Capital	498	140	197
Fixed Assets	5	6	7
Current Assets	2m	2m	1m

Fitlock Systems Ltd
10 Albert Street, Halifax, HX1 5NW
Tel: 01422-354286 **Fax:** 01484-714538
E-mail: elaine.whatley@fitlocksystems.com
Website: http://www.fitlocksystems.com
Managers: E. Whatley (Mgr)
Immediate Holding Company: FIT-LOCK SYSTEMS LIMITED
Registration no: 03091603 **VAT No.:** GB 639 0169 31
Date established: 1995 **Turnover:** £250,000 - £500,000
No.of Employees: 1 - 10 **Product Groups:** 35, 66

Date of Accounts	Aug 11	Aug 10	Aug 09
Working Capital	886	857	685
Fixed Assets	844	915	951
Current Assets	2m	2m	1m
Current Liabilities	N/A	600	N/A

G B F
Unit 5 Bandwalk Industrial Estate Saddleworth Road, Greetland, Halifax, HX4 8BA
Tel: 01422-313542 **Fax:** 01422-372992
E-mail: g.bateman@btconnect.com
Directors: T. Marsh (Prop)
Immediate Holding Company: G BATEMAN FABRICATIONS LTD
Registration no: 05626882 **Date established:** 2005
No.of Employees: 1 - 10 **Product Groups:** 35

Date of Accounts	Nov 11	Nov 10	Nov 09
Working Capital	164	127	82
Fixed Assets	9	16	24
Current Assets	315	252	210

James Garside & Son Ltd
Grantham Works Grantham Road, Halifax, HX3 6PL
Tel: 01422-347212 **Fax:** 01422-349465
E-mail: jamesgarsideltd@hotmail.com
Website: http://www.jamesgarsideltd.com
Bank(s): Barclays
Directors: C. Garside (Dir)
Immediate Holding Company: JAMES GARSIDE & SON LIMITED
Registration no: 00382596 **VAT No.:** GB 183 7059 44
Date established: 1943 **Turnover:** Up to £250,000
No.of Employees: 11 - 20 **Product Groups:** 72

Date of Accounts	Feb 12	Feb 11	Feb 10
Working Capital	145	118	124
Fixed Assets	760	759	798
Current Assets	298	256	231

Ernest Gill & Son
Hope Street, Halifax, HX1 5DW
Tel: 01422-330037 **Fax:** 01422-399747
E-mail: enquiries@ernestgill.co.uk
Website: http://www.ernestgill.co.uk
Managers: S. Gill (Mgr)
No.of Employees: 21 - 50 **Product Groups:** 26, 67

Glendale Filtration
3 Epsom Grove Southowram, Halifax, HX3 9NQ
Tel: 01422-345923 **Fax:** 01422-345923
Directors: A. Holsworth (Ptnr)
No.of Employees: 1 - 10 **Product Groups:** 40, 66

Graham
Wade Street, Halifax, HX1 1SN
Tel: 01422-359141 **Fax:** 01422-381032
Website: http://www.graham-group.co.uk
Managers: R. Knowles (Mgr)
Ultimate Holding Company: SAINT-GOBAIN PLC
Immediate Holding Company: GRAHAM GROUP LTD
Registration no: 00066738 **VAT No.:** GB 394 1212 63
No.of Employees: 1 - 10 **Product Groups:** 66

Halifax Air Systems Ltd
98-100 Spring Hall Lane, Halifax, HX1 4TW
Tel: 01422-364621 **Fax:** 01422-364622
E-mail: info@halifaxairsystems.co.uk
Website: http://www.halifaxairsystems.co.uk
Directors: M. Cooper (Fin), R. Cooper (MD)
Immediate Holding Company: HALIFAX AIR SYSTEMS LIMITED
Registration no: 01285384 **VAT No.:** GB 184 8705 28
Date established: 1976 **Turnover:** £250,000 - £500,000
No.of Employees: 1 - 10 **Product Groups:** 40, 52, 54

Date of Accounts	May 11	May 10	May 09
Working Capital	7	7	-42
Fixed Assets	27	14	21
Current Assets	113	98	92

Halifax Numerical Controls Ltd
Holmfield Works Shay Lane, Halifax, HX3 6RS
Tel: 01422-360607 **Fax:** 01422-360614
E-mail: mike.d@hnc.ltd.uk
Website: http://hncl.co.uk
Directors: M. Diskin (MD)
Immediate Holding Company: HALIFAX NUMERICAL CONTROLS LIMITED
Registration no: 03519696 **Date established:** 1998
No.of Employees: 1 - 10 **Product Groups:** 37, 38, 44, 46, 48, 67, 84

Date of Accounts	Mar 11	Mar 10	Mar 09
Working Capital	98	163	167
Fixed Assets	16	26	41
Current Assets	298	342	373

Halifax Process Engineering Ltd
4 Shay Lane Works Shay Lane, Ovenden, Halifax, HX3 6SF
Tel: 01422-367931 **Fax:** 01422- 349023
E-mail: andy@halifaxprocess.co.uk
Website: http://www.halifaxprocess.co.uk
Directors: A. Brown (Dir)
Immediate Holding Company: HALIFAX PROCESS ENGINEERING LIMITED
Registration no: 01476926 **VAT No.:** 333 6286 57 **Date established:** 1980
Turnover: £500,000 - £1m **No.of Employees:** 1 - 10 **Product Groups:** 45

Date of Accounts	Aug 09	Aug 08	Aug 07
Working Capital	-26	33	-8
Fixed Assets	16	21	26
Current Assets	105	186	169

Halifax Sheet Metal & Ventilation
Pellon Industrial Estate Queens Road, Halifax, HX1 4PR
Tel: 01422-362361 **Fax:** 01422-340591
E-mail: m.fitzgerald@hsmv.co.uk
Website: http://www.hsmv.co.uk
Directors: M. Fitzgerald (MD)
Ultimate Holding Company: DEALCATER TRADING LTD
Immediate Holding Company: LEO GROUP LTD
Registration no: 06759315 **VAT No.:** GB 183 4460 58
Date established: 2008 **Turnover:** £1m - £2m **No.of Employees:** 1 - 10
Product Groups: 35, 36, 52

Date of Accounts	Apr 08	Apr 07	Apr 06
Working Capital	107	71	112
Fixed Assets	256	264	272
Current Assets	418	241	274
Current Liabilities	311	170	163
Total Share Capital	163	163	163

Hargreaves Foundry Drainage Ltd
Carr House Water Lane, Halifax, HX3 9HG
Tel: 01422-330607 **Fax:** 01422-320349
E-mail: info@hargreavesfoundry.co.uk
Website: http://www.hargreavesfoundry.co.uk
Bank(s): Barclays
Directors: H. Thornber (Fin), M. Hinchliffe (MD)
Managers: N. Stokes (Comm), I. Eglin (Purch Mgr), J. Murphey (Personnel)
Ultimate Holding Company: A. DYSON & SON (PATTERNS) LIMITED
Immediate Holding Company: HARGREAVES FOUNDRY DRAINAGE LIMITED
Registration no: 03428346 **Date established:** 1997 **Turnover:** £2m - £5m
No.of Employees: 51 - 100 **Product Groups:** 26, 34, 35, 36, 39, 41

Date of Accounts	Mar 11	Mar 10	Mar 09
Working Capital	829	782	586
Current Assets	2m	2m	2m

Harrison Associates
Glendale Red Beck Road, Halifax, HX3 6XL
Tel: 01422-361122 **Fax:** 01422-360062
Directors: S. Harrison (Prop)
Date established: 1997 **No.of Employees:** 1 - 10 **Product Groups:** 35

Hartley & Sugden
Atlas Works Gibbet Street, Halifax, HX1 4DB
Tel: 01422-355651 **Fax:** 01422-359636
E-mail: paulcooper@ormandyltd.com
Website: http://www.hartleyandsugden.co.uk
Directors: P. Cooper (MD)
Ultimate Holding Company: ORMANDY LIMITED
Immediate Holding Company: ORMANDY LIMITED
Registration no: 06086786 **VAT No.:** GB 118 9261 58
Date established: 2000 **Turnover:** £10m - £20m **No.of Employees:** 1 - 10
Product Groups: 40

Date of Accounts	Jun 11	Jun 10	Jun 09
Sales Turnover	24m	24m	22m
Pre Tax Profit/Loss	30	303	1m
Working Capital	771	656	431
Fixed Assets	1m	1m	1m
Current Assets	8m	7m	7m
Current Liabilities	3m	3m	3m

James H Heal & Co. Ltd
Richmond Works Lake View, Halifax, HX3 6EP
Tel: 01422-366355 **Fax:** 01422-352440
E-mail: info@james-heal.co.uk
Website: http://www.james-heal.co.uk
Bank(s): HSBC
Directors: E. Rich (Dir), M. Minich (Fin), A. Watson (Dir)
Managers: K. Taylor, J. Ingam (Tech Serv Mgr), J. Klose (Mats Contrlr)
Immediate Holding Company: JAMES H.HEAL AND COMPANY LIMITED
Registration no: 00414668 **VAT No.:** 525 7385 29 **Date established:** 1946
Turnover: £5m - £10m **No.of Employees:** 51 - 100 **Product Groups:** 38

Date of Accounts	Oct 11	Oct 10	Oct 09
Sales Turnover	9m	8m	7m
Pre Tax Profit/Loss	617	568	371
Working Capital	3m	2m	2m
Fixed Assets	2m	2m	1m
Current Assets	4m	4m	3m
Current Liabilities	320	307	226

Hebble Plastic Coatings
Unit 36a Phoebe Lane Industrial Estate, Halifax, HX3 9EX
Tel: 01422-341948 **Fax:** 01422-341948
E-mail: hebbleplasticcoatings@gmail.com
Directors: D. Smith (Prop)
Date established: 1998 **No.of Employees:** 1 - 10 **Product Groups:** 46, 48

Heritage Cashmere UK Ltd
White Rose Mill Holdsworth Road, Halifax, HX3 6SN
Tel: 01422-247800 **Fax:** 01422-247544
E-mail: info@heritage-cashmere.co.uk
Website: http://www.heritage-cashmere.co.uk
Bank(s): Barclays
Directors: J. Kaye (MD)
Immediate Holding Company: HERITAGE CASHMERE UK LIMITED
Registration no: 06904570 **VAT No.:** GB 698 0128 09
Date established: 2009 **Turnover:** £2m - £5m **No.of Employees:** 11 - 20
Product Groups: 23, 66

Date of Accounts	Dec 11	Dec 10	Dec 09
Working Capital	24	12	30
Fixed Assets	100	119	109
Current Assets	1m	761	604

Holt Bros Halifax Ltd
Hope Street, Halifax, HX1 5BT
Tel: 01422-360341 **Fax:** 01422-355039
E-mail: vladimir1@tesco.net
Website: http://www.holtbros-heat-treatment.co.uk
Bank(s): Lloyds TSB Bank plc
Directors: P. Fletcher (MD)
Ultimate Holding Company: ELLIS FISH HOLDINGS LIMITED
Immediate Holding Company: HOLT BROTHERS(HALIFAX)LIMITED
Registration no: 00179506 **Date established:** 2022 **Turnover:** £1m - £2m
No.of Employees: 11 - 20 **Product Groups:** 48

Date of Accounts	Sep 11	Sep 10	Sep 09
Working Capital	257	255	670
Fixed Assets	126	65	89
Current Assets	470	997	1m

John Horsfall & Sons Ltd
West Vale Works Greetland, Halifax, HX4 8BB
Tel: 01422-372237 **Fax:** 01422-310105
E-mail: info@johnhorsfall.co.uk
Website: http://www.johnhorsfall.co.uk
Directors: D. Deakin (Sales), R. Currie (Fin)
Ultimate Holding Company: JOHN HORSFALL & SONS(GREETLAND),LIMITED
Immediate Holding Company: JOHN HORSFALL & SONS(GREETLAND),LIMITED
Registration no: 00083425 **VAT No.:** GB 184 1032 88
Date established: 2005 **Turnover:** £10m - £20m **No.of Employees:** 1 - 10
Product Groups: 23, 24

Date of Accounts	Dec 11	Dec 10	Dec 09
Sales Turnover	16m	12m	12m
Pre Tax Profit/Loss	2m	1m	917
Working Capital	3m	2m	2m
Fixed Assets	2m	2m	2m
Current Assets	7m	5m	4m
Current Liabilities	2m	2m	2m

Imago Metal Ltd
Victoria House Victoria Road, Halifax, HX1 5PT
Tel: 01422-359777 **Fax:** 01422-357799
E-mail: harvey@imago-metal.co.uk
Website: http://www.imago-metal.co.uk
Directors: H. Shaw (Dir), R. Shaw (Dir)
Immediate Holding Company: IMAGO METAL LIMITED
Registration no: 05030833 **Date established:** 2004
No.of Employees: 21 - 50 **Product Groups:** 46, 48

Date of Accounts	Feb 08	Feb 07	Feb 06
Sales Turnover	N/A	N/A	695
Pre Tax Profit/Loss	N/A	N/A	87
Working Capital	107	106	23
Fixed Assets	99	110	89
Current Assets	360	302	265
Current Liabilities	254	196	242
ROCE% (Return on Capital Employed)			77.0
ROT% (Return on Turnover)			12.5

Interface Europe Ltd
Shelf Mills, Halifax, HX3 7PA
Tel: 08705-304030 **Fax:** 01274-694095
E-mail: info@interface.com
Website: http://www.interfaceflor.eu
Bank(s): National Westminster Bank Plc
Directors: S. Carlton (Co Sec)
Managers: A. Dunn (Tech Serv Mgr), D. Handcombe (Fin Mgr), A. Kellett (Mktg Serv Mgr)
Ultimate Holding Company: INTERFACE INC (USA)
Immediate Holding Company: INTERFACE EUROPE SHARE PARTICIPATION TRUSTEES LIMITED
Registration no: 03369703 **Date established:** 1997
Turnover: £75m - £125m **No.of Employees:** 251 - 500
Product Groups: 23

Iron Designs
Unit 51 Bowers Mill Branch Road, Barkisland, Halifax, HX4 0AD
Tel: 01422-377555 **Fax:** 01422-377555
Directors: C. Wood (Prop)
Immediate Holding Company: IRON DESIGNS (HALIFAX) LTD
Registration no: 07109287 **Date established:** 2009
Turnover: £250,000 - £500,000 **No.of Employees:** 1 - 10
Product Groups: 35, 46, 49

Date of Accounts	Dec 11	Dec 10
Working Capital	-8	-11
Fixed Assets	10	16
Current Assets	1	9

J B S Fireworks
South Mill White Rose Mill Holdsworth Road, Halifax, HX3 6SN
Tel: 0783-016 8518
E-mail: info@jbsfireworks.co.uk
Website: http://www.jbsfireworks.co.uk
Directors: M. Bell (Prop)
Immediate Holding Company: M.A. ESTATES LIMITED
Registration no: 04039266 **Date established:** 1998
No.of Employees: 1 - 10 **Product Groups:** 32, 81, 89

Date of Accounts	Feb 11	Feb 10	Feb 09
Working Capital	1m	1m	1m
Fixed Assets	286	182	200
Current Assets	3m	2m	2m

J G Harrison & Sons Ltd
New Brunswick Street Off Gibbett Street, Halifax, HX1 5BW
Tel: 01422-363525 **Fax:** 01422-343070
E-mail: sales@jgharrison.co.uk
Website: http://www.harrisonlighting.co.uk
Directors: J. Harrison (MD)
Immediate Holding Company: J.G. HARRISON & SONS LIMITED
Registration no: 01949903 **Date established:** 1985 **Turnover:** £1m - £2m
No.of Employees: 11 - 20 **Product Groups:** 67, 77

Date of Accounts	Dec 11	Dec 10	Dec 09
Working Capital	255	333	319
Fixed Assets	574	605	619
Current Assets	1m	1m	900

J B G Computer Services
Civic Hall Rochdale Road, Greetland, Halifax, HX4 8AH
Tel: 01422-311111 **Fax:** 01422-311133
E-mail: sales@jbg.co.uk
Website: http://www.jbg.co.uk
Directors: J. Greenway (Dir), R. Chanthek (MD), R. Tschanschek (Dir), R. Tschanschek (Fin)
Managers: L. Greenaway (Admin Off)
Immediate Holding Company: J.B.G. COMPUTER SERVICES LIMITED
Registration no: 02280339 **Date established:** 1988
Turnover: £250,000 - £500,000 **No.of Employees:** 1 - 10
Product Groups: 67

Date of Accounts	Dec 08	Dec 07	Dec 06
Working Capital	35	46	69
Fixed Assets	342	344	347
Current Assets	131	116	133
Current Liabilities	95	70	64

K T Hydraulic Ltd
Hope Hall Mill Union Street South, Halifax, HX1 2LB
Tel: 01422-358885 **Fax:** 01422-359512
E-mail: roger.fish@kt-hydraulics.co.uk
Website: http://www.kthydraulics.com
Directors: R. Fish (Fin)
Immediate Holding Company: K T HYDRAULICS LIMITED
Registration no: 01950662 **VAT No.:** GB 427 3546 47
Date established: 1985 **Turnover:** £1m - £2m **No.of Employees:** 11 - 20
Product Groups: 38, 40

Date of Accounts	Sep 11	Sep 10	Sep 09
Working Capital	2m	2m	1m
Fixed Assets	179	27	30
Current Assets	4m	3m	2m

Kellett Engineering Co. Ltd
Jasper Street, Halifax, HX1 4NT
Tel: 0113-263 9041 **Fax:** 0113-231 0717
E-mail: sales@kellettwindows.co.uk
Website: http://www.kellettwindows.co.uk

see next page

***Kellett Engineering Co. Ltd** - Cont'd*

Directors: V. Inman (Dir)
Ultimate Holding Company: ENVOYJADE LIMITED
Immediate Holding Company: KELLETT ENGINEERING COMPANY LIMITED
Registration no: 00402740 **VAT No.:** GB 461 2499 43
Date established: 1946 **Turnover:** £500,000 - £1m
No.of Employees: 1 - 10 **Product Groups:** 39

Date of Accounts	May 11	May 10	May 09
Working Capital	233	238	252
Fixed Assets	4	7	2
Current Assets	259	269	288

Kluber Lubrication

Bradford Road, Halifax, HX3 7BN
Tel: 01422-205115 **Fax:** 01422-206073
E-mail: sales@uk.klueber.com
Website: http://www.klueber.com
Bank(s): Barclays
Directors: P. Webster (MD)
Managers: E. Janes (Mktg Serv Mgr), J. Haddock (Fin Mgr)
Immediate Holding Company: KLUBER LUBRICATION GREAT BRITAIN LIMITED
Registration no: 01056913 **Date established:** 1972 **Turnover:** £5m - £10m
No.of Employees: 11 - 20 **Product Groups:** 30, 31, 32, 35, 36, 66, 86

Date of Accounts	Dec 11	Dec 10	Dec 09
Sales Turnover	7m	7m	7m
Pre Tax Profit/Loss	2m	1m	1m
Working Capital	936	593	664
Fixed Assets	214	219	229
Current Assets	2m	2m	2m
Current Liabilities	659	699	544

L B Freight Ltd

36 Prescott Street, Halifax, HX1 2QW
Tel: 01422-351217 **Fax:** 01422-330209
E-mail: sales@lbfreight.co.uk
Website: http://www.lbfreight.co.uk
Directors: H. Blues (MD)
Immediate Holding Company: L.B. FREIGHT LIMITED
Registration no: 01404126 **Date established:** 1978 **Turnover:** £1m - £2m
No.of Employees: 1 - 10 **Product Groups:** 75, 76

Date of Accounts	Mar 12	Mar 11	Mar 10
Working Capital	33	33	22
Fixed Assets	29	37	34
Current Assets	103	138	106

Lynwood Products Ltd

Ridings Business Park Hopwood Lane, Halifax, HX1 3TT
Tel: 01422-343257 **Fax:** 01422-347524
Website: http://www.lynwoodproducts.co.uk
Directors: H. Waghorn (MD)
Managers: C. Wilby (Personnel), J. Aspden (Mktg Serv Mgr)
Immediate Holding Company: Lynwood Group Holdings Ltd
Registration no: 04568404 **Date established:** 2002 **Turnover:** £2m - £5m
No.of Employees: 21 - 50 **Product Groups:** 36, 49

Date of Accounts	Mar 10	Mar 09	Mar 08
Sales Turnover	6m	5m	5m
Pre Tax Profit/Loss	-1m	-3m	-926
Working Capital	3m	1m	1m
Fixed Assets	544	2m	3m
Current Assets	5m	3m	3m
Current Liabilities	1m	705	1m

Martins Mill Packaging

Unit 42 Empire Business Centre Shay Lane, Halifax, HX3 6SG
Tel: 01422-363935 **Fax:** 01422-300800
E-mail: rmatmmp@aol.com
Directors: R. Moroney (Prop)
Immediate Holding Company: MARTINS MILL PACKAGING LTD
Registration no: 06681281 **Date established:** 2008
Turnover: £250,000 - £500,000 **No.of Employees:** 1 - 10
Product Groups: 23, 24, 27, 30, 63, 66

Date of Accounts	Aug 11	Aug 10	Aug 09
Working Capital	-4	-5	-14
Fixed Assets	18	18	18
Current Assets	176	119	92

Merlin Precision Engineering Ltd

Eldon Street, Halifax, HX3 6DW
Tel: 01422-300420 **Fax:** 01422-300420
E-mail: gary@merlin-printing.co.uk
Website: http://www.merlin-printing.co.uk
Directors: G. Murphy (MD)
Immediate Holding Company: MERLIN PRECISION ENGINEERING LIMITED
Registration no: 04048314 **Date established:** 2000
No.of Employees: 1 - 10 **Product Groups:** 44, 48, 67

Date of Accounts	Aug 11	Aug 10	Aug 09
Working Capital	-26	-11	-0
Fixed Assets	67	63	62
Current Assets	33	36	50

Northern Filter Supplies

Pear Street, Halifax, HX1 3UA
Tel: 01422-359821 **Fax:** 01422-344324
E-mail: sales@northernfilters.co.uk
Website: http://www.northernfilters.co.uk
Directors: T. Dubaj (Prop)
Date established: 1981 **No.of Employees:** 1 - 10 **Product Groups:** 38, 42

Northern Installations Ltd

Lumbrook Mills Westercroft Lane, Halifax, HX3 7TY
Tel: 01422-202777 **Fax:** 01422-202888
E-mail: kevin@northerninstallations.co.uk
Website: http://www.northerninstallations.co.uk
Directors: K. Johnson (Snr Part)
Managers: G. Kemp (Fin Mgr), M. Hubball (Purch Mgr)
Immediate Holding Company: NORTHERN ESCALATOR INSTALLATIONS LLP
Registration no: OC359652 **Date established:** 2010
No.of Employees: 21 - 50 **Product Groups:** 45, 72

Date of Accounts	Nov 11
Working Capital	1m
Fixed Assets	4m
Current Assets	2m

P C Lifting Services

4 Market Business Centre Hanson Lane, Halifax, HX1 5PF
Tel: 01422-342318 **Fax:** 01422-314319
E-mail: paul.carter@pclifting.co.uk
Website: http://www.pclifting.co.uk
Directors: P. Carter (Prop)
Immediate Holding Company: P C LIFTING SERVICES LTD
Registration no: 04940118 **Date established:** 2003
No.of Employees: 1 - 10 **Product Groups:** 35, 39, 45

Date of Accounts	Oct 11	Oct 10	Oct 09
Working Capital	19	17	18
Fixed Assets	16	11	N/A
Current Assets	19	15	13

P O S Ltd

Phoebe Lane Industrial Estate, Halifax, HX3 9EX
Tel: 01422-349083
E-mail: sales@poslogistics.co.uk
Website: http://www.poslogistics.co.uk
Directors: K. Hartley (Dir)
Immediate Holding Company: POS LIMITED
Registration no: 01831160 **Date established:** 1984
No.of Employees: 1 - 10 **Product Groups:** 44

Date of Accounts	Sep 11	Sep 10	Sep 09
Working Capital	301	294	250
Fixed Assets	36	34	81
Current Assets	345	454	351

Park Metal Polishing

Unit 22-23 Calder Workshops Gibbet Street, Halifax, HX1 4JQ
Tel: 01422-345404 **Fax:** 01422-345404
Website: http://www.parkmetalpolishing.co.uk
Directors: G. Park (Prop)
Date established: 1987 **No.of Employees:** 1 - 10 **Product Groups:** 46, 48

Pegasus Fire Protection

8 Southedge Close Hipperholme, Halifax, HX3 8DW
Tel: 01422-206076 **Fax:** 01422-206076
Website: http://www.dryriser.co.uk
Directors: F. Quinn (Prop)
Date established: 1980 **No.of Employees:** 1 - 10 **Product Groups:** 38, 42

Date of Accounts	Jul 10	Jul 09	Jul 08
Working Capital	-4	-23	-18
Fixed Assets	20	24	25
Current Assets	55	46	47
Current Liabilities	24	17	18

Pennine Automation Spares Ltd

Brookwoods Industrial Estate Burrwood Way, Holywell Green, Halifax, HX4 9BH
Tel: 01422-310259 **Fax:** 01422-371338
E-mail: neil@pennineuk.com
Website: http://www.pennineuk.com
Directors: N. Ginley (MD)
Ultimate Holding Company: PENNINE ENGINEERING GROUP LIMITED
Immediate Holding Company: PENNINE AUTOMATION LIMITED
Registration no: 01622438 **VAT No.:** GB 361 5510 74
Date established: 1982 **Turnover:** £1m - £2m **No.of Employees:** 1 - 10
Product Groups: 37, 67

Date of Accounts	May 11	Mar 10	Mar 09
Working Capital	160	297	282
Fixed Assets	N/A	N/A	71
Current Assets	160	445	472

Pickles Wood Tools

1 Rocks Road, Halifax, HX3 0HR
Tel: 01422-361838 **Fax:** 01422-348288
E-mail: pickleswoodtools@aol.com
Directors: J. Pickles (Prop)
Date established: 1982 **No.of Employees:** 1 - 10 **Product Groups:** 46

Portway Press Ltd

Timeform House Northgate, Halifax, HX1 1XF
Tel: 01422-330330 **Fax:** 01422-398017
E-mail: peter.bell@timeform.com
Website: http://www.timeform.com
Bank(s): National Westminster
Directors: M. Cruddace (Co Sec)
Managers: L. Tomlinson (Sales Admin), C. Wright (Tech Serv Mgr), D. Cracknell, K. Packman
Ultimate Holding Company: BETFAIR GROUP PLC
Immediate Holding Company: PORTWAY PRESS,LIMITED
Registration no: 00477913 **VAT No.:** GB 183 740747
Date established: 1950 **Turnover:** £2m - £5m **No.of Employees:** 51 - 100
Product Groups: 28

Date of Accounts	Apr 11	Apr 10	Apr 09
Sales Turnover	3m	3m	3m
Pre Tax Profit/Loss	-362	-202	-966
Working Capital	-237	57	226
Fixed Assets	758	827	860
Current Assets	407	801	1m
Current Liabilities	494	586	724

Pulsonic Technologies Ltd

Riverside House North Dean Business Park Stainland Road, Greetland, Halifax, HX4 8LR
Tel: 01422-363462 **Fax:** 08709-224026
E-mail: sales@pulsonictechnologies.com
Website: http://www.pulsonictechnologies.com
Directors: J. Duffy (MD)
Managers: N. Nicoll (Chief Acct)
Immediate Holding Company: PULSONIC TECHNOLOGIES LIMITED
Registration no: 02345885 **Date established:** 1989
Turnover: Up to £250,000 **No.of Employees:** 1 - 10 **Product Groups:** 38, 85

Date of Accounts	Jun 11	Jun 10	Jun 09
Working Capital	54	-194	-194
Fixed Assets	433	449	454
Current Assets	158	107	71

R J Mobility Ltd

Boxtree Mills, Halifax, HX3 5AE
Tel: 01422-358888 **Fax:** 01422-355924
E-mail: rgreenway@boxford.co.uk
Website: http://www.rjmobility.com
Bank(s): Lloyds
Directors: R. Greenway (Fin)
Immediate Holding Company: R. J. MOBILITY LIMITED
Registration no: 02481950 **VAT No.:** GB 520 2579 71
Date established: 1990 **Turnover:** £2m - £5m **No.of Employees:** 21 - 50
Product Groups: 26, 39

Date of Accounts	Apr 11	Apr 10	Apr 09
Working Capital	491	485	481
Fixed Assets	N/A	N/A	2
Current Assets	514	523	541

Reflecting Roadstuds Ltd

1 Mill Lane, Halifax, HX3 6TR
Tel: 01422-360208 **Fax:** 01422-349075
E-mail: ts@craglands.demon.co.uk
Website: http://www.percyshawcatseyes.com
Directors: J. Horton (Fin), T. Shaw (MD)
Immediate Holding Company: REFLECTING ROADSTUDS LIMITED
Registration no: 00298350 **VAT No.:** GB 183 4795 27
Date established: 1935 **Turnover:** £1m - £2m **No.of Employees:** 1 - 10
Product Groups: 29, 34

Date of Accounts	Mar 12	Mar 11	Mar 10
Working Capital	2m	2m	2m
Fixed Assets	155	160	156
Current Assets	2m	2m	2m

Renold High Tech Couplings

112 Parkinson Lane, Halifax, HX1 3QH
Tel: 01422-255000 **Fax:** 01422-320273
E-mail: paul.shuffleton@renold.com
Website: http://www.renold.com
Directors: P. Shuffleton (MD)
Managers: H. Byrne (Personnel), S. Thornton, T. Wright (Fin Mgr), A. Dean (Sales & Mktg Mg), R. Kain (Buyer)
Immediate Holding Company: RENOLD P.L.C
Date established: 1952 **Turnover:** £5m - £10m
No.of Employees: 51 - 100 **Product Groups:** 29, 35, 39

Restore Tile & Grout Ltd

Bailey Hall Business Park Bailey Hall Road, Halifax, HX3 9XJ
Tel: 01422-346464
E-mail: sales@restoretileandgrout.co.uk
Website: http://www.restoretileandgrout.co.uk
Directors: L. Rogers (Dir)
Immediate Holding Company: ALPINE RESTORATIONS LTD
Registration no: 06522429 **Date established:** 2008
No.of Employees: 1 - 10 **Product Groups:** 40, 52, 64, 83

Rogerson Yarns Ltd

30 Clifton Road, Halifax, HX3 0BT
Tel: 01422-364088 **Fax:** 01422-348709
E-mail: jonathan@rogersonyarnsltd.co.uk
Directors: J. Rogerson (MD), A. Rogerson (Fin)
Immediate Holding Company: ROGERSON (YARNS) LIMITED
Registration no: 01645040 **VAT No.:** GB 361 5628 51
Date established: 1982 **Turnover:** Up to £250,000
No.of Employees: 1 - 10 **Product Groups:** 23

Date of Accounts	Mar 11	Mar 10	Mar 09
Sales Turnover	N/A	29	N/A
Working Capital	11	7	6
Fixed Assets	2	3	3
Current Assets	63	35	14
Current Liabilities	43	N/A	8

S & S Marketing

B8-B10 Unit Tenterfields Business Park Burnley Road, Luddendenfoot, Halifax, HX2 6EQ
Tel: 01422-882754 **Fax:** 01422-884978
E-mail: sales@sandsmarketing.co.uk
Website: http://www.sandsmarketing.co.uk
Directors: S. Smith (Ptnr)
Turnover: Up to £250,000 **No.of Employees:** 1 - 10 **Product Groups:** 20, 40, 41

Shop & Bakery Equipment Ltd

Adelaide Street, Halifax, HX1 4LY
Tel: 01422-356034 **Fax:** 01422-321113
E-mail: info@sabelhfx.demon.co.uk
Directors: K. Scofield (MD)
Immediate Holding Company: SHOP & BAKERY EQUIPMENT LIMITED
Registration no: 01126255 **Date established:** 1973
No.of Employees: 1 - 10 **Product Groups:** 20, 40, 41

Date of Accounts	Feb 11	Feb 10	Feb 09
Working Capital	141	84	75
Fixed Assets	33	76	83
Current Assets	494	454	391
Current Liabilities	N/A	N/A	77

Siddall & Hilton

Holmfield Industrial Estate Holmfield, Halifax, HX2 9TN
Tel: 01422-233100 **Fax:** 01422-233111
E-mail: sales@siddall.com
Website: http://siddallandhilton.com
Directors: P. Siddall (MD), A. Siddall (Grp Chief Exec), J. Firth (Fin)
Ultimate Holding Company: SIDDALL GROUP LIMITED
Immediate Holding Company: SIDDALL AND HILTON,LIMITED
Registration no: 00058588 **Date established:** 1998 **Turnover:** £1m - £2m
No.of Employees: 1 - 10 **Product Groups:** 24, 38, 67

Date of Accounts	Dec 10	Dec 09	Dec 08
Sales Turnover	2m	2m	2m
Pre Tax Profit/Loss	3m	5m	1m
Working Capital	-7m	-6m	-5m
Fixed Assets	18m	17m	16m
Current Assets	1m	883	1m
Current Liabilities	5m	4m	1m

Simms Platers

Unit 2a Wellington Street West, Halifax, HX1 2TQ
Tel: 01422-360232 **Fax:** 01422-360232
Directors: C. Hinchliffe (Ptnr)
Date established: 1986 **No.of Employees:** 1 - 10 **Product Groups:** 46, 48

Robert Skinner

Bay 4 Shay Lane Works Shay Lane, Ovenden, Halifax, HX3 6SF
Tel: 01422-365872 **Fax:** 01422-349171
Directors: R. Pickles (Prop)
Date established: 1987 **No.of Employees:** 1 - 10 **Product Groups:** 48

Sonoco Re-Cycling (a member of Sonoco International)

Stainland Board Mills Holywell Green, Halifax, HX4 9PY
Tel: 01422-374705 **Fax:** 01422-371495
E-mail: phil.woolley@sonoco-alcore.net
Website: http://www.sonoco-alcore.net
Bank(s): Barclays
Managers: B. Rhodes (Transport)
Immediate Holding Company: SONOCO PRODUCTS CO. (USA)
Registration no: 00082196 **Turnover:** £20m - £50m
No.of Employees: 51 - 100 **Product Groups:** 25, 27

W B Swift Ltd

Leafland Street, Halifax, HX1 4LX
Tel: 01422-358073 **Fax:** 01422-330360
E-mail: lisa.charlton@wbswift.co.uk
Website: http://www.wbswift.co.uk
Managers: L. Charlton (Sales Admin)
Immediate Holding Company: WILLIAM B. SWIFT LTD
Registration no: 00496924 **VAT No.:** GB 183 8802 36
Date established: 1951 **Turnover:** £250,000 - £500,000
No.of Employees: 1 - 10 **Product Groups:** 35, 43

Technolube Lubrication Systems

Unit 17 Calder Workshops Gibbet Street, Halifax, HX1 4JQ
Tel: 01422-320784 **Fax:** 01422-346047
Website: http://www.technolube.co.uk
Directors: G. Rooke (Prop)
Immediate Holding Company: BODY BLISS LADIES GYM LIMITED
Registration no: 06881197 **Date established:** 2012
No.of Employees: 1 - 10 **Product Groups:** 38, 42

Tekniform

Unit 9 Lee Bridge Industrial Estate, Halifax, HX3 5HE
Tel: 01422-354455 **Fax:** 01422- 354499
E-mail: sales@tekniform.com
Website: http://www.tekniform.com
Directors: J. Stanley (MD)
Immediate Holding Company: TEKNIFORM LIMITED
Registration no: 04966369 **Date established:** 2003
No.of Employees: 1 - 10 **Product Groups:** 33

Date of Accounts	Dec 07	Dec 06	Dec 05
Working Capital	-61	-67	-59
Fixed Assets	54	72	76
Current Assets	106	250	175
Current Liabilities	167	317	234

Testrite Ltd

Woodfield Works Old Lane, Halifax, HX3 6TF
Tel: 01422-366963 **Fax:** 01422-345431
E-mail: info@testrite.co.uk
Website: http://www.testrite.co.uk
Directors: K. Nichols (MD)
Immediate Holding Company: TESTRITE LIMITED
Registration no: 00753319 **VAT No.:** GB 183 8775 13
Date established: 1963 **Turnover:** £250,000 - £500,000
No.of Employees: 1 - 10 **Product Groups:** 38

Date of Accounts	Apr 12	Apr 11	Apr 10
Working Capital	2	81	80
Fixed Assets	143	61	67
Current Assets	150	137	125

Ultra Fabrications

Brook Mills Saddleworth Road, Greetland, Halifax, HX4 8LZ
Tel: 01422-387387 **Fax:** 01422-387387
E-mail: ultrafab@btconnect.com
Website: http://www.ultrafabrications.co.uk
Directors: M. Ozanne (Prop)
Date established: 2002 **No.of Employees:** 1 - 10 **Product Groups:** 35

V T L Automotors Ltd

Ellen Holme Luddendenfoot, Halifax, HX2 6EL
Tel: 01422-882561 **Fax:** 01422-883323
E-mail: bruno.jouan@vtl-group.com
Website: http://www.vtl-group.com
Bank(s): Lloyds TSB, Reading
Directors: D. Clegg (Sales & Tech), B. Jouan (Fin), C. Elliot (Chief Op Offcr)
Managers: L. Zeiller (Systems Mgr), S. Willard (Buyer), S. Sayers (Quality Control), M. Loraine (Sales Prom Mgr)
Ultimate Holding Company: VTL (HOLDINGS) LIMITED
Immediate Holding Company: VTL (EUROPE) LIMITED
Registration no: 03452426 **Date established:** 1997 **Turnover:** £5m - £10m
No.of Employees: 51 - 100 **Product Groups:** 66

Date of Accounts	Dec 10	Dec 09	Dec 08
Sales Turnover	27m	10m	N/A
Pre Tax Profit/Loss	3m	1m	1m
Working Capital	-1m	-3m	3m
Fixed Assets	4m	5m	854
Current Assets	7m	12m	7m
Current Liabilities	4m	2m	773

Vandalite Lighting

Dunkirk Mills Dunkirk Street, Halifax, HX1 3TB
Tel: 01422-354254 **Fax:** 01422-356066
E-mail: enquiries@vandalite.com
Website: http://www.vandalite.com
Directors: B. Hooson (Dir)
Managers: P. Ling (Fin Mgr)
Immediate Holding Company: PRIME FABRICATIONS UK LIMITED
Registration no: 06043255 **Date established:** 2007
Turnover: Up to £250,000 **No.of Employees:** 21 - 50 **Product Groups:** 37

Videre Solutions

Brian Royd Business Centre Saddleworth Road, Greetland, Halifax, HX4 8NF
Tel: 01422-374770 **Fax:** 01422-371913
E-mail: info@displayit.co.uk
Website: http://www.displayit.co.uk
Directors: S. Crowe (Co Sec), A. Crowe (Dir)
Immediate Holding Company: VIDERE SOLUTIONS LIMITED
Registration no: 05531690 **Date established:** 2005
No.of Employees: 1 - 10 **Product Groups:** 84

Date of Accounts	Mar 11	Mar 10	Mar 07
Working Capital	-23	-23	-25
Fixed Assets	30	30	31
Current Assets	N/A	N/A	5
Current Liabilities	23	23	N/A

Walker Singleton Chartered Surveyors

13 Lister Lane Property House, Halifax, HX1 5AS
Tel: 01422-430000 **Fax:** 01422-430010
E-mail: david.heap@walkersingleton.co.uk
Website: http://www.walkersingleton.co.uk
Bank(s): The Royal Bank of Scotland
Directors: D. Heap (Dir), H. Eastwood (MD), R. Smith (Fin)
Immediate Holding Company: WALKER SINGLETON (RESIDENTIAL) LIMITED
Registration no: 03754495 **VAT No.:** GB 686 6644 77
Date established: 1999 **Turnover:** £2m - £5m **No.of Employees:** 21 - 50
Product Groups: 61, 80

Date of Accounts	Apr 12	Apr 11	Apr 10
Working Capital	-37	-84	-2
Current Assets	63	35	32

Weld-AC Supplies Ltd

Unit 3 Arden Works Fenton Road, Halifax, HX1 3PP
Tel: 01422-346536 **Fax:** 01422-364994
E-mail: sales@weldac.co.uk
Website: http://www.weldac.co.uk
Directors: R. Wright (Dir)
Immediate Holding Company: WELD-AC SUPPLIES LIMITED
Registration no: 02231340 **Date established:** 1988
No.of Employees: 1 - 10 **Product Groups:** 46

Date of Accounts	Oct 11	Oct 10	Oct 09
Working Capital	81	74	78
Fixed Assets	3	4	5
Current Assets	149	141	132

White Rose Non Wovens Ltd

12 West Parade, Halifax, HX1 2TA
Tel: 01422-347140 **Fax:** 01422-346709
E-mail: sales@wrnw.co.uk
Website: http://www.whiterosenonwovensltd.co.uk
Directors: P. Enright (MD)
Immediate Holding Company: WHITE ROSE NON WOVENS LIMITED
Registration no: 02674698 **Date established:** 1991
Turnover: £500,000 - £1m **No.of Employees:** 1 - 10 **Product Groups:** 38, 42

Date of Accounts	Jan 12	Jan 11	Jan 10
Working Capital	134	141	125
Fixed Assets	106	109	113
Current Assets	219	271	258

Whiteley Sheet Metal Work Ltd

Boxtree Mill Boy Lane, Wheatley, Halifax, HX3 5AF
Tel: 01422-330194 **Fax:** 01422-355924
E-mail: michaeljames@boxford.co.uk
Website: http://www.boxford.co.uk
Bank(s): Lloyds TSB
Directors: R. Greenway (Prop), R. Greenway (MD)
Managers: M. Frier (Purch Mgr), M. James (Mgr)
Immediate Holding Company: WHITELEY SHEET METALWORK LIMITED
Registration no: 01699245 **VAT No.:** GB 361 7295 42
Date established: 1983 **Turnover:** £500,000 - £1m
No.of Employees: 11 - 20 **Product Groups:** 48

Date of Accounts	Apr 08	Apr 07	Apr 06
Working Capital	219	227	207
Fixed Assets	88	78	114
Current Assets	229	236	218
Current Liabilities	10	9	11

Yorkshire Cleaning Fabrics

Drakes Industrial Estate Shay Lane, Ovenden, Halifax, HX3 6RL
Tel: 01422-358286 **Fax:** 01422-346891
E-mail: info@ycfcleaning.co.uk
Website: http://www.ycs.net
Bank(s): Barclays
Directors: Wood (Prop)
Immediate Holding Company: YORKSHIRE CLEANING FABRICS LIMITED
Registration no: 01063000 **VAT No.:** GB 184 0583 56
Date established: 1972 **Turnover:** £500,000 - £1m
No.of Employees: 21 - 50 **Product Groups:** 23, 24

Date of Accounts	Jul 11	Jul 10	Jul 09
Working Capital	190	162	158
Fixed Assets	222	122	113
Current Assets	547	449	407

Yorkshire Refractory Products Ltd

Unit 9 Lee Bridge Industrial Estate, Halifax, HX3 5HE
Tel: 01422-353344 **Fax:** 01422-353366
E-mail: sales@yrpl.com
Website: http://www.yorkshirerefractoryproducts.com
Directors: M. Mollet (Sales), P. Diston (Sales & Mktg), M. Mollett (MD)
Managers: C. Mollitt (I.T. Exec), L. Mollett (Sales Admin)
Immediate Holding Company: YORKSHIRE REFRACTORY PRODUCTS LIMITED
Registration no: 03663634 **Date established:** 1998 **Turnover:** £5m - £10m
No.of Employees: 1 - 10 **Product Groups:** 17, 25, 27, 32, 33, 40, 48, 52, 66, 67, 84

Date of Accounts	Dec 07	Dec 06	Dec 05
Working Capital	-7	-44	-77
Fixed Assets	366	388	359
Current Assets	2060	2356	1829
Current Liabilities	2067	2399	1906
Total Share Capital	5	5	5

Zip Heaters Manufacturers UK Ltd

R4 Unit Tenterfields Business Park Burnley Road, Luddendenfoot, Halifax, HX2 6EQ
Tel: 01422-886214
Website: http://www.zipindustries.com
Directors: M. Crouch (MD)
Managers: C. Binnie (Chief Acct)
Ultimate Holding Company: ZIP INDUSTRIES (Aust) PTY LTD (AUSTRALIA
Immediate Holding Company: ZIP HEATERS (UK) LIMITED
Registration no: 02649782 **Date established:** 1991
No.of Employees: 1 - 10 **Product Groups:** 40, 42, 66

Date of Accounts	Jun 11	Jun 10	Jun 09
Pre Tax Profit/Loss	2m	2m	870
Working Capital	5m	4m	3m
Fixed Assets	207	163	253
Current Assets	9m	8m	7m
Current Liabilities	3m	3m	2m

Hebden Bridge

Blackwood Communications

2a New Road Mytholmroyd, Hebden Bridge, HX7 5DZ
Tel: 01422-883688 **Fax:** 01422-881376
E-mail: info@blackwood-pr.co.uk
Directors: B. Hodgson (Prop)
Date established: 1991 **Turnover:** Up to £250,000
No.of Employees: 1 - 10 **Product Groups:** 81

Calrec Audio Ltd

Nutclough Mill, Hebden Bridge, HX7 8EZ
Tel: 01422-842159 **Fax:** 01422-845244
E-mail: enquiries@calrec.com
Website: http://www.calrec.com
Bank(s): Yorkshire Bank PLC
Directors: G. Warren (Fin), K. Edwards (Fin)
Managers: B. Duffy (Purch Mgr), B. Eccles (Tech Serv Mgr), H. Goodman (Sales & Mktg Mg), T. McNelly (Personnel)
Immediate Holding Company: CALREC AUDIO LIMITED
Registration no: 02392336 **VAT No.:** GB 516 3094 61
Date established: 1989 **Turnover:** £10m - £20m
No.of Employees: 101 - 250 **Product Groups:** 37

Date of Accounts	Mar 11	Mar 10	Mar 09
Sales Turnover	15m	9m	15m
Pre Tax Profit/Loss	3m	833	4m
Working Capital	13m	11m	11m
Fixed Assets	1m	174	89
Current Assets	19m	15m	15m
Current Liabilities	4m	3m	3m

High Viz Shop Ltd

Unit 2 Greenhill Mills Greenhill Industrial Estate, Mytholmroyd, Hebden Bridge, HX7 5QF
Tel: 01422-881287 **Fax:** 01422-882366
E-mail: sales@highvizshop.co.uk
Website: http://www.highvizshop.co.uk
Managers: S. Mitchell (Mgr)
No.of Employees: 1 - 10 **Product Groups:** 24

M S L Woodworking Machinery Ltd

Unit 3 White Lee Burnley Road, Mytholmroyd, Hebden Bridge, HX7 5QL
Tel: 01422-886542 **Fax:** 01422-886542
Directors: M. Swann (MD)
Immediate Holding Company: MSL WOODWORKING MACHINERY LIMITED
Registration no: 04478124 **Date established:** 2002
No.of Employees: 1 - 10 **Product Groups:** 46

Date of Accounts	Jul 12	Jul 11	Jul 10
Working Capital	9	7	2
Fixed Assets	2	2	3
Current Assets	42	26	27

Megaman

Unit 2 Topland Country Business Park, Cragg Vale, Hebden Bridge, HX7 5RW
Tel: 01422-888525 **Fax:** 01422-888526
E-mail: sales@megamanuk.com
Website: http://www.megamanuk.com
Directors: J. Murphy (MD)
Registration no: 01500788 **Date established:** 1980
Turnover: Up to £250,000 **No.of Employees:** 1 - 10 **Product Groups:** 36, 37, 67

Sutcliffe Farrar & Co. Ltd

Banksfield Works Mytholmroyd, Hebden Bridge, HX7 5LT
Tel: 01422-883363 **Fax:** 01422-885479
E-mail: sales@fieldclassics.co.uk
Website: http://www.fieldclassics.co.uk
Directors: J. Farrar (Dir)
Immediate Holding Company: SUTCLIFFE,FARRAR & CO.LIMITED
Registration no: 00379182 **VAT No.:** GB 183 8845 18
Date established: 1943 **Turnover:** £500,000 - £1m
No.of Employees: 1 - 10 **Product Groups:** 24

Date of Accounts	Mar 12	Mar 11	Mar 10
Working Capital	5	32	48
Fixed Assets	9	11	13
Current Assets	98	123	113

Heckmondwike

600 Group plc

PO Box 20, Heckmondwike, WF16 0HN
Tel: 01924-415000 **Fax:** 01924-415015
E-mail: mail@600group.com
Website: http://www.600group.com
Directors: M. Berry (MD)
Immediate Holding Company: 600 GROUP PUBLIC LIMITED COMPANY(THE)
Registration no: 00196730 **Date established:** 2024
Turnover: £20m - £50m **No.of Employees:** 101 - 250
Product Groups: 46, 67

A M O Security Roller Systems Ltd

Unit 6 Sycamore Industrial Estate Walkley Lane, Heckmondwike, WF16 0NL
Tel: 01924-412666 **Fax:** 01924-412233
E-mail: sales@amosecurity.co.uk
Website: http://www.amosecurity.co.uk
Directors: A. Crookes (MD)
Immediate Holding Company: AMO SECURITY ROLLER SYSTEMS LIMITED
Registration no: 03011888 **Date established:** 1995
No.of Employees: 11 - 20 **Product Groups:** 25, 30, 35, 36, 66

Date of Accounts	Mar 12	Mar 11	Mar 10
Working Capital	28	34	6
Fixed Assets	87	20	26
Current Assets	181	197	160

Betech 100 P T Ltd
Four Square Building Thomas Street, Heckmondwike, WF16 0LS
Tel: 08707-573344 **Fax:** 08707-573388
E-mail: sales@betech.co.uk
Website: http://www.betech.co.uk
Directors: A. Benson (Fin)
Immediate Holding Company: BETECH 100PT LTD.
Registration no: 02404937 **Date established:** 1989
Turnover: £500,000 - £1m **No.of Employees:** 1 - 10 **Product Groups:** 37

Date of Accounts	Dec 10	Dec 09	Dec 08
Working Capital	72	25	-0
Fixed Assets	83	98	101
Current Assets	369	267	294

Burgess & Co. Ltd
New North Road, Heckmondwike, WF16 9DP
Tel: 01924-402406 **Fax:** 01924-410175
E-mail: info@cburgess.co.uk
Website: http://www.cburgess.co.uk
Directors: C. Burgess (Dir)
Immediate Holding Company: C. BURGESS & CO. LIMITED
Registration no: 01400245 **VAT No.:** GB 185 2218 63
Date established: 1978 **Turnover:** £250,000 - £500,000
No.of Employees: 1 - 10 **Product Groups:** 48

Date of Accounts	Dec 11	Dec 10	Dec 09
Working Capital	-36	-57	-18
Fixed Assets	88	99	110
Current Assets	142	115	155

Bysel Ltd
Selby House 27a Batley Road, Heckmondwike, WF16 9ND
Tel: 01924-403857 **Fax:** 01924-405368
E-mail: info@byselcandy.com
Website: http://www.byselcandy.com
Bank(s): Barclays, Dewsbury
Directors: C. Bottomley (MD)
Managers: D. Powell (Sales Prom Mgr), L. Moorhouse (Sales Admin)
Immediate Holding Company: BYSEL LIMITED
Registration no: 00393298 **VAT No.:** GB 183 4385 46
Date established: 1945 **Turnover:** £2m - £5m **No.of Employees:** 21 - 50
Product Groups: 20

Date of Accounts	Apr 11	Apr 10	Apr 09
Working Capital	2m	2m	2m
Fixed Assets	584	620	637
Current Assets	2m	3m	2m

Carnation Designs Ltd
Unit 1 Smithies Lane Beehive Business Park, Heckmondwike, WF16 0PN
Tel: 01924-411211
E-mail: sales@carnationdesigns.co.uk
Website: http://www.carnationdesigns.co.uk
Directors: G. Spink (Dir)
Ultimate Holding Company: ELEKTRON TECHNOLOGY PLC
Immediate Holding Company: CARNATION DESIGNS LIMITED
Registration no: 03076362 **Date established:** 1995 **Turnover:** £2m - £5m
No.of Employees: 11 - 20 **Product Groups:** 40, 68

Date of Accounts	Mar 10	Mar 09	Mar 08
Sales Turnover	2m	2m	2m
Pre Tax Profit/Loss	391	133	85
Working Capital	-144	-460	-633
Fixed Assets	38	73	111
Current Assets	878	865	713
Current Liabilities	282	106	117

Colchester Lathe Co. Ltd
PO Box 20, Heckmondwike, WF16 0HN
Tel: 01924-415000 **Fax:** 01924-412604
E-mail: mail@600uk.com
Website: http://www.600uk.com
Bank(s): National Westminster, 64 Knightsbridge, London SW16 7LG
Directors: D. Norman (Grp Chief Exec), R. Taylor (Fin)
Managers: C. Parker (Purch Mgr), H. Bamsorth (Sales Prom Mgr), P. Weaver (Buyer), P. Cullen (Mktg Serv Mgr), M. Ledgard
Ultimate Holding Company: 600 GROUP PUBLIC LIMITED COMPANY(THE)
Immediate Holding Company: COLCHESTER LATHE CO. LIMITED
Registration no: 00375668 **VAT No.:** GB 226 2185 65
Date established: 1942 **No.of Employees:** 51 - 100 **Product Groups:** 46

Date of Accounts	Mar 09	Apr 10	Apr 11
Working Capital	368	368	40
Current Assets	7m	7m	6m

Consultant Services Group Ltd
Station Lane, Heckmondwike, WF16 0NF
Tel: 01924-409988 **Fax:** 0191-491 1122
E-mail: info@consultant-services.co.uk
Website: http://www.consultant-services.co.uk
Directors: N. Wilson (Dir), L. Butterworth (Fin)
Managers: S. Hansord (Tech Serv Mgr), C. Holder (Personnel)
Immediate Holding Company: CONSULTANT SERVICES GROUP LIMITED
Registration no: 00965415 **Date established:** 1969
Turnover: £20m - £50m **No.of Employees:** 1 - 10 **Product Groups:** 52

Date of Accounts	May 11	May 10	May 09
Sales Turnover	21m	23m	25m
Pre Tax Profit/Loss	131	267	1m
Working Capital	3m	3m	3m
Fixed Assets	3m	2m	3m
Current Assets	6m	6m	6m
Current Liabilities	2m	2m	2m

Dave Dalby Woodturning
143 Halifax Road, Heckmondwike, WF16 0DR
Tel: 01924-410381 **Fax:** 01924-406006
E-mail: davedalby@ntlworld.com
Website: http://www.davedalbywoodturning.co.uk
Turnover: Up to £250,000 **No.of Employees:** 1 - 10 **Product Groups:** 25, 26, 36, 47, 48, 63, 66, 67

Denley Hydraulics Ltd
Spen Vale Street, Heckmondwike, WF16 0NQ
Tel: 01924-413400 **Fax:** 01924-410109
E-mail: jon.n@denleyhydraulics.co.uk
Website: http://www.denleyhydraulics.co.uk
Directors: J. Nock (MD), K. Ludi (Sales)
Immediate Holding Company: DENLEY HYDRAULICS LIMITED
Registration no: 04063402 **Date established:** 2000 **Turnover:** £2m - £5m
No.of Employees: 21 - 50 **Product Groups:** 35, 36, 38, 39, 40, 45, 46

Date of Accounts	Nov 11	Nov 10	Nov 09
Working Capital	1m	1m	1m
Fixed Assets	160	190	231
Current Assets	2m	2m	2m

T S Harrison & Sons Ltd
Union Works Union Street, Heckmondwike, WF16 0HL
Tel: 01924-415000 **Fax:** 01924-415011
E-mail: mail@600lathes.co.uk
Website: http://www.600uk.co
Directors: D. Smith (Sales)
Managers: H. Bamforth (Sales Off Mgr), M. Aston (Purch Mgr)
Ultimate Holding Company: 00196730
Immediate Holding Company: T. S. HARRISON & SONS LIMITED
Registration no: 01469020 **VAT No.:** GB 226 5185 65
Date established: 1979 **Turnover:** £75m - £125m
No.of Employees: 101 - 250 **Product Groups:** 46, 67

Arthur Heaton & Co. Ltd
Station Lane, Heckmondwike, WF16 0NF
Tel: 01924-403731 **Fax:** 01924-410069
Directors: A. Miller (Dir)
Ultimate Holding Company: MILBUCON (HOLDINGS) LIMITED
Immediate Holding Company: ARTHUR HEATON & CO. LIMITED
Registration no: 01538359 **VAT No.:** GB 333 7865 36
Date established: 1981 **Turnover:** £500,000 - £1m
No.of Employees: 1 - 10 **Product Groups:** 23, 30, 35, 43, 49

Date of Accounts	Apr 12	Apr 11	Apr 10
Working Capital	83	91	93
Fixed Assets	2	N/A	N/A
Current Assets	92	105	108

Lamplast Industrial Plastics
Unit G Spen Vale Street, Heckmondwike, WF16 0NQ
Tel: 01924-400123 **Fax:** 01924-400155
E-mail: les@lamplast.co.uk
Website: http://www.lamplast.co.uk
Directors: L. Tingle (MD)
Immediate Holding Company: DENLEY HYDRAULICS LIMITED
Date established: 2000 **No.of Employees:** 1 - 10 **Product Groups:** 22, 23, 25, 26, 30, 32, 33, 35, 37, 38, 39, 40, 42, 48, 49, 52, 66

Date of Accounts	Oct 11	Oct 10	Oct 09
Working Capital	156	169	66
Fixed Assets	270	206	245
Current Assets	477	577	1m

Mileta Ltd
Spen Vale Mills Station Lane, Heckmondwike, WF16 0NQ
Tel: 01924-409311 **Fax:** 01924-409839
E-mail: brianward@tog24.com
Website: http://www.tog24.com
Bank(s): HSBC
Directors: I. Ward (MD)
Immediate Holding Company: MILETA SPORTS LIMITED
Registration no: 01132951 **VAT No.:** GB 185 2013 81
Date established: 1973 **Turnover:** £10m - £20m
No.of Employees: 21 - 50 **Product Groups:** 24

Date of Accounts	Jun 08	Jun 09	Jun 10
Sales Turnover	18m	18m	18m
Pre Tax Profit/Loss	3m	100	-348
Working Capital	8m	8m	7m
Fixed Assets	1m	1m	993
Current Assets	10m	10m	9m
Current Liabilities	1m	723	653

R J H Finishing Systems Ltd
Artillery Street, Heckmondwike, WF16 0NR
Tel: 01924-402490 **Fax:** 01924-404635
E-mail: sales@rjhfinishing.co.uk
Website: http://www.rjhfinishing.co.uk
Bank(s): National Westminster Bank Plc
Directors: G. Minton (MD)
Immediate Holding Company: RJH MORRISFLEX HOLDINGS LIMITED
Registration no: 04210091 **VAT No.:** GB 526 0475 57
Date established: 2001 **Turnover:** £1m - £2m **No.of Employees:** 11 - 20
Product Groups: 35, 36, 40, 46

Date of Accounts	Oct 11	Oct 10	Oct 09
Working Capital	N/A	114	N/A
Fixed Assets	114	N/A	114
Current Assets	N/A	114	N/A

Rieter Automotive Great Britain Ltd
Flushmill West Gate, Heckmondwike, WF16 0EP
Tel: 08706-066608 **Fax:** 01924-236340
E-mail: roger.lacey@rieterauto.com
Website: http://www.riter.com
Directors: U. Leinhauser (Fin)
Managers: M. Holt (Fin Mgr), R. Lacey (Personnel)
Ultimate Holding Company: RIETER HOLDING AG (SWITZERLAND).
Immediate Holding Company: AUTONEUM GREAT BRITAIN LIMITED
Registration no: 02248334 **VAT No.:** GB 406 4891 45
Date established: 1988 **Turnover:** £50m - £75m
No.of Employees: 51 - 100 **Product Groups:** 23, 40, 68

Date of Accounts	Dec 11	Dec 10	Dec 09
Sales Turnover	55m	49m	38m
Pre Tax Profit/Loss	-7m	-6m	-9m
Working Capital	-13m	-7m	-11m
Fixed Assets	12m	13m	15m
Current Assets	18m	14m	10m
Current Liabilities	1m	322	238

Seddon Manufacturing Ltd
Premises Swallow Street, Heckmondwike, WF16 0LA
Tel: 01924-410040 **Fax:** 01924-411944
Directors: R. Feddon (MD)
Immediate Holding Company: SEDDON MANUFACTURING LIMITED
Registration no: 03934181 **Date established:** 2000
No.of Employees: 1 - 10 **Product Groups:** 22, 27, 30

Date of Accounts	Jun 11	Jun 10	Jun 09
Working Capital	-7	-9	-5
Fixed Assets	5	7	8
Current Assets	104	96	64

Signshere
1 Gomersal Road, Heckmondwike, WF16 9BU
Tel: 01924-412777 **Fax:** 01924-410077
E-mail: info@signshere.co.uk
Website: http://www.signshere.co.uk
Directors: G. Crosland (Dir)
No.of Employees: 1 - 10 **Product Groups:** 28, 30, 44, 84

Videcon plc
Unit 1 Concept Business Park Smithies Lane, Heckmondwike, WF16 0PN
Tel: 01924-528000
E-mail: sales@videcon.co.uk
Website: http://www.videcon.co.uk
Directors: A. Croston (Sales)
Managers: J. English (Ops Mgr), S. Newsome (Sales Prom Mgr), R. Watson (Mktg Serv Mgr), M. Foster
Immediate Holding Company: VIDECON PUBLIC LIMITED COMPANY
Registration no: 03085668 **Date established:** 1995
Turnover: £10m - £20m **No.of Employees:** 21 - 50 **Product Groups:** 37, 38

Date of Accounts	Aug 11	Aug 10	Aug 09
Sales Turnover	11m	11m	11m
Pre Tax Profit/Loss	738	589	856
Working Capital	3m	3m	3m
Fixed Assets	319	387	403
Current Assets	6m	4m	4m
Current Liabilities	2m	478	1m

W Knowles Ltd
6 Chapel Lane, Heckmondwike, WF16 9JT
Tel: 01924-402208 **Fax:** 01924-406895
E-mail: knowles@btconnect.com
Website: http://www.wilsonknowlesandsons.co.uk
Directors: C. Knowles (MD)
Immediate Holding Company: W KNOWLES LIMITED
Registration no: 04079984 **Date established:** 2000
No.of Employees: 1 - 10 **Product Groups:** 43

Date of Accounts	Aug 11	Aug 10	Aug 09
Working Capital	216	223	206
Fixed Assets	35	35	35
Current Assets	466	355	353

Holmfirth

Bower Roebuck & Co. Ltd
Glendale Mills New Mill, Holmfirth, HD9 7EN
Tel: 01484-682181 **Fax:** 01484-683469
E-mail: info@bowerroebuck.com
Website: http://www.bowerroebuck.co.uk
Directors: S. Taylor (Fin), J. Taylor (Fin), R. Hall (MD)
Ultimate Holding Company: SCABAL SA (BELGIUM)
Immediate Holding Company: BOWER ROEBUCK & CO.,LIMITED
Registration no: 00062048 **Date established:** 1999 **Turnover:** £5m - £10m
No.of Employees: 51 - 100 **Product Groups:** 23

Date of Accounts	Dec 11	Dec 10	Dec 09
Sales Turnover	7m	7m	6m
Pre Tax Profit/Loss	233	-20	-44
Working Capital	3m	2m	3m
Fixed Assets	1m	1m	2m
Current Assets	5m	4m	3m
Current Liabilities	183	214	104

Briton Engineering Devlop Ltd
Unit 1 Lee Mills Industrial Estate, Scholes, Holmfirth, HD9 1RT
Tel: 01484-689933 **Fax:** 01484-689944
E-mail: info@snowflex.com
Website: http://www.snowflex.com
Directors: S. Waddingham (Dir), S. Thomas (Co Sec)
Immediate Holding Company: BRITON ENGINEERING DEVELOPMENTS LIMITED
Registration no: 01444879 **Date established:** 1979
Turnover: £500,000 - £1m **No.of Employees:** 1 - 10 **Product Groups:** 39, 49

Date of Accounts	Dec 11	Dec 10	Dec 09
Working Capital	1m	1m	1m
Fixed Assets	43	40	30
Current Assets	1m	2m	2m

Bronte Natural Spring Water Ltd
Bridge Works Woodhead Road, Honley, Holmfirth, HD9 6PW
Tel: 08451-300469 **Fax:** 01484-662288
Website: http://www.brontewater.co.uk
Directors: T. Saville (Dir)
Immediate Holding Company: BRONTE WATER COOLERS LIMITED
Date established: 1997 **Turnover:** £2m - £5m **No.of Employees:** 1 - 10
Product Groups: 40, 66

Date of Accounts	Mar 12	Mar 11	Mar 10
Working Capital	143	96	151
Fixed Assets	68	74	75
Current Assets	248	205	387

Broomfield Carbide Gauges Ltd
Brigg Mills 3 The Cobbles, Meltham, Holmfirth, HD9 5QQ
Tel: 01484-665599 **Fax:** 0844-504 6692
E-mail: info@broomfieldgauges.com
Website: http://www.broomfieldgauges.com
Directors: D. Pearson (MD)
Immediate Holding Company: BROOMFIELD CARBIDE GAUGES LIMITED
Registration no: 01352774 **VAT No.:** GB 185 0897 27
Date established: 1978 **Turnover:** £500,000 - £1m
No.of Employees: 1 - 10 **Product Groups:** 38, 48

Date of Accounts	Feb 11	Feb 10	Feb 09
Working Capital	-3	-6	-5
Fixed Assets	22	20	20
Current Assets	44	38	42

Burton Safes Ltd
Unit 28 Brockholes Industrial Park Brockholes, Holmfirth, HD9 7BN
Tel: 01484-663388 **Fax:** 01484-666338
E-mail: enquiries@burtonsafes.co.uk
Website: http://www.burtonsafes.co.uk
Directors: J. Elson (Chief Op Offcr)
Immediate Holding Company: BURTON SAFES LIMITED
Registration no: 04744621 **Date established:** 2003 **Turnover:** £1m - £2m
No.of Employees: 11 - 20 **Product Groups:** 26, 33, 36, 40, 41, 52, 66, 67, 81

Date of Accounts	Apr 12	Apr 11	Apr 10
Working Capital	435	402	347
Fixed Assets	78	113	126
Current Assets	1m	1m	856

Butterworth & Roberts Ltd (a division of Gama Beta Holdings Ltd)
Yewtree Mills Holmbridge, Holmfirth, HD9 2NN
Tel: 01484-691500 **Fax:** 01484-681783
E-mail: sales@butterworthroberts.co.uk
Website: http://www.butterworthroberts.co.uk
Bank(s): HSBC Bank plc
Directors: R. Mattock (MD)
Ultimate Holding Company: GAMMA BETA INVESTMENTS LTD (ISLE OF MAN)
Immediate Holding Company: W. WHITEHEAD & SONS LIMITED
Registration no: 02860520 **VAT No.:** GB 183 3205 79
Date established: 1993 **Turnover:** £2m - £5m **No.of Employees:** 21 - 50
Product Groups: 23

Date of Accounts	Apr 11	Apr 10	Apr 09
Sales Turnover	5m	5m	N/A
Pre Tax Profit/Loss	96	89	N/A
Working Capital	708	2m	2m
Fixed Assets	1m	829	895
Current Assets	6m	7m	6m
Current Liabilities	830	78	N/A

Richard Carter Ltd
Neiley Works 72 New Mill Road, Honley, Holmfirth, HD9 6QQ
Tel: 01484-666806 **Fax:** 01484-666802
E-mail: richard.carter@richardcarterltd.co.uk
Website: http://www.richardcarterltd.co.uk
Directors: R. Carter (Dir)
Managers: A. Pullan (Sales Prom Mgr)
Immediate Holding Company: RICHARD CARTER,LIMITED
Registration no: 00106624 **Date established:** 2009
No.of Employees: 21 - 50 **Product Groups:** 25, 30, 33, 36, 41, 42, 45, 49, 67

Date of Accounts	Dec 11	Dec 10	Dec 09
Working Capital	1m	808	504
Fixed Assets	465	435	438
Current Assets	2m	2m	1m

Colour Anodisers
29 Dean Brook Road Netherthong, Holmfirth, HD9 3UF
Tel: 01484-680191 **Fax:** 01484-680191
E-mail: info@colouranodisers.co.uk
Website: http://www.colouranodisers.co.uk
Directors: T. Leech (Prop)
Date established: 1998 **No.of Employees:** 1 - 10 **Product Groups:** 46, 48

Co-op
50-52 Wooldale Road, Holmfirth, HD9 1QJ
Tel: 01484-690720 **Fax:** 01484-690721
E-mail: central@wooldale.coop
Website: http://www.co-operative.coop
Managers: C. Davis (Chief Acct), S. Roberts
Immediate Holding Company: THE ACTION STATION UK LTD
Registration no: 05834038 **Date established:** 2006 **Turnover:** £2m - £5m
No.of Employees: 1 - 10 **Product Groups:** 61

Date of Accounts	Mar 12	Mar 11	Mar 10
Sales Turnover	1445m	1421m	1439m
Pre Tax Profit/Loss	22m	35m	68m
Working Capital	-611m	-569m	-549m
Fixed Assets	849m	862m	859m
Current Assets	477m	417m	454m
Current Liabilities	95m	112m	112m

Dathan Tool & Gauge Co. Ltd
Mean Lane Meltham, Holmfirth, HD9 5RU
Tel: 01484-851207 **Fax:** 01484-852271
E-mail: sales@dathan.co.uk
Website: http://www.dathan.co.uk
Bank(s): Lloyds TSB Bank plc
Directors: E. Moorhouse (Dir), R. Moorhouse (Comm)
Immediate Holding Company: DATHAN TOOL & GAUGE CO LIMITED
Registration no: 00815148 **VAT No.:** GB 183 5363 51
Date established: 1964 **Turnover:** £2m - £5m **No.of Employees:** 21 - 50
Product Groups: 46

Date of Accounts	Sep 11	Sep 10	Sep 09
Working Capital	1m	1m	1m
Fixed Assets	844	809	750
Current Assets	2m	2m	2m

Dunsley Heat Ltd
Bridge Mills Holmfirth, Holmfirth, HD9 3TW
Tel: 01484-682635 **Fax:** 01484-688428
E-mail: sales@dunsleyheat.co.uk
Website: http://www.dunsleyheat.co.uk
Bank(s): Lloyds
Directors: J. Broadbent (MD), R. Broadbent (MD)
Immediate Holding Company: DUNSLEY HEAT LIMITED
Registration no: 01858931 **VAT No.:** GB 183 3182 65
Date established: 1984 **No.of Employees:** 11 - 20 **Product Groups:** 35, 40

Date of Accounts	Jan 11	Jan 10	Jan 09
Working Capital	1m	1m	828
Fixed Assets	28	33	38
Current Assets	2m	1m	1m

Peter Dyson & Son Ltd
3 Cuckoo Lane Honley, Holmfirth, HD9 6AS
Tel: 01484-661062 **Fax:** 01484-663709
E-mail: peter.dyson@peterdyson.co.uk
Website: http://www.peterdyson.co.uk
Directors: P. Dyson (MD), A. Dyson (Co Sec)
Immediate Holding Company: PETER DYSON & SON LIMITED
Registration no: 01013883 **Date established:** 1971
Turnover: Up to £250,000 **No.of Employees:** 1 - 10 **Product Groups:** 36, 39, 40

Date of Accounts	Mar 11	Mar 10	Mar 09
Working Capital	16	17	27
Fixed Assets	193	193	194
Current Assets	35	42	49

Fisher
Bent Ley Industrial Estate Bent Ley Road, Meltham, Holmfirth, HD9 4AP
Tel: 01484-854321 **Fax:** 01484-854244
E-mail: jeff.monks@fisherplastics.co.uk
Website: http://www.fisherplastics.co.uk
Bank(s): National Westminster Bank Plc
Directors: E. Mitchell (Works), I. Rendell (MD), J. Greenhalgh (Tech Serv), J. Monks (MD), P. Moores (Sales)
Ultimate Holding Company: MOON FACE LIMITED
Immediate Holding Company: HAROLD FISHER (PLASTICS) LIMITED
Registration no: 00587664 **VAT No.:** GB 183 5587 29
Date established: 1957 **Turnover:** £1m - £2m **No.of Employees:** 21 - 50
Product Groups: 30, 31, 42, 45, 48

Date of Accounts	Oct 09	Oct 08	Oct 07
Sales Turnover	375	353	280
Pre Tax Profit/Loss	1	16	8
Working Capital	-25	-17	5
Fixed Assets	309	308	290
Current Assets	33	31	33
Current Liabilities	11	18	11

I W B Train
Ford Farm Cottage Totties, Holmfirth, HD9 1UW
Tel: 07534-649743
E-mail: peter.nicholson15@btopenworld.com
Website: http://www.iwbtrain.com
Directors: P. Nicholson (Prop)
Immediate Holding Company: MONARCH FARMS LIMITED
Date established: 2003 **No.of Employees:** 1 - 10 **Product Groups:** 44

Date of Accounts	Jul 11	Jul 10	Jul 09
Working Capital	-256	-234	-248
Fixed Assets	150	131	143
Current Assets	97	80	52

J & J W Longbottom (Incorporating Sloan & Davidson Ltd)
Bridge Foundries, Holmfirth, HD9 7AW
Tel: 01484-682141 **Fax:** 01484-681513
Directors: R. Gudgeon (MD)
Immediate Holding Company: J. & J.W. LONGBOTTOM LIMITED
Registration no: 00153972 **Date established:** 2019
Turnover: £500,000 - £1m **No.of Employees:** 1 - 10 **Product Groups:** 34

Date of Accounts	Mar 11	Mar 10	Mar 09
Working Capital	307	298	258
Fixed Assets	180	196	241
Current Assets	1m	1m	945

J T Knitting Ltd
Dobroyd Mills New Mill, Holmfirth, HD9 1AF
Tel: 01484-685415 **Fax:** 01484-686119
E-mail: sales@jtknitting.plus.com
Directors: M. Metcalfe (Dir)
Immediate Holding Company: JT KNITTING LIMITED
Registration no: 02396334 **VAT No.:** GB 516 3645 50
Date established: 1989 **Turnover:** £500,000 - £1m
No.of Employees: 1 - 10 **Product Groups:** 23

Date of Accounts	Sep 11	Sep 10	Sep 09
Working Capital	70	71	75
Fixed Assets	2	2	3
Current Assets	219	115	131

Jewson Ltd
12 New Mill Road Honley, Holmfirth, HD9 6PL
Tel: 01484-666940 **Fax:** 01484-664034
Website: http://www.jewson.co.uk
Directors: C. Kenward (Fin), T. Newman (Sales), P. Hindle (MD)
Managers: S. Gryce, L. Whitehead (District Mgr), R. Dyson (Chief Acct)
Ultimate Holding Company: COMPAGNIE DE SAINT GOBAIN (FRANCE)
Immediate Holding Company: JEWSON LIMITED
Registration no: 00348407 **Date established:** 1939
Turnover: £500m - £1,000m **No.of Employees:** 1 - 10
Product Groups: 66

Date of Accounts	Dec 11	Dec 10	Dec 09
Sales Turnover	1606m	1547m	1485m
Pre Tax Profit/Loss	18m	100m	45m
Working Capital	-345m	-250m	-349m
Fixed Assets	496m	387m	461m
Current Assets	657m	1005m	1320m
Current Liabilities	66m	120m	64m

Kenworth Products Ltd
Unit 2 Honley Business Centre New Mill Road, Honley, Holmfirth, HD9 6QB
Tel: 01484-660222 **Fax:** 01484- 660333
E-mail: enquiries@kenworthproducts.co.uk
Website: http://www.kenworthproducts.co.uk
Directors: D. Stanley (Dir), A. Burt (Fin), R. Askey (Dir)
Immediate Holding Company: KENWORTH PRODUCTS LIMITED
Registration no: 02722732 **Date established:** 1992
No.of Employees: 1 - 10 **Product Groups:** 67, 83

Date of Accounts	Feb 08	Feb 11	Feb 10
Working Capital	165	209	165
Fixed Assets	27	23	18
Current Assets	456	458	340

Laser Products UK Ltd
Phoenix Works Hope Bank Honley, Honley, Holmfirth, HD9 6PR
Tel: 01484-665870 **Fax:** 01484-663581
E-mail: sales@laserproductsuk.com
Website: http://www.laserproductsuk.com
Directors: A. Ryder (Dir)
Immediate Holding Company: LASER PRODUCTS UK LTD.
Registration no: 05260204 **Date established:** 2004
No.of Employees: 1 - 10 **Product Groups:** 46, 47

Date of Accounts	Mar 11	Mar 10	Mar 09
Working Capital	63	49	115
Fixed Assets	279	363	452
Current Assets	775	687	509

Lightowlers Yarns Ltd
Brigg House Mills 7 The Cobbles, Meltham, Holmfirth, HD9 5QQ
Tel: 01484-850908 **Fax:** 01484-850424
E-mail: lighthowlersyarns@aol.com
Bank(s): Royal Bank of Scotland
Directors: J. Lightowlers (MD), J. Mark (MD)
Managers: A. Lightowlers (Tech Serv Mgr)
Immediate Holding Company: LIGHTOWLERS YARNS LIMITED
Registration no: 00656660 **VAT No.:** 183 6902 42 **Date established:** 1960
Turnover: £1m - £2m **No.of Employees:** 21 - 50 **Product Groups:** 23

Date of Accounts	Apr 12	Apr 11	Apr 10
Working Capital	374	310	234
Fixed Assets	180	186	173
Current Assets	1m	910	555

Philip Lodge Ltd
Machine Works New Mill Road, Brockholes, Holmfirth, HD9 7AE
Tel: 01484-661143 **Fax:** 01484-661164
Directors: P. Lodge (MD)
Immediate Holding Company: PHILIP LODGE LIMITED
Registration no: 03666766 **VAT No.:** GB 183 5075 56
Date established: 1998 **Turnover:** £500,000 - £1m
No.of Employees: 1 - 10 **Product Groups:** 43, 48

Date of Accounts	Nov 11	Nov 10	Nov 09
Working Capital	17	15	13
Fixed Assets	1	1	1
Current Assets	53	47	42

Norwood Instruments Ltd
New Mill Road Honley, Holmfirth, HD9 6QD
Tel: 01484-661318 **Fax:** 01484-661319
Bank(s): Lloyds TSB
Directors: M. Dickinson (Fin)
Immediate Holding Company: NORWOOD INSTRUMENTS LIMITED
Registration no: 00552437 **VAT No.:** GB 183 7346 41
Date established: 1955 **Turnover:** £500,000 - £1m
No.of Employees: 21 - 50 **Product Groups:** 28, 38

Date of Accounts	Aug 11	Aug 10	Aug 09
Working Capital	215	198	182
Fixed Assets	561	542	549
Current Assets	270	283	285

P D A Ltd
Woodfield Holmfirth Road, New Mill, Holmfirth, HD9 7LX
Tel: 01484-685879 **Fax:** 01484-687592
E-mail: admin@pdainternational.com
Website: http://www.pdainternational.com
Bank(s): National Westminster
Directors: P. Downing (MD), P. Downing (MD)
Immediate Holding Company: P D A LIMITED
Registration no: 02942302 **VAT No.:** GB 361 6558 41
Date established: 1994 **Turnover:** Up to £250,000
No.of Employees: 11 - 20 **Product Groups:** 80, 86

Date of Accounts	Jul 11	Jul 10	Jul 09
Sales Turnover	62	77	60
Pre Tax Profit/Loss	3	6	1
Working Capital	-197	-196	-186
Fixed Assets	193	195	193
Current Assets	122	100	58
Current Liabilities	7	8	12

Sentra Access Engineering Ltd
Unit D13 Meltham Mills Industrial Estate Meltham, Holmfirth, HD9 4DS
Tel: 01484-851222 **Fax:** 01484-851333
E-mail: sentra@btconnect.com
Website: http://www.sentra-online.co.uk
Directors: G. Woollin (MD), S. Jones (Fin)
Immediate Holding Company: SENTRA ACCESS ENGINEERING LIMITED
Registration no: 03889579 **Date established:** 1999
No.of Employees: 1 - 10 **Product Groups:** 26, 35

Date of Accounts	Jan 12	Jan 11	Jan 10
Working Capital	47	47	35
Fixed Assets	27	32	43
Current Assets	123	110	105

Simplast Plastics
Reins Mill Reins, Honley, Holmfirth, HD9 6NB
Tel: 01484-666140 **Fax:** 01484-667653
E-mail: enquiries@simplast.co.uk
Website: http://www.simplast.co.uk
Directors: C. Watson (Prop)
Registration no: 04799287 **VAT No.:** GB 333 7718 49
Date established: 2003 **Turnover:** £500,000 - £1m
No.of Employees: 1 - 10 **Product Groups:** 30

Sovereign Agricultural Services
Sheffield Road Hepworth, Holmfirth, HD9 7TT
Tel: 01484-689986 **Fax:** 01484-689986
Directors: T. Bennett (Ptnr)
No.of Employees: 1 - 10 **Product Groups:** 41

T C W Services Controls Ltd
293 New Mill Road Brockholes, Holmfirth, HD9 7AL
Tel: 01484-662865 **Fax:** 01484-667574
E-mail: sales@tcw-services.co.uk
Website: http://www.tcw-services.co.uk
Directors: J. Williams (MD)
Immediate Holding Company: T.C.W. SERVICES (CONTROLS) LIMITED
Registration no: 01165736 **VAT No.:** GB 184 4184 50
Date established: 1974 **No.of Employees:** 1 - 10 **Product Groups:** 40

Date of Accounts	Apr 11	Apr 10	Apr 09
Working Capital	197	194	141
Fixed Assets	264	267	321
Current Assets	252	359	530

George Vyner Ltd
Simplex House Mytholmbridge Mills, Holmfirth, HD9 7TZ
Tel: 01484-685221 **Fax:** 01484-688538
Bank(s): Barclays
Directors: G. Scott (Dir)
Ultimate Holding Company: GEORGE VYNER LIMITED
Immediate Holding Company: GEORGE VYNER(DISTRIBUTORS)LIMITED
Registration no: 00929814 **VAT No.:** GB 183 8619 27
Date established: 1968 **Turnover:** £500,000 - £1m
No.of Employees: 11 - 20 **Product Groups:** 27

Sam Weller Holdings Ltd
Pickwick Mill Huddersfield Road Holmfirth, Thongsbridge, Holmfirth, HD9 3JL
Tel: 01484-683201 **Fax:** 01484-689700
E-mail: info@samwellerltd.co.uk
Website: http://www.samwellerltd.co.uk
Directors: C. Weller (MD)
Managers: A. Weller (Sales Prom Mgr), C. Weller (Accounts)
Immediate Holding Company: SAM WELLER HOLDINGS LIMITED
Registration no: 03738161 **VAT No.:** GB 763 7423 15
Date established: 1999 **Turnover:** £1m - £2m **No.of Employees:** 1 - 10
Product Groups: 23, 24, 43, 66

Date of Accounts	Dec 11	Dec 10	Dec 09
Working Capital	-111	-335	-124
Fixed Assets	3m	3m	3m
Current Assets	122	7	13

T C Williams Burners Ltd

Bradshaw Works Bradshaw Road, Honley, Holmfirth, HD9 6DT
Tel: 01484-662185 **Fax:** 01484-667574
E-mail: tcw_burners@yahoo.co.uk
Website: http://www.burnerspares.com
Directors: P. Broadbent (MD)
Immediate Holding Company: T.C. WILLIAMS (BURNERS) LIMITED
Registration no: 01617314 **Date established:** 1982
No.of Employees: 1 - 10 **Product Groups:** 40, 42, 46

Date of Accounts	Apr 11	Apr 10	Apr 09
Working Capital	-20	-17	-17
Fixed Assets	1	N/A	3
Current Assets	41	63	84

Wright Publications Ltd

River House Miry Lane, Thongsbridge, Holmfirth, HD9 7SA
Tel: 01484-681328 **Fax:** 01484-688124
E-mail: info@wrights.co.uk
Website: http://www.wrights.co.uk
Directors: A. Wright (Fin)
Immediate Holding Company: WRIGHT PUBLICATIONS LIMITED
Registration no: 02552337 **Date established:** 1990
Turnover: £500,000 - £1m **No.of Employees:** 11 - 20
Product Groups: 28, 80

Date of Accounts	Dec 11	Dec 10	Dec 09
Working Capital	2m	1m	1m
Fixed Assets	63	81	67
Current Assets	2m	2m	2m

WSI E-Biz Solutions

The Old Post Office Burnlee Road, Holmfirth, HD9 2PS
Tel: 08450-563561
E-mail: steve@wsi-ebizsolutions.biz
Website: http://wsi-ebizsolutions.biz
Directors: S. Harvey-Franklin (Prop)
Immediate Holding Company: W S I [N. I.] LTD
Registration no: NI611695 **Date established:** 2012
No.of Employees: 1 - 10 **Product Groups:** 44

Huddersfield

Aircon Direct Easy Computers

Neptune Way Off Leeds Road, Deighton, Huddersfield, HD2 1UA
Tel: 08444-124540 **Fax:** 01484-319801
E-mail: nick@easycom.co.uk
Website: http://www.aircondirect.co.uk
Managers: D. Clarkson
Ultimate Holding Company: TRADEHOLD LTD (SOUTH AFRICA)
Immediate Holding Company: NORTH SHOE LIMITED
Registration no: 03746291 **Date established:** 1975
Turnover: Over £1,000m **No.of Employees:** 1 - 10 **Product Groups:** 40, 42, 66

Alarm Doctors

18 High Street Clayton West, Huddersfield, HD8 9PD
Tel: 01484-866307
E-mail: sales@alarm-doctors.co.uk
Website: http://www.alarm-doctors.co.uk
Directors: M. Willson (Dir)
Immediate Holding Company: ALARM DOCTORS LIMITED
Registration no: 05565938 **Date established:** 2005
No.of Employees: 1 - 10 **Product Groups:** 40, 52, 67

Anything Iron

1 Heath House Mill Heath House Lane, Golcar, Huddersfield, HD7 4JW
Tel: 01484-644111 **Fax:** 01484-644111
E-mail: jim@anythingiron.wanadoo.co.uk
Website: http://www.anythingiron.co.uk
Directors: J. Finch (Prop)
Date established: 1998 **No.of Employees:** 1 - 10 **Product Groups:** 26, 35

Aqua 3

International House Penistone Road, Fenay Bridge, Huddersfield, HD8 0LE
Tel: 08452-308105 **Fax:** 01484-340900
E-mail: sales@brewfit.com
Website: http://www.aqua3water.com
Managers: E. Turner (Sales Prom Mgr)
Ultimate Holding Company: PAXMAN GROUP LIMITED
Immediate Holding Company: PAXMAN COOLERS LIMITED
Date established: 1997 **No.of Employees:** 21 - 50 **Product Groups:** 40, 66

Date of Accounts	Sep 11	Sep 10	Sep 09
Working Capital	284	306	277
Fixed Assets	919	880	906
Current Assets	1m	1m	1m

Associated Utility Supplies Ltd

Unit 1 Park Mill Way Clayton West, Huddersfield, HD8 9XJ
Tel: 01484-860575 **Fax:** 01484-860576
E-mail: paul@aus.co.uk
Website: http://www.aus.co.uk
Directors: P. Hornby (Dir)
Immediate Holding Company: ASSOCIATED UTILITY SUPPLIES LIMITED
Registration no: 03492030 **Date established:** 1998
No.of Employees: 11 - 20 **Product Groups:** 35, 39, 45

Date of Accounts	Apr 12	Apr 11	Apr 10
Working Capital	1m	931	802
Fixed Assets	146	154	178
Current Assets	3m	2m	2m

Batoyle Holdings plc

Colne Vale Road, Huddersfield, HD3 4NY
Tel: 01484-653015 **Fax:** 01484-460078
E-mail: donald.brett@batoyle.co.uk
Website: http://www.batoyle.co.uk
Bank(s): Barclays
Directors: D. Brett (MD), D. Burton-bullard (Fin)
Managers: N. Young (Purch Mgr)
Immediate Holding Company: BATOYLE HOLDINGS LIMITED
Registration no: 02377929 **VAT No.:** GB 183 5273 52
Date established: 1989 **Turnover:** £10m - £20m
No.of Employees: 51 - 100 **Product Groups:** 31, 32, 40, 66

Date of Accounts	Jun 11	Jun 10	Jun 09
Sales Turnover	13m	11m	11m
Pre Tax Profit/Loss	409	528	307
Working Capital	11	-74	-246
Fixed Assets	2m	2m	3m
Current Assets	3m	2m	2m
Current Liabilities	464	763	544

Beaver Sports Yorkshire Ltd

Flint Street, Huddersfield, HD1 6LG
Tel: 01484-512354 **Fax:** 01484-434995
E-mail: info@beaversports.co.uk
Website: http://www.beaversports.co.uk
Bank(s): National Westminster Bank Plc
Directors: N. Stockhill (MD)
Immediate Holding Company: BEAVER SPORTS (YORKSHIRE) LTD
Registration no: 01376011 **VAT No.:** GB 185 1608 55
Date established: 1978 **Turnover:** £2m - £5m **No.of Employees:** 11 - 20
Product Groups: 39, 51, 68

Date of Accounts	Dec 11	Dec 10	Dec 09
Working Capital	2m	2m	1m
Fixed Assets	2m	2m	2m
Current Assets	2m	2m	1m

Bespoke Stairlifts

Unit 8 Fieldhouse Park Old Fieldhouse Lane, Huddersfield, HD2 1FA
Tel: 01484-516777 **Fax:** 01484-559161
E-mail: david@bespokestairlifts.co.uk
Website: http://www.bespokestairlifts.co.uk
Directors: D. Burns (Ptnr)
Date established: 2004 **No.of Employees:** 11 - 20 **Product Groups:** 35, 39, 45

Black Cat Fireworks Ltd

Crosland Hill, Huddersfield, HD4 7AD
Tel: 01484-640640 **Fax:** 01484-658039
E-mail: sales@blackcatfireworks.co.uk
Website: http://www.blackcatfireworks.co.uk
Bank(s): HSBC Bank plc
Directors: A. Brown (MD), D. Sayers (Sales & Mktg), J. Armitage (Fin)
Managers: G. Williams (I.T. Exec), M. Broad (Tech Serv Mgr), H. Lovack (Personnel), D. Coates (Comptroller), H. Ashton (Sales & Mktg Mg), K. Drury (Personnel)
Ultimate Holding Company: LI & FUNG LIMITED (BERMUDA)
Immediate Holding Company: BLACK CAT FIREWORKS LIMITED
Registration no: 01900841 **VAT No.:** GB 419 8450 30
Date established: 1985 **Turnover:** £10m - £20m
No.of Employees: 21 - 50 **Product Groups:** 32

Date of Accounts	Dec 11	Dec 10	Dec 09
Sales Turnover	8m	8m	9m
Pre Tax Profit/Loss	1m	2m	2m
Working Capital	4m	4m	-12m
Fixed Assets	2m	2m	2m
Current Assets	5m	6m	4m
Current Liabilities	2m	2m	965

C Booth & Sons

Sheffield House 13 Cross Church Street, Huddersfield, HD1 2PY
Tel: 01484-530457
E-mail: sales@chaboogroup.co.uk
Website: http://www.chaboo.com
Directors: S. Green (Prop)
Date established: 1985 **No.of Employees:** 1 - 10 **Product Groups:** 36

J Bradbury & Co. Ltd

Britannia Mills Stoney Battery, Huddersfield, HD1 4TW
Tel: 01484-648182 **Fax:** 01484-648669
E-mail: sales@bradburyfabrics.com
Website: http://www.bradburyfabrics.com
Bank(s): National Westminster Bank Plc
Directors: R. Hill (Sales), S. Waite (MD), S. Oxley (Fin)
Immediate Holding Company: J.BRADBURY & COMPANY(SADDLEWORTH),LIMITED
Registration no: 00171961 **Date established:** 2020 **Turnover:** £1m - £2m
No.of Employees: 21 - 50 **Product Groups:** 23, 24, 40

Date of Accounts	Mar 12	Mar 11	Mar 10
Working Capital	411	352	327
Fixed Assets	242	278	329
Current Assets	2m	2m	2m
Current Liabilities	N/A	N/A	1m

Brierley Bros Ltd

Albert Mills Albert Street, Huddersfield, HD1 3PZ
Tel: 01484-426511 **Fax:** 01484-430244
E-mail: robin@brierleybrothers.com
Bank(s): HSBC Bank plc
Directors: R. Gledhill (Dir)
Ultimate Holding Company: BRIERLEY BROTHERS HOLDINGS LIMITED
Immediate Holding Company: BRIERLEY BROTHERS,LIMITED
Registration no: 00049371 **VAT No.:** GB 183 3674 44
Date established: 1996 **Turnover:** £2m - £5m **No.of Employees:** 11 - 20
Product Groups: 23

Date of Accounts	Dec 11	Dec 10	Dec 09
Working Capital	210	72	-137
Fixed Assets	174	167	132
Current Assets	917	532	461

John L Brierley Ltd

Turnbridge Mills, Huddersfield, HD1 6QT
Tel: 01484-435555 **Fax:** 01484-435159
E-mail: sales@johnlbrierley.com
Website: http://www.johnlbrierley.com
Bank(s): HSBC, Cloth Hall Street
Directors: I. Brierley (Dir)
Immediate Holding Company: JOHN L. BRIERLEY LIMITED
Registration no: 00205472 **Date established:** 2025
Turnover: £10m - £20m **No.of Employees:** 51 - 100 **Product Groups:** 23, 63

Date of Accounts	Mar 11	Mar 10	Mar 09
Sales Turnover	10m	10m	N/A
Pre Tax Profit/Loss	715	347	486
Working Capital	6m	6m	4m
Fixed Assets	1m	1m	2m
Current Assets	8m	7m	5m
Current Liabilities	839	614	341

Thomas Broadbent & Sons Ltd (a division of Thomas Broadbent & Sons Ltd)

Queen Street South, Huddersfield, HD1 3EA
Tel: 01484-477200 **Fax:** 01484-516142
E-mail: sbroadbent@broadbent.co.uk
Website: http://www.broadbent.co.uk
Bank(s): HSBC Bank plc
Directors: J. Wright (Sales), S. Broadbent (MD), J. Knapp (Fin)
Managers: N. Wareham, P. Thompson (Buyer), S. Shaw (Personnel)
Immediate Holding Company: THOMAS BROADBENT & SONS,LIMITED
Registration no: 00043017 **VAT No.:** GB 183 4802 56
Date established: 1995 **Turnover:** £20m - £50m
No.of Employees: 101 - 250 **Product Groups:** 40

Date of Accounts	Sep 11	Sep 10	Sep 09
Sales Turnover	21m	19m	21m
Pre Tax Profit/Loss	797	511	-765
Working Capital	1m	370	-186
Fixed Assets	5m	5m	5m
Current Assets	11m	10m	7m
Current Liabilities	8m	4m	4m

Brook Crompton UK Ltd

St Thomas' Road, Huddersfield, HD1 3LJ
Tel: 01484-557200 **Fax:** 01484-557201
E-mail: paul.hopley@brookcrompton.com
Website: http://www.brookcrompton.com
Bank(s): Barclays, Market Place, 28 George Street, Luton
Directors: P. Hopley (Dir)
Managers: C. Lawton, D. Hirst (Personnel)
Ultimate Holding Company: A-TEC INDUSTRIES GMBH (AUSTRIA)
Immediate Holding Company: BROOK CROMPTON UK LIMITED
Registration no: 04305426 **VAT No.:** GB 242 3380 87
Date established: 2001 **Turnover:** £2m - £5m **No.of Employees:** 21 - 50
Product Groups: 37, 48

Date of Accounts	Dec 10	Dec 09	Dec 08
Sales Turnover	4m	N/A	N/A
Pre Tax Profit/Loss	2m	N/A	N/A
Working Capital	-4m	-2m	-2m
Fixed Assets	9m	N/A	N/A
Current Assets	5m	N/A	N/A
Current Liabilities	268	N/A	N/A

Brook Dyeing Co. Ltd

Slaithwaite Dyeworks Britannia Mills, Slaithwaite, Huddersfield, HD7 5HE
Tel: 01484-842345 **Fax:** 01484-843640
E-mail: brook@dyeing.fsnet.co.uk
Bank(s): HSBC Bank plc
Directors: D. Johnson (Div), T. Gledhill (MD)
Immediate Holding Company: HEALEY DYEING LIMITED
Registration no: 00612546 **VAT No.:** GB 183 3674 44
Date established: 1958 **Turnover:** £2m - £5m **No.of Employees:** 21 - 50
Product Groups: 23, 43

Date of Accounts	Dec 06	Dec 05
Working Capital	-517	-131
Fixed Assets	129	249
Current Assets	402	532
Current Liabilities	919	663
Total Share Capital	40	40

John Brooke & Sons Ltd

Unit 19 Brookes Mill Office Park Armitage Bridge, Huddersfield, HD4 7NR
Tel: 01484-340000 **Fax:** 01484-340001
E-mail: office@brookesmill.co.uk
Website: http://www.brookesmill.co.uk
Managers: M. Irving (Sales Admin)
Ultimate Holding Company: JOHN BROOKE & SONS HOLDINGS LIMITED
Immediate Holding Company: JOHN BROOKE & SONS LTD
Registration no: 00056189 **VAT No.:** GB 183 3673 46
Date established: 1998 **Turnover:** £250,000 - £500,000
No.of Employees: 1 - 10 **Product Groups:** 80

Date of Accounts	Mar 12	Mar 11	Mar 10
Working Capital	1m	1m	1m
Fixed Assets	5m	6m	6m
Current Assets	1m	1m	1m

Buck & Hickman Ltd

Unit 19 Ringway Industrial Estate Beck Road, Huddersfield, HD1 5DG
Tel: 01484-426611 **Fax:** 01484-435368
E-mail: john@buckhickman.com
Website: http://www.buckhickman.com
Managers: P. Harrison (District Mgr)
Ultimate Holding Company: TRAVIS PERKINS PLC
Immediate Holding Company: BOSTON (2011) LIMITED
Registration no: 06028304 **Date established:** 2006
No.of Employees: 1 - 10 **Product Groups:** 24, 36, 37, 46

Date of Accounts	Dec 10	Mar 10	Mar 09
Working Capital	6m	6m	6m
Current Assets	27m	27m	27m

C M S Vocational Training Ltd

29 Green Street, Huddersfield, HD1 5DQ
Tel: 01484-434800 **Fax:** 01484-515268
E-mail: enquiries@cmsvoc.co.uk
Website: http://www.cmsvoc.co.uk
Bank(s): Barclays
Directors: R. Triggs (MD)
Immediate Holding Company: C.M.S. VOCATIONAL TRAINING LIMITED
Registration no: 04108137 **VAT No.:** GB 361 6124 74
Date established: 2000 **Turnover:** £500,000 - £1m
No.of Employees: 11 - 20 **Product Groups:** 86

Date of Accounts	Jul 11	Jul 10	Jul 09
Working Capital	110	109	104
Fixed Assets	88	96	85
Current Assets	211	215	178

Central C N C Machinery Ltd

Unit 12b Scar Lane Milnsbridge, Huddersfield, HD3 4PE
Tel: 01484-641641 **Fax:** 01484-460101
E-mail: enquiries@centralcnc.co.uk
Website: http://www.centralcnc.co.uk
Directors: S. Merewood (Sales)
Immediate Holding Company: CENTRAL C.N.C. MACHINERY LIMITED
Registration no: 03559308 **Date established:** 1998
No.of Employees: 1 - 10 **Product Groups:** 36, 37, 44, 46, 47, 48, 66, 67, 84, 86

Date of Accounts	Dec 11	Dec 10	Dec 09
Working Capital	20	22	24
Fixed Assets	17	7	9
Current Assets	113	111	110
Current Liabilities	1	N/A	N/A

Cole & Wilson Ltd

Nabbs Lane Chemical Works Slaithwaite, Huddersfield, HD7 5AT
Tel: 01484-842353 **Fax:** 01484-843598
E-mail: info@colewilson.co.uk
Website: http://www.colewilson.co.uk

Directors: R. Cole (Dir)
Immediate Holding Company: COLE & WILSON,LIMITED
Registration no: 00223156 **VAT No.:** GB 183 3083 67
Date established: 2027 **Turnover:** £1m - £2m **No.of Employees:** 1 - 10
Product Groups: 32

Date of Accounts	Mar 11	Mar 10	Mar 09
Working Capital	128	26	-10
Fixed Assets	16	269	287
Current Assets	295	221	232
Current Liabilities	1	N/A	N/A

Colne Valley Rubber Ltd

Bankgate Mills Bankgate Slaithwaite, Huddersfield, HD7 5DL
Tel: 01484-845239 **Fax:** 01484-842900
E-mail: admin@colnevalleyrubber.co.uk
Website: http://www.colnevalleyrubber.co.uk
Managers: A. Randall
Immediate Holding Company: COLNE VALLEY RUBBER LIMITED
Registration no: 02912741 **VAT No.:** GB 721 2804 68
Date established: 1994 **No.of Employees:** 1 - 10 **Product Groups:** 29, 66

Date of Accounts	Dec 11	Dec 10	Dec 09
Working Capital	31	8	22
Fixed Assets	N/A	1	1
Current Assets	123	63	76

Commercial Transport Export Ltd

6 Dryclough Road, Huddersfield, HD4 5HU
Tel: 01484-653662 **Fax:** 01484-653662
E-mail: sales@commercialtransportexport.com
Website: http://www.commercialtransportexport.com
Directors: M. Riaz (MD), N. Riaz (Fin)
Immediate Holding Company: COMMERCIAL TRANSPORT EXPORT LIMITED
Registration no: 03650327 **Date established:** 1998
No.of Employees: 1 - 10 **Product Groups:** 42

Date of Accounts	Mar 11	Mar 10	Mar 09
Working Capital	425	284	259
Fixed Assets	2	2	2
Current Assets	462	426	487

Continental Sports Ltd

Millgate, Huddersfield, HD1 4SD
Tel: 01484-542051 **Fax:** 01484-539148
E-mail: sales@continentalsports.co.uk
Website: http://www.continentalsports.co.uk
Bank(s): HSBC Bank plc
Directors: N. Booth (MD), N. Booth (MD)
Managers: M. Hunsley, S. McLoughlin (Tech Serv Mgr), E. Rothery (Personnel)
Immediate Holding Company: CONTINENTAL SPORTS LIMITED
Registration no: 00830200 **VAT No.:** GB 516 3500 76
Date established: 1964 **Turnover:** £5m - £10m
No.of Employees: 101 - 250 **Product Groups:** 26, 49

Date of Accounts	Dec 11	Dec 10	Dec 09
Sales Turnover	8m	7m	8m
Pre Tax Profit/Loss	591	443	-281
Working Capital	2m	2m	2m
Fixed Assets	872	896	958
Current Assets	5m	4m	4m
Current Liabilities	838	532	806

Continental Wines & Foods Ltd

Trafalgar Mills Leeds Road, Huddersfield, HD2 1YY
Tel: 01484-538333 **Fax:** 01484-544734
E-mail: info@continental-wine.co.uk
Website: http://www.continental-wine.co.uk
Directors: S. Bartolini (Sales), J. Shinwell (MD), P. Taylor (Fin), P. Taylor (Fin)
Managers: L. Teal (Purch Mgr), V. Lee (Mktg Serv Mgr), S. Makin (I.T. Exec), C. Telford (Tech Serv Mgr), M. Holmes (Purch Mgr), V. Swales (Mktg Serv Mgr)
Immediate Holding Company: CONTINENTAL WINE & FOOD LIMITED
Registration no: 00678941 **VAT No.:** GB 361 5349 55
Date established: 1960 **Turnover:** £50m - £75m
No.of Employees: 101 - 250 **Product Groups:** 61

Date of Accounts	Mar 12	Mar 11	Mar 10
Sales Turnover	64m	57m	49m
Pre Tax Profit/Loss	5m	4m	3m
Working Capital	10m	7m	5m
Fixed Assets	3m	3m	3m
Current Assets	22m	18m	14m
Current Liabilities	7m	6m	5m

Contraband

Unit 35 Union Mills Tanyard Road, Milnsbridge, Huddersfield, HD3 4NB
Tel: 08454-601800 **Fax:** 01484-460171
E-mail: info@carefromcontraband.com
Website: http://www.carefromcontraband.com
Directors: C. Beaumont (Dir), E. Jackson (Co Sec), E. Jackson (Fin)
Managers: J. Beaumont (Sales Prom Mgr)
Registration no: 02247991 **VAT No.:** 477 0981 09 **Turnover:** £1m - £2m
No.of Employees: 11 - 20 **Product Groups:** 65, 81

Cummins Turbo Technologies Ltd

St Andrews Road, Huddersfield, HD1 6RA
Tel: 01484-422244 **Fax:** 01484-511680
E-mail: gillian.murray@cummins.com
Website: http://www.cummins.com/turbos
Bank(s): National Westminster Bank Plc
Directors: I. Smith (Fin), J. Stephenson (MD), P. Hibbertson (MD), M. Miller (Fin)
Managers: G. Murray, S. Robinson (Sales & Mktg Mg), M. Cooke (I.T. Exec), A. Turner (Mats Contrlr)
Ultimate Holding Company: CUMMINS INC (USA)
Immediate Holding Company: CUMMINS TURBO TECHNOLOGIES LIMITED
Registration no: 00506282 **VAT No.:** GB 185 2243 64
Date established: 1952 **Turnover:** £75m - £125m
No.of Employees: 501 - 1000 **Product Groups:** 40, 68

Date of Accounts	Dec 10	Dec 09	Dec 08
Sales Turnover	94m	115m	217m
Pre Tax Profit/Loss	90m	-16m	4m
Working Capital	54m	-39m	-16m
Fixed Assets	1m	26m	25m
Current Assets	54m	27m	44m
Current Liabilities	N/A	8m	10m

D G R Designs

388 Leymoor Road Golcar, Huddersfield, HD7 4QF
Tel: 01484-656111 **Fax:** 01484-656111
E-mail: sales@dgrdesigns.co.uk
Website: http://www.dgrdesigns.co.uk
Directors: D. Ribbons (Prop)
Turnover: Up to £250,000 **No.of Employees:** 1 - 10 **Product Groups:** 46

D W Dyson Firarms Consultants Ltd

Wood Lea Shepley, Huddersfield, HD8 8ES
Tel: 01484-607331
E-mail: dwdyson@hotmail.com
Website: http://www.firearmsexperts.co.uk
Directors: D. Dyson (Prop)
Date established: 1973 **No.of Employees:** 1 - 10 **Product Groups:** 36, 39, 40

David Brown Gear Systems

Park Works Lockwood, Crosland Moor, Huddersfield, HD4 5DD
Tel: 01484-465500 **Fax:** 01484-465586
E-mail: sales@davidbrown.textron.com
Website: http://www.textronpt.com
Bank(s): HSBC
Directors: K. Bancroft (Pers)
Ultimate Holding Company: CLYDE BLOWERS CAPITAL FUND II LP (SCOTLAND)
Immediate Holding Company: DAVID BROWN GEAR SYSTEMS LIMITED
Registration no: 06624684 **VAT No.:** GB 183 7490 34
Date established: 2008 **Turnover:** £20m - £50m
No.of Employees: 251 - 500 **Product Groups:** 35, 39

Date of Accounts	Dec 11	Dec 10	Dec 09
Sales Turnover	31m	39m	54m
Pre Tax Profit/Loss	-2m	5m	808
Working Capital	15m	23m	16m
Fixed Assets	20m	19m	23m
Current Assets	44m	39m	35m
Current Liabilities	8m	5m	10m

Design Paradigm Ltd

Platt Mill New Street, Slaithwaite, Huddersfield, HD7 5AB
Tel: 01484-844882 **Fax:** 01484-841200
E-mail: colin@design-paradigm.co.uk
Website: http://www.design-paradigm.co.uk
Directors: C. Findlay (Dir), M. Critchley (Fin)
Immediate Holding Company: DESIGN PARADIGM LIMITED
Registration no: 03489556 **Date established:** 1998
Turnover: £250,000 - £500,000 **No.of Employees:** 1 - 10
Product Groups: 44

Date of Accounts	Jul 07	Apr 07	Apr 06
Sales Turnover	119	316	280
Pre Tax Profit/Loss	42	132	103
Working Capital	86	118	91
Fixed Assets	13	15	21
Current Assets	214	259	167
Current Liabilities	129	141	76
ROCE% (Return on Capital Employed)	42.6	99.5	92.6
ROT% (Return on Turnover)	35.4	41.7	36.9

Direct Voice & Data Ltd

Direct House 16 Commercial Road, Skelmanthorpe, Huddersfield, HD8 9DA
Tel: 01484-867867 **Fax:** 01484-867860
E-mail: info@direct-voiceanddata.com
Website: http://www.direct-voiceanddata.com
Directors: K. Henderson (Dir)
Immediate Holding Company: DIRECT VOICE AND DATA LTD
Registration no: 06960833 **Date established:** 2009 **Turnover:** £1m - £2m
No.of Employees: 11 - 20 **Product Groups:** 37, 44, 48, 67, 79

Date of Accounts	Jul 10
Working Capital	1
Current Assets	1

Don Robinson

19a Mark Street, Huddersfield, HD1 4ST
Tel: 01484-421362
Website: http://www.guns4u2.co.uk
Directors: D. Robinson (Prop)
No.of Employees: 1 - 10 **Product Groups:** 36, 39, 40

H Downs & Sons Huddersfield Ltd

Peacock Works Leeds Road, Huddersfield, HD2 1XR
Tel: 01484-428203 **Fax:** 01484-546993
E-mail: sales@hdowns.co.uk
Website: http://www.hdowns.co.uk
Bank(s): Lloyds TSB Bank plc
Directors: T. Thompson (Co Sec), R. Downs (Dir), D. Downs (Dir), N. Downs (Dir)
Immediate Holding Company: H. DOWNS & SONS (HUDDERSFIELD) LIMITED
Registration no: 00578623 **VAT No.:** GB 183 5374 46
Date established: 1957 **Turnover:** £1m - £2m **No.of Employees:** 21 - 50
Product Groups: 34

Date of Accounts	Mar 12	Mar 11	Mar 10
Working Capital	386	326	208
Fixed Assets	856	827	849
Current Assets	818	689	569

Dugdale Bros & Co. Ltd

5 Northumberland Street, Huddersfield, HD1 1RL
Tel: 01484-421772 **Fax:** 01484-435469
E-mail: sales@dugdalebros.com
Website: http://www.dugdale-bros.com
Directors: R. Charnock (MD), S. Charnock (Fin)
Immediate Holding Company: DUGDALE BROS. & CO. LIMITED
Registration no: 00561828 **Date established:** 1956
No.of Employees: 1 - 10 **Product Groups:** 23

Date of Accounts	Dec 11	Dec 10	Dec 09
Working Capital	690	518	428
Fixed Assets	876	857	845
Current Assets	2m	2m	1m

James Dyson Ltd

Hoyle Ing Dyeworks Linthwaite, Huddersfield, HD7 5RU
Tel: 01484-842456 **Fax:** 01484-847253
E-mail: enquiries@jamesdyson.co.uk
Website: http://www.jamesdyson.co.uk
Bank(s): The Royal Bank of Scotland
Directors: J. Pattison (Co Sec), S. Gledhill (MD), K. Gledhill (Co Sec)
Managers: J. Cooper (Sales Admin), L. McMair, G. Littlewood (Sales Admin), H. Patterson

Registration no: 02351975 **VAT No.:** GB 183 3314 74
Date established: 1989 **Turnover:** £2m - £5m **No.of Employees:** 21 - 50
Product Groups: 23

Date of Accounts	Mar 08	Mar 07	Mar 06
Working Capital	92	101	160
Fixed Assets	41	51	64
Current Assets	283	358	446
Current Liabilities	191	257	286
Total Share Capital	3	3	3

Easilift Loading Sytems Ltd

Pembroke House Penistone Road, Fenay Bridge, Huddersfield, HD8 0LF
Tel: 01484-601400 **Fax:** 01628-668858
E-mail: sales@loading-systems.co.uk
Website: http://www.loading-systems.co.uk
Bank(s): Barclays Bank
Directors: D. Whyatt (Sales & Mktg), R. Fay (MD)
Managers: D. Tyman (Ops Mgr), G. Hepworth (Chief Acct)
Ultimate Holding Company: ROHAKA BV (NETHERLANDS)
Immediate Holding Company: EASILIFT LOADING SYSTEMS LIMITED
Registration no: 01258026 **Date established:** 1976 **Turnover:** £2m - £5m
No.of Employees: 51 - 100 **Product Groups:** 29, 30, 35, 45

Date of Accounts	Dec 11	Dec 10	Dec 09
Sales Turnover	20m	15m	15m
Pre Tax Profit/Loss	2m	600	1m
Working Capital	2m	2m	1m
Fixed Assets	700	153	172
Current Assets	5m	6m	4m
Current Liabilities	2m	3m	2m

Eastman Staples Ltd (Eastman Machine Co. Ltd)

Lockwood Road, Huddersfield, HD1 3QW
Tel: 01484-888888 **Fax:** 01484-888800
E-mail: c.werb@eastman.co.uk
Website: http://www.eastman.co.uk
Bank(s): National Westminster Bank Plc
Directors: C. Werb (MD), T. Houghton (Co Sec)
Ultimate Holding Company: VOLTEX HOLDINGS LTD (SOUTH AFRICA)
Immediate Holding Company: EASTMAN LIMITED
Registration no: 01892279 **Date established:** 1985 **Turnover:** £5m - £10m
No.of Employees: 21 - 50 **Product Groups:** 38, 43, 48, 67

Elegance & Infinity

Unit 3c Spa Fields Industrial Estate New Street, Slaithwaite, Huddersfield, HD7 5BB
Tel: 01484-847314 **Fax:** 01484-847314
E-mail: dean.parkinson@eleganceandinfinity.co.uk
Website: http://www.eleganceandinfinity.co.uk
Directors: D. Parkinson (Ptnr), C. Parkins (Ptnr), C. Parkinson (Ptnr)
Immediate Holding Company: HYSTAT SYSTEMS LIMITED
Registration no: 03691572 **Date established:** 1976
No.of Employees: 1 - 10 **Product Groups:** 25, 30, 35

J T Ellis & Co. Ltd

Crown Works Silver Street, Huddersfield, HD5 9BA
Tel: 01484-514212 **Fax:** 01484-456433
E-mail: sales@ellisfurniture.co.uk
Website: http://www.ellisfurniture.co.uk
Bank(s): National Westminster Bank Plc
Directors: T. Ellis (Dir), P. Wade (Sales)
Managers: J. Morgan (Tech Serv Mgr), R. Bundey (Fin Mgr), R. Fitz-maurice (Mktg Serv Mgr), A. Eyles (Purch Mgr)
Immediate Holding Company: J.T.ELLIS AND COMPANY LIMITED
Registration no: 00075269 **VAT No.:** GB 183 6312 63
Date established: 2002 **Turnover:** £10m - £20m
No.of Employees: 101 - 250 **Product Groups:** 26

Date of Accounts	Jun 11	Jun 10	Jun 09
Sales Turnover	15m	16m	17m
Pre Tax Profit/Loss	771	2m	2m
Working Capital	10m	9m	25m
Fixed Assets	969	1m	2m
Current Assets	12m	11m	26m
Current Liabilities	884	1m	761

European O G D Ltd

Nortonthorpe Mills Wakefield Road, Scissett, Huddersfield, HD8 9LA
Tel: 01484-865228 **Fax:** 01484-861887
E-mail: info@eogd.co.uk
Website: http://www.eogd.co.uk
Directors: R. Lee (Dir)
Managers: C. Yang (Sales Prom Mgr)
Immediate Holding Company: EUROPEAN OGD LIMITED
Registration no: 02819343 **VAT No.:** GB 567 1021 57
Date established: 1993 **Turnover:** £1m - £2m **No.of Employees:** 1 - 10
Product Groups: 32

Date of Accounts	Dec 11	Dec 10	Dec 09
Working Capital	-108	-100	-100
Fixed Assets	7	9	N/A
Current Assets	333	305	364

Event Equipment Hire

77 Cliffe End Road, Huddersfield, HD3 4FG
Tel: 01422-200960 **Fax:** 08704-902509
E-mail: sales@eventequipmenthire.co.uk
Website: http://www.eventequipmenthire.co.uk
Directors: R. Haigh (Prop)
Immediate Holding Company: EVENT EQUIPMENT HIRE LIMITED
Registration no: 05942165 **Date established:** 2006
Turnover: Up to £250,000 **No.of Employees:** 1 - 10 **Product Groups:** 23, 24, 83

Date of Accounts	Sep 11	Sep 10	Sep 09
Working Capital	-13	-13	1
Fixed Assets	48	48	22
Current Assets	15	15	14

Express Alloys Ltd

Unit 1 Nortonthorpe Mills Wakefield Road, Scissett, Huddersfield, HD8 9LA
Tel: 01484-866860 **Fax:** 01484-866861
E-mail: sales@expressalloys.com
Website: http://www.expressalloys.com
Directors: A. Swift (MD)
Immediate Holding Company: EXPRESS ALLOYS LTD
Registration no: 03636760 **VAT No.:** GB 721 2218 81
Date established: 1998 **Turnover:** Up to £250,000
No.of Employees: 1 - 10 **Product Groups:** 34, 36

Date of Accounts	Dec 11	Dec 10	Dec 09
Working Capital	85	162	278
Fixed Assets	24	15	32

see next page

Express Alloys Ltd - Cont'd

Current Assets	218	259	340

Extract Technology
Bradley Junction Industrial Estate Leeds Road, Huddersfield, HD2 1UR
Tel: 01484-432727 **Fax:** 01484-432659
E-mail: awainwright@extract-technology.com
Website: http://www.extract-technology.com
Bank(s): Lloyds
Managers: J. Armitage (Comptroller), S. Carpmail (Sales & Mktg Mg), G. Singh, G. Turner (Buyer), A. Wainwright (Chief Mgr), J. Larder (Personnel)
Ultimate Holding Company: TETRA LAVAL HOLDINGS BV (NETHERLANDS)
Immediate Holding Company: TETRA PAK CPS LIMITED
Registration no: 01579033 **Date established:** 1981 **Turnover:** £5m - £10m
No.of Employees: 51 - 100 **Product Groups:** 40

Date of Accounts	Dec 11	Dec 10	Dec 09
Sales Turnover	10m	10m	14m
Pre Tax Profit/Loss	-267	437	670
Working Capital	3m	3m	3m
Fixed Assets	634	712	650
Current Assets	5m	6m	7m
Current Liabilities	885	2m	3m

Fabtec Manufacturing Ltd
Unit 7 Kiln Hill Industrial Estate Slaithwaite, Huddersfield, HD7 5JS
Tel: 01484-844969
Directors: S. McEvoy (Co Sec)
Immediate Holding Company: FABTEC MANUFACTURING LIMITED
Registration no: 02949732 **Date established:** 1994
No.of Employees: 1 - 10 **Product Groups:** 36, 49, 65

Date of Accounts	Jul 12	Jul 11	Jul 10
Working Capital	65	42	35
Fixed Assets	4	4	5
Current Assets	136	120	89

Fireplace World (Fired Up Group)
St Thomas's Road, Huddersfield, HD1 3LF
Tel: 08448-809393 **Fax:** 01484-854867
E-mail: info@fireplaceworld.co.uk
Website: http://www.fireplaceworld.co.uk
Managers: I. Holling (Personnel)
Immediate Holding Company: FIREPLACE WORLD (UK) LIMITED
Registration no: 04629581 **Date established:** 2003
Turnover: £10m - £20m **No.of Employees:** 251 - 500
Product Groups: 33, 40, 66

Date of Accounts	Dec 08
Working Capital	38
Current Assets	86

Forteq UK Ltd
Tandem Industrial Estate Wakefield Road, Tandem, Huddersfield, HD5 0QR
Tel: 01484-424384 **Fax:** 01484-535053
E-mail: paul.w@forteq-group.com
Website: http://www.forteq-group.com
Bank(s): Barclays
Directors: P. Wallis (MD)
Managers: I. Littlewood (Fin Mgr), M. Derrick (Tech Serv Mgr), G. Sykes (Personnel)
Ultimate Holding Company: TRANSMISSION TECHNOLOGY HOLDING AG (SWITZERLAND)
Immediate Holding Company: FORTEQ (UK) LIMITED
Registration no: 00304968 **Date established:** 1935 **Turnover:** £5m - £10m
No.of Employees: 51 - 100 **Product Groups:** 30, 35

Date of Accounts	Dec 11	Dec 10	Dec 09
Sales Turnover	9m	8m	7m
Pre Tax Profit/Loss	685	578	130
Working Capital	2m	2m	2m
Fixed Assets	2m	2m	2m
Current Assets	4m	4m	3m
Current Liabilities	798	712	366

Future Technologies
975 Leeds Road, Huddersfield, HD2 1UP
Tel: 08708-303966 **Fax:** 01484-345409
E-mail: paul@futuretechnologies.co.uk
Website: http://www.FutureTechnologies.co.uk
Directors: P. Duley (Ptnr)
No.of Employees: 1 - 10 **Product Groups:** 37, 40, 48, 67

Gardner & Newton Ltd
Queens Mill Road Lockwood, Huddersfield, HD1 3PG
Tel: 01484-517010 **Fax:** 01484-517050
E-mail: sales@n-gn.co.uk
Website: http://www.glassbending.co.uk
Bank(s): HSBC Bank Plc, Merseyside
Directors: G. Smith (Co Sec), K. Woodcock (MD)
Immediate Holding Company: J.M. Newton Ltd
Registration no: 06499505 **VAT No.:** GB 151 9631 65
Turnover: £500,000 - £1m **No.of Employees:** 21 - 50
Product Groups: 33, 35

Garrards Timber Merchants
Great Northern Street, Huddersfield, HD1 6BR
Tel: 01484-428321 **Fax:** 01484-512403
E-mail: sales@garrards-timber.co.uk
Website: http://www.garrards-timber.co.uk
Bank(s): National Westminster, Huddersfield
Directors: G. Roebuck (Fin)
Managers: S. Chapman (Chief Mgr)
Immediate Holding Company: VIEWSTONE LTD
Registration no: 04051352 **VAT No.:** GB 185 0114 85
No.of Employees: 21 - 50 **Product Groups:** 25

David Harrison & Sons Ltd
Canal Mills Hillhouse Lane, Huddersfield, HD1 1ED
Tel: 01484-533391 **Fax:** 01484-434934
E-mail: sales@dharrisonandsons.co.uk
Website: http://www.dharrisonandsons.co.uk
Bank(s): National Westminster Bank Plc
Directors: N. Harrison (MD)
Immediate Holding Company: DAVID HARRISON & SONS LIMITED
Registration no: 01287828 **VAT No.:** GB 427 3853 38
Date established: 1976 **Turnover:** £2m - £5m **No.of Employees:** 21 - 50
Product Groups: 37, 40, 63

Date of Accounts	Dec 11	Dec 10	Dec 09
Working Capital	2m	2m	2m
Fixed Assets	658	648	655
Current Assets	2m	2m	2m

Hartwell Ford
St Andrews Road, Huddersfield, HD1 6RJ
Tel: 08704-134565 **Fax:** 01484-538811
E-mail: ernie.hodgson@hartwell.co.uk
Website: http://www.hartwell.co.uk
Directors: A. Mikkelson (Ch), M. Nafoosi (Grp Chief Exec)
Managers: C. Shipley (Fin Mgr), E. Hodgson (Sales Prom Mgr), F. Colin (Chief Mgr), S. Dooler (Cust Serv Mgr)
Immediate Holding Company: HARTWELL PLC
Registration no: 00155302 **VAT No.:** GB 176 0950 50
Date established: 1919 **Turnover:** £50m - £75m **No.of Employees:** 1 - 10
Product Groups: 39, 68, 72

Hebble Hydraulic Services Ltd
Spa Fields Industrial Estate New Street, Slaithwaite, Huddersfield, HD7 5BB
Tel: 01484-846688 **Fax:** 01484-847701
E-mail: lee@hebblehydraulics.com
Website: http://www.hebblehydraulics.com
Directors: J. Conroy (Fin), L. Conroy (Fab)
Immediate Holding Company: HEBBLE HYDRAULIC SERVICES LIMITED
Registration no: 01916608 **VAT No.:** GB 399 4844 78
Date established: 1985 **Turnover:** £250,000 - £500,000
No.of Employees: 11 - 20 **Product Groups:** 48

Date of Accounts	Mar 12	Mar 11	Mar 10
Working Capital	147	70	75
Fixed Assets	106	109	83
Current Assets	359	248	190

Heppenstalls
135 Armitage Road Milnsbridge, Huddersfield, HD3 4JY
Tel: 01484-658411 **Fax:** 01484-647320
E-mail: enquiries@heppenstalls.net
Website: http://www.happenstalls.net
Directors: A. Coldwell (Dir)
Immediate Holding Company: NOEL HEPPENSTALL LIMITED
Registration no: 02102863 **VAT No.:** GB 183 4290 57
Date established: 1987 **Turnover:** Up to £250,000
No.of Employees: 1 - 10 **Product Groups:** 80, 84

Date of Accounts	Apr 11	Apr 10	Apr 09
Working Capital	162	172	204
Fixed Assets	9	15	19
Current Assets	204	214	245

Hillbrook Printing Inks Ltd
New Street Slaithwaite, Huddersfield, HD7 5BB
Tel: 01484-843535 **Fax:** 01484-840031
Website: http://www.hillbrook.co.uk
Directors: P. Leadbeater (Pers), J. Hill (Fin), A. Hill (Dir)
Managers: C. Leadbeater
Immediate Holding Company: HILLBROOK PRINTING INKS LIMITED
Registration no: 01105264 **Date established:** 1973
No.of Employees: 21 - 50 **Product Groups:** 32

Date of Accounts	Dec 09	Dec 08	Dec 07
Pre Tax Profit/Loss	-192	56	268
Working Capital	905	1m	1m
Fixed Assets	1m	1m	1m
Current Assets	2m	2m	2m
Current Liabilities	298	329	272

Z Hinchliffe & Sons Ltd
Hartcliffe Mills Denby Dale, Huddersfield, HD8 8QL
Tel: 01484-862207 **Fax:** 01484-865227
E-mail: office@zhinchliffe.co.uk
Website: http://www.zhinchliffe.co.uk
Bank(s): HSBC
Directors: G. Ross (Fin)
Ultimate Holding Company: HAROLD HINCHLIFFE LIMITED
Immediate Holding Company: Z.HINCHLIFFE & SONS LIMITED
Registration no: 00078708 **VAT No.:** GB 183 4735 45
Date established: 2003 **Turnover:** £10m - £20m
No.of Employees: 101 - 250 **Product Groups:** 23, 63

Date of Accounts	Jun 11	Jun 10	Jun 09
Sales Turnover	18m	16m	15m
Pre Tax Profit/Loss	977	-390	-801
Working Capital	19m	18m	19m
Fixed Assets	3m	3m	3m
Current Assets	20m	19m	25m
Current Liabilities	902	566	859

Horizon Signs UK Ltd
Unit 15b Holme Mills Britannia Road, Huddersfield, HD3 4QF
Tel: 01484-460909 **Fax:** 01484-460472
E-mail: keith.ball@horizonprint.co.uk
Website: http://www.horizon-signs.com
Bank(s): Yorkshire Bank PLC
Directors: K. Ball (MD)
Ultimate Holding Company: HORIZON MARKETING (UK) LIMITED
Immediate Holding Company: HORIZON-GROUP LIMITED
Registration no: 02921592 **VAT No.:** GB 567 2745 10
Date established: 1994 **Turnover:** £1m - £2m **No.of Employees:** 11 - 20
Product Groups: 49

Date of Accounts	Mar 12	Mar 11	Mar 10
Working Capital	48	64	-25
Fixed Assets	48	42	38
Current Assets	542	482	429

Huddersfield & District Textile Training Co. Ltd
Textile House Red Doles Lane, Huddersfield, HD2 1YF
Tel: 01484-346500 **Fax:** 01484-346501
E-mail: reception@textile-training.com
Website: http://www.textilehouse.co.uk
Directors: B. Macbeth (MD)
Immediate Holding Company: HUDDERSFIELD & DISTRICT TEXTILE TRAINING COMPANY LIMITED
Registration no: 03485552 **Date established:** 1997 **Turnover:** £1m - £2m
No.of Employees: 21 - 50 **Product Groups:** 86

Date of Accounts	Dec 11	Dec 10	Dec 09
Sales Turnover	2m	2m	2m
Pre Tax Profit/Loss	-166	-84	7
Working Capital	117	262	319
Fixed Assets	3m	3m	1m
Current Assets	387	578	537
Current Liabilities	97	144	182

Huddersfield Dyeing Co. Ltd
Canal Street, Huddersfield, HD1 6NY
Tel: 01484-535353 **Fax:** 01484-430426
E-mail: info@huddersfielddyeing.co.uk
Bank(s): HSBC Bank plc
Directors: J. Brook (MD), T. Gledhill (Fin)
Immediate Holding Company: HUDDERSFIELD DYEING COMPANY LIMITED
Registration no: 04923072 **VAT No.:** GB 183 3674 44
Date established: 2003 **Turnover:** £1m - £2m **No.of Employees:** 21 - 50
Product Groups: 23

Date of Accounts	Dec 11	Dec 10	Dec 09
Working Capital	-19	-100	-169
Fixed Assets	91	162	223
Current Assets	524	607	761

Hystat Systems Ltd
Spa Fields Industrial Estate New Street, Slaithwaite, Huddersfield, HD7 5BB
Tel: 01484-845740 **Fax:** 01484-842254
E-mail: info@hystat.co.uk
Website: http://www.hystat.co.uk
Bank(s): Lloyds TSB Bank plc
Directors: R. Wadsworth (MD), S. Wadsworth (Co Sec)
Managers: C. Watson (Mktg Serv Mgr), M. Richardson (Buyer)
Immediate Holding Company: HYSTAT SYSTEMS LIMITED
Registration no: 01244978 **VAT No.:** GB 184 7392 28
Date established: 1976 **Turnover:** £5m - £10m
No.of Employees: 51 - 100 **Product Groups:** 35, 38, 40

Date of Accounts	Feb 11	Feb 10	Feb 09
Sales Turnover	8m	8m	N/A
Pre Tax Profit/Loss	-167	226	N/A
Working Capital	-126	36	-273
Fixed Assets	1m	1m	2m
Current Assets	3m	3m	3m
Current Liabilities	1m	1m	N/A

W T Johnson & Sons Huddersfield Ltd
Bankfield Mills Moldgreen, Huddersfield, HD5 9BB
Tel: 01484-549965 **Fax:** 01484-448106
E-mail: reception@wtjohnson.co.uk
Website: http://www.wtjohnson.co.uk
Bank(s): Barclays
Directors: D. Johnson (Fin), P. Johnson (Dir)
Managers: A. Broadbent, J. McKinnel (Tech Serv Mgr), V. Ayres
Immediate Holding Company: W.T.JOHNSON & SONS(HUDDERSFIELD)LIMITED
Registration no: 00531016 **VAT No.:** GB 184 5131 66
Date established: 1954 **Turnover:** £2m - £5m **No.of Employees:** 51 - 100
Product Groups: 23

Date of Accounts	Apr 11	Apr 10	Apr 09
Sales Turnover	5m	N/A	4m
Pre Tax Profit/Loss	74	N/A	-110
Working Capital	-279	161	650
Fixed Assets	7m	7m	7m
Current Assets	2m	2m	2m
Current Liabilities	530	N/A	348

Jones Steel Ltd
PO Box 66, Huddersfield, HD1 1YQ
Tel: 01484-513888 **Fax:** 01484-513999
E-mail: sales@jonessteel.com
Website: http://www.jonessteel.com
Directors: S. Yildiz (Fin), C. Jones (MD)
Immediate Holding Company: JONES STEEL LIMITED
Registration no: 02956139 **VAT No.:** GB 651 3643 48
Date established: 1994 **Turnover:** £1m - £2m **No.of Employees:** 1 - 10
Product Groups: 23, 34, 35, 36, 39, 45, 54, 61, 66, 67

Date of Accounts	Aug 11	Aug 10	Aug 09
Working Capital	153	155	183
Fixed Assets	28	39	30
Current Assets	410	363	332

Keogh Fabrications Ltd
Unit 1 Bridgecroft, Huddersfield, HD3 4NF
Tel: 01484-460060 **Fax:** 01484-642988
E-mail: keoghpkeogh@aol.com
Directors: P. Keogh (Dir)
Ultimate Holding Company: LODGE JOINERY & TIMBER COMPANY LIMITED
Immediate Holding Company: KEOGH FABRICATIONS LIMITED
Registration no: 05133808 **Date established:** 2004
No.of Employees: 11 - 20 **Product Groups:** 26, 35

Date of Accounts	May 11	May 10	May 09
Working Capital	-80	57	42
Fixed Assets	21	48	61
Current Assets	135	146	154
Current Liabilities	N/A	25	30

Kilner Hutchinson Ltd
Emerald Street, Huddersfield, HD1 6BY
Tel: 01484-426646 **Fax:** 01484-542931
E-mail: andrew@kilnerhutchinson.co.uk
Website: http://www.kilnerhutchinsonfoundries.co.uk
Bank(s): HSBC
Directors: A. Kilner (Dir), K. Hutchinson (Dir)
Immediate Holding Company: KILNER & HUTCHINSON LIMITED
Registration no: 06003220 **VAT No.:** GB 183 9630 34
Date established: 2006 **Turnover:** £500,000 - £1m
No.of Employees: 11 - 20 **Product Groups:** 34

Date of Accounts	Jul 11	Jul 10	Jul 09
Working Capital	302	292	233
Fixed Assets	231	253	279
Current Assets	747	531	613

Kirklees College Huddersfield Centre
37 New North Road, Huddersfield, HD1 5NN
Tel: 01484-437077 **Fax:** 01484-511885
E-mail: info@kirkleescollege.ac.uk
Website: http://www.huddcoll.ac.uk
Directors: P. Mccann (Head)
Managers: M. Deans, G. Higgs
Date established: 1964 **No.of Employees:** 1 - 10 **Product Groups:** 86

Kirklees Guns
17 Lord Street, Huddersfield, HD1 1QA
Tel: 01484-544600 **Fax:** 01484-512704
E-mail: info@kirklees-guns.co.uk
Website: http://www.kirklees-guns.co.uk
Directors: M. Wood (Prop)
Date established: 1988 **No.of Employees:** 1 - 10 **Product Groups:** 36, 39, 40

L W E Arms
Mirfield Rifle Range Paul Lane, Huddersfield, HD5 0PU
Tel: 01924-492458 **Fax:** 01924-515434

Directors: J. Ellin (Prop)
Date established: 1987 **No.of Employees:** 1 - 10 **Product Groups:** 36, 39, 40

Lantech Solutions Ltd

Unit 11 Bradley Mills Bradley Mills Road, Huddersfield, HD1 6PQ
Tel: 01484-423913 **Fax:** 01484-840622
E-mail: sales@lantechsolutions.co.uk
Website: http://www.lantechsolutions.co.uk
Directors: L. Lemon (MD)
Immediate Holding Company: LANTECH SOLUTIONS LIMITED
Registration no: 04861663 **Date established:** 2003
No.of Employees: 1 - 10 **Product Groups:** 29, 30, 36

Date of Accounts	Jul 10	Jul 09	Apr 12
Working Capital	25	15	86
Fixed Assets	6	6	5
Current Assets	166	142	269
Current Liabilities	N/A	N/A	99

Lexcast Ltd

Ashbrow Mills Ashbrow Road, Huddersfield, HD2 1DU
Tel: 01484-513833 **Fax:** 01484-534131
E-mail: malcolm@lexcast.co.uk
Website: http://www.lexcast.co.uk
Bank(s): Barclays
Directors: D. Hirst (Co Sec), M. Senior (MD), A. Mosley (Dir)
Ultimate Holding Company: HARTFORD TRADING LIMITED
Immediate Holding Company: LEXCAST LIMITED
Registration no: 01490138 **VAT No.:** GB 525 8096 31
Date established: 1980 **Turnover:** £2m - £5m **No.of Employees:** 21 - 50
Product Groups: 30

Date of Accounts	Apr 11	Apr 10	Apr 09
Working Capital	2m	2m	2m
Fixed Assets	1	1	1
Current Assets	3m	3m	2m

Lila Hirst TCW Ltd

Holme Mills West Slaithwaite Road, Huddersfield, HD7 6LS
Tel: 01484-844012 **Fax:** 01484-847155
Directors: F. Townend (Dir), M. Martin (Fin)
Immediate Holding Company: LILA HIRST (TCW) LIMITED
Registration no: 06499023 **Date established:** 2008
No.of Employees: 11 - 20 **Product Groups:** 43

Date of Accounts	Jan 12	Jan 11	Jan 10
Working Capital	-16	-11	-21
Fixed Assets	26	20	23
Current Assets	335	157	179

Mamas & Papas (Stores) Ltd

Colne Bridge Road, Huddersfield, HD5 0RH
Tel: 08452-682000 **Fax:** 01484-438210
E-mail: sales@mamasandpapas.co.uk
Website: http://www.mamasandpapas.com
Bank(s): Royal bank of Scotland
Directors: J. Greenwood (Co Sec), R. Spychalski (Chief Op Offcr), C. Drury (Mkt Research)
Managers: C. Brown (Personnel), P. Flirett, H. Robinson (Sales Prom Mgr), C. Austin (Mktg Serv Mgr)
Ultimate Holding Company: MAMAS & PAPAS (HOLDINGS) LIMITED
Immediate Holding Company: MAMAS & PAPAS (PROPERTY) LIMITED
Registration no: 02625814 **Date established:** 1991
Turnover: £75m - £125m **No.of Employees:** 501 - 1000
Product Groups: 26, 65

Date of Accounts	Mar 08	Mar 09	Apr 10
Sales Turnover	485	900	900
Pre Tax Profit/Loss	-296	200	604
Working Capital	-202	-517	N/A
Fixed Assets	9m	9m	N/A
Current Assets	121	530	N/A
Current Liabilities	46	236	N/A

Mentor Business Systems Ltd

19-27 Thistle Street, Huddersfield, HD1 6PU
Tel: 08448-791690 **Fax:** 01484-513747
E-mail: andy.carter@mentorbs.com
Website: http://www.mentorbs.com
Bank(s): Lloyds TSB Bank plc
Directors: B. Lindroth (Dir), M. Moore (Co Sec), L. Hill (Fin)
Managers: A. Carter (Chief Mgr), K. Hatfield (Chief Mgr), P. Clegg (Sales Prom Mgr)
Ultimate Holding Company: UNITED TECHNOLOGIES CORP INC (USA)
Immediate Holding Company: MENTOR BUSINESS SYSTEMS LIMITED
Registration no: 01892391 **VAT No.:** GB 399 2228 13
Date established: 1985 **Turnover:** £500,000 - £1m
No.of Employees: 11 - 20 **Product Groups:** 40, 44

Date of Accounts	Dec 10	Dec 09	Dec 08
Sales Turnover	1m	982	840
Pre Tax Profit/Loss	248	299	142
Working Capital	245	295	420
Fixed Assets	5	5	8
Current Assets	489	559	593
Current Liabilities	122	107	119

Metrodent Ltd

PO Box B29, Huddersfield, HD3 4EP
Tel: 01484-461616 **Fax:** 01484-462700
E-mail: sales@metrodent.com
Website: http://www.metrodent.com
Bank(s): National Westminster
Directors: G. Needham (Mkt Research), G. Needham (MD), M. Toon (Dir)
Immediate Holding Company: METRODENT LIMITED
Registration no: 00320774 **VAT No.:** GB 183 4637 45
Date established: 1936 **No.of Employees:** 21 - 50 **Product Groups:** 32, 38, 40

Date of Accounts	Dec 11	Dec 10	Dec 09
Working Capital	2m	2m	2m
Fixed Assets	308	315	330
Current Assets	2m	2m	2m

Michael George Manufacturing Ltd

236 Lockwood Road, Huddersfield, HD1 3TG
Tel: 01484-533787 **Fax:** 01484-549147
E-mail: enquiries@micheal-george.co.uk
Directors: B. Rutter (MD), M. Boot (Sales & Mktg), R. Rutter (MD)
Managers: V. Haycock (Chief Acct)
Immediate Holding Company: MICHAEL GEORGE MANUFACTURING LIMITED
Registration no: 06795819 **Date established:** 2009
Turnover: £250,000 - £500,000 **No.of Employees:** 11 - 20
Product Groups: 24, 63

Date of Accounts	Mar 12	Mar 11	Mar 10
Working Capital	5	8	13
Fixed Assets	15	12	7
Current Assets	188	131	99

Midland Automation Ltd

P O Box 395, Huddersfield, HD3 4NY
Tel: 01484-461133 **Fax:** 01484-461123
E-mail: richard_regan@midlandjay.co.uk
Website: http://www.midlandjay.co.uk
Directors: R. Reagan (MD), R. Regan (MD)
Immediate Holding Company: MIDLAND AUTOMATION LIMITED
Registration no: 01000123 **Date established:** 1971
Turnover: £500,000 - £1m **No.of Employees:** 1 - 10 **Product Groups:** 37

Date of Accounts	Mar 08	Mar 07	Mar 06
Working Capital	1207	1006	922
Fixed Assets	233	236	116
Current Assets	2466	2009	1972
Current Liabilities	1259	1003	1050
Total Share Capital	794	794	794

M N S Textiles Ltd

Unit 3-4 Pollard Street South Milnsbridge, Huddersfield, HD3 4NB
Tel: 01484-645022
E-mail: page8824@tiscali.co.uk
Directors: M. Akhtar (MD)
Immediate Holding Company: M.N.S. TEXTILES LIMITED
Registration no: 05190175 **Date established:** 2004 **Turnover:** £5m - £10m
No.of Employees: 1 - 10 **Product Groups:** 23

Date of Accounts	Dec 11	Dec 10	Dec 09
Working Capital	2m	2m	2m
Fixed Assets	583	458	408
Current Assets	3m	3m	2m

Mobile Concrete Pumps Ltd

Red Doles Lane, Huddersfield, HD2 1YD
Tel: 01484-558448 **Fax:** 01484-558255
E-mail: info@myersgroup.co.uk
Website: http://www.readymix-huddersfield.co.uk/mcp
Directors: A. Berry (MD)
Managers: M. Hall (Fin Mgr), M. Wilkinson (Tech Serv Mgr)
Ultimate Holding Company: ISAAC TIMMINS LIMITED
Immediate Holding Company: MOBILE CONCRETE PUMPS LIMITED
Registration no: 00951630 **Date established:** 1969
Turnover: £250,000 - £500,000 **No.of Employees:** 1 - 10
Product Groups: 33, 40, 52, 66

Date of Accounts	Jun 11	Jun 10	Jun 09
Working Capital	N/A	N/A	110
Current Assets	N/A	N/A	110

Modern Handling Services Ltd

Unit 21 George Street, Milnsbridge, Huddersfield, HD3 4JD
Tel: 01484-461043 **Fax:** 01484-461042
E-mail: themhsltd@aol.com
Website: http://www.modernhandling.co.uk
Directors: C. Callaghan (MD)
Immediate Holding Company: MODERN HANDLING SERVICES LIMITED
Registration no: 00639118 **VAT No.:** GB 183 8084 40
Date established: 1959 **Turnover:** £250,000 - £500,000
No.of Employees: 1 - 10 **Product Groups:** 25, 26, 30, 36, 39, 45

Date of Accounts	Jun 11	Jun 10	Jun 09
Working Capital	6	-10	-26
Fixed Assets	14	16	18
Current Assets	47	43	48

Nelson Roller & Rubber

Unit at Bargate Bargate Manchester Road, Linthwaite, Huddersfield, HD7 5QX
Tel: 01484-845015 **Fax:** 01484-842732
E-mail: info@nelsonroller.co.uk
Website: http://www.nelsonroller.co.uk
Directors: J. Cusworth (Prop)
Immediate Holding Company: NELSON ROLLER & RUBBER CO. LIMITED
Registration no: 00346134 **VAT No.:** GB 860 0217 63
Date established: 1938 **Turnover:** £500,000 - £1m
No.of Employees: 1 - 10 **Product Groups:** 23, 29, 37, 44

Date of Accounts	Dec 11	Dec 10	Dec 09
Working Capital	107	69	61
Fixed Assets	33	36	46
Current Assets	172	127	121

Oakwood Doors

Unit 7a Riverside Works Bradley Mills Road, Huddersfield, HD1 6PQ
Tel: 01484-432917 **Fax:** 01484-452112
E-mail: oakwooddoor@aol.com
Website: http://www.online-doors.co.uk
Directors: M. Joyce (Prop)
No.of Employees: 1 - 10 **Product Groups:** 25, 33, 35, 36, 66

Olympus Technologies Ltd

Melbourne Works 8 Firth Street, Huddersfield, HD1 3BA
Tel: 01484-514513 **Fax:** 01484-435027
E-mail: info@olympustechnologies.co.uk
Website: http://www.olympustechnologies.co.uk
Directors: J. Smith (Prop)
Immediate Holding Company: OLYMPUS TECHNOLOGIES LIMITED
Registration no: 02134805 **Date established:** 1987
No.of Employees: 1 - 10 **Product Groups:** 24, 30, 32, 33, 34

Date of Accounts	Mar 12	Mar 11	Mar 10
Working Capital	124	134	127
Fixed Assets	3	4	6
Current Assets	221	233	200

P H Europe Ltd

Ellerslie House Queens Road, Huddersfield, HD2 2AG
Tel: 01484-351070 **Fax:** 01484-351080
E-mail: info@pheurope.com
Website: http://www.pheurope.com
Directors: E. Ivanova (Sales)
Immediate Holding Company: PH EUROPE LIMITED
Registration no: 03181526 **Date established:** 1996
No.of Employees: 1 - 10 **Product Groups:** 30, 35

Date of Accounts	Mar 12	Mar 11	Mar 10
Working Capital	145	61	44
Fixed Assets	5	9	13
Current Assets	407	322	320

P.P.L Pollution Prevention

New Mills Brougham Road, Marsden, Huddersfield, HD7 6AZ
Tel: 01484-845000 **Fax:** 01484-845222
E-mail: help@pollutionprevention.co.uk
Website: http://www.pollutionprevention.co.uk
Turnover: £5m - £10m **No.of Employees:** 51 - 100 **Product Groups:** 30, 32, 35, 36, 38, 39, 40, 42, 44, 45, 51, 52, 54, 66, 74, 85

Pennine Radio Ltd

82 Fitzwilliam Street, Huddersfield, HD1 5BE
Tel: 01484-538211 **Fax:** 01484-542004
E-mail: info@pr1.co.uk
Website: http://www.prl.co.uk
Bank(s): HSBC
Directors: J. Taylor (Dir)
Immediate Holding Company: PENNINE RADIO LIMITED
Registration no: 00607458 **VAT No.:** GB 183 7303 59
Date established: 1958 **Turnover:** £500,000 - £1m
No.of Employees: 11 - 20 **Product Groups:** 37, 48

Date of Accounts	Jun 11	Jun 10	Jun 09
Working Capital	-211	-212	-149
Fixed Assets	200	230	258
Current Assets	171	177	212

Phoenox Textiles Ltd

Spring Grove Mills Scissett, Clayton West, Huddersfield, HD8 9HH
Tel: 01484-863227 **Fax:** 01484-865352
E-mail: sales@phoenox.co.uk
Website: http://www.phoenox.co.uk
Bank(s): Midland, Penistone
Directors: S. Hirst (Fin)
Immediate Holding Company: PHOENOX TEXTILES LIMITED
Registration no: 00528027 **VAT No.:** GB 183 3706 57
Date established: 1954 **Turnover:** £5m - £10m **No.of Employees:** 21 - 50
Product Groups: 23

Date of Accounts	Dec 11	Dec 10	Dec 09
Working Capital	3m	3m	3m
Fixed Assets	1m	2m	2m
Current Assets	4m	3m	4m

Pod Space Ltd.

1 Camp Hill, Scammonden, Huddersfield, HD3 3FR
Tel: 01484-841167
E-mail: info@pod-space.co.uk
Website: http://www.pod-space.co.uk
Directors: B. Lord (Dir)
Registration no: 06260285 **Date established:** 2006
Turnover: £250,000 - £500,000 **No.of Employees:** 1 - 10
Product Groups: 25

Poundstretcher Ltd

Trident Business Park Leeds Road, Huddersfield, HD2 1UA
Tel: 01484-431444 **Fax:** 0113-254 9371
E-mail: customercare@poundstretcher.co.uk
Website: http://www.poundstretcher.co.uk
Bank(s): HSBC
Directors: S. Tayub (Ch), M. Collinson (Pers), R. Ellis (Fin)
Managers: D. Chew, J. McNae, M. Allan, A. Crowe (Mktg Serv Mgr)
Ultimate Holding Company: CROWN CREST GROUP LIMITED
Immediate Holding Company: POUNDSTRETCHER LIMITED
Registration no: 00553014 **Date established:** 1955
Turnover: £250m - £500m **No.of Employees:** 251 - 500
Product Groups: 61

Date of Accounts	Feb 09	Apr 10	Apr 11
Sales Turnover	296m	328m	308m
Pre Tax Profit/Loss	-9m	-7m	1m
Working Capital	1m	2m	-305
Fixed Assets	25m	20m	22m
Current Assets	65m	62m	79m
Current Liabilities	21m	18m	12m

Presscut Machinery Yorkshire Ltd

2 near Bank Shelley, Huddersfield, HD8 8LS
Tel: 01484-609000 **Fax:** 01484-609383
Website: http://www.presscutmachinery.com
Directors: A. Bennett (Dir), S. Bennett (Fin)
Immediate Holding Company: PRESS CUT MACHINERY (YORKSHIRE) LIMITED
Registration no: 03569833 **Date established:** 1998
No.of Employees: 1 - 10 **Product Groups:** 46

Date of Accounts	Jun 12	Jun 11	Jun 10
Working Capital	10	7	2
Fixed Assets	1	1	N/A
Current Assets	64	75	64

Price Carnell Ltd

254 Wakefield Road Denby Dale, Huddersfield, HD8 8SU
Tel: 01484-861478 **Fax:** 0113-244 2799
E-mail: denby@pricecarnell.com
Website: http://www.pricecarnell.com
Directors: J. Price (Dir)
Immediate Holding Company: PRICE CARNELL LIMITED
Registration no: 04038193 **Date established:** 2000
Turnover: Up to £250,000 **No.of Employees:** 1 - 10 **Product Groups:** 80

Date of Accounts	Aug 11	Aug 10	Aug 09
Working Capital	49	38	50
Fixed Assets	1	N/A	N/A
Current Assets	50	43	52
Current Liabilities	2	5	2

Prima Packaging Ltd

Unit 2 & 3 Bradley Junction Industrial Estate Leeds Road, Huddersfield, HD2 1UR
Tel: 01484-429937 **Fax:** 0845-475 4027
E-mail: vicky@primapackaging.co.uk
Website: http://www.primapackaging.co.uk
Directors: V. Dupont (MD)
Immediate Holding Company: PRIMA PACKAGING LIMITED
Registration no: 03453383 **Date established:** 1997
No.of Employees: 21 - 50 **Product Groups:** 20, 27, 30, 48, 84

Date of Accounts	Mar 12	Mar 11	Mar 10
Working Capital	170	115	136
Fixed Assets	49	73	56
Current Assets	289	254	224

Provalve
Automation Works 656 Leeds Road, Deighton, Huddersfield, HD2 1UB
Tel: 01484-424676 **Fax:** 01484-424622
E-mail: paulh@provalve.co.uk
Website: http://www.provalve.co.uk
Directors: P. Hunter (MD)
Immediate Holding Company: PROVALVE LIMITED
Registration no: 03961901 **Date established:** 2000
No.of Employees: 11 - 20 **Product Groups:** 36, 37, 38

Date of Accounts	May 11	May 10	May 09
Working Capital	-0	-183	-324
Fixed Assets	738	715	706
Current Assets	660	633	347
Current Liabilities	295	N/A	N/A

Ramsden Bros Huddersfield Ltd
Crossland Moor Mills, Huddersfield, HD4 5AH
Tel: 01484-421042 **Fax:** 01484-559236
Bank(s): Lloyds
Directors: I. Mackenzie (Dir)
Immediate Holding Company: RAMSDEN BROS. (HUDDERSFIELD) LIMITED
Registration no: 00362196 **VAT No.:** GB 184 1162 75
Date established: 1940 **Turnover:** £250,000 - £500,000
No.of Employees: 11 - 20 **Product Groups:** 23

Date of Accounts	Dec 11	Dec 10	Dec 09
Working Capital	172	198	208
Fixed Assets	89	95	100
Current Assets	285	289	279

Readymix Huddersfield Ltd
Red Doles Lane Leeds Road, Huddersfield, HD2 1YD
Tel: 01484-535311 **Fax:** 01484-558255
E-mail: concrete@readymix-huddersfield.co.uk
Website: http://www.readymix-huddersfield.co.uk
Bank(s): National Westminster
Directors: J. Myers (MD), R. Whittaker (Co Sec), J. Berrie (Dir)
Managers: A. Hodges (Buyer), I. Valentine (Sales Prom Mgr), M. Riley (Chief Mgr), M. Wilkinson (I.T. Exec)
Immediate Holding Company: Readymix Industrial Group
Registration no: 00446451 **VAT No.:** GB 183 8849 10
Turnover: £10m - £20m **No.of Employees:** 51 - 100 **Product Groups:** 33, 66

Reliance Precision (Reliance Precision Ltd)
Rowley Mills Penistone Road Penistone Road, Fenay Bridge, Huddersfield, HD8 0LE
Tel: 01484-601000 **Fax:** 01484-601001
E-mail: sales@reliance.co.uk
Website: http://www.reliance.co.uk
Bank(s): HSBC Bank plc
Directors: I. Walter (Fin), J. O'Brien (Ch), R. Kenworthy (MD)
Managers: S. Sheard (Tech Serv Mgr), J. Coffey, K. Jolly (Purch Mgr), R. Barrett (Publicity)
Immediate Holding Company: RELIANCE PRECISION LIMITED
Registration no: 00171578 **VAT No.:** GB 333 7596 37
Date established: 2020 **Turnover:** £10m - £20m
No.of Employees: 51 - 100 **Product Groups:** 35, 48, 67

Date of Accounts	Mar 12	Mar 11	Mar 10
Sales Turnover	20m	18m	15m
Pre Tax Profit/Loss	3m	2m	254
Working Capital	7m	6m	4m
Fixed Assets	5m	6m	7m
Current Assets	9m	9m	7m
Current Liabilities	2m	2m	1m

Right Lines Ltd
Waverley House Waverley Road, Huddersfield, HD1 5NA
Tel: 01484-544111 **Fax:** 01484-549111
E-mail: enquiries@rightlines.ltd.uk
Website: http://www.rightlines.ltd.uk
Directors: J. Robbins (Fin), R. Robbins (MD)
Immediate Holding Company: RIGHT LINES LIMITED
Registration no: 04819548 **Date established:** 2003
Turnover: Up to £250,000 **No.of Employees:** 1 - 10 **Product Groups:** 33, 36

Date of Accounts	Mar 11	Mar 10	Mar 09
Working Capital	37	21	-5
Fixed Assets	2	1	1
Current Assets	137	126	88

Riley Dunn & Wilson Ltd
Red Doles Lane Leeds Road, Huddersfield, HD2 1YE
Tel: 01484-534323 **Fax:** 01484-435048
E-mail: charles.dunn@rdw.co.uk
Website: http://www.rdw.co.uk
Bank(s): The Bank of Scotland
Directors: C. Dunn (MD), J. Mills (Fin)
Immediate Holding Company: RILEY DUNN & WILSON LIMITED
Registration no: 06237537 **VAT No.:** GB 482 1971 30
Date established: 2007 **Turnover:** £2m - £5m **No.of Employees:** 21 - 50
Product Groups: 28

Date of Accounts	Apr 11	Apr 10	Apr 09
Working Capital	-21	41	42
Fixed Assets	99	147	201
Current Assets	415	424	534

S 2 S Electronic
Tunbridge Mills Quay Street, Huddersfield, HD1 6QX
Tel: 01484-530893 **Fax:** 01484-550500
E-mail: alarna.drivedale@s2s.uk.com
Website: http://www.s2s.uk.com
Directors: A. Dukinfield (MD), K. Waugh (Contracts)
Managers: A. Drivedale (Mktg Serv Mgr)
Ultimate Holding Company: CHADLAW S2S LIMITED
Immediate Holding Company: S2S ELECTRONICS LTD
Registration no: 02199121 **Date established:** 1987 **Turnover:** £2m - £5m
No.of Employees: 21 - 50 **Product Groups:** 28, 30, 34, 35, 37, 44, 84, 85

Date of Accounts	Dec 10	Dec 09	Dec 08
Working Capital	1m	1m	1m
Fixed Assets	111	45	64
Current Assets	2m	2m	2m

Schofield & Smith Huddersfield Ltd
Unit 26 Upper Mills Slaithwaite, Huddersfield, HD7 5HA
Tel: 01484-842471 **Fax:** 01484-842684
E-mail: sales@schofieldandsmith.co.uk
Website: http://www.schofieldandsmith.co.uk
Directors: J. Sykes (Fin), O. Franco (MD)
Ultimate Holding Company: HARROLDS HOLDINGS LIMITED (GUERNSEY)
Immediate Holding Company: SCHOFIELD & SMITH (HUDDERSFIELD) LIMITED
Registration no: 00482361 **VAT No.:** GB 183 9235 40
Date established: 1950 **Turnover:** £2m - £5m **No.of Employees:** 1 - 10
Product Groups: 23

Date of Accounts	Dec 11	Dec 10	Dec 09
Working Capital	1m	983	1m
Fixed Assets	7	8	311
Current Assets	1m	1m	1m

Scientific Lubricants Ltd
Glendene Depot New Hey Road, Huddersfield, HD3 3YW
Tel: 01422-375401 **Fax:** 01422-379666
E-mail: sales@scientificoil.co.uk
Website: http://www.scientificoil.co.uk
Directors: J. Cowgill (MD)
Immediate Holding Company: SCIENTIFIC LUBRICANTS LIMITED
Registration no: 00985021 **Date established:** 1970
Turnover: £250,000 - £500,000 **No.of Employees:** 1 - 10
Product Groups: 66

Date of Accounts	Jul 11	Jul 10	Jul 09
Working Capital	111	138	146
Fixed Assets	120	120	127
Current Assets	239	262	265

Scrollformer Wrought Ironwork
Chapel Street Moldgreen, Huddersfield, HD5 9BQ
Tel: 01484-422457
Directors: M. Oakes (Prop)
Date established: 1996 **No.of Employees:** 1 - 10 **Product Groups:** 26, 35

Sellers Engineers
Trident Business Park Neptune Way, Huddersfield, HD2 1UA
Tel: 01484-540101 **Fax:** 01484-544457
E-mail: admin@sellersengineers.com
Website: http://www.sellersengineers.com
Bank(s): National Westminster Bank Plc
Directors: I. Shaw (Works), N. Miller (Sales)
Managers: F. Graham, U. Hobson
Ultimate Holding Company: TRADEHOLD LTD (SOUTH AFRICA)
Immediate Holding Company: NORTH SHOE LIMITED
Registration no: 05581766 **VAT No.:** GB 427 3140 75
Date established: 1975 **Turnover:** £5m - £10m
No.of Employees: 51 - 100 **Product Groups:** 43, 46

Service Engineering
Unit 8 Station Court Park Mill Way, Clayton West, Huddersfield, HD8 9XJ
Tel: 01484-866846 **Fax:** 01484-862159
E-mail: info@serviceengineering.co.uk
Website: http://www.serviceengineering.co.uk
Directors: S. Garbiak (Co Sec)
Immediate Holding Company: SERVICE ENGINEERING CNC LIMITED
Registration no: 04587623 **Date established:** 2002
No.of Employees: 1 - 10 **Product Groups:** 46

Date of Accounts	Dec 11	Dec 10	Dec 09
Working Capital	17	17	43
Fixed Assets	3	4	1
Current Assets	30	30	45

Sesame Ltd
Independence House Holly Bank Road, Huddersfield, HD3 3HN
Tel: 01484-422224 **Fax:** 01484-426152
E-mail: contactcentre@sesame.co.uk
Website: http://www.sesame.co.uk
Managers: M. Couzens
Ultimate Holding Company: RESOLUTION LTD (GUERNSEY)
Immediate Holding Company: SESAME LIMITED
Registration no: 02844161 **Date established:** 1993
Turnover: £75m - £125m **No.of Employees:** 251 - 500
Product Groups: 80, 82

Date of Accounts	Dec 11	Dec 10	Dec 09
Sales Turnover	170m	163m	157m
Pre Tax Profit/Loss	-2m	1m	-259
Working Capital	121m	123m	127m
Current Assets	148m	160m	169m
Current Liabilities	23m	24m	21m

Severn Unival Ltd
Milford Buildings Milford Street, Huddersfield, HD1 3DY
Tel: 01484-518080 **Fax:** 01484-518087
Website: http://www.severnglocon.com
Directors: M. Critchley (Fin), C. Findlay (Dir)
Managers: N. Clarke, S. Aveyard, S. Geldart (Fin Mgr), S. North (Personnel), R. Goward (Tech Buyer)
Ultimate Holding Company: SEVERN GLOCON GROUP PLC
Immediate Holding Company: SEVERN UNIVAL LIMITED
Registration no: 01564220 **Date established:** 1981
Turnover: £10m - £20m **No.of Employees:** 101 - 250
Product Groups: 36, 37, 38

Date of Accounts	Dec 11	Dec 10	Dec 09
Sales Turnover	18m	16m	18m
Pre Tax Profit/Loss	2m	2m	2m
Working Capital	4m	2m	3m
Fixed Assets	428	446	421
Current Assets	8m	5m	6m
Current Liabilities	2m	849	1m

Shaw Bros
Viaduct Works Clay Lane, Slaithwaite, Huddersfield, HD7 5BG
Tel: 01484-846442 **Fax:** 01484-847774
E-mail: carole@shawbros.fsnet.co.uk
Website: http://www.shaw-bros.co.uk
Directors: D. Shaw (Ptnr)
No.of Employees: 1 - 10 **Product Groups:** 25, 35, 39

Shaw Pallet Ltd
Bridge Street Slaithwaite, Huddersfield, HD7 5JN
Tel: 01484-848400 **Fax:** 01484-848410
E-mail: info@shawpallet.com
Website: http://www.shawpallet.com
Bank(s): National Westminster
Directors: C. Hillaby (Ch), J. Coupland (Sales & Mktg), M. Dragicevic (Fin), S. Quarmby (Dir)
Ultimate Holding Company: SHAW PALLET (HOLDINGS) LIMITED
Immediate Holding Company: SHAW PALLET LIMITED
Registration no: 01150422 **VAT No.:** GB 184 3961 35
Date established: 1973 **Turnover:** £5m - £10m **No.of Employees:** 21 - 50
Product Groups: 45

Date of Accounts	Mar 12	Mar 11	Mar 10
Sales Turnover	6m	N/A	N/A
Pre Tax Profit/Loss	357	N/A	N/A
Working Capital	2m	2m	1m
Fixed Assets	180	231	251
Current Assets	3m	3m	3m
Current Liabilities	323	N/A	N/A

Shaws Petroleum Ltd
Manor Road Farnley Tyas, Huddersfield, HD4 6UL
Tel: 01484-667744 **Fax:** 01484-662244
E-mail: paulsykes@shawspetroleum.co.uk
Website: http://www.shawspetroleum.co.uk
Directors: L. Greaves (Pers), P. Sykes (MD), S. Alder (Fin)
Immediate Holding Company: SHAWS PETROLEUM LIMITED
Registration no: 00855613 **VAT No.:** GB 427 4390 47
Date established: 1965 **Turnover:** £20m - £50m **No.of Employees:** 1 - 10
Product Groups: 66

Date of Accounts	Jun 11	Jun 10	Jun 09
Sales Turnover	32m	31m	33m
Pre Tax Profit/Loss	17	24	-70
Working Capital	-1m	-1m	-2m
Fixed Assets	9m	9m	9m
Current Assets	2m	2m	1m
Current Liabilities	147	282	599

Sicame Electrical Developments Ltd
843-855 Leeds Road, Huddersfield, HD2 1WA
Tel: 01484-681115 **Fax:** 01484-687352
E-mail: jim.henderson@sicame.co.uk
Website: http://www.sicame.co.uk
Bank(s): Barclays, Bradford
Directors: A. Noble (Fin), J. Henderson (MD)
Managers: P. Croton (Tech Serv Mgr), T. Atkinson, D. Hodgkiss (Purch Mgr)
Ultimate Holding Company: SICAME SA (FRANCE)
Immediate Holding Company: SICAME ELECTRICAL DEVELOPMENTS LIMITED
Registration no: 00686246 **VAT No.:** GB 526 0385 58
Date established: 1961 **Turnover:** £10m - £20m
No.of Employees: 101 - 250 **Product Groups:** 36, 37, 39, 40, 51

Date of Accounts	Dec 11	Dec 10	Dec 09
Sales Turnover	13m	13m	11m
Pre Tax Profit/Loss	-519	-107	-382
Working Capital	2m	2m	2m
Fixed Assets	2m	1m	1m
Current Assets	7m	7m	5m
Current Liabilities	1m	245	435

Sign A Rama Ltd
20 Viaduct Street, Huddersfield, HD1 6AJ
Tel: 01484-517070 **Fax:** 01484-517171
E-mail: huddersfield@sign-a-rama.co.uk
Website: http://www.sign-a-rama.co.uk
Directors: K. Ingle (Ptnr)
Immediate Holding Company: SIGNARAMA (BIRMINGHAM WEST) LTD
Registration no: 07106075 **Date established:** 2009
No.of Employees: 1 - 10 **Product Groups:** 30, 39, 40, 80

Spectrum Yarns Ltd
Spa Mill New Street, Slaithwaite, Huddersfield, HD7 5BB
Tel: 01484-843732 **Fax:** 01484-847784
E-mail: enquiries@spectrumyarns.co.uk
Website: http://www.spectrumyarns.co.uk
Bank(s): Lloyds TSB Bank plc
Directors: I. Porter (Fin), R. Brown (MD)
Managers: P. Holt (Sales Prom Mgr), D. Taylor
Immediate Holding Company: SPECTRUM YARNS LIMITED
Registration no: 01142407 **VAT No.:** GB 184 4153 61
Date established: 1973 **Turnover:** £10m - £20m
No.of Employees: 51 - 100 **Product Groups:** 23

Date of Accounts	Mar 12	Mar 11	Mar 10
Sales Turnover	15m	14m	12m
Pre Tax Profit/Loss	354	415	-307
Working Capital	5m	5m	4m
Fixed Assets	976	1m	1m
Current Assets	9m	8m	7m
Current Liabilities	1m	1m	1m

R V Spivey & Sons
Rear of Croft Street, Huddersfield, HD1 4UH
Tel: 01484-543508 **Fax:** 01484-543508
Directors: R. Spivey (Prop)
Date established: 1965 **No.of Employees:** 1 - 10 **Product Groups:** 43

Stork Brothers Ltd
Bay Hall Mills Bay Hall Common Road, Huddersfield, HD1 5EP
Tel: 01484-424283 **Fax:** 01484-542876
E-mail: enquiries@storkbrothers.co.uk
Website: http://www.storkbrothers.co.uk
Bank(s): HSBC
Directors: S. Moorhouse (MD), J. Fleming (Fin)
Managers: M. Brown (Chief Acct)
Ultimate Holding Company: FLYING MAGIC LIMITED
Immediate Holding Company: STORK BROTHERS LIMITED
Registration no: 00187655 **VAT No.:** GB 183 6967 14
Date established: 2023 **Turnover:** £5m - £10m
No.of Employees: 51 - 100 **Product Groups:** 23

Date of Accounts	Apr 12	Apr 11	Apr 10
Working Capital	990	986	997
Fixed Assets	88	99	54
Current Assets	2m	2m	2m
Current Liabilities	210	N/A	175

T G Plastics Ltd
Britannia Mills Stoney Battery, Huddersfield, HD1 4TL
Tel: 01484-655221 **Fax:** 01484-644779
E-mail: tom.tgeng@btconnect.com
Bank(s): Barclays
Directors: J. Walsh (Fin)
Immediate Holding Company: TG PLASTICS LIMITED
Registration no: 06734069 **VAT No.:** GB 721 2742 64
Date established: 2008 **Turnover:** Up to £250,000
No.of Employees: 11 - 20 **Product Groups:** 30

Date of Accounts	Oct 11	Oct 10	Oct 09
Sales Turnover	1m	374	631
Pre Tax Profit/Loss	43	21	-21
Working Capital	6	-45	-79
Fixed Assets	64	43	58
Current Assets	21	69	167
Current Liabilities	15	4	29

Targon Technology
Forland Mills Slades Road, Golcar, Huddersfield, HD7 4JS
Tel: 08450-719115 **Fax:** 01484-640466
E-mail: sales@targon.co.uk
Website: http://www.openviewgroup.com
Managers: A. Brown (Mgr)
Registration no: 02198706 **Date established:** 1987
No.of Employees: 1 - 10 **Product Groups:** 35, 37, 40, 48, 52, 67

Taylor & Jones Ltd
Crosland Road Industrial Estate Netherton, Huddersfield, HD4 7DQ
Tel: 01484-665321 **Fax:** 01484-666952
E-mail: kevin@taylorandjones.co.uk
Website: http://www.taylorandjones.co.uk
Managers: K. Clegg (Mgr)
Immediate Holding Company: TAYLOR AND JONES LIMITED
Registration no: 05297450 **VAT No.:** GB 183 3080 73
Date established: 2004 **Turnover:** £500,000 - £1m
No.of Employees: 1 - 10 **Product Groups:** 46

Date of Accounts	Feb 08	Feb 11	Feb 10
Sales Turnover	N/A	811	699
Pre Tax Profit/Loss	N/A	43	-28
Working Capital	172	199	163
Fixed Assets	368	178	228
Current Assets	802	421	426
Current Liabilities	N/A	77	88

Taylor & Lodge (t/a Taylor & Lodge)
Rashcliffe Mills Albert Street, Huddersfield, HD1 3PE
Tel: 01484-423231 **Fax:** 01484-435313
E-mail: headoffice@taylorandlodge.co.uk
Website: http://www.taylorandlodge.co.uk
Bank(s): Lloyds TSB
Directors: B. Haigh (MD), R. McQuillan (Sales)
Immediate Holding Company: TAYLOR LODGE
Registration no: 07493567 **VAT No.:** GB 184 4696 23
Date established: 2011 **Turnover:** £2m - £5m **No.of Employees:** 21 - 50
Product Groups: 23, 63

Taylor Shaw (Shaw Son & Greenhalgh Ltd)
St Thomas' Road, Huddersfield, HD1 3LG
Tel: 01484-651177 **Fax:** 01484-645854
E-mail: sales@taylorshaw.co.uk
Website: http://www.taylorshaw.co.uk
Bank(s): National Westminster Bank Plc
Directors: I. Johnson (MD), M. Greenhalgh (Dir), M. Sanderson (Sales)
Immediate Holding Company: Flow System Technologies Ltd
Registration no: 06576188 **VAT No.:** GB 183 7192 42
Date established: 1905 **Turnover:** £2m - £5m **No.of Employees:** 21 - 50
Product Groups: 36, 48

Taylorshaw Valves Ltd
St Thomas' Road, Huddersfield, HD1 3LG
Tel: 01484-484880 **Fax:** 01484-645854
E-mail: sales@shawvalves.co.uk
Website: http://www.shawvalves.co.uk
Directors: N. Horn (Co Sec)
Immediate Holding Company: Flow System Technologies Ltd
Registration no: 06326871 **No.of Employees:** 51 - 100
Product Groups: 36, 37, 38

Telebits
28 Rowlands Avenue, Huddersfield, HD5 9YA
Tel: 01484-300889
E-mail: sales@telebits.co.uk
Website: http://www.telebits.co.uk
Directors: G. Hadley (Prop)
Turnover: Up to £250,000 **No.of Employees:** 1 - 10 **Product Groups:** 37

Thorite
Barge Street, Huddersfield, HD1 3LN
Tel: 01484-534245 **Fax:** 01484-435023
E-mail: huddersfield@thorite.co.uk
Website: http://www.thorite.co.uk
Managers: J. Fletcher
Immediate Holding Company: THOMAS WRIGHT/THORITE GROUP LTD
Registration no: 00177707 **VAT No.:** GB 179 3058 37
Date established: 1850 **Turnover:** £5m - £10m **No.of Employees:** 1 - 10
Product Groups: 38, 40

Thornton & Ross Ltd
Linthwaite Laboratories Manchester Road, Linthwaite, Huddersfield, HD7 5QH
Tel: 01484-842217 **Fax:** 01484-847301
E-mail: jonathanthornton@thorntonross.com
Website: http://www.thorntonross.com
Bank(s): Barclays
Directors: B. Draude (Sales), G. Adams (Fin), J. Thornton (MD), J. Alpin (Fin)
Managers: M. Davies, R. Foster (Tech Serv Mgr), C. Wheeler (Mktg Serv Mgr), N. Shewring (Personnel)
Immediate Holding Company: SUNDROPS LIMITED
Registration no: 00338772 **Date established:** 1938
Turnover: £50m - £75m **No.of Employees:** 251 - 500
Product Groups: 31, 32

Date of Accounts	Mar 09	Mar 08	Mar 10
Working Capital	2m	885	2m
Fixed Assets	1	1	1
Current Assets	2m	1m	2m

Trojan Plastics Ltd
Ramsden Mills Britannia Road, Huddersfield, HD3 4QG
Tel: 01484-648181 **Fax:** 01484-657098
E-mail: sales@trojanplastics.co.uk
Website: http://www.trojanplastics.co.uk
Bank(s): Barclays
Directors: J. Mosley (MD), D. Hirst (Fin)
Ultimate Holding Company: HARTFORD HOLDINGS LIMITED
Immediate Holding Company: TROJAN PLASTICS LIMITED
Registration no: 01995822 **VAT No.:** GB 525 8096 31
Date established: 1986 **Turnover:** £10m - £20m
No.of Employees: 101 - 250 **Product Groups:** 30

Date of Accounts	Apr 11	Apr 10	Apr 09
Sales Turnover	18m	19m	16m
Pre Tax Profit/Loss	716	794	125
Working Capital	5m	4m	7m
Fixed Assets	1	1	1
Current Assets	7m	7m	10m
Current Liabilities	879	747	757

Tyreseal UK
6 Chapel Hill, Huddersfield, HD1 3EB
Tel: 01484-539411 **Fax:** 01484-349518
E-mail: sultana.shafi@tyreseal.co.uk
Website: http://www.tyreseal.co.uk
Directors: M. Shafi (Fin), S. Shafi (MD)
Immediate Holding Company: TYRESEAL LIMITED
Registration no: 04225819 **Date established:** 2012
Turnover: Up to £250,000 **No.of Employees:** 11 - 20 **Product Groups:** 68

Date of Accounts	May 07	May 06
Working Capital	N/A	-10
Fixed Assets	4	5
Current Assets	31	15
Current Liabilities	32	25

United Anodisers
Field Mills Red Doles Lane, Huddersfield, HD2 1YG
Tel: 01484-533142 **Fax:** 01484-435175
E-mail: sales@hmfltd.co.uk
Website: http://home.scarlet.be
Directors: P. Watts (MD), T. Hutton (Dir), A. Smith (Fin)
Managers: A. Robinson (Comm), K. Nurse (Purch Mgr)
Ultimate Holding Company: COIL S A/N V (BELGIUM)
Immediate Holding Company: UNITED ANODISERS LIMITED
Registration no: 04203034 **VAT No.:** GB 119 7195 49
Date established: 2001 **Turnover:** £2m - £5m **No.of Employees:** 51 - 100
Product Groups: 46, 48

Date of Accounts	Dec 11	Dec 10	Dec 09
Sales Turnover	7m	4m	3m
Pre Tax Profit/Loss	743	-860	-19
Working Capital	288	-2m	-151
Fixed Assets	2m	2m	2m
Current Assets	3m	1m	839
Current Liabilities	527	353	209

Universal Engineering Workholding Ltd
New Street Netherton, Huddersfield, HD4 7EZ
Tel: 01484-663018 **Fax:** 01484-663758
E-mail: sales@uew.co.uk
Website: http://www.uew.co.uk
Directors: M. Adams (MD)
Immediate Holding Company: UNIVERSAL ENGINEERING WORKHOLDING LIMITED
Registration no: 00368226 **VAT No.:** GB 184 8715 25
Date established: 1941 **Turnover:** £1m - £2m **No.of Employees:** 1 - 10
Product Groups: 35, 46

Date of Accounts	Dec 11	Dec 10	Dec 09
Working Capital	68	-100	-81
Fixed Assets	521	482	515
Current Assets	392	284	227

Vivimed Labs Europe Ltd
PO Box b3, Huddersfield, HD1 6BU
Tel: 01484-320500 **Fax:** 01484-320300
E-mail: sales@vivimedlabs.com
Website: http://www.vivimedlabs.com
Bank(s): National Westminster Bank Plc
Directors: L. Crascall (Sales & Mktg), R. Smith (MD)
Managers: I. Wilkinson (Tech Serv Mgr), R. Blakey (Fin Mgr), K. Parr (Personnel)
Ultimate Holding Company: YULE CATTO & CO PUBLIC LIMITED COMPANY
Immediate Holding Company: VIVIMED LABS EUROPE LTD
Registration no: 00069842 **VAT No.:** GB 517 1160 00
Date established: 2001 **Turnover:** £10m - £20m
No.of Employees: 21 - 50 **Product Groups:** 32

Date of Accounts	Dec 07	Mar 11	Mar 10
Sales Turnover	8m	12m	16m
Pre Tax Profit/Loss	-335	1m	2m
Working Capital	257	3m	2m
Fixed Assets	502	1m	2m
Current Assets	3m	6m	5m
Current Liabilities	934	707	900

Wakefield Brush UK Ltd
Unit 8 Newhaven Business Park Lowergate, Milnsbridge, Huddersfield, HD3 4HS
Tel: 01484-642555 **Fax:** 01484-642888
E-mail: sales@wakefieldbrushcompany.co.uk
Website: http://www.wakefieldbrushcompany.co.uk
Directors: G. Brooke (MD)
Immediate Holding Company: WAKEFIELD BRUSH UK LIMITED
Registration no: 05273834 **VAT No.:** GB 464 2376 41
Date established: 2004 **Turnover:** Up to £250,000
No.of Employees: 1 - 10 **Product Groups:** 40

Date of Accounts	Dec 11	Dec 10	Dec 09
Working Capital	25	18	3
Fixed Assets	1	1	1
Current Assets	37	33	32

Westin W S Ltd
Phoenix Mill Leeds Road, Huddersfield, HD1 6NG
Tel: 01484-421585 **Fax:** 01484-432420
E-mail: sales@westin.co.uk
Website: http://www.westin.co.uk
Bank(s): Barclays
Directors: H. Blackburn (Dir), D. Pratt (Fin)
Managers: M. Sharpe (Buyer), A. Phillips (Mktg Serv Mgr)
Immediate Holding Company: W. S. WESTIN GROUP LIMITED
Registration no: 00352890 **VAT No.:** 183 8044 52 **Date established:** 1939
Turnover: £1m - £2m **No.of Employees:** 21 - 50 **Product Groups:** 26, 30, 33, 35, 40

Date of Accounts	Mar 12	Mar 11	Mar 10
Working Capital	-225	-305	-210
Fixed Assets	2m	1m	1m
Current Assets	103	8	56

Willow Models
4 Willow Grove Golcar, Huddersfield, HD7 4RX
Tel: 01484-658832 **Fax:** 01484-658832
E-mail: info@willowmodels.com
Website: http://www.willowmodels.com
Directors: M. Pearce (Prop)
Date established: 1998 **No.of Employees:** 1 - 10 **Product Groups:** 49, 65

Wood Auto Supplies Ltd
Colne Road, Huddersfield, HD1 3ES
Tel: 01484-428261 **Fax:** 01484-434933
E-mail: sales@woodauto.co.uk
Website: http://www.woodauto.com
Bank(s): National Westminster Bank Plc
Directors: R. Heywood (Ch), A. Stead (Fin), G. Heywood (MD)
Managers: C. Fountain (Purch Mgr)
Ultimate Holding Company: WOOD AUTO (HOLDINGS) LIMITED
Immediate Holding Company: WOOD AUTO SUPPLIES LIMITED
Registration no: 00851509 **VAT No.:** GB 183 3174 64
Date established: 1965 **Turnover:** £5m - £10m
No.of Employees: 51 - 100 **Product Groups:** 39, 68

Date of Accounts	Mar 11	Mar 10	Mar 09
Sales Turnover	8m	7m	N/A
Pre Tax Profit/Loss	28	16	243
Working Capital	3m	3m	3m
Fixed Assets	534	505	526
Current Assets	4m	4m	4m
Current Liabilities	218	151	139

Woodcock & Wilson Ltd
Airstream Works Blackmoorfoot Road, Huddersfield, HD4 7AA
Tel: 01484-461973 **Fax:** 01484-462888
E-mail: sales@fanmanufacturers.com
Website: http://www.fanmanufacturers.com
Directors: M. Jones (MD), P. Hebden (Fin)
Managers: M. Crouch (Contracts Mgr), V. Phillips (Sales Prom Mgr)
Ultimate Holding Company: MATCHEXTRA LIMITED
Immediate Holding Company: WOODCOCK & WILSON LIMITED
Registration no: 01353953 **Date established:** 1978 **Turnover:** £2m - £5m
No.of Employees: 21 - 50 **Product Groups:** 39, 40, 48, 66

Date of Accounts	Mar 11	Mar 10	Mar 09
Working Capital	2m	1m	1m
Fixed Assets	142	141	153
Current Assets	2m	2m	2m

H Young Transport Ltd
Red Doles Lane, Huddersfield, HD2 1YF
Tel: 01484-535677 **Fax:** 01484-516005
Website: http://www.hyoung-transport.co.uk
Managers: J. Law (Mgr)
Ultimate Holding Company: H YOUNG LOGISTICS LIMITED
Immediate Holding Company: H. YOUNG TRANSPORT LIMITED
Registration no: 05673182 **Date established:** 2006 **Turnover:** £5m - £10m
No.of Employees: 21 - 50 **Product Groups:** 77

Date of Accounts	Mar 11	Mar 10	Mar 09
Working Capital	15	-193	-240
Fixed Assets	264	403	519
Current Assets	1m	1m	1m

Ilkley

Alexika Ltd
Communication House 93 Main Street, Addingham, Ilkley, LS29 0PD
Tel: 01943-839227 **Fax:** 01943-830279
E-mail: mail@alexika.com
Website: http://www.alexika.com
Directors: M. Robinson (MD)
Immediate Holding Company: ALEXIKA LIMITED
Registration no: 03773506 **VAT No.:** GB 721 6422 62
Date established: 1999 **No.of Employees:** 1 - 10 **Product Groups:** 80

Date of Accounts	Sep 11	Sep 10	Sep 09
Working Capital	71	75	84
Fixed Assets	42	49	50
Current Assets	108	115	115

Ilkley Stove Centre
301 Leeds Road, Ilkley, LS29 8NF
Tel: 01943-602003 **Fax:** 01943-817003
E-mail: anni.js@hotmail.com
Website: http://www.ilkleystovecentre.co.uk
Directors: I. Stokoe (Prop)
Immediate Holding Company: GLOBALCROWN LIMITED
Registration no: 04607836 **Date established:** 1979
No.of Employees: 11 - 20 **Product Groups:** 40

Date of Accounts	Jul 11	Jul 10	Jul 09
Working Capital	258	258	246
Fixed Assets	19	25	27
Current Assets	371	389	345

Instrumentation Systems & Services Ltd
PO Box 1, Ilkley, LS29 8EU
Tel: 01943-602001 **Fax:** 01943-816796
E-mail: admin@issltd.co.uk
Website: http://www.issltd.co.uk
Managers: S. Kelly (Sales Prom Mgr)
Immediate Holding Company: INSTRUMENTATION SYSTEMS & SERVICES LIMITED
Registration no: 02612775 **Date established:** 1991
No.of Employees: 1 - 10 **Product Groups:** 37, 38

Date of Accounts	May 11	May 10	May 09
Working Capital	204	176	180
Fixed Assets	44	33	53
Current Assets	369	335	354

Mico Dry Ice Cleaning
46 Long Meadows Burley in Wharfedale, Ilkley, LS29 7RY
Tel: 01943-864992
E-mail: sales@mico-services.co.uk
Website: http://www.mico-services.co.uk
Directors: P. Smith (Prop)
Managers: M. Coelho (Chief Mgr), N. Basic (Mktg Serv Mgr)
Turnover: Up to £250,000 **No.of Employees:** 1 - 10 **Product Groups:** 52

N G Bailey
Denton, Ilkley, LS29 0HH
Tel: 01943-601933 **Fax:** 01943-816117
E-mail: generalenquiries@ngbailey.co.uk
Website: http://www.ngbailey.co.uk
Directors: M. Andrews (Ch), M. Bailey (MD), N. Bailey (Dir), L. Ashman (Fin)
Managers: J. Earl
Immediate Holding Company: SCOTIA PROPERTY HEATING (DOMESTIC) LIMITED
Registration no: SC153584 **VAT No.:** GB 179 3966 02
Date established: 1994 **Turnover:** £1m - £2m **No.of Employees:** 1 - 10
Product Groups: 52

Parmley Graham Ltd

St Johns Hall Burley Lane, Menston, Ilkley, LS29 6EU
Tel: 01943-870400 **Fax:** 01943-870067
E-mail: leeds@parmley-graham.co.uk
Website: http://www.parmley-graham.co.uk
Managers: A. Ambridge (Mgr)
Immediate Holding Company: PARMLEY GRAHAM LIMITED
Registration no: 00172842 **VAT No.:** GB 176 7006 54
Date established: 2021 **Turnover:** £20m - £50m **No.of Employees:** 1 - 10
Product Groups: 37

Date of Accounts	Dec 11	Dec 10	Dec 09
Sales Turnover	34m	33m	26m
Pre Tax Profit/Loss	1m	910	353
Working Capital	4m	4m	3m
Fixed Assets	1m	1m	1m
Current Assets	10m	9m	7m
Current Liabilities	1m	900	415

PlanIT Inks Ltd

9 Crossbank Road Addingham, Ilkley, LS29 0JZ
Tel: 07999-641777
E-mail: sales@planitinks.com
Website: http://www.planitinks.com
Directors: J. Heptonstall (Procurement), P. Heptonstall (Dir)
Managers: D. Parsley (Sales Prom Mgr)
Immediate Holding Company: SPECIALIST DUCTING SUPPLIES LIMITED
Registration no: 02010194 **Date established:** 1986
No.of Employees: 1 - 10 **Product Groups:** 30

Date of Accounts	Dec 09	Dec 08	Dec 07
Working Capital	-10	-10	-26
Fixed Assets	19	21	24
Current Assets	25	43	15

Professional Fitness & Education

9a Cleasby Road Menston, Ilkley, LS29 6JE
Tel: 01943-879816 **Fax:** 01943-870887
E-mail: christine.north@northernfitness.co.uk
Website: http://www.nothernfitness.co.uk
Directors: E. Butler (Fin), C. North (MD)
Immediate Holding Company: NORTHERN FITNESS & EDUCATION LIMITED
Registration no: 03817367 **VAT No.:** GB 654 0427 51
Date established: 1999 **Turnover:** Up to £250,000
No.of Employees: 1 - 10 **Product Groups:** 67

Date of Accounts	Jul 12	Jul 11	Jul 10
Working Capital	N/A	1	-22
Fixed Assets	N/A	N/A	22
Current Assets	N/A	2	56

R B Labels Ltd

37 Grove Road, Ilkley, LS29 9PF
Tel: 01943-468302 **Fax:** 01943-850406
E-mail: sales@rblabels.co.uk
Website: http://www.rblabels.co.uk
Directors: M. Wade (MD), P. Wade (Fin)
Immediate Holding Company: R.B. LABELS LIMITED
Registration no: 03000351 **VAT No.:** GB 500 2623 11
Date established: 1994 **Turnover:** £500,000 - £1m
No.of Employees: 1 - 10 **Product Groups:** 27, 28, 42

Date of Accounts	Mar 11	Mar 10	Mar 09
Working Capital	N/A	1	5
Current Assets	6	7	11

Readshaw Timber Ltd

High House Farm Turner Lane, Addingham, Ilkley, LS29 0LJ
Tel: 01943-830037 **Fax:** 01943-830440
E-mail: carl@readshawtimber.co.uk
Website: http://www.readshawtimber.co.uk
Directors: C. Readshaw (Fin), C. Readshaw (MD)
Immediate Holding Company: READSHAW TIMBER LIMITED
Registration no: 04384710 **Date established:** 2002
No.of Employees: 1 - 10 **Product Groups:** 25, 36, 38, 39, 41, 45, 46, 47, 66, 83

Date of Accounts	Mar 11	Mar 10	Mar 09
Working Capital	-3	-36	-2
Fixed Assets	140	159	183
Current Assets	77	64	80

Silkscreen Europe Ltd

PO Box 229, Ilkley, LS29 1AA
Tel: 01943-605650 **Fax:** 0870-855 5550
E-mail: info@sseworldwide.co.uk
Website: http://www.sseworldwide.co.uk
Directors: S. Armitage (MD)
Immediate Holding Company: SILKSCREEN EUROPE LIMITED
Registration no: 02972597 **Date established:** 1994
Turnover: £500,000 - £1m **No.of Employees:** 1 - 10 **Product Groups:** 44

Date of Accounts	Apr 11	Apr 10	Apr 09
Working Capital	152	81	96
Fixed Assets	3	1	2
Current Assets	295	162	148

Spooner Industries Ltd

Moorland Engineering Works Railway Road, Ilkley, LS29 8JB
Tel: 01943-609505 **Fax:** 01943-603190
E-mail: mbrook@spooner.co.uk
Website: http://www.spooner.co.uk
Directors: J. Muggleston (Co Sec), M. Brook (MD), S. Newell (Sales)
Managers: C. Eastham (Purch Mgr), D. Acrid (Tech Serv Mgr)
Ultimate Holding Company: AEGEUS INDUSTRIES LIMITED
Immediate Holding Company: SPOONER INDUSTRIES LIMITED
Registration no: 00643047 **VAT No.:** GB 427 8288 18
Date established: 1959 **Turnover:** £20m - £50m
No.of Employees: 51 - 100 **Product Groups:** 40, 41, 43, 44, 46

Date of Accounts	Jun 11	Jun 10	Jun 09
Sales Turnover	23m	13m	15m
Pre Tax Profit/Loss	1m	402	838
Working Capital	4m	3m	3m
Fixed Assets	3m	4m	4m
Current Assets	11m	8m	6m
Current Liabilities	4m	3m	2m

Keighley

A C E Elevators Ltd

Beckside House Pitt Street, Keighley, BD21 4PF
Tel: 01535-602239 **Fax:** 01535-661268
E-mail: francisco.mateo@orona.co.uk
Website: http://www.orona.co.uk
Directors: F. Mateo (MD)
Immediate Holding Company: ACE ELEVATORS LIMITED
Registration no: 07092845 **VAT No.:** GB 303 4835 81
Date established: 2009 **Turnover:** £2m - £5m **No.of Employees:** 1 - 10
Product Groups: 45

A1 Roper Ltd

Crown Works Worth Way, Keighley, BD21 5LR
Tel: 01535-604215 **Fax:** 01535-602689
E-mail: admin@a1-roper.com
Website: http://www.a1-roper.com
Bank(s): The Royal Bank of Scotland
Directors: G. Richardson (MD)
Immediate Holding Company: A1 ROPER LTD
Registration no: 05454369 **Date established:** 2005
Turnover: £500,000 - £1m **No.of Employees:** 11 - 20
Product Groups: 36, 39, 40, 42, 45, 46

Date of Accounts	Dec 11	Dec 10	Dec 09
Working Capital	152	145	128
Fixed Assets	82	89	93
Current Assets	351	339	260

Acetarc Welding & Engineering Co. Ltd

Atley Works Dalton Lane, Keighley, BD21 4HT
Tel: 01535-607323 **Fax:** 01535-602522
E-mail: sales@acetarc.co.uk
Website: http://www.acetarc.co.uk
Bank(s): Barclays
Directors: P. Burrell (Sales), S. Harker (I.T. Dir)
Immediate Holding Company: ACETARC WELDING & ENGINEERING COMPANY LIMITED
Registration no: 00981662 **VAT No.:** GB 179 3664 18
Date established: 1970 **Turnover:** £250,000 - £500,000
No.of Employees: 11 - 20 **Product Groups:** 39, 45, 46

Date of Accounts	Sep 11	Sep 10	Sep 09
Working Capital	193	219	223
Fixed Assets	79	26	31
Current Assets	390	332	300

Aero Vac Systems

500 Bradford Road Sandbeds, Keighley, BD20 5NG
Tel: 01274-550500 **Fax:** 01274-550501
E-mail: sales@aerovac.com
Website: http://www.aerovac.com
Bank(s): Lloyds
Directors: S. Bowers (Co Sec), M. Goldstein (Fin), J. Jaggar (Comm), L. Edenbrow (Fin)
Managers: M. Woodhouse (Buyer)
Ultimate Holding Company: UMECO LIMITED
Immediate Holding Company: UMECO PROCESS MATERIALS LIMITED
Registration no: 01472714 **VAT No.:** GB 343 4003 01
Date established: 1980 **Turnover:** £10m - £20m
No.of Employees: 21 - 50 **Product Groups:** 39

Date of Accounts	Mar 12	Mar 11	Mar 10
Sales Turnover	18m	16m	12m
Pre Tax Profit/Loss	3m	3m	2m
Working Capital	13m	11m	8m
Fixed Assets	2m	2m	2m
Current Assets	17m	15m	11m
Current Liabilities	755	853	452

Airedale 3D

9 Craven Road Bradford Road, Keighley, BD21 4AR
Tel: 01535-665858
E-mail: ian@airedale3d.co.uk
Website: http://www.airedale3d.co.uk
Directors: I. Watkin (Ptnr)
Date established: 2003 **Turnover:** Up to £250,000
No.of Employees: 1 - 10 **Product Groups:** 44, 79

Airedale Springs

The Spring Works Bridgehouse Lane, Haworth, Keighley, BD22 8PA
Tel: 01535-643456 **Fax:** 01535-645392
E-mail: sales@airedalesprings.co.uk
Website: http://www.airedalesprings.co.uk
Bank(s): Barclays, Skipton
Directors: T. Parkinson (Ch)
Managers: S. Parkinson (Tech Serv Mgr), S. Brook (Mktg Serv Mgr), S. Ibbotson
Immediate Holding Company: AIREDALE SPRINGS LIMITED
Registration no: 00395974 **Date established:** 1945 **Turnover:** £2m - £5m
No.of Employees: 21 - 50 **Product Groups:** 34, 35, 36, 38, 39, 49, 68, 85

Date of Accounts	Dec 11	Dec 10	Dec 09
Working Capital	2m	4m	268
Fixed Assets	2m	233	391
Current Assets	2m	5m	480

Alfran Fasteners Ltd

Central Ironworks Parson Street, Keighley, BD21 3HD
Tel: 01535-664993 **Fax:** 01535-664994
E-mail: sales@alfranfasteners.co.uk
Website: http://www.andaray.co.uk
Bank(s): HSBC Bank plc
Directors: A. Costello (MD)
Ultimate Holding Company: NORTHERN ENDEAVOUR LIMITED
Immediate Holding Company: ALFRAN FASTENERS LIMITED
Registration no: 03242120 **VAT No.:** GB 181 0388 72
Date established: 1996 **No.of Employees:** 11 - 20 **Product Groups:** 35, 66

Date of Accounts	Feb 08	Feb 11	Feb 10
Working Capital	163	402	377
Fixed Assets	31	22	27
Current Assets	802	834	1m

Ammeraal Beltech Ltd

Parkwood Street, Keighley, BD21 4PL
Tel: 01535-667015 **Fax:** 01535-610250
E-mail: keighley@ammeraalbeltech.co.uk
Website: http://www.ammeraalbeltech.com
Bank(s): Lloyds TSB, North Street
Managers: G. Marsh (Product)
Ultimate Holding Company: GAMMA HOLDING NV (NETHERLANDS)
Immediate Holding Company: AMMERAAL BELTECH LIMITED
Registration no: 01163300 **VAT No.:** GB 500 5844 77
Date established: 1974 **Turnover:** £2m - £5m **No.of Employees:** 21 - 50
Product Groups: 22, 23, 29, 30, 35

Date of Accounts	Dec 11	Dec 10	Dec 09
Sales Turnover	17m	15m	12m
Pre Tax Profit/Loss	2m	1m	652
Working Capital	819	941	108
Fixed Assets	2m	2m	2m
Current Assets	8m	6m	5m
Current Liabilities	3m	2m	2m

Autoclaves Ltd

Crown Works Worth Way, Keighley, BD21 5LR
Tel: 01535-687450 **Fax:** 01274-564525
E-mail: info@autoclavesgroup.com
Website: http://www.autoclavesgroup.com
Managers: A. Leatt (Sales Prom Mgr)
Immediate Holding Company: AUTOCLAVES LIMITED
Registration no: 03474110 **Date established:** 1997 **Turnover:** £1m - £2m
No.of Employees: 21 - 50 **Product Groups:** 29, 38, 40, 41, 42, 43

Date of Accounts	Jan 12	Jan 11	Jan 10
Working Capital	141	-2	411
Fixed Assets	196	429	184
Current Assets	667	594	1m

L E Ayrton

Hawkcliffe Farm Keighley Road, Steeton, Keighley, BD20 6QR
Tel: 01535-656147
Directors: L. Ayrton (Prop)
Date established: 1983 **No.of Employees:** 1 - 10 **Product Groups:** 41

B T A L Incorporating Kadtal

Universal Mills Bradford Road, Keighley, BD21 4BW
Tel: 01274-668149 **Fax:** 01535- 609998
E-mail: info@btal.co.uk
Website: http://www.btal.co.uk
Directors: J. Lister (Co Sec), J. Igle (MD)
Managers: C. Jollife (Sales Prom Mgr), J. Acrid (Sales Admin)
Ultimate Holding Company: APPRIS CHARITY LIMITED
Immediate Holding Company: APPRIS MANAGEMENT LIMITED
Registration no: 03335776 **Date established:** 1997
Turnover: £500,000 - £1m **No.of Employees:** 11 - 20 **Product Groups:** 86

Date of Accounts	Aug 09	Aug 08	Aug 07
Working Capital	-17	-19	-88
Fixed Assets	36	35	34
Current Assets	715	607	312

Bethel Rhodes & Sons Ltd

5 Alice Street, Keighley, BD21 3JD
Tel: 01535-602532 **Fax:** 01535-610067
E-mail: enquiries@bethelrhodes.co.uk
Website: http://www.bethelrhodes.co.uk
Directors: A. Trowers (MD)
Immediate Holding Company: BETHEL RHODES & SONS (WIREWORKERS) LIMITED
Registration no: 00679113 **VAT No.:** GB 180 1338 88
Date established: 1960 **Turnover:** £1m - £2m **No.of Employees:** 1 - 10
Product Groups: 30, 35, 49, 52, 66

Date of Accounts	Dec 11	Dec 10	Dec 09
Working Capital	1m	1m	1m
Fixed Assets	305	319	353
Current Assets	1m	1m	1m

Brenmoor Ltd

Summit House Riparian Way, Cross Hills, Keighley, BD20 7BW
Tel: 01535-633088 **Fax:** 01535-636911
E-mail: info@brenmoor.com
Website: http://www.brenmoor.com
Directors: M. Moorhouse (MD)
Immediate Holding Company: BRENMOOR LTD
Registration no: 05445872 **Date established:** 2005
Turnover: £500,000 - £1m **No.of Employees:** 1 - 10 **Product Groups:** 30

Date of Accounts	Jul 12	Jul 11	Jul 10
Working Capital	37	20	37
Fixed Assets	76	68	92
Current Assets	164	140	225

British Thornton E S F Ltd

Prospect Works South Street, Keighley, BD21 5AA
Tel: 01535-683250 **Fax:** 01535-680226
E-mail: stuartl@british-thornton.co.uk
Website: http://www.british-thornton.co.uk
Bank(s): Co-operative, Bradford
Directors: S. Little (MD), G. Wilks (Fin), D. Jevons (MD), D. Jeavons (MD)
Managers: S. Little (Ops Mgr), A. Henry (Nat Sales Mgr), A. Cunningham (Sales Prom Mgr)
Ultimate Holding Company: THORNTON EME GROUP LIMITED
Immediate Holding Company: BRITISH THORNTON LIMITED
Registration no: 00088812 **VAT No.:** GB 647 6552 07
Date established: 2006 **Turnover:** £10m - £20m
No.of Employees: 101 - 250 **Product Groups:** 26, 49

Date of Accounts	Dec 10	Dec 09	Dec 08
Working Capital	-19	-19	N/A

Brook International

Flagship House Riparian Way, Cross Hills, Keighley, BD20 7BW
Tel: 01535-639020 **Fax:** 01535-639029
E-mail: abrook@brookinternational.com
Website: http://www.brookinternational.com
Bank(s): Barclays
Directors: A. Brook (MD)
Ultimate Holding Company: JODA HOLDINGS LIMITED
Immediate Holding Company: JODA FREIGHT LIMITED
Registration no: 03456284 **VAT No.:** GB 168 9677 89
Date established: 1997 **Turnover:** £2m - £5m **No.of Employees:** 11 - 20
Product Groups: 23, 63

Byworth Boilers

Parkwood Boiler Works Parkwood Street, Keighley, BD21 4NW
Tel: 01535-665225 **Fax:** 01535-607550
E-mail: sales@byworth.co.uk
Website: http://www.byworth.co.uk
Directors: P. Baldwin (MD), A. Parker (Fin)
Ultimate Holding Company: DENNIS BALDWIN GROUP LTD
Immediate Holding Company: BYWORTH BOILERS LTD
Registration no: 07398810 **Date established:** 2010 **Turnover:** £5m - £10m
No.of Employees: 21 - 50 **Product Groups:** 40, 48, 52

Date of Accounts	Dec 11	Dec 10
Sales Turnover	7m	N/A
Pre Tax Profit/Loss	284	N/A
Working Capital	901	1
Fixed Assets	403	N/A
Current Assets	2m	1
Current Liabilities	482	N/A

Caremor Stairlift Services Ltd
26 North Street, Keighley, BD21 3SE
Tel: 01535-690086 **Fax:** 01535-690123
E-mail: sales@caremorestairlifts.co.uk
Website: http://www.caremorstairlifts.co.uk
Directors: M. Rattle (MD)
Immediate Holding Company: CAREMOR STAIRLIFT SERVICES LIMITED
Registration no: 03440041 **Date established:** 1997
No.of Employees: 1 - 10 **Product Groups:** 35, 39, 45

Date of Accounts	Sep 08	Sep 07	Sep 06
Working Capital	-18	-15	-47
Fixed Assets	5	6	8
Current Assets	218	224	144

Cinetic Landis Ltd
Skipton Road Cross Hills, Keighley, BD20 7SD
Tel: 01535-633211 **Fax:** 01535-635493
E-mail: rcoverdale@cinetic-landis.co.uk
Website: http://www.cinetic-landis.com
Bank(s): Barclays
Directors: S. Coverdale (MD)
Managers: D. Hixon (Purch Mgr), M. Molyneux (Fin Mgr)
Immediate Holding Company: CINETIC LANDIS LIMITED
Registration no: 05577045 **VAT No.:** GB 179 3827 16
Date established: 2005 **Turnover:** £20m - £50m
No.of Employees: 251 - 500 **Product Groups:** 46

Date of Accounts	Dec 11	Dec 10	Dec 09
Sales Turnover	40m	39m	36m
Pre Tax Profit/Loss	4m	5m	4m
Working Capital	19m	19m	17m
Fixed Assets	13m	14m	14m
Current Assets	41m	33m	29m
Current Liabilities	14m	5m	7m

Cirteq Ltd
Hayfield Colne Road, Glusburn, Keighley, BD20 8QP
Tel: 01535-633333 **Fax:** 01535-632966
E-mail: mail@cirteq.com
Website: http://www.cirteq.com
Bank(s): The Royal Bank of Scotland plc
Directors: V. Stevens (Prop)
Ultimate Holding Company: GLUSBURN HOLDINGS LIMITED
Immediate Holding Company: CIRTEQ LIMITED
Registration no: 03062174 **VAT No.:** GB 381 1425 71
Date established: 1995 **Turnover:** £10m - £20m
No.of Employees: 101 - 250 **Product Groups:** 35

Date of Accounts	Mar 11	Mar 10	Mar 09
Sales Turnover	18m	10m	15m
Pre Tax Profit/Loss	2m	-2m	159
Working Capital	6m	3m	4m
Fixed Assets	N/A	799	926
Current Assets	9m	6m	8m
Current Liabilities	558	363	322

David Petyt Ltd
8 Hanover Street, Keighley, BD21 3QJ
Tel: 01535-604853
E-mail: info@davidpetytmenswear.co.uk
Website: http://www.petyt.co.uk
Directors: V. Patel (MD)
No.of Employees: 1 - 10 **Product Groups:** 24, 63, 83

Dean Smith & Grace Lathes Ltd
PO Box 15, Keighley, BD21 4PG
Tel: 01535-605261 **Fax:** 01535-680921
E-mail: robert@deansmithandgrace.co.uk
Website: http://www.deansmithandgrace.co.uk
Bank(s): Barclays
Directors: R. Newton (Dir)
Immediate Holding Company: DSG LATHES LTD
Registration no: 02781762 **VAT No.:** GB 607 0903 62
Date established: 2003 **Turnover:** £5m - £10m **No.of Employees:** 11 - 20
Product Groups: 46, 47, 67

Date of Accounts	Mar 07	Mar 06
Sales Turnover	N/A	1713
Pre Tax Profit/Loss	N/A	131
Working Capital	-267	33
Fixed Assets	487	215
Current Assets	987	1178
Current Liabilities	1254	1146
Total Share Capital	10	10
ROCE% (Return on Capital Employed)		53.0
ROT% (Return on Turnover)		7.7

E Dobson & Co Gaskets Ltd
Oakworth Road, Keighley, BD21 1QQ
Tel: 01535-607257 **Fax:** 01535-608171
E-mail: robert.jeffrey@dobsongasket.com
Website: http://www.dobsongasket.com
Bank(s): Barclays, 77 North St
Directors: A. Jeffrey (Sales), R. Jeffrey (Fin)
Immediate Holding Company: E DOBSON & COMPANY (GASKETS) LIMITED
Registration no: 00752326 **VAT No.:** 179 6900 17 **Date established:** 1963
Turnover: £1m - £2m **No.of Employees:** 21 - 50 **Product Groups:** 29, 30, 33

Date of Accounts	Mar 11	Mar 10	Mar 09
Working Capital	60	-49	-40
Fixed Assets	873	945	341
Current Assets	577	444	447

Dolphin Stairlift North Yorkshire
11 Lawcliffe Crescent Haworth, Keighley, BD22 8RD
Tel: 01535-647744 **Fax:** 01535-647744
E-mail: gareth@dolphin-mobility.co.uk
Website: http://www.dolphinstairlifts.com
Directors: G. Watkinson (Prop), J. Petty (Prop), J. Peppy (Prop)
Date established: 2001 **No.of Employees:** 1 - 10 **Product Groups:** 35, 39, 45

Eclipse Engineering
Victoria Works Cherry Street, Keighley, BD21 4JX
Tel: 01535-691094
E-mail: rclough@eclipse.co.uk
Website: http://www.eclipse.co.uk
Directors: R. Clough (Prop)
Date established: 1990 **No.of Employees:** 1 - 10 **Product Groups:** 35

Colin Farrar Brewery Services Colin Farrar Brewery Services
1 Progress Works Parkwood Street, Keighley, BD21 4NX
Tel: 01535-681839 **Fax:** 01535-681887
E-mail: mail@cfbs.co.uk
Website: http://www.cfbsonline.co.uk
Directors: C. Farrar (Prop)
Registration no: 02932949 **Date established:** 1994
No.of Employees: 11 - 20 **Product Groups:** 36, 40, 41, 65, 67

R & L Fawcett Engineering
Craven Road Bradford Road, Keighley, BD21 4AR
Tel: 01535-669894 **Fax:** 01535-669894
E-mail: sales@fawcettengineering.co.uk
Directors: K. Smith (Prop)
Date established: 1979 **No.of Employees:** 1 - 10 **Product Groups:** 35

First Choice Rentals
Unit 4 Mandale Industrial Estate South Street, Keighley, BD21 1DB
Tel: 01535-609200
Directors: S. Addy (Ptnr)
Immediate Holding Company: FIRST CHOICE RENTAL LTD
Registration no: 07509135 **Date established:** 2011
No.of Employees: 1 - 10 **Product Groups:** 43

Freeway Washers Ltd
Prospect Works Deal Street, Keighley, BD21 4LA
Tel: 01535-610600 **Fax:** 01535-610700
E-mail: info@freewaywasher.com
Website: http://www.freewaywasher.com
Managers: A. Harland
Ultimate Holding Company: FREEWAY WASHERS INC (CANADA)
Immediate Holding Company: FREEWAY WASHER LIMITED
Registration no: 04232964 **Date established:** 2001
No.of Employees: 1 - 10 **Product Groups:** 22, 23, 25, 27, 29, 30, 31, 33, 34, 35, 37, 39, 40, 45, 46, 47, 48, 49, 51, 52, 66, 67, 68

Date of Accounts	Dec 11	Dec 10	Dec 09
Working Capital	412	358	174
Fixed Assets	238	257	384
Current Assets	604	593	306

Genesis Construction Machinery Ltd
Unit 2 Parkside Works Parkwood Street, Keighley, BD21 4PJ
Tel: 01535-661234 **Fax:** 01535-608765
E-mail: info@genesisequipment.co.uk
Website: http://www.genesiscms.co.uk
Directors: A. Clough (Dir)
Immediate Holding Company: GENESIS CONSTRUCTION MACHINERY SALES LIMITED
Registration no: 04679086 **Date established:** 2003
No.of Employees: 11 - 20 **Product Groups:** 45

Date of Accounts	Mar 12	Mar 11	Mar 10
Working Capital	-26	-32	-23
Fixed Assets	41	48	28
Current Assets	47	33	48

George Emmott Pawsons Ltd
Wadsworth Mill Oxenhope, Keighley, BD22 9NE
Tel: 01535-643733 **Fax:** 01535-642108
E-mail: mail@emmottsprings.co.uk
Website: http://www.emmottsprings.co.uk
Bank(s): Barclays Bank PLC
Directors: S. Clayton (MD)
Ultimate Holding Company: EMMOTT PAWSONS HOLDINGS LIMITED
Immediate Holding Company: GEORGE EMMOTT (PAWSONS) LIMITED
Registration no: 00248018 **Date established:** 1930 **Turnover:** £2m - £5m
No.of Employees: 11 - 20 **Product Groups:** 35, 36, 38, 39, 45, 48, 49, 66

Date of Accounts	Mar 11	Mar 10	Mar 09
Working Capital	219	238	229
Fixed Assets	115	129	148
Current Assets	683	588	578
Current Liabilities	146	248	115

Gesipa Blind Riveting Systems Ltd
Dalton Lane, Keighley, BD21 4JU
Tel: 01535-212200 **Fax:** 01535-212232
E-mail: n.anand@gesipa.co.uk
Website: http://www.gesipa.co.uk
Directors: M. Diesendorff (MD)
Managers: N. Anand (Mktg Serv Mgr)
Immediate Holding Company: GESIPA Blindniettechnik GmbH
Registration no: 00926257 **Date established:** 1971 **Turnover:** £5m - £10m
No.of Employees: 51 - 100 **Product Groups:** 35, 36, 37, 46, 66

Date of Accounts	Dec 11	Dec 10	Dec 09
Sales Turnover	7m	6m	5m
Pre Tax Profit/Loss	374	223	-5
Working Capital	2m	1m	1m
Fixed Assets	3m	2m	2m
Current Assets	3m	3m	2m
Current Liabilities	411	330	313

George Green Keighley
Parkwood Works Parkwood Street, Keighley, BD21 4PN
Tel: 01535-603728 **Fax:** 01535-610340
E-mail: enquiries@georgegreen-uk.com
Website: http://www.georgegreen-uk.com
Bank(s): Yorkshire Bank PLC
Directors: A. Curtis (Works)
Immediate Holding Company: GEORGE GREEN (KEIGHLEY) LIMITED
Registration no: 01351390 **VAT No.:** GB 303 3911 96
Date established: 1978 **No.of Employees:** 11 - 20 **Product Groups:** 35, 36, 40, 46, 48

Date of Accounts	May 12	May 11	May 10
Working Capital	172	105	137
Fixed Assets	391	397	305
Current Assets	660	442	610

Guardian Security Installations Ltd
73 South Street, Keighley, BD21 1AD
Tel: 01535-600677 **Fax:** 01535-600677
E-mail: guardian.security@virgin.net
Website: http://gsiltd.co.uk
Directors: W. heggarty (Dir), S. emsley (Dir)
Immediate Holding Company: GUARDIAN SECURITY INSTALLATIONS LIMITED
Registration no: 05732703 **Date established:** 2006
No.of Employees: 1 - 10 **Product Groups:** 37, 40, 67

Habasit Rossi Ltd
Habegger House
Keighley Road
Silsden, Keighley, BD20 0EA
Tel: 0844-835 9555 **Fax:** 0844-835 9669
E-mail: sales.uk@habasitrossi.com
Website: http://www.habasit.co.uk
Bank(s): Barclays, National Westminster
Managers: R. Smith (Mgr), R. Smith (Chief Mgr)
Ultimate Holding Company: HABASIT HOLDING AG (SWITZERLAND)
Immediate Holding Company: HABASIT ROSSI LIMITED
Registration no: 03712188 **VAT No.:** GB 259 9015 31
Date established: 1999 **Turnover:** £10m - £20m
No.of Employees: 51 - 100 **Product Groups:** 23, 29, 30, 35, 45, 48

Date of Accounts	Jul 11	Jul 10	Jul 09
Working Capital	61	59	40
Fixed Assets	61	86	70
Current Assets	328	312	300

Hattersley Aladdin Ltd
Greengate Shed Greengates, Keighley, BD21 5JL
Tel: 01535-681205 **Fax:** 01535-610195
E-mail: sales@hattersley.co.uk
Website: http://www.hattersley.co.uk
Bank(s): Barclays, 77 North Street
Directors: D. Batty (MD), T. Joint (Fin)
Ultimate Holding Company: GEORGE HATTERSLEY (1985) LIMITED
Immediate Holding Company: HATTERSLEY ALADDIN LIMITED
Registration no: 01016110 **Date established:** 1971 **Turnover:** £2m - £5m
No.of Employees: 21 - 50 **Product Groups:** 36, 40

Date of Accounts	Jun 11	Jun 10	Jun 09
Working Capital	1m	1m	1m
Fixed Assets	158	174	187
Current Assets	2m	2m	2m

Hewitt & Topham Ltd
Royd Way, Keighley, BD21 3LG
Tel: 01535-602587 **Fax:** 01535-680587
E-mail: brian@hewitt-topham.co.uk
Website: http://www.hewitt-topham.co.uk
Directors: B. Clough (Dir), B. Clough (MD)
Immediate Holding Company: HEWITT & TOPHAM LIMITED
Registration no: 01098508 **VAT No.:** GB 180 8345 56
Date established: 1973 **Turnover:** £500,000 - £1m
No.of Employees: 11 - 20 **Product Groups:** 35, 48, 66

Date of Accounts	Mar 11	Mar 10	Mar 09
Working Capital	113	127	127
Fixed Assets	518	538	538
Current Assets	249	194	227

Just-clips (Just-Products)
The Old Coach House, Low Fold Station Road, Steeton, Keighley, BD20 6RL
Tel: 01535-653635 **Fax:** 01535-653685
E-mail: sales@just-products.co.uk
Website: http://www.just-clips.co.uk
Directors: G. Lloyd (Prop)
Turnover: Up to £250,000 **No.of Employees:** 1 - 10 **Product Groups:** 30, 36, 49

Keighley Laboratories Ltd
Croft House South Street, Keighley, BD21 1EG
Tel: 01535-664211 **Fax:** 01535-680604
E-mail: debbie@keighleylabs.co.uk
Website: http://www.keighleylabs.co.uk
Bank(s): National Westminster Bank Plc
Directors: D. Mellor (MD)
Ultimate Holding Company: KEIGHLEY LABORATORIES GROUP LIMITED
Immediate Holding Company: KEIGHLEY LABORATORIES,LIMITED
Registration no: 00164811 **VAT No.:** GB 500 3496 84
Date established: 2020 **Turnover:** £2m - £5m **No.of Employees:** 51 - 100
Product Groups: 38, 48, 84, 85

Date of Accounts	Mar 11	Mar 10	Mar 09
Sales Turnover	3m	2m	3m
Pre Tax Profit/Loss	147	-66	14
Working Capital	937	778	752
Fixed Assets	1m	1m	1m
Current Assets	2m	1m	2m
Current Liabilities	233	296	588

Keylighting Ltd
Northbrook Works Alkincote Street, Keighley, BD21 5JT
Tel: 01535-616300 **Fax:** 01535-616301
E-mail: nick.robinson@keylighting.co.uk
Website: http://www.keylighting.co.uk
Bank(s): National Westminster Bank Plc
Directors: B. Robinson (Fin), N. Robinson (MD)
Managers: A. Hussain (Mktg Serv Mgr), D. Bailey (Buyer), T. Collins (Sales Prom Mgr)
Immediate Holding Company: KEYLIGHTING LIMITED
Registration no: 01810394 **VAT No.:** GB 405 9658 32
Date established: 1984 **Turnover:** £1m - £2m **No.of Employees:** 51 - 100
Product Groups: 37

Date of Accounts	Jan 11	Jan 10	Jan 09
Working Capital	811	762	673
Fixed Assets	489	499	545
Current Assets	2m	2m	1m

Kone plc
Worthdale House Worth Bridge Road, Keighley, BD21 4YA
Tel: 0800-652 0692 **Fax:** 0151-546 3244
E-mail: salesandmarketing@kone.com
Website: http://www.kone.com
Directors: A. Todd (Sales), P. Chamberlain (MD), S. Dow (Mkt Research)
Managers: I. Charman (Mgr)
Immediate Holding Company: KONE PUBLIC LIMITED COMPANY
Registration no: 01372978 **Date established:** 1978
Turnover: £50m - £75m **No.of Employees:** 51 - 100 **Product Groups:** 37, 45

Lambert Machine Tool Co. Ltd (H.O./Factory)
Riverside, Keighley, BD21 4JP
Tel: 01535-611996 **Fax:** 01535-610771
E-mail: info@lambertmt.co.uk
Website: http://www.lambertmt.co.uk
Directors: S. Raistrick (Co Sec), R. Lambert (MD)
Immediate Holding Company: LAMBERT MACHINE TOOL COMPANY LIMITED
Registration no: 02662585 **Date established:** 1991
Turnover: Up to £250,000 **No.of Employees:** 1 - 10 **Product Groups:** 46, 48, 67

Date of Accounts	Dec 11	Dec 10	Dec 09
Working Capital	-94	-49	-59
Fixed Assets	4	10	25
Current Assets	14	67	35

Lamik Enterprises Ltd
Unit 6 Newbridge Industrial Estate Pitt Street, Keighley, BD21 4PQ
Tel: 01535-610977 **Fax:** 01535-610418
Directors: S. Robinson (MD), S. Robertson (Fin)
Immediate Holding Company: LAMIK ENTERPRISES LIMITED
Registration no: 03230493 **Date established:** 1996
No.of Employees: 1 - 10 **Product Groups:** 35, 48

Date of Accounts	Jul 11	Jul 10	Jul 09
Working Capital	-27	-53	25
Fixed Assets	4	5	8
Current Assets	114	90	131

Lateral Design Concepts Ltd
Unit 2 River Technology Park Brewery Street, Keighley, BD21 4JQ
Tel: 01535-662244 **Fax:** 01535-662264
E-mail: info@lateraldc.co.uk
Website: http://www.lateraldc.co.uk
Directors: I. Greenwood (Fin), S. Greenwood (MD)
Managers: D. Waddington (Comptroller), J. Holgate (Purch Mgr), H. Carson (Mgr), R. Yates (Sales & Mktg Mg)
Immediate Holding Company: LATERAL DESIGN CONCEPTS LIMITED
Registration no: 04400617 **Date established:** 2002
No.of Employees: 21 - 50 **Product Groups:** 35, 39, 45

Date of Accounts	Mar 11	Mar 10	Mar 09
Working Capital	372	168	-75
Fixed Assets	734	748	540
Current Assets	1m	879	487

Leach & Thompson Ltd
Chapel Foundry Dalton Lane, Keighley, BD21 4JU
Tel: 01535-602452 **Fax:** 01535-669183
E-mail: info@smallcastings.co.uk
Website: http://www.smallcastings.co.uk
Bank(s): Yorkshire Bank PLC
Directors: R. Milner (Dir)
Immediate Holding Company: LEACH & THOMPSON LIMITED
Registration no: 00357338 **VAT No.:** GB 179 4831 20
Date established: 1939 **Turnover:** £500,000 - £1m
No.of Employees: 11 - 20 **Product Groups:** 34, 36, 45, 49

Date of Accounts	Sep 11	Sep 10	Sep 09
Working Capital	239	273	250
Fixed Assets	129	50	55
Current Assets	447	440	352

John Leighton C N C Services Ltd
13 Valley Road, Keighley, BD21 4LZ
Tel: 01535-607941 **Fax:** 01535-691177
E-mail: johnleightoncnc@aol.com
Website: http://www.projectitservices.co.uk
Directors: M. Lajszczuk (Fin), J. Leighton (Dir)
Immediate Holding Company: JOHN LEIGHTON C.N.C. SERVICES LIMITED
Registration no: 01683292 **Date established:** 1982
No.of Employees: 1 - 10 **Product Groups:** 37

Date of Accounts	Jun 11	Jun 10	Jun 09
Working Capital	1	26	-13
Fixed Assets	5	6	6
Current Assets	14	67	65

Linear Composites
Vale Mills Oakworth, Keighley, BD22 0EB
Tel: 01535-643363 **Fax:** 01535-643605
E-mail: sales@linearcomposites.com
Website: http://www.linearcomposites.com
Directors: I. Prince (Fin), S. Miller (Comm)
Managers: C. Prevett (Tech Serv Mgr), L. Collis (Purch Mgr)
Ultimate Holding Company: SECI SPA (ITALY)
Immediate Holding Company: LINEAR COMPOSITES LIMITED
Registration no: 02380921 **Date established:** 1989 **Turnover:** £5m - £10m
No.of Employees: 21 - 50 **Product Groups:** 23

Date of Accounts	Dec 11	Dec 10	Dec 09
Sales Turnover	6m	6m	5m
Pre Tax Profit/Loss	1m	964	642
Working Capital	2m	835	1m
Fixed Assets	114	136	154
Current Assets	4m	2m	3m
Current Liabilities	537	205	208

Marrose Engineering Ltd Abrasive Wheel Manufacturing Division
North Beck Mills Becks Road, Keighley, BD21 1SD
Tel: 01535-602364 **Fax:** 01535-610095
E-mail: marrose@csi.com
Website: http://www.marrose.com
Bank(s): Barclays Bank PLC
Directors: T. Day (Dir)
Immediate Holding Company: MARROSE ENGINEERING LIMITED
Registration no: 01278149 **VAT No.:** GB 108 8402 78
Date established: 1976 **Turnover:** £500,000 - £1m
No.of Employees: 11 - 20 **Product Groups:** 33, 45

Date of Accounts	Mar 11	Mar 10	Mar 09
Working Capital	96	95	43
Fixed Assets	841	882	963
Current Assets	377	324	395

Martens Conveyors
72 Wheathead Lane, Keighley, BD22 6NN
Tel: 01535-609028 **Fax:** 01535-605425
E-mail: martensbelts@btconnect.com
Website: http://www.maertens.de

Managers: D. Lee (Sales Prom Mgr)
Registration no: 03683627 **Date established:** 2006
No.of Employees: 1 - 10 **Product Groups:** 29, 30, 33, 35, 45

Mayr Transmissions Ltd
Unit 10-11 Valley Road, Keighley, BD21 4LZ
Tel: 01535-663900 **Fax:** 01535-663261
E-mail: sales@mayr.co.uk
Website: http://www.mayr.co.uk
Managers: A. Nicoll (Chief Mgr)
Ultimate Holding Company: CHR MAYR GMBH AND CO KG (GERMANY)
Immediate Holding Company: MAYR TRANSMISSIONS LIMITED
Registration no: 01844475 **VAT No.:** GB 406 0400 13
Date established: 1984 **Turnover:** £1m - £2m **No.of Employees:** 1 - 10
Product Groups: 29, 35

Date of Accounts	Dec 11	Dec 10	Dec 09
Working Capital	948	871	839
Fixed Assets	32	5	11
Current Assets	1m	979	1m

N S F Controls Ltd
Ingrow Bridge Works Ingrow Lane, Keighley, BD21 5EF
Tel: 01535-661144 **Fax:** 01535-661474
E-mail: info@nsfcontrols.co.uk
Website: http://www.nsfcontrols.co.uk
Bank(s): Lloyds TSB Bank plc
Directors: D. Priestley (MD), R. Griffiths (Fin)
Managers: R. Whitaker (Comm), S. Wright (Buyer), S. Winteridge (Tech Serv Mgr)
Ultimate Holding Company: INGROW ESTATES LIMITED
Immediate Holding Company: NSF CONTROLS LIMITED
Registration no: 03378269 **VAT No.:** GB 807 9761 85
Date established: 1997 **Turnover:** £2m - £5m **No.of Employees:** 51 - 100
Product Groups: 37, 38

Date of Accounts	Jun 11	Jun 10	Jun 09
Working Capital	1m	912	783
Fixed Assets	115	31	12
Current Assets	2m	2m	1m

Neophix Engineering Co. Ltd
Devonshire House West Lane, Keighley, BD21 2LP
Tel: 01535-667382 **Fax:** 01535-680825
E-mail: info@neophix.co.uk
Website: http://www.neophix.co.uk
Bank(s): Yorkshire Bank PLC
Directors: J. Driver (Dir), L. Driver (Dir)
Managers: F. Driver
Ultimate Holding Company: TECHNO CLAMP COMPANY LIMITED
Immediate Holding Company: NEOPHIX ENGINEERING CO. LIMITED
Registration no: 01294445 **Date established:** 1977 **Turnover:** £1m - £2m
No.of Employees: 11 - 20 **Product Groups:** 35, 36, 48

Date of Accounts	Dec 11	Dec 10	Dec 09
Working Capital	2m	2m	2m
Fixed Assets	498	506	515
Current Assets	2m	2m	2m

Office Interiors Wholesale Ltd
Eagle Mill Dalton Lane, Keighley, BD21 4HT
Tel: 01535-601100 **Fax:** 08707-898444
E-mail: info@officeinteriorsltd.co.uk
Website: http://www.officeinteriorsltd.co.uk
Directors: M. Loch (MD)
Immediate Holding Company: OFFICE INTERIORS WHOLESALE LIMITED
Registration no: 01714179 **Date established:** 1983
No.of Employees: 11 - 20 **Product Groups:** 26, 35, 44, 49, 52, 67, 72, 83

Date of Accounts	Apr 11	Apr 10	Apr 09
Working Capital	-69	-56	8
Fixed Assets	854	790	764
Current Assets	402	459	332

Ogden Fibres Ltd
Becks Mill Becks Road, Keighley, BD21 1SD
Tel: 01535-690222 **Fax:** 01535-690111
E-mail: mail@ogdenfibres.com
Website: http://www.ogdenfibres.com
Bank(s): National Westminster Bank Plc
Directors: G. Ogden (MD), E. Golding (Fin)
Ultimate Holding Company: JOSEPH OGDEN LIMITED
Immediate Holding Company: OGDEN FIBRES LIMITED
Registration no: 00173055 **Date established:** 2021 **Turnover:** £2m - £5m
No.of Employees: 21 - 50 **Product Groups:** 23

Date of Accounts	Mar 12	Mar 11	Mar 10
Working Capital	957	956	750
Fixed Assets	81	65	72
Current Assets	2m	2m	1m

Oil-Line Heating Services
Sweetbrow Cottage Cowling, Keighley, BD22 0LN
Tel: 07739-390993
E-mail: service@oilline.co.uk
Website: http://www.oilline.co.uk
Directors: M. Platt (Prop)
No.of Employees: 1 - 10 **Product Groups:** 40, 42, 48, 52

Peter Black Footwear & Accessories
Lawkholme Lane, Keighley, BD21 3BB
Tel: 01535-612222 **Fax:** 01535-609973
E-mail: pbh@peterblack.co.uk
Website: http://www.peterblack.co.uk
Directors: B. Pool (Dir), C. Kershaw (Co Sec)
Ultimate Holding Company: LI & FUNG LIMITED (BERMUDA)
Immediate Holding Company: PETER BLACK EUROPE LIMITED
Registration no: 00702417 **VAT No.:** GB 303 3834 85
Date established: 1961 **Turnover:** £125m - £250m
No.of Employees: 1 - 10 **Product Groups:** 22, 49, 66

Date of Accounts	Dec 11	Dec 10	Dec 09
Sales Turnover	59m	70m	93m
Pre Tax Profit/Loss	989	3m	3m
Working Capital	9m	19m	17m
Fixed Assets	305	333	413
Current Assets	29m	36m	41m
Current Liabilities	5m	6m	13m

Peter Black Footwear & Accessories Keighley Ltd
Airedale Mill Lawkholme Lane, Keighley, BD21 3JQ
Tel: 01535-661177 **Fax:** 01535-611643
Website: http://www.peterblack.co.uk

Directors: S. Lister (Grp Chief Exec), N. Cottrell (Fin), G. Cierpiol (MD), S. Davies (Dir), P. Black (Prop)
Immediate Holding Company: PETER BLACK FOOTWEAR & ACCESSORIES LIMITED
Registration no: 00443567 **Date established:** 1947
Turnover: £75m - £125m **No.of Employees:** 51 - 100
Product Groups: 22, 29

Date of Accounts	Dec 07
Pre Tax Profit/Loss	-2940
Working Capital	-21890
Fixed Assets	39060
Current Assets	190
Current Liabilities	22080
ROCE% (Return on Capital Employed)	-17.1

The Polished Plaster Company
Unit 7-9 Valley Road Business Park Gas Works Road, Keighley, BD21 4LZ
Tel: 01535-667038
E-mail: info@polishedplastercompany.co.uk
Website: http://www.polishedplastercompany.co.uk
Registration no: 07048394 **Turnover:** Up to £250,000
No.of Employees: 1 - 10 **Product Groups:** 27, 45, 52, 65, 66

Polyan Covers
5 Bainbridge Wharf Farnhill, Keighley, BD20 9BX
Tel: 01535-631212 **Fax:** 01535-631313
Directors: D. Greenwood (Prop)
Date established: 1996 **No.of Employees:** 1 - 10 **Product Groups:** 30

Premier Arms Co.
153 Keighley Road Cowling, Keighley, BD22 0AH
Tel: 01535-634088
Directors: S. Andrews (Prop)
Date established: 1990 **No.of Employees:** 1 - 10 **Product Groups:** 36, 39, 40

Rippon Farm Services Ltd
Dalesgate Works Skipton Road, Cross Hills, Keighley, BD20 7BX
Tel: 01535-632661 **Fax:** 01535-633752
E-mail: sales@r-f-s.com
Website: http://www.r-f-s.com
Directors: G. Brown (MD), W. Houseman (Co Sec)
Ultimate Holding Company: RIPON FARM SERVICES LIMITED
Immediate Holding Company: SMITH BROS. (KEIGHLEY) LIMITED
Registration no: 00476216 **Date established:** 1949
No.of Employees: 11 - 20 **Product Groups:** 41

Date of Accounts	Oct 11	Oct 10	Oct 09
Working Capital	6	6	6
Current Assets	6	6	6

Sabre Stairlift Systems Ltd
Unit 66 Mantra House South Street, Keighley, BD21 1SX
Tel: 01535-681867 **Fax:** 01535-681885
E-mail: info@sabre-stairlifts.co.uk
Website: http://www.sabre-stairlifts.co.uk
Directors: C. Hartley (Fin), J. Sugden (MD)
Immediate Holding Company: SABRE STAIRLIFT SYSTEMS LIMITED
Registration no: 03104340 **Date established:** 1995
Turnover: Up to £250,000 **No.of Employees:** 1 - 10 **Product Groups:** 35, 39, 45

Date of Accounts	Sep 11	Sep 10	Sep 09
Working Capital	-27	-29	-19
Fixed Assets	40	40	24
Current Assets	29	23	42

Sealand Engineering Keighley Ltd
Devonshire Works Pitt Street, Keighley, BD21 4PF
Tel: 01535-610345 **Fax:** 01535-605492
E-mail: sales@sealandengineering.co.uk
Website: http://www.sealandengineering.co.uk
Bank(s): Secure Trust plc
Directors: R. Whitaker (MD)
Immediate Holding Company: SEALAND ENGINEERING (KEIGHLEY) LIMITED
Registration no: 00526337 **VAT No.:** GB 180 0445 92
Date established: 1953 **Turnover:** £250,000 - £500,000
No.of Employees: 11 - 20 **Product Groups:** 36

Date of Accounts	Nov 11	Nov 10	Nov 09
Working Capital	122	138	98
Fixed Assets	42	36	36
Current Assets	391	401	351

Seba Developments
Unit 1 Keighley Industrial Park Royd Ings Avenue, Keighley, BD21 4DZ
Tel: 01535-687799 **Fax:** 01535-687798
E-mail: info@seba.co.uk
Website: http://www.seba.co.uk
Bank(s): Barclays
Directors: M. Johnson (MD)
Registration no: 01068223 **VAT No.:** GB 343 0341 01
Date established: 1972 **Turnover:** £500,000 - £1m
No.of Employees: 11 - 20 **Product Groups:** 37, 38, 40, 42, 46, 47, 66

Skipton Properties
Grove House Red Holt Drive, Keighley, BD21 5EG
Tel: 01535-639620 **Fax:** 01535-636783
E-mail: info@skiptonproperties.com
Website: http://www.skiptonproperties.com
Directors: S. Barraclough (Dir)
Managers: J. Campbell (Sales Admin), A. Trowell (Buyer)
Ultimate Holding Company: JODA HOLDINGS LIMITED
Immediate Holding Company: SKIPTON PROPERTIES LIMITED
Registration no: 02158429 **Date established:** 1987 **Turnover:** £5m - £10m
No.of Employees: 21 - 50 **Product Groups:** 80

Date of Accounts	Jun 11	Jun 10	Jun 09
Sales Turnover	6m	16m	10m
Pre Tax Profit/Loss	-617	735	-2m
Working Capital	3m	4m	6m
Fixed Assets	1m	1m	2m
Current Assets	15m	21m	23m
Current Liabilities	1m	3m	2m

Specialist Technical Solutions Ltd
PO Box 312, Keighley, BD22 9YA
Tel: 01535-647200 **Fax:** 01535-647300
E-mail: paul@specialist-technical-solutions.co.uk
Website: http://www.specialist-technical-solutions.co.uk

Directors: S. Hill (Co Sec)
Immediate Holding Company: THE ROWAN CONCEPT LIMITED
Registration no: 04192624 **Date established:** 2001
No.of Employees: 1 - 10 **Product Groups:** 41

Date of Accounts	Oct 10	Oct 08	Oct 11
Working Capital	-27	-11	-26
Fixed Assets	1	2	1
Current Assets	3	5	2

Spencer Fabrications

Victoria Works Cherry Street, Keighley, BD21 4JX
Tel: 01535-690268
Directors: D. Spencer (Prop)
Date established: 1988 **No.of Employees:** 1 - 10 **Product Groups:** 35

Stylecraft

PO Box 62, Keighley, BD21 1PP
Tel: 01535-609798 **Fax:** 01535-669952
E-mail: info@stylecraftltd.co.uk
Website: http://www.stylecraft-yarns.co.uk
Directors: J. Frankish (Dir)
Immediate Holding Company: SPECTRUM YARNS
Registration no: 01142407 **VAT No.:** GB 265 5140 65
Date established: 1990 **Turnover:** £250,000 - £500,000
No.of Employees: 1 - 10 **Product Groups:** 23

Date of Accounts	Mar 99	Sep 97
Working Capital	-0	-0

Teconnex Ltd

Bronte Warehouse Chesham Street, Keighley, BD21 4LG
Tel: 01535-691122 **Fax:** 01535-691133
E-mail: sales@teconnex.com
Website: http://www.teconnex.com
Bank(s): National Westminster Bank Plc
Directors: D. Milles (Ch), M. Galey (Co Sec)
Ultimate Holding Company: HEXADEX LIMITED
Immediate Holding Company: TECONNEX LIMITED
Registration no: 01447529 **VAT No.:** GB 180 0261 05
Date established: 1979 **Turnover:** £5m - £10m
No.of Employees: 101 - 250 **Product Groups:** 30, 35, 36

Date of Accounts	Dec 11	Dec 10	Dec 09
Sales Turnover	16m	12m	8m
Pre Tax Profit/Loss	3m	3m	2m
Working Capital	5m	4m	4m
Fixed Assets	968	842	826
Current Assets	7m	6m	5m
Current Liabilities	773	418	416

Woodrow Universal Ltd

Junction Mills Skipton Road, Cross Hills, Keighley, BD20 7SE
Tel: 01535-633364 **Fax:** 01535-634439
E-mail: elwyn.jones@woodrowuniversal.co.uk
Website: http://www.woodrowuniversal.co.uk
Bank(s): Barclays
Directors: E. Jones (Fin), J. Jones (Fin), D. Catteral (Sales)
Managers: A. Cirns (Fin Mgr)
Ultimate Holding Company: BURBERRY GROUP PLC
Immediate Holding Company: WOODROW-UNIVERSAL LIMITED
Registration no: 00296252 **VAT No.:** GB 447 6784 02
Date established: 1935 **Turnover:** £5m - £10m
No.of Employees: 51 - 100 **Product Groups:** 23, 63

Date of Accounts	Mar 11	Mar 10	Mar 09
Sales Turnover	8m	6m	7m
Pre Tax Profit/Loss	-301	-358	-666
Working Capital	4m	-963	-958
Fixed Assets	1m	1m	2m
Current Assets	6m	4m	5m
Current Liabilities	210	227	476

Knottingley

Allied Glass Containers Ltd

Hope Glass Works Fearnley Green Road, Knottingley, WF11 8DH
Tel: 01977-672661 **Fax:** 01977-607116
E-mail: admin@allied-glass.com
Website: http://www.allied-glass.com
Bank(s): National Westminster Bank Plc
Directors: A. Henderson (MD), J. Hart (Fin), J. Firth (Fin)
Managers: R. Bavester (I.T. Exec), T. Sharkey (Personnel), R. Bavester (Tech Serv Mgr), P. Cogill (Purch Mgr)
Ultimate Holding Company: ALLIED GLASS GROUP LIMITED
Immediate Holding Company: ALLIED GLASS CONTAINERS LIMITED
Registration no: 03846688 **VAT No.:** GB 181 4955 43
Date established: 1999 **Turnover:** £10m - £20m
No.of Employees: 251 - 500 **Product Groups:** 33

Date of Accounts	Dec 08	Dec 09	Dec 10
Sales Turnover	76m	78m	86m
Pre Tax Profit/Loss	7m	8m	10m
Working Capital	12m	13m	10m
Fixed Assets	36m	37m	36m
Current Assets	38m	31m	34m
Current Liabilities	6m	5m	6m

Ardagh Glass Ltd

Headlands Lane, Knottingley, WF11 0HP
Tel: 01977-674111 **Fax:** 01977-635821
E-mail: marketing@rockware.co.uk
Website: http://www.ardaghglass.com
Bank(s): National Westminster Bank Plc
Directors: A. Robertson (Sales), J. Riordan (Fin), K. Swindell (MD)
Managers: L. Mantell (Comm)
Ultimate Holding Company: ARDAGH GLASS GROUP SA (LUXEMBOURG)
Immediate Holding Company: ARDAGH GLASS LIMITED
Registration no: 00567801 **VAT No.:** GB 698 3696 54
Date established: 1956 **Turnover:** £250m - £500m
No.of Employees: 251 - 500 **Product Groups:** 33, 44, 76, 84

Date of Accounts	Dec 11	Dec 10	Dec 09
Sales Turnover	297m	288m	283m
Pre Tax Profit/Loss	29m	46m	24m
Working Capital	326m	313m	153m
Fixed Assets	114m	124m	132m
Current Assets	406m	378m	224m
Current Liabilities	27m	27m	9m

C & C Fabrications

Great North Road, Knottingley, WF11 8PG
Tel: 01977-670067 **Fax:** 01977-670066
E-mail: info@candcfabrications.co.uk
Website: http://www.candcfabrications.co.uk
Directors: C. Butler (Prop)
No.of Employees: 11 - 20 **Product Groups:** 35

Howe Cool

The Cottage Low Street, Brotherton, Knottingley, WF11 9HQ
Tel: 01977-677077 **Fax:** 01977-677077
E-mail: cliff@howecool.com
Website: http://www.howecool.com
Directors: C. Howe (Prop)
Date established: 2000 **Turnover:** £250,000 - £500,000
No.of Employees: 1 - 10 **Product Groups:** 38, 40, 52, 66

Linpac Packaging Ltd

A1 Business Park Knottingley Road, Knottingley, WF11 0BL
Tel: 01977-671111 **Fax:** 01977- 670670
E-mail: info@linpacpackaging.com
Website: http://www.linpac.com
Directors: J. Jones (Dir), S. Salter (Tech Serv), R. Paul (Fin), R. Fensome (Dir), A. Cockrem (Dir), A. Creese (MD), A. Heap (Dir), P. Thumerel (Dir)
Managers: T. Komaromy (Mktg Serv Mgr), R. Langfield (I.T. Exec), B. Laing (Mktg Serv Mgr)
Ultimate Holding Company: LINPAC SENIOR HOLDINGS LIMITED
Immediate Holding Company: LINPAC PACKAGING LIMITED
Registration no: 00949597 **VAT No.:** GB 482 0964 32
Date established: 1969 **Turnover:** £75m - £125m
No.of Employees: 21 - 50 **Product Groups:** 30

Date of Accounts	Dec 10	Dec 09	Dec 08
Sales Turnover	97m	92m	89m
Pre Tax Profit/Loss	5m	6m	-18m
Working Capital	212m	217m	217m
Fixed Assets	56m	38m	38m
Current Assets	248m	266m	266m
Current Liabilities	7m	14m	14m

Plasmor Ltd

PO Box 44, Knottingley, WF11 0DN
Tel: 01977-673221 **Fax:** 01977-607071
E-mail: jslater@plasmor.co.uk
Website: http://www.plasmor.co.uk
Bank(s): Lloyds, Doncaster
Directors: J. Swain (Sales), J. Slater (MD), N. Marwood (Fin)
Immediate Holding Company: PLASMOR LIMITED
Registration no: 00642173 **Date established:** 1959
Turnover: £20m - £50m **No.of Employees:** 251 - 500
Product Groups: 14, 33

Date of Accounts	Aug 11	Aug 10	Aug 09
Sales Turnover	49m	47m	41m
Pre Tax Profit/Loss	-795	514	-1m
Working Capital	15m	16m	14m
Fixed Assets	22m	22m	23m
Current Assets	24m	25m	21m
Current Liabilities	3m	3m	3m

Translift Freight Ltd

PO Box 44, Knottingley, WF11 0DN
Tel: 01977-672301 **Fax:** 01977-607071
E-mail: john.hardstaff@plasmor.co.uk
Website: http://www.plasmor.co.uk
Bank(s): Lloyds
Managers: J. Hardstaff (Chief Mgr)
Ultimate Holding Company: PLASMOR LIMITED
Immediate Holding Company: TRANSLIFT FREIGHT LIMITED
Registration no: 00332953 **Date established:** 1937 **Turnover:** £5m - £10m
No.of Employees: 51 - 100 **Product Groups:** 72

Date of Accounts	Aug 11	Aug 10	Aug 09
Sales Turnover	8m	7m	6m
Pre Tax Profit/Loss	-117	111	281
Working Capital	675	779	484
Fixed Assets	2m	2m	2m
Current Assets	2m	2m	1m
Current Liabilities	137	190	313

Leeds

A Andrews & Sons Marbles & Tiles Ltd

324-330 Meanwood Road, Leeds, LS7 2JE
Tel: 0113-262 4751 **Fax:** 0113-262 3337
E-mail: sales@andrews-tiles.co.uk
Website: http://www.andrews-tiles.co.uk
Bank(s): Yorkshire, Leeds
Directors: R. Horton (Co Sec), D. Clough (MD), P. Waite (Contracts)
Managers: C. Wood (Buyer)
Ultimate Holding Company: A. ANDREWS & SONS (MARBLES & TILES) LIMITED
Immediate Holding Company: A. ANDREWS TRUSTEE LIMITED
Registration no: 03697011 **VAT No.:** GB 169 1098 42
Date established: 1999 **Turnover:** £10m - £20m
No.of Employees: 21 - 50 **Product Groups:** 30, 33

ADT Fire & Security plc

1-3 Bowling Green Terrace, Leeds, LS11 9SP
Tel: 0113-291 1139 **Fax:** 0113-242 5933
Website: http://www.adt.co.uk
Managers: S. Gilkes
Ultimate Holding Company: TYCO INTERNATIONAL LIMITED (SWITZERLAND)
Immediate Holding Company: ADT FIRE AND SECURITY PLC
Registration no: 01161045 **Date established:** 1974
No.of Employees: 1 - 10 **Product Groups:** 37, 38, 39, 40, 47, 52, 81

Date of Accounts	Sep 11	Sep 08	Sep 09
Sales Turnover	363m	414m	384m
Pre Tax Profit/Loss	18m	4m	10m
Working Capital	450m	618m	561m
Fixed Assets	120m	193m	171m
Current Assets	710m	765m	722m
Current Liabilities	81m	57m	42m

A T P

Elmete House Elmete Lane, Leeds, LS8 2LJ
Tel: 0113-273 8555 **Fax:** 0113-273 8666
E-mail: info@atpadvertising.com
Website: http://www.atpadvertising.com
Bank(s): Bank of Scotland
Directors: I. Ruddock (MD)
Immediate Holding Company: A.T.P. ADVERTISING & MARKETING LIMITED
Registration no: 02684007 **VAT No.:** GB 613 0680 73
Date established: 1992 **No.of Employees:** 11 - 20 **Product Groups:** 81

Date of Accounts	May 11	May 10	May 09
Working Capital	135	120	134
Fixed Assets	31	42	50
Current Assets	429	382	480

Aalco Metals Ltd

1 Revie Road, Leeds, LS11 8JG
Tel: 0113-276 3300 **Fax:** 0113-276 0382
E-mail: leeds@aalco.co.uk
Website: http://www.aalco.co.uk
Bank(s): National Westminster Bank Plc
Managers: G. Pollitt (Chief Mgr)
Ultimate Holding Company: HENLEY MANAGEMENT COMPANY (USA)
Immediate Holding Company: AALCO METALS LIMITED
Registration no: 03551533 **Date established:** 1998
Turnover: £125m - £250m **No.of Employees:** 11 - 20
Product Groups: 34, 35, 36, 66

Date of Accounts	Dec 11	Dec 10	Dec 09
Sales Turnover	360m	309m	244m
Pre Tax Profit/Loss	12m	12m	5m
Working Capital	165m	113m	103m
Fixed Assets	13m	13m	14m
Current Assets	252m	226m	202m
Current Liabilities	13m	14m	7m

Abbey Crest Plc

4100 Park Approach, Leeds, LS15 8GB
Tel: 0113-245 3804 **Fax:** 0113-284 5708
E-mail: reccrutment5@abbeycrest.co.uk
Website: http://www.abbeycrest.co.uk
Bank(s): Barclays
Directors: M. Adamson (Prop), M. Adamson (Ch), P. Walker (Grp Chief Exec)
Managers: S. Robinson (Mktg Serv Mgr), D. Hatfield (I.T. Exec)
Immediate Holding Company: ABBEYCREST PLC
Registration no: 01411796 **VAT No.:** GB 431 0391 94
Date established: 1979 **Turnover:** £20m - £50m
No.of Employees: 11 - 20 **Product Groups:** 65

Date of Accounts	Feb 08
Sales Turnover	61940
Pre Tax Profit/Loss	-3530
Working Capital	7850
Fixed Assets	6970
Current Assets	27530
Current Liabilities	19680
Total Share Capital	2660
ROCE% (Return on Capital Employed)	-23.8

Ace Engineers Ltd

Albert Road Morley, Leeds, LS27 8LD
Tel: 0113-252 2611 **Fax:** 0113-238 0274
E-mail: sales@ace-engineers.co.uk
Website: http://www.ace-engineers.co.uk
Directors: N. Tappin (Sales), D. Preston (Dir)
Immediate Holding Company: ACE ENGINEERS (MORLEY) LIMITED
Registration no: 02690654 **Date established:** 1992
Turnover: Up to £250,000 **No.of Employees:** 21 - 50 **Product Groups:** 66

Date of Accounts	Feb 08	Feb 11	Feb 10
Working Capital	234	-76	-84
Fixed Assets	815	736	765
Current Assets	821	923	752

Addleshaw Goddard

Soverign Street, Leeds, LS1 1HQ
Tel: 0113-209 2000 **Fax:** 0113-209 2060
E-mail: monica.burch@addleshawgoddard.com
Website: http://www.addleshawgoddard.com
Directors: M. Burch (Snr Part)
Registration no: 02902418 **VAT No.:** 686 1261 21
No.of Employees: 251 - 500 **Product Groups:** 80

Advanced Tooling Technology

Unit 10 Swordfish Way Sherburn in Elmet, Leeds, LS25 6NG
Tel: 01977-684486 **Fax:** 01977-684459
E-mail: sales@advancedtooling.co.uk
Website: http://www.advancedtooling.co.uk
Directors: I. Wilkins (Dir), R. Stopforth (Fin)
Ultimate Holding Company: HARDMETAL PRODUCTS LIMITED
Immediate Holding Company: ADVANCED TOOLING TECHNOLOGY LIMITED
Registration no: 04666709 **Date established:** 2003
Turnover: £250,000 - £500,000 **No.of Employees:** 1 - 10
Product Groups: 46

Date of Accounts	Mar 11	Mar 10	Mar 09
Sales Turnover	N/A	N/A	361
Pre Tax Profit/Loss	N/A	N/A	171
Working Capital	115	110	70
Fixed Assets	36	55	74
Current Assets	169	149	123
Current Liabilities	N/A	N/A	49

AETC Ltd

Victoria Avenue Yeadon, Leeds, LS19 7AW
Tel: 0113-250 5151 **Fax:** 0113-238 6006
Website: http://www.aetc.co.uk
Bank(s): America
Directors: J. Sloboda (Fin)
Managers: C. Nicholson (Comptroller), P. Mildenhall (Tech Serv Mgr), G. Curtis (Purch Mgr)
Ultimate Holding Company: PRECISION CASTPARTS CORP (USA)
Immediate Holding Company: AETC LIMITED
Registration no: 03206792 **VAT No.:** GB 647 5921 07
Date established: 1996 **Turnover:** £50m - £75m
No.of Employees: 501 - 1000 **Product Groups:** 34, 39, 40, 48

Date of Accounts	Mar 08	Mar 09	Mar 10
Sales Turnover	81m	99m	79m
Pre Tax Profit/Loss	5m	18m	7m
Working Capital	11m	27m	8m
Fixed Assets	34m	26m	19m
Current Assets	40m	58m	38m
Current Liabilities	7m	7m	3m

Airedale Environmental Services Ltd
The Old Bank 7-9 Harrogate Road Rawdon, Leeds, LS19 6HW
Tel: 0113-250 2459 **Fax:** 0113-250 1858
E-mail: jenny.markham@airedale-es.co.uk
Website: http://www.airedale-cleanrooms.co.uk
Directors: J. Markham (Co Sec)
Immediate Holding Company: AIREDALE ENVIRONMENTAL SERVICES LTD.
Registration no: 02869912 **Date established:** 1993 **Turnover:** £1m - £2m
No.of Employees: 1 - 10 **Product Groups:** 40, 52, 67

Date of Accounts	Mar 08	Mar 07	Mar 06
Working Capital	-183	-342	-52
Fixed Assets	345	599	593
Current Assets	632	707	780

Airedale International Air Conditioning Ltd
Leeds Road Rawdon, Leeds, LS19 6JY
Tel: 0113-239 1000 **Fax:** 0113-250 7219
E-mail: enquiries@airedale.com
Website: http://www.airedale.com
Bank(s): Barclays
Directors: S. Joyce (Pers), C. Parkman (MD), J. Clegg (Co Sec)
Managers: C. Coates (Buyer), S. Reading (Tech Serv Mgr), F. Farrelly
Ultimate Holding Company: MODINE MANUFACTURING CO. (USA)
Immediate Holding Company: AIREDALE INTERNATIONAL AIR CONDITIONING LIMITED
Registration no: 01173149 **Date established:** 1974
Turnover: £20m - £50m **No.of Employees:** 251 - 500
Product Groups: 38, 40, 52, 66

Date of Accounts	Mar 11	Mar 10	Mar 09
Sales Turnover	36m	33m	39m
Pre Tax Profit/Loss	4m	3m	3m
Working Capital	3m	4m	1m
Fixed Assets	2m	2m	2m
Current Assets	14m	14m	12m
Current Liabilities	3m	3m	3m

Airedale Signs & Graphics
Meanwood Road, Leeds, LS1 1AA
Tel: 0800-012 6752
E-mail: info@airedalesigns.co.uk
Website: http://www.airedalesigns.co.uk
Directors: P. Smith (Dir)
Date established: 1992 **No.of Employees:** 1 - 10 **Product Groups:** 30, 39, 49

Allegro Promotional Products
16 West Park Road, Leeds, LS8 2HB
Tel: 0113-266 4394 **Fax:** 0113-226 7438
E-mail: sales@app.uk.com
Website: http://www.app.uk.com
Directors: E. Storey (Fin), J. Storey (Ptnr)
Immediate Holding Company: ALLEGRO PROMOTIONAL PRODUCTS LIMITED
Registration no: 04748309 **VAT No.:** GB 349 5674 10
Date established: 2003 **Turnover:** £500,000 - £1m
No.of Employees: 1 - 10 **Product Groups:** 66

Allenbuild Ltd North West
7 Hawthorn Park Coal Road, Leeds, LS14 1PQ
Tel: 01484-412910 **Fax:** 0113-237 5601
E-mail: steve.clarkson@allenbuild.co.uk
Website: http://www.allenbuild.co.uk
Directors: D. Stewart (MD), E. Carlisle (Fin), J. Eastwood (Tech Serv), S. Clarkson (MD)
Immediate Holding Company: ALLENBUILD LIMITED
Registration no: 01248351 **VAT No.:** GB 180 5975 38
Date established: 1976 **Turnover:** £125m - £250m
No.of Employees: 11 - 20 **Product Groups:** 52

Allied Fabrication Services
Unit 23 Asquith Avenue Morley, Leeds, LS27 9QS
Tel: 0113-218 9800 **Fax:** 0113-218 9400
Directors: A. Richardson (Ptnr)
Registration no: 03128399 **Date established:** 1995
No.of Employees: 1 - 10 **Product Groups:** 35

Allied Glass Containers Ltd
69 South Accommodation Road, Leeds, LS10 1NQ
Tel: 0113-245 1568 **Fax:** 0113-244 9349
E-mail: admin@allied-glass.com
Website: http://www.allied-glass.com
Bank(s): Lloyds, London
Directors: P. Morrison (Sales & Mktg), J. Firth (Fin), A. Henderson (MD), J. Hart (Fin)
Managers: C. Sharkey (Personnel), R. Bavester (Tech Serv Mgr), G. Law
Ultimate Holding Company: ALLIED GLASS GROUP LIMITED
Immediate Holding Company: ALLIED GLASS CONTAINERS LIMITED
Registration no: 03846688 **VAT No.:** GB 758 4092 04
Date established: 1999 **Turnover:** £75m - £125m
No.of Employees: 501 - 1000 **Product Groups:** 45, 66

Date of Accounts	Dec 08	Dec 09	Dec 10
Sales Turnover	76m	78m	86m
Pre Tax Profit/Loss	7m	8m	10m
Working Capital	12m	13m	10m
Fixed Assets	36m	37m	36m
Current Assets	38m	31m	34m
Current Liabilities	6m	5m	6m

AMB Industrial Services Ltd
78 Scotchman Lane Morley, Leeds, LS27 0BJ
Tel: 0113-349 1765 **Fax:** 0113-322 0429
E-mail: service@ambindustrial.co.uk
Website: http://www.ambindustrial.co.uk
Directors: A. Bayliss (Dir), C. Newsome (Fin)
Registration no: 06523011 **Date established:** 2008
Turnover: Up to £250,000 **No.of Employees:** 1 - 10 **Product Groups:** 40, 67, 83

Andjon Metal Fabrications
Unit 1 Victoria Mills Elder Road, Leeds, LS13 4DL
Tel: 0113-255 9090
Website: http://www.andjon.co.uk
Directors: A. Woodfine (Prop)
Ultimate Holding Company: BEAVER LEEDS (HOLDINGS) LIMITED
Immediate Holding Company: BEAVER LEEDS LTD
Registration no: 03760311 **Date established:** 1999
No.of Employees: 1 - 10 **Product Groups:** 35

Date of Accounts	Jul 11	Jul 10	Jul 09
Working Capital	387	342	298
Fixed Assets	71	84	37
Current Assets	666	520	458

Andrews Fasteners Ltd
Unit 8 Latchmore Industrial Park Low Fields Road, Leeds, LS12 6DN
Tel: 0113-246 9992 **Fax:** 0113-243 6463
E-mail: sales@andrewsfasteners.co.uk
Website: http://www.andrewsfasteners.co.uk
Directors: P. Krause (Dir)
Immediate Holding Company: ANDREWS FASTENERS LIMITED
Registration no: 01531702 **VAT No.:** GB 797 1512 01
Date established: 1980 **Turnover:** £2m - £5m **No.of Employees:** 11 - 20
Product Groups: 35

Date of Accounts	Dec 11	Dec 10	Dec 09
Working Capital	504	521	590
Fixed Assets	8	17	29
Current Assets	2m	2m	1m

Andrews Sykes Hire Ltd
Unit 1 National Road Hunslet Business Park, Leeds, LS10 1TE
Tel: 0113-276 1444 **Fax:** 0114-269 5522
E-mail: jon.pryce@andrews-sykes.com
Website: http://www.andrews-sykes.com
Managers: J. Pryce (Mgr)
Immediate Holding Company: ANDREWS SYKES HIRE LIMITED
Registration no: 02985657 **VAT No.:** GB 100 4295 24
Date established: 1994 **Turnover:** £5m - £10m **No.of Employees:** 1 - 10
Product Groups: 40

Date of Accounts	Dec 11	Dec 10	Dec 09
Sales Turnover	35m	36m	34m
Pre Tax Profit/Loss	10m	10m	8m
Working Capital	8m	6m	2m
Fixed Assets	7m	7m	9m
Current Assets	33m	35m	35m
Current Liabilities	7m	7m	5m

Apollo Lighting Ltd
Unit D9 Cross Green Approach, Leeds, LS9 0SG
Tel: 0113-240 5511 **Fax:** 0113-240 5151
E-mail: sales@apollolighting.co.uk
Website: http://www.apollolighting.co.uk
Directors: G. Falkingham (Ch), S. Goldberg (MD), J. Jackson (Fin)
Managers: L. Parker (Comm), D. Hawkshaw
Immediate Holding Company: APOLLO LIGHTING LIMITED
Registration no: 01518386 **Date established:** 1980 **Turnover:** £2m - £5m
No.of Employees: 21 - 50 **Product Groups:** 37

Date of Accounts	Jul 11	Jul 10	Jul 09
Working Capital	237	187	296
Fixed Assets	60	59	82
Current Assets	906	975	1m

Applied Metal Technology Ltd
3 Ashfield Close Whitehall Industrial Estate Whitehall Road, Leeds, LS12 5JB
Tel: 0113-279 3708 **Fax:** 0113-279 3816
E-mail: iantaylor@appliedmetal.co.uk
Website: http://www.appliedmetal.co.uk
Directors: D. Hopton (I.T. Dir), I. Taylor (MD)
Immediate Holding Company: APPLIED METAL TECHNOLOGY LIMITED
Registration no: 04760264 **Date established:** 2003
No.of Employees: 11 - 20 **Product Groups:** 26, 35, 36, 39, 46, 48, 84

Date of Accounts	Jul 11	Jul 10	Jul 09
Working Capital	343	224	155
Fixed Assets	113	114	69
Current Assets	642	515	339

Aqualand Ltd
Stonebridge Mills Stonebridge Lane, Leeds, LS12 4QL
Tel: 0113-263 1451 **Fax:** 0113- 2792472
E-mail: charlotte.hurdman@aqualandlimited.com
Website: http://www.aqualandlimited.com
Directors: R. Hurdman (Dir), C. Hurdman (Fin)
Ultimate Holding Company: AQUALAND HOLDINGS LIMITED
Immediate Holding Company: AQUALAND LIMITED
Registration no: 02690043 **VAT No.:** GB 613 0577 66
Date established: 1992 **Turnover:** £1m - £2m **No.of Employees:** 11 - 20
Product Groups: 24

Date of Accounts	Mar 11	Mar 10	Mar 09
Working Capital	310	326	309
Fixed Assets	45	47	53
Current Assets	564	517	454

Arc International Tableware UK Ltd
Suite 52 Concourse House Oakhurst Avenue, Leeds, LS11 7DF
Tel: 0113-271 0033 **Fax:** 0113-276 3433
E-mail: peter.oakden@arctableware.com
Website: http://www.arctableware.com
Managers: P. Oakden (Mgr)
Ultimate Holding Company: ARC INTERNATIONAL SA (FRANCE)
Immediate Holding Company: ARC INTERNATIONAL TABLEWARE UK LIMITED
Registration no: 01567500 **Date established:** 1981
Turnover: £10m - £20m **No.of Employees:** 1 - 10 **Product Groups:** 49, 63

Date of Accounts	Dec 09	Dec 08	Dec 07
Sales Turnover	10m	14m	17m
Pre Tax Profit/Loss	-983	-3m	-4m
Working Capital	-9m	-8m	-5m
Fixed Assets	57	116	175
Current Assets	3m	7m	12m
Current Liabilities	1m	1m	2m

Archbold Logistics Ltd
Albert Road Morley, Leeds, LS27 8TT
Tel: 0113-252 2333 **Fax:** 0113-252 7915
E-mail: ian.matthews@archbold.co.uk
Website: http://www.archbold.co.uk
Bank(s): National Westminster
Directors: A. Maher (MD), B. Ashford (Fin), D. Archbold (Ch), G. Cox (Non Exec), S. Hutchison (MD)
Managers: K. Armitage (Sec)
Immediate Holding Company: ARCHBOLD LOGISTICS LIMITED
Registration no: 01146071 **Date established:** 1973
Turnover: £10m - £20m **No.of Employees:** 101 - 250
Product Groups: 72, 77

Date of Accounts	Dec 09	Dec 08	Dec 07
Sales Turnover	18m	18m	16m
Pre Tax Profit/Loss	-35	59	-210
Working Capital	-225	-288	937
Fixed Assets	4m	5m	3m
Current Assets	5m	5m	5m
Current Liabilities	905	758	929

Arctic Products Ltd
Nina Works Gelderd Road, Leeds, LS12 6NA
Tel: 08448-718461 **Fax:** 01536-264900
E-mail: sales@arctic-products.co.uk
Website: http://www.arctic-products.co.uk
Directors: K. Dallimore (Comm)
Ultimate Holding Company: VOLVOX GROUP (LEEDS) LIMITED
Immediate Holding Company: ARCTIC PRODUCTS LIMITED
Registration no: 01582704 **VAT No.:** GB 359 9018 17
Date established: 1981 **Turnover:** £2m - £5m **No.of Employees:** 1 - 10
Product Groups: 30, 34

Date of Accounts	Sep 11	Sep 10	Sep 09
Sales Turnover	3m	2m	2m
Pre Tax Profit/Loss	190	360	300
Working Capital	1m	1m	868
Fixed Assets	36	39	36
Current Assets	2m	2m	1m
Current Liabilities	157	161	206

Arla Foods plc
4 Savannah Way Leeds Valley Park, Leeds, LS10 1AB
Tel: 0113-382 7000 **Fax:** 0113-382 7030
E-mail: trademarks@arlafoods.com
Website: http://www.arlafoods.com
Directors: N. Davidson (Dir)
Ultimate Holding Company: ARLA FOODS AMBA (DENMARK)
Immediate Holding Company: ARLA FOODS LIMITED
Registration no: 02143253 **Date established:** 1987
Turnover: Over £1,000m **No.of Employees:** 251 - 500
Product Groups: 20

Date of Accounts	Dec 11	Dec 10	Dec 09
Sales Turnover	1587m	1482m	1435m
Pre Tax Profit/Loss	31m	31m	29m
Working Capital	31m	67m	79m
Fixed Assets	310m	297m	276m
Current Assets	229m	289m	317m
Current Liabilities	11m	5m	158m

Arup
78 East Street, Leeds, LS9 8EE
Tel: 0113-242 8498 **Fax:** 0113-242 8573
E-mail: kay.fisher@arup.com
Website: http://www.arup.com
Managers: K. Fisher (Sales Admin), K. Walters (Mktg Serv Mgr), K. Ellite (Personnel), V. Porter (Fin Mgr)
Immediate Holding Company: ARUP GROUP LTD
Registration no: SC062237 **Turnover:** £75m - £125m
No.of Employees: 101 - 250 **Product Groups:** 87

Asd Metal Services plc
Valley Farm Road Stourton, Leeds, LS10 1SD
Tel: 0113-254 0711 **Fax:** 01482-633370
E-mail: enquiries@asdmetalservices.co.uk
Website: http://www.asdmetalservices.co.uk
Bank(s): Barclays
Directors: M. Joyce (Fin)
Managers: A. Hobson (Buyer), A. Hobson (Sales Prom Mgr), K. Avaliani
Ultimate Holding Company: KLOCKNER & CO SE (GERMANY)
Immediate Holding Company: ASD METAL SERVICES LIMITED
Registration no: 02680562 **Date established:** 1992
Turnover: Over £1,000m **No.of Employees:** 101 - 250
Product Groups: 66

Date of Accounts	Dec 11	Dec 08
Working Capital	2	2
Current Assets	2	2

Asda Stores Ltd
Asda House Southbank Great Wilson Street, Leeds, LS11 5AD
Tel: 0113-243 5435 **Fax:** 0113-241 8666
Website: http://www.asda.com
Directors: D. Gurr (Dir), A. Spindler (Dir)
Ultimate Holding Company: WAL-MART STORES INC (USA)
Immediate Holding Company: ASDA STORES LIMITED
Registration no: 00464777 **VAT No.:** GB 362 0127 92
Date established: 1949 **Turnover:** Over £1,000m
No.of Employees: 1501 & over **Product Groups:** 61

Date of Accounts	Dec 11	Dec 10	Dec 09
Sales Turnover	21660m	20535m	19819m
Pre Tax Profit/Loss	507m	492m	571m
Working Capital	-294m	307m	87m
Fixed Assets	5319m	4431m	4347m
Current Assets	3707m	3739m	5203m
Current Liabilities	821m	764m	720m

Ashby & Anderson
191 Whitehall Road, Leeds, LS12 6EW
Tel: 0113-387 5951 **Fax:** 0113-231 0267
E-mail: info@wgsearch.co.uk
Website: http://www.wgsearch.co.uk
Directors: R. Search (MD)
Ultimate Holding Company: SEARCH GROUP HOLDINGS LIMITED
Immediate Holding Company: ASHBY & ANDERSON,LIMITED
Registration no: 00193866 **Date established:** 2023
No.of Employees: 1 - 10 **Product Groups:** 31, 45, 49

Date of Accounts	Dec 99	Dec 11	Dec 10
Working Capital	6	6	6
Current Assets	6	6	6

Ashdale Electrical Testing Installation & Appliance Testing
61 Manston Crescent, Leeds, LS15 8BN
Tel: 0113-260 0527 **Fax:** 0113-260 0527
E-mail: ashdalepat@hotmail.co.uk
Website: http://www.ashdale-electricaltesting.co.uk
Directors: G. Ruane (Prop)
Turnover: Up to £250,000 **No.of Employees:** 1 - 10 **Product Groups:** 38, 67, 85

Ashworth Leeds
Jawbone Industrial Estate Wood Lane, Rothwell, Leeds, LS26 0RS
Tel: 0113-282 0002 **Fax:** 0113-282 5572
E-mail: info@ashworth-frazer.co.uk
Website: http://www.ashworth.eu.com

Managers: D. Kaye (Mgr), M. Culley (Mktg Serv Mgr)
Immediate Holding Company: OLIVER ASHWORTH GROUP
Registration no: 00002733 **Turnover:** £75m - £125m
No.of Employees: 11 - 20 **Product Groups:** 30, 32

Aspli Safety Equipment Centre Ltd

211 Hunslet Road, Leeds, LS10 1PF
Tel: 0113-246 1550 **Fax:** 0113-246 1560
E-mail: sales@aspli.com
Website: http://www.aspli.com
Directors: J. Heaton (MD)
Registration no: 01387726 **VAT No.:** 184 7500 51 **Turnover:** £1m - £2m
No.of Employees: 1 - 10 **Product Groups:** 22, 39, 40

Date of Accounts	Dec 07	Dec 06	Dec 05
Working Capital	101	75	107
Fixed Assets	515	328	264
Current Assets	422	400	393
Current Liabilities	321	326	286

Avanta UK Ltd

Unit B1 Astra Park Parkside Lane, Leeds, LS11 5SZ
Tel: 0113-384 8777 **Fax:** 0113-384 8778
E-mail: sales@avantauk.com
Website: http://www.avantauk.com
Directors: D. Beattie (MD), A. Chipp (Fin)
Immediate Holding Company: AVANTA UK LIMITED
Registration no: 03962158 **Date established:** 2000
No.of Employees: 1 - 10 **Product Groups:** 35, 77

Date of Accounts	Jun 11	Jun 10	Jun 09
Working Capital	-111	-78	-56
Fixed Assets	412	441	483
Current Assets	908	638	593
Current Liabilities	205	120	143

Awesome Merchandise Ltd

Barkston House Croydon Street, Leeds, LS11 9RT
Tel: 0113-243 5667
E-mail: info@awesomemerchandise.co.uk
Website: http://www.awesomemerchandise.co.uk
Directors: L. Hodson (Prop)
Immediate Holding Company: AWESOME MERCHANDISE LTD
Registration no: 07042508 **Date established:** 2009
No.of Employees: 1 - 10 **Product Groups:** 23, 24, 27, 65

Date of Accounts	Oct 11	Oct 10
Working Capital	-48	47
Fixed Assets	116	56
Current Assets	120	78

B C S Electrics Ltd

40 Charlton Grove, Leeds, LS9 9JT
Tel: 0113-235 0400 **Fax:** 0113-235 0416
E-mail: info@bcselectrics.co.uk
Website: http://www.bcselectrics.co.uk
Directors: M. Thomas (MD), M. Furness (Co Sec)
Managers: R. Kay (Admin Off)
Ultimate Holding Company: B.C.S. ELECTRICS (HOLDINGS) LIMITED
Immediate Holding Company: B.C.S.ELECTRICS LIMITED
Registration no: 00406364 **VAT No.:** GB 169 2131 65
Date established: 1946 **No.of Employees:** 21 - 50 **Product Groups:** 52

Date of Accounts	Feb 08	Feb 11	Feb 10
Working Capital	236	158	316
Fixed Assets	199	55	150
Current Assets	1m	827	893

B O M Engineering Ltd

Station Road Morley, Leeds, LS27 8JT
Tel: 0113-253 7544 **Fax:** 0113-252 7851
E-mail: sales@bomeng.co.uk
Website: http://www.bomengineering.co.uk
Directors: M. Brook (MD)
Immediate Holding Company: B.O.M. LIGHT ENGINEERING LIMITED
Registration no: 01118477 **VAT No.:** GB 171 3430 91
Date established: 1973 **Turnover:** £250,000 - £500,000
No.of Employees: 1 - 10 **Product Groups:** 35, 48

Date of Accounts	Aug 11	Aug 10	Aug 09
Working Capital	23	25	24
Fixed Assets	25	25	26
Current Assets	24	28	27

B T T G Ltd

Ring Road West Park, Leeds, LS16 6QL
Tel: 0113-259 1999 **Fax:** 0113-278 0306
E-mail: sdonnelly@bttg.co.uk
Website: http://www.bttg.co.uk
Bank(s): Bank of Scotland
Directors: S. Donnelly (Comm)
Ultimate Holding Company: BTTG HOLDINGS LIMITED
Immediate Holding Company: BTTG LIMITED
Registration no: 04628697 **VAT No.:** GB 145 9206 63
Date established: 2003 **Turnover:** Up to £250,000
No.of Employees: 11 - 20 **Product Groups:** 85

Date of Accounts	Nov 10	Sep 11	Sep 09
Sales Turnover	N/A	N/A	68
Pre Tax Profit/Loss	N/A	N/A	-35
Working Capital	49	-26	20
Fixed Assets	210	211	720
Current Assets	107	84	64
Current Liabilities	N/A	N/A	5

BAB Industrial & Commercial

7 Stainburn Avenue, Leeds, LS17 6PQ
Tel: 0113-269 5936 **Fax:** 0113-269 5936
E-mail: brian@boardman-online.co.uk
Website: http://www.firstnet.co.uk
Directors: B. Boardman (Prop)
Turnover: £250,000 - £500,000 **No.of Employees:** 1 - 10
Product Groups: 33, 40

Bailey Teswaine

7 Brown Lane West, Leeds, LS12 6EH
Tel: 0113-243 9921 **Fax:** 08451-828128
E-mail: enquiries@baileyteswaine.co.uk
Website: http://www.baileyteswaine.co.uk
Bank(s): HSBC Bank plc
Directors: B. Cowell (Co Sec), D. Lane (Dir), Patsalides (MD), G. Stow (Mkt Research)
Managers: C. Dean, S. Bostock (Tech Supp Mgr), C. Bailey (Nat Sales Mgr)
Ultimate Holding Company: NG BAILEY LIMITED
Immediate Holding Company: NG BAILEY IT SERVICES LIMITED
Registration no: 02338401 **Date established:** 1989
Turnover: £20m - £50m **No.of Employees:** 251 - 500
Product Groups: 37, 44, 52

Date of Accounts	Feb 08	Feb 09	Feb 10
Sales Turnover	66m	55m	46m
Pre Tax Profit/Loss	-4m	-12m	-5m
Working Capital	-11m	-7m	195
Fixed Assets	17m	8m	951
Current Assets	22m	18m	18m
Current Liabilities	4m	4m	2m

Barkston Plastics Engineering Ltd

221 Pontefract Lane, Leeds, LS9 0DX
Tel: 0113-249 2200 **Fax:** 01942-842844
E-mail: jenny.duxbury@barkstonltd.co.uk
Website: http://www.barkstonltd.co.uk
Bank(s): HSBC Bank plc
Directors: J. Duxbury (Dir)
Ultimate Holding Company: L.A.R. HOLDINGS LIMITED
Immediate Holding Company: BARKSTON PLASTICS LTD
Registration no: 00959719 **VAT No.:** GB 545 4817 27
Date established: 1969 **Turnover:** £2m - £5m **No.of Employees:** 51 - 100
Product Groups: 35, 40, 48, 66

Date of Accounts	Nov 11	Nov 10	Nov 09
Working Capital	406	480	514
Fixed Assets	78	98	83
Current Assets	2m	2m	2m
Current Liabilities	N/A	464	422

Barraclough Packaging Services Ltd

397 Harrogate Road, Leeds, LS17 6DJ
Tel: 0113-240 5421 **Fax:** 0113-240 5421
Directors: D. Barraclough (Fin)
Immediate Holding Company: BARRACLOUGH PACKAGING SERVICES LIMITED
Registration no: 02139921 **Date established:** 1987
No.of Employees: 1 - 10 **Product Groups:** 38, 42

Date of Accounts	Dec 10	Dec 09	Dec 08
Working Capital	-69	-36	-23
Fixed Assets	10	9	9
Current Assets	33	15	21

Batleys Cash & Carry

Skelton Grange Road, Leeds, LS10 1RZ
Tel: 0113-277 1313 **Fax:** 0113-272 0495
Website: http://www.batleys.co.uk
Bank(s): HSBC Bank plc
Managers: B. Routledge (Chief Mgr)
Immediate Holding Company: L. BATLEY HOLDINGS LTD
Registration no: 00675326 **Turnover:** Up to £250,000
No.of Employees: 51 - 100 **Product Groups:** 61

Battery Equipment Services Ltd

Unit 81 Barkston House Croydon Street, Leeds, LS11 9RT
Tel: 0113-243 6111 **Fax:** 0113-234 0917
E-mail: admin@besltd.f9.co.uk
Website: http://www.batteryequipmentservices.co.uk
Directors: M. Jackson (Dir)
Immediate Holding Company: BATTERY EQUIPMENT SERVICES LIMITED
Registration no: 01965702 **VAT No.:** GB 388 0153 41
Date established: 1985 **Turnover:** £500,000 - £1m
No.of Employees: 1 - 10 **Product Groups:** 37

Date of Accounts	Dec 10	Dec 09	Dec 08
Working Capital	462	439	489
Fixed Assets	16	23	23
Current Assets	548	481	543

Bemco Ltd

Unit 1 Royds Park, Leeds, LS12 4TU
Tel: 0113-263 3995 **Fax:** 0113-263 2658
E-mail: accounts@bemco.co.uk
Website: http://www.bemco.co.uk
Directors: O. Bennett (Fin), S. Barkes (MD)
Immediate Holding Company: BEMCO LIMITED
Registration no: 04851594 **VAT No.:** GB 175 8013 58
Date established: 2003 **Turnover:** £5m - £10m **No.of Employees:** 1 - 10
Product Groups: 67

Date of Accounts	May 12	May 11	May 10
Working Capital	16	26	34
Fixed Assets	7	9	9
Current Assets	28	38	49

Berwin & Berwin Ltd

Roseville Road, Leeds, LS8 5EE
Tel: 0113-244 2244 **Fax:** 0113-242 4398
E-mail: sales@berwinberwin.co.uk
Website: http://www.berwinberwin.co.uk
Directors: C. Bower (Sales)
Managers: L. Hector
Ultimate Holding Company: BERWIN HOLDINGS LIMITED
Immediate Holding Company: BERWIN & BERWIN LIMITED
Registration no: 00529000 **Date established:** 1954
Turnover: £20m - £50m **No.of Employees:** 51 - 100 **Product Groups:** 24

Date of Accounts	Dec 11	Dec 10	Dec 09
Sales Turnover	47m	41m	37m
Pre Tax Profit/Loss	1m	1m	670
Working Capital	3m	2m	649
Fixed Assets	2m	3m	3m
Current Assets	23m	21m	15m
Current Liabilities	5m	5m	4m

Bicknell Control Systems Ltd

Union Mills Dawson Hill, Morley, Leeds, LS27 9JS
Tel: 0113-238 1661 **Fax:** 0113-238 1640
E-mail: bicknellcontrols@btconnect.com
Managers: D. Mcnally (Mgr)
Immediate Holding Company: BICKNELL CONTROL SYSTEMS LIMITED
Registration no: 01767305 **VAT No.:** GB 333 7115 79
Date established: 1983 **Turnover:** £1m - £2m **No.of Employees:** 11 - 20
Product Groups: 38

Date of Accounts	Apr 11	Apr 10	Apr 09
Working Capital	210	103	137
Fixed Assets	159	168	118
Current Assets	545	433	432

Biffa Waste Services Ltd

10 Queen Street Woodlesford, Leeds, LS26 8AL
Tel: 0800-601601 **Fax:** 0113-287 7419
E-mail: peter.hass@biffa.co.uk
Website: http://www.biffa.co.uk
Managers: A. Oates (Depot Mgr)
Immediate Holding Company: BIFFA WASTE SERVICES LIMITED
Registration no: 00946107 **Date established:** 1969
No.of Employees: 21 - 50 **Product Groups:** 32, 54

Date of Accounts	Mar 08	Mar 09	Apr 10
Sales Turnover	555m	574m	492m
Pre Tax Profit/Loss	23m	50m	30m
Working Capital	229m	271m	293m
Fixed Assets	371m	360m	378m
Current Assets	409m	534m	609m
Current Liabilities	50m	100m	115m

Bindoff

23 Linton Crescent, Leeds, LS17 8PZ
Tel: 0113-268 1526
E-mail: hello@bindoff.co.uk
Website: http://www.bindoff.co.uk
Directors: M. Bindoff (Prop)
Immediate Holding Company: BINDOFF MEDIA LTD
Registration no: 07092213 **Date established:** 2009
Turnover: Up to £250,000 **No.of Employees:** 1 - 10 **Product Groups:** 37, 44, 79

Date of Accounts	Dec 11	Dec 10
Working Capital	-0	2
Fixed Assets	2	2
Current Assets	7	2

K Bins Ltd

Westfield Mills Kirk Lane, Yeadon, Leeds, LS19 7LX
Tel: 0113-250 9777 **Fax:** 0113-250 6700
E-mail: sales@kbins.com
Website: http://www.kbins.com
Bank(s): Yorkshire Bank
Directors: C. Dalton (Dir)
Ultimate Holding Company: GKF GROUP LIMITED
Immediate Holding Company: K-BINS LIMITED
Registration no: 02608881 **VAT No.:** 557 2130 54 **Date established:** 1991
Turnover: £250,000 - £500,000 **No.of Employees:** 11 - 20
Product Groups: 30, 77

Date of Accounts	Mar 11	Mar 10	Mar 09
Working Capital	1m	1m	1m
Fixed Assets	138	133	2
Current Assets	2m	2m	1m

Binson Bearing Co.

335a Roundhay Road, Leeds, LS8 4HT
Tel: 0113-249 0251 **Fax:** 0113-235 0375
E-mail: sales@binsonbearings.ssnet.co.uk
Website: http://www.binsonbearings.co.uk
Managers: M. Robinson (Mgr)
No.of Employees: 1 - 10 **Product Groups:** 35, 40, 45, 66, 67

Blind Factory Leeds Ltd

28 Penraevon Street Penraevon Industrial Estate, Leeds, LS7 2AW
Tel: 0113-262 6660 **Fax:** 0113-262 6669
E-mail: brian@theblindfactoryleeds.co.uk
Website: http://www.theblindfactoryleeds.co.uk
Directors: B. Roberts (Fin)
Immediate Holding Company: THE BLIND FACTORY (LEEDS) LIMITED
Registration no: 04370451 **Date established:** 2002
No.of Employees: 1 - 10 **Product Groups:** 30, 63, 66

Date of Accounts	Feb 11	Feb 10	Feb 09
Working Capital	-45	-46	-20
Fixed Assets	N/A	1	2
Current Assets	14	6	18

Bloctube Marine Services Ltd

Unit 5, Felnex Close, Leeds, LS9 0SR
Tel: 0113-248 4827 **Fax:** 0113-240 3351
E-mail: bloctube@aol.com
Website: http://www.bloctube.co.uk
Directors: S. Merritt (MD), S. O'Brien (Fin)
Managers: S. Keeligan (Tech Serv Mgr)
Immediate Holding Company: BLOCTUBE MARINE SERVICES LIMITED
Registration no: 04001743 **VAT No.:** GB 168 8456 13
Date established: 2000 **Turnover:** Up to £250,000
No.of Employees: 1 - 10 **Product Groups:** 37, 38, 39, 40

Date of Accounts	Jun 11	Jun 10	Jun 09
Sales Turnover	183	227	215
Pre Tax Profit/Loss	11	-22	-12
Working Capital	-21	-38	-22
Fixed Assets	8	9	14
Current Assets	71	37	53
Current Liabilities	5	6	N/A

Booker Wellman Ltd

Sizers Court Henshaw Lane, Yeadon, Leeds, LS19 7DP
Tel: 0113-250 3829 **Fax:** 0113-250 9416
Managers: G. Williams (Mgr)
Immediate Holding Company: BOOKER WELLMAN (HOLDINGS) LIMITED
Registration no: 01503416 **VAT No.:** GB 179 5962 00
Date established: 1980 **Turnover:** £500,000 - £1m
No.of Employees: 11 - 20 **Product Groups:** 35, 48

Date of Accounts	Dec 11	Dec 10	Dec 09
Working Capital	-393	-308	-68
Fixed Assets	1m	1m	949
Current Assets	72	140	53

B P A UK Ltd (Vacuum Pumps & Blowers)

Unit A6 Astra Park Parkside Lane, Leeds, LS11 5SZ
Tel: 0113-276 5000 **Fax:** 0113-271 5880
E-mail: sales@bpauk.com
Website: http://www.bpauk.com
Directors: T. Hartley (MD)
Immediate Holding Company: BPA (UK) LIMITED
Registration no: 04583110 **VAT No.:** GB 804 6841 30
Date established: 2002 **No.of Employees:** 1 - 10 **Product Groups:** 40, 41, 42, 48, 66, 67

Date of Accounts	Nov 11	Nov 10	Nov 09
Working Capital	167	172	189
Fixed Assets	90	89	99
Current Assets	373	340	364

Braime Elevator Components Ltd
Hunslet Road, Leeds, LS10 1JZ
Tel: 0113-246 1800 **Fax:** 0113-243 5021
E-mail: 4b-uk@go4b.com
Website: http://www.go4b.com
Bank(s): National Westminster Bank Plc
Directors: O. Braime (Sales), D. Brown (Fin), M. Mills (Fin)
Managers: A. Braime (Tech Serv Mgr), L. Stockhill (Sales Prom Mgr), S. Biock (Mktg Serv Mgr)
Ultimate Holding Company: T.F. & J.H. BRAIME (HOLDINGS) P.L.C.
Immediate Holding Company: BRAIME ELEVATOR COMPONENTS LIMITED
Registration no: 01171825 **VAT No.:** GB 168 9597 87
Date established: 1974 **Turnover:** £5m - £10m **No.of Employees:** 11 - 20
Product Groups: 35, 38, 41, 45

Date of Accounts	Dec 11	Dec 10	Dec 09
Sales Turnover	7m	6m	5m
Pre Tax Profit/Loss	514	420	241
Working Capital	5m	4m	4m
Fixed Assets	107	16	29
Current Assets	6m	5m	5m
Current Liabilities	350	281	160

Bramley Garage Doors
Britannia Road Morley, Leeds, LS27 0DN
Tel: 0113-253 9734 **Fax:** 0113-253 7437
E-mail: bramleygaragedoors@btopenworld.com
Website: http://www.bramleygaragedoors.co.uk
Directors: R. Davidson (Prop)
Registration no: 04788867 **Date established:** 2003
No.of Employees: 1 - 10 **Product Groups:** 25, 30, 35, 36, 52

Brandenburg Gates
27-29 Cross Green Lane, Leeds, LS9 8LJ
Tel: 0113-244 4442 **Fax:** 0113-242 4445
Directors: G. Dunbar (Ptnr)
Immediate Holding Company: BRANDENBURG GATES LIMITED
Registration no: 06350271 **Date established:** 2007
No.of Employees: 1 - 10 **Product Groups:** 26, 35

Date of Accounts	Aug 11	Aug 10	Aug 09
Working Capital	19	-10	-4
Fixed Assets	6	11	16
Current Assets	19	9	21

Brandon Medical Company Ltd
Holme Well Road, Leeds, LS10 4TQ
Tel: 0113-277 7393 **Fax:** 0113-272 8844
E-mail: enquiries@brandon-medical.com
Website: http://www.brandon-medical.com
Directors: G. Hall (Dir)
Managers: N. Smithson
Ultimate Holding Company: BRANDON GROUP LIMITED
Immediate Holding Company: BRANDON MEDICAL COMPANY LIMITED
Registration no: 02827189 **Date established:** 1993 **Turnover:** £2m - £5m
No.of Employees: 21 - 50 **Product Groups:** 37, 38

Date of Accounts	Oct 11	Oct 10	Oct 09
Working Capital	934	783	929
Fixed Assets	775	852	712
Current Assets	2m	3m	2m

Brass
9a Alma Road, Leeds, LS6 2AH
Tel: 0113-230 4000 **Fax:** 0113-230 2332
E-mail: hello@brassagency.com
Website: http://www.brassagency.com
Directors: J. Morgan (Grp Chief Exec)
Managers: R. Page (Mktg Serv Mgr), C. Beer (Fin Mgr), M. Richmond (Tech Serv Mgr), M. Myers (Personnel)
Immediate Holding Company: BRAHM LIMITED
Registration no: 01708346 **Date established:** 1983
Turnover: £10m - £20m **No.of Employees:** 101 - 250 **Product Groups:** 81

Date of Accounts	Jul 11	Jul 10	Jul 09
Sales Turnover	16m	16m	17m
Pre Tax Profit/Loss	325	558	465
Working Capital	-1m	-989	-386
Fixed Assets	6m	6m	6m
Current Assets	3m	4m	4m
Current Liabilities	3m	3m	3m

Brenntag Albion Colours
Unit 1 Albion House Rawdon Park, Yeadon, Leeds, LS19 7XX
Tel: 0113-387 9200 **Fax:** 0113-387 9290
E-mail: enquiry@brenntag.co.uk
Website: http://www.brenntag.co.uk
Bank(s): Lloyds TSB Bank plc
Directors: P. Savage (Ch), S. Holland (Dir)
Ultimate Holding Company: BRENNTAG AG (GERMANY)
Immediate Holding Company: BRENNTAG UK LIMITED
Registration no: 05262170 **Date established:** 2004
Turnover: £250m - £500m **No.of Employees:** 51 - 100
Product Groups: 32, 62

Date of Accounts	Dec 11	Dec 10	Dec 09
Sales Turnover	266m	234m	208m
Pre Tax Profit/Loss	29m	29m	21m
Working Capital	152m	114m	102m
Fixed Assets	59m	62m	63m
Current Assets	220m	176m	152m
Current Liabilities	27m	24m	20m

Bright Screw Co. Ltd
Bagley Lane Rodley, Leeds, LS13 1JB
Tel: 0113-256 4166 **Fax:** 0113-239 3480
E-mail: sales@brightscrew.co.uk
Website: http://www.brightscrew.co.uk
Bank(s): National Westminster
Directors: H. Brown (Fin), N. Brown (MD)
Managers: J. Goodwin, T. McDonald (Buyer)
Immediate Holding Company: BRIGHT SCREW COMPANY LIMITED(THE)
Registration no: 00365862 **VAT No.:** GB 168 8554 13
Date established: 1941 **No.of Employees:** 51 - 100 **Product Groups:** 35

Date of Accounts	Dec 11	Dec 10	Dec 09
Pre Tax Profit/Loss	501	500	457
Working Capital	662	705	839
Fixed Assets	1m	1m	2m
Current Assets	3m	2m	2m
Current Liabilities	792	674	400

Brooke North Solicitors
Crown House 81-89 Great George Street, Leeds, LS1 3BR
Tel: 0113-283 2100 **Fax:** 0113-283 3999
E-mail: gw@brookenorth.co.uk
Website: http://www.brookenorth.co.uk
Bank(s): Royal bank of Scotland; Bank of Ireland
Directors: S. Morgan (Ptnr), R. Dalton (Ptnr), N. Middleman (MD), G. Watson (Ptnr), G. Watson (Snr Part), S. Frith (Ptnr), P. Butler (Co Sec), S. Lopeman (Ptnr), S. Frieze (Ptnr), S. Thomas (Ptnr), R. Parr (Ptnr), R. Meadows (Ptnr), N. Hoyle (Ptnr), N. Middlemass (Fin), N. Middlemas (Ptnr), J. Pearlman (Ptnr), H. Middlemass (Ptnr), R. Stockdale (Ptnr)
Managers: T. Knight, T. Knight (Personnel)
Immediate Holding Company: BROOKE NORTH LLP
Registration no: OC317798 **Date established:** 2006 **Turnover:** £2m - £5m
No.of Employees: 21 - 50 **Product Groups:** 80

Date of Accounts	Mar 11	Mar 10	Mar 09
Working Capital	204	11	173
Fixed Assets	357	421	477
Current Assets	2m	2m	2m

Browns Fasteners Ltd
Deanfield Mills Asquith Avenue, Morley, Leeds, LS27 9QS
Tel: 0113-252 2185 **Fax:** 0113-252 0826
E-mail: sales@brownsfasteners.co.uk
Website: http://www.brownsfasteners.co.uk
Bank(s): The Royal Bank of Scotland
Directors: T. Wilber (MD)
Immediate Holding Company: BROWNS FASTENERS LIMITED
Registration no: 00521228 **VAT No.:** GB 169 1997 08
Date established: 1953 **Turnover:** £2m - £5m **No.of Employees:** 11 - 20
Product Groups: 35, 66

Date of Accounts	Mar 11	Mar 10	Mar 09
Working Capital	389	355	337
Fixed Assets	155	150	99
Current Assets	1m	1m	1m

Buck & Hickman Ltd
Unit 1 Gloucester Court Gloucester Terrace, Leeds, LS12 2ER
Tel: 0113-246 0911 **Fax:** 0113-244 6888
E-mail: leeds@buckandhickman.com
Website: http://www.buckhickman.co.uk
Managers: P. Churchill (District Mgr)
Ultimate Holding Company: TRAVIS PERKINS PLC
Immediate Holding Company: BOSTON (2011) LIMITED
Registration no: 06028304 **Date established:** 2006
Turnover: £75m - £125m **No.of Employees:** 1 - 10 **Product Groups:** 24, 29, 30, 33, 36, 37, 41, 46

Date of Accounts	Dec 10	Mar 10	Mar 09
Working Capital	6m	6m	6m
Current Assets	27m	27m	27m

Burns Welding Services
Woodcock Farm Back Lane, Leeds, LS12 5HJ
Tel: 0113-287 7929 **Fax:** 0113-290 9471
E-mail: sales@burnswelding.co.uk
Website: http://www.burnswelding.co.uk
Directors: C. Burn (Prop)
Date established: 1998 **No.of Employees:** 1 - 10 **Product Groups:** 46

C B Associates
Unit 8 Southfield Mills Topcliffe Lane, Morley, Leeds, LS27 0HW
Tel: 0113-252 6848 **Fax:** 0113-252 6959
E-mail: cbassociates@surfree.co.uk
Directors: C. Brocklesby (Ptnr)
Date established: 2001 **No.of Employees:** 1 - 10 **Product Groups:** 38, 42

C B M Construction
Goodman House Goodman Street, Leeds, LS10 1NY
Tel: 0113-271 0200 **Fax:** 0113-271 2446
E-mail: info@cbm-construction.co.uk
Website: http://www.cbm-construction.co.uk
Directors: A. Bashforth (MD)
Immediate Holding Company: CBM CONSTRUCTION GROUP LIMITED
Registration no: 03192679 **VAT No.:** GB 660 2627 50
Date established: 1996 **Turnover:** £1m - £2m **No.of Employees:** 1 - 10
Product Groups: 52

Date of Accounts	Sep 11	Sep 10	Sep 09
Working Capital	97	233	652
Fixed Assets	258	261	21
Current Assets	771	1m	1m

C C L Veloduct Ltd
5 Emmanuel Trading Estate Springwell Road, Leeds, LS12 1AT
Tel: 0113-234 0511
Website: http://www.veloduct.co.uk
Managers: D. Longhorn (Mgr)
Ultimate Holding Company: FP009344
Immediate Holding Company: LINDAB LIMITED
Registration no: 01641399 **Date established:** 1982
Turnover: £50m - £75m **No.of Employees:** 1 - 10 **Product Groups:** 40, 66

C C S (a division of Consumerdata Ltd)
3 Armley Court Armley Road, Leeds, LS12 2LB
Tel: 0113-242 0520 **Fax:** 0113- 2420050
E-mail: info@consumersketch.co.uk
Website: http://www.consumerdata.com
Bank(s): HSBC Bank plc
Directors: B. Ingham (MD), P. Ingham (MD)
Managers: T. Brock (Chief Mgr)
Immediate Holding Company: CONSUMERDATA LIMITED
Registration no: 02800504 **VAT No.:** GB 576 8434 93
Date established: 1993 **No.of Employees:** 11 - 20 **Product Groups:** 44, 80, 81

Cad Fab Ltd
7 The Courtyards Victoria Road, Leeds, LS14 2LB
Tel: 0113-265 5010 **Fax:** 0113-265 5012
E-mail: cadfab@aol.com
Directors: J. Clarke (MD)
Immediate Holding Company: CAD-FAB LIMITED
Registration no: 02517337 **VAT No.:** GB 556 9991 70
Date established: 1990 **Turnover:** £250,000 - £500,000
No.of Employees: 1 - 10 **Product Groups:** 48

Date of Accounts	Jul 11	Jul 10	Jul 09
Working Capital	-2	11	-4
Fixed Assets	321	351	367
Current Assets	112	105	79

Caffe Society
2 Lincoln Way Sherburn In Elmet, Leeds, LS25 6PJ
Tel: 01977-687580 **Fax:** 0845-450 0499
E-mail: info@caffesociety.co.uk
Website: http://caffesociety.co.uk
Directors: S. Mooring (Dir), S. Mooring (Dir)
Managers: D. Ferguson
Immediate Holding Company: CAFFE SOCIETY LTD.
Registration no: 04227424 **Date established:** 2001
No.of Employees: 21 - 50 **Product Groups:** 20

Date of Accounts	Aug 11	Aug 10	Aug 09
Working Capital	187	236	75
Fixed Assets	569	542	538
Current Assets	710	780	769

Calderys UK Ltd
Unit 5-8 Ashfield Way Whitehall Industrial Estate Whitehall Road, Leeds, LS12 5JB
Tel: 0113-263 6268 **Fax:** 0113-279 0539
E-mail: enquiry@lafarge.co.uk
Website: http://www.calderys.com
Managers: C. Sylvester (Comptroller), C. Sylvester (Comptroller)
Ultimate Holding Company: IMERYS SA (FRANCE)
Immediate Holding Company: CALDERYS UK LTD
Registration no: 01039428 **VAT No.:** GB 170 2474 82
Date established: 1972 **Turnover:** £5m - £10m **No.of Employees:** 21 - 50
Product Groups: 33

Date of Accounts	Dec 11	Dec 10	Dec 09
Sales Turnover	10m	9m	11m
Pre Tax Profit/Loss	-1m	-244	-179
Working Capital	3m	3m	3m
Fixed Assets	353	2m	2m
Current Assets	8m	6m	16m
Current Liabilities	1m	680	863

Calomax Ltd
Calomax House Lupton Avenue, Leeds, LS9 7DD
Tel: 0113-249 6681 **Fax:** 0113-235 0358
E-mail: sales@calomax.co.uk
Website: http://www.calomax.co.uk
Bank(s): Yorkshire Bank
Directors: G. Pearson (Co Sec), P. Bowers (Sales & Mktg)
Ultimate Holding Company: CALOMAX LIMITED
Immediate Holding Company: CALOMAX LIMITED
Registration no: 02617748 **VAT No.:** GB 168 9432 22
Date established: 1991 **Turnover:** £1m - £2m **No.of Employees:** 11 - 20
Product Groups: 40

Date of Accounts	Sep 08	Oct 09	Oct 10
Working Capital	430	498	518
Fixed Assets	595	595	580
Current Assets	662	654	629

Calverley Control Installations Ltd
Blacup House Royds Close, Leeds, LS12 6LL
Tel: 0113-279 6611 **Fax:** 0113-231 0391
E-mail: info@calverley.biz
Website: http://www.calverley.biz
Directors: S. Collins (MD)
Immediate Holding Company: CALVERLEY CONTROL INSTALLATIONS LIMITED
Registration no: 02466655 **Date established:** 1990
Turnover: £500,000 - £1m **No.of Employees:** 11 - 20
Product Groups: 52, 84

Date of Accounts	Dec 11	Dec 10	Dec 09
Working Capital	-36	10	5
Fixed Assets	96	68	54
Current Assets	410	465	282

Carolina Blinds
44 Stainburn Road, Leeds, LS17 6NN
Tel: 0113-307 0456 **Fax:** 0113-268 7974
E-mail: info@blindsleeds.com
Website: http://www.blindsleeds.com
Directors: M. Cardis (Prop)
Managers: M. Cardis (Sales Admin)
Immediate Holding Company: THE CAROLINA BLIND COMPANY LIMITED
Registration no: 04693159 **Date established:** 2003
Turnover: Up to £250,000 **No.of Employees:** 1 - 10 **Product Groups:** 23, 24, 30, 35, 63, 66

Peter Cassidy Leeds Ltd
Holbeck Lane, Leeds, LS11 9XA
Tel: 0113-245 5457 **Fax:** 0113-242 6456
E-mail: brian.houlding@petercassidy.co.uk
Website: http://www.petercassidy.co.uk
Directors: B. Houlding (Sales)
Ultimate Holding Company: MAINRIM LIMITED
Immediate Holding Company: PETER CASSIDY (LEEDS) LIMITED
Registration no: 00945299 **VAT No.:** GB 450 6660 55
Date established: 1969 **Turnover:** £2m - £5m **No.of Employees:** 1 - 10
Product Groups: 45

Date of Accounts	Dec 11	Dec 10	Dec 09
Working Capital	378	284	277
Fixed Assets	58	63	75
Current Assets	559	460	454

Ceramique International Ltd
Unit 1 Royds Lane, Leeds, LS12 6DU
Tel: 0113-231 0218 **Fax:** 0113-231 0353
E-mail: cameron@ceramiqueinternationale.co.uk
Website: http://www.tilesandmosaics.co.uk
Directors: C. Fraser (Comm), P. Vann (Chief Op Offcr), C. Fraser (Dir), J. Greaves (MD), N. Greaves (Dir)
Immediate Holding Company: CERAMIQUE INTERNATIONALE LIMITED
Registration no: 01171559 **VAT No.:** GB 500 4072 12
Date established: 1974 **Turnover:** £2m - £5m **No.of Employees:** 11 - 20
Product Groups: 33

Chippindale Plant Ltd (Head Office)
Butterbowl Works Ring Road, Lower Wortley, Leeds, LS12 5AJ
Tel: 0113-263 2344 **Fax:** 0113-279 1710
E-mail: nigel@chippindale-plant.co.uk
Website: http://www.chippindale-plant.co.uk
Bank(s): HSBC Bank plc
Directors: N. Chippindale (MD), T. Robinson (Sales)
Immediate Holding Company: CHIPPINDALE PLANT LIMITED
Registration no: 00467731 **VAT No.:** GB 168 8251 31
Date established: 1949 **Turnover:** £5m - £10m
No.of Employees: 51 - 100 **Product Groups:** 45

Date of Accounts	Apr 11	Apr 10	Apr 09
Sales Turnover	7m	7m	7m
Pre Tax Profit/Loss	260	210	215
Working Capital	-890	-1m	-2m
Fixed Assets	7m	7m	7m
Current Assets	2m	2m	1m
Current Liabilities	685	488	316

Chubb Fire Limited

5 Canal Place, Leeds, LS12 2DU
Tel: 0844-8791820 **Fax:** 0113-243 8704
Website: http://www.chubb.co.uk
Bank(s): National Westminster Bank Plc
Managers: D. Kerr (District Mgr), M. Cane, P. Scurrah (District Mgr), L. Hutchinson (Admin Off)
Immediate Holding Company: Chubb Group Security Ltd
Registration no: 00134210 **VAT No.:** GB 609 0284 52
Date established: 1981 **Turnover:** £50m - £75m
No.of Employees: 11 - 20 **Product Groups:** 81

Citibase

100 Wellington Street, Leeds, LS1 4LT
Tel: 0113-242 2444 **Fax:** 0113-242 2433
E-mail: leeds.ws@citibase.co.uk
Website: http://www.citibase.co.uk
Managers: L. Slater
Immediate Holding Company: SYMBIANT LIMITED
Registration no: 02767719 **Date established:** 2003
No.of Employees: 1 - 10 **Product Groups:** 80

Date of Accounts	May 11	May 10	May 09
Working Capital	59	49	201
Fixed Assets	59	83	56
Current Assets	132	209	459

Clantex Ltd

The Moorings Waterside Industrial Park Waterside Road, Leeds, LS10 1DG
Tel: 0113-200 8200 **Fax:** 0113-200 8202
E-mail: khoulbrook@clantex.co.uk
Website: http://www.clantex.co.uk
Directors: K. Houlbrook (MD), K. Howbrook (MD)
Immediate Holding Company: CLANTEX LIMITED
Registration no: 06202743 **Date established:** 2007 **Turnover:** £1m - £2m
No.of Employees: 11 - 20 **Product Groups:** 40

Date of Accounts	Dec 10	Dec 09	Dec 08
Working Capital	672	355	396
Fixed Assets	76	156	429
Current Assets	1m	728	799
Current Liabilities	N/A	N/A	42

Cohen & Wilks International Ltd

Aquatite House Mabgate, Leeds, LS9 7DR
Tel: 0113-245 0804 **Fax:** 0113-391 7858
E-mail: reception@cwil.co.uk
Website: http://www.cohenandwilks.co.uk
Directors: P. Lacey (Sales), M. Foxall (Dir), J. Barrow (Fin), M. Crompton (Ch)
Managers: J. Fox (Personnel)
Ultimate Holding Company: MITSUI & CO LIMITED (JAPAN)
Immediate Holding Company: COHEN & WILKS INTERNATIONAL LIMITED
Registration no: 01188155 **Date established:** 1974
Turnover: £20m - £50m **No.of Employees:** 51 - 100 **Product Groups:** 61

Date of Accounts	Mar 12	Mar 11	Mar 10
Sales Turnover	26m	23m	26m
Pre Tax Profit/Loss	663	637	2m
Working Capital	6m	6m	6m
Fixed Assets	2m	2m	2m
Current Assets	11m	11m	9m
Current Liabilities	3m	2m	754

Colliers International UK plc

15-16 Park Row, Leeds, LS1 5HD
Tel: 0113-200 1800 **Fax:** 0113-200 1889
E-mail: sophie.latimer@colliersce.co.uk
Website: http://www.colliers.com
Directors: G. Styles (Prop)
Immediate Holding Company: COLLIERS INTERNATIONAL UK PLC
Registration no: 04195561 **Date established:** 2001 **Turnover:** £2m - £5m
No.of Employees: 21 - 50 **Product Groups:** 80, 82, 84

Date of Accounts	Dec 10	Dec 09	Dec 08
Sales Turnover	66m	58m	78m
Pre Tax Profit/Loss	-8m	-40m	-11m
Working Capital	11m	14m	-65
Fixed Assets	39m	40m	67m
Current Assets	23m	24m	35m
Current Liabilities	10m	9m	13m

Companion Stairlifts

24b Oxford Road Guiseley, Leeds, LS20 9AS
Tel: 01943-882000 **Fax:** 01943-874953
E-mail: info@helptheaged.org.uk
Website: http://www.helptheaged.org.uk
Directors: M. Loftus (MD)
Registration no: 04728243 **Date established:** 2001
No.of Employees: 11 - 20 **Product Groups:** 35, 39, 45

Computerpower Consultants Ltd

21 Mount Pleasant Guiseley, Leeds, LS20 9EB
Tel: 01943-870070 **Fax:** 01943-879186
E-mail: alan.g@computer-power.co.uk
Directors: E. Gordon (Fin), A. Gordon (MD)
Immediate Holding Company: COMPUTERPOWER (CONSULTANTS) LIMITED
Registration no: 02548655 **VAT No.:** GB 557 0769 13
Date established: 1990 **Turnover:** £500,000 - £1m
No.of Employees: 1 - 10 **Product Groups:** 37, 38, 44

Date of Accounts	Oct 11	Oct 10	Oct 09
Working Capital	109	131	119
Fixed Assets	9	12	14
Current Assets	200	234	234

Conservatories By Design Ltd

Unit 10 Rossett Business Park Rodley Lane, Leeds, LS13 1BQ
Tel: 0113-236 1908 **Fax:** 0113-236 1522
E-mail: p.clarke.cbd@btconnect.com
Website: http://www.conservatoriesbydesign.net
Directors: P. Clarke (Prop)
Immediate Holding Company: CONSERVATORIES BY DESIGN (ROOFKITS) LIMITED
Registration no: 07088572 **Date established:** 2009
No.of Employees: 1 - 10 **Product Groups:** 25, 30, 35, 40

Date of Accounts	Feb 11	Feb 10
Working Capital	-48	N/A
Fixed Assets	13	N/A
Current Assets	78	N/A

Constar International UK Ltd

Moor Lane Trading Estate Sherburn in Elmet, Leeds, LS25 6ES
Tel: 01977-882000 **Fax:** 01977-882092
E-mail: iatkinson@constar.net
Website: http://www.constar.net
Bank(s): National Westminster Bank Plc
Directors: C. Phelan (MD), I. Atkinson (Fin)
Managers: J. Crowley (Sales & Mktg Mg), A. Whale (Personnel), G. Hall (Purch Mgr)
Ultimate Holding Company: CONSTAR INTERNATIONAL INC (UNITED STATES)
Immediate Holding Company: CONSTAR INTERNATIONAL U.K. LIMITED
Registration no: 02407933 **VAT No.:** GB 545 3400 65
Date established: 1989 **Turnover:** £50m - £75m
No.of Employees: 101 - 250 **Product Groups:** 25, 30, 31, 66

Date of Accounts	Dec 11	Dec 10	Dec 09
Sales Turnover	83m	74m	74m
Pre Tax Profit/Loss	812	-852	2m
Working Capital	-15m	-17m	-16m
Fixed Assets	7m	8m	9m
Current Assets	13m	12m	12m
Current Liabilities	2m	9m	3m

Peter Cook International

Aneal Business Centre Cross Green Approach, Leeds, LS9 0SG
Tel: 0113-235 1111 **Fax:** 0113-235 0034
E-mail: sales@petercookint.com
Website: http://www.petercookint.com
Bank(s): Barclays
Directors: C. Pickup (MD)
Immediate Holding Company: ANEAL DEVELOPMENTS LLP
Registration no: 01309498 **VAT No.:** GB 533 1933 59
Date established: 2004 **Turnover:** Up to £250,000
No.of Employees: 11 - 20 **Product Groups:** 25, 29

Leonard Cooper Ltd

Balm Road, Leeds, LS10 2JR
Tel: 0113-270 5441 **Fax:** 0113-276 0659
E-mail: rowland.ingram@leonardcooperltd.co.uk
Website: http://www.leonardcooperltd.co.uk
Bank(s): National Westminster, Leeds
Directors: R. Ingram (MD), A. Lowther (Co Sec), D. Hobson (Dir)
Immediate Holding Company: LEONARD COOPER LIMITED
Registration no: 00157872 **VAT No.:** 168 8732 15 **Date established:** 2019
Turnover: £2m - £5m **No.of Employees:** 21 - 50 **Product Groups:** 30, 35, 36, 45

Date of Accounts	Mar 12	Mar 11	Mar 10
Working Capital	93	93	258
Fixed Assets	630	452	476
Current Assets	969	721	576

Co-Optimize Marketing Ltd

31 Fieldhead Drive Barwick In Elmet, Leeds, LS15 4EE
Tel: 0113-393 5116 **Fax:** 0113-267 8720
E-mail: chris.allcoat@co-optimize.co.uk
Website: http://www.co-optimize.co.uk
Directors: C. Allcoat (Dir)
Immediate Holding Company: CO-OPTIMIZE MARKETING LIMITED
Registration no: 04620951 **Date established:** 2002
Turnover: Up to £250,000 **No.of Employees:** 1 - 10 **Product Groups:** 49

Date of Accounts	Mar 12	Mar 11	Mar 10
Working Capital	5	1	N/A
Current Assets	15	26	9

Corporate Document Services Ltd

7 Eastgate, Leeds, LS2 7LY
Tel: 0113-399 4000 **Fax:** 0113-399 4202
E-mail: info@cds.co.uk
Website: http://www.cds.co.uk
Directors: L. White (Fin)
Managers: F. Bally (Mgr), M. Smith, P. Meersman (Mktg Serv Mgr)
Ultimate Holding Company: The Baird Group Limited
Immediate Holding Company: CORPORATE DOCUMENT SERVICES LIMITED
Registration no: 02925653 **Date established:** 1994
Turnover: £20m - £50m **No.of Employees:** 21 - 50 **Product Groups:** 81

Date of Accounts	Dec 11	Dec 10	Dec 09
Sales Turnover	23m	26m	27m
Pre Tax Profit/Loss	160	169	491
Working Capital	3m	3m	3m
Fixed Assets	946	1m	1m
Current Assets	7m	7m	7m
Current Liabilities	1m	2m	2m

Cover Structure

Blue Zone Newmarket Approach, Leeds, LS9 0RJ
Tel: 0113-235 0088 **Fax:** 0113-235 0333
E-mail: info@coverstructure.com
Website: http://www.coverstructure.com
Directors: J. Harrison (Fin), G. Quinlan (MD)
Managers: A. Dwyer, G. Dennett (Buyer)
Immediate Holding Company: COVER STRUCTURE LIMITED
Registration no: 02762144 **Date established:** 1992
No.of Employees: 21 - 50 **Product Groups:** 52

Date of Accounts	Dec 11	Dec 10	Dec 09
Working Capital	516	736	702
Fixed Assets	66	100	126
Current Assets	2m	2m	1m

Peter Cox Ltd

John O Gaunts Trading Estate Leeds Road, Rothwell, Leeds, LS26 0JB
Tel: 0113-282 5316 **Fax:** 0113-393 4927
E-mail: headoffice@petercox.com
Website: http://www.petercox.com
Managers: J. Haran (District Mgr)
Ultimate Holding Company: GERALDTON SERVICES INC (USA)
Immediate Holding Company: PETER COX LIMITED
Registration no: 02438126 **Date established:** 1989
No.of Employees: 21 - 50 **Product Groups:** 07, 32, 52, 66

Date of Accounts	Dec 11	Dec 10	Dec 09
Sales Turnover	15m	15m	14m
Pre Tax Profit/Loss	645	282	-350
Working Capital	3m	3m	2m
Fixed Assets	459	542	643
Current Assets	6m	5m	4m
Current Liabilities	2m	2m	961

C P L Petroleum

Queen Street Woodlesford, Leeds, LS26 8AL
Tel: 0113-235 0450 **Fax:** 0113-235 0351
E-mail: leeds@cplpetroleum.co.uk
Website: http://www.cplpetroleum.co.uk
Managers: A. Storey (District Mgr), A. Story (Mgr), M. Burton (Mgr)
Ultimate Holding Company: CPL INDUSTRIES HOLDINGS LIMITED
Immediate Holding Company: CPL PETROLEUM LIMITED
Registration no: 03003860 **VAT No.:** GB 721 5764 39
Date established: 1994 **No.of Employees:** 1 - 10 **Product Groups:** 66

Date of Accounts	Mar 12	Mar 11	Mar 10
Pre Tax Profit/Loss	N/A	878	904
Working Capital	31	30m	30m
Fixed Assets	26	26m	26m
Current Assets	57	56m	56m
Current Liabilities	26	246	253

Craftwork Upholstery Ltd

Premier House Barras Street, Leeds, LS12 4JS
Tel: 0113-279 0429 **Fax:** 0113-203 8080
E-mail: michael@craftworkupholstery.com
Website: http://www.craftworkupholstery.com
Directors: M. Hopkinson (Dir), H. Cook (Co Sec)
Managers: D. Knowles (Buyer), M. Hughes (Factory Mgr), C. Peck-russell (Comptroller)
Immediate Holding Company: CRAFTWORK UPHOLSTERY LIMITED
Registration no: 05349438 **Date established:** 2005
No.of Employees: 21 - 50 **Product Groups:** 26

Date of Accounts	May 12	May 11	May 10
Working Capital	696	485	418
Fixed Assets	357	459	516
Current Assets	1m	1m	831

Crispin Orthotics

Unit 5 Revie Road, Leeds, LS11 8JG
Tel: 0113-271 7117 **Fax:** 0113-271 3434
Website: http://www.crispinorthotics.com
Directors: H. Turner (Fin), M. Thaxter (Prop)
Immediate Holding Company: CRISPIN ORTHOTICS LTD
Registration no: 04766565 **Date established:** 2003
No.of Employees: 21 - 50 **Product Groups:** 38, 67

Cronapress Ltd

Parkside Works Otley Road, Guiseley, Leeds, LS20 8BH
Tel: 01943-876600 **Fax:** 01943-870088
E-mail: sales@cronapress.co.uk
Website: http://www.cronapress.co.uk
Directors: C. Butler (MD)
Immediate Holding Company: CRONAPRESS LIMITED
Registration no: 02395908 **Date established:** 1989
Turnover: £250,000 - £500,000 **No.of Employees:** 1 - 10
Product Groups: 40

Date of Accounts	Mar 11	Mar 10	Mar 09
Working Capital	109	106	-31
Fixed Assets	160	163	164
Current Assets	355	309	170

Cy-Nap

Studio 28 Dock Street, Leeds, LS10 1JF
Tel: 0113-234 2111 **Fax:** 0113-243 9289
E-mail: smccann@txttools.co.uk
Website: http://www.txttools.co.uk
Directors: S. Mccan (Prop), S. McCann (MD), S. Sidaway (Mkt Research)
Immediate Holding Company: FIVE STAR EMPLOYMENT SERVICES LIMITED
Registration no: 04643020 **Date established:** 1990
Turnover: £500,000 - £1m **No.of Employees:** 11 - 20 **Product Groups:** 44

D L A Piper UK Llp

2 Princes Square Princes Exchange, Leeds, LS1 4BY
Tel: 08700-111111 **Fax:** 0113-369 2396
E-mail: daniel.pollick@dlapiper.com
Website: http://www.dlapiper.com
Directors: D. Pollick (I.T. Dir)
Ultimate Holding Company: DLA PIPER INTERNATIONAL LLP
Immediate Holding Company: DLA PIPER UK LLP
Registration no: OC307847 **Date established:** 2004
Turnover: £250,000 - £500,000 **No.of Employees:** 101 - 250
Product Groups: 80

Date of Accounts	Apr 11	Apr 10	Apr 09
Sales Turnover	368m	360m	382m
Pre Tax Profit/Loss	120m	112m	124m
Working Capital	107m	98m	119m
Fixed Assets	21m	27m	30m
Current Assets	296m	277m	273m
Current Liabilities	42m	30m	28m

Dale Carnegie Training Ltd

1200 Century Way Thorpe Park, Leeds, LS15 8ZA
Tel: 0113-251 5116
Website: http://www.dale-carnegie.co.uk
Managers: J. Dennet (Mgr)
Immediate Holding Company: WORKSAFE CONSULTANCY SERVICES LIMITED
Date established: 1995 **Turnover:** £1m - £2m **No.of Employees:** 1 - 10
Product Groups: 86

Date of Accounts	Sep 11
Sales Turnover	46
Pre Tax Profit/Loss	34
Working Capital	22
Fixed Assets	7
Current Assets	51
Current Liabilities	17

Daniels Group

Waterside Road Waterside Industrial Park, Leeds, LS10 1RW
Tel: 0113-202 5160 **Fax:** 0113-276 1956
Website: http://www.danielsgroup.eu
Managers: P. Gledhill (Chief Mgr), S. Hill (Purch Mgr)
Registration no: 02049893 **No.of Employees:** 251 - 500
Product Groups: 20, 21

Date of Accounts	Dec 07	Dec 06	Dec 05
Sales Turnover	90972	79074	65340
Pre Tax Profit/Loss	6890	6069	4651

see next page

Daniels Group - Cont'd

Working Capital	-7017	-9224	-8677
Fixed Assets	26505	27927	19895
Current Assets	20752	17654	14323
Current Liabilities	27769	26878	23000
Total Share Capital	1	1	1
ROCE% (Return on Capital Employed)	35.4	32.4	41.5
ROT% (Return on Turnover)	7.6	7.7	7.1

Dantherm Filtration Ltd

Limewood Approach, Leeds, LS14 1NG
Tel: 0113-273 9400 **Fax:** 0113-265 0735
E-mail: rh@danthermfiltration.com
Website: http://www.danthermfiltration.com
Bank(s): Danske Bank
Directors: A. Whiteside (Fab), J. Blake (Sales), J. Watson (Sales), D. Proud (MD), D. Wood (Co Sec), R. Halliwell (MD), S. Lusty (MD)
Managers: C. Johnson (Mktg Serv Mgr), A. Bishop (Mktg Serv Mgr), A. Bishop (Tech Serv Mgr), P. Bamforth (I.T. Exec), P. Innes (Export Sales Mg), J. Turner (Buyer)
Immediate Holding Company: DANTHERM FILTRATION LTD
Registration no: 00562216 **VAT No.:** GB 169 7754 04
Date established: 1956 **Turnover:** £2m - £5m **No.of Employees:** 21 - 50
Product Groups: 40, 42, 48, 52, 54

Date of Accounts	Dec 07	Dec 06	Dec 05
Sales Turnover	5542	5338	4946
Pre Tax Profit/Loss	341	286	156
Working Capital	1159	420	160
Fixed Assets	289	342	315
Current Assets	2552	1792	1111
Current Liabilities	1393	1372	951
Total Share Capital	2068	2068	2068
ROCE% (Return on Capital Employed)	23.6	37.6	32.7
ROT% (Return on Turnover)	6.2	5.4	3.1

Dapaa Tints - Mobile Window Tinting Specialists

14 Dawson Road, Leeds, LS11 7AS
Tel: 0113-228 0073
E-mail: info@dapaatints.co.uk
Website: http://www.dapaatints.co.uk
Directors: M. Khan (Prop)
No.of Employees: 1 - 10 **Product Groups:** 39, 68

Darnton E G S Ltd

Monk Fryston Hall Monk Fryston, Leeds, LS25 5DU
Tel: 01977-681001 **Fax:** 01977-681006
E-mail: alistair.hamilton@darntonegs.com
Website: http://www.darntonelgee.com
Bank(s): The Royal Bank of Scotland
Directors: A. Lodge (Sales & Mktg), A. Hamilton (MD)
Managers: B. Portela (Tech Serv Mgr), E. Longhurst (Fin Mgr)
Immediate Holding Company: DARNTON EGS LIMITED
Registration no: 06617944 **VAT No.:** GB 613 0924 71
Date established: 2008 **Turnover:** £1m - £2m **No.of Employees:** 21 - 50
Product Groups: 44, 81, 84

Date of Accounts	Sep 11	Sep 10	Sep 09
Working Capital	1m	1m	1m
Fixed Assets	172	133	155
Current Assets	2m	2m	2m

David Fox Design Ltd

23 East View Yeadon, Leeds, LS19 7AD
Tel: 0113-250 2800 **Fax:** 01302-849299
E-mail: info@davidfoxdesign.com
Website: http://www.davidfoxdesign.com
Directors: D. Fox (Dir)
Registration no: 07097688 **No.of Employees:** 1 - 10 **Product Groups:** 85

Dawson Rentals Materials Handling Equipment Ltd

Aberford Road Garforth, Leeds, LS25 2ET
Tel: 0113-287 4874 **Fax:** 0113-286 9158
E-mail: info@dawsongroup.co.uk
Website: http://www.dawsongroup.co.uk
Bank(s): Barclays
Directors: A. Cooper (MD)
Managers: P. Shires (Fin Mgr)
Ultimate Holding Company: DAWSONGROUP PLC
Immediate Holding Company: DAWSONRENTALS MATERIALS HANDLING EQUIPMENT LIMITED
Registration no: 02652091 **VAT No.:** GB 420 8677 49
Date established: 1991 **No.of Employees:** 21 - 50 **Product Groups:** 45, 83

Date of Accounts	Dec 11	Dec 10	Dec 09
Sales Turnover	13m	14m	14m
Pre Tax Profit/Loss	2m	2m	814
Working Capital	-5m	-3m	-6m
Fixed Assets	21m	19m	25m
Current Assets	2m	6m	4m
Current Liabilities	5m	7m	8m

Denison Mayes Group Ltd

Unit 14 Enterprise Park Moorhouse Avenue, Leeds, LS11 8HA
Tel: 0113-270 8011 **Fax:** 0113-271 2850
E-mail: sales@denisonmayesgroup.com
Website: http://www.denisonmayesgroup.com
Bank(s): Bank of Scotland
Directors: P. Rothera (MD), R. Rothera (Dir), S. Willett (Chief Op Offcr)
Immediate Holding Company: DENISON MAYES GROUP LIMITED
Registration no: 03598085 **Date established:** 1998 **Turnover:** £2m - £5m
No.of Employees: 21 - 50 **Product Groups:** 38, 85

Date of Accounts	Jun 12	Jun 11	Jun 10
Working Capital	-126	-169	-195
Fixed Assets	218	228	257
Current Assets	505	471	454

Depuy International (a division of Johnson & Johnson Co.)

St Anthonys Road Beeston, Leeds, LS11 8DT
Tel: 0113-270 0461 **Fax:** 0113-272 4101
E-mail: depuy@dpygb.jnj.com
Website: http://www.depuy.com
Directors: P. Wells (Co Sec), R. Twomey (Dir)
Ultimate Holding Company: JOHNSON & JOHNSON (USA)
Immediate Holding Company: DEPUY INTERNATIONAL (HOLDINGS) LIMITED
Registration no: 03331107 **VAT No.:** GB 686 9141 88
Date established: 1997 **Turnover:** £5m - £10m
No.of Employees: 501 - 1000 **Product Groups:** 38, 67

Date of Accounts	Dec 08	Jan 10	Jan 11
Pre Tax Profit/Loss	6m	6m	6m
Working Capital	163m	167m	171m
Current Assets	183m	188m	194m
Current Liabilities	2m	2m	860

Direct Heating Installations

11 Wolley Avenue, Leeds, LS12 5DX
Tel: 0113-229 7602
E-mail: directheatinginstallations@yahoo.co.uk
Website: http://www.directheatingionstallation.co.uk
Directors: M. Baran (Prop)
Date established: 2006 **No.of Employees:** 1 - 10 **Product Groups:** 37, 40, 48

Oliver Douglas Ltd

Amberley Works Chelsea Close, Leeds, LS12 4HP
Tel: 0113-279 7373 **Fax:** 0113-279 1014
E-mail: admin@oliver-douglas.co.uk
Website: http://www.oliverdouglas.com
Managers: J. Robinson (Sales Admin)
Ultimate Holding Company: NEWSMITH STAINLESS LIMITED
Immediate Holding Company: OLIVER DOUGLAS LIMITED
Registration no: 02136843 **VAT No.:** GB 444 3565 47
Date established: 1987 **Turnover:** £500,000 - £1m
No.of Employees: 1 - 10 **Product Groups:** 40

Date of Accounts	Jun 11	Jun 10	Jun 09
Working Capital	530	550	520
Fixed Assets	17	22	52
Current Assets	652	628	642

Dr Oetker

4600 Park Approach Thorpe Park, Leeds, LS15 8GB
Tel: 0113-823 1400 **Fax:** 0113-823 1401
E-mail: info@oetker.co.uk
Website: http://www.oetker.co.uk
Managers: C. Dennis (Admin Off)
Ultimate Holding Company: DR AUGUST OETKER KG (GERMANY)
Immediate Holding Company: DR. OETKER (UK) LIMITED
Registration no: 04293376 **Date established:** 2001
No.of Employees: 1 - 10 **Product Groups:** 20

Date of Accounts	Dec 11	Dec 10	Dec 09
Sales Turnover	137m	189m	182m
Pre Tax Profit/Loss	19m	-5m	-5m
Working Capital	16m	-9m	-12m
Fixed Assets	59m	70m	79m
Current Assets	43m	56m	52m
Current Liabilities	8m	19m	12m

Drawn Metal Ltd

Anchor Works Swinnow Lane, Leeds, LS13 4NE
Tel: 0113-256 5661 **Fax:** 0113-239 3194
E-mail: r.copping@drawnmetal.co.uk
Website: http://drawnmetal.co.uk
Bank(s): HSBC, Pudsey
Directors: C. Murray (Sales), J. Wilson (Co Sec), R. Copping (Dir), K. Willows (Sales & Mktg)
Managers: J. Grundy, G. Cockroft
Ultimate Holding Company: DRAWN METAL HOLDINGS LIMITED
Immediate Holding Company: DRAWN METAL,LIMITED
Registration no: 00201877 **VAT No.:** GB 169 1246 53
Date established: 2024 **Turnover:** £2m - £5m **No.of Employees:** 21 - 50
Product Groups: 26, 35, 36

Date of Accounts	Apr 11	Apr 10	Apr 09
Sales Turnover	3m	8m	9m
Pre Tax Profit/Loss	N/A	703	333
Working Capital	2m	2m	2m
Fixed Assets	1m	968	773
Current Assets	3m	4m	6m
Current Liabilities	630	1m	1m

Duffield Printers

421 Kirkstall Road, Leeds, LS4 2HA
Tel: 0113-279 3011 **Fax:** 0113-231 0098
E-mail: martyn@duffieldprinters.co.uk
Website: http://www.duffieldprinters.co.uk
Bank(s): National Westminster
Directors: M. Duffield (MD), J. Broadbent (Fin)
Immediate Holding Company: MAC2PRINT LIMITED
Registration no: 04247520 **VAT No.:** GB 168 8379 05
Date established: 2001 **No.of Employees:** 21 - 50 **Product Groups:** 27, 28

Dunbar & Boardman Partnership

Westgate House 100 Wellington Street, Leeds, LS1 4LT
Tel: 0113-237 3067 **Fax:** 0113-237 3069
E-mail: mail@dunbarboardman.com
Website: http://www.dunbarboardman.com
Managers: J. Spragg (Mgr)
Immediate Holding Company: SYMBIANT LIMITED
Date established: 2003 **No.of Employees:** 1 - 10 **Product Groups:** 35, 39, 45

Date of Accounts	May 11	May 10	May 09
Working Capital	59	49	201
Fixed Assets	59	83	56
Current Assets	132	209	459

Easaway Drain Care UK Ltd

Four Seasons House Railway Road Cross Gates, Crossgates, Leeds, LS15 8EL
Tel: 0113-260 6767 **Fax:** 0113-260 3939
E-mail: enquiries@easawaydraincare.com
Website: http://www.easawaydraincare.com
Directors: T. Phillips (MD), T. Phillips (Fin)
Immediate Holding Company: EASAWAY DRAIN CARE (UK) LIMITED
Registration no: 04914032 **Date established:** 2003
Turnover: £250,000 - £500,000 **No.of Employees:** 21 - 50
Product Groups: 52

Date of Accounts	Sep 11	Sep 10	Sep 09
Working Capital	45	97	46
Fixed Assets	91	116	130
Current Assets	205	245	150

Eco Lab

Lotherton Way Garforth, Leeds, LS25 2JY
Tel: 0113-232 0066 **Fax:** 0113-287 1317
Website: http://www.adams-healthcare.co.uk
Directors: A. Newson (Dir)
Immediate Holding Company: WHEATLEY M & E SERVICES LIMITED
Date established: 1997 **No.of Employees:** 51 - 100 **Product Groups:** 31, 63, 69, 84

Date of Accounts	Feb 09	Feb 10	Feb 11
Sales Turnover	17m	17m	19m
Pre Tax Profit/Loss	2m	2m	2m
Working Capital	9m	9m	10m
Fixed Assets	845	793	840
Current Assets	12m	12m	13m
Current Liabilities	2m	2m	2m

Electric Center

Gibraltar Island Road Old Mill Business Park, Leeds, LS10 1RJ
Tel: 0113-385 2700 **Fax:** 0113-385 2707
Website: http://www.electric-center.co.uk
Managers: N. Scott (District Mgr)
Ultimate Holding Company: WOLSELEY PLC (JERSEY)
Immediate Holding Company: A.C. ELECTRICAL WHOLESALE LIMITED
Registration no: 01204867 **Date established:** 1975 **Turnover:** £2m - £5m
No.of Employees: 11 - 20 **Product Groups:** 37, 63, 67

Date of Accounts	Jul 11	Jul 10	Jul 09
Pre Tax Profit/Loss	315	292	891
Working Capital	20m	20m	20m
Current Assets	20m	20m	20m

Elmwood

Ghyll Royd Guiseley, Leeds, LS20 9LT
Tel: 01943-870229 **Fax:** 01943-870191
E-mail: jonathan.sands@elmwood.co.uk
Website: http://www.elmwood.com
Directors: D. Longbottom (Fin), J. Sands (Ch), D. Bootland (Tech Serv)
Managers: R. Peel (Mktg Serv Mgr), P. Harrison (Sales Admin)
Immediate Holding Company: ELMWOOD DESIGN LIMITED
Registration no: 02360152 **Date established:** 1989
Turnover: £10m - £20m **No.of Employees:** 51 - 100 **Product Groups:** 44, 81

Date of Accounts	Dec 11	Dec 10	Dec 09
Sales Turnover	11m	11m	9m
Pre Tax Profit/Loss	284	288	558
Working Capital	2m	2m	2m
Fixed Assets	1m	1m	1m
Current Assets	5m	4m	4m
Current Liabilities	2m	1m	2m

Emergi Lite Safety Systems Ltd

Bruntcliffe Lane Morley, Leeds, LS27 9LL
Tel: 0113-281 0600 **Fax:** 0113-281 0601
E-mail: emergi-lite_sales@tnb.com
Website: http://www.emergi-lite.co.uk
Bank(s): Barclays, National Westminster
Directors: J. Claire (Mkt Research), J. Clare (Sales & Mktg), J. Smith (MD), P. Turnbow (Co Sec)
Managers: K. Herbert (I.T. Exec), M. Eatherington (Mgr), N. Makin (Buyer), J. Burlow (), J. Burlow
Immediate Holding Company: Kaufel (U.K.) Ltd
Registration no: 02135118 **Date established:** 1987
Turnover: £10m - £20m **No.of Employees:** 21 - 50 **Product Groups:** 37, 67

Emmerson Doors Ltd

Unit 1a Enterprise Way Salerburn In Elmet, Sherburn In Elmet, Leeds, LS25 6NA
Tel: 01977-685566 **Fax:** 01977-681981
E-mail: sales@emmerson-doors.co.uk
Website: http://www.emmerson-doors.co.uk
Directors: E. Clark (Co Sec), P. Emmerson (MD)
Managers: S. Emmerson (Transport), J. Foster
Immediate Holding Company: EMMERSON DOORS LTD
Registration no: 06542787 **VAT No.:** GB 482 1842 41
Date established: 2008 **Turnover:** £2m - £5m **No.of Employees:** 21 - 50
Product Groups: 30, 35, 36, 48

Date of Accounts	Mar 12	Mar 11	Mar 10
Working Capital	16	13	-11
Fixed Assets	80	98	116
Current Assets	740	650	630

Encase Ltd

2 Yeadon Airport Industrial Estate Harrogate Road, Yeadon, Leeds, LS19 7WP
Tel: 0113-250 5616 **Fax:** 0113-239 1145
E-mail: info@encase.co.uk
Website: http://www.encase.co.uk
Bank(s): HSBC
Directors: J. Wilks (Co Sec), P. Lockwood (Chief Op Offcr)
Managers: B. Wray (Sales Prom Mgr), D. Moon (Tech Serv Mgr), H. Lowe (Personnel)
Ultimate Holding Company: CANADIAN OVERSEAS PACKAGING INDUSTRIES LTD (CANADA)
Immediate Holding Company: ENCASE LIMITED
Registration no: 00852604 **VAT No.:** GB 179 9285 93
Date established: 1965 **Turnover:** £10m - £20m
No.of Employees: 101 - 250 **Product Groups:** 27

Date of Accounts	Jun 12	Jun 11	Jun 10
Sales Turnover	33m	32m	26m
Pre Tax Profit/Loss	1m	138	186
Working Capital	1m	-1m	-2m
Fixed Assets	5m	5m	6m
Current Assets	12m	14m	12m
Current Liabilities	2m	2m	2m

Endon Lighting Ltd

1-3 Cross Green Way, Leeds, LS9 0SE
Tel: 0113-380 5700 **Fax:** 0113-248 4519
E-mail: neil.baldwin@endon.co.uk
Website: http://www.endon.co.uk
Directors: C. Dodd (Fin), N. Baldwin (MD), T. Hayfield (Sales)
Managers: D. Clark (Purch Ledg Mgr), I. Macdonald (Tech Serv Mgr)
Ultimate Holding Company: THE NATIONAL LIGHTING COMPANY LIMITED
Immediate Holding Company: THE UK LIGHTING COMPANY LIMITED
Registration no: 02782682 **VAT No.:** GB 170 4743 71
Date established: 1993 **Turnover:** £20m - £50m
No.of Employees: 51 - 100 **Product Groups:** 37, 61

Date of Accounts	Dec 10	Dec 09	Dec 07
Working Capital	557	557	557
Current Assets	754	754	754
Current Liabilities	N/A	N/A	197

Entech Ltd
Bond House 3 The Bourse, Leeds, LS1 5EN
Tel: 0113-234 4048 **Fax:** 0113-234 3383
E-mail: richard@entech.us
Website: http://www.entech.us
Directors: R. Pickles (Dir)
Managers: J. Sampson (Comptroller)
Immediate Holding Company: ENTECH LIMITED
Registration no: 02521027 **Date established:** 1990
No.of Employees: 11 - 20 **Product Groups:** 38, 44, 54, 67, 80

Date of Accounts	Mar 11	Mar 10	Mar 09
Working Capital	N/A	54	-7
Fixed Assets	1	1	2
Current Assets	228	267	103

Epco Ltd
Felnex Square Cross Green Industrial Estate, Leeds, LS9 0ST
Tel: 0113-249 1155 **Fax:** 0113-249 1166
E-mail: sales@epco-plastics.com
Website: http://www.epco-plastics.com
Directors: A. Knowles (Fin), C. Knowles (MD)
Immediate Holding Company: EPCO LIMITED
Registration no: 02956652 **Date established:** 1994 **Turnover:** £1m - £2m
No.of Employees: 1 - 10 **Product Groups:** 30

Date of Accounts	Mar 12	Mar 11	Mar 10
Working Capital	429	351	376
Fixed Assets	52	58	30
Current Assets	1m	1m	969

Epilepsy Action
New Anstey House Gateway Drive, Yeadon, Leeds, LS19 7LY
Tel: 0113-210 8800 **Fax:** 0113-391 0300
E-mail: p.lee@epilepsy.org.uk
Website: http://www.epilepsy.org.uk
Bank(s): Yorkshire Bank PLC
Directors: P. Lee (Grp Chief Exec)
Immediate Holding Company: BRITISH EPILEPSY ASSOCIATION
Registration no: 00797997 **Date established:** 1964 **Turnover:** £2m - £5m
No.of Employees: 51 - 100 **Product Groups:** 80, 87

Date of Accounts	Dec 11	Dec 10	Dec 09
Sales Turnover	3m	3m	3m
Pre Tax Profit/Loss	-469	142	452
Working Capital	1m	1m	1m
Fixed Assets	2m	2m	2m
Current Assets	2m	2m	2m
Current Liabilities	473	501	371

Eriks UK (Leeds Electro Mechanical)
New Craven Gate, Leeds, LS11 5NJ
Tel: 0113-243 8846 **Fax:** 0113-246 0788
E-mail: leeds.repair@eriks.co.uk
Website: http://www.eriks.co.uk
Managers: A. Sly, D. Richards (Mgr), B. Taylor (District Mgr)
Date established: 1999 **No.of Employees:** 11 - 20 **Product Groups:** 35

Euro Machines Ltd
The White House Rawdon, Leeds, LS19 6PU
Tel: 01756-710588 **Fax:** 01756-710234
E-mail: sales@euro-machine.com
Website: http://www.euro-machines.com
Bank(s): Barclays, Bradford
Directors: J. Alderson (Ch), D. Bonne (Co Sec)
Registration no: 00988431 **VAT No.:** GB 172 1810 85
Turnover: £1m - £2m **No.of Employees:** 11 - 20 **Product Groups:** 48, 67

Evans Easyspace Ltd
Millshaw, Leeds, LS11 8EG
Tel: 0113-271 1888 **Fax:** 0113-271 8487
E-mail: info@evanspropertygroup.com
Website: http://www.evanspropertygroup.com
Directors: A. Evans (Dir), P. Millington (Fin), P. Horsborough (Pers)
Ultimate Holding Company: DRACHS INVESTMENTS NO 3 LIMITED (JERSEY)
Immediate Holding Company: EVANS EASYSPACE LIMITED
Registration no: 04844882 **Date established:** 2003 **Turnover:** £2m - £5m
No.of Employees: 51 - 100 **Product Groups:** 80

Date of Accounts	Dec 11	Dec 10	Dec 09
Working Capital	17	8	8
Current Assets	3m	3m	3m

Evans Halshaw Motors Ltd
Roseville Road, Leeds, LS8 5QP
Tel: 0113-280 0200 **Fax:** 0113-220 7609
Website: http://www.evanshalshaw.co.uk
Managers: G. Dickins (Sales Prom Mgr), P. Rumney, N. Brown (Chief Acct)
Ultimate Holding Company: PENDRAGON PLC
Immediate Holding Company: EVANS HALSHAW MOTORS LIMITED
Registration no: 01359849 **Date established:** 1978
Turnover: £20m - £50m **No.of Employees:** 101 - 250 **Product Groups:** 68

Date of Accounts	Dec 11	Dec 10	Dec 09
Working Capital	11m	11m	11m
Fixed Assets	9m	9m	9m
Current Assets	14m	14m	14m
Current Liabilities	3m	4m	4m

Everbuild Building Products Ltd
41 Knowsthorpe Way Cross Green Industrial Estate, Leeds, LS9 0SW
Tel: 0113-240 3456 **Fax:** 0113-240 0024
E-mail: reception@everbuild.co.uk
Website: http://www.everbuild.co.uk
Directors: G. Senior (Sales), K. Morris (Purch), D. Seymour (MD), G. Mercer (Fin)
Managers: S. Howard (Personnel), T. Round (Tech Serv Mgr), H. Kirby (Mktg Serv Mgr)
Immediate Holding Company: EVERBUILD BUILDING PRODUCTS LIMITED
Registration no: 02890352 **Date established:** 1994
Turnover: £50m - £75m **No.of Employees:** 101 - 250 **Product Groups:** 32

Date of Accounts	Feb 12	Feb 11	Feb 10
Sales Turnover	60m	53m	45m
Pre Tax Profit/Loss	3m	3m	1m
Working Capital	5m	4m	3m
Fixed Assets	12m	12m	12m
Current Assets	18m	17m	14m
Current Liabilities	2m	2m	2m

Eversheds
Bridgewater Place Water Lane, Leeds, LS11 5DR
Tel: 0113-243 0391 **Fax:** 0113-245 6188
E-mail: d-gray@eversheds.com
Website: http://www.eversheds.com
Bank(s): Barclays
Directors: M. Smith (Fin), L. Bennett (Mkt Research)
Managers: A. Scott, C. Briant (I.T. Exec), M. Naylor (Personnel)
Immediate Holding Company: TAILORS DIRECT LTD
Registration no: OC304065 **Date established:** 2002
Turnover: £20m - £50m **No.of Employees:** 501 - 1000
Product Groups: 80

Excelsior Air Conditioning Ltd
Unit 4 Globe Road, Leeds, LS11 5QG
Tel: 0113-244 5732 **Fax:** 0113-243 6824
Directors: C. Sonden (Dir)
Immediate Holding Company: ABLE EXHIBITIONS LIMITED
Date established: 1982 **No.of Employees:** 11 - 20 **Product Groups:** 40, 66

Express Bi Folding Doors Ltd
1 Phoenix Court Lotherton Way, Garforth, Leeds, LS25 2GY
Tel: 0113-286 9191
E-mail: sales@expressbifoldingdoors.co.uk
Website: http://www.expressbifoldingdoors.co.uk
Directors: S. Bromberg (Dir)
Managers: A. Mutch (Sales & Mktg Mg), S. Longstaff (Ops Mgr)
Immediate Holding Company: EXPRESS BI FOLDING DOORS LIMITED
Registration no: 06177269 **Date established:** 2007
No.of Employees: 51 - 100 **Product Groups:** 25, 35

Date of Accounts	Aug 11	Aug 10	Aug 09
Working Capital	-190	-8	239
Fixed Assets	1m	484	176
Current Assets	2m	1m	909

F T L Company Ltd
Howley Park Road Morley, Leeds, LS27 0QS
Tel: 0113-253 0331 **Fax:** 0113-252 7528
E-mail: info@ftlsolutions.co.uk
Website: http://www.ftlsolutions.co.uk
Bank(s): Barclays, Bradford
Directors: S. Reed (MD), S. Jones (Fin), S. Jones (Dir), M. Armitage (Dir), K. Runton (Ch)
Ultimate Holding Company: F.T.L. HOLDINGS LIMITED
Immediate Holding Company: F.T.L. HOLDINGS LIMITED
Registration no: 01804205 **VAT No.:** GB 525 9019 44
Date established: 1984 **Turnover:** £2m - £5m **No.of Employees:** 51 - 100
Product Groups: 29, 30, 36, 37

Date of Accounts	Dec 10	Dec 09	Dec 08
Sales Turnover	5m	4m	5m
Pre Tax Profit/Loss	366	217	-322
Working Capital	3m	3m	3m
Fixed Assets	3m	3m	3m
Current Assets	4m	4m	4m
Current Liabilities	601	1m	379

Facultatieve Technologies Ltd
Moor Road, Leeds, LS10 2DD
Tel: 0113-276 8888 **Fax:** 0113-271 8188
E-mail: info@facultatieve-technologies.co.uk
Website: http://www.facultatieve-technologies.co.uk
Bank(s): Barclays
Directors: J. Wood (Fin), J. Keizer (Grp Chief Exec)
Managers: J. Stratton (Personnel), J. Tempest (Purch Mgr), T. Brooks (Sales Prom Mgr), N. Field (Tech Serv Mgr)
Ultimate Holding Company: BV BEHEERMIJ DE FACULTATIEVE (NETHERLANDS)
Immediate Holding Company: FACULTATIEVE TECHNOLOGIES LIMITED
Registration no: 00633222 **VAT No.:** GB 169 2853 27
Date established: 1959 **Turnover:** £20m - £50m
No.of Employees: 21 - 50 **Product Groups:** 33, 40, 42, 48, 84

Date of Accounts	Dec 11	Dec 10	Dec 09
Sales Turnover	31m	28m	20m
Pre Tax Profit/Loss	3m	2m	1m
Working Capital	6m	8m	6m
Fixed Assets	363	186	214
Current Assets	15m	16m	13m
Current Liabilities	5m	4m	3m

Fairhurst
51a St Pauls Street, Leeds, LS1 2TE
Tel: 0113-243 4671 **Fax:** 0113-242 3863
E-mail: leeds@fairhurst.co.uk
Website: http://www.fairhurst.co.uk
Bank(s): Royal Bank of Scotland, 98 Buchanan Street, Glasgow G1 3BA
Directors: P. Ward (Ptnr)
Immediate Holding Company: W.A. FAIRHURST (U.K.) LIMITED
Registration no: SC159839 **VAT No.:** GB 259 9411 23
Date established: 1995 **Turnover:** £10m - £20m
No.of Employees: 21 - 50 **Product Groups:** 54, 81, 84

Farason Ltd
Low Hall Road Horsforth, Leeds, LS18 4EF
Tel: 0113-258 6538 **Fax:** 0113-258 7149
E-mail: kdmcinnes@aol.com
Website: http://www.farasonltd.co.uk
Directors: K. Mcinnes (Prop)
Immediate Holding Company: FARASON LIMITED
Registration no: 00683734 **VAT No.:** GB 170 5410 39
Date established: 1961 **Turnover:** £1m - £2m **No.of Employees:** 11 - 20
Product Groups: 42

Date of Accounts	Mar 12	Mar 11	Mar 10
Working Capital	140	119	169
Fixed Assets	4	33	9
Current Assets	292	212	284

Fenner Drives Ltd
Hudson Road, Leeds, LS9 7DF
Tel: 0870-7577007 **Fax:** 0113-248 9656
E-mail: sales@fennerdrives.com
Website: http://www.fennerdrives.com
Bank(s): Barclays
Directors: D. Fanthorpe (MD)
Managers: D. Gornall (Sales Prom Mgr), S. Bennett (Buyer), R. Bainbridge (Tech Serv Mgr), N. Fowler (Mktg Serv Mgr)
Ultimate Holding Company: Fenner PLC
Immediate Holding Company: Fenner P.L.C.
Registration no: 00465606 **Date established:** 1949 **Turnover:** £2m - £5m
No.of Employees: 51 - 100 **Product Groups:** 23, 29, 30, 35, 45

Ferguss Home Leisure
Deneswood House High Close, Rawdon, Leeds, LS19 6HF
Tel: 0113-250 2213 **Fax:** 0113-250 2746
E-mail: neil@ferguss.com
Website: http://www.ferguss.com
Directors: N. Broom (Prop), N. Broome (Ptnr)
Turnover: Up to £250,000 **No.of Employees:** 1 - 10 **Product Groups:** 26, 27, 30, 37

Findley House Interiors
401b Selby Road, Leeds, LS15 7AY
Tel: 0113-260 0828 **Fax:** 0113-264 1800
E-mail: sales@findleyhouse.co.uk
Website: http://www.findleyhouse.co.uk
Directors: J. Wordworth (Prop)
No.of Employees: 1 - 10 **Product Groups:** 26, 33, 35, 40, 49, 66

Finning UK Ltd
Gelderd Road Morley, Leeds, LS27 7JS
Tel: 0113-253 4221 **Fax:** 0113-253 1452
E-mail: leeds@finning.co.uk
Website: http://www.finning.co.uk
Managers: R. Leeming (Reg Mgr)
Ultimate Holding Company: FINNING INTERNATIONAL INC (CANADA)
Immediate Holding Company: FINNING (UK) LTD.
Registration no: 00367090 **Date established:** 1941
No.of Employees: 101 - 250 **Product Groups:** 39, 45

Date of Accounts	Dec 11	Dec 10	Dec 09
Sales Turnover	522m	413m	334m
Pre Tax Profit/Loss	31m	10m	8m
Working Capital	98m	79m	49m
Fixed Assets	71m	81m	77m
Current Assets	236m	207m	170m
Current Liabilities	70m	38m	34m

First Group plc
Kirkstall Road, Leeds, LS3 1LH
Tel: 08456-045460 **Fax:** 0113- 3815097
E-mail: info@firstleeds.co.uk
Website: http://www.firstgroup.com
Directors: R. Harris (Comm)
Managers: C. Donnelly (Mgr), I. Hurst (Design Eng)
Immediate Holding Company: FIRSTGROUP PLC
Registration no: SC157176 **VAT No.:** GB 464 6445 28
Date established: 1995 **Turnover:** £75m - £125m
No.of Employees: 251 - 500 **Product Groups:** 72

Date of Accounts	Mar 11	Mar 10	Mar 09
Sales Turnover	6429m	6319m	6187m
Pre Tax Profit/Loss	127m	180m	200m
Working Capital	-322m	-284m	-712m
Fixed Assets	4162m	4526m	4871m
Current Assets	1105m	1066m	1046m
Current Liabilities	979m	230m	1198m

Firstneat Ltd
99 Mabgate, Leeds, LS9 7DR
Tel: 0113-245 4039 **Fax:** 0113-245 4039
Website: http://www.firstneatclothing.co.uk
Directors: B. Berry (Fab)
Immediate Holding Company: FIRSTNEAT LIMITED
Registration no: 01821948 **Date established:** 1984
Turnover: £500,000 - £1m **No.of Employees:** 21 - 50 **Product Groups:** 24

Date of Accounts	Jul 09	Jul 08	May 11
Working Capital	56	64	-10
Fixed Assets	5	6	3
Current Assets	135	120	124

Firth Powerfix
71 Gelderd Road, Leeds, LS12 6HF
Tel: 0113-245 1626 **Fax:** 0113-242 3887
E-mail: sales@powerfixonline.co.uk
Website: http://www.powerfixonline.co.uk
Bank(s): National Westminster Bank Plc
Directors: D. Young (Sales), I. Firth (MD)
Managers: N. Firth (Purch Mgr), M. Noble (I.T. Exec), M. Nobel (Mgr), F. Nicole
Ultimate Holding Company: SIG PLC
Immediate Holding Company: SIG TRADING LTD
Registration no: 01810489 **VAT No.:** GB 183 4433 61
Date established: 2005 **Turnover:** £5m - £10m **No.of Employees:** 21 - 50
Product Groups: 35, 37

Date of Accounts	Dec 10	Dec 09	Dec 08
Working Capital	N/A	N/A	200
Current Assets	N/A	N/A	200

Fishing With Style
40 Aire Grove Yeadon, Leeds, LS19 7TY
Tel: 0113-250 7244
E-mail: sales@fishingwithstyle.co.uk
Website: http://www.fishingwithstyle.co.uk
Directors: S. Cheetham (Ptnr)
No.of Employees: 1 - 10 **Product Groups:** 23, 49

Flow Training
Unity Business Centre 26 Roundhay Road, Leeds, LS7 1AB
Tel: 08450-176076
E-mail: info@flowtraining.co.uk
Website: http://www.flowtraining.co.uk
Directors: C. Nunnington (MD), C. Nunnington (Prop)
Immediate Holding Company: FLOW TRAINING CIC
Registration no: 06208424 **Date established:** 2007
Turnover: Up to £250,000 **No.of Employees:** 1 - 10 **Product Groups:** 80, 86

Date of Accounts	Jul 09	Jul 08
Sales Turnover	N/A	4
Pre Tax Profit/Loss	N/A	-0
Working Capital	-1	-0
Current Assets	2	2
Current Liabilities	N/A	3

Foster Enterprises
2 Whingate, Leeds, LS12 3BL
Tel: 0113-279 7075 **Fax:** 0113-279 8493
Directors: P. Foster (Prop)
Immediate Holding Company: NEW ARMLEY CARS LIMITED
Registration no: 04316649 **Date established:** 2001
Turnover: Up to £250,000 **No.of Employees:** 1 - 10 **Product Groups:** 24, 66

see next page

Foster Enterprises - Cont'd

Date of Accounts	Nov 10	Nov 09	Nov 08
Sales Turnover	N/A	N/A	66
Pre Tax Profit/Loss	N/A	N/A	-24
Working Capital	-30	-66	-66
Fixed Assets	6	26	33
Current Assets	3	N/A	N/A
Current Liabilities	N/A	N/A	67

Foundrometers Instrumentation Ltd
Unit 17 Enterprise Court Pit Lane, Micklefield, Leeds, LS25 4BU
Tel: 0113-287 4411 **Fax:** 0113-287 4422
E-mail: p.hargraves@foundrometers.co.uk
Website: http://www.foundrometers.co.uk
Directors: P. Hargraves (Co Sec)
Immediate Holding Company: FOUNDROMETERS INSTRUMENTATION LIMITED
Registration no: 02431393 **VAT No.:** GB 556 8613 10
Date established: 1989 **Turnover:** £500,000 - £1m
No.of Employees: 1 - 10 **Product Groups:** 37, 38, 39, 40, 44, 45, 49, 67, 84

Date of Accounts	Dec 11	Dec 10	Dec 09
Working Capital	13	26	N/A
Fixed Assets	110	110	122
Current Assets	225	177	161

Four Square Innovations
6 Hawksworth Grove, Leeds, LS5 3NB
Tel: 08444-93699 **Fax:** 08701-326527
E-mail: training@foursquareinnovations.co.uk
Website: http://foursquareinnovations.co.uk
Directors: C. Boswell (MD)
Immediate Holding Company: SQUARELODGE LLP
Registration no: OC309102 **Date established:** 2004
Turnover: Up to £250,000 **No.of Employees:** 1 - 10 **Product Groups:** 44

Date of Accounts	Apr 10	Apr 09	Aug 07
Sales Turnover	N/A	34	N/A
Pre Tax Profit/Loss	N/A	33	N/A
Working Capital	12	10	11
Fixed Assets	1	1	1
Current Assets	18	15	4
Current Liabilities	2	N/A	N/A

Freud Tooling UK Ltd
Unit 6 Whitehall Cross, Leeds, LS12 5XE
Tel: 08707-704275 **Fax:** 0870-770 4274
E-mail: sales@freudtooling.co.uk
Website: http://www.freudtooling.co.uk
Directors: S. Hendlesby (MD)
Ultimate Holding Company: FREUD POZZO SPA (ITALY)
Immediate Holding Company: FREUD TOOLING U.K. LIMITED
Registration no: 02133230 **VAT No.:** GB 461 1364 71
Date established: 1987 **Turnover:** £1m - £2m **No.of Employees:** 1 - 10
Product Groups: 36, 37

Date of Accounts	Dec 11	Dec 10	Dec 09
Sales Turnover	2m	1m	1m
Pre Tax Profit/Loss	-346	3	-27
Working Capital	276	592	603
Fixed Assets	N/A	39	58
Current Assets	387	1m	2m
Current Liabilities	77	119	75

Fusion Unlimited
Devonshire Hall Devonshire Avenue, Leeds, LS8 1AW
Tel: 0113-226 2202 **Fax:** 0113-288 8205
E-mail: kc@fusionunlimited.co.uk
Website: http://www.fusionunlimited.co.uk
Managers: D. Hall (Tech Serv Mgr), M. Curtis, E. Tuner-hardy (Personnel), J. Whitehead (Comptroller), J. Blake
Ultimate Holding Company: ADVERTISING PRINCIPLES (GROUP) LIMITED
Immediate Holding Company: THREE FALLING LIMITED
Registration no: 03364812 **Date established:** 2001
No.of Employees: 51 - 100 **Product Groups:** 81

Date of Accounts	Mar 12	Mar 11	Mar 10
Working Capital	-0	-0	-0

G D S Technologies Ltd
1 Fusion Point Ash Lane, Garforth, Leeds, LS25 2GA
Tel: 0113-286 0166 **Fax:** 0113-286 4073
E-mail: admin@gds-technologies.co.uk
Website: http://www.gds-technologies.co.uk
Directors: A. Utley (Fin), S. Utley (MD)
Immediate Holding Company: GDS TECHNOLOGIES LIMITED
Registration no: 03529380 **VAT No.:** GB 481 8400 44
Date established: 1998 **Turnover:** £500,000 - £1m
No.of Employees: 11 - 20 **Product Groups:** 38

Date of Accounts	May 11	May 10	May 09
Working Capital	205	135	203
Fixed Assets	1m	1m	1m
Current Assets	568	376	428

G K D UK Ltd
Unit 14 Bypass Park Estate, Sherburn In Elmet, Leeds, LS25 6EP
Tel: 01977-686410 **Fax:** 01977-686411
E-mail: info@gkd.de
Website: http://www.gkd.de
Directors: P. Kaschula (Fin)
Ultimate Holding Company: GKD-GERB KUFFERATH AG (GERMANY)
Immediate Holding Company: GKD (UK) LIMITED
Registration no: 03641916 **Date established:** 1998
No.of Employees: 11 - 20 **Product Groups:** 35

Date of Accounts	Dec 11	Dec 10	Dec 09
Working Capital	302	95	127
Fixed Assets	252	226	256
Current Assets	993	674	603

G M T Rubber Metal Technic Ltd
9 The Sidings Station Road, Guiseley, Leeds, LS20 8BX
Tel: 01943-870670 **Fax:** 01943-870631
E-mail: sales@gmt.gb.com
Website: http://www.gmt.gb.com
Directors: J. Twigden (Co Sec)
Managers: S. Melville (Chief Mgr)
Ultimate Holding Company: GUMMI-METALL-TECHNIC GMBH (GERMANY)
Immediate Holding Company: G. M. T. RUBBER-METAL-TECHNIC LIMITED
Registration no: 01878734 **Date established:** 1985
Turnover: £75m - £125m **No.of Employees:** 1 - 10 **Product Groups:** 29, 31, 35, 39, 40, 61, 68

Date of Accounts	Dec 11	Dec 10	Dec 09
Working Capital	586	418	401
Fixed Assets	31	48	51
Current Assets	1m	1m	675

G P Catering Equipment Manufacturers
Whitehall Industrial Estate Whitehall Road, Leeds, LS12 5JB
Tel: 0113-279 8558 **Fax:** 0113-279 8558
Directors: D. Wilson (Prop), G. Parker (Prop)
Date established: 1984 **No.of Employees:** 1 - 10 **Product Groups:** 20, 40, 41

Games Tec Ltd
Low Lane Horsforth, Leeds, LS18 4ER
Tel: 08456-044044 **Fax:** 0113-239 0072
E-mail: chrisbutler@gamestec.co.uk
Website: http://www.gamestec.co.uk
Bank(s): HSBC Bank plc
Directors: C. Butler (Dir)
Ultimate Holding Company: DANOPTRA LIMITED
Immediate Holding Company: GAMESTEC LIMITED
Registration no: 08142400 **Date established:** 2012
Turnover: £50m - £75m **No.of Employees:** 51 - 100 **Product Groups:** 49

Garcross Engineering
Brandon Building Pepper Road, Leeds, LS10 2RU
Tel: 0113-271 4230 **Fax:** 0113-271 4240
E-mail: david@garcross.co.uk
Website: http://www.garcross.co.uk
Directors: D. Crossland (MD), M. Crossland (Co Sec)
Immediate Holding Company: GARCROSS ENGINEERING LIMITED
Registration no: 04617725 **Date established:** 2002
No.of Employees: 1 - 10 **Product Groups:** 35

Date of Accounts	Mar 11	Mar 10	Mar 09
Working Capital	447	724	663
Fixed Assets	1m	1m	1m
Current Assets	1m	1m	1m

Gates R Us
Unit 17 Rossett Business Park Rodley Lane, Leeds, LS13 1BG
Tel: 0113-257 1010
Directors: A. Brooke (Prop)
Date established: 2002 **No.of Employees:** 1 - 10 **Product Groups:** 35

Geofabrics
Skelton Grange Road, Leeds, LS10 1RZ
Tel: 0113-202 5678 **Fax:** 0113-202 5655
E-mail: info@geofabrics.com
Website: http://www.geofabrics.com
Bank(s): Barclays
Directors: G. Donald (MD)
Ultimate Holding Company: GRANWOOD HOLDINGS LTD
Immediate Holding Company: HECKMONDWIKE F.B. LTD
Registration no: 02486205 **Date established:** 1990 **Turnover:** £2m - £5m
No.of Employees: 21 - 50 **Product Groups:** 23, 30

Date of Accounts	Dec 07	Dec 06	Dec 05
Pre Tax Profit/Loss	764	783	737
Working Capital	1927	1296	1098
Fixed Assets	1260	1344	1416
Current Assets	3945	2805	2805
Current Liabilities	2018	1509	1707
Total Share Capital	1500	1500	1500
ROCE% (Return on Capital Employed)	24.0	29.7	29.3

Gledco Engineered Materials Ltd
Bankfield Terrace, Leeds, LS4 2JR
Tel: 0113-275 1144 **Fax:** 0113-230 4724
E-mail: sales@usggledco.co.uk
Website: http://www.usggledco.co.uk
Bank(s): Barclays
Directors: R. Gledhill (MD)
Immediate Holding Company: USG-GLEDCO LTD
Registration no: 03135546 **VAT No.:** GB 686 8061 91
Date established: 1995 **Turnover:** £5m - £10m **No.of Employees:** 21 - 50
Product Groups: 33

Date of Accounts	Apr 11	Apr 10	Apr 09
Sales Turnover	5m	5m	5m
Pre Tax Profit/Loss	193	-189	-34
Working Capital	-535	-609	-395
Fixed Assets	2m	2m	2m
Current Assets	2m	2m	2m
Current Liabilities	2m	1m	1m

Goldfinch
The Old Barn King Lane Farm King Lane, Leeds, LS17 5PS
Tel: 0113-285 7990 **Fax:** 0113-285 7991
E-mail: medical@goldfinch.uk.com
Website: http://www.goldfinch.uk.com
Managers: M. Finch
Immediate Holding Company: S&S LIVING LIMITED
Date established: 2012 **No.of Employees:** 1 - 10 **Product Groups:** 75

J Gorstige Ltd
Unit 10 Carlton Mill Pickering Street, Leeds, LS12 2QG
Tel: 0113-279 5200 **Fax:** 0113-279 5200
Directors: J. Greenwood (MD), C. Greenwood (MD)
Immediate Holding Company: J. GORSTIGE LIMITED
Registration no: 00205019 **Date established:** 1925
Turnover: Up to £250,000 **No.of Employees:** 1 - 10 **Product Groups:** 25, 35

Date of Accounts	Dec 09	Dec 08	Dec 07
Sales Turnover	N/A	65	59
Pre Tax Profit/Loss	N/A	-15	-19
Working Capital	-72	-56	-41
Fixed Assets	N/A	1	1
Current Assets	26	26	32
Current Liabilities	N/A	63	58

Graham
22 Brown Lane West, Leeds, LS11 0DN
Tel: 0113-245 1200 **Fax:** 0113-234 0568
Website: http://www.graham-group.co.uk
Bank(s): HSBC Bank plc
Managers: P. Teesedale (Mgr)
Ultimate Holding Company: SAINT GOBAIN (FRANCE)
Immediate Holding Company: JEWSON LTD
Registration no: 00348407 **VAT No.:** GB 394 1212 63
Turnover: £500m - £1,000m **No.of Employees:** 11 - 20
Product Groups: 66

Graticule
2 Blenheim Court, Leeds, LS2 9AE
Tel: 0113-234 4000 **Fax:** 0113-246 5071
E-mail: sales@graticule.com
Website: http://www.graticule.com
Directors: J. Hogg (MD)
Immediate Holding Company: GEOSOFT LTD T/A GRATICULE
Registration no: 02544125 **VAT No.:** GB 545 6606 30
Turnover: Up to £250,000 **No.of Employees:** 1 - 10 **Product Groups:** 44

Greencore Frozen Foods
Midland Road Hunslet, Leeds, LS10 2RJ
Tel: 0113-297 6000 **Fax:** 0113-297 6001
E-mail: info@greencore.com
Website: http://www.greencore.com
Ultimate Holding Company: GREENCORE GROUP PUBLIC LIMITED COMPANY
Immediate Holding Company: LEEDS REMOVALS LTD.
Registration no: 02364956 **Date established:** 2008
Turnover: £10m - £20m **No.of Employees:** 1 - 10 **Product Groups:** 20, 62

Date of Accounts	Sep 11	Sep 10	Sep 09
Working Capital	-12	-22	-1
Fixed Assets	33	27	3
Current Assets	105	61	49

Grontmij International Ltd
Newton House 9-13 Newton Road, Leeds, LS7 4DN
Tel: 0113-237 4073 **Fax:** 0113- 2620737
E-mail: roger.pyle@grontmij.co.uk
Website: http://www.carlbro.co.uk
Directors: D. Sadler (Fin), J. Pyle (MD)
Ultimate Holding Company: GRONTMIJ NV (NETHERLANDS)
Immediate Holding Company: GRONTMIJ SERVICES LIMITED
Registration no: 02707426 **VAT No.:** GB 418 0640 71
Date established: 1992 **Turnover:** Up to £250,000
No.of Employees: 1 - 10 **Product Groups:** 80

Date of Accounts	Dec 11	Dec 10	Dec 09
Sales Turnover	46m	37m	42m
Working Capital	-717	-1m	-2m
Fixed Assets	2m	2m	3m
Current Assets	11m	14m	9m
Current Liabilities	6m	4m	4m

Guyson International Ltd (Hose and Couplings Division)
Southview Business Park Ghyll Royd, Guiseley, Leeds, LS20 9PR
Tel: 01943-870044 **Fax:** 01943-870066
E-mail: leeds@guyson.co.uk
Website: http://www.guyson.co.uk
Bank(s): HSBC Bank plc
Directors: T. Thomson (Fin), J. Thomson (Dir)
Immediate Holding Company: GUYSON INTERNATIONAL LIMITED
Registration no: 01549447 **VAT No.:** GB 168 9614 16
Date established: 1981 **Turnover:** £10m - £20m
No.of Employees: 21 - 50 **Product Groups:** 29, 30, 36

Date of Accounts	May 11	May 10	May 09
Sales Turnover	17m	14m	14m
Pre Tax Profit/Loss	938	-138	-286
Working Capital	7m	6m	5m
Fixed Assets	2m	2m	2m
Current Assets	10m	9m	8m
Current Liabilities	2m	1m	1m

H B Aluminium Fabrications Ltd
California House Leathley Road, Leeds, LS10 1BG
Tel: 0113-243 8195 **Fax:** 0113-242 2561
E-mail: admin@hb-aluminium.co.uk
Website: http://www.hb-aluminium.co.uk
Directors: I. Dewhirst (MD)
Ultimate Holding Company: H B ALUMINIUM FABRICATIONS HOLDINGS LIMITED
Immediate Holding Company: HB ALUMINIUM FABRICATIONS LIMITED
Registration no: 01548439 **VAT No.:** GB 362 0458 69
Date established: 1981 **Turnover:** £1m - £2m **No.of Employees:** 11 - 20
Product Groups: 35, 52

Date of Accounts	Apr 12	Apr 11	Apr 10
Working Capital	279	300	414
Fixed Assets	106	110	104
Current Assets	483	524	705

H L N Supplies
67 Upper Accommodation Road, Leeds, LS9 8JP
Tel: 0113-240 2000 **Fax:** 0113-240 4000
E-mail: sales@hlnsupplies.co.uk
Website: http://www.hlnsupplies.co.uk
Bank(s): National Westminster
Directors: W. Mitchell (Co Sec), H. Mitchell (Dir)
Managers: M. Egan (Tech Serv Mgr)
Registration no: 01762733 **Date established:** 1983 **Turnover:** £1m - £2m
No.of Employees: 21 - 50 **Product Groups:** 30, 49

Halcrow Group Ltd
Arndale House Otley Road Headingley, Leeds, LS6 2UL
Tel: 0113-220 8220 **Fax:** 0113-274 2924
Website: http://www.halcrow.com
Bank(s): HSBC
Managers: S. Watt (Sales Admin)
Ultimate Holding Company: HALCROW HOLDINGS LIMITED
Immediate Holding Company: HALCROW GROUP LIMITED
Registration no: 03415971 **VAT No.:** GB 169 8443 16
Date established: 1997 **Turnover:** £2m - £5m **No.of Employees:** 51 - 100
Product Groups: 84

Date of Accounts	Dec 10	Dec 09	Dec 08
Sales Turnover	331m	379m	366m
Pre Tax Profit/Loss	17m	27m	22m
Working Capital	70m	58m	-1m
Fixed Assets	29m	26m	78m
Current Assets	173m	163m	134m
Current Liabilities	55m	75m	76m

Hansen Facades Ltd
6 Mill Lane, Leeds, LS13 3HE
Tel: 0113-255 5111 **Fax:** 0161-643 1167
E-mail: sales@maghansen.com
Website: http://www.hansenfacades.co.uk

Directors: P. Nordestgaard (Co Sec), C. Addy (Fin), C. Bailey (Sales)
Managers: M. Richards (Sales Prom Mgr)
Ultimate Holding Company: HANSENGROUP A/S (DENMARK)
Immediate Holding Company: MAGHANSEN LIMITED
Registration no: 02737254 **Date established:** 1992 **Turnover:** £5m - £10m
No.of Employees: 1 - 10 **Product Groups:** 26, 35

Date of Accounts	Jun 10	Jun 09	Jun 08
Sales Turnover	8m	12m	15m
Pre Tax Profit/Loss	15	-266	-3m
Working Capital	3m	3m	1m
Fixed Assets	N/A	94	441
Current Assets	9m	7m	8m
Current Liabilities	267	323	745

James Hare Ltd
Monarch House Queen Street, Leeds, LS1 1LX
Tel: 0113-243 1204 **Fax:** 0113-234 7648
E-mail: sales@james-hare.com
Website: http://www.james-hare.com
Bank(s): HSBC Bank plc
Directors: J. Hare (MD), S. Quinn (Sales), M. Ripley (Fin), S. Hare (Sales)
Immediate Holding Company: JAMES HARE,LIMITED
Registration no: 00073195 **Date established:** 2002
Turnover: Up to £250,000 **No.of Employees:** 21 - 50 **Product Groups:** 63

Date of Accounts	Dec 11	Dec 10	Dec 09
Working Capital	-1m	-528	-645
Fixed Assets	6m	3m	3m
Current Assets	3m	4m	3m

Harewood House Trust Ltd
Harewood House Harewood, Leeds, LS17 9LG
Tel: 0113-218 1010 **Fax:** 0113-218 1002
E-mail: info@harewood.org
Website: http://www.harewood.org
Bank(s): National Westminster Bank Plc
Directors: M. Schafer (Grp Chief Exec)
Immediate Holding Company: HAREWOOD HOUSE TRUST LIMITED
Registration no: 02004021 **Date established:** 1986 **Turnover:** £2m - £5m
No.of Employees: 101 - 250 **Product Groups:** 80

Date of Accounts	Dec 11	Dec 10
Working Capital	-190	-347
Fixed Assets	240	417
Current Assets	463	546

Harrison Thompson & Co. Ltd
Yeoman House Whitehall Industrial Estate Whitehall Road, Leeds, LS12 5JB
Tel: 0113-279 5854 **Fax:** 0113-231 0406
E-mail: info@yeomanshield.com
Website: http://www.yeomanshield.com
Directors: S. Russell (Sales), A. Starkey (Fin)
Managers: M. Macloughlan (Buyer), S. Moores
Immediate Holding Company: HARRISON THOMPSON AND COMPANY LIMITED
Registration no: 02669275 **VAT No.:** GB 169 3105 61
Date established: 1991 **Turnover:** £5m - £10m
No.of Employees: 51 - 100 **Product Groups:** 23, 25, 26, 29, 30, 33, 34, 35, 36, 39, 52

Date of Accounts	Jan 12	Jan 11	Jan 10
Sales Turnover	7m	7m	8m
Pre Tax Profit/Loss	303	125	1m
Working Capital	2m	2m	1m
Fixed Assets	2m	2m	2m
Current Assets	3m	2m	3m
Current Liabilities	786	579	921

Albert Haywood & Sons Ltd
16 Ring Road West Park, Leeds, LS16 6QS
Tel: 0113-230 4050 **Fax:** 0113-278 3843
E-mail: mjh@haywoodsltd.co.uk
Website: http://www.haywoodleeds.co.uk
Directors: M. Haywood (MD)
Ultimate Holding Company: AHS HOLDINGS LIMITED
Immediate Holding Company: ALBERT HAYWOOD & SONS LIMITED
Registration no: 00948233 **VAT No.:** GB 168 9629 03
Date established: 1969 **Turnover:** £2m - £5m **No.of Employees:** 1 - 10
Product Groups: 24

Date of Accounts	Dec 11	Dec 10	Feb 10
Working Capital	511	519	428
Fixed Assets	161	167	177
Current Assets	1m	1m	1m
Current Liabilities	174	N/A	N/A

Hazel Products
Brancepeth Place, Leeds, LS12 2EG
Tel: 0113-242 6999 **Fax:** 0113-245 2954
Website: http://www.hazelproducts.com
Directors: G. Christie (Prop)
Immediate Holding Company: HAZEL PRODUCTS UK LIMITED
Registration no: 07560146 **Date established:** 2011
No.of Employees: 21 - 50 **Product Groups:** 38, 42

Heath Lambert Group
Minerva House 29 East Parade, Leeds, LS1 5PS
Tel: 0113-246 1313 **Fax:** 020-7560 3540
E-mail: jdakin@heathlambert.co.uk
Website: http://www.heathlambert.com
Directors: D. Morgan (MD), M. Slater (MD)
Managers: J. Dakin, S. Doyle (Mktg Serv Mgr)
Ultimate Holding Company: SPORTS AID YORKSHIRE AND HUMBERSIDE
Immediate Holding Company: HEATH LAMBERT LIMITED
Registration no: 01199129 **Date established:** 1975
Turnover: Up to £250,000 **No.of Employees:** 11 - 20 **Product Groups:** 80, 82

High Technology Lighting Ltd
Unit 3 Lockwood Court, Leeds, LS11 5TY
Tel: 0113-277 8077 **Fax:** 0113-277 6937
E-mail: info@high-technology-lighting.co.uk
Website: http://www.high-technology-lighting.co.uk
Bank(s): The Royal Bank of Scotland
Directors: G. Kemp (MD)
Immediate Holding Company: HIGH TECHNOLOGY LIGHTING LIMITED
Registration no: 01608563 **VAT No.:** GB 371 9404 46
Date established: 1982 **Turnover:** £1m - £2m **No.of Employees:** 11 - 20
Product Groups: 37

Date of Accounts	Mar 12	Mar 11	Mar 10
Working Capital	81	39	1m
Fixed Assets	19	17	16
Current Assets	1m	1m	1m

Hoare Lea & Partners
6th Floor Town Centre House Merrion Centre, Leeds, LS2 8LY
Tel: 0113-245 7550 **Fax:** 0113-244 3113
E-mail: iancowley@hoarelea.com
Website: http://www.hoarelea.com
Directors: I. Cowley (Ptnr)
Managers: N. Trigg, B. Richardson
Ultimate Holding Company: TOWN CENTRE SECURITIES PLC
Immediate Holding Company: TCS TRUSTEES LIMITED
Registration no: 01854244 **Date established:** 1995 **Turnover:** £1m - £2m
No.of Employees: 21 - 50 **Product Groups:** 84

C B Horne
1a Coteroyd Avenue Churwellmorley, Morley, Leeds, LS27 7TU
Tel: 0774-808 6633
Directors: C. Horn (Prop)
No.of Employees: 1 - 10 **Product Groups:** 23, 33, 52, 66

Howard Marketing
17 Bramley Business Park Railsfield Rise Bramley, Leeds, LS13 3SA
Tel: 0113-255 8533 **Fax:** 0113-255 8540
E-mail: webenquirry@howardmarketing.co.uk
Website: http://www.howardmarketing.co.uk
Directors: G. Sharp (Prop)
Registration no: 03097727 **Date established:** 1995
No.of Employees: 1 - 10 **Product Groups:** 22

Howarth Timber & Building Supplies Ltd
Prince Edwards Works Pontefract Lane, Leeds, LS9 0RA
Tel: 0113-200 0100 **Fax:** 0113-248 8474
E-mail: gfroggatt@howarth-timber.co.uk
Website: http://www.howarthtimber.co.uk
Bank(s): HSBC Bank plc
Managers: A. Smith, D. Scoffield (District Mgr)
Immediate Holding Company: HOWARTH TIMBER GROUP LIMITED
Registration no: 00067025 **VAT No.:** GB 169 3852 24
Date established: 2000 **Turnover:** £75m - £125m
No.of Employees: 11 - 20 **Product Groups:** 25, 26, 32, 33, 35, 36, 48, 49, 61, 63, 66

Date of Accounts	Mar 12	Mar 11	Mar 10
Sales Turnover	121m	121m	107m
Pre Tax Profit/Loss	1m	1m	944
Working Capital	22m	20m	20m
Fixed Assets	23m	24m	25m
Current Assets	43m	41m	38m
Current Liabilities	9m	8m	12m

Howgate Sable
1200 Century Way Thorpe Park, Leeds, LS15 8ZA
Tel: 0113-251 5033 **Fax:** 0113-251 5466
E-mail: leeds@howgate-sable.com
Website: http://www.howgate-sable.com
Directors: M. Boyle (Ptnr)
Immediate Holding Company: WORKSAFE CONSULTANCY SERVICES LIMITED
Registration no: 07213776 **VAT No.:** GB 451 5949 30
Date established: 1995 **Turnover:** £2m - £5m **No.of Employees:** 1 - 10
Product Groups: 80

Date of Accounts	Sep 11
Sales Turnover	46
Pre Tax Profit/Loss	34
Working Capital	22
Fixed Assets	7
Current Assets	51
Current Liabilities	17

D J Hudson
Fenton Dene Farm Fenton Lane, Sherburn in Elmet, Leeds, LS25 6EZ
Tel: 01937-557285
Directors: D. Hudson (Prop)
Date established: 1977 **No.of Employees:** 1 - 10 **Product Groups:** 35

Hydraulic Analysis Ltd
Mill House Hawksworth Road, Horsforth, Leeds, LS18 4JP
Tel: 0113-258 1622 **Fax:** 0113-259 0863
E-mail: a.keech@hydraulic-analysis.com
Website: http://www.hydraulic-analysis.com
Bank(s): Barclays
Directors: A. Keech (MD)
Managers: T. Lobb (Sales & Mktg Mg), E. Mullins (Fin Mgr), R. Sheller (Tech Serv Mgr)
Ultimate Holding Company: HYDRAULIC ANALYSIS GROUP LIMITED
Immediate Holding Company: HYDRAULIC ANALYSIS LIMITED
Registration no: 06930187 **VAT No.:** GB 171 4919 54
Date established: 2009 **Turnover:** £1m - £2m **No.of Employees:** 21 - 50
Product Groups: 37, 38, 39, 42

Date of Accounts	Sep 11	Sep 10
Working Capital	24	23
Fixed Assets	10	14
Current Assets	451	485

I C Blue Electronics Ltd
43-51 Cookridge Street, Leeds, LS2 3AW
Tel: 08456-440914 **Fax:** 0845-644 0916
E-mail: sales@icblue-electronics.com
Website: http://www.icblue-electronics.com
Directors: A. Lucas (MD)
Immediate Holding Company: IC BLUE LIMITED
Registration no: 04415750 **Date established:** 2002 **Turnover:** £2m - £5m
No.of Employees: 11 - 20 **Product Groups:** 67

Date of Accounts	Aug 11	Aug 10	Aug 09
Working Capital	171	188	39
Fixed Assets	174	177	15
Current Assets	1m	1m	663

I M A Ltd
Parkwell House Otley Road, Guiseley, Leeds, LS20 8BH
Tel: 01943-878877 **Fax:** 01943-879988
E-mail: sales@ima.co.uk
Website: http://www.ima.co.uk
Directors: D. Parker (MD)
Immediate Holding Company: INTERNATIONAL MOISTURE ANALYSERS LIMITED
Registration no: 03139430 **VAT No.:** GB 641 9635 24
Date established: 1995 **Turnover:** £1m - £2m **No.of Employees:** 1 - 10
Product Groups: 38, 85

Date of Accounts	Dec 07	Jun 11	Jun 10
Working Capital	-19	-108	-89
Fixed Assets	384	383	388
Current Assets	82	373	477

I M I Watson Smith Ltd
Cross Chancellor Street, Leeds, LS6 2RT
Tel: 0113-245 7587 **Fax:** 0113-246 5735
E-mail: aaith@northen.com
Website: http://www.watsonsmith.com
Bank(s): Lloyds TSB Bank plc
Directors: P. Hartley (MD), A. Haigh (Fin)
Managers: D. Rhodes (Tech), L. Blackburn (Export Sales Mg)
Ultimate Holding Company: IMI PLC
Immediate Holding Company: IMI WATSON SMITH LIMITED
Registration no: 01691122 **Date established:** 1983
No.of Employees: 51 - 100 **Product Groups:** 38

Date of Accounts	Dec 10	Dec 09	Dec 08
Pre Tax Profit/Loss	98	156	262
Working Capital	5m	5m	5m
Current Assets	5m	5m	5m
Current Liabilities	27	44	75

ibm247
Unit 2 Castle Grove Studios 18 Castle Grove Drive, Leeds, LS6 4BR
Tel: 0845-345 7859 **Fax:** 0845-3457897
E-mail: sales@ibm247.co.uk
Website: http://www.ibm247.co.uk
Managers: P. Waite (Admin Off)
Registration no: 05131766 **Date established:** 2003
Turnover: £250,000 - £500,000 **No.of Employees:** 1 - 10
Product Groups: 44

Ice Signs & Engraving
Marcon House Wyther Lane, Leeds, LS5 3BT
Tel: 0113-224 2124 **Fax:** 0113-224 2110
E-mail: sales@icesigns.co.uk
Website: http://www.icesigns.co.uk
Directors: P. Bairstow (Fin), S. Bairstow (Sales)
Immediate Holding Company: ICE SIGNS & ENGRAVING LIMITED
Registration no: 04810561 **Date established:** 2003
No.of Employees: 1 - 10 **Product Groups:** 28, 30, 39, 40, 48

Date of Accounts	Jul 11	Jul 10	Jul 09
Working Capital	58	64	58
Fixed Assets	43	41	51
Current Assets	251	220	211

Imagination Technology
Canal Wharf, Leeds, LS11 5DB
Tel: 0113-242 9814 **Fax:** 0113-242 6163
E-mail: info@imgtec.com
Website: http://www.imgtec.com
Managers: J. Stephenson (Admin Off), J. Steveson (Mgr)
Immediate Holding Company: SEGA ENTERPRISES LTD (JAPAN)
Registration no: 01306335 **VAT No.:** 613 4955 40
No.of Employees: 21 - 50 **Product Groups:** 44

Indespension Ltd
National Road Hunslet Business Park, Leeds, LS10 1TD
Tel: 0113-270 7444 **Fax:** 0113-270 8282
E-mail: leeds@indespension.com
Website: http://www.indespension.co.uk
Managers: M. Phillips (Mgr)
Ultimate Holding Company: D.R.A. LTD
Immediate Holding Company: INDESPENSION LTD
Registration no: 02125263 **Date established:** 1987
No.of Employees: 1 - 10 **Product Groups:** 39

Date of Accounts	Jun 11	Jun 10	Jun 09
Sales Turnover	17m	15m	19m
Pre Tax Profit/Loss	550	192	137
Working Capital	2m	1m	2m
Fixed Assets	4m	5m	6m
Current Assets	8m	8m	8m
Current Liabilities	3m	527	783

Industria Bearings & Transmissions Ltd
Unit 17 Enterprise Park Moorhouse Avenue, Leeds, LS11 8HA
Tel: 0113-272 3777 **Fax:** 0113-272 3888
E-mail: industria@leeds.co.uk
Website: http://www.industria.co.uk
Managers: A. Townend (Mgr)
Ultimate Holding Company: ARPOADOR LIMITED
Immediate Holding Company: INDUSTRIA BEARINGS AND TRANSMISSIONS LIMITED
Registration no: 06006121 **Date established:** 2006 **Turnover:** £2m - £5m
No.of Employees: 1 - 10 **Product Groups:** 35

Date of Accounts	Oct 11	Oct 10	Oct 09
Working Capital	654	565	493
Fixed Assets	148	157	N/A
Current Assets	2m	2m	1m

Initial Cleaning Services
6 Maple Park Lowfields Avenue, Leeds, LS12 6HH
Tel: 0113-272 1122 **Fax:** 0113-270 4703
E-mail: leeds@initialcleaning.co.uk
Website: http://www.rentokillintial.com
Directors: J. Naylor (Sales)
Managers: A. Mumford (Mgr)
Ultimate Holding Company: RENTOKIL INITIAL PLC
Immediate Holding Company: RENTOKIL INITIAL FACILITIES SERVICES (UK) LIMITED
Registration no: 02329448 **Date established:** 1988
Turnover: £75m - £125m **No.of Employees:** 101 - 250
Product Groups: 52

Date of Accounts	Dec 11	Dec 10	Dec 09
Sales Turnover	206m	199m	191m
Pre Tax Profit/Loss	5m	2m	648
Working Capital	-23m	-22m	-14m
Fixed Assets	63m	54m	37m
Current Assets	122m	47m	59m
Current Liabilities	33m	28m	20m

Albert Innes Ltd
Beckett House Enfield Avenue, Leeds, LS7 1QN
Tel: 0113-242 4949 **Fax:** 0113-242 6331
E-mail: geoffinnes@albertinnes.co.uk
Website: http://www.albertinns.co.uk

see next page

***Albert Innes Ltd** - Cont'd*
Directors: G. Innes (MD)
Managers: S. Young (Buyer)
Immediate Holding Company: ALBERT INNES LIMITED
Registration no: 00353716 **VAT No.:** GB 169 2567 28
Date established: 1939 **Turnover:** £1m - £2m **No.of Employees:** 21 - 50
Product Groups: 37

Date of Accounts	Mar 11	Mar 10	Mar 09
Working Capital	197	189	174
Fixed Assets	65	101	125
Current Assets	602	532	557

Invicta
Westland Square, Leeds, LS11 5SS
Tel: 0113-277 1222 **Fax:** 0113-271 6860
E-mail: sales@invictaforks.co.uk
Website: http://www.invictaforks.co.uk
Directors: P. Sharpe (Dir)
Immediate Holding Company: RICHARD WILSON (DENCOL) LIMITED
Registration no: 01183015 **VAT No.:** GB 405 1434 94
Date established: 1974 **Turnover:** Up to £250,000
No.of Employees: 21 - 50 **Product Groups:** 34, 35

Date of Accounts	Jan 08	Jan 07	Jan 06
Working Capital	-845	20	-69
Fixed Assets	55	34	60
Current Assets	452	864	270

Irwins Ltd
Low Hall Road Horsforth, Leeds, LS18 4EW
Tel: 0113-250 6811 **Fax:** 0113-250 6933
E-mail: paul.worcester@irwins.co.uk
Website: http://www.irwins.co.uk
Bank(s): Barclays, Leeds
Directors: D. Hutchinson (Dir), P. Worcester (Ch), P. Worcester (Dir), A. Worcester (Ch), P. Moorhouse (Dir), I. Nelson (Dir)
Ultimate Holding Company: IRWINS HOLDINGS LIMITED
Immediate Holding Company: IRWINS LIMITED
Registration no: 03145905 **VAT No.:** GB 665 3769 92
Date established: 1996 **Turnover:** £20m - £50m
No.of Employees: 101 - 250 **Product Groups:** 52

Date of Accounts	Mar 09	Mar 08	Sep 07
Sales Turnover	24m	14m	27m
Pre Tax Profit/Loss	209	80	-1m
Working Capital	800	560	-321
Fixed Assets	139	143	126
Current Assets	5m	9m	7m
Current Liabilities	2m	5m	3m

J B C Industrial Services Ltd
Howley Park Road East Morley, Leeds, LS27 0SW
Tel: 0113-220 3830 **Fax:** 0113-252 1407
E-mail: info@jbcmail.co.uk
Website: http://www.jbcindserv.co.uk
Directors: D. Parker (MD), R. Berry (Co Sec)
Immediate Holding Company: JBC Group Ltd
Registration no: 01990987 **VAT No.:** GB 301 4657 91
No.of Employees: 11 - 20 **Product Groups:** 52

Date of Accounts	Jun 08	Jun 07	Jun 06
Working Capital	310	344	267
Fixed Assets	336	265	199
Current Assets	1686	1276	1074
Current Liabilities	1376	932	807

J Hirst Electrical Engineers Ltd
New Bank Street Morley, Leeds, LS27 8NT
Tel: 0113-253 4679 **Fax:** 0113-201 2977
E-mail: sales@jhirst.co.uk
Website: http://www.jhirst.co.uk
Managers: J. Fellowes (Mgr)
Immediate Holding Company: J. HIRST ELECTRICAL ENGINEERS LIMITED
Registration no: 06579647 **VAT No.:** GB 171 6109 79
Date established: 2008 **Turnover:** £500,000 - £1m
No.of Employees: 1 - 10 **Product Groups:** 48

Date of Accounts	May 12	May 11	May 10
Working Capital	50	50	38
Fixed Assets	49	49	35
Current Assets	159	159	134
Current Liabilities	34	34	24

Jewson Ltd
Gibraltar Island Road Old Mill Business Park, Leeds, LS10 1RJ
Tel: 0113-270 2717 **Fax:** 0113-276 0691
E-mail: steve.king@jewson.co.uk
Website: http://www.jewson.co.uk
Managers: S. King (District Mgr)
Ultimate Holding Company: COMPAGNIE DE SAINT GOBAIN (FRANCE)
Immediate Holding Company: JEWSON LIMITED
Registration no: 00348407 **VAT No.:** GB 497 7184 33
Date established: 1939 **Turnover:** £2m - £5m **No.of Employees:** 11 - 20
Product Groups: 66

Date of Accounts	Dec 11	Dec 10	Dec 09
Sales Turnover	1606m	1547m	1485m
Pre Tax Profit/Loss	18m	100m	45m
Working Capital	-345m	-250m	-349m
Fixed Assets	496m	387m	461m
Current Assets	657m	1005m	1320m
Current Liabilities	66m	120m	64m

Jewson Ltd
Britannia Road Morley, Leeds, LS27 0NJ
Tel: 0113-253 8882 **Fax:** 0113-253 2824
E-mail: andy.donaldson@jewson.co.uk
Website: http://www.jewson.co.uk
Managers: A. Donaldson (District Mgr)
Ultimate Holding Company: COMPAGNIE DE SAINT GOBAIN (FRANCE)
Immediate Holding Company: JEWSON LIMITED
Registration no: 00348407 **VAT No.:** GB 497 7184 83
Date established: 1939 **No.of Employees:** 1 - 10 **Product Groups:** 66

Date of Accounts	Dec 11	Dec 10	Dec 09
Sales Turnover	1606m	1547m	1485m
Pre Tax Profit/Loss	18m	100m	45m
Working Capital	-345m	-250m	-349m
Fixed Assets	496m	387m	461m
Current Assets	657m	1005m	1320m
Current Liabilities	66m	120m	64m

Jo Malone
15-17 Queen Victoria Street, Leeds, LS1 6BD
Tel: 08701-925141 **Fax:** 0113-234 5724
E-mail: janeb@jomalone.co.uk
Website: http://www.jomalone.co.uk
Managers: J. Bromwell (Mgr)
No.of Employees: 1 - 10 **Product Groups:** 32, 63

John Hornby Skewes & Co. Ltd
Salem House Parkinson Approach, Garforth, Leeds, LS25 2HR
Tel: 0113-286 5381 **Fax:** 0113-286 8515
E-mail: info@jhs.co.uk
Website: http://www.jhs.co.uk
Bank(s): Yorkshire Bank PLC
Directors: L. Drumm (Dir)
Immediate Holding Company: JOHN HORNBY SKEWES AND COMPANY LIMITED
Registration no: 00863562 **VAT No.:** GB 168 8416 25
Date established: 1965 **Turnover:** £10m - £20m
No.of Employees: 51 - 100 **Product Groups:** 65

Date of Accounts	Mar 12	Mar 11	Mar 10
Sales Turnover	12m	12m	14m
Pre Tax Profit/Loss	-48	115	392
Working Capital	7m	7m	7m
Fixed Assets	447	409	428
Current Assets	8m	8m	8m
Current Liabilities	671	846	1m

Jones Myers LLP
St Pauls House 23 Park Square South, Leeds, LS1 2ND
Tel: 0113-246 0055 **Fax:** 0113-246 7446
E-mail: info@jonesmyers.co.uk
Website: http://www.jonesmyers.co.uk
Directors: P. Jones (Snr Part)
Immediate Holding Company: JONES MYERS LLP
Registration no: OC348053 **Date established:** 2009 **Turnover:** £2m - £5m
No.of Employees: 21 - 50 **Product Groups:** 80, 82

Date of Accounts	Mar 11	Mar 10
Working Capital	625	576
Fixed Assets	132	151
Current Assets	946	962

Jowett & Sowry Ltd
Barbondale Mill Lane, Bardsey, Leeds, LS17 9AN
Tel: 0113-263 5317 **Fax:** 0113-289 0429
E-mail: nick@jowettandsowry.co.uk
Website: http://www.jowettandsowryltd.co.uk
Directors: G. Sheard (Sales), D. Gregory (Prop), N. Ashley (MD)
Immediate Holding Company: PLANNED OFFICES LIMITED
Registration no: 00150064 **VAT No.:** GB 171 5820 68
Date established: 2018 **Turnover:** £2m - £5m **No.of Employees:** 1 - 10
Product Groups: 26, 67

Date of Accounts	Apr 11	Apr 10	Apr 09
Working Capital	-91	-25	N/A
Fixed Assets	254	307	328
Current Assets	106	140	125

K & L Fabrications
Unit 2 Aire Place Mills Kirkstall Road, Leeds, LS3 1JL
Tel: 0113-234 2359 **Fax:** 0113-271 3111
Directors: K. Shackleton (Ptnr)
No.of Employees: 1 - 10 **Product Groups:** 35

K T S Wire
Howley Park Road Morley, Leeds, LS27 0BN
Tel: 0113-253 2421 **Fax:** 0113-307 6868
E-mail: sales@ktswire.com
Website: http://www.ktswire.com
Directors: P. Hobson (Fin), S. Longbottom (MD)
Managers: K. Wiloch, T. Farley (Sales Prom Mgr)
Immediate Holding Company: KTS WIRE LIMITED
Registration no: 06748460 **VAT No.:** GB 764 2448 18
Date established: 2008 **Turnover:** £5m - £10m **No.of Employees:** 21 - 50
Product Groups: 35

Date of Accounts	Dec 11	Dec 10	Dec 09
Working Capital	-1m	-1m	-1m
Fixed Assets	513	371	350
Current Assets	2m	1m	777

Kelson Interiors
Topcliffe Lane Morley, Leeds, LS27 0HW
Tel: 0113-252 7900 **Fax:** 0113-252 7977
E-mail: info@kelson.co.uk
Website: http://www.kelson.co.uk
Directors: P. Kelly (MD)
Immediate Holding Company: KELSON INTERIORS LIMITED
Registration no: 02966549 **Date established:** 1994
No.of Employees: 1 - 10 **Product Groups:** 52

Date of Accounts	Nov 11	Nov 10	Nov 09
Working Capital	9	6	10
Fixed Assets	2	2	3
Current Assets	99	128	106

Kingfisher Lubrication
136 Meanwood Road, Leeds, LS7 2BT
Tel: 0113-209 8989 **Fax:** 0113-237 4027
E-mail: info@kingfisherlub.co.uk
Website: http://www.kingfisherlub.co.uk
Bank(s): Lloyds TSB Bank plc
Directors: J. Fisher (MD), R. Holt (Tech Serv), J. Dunne (Fin)
Immediate Holding Company: KINGFISHER (LUBRICATION) LIMITED
Registration no: 00519472 **VAT No.:** GB 169 9895 73
Date established: 1953 **Turnover:** £1m - £2m **No.of Employees:** 21 - 50
Product Groups: 36, 39, 40, 84

Date of Accounts	May 12	May 11	May 10
Sales Turnover	N/A	N/A	2m
Pre Tax Profit/Loss	N/A	N/A	-195
Working Capital	1m	1m	1m
Fixed Assets	2m	2m	3m
Current Assets	2m	1m	1m
Current Liabilities	N/A	N/A	72

Kodak Morley
Howley Park Estate Morley, Leeds, LS27 0QT
Tel: 0113-253 7711 **Fax:** 0113-283 0499
E-mail: hardingm@kpgraphics.com
Website: http://www.kodak.com
Bank(s): National Westminster Bank Plc
Directors: M. Harding (MD), P. Ball (Dir), T. Baber (MD)
Managers: D. Beech (Purch Mgr), M. Harding (Mgr)
Immediate Holding Company: KODAK P.L.C.
Registration no: 00031919 **VAT No.:** GB 349 5184 27
Turnover: £75m - £125m **No.of Employees:** 101 - 250
Product Groups: 28

KPMG UK Ltd
1 The Embankment Neville Street, Leeds, LS1 4DW
Tel: 0113-231 3000 **Fax:** 0113-231 3200
Website: http://www.kpmg.co.uk
Managers: S. Nelson (Mktg Serv Mgr), M. Stopps (I.T. Exec), J. McLaughlin (Purch Mgr)
Ultimate Holding Company: KPMG EUROPE LLP
Immediate Holding Company: KPMG UK LIMITED
Registration no: 03580549 **Date established:** 1998
Turnover: £20m - £50m **No.of Employees:** 501 - 1000
Product Groups: 80

Date of Accounts	Sep 11	Sep 10	Sep 09
Sales Turnover	698m	632m	624m
Pre Tax Profit/Loss	655	593	584
Working Capital	1m	847	419
Current Assets	23m	21m	25m
Current Liabilities	22m	20m	20m

Kuwait Petroleum International Lubricants UK Ltd
Kuwait Petroleum Lubricants Knowsthorpe Gate, Leeds, LS9 0NP
Tel: 0113-235 0555 **Fax:** 0113-248 5026
E-mail: stuart.drom@kuwaitoils.com
Website: http://www.q8oils.com
Directors: S. Drom (MD)
Managers: J. Auld (Fin Mgr), S. Hawkhead (Personnel), L. Brunyee, C. Eames, S. Haigh (Purch Mgr)
Ultimate Holding Company: KUWAIT PETROLEUM CORPORATION
Immediate Holding Company: KUWAIT PETROLEUM INTERNATIONAL LUBRICANTS (UK) LIMITED
Registration no: 02073564 **Date established:** 1986
Turnover: £20m - £50m **No.of Employees:** 51 - 100 **Product Groups:** 31

Date of Accounts	Mar 12	Mar 11	Mar 10
Sales Turnover	53m	47m	32m
Pre Tax Profit/Loss	-63	-876	-303
Working Capital	4m	4m	4m
Fixed Assets	1m	1m	1m
Current Assets	15m	14m	10m
Current Liabilities	2m	3m	2m

L P Import Export Supplies Ltd
Chartists Way Morley, Leeds, LS27 9ET
Tel: 0113-252 4999 **Fax:** 0113-238 0769
E-mail: orders@lpssupplies.com
Website: http://www.lpssupplies.com
Directors: L. Stephenson (Fin)
Immediate Holding Company: L.P. (IMPORT-EXPORT) SUPPLIES LIMITED
Registration no: 01375096 **Date established:** 1978
No.of Employees: 11 - 20 **Product Groups:** 66

Date of Accounts	Dec 11	Dec 10	Dec 09
Working Capital	2m	2m	2m
Fixed Assets	1	1	1
Current Assets	2m	2m	2m

L P M Cleaning
Cross Green Way, Leeds, LS9 0SE
Tel: 0113-248 6000 **Fax:** 01691-654789
E-mail: info@morrisholdings.co.uk
Website: http://www.morrisholdings.co.uk
Directors: N. Wilson (Dir), S. Dudley (Fin)
Managers: E. Norton (Personnel)
Ultimate Holding Company: LPM GROUP LIMITED
Immediate Holding Company: DEPENDABLE SERVICES LIMITED
Registration no: 01170023 **Date established:** 1984 **Turnover:** £5m - £10m
No.of Employees: 11 - 20 **Product Groups:** 52

Leeds Bradford International Airport Ltd
White House Lane Yeadon, Leeds, LS19 7TU
Tel: 0113-250 9696 **Fax:** 0113-250 5426
E-mail: sales@lbia.co.uk
Website: http://www.lbia.co.uk
Bank(s): National Westminster Bank Plc
Directors: A. Williams (Dir)
Managers: J. Broughton (Sales & Mktg Mg), S. Brown (Fin Mgr)
Ultimate Holding Company: LBIA HOLDING LIMITED
Immediate Holding Company: LEEDS BRADFORD INTERNATIONAL AIRPORT LIMITED
Registration no: 02065958 **VAT No.:** GB 431 0911 94
Date established: 1986 **Turnover:** £20m - £50m
No.of Employees: 101 - 250 **Product Groups:** 71

Date of Accounts	Mar 11	Mar 10	Mar 09
Sales Turnover	21m	20m	21m
Pre Tax Profit/Loss	-11m	-5m	-3m
Working Capital	11m	7m	2m
Fixed Assets	132m	136m	134m
Current Assets	19m	17m	11m
Current Liabilities	7m	9m	7m

Leeds Bronze Engineering Ltd
14 Westland Square Dewsbury Road, Leeds, LS11 5UB
Tel: 0113-271 8711 **Fax:** 0113-277 2145
E-mail: m.anwar@leedsbronze.co.uk
Website: http://www.leedsbronze.co.uk
Directors: P. Binnie (MD)
Ultimate Holding Company: Calder P.L.C.
Registration no: 00208173 **Date established:** 1974
Turnover: £50m - £75m **No.of Employees:** 51 - 100 **Product Groups:** 34, 35, 36, 66

Date of Accounts	May 11	May 10	May 09
Sales Turnover	14m	9m	11m
Pre Tax Profit/Loss	2m	767	1m
Working Capital	7m	10m	9m
Fixed Assets	798	815	968
Current Assets	11m	12m	11m
Current Liabilities	582	486	527

Leeds Equipment Service
Barrack Road, Leeds, LS7 4AB
Tel: 0113-247 7387 **Fax:** 0113-247 7392
Managers: E. Cryer (Admin Off), T. Gregson (Mgr)
No.of Employees: 21 - 50 **Product Groups:** 38, 67

Leeds Pipe Centre
7 Gelderd Trading Estate West Vale, Leeds, LS12 6BD
Tel: 0113-244 2161 **Fax:** 0113-204 8201
Website: http://www.centers.co.uk
Managers: C. Webb (District Mgr), A. Crowther (Mgr), A. Crowther (District Mgr), I. King (Mgr)
Immediate Holding Company: Wolseley Holdings P.L.C.
Registration no: 06346445 **Date established:** 1996
Turnover: £500,000 - £1m **No.of Employees:** 11 - 20 **Product Groups:** 66

Leeds Transformer Co. Ltd
Larchfield Road, Leeds, LS10 1QP
Tel: 0113-270 5596 **Fax:** 0113-272 1458
E-mail: sales@leedstransformer.co.uk
Website: http://www.leedstransformer.co.uk
Bank(s): Yorkshire Bank
Directors: N. Wilkes (Dir)
Managers: S. Cooper
Immediate Holding Company: LEEDS TRANSFORMER CO.LIMITED
Registration no: 00813216 **VAT No.:** GB 170 0805 95
Date established: 1964 **Turnover:** £500,000 - £1m
No.of Employees: 21 - 50 **Product Groups:** 37

Date of Accounts	Jul 11	Jul 10	Jul 09
Working Capital	381	318	238
Fixed Assets	148	149	81
Current Assets	504	543	580

Leeds Vacuum Formers Ltd
4 National Road Hunslet Business Park, Leeds, LS10 1TD
Tel: 0113-277 3800 **Fax:** 0113-277 5263
E-mail: nigel@leedsvacform.com
Website: http://www.leedsvacform.com
Directors: N. Coates (MD)
Immediate Holding Company: LEEDS VACUUM FORMERS LIMITED
Registration no: 03769841 **VAT No.:** GB 418 0383 65
Date established: 1999 **Turnover:** £1m - £2m **No.of Employees:** 21 - 50
Product Groups: 30

Date of Accounts	Dec 11	Dec 10	Dec 09
Working Capital	317	136	34
Fixed Assets	410	442	559
Current Assets	1m	682	992

Leeds Welding Co. Ltd
Westland Square, Leeds, LS11 5SS
Tel: 0113-271 1000 **Fax:** 0113-271 1023
E-mail: sales@leedswelding.co.uk
Website: http://www.leedswelding.co.uk
Bank(s): National Westminster Bank Plc
Directors: G. Almond (Fin), R. Eaglen (Dir), S. Addison (Dir)
Immediate Holding Company: LEEDS WELDING COMPANY LIMITED(THE)
Registration no: 00388598 **VAT No.:** GB 169 6678 96
Date established: 1944 **Turnover:** £5m - £10m **No.of Employees:** 21 - 50
Product Groups: 48

Date of Accounts	Dec 11	Dec 10	Dec 09
Sales Turnover	8m	7m	5m
Pre Tax Profit/Loss	349	267	179
Working Capital	424	391	478
Fixed Assets	501	623	680
Current Assets	3m	2m	2m
Current Liabilities	806	749	390

Leeds York & North Yorkshire Chamber Of Commerce
White Rose House 28a York Place, Leeds, LS1 2EZ
Tel: 0113-247 0000 **Fax:** 0113-247 1111
E-mail: info@yourchamber.org.uk
Website: http://www.yourchamber.org.uk
Directors: G. Williamson (Grp Chief Exec)
Immediate Holding Company: LEEDS, YORK AND NORTH YORKSHIRE CHAMBER OF COMMERCE AND INDUSTRY
Registration no: 00014183 **Date established:** 1980 **Turnover:** £2m - £5m
No.of Employees: 21 - 50 **Product Groups:** 80

Date of Accounts	Mar 11	Mar 10	Mar 09
Sales Turnover	2m	2m	2m
Pre Tax Profit/Loss	-162	5	-214
Working Capital	801	732	776
Fixed Assets	77	100	45
Current Assets	1m	1m	2m
Current Liabilities	258	459	723

Lettershop Group
Whitehall Park Whitehall Road, Leeds, LS12 5XX
Tel: 0113-231 1113 **Fax:** 0113-231 1444
E-mail: info@tlg.co.uk
Website: http://www.tlg.co.uk
Bank(s): National Westminster Bank Plc
Directors: D. McGolpin (Mkt Research)
Managers: D. Vickers (Tech Serv Mgr), I. Hopps, I. Hopps, J. Hornby
Ultimate Holding Company: W.A. SMITH (LEEDS) LIMITED
Immediate Holding Company: T.L.G. PROPERTIES LIMITED
Registration no: 00165672 **Date established:** 1995
Turnover: £20m - £50m **No.of Employees:** 101 - 250
Product Groups: 28, 81

Date of Accounts	Jan 12	Jan 11	Jan 10
Sales Turnover	23m	24m	25m
Pre Tax Profit/Loss	-916	-1m	-852
Working Capital	4m	4m	4m
Fixed Assets	5m	6m	7m
Current Assets	8m	9m	9m
Current Liabilities	2m	2m	2m

Linnet Technology
Unit 4 Enterprise Court Pit Lane, Micklefield, Leeds, LS25 4BU
Tel: 0113-287 7536 **Fax:** 0113-287 2945
E-mail: agrey@linnet-tec.co.uk
Website: http://www.linnet-tec.co.uk
Directors: J. Dornan (MD)
Managers: C. Rhodes (Mgr)
Registration no: 05372669 **Date established:** 2005
No.of Employees: 1 - 10 **Product Groups:** 37, 48, 51

Litetask Ltd
1 The Courtyards Victoria Road, Leeds, LS14 2LB
Tel: 0113-265 2651 **Fax:** 0113-265 2652
E-mail: info@litetask.co.uk
Website: http://www.litetask.co.uk
Directors: J. Barnes (MD)
Ultimate Holding Company: LEEDS KINDLY LIGHT LIMITED
Immediate Holding Company: LITETASK LIMITED
Registration no: 01029566 **Date established:** 1971 **Turnover:** £2m - £5m
No.of Employees: 11 - 20 **Product Groups:** 37, 84

Date of Accounts	Dec 11	Dec 10	Dec 09
Working Capital	224	260	281
Fixed Assets	137	183	101
Current Assets	991	1m	957
Current Liabilities	N/A	521	N/A

Lord Of The Linens
26 Kirkstall Lane, Leeds, LS5 3BH
Tel: 0113-274 2727 **Fax:** 0113-230 6541
E-mail: sales@clearancestockonline.com
Website: http://www.clearancestockonline.com
Directors: L. Manley (Ptnr)
No.of Employees: 11 - 20 **Product Groups:** 36, 49

Lorien Holdings Ltd
West One 114 Wellington Street, Leeds, LS1 1BA
Tel: 0113-245 5911 **Fax:** 0113-200 2271
E-mail: info@lorien.co.uk
Website: http://www.lorienresourcing.co.uk
Directors: D. O'Neill (Fin)
Managers: K. Sarll (Mktg Serv Mgr), R. Gorman (Personnel), S. Leyland (Tech Serv Mgr)
Ultimate Holding Company: LORIEN LIMITED
Immediate Holding Company: LORIEN RESOURCING LIMITED
Registration no: 01333388 **VAT No.:** GB 613 0779 54
Date established: 1977 **Turnover:** £125m - £250m
No.of Employees: 51 - 100 **Product Groups:** 80

Date of Accounts	Jan 12	Jan 11	Jan 10
Sales Turnover	203m	204m	165m
Pre Tax Profit/Loss	3m	3m	2m
Working Capital	4m	4m	3m
Fixed Assets	466	731	964
Current Assets	48m	56m	47m
Current Liabilities	24m	29m	26m

Lowe Engineering Ltd
Unit 5 Lockwood Park Parkside Lane, Leeds, LS11 5UX
Tel: 0113-276 0001 **Fax:** 0113-276 2848
E-mail: graeme.walker@loweengineering.com
Website: http://www.loweengineering.com
Directors: T. Lister (Sales), G. Walker (Chief Op Offcr), G. Walker (MD)
Immediate Holding Company: LOWE ENGINEERING LIMITED
Registration no: 04751609 **Date established:** 2003
No.of Employees: 11 - 20 **Product Groups:** 37, 54

Date of Accounts	Oct 09	Oct 08	Oct 07
Working Capital	-34	-5	-59
Fixed Assets	15	15	32
Current Assets	316	335	332

Lubetec UK
Airforce House Springwell Road, Leeds, LS12 1BH
Tel: 0113-246 9333 **Fax:** 0113-246 0555
E-mail: sales@lubetec.co.uk
Website: http://www.lubetec.co.uk
Managers: B. Potter
Immediate Holding Company: LUBETEC UK LIMITED
Registration no: 05151672 **VAT No.:** GB 412 1475 91
Date established: 2004 **Turnover:** £1m - £2m **No.of Employees:** 1 - 10
Product Groups: 35, 36, 39, 40, 42, 46

Date of Accounts	Aug 11	Aug 10	Aug 09
Working Capital	225	142	94
Fixed Assets	2	2	1
Current Assets	364	262	163

M F Hire Ltd
Howley Park Road East Morley, Leeds, LS27 0SW
Tel: 0113-238 0646 **Fax:** 0113-238 0582
E-mail: enq@mfhgroup.co.uk
Website: http://www.mfhgroup.co.uk
Managers: W. Twitchett (Mgr)
Ultimate Holding Company: M.F.H. ENGINEERING (HOLDINGS) LIMITED
Immediate Holding Company: M.F. HIRE LIMITED
Registration no: 01362202 **Date established:** 1978
Turnover: £10m - £20m **No.of Employees:** 1 - 10 **Product Groups:** 45, 83

Date of Accounts	Mar 12	Mar 11	Mar 10
Working Capital	365	349	328
Fixed Assets	145	166	210
Current Assets	531	532	480

M S S Fieldside Ltd
City Mills Peel Street, Morley, Leeds, LS27 8QL
Tel: 0113-252 4868 **Fax:** 0113-238 0182
Directors: A. Senior (MD)
Immediate Holding Company: MSS WORKSHOP LIMITED
Registration no: 05302385 **Date established:** 2005
No.of Employees: 1 - 10 **Product Groups:** 46, 48

Date of Accounts	Dec 10	Dec 09	Dec 08
Working Capital	-21	-20	-21
Fixed Assets	28	34	41
Current Assets	103	98	98

M S Welding
Unit 16b Deanfield Mills Asquith Avenue, Morley, Leeds, LS27 9QS
Tel: 0113-252 1763 **Fax:** 0113-218 9100
E-mail: sales@mswelding.co.uk
Website: http://www.mswelding.co.uk
Directors: M. Steel (Ptnr)
Registration no: 03128399 **Date established:** 1995
No.of Employees: 1 - 10 **Product Groups:** 46

M T R Partnership Ltd
196 Selby Road, Leeds, LS15 0LF
Tel: 0113-228 8180
E-mail: info@mtrp.co.uk
Website: http://www.mtrp.co.uk
Directors: R. Mackertich (Dir)
Immediate Holding Company: MTRP LTD
Registration no: 04310022 **Date established:** 2001
No.of Employees: 1 - 10 **Product Groups:** 80

Date of Accounts	Oct 11	Oct 10	Oct 09
Working Capital	-1	-1	1
Fixed Assets	4	4	5
Current Assets	65	69	35
Current Liabilities	66	N/A	N/A

Mckenna's Microwaves
7 Harley Drive, Leeds, LS13 4QY
Tel: 0113-257 0376
Directors: G. Miles (Prop)
No.of Employees: 1 - 10 **Product Groups:** 36, 40

Mackenzie Stuart Ltd
Fountain House 3Rd Floor, 4 South Parade, Leeds, LS1 5QX
Tel: 0113-367 2720 **Fax:** 0113-367 2721
E-mail: info@mackenziestuart.com
Website: http://www.mackenziestuart.com
Directors: I. Cundale (MD), S. Fairbank (MD)
Immediate Holding Company: Ms Realisations Leeds plc
Registration no: 06443393 **Date established:** 2007 **Turnover:** £2m - £5m
No.of Employees: 51 - 100 **Product Groups:** 80

Date of Accounts	Apr 08	Apr 07	Apr 06
Sales Turnover	3989	3507	1269
Pre Tax Profit/Loss	128	745	135
Working Capital	316	199	50
Fixed Assets	283	346	117
Current Assets	877	1087	538
Current Liabilities	561	888	487
Total Share Capital	50	50	50
ROCE% (Return on Capital Employed)	21.3	136.7	80.6
ROT% (Return on Turnover)	3.2	21.2	10.6

Maplin Electronics Ltd
3 Regent Street, Leeds, LS2 7QA
Tel: 0113-244 9200 **Fax:** 0113-243 0210
Website: http://www.maplin.co.uk
Managers: J. Featherstone (Mgr)
Ultimate Holding Company: MONTAGU PRIVATE EQUITY LLP
Immediate Holding Company: MAPLIN ELECTRONICS LIMITED
Registration no: 01264385 **Date established:** 1976
Turnover: £125m - £250m **No.of Employees:** 21 - 50
Product Groups: 37, 61

Date of Accounts	Dec 11	Dec 08	Dec 09
Sales Turnover	205m	204m	204m
Pre Tax Profit/Loss	25m	32m	35m
Working Capital	118m	49m	75m
Fixed Assets	27m	28m	28m
Current Assets	207m	108m	142m
Current Liabilities	78m	51m	59m

Marchington Properties Ltd
Millshaw, Leeds, LS11 8EG
Tel: 0113-271 1888 **Fax:** 0113-271 8487
E-mail: info@evanspropertygroup.com
Website: http://www.evanspropertygroup.com
Directors: D. Evans (Dir), D. Helliwell (Dir), R. Evans (Dir)
Registration no: SC001376 **Turnover:** £500,000 - £1m
No.of Employees: 51 - 100 **Product Groups:** 80

Markel UK Ltd
Riverside West Whitehall Road, Leeds, LS1 4AW
Tel: 08453-512600 **Fax:** 0113-245 0924
Website: http://www.markeluk.com
Managers: K. Hill (Reg Mgr), G. Wilburn (Chief Mgr)
Ultimate Holding Company: MARKEL CORP (USA)
Immediate Holding Company: MARKEL (UK) LIMITED
Registration no: 02430992 **Date established:** 1989
Turnover: £250,000 - £500,000 **No.of Employees:** 21 - 50
Product Groups: 82

Date of Accounts	Dec 11	Dec 10	Dec 09
Current Assets	601	534	479
Current Liabilities	N/A	534	479

Matrix Control Solutions
38a Main Street Garforth, Leeds, LS25 1AA
Tel: 0113-286 1420 **Fax:** 0113-287 1820
Website: http://www.matrixcontrolsolutions.com
Managers: P. Burroughs (Mgr)
No.of Employees: 11 - 20 **Product Groups:** 38, 54

Mitchell Fox & Co. Ltd
9 Whitehouse Street, Leeds, LS10 1AD
Tel: 0113-246 1000 **Fax:** 0113-246 5000
E-mail: sales@mitchellfox.co.uk
Website: http://www.mitchellfoxgroup.com
Directors: R. Hazeldine (Dir)
Immediate Holding Company: MITCHELL,FOX & COMPANY LIMITED
Registration no: 00306473 **VAT No.:** GB 169 8700 22
Date established: 1935 **Turnover:** £2m - £5m **No.of Employees:** 11 - 20
Product Groups: 67

Date of Accounts	Oct 11	Oct 10	Oct 09
Working Capital	1m	884	871
Fixed Assets	136	140	151
Current Assets	1m	1m	1m

Molson Coors Brewing Company
Headingley Office Park 8 Victoria Road, Leeds, LS6 1LG
Tel: 0113-274 4444 **Fax:** 0113-280 4403
Website: http://www.molsoncoors.co.uk
Directors: E. Reddington (MD), P. Holmes (I.T. Dir), K. Derry (Pers)
Immediate Holding Company: Coors Holdings Ltd
Registration no: 00026018 **No.of Employees:** 251 - 500
Product Groups: 21, 62

Molton Brown Emporium
41-43 County Arcade, Leeds, LS1 6BH
Tel: 08702-243942 **Fax:** 0113-242 6258
Website: http://www.moltonbrown.co.uk
Directors: M. Oldroydd (Dir)
Ultimate Holding Company: KAO CORPORATION (JAPAN)
Immediate Holding Company: MOLTON BROWN LIMITED
Registration no: 02414997 **Date established:** 1989
No.of Employees: 1 - 10 **Product Groups:** 32, 63

Date of Accounts	Dec 11	Dec 10	Dec 09
Sales Turnover	57m	57m	58m
Pre Tax Profit/Loss	2m	6m	4m
Working Capital	42m	40m	36m
Fixed Assets	6m	6m	7m
Current Assets	53m	54m	49m
Current Liabilities	5m	5m	6m

Abraham Moon & Sons Ltd
Netherfield Mills Guiseley, Leeds, LS20 9PA
Tel: 01943-873181 **Fax:** 01943-870182
E-mail: sales@moons.co.uk
Website: http://www.moon.co.uk
Bank(s): HSBC Bank plc
Directors: J. Walsh (MD)
Ultimate Holding Company: ABRAHAM MOON HOLDINGS LIMITED
Immediate Holding Company: ABRAHAM MOON & SONS LIMITED
Registration no: 00163364 **VAT No.:** GB 179 3828 14
Date established: 2020 **Turnover:** £10m - £20m
No.of Employees: 101 - 250 **Product Groups:** 23

Date of Accounts	Dec 11	Dec 10	Dec 09
Sales Turnover	15m	12m	10m
Pre Tax Profit/Loss	3m	1m	-358
Working Capital	6m	3m	3m
Fixed Assets	2m	3m	2m
Current Assets	11m	8m	6m
Current Liabilities	5m	4m	2m

Multimount
Unit D5 Wyther Lane Industrial Estate Wyther Lane, Leeds, LS5 3BT
Tel: 0113-230 2046 **Fax:** 0113-224 2046
E-mail: sales@multimount.com
Website: http://www.multimount.com
Directors: D. Rose (Fin)
Managers: P. Rose (Mgr)
Immediate Holding Company: MULTIMOUNT LIMITED
Registration no: 03197267 **Date established:** 1996
No.of Employees: 11 - 20 **Product Groups:** 25, 26, 28, 30, 36, 38, 39, 42, 46, 48, 49, 51, 52, 67, 68, 81, 84

Date of Accounts	May 10	May 09	May 08
Working Capital	-92	-35	12
Fixed Assets	62	113	106
Current Assets	287	191	311

N J Metals
270 Abbey Road, Leeds, LS5 3NE
Tel: 0113-258 2611 **Fax:** 0113-258 2886
Website: http://www.njmetals.com
Directors: N. Joy (Prop)
Immediate Holding Company: N.J. METALS & SONS LTD
Registration no: 04220235 **No.of Employees:** 1 - 10 **Product Groups:** 35, 49, 66

Nampak Carton
Cockburn Fields Middleton Grove, Leeds, LS11 5LX
Tel: 0113-276 0730 **Fax:** 0113-276 0165
E-mail: cartons@eu.nampak.com
Website: http://www.mypackaging.com
Directors: A. Bridge (I.T. Dir)
Managers: P. Taylor (Purch Mgr)
Turnover: £75m - £125m **No.of Employees:** 251 - 500
Product Groups: 27, 28

Narla Engineering & Imports Ltd
64 Danby Walk, Leeds, LS9 8JF
Tel: 0113-248 2028 **Fax:** 0113-240 5518
E-mail: paullindley@narlaengineering.com
Website: http://www.narlaengineering.com
Directors: H. Hollifield (Fin), P. Lindley (Dir)
Managers: I. Fairburn (Buyer), T. Burrow (Mktg Serv Mgr), J. O'Connor (Personnel)
Immediate Holding Company: NARLA ENGINEERING & IMPORTS LIMITED
Registration no: 00735406 **Date established:** 1962
No.of Employees: 21 - 50 **Product Groups:** 46, 48

Date of Accounts	Mar 11	Mar 10	Mar 09
Working Capital	67	151	260
Fixed Assets	223	216	297
Current Assets	493	503	913

National Holidays
Low Fields Road, Leeds, LS12 6DN
Tel: 0113-279 3000 **Fax:** 01924-898855
E-mail: m.lock@nationalholidays.com
Website: http://www.nationalholidays.com
Managers: M. Lock (Mgr)
Immediate Holding Company: NATIONWIDE ACCESS LIMITED
Registration no: 04405299 **Date established:** 2002
Turnover: £20m - £50m **No.of Employees:** 11 - 20 **Product Groups:** 45, 83

Naturelli Stone
The Ronson Building, Outer Ring Road Limewood Approach, Seacroft, Leeds, LS14 1NG
Tel: 0113-218 88 87 **Fax:** 0113-218 8966
E-mail: info@naturelli.com
Website: http://www.naturelli.com
Directors: A. warden (Sales)
Registration no: 05211315 **Date established:** 1996 **Turnover:** £2m - £5m
No.of Employees: 11 - 20 **Product Groups:** 33

Neva Consultants Car Leasing Leeds
55 Linton Rise, Leeds, LS17 8QW
Tel: 08452-062277 **Fax:** 0845-207 2277
E-mail: howard.mostyn@nevaplc.co.uk
Website: http://www.business-contract-hire.co.uk
Directors: H. Mostyn (Prop)
Registration no: OC317044 **No.of Employees:** 1 - 10 **Product Groups:** 72

Newross Impex Ltd (t/a Skopes)
New Skopes House 2 Cross Green Garth, Cross Green Industrial Estate, Leeds, LS9 0SF
Tel: 0113-240 2211 **Fax:** 0113-248 9544
E-mail: info@skopes.com
Website: http://www.skopes.com
Bank(s): Yorkshire Bank PLC
Directors: C. Hartley (Fin), S. Cope (MD)
Managers: R. Siswick
Registration no: 01530324 **VAT No.:** GB 349 4874 07
Turnover: £2m - £5m **No.of Employees:** 51 - 100 **Product Groups:** 24

Date of Accounts	Dec 09	Dec 08	Dec 07
Sales Turnover	8m	9m	8m
Pre Tax Profit/Loss	36	50	327
Working Capital	3m	3m	3m
Fixed Assets	178	137	160
Current Assets	3m	4m	4m
Current Liabilities	203	298	438

Harold Newsome Ltd
Paragon Works Elder Road, Leeds, LS13 4DJ
Tel: 0113-257 0156 **Fax:** 0113-256 4095
E-mail: clive.h.newsome@btconnect.com
Bank(s): HSBC Bank plc
Directors: H. Steward (Fin), C. Newsome (Dir)
Managers: S. Hartley (Tech Serv Mgr), M. Warhurst (Chief Buyer)
Immediate Holding Company: HAROLD NEWSOME LIMITED
Registration no: 00327454 **VAT No.:** GB 170 7368 56
Date established: 1937 **Turnover:** £2m - £5m **No.of Employees:** 21 - 50
Product Groups: 35

Date of Accounts	Mar 11	Mar 10	Mar 09
Sales Turnover	N/A	4m	6m
Pre Tax Profit/Loss	N/A	380	1m
Working Capital	4m	4m	5m
Fixed Assets	251	259	270
Current Assets	5m	6m	6m
Current Liabilities	N/A	297	773

N M P Electrics
Morley, Leeds, LS27 0ZR
Tel: 0113-204 9381 **Fax:** 0113-204 9381
E-mail: info@nmpelectrics.co.uk
Website: http://www.nmpelectrics.co.uk
Directors: N. Pope (Prop)
No.of Employees: 1 - 10 **Product Groups:** 38, 52, 67, 85

Northern Containers Ltd
Haigh Park Road, Leeds, LS10 1RT
Tel: 0113-270 8515 **Fax:** 0113-271 9687
E-mail: info@norcon.co.uk
Website: http://www.nor-com.co.uk
Bank(s): National Westminster
Directors: P. Coghlan (MD)
Ultimate Holding Company: C.H.P. HOLDINGS LIMITED
Immediate Holding Company: NORTHERN CONTAINERS LIMITED
Registration no: 02361752 **VAT No.:** GB 482 1407 59
Date established: 1989 **Turnover:** £1m - £2m **No.of Employees:** 11 - 20
Product Groups: 39, 48

Date of Accounts	Jun 11	Jun 10	Jun 09
Working Capital	702	702	682
Fixed Assets	122	153	188
Current Assets	951	1m	950

Northern Radiators Ltd
Unit J Apex Industrial Estate Parkfield Street, Leeds, LS11 5PH
Tel: 0113-243 5051 **Fax:** 0113-245 7486
E-mail: info@northernradiators.co.uk
Website: http://www.northernradiators.co.uk
Directors: N. White (Prop)
Immediate Holding Company: NORTHERN RADIATORS LIMITED
Registration no: 00168201 **VAT No.:** GB 169 5147 35
Date established: 2020 **Turnover:** £1m - £2m **No.of Employees:** 1 - 10
Product Groups: 39, 40

Date of Accounts	Sep 11	Sep 10	Sep 09
Working Capital	361	311	552
Fixed Assets	1m	1m	1m
Current Assets	512	455	658

Oddy Hydraulics Ltd
Tristran Centre Brown Lane West, Leeds, LS12 6BF
Tel: 0113-244 8787 **Fax:** 0113-244 9786
E-mail: sales@oddy-hyds.com
Website: http://www.oddy-hyds.com
Directors: M. Kane (Dir)
Immediate Holding Company: ODDY HYDRAULICS LIMITED
Registration no: 01963171 **Date established:** 1985 **Turnover:** £1m - £2m
No.of Employees: 1 - 10 **Product Groups:** 40, 45, 47

Date of Accounts	Mar 12	Mar 11	Mar 10
Working Capital	503	417	449
Fixed Assets	18	25	30
Current Assets	796	619	672
Current Liabilities	6	N/A	N/A

Oilgear Towler Ltd
37 Burley Road, Leeds, LS3 1JT
Tel: 0113-394 7300 **Fax:** 0113-394 7301
E-mail: enquiries@oilgear-towler.co.uk
Website: http://www.oilgear-towler.co.uk
Directors: A. McAleavy (Co Sec), F. Masure (Dir)
Ultimate Holding Company: OILGEAR CO (USA), THE
Immediate Holding Company: OILGEAR EUROPEAN HOLDINGS LIMITED
Registration no: 06119895 **Date established:** 2007
Turnover: £250,000 - £500,000 **No.of Employees:** 1 - 10
Product Groups: 40, 45

Date of Accounts	Dec 11	Dec 10	Dec 09
Pre Tax Profit/Loss	1m	1m	-257
Working Capital	3m	2m	-5m
Fixed Assets	10m	10m	10m
Current Assets	3m	2m	N/A
Current Liabilities	26	10	N/A

Optare Group Ltd
Hurricane Way South Sherburn In Elmet, Leeds, LS25 6PT
Tel: 0113-264 5182 **Fax:** 0113-260 6635
E-mail: info@optare.com
Website: http://www.optare.com
Bank(s): HSBC Bank plc
Directors: M. Dunn (Co Sec)
Managers: C. Wise, S. Martindale (Personnel), S. Johnson (Mktg Serv Mgr)
Ultimate Holding Company: AMAS HOLDING SA (LUXEMBOURG)
Immediate Holding Company: OPTARE GROUP LTD
Registration no: 01818255 **Date established:** 1984
Turnover: £20m - £50m **No.of Employees:** 101 - 250
Product Groups: 37, 39, 68, 84

Date of Accounts	Dec 10	Dec 09	Dec 08
Sales Turnover	46m	53m	63m
Pre Tax Profit/Loss	-1m	-6m	-4m
Working Capital	-2m	5m	6m
Fixed Assets	7m	6m	8m
Current Assets	29m	30m	35m
Current Liabilities	2m	5m	2m

Paperfix UK
33 Westway Garforth, Leeds, LS25 1DA
Tel: 0845-601 7376 **Fax:** 0845-601 8536
E-mail: chris.linton@paperfix.co.uk
Website: http://www.paperfix.co.uk
Directors: C. Linton (Dir), H. Linton (Fin)
Immediate Holding Company: PAPERFIX UK LIMITED
Registration no: 06088047 **Date established:** 2007
Turnover: Up to £250,000 **No.of Employees:** 1 - 10 **Product Groups:** 28

Date of Accounts	Mar 11	Mar 10	Mar 09
Sales Turnover	N/A	N/A	86
Pre Tax Profit/Loss	N/A	N/A	8
Working Capital	17	6	5
Fixed Assets	24	24	25
Current Assets	68	49	26
Current Liabilities	14	7	5

Parker Merchanting Ltd
John O Gaunts Trading Estate Leeds Road, Rothwell, Leeds, LS26 0DU
Tel: 08451-202454 **Fax:** 0121-503 4501
E-mail: pclarney@parker-merchanting.co.uk
Website: http://www.parker-merchanting.com
Bank(s): Barclays
Directors: N. Brook (Comm), R. Williams (Sales), L. Pattinson (MD)
Managers: F. Galvin (District Mgr), C. Homes (Mgr), P. Clarney (Chief Mgr), L. Young (Mktg Serv Mgr), P. Swain (Comm)
Ultimate Holding Company: RAY INVESTMENT SARL (LUXEMBOURG)
Immediate Holding Company: PARKER MERCHANTING LIMITED
Registration no: 00224779 **VAT No.:** GB 614 2136 80
Date established: 1927 **Turnover:** £75m - £125m
No.of Employees: 51 - 100 **Product Groups:** 22, 23, 24, 29, 30, 32, 33, 37, 39, 40, 45, 63, 66, 68

Date of Accounts	Dec 10	Dec 09	Dec 08
Working Capital	51	51	51
Current Assets	51	51	51

Pennine Castings Ltd
Pennine Industrial Estate Modder Place, Armley, Leeds, LS12 3ES
Tel: 0113-263 8755 **Fax:** 0113-279 1134
E-mail: info@penninecastings.co.uk
Website: http://www.penninecastings.co.uk
Bank(s): Royal Bank of Scotland
Directors: P. Black (Dir)
Managers: A. Brittain (Sales Prom Mgr), G. Hutchins
Immediate Holding Company: PENNINE CASTINGS LIMITED
Registration no: 02237282 **VAT No.:** GB 481 8616 21
Date established: 1988 **Turnover:** £1m - £2m **No.of Employees:** 21 - 50
Product Groups: 34

Date of Accounts	May 11	May 10	May 09
Working Capital	732	728	677
Fixed Assets	200	222	252
Current Assets	949	983	850

Pharmaceutical Packaging Leeds Ltd
129 Water Lane, Leeds, LS11 9UD
Tel: 0113-213 4343 **Fax:** 0113-213 4345
E-mail: sales@ppl-leeds.co.uk
Website: http://www.ppl-leeds.co.uk
Directors: P. McVicker (Sales & Mktg), P. Bond (Ch)
Managers: M. Bond (Sales Admin)
Immediate Holding Company: PHARMACEUTICAL PACKAGING (LEEDS) LIMITED
Registration no: 02169560 **VAT No.:** GB 477 0416 40
Date established: 1987 **Turnover:** £2m - £5m **No.of Employees:** 21 - 50
Product Groups: 30, 44

Date of Accounts	Oct 11	Oct 10	Oct 09
Working Capital	-104	-226	-138
Fixed Assets	64	95	131
Current Assets	1m	2m	2m

The Pipe Centre
7 Gelderd Trading Estate West Vale, Leeds, LS12 6BD
Tel: 01274-726058 **Fax:** 01274-726395
Website: http://www.pipecenter.co.uk
Managers: A. Crowder (Mgr), A. Crowther (District Mgr), J. Hoy (District Mgr)
Registration no: 00636445 **Turnover:** £50m - £75m
No.of Employees: 11 - 20 **Product Groups:** 40

Plastic Art Company
Unit 7 Glover Way Parkside Industrial Estate, Leeds, LS11 5JP
Tel: 0113-271 7744 **Fax:** 0113-271 9590
E-mail: info@plasticart.co
Website: http://www.plasticart.co
Directors: B. Paterson (Prop)
Immediate Holding Company: THE PLASTIC ART COMPANY (LEEDS) LIMITED
Registration no: 02459662 **VAT No.:** GB 542 3808 33
Date established: 1990 **Turnover:** £1m - £2m **No.of Employees:** 1 - 10
Product Groups: 42, 44

Date of Accounts	Jun 11	Jun 10	Jun 09
Working Capital	66	87	107
Fixed Assets	30	38	43
Current Assets	162	173	198

Ploverhill Ltd
Scotch Park Trading Estate Forge Lane, Leeds, LS12 2PY
Tel: 0113-279 4200 **Fax:** 0113-231 0956
E-mail: sales@ploverhill.co.uk
Website: http://www.ploverhill.com
Directors: V. Arthurs (Fin), R. Arthurs (Dir)
Ultimate Holding Company: SALEM GROUP HOLDINGS LTD
Immediate Holding Company: PLOVERHILL LIMITED
Registration no: 01558532 **VAT No.:** GB 362 0672 67
Date established: 1981 **Turnover:** £500,000 - £1m
No.of Employees: 1 - 10 **Product Groups:** 48

Date of Accounts	Aug 11	Aug 10	Aug 09
Working Capital	235	281	307
Fixed Assets	265	28	35
Current Assets	637	629	536

Polestar Petty
Petty House Whitehall Road, Leeds, LS12 1BD
Tel: 0113-243 2341 **Fax:** 0113-237 7924
E-mail: info@digitalprint.co.uk
Website: http://www.polestar-group.com
Bank(s): Lloyds TSB Bank plc
Directors: A. Goodwin (Co Sec), P. McMorrine (Sales), L. Atkinson (MD), B. Hibbert (Grp Chief Exec), C. Bowen (MD)
Managers: M. Thomas (Personnel), D. Craig (Purch Mgr), A. Goldthorpe (I.T. Exec)
Ultimate Holding Company: INK ACQUISITIONS LTD (CAYMAN IS)
Immediate Holding Company: TERMINUS 3 LIMITED
Registration no: 02349434 **VAT No.:** GB 545 3881 23
Date established: 1989 **Turnover:** £2m - £5m
No.of Employees: 251 - 500 **Product Groups:** 28

Date of Accounts	Sep 08	Sep 07
Pre Tax Profit/Loss	-193520	N/A
Working Capital	-145920	500
Fixed Assets	193650	240750
Current Assets	N/A	500
Current Liabilities	145920	N/A
Total Share Capital	215000	215000
ROCE% (Return on Capital Employed)	-405.4	

Portakabin Ltd (Leeds Hire Centre)
Gelderd Road, Leeds, LS12 6LZ
Tel: 0113-263 3910 **Fax:** 0113-263 3909
E-mail: james.pow@portakabin.com
Website: http://www.portakabin.co.uk
Managers: J. Pow (Mgr)
Immediate Holding Company: PORTAKABIN LIMITED
Registration no: 00685303 **Date established:** 1961
No.of Employees: 1 - 10 **Product Groups:** 35, 39

Date of Accounts	Jun 11	Jun 10	Jun 09
Sales Turnover	171m	174m	202m
Pre Tax Profit/Loss	27m	26m	30m
Working Capital	35m	25m	8m
Fixed Assets	104m	103m	113m
Current Assets	79m	76m	67m
Current Liabilities	27m	35m	29m

Poulter Partners
Rose Wharfe East Street, Leeds, LS9 8EE
Tel: 0113-285 6500 **Fax:** 0113-285 6501
E-mail: sales@poulterpartners.com
Website: http://www.poulterpartners.com
Bank(s): Lloyds TSB
Directors: M. Shaw (Dir)
Immediate Holding Company: POULTER GROUP LIMITED
Registration no: 03504088 **Date established:** 1998
Turnover: £500,000 - £1m **No.of Employees:** 51 - 100
Product Groups: 81

Powerlite Lighting Solutions Ltd
Units H34 Gildersome Spur Morley, Leeds, LS27 7JZ
Tel: 0113-289 7832 **Fax:** 0113-259 7917
E-mail: info@powerlite-lighting.com
Website: http://www.powerlite-lighting.com
Directors: A. Moss (MD), S. Thompson (Dir)
Managers: L. Bingham (Fin Mgr)
Immediate Holding Company: POWERLITE LIGHTING SOLUTIONS LIMITED
Registration no: 06892702 **Date established:** 2009
Turnover: £250,000 - £500,000 **No.of Employees:** 21 - 50
Product Groups: 37, 67

Date of Accounts	Apr 12	Apr 11	Apr 10
Working Capital	53	152	216
Fixed Assets	19	19	24
Current Assets	1m	1m	1m

Presmore Services
108 Fairfield Crescent, Leeds, LS13 3EB
Tel: 0113-255 7830
E-mail: presmore-cleaning@hotmail.co.uk
Directors: K. Perston (Prop)
Immediate Holding Company: PRESMORE CLEANING SERVICES LIMITED
Registration no: 06351606 **Date established:** 2007
No.of Employees: 1 - 10 **Product Groups:** 23, 40, 49, 52

Prime Safe Ltd
Forster Street, Leeds, LS10 1PW
Tel: 0113-276 2626 **Fax:** 0113-271 8750
E-mail: cliveh@corricoat.com
Website: http://www.corrocoat.com
Directors: C. Harper (Fin)
Immediate Holding Company: PRIME SAFE LIMITED
Registration no: 01634383 **Date established:** 1982
No.of Employees: 51 - 100 **Product Groups:** 46, 48

Date of Accounts	Jun 05	Jun 04	Jun 03
Working Capital	N/A	49	49
Current Assets	N/A	49	49

Pro2col Debt Collection
Unity Business Centre 33 Roundhay Road, Leeds, LS7 1AB
Tel: 0113-243 6969 **Fax:** 0113-322 6252
E-mail: info@pro2col.co.uk
Website: http://www.pro2col.co.uk
Directors: B. Rogers (MD)
Date established: 2005 **Turnover:** Up to £250,000
No.of Employees: 11 - 20 **Product Groups:** 44, 82

Procter Fencing
Isabella Road Garforth, Leeds, LS25 2DY
Tel: 0113-287 2777 **Fax:** 0113-242 2649
E-mail: enquiries@procterfencing.co.uk
Website: http://www.procterfencing.co.uk
Bank(s): Lloyds
Directors: J. Procter (MD), K. Kerwin (Fin)
Managers: A. Davies (Tech Serv Mgr)
Immediate Holding Company: PROCTER BROS. LIMITED
Registration no: 00144614 **VAT No.:** GB 168 8218 29
Date established: 2016 **Turnover:** £10m - £20m
No.of Employees: 101 - 250 **Product Groups:** 35, 40

Date of Accounts	Dec 11	Dec 10	Dec 09
Sales Turnover	16m	14m	14m
Pre Tax Profit/Loss	-326	-678	34
Working Capital	839	1m	2m
Fixed Assets	3m	2m	2m
Current Assets	6m	4m	4m
Current Liabilities	2m	1m	1m

ProWeigh (Yorkshire) Ltd
Garforth, Leeds, LS25 2EG
Tel: 0113-287 4336 **Fax:** 0113-287 4336
E-mail: info@proweigh.co.uk
Website: http://www.proweigh.co.uk
Directors: K. Franks (Sales)
Registration no: 04687719 **Turnover:** £500,000 - £1m
No.of Employees: 1 - 10 **Product Groups:** 38, 83

P T S Plumbing Trade Supplies Ltd
Unit 4 Gibraltar Island Road Old Mill Business Park, Leeds, LS10 1RJ
Tel: 0113-201 6900 **Fax:** 0113-201 6996
E-mail: 4209.sales@bssgroup.com
Website: http://www.ptsplumbing.co.uk
Managers: S. Jenning (Mgr)
Ultimate Holding Company: TRAVIS PERKINS PLC
Immediate Holding Company: P.T.S. PLUMBING TRADE SUPPLIES LIMITED
Registration no: 01851210 **Date established:** 1984
No.of Employees: 11 - 20 **Product Groups:** 33, 36, 40

Date of Accounts	Dec 10	Mar 10	Mar 09
Working Capital	1m	1m	1m
Current Assets	1m	1m	1m

Pudsey Transport Ltd
Howley Park Road Morley, Leeds, LS27 0BN
Tel: 08452-302130 **Fax:** 0113-236 1482
E-mail: sales@pudseytransport.co.uk
Website: http://www.pudseytransport.co.uk
Directors: J. Thompson (Co Sec), G. Thompson (Trans)
Immediate Holding Company: PUDSEY TRANSPORT LIMITED
Registration no: 02463545 **Date established:** 1990 **Turnover:** £1m - £2m
No.of Employees: 21 - 50 **Product Groups:** 72, 80, 84

Date of Accounts	Jan 12	Jan 11	Jan 10
Working Capital	81	66	-6
Fixed Assets	307	239	327
Current Assets	366	404	289

Qualitest Equipment Sales
83 The Avenue Alwoodley, Leeds, LS17 7NP
Tel: 0113-267 3035 **Fax:** 0113-230 0355
E-mail: graham.keeble@btconnect.com
Directors: G. Keeble (Prop)
Turnover: £250,000 - £500,000 **No.of Employees:** 1 - 10
Product Groups: 37

Quarmby Promotions Ltd (Katz Quarmby)
Creative House 22-23 Howley Park Business Village Pullan Way, Morley, Leeds, LS27 0BZ
Tel: 0113-393 6390
E-mail: info@thekatzgroup.com
Website: http://www.thekatzgroup.com
Directors: G. Hobson (Dir)
Ultimate Holding Company: PAPIERFABRIK AUGUST KOEHLER AG (GERMANY)
Immediate Holding Company: QUARMBY PROMOTIONS LIMITED
Registration no: 04229053 **Date established:** 2001 **Turnover:** £5m - £10m
No.of Employees: 1 - 10 **Product Groups:** 27, 28, 49, 81

Date of Accounts	Dec 10	Dec 09	Dec 08
Pre Tax Profit/Loss	N/A	N/A	-2m
Working Capital	736	738	-92
Fixed Assets	2	5	20
Current Assets	2m	1m	3m
Current Liabilities	N/A	N/A	433

R H Freight Services Ltd
Unit B Millshaw Business Living Global Avenue, Leeds, LS11 8PR
Tel: 0113-200 8000 **Fax:** 0113-200 8080
E-mail: leeds2@rhgroup.co.uk
Website: http://www.rhfreight.com
Bank(s): Barclays
Managers: D. Dallyn (District Mgr)
Ultimate Holding Company: RENNIES FREIGHT SERVICES LIMITED
Immediate Holding Company: RH FREIGHT SERVICES LIMITED
Registration no: 01336260 **Date established:** 1977
No.of Employees: 11 - 20 **Product Groups:** 72, 74, 76, 84

Date of Accounts	Dec 11	Dec 10	Dec 09
Sales Turnover	111m	106m	96m
Pre Tax Profit/Loss	800	3m	3m
Working Capital	3m	730	-148
Fixed Assets	N/A	2m	3m
Current Assets	3m	2m	3m
Current Liabilities	N/A	665	2m

R & L Enterprises Ltd
Swinnow View, Leeds, LS13 4NA
Tel: 0113-257 4208 **Fax:** 0113-256 0876
E-mail: admin@rexaloy.co.uk
Website: http://www.rexaloy.co.uk
Bank(s): HSBC
Directors: J. Bell (Dir), R. Roope (Dir)
Immediate Holding Company: R.& L.ENTERPRISES LIMITED
Registration no: 00375613 **VAT No.:** GB 169 7185 17
Date established: 1942 **Turnover:** £1m - £2m **No.of Employees:** 21 - 50
Product Groups: 42

Date of Accounts	Sep 11	Sep 10	Sep 09
Working Capital	56	7	-59
Fixed Assets	324	231	287
Current Assets	691	595	688

R S L Steeper
Unit 7 Hunslet Trading Estate Severn Road, Hunslet, Leeds, LS10 1BL
Tel: 0113-270 4841 **Fax:** 0113-271 5444
E-mail: enquiries@rslsteeper.com
Website: http://www.rslsteeper.com
Bank(s): Midland
Managers: D. Sheard (Mgr)
Immediate Holding Company: RSL STEEPER TRUSTEES LIMITED
Registration no: 06343461 **VAT No.:** GB 216 3052 04
Date established: 2007 **Turnover:** £20m - £50m
No.of Employees: 21 - 50 **Product Groups:** 38

Rackingplus Com Ltd
Systems House 4 Gelderd Buisness Park, Leeds, LS12 6QB
Tel: 0800-026 2062 **Fax:** 0113-387 4141
E-mail: mh@rackingplus.com
Website: http://www.rackingplus.com
Directors: A. Jagger (Sales), N. Procter (Sales), S. Bell-Procter (MD)
Registration no: 02421313 **No.of Employees:** 21 - 50
Product Groups: 28, 45

Rakusens Ltd
Rakusen House Clayton Wood Rise, Leeds, LS16 6QN
Tel: 0113-278 4821 **Fax:** 0113-278 4064
E-mail: reception@rakusens.co.uk
Website: http://www.rakusens.co.uk
Directors: J. Bowman (Fin), G. Knapton (Chief Op Offcr), A. Pridmore (MD), C. Pridmore (MD)
Managers: M. Gazanayi (Personnel)
Ultimate Holding Company: CAPMAC LIMITED
Immediate Holding Company: RAKUSEN'S LIMITED
Registration no: 02385824 **Date established:** 1989 **Turnover:** £5m - £10m
No.of Employees: 51 - 100 **Product Groups:** 62

Date of Accounts	Jun 12	Jun 11	Jun 10
Working Capital	503	360	212
Fixed Assets	1m	1m	1m
Current Assets	2m	2m	1m

Ramada
Mill Green View, Leeds, LS14 5QF
Tel: 08448-159108 **Fax:** 0113-232 3018
E-mail: sales.leedsnorth@ramadajarvis.co.uk
Website: http://www.ramadajarvis.co.uk
Managers: E. Cox (Chief Mgr)
Ultimate Holding Company: LEAF HOTELS LIMITED
Immediate Holding Company: EUROLANTIC LEISURE LIMITED
Registration no: 04329157 **VAT No.:** GB 260 5666 57
Date established: 2001 **Turnover:** £2m - £5m **No.of Employees:** 21 - 50
Product Groups: 69

Date of Accounts	Mar 11	Mar 10	Mar 09
Sales Turnover	2m	2m	955
Pre Tax Profit/Loss	393	382	236
Working Capital	390	470	582
Fixed Assets	8m	7m	7m
Current Assets	1m	1m	1m
Current Liabilities	95	142	211

Ratcliff Palfinger Ltd
Lotherton Way Garforth, Leeds, LS25 2JY
Tel: 0113-232 2200 **Fax:** 0113-286 5075
E-mail: barry@ratcliffe.co.uk
Website: http://www.ratcliffpalfinger.co.uk
Managers: B. Lynn (Mgr)
Ultimate Holding Company: PALFINGER AG (AUSTRIA)
Immediate Holding Company: RATCLIFF PALFINGER LIMITED
Registration no: 01019643 **Date established:** 1971
Turnover: £10m - £20m **No.of Employees:** 11 - 20 **Product Groups:** 35, 39, 45

Date of Accounts	Dec 11	Dec 10	Dec 09
Sales Turnover	15m	12m	11m
Pre Tax Profit/Loss	-780	-393	-609
Working Capital	-614	1m	1m
Fixed Assets	1m	508	528
Current Assets	6m	5m	4m
Current Liabilities	1m	643	635

Reactfast Ackroyd Plumbing and Drainage Ltd
King George Avenue Morley, Leeds, LS27 8NJ
Tel: 0113-271 9870
E-mail: apdltd@hotmail.co.uk
Ultimate Holding Company: HOMESERVE PLC
Immediate Holding Company: 001 REACTFAST SOLUTIONS LIMITED
Registration no: 04101446 **Date established:** 2000
Turnover: Up to £250,000 **No.of Employees:** 1 - 10 **Product Groups:** 36, 66

Date of Accounts	Dec 08	Dec 07	Dec 06
Sales Turnover	10m	11m	13m
Pre Tax Profit/Loss	111	-19	-493
Working Capital	-79	-218	-230
Fixed Assets	457	520	738
Current Assets	2m	2m	3m
Current Liabilities	943	950	1m

Reed Accountancy Personnel Ltd
24-26 Lands Lane, Leeds, LS1 6LB
Tel: 0113-245 9181 **Fax:** 0113-243 1845
E-mail: rapleeds@reed.co.uk
Website: http://www.reed.co.uk
Directors: J. Reed (MD)
Managers: S. Wake (Mgr), S. Wake (District Mgr)
Immediate Holding Company: Reed Personnel Services Ltd
Registration no: 00973629 **Turnover:** £125m - £250m
No.of Employees: 21 - 50 **Product Groups:** 80

Reed Social Care
5 & 5a South Parade, Leeds, LS1 5QX
Tel: 0113-394 2940 **Fax:** 0113-394 2941
E-mail: gladys.wright@reedglobal.com
Website: http://www.reed.co.uk
Directors: J. Reed (MD)
Managers: G. Wright (Comm), G. Wright (Mgr)
Registration no: 03974512 **Date established:** 1985
Turnover: £250m - £500m **No.of Employees:** 11 - 20 **Product Groups:** 80

Rehabilitation Services Ltd
Unit 7 Hunslet Trading Estate, Severn Road, Leeds, LS10 1BL
Tel: 0113-270 4841 **Fax:** 020-8785 6339
E-mail: enquiries@rslsteeper.com
Website: http://www.rslsteeper.com
Managers: S. East (Chief Mgr)
Ultimate Holding Company: RSL Steeper Holdings Ltd
Immediate Holding Company: Meditech Group Ltd
Registration no: 02110996 **No.of Employees:** 21 - 50
Product Groups: 38, 67

Reinforcements Northern
Unit 2 Moor Lane Trading Estate Sherburn In Elmet, Leeds, LS25 6ES
Tel: 01977-685411 **Fax:** 01977-684881
E-mail: hoard.robinson@theroegroup.com
Managers: H. Robinson (Mgr)
No.of Employees: 11 - 20 **Product Groups:** 35

Rema Tip Top UK Ltd
Westland Square, Leeds, LS11 5XS
Tel: 0113-277 0044 **Fax:** 0113-277 2139
E-mail: info@tip-top.co.uk
Website: http://www.rema-tiptop.co.uk
Directors: G. Mangham (Fin), E. Mason (Pers), C. Jones (Dir)
Managers: C. Gillett (Buyer), A. Smith
Ultimate Holding Company: STAHLGRUBER OTTO GRUBER GMBH & CO (GERMANY)
Immediate Holding Company: REMA TIP TOP AUTOMOTIVE UK LIMITED
Registration no: 00756475 **Date established:** 1963 **Turnover:** £5m - £10m
No.of Employees: 101 - 250 **Product Groups:** 63, 66

see next page

Rema Tip Top UK Ltd - Cont'd

Date of Accounts	Dec 11	Dec 10	Dec 09
Sales Turnover	9m	9m	9m
Pre Tax Profit/Loss	519	620	110
Working Capital	8m	8m	8m
Fixed Assets	353	385	433
Current Assets	10m	10m	9m
Current Liabilities	797	1m	845

Remploy Ltd
Manor Mill Lane, Leeds, LS11 8DF
Tel: 0113-272 6900 **Fax:** 0113-277 9170
E-mail: alan.hill@remploy.co.uk
Website: http://www.remploy.co.uk
Bank(s): National Westminster Bank Plc
Managers: A. Hill (Mgr)
Immediate Holding Company: REMPLOY LIMITED
Registration no: NF003194 **VAT No.:** GB 226 5029 79
Date established: 1995 **Turnover:** £5m - £10m
No.of Employees: 51 - 100 **Product Groups:** 29, 30, 38, 39

Rexel UK Limited
John O'Gaunts Industrial Estate, Leeds, LS26 0DU
Tel: 0113-205 9000 **Fax:** 0113-244 1523
E-mail: industrial.leeds@hagemeyer.co.uk
Website: http://www.rexel.co.uk
Bank(s): Barclays
Directors: Rose (MD)
Managers: R. Wainwright (Chief Buyer), A. Smith (Chief Buyer), C. Stockdale (District Mgr), R. Lethbridge (District Mgr), T. Beston (District Mgr)
Immediate Holding Company: W F Electrical
Registration no: 00434724 **VAT No.:** GB 171 7067 64
Date established: 1974 **Turnover:** £2m - £5m **No.of Employees:** 21 - 50
Product Groups: 67

Rhodia UK Ltd
Wortley Low Mills, Leeds, LS12 4RF
Tel: 0113-259 8000 **Fax:** 0113-259 8052
Website: http://www.rhodia.com
Directors: R. Tyler (MD)
Managers: B. Milner (Site Co-ord)
Ultimate Holding Company: RHODIA SA (FRANCE)
Immediate Holding Company: RHODIA UK LIMITED
Registration no: 00036833 **Date established:** 1992
No.of Employees: 1 - 10 **Product Groups:** 31, 32

Date of Accounts	Dec 10	Dec 09	Dec 08
Sales Turnover	111m	86m	131m
Pre Tax Profit/Loss	-19m	-21m	-603
Working Capital	1m	23m	53m
Fixed Assets	77m	76m	71m
Current Assets	46m	318m	301m
Current Liabilities	4m	5m	3m

Richard Wilson Dencol Ltd
Westland Square, Leeds, LS11 5SS
Tel: 0113-271 7588 **Fax:** 0113-277 5124
E-mail: d.wilson@leedsbronze.co.uk
Website: http://www.wilsondencol.co.uk
Bank(s): HSBC Bank plc
Directors: S. Wilson (MD), S. Deuce (Fin), C. Wilson (Fin), D. Wilson (MD)
Managers: A. Flanagan (Mktg Serv Mgr), T. Hall (Personnel)
Immediate Holding Company: RICHARD WILSON (DENCOL) LIMITED
Registration no: 01183015 **Date established:** 1974 **Turnover:** £2m - £5m
No.of Employees: 21 - 50 **Product Groups:** 37, 67

Date of Accounts	Oct 11	Oct 10	Oct 09
Working Capital	1m	683	670
Fixed Assets	N/A	116	146
Current Assets	1m	2m	2m

J A Richardson Electrical Ltd
37 St Michaels Lane, Leeds, LS6 3BR
Tel: 0113-275 9191 **Fax:** 0113-278 3872
E-mail: enq@richardsonelectrical.co.uk
Website: http://www.richardsonelectrical.co.uk
Directors: L. Richardson (MD), N. Richardson (Dir)
Managers: R. Carter (Fin Mgr), D. Baker (Buyer)
Immediate Holding Company: J.A. RICHARDSON (ELECTRICAL) LIMITED
Registration no: 00761378 **Date established:** 1963 **Turnover:** £5m - £10m
No.of Employees: 51 - 100 **Product Groups:** 52

Date of Accounts	Mar 12	Mar 11	Mar 10
Working Capital	1m	1m	1m
Fixed Assets	173	133	160
Current Assets	2m	3m	2m

Ringways Garages Leeds Ltd
Whitehall Road, Leeds, LS12 5NL
Tel: 0113-263 4222 **Fax:** 0113-279 8146
E-mail: stephen.russell@ringways.co.uk
Website: http://www.ringways.co.uk
Directors: S. Russell (MD)
Ultimate Holding Company: WORTLEA ESTATES (LEEDS) LIMITED
Immediate Holding Company: RINGWAYS GARAGES (CREWE) LTD
Registration no: 01242656 **Date established:** 1976
Turnover: £20m - £50m **No.of Employees:** 51 - 100 **Product Groups:** 82

Date of Accounts	Dec 09	Dec 08
Working Capital	-2m	-2m

Rocom
Unit 6 First Floor Temple Point Finch Drive, Leeds, LS15 9JQ
Tel: 01937-847777 **Fax:** 01937-847788
E-mail: enquiries@rocom.co.uk
Website: http://www.rocom.co.uk
Bank(s): HSBC
Directors: C. Gee (Fin)
Managers: L. Howard (Tech Serv Mgr)
Ultimate Holding Company: NYCOMM HOLDINGS LIMITED
Immediate Holding Company: MOCOR LIMITED
Registration no: 01543832 **VAT No.:** GB 349 5131 48
Date established: 1981 **Turnover:** £10m - £20m
No.of Employees: 51 - 100 **Product Groups:** 37, 79

Date of Accounts	Dec 09	Dec 08	Dec 07
Sales Turnover	43m	47m	49m
Pre Tax Profit/Loss	-378	2m	3m
Working Capital	252	4m	9m
Fixed Assets	67	249	424
Current Assets	10m	17m	21m
Current Liabilities	5m	2m	2m

Rodley Boat Centre
Canal Wharf Canal Road, Leeds, LS13 1LP
Tel: 0113-257 6132 **Fax:** 0113-257 6132
E-mail: sales@rodleyboatcentre.co.uk
Directors: C. Snowden (Ptnr)
Date established: 1969 **No.of Employees:** 1 - 10 **Product Groups:** 35, 36, 39

Rolling Center UK Ltd
Unit 5 South Leeds Trade Centre Belle Isle Road, Leeds, LS10 2DL
Tel: 08448-467320 **Fax:** 0113-201 6688
E-mail: info@rollingcenter.co.uk
Website: http://www.rollingcenter.co.uk
Managers: S. Choudhury (Sales Admin)
Immediate Holding Company: ROLLING CENTER LIMITED
Registration no: 04725217 **Date established:** 2003
No.of Employees: 1 - 10 **Product Groups:** 35

Date of Accounts	Apr 11	Apr 10	Apr 09
Working Capital	96	58	45
Fixed Assets	66	53	62
Current Assets	442	367	263

Rollo UK Ltd
2 Balm Road Industrial Estate Beza Street, Leeds, LS10 2BG
Tel: 0113-272 0444 **Fax:** 0113-272 0499
E-mail: r.evans@rollouk.com
Managers: D. Hesseldine (Chief Mgr), N. Craven (Mgr), P. Rennie (Sales Prom Mgr), R. Evans (Serv Mgr), R. Barker (Admin Off)
Ultimate Holding Company: Man Rollo BV
Immediate Holding Company: ROLLO UK LTD
Registration no: 01343019 **VAT No.:** GB 391 3015 73
Date established: 1977 **Turnover:** £2m - £5m **No.of Employees:** 1 - 10
Product Groups: 37, 67

Romar Packaging Ltd
New Market Lane, Leeds, LS9 0SH
Tel: 0113-249 4543 **Fax:** 0113-249 1803
E-mail: info@romar-packaging.co.uk
Website: http://www.romar-packaging.co.uk
Bank(s): HSBC Bank plc
Directors: K. Ellis (Fin)
Ultimate Holding Company: ROBERTS, MART (HOLDINGS) CO. LTD.
Immediate Holding Company: ROMAR PACKAGING LIMITED
Registration no: 01670321 **VAT No.:** GB 361 7472 46
Date established: 1982 **Turnover:** £5m - £10m **No.of Employees:** 21 - 50
Product Groups: 30, 31

Date of Accounts	Dec 11	Dec 10	Dec 09
Sales Turnover	10m	10m	8m
Pre Tax Profit/Loss	97	85	108
Working Capital	892	754	664
Fixed Assets	100	167	195
Current Assets	4m	4m	3m
Current Liabilities	360	185	166

Rosemont Pharmaceuticals
Rosemont House Yorkdale Industrial Park Braithwaite Street, Leeds, LS11 9XE
Tel: 0113-244 1400 **Fax:** 0113-245 3567
E-mail: infodesk@rosemontpharma.com
Website: http://www.rosemontpharma.com
Bank(s): Barclays
Directors: J. Blythe (MD), N. Salvin (Fin)
Ultimate Holding Company: ROSEMONT HOLDINGS LIMITED
Immediate Holding Company: ROSEMONT PHARMACEUTICALS LIMITED
Registration no: 00924648 **VAT No.:** GB 170 6046 83
Date established: 1967 **Turnover:** £20m - £50m
No.of Employees: 101 - 250 **Product Groups:** 31

Date of Accounts	Dec 11	Dec 10	Dec 09
Sales Turnover	36m	39m	37m
Pre Tax Profit/Loss	15m	17m	17m
Working Capital	70m	57m	39m
Fixed Assets	8m	8m	9m
Current Assets	77m	64m	46m
Current Liabilities	4m	4m	4m

Ross Care Centres Ltd
3 Royal London Industrial Estate Old Lane, Leeds, LS11 8AG
Tel: 0113-277 7007 **Fax:** 0113-277 7040
E-mail: brian.murphy@rosscare.co.uk
Directors: S. Dean (Dir)
Managers: G. Murphy (Mgr), B. Murphy (Ops Mgr)
No.of Employees: 11 - 20 **Product Groups:** 38, 67

Rotary Ltd
4-5 Buslingthorpe Green, Leeds, LS7 2HG
Tel: 0113-262 0911 **Fax:** 0113-262 6342
E-mail: john.dunwell@rotary.co.uk
Website: http://www.rotarygroup.com
Bank(s): HSBC
Directors: J. Dunwell (MD)
Managers: T. Bradder (I.T. Exec), B. Trafford, S. Musgrave
Ultimate Holding Company: HASTIE GROUP LIMITED (AUSTRALIA)
Immediate Holding Company: ROTARY YORKSHIRE LIMITED
Registration no: 00480195 **VAT No.:** GB 169 7448 11
Date established: 1950 **Turnover:** £20m - £50m
No.of Employees: 51 - 100 **Product Groups:** 52

Date of Accounts	Jun 11	Jun 10	Jun 09
Sales Turnover	32m	25m	22m
Pre Tax Profit/Loss	1m	381	741
Working Capital	4m	2m	2m
Fixed Assets	243	252	312
Current Assets	22m	18m	18m
Current Liabilities	816	776	590

Rothera & Berenton Ltd
Fairfield House 186 Armley Road, Leeds, LS12 2QH
Tel: 0113-263 2541 **Fax:** 0113-387 4820
E-mail: simon.west@paperco.co.uk
Website: http://www.paperco.co.uk
Bank(s): National Westminster Bank Plc
Directors: C. Nearing (Dir), S. Dooley (Sales & Mktg)
Managers: S. West (Sales Admin), J. Whitley (Sales Admin), K. Falcon (Comm), P. Schofield (I.T. Exec)
Ultimate Holding Company: BUNZL P.L.C.
Immediate Holding Company: BUNZL FINE PAPER
Registration no: 00783100 **Turnover:** £20m - £50m
No.of Employees: 51 - 100 **Product Groups:** 66

Sandring Ltd
224 Burley Road, Leeds, LS4 2EU
Tel: 0113-274 4488 **Fax:** 0113-275 8030
E-mail: sales@sandring.co.uk
Website: http://www.sandring.co.uk
Directors: R. Booth (MD)
Immediate Holding Company: SANDRING LIMITED
Registration no: 01393876 **VAT No.:** GB 313 5629 72
Date established: 1978 **Turnover:** Up to £250,000
No.of Employees: 1 - 10 **Product Groups:** 35, 67

Date of Accounts	Nov 10	Nov 09	Nov 08
Sales Turnover	197	269	381
Pre Tax Profit/Loss	-32	-9	-134
Working Capital	128	-40	-31
Fixed Assets	9	9	10
Current Assets	197	50	28
Current Liabilities	31	51	12

Scagliola Co.
Business Centre 231 Chapeltown Road, Leeds, LS7 3DX
Tel: 0113-262 6811 **Fax:** 0113-262 5448
E-mail: info@scagliolaco.com
Website: http://www.scagliolaco.com
Directors: M. Koumbouzis (Prop)
Immediate Holding Company: ETHICAL HOMECARE SOLUTIONS LTD
Date established: 2011 **No.of Employees:** 1 - 10 **Product Groups:** 52

Scattergood & Johnson Ltd
Lowfields Road, Leeds, LS12 6ET
Tel: 0113-243 0203 **Fax:** 0113-242 0959
E-mail: info@scatts.co.uk
Website: http://www.scatts.co.uk
Directors: I. Manson (Fin), R. Hargreaves (MD)
Ultimate Holding Company: S & J INDUSTRIES LIMITED
Immediate Holding Company: SCATTERGOOD & JOHNSON LIMITED
Registration no: 00199809 **VAT No.:** GB 613 1905 70
Date established: 2024 **Turnover:** £20m - £50m
No.of Employees: 51 - 100 **Product Groups:** 67

Date of Accounts	Apr 11	Apr 10	Apr 09
Sales Turnover	24m	19m	20m
Pre Tax Profit/Loss	423	494	318
Working Capital	3m	3m	3m
Fixed Assets	245	268	282
Current Assets	11m	10m	9m
Current Liabilities	2m	1m	1m

Schneider Electric Ltd
123 Jack Lane, Leeds, LS10 1BS
Tel: 0113-290 3500 **Fax:** 0113-290 3710
E-mail: chris.gallagher@schneider-electric.com
Website: http://www.schneider-electric.com
Managers: C. Gallagher (Chief Mgr)
Ultimate Holding Company: SCHNEIDER ELECTRIC SA (FRANCE)
Immediate Holding Company: SCHNEIDER ELECTRIC LIMITED
Registration no: 01407228 **Date established:** 1978
Turnover: £20m - £50m **No.of Employees:** 251 - 500
Product Groups: 37, 38, 40, 49, 67

Date of Accounts	Dec 11	Dec 10	Dec 09
Sales Turnover	444m	407m	357m
Pre Tax Profit/Loss	28m	37m	38m
Working Capital	188m	164m	124m
Fixed Assets	35m	32m	20m
Current Assets	314m	263m	219m
Current Liabilities	48m	39m	34m

Scientific Games International Ltd
3 George Mann Road, Leeds, LS10 1DJ
Tel: 0113-385 5000 **Fax:** 0113-385 5200
E-mail: sales@scigames.co.uk
Website: http://www.sciconnections.com
Bank(s): Barclays
Directors: T. McQueen (Fin), M. Scholey (MD)
Managers: K. Loughlin (Personnel), P. McGeever (Tech Serv Mgr), C. Allen (Mktg Serv Mgr), P. Bosworth
Ultimate Holding Company: SCIENTIFIC GAMES CORP (USA)
Immediate Holding Company: SCIENTIFIC GAMES INTERNATIONAL LIMITED
Registration no: 01754767 **Date established:** 1983
Turnover: £50m - £75m **No.of Employees:** 251 - 500 **Product Groups:** 28

Date of Accounts	Dec 11	Dec 10	Dec 09
Sales Turnover	51m	55m	52m
Pre Tax Profit/Loss	17m	20m	11m
Working Capital	53m	39m	22m
Fixed Assets	43m	43m	22m
Current Assets	66m	50m	32m
Current Liabilities	4m	4m	3m

Seaquist Closures Ltd
Leeds Twenty-Seven Industrial Estate 5 Bruntcliffe Avenue, Morley, Leeds, LS27 0LL
Tel: 0113-220 3200 **Fax:** 0113-289 7323
E-mail: brian.laurance@seaquistclosures.com
Website: http://www.seaquistclosures.eu
Directors: B. Laurance (MD), P. Glew (Co Sec)
Ultimate Holding Company: APTAR GROUP INC (USA)
Immediate Holding Company: SEAQUIST CLOSURES LIMITED
Registration no: 03005535 **Date established:** 1994
Turnover: £10m - £20m **No.of Employees:** 51 - 100 **Product Groups:** 35, 45

Date of Accounts	Dec 10	Dec 09	Dec 08
Sales Turnover	11m	11m	11m
Pre Tax Profit/Loss	-15	637	129
Working Capital	2m	3m	2m
Fixed Assets	2m	1m	1m
Current Assets	4m	4m	4m
Current Liabilities	967	853	540

Secure Welding Ltd
Unit 9 Upper Wortley Drive, Leeds, LS12 4JA
Tel: 0113-289 0999
E-mail: securewelding@btopenworld.com
Website: http://www.securewelding.co.uk
Directors: W. Diffy (MD), C. Boorman (Fin)
Immediate Holding Company: LEEDS GATES LIMITED
Registration no: 04598266 **Date established:** 2002
No.of Employees: 1 - 10 **Product Groups:** 26, 35

Date of Accounts	Dec 10	Dec 08	Dec 06
Working Capital	-1	-1	-3
Fixed Assets	4	4	6
Current Assets	4	5	5

Securerail Ltd
Unit 16 Swordfish Way Sherburn in Elmet, Leeds, LS25 6NG
Tel: 01977-681683 **Fax:** 01977-681684
E-mail: srl@securerail.co.uk
Website: http://www.securerail.co.uk
Directors: M. Hutton (Dir)
Immediate Holding Company: SECURERAIL LIMITED
Registration no: 03152204 **Date established:** 1996
No.of Employees: 1 - 10 **Product Groups:** 26, 35

Date of Accounts	Feb 12	Feb 11	Feb 10
Working Capital	-31	-22	19
Fixed Assets	738	759	782
Current Assets	130	199	173

Selby Engineering & Lifting Safety Ltd (SELS)
3 Lincoln Way Sherburn in Elmet, Leeds, LS25 6PJ
Tel: 01977-684600 **Fax:** 01977-685300
E-mail: sales@liftingsafety.co.uk
Website: http://www.liftingsafety.co.uk
Directors: D. Atkinson (MD), J. Lanagham (Fin)
Immediate Holding Company: SELBY ENGINEERING & LIFTING SERVICES LIMITED
Registration no: 05879913 **Date established:** 2006
No.of Employees: 1 - 10 **Product Groups:** 23, 25, 35, 36, 37, 38, 39, 40, 41, 43, 45, 48, 51, 66, 67, 68, 83, 84, 86

Server Parts Ltd
Unit 3 Castle Grove Studios 20 Castle Grove Drive, Leeds, LS6 4BR
Tel: 08453-457875 **Fax:** 0845-345 7897
E-mail: sales@serverparts.co.uk
Website: http://www.serverparts.co.uk
Directors: P. Wilby (MD)
Immediate Holding Company: SERVER PARTS LIMITED
Registration no: 04848373 **Date established:** 2003
Turnover: £500,000 - £1m **No.of Employees:** 1 - 10 **Product Groups:** 44

Date of Accounts	Jul 11	Jul 10	Jul 09
Working Capital	104	99	34
Fixed Assets	N/A	2	4
Current Assets	361	317	254

Sherps Fabric Printers Ltd
Unit 2b Westfield Mills Kirk Lane, Yeadon, Leeds, LS19 7LX
Tel: 0113-250 6521 **Fax:** 0113-250 6264
E-mail: ross@sharpsfabricprinters.co.uk
Website: http://www.printerfuel.com
Directors: R. Thackray (MD)
Immediate Holding Company: SHARPS FABRIC PRINTERS LIMITED
Registration no: 04395723 **VAT No.:** 796 6024 92 **Date established:** 2002
Turnover: £1m - £2m **No.of Employees:** 1 - 10 **Product Groups:** 23

Date of Accounts	Sep 11	Sep 10	Sep 09
Working Capital	215	240	206
Fixed Assets	91	101	233
Current Assets	388	440	503

Shreyas Limited
37 Stonelea Court, Meanwood, Leeds, LS7 2UH
Tel: 0113-275 2645 **Fax:** 0113-275 2645
E-mail: support@shreyas.co.uk
Website: http://www.shreyas.co.uk
Managers: S. Patchimalla (Cust Serv Mgr)
Registration no: 05231798 **Date established:** 2004
Turnover: Up to £250,000 **No.of Employees:** 21 - 50 **Product Groups:** 44

Date of Accounts	Sep 09	Sep 08	Sep 07
Working Capital	-0	-0	3
Fixed Assets	2	2	2
Current Assets	52	79	52

Signs Express
Unit 2 Leodis Court, Leeds, LS11 5JJ
Tel: 0113-243 6711 **Fax:** 0113-243 6744
E-mail: leeds@signsexpress.co.uk
Website: http://www.signsexpress.co.uk
Directors: D. Nurse (MD)
Immediate Holding Company: SIGNS EXPRESS LIMITED
Registration no: 02375913 **Date established:** 1989
No.of Employees: 1 - 10 **Product Groups:** 30, 39, 40, 80, 81, 84

Silchrome Plating Ltd
Barras Garth Road, Leeds, LS12 4JW
Tel: 0113-263 7808 **Fax:** 0113-263 2682
E-mail: sales@silchrome.co.uk
Website: http://www.silchrome.co.uk
Bank(s): National Westminster
Directors: A. Thwaite (MD)
Managers: M. Rogers (Fin Mgr)
Ultimate Holding Company: SILCHROME HOLDINGS LIMITED
Immediate Holding Company: SILCHROME PLATING LIMITED
Registration no: 03214889 **VAT No.:** GB 675 2444 21
Date established: 1996 **Turnover:** £1m - £2m **No.of Employees:** 21 - 50
Product Groups: 48

Date of Accounts	Mar 11	Mar 10	Mar 09
Working Capital	238	281	284
Fixed Assets	297	312	325
Current Assets	836	831	798

SKF Economos UK Ltd Leeds Branch
Unit 5-6, Armley Link Armley Road, Leeds, LS12 2QN
Tel: 0113-231 0303 **Fax:** 0113-231 0395
E-mail: leeds@economos.com
Website: http://www.economos.com
Directors: R. Kumra (MD), P. Chambers (MD)
Ultimate Holding Company: Economos AG (Austria)
Immediate Holding Company: Economos Ltd
Registration no: 02414449 **VAT No.:** GB 532 1465 72
Turnover: £2m - £5m **No.of Employees:** 1 - 10 **Product Groups:** 29, 30, 33, 40, 42, 48

Specialist Computer Centres Ltd
Applied House Killingbeck Drive, York Road, Leeds, LS14 6UF
Tel: 0113-240 5250 **Fax:** 0113-240 1093
Website: http://www.scc.com
Bank(s): HSBC Bank plc
Directors: I. Scott (Sales), D. Lewis (MD), P. Rigby (Ch)
Managers: L. Hatersly (Sales Prom Mgr), A. Sadler (Sales Prom Mgr), R. Boardall
Immediate Holding Company: SPECIALIST COMPUTER HOLDINGS LTD
Registration no: 01206327 **Turnover:** £5m - £10m
No.of Employees: 11 - 20 **Product Groups:** 26, 44, 67, 81

Specialist Switchgear Systems Ltd
Unit 2 Royds Park, Leeds, LS12 4TU
Tel: 0113-231 9911 **Fax:** 0113-231 9900
Directors: G. Hoy (MD)
Immediate Holding Company: SPECIALIST SWITCHGEAR SYSTEMS LIMITED
Registration no: 01853261 **Date established:** 1984
No.of Employees: 1 - 10 **Product Groups:** 36, 40

Date of Accounts	Dec 11	Dec 10	Dec 09
Working Capital	1m	1m	1m
Fixed Assets	120	127	136
Current Assets	2m	1m	1m

Speedy Survey
Westgate Link Wellington Bridge Street, Leeds, LS3 1LW
Tel: 0113-244 8555 **Fax:** 0113-247 1977
E-mail: darren.hallas@speedyservices.com
Website: http://www.speedyhire.com
Managers: D. Hallas (Reg Mgr)
Immediate Holding Company: JLS (OXFORD COURT) LIMITED
Registration no: SC046005 **Date established:** 2004 **Turnover:** £2m - £5m
No.of Employees: 21 - 50 **Product Groups:** 83

Spentex B C A Ltd
Unit 7 First Avenue Sherburn In Elmet, Leeds, LS25 6PD
Tel: 01977-680697 **Fax:** 01937-541237
E-mail: sales@spentex.co.uk
Website: http://www.spentex.co.uk
Directors: S. Spencer (MD)
Immediate Holding Company: SPENTEX B.C.A. LIMITED
Registration no: 01554450 **VAT No.:** GB 687 0834 96
Date established: 1981 **Turnover:** £500,000 - £1m
No.of Employees: 1 - 10 **Product Groups:** 24, 32, 63

Date of Accounts	Jun 11	Jun 10	Jun 09
Working Capital	8	24	23
Fixed Assets	30	32	31
Current Assets	135	135	142

David Spirett
Stone Barn Workshops Park House Farm, Aberford, Leeds, LS25 3DH
Tel: 0113-281 3338 **Fax:** 0113-393 5582
E-mail: davidspirett@btconnect.com
Website: http://www.landrovermad.co.uk
Directors: D. Spirett (Prop)
Immediate Holding Company: AWESUM LTD
Date established: 2010 **No.of Employees:** 1 - 10 **Product Groups:** 41

Date of Accounts	Jun 11
Working Capital	-9
Fixed Assets	1
Current Assets	10

Sports Coach UK
114 Cardigan Road, Leeds, LS6 3BJ
Tel: 0113-274 4802 **Fax:** 0113-275 5019
E-mail: tbyrne@sportscoachuk.org
Website: http://www.sportscoachuk.org
Bank(s): Nat West
Directors: T. Byrne (Grp Chief Exec), C. Hawe (MD), B. Smith (Dir)
Managers: G. Bishop (Mgr), Z. Marlow (Mktg Serv Mgr)
Immediate Holding Company: NATIONAL COACHING FOUNDATION(THE)
Registration no: 02092919 **VAT No.:** GB 482 0643 52
Date established: 1987 **Turnover:** £5m - £10m
No.of Employees: 51 - 100 **Product Groups:** 87

Date of Accounts	Mar 08	Mar 07	Mar 06
Sales Turnover	9013	7734	6942
Pre Tax Profit/Loss	1151	202	532
Working Capital	2983	1345	895
Fixed Assets	405	1077	1511
Current Assets	7531	6099	5675
Current Liabilities	4548	4754	4780
ROCE% (Return on Capital Employed)	34.0	8.3	22.1
ROT% (Return on Turnover)	12.8	2.6	7.7

Spray Plant
17 Hales Road, Leeds, LS12 4PL
Tel: 0113-231 0500 **Fax:** 0113-231 0102
E-mail: trevor@sprayplant.co.uk
Website: http://www.sprayplant.co.uk
Directors: T. Smith (MD)
Immediate Holding Company: SPRAY PLANT (UK) LIMITED
Registration no: 02906793 **Date established:** 1994
No.of Employees: 11 - 20 **Product Groups:** 38, 42

Date of Accounts	Apr 11	Apr 10	Apr 09
Working Capital	315	218	169
Fixed Assets	192	213	267
Current Assets	703	594	572

Squeak & Bubbles Leeds Window Cleaners
23 Darkwood Way Shadwell, Leeds, LS17 8BQ
Tel: 0113-266 9639
E-mail: info@squeakandbubbles.co.uk
Website: http://www.squeakandbubbles.co.uk
Directors: D. Pryce (Prop)
Date established: 2008 **No.of Employees:** 1 - 10 **Product Groups:** 52

Stalum Engineering Ltd
3 Darnall Works Leathley Road, Leeds, LS10 1BG
Tel: 0113-242 2289 **Fax:** 0113-234 7951
E-mail: enquiries@stalum.co.uk
Website: http://www.stalum.co.uk
Directors: D. Quin Collinson (Fin), C. Collinson (Dir)
Immediate Holding Company: STALUM ENGINEERING LIMITED
Registration no: 02715298 **Date established:** 1992
Turnover: £500,000 - £1m **No.of Employees:** 1 - 10 **Product Groups:** 45, 84

Date of Accounts	May 12	May 11	May 10
Working Capital	5	1	1
Fixed Assets	6	8	7
Current Assets	154	169	143

Stanley Decorating Products
135 Gelderd Road, Leeds, LS12 6BE
Tel: 0113-251 1450 **Fax:** 0113-243 3910
Website: http://www.stanleyworks.com
Bank(s): Barclays
Managers: W. Dowgill (Plant)
Immediate Holding Company: Stanley UK Ltd
Registration no: 00170466 **VAT No.:** GB 613 4028 79
Turnover: £20m - £50m **No.of Employees:** 101 - 250 **Product Groups:** 49

Charles F Stead & Co. Ltd
Tannery Sheepscar Street North, Leeds, LS7 2BY
Tel: 0113-262 1005 **Fax:** 0113-262 6309
E-mail: johnt@cfstead.com
Website: http://www.cfstead.com
Bank(s): National Westminster Bank Plc
Directors: J. Thompson (Fin), C. Hodgson (Chief Op Offcr), D. Bailey (Sales)
Managers: M. Harris (Tech Serv Mgr)
Ultimate Holding Company: CHARLES F STEAD (HOLDINGS) LIMITED
Immediate Holding Company: CHARLES F.STEAD & COMPANY,LIMITED
Registration no: 00080604 **VAT No.:** GB 168 8090 29
Date established: 2004 **Turnover:** £10m - £20m
No.of Employees: 51 - 100 **Product Groups:** 22

Date of Accounts	Dec 11	Dec 10	Dec 09
Sales Turnover	12m	11m	7m
Pre Tax Profit/Loss	-354	1m	301
Working Capital	6m	5m	5m
Fixed Assets	1m	2m	1m
Current Assets	7m	6m	5m
Current Liabilities	698	504	206

Steel Product Supplies
Unit 5 South Leeds Trade Centre Belle Isle Road, Hunslet, Leeds, LS10 2DL
Tel: 0113-201 6677 **Fax:** 0113-201 6688
E-mail: info@steelproductsupplies.co.uk
Website: http://www.steelproductsupplies.co.uk
Directors: S. Smith (MD)
Registration no: 06384063 **Date established:** 2007
No.of Employees: 1 - 10 **Product Groups:** 34, 49

Stonebridge Chinese Services Ltd
131 Stonebridge Lane Farnley, Leeds, LS12 5AQ
Tel: 0113-229 8786
E-mail: info@s-c-s-uk.com
Website: http://www.s-c-s-uk.com
Directors: J. Twyman (MD), P. Twyman (Fin)
Immediate Holding Company: STONEBRIDGE CHINESE SERVICES LIMITED
Registration no: 05257797 **Date established:** 2004
No.of Employees: 1 - 10 **Product Groups:** 86

Date of Accounts	Oct 11	Oct 10	Oct 09
Working Capital	-3	-4	-2
Fixed Assets	6	6	4
Current Assets	4	3	1

Stuart Hirst Ltd
Chelwood House Chelwood Drive, Leeds, LS8 2AT
Tel: 0113-246 3060 **Fax:** 0113-236 9977
E-mail: adverts@stuarthirst.co.uk
Website: http://www.stuarthirst.co.uk
Directors: A. Jackson (Fin), M. Wappett (Dir)
Immediate Holding Company: STUART HIRST LIMITED
Registration no: 02273942 **Date established:** 1988
No.of Employees: 1 - 10 **Product Groups:** 81

Date of Accounts	Oct 11	Oct 10	Oct 09
Working Capital	272	271	219
Fixed Assets	37	38	38
Current Assets	407	456	424

Sub Scan
Unit 15 Silver Court Intercity Way, Leeds, LS13 4LY
Tel: 0113-257 1444 **Fax:** 0113-219 4919
E-mail: sales@subscan.com
Website: http://www.subscan.com
Directors: R. Mason (Dir)
Immediate Holding Company: SUBSCAN (SUB-SITE) SURVEYS LIMITED
Registration no: 05812307 **Date established:** 2006
No.of Employees: 1 - 10 **Product Groups:** 30, 32, 33, 35, 36, 38, 39, 40, 41, 45, 47, 48, 51, 52, 54, 66, 72, 80, 84, 85

Date of Accounts	May 11	May 10	May 09
Working Capital	-0	-0	-0
Current Assets	4	4	4
Current Liabilities	4	N/A	N/A

Sun 247 (a division of Ware247 Ltd)
Unit 2 Castle Grove Studios 18 Castle Grove Drive, Leeds, LS6 4BR
Tel: 0845-3457859 **Fax:** 0845-3457897
E-mail: sales@sun247.co.uk
Website: http://www.sun247.co.uk
Managers: P. Waite (Sales Prom)
Registration no: 05131766 **Date established:** 2006
Turnover: £250,000 - £500,000 **No.of Employees:** 1 - 10
Product Groups: 44

Sunglassesuk.com
FREEPOST NEA9470, Leeds, LS1 1YY
Tel: 0845-6772219
E-mail: info@sunglassesuk.com
Website: http://www.sunglassesuk.com
Registration no: 03936204 **Product Groups:** 38, 65

Supasplit Ltd
5 Highcliffe Industrial Estate Bruntcliffe Lane, Morley, Leeds, LS27 9LR
Tel: 0113-252 2033 **Fax:** 0113-253 4102
E-mail: sales@supasplit.com
Website: http://www.supasplit.com
Directors: R. Holmes (Dir)
Ultimate Holding Company: KIVETON PARK (HOLDINGS) LIMITED
Immediate Holding Company: KIVETON PARK (SUPASPLIT) LIMITED
Registration no: 01590807 **VAT No.:** GB 034 5885 94
Date established: 1981 **Turnover:** £250,000 - £500,000
No.of Employees: 1 - 10 **Product Groups:** 33, 36, 37, 42, 43

Date of Accounts	Jun 11	Jun 10	Jun 08
Working Capital	7	7	48
Fixed Assets	N/A	N/A	19
Current Assets	29	29	79

Superequip Catering Equipment
Millshaw Park Avenue, Leeds, LS11 0LR
Tel: 0113-270 7303 **Fax:** 0113-270 9198
Website: http://www.dwm-uk.com

see next page

Superequip Catering Equipment - Cont'd

Directors: P. Wood (Dir), Y. Sahin (Fin)
Immediate Holding Company: SUPEREQUIP LIMITED
Registration no: 04288673 **Date established:** 2001
No.of Employees: 1 - 10 **Product Groups:** 20, 40, 41

Date of Accounts	Dec 11	Dec 10	Dec 09
Working Capital	146	169	149
Fixed Assets	4	6	8
Current Assets	420	416	368

Surface Technology plc

Long Causeway, Leeds, LS9 0NY
Tel: 0113-248 0555 **Fax:** 0113-235 0169
E-mail: martinc@armourcote.co.uk
Website: http://www.surfacetechnology.co.uk
Directors: A. Millington (MD)
Ultimate Holding Company: NORMAN HAY PLC
Immediate Holding Company: SURFACE TECHNOLOGY PLC
Registration no: 04021109 **Date established:** 2000
No.of Employees: 21 - 50 **Product Groups:** 48

Date of Accounts	Dec 11	Dec 10	Dec 09
Sales Turnover	23m	19m	15m
Pre Tax Profit/Loss	2m	1m	1m
Working Capital	7m	6m	6m
Fixed Assets	3m	3m	3m
Current Assets	17m	13m	13m
Current Liabilities	5m	3m	4m

Surfachem Ltd

2 The Embankment Sovereign Street, Leeds, LS1 4BP
Tel: 0113-394 9200 **Fax:** 0113-244 5910
E-mail: enquiries@surfachem.com
Website: http://www.surfachem.com
Directors: M. Briggs (Fin), N. Hall (MD), M. Kessler (MD), P. Sumpter (Export)
Ultimate Holding Company: 2M GROUP LIMITED
Immediate Holding Company: SURFACHEM LIMITED
Registration no: 01565953 **VAT No.:** GB 461 3886 31
Date established: 1981 **Turnover:** £20m - £50m
No.of Employees: 21 - 50 **Product Groups:** 66

Date of Accounts	Apr 12	Apr 11	Apr 10
Sales Turnover	50m	49m	44m
Pre Tax Profit/Loss	4m	4m	4m
Working Capital	14m	12m	10m
Fixed Assets	215	281	310
Current Assets	34m	26m	25m
Current Liabilities	2m	3m	2m

Sword Group Ltd

Enfield Street, Leeds, LS7 1RF
Tel: 08716-209173 **Fax:** 0113-244 4201
E-mail: mail@intechsolutions.co.uk
Website: http://www.sword-group.com
Managers: J. Brill (Sales Admin)
Immediate Holding Company: LIME TREE FOODS LIMITED
Registration no: 04094000 **Date established:** 2000 **Turnover:** £5m - £10m
No.of Employees: 1 - 10 **Product Groups:** 44

Date of Accounts	Dec 11	Dec 10	Dec 09
Working Capital	520	361	83
Fixed Assets	476	450	502
Current Assets	988	814	803

Sydney Beaumont Leeds Ltd

Unit 5 Sydenham Road, Leeds, LS11 9RU
Tel: 0113-245 8729 **Fax:** 0113-242 8524
E-mail: info@sydb.co.uk
Website: http://www.sydb.co.uk
Directors: K. Hudson (Fin), G. Leigh (MD)
Immediate Holding Company: SYDNEY BEAUMONT (LEEDS) LIMITED
Registration no: 00919268 **VAT No.:** GB 168 8353 23
Date established: 1967 **Turnover:** £500,000 - £1m
No.of Employees: 1 - 10 **Product Groups:** 27, 66

Date of Accounts	Sep 11	Sep 10	Sep 09
Working Capital	28	43	55
Fixed Assets	144	145	148
Current Assets	228	233	228

The Symphony Group plc

Gelderd Lane, Leeds, LS12 6AL
Tel: 0113-230 8000 **Fax:** 0113-231 0138
Website: http://www.symphony-group.co.uk
Directors: G. Smith (Fin), M. Davies (MD), P. Kettlewell (Sales)
Ultimate Holding Company: Berkley Ltd
Immediate Holding Company: Symphony Holdings Ltd
Registration no: 01022506 **VAT No.:** GB 169 1502 61
Date established: 1971 **Turnover:** £75m - £125m
No.of Employees: 1001 - 1500 **Product Groups:** 26

Date of Accounts	Dec 07
Sales Turnover	134430
Pre Tax Profit/Loss	14130
Working Capital	45820
Fixed Assets	5370
Current Assets	72960
Current Liabilities	27140
Total Share Capital	250
ROCE% (Return on Capital Employed)	27.6

T L A Catering Engineers Ltd

Derwent Avenue Garforth, Leeds, LS25 1HN
Tel: 0113-287 4448 **Fax:** 0113-287 7400
Website: http://www.tlacateringengineers.co.uk
Directors: A. Thackery (Prop)
Immediate Holding Company: T L A CATERING ENGINEERS LIMITED
Registration no: 06627445 **Date established:** 2008
No.of Employees: 1 - 10 **Product Groups:** 20, 40, 41

Date of Accounts	Mar 12	Mar 11	Mar 10
Working Capital	42	27	14
Fixed Assets	4	5	6
Current Assets	89	77	64

T M P Worldwide

Minerva House 29 East Parade, Leeds, LS1 5PS
Tel: 0113-368 5000 **Fax:** 0113-368 5001
E-mail: samantha.ward@tmpw.co.uk
Website: http://www.tmpw.co.uk
Managers: J. Beddow (Mgr)
Immediate Holding Company: GLENTROOL ESTATES GROUP LIMITED
Registration no: 06594482 **VAT No.:** GB 420 3267 93
Date established: 1999 **No.of Employees:** 1 - 10 **Product Groups:** 80, 81, 86

T Shirt Printers Ltd

Baker Street Morley, Leeds, LS27 0AB
Tel: 0113-238 1644 **Fax:** 0113-238 1637
E-mail: catherine@tshirtprinters.ltd.uk
Website: http://www.tshirtprinters.ltd.uk
Directors: C. Atkinson (Fin)
Immediate Holding Company: T. SHIRT PRINTERS LIMITED
Registration no: 04130450 **Date established:** 2000
No.of Employees: 21 - 50 **Product Groups:** 23, 24, 84

Tanda Engineering

98 Henshaw Lane Yeadon, Leeds, LS19 7RZ
Tel: 0113-250 2917 **Fax:** 0113-250 5160
E-mail: enquiries@tandaengineering.co.uk
Website: http://www.tandaengineering.co.uk
Directors: R. Noutch (Prop)
Immediate Holding Company: TANDA ENGINEERING (YORKSHIRE) LIMITED
Registration no: 07761643 **VAT No.:** 169 1246 53 **Date established:** 2011
Turnover: £250,000 - £500,000 **No.of Employees:** 1 - 10
Product Groups: 35, 41, 67

Tata Steel

11 Oldfield Lane, Leeds, LS12 4DH
Tel: 0113-230 8501 **Fax:** 0113-272 7197
E-mail: angela.barnard@corusgroup.com
Website: http://www.tatasteel.com
Managers: J. Eyre (Mgr)
Ultimate Holding Company: TATA STEEL LIMITED (INDIA)
Immediate Holding Company: CORUS GROUP LIMITED
Registration no: 03811373 **Date established:** 1999
No.of Employees: 21 - 50 **Product Groups:** 34

Taybell Alarms Ltd

The Security Centre 5 Stonegate Road, Leeds, LS6 4HZ
Tel: 01423-701122 **Fax:** 0113-274 3680
E-mail: sales@taybell.co.uk
Website: http://www.taybell.co.uk
Bank(s): Yorkshire Bank
Directors: D. Scaife (Dir), G. Whitehead (Co Sec), M. Thorley (Dir)
Immediate Holding Company: TAYBELL ALARMS LIMITED
Registration no: 02041257 **VAT No.:** GB 430 9583 46
Date established: 1986 **Turnover:** £500,000 - £1m
No.of Employees: 11 - 20 **Product Groups:** 37, 38, 40, 47

Date of Accounts	Aug 11	Aug 10	Aug 09
Working Capital	-77	-92	-89
Fixed Assets	128	147	149
Current Assets	140	108	128

A Taylor & Sons Leeds Ltd

Pennine Industrial Estate Modder Place, Armley, Leeds, LS12 3ES
Tel: 0113-279 3155
E-mail: sales@ataylor.co.uk
Website: http://www.ataylor.co.uk
Managers: C. Smith
Immediate Holding Company: PENNINE CASTINGS LIMITED
Registration no: 02237282 **Date established:** 1988
No.of Employees: 11 - 20 **Product Groups:** 35

Date of Accounts	May 11	May 10	May 09
Working Capital	732	728	677
Fixed Assets	200	222	252
Current Assets	949	983	850

Telaer Services Ltd

10-11 Howley Park Business Village Pullan Way, Morley, Leeds, LS27 0BZ
Tel: 0113-253 0655 **Fax:** 0113-253 0665
E-mail: tel-aer@virgin.net
Website: http://www.telaer.tv
Directors: S. Ramsey (MD), G. Hirst (Dir), S. Howard (Dir)
Immediate Holding Company: TELAER SERVICES LIMITED
Registration no: 01165216 **VAT No.:** 171 6031 90 **Date established:** 1974
Turnover: £250,000 - £500,000 **No.of Employees:** 21 - 50
Product Groups: 79

Date of Accounts	Dec 09	Apr 09	Apr 08
Working Capital	108	4	59
Fixed Assets	101	109	88
Current Assets	823	525	383

Thackers Commercial Ltd

Westland Square, Leeds, LS11 5SS
Tel: 0113-271 8448 **Fax:** 0113-277 8124
E-mail: info@thackerscommercial.co.uk
Website: http://www.thackerscommercial.co.uk
Directors: A. Wilkinson (MD), C. Wilkinson (Fin)
Ultimate Holding Company: THACKERS COMMERCIAL (HOLDINGS) LIMITED
Immediate Holding Company: THACKERS (COMMERCIAL) LIMITED
Registration no: 03402026 **Date established:** 1997
No.of Employees: 1 - 10 **Product Groups:** 37, 46, 48

Date of Accounts	Jun 12	Jun 11	Jun 10
Working Capital	1	14	63
Fixed Assets	170	142	150
Current Assets	232	264	276

Thomas Bros Leeds Ltd

Stanningley Field Close, Leeds, LS13 4QG
Tel: 0113-256 7210 **Fax:** 0113-256 9199
E-mail: info@tbleeds.com
Website: http://www.tbleeds.com
Directors: W. Thomas (MD), S. Thomas (Jt MD), A. Thomas (Fin), A. Thomas (Jt MD)
Managers: D. Crampton (Foundry Mgr), R. Hutchinson (I.T. Exec)
Immediate Holding Company: THOMAS BROTHERS (LEEDS) LIMITED
Registration no: 03705005 **VAT No.:** GB 171 8856 32
Date established: 1999 **No.of Employees:** 21 - 50 **Product Groups:** 48

Date of Accounts	Apr 11	Apr 10	Apr 09
Working Capital	429	527	794
Fixed Assets	N/A	N/A	273
Current Assets	429	749	1m

Thoroughbred Covers Ltd

349 Kirkstall Road, Leeds, LS4 2HD
Tel: 0113-279 5079 **Fax:** 0113-231 0835
E-mail: sales@thoroughbred-covers.co.uk
Website: http://www.thoroughbred-covers.co.uk
Directors: A. Parker (Dir)
Immediate Holding Company: THOROUGHBRED COVERS LIMITED
Registration no: 02520921 **Date established:** 1990
No.of Employees: 1 - 10 **Product Groups:** 27, 30

Date of Accounts	Jun 11	Jun 10	Jun 09
Working Capital	-41	-34	-31
Fixed Assets	2	2	3
Current Assets	5	3	5
Current Liabilities	30	N/A	21

Thyssenkrupp Bilstein Woodhead

177 Kirkstall Road, Leeds, LS4 2AQ
Tel: 0113-244 1202 **Fax:** 0113-234 7738
E-mail: jonathan.sandground@tka-wo.thyssenkrupp.com
Website: http://www.thyssenkrupp.com
Bank(s): National Westminster Bank Plc
Directors: P. Bearfield (Fin), J. Sandground (MD)
Managers: A. Welsh (Sales Prom Mgr), E. Cooke, G. Taylor (Tech Serv Mgr)
Ultimate Holding Company: THYSSEN KRUPP AG (GERMANY)
Immediate Holding Company: THYSSENKRUPP BILSTEIN WOODHEAD LIMITED
Registration no: 02479379 **Date established:** 1990
Turnover: £20m - £50m **No.of Employees:** 51 - 100 **Product Groups:** 35

Date of Accounts	Sep 11	Sep 10	Sep 09
Sales Turnover	26m	21m	17m
Pre Tax Profit/Loss	4m	3m	1m
Working Capital	7m	7m	6m
Fixed Assets	6m	6m	6m
Current Assets	15m	16m	14m
Current Liabilities	3m	3m	2m

Till & Whitehead (t/a L Birkinshaw)

Till & Whitehead Main 37 Ings Road, Leeds, LS9 9HG
Tel: 0113-249 6641 **Fax:** 0113-248 8968
E-mail: leeds@tillwite.com
Website: http://www.tillwite.com
Managers: M. Dunn (Chief Mgr)
Registration no: 00046963 **VAT No.:** GB 169 0521 62
No.of Employees: 1 - 10 **Product Groups:** 25, 36

Timberwise UK Ltd

Kirkfields Business Centre Kirk Lane, Yeadon, Leeds, LS19 7ET
Tel: 0113-250 4402 **Fax:** 0113-250 9931
E-mail: leeds@timberwise.co.uk
Website: http://www.timberwise.co.uk
Directors: N. Hartley (Dir)
Ultimate Holding Company: TIMBERWISE HOLDINGS LIMITED
Immediate Holding Company: TIMBERWISE (UK) LIMITED
Registration no: 03230356 **Date established:** 1996
No.of Employees: 11 - 20 **Product Groups:** 07, 32, 52

Date of Accounts	Dec 11	Dec 10	Dec 09
Sales Turnover	N/A	N/A	5m
Pre Tax Profit/Loss	N/A	N/A	214
Working Capital	397	343	326
Fixed Assets	265	291	301
Current Assets	1m	1m	1m
Current Liabilities	N/A	N/A	585

Tornado Construction Products (Supply & Distribution Depot)

28 Donisthorpe Street, Leeds, LS10 1PL
Tel: 0113-242 4342 **Fax:** 0113-246 0272
E-mail: sales@tornado-fixings.co.uk
Website: http://www.tornado-fixings.co.uk
Managers: P. Fergie (Warehouse Mgr)
Immediate Holding Company: TORNADO FIXINGS LIMITED
Registration no: 02319045 **VAT No.:** GB 392 1816 43
Date established: 1988 **Turnover:** £500,000 - £1m
No.of Employees: 1 - 10 **Product Groups:** 66

Date of Accounts	Dec 11	Dec 10	Dec 09
Working Capital	105	137	125
Fixed Assets	127	135	172
Current Assets	276	308	337

Town End Leeds plc

Unit 17 Silver Court Intercity Way, Leeds, LS13 4LY
Tel: 0113-256 4251 **Fax:** 0113-239 3315
E-mail: sales@dyes.co.uk
Website: http://www.dyes.co.uk
Bank(s): Barclays
Directors: A. Hayes (I.T. Dir), C. Watson (MD), J. Carlisle (Fin), M. Walker (Pers)
Immediate Holding Company: TOWN END (LEEDS) PLC
Registration no: 00294907 **VAT No.:** GB 168 8156 25
Date established: 1934 **Turnover:** £2m - £5m **No.of Employees:** 11 - 20
Product Groups: 31, 32

Date of Accounts	Mar 12	Mar 11	Mar 10
Sales Turnover	4m	4m	3m
Pre Tax Profit/Loss	102	64	25
Working Capital	701	666	643
Fixed Assets	188	133	106
Current Assets	1m	1m	1m
Current Liabilities	226	263	218

Towry

55 St Pauls Street, Leeds, LS1 2TE
Tel: 0113-244 5911 **Fax:** 01937-584371
E-mail: enquiries@towrylaw.com
Website: http://www.edwardjones.com
Bank(s): Barclays
Directors: M. Standish (Div), S. Nichols (Dir)
Managers: A. Brooke (Mgr), T. Clayton (Mgr), A. Springall (District Mgr), K. Croxford (District Mgr)
Ultimate Holding Company: Towry Holdings Ltd
Immediate Holding Company: TOWRY LIMITED
Registration no: 00607039 **Date established:** 1958 **Turnover:** £2m - £5m
No.of Employees: 21 - 50 **Product Groups:** 82

Date of Accounts	Dec 07	Dec 06	Dec 05
Sales Turnover	32497	30193	30502
Pre Tax Profit/Loss	3337	2959	1652

Working Capital	23159	19259	15688
Fixed Assets	3422	1744	1497
Current Assets	23655	19594	17910
Current Liabilities	496	335	2222
Total Share Capital	21933	21933	21933
ROCE% (Return on Capital Employed)	12.6	14.1	9.6
ROT% (Return on Turnover)	10.3	9.8	5.4

Ullmann International Ltd

The Business Centre 4 Kingsmead Drive, Leeds, LS14 1AH
Tel: 0113-201 8844 **Fax:** 0113-201 8855
E-mail: info@ullmann.co.uk
Website: http://www.ullmann.co.uk
Directors: A. Ullmann (MD)
Immediate Holding Company: ULLMANN INTERNATIONAL LIMITED
Registration no: 07572741 **VAT No.:** GB 430 9855 39
Date established: 2011 **Turnover:** £500,000 - £1m
No.of Employees: 1 - 10 **Product Groups:** 23, 63

Ultrasonic Cleaning Services UK Ltd

Unit 4 10 Pepper Road, Leeds, LS10 2PP
Tel: 0113-271 5807 **Fax:** 0113-271 5722
E-mail: graham@ultrasonicuk.com
Website: http://www.ultrasonicuk.com
Directors: G. Wilkinson (MD)
Immediate Holding Company: ULTRASONIC CLEANING SERVICES (U.K.) LIMITED
Registration no: 01222000 **Date established:** 1975
No.of Employees: 1 - 10 **Product Groups:** 46, 48

Date of Accounts	Dec 11	Dec 10	Dec 09
Working Capital	7	27	29
Fixed Assets	9	11	10
Current Assets	35	56	58

Union Industries (Ralf Ellerker Ltd)

Whitehouse Street, Leeds, LS10 1AD
Tel: 0113-244 8393 **Fax:** 0113-242 1307
E-mail: sales@unionindustries.co.uk
Website: http://www.unionindustries.co.uk
Bank(s): Lloyds TSB Bank plc
Directors: M. Schofiled (Ch), C. Schofield (Co Sec)
Managers: A. Huft (Nat Sales Mgr), C. Whittaker (Nat Sales Mgr), B. Byard (Chief Acct)
Ultimate Holding Company: VERDER INTERNATIONAL BV (NETHERLANDS)
Immediate Holding Company: UNION INDUSTRIES LIMITED
Registration no: 03389635 **VAT No.:** GB 172 0279 78
Date established: 1997 **Turnover:** £5m - £10m
No.of Employees: 51 - 100 **Product Groups:** 30, 39, 40, 45, 46

Universal Glazing Ltd

Unit 12 Silver Court Intercity Way, Leeds, LS13 4LY
Tel: 0113-257 2021 **Fax:** 0113-239 3317
E-mail: universal@unit12.fsnet.co.uk
Directors: J. Hargreaves (Dir)
Immediate Holding Company: UNIVERSAL GLAZING LIMITED
Registration no: 02884083 **VAT No.:** 607 2531 63 **Date established:** 1994
Turnover: £1m - £2m **No.of Employees:** 1 - 10 **Product Groups:** 35

Date of Accounts	Mar 11	Mar 10	Mar 09
Working Capital	32	8	-15
Fixed Assets	21	28	20
Current Assets	110	177	285

University Of Leeds (Subsidiary of University of Leeds)

Woodhouse Lane, Leeds, LS2 9JT
Tel: 0113-243 1751 **Fax:** 0113-244 3923
E-mail: m.j.p.arthur@adm.leeds.ac.uk
Website: http://www.leeds.ac.uk
Bank(s): National Westminster Bank Plc
Directors: M. Arther (Grp Chief Exec), R. Wolson (Fin)
Managers: M. Arthur, K. Mapp (Mktg Serv Mgr)
Ultimate Holding Company: UNIVERSITY OF LEEDS (UK)
Immediate Holding Company: UNIVERSITY OF LEEDS IP LIMITED
Registration no: 04582496 **Date established:** 2002
Turnover: £500,000 - £1m **No.of Employees:** 1501 & over
Product Groups: 40, 42, 44, 48, 54, 80, 81, 84, 85, 86, 87

Date of Accounts	Jul 11	Jul 10	Jul 09
Sales Turnover	1m	732	631
Pre Tax Profit/Loss	-14	38	5
Working Capital	58	72	34
Current Assets	909	369	218
Current Liabilities	384	130	109

Urquhart Dykes & Lord

Tower North Central Merrion Way, Leeds, LS2 8PA
Tel: 0113-245 2388 **Fax:** 0113-243 0446
E-mail: email@udl.co.uk
Website: http://www.udl.co.uk
Managers: S. Firth
Immediate Holding Company: URQUHART-DYKES & LORD LLP
Registration no: OC307196 **VAT No.:** GB 239 3059 55
Date established: 2004 **Turnover:** £10m - £20m
No.of Employees: 21 - 50 **Product Groups:** 80

Date of Accounts	Apr 12	Apr 11	Apr 10
Sales Turnover	16m	16m	15m
Pre Tax Profit/Loss	3m	3m	6m
Working Capital	5m	4m	7m
Fixed Assets	232	217	347
Current Assets	7m	6m	9m
Current Liabilities	875	1m	737

Vallectric Ltd

Sweet Street, Leeds, LS11 9DB
Tel: 0113-242 3800 **Fax:** 0113-242 4960
E-mail: andrew.ball@vallectric.co.uk
Website: http://www.vallectric.co.uk
Bank(s): Bank of Scotland
Directors: A. Gardner (MD), A. Ball (Dir), A. Gardener (MD), A. Gardner (Co Sec), C. Novotny (Ch), D. Allen (Dir), D. Lawton (Chief Op Offcr)
Immediate Holding Company: VALLECTRIC LIMITED
Registration no: 00639416 **VAT No.:** GB 545 4862 22
Date established: 1959 **Turnover:** £5m - £10m
No.of Employees: 101 - 250 **Product Groups:** 52

Date of Accounts	Mar 09	Mar 08	Mar 07
Sales Turnover	14m	14m	16m
Pre Tax Profit/Loss	224	281	415

Working Capital	2m	2m	2m
Fixed Assets	9	16	20
Current Assets	4m	6m	5m
Current Liabilities	2m	4m	3m
Total Share Capital	74	74	74

Benjamin R Vickers & Sons Ltd

Clarence Road, Leeds, LS10 1ND
Tel: 0113-386 7654 **Fax:** 0113-386 7676
E-mail: inbox@vickers-oil.com
Website: http://www.vickers-oil.com
Bank(s): National Westminster Bank Plc
Directors: P. Vickers (MD), R. Brophy (Fin)
Immediate Holding Company: VICKERS (LEEDS) LIMITED
Registration no: 00145215 **VAT No.:** GB 169 2805 38
Date established: 2016 **Turnover:** £2m - £5m **No.of Employees:** 21 - 50
Product Groups: 31, 32, 66

Date of Accounts	Oct 04	Oct 03
Working Capital	5	5
Current Assets	5	5

Vinceremos Wines & Spirits Ltd

Royal House 28 Sovereign Street, Leeds, LS1 4BJ
Tel: 0113-244 0002 **Fax:** 0113-288 4566
E-mail: info@vinceremos.co.uk
Website: http://www.vinceremos.co.uk
Directors: J. Gardener (MD)
Immediate Holding Company: VINCEREMOS WINES & SPIRITS LIMITED
Registration no: 02626530 **Date established:** 1991
Turnover: £500,000 - £1m **No.of Employees:** 1 - 10 **Product Groups:** 21, 62

Date of Accounts	Aug 11	Aug 10	Aug 09
Working Capital	164	179	174
Fixed Assets	5	10	11
Current Assets	416	402	382

Visa Hand Tools Ltd

Gibson House Barrowby Lane, Garforth, Leeds, LS25 1NG
Tel: 0113-286 9245 **Fax:** 0113-286 6859
E-mail: sales@visatools.co.uk
Website: http://www.visatools.co.uk
Bank(s): National Westminster
Directors: C. Timmins (MD)
Immediate Holding Company: VISA HAND TOOLS LIMITED
Registration no: 01496508 **VAT No.:** GB 287 6085 16
Date established: 1980 **Turnover:** £250,000 - £500,000
No.of Employees: 11 - 20 **Product Groups:** 36

Date of Accounts	Mar 11	Mar 10	Mar 09
Working Capital	18	12	10
Fixed Assets	3	3	5
Current Assets	227	205	149

Visper Technical

47 Kentmere Avenue, Leeds, LS14 6QD
Tel: 0113-212 0613 **Fax:** 0870-900 5919
E-mail: melanie.harper@vispertechnical.co.uk
Website: http://www.vispertechnical.co.uk
Directors: M. Harper (MD), M. Harper (Prop)
Date established: 2008 **Turnover:** Up to £250,000
No.of Employees: 1 - 10 **Product Groups:** 80

W K H Fabrications Ltd

Cemetery Road Yeadon, Leeds, LS19 7BD
Tel: 0113-239 1909 **Fax:** 0113-250 0773
Website: http://www.wkhgroup.co.uk
Directors: W. Huddleston (MD)
Immediate Holding Company: WKH FABRICATIONS LIMITED
Registration no: 07537745 **Date established:** 2011
No.of Employees: 11 - 20 **Product Groups:** 30, 41, 42

Date of Accounts	Mar 12
Working Capital	-546
Fixed Assets	801
Current Assets	442

W S Atkins

3100 Century Way Thorpe Park, Leeds, LS15 8ZB
Tel: 0113-306 6000 **Fax:** 0113-306 6001
E-mail: david.boldra@fgould.com
Website: http://www.atkinsglobal.com
Bank(s): Nat West
Managers: D. Boldra (Mgr), S. Mitchell
Immediate Holding Company: W.S. ATKINS LTD
Registration no: 00755613 **VAT No.:** GB 209 8612 53
Turnover: £75m - £125m **No.of Employees:** 501 - 1000
Product Groups: 84

W S H Services Ltd

Tarn House 77 High Street, Yeadon, Leeds, LS19 7SP
Tel: 0113-250 2946
E-mail: sales@wshservices.co.uk
Website: http://www.wshservices.co.uk/index.htm
Directors: W. Hargreaves (MD)
Immediate Holding Company: WSH SERVICES LIMITED
Registration no: 06371180 **Date established:** 2007
Turnover: £250,000 - £500,000 **No.of Employees:** 1 - 10
Product Groups: 08

Date of Accounts	Sep 11	Sep 10	Sep 09
Working Capital	11	3	-3
Fixed Assets	84	97	118
Current Assets	40	21	14

W T Products Ltd

Unit 3 Cedar Terrace, Leeds, LS12 1TQ
Tel: 0113-279 7345 **Fax:** 0113-231 0725
E-mail: wtproducts1@btconnect.com
Website: http://www.wtproducts.co.uk
Bank(s): National Westminster Bank Plc
Directors: S. Hewitt (Co Sec), B. Willis (MD)
Immediate Holding Company: W.T. PRODUCTS LIMITED
Registration no: 03490801 **VAT No.:** GB 343 0352 93
Date established: 1998 **Turnover:** £500,000 - £1m
No.of Employees: 11 - 20 **Product Groups:** 37

Date of Accounts	Jun 11	Jun 10	Jun 09
Working Capital	-32	-28	-14
Fixed Assets	50	60	60
Current Assets	162	147	130

Warrens Display Ltd

359 Burley Road, Leeds, LS4 2PX
Tel: 0113-278 3614 **Fax:** 0113-274 4300
E-mail: sales@warrens.co.uk
Website: http://www.warrens.co.uk
Directors: A. Leal (MD)
Immediate Holding Company: WARRENS DISPLAY LIMITED
Registration no: 03125257 **Date established:** 1995 **Turnover:** £2m - £5m
No.of Employees: 11 - 20 **Product Groups:** 81

Date of Accounts	Mar 11	Mar 10	Mar 09
Working Capital	-20	-20	37
Fixed Assets	44	46	58
Current Assets	-20	443	335

Watershed Packaging Ltd

Westland Square, Leeds, LS11 5SS
Tel: 0113-277 0606 **Fax:** 0113-277 7174
E-mail: sales@watershed-packaging.co.uk
Website: http://www.watershed-packaging.co.uk
Bank(s): National Westminster
Directors: S. Walker (MD)
Immediate Holding Company: WATERSHED PACKAGING LIMITED
Registration no: 02877836 **VAT No.:** GB 548 7934 87
Date established: 1993 **Turnover:** £5m - £10m
No.of Employees: 51 - 100 **Product Groups:** 27, 42

Date of Accounts	Dec 11	Dec 10	Dec 09
Sales Turnover	8m	N/A	N/A
Pre Tax Profit/Loss	107	N/A	N/A
Working Capital	142	198	80
Fixed Assets	1m	1m	1m
Current Assets	3m	2m	2m
Current Liabilities	1m	N/A	N/A

WEJ Secretarial Services

8 Greenfield Avenue Kippax, Leeds, LS25 7PS
Tel: 07708-359511
E-mail: wej3931@btinternet.com
Website: http://www.wejsecretarial.co.uk
Directors: W. Jones (Prop)
Date established: 2008 **No.of Employees:** 1 - 10 **Product Groups:** 80

Wellman Booth

2 Kirkfields Industrial Centre Kirk Lane, Yeadon, Leeds, LS19 7LX
Tel: 0113-387 9730 **Fax:** 0113-250 6180
E-mail: maureen.sharman@wellmanbooth.co.uk
Website: http://www.wellmanbooth.co.uk
Bank(s): Barclays
Managers: K. Finnemore (Mgr)
Ultimate Holding Company: LANGLEY HOLDINGS PLC
Immediate Holding Company: CLARKE CHAPMAN GROUP
Registration no: 00120644 **VAT No.:** 439 5293 21 **Date established:** 1977
Turnover: £10m - £20m **No.of Employees:** 11 - 20 **Product Groups:** 45

West Yorkshire Drawing Office Services Ltd

Swallow Hill Mills Tong Road, Leeds, LS12 4QG
Tel: 0113-220 5400 **Fax:** 0113-231 0615
E-mail: stuart@wydos.co.uk
Website: http://www.wydos.co.uk
Directors: E. Palm (Dir)
Immediate Holding Company: WEST YORKSHIRE DRAWING OFFICE SERVICES LIMITED
Registration no: 01048460 **VAT No.:** GB 170 4392 74
Date established: 1972 **Turnover:** £500,000 - £1m
No.of Employees: 1 - 10 **Product Groups:** 64

Date of Accounts	Mar 12	Mar 11	Mar 10
Working Capital	144	158	152
Fixed Assets	354	358	360
Current Assets	186	206	229

Westminster Controls Ltd

Unit 3 Pym Street, Leeds, LS10 1PG
Tel: 0113-288 4500 **Fax:** 0113-246 0791
E-mail: info@westminstercontrols.com
Website: http://www.westminstercontrols.com
Bank(s): Yorkshire Bank
Directors: J. Quinn (MD)
Immediate Holding Company: WESTMINSTER CONTROLS LIMITED
Registration no: 01621972 **VAT No.:** GB 371 9917 17
Date established: 1982 **Turnover:** £1m - £2m **No.of Employees:** 11 - 20
Product Groups: 52

Date of Accounts	Mar 09	Mar 08	Sep 11
Working Capital	218	169	208
Fixed Assets	182	176	64
Current Assets	2m	1m	1m

Wheelhouse & Noble

Energy House Hales Road, Leeds, LS12 4PL
Tel: 0113-263 1513 **Fax:** 0113-231 1891
E-mail: karen@wne.org.uk
Website: http://www.wne.org.uk
Bank(s): Yorkshire
Directors: K. Wheelhouse (Dir), J. White (Dir), K. Lickley (Co Sec), K. Lickley (Fin)
Immediate Holding Company: WHEELHOUSE & NOBLE LIMITED
Registration no: 01104058 **VAT No.:** GB 170 9972 31
Date established: 1973 **Turnover:** £2m - £5m **No.of Employees:** 11 - 20
Product Groups: 52

Date of Accounts	Dec 07	Dec 06	Dec 05
Working Capital	-3	-31	-6
Fixed Assets	311	330	276
Current Assets	321	407	300
Current Liabilities	324	438	305
Total Share Capital	1	1	1

White Young Green

Arndale Court Headingley, Leeds, LS6 2UJ
Tel: 0113-278 7111 **Fax:** 0113-278 3487
E-mail: enquiries@wyg.com
Website: http://www.wyg.com
Bank(s): Lloyds TSB Bank plc
Directors: A. Higgs (Dir), J. Purvis (Grp Chief Exec), M. Procter (MD), R. Hare (Dir), R. Hartley (Co Sec), S. Carruthers (Dir), W. Brayson (Ch), S. Basso (Sales & Mktg), C. Farbridge (Co Sec)
Managers: S. Green (Sales & Mktg Mg), H. Jones (Personnel)
Immediate Holding Company: Wyg plc
Registration no: 05111508 **VAT No.:** GB 431 0326 08
Date established: 1999 **Turnover:** £50m - £75m
No.of Employees: 251 - 500 **Product Groups:** 80, 84

William G Search Ltd
Whitehall Road, Leeds, LS12 6EP
Tel: 0113-263 9081 **Fax:** 0151-549 1914
E-mail: info@wgsearch.co.uk
Website: http://www.wgsearch.co.uk
Bank(s): Midland
Directors: R. Search (MD), R. Search (MD)
Managers: L. Gaunt (Tech Serv Mgr), S. Renton, D. Austin (Purch Mgr)
Ultimate Holding Company: SEARCH GROUP HOLDINGS LIMITED
Immediate Holding Company: WILLIAM G. SEARCH LIMITED
Registration no: 00407145 **VAT No.:** GB 477 0776 10
Date established: 1946 **Turnover:** £10m - £20m
No.of Employees: 21 - 50 **Product Groups:** 35, 37, 40, 45

Date of Accounts	Dec 11	Dec 10	Dec 09
Sales Turnover	11m	11m	10m
Pre Tax Profit/Loss	140	196	101
Working Capital	-593	-547	-518
Fixed Assets	6m	7m	7m
Current Assets	2m	2m	2m
Current Liabilities	590	590	610

William Hill
PO Box 170, Leeds, LS2 8JF
Tel: 0113-291 2000 **Fax:** 0113-291 2282
E-mail: humanresources-leeds@williamhill.co.uk
Website: http://www.williamhill.co.uk
Directors: S. Lane (Dir)
Managers: A. Alderson, J. Lahive (Fin Mgr), K. White (Purch Mgr)
Immediate Holding Company: NOMURA
Registration no: 00278208 **No.of Employees:** 1 - 10 **Product Groups:** 89

Willmott Dixon Construction Ltd
Unit 3 Cliffe Park Bruntcliffe Road, Morley, Leeds, LS27 0RY
Tel: 0113-238 3283 **Fax:** 0113-238 0268
E-mail: mark.pheasey@willmottdixon.co.uk
Website: http://www.willmotdixon.co.uk
Bank(s): HSBC Bank plc
Directors: M. Pheasey (Trans)
Ultimate Holding Company: HARDWICKE INVESTMENTS LIMITED
Immediate Holding Company: WILLMOTT DIXON CONSTRUCTION LIMITED
Registration no: 00768173 **VAT No.:** GB 197 7377 96
Date established: 1963 **Turnover:** £10m - £20m
No.of Employees: 51 - 100 **Product Groups:** 52

Date of Accounts	Dec 11	Dec 10	Dec 09
Sales Turnover	682m	661m	690m
Pre Tax Profit/Loss	28m	27m	27m
Working Capital	20m	19m	17m
Fixed Assets	915	843	1m
Current Assets	203m	196m	197m
Current Liabilities	40m	42m	49m

Wright & Shields
Town Street Bramley, Leeds, LS13 3JT
Tel: 0113-256 8844 **Fax:** 0113-255 9182
E-mail: sales@wrightandshields.co.uk
Website: http://www.wrightandshields.co.uk
Directors: M. Shields (Prop)
Immediate Holding Company: WRIGHT & SHIELDS LIMITED
Registration no: 08006491 **Date established:** 2012
No.of Employees: 1 - 10 **Product Groups:** 40

John Wyatt Ltd
Braithwaite Street, Leeds, LS11 9XE
Tel: 0113-244 4151 **Fax:** 0113-242 3186
E-mail: simon@johnwyattltd.co.uk
Website: http://www.johnwyattltd.com
Bank(s): Lloyds TSB Bank plc
Directors: S. Wyatt (MD)
Managers: J. Mennell (Chief Acct)
Immediate Holding Company: JOHN WYATT LIMITED
Registration no: 00286241 **VAT No.:** GB 169 9022 35
Date established: 1934 **Turnover:** £10m - £20m
No.of Employees: 21 - 50 **Product Groups:** 20, 62

Date of Accounts	Dec 11	Dec 10	Dec 09
Sales Turnover	N/A	13m	17m
Pre Tax Profit/Loss	N/A	-548	-6
Working Capital	351	-439	-147
Fixed Assets	933	1m	2m
Current Assets	2m	1m	887
Current Liabilities	N/A	223	126

Xrio Ltd
357 Roundhay Road, Leeds, LS8 4BU
Tel: 08456-443226
E-mail: sales@xrio.com
Website: http://www.xrio.com
Managers: M. Rushworth (Consultant)
Ultimate Holding Company: ENTERPRISE TRADING LTD
Immediate Holding Company: XRIO LIMITED
Registration no: 04516148 **Date established:** 2002
No.of Employees: 1 - 10 **Product Groups:** 37

Date of Accounts	Dec 10	Dec 09	Dec 08
Working Capital	-13	33	18
Fixed Assets	122	144	167
Current Assets	90	108	93

Y C S Computers C I C
124 Roundhay Road, Leeds, LS8 5NA
Tel: 0113-235 0174 **Fax:** 0113-235 0174
E-mail: info@ycscomputers.com
Website: http://www.ycscomputers.com
Directors: R. Sanyang (MD)
Immediate Holding Company: YCS COMPUTERS C.I.C.
Registration no: 05001393 **Date established:** 2003
Turnover: Up to £250,000 **No.of Employees:** 1 - 10 **Product Groups:** 44

Date of Accounts	Dec 11	Dec 10	Dec 09
Sales Turnover	59	N/A	N/A
Pre Tax Profit/Loss	-1	N/A	N/A
Working Capital	1	1	-2
Fixed Assets	6	7	9
Current Assets	3	2	N/A
Current Liabilities	1	N/A	N/A

Yamato Scale Dataweigh UK Ltd (Yamato Scale Japan)
5 Maple Park Lowfields Avenue, Leeds, LS12 6HH
Tel: 0113-322 1546 **Fax:** 0113-271 7012
E-mail: andrea.spencer@yamatoscale.co.uk
Website: http://www.yamatoscale.co.uk
Directors: N. Fowel (Dir)
Ultimate Holding Company: YAMATO SCALE COMPANY LIMITED (JAPAN)
Immediate Holding Company: YAMATO SCALE DATAWEIGH (UK) LTD.
Registration no: 02919226 **Date established:** 1994 **Turnover:** £5m - £10m
No.of Employees: 1 - 10 **Product Groups:** 38, 42, 67

Date of Accounts	Dec 11	Dec 10	Dec 09
Sales Turnover	6m	6m	6m
Pre Tax Profit/Loss	31	56	100
Working Capital	739	723	727
Fixed Assets	138	141	125
Current Assets	3m	3m	3m
Current Liabilities	730	826	573

Yorkshire Post
Wellington Street, Leeds, LS1 1RF
Tel: 0113-243 2701 **Fax:** 01274-370165
Website: http://www.yorkshireposttoday.co.uk
Directors: S. Green (MD), P. Mccall (Co Sec), D. Sweeney (Adv), C. Green (Dir), D. McLoughlin (Sales & Mktg), P. Cooper (Co Sec)
Managers: K. Armitage (Chief Mgr), L. Murfin (Mgr), P. Johnson (I.T. Exec)
Ultimate Holding Company: SC015382
Immediate Holding Company: YORKSHIRE POST MAGAZINES LIMITED
Registration no: 02773199 **Date established:** 1992
Turnover: £10m - £20m **No.of Employees:** 1 - 10 **Product Groups:** 28, 79

Date of Accounts	Jan 10	Dec 08	Dec 07
Sales Turnover	16m	19m	20m
Working Capital	89m	89m	89m
Current Assets	89m	89m	89m

Liversedge

Auto Paint
4b Union Road, Liversedge, WF15 7HW
Tel: 01924-410125 **Fax:** 01924-501555
Directors: G. Simpson (Prop)
Immediate Holding Company: AUTOBLEND LIMITED
Registration no: 02197810 **Date established:** 1987
No.of Employees: 1 - 10 **Product Groups:** 38, 42

Date of Accounts	Nov 11	Nov 10	Nov 09
Working Capital	1	5	14
Fixed Assets	3	4	1
Current Assets	45	44	46

B Kemp Grinders
Green Road, Liversedge, WF15 6DN
Tel: 01924-408832 **Fax:** 01924-408832
Website: http://www.bkempgrinders.co.uk
Directors: J. Kemp (Prop)
Date established: 1991 **No.of Employees:** 1 - 10 **Product Groups:** 48

Birkbys Plastics Ltd
Headlands Road, Liversedge, WF15 6QA
Tel: 01924-414200 **Fax:** 01924-400051
E-mail: marketing@birkbys.co.uk
Website: http://www.birkbys.co.uk
Bank(s): National Westminster Bank Plc
Directors: N. Rose (Fin), M. Flanigan (Sales), I. Parker (Dir), F. Jones (Pers)
Managers: H. Pickford (Buyer)
Ultimate Holding Company: VERVE INDUSTRIES LIMITED
Immediate Holding Company: BIRKBY'S PLASTICS LIMITED
Registration no: 02486780 **Date established:** 1990
Turnover: £20m - £50m **No.of Employees:** 251 - 500 **Product Groups:** 30

Date of Accounts	Mar 08	Mar 09	Mar 10
Sales Turnover	38m	29m	24m
Pre Tax Profit/Loss	4m	-1m	-816
Working Capital	4m	3m	2m
Fixed Assets	4m	4m	4m
Current Assets	11m	6m	8m
Current Liabilities	2m	2m	2m

Charles E Dickinson & Co
Triton House Hare Park Lane, Liversedge, WF15 8HN
Tel: 01274-876797 **Fax:** 01274-851087
Website: http://www.cedickinson.co.uk
Directors: J. Wilson (Sales), R. Wilson (MD)
Managers: L. Wilson-Pieri (Admin Off)
Immediate Holding Company: THE EARTH COLLECTION LIMITED
Registration no: 06073626 **VAT No.:** GB 180 1723 85
Date established: 2003 **Turnover:** £5m - £10m **No.of Employees:** 1 - 10
Product Groups: 23

County Scales North
1 Frost Hill Business Park Rhodes Street, Liversedge, WF15 6BG
Tel: 01924-412202 **Fax:** 01924-412282
E-mail: stevegoodwin1960@gmail.com
Website: http://www.county-scales.co.uk
Directors: S. Goodwin (Prop)
Date established: 1997 **No.of Employees:** 1 - 10 **Product Groups:** 38, 42

G N G Convertors
Units 60-70 B M K Industrial Estate Wakefield Road, Liversedge, WF15 6BS
Tel: 01924-400501
E-mail: info@gng-group.co.uk
Website: http://www.gng-group.co.uk
Directors: N. Spencer (MD), P. Whittel (MD)
Managers: J. Knowles (Personnel), H. White (Comptroller)
No.of Employees: 21 - 50 **Product Groups:** 26, 29, 49

Heckmondwike FB
PO Box 7, Liversedge, WF15 7FH
Tel: 01924-410544 **Fax:** 01924-413613
E-mail: sales@heckmondwike-fb.co.uk
Website: http://www.heckmondwike-fb.co.uk
Bank(s): Barclays
Directors: R. Mortimer (Sales)
Immediate Holding Company: HECKMONDWIKE FB LIMITED
Registration no: 01538817 **Date established:** 1981
Turnover: £10m - £20m **No.of Employees:** 101 - 250
Product Groups: 23, 24, 25, 31, 33, 36, 43, 44, 49, 52, 66

Newsmith Stainless Ltd
Fountain Works Child Lane, Liversedge, WF15 7PH
Tel: 01924-405988 **Fax:** 01924-403304
E-mail: john.chappell@newsmith.co.uk
Website: http://www.newsmith.co.uk
Directors: B. Patel (Tech Serv), J. Chappell (Co Sec)
Managers: R. Woffindin (Mktg Serv Mgr)
Immediate Holding Company: NEWSMITH STAINLESS LIMITED
Registration no: 00968816 **Date established:** 1969
Turnover: £10m - £20m **No.of Employees:** 51 - 100 **Product Groups:** 40, 41, 45, 46

Date of Accounts	Jun 11	Jun 10	Jun 09
Sales Turnover	15m	15m	14m
Pre Tax Profit/Loss	-388	392	460
Working Capital	-151	-407	-663
Fixed Assets	5m	6m	6m
Current Assets	5m	5m	4m
Current Liabilities	2m	2m	2m

Play Rite
Wellington Mills Huddersfield Road, Liversedge, WF15 7FH
Tel: 01924-412488 **Fax:** 01924-412337
E-mail: info@playrite.co.uk
Website: http://www.playrite.co.uk
Bank(s): Barclays, Loughborough
Directors: J. Walker (Fin), M. Pass (Ch)
Ultimate Holding Company: NATIONAL FLOOR COVERINGS LTD
Immediate Holding Company: HECKMONDWIKE F B LTD
Registration no: 00545333 **Date established:** 1991 **Turnover:** £1m - £2m
No.of Employees: 21 - 50 **Product Groups:** 29, 49

Wrought Craft
2 Rouse Street, Liversedge, WF15 6LG
Tel: 01274-855516
Directors: C. Clare (Ptnr)
Date established: 1990 **No.of Employees:** 1 - 10 **Product Groups:** 26, 35

Yorkshire Rubber Linings Ltd
Preistley House Spenborough Industrial Estate Union Road, Liversedge, WF15 7JZ
Tel: 01924-410414 **Fax:** 01924-410413
E-mail: sales@rubberlinings.co.uk
Website: http://www.rubberlinings.co.uk
Bank(s): Lloyds TSB Bank plc
Directors: M. Holroyd (MD)
Immediate Holding Company: YORKSHIRE RUBBER LININGS LIMITED
Registration no: 02407401 **VAT No.:** GB 516 4820 53
Date established: 1989 **Turnover:** £2m - £5m **No.of Employees:** 11 - 20
Product Groups: 29, 31, 36, 39, 40, 41, 42, 48, 49, 51, 63, 66

Date of Accounts	Mar 11	Mar 10	Mar 09
Working Capital	114	53	61
Fixed Assets	43	52	64
Current Assets	278	208	273

Mirfield

James Walker Textiles Ltd
Station Road, Mirfield, WF14 8NA
Tel: 01924-492277 **Fax:** 01924-480263
E-mail: sales@jwalker.co.uk
Website: http://www.jwalker.co.uk
Directors: J. Walker (MD)
Ultimate Holding Company: JAMES WALKER TEXTILES LIMITED
Immediate Holding Company: JAMES WALKER TEXTILES LIMITED
Registration no: 06382867 **Date established:** 2007 **Turnover:** £2m - £5m
No.of Employees: 1 - 10 **Product Groups:** 24

Date of Accounts	Jan 12	Jan 11	Jan 10
Working Capital	2m	2m	2m
Fixed Assets	334	360	375
Current Assets	2m	2m	2m

Pakprint Tapes Ltd
Unit 19 Bankfield Business Park, Huddersfield Road, Mirfield, WF14 9DD
Tel: 01924-483000 **Fax:** 01924-483009
E-mail: sales@pakprint.co.uk
Website: http://www.pakprint.co.uk
Directors: R. Tunnacliffe (I.T. Dir), M. Sykes (Fin)
Registration no: 01566487 **Date established:** 1981
No.of Employees: 1 - 10 **Product Groups:** 38, 42

Date of Accounts	Dec 09	Dec 08	Dec 07
Working Capital	142	104	130
Fixed Assets	22	46	62
Current Assets	289	354	350

Premier Fork Truck Services Ltd
Butt End Mills Chadwick Fold Lane, Mirfield, WF14 8PW
Tel: 01924-495745 **Fax:** 01924- 499257
Directors: J. Bould (Prop)
Registration no: 06228696 **Date established:** 1976
No.of Employees: 1 - 10 **Product Groups:** 35, 39, 45

Normanton

Bosch Rexroth Ltd
Foxbridge Way Normanton Industrial Estate, Normanton, WF6 1TN
Tel: 01924-220100 **Fax:** 01924-890111
E-mail: tony.kay@uk.hagglunds.com
Website: http://www.hagglund.com
Directors: S. Clark (Co Sec)
Managers: P. Bowden (Mgr)
Ultimate Holding Company: ROBERT BOSCH GMBH (GERMANY)
Immediate Holding Company: HAGGLUNDS DRIVES LIMITED
Registration no: 02682886 **Date established:** 1992 **Turnover:** £2m - £5m
No.of Employees: 21 - 50 **Product Groups:** 35, 37, 38, 40, 66, 67

Date of Accounts	Dec 11	Dec 10	Dec 09
Sales Turnover	4m	8m	6m
Pre Tax Profit/Loss	125	309	9
Working Capital	2m	2m	1m
Fixed Assets	N/A	142	186
Current Assets	2m	4m	2m
Current Liabilities	N/A	718	522

Choice Electrical Installations
1 Beverley Close, Normanton, WF6 1BU
Tel: 01924-891759
Website: http://www.choice-electrical.com

Directors: G. Briscoe (Prop)
No.of Employees: 1 - 10 **Product Groups:** 37, 52, 84

D Benson Controls Ltd

Normanton Industrial Estate, Normanton, WF6 1QS
Tel: 01924-894162 **Fax:** 01924-896518
E-mail: reception@dbensoncontrols.co.uk
Website: http://www.dbensoncontrols.co.uk
Bank(s): HSBC Bank plc
Directors: J. Williams (Fin), H. Culloden (Dir), K. Williams (MD)
Managers: S. Rhodes (Est), M. Burgess (Est), P. Kenyon (Purch Mgr)
Immediate Holding Company: D. BENSON & CO. LIMITED
Registration no: 00665627 **VAT No.:** GB 182 6870 35
Date established: 1960 **Turnover:** £2m - £5m **No.of Employees:** 21 - 50
Product Groups: 35, 37

Date of Accounts	Sep 11	Sep 10	Sep 08
Working Capital	-13	-13	-10
Fixed Assets	480	480	480
Current Assets	5	6	6

Dispo International

Express Way Wakefield Europort, Normanton, WF6 2TZ
Tel: 01924-891462 **Fax:** 01924-896568
E-mail: sales@dispo.co.uk
Website: http://www.dispo.co.uk
Directors: R. Hall (Dir), A. Verheyen (Dir)
Immediate Holding Company: PAPERWORK (PAPER CONVERTERS) LTD
Registration no: 02660315 **Turnover:** £2m - £5m
No.of Employees: 11 - 20 **Product Groups:** 30

Jubilee Model & Minature Fittings

17 Altofts Lodge Drive, Normanton, WF6 2LB
Tel: 01924-890596
Directors: D. English (Prop)
Date established: 1980 **No.of Employees:** 1 - 10 **Product Groups:** 35

L P A Excil Electronics

Ripley Drive Normanton Industrial Estate, Normanton, WF6 1QT
Tel: 01924-224100 **Fax:** 01924-224111
E-mail: enquiries@lpa-excil.com
Website: http://www.lpa-group.com
Bank(s): Bank of Scotland
Directors: T. Abel (Fin), J. Heskth (MD), D. Cunningham (Sales), J. Hesketh (Tech Serv)
Managers: G. Rourke
Ultimate Holding Company: LPA GROUP PLC
Immediate Holding Company: EXCIL ELECTRONICS LIMITED
Registration no: 01675128 **VAT No.:** GB 361 6439 49
Date established: 1982 **Turnover:** £2m - £5m **No.of Employees:** 51 - 100
Product Groups: 84

Date of Accounts	Sep 11	Sep 10	Sep 09
Sales Turnover	5m	4m	3m
Pre Tax Profit/Loss	251	-161	-200
Working Capital	870	532	656
Fixed Assets	345	335	373
Current Assets	2m	2m	1m
Current Liabilities	173	142	110

Parkside Flexible Europe Ltd

Tyler Close Normanton Industrial Estate, Normanton, WF6 1RL
Tel: 01924-898074 **Fax:** 01924-893236
E-mail: chris.kozlik@parksideflex.com
Website: http://www.parksideflex.com
Directors: C. Kozlik (Sales), R. Grace (Pers), L. Dall (Ch), D. Needham (Fin), S. Chawner (Fin)
Managers: A. Fox (Tech Serv Mgr), L. Elliott
Ultimate Holding Company: BUSHMAN LIMITED (ANGUILLA)
Immediate Holding Company: PARKSIDE FLEXIBLES (EUROPE) LIMITED
Registration no: 05325366 **Date established:** 2005
Turnover: £20m - £50m **No.of Employees:** 101 - 250
Product Groups: 38, 42

Date of Accounts	Dec 11	Dec 10	Dec 09
Sales Turnover	25m	19m	17m
Pre Tax Profit/Loss	3m	576	829
Working Capital	2m	428	-461
Fixed Assets	3m	3m	3m
Current Assets	6m	3m	3m
Current Liabilities	2m	1m	2m

Plastiflex UK Ltd

Ripley Close Normanton Indl-Est, Normanton, WF6 1TB
Tel: 01924-783600 **Fax:** 01924-896715
E-mail: ian.howe@plastiflex.co.uk
Website: http://www.plastiflex.co.uk
Directors: I. Howe (Co Sec), M. James (MD)
Managers: I. Howe (Chief Mgr), J. Carr (Accounts), H. Gaunt, H. Daunt (Sales Prom Mgr), A. Blair (Purch Mgr)
Immediate Holding Company: PLASTIFLEX (UK) LIMITED
Registration no: 02639300 **VAT No.:** GB 590 0685 70
Date established: 1991 **Turnover:** £5m - £10m **No.of Employees:** 21 - 50
Product Groups: 30

Date of Accounts	Dec 10	Dec 09	Dec 08
Working Capital	567	592	592
Fixed Assets	70	70	72
Current Assets	1m	805	855

The Proton Group Ltd

Ripley Drive Normanton Industrial Estate, Normanton, WF6 1QT
Tel: 01924-892834 **Fax:** 01924-220213
E-mail: mail@proton-group.co.uk
Website: http://www.proton-group.co.uk
Bank(s): Yorkshire Bank PLC
Directors: M. Angus (MD), P. Shakespeare (Co Sec)
Managers: R. Burton (Personnel)
Ultimate Holding Company: PROTON HOLDINGS LIMITED
Immediate Holding Company: THE PROTON GROUP LIMITED
Registration no: 01000982 **Date established:** 1971 **Turnover:** £2m - £5m
No.of Employees: 21 - 50 **Product Groups:** 31, 32, 41, 66

Date of Accounts	Aug 11	Aug 10	Aug 09
Sales Turnover	3m	4m	3m
Pre Tax Profit/Loss	102	261	224
Working Capital	3m	3m	2m
Fixed Assets	80	114	145
Current Assets	4m	3m	3m
Current Liabilities	163	160	138

Really Useful Products Ltd

Unit 2 Foxbridge Way Normanton Industrial Estate, Normanton, WF6 1TN
Tel: 01924-898477
E-mail: cb@reallyusefulproducts.com
Website: http://www.reallyusefulproducts.co.uk
Directors: M. Pickles (MD), C. Crawford (Fin)
Managers: J. Walker, C. Haw
Immediate Holding Company: REALLY USEFUL PRODUCTS LTD
Registration no: 03899123 **Date established:** 1999
Turnover: £20m - £50m **No.of Employees:** 101 - 250
Product Groups: 26, 30

Date of Accounts	May 11	May 10	May 09
Sales Turnover	25m	22m	16m
Pre Tax Profit/Loss	256	1m	501
Working Capital	-2m	-1m	-1m
Fixed Assets	10m	8m	7m
Current Assets	8m	7m	5m
Current Liabilities	2m	2m	2m

Renshaw Napier Ltd

Ripley Drive Normanton Industrial Estate, Normanton, WF6 1RY
Tel: 01924-895485 **Fax:** 01924-220046
E-mail: info@renshawnapier.co.uk
Website: http://www.renshawnapierltd.co.uk
Bank(s): HSBC Bank plc
Directors: H. Billington (Pers), A. Brown (Dir), S. DeLaat (Sales), M. O'Donough (I.T. Dir), D. Shayes (MD), J. Janssis (MD), M. Stone (Ch), G. Wither (Fin), D. Barratt (Ch)
Managers: A. Williams (Mats Contrlr), P. Allan (Mgr)
Immediate Holding Company: RENSHAWNAPIER LIMITED
Registration no: 01665672 **VAT No.:** GB 623 1180 81
Date established: 1982 **Turnover:** £75m - £125m
No.of Employees: 101 - 250 **Product Groups:** 62

Rontec Ltd

Unit 11 Beckbridge Road, Normanton Industrial Estate, Normanton, WF6 1TE
Tel: 01924-898209 **Fax:** 01924-899854
E-mail: richard.ashworth@rontec.co.uk
Website: http://www.rontec.co.uk
Directors: J. Costima (MD), R. Ashworth (Ch)
Immediate Holding Company: RONTEC LIMITED
Registration no: 00936452 **VAT No.:** GB 170 0048 12
Date established: 1968 **Turnover:** Up to £250,000
No.of Employees: 1 - 10 **Product Groups:** 37, 38, 44

Date of Accounts	Aug 09	Aug 08	Aug 07
Working Capital	-41	55	-30
Fixed Assets	8	5	6
Current Assets	49	55	58

S E W Eurodrive Ltd

Beckbridge Road Normanton Industrial Estate, Normanton, WF6 1QR
Tel: 01924-893855 **Fax:** 01924-893702
E-mail: info@sew-eurodrive.co.uk
Website: http://www.sew-eurodrive.com
Bank(s): HSBC, Wakefield
Directors: J. Pickup (Co Sec), M. Holmes (MD)
Managers: H. Roberts (Sales & Mktg Mg), S. Horner (Tech Serv Mgr)
Ultimate Holding Company: BV BETEILGUNG GMBH & CO KG
Immediate Holding Company: SEW-EURODRIVE LIMITED
Registration no: 00947360 **Date established:** 1969
Turnover: £20m - £50m **No.of Employees:** 101 - 250
Product Groups: 35, 37, 39, 45, 48, 67, 84

Date of Accounts	Feb 08	Feb 11	Feb 10
Sales Turnover	25m	27m	22m
Pre Tax Profit/Loss	5m	5m	2m
Working Capital	11m	11m	9m
Fixed Assets	2m	8m	6m
Current Assets	14m	16m	14m
Current Liabilities	1m	2m	367

Tri Wire Ltd Electrical Wires Division

Good Hope Close Normanton Indl-Est, Normanton, WF6 1TR
Tel: 01924-224200 **Fax:** 01924-220098
E-mail: maria.davis@nexans.com
Website: http://www.nexans.co.uk/triwire
Bank(s): Barclays
Managers: D. Goldthorpe (Purch Mgr), M. Spurr (Quality Control), R. Weir (Mgr), W. Placke (Legal), M. Davis (Fin Mgr)
Ultimate Holding Company: NEXANS PARTICIPATIONS SA (FRANCE)
Immediate Holding Company: TRI-WIRE LIMITED
Registration no: 02279142 **VAT No.:** GB 464 3332 56
Date established: 1988 **Turnover:** £20m - £50m
No.of Employees: 21 - 50 **Product Groups:** 35, 37

Date of Accounts	Dec 10	Dec 09	Dec 08
Sales Turnover	48m	32m	43m
Pre Tax Profit/Loss	-238	-24	-2m
Working Capital	1m	1m	1m
Fixed Assets	1m	1m	2m
Current Assets	13m	10m	6m
Current Liabilities	7m	5m	3m

VAPLAS Ltd

Unit 5 Tuscany Court Express Way, Normanton, WF6 2AE
Tel: 01924-220050 **Fax:** 01977-559988
E-mail: sales@vaplas.com
Website: http://www.vaplas.com
Directors: L. Baker (Fin)
Immediate Holding Company: VAPLAS LIMITED
Registration no: 02878509 **VAT No.:** GB 642 6247 42
Date established: 1993 **Turnover:** £500,000 - £1m
No.of Employees: 1 - 10 **Product Groups:** 30, 40, 42, 48, 66, 84

Date of Accounts	Dec 11	Dec 10	Dec 09
Working Capital	-30	-23	-23
Fixed Assets	116	152	146
Current Assets	317	317	310

York Lift Trucks Ltd

Unit 1 Beckridge Industrial Estate Ripley Drive, Normanton Industrial Estate, Normanton, WF6 1JD
Tel: 01924-266776 **Fax:** 01924-266701
E-mail: m.ovenden123@btinternet.com
Website: http://www.manleyflts.fsnet.co.uk
Directors: M. Ovenden (Dir)
Immediate Holding Company: YORK LIFT TRUCKS LIMITED
Registration no: 03526163 **Date established:** 1998
No.of Employees: 1 - 10 **Product Groups:** 35, 39, 45

Date of Accounts	Mar 11	Mar 10	Mar 09
Working Capital	127	87	33
Fixed Assets	70	85	35
Current Assets	164	143	65

Ossett

A I P Compressor Services Ltd

Logic Works Dewsbury Road, Ossett, WF5 9QF
Tel: 01924-264217 **Fax:** 01924-281004
E-mail: sales@aipcompressors.co.uk
Website: http://www.aipcompressors.co.uk
Directors: A. Williams (MD)
Immediate Holding Company: A.I.P. COMPRESSOR SERVICES LIMITED
Registration no: 01586786 **Date established:** 1981 **Turnover:** £1m - £2m
No.of Employees: 1 - 10 **Product Groups:** 31, 35, 40, 46

Date of Accounts	Sep 11	Sep 10	Sep 09
Working Capital	135	108	111
Fixed Assets	114	100	124
Current Assets	251	267	239

Ask

5 Parkway House Ashley Industrial Estate Wakefield Road, Ossett, WF5 9JD
Tel: 01924-270333 **Fax:** 01924-270888
Directors: K. Ashton (Prop)
Immediate Holding Company: ASK MATERIALS HANDLING LIMITED
Registration no: 08121749 **Date established:** 2012
No.of Employees: 1 - 10 **Product Groups:** 35, 39, 45

L A Brook Ltd

Royds Mill Leeds Road, Ossett, WF5 9YA
Tel: 01924-277026 **Fax:** 01924-262074
E-mail: sales@labrook.com
Website: http://www.labrooks.com
Directors: K. Campbell (Sales), P. Brook (MD), R. Brook (Co Sec)
Immediate Holding Company: L.A. BROOK LIMITED
Registration no: 00640746 **VAT No.:** GB 168 9051 34
Date established: 1959 **Turnover:** £1m - £2m **No.of Employees:** 11 - 20
Product Groups: 27, 32, 66

Date of Accounts	Oct 11	Oct 10	Oct 09
Working Capital	431	425	441
Fixed Assets	87	90	87
Current Assets	650	660	700

The Burmatex

Victoria Mills The Green, Ossett, WF5 0AN
Tel: 01924-263718 **Fax:** 01924-264004
E-mail: info@burmatex.co.uk
Website: http://www.burmatex.co.uk
Bank(s): Barclays
Directors: R. Salt (Fin), N. Rylands (MD), N. Brook (Grp Sales)
Managers: S. Holroyd (Purch Mgr), C. Huby (Mktg Serv Mgr)
Ultimate Holding Company: AIREA PLC
Immediate Holding Company: BURMATEX LIMITED
Registration no: 00596538 **Date established:** 1958
Turnover: £10m - £20m **No.of Employees:** 51 - 100 **Product Groups:** 23

Date of Accounts	Jun 11	Jun 10	Jun 09
Sales Turnover	18m	18m	20m
Pre Tax Profit/Loss	-233	863	-1m
Working Capital	5m	5m	5m
Fixed Assets	3m	3m	4m
Current Assets	10m	10m	9m
Current Liabilities	1m	1m	915

C M Healthcare

Sunnybank Works Sunnybank Street, Ossett, WF5 8PE
Tel: 01924-283336 **Fax:** 01924-283337
E-mail: cmhealthcare@btconnect.com
Website: http://www.cmhealthcare.co.uk
Managers: P. Korn (Mgr)
Immediate Holding Company: GREMEDIA SCREENPRINT LTD
Registration no: 02365476 **Date established:** 1989
No.of Employees: 1 - 10 **Product Groups:** 24, 38, 86

Date of Accounts	Jun 11	Jun 10	Jun 09
Working Capital	-33	-35	-15
Fixed Assets	37	44	32
Current Assets	21	17	15

Carclo plc

88, Ossett, WF5 9LR
Tel: 01924-268040 **Fax:** 01924-283226
E-mail: investor.relations@carclo-plc.com
Website: http://www.carclo-plc.com
Directors: R. Brooksbank (Fin)
Managers: I. Williamson
Immediate Holding Company: CARCLO PLC
Registration no: 00196249 **VAT No.:** GB 183 5627 43
Date established: 2024 **Turnover:** £75m - £125m
No.of Employees: 1 - 10 **Product Groups:** 30, 66

Date of Accounts	Mar 12	Mar 11	Mar 10
Sales Turnover	93m	89m	81m
Pre Tax Profit/Loss	5m	6m	5m
Working Capital	13m	14m	17m
Fixed Assets	80m	73m	71m
Current Assets	38m	42m	41m
Current Liabilities	8m	8m	8m

Crossling Pipeline

Unit 9a Roundwood Industrial Estate, Ossett, WF5 9SQ
Tel: 01924-371666 **Fax:** 01924-234690
E-mail: paul.clayton@crossling.co.uk
Website: http://www.crossling.co.uk
Bank(s): Yorkshire Bank PLC
Managers: P. Clayton (District Mgr)
Ultimate Holding Company: C. BANCROFT LTD
Registration no: 00107189 **VAT No.:** GB 183 4426 58
Turnover: £50m - £75m **No.of Employees:** 11 - 20 **Product Groups:** 36

Danoil Lubricants Ltd

94 Owl Lane, Ossett, WF5 9AU
Tel: 01924-263128 **Fax:** 01924-264078
E-mail: richard@chappellfuels.co.uk
Website: http://www.chappellfuels.co.uk
Directors: B. Chappell (Dir)
Immediate Holding Company: DANOIL LUBRICANTS LIMITED
Registration no: 03201039 **Date established:** 1996
Turnover: £500,000 - £1m **No.of Employees:** 1 - 10 **Product Groups:** 31, 32

see next page

Danoil Lubricants Ltd - Cont'd

Date of Accounts	Jun 11	Jun 09	Jun 08
Working Capital	20	24	23
Fixed Assets	8	5	6
Current Assets	78	53	56

Dave Dickinson & Associates Ltd

RCM Business Centre Sandbeds Trading Estate, Ossett, WF5 9ND
Tel: 01924-265757 **Fax:** 01924-275117
E-mail: reception@ddaltd.co.uk
Website: http://www.ddaltd.co.uk
Bank(s): Yorkshire Bank PLC
Directors: P. Guest (MD), C. Guest (Co Sec)
Managers: A. Greenwood (Tech Serv Mgr), L. Davies (Admin Off)
Ultimate Holding Company: D D A CONSULTING ENGINEERS LIMITED
Immediate Holding Company: DAVE DICKINSON & ASSOCIATES LIMITED
Registration no: 02377576 **VAT No.:** GB 518 2407 59
Date established: 1989 **Turnover:** £1m - £2m **No.of Employees:** 21 - 50
Product Groups: 84

Date of Accounts	Mar 12	Mar 11	Mar 10
Working Capital	586	744	2m
Fixed Assets	22	40	26
Current Assets	1m	1m	2m

Drive Computer Services Ltd

251 Dewsbury Road, Ossett, WF5 9QF
Tel: 01924-280388 **Fax:** 01924-280117
E-mail: enquiries@drivecomputing.co.uk
Website: http://www.drivecomputing.co.uk
Directors: R. Grant (Fin), R. Holderness (Dir)
Immediate Holding Company: DRIVE COMPUTER SERVICES LIMITED
Registration no: 03513758 **Date established:** 1998 **Turnover:** £1m - £2m
No.of Employees: 21 - 50 **Product Groups:** 28, 37, 40, 44

Date of Accounts	Mar 11	Mar 10	Mar 09
Working Capital	160	157	152
Fixed Assets	140	131	127
Current Assets	739	697	685

Elite Ironwork Wrought Iron

58 Swithenbank Avenue, Ossett, WF5 9RR
Tel: 01924-211470
Website: http://www.eliteironwork.co.uk
Directors: L. Bomount (Prop)
Date established: 2005 **No.of Employees:** 1 - 10 **Product Groups:** 26, 35

Feature Metal Work

Kingsway, Ossett, WF5 8DN
Tel: 01924-274134 **Fax:** 01924-274134
Directors: P. Summerscales (Prop)
Date established: 1995 **No.of Employees:** 1 - 10 **Product Groups:** 26, 35

Global Doors Ltd

Unit 4 Roundwood Industrial Estate, Ossett, WF5 9SQ
Tel: 01924-283004 **Fax:** 01924-264329
E-mail: dale@globaldoorsltd.co.uk
Website: http://www.globaldoorsltd.co.uk
Directors: B. Woodhouse (MD)
Managers: M. Fletcher (Sales Prom Mgr)
Immediate Holding Company: GLOBAL DOORS LIMITED
Registration no: 04556829 **Date established:** 1993 **No.of Employees:** 16
Product Groups: 25, 26, 30, 33, 35, 36

Date of Accounts	Dec 11	Dec 10	Dec 09
Working Capital	476	386	424
Fixed Assets	133	95	100
Current Assets	700	544	616

Global Logistics

88 Wakefield Road, Ossett, WF5 9JX
Tel: 01924-266609 **Fax:** 01924-266610
E-mail: globelogistics@talk21.com
Website: http://www.globelogistics.co.uk
Directors: A. Teal (Trans)
Immediate Holding Company: GB POWER STEERING LIMITED
Date established: 2011 **Turnover:** £500,000 - £1m
No.of Employees: 1 - 10 **Product Groups:** 72, 76, 84

Grinding Services

Unit 9b Roundwood Industrial Estate, Ossett, WF5 9SQ
Tel: 01924-280075 **Fax:** 01924-239408
E-mail: sales@grindingservices.co.uk
Website: http://www.grindingservices.co.uk
Directors: R. Traynor (Prop)
Immediate Holding Company: REDWALL MARKETING SERVICES LIMITED
Date established: 1999 **No.of Employees:** 1 - 10 **Product Groups:** 29, 33, 36, 42, 48

Hydro Building Systems Ltd

H B S Centre Albert Drive, Ossett, WF5 9TG
Tel: 01924-232323 **Fax:** 01256-724949
E-mail: info@technal.co.uk
Website: http://www.technal.co.uk
Managers: R. Mousley (Ops Mgr)
Ultimate Holding Company: NORSK HYDRO ASA (NORWAY)
Immediate Holding Company: HYDRO BUILDING SYSTEMS LIMITED
Registration no: 01420752 **Date established:** 1979
No.of Employees: 21 - 50 **Product Groups:** 13, 18, 30, 31, 32, 34, 37, 66, 67, 87

Date of Accounts	Dec 11	Dec 10	Dec 09
Sales Turnover	17m	18m	21m
Pre Tax Profit/Loss	-944	-33	123
Working Capital	4m	4m	5m
Fixed Assets	458	554	638
Current Assets	7m	8m	8m
Current Liabilities	349	442	653

Hydro Fire Ltd

Fire Protection House 9 Kings Close, Ossett, WF5 8QU
Tel: 01924-264074 **Fax:** 01924-264074
E-mail: sales@hydrofire.co.uk
Website: http://www.hydrofire.co.uk
Directors: C. Wardman (Dir)
Immediate Holding Company: HYDRO FIRE LIMITED
Registration no: 05713463 **Date established:** 2006
No.of Employees: 1 - 10 **Product Groups:** 30, 35, 36, 37, 38, 39, 40, 52, 67, 86

Date of Accounts	Mar 11	Mar 10	Mar 09
Working Capital	34	27	16
Fixed Assets	31	27	28
Current Assets	93	50	55

Ice Arets Ltd

130 Kingsway, Ossett, WF5 8DQ
Tel: 01924-280905 **Fax:** 0113-276 1921
Website: http://www.arets.com
Directors: J. Poyner (MD)
Immediate Holding Company: ICE ARETS UK LIMITED
Registration no: 05814235 **Date established:** 2006 **Turnover:** £2m - £5m
No.of Employees: 1 - 10 **Product Groups:** 32

Date of Accounts	Dec 11	Dec 10	Dec 09
Sales Turnover	4m	6m	N/A
Pre Tax Profit/Loss	-894	-757	N/A
Working Capital	-1m	-868	-463
Fixed Assets	292	382	457
Current Assets	2m	3m	3m
Current Liabilities	1m	1m	2m

James Latham plc

Longlands Milner Way, Ossett, WF5 9JE
Tel: 01924-276111 **Fax:** 01924-275156
E-mail: plywood.north@lathams.co.uk
Website: http://www.lathamtimber.co.uk
Bank(s): National Westminster Bank Plc
Directors: A. Wright (Dir)
Ultimate Holding Company: QUEENSBRIDGE HOLDINGS LIMITED
Immediate Holding Company: JAMES LATHAM PUBLIC LIMITED COMPANY
Registration no: 00065619 **VAT No.:** GB 169 6943 06
Date established: 2000 **Turnover:** £20m - £50m
No.of Employees: 21 - 50 **Product Groups:** 25, 66

Date of Accounts	Mar 12	Mar 11	Mar 10
Sales Turnover	144m	130m	115m
Pre Tax Profit/Loss	7m	8m	6m
Working Capital	40m	39m	36m
Fixed Assets	23m	19m	19m
Current Assets	62m	60m	53m
Current Liabilities	5m	7m	5m

Killgerm Group Ltd

PO Box 2 Denholme Drive, Ossett, WF5 9NA
Tel: 01924-268400 **Fax:** 01924-274385
E-mail: sales@killgerm.com
Website: http://www.killgerm.com
Bank(s): National Westminster Bank Plc
Directors: G. Ward (Dir), J. Peck (Ch), J. Warren (Fin), P. Dalgliesh (Dir), P. Kitson (Co Sec)
Managers: D. Hall (I.T. Exec), E. Fearan (Mktg Serv Mgr)
Ultimate Holding Company: Killgerm Group Ltd
Immediate Holding Company: KILLGERM GROUP LIMITED
Registration no: 01272745 **VAT No.:** GB 361 5592 46
Date established: 1976 **Turnover:** £20m - £50m
No.of Employees: 21 - 50 **Product Groups:** 31, 32

Date of Accounts	Dec 08	Dec 07	Dec 06
Pre Tax Profit/Loss	64	-10	-139
Working Capital	-76	-151	-324
Fixed Assets	3073	2876	2972
Current Assets	2317	1176	1059
Current Liabilities	2393	1326	1383
Total Share Capital	120	120	120
ROCE% (Return on Capital Employed)	2.1	-0.4	-5.2

Mailopeners Ltd

6 Heath House Chancery Road, Ossett, WF5 9RZ
Tel: 01924-281812 **Fax:** 01924-263131
E-mail: mailopening@btconnect.com
Website: http://www.mailopeners.com
Directors: S. Bleasdale (Fin), J. Holland (Dir)
Immediate Holding Company: MAILOPENERS LIMITED
Registration no: 05169844 **Date established:** 2004
No.of Employees: 1 - 10 **Product Groups:** 44, 49

Date of Accounts	Sep 06	Sep 05
Working Capital	-26	N/A
Fixed Assets	14	N/A
Current Assets	66	N/A

Nettletons & Porters Ltd

Wakefield Road, Ossett, WF5 9JX
Tel: 01924-273047 **Fax:** 01924-280584
E-mail: jtorrents@nettletons.co.uk
Bank(s): National Westminster Bank Plc
Directors: G. Greer (Fin), J. Torrents (MD)
Managers: T. Hall (Works Gen Mgr), M. Potts (Sales Admin)
Ultimate Holding Company: COLOMER Y MUNMANY SA (SPAIN)
Immediate Holding Company: NETTLETONS & PORTERS LIMITED
Registration no: 00238605 **VAT No.:** GB 169 3340 51
Date established: 1929 **Turnover:** £5m - £10m **No.of Employees:** 11 - 20
Product Groups: 22, 66

Date of Accounts	Dec 10	Dec 09	Dec 08
Sales Turnover	4m	8m	7m
Pre Tax Profit/Loss	309	69	187
Working Capital	2m	2m	1m
Fixed Assets	813	1m	1m
Current Assets	2m	2m	2m
Current Liabilities	187	116	177

Ossett Industrial Projects Ltd

31 South Parade, Ossett, WF5 0EF
Tel: 01924-281389 **Fax:** 01924-281394
E-mail: sales@oipleisure.co.uk
Website: http://www.oipleisure.co.uk
Directors: M. Linford (Fin)
Immediate Holding Company: OSSETT INDUSTRIAL PROJECTS LIMITED
Registration no: 02968463 **VAT No.:** GB 591 0901 47
Date established: 1994 **Turnover:** Up to £250,000
No.of Employees: 1 - 10 **Product Groups:** 37

Date of Accounts	Mar 12	Mar 11	Sep 10
Working Capital	131	90	107
Fixed Assets	25	34	66
Current Assets	185	142	211

Parker Hannisin plc

66 Wakefield Road, Ossett, WF5 9JS
Tel: 01924-282200 **Fax:** 01924-282299
E-mail: info@parker.com
Website: http://www.parker.com
Bank(s): Lloyds TSB, Gillingham Branch
Managers: D. Balls (District Mgr)
Ultimate Holding Company: PARKER HANNIFIN (HOLDINGS) LTD
Immediate Holding Company: PARKER HANNIFIN (GB) LTD
Registration no: 04806503 **VAT No.:** GB 449 6529 06
Date established: 1950 **Turnover:** £5m - £10m **No.of Employees:** 11 - 20
Product Groups: 36, 38, 39, 40, 46, 48, 67, 84

Powermaster

Springfield Mills Spa Street, Ossett, WF5 0HW
Tel: 01924-272696 **Fax:** 01924-272711
E-mail: sales@power-master.co.uk
Website: http://www.power-master.co.uk
Directors: J. Wrenshaw (MD), J. Moffatt (MD)
Managers: M. Hey
Immediate Holding Company: POWERMASTER (WAKEFIELD) LIMITED
Registration no: 03141416 **Date established:** 1995
No.of Employees: 1 - 10 **Product Groups:** 37

Date of Accounts	Jan 11	Jan 10	Jan 09
Working Capital	-10	22	29
Fixed Assets	8	9	11
Current Assets	114	102	107

Techweld Supplies

Unit A Nova Scotia Works Dale Street, Ossett, WF5 9HQ
Tel: 01924-281291 **Fax:** 01924-277871
Directors: M. Cross (Prop)
No.of Employees: 1 - 10 **Product Groups:** 46

West Yorkshire Printing Co. Ltd

Wyprint House Smith Way, Wakefield Road, Ossett, WF5 9JZ
Tel: 01924-280522 **Fax:** 01924-280145
E-mail: sales@westyorkshireprinting.co.uk
Website: http://www.wyprint.co.uk
Bank(s): Barclays
Directors: J. Dixon (Ch), M. Waller (Dir)
Managers: D. Pool (Develop Mgr), J. Falkirk (Sales Prom)
Immediate Holding Company: West Yorkshire Printing Company Ltd
Registration no: 00012592 **VAT No.:** GB 169 1360 55
Date established: 1831 **Turnover:** £5m - £10m **No.of Employees:** 21 - 50
Product Groups: 23, 27, 28, 30

Date of Accounts	Dec 07	Dec 06	Dec 05
Pre Tax Profit/Loss	N/A	N/A	-274
Working Capital	2071	2072	2067
Fixed Assets	2071	2217	2453
Current Assets	2392	2432	2391
Current Liabilities	321	360	324
Total Share Capital	121	121	121
ROCE% (Return on Capital Employed)			-6.1

Otley

Aire Services

PO Box 87, Otley, LS21 1TG
Tel: 01943-858409
E-mail: info@aireservices.co.uk
Website: http://www.aireservices.co.uk
Directors: W. Mitchell (Prop)
Immediate Holding Company: AIRE SERVICES LIMITED
Registration no: 04882610 **Date established:** 2003
No.of Employees: 1 - 10 **Product Groups:** 37, 40

Craftsman Tools Ltd

Side Copse, Otley, LS21 1JE
Tel: 01943-466788 **Fax:** 01943-850144
E-mail: sales@craftsmantools.com
Website: http://www.craftsmantools.com
Bank(s): Lloyds
Directors: R. Johnson (Dir)
Managers: T. Gillet (Comptroller)
Ultimate Holding Company: CRAFTSMAN TOOLS LIMITED
Immediate Holding Company: CRAFTSMAN TOOLS LIMITED
Registration no: 00518142 **VAT No.:** GB 168 8408 24
Date established: 1953 **Turnover:** £2m - £5m **No.of Employees:** 51 - 100
Product Groups: 35, 39, 46

Date of Accounts	Jan 12	Jan 11	Jan 10
Sales Turnover	5m	4m	4m
Pre Tax Profit/Loss	278	-102	30
Working Capital	1m	1m	1m
Fixed Assets	2m	2m	2m
Current Assets	2m	2m	2m
Current Liabilities	289	281	192

Penmann Climatic Systems Ltd

Highfield Pool Road, Pool in Wharfedale, Otley, LS21 1EG
Tel: 0113-202 7300 **Fax:** 0113-202 7301
E-mail: office@penmann.co.uk
Website: http://www.penmann.co.uk
Directors: J. Kirwin (Comm)
Immediate Holding Company: PENMANN CLIMATIC SYSTEMS LTD
Registration no: 01463993 **VAT No.:** 500 2827 92 **Date established:** 1979
Turnover: £250,000 - £500,000 **No.of Employees:** 1 - 10
Product Groups: 52, 87

Date of Accounts	Mar 11	Mar 10	Mar 09
Working Capital	-30	44	24
Fixed Assets	61	43	57
Current Assets	168	387	324

William Sinclair & Sons Stationers Ltd

PO Box 1, Otley, LS21 1QF
Tel: 01943-461144 **Fax:** 01943-850017
E-mail: enquiries@sinclairsproducts.com
Website: http://www.silvine.com
Directors: P. Howard (Dir), A. Howard (Fin)
Managers: R. Padden (Tech Serv Mgr), S. Medley (Mktg Serv Mgr)
Immediate Holding Company: WILLIAM SINCLAIR & SONS (STATIONERS) LIMITED
Registration no: 00602428 **VAT No.:** GB 169 7900 25
Date established: 1958 **Turnover:** £10m - £20m
No.of Employees: 101 - 250 **Product Groups:** 27

Date of Accounts	Aug 11	Aug 10	Aug 09
Sales Turnover	14m	13m	13m
Pre Tax Profit/Loss	402	862	834
Working Capital	11m	11m	11m
Fixed Assets	4m	3m	3m
Current Assets	13m	13m	12m
Current Liabilities	946	1m	858

Weidmann Whiteley Ltd
Pool In Wharfedale, Otley, LS21 1RP
Tel: 0113-284 2121 **Fax:** 0113-284 2272
E-mail: paul.hirst@wicor.com
Website: http://www.wicor.com
Bank(s): National Westminster, Otley
Directors: P. Hirst (MD)
Ultimate Holding Company: WICOR HOLDING AG (SWITZERLAND)
Immediate Holding Company: WEIDMANN WHITELEY LIMITED
Registration no: 01531157 **VAT No.:** GB 243 1990 56
Date established: 1980 **Turnover:** £10m - £20m
No.of Employees: 101 - 250 **Product Groups:** 23, 27, 29

Date of Accounts	Dec 11	Dec 10	Dec 09
Sales Turnover	17m	14m	14m
Pre Tax Profit/Loss	431	155	223
Working Capital	4m	4m	5m
Fixed Assets	8m	9m	9m
Current Assets	7m	7m	7m
Current Liabilities	226	390	233

Pontefract

Active Aerials
3 Hacking Lane South Elmsall, Pontefract, WF9 2SU
Tel: 01977-647349
Directors: M. Senior (Prop)
No.of Employees: 1 - 10 **Product Groups:** 26, 37, 39, 67

Advanced Diesel Engineering
14 Langthwaite Grange Business Park South Kirby, Pontefract, WF9 3AP
Tel: 01977-658100 **Fax:** 01977-608111
E-mail: dan.willows@adeltd.co.uk
Website: http://www.adeltd.co.uk
Product Groups: 37, 38, 39, 40, 42, 52, 67, 83

Date of Accounts	Jul 11	Jul 10	Jul 09
Sales Turnover	13m	12m	N/A
Pre Tax Profit/Loss	366	606	1m
Working Capital	656	732	672
Fixed Assets	2m	2m	2m
Current Assets	5m	5m	4m
Current Liabilities	1m	868	679

Allen Fabrications
28 Lidgate Crescent Langthwaite Grange Industrial Estsou, South Kirkby, Pontefract, WF9 3NR
Tel: 01977-640860 **Fax:** 01977-651452
Website: http://www.allenfabrications.co.uk
Directors: W. Allen (MD)
Immediate Holding Company: ALLEN FABRICATIONS & SONS LTD
Registration no: 05269273 **Date established:** 2004
No.of Employees: 11 - 20 **Product Groups:** 35

Date of Accounts	Dec 11	Dec 10	Dec 09
Working Capital	53	18	82
Fixed Assets	46	59	78
Current Assets	149	90	131
Current Liabilities	N/A	12	23

Chiorino UK Ltd
Phoenix Avenue Featherstone, Pontefract, WF7 6EP
Tel: 01977-691880 **Fax:** 0870-606 5061
E-mail: sales@chiorino.co.uk
Website: http://www.chiorino.co.uk
Bank(s): Barclays, Leeds
Managers: M. Bull (Mgr)
Ultimate Holding Company: CHIORINO PARTICIPATIONS SA (LUXEMBOURG)
Immediate Holding Company: CHIORINO U.K. LIMITED
Registration no: 01196087 **Date established:** 1975 **Turnover:** £2m - £5m
No.of Employees: 21 - 50 **Product Groups:** 22, 23, 25, 29

Date of Accounts	Dec 11	Dec 10	Dec 09
Sales Turnover	5m	4m	4m
Pre Tax Profit/Loss	445	326	10
Working Capital	2m	2m	1m
Fixed Assets	2m	2m	2m
Current Assets	3m	3m	2m
Current Liabilities	1m	1m	903

Coils Ltd
36 Lidgate Crescent Langthwaite Grange Industrial Estate, South Kirkby, Pontefract, WF9 3NR
Tel: 01977-641757 **Fax:** 01977-641688
E-mail: sales@handccoils.co.uk
Website: http://www.handccoils.co.uk
Directors: W. Galloway (Dir), P. Galloway (Dir)
Ultimate Holding Company: C.G.H. HOLDINGS LIMITED
Immediate Holding Company: HEATING & COOLING COILS LIMITED
Registration no: 01819970 **Date established:** 1984
No.of Employees: 1 - 10 **Product Groups:** 40

Date of Accounts	Dec 07	Dec 06	Dec 05
Working Capital	18	10	10
Current Assets	133	41	41
Current Liabilities	N/A	31	N/A

Colour Rite
Acton Hall Enterprise Park Station Lane, Featherstone, Pontefract, WF7 6EQ
Tel: 01977-798877 **Fax:** 01977-798877
Directors: A. Carr (Prop)
Immediate Holding Company: FIRST AID FIRST DIRECT LTD
Date established: 2008 **No.of Employees:** 1 - 10 **Product Groups:** 38, 42

M & T Crossley Tordoff
Jubilee Way, Pontefract, WF8 1DH
Tel: 01977-702002 **Fax:** 01977-600002
E-mail: info@ctski.co.uk
Website: http://www.ctski.co.uk
Directors: T. Tordoff (Prop), T. Tordoff (Prop)
VAT No.: GB 181 8325 56 **Date established:** 1962
Turnover: Up to £250,000 **No.of Employees:** 1 - 10 **Product Groups:** 40, 61

D S Smith Corrugated
Common Side Lane Featherstone, Pontefract, WF7 5DF
Tel: 01977-781100 **Fax:** 01977-780356
E-mail: brian.lister@dssp.com
Website: http://www.dssmith-packaging.com
Directors: J. Anderson (MD)
Managers: D. Wood (Personnel), M. Daniels (Tech Serv Mgr), J. Dennison (Personnel), G. Tomlinson (I.T. Exec), M. Webster (Comptroller)
Immediate Holding Company: LINPAC CONTAINERS INTERNATIONAL LTD
Registration no: 01230693 **Date established:** 1973 **Turnover:** £1m - £2m
No.of Employees: 251 - 500 **Product Groups:** 27

Dempsey Dyer Ltd
Langthwaite Grange Business Park South Kirkby, Pontefract, WF9 3AP
Tel: 01977-649641 **Fax:** 01977-653041
E-mail: sales@dempseydyer.co.uk
Website: http://www.dempseydyer.co.uk
Directors: A. Dyer (Fin), C. Worley (Fin), P. Dyer (Dir), T. Dyer (MD)
Managers: A. Mills (Personnel), J. Bratley (Tech Serv Mgr)
Immediate Holding Company: DEMPSEY DYER LIMITED
Registration no: 01309583 **Date established:** 1977 **Turnover:** £5m - £10m
No.of Employees: 51 - 100 **Product Groups:** 25, 30, 36

Date of Accounts	Mar 11	Mar 10	Mar 09
Sales Turnover	7m	5m	N/A
Pre Tax Profit/Loss	3	-386	-128
Working Capital	2m	2m	3m
Fixed Assets	973	1m	979
Current Assets	3m	3m	3m
Current Liabilities	173	121	193

Digital Metal Ltd
The Church Gatehouse Skinner Lane, Pontefract, WF8 1HG
Tel: 01977-706121 **Fax:** 01977-705226
E-mail: info@digimetal.co.uk
Website: http://www.digimetal.co.uk
Directors: S. Warner (MD)
Managers: S. Monaghan (Mktg Serv Mgr)
Registration no: 04033790 **Turnover:** Up to £250,000
No.of Employees: 1 - 10 **Product Groups:** 44

Date of Accounts	Jul 09	Jul 08	Jul 07
Working Capital	-0	-1	-1
Fixed Assets	N/A	1	1
Current Assets	5	6	8

Direct Fabrications
Unit 45f-G Lidgate Crescent Langthwaite Grange Industrial Estate, South Kirkby, Pontefract, WF9 3NR
Tel: 01977-651501 **Fax:** 01977-641697
E-mail: paulcopley@directfabrications.net
Website: http://www.directfabrications.net
Directors: P. Copley (Prop), P. Coppley (Prop)
Date established: 1999 **No.of Employees:** 1 - 10 **Product Groups:** 35

Hanson Myrefield
Warren Road Featherstone, Pontefract, WF7 6EL
Tel: 01977-695111 **Fax:** 01977-695151
E-mail: andrew.sheard@hansongarages.co.uk
Website: http://www.hansonconcretegarages.co.uk
Directors: G. Hanson (MD)
Managers: A. Taggert (Ops Mgr), A. Sheard (Ops Mgr), A. Roberts (Sales Prom Mg), S. Abbott
Immediate Holding Company: HANSON-MYREFIELD-LIMITED
Registration no: 02927821 **Date established:** 1994
No.of Employees: 21 - 50 **Product Groups:** 25, 30, 33

Date of Accounts	Dec 11	Dec 10	Dec 09
Working Capital	25	219	258
Fixed Assets	750	399	407
Current Assets	986	911	931

Ironcraft
Sunnybank Waggon Lane, Upton, Pontefract, WF9 1JT
Tel: 01977-648991
Directors: R. Corly (Prop)
Date established: 1998 **No.of Employees:** 1 - 10 **Product Groups:** 26, 35

Moran Metalcraft
Unit 10 Britannia Works Skinner Lane, Pontefract, WF8 1NA
Tel: 01977-702558 **Fax:** 01977-702558
Directors: A. Moran (Prop)
Immediate Holding Company: DIGITAL METAL LIMITED
Registration no: 04033790 **Date established:** 2000
No.of Employees: 1 - 10 **Product Groups:** 26, 35

Northern Spares & Services
Chapel Works Wakefield Road, Fitzwilliam, Pontefract, WF9 5BP
Tel: 01977-610187 **Fax:** 01977-610012
E-mail: crusherclarke@aol.com
Directors: R. Clarke (MD)
Immediate Holding Company: KINSLEY AND FITZWILLIAM LEARNING AND COMMUNITY CENTRE
Registration no: 04676691 **Date established:** 1999
No.of Employees: 1 - 10 **Product Groups:** 42, 45, 48

Date of Accounts	Mar 11	Mar 10	Mar 09
Working Capital	113	85	29
Fixed Assets	163	41	43
Current Assets	121	94	67

Opti-Pharma UK
Lynwood House 56 Lynwood Crescent, Pontefract, WF8 3QX
Tel: 01977-791302 **Fax:** 01977-791302
E-mail: info@optipharmauk.co.uk
Website: http://www.optipharmauk.co.uk
Product Groups: 40, 42, 66, 85

Power Plant Services
22 Langthwaite Road Langthwaite Grange Industrial Estate, South Kirkby, Pontefract, WF9 3AP
Tel: 01977-641144 **Fax:** 01977-648180
E-mail: tony@ppspower.com
Website: http://www.ppspower.com
Directors: A. Jenkinson (Sales), G. Wrigglesworth (Fin), T. Brimbell (Dir), T. Brimble (MD), T. Brimele (MD)
Managers: T. Coulthard (Sales Prom Mgr)
Immediate Holding Company: THE ICE CO LOGISTICS LIMITED
Registration no: 06023494 **Date established:** 2006
No.of Employees: 21 - 50 **Product Groups:** 37, 40, 48, 83

Precision Engineers Pontefract Ltd
South Baileygate, Pontefract, WF8 2JL
Tel: 01977-702439 **Fax:** 01977-600284
E-mail: thorpemartin@pel-ltd.co.uk
Bank(s): Yorkshire
Directors: M. Thorpe (Dir), M. Carey-Topping (MD), R. Whittaker (Dir)
Immediate Holding Company: Precision Engineers (Pontefract) Ltd.
Registration no: 00682262 **VAT No.:** GB 181 9098 36
Date established: 1961 **Turnover:** £1m - £2m **No.of Employees:** 11 - 20
Product Groups: 48, 84, 85

Date of Accounts	Dec 11	Dec 10	Dec 09
Working Capital	168	38	13
Fixed Assets	168	145	128
Current Assets	637	462	251

Prestige Pumps Ltd
Unit 9 Innovation Square Green Lane, Featherstone, Pontefract, WF7 6NX
Tel: 01977-602200 **Fax:** 01924-379953
E-mail: sales@prestigepumps.co.uk
Website: http://www.prestigepumps.co.uk
Directors: D. Moxon (MD), M. Walker (Fin)
Immediate Holding Company: PRESTIGE PUMPS LIMITED
Registration no: 03528153 **Date established:** 1998
No.of Employees: 11 - 20 **Product Groups:** 39, 40, 41, 42, 43, 45, 46, 48, 49, 67, 68, 83

Date of Accounts	Mar 12	Mar 11	Mar 10
Working Capital	214	199	150
Fixed Assets	87	71	79
Current Assets	627	592	371

Randalls Fabrications Ltd
Hoyle Mill Road Kinsley, Pontefract, WF9 5JB
Tel: 01977-615132 **Fax:** 01977-610059
E-mail: info@randallsfabrications.co.uk
Website: http://www.randallsfabrications.co.uk
Bank(s): The Royal Bank of Scotland
Directors: R. Wake (Fin), A. Muirhead (MD), M. Hampson (Sales)
Ultimate Holding Company: RAMSHORN LIMITED
Immediate Holding Company: RANDALLS FABRICATIONS LIMITED
Registration no: 01312065 **VAT No.:** GB 734 5383 26
Date established: 1977 **Turnover:** Up to £250,000
No.of Employees: 21 - 50 **Product Groups:** 42, 45, 54

Date of Accounts	May 12	May 11	May 10
Working Capital	2m	1m	1m
Fixed Assets	531	531	537
Current Assets	10m	6m	6m

Ripon Farm Services Ltd
Great North Road Darrington, Pontefract, WF8 3BW
Tel: 01977-795241 **Fax:** 01977-798074
E-mail: sales@riponfarmservices.co.uk
Website: http://www.riponfarmservices.co.uk
Directors: G. Brown (MD)
Immediate Holding Company: RIPON FARM SERVICES LIMITED
Registration no: 01667383 **Date established:** 1982
No.of Employees: 11 - 20 **Product Groups:** 41

Date of Accounts	Jan 12	Jan 11	Jan 10
Sales Turnover	73m	69m	56m
Pre Tax Profit/Loss	1m	1m	705
Working Capital	7m	7m	3m
Fixed Assets	5m	5m	5m
Current Assets	23m	17m	17m
Current Liabilities	678	1m	581

S C F Supplies
3 Lister Park Featherstone, Pontefract, WF7 6FE
Tel: 01977-700030 **Fax:** 01977-700074
E-mail: sales@scfsupplies.co.uk
Website: http://www.scfsupplies.co.uk
Directors: S. Ferres (Prop)
No.of Employees: 1 - 10 **Product Groups:** 35

The Tambour Company Ltd
Warren Road Green Lane Business Park, Featherstone, Pontefract, WF7 6EL
Tel: 01977-600026 **Fax:** 01977-600991
E-mail: william.wesson@tambour.co.uk
Website: http://www.tambour.co.uk
Directors: W. Wesson (MD), W. Wesson (Fin)
Immediate Holding Company: THE TAMBOUR COMPANY LTD.
Registration no: 02909715 **VAT No.:** GB 642 6879 05
Date established: 1994 **Turnover:** £1m - £2m **No.of Employees:** 1 - 10
Product Groups: 25

Date of Accounts	Mar 08	Mar 07	Mar 06
Working Capital	530	-314	-141
Fixed Assets	1038	1084	1130
Current Assets	1198	443	518
Current Liabilities	668	758	659
Total Share Capital	10	10	10

Pudsey

A & S Fabrications
Grangefield Mill Grangefield Road, Stanningley, Pudsey, LS28 6JT
Tel: 0113-279 3868 **Fax:** 0113-263 1113
E-mail: sales@asfabs.co.uk
Website: http://www.asfabs.co.uk
Directors: A. Hughes (Fin), S. Hughes (MD)
Immediate Holding Company: A & S FABRICATIONS (LEEDS) LIMITED
Registration no: 04142782 **Date established:** 2001
Turnover: Up to £250,000 **No.of Employees:** 1 - 10 **Product Groups:** 35

Date of Accounts	Dec 10	Dec 09	Dec 08
Sales Turnover	101	148	183
Pre Tax Profit/Loss	-1	10	6
Working Capital	-38	-33	-40
Fixed Assets	80	78	81
Current Assets	-26	-29	-38
Current Liabilities	12	4	2

Acrivarn Ltd
South Park Mills Hare Lane, Pudsey, LS28 8DR
Tel: 0113-257 8875 **Fax:** 0113-257 7564
E-mail: sales@acrivarn.co.uk
Website: http://www.acrivarn.co.uk
Bank(s): HSBC
Directors: S. Cope (MD)
Immediate Holding Company: ACRIVARN LIMITED
Registration no: 00900220 **VAT No.:** GB 179 3251 43
Date established: 1967 **Turnover:** £1m - £2m **No.of Employees:** 11 - 20
Product Groups: 41

see next page

Acrivarn Ltd - Cont'd

Date of Accounts	Apr 12	Apr 11	Apr 10
Working Capital	103	48	100
Fixed Assets	138	136	134
Current Assets	499	468	432

Aire Bearings

34 Bradford Road Stanningley, Pudsey, LS28 6DD
Tel: 0113-256 5676 **Fax:** 0113-255 4894
E-mail: sales@airebearings.co.uk
Website: http://www.airebearings.co.uk
Directors: D. Richards (Co Sec)
Immediate Holding Company: AIRE BEARINGS LIMITED
Registration no: 04650086 **Date established:** 2003
No.of Employees: 1 - 10 **Product Groups:** 35

Date of Accounts	Apr 12	Apr 11	Apr 10
Working Capital	27	2	-0
Fixed Assets	8	1	2
Current Assets	158	111	187

I G Atkinson Leeds Ltd

13 Nether Street Farsley, Pudsey, LS28 5LN
Tel: 0113-255 6848 **Fax:** 0113-257 4892
E-mail: ian@igatkinson.co.uk
Website: http://www.igatkinson.co.uk
Directors: J. Noblett (Fin), I. Atkinson (MD)
Immediate Holding Company: I.G. ATKINSON (LEEDS) LIMITED
Registration no: 01568687 **Date established:** 1981
Turnover: £250,000 - £500,000 **No.of Employees:** 11 - 20
Product Groups: 52

Date of Accounts	Jul 11	Jul 10	Jul 09
Working Capital	113	117	103
Fixed Assets	360	364	490
Current Assets	286	214	270

Bell Bros Pudsey Ltd

Green Lane, Pudsey, LS28 8JN
Tel: 0113-256 5715 **Fax:** 0113-256 9255
E-mail: info@bellbros.com
Website: http://www.bellbros.com
Bank(s): Barclays
Directors: C. Bell (MD), P. Bell (MD), J. Bell (MD)
Managers: T. Bradbury (Chief Mgr)
Immediate Holding Company: BELL BROS (PUDSEY) LIMITED
Registration no: 00367423 **VAT No.:** GB 179 3646 20
Date established: 1941 **Turnover:** £1m - £2m **No.of Employees:** 11 - 20
Product Groups: 45, 48

Date of Accounts	Mar 11	Mar 10	Mar 09
Working Capital	57	120	431
Fixed Assets	623	4m	184
Current Assets	185	239	556

Bolt & Nut Supplies Ltd

35-37 Chapeltown, Pudsey, LS28 7RZ
Tel: 0113-255 6336 **Fax:** 0113-256 9242
Directors: D. Hall (Dir)
Immediate Holding Company: BOLT AND NUT SUPPLIES LIMITED
Registration no: 01465656 **VAT No.:** GB 343 0008 11
Date established: 1979 **Turnover:** £500,000 - £1m
No.of Employees: 1 - 10 **Product Groups:** 63, 66

Date of Accounts	Sep 11	Sep 10	Sep 09
Working Capital	117	170	197
Fixed Assets	30	24	27
Current Assets	507	490	423

Caters

The Old Mill Sunfield Place, Stanningley, Pudsey, LS28 6DR
Tel: 0113-257 5757 **Fax:** 0113-255 5100
E-mail: mike@caters.net
Website: http://www.caters.net
Bank(s): Yorkshire Bank PLC
Directors: M. Cater (MD)
Ultimate Holding Company: MICHAEL CATER HOLDINGS LIMITED
Immediate Holding Company: MICHAEL CATER & ASSOCIATES LIMITED
Registration no: 01681040 **VAT No.:** GB 372 0767 49
Date established: 1982 **Turnover:** £250,000 - £500,000
No.of Employees: 11 - 20 **Product Groups:** 81

Date of Accounts	Mar 12	Mar 11	Mar 10
Working Capital	187	177	174
Fixed Assets	47	42	11
Current Assets	428	513	416

Computer Services Consultants UK Ltd

Yeadon House New Street, Pudsey, LS28 8AQ
Tel: 0113-239 3000 **Fax:** 0113-255 3917
E-mail: simon.bellwood@cscworld.com
Website: http://www.cscworld.com
Bank(s): HSBC Bank plc
Directors: M. Roberts (Dir), M. Roberts (Sales), S. Bellwood (Fin)
Managers: S. Peat ()
Ultimate Holding Company: COBCO 867 LIMITED
Immediate Holding Company: COMPUTER SERVICES CONSULTANTS (U.K.) LIMITED
Registration no: 02237053 **VAT No.:** GB 172 2450 84
Date established: 1988 **Turnover:** £5m - £10m **No.of Employees:** 21 - 50
Product Groups: 44

Date of Accounts	Mar 11	Mar 10	Mar 09
Sales Turnover	N/A	N/A	5m
Pre Tax Profit/Loss	N/A	N/A	2m
Working Capital	2m	974	360
Fixed Assets	537	760	945
Current Assets	6m	4m	2m
Current Liabilities	N/A	N/A	2m

D T Power Tool Services

153 Richardshaw Lane Stanningley, Pudsey, LS28 6AA
Tel: 0113-239 3477 **Fax:** 0113-239 3477
Directors: D. Thompson (Prop)
Date established: 1992 **No.of Employees:** 1 - 10 **Product Groups:** 37

Daletech Electronics Ltd

Regency House Valley Road, Pudsey, LS28 9EN
Tel: 0113-239 4220 **Fax:** 0113-255 3583
E-mail: sales@daletech.co.uk
Website: http://www.daletech.co.uk
Bank(s): TSB, Leeds
Directors: C. Dawson (MD)
Immediate Holding Company: DALETECH ELECTRONICS LIMITED
Registration no: 02092372 **VAT No.:** GB 444 3076 62
Date established: 1987 **Turnover:** £250,000 - £500,000
No.of Employees: 11 - 20 **Product Groups:** 38, 85

Date of Accounts	Mar 12	Mar 11	Mar 10
Working Capital	152	163	134
Fixed Assets	260	265	274
Current Assets	289	339	299

Dytel Technologies Ltd

1 Stanningley Industrial Centre Varley Street, Stanningley, Pudsey, LS28 6AN
Tel: 0113-236 0980 **Fax:** 0113-236 1040
E-mail: charles@dytel.co.uk
Website: http://www.dytel.co.uk
Directors: C. Adams (MD)
Immediate Holding Company: DYTEL TECHNOLOGIES LIMITED
Registration no: 02540241 **Date established:** 1990
No.of Employees: 1 - 10 **Product Groups:** 84

Date of Accounts	Mar 11	Mar 10	Mar 09
Working Capital	21	16	-27
Fixed Assets	45	48	53
Current Assets	196	16	180

Emmark UK Ltd

Emmark House 5 Carlisle Drive, Pudsey, LS28 8QS
Tel: 0113-255 2344 **Fax:** 0113-239 3856
E-mail: mtillotson@emmark.co.uk
Website: http://www.emmarkuk.co.uk
Bank(s): National Westminster Bank Plc
Directors: M. Tillotson (Dir)
Immediate Holding Company: EMMARK UK LIMITED
Registration no: 02283060 **Date established:** 1988 **Turnover:** £2m - £5m
No.of Employees: 11 - 20 **Product Groups:** 41, 67

Date of Accounts	Oct 11	Oct 10	Oct 09
Working Capital	2m	1m	1m
Fixed Assets	28	37	29
Current Assets	2m	2m	2m

Fibretex Mouldings

Waterloo Road, Pudsey, LS28 8DQ
Tel: 0113-236 1094 **Fax:** 0113-255 5345
Directors: C. Nettleton (Prop)
Immediate Holding Company: CRESCO INDUSTRIAL SUPPLIES LIMITED
Date established: 1995 **Turnover:** Up to £250,000
No.of Employees: 1 - 10 **Product Groups:** 30, 33

Four Seasons France Ltd

19 Carr Road Calverley, Pudsey, LS28 5NE
Tel: 0113-256 4373 **Fax:** 0113-255 5923
E-mail: info@fourseasonsfrance.co.uk
Website: http://www.fourseasons.uk.net
Directors: D. Illingworth (Sales & Mktg), D. Illingworth (Dir), D. Eccles (Co Sec), J. Wilkinson (Dir)
Immediate Holding Company: FOUR SEASONS (LEISURE) LIMITED
Registration no: 01016997 **Date established:** 1971
No.of Employees: 1 - 10 **Product Groups:** 69

Date of Accounts	Dec 09	Dec 08	Dec 07
Working Capital	-17	-14	-9
Fixed Assets	2	2	3
Current Assets	1	1	21

Fulwith Textiles

Sunny Bank Mills Farsley, Pudsey, LS28 5UJ
Tel: 0113-257 9811 **Fax:** 0113-257 7064
Directors: N. Hesp (Prop)
Immediate Holding Company: FULWITH TEXTILES LIMITED
Registration no: 03944292 **Date established:** 2000
Turnover: £250,000 - £500,000 **No.of Employees:** 1 - 10
Product Groups: 63

Date of Accounts	Mar 11	Mar 10	Mar 08
Working Capital	-1	7	6
Fixed Assets	2	2	3
Current Assets	76	90	69

G R P Leeds

Springfield Works Bagley Lane, Farsley, Pudsey, LS28 5LL
Tel: 0113-255 4664 **Fax:** 0113-239 3215
E-mail: sales@grp-group.co.uk
Website: http://www.grp-group.co.uk
Directors: D. Barnes (Fab), D. Read (MD), L. Ness (Sales), K. Reynolds Jones (Mkt Research)
Ultimate Holding Company: GRP LEEDS LIMITED
Immediate Holding Company: GRP ENTERPRISES LIMITED
Registration no: 01488290 **VAT No.:** GB 651 7880 14
Date established: 1980 **No.of Employees:** 21 - 50 **Product Groups:** 39

Date of Accounts	Mar 12	Mar 11	Mar 10
Working Capital	228	199	197
Fixed Assets	N/A	96	49
Current Assets	328	686	666
Current Liabilities	100	N/A	N/A

Hainsworth Industrial Textiles

Spring Valley Stanningley, Pudsey, LS28 6DW
Tel: 0113-257 0391 **Fax:** 0113-395 5686
E-mail: sales@hainsworth.co.uk
Website: http://www.hainsworth.co.uk
Bank(s): Lloyds TSB Bank plc
Directors: T. Hainsworth (MD), D. Simpson (Sales)
Managers: I. Turba (Mktg Serv Mgr), A. Hainsworth (Comptroller), S. Fowler (Purch Mgr), W. Wasley (Tech Serv Mgr), A. Wilson (Personnel)
Immediate Holding Company: A.W. HAINSWORTH PROPERTY LIMITED
Registration no: 06552921 **VAT No.:** GB 707 9294 08
Date established: 2008 **Turnover:** £10m - £20m
No.of Employees: 101 - 250 **Product Groups:** 23, 24, 30, 49, 63

Date of Accounts	Mar 12	Mar 11	Mar 10
Sales Turnover	163	N/A	N/A
Pre Tax Profit/Loss	119	N/A	N/A
Working Capital	135	156	91
Fixed Assets	526	557	588
Current Assets	168	159	139
Current Liabilities	32	N/A	N/A

Hopkins Catering Equipment Ltd

Valley Mills 151 Kent Road, Pudsey, LS28 9NF
Tel: 0113-257 7934 **Fax:** 0113-257 6759
E-mail: info@hopkins.biz
Website: http://www.hopkins.biz
Bank(s): National Westminster Bank Plc
Directors: C. Hopkins (MD), V. Hopkins (Dir), B. Stacey (Co Sec)
Managers: M. Jafrape (Purch Mgr)
Immediate Holding Company: HOPKINS X L HOLDINGS LIMITED
Registration no: 00635524 **VAT No.:** GB 500 2553 06
Date established: 1959 **Turnover:** Up to £250,000
No.of Employees: 51 - 100 **Product Groups:** 30, 40

Date of Accounts	Aug 11	Aug 10	Aug 09
Working Capital	460	460	460
Fixed Assets	51	51	51
Current Assets	473	474	474

Horrocks Diesel Services

3 Slaters Road Stanningley, Pudsey, LS28 6EY
Tel: 0113-236 3298 **Fax:** 0113-236 3298
Directors: D. Horrocks (Prop)
Date established: 1993 **No.of Employees:** 1 - 10 **Product Groups:** 40

Industrial Plastic Supplies Ltd

3 Milestone Court Business Park Town Street, Stanningley, Pudsey, LS28 6HE
Tel: 0113-257 9000 **Fax:** 0113-257 2222
E-mail: info@industrialplastics.co.uk
Website: http://www.industrialplastics.co.uk
Directors: C. Luty (MD)
Immediate Holding Company: INDUSTRIAL PLASTIC SUPPLIES LIMITED
Registration no: 01957648 **Date established:** 1985 **Turnover:** £2m - £5m
No.of Employees: 1 - 10 **Product Groups:** 30, 66

Date of Accounts	Dec 11	Dec 10	Dec 09
Working Capital	247	197	145
Fixed Assets	16	3	8
Current Assets	449	411	279

J T M Service Ltd

6 Milestone Court Stanningley, Pudsey, LS28 6HE
Tel: 0113-257 2221 **Fax:** 0113-257 3360
E-mail: john@jtmservice.com
Website: http://www.jtmservice.com
Directors: J. Middleton (MD), M. Tomlinson (Fin)
Immediate Holding Company: JTM SERVICE LIMITED
Registration no: 02471804 **Date established:** 1990
No.of Employees: 11 - 20 **Product Groups:** 32, 40, 48

Date of Accounts	Oct 11	Oct 10	Oct 09
Working Capital	339	324	311
Fixed Assets	96	124	108
Current Assets	728	786	772

L B B C Technologies

Beechwood Street Stanningley, Pudsey, LS28 6PT
Tel: 0113-205 7400 **Fax:** 0113-256 3509
E-mail: sales@lbbc.co.uk
Website: http://www.lbbc.co.uk
Directors: H. Pickard (MD)
Managers: D. Forrell (Buyer)
Immediate Holding Company: LBBC TECHNOLOGIES LIMITED
Registration no: 07125859 **VAT No.:** 179 8662 94 **Date established:** 2010
Turnover: £2m - £5m **No.of Employees:** 1 - 10 **Product Groups:** 40

Leigh House Facilities Management Ltd

Leigh House Varley Street, Stanningley, Pudsey, LS28 6AN
Tel: 0113-255 7979 **Fax:** 0113-255 7970
E-mail: mail@leighhouse.com
Website: http://www.leighhouse.com
Managers: S. Padgett (Sales Admin)
Immediate Holding Company: LEIGH HOUSE FACILITIES MANAGEMENT LIMITED
Registration no: 02758215 **Date established:** 1992
Turnover: £500,000 - £1m **No.of Employees:** 1 - 10 **Product Groups:** 80

Date of Accounts	May 11	May 10	May 09
Working Capital	-0	N/A	N/A
Fixed Assets	1	N/A	N/A
Current Assets	42	N/A	N/A

London Oil Refining Co

Richardshaw Road Grangefield Industrial Estate, Stanningley, Pudsey, LS28 6QZ
Tel: 0113-236 0036 **Fax:** 0113-236 0038
E-mail: info@astonish.co.uk
Website: http://www.astonishcleaners.com
Bank(s): HSBC Bank plc
Directors: A. Moss (Ch), M. Moss (Fin), M. Moss (Co Sec)
Managers: H. Moss (Mgr)
Ultimate Holding Company: 03422443
Immediate Holding Company: THE LONDON OIL REFINING CO. LIMITED
Registration no: 02587314 **Date established:** 1991
Turnover: £10m - £20m **No.of Employees:** 21 - 50 **Product Groups:** 31, 32, 36

Date of Accounts	May 08	May 07	May 06
Sales Turnover	8374	7945	7368
Pre Tax Profit/Loss	351	236	264
Working Capital	934	694	496
Fixed Assets	1478	1561	1669
Current Assets	2656	2285	2340
Current Liabilities	1722	1591	1844
Total Share Capital	70	70	70
ROCE% (Return on Capital Employed)	14.6	10.5	12.2
ROT% (Return on Turnover)	4.2	3.0	3.6

Newton Derby Ltd

Grangefield House Richardshaw Road, Pudsey, LS28 6QS
Tel: 0113-218 0717 **Fax:** 0113-257 2206
E-mail: sales@newtonderby.co.uk
Website: http://www.newtonderby.co.uk
Bank(s): National Westminster, Ipswich
Directors: S. Wood (MD), C. Lacey (Co Sec)
Managers: M. Nolan (Mgr), I. Forsey (Sales Prom Mgr)
Immediate Holding Company: M P Industries Ltd
Registration no: 05485104 **VAT No.:** 710 2063 00 **Date established:** 1899
Turnover: £1m - £2m **No.of Employees:** 11 - 20 **Product Groups:** 37, 39

Ogden Transteel Ltd

Stanningley Works Butler Way, Stanningley, Pudsey, LS28 6EA
Tel: 0113-257 8221 **Fax:** 0113-236 2340
E-mail: ogdensteel@hotmail.co.uk
Website: http://www.ogdentransteelleeds.co.uk
Managers: P. Hill (Sales Prom Mgr)
Immediate Holding Company: OGDEN (TRANSTEEL) LIMITED
Registration no: 02141205 **Date established:** 1987
Turnover: £500,000 - £1m **No.of Employees:** 1 - 10 **Product Groups:** 66

Date of Accounts	May 12	May 11	May 10
Working Capital	188	-97	-97
Fixed Assets	493	504	490

Current Assets	638	367	280

Protier Lifting Services Ltd
Atlas Works Richardshaw Road, Stanningley, Pudsey, LS28 6RG
Tel: 0113-236 1811 **Fax:** 0113-236 2044
E-mail: sales@protier.co.uk
Website: http://www.protier.co.uk
Directors: P. Jackson (MD), G. Town (Fin)
Immediate Holding Company: PROTIER LIMITED
Registration no: 01374186 **Date established:** 1978
Turnover: £500,000 - £1m **No.of Employees:** 11 - 20
Product Groups: 30, 35, 37, 45

Date of Accounts	Jun 12	Jun 11	Jun 10
Working Capital	183	171	153
Fixed Assets	511	464	464
Current Assets	428	441	424

Pudsey Plant Hire Ltd
Lumby Lane, Pudsey, LS28 9JF
Tel: 0113-257 6116 **Fax:** 0113-236 1360
E-mail: mail@pudseyplanthire.co.uk
Website: http://www.pudseyplanthire.co.uk
Bank(s): Yorkshire
Directors: P. Vipond (MD)
Immediate Holding Company: PUDSEY PLANT HIRE LIMITED
Registration no: 00892254 **VAT No.:** GB 665 3573 12
Date established: 1966 **Turnover:** £1m - £2m **No.of Employees:** 21 - 50
Product Groups: 83

Date of Accounts	Dec 11	Dec 10	Dec 09
Working Capital	8	73	118
Fixed Assets	358	432	448
Current Assets	212	279	267

Schunk UK Ltd
Richardshaw Drive, Pudsey, LS28 6QR
Tel: 0113-256 7238 **Fax:** 0113-255 2017
E-mail: schunk.uk.sales@schunk-group.com
Website: http://www.schunk-group.com
Bank(s): Lloyds TSB Bank plc
Directors: W. Seidt (MD), T. Wilson (Fin)
Immediate Holding Company: SCHUNK U.K. LIMITED
Registration no: 00737825 **VAT No.:** GB 239 5270 49
Date established: 1962 **Turnover:** £2m - £5m **No.of Employees:** 21 - 50
Product Groups: 30, 33, 34, 36, 37, 38, 40, 42, 67

Date of Accounts	Dec 11	Dec 10	Dec 09
Working Capital	940	879	1m
Fixed Assets	369	422	379
Current Assets	1m	1m	1m

Selective Edge Ltd
Westbourne House Bagley Lane, Farsley, Pudsey, LS28 5LY
Tel: 08452-574444 **Fax:** 0845-257 4429
E-mail: info@selectiveedge.com
Website: http://www.selectiveedge.com
Directors: S. Robertson (Dir)
Immediate Holding Company: SELECTIVE EDGE LIMITED
Registration no: 05558354 **Date established:** 2005
Turnover: £250,000 - £500,000 **No.of Employees:** 1 - 10
Product Groups: 80, 86, 87

Date of Accounts	Dec 10	Dec 09	Dec 08
Working Capital	-32	-42	33
Fixed Assets	5	7	8
Current Assets	12	24	77

U S Marine & Industrial Pump Repair Ltd
Site 20 Grangefield Industrial Estate Richardshaw Lane, Pudsey, LS28 6QW
Tel: 0113-256 3721 **Fax:** 0113-255 9820
E-mail: sales@usmarine.co.uk
Website: http://www.usmarine.co.uk
Bank(s): The Yorkshire Bank, Armley, Leeds
Directors: S. Tunstall (MD)
Immediate Holding Company: VICKERS LABORATORIES (HOLDINGS) LIMITED
Registration no: 01016531 **VAT No.:** GB 171 6844 49
Date established: 2010 **Turnover:** £2m - £5m **No.of Employees:** 11 - 20
Product Groups: 39

Date of Accounts	May 11	May 10	May 09
Sales Turnover	N/A	N/A	2m
Pre Tax Profit/Loss	N/A	N/A	93
Working Capital	1m	121	269
Fixed Assets	341	743	715
Current Assets	1m	662	739
Current Liabilities	N/A	N/A	135

Vickers Laboratories Ltd
Grangefield Industrial Estate Richardshaw Road, Pudsey, LS28 6QW
Tel: 0113-236 2811 **Fax:** 0113-236 2703
E-mail: info@viclabs.co.uk
Website: http://www.viclabs.co.uk
Bank(s): Barclays, Otley
Directors: J. Driver (Grp Chief Exec), H. Thornley (Fin)
Ultimate Holding Company: VICKERS LABORATORIES (HOLDINGS) LIMITED
Immediate Holding Company: VICKERS LABORATORIES LIMITED
Registration no: 01016531 **VAT No.:** GB 180 1773 70
Date established: 1971 **Turnover:** £2m - £5m **No.of Employees:** 21 - 50
Product Groups: 31, 32, 38, 61, 66

Date of Accounts	May 11	May 10	May 09
Sales Turnover	N/A	N/A	2m
Pre Tax Profit/Loss	N/A	N/A	93
Working Capital	1m	121	269
Fixed Assets	341	743	715
Current Assets	1m	662	739
Current Liabilities	N/A	N/A	135

W D S
Richardshaw Road Grangefield Industrial Estate, Pudsey, LS28 6LE
Tel: 0113-290 9852 **Fax:** 08456-011173
E-mail: sales@wdsltd.co.uk
Website: http://www.wdsltd.co.uk
Bank(s): Lloyds, Reading
Directors: P. Crowder (MD)
Immediate Holding Company: WDS COMPONENT PARTS LIMITED
Registration no: 06819551 **Date established:** 2009 **Turnover:** £5m - £10m
No.of Employees: 21 - 50 **Product Groups:** 34, 46

Date of Accounts	Mar 11	Mar 10
Working Capital	929	711
Fixed Assets	2m	2m
Current Assets	3m	2m

Y P S Valves Ltd
Richardshaw Road Grangefield Industrial Estate, Pudsey, LS28 6QW
Tel: 0113-256 7725 **Fax:** 0113-255 1275
E-mail: info@yps-valves.co.uk
Website: http://www.yps-valves.co.uk
Bank(s): H S B C
Directors: S. Barraclough (Dir), R. Wormald (Fin)
Immediate Holding Company: YPS VALVES LIMITED
Registration no: 01307137 **Date established:** 1977 **Turnover:** £5m - £10m
No.of Employees: 21 - 50 **Product Groups:** 36

Date of Accounts	Dec 11	Dec 10	Dec 09
Working Capital	3m	3m	3m
Fixed Assets	842	862	935
Current Assets	4m	4m	4m

Shipley

Acorn Mobility Services Ltd
Spring Mills Norwood Avenue, Shipley, BD18 2AX
Tel: 01274-590101 **Fax:** 01274-533129
E-mail: info@acornstairlifts.com
Website: http://www.acornstairlifts.com
Directors: J. Allen (Dir)
Immediate Holding Company: ACORN MOBILITY SERVICES LTD.
Registration no: 02593771 **Date established:** 1991
No.of Employees: 1001 - 1500 **Product Groups:** 35, 39, 45

Date of Accounts	Sep 11	Sep 10	Sep 09
Sales Turnover	89m	72m	65m
Pre Tax Profit/Loss	7m	4m	642
Working Capital	3m	7m	4m
Fixed Assets	15m	5m	5m
Current Assets	26m	20m	18m
Current Liabilities	18m	9m	10m

B Fletcher
55 Coach Road Baildon, Shipley, BD17 5HS
Tel: 01274-582891
Directors: B. Fletcher (Prop)
No.of Employees: 1 - 10 **Product Groups:** 26, 35

Camline Products & Services
Unit 4 Jubilee Way, Shipley, BD18 1QG
Tel: 01274-594488 **Fax:** 01274-598694
E-mail: sales@camlineproducts.co.uk
Website: http://www.camlineproducts.co.uk
Directors: M. Mchale (Dir), J. Scott (Fin)
Immediate Holding Company: CAMLINE PRODUCTS & SERVICES LIMITED
Registration no: 04757302 **Date established:** 2003
No.of Employees: 11 - 20 **Product Groups:** 35, 39, 45

Date of Accounts	Mar 11	Mar 10	Mar 09
Working Capital	56	45	13
Fixed Assets	6	5	7
Current Assets	248	133	73

Cardinal Shopfitting Ltd
Systems House Ives Street, Shipley, BD17 7DZ
Tel: 01274-200900 **Fax:** 01274-588811
E-mail: barnardm@cardinal.ltd.uk
Website: http://www.cardinal.ltd.uk
Directors: M. Barnard (Fin)
Ultimate Holding Company: CARDINAL LIMITED
Immediate Holding Company: FERN HILL HOLDINGS LIMITED
Registration no: 03090199 **VAT No.:** GB 556 8042 27
Date established: 1995 **Turnover:** £500,000 - £1m
No.of Employees: 251 - 500 **Product Groups:** 26, 52

Date of Accounts	Dec 11	Dec 10	Dec 09
Sales Turnover	N/A	870	892
Pre Tax Profit/Loss	N/A	282	350
Working Capital	-767	-2m	-2m
Fixed Assets	5m	6m	6m
Current Assets	950	926	1m
Current Liabilities	N/A	2m	3m

Carnaud Metal Box Engineering
Dockfield Road, Shipley, BD17 7AY
Tel: 01274-846200 **Fax:** 01274-846201
E-mail: info@carnaudmetalboxengineering.com
Website: http://www.carnaudmetalboxengineering.com
Bank(s): National Westminster Bank Plc
Directors: I. Scholiey (MD), P. Leeming (Fin)
Ultimate Holding Company: CROWN HOLDINGS INC (USA)
Immediate Holding Company: CARNAUDMETALBOX ENGINEERING LIMITED
Registration no: 00472767 **Date established:** 1949
Turnover: £75m - £125m **No.of Employees:** 101 - 250
Product Groups: 46

Date of Accounts	Dec 11	Dec 10	Dec 09
Sales Turnover	96m	55m	41m
Pre Tax Profit/Loss	15m	5m	366
Working Capital	18m	11m	8m
Fixed Assets	3m	2m	2m
Current Assets	51m	46m	21m
Current Liabilities	22m	22m	8m

Centa Transmissions
Thackley Court Thackley Old Road, Shipley, BD18 1BW
Tel: 01274-531034 **Fax:** 01274-531159
E-mail: post@centa-uk.co.uk
Website: http://www.centa-uk.co.uk
Bank(s): Barclays
Directors: R. Arnott (MD)
Managers: G. Noake (Mktg Serv Mgr), J. Hardy
Immediate Holding Company: CENTA TRANSMISSIONS LIMITED
Registration no: 01435941 **Date established:** 1979 **Turnover:** £2m - £5m
No.of Employees: 11 - 20 **Product Groups:** 35

Date of Accounts	Dec 11	Dec 10	Dec 09
Working Capital	2m	2m	2m
Fixed Assets	916	739	715
Current Assets	3m	3m	2m

Chemspec Europe Ltd
Unit 36c Tong Park Works Tong Park, Baildon, Shipley, BD17 7QD
Tel: 01274-597333 **Fax:** 01274-597444
E-mail: info@chemspec-europe.com
Website: http://www.chemspec-europe.com
Directors: R. Sudall (Co Sec)
Ultimate Holding Company: RPM INC (USA)
Immediate Holding Company: CHEMSPEC EUROPE LIMITED
Registration no: 02225091 **Date established:** 1988
Turnover: £500,000 - £1m **No.of Employees:** 1 - 10 **Product Groups:** 32

Date of Accounts	May 12	May 11	May 10
Sales Turnover	699	688	778
Pre Tax Profit/Loss	-8	46	-44
Working Capital	1m	1m	1m
Current Assets	1m	1m	1m
Current Liabilities	21	7	3

Cryotherm Insulation Ltd
Hirst Wood Road, Shipley, BD18 4BU
Tel: 01274-589175 **Fax:** 01274-593315
E-mail: enquiries@cryotherm.co.uk
Website: http://www.cryotherm.co.uk
Directors: D. Godfrey (MD)
Ultimate Holding Company: BRACEFILL LIMITED
Immediate Holding Company: CRYOTHERM INSULATION LIMITED
Registration no: 01306743 **VAT No.:** GB 606 8251 45
Date established: 1977 **Turnover:** £500,000 - £1m
No.of Employees: 1 - 10 **Product Groups:** 33

Date of Accounts	Jul 12	Jul 11	Jul 10
Working Capital	184	174	897
Fixed Assets	403	397	492
Current Assets	307	272	998

D & E Metal Fabrications
1 County Workshops Dockfield Road, Shipley, BD17 7AR
Tel: 01274-532410 **Fax:** 01274-532410
Directors: M. Domanski (Ptnr)
Date established: 1991 **No.of Employees:** 1 - 10 **Product Groups:** 35

Denso Marston Ltd
Otley Road Baildon, Charlestown, Shipley, BD17 7JR
Tel: 01274-582266 **Fax:** 01274-597165
E-mail: martin.mcnally@uk.fujitsu.com
Website: http://www.denso-europe.com
Bank(s): Lloyds TSB Bank plc
Directors: M. Kako (Dir)
Managers: B. Sagar (Personnel), G. Littlewood, M. Foster (Tech Serv Mgr), W. Faulding (Fin Mgr)
Ultimate Holding Company: DENSO CORPORATION (JAPAN)
Immediate Holding Company: DENSO MARSTON LTD
Registration no: 00305275 **VAT No.:** GB 168 9498 89
Date established: 1935 **Turnover:** £75m - £125m
No.of Employees: 501 - 1000 **Product Groups:** 40

Date of Accounts	Mar 11	Mar 10	Mar 09
Sales Turnover	79m	50m	81m
Pre Tax Profit/Loss	7m	20	4m
Working Capital	1m	-10	5m
Fixed Assets	28m	24m	30m
Current Assets	26m	16m	24m
Current Liabilities	2m	2m	3m

Don Whitley Scientific Ltd
14 Otley Road, Shipley, BD17 7SE
Tel: 01274-595728 **Fax:** 01274-531197
E-mail: sales@dwscientific.co.uk
Website: http://www.dwscientific.co.uk
Bank(s): Allied Irish Bank (GB)
Directors: N. Kosmirak (Fin), P. Walton (MD)
Managers: D. Robinson (Mktg Serv Mgr), S. Parry (Mats Contrlr)
Immediate Holding Company: DON WHITLEY SCIENTIFIC LIMITED
Registration no: 01342672 **VAT No.:** GB 303 3503 14
Date established: 1977 **Turnover:** £2m - £5m **No.of Employees:** 21 - 50
Product Groups: 38, 42, 67, 84, 88

Date of Accounts	Dec 10	Dec 09	Dec 08
Working Capital	271	250	267
Fixed Assets	260	271	320
Current Assets	2m	2m	2m

Fabreeka International Inc
Units 8-12 Jubilee Way, Shipley, BD18 1QG
Tel: 01274-531333 **Fax:** 01274-531717
E-mail: info@fabreeka-uk.com
Website: http://www.fabreeka.co.uk
Directors: A. McGuire (Co Sec)
Managers: R. Naranbhai (Mktg Serv Mgr)
Immediate Holding Company: FABREEKA INTERNATIONAL INC.
Registration no: FC005296 **Date established:** 1963
Turnover: £20m - £50m **No.of Employees:** 1 - 10 **Product Groups:** 29, 30, 37, 38

H C Slingsby plc
Otley Road Baildon, Shipley, BD17 7LW
Tel: 01274-535030 **Fax:** 01274-723044
E-mail: info@slingsby.com
Website: http://www.slingsby.com
Bank(s): HSBC Bank plc
Directors: D. Slingsby (Dir), R. Hudson (Fin), C. Slingsby (Sales), L. Wright (Mkt Research)
Managers: S. Ripley (Buyer), M. Tearne (Personnel), M. Green (Tech Serv Mgr)
Immediate Holding Company: H C SLINGSBY P L C
Registration no: 00452716 **VAT No.:** GB 179 3280 36
Date established: 1948 **Turnover:** £10m - £20m
No.of Employees: 101 - 250 **Product Groups:** 26, 35, 39, 40, 41, 45, 67

Date of Accounts	Dec 11	Dec 10	Dec 09
Sales Turnover	15m	17m	16m
Pre Tax Profit/Loss	422	1m	1m
Working Capital	5m	5m	5m
Fixed Assets	8m	8m	8m
Current Assets	7m	8m	7m
Current Liabilities	868	1m	721

Kay Dee Engineering Plastics Ltd
2 Jubilee Court Thackley Old Road, Shipley, BD18 1QF
Tel: 01274-590824 **Fax:** 01274-531409
E-mail: info@kaylan.co.uk
Website: http://www.kaylan.co.uk
Bank(s): Barclays
Directors: S. Ward (Dir), J. Ward (Sales)
Immediate Holding Company: KAY DEE ENGINEERING (PLASTICS) LIMITED
Registration no: 01407276 **VAT No.:** GB 325 4222 88
Date established: 1979 **Turnover:** £1m - £2m **No.of Employees:** 21 - 50
Product Groups: 30, 48, 66

see next page

Kay Dee Engineering Plastics Ltd - Cont'd

Date of Accounts	Dec 11	Dec 10	Dec 09
Working Capital	622	533	353
Fixed Assets	2m	2m	2m
Current Assets	1m	999	619

Manor Coating Systems

Otley Road Charlestown, Shipley, BD17 7DP
Tel: 01274-587351 **Fax:** 01274-531360
E-mail: sales@manorcoatingsystems.co.uk
Website: http://www.manorcoatingsystems.co.uk
Directors: M. Brennan (Fab), P. Smith (Mkt Research)
Immediate Holding Company: SHIPLEY PAINT LIMITED
Registration no: 04886138 **VAT No.:** GB 180 4257 93
Date established: 2003 **Turnover:** £5m - £10m
No.of Employees: 51 - 100 **Product Groups:** 23, 32

Nicholl Packaging Ltd

4 Thackley Court Thackley Old Road, Shipley, BD18 1BW
Tel: 01274-580563 **Fax:** 01274-531675
E-mail: sales@nichollpackaging.co.uk
Website: http://www.nichollpackaging.co.uk
Directors: K. Nicholl (MD)
Managers: K. Shaw (Sales Prom Mgr)
Immediate Holding Company: NICHOLL PACKAGING LIMITED
Registration no: 01505138 **VAT No.:** GB 343 4876 39
Date established: 1980 **Turnover:** £250,000 - £500,000
No.of Employees: 1 - 10 **Product Groups:** 30, 45

Date of Accounts	Aug 11	Aug 10	Aug 09
Working Capital	45	37	34
Fixed Assets	12	15	10
Current Assets	131	124	108

Pace plc

Victoria Mills Victoria Road, Saltaire, Shipley, BD18 3LF
Tel: 01274-532000 **Fax:** 01274-532010
E-mail: info@pace.com
Website: http://www.pace.com
Directors: A. Dixon (Co Sec)
Managers: T. Hargrave, J. Ezard (Personnel)
Immediate Holding Company: PACE PLC
Registration no: 01672847 **VAT No.:** GB 333 4504 83
Date established: 1982 **Turnover:** Over £1,000m
No.of Employees: 501 - 1000 **Product Groups:** 37

Date of Accounts	Dec 09	Dec 08
Sales Turnover	1133m	745m
Pre Tax Profit/Loss	70m	14m
Working Capital	93m	29m
Fixed Assets	139m	148m
Current Assets	375m	326m
Current Liabilities	65m	65m

Sydney Packett & Sons Ltd

Salts Wharfashley Lane, Shipley, BD17 7DB
Tel: 01274-206500 **Fax:** 01274-206506
E-mail: mail@packetts.com
Website: http://www.packetts.com
Bank(s): Lloyds TSB
Directors: A. Packett (Dir), P. Barrett (Co Sec)
Immediate Holding Company: SYDNEY PACKETT & SONS LIMITED
Registration no: 00371448 **Date established:** 1941 **Turnover:** £1m - £2m
No.of Employees: 21 - 50 **Product Groups:** 82

Date of Accounts	Nov 11	Nov 10	Nov 09
Working Capital	299	291	275
Fixed Assets	84	73	78
Current Assets	2m	3m	2m

John Peel & Son Ltd

Baildon Mills Northgate, Baildon, Shipley, BD17 6JY
Tel: 01274-583276 **Fax:** 01274-598533
E-mail: robert.askew@peelflock.com
Website: http://www.peelflock.com
Directors: R. Askew (Fin)
Immediate Holding Company: JOHN PEEL & SON LIMITED
Registration no: 00164770 **Date established:** 2020
Turnover: £500,000 - £1m **No.of Employees:** 1 - 10 **Product Groups:** 23

Date of Accounts	Dec 11	Dec 10	Dec 09
Working Capital	332	328	323
Fixed Assets	25	29	35
Current Assets	407	405	388

Pennine Mobility Ltd

6 Nab Wood Drive, Shipley, BD18 4EJ
Tel: 01274-585898 **Fax:** 01274-585898
Website: http://www.penninemobility.co.uk
Directors: C. Williamson (Fin)
Immediate Holding Company: PENNINE MOBILITY LIMITED
Registration no: 03010984 **Date established:** 1995
Turnover: Up to £250,000 **No.of Employees:** 1 - 10 **Product Groups:** 35, 39, 45

Date of Accounts	Apr 11	Apr 10	Apr 09
Sales Turnover	147	153	162
Pre Tax Profit/Loss	-3	1	2
Working Capital	17	19	16
Fixed Assets	4	5	7
Current Assets	43	43	49
Current Liabilities	24	24	33

Jack Pennington Ltd

2 Hird Street, Shipley, BD17 7ED
Tel: 01274-534444 **Fax:** 01274-534433
E-mail: sales@pennington.co.uk
Website: http://www.pennington.co.uk
Bank(s): Barclays
Directors: S. Mettrick (Chief Op Offcr), A. Simpson (Fin), C. Simpson (Dir)
Managers: G. Wiles (Purch Mgr), M. Elliott (Personnel)
Immediate Holding Company: JACK PENNINGTON LIMITED
Registration no: 01168331 **VAT No.:** GB 180 9606 49
Date established: 1974 **Turnover:** £10m - £20m
No.of Employees: 51 - 100 **Product Groups:** 35, 37, 66, 83

Date of Accounts	Jun 11	Jun 10	Jun 09
Sales Turnover	10m	8m	9m
Pre Tax Profit/Loss	286	278	116
Working Capital	2m	1m	902
Fixed Assets	1m	2m	2m
Current Assets	4m	3m	3m
Current Liabilities	247	272	464

Purification Products Ltd

Reliance Works Saltaire Road, Shipley, BD18 3HL
Tel: 01274-530155 **Fax:** 01274-580453
E-mail: sales@purification.co.uk
Website: http://www.purification.co.uk
Bank(s): Barclays, Bradford
Directors: R. Mellor (Tech Serv), B. Moakes (Sales), Q. Mackenzie (Dir)
Immediate Holding Company: PURIFICATION PRODUCTS LIMITED
Registration no: 02476877 **VAT No.:** GB 556 9870 82
Date established: 1990 **Turnover:** £2m - £5m **No.of Employees:** 21 - 50
Product Groups: 22, 31, 32, 33, 42

Date of Accounts	May 11	May 10	May 09
Working Capital	436	434	351
Fixed Assets	147	168	190
Current Assets	560	616	568

Quality Freight Services

Unit 1,Peel House Taunton Street, Shipley, BD18 3NA
Tel: 01274-580866 **Fax:** 01274-580992
E-mail: steve@qualityfreight.co.uk
Website: http://www.qualityfreight.co.uk
Directors: M. Johnson (Dir)
Managers: C. Magson
Immediate Holding Company: Quality Freight Services Ltd
Registration no: 03090860 **Date established:** 1995 **Turnover:** £2m - £5m
No.of Employees: 11 - 20 **Product Groups:** 39, 45, 76, 79

Date of Accounts	Aug 10	Aug 09	Aug 08
Working Capital	139	117	30
Fixed Assets	136	98	126
Current Assets	724	601	657

Rushtons Insolvency Services

Merchants Quay Ashley Lane, Shipley, BD17 7DB
Tel: 01274-598585 **Fax:** 01274-599474
E-mail: rushtonsinsol@btinternet.com
Website: http://www.rushtonsinsol.com
Directors: R. Clauchton (Ptnr)
Immediate Holding Company: SHREWTON STEAM LAUNDRIES LIMITED
Registration no: 03089949 **Date established:** 1944
Turnover: £500,000 - £1m **No.of Employees:** 1 - 10 **Product Groups:** 80, 81, 82

Date of Accounts	Mar 09	Mar 08	Mar 07
Working Capital	-12	-8	-6
Fixed Assets	198	54	66
Current Assets	62	68	69

Sowerby Bridge

A & R Control Systems Ltd

SDH Indl-Est West Street, Sowerby Bridge, HX6 3BS
Tel: 01422-833585 **Fax:** 01422-833773
E-mail: automation@aarcs.co.uk
Website: http://www.aarcs.co.uk
Bank(s): Lloyds TSB
Directors: A. White (Comm), A. White (Fin), R. Lister (Fab), R. Lister (MD)
Immediate Holding Company: A & R CONTROL SYSTEMS LTD
Registration no: 03896995 **VAT No.:** GB 566 9066 01
Date established: 1999 **Turnover:** £500,000 - £1m
No.of Employees: 11 - 20 **Product Groups:** 38

Date of Accounts	Mar 11	Mar 10	Mar 09
Working Capital	8	-0	19
Fixed Assets	5	7	10
Current Assets	253	179	129

Aflex Hose Ltd

Spring Bank Industrial Estate Watson Mill Lane, Sowerby Bridge, HX6 3BW
Tel: 01422-317200 **Fax:** 01422-836000
E-mail: rod.anderson@aflex-hose.co.uk
Website: http://www.aflex-hose.co.uk
Bank(s): The Royal Bank of Scotland
Directors: R. Anderson (MD)
Managers: C. Manley (Buyer), T. Firth (Personnel), M. Watson (Tech Serv Mgr), A. Gibson (Chief Acct), A. Keene
Immediate Holding Company: AFLEX HOSE LIMITED
Registration no: 01088141 **Date established:** 1972
Turnover: £10m - £20m **No.of Employees:** 101 - 250
Product Groups: 29, 30, 36

Date of Accounts	Aug 11	Aug 10	Aug 09
Sales Turnover	18m	14m	11m
Pre Tax Profit/Loss	3m	1m	881
Working Capital	3m	2m	804
Fixed Assets	2m	2m	2m
Current Assets	9m	8m	6m
Current Liabilities	3m	3m	2m

B B N Sutcliffe

Clifton Warehouse Lower Clifton Street, Sowerby Bridge, HX6 2BY
Tel: 01422-831038 **Fax:** 01422-839841
E-mail: sales@bbn.co.uk
Website: http://www.bbn.co.uk
Managers: R. Aitchison (District Mgr)
Immediate Holding Company: B B N GROUP
Registration no: 01052651 **VAT No.:** GB 183 5092 56
Turnover: £500,000 - £1m **No.of Employees:** 1 - 10 **Product Groups:** 66

Benson Payne Ltd

Sleepy Willow 2 Willow Clough, Ripponden, Sowerby Bridge, HX6 4SA
Tel: 07973-207631 **Fax:** 01422-203540
E-mail: mike@bensonpayne.co.uk
Website: http://www.bensonpayne.co.uk
Directors: M. Payne (MD)
Immediate Holding Company: BENSON PAYNE LIMITED
Registration no: 02458482 **VAT No.:** 516 4690 40 **Date established:** 1990
Turnover: £500,000 - £1m **No.of Employees:** 1 - 10 **Product Groups:** 80, 81, 86

Date of Accounts	Dec 08	Dec 07	Mar 11
Working Capital	172	161	32
Fixed Assets	15	14	5
Current Assets	256	240	71
Current Liabilities	N/A	N/A	39

Contrec Europe Ltd

P.o. box 436, Sowerby Bridge, HX6 3YA
Tel: 01422-829940 **Fax:** 01422-829941
E-mail: sales@contrec.co.uk
Website: http://www.contreceurope.eu
Directors: C. Naylor (Dir), R. Bancroft (Fin), R. Bancroft (Dir)
Managers: L. Bancroft (Mktg Serv Mgr)
Immediate Holding Company: Contrec Systems Pty
Registration no: 03488139 **Turnover:** £500,000 - £1m
No.of Employees: 1 - 10 **Product Groups:** 38, 39, 42, 44, 67

Date of Accounts	Dec 07	Dec 06	Dec 05
Sales Turnover	767	763	696
Pre Tax Profit/Loss	51	15	7
Working Capital	140	104	86
Fixed Assets	2	3	12
Current Assets	253	248	225
Current Liabilities	113	144	139
ROCE% (Return on Capital Employed)	35.9	13.9	7.4
ROT% (Return on Turnover)	6.7	2.0	1.0

Cotesi UK Ltd

Suite 7 Harley House Mill Fold, Sowerby Bridge, HX6 4DJ
Tel: 01422-821000 **Fax:** 01422-821007
E-mail: enquiries@cotesi.co.uk
Website: http://www.cotesi.co.uk
Directors: M. Ruck (MD)
Ultimate Holding Company: VIOLAS-SOCIEDADE GESTORA DE PARTICIPACOES SOCIAIS (POR)
Immediate Holding Company: COTESI (UK) LIMITED
Registration no: 02216297 **VAT No.:** GB 641 4426 60
Date established: 1988 **Turnover:** £2m - £5m **No.of Employees:** 1 - 10
Product Groups: 23, 35, 63

Date of Accounts	Dec 11	Dec 10	Dec 09
Working Capital	-774	-634	-581
Fixed Assets	11	15	10
Current Assets	2m	2m	2m

Denroyd Ltd

Lockhill Mills Holmes Road, Sowerby Bridge, HX6 3LD
Tel: 01422-833147 **Fax:** 01422-833615
E-mail: sales@denroyd.co.uk
Website: http://www.denroyd.co.uk
Bank(s): Yorkshire Bank PLC
Directors: A. Plant (MD)
Immediate Holding Company: DENROYD LIMITED
Registration no: 01662578 **VAT No.:** GB 361 6031 81
Date established: 1982 **Turnover:** £1m - £2m **No.of Employees:** 21 - 50
Product Groups: 30

Date of Accounts	Aug 11	Aug 10	Aug 09
Working Capital	947	866	771
Fixed Assets	355	389	388
Current Assets	1m	1m	978

Dugdale plc

Valley Mill Holmes Road, Sowerby Bridge, HX6 2AA
Tel: 01422-832501 **Fax:** 01422-833401
E-mail: d.outen@dugdaleplc.com
Website: http://www.dugdaleplc.com
Bank(s): Lloyds TSB Bank plc
Directors: D. Rowell (Fin), D. Outen (MD), D. Outen (MD), R. Bickerton (Fin)
Immediate Holding Company: DUGDALE PLC
Registration no: 04116131 **VAT No.:** GB 183 3291 60
Date established: 2000 **Turnover:** £20m - £50m
No.of Employees: 51 - 100 **Product Groups:** 30

Date of Accounts	Dec 11	Dec 10	Dec 09
Sales Turnover	25m	22m	19m
Pre Tax Profit/Loss	225	168	365
Working Capital	2m	2m	2m
Fixed Assets	2m	2m	2m
Current Assets	8m	7m	6m
Current Liabilities	3m	2m	865

Eagle Power Energy Ltd

Greave Head Farm Ripponden, Sowerby Bridge, HX6 4NU
Tel: 01422-823360 **Fax:** 01422-823623
E-mail: info@eaglepower.co.uk
Website: http://www.eaglepower.co.uk
Directors: S. Gumbley (Fin), J. Gumbley (Prop)
Immediate Holding Company: EAGLE POWER ENERGY LTD.
Registration no: 01644240 **VAT No.:** GB 361 5805 55
Date established: 1982 **Turnover:** £2m - £5m **No.of Employees:** 1 - 10
Product Groups: 32, 61, 62

Date of Accounts	Jul 10	Jul 09	Jul 08
Working Capital	253	217	155
Fixed Assets	12	21	13
Current Assets	428	371	363

Flowhire

Riverside Canal Road, Sowerby Bridge, HX6 2AY
Tel: 01422-829930 **Fax:** 07000-356944
E-mail: info@flowhire.co.uk
Website: http://www.flowhire.co.uk
Managers: M. Bancroft (Mgr)
Immediate Holding Company: FLOWHIRE LIMITED
Registration no: 03488133 **Date established:** 1998 **Turnover:** £1m - £2m
No.of Employees: 1 - 10 **Product Groups:** 38

Date of Accounts	Mar 11	Mar 10	Mar 09
Working Capital	27	68	27
Fixed Assets	99	107	59
Current Assets	56	154	84

Garrison Associates

2 Warehouse, Sowerby Bridge, HX6 2AG
Tel: 01422-316160 **Fax:** 01422-316400
E-mail: garrisonassoc@tiscali.co.uk
Directors: M. Gardner (Dir)
Immediate Holding Company: GARRISON PROPERTIES LIMITED
Registration no: 03279570 **Date established:** 1996
No.of Employees: 1 - 10 **Product Groups:** 35

Date of Accounts	Jun 11	Jun 10	Jun 09
Working Capital	74	78	83
Fixed Assets	449	449	449
Current Assets	127	128	127

J L A

Meadowcroft Lane Ripponden, Sowerby Bridge, HX6 4AJ
Tel: 0800-591903 **Fax:** 01507-611132
E-mail: info@jla.com
Website: http://www.jla.com
Managers: K. Humpleby (Mktg Serv Mgr)
Ultimate Holding Company: JLA EQUITYCO LIMITED
Immediate Holding Company: JLA EQUITYCO LIMITED
Registration no: 07195122 **Date established:** 2010
Turnover: £20m - £50m **No.of Employees:** 251 - 500
Product Groups: 23, 40, 48, 84

Date of Accounts	Oct 11	Oct 10
Sales Turnover	55m	29m
Pre Tax Profit/Loss	-16m	-8m
Working Capital	6m	12m
Fixed Assets	145m	147m
Current Assets	20m	24m
Current Liabilities	13m	8m

Frank Langfield Ltd

Hollins Mill Lane, Sowerby Bridge, HX6 2RF
Tel: 01422-835388 **Fax:** 01422-834452
E-mail: dave@langfieldwelding.com
Website: http://www.langfieldwelding.com
Directors: D. Langfield (MD)
Immediate Holding Company: FRANK LANGFIELD LIMITED
Registration no: 02925381 **Date established:** 1994
No.of Employees: 1 - 10 **Product Groups:** 32, 33, 34, 35, 40

Date of Accounts	Dec 11	Dec 10	Dec 09
Working Capital	746	680	604
Fixed Assets	311	328	339
Current Assets	798	736	650

M G Metal Finishers

Burnley Road, Sowerby Bridge, HX6 2TL
Tel: 01422-831916 **Fax:** 01422-831916
E-mail: amthea@mgmetalpolishing.co.uk
Website: http://www.mgmetalpolishing.co.uk
Directors: D. Gee (Prop)
Immediate Holding Company: M AND G METAL FINISHERS LIMITED
Registration no: 04680781 **Date established:** 2003
Turnover: Up to £250,000 **No.of Employees:** 1 - 10 **Product Groups:** 46, 48

Date of Accounts	Mar 12	Mar 11	Mar 10
Sales Turnover	N/A	43	44
Pre Tax Profit/Loss	N/A	14	14
Working Capital	-8	-9	-11
Fixed Assets	11	12	13
Current Assets	11	11	6
Current Liabilities	N/A	11	6

Rose Hill Polymers Ltd

Watson Mill Lane, Sowerby Bridge, HX6 3BW
Tel: 01422-839456 **Fax:** 01422-316952
E-mail: sales@rosehillpolymers.com
Website: http://www.rosehillpolymers.com
Directors: M. Hopkinson (Ch), J. Longbottom (MD)
Managers: J. Garside (Comptroller), G. Harris (Sales Admin), M. Luby (Mktg Serv Mgr), A. Robinson (Chief Mgr), S. Wilson (Sales & Mktg Mg)
Ultimate Holding Company: TECHNOPOLYMER LIMITED
Immediate Holding Company: ROSEHILL POLYMERS LTD
Registration no: 02283308 **Date established:** 1988
No.of Employees: 51 - 100 **Product Groups:** 30, 49, 52

Date of Accounts	Mar 12	Mar 11	Mar 10
Sales Turnover	21m	17m	16m
Pre Tax Profit/Loss	344	108	276
Working Capital	-323	-772	-619
Fixed Assets	7m	7m	6m
Current Assets	8m	7m	6m
Current Liabilities	3m	3m	2m

Ryburn Machinery Ripponden Ltd

Oldham Road Ripponden, Sowerby Bridge, HX6 4EL
Tel: 01422-823132 **Fax:** 01422- 823819
E-mail: ryburnpoly@tiscali.co.uk
Website: http://www.rypak.com
Directors: M. Oldham (Fin)
Immediate Holding Company: RYBURN MACHINERY (RIPPONDEN) LIMITED
Registration no: 01345136 **Date established:** 1977
No.of Employees: 1 - 10 **Product Groups:** 38, 42

Date of Accounts	Dec 08	Dec 07	Dec 06
Working Capital	13	18	12
Fixed Assets	4	6	7
Current Assets	64	73	70
Current Liabilities	N/A	46	44

Ryburn Rubber Ltd

Watson Mill Lane, Sowerby Bridge, HX6 3BW
Tel: 01422-316323 **Fax:** 01422-835898
E-mail: sales@ryburnrubber.co.uk
Website: http://www.ryburnrubber.co.uk
Directors: J. Hopkinson (Fin), H. Hopkinson (MD)
Managers: A. Robinson (Chief Mgr)
Immediate Holding Company: RYBURN RUBBER LTD
Registration no: 03137709 **Date established:** 1995
No.of Employees: 11 - 20 **Product Groups:** 29, 63, 66

Date of Accounts	Feb 08	Feb 07	Feb 06
Working Capital	-28	92	65
Fixed Assets	282	275	243
Current Assets	143	353	379
Current Liabilities	171	262	314
Total Share Capital	260	260	260

J & S Taylor Ltd

Corporation Mill Corporation Street, Sowerby Bridge, HX6 2QQ
Tel: 01422-832616 **Fax:** 01422-833686
E-mail: jands.taylor@btinternet.com
Website: http://www.taylorsdirect.co.uk
Directors: N. Whitworth (Dir)
Immediate Holding Company: J & S TAYLOR LIMITED
Registration no: 02609872 **VAT No.:** GB 183 4006 80
Date established: 1991 **No.of Employees:** 1 - 10 **Product Groups:** 23

Date of Accounts	Mar 12	Mar 11	Mar 10
Working Capital	116	115	115
Fixed Assets	101	102	102
Current Assets	168	180	157

Tubend

Stanley Street, Sowerby Bridge, HX6 2AH
Tel: 01422-833461 **Fax:** 01422-835319
E-mail: tubenduk@aol.com
Directors: P. Whitworth (Ptnr)
Date established: 1977 **Turnover:** Up to £250,000
No.of Employees: 1 - 10 **Product Groups:** 48

Wightman Stewart Water Jet Ltd

Oldham Road, Sowerby Bridge, HX6 4EH
Tel: 01422-823801 **Fax:** 01422-824031
E-mail: info@wightmanstewart.co.uk
Website: http://www.wightmanstewart.co.uk
Directors: S. Fitton (MD), P. Dewar Fitton (Fin)
Immediate Holding Company: WIGHTMAN STEWART LIMITED
Registration no: 02138733 **Date established:** 1987
Turnover: Up to £250,000 **No.of Employees:** 1 - 10 **Product Groups:** 46

Date of Accounts	Aug 08	Aug 07	Aug 10
Working Capital	350	302	328
Fixed Assets	42	42	30
Current Assets	1m	671	766

W S Ursviken

1 Commercial Mills Oldham Road, Sowerby Bridge, HX6 4EH
Tel: 01422-820701 **Fax:** 01422-824031
E-mail: info@wightmanstewart.co.uk
Website: http://www.wightmanstewart.com
Directors: S. Fitton (MD)
Date established: 1987 **No.of Employees:** 1 - 10 **Product Groups:** 46

Zodion Ltd

Zodion House Station Road, Sowerby Bridge, HX6 3AF
Tel: 01422-317337 **Fax:** 01422-836717
E-mail: info@lucyzodion.com
Website: http://www.zodionltd.eu.com
Bank(s): The Royal Bank of Scotland
Directors: J. Fox (Tech Serv), J. Fox (MD), P. Griffith (Sales), C. Scott (Dir)
Immediate Holding Company: ZODION LIMITED
Registration no: 07448407 **VAT No.:** GB 704 0387 64
Date established: 2010 **Turnover:** £2m - £5m **No.of Employees:** 51 - 100
Product Groups: 30, 37, 38, 39, 49, 67, 68

Date of Accounts	Dec 07	Dec 06	Dec 05
Sales Turnover	5408	4632	4541
Pre Tax Profit/Loss	730	567	476
Working Capital	3199	2583	2228
Fixed Assets	386	447	363
Current Assets	5390	4632	4269
Current Liabilities	2191	2049	2041
Total Share Capital	1275	1275	1275
ROCE% (Return on Capital Employed)	20.4	18.7	18.4
ROT% (Return on Turnover)	13.5	12.2	10.5

Wakefield

A P P Steel Structure Ltd

Unit 14 & 15 Flanshaw Way, Wakefield, WF2 9LP
Tel: 01924-367447 **Fax:** 01924-366593
E-mail: alan@appsteel.co.uk
Website: http://www.appsteel.co.uk
Bank(s): Royal Bank of Scotland
Directors: A. Holroyd (Dir)
Managers: G. Jones (Chief Acct)
Immediate Holding Company: M.A.P. STRUCTURAL STEEL SERVICES LIMITED
Registration no: 03958103 **VAT No.:** GB 436 5386 32
Date established: 2000 **Turnover:** £5m - £10m **No.of Employees:** 21 - 50
Product Groups: 35, 51

Date of Accounts	Dec 07	Dec 06	Dec 05
Pre Tax Profit/Loss	289	357	N/A
Working Capital	-476	-163	-275
Fixed Assets	749	786	805
Current Assets	2m	1m	943
Current Liabilities	398	340	N/A

A S D Westok Ltd

Horbury Junction Industrial Estate Calder Vale Road, Horbury, Wakefield, WF4 5ER
Tel: 01924-264121 **Fax:** 01924-280030
E-mail: info@asdwestok.co.uk
Website: http://www.asdwestok.co.uk
Directors: K. Devonport (Co Sec), A. Earnshaw (Fab), A. Holmes (MD), M. Hawes (Dir), M. Clarke (MD), M. Hawes (I.T. Dir)
Ultimate Holding Company: KLOCKNER & CO SE (GERMANY)
Immediate Holding Company: ASD WESTOK LIMITED
Registration no: 04486009 **Date established:** 2002
Turnover: £10m - £20m **No.of Employees:** 21 - 50 **Product Groups:** 48

Date of Accounts	Dec 10	Feb 08	Feb 10
Sales Turnover	11m	24m	11m
Pre Tax Profit/Loss	961	4m	304
Working Capital	8m	2m	7m
Fixed Assets	3m	3m	3m
Current Assets	9m	8m	7m
Current Liabilities	337	2m	368

Acoustic Applications Ltd

Unit 8 Caldervale Road Horbury Junction Industrial Estate, Horbury, Wakefield, WF4 5ER
Tel: 01924-283610 **Fax:** 01924-264817
E-mail: sales@acousticapplications.co.uk
Website: http://www.acousticapplications.co.uk
Directors: S. Lynsey (MD), C. Foster (Eng Serv), S. Lindsay (MD)
Immediate Holding Company: ACOUSTIC APPLICATIONS LIMITED
Registration no: 01601123 **VAT No.:** GB 361 4825 54
Date established: 1981 **Turnover:** £500,000 - £1m
No.of Employees: 1 - 10 **Product Groups:** 52, 54

Date of Accounts	Dec 08	Dec 07	Dec 06
Working Capital	-91	134	149
Fixed Assets	113	99	106
Current Assets	152	394	323
Current Liabilities	N/A	2	N/A

Alternative Finishes Ltd

Unit W Wakefield Commercial Park Bridge Road, Horbury, Wakefield, WF4 5NW
Tel: 01924-267803 **Fax:** 01924-277070
E-mail: info@alternativelimited.co.uk
Website: http://www.alternativelimited.co.uk
Directors: M. Kenna (MD)
Immediate Holding Company: ALTERNATIVE FINISHES LIMITED
Registration no: 03892427 **Date established:** 1999
No.of Employees: 1 - 10 **Product Groups:** 46, 48

Date of Accounts	Mar 11	Mar 10	Mar 09
Working Capital	149	179	166
Fixed Assets	55	34	37
Current Assets	292	311	271

Assyst Bullmer Ltd

3 South Park Way Wakefield 41 Business Park, Wakefield, WF2 0XJ
Tel: 01924-373900 **Fax:** 01924-374044
E-mail: info@assystbullmer.co.uk
Website: http://www.assystbullmer.co.uk
Directors: D. Bell (MD), G. Ward (Fin)
Immediate Holding Company: ASSYST BULLMER LIMITED
Registration no: 02149996 **VAT No.:** GB 464 2772 33
Date established: 1987 **Turnover:** £500,000 - £1m
No.of Employees: 1 - 10 **Product Groups:** 23, 24, 42, 43, 44, 46, 47, 48, 67, 68, 81, 84

Date of Accounts	Dec 11	Dec 10	Dec 09
Sales Turnover	N/A	891	912
Pre Tax Profit/Loss	N/A	47	14
Working Capital	240	193	171
Fixed Assets	30	41	49
Current Assets	677	371	445
Current Liabilities	N/A	118	216

Atlas Machinery

Unit 1 Flanshaw Way, Wakefield, WF2 9LP
Tel: 01924-381999 **Fax:** 01924-378999
E-mail: info@atlasuk.com
Website: http://www.atlasuk.com
Directors: S. Lamb (MD)
Immediate Holding Company: ATLAS MACHINERY (U.K.) LIMITED
Registration no: 02664325 **Date established:** 1991
No.of Employees: 11 - 20 **Product Groups:** 67

Date of Accounts	Nov 11	Nov 10	Nov 09
Working Capital	641	762	743
Fixed Assets	90	80	75
Current Assets	2m	3m	2m

Avery Berkel UK

Monkton Industrial Estate Denby Dale Road, Wakefield, WF2 7BP
Tel: 08709-050081
Website: http://www.averyweigh-tronix.com
Registration no: NF001015 **Date established:** 1958
No.of Employees: 11 - 20 **Product Groups:** 38, 67, 83

AZCARPARTS UK

2A DEWSBURY ROAD WESTGATE WAKEFIELD WF2 9BS 2A DEWSBURY ROAD, WESTGATE, Wakefield, WF2 9BS
Tel: 01924-369000 **Fax:** 01924-298625
E-mail: azar@azcarparts.vo.uk
Website: http://WWW.AZCARPARTS.CO.UK
Directors: A. KHALIQ (Dir)
Date established: 1997 **Turnover:** £500,000 - £1m
No.of Employees: 1 - 10 **Product Groups:** 68, 83

B C Services

Wyngarth Bradford Road, Tingley, Wakefield, WF3 1QN
Tel: 0113-238 3783 **Fax:** 0113-238 3783
Directors: B. Cooper (Prop)
Immediate Holding Company: B-C (MACHINERY) SERVICES LIMITED
Registration no: 04630182 **Date established:** 2003
No.of Employees: 1 - 10 **Product Groups:** 46

Date of Accounts	Mar 12	Mar 11	Mar 10
Working Capital	67	64	63
Fixed Assets	5	6	7
Current Assets	95	96	96

B S P Hydraulics

Unit 51 Monckton Road Industrial Estate, Wakefield, WF2 7AL
Tel: 01924-332491 **Fax:** 01924-332493
E-mail: sales@bsphydraulics.co.uk
Website: http://www.bsphydraulics.co.uk
Directors: D. Conyers (Prop)
Immediate Holding Company: BSP HYDRAULICS LIMITED
Registration no: 04399415 **Date established:** 2002
No.of Employees: 1 - 10 **Product Groups:** 29, 30, 35, 36, 37, 38, 40, 41, 45, 46, 48, 61, 67, 84

Date of Accounts	Mar 11	Mar 10	Mar 09
Working Capital	62	65	66
Fixed Assets	13	4	5
Current Assets	330	213	224

Bezier Creative Printers

Balne Lane, Wakefield, WF2 0DF
Tel: 01924-362921 **Fax:** 01924-372615
E-mail: enquiries@bezier.co.uk
Website: http://www.bezier.com
Bank(s): National Westminster Bank Plc
Directors: A. Lamb (Fin), L. Elrod (Sales), A. Woolley (Pers), J. Lees (Sales & Mktg)
Managers: C. Darce (Personnel), P. Pateman (Purch Mgr), M. Waddington (Tech Serv Mgr), J. Stirling (Comptroller)
Ultimate Holding Company: BEZIER ACQUISITIONS LIMITED
Immediate Holding Company: BEZIER LIMITED
Registration no: 01044825 **Date established:** 1972
Turnover: £125m - £250m **No.of Employees:** 251 - 500
Product Groups: 23, 49

Biffa Waste Services Ltd

Calder Vale Road, Wakefield, WF1 5PJ
Tel: 01924-200212 **Fax:** 01924-376718
E-mail: marketing@biffa.co.uk
Website: http://www.biffa.co.uk
Managers: C. Forward (Ops Mgr)
Immediate Holding Company: BIFFA WASTE SERVICES LIMITED
Registration no: 00946107 **Date established:** 1969
No.of Employees: 1 - 10 **Product Groups:** 32, 54

Date of Accounts	Mar 08	Mar 09	Apr 10
Sales Turnover	555m	574m	492m
Pre Tax Profit/Loss	23m	50m	30m
Working Capital	229m	271m	293m
Fixed Assets	371m	360m	378m
Current Assets	409m	534m	609m
Current Liabilities	50m	100m	115m

Bon Marche Ltd

Jubilee Way Grange Moor, Wakefield, WF4 4SJ
Tel: 01924-700100 **Fax:** 01924-700249
E-mail: info@bonmarche.co.uk
Website: http://www.bonmarche.co.uk

see next page

Bon Marche Ltd - Cont'd

Directors: S. Alldridge (Fin), B. Butterwick (MD)
Managers: D. Fearnsides (Tech Serv Mgr), L. Compston (Personnel)
Immediate Holding Company: BONMARCHE LIMITED
Registration no: 04099886 **Date established:** 2012
Turnover: £125m - £250m **No.of Employees:** 1 - 10 **Product Groups:** 24, 61

Brotherton Esseco Ltd

Calder Vale Road, Wakefield, WF1 5PH
Tel: 01924-371919 **Fax:** 01924-290408
E-mail: russel.etherington@brothertonesseco.com
Website: http://www.brothertonesseco.com
Bank(s): Lloyds TSB Bank plc
Directors: R. Grant (Fin), R. Cheney (Co Sec), R. Perry (MD), R. Mills (MD)
Managers: R. Sykes (Comm), R. Sykes (Mktg Serv Mgr), L. Edwards (Tech Serv Mgr), R. Grant (Accounts), C. Robertshaw (Prod Mgr), R. Etherington (Sales Prom Mgr)
Ultimate Holding Company: CHURCH AND DWIGHT CO INC (USA)
Immediate Holding Company: BROTHERTON ESSECO LIMITED
Registration no: 01903619 **VAT No.:** GB 419 5272 36
Date established: 1878 **Turnover:** £20m - £50m **No.of Employees:** 100
Product Groups: 31, 32, 42, 62, 66, 67, 68

Date of Accounts	Dec 11	Dec 10	Dec 09
Sales Turnover	20m	29m	22m
Pre Tax Profit/Loss	2m	4m	3m
Working Capital	3m	4m	4m
Fixed Assets	10m	9m	5m
Current Assets	8m	12m	9m
Current Liabilities	1m	3m	2m

Calder Catering Equipment Services

Unit 1 Grey Street, Wakefield, WF1 3HQ
Tel: 01924-872972 **Fax:** 01924-872962
E-mail: nigel@caldercatering.co.uk
Website: http://www.caldercatering.co.uk
Directors: N. Hubert (Ptnr)
Immediate Holding Company: CALDER CATERING EQUIPMENT SERVICES LIMITED
Registration no: 05748583 **Date established:** 2006
Turnover: Up to £250,000 **No.of Employees:** 1 - 10 **Product Groups:** 37, 38, 40, 63, 66

Date of Accounts	Mar 11	Mar 10	Mar 09
Working Capital	40	36	72
Fixed Assets	58	63	69
Current Assets	282	275	359
Current Liabilities	N/A	94	N/A

Cava

Kirkgate Commercial Centre, Wakefield, WF1 5DJ
Tel: 01924-374433 **Fax:** 01924-374499
Website: http://www.cava-uk.com
Directors: C. Robshaw (MD)
Ultimate Holding Company: GRAFITEC HOLDINGS LIMITED
Immediate Holding Company: BALUN LIMITED
Registration no: 05192689 **Date established:** 2004
Turnover: Up to £250,000 **No.of Employees:** 1 - 10 **Product Groups:** 38, 42

CBM Logix

New City Chambers 36 Wood Street, Wakefield, WF1 2HB
Tel: 0786-787 4857
E-mail: contact@cbm-logix.com
Website: http://www.cbm-logix.com
Registration no: 05285089 **Product Groups:** 37, 38, 42, 44, 49, 54, 66, 67, 80, 84

Date of Accounts	Mar 07	Mar 06
Working Capital	19	16
Fixed Assets	4	2
Current Assets	47	53
Current Liabilities	28	37

Certex UK Ltd

Flanshaw Way Industrial Estate Flanshaw Way, Wakefield, WF2 9LP
Tel: 01924-375431 **Fax:** 01924-290538
E-mail: sales@certex.co.uk
Website: http://www.certex.co.uk
Directors: T. Stringer (MD)
Managers: D. Blakey (District Mgr), D. Blakley (Mgr)
Immediate Holding Company: CERTEX (UK) LIMITED
Registration no: 00928803 **Date established:** 1968
Turnover: Up to £250,000 **No.of Employees:** 1 - 10 **Product Groups:** 23, 30, 35

Counter Corrosion Engineers Ltd

44 Thornes Lane, Wakefield, WF1 5RR
Tel: 01924-380002 **Fax:** 01924-458019
Directors: M. Smith (Dir)
No.of Employees: 1 - 10 **Product Groups:** 46, 48

Crompton Controls Ltd

Monckton Road Industrial Estate, Wakefield, WF2 7AL
Tel: 01924-368251 **Fax:** 01924-367274
E-mail: sales@cromptoncontrols.co.uk
Website: http://www.cromptoncontrols.co.uk
Directors: J. Bradley (MD), J. Adams (Fin)
Immediate Holding Company: CROMPTON CONTROLS LIMITED
Registration no: 08152297 **Date established:** 2012
Turnover: Up to £250,000 **No.of Employees:** 21 - 50 **Product Groups:** 37, 38, 40, 46, 66, 67, 85

Date of Accounts	Dec 08	Dec 07	Dec 06
Sales Turnover	4m	4m	4m
Pre Tax Profit/Loss	-64	163	130
Working Capital	-1m	-1m	-775
Fixed Assets	2m	3m	3m
Current Assets	2m	1m	1m
Current Liabilities	648	354	297

D M F Ltd

2 Dewsbury Road, Wakefield, WF2 9BS
Tel: 01924-370685 **Fax:** 01924-364160
E-mail: sales@dmfwakefield.co.uk
Website: http://www.dmfwakefield.co.uk
Bank(s): HSBC, Wakefield
Directors: J. Martin (Sales), M. Francis (MD), A. Lawson (MD)
Immediate Holding Company: D.M.F. (WAKEFIELD) LIMITED
Registration no: 01252914 **VAT No.:** GB 182 7436 46
Date established: 1976 **Turnover:** £2m - £5m **No.of Employees:** 21 - 50
Product Groups: 40, 68

Date of Accounts	Apr 12	Apr 11	Apr 10
Working Capital	148	44	263
Fixed Assets	92	139	161
Current Assets	937	1m	1m

D & M Machinery

40 Thornes Lane, Wakefield, WF1 5RR
Tel: 01924-290206 **Fax:** 01924-371852
E-mail: info@dmmachinery.co.uk
Website: http://www.dmmachinery.co.uk
Directors: A. Johnson (Prop)
Registration no: 359 4193 **Date established:** 1982
No.of Employees: 11 - 20 **Product Groups:** 42, 67

Dearnleys Ltd

120-128 Wrenthorpe Road Wrenthorpe, Wakefield, WF2 0JN
Tel: 01924-371791 **Fax:** 01924-386001
E-mail: info@dearnleys.com
Website: http://www.dearnleys.com
Bank(s): Barclays
Directors: A. McHale (MD)
Managers: J. Deegan (Tech Serv Mgr), R. McHale (Comptroller)
Ultimate Holding Company: Mayo (Holdings) Ltd
Immediate Holding Company: Mayo (Holdings) Ltd
Registration no: 01224188 **VAT No.:** GB 565 5401 39
Date established: 1975 **Turnover:** £1m - £2m **No.of Employees:** 21 - 50
Product Groups: 24, 29, 30

Date of Accounts	Mar 10	Mar 09	Mar 08
Working Capital	466	489	975
Fixed Assets	204	241	265
Current Assets	985	2m	3m

Deborah Services Ltd

Thornes Moor Road, Wakefield, WF2 8PT
Tel: 01924-378222 **Fax:** 01924-366250
E-mail: steveflounders@deborahservices.co.uk
Website: http://www.deborahservices.co.uk
Bank(s): National Westminster Bank Plc
Directors: S. Flounders (MD), L. Spring (Fin), J. Neal (Fin)
Managers: E. Brass (Personnel), S. Magaldi (Purch Mgr), G. Scott (Tech Serv Mgr), L. Tazzyman (Mktg Serv Mgr)
Immediate Holding Company: DEBORAH SERVICES LIMITED
Registration no: 04013621 **VAT No.:** GB 518 2433 58
Date established: 2000 **Turnover:** £75m - £125m
No.of Employees: 1501 & over **Product Groups:** 29, 52, 54, 83

Date of Accounts	Apr 11	Apr 10	Apr 09
Sales Turnover	81m	70m	88m
Pre Tax Profit/Loss	3m	71	2m
Working Capital	5m	8m	8m
Fixed Assets	25m	14m	16m
Current Assets	25m	25m	26m
Current Liabilities	10m	8m	8m

Denby Catering Equipment

Unit 2 Thornes Trading Estate Chantry Bridge Industrial Estate, Wakefield, WF1 5QN
Tel: 01924-200567 **Fax:** 01924-200311
E-mail: info@dceonline.co.uk
Website: http://www.denbycatering.co.uk
Directors: G. Hartley (Dir)
Immediate Holding Company: DENBY CATERING EQUIPMENT LIMITED
Registration no: 04399476 **Date established:** 2002
No.of Employees: 1 - 10 **Product Groups:** 20, 40, 41

Date of Accounts	Mar 11	Mar 10	Mar 09
Working Capital	22	18	7
Fixed Assets	16	15	22
Current Assets	296	213	244

Double Two Ltd

PO Box 1, Wakefield, WF1 5RQ
Tel: 01924-375651 **Fax:** 01924-290096
E-mail: kevin.mellor@wsg.co.uk
Website: http://www.wsg.co.uk
Bank(s): HSBC Bank plc
Directors: K. Mellor (Fin)
Managers: J. Thompson (Tech Serv Mgr), B. Lawton (Personnel), J. Geddes, P. Gibbons (Sales Prom Mgr)
Ultimate Holding Company: WAKEFIELD SHIRT COMPANY LIMITED(THE)
Immediate Holding Company: DOUBLE TWO LIMITED
Registration no: 00540034 **VAT No.:** GB 404 7327 71
Date established: 1954 **Turnover:** £10m - £20m
No.of Employees: 51 - 100 **Product Groups:** 24, 63

Date of Accounts	Dec 11	Dec 10	Dec 09
Sales Turnover	20m	11m	10m
Pre Tax Profit/Loss	469	241	97
Working Capital	2m	2m	1m
Fixed Assets	279	337	388
Current Assets	6m	5m	4m
Current Liabilities	307	246	199

The Drinks Menu

238 Barnsley Road Sandal, Wakefield, WF2 6EL
Tel: 01924-240 011
E-mail: contact@thedrinksmenu.co.uk
Website: http://www.thedrinksmenu.co.uk
Directors: R. Chambers (MD), M. Singh (Export)
Managers: A. Ling (Sales Prom Mgr)
Registration no: 06701510 **Date established:** 2008
Turnover: £250,000 - £500,000 **No.of Employees:** 1 - 10
Product Groups: 21

Earthmover Tyres Wakefield Ltd

Flanshaw Industrial Estate Flanshaw Way, Wakefield, WF2 9LP
Tel: 01924-363821 **Fax:** 01924-382365
E-mail: gordon@earthmovertyres.com
Website: http://www.earthmovertyres.com
Directors: G. Wood (MD)
Immediate Holding Company: EARTHMOVER TYRES (WAKEFIELD) LIMITED
Registration no: 05168678 **Date established:** 2004
Turnover: £500,000 - £1m **No.of Employees:** 11 - 20 **Product Groups:** 39

Date of Accounts	May 11	May 10	May 09
Working Capital	431	405	435
Fixed Assets	106	138	133
Current Assets	1m	673	637

Eddison & Wanless Ltd

Unit 1 Mallard Industrial Park Charles Street, Horbury, Wakefield, WF4 5FD
Tel: 01924-271128 **Fax:** 01924-271251
E-mail: info@eddisonwanless.co.uk
Website: http://www.eddisonwanless.co.uk
Bank(s): National Westminster
Directors: A. Benson (MD)
Immediate Holding Company: EDDISON & WANLESS LIMITED
Registration no: 02433778 **VAT No.:** GB 536 8823 13
Date established: 1989 **Turnover:** £2m - £5m **No.of Employees:** 21 - 50
Product Groups: 37, 48

Date of Accounts	Dec 11	Dec 10	Dec 09
Sales Turnover	N/A	4m	4m
Pre Tax Profit/Loss	N/A	233	633
Working Capital	130	136	317
Fixed Assets	3m	3m	3m
Current Assets	1m	1m	1m
Current Liabilities	N/A	257	331

Egon Publishers Ltd

618 Leeds Road Outwood, Wakefield, WF1 2LT
Tel: 01924-871697 **Fax:** 01924-871697
E-mail: information@egon.co.uk
Website: http://www.omega-cottage.eu
Directors: R. Redman (Co Sec)
Registration no: 01336483 **Date established:** 1977
Turnover: Up to £250,000 **No.of Employees:** 1 - 10 **Product Groups:** 28

Elite Energy - The Specialist Energy Consultancy

Unit 1 Mariner Court Durkar, Wakefield, WF4 3FL
Tel: 0800-043 8100
E-mail: enquiries@eliteenergy.org.uk
Website: http://www.eliteenergy.org.uk
Directors: C. Evans (MD)
Immediate Holding Company: MAXAIM LLP
Registration no: 06728970 **Date established:** 2009
Turnover: £500,000 - £1m **No.of Employees:** 11 - 20 **Product Groups:** 80

Elliott Hire Ltd

Seckar Wood Industrial Park Barnsley Road, Newmillerdam, Wakefield, WF2 6QW
Tel: 01924-254 4420 **Fax:** 01924-241959
E-mail: paul.askey@elliott-algeco.com
Website: http://www.elliotthire.co.uk
Directors: G. Underhill (MD)
Managers: J. Mellars (District Mgr), J. Mellers (Mgr), J. Moore (Eng Exec), P. Askey (District Mgr)
Ultimate Holding Company: ELLIOTT GROUP HOLDINGS UK LTD
Immediate Holding Company: ELLIOTT GROUP HOLDINGS LTD
Registration no: 00147207 **No.of Employees:** 11 - 20
Product Groups: 35, 39, 77, 83

Date of Accounts	Dec 10	Dec 09	Dec 08
Pre Tax Profit/Loss	-26m	-30m	-228m
Working Capital	-1m	-56m	-6m
Fixed Assets	403m	456m	456m
Current Assets	6m	6m	4m
Current Liabilities	5m	846	2m

Eurometals UK Ltd

16a Forge Lane Horbury, Wakefield, WF4 5EH
Tel: 01924-262020 **Fax:** 01924-266822
E-mail: eurometals@easynet.co.uk
Website: http://www.easynet.co.uk
Directors: F. Fleuret (MD), J. Flemington (Fin)
Immediate Holding Company: EUROMETALS (UK) LIMITED
Registration no: 03231707 **Date established:** 1996 **Turnover:** £1m - £2m
No.of Employees: 1 - 10 **Product Groups:** 29, 30, 34, 35, 36, 37, 40, 42, 43, 44, 45, 46, 47, 66, 67

Date of Accounts	Dec 11	Dec 10	Dec 09
Working Capital	168	145	77
Fixed Assets	4	6	2
Current Assets	463	487	271

Fit Feet

67 Dewsbury Road, Wakefield, WF2 9BL
Tel: 01924-375400
E-mail: i.harvey1@btinternet.com
Website: http://www.ukfitfeet.co.uk
Directors: I. Harvey (Prop)
Turnover: Up to £250,000 **No.of Employees:** 1 - 10 **Product Groups:** 88

Grass Concrete Ltd

Duncan House 142 Thornes Lane, Thornes, Wakefield, WF2 7RE
Tel: 01924-379443 **Fax:** 01924-290289
E-mail: bob@grasscrete.com
Website: http://www.grasscrete.com
Directors: R. Howden FRSA (MD), R. Walker (Ch)
Managers: J. Roberts (Sales Prom Mgr), A. Dickinson (Accounts)
Ultimate Holding Company: Ongoing Developments Ltd
Registration no: 00987037 **VAT No.:** GB 169 6706 20
Date established: 1970 **Turnover:** £2m - £5m **No.of Employees:** 1 - 10
Product Groups: 23, 30, 33, 35, 38, 39, 40, 45, 48, 51, 52, 66

Date of Accounts	Mar 12	Mar 11	Mar 10
Working Capital	509	464	396
Current Assets	591	563	502

Hamuel-Reichenbacher Ltd

7 Halifax Road Dewsbury, Wakefield, WF13 2OH
Tel: 01924-950600 **Fax:** 01924-455592
E-mail: bob.mcdermott@reichenbacher.co.uk
Website: http://www.reichenbacher.co.uk
Directors: A. Thompson (Sales), B. McDermott (Grp Chief Exec), D. Müller (Sales)
Immediate Holding Company: Hamuel Reichenbacher Ltd
Registration no: 05535794 **Date established:** 2003
Turnover: £250m - £500m **No.of Employees:** 1 - 10 **Product Groups:** 30, 38, 42, 46, 47, 48, 67

Date of Accounts	Dec 11	Dec 10	Dec 09
Working Capital	250	159	-406
Fixed Assets	34	30	25
Current Assets	439	206	619

Harvard Engineering Ltd

Tyler Close Normanton, Wakefield, WF6 1RL
Tel: 0113-383 1091 **Fax:** 0113-383 1010
E-mail: jamesosborne@harvardeng.com
Website: http://www.harvardeng.com

Directors: S. Cotton (Sales), M. Baum (Fin), M. Baum (Co Sec), J. McDonnell (MD), J. McDonald (MD)
Managers: M. Tennyson (Buyer), N. Sheppard (Sales Prom Mgr), M. McDonnell (Sales Prom Mgr)
Immediate Holding Company: HARVARD ENGINEERING PLC
Registration no: 02866874 **Date established:** 1993 **Turnover:** £5m - £10m
No.of Employees: 101 - 250 **Product Groups:** 37

Date of Accounts	Oct 11	Oct 10	Oct 09
Sales Turnover	21m	14m	8m
Pre Tax Profit/Loss	4m	1m	436
Working Capital	4m	2m	2m
Fixed Assets	2m	975	495
Current Assets	10m	7m	3m
Current Liabilities	3m	2m	547

Heath Lambert Insurance Services Ltd

Phoenix Court Jacobs Well Lane, Wakefield, WF1 3NT
Tel: 01924-207000 **Fax:** 01924-366813
E-mail: keyconnect@heathlambert.co.uk
Website: http://www.heathlambert.com
Directors: P. Smith (Dir)
Managers: P. Augur (Mgr), P. Hickman (Chief Mgr)
Immediate Holding Company: HEATH LAMBERT INSURANCE SERVICES LIMITED
Registration no: 00308512 **Date established:** 1935
Turnover: £125m - £250m **No.of Employees:** 101 - 250
Product Groups: 80, 82

Hedley Hydraulics Ltd

High Street Crigglestone, Wakefield, WF4 3HT
Tel: 01924-259999 **Fax:** 01924-252211
E-mail: sales@hedley-hyd.com
Website: http://www.hedley-hyd.com
Directors: J. Booker (MD), J. Massey (Dir), S. Davies (Dir), D. Oldfield (MD)
Ultimate Holding Company: HEDLEY DMB LIMITED
Immediate Holding Company: HEDLEY HYDRAULICS LIMITED
Registration no: 01244285 **Date established:** 1976 **Turnover:** £2m - £5m
No.of Employees: 21 - 50 **Product Groups:** 40

Date of Accounts	Jan 12	Jan 11	Jan 10
Working Capital	653	594	503
Fixed Assets	100	87	96
Current Assets	2m	1m	1m

Ibstock Brick Ltd

Swine Lane Nostell, Wakefield, WF4 1QH
Tel: 01924-866123 **Fax:** 01924-866101
E-mail: d.humphrey@ibstock.co.uk
Website: http://www.ibstock.co.uk
Managers: D. Humphrey (Mgr)
Ultimate Holding Company: CRH PUBLIC LIMITED COMPANY
Immediate Holding Company: IBSTOCK BRICK LIMITED
Registration no: 00063230 **Date established:** 1999
No.of Employees: 21 - 50 **Product Groups:** 33

Date of Accounts	Dec 11	Dec 10	Dec 09
Sales Turnover	163m	156m	125m
Pre Tax Profit/Loss	15m	7m	4m
Working Capital	67m	57m	69m
Fixed Assets	269m	276m	282m
Current Assets	94m	84m	90m
Current Liabilities	10m	12m	10m

Images Hair Studio

576 Leeds Road, Wakefield, WF1 2DT
Tel: 01924-823241
Directors: J. Carter (Prop)
Turnover: Up to £250,000 **No.of Employees:** 1 - 10 **Product Groups:** 35, 46, 49

Iot PRC

Northern House Moor Knoll Lane, East Ardsley, Wakefield, WF3 2EE
Tel: 01924-823455 **Fax:** 01924-820433
E-mail: enquiries@iotplc.com
Website: http://www.iotplc.com
Bank(s): Barclays
Directors: M. Mccarney (Dir), S. Wren (Co Sec)
Ultimate Holding Company: SHARP CORP (JAPAN)
Immediate Holding Company: EUROCOPY VEHICLE LEASING LIMITED
Registration no: 03075460 **VAT No.:** GB 420 5577 68
Date established: 1995 **Turnover:** £250,000 - £500,000
No.of Employees: 51 - 100 **Product Groups:** 48

Date of Accounts	Mar 12	Sep 10	Sep 09
Sales Turnover	31m	18m	20m
Pre Tax Profit/Loss	2m	3m	2m
Working Capital	16m	14m	12m
Fixed Assets	355	822	981
Current Assets	20m	19m	17m
Current Liabilities	2m	3m	3m

J C P Services Ltd

Unit 50 Wakefield Commercial Park Bridge Road, Horbury, Wakefield, WF4 5NW
Tel: 01924-278585 **Fax:** 01924-278585
Website: http://www.jcpservicesltd.org.uk
Directors: C. Penn (Fin), J. Penn (MD)
Immediate Holding Company: JCP SERVICES LIMITED
Registration no: 05368168 **Date established:** 2005
No.of Employees: 1 - 10 **Product Groups:** 26, 35

Date of Accounts	Feb 11	Feb 10	Feb 09
Working Capital	-4	-4	-6
Fixed Assets	7	5	7
Current Assets	45	31	24

Jomu Ltd

Unit 16 Navigation Court, Wakefield, WF2 7BJ
Tel: 0800-634 8646 **Fax:** 0870-125 5470
E-mail: info@jomu.co.uk
Website: http://www.jomu.co.uk
Directors: A. Jones (MD)
Immediate Holding Company: JOMU LTD
Registration no: 05469572 **Date established:** 2005
No.of Employees: 1 - 10 **Product Groups:** 80

Date of Accounts	Jun 11	Jun 10	Jun 09
Working Capital	2	2	-0
Fixed Assets	2	3	2
Current Assets	79	79	45

KCOM Group Public Limited Company

Melbourne House Brandy Carr Road, Wrenthorpe, Wakefield, WF2 0UG
Tel: 0800-915 5226 **Fax:** 01482-602100
E-mail: me@kcom.com
Website: http://www.kcom.com
Directors: G. Young (Sales), N. Gower (MD)
Managers: M. Lloydd (Sec)
Registration no: 02150618 **Product Groups:** 37, 38, 44, 48, 52, 67, 79, 80, 81, 84, 86

K S W Engineering

Unit 1 Grantley Way, Wakefield, WF1 4PY
Tel: 01924-565422
E-mail: kielward@aol.com
Website: http://www.kswengineering.org.uk
Directors: K. Ward (Prop)
Immediate Holding Company: K S W ENGINEERING (YORKSHIRE) LTD
Registration no: 07840167 **Date established:** 2011
No.of Employees: 11 - 20 **Product Groups:** 26, 35

Lar

Bradford Road East Ardsley, Wakefield, WF3 2DN
Tel: 0113-252 4586 **Fax:** 0113- 2536621
E-mail: m5lar@qsl.net
Website: http://www.larcomms.co.uk
Directors: S. Pounder (Prop)
Turnover: Up to £250,000 **No.of Employees:** 1 - 10 **Product Groups:** 37

Lincoln Cleaning Technology

179, Batley Road,, Wakefield, WF2 0AH
Tel: 01924-820876 **Fax:** 01924-826830
E-mail: info@lincolncleaningtechnology.co.uk
Website: http://www.lincolncleaningtechnology.co.uk
Managers: M. Pearson (Sales Prom Mgr)
Date established: 1989 **No.of Employees:** 1 - 10 **Product Groups:** 40

M & S Lift Trucks

1240 Dewsbury Road Tingley, Wakefield, WF3 1LX
Tel: 0113-259 7909 **Fax:** 0113-252 9072
Directors: S. Crosswaite (Snr Part)
Immediate Holding Company: M S LIFT-TRUCK LIMITED
Registration no: 05068726 **Date established:** 2004
No.of Employees: 1 - 10 **Product Groups:** 35, 39, 45

Multi Marque Production Engineering Ltd

Unit 33 Monckton Road Industrial Estate, Wakefield, WF2 7AL
Tel: 01924-290231 **Fax:** 01924-382241
E-mail: enquiries@multi-marque.co.uk
Website: http://www.multi-marque.co.uk
Bank(s): Midland
Directors: J. Barrett (MD)
Immediate Holding Company: MULTI MARQUE PRODUCTION ENGINEERING LIMITED
Registration no: 02578389 **VAT No.:** GB 590 6138 32
Date established: 1991 **Turnover:** £250,000 - £500,000
No.of Employees: 11 - 20 **Product Groups:** 42, 45, 48

Date of Accounts	Apr 11	Apr 10	Apr 09
Working Capital	432	398	345
Fixed Assets	70	69	87
Current Assets	509	470	466

Northern Sideloaders Ltd

Colliery Approach Lofthouse, Wakefield, WF3 3JG
Tel: 01924-827400 **Fax:** 01924-828883
E-mail: ian@northernsideloaders.co.uk
Website: http://www.northernsideloaders.com
Directors: I. Platts (MD)
Immediate Holding Company: NORTHERN SIDELOADERS LIMITED
Registration no: 02857769 **Date established:** 1993
No.of Employees: 11 - 20 **Product Groups:** 35, 39, 45

Date of Accounts	Oct 11	Oct 10	Oct 09
Working Capital	114	90	15
Fixed Assets	1m	1m	1m
Current Assets	428	333	270

Orbit Divers

76 Thirlmere Road, Wakefield, WF2 9ER
Tel: 01924-332345 **Fax:** 01924- 380839
Website: http://www.orbitdivers.co.uk
Directors: S. Moulson (Prop)
No.of Employees: 1 - 10 **Product Groups:** 40, 74, 80

Orchard Drawing Boards

Union Square, Wakefield, WF1 1TT
Tel: 01924-291333 **Fax:** 01924-290909
E-mail: vicky@thebigorchard.com
Website: http://www.thebigorchard.com
Directors: V. Tindall (Fin)
Immediate Holding Company: ORCHARD DRAWING BOARDS LIMITED
Registration no: 05517435 **Date established:** 2005
Turnover: £500,000 - £1m **No.of Employees:** 1 - 10 **Product Groups:** 25, 26, 27, 30, 35, 37, 38, 39, 40, 42, 44, 46, 49, 64, 67, 81, 83, 84, 86

Date of Accounts	Dec 11	Dec 10	Dec 09
Working Capital	-79	-37	-34
Fixed Assets	137	156	157
Current Assets	185	212	194

Pallet Truck Services

3 Blackgates Court Tingley, Wakefield, WF3 1TH
Tel: 0113-252 7852 **Fax:** 0113-252 7852
Directors: P. Robinson (Ptnr)
Date established: 1987 **No.of Employees:** 1 - 10 **Product Groups:** 35, 39, 45

Pickerings Europe Ltd

77-81 Dewsbury Road Tingley, Wakefield, WF3 1LE
Tel: 0113-252 2678 **Fax:** 0113-252 6851
Website: http://www.pickerings.co.uk
Managers: L. Mann (Mgr)
Ultimate Holding Company: KIPLUN LIMITED
Immediate Holding Company: PICKERINGS EUROPE LIMITED
Registration no: 03217853 **Date established:** 1996
No.of Employees: 21 - 50 **Product Groups:** 35, 39, 45

Date of Accounts	Dec 11	Dec 10	Dec 09
Sales Turnover	22m	20m	23m
Pre Tax Profit/Loss	3m	35m	5m
Working Capital	25m	25m	19m
Fixed Assets	11m	9m	9m
Current Assets	31m	30m	24m
Current Liabilities	4m	4m	3m

Planet Platforms (Northern) Ltd

Brunel Close Century Park Wakefield, Wakefield 41 Industrial Estate, Wakefield, WF2 0XG
Tel: 01924-829771 **Fax:** 01924-267090
E-mail: info@planetplatforms.co.uk
Website: http://www.planetplatform.co.uk
Directors: G. Armitage (Fin), P. Pemberton (MD)
Ultimate Holding Company: PLANET PLATFORMS (HOLDINGS) LIMITED
Immediate Holding Company: PLANET PLATFORMS (NORTHERN) LIMITED
Registration no: 03906183 **Date established:** 2000 **Turnover:** £5m - £10m
No.of Employees: 1 - 10 **Product Groups:** 35, 39, 45

Date of Accounts	Mar 11	Mar 10	Mar 09
Working Capital	4	10	18
Fixed Assets	N/A	20	27
Current Assets	148	157	596

Plaster WRX

158 Bridge Road Horbury, Wakefield, WF4 5NR
Tel: 07973-416072
E-mail: info@plasterwrx.com
Website: http://www.plasterwrx.com
Directors: A. Graystock (Prop)
Registration no: 06543257 **Date established:** 2005
No.of Employees: 1 - 10 **Product Groups:** 30, 52, 66

Polar Ford Wakefield

Calder Island Way, Wakefield, WF2 7AW
Tel: 01924-290290 **Fax:** 01226-732867
E-mail: glen.kenington@polar-motor.co.uk
Website: http://www.ford.co.uk
Directors: A. Murphy (Co Sec), S. Taylor (Dir & Gen Mgr), B. Rucker (Mkt Research)
Managers: D. Rhodes (Sec), B. Rooker (Mktg Serv Mgr), I. Wilson, G. Kenington (District Mgr), T. Chrispmas
Immediate Holding Company: FRIARS 676 LIMITED
Registration no: 00191596 **Date established:** 2012
No.of Employees: 21 - 50 **Product Groups:** 68

Date of Accounts	May 07	May 06	May 05
Working Capital	-2	-8	28
Fixed Assets	13	10	1
Current Assets	13	30	42

Polygraphica Equipment Ltd

1 Benton Office Park Bennett Avenue, Horbury, Wakefield, WF4 5RA
Tel: 01924-200444 **Fax:** 01924-363714
E-mail: sales@polygraphica.com
Website: http://www.polygraphica.com
Directors: D. Hartshorne (Fin), A. Lapish (Dir)
Immediate Holding Company: POLYGRAPHICA EQUIPMENT LIMITED
Registration no: 02810640 **Date established:** 1993
No.of Employees: 1 - 10 **Product Groups:** 24, 42, 43, 44, 67

Date of Accounts	Mar 12	Mar 11	Mar 10
Working Capital	166	166	166
Fixed Assets	16	21	29
Current Assets	335	745	317

Polypal

Polypal House Monckton Road Industrial Estate, Wakefield, WF2 7AL
Tel: 01924-200015 **Fax:** 01924-201160
E-mail: dmcqueen@polypal.co.uk
Website: http://www.polypal.co.uk
Bank(s): Lloyds
Directors: D. Mcqueen (MD), J. Youle (Sales & Mktg), J. Youle (Sales & Mktg), S. Walker (Chief Op Offcr)
Managers: K. Worrall
Immediate Holding Company: DAVID GEE ASSOCIATES LIMITED
Registration no: 03319007 **VAT No.:** GB 277 4158 32
Date established: 1997 **Turnover:** Up to £250,000
No.of Employees: 21 - 50 **Product Groups:** 26

Date of Accounts	Mar 09	Sep 11	Sep 10
Pre Tax Profit/Loss	889	N/A	N/A
Working Capital	5m	2m	2m
Fixed Assets	316	4m	3m
Current Assets	5m	2m	2m
Current Liabilities	354	N/A	N/A

Polyurethane Progress Ltd

Church Street, Wakefield, WF1 5QY
Tel: 01924-387310 **Fax:** 01924-382951
E-mail: office@polyprog.co.uk
Website: http://www.polyprog.co.uk
Bank(s): HSBC
Directors: J. Gladwin (Fin)
Managers: B. Cookson (Sales Prom Mgr)
Immediate Holding Company: POLYURETHANE PROGRESS LIMITED
Registration no: 01961972 **VAT No.:** GB 436 5405 54
Date established: 1985 **Turnover:** £1m - £2m **No.of Employees:** 21 - 50
Product Groups: 29, 30, 31

Date of Accounts	Feb 12	Feb 11	Feb 10
Sales Turnover	N/A	N/A	1m
Working Capital	362	381	355
Fixed Assets	334	317	349
Current Assets	604	604	537

R C M Stainless

48 Thornes Lane, Wakefield, WF1 5RR
Tel: 01924-366246 **Fax:** 01924-368146
Managers: S. Thompson (Mgr)
Date established: 2003 **No.of Employees:** 21 - 50 **Product Groups:** 37, 40, 48

R G Fabrication

4 Flanshaw Works Flanshaw Lane, Wakefield, WF2 9JF
Tel: 01924-376265 **Fax:** 01924-376265
Directors: R. Green (Prop)
Date established: 2003 **No.of Employees:** 1 - 10 **Product Groups:** 26, 35

Range Cylinders Ltd

Tadman Street, Wakefield, WF1 5QU
Tel: 01924-234500 **Fax:** 01924-385015
Website: http://www.range-cylinders.co.uk
Directors: N. Crowe (Dir)
Ultimate Holding Company: KINGSPAN GROUP PUBLIC LIMITED COMPANY
Immediate Holding Company: KINGSPAN HOT WATER SYSTEMS LIMITED

see next page

Range Cylinders Ltd - Cont'd
Registration no: 04357772 **VAT No.:** GB 562 3227 57
Date established: 2002 **Turnover:** £50m - £75m
No.of Employees: 101 - 250 **Product Groups:** 35, 85

Date of Accounts	Dec 11	Dec 10	Dec 09
Sales Turnover	54m	52m	47m
Pre Tax Profit/Loss	1m	3m	2m
Working Capital	-599	-1m	-5m
Fixed Assets	11m	13m	13m
Current Assets	29m	26m	27m
Current Liabilities	6m	5m	6m

Rawson Carpets Ltd
Castlebank Mills Portobello Road, Wakefield, WF1 5PS
Tel: 01924-373421 **Fax:** 01924-290334
E-mail: sales@rawsoncarpets.co.uk
Website: http://www.rawsoncarpets.co.uk
Directors: A. Johnson (Dir), D. Whittingham (Fin)
Managers: A. Fuant (Personnel), D. Hudson (Nat Sales Mgr), J. Dickins (Tech Serv Mgr), N. Pentecost (Buyer)
Ultimate Holding Company: BRAVESHIRE LIMITED
Immediate Holding Company: RAWSON CARPETS LIMITED
Registration no: 01665381 **VAT No.:** GB 381 4505 58
Date established: 1982 **Turnover:** £5m - £10m
No.of Employees: 101 - 250 **Product Groups:** 23

Date of Accounts	Jun 11	Jun 10	Jun 09
Sales Turnover	6m	6m	5m
Pre Tax Profit/Loss	70	366	419
Working Capital	2m	2m	1m
Current Assets	3m	3m	2m
Current Liabilities	145	122	143

W E Rawson Ltd
Castlebank Mills Portobello Road, Wakefield, WF1 5PS
Tel: 01924-373421 **Fax:** 01924-290334
E-mail: reception@werawson.co.uk
Website: http://www.rawsoncarpets.co.uk
Bank(s): Barclays
Directors: N. Penn (Sales), D. Whittingham (Fin)
Managers: J. Dickens (Tech Serv Mgr), N. Pentecost (Purch Mgr), D. Hudson (Sales & Mktg Mg), A. Faung (Personnel)
Ultimate Holding Company: BRAVESHIRE LIMITED
Immediate Holding Company: W.E.RAWSON LIMITED
Registration no: 00248570 **VAT No.:** GB 381 4505 58
Date established: 1930 **Turnover:** £20m - £50m
No.of Employees: 101 - 250 **Product Groups:** 23

Date of Accounts	Jun 11	Jun 10	Jun 09
Sales Turnover	21m	21m	21m
Pre Tax Profit/Loss	151	2m	2m
Working Capital	1m	1m	281
Fixed Assets	9m	10m	9m
Current Assets	15m	14m	13m
Current Liabilities	1m	1m	1m

Redbeck Farm Shop
339 Doncaster Road Crofton, Wakefield, WF4 1RT
Tel: 01924-862037
E-mail: info@redbeckshooting.com
Website: http://www.redbeckshooting.com
Directors: D. Baines (Prop)
Immediate Holding Company: REDBECK SHOOTING SUPPLIES LIMITED
Registration no: 06863362 **Date established:** 2009
No.of Employees: 1 - 10 **Product Groups:** 36, 39, 40

Date of Accounts	Mar 11	Mar 10
Working Capital	88	40
Fixed Assets	5	3
Current Assets	210	142

Renotex Ltd
Pollard Street Lofthouse, Wakefield, WF3 3HG
Tel: 01924-820003 **Fax:** 01924-829529
E-mail: sales@renotex.co.uk
Website: http://www.renotex.co.uk
Directors: D. Scott (Fin)
Immediate Holding Company: RENOTEX LIMITED
Registration no: 02810671 **Date established:** 1993
No.of Employees: 11 - 20 **Product Groups:** 46, 48

Date of Accounts	Mar 12	Mar 11	Mar 10
Working Capital	50	20	17
Current Assets	92	69	84

Joseph Rhodes Ltd
Bell Vue Elm Tree Street, Wakefield, WF1 5EQ
Tel: 01924-371161 **Fax:** 01924-370928
E-mail: sales@grouprhodes.co.uk
Website: http://www.josephrhodes.co.uk
Bank(s): Barclays
Directors: B. Richardson (Sales), A. Khan (Mkt Research)
Managers: T. Kerridge (Tech Serv Mgr), H. Malcolm (Personnel), A. Cooper (Comptroller), P. Hurst (Buyer)
Immediate Holding Company: JOSEPH RHODES LIMITED
Registration no: 00063294 **VAT No.:** GB 419 3585 32
Date established: 1999 **Turnover:** £10m - £20m
No.of Employees: 101 - 250 **Product Groups:** 46

Date of Accounts	Feb 08	Feb 11	Feb 10
Sales Turnover	N/A	17m	14m
Pre Tax Profit/Loss	141	533	264
Working Capital	929	2m	1m
Fixed Assets	6m	5m	5m
Current Assets	7m	10m	9m
Current Liabilities	2m	4m	3m

S K F UK Ltd
Wakefield Industrial Estate Brindley Houe, Wakefield 41 Industrial Estate, Wakefield, WF2 0XQ
Tel: 01924-870211 **Fax:** 01924-870184
E-mail: michelle.large@skf.co.uk
Website: http://www.skf.co.uk
Managers: M. Large
Ultimate Holding Company: AKTIEBOLAGET SKF (SWEDEN)
Immediate Holding Company: SKF (U.K) LIMITED
Registration no: 00107367 **Date established:** 2010
No.of Employees: 1 - 10 **Product Groups:** 35, 45

Date of Accounts	Dec 11	Dec 10	Dec 09
Sales Turnover	251m	203m	182m
Pre Tax Profit/Loss	54m	35m	21m
Working Capital	83m	64m	76m
Fixed Assets	19m	20m	18m
Current Assets	120m	97m	107m
Current Liabilities	19m	16m	16m

S W L Engineering
3 Holmfield Chase Stanley, Wakefield, WF3 4QZ
Tel: 07961-170212 **Fax:** 01924-824950
E-mail: steve@flown.freeserve.co.uk
Directors: S. Lown (Dir)
No.of Employees: 1 - 10 **Product Groups:** 35, 66

Peter Sandham Associates
Towers Lane Crofton, Wakefield, WF4 1PT
Tel: 01924-865565 **Fax:** 01977-723948
E-mail: petersandham@totalise.co.uk
Website: http://www.totalise.co.uk
Directors: P. Sandham (Prop)
Immediate Holding Company: PINDER PLANT LIMITED
Registration no: 01910915 **Date established:** 1985
No.of Employees: 1 - 10 **Product Groups:** 35

Sirdar Spinning Ltd
PO Box 31, Wakefield, WF2 9ND
Tel: 01924-371501 **Fax:** 01924-290506
E-mail: enquiries@sirdar.co.uk
Website: http://www.sirdar.co.uk
Bank(s): Barclays
Directors: I. Stead (Fin), R. Morris (Dir)
Managers: R. Young (Tech Serv Mgr), C. Powell (Mktg Serv Mgr), L. Rattigan (Personnel)
Ultimate Holding Company: SIRDAR HOLDINGS LIMITED
Immediate Holding Company: HAYFIELD TEXTILES LIMITED
Registration no: 00194421 **VAT No.:** GB 170 3762 72
Date established: 2023 **Turnover:** £20m - £50m
No.of Employees: 51 - 100 **Product Groups:** 23

Date of Accounts	Jun 11	Jun 10	Jun 09
Pre Tax Profit/Loss	N/A	-4	-4
Working Capital	400	844	848
Current Assets	400	848	852
Current Liabilities	N/A	4	4

Slater & Crabtree Ltd
Thornes Lane, Wakefield, WF1 5RW
Tel: 01924-374874 **Fax:** 01924-378288
E-mail: sales@slatercrabtree.co.uk
Website: http://www.slatercrabtree.co.uk
Bank(s): National Westminster, Barnsley
Directors: C. Ridgway (Ch), D. Slater (Fin)
Immediate Holding Company: SLATER & CRABTREE LIMITED
Registration no: 00223606 **Date established:** 2027
No.of Employees: 21 - 50 **Product Groups:** 46, 47, 48

Date of Accounts	Mar 10	Mar 09	Mar 08
Working Capital	1m	1m	1m
Fixed Assets	725	771	854
Current Assets	1m	2m	2m

Star Sportswear Ltd Pro Star
PO Box 20, Wakefield, WF2 7AJ
Tel: 01924-291441 **Fax:** 01924-384495
E-mail: sales@prostar.co.uk
Website: http://www.prostar.co.uk
Bank(s): Barclays
Directors: P. Archbell (MD), R. Archbell (Ch), D. Bedford (Dir)
Managers: G. Kilkenny (Accounts), L. Lawton
Immediate Holding Company: Global Star Holdings Ltd
Registration no: 00071811 **Date established:** 1990
Turnover: £10m - £20m **No.of Employees:** 101 - 250 **Product Groups:** 24

Date of Accounts	Nov 07	Nov 06	Nov 05
Sales Turnover	10784	10626	11111
Pre Tax Profit/Loss	474	624	823
Working Capital	5035	4578	4207
Fixed Assets	437	816	931
Current Assets	6974	6324	6346
Current Liabilities	1940	1746	2140
Total Share Capital	60	60	60
ROCE% (Return on Capital Employed)	8.7	11.6	16.0
ROT% (Return on Turnover)	4.4	5.9	7.4

T E I Ltd
PO Box 80, Wakefield, WF1 5YS
Tel: 01924-780000 **Fax:** 01924-201901
E-mail: dowt@tei.co.uk
Website: http://www.tei.co.uk
Bank(s): HSBC, London
Directors: T. Dow (Sales), J. Budby (Co Sec)
Managers: C. Drury, S. Dolan (Tech Serv Mgr)
Ultimate Holding Company: S.E.S. HOLDINGS (UK) LIMITED
Immediate Holding Company: TEI LIMITED
Registration no: 05236072 **VAT No.:** GB 169 6379 09
Date established: 2004 **Turnover:** £10m - £20m
No.of Employees: 251 - 500 **Product Groups:** 36, 39, 40, 48

Date of Accounts	Mar 12	Mar 11	Mar 10
Sales Turnover	24m	18m	24m
Pre Tax Profit/Loss	265	93	1m
Working Capital	2m	2m	2m
Fixed Assets	132	72	91
Current Assets	9m	6m	5m
Current Liabilities	3m	3m	2m

Touch A V Ltd
22 Johns Avenue Lofthouse, Wakefield, WF3 3LU
Tel: 0845-475 2113 **Fax:** 0870-836 2113
E-mail: install@touchav.co.uk
Website: http://www.touchaudiovisual.co.uk
Directors: D. Wilson (Prop)
Immediate Holding Company: TOUCH AV LTD
Registration no: 05825387 **Date established:** 2006
Turnover: £250,000 - £500,000 **No.of Employees:** 1 - 10
Product Groups: 38, 48, 81, 84

Date of Accounts	May 11	May 10	May 09
Sales Turnover	N/A	N/A	154
Working Capital	8	7	13
Fixed Assets	7	9	11
Current Assets	82	69	65
Current Liabilities	N/A	57	N/A

TQ Environmental Plc
Flanshaw way, Wakefield, WF2 9LP
Tel: 01924-380700 **Fax:** 01924-361700
E-mail: sales@tqplc.com
Website: http://www.tqplc.com
Bank(s): Lloyds Bank
Directors: N. Andrews (MD)
Managers: G. Hall (Sales & Mktg Mg)
Registration no: 02518328 **VAT No.:** GB 590 6563 17
Date established: 1990 **Turnover:** £1m - £2m **No.of Employees:** 20
Product Groups: 38, 84

Date of Accounts	Sep 11	Sep 10	Sep 09
Sales Turnover	1m	1m	2m
Pre Tax Profit/Loss	-17	-2	-4
Working Capital	195	206	9
Fixed Assets	374	380	389
Current Assets	501	590	519
Current Liabilities	143	140	313

V & B Catering Equipment
The Yard Industrial Street, Wakefield, WF1 3NG
Tel: 01924-369866 **Fax:** 01924-369866
Directors: B. Harding (Prop)
Date established: 1990 **No.of Employees:** 1 - 10 **Product Groups:** 20, 40, 41

The Wakefield Shirt Company Limited
Thornes Lane Wharf, Wakefield, WF1 5RL
Tel: 01924-375651 **Fax:** 01924-290096
E-mail: marketing@wsg.co.uk
Website: http://www.wsg.co.uk
Directors: R. Donner (MD), T. Roehricht (Sales & Mktg)
Managers: J. Thompson (Computer Mgr), P. Thompson (Grp Purch Mgr), S. Oxley (Mktg Serv Mgr)
Registration no: 00361629 **Turnover:** £20m - £50m
No.of Employees: 251 - 500 **Product Groups:** 24, 29, 40

Date of Accounts	Dec 07	Dec 06
Sales Turnover	17320	15170
Pre Tax Profit/Loss	420	330
Working Capital	4180	3800
Fixed Assets	8390	8410
Current Assets	8400	7980
Current Liabilities	4220	4180
Total Share Capital	1170	1170
ROCE% (Return on Capital Employed)	3.3	2.7
ROT% (Return on Turnover)	2.4	2.2

Waterhouse Building Refurbishment & Interiors
98 Bradford Road East Ardsley, Wakefield, WF3 2JL
Tel: 01924-822274 **Fax:** 01924-823951
E-mail: info@waterhouse-ideas.co.uk
Website: http://www.waterhouse-ideas.co.uk
Bank(s): Barclays
Directors: T. Waterhouse (Co Sec), W. Waterhouse (MD), P. Thompson (Contracts), L. Wdowzyk (Sales), J. Waterhouse (MD), P. Morrish (Dir)
Managers: L. Wdowczyk (Sales Prom Mgr), C. Simpson
Immediate Holding Company: H. WATERHOUSE & SONS (WAKEFIELD) LIMITED
Registration no: 01199343 **VAT No.:** GB 171 8430 66
Date established: 1975 **Turnover:** £2m - £5m **No.of Employees:** 21 - 50
Product Groups: 52

Date of Accounts	Mar 11	Mar 10	Mar 09
Working Capital	379	331	400
Fixed Assets	90	54	75
Current Assets	2m	1m	1m

Wra Metal Finishing Services
Sherwood Industrial Estate Robin Hood, Wakefield, WF3 3EL
Tel: 0113-282 8231 **Fax:** 0113-280 0211
Website: http://www.wracoatings.co.uk
Directors: A. Smith (Prop)
Immediate Holding Company: F. KNOWLES & SON LIMITED
Registration no: 01359682 **Date established:** 1978
No.of Employees: 1 - 10 **Product Groups:** 46, 48

Date of Accounts	Mar 12	Mar 11	Mar 10
Working Capital	60	26	-156
Fixed Assets	381	362	541
Current Assets	212	201	246

Wren General Merchants Ltd
Waterfront House New Brunswick Street, Wakefield, WF1 5QR
Tel: 01924-366383 **Fax:** 01924-298055
E-mail: info@perfectalgarve.com
Website: http://www.perfectalgarve.com
Directors: P. Lawes (MD)
Immediate Holding Company: WREN GENERAL MERCHANTS LIMITED
Registration no: 00696609 **Date established:** 1961
No.of Employees: 1 - 10 **Product Groups:** 66

Date of Accounts	Dec 11	Dec 10	Dec 09
Working Capital	1m	1m	1m
Fixed Assets	482	482	485
Current Assets	1m	1m	1m

Wetherby

Arville Textiles
Sandbeck Lane, Wetherby, LS22 7DQ
Tel: 01937-582735 **Fax:** 01937-580196
E-mail: graham.ford@arville.com
Website: http://www.arville.com
Bank(s): Barclays
Directors: G. Ford (MD), R. Wight (Fin)
Managers: N. Sykes (Sales & Mktg Mg), N. Hull (Prod Mgr)
Ultimate Holding Company: ARVILLE HOLDINGS LIMITED
Immediate Holding Company: HEATHERMIST LTD
Registration no: 00655331 **VAT No.:** GB 482 0055 69
Date established: 1960 **Turnover:** £5m - £10m **No.of Employees:** 11 - 20
Product Groups: 23, 63

Date of Accounts	May 08	May 09	May 10
Sales Turnover	N/A	7m	6m
Pre Tax Profit/Loss	-61	99	-1
Working Capital	2m	6m	6m
Fixed Assets	6m	2m	2m
Current Assets	2m	7m	7m
Current Liabilities	N/A	327	314

Bayford & Co. Ltd
Bowcliffe Hall Bramham, Wetherby, LS23 6LP
Tel: 01937-541111 **Fax:** 01937-841465
E-mail: sales@bayford.co.uk
Website: http://www.bayford.co.uk

Directors: D. Turner (Ch), J. Turner (MD), P. Hall (Fin)
Managers: A. Walsh (Mktg Serv Mgr)
Immediate Holding Company: Fambo Ltd
Registration no: 04928440 **Date established:** 1937
Turnover: £250m - £500m **No.of Employees:** 101 - 250
Product Groups: 31

Date of Accounts	Jun 08
Sales Turnover	452260
Pre Tax Profit/Loss	2250
Working Capital	-3220
Fixed Assets	20210
Current Assets	54920
Current Liabilities	58140
Total Share Capital	2420
ROCE% (Return on Capital Employed)	13.2

British Library
Boston Spa, Wetherby, LS23 7BQ
Tel: 01937-546000 **Fax:** 01937-546333
E-mail: dsc-customer-services@bl.uk
Website: http://www.bl.uk
Directors: L. Brinley (Grp Chief Exec)
No.of Employees: 1 - 10 **Product Groups:** 80

Britton Price Ltd
169 High Street Boston Spa, Wetherby, LS23 6BH
Tel: 01937-849494 **Fax:** 01937-541127
Website: http://www.brittonprice.co.uk
Directors: P. Crosby (Sales)
Immediate Holding Company: BRITTON PRICE LIMITED
Registration no: 03247545 **Date established:** 1996
No.of Employees: 1 - 10 **Product Groups:** 35, 39, 45

Date of Accounts	Dec 11	Dec 10	Dec 09
Sales Turnover	5m	5m	4m
Pre Tax Profit/Loss	591	342	228
Working Capital	987	699	611
Fixed Assets	31	22	40
Current Assets	2m	2m	1m
Current Liabilities	745	661	478

Encon Insulation Ltd (Head Office)
Brunswick House 1 Deighton Close, Wetherby, LS22 7GZ
Tel: 01937-524200 **Fax:** 01937-524222
E-mail: info@encon.co.uk
Website: http://www.encon.co.uk
Bank(s): Bank of Scotland
Directors: M. Neville (Dir), P. Kirk (Fin), S. Moore (MD), S. Moore (Chief Op Offcr), G. MacDonald (MD), G. Fallows (MD), P. Proom (Div)
Managers: B. Sudlow (Sales Admin), D. Simpson (Sales Prom Mgr), D. Truswell (Purch Mgr)
Ultimate Holding Company: WOLSELEY PLC (JERSEY)
Immediate Holding Company: ENCON LIMITED
Registration no: 03411533 **Date established:** 1997
Turnover: £125m - £250m **No.of Employees:** 21 - 50
Product Groups: 14, 25, 30, 33

Goldenfry Foods Ltd
Sandbeck Way, Wetherby, LS22 7DW
Tel: 01937-583631 **Fax:** 01937-580024
E-mail: johnh@goldenfry.co.uk
Bank(s): HSBC
Directors: J. Herridge (Co Sec)
Ultimate Holding Company: GOLDENFRY LIMITED
Immediate Holding Company: GOLDENFRY LIMITED
Registration no: 02404748 **Date established:** 1989
Turnover: £20m - £50m **No.of Employees:** 101 - 250 **Product Groups:** 20

Date of Accounts	Dec 10	Dec 09	Dec 08
Sales Turnover	25m	23m	22m
Pre Tax Profit/Loss	-155	-830	-2m
Working Capital	4m	5m	6m
Fixed Assets	5m	5m	5m
Current Assets	10m	10m	13m
Current Liabilities	3m	3m	4m

Hanson Aggregates
Clifford House York Road, Wetherby, LS22 7NS
Tel: 08456-006616 **Fax:** 01937-545889
E-mail: sales.orderswest@hanson-aggregates-n.com
Website: http://www.hanson.co.uk
Bank(s): Barclays
Directors: A. Eyles (Dir)
Managers: T. Williams
Ultimate Holding Company: HEIDELBERG CEMENT AG (GERMANY)
Immediate Holding Company: HANSON AGGREGATES LIMITED
Registration no: 02565390 **VAT No.:** GB 238 7665 22
Date established: 1990 **Turnover:** £75m - £125m
No.of Employees: 21 - 50 **Product Groups:** 14, 17, 33

Date of Accounts	Dec 11	Dec 10	Dec 09
Working Capital	82m	82m	82m
Current Assets	82m	82m	82m

Inspirepac Ltd
Sandbeck Lane, Wetherby, LS22 7YD
Tel: 01937-868200 **Fax:** 01937-868247
E-mail: chris.munroe@inspirepac.com
Website: http://www.inspirepac.com
Directors: C. Munroe (Fin), K. Smith (Sales)
Managers: D. Bealby (Tech Serv Mgr), D. Aris (Personnel)
Ultimate Holding Company: INSPIREPAC LIMITED
Immediate Holding Company: INSPIREPAC SAFEPACK LIMITED
Registration no: 01058698 **Date established:** 1972
No.of Employees: 101 - 250 **Product Groups:** 27

Date of Accounts	Jan 09	Jan 08	Jan 07
Sales Turnover	N/A	N/A	16m
Pre Tax Profit/Loss	N/A	N/A	3m
Working Capital	3m	3m	3m
Current Assets	3m	3m	3m

Keller Geo Technique
Unit 611 Avenue D Thorp Arch Estate, Wetherby, LS23 7FS
Tel: 01937-541118 **Fax:** 01937-541371
E-mail: info@keller-ge.co.uk
Website: http://www.keller-geotechnique.co.uk
Bank(s): Bank of Scotland
Directors: R. Barratt (Fin), M. Martin (Dir), A. Bell (Ch), M. Edwards (Contracts)
Managers: T. Hughes (Comm), S. Goldsworth (Buyer), S. Jastak (Purch Mgr), D. Cromber, D. Cromber (Personnel)
Immediate Holding Company: KELLER COLCRETE LIMITED
Registration no: 00323483 **Date established:** 1937
No.of Employees: 21 - 50 **Product Groups:** 51, 52

M C M
Rudgate Thorp Arch Estate, Wetherby, LS23 7AT
Tel: 01937-844000 **Fax:** 01937-842524
E-mail: sales@mcm-moisture.com
Website: http://www.mcm-moisture.com
Directors: N. Wallis (Dir)
Ultimate Holding Company: MCM (HOLDINGS) LIMITED
Immediate Holding Company: MOISTURE CONTROL AND MEASUREMENT (U.K.) LIMITED
Registration no: 02293943 **Date established:** 1988 **Turnover:** £2m - £5m
No.of Employees: 11 - 20 **Product Groups:** 38, 42

Date of Accounts	Oct 11	Oct 10	Oct 09
Working Capital	4	4	4
Current Assets	10	10	10

Moores Furniture Group
Unit 350 Thorp Arch Trading Estate, Thorp Arch Estate, Wetherby, LS23 7DD
Tel: 01937-842394 **Fax:** 01937-845396
E-mail: marketing@moores.co.uk
Website: http://www.moores.co.uk
Bank(s): Barclays
Directors: A. Calvert (Fin), K. Tolson (Sales & Mktg), J. Cahill (Sales), A. Radcliffe (Fin)
Managers: P. Carse (Purch Mgr), T. Waltasaari, S. Thompson (Personnel), S. Swan (Tech Serv Mgr)
Ultimate Holding Company: MASCO CORP INC (USA)
Immediate Holding Company: MOORES FURNITURE GROUP LIMITED
Registration no: 01083749 **VAT No.:** GB 613 3661 62
Date established: 1972 **Turnover:** £50m - £75m
No.of Employees: 501 - 1000 **Product Groups:** 26

Date of Accounts	Dec 11	Dec 10	Dec 09
Sales Turnover	50m	56m	59m
Pre Tax Profit/Loss	-6m	-7m	-2m
Working Capital	10m	17m	23m
Fixed Assets	4m	5m	6m
Current Assets	25m	27m	33m
Current Liabilities	3m	3m	3m

N T R Ltd
Unit 372a Thorp Arch Estate Thorp Arch Estate, Wetherby, LS23 7BJ
Tel: 01937-845112 **Fax:** 01937-845467
E-mail: info@ntrltd.co.uk
Website: http://www.ntrltd.co.uk
Bank(s): National Westminster Bank Plc
Directors: D. Atkinson (Fin), C. Broadley Naylor (MD)
Managers: S. Tatham (Chief Acct)
Ultimate Holding Company: MEADWAY HOLDINGS LIMITED
Immediate Holding Company: N T R LTD
Registration no: 01433038 **VAT No.:** GB 332 2651 86
Date established: 1979 **Turnover:** £1m - £2m **No.of Employees:** 21 - 50
Product Groups: 33, 36

Date of Accounts	Mar 12	Mar 11	Mar 10
Working Capital	196	111	108
Fixed Assets	57	52	78
Current Assets	483	394	360

Peter Smith Associates
209 High Street Boston Spa, Wetherby, LS23 6AA
Tel: 01937-842588 **Fax:** 01937-842588
E-mail: petersmith209@tiscali.co.uk
Directors: P. Smith (Prop)
Date established: 2002 **No.of Employees:** 1 - 10 **Product Groups:** 35

Rhino Barrier Systems Ltd
Equinox 1 Audby Lane, Wetherby, LS22 7RD
Tel: 01937-580033 **Fax:** 01937-583322
E-mail: info@rhinobarriers.com
Website: http://www.rhinobarriers.com
Directors: R. Macrae (Fin)
Managers: N. Jewitt
Immediate Holding Company: RHINO BARRIER SYSTEMS LTD
Registration no: 03818746 **Date established:** 1999
No.of Employees: 1 - 10 **Product Groups:** 42, 45

Date of Accounts	Oct 07	Oct 06	Oct 05
Working Capital	215	167	122
Fixed Assets	9	12	10
Current Assets	428	222	273
Current Liabilities	212	54	151
Total Share Capital	N/A	8	8

Robinson & Birdsell Ltd
Audby House Audby Lane, Wetherby, LS22 7FD
Tel: 01937-548800 **Fax:** 01937-548801
E-mail: dem@robinson-birdsell.co.uk
Website: http://www.robinson-birdsell.co.uk
Bank(s): HSBC Bank plc
Directors: D. Catchpole (MD)
Managers: B. Atkinson, S. Whitley (Chief Acct), S. Whiteley (Chief Acct)
Immediate Holding Company: ROBINSON & BIRDSELL LIMITED
Registration no: 00576778 **Date established:** 1957
Turnover: £10m - £20m **No.of Employees:** 21 - 50 **Product Groups:** 51

Say Scaffolding Ltd
Unit 2-3 & Offices Woodgate Business Business Centre Rudgate, Thorp Arch, Wetherby, LS23 7AU
Tel: 01937-848480 **Fax:** 01904-737702
E-mail: info@sayltd.co.uk
Website: http://www.sayltd.co.uk
Directors: P. Wetten (MD)
Managers: H. Watson (Chief Acct), S. Magson (Personnel), S. Burns (Tech Serv Mgr)
Immediate Holding Company: SAY SCAFFOLDING LIMITED
Registration no: 05314071 **Date established:** 2004
No.of Employees: 21 - 50 **Product Groups:** 25, 35, 36, 39, 40, 45, 48, 52, 66, 83

Date of Accounts	May 11	May 10	May 09
Working Capital	-46	-499	-555
Fixed Assets	1m	1m	1m
Current Assets	647	491	411

Swift Research Ltd
Concept House Sandbeck Way, Wetherby, LS22 7DN
Tel: 01937-543600 **Fax:** 01937-543610
E-mail: info@swift-research.co.uk
Website: http://www.swift-research.co.uk
Directors: K. France (Dir), N. Mellor (Chief Op Offcr), M. Penfold (Fin)
Managers: G. Stewart (Develop Mgr)
Ultimate Holding Company: SANDMARTEN HOLDINGS LIMITED
Immediate Holding Company: SWIFT RESEARCH LIMITED
Registration no: 03151774 **Date established:** 1996 **Turnover:** £1m - £2m
No.of Employees: 51 - 100 **Product Groups:** 81

Date of Accounts	Feb 12	Feb 11	Feb 10
Working Capital	133	15	-45
Fixed Assets	255	466	483
Current Assets	890	827	989

Taegutec UK Ltd
Wetherby Grange Park Boston Road, Wetherby, LS22 5NB
Tel: 01937-589828 **Fax:** 01937-589996
E-mail: sales@taegutec.co.uk
Website: http://www.taegutec.co.uk
Managers: S. Taylor (Fin Mgr)
Ultimate Holding Company: BERKSHIRE HATHAWAY INC (USA)
Immediate Holding Company: TAEGUTEC UK LIMITED
Registration no: 03915895 **Date established:** 2000 **Turnover:** £2m - £5m
No.of Employees: 1 - 10 **Product Groups:** 45

Date of Accounts	Dec 11	Dec 10	Dec 09
Sales Turnover	4m	3m	2m
Pre Tax Profit/Loss	90	74	-67
Working Capital	-46	-92	-135
Fixed Assets	45	29	23
Current Assets	2m	1m	853
Current Liabilities	239	194	135

Thorp Arch Powder Coatings
Unit 185 Thorp Arch Trading Estate Thorp Arch Estate, Wetherby, LS23 7BJ
Tel: 01937-541267 **Fax:** 01937-541267
Directors: I. Wilson (Prop)
Date established: 1981 **No.of Employees:** 1 - 10 **Product Groups:** 46, 48

West Yorkshire Steel Co. Ltd
Sandbeck Works Sandbeck Way, Wetherby, LS22 7DN
Tel: 01937-584440 **Fax:** 01937-580128
E-mail: sales@westyorkssteel.com
Website: http://www.westyorkssteel.com
Directors: D. Ellis (Dir)
Immediate Holding Company: WEST YORKSHIRE STEEL CO. LIMITED
Registration no: 01229647 **VAT No.:** GB 172 0259 84
Date established: 1975 **No.of Employees:** 1 - 10 **Product Groups:** 34, 35, 36, 48, 61, 66

Date of Accounts	Nov 11	Nov 10	Nov 09
Working Capital	62	-16	-26
Fixed Assets	86	60	49
Current Assets	261	225	311

X L Marking Systems
7 Cedar Covert, Wetherby, LS22 7XW
Tel: 01937-580148 **Fax:** 01937-842137
Directors: L. Harding (Prop)
Date established: 1988 **No.of Employees:** 1 - 10 **Product Groups:** 37

Zinsser UK
Wetherby House 7 Market Place, Wetherby, LS22 6LG
Tel: 01937-584422 **Fax:** 01937-584422
Website: http://www.zinsseruk.com
Managers: I. Prest (Mgr)
No.of Employees: 1 - 10 **Product Groups:** 27, 32

CHANNEL ISLANDS

Guernsey

The Butterfield Fulcrum
PO Box 211, Guernsey, GY1 3NQ
Tel: 01481-720321 **Fax:** 01481-714533
E-mail: guernsey@butterfieldgroup.com
Website: http://www.bfgl.com
Directors: A. Howard (MD)
Managers: K. Mccarney
No.of Employees: 21 - 50 **Product Groups:** 80, 82

Caplain Glasshouse Services Ltd
Petit Marais Vale, Guernsey, GY3 5DH
Tel: 01481-244159 **Fax:** 01481-248491
E-mail: caplainglass@guernsey.net
Website: http://www.caplaingreenhouses.com
Directors: E. Caplain (Prop)
Date established: 1982 **No.of Employees:** 1 - 10 **Product Groups:** 26, 35

Channel Distribution Services Ltd
Pointes Lane St Andrew, Guernsey, GY6 8UH
Tel: 01481-235631 **Fax:** 01481-235094
Managers: P. Le Lievre (Mgr)
Turnover: Up to £250,000 **No.of Employees:** 1 - 10 **Product Groups:** 30, 66

Condor Logistics
Longue Hougue Lane St Sampson, Guernsey, GY2 4JN
Tel: 01481-242020 **Fax:** 01481-245074
E-mail: paul.wilson@condorlogistics.co.uk
Website: http://www.condorlogistics.co.uk
Bank(s): Lloyds TSB Bank plc
Managers: D. Le Sauvage (Mgr)
Turnover: £125m - £250m **No.of Employees:** 21 - 50
Product Groups: 71, 72, 76, 77

Creaseys Ltd
9-25 High Street St Peter Port, Guernsey, GY1 2JZ
Tel: 01481-720203 **Fax:** 01481-712102
E-mail: mail@creaseys.com
Website: http://www.creaseys.com
Directors: P. Creasey (Co Sec)
Managers: A. Pinsard, L. Dodd (Personnel)
Date established: 1899 **No.of Employees:** 1 - 10 **Product Groups:** 61

Cyclo Systems Ltd
Rue Sauvage St Sampson, Guernsey, GY2 4WN
Tel: 07781-111688
E-mail: sales@cyclosystems.com
Website: http://www.cyclosystems.com
Directors: J. Queripel (MD)
No.of Employees: 1 - 10 **Product Groups:** 36, 54

GO Enterprise
Po Box 398, Guernsey, GY1 3FT
Tel: 07781-414844
E-mail: info@goe.gg
Website: http://www.goenterprise.co.uk
Managers: A. LH (Develop Mgr)
Registration no: 07636960 **Date established:** 2009
Turnover: Up to £250,000 **No.of Employees:** 1 - 10 **Product Groups:** 44, 61, 79, 80

Guernsey Freight Services
Airport Complex Forest, Guernsey, GY8 0DJ
Tel: 01481-238180 **Fax:** 01481-235479
E-mail: info@guernseyfreight.com
Website: http://www.guernsey-airport.gov.gg
Directors: R. Brache (Grp Chief Exec)
No.of Employees: 21 - 50 **Product Groups:** 76

Guernsey Wood Carvers Ltd
Rue Des Issues St. Saviour, Guernsey, GY7 9FS
Tel: 01481-265373 **Fax:** 01481-265649
Website: http://www.cwgsy.net
No.of Employees: 1 - 10 **Product Groups:** 25, 37, 84

Interseals Guernsey Ltd
Lowlands Industrial Estate Braye Road, Vale, Guernsey, GY3 5XG
Tel: 01481-246364 **Fax:** 01481-248235
E-mail: sales@interseals.co.uk
Website: http://www.interseal.co.uk
Directors: T. Walkington (MD)
Registration no: 00004776 **Turnover:** £1m - £2m
No.of Employees: 1 - 10 **Product Groups:** 22, 23, 30, 33

Lawrence Engineering
Andykbarkerhotmailcouk La Mazotte, Vale, Guernsey, GY3 5LF
Tel: 01481-241277 **Fax:** 01481-241257
Website: http://www.cwgsy.net
Managers: S. Page (Mgr)
No.of Employees: 1 - 10 **Product Groups:** 37, 84

Mainbrayce Ltd
Inner Harbour Alderney, Guernsey, GY9 3DL
Tel: 01481-822772 **Fax:** 01481-823683
E-mail: info@mainbrayce.co.uk
Website: http://www.mainbrayce.co.uk
Directors: P. Hutton (Dir)
Date established: 1970 **No.of Employees:** 1 - 10 **Product Groups:** 35, 36, 39

Marine & General Engineers Ltd (Head Office)
PO Box 470, Guernsey, GY1 6AT
Tel: 01481-243048 **Fax:** 01481-248765
E-mail: sales@mge.gg
Website: http://www.mge.gg
Bank(s): National Westminster Bank Plc
Directors: A. Way (Dir), D. Coleman (Fin), D. Norman (MD)
Managers: C. Tanguy, S. Bougourd (Tech Serv Mgr)
Registration no: 00004033 **Turnover:** £2m - £5m
No.of Employees: 21 - 50 **Product Groups:** 39

Norman Piette Ltd
PO Box 88, Guernsey, GY1 3EE
Tel: 01481-245801 **Fax:** 01481-428542
E-mail: sales@norman-piette.com
Website: http://www.norman-piette.com
Bank(s): National Westminster, Guernsey
Directors: C. Fenner (MD), T. Gallienne (Fin)
Managers: L. Robert (Personnel), L. Forman (Buyer), B. Borgod (Tech Serv Mgr), B. Borgod (I.T. Exec), S. Pow (Sales Prom Mgr)
Turnover: £1m - £2m **No.of Employees:** 101 - 250 **Product Groups:** 66, 67

Polar Instruments Ltd
Garenne Park St Sampson, Guernsey, GY2 4AF
Tel: 01481-253081 **Fax:** 01481-252476
E-mail: mail@polarinstruments.com
Website: http://www.polarinstruments.com
Directors: M. Gaudion (Grp Chief Exec)
No.of Employees: 1 - 10 **Product Groups:** 37, 84, 85

Rue Maze Practice
Rue Maze St Martin, Guernsey, GY4 6LJ
Tel: 01481-236236
Website: http://www.rmd.gg
Managers: M. Driscoll (Mgr)
No.of Employees: 11 - 20 **Product Groups:** 32, 38, 88

Sea Tech
Clock Tower Weighbridge, St. Peter Port, Guernsey, GY1 2ND
Tel: 07781-123121 **Fax:** 01481-710999
Website: http://www.cwgsy.net
Directors: I. Hoskins (Prop)
No.of Employees: 1 - 10 **Product Groups:** 37, 84

Sidlocks Of Guernsey
Pitronnerie Road St Peter Port, Guernsey, GY1 2RN
Tel: 01481-713883 **Fax:** 01481-726800
E-mail: roy@sidlocks.co.uk
Website: http://www.sidlocks.co.uk
Directors: R. Kilpatrick (MD)
Date established: 1987 **No.of Employees:** 1 - 10 **Product Groups:** 20, 40, 41

Siteweld Ltd
West View Bunker Hill, Vale, Guernsey, GY3 5JU
Tel: 01481-246210 **Fax:** 01481-243167
E-mail: siteweldltd@cwgsy.net
Website: http://www.siteweld.co.uk
Directors: T. Martel (MD)
Date established: 1901 **No.of Employees:** 1 - 10 **Product Groups:** 35

Stainless Steel Fabrications
Southside St Sampson, Guernsey, GY2 4QJ
Tel: 01481-248146 **Fax:** 01481-247187
E-mail: actourtel@guernsey.net
Website: http://www.ssf.gg
Directors: A. Tourtel (Prop)
Date established: 2004 **No.of Employees:** 1 - 10 **Product Groups:** 35

Jersey

Air Heating & Manufacturing
6 Seaton Lane St Helier, Jersey, JE2 3QJ
Tel: 01534-734830 **Fax:** 01534-767681
E-mail: airheating@hotmail.com
Directors: B. Mccarthy (Ptnr)
Date established: 1982 **Turnover:** Up to £250,000
No.of Employees: 1 - 10 **Product Groups:** 35, 36, 48

Aviation Jersey Ltd
2 Seacroft Stores La Grande Route De Lane Cote, St Clement, Jersey, JE2 6SB
Tel: 01534-725301 **Fax:** 01534-759449
E-mail: info@aviationjersey.com
Website: http://www.aviationjersey.com
Directors: P. Halksworth (MD)
Registration no: 00000389 **Turnover:** £1m - £2m
No.of Employees: 1 - 10 **Product Groups:** 39

Brady & Gallagher
15-17 James Street St Helier, Jersey, JE2 4TT
Tel: 01534-758267 **Fax:** 01534-759218
E-mail: enquiries@bradyandgallagher.com
Directors: F. Brady (MD)
No.of Employees: 21 - 50 **Product Groups:** 40, 52, 66

Bull & Co.
St Ives La Colomberie, St Helier, Jersey, JE2 4QA
Tel: 01534-866688 **Fax:** 01534-866699
E-mail: enquiries@bullandcompany.com
Website: http://www.bullandcompany.com
Directors: D. Letto (MD)
Turnover: Up to £250,000 **No.of Employees:** 1 - 10 **Product Groups:** 80

C B Richard Ellis Ltd
45 Century Building, Jersey, JE2 3AD
Tel: 01534-874141 **Fax:** 01534-874488
Website: http://www.cbre.co.uk
Directors: B. Sarre (Dir), J. Carter (MD)
Registration no: 03536032 **VAT No.:** GB 245 0595 63
Turnover: £20m - £50m **No.of Employees:** 1 - 10 **Product Groups:** 80

Channel Shutter & Door Co. Ltd
3 Les Serres Route De Longueville St Saviour, Jersey, JE2 7RZ
Tel: 01534-285916 **Fax:** 01534-736490
E-mail: info@channeldoors.com
Website: http://www.channeldoors.com
Directors: M. Cowen (MD)
No.of Employees: 1 - 10 **Product Groups:** 26, 35

D K Collins Marine Ltd
South Pier Commercial Buildings, St Helier, Jersey, JE2 3NB
Tel: 01534-732415 **Fax:** 01534-767332
E-mail: dkcollmar@localdial.com
Website: http://www.localdial.com
Directors: R. Billot (MD)
No.of Employees: 11 - 20 **Product Groups:** 35, 36, 39

Deveau Commercials
La Rue De Bechet Trinity, Jersey, JE3 5BE
Tel: 01534-865940 **Fax:** 01534-865941

Directors: P. Deveau (Prop)
Date established: 2000 **No.of Employees:** 1 - 10 **Product Groups:** 35, 39, 45

Four Seasons Roofing
PO Box 200, Jersey, JE4 0QJ
Tel: 07797-799125 **Fax:** 01534-727616
E-mail: jamie_oneill@hotmail.com
Website: http://www.fourseasonsonline.co.uk
No.of Employees: 1 - 10 **Product Groups:** 37, 52

Full Service Centre
3 Oaks Lane Grande Route De St Laurent St Lawrence, Jersey, JE3 1NG
Tel: 01534-625911 **Fax:** 01534-723904
E-mail: c.kershaw@citicabs.co.uk
Website: http://www.citicabs.co.uk
Directors: R. Hannah (Prop)
No.of Employees: 1 - 10 **Product Groups:** 25, 35, 48

The Guiton Group Ltd
Guiton House Five Oaks, Jersey, JE4 8XQ
Tel: 01534-611611 **Fax:** 01534-611825
E-mail: editorial@thisisjersey.com
Website: http://www.thisisjersey.com
Directors: P. Carter (MD)
Turnover: £10m - £20m **No.of Employees:** 101 - 250 **Product Groups:** 44

Healthspan Ltd
47 King Street St Helier, Jersey, JE2 4WE
Tel: 01534-758391
E-mail: sales@healthspan.com
Website: http://www.healthspan.com
Managers: C. Knight
Date established: 2004 **No.of Employees:** 1 - 10 **Product Groups:** 31, 32

Jackson Yacht Services
Le Boulevard St Brelade, Jersey, JE3 8AB
Tel: 01534-743819 **Fax:** 01534-745952
E-mail: sales@jacksonyacht.com
Website: http://www.jacksonyacht.com
Directors: M. Jackson (MD)
Immediate Holding Company: M.K. JACKSON LTD
Turnover: £500,000 - £1m **No.of Employees:** 1 - 10 **Product Groups:** 23, 39, 74

Jersey Deep Freeze Ltd
Block D 19 Oxford Road, St Helier, Jersey, JE2 4LJ
Tel: 01534-768621
Directors: A. Duquemin (MD)
No.of Employees: 1 - 10 **Product Groups:** 40, 66

The Jersey Pottery Ltd
Gorey Village Main Road Grouville, Jersey, JE3 9EP
Tel: 01534-850850 **Fax:** 01534-856403
E-mail: office@jerseypottery.com
Website: http://www.jerseypottery.com
Directors: J. Jones (Dir), M. Jones (Design)
Managers: A. Sinel (Chief Acct)
No.of Employees: 21 - 50 **Product Groups:** 33

Le Lievre's
Don Street St Helier, Jersey, JE2 4TQ
Tel: 01534-635300 **Fax:** 01534-635301
E-mail: sales@lelievres.com
Website: http://www.lelievres.com
Directors: R. Lievre (Prop)
Managers: C. Lemarquand (Mgr)
Date established: 1995 **No.of Employees:** 21 - 50 **Product Groups:** 20, 40, 41

John McGranahan Electrical Contractors
Mon Reve Victoria Avenue, St Helier, Jersey, JE2 3LU
Tel: 07797-762492 **Fax:** 01534-726544
E-mail: johnmcgranahan@hotmail.com
Website: http://www.johnmcgranahan-electricalcontractors.co.uk
Directors: J. McGranahan (Dir)
Date established: 2000 **No.of Employees:** 1 - 10 **Product Groups:** 52

Mercury Distribution
La Rue De Lane Chesnaie St John, Jersey, JE3 4FW
Tel: 01534-762200 **Fax:** 01534-762201
E-mail: sales@mercurydistribution.com
Website: http://www.mercurydeliver.com
Directors: B. Dempsey (Dir), H. Buesnel (Dir), J. Jordan (Dir)
No.of Employees: 21 - 50 **Product Groups:** 21, 32, 48

Morris Marine
Unit 2 Woodlands Farm La Rue De Maupertuis, St Helier, Jersey, JE2 3HG
Tel: 07797-767100
Directors: D. Morris (Prop)
No.of Employees: 1 - 10 **Product Groups:** 35, 36, 39

Network Distribution Ltd
Vine St Chambers 16 Vine Street, St Helier, Jersey, JE2 4WB
Tel: 01534-725025 **Fax:** 01534-729890
E-mail: sales@stillage.net
Website: http://www.stillage.net
Directors: D. Jenkins (MD)
Ultimate Holding Company: BRAMBLES PROPERTY SERVICES LTD
Immediate Holding Company: NOVA TRAINING LTD
Registration no: 04454714 **No.of Employees:** 1 - 10 **Product Groups:** 35, 39, 45

Date of Accounts	**Oct 07**	**Oct 06**	**Oct 05**
Working Capital	-274	-274	-274
Current Liabilities	274	274	274

Normans
Queen's Road St Helier, Jersey, JE2 3GR
Tel: 01534-883388 **Fax:** 01534-883334
E-mail: sales@normans.je
Directors: M. Trigg (Mkt Research), N. Radcliffe (MD)
Managers: N. Queree (I.T. Exec), S. Venables (Purch Mgr)
Registration no: 01553802 **No.of Employees:** 1 - 10 **Product Groups:** 35, 66

Date of Accounts	**Mar 08**	**Mar 07**	**Mar 06**
Working Capital	1	1	1
Current Assets	1	1	1

P & R Marketing
4 Roussel Court Roussel Mews, St Helier, Jersey, JE2 3PQ
Tel: 07797-715334
Directors: P. Hudson (Dir)
No.of Employees: 1 - 10 **Product Groups:** 40, 66

Pallot
La Rue De Bechet Trinity, Jersey, JE3 5BE
Tel: 01534-863888 **Fax:** 01534-863889
E-mail: info@lcpallot.je
Website: http://www.lcpallot.je
Directors: S. Pallot (Ptnr)
Date established: 1938 **No.of Employees:** 1 - 10 **Product Groups:** 41

Precision Plastics Jersey Ltd
30-32 Devonshire Place St Helier, Jersey, JE2 3RD
Tel: 01534-737491
Directors: I. Curwood (Sales)
No.of Employees: 1 - 10 **Product Groups:** 30

Raffray Ltd
La Rue Sinnatt La Rue Des Pres Trading Estate, St Saviour, Jersey, JE2 7QT
Tel: 01534-723151 **Fax:** 01534-769489
E-mail: michaelallo@hotmail.com
Website: http://www.raffray.co.uk
Bank(s): HSBC
Managers: M. Allo (Mgr)
Date established: 1850 **No.of Employees:** 11 - 20 **Product Groups:** 35, 46

St Helier Ironworks
5 Le Breton Lane St Helier, Jersey, JE2 4QP
Tel: 01534-735622
Directors: M. Davey (MD)
Date established: 1967 **No.of Employees:** 1 - 10 **Product Groups:** 26, 35

Seahorse Pools Ltd
Le Pavillion De Bel Air La Rue De Bel-Air, St Mary, Jersey, JE3 3ED
Tel: 01534-484449 **Fax:** 01534-484458
Directors: D. Lee (MD)
Registration no: 00001131 **Date established:** 1968
Turnover: £250,000 - £500,000 **No.of Employees:** 1 - 10
Product Groups: 33, 52

Smail & Richards Ltd
Halcyon House West Hill, St Helier, Jersey, JE2 3HB
Tel: 01534-723503 **Fax:** 01534-780480
E-mail: brichards@smailandrichards.co.uk
Website: http://www.smailandrichards.co.uk
Directors: T. O'halloran (MD)
Date established: 1970 **Turnover:** £2m - £5m **No.of Employees:** 11 - 20
Product Groups: 37, 40, 52

Storaway Services Ltd
Broadlands La Rue De Mahaut, St Ouen, Jersey, JE3 2GF
Tel: 01534-485091 **Fax:** 01534-485091
E-mail: storaway@jerseymail.co.uk
Website: http://www.storawayjersey.com
Directors: R. Vibert (Prop)
No.of Employees: 1 - 10 **Product Groups:** 35, 42, 45

WALES

Dyfed

Aberaeron

Alan James Raddon
Clifton House Aberarth, Aberaeron, SA46 0LW
Tel: 01545-570904
E-mail: alraddon@aol.com
Directors: A. Raddon (Prop)
No.of Employees: 1 - 10 **Product Groups:** 22

Mid-Glamorgan

Aberdare

Celtic Energy Ltd
Heol Ty Aberaman Aberaman, Aberdare, CF44 6RF
Tel: 01685-874 201 **Fax:** 01685-878 105
E-mail: info@coal.com
Website: http://cgi.www.coal.com
Directors: D. Lee (Fin), D. Warren (Co Sec), J. Greenhalgh (Dir), L. Humphreys (Fin), L. Humphrys (Fin), M. Thomas (Grp Chief Exec)
Managers: R. Morris (Mktg Serv Mgr), R. Sharp (I.T. Exec)
Ultimate Holding Company: Celtic Mining Group Ltd
Immediate Holding Company: Celtic Mining Group Ltd
Registration no: 02997376 **VAT No.:** GB 648 4315 25
Date established: 1995 **Turnover:** £50m - £75m **No.of Employees:** 1 - 10
Product Groups: 51

Date of Accounts	Mar 08	Mar 07
Sales Turnover	50980	50780
Pre Tax Profit/Loss	5830	1610
Working Capital	85840	71640
Fixed Assets	60070	59910
Current Assets	99020	84940
Current Liabilities	13180	13300
ROCE% (Return on Capital Employed)	4.0	1.2
ROT% (Return on Turnover)	11.4	3.2

Eftec Ltd
Rhigos, Aberdare, CF44 9UE
Tel: 01685-815400 **Fax:** 01685-813997
E-mail: colin.thomas@efteclTd.co.uk
Website: http://www.eftecltd.co.uk
Bank(s): Lloyds TSB
Managers: I. Davies (Sales & Mktg Mg), S. Reynolds (Buyer), J. Thomas (Fin Mgr), M. Phillips (Comptroller)
Ultimate Holding Company: EMS-CHEMIE HOLDING AG (SWITZERLAND)
Immediate Holding Company: EFTEC LIMITED
Registration no: 01406940 **Date established:** 1978
Turnover: £20m - £50m **No.of Employees:** 21 - 50 **Product Groups:** 31, 32

Date of Accounts	Dec 11	Dec 10	Dec 09
Sales Turnover	26m	24m	22m
Pre Tax Profit/Loss	1m	965	3m
Working Capital	4m	3m	4m
Fixed Assets	2m	2m	3m
Current Assets	7m	6m	7m
Current Liabilities	376	330	586

Jewson Ltd
Cwmbach Road, Aberdare, CF44 0NE
Tel: 01685-873456 **Fax:** 01685-881316
Website: http://www.jewson.co.uk
Managers: G. Davies (Mgr)
Ultimate Holding Company: COMPAGNIE DE SAINT GOBAIN (FRANCE)
Immediate Holding Company: JEWSON LIMITED
Registration no: 00348407 **Date established:** 1939
Turnover: Over £1,000m **No.of Employees:** 1 - 10 **Product Groups:** 66

Date of Accounts	Dec 11	Dec 10	Dec 09
Sales Turnover	1606m	1547m	1485m
Pre Tax Profit/Loss	18m	100m	45m
Working Capital	-345m	-250m	-349m
Fixed Assets	496m	387m	461m
Current Assets	657m	1005m	1320m
Current Liabilities	66m	120m	64m

M P E Ltd
Unit 6-7 Hirwaun Industrial Estate Hirwaun, Aberdare, CF44 9UP
Tel: 01685-812765 **Fax:** 01685-810072
E-mail: sales@mpelimited.co.uk
Website: http://www.mpelimited.co.uk
Directors: C. Owen (MD)
Immediate Holding Company: WILLOWCHEM TECHNOLOGY LIMITED
Registration no: 05721460 **Date established:** 2006
Turnover: £500,000 - £1m **No.of Employees:** 1 - 10 **Product Groups:** 46, 48

Date of Accounts	Feb 08	Feb 11	Feb 10
Working Capital	2	4	4
Fixed Assets	1	N/A	N/A
Current Assets	32	11	19
Current Liabilities	5	5	N/A

Secure-IT-Vision
99 Fforchaman Road Cwmaman, Aberdare, CF44 6NF
Tel: 01685-881978
E-mail: secureitvision@btinternet.com
Website: http://www.secureitvision.vpweb.co.uk
Directors: L. Jones (Prop)
Immediate Holding Company: SECURE-IT-VISION LTD
Registration no: 06568026 **Date established:** 2008
Turnover: Up to £250,000 **No.of Employees:** 1 - 10 **Product Groups:** 35, 36, 40, 44

Tectonic International Ltd
The Old School Merthyr Road, Llwydcoed, Aberdare, CF44 0UT
Tel: 01685-722225 **Fax:** 01685-722321
E-mail: sales@tectonicinternational.com
Website: http://www.tectonicinternational.com
Directors: S. Haper (MD)
Managers: R. Crichton (Chief Acct)
Immediate Holding Company: TECTONIC INTERNATIONAL LIMITED
Registration no: 03696680 **VAT No.:** GB 558 2367 17
Date established: 1999 **Turnover:** £2m - £5m **No.of Employees:** 11 - 20
Product Groups: 28, 32, 44

Date of Accounts	Dec 11	Dec 10	Dec 09
Working Capital	118	75	152
Fixed Assets	307	307	137
Current Assets	404	180	216

Tubex Ltd
Aberaman Industrial Estate Aberaman, Aberdare, CF44 6DA
Tel: 01685-883833 **Fax:** 01685-888001
E-mail: simonwhite@tubex.com
Website: http://www.tubex.com
Directors: A. Green (Chief Op Offcr), S. White (Comm)
Managers: A. Jones (Admin Off), G. Jones (Comptroller), J. Sessions (Mktg Serv Mgr)
Immediate Holding Company: TUBEX LIMITED
Registration no: 04537236 **Date established:** 2002 **Turnover:** £5m - £10m
No.of Employees: 51 - 100 **Product Groups:** 29, 30, 31, 42

Date of Accounts	Jun 10	Jun 09	Jun 08
Sales Turnover	5m	6m	6m
Pre Tax Profit/Loss	485	230	227
Working Capital	767	384	261
Fixed Assets	992	1m	1m
Current Assets	2m	2m	2m
Current Liabilities	373	368	840

Gwent

Abergavenny

Abergavenny Guns & Tackle
9 Brecon Road, Abergavenny, NP7 5UH
Tel: 01873-853708 **Fax:** 01873- 858846
Directors: D. Gush (Prop)
Date established: 2002 **No.of Employees:** 1 - 10 **Product Groups:** 36, 39, 40

A-Plant Ltd
Union Road, Abergavenny, NP7 7RL
Tel: 01873-854521 **Fax:** 01873-859012
Website: http://www.toolhireshops.com
Bank(s): Lloyds TSB Bank plc
Managers: A. Peckham (Chief Mgr), A. Pemberton (Mgr)
Immediate Holding Company: A.PLANT LIMITED
Registration no: 05407712 **VAT No.:** GB 215 5687 37
Date established: 2005 **Turnover:** £20m - £50m
No.of Employees: 11 - 20 **Product Groups:** 83

Border Refrigeration & Domestics
Heads of The Valley Training Centre Ty-Mawr Road, Gilwern, Abergavenny, NP7 0EB
Tel: 01873-831828 **Fax:** 01873-831828
Directors: F. Probert (MD), L. Probert (Fin)
Immediate Holding Company: BORDER REFRIGERATION SERVICES LIMITED
Registration no: 04659082 **Date established:** 2003
No.of Employees: 1 - 10 **Product Groups:** 36, 40

Date of Accounts	Mar 08	Mar 07	Mar 06
Working Capital	77	46	102
Fixed Assets	192	188	191
Current Assets	106	81	138
Current Liabilities	N/A	32	35

Business Language Services
Westgate House 2 Union Road East, Abergavenny, NP7 5UW
Tel: 01873-856762 **Fax:** 01873-855006
E-mail: info@businesslanguageservices.co.uk
Website: http://www.businesslanguageservices.co.uk
Product Groups: 28, 80

Date of Accounts	Feb 09	Oct 07	Oct 06
Working Capital	35	114	116
Fixed Assets	79	5	6
Current Assets	112	236	199
Current Liabilities	77	122	83

Evanselect Ltd
5 Hastings Close Ysbytty Fields Ysbytty Fields, Abergavenny, NP7 9JD
Tel: 01873-851046 **Fax:** 01873-777302
E-mail: sales@evanselect.com
Website: http://www.evanselect.com
Directors: D. Evans (Fin), R. Evans (MD)
Registration no: 05252735 **Turnover:** Up to £250,000
No.of Employees: 1 - 10 **Product Groups:** 52

Date of Accounts	Oct 08	Oct 07	Oct 06
Working Capital	-11	-8	-1
Fixed Assets	7	10	4
Current Assets	9	16	18
Current Liabilities	21	23	19

Jerboa
Grofield Baker Street, Abergavenny, NP7 5BB
Tel: 0800-043 2190
E-mail: info@jerboadesign.com
Website: http://www.jerboadesign.com
Managers: A. Jones (Mgr)
Turnover: Up to £250,000 **No.of Employees:** 1 - 10 **Product Groups:** 27, 28, 37, 44, 49, 64, 67, 79, 81

John Cranna
39 Lower Monk Street, Abergavenny, NP7 5LU
Tel: 01873-855541 **Fax:** 01873-855541
E-mail: john.cranna@btconnect.com
Website: http://www.johncranna.co.uk
Directors: J. Cranna (Prop)
Date established: 1993 **No.of Employees:** 1 - 10 **Product Groups:** 35

Milsteel Fabrications
Swan Meadow Monmouth Road, Abergavenny, NP7 5HF
Tel: 01873-858225 **Fax:** 01873-859808
Directors: R. Hookham (Ptnr)
No.of Employees: 1 - 10 **Product Groups:** 26, 35

Speake & Co Llanfapley
6 Firs Road Llanvapley, Abergavenny, NP7 8SL
Tel: 01600-780150 **Fax:** 01600-780150
E-mail: billspeake@btconnect.com
Website: http://www.speakesensors.com
Directors: B. Speake (Ptnr)
Turnover: Up to £250,000 **No.of Employees:** 1 - 10 **Product Groups:** 37, 38

Studio 49 Photography
Woodvale Common Road, Gilwern, Abergavenny, NP7 0DR
Tel: 01873-831155
E-mail: info@studio49photography.co.uk
Website: http://www.studio49photography.co.uk

Directors: M. Taylor (Dir), M. Taylor (Prop)
Turnover: Up to £250,000 **No.of Employees:** 1 - 10 **Product Groups:** 81

Worcester Electrical Distributors Ltd

Mill Street, Abergavenny, NP7 5HE
Tel: 01873-850062 **Fax:** 01873-850082
E-mail: abergavenny@worcesterelectrical.co.uk
Website: http://www.worcesterelectrical.co.uk
Managers: M. Silver (Mgr)
Immediate Holding Company: WORCESTER ELECTRICAL DISTRIBUTORS LIMITED
Registration no: 02203536 **Date established:** 1987
No.of Employees: 1 - 10 **Product Groups:** 37, 38, 67

Date of Accounts	Mar 12	Mar 11	Mar 10
Sales Turnover	13m	11m	8m
Pre Tax Profit/Loss	583	252	-153
Working Capital	436	76	-192
Fixed Assets	249	231	307
Current Assets	5m	4m	3m
Current Liabilities	1m	192	1m

Clwyd

Abergele

Abergele Mobility

Rhuddlan Road, Abergele, LL22 7HF
Tel: 01745-827990 **Fax:** 01745-827990
E-mail: info@abergele-mobility.co.uk
Website: http://www.abergele-mobility.co.uk
Managers: M. Rose (Mgr)
No.of Employees: 1 - 10 **Product Groups:** 39, 45, 67, 85

Slaters Of Abergele Ltd

Market Street, Abergele, LL22 7AL
Tel: 01745-828282 **Fax:** 01745-825390
E-mail: action@slaters.com
Website: http://www.slaters.com
Bank(s): Barclays
Directors: N. Knowlson (Sales), P. Martindale (Fin), P. Taverner (MD), P. Tavernor (MD)
Managers: L. Potts (Tech Serv Mgr), D. Macrae (Personnel), E. Knowlson-roberts (Mktg Serv Mgr)
Immediate Holding Company: SLATERS OF ABERGELE LIMITED
Registration no: 00488334 **VAT No.:** GB 159 1960 38
Date established: 1950 **Turnover:** £50m - £75m
No.of Employees: 21 - 50 **Product Groups:** 68

Date of Accounts	Sep 11	Sep 10	Sep 09
Sales Turnover	66m	41m	50m
Pre Tax Profit/Loss	-420	-635	-359
Working Capital	-2m	-1m	224
Fixed Assets	8m	7m	8m
Current Assets	13m	7m	9m
Current Liabilities	1m	725	1m

Gwent

Abertillery

Blackwood Engineering

Glandwr Industrial Estate Aberbeeg, Abertillery, NP13 2LN
Tel: 01495-214331 **Fax:** 01495-217309
E-mail: darren.kelly@bweng.com
Website: http://www.bweng.com
Bank(s): Barclays
Directors: S. Kerr (Fin)
Managers: D. Kelly, C. Simner (Buyer)
Ultimate Holding Company: BIRDEL LIMITED
Immediate Holding Company: BLACKWOOD ENGINEERING LIMITED
Registration no: 00423178 **VAT No.:** GB 648 3506 23
Date established: 1946 **Turnover:** £10m - £20m
No.of Employees: 21 - 50 **Product Groups:** 34, 45

Date of Accounts	Apr 11	Apr 10	Apr 09
Sales Turnover	19m	10m	16m
Pre Tax Profit/Loss	256	288	295
Working Capital	2m	1m	2m
Fixed Assets	199	169	161
Current Assets	8m	5m	5m
Current Liabilities	2m	996	2m

Customer Service

Kings Head Buildings Oak Street, Abertillery, NP13 1TN
Tel: 01495-325325 **Fax:** 08709-909741
E-mail: enquiries@customerservices.uk.com
Website: http://www.customerservice.uk.com
Directors: J. Griffiths (Grp Chief Exec)
No.of Employees: 1 - 10 **Product Groups:** 79

Global Laser Technology Solutions

Cwmtillery Industrial Estate Cwmtillery, Abertillery, NP13 1LZ
Tel: 01495-212213 **Fax:** 01495-212004
E-mail: davidb@globallasertech.com
Website: http://www.globallasertech.com
Directors: J. Miller (MD)
Managers: J. White (Mktg Serv Mgr)
Immediate Holding Company: Lasercom Systems Ltd
Registration no: 04528745 **Date established:** 2002
No.of Employees: 11 - 20 **Product Groups:** 37, 38, 46, 48

Date of Accounts	Jun 10	Oct 09	Oct 08
Working Capital	38	-0	102
Fixed Assets	27	41	58
Current Assets	424	419	516

Dyfed

Aberystwyth

Deckscape Decking (Incorporating The Welsh Hot Tub Company)

Oak Dale Goginan, Aberystwyth, SY23 3PB
Tel: 01970-624421
E-mail: enquiries@thedeckcompany.co.uk
Website: http://www.thedeckcompany.co.uk
Directors: S. Baxter (Prop)
Immediate Holding Company: THE DECK COMPANY LTD
Registration no: 05443240 **Date established:** 2005
No.of Employees: 1 - 10 **Product Groups:** 25, 38

Hydroclean

1 Parcycwm Glan Yr Afon Industrial Estate, Llanbadarn Fawr, Aberystwyth, SY23 3JQ
Tel: 01970-636603 **Fax:** 01970-612588
E-mail: henry-hydroclean@tiscali.co.uk
Website: http://www.wynfordwilliamscars.co.uk
Managers: K. Jones (Mgr)
No.of Employees: 1 - 10 **Product Groups:** 23, 26, 40, 52

Kanda

Canolafan Llanafan, Aberystwyth, SY23 4AY
Tel: 01974-261273 **Fax:** 01974-261 273
E-mail: sales@kanda.com
Website: http://www.kanda.com
Directors: A. Davies (MD)
Immediate Holding Company: EMBEDDED RESULTS LIMITED
Registration no: 04514011 **Date established:** 2002
Turnover: £250,000 - £500,000 **No.of Employees:** 1 - 10
Product Groups: 37, 38, 44, 67

Date of Accounts	Aug 11	Aug 10	Aug 09
Working Capital	-27	-1	-45
Fixed Assets	5	11	13
Current Assets	68	102	54

Lewis Gareth Architects Penseiri

34 Terrace Road, Aberystwyth, SY23 2AE
Tel: 01970-624624 **Fax:** 01970-625559
E-mail: he@glewis.plus.com
Directors: G. Lewis (Prop)
Turnover: £500,000 - £1m **No.of Employees:** 1 - 10 **Product Groups:** 84

N H Picture Frames

The Market Hall, Aberystwyth, SY23 1TW
Tel: 01970-615512
E-mail: kyleireland@hotmail.com
Website: http://www.nicelyhungpictureframes.com
Directors: J. Ireland (Ptnr)
No.of Employees: 1 - 10 **Product Groups:** 25, 26, 36, 49

Gwynedd

Amlwch

Rehau Ltd

Site 8 Amlwch Business Park, Amlwch, LL68 9BX
Tel: 01407-833200 **Fax:** 01407-833201
E-mail: peter.ault@rehau.com
Website: http://www.rehau.com
Managers: P. Ault (Mgr), T. Wright (Personnel)
Ultimate Holding Company: WAGNER HOLDING AG (SWITZERLAND)
Immediate Holding Company: REHAU LIMITED
Registration no: 00722004 **Date established:** 1962
No.of Employees: 51 - 100 **Product Groups:** 38, 42

Date of Accounts	Dec 11	Dec 10	Dec 09
Sales Turnover	84m	89m	89m
Pre Tax Profit/Loss	-249	-3m	-1m
Working Capital	17m	15m	17m
Fixed Assets	20m	22m	25m
Current Assets	24m	25m	27m
Current Liabilities	3m	3m	N/A

Dyfed

Ammanford

Aalco Dyfed

Unit 3-4 Capel Hendre Industrial Estate, Ammanford, SA18 3SJ
Tel: 01269-842044 **Fax:** 01269-845276
E-mail: dyfed@aalco.co.uk
Website: http://www.aalco.co.uk
Managers: L. Williams (Mgr)
Ultimate Holding Company: UK STEELSTOCK LTD
Immediate Holding Company: AMARI METALS LTD
Registration no: 03551533 **Date established:** 1968
Turnover: £125m - £250m **No.of Employees:** 1 - 10 **Product Groups:** 34, 35, 36, 66

Airdancer Wales

Unit D1 Capel Hendre Industrial Estate, Ammanford, SA18 3SJ
Tel: 01269-268086
E-mail: info@airdancerwales.co.uk
Website: http://www.airdancerwales.co.uk
Directors: P. Powell (Prop)
Date established: 2008 **Turnover:** Up to £250,000
No.of Employees: 1 - 10 **Product Groups:** 29

Amman Catering Equipment Ltd

Unit 7 Glanamman Workshops Tabernacle Road, Glanamman, Ammanford, SA18 2YB
Tel: 01269-822833 **Fax:** 01269-824640
E-mail: info@acewales.co.uk
Website: http://www.amman-catering.com
Directors: D. Rees (Dir)
Immediate Holding Company: AMMAN CATERING EQUIPMENT LIMITED
Registration no: 04847159 **Date established:** 2003
No.of Employees: 1 - 10 **Product Groups:** 40, 42, 67

C R Clarke & Co UK Ltd

Unit 3 Betws Industrial Park, Ammanford, SA18 2LS
Tel: 01269-590530 **Fax:** 01269-590540
E-mail: laurence@crclarke.co.uk
Website: http://www.crclarke.com
Bank(s): HSBC Bank plc
Directors: M. Clarke (Dir)
Managers: B. Thomas, A. Davies (Purch Mgr)
Immediate Holding Company: C.R. CLARKE & CO. (UK) LIMITED
Registration no: 02022077 **VAT No.:** GB 840 4425 50
Date established: 1986 **Turnover:** £1m - £2m **No.of Employees:** 21 - 50
Product Groups: 40, 42, 67

Date of Accounts	Dec 11	Dec 10	Dec 09
Working Capital	220	326	340
Fixed Assets	550	619	556
Current Assets	755	890	899

Chorus Panel & Profiles

Llandybie, Ammanford, SA18 3JG
Tel: 01269-850691 **Fax:** 01269-851081
Website: http://www.coruspanelsandprofiles.co.uk
Bank(s): National Westminster
Directors: M. Boyles (Ch), S. Horton (MD)
Managers: G. Owen (Fin Mgr)
Ultimate Holding Company: MORGAN GRP LIMITED
Immediate Holding Company: ENVICO HOLDINGS LIMITED
Registration no: 22840000 **VAT No.:** 238 7122 60 **Date established:** 2008
Turnover: £20m - £50m **No.of Employees:** 101 - 250 **Product Groups:** 34

William Corbett & Co. Ltd

Pantyffynnon Road, Ammanford, SA18 3HN
Tel: 01269-593215 **Fax:** 01269-591929
E-mail: jonathan.jennings@williamcorbett.co.uk
Website: http://williamcorbett.co.uk
Directors: J. Jennings (MD)
Immediate Holding Company: WILLIAM CORBETT & CO. LIMITED
Registration no: 02596116 **VAT No.:** GB 587 9758 49
Date established: 1991 **No.of Employees:** 1 - 10 **Product Groups:** 34

Date of Accounts	Mar 11	Mar 10	Mar 09
Working Capital	4m	4m	4m
Fixed Assets	214	240	168
Current Assets	4m	4m	4m

Integrated Business Services Ltd

Anedd Wen Wernddu Road, Ammanford, SA18 2UR
Tel: 01269-592427 **Fax:** 01269-594853
E-mail: wynpryce@aol.com
Website: http://www.integra-cymru.com
Directors: W. Pryce (Dir), E. Pryce (Fin)
Immediate Holding Company: INTEGRATED BUSINESS SERVICES LIMITED
Registration no: 02421707 **Date established:** 1989 **Turnover:** £1m - £2m
No.of Employees: 1 - 10 **Product Groups:** 82, 84, 86

Date of Accounts	Mar 11	Mar 10	Mar 09
Working Capital	-6	-4	33
Fixed Assets	8	8	13
Current Assets	29	175	208

Morgan Marine Ltd

Cilyrychen Industrial Estate Llandybie, Ammanford, SA18 3GY
Tel: 01269-850437 **Fax:** 01269-850656
E-mail: sales@morgan-marine.com
Website: http://www.morgan-marine.com
Bank(s): Barclays
Directors: S. Paton (Sales)
Managers: S. Pugh (Purch Mgr), S. Evans, K. Davies (Tech Serv Mgr), S. Davids (Personnel)
Immediate Holding Company: MORGAN MARINE LIMITED
Registration no: 00856716 **VAT No.:** GB 124 4035 12
Date established: 1965 **Turnover:** £5m - £10m
No.of Employees: 101 - 250 **Product Groups:** 30, 35, 37, 84

Date of Accounts	Jun 12	Jun 11	Jun 10
Sales Turnover	10m	7m	7m
Pre Tax Profit/Loss	675	266	255
Working Capital	773	648	603
Fixed Assets	1m	1m	1m
Current Assets	4m	3m	3m
Current Liabilities	916	767	724

P D Eden Hall

Heol Ddu Tycroes, Ammanford, SA18 3SP
Tel: 01269-592911 **Fax:** 01269-596653
Website: http://www.pd-edenhall.co.uk
Managers: D. Kedward (Mgr)
Immediate Holding Company: HANSON GROUP
Registration no: 00615899 **VAT No.:** GB 302 9823 69
Turnover: £1m - £2m **No.of Employees:** 1 - 10 **Product Groups:** 33

Quinshield Ltd

Unit 27-28 Capel Hendre Industrial Estate, Ammanford, SA18 3SJ
Tel: 01269-832220 **Fax:** 01269-832221
E-mail: sales@quinshield.co.uk
Website: http://www.quinshield.com
Bank(s): Bank of Wales PLC
Directors: D. Jenkins (Fin), D. Jenkins (MD)
Managers: I. Young (Sales Prom Mgr), K. Wainwright
Immediate Holding Company: QUINSHIELD LIMITED
Registration no: 02767033 **VAT No.:** GB 558 0590 24
Date established: 1992 **Turnover:** £5m - £10m
No.of Employees: 51 - 100 **Product Groups:** 30

Date of Accounts	Dec 11	Dec 10	Dec 09
Sales Turnover	N/A	N/A	6m
Pre Tax Profit/Loss	N/A	N/A	592
Working Capital	2m	2m	2m
Fixed Assets	277	328	300
Current Assets	3m	2m	2m
Current Liabilities	N/A	N/A	373

Gwynedd

Bala

County Press
County Press Buildings Station Road, Bala, LL23 7PG
Tel: 01678-520262 **Fax:** 01678-521251
E-mail: budgerigarworld@msn.com
Website: http://www.budgerigarworld.com
Managers: G. Evans (Mgr)
Registration no: 01659803 **VAT No.:** GB 159 3836 29
No.of Employees: 1 - 10 **Product Groups:** 28

Get Wet The Adventure Company Ltd
2 Arenig Street, Bala, LL23 7AH
Tel: 07775-658335
E-mail: admin@getwettheadventurecompany.com
Website: http://www.get-wet.co.uk
Directors: J. Smith (Dir), J. Smith (Prop), T. Vollum (Dir)
Immediate Holding Company: GET WET THE ADVENTURE COMPANY LIMITED
Registration no: 05983536 **Date established:** 2006
Turnover: Up to £250,000 **No.of Employees:** 1 - 10 **Product Groups:** 89

Date of Accounts	Mar 11	Mar 10	Mar 09
Working Capital	-54	-39	-42
Fixed Assets	21	25	29
Current Assets	1	5	1

Sensotec 4-Warn Ltd
Unit 7 Industrial Estate, Bala, LL23 7NL
Tel: 08700-711444 **Fax:** 0870-074 0000
E-mail: rob@4-warn.com
Website: http://www.sensortec.co.uk
Directors: P. Hall (Sales)
Ultimate Holding Company: WHITE ROCK SECURITY (EUROPE) LTD
Immediate Holding Company: SENSOTEC 4-WARN LIMITED
Registration no: 03100457 **Date established:** 1995
No.of Employees: 1 - 10 **Product Groups:** 38, 40, 67

Date of Accounts	Dec 07	Dec 06	Dec 05
Working Capital	-96	-92	-91
Current Assets	7	6	7
Current Liabilities	103	98	98

Gwynedd

Bangor

C P L Petroleum Ltd
Unit 7 Llandygai Industrial Estate, Llandygai, Bangor, LL57 4YH
Tel: 01248-352768 **Fax:** 01248-352048
E-mail: andrea.wardle@cambriaoil.co.uk
Website: http://www.cplpetroleum.co.uk
Managers: A. Wardle (District Mgr)
Ultimate Holding Company: CPL INDUSTRIES HOLDINGS LIMITED
Immediate Holding Company: CPL PETROLEUM LIMITED
Registration no: 03003860 **VAT No.:** GB 721 5764 39
Date established: 1994 **Turnover:** £5m - £10m **No.of Employees:** 1 - 10
Product Groups: 44, 66

Date of Accounts	Mar 12	Mar 11	Mar 10
Pre Tax Profit/Loss	N/A	878	904
Working Capital	31	30m	30m
Fixed Assets	26	26m	26m
Current Assets	57	56m	56m
Current Liabilities	26	246	253

Huws Gray
Unit 11 Llandygai Industrial Estate Llandygai, Bangor, LL57 4YH
Tel: 01248-362247 **Fax:** 01248-362248
Bank(s): HSBC
Directors: T. Owen (Co Sec)
Managers: D. Parry (Mgr)
Immediate Holding Company: HUWS GRAY LIMITED
Registration no: 02506633 **VAT No.:** GB 713 6074 54
Date established: 1990 **Turnover:** £50m - £75m
No.of Employees: 11 - 20 **Product Groups:** 35, 66

Date of Accounts	Dec 11	Dec 10	Dec 09
Sales Turnover	72m	66m	59m
Pre Tax Profit/Loss	8m	8m	6m
Working Capital	18m	16m	12m
Fixed Assets	25m	23m	21m
Current Assets	28m	24m	20m
Current Liabilities	4m	4m	3m

N W Fencing Co.
Cefn Coed Llandygai, Bangor, LL57 4BG
Tel: 01248-364673 **Fax:** 01248-354166
E-mail: info@nwfencingco.com
Website: http://www.nwfencingco.com
Directors: J. Blackburn (MD)
Managers: P. Blackburn (Admin Off), H. Clinton (Sales Admin)
Ultimate Holding Company: ACHNASHEAN HOLDINGS LIMITED
Immediate Holding Company: ACHNASHEAN FENCING LIMITED
Registration no: 03772307 **Date established:** 1999 **Turnover:** £2m - £5m
No.of Employees: 21 - 50 **Product Groups:** 25, 33, 35

Date of Accounts	Oct 11	Oct 10	Oct 09
Working Capital	-102	-23	5
Fixed Assets	182	179	178
Current Assets	662	766	857

Owen & Palmer Ltd
Unit 12 Llandygai Industrial Estate Llandygai, Bangor, LL57 4YH
Tel: 01248-353515 **Fax:** 01248-353736
E-mail: accounts@owenandpalmer.co.uk
Website: http://www.opalcom.co.uk
Bank(s): Basford, Nottingham
Directors: A. Basham (MD), P. Roberts (Fin)
Immediate Holding Company: OWEN & PALMER LIMITED
Registration no: 01101421 **VAT No.:** GB 520 7693 48
Date established: 1973 **Turnover:** £1m - £2m **No.of Employees:** 21 - 50
Product Groups: 48

Date of Accounts	Oct 11	Oct 10	Oct 09
Working Capital	501	450	402
Fixed Assets	57	68	39
Current Assets	1m	841	863

Regional Engineering Fabrication
Ogwen House Llwyn Bleddyn, Llanllechid, Bangor, LL57 3EF
Tel: 01248-601500 **Fax:** 01248-605394
Directors: P. Hargreaves (Prop)
Date established: 1988 **No.of Employees:** 1 - 10 **Product Groups:** 35

Stockwell Steel
Goods Yard, Bangor, LL57 2TX
Tel: 01248-364041 **Fax:** 01248-353100
E-mail: bangor@bmsteel.co.uk
Website: http://www.bmsteel.co.uk
Bank(s): Bank of Scotland
Directors: J. Walker (MD)
Managers: S. Stockwell (Chief Mgr), S. Stockwell (Mgr)
Immediate Holding Company: BARCLAY MATTIESON
Registration no: 00030987 **VAT No.:** GB 723 9322 39
Date established: 1983 **Turnover:** £500,000 - £1m
No.of Employees: 11 - 20 **Product Groups:** 34, 35

Austin Taylor Communications
Bethesda, Bangor, LL57 3BX
Tel: 01248-600561 **Fax:** 01248-601674
E-mail: phil.griffith@austin-taylor.co.uk
Website: http://www.austin-taylor.co.uk
Managers: P. Griffith (Ops Mgr)
Ultimate Holding Company: COMMUNICATIONS SYSTEMS INC (USA)
Immediate Holding Company: AUSTIN TAYLOR COMMUNICATIONS LIMITED
Registration no: 00425286 **VAT No.:** GB 489 9470 67
Date established: 1946 **Turnover:** £1m - £2m **No.of Employees:** 1 - 10
Product Groups: 37

Date of Accounts	Dec 11	Dec 10	Dec 09
Sales Turnover	2m	2m	2m
Pre Tax Profit/Loss	-920	-808	-597
Working Capital	-2m	-1m	-251
Fixed Assets	102	337	251
Current Assets	987	1m	2m
Current Liabilities	173	81	41

Watkin Jones & Son Ltd
Llandygai Industrial Estate Llandygai, Bangor, LL57 4YH
Tel: 01248-362516 **Fax:** 01248-352860
E-mail: mark.watkinjones@watkinjones.com
Website: http://www.watkinjones.com
Directors: M. Watkin Jones (MD), P. Byrom (Co Sec)
Managers: R. De'ath (Tech Serv Mgr), J. Smith (Personnel), S. Griffiths (Mktg Serv Mgr)
Ultimate Holding Company: WATKIN JONES GROUP LIMITED
Immediate Holding Company: WATKIN JONES & SON LIMITED
Registration no: 02539870 **Date established:** 1990
Turnover: £75m - £125m **No.of Employees:** 51 - 100 **Product Groups:** 80

Date of Accounts	Sep 11	Sep 10	Sep 09
Sales Turnover	125m	113m	144m
Pre Tax Profit/Loss	18m	12m	12m
Working Capital	74m	65m	150m
Fixed Assets	8m	2m	2m
Current Assets	171m	207m	201m
Current Liabilities	N/A	18m	22m

Welsh Slates
Penrhyn Quarry Bethesda, Bangor, LL57 4YG
Tel: 01248-600656 **Fax:** 01248-601171
E-mail: enquiries@welshslate.com
Website: http://www.welshslate.com
Bank(s): HSBC
Directors: N. Oakes (Fin)
Managers: R. Williams (Personnel), J. Owen (Mktg Serv Mgr), E. Griffiths (Purch Mgr), S. Garner (Mgr)
Immediate Holding Company: WELSH SLATE LIMITED
Registration no: 06391123 **VAT No.:** GB 159 3703 48
Date established: 2007 **Turnover:** £10m - £20m
No.of Employees: 101 - 250 **Product Groups:** 12, 14

Date of Accounts	Dec 11	Dec 10	Dec 09
Sales Turnover	18m	18m	18m
Pre Tax Profit/Loss	273	-1m	-7m
Working Capital	-15m	-15m	-15m
Fixed Assets	23m	24m	26m
Current Assets	6m	5m	5m
Current Liabilities	15m	1m	1m

Mid-Glamorgan

Bargoed

A P T (Advanced Pro Tools Ltd)
27 Pant-Y-Fid Road Aberbargoed, Bargoed, CF81 9DT
Tel: 01443-835086 **Fax:** 01443-835086
E-mail: sales@handtools.org.uk
Website: http://www.handtools.org.uk
Directors: D. Jones (Fin), S. Jones (Dir)
Immediate Holding Company: ALLIED PROFESIONAL TRADES
Registration no: 03593513 **Date established:** 1998
Turnover: Up to £250,000 **No.of Employees:** 1 - 10 **Product Groups:** 36, 47, 66

Aber Wrought Iron
Unit 15-17 Bowen Indl-Est Aberbargoed, Bargoed, CF81 9EP
Tel: 01443-822029 **Fax:** 01443-822029
Directors: J. Aston (MD), L. Aston (Fin)
Immediate Holding Company: ABER WROUGHT IRON LIMITED
Registration no: 05337391 **Date established:** 2005
No.of Employees: 11 - 20 **Product Groups:** 26, 35

Date of Accounts	Apr 11	Apr 09	Apr 08
Working Capital	102	61	89
Fixed Assets	105	108	114
Current Assets	240	160	201

Tom Evans Audio Design
St Margarets Park Main Entrance Pengam Road, Aberbargoed, Bargoed, CF81 9FW
Tel: 01443-833570 **Fax:** 01443-839977
E-mail: sales@audiodesign.co.uk
Website: http://www.audiodesign.co.uk
Directors: T. Evans (Prop)
Immediate Holding Company: CRIMPFIL LIMITED
Registration no: 00946365 **Date established:** 1969
Turnover: £10m - £20m **No.of Employees:** 1 - 10 **Product Groups:** 37

South Glamorgan

Barry

Alembic Ltd
Unit 6 Wimbourne Buildings, Barry, CF63 3RA
Tel: 01446-733174 **Fax:** 01446-733184
E-mail: david@alembic.freeserve.co.uk
Directors: D. Randall (Prop)
Immediate Holding Company: ALEMBIC LIMITED
Registration no: 02429212 **Date established:** 1989 **Turnover:** £2m - £5m
No.of Employees: 1 - 10 **Product Groups:** 31

Date of Accounts	Dec 11	Dec 10	Dec 09
Working Capital	935	917	1m
Fixed Assets	305	306	308
Current Assets	1m	1m	1m

Assaultsystems Gunsmiths
Romanwell Road, Barry, CF62 5TH
Tel: 01446-746375 **Fax:** 01633-860303
Managers: N. Thommas (Mgr)
No.of Employees: 1 - 10 **Product Groups:** 36, 39, 40

C O S Group
Ty Verlon Industrial Estate, Barry, CF63 2BE
Tel: 01446-418000 **Fax:** 01446-418009
E-mail: sales@cosgroup.co.uk
Website: http://www.cosgroup.co.uk
Directors: D. Emery (Dir), J. Jones (Fin)
Managers: A. Danks
Immediate Holding Company: THE C.O.S. GROUP LIMITED
Registration no: 03383225 **Date established:** 1997
No.of Employees: 21 - 50 **Product Groups:** 64, 66

Date of Accounts	Mar 11	Mar 10	Mar 09
Working Capital	287	276	371
Fixed Assets	323	321	356
Current Assets	1m	1m	1m

Circatek Design Solutions
8 Pearce Court, Barry, CF63 1QD
Tel: 08453-920144
E-mail: sales@circatek.co.uk
Website: http://www.circatek.co.uk
Directors: N. Evans (Prop)
Turnover: Up to £250,000 **No.of Employees:** 1 - 10 **Product Groups:** 37, 44, 84

David Evans Agricultural Ltd
Old Middle Hill Llancarfan, Barry, CF62 3AD
Tel: 01446-781711 **Fax:** 01446-781713
E-mail: info@davidevansagricultural.co.uk
Website: http://www.davidevansagricultural.co.uk
Directors: D. Evans (Prop)
Immediate Holding Company: DAVID EVANS AGRICULTURAL LIMITED
Registration no: 04420870 **Date established:** 2002
No.of Employees: 1 - 10 **Product Groups:** 41

Date of Accounts	Mar 11	Mar 10	Mar 09
Working Capital	262	72	67
Fixed Assets	206	218	223
Current Assets	1m	984	1m

Dow Corning Ltd
Cardiff Road, Barry, CF63 2YL
Tel: 01446-732350 **Fax:** 01446-730495
E-mail: henry.ott@dowcorning.com
Website: http://www.dowcorning.com
Bank(s): Barclays
Managers: G. Cole (Fin Mgr), D. Ott (Site Co-ord), L. Evans (Personnel), S. Williams
Ultimate Holding Company: DOW CORNING CORP (USA)
Immediate Holding Company: DOW CORNING LIMITED
Registration no: 00486170 **VAT No.:** GB 134 0237 13
Date established: 1950 **Turnover:** £500m - £1,000m
No.of Employees: 501 - 1000 **Product Groups:** 38, 67, 84, 85, 88

Date of Accounts	Dec 11	Dec 10	Dec 09
Sales Turnover	507m	440m	391m
Pre Tax Profit/Loss	12m	9m	-4m
Working Capital	8m	-36m	-15m
Fixed Assets	193m	191m	197m
Current Assets	233m	265m	225m
Current Liabilities	25m	19m	23m

E T B
Cardiff Road, Barry, CF63 2QW
Tel: 01446-733167 **Fax:** 01446-733167
E-mail: shaun.hurley2@ntlworld.com
Managers: S. Hurley (Mgr)
Immediate Holding Company: ETB LTD
Registration no: 00934694 **Date established:** 1968
No.of Employees: 1 - 10 **Product Groups:** 29, 68

Edmundson Electrical Ltd
Units 13 & 14 Ty-Verlon Industrial Estate, Barry, CF63 2BE
Tel: 01446-701107 **Fax:** 01446-701104
E-mail: barry.381@eel.co.uk
Website: http://www.edmundson-electrical.co.uk/
Managers: J. Farrugia (District Mgr)
Ultimate Holding Company: BLACKFRIARS CORP (USA)
Immediate Holding Company: EDMUNDSON ELECTRICAL LIMITED
Registration no: 02667012 **VAT No.:** GB 579 9948 39
Date established: 1991 **No.of Employees:** 1 - 10 **Product Groups:** 87

Date of Accounts	Dec 11	Dec 10	Dec 09
Sales Turnover	1023m	852m	788m
Pre Tax Profit/Loss	57m	53m	45m

Working Capital	256m	225m	184m
Fixed Assets	17m	3m	4m
Current Assets	439m	358m	298m
Current Liabilities	59m	38m	37m

Eriks Industrial Services Ltd (Cardiff Electro Mechanical)

Unit A T Y Verlon Industrial Estate, Barry, CF63 2BE
Tel: 01446-737748 **Fax:** 01446-737769
E-mail: simon.oleary@eriks.co.uk
Website: http://www.eriks.com
Managers: S. Oleary (District Mgr)
Ultimate Holding Company: SHV HOLDINGS NV (NETHERLANDS)
Immediate Holding Company: ERIKS INDUSTRIAL SERVICES LIMITED
Registration no: 03142338 **Date established:** 1995
Turnover: £250m - £500m **No.of Employees:** 1 - 10 **Product Groups:** 35

Date of Accounts	Dec 11	Dec 10	Dec 09
Sales Turnover	231m	216m	210m
Pre Tax Profit/Loss	16m	10m	4m
Working Capital	35m	31m	22m
Fixed Assets	9m	10m	11m
Current Assets	101m	93m	80m
Current Liabilities	16m	13m	8m

Fabmec Ltd

Biglis House Ty Verlon Industrial Estate Cardiff Road, Barry, CF63 2BE
Tel: 01446-720000 **Fax:** 01446-746548
E-mail: info@fabmec.co.uk
Website: http://www.fabmec.co.uk
Directors: P. Hunt (Dir)
Immediate Holding Company: FABMEC LIMITED
Registration no: 02105482 **Date established:** 1987
No.of Employees: 1 - 10 **Product Groups:** 35, 39, 45

Date of Accounts	May 11	May 10	May 09
Working Capital	30	12	45
Fixed Assets	11	15	19
Current Assets	129	95	96

G H Stationers Ltd

Unit D 3 Atlantic Gate Atlantic Trading Estate, Barry, CF63 3RF
Tel: 01446-749222 **Fax:** 01446-742999
E-mail: sales@ghstationers.com
Website: http://www.ghstationers.com
Directors: G. Kent (MD)
Immediate Holding Company: G.H. STATIONERS LIMITED
Registration no: 03879238 **Date established:** 1999
Turnover: £50m - £75m **No.of Employees:** 1 - 10 **Product Groups:** 27

Date of Accounts	Nov 11	Nov 10	Nov 09
Working Capital	1	9	-3
Fixed Assets	163	161	160
Current Assets	86	138	102

Garden Fencing Services

104 Pontypridd Road, Barry, CF62 7LT
Tel: 01446-419428
Directors: A. Neilson (Prop)
Date established: 2006 **No.of Employees:** 1 - 10 **Product Groups:** 26, 35

Genero Productions

Unit 4 Ty Verlon Industrial Estate, Barry, CF63 2BE
Tel: 01446-740043 **Fax:** 0870-163 0701
E-mail: info@genero-productions.co.uk
Website: http://www.genero-productions.co.uk
Directors: P. Leckie (MD)
Immediate Holding Company: GENERO PRODUCTIONS LIMITED
Registration no: 05807065 **Date established:** 2006
Turnover: Up to £250,000 **No.of Employees:** 11 - 20 **Product Groups:** 83

Date of Accounts	May 11	May 10	May 09
Working Capital	-94	-104	-105
Fixed Assets	188	165	248
Current Assets	111	82	67

Harris Pye Group Ltd

David Davies Road No 2 Barry Dock, Barry, CF63 4AB
Tel: 01446-720066 **Fax:** 01446-700801
E-mail: christopher.trigg@harris-pye.com
Website: http://www.harrispyegroup.com
Bank(s): HSBC, Cardiff
Directors: C. Trigg (Fin)
Managers: C. Chandoler (Purch Mgr), D. Batters (Tech Serv Mgr), W. Davis (Personnel), J. Batters (Mktg Serv Mgr)
Ultimate Holding Company: HARRIS PYE GROUP LIMITED
Immediate Holding Company: HARRIS PYE 2006 LIMITED
Registration no: 02359988 **VAT No.:** GB 484 1925 25
Date established: 1989 **Turnover:** £1m - £2m
No.of Employees: 251 - 500 **Product Groups:** 36, 39, 40, 48, 84

Date of Accounts	Dec 11	Dec 10	Dec 09
Sales Turnover	N/A	N/A	1m
Pre Tax Profit/Loss	5m	N/A	1m
Working Capital	-191	-191	-191
Fixed Assets	900	900	900
Current Assets	5m	N/A	N/A

Ornamental Fabrications

Unit 8 Atlantic Trading Estate, Barry, CF63 3RF
Tel: 01446-721168 **Fax:** 01446-732360
E-mail: info@ornfab.co.uk
Website: http://www.ornfab.co.uk
Directors: S. Collier (MD)
Immediate Holding Company: ORNAMENTAL IRON LIMITED
Registration no: 03524416 **Date established:** 1998
No.of Employees: 1 - 10 **Product Groups:** 26, 35

Date of Accounts	Mar 09	Mar 08	Mar 07
Working Capital	55	37	102
Fixed Assets	49	61	64
Current Assets	221	192	294

Scafftag

Wimbourne Road, Barry, CF63 3DH
Tel: 01446-721029 **Fax:** 01446-743994
E-mail: customer.services@scafftag.com
Website: http://www.scafftag.com
Bank(s): Lloyds, Barry
Directors: A. Walsham (Co Sec), F. Jaehnert (Dir)
Ultimate Holding Company: BRADY CORP (USA)
Immediate Holding Company: SCAFFTAG LIMITED
Registration no: 01434887 **VAT No.:** 402 3419 01 **Date established:** 1979
Turnover: £250,000 - £500,000 **No.of Employees:** 21 - 50
Product Groups: 40

Date of Accounts	Jul 11	Jul 10	Jul 09
Sales Turnover	N/A	N/A	279
Pre Tax Profit/Loss	N/A	2	2m
Working Capital	7m	7m	7m
Current Assets	7m	7m	7m

Spartan Engine & Plant Repairs Ltd

Unit 16 Atlantic Trading Estate, Barry, CF63 3RF
Tel: 01446-701133 **Fax:** 01446-701233
E-mail: r.g.bailey@hotmail.co.uk
Directors: R. Bailey (Dir)
Ultimate Holding Company: SPARTAN HOLDINGS LIMITED
Immediate Holding Company: SPARTAN ENGINE AND PLANT REPAIRS LIMITED
Registration no: 01974188 **Date established:** 1985
No.of Employees: 1 - 10 **Product Groups:** 42, 45

Date of Accounts	Mar 12	Mar 11	Mar 10
Working Capital	139	181	142
Fixed Assets	141	155	197
Current Assets	263	297	199

Techni Flow UK Ltd

Unit 8I Atlantic Trading Estate, Barry, CF63 3RF
Tel: 01446-701122 **Fax:** 01446-736332
E-mail: sales@pumpengineering.co.uk
Website: http://www.pumpengineering.co.uk
Directors: P. Hilldrup (Co Sec), P. Hildrup (Dir), S. Fry (MD), D. Hilldrup (MD)
Managers: S. Fry (I.T. Exec)
Immediate Holding Company: TECHNI-FLOW (UK) LIMITED
Registration no: 02730717 **VAT No.:** 648 3631 20 **Date established:** 1992
Turnover: Up to £250,000 **No.of Employees:** 1 - 10 **Product Groups:** 67

Date of Accounts	Jul 11	Jul 10	Jul 09
Working Capital	9	-13	-15
Fixed Assets	3	3	3
Current Assets	69	32	29

Western Welding & Engineering Co. Ltd

Unit 9 Atlantic Trading Estate, Barry, CF63 3XA
Tel: 01446-733466 **Fax:** 01446-720993
Website: http://www.westernwelding.co.uk
Bank(s): Lloyds
Directors: D. Smele (MD)
Immediate Holding Company: WESTERN WELDING & ENGINEERING COMPANY LIMITED
Registration no: 00509386 **VAT No.:** GB 133 5492 75
Date established: 1952 **Turnover:** £500,000 - £1m
No.of Employees: 11 - 20 **Product Groups:** 35, 48

Date of Accounts	Sep 11	Sep 10	Sep 09
Sales Turnover	N/A	675	1m
Pre Tax Profit/Loss	N/A	-95	122
Working Capital	828	600	685
Fixed Assets	N/A	348	360
Current Assets	1m	994	1m
Current Liabilities	N/A	132	224

William Hill

102 Barry Road, Barry, CF63 1BB
Tel: 0800-223311 **Fax:** 01446-700395
E-mail: sales@alanwilliams.co.uk
Website: http://www.williamhill.com
Directors: A. Williams (Fin), A. Williams (MD)
Managers: D. James (Sales Prom Mgr), J. Watts (Accounts), M. Cox (Sales Eng)
Immediate Holding Company: ALAN WILLIAMS & CO (WALES) LTD
Registration no: 04728575 **VAT No.:** GB 136 4691 56
Date established: 2003 **Turnover:** £2m - £5m **No.of Employees:** 1 - 10
Product Groups: 40, 66

Gwent

Blackwood

CBI & Reassurance Service Care

4 Small Business Centre Penmaen Road, Pontllanfraith, Blackwood, NP12 2DZ
Tel: 01495-227999 **Fax:** 01495-227999
Directors: A. Taylor (Prop)
Immediate Holding Company: ICSNET UK LIMITED
Date established: 2007 **No.of Employees:** 1 - 10 **Product Groups:** 43

Frontier Medical Group

Newbridge Industrial Estate Newbridge Road, Pontllanfraith, Blackwood, NP12 2YN
Tel: 01495-235800 **Fax:** 01495-235808
E-mail: info@sharpsafe.co.uk
Website: http://www.sharpsafe.co.uk
Directors: N. Davis (MD)
Managers: M. Tudor (Product), H. Salmon (Personnel), H. Briggs (Purch Mgr), J. Wilson (Chief Acct), A. Timpany (Sales Prom Mgr), S. Coombes (Tech Serv Mgr)
Ultimate Holding Company: FRONTIER MEDICAL PRODUCTS LIMITED
Immediate Holding Company: FRONTIER PLASTICS LIMITED
Registration no: 00869871 **Date established:** 1966
Turnover: £10m - £20m **No.of Employees:** 101 - 250
Product Groups: 30, 38

Date of Accounts	Mar 11	Mar 10	Mar 09
Sales Turnover	16m	16m	N/A
Pre Tax Profit/Loss	509	5m	821
Working Capital	5m	5m	3m
Fixed Assets	6m	5m	5m
Current Assets	7m	7m	5m
Current Liabilities	771	1m	647

General Dynamics

Unit 2-3 Bryn Brithdir, Oakdale Business Park, Blackwood, NP12 4AA
Tel: 01495-236300 **Fax:** 01495-236400
E-mail: sales@generaldynamics.uk.com
Website: http://www.generaldynamics.uk.com
Directors: Z. Mitchell (Dir)
Ultimate Holding Company: GENERAL DYNAMICS CORP (USA)
Immediate Holding Company: GENERAL DYNAMICS UNITED KINGDOM LIMITED
Registration no: 01911653 **Date established:** 1985
Turnover: £250m - £500m **No.of Employees:** 1001 - 1500
Product Groups: 36, 37

Date of Accounts	Dec 11	Dec 10	Dec 09
Sales Turnover	407m	372m	349m
Pre Tax Profit/Loss	58m	54m	44m
Working Capital	113m	93m	106m
Fixed Assets	72m	62m	10m
Current Assets	278m	239m	239m
Current Liabilities	108m	110m	118m

Hazrem Environmental

Unit C Chambers House 49 Blackwood Road, Pontllanfraith, Blackwood, NP12 2BW
Tel: 01495-233400
E-mail: sales@hazrem.co.uk
Website: http://www.hazrem.co.uk
Directors: P. Goddard (Dir)
Immediate Holding Company: HAZREM ENVIRONMENTAL LTD
Registration no: 05064100 **Date established:** 2004
Turnover: £250,000 - £500,000 **No.of Employees:** 1 - 10
Product Groups: 32, 54

Date of Accounts	Mar 11	Mar 10	Mar 09
Working Capital	52	40	4
Fixed Assets	122	54	14
Current Assets	223	128	57

Gus Jones

109 High Street, Blackwood, NP12 1AD
Tel: 01495-223338 **Fax:** 01495-224220
E-mail: michael@royalmasonic.herts.sch.uk
Website: http://www.gusjonesjewellers.co.uk
Directors: M. Jones (Dir)
Immediate Holding Company: GUS JONES (JEWELLERS) LIMITED
Registration no: 01290871 **Date established:** 1976 **Turnover:** £1m - £2m
No.of Employees: 11 - 20 **Product Groups:** 61

Date of Accounts	Mar 11	Mar 10	Mar 09
Sales Turnover	2m	2m	1m
Pre Tax Profit/Loss	-28	61	-2
Working Capital	709	719	666
Fixed Assets	396	403	411
Current Assets	819	856	813
Current Liabilities	65	76	100

L & L Welding

Unit 1e St Davids Industrial Estate, Pengam, Blackwood, NP12 3SW
Tel: 01443-832000 **Fax:** 01443-832000
E-mail: marklewiswales@yahoo.co.uk
Website: http://www.arfonironworks.co.uk
Directors: M. Lewis (Prop)
No.of Employees: 1 - 10 **Product Groups:** 35, 36, 39, 40

Motion29 Ltd

U29 Woodfieldside Business Park Penmaen Road Pontllanfraith, Blackwood, NP12 2DG
Tel: 01495-227603 **Fax:** 08450-942520
E-mail: sales@motion29.co.uk
Website: http://www.motion29.com
Directors: S. Fisher (Dir)
Immediate Holding Company: MOTION29 LIMITED
Registration no: 05681361 **Date established:** 2006
Turnover: £250,000 - £500,000 **No.of Employees:** 1 - 10
Product Groups: 37, 40

Date of Accounts	Jun 12	Jun 11	Jun 10
Working Capital	102	51	23
Fixed Assets	11	6	6
Current Assets	262	149	130

Moulded Foams Ltd

2 Hawtin Park Gellihaf, Blackwood, NP12 2EU
Tel: 01443-441491 **Fax:** 01443-441453
E-mail: sales@mouldedfoams.com
Website: http://www.mouldedfoams.com
Managers: A. Trousdell (Comptroller), J. Dando (Sales Prom Mgr), J. Granville (Tech Serv Mgr)
Ultimate Holding Company: MOULDED FOAMS (SCOTLAND) LTD
Immediate Holding Company: MOULDED FOAMS LIMITED
Registration no: SC146277 **Date established:** 1993
No.of Employees: 21 - 50 **Product Groups:** 30, 48, 76, 84

Date of Accounts	Dec 11	Dec 10	Dec 09
Sales Turnover	11m	10m	9m
Pre Tax Profit/Loss	190	618	154
Working Capital	362	778	20
Fixed Assets	4m	3m	3m
Current Assets	3m	3m	3m
Current Liabilities	1m	487	612

Reesman Transport

Rees House The Rock, Blackwood, NP12 1DA
Tel: 01495-220114 **Fax:** 01495-231056
E-mail: sales@reesmanrefrigeration.com
Website: http://www.reesmanrefrigeration.com
Directors: D. Daly (MD)
Immediate Holding Company: DALE REES SERVICES LIMITED
Registration no: 04487709 **Date established:** 2002
Turnover: Up to £250,000 **No.of Employees:** 1 - 10 **Product Groups:** 36, 40

Date of Accounts	Jul 11	Jul 10	Jul 09
Sales Turnover	N/A	144	123
Pre Tax Profit/Loss	N/A	20	3
Working Capital	11	3	4
Fixed Assets	33	19	16
Current Assets	96	64	45
Current Liabilities	N/A	11	12

S Z Gears Ltd

Unit 2 Bryn Brithdir Oakdale Business Park, Blackwood, NP12 4AA
Tel: 01495-245008 **Fax:** 01633-612626
E-mail: sales@szgears.co.uk
Website: http://www.szgears.co.uk
Directors: S. Davies (MD)
Ultimate Holding Company: MC232 LIMITED
Immediate Holding Company: S.Z. GEARS LIMITED
Registration no: 01249262 **Date established:** 1976
No.of Employees: 11 - 20 **Product Groups:** 35, 45

Date of Accounts	Mar 11	Mar 10	Mar 09
Working Capital	299	256	350
Fixed Assets	156	81	127
Current Assets	700	560	520

Standard Specialised Fasteners Ltd
Unit H St Davids Industrial Estate Pengam, Blackwood, NP12 3SW
Tel: 01443-830810 **Fax:** 01443-838124
E-mail: nwilliams@sasfast.com
Website: http://www.sasfast.com
Directors: N. Williams (Fin)
Immediate Holding Company: STANDARD AND SPECIALISED FASTENERS LIMITED
Registration no: 01886761 **VAT No.:** GB 402 5896 54
Date established: 1985 **No.of Employees:** 1 - 10 **Product Groups:** 35, 37, 66

Date of Accounts	Apr 11	Apr 10	Apr 09
Working Capital	127	125	130
Fixed Assets	37	41	45
Current Assets	304	277	281

Utility Training Services Ltd
Unit 14 Oakdale Court Bryn Brithdir, Oakdale Business Park, Blackwood, NP12 4AD
Tel: 01495-245364
E-mail: paul@utilitytrainingservices.co.uk
Website: http://www.utilitytrainingservices.co.uk
Directors: P. Williams (Dir)
Immediate Holding Company: UTILITY TRAINING SERVICES LTD
Registration no: 06481563 **Date established:** 2008
Turnover: Up to £250,000 **No.of Employees:** 1 - 10 **Product Groups:** 86

Date of Accounts	Jan 12	Jan 11	Jan 10
Working Capital	91	17	18
Fixed Assets	46	47	41
Current Assets	204	48	52

Gwynedd

Blaenau Ffestiniog

Greaves Welsh Slate Co. Ltd
Llechwedd Slate Mines, Blaenau Ffestiniog, LL41 3NB
Tel: 01766-830522 **Fax:** 01766-830711
E-mail: llechwedd@aol.com
Website: http://www.welsh-slate.com
Bank(s): HSBC
Directors: J. Nagy Livingstone Learmonth (Dir), D. Hicken (Co Sec)
Managers: G. Wilkes (Fin Mgr)
Immediate Holding Company: GREAVES WELSH SLATE COMPANY LIMITED
Registration no: 01761719 **VAT No.:** GB 401 3822 02
Date established: 1983 **Turnover:** £250,000 - £500,000
No.of Employees: 51 - 100 **Product Groups:** 14, 33, 52

Date of Accounts	Sep 11	Sep 10	Sep 09
Working Capital	-344	-398	-517
Fixed Assets	27	40	30
Current Assets	608	514	490

Metcalfe Catering Equipment Ltd
Haygarth Park, Blaenau Ffestiniog, LL41 3PF
Tel: 01766-830456 **Fax:** 01766-831170
E-mail: info@metcalfecatering.co.uk
Website: http://www.metcalfecatering.com
Bank(s): HSBC Bank plc
Directors: J. Brooke (Fin), N. Richards (Dir)
Immediate Holding Company: METCALFE CATERING EQUIPMENT LIMITED
Registration no: 00386634 **VAT No.:** GB 741 6318 43
Date established: 1944 **Turnover:** £1m - £2m **No.of Employees:** 11 - 20
Product Groups: 38, 40

Date of Accounts	Dec 11	Dec 10	Dec 09
Working Capital	301	263	235
Fixed Assets	257	252	219
Current Assets	1m	793	887

Quarry Tours Ltd
Llechwedd Slate Caverns, Blaenau Ffestiniog, LL41 3NB
Tel: 01766-830306 **Fax:** 01766-831260
E-mail: bookings@llechwedd.co.uk
Website: http://www.llechwedd-slate-caverns.co.uk
Directors: D. Hicken (Fin), M. Bewick (Dir)
Managers: M. Bewick (Buyer)
Ultimate Holding Company: J.W.GREAVES & SONS,LIMITED
Immediate Holding Company: QUARRY TOURS LIMITED
Registration no: 01009327 **Date established:** 1971
No.of Employees: 21 - 50 **Product Groups:** 69

Date of Accounts	Sep 11	Sep 10	Sep 09
Working Capital	339	452	516
Fixed Assets	406	412	436
Current Assets	518	645	681

Dyfed

Boncath

W Y N Thomas & Son
Lleine Lan Blaenffos, Boncath, SA37 0JF
Tel: 01239-841237 **Fax:** 01239-841807
Directors: W. Thomas (Prop)
Date established: 1967 **No.of Employees:** 1 - 10 **Product Groups:** 41

Dyfed

Bow Street

Builder Center Ltd
Station Yard, Bow Street, SY24 5AT
Tel: 01970-820026 **Fax:** 01970-820263
Website: http://www.buildercentre.co.uk
Managers: I. Lewis (District Mgr)
Ultimate Holding Company: 00029846
Immediate Holding Company: BUILD CENTER LIMITED
Registration no: 00462397 **VAT No.:** GB 222 8284 72
Date established: 1948 **No.of Employees:** 1 - 10 **Product Groups:** 14, 25, 33, 63, 66

Powys

Brecon

Ian Dennis Partnership
Ynys Clydach Sennybridge, Brecon, LD3 8TY
Tel: 01874-636535 **Fax:** 01874-636535
E-mail: veradennis@hotmail.co.uk
Directors: I. Dennis (Prop)
Date established: 1990 **No.of Employees:** 1 - 10 **Product Groups:** 26, 35

Fire & Stove Shop
5 St Marys Street, Brecon, LD3 7AA
Tel: 01874-622088 **Fax:** 029-2081 3347
E-mail: brecon@decoheat.co.uk
Website: http://www.decorativeheating.co.uk
Directors: J. Portsmouth (Prop)
Immediate Holding Company: THE FIRE AND STOVE SHOP LTD
Registration no: 07494983 **Date established:** 2011
No.of Employees: 1 - 10 **Product Groups:** 40

Ted Hopkins
Brecon Enterprise Park, Brecon, LD3 8BT
Tel: 01874-623322 **Fax:** 01874-620082
E-mail: brecon@tedhopkins.co.uk
Website: http://www.tedhopkins.co.uk
Managers: R. Jones (Mgr)
Registration no: 02338612 **Date established:** 1989
No.of Employees: 1 - 10 **Product Groups:** 41

King Morter Proud & Co.
Kings Arms Vaults The Watton, Brecon, LD3 7EF
Tel: 01874-625353 **Fax:** 01874-624384
E-mail: admin@kmpbrecon.co.uk
Directors: J. Bromley (Ptnr)
Immediate Holding Company: KING MORTER PROUD & CO LIMITED
Registration no: 07461356 **VAT No.:** GB 134 3258 87
Date established: 2010 **No.of Employees:** 1 - 10 **Product Groups:** 80

Date of Accounts	Mar 12
Working Capital	182
Fixed Assets	256
Current Assets	320

Paul Dennis Metal Works
Penllwyn Hendy Senni, Brecon, LD3 8SU
Tel: 01874-636636 **Fax:** 01874-638970
E-mail: info@pauldennismetalworks.co.uk
Directors: R. Pinhore (Dir)
Immediate Holding Company: PAUL DENNIS ASSOCIATES SENNYBRIDGE COMPANY LTD
Registration no: 03150334 **Date established:** 1996
No.of Employees: 1 - 10 **Product Groups:** 26, 35

Date of Accounts	Jan 11	Jan 10	Jan 09
Working Capital	-12	3	29
Fixed Assets	17	7	4
Current Assets	167	100	89

Rodell Chimneys Ltd
Ffrwdgrech Industrial Estate, Brecon, LD3 8LA
Tel: 01874-623723 **Fax:** 01874-623725
E-mail: rcltd1@btconnect.com
Website: http://www.rodell-chimneys.co.uk
Bank(s): HSBC
Directors: J. Rodell (MD)
Immediate Holding Company: RODELL CHIMNEYS LIMITED
Registration no: 00961183 **VAT No.:** GB 135 0352 07
Date established: 1969 **Turnover:** £500,000 - £1m
No.of Employees: 11 - 20 **Product Groups:** 35, 36, 42, 51, 52

Date of Accounts	Mar 11	Feb 08	Feb 10
Working Capital	106	101	103
Fixed Assets	164	168	162
Current Assets	308	247	287

Winslow Adaptics Ltd
Unit 11 Brecon Enterprise Park, Brecon, LD3 8BT
Tel: 01874-625555 **Fax:** 01874-625500
E-mail: sales@winslowadaptics.com
Website: http://www.winslowadaptics.com
Bank(s): Midland
Directors: L. Winslow (Fin), L. Winslow (Fin)
Managers: R. Davies (Ops Mgr), M. Garside (Tech Serv Mgr)
Immediate Holding Company: WINSLOW ADAPTICS LIMITED
Registration no: 02338612 **VAT No.:** 484 5822 15 **Date established:** 1989
Turnover: £1m - £2m **No.of Employees:** 11 - 20 **Product Groups:** 37

Date of Accounts	Mar 11	Mar 10	Mar 09
Working Capital	37	1	-119
Fixed Assets	284	313	341
Current Assets	341	264	329

Mid-Glamorgan

Bridgend

A C E Roofing Services
7 Llynfi Street, Bridgend, CF31 1SY
Tel: 01656-668649
Directors: M. Butler (Prop)
No.of Employees: 1 - 10 **Product Groups:** 26, 35

Abril Industrial Waxes Ltd
Sturmi Way Village Farm Industrial Estate, Pyle, Bridgend, CF33 6BZ
Tel: 01656-744896 **Fax:** 01656-744887
E-mail: info@abrilindustrialwaxes.co.uk
Website: http://www.abril.co.uk
Directors: P. Brandon (Co Sec), B. Cooke (Dir)
Immediate Holding Company: ABRIL INDUSTRIAL WAXES LIMITED
Registration no: 04646926 **VAT No.:** GB 540 9519 40
Date established: 2003 **Turnover:** £2m - £5m **No.of Employees:** 1 - 10
Product Groups: 20, 31, 32, 48, 49, 66

Date of Accounts	Aug 11	Aug 10	Feb 09
Working Capital	710	427	224
Fixed Assets	170	164	1m
Current Assets	849	519	354

Aircraft Maintenance Ltd
Eagle House Village Farm Industrial Estate, Pyle, Bridgend, CF33 6NU
Tel: 01656-743700 **Fax:** 01656-744265
E-mail: office@amss.co
Website: http://www.amss.co
Bank(s): Barclays
Directors: D. Barber (Ch), S. Harries (Fin), V. Reitze (Comm)
Managers: D. Evans (Purch Mgr), S. Barber (Eng Serv Mgr), C. Wellings (Fin Mgr)
Ultimate Holding Company: BARBER HOLDINGS LIMITED
Immediate Holding Company: AIRCRAFT MAINTENANCE SUPPORT SERVICES LIMITED
Registration no: 01402826 **VAT No.:** GB 331 0732 05
Date established: 1978 **Turnover:** £10m - £20m
No.of Employees: 51 - 100 **Product Groups:** 39

Date of Accounts	Dec 11	Dec 10	Dec 09
Sales Turnover	14m	10m	11m
Pre Tax Profit/Loss	444	324	2m
Working Capital	2m	2m	1m
Fixed Assets	512	310	336
Current Assets	7m	6m	6m
Current Liabilities	3m	2m	3m

Antifriction Components Ltd
Unit 5 North Point Western Avenue, Bridgend Industrial Estate, Bridgend, CF31 3RX
Tel: 01656-651292 **Fax:** 01656-651620
Website: http://www.afc-uk.com
Managers: A. Lewis (Mgr)
Ultimate Holding Company: KOWLOON INVESTMENTS LIMITED (MAURITIUS)
Immediate Holding Company: ANTI-FRICTION COMPONENTS LIMITED
Registration no: 01275175 **Date established:** 1976
No.of Employees: 1 - 10 **Product Groups:** 35, 45

Date of Accounts	Sep 11	Sep 10	Sep 09
Sales Turnover	12m	11m	9m
Pre Tax Profit/Loss	427	231	93
Working Capital	592	357	275
Fixed Assets	206	17	28
Current Assets	4m	4m	3m
Current Liabilities	1m	1m	1m

B.A.S.S (Bridgend Audio Security Systems)
35 Brynderi, Bridgend, CF31 4EN
Tel: 07973-498637
E-mail: sales@b-a-s-s.co.uk
Website: http://b-a-s-s.co.uk
Turnover: Up to £250,000 **No.of Employees:** 1 - 10 **Product Groups:** 37, 67

B G Lubrication & Pipework Services Ltd
Heol Y Llyfrau Aberkenfig, Bridgend, CF32 9PL
Tel: 01656-722344 **Fax:** 01656-720090
Directors: R. Gordon (Dir), D. Gordon (Co Sec)
Immediate Holding Company: B.G. LUBRICATION & PIPEWORK SERVICES LIMITED
Registration no: 02141889 **Date established:** 1987
No.of Employees: 1 - 10 **Product Groups:** 38, 42

Date of Accounts	Sep 10	Sep 09	Sep 08
Working Capital	34	7	24
Fixed Assets	7	79	82
Current Assets	44	21	70

Biomet UK Ltd
Waterton Industrial Estate, Bridgend, CF31 3XA
Tel: 01656-655221 **Fax:** 01656-645454
E-mail: mike.thompson@biomet.com
Website: http://www.biomet.com
Bank(s): Barclays
Directors: C. McMahon (Fin), K. Brownhill (Fin), M. Thompson (MD)
Managers: A. Radmore (Tech Serv Mgr), R. Downs (Mktg Serv Mgr), R. Downs (Mktg Serv Mgr)
Ultimate Holding Company: BIOMET INC (USA)
Immediate Holding Company: BIOMET UK LIMITED
Registration no: 01019715 **VAT No.:** GB 194 8140 43
Date established: 1971 **Turnover:** £75m - £125m
No.of Employees: 501 - 1000 **Product Groups:** 22, 38

Date of Accounts	May 11	May 10	May 09
Sales Turnover	101m	177m	157m
Pre Tax Profit/Loss	23m	49m	43m
Working Capital	31m	20m	47m
Fixed Assets	16m	13m	11m
Current Assets	44m	48m	78m
Current Liabilities	5m	9m	12m

Brackla Patio Centre
Unit 2 Heol Ffaldau, Brackla Industrial Estate, Bridgend, CF31 2AJ
Tel: 01656-647595
E-mail: sales@bracklapatiocentre.co.uk
Website: http://www.bracklapatiocentre.co.uk
Directors: C. Davies (Prop)
Date established: 1993 **Turnover:** Up to £250,000
No.of Employees: 1 - 10 **Product Groups:** 07, 33

Brynol Chrome Ltd
76 Village Farm Road Village Farm Industrial Estate, Pyle, Bridgend, CF33 6BN
Tel: 01656-744606 **Fax:** 01656-746744
E-mail: sales@brynolengineering.co.uk
Website: http://www.brynolengineering.co.uk
Directors: N. Skidmore (MD)
Immediate Holding Company: BRYNOL CHROME LIMITED
Registration no: 05070000 **Date established:** 2004
No.of Employees: 1 - 10 **Product Groups:** 46, 48

Date of Accounts	Mar 11	Mar 10	Mar 09
Working Capital	-67	-50	-75
Fixed Assets	164	170	174
Current Assets	42	74	60

Business In Focus Ltd
Enterprise Centre Bryn Road Aberkenfig, Bridgend, CF32 9BS
Tel: 01656-724414 **Fax:** 01656-748401
E-mail: info@businessinfocus.co.uk
Website: http://www.businessinfocus.co.uk
Bank(s): National Westminster, Bridgend
Directors: G. Bray (MD)
Managers: G. Jones (Property Mgr), E. Ellis (Fin Mgr)
Immediate Holding Company: BUSINESS IN FOCUS LIMITED
Registration no: 02553654 **VAT No.:** GB 540 8347 48
Date established: 1990 **Turnover:** £1m - £2m **No.of Employees:** 11 - 20
Product Groups: 80, 86

Date of Accounts	Mar 12	Mar 11	Mar 10
Working Capital	-94	-201	-278
Fixed Assets	10m	9m	8m
Current Assets	540	425	329

Celtic Tyres Services Bridgend Ltd
Princes Way Bridgend Industrial Estate, Bridgend, CF31 3TT
Tel: 01656-657424 **Fax:** 01656-647743
E-mail: enquiries@celtictyres.co.uk
Website: http://www.celtictyres.co.uk
Bank(s): Barclays, Port Talbot
Directors: R. Jenkins (MD)
Ultimate Holding Company: CELTIC TYRE SERVICES (HOLDINGS) LIMITED
Immediate Holding Company: CELTIC TYRE SERVICES (MAESTEG) LIMITED
Registration no: 01071945 **VAT No.:** GB 133 5275 83
Date established: 1972 **Turnover:** £5m - £10m **No.of Employees:** 11 - 20
Product Groups: 29, 37, 39

Date of Accounts	Nov 11	Nov 10	Nov 09
Working Capital	-110	-90	-82
Current Assets	3	11	10
Current Liabilities	104	N/A	N/A

Chauffeurs For You
36 Walters Road Ogmore Vale, Bridgend, CF32 7DN
Tel: 01656-841353 **Fax:** 01656-841353
E-mail: info@chauffeursforyou.co.uk
Website: http://www.chauffeursforyou.co.uk
Directors: G. Tuck (Prop)
Date established: 2001 **No.of Employees:** 1 - 10 **Product Groups:** 72

Computer Services Group
C S G House 7 George Thomas Avenue, Brynmenyn, Bridgend, CF32 9SQ
Tel: 01656-725505 **Fax:** 01656-725999
E-mail: sales@csgrp.co.uk
Website: http://www.csgrp.co.uk
Bank(s): Lloyds TSB Bank plc
Directors: R. Vise (MD)
Immediate Holding Company: CSG COMPUTER SERVICES LTD
Registration no: 04712129 **VAT No.:** GB 433 2831 70
Date established: 2003 **No.of Employees:** 11 - 20 **Product Groups:** 44

Date of Accounts	Sep 11	Sep 10	Sep 09
Working Capital	33	-91	-85
Fixed Assets	872	912	958
Current Assets	332	331	323

Control 2K Ltd
Waterton Industrial Estate, Bridgend, CF31 3WT
Tel: 01656-646404 **Fax:** 01656-673925
E-mail: admin@control2k.co.uk
Website: http://www.control2k.co.uk
Directors: S. Osborne (Tech Serv), D. Bowen (Fin)
Managers: A. Jordan (Sales & Mktg Mg)
Registration no: 03709130 **No.of Employees:** 11 - 20
Product Groups: 44, 79

Days Health Care (DMA Ltd)
North Road Bridgend Industrial Estate, Bridgend, CF31 3TP
Tel: 01656-664700 **Fax:** 01656-767178
E-mail: info@dayshealthcare.com
Website: http://www.daysmedical.com
Directors: B. O'Neill (MD), C. Costigan (Dir), R. Jones (Dir), V. Dikov (I.T. Dir)
Managers: C. Morgan (Purch Mgr), L. Reeves (Works Gen Mgr), M. Hermolle (Personnel), R. Mainwaring, R. Mainwaring ()
Immediate Holding Company: A. N. SUPPLIES (WHOLESALE ELECTRICAL DISTRIBUTORS) LIMITED
Registration no: 01120623 **Date established:** 1976
Turnover: £10m - £20m **No.of Employees:** 51 - 100 **Product Groups:** 26, 36

Date of Accounts	Dec 10	Dec 09	Dec 08
Working Capital	362	385	391
Fixed Assets	297	187	206
Current Assets	2m	2m	2m
Current Liabilities	N/A	135	107

Dialog Technivac Ltd
Unit 5 Raven Close, Bridgend Industrial Estate, Bridgend, CF31 3RF
Tel: 01656-645856 **Fax:** 01656-646541
E-mail: info@technivac.co.uk
Website: http://www.technivac.co.uk
Bank(s): HSBC
Directors: C. Mathias (Fin)
Ultimate Holding Company: DIALOG GROUP BERHAD (MALAYSIA)
Immediate Holding Company: DIALOG TECHNIVAC LIMITED
Registration no: 01918943 **VAT No.:** 438 5809 18 **Date established:** 1985
Turnover: £1m - £2m **No.of Employees:** 11 - 20 **Product Groups:** 42

Date of Accounts	Jun 11	Jun 10	Jun 09
Working Capital	188	85	240
Fixed Assets	210	200	229
Current Assets	1m	1m	1m

Easi Care Mobility
Unit 1-3 Sturmi Way Village Farm Industrial Estate, Pyle, Bridgend, CF33 6BZ
Tel: 01656-670472 **Fax:** 01656-670492
Website: http://www.easicaremobility.co.uk
Directors: A. Bowen (Prop), A. Bowen (Sales)
Immediate Holding Company: EASI CARE MOBILITY LIMITED
Registration no: 04943144 **Date established:** 2003
Turnover: £250,000 - £500,000 **No.of Employees:** 1 - 10
Product Groups: 38, 67

En-Quest Environmental UK
Litchard Industrial Estate, Bridgend, CF31 2AL
Tel: 01656-766668 **Fax:** 01656-648747
Directors: M. Miers (MD)
Managers: C. Drake, L. Glenney (Sales Admin)
Immediate Holding Company: EN-QUEST ENVIRONMENTAL (UK) LIMITED
Registration no: 05137251 **Date established:** 2004
No.of Employees: 1 - 10 **Product Groups:** 54

Date of Accounts	May 08	May 07	May 06
Working Capital	-6	-6	-3
Fixed Assets	1	2	2
Current Assets	11	13	56
Current Liabilities	17	19	59

Excel Power Construction
Unit 5b2 Ewenny Industrial Estate, Bridgend, CF31 3EX
Tel: 01656-661188 **Fax:** 01656-661155
E-mail: info@excelpower.co.uk
Website: http://www.excelpower.co.uk
Directors: D. James (Dir), W. James (Prop)
Immediate Holding Company: EXCEL POWER CONSTRUCTION LTD
Registration no: 03701161 **Date established:** 1999
No.of Employees: 21 - 50 **Product Groups:** 35

Date of Accounts	Jan 11	Jan 10	Jan 09
Working Capital	-194	-171	-210
Fixed Assets	251	267	275
Current Assets	295	243	225

F T M Materials Handling Ltd
Unit 1 Ewenny Industrial Estate, Bridgend, CF31 3EX
Tel: 01656-766200 **Fax:** 01656-767976
E-mail: admin@ftmbridgend.co.uk
Website: http://www.ftmbridgend.co.uk
Directors: B. Radley (Fin), K. Donoghue (Dir)
Immediate Holding Company: FTM MATERIALS HANDLING LIMITED
Registration no: 02007156 **Date established:** 1986 **Turnover:** £2m - £5m
No.of Employees: 21 - 50 **Product Groups:** 67

Date of Accounts	Mar 12	Mar 11	Mar 10
Working Capital	2m	1m	1m
Fixed Assets	1m	1m	2m
Current Assets	3m	2m	2m

Fiskars Brands UK Ltd
Newlands Avenue Brackla Indl-Est, Litchard Indl-Est, Bridgend, CF31 2XA
Tel: 01656-655595 **Fax:** 01656- 659582
E-mail: sales@fiskars.com
Website: http://www.fiskars.com
Bank(s): Union Bank of Finland
Directors: D. Perry (Mkt Research), V. Treves (Fin), A. Smith (MD), M. Prosser (MD), G. Davies (Dep Pres)
Managers: G. Colledge (Ops Mgr), D. Morgan (Fin Mgr), N. Gazzard (Buyer), N. Gold (I.T. Exec), J. Davies (Purch Mgr), R. Hawkes (Sales Prom Mgr), J. Wilks (Sales Prom Mgr), A. Jones, H. Robert (Export Sales Mg)
Ultimate Holding Company: FISKARS OY AB (FINLAND)
Registration no: 02542030 **Date established:** 1990
Turnover: £10m - £20m **No.of Employees:** 21 - 50 **Product Groups:** 30

Date of Accounts	Dec 09	Dec 08	Dec 07
Working Capital	3m	3m	3m
Current Assets	3m	3m	3m

Gee Construction Ltd
New Street Bridgend Industrial Estate, Bridgend, CF31 3UD
Tel: 01656-653541 **Fax:** 01656-657717
E-mail: bridgend@geeconstruction.co.uk
Website: http://www.geeconstruction.co.uk
Bank(s): Barclays
Directors: I. Simpson (Fin), J. Newbury (Ch)
Managers: M. Whelton (Mktg Serv Mgr)
Ultimate Holding Company: HEADCROWN GROUP PLC
Immediate Holding Company: GEE CONSTRUCTION LTD
Registration no: 02493640 **Date established:** 1990
Turnover: £10m - £20m **No.of Employees:** 21 - 50 **Product Groups:** 52, 84

Date of Accounts	Sep 11	Sep 10	Sep 09
Sales Turnover	26m	25m	29m
Pre Tax Profit/Loss	371	511	-2m
Working Capital	3m	3m	3m
Fixed Assets	5m	7m	8m
Current Assets	15m	15m	14m
Current Liabilities	7m	6m	6m

Glamorgan Gazette
2 Brackla St Centre, Bridgend, CF31 1DD
Tel: 01656-304900 **Fax:** 01656-304904
E-mail: glamorgan.gazette@wme.co.uk
Website: http://www.mediawales.co.uk
Bank(s): National Westminster Bank Plc
Directors: K. Dye (MD)
Managers: P. Curran (Accounts), P. Jones (Publishing), D. Rees, L. Cardwell (Sales Prom Mgr), D. Rees (Publishing)
Immediate Holding Company: Western Mail & Echo Ltd
Registration no: 00150249 **Turnover:** £2m - £5m
No.of Employees: 11 - 20 **Product Groups:** 28

Harman International
Bennett Street Bridgend Industrial Estate, Bridgend, CF31 3SH
Tel: 01656-645441 **Fax:** 01656-650327
E-mail: info@harman.com
Website: http://www.harman.com
Directors: P. Selby (MD)
Managers: H. Lewis (Personnel), C. Thompson (I.T. Exec), K. Mcmahon (Fin Mgr), R. Hemming (Purch Mgr)
Ultimate Holding Company: HARMAN INTERNATIONAL INDUSTRIES, INCORPORATED
Immediate Holding Company: HARMAN UK LIMITED
Registration no: 02123223 **VAT No.:** GB 220 5465 95
Date established: 1980 **Turnover:** £75m - £125m
No.of Employees: 51 - 100 **Product Groups:** 37

Date of Accounts	Mar 11	Mar 09	Mar 08
Working Capital	150	89	97
Fixed Assets	12	20	21
Current Assets	206	108	116

Hilf Supply Chain Solutions Ltd
3 Heol Bryncwtyn Pencoed, Bridgend, CF35 5PX
Tel: 029-2125 0390 **Fax:** 01656-864314
E-mail: info@hilf.co.uk
Website: http://www.hilf.co.uk

Directors: L. Harding (MD), H. Harding (Co Sec)
Registration no: 04471863 **Date established:** 1902
No.of Employees: 1 - 10 **Product Groups:** 80

Invacare Ltd
Pencoed Technology Park, Bridgend, CF35 5HZ
Tel: 01656-776200 **Fax:** 01656-667532
E-mail: mprosser@invacare.com
Website: http://www.invacare.co.uk
Directors: J. Lewis (MD), S. Morgan (Co Sec), R. Hawkes (Sales & Mktg), M. Prosser (MD)
Managers: N. Morris (I.T. Exec)
Ultimate Holding Company: INVACARE CORPORATION (USA)
Immediate Holding Company: INVACARE LIMITED
Registration no: 05178693 **Date established:** 2004
Turnover: £50m - £75m **No.of Employees:** 101 - 250
Product Groups: 26, 39

Date of Accounts	Nov 10	Nov 09	Nov 08
Sales Turnover	6m	6m	6m
Pre Tax Profit/Loss	267	-4m	267
Working Capital	-553	-301	-6m
Fixed Assets	5m	5m	14m
Current Assets	2m	2m	2m
Current Liabilities	1m	790	797

Jenstar Ltd
Sturmi Way Village Farm Industrial Estate, Pyle, Bridgend, CF33 6BZ
Tel: 01656-745818 **Fax:** 01656-745818
Website: http://www.jenstar.co.uk
Directors: B. Jennings (MD), K. Jennings (Co Sec)
Immediate Holding Company: JENSTAR LIMITED
Registration no: 01018785 **VAT No.:** GB 133 5238 89
Date established: 1971 **Turnover:** £250,000 - £500,000
No.of Employees: 1 - 10 **Product Groups:** 37

Date of Accounts	Dec 11	Dec 10	Dec 09
Working Capital	168	204	211
Fixed Assets	62	56	59
Current Assets	182	214	223

John Raymond Transport Ltd
Ewenny Industrial Estate Waterton, Bridgend, CF31 3EZ
Tel: 01656-666800 **Fax:** 01656-666801
E-mail: customers@jrt.co.uk
Website: http://www.jrt.co.uk
Bank(s): National Westminster Bank Plc
Directors: A. Raymond (Fin), P. Johns (MD)
Ultimate Holding Company: JRT HOLDINGS LIMITED
Immediate Holding Company: JOHN RAYMOND TRANSPORT LIMITED
Registration no: 00400527 **Date established:** 1945
Turnover: £20m - £50m **No.of Employees:** 101 - 250
Product Groups: 72, 77

Date of Accounts	Sep 11	Sep 10	Sep 09
Sales Turnover	21m	20m	20m
Pre Tax Profit/Loss	19	-315	12
Working Capital	-1m	-956	-527
Fixed Assets	3m	3m	4m
Current Assets	4m	4m	4m
Current Liabilities	3m	3m	3m

Joseph Ash Galvanising
Bridgend Galvanisors Princes Way, Bridgend Industrial Estate, Bridgend, CF31 3AQ
Tel: 01656-668735 **Fax:** 01656-767139
E-mail: davids@josephash.co.uk
Website: http://www.josephash.co.uk
Managers: D. Satterwaite (Mgr)
Immediate Holding Company: CPP-ELEC LIMITED
Registration no: 05807499 **Date established:** 2005
Turnover: £10m - £20m **No.of Employees:** 11 - 20 **Product Groups:** 48

Date of Accounts	Feb 08	Feb 11	Feb 10
Sales Turnover	160	N/A	153
Pre Tax Profit/Loss	N/A	N/A	1
Working Capital	-39	-21	-30
Fixed Assets	33	20	24
Current Assets	22	46	39
Current Liabilities	30	N/A	34

Keens Guns
117 Bridgend Road Aberkenfig, Bridgend, CF32 9AP
Tel: 01656-720807 **Fax:** 01656-724889
E-mail: sales@keenstackleandguns.co.uk
Website: http://www.keenstackleandguns.co.uk
Directors: P. Keens (Prop)
No.of Employees: 1 - 10 **Product Groups:** 22, 32, 36, 38, 49, 68

Keith Lealand Services
41 Heol Morfa Village Farm Industrial Estate Pyle, Bridgend, CF33 6BP
Tel: 01656-742555 **Fax:** 01656-744261
Directors: K. Lealand (Prop)
Immediate Holding Company: TDH LOGISTICS LIMITED
Registration no: 06875907 **Date established:** 2011
Turnover: Up to £250,000 **No.of Employees:** 11 - 20 **Product Groups:** 22, 29, 30, 36, 37, 39, 49

M & M Catering Equipment
Unit 3 & 4 Heol Ffaldau, Brackla Industrial Estate, Bridgend, CF31 2AJ
Tel: 01656-654003
E-mail: steve@mmcatering.co.uk
Website: http://www.mmcatering.co.uk
Directors: S. Morris (Dir)
Immediate Holding Company: ON SITE PLUMBING LIMITED
Registration no: 03843083 **Date established:** 1999
No.of Employees: 1 - 10 **Product Groups:** 20, 40, 41

M P N Upvc Windowsdoors & Conservatories
10A EWENNY ROAD, Bridgend, CF31 3HL
Tel: 01656-648464 **Fax:** 01639-851287
E-mail: mpnwindows@aol.com
Website: http://www.mpn.com
Directors: P. Webster (Prop)
Registration no: 07048166 **Date established:** 1995 **Turnover:** £1m - £2m
No.of Employees: 51 - 100 **Product Groups:** 30, 33, 52

Metal Goods Wales Ltd
North Road Bridgend Industrial Estate, Bridgend, CF31 3TP
Tel: 01656-647755 **Fax:** 01656-647744
E-mail: sales@metalgoods.co.uk

see next page

***Metal Goods Wales Ltd** - Cont'd*

Directors: W. David (MD)
Immediate Holding Company: METAL GOODS (WALES) LIMITED
Registration no: 03169967 **VAT No.:** GB 666 9392 77
Date established: 1996 **No.of Employees:** 1 - 10 **Product Groups:** 66

Date of Accounts	May 12	May 11	May 10
Working Capital	398	352	370
Fixed Assets	37	42	30
Current Assets	906	885	819

Morplas Ltd

Unit 32 Sturmi Way Village Farm Industrial Estate, Pyle, Bridgend, CF33 6BZ
Tel: 01656-670650 **Fax:** 01656-670650
E-mail: morplas@aol.com
Website: http://www.morplas.co.uk
Directors: N. Morgan (MD)
Immediate Holding Company: MORPLAS LIMITED
Registration no: 05700522 **Date established:** 2006
No.of Employees: 1 - 10 **Product Groups:** 30, 48

Date of Accounts	Apr 11	Apr 10	Apr 09
Working Capital	-17	-0	-6
Fixed Assets	14	14	16
Current Assets	30	46	39

J W & E Morris & Son Ltd

South Road Bridgend Industrial Estate, Bridgend, CF31 3RB
Tel: 01656-653705 **Fax:** 01656-767187
E-mail: winston.hall@jwmorris.co.uk
Website: http://www.morrisgroup.co.uk
Directors: D. Kearle (MD), J. Kearle (Fin)
Managers: S. Thomas (Buyer), C. Willis (Mktg Serv Mgr)
Ultimate Holding Company: MORRIS MCLELLAN LIMITED
Immediate Holding Company: J.W. & E. MORRIS & SON LIMITED
Registration no: 01505158 **VAT No.:** GB 282 6871 25
Date established: 1980 **Turnover:** £20m - £50m
No.of Employees: 251 - 500 **Product Groups:** 35, 37, 38

Date of Accounts	Jun 11	Jun 10	Jun 09
Sales Turnover	25m	27m	30m
Pre Tax Profit/Loss	747	344	437
Working Capital	9m	8m	8m
Fixed Assets	1m	1m	1m
Current Assets	14m	12m	15m
Current Liabilities	1m	1m	2m

Morris Line Engineering

Main Avenue Brackla Industrial Estate, Bridgend, CF31 2AG
Tel: 01656-650680 **Fax:** 01656-768209
E-mail: brian.jones@morrisline.co.uk
Website: http://www.morrisline.co.uk
Bank(s): Barclays
Directors: B. Jones (Div)
Managers: R. Gray (Sales Prom Mgr), K. Wills, N. Jones
Immediate Holding Company: BRIDGEND CAR AUCTIONS LTD
Registration no: 05350131 **Date established:** 2005 **Turnover:** £2m - £5m
No.of Employees: 21 - 50 **Product Groups:** 37

Date of Accounts	Feb 11	Feb 10	Feb 09
Working Capital	8	17	20
Fixed Assets	1	1	1
Current Assets	22	20	26

Nodor International Ltd

Nodor House South Road, Bridgend Industrial Estate, Bridgend, CF31 3PT
Tel: 01656-653553 **Fax:** 01656-650468
E-mail: info@nodor-darts.co.uk
Website: http://www.reddragon.com
Bank(s): National Westminster
Directors: V. Bluck (MD)
Managers: C. James (Sales Admin)
Immediate Holding Company: NODOR INTERNATIONAL LIMITED
Registration no: 02886136 **VAT No.:** GB 133 4526 89
Date established: 1994 **Turnover:** £2m - £5m **No.of Employees:** 21 - 50
Product Groups: 49

Date of Accounts	Dec 11	Dec 10	Dec 09
Working Capital	1m	1m	1m
Fixed Assets	555	552	522
Current Assets	4m	4m	4m

P C M Business Improvement Ltd

2 Ty Merchant Pencoed, Bridgend, CF35 6PN
Tel: 01656-862916
E-mail: enquiries@pcmbusinessimprovement.co.uk
Website: http://www.pcmbusinessimprovement.co.uk
Directors: P. Mendez (Fin), P. Mendez (Dir)
Immediate Holding Company: PCM BUSINESS IMPROVEMENT LIMITED
Registration no: 06645368 **VAT No.:** GB 783 4783 83
Date established: 2008 **No.of Employees:** 1 - 10 **Product Groups:** 80

Date of Accounts	Mar 12	Mar 11	Mar 10
Working Capital	-18	-14	-25
Fixed Assets	20	23	26
Current Assets	12	16	12

Pencoed Refrigeration

15 Redlands Close Pencoed, Bridgend, CF35 6YU
Tel: 01656-862287
E-mail: frank.hughes1@virgin.net
Directors: F. Hughes (Prop)
Immediate Holding Company: BRIDGEND REFRIGERATION LIMITED
Registration no: 04555363 **Date established:** 2002
No.of Employees: 1 - 10 **Product Groups:** 36, 40

Photronics UK Ltd

1 Technology Drive, Bridgend, CF31 3LU
Tel: 01656-662171 **Fax:** 01656-656183
E-mail: wales@photronics.com
Website: http://www.photronics.com
Bank(s): National Westminster Bank Plc
Directors: R. Lloyd (Dir)
Ultimate Holding Company: PHOTRONICS INC (USA)
Immediate Holding Company: PHOTRONICS (UK) LIMITED
Registration no: 03121018 **VAT No.:** GB 438 6789 90
Date established: 1995 **Turnover:** £20m - £50m
No.of Employees: 101 - 250 **Product Groups:** 47

Date of Accounts	Oct 10	Oct 11	Nov 08
Sales Turnover	23m	27m	25m
Pre Tax Profit/Loss	5m	6m	3m
Working Capital	5m	6m	-12m
Fixed Assets	6m	6m	11m
Current Assets	10m	11m	14m
Current Liabilities	1m	2m	2m

Plascon Manufacturing

Brackla Industrial Estate, Bridgend, CF31 2AD
Tel: 01656-769761 **Fax:** 01656-769762
E-mail: stplynne@aol.com
Website: http://www.kellysearch.com/gb-company-5691049.html
Directors: L. Stephens (Dir)
Immediate Holding Company: PLASCON MANUFACTURING LIMITED
Registration no: 05005803 **VAT No.:** GB 826 6911 09
Date established: 2004 **Turnover:** £500,000 - £1m
No.of Employees: 1 - 10 **Product Groups:** 30

Date of Accounts	Mar 11	Mar 10	Mar 09
Working Capital	-145	-140	-105
Fixed Assets	48	38	13
Current Assets	144	164	132

Pressrite Engineering & Promotional Products Ltd

24 Ogmore Crescent Bridgend Industrial Estate, Bridgend, CF31 3TE
Tel: 01656-657067 **Fax:** 01656-645857
E-mail: pressrite@yahoo.co.uk
Website: http://www.pressrite.co.uk
Directors: M. Phillips (Dir)
Immediate Holding Company: PRESSRITE ENGINEERING LIMITED
Registration no: 01247226 **Date established:** 1976
No.of Employees: 11 - 20 **Product Groups:** 36, 37, 38

Date of Accounts	Apr 12	Apr 11	Apr 10
Working Capital	88	108	135
Fixed Assets	141	169	157
Current Assets	186	292	329

R P M Shopfront Manufacturers Ltd

14 Millers Avenue Brynmenyn Industrial Estate, Brynmenyn, Bridgend, CF32 9TD
Tel: 01656-724704 **Fax:** 01656-725924
E-mail: johnm@rpmshopfronts.co.uk
Website: http://www.rpmshopfronts.co.uk
Directors: J. Mitchell (MD)
Immediate Holding Company: R.P.M. SHOPFRONT MANUFACTURERS LIMITED
Registration no: 00988702 **Date established:** 1970
No.of Employees: 1 - 10 **Product Groups:** 26, 35

Date of Accounts	Aug 11	Aug 10	Aug 09
Working Capital	210	272	245
Fixed Assets	234	225	236
Current Assets	301	398	304

Ravenstock MSG Ltd

North Road Bridgend Industrial Estate, Bridgend, CF31 3TP
Tel: 01656-668713 **Fax:** 01656-767719
E-mail: info@ravenstock.co.uk
Website: http://www.ravenstock.co.uk
Directors: J. Robertson (Dir), R. Cogbill (Cust Serv)
Immediate Holding Company: RAVENSTOCK MSG LIMITED
Registration no: 04283040 **VAT No.:** GB 727 2893 07
Date established: 2001 **Turnover:** £500,000 - £1m
No.of Employees: 21 - 50 **Product Groups:** 35, 83

Renowheel Ltd

Block D Unit 2 Brackla Industrial Estate, Bridgend, CF31 2DB
Tel: 01656-657993 **Fax:** 01656-657993
E-mail: enquiries@renowheel.co.uk
Website: http://www.renowheel.co.uk
Directors: S. Rudd (Dir)
Immediate Holding Company: RENOWHEEL LIMITED
Registration no: 05596715 **Date established:** 2005
No.of Employees: 1 - 10 **Product Groups:** 46, 48

Date of Accounts	Sep 11	Sep 10	Sep 09
Working Capital	3	-3	-1
Fixed Assets	31	31	32
Current Assets	20	9	62

Rockit Specialists Ltd

Waterton Park Waterton, Bridgend, CF31 3PH
Tel: 01656-767222 **Fax:** 01656-769333
E-mail: info@rockitspecialists.com
Website: http://www.rockitspecialists.com
Directors: R. Dance (Dir)
Immediate Holding Company: ROCK I.T. SPECIALISTS LIMITED
Registration no: 06583990 **Date established:** 2008
Turnover: £250,000 - £500,000 **No.of Employees:** 21 - 50
Product Groups: 44, 85

Date of Accounts	May 11	May 10	May 09
Working Capital	18	14	3
Fixed Assets	16	6	7
Current Assets	93	68	26

Rockwool Rockpanel B V

Wern Tarw Rhiwceiliog Pencoed, Bridgend, CF35 6NY
Tel: 01656-863210 **Fax:** 01656-863611
E-mail: info@rockwool.co.uk
Website: http://www.rockpanel.co.uk
Directors: B. Roberts (MD), G. Rees (Fin)
Managers: J. Thomas (Purch Mgr), K. Bollington (Computer Mgr), C. Bligh (Publicity)
Ultimate Holding Company: ROCKWOOL INTERNATIONAL A/S (DENMARK)
Immediate Holding Company: ROCKWOOL LIMITED
Registration no: 00972252 **VAT No.:** GB 540 7071 68
Date established: 1970 **Turnover:** £75m - £125m
No.of Employees: 1 - 10 **Product Groups:** 33

Date of Accounts	Dec 11	Dec 10	Dec 09
Sales Turnover	97m	79m	82m
Pre Tax Profit/Loss	-4m	-11m	-19m
Working Capital	8m	4m	640
Fixed Assets	73m	81m	89m
Current Assets	24m	18m	19m
Current Liabilities	5m	5m	6m

Roma Medical Aids Ltd

York Road Bridgend Industrial Estate, Bridgend, CF31 3TB
Tel: 01656-674488 **Fax:** 01656-674499
E-mail: sales@romamedical.co.uk
Website: http://www.romamedical.co.uk
Bank(s): Midland, Bridgend
Directors: S. Dalton (MD), S. Dolton (MD)
Managers: S. Hughes, P. Prentice (Prod Mgr)
Ultimate Holding Company: INVAMED GROUP LIMITED
Immediate Holding Company: ROMA MEDICAL AIDS LIMITED
Registration no: 01869285 **VAT No.:** 763 0039 51 **Date established:** 1984
Turnover: £10m - £20m **No.of Employees:** 51 - 100 **Product Groups:** 26, 36, 38, 39

Date of Accounts	Nov 11	Nov 10	Nov 09
Sales Turnover	12m	12m	12m
Pre Tax Profit/Loss	219	383	477
Working Capital	7m	7m	7m
Fixed Assets	442	480	452
Current Assets	8m	8m	9m
Current Liabilities	233	219	189

RSS Group

Unit 32A/32B Village Farm Industrial Estate Pyle, Bridgend, CF33 6BL
Tel: 01656-740074 **Fax:** 01656-747057
E-mail: steve@rssgroup.co.uk
Website: http://www.rssgroup.co.uk
No.of Employees: 11 - 20 **Product Groups:** 23, 30, 35, 37, 38, 39, 45, 48, 52, 66, 67, 84, 85, 86

Severn Trent Services

2 Technology Drive, Bridgend, CF31 3NA
Tel: 01656-647557 **Fax:** 01656-646525
E-mail: tim.down@stl-analytical.co.uk
Website: http://www.stsanalytical.com
Managers: J. Rogers (Mgr)
Ultimate Holding Company: HYDER P.L.C.
Registration no: 02212959 **Date established:** 1992
No.of Employees: 51 - 100 **Product Groups:** 54, 85

Sony Manufacturing

Pencoed Technology Park, Bridgend, CF35 5HZ
Tel: 01656-860666 **Fax:** 01656-861122
E-mail: info@sony.com
Website: http://www.solidisk.com
Managers: C. Norris (Purch Mgr), D. Lewis-whelan (Personnel), W. Langdon (Fin Mgr), G. Kelly (Chief Mgr), D. Morgan (Tech Serv Mgr)
Immediate Holding Company: 10 LIMITED
Registration no: 06493647 **Date established:** 1997
Turnover: £250,000 - £500,000 **No.of Employees:** 251 - 500
Product Groups: 37

Date of Accounts	Dec 10	Dec 09	Dec 08
Working Capital	92	109	21
Fixed Assets	4	2	28
Current Assets	128	194	135
Current Liabilities	N/A	N/A	63

Spectrum Technologies Ltd

Western Avenue Bridgend Industrial Estate, Bridgend, CF31 3RT
Tel: 01656-655437 **Fax:** 01656-655920
E-mail: sales@spectrumtech.com
Website: http://www.spectrumtech.com
Bank(s): Lloyds
Directors: P. Dickenson (Dir), J. Mehan (Sales & Mktg)
Managers: L. Hopkins (Purch Mgr), R. Briggs (Fin Mgr)
Immediate Holding Company: SPECTRUM TECHNOLOGIES PLC
Registration no: 02385991 **VAT No.:** 530 1463 88 **Date established:** 1989
Turnover: £5m - £10m **No.of Employees:** 51 - 100 **Product Groups:** 37, 38, 44, 46

Date of Accounts	Dec 09	Dec 08	Mar 12
Sales Turnover	8m	7m	8m
Pre Tax Profit/Loss	452	257	809
Working Capital	2m	2m	4m
Fixed Assets	738	912	599
Current Assets	5m	5m	5m
Current Liabilities	1m	1m	1m

Steel Design Services

Unit 21 Ogmore Cresent Bridgend Industrial Estate, Bridgend, CF31 3TE
Tel: 01656-657227 **Fax:** 01656-657163
Directors: J. Cattle (Jt MD), H. Prescott (Fin), J. Prescott (Dir), S. Prescott (Jt MD)
Immediate Holding Company: MIRROR IMAGE PAINT SPECIALISTS LTD
Registration no: 01241350 **Date established:** 2011
Turnover: Up to £250,000 **No.of Employees:** 1 - 10 **Product Groups:** 48, 51, 84

Sulzer Dowding & Mills

Unit A39 Kent Road Bridgend Industrial Estate, Bridgend, CF31 3TU
Tel: 01656-645013 **Fax:** 01656-655080
E-mail: darren.steward@sulzer.com
Website: http://www.sulzer.com
Managers: D. Steward (Mgr), P. Warlock (District Mgr)
Immediate Holding Company: CASTLE SUPPORT SERVICES PLC
Registration no: 00160837 **Date established:** 1997
Turnover: £250,000 - £500,000 **No.of Employees:** 21 - 50
Product Groups: 37, 44, 45, 48, 84, 85

Truplate Ltd

25 Ogmore Crescent Bridgend Industrial Estate, Bridgend, CF31 3TE
Tel: 01656-655499 **Fax:** 01656-655960
E-mail: trueplates@aol.com
Directors: C. Storey (MD)
Immediate Holding Company: TRUPLATE LIMITED
Registration no: 03447588 **Date established:** 1997
No.of Employees: 1 - 10 **Product Groups:** 46, 48

Date of Accounts	Oct 11	Oct 10	Oct 09
Working Capital	61	67	64
Fixed Assets	37	19	11
Current Assets	96	101	93

Tudor Signs

6 CWRT Y Coed Brackla, Bridgend, CF31 2ST
Tel: 01656-650901 **Fax:** 01656-650901
Website: http://www.tudorsigns.co.uk
Directors: L. Willey (Prop)
Date established: 2000 **No.of Employees:** 1 - 10 **Product Groups:** 30, 39, 40

Tyco Waterworks Atlantic Plastics Ltd

Coytrahene Close Brackla Industrial Estate, Bridgend, CF31 2AX
Tel: 01656-654067 **Fax:** 01656-768705
E-mail: info@atlantic-plastics.co.uk
Website: http://www.tyco-valves.com
Directors: J. Fry (Fin), J. Van Ooijen (Dir)
Managers: K. Williams (Personnel), W. Elms (Purch Mgr), P. Hurn (Mktg Serv Mgr)

Immediate Holding Company: EDWARD BARBER & COMPANY LTD
Registration no: 01154347 **Turnover:** £20m - £50m
No.of Employees: 251 - 500 **Product Groups:** 30, 48, 66

Venteckductwork Services

Unit 60 Village Farm Road Village Farm Industrial Estate, Pyle, Bridgend, CF33 6BL
Tel: 01656-749749 **Fax:** 01656-749751
E-mail: venteck@lineone.net
Directors: S. Davies (Ptnr)
Immediate Holding Company: GUARDIAN GLOBAL TECHNOLOGY GROUP LTD
Date established: 2003 **No.of Employees:** 11 - 20 **Product Groups:** 37, 40, 48

Williams Fasteners Wales

Unit 1-2 Green Court Village Farm Road Village Farm Industrial Estate, Pyle, Bridgend, CF33 6BN
Tel: 01656-745155 **Fax:** 01656-746227
E-mail: sales@williamsfasteners.com
Website: http://www.williamsfasteners.com
Managers: L. Morrissey (District Mgr)
Ultimate Holding Company: REDWINGER HOLDINGS LIMITED
Immediate Holding Company: J. J. WILLIAMS (PAINTING SERVICES) LIMITED
Date established: 1984 **No.of Employees:** 1 - 10 **Product Groups:** 35

Winmau Dartboard Co. Ltd

South Road Bridgend Industrial Estate, Bridgend, CF31 3PT
Tel: 01656-767042 **Fax:** 01656-650468
E-mail: info@winmau.com
Website: http://www.winmau.com
Directors: V. Bluck (Grp Chief Exec)
Managers: S. Clinckenburg (Admin Off), A. Milton (District Mgr)
Ultimate Holding Company: WINMAU HOLDINGS LIMITED
Immediate Holding Company: WINMAU DARTBOARD COMPANY LIMITED
Registration no: 00624584 **Date established:** 1959 **Turnover:** £2m - £5m
No.of Employees: 21 - 50 **Product Groups:** 49

Date of Accounts	Dec 11	Dec 10	Dec 09
Working Capital	857	770	712
Current Assets	2m	2m	2m

Wolseley Drain Centre (a division of Wolseley)

Unit 35-36 Bennett Street Bridgend Industrial Estate, Bridgend, CF31 3SH
Tel: 01656-661331 **Fax:** 01656-767210
E-mail: mark.williams@wolseley.co.uk
Website: http://www.wolseley.co.uk
Managers: M. Williams (Sales Prom Mgr)
Immediate Holding Company: DRAIN CENTER LIMITED
Registration no: 00424702 **Date established:** 1946 **Turnover:** £2m - £5m
No.of Employees: 1 - 10 **Product Groups:** 30, 31, 36

Wrekin Construction Co. Ltd

49 Main Avenue Brackla Industrial Estate, Bridgend, CF31 2XJ
Tel: 01656-668018 **Fax:** 01656- 768148
E-mail: postmaster@wrekin.co.uk
Website: http://www.wrekin.co.uk
Directors: D. N'neill (Dir)
Immediate Holding Company: NARBETH'S MECHANICAL SERVICES LIMITED
Registration no: 00664676 **Date established:** 1998
Turnover: £75m - £125m **No.of Employees:** 1 - 10 **Product Groups:** 51

Date of Accounts	Jun 12	Jun 11	Jun 10
Working Capital	60	-56	-67
Fixed Assets	118	128	139
Current Assets	584	704	754

Gwynedd

Brynteg

Dragon Fire

Bryn Mair Yard, Brynteg, LL78 8QA
Tel: 01248-853399 **Fax:** 01248-853374
E-mail: sales@dragonfirewales.co.uk
Website: http://www.dragonfirewales.co.uk
Directors: J. Smart (Prop)
Date established: 1998 **No.of Employees:** 1 - 10 **Product Groups:** 38, 42

Clwyd

Buckley

Buckley Industrial

1 Catheralls Industrial Estate Brookhill Way, Buckley, CH7 3PS
Tel: 01244-544080 **Fax:** 01244-549999
E-mail: sales@buckley-industrial.co.uk
Website: http://www.buckley-industrial.co.uk
Managers: S. Dransfield (Chief Mgr)
No.of Employees: 1 - 10 **Product Groups:** 36, 38, 51, 66

D B E Sales

Unit C1 Spencer Industrial Estate Liverpool Road, Buckley, CH7 3LY
Tel: 01244-540400 **Fax:** 01244-540400
E-mail: simonj.jones@yahoo.co.uk
Directors: S. Jones (Prop)
Immediate Holding Company: INDUSTRIAL STEEL SUPPLIERS LIMITED
Date established: 1989 **No.of Employees:** 1 - 10 **Product Groups:** 35

North West Enamellers

Catheralls Industrial Estate Brookhill Way, Buckley, CH7 3PS
Tel: 01244-549185 **Fax:** 01244-544739
E-mail: sales@northwestenamellers.co.uk
Website: http://www.northwestenamellers.co.uk

Directors: S. Jones (Ptnr)
Immediate Holding Company: MIL-TEK EXPRESS LIMITED
Registration no: 01476869 **Date established:** 2000
Turnover: Up to £250,000 **No.of Employees:** 1 - 10 **Product Groups:** 46, 48

Date of Accounts	Jan 12	Jan 11	Jan 10
Working Capital	626	1m	1m
Fixed Assets	953	981	874
Current Assets	688	2m	2m

Powys

Builth Wells

D M Morgan Ltd

4 Penybryn, Builth Wells, LD2 3LF
Tel: 01982-552712
E-mail: lindymogs@yahoo.co.uk
Directors: D. Morgan (MD)
Immediate Holding Company: D.M. MORGAN (MOGS) LIMITED
Registration no: 04713518 **Date established:** 2003
No.of Employees: 1 - 10 **Product Groups:** 35

Date of Accounts	Mar 11	Mar 10	Mar 08
Working Capital	17	32	22
Fixed Assets	5	6	9
Current Assets	110	85	66

N J Guns

2a High Street, Builth Wells, LD2 3DN
Tel: 01982-552174 **Fax:** 01982-553602
E-mail: enquiries@njguns.co.uk
Website: http://www.njguns.co.uk
Directors: N. Jones (Prop)
Date established: 1982 **No.of Employees:** 1 - 10 **Product Groups:** 36, 39, 40

Dyfed

Burry Port

Huntingdon Fusion Techniques

Stukeley Meadow Gwscwm Road, Burry Port, SA16 0BU
Tel: 01554-836836 **Fax:** 01554-836837
E-mail: jonlewis@huntingdonfusion.com
Website: http://www.huntingdonfusion.com
Directors: J. Lewis (MD)
Registration no: 01289542 **Date established:** 2001 **Turnover:** £2m - £5m
No.of Employees: 1 - 10 **Product Groups:** 34, 35, 46, 48, 67

Date of Accounts	Jun 08	Jun 07	Jun 06
Working Capital	90	72	53
Fixed Assets	283	289	240
Current Assets	326	330	288
Current Liabilities	237	258	235
Total Share Capital	5	5	5

Pipestoppers

Stukeley Meadow, Burry Port, SA16 0BU
Tel: 01554-836836 **Fax:** 01554-836837
E-mail: pipe@pipestoppers.net
Website: http://www.pipestoppers.net
Directors: D. Sewell (MD)
Registration no: 01289542 **No.of Employees:** 1 - 10 **Product Groups:** 29, 35, 46, 66

Date of Accounts	Jan 08	Jan 07	Jan 06
Working Capital	-95	36	-19
Fixed Assets	67	59	69
Current Assets	170	143	136
Current Liabilities	264	107	155
Total Share Capital	30	30	30

Seaswan Products

Unit 1.12 Parc Dyfatty Park, Burry Port, SA16 0FB
Tel: 01554-834884 **Fax:** 01554-772500
E-mail: sales@seaswan.co.uk
Website: http://www.seaswan.co.uk
Managers: M. Hofton (Mgr)
Immediate Holding Company: H QUBED LIMITED
Registration no: 04680870 **Date established:** 2003
No.of Employees: 1 - 10 **Product Groups:** 24, 40, 83

Date of Accounts	Mar 11	Mar 10	Mar 09
Working Capital	6	-11	-9
Fixed Assets	6	8	6
Current Assets	29	28	43

Gwynedd

Caernarfon

Arfon Dwyfor Training Ltd

Maesincla, Caernarfon, LL55 1RS
Tel: 01286-677275 **Fax:** 01286-677250
E-mail: enquiry@adt-ltd.com
Website: http://www.adt-ltd.com
Directors: J. Roberts (MD), D. Evans (Dir)
Managers: B. Jones (Contracts Mgr)
Immediate Holding Company: ARFON DWYFOR TRAINING LIMITED
Registration no: 01751129 **VAT No.:** GB 420 0309 21
Date established: 1983 **No.of Employees:** 21 - 50 **Product Groups:** 86, 87

Date of Accounts	Jul 11	Jul 10	Jul 09
Working Capital	3m	3m	3m
Fixed Assets	106	123	148
Current Assets	4m	3m	3m

Castle Marine Ltd

Castle Boatyard The Harbour, Caernarfon, LL54 5RS
Tel: 01286-674322 **Fax:** 01286-678094
Website: http://www.castlemarine.co.uk
Directors: C. Williams (MD)
Immediate Holding Company: CASTLE MARINE LIMITED
Registration no: 05561887 **Date established:** 2005
No.of Employees: 1 - 10 **Product Groups:** 35, 36, 39

Date of Accounts	Mar 12	Mar 11	Sep 08
Working Capital	14	7	N/A
Current Assets	33	18	N/A

Designer Signs

Unit 7 Penygroes Industrial Estate Penygroes, Caernarfon, LL54 6DB
Tel: 01286-882222 **Fax:** 01286-882222
Website: http://www.designersigns.uk.com
Directors: M. Thatcher (Prop)
Immediate Holding Company: DESIGNER SIGNS UK LIMITED
Registration no: 06535503 **Date established:** 2008
No.of Employees: 1 - 10 **Product Groups:** 27, 30, 31

Date of Accounts	Mar 11	Mar 10	Mar 09
Working Capital	-66	-51	-45
Fixed Assets	74	66	67
Current Assets	53	33	15

Dragon Safety Systems

Brynrefail, Caernarfon, LL55 3NR
Tel: 01286-685470 **Fax:** 01286-685473
E-mail: info@rat-uk.com
Website: http://www.rat.ca
Managers: J. Arkless
Immediate Holding Company: DRAGON SAFETY SYSTEMS UK LIMITED
Registration no: 05701552 **Date established:** 2006
No.of Employees: 1 - 10 **Product Groups:** 40, 54, 84, 86

Date of Accounts	Dec 08	Dec 07	Feb 11
Working Capital	-27	N/A	1
Fixed Assets	27	N/A	13
Current Assets	18	N/A	35

Snowdonia Windows & Doors Gwynedd Ltd

Old PO Garage Crown Street, Caernarfon, LL55 1SY
Tel: 01286-672935 **Fax:** 01286-677751
E-mail: wynne@snowdoniawindows.wanadoo.co.uk
Website: http://www.snowdoniawindows.co.uk
Directors: R. Griffiths (MD)
Immediate Holding Company: SNOWDONIA WINDOWS & DOORS (GWYNEDD) LIMITED
Registration no: 02227340 **VAT No.:** GB 179 0940 11
Date established: 1988 **Turnover:** £2m - £5m **No.of Employees:** 1 - 10
Product Groups: 30

Date of Accounts	Mar 11	Mar 10	Mar 09
Working Capital	-137	-126	-122
Fixed Assets	248	246	251
Current Assets	78	126	132

Weldpar Cymru Wales

Pant-Y-Waun Waunfawr, Caernarfon, LL55 4YY
Tel: 01286-650720 **Fax:** 01286-650720
E-mail: info@weldpar.co.uk
Website: http://www.weldpar.co.uk
Directors: S. Parry (Prop)
Date established: 1992 **No.of Employees:** 1 - 10 **Product Groups:** 46

Mid-Glamorgan

Caerphilly

AE&E MII Ltd

Unit 20 Plant Glas Industrial Estate, Bedwas, Caerphilly, CF83 8DR
Tel: 029-2085 7800 **Fax:** 029-2085 7839
E-mail: info@aee-mii.co.uk
Website: http://www.aee-group.com
Bank(s): Barclays, London
Directors: P. Lewis (Co Sec), D. Porter (Sales), M. Wilkins (MD), P. Lewis (Co Sec)
Managers: G. Banhan (I.T. Exec)
Immediate Holding Company: BLUE BOX LTD
Registration no: 01817547 **Date established:** 1999
Turnover: £50m - £75m **No.of Employees:** 11 - 20 **Product Groups:** 40, 42, 84

Date of Accounts	Sep 99	Sep 98	Sep 97
Sales Turnover	N/A	N/A	21
Pre Tax Profit/Loss	-1	-1	2
Working Capital	35	36	37
Current Assets	36	36	49
Current Liabilities	1	1	12

Air Conditioning Systems Wales Ltd

Bedwas House Greenway, Bedwas, Caerphilly, CF83 8DW
Tel: 029-2086 6700
E-mail: jamiedownes@btconnect.com
Website: http://www.airconditioningwales.co
Directors: J. Rees (Co Sec), C. Lane (Dir)
Immediate Holding Company: AIR CONDITIONING SYSTEMS WALES LIMITED
Registration no: 05502827 **Date established:** 2005
No.of Employees: 1 - 10 **Product Groups:** 40, 66

Date of Accounts	Jul 11	Jul 10	Jul 09
Working Capital	19	18	28
Fixed Assets	8	12	16
Current Assets	47	56	67
Current Liabilities	14	6	4

Angel

Pantglas Industrial Estate Bedwas, Caerphilly, CF83 8XD
Tel: 029-2088 4444 **Fax:** 029-2088 7005
E-mail: jeremy.procter@procterbedwas.co.uk
Directors: J. Procter (MD)
Date established: 2000 **No.of Employees:** 21 - 50 **Product Groups:** 26, 35

ATM Wales Ltd

17 & 18 Venture Wales Drive Bedwas House Industrial Estate, Bedwas, Caerphilly, CF83 8GF
Tel: 029-2085 2112
E-mail: andrew@a-t-m.org.uk
Website: http://www.hottubsandthings.co.uk
Directors: M. Evans Jones (Fin), A. Evans Jones (MD)
Immediate Holding Company: ATM (WALES) LIMITED
Registration no: 04996615 **Date established:** 2003
Turnover: £250,000 - £500,000 **No.of Employees:** 1 - 10
Product Groups: 25, 30, 38, 52, 66

Date of Accounts	Mar 11	Mar 10	Mar 09
Working Capital	9	7	10
Fixed Assets	2	3	4
Current Assets	49	42	56

Caerphilly Metal Polishers

1 The Rhos Bedwas Road, Caerphilly, CF83 3AU
Tel: 029-2086 7837 **Fax:** 029-2086 7837
Directors: P. Skym (Prop)
Date established: 1971 **Turnover:** Up to £250,000
No.of Employees: 1 - 10 **Product Groups:** 48

Checkfire

Unit 12 Pontygwindy Industrial Estate, Caerphilly, CF83 3HU
Tel: 029-2086 8333 **Fax:** 029-2085 0627
E-mail: sales@checkfire.co.uk
Website: http://www.checkfire.co.uk
Bank(s): Barclays, Cardiff
Directors: A. Robins (Snr Part), D. Robins (Ptnr)
Ultimate Holding Company: P H GLATFELTER CAERPHILLY INC (USA)
Immediate Holding Company: P H GLATFELTER CAERPHILLY LIMITED
Registration no: 05285231 **VAT No.:** GB 282 5922 39
Date established: 2004 **Turnover:** £20m - £50m
No.of Employees: 11 - 20 **Product Groups:** 32, 40, 49, 52

Date of Accounts	Dec 11	Dec 10	Dec 09
Sales Turnover	31m	31m	27m
Pre Tax Profit/Loss	-464	88	-3m
Working Capital	5m	5m	4m
Fixed Assets	4m	4m	4m
Current Assets	9m	8m	9m
Current Liabilities	501	604	476

D S Smith Recycling

Unit 2 Pantglas Industrial Estate Bedwas, Caerphilly, CF83 8DR
Tel: 029-2086 7804 **Fax:** 029-2086 7437
E-mail: phil.herbert@severnside.com
Website: http://www.7side.com
Bank(s): National Westminster
Managers: P. Herbert (Mgr)
Ultimate Holding Company: DS SMITH PLC
Immediate Holding Company: DS SMITH HOLDINGS LTD
Registration no: 00489560 **VAT No.:** GB 479 5202 22
Turnover: £20m - £50m **No.of Employees:** 21 - 50 **Product Groups:** 27, 66

D S Smith Recycling

Ty Gwyrdd 11 Beddau Way, Caerphilly, CF83 2AX
Tel: 029-2071 8400 **Fax:** 029-2069 2120
E-mail: enquire@dssmithrecycling.com
Website: http://www.dssmithrecycling.com
Bank(s): Barclays
Directors: P. Mcguinness (MD), A. Steele (Fin), F. Patel (Pers)
Managers: T. Price (Mktg Serv Mgr), C. Jones (Tech Serv Mgr), D. Evans (Comptroller), J. Malone
Immediate Holding Company: BPB PAPER BOARD
Registration no: SC034256 **VAT No.:** GB 438 3065 50
No.of Employees: 51 - 100 **Product Groups:** 27, 66

D & T Mobility Services

112 Mill Road, Caerphilly, CF83 3FE
Tel: 029-2088 1341 **Fax:** 029-2085 1116
E-mail: david@stairlifts-wales.co.uk
Website: http://www.stairlifts-wales.co.uk
Directors: D. Dodge (Prop)
No.of Employees: 1 - 10 **Product Groups:** 24, 30, 38

Direct Plant Supplies Ltd

2 Pen-Y-Dre, Caerphilly, CF83 2NZ
Tel: 029-2088 0088 **Fax:** 029-2085 0088
E-mail: info@directplant.co.uk
Website: http://www.directplant.co.uk
Directors: P. Taylor (Fin)
Immediate Holding Company: DIRECT PLANT SUPPLIES LIMITED
Registration no: 04124995 **Date established:** 2000
No.of Employees: 1 - 10 **Product Groups:** 37

Date of Accounts	Jan 12	Jan 11	Jan 10
Working Capital	8	N/A	-9
Fixed Assets	4	5	10
Current Assets	51	40	55

DS Smith Paper Limited

Ty Gwyrdd 11 Beddau Way, Caerphilly, CF83 2AX
Tel: 029-2071 8400 **Fax:** 0114-243 7208
E-mail: sales@sevenside.com
Website: http://www.dssmithrecycling.com
Bank(s): National Westminer
Directors: J. Malone (Sales), P. McGuinness (MD)
Managers: S. Leak (Mgr)
Ultimate Holding Company: David S. Smith P.L.C.
Immediate Holding Company: St. Regis Paper Co Ltd
Registration no: 00058614 **VAT No.:** GB 479 5202 22
Turnover: £20m - £50m **No.of Employees:** 21 - 50 **Product Groups:** 66

Ecolab Ltd

Caerphilly Business Park, Caerphilly, CF83 3ED
Tel: 029-2085 2000 **Fax:** 029-2086 5969
Website: http://www.ecolab.com
Directors: T. Browne (Dir)
Managers: S. Carol (Chief Acct)
Ultimate Holding Company: ECOLAB INC (USA)
Immediate Holding Company: ECOLAB LIMITED
Registration no: 00649192 **Date established:** 1960
No.of Employees: 21 - 50 **Product Groups:** 07, 32, 52

Date of Accounts	Nov 11	Nov 10	Nov 09
Sales Turnover	107m	104m	100m
Pre Tax Profit/Loss	-499	-589	-4m
Working Capital	931	4m	3m
Fixed Assets	27m	30m	34m
Current Assets	45m	45m	38m
Current Liabilities	18m	16m	16m

Eriez Magnetics Europe Ltd

Bedwas House Industrial Estate Bedwas, Caerphilly, CF83 8YG
Tel: 029-2086 8501 **Fax:** 029-2085 1314
E-mail: info@eriezeurope.co.uk
Website: http://www.eriez.com
Bank(s): HSBC
Directors: J. Jamieson (Fin), J. Curwen (MD)
Managers: G. Canhan (Chief Buyer), G. Meese (Sales Prom Mgr), C. Little (Personnel), D. Lloyd (Mktg Serv Mgr)
Ultimate Holding Company: ERIEZ MANUFACTURING CO (USA)
Immediate Holding Company: ERIEZ MAGNETICS EUROPE LIMITED
Registration no: 01397255 **VAT No.:** GB 315 3491 73
Date established: 1978 **Turnover:** £10m - £20m
No.of Employees: 101 - 250 **Product Groups:** 37, 38, 42, 45, 67

Date of Accounts	Dec 11	Dec 10	Dec 09
Sales Turnover	16m	12m	13m
Pre Tax Profit/Loss	2m	1m	2m
Working Capital	6m	6m	5m
Fixed Assets	1m	2m	2m
Current Assets	9m	7m	6m
Current Liabilities	3m	900	880

Fireshield Sprinklers

Unit 10 Poplar Road, Caerphilly, CF83 1LF
Tel: 029-2088 4000 **Fax:** 029-2085 0851
Directors: J. Soos (Dir)
Immediate Holding Company: FIRESHIELD SPRINKLERS LIMITED
Registration no: 04577738 **Date established:** 2002
No.of Employees: 1 - 10 **Product Groups:** 38, 42

Date of Accounts	Oct 11	Oct 10	Oct 09
Working Capital	-5	-6	32
Fixed Assets	27	29	37
Current Assets	194	140	145

Garran Lockers Ltd

Garran House Nantgarw Road, Caerphilly, CF83 1AQ
Tel: 08456-588600 **Fax:** 08456-588601
E-mail: info@garran-lockers.co.uk
Website: http://www.garran-lockers.co.uk
Bank(s): National Westminster Bank Plc
Directors: N. Duggan (Fin)
Managers: D. Phelps, J. Gloria
Immediate Holding Company: GARRAN LOCKERS LIMITED
Registration no: 03344995 **VAT No.:** GB 133 4076 94
Date established: 1997 **Turnover:** £5m - £10m
No.of Employees: 51 - 100 **Product Groups:** 26, 35, 36, 49

Date of Accounts	Apr 11	Apr 10	Apr 09
Sales Turnover	N/A	N/A	6m
Pre Tax Profit/Loss	N/A	N/A	110
Working Capital	-470	-426	-343
Fixed Assets	2m	2m	2m
Current Assets	2m	1m	1m
Current Liabilities	N/A	N/A	703

Hydro Aluminium Extrusion Ltd

Pantglas Industrial Estate Bedwas, Caerphilly, CF83 8DR
Tel: 029-2085 4600 **Fax:** 029-2086 3728
E-mail: tracey.gifford@hydro.com
Website: http://www.hydro.com/extrusion/uk
Directors: P. Randle (Pers), H. Hargen (MD)
Managers: J. Norman, T. Gifford (Mktg Serv Mgr)
Ultimate Holding Company: NORSK HYDRO ASA (NORWAY)
Immediate Holding Company: HYDRO ALUMINIUM EXTRUSION LIMITED
Registration no: 00961843 **VAT No.:** GB 134 6357 70
Date established: 1969 **Turnover:** £50m - £75m
No.of Employees: 101 - 250 **Product Groups:** 34, 38, 44, 46, 48, 84

Date of Accounts	Dec 11	Dec 10	Dec 09
Sales Turnover	73m	67m	61m
Pre Tax Profit/Loss	-1m	-2m	-6m
Working Capital	11m	12m	12m
Fixed Assets	7m	7m	9m
Current Assets	29m	31m	28m
Current Liabilities	3m	3m	4m

J J Castings Investments (Heat Treatment) Ltd

Caerphilly Business Park Van Road, Caerphilly, CF83 3EL
Tel: 029-2088 7837 **Fax:** 029-2086 1900
E-mail: accounts@jjcastings.com
Website: http://www.jjcastings.co.uk
Bank(s): Barclays
Directors: I. Bermudez (Dir)
Immediate Holding Company: J.J.CASTINGS INVESTMENTS(HEAT TREATMENT)LIMITED
Registration no: 00740897 **VAT No.:** GB 615 7984 06
Date established: 1962 **Turnover:** £2m - £5m **No.of Employees:** 11 - 20
Product Groups: 48

Date of Accounts	Apr 12	Apr 11	Apr 10
Working Capital	285	287	289
Fixed Assets	290	287	305
Current Assets	355	351	339

J R Industries Ltd

1 Sir Alfred Owen Way Pontygwindy Industrial Estate, Caerphilly, CF83 3HU
Tel: 029-2085 7630 **Fax:** 029-2085 7633
E-mail: julial@jrindustries.co.uk
Website: http://www.jrindustries.co.uk
Bank(s): Barclays
Directors: R. Howard (Fin), J. Lovegrove (Co Sec)
Managers: K. Hopkins (Tech Serv Mgr), P. Challoner (Sales Prom Mgr), A. Edwards (Purch Mgr)
Ultimate Holding Company: CAXTON PLACE HOLDINGS LIMITED
Immediate Holding Company: JR INDUSTRIES HOLDINGS LIMITED
Registration no: 03761528 **VAT No.:** GB 133 4081 04
Date established: 1999 **Turnover:** £5m - £10m
No.of Employees: 51 - 100 **Product Groups:** 35, 39

Date of Accounts	Dec 11	Dec 10	Dec 09
Pre Tax Profit/Loss	N/A	N/A	500
Working Capital	-29	-29	-29
Fixed Assets	5m	5m	5m

Kenton Flooring

Woodpecker House 29 Pantglas Industrial Estate, Bedwas, Caerphilly, CF83 8DR
Tel: 029-2088 8223 **Fax:** 029-2088 1694
E-mail: info@kentonfloors.co.uk
Website: http://www.woodpeckerflooring.co.uk
Directors: N. Ker (MD)
Immediate Holding Company: WOODPECKER TRADING CO LIMITED
Date established: 1996 **No.of Employees:** 11 - 20 **Product Groups:** 36, 40

Date of Accounts	Jul 11	Jul 10	Jul 09
Working Capital	650	635	599
Fixed Assets	985	967	1m
Current Assets	2m	1m	1m

Lenstec Ltd

Unit 8 Bedwas Business Centre Bedwas, Caerphilly, CF83 8DU
Tel: 029-2088 3009 **Fax:** 029-2088 9798
E-mail: sales@lenstec.co.uk
Website: http://www.lenstec.co.uk
Directors: E. Arbuthnot (Fin), M. Burroughs (Sales)
Managers: G. Donovan (Chief Acct), P. Bennett (Tech Serv Mgr)
Immediate Holding Company: LENSTEC LIMITED
Registration no: 01734416 **Date established:** 1983
Turnover: £10m - £20m **No.of Employees:** 51 - 100 **Product Groups:** 37, 38, 65

Date of Accounts	Apr 12	Apr 11	Apr 10
Sales Turnover	17m	11m	N/A
Pre Tax Profit/Loss	746	318	N/A
Working Capital	804	193	372
Fixed Assets	1m	1m	798
Current Assets	6m	5m	2m
Current Liabilities	3m	2m	N/A

Nuaire Ltd

Western Industrial Estate Lon-Y-Llyn, Caerphilly, CF83 1NA
Tel: 029-2088 5911 **Fax:** 029-2088 7033
E-mail: info@nuaire.co.uk
Website: http://www.nuaire.co.uk
Bank(s): Barclays
Managers: M. Huxtable
Ultimate Holding Company: NU-OVAL ACQUISITIONS 1 LIMITED
Immediate Holding Company: NUAIRE LIMITED
Registration no: 00877308 **VAT No.:** GB 615 9079 25
Date established: 1966 **Turnover:** £20m - £50m
No.of Employees: 251 - 500 **Product Groups:** 40

Date of Accounts	Sep 11	Sep 10	Sep 09
Sales Turnover	52m	45m	47m
Pre Tax Profit/Loss	7m	7m	8m
Working Capital	52m	44m	37m
Fixed Assets	10m	11m	11m
Current Assets	64m	53m	46m
Current Liabilities	4m	2m	2m

Pregis Rigid Packaging Ltd

10 Sir Alfred Owen Way Pontygwindy Industrial Estate, Caerphilly, CF83 2WL
Tel: 029-2085 8900 **Fax:** 029-2085 8909
E-mail: nbridge@pregis.com
Website: http://www.pregis.com
Bank(s): National Westminster Bank Plc
Managers: N. Bridge (Factory Mgr)
Immediate Holding Company: PREGIS RIGID PACKAGING LIMITED
Registration no: SC121847 **Date established:** 1989
No.of Employees: 21 - 50 **Product Groups:** 27, 30, 35, 40, 42, 48, 66

Procter Machinery Guarding Ltd

11 Pantglas Indl-Est Bedwas, Caerphilly, CF83 8XD
Tel: 029-2088 2222 **Fax:** 029- 20887005
E-mail: jeremy.procter@procterbedwas.co.uk
Website: http://www.machinesafety.co.uk
Directors: J. Procter (MD), J. Lamb (Mkt Research), J. Proctor (MD)
Managers: A. Davies (I.T. Exec), N. Fitzgerald (Purch Mgr), A. Simmons (Sales & Mktg Mg)
No.of Employees: 51 - 100 **Product Groups:** 30, 35, 40, 49

Remar Safety Services Ltd

Unit 1 Poplar Road, Caerphilly, CF83 1LF
Tel: 029-2086 0416 **Fax:** 029-2088 9194
E-mail: gregjewell@tiscali.co.uk
Directors: G. Jewell (Dir)
Immediate Holding Company: REMAR (SAFETY SERVICES) LIMITED
Registration no: 01330649 **VAT No.:** GB 315 0065 08
Date established: 1977 **Turnover:** Up to £250,000
No.of Employees: 1 - 10 **Product Groups:** 24, 35, 39, 40, 49, 54

Date of Accounts	Dec 11	Dec 10	Dec 09
Sales Turnover	N/A	N/A	235
Pre Tax Profit/Loss	N/A	N/A	34
Working Capital	38	10	-32
Fixed Assets	90	74	78
Current Assets	103	52	27
Current Liabilities	N/A	N/A	15

Safecontractor

Brecon House, Caerphilly Business Park, Caerphilly, CF83 3GG
Tel: 029-2026 6242 **Fax:** 029-2080 8547
E-mail: sc.contractorsales@safecontractor.com
Website: http://www.safecontractor.com
Managers: K. Townley ()
Registration no: 07181296 **Date established:** 2003 **Turnover:**
No.of Employees: 51 - 100 **Product Groups:** 80, 84

Spotnails Ltd

14 Pantglas Industrial Estate Bedwas, Caerphilly, CF83 8DR
Tel: 029-2086 0222 **Fax:** 029-2086 0222
E-mail: sales@spotnails.co.uk
Website: http://www.spotnails.co.uk
Bank(s): Bank of Wales Plc
Directors: K. Stephen (MD)
Managers: P. Thorncroft (Sales Admin), J. Quaife (Sales Prom Mgr)
Ultimate Holding Company: SPOTNAILS LIMITED
Immediate Holding Company: SPOTNAILS MAESTRI LTD
Registration no: 00535654 **VAT No.:** GB 465 0384 46
Date established: 1954 **Turnover:** £2m - £5m **No.of Employees:** 21 - 50
Product Groups: 35, 36, 37, 49

Sutherland Trading Co.
Unit 3 Greenway Bedwas House Industrial Estate, Bedwas, Caerphilly, CF83 8XQ
Tel: 029-2088 7337 **Fax:** 029-2085 1056
E-mail: sales@sutherlandtrading.com
Website: http://www.sutherlandtrading.com
Bank(s): National Westminster
Directors: G. Jones (MD)
Managers: M. Hudd (Sales Prom Mgr), J. Isaac
Immediate Holding Company: SUTHERLAND TRADING COMPANY LIMITED
Registration no: 04112976 **VAT No.:** 437 1481 52 **Date established:** 2000
Turnover: £5m - £10m **No.of Employees:** 21 - 50 **Product Groups:** 65

Date of Accounts	Mar 12	Mar 11	Mar 10
Sales Turnover	N/A	N/A	6m
Pre Tax Profit/Loss	N/A	N/A	-171
Working Capital	1m	1m	1m
Fixed Assets	746	830	873
Current Assets	2m	2m	3m
Current Liabilities	N/A	N/A	964

Zonner Industries Ltd
Block A Van Court, Caerphilly, CF83 3ED
Tel: 029-2085 5200 **Fax:** 029-2085 5209
E-mail: steveg@zonner.co.uk
Bank(s): HSBC
Directors: S. Griffith (Dir), S. Griffiths (Dir), R. Shewell (MD), C. Jones (MD)
Managers: S. Griffiths (Char Surv)
Immediate Holding Company: ZONNER INDUSTRIES LIMITED
Registration no: 06411122 **VAT No.:** GB 402 3814 92
Date established: 2007 **Turnover:** £1m - £2m **No.of Employees:** 21 - 50
Product Groups: 48

Date of Accounts	Apr 10	Apr 09	Apr 08
Working Capital	-43	47	27
Fixed Assets	1m	1m	1m
Current Assets	526	679	977

Powys

Caersws

Griffiths & Evans
New Depot Workshop Llanwnog, Caersws, SY17 5JG
Tel: 01686-688567 **Fax:** 01686- 688758
Directors: I. Jones (Prop)
Date established: 1995 **No.of Employees:** 1 - 10 **Product Groups:** 35

J I Morgan
Wern Llawr Y Glyn Llawr-y-Glyn, Caersws, SY17 5RH
Tel: 01686-430275
Directors: J. Morgan (Prop)
Immediate Holding Company: P L WESTON LTD
Date established: 2011 **No.of Employees:** 1 - 10 **Product Groups:** 41

Gwent

Caldicot

A J Access Platforms Ltd
Unit 10 Pill Way, Portskewett, Caldicot, NP26 5PU
Tel: 01291-421155 **Fax:** 01291-423930
E-mail: info@accessplatforms.com
Website: http://www.accessplatforms.com
Bank(s): Barclays
Directors: A. Mort (MD)
Ultimate Holding Company: AFI HOLDINGS LIMITED
Immediate Holding Company: A J RENTALS LIMITED
Registration no: 02565326 **VAT No.:** GB 542 7706 39
Date established: 1990 **Turnover:** £5m - £10m **No.of Employees:** 21 - 50
Product Groups: 45, 83

Date of Accounts	May 10	May 09	May 08
Sales Turnover	8m	11m	9m
Pre Tax Profit/Loss	290	120	205
Working Capital	-2m	-2m	-2m
Fixed Assets	6m	7m	7m
Current Assets	1m	3m	3m
Current Liabilities	263	542	1m

Caldi Castle Hire
2 Ferneycross Caldicot, Caldicot, NP26 4QY
Tel: 0774-739 9541
E-mail: mrk_cochrane@yahoo.com
Directors: M. Cochrane (Prop)
Date established: 2008 **Turnover:** Up to £250,000
No.of Employees: 1 - 10 **Product Groups:**

County Welding & Brazing Supplies Ltd
Unit 21 Beacon Business Park Norman Way, Portskewett, Caldicot, NP26 5PY
Tel: 01291-431373 **Fax:** 01291-431374
Website: http://www.cwbwholesale.com
Directors: D. Cosgrove (Dir), D. Cosgrove (MD)
Registration no: 06080449 **Date established:** 2007
No.of Employees: 1 - 10 **Product Groups:** 46

Date of Accounts	Dec 07	Dec 06	Dec 05
Working Capital	73	49	46
Fixed Assets	35	19	20
Current Assets	316	172	142
Current Liabilities	243	123	95
Total Share Capital	50	50	50

Meridian Metal Trading Ltd
The Square Magor, Caldicot, NP26 3HY
Tel: 01633-882700 **Fax:** 01633-882713
E-mail: steves@meridianmetals.com
Website: http://www.meridianmetals.com
Directors: S. Savigar (Sales)
Immediate Holding Company: MERIDIAN METAL TRADING LIMITED
Registration no: 02052884 **Date established:** 1986
Turnover: £50m - £75m **No.of Employees:** 1 - 10 **Product Groups:** 34

Date of Accounts	May 11	May 10	May 09
Sales Turnover	76m	64m	53m
Pre Tax Profit/Loss	2m	2m	700
Working Capital	-5m	-4m	-2m
Fixed Assets	17m	15m	12m
Current Assets	40m	39m	26m
Current Liabilities	2m	2m	2m

Mitel Networks
Castlegate Business Park, Caldicot, NP26 5YR
Tel: 08709-092020 **Fax:** 08709-094040
E-mail: graham_bevington@mitel.com
Website: http://www.mitel.com
Bank(s): Lloyds TSB Bank plc
Directors: G. Bevington (MD), J. Evans (Fin)
Ultimate Holding Company: MITEL NETWORKS CORP (CANADA)
Immediate Holding Company: MITEL NETWORKS LIMITED
Registration no: 01309629 **Date established:** 1977
Turnover: £75m - £125m **No.of Employees:** 101 - 250
Product Groups: 37

Date of Accounts	Apr 11	Apr 10	Apr 09
Sales Turnover	105m	98m	100m
Pre Tax Profit/Loss	2m	566	-11m
Working Capital	64m	62m	62m
Fixed Assets	11m	11m	10m
Current Assets	99m	137m	107m
Current Liabilities	17m	17m	16m

P D Edenhall
Caldicot Road Rogiet, Caldicot, NP26 3TF
Tel: 01291-426700 **Fax:** 01291-425463
E-mail: steve.kitchen@pd-edenhall.co.uk
Website: http://www.pd-edenhall.co.uk
Managers: S. Kitchen (Est)
Immediate Holding Company: CALDICOT BUILDING SUPPLIES LTD
Registration no: 04112008 **Date established:** 2000
Turnover: £500,000 - £1m **No.of Employees:** 1 - 10 **Product Groups:** 33

Date of Accounts	Mar 11	Mar 10	Mar 09
Sales Turnover	N/A	N/A	796
Pre Tax Profit/Loss	N/A	N/A	-17
Working Capital	-8	29	-4
Fixed Assets	6	7	21
Current Assets	103	140	232
Current Liabilities	N/A	N/A	47

Quadratec Ltd
Lodge House Lodge Way Severn Bridge Industrial Estate, Portskewett, Caldicot, NP26 5PS
Tel: 01291-424390 **Fax:** 01291-425133
E-mail: info@quadratec-ltd.co.uk
Website: http://www.quadratec-ltd.co.uk
Directors: M. Thatcher (MD), J. Thatcher (Fin)
Immediate Holding Company: QUADRATEC LIMITED
Registration no: 03100452 **Date established:** 1995
Turnover: £250,000 - £500,000 **No.of Employees:** 1 - 10
Product Groups: 37, 38, 39, 40, 41, 44, 45, 46, 47, 48, 67, 68, 81, 84, 85

Date of Accounts	Dec 11	Dec 10	Dec 09
Working Capital	-6	-2	-10
Fixed Assets	12	9	10
Current Assets	271	153	155

Sensemaster Ltd
Unit 1 Severn Bridge Symondscliffe Way Portskewett, Caldicot, NP26 5PW
Tel: 01291-422022 **Fax:** 01291-420022
E-mail: mail@sensemaster.co.uk
Website: http://www.sensemaster.co.uk
Directors: S. Davies (Dir)
Immediate Holding Company: SENSEMASTER LIMITED
Registration no: 01852673 **VAT No.:** GB 412 7819 55
Date established: 1984 **Turnover:** £250,000 - £500,000
No.of Employees: 1 - 10 **Product Groups:** 37, 38, 44

Date of Accounts	Mar 12	Mar 11	Mar 10
Working Capital	86	62	45
Fixed Assets	11	10	13
Current Assets	202	148	121

Severn Fuels & Production Lubricants Ltd
Progress Industrial Estate Station Road, Rogiet, Caldicot, NP26 3UE
Tel: 01594-844447 **Fax:** 01291-426940
E-mail: sales@severnfuels.co.uk
Website: http://www.severnfuels.co.uk
Bank(s): Lloyds TSB Bank plc
Directors: A. Mould (MD)
Managers: K. Harford (Sales Prom Mgr)
Immediate Holding Company: SEVERN ESTUARY INVESTMENTS LTD.
Registration no: 03168895 **VAT No.:** GB 356 4868 13
Date established: 1996 **Turnover:** £10m - £20m
No.of Employees: 51 - 100 **Product Groups:** 30, 31, 32, 35, 38, 66

Date of Accounts	Aug 11	Aug 10	Aug 09
Working Capital	-135	1	1
Fixed Assets	151	151	151
Current Assets	1	1	1
Current Liabilities	136	N/A	N/A

Severn Machine Tools Ltd
8 Castle Way Severn Bridge Industrial Estate, Portskewett, Caldicot, NP26 5PR
Tel: 01291-424373 **Fax:** 01291-423455
E-mail: sales@severnmachinetools.com
Website: http://www.severnmachinetools.com
Directors: W. Gerrard (Fin)
Immediate Holding Company: SEVERN MACHINE TOOLS LIMITED
Registration no: 02891101 **VAT No.:** 615 9538 19 **Date established:** 1994
Turnover: £1m - £2m **No.of Employees:** 1 - 10 **Product Groups:** 48, 67

Date of Accounts	Jun 11	Jun 10	Jun 09
Working Capital	123	133	214
Fixed Assets	2	4	38
Current Assets	466	480	601
Current Liabilities	N/A	N/A	21

Tata Steel
Unit 4 Symondscliffe Way Portskewett, Caldicot, NP26 5PW
Tel: 01291-421732 **Fax:** 01291-425085
E-mail: chris.terrell@corusgroup.com
Website: http://www.corusgroup.com
Managers: C. Terrell (Mgr), A. Hooper, J. Brace (Personnel)
Ultimate Holding Company: TATA STEEL LIMITED (INDIA)
Immediate Holding Company: CORUS GROUP LIMITED
Registration no: 03811373 **Date established:** 1999
No.of Employees: 21 - 50 **Product Groups:** 66

Date of Accounts	Apr 12	Apr 11	Apr 10
Working Capital	421	386	348
Fixed Assets	6	9	4
Current Assets	557	461	424

South Glamorgan

Cardiff

ADT Fire & Security plc
A D T House Copse Walk Cardiff Gate Business Park, Pontprennau, Cardiff, CF23 8RB
Tel: 0800-542 3108 **Fax:** 029-2042 2750
Website: http://www.adt.co.uk
Managers: J. Ambler (Chief Mgr)
Ultimate Holding Company: TYCO INTERNATIONAL LIMITED (SWITZERLAND)
Immediate Holding Company: ADT FIRE AND SECURITY PLC
Registration no: 01161045 **Date established:** 1974
No.of Employees: 21 - 50 **Product Groups:** 37, 38, 39, 40, 47, 52, 81

Date of Accounts	Sep 11	Sep 08	Sep 09
Sales Turnover	363m	414m	384m
Pre Tax Profit/Loss	18m	4m	10m
Working Capital	450m	618m	561m
Fixed Assets	120m	193m	171m
Current Assets	710m	765m	722m
Current Liabilities	81m	57m	42m

A M T Marine & Industrial Engineering Ltd
3 Brindley Road, Cardiff, CF11 8TX
Tel: 029-2037 7022
E-mail: sales@amtmarine.co.uk
Website: http://www.amtmarine.co.uk
Directors: J. Wilson (Fin), M. Thomas (MD)
Immediate Holding Company: A.M.T. MARINE AND INDUSTRIAL ENGINEERING LIMITED
Registration no: 02362540 **Date established:** 1989 **Turnover:** £1m - £2m
No.of Employees: 1 - 10 **Product Groups:** 35, 36, 39

Date of Accounts	Sep 11	Sep 10	Sep 09
Sales Turnover	N/A	1m	2m
Pre Tax Profit/Loss	N/A	73	92
Working Capital	117	107	55
Fixed Assets	28	21	16
Current Assets	199	272	244
Current Liabilities	N/A	136	147

A S D Metal Services Cardiff
East Moors Road, Cardiff, CF24 5EE
Tel: 029-2046 0622 **Fax:** 029-2049 0105
E-mail: cardiff@asdmetalservices.co.uk
Website: http://www.asdmetalservices.co.uk
Bank(s): Barclays
Managers: C. Whittle (Sales & Mktg Mg), M. Roberts (Chief Mgr)
Immediate Holding Company: METAL FABRICATION COMPANY (CARDIFF) LIMITED
Registration no: 00552565 **VAT No.:** GB 412 1831 95
Date established: 1955 **Turnover:** £5m - £10m **No.of Employees:** 21 - 50
Product Groups: 34

Date of Accounts	Aug 11	Aug 10	Aug 09
Working Capital	1m	1m	2m
Fixed Assets	924	471	471
Current Assets	1m	1m	2m

A T L Telecommunications Ltd
Fountain House Fountain Lane, St Mellons, Cardiff, CF3 0FB
Tel: 029-2050 0700 **Fax:** 029-2050 0701
E-mail: sales@atltelecom.com
Website: http://www.atltelecom.com
Bank(s): National Westminster Bank Plc
Directors: J. Clarke (Prop)
Ultimate Holding Company: WESTLEIGH INVESTMENTS HOLDINGS LIMITED
Immediate Holding Company: ATL TELECOM LIMITED
Registration no: 04335781 **VAT No.:** GB 542 6841 38
Date established: 2001 **Turnover:** £5m - £10m **No.of Employees:** 21 - 50
Product Groups: 37, 38, 44

Date of Accounts	Aug 11	Aug 10	Aug 09
Working Capital	631	709	1m
Fixed Assets	4	9	45
Current Assets	900	1m	2m

A T S Business Machines
1 Brithdir Street, Cardiff, CF24 4LE
Tel: 029-2037 7455 **Fax:** 029-2037 7455
E-mail: info@atsbm-group.com
Website: http://www.atsbm-group.com
Directors: B. Adams (Ptnr)
Managers: V. Lockwood
Date established: 1969 **No.of Employees:** 1 - 10 **Product Groups:** 44

A W E Ltd
Unit R04-R05 Cardiff Bay Business Centre, Cardiff, CF24 5EL
Tel: 029-2049 2848 **Fax:** 029-2049 1369
E-mail: water@aweltd.co.uk
Website: http://www.aweltd.co.uk
Directors: J. Peckham (Fin), P. Peckham (MD)
Immediate Holding Company: A.W.E. (ANDERSON WATER EQUIPMENT) LIMITED
Registration no: 01764097 **VAT No.:** GB 412 7154 81
Date established: 1983 **Turnover:** £1m - £2m **No.of Employees:** 1 - 10
Product Groups: 17, 30, 32, 36, 37, 40, 42, 52, 54, 84

Date of Accounts	Oct 11	Oct 10	Oct 09
Working Capital	365	340	338
Fixed Assets	46	19	22
Current Assets	477	540	475

Abbey Lifts Ltd
28 South Luton Place, Cardiff, CF24 0EX
Tel: 029-2049 4200 **Fax:** 029-2047 1600
E-mail: info@abbeylifts.co.uk
Website: http://www.abbeylifts.co.uk
Directors: J. Taylor (Dir)
Immediate Holding Company: ABBEY LIFTS LIMITED
Registration no: 01667840 **Date established:** 1982
No.of Employees: 11 - 20 **Product Groups:** 35, 39, 45

see next page

Abbey Lifts Ltd - *Cont'd*

Date of Accounts	Feb 12	Feb 11	Feb 10
Working Capital	-4	-6	136
Fixed Assets	16	14	20
Current Assets	112	117	253

Adenhart Wales Ltd
Unit 1 Guest Road, Cardiff, CF24 5JS
Tel: 029-2048 1414 **Fax:** 029-2048 2051
E-mail: info@adenhart.co.uk
Website: http://www.adenhart.co.uk
Directors: M. Allen (MD)
Ultimate Holding Company: ADENHART (CARDIFF) LIMITED
Immediate Holding Company: ADENHART (WALES) LIMITED
Registration no: 07192381 **Date established:** 2010
No.of Employees: 1 - 10 **Product Groups:** 26, 35

Date of Accounts	Mar 11
Working Capital	15
Fixed Assets	32
Current Assets	155

Alpha Cash Registers
108 Cathays Terrace, Cardiff, CF24 4HY
Tel: 029-2023 9259
Website: http://www.alphatillsandscales.co.uk
Directors: T. Jones (Prop)
Date established: 1994 **No.of Employees:** 1 - 10 **Product Groups:** 38, 42

Ametek Prestolight
Regal Works Ipswich Road, Cardiff, CF23 9XP
Tel: 029-2049 6763 **Fax:** 029-2046 2337
E-mail: chris.jenkins@ametek.co.uk
Website: http://www.ametek.co.uk
Directors: J. Walker (Co Sec), M. Lea (Dir)
Managers: C. Jenkins (Sales & Mktg Mg), C. Jenkins (Mgr), N. Furnish (Ops Mgr), D. Kelly (Buyer)
Ultimate Holding Company: AMETEK INC., USA
Immediate Holding Company: LLOYD INSTRUMENTS LTD., FAREHAM UK
VAT No.: GB 568 3389 920 002 **Turnover:** £5m - £10m
No.of Employees: 1 - 10 **Product Groups:** 37, 39

Anstee & Ware Ltd
New Building Foreshaw Road, Cardiff, CF10 4DF
Tel: 029-2048 1831 **Fax:** 029-2049 6592
E-mail: paul.holbrook@ansteeware.co.uk
Website: http://www.ansteeware.co.uk
Bank(s): Barclays
Directors: M. Trigg (MD)
Ultimate Holding Company: A W HOLDING COMPANY LIMITED
Immediate Holding Company: ANSTEE & WARE LIMITED
Registration no: 00477097 **Date established:** 1950 **Turnover:** £2m - £5m
No.of Employees: 21 - 50 **Product Groups:** 35, 37, 40, 44, 48, 67

Date of Accounts	Dec 11	Dec 10	Dec 09
Sales Turnover	19m	16m	15m
Pre Tax Profit/Loss	842	713	183
Working Capital	2m	1m	911
Fixed Assets	1m	1m	1m
Current Assets	8m	6m	6m
Current Liabilities	4m	3m	4m

Applemed Exhibitions
Unit 2 Pacific Business Park Pacific Road, Cardiff, CF24 5HJ
Tel: 029-2043 7720 **Fax:** 029-2043 7721
E-mail: exhibitions@applemed.co.uk
Website: http://www.applemed.co.uk
Directors: P. Walker (Prop)
Immediate Holding Company: PRINT PARTNERSHIP SOLUTIONS LIMITED
Registration no: 06305568 **Date established:** 2002
No.of Employees: 1 - 10 **Product Groups:** 26, 30, 35, 37, 38, 39, 49, 52, 65, 66, 67, 69, 72, 80, 81, 83, 84, 86

Applied Automation UK Ltd
Ipswich Road, Cardiff, CF23 9AQ
Tel: 029-2049 4551 **Fax:** 029-2048 1955
E-mail: jon-paul@x-stk.com
Website: http://www.appliedautomation.co.uk
Directors: V. Rowe (Co Sec)
Managers: J. Kelleher (Sales Admin), J. Kelleher (Sales Admin)
Ultimate Holding Company: TOTAL FILTRATION LIMITED
Immediate Holding Company: APPLIED AUTOMATION (UK) LIMITED
Registration no: 02532117 **VAT No.:** GB 135 6608 65
Date established: 1990 **Turnover:** £1m - £2m **No.of Employees:** 1 - 10
Product Groups: 35, 36, 38

Date of Accounts	Mar 12	Mar 11	Mar 10
Sales Turnover	10m	8m	6m
Pre Tax Profit/Loss	526	434	171
Working Capital	805	589	414
Fixed Assets	2m	2m	1m
Current Assets	3m	3m	3m
Current Liabilities	957	645	776

Argonaut Systems Ltd
Guildford House 3-4 Guildford Crescent, Cardiff, CF10 2HJ
Tel: 0845-643 1881
E-mail: mail@argonautsystems.com
Website: http://www.argonautsystems.com
Directors: S. Coleman (MD)
Managers: R. Harford (Develop Mgr)
Registration no: 06254134 **Date established:** 2007
Turnover: Up to £250,000 **No.of Employees:** 1 - 10 **Product Groups:** 44

Date of Accounts	May 08
Working Capital	2
Fixed Assets	5
Current Assets	18
Current Liabilities	16
Total Share Capital	1

Arup
4 Pierhead Street Capital Waterside, Cardiff, CF10 4QP
Tel: 029-2047 3727 **Fax:** 029-2047 2277
E-mail: cardiff@arup.com
Website: http://www.arup.com
Directors: S. Luke (Dir)
Immediate Holding Company: ARUP GROUP LTD
Registration no: SC062237 **No.of Employees:** 101 - 250
Product Groups: 44

W S Atkins Ltd
Level 4 Longcross Court 47 Newport Road, Cardiff, CF24 0AD
Tel: 029-2048 5159 **Fax:** 029-2048 5138
E-mail: mark.bogler@fgould.com
Website: http://www.atkinsglobal.com
Managers: M. Bogler
Immediate Holding Company: SIGNWALES CBC
Registration no: 00688424 **VAT No.:** GB 209 8612 53
Date established: 2005 **Turnover:** Up to £250,000
No.of Employees: 51 - 100 **Product Groups:** 84

Atradius
3 Harbour Drive Capital Waterside, Cardiff, CF10 4WZ
Tel: 029-2082 4000 **Fax:** 029-2082 4003
E-mail: pam.james@atradius.com
Website: http://www.atradius.co.uk
Managers: P. James (Mktg Serv Mgr), A. Hamilton (Comptroller), C. Tibbs (Sales Admin), J. Dartnell, A. Middleton (Personnel), K. Nie (Sales & Mktg Mg)
Ultimate Holding Company: ATRADIUS NV (NETHERLANDS)
Immediate Holding Company: ATRADIUS COLLECTIONS LIMITED
Registration no: 03429221 **Date established:** 1997 **Turnover:** £2m - £5m
No.of Employees: 251 - 500 **Product Groups:** 82

Date of Accounts	Dec 11	Dec 10	Dec 09
Sales Turnover	2m	3m	5m
Pre Tax Profit/Loss	-861	-139	168
Working Capital	-2	845	852
Current Assets	2m	2m	6m
Current Liabilities	293	302	694

B A Cash & Carry Ltd
24 Hadfield Road, Cardiff, CF11 8AQ
Tel: 029-2022 9962 **Fax:** 029-2023 8581
E-mail: cardiff@ba-cc.co.uk
Website: http://www.ba-cc.co.uk
Directors: Z. Ahmed (Dir)
Ultimate Holding Company: B.A. CASH & CARRY (CARDIFF) LIMITED
Immediate Holding Company: B.A. CASH & CARRY (CARDIFF) LIMITED
Registration no: 01429865 **Date established:** 1979
Turnover: £75m - £125m **No.of Employees:** 101 - 250
Product Groups: 61

Date of Accounts	Feb 12	Feb 11	Feb 10
Sales Turnover	96m	97m	99m
Pre Tax Profit/Loss	871	597	460
Working Capital	-3m	-4m	-4m
Fixed Assets	9m	10m	10m
Current Assets	9m	7m	8m
Current Liabilities	1m	1m	548

B & B Industrial Doors
Curran House Curran Industrial Estate Curran Road, Cardiff, CF10 5DF
Tel: 029-2036 2580 **Fax:** 029-2036 2590
E-mail: info@bandbdoors.co.uk
Website: http://www.bandbdoors.co.uk
Directors: A. Hurford (Dir)
Immediate Holding Company: B & B INDUSTRIAL DOORS (UK) LIMITED
Registration no: 03429038 **Date established:** 2010
No.of Employees: 1 - 10 **Product Groups:** 35, 36, 39, 48

Date of Accounts	Jun 11	Jun 10
Working Capital	2	3
Current Assets	3	66

B C B International Ltd
Units 7-8 Clydesmuir Road Industrial Estate, Cardiff, CF24 2QS
Tel: 029-2043 3700 **Fax:** 029-2043 3701
E-mail: info@bcbin.com
Website: http://www.bcbin.com
Bank(s): Bank of Wales PLC
Managers: A. Jarvis (Comptroller)
Immediate Holding Company: B.C.B. INTERNATIONAL LIMITED
Registration no: 01442485 **VAT No.:** GB 402 5592 74
Date established: 1979 **Turnover:** £2m - £5m **No.of Employees:** 21 - 50
Product Groups: 20, 23, 38, 39, 40, 48, 67, 76

Date of Accounts	Jun 11	Jun 10	Jun 09
Working Capital	888	885	585
Fixed Assets	751	832	820
Current Assets	3m	2m	3m

Balmain Mail Order
63-67 Wellfield Road, Cardiff, CF24 3PA
Tel: 029-2043 7343 **Fax:** 029-2043 7342
Directors: R. Aggarwal (MD)
No.of Employees: 21 - 50 **Product Groups:** 32, 63

Bank of Scotland plc
1 Kingsway, Cardiff, CF10 3YB
Tel: 029-2080 0800 **Fax:** 029-2080 0826
E-mail: terry_white@bankofscotland.co.uk
Website: http://www.bankofscotland.co.uk
Directors: P. Shaw (Sales)
Managers: T. White (Mgr), F. Brinston (Mgr)
Immediate Holding Company: BANK OF SCOTLAND PLC
Registration no: SC327000 **VAT No.:** GB 270 1467 76
Date established: 2007 **Turnover:** £50m - £75m
No.of Employees: 11 - 20 **Product Groups:** 82

Barloworld Handling Ltd
Ocean Way, Cardiff, CF24 5BH
Tel: 029-2045 4900 **Fax:** 029-2045 4908
E-mail: cardiff@handling.barloworld.co.uk
Website: http://www.barloworld.co.uk
Directors: G. Newell (Sales)
Managers: D. Beddard (Reg Mgr)
Ultimate Holding Company: BARLOWORLD LIMITED (SOUTH AFRICA)
Immediate Holding Company: BARLOWORLD HANDLING LIMITED
Registration no: 00564646 **Date established:** 1956
No.of Employees: 1 - 10 **Product Groups:** 35, 39, 45

Date of Accounts	Sep 11	Sep 10	Sep 09
Sales Turnover	106m	96m	96m
Pre Tax Profit/Loss	-3m	-2m	-5m
Working Capital	-20m	10m	-18m
Fixed Assets	37m	55m	46m
Current Assets	33m	55m	23m
Current Liabilities	6m	6m	18m

Batt Cables plc
66 Albany Road, Cardiff, CF24 3RR
Tel: 029-2045 0044 **Fax:** 029-2046 4724
E-mail: jeff.wright@batt.co.uk
Website: http://www.batt.co.uk
Managers: J. Wright (Mgr)
Immediate Holding Company: BATT CABLES PLC
Registration no: 01353688 **Date established:** 1978
No.of Employees: 1 - 10 **Product Groups:** 30, 35, 36, 37, 38, 44, 66, 67

Date of Accounts	Mar 12	Mar 11	Mar 10
Sales Turnover	106m	98m	84m
Pre Tax Profit/Loss	8m	9m	5m
Working Capital	41m	36m	31m
Fixed Assets	8m	9m	8m
Current Assets	69m	60m	54m
Current Liabilities	3m	3m	2m

Beldam Burgmann
Unit P6 South Point Clos Marion, Cardiff, CF10 4LQ
Tel: 029-2048 7646 **Fax:** 029- 20481133
Website: http://www.beldamburgmann.com
Directors: V. Butcher (Dir), M. Seekings (MD), M. Seeking (MD)
Managers: S. Winfield (Sales Prom)
Immediate Holding Company: PEXION LTD
Registration no: 00137350 **Turnover:** £10m - £20m
No.of Employees: 1 - 10 **Product Groups:** 22, 24, 29, 30

Biffa Waste Services Ltd
Curran Embankment, Cardiff, CF10 5FX
Tel: 029-2022 1862 **Fax:** 029-2047 1605
E-mail: marketing@biffa.co.uk
Website: http://www.biffa.co.uk
Managers: P. Rann (Mgr)
Immediate Holding Company: BIFFA WASTE SERVICES LIMITED
Registration no: 00946107 **Date established:** 1969
No.of Employees: 1 - 10 **Product Groups:** 32, 54

Date of Accounts	Mar 08	Mar 09	Apr 10
Sales Turnover	555m	574m	492m
Pre Tax Profit/Loss	23m	50m	30m
Working Capital	229m	271m	293m
Fixed Assets	371m	360m	378m
Current Assets	409m	534m	609m
Current Liabilities	50m	100m	115m

Biocatalysts Ltd
Unit 1 Cefn Coed Nantgarw, Cardiff, CF15 7QQ
Tel: 01443-843712 **Fax:** 01443-846500
E-mail: sales@biocats.com
Website: http://www.biocatalysts.com
Bank(s): Barclays
Directors: S. West (MD), T. Cannon (Pers)
Managers: C. West (Mktg Serv Mgr), E. Finlay, K. Hilditch
Immediate Holding Company: BIOCATALYSTS LIMITED
Registration no: 02570883 **VAT No.:** GB 477 6791 81
Date established: 1990 **Turnover:** £2m - £5m **No.of Employees:** 21 - 50
Product Groups: 31

Date of Accounts	Sep 11	Sep 10	Sep 09
Working Capital	1m	1m	1m
Fixed Assets	3m	3m	3m
Current Assets	2m	3m	2m

Bogod & Company Ltd
Fortran Road St. Mellons, Cardiff, CF3 0WJ
Tel: 029-2079 2079
Directors: H. Bogod (Prop), N. Davey (Fin), R. Bogod (Prop), S. Bogod (Prop)
Immediate Holding Company: BOGOD & COMPANY LIMITED
Registration no: 00600493 **Date established:** 1958 **Turnover:** £5m - £10m
No.of Employees: 21 - 50 **Product Groups:** 43, 82

Date of Accounts	Mar 08	Mar 07	Mar 06
Sales Turnover	5400	6263	6231
Pre Tax Profit/Loss	115	177	115
Working Capital	2679	2560	2419
Fixed Assets	108	130	142
Current Assets	3499	3578	3176
Current Liabilities	820	1018	757
ROCE% (Return on Capital Employed)	4.1	6.6	4.5
ROT% (Return on Turnover)	2.1	2.8	1.9

Buck & Hickman Ltd
Neptune Point Vanguard Way, Cardiff, CF24 5PG
Tel: 029-2030 6080 **Fax:** 029-2030 6030
E-mail: cardiff@buckandhickman.com
Website: http://www.buckandhickman.com
Managers: S. Wright (Ops Mgr)
Ultimate Holding Company: TRAVIS PERKINS PLC
Immediate Holding Company: BOSTON (2011) LIMITED
Registration no: 06028304 **Date established:** 2006
No.of Employees: 21 - 50 **Product Groups:** 23, 24, 33, 36, 37, 41, 46

Date of Accounts	Dec 10	Mar 10	Mar 09
Working Capital	6m	6m	6m
Current Assets	27m	27m	27m

Business In Focus Ltd
Enterprise House 127-129 Bute Street, Cardiff, CF10 5LE
Tel: 029-2049 4411 **Fax:** 029-2048 1623
E-mail: phil@diamond-discovery.co.uk
Website: http://www.businessinfocus.co.uk
Bank(s): National Westminster Bank Plc
Directors: G. Rees (Dir), J. Evens (Dep Ch), J. Harrison (Dir), J. Sainsbury (Dir), J. Huish (Dir), G. Bray (Grp Chief Exec), W. Snowdon (Dir), B. Foday (Dir), R. Forster (Dir)
Managers: M. Cross (Develop Mgr), H. Mills (Sales Prom Mgr), E. Williams (Comptroller), E. Williams (Sales Admin), T. Thomas, T. Thomas (Personnel)
Immediate Holding Company: BUSINESS IN FOCUS LIMITED
Registration no: 02553654 **Date established:** 1990
Turnover: £500,000 - £1m **No.of Employees:** 21 - 50
Product Groups: 80, 86

Capital Coated Steel Ltd
East Tyndall Street, Cardiff, CF24 5DA
Tel: 029-2043 6000 **Fax:** 029-2048 8687
E-mail: email@capitalcs.com
Website: http://www.capitalcs.com
Bank(s): National Westminster Bank Plc
Directors: C. O'Sullivan (Sales & Mktg), G. Hunt (MD), G. Asprou (Fin)
Managers: S. Nurse (Ops Mgr), S. Roberts, T. Cisuelo (Personnel)
Ultimate Holding Company: CAPITAL COATED STEEL LIMITED
Immediate Holding Company: CAPITAL COATED STEEL LIMITED
Registration no: 01066357 **Date established:** 1972
Turnover: £20m - £50m **No.of Employees:** 21 - 50 **Product Groups:** 34

Date of Accounts	Mar 11	Mar 10	Mar 09
Sales Turnover	27m	21m	19m
Pre Tax Profit/Loss	256	163	137

Working Capital	3m	3m	3m
Fixed Assets	3m	3m	4m
Current Assets	12m	10m	7m
Current Liabilities	2m	2m	1m

Cardiff Chemicals Ltd

65 King George V Drive West, Cardiff, CF14 4EF
Tel: 029-2077 9612 **Fax:** 029-2077 9612
E-mail: info@cardiff-chemicals.com
Website: http://www.cardiff-chemicals.com
Directors: C. Pant (MD)
Immediate Holding Company: CARDIFF CHEMICALS LIMITED
Registration no: 02428904 **Date established:** 1989
Turnover: £500,000 - £1m **No.of Employees:** 1 - 10 **Product Groups:** 32, 42

Date of Accounts	Mar 11	Mar 10	Mar 09
Working Capital	5	-14	-15
Fixed Assets	63	86	89
Current Assets	15	21	22

Cardiff Galvanizers

Cambria House East Moors Road, Cardiff, CF24 5EG
Tel: 029-2048 0321 **Fax:** 029-2048 3728
E-mail: info@cardiffgalvanizers.co.uk
Website: http://www.cardiffgalvanizers.co.uk
Bank(s): HSBC Bank plc
Directors: R. Evans (MD)
Ultimate Holding Company: CARDIFF GALVANIZERS HOLDINGS LIMITED
Immediate Holding Company: CARDIFF GALVANIZERS (1969) LIMITED
Registration no: 00964827 **VAT No.:** GB 134 6185 73
Date established: 1969 **No.of Employees:** 51 - 100 **Product Groups:** 46

Date of Accounts	Sep 11	Sep 10	Sep 09
Working Capital	391	440	400
Fixed Assets	195	198	490
Current Assets	1m	1m	996

Cardiff Management & Language Academy

16-17 High Street, Cardiff, CF10 1AX
Tel: 029-2022 6047 **Fax:** 029-2037 2281
E-mail: info@cmla.uk.com
Website: http://www.cmla.uk.com
Directors: H. Mohamed (MD), Z. Nasir (Fin), E. Hamilton (Fin)
Immediate Holding Company: CARDIFF MANAGEMENT & LANGUAGES ACADEMY LIMITED
Registration no: 05741909 **Date established:** 2006
Turnover: £250,000 - £500,000 **No.of Employees:** 1 - 10
Product Groups: 86

Date of Accounts	Mar 11	Mar 10	Mar 09
Sales Turnover	328	451	301
Working Capital	-12	38	-12
Fixed Assets	22	16	4
Current Assets	24	74	34

Cardiff Metropolitan University

Cyncoed Campus Cyncoed Road, Cardiff, CF23 6XD
Tel: 029-2041 6070 **Fax:** 029-2076 5569
E-mail: info@uwic.ac.uk
Website: http://www.uwic.ac.uk
Bank(s): National Westminster Bank Plc
Managers: M. Davis
Immediate Holding Company: FUTURA LETTINGS LIMITED
Registration no: 02656744 **VAT No.:** GB 542 9157 36
Date established: 2009 **Turnover:** £2m - £5m
No.of Employees: 101 - 250 **Product Groups:** 85, 86

Cartridge World Ltd

121 Clifton Street, Cardiff, CF24 1LW
Tel: 029-2049 4956 **Fax:** 029-2049 4956
Website: http://www.cartridgeworld.org
Directors: D. Cleaver (Dir)
Registration no: 04124067 **Date established:** 2000 **Turnover:** £5m - £10m
No.of Employees: 1 - 10 **Product Groups:** 28, 30, 44, 64

Cartridge World Ltd

49 Whitchurch Road, Cardiff, CF14 3JP
Tel: 029-2065 0573 **Fax:** 029-2065 0571
Website: http://www.cardiff.cartridgeworld.co.uk
Directors: E. Mustafa (Prop)
Immediate Holding Company: CARTRIDGE WORLD LIMITED
Registration no: 04124067 **Date established:** 2000 **Turnover:** £5m - £10m
No.of Employees: 1 - 10 **Product Groups:** 28, 30, 44

Date of Accounts	Dec 11	Dec 10	Dec 09
Sales Turnover	6m	7m	8m
Pre Tax Profit/Loss	373	164	210
Working Capital	1m	967	878
Fixed Assets	403	455	524
Current Assets	7m	7m	6m
Current Liabilities	4m	1m	2m

Celtic Tyre Services Cardiff Ltd

Brindley Road, Cardiff, CF11 8TX
Tel: 029-2022 1201 **Fax:** 029-2066 4985
E-mail: enquiries@celtictyres.co.uk
Website: http://www.celtictyres.co.uk
Bank(s): Barclays
Directors: R. Jenkins (MD)
Ultimate Holding Company: CELTIC TYRE SERVICES (HOLDINGS) LIMITED
Immediate Holding Company: CELTIC TYRE SERVICES (CARDIFF) LIMITED
Registration no: 00938580 **VAT No.:** GB 133 5276 81
Date established: 1968 **Turnover:** £1m - £2m **No.of Employees:** 11 - 20
Product Groups: 68

Date of Accounts	Nov 11	Nov 10	Nov 09
Working Capital	269	260	343
Fixed Assets	40	64	37
Current Assets	906	736	801

Commercial Kitchen Maintenance Ltd

6a Dalcross Street, Cardiff, CF24 4UB
Tel: 029-2049 2884 **Fax:** 029-2049 8361
E-mail: service@ckmltd.co.uk
Website: http://www.ckmltd.co.uk
Bank(s): HSBC Bank plc
Directors: F. Wickland (Sales), J. Bradley (Dir)
Immediate Holding Company: COMMERCIAL KITCHEN MAINTENANCE LIMITED
Registration no: 00903083 **VAT No.:** GB 133 4336 94
Date established: 1967 **Turnover:** £1m - £2m **No.of Employees:** 21 - 50
Product Groups: 48, 67

Date of Accounts	Apr 11	Apr 10	Apr 09
Working Capital	123	199	135
Fixed Assets	367	347	331
Current Assets	822	960	618

Company Searches

Crwys House 33 Crwys Road, Cardiff, CF24 4YF
Tel: 0800-072 0144 **Fax:** 029-2039 5561
E-mail: customerservices@companysearches.co.uk
Website: http://www.companysearches.co.uk
Managers: H. John (Mgr), H. John, H. John (Cust Serv Mgr), A. Tilly (Chief Acct), M. Hart (Mgr)
Immediate Holding Company: OFFSHORE STAINLESS SUPPLIES LIMITED
Registration no: 03885245 **Date established:** 1999
No.of Employees: 1 - 10 **Product Groups:** 82

Conka Design Ltd

Coal Exchange Building Mount Stuart Square, Cardiff, CF10 5EB
Tel: 08448-009727 **Fax:** 0845-862 2127
E-mail: info@conkadesign.co.uk
Website: http://www.conkadesign.co.uk
Directors: D. Ashman (Dir)
Immediate Holding Company: CONKA DESIGN LTD
Registration no: 05898603 **Date established:** 2006
No.of Employees: 1 - 10 **Product Groups:** 84

Date of Accounts	Oct 11	Oct 10	Oct 09
Working Capital	15	3	-9
Fixed Assets	10	14	1
Current Assets	175	53	14

Cooke & Arkwright (Chartered Surveyors)

7-8 Windsor Place, Cardiff, CF10 3SX
Tel: 029-2034 6346 **Fax:** 029-2034 6300
E-mail: cardiff@coark.com
Website: http://www.coark.com
Directors: L. Gronning (Co Sec), M. Lawley (Ch)
Immediate Holding Company: COOKE & ARKWRIGHT LIMITED
Registration no: 02618062 **Date established:** 1991 **Turnover:** £2m - £5m
No.of Employees: 21 - 50 **Product Groups:** 80

Date of Accounts	Sep 11	Sep 10	Sep 09
Working Capital	591	597	595
Fixed Assets	8	14	15
Current Assets	1m	1m	1m

Coors Brewers Ltd

Copse Walk Cardiff Gate Business Park, Pontprennau, Cardiff, CF23 8BB
Tel: 029-2054 5500 **Fax:** 029-2054 5550
E-mail: sales@coors.com
Website: http://www.molsoncoors.com
Bank(s): Lloyds TSB Bank plc
Directors: M. Cousins (Sales), N. Moir (MD)
Managers: P. Doubler, L. James (Sec)
Ultimate Holding Company: MOLSON COORS BREWING COMPANY (U.S.A)
Immediate Holding Company: COORS BREWERS LIMITED
Registration no: 06824686 **Date established:** 2009
No.of Employees: 51 - 100 **Product Groups:** 21

The Costa Rica Coffee Co. Ltd

85 Pontcanna Street, Cardiff, CF11 9HS
Tel: 029-2022 6554 **Fax:** 029-2066 7600
E-mail: martin.borg@costaricacoffee.co.uk
Website: http://www.costaricacoffee.co.uk
Directors: M. Borg (MD)
Managers: M. Rees (Sales Prom Mgr)
Immediate Holding Company: COSTA RICA COFFEE COMPANY LIMITED
Registration no: 04419968 **VAT No.:** GB 483 9797 71
Date established: 2002 **Turnover:** £250,000 - £500,000
No.of Employees: 1 - 10 **Product Groups:** 62

Date of Accounts	Apr 08	Apr 07	Apr 06
Working Capital	-9	-8	-2
Fixed Assets	13	14	13
Current Assets	10	12	20
Current Liabilities	19	20	22
Total Share Capital	1	1	1

C P L Petroleum Ltd

Roeth Dock, Cardiff, CF10 4UX
Tel: 01495-247400 **Fax:** 01495-243954
E-mail: abercarn@cplpetroleum.co.uk
Website: http://www.cplpetroleum.co.uk
Managers: J. Bradley
Ultimate Holding Company: CPL INDUSTRIES HOLDINGS LIMITED
Immediate Holding Company: CPL PETROLEUM LIMITED
Registration no: 03003860 **VAT No.:** GB 275 0972 38
Date established: 1994 **Turnover:** £500m - £1,000m
No.of Employees: 1 - 10 **Product Groups:** 66

Date of Accounts	Mar 12	Mar 11	Mar 10
Pre Tax Profit/Loss	N/A	878	904
Working Capital	31	30m	30m
Fixed Assets	26	26m	26m
Current Assets	57	56m	56m
Current Liabilities	26	246	253

Crowning Glory Silk Veils

96 Everest Avenue, Cardiff, CF14 5AR
Tel: 029-2075 0723
E-mail: info@silkveil.com
Website: http://www.silkveil.com
Directors: A. Guise (MD), A. Guise (Prop)
No.of Employees: 1 - 10 **Product Groups:** 23

Crwys Electrics Ltd

32 Crwys Road, Cardiff, CF24 4NL
Tel: 029-2022 7095 **Fax:** 029-2023 1462
Website: http://www.crwyselectrics.co.uk
Directors: P. Edwards (Dir)
Immediate Holding Company: CRWYS ELECTRICS LIMITED
Registration no: 00809939 **Date established:** 1964
No.of Employees: 1 - 10 **Product Groups:** 36, 40

Date of Accounts	Apr 11	Apr 10	Apr 09
Working Capital	35	30	30
Fixed Assets	15	2	3
Current Assets	80	70	77

Culver Holdings plc

Llanmaes St Fagans, Cardiff, CF5 6DU
Tel: 029-2067 5204 **Fax:** 029-2057 6290
E-mail: enquiries@culver.uk.com
Website: http://www.culverholdings.com
Directors: A. Viles (Grp Chief Exec), G. Collison (Fin)
Managers: R. Biles (Tech Serv Mgr), V. Yates
Immediate Holding Company: CULVER HOLDINGS PLC
Registration no: 02611363 **Date established:** 1991 **Turnover:** £2m - £5m
No.of Employees: 21 - 50 **Product Groups:** 69

Date of Accounts	Dec 10	Dec 09	Dec 08
Sales Turnover	2m	1m	1m
Pre Tax Profit/Loss	-824	-1m	-1m
Working Capital	-3m	-2m	-904
Fixed Assets	317	575	593
Current Assets	136	925	1m
Current Liabilities	3m	2m	953

Cymru-Web Net Ltd

Cymru Web House 22 Denton Road, Cardiff, CF5 1PE
Tel: 029-2031 5817 **Fax:** 029-2031 5817
E-mail: enquiries@cymru-web.net
Website: http://www.cymru-web.net
Directors: E. Pearson (Fin)
Managers: K. Crampton
Immediate Holding Company: Propona Ltd
Registration no: 04208811 **Date established:** 2001
Turnover: Up to £250,000 **No.of Employees:** 1 - 10 **Product Groups:** 44

Date of Accounts	May 08
Working Capital	13
Fixed Assets	2
Current Assets	52
Current Liabilities	39

Cyrus R W Group Ltd

Alfred Cook Building Canal Parade, Cardiff, CF10 5RD
Tel: 029-2034 4400 **Fax:** 029-2034 4477
E-mail: info@cyrus-rw.co.uk
Website: http://www.cyrus-rw.co.uk
Bank(s): Barclays
Directors: G. Waite (Sales), I. Watkins (Ch), P. Lewis (I.T. Dir)
Ultimate Holding Company: CYRUS R W HOLDINGS LIMITED
Immediate Holding Company: CYRUS - RW GROUP LIMITED
Registration no: 03066431 **VAT No.:** GB 655 7932 94
Date established: 1995 **Turnover:** £5m - £10m
No.of Employees: 51 - 100 **Product Groups:** 46, 48

Date of Accounts	Dec 11	Dec 10	Dec 09
Sales Turnover	9m	9m	7m
Pre Tax Profit/Loss	917	827	659
Working Capital	974	581	894
Fixed Assets	4m	3m	3m
Current Assets	6m	5m	5m
Current Liabilities	3m	3m	2m

D Brash & Sons Ltd

Calibra House Splott Industrial Estate, Cardiff, CF24 5FF
Tel: 029-2048 8124 **Fax:** 029-2048 1115
E-mail: sales@brash-scales.co.uk
Website: http://www.dbrash.com
Managers: R. Park (District Mgr)
Registration no: SC056784 **Date established:** 1879 **Turnover:** £1m - £2m
No.of Employees: 11 - 20 **Product Groups:** 26, 38

D T Z

Marchmount House Dumfries Place, Cardiff, CF10 3RJ
Tel: 029-2026 2200 **Fax:** 029-2039 5379
E-mail: info@dtz.com
Website: http://www.dtz.com
Managers: R. James
Immediate Holding Company: DTZ MCCOMBE PIERCE LLP
Registration no: NC000516 **Date established:** 2009
No.of Employees: 21 - 50 **Product Groups:** 54, 80, 84

Date of Accounts	Apr 12	Apr 11	Apr 10
Working Capital	544	613	968
Fixed Assets	68	105	156
Current Assets	1m	1m	3m

Dalcross Tyre Services Ltd

Dalcross Street, Cardiff, CF24 4SD
Tel: 029-2049 7394 **Fax:** 029-2049 8897
E-mail: dalcrosstyres@hotmail.com
Website: http://www.dalcrosstyres.co.uk
Directors: V. Kempton (MD)
Immediate Holding Company: DALCROSS TYRE SERVICES LIMITED
Registration no: 01000021 **VAT No.:** GB 133 4490 84
Date established: 1971 **Turnover:** £250,000 - £500,000
No.of Employees: 1 - 10 **Product Groups:** 29, 68

Date of Accounts	Dec 11	Dec 10	Dec 09
Working Capital	121	131	138
Fixed Assets	16	12	14
Current Assets	226	222	216

Data Powertools Ltd

427 Cowbridge Road West, Cardiff, CF5 5TF
Tel: 029-2059 5710 **Fax:** 029-2059 1540
E-mail: sales@datapowertools.co.uk
Website: http://www.datapowertools.co.uk
Bank(s): HSBC Bank plc
Directors: M. Dando (MD), L. Dando (Fin)
Managers: M. Coleman (Sales Admin), M. Dando (Tech Serv Mgr)
Immediate Holding Company: DATA POWERTOOLS LIMITED
Registration no: 01352164 **VAT No.:** GB 393 9542 08
Date established: 1978 **Turnover:** £500,000 - £1m
No.of Employees: 11 - 20 **Product Groups:** 66

Date of Accounts	Mar 11	Mar 10	Mar 09
Working Capital	41	113	181
Fixed Assets	691	722	751
Current Assets	627	595	669

T B Davies Ltd

Penarth Road Llandough Trading Estate, Cardiff, CF11 8TD
Tel: 029-2071 3000 **Fax:** 029-2070 2386
E-mail: sales@tbdavies.co.uk
Website: http://www.tbdavies.co.uk
Bank(s): National Westminster

see next page

***T B Davies Ltd** - Cont'd*

Directors: D. Gray (Dir), J. Gray (Dir)
Managers: F. Camilleri (Sales Prom Mgr)
Ultimate Holding Company: T B DAVIES (HOLDINGS) LIMITED
Immediate Holding Company: T B DAVIES (CARDIFF) LIMITED
Registration no: 00534073 **VAT No.:** 134 1442 07 **Date established:** 1954
Turnover: £2m - £5m **No.of Employees:** 11 - 20 **Product Groups:** 34, 35

Date of Accounts	Dec 11	Dec 10	Dec 09
Sales Turnover	5m	4m	5m
Pre Tax Profit/Loss	12	-29	-69
Working Capital	140	177	185
Fixed Assets	490	429	490
Current Assets	1m	881	1m
Current Liabilities	174	151	182

Delaval

Oak House Pascal Close, St Mellons, Cardiff, CF3 0LW
Tel: 029-2077 5800 **Fax:** 01633-838054
E-mail: info@delaval.co.uk
Website: http://www.delaval.com
Directors: A. Reece (MD), N. Pattemore (Fin)
Managers: T. Burns (Personnel), B. Ellis (Mktg Serv Mgr)
Ultimate Holding Company: TETRA LAVAL HOLDINGS BV (NETHERLANDS)
Immediate Holding Company: DELAVAL LIMITED
Registration no: 01945075 **VAT No.:** GB 433 1481 76
Date established: 1985 **Turnover:** £10m - £20m
No.of Employees: 21 - 50 **Product Groups:** 41

Date of Accounts	Dec 11	Dec 10	Dec 09
Sales Turnover	12m	12m	12m
Pre Tax Profit/Loss	371	31	282
Working Capital	1m	2m	2m
Fixed Assets	586	605	666
Current Assets	3m	4m	3m
Current Liabilities	2m	2m	1m

designdough ltd

Studio 10 The Coal Exchange Mount Stuart Square, Cardiff, CF10 5EB
Tel: 029-2000 8834
E-mail: studio@designdough.co.uk
Website: http://www.designdough.co.uk
Directors: J. Brown (MD)
Immediate Holding Company: DESIGN DOUGH LTD
Registration no: 06017344 **Date established:** 2006
Turnover: Up to £250,000 **No.of Employees:** 1 - 10 **Product Groups:** 81

Date of Accounts	Dec 11	Dec 10	Dec 09
Working Capital	-6	-1	1
Fixed Assets	10	1	N/A
Current Assets	16	15	10

Door Maintenance Co. Ltd

8 Curran Industrial Estate Curran Road, Cardiff, CF10 5DF
Tel: 029-2066 5539 **Fax:** 029-2066 8207
E-mail: rsmith@pme.co.uk
Website: http://www.doormaintenance.net
Bank(s): Barclays
Directors: J. O'Sullivan (MD), R. Pickford (Sales & Mktg), R. Pickford (MD), R. Smith (Dir), R. Smith (Tech Serv)
Ultimate Holding Company: 00933443
Immediate Holding Company: DOOR MAINTENANCE CO. LIMITED
Registration no: 01783555 **VAT No.:** GB 298 5463 02
Date established: 1984 **Turnover:** £2m - £5m **No.of Employees:** 21 - 50
Product Groups: 35, 48

Date of Accounts	Jun 08	Jun 07	Jun 06
Working Capital	365	358	356
Current Assets	1121	1317	1273
Current Liabilities	756	959	917

Dunbar & Boardman

Victoria House Andrews Road, Cardiff, CF14 2JP
Tel: 029-2056 7673 **Fax:** 029-2056 7758
E-mail: seymour.associates@virgin.net
Website: http://www.dunbarboardman.com
Managers: F. Seymour (Mgr)
Immediate Holding Company: CHARLESWORTH PROPERTY HOLDINGS LIMITED
Registration no: 03380549 **Date established:** 1997
No.of Employees: 1 - 10 **Product Groups:** 35, 39, 45

Date of Accounts	Dec 10	Dec 09	Dec 08
Working Capital	392	397	416
Current Assets	425	430	456

Dynic UK

Unit 7 Trident Trade Park Glass Avenue, Cardiff, CF24 5EP
Tel: 029-2048 3973 **Fax:** 029-2048 6706
E-mail: ian@dynic.co.uk
Website: http://www.dynic.co.uk
Directors: S. Jones (Co Sec)
Managers: I. Williams (Chief Mgr), J. Parker
Ultimate Holding Company: DYNIC CORPORATION (JAPAN)
Immediate Holding Company: DYNIC (UK) LTD
Registration no: 02419798 **Date established:** 1989 **Turnover:** £5m - £10m
No.of Employees: 21 - 50 **Product Groups:** 23, 30, 40

Date of Accounts	Dec 11	Dec 10	Dec 09
Sales Turnover	9m	9m	8m
Pre Tax Profit/Loss	113	50	224
Working Capital	2m	2m	2m
Fixed Assets	219	53	89
Current Assets	5m	5m	4m
Current Liabilities	130	107	202

E C D Castings

Wentloog Road Rumney, Cardiff, CF3 1XH
Tel: 029-2036 2333 **Fax:** 029-2036 2216
E-mail: ecd@ecdcastingsltd.co.uk
Website: http://www.ecdcastingsltd.co.uk
Immediate Holding Company: ECD CASTINGS LTD
Registration no: 05344280 **Date established:** 2005
No.of Employees: 11 - 20 **Product Groups:** 37, 40

Date of Accounts	Jun 11	Jun 10	Jun 09
Working Capital	105	5	-102
Fixed Assets	314	349	367
Current Assets	1m	1m	1m

E Turner & Sons

32 Cathedral Road, Cardiff, CF11 9UQ
Tel: 029-2022 1002 **Fax:** 029-2038 8206
E-mail: construction.turner@willmottdixon.co.uk
Website: http://www.willmottdixon.co.uk
Bank(s): HSBC, London
Directors: A. Brewer (Dir), R. Willmott (Ch), B. Drysdale (MD)
Ultimate Holding Company: Willmott Dixon Ltd
Immediate Holding Company: Willmott Dixon Construction Ltd
Registration no: 00768173 **VAT No.:** GB 197 7377 96
Date established: 1992 **Turnover:** £20m - £50m
No.of Employees: 51 - 100 **Product Groups:** 52

Earthmonkey Media

Indycuee Media Centre Culverhouse Cross, Cardiff, CF5 6XJ
Tel: 08456-436261 **Fax:** 01443-231434
E-mail: info@earthmonkey.co.uk
Website: http://www.earthmonkey.co.uk
Directors: J. Daniel (Dir)
Immediate Holding Company: EARTHMONKEY MEDIA LIMITED
Registration no: 06183868 **Date established:** 2007
No.of Employees: 1 - 10 **Product Groups:** 81

Date of Accounts	Mar 12	Mar 11	Mar 10
Sales Turnover	N/A	28	N/A
Working Capital	9	1	-2
Fixed Assets	N/A	N/A	1
Current Assets	18	9	4

Electrostatic Coatings

Unit 5a Charnwood Park Clos Marion, Cardiff, CF10 4LJ
Tel: 029-2048 0800 **Fax:** 01925-228773
Website: http://www.vandacoatings.co.uk
Directors: E. Shaw (Prop)
Managers: R. Jenkins (Mgr)
Immediate Holding Company: ELECTROSTATICS LIMITED
Registration no: 04784367 **Date established:** 2003
No.of Employees: 21 - 50 **Product Groups:** 46, 48

Elmatic Cardiff Ltd

Wentloog Road Rumney, Cardiff, CF3 1XH
Tel: 029-2077 8727 **Fax:** 029-2079 2297
E-mail: sales@elmatic.co.uk
Website: http://www.elmatic.co.uk
Bank(s): National Westminster Bank Plc
Directors: A. Hodges (MD)
Managers: P. Crisp (Sales Prom Mgr), M. Lamble, A. Jones (Fin Mgr), C. Crisp (Sales Admin)
Ultimate Holding Company: ELMATIC (CARDIFF) LIMITED
Registration no: 00712687 **VAT No.:** GB 134 7201 96
Date established: 1962 **Turnover:** £5m - £10m
No.of Employees: 51 - 100 **Product Groups:** 37, 38, 40

Date of Accounts	Jun 11	Jun 10	Jun 09
Working Capital	105	5	-102
Fixed Assets	314	349	367
Current Assets	1m	1m	1m

Euro Quality Coatings Ltd

Wentloog Corporate Park Wentloog Road, Rumney, Cardiff, CF3 2ER
Tel: 029-2036 2999 **Fax:** 029-2079 0785
E-mail: info@eqcltd.co.uk
Website: http://www.euroqualitycoatings.co.uk
Directors: J. Morse (Fin), S. Rosher (MD), S. Rosher (MD)
Managers: A. Phillips (Chief Acct)
Immediate Holding Company: EURO QUALITY COATINGS LIMITED
Registration no: 02901157 **Date established:** 1994 **Turnover:** £2m - £5m
No.of Employees: 21 - 50 **Product Groups:** 46

Date of Accounts	Jul 11	Jul 10	Jul 09
Working Capital	419	484	332
Fixed Assets	545	233	279
Current Assets	1m	1m	836

Eurobond Laminates Ltd

Wentloog Corporate Park Wentloog Road, Rumney, Cardiff, CF3 2ER
Tel: 029-2077 6677 **Fax:** 029-2036 9161
E-mail: sales@eurobond.co.uk
Website: http://www.eurobond.co.uk
Bank(s): National Westminster, Cardiff
Directors: M. Rees (Fin), J. Hunter (Pers)
Managers: D. Hurley (Tech Serv Mgr)
Ultimate Holding Company: SPEYSIDE LTD
Immediate Holding Company: EUROBOND LIMITED
Registration no: 03885985 **VAT No.:** GB 615 6301 65
Date established: 1999 **Turnover:** £10m - £20m
No.of Employees: 101 - 250 **Product Groups:** 33, 35

Date of Accounts	Dec 10	Dec 09	Dec 08
Working Capital	374	394	374
Fixed Assets	N/A	2	4
Current Assets	511	484	459
Current Liabilities	87	39	N/A

Euroclad Ltd

Wentloog Corporate Park Wentloog Road, Rumney, Cardiff, CF3 2ER
Tel: 029-2079 0722 **Fax:** 029-2036 0187
E-mail: sales@euroclad.com
Website: http://www.euroclad.com
Bank(s): Barclays
Directors: P. Cook (MD), T. Phillips (Ch), A. Phillips (Fin)
Managers: A. Hickin (Mktg Serv Mgr), I. Barkley (Sales Prom Mgr)
Ultimate Holding Company: EURO CLAD (INVESTMENTS) LIMITED
Immediate Holding Company: EURO CLAD (HOLDINGS) LIMITED
Registration no: 02427748 **VAT No.:** GB 535 2654 46
Date established: 1989 **Turnover:** £20m - £50m
No.of Employees: 101 - 250 **Product Groups:** 35

Date of Accounts	Dec 10	Dec 09	Dec 08
Sales Turnover	23m	24m	35m
Pre Tax Profit/Loss	122	-222	33
Working Capital	2m	2m	2m
Fixed Assets	2m	3m	3m
Current Assets	8m	7m	8m
Current Liabilities	1m	2m	2m

European Metals Recycling Ltd

Dowlais Wharf Roath Dock, Cardiff, CF10 4ED
Tel: 029-2048 8522 **Fax:** 029-2046 0790
E-mail: victoria.dommett@elrltd.com
Website: http://www.elrltd.com
Directors: V. Dommett (Co Sec)
Immediate Holding Company: EUROPEAN METAL RECYCLING LIMITED
Registration no: 02954623 **Date established:** 1994
Turnover: £10m - £20m **No.of Employees:** 1 - 10 **Product Groups:** 42, 66

Date of Accounts	Dec 11	Dec 10	Dec 09
Sales Turnover	3032m	2431m	1843m
Pre Tax Profit/Loss	116m	155m	91m
Working Capital	414m	371m	167m
Fixed Assets	518m	483m	480m
Current Assets	1027m	717m	557m
Current Liabilities	124m	118m	185m

Fairhill Solutions

Unit C4 Garth Works Taffs Well, Cardiff, CF15 7YF
Tel: 01443-887832 **Fax:** 08456-529924
E-mail: contactus@fairhillsolutions.co.uk
Website: http://www.fairhillsolutions.co.uk
Directors: P. Stephens (Prop)
Immediate Holding Company: FAIRHILL SOLUTIONS LIMITED
Registration no: 06506356 **Date established:** 2008
No.of Employees: 1 - 10 **Product Groups:** 44

Date of Accounts	Mar 12	Mar 11	Mar 10
Working Capital	-12	1	-1
Fixed Assets	3	2	2
Current Assets	8	8	3

FineCal (Cymru) Ltd

3 Rhymney River Bridge Road Rumney, Cardiff, CF23 9AF
Tel: 029-2046 2644 **Fax:** 029-2048 4522
E-mail: sales@finecal.co.uk
Website: http://www.finecal.co.uk
Bank(s): Barclays
Directors: N. Gough (Ch), S. Gough (MD)
Managers: D. Greening (Cust Serv Mgr), T. Eagle (Mktg Serv Mgr)
Immediate Holding Company: Finecal Cymru 2010 Ltd
Registration no: 07127264 **Date established:** 1979 **Turnover:** £1m - £2m
No.of Employees: 11 - 20 **Product Groups:** 23, 27, 30, 32, 37, 42

Fire & Stove Shop (Decorative Heating Ltd)

The Ton Garage Merthyr Road Tongwynlais, Cardiff, CF15 7XW
Tel: 029-2081 1478 **Fax:** 029-2086 1576
E-mail: cardiff@decorativeheating.co.uk
Website: http://www.decorativeheating.co.uk
Directors: J. Portsmouth (MD)
Immediate Holding Company: DECORATIVE HEATING LIMITED
Registration no: 04804011 **Date established:** 2003
Turnover: £500,000 - £1m **No.of Employees:** 11 - 20
Product Groups: 35, 36, 52, 66

Date of Accounts	Jun 11	Jun 10	Jun 09
Working Capital	29	20	30
Fixed Assets	127	115	87
Current Assets	293	210	176

Forgemasters Ltd

Garth Works Taffs Well, Cardiff, CF15 7YF
Tel: 029-2081 0341 **Fax:** 029-2081 0108
E-mail: info@swforgemasters.co.uk
Website: http://www.swforgemasters.co.uk
Directors: P. Brabban (Dir), I. Davies (Fin)
Ultimate Holding Company: CASTELL INTERNATIONAL LIMITED
Immediate Holding Company: FORGEMASTERS LIMITED
Registration no: 02103640 **Date established:** 1987 **Turnover:** £2m - £5m
No.of Employees: 21 - 50 **Product Groups:** 48

Date of Accounts	Mar 11	Mar 10	Mar 09
Working Capital	162	69	35
Fixed Assets	153	225	302
Current Assets	545	772	723

Fusion Workshop

Quebec House Cowbridge Road East, Cardiff, CF11 9AB
Tel: 029-2066 6655 **Fax:** 029-2066 6644
E-mail: chris.short@fusionworkshop.com
Website: http://www.fusionworkshop.co.uk
Directors: C. Short (Grp Chief Exec)
Immediate Holding Company: FUSION WORKSHOP LIMITED
Registration no: 03749987 **Date established:** 1999
Turnover: £250,000 - £500,000 **No.of Employees:** 21 - 50
Product Groups: 44, 79, 80

Date of Accounts	Mar 12	Mar 11	Mar 10
Working Capital	211	186	181
Fixed Assets	53	71	76
Current Assets	541	542	487

G M A C (Head Office)

Unit 6.1 Heol Y Gamlas Parc Nantgarw, Nantgarw, Cardiff, CF15 7QU
Tel: 08448-712222 **Fax:** 01273-771501
E-mail: erhard.paulat@gmacfs.com
Website: http://www.gmacfs.co.uk
Bank(s): Lloyds TSB Bank plc
Directors: E. Paulat (MD)
Ultimate Holding Company: ALLY FINANCIAL INC (USA)
Immediate Holding Company: GMAC UK FINANCE PLC
Registration no: 01881045 **Date established:** 1985 **Turnover:** £1m - £2m
No.of Employees: 501 - 1000 **Product Groups:** 82

Date of Accounts	Dec 10	Dec 09	Dec 08
Sales Turnover	1m	898	3m
Pre Tax Profit/Loss	1m	765	863
Working Capital	6m	6m	5m
Current Assets	12m	14m	22m
Current Liabilities	506	214	712

Geldards LLP

Dumfries House Dumfries Place, Cardiff, CF10 3ZF
Tel: 029-2023 8239 **Fax:** 029-2023 7268
E-mail: info@geldards.com
Website: http://www.geldards.com
Directors: J. Pearson (Grp Chief Exec), J. Dancey (Fin)
Managers: M. Boudier (Personnel), H. Wigley
Immediate Holding Company: GELDARDS LLP
Registration no: OC313172 **VAT No.:** GB 134 0218 17
Date established: 2005 **Turnover:** £10m - £20m
No.of Employees: 101 - 250 **Product Groups:** 80

Date of Accounts	Jul 11	Jul 10	Jul 09
Sales Turnover	N/A	20m	22m
Pre Tax Profit/Loss	4m	5m	5m
Working Capital	5m	6m	6m
Fixed Assets	997	1m	1m
Current Assets	10m	11m	11m
Current Liabilities	1m	1m	1m

Gnashers Dental Technicians

90 Woodville Road, Cardiff, CF24 4ED
Tel: 029-2023 6268 **Fax:** 029-2023 6268
Website: http://www.gnashers.uk.com
Directors: D. Morgan (Fin), B. Williams (Prop), B. Williams (Ptnr)
No.of Employees: 1 - 10 **Product Groups:** 38, 67

Graig Shipping
1 Caspian Point Caspian Way, Cardiff, CF10 4DQ
Tel: 029-2044 0200 **Fax:** 029-2044 0207
E-mail: mail@graig.com
Website: http://www.graig.com
Directors: C. Davies (Fin), C. Williams (Mkt Research), H. Williams (Grp Chief Exec)
Managers: K. Treharne (Tech Serv Mgr), N. Owens (Purch Mgr), V. Dwyer
Ultimate Holding Company: IDWAL WILLIAMS AND COMPANY LIMITED
Immediate Holding Company: GRAIG CARDIFF SHIPPING LTD
Registration no: 07281436 **Date established:** 2010
Turnover: £50m - £75m **No.of Employees:** 21 - 50 **Product Groups:** 74, 80

Date of Accounts	Dec 11	Dec 10
Pre Tax Profit/Loss	-7	19
Working Capital	261	4m
Fixed Assets	17m	8m
Current Assets	467	4m
Current Liabilities	96	N/A

Green Light Products Ltd
Capital Business Park Parkway, Cardiff, CF3 2PX
Tel: 029-2079 0880 **Fax:** 029-2079 2470
E-mail: sales@greenlightproducts.co.uk
Website: http://www.greenlightproducts.co.uk
Managers: S. Douglas (Contrlr)
Immediate Holding Company: GREEN LIGHT PRODUCTS LIMITED
Registration no: 02926851 **Date established:** 1994
Turnover: £250,000 - £500,000 **No.of Employees:** 11 - 20
Product Groups: 27, 30, 67

Date of Accounts	Dec 11	Dec 10	Dec 09
Working Capital	604	597	418
Fixed Assets	504	473	505
Current Assets	1m	1m	1m

greenfield media solutions limited
The Television Centre Culverhouse Cross, Cardiff, CF5 6XJ
Tel: 029-2059 0334 **Fax:** 029-2059 0335
E-mail: info@greenfieldmedia.com
Website: http://www.greenfieldmedia.com
Directors: W. Innes (MD)
Registration no: 05346982 **Date established:** 2005
No.of Employees: 1 - 10 **Product Groups:** 80, 81

Date of Accounts	Dec 09	Dec 08	Dec 07
Working Capital	49	6	-19
Fixed Assets	45	62	49
Current Assets	248	316	532

J D Griffiths
Fford Cottage St George's-Super-Ely, Cardiff, CF5 6ET
Tel: 01446-760867 **Fax:** 01446-760082
E-mail: jdgriffiths@btconnect.com
Directors: J. Griffiths (Prop)
Date established: 1980 **No.of Employees:** 1 - 10 **Product Groups:** 41

Hall Fabrications
Lamby Workshops Lamby Way, Rumney, Cardiff, CF3 2EQ
Tel: 029-2036 0686 **Fax:** 029-2036 0686
E-mail: tonyhall1@btconnect.com
Directors: A. Hall (Prop)
Immediate Holding Company: PROPCO INVESTMENTS LIMITED
Registration no: 04715299 **Date established:** 2007
No.of Employees: 1 - 10 **Product Groups:** 35

Harlech Doors Ltd
8 Curran Industrial Estate Curran Road, Cardiff, CF10 5DF
Tel: 029-2066 5539 **Fax:** 029-2066 5518
E-mail: rsmith@pme.co.uk
Website: http://www.doormaintenance.net
Directors: R. Smith (Dir)
Managers: J. Butler (Chief Mgr), P. Wilcock (Buyer)
Ultimate Holding Company: DOOR MAINTENANCE HOLDINGS COMPANY LIMITED
Immediate Holding Company: DOOR MAINTENANCE CO. LIMITED
Registration no: 01783555 **Date established:** 1984
No.of Employees: 21 - 50 **Product Groups:** 26, 35

Date of Accounts	Jun 11	Jun 10	Jun 09
Working Capital	-42	-16	377
Fixed Assets	147	117	10
Current Assets	409	763	1m

Heatforce
10 Lambourne Crescent Llanishen, Cardiff, CF14 5GP
Tel: 08452-600321 **Fax:** 08452-600322
E-mail: enquiries@heatforce.co.uk
Website: http://www.heatforce.co.uk
Directors: N. Williams (Fin), P. Maddocks (Prop)
Immediate Holding Company: HEATFORCE (WALES) LIMITED
Registration no: 04261333 **Date established:** 2001
No.of Employees: 51 - 100 **Product Groups:** 25, 26, 52

Date of Accounts	Sep 11	Sep 10	Sep 09
Working Capital	209	346	367
Fixed Assets	1m	973	1m
Current Assets	2m	1m	1m

High Motive Ltd
Unit 10 Wroughton Place Ely, Cardiff, CF5 4AB
Tel: 029-2056 3366 **Fax:** 029-2056 3606
E-mail: phil@highmotive.co.uk
Website: http://www.highmotive.co.uk
Directors: P. Miles (MD)
Immediate Holding Company: HIGH MOTIVE LIMITED
Registration no: 04048390 **Date established:** 2000
Turnover: Up to £250,000 **No.of Employees:** 11 - 20 **Product Groups:** 79, 80

Date of Accounts	Aug 12	Aug 11	Aug 10
Sales Turnover	753	N/A	N/A
Pre Tax Profit/Loss	173	N/A	N/A
Working Capital	-250	-70	-35
Fixed Assets	423	108	63
Current Assets	211	143	121
Current Liabilities	404	N/A	N/A

Hilti GT Britain Ltd
4 Rhymney River Bridge Road, Cardiff, CF23 9AF
Tel: 0800-886100 **Fax:** 0800-886200
Website: http://www.hilti.co.uk
Ultimate Holding Company: HILTI AG (LIECHTENSTEIN)
Immediate Holding Company: HILTI (GT.BRITAIN) LIMITED
Registration no: 00479786 **Date established:** 1950
Turnover: £75m - £125m **No.of Employees:** 1 - 10 **Product Groups:** 35, 37, 48

Date of Accounts	Dec 10	Dec 09	Dec 08
Sales Turnover	65m	66m	79m
Pre Tax Profit/Loss	766	-379	-48
Working Capital	12m	15m	12m
Fixed Assets	5m	5m	6m
Current Assets	33m	25m	23m
Current Liabilities	6m	4m	5m

Hoare Lea & Partners
Charterhouse Links Business Park Fortran Road, St Mellons, Cardiff, CF3 0LT
Tel: 029-2053 5050 **Fax:** 029-2053 5053
E-mail: johnrhoden@hoarelea.com
Website: http://www.hoarelea.com
Directors: J. Rhoden (Snr Part)
Immediate Holding Company: HOARE LEA LIMITED
Registration no: 07088478 **Date established:** 2009
Turnover: £10m - £20m **No.of Employees:** 21 - 50 **Product Groups:** 84

Holder Mathias Architects
The Bonded Warehouse Atlantic Wharf, Cardiff, CF10 4HF
Tel: 029-2049 8681 **Fax:** 029-2046 1337
E-mail: enquiries@holdermathias.com
Website: http://www.holdermathias.com
Bank(s): Lloyds TSB Bank plc
Directors: K. Hobbs (Fin)
Managers: S. Mead (Tech Serv Mgr), L. Shellhard (Mktg Serv Mgr), J. Devenney, L. Shellard (Mktg Serv Mgr)
Ultimate Holding Company: HOLDER MATHIAS LLP
Immediate Holding Company: HOLDER MATHIAS ARCHITECTS LIMITED
Registration no: 02108133 **VAT No.:** GB 402 5175 90
Date established: 1987 **Turnover:** £2m - £5m **No.of Employees:** 51 - 100
Product Groups: 84

Date of Accounts	Jun 11	Jun 10	Jun 09
Sales Turnover	N/A	4m	5m
Pre Tax Profit/Loss	N/A	8	38
Working Capital	895	851	835
Fixed Assets	50	109	174
Current Assets	2m	2m	2m
Current Liabilities	310	489	549

Horseley Bridge
Garth Works Taffs Well, Cardiff, CF15 7YF
Tel: 029-2081 5270 **Fax:** 029-2081 5275
E-mail: dewaters@connect-2.co.uk
Website: http://www.horseleybridgetanks.com
Managers: A. McDonagh (Chief Mgr)
Ultimate Holding Company: CASTELL INTERNATIONAL LIMITED
Immediate Holding Company: FORGEMASTERS LIMITED
Registration no: 02103640 **Date established:** 1987
No.of Employees: 21 - 50 **Product Groups:** 30, 35

Date of Accounts	Mar 11	Mar 10	Mar 09
Working Capital	162	69	35
Fixed Assets	153	225	302
Current Assets	545	772	723

Huntleigh Healthcare
Unit 35 Portmanmoor Road Industrial Estate, Cardiff, CF24 5HB
Tel: 029-2048 5885 **Fax:** 029-2049 2520
E-mail: sales@huntleigh-diagnostics.co.uk
Website: http://www.huntleigh-diagnostics.co.uk
Bank(s): Barclays, Boreham Wood
Directors: P. Cashim (MD)
Managers: A. Roberts (Nat Sales Mgr), D. Meilak (Mktg Serv Mgr)
Ultimate Holding Company: HUNTLEIGH TECHNOLOGY P.L.C.
Registration no: 02510171 **VAT No.:** GB 615 5585 30
Turnover: £5m - £10m **No.of Employees:** 101 - 250 **Product Groups:** 31, 37, 38

I Q E plc
Cypress Drive St Mellons, Cardiff, CF3 0EG
Tel: 029-2083 9400 **Fax:** 029- 20839401
E-mail: info@iqep.com
Website: http://www.iqep.com
Directors: P. Rasmussen (Co Sec), G. Ainsworth (Ch)
Immediate Holding Company: IQE PLC
Registration no: 03745726 **Date established:** 1999
Turnover: £75m - £125m **No.of Employees:** 251 - 500
Product Groups: 37, 40

Date of Accounts	Dec 11	Dec 10	Dec 09
Sales Turnover	75m	73m	53m
Pre Tax Profit/Loss	7m	6m	2m
Working Capital	9m	17m	5m
Fixed Assets	72m	55m	41m
Current Assets	33m	41m	28m
Current Liabilities	12m	8m	12m

I T V Wales plc
The Television Centre Culverhouse Cross, Cardiff, CF5 6XJ
Tel: 08448-810100 **Fax:** 029-2059 7183
E-mail: phil.henfrey@itv.com
Website: http://www.itv.com
Directors: A. Evans (Sales), M. McCullagh (Fin), H. Tautz (Co Sec)
Managers: P. Henfrey
Ultimate Holding Company: ITV PLC
Immediate Holding Company: ITV WALES & WEST LIMITED
Registration no: 02272112 **Date established:** 1988
Turnover: £20m - £50m **No.of Employees:** 51 - 100 **Product Groups:** 89

Date of Accounts	Dec 08	Dec 07
Sales Turnover	N/A	22m
Pre Tax Profit/Loss	279	148m
Working Capital	N/A	9m
Current Assets	N/A	9m

Imaginet Ltd
Greyfriars House Greyfriars Road, Cardiff, CF10 3AL
Tel: 029-2057 4500 **Fax:** 029-2025 5535
E-mail: sales@imaginet.co.uk
Website: http://www.imaginet.co.uk
Directors: N. Roberts (MD)
Managers: P. Dauncey (Sales Prom Mgr)
Immediate Holding Company: IMAGINET LIMITED
Registration no: 03042421 **Date established:** 1995 **Turnover:** £2m - £5m
No.of Employees: 11 - 20 **Product Groups:** 44, 79, 80

Date of Accounts	Apr 11	Apr 10	Apr 09
Working Capital	-151	-188	-273
Fixed Assets	241	231	221
Current Assets	249	277	185

Industrial Catering Industries Ltd
Sterling Works Clarence Road, Cardiff, CF10 5FA
Tel: 029-2049 8498 **Fax:** 029-2048 8838
E-mail: mail@protect-u.co.uk
Website: http://www.protect-u.co.uk
Directors: C. Duddridge (Dir)
Immediate Holding Company: INDUSTRIAL AND CATERING INDUSTRIES LIMITED
Registration no: 02727570 **VAT No.:** GB 543 0496 53
Date established: 1992 **Turnover:** Up to £250,000
No.of Employees: 1 - 10 **Product Groups:** 63, 67

Date of Accounts	Aug 10	Aug 09	Aug 08
Working Capital	-19	-26	-27
Fixed Assets	46	48	49
Current Assets	98	104	124

Industrial Friction Materials Ltd
Unit 7 East Moors Business Park East Moors Road, Cardiff, CF24 5JX
Tel: 029-2049 9111 **Fax:** 029-2049 0011
E-mail: mail@industrialfriction.com
Website: http://www.industrialfriction.com
Directors: J. Price (MD)
Immediate Holding Company: INDUSTRIAL FRICTION MATERIALS LIMITED
Registration no: 01197141 **VAT No.:** GB 282 4218 63
Date established: 1975 **Turnover:** Up to £250,000
No.of Employees: 1 - 10 **Product Groups:** 35

Date of Accounts	Mar 11	Mar 10	Mar 09
Working Capital	-33	-34	-20
Fixed Assets	3	2	7
Current Assets	73	51	41

Insteng Process Automation Ltd
Unit 3 Moy Road Industrial Estate Taffs Well, Cardiff, CF15 7QR
Tel: 029-2081 5000 **Fax:** 029-2081 3051
E-mail: sylviaburris@insteng.co.uk
Website: http://www.insteng.co.uk
Bank(s): National Westminster Bank Plc
Directors: S. Burris (Dir), S. Read (Chief Op Offcr), S. Burris (Dir)
Managers: D. John (Tech Serv Mgr)
Immediate Holding Company: INSTENG PROCESS AUTOMATION LIMITED
Registration no: 01165037 **VAT No.:** GB 137 1324 92
Date established: 1974 **Turnover:** £2m - £5m **No.of Employees:** 11 - 20
Product Groups: 37, 38, 39, 40, 44

Date of Accounts	May 12	May 11	May 10
Working Capital	174	144	151
Fixed Assets	105	128	136
Current Assets	797	558	653
Current Liabilities	225	155	N/A

Institute Of Chartered Accountants
Regus House Falcon Drive, Cardiff, CF10 4RU
Tel: 020-7920 8100 **Fax:** 020-7920 0547
E-mail: feedback@icaew.co.uk
Website: http://www.icaew.com
Directors: A. Fagg (Fin), B. Wilson (Tech Serv), M. Owens (Pers), S. Best (Mkt Research)
Managers: S. Fernley (Sales Admin)
Immediate Holding Company: FUSION LAW COSTS CONSULTANTS LIMITED
Registration no: 00608198 **Date established:** 2002
Turnover: £20m - £50m **No.of Employees:** 101 - 250 **Product Groups:** 87

Date of Accounts	Apr 04	Apr 03
Working Capital	57	-3
Fixed Assets	9	11
Current Assets	93	49

Integrated Vision Systems Ltd
38 Mill Road Ely, Cardiff, CF5 4AG
Tel: 0808-202 6666 **Fax:** 0871-277 1909
Directors: J. Owen (Fin), R. Grigg (MD)
Registration no: 05189851 **Date established:** 2004
Turnover: £250,000 - £500,000 **No.of Employees:** 1 - 10
Product Groups: 44

Jewson Ltd
East Moors Road, Cardiff, CF24 5EE
Tel: 029-2046 0511 **Fax:** 029-2048 7984
E-mail: richerdm.roberts@jewson.co.uk
Website: http://www.jewson.co.uk
Bank(s): Barclays
Managers: G. Owens (Mgr)
Ultimate Holding Company: COMPAGNIE DE SAINT GOBAIN (FRANCE)
Immediate Holding Company: JEWSON LIMITED
Registration no: 00348407 **VAT No.:** GB 394 1212 63
Date established: 1939 **Turnover:** Up to £250,000
No.of Employees: 21 - 50 **Product Groups:** 66

Date of Accounts	Dec 11	Dec 10	Dec 09
Sales Turnover	1606m	1547m	1485m
Pre Tax Profit/Loss	18m	100m	45m
Working Capital	-345m	-250m	-349m
Fixed Assets	496m	387m	461m
Current Assets	657m	1005m	1320m
Current Liabilities	66m	120m	64m

William Jones Packaging
Unit B5 South Point Foreshore Road, Cardiff, CF10 4SP
Tel: 029-2048 6262 **Fax:** 029-2048 1230
E-mail: sales@wjpackaging.co.uk
Website: http://www.wjpackaging.co.uk
Directors: R. Austin (MD)
Immediate Holding Company: WILLIAM JONES PACKAGING LIMITED
Registration no: 03401516 **VAT No.:** GB 133 4410 11
Date established: 1997 **Turnover:** £2m - £5m **No.of Employees:** 1 - 10
Product Groups: 27, 30, 48

Date of Accounts	Jul 11	Jul 10	Jul 09
Working Capital	282	226	222
Fixed Assets	16	16	19
Current Assets	445	412	397

Kennedy James Griffiths Architects
Unit 7 Oak Tree Court Mulberry Drive Cardiff Gate Business Park, Pontprennau, Cardiff, CF23 8RS
Tel: 029-2054 5100 **Fax:** 029-2054 6216
E-mail: ceri@kennedyjamesgriffiths.co.uk
Website: http://www.kennedyjamesgriffiths.co.uk
Directors: C. Griffiths (Ptnr)
Date established: 2000 **Turnover:** £1m - £2m **No.of Employees:** 1 - 10
Product Groups: 84

Knight Fire & Security
84 Seawall Road Seawall Road, Cardiff, CF24 5PH
Tel: 029-2048 8129 **Fax:** 029-2048 9132
E-mail: sales@knightplastics.com
Website: http://www.knightfireandsecurity.com
Bank(s): HSBC
Directors: C. Wegener (MD), T. Wegener (Fin), C. Wegener (MD)
Managers: M. Wegener (Sales & Mktg Mg)
Immediate Holding Company: PONTYPOOL PRECISION ENGINEERING LTD
Registration no: 01787348 **Date established:** 2011 **Turnover:** £2m - £5m
No.of Employees: 51 - 100 **Product Groups:** 30

Date of Accounts	Jan 08	Dec 07	Dec 06
Pre Tax Profit/Loss	N/A	N/A	489
Working Capital	722	745	1024
Fixed Assets	290	286	369
Current Assets	1496	1537	1584
Current Liabilities	773	793	561
Total Share Capital	5	5	105
ROCE% (Return on Capital Employed)			35.1

KPMG UK Ltd
3 Assembly Square Britannia Quay, Cardiff, CF10 4PL
Tel: 029-2046 8000 **Fax:** 029-2046 8200
E-mail: simon.jones@kpmg.co.uk
Website: http://www.kpmg.co.uk
Directors: S. Jones (Snr Part)
Ultimate Holding Company: KPMG EUROPE LLP
Immediate Holding Company: KPMG UK LIMITED
Registration no: 03580549 **Date established:** 1998
No.of Employees: 21 - 50 **Product Groups:** 80

Date of Accounts	Sep 11	Sep 10	Sep 09
Sales Turnover	698m	632m	624m
Pre Tax Profit/Loss	655	593	584
Working Capital	1m	847	419
Current Assets	23m	21m	25m
Current Liabilities	22m	20m	20m

Kwik-Fit GB Ltd
113-115 North Road, Cardiff, CF14 3AD
Tel: 029-2062 0022
Website: http://www.kwik-fit.com
Managers: D. Hughes (Mgr)
Ultimate Holding Company: FINANCIERE DAUNOU 2 SA (LUXEMBOURG)
Immediate Holding Company: KWIK-FIT (GB) LIMITED
Registration no: 01009184 **Date established:** 1971
No.of Employees: 1 - 10 **Product Groups:** 29, 39, 85

Date of Accounts	Dec 10	Dec 09	Dec 08
Sales Turnover	527m	495m	449m
Pre Tax Profit/Loss	269m	56m	97m
Working Capital	197m	201m	154m
Fixed Assets	106m	115m	110m
Current Assets	375m	368m	329m
Current Liabilities	36m	36m	38m

L W T Marketing Services
3 Bishops Road Whitchurch, Cardiff, CF14 1LT
Tel: 029-2061 8085 **Fax:** 029-2069 1797
E-mail: lyndon@lwtmarketing.co.uk
Website: http://www.lwtmarketing.co.uk
Directors: L. Thomas (Prop), S. Thomas (Fin)
Immediate Holding Company: BMAC DESIGN & DEVELOPMENTS LTD
Registration no: 02953482 **VAT No.:** GB 380 8742 30
Date established: 2012 **Turnover:** £250,000 - £500,000
No.of Employees: 1 - 10 **Product Groups:** 81

Date of Accounts	Dec 06	Dec 05
Working Capital	-76	-72
Fixed Assets	4	6
Current Assets	24	32
Current Liabilities	100	104
Total Share Capital	1	1

Major Motor Services Ltd
City House 64 Sloper Road, Cardiff, CF11 8AB
Tel: 029-2037 2688 **Fax:** 029-2022 3172
E-mail: sales@majormotors.co.uk
Website: http://www.majormotors.co.uk
Bank(s): National Westminster Bank Plc
Directors: J. Senior (Dir)
Immediate Holding Company: MAJOR MOTOR SERVICES LIMITED
Registration no: 02525083 **VAT No.:** GB 483 9584 88
Date established: 1990 **Turnover:** £1m - £2m **No.of Employees:** 11 - 20
Product Groups: 38, 39, 40, 48

Date of Accounts	Jul 11	Jul 10	Jul 09
Working Capital	37	34	70
Fixed Assets	663	673	326
Current Assets	261	243	232

Mele & Co.
Sanatorium Road, Cardiff, CF11 8PN
Tel: 029-2022 1331 **Fax:** 029-2022 2409
E-mail: business@meleandco.com
Website: http://www.meleandco.com
Directors: W. Caddick (MD)
Immediate Holding Company: LIONITE MELE LIMITED
Registration no: 00928127 **VAT No.:** GB 134 0868 75
Date established: 1968 **No.of Employees:** 11 - 20 **Product Groups:** 22, 25, 26, 27, 33, 35, 49, 65

Date of Accounts	Dec 11	Dec 10	Dec 09
Working Capital	805	715	348
Fixed Assets	29	41	28
Current Assets	1m	827	1m

Metal Fabrication Co Cardiff Ltd
East Moors Road, Cardiff, CF24 5EE
Tel: 029-2048 9767 **Fax:** 029-2048 0407
E-mail: sales@metal-fab.co.uk
Website: http://www.metal-fab.co.uk
Bank(s): National Westminster
Directors: R. Porter (MD), R. Porter (MD), G. Mayze (Fin)
Managers: M. Porter (Est), R. Allen (Buyer)
Immediate Holding Company: METAL FABRICATION COMPANY (CARDIFF) LIMITED
Registration no: 00552565 **VAT No.:** GB 135 0855 78
Date established: 1955 **Turnover:** £1m - £2m **No.of Employees:** 21 - 50
Product Groups: 35, 36, 52

Date of Accounts	Aug 11	Aug 10	Aug 09
Working Capital	1m	1m	2m
Fixed Assets	924	471	471
Current Assets	1m	1m	2m

Metal Skills
31 Ruskin Close Llanrumney, Cardiff, CF3 5LA
Tel: 029-2048 2500 **Fax:** 029-2048 2500
Directors: C. Sullivan (Prop)
No.of Employees: 1 - 10 **Product Groups:** 35, 49, 66

Metalcraft Products Cardiff Ltd
206 Titan House Cardiff Bay Business Centre Titan Road, Cardiff, CF24 5BS
Tel: 029-2046 5465 **Fax:** 029-2048 2255
E-mail: info@metalcraftproducts.co.uk
Website: http://www.metalcraftproducts.co.uk
Directors: D. Toye (MD), L. Toye (Fin)
Ultimate Holding Company: METALCRAFT HOLDINGS (CARDIFF) LIMITED
Immediate Holding Company: METALCRAFT PRODUCTS (CARDIFF) LIMITED
Registration no: 00438857 **VAT No.:** GB 133 6548 69
Date established: 1947 **Turnover:** £1m - £2m **No.of Employees:** 1 - 10
Product Groups: 45

Date of Accounts	Aug 11	Aug 10	Aug 09
Working Capital	-43	-70	-89
Current Assets	106	96	84

Metrad International (UK) Ltd.
168 Clare Road, Cardiff, CF11 6RX
Tel: 029-2125 0955 **Fax:** 029-2025 8255
E-mail: purchases@metradinternational.co.uk
Website: http://metradinternational.com
Directors: V. Sangani (Dir)
Registration no: 06681117 **Date established:** 2008
No.of Employees: 1 - 10 **Product Groups:** 34, 66

Metroweld Wales Ltd
Unit M106 Cardiff Bay Business Centre Titan Road, Cardiff, CF24 5EJ
Tel: 029-2048 6384 **Fax:** 029-2046 5196
E-mail: j_norman@btconnect.com
Directors: J. Norman (Dir)
Immediate Holding Company: METROWELD WALES LIMITED
Registration no: 02526469 **Date established:** 1990
No.of Employees: 1 - 10 **Product Groups:** 46

Date of Accounts	Mar 11	Mar 10	Mar 09
Working Capital	48	31	34
Fixed Assets	3	4	5
Current Assets	143	122	95

Microwave Repairs
53 Ely Road, Cardiff, CF5 2JF
Tel: 029-2055 4369
Directors: J. Hayward (Prop)
No.of Employees: 1 - 10 **Product Groups:** 36, 40

Mildef Ltd
Units 1.11-1.12 Cardiff Business Technology Centre Senghennydd Road, Cardiff, CF24 4AY
Tel: 029-2064 7040
E-mail: sales@mildef.co.uk
Website: http://www.mildef.co.uk
Directors: D. Skinner (MD)
Immediate Holding Company: TERRALOGIC LTD
Registration no: 03845454 **Date established:** 1999 **Turnover:** £1m - £2m
No.of Employees: 1 - 10 **Product Groups:** 44, 67

Date of Accounts	Mar 11	Mar 10	Mar 09
Working Capital	83	91	43
Fixed Assets	1m	1m	1m
Current Assets	298	373	879

Minerva Laboratories Ltd
Unit 13 Eastgate Business Park Wentloog Avenue, Cardiff, CF3 2EY
Tel: 08453-453912 **Fax:** 029-2046 0337
E-mail: info@minervalabs.co.uk
Website: http://www.minervalabs.co.uk
Directors: A. Beresford (Fin), K. Davies (Chief Op Offcr), J. Melville (MD)
Managers: N. Watkins (Personnel), L. Kennedy (Sales & Mktg Mg)
Ultimate Holding Company: HYGEA HOLDINGS LIMITED
Immediate Holding Company: MINERVA LABORATORIES LIMITED
Registration no: 00246797 **Date established:** 1930 **Turnover:** £1m - £2m
No.of Employees: 21 - 50 **Product Groups:** 29, 38, 40

Date of Accounts	Oct 11	Oct 10	Oct 09
Sales Turnover	1m	1m	1m
Pre Tax Profit/Loss	128	175	148
Working Capital	696	823	835
Fixed Assets	166	150	161
Current Assets	1m	1m	1m
Current Liabilities	203	161	180

Minton Treharne & Davies Ltd
Merton House The Avenue Industrial Park Croescadarn Close, Cardiff, CF23 8HF
Tel: 029-2054 0000 **Fax:** 029-2054 0111
E-mail: john.minton@minton.co.uk
Website: http://www.minton.co.uk
Directors: J. Minton (Dir), J. Minton (Fin)
Immediate Holding Company: MINTON,TREHARNE & DAVIES LIMITED
Registration no: 00435262 **Date established:** 1947 **Turnover:** £5m - £10m
No.of Employees: 51 - 100 **Product Groups:** 54, 84, 85

Date of Accounts	Mar 11	Mar 10	Mar 09
Sales Turnover	10m	10m	6m
Pre Tax Profit/Loss	834	836	502
Working Capital	4m	3m	1m
Fixed Assets	5m	5m	2m
Current Assets	6m	5m	3m
Current Liabilities	2m	1m	672

Monks & Crane Industrial Group Ltd
Seawall Road, Cardiff, CF24 5XG
Tel: 029-2043 6400 **Fax:** 029-2048 9910
E-mail: sgh@mcrane.co.uk
Website: http://www.mcrane.co.uk
Bank(s): Barclays
Managers: S. Hill (Mgr)
Ultimate Holding Company: ADOLF WURTH GMBH & CO KG (GERMANY)
Immediate Holding Company: MONKS & CRANE INDUSTRIAL GROUP LIMITED
Registration no: 00342072 **VAT No.:** GB 368 1843 25
Date established: 1938 **Turnover:** £2m - £5m **No.of Employees:** 11 - 20
Product Groups: 40, 46

Date of Accounts	Dec 11	Dec 10	Dec 09
Sales Turnover	45m	43m	48m
Pre Tax Profit/Loss	-2m	-1m	-2m
Working Capital	2m	3m	3m
Fixed Assets	553	701	556
Current Assets	16m	15m	17m
Current Liabilities	1m	1m	2m

Morgan Cole
Bradley Court 11 Park Place, Cardiff, CF10 3DR
Tel: 029-2038 5385 **Fax:** 029-2038 5300
E-mail: info@morgan-cole.com
Website: http://www.morgan-cole.com
Bank(s): HSBC Bank plc
Directors: C. Bray (Fin), B. Potter (Ch)
Managers: J. Jones (Personnel), J. Wright (Tech Serv Mgr), I. Emery (Mktg Serv Mgr)
Immediate Holding Company: MORGAN COLE SERVICES LIMITED
Registration no: 03618502 **Date established:** 1998
No.of Employees: 51 - 100 **Product Groups:** 80

Motorpoint Arena
Mary Ann Street, Cardiff, CF10 2EQ
Tel: 029-2022 4488 **Fax:** 029-2023 4501
E-mail: cia.sales@livenation.co.uk
Website: http://www.livenation.co.uk/cardiff
Managers: J. Knowles (Mgr)
Immediate Holding Company: EVENT WIZARDS LIMITED
Registration no: 05818186 **Date established:** 2009
Turnover: £250,000 - £500,000 **No.of Employees:** 21 - 50
Product Groups: 69, 80, 87

Date of Accounts	Dec 11	May 11	May 10
Working Capital	-33	-125	-74
Fixed Assets	172	130	181
Current Assets	5	199	11

N & C Building Products Ltd
325-327 Penarth Road, Cardiff, CF11 8TT
Tel: 029-2039 0146 **Fax:** 029-2022 4356
E-mail: rob.hodder@nichollsandclarke.com
Website: http://www.ncdirect.com
Bank(s): National Westminster Bank Plc
Directors: R. Knight (Fin)
Managers: R. Hodder (Mgr)
Ultimate Holding Company: NICHOLLS & CLARKE LIMITED
Immediate Holding Company: N & C BUILDING PRODUCTS LIMITED
Registration no: 00000140 **VAT No.:** GB 243 1639 76
Date established: 1956 **Turnover:** £2m - £5m **No.of Employees:** 11 - 20
Product Groups: 26, 30, 32, 33, 36

Date of Accounts	Dec 11	Dec 10	Dec 09
Sales Turnover	42m	38m	38m
Pre Tax Profit/Loss	1m	618	314
Working Capital	624	236	-491
Fixed Assets	1m	1m	2m
Current Assets	18m	15m	15m
Current Liabilities	2m	1m	1m

Nationwide Platforms
Castle Works East Moors Road, Cardiff, CF24 5NN
Tel: 029-2049 7242 **Fax:** 029-2045 5033
E-mail: cardiff@nationwideplatforms.co.uk
Website: http://www.nationwideplatforms.co.uk
Managers: A. Stokes (Chief Mgr)
Immediate Holding Company: NATIONWIDE ACCESS LIMITED
Registration no: 04405299 **Date established:** 2002
Turnover: £20m - £50m **No.of Employees:** 11 - 20 **Product Groups:** 45, 83

Opus International Consultants UK Ltd
Unit 2 Fountain Court Fountain Lane, St Mellons, Cardiff, CF3 0FB
Tel: 029-2077 7373
E-mail: cardiff@opusinternational.co.uk
Website: http://www.opusinternational.co.uk
Bank(s): Lloyds
Directors: D. Mills (Dir)
Ultimate Holding Company: KHAZANAH NASIONAL BERHAD (MALAYSIA)
Immediate Holding Company: OPUS INTERNATIONAL CONSULTANTS (UK) LIMITED
Registration no: 02847568 **Date established:** 1993
Turnover: £10m - £20m **No.of Employees:** 21 - 50 **Product Groups:** 54, 80, 84, 85

Date of Accounts	Dec 11	Dec 10	Dec 09
Sales Turnover	7m	8m	8m
Pre Tax Profit/Loss	-1m	230	-992
Working Capital	1m	2m	2m
Fixed Assets	140	161	215
Current Assets	8m	7m	8m
Current Liabilities	1m	819	504

Owen Pittard
7 Elgar CR Llanrumney, Cardiff, CF3 5RT
Tel: 029-2079 3710 **Fax:** 029-2079 3710
E-mail: owenpittard@hotmail.co.uk
Directors: O. Pittard (Prop)
Date established: 1991 **No.of Employees:** 1 - 10 **Product Groups:** 46

P D R
Uwic Western Avenue, Cardiff, CF5 2YB
Tel: 029-2041 6725 **Fax:** 029-2041 6973
E-mail: info@pdronline.co.uk
Website: http://www.pdronline.co.uk
Directors: J. Evans (Comm)
Registration no: 03819227 **No.of Employees:** 21 - 50 **Product Groups:** 85

P & P Supplies Ltd
Units 9 10 & 11 Ely Distribution Centre Argyle Way, Cardiff, CF5 5NJ
Tel: 029-2059 7593 **Fax:** 029-2059 1268
E-mail: info@pandpsupplies.co.uk
Website: http://www.pandpsupplies.co.uk
Bank(s): Lloyds TSB Bank plc

Directors: J. Ward (Fin)
Ultimate Holding Company: P & P SUPPLIES (HOLDINGS) LIMITED
Immediate Holding Company: P AND P SUPPLIES LIMITED
Registration no: 01842880 **VAT No.:** GB 402 4930 85
Date established: 1984 **Turnover:** £1m - £2m **No.of Employees:** 11 - 20
Product Groups: 48, 66

Date of Accounts	Jan 11	Jan 10	Jan 09
Working Capital	123	17	-15
Fixed Assets	405	383	524
Current Assets	513	414	408

Papergraphics
9 Pantgwynlais Tongwynlais, Cardiff, CF15 7LS
Tel: 029-2081 3995 **Fax:** 01245-237178
E-mail: clive.turner@paper-graphics.com
Website: http://www.paper-graphics.com
Managers: C. Turner (Mgr)
No.of Employees: 51 - 100 **Product Groups:** 27, 30

Parsons Brinckerhoff
27-29 Cathedral Road, Cardiff, CF11 9HA
Tel: 029-2082 7000 **Fax:** 029-2082 7001
Website: http://www.pbworld.com
Directors: K. Jenkins (Tech Serv)
Ultimate Holding Company: BALFOUR BEATTY PLC
Immediate Holding Company: PARSONS BRINCKERHOFF LTD
Registration no: 02554514 **VAT No.:** GB 137 9914 31
Date established: 1990 **No.of Employees:** 51 - 100 **Product Groups:** 84, 87

Pelican Healthcare Ltd
Quadrant Centre Cardiff Business Park, Cardiff, CF14 5WF
Tel: 029-2074 7000 **Fax:** 029-2074 7001
E-mail: mailroom@pelicanhealthcare.co.uk
Website: http://www.pelicanhealthcare.co.uk
Bank(s): Barclays
Directors: N. Jones (Fin), J. Lewis (Fin), P. Eakin (MD)
Managers: M. Gregory (Buyer), G. Sims (Sales & Mktg Mg), T. Higgins (Personnel), S. Charitos (Tech Serv Mgr)
Ultimate Holding Company: EAKIN HOLDINGS LIMITED
Immediate Holding Company: PELICAN HEALTHCARE LIMITED
Registration no: 02648823 **VAT No.:** 615 5088 44 **Date established:** 1991
Turnover: £20m - £50m **No.of Employees:** 101 - 250
Product Groups: 27, 30

Date of Accounts	Mar 11	Mar 10	Mar 09
Sales Turnover	24m	18m	15m
Pre Tax Profit/Loss	6m	4m	3m
Working Capital	7m	4m	3m
Fixed Assets	5m	4m	3m
Current Assets	11m	7m	6m
Current Liabilities	2m	996	920

Penarth Industrial Services
8 Gripoly Mills Sloper Road, Cardiff, CF11 8AA
Tel: 029-2064 1555 **Fax:** 029-2064 1899
E-mail: info@pisltd.com
Website: http://www.tema-engineering.co.uk
Bank(s): Lloyds TSB
Directors: A. Rowles (Fin), A. Marrinof (Prop)
Immediate Holding Company: PENARTH INDUSTRIAL SERVICES LIMITED
Registration no: 01158345 **VAT No.:** GB 137 1254 87
Date established: 1974 **Turnover:** £10m - £20m
No.of Employees: 51 - 100 **Product Groups:** 48

Date of Accounts	Mar 11	Mar 10	Mar 09
Sales Turnover	11m	13m	7m
Pre Tax Profit/Loss	101	199	718
Working Capital	217	-507	548
Fixed Assets	593	1m	709
Current Assets	3m	4m	2m
Current Liabilities	2m	2m	761

Perman Bath Coatings
59 Beulah Road, Cardiff, CF14 6LW
Tel: 029-2069 3340 **Fax:** 029-2069 3340
E-mail: pjgould@btinternet.com
Directors: P. Gould (Dir)
Immediate Holding Company: PERMAN8 BATH COATINGS LIMITED
Registration no: 04644833 **Date established:** 2003
No.of Employees: 1 - 10 **Product Groups:** 46, 48

Date of Accounts	Mar 11	Mar 10	Mar 09
Working Capital	1	2	3
Fixed Assets	3	4	1
Current Assets	5	5	6

Phoenix Saxton Ltd
Pomeroy Works Clarence Road, Cardiff, CF10 5FA
Tel: 029-2048 7848 **Fax:** 029-2049 3493
E-mail: mike@phoenixsaxton.com
Website: http://www.phoenix-saxton.co.uk
Directors: M. Williams (MD)
Immediate Holding Company: PHOENIX-SAXTON LIMITED
Registration no: 01772966 **VAT No.:** GB 402 4013 23
Date established: 1983 **Turnover:** £500,000 - £1m
No.of Employees: 1 - 10 **Product Groups:** 66

Date of Accounts	Dec 11	Dec 10	Dec 09
Working Capital	309	326	297
Fixed Assets	146	148	165
Current Assets	652	640	670

Phoenix Surveying & Safety Equipment
Unit 17 Swift Business Centre East Moors Industrial Estate Keen Road, Cardiff, CF24 5JR
Tel: 029-2047 0776 **Fax:** 029-2047 0779
E-mail: sales@phoenixse.com
Website: http://www.phoenixse.com
Managers: C. Griffiths (Sales Admin)
Immediate Holding Company: PHOENIX SURVEYING EQUIPMENT LIMITED
Registration no: 01336159 **Date established:** 1977 **Turnover:** £1m - £2m
No.of Employees: 1 - 10 **Product Groups:** 38

Date of Accounts	Mar 08
Current Assets	3
Current Liabilities	3

Poeton Cardiff Ltd
283 Penarth Road, Cardiff, CF11 8UL
Tel: 029-2038 8182 **Fax:** 029-2038 8185
E-mail: sales@poetoncardiff.co.uk
Website: http://www.poeton.co.uk
Bank(s): Barclays, Bristol
Directors: S. Elliot Mead (Fin), D. Bignell (Fin), T. Amos (Develop)
Managers: M. Holmes (Chief Mgr)
Ultimate Holding Company: A.T. POETON & SON LIMITED
Immediate Holding Company: POETON (CARDIFF) LIMITED
Registration no: 00518848 **VAT No.:** GB 435 4192 56
Date established: 1953 **Turnover:** £2m - £5m **No.of Employees:** 21 - 50
Product Groups: 48, 85

Polymed Systems Ltd
Unit 1 Gabalfa Workshops Clos Menter Excelsior Industrial Estate, Cardiff, CF14 3AY
Tel: 029-2052 1234 **Fax:** 029-2052 1221
E-mail: sales@polymed.co.uk
Website: http://www.polymed.co.uk
Directors: B. Quilter (Co Sec)
Immediate Holding Company: POLYMED LIMITED
Registration no: 01946437 **VAT No.:** GB 433 2626 71
Date established: 1985 **Turnover:** £250,000 - £500,000
No.of Employees: 1 - 10 **Product Groups:** 31, 32, 48, 85

Date of Accounts	Dec 11	Dec 10	Dec 09
Working Capital	160	124	109
Fixed Assets	14	18	19
Current Assets	234	162	143

Port Painters Ltd
Unit 3 Ringside Business Centre Heol Y Rhosog, Rumney, Cardiff, CF3 2EW
Tel: 029-2077 7070 **Fax:** 029-2036 3023
E-mail: enquiries@portpainters.com
Website: http://www.portpainters.com
Directors: N. Curtis (Fin)
Managers: T. Cummings (Contracts Mgr)
Immediate Holding Company: PORT PAINTERS LIMITED
Registration no: 01036437 **Date established:** 1971 **Turnover:** £1m - £2m
No.of Employees: 21 - 50 **Product Groups:** 46, 48

Date of Accounts	Dec 11	Dec 10	Dec 09
Sales Turnover	1m	1m	1m
Pre Tax Profit/Loss	-48	110	-13
Working Capital	131	162	198
Fixed Assets	14	24	29
Current Assets	347	264	335
Current Liabilities	110	65	43

Portman Travel Ltd (Head Office)
Capital Tower Greyfriars Road, Cardiff, CF10 3PN
Tel: 029-2040 2600 **Fax:** 01792-653101
Website: http://www.portmantravel.com
Bank(s): Lloyds TSB Bank plc
Directors: A. Larby (Ch)
Managers: R. Harris (Reg Mgr), K. David (Mgr)
Ultimate Holding Company: SUPER SELECTOR SARL
Immediate Holding Company: PORTMAN TRAVEL LIMITED
Registration no: 00620104 **VAT No.:** GB 680 4034 53
Date established: 1959 **Turnover:** £10m - £20m
No.of Employees: 11 - 20 **Product Groups:** 69, 76

Practice Net Ltd
Cardiff Business Technology Centre 2 Capital Business Park Par, Cardiff, CF3 2PX
Tel: 029-2083 7410 **Fax:** 029-2083 7427
E-mail: dalerogers@practicenet.co.uk
Website: http://www.practicenet.co.uk
Directors: D. Rogers (Dir)
Ultimate Holding Company: RADIUS PROFESSIONAL LIMITED
Immediate Holding Company: PRACTICE NET LIMITED
Registration no: 00864089 **Date established:** 1965 **Turnover:** £1m - £2m
No.of Employees: 1 - 10 **Product Groups:** 67

Date of Accounts	Feb 12	Feb 11	Feb 10
Working Capital	97	75	66
Current Assets	140	152	124

Preston & Thomas Ltd
Unit 3 Heron Road Rumney, Cardiff, CF3 3JE
Tel: 029-2079 3331 **Fax:** 029-2077 9195
E-mail: davidthomas@prestonandthomas.co.uk
Website: http://www.prestonandthomas.co.uk
Bank(s): National Westminster, 17 St Mary St, Cardiff
Directors: D. Thomas (Dir), S. Preston (Dir)
Managers: B. Simmons (Buyer), I. Guy (Chief Mgr)
Immediate Holding Company: PRESTON AND THOMAS LIMITED
Registration no: 00239002 **VAT No.:** GB 134 1873 77
Date established: 2029 **Turnover:** £1m - £2m **No.of Employees:** 21 - 50
Product Groups: 40

Date of Accounts	Mar 11	Mar 10	Mar 09
Working Capital	-231	-183	30
Fixed Assets	598	693	668
Current Assets	298	346	529

Principality Building Society
PO Box 89, Cardiff, CF10 1UA
Tel: 08450-450452 **Fax:** 029-2023 4427
E-mail: enquiries@principality.co.uk
Website: http://www.principality.co.uk
Directors: S. Allen (Pers), G. Thomas (Fin), I. Brown (Tech Serv), P. Griffiths (Grp Chief Exec)
Immediate Holding Company: PRINCIPALITY LIMITED
Registration no: 03363851 **Date established:** 1997
Turnover: £250m - £500m **No.of Employees:** 501 - 1000
Product Groups: 82

Propona
Mount Stuart Square Cardiff Bay, Cardiff, CF10 5LR
Tel: 029-2044 4777
E-mail: enquiries@propona.co.uk
Website: http://www.propona.co.uk
Directors: C. Sully (Dir)
Immediate Holding Company: CULTURE RECORDS LIMITED
Registration no: 04208811 **Date established:** 2003
No.of Employees: 1 - 10 **Product Groups:** 44

Date of Accounts	Jul 11
Working Capital	17
Current Assets	17

PSI Ltd (Skiweb UK)
Llantrisant Road Capel Llanilltern, Cardiff, CF5 6JR
Tel: 029-2089 0800 **Fax:** 029-2089 0800
E-mail: info@skiweb.uk.com
Website: http://www.skiweb.uk.com
Directors: S. Brooks (Dir)
Registration no: 05381127 **Date established:** 2004
Turnover: £250,000 - £500,000 **No.of Employees:** 1 - 10
Product Groups: 65

Quality Laser Optics Ltd
2 Alexandra Gate, Ffordd Pengam,, Cardiff, CF24 2SA,
Tel: 029-2089 4751 **Fax:** 01624-827166
E-mail: custserv@optics.org
Website: http://optics.org
Directors: G. Thomas (MD)
No.of Employees: 11 - 20 **Product Groups:** 37, 38, 65

M A Rapport & Co. Ltd
Ivor House Bridge Street, Cardiff, CF10 2TH
Tel: 029-2037 3737 **Fax:** 029-2022 0121
E-mail: info@rapportlondon.com
Website: http://www.rapportlondon.com
Bank(s): Lloyds TSB Bank plc
Directors: O. Rapport (Dir)
Managers: B. Barton (Sales Prom Mgr)
Immediate Holding Company: M.A.RAPPORT & CO.LIMITED.
Registration no: 00180941 **VAT No.:** GB 134 0001 42
Date established: 2022 **Turnover:** £1m - £2m **No.of Employees:** 21 - 50
Product Groups: 49

Date of Accounts	Jan 12	Jan 11	Jan 10
Working Capital	605	629	693
Fixed Assets	246	253	153
Current Assets	1m	1m	1m

Reed Accountancy
4 Working Street, Cardiff, CF10 1GN
Tel: 029-2038 8466 **Fax:** 029-2038 6500
E-mail: steven.smith@reedglobal.com
Website: http://www.reed.co.uk
Managers: S. Smith (Comm)
Immediate Holding Company: REED PERSONNEL SERVICES LTD
Registration no: 00973629 **Date established:** 1994
Turnover: £125m - £250m **No.of Employees:** 1 - 10 **Product Groups:** 80

Reed Employment Ltd
4 Working Street, Cardiff, CF10 1GN
Tel: 029-2039 9633 **Fax:** 01792-484861
E-mail: cardiff@reed.co.uk
Website: http://www.reed.co.uk
Managers: R. Hole
Ultimate Holding Company: REED GLOBAL LTD (MALTA)
Immediate Holding Company: REED EMPLOYMENT LIMITED
Registration no: 00669854 **Date established:** 1960
Turnover: £75m - £125m **No.of Employees:** 1 - 10 **Product Groups:** 80

Date of Accounts	Jun 11	Jun 10	Dec 07
Sales Turnover	618	450	287m
Pre Tax Profit/Loss	-2m	310	8m
Working Capital	23m	28m	28m
Fixed Assets	31	36	5m
Current Assets	28m	30m	74m
Current Liabilities	37	29	21m

Reliance Security Group Limited
Unit 1, Talbot Green Business Park, Heol Y Twyn Talbot Green, PontyClun, Cardiff, CF72 9FG
Tel: 0870-6068999 **Fax:** 029-2036 9938
E-mail: info@reliancesecurity.co.uk
Website: http://www.reliancesecurity.co.uk
Directors: T. Roice (MD)
Managers: M. Tuckwell (Mgr)
Ultimate Holding Company: Barclays plc
Immediate Holding Company: Reliance Security Group Ltd
Registration no: 01473721 **No.of Employees:** 11 - 20 **Product Groups:** 81

Renold Clutches & Couplings Ltd
Newlands Road, Cardiff, CF11 2EU
Tel: 029-2079 2737 **Fax:** 029-2079 1360
E-mail: martin.slade@renold.com
Website: http://www.renold.com
Bank(s): RBS
Directors: M. Slade (Sales)
Managers: J. Canning, P. Tobin, G. Johns (Tech Serv Mgr), G. Johns (I.T. Exec), P. Tobin
Turnover: £5m - £10m **No.of Employees:** 51 - 100 **Product Groups:** 29, 35, 38, 39, 41, 43, 45, 46, 84

Research & Marketing Group
Trefor House Galdames Place, Cardiff, CF24 5RE
Tel: 029-2043 5800 **Fax:** 029-2048 3540
E-mail: phil.evans@rmg-uk.co.uk
Website: http://www.rmltd.net
Bank(s): Bank of Wales PLC
Managers: P. Evans
Ultimate Holding Company: RESEARCH AND MARKETING HOLDINGS LIMITED
Immediate Holding Company: RESEARCH AND MARKETING LIMITED
Registration no: 01026815 **VAT No.:** GB 691 7376 94
Date established: 1971 **No.of Employees:** 51 - 100 **Product Groups:** 81

Date of Accounts	Sep 11	Sep 10	Sep 09
Working Capital	261	280	274
Fixed Assets	101	112	76
Current Assets	555	603	515

Rhys Davies Freight Logistics Ltd
Unit 1 Moy Road Industrial Estate, Taffs Well, Cardiff, CF15 7QR
Tel: 029-2081 0587 **Fax:** 029-2081 0717
E-mail: info@rhysdavies.co.uk
Website: http://www.rhysdavies.co.uk
Bank(s): National Westminster
Directors: M. Richmond (MD)
Ultimate Holding Company: PENNBORO LIMITED
Immediate Holding Company: RHYS DAVIES & SONS LIMITED
Registration no: 01718283 **Date established:** 1983
Turnover: £20m - £50m **No.of Employees:** 51 - 100 **Product Groups:** 72

Date of Accounts	Aug 11	Aug 10	Aug 09
Sales Turnover	36m	35m	33m
Pre Tax Profit/Loss	668	708	492
Working Capital	4m	3m	2m
Fixed Assets	5m	4m	4m
Current Assets	13m	12m	11m
Current Liabilities	5m	6m	6m

Richard H Powell & Partners Ltd (Richard H. Powell & Partners Ltd)
1 Tollgate Close, Cardiff, CF11 8UE
Tel: 029-2023 2323 **Fax:** 029-2039 8110
E-mail: mail@powell.co.uk
Website: http://www.powell.co.uk
Bank(s): Barclays
Directors: R. Powell (MD)
Immediate Holding Company: POWELL.CO.UK LIMITED
Registration no: 03875665 **Date established:** 1999 **Turnover:** £2m - £5m
No.of Employees: 11 - 20 **Product Groups:** 26, 35, 52, 84

Rockall Recruitment
Unit 9 Lambourne Crescent Cardiff Business Park, Llanishen, Cardiff, CF14 5GF
Tel: 029-2074 7748 **Fax:** 029-2074 7874
E-mail: admin@rockall.co.uk
Website: http://www.rockallrecruitment.co.uk
Directors: K. Murphy (Fin), R. Murphy (MD)
Ultimate Holding Company: ROCKALL HOLDINGS LIMITED
Immediate Holding Company: ROCKALL RECRUITMENT LIMITED
Registration no: 03300264 **Date established:** 1997
No.of Employees: 1 - 10 **Product Groups:** 80

Date of Accounts	May 11	May 10	May 09
Working Capital	-55	-16	84
Fixed Assets	18	26	65
Current Assets	168	225	666

Royal Society Of Architects In Wales
4 Cathedral Road, Cardiff, CF11 9LJ
Tel: 029-2022 8987 **Fax:** 029-2023 0030
E-mail: rsaw@inst.riba.org
Website: http://www.architecture.com
Directors: L. Walder (MD)
Immediate Holding Company: LACEGROVE (INVESTMENTS) LLP
Registration no: RC000484 **VAT No.:** GB 232 3518 91
Date established: 2011 **No.of Employees:** 1 - 10 **Product Groups:** 84

Date of Accounts	Dec 11	Dec 10	Dec 09
Working Capital	-689	223	99
Fixed Assets	5m	4m	4m
Current Assets	109	376	272

Ryan Transport Ltd
Coldstores Road Queen Alexandra Dock, Cardiff, CF10 4LL
Tel: 029-2047 1558 **Fax:** 029-2048 9547
E-mail: maryrichards@btconnect.com
Bank(s): Barclays
Directors: M. Newell (Fin)
Managers: M. Richards, L. Davies (Purch Mgr)
Ultimate Holding Company: CARGO SERVICES (UK) LIMITED
Immediate Holding Company: RYAN TRANSPORT LIMITED
Registration no: 00461229 **VAT No.:** GB 656 0911 34
Date established: 1948 **Turnover:** £5m - £10m **No.of Employees:** 21 - 50
Product Groups: 72

Date of Accounts	Dec 11	Dec 10	Dec 09
Working Capital	-85	-209	66
Fixed Assets	1m	1m	850
Current Assets	2m	1m	2m
Current Liabilities	N/A	458	474

Rycon Steels Ltd
2 Alexandra Industrial Estate Wentloog Road, Rumney, Cardiff, CF3 1EY
Tel: 029-2036 2311 **Fax:** 029-2036 2322
E-mail: dudley@ryconsteels.co.uk
Website: http://www.ryconsteels.co.uk
Directors: D. Brown (Fin)
Ultimate Holding Company: RYCON HOLDINGS LIMITED
Immediate Holding Company: RYCON STEELS LIMITED
Registration no: 01029551 **VAT No.:** 134 6516 76 **Date established:** 1971
Turnover: £2m - £5m **No.of Employees:** 11 - 20 **Product Groups:** 66

Date of Accounts	Sep 11	Sep 10	Sep 09
Sales Turnover	N/A	2m	2m
Pre Tax Profit/Loss	N/A	20	-14
Working Capital	3	18	23
Fixed Assets	81	91	101
Current Assets	854	782	666
Current Liabilities	N/A	35	255

S A Brain & Co. Ltd
Crawshay Street, Cardiff, CF10 5DS
Tel: 029-2040 2060 **Fax:** 029-2040 3344
E-mail: colin.gin@sabrain.com
Website: http://www.sabrain.com
Bank(s): Lloyds TSB
Directors: R. Davies (Sales & Mktg), M. Reed (Fin)
Managers: C. Gin, T. Dickinson (Personnel), K. Roche (Tech Serv Mgr)
Immediate Holding Company: S.A.BRAIN & COMPANY,LIMITED
Registration no: 00052099 **Date established:** 1997
Turnover: £50m - £75m **No.of Employees:** 101 - 250
Product Groups: 21, 62

Date of Accounts	Sep 08	Sep 09	Sep 10
Sales Turnover	113m	103m	99m
Pre Tax Profit/Loss	6m	10m	3m
Working Capital	-15m	582	115
Fixed Assets	148m	142m	138m
Current Assets	15m	31m	30m
Current Liabilities	10m	14m	14m

S & A Industrial Equipment
Ipswich Road, Cardiff, CF23 9AQ
Tel: 029-2045 0128 **Fax:** 029-2048 7907
E-mail: sales@bluetrolley.com
Website: http://www.bluetrolley.com
Directors: M. Rosser (MD), A. Hancock (MD), H. Hancock (Dir)
Ultimate Holding Company: 00543205
Immediate Holding Company: S AND A INDUSTRIAL EQUIPMENT LIMITED
Registration no: 01396095 **Date established:** 1978
No.of Employees: 21 - 50 **Product Groups:** 26, 35, 39, 45

Date of Accounts	Dec 07	Dec 06	Dec 05
Working Capital	284	244	176
Fixed Assets	43	28	22
Current Assets	1487	1451	1198
Current Liabilities	1204	1207	1021
Total Share Capital	51	51	51

Seal Masters
Unit 4 Batchelor Road Excelsior Industrial Estate, Cardiff, CF14 3AX
Tel: 029-2061 7005 **Fax:** 029-2061 1006
E-mail: sales@sealmasters.co.uk
Website: http://www.sealmasters.co.uk
Directors: J. Stagg (Prop), C. Morris (Prop), S. McClymont (Sales), C. Morris (MD)
Immediate Holding Company: SEALMASTERS LIMITED
Registration no: 02448846 **VAT No.:** GB 542 7539 32
Date established: 1989 **Turnover:** £500,000 - £1m
No.of Employees: 1 - 10 **Product Groups:** 22, 29, 30, 31, 32, 33, 36, 38, 39, 40

Date of Accounts	Mar 10	Mar 09	Mar 08
Working Capital	115	79	60
Fixed Assets	10	16	17
Current Assets	368	366	413
Current Liabilities	153	136	149

Semaphore Cardiff Ltd
28 Bessemer Road, Cardiff, CF11 8BA
Tel: 029-2022 4111 **Fax:** 029-2022 5401
E-mail: sales@semaphoredisplay.co.uk
Website: http://www.semaphoredisplay.co.uk
Directors: J. Marshall (Sales)
Ultimate Holding Company: SEMAPHORE HOLDINGS LIMITED
Immediate Holding Company: SEMAPHORE (CARDIFF) LIMITED
Registration no: 01934640 **Date established:** 1985 **Turnover:** £1m - £2m
No.of Employees: 11 - 20 **Product Groups:** 28, 30, 39, 40

Date of Accounts	Aug 11	Aug 10	Aug 09
Working Capital	-18	13	25
Fixed Assets	33	39	47
Current Assets	140	227	224

Servonetic Control Instruments Ltd
Viaduct Road Gwaelod-Y-Garth, Cardiff, CF15 9JN
Tel: 029-2081 0209 **Fax:** 029-2081 3609
E-mail: andy@servonetic.fsnet.co.uk
Directors: A. Abbott (MD), C. Abbott (Fin)
Immediate Holding Company: SERVONETIC CONTROL INSTRUMENTS LIMITED
Registration no: 00658853 **VAT No.:** GB 329 0829 46
Date established: 1960 **Turnover:** Up to £250,000
No.of Employees: 1 - 10 **Product Groups:** 38

Date of Accounts	Nov 11	Nov 10	Nov 09
Working Capital	11	11	-12
Fixed Assets	30	30	30
Current Assets	50	50	43

Soundkit Ltd
12 Earle Place, Cardiff, CF5 1NZ
Tel: 029-2034 2907 **Fax:** 029-2023 1235
E-mail: david@soundkit.co.uk
Website: http://www.soundkit.co.uk
Directors: J. Richards (Fin), M. Richards (MD)
Immediate Holding Company: SOUNDKIT LIMITED
Registration no: 04473561 **Date established:** 2002
Turnover: £250,000 - £500,000 **No.of Employees:** 1 - 10
Product Groups: 37

Date of Accounts	Jul 11	Jul 10	Jul 09
Working Capital	25	27	14
Fixed Assets	4	2	3
Current Assets	115	84	60

South Wales Filters
82 Lascelles Drive Pontprennau, Cardiff, CF23 8NQ
Tel: 029-2073 3337
E-mail: sales@swfilters.demon.co.uk
Website: http://www.swfilter.co.uk
Directors: P. Stevens (Prop)
Date established: 1989 **No.of Employees:** 1 - 10 **Product Groups:** 38, 42

South Wales Fork Trucks Hire Ltd
5 Park Street, Cardiff, CF10 1NT
Tel: 029-2037 7977 **Fax:** 01639-750612
E-mail: sales@southwalesforktrucks.co.uk
Website: http://www.southwalesforktrucks.co.uk
Directors: E. Selby (Dir), B. Selby (MD)
Immediate Holding Company: SOUTH WALES FORK TRUCKS HIRE LIMITED
Registration no: 06429383 **Date established:** 2007
No.of Employees: 21 - 50 **Product Groups:** 35, 39, 45

Date of Accounts	Mar 11	Mar 10	Mar 09
Working Capital	19	44	44
Fixed Assets	449	399	414
Current Assets	229	233	264

Speedy Services
Unit 47 Portmanmoor Road Industrial Estate, Cardiff, CF24 5HB
Tel: 029-2066 8777 **Fax:** 029-2066 8778
E-mail: tim.burford@speedyhire.co.uk
Website: http://www.speedyservices.com
Managers: T. Burford (Mgr)
Immediate Holding Company: SPEEDY HIRE PLC
Registration no: 00927680 **Date established:** 1968
No.of Employees: 1 - 10 **Product Groups:** 35, 39, 45

Starcke Abrasives Ltd
2 Alexandra Gate Ffordd Pengam, Cardiff, CF24 2SA
Tel: 029-2089 4828 **Fax:** 029-2048 7410
E-mail: info@starckeuk.com
Website: http://www.starckeuk.com
Directors: L. Colley (Fin)
Ultimate Holding Company: STARKE GMBH
Immediate Holding Company: STARCKE ABRASIVES UK LIMITED
Registration no: 00498637 **Date established:** 1951
Turnover: £500,000 - £1m **No.of Employees:** 1 - 10 **Product Groups:** 33

Date of Accounts	Dec 11	Dec 10	Dec 09
Working Capital	386	381	374
Fixed Assets	42	27	30
Current Assets	833	977	825

Swanson Mackay
Unit C4 West Point Industrial Estate Penarth Road, Cardiff, CF11 8JQ
Tel: 029-2070 6400 **Fax:** 029-2071 3929
E-mail: sales@swansonmackay.co.uk
Directors: P. Williams (MD)
Registration no: 01849184 **VAT No.:** GB 329 0645 56
Date established: 2005 **Turnover:** £1m - £2m **No.of Employees:** 1 - 10
Product Groups: 77

Date of Accounts	Jun 08	Jun 07
Working Capital	220	140
Fixed Assets	35	41
Current Assets	752	754
Current Liabilities	532	614
Total Share Capital	50	50

T A C P Landscape Architects
10 Park Grove, Cardiff, CF10 3BN
Tel: 029-2022 8966 **Fax:** 029-2039 4776
E-mail: admin@tacp.co.uk
Website: http://www.tacp.uk.com
Bank(s): Midland
Directors: G. West (Snr Part)
Immediate Holding Company: TACP LIMITED LIABILITY PARTNERSHIP
Registration no: OC308486 **VAT No.:** GB 164 8037 57
Date established: 2004 **Turnover:** £1m - £2m **No.of Employees:** 11 - 20
Product Groups: 07, 84

Date of Accounts	Jun 11	Jun 10	Jun 09
Sales Turnover	N/A	2m	N/A
Pre Tax Profit/Loss	N/A	441	N/A
Working Capital	37	223	144
Fixed Assets	186	228	246
Current Assets	392	544	535
Current Liabilities	N/A	151	226

Tarmac Building Products Ltd
Viking Place Off Rover Way, Cardiff, CF24 2RX
Tel: 029-2046 5969 **Fax:** 029-2046 4407
E-mail: m.simpson@tarmac.co.uk
Website: http://www.tarmac.co.uk
Managers: M. O'donnel (Mgr), M. O'donnell (Site Co-ord)
Ultimate Holding Company: REGINALD ATKIN (HOLDINGS) LIMITED
Immediate Holding Company: TARMAC BUILDING PRODUCTS LIMITED
Registration no: 04026569 **Date established:** 2000
No.of Employees: 1 - 10 **Product Groups:** 33

Date of Accounts	Dec 11	Dec 10	Dec 09
Sales Turnover	170m	97m	N/A
Pre Tax Profit/Loss	-60m	-40m	N/A
Working Capital	-833	13m	N/A
Fixed Assets	18m	57m	N/A
Current Assets	40m	51m	N/A
Current Liabilities	14m	13m	N/A

Taylors Etc
143 Colchester Avenue Penylan, Cardiff, CF23 9AN
Tel: 029-2035 8400 **Fax:** 029-2035 8409
E-mail: info@taylorsetc.co.uk
Website: http://www.taylorsetc.co.uk
Directors: L. Taylor (Dir)
Immediate Holding Company: TAYLORS ETC DESIGN LTD
Registration no: 07023874 **VAT No.:** GB 655 5709 10
Date established: 2009 **Turnover:** £2m - £5m **No.of Employees:** 1 - 10
Product Groups: 33

Date of Accounts	Jul 11	Jul 10
Working Capital	-1	-21
Fixed Assets	56	52
Current Assets	312	173

Thomas Hosking Ltd
Unit 4 Dumballs Road, Cardiff, CF10 5FE
Tel: 029-2048 0324 **Fax:** 029-2049 2075
E-mail: thomashosking@btconnect.com
Website: http://www.thomashosking.com
Directors: D. Hosking (Dir)
Immediate Holding Company: THOMAS HOSKING LIMITED
Registration no: 05402693 **VAT No.:** GB 133 8099 62
Date established: 2005 **Turnover:** £500,000 - £1m
No.of Employees: 1 - 10 **Product Groups:** 39, 45

Date of Accounts	Mar 12	Mar 11	Mar 10
Working Capital	-49	-5	89
Fixed Assets	2	2	7
Current Assets	98	87	304

Timberwise (UK) Ltd
The Cottage, Mill Farm St Mellons Road, Lisvane, Cardiff, CF14 0SH
Tel: 029-2075 5506 **Fax:** 029-2076 1004
E-mail: cardiff@timberwise.co.uk
Website: http://www.timberwise.co.uk
Registration no: 03230356 **Product Groups:** 07, 32, 52

Torgy Atlantic Engineering
3 Llandough Trading Estate Penarth Road, Cardiff, CF11 8RR
Tel: 029-2070 8461 **Fax:** 029-2035 0437
E-mail: sales@torgy-atlantic.co.uk
Website: http://www.torgy-atlantic.co.uk
Directors: P. Evan (MD)
Immediate Holding Company: ATLANTIC GROUP P.L.C.
Registration no: 03462217 **VAT No.:** GB 692 0821 31
No.of Employees: 1 - 10 **Product Groups:** 30

Date of Accounts	Dec 07	Dec 06	Dec 05
Working Capital	297	123	152
Fixed Assets	38	33	42
Current Assets	991	173	884
Current Liabilities	694	50	732

Total Filtration Ltd
Ipswich Road, Cardiff, CF23 9AQ
Tel: 029-2049 7612 **Fax:** 029-2047 1110
E-mail: sales@totalfiltration.com
Website: http://www.totalfiltration.com
Bank(s): HSBC Bank plc
Directors: C. Lewis (Fin), J. Mounsher (MD)
Immediate Holding Company: TOTAL FILTRATION LIMITED
Registration no: 00970096 **VAT No.:** GB 666 5465 96
Date established: 1970 **Turnover:** £2m - £5m **No.of Employees:** 11 - 20
Product Groups: 33, 34, 35, 36, 38, 40

Date of Accounts	Mar 11	Mar 10	Mar 09
Working Capital	230	298	442
Fixed Assets	9	14	27
Current Assets	426	539	658

Travis Perkins plc
Roath Dock, Cardiff, CF10 4ED
Tel: 029-2049 1100 **Fax:** 029-2046 2193
Website: http://www.travisperkins.co.uk

Directors: M. Britton (Fin), D. Curtin (Dir), C. Huxtable (Dir), B. Britton (Dir)
Managers: D. Finch (Gen Contact)
Immediate Holding Company: TRAVIS PERKINS PLC
Registration no: 00824821 **Date established:** 1964
No.of Employees: 51 - 100 **Product Groups:** 66

Tricho-Tech

Unit 1 Pentwyn Business Centre Wharfedale Road, Cardiff, CF23 7HB
Tel: 029-2054 0542 **Fax:** 029-2073 5036
E-mail: info@concateno.com
Website: http://www.concateno.com
Managers: K. Blackwell
Immediate Holding Company: CONCATENO PLC
Registration no: 03276164 **VAT No.:** 682 6687 83
Turnover: £250,000 - £500,000 **No.of Employees:** 51 - 100
Product Groups: 63, 84

Date of Accounts	Dec 07	Dec 06	Dec 05
Sales Turnover	3980	N/A	N/A
Pre Tax Profit/Loss	989	N/A	N/A
Working Capital	793	23	-68
Fixed Assets	462	588	486
Current Assets	2075	937	713
Current Liabilities	1282	914	781
Total Share Capital	1	1	1
ROCE% (Return on Capital Employed)	78.8		
ROT% (Return on Turnover)	24.8		

Ultrawave Ltd

Unit 14-15 Eastgate Business Park Wentloog Avenue, Cardiff, CF3 2EY
Tel: 029-2083 7337 **Fax:** 0845-330 4231
E-mail: admin@ultrawave.co.uk
Website: http://www.ultrawave.co.uk
Bank(s): Lloyds TSB Bank plc
Directors: C. Czyrko (Sales & Mktg)
Ultimate Holding Company: HYGEA HOLDINGS LIMITED
Immediate Holding Company: ULTRAWAVE LIMITED
Registration no: 02558071 **VAT No.:** GB 542 7279 32
Date established: 1990 **Turnover:** £2m - £5m **No.of Employees:** 21 - 50
Product Groups: 32, 37, 38, 47

Date of Accounts	Oct 11	Oct 10	Oct 09
Sales Turnover	2m	2m	2m
Pre Tax Profit/Loss	10	4	51
Working Capital	151	131	135
Fixed Assets	56	73	63
Current Assets	958	963	967
Current Liabilities	166	253	133

Vanda Coatings

Unit 5a Charnwood Park Clos Marion, Cardiff, CF10 4LJ
Tel: 029-2048 0800 **Fax:** 029-2045 7600
E-mail: andrew@vandacoatings.co.uk
Website: http://www.vandacoatings.co.uk
Directors: A. Morgan (Fin)
Immediate Holding Company: V & A COATINGS LIMITED
Registration no: 04341564 **Date established:** 2001
No.of Employees: 1 - 10 **Product Groups:** 46, 48

Date of Accounts	Dec 11	Dec 10	Dec 09
Working Capital	-0	-0	-0
Current Assets	3	3	3

Vespa Classics UK

32 Inglefield Avenue, Cardiff, CF14 3PZ
Tel: 0791-433 4271
E-mail: info@vespaclassics.com
Website: http://www.vespaclassics.com
Directors: L. Spear (Prop)
Date established: 1999 **Turnover:** £250,000 - £500,000
No.of Employees: 1 - 10 **Product Groups:** 39

Vincent Charles Executive Search Ltd

43 Cheriton Drive, Cardiff, CF14 9DF
Tel: 029-2076 2005
E-mail: partner@vincentcharles.co.uk
Website: http://www.vincentcharles.co.uk
Registration no: 06096826 **Date established:** 1997
No.of Employees: 1 - 10 **Product Groups:** 80

W C T S Building Services Ltd

Unit 7 Curran Road, Cardiff, CF10 5DF
Tel: 01656-331261 **Fax:** 01656-655969
E-mail: enquiries@wctslimited.co.uk
Website: http://www.wctslimited.co.uk
Directors: J. Budd (Dir)
Immediate Holding Company: WCTS LIMITED
Registration no: 04572208 **Date established:** 2002
No.of Employees: 11 - 20 **Product Groups:** 35, 40, 86

Date of Accounts	Dec 08	Dec 07	Dec 06
Sales Turnover	N/A	N/A	632
Pre Tax Profit/Loss	N/A	N/A	108
Working Capital	28	99	83
Fixed Assets	19	38	69
Current Assets	128	139	165
Current Liabilities	N/A	34	34

Waterspace Developments Limited

Unit K5 South Point Clos Marian, Cardiff, CF10 4LQ
Tel: 07860-734600
E-mail: steve.evans@floating-offices.co.uk
Website: http://www.floating-offices.co.uk
Directors: S. Evans (Sales), G. Davidson (Fin)
Registration no: 06670221 **Date established:** 2008
Turnover: Up to £250,000 **No.of Employees:** 1 - 10 **Product Groups:** 25

Westdale Press Ltd

Unit 70 Portmanmoor Road Industrial Estate, Cardiff, CF24 5HB
Tel: 029-2066 2600 **Fax:** 029-2066 2608
E-mail: enquiries@westdale.co.uk
Website: http://www.westdale.co.uk
Directors: B. Atkins (Fin), J. Cundy (Comm)
Ultimate Holding Company: WESTDALE PRINTING GROUP LIMITED
Immediate Holding Company: WESTDALE LIMITED
Registration no: 04720463 **Date established:** 2003
Turnover: £10m - £20m **No.of Employees:** 101 - 250 **Product Groups:** 28

Wizmark Computers

40 Meadvale Road, Cardiff, CF3 1UG
Tel: 029-2079 7767
E-mail: enquiries@wizmarkcomputers.co.uk
Website: http://www.wizmarkcomputers.co.uk

Directors: M. Bridges (Prop)
No.of Employees: 1 - 10 **Product Groups:** 44, 67

W R Refrigeration Ltd

Unit 1 Malvern Drive, Llanishen, Cardiff, CF14 5DR
Tel: 029-2076 2519 **Fax:** 029-2076 5001
E-mail: sales@wrrefrigeration.co.uk
Website: http://www.wrref.com
Directors: H. Cole (MD)
Managers: N. McGrath (Sales Prom Mgr), K. Mills (Mgr), T. Weed (Serv Mgr)
Ultimate Holding Company: HUURRE GROUP OY (FINLAND)
Immediate Holding Company: WR REFRIGERATION LIMITED
Registration no: 00594746 **VAT No.:** GB 485 4284 16
Date established: 1957 **No.of Employees:** 1 - 10 **Product Groups:** 29, 40, 41, 48, 52

Date of Accounts	Dec 11	Dec 10	Dec 09
Sales Turnover	45m	44m	57m
Pre Tax Profit/Loss	412	-2m	1m
Working Capital	29m	21m	23m
Fixed Assets	3m	4m	3m
Current Assets	52m	45m	36m
Current Liabilities	4m	2m	2m

Wrought Iron Centre

Parkfield Place, Cardiff, CF14 3AR
Tel: 029-2062 1003
Directors: S. Preece (Prop)
Date established: 1960 **No.of Employees:** 1 - 10 **Product Groups:** 26, 35

YODspica

26 Whitworth Court Tudor Street Cardiff, Cardiff, CF11 6AD
Tel: 029-2022 7199
E-mail: contact@yodspica.com
Website: http://www.yodspica.com
Managers: E. Assuncao
Immediate Holding Company: YODSPICA LTD
Registration no: 06800692 **Date established:** 2009
Turnover: Up to £250,000 **No.of Employees:** 1 - 10 **Product Groups:** 61, 84

Date of Accounts	Jan 11	Jan 10
Fixed Assets	3	2

Dyfed

Cardigan

C T P Fabrications

Unit 31 Pentood Industrial Estate, Cardigan, SA43 3AG
Tel: 01239-621005 **Fax:** 01239-615272
Directors: R. Gordon (Prop)
No.of Employees: 1 - 10 **Product Groups:** 26, 35

Cardigan Sand & Gravel Co. Ltd

CNWC Y Saeson Penparc, Cardigan, SA43 1RB
Tel: 01239-612342 **Fax:** 01239-615238
E-mail: info@cardigansand.co.uk
Website: http://www.cardigansand.co.uk
Directors: M. Mcgee (MD)
Immediate Holding Company: CARDIGAN SAND AND GRAVEL COMPANY LIMITED
Registration no: 00631623 **Date established:** 1959
No.of Employees: 11 - 20 **Product Groups:** 14, 51

Date of Accounts	Mar 11	Mar 10	Mar 09
Working Capital	1m	1m	911
Fixed Assets	741	824	955
Current Assets	2m	2m	1m

Granant Precast Concrete

Grannant Uchaf St Dogmaels, Cardigan, SA43 3LY
Tel: 01239-881232 **Fax:** 01239-881269
E-mail: granant.precast1@btconnect.com
Website: http://www.agregister.co.uk/company-75056746.html
Directors: R. Morris (MD)
Turnover: £500,000 - £1m **No.of Employees:** 1 - 10 **Product Groups:** 33, 35

Jewson Ltd

Station Road, Cardigan, SA43 3AD
Tel: 01239-613511 **Fax:** 01239-614676
E-mail: debbie.rogers@jewson.co.uk
Website: http://www.jewson.co.uk
Managers: D. Rogers (District Mgr)
Ultimate Holding Company: COMPAGNIE DE SAINT GOBAIN (FRANCE)
Immediate Holding Company: JEWSON LIMITED
Registration no: 00348407 **Date established:** 1939
Turnover: Over £1,000m **No.of Employees:** 1 - 10 **Product Groups:** 66

Date of Accounts	Dec 11	Dec 10	Dec 09
Sales Turnover	1606m	1547m	1485m
Pre Tax Profit/Loss	18m	100m	45m
Working Capital	-345m	-250m	-349m
Fixed Assets	496m	387m	461m
Current Assets	657m	1005m	1320m
Current Liabilities	66m	120m	64m

Dyfed

Carmarthen

BJP Property Estate Agents

104 Lammas Street, Carmarthen, SA31 3AP
Tel: 01267-236363 **Fax:** 01267-236344
E-mail: carmarthen@bjpco.com
Website: http://www.bjpco.com/
Managers: D. Phillips (I.T. Exec)
Date established: 1988 **No.of Employees:** 11 - 20 **Product Groups:** 80

C P L Petroleum Ltd

Station Road St Clears, Carmarthen, SA33 4BN
Tel: 01554-772948 **Fax:** 01554-758742
E-mail: dyfed@cplpetroleum.co.uk
Website: http://www.cplpetroleum.co.uk
Bank(s): National Westminster
Managers: L. O'Shea (Reg Mgr), S. Pocock (District Mgr)
Ultimate Holding Company: CPL Industries Holdings Ltd
Immediate Holding Company: CPL PETROLEUM LIMITED
Registration no: 03003860 **VAT No.:** GB 721 5764 39
Date established: 1994 **Turnover:** £500m - £1,000m
No.of Employees: 21 - 50 **Product Groups:** 66

Comfort Zone

Cambrian Way John Street, Carmarthen, SA31 1QN
Tel: 01267-229393 **Fax:** 01267-234082
No.of Employees: 1 - 10 **Product Groups:** 38

Eco Technology Ltd

Amex Park Llansteffan Road, Johnstown, Carmarthen, SA31 3NF
Tel: 01267-236417 **Fax:** 01267-233034
E-mail: enquiries@ecotechnology.ltd.uk
Website: http://www.ecotechnology.ltd.uk
Directors: P. Mellor (MD)
Managers: R. White (Mktg Serv Mgr)
Immediate Holding Company: ECO TECHNOLOGY LTD.
Registration no: 02832828 **Date established:** 1993
No.of Employees: 21 - 50 **Product Groups:** 54

Date of Accounts	Jul 08	Jul 07	Jul 06
Working Capital	350	301	112
Fixed Assets	56	28	37
Current Assets	728	565	339
Current Liabilities	377	263	227

Cled Evans Construction Ltd

Ffordd Works Llangynog Road, Johnstown, Carmarthen, SA33 5BL
Tel: 01267-232827 **Fax:** 01267-232933
E-mail: carol@cledevans.co.uk
Website: http://www.cledevans.co.uk
Directors: C. Evans (Dir), C. Evans (Fin)
Immediate Holding Company: CLED EVANS CONSTRUCTION LTD
Registration no: 06544462 **Date established:** 2008
No.of Employees: 21 - 50 **Product Groups:** 35

Date of Accounts	Dec 11	Dec 10	Dec 09
Working Capital	-5	19	-34
Fixed Assets	50	68	66
Current Assets	327	358	489

D A G Jones

Uplands, Carmarthen, SA32 8EA
Tel: 01267-267313 **Fax:** 01267-267841
Directors: D. Jones (Prop)
Date established: 1967 **No.of Employees:** 1 - 10 **Product Groups:** 26, 35

Gwili Jones & Sons

Hafod Peniel, Carmarthen, SA32 7AD
Tel: 01267-235827 **Fax:** 01267-233583
E-mail: huw@gwilitractors.co.uk
Website: http://www.gwilitractors.co.uk
Directors: H. Jones (Ptnr)
No.of Employees: 1 - 10 **Product Groups:** 34, 67

H J Lodwig

Gwaefi Farm Bridge Street, St Clears, Carmarthen, SA33 4EW
Tel: 01994-230347 **Fax:** 01994-230347
Directors: J. Lodwig (Prop), H. Lodwig (Prop)
Date established: 1963 **No.of Employees:** 1 - 10 **Product Groups:** 41

O J Williams Fuel Distributor

Station Road St Clears, Carmarthen, SA33 4BN
Tel: 01994-230355 **Fax:** 01994-230732
E-mail: andrea.whittle@ojwilliams.co.uk
Website: http://www.owenfuelsojwilliams.co.uk
Bank(s): National Westminster Bank Plc
Directors: B. Zaza (Co Sec)
Managers: A. Whittle (Mgr)
Registration no: 01512959 **VAT No.:** GB 124 5411 05
Turnover: £20m - £50m **No.of Employees:** 21 - 50 **Product Groups:** 66

Sarah Macbean Estate Agents

28 King Street, Carmarthen, SA31 1BS
Tel: 01267-230423 **Fax:** 01267-230623
E-mail: cherbert@francissant.com
Website: http://www.sarahmacbean.co.uk
Directors: C. Herbert (Dir)
No.of Employees: 1 - 10 **Product Groups:** 80

Source For Me Limited

Glen Farm Llanddarog Road, Carmarthen, SA32 8AP
Tel: 0845-8037769
E-mail: info@source4me.co.uk
Website: http://www.source4me.co.uk/
Directors: M. Foreman (Dir)
Registration no: 06017114 **Date established:** 2006
Turnover: £250,000 - £500,000 **No.of Employees:** 1 - 10
Product Groups: 66

Date of Accounts	Dec 09	Dec 08	Dec 07
Working Capital	1	-15	-3
Fixed Assets	1	N/A	N/A
Current Assets	23	8	6
Current Liabilities	N/A	5	N/A

Travis Perkins plc

Station Road St Clears, Carmarthen, SA33 4BN
Tel: 01994-230006 **Fax:** 01994-230732
E-mail: martin.rice@travisperkins.co.uk
Website: http://www.travisperkins.co.uk
Managers: M. Rice (District Mgr)
Immediate Holding Company: TRAVIS PERKINS PLC
Registration no: 00824821 **Date established:** 1964
Turnover: Up to £250,000 **No.of Employees:** 1 - 10 **Product Groups:** 66

Date of Accounts	Dec 11	Dec 10	Dec 09
Sales Turnover	4779m	3153m	2931m
Pre Tax Profit/Loss	270m	197m	213m
Working Capital	133m	159m	248m
Fixed Assets	2771m	2749m	2108m
Current Assets	1421m	1329m	1035m
Current Liabilities	473m	412m	109m

Gwent

Chepstow

Aalco
Avenue West Newhouse Farm Industrial Estate, Mathern, Chepstow, NP16 6UD
Tel: 01291-638638 **Fax:** 01291-638600
E-mail: chepstow@aalco.co.uk
Website: http://www.aalco.co.uk
Bank(s): National Westminster Bank Plc
Managers: J. Whitehead (District Mgr), D. Blackford, W. Bligh
Ultimate Holding Company: UK STEELSTOCK LTD
Immediate Holding Company: AMARI METALS LTD
Registration no: 03551533 **Date established:** 1997
Turnover: £125m - £250m **No.of Employees:** 21 - 50
Product Groups: 34, 35, 36, 66

Bristol Business College
3a Moor Street, Chepstow, NP16 5DF
Tel: 08455-551030
E-mail: info@bristolbusinesscollege.com
Website: http://www.bristolbusinesscollege.com
Directors: R. Rigby (Fin), P. Brady (Dir), P. Brady (MD)
Immediate Holding Company: BRISTOL BUSINESS COLLEGE LTD
Registration no: 06114281 **Date established:** 2007
No.of Employees: 1 - 10 **Product Groups:** 86

Date of Accounts	Mar 11	Mar 10	Mar 09
Working Capital	-70	-56	-62
Fixed Assets	2	3	4
Current Assets	8	6	4

C P L Petroleum Ltd
Brockweir, Chepstow, NP16 7NG
Tel: 01291-689268 **Fax:** 01291-689835
E-mail: sales@cplpetroleum.co.uk
Website: http://www.cplpetroleum.co.uk
Managers: R. Taylor (District Mgr), L. Linley (Mgr), L. Linley
Ultimate Holding Company: CPL INDUSTRIES HOLDINGS LIMITED
Immediate Holding Company: CPL PETROLEUM LIMITED
Registration no: 03003860 **VAT No.:** GB 275 0972 38
Date established: 1994 **Turnover:** £250m - £500m
No.of Employees: 1 - 10 **Product Groups:** 66

Date of Accounts	Mar 11	Mar 10	Mar 09
Pre Tax Profit/Loss	878	904	N/A
Working Capital	30m	30m	29m
Fixed Assets	26m	26m	26m
Current Assets	56m	56m	55m
Current Liabilities	246	253	N/A

Comet Home Delivery
Unit 12 Severn Link Distribution Centre Newhouse Farm Industrial Es, Mathern, Chepstow, NP16 6UN
Tel: 01482-320681 **Fax:** 01291-630757
E-mail: graham.roberts@comet.co.uk
Website: http://www.comet.co.uk
Managers: G. Roberts (Mgr)
Ultimate Holding Company: STUDWELDERS HOLDINGS LIMITED
Registration no: 05677482 **Date established:** 2006
No.of Employees: 51 - 100 **Product Groups:** 30, 49, 72

Eden Rose Lifestyle
11 St Mary Street, Chepstow, NP16 5EW
Tel: 01291-627340 **Fax:** 01291-431636
E-mail: info@edenroselifestyle.co.uk
Website: http://www.edenroselifestyle.co.uk
Directors: L. Jones (Prop)
Date established: 1985 **Turnover:** Up to £250,000
No.of Employees: 1 - 10 **Product Groups:** 24, 52, 81, 84

Enviropower Ltd
PO Box 6, Chepstow, NP16 7EY
Tel: 01291-630595 **Fax:** 01291-624570
E-mail: info@enviropower.org.uk
Website: http://www.enviropower.org.uk
Directors: A. Speechley (MD), L. Davies (Fin), M. Chesshire (Non Exec)
Immediate Holding Company: ENVIROPOWER LTD
Registration no: 05836498 **VAT No.:** GB 540 6993 27
Date established: 2006 **Turnover:** Up to £250,000
No.of Employees: 1 - 10 **Product Groups:** 37

Forget Me Not Regalia
PO Box 112, Chepstow, NP16 5WD
Tel: 01291-621126 **Fax:** 01291-621126
E-mail: forgetmenot_regalia@yahoo.co.uk
Website: http://www.forgetmenotregalia.co.uk
Managers: K. Jones (Mgr)
Date established: 1992 **No.of Employees:** 1 - 10 **Product Groups:** 49

Furniture Lighting Centre
22 Mount Way, Chepstow, NP16 5NF
Tel: 0800-043 6342
E-mail: sales@outdoor-lighting-centre.co.uk
Website: http://www.outdoor-lighting-centre.co.uk
Directors: L. Bhangoo (Ptnr)
Immediate Holding Company: DIRECT TO YOU ONLINE LIMITED
Registration no: 07175943 **Date established:** 2010
No.of Employees: 1 - 10 **Product Groups:** 37

Date of Accounts	Mar 11
Working Capital	-6
Fixed Assets	8
Current Assets	17
Current Liabilities	13

Marriott St Pierre Hotel & Country Club
St Pierre Park, Chepstow, NP16 6YA
Tel: 01291-625261 **Fax:** 01291-629975
E-mail: richard.lansberry@marriotthotels.com
Website: http://www.marriott.com
Bank(s): Girobank
Managers: S. Jones (Sales & Mktg Mg), R. Lansberry (Chief Mgr), J. Ayling (Personnel), L. Baker (Personnel), N. Heal (Fin Mgr)
Ultimate Holding Company: WHITBREAD HOTELS GROUP
VAT No.: GB 243 2928 64 **Turnover:** £75m - £125m
No.of Employees: 251 - 500 **Product Groups:** 69, 89

Osborn Unipol Ltd
Dendix House Lower Church Street, Chepstow, NP16 5XT
Tel: 01291-634000 **Fax:** 01291-634098
E-mail: lpainter@osborn-unipol.co.uk
Website: http://www.osborn.de
Directors: J. Reavey-Sutter (MD), L. Painter (Fin), L. Painter (Co Sec)
Ultimate Holding Company: FP050504
Immediate Holding Company: OSBORN-UNIPOL (UK) LIMITED
Registration no: 00365565 **Date established:** 1941 **Turnover:** £5m - £10m
No.of Employees: 51 - 100 **Product Groups:** 32, 33

Date of Accounts	Dec 07
Sales Turnover	5060
Pre Tax Profit/Loss	1060
Working Capital	2942
Fixed Assets	322
Current Assets	4510
Current Liabilities	1568
Total Share Capital	870
ROCE% (Return on Capital Employed)	32.5

Policycheck Ltd
10 Moor Street, Chepstow, NP16 5DD
Tel: 01291-626779
E-mail: info@policycheck.co.uk
Website: http://www.policycheck.co.uk
Managers: M. Isaac
Immediate Holding Company: POLICY CHECK LIMITED
Registration no: 05228096 **Date established:** 2004
Turnover: £250,000 - £500,000 **No.of Employees:** 1 - 10
Product Groups: 82

Date of Accounts	Jun 11	Jun 10	Jun 09
Working Capital	-7	-5	9
Fixed Assets	1	2	1
Current Assets	11	8	34

R P S Planning & Development Ltd
Conrad House Beaufort Square, Chepstow, NP16 5EP
Tel: 01291-621821 **Fax:** 01291-627827
E-mail: cliftona@rpsgroup.com
Website: http://www.rpsgroup.com
Directors: A. Clifton (MD), D. Terry (Fin)
Ultimate Holding Company: R P S GROUP PLC
Immediate Holding Company: RPS PLANNING & DEVELOPMENT LIMITED
Registration no: 02947164 **Date established:** 1994
Turnover: £250m - £500m **No.of Employees:** 21 - 50
Product Groups: 51, 81, 84

Date of Accounts	Dec 11	Dec 10	Dec 09
Sales Turnover	87m	83m	87m
Pre Tax Profit/Loss	9m	9m	23m
Working Capital	-2m	-2m	-9m
Fixed Assets	37m	28m	29m
Current Assets	31m	27m	21m
Current Liabilities	11m	9m	15m

Reid Lifting Ltd
Unit 1 Severnlink Distribution Centre Newhouse Farm Industrial Estate, Mathern, Chepstow, NP16 6UN
Tel: 01291-620796 **Fax:** 01291-626490
E-mail: enquiries@reidlifting.com
Website: http://www.reidlifting.com
Directors: E. Battersby (Fin)
Managers: J. Bird (Sales Admin)
Immediate Holding Company: REID LIFTING LIMITED
Registration no: 03896652 **Date established:** 1999
No.of Employees: 11 - 20 **Product Groups:** 35, 39, 45

Date of Accounts	Apr 11	Apr 10	Apr 09
Working Capital	1m	1m	1m
Fixed Assets	882	618	434
Current Assets	1m	1m	1m

Studwelders Composite Floor Decks Ltd
Millennium House Severn Link Distribution Centre, Mathern, Chepstow, NP16 6UN
Tel: 01291-626048 **Fax:** 01291-629979
E-mail: info@studwelders.co.uk
Website: http://www.studwelders.co.uk
Bank(s): Barclays
Directors: S. Haines (Chief Op Offcr)
Ultimate Holding Company: STUDWELDERS HOLDINGS LIMITED
Immediate Holding Company: PRECAMBER LTD
Registration no: 00545832 **VAT No.:** GB 315 1259 87
Date established: 1955 **Turnover:** £20m - £50m
No.of Employees: 21 - 50 **Product Groups:** 35, 48, 83

Date of Accounts	Dec 05	Mar 09	Mar 08
Sales Turnover	10m	20m	19m
Pre Tax Profit/Loss	459	321	68
Working Capital	1m	557	1m
Fixed Assets	589	558	517
Current Assets	5m	11m	7m
Current Liabilities	738	2m	2m

Touch Print Ltd
49 Maple Avenue Bulwark, Chepstow, NP16 5RG
Tel: 01291-621401 **Fax:** 01291-621403
E-mail: sales@touchprint.co.uk
Website: http://www.touchprint.co.uk
Directors: B. Davies (MD), S. Davies (Fin)
Immediate Holding Company: DAVIES BUSINESS SERVICES (CHEPSTOW) LIMITED
Registration no: 03262796 **Date established:** 1996
Turnover: Up to £250,000 **No.of Employees:** 1 - 10 **Product Groups:** 38, 42

Date of Accounts	Dec 10	Dec 09	Dec 08
Working Capital	52	50	43
Fixed Assets	2	3	4
Current Assets	97	122	163
Current Liabilities	11	9	24

H J Weir Engineering Co. Ltd
Bulwark Industrial Estate Bulwark, Chepstow, NP16 5QZ
Tel: 01291-622036 **Fax:** 01291-627350
E-mail: sales@h-j-weir.co.uk
Website: http://www.hjweir.co.uk
Bank(s): HSBC Bank plc
Directors: M. Griffiths (Fin)
Managers: A. Oliver (Tech Serv Mgr), B. Morgan (Personnel), J. Luckhurst, R. Weir (Mktg Serv Mgr)
Immediate Holding Company: H.J.WEIR ENGINEERING COMPANY LIMITED
Registration no: 00697804 **VAT No.:** GB 134 6875 48
Date established: 1961 **Turnover:** £2m - £5m **No.of Employees:** 51 - 100
Product Groups: 40, 43

Date of Accounts	Sep 11	Sep 10	Sep 09
Sales Turnover	4m	4m	3m
Pre Tax Profit/Loss	916	414	-299
Working Capital	4m	2m	2m
Fixed Assets	2m	2m	1m
Current Assets	4m	3m	2m
Current Liabilities	195	202	117

Clwyd

Colwyn Bay

Dva Controls
1 Sunningdale Grove, Colwyn Bay, LL29 6DG
Tel: 01492-534937
E-mail: allan@dva-controls.co.uk
Website: http://www.dva.co.uk
Directors: A. Patrick (Prop)
Turnover: Up to £250,000 **No.of Employees:** 1 - 10 **Product Groups:** 37

Fixit Power Tools
5 Llewelyn Road, Colwyn Bay, LL29 7AP
Tel: 01492-530391 **Fax:** 01492-531999
E-mail: shopsales@tools-uk.co.uk
Website: http://www.tools-uk.co.uk
Directors: N. Hollsworth (Prop)
Date established: 1988 **No.of Employees:** 1 - 10 **Product Groups:** 37

Indtel Telecommunication Consultants (Global Telecoms Partnership)
Garth Road Glan Conwy, Colwyn Bay, LL28 5TD
Tel: 08452-263532
E-mail: steve.markham@indtel.net
Website: http://www.indtel.net
Directors: M. Bedourt (MD), S. Markham (Prop)
Date established: 1994 **Turnover:** £500,000 - £1m
No.of Employees: 1 - 10 **Product Groups:** 37, 52, 67, 79

Jennings Building & Civil Engineering Ltd
Bod Hyfryd Tanygraig Road, Llysfaen, Colwyn Bay, LL29 8TH
Tel: 01492-514006 **Fax:** 01492-512820
E-mail: reception@jenningsbce.co.uk
Website: http://www.jennings-construction.co.uk
Directors: D. Jones (Dir), E. Jones (Co Sec)
Managers: A. Evans (Comptroller)
Immediate Holding Company: JENNINGS BUILDING & CIVIL ENGINEERING LIMITED
Registration no: 01836048 **Date established:** 1984 **Turnover:** £2m - £5m
No.of Employees: 21 - 50 **Product Groups:** 83

Date of Accounts	Mar 11	Mar 10	Mar 09
Sales Turnover	4m	5m	N/A
Pre Tax Profit/Loss	104	209	302
Working Capital	1m	956	647
Fixed Assets	707	818	1m
Current Assets	2m	2m	2m
Current Liabilities	268	189	465

Mott Macdonald Wales Ltd
Ty Mott Mcdonald 5 Woodland Road West, Colwyn Bay, LL29 7DH
Tel: 01492-534601 **Fax:** 01492-533063
E-mail: richard.griffiths@mottmac.com
Website: http://www.mottmac.com
Directors: R. Griffiths (Prop)
Immediate Holding Company: MOTT MACDONALD GROUP LTD
Registration no: 01243967 **Date established:** 1973
Turnover: £75m - £125m **No.of Employees:** 11 - 20 **Product Groups:** 42, 54, 84, 85

North Wales Training Ltd
Swan Road Mochdre Business Park Mochdre, Colwyn Bay, LL28 5HB
Tel: 01492-543431 **Fax:** 01492-544292
E-mail: info@nwtraining.co.uk
Website: http://www.nwtraining.co.uk
Bank(s): National Westminster
Directors: S. Denten (Grp Chief Exec), M. Roberts (Fin)
Managers: P. Evans, G. Herridge
Immediate Holding Company: NORTH WALES TRAINING LTD.
Registration no: 02065604 **VAT No.:** GB 456 9217 21
Date established: 1986 **Turnover:** £2m - £5m **No.of Employees:** 21 - 50
Product Groups: 86

Date of Accounts	Jul 11	Jul 10	Jul 09
Working Capital	796	754	705
Fixed Assets	646	452	428
Current Assets	1m	1m	986

E Poppleton & Son Ltd
Conway Road, Colwyn Bay, LL28 5BS
Tel: 01492-546061 **Fax:** 01492-544076
E-mail: edgar@poppleton.co.uk
Website: http://www.poppleton.co.uk
Directors: S. Vaughan (Chief Op Offcr), G. Vaughan (MD)
Immediate Holding Company: E.POPPLETON & SON LIMITED
Registration no: 00683842 **VAT No.:** GB 159 3534 45
Date established: 1961 **Turnover:** £1m - £2m **No.of Employees:** 21 - 50
Product Groups: 35, 36

Date of Accounts	Mar 11	Mar 10	Mar 09
Working Capital	1m	1m	867
Fixed Assets	812	796	814
Current Assets	1m	2m	1m

Gwynedd

Conwy

J N R Security
45 Pengarth, Conwy, LL32 8RP
Tel: 01492-596406
E-mail: sales@jnrsecurity.co.uk
Website: http://www.jnrsecurity.co.uk
Directors: J. Roberts (Prop)
Turnover: Up to £250,000 **No.of Employees:** 1 - 10 **Product Groups:** 37, 40, 67

Network Conwy
Conwy Marina Ellis Way, Conwy, LL32 8GU
Tel: 01492-580001 **Fax:** 01492-580004
E-mail: info@nybconwy.co.uk
Website: http://www.nybconwy.co.uk
Directors: R. Wooward (Dir)
Immediate Holding Company: NETWORK NORTH WALES (CONWY) LIMITED
Registration no: 04003743 **Date established:** 2000
No.of Employees: 1 - 10 **Product Groups:** 24, 39, 68, 82

Date of Accounts	May 12	May 11	May 10
Working Capital	1	11	233
Fixed Assets	56	76	78
Current Assets	229	540	686

Network Yacht Chandlery
Conwy Marina Ellis Way, Conwy, LL32 8GU
Tel: 01492-572777
E-mail: info@nybconway.co.uk
Website: http://www.yatchchandlers.co.uk
Managers: K. Woodward (Mgr)
Immediate Holding Company: NETWORK NORTH WALES (CONWY) LIMITED
Registration no: 04003743 **Date established:** 2000
No.of Employees: 1 - 10 **Product Groups:** 37, 67

Date of Accounts	May 12	May 11	May 10
Working Capital	1	11	233
Fixed Assets	56	76	78
Current Assets	229	540	686

Richard Doble
Marianglas Chapel Street, Conwy, LL32 8BH
Tel: 01492-576905
E-mail: rdobleip@gmail.com
Website: http://www.europeanpatentattorney.co.uk
Directors: R. Doble (Prop)
Date established: 2007 **No.of Employees:** 1 - 10 **Product Groups:** 80

Robertson Geologging Ltd
York Road Deganwy, Conwy, LL31 9PX
Tel: 01492-582323 **Fax:** 01492-582322
E-mail: sales@geologging.com
Website: http://www.geologging.com
Bank(s): HSBC
Directors: S. Parry (Sales & Mktg), S. Parry (Sales & Mktg), D. Merton Lyn (MD)
Ultimate Holding Company: OYO CORPORATION (JAPAN)
Immediate Holding Company: ROBERTSON GEOLOGGING LIMITED
Registration no: 02059684 **VAT No.:** GB 420 0965 84
Date established: 1986 **Turnover:** £5m - £10m **No.of Employees:** 21 - 50
Product Groups: 38, 84

Date of Accounts	Sep 11	Sep 10	Sep 09
Sales Turnover	5m	5m	5m
Pre Tax Profit/Loss	796	536	501
Working Capital	2m	2m	1m
Fixed Assets	469	521	560
Current Assets	4m	3m	2m
Current Liabilities	1m	812	776

Clwyd

Corwen

Alwen Garage
Llanfihangel Glyn Myfyr, Corwen, LL21 9UH
Tel: 01490-420567 **Fax:** 01490-420418
Directors: K. Roberts (Prop)
Date established: 1979 **Turnover:** Up to £250,000
No.of Employees: 1 - 10 **Product Groups:** 07, 29, 39, 41, 48, 67

Cerrig Furniture
Cae Bryn Cerrigydrudion, Corwen, LL21 9SW
Tel: 01490-420372
Website: http://www.uwchaled.conwy.sch.uk
Directors: R. Hall (Prop)
Date established: 1983 **Turnover:** Up to £250,000
No.of Employees: 1 - 10 **Product Groups:** 25, 26, 63

Ruth Lee Ltd
London Road, Corwen, LL21 0RZ
Tel: 01490-413282 **Fax:** 01490-413091
E-mail: mail@ruthlee.co.uk
Website: http://www.ruthlee.co.uk
Directors: S. Edwards (Dir), R. Lee (Co Sec)
Immediate Holding Company: RUTH LEE LIMITED
Registration no: 03814906 **Date established:** 1999
No.of Employees: 21 - 50 **Product Groups:** 38, 42

Date of Accounts	Apr 11	Apr 10	Apr 09
Working Capital	212	122	170
Fixed Assets	272	344	349
Current Assets	350	377	237

Outside In Designs UK Ltd
Phoenix House London Road, Corwen, LL21 0DR
Tel: 01490-413322 **Fax:** 01490-413336
E-mail: mail@westmeters.co.uk
Website: http://www.westmeters.co.uk
Managers: M. Grimes (Mktg Serv Mgr)
Immediate Holding Company: OUTSIDE IN DESIGNS (UK) LTD
Registration no: 07974130 **VAT No.:** GB 288 2876 96
Date established: 2012 **Turnover:** £500,000 - £1m
No.of Employees: 1 - 10 **Product Groups:** 38, 49

Date of Accounts	Mar 08	Mar 07	Mar 06
Sales Turnover	2119	N/A	N/A
Pre Tax Profit/Loss	76	N/A	N/A
Working Capital	326	71	104
Fixed Assets	112	181	156
Current Assets	1238	1040	891
Current Liabilities	912	969	787
Total Share Capital	9	9	9
ROCE% (Return on Capital Employed)	17.3		
ROT% (Return on Turnover)	3.6		

Wholebake Ltd
Ty'N Llidiart Industrial Estate, Corwen, LL21 9RR
Tel: 01490-412297 **Fax:** 01490-412053
E-mail: info@wholebake.co.uk
Website: http://www.wholebake.co.uk
Directors: M. Gould (MD), J. Gibson (Co Sec)
Immediate Holding Company: WHOLEBAKE LIMITED
Registration no: 03292581 **Date established:** 1996 **Turnover:** £1m - £2m
No.of Employees: 21 - 50 **Product Groups:** 20

Date of Accounts	Mar 12	Mar 11	Mar 10
Working Capital	504	-111	-337
Fixed Assets	705	515	397
Current Assets	2m	1m	652

Ifor Williams Trailers Ltd
The Smithy Cynwyd, Corwen, LL21 0LB
Tel: 01490-412626 **Fax:** 01490-412770
E-mail: philip.evans@iwt.co.uk
Website: http://www.iwt.co.uk
Bank(s): HSBC, Wrexham
Managers: D. Royall, G. Burns (Personnel), J. Connell (Fin Mgr), P. Evans, S. Adey (Tech Serv Mgr)
Ultimate Holding Company: IWT HOLDINGS LTD (JERSEY)
Immediate Holding Company: IFOR WILLIAMS TRAILERS LIMITED
Registration no: 01206036 **Date established:** 1975
Turnover: £20m - £50m **No.of Employees:** 251 - 500
Product Groups: 39, 41, 45

Date of Accounts	Mar 11	Mar 10	Mar 09
Sales Turnover	46m	43m	47m
Pre Tax Profit/Loss	3m	3m	1m
Working Capital	13m	11m	10m
Fixed Assets	4m	4m	4m
Current Assets	20m	16m	15m
Current Liabilities	1m	822	435

South Glamorgan

Cowbridge

Ace Skip Hire & Recycling
Llandow Trading Estate Llandow, Cowbridge, CF71 7PB
Tel: 01446-732731 **Fax:** 01446-732731
E-mail: sales@valerecycling.co.uk
Website: http://www.valerecycling.co.uk
Directors: J. Ellise (Ptnr)
Managers: M. Hendy (Ops Mgr)
Immediate Holding Company: HAFREN CONTRACTS LIMITED
Registration no: 06765100 **Date established:** 2008
No.of Employees: 1 - 10 **Product Groups:** 27, 33

Bus Shelters Ltd
Unit 60 Llantwit Major Road, Llandow, Cowbridge, CF71 7PY
Tel: 01446-795444 **Fax:** 01446-793344
E-mail: lisa.brown@shelters.co.uk
Website: http://www.shelters.co.uk
Bank(s): Bridgend
Directors: R. James (Dir), R. Spence (MD), W. Brian (Sales)
Managers: R. Thomas (Sales Prom Mgr), L. Brown (Sales Prom Mgr)
Immediate Holding Company: BUS SHELTERS LTD.
Registration no: 01822681 **VAT No.:** GB 588 0940 02
Date established: 1984 **Turnover:** £5m - £10m
No.of Employees: 51 - 100 **Product Groups:** 25, 33, 35

Contar Ltd
62 Vale Business Park Llandow, Cowbridge, CF71 7PF
Tel: 01446-773542 **Fax:** 01446-774113
E-mail: info@contarflooring.com
Website: http://www.contarflooring.com
Directors: D. Thomas (Dir), P. Chinn (Co Sec)
Immediate Holding Company: CONTAR LIMITED
Registration no: 02242796 **VAT No.:** GB 484 0632 45
Date established: 1988 **Turnover:** Up to £250,000
No.of Employees: 1 - 10 **Product Groups:** 30

Date of Accounts	Mar 11	Mar 10	Mar 09
Working Capital	-89	-47	-69
Fixed Assets	8	4	6
Current Assets	219	372	254

Fasteners & Engineering Supplies Ltd
5 Westgate, Cowbridge, CF71 7AQ
Tel: 01446-774888 **Fax:** 01446-773778
E-mail: sales@f-e-s.co.uk
Website: http://www.f-e-s.co.uk
Directors: I. Thomas (Prop)
Immediate Holding Company: FASTENERS AND ENGINEERING SUPPLIES LIMITED
Registration no: 01558363 **Date established:** 1981
Turnover: £250,000 - £500,000 **No.of Employees:** 1 - 10
Product Groups: 25, 27, 30, 35, 39, 66

Date of Accounts	Jul 11	Jul 10	Jul 09
Working Capital	18	17	24
Fixed Assets	21	26	17
Current Assets	147	129	128

J W B Recycling Ltd
Unit 3 Llandow Trading Estate Llandow, Cowbridge, CF71 7PB
Tel: 01446-795500 **Fax:** 01446-793838
E-mail: info@jwbrecycling.co.uk
Website: http://www.jwbrecycling.co.uk
Directors: J. Bremner (Dir)
Immediate Holding Company: J.W.B. RECYCLING LIMITED
Registration no: 04767659 **Date established:** 2003
No.of Employees: 1 - 10 **Product Groups:** 31, 32, 34, 35, 38, 40, 48, 49, 54, 66

Date of Accounts	May 11	May 10	May 09
Working Capital	2m	1m	673
Fixed Assets	44	54	47
Current Assets	2m	1m	874

Metrology Systems Wales
21 Bessant Close, Cowbridge, CF71 7HP
Tel: 01446-772926 **Fax:** 01446-772926
E-mail: alun@metrologysystems.co.uk
Website: http://www.metrologysystems.co.uk
Directors: G. Armstrong (Ptnr), A. Armstrong (MD)
Managers: D. Armstrong (Chief Mgr)
Turnover: Up to £250,000 **No.of Employees:** 1 - 10 **Product Groups:** 38

P P Composites Ltd
Unit 38 Vale Business Park, Llandow, Cowbridge, CF71 7PF
Tel: 01446-775885 **Fax:** 01446-775822
E-mail: sales@ppcomposites.ltd.uk
Directors: P. Devonish Turner (Dir), P. Devonish Turner (MD)
Immediate Holding Company: P P COMPOSITES LIMITED
Registration no: 01766051 **VAT No.:** GB 402 3230 21
Date established: 1983 **Turnover:** Up to £250,000
No.of Employees: 1 - 10 **Product Groups:** 30, 32, 33, 48

Date of Accounts	Sep 07	Sep 06	Sep 05
Working Capital	70	22	16
Fixed Assets	9	11	12
Current Assets	110	93	97
Current Liabilities	N/A	N/A	10

Shor Line
Units 39a Vale Business Park Llandow, Cowbridge, CF71 7PF
Tel: 01446-773668
E-mail: quality@shor-line.co.uk
Website: http://www.shor-line.co.uk
Directors: J. Schroer (Co Sec), R. Donahue (Dir)
Immediate Holding Company: SHOR-LINE LIMITED
Registration no: 01886341 **Date established:** 1985 **Turnover:** £1m - £2m
No.of Employees: 1 - 10 **Product Groups:** 27, 29, 31, 36, 37, 38, 67, 68, 83

Date of Accounts	Dec 11	Dec 10	Dec 09
Working Capital	29	-183	-349
Fixed Assets	59	39	45
Current Assets	777	473	329

Solideal UK Ltd
Vale Business Park Llandow, Cowbridge, CF71 7PF
Tel: 01446-774914 **Fax:** 01446-775410
E-mail: len.sambrook@solidealuk.com
Website: http://www.solidealuk.com
Bank(s): National Westminster
Directors: A. Barnaby (Co Sec), L. Sambrook (MD)
Ultimate Holding Company: CAMOPLAST SOLIDEAL INC (CANADA)
Immediate Holding Company: SOLIDEAL UK LIMITED
Registration no: 02589003 **VAT No.:** GB 587 9176 71
Date established: 1991 **Turnover:** £10m - £20m
No.of Employees: 21 - 50 **Product Groups:** 29

Date of Accounts	Mar 12	Mar 11	Mar 10
Sales Turnover	20m	15m	9m
Pre Tax Profit/Loss	1m	889	22
Working Capital	3m	2m	2m
Fixed Assets	377	391	369
Current Assets	10m	7m	4m
Current Liabilities	593	785	284

Storage Design Ltd
Primrose Hill House Primrose Hill, Cowbridge, CF71 7DU
Tel: 01446-772614 **Fax:** 01446-774770
E-mail: info@storage-design.co.uk
Website: http://www.storage-design.co.uk
Directors: C. Bird (Fin)
Managers: T. Bird (Sales Prom Mgr)
Immediate Holding Company: STORAGE DESIGN LIMITED
Registration no: 03184634 **Date established:** 1996
No.of Employees: 1 - 10 **Product Groups:** 25, 26, 27, 30, 35, 36, 40, 45, 67, 77

Date of Accounts	Apr 12	Apr 11	Apr 10
Working Capital	53	46	55
Fixed Assets	7	10	13
Current Assets	118	110	118

Vale Contractors Wales Ltd
Unit 45 Llandow Trading Estate Llandow, Cowbridge, CF71 7PB
Tel: 01446-793562 **Fax:** 01446-795231
E-mail: g.j.sivyer@valecontractors.co.uk
Website: http://www.valecontractors.co.uk
Directors: G. Sivyer (MD)
Immediate Holding Company: VALE CONTRACTORS (SOUTH WALES) LIMITED
Registration no: 01647618 **Date established:** 1982
No.of Employees: 1 - 10 **Product Groups:** 33, 84

Date of Accounts	Mar 06	Jun 09	Jun 08
Working Capital	10	-52	15
Fixed Assets	173	111	44
Current Assets	304	382	236

Powys

Crickhowell

C M D Consultants
1 Llanbedr Road, Crickhowell, NP8 1BT
Tel: 01873-811146
Website: http://www.culturetraining.co.uk
Directors: C. Ditz (Prop)
Immediate Holding Company: CRICKHOWELL SAFETY SOLUTIONS LIMITED
Date established: 2003 **No.of Employees:** 1 - 10 **Product Groups:** 80

Cab Parts & Accessories

Humphreys House Elvicta Estates, Crickhowell, NP8 1DF
Tel: 01873-811810 **Fax:** 01873-811401
E-mail: cpa_wales@btconnect.com
Website: http://www.cabparts.co.uk
Directors: F. Dickinson (Fin), S. Dickinson (Dir)
Immediate Holding Company: CAB PARTS & ACCESSORIES LIMITED
Registration no: 01616572 **VAT No.:** GB 349 1608 43
Date established: 1982 **Turnover:** £500,000 - £1m
No.of Employees: 1 - 10 **Product Groups:** 41

Date of Accounts	Oct 10	May 09	May 08
Working Capital	301	137	138
Fixed Assets	9	10	8
Current Assets	658	339	375

Dyfed

Crymych

Wim Rutjes Catering Equipment Repairs

Penyllyn Brynberian, Crymych, SA41 3TL
Tel: 01239-891580 **Fax:** 01239-891580
E-mail: wim.rutjes@indigoswitch.co.uk
Website: http://www.wimrutjes.co.uk
Directors: W. Rutjes (Prop)
Date established: 1992 **No.of Employees:** 1 - 10 **Product Groups:** 20, 40, 41

Gwent

Cwmbran

A M F Polymers Ltd

Avondale Way Avondale Industrial Estate, Pontrhydyrun, Cwmbran, NP44 1TS
Tel: 01633-873229 **Fax:** 01633-866600
Directors: P. Flynn (Fin), A. Flynn (MD)
Immediate Holding Company: A M F POLYMERS (CWMBRAN) LIMITED
Registration no: 03183757 **VAT No.:** GB 516 9369 26
Date established: 1996 **Turnover:** £250,000 - £500,000
No.of Employees: 1 - 10 **Product Groups:** 30, 42

Date of Accounts	Dec 10	Dec 09	Dec 07
Working Capital	-51	-63	-84
Fixed Assets	151	151	151
Current Assets	14	15	14

ALR Services Wales Office

Oldbury Business Centre Oldbury Road, Cwmbran, NP44 3JU
Tel: 01633-838811 **Fax:** 01633-838834
E-mail: sales@alrwales.co.uk
Website: http://www.alrwales.co.uk
Directors: I. Jeramiah (Dir)
No.of Employees: 1 - 10 **Product Groups:** 37, 84

Antifriction Components Ltd

Unit 45 Llantarnam Industrial Park, Cwmbran, NP44 3AW
Tel: 01633-872126 **Fax:** 01633-872039
E-mail: cwmbransales@afc-uk.com
Website: http://www.afc-uk.com
Directors: C. Littler (Dir)
Ultimate Holding Company: KOWLOON INVESTMENTS LIMITED (MAURITIUS)
Immediate Holding Company: ANTI-FRICTION COMPONENTS LIMITED
Registration no: 01275175 **VAT No.:** GB 140 4857 77
Date established: 1976 **Turnover:** £2m - £5m **No.of Employees:** 1 - 10
Product Groups: 67

Date of Accounts	Sep 11	Sep 10	Sep 09
Sales Turnover	12m	11m	9m
Pre Tax Profit/Loss	427	231	93
Working Capital	592	357	275
Fixed Assets	206	17	28
Current Assets	4m	4m	3m
Current Liabilities	1m	1m	1m

Bell Hydraulics Ltd

Edlogan Works Chapel Lane, Croesyceiliog, Cwmbran, NP44 2PP
Tel: 01633-861423 **Fax:** 01633-864472
E-mail: mary.bell@bellhydraulics.co.uk
Website: http://www.bellhydraulics.co.uk
Directors: M. Bell (MD)
Immediate Holding Company: BELL HYDRAULICS LIMITED
Registration no: 06088875 **VAT No.:** GB 282 6289 30
Date established: 2007 **Turnover:** £500,000 - £1m
No.of Employees: 1 - 10 **Product Groups:** 38, 40

Date of Accounts	Feb 12	Feb 11	Feb 10
Working Capital	29	24	9
Fixed Assets	10	14	14
Current Assets	121	107	64

Belmey Industrial Supplies

Unit 12 & 17 Oldbury Business Centre Oldbury Road, Cwmbran, NP44 3JU
Tel: 01633-872474 **Fax:** 01633-875557
E-mail: mike@belmey.co.uk
Website: http://www.belmey.co.uk
Directors: M. Bell (Ptnr)
Registration no: 03056649 **VAT No.:** GB 535 1771 47
Turnover: £500,000 - £1m **No.of Employees:** 1 - 10 **Product Groups:** 30, 35, 36, 37, 40

C C F UK Ltd

Unit 1 Avondale House Avondale Road, Pontrhydyrun, Cwmbran, NP44 1TT
Tel: 01633-877366 **Fax:** 01633-875666
E-mail: info@conceptfabs.co.uk
Website: http://www.diamondfabrications.co.uk
Managers: M. Fisher (Mgr)
Immediate Holding Company: CONCEPT CATERING FABRICATIONS LIMITED
Registration no: 07156360 **Date established:** 2010
No.of Employees: 1 - 10 **Product Groups:** 33, 40, 48, 67, 69, 84

Date of Accounts	Oct 08	Oct 07	Oct 06
Sales Turnover	735	512	330
Pre Tax Profit/Loss	104	122	87
Working Capital	-33	1	-44
Fixed Assets	103	89	87
Current Assets	317	259	176
Current Liabilities	350	258	220
Total Share Capital	25	25	25

Cooper Controls Ltd

Usk House Lakeside, Llantarnam Industrial Park, Cwmbran, NP44 3HD
Tel: 01633-838088 **Fax:** 01633-867880
E-mail: info@zero88.com
Website: http://www.coopercontrols.com
Bank(s): Barclays
Directors: C. Clayton (Dir), R. Davies (Fin)
Managers: C. House (Mktg Serv Mgr), C. House (Mktg Serv Mgr), T. Harris, D. West (I.T. Exec), D. West (Tech Serv Mgr), G. Heales (Sales Prom Mgr), S. Lloyd (Purch Mgr)
Ultimate Holding Company: COOPER INDUSTRIES LTD (BERMUDA)
Immediate Holding Company: ZERO 88 LIGHTING LIMITED
Registration no: 03586095 **VAT No.:** 227 2069 76 **Date established:** 1998
Turnover: £2m - £5m **No.of Employees:** 51 - 100 **Product Groups:** 37, 67

Date of Accounts	Dec 10	Dec 09	Dec 07
Sales Turnover	N/A	N/A	4m
Pre Tax Profit/Loss	N/A	N/A	205
Working Capital	390	390	390
Current Assets	390	390	390

Crane Process Flow Technology Ltd

Grange Road, Cwmbran, NP44 3XX
Tel: 01633-486666 **Fax:** 01633-486777
E-mail: technical.sales@craneflow.com
Website: http://www.saundersvalves.com
Bank(s): HSBC Bank plc
Directors: P. Wilson (MD)
Managers: H. Buckley, D. Birch (Sales Prom Mgr), D. Maile (Fin Mgr), M. Gadd, M. Warner (Tech Serv Mgr), P. Nicholas (Personnel)
Ultimate Holding Company: CRANE CO. (USA)
Immediate Holding Company: CRANE PROCESS FLOW TECHNOLOGIES LTD
Registration no: 00447239 **VAT No.:** GB 134 3518 87
Date established: 1947 **Turnover:** £20m - £50m
No.of Employees: 251 - 500 **Product Groups:** 30, 36, 38, 39, 40

Date of Accounts	Dec 11	Dec 10	Dec 09
Sales Turnover	21m	22m	17m
Pre Tax Profit/Loss	2m	3m	-311
Working Capital	5m	4m	3m
Fixed Assets	3m	2m	2m
Current Assets	8m	8m	7m
Current Liabilities	2m	2m	1m

Crossford Oil & Tool Supplies Ltd

Unit 94 Springvale Industrial Estate, Cwmbran, NP44 5BH
Tel: 01633-873612 **Fax:** 01633-864884
E-mail: sales@crossfords.co.uk
Website: http://www.crossfords.co.uk
Directors: G. Hurford (Dir)
Immediate Holding Company: CROSSFORD OIL & TOOL SUPPLIES LTD
Registration no: 01561550 **VAT No.:** GB 356 4678 18
Date established: 1981 **Turnover:** £250,000 - £500,000
No.of Employees: 1 - 10 **Product Groups:** 66

Date of Accounts	May 12	May 11	May 10
Working Capital	73	57	34
Fixed Assets	47	24	47
Current Assets	220	199	162

Custom Design Mouldings Ltd

Unit 212-215 Springvale Industrial Estate, Cwmbran, NP44 5BJ
Tel: 01633-861441 **Fax:** 01633-876412
E-mail: info@cdg-uk.com
Website: http://www.cdg-uk.com
Bank(s): Lloyds
Directors: A. Reece (MD)
Immediate Holding Company: CUSTOM DESIGN MOULDINGS LIMITED
Registration no: 01254136 **VAT No.:** GB 288 9165 94
Date established: 1976 **Turnover:** £500,000 - £1m
No.of Employees: 11 - 20 **Product Groups:** 37

Date of Accounts	Mar 12	Mar 11	Mar 10
Working Capital	17	-80	2
Fixed Assets	238	216	162
Current Assets	407	378	389

Cwmbran Engineering Services

Unit 37 John Baker Close Llantarnam Industrial Park, Cwmbran, NP44 3AX
Tel: 01633-871616 **Fax:** 01633-861052
E-mail: sales@cesmoulds.co.uk
Website: http://www.cesmoulds.co.uk
Directors: I. Bode (Dir)
Immediate Holding Company: CWMBRAN ENGINEERING SERVICES (C.E.S.) LIMITED
Registration no: 02169057 **Date established:** 1987
Turnover: £500,000 - £1m **No.of Employees:** 11 - 20
Product Groups: 30, 31, 48

Date of Accounts	Mar 12	Mar 11	Mar 10
Working Capital	11	-1	-6
Fixed Assets	2	4	6
Current Assets	148	111	146

D J Refrigeration & Air Conditioning

Unit 6 Lakeside Park, Llantarnam Industrial Park, Cwmbran, NP44 3XS
Tel: 01633-486260 **Fax:** 01633-486292
E-mail: info@djsrefrigeration.co.uk
Website: http://www.djsrefrigeration.co.uk
Managers: D. Moss (Mgr)
Immediate Holding Company: DJ'S REFRIGERATION LTD
Registration no: 07722047 **Date established:** 2011 **Turnover:** £1m - £2m
No.of Employees: 21 - 50 **Product Groups:** 39, 40

Duradec Wales Ltd

30 Ellwood Path St Dials, Cwmbran, NP44 4RD
Tel: 01633-485309 **Fax:** 01633-863949
Directors: C. Cousins (Fin), R. Cousins (MD)
Immediate Holding Company: DURADEC (WALES) LIMITED
Registration no: 00819651 **Date established:** 1964
Turnover: Up to £250,000 **No.of Employees:** 1 - 10 **Product Groups:** 30

Date of Accounts	Jun 09	Jun 08	Jun 07
Working Capital	-3	-3	-1
Fixed Assets	1	1	1
Current Assets	N/A	N/A	1

E R H Communications Ltd

Grange Industrial Estate, Cwmbran, NP44 8HQ
Tel: 01633-484343 **Fax:** 01633-483773
E-mail: dave.jones@erh.co.uk
Website: http://www.erh.co.uk
Directors: S. Butler (Comm), E. Warlock (Pers), D. Jones (MD)
Managers: G. Smith
Ultimate Holding Company: E R H (HOLDINGS) LIMITED
Immediate Holding Company: ERH COMMUNICATIONS LIMITED
Registration no: 02697046 **Date established:** 1992
No.of Employees: 21 - 50 **Product Groups:** 37, 39, 49, 51

Date of Accounts	Dec 11	Dec 10	Dec 09
Sales Turnover	16m	19m	14m
Pre Tax Profit/Loss	327	454	491
Working Capital	833	584	382
Current Assets	5m	5m	4m
Current Liabilities	938	2m	929

Electroservices Ltd (Electroservices Group)

William Brown Close Llantarnam Industrial Park, Cwmbran, NP44 3AB
Tel: 01633-486920 **Fax:** 01633-486921
E-mail: sales@e-sltd.co.uk
Website: http://www.electro-services.com
Bank(s): Barclays
Managers: R. Bradley (Chief Mgr), A. Pugh (Chief Mgr)
Immediate Holding Company: ELECTRO SERVICES LIMITED
Registration no: 02741136 **VAT No.:** GB 282 6374 39
Date established: 1992 **Turnover:** £5m - £10m **No.of Employees:** 21 - 50
Product Groups: 39, 48, 85

L H Evans Ltd

Unit 53 Springvale Industrial Estate, Cwmbran, NP44 5BB
Tel: 01633-873236 **Fax:** 01633-874427
E-mail: andrew.evans@lhevans.co.uk
Directors: E. Phillips (Fin), A. Evans (MD)
Managers: S. Henbury (Personnel), N. Chaple
Ultimate Holding Company: L. H. EVANS HOLDINGS LIMITED
Immediate Holding Company: L.H. EVANS LIMITED
Registration no: 01242420 **Date established:** 1976 **Turnover:** £5m - £10m
No.of Employees: 1 - 10 **Product Groups:** 36, 40

Date of Accounts	Mar 11	Mar 10	Mar 09
Sales Turnover	9m	9m	N/A
Pre Tax Profit/Loss	-469	-394	101
Working Capital	1m	2m	2m
Fixed Assets	957	559	637
Current Assets	4m	4m	4m
Current Liabilities	546	105	123

Fike Safety Technology Ltd

Unit 31 Springvale Industrial Estate, Cwmbran, NP44 5BD
Tel: 01633-865558 **Fax:** 01633-866656
E-mail: fstinfo@fike.com
Website: http://www.fikesafetytechnology.co.uk
Directors: J. Bosworth (MD)
Managers: I. Morgan-jones (Purch Mgr), S. Abraham (Develop Eng), M. Dew (Personnel), S. Linney (Comptroller)
Ultimate Holding Company: FIKE CORPORATION (USA)
Immediate Holding Company: FIKE SAFETY TECHNOLOGY LTD
Registration no: 02995414 **Date established:** 1994 **Turnover:** £2m - £5m
No.of Employees: 51 - 100 **Product Groups:** 38, 40, 67, 84

Date of Accounts	Dec 11	Dec 10	Dec 09
Sales Turnover	4m	5m	4m
Pre Tax Profit/Loss	-577	-167	-731
Working Capital	-2m	-2m	-1m
Fixed Assets	2m	2m	2m
Current Assets	2m	3m	2m
Current Liabilities	213	223	211

Fulleon

Llantarnam Industrial Park, Cwmbran, NP44 3AW
Tel: 01633-628500 **Fax:** 01633-866346
E-mail: info@fulleon.co.uk
Website: http://www.fulleon.co.uk
Bank(s): National Westminster Bank Plc
Directors: G. Gawronski (Dir), J. Lee (Fin), T. Helz (Co Sec)
Managers: M. Griffiths (Mktg Serv Mgr), T. Smith (Purch Mgr), L. Danby (Mktg Serv Mgr)
Ultimate Holding Company: COOPER INDUSTRIES LTD (BERMUDA)
Immediate Holding Company: COOPER FULLEON LIMITED
Registration no: 01342230 **VAT No.:** GB 302 4741 96
Date established: 1977 **Turnover:** £10m - £20m
No.of Employees: 51 - 100 **Product Groups:** 37, 40

Date of Accounts	Dec 11	Dec 10	Dec 09
Sales Turnover	19m	17m	16m
Pre Tax Profit/Loss	3m	3m	3m
Working Capital	4m	973	13m
Fixed Assets	2m	2m	2m
Current Assets	9m	5m	28m
Current Liabilities	2m	1m	1m

G A C UK Ltd

56 Llantarnam Park Llantarnam Industrial Park, Cwmbran, NP44 3AW
Tel: 01633-861411 **Fax:** 01633-838306
Website: http://www.goodmarkgroup.com
Bank(s): National Westminster, 36-37 Gwent Square, Cwmbran
Directors: C. Gent (Dir), T. Davies (MD)
Managers: G. Williams (Purch Mgr), S. Twells (Sales Prom Mgr), S. Elliott
Ultimate Holding Company: ORIANDA LIMITED {ISLE OF MAN}
Immediate Holding Company: GAC (UK) LIMITED
Registration no: 03005158 **VAT No.:** GB 655 4658 06
Date established: 1994 **Turnover:** £5m - £10m **No.of Employees:** 21 - 50
Product Groups: 31, 49

Date of Accounts	Jun 11	Jun 10	Jun 09
Sales Turnover	9m	9m	8m
Pre Tax Profit/Loss	188	352	364
Working Capital	1m	1m	1m
Fixed Assets	129	90	83
Current Assets	3m	3m	3m
Current Liabilities	227	489	519

Gwent Cables Ltd

Unit 1 John Baker Close Llantarnam Industrial Park, Cwmbran, NP44 3AX
Tel: 01633-838068 **Fax:** 01633-645990
E-mail: info@gwentcables.com
Website: http://www.gwentcables.com
Directors: K. Gibbons (Dir), Y. Gibbons (Fin)
Immediate Holding Company: GWENT CABLES LIMITED
Registration no: 05684672 **Date established:** 2006
Turnover: £500,000 - £1m **No.of Employees:** 11 - 20 **Product Groups:** 37

Date of Accounts	Mar 12	Mar 11	Mar 10
Working Capital	142	131	44
Fixed Assets	51	64	46
Current Assets	328	322	167

Gwent Powder Coatings Ltd
Unit 37 Springvale Industrial Estate, Cwmbran, NP44 5BD
Tel: 01633-860901 **Fax:** 01633- 872030
E-mail: gpowdercoatings@btconnect.com
Directors: S. Walley (Fin), K. Walley (MD)
Registration no: 01899762 **VAT No.:** GB 402 6015 10
Date established: 1985 **Turnover:** £500,000 - £1m
No.of Employees: 1 - 10 **Product Groups:** 46

Date of Accounts	May 07	May 06
Working Capital	19	21
Fixed Assets	30	43
Current Assets	74	85
Current Liabilities	55	64
Total Share Capital	25	25

Habonim UK Ltd
Pembroke House Ty Coch Lane Llantarnam Park Way, Cwmbran, NP44 3AU
Tel: 01633-484554 **Fax:** 01633-482252
E-mail: sales@habonimuk.com
Website: http://www.habonim.com
Directors: G. Jones (MD)
Immediate Holding Company: HABONIM UK LIMITED
Registration no: 06050986 **Date established:** 2007
No.of Employees: 1 - 10 **Product Groups:** 36, 37, 38

Date of Accounts	Dec 11	Dec 10	Dec 09
Working Capital	-1	-2	-0
Fixed Assets	1	2	1
Current Assets	23	21	34

Hamilton Beverstock Ltd
Grange Industrial Estate, Cwmbran, NP44 8HQ
Tel: 01633-838900 **Fax:** 01633-873803
E-mail: sales@hamiltonbeverstock.com
Website: http://www.hamiltonbeverstock.com
Directors: S. Beverstock (Dir)
Immediate Holding Company: HAMILTON BEVERSTOCK LTD
Registration no: 01851620 **Date established:** 1984 **Turnover:** £1m - £2m
No.of Employees: 1 - 10 **Product Groups:** 48

Date of Accounts	Mar 11	Mar 10	Mar 09
Working Capital	-7	-24	-24
Fixed Assets	76	93	112
Current Assets	115	106	97

Hempel UK Ltd
Llantarnam Industrial Park, Cwmbran, NP44 3XF
Tel: 01633-874024 **Fax:** 01633-489089
E-mail: sales.uk@hempel.com
Website: http://www.hempel.com
Directors: N. Frowen (MD)
Managers: C. Peterson (Personnel), D. Nuttall (Tech Serv Mgr), P. Penfold (Comptroller)
Ultimate Holding Company: HEMPEL'S MARINE PAINTS AS (DENMARK)
Immediate Holding Company: HEMPEL UK LTD.
Registration no: 00395704 **VAT No.:** GB 239 1132 81
Date established: 1945 **Turnover:** £10m - £20m
No.of Employees: 21 - 50 **Product Groups:** 32

Date of Accounts	Dec 11	Dec 10	Dec 09
Sales Turnover	14m	14m	15m
Pre Tax Profit/Loss	-239	509	-143
Working Capital	2m	4m	3m
Fixed Assets	1m	2m	2m
Current Assets	5m	7m	8m
Current Liabilities	836	1m	884

Holliday's Packaging
1 Greenhill Road, Cwmbran, NP44 3DQ
Tel: 01633-485593 **Fax:** 01633-872114
E-mail: mark@hollidayspackaging.com
Website: http://www.hollidayspackaging.co.uk
Directors: M. Holliday (Prop)
Date established: 1961 **No.of Employees:** 1 - 10 **Product Groups:** 38, 42

Ideal Presentations Ltd
Unit 10 Avondale Industrial Estate, Cwmbran, NP44 1UF
Tel: 01633-508037 **Fax:** 01633-508458
E-mail: support@idealpresentations.com
Website: http://www.idealpresentations.com
Directors: A. Byers (MD), G. Froude (Chief Op Offcr)
Registration no: 05427414 **Date established:** 2004
No.of Employees: 1 - 10 **Product Groups:** 37

Date of Accounts	Apr 08	Apr 07	Apr 06
Sales Turnover	27	17	N/A
Working Capital	-2	5	1
Fixed Assets	9	3	N/A
Current Assets	11	5	1
Current Liabilities	13	N/A	N/A
Total Share Capital	25	N/A	N/A

Ironspray Ltd
Ty Coch Way, Cwmbran, NP44 7HB
Tel: 01633-872024 **Fax:** 01633-876536
E-mail: elizabeth@ironspray.co.uk
Website: http://www.ironspray.co.uk
Bank(s): Midland
Directors: E. Calder (MD)
Managers: S. Compton (Sales Admin)
Immediate Holding Company: IRONSPRAY LIMITED
Registration no: 01773912 **VAT No.:** GB 394 0854 28
Date established: 1983 **No.of Employees:** 21 - 50 **Product Groups:** 43

Date of Accounts	Apr 11	Apr 10	Apr 09
Working Capital	100	165	168
Fixed Assets	408	452	476
Current Assets	445	485	481

Isotemp Ductwork Ltd
Court Road Industrial Estate, Cwmbran, NP44 3XE
Tel: 01633-867421 **Fax:** 01633- 868419
E-mail: enquiries@isotemp.co.uk
Website: http://www.isotemp.co.uk
Bank(s): Lloyds TSB Bank plc
Directors: A. Curran (Dir)
Ultimate Holding Company: ISOTEMP ENGINEERING LIMITED
Immediate Holding Company: ISOTEMP DUCTWORK LIMITED
Registration no: 01368900 **Date established:** 1978 **Turnover:** £5m - £10m
No.of Employees: 51 - 100 **Product Groups:** 30, 36

Date of Accounts	Dec 09	Dec 08	Dec 07
Sales Turnover	7m	7m	N/A
Pre Tax Profit/Loss	-418	-284	N/A
Working Capital	-558	-97	245
Fixed Assets	853	1m	1m
Current Assets	2m	2m	2m
Current Liabilities	690	902	N/A

Just Rollers
Unit 25 Somerset Industrial Estate, Cwmbran, NP44 1QX
Tel: 01633-869436 **Fax:** 01633-860046
E-mail: sales@justrollers.com
Website: http://www.justrollers.com
Bank(s): Barclays
Directors: G. Davis (MD)
Ultimate Holding Company: JUST HOLDINGS LIMITED
Immediate Holding Company: JUST ROLLERS PLC
Registration no: 00969967 **VAT No.:** GB 194 9651 13
Date established: 1970 **Turnover:** £5m - £10m
No.of Employees: 51 - 100 **Product Groups:** 29

Date of Accounts	Sep 11	Sep 10	Sep 09
Sales Turnover	7m	6m	6m
Pre Tax Profit/Loss	483	231	216
Working Capital	2m	2m	2m
Fixed Assets	442	359	362
Current Assets	3m	3m	3m
Current Liabilities	347	375	212

Cyril Luff Metal Decorators Ltd
57-58 Springvale Industrial Estate, Cwmbran, NP44 5BD
Tel: 01633-869531 **Fax:** 01633-865046
E-mail: info@cyrilluff.co.uk
Website: http://www.cyrilluff.co.uk
Bank(s): Barclays
Directors: B. Luff (MD)
Ultimate Holding Company: CLMD HOLDINGS LIMITED
Immediate Holding Company: CYRIL LUFF (METAL DECORATORS) LIMITED
Registration no: 01411397 **VAT No.:** GB 328 8284 28
Date established: 1979 **Turnover:** £2m - £5m **No.of Employees:** 21 - 50
Product Groups: 28

Date of Accounts	May 11	May 10	May 09
Working Capital	811	867	834
Fixed Assets	237	186	220
Current Assets	1m	1m	1m

Nortech Control Systems Ltd
Brecon House William Brown Close, Llantarnam Industrial Park, Cwmbran, NP44 3AB
Tel: 01633-485533 **Fax:** 01633-485666
E-mail: sales@nortechcontrol.com
Website: http://www.nortechcontrol.com
Directors: S. Blackler (MD)
Immediate Holding Company: NORTECH CONTROL SYSTEMS LIMITED
Registration no: 02737572 **Date established:** 1992
No.of Employees: 11 - 20 **Product Groups:** 36, 37, 38, 39, 40, 44, 68, 81, 84

Date of Accounts	Dec 11	Dec 10	Dec 09
Working Capital	267	260	220
Fixed Assets	3	18	17
Current Assets	543	481	459

P C Pallets Ltd
The Yard Llandowlais Street, Oakfield, Cwmbran, NP44 7HD
Tel: 01633-865069 **Fax:** 01633-865069
E-mail: pandc.pallets@btconnect.com
Website: http://www.pcpallets.co.uk
Directors: P. Charley (MD)
Immediate Holding Company: PC PALLETS LTD
Registration no: 06917343 **Date established:** 2009
Turnover: £500,000 - £1m **No.of Employees:** 1 - 10 **Product Groups:** 25, 42, 45, 67, 76

Date of Accounts	May 10
Working Capital	-8
Fixed Assets	9
Current Assets	118

Ringtel Electronics UK Ltd
Ringtel House Lake View, Llantarnam Industrial Park, Cwmbran, NP44 3HP
Tel: 01633-489550 **Fax:** 01633-489570
E-mail: sales@ringtel.com
Website: http://www.ringtel.com
Directors: J. Coop-Franklin (MD)
Immediate Holding Company: RINGTEL ELECTRONICS (UK) LIMITED
Registration no: 03003557 **VAT No.:** GB 650 9339 27
Date established: 1994 **Turnover:** £2m - £5m **No.of Employees:** 1 - 10
Product Groups: 37

Date of Accounts	Dec 11	Dec 10	Dec 09
Working Capital	681	893	821
Fixed Assets	58	55	105
Current Assets	797	1m	1m

S D C Technologies Ltd
Unit 6 Llantarnam Industrial Park Llantarnam Industrial Park, Cwmbran, NP44 3AW
Tel: 01633-627030 **Fax:** 01633-627031
E-mail: info@sdctech.com
Website: http://www.sdctech.com
Directors: F. Bassoff (Co Sec)
Managers: D. Aviss
Immediate Holding Company: SDC TECHNOLOGIES INC.
Registration no: FC018866 **Date established:** 1995
Turnover: £20m - £50m **No.of Employees:** 1 - 10 **Product Groups:** 46, 48

Schaltbau Machine Electrics Ltd
Unit 335-336 Woodside Way Springvale Industrial Estate, Cwmbran, NP44 5BR
Tel: 01633-877555 **Fax:** 01633-873366
E-mail: sales@schaltbau-me.com
Website: http://www.schaltbau-me.com
Directors: T. Fox (MD)
Ultimate Holding Company: SCHALTBAU HOLDING AG (GERMANY)
Immediate Holding Company: TRUKAIDS LIMITED
Registration no: 01507048 **Date established:** 1980 **Turnover:** £2m - £5m
No.of Employees: 21 - 50 **Product Groups:** 37, 39, 48, 67, 83

Date of Accounts	Dec 10	Dec 09	Dec 08

Shoreheat Ltd
Unit 25 Court Road Industrial Estate, Cwmbran, NP44 3AS
Tel: 01633-869329 **Fax:** 01633-485623
Website: http://www.shoreheat.co.uk
Managers: S. Oakerbee (District Mgr)
Ultimate Holding Company: PROGRESS GROUP LIMITED
Immediate Holding Company: SHOREHEAT LIMITED
Registration no: 01566154 **Date established:** 1981 **Turnover:** £5m - £10m
No.of Employees: 1 - 10 **Product Groups:** 36, 38, 40

Date of Accounts	Dec 11	Dec 10	Dec 09
Sales Turnover	14m	17m	13m
Pre Tax Profit/Loss	28	540	327
Working Capital	2m	2m	2m
Fixed Assets	560	461	505
Current Assets	6m	6m	6m
Current Liabilities	247	480	388

Stagecoach In South Wales
1 St Davids Road, Cwmbran, NP44 1PD
Tel: 01633-838856 **Fax:** 01633-865299
E-mail: angie.williams@stagecoachbus.com
Website: http://www.stagecoachbus.com
Directors: J. Gould (MD)
Managers: M. Tunstall (Ops Mgr)
Ultimate Holding Company: STAGECOACH GROUP PLC
Immediate Holding Company: STAGECOACH TRANSPORT HOLDINGS PLC
Registration no: 03092390 **Turnover:** £10m - £20m
No.of Employees: 101 - 250 **Product Groups:** 72

Teledyne Reynolds Ltd
Caldicot Way Pontrhydyrun, Cwmbran, NP44 1UF
Tel: 01633-863673 **Fax:** 01635-262244
Website: http://www.reynoldsindustries.ltd.uk
Managers: I. Davis (Mgr)
Ultimate Holding Company: TELEDYNE TECHNOLOGIES INC (USA)
Registration no: 01607550 **Date established:** 1982 **Turnover:** £5m - £10m
No.of Employees: 1 - 10 **Product Groups:** 37

Vision Computer Centre Ltd
Unit 116 Springvale Industrial Estate, Cwmbran, NP44 5BG
Tel: 01633-864444 **Fax:** 01633-877834
E-mail: mark.morgan@visionwales.com
Website: http://www.visioncomputercentre.co.uk
Directors: M. Morgan (MD)
Immediate Holding Company: VISION COMPUTER CENTRE LIMITED
Registration no: 04630049 **Date established:** 2003
No.of Employees: 1 - 10 **Product Groups:** 26, 27, 30, 32, 34, 35, 36, 37, 38, 40, 44, 45, 46, 47, 48, 49, 52, 61, 67, 69, 79, 84, 86

Date of Accounts	Jan 11	Jan 10	Jan 09
Working Capital	76	8	-12
Fixed Assets	63	15	16
Current Assets	173	65	84

Clwyd

Deeside

Aber Roof Truss Ltd (Gang-Nail Systems Ltd)
Off Babbage Road Engineer Park, Sandycroft, Deeside, CH5 2QD
Tel: 01244-539165 **Fax:** 01244-539166
E-mail: info@aberrooftruss.co.uk
Website: http://www.aberrooftruss.co.uk
Directors: K. Dunbebin (Co Sec)
Immediate Holding Company: ABER ROOF TRUSS LIMITED
Registration no: 03521094 **Date established:** 1998
No.of Employees: 11 - 20 **Product Groups:** 35, 66

Date of Accounts	Dec 07	Jun 11	Jun 10
Working Capital	21	99	87
Fixed Assets	513	410	431
Current Assets	422	327	300

Accuromm UK Ltd
20 Welsh Road Garden City, Deeside, CH5 2RA
Tel: 01244-836385 **Fax:** 01244-241100
E-mail: info@accurommuk.com
Website: http://www.accurommuk.com
Directors: T. Harashima (Dir)
Ultimate Holding Company: FUJI SEIKO LTD (JAPAN)
Immediate Holding Company: ACCUROMM (U.K.) LIMITED
Registration no: 02138730 **VAT No.:** GB 485 8702 04
Date established: 1987 **Turnover:** £250,000 - £500,000
No.of Employees: 1 - 10 **Product Groups:** 33, 46

Date of Accounts	Dec 11	Dec 10	Dec 09
Sales Turnover	413	313	327
Pre Tax Profit/Loss	8	-1	19
Working Capital	1m	1m	1m
Fixed Assets	2	3	4
Current Assets	1m	1m	1m
Current Liabilities	12	16	14

Allsorts
82 Chester Road West Shotton, Deeside, CH5 1BZ
Tel: 01244-811888 **Fax:** 01244-811888
E-mail: enquiries@secondhandheaven.co.uk
Website: http://www.secondhandheaven.co.uk
Directors: G. Laugharne (Prop)
Turnover: Up to £250,000 **No.of Employees:** 1 - 10 **Product Groups:** 26, 34, 51

B A S S Hydro Coatings Ltd
Unit 101 Tenth Avenue Deeside Industrial Park, Deeside, CH5 2UA
Tel: 01244-281315 **Fax:** 01244-281316
Website: http://www.bass.co.uk
Directors: A. Holt (Co Sec)
Managers: D. Thomas (Mktg Serv Mgr), D. Thomas (Mktg Serv Mgr)
Ultimate Holding Company: SYSTEMS LABELLING LIMITED
Immediate Holding Company: BUSINESS SUPPLIES (NORTH WALES) LIMITED
Registration no: 02484831 **Date established:** 1996
Turnover: £10m - £20m **No.of Employees:** 51 - 100 **Product Groups:** 32

Date of Accounts	Dec 11	Dec 10	Dec 09
Working Capital	-2	-14	9
Fixed Assets	20	27	2
Current Assets	84	76	91

Ball Packaging Europe
Sixth Avenue Deeside Industrial Park, Deeside, CH5 2LB
Tel: 01244-280464 **Fax:** 01244-281745
E-mail: kevin.blackwell@ball.com
Website: http://www.ball-europe.com
Managers: J. Birchall (Purch Mgr), L. Evanova-chamberlain (Personnel), M. Lemoyne (Plant), N. Sutherland (Tech Serv Mgr), J. Jones (Comptroller)
No.of Employees: 101 - 250 **Product Groups:** 35, 45

Chem Oil Engineering Ltd
Rectors Lane Pentre, Deeside, CH5 2DN
Tel: 01244-535262 **Fax:** 01244-534277
E-mail: office@chemoil.u-net.com
Website: http://www.chemoil.u-net.com
Bank(s): HSBC Bank plc
Directors: D. Bond (Dir), D. Bond (MD), I. Phoenix (Dir)
Managers: C. Eardley (Chief Acct)
Immediate Holding Company: CHEM-OIL ENGINEERING LIMITED
Registration no: 05413637 **Date established:** 2005 **Turnover:** £2m - £5m
No.of Employees: 11 - 20 **Product Groups:** 37, 46

Date of Accounts	Apr 11	Apr 10	Apr 09
Working Capital	204	101	61
Fixed Assets	7	10	12
Current Assets	390	287	320

Colour Coatings Ltd
50-51 Deeside Industrial Estate Welsh Road, Deeside, CH5 2LR
Tel: 01244-281555 **Fax:** 01244-281555
E-mail: info@colourcoatings.co.uk
Website: http://www.colourcoatings.co.uk
Directors: A. Butt (MD)
Immediate Holding Company: COLOUR COATINGS LIMITED
Registration no: 03722356 **Date established:** 1999
No.of Employees: 1 - 10 **Product Groups:** 46, 48

Date of Accounts	Mar 12	Mar 11	Mar 10
Working Capital	30	57	57
Fixed Assets	28	31	34
Current Assets	108	152	118
Current Liabilities	N/A	35	N/A

D R B Group
First Avenue Deeside Industrial Park, Deeside, CH5 2QR
Tel: 01244-280280 **Fax:** 01244-390899
E-mail: sales@drbgroup.co.uk
Website: http://www.drbgroup.co.uk
Directors: Bennett (MD)
Managers: G. Kelly (Sales & Mktg Mg), K. Vivian (Personnel), N. Parry (Tech Serv Mgr)
Ultimate Holding Company: FLETCHER,LANGLEY LIMITED
Immediate Holding Company: DRB GROUP LIMITED
Registration no: 05488481 **Date established:** 2005 **Turnover:** £2m - £5m
No.of Employees: 101 - 250 **Product Groups:** 35, 67

Deeside Property Improvments - D P I
Sealand Road Sealand, Deeside, CH5 2RH
Tel: 01244-823232 **Fax:** 01244-823217
E-mail: sales@dpimprovements.net
Website: http://www.dpimprovements.net
Directors: J. Fleet (Prop)
No.of Employees: 1 - 10 **Product Groups:** 25, 33, 35, 66

Dixon Bate Ltd
Unit 45 First Avenue Deeside Industrial Park, Deeside, CH5 2LG
Tel: 01244-288925 **Fax:** 01244-288462
E-mail: technical@dixonbate.co.uk
Website: http://www.dixonbate.co.uk
Bank(s): The Royal Bank of Scotland
Directors: P. Miles (Sales), T. Barnes (MD), L. Arnott (Fin), P. Stanton (Pers)
Managers: P. Ashley (Prod Mgr)
Immediate Holding Company: Bradley Industries Ltd
Registration no: 00971984 **VAT No.:** GB 406 1792 62
Date established: 1984 **Turnover:** £2m - £5m **No.of Employees:** 21 - 50
Product Groups: 33, 35, 36, 39, 68

Emergency Planning Solutions
34 Chester Road Dobshill, Deeside, CH5 3LZ
Tel: 01244-550253
E-mail: davidashford@epstraining.co.uk
Website: http://www.epstraining.co.uk
Directors: D. Ashford (Prop)
Date established: 2009 **Turnover:** Up to £250,000
No.of Employees: 1 - 10 **Product Groups:** 86

Eriks
Weighbridge Road Deeside Industrial Park, Deeside, CH5 2LL
Tel: 01244-284492 **Fax:** 01244-285021
E-mail: tony.lamont@eriks.co.uk
Website: http://www.eriks.co.uk
Managers: T. Lamont (Site Co-ord)
Registration no: 03142338 **No.of Employees:** 1 - 10 **Product Groups:** 30

Excelsior Technolgies
Parkway Deeside Industrial Park, Deeside, CH5 2NS
Tel: 01244-833230 **Fax:** 01352-734539
E-mail: admin@exceltechuk.com
Website: http://www.exceltechuk.com
Bank(s): Lloyds TSB Bank plc
Directors: T. McInnes (Fin)
Managers: L. Edwards, S. Sutton (Personnel), M. Beresford (Tech Serv Mgr), B. Shaw, J. Eller (Sales Prom Mgr)
Immediate Holding Company: EXCELSIOR TECHNOLOGIES LIMITED
Registration no: 05188170 **Date established:** 2004
Turnover: £20m - £50m **No.of Employees:** 101 - 250 **Product Groups:** 30

Date of Accounts	Dec 11	Dec 10	Dec 09
Sales Turnover	40m	38m	31m
Pre Tax Profit/Loss	-212	1m	703
Working Capital	-3m	-3m	-3m
Fixed Assets	16m	15m	11m
Current Assets	14m	15m	11m
Current Liabilities	9m	3m	3m

Fabricom Janus Neill Ltd
5 Deva Industrial Park Factory Road, Sandycroft, Deeside, CH5 2QJ
Tel: 01244-529030 **Fax:** 01244-538531
E-mail: keith.pearson@fabricon-gdfsuez.co.uk
Website: http://www.fabricom-gdfsuez.co.uk
Directors: K. Pearson (Dir)
Immediate Holding Company: FABRICOM JANUS NEILL LIMITED
Registration no: 07876330 **Date established:** 2011
No.of Employees: 21 - 50 **Product Groups:** 37, 40, 48

Date of Accounts	Dec 10	Dec 09	Dec 08
Working Capital	-8	-8	-7
Fixed Assets	9	10	10

Fawcett Christie Hydraulics Ltd
Sandycroft Industrial Estate Chester Road, Sandycroft, Deeside, CH5 2QP
Tel: 01244-535515 **Fax:** 01244-533002
E-mail: sales@fch.co.uk
Website: http://www.fch.co.uk
Bank(s): Lloyds TSB Bank plc
Directors: D. Jones (Fin)
Managers: H. Freeman (Mktg Serv Mgr), I. Anderson (Tech Serv Mgr), R. Wheat (Purch Mgr), C. Conway (Personnel)
Ultimate Holding Company: OLAER GROUP LIMITED
Immediate Holding Company: OLAER FAWCETT CHRISTIE LIMITED
Registration no: 01114923 **VAT No.:** GB 439 7434 19
Date established: 1973 **Turnover:** £10m - £20m
No.of Employees: 51 - 100 **Product Groups:** 33, 35, 36, 38, 40, 42, 48, 63, 66, 67, 84, 85

Date of Accounts	Dec 11	Dec 10	Dec 09
Sales Turnover	16m	13m	12m
Pre Tax Profit/Loss	1m	1m	797
Working Capital	4m	3m	2m
Fixed Assets	709	653	763
Current Assets	7m	6m	5m
Current Liabilities	2m	1m	857

Fireprotect Chester Ltd
Factory Road Sandycroft, Deeside, CH5 2QJ
Tel: 01244-536595 **Fax:** 01244-533592
E-mail: info@fireprotect.co.uk
Website: http://www.fireprotect.co.uk
Directors: N. Baker (MD)
Immediate Holding Company: FIREPROTECT (CHESTER) LIMITED
Registration no: 01593061 **Date established:** 1981 **Turnover:** £1m - £2m
No.of Employees: 1 - 10 **Product Groups:** 23, 26, 27, 30, 32, 33, 39, 45, 66, 84, 85

Date of Accounts	Oct 11	Oct 10	Oct 09
Working Capital	6	9	3
Fixed Assets	11	9	13
Current Assets	78	100	73

James Fisher Inspection & Measurement Services Ltd (t/a N D T Radiography)
Factory Road Sandycroft, Deeside, CH5 2QJ
Tel: 01244-520058 **Fax:** 01244-535440
E-mail: contact@jfims.co.uk
Website: http://www.jfims.co.uk
Bank(s): HSBC Bank plc
Directors: A. Lewis (Sales), N. Troughton (Mkt Research)
Managers: A. Chappele (Ops Mgr), S. Denney (Personnel)
Ultimate Holding Company: JAMES FISHER AND SONS PUBLIC LIMITED COMPANY
Immediate Holding Company: JAMES FISHER INSPECTION AND MEASUREMENT SERVICES LIMITED
Registration no: 05915488 **Date established:** 2006 **Turnover:** £2m - £5m
No.of Employees: 21 - 50 **Product Groups:** 51, 54, 84, 85

Date of Accounts	Dec 11	Dec 10	Dec 09
Sales Turnover	N/A	4m	8m
Pre Tax Profit/Loss	N/A	-16	337
Working Capital	2	129	-712
Fixed Assets	N/A	N/A	886
Current Assets	2	129	4m
Current Liabilities	N/A	N/A	1m

Gainland International Ltd
Factory Road Sandycroft, Deeside, CH5 2QJ
Tel: 01244-536326 **Fax:** 01244-531254
E-mail: lynne.ball@gccdiagnostics.com
Website: http://www.gccdiagnostics.com
Directors: G. Ball (Fin), L. Ball (Co Sec)
Immediate Holding Company: GAINLAND (INTERNATIONAL) LIMITED
Registration no: 01765938 **VAT No.:** GB 406 1171 94
Date established: 1983 **Turnover:** £500,000 - £1m
No.of Employees: 1 - 10 **Product Groups:** 27, 31, 32, 66

Date of Accounts	Dec 11	Dec 10	Dec 09
Working Capital	107	45	33
Fixed Assets	17	13	17
Current Assets	207	103	80

Gem Engineering Ltd
Engineers Park Factory Road, Sandycroft, Deeside, CH5 2QJ
Tel: 01244-520859 **Fax:** 01244-520328
E-mail: reception@gemengineering.co.uk
Website: http://www.gemengineering.co.uk
Bank(s): T.S.B., London
Directors: G. Thomas (MD), O. Gray (Fin)
Managers: R. Sullivan (Buyer)
Immediate Holding Company: GEM ENGINEERING LTD
Registration no: 01435014 **VAT No.:** GB 310 5510 18
Date established: 1979 **Turnover:** £2m - £5m **No.of Employees:** 21 - 50
Product Groups: 35, 48, 66

Date of Accounts	Dec 11	Dec 10	Dec 09
Working Capital	312	111	85
Fixed Assets	667	735	742
Current Assets	1m	1m	1m

Griffiths & Son
Unit 4 Plot 34 Clwyd Close Manor Lane Hawarden Industrial Park Manor Lane, Hawarden, Deeside, CH5 3PZ
Tel: 01244-537800 **Fax:** 01244-537757
E-mail: griffiths-son@btinternet.com
Directors: E. Griffiths (Prop)
Immediate Holding Company: REFRIGERATION NORWEST(CHESTER) LIMITED
Registration no: 00979895 **VAT No.:** GB 160 9359 54
Date established: 1970 **Turnover:** £1m - £2m **No.of Employees:** 1 - 10
Product Groups: 37, 40, 48, 52, 83

Date of Accounts	Dec 11	Dec 10	Dec 09
Sales Turnover	9m	11m	12m
Pre Tax Profit/Loss	288	455	302
Working Capital	4m	4m	3m
Fixed Assets	1m	1m	1m
Current Assets	6m	6m	6m
Current Liabilities	689	683	1m

Henrob Ltd
Second Avenue Deeside Industrial Park, Deeside, CH5 2NX
Tel: 01244-837220 **Fax:** 01244-837222
E-mail: sales@henrob.com
Website: http://www.henrob.com
Bank(s): National Westminster Bank Plc
Directors: P. Halsall (Develop), P. Whitehead (Dir)
Managers: E. Lancaster-williams (Personnel), J. Denny (Tech Serv Mgr)
Immediate Holding Company: HENROB LIMITED
Registration no: 01873269 **VAT No.:** GB 431 5103 03
Date established: 1984 **Turnover:** £10m - £20m
No.of Employees: 51 - 100 **Product Groups:** 35, 37, 46

Date of Accounts	Dec 11	Dec 10	Dec 09
Sales Turnover	18m	12m	8m
Pre Tax Profit/Loss	2m	1m	137
Working Capital	4m	3m	1m
Fixed Assets	5m	5m	5m
Current Assets	8m	5m	5m
Current Liabilities	2m	701	2m

J R Webster & Co. Ltd
Prince William Avenue Sandycroft, Deeside, CH5 2QZ
Tel: 01244-520373 **Fax:** 01244-535866
E-mail: sales@jrwebster.co.uk
Website: http://www.jrwebster.co.uk
Bank(s): Bank of Wales PLC
Directors: P. Lee (MD)
Managers: K. Walker (Chief Acct)
Immediate Holding Company: J.R. WEBSTER AND COMPANY LIMITED
Registration no: 01349584 **VAT No.:** GB 310 2350 29
Date established: 1978 **Turnover:** £5m - £10m **No.of Employees:** 11 - 20
Product Groups: 35

Date of Accounts	May 11	May 10	May 09
Sales Turnover	6m	5m	5m
Pre Tax Profit/Loss	732	267	463
Working Capital	3m	2m	2m
Fixed Assets	3m	4m	4m
Current Assets	4m	3m	3m
Current Liabilities	391	265	214

L & G Engineering
Unit 6 Factory Road, Sandycroft, Deeside, CH5 2QJ
Tel: 01244-536410 **Fax:** 01244-537643
Directors: G. Roberts (Dir), G. Roberts (Prop)
Immediate Holding Company: TRAVELSHIELD LIMITED
Registration no: 05851941 **Date established:** 1986
No.of Employees: 1 - 10 **Product Groups:** 46

Date of Accounts	Sep 07
Working Capital	-8
Fixed Assets	32
Current Assets	164
Current Liabilities	172

M J Maillis
Shotton Works Deeside Industrial Park, Deeside, CH5 2NH
Tel: 01244-836290 **Fax:** 01244-836291
E-mail: kevin.lambert@maillis.co.uk
Website: http://www.mjmaillis.co.uk
Directors: M. Maillis (Prop)
Date established: 2003 **No.of Employees:** 1 - 10 **Product Groups:** 38, 42

Mayr Melnhof Packaging UK Ltd
Fourth Avenue Deeside Industrial Park, Deeside, CH5 2NR
Tel: 01244-289885 **Fax:** 01244-281223
E-mail: wayne.fitzpatrick@mm-packaging.com
Website: http://www.mm-packaging.com
Directors: W. Fitzpatrick (Sales), J. Stansfield (Pers), M. Brown (Tech Serv)
Ultimate Holding Company: MAYR-MELNHOF KARTON AG (AUSTRIA)
Immediate Holding Company: MAYR-MELNHOF PACKAGING UK LIMITED
Registration no: 02729350 **VAT No.:** GB 162 7876 32
Date established: 1992 **Turnover:** £50m - £75m
No.of Employees: 101 - 250 **Product Groups:** 27, 28

Date of Accounts	Dec 11	Dec 10	Dec 09
Sales Turnover	79m	73m	72m
Pre Tax Profit/Loss	3m	4m	2m
Working Capital	19m	14m	11m
Fixed Assets	7m	8m	9m
Current Assets	35m	36m	26m
Current Liabilities	4m	4m	4m

Allan Morris Transport Ltd
Factory Road Sandycroft, Deeside, CH5 2QJ
Tel: 01244-520668 **Fax:** 01244-533766
E-mail: enq@allanmorris.co.uk
Website: http://www.allanmorris.co.uk
Managers: D. Brockhurst
Immediate Holding Company: ALLAN MORRIS TRANSPORT LIMITED
Registration no: 01672709 **Date established:** 1982 **Turnover:** £2m - £5m
No.of Employees: 1 - 10 **Product Groups:** 72

Date of Accounts	Mar 12	Mar 11	Mar 10
Sales Turnover	N/A	N/A	5m
Pre Tax Profit/Loss	N/A	N/A	-276
Working Capital	-869	-1m	-1m
Fixed Assets	1m	2m	2m
Current Assets	1m	1m	1m
Current Liabilities	N/A	N/A	903

N W P Power Systems
Delta House Tenth Avenue Zone 3 Deeside Industrial Park, Deeside, CH5 2UA
Tel: 01244-288288
E-mail: info@nwpltd.com
Website: http://www.nwpltd.com
Directors: G. Wilcox (Chief Op Offcr)
Ultimate Holding Company: CILANTRO LUXEMBOURG SARL (LUXEMBOURG)
Immediate Holding Company: NWP ELECTRICAL LIMITED
Registration no: 03201210 **Date established:** 1996 **Turnover:** £2m - £5m
No.of Employees: 51 - 100 **Product Groups:** 37, 52

Date of Accounts	Jun 09	Jun 08	Apr 11
Sales Turnover	7m	N/A	N/A
Pre Tax Profit/Loss	-2	275	N/A
Working Capital	188	49	2m
Fixed Assets	783	1m	N/A
Current Assets	2m	2m	2m
Current Liabilities	419	1m	N/A

North Wales Controls
Unit 28-29 Garden City Industrial Estate Sealand Avenue, Deeside, CH5 2HW
Tel: 01244-812828 **Fax:** 01244-812829
E-mail: sales@northwalescontrols.co.uk
Website: http://www.northwalescontrols.co.uk
Directors: N. Holland (Prop)
No.of Employees: 1 - 10 **Product Groups:** 36, 37, 38

Peter Cox Ltd
Unit 17 Engineer Park, Sandycroft, Deeside, CH5 2QB
Tel: 01244-538610 **Fax:** 01244-534720
Website: http://www.petercox.com
Immediate Holding Company: PETER COX LIMITED
Registration no: 02438126 **Date established:** 1989
No.of Employees: 1 - 10 **Product Groups:** 07, 32, 52, 66

Remsdaq Ltd
Parkway Deeside Industrial Park, Deeside, CH5 2NL
Tel: 01244-286495 **Fax:** 01244-286496
E-mail: reception@remsdaq.com
Website: http://www.remsdaq.com
Bank(s): Barclays
Directors: P. Napier (Fin), T. Breen (MD)
Managers: C. Taylor (Tech Serv Mgr), S. Peers (Purch Mgr), A. Williams (Personnel), H. Williams (Mktg Serv Mgr)
Immediate Holding Company: REMSDAQ LIMITED
Registration no: 03417251 **VAT No.:** GB 162 6316 75
Date established: 1997 **Turnover:** £20m - £50m
No.of Employees: 51 - 100 **Product Groups:** 36, 37, 38, 39, 40, 44, 52, 67, 83, 84, 86

Date of Accounts	May 11	May 10	May 09
Sales Turnover	21m	22m	14m
Pre Tax Profit/Loss	1m	1m	739
Working Capital	3m	2m	1m
Fixed Assets	3m	3m	3m
Current Assets	9m	10m	7m
Current Liabilities	4m	4m	4m

V Roberts
12 Sutton Close Connah's Quay, Deeside, CH5 4FZ
Tel: 01244-811400 **Fax:** 01244- 811400
E-mail: enquiries@websorceress.co.uk
Directors: V. Roberts (Prop)
No.of Employees: 1 - 10 **Product Groups:** 35

Samarind Ltd
Parkway Business Centre Parkway, Deeside Industrial Park, Deeside, CH5 2LE
Tel: 01244-288281 **Fax:** 01244-288820
E-mail: info@samarind.co.uk
Website: http://www.samarind.co.uk
Directors: S. Pothiawala (Dir), M. Pothiawala (Dir)
Immediate Holding Company: SAMARIND LIMITED
Registration no: 02105894 **Date established:** 1987
No.of Employees: 21 - 50 **Product Groups:** 44

Date of Accounts	Mar 12	Mar 11	Mar 10
Working Capital	203	205	177
Fixed Assets	23	28	34
Current Assets	500	432	379

Specialist Supplies
19 Garden City Industrial Estate Sealand Avenue, Deeside, CH5 2HW
Tel: 01244-836600 **Fax:** 01244- 836600
Directors: P. Satchwell (Prop)
Date established: 2000 **No.of Employees:** 1 - 10 **Product Groups:** 36, 40

Thermographic Measurements Ltd
Riverside Buildings Dock Road, Connah's Quay, Deeside, CH5 4DS
Tel: 01244-818348 **Fax:** 01244-818502
E-mail: sales@tmchallcrest.com
Website: http://www.t-m-c.com
Bank(s): HSBC Bank plc
Managers: N. Skevington (Purch Mgr), L. Booth (Mktg Serv Mgr)
Ultimate Holding Company: Altonover Enterprises Ltd
Registration no: 01161376 **Date established:** 1969 **Turnover:** £2m - £5m
No.of Employees: 21 - 50 **Product Groups:** 38

Thrislington Cubicles Ltd
Prince William Avnorth Wales Trade Centre Sandycroft, Deeside, CH5 2QZ
Tel: 01244-520677 **Fax:** 01244-535670
E-mail: info@thrislingtoncubicles.com
Website: http://www.thrislingtoncubicles.com
Bank(s): Royal Bank of Scotland, 1 Dale St, Liverpool
Directors: P. Wilson (MD), M. Elwine (MD)
Ultimate Holding Company: STRATA GROUP HOLDINGS (SCOTLAND) LIMITED
Immediate Holding Company: THRISLINGTON CUBICLES LIMITED
Registration no: 03020465 **VAT No.:** GB 656 0109 53
Date established: 1995 **Turnover:** £2m - £5m **No.of Employees:** 51 - 100
Product Groups: 83

Date of Accounts	Dec 11	Dec 10	Dec 09
Sales Turnover	8m	7m	4m
Pre Tax Profit/Loss	374	893	618
Working Capital	2m	2m	1m
Fixed Assets	180	214	270
Current Assets	4m	3m	2m
Current Liabilities	636	338	308

Turnstone Patio Centre Ltd (Concrete Paving Manufacturers)
Rectors Lane Pentre, Deeside, CH5 2DN
Tel: 01244-539601 **Fax:** 01244-539691
E-mail: info@pavingslabs.net
Website: http://www.pavingslabs.net
Directors: M. Russell (MD)
Immediate Holding Company: CHEM-OIL (ENGINEERING PROJECTS) LIMITED
Registration no: 07094098 **Date established:** 1981
No.of Employees: 1 - 10 **Product Groups:** 33, 52, 65, 66

Date of Accounts	Apr 11	Apr 10	Apr 09
Working Capital	29	49	55
Fixed Assets	107	109	111
Current Assets	43	58	67

Westway
Unit 1, Floodsyard Rectors Lanepentre, Deeside, CH5 2DH
Tel: 0870-8509436 **Fax:** 0151-355 7673
E-mail: sales@west-way.com
Website: http://www.west-way.com
Managers: E. Callan (Develop Mgr)
Registration no: 03072231 **Date established:** 1990
Turnover: £250,000 - £500,000 **No.of Employees:** 1 - 10
Product Groups: 26

Date of Accounts	Jul 07	Jul 06	Jul 05
Working Capital	231	162	260
Fixed Assets	263	116	117
Current Assets	294	409	474
Current Liabilities	63	247	215

Willacy Oil Services Ltd
Whittle Close Engineer Park, Sandycroft, Deeside, CH5 2QE
Tel: 01244-520122 **Fax:** 01244-520283
E-mail: sales@willacyoil.com
Website: http://www.willacyoil.com
Bank(s): Royal bank of scotland
Directors: A. Planellas (Dir), R. Allan (Fin)
Managers: A. Patterson (Personnel), M. Barlow (Tech Serv Mgr)
Ultimate Holding Company: GRUPO TRADEBE (SPAIN)
Immediate Holding Company: TRADEBE REFINERY SERVICES LIMITED
Registration no: 02369873 **Date established:** 1989 **Turnover:** £5m - £10m
No.of Employees: 11 - 20 **Product Groups:** 39, 40, 42

Date of Accounts	Dec 11	Dec 10	Dec 09
Sales Turnover	5m	5m	5m
Pre Tax Profit/Loss	-54	-225	-375
Working Capital	463	237	221
Fixed Assets	2m	2m	2m
Current Assets	6m	5m	5m
Current Liabilities	575	199	106

William Hall & Company
The Estate Office Hawarden, Deeside, CH5 3NX
Tel: 01244-531547 **Fax:** 0161-436 4855
E-mail: enquiries@williamhallandco.com
Website: http://www.williamhallandco.com
Directors: W. Hall (Ptnr)
Immediate Holding Company: CHERRY ORCHARD FARM LIMITED
Registration no: 00416317 **Date established:** 1997
Turnover: Up to £250,000 **No.of Employees:** 1 - 10 **Product Groups:** 23

Date of Accounts	Mar 11	Mar 10	Mar 09
Working Capital	-370	-278	-230
Fixed Assets	321	321	295
Current Assets	114	104	85

Wirral Fospray Ltd
Clwyd Close Manor Lane Hawarden, Deeside, CH5 3PZ
Tel: 01244-520202 **Fax:** 01244-520363
E-mail: admin@wirralfospray.com
Website: http://www.wirralfospray.com
Bank(s): National Westminster Bank Plc
Directors: C. Schwarz (Dir)
Ultimate Holding Company: SCHWARZ HOLDINGS LIMITED
Immediate Holding Company: WIRRAL FOSPRAY LIMITED
Registration no: 01251988 **VAT No.:** GB 163 2372 79
Date established: 1976 **Turnover:** £2m - £5m **No.of Employees:** 11 - 20
Product Groups: 32

Date of Accounts	Jul 11	Jul 10	Jul 09
Working Capital	184	463	432
Fixed Assets	33	57	56
Current Assets	502	774	779
Current Liabilities	119	143	93

C P Witter Ltd
Unit 1 Drome Road, Deeside Industrial Park, Deeside, CH5 2NY
Tel: 01244-284500
Website: http://www.wittertowbar.co.uk
Bank(s): HSBC Bank plc
Directors: B. Witter (Ch), J. Bedford (Dir), J. Hinchliffe (MD), K. Colder (Dir)
Managers: D. Vaughan-Williams (I.T. Exec), M. Clarke
Immediate Holding Company: C.P. Witter Ltd
Registration no: 01362420 **Date established:** 1950 **Turnover:** £5m - £10m
No.of Employees: 51 - 100 **Product Groups:** 39

Date of Accounts	Jan 08	Jan 07	Jan 06
Sales Turnover	12553	12052	11791
Pre Tax Profit/Loss	750	518	1013
Working Capital	5305	5106	4532
Fixed Assets	1988	1937	2130
Current Assets	6783	6234	6483
Current Liabilities	1478	1129	1951
Total Share Capital	30	30	30
ROCE% (Return on Capital Employed)	10.3	7.3	15.2
ROT% (Return on Turnover)	6.0	4.3	8.6

Worldwide Marine Technology
Dee House Parkway Deeside Industrial Estate Deeside Industrial Park, Deeside, CH5 2NS
Tel: 01244-287850 **Fax:** 01244-288 609
E-mail: info@wmtmarine.com
Website: http://www.wmtmarine.com
Directors: G. Hayes (MD)
Immediate Holding Company: WORLDWIDE MARINE TECHNOLOGY LIMITED
Registration no: 02858650 **Date established:** 1993
No.of Employees: 21 - 50 **Product Groups:** 35, 36, 39

Date of Accounts	May 11	May 10	May 09
Working Capital	746	674	540
Fixed Assets	20	22	30
Current Assets	1m	977	1m

Clwyd

Denbigh

Catalyst Systems North Wales Ltd
Unit 15b Colomendy Industrial Estate Rhyl Road, Denbigh, LL16 5TA
Tel: 01745-816611 **Fax:** 01745-816088
E-mail: enquiries@catsystems.co.uk
Website: http://www.catsystems.co.uk
Directors: F. McGough (Fin), R. Mcgough (MD)
Immediate Holding Company: CATALYST SYSTEMS (NORTH WALES) LIMITED
Registration no: 04083111 **VAT No.:** GB 489 9275 65
Date established: 2000 **Turnover:** £250,000 - £500,000
No.of Employees: 1 - 10 **Product Groups:** 44

Date of Accounts	Dec 11	Dec 10	Dec 09
Working Capital	-9	-5	-12
Fixed Assets	11	12	17
Current Assets	106	103	80

Denbigh Building Plastics Ltd
Unit 7 Colomendy Industrial Estate Rhyl Road, Denbigh, LL16 5TA
Tel: 01745-813598 **Fax:** 01745-817267
E-mail: dbp_ltd@btconnect.com
Website: http://www.dbpltd.co.uk
Directors: S. Gough-Roberts (Dir), M. Hargrave (Sales)
Immediate Holding Company: DENBIGH BUILDING PLASTICS LTD
Registration no: 05067328 **Date established:** 2004
Turnover: £250,000 - £500,000 **No.of Employees:** 11 - 20
Product Groups: 66

Date of Accounts	Mar 12	Mar 11	Mar 10
Working Capital	-13	-44	-10
Fixed Assets	156	167	134
Current Assets	237	209	253

Jewson Ltd
Colomendy Industrial Estate Rhyl Road, Denbigh, LL16 5TA
Tel: 01745-812606 **Fax:** 01745-812543
Website: http://www.jewson.co.uk
Managers: A. Jones (Asst Gen Mgr), G. Roberts (District Mgr), H. Schrimshaw (Mgr)
Ultimate Holding Company: COMPAGNIE DE SAINT GOBAIN (FRANCE)
Immediate Holding Company: JEWSON LIMITED
Registration no: 00348407 **VAT No.:** GB 497 7184 83
Date established: 1939 **No.of Employees:** 1 - 10 **Product Groups:** 66

Date of Accounts	Dec 11	Dec 10	Dec 09
Sales Turnover	1606m	1547m	1485m
Pre Tax Profit/Loss	18m	100m	45m
Working Capital	-345m	-250m	-349m
Fixed Assets	496m	387m	461m
Current Assets	657m	1005m	1320m
Current Liabilities	66m	120m	64m

Oelheld UK Ltd
Unit 16 Colomendy Business Park Rhyl Road, Denbigh, LL16 5TA
Tel: 01745-814777 **Fax:** 01745-813222
E-mail: sales@oelheldgroup.co.uk
Website: http://www.oelheld.com
Directors: P. Hayter (MD), S. Hayter (Co Sec)
Immediate Holding Company: OEL-HELD (UK) LIMITED
Registration no: 03508723 **Date established:** 1998
No.of Employees: 1 - 10 **Product Groups:** 49

Date of Accounts	Mar 12	Mar 11	Mar 10
Working Capital	107	76	40
Fixed Assets	32	36	22
Current Assets	671	551	443

Shorecliffe Training Ltd
Unit 27a Colomendy Industrial Estate Rhyl Road, Denbigh, LL16 5TA
Tel: 01745-815977 **Fax:** 01745-815790
E-mail: office@shorecliffe-training.co.uk
Website: http://www.shorecliffe-training.co.uk
Bank(s): Barclays
Directors: S. Williams (MD)
Immediate Holding Company: SHORECLIFFE TRAINING LIMITED
Registration no: 03684374 **VAT No.:** 720 9771 28 **Date established:** 1998
No.of Employees: 11 - 20 **Product Groups:** 86

Date of Accounts	Mar 11	Mar 10	Mar 09
Working Capital	176	169	132
Fixed Assets	74	64	69
Current Assets	243	238	171

Technical Fabrics UK Ltd
Unit 31 Colomendy Industrial Estate Rhyl Road, Denbigh, LL16 5TA
Tel: 01745-816166 **Fax:** 01745-816168
E-mail: info@filterbag.co.uk
Website: http://www.filterbag.co.uk
Directors: R. Marchetti (Co Sec)
Managers: D. Cookson (Chief Mgr)
Immediate Holding Company: TECHNICAL FABRICS (U.K.) LIMITED
Registration no: 03118062 **VAT No.:** GB 643 9844 03
Date established: 1995 **Turnover:** £500,000 - £1m
No.of Employees: 1 - 10 **Product Groups:** 23, 34, 35, 42, 48, 63

Date of Accounts	Oct 11	Oct 10	Oct 09
Working Capital	54	37	35
Fixed Assets	19	22	22
Current Assets	148	173	149

Travis Perkins plc
Plot 10c Colomendy Industrial Estate, Denbigh, LL16 5TA
Tel: 01745-813332 **Fax:** 01745-816382
E-mail: denbigh@travisperkins.co.uk
Website: http://www.travisperkins.co.uk
Managers: R. Harman (Mgr)
Immediate Holding Company: TRAVIS PERKINS PLC
Registration no: 00824821 **VAT No.:** GB 408 5567 37
Date established: 1964 **No.of Employees:** 1 - 10 **Product Groups:** 66

Date of Accounts	Dec 11	Dec 10	Dec 09
Sales Turnover	4779m	3153m	2931m
Pre Tax Profit/Loss	270m	197m	213m
Working Capital	133m	159m	248m
Fixed Assets	2771m	2749m	2108m
Current Assets	1421m	1329m	1035m
Current Liabilities	473m	412m	109m

Gwynedd

Dolgellau

J L L Edwards
Cefn Braich Rhydymain, Dolgellau, LL40 2BP
Tel: 01341-450688 **Fax:** 01341-450688
Directors: J. Edwards (Ptnr)
Date established: 1985 **No.of Employees:** 1 - 10 **Product Groups:** 35

The Milliput Co.

Unit 8 Marian Mawr Industrial Estate, Dolgellau, LL40 1UU
Tel: 01341-422562 **Fax:** 01341-422562
E-mail: info@milliput.demon.co.uk
Website: http://www.milliput.com
Directors: E. Atherton (Prop)
Registration no: 00921630 **VAT No.:** GB 147 6116 67
Turnover: £250,000 - £500,000 **No.of Employees:** 1 - 10
Product Groups: 32

Gwynedd

Dulas

Fybertec Upholstery Cleaners

Llys Dulas, Dulas, LL70 9LX
Tel: 01248-410307 **Fax:** 01248-410893
E-mail: jamieledingham@aol.co.uk
Website: http://www.fybertec.co.uk
Directors: J. Ledingham (Prop)
Immediate Holding Company: FYBERTEC LIMITED
Registration no: 05091501 **Date established:** 2004
No.of Employees: 1 - 10 **Product Groups:** 23

Date of Accounts	Jun 11	Jun 10	Jun 09
Working Capital	-2m	-2m	-2m
Fixed Assets	4m	4m	3m
Current Assets	482	511	319

Gwent

Ebbw Vale

A B Cardinal Packaging Ltd

Unit 29 Rassau Industrial Estate Rassau, Ebbw Vale, NP23 5SD
Tel: 01495-308800 **Fax:** 01495-301776
E-mail: sales@cardinal-pkg.co.uk
Website: http://www.cardinalpackaging.co.uk
Directors: D. Williams (Fin), B. Tucker (MD)
Managers: J. Tucker (Mktg Serv Mgr), R. Tucker (I.T. Exec)
Immediate Holding Company: A.B. CARDINAL PACKAGING LIMITED
Registration no: 07310060 **Date established:** 2010
Turnover: Up to £250,000 **No.of Employees:** 21 - 50 **Product Groups:** 27, 30

Date of Accounts	Feb 11
Working Capital	-1m
Fixed Assets	1m
Current Assets	2m

A D M Services

2 Barleyfield Industrial Estate Barleyfield Way, Nantyglo, Ebbw Vale, NP23 4LU
Tel: 01495-315040 **Fax:** 01495-315448
E-mail: andrew.metcalfe@tiscali.co.uk
Directors: A. Metcalfe (Dir)
Immediate Holding Company: A D METCALFE (SERVICES) LIMITED
Registration no: 07105334 **Date established:** 2009
No.of Employees: 1 - 10 **Product Groups:** 30, 35, 36, 40, 46, 52, 66

Date of Accounts	Mar 11
Working Capital	7
Fixed Assets	48
Current Assets	134

Base Handling Products Ltd

Unit 20 Barleyfield Industrial Estate Barleyfield Way, Nantyglo, Ebbw Vale, NP23 4YF
Tel: 01495-312172 **Fax:** 01495-312089
E-mail: info@basehandling.co.uk
Website: http://www.basehandling.co.uk
Bank(s): National Westminster
Directors: A. Pitt (Sales), E. Pitt (MD)
Immediate Holding Company: BASE HANDLING PRODUCTS LTD
Registration no: 04325394 **VAT No.:** GB 615 7956 11
Date established: 2001 **Turnover:** £500,000 - £1m
No.of Employees: 21 - 50 **Product Groups:** 84

Date of Accounts	Feb 12	Feb 11	Feb 10
Working Capital	-81	-122	-111
Fixed Assets	145	127	153
Current Assets	395	156	196
Current Liabilities	177	60	131

Bewa UK Ltd

Noble Square Brynmawr, Ebbw Vale, NP23 4BS
Tel: 01495-310170 **Fax:** 01495-311816
E-mail: bewauk@yahoo.co.uk
Directors: R. Thomas (MD)
Immediate Holding Company: B.E.W.A. (U.K.) LIMITED
Registration no: 01211298 **VAT No.:** GB 282 6685 22
Date established: 1975 **Turnover:** £500,000 - £1m
No.of Employees: 1 - 10 **Product Groups:** 36, 37, 39, 45, 84

Date of Accounts	Dec 11	Dec 10	Dec 09
Working Capital	53	33	4
Fixed Assets	45	47	50
Current Assets	81	120	80

Blackwood Welding & Safety Supplies

Unit 1 CWM Small Business Centre Marine Street, Cwm, Ebbw Vale, NP23 7TB
Tel: 01495-371066 **Fax:** 01495-371425
E-mail: stevebwss@gmail.com
Directors: S. Evans (Prop)
Immediate Holding Company: BLACKWOOD WELDING & SAFETY SUPPLIES LIMITED
Registration no: 06548136 **Date established:** 2008
No.of Employees: 1 - 10 **Product Groups:** 46

Date of Accounts	Mar 12	Mar 11	Mar 10
Working Capital	-159	-152	-156
Fixed Assets	174	160	164
Current Assets	262	241	254

Bottcher UK Ltd

Cwmdraw Industrial Estate Newtown, Ebbw Vale, NP23 5AE
Tel: 01495-350300 **Fax:** 01495-350064
E-mail: stephen.hannon@bottcher-systems.com
Website: http://www.boettcher.de
Bank(s): Barclays, 54 Lombard St, London EC3V 0BB
Directors: D. Neal (Co Sec), J. Wilcox (Co Sec), S. Hannon (MD)
Ultimate Holding Company: FELIX BOTTCHER GMBH & CO KG (GERMANY)
Immediate Holding Company: BOTTCHER U.K. LIMITED
Registration no: 01093864 **VAT No.:** GB 224 4428 82
Date established: 1973 **Turnover:** £5m - £10m
No.of Employees: 51 - 100 **Product Groups:** 29, 30, 43, 44

Date of Accounts	Dec 10	Dec 09	Dec 08
Sales Turnover	6m	6m	7m
Pre Tax Profit/Loss	64	-66	176
Working Capital	3m	3m	3m
Fixed Assets	1m	1m	2m
Current Assets	4m	4m	4m
Current Liabilities	445	323	338

Design Environmental Ltd

Unit 32 Rassau Industrial Estate Rassau, Ebbw Vale, NP23 5SD
Tel: 01495-305555 **Fax:** 01495-303595
E-mail: sales@designenvironmental.co.uk
Website: http://www.designenvironmental.co.uk
Managers: S. Willis (Fin Mgr), W. Bainton (Purch Mgr), K. Barber (Sales Prom Mgr), A. Morris (Personnel)
Immediate Holding Company: DESIGN ENVIRONMENTAL LIMITED
Registration no: 01943056 **VAT No.:** GB 430 8314 78
Date established: 1985 **Turnover:** £5m - £10m
No.of Employees: 51 - 100 **Product Groups:** 38, 85

Date of Accounts	Dec 11	Dec 10	Dec 09
Sales Turnover	7m	5m	5m
Pre Tax Profit/Loss	572	200	199
Working Capital	711	551	386
Fixed Assets	400	330	374
Current Assets	2m	2m	2m
Current Liabilities	1m	1m	922

Express Contracts Drying Ltd

Unit 8 Rassau Industrial Estate Rassau, Ebbw Vale, NP23 5SD
Tel: 01495-303363 **Fax:** 01495-308683
E-mail: pdl@spraypro.com
Website: http://www.spraypro.com
Directors: D. Mcdermott (MD)
Immediate Holding Company: SPRAY PROCESSES LTD
Registration no: 03216491 **Turnover:** £250,000 - £500,000
No.of Employees: 21 - 50 **Product Groups:** 20, 32, 84

G T S Flexible Materials Ltd

Unit 41 Rassau Industrial Estate Rassau, Ebbw Vale, NP23 5SD
Tel: 01495-307060 **Fax:** 01495-306333
E-mail: mail@gts-flexible.co.uk
Website: http://www.gts-flexible.co.uk
Directors: G. Farmer (MD)
Managers: T. Wright (Personnel), O. Brian (Fin Mgr)
Immediate Holding Company: G T S FLEXIBLE MATERIALS LIMITED
Registration no: 01336286 **Date established:** 1977
Turnover: £10m - £20m **No.of Employees:** 21 - 50 **Product Groups:** 27, 30, 32, 48

Date of Accounts	Nov 11	Nov 10	Nov 09
Sales Turnover	12m	8m	5m
Pre Tax Profit/Loss	3m	2m	450
Working Capital	7m	4m	3m
Fixed Assets	764	828	885
Current Assets	8m	6m	4m
Current Liabilities	973	843	258

L C R Capacitors Eu Ltd

Unit 18 Rassau Industrial Estate Rassau, Ebbw Vale, NP23 5SD
Tel: 01495-307070 **Fax:** 01495-306965
E-mail: peter.balz@capacitors.com
Website: http://www.lcrcapacitors.co.uk
Bank(s): Barclays
Directors: J. Balz (Co Sec), D. Haines-jones (Fin), P. Balz (MD)
Ultimate Holding Company: LCR CAPACITORS HOLDINGS LIMITED
Immediate Holding Company: L.C.R. CAPACITORS LIMITED
Registration no: 01524434 **VAT No.:** GB 359 6950 00
Date established: 1980 **Turnover:** £1m - £2m **No.of Employees:** 21 - 50
Product Groups: 37

Date of Accounts	Jul 11	Jul 10	Jul 09
Working Capital	661	812	813
Fixed Assets	2m	2m	2m
Current Assets	663	814	815

Metalweld Fabrications

Beacon Works Blaenant Industrial Estate, Brynmawr, Ebbw Vale, NP23 4AZ
Tel: 01495-310800
E-mail: nprice@ts-ltd.co.uk
Directors: N. Price (Prop)
Date established: 1998 **No.of Employees:** 1 - 10 **Product Groups:** 35

Sears Manufacturing Company Europe Ltd

Unit 33 Rassau Industrial Estate Rassau, Ebbw Vale, NP23 5SD
Tel: 01495-304518 **Fax:** 01495-304452
E-mail: info@searsseating.co.uk
Website: http://www.searsseating.net
Bank(s): National Westminster Bank Plc
Directors: K. Wichelt (MD), P. Jones (Fin)
Managers: M. Madeley (Purch Mgr), G. Davies (Personnel), C. Harris, A. Glick, C. Davies
Ultimate Holding Company: SEARS MANUFACTURING COMPANY (USA)
Immediate Holding Company: SEARS MANUFACTURING CO. (EUROPE) LIMITED
Registration no: 01275439 **VAT No.:** GB 273 9032 53
Date established: 1976 **Turnover:** £10m - £20m
No.of Employees: 51 - 100 **Product Groups:** 26, 39, 41, 45, 48, 67, 83, 84

Date of Accounts	Dec 11	Dec 10	Dec 09
Sales Turnover	18m	12m	8m
Pre Tax Profit/Loss	132	-615	-2m
Working Capital	1m	591	1m
Fixed Assets	1m	809	848
Current Assets	6m	4m	3m
Current Liabilities	357	424	252

T S A Ltd

Blaenant Industrial Estate Blaenavon Road, Brynmawr, Ebbw Vale, NP23 4BX
Tel: 01495-312666 **Fax:** 01495-312819
E-mail: info@tsa-ltd.co.uk
Website: http://www.tsa-ltd.co.uk
Directors: R. Warr (MD), A. Francis (Sales), K. Wilson (Fin), N. Price (Fab)
Managers: M. Poyntz, G. Bowden (I.T. Exec), J. Williams (Sales Admin)
Ultimate Holding Company: TEXTILE SHAPES AND ASSEMBLIES (EUROPE) LIMITED
Immediate Holding Company: WHOLESALE MEAT SALE (TELFORD) LIMITED
Registration no: 06540029 **Date established:** 2008
No.of Employees: 51 - 100 **Product Groups:** 23, 27, 29, 30, 33, 36, 39, 40, 42, 44, 48, 66, 68

Date of Accounts	Jun 09
Working Capital	-45
Fixed Assets	17
Current Assets	66

Yuasa Battery UK Ltd

Unit 22 Rassau Industrial Estate Rassau, Ebbw Vale, NP23 5SD
Tel: 01495-350121 **Fax:** 01495-350661
E-mail: akio.furukawa@yuasaeurope.com
Website: http://www.yuasa-battery.co.uk
Bank(s): Lloyds TSB Bank plc
Directors: P. Groves (Co Sec), A. Furukawa (Dir)
Managers: J. Cook (Tech Serv Mgr), W. Carter (Personnel), A. Taylor, T. Williams
Ultimate Holding Company: GS YUASA CORPORATION (JAPAN)
Immediate Holding Company: YUASA BATTERY (UK) LIMITED
Registration no: 01561536 **Date established:** 1981
Turnover: £75m - £125m **No.of Employees:** 251 - 500
Product Groups: 37

Date of Accounts	Dec 11	Dec 10	Dec 09
Sales Turnover	117m	79m	63m
Pre Tax Profit/Loss	138	-570	215
Working Capital	11m	12m	13m
Fixed Assets	9m	9m	8m
Current Assets	67m	33m	34m
Current Liabilities	1m	1m	1m

Mid-Glamorgan

Ferndale

Kingsward Ltd

15 Oaklands Business Park, Ferndale, CF43 4UG
Tel: 01443-732088 **Fax:** 01443-733590
Website: http://www.kingsward.co.uk
Directors: A. Keetch (MD)
Immediate Holding Company: KINGSWARD LIMITED
Registration no: 02469567 **Date established:** 1990
No.of Employees: 21 - 50 **Product Groups:** 36, 48, 66

Date of Accounts	Aug 11	Aug 10	Aug 09
Working Capital	525	450	522
Fixed Assets	41	68	94
Current Assets	733	700	758

Pontypridd Precision Engineering Ltd

Unit 1-7 Maerdy Industrial Estate Maerdy Road, Ferndale, CF43 4AB
Tel: 01443-756995 **Fax:** 01443-755997
E-mail: sitesub@ppelimited.co.uk
Website: http://www.pplimited.com
Directors: M. Price (MD)
Managers: M. Price
Immediate Holding Company: PONTYPRIDD PRECISION ENGINEERING LIMITED
Registration no: 02261825 **Date established:** 1988 **Turnover:** £1m - £2m
No.of Employees: 21 - 50 **Product Groups:** 46

Date of Accounts	Oct 11	Oct 10	Oct 09
Working Capital	-71	-80	-107
Fixed Assets	489	514	567
Current Assets	246	344	291

Sapphire Research & Electronics Ltd

Amerena House Morris Terrace, Ferndale, CF43 4ST
Tel: 01443-730782 **Fax:** 01443-730035
E-mail: sales@sapphireresearch.com
Website: http://www.sapphireresearch.com
Directors: R. Parker (MD), C. Parker (Fin)
Immediate Holding Company: SAPPHIRE RESEARCH AND ELECTRONICS LIMITED
Registration no: 00898153 **VAT No.:** GB 135 1662 84
Date established: 1967 **Turnover:** £500,000 - £1m
No.of Employees: 1 - 10 **Product Groups:** 37, 38

Date of Accounts	Mar 12	Mar 11	Mar 10
Working Capital	298	317	303
Fixed Assets	106	103	106
Current Assets	359	359	355

Dyfed

Fishguard

Catering Supplies & Equipment

6b Feidr Castell, Fishguard, SA65 9BB
Tel: 01348-875587 **Fax:** 01348-875613
E-mail: info@csehire.co.uk
Directors: S. Cookson (Prop)
Immediate Holding Company: PAUL JENKINS AND SONS LIMITED
Date established: 2010 **No.of Employees:** 1 - 10 **Product Groups:** 20, 40, 41

Date of Accounts	Jan 12
Working Capital	-90
Fixed Assets	175
Current Assets	118

Clwyd

Flint

E P E UK Ltd
16 Manor Industrial Estate, Flint, CH6 5UY
Tel: 01352-730720 **Fax:** 01352-730820
E-mail: a.fairclough@epe-uk.com
Website: http://www.epe-uk.com
Directors: A. Fairclough (MD)
Immediate Holding Company: E P E (UK) LIMITED
Registration no: 02157154 **VAT No.:** GB 479 5841 85
Date established: 1987 **Turnover:** £500,000 - £1m
No.of Employees: 1 - 10 **Product Groups:** 33, 35, 36, 39, 40, 42, 44

Date of Accounts	Dec 11	Dec 10	Dec 09
Working Capital	113	56	66
Fixed Assets	165	176	189
Current Assets	271	202	212
Current Liabilities	N/A	9	N/A

Electrical Wholesale Supplies
Unit 5 Heinzel Park Aber Park Aber Road, Flint, CH6 5EX
Tel: 01352-733200
Directors: D. Halliwell (MD), D. Halliwell (Prop)
Immediate Holding Company: ELECTRICAL WHOLESALE SUPPLIES (FLINT) LIMITED
Registration no: 04748163 **Date established:** 2003
No.of Employees: 1 - 10 **Product Groups:** 36, 40

Date of Accounts	Apr 11	Apr 10	Apr 09
Working Capital	242	231	208
Fixed Assets	17	20	31
Current Assets	348	339	311

Global Lift Equipment Ltd
Unit H42-H43 Ashmount Enterprise Park Aber Road, Flint, CH6 5YL
Tel: 01352-735400 **Fax:** 01352-735733
E-mail: sales@global-lift.com
Website: http://www.global-lift.com
Directors: H. Roberts (Dir)
Immediate Holding Company: GLOBAL LIFT EQUIPMENT LIMITED
Registration no: 02944884 **Date established:** 1994
No.of Employees: 11 - 20 **Product Groups:** 35, 39, 45

Date of Accounts	Oct 11	Oct 10	Oct 09
Working Capital	527	326	202
Fixed Assets	16	23	31
Current Assets	2m	2m	2m

Instant Crusher Spares Ltd
24 Castle Park Industrial Estate, Flint, CH6 5XA
Tel: 01352-732284 **Fax:** 01352-734633
E-mail: enquiries@instcrush.com
Website: http://www.instantcrusherspares.co.uk
Directors: W. Roberts (Dir)
Immediate Holding Company: INSTANT CRUSHER SPARES LIMITED
Registration no: 02571073 **Date established:** 1991
Turnover: £250,000 - £500,000 **No.of Employees:** 1 - 10
Product Groups: 33, 45

Date of Accounts	Jul 11	Jul 10	Jul 09
Working Capital	212	200	231
Fixed Assets	96	86	115
Current Assets	868	716	575

Liftstore Ltd
Unit 15 Manor Farm Industrial Estate, Flint, CH6 5UY
Tel: 01352-793222 **Fax:** 01352-793255
E-mail: r.young@liftstore.com
Website: http://www.liftstore.com
Directors: R. Young (MD), E. Reid (Sales)
Immediate Holding Company: LIFTSTORE LTD
Registration no: 02931013 **Date established:** 1994 **Turnover:** £5m - £10m
No.of Employees: 101 - 250 **Product Groups:** 38, 39, 40, 45

Polyroof Products Ltd
Castle Park Industrial Estate Evans Street, Flint, CH6 5XA
Tel: 01352-735135 **Fax:** 01352-735182
E-mail: info@polyroof.co.uk
Website: http://www.polyroof.co.uk
Bank(s): HSBC, Lancaster
Directors: D. Roberts (MD), N. Roberts (Sales & Mktg)
Immediate Holding Company: POLYROOF PRODUCTS LIMITED
Registration no: 01857434 **Date established:** 1984 **Turnover:** £2m - £5m
No.of Employees: 21 - 50 **Product Groups:** 30

Date of Accounts	Mar 11	Mar 10	Mar 09
Working Capital	647	549	601
Fixed Assets	72	76	387
Current Assets	2m	1m	2m

Saluss Ltd
Unit 7 Acorn Business Park, Flint, CH6 5YN
Tel: 01352-736558
Website: http://www.saluss.co.uk
Directors: M. Davies (Dir)
Registration no: 04497337 **Date established:** 2002
No.of Employees: 11 - 20 **Product Groups:** 38, 39, 45, 48

Solon Security Ltd
Unit 40 Manor Industrial Estate, Flint, CH6 5UY
Tel: 01352-762266
E-mail: sales@solonsecurity.co.uk
Website: http://www.solonsecurity.co.uk
Directors: A. Fearnall (MD)
Managers: M. Fleming (Chief Mgr)
Immediate Holding Company: SOLON SECURITY LTD
Registration no: 03065075 **Date established:** 1995
No.of Employees: 11 - 20 **Product Groups:** 24, 37, 38

Date of Accounts	Sep 11	Sep 10	Sep 09
Working Capital	870	616	1m
Fixed Assets	613	615	595
Current Assets	2m	2m	2m

Gwynedd

Gaerwen

Gwynedd Industrial & Welding Supplies Ltd
Unit 9 Gaerwen Industrial Estate, Gaerwen, LL60 6HR
Tel: 01248-422190 **Fax:** 01248-422193
E-mail: nick.collier@boc.com
Website: http://www.leengate.com
Directors: N. Collier (Dir)
Ultimate Holding Company: LINDE AG (GERMANY)
Immediate Holding Company: GWYNEDD INDUSTRIAL AND WELDING SUPPLIES LIMITED
Registration no: 06746339 **Date established:** 2008
No.of Employees: 1 - 10 **Product Groups:** 46

Date of Accounts	Dec 11	Dec 10	Dec 09
Sales Turnover	913	864	427
Pre Tax Profit/Loss	-97	-81	-25
Working Capital	-168	-100	-41
Fixed Assets	225	259	253
Current Assets	259	302	295
Current Liabilities	26	128	113

Heritage Hardwood
Star Crossroads Star, Gaerwen, LL60 6AL
Tel: 01248-715280 **Fax:** 01248-713383
E-mail: sales@heritage-hardwood.co.uk
Website: http://www.heritage-hardwood.co.uk
Directors: K. Grayson (MD)
Immediate Holding Company: HERITAGE HARDWOOD CONSERVATORIES LIMITED
Registration no: 04952677 **Date established:** 2003
No.of Employees: 21 - 50 **Product Groups:** 25, 35, 51, 52

Date of Accounts	Jan 12	Jan 11	Jan 08
Working Capital	15	15	20
Fixed Assets	2	3	7
Current Assets	57	41	48

Welsh Country Foods Ltd
Gaerwen Industrial Estate, Gaerwen, LL60 6HR
Tel: 01248-421111 **Fax:** 01248-423270
E-mail: jowen@gcfg.com
Website: http://www.gcfg.com
Bank(s): Bank of Scotland, Aberdeen
Directors: R. Guth (Sales), P. Morgan (Procurement), E. Ennis (MD)
Managers: T. Williams (Chief Acct), E. Josse (Personnel), W. Owen (Tech Serv Mgr), B. Flynn (Purch Mgr)
Ultimate Holding Company: GRAMPIAN COUNTRY FOODS LIMITED
Immediate Holding Company: A.A.C. WATERPROOFING LIMITED
Registration no: 02732585 **Date established:** 1989
Turnover: £75m - £125m **No.of Employees:** 251 - 500
Product Groups: 62

Date of Accounts	Jul 11	Jul 10	Jul 09
Working Capital	224	21	29
Fixed Assets	252	258	276
Current Assets	786	388	383

Dyfed

Goodwick

Jewson Ltd
Wern Road, Goodwick, SA64 0AA
Tel: 01348-872238 **Fax:** 01348-874041
E-mail: mike.hillen@jewson.co.uk
Website: http://www.jewson.co.uk
Managers: M. Hillen (Mgr)
Ultimate Holding Company: COMPAGNIE DE SAINT GOBAIN (FRANCE)
Immediate Holding Company: JEWSON LIMITED
Registration no: 00348407 **VAT No.:** GB 497 7184 83
Date established: 1939 **Turnover:** Over £1,000m **No.of Employees:** 1 - 10
Product Groups: 66

Date of Accounts	Dec 11	Dec 10	Dec 09
Sales Turnover	1606m	1547m	1485m
Pre Tax Profit/Loss	18m	100m	45m
Working Capital	-345m	-250m	-349m
Fixed Assets	496m	387m	461m
Current Assets	657m	1005m	1320m
Current Liabilities	66m	120m	64m

Dyfed

Haverfordwest

Cmaine Shipping Ltd
22 Ruther Park, Haverfordwest, SA61 1DH
Tel: 01437-769922 **Fax:** 01437-766797
E-mail: cmaine@btinternet.com
Directors: J. Couceiro (Fin)
Managers: K. Couceiro (Sales Prom Mgr), A. Barker (Sales Admin)
Ultimate Holding Company: 01613551
Immediate Holding Company: CMAINE (SHIPPING) LIMITED
Registration no: 01720004 **VAT No.:** GB 656 0192 40
Date established: 1983 **Turnover:** Up to £250,000
No.of Employees: 1 - 10 **Product Groups:** 74, 76

T H Davies
Westlands Pembroke Road, Haverfordwest, SA62 4LA
Tel: 01437-764100 **Fax:** 01437-764100
Directors: T. Davies (Prop)
Date established: 1979 **No.of Employees:** 1 - 10 **Product Groups:** 41

The Development Company UK Ltd
No 1 Panteg Road Solva, Haverfordwest, SA62 6TN
Tel: 01437-721879 **Fax:** 01437-720918
E-mail: info@developmentco.com
Website: http://www.developmentco.com
Directors: M. Hopkins (MD), R. Hopkins (Fin)
Immediate Holding Company: THE DEVELOPMENT COMPANY UK LIMITED
Registration no: 04069698 **Date established:** 2000
Turnover: Up to £250,000 **No.of Employees:** 1 - 10 **Product Groups:** 86

Date of Accounts	Sep 11	Sep 10	Sep 09
Working Capital	59	48	61
Fixed Assets	26	81	87
Current Assets	101	111	103

Jewson Ltd
Old Hakin Road, Haverfordwest, SA61 1XE
Tel: 01437-765231 **Fax:** 01437-760856
Website: http://www.jewson.co.uk
Managers: H. Lewis (Mgr)
Ultimate Holding Company: COMPAGNIE DE SAINT GOBAIN (FRANCE)
Immediate Holding Company: JEWSON LIMITED
Registration no: 00348407 **VAT No.:** GB 394 1212 63
Date established: 1939 **Turnover:** £250m - £500m
No.of Employees: 11 - 20 **Product Groups:** 66

Date of Accounts	Dec 11	Dec 10	Dec 09
Sales Turnover	1606m	1547m	1485m
Pre Tax Profit/Loss	18m	100m	45m
Working Capital	-345m	-250m	-349m
Fixed Assets	496m	387m	461m
Current Assets	657m	1005m	1320m
Current Liabilities	66m	120m	64m

Kestrel Publishing
12 Lower Quay Road Hook, Haverfordwest, SA62 4LR
Tel: 01437-891090
E-mail: enquiry@kestrelpublishing.co.uk
Website: http://www.kestrelpublishing.co.uk/
Directors: D. Philip (Prop), D. Phillips (Dir)
Date established: 1994 **No.of Employees:** 1 - 10 **Product Groups:** 44

Mainport Training Ltd
Unit 11 Lodge Estate Withybush Road, Haverfordwest, SA62 4BW
Tel: 01437-779733 **Fax:** 020-7987 8193
E-mail: info@prt.uk.com
Website: http://www.mainporttraining.com
Directors: C. Hancock (Dir)
Immediate Holding Company: MAINPORT TRAINING (WALES) LIMITED
Registration no: 02744972 **Date established:** 1992
No.of Employees: 1 - 10 **Product Groups:** 35, 39, 45

Date of Accounts	Apr 11	Apr 10	Apr 09
Working Capital	215	187	88
Fixed Assets	72	81	65
Current Assets	548	497	509

Melin Tregwynt
Tregwynt Mill Castle Morris, Haverfordwest, SA62 5UX
Tel: 01348-891225 **Fax:** 01348-891694
E-mail: info@melintregwynt.co.uk
Website: http://www.melintregwynt.co.uk
Bank(s): Barclays, Fishguard
Directors: E. Griffiths (Ptnr), A. Griffiths (Ptnr)
VAT No.: GB 122 2555 08 **Turnover:** £1m - £2m **No.of Employees:** 11 - 20
Product Groups: 24, 61

Paul Morafon
Kerrigwyn Rectory Road, Llangwm, Haverfordwest, SA62 4JA
Tel: 01437-891318
E-mail: paulmorafon@hotmail.co.uk
Website: http://www.countec21.com
Directors: P. Morafon (Prop)
Date established: 1978 **No.of Employees:** 1 - 10 **Product Groups:** 26, 35

W E Morse & Son
The Workshop Wolfscastle, Haverfordwest, SA62 5LU
Tel: 01437-741655 **Fax:** 01437-741317
Directors: R. Morse (Prop)
Immediate Holding Company: W E MORSE & SON LTD
Registration no: 04984233 **Date established:** 2003
No.of Employees: 1 - 10 **Product Groups:** 35

Date of Accounts	Dec 11	Dec 10	Dec 09
Working Capital	117	145	173
Fixed Assets	151	154	156
Current Assets	119	149	181

Paul Williams
Abernant Lodge Llandeloy, Haverfordwest, SA62 6ND
Tel: 01348-831958 **Fax:** 01348-831958
Directors: P. Williams (Prop)
Date established: 2002 **No.of Employees:** 1 - 10 **Product Groups:** 26, 35

Mid-Glamorgan

Hengoed

Carpenter Ltd
15 North Road Penallta Industrial Estate, Penallta, Hengoed, CF82 7SS
Tel: 01443-816565 **Fax:** 01443-813943
E-mail: sales.uk@carpenter.com
Website: http://www.carpenter.ltd.uk
Bank(s): National Westminster
Managers: R. Peachey (District Mgr)
Ultimate Holding Company: CARPENTER CO INC (USA)
Immediate Holding Company: CARPENTER LIMITED
Registration no: 00214781 **Date established:** 2026 **Turnover:** £1m - £2m
No.of Employees: 21 - 50 **Product Groups:** 26, 30

Date of Accounts	Dec 11	Dec 10	Dec 09
Sales Turnover	84m	84m	75m
Pre Tax Profit/Loss	6m	8m	9m
Working Capital	36m	30m	25m
Fixed Assets	19m	21m	22m
Current Assets	44m	39m	33m
Current Liabilities	3m	3m	2m

Dragon Welding

Unit 2 Duffryn Industrial Estate Ystrad Mynach, Hengoed, CF82 7RJ
Tel: 01443-862112 **Fax:** 01443-862112
Directors: T. Carman (Prop)
Ultimate Holding Company: BIOTAGE AB (SWEDEN)
Immediate Holding Company: BIOTAGE GB LIMITED
Registration no: 01033865 **Date established:** 1971 **Turnover:** £2m - £5m
No.of Employees: 1 - 10 **Product Groups:** 26, 35

Date of Accounts	Dec 11	Dec 10	Dec 09
Sales Turnover	6m	6m	5m
Pre Tax Profit/Loss	817	921	422
Working Capital	7m	6m	6m
Fixed Assets	2m	2m	2m
Current Assets	8m	7m	6m
Current Liabilities	389	483	353

Ecoflor Ltd

PO Box 26, Hengoed, CF82 7YD
Tel: 03331-234385 **Fax:** 08443-104561
E-mail: info@ecoflor.co.uk
Website: http://www.resinflooring.com
Directors: N. Davies (Dir)
Immediate Holding Company: ECOFLOR LIMITED
Registration no: 05315250 **Date established:** 2004
No.of Employees: 1 - 10 **Product Groups:** 30

Date of Accounts	May 11	May 10	May 09
Sales Turnover	351	327	N/A
Pre Tax Profit/Loss	12	62	N/A
Working Capital	-9	-25	14
Fixed Assets	64	81	8
Current Assets	54	130	56
Current Liabilities	42	29	N/A

Fork Truck Express Services

Unit 2 Duffryn Square Distribution Way Ystrad Mynach, Hengoed, CF82 7TS
Tel: 01443-816171 **Fax:** 01443-816540
E-mail: ftes_2000@yahoo.co.uk
Website: http://www.forktruckexpress.co.uk
Directors: D. Moseley (Dir), D. James (Fin)
Immediate Holding Company: FORK TRUCK EXPRESS SERVICES LIMITED
Registration no: 04528017 **Date established:** 2002
No.of Employees: 1 - 10 **Product Groups:** 35, 39, 45

Date of Accounts	Jun 11	Jun 10	Jun 09
Working Capital	4	19	19
Fixed Assets	49	35	34
Current Assets	65	73	62
Current Liabilities	N/A	N/A	21

Gittins & Hayter Ltd

Raglan Engineering Works Raglan Road, Hengoed, CF82 7LY
Tel: 01443-813229 **Fax:** 01443-813379
E-mail: sales@gittinsandhayter.co.uk
Website: http://www.gittinsandhayter.co.uk
Directors: M. Hayter (Co Sec), P. Hayter (MD)
Immediate Holding Company: GITTENS AND HAYTER LIMITED
Registration no: 00858499 **VAT No.:** GB 134 1401 21
Date established: 1965 **Turnover:** £500,000 - £1m
No.of Employees: 1 - 10 **Product Groups:** 48

Date of Accounts	Sep 11	Sep 10	Sep 09
Working Capital	119	122	125
Fixed Assets	59	63	68
Current Assets	175	165	161

Lunar Computers

53 Brynavon Terrace, Hengoed, CF82 7LZ
Tel: 01443-816500
E-mail: sales@lunar-computers.com
Website: http://www.lunar-computers.com
Directors: I. Monico (Prop)
Date established: 2002 **No.of Employees:** 1 - 10 **Product Groups:** 44, 61, 64, 67, 83

Newlook Upholstery Ltd

Old Cinema Raglan Road, Hengoed, CF82 7LY
Tel: 029-2045 7575
E-mail: salesteam@newlookupholstery.com
Website: http://www.newlookupholstery.com
Directors: Y. Ingram (MD), P. Ingram (Fin)
Immediate Holding Company: NEWLOOK UPHOLSTERY LIMITED
Registration no: 03723872 **Date established:** 1999
Turnover: Up to £250,000 **No.of Employees:** 1 - 10 **Product Groups:** 22, 24, 26

Date of Accounts	Apr 11	Apr 10	Apr 09
Sales Turnover	174	164	N/A
Pre Tax Profit/Loss	26	27	N/A
Working Capital	6	4	-4
Fixed Assets	2	3	5
Current Assets	41	29	43
Current Liabilities	16	20	N/A

Smoke Control Services Ltd

The Innovation Centre Ystrad Mynach, Hengoed, CF82 7FN
Tel: 08702-406460 **Fax:** 01443-819119
E-mail: a.meek@smokecontrol.co.uk
Website: http://www.smokecontrol.co.uk
Bank(s): Barclays
Directors: A. Meek (MD)
Managers: L. Dew (Fin Mgr)
Immediate Holding Company: SMOKE CONTROL SERVICES LIMITED
Registration no: 02776224 **VAT No.:** GB 615 7310 59
Date established: 1992 **Turnover:** £2m - £5m **No.of Employees:** 21 - 50
Product Groups: 40

Date of Accounts	Mar 12	Mar 11	Mar 10
Working Capital	276	103	112
Fixed Assets	55	51	29
Current Assets	2m	1m	1m

Venture Wales

Tredomen Business & Technology Centre Tredomen Park, Ystrad Mynach, Hengoed, CF82 7FN
Tel: 01443-866250 **Fax:** 01443-866254
E-mail: info@venturewales.com
Website: http://www.venturewales.com
Managers: J. Gorin (Reg Mgr)
Ultimate Holding Company: VENTURE WALES BUSINESS COMPANY
Registration no: 01716838 **Date established:** 2002
Turnover: £500,000 - £1m **No.of Employees:** 1 - 10 **Product Groups:** 80

Gwynedd

Holyhead

Anglesey Aluminium Metal Ltd

PO Box 4, Holyhead, LL65 2UJ
Tel: 01407-725000 **Fax:** 01407-725001
Website: http://www.angleseyaluminium.co.uk
Directors: B. King (Works), R. Brennan (Fin)
Managers: C. Kennedy
Immediate Holding Company: ANGLESEY ALUMINIUM METAL LIMITED
Registration no: 00909645 **Date established:** 1967
Turnover: £125m - £250m **No.of Employees:** 501 - 1000
Product Groups: 46

Date of Accounts	Dec 11	Dec 10	Dec 08
Sales Turnover	140m	136m	175m
Pre Tax Profit/Loss	N/A	-17m	7m
Working Capital	31m	34m	69m
Fixed Assets	5m	5m	8m
Current Assets	38m	42m	100m
Current Liabilities	460	471	5m

Diving Services Anglesey

Heather Cliffe Ravenspoint Road, Trearddur Bay, Holyhead, LL65 2AQ
Tel: 01407-860318 **Fax:** 01407-860318
Directors: M. McGee (Prop)
Date established: 1982 **Turnover:** Up to £250,000
No.of Employees: 1 - 10 **Product Groups:** 24, 35, 37, 39, 40, 49, 51

Eaton Electric Ltd

Turkey Shore, Holyhead, LL65 2DH
Tel: 01407-766300 **Fax:** 01407-766336
E-mail: sales@memonline.com
Website: http://www.memonline.com
Directors: I. Yule (Co Sec)
Ultimate Holding Company: EATON CORPORATION (USA)
Immediate Holding Company: EATON ELECTRIC LIMITED
Registration no: 04617032 **Date established:** 2002
Turnover: £50m - £75m **No.of Employees:** 501 - 1000
Product Groups: 36, 40

Date of Accounts	Dec 11	Dec 10	Dec 09
Sales Turnover	72m	67m	63m
Pre Tax Profit/Loss	-10m	-16m	-10m
Working Capital	-4m	270	10m
Fixed Assets	13m	15m	21m
Current Assets	33m	36m	38m
Current Liabilities	5m	7m	6m

Facilities Management Online Ltd

Cefn Tew Tynlon, Holyhead, LL65 4UA
Tel: 08454-688688 **Fax:** 01248-470003
E-mail: james@fmonline.co.uk
Website: http://www.fmonline.co.uk
Directors: E. Brunson (Fin), J. Brunson (MD)
Immediate Holding Company: FACILITIES MANAGEMENT ONLINE LIMITED
Registration no: 03862464 **Date established:** 1999
No.of Employees: 1 - 10 **Product Groups:** 81

Date of Accounts	Oct 11	Oct 10	Oct 09
Working Capital	-34	-20	-3
Fixed Assets	1	1	2
Current Assets	32	23	24

Gwynedd Shipping Ltd

London Road, Holyhead, LL65 2PB
Tel: 01407-760232 **Fax:** 01407-765344
E-mail: info@gwyneddshipping.com
Website: http://gwyneddshipping.com
Bank(s): National Westminster
Directors: A. Kinsella (MD), P. Arnold (Sales), M. Cunnew (MD), K. Mallone (Dir)
Managers: I. McBain (I.T. Exec)
Ultimate Holding Company: GLENBALLY LTD (EIRE)
Immediate Holding Company: GWYNEDD SHIPPING LIMITED
Registration no: 01848682 **VAT No.:** GB 401 4178 95
Date established: 1984 **Turnover:** £10m - £20m
No.of Employees: 21 - 50 **Product Groups:** 45

Date of Accounts	May 11	May 10	May 09
Sales Turnover	13m	13m	N/A
Pre Tax Profit/Loss	-341	-422	-80
Working Capital	-484	-935	-900
Fixed Assets	3m	4m	5m
Current Assets	3m	3m	3m
Current Liabilities	418	684	802

Hanson Aggregates Ltd

Caer Glaw Quarry Gwalchmai, Holyhead, LL65 4PW
Tel: 01407-720292 **Fax:** 01407-720106
Website: http://www.hanson-aggregates.com
Directors: R. Chambers (Grp Chief Exec)
Managers: G. Kitson (District Mgr), A. Roberts (Mgr)
Ultimate Holding Company: HEIDELBERG CEMENT AG (GERMANY)
Immediate Holding Company: HANSON AGGREGATES LIMITED
Registration no: 02565390 **Date established:** 1990
No.of Employees: 1 - 10 **Product Groups:** 33, 45, 67

Date of Accounts	Dec 10	Dec 09	Dec 08
Working Capital	82m	82m	82m
Current Assets	82m	82m	82m

Irish Ferries Freight Line

Salt Island, Holyhead, LL65 1DR
Tel: 08717-300200 **Fax:** 01407-760340
E-mail: ianfenwick@irishferries.co.uk
Website: http://www.irishferries.co.uk
Bank(s): H S B C
Managers: D. Roberts (Fin Mgr), I. Fenwick
Immediate Holding Company: IRISH CONTINENTAL GROUP, DUBLIN
Registration no: 01019995 **No.of Employees:** 21 - 50 **Product Groups:** 74

Stena Line Ltd

Stena House Station Approach, Holyhead, LL65 1DQ
Tel: 01407-606666 **Fax:** 01407-606604
E-mail: vic.goodwin@stenaline.com
Website: http://www.stenaline.co.uk
Directors: V. Goodwin (Dir), R. Stracey (Legal), G. Bomdahl (MD)
Managers: S. Mcbride (Personnel), W. Parry, W. Parry, O. Noonan (Mktg Serv Mgr), C. Parry, R. Buhlman (I.T. Exec), P. Grant (Nat Sales Mgr), D. Breed (I.T. Exec), C. Parry
Immediate Holding Company: STENA LINE HOLIDAYS LIMITED
Registration no: NF002606 **VAT No.:** GB 404 5171 86
Date established: 1985 **Turnover:** £125m - £250m
No.of Employees: 1 - 10 **Product Groups:** 74, 76

Date of Accounts	Dec 07	Dec 06
Sales Turnover	198900	191500
Pre Tax Profit/Loss	11100	9000
Working Capital	38200	54100
Fixed Assets	11100	9400
Current Assets	102300	82500
Current Liabilities	64100	28400
Total Share Capital	59000	34000
ROCE% (Return on Capital Employed)	22.5	14.2
ROT% (Return on Turnover)	5.6	4.7

Valley Forge

Old Smithy Field Street, Valley, Holyhead, LL65 3EG
Tel: 01407-741445 **Fax:** 01407-742060
E-mail: dave@valleyforge.fsnet.co.uk
Directors: D. North (Prop)
Date established: 1996 **No.of Employees:** 1 - 10 **Product Groups:** 26, 35

Clwyd

Holywell

AMRI (UK) Limited

Mostyn Road, Holywell, CH8 9DN
Tel: 01352-717100 **Fax:** 01352-717171
E-mail: info@amriglobal.com
Website: http://www.amriglobal.com
Directors: A. Frederick (Fin), D. Rowles (MD), M. Comrie (MD)
Managers: D. Rowles (Site Co-ord), P. Cotterill, S. Jones (Admin Off), B. Williams (I.T. Exec), C. Mills (Comm), P. Cotterill (Develop Mgr), R. Alsop (Fin Mgr)
Ultimate Holding Company: Great Lakes Chemical Corporation
Immediate Holding Company: Great Lakes (UK) Ltd
Registration no: 02242758 **VAT No.:** GB 726 9331 20
Date established: 1987 **Turnover:** £5m - £10m **No.of Employees:** 1 - 10
Product Groups: 66, 84

Date of Accounts	May 08	May 07	May 06
Sales Turnover	14319	11568	1091
Pre Tax Profit/Loss	-407	-2738	-241
Working Capital	-1379	-1519	415
Fixed Assets	568	257	253
Current Assets	2827	3069	1270
Current Liabilities	4206	4588	855
Total Share Capital	1142	1013	695
ROCE% (Return on Capital Employed)	50.2	217.0	-36.1
ROT% (Return on Turnover)	-2.8	-23.7	-22.1

Amri UK

Mostyn Road, Holywell, CH8 9DN
Tel: 01352-717100 **Fax:** 01352-717171
Website: http://www.amriglobal.com
Directors: D. Rowles (Dir), K. Gilmour (MD)
Managers: J. Scott (Sales Prom Mgr)
Immediate Holding Company: Albany Molecular Research Ltd
Registration no: 02242758 **VAT No.:** GB 496 0980 03
Date established: 1996 **Turnover:** £1m - £2m **No.of Employees:** 51 - 100
Product Groups: 40, 41, 42

Kingspan Ltd

Unit 2-4 Greenfield Business Park 2 Bagillt Road, Greenfield, Holywell, CH8 7GJ
Tel: 01352-716100 **Fax:** 01352-710161
E-mail: tom.mcguinness@kingspan.com
Website: http://www.kingspanpanels.co.uk
Bank(s): Barclays
Directors: T. Mcguinness (Dir), P. Bullough (Fin)
Managers: C. Cartwright, T. Clarke (Personnel), M. Jones (Purch Mgr), V. Rae (Mktg Serv Mgr), C. Jackson (Tech Serv Mgr)
Ultimate Holding Company: KINGSPAN GROUP PUBLIC LIMITED COMPANY
Immediate Holding Company: KINGSPAN LIMITED
Registration no: 01037468 **VAT No.:** GB 388 5318 10
Date established: 1972 **Turnover:** £125m - £250m
No.of Employees: 501 - 1000 **Product Groups:** 35

Date of Accounts	Dec 11	Dec 10	Dec 09
Sales Turnover	282m	227m	211m
Pre Tax Profit/Loss	16m	17m	12m
Working Capital	63m	86m	37m
Fixed Assets	57m	66m	73m
Current Assets	109m	165m	125m
Current Liabilities	20m	19m	12m

Knitmesh Technologies Ltd

Coast Road Llanerch-Y-Mor, Holywell, CH8 9DP
Tel: 01352-712058 **Fax:** 01352-714909
E-mail: sales@knitmeshtechnologies.com
Website: http://www.knitmeshtechnologies.com
Managers: P. Evans (Site Co-ord)
Immediate Holding Company: KNITMESH TECHNOLOGIES LIMITED
Registration no: 06287783 **Date established:** 2007 **Turnover:** £5m - £10m
No.of Employees: 51 - 100 **Product Groups:** 33, 35, 36, 37, 39, 40, 42

La Cafetiere

Coast Road Greenfield Llanerch-Y-Mor, Holywell, CH8 9DP
Tel: 01352-717555 **Fax:** 01352-715699
E-mail: john.jackson@lacafetiere.com
Website: http://www.lacafetiere.com
Directors: J. Jackson (Sales & Mktg), S. Nicol (Fin)
Ultimate Holding Company: THE GREENFIELD GROUP LTD
Immediate Holding Company: HOUSEHOLD ARTICLES LTD
Registration no: 04666356 **VAT No.:** GB 218 1680 70
Date established: 2003 **Turnover:** £2m - £5m **No.of Employees:** 21 - 50
Product Groups: 30, 36, 40

Onyx Total Waste Management Ltd

Crown Church Quarry Trelogan, Holywell, CH8 9BD
Tel: 01745-560320 **Fax:** 01745-561308
Website: http://www.onyxgroup.co.uk

Managers: T. Ynn (District Mgr), T. Wynn (District Mgr)
Immediate Holding Company: DIRECT FLOWERS (WHOLESALE) LIMITED
Registration no: 02202133 **Date established:** 2003
No.of Employees: 21 - 50 **Product Groups:** 34, 39, 42, 54

M D Ponton & Son

Sefton Workshop Babell, Holywell, CH8 8QD
Tel: 01352-720131 **Fax:** 01352-721053
Directors: M. Ponton (Ptnr)
Immediate Holding Company: M D PONTON & SON LIMITED
Registration no: 06104916 **Date established:** 2007
No.of Employees: 1 - 10 **Product Groups:** 41

Date of Accounts	Mar 11	Mar 10	Mar 09
Working Capital	-5	-13	-7
Fixed Assets	8	11	9
Current Assets	71	52	38

Shotblast Engineering Services plc

Park Works Bagillt Road, Greenfield, Holywell, CH8 7EP
Tel: 01352-712412 **Fax:** 01352-710937
E-mail: gen.office_ses@btconnect.com
Website: http://www.shotblast-services-plc.co.uk
Bank(s): Royal Bank of Scotland, Liverpool
Directors: C. Burgess (Comm), A. Feliciello (MD), B. Palmer (Co Sec), P. Griffiths (Sales)
Immediate Holding Company: SHOTBLAST ENGINEERING SERVICES LIMITED
Registration no: 01173264 **Date established:** 1974 **Turnover:** £2m - £5m
No.of Employees: 21 - 50 **Product Groups:** 40, 42, 45, 46, 48, 52

Date of Accounts	Nov 11	Nov 10	Nov 09
Working Capital	202	416	472
Fixed Assets	1m	1m	1m
Current Assets	837	876	780

Warwick Chemicals

Coast Road Mostyn, Holywell, CH8 9HE
Tel: 01745-560651 **Fax:** 01745-561353
E-mail: sales@warwickchem.com
Website: http://www.warwickchem.com
Managers: R. Prosser (Tech Serv Mgr), S. Pipe, S. Williams (Comptroller), P. Baxter, P. Kelsall (Personnel)
Ultimate Holding Company: WARWICK INTERNATIONAL HOLDINGS LIMITED
Immediate Holding Company: WARWICK INTERNATIONAL LIMITED
Registration no: 02386927 **VAT No.:** 559 8688 58 **Date established:** 1989
No.of Employees: 101 - 250 **Product Groups:** 32

Dyfed

Kilgetty

M J Parry & Company Ltd

Woodview Loveston, Kilgetty, SA68 0PA
Tel: 01834-891614 **Fax:** 01834-891614
Directors: M. Parry (MD)
Immediate Holding Company: M.J. PARRY & COMPANY LIMITED
Registration no: 06193304 **Date established:** 2007
No.of Employees: 1 - 10 **Product Groups:** 41

Date of Accounts	Mar 11	Mar 10	Mar 09
Working Capital	52	50	69
Fixed Assets	14	17	20
Current Assets	151	162	190

Powys

Knighton

Clayton Engineering Ltd

Ludlow Road, Knighton, LD7 1LP
Tel: 01547-520585 **Fax:** 01547-520507
E-mail: enquiries@claytonengineering.co.uk
Website: http://www.claytonengineering.co.uk
Bank(s): Barclays
Directors: B. Hughes (Eng Serv), S. Allen (Co Sec), S. Allan (Fin)
Ultimate Holding Company: C E L HOLDINGS LIMITED
Immediate Holding Company: CLAYTON ENGINEERING LIMITED
Registration no: 01274923 **VAT No.:** GB 661 5410 54
Date established: 1976 **Turnover:** £500,000 - £1m
No.of Employees: 21 - 50 **Product Groups:** 39, 45

Date of Accounts	Dec 11	Dec 10	Dec 09
Working Capital	628	445	392
Fixed Assets	731	771	805
Current Assets	1m	1m	1m

Teme Valley Tractor Ltd

Station Yard Station Road, Knighton, LD7 1DT
Tel: 01547-528351 **Fax:** 01547-520517
E-mail: graham.tvtknighton@yahoo.co.uk
Website: http://www.temevalleytractors.co.uk
Directors: B. Smart (Dir), G. Probert (Dir)
Immediate Holding Company: TEME VALLEY TRACTORS LIMITED
Registration no: 01717662 **Date established:** 1983
Turnover: £500,000 - £1m **No.of Employees:** 21 - 50 **Product Groups:** 41

Date of Accounts	Dec 11	Dec 10	Dec 09
Sales Turnover	903	869	845
Pre Tax Profit/Loss	150	135	132
Working Capital	1m	1m	1m
Fixed Assets	87	97	118
Current Assets	3m	3m	3m
Current Liabilities	156	185	169

Western Tractors

Station Road, Knighton, LD7 1DT
Tel: 01547-520132 **Fax:** 01547-520132
E-mail: richard@westerntractors.co.uk
Website: http://www.westerntractors.co.uk
Directors: R. Williams (Prop)
Ultimate Holding Company: M A EVANS TRANSPORT LIMITED
Immediate Holding Company: KNIGHTON TRUCK COMPANY LIMITED(THE)
Registration no: 01877475 **Date established:** 1985
Turnover: Up to £250,000 **No.of Employees:** 1 - 10 **Product Groups:** 41

Date of Accounts	Dec 10	Dec 09	Dec 08
Working Capital	68	80	79
Current Assets	88	99	89

Dyfed

Lampeter

Lampeter Shooting Supplies

Market Street, Lampeter, SA48 7DS
Tel: 01570-422174 **Fax:** 01570-422333
E-mail: d-jones@gunshop.uk.com
Website: http://www.shotgunuk.com
Directors: L. Jones (Prop)
Date established: 1992 **No.of Employees:** 1 - 10 **Product Groups:** 36, 39, 40

Dyfed

Llandovery

Muller South Wales Ltd (Part of Muller England Ltd)

Heol Pluguffan Church Bank, Llandovery, SA20 0AZ
Tel: 01550-720883 **Fax:** 01550-721206
E-mail: southwales@muller-england.co.uk
Website: http://www.muller-england.co.uk
Managers: P. Lawlor (Mgr)
Ultimate Holding Company: MULLER HOLDINGS LIMITED
Immediate Holding Company: MULLER SOUTH WALES LIMITED
Registration no: 01470211 **Date established:** 1979
Turnover: £500,000 - £1m **No.of Employees:** 1 - 10 **Product Groups:** 48

Record Industrial Brushes Ltd

Unit 1-12 Industrial Estate Church Bank, Llandovery, SA20 0DT
Tel: 01550-720077 **Fax:** 01550-720911
E-mail: info@rib-uk.co.uk
Website: http://www.rib-uk.co.uk
Bank(s): Bank of Wales PLC
Directors: A. Bruhn (Fin), D. Johns (Dir)
Managers: P. Griffiths (Sales Prom Mgr)
Ultimate Holding Company: KULLEN GMBH & CO KG (GERMANY)
Immediate Holding Company: R.I.B. - KOTI LIMITED
Registration no: 01214442 **Date established:** 1975
No.of Employees: 51 - 100 **Product Groups:** 35, 37, 38, 43, 46, 49, 66

Date of Accounts	Mar 11	Mar 10	Mar 09
Pre Tax Profit/Loss	243	-11	128
Working Capital	1m	1m	959
Fixed Assets	541	576	365
Current Assets	1m	1m	1m
Current Liabilities	96	40	66

Warehouse & Industrial Development Ltd

Abercrychan Mill, Llandovery, SA20 0YW
Tel: 01550-720259 **Fax:** 01550-721369
E-mail: info@mccannsgroup.com
Website: http://www.w-i-d.co.uk
Directors: J. Mccann (MD), D. O Hehir (Fin)
Immediate Holding Company: WAREHOUSE & INDUSTRIAL DEVELOPMENTS LIMITED
Registration no: 01902223 **Date established:** 1985 **Turnover:** £1m - £2m
No.of Employees: 11 - 20 **Product Groups:** 35, 42, 45

Date of Accounts	Dec 09	Dec 08	Dec 07
Sales Turnover	N/A	2m	1m
Pre Tax Profit/Loss	N/A	125	108
Working Capital	208	168	166
Fixed Assets	946	290	289
Current Assets	624	345	460
Current Liabilities	N/A	52	52

Powys

Llandrindod Wells

Dilwyns

Oxford Chambers Temple Street, Llandrindod Wells, LD1 5DL
Tel: 01597-822707 **Fax:** 01597-824085
E-mail: peter@dilwyns-solicitors.co.uk
Website: http://www.dilwyns-solicitors.co.uk
Directors: P. Wilcox-Jones (Snr Part)
Immediate Holding Company: NEW DYNANT LIMITED
Registration no: 05770068 **VAT No.:** GB 122 3684 89
Date established: 2003 **Turnover:** £250,000 - £500,000
No.of Employees: 1 - 10 **Product Groups:** 80

Date of Accounts	Dec 10	Dec 09
Pre Tax Profit/Loss	-0	-0
Working Capital	-2	-1
Current Liabilities	2	N/A

Faire Bros & Co. Ltd

Elan House Waterloo Road, Llandrindod Wells, LD1 6BH
Tel: 01597-827800 **Fax:** 01597-827 899
E-mail: sales@fairebros.co.uk
Website: http://www.fairebros.co.uk
Directors: G. Goodchild (Co Sec)
Immediate Holding Company: FAIRE BROS. & CO. LIMITED
Registration no: 01661940 **Date established:** 1982 **Turnover:** £2m - £5m
No.of Employees: 1 - 10 **Product Groups:** 22, 23, 35

Date of Accounts	Dec 11	Dec 10	Dec 09
Working Capital	120	-13	65
Fixed Assets	97	122	85
Current Assets	541	392	394

J R C & S J Wyatt Construction Ltd

New Forge Ddole Road Industrial Estate, Llandrindod Wells, LD1 6DF
Tel: 01597-822722 **Fax:** 01597-824930
E-mail: jrcwyatt@aol.com
Website: http://www.jrcwyattconstructionltd.com
Directors: J. Wyatt (Dir)
Immediate Holding Company: JRC & SJ WYATT CONSTRUCTION LIMITED
Registration no: 06386505 **Date established:** 2007
Turnover: £500,000 - £1m **No.of Employees:** 1 - 10 **Product Groups:** 35

Date of Accounts	Oct 10	Oct 09	Oct 08
Sales Turnover	460	431	897
Pre Tax Profit/Loss	-104	-0	N/A
Working Capital	-105	-0	N/A
Current Assets	57	33	N/A
Current Liabilities	4	21	N/A

Mervyn Price

Graig Fawr Farm Bettws Hundred House, Llandrindod Wells, LD1 5RP
Tel: 01982-570338 **Fax:** 01982-570338
Directors: M. Price (Prop)
Date established: 1969 **No.of Employees:** 1 - 10 **Product Groups:** 41

Setten Ixl Ltd

Waterloo Road, Llandrindod Wells, LD1 6BH
Tel: 01597-827800 **Fax:** 01597-827847
E-mail: admin@ixl.uk.com
Website: http://www.ixl.uk.com
Bank(s): HSBC
Directors: A. Morris (Prop), J. Fox (Ch), K. Trenberth (Sales & Mktg), M. Stone (Fin), M. Thorn (Fin), P. Ross (MD), S. Gordon (Sales & Mktg)
Managers: B. Bibb (I.T. Exec), C. Cozens (Sales & Mktg Mg), C. Cozens (Mktg Serv Mgr), G. Webster (Mktg Serv Mgr), J. Evans (Ops Mgr), C. Jones (Personnel)
Immediate Holding Company: Ixl 2008 Ltd
Registration no: 04506868 **VAT No.:** GB 594 3960 95
Date established: 2002 **Turnover:** £20m - £50m
No.of Employees: 51 - 100 **Product Groups:** 27, 28, 30, 35, 49

Date of Accounts	Mar 10	Mar 09	Dec 07
Working Capital	-367	-109	11
Fixed Assets	444	486	N/A
Current Assets	2m	2m	12

Skye Instruments Ltd

Unit 21 Ddole Road Industrial Estate, Llandrindod Wells, LD1 6DF
Tel: 01597-824811 **Fax:** 01597-824812
E-mail: skyemail@skyeinstruments.com
Website: http://www.skyeinstruments.com
Bank(s): HSBC/Barclays
Directors: G. Wilde (MD)
Immediate Holding Company: SKYE INSTRUMENTS LIMITED
Registration no: 01705412 **VAT No.:** GB 384 6246 28
Date established: 1983 **Turnover:** £500,000 - £1m
No.of Employees: 11 - 20 **Product Groups:** 67

Date of Accounts	Jun 11	Jun 10	Jun 09
Working Capital	275	254	220
Fixed Assets	420	433	209
Current Assets	399	335	281

Gwynedd

Llandudno

The Diamond Stylus Company Ltd

Council Street West, Llandudno, LL30 1ED
Tel: 01492-860880 **Fax:** 01492-860653
E-mail: sales@diamondstylus.co.uk
Website: http://www.diamondstylus.co.uk
Bank(s): Barclays
Directors: R. Blakeley (Ch), R. Bleakley (Fin), T. Rickards (MD)
Immediate Holding Company: Sumners Caterers Ltd
Registration no: 02465419 **VAT No.:** GB 490 1723 54
Date established: 1952 **Turnover:** £2m - £5m **No.of Employees:** 21 - 50
Product Groups: 26, 37

Date of Accounts	Mar 08	Mar 07	Mar 06
Working Capital	547	599	565
Fixed Assets	54	60	76
Current Assets	1003	1079	999
Current Liabilities	457	480	433
Total Share Capital	300	300	300

J Mckernon & Co. Ltd

9 Lloyd Street, Llandudno, LL30 2UU
Tel: 01492-873718 **Fax:** 01492-873718
Directors: J. Mckernon (Dir)
Immediate Holding Company: J MCKERNON & CO LTD
Registration no: 06185094 **Date established:** 2007
No.of Employees: 1 - 10 **Product Groups:** 35

Date of Accounts	Mar 11	Mar 09	Mar 08
Working Capital	6	-0	-0
Fixed Assets	1	2	2
Current Assets	23	11	18

Jewson Ltd

Council Street West, Llandudno, LL30 1ED
Tel: 01492-874848 **Fax:** 01492-860178
E-mail: phillipdolan@jewson.co.uk
Website: http://www.jewson.co.uk
Managers: S. Howell (Mgr)
Ultimate Holding Company: COMPAGNIE DE SAINT GOBAIN (FRANCE)
Immediate Holding Company: JEWSON LIMITED
Registration no: 00348407 **VAT No.:** GB 497 7184 83
Date established: 1939 **Turnover:** Up to £250,000
No.of Employees: 1 - 10 **Product Groups:** 66

Date of Accounts	Dec 11	Dec 10	Dec 09
Sales Turnover	1606m	1547m	1485m
Pre Tax Profit/Loss	18m	100m	45m
Working Capital	-345m	-250m	-349m
Fixed Assets	496m	387m	461m
Current Assets	657m	1005m	1320m
Current Liabilities	66m	120m	64m

North West Dental Equipment
11 St Annes Gardens, Llandudno, LL30 1SD
Tel: 01492-582404
E-mail: info@dental-chairs.co.uk
Website: http://www.dental-chairs.co.uk
Directors: J. Roberts (Prop)
Date established: 1998 **Turnover:** £500,000 - £1m
No.of Employees: 1 - 10 **Product Groups:** 67, 83

Old Smithy Gate Company
Conwy Road, Llandudno, LL31 9BA
Tel: 01492-592777
E-mail: theoldsmithygatecompany@btconnect.com
Website: http://www.theoldsmithygatecompany.co.uk
Directors: I. Young (Prop)
Immediate Holding Company: CASTLE CABS (CONWY) LIMITED
Registration no: 06257173 **Date established:** 2001
No.of Employees: 1 - 10 **Product Groups:** 26, 35

Phoenix Catering Engineers
19 Tal Y Sarn Tremarl Industrial Estate, Llandudno, LL31 9PW
Tel: 01492-593988 **Fax:** 01492- 593988
Website: http://www.phoenixtalysarn.co.uk
Directors: M. Woodcock (Ptnr)
Immediate Holding Company: PHOENIX CATERING ENGINEERS LIMITED
Registration no: 05429398 **Date established:** 2005
No.of Employees: 1 - 10 **Product Groups:** 20, 40, 41

The Risc Group Ltd
Church Walks, Llandudno, LL30 2HL
Tel: 08448-420100 **Fax:** 0870-050 3201
E-mail: information@risc-group.com
Website: http://www.clunkclick.net
Managers: F. Burton (Sales & Mktg Mg)
Immediate Holding Company: KWIK TECHNOLOGY LIMITED
Registration no: 03935051 **Date established:** 2010
No.of Employees: 1 - 10 **Product Groups:** 44

Date of Accounts	Feb 08	Feb 07	Feb 06
Working Capital	-21	-89	-97
Fixed Assets	66	60	62
Current Assets	161	88	88
Current Liabilities	182	177	185

Seaga UK
Unit 8 Cae Bach Builder Street, Llandudno, LL30 1DR
Tel: 01492-874010
E-mail: lhewlett@seaga.co.uk
Website: http://www.seaga.co.uk
Managers: L. Hewlett (Comptroller)
Immediate Holding Company: SEAGA UK LIMITED
Registration no: 05066744 **Date established:** 2004
No.of Employees: 1 - 10 **Product Groups:** 38, 42

Date of Accounts	Dec 10	Dec 09	Dec 08
Working Capital	453	-670	-632
Fixed Assets	16	23	20
Current Assets	607	461	521

Sugro Robertson Ltd
Tynycoed Llanrhos, Llandudno, LL30 1SA
Tel: 01492-581811 **Fax:** 01492-583416
E-mail: richard.fowler@robresint.co.uk
Website: http://www.robresint.co.uk
Bank(s): Bank of Scotland
Directors: C. Burgess (MD)
Ultimate Holding Company: FUGRO NV (NETHERLANDS)
Immediate Holding Company: ROBERTSON RESEARCH INTERNATIONAL LIMITED
Registration no: 05019270 **VAT No.:** GB 654 0663 39
Date established: 2004 **Turnover:** £2m - £5m
No.of Employees: 251 - 500 **Product Groups:** 51, 84

Town & Country Carpets
20 Mostyn Avenue, Llandudno, LL30 1YY
Tel: 01492-872400
E-mail: hughes9uw@btinternet.com
Website: http://www.townandcountry-carpets.co.uk
Directors: S. Hughes (Prop)
No.of Employees: 1 - 10 **Product Groups:** 23, 25, 30, 31, 33, 35, 63, 66

Universal Auto Electrical & Fuel Injection Services
Unit 5 Builder Street, Llandudno, LL30 1DR
Tel: 01492-876583 **Fax:** 01492-860290
E-mail: shaun.hurley@lineone.net
Directors: C. Hughes (Ptnr)
No.of Employees: 1 - 10 **Product Groups:** 40

David Williams Llandudno Ltd
4 Builder Street, Llandudno, LL30 1DR
Tel: 01492-876869 **Fax:** 01492-870664
E-mail: williamswelders@hotmail.co.uk
Website: http://www.davidwilliamsllandudno.co.uk
Directors: G. Williams (Dir)
Immediate Holding Company: DAVID WILLIAMS (LLANDUDNO) LIMITED
Registration no: 00456404 **VAT No.:** GB 161 4840 74
Date established: 1948 **Turnover:** £250,000 - £500,000
No.of Employees: 1 - 10 **Product Groups:** 48

Date of Accounts	Sep 11	Sep 10	Sep 09
Working Capital	-55	-8	23
Fixed Assets	85	88	94
Current Assets	83	79	111

Dyfed

Llandysul

Derlwyn Drums
Henbant Fawr Derlwyn, Capel Dewi, Llandysul, SA44 4PQ
Tel: 01559-362583
Directors: J. Moseley (Prop)
Date established: 1968 **No.of Employees:** 1 - 10 **Product Groups:** 35, 36, 45

J D Wigley
Gweithdu Metal Works Velindre, Llandysul, SA44 5YA
Tel: 01559-370075 **Fax:** 01559-370116
E-mail: jdw47@supanet.com
Directors: J. Wigley (Prop)
Date established: 1995 **No.of Employees:** 1 - 10 **Product Groups:** 26, 35

Dyfed

Llanelli

A M G Resources Ltd
Nevills Dock, Llanelli, SA15 2HD
Tel: 01554-750791 **Fax:** 01554-752625
E-mail: phil.kultschar@amgindustries.co.uk
Website: http://www.birmingham.co.uk/amg/
Bank(s): National Westminster Bank Plc
Directors: T. Banks (Fin)
Managers: P. Kultschar (Works Gen Mgr), L. Burley (Sales Admin)
Ultimate Holding Company: AMG INDUSTRIES CORPORATION (USA)
Immediate Holding Company: AMG RESOURCES LIMITED
Registration no: 01516685 **Date established:** 1980
Turnover: £10m - £20m **No.of Employees:** 21 - 50 **Product Groups:** 34, 46, 66

Date of Accounts	Dec 11	Dec 10	Dec 09
Sales Turnover	20m	18m	15m
Pre Tax Profit/Loss	34	70	433
Working Capital	4m	4m	4m
Fixed Assets	2m	1m	1m
Current Assets	9m	9m	8m
Current Liabilities	2m	3m	3m

A P Financial Services UK Ltd
3 John Street, Llanelli, SA15 1UN
Tel: 01554-775618 **Fax:** 01554-777708
E-mail: davidasher@pella-associates.co.uk
Website: http://www.ap-financialservices.co.uk
Directors: D. Asher (MD)
Immediate Holding Company: A.P. FINANCIAL SERVICES UK LTD
Registration no: 04527173 **Date established:** 2002
Turnover: Up to £250,000 **No.of Employees:** 1 - 10 **Product Groups:** 80, 82

Date of Accounts	Jan 12	Jan 11	Jan 10
Sales Turnover	N/A	N/A	188
Pre Tax Profit/Loss	N/A	N/A	3
Working Capital	10	24	14
Fixed Assets	74	74	1
Current Assets	14	72	63
Current Liabilities	N/A	4	1

Avon Inflatables Ltd
Dafen, Llanelli, SA14 8NA
Tel: 01554-882000 **Fax:** 01554-882039
E-mail: alan.morgan@zmp-zodiac.com
Website: http://www.avoninflatables.co.uk
Bank(s): Barclays
Directors: A. Morgan (Dir), K. Protheroe (MD)
Managers: P. Pritchard (Tech Serv Mgr), S. Lang (Mktg Serv Mgr), T. Win (Comptroller)
Ultimate Holding Company: THE CARLYLE GROUP LLC (USA)
Immediate Holding Company: AVON INFLATABLES LIMITED
Registration no: 00259668 **Date established:** 1931 **Turnover:** £5m - £10m
No.of Employees: 51 - 100 **Product Groups:** 29, 39, 40

Date of Accounts	Sep 11	Sep 10	Sep 09
Sales Turnover	3m	6m	6m
Pre Tax Profit/Loss	-779	-523	-791
Working Capital	486	1m	2m
Fixed Assets	351	362	368
Current Assets	3m	3m	4m
Current Liabilities	268	582	225

Combidrive Ltd
Unit 6 Parc Menter, Cross Hands, Llanelli, SA14 6RA
Tel: 01269-834848 **Fax:** 01269-834850
E-mail: jason@combidrive.com
Website: http://www.combidrive.com
Directors: E. Jones (MD)
Immediate Holding Company: COMBIDRIVE LIMITED
Registration no: 01200180 **VAT No.:** GB 200 5351 27
Date established: 1975 **Turnover:** £1m - £2m **No.of Employees:** 1 - 10
Product Groups: 35, 37, 39

Date of Accounts	Mar 11	Mar 10	Mar 09
Working Capital	13	1	5
Fixed Assets	7	10	14
Current Assets	150	107	103

Crane Aid Service Company Ltd
Unit 2012 North Avenue Trostre Business Park, Llanelli, SA14 9UU
Tel: 01554-751862 **Fax:** 01554-751664
E-mail: info@craneaid.co.uk
Website: http://www.craneaid.co.uk
Directors: J. Swift (Dir)
Immediate Holding Company: CRANE AID SERVICE COMPANY LIMITED
Registration no: 04761922 **Date established:** 2003
No.of Employees: 1 - 10 **Product Groups:** 35, 39, 45

Date of Accounts	Mar 11	Mar 10	Mar 09
Working Capital	84	86	67
Fixed Assets	39	52	68
Current Assets	202	161	130

Daniels Fans Ltd
Heol Gors Dafen Industrial Estate, Dafen, Llanelli, SA14 8QR
Tel: 01554-752148 **Fax:** 01554-741109
E-mail: sales@danielsfans.ltd.uk
Website: http://www.danielsfans.ltd.uk
Bank(s): Barclays
Directors: J. Daniels (MD), R. Williams (Fin), N. Daniels (MD)
Managers: M. Daniels (Works Gen Mgr)
Immediate Holding Company: DANIELS FANS LIMITED
Registration no: 01326006 **VAT No.:** GB 124 9690 52
Date established: 1977 **Turnover:** £1m - £2m **No.of Employees:** 21 - 50
Product Groups: 40

Date of Accounts	Sep 11	Sep 10	Sep 09
Working Capital	14	-57	27
Fixed Assets	1m	1m	1m
Current Assets	842	906	575

Dawn Group Ltd
Heol Ty Newydd Cross Hands Food Park, Cross Hands, Llanelli, SA14 6RF
Tel: 01269-846400 **Fax:** 01269-846402
Website: http://www.dawnmeats.com
Directors: D. Browne (Dir), J. Kelly (Dir), P. Queally (Dir)
Ultimate Holding Company: QDB HOLDINGS
Immediate Holding Company: DAWN HOLDINGS
Registration no: 02297659 **VAT No.:** GB 557 8830 93
Date established: 1988 **Turnover:** £250m - £500m
No.of Employees: 501 - 1000 **Product Groups:** 20

Date of Accounts	Dec 11	Dec 10	Dec 09
Working Capital	2m	1m	1m
Fixed Assets	50	55	55
Current Assets	2m	1m	1m

Dyfed Recycling Services Ltd
Dafen Industrial Estate Dafen, Llanelli, SA14 8QE
Tel: 0800-072 7278 **Fax:** 01554-770729
E-mail: recycling@owens-logistics.com
Website: http://www.dyfedrecycling.com
Directors: B. Evans (Prop)
Ultimate Holding Company: OWENS (ROAD SERVICES) LIMITED
Immediate Holding Company: ORS CONTRACT MANAGEMENT LIMITED
Date established: 1989 **Turnover:** £5m - £10m **No.of Employees:** 11 - 20
Product Groups: 83

Date of Accounts	Jun 11	Jun 10	Jun 09
Sales Turnover	33m	30m	28m
Pre Tax Profit/Loss	-13	-163	-492
Working Capital	-4m	-4m	-3m
Fixed Assets	11m	11m	13m
Current Assets	7m	8m	6m
Current Liabilities	7m	7m	5m

Dyfed Steels
Tube Works Maescanner Road Dafen, Llanelli, SA14 8NS
Tel: 01554-757241 **Fax:** 01554-777701
E-mail: dyfedsteels@netscapeonline.co.uk
Website: http://www.dyfedsteel.co.uk
Bank(s): HSBC
Directors: D. Thomas (Dir), J. Schofield (Fin), A. Morgan (Co Sec)
Managers: D. Allender (Tech Serv Mgr)
Immediate Holding Company: DYFED STEELS LIMITED
Registration no: 01287461 **VAT No.:** GB 124 8861 56
Date established: 1976 **Turnover:** £50m - £75m
No.of Employees: 101 - 250 **Product Groups:** 66

Date of Accounts	Jan 12	Jan 11	Jan 10
Sales Turnover	64m	57m	38m
Pre Tax Profit/Loss	146	2m	-896
Working Capital	6m	6m	6m
Fixed Assets	9m	9m	9m
Current Assets	31m	30m	20m
Current Liabilities	11m	12m	7m

Felinfoel Brewery Co. Ltd
Farmers Row, Llanelli, SA14 8LB
Tel: 01554-773357 **Fax:** 01554-752452
E-mail: info@felinfoel-brewery.com
Website: http://www.felinfoel-brewery.com
Bank(s): Giro Bank
Directors: N. Tinnuche (Co Sec), P. Lewis (Dir)
Managers: L. Williams (Mktg Serv Mgr)
Immediate Holding Company: FELINFOEL BREWERY COMPANY LIMITED(THE)
Registration no: 00090279 **VAT No.:** GB 121 9365 81
Date established: 2006 **Turnover:** £2m - £5m **No.of Employees:** 21 - 50
Product Groups: 21

Date of Accounts	Mar 12	Mar 11	Mar 10
Pre Tax Profit/Loss	7	N/A	N/A
Working Capital	170	N/A	N/A
Fixed Assets	4m	4m	4m
Current Assets	1m	1m	1m
Current Liabilities	532	N/A	N/A

Geo Laboratory Testing Services Ltd
Unit 23-26 The Foothold Enterprise Village Burry Road, Llanelli, SA15 2DS
Tel: 01554-757734 **Fax:** 01554-775107
E-mail: info@geo.uk.com
Website: http://www.geo.uk.com
Managers: B. Sharp
Immediate Holding Company: GEO LABORATORY TESTING SERVICES LIMITED
Registration no: 05160855 **Date established:** 2004
No.of Employees: 1 - 10 **Product Groups:** 85

Date of Accounts	Jun 10	Jun 09	Jun 08
Working Capital	105	136	17
Fixed Assets	258	111	133
Current Assets	546	455	386

Jewson Ltd
Trinity Road, Llanelli, SA15 2AB
Tel: 01554-774655 **Fax:** 01554-759646
E-mail: davee.jackson@jewson.co.uk
Website: http://www.jewson.co.uk
Managers: A. Carlyon (Sales Prom Mgr), D. Jackson (Mgr)
Ultimate Holding Company: COMPAGNIE DE SAINT GOBAIN (FRANCE)
Immediate Holding Company: JEWSON LIMITED
Registration no: 00348407 **VAT No.:** GB 497 7184 33
Date established: 1939 **Turnover:** £5m - £10m **No.of Employees:** 1 - 10
Product Groups: 66

Date of Accounts	Dec 11	Dec 10	Dec 09
Sales Turnover	1606m	1547m	1485m
Pre Tax Profit/Loss	18m	100m	45m
Working Capital	-345m	-250m	-349m
Fixed Assets	496m	387m	461m
Current Assets	657m	1005m	1320m
Current Liabilities	66m	120m	64m

Peter Luck
24 Havard Road, Llanelli, SA14 8SB
Tel: 01554-771205
Directors: P. Luck (Prop)
Date established: 1982 **No.of Employees:** 1 - 10 **Product Groups:** 35

Moseley Brothers Ltd
Unit 5 Heol Aur Dafen, Llanelli, SA14 8QN
Tel: 01554-755565 **Fax:** 01554-753982
E-mail: jcooper.semtek@btconnect.com
Website: http://www.moseleybrothers.co.uk

Directors: J. Cooper (Chief Op Offcr)
Immediate Holding Company: SEMTEK TOOLS LIMITED
Registration no: 05382139 **Date established:** 2005
No.of Employees: 1 - 10 **Product Groups:** 46

Date of Accounts	Mar 06	Sep 09	Sep 08
Working Capital	-124	-300	-260
Fixed Assets	371	415	434
Current Assets	399	400	582

Pontrilas Group Packaging Ltd

Trosserch Road Llangennech, Llanelli, SA14 8DZ
Tel: 01554-823100 **Fax:** 01554-821822
E-mail: sales@pgppallets.co.uk
Website: http://www.pgppallets.co.uk
Bank(s): HSBC Bank plc
Directors: E. Hilton (Fin), S. Poynton (Sales), V. Hickman (Sales)
Managers: A. Gordon (Tech Serv Mgr), D. Turner
Ultimate Holding Company: PONTRILAS GROUP LIMITED
Immediate Holding Company: PONTRILAS PACKAGING LIMITED
Registration no: 02379869 **Date established:** 1989
Turnover: £10m - £20m **No.of Employees:** 51 - 100 **Product Groups:** 25, 27, 30, 31, 35, 45, 66

Date of Accounts	Jul 11	Jul 10	Jul 09
Sales Turnover	12m	10m	10m
Pre Tax Profit/Loss	10	204	N/A
Working Capital	63	59	-214
Fixed Assets	573	578	649
Current Assets	4m	4m	3m
Current Liabilities	2m	1m	899

Quantum Geotechnical Ltd

Heol Y Bwlch Bynea, Llanelli, SA14 9ST
Tel: 01554-744880 **Fax:** 01554-746150
E-mail: enquiries@quantum-gb.co.uk
Website: http://www.quantum-gb.co.uk
Directors: J. Goodfellow (Dir)
Immediate Holding Company: QUANTUM LIMITED
Registration no: 01592381 **Date established:** 1981 **Turnover:** £1m - £2m
No.of Employees: 11 - 20 **Product Groups:** 45, 51, 52, 84

Date of Accounts	Mar 11	Mar 10	Mar 09
Working Capital	522	161	79
Fixed Assets	222	542	542
Current Assets	649	278	243

Schaeffler UK Ltd

Yspitty Road, Llanelli, SA14 9TG
Tel: 01554-772288 **Fax:** 01554-771201
E-mail: info.uk@schaeffler.com
Website: http://www.schaeffler.co.uk
Directors: R. Evans (Dir), A. Brock (Fin), A. Roberts (Pers)
Managers: A. Parkhouse (Tech Serv Mgr), P. Evans (Buyer)
Ultimate Holding Company: INA HOLDING SCHAEFFLER KG (GERMANY)
Immediate Holding Company: SCHAEFFLER (UK) LIMITED
Registration no: 00556493 **Date established:** 1955
No.of Employees: 101 - 250 **Product Groups:** 35, 45

Date of Accounts	Dec 11	Dec 10	Dec 09
Sales Turnover	62m	58m	59m
Pre Tax Profit/Loss	5m	1m	4m
Working Capital	4m	6m	12m
Fixed Assets	18m	13m	9m
Current Assets	24m	21m	22m
Current Liabilities	20m	3m	10m

Sheds N Chalets Ltd

Lower Trostre Road, Llanelli, SA15 2EA
Tel: 01554-759472 **Fax:** 01554-775022
E-mail: sales@shedsnchalets.com
Website: http://www.shedsnchalets.co.uk
Directors: M. Neve (Prop)
Immediate Holding Company: SHEDS N CHALETS LIMITED
Registration no: 04452977 **Date established:** 2002
No.of Employees: 1 - 10 **Product Groups:** 25, 35, 38, 41, 66

Date of Accounts	May 12	May 11	May 10
Working Capital	-1	-10	-25
Fixed Assets	25	31	33
Current Assets	84	89	76

Swift Circuits Ltd

Unit 38 Enterprise Workshops Lower Trostre Road, Llanelli, SA15 2EA
Tel: 01554-775333 **Fax:** 01554-775458
E-mail: sales@swiftcircuits.co.uk
Website: http://www.swiftcircuits.co.uk
Bank(s): Lloyds TSB Bank plc
Directors: R. Millbery (Fin), J. Millbery (Sales)
Managers: G. Jaggard (Admin Off)
Immediate Holding Company: SWIFT CIRCUITS LIMITED
Registration no: 01946011 **VAT No.:** GB 413 5575 61
Date established: 1985 **Turnover:** £500,000 - £1m
No.of Employees: 11 - 20 **Product Groups:** 37

Date of Accounts	Mar 11	Mar 10	Mar 09
Sales Turnover	803	801	905
Pre Tax Profit/Loss	18	11	-3
Working Capital	40	30	-6
Fixed Assets	65	72	90
Current Assets	325	285	296
Current Liabilities	175	155	207

Welsh Chocolate Fountains

6 Llwyn Cyfarthwch Near Swansea, Llanelli, SA15 1GY
Tel: 01554-778516
E-mail: info@welshchocolatefountains.com
Website: http://www.welshchocolatefountains.com
Directors: A. Bowen (Prop)
Date established: 2006 **No.of Employees:** 1 - 10 **Product Groups:** 83

West Wales Marble & Granite

Units 9-11 Industrial Estate Church Road, Gorslas, Llanelli, SA14 7NN
Tel: 01269-832868 **Fax:** 01267-238525
E-mail: mail@westwalesmarbleandgranite.com
Website: http://www.west-walesmarbleandgranite.co.uk
Directors: R. Walton (Ptnr)
Date established: 1988 **No.of Employees:** 1 - 10 **Product Groups:** 26, 33

Gwynedd

Llanerchymedd

Small Holder Services

The Barns Neuadd Wen, Mynydd Bodafon, Llanerchymedd, LL71 8BL
Tel: 01248-410102
E-mail: office@smallholderservices.co.uk
Website: http://www.smallholderservices.co.uk
Managers: C. Brassey (Sales Prom Mgr)
Date established: 2002 **Turnover:** Up to £250,000
No.of Employees: 1 - 10 **Product Groups:** 07

Powys

Llanfyllin

Gareth Lewis

The Mount, Llanfyllin, SY22 5LE
Tel: 01691-648411 **Fax:** 01691-648163
E-mail: admin@gareth-lewis.com
Website: http://www.gareth-lewis.com
Directors: T. Jones (Prop)
Registration no: 06431456 **Date established:** 1970
No.of Employees: 1 - 10 **Product Groups:** 41

Pentangle Puzzles & Games

PO Box 5, Llanfyllin, SY22 5WD
Tel: 01691-649123 **Fax:** 01691-649926
E-mail: info@pentangle-puzzles.co.uk
Website: http://www.pentangle-puzzles.co.uk
Directors: T. Dixon (Dir)
Immediate Holding Company: PENTANGLE PUZZLES LIMITED
Registration no: 03959027 **VAT No.:** GB 189 4452 21
Date established: 2000 **Turnover:** Up to £250,000
No.of Employees: 1 - 10 **Product Groups:** 28

Date of Accounts	Jun 11	Jun 10	Jun 09
Sales Turnover	N/A	48	N/A
Pre Tax Profit/Loss	N/A	2	N/A
Working Capital	5	4	1
Fixed Assets	17	16	17
Current Assets	79	82	62
Current Liabilities	66	1	N/A

Emyr Roberts

Cefn Coed Uchaf Llanfihangel, Llanfyllin, SY22 5JF
Tel: 01691-648717
Directors: E. Roberts (Prop)
Immediate Holding Company: EMYR ROBERTS LTD
Registration no: 07812730 **Date established:** 2011
No.of Employees: 1 - 10 **Product Groups:** 41

Dyfed

Llanfyrnach

Sterling Machanical Services

Henffordd Tegryn, Llanfyrnach, SA35 0DN
Tel: 01239-698289 **Fax:** 01239-698316
Managers: A. Johnson (Mgr)
Date established: 1989 **No.of Employees:** 1 - 10 **Product Groups:** 46

Gwynedd

Llangefni

All Meck Services

Tyn Llan Farm Llangwyllog, Llangefni, LL77 7HX
Tel: 01248-751270 **Fax:** 01248-751276
E-mail: info@allmeck.com
Website: http://www.allmeck.com
Directors: G. Spencer (Dir)
Immediate Holding Company: ALLMECK SERVICES LTD
Registration no: 04834870 **Date established:** 2003
Turnover: £250,000 - £500,000 **No.of Employees:** 11 - 20
Product Groups: 35

Date of Accounts	Jul 11	Jul 10	Jul 09
Sales Turnover	N/A	352	392
Pre Tax Profit/Loss	N/A	-46	18
Working Capital	5	28	9
Fixed Assets	92	2	72
Current Assets	19	86	166
Current Liabilities	N/A	47	149

Campbell Grindlay Engineering Limited

Dafarn Newydd Ffordd Penmynydd, Llangefni, LL77 7SD
Tel: 01248-723569 **Fax:** 01248-750412
E-mail: cg@cgeng.co.uk
Website: http://www.campbellgrindlayengineering.com
Directors: C. Grindlay (Prop)
Registration no: 05630228 **Date established:** 1996
No.of Employees: 1 - 10 **Product Groups:** 31, 32, 33, 40

Faun Municipal Vehicles Ltd

Unit 4 Bryn Cefni Industrial Park, Llangefni, LL77 7XA
Tel: 01248-722777 **Fax:** 01248-750220
E-mail: sales@faun.demon.co.uk
Website: http://www.faun.com
Bank(s): Barclays
Directors: J. Jones (MD), S. Ball (Fin)
Managers: R. Hobbs, C. Jones, E. Stott (Personnel)
Ultimate Holding Company: FAUN UMWELTTECHNIK GMBH (GERMANY)
Immediate Holding Company: FAUN ZOELLER (UK) LIMITED
Registration no: 00751804 **VAT No.:** GB 159 9051 35
Date established: 1963 **Turnover:** £20m - £50m
No.of Employees: 21 - 50 **Product Groups:** 39

Date of Accounts	Dec 11	Dec 10	Dec 09
Sales Turnover	25m	30m	25m
Pre Tax Profit/Loss	-5m	722	242
Working Capital	-8m	-821	-1m
Fixed Assets	5m	3m	3m
Current Assets	11m	18m	7m
Current Liabilities	4m	3m	5m

Mona Lifting Ltd

Unit 5 Bryn Cefni Industrial Park, Llangefni, LL77 7XA
Tel: 01248-751300 **Fax:** 01248-751304
Directors: S. Jones (Prop)
Immediate Holding Company: MONA LIFTING LIMITED
Registration no: 05262191 **Date established:** 2004
No.of Employees: 1 - 10 **Product Groups:** 35, 39, 45

Date of Accounts	Dec 11	Dec 10	Dec 09
Working Capital	-39	82	130
Fixed Assets	763	689	164
Current Assets	198	211	313

Clwyd

Llangollen

Davies Brothers Construtions Ltd

Cross Lane, Llangollen, LL20 8HU
Tel: 01978-860691 **Fax:** 01978-860785
E-mail: mail@daviesbrothers.org.uk
Website: http://www.daviesbrothers.org.uk
Directors: N. Davies (Dir)
Immediate Holding Company: DAVIES BROTHERS CONSTRUCTION LIMITED
Registration no: 06159518 **Date established:** 2007
No.of Employees: 11 - 20 **Product Groups:** 41

Date of Accounts	Oct 11	Oct 10	Oct 09
Working Capital	-29	-98	-108
Fixed Assets	498	536	536
Current Assets	259	227	285

Dobson & Crowther

New Berwyn Works Berwyn Road, Llangollen, LL20 8AE
Tel: 01978-862100 **Fax:** 01978-860410
E-mail: sales@dobsonandcrowther.com
Website: http://www.dobsonandcrowther.com
Directors: P. Holden (Prop)
Managers: T. Dart (Nat Sales Mgr), N. Thomas (Fin Mgr), J. Wattss (Personnel), C. Morris (Tech Serv Mgr), W. Morris (Buyer)
Immediate Holding Company: DOBSON & CROWTHER LIMITED
Registration no: 05622782 **Date established:** 2005
Turnover: £10m - £20m **No.of Employees:** 101 - 250
Product Groups: 27, 28

Date of Accounts	Dec 11	Dec 10	Dec 09
Sales Turnover	11m	11m	10m
Pre Tax Profit/Loss	138	116	-213
Working Capital	-1m	-1m	-1m
Fixed Assets	3m	3m	4m
Current Assets	5m	4m	4m
Current Liabilities	3m	3m	3m

Powys

Llanidloes

Llanisolar Ltd

Unit 5d Parc Derwen Fawr, Llanidloes, SY18 6FE
Tel: 01686-412552 **Fax:** 01686-412552
E-mail: info@llanisolar.co.uk
Website: http://www.llanisolar.co.uk
Directors: M. Wells (Fin), C. Lord Smith (Dir)
Immediate Holding Company: LLANISOLAR LTD
Registration no: 05491144 **Date established:** 2005
No.of Employees: 1 - 10 **Product Groups:** 37, 40

Date of Accounts	Mar 11	Mar 10	Mar 09
Working Capital	-12	-2	N/A
Fixed Assets	12	6	6
Current Assets	88	51	66

Gwynedd

Llanrwst

Danline International Ltd

Nebo Road, Llanrwst, LL26 0SE
Tel: 01492-640651 **Fax:** 01492-641601
E-mail: sales@danline.co.uk
Website: http://www.danline.co.uk
Bank(s): Bank of Scotland
Directors: T. Hufton (Co Sec), J. Jones (Dir), E. Williams (MD)
Managers: A. Peake (Sales Prom Mgr)
Ultimate Holding Company: H.N.H. HOLDINGS LIMITED
Immediate Holding Company: Danline International Limited
Registration no: 01144263 **VAT No.:** GB 352 4021 95
Date established: 1973 **Turnover:** £2m - £5m **No.of Employees:** 21 - 50
Product Groups: 49

Date of Accounts	Aug 11	Aug 10	Aug 09
Working Capital	-7	-115	-260
Fixed Assets	79	76	71
Current Assets	861	909	884
Current Liabilities	2	340	207

Powys

Llansantffraid

Wynnstay Group plc
Eagle House, Llansantffraid, SY22 6AQ
Tel: 01691-828512 **Fax:** 01691-828690
E-mail: kenneth.greetham@wynnstay.co.uk
Website: http://www.wynnstay.co.uk
Directors: B. Harris (MD), M. Jones (Sales), K. Greetham (MD), E. Hughes (Dir), Harris (MD), J. Davies (Ch)
Managers: P. Godwin (Purch Mgr), S. Roberts (Personnel), A. Evans (Mktg Serv Mgr), I. Davies (I.T. Exec)
Immediate Holding Company: WYNNSTAY GROUP P.L.C.
Registration no: 02704051 **VAT No.:** GB 159 1866 30
Date established: 1992 **Turnover:** £125m - £250m
No.of Employees: 1 - 10 **Product Groups:** 62

Date of Accounts	Oct 11	Oct 10	Oct 09
Sales Turnover	346m	244m	215m
Pre Tax Profit/Loss	7m	6m	5m
Working Capital	20m	18m	15m
Fixed Assets	36m	32m	28m
Current Assets	75m	60m	44m
Current Liabilities	11m	11m	7m

South Glamorgan

Llantwit Major

L D L Engineering Services
9 Heritage Business Park Wick Road, Llantwit Major, CF61 1YU
Tel: 01446-794434 **Fax:** 01446-794448
Directors: L. Llewellyn (Prop)
Date established: 1992 **No.of Employees:** 1 - 10 **Product Groups:** 35

Dyfed

Llanwrda

M H Evans
Riverside, Llanwrda, SA19 8AL
Tel: 01550-777516
Directors: M. Evans (Prop)
Date established: 1973 **No.of Employees:** 1 - 10 **Product Groups:** 35

Turbine Technologies
Unit 2 Dulais Store, Llanwrda, SA19 8AL
Tel: 01550-777491
E-mail: admin@turbinetec.co.uk
Website: http://www.turbinetec.co.uk
Directors: R. Manning (Prop)
No.of Employees: 1 - 10 **Product Groups:** 32, 40, 41

Powys

Llanwrtyd Wells

Neuadd Bwll Framing
Neuadd Bwll, Llanwrtyd Wells, LD5 4AD
Tel: 01591-610861
E-mail: mike@welshframing.com
Website: http://www.welshframing.com
No.of Employees: 1 - 10 **Product Groups:** 25, 26, 36

Powys

Llanymynech

Ascott Smallholding Supplies Ltd
The Creamery Four Crosses, Llanymynech, SY22 6RH
Tel: 01691-839904 **Fax:** 0870-7740140
E-mail: phil@ascott-shop.com
Website: http://www.ascott.biz
Directors: K. Self (Dir)
Managers: P. Pointon (Mgr)
Immediate Holding Company: ASCOTT SMALLHOLDING SUPPLIES LTD
Registration no: 04505585 **Date established:** 2002
No.of Employees: 1 - 10 **Product Groups:** 20, 32, 41

Powys

Machynlleth

Dulas Valley Tipis
Ceinws, Machynlleth, SY20 9EX
Tel: 01654-761542 **Fax:** 01654-761542
E-mail: info@tipis.co.uk
Website: http://www.tipis.co.uk
Directors: L. Davidson (Dir)
No.of Employees: 1 - 10 **Product Groups:** 24

Deri Jones & Associates Ltd
Plas Machynlleth, Machynlleth, SY20 8ER
Tel: 01654-702001 **Fax:** 0870-762 0089
E-mail: info@djaweb.co.uk
Website: http://www.djaweb.co.uk
Directors: D. Jones (Dir)
Immediate Holding Company: DERI JONES & ASSOCIATES LIMITED
Registration no: 04867436 **Date established:** 2003
Turnover: Up to £250,000 **No.of Employees:** 1 - 10 **Product Groups:** 39, 44, 80, 84

Date of Accounts	Aug 11	Aug 10	Aug 09
Sales Turnover	N/A	N/A	54
Pre Tax Profit/Loss	N/A	N/A	-32
Working Capital	3	-17	-4
Fixed Assets	11	14	17
Current Assets	24	27	22
Current Liabilities	N/A	N/A	12

K P Fire
Ty Gwyn Commins Coch, Machynlleth, SY20 8LG
Tel: 01650-511258 **Fax:** 01650-511258
E-mail: kpfire@aol.com
Directors: G. Lewinton (Prop)
Date established: 2000 **No.of Employees:** 1 - 10 **Product Groups:** 38, 42

Mid Wales Tourism
The Station, Machynlleth, SY20 8TG
Tel: 01654-702653 **Fax:** 01654-703235
E-mail: valerie.hawkins@midwalestourism.co.uk
Website: http://www.midwalestourism.co.uk
Directors: V. Hawkins (Grp Chief Exec)
Immediate Holding Company: TOURISM WALES LIMITED
Registration no: 05108416 **VAT No.:** GB 549 8245 02
Date established: 2004 **Turnover:** £500,000 - £1m
No.of Employees: 1 - 10 **Product Groups:** 84, 87

Pressurefast
Forge Road, Machynlleth, SY20 8EG
Tel: 01654-702865 **Fax:** 01654-703450
E-mail: sales@pressurefast.com
Website: http://www.pressurefast.com
Directors: C. Stanley (Dir)
Immediate Holding Company: PRESSUREFAST LIMITED
Registration no: 02362159 **VAT No.:** GB 48 2182 10
Date established: 1989 **Turnover:** £500,000 - £1m
No.of Employees: 1 - 10 **Product Groups:** 36, 40

Date of Accounts	Mar 06
Working Capital	180
Fixed Assets	5
Current Assets	208

Mid-Glamorgan

Maesteg

Celtic Tyre Services Maesteg Ltd
Rear of Talbot Street, Maesteg, CF34 9BT
Tel: 01656-733514 **Fax:** 01656-733514
E-mail: rob237197@aol.com
Website: http://www.celtictyres.co.uk
Directors: R. Jenkins (MD)
Managers: R. Bevan (Depot Mgr), R. Bevan (District Mgr)
Ultimate Holding Company: 00938581
Immediate Holding Company: CELTIC TYRE SERVICES (MAESTEG) LIMITED
Registration no: 01071945 **VAT No.:** GB 133 5273 87
Date established: 1972 **No.of Employees:** 1 - 10 **Product Groups:** 68

Date of Accounts	Nov 07	Nov 06
Working Capital	-75	-70
Current Assets	9	7
Current Liabilities	84	77

Gardner Aerospace Wales Ltd
Forge Industrial Estate, Maesteg, CF34 0AY
Tel: 01656-812100 **Fax:** 01656-812101
E-mail: wales@gardner-aerospace.com
Website: http://www.gardner-aerospace.com
Bank(s): Lloyds
Directors: G. Evans (MD), M. Cooper (Dir), S. Butler (MD)
Managers: D. Walters (Purch Mgr), J. Moore (Export Sales Mg), N. Edwards (I.T. Exec), D. Goodall (Personnel)
Ultimate Holding Company: Ggl3 Ltd
Immediate Holding Company: Gardner Group Ltd
Registration no: 00956749 **VAT No.:** 500 9463 69 **Date established:** 1969
Turnover: £5m - £10m **No.of Employees:** 51 - 100 **Product Groups:** 25, 33

K Morgan & Son
1 Gelli Siriol Llangynwyd, Maesteg, CF34 9RW
Tel: 07970-025691 **Fax:** 01656-734451
Directors: K. Morgan (Ptnr)
Date established: 1980 **No.of Employees:** 1 - 10 **Product Groups:** 41

Knott-Avonride Ltd
Unit 4 Spelter Site, Caerau, Maesteg, CF34 0AQ
Tel: 01656-739111 **Fax:** 01656-737677
E-mail: rmorgan@knottuk.com
Website: http://www.knottuk.com
Bank(s): HSBC Bank plc
Directors: N. Collins (Co Sec)
Managers: R. Morgan (Mgr)
Ultimate Holding Company: KNOTT HOLDING GMBH (GERMANY)
Immediate Holding Company: AVONRIDE LIMITED
Registration no: 01649441 **Date established:** 1982 **Turnover:** £2m - £5m
No.of Employees: 21 - 50 **Product Groups:** 39, 41, 45

Date of Accounts	Dec 11	Dec 10	Dec 09
Working Capital	50	50	50
Current Assets	50	50	50

Gwynedd

Menai Bridge

Good Designs
60 Mill Bank Estate Llandegfan, Menai Bridge, LL59 5RD
Tel: 01248-713624 **Fax:** 01248-713624
E-mail: info@disabledcycling.f2s.com
Website: http://www.disabledcycling.f2s.com
Directors: D. Good (Prop)
Turnover: Up to £250,000 **No.of Employees:** 1 - 10 **Product Groups:** 39, 45, 67, 85

Mid-Glamorgan

Merthyr Tydfil

Amnitec Ltd
Abercanaid, Merthyr Tydfil, CF48 1UX
Tel: 01685-385641 **Fax:** 01685-389683
E-mail: sales@amnitec.co.uk
Website: http://www.amnitec.co.uk
Bank(s): Midland
Managers: K. Rogers (Ops Mgr)
Ultimate Holding Company: INTERNATIONAL HOSE HOLDING COMPANY LLC (UNITED STATES)
Immediate Holding Company: AMNITEC LIMITED
Registration no: 00587472 **Date established:** 1957 **Turnover:** £5m - £10m
No.of Employees: 51 - 100 **Product Groups:** 30, 35, 36

Date of Accounts	Dec 11	Dec 10	Dec 09
Sales Turnover	9m	9m	8m
Pre Tax Profit/Loss	433	99	-986
Working Capital	211	-307	-516
Fixed Assets	178	261	371
Current Assets	7m	7m	11m
Current Liabilities	2m	2m	4m

Beaver Power Ltd
Goat Mill Road Dowlais, Merthyr Tydfil, CF48 3TF
Tel: 01685-353270 **Fax:** 01685-353271
E-mail: paulbeaton@mayphil.co.uk
Website: http://www.beaverpower.co.uk
Directors: P. Beaton (Fin)
Immediate Holding Company: BEAVER POWER LIMITED
Registration no: 03637769 **VAT No.:** GB 411 2198 92
Date established: 1998 **Turnover:** £1m - £2m **No.of Employees:** 1 - 10
Product Groups: 37, 67

Date of Accounts	Mar 12	Mar 11	Mar 10
Working Capital	2	3	3
Fixed Assets	N/A	5	3
Current Assets	967	1m	298

Biffa Waste Services Ltd
Trecatti Landfill Site Pant-y-Waun, Merthyr Tydfil, CF48 4AB
Tel: 01685-721882 **Fax:** 01685-387285
E-mail: chris.jones@biffa.co.uk
Website: http://www.biffa.co.uk
Managers: C. Jones (Ops Mgr)
Immediate Holding Company: BIFFA WASTE SERVICES LIMITED
Registration no: 00946107 **Date established:** 1969
No.of Employees: 11 - 20 **Product Groups:** 54

Date of Accounts	Mar 08	Mar 09	Apr 10
Sales Turnover	555m	574m	492m
Pre Tax Profit/Loss	23m	50m	30m
Working Capital	229m	271m	293m
Fixed Assets	371m	360m	378m
Current Assets	409m	534m	609m
Current Liabilities	50m	100m	115m

CORDS Duaflex Ltd
Mayphil Industrial Estate Goatmill Road, Dowlais, Merthyr Tydfil, CF48 3TF
Tel: 01685-353240 **Fax:** 01685-353241
E-mail: sales@mayphil.co.uk
Website: http://www.mayphil.co.uk
Directors: P. Beaton (Fin), R. Medora (MD)
Ultimate Holding Company: MAYPHIL (UK) LTD.
Immediate Holding Company: CORDS DUAFLEX LIMITED
Registration no: 03779861 **Date established:** 1999
No.of Employees: 21 - 50 **Product Groups:** 30, 39, 40, 68

Date of Accounts	Mar 12	Mar 11	Mar 10
Working Capital	3	-13	-69
Current Assets	43	39	118

Cynon Valley Leader
52-53 Glebeland Street, Merthyr Tydfil, CF47 8AT
Tel: 01685-884406 **Fax:** 01685-884312
E-mail: cynon.valley.leader@wme.co.uk
Bank(s): Bank of Scotland
Managers: G. Marsh (Publishing), G. Marsh, L. Ilies ()
Immediate Holding Company: WESTERN MAIL ECHO LTD
No.of Employees: 11 - 20 **Product Groups:** 28

Evans Halshaw Merthyr Tydfil
Pentrebach Road, Merthyr Tydfil, CF48 1YA
Tel: 01685-374111 **Fax:** 01685-383038
Website: http://www.kia.co.uk
Bank(s): Barclays
Managers: B. Neale (Comm), C. Cusak (Admin Off), J. Browne (Mgr), L. Wood
Ultimate Holding Company: MC 478 LIMITED
Immediate Holding Company: CWMBRAN MOTORS LIMITED
Registration no: 01359849 **Date established:** 1973
Turnover: £10m - £20m **No.of Employees:** 51 - 100 **Product Groups:** 68

Date of Accounts	Dec 11	Dec 10	Dec 09
Working Capital	-132	10	10
Fixed Assets	142	N/A	N/A
Current Assets	10	10	10
Current Liabilities	142	N/A	N/A

Forklift Training
Pant Industrial Estate Dowlais, Merthyr Tydfil, CF48 2SR
Tel: 01685-359990
E-mail: gwentforklifttraining@hotmail.co.uk
Website: http://www.forklifttrainingsouthwales.co.uk
Directors: S. Bills (Prop)
Immediate Holding Company: WHOLESNAX (NATURAL PRODUCTS) LIMITED
Registration no: 03764695 **Date established:** 2005
No.of Employees: 1 - 10 **Product Groups:** 45, 67, 86

Date of Accounts	Sep 11	Sep 10	Sep 09
Working Capital	-93	-33	15
Fixed Assets	232	28	41
Current Assets	15	17	61

Functional Foam Beacons Products Ltd (t/a Functional Foam & Beacons Leisure)
Efi Industrial Estate Brecon Road, Merthyr Tydfil, CF47 8RB
Tel: 01685-350011 **Fax:** 01685-388396
E-mail: sales@beaconsproducts.co.uk
Website: http://www.beaconsproducts.co.uk
Directors: A. Stammers (MD), A. Stammers (MD)
Managers: T. Barton, T. Barton, N. Bosanko (Sales & Mktg Mg)
Immediate Holding Company: BEACONS PRODUCTS LIMITED
Registration no: 02621076 **VAT No.:** GB 438 6898 85
Date established: 1991 **Turnover:** £1m - £2m **No.of Employees:** 11 - 20
Product Groups: 23, 26, 27, 29, 30, 31, 42, 49, 65, 68

Date of Accounts	Nov 11	Nov 10	Nov 09
Working Capital	402	241	134
Fixed Assets	394	374	194
Current Assets	632	471	377

K Hamer
Unit A2 Enterprise Centre Pentrebach, Merthyr Tydfil, CF48 4DR
Tel: 01443-693506
Directors: K. Hamer (Prop)
Ultimate Holding Company: ALGORITHME PHARMA HOLDINGS INC (CANADA)
Immediate Holding Company: SYSTEMS ELECTRICAL ENGINEERING LIMITED
Registration no: 06644895 **Date established:** 1993
Turnover: £250,000 - £500,000 **No.of Employees:** 1 - 10
Product Groups: 35, 36

Date of Accounts	Aug 06	Aug 05	Aug 04
Working Capital	-13	-16	N/A
Current Assets	1	1	6

Hoover Ltd
Pentrebach, Merthyr Tydfil, CF48 4TU
Tel: 01685-721222 **Fax:** 01685-382946
E-mail: a.bertali@hoovercandy.com
Website: http://www.hoover.co.uk
Bank(s): National Westminster Bank Plc
Managers: R. Mudie
Ultimate Holding Company: CANDY SPA (ITALY)
Immediate Holding Company: HOOVER LIMITED
Registration no: 02521528 **VAT No.:** GB 228 6866 24
Date established: 1990 **Turnover:** £125m - £250m
No.of Employees: 101 - 250 **Product Groups:** 40

Date of Accounts	Dec 11	Dec 10	Dec 09
Sales Turnover	187m	215m	216m
Pre Tax Profit/Loss	1m	13m	-642
Working Capital	54m	53m	41m
Fixed Assets	11m	11m	12m
Current Assets	108m	112m	98m
Current Liabilities	32m	38m	37m

King David Tyres
Pentrebach Road, Merthyr Tydfil, CF48 1YA
Tel: 01685-723460 **Fax:** 01685-723460
Directors: B. Dix (Prop)
Ultimate Holding Company: MC 478 LIMITED
Immediate Holding Company: CWMBRAN MOTORS LIMITED
Registration no: 01151029 **Date established:** 1973
No.of Employees: 1 - 10 **Product Groups:** 29, 68

Date of Accounts	Dec 11	Dec 10	Dec 09
Working Capital	-132	10	10
Fixed Assets	142	N/A	N/A
Current Assets	10	10	10
Current Liabilities	142	N/A	N/A

Leebeesley plc
Pant Industrial Estate Dowlais, Merthyr Tydfil, CF48 2SS
Tel: 01685-385524 **Fax:** 01685-723006
E-mail: bwoolley@leebeesley.co.uk
Website: http://www.leebeesley.co.uk
Bank(s): Barclays, Queens Square, Wolverhampton
Managers: B. Woolley, M. Day (Sales Admin)
Immediate Holding Company: LEE BEESLEY HOLDINGS LIMITED
Registration no: 01234891 **VAT No.:** GB 545 1884 27
Date established: 1975 **Turnover:** £20m - £50m
No.of Employees: 21 - 50 **Product Groups:** 40, 48, 52, 84

Linde Heavy Truck Division (Linde Material Handling Division)
Linde Industrial Park Pentrebach, Merthyr Tydfil, CF48 4LA
Tel: 01443-624200 **Fax:** 01443-624300
E-mail: info@linde.com
Website: http://www.linde-htd.com
Bank(s): Barclays, Swansea
Managers: M. Taylor (Personnel), R. Smart (Comptroller), T. Edmunds (Tech Serv Mgr), C. Flint, D. Shyne (Purch Mgr), D. Bertozi, D. Bridge (Personnel)
Ultimate Holding Company: SUPERLIFT HOLDINGS SARL (LUXEMBOURG)
Immediate Holding Company: LINDE HEAVY TRUCK DIVISION LIMITED
Registration no: 00804058 **VAT No.:** GB 587 9293 67
Date established: 1964 **Turnover:** £50m - £75m
No.of Employees: 101 - 250 **Product Groups:** 45, 61, 67, 83

Date of Accounts	Dec 11	Dec 10	Dec 09
Sales Turnover	76m	66m	59m
Pre Tax Profit/Loss	-17m	-12m	-20m
Working Capital	3m	1	-14m
Fixed Assets	12m	12m	12m
Current Assets	40m	54m	28m
Current Liabilities	6m	4m	3m

Mayphil Pistons Ltd
Goat Mill Road Dowlais, Merthyr Tydfil, CF48 3TF
Tel: 01685-353220 **Fax:** 01685-353221
E-mail: mayuk@aol.com
Website: http://www.mayphil.co.uk
Directors: R. Gibson (Works), R. Medora (MD), P. Manchanda (Chief Op Offcr), P. Beaton (Fin), V. Medora (MD), R. Williams (Comm), N. Padfield (Co Sec)
Managers: R. Hall (Ops Mgr), M. Andrew (Sales Admin)
Immediate Holding Company: MAYPHIL (UK) LTD.
Registration no: 01158616 **VAT No.:** GB 272 6585 33
Date established: 1974 **Turnover:** £1m - £2m **No.of Employees:** 1 - 10
Product Groups: 39

Merthyr Motor Auctions Ltd (t/a M.M.A.)
Red Barrel House Pant Road, Dowlais, Merthyr Tydfil, CF48 3SH
Tel: 01685-377818 **Fax:** 01685-722715
E-mail: sales@auctioneers.co.uk
Website: http://www.auctioneers.co.uk
Bank(s): National Westminster
Directors: A. Davies (MD)
Immediate Holding Company: MERTHYR TYDFIL CAR AUCTION LIMITED
Registration no: 01438339 **VAT No.:** 337 8232 46 **Date established:** 1979
Turnover: £2m - £5m **No.of Employees:** 21 - 50 **Product Groups:** 61, 68

Date of Accounts	Mar 12	Mar 11	Mar 10
Sales Turnover	4m	4m	4m
Pre Tax Profit/Loss	289	151	268
Working Capital	1m	928	1m
Fixed Assets	397	398	476
Current Assets	2m	2m	2m
Current Liabilities	438	442	494

Micromotors
Cyfartha Industrial Estate Merthyr, Merthyr Tydfil, CF47 8PE
Tel: 01685-723571 **Fax:** 01685-359625
E-mail: enquiries@micromotors.co.uk
Website: http://www.micromotors.co.uk
Bank(s): Barclays
Directors: M. Powell (MD), M. Powell (Chief Op Offcr)
Immediate Holding Company: Jamal Dynamics Ltd
Registration no: 01343013 **VAT No.:** GB 315 3693 61
Date established: 1982 **Turnover:** £2m - £5m **No.of Employees:** 51 - 100
Product Groups: 37, 40

Mitre Linen
1 Goat Mill Road Dowlais, Merthyr Tydfil, CF48 3TD
Tel: 01685-353456 **Fax:** 01254-614222
E-mail: sales@mitrehallandletts.com
Website: http://www.mitrelinen.com
Bank(s): Barclays
Directors: S. Broadhurst (Dir)
Managers: L. Vokins (Sales & Mktg Mg), P. James (Buyer)
Immediate Holding Company: 4JNG PROPERTIES LIMITED
Registration no: 02070285 **VAT No.:** GB 245 4062 78
Date established: 2011 **Turnover:** £2m - £5m **No.of Employees:** 51 - 100
Product Groups: 23

Netlog Technology
Pant Industrial Estate Dowlais, Merthyr Tydfil, CF48 2SR
Tel: 01685-384654 **Fax:** 01685-384674
E-mail: info@netlogtec.com
Website: http://www.netlogtec.com
Directors: N. James (Co Sec), G. James (Dir)
Immediate Holding Company: NETLOG TECHNOLOGY LIMITED
Registration no: 03186000 **Date established:** 1996
Turnover: Up to £250,000 **No.of Employees:** 1 - 10 **Product Groups:** 37, 44, 67, 80

Date of Accounts	Jun 10	Jun 09	Jun 08
Working Capital	-85	-60	-38
Fixed Assets	175	182	188
Current Assets	66	41	52

O P Chocolate Ltd
High Street Dowlais, Merthyr Tydfil, CF48 3TB
Tel: 01685-352560 **Fax:** 01685-352599
E-mail: sales@opchocolate.com
Website: http://www.opchocolate.com
Directors: T. Caccavale (Fin), D. Bevan (Fin)
Managers: P. McNally (Purch Mgr), A. Lee, G. Thomas (Personnel)
Ultimate Holding Company: CEMOI SA (FRANCE)
Immediate Holding Company: O.P. CHOCOLATE LIMITED
Registration no: 02557248 **Date established:** 1990
Turnover: £20m - £50m **No.of Employees:** 251 - 500
Product Groups: 20, 62

Date of Accounts	Dec 11	Dec 10	Dec 09
Sales Turnover	35m	32m	31m
Pre Tax Profit/Loss	904	2m	3m
Working Capital	-4m	-4m	-4m
Fixed Assets	10m	7m	6m
Current Assets	11m	10m	8m
Current Liabilities	2m	2m	1m

Rack International UK Ltd
Pant Industrial Estate Dowlais, Merthyr Tydfil, CF48 2SR
Tel: 01685-383133 **Fax:** 01685-383836
E-mail: sales@rackinternational.com
Website: http://www.rackinternational.com
Directors: S. Goldsworthy (Fin), A. Grainger (MD)
Managers: A. Cobley (Tech Serv Mgr)
Registration no: 03764695 **VAT No.:** GB 541 0952 65
Date established: 1999 **Turnover:** £500,000 - £1m
No.of Employees: 1 - 10 **Product Groups:** 26, 34, 35, 67

Date of Accounts	Jun 07	Jun 06
Working Capital	-76	-129
Fixed Assets	76	71
Current Assets	2170	1788
Current Liabilities	2246	1917

Rokel Engineering Ltd
Unit 18 Pant Industrial Estate Dowlais, Merthyr Tydfil, CF48 2SR
Tel: 01685-370622 **Fax:** 01685-721802
E-mail: kelvin.wooldridge@rokelengineering.co.uk
Website: http://www.rokelengineering.co.uk
Directors: A. Meek (MD)
Immediate Holding Company: ROKEL ENGINEERING LIMITED
Registration no: 07928585 **Date established:** 2012
No.of Employees: 1 - 10 **Product Groups:** 35

Simbec Research Ltd
Merthyr Industrial Park Pentrebach, Merthyr Tydfil, CF48 4DR
Tel: 01443-690977 **Fax:** 01443-692494
E-mail: alan.woodward@simbec.co.uk
Website: http://www.simbecresearch.co.uk
Directors: J. Maddock (MD), B. Hallisey (Co Sec)
Managers: S. Febbraro, A. Woodward (Develop Mgr)
Ultimate Holding Company: ALGORITHME PHARMA HOLDINGS INC (CANADA)
Immediate Holding Company: SIMBEC RESEARCH LIMITED
Registration no: 01191772 **VAT No.:** GB 289 0833 21
Date established: 1974 **Turnover:** £5m - £10m **No.of Employees:** 1 - 10
Product Groups: 84, 85

Date of Accounts	Jul 08	Sep 11	Sep 10
Sales Turnover	9m	7m	7m
Pre Tax Profit/Loss	381	-967	-68
Working Capital	1m	24	1m
Fixed Assets	3m	3m	3m
Current Assets	2m	2m	3m
Current Liabilities	251	1m	955

Stephens & George Print Group
Goat Mill Road Dowlais, Merthyr Tydfil, CF48 3TD
Tel: 01685-388888 **Fax:** 01685-385732
E-mail: sales@stephensandgeorge.co.uk
Website: http://www.stephensandgeorge.co.uk
Bank(s): Bank of Wales
Directors: D. Debattista (Fin), A. Jones (MD)
Managers: S. Price (Tech Serv Mgr), B. Powell (Mktg Serv Mgr), S. Downs, V. Jones (Personnel)
Ultimate Holding Company: STEPHENS AND GEORGE LIMITED
Immediate Holding Company: STEPHENS & GEORGE COMMERCIAL LIMITED
Registration no: 02229134 **VAT No.:** GB 666 6282 02
Date established: 1988 **Turnover:** £10m - £20m
No.of Employees: 101 - 250 **Product Groups:** 28

Supac Ltd
Unit 3 Goatmill Road Industrial Estate, Merthyr Tydfil, CF48 3TD
Tel: 01685-729850 **Fax:** 01685-729855
E-mail: sales@supac.co.uk
Website: http://www.supac.co.uk
Directors: C. Morgan (Dir), D. Morgan (MD), G. Morgan (MD), R. Morgan (Dir), S. Morgan (Sales)
Managers: N. Morgan (I.T. Exec)
Immediate Holding Company: Supac Ltd
Registration no: 00508062 **VAT No.:** GB 135 6578 48
Date established: 1952 **Turnover:** Up to £250,000
No.of Employees: 1 - 10 **Product Groups:** 37

Date of Accounts	Mar 10	Mar 09	Mar 08
Working Capital	1m	1m	1m
Fixed Assets	856	865	196
Current Assets	2m	2m	2m

Swift Credit Services Ltd
Hazeldene High Street Penydarren, Merthyr Tydfil, CF47 9AH
Tel: 08445-466910 **Fax:** 08700-006210
E-mail: sales@swift-credit.com
Website: http://www.swiftcredit.co.uk
Directors: H. Lloyd-Lewis (MD)
Immediate Holding Company: SWIFT CREDIT SERVICES LIMITED
Registration no: 01159954 **Date established:** 1974 **Turnover:** £2m - £5m
No.of Employees: 11 - 20 **Product Groups:** 82

Date of Accounts	Mar 11	Mar 10	Mar 09
Working Capital	384	261	143
Fixed Assets	87	125	160
Current Assets	997	1m	837

Triumph Furniture (t/a Triumph Business Systems)
The Willows, Merthyr Tydfil, CF48 1YH
Tel: 01685-384041 **Fax:** 01685-352202
E-mail: info@triumphstorage.com
Website: http://www.triumphstorage.com
Bank(s): Lloyds, Queen Street, Cardiff
Directors: C. Jackson (MD), P. Morgan (Co Sec)
Ultimate Holding Company: T.B.S (SOUTH WALES) HOLDINGS LIMITED
Immediate Holding Company: SEKALB NINE LIMITED
Registration no: 00368525 **Date established:** 1941
Turnover: £20m - £50m **No.of Employees:** 101 - 250
Product Groups: 26, 38, 49

Date of Accounts	Apr 08	Apr 07	May 09
Sales Turnover	20m	19m	24m
Pre Tax Profit/Loss	9	137	663
Working Capital	2m	2m	2m
Fixed Assets	3m	3m	3m
Current Assets	11m	11m	13m
Current Liabilities	4m	3m	4m

Z-Laser Uk Sales Office
PO Box 55, Merthyr Tydfil, NP11 9AB
Tel: 07515-574756
E-mail: rees@z-laser.com
Website: http://www.z-laser.com
Managers: G. Rees (Sales Prom Mgr)
Registration no: DE14211564 **Date established:** 1985
Turnover: £5m - £10m **No.of Employees:** 51 - 100 **Product Groups:** 67

Dyfed

Milford Haven

Ashdale Engineering Ltd
14 Orion House Nelson Quay, Milford Haven, SA73 3AZ
Tel: 01646-693570
E-mail: contracts@ashdale-engineering.com
Website: http://www.ashdale-engineering.com
Directors: M. Mead (Dir)
Immediate Holding Company: ASHDALE ENGINEERING UK LTD
Registration no: 06013500 **Date established:** 2006 **Turnover:** £2m - £5m
No.of Employees: 1 - 10 **Product Groups:** 35, 45

Date of Accounts	Jul 11	Jul 10	Jul 09
Working Capital	417	273	353
Fixed Assets	36	30	27

see next page

Ashdale Engineering Ltd - Cont'd

Current Assets	660	752	645
Current Liabilities	218	N/A	N/A

C A C Industrial Products Ltd
Thornton Industrial Trading Estate, Milford Haven, SA73 2RU
Tel: 01646-692626 **Fax:** 01646-690144
E-mail: sales@cac-industrial.co.uk
Website: http://www.cac-industrial.co.uk
Bank(s): Barclays
Directors: G. Parish (Works)
Immediate Holding Company: C.A.C. INDUSTRIAL PRODUCTS LIMITED
Registration no: 00691418 **VAT No.:** GB 647 8307 10
Date established: 1961 **Turnover:** £1m - £2m **No.of Employees:** 11 - 20
Product Groups: 22, 24, 40, 63, 67

Date of Accounts	Apr 11	Apr 10	Apr 09
Working Capital	201	180	233
Fixed Assets	43	51	41
Current Assets	311	279	357

C B L Ceramics Ltd
Marble Hall Road Steynton, Milford Haven, SA73 2PP
Tel: 01646-697681 **Fax:** 01646-690053
Bank(s): HSBC Bank plc
Managers: S. Jones (Plant)
Immediate Holding Company: CBL CERAMICS LIMITED
Registration no: 02736169 **VAT No.:** GB 122 0717 18
Date established: 1992 **Turnover:** £2m - £5m **No.of Employees:** 21 - 50
Product Groups: 31, 33, 37

Date of Accounts	Dec 11	Dec 10	Dec 09
Sales Turnover	N/A	N/A	3m
Pre Tax Profit/Loss	N/A	N/A	526
Working Capital	4m	3m	3m
Fixed Assets	181	162	280
Current Assets	5m	5m	4m
Current Liabilities	N/A	N/A	964

Celtic SMR Ltd
Unit 9-10 Dolphin Court Brunel Quay, Neyland, Milford Haven, SA73 1PY
Tel: 01646-603150 **Fax:** 01646-603159
E-mail: gmacphail@celticsmr.co.uk
Website: http://www.celticsmr.co.uk
Directors: M. Howe (MD)
Immediate Holding Company: CELTIC SMR LIMITED
Registration no: 01795571 **VAT No.:** GB 155 5102 88
Date established: 1984 **Turnover:** Up to £250,000
No.of Employees: 1 - 10 **Product Groups:** 37

Date of Accounts	Dec 11	Dec 10	Dec 09
Working Capital	398	370	439
Fixed Assets	179	136	68
Current Assets	1m	1m	861

Consort Equipment Products
Thornton Industrial Estate, Milford Haven, SA73 2RT
Tel: 01646-692172 **Fax:** 01646-695195
E-mail: enquiries@consortepl.com
Website: http://www.consortepl.com
Bank(s): HSBC Bank plc
Directors: C. Baggs (Mats), E. Spankie (MD)
Managers: R. Griffiths
Ultimate Holding Company: CONSORT (1996) LIMITED
Immediate Holding Company: CONSORT EQUIPMENT PRODUCTS LIMITED
Registration no: 03160980 **VAT No.:** GB 666 8400 12
Date established: 1996 **No.of Employees:** 51 - 100 **Product Groups:** 40, 66

Date of Accounts	Dec 08	Dec 07	Mar 11
Sales Turnover	N/A	4m	N/A
Pre Tax Profit/Loss	N/A	-70	N/A
Working Capital	708	917	1m
Fixed Assets	613	838	371
Current Assets	2m	2m	2m
Current Liabilities	N/A	256	N/A

Cory Brothers Shipping Agency Ltd
20 Temeraire House Nelson Quay, Milford Haven, SA73 3BN
Tel: 01646-692472 **Fax:** 01646-690023
E-mail: corymhaven@cory.co.uk
Website: http://www.cory.co.uk
Directors: K. Gorman (Dir)
Managers: A. Lewis (Mgr)
Ultimate Holding Company: BRAEMAR SHIPPING SERVICES PLC
Immediate Holding Company: CORY BROTHERS SHIPPING AGENCY LIMITED
Registration no: 04717201 **VAT No.:** GB 244 0497 69
Date established: 2003 **Turnover:** £500,000 - £1m
No.of Employees: 1 - 10 **Product Groups:** 76

Date of Accounts	Feb 12	Feb 12	Feb 11
Sales Turnover	30m	30m	28m
Pre Tax Profit/Loss	2m	2m	949
Working Capital	-2m	-2m	-2m
Fixed Assets	5m	5m	6m
Current Assets	12m	12m	13m
Current Liabilities	3m	3m	3m

Genpower Ltd
Unit 1 Dowty Park Thornton Road, Milford Haven, SA73 2RS
Tel: 08450-942452 **Fax:** 0845-094 2453
E-mail: sales@genpoweruk.com
Website: http://www.genpoweruk.co.uk
Directors: R. Llewelyn (Prop)
Immediate Holding Company: GENPOWER LTD
Registration no: 05758983 **Date established:** 2006
Turnover: Up to £250,000 **No.of Employees:** 1 - 10 **Product Groups:** 37

Date of Accounts	Mar 12	Mar 11	Mar 10
Working Capital	361	227	93
Fixed Assets	18	18	23
Current Assets	828	543	297
Current Liabilities	39	34	N/A

Manderwood Timber Engineering Ltd
Unit 5 Great Honeyborough Trading Estate, Neyland, Milford Haven, SA73 1SE
Tel: 01646-600621 **Fax:** 01646-600784
E-mail: sales@manderwood.co.uk
Website: http://www.manderwood.co.uk
Bank(s): Barclays, Haverfordwest
Directors: C. Tansey (MD)
Immediate Holding Company: MANDERWOOD TIMBER ENGINEERING LIMITED
Registration no: 01339715 **VAT No.:** GB 326 8602 52
Date established: 1977 **Turnover:** £2m - £5m **No.of Employees:** 11 - 20
Product Groups: 25

Date of Accounts	Mar 12	Mar 11	Mar 10
Working Capital	914	653	567
Fixed Assets	414	433	442
Current Assets	1m	894	787

Milford Haven Ship Repairers
The Docks, Milford Haven, SA73 3DJ
Tel: 01646-696320 **Fax:** 01646-696321
E-mail: tudor.symmonds@mhpa.co.uk
Website: http://www.milford-docks.co.uk
Bank(s): Barclays
Managers: T. Symmonds (Mgr)
Ultimate Holding Company: MILFORD HAVEN PORT AUTHORITY GROUP
Immediate Holding Company: MILFORD DOCKS CO.
Registration no: 03219710 **VAT No.:** GB 647 8607 95
Date established: 1996 **Turnover:** £500,000 - £1m
No.of Employees: 21 - 50 **Product Groups:** 39

Milford Steel Fabricators
Unit 81 Waterston Industrial Estate Main Road, Waterston, Milford Haven, SA73 1DP
Tel: 01646-695019 **Fax:** 01646-697809
E-mail: milfordsteel@btconnect.com
Website: http://www.milfordsteel.com
Directors: I. John (Prop)
Registration no: 05606978 **Date established:** 2005
No.of Employees: 1 - 10 **Product Groups:** 35

R & R Windows
Unit 12 Thornton Business Park, Milford Haven, SA73 2RY
Tel: 01646-693383 **Fax:** 01646-694833
Directors: A. Richards (MD)
Date established: 2002 **No.of Employees:** 1 - 10 **Product Groups:** 46

S & M Thomas
4 James Street Neyland, Milford Haven, SA73 1RP
Tel: 01646-600272 **Fax:** 01646-600272
Directors: S. Thomas (Dir)
Date established: 1986 **No.of Employees:** 1 - 10 **Product Groups:** 20, 40, 41

Walters Group Ltd
The Old Customs House The Docks, Milford Haven, SA73 3AA
Tel: 01646-698218 **Fax:** 01646-698846
E-mail: enquiries@thewaltersgroup.co.uk
Website: http://www.thewaltersgroup.co.uk
Directors: R. Edwards (Fin), D. Walters (MD)
Immediate Holding Company: WALTERS GENERAL LTD.
Registration no: 03304589 **Date established:** 1997
Turnover: £250,000 - £500,000 **No.of Employees:** 1 - 10
Product Groups: 36, 40, 49, 66

Date of Accounts	Jan 11	Jan 10	Jan 09
Sales Turnover	317	254	353
Pre Tax Profit/Loss	130	36	95
Working Capital	287	202	186
Fixed Assets	62	62	62
Current Assets	299	215	205
Current Liabilities	11	N/A	4

Clwyd

Mold

24 7 Roller Shutters
The Old Chapel Denbigh Road, Hendre, Mold, CH7 5QL
Tel: 01352-741320 **Fax:** 0151- 4275709
E-mail: enquiries@20four7.co.uk
Website: http://www.20four7.co.uk
Directors: K. Jolliffe (Dir), P. Caza (Dir)
Managers: E. Winter (Admin Off)
Immediate Holding Company: ABSOLUTE DOOR SYSTEMS LLP
Registration no: OC306879 **Date established:** 2004
No.of Employees: 1 - 10 **Product Groups:** 26, 35

Date of Accounts	Dec 07	Dec 06
Working Capital	21	5
Fixed Assets	232	257
Current Assets	194	126
Current Liabilities	173	122

Brockley Motors
Pant Y Buarth Depot Pant Y Buarth, Gwernaffield, Mold, CH7 5ER
Tel: 01352-741160 **Fax:** 01352- 741160
Directors: D. Brockley (Ptnr), K. Brockley (Ptnr)
Date established: 1970 **No.of Employees:** 1 - 10 **Product Groups:** 40

Crystal Clear
Highfield House County Road, Leeswood, Mold, CH7 4RF
Tel: 01352-771426
E-mail: johnscrystalwc@aol.com
Directors: J. Clancey (Prop)
Turnover: Up to £250,000 **No.of Employees:** 1 - 10 **Product Groups:** 52

G C Hahn & Co. Ltd
Maes Gwern Mold Business Park, Mold, CH7 1XW
Tel: 01352-705500 **Fax:** 01352-705555
E-mail: caroline.pender@gchahn.com
Website: http://www.gchahn.co.uk
Directors: P. Prendergast (Mkt Research), P. Prendergast (MD)
Managers: C. Pender (Sec), C. Pender
Ultimate Holding Company: 00076535
Immediate Holding Company: G. C. HAHN AND COMPANY LIMITED
Registration no: 01871654 **VAT No.:** GB 413 0942 85
Date established: 1984 **Turnover:** £20m - £50m
No.of Employees: 51 - 100 **Product Groups:** 32

Date of Accounts	Mar 08	Mar 07	Dec 06
Sales Turnover	16642	3752	16293
Pre Tax Profit/Loss	834	252	1153
Working Capital	2560	2496	2112
Fixed Assets	2136	2005	1890
Current Assets	6139	5193	5005
Current Liabilities	3579	2697	2893
Total Share Capital	100	100	100
ROCE% (Return on Capital Employed)	17.8	5.6	28.8
ROT% (Return on Turnover)	5.0	6.7	7.1

N W N Media Ltd
Mold Business Park Wrexham Road, Mold, CH7 1XY
Tel: 01352-707707 **Fax:** 01978-311421
E-mail: david.faulkner@nwn.co.uk
Website: http://www.nwn.co.uk
Directors: D. Faulkner (MD)
Immediate Holding Company: NWN MEDIA LIMITED
Registration no: 00167825 **VAT No.:** GB 158 9070 37
Date established: 2020 **Turnover:** £10m - £20m **No.of Employees:** 1 - 10
Product Groups: 28

Date of Accounts	Mar 11	Mar 10	Mar 09
Sales Turnover	15m	15m	16m
Pre Tax Profit/Loss	340	375	225
Working Capital	775	1m	1m
Fixed Assets	15m	15m	16m
Current Assets	3m	4m	4m
Current Liabilities	1m	1m	1m

Nu Image Packaging - Clwyd Ltd
Pontybodkin Hill Leeswood, Mold, CH7 4RY
Tel: 01352-779000 **Fax:** 01352-779091
E-mail: sales@nu-image.co.uk
Website: http://www.nu-image.co.uk
Directors: R. Nunn (MD)
Immediate Holding Company: NU-IMAGE PACKAGING (CLWYD) LIMITED
Registration no: 02466316 **Date established:** 1990
Turnover: £500,000 - £1m **No.of Employees:** 1 - 10 **Product Groups:** 31, 48, 76, 84

Date of Accounts	Mar 11	Mar 10	Mar 09
Working Capital	780	703	714
Fixed Assets	128	160	56
Current Assets	1m	998	930

P & A Group of Companies
Mold Industrial Estate Wrexham Road, Mold, CH7 4HE
Tel: 01352-752555 **Fax:** 01352-755200
E-mail: sales@p-a-group.com
Website: http://www.p-a-group.com
Bank(s): Midland
Directors: S. Morgan (MD)
Managers: N. Roberts (Mktg Serv Mgr)
Registration no: 01880477 **Date established:** 1975 **Turnover:** £2m - £5m
Product Groups: 25, 27, 45

Seasonal Reflections Ltd
30 High Street, Mold, CH7 1BH
Tel: 01352-756070 **Fax:** 01352-757011
E-mail: helen.jones@xinetica.com
Website: http://partyshop-mold.co.uk
Directors: K. Duplop (MD), H. Perry (MD), H. Perry (Prop), J. Edwards (Fin)
Immediate Holding Company: SEASONAL REFLECTIONS LIMITED
Registration no: 04380043 **Date established:** 2002
No.of Employees: 1 - 10 **Product Groups:** 24, 29, 49

Date of Accounts	Mar 11	Mar 10	Mar 09
Working Capital	72	79	75
Fixed Assets	2	3	3
Current Assets	85	92	92

Sprint Fastening Systems Ltd
1 Rhodfa Mynydd, Mold, CH7 1GQ
Tel: 01244-534100 **Fax:** 01244-539038
E-mail: info@sprint-fastenings.co.uk
Website: http://www.sprint-fastenings.com
Directors: J. Bates (Dir)
Immediate Holding Company: SPRINT FASTENING SYSTEMS LIMITED
Registration no: 04421756 **Date established:** 2002
Turnover: Up to £250,000 **No.of Employees:** 1 - 10 **Product Groups:** 35, 39, 46

Date of Accounts	Dec 11	Dec 10	Dec 09
Sales Turnover	143	80	42
Pre Tax Profit/Loss	8	-0	-2
Working Capital	-20	-19	-5
Fixed Assets	74	80	87
Current Assets	153	28	29
Current Liabilities	133	41	23

Synthite Ltd
Alyn Works Denbigh Road, Mold, CH7 1BT
Tel: 01352-752521 **Fax:** 01352-700182
E-mail: sales@synthite.co.uk
Website: http://www.synthite.co.uk
Bank(s): Barclays, West Bromwich
Directors: K. Jones (MD), D. Kelso (Fin)
Managers: S. Morton (Tech Serv Mgr), S. Tomlinson (Personnel), S. Niazi (Sales & Mktg Mg), M. Powell (Comm)
Ultimate Holding Company: TENNANTS CONSOLIDATED LIMITED
Immediate Holding Company: SYNTHITE LIMITED
Registration no: 00164640 **VAT No.:** GB 276 9988 69
Date established: 2020 **Turnover:** £50m - £75m
No.of Employees: 101 - 250 **Product Groups:** 31, 32

Date of Accounts	Dec 11	Dec 10	Dec 09
Sales Turnover	63m	58m	39m
Pre Tax Profit/Loss	4m	4m	4m
Working Capital	15m	17m	15m
Fixed Assets	8m	5m	4m
Current Assets	19m	21m	19m
Current Liabilities	1m	1m	966

Tiger Tim Products Ltd
Industrial Estate Rhosesmor, Mold, CH7 6PZ
Tel: 01352-780861 **Fax:** 01352-781294
E-mail: sales@tigertimproducts.co.uk
Website: http://www.tigertimproducts.co.uk
Bank(s): Barclays
Directors: A. Price (Dir), P. Thomas (Fin), S. Keidel (Purch)
Managers: K. Grant (Personnel)
Ultimate Holding Company: THE FLAME GROUP LIMITED
Immediate Holding Company: TIGER TIM PRODUCTS LIMITED
Registration no: 01393841 **VAT No.:** GB 401 4292 00
Date established: 1978 **Turnover:** £20m - £50m
No.of Employees: 51 - 100 **Product Groups:** 40

Date of Accounts	Mar 11	Mar 10	Mar 09
Sales Turnover	21m	20m	21m
Pre Tax Profit/Loss	973	2m	1m
Working Capital	4m	3m	1m
Fixed Assets	2m	2m	2m
Current Assets	9m	8m	9m
Current Liabilities	300	348	528

Tweeds
St Andrews Park Queens Lane, Bromfield Industrial Estate, Mold, CH7 1XB
Tel: 01352-756161 **Fax:** 01352-756166
E-mail: l.morley@tweeds.co.uk
Website: http://www.tweeds.co.uk
Directors: L. Morley (Reg), L. Morley (Dir)
Managers: A. Piercy (Sec)
Registration no: 04846533 **Date established:** 2003
Turnover: £500,000 - £1m **No.of Employees:** 1 - 10 **Product Groups:** 84

Zest 4 Leisure
St Andrews Park Queens Lane, Bromfield Industrial Estate, Mold, CH7 1XB
Tel: 01352-752555 **Fax:** 08702-002357
E-mail: sales@zest4leisure.co.uk
Website: http://www.zest4leisure.co.uk
Managers: A. Williams (Mgr)
Immediate Holding Company: ZEST FOR LEISURE LIMITED
Registration no: 05180716 **Date established:** 2004
No.of Employees: 51 - 100 **Product Groups:** 25, 26, 35, 41, 49

Gwent

Monmouth

Codel Ltd
Watery Lane, Monmouth, NP25 5AT
Tel: 01600-772023 **Fax:** 01443-843460
Website: http://www.codelmark.com
Bank(s): Barclays, Caerphilly
Directors: M. Warner (Sales)
Immediate Holding Company: CODEL LIMITED
Registration no: 03916780 **VAT No.:** GB 402 5179 82
Date established: 2000 **Turnover:** £2m - £5m **No.of Employees:** 11 - 20
Product Groups: 66, 85

E2l Ltd
19 White Swan Court, Monmouth, NP25 3NY
Tel: 01600-714856
E-mail: info@e2l.uk.com
Website: http://www.e2l.uk.com
Directors: L. Owen (MD)
Ultimate Holding Company: E2L HOLDINGS LIMITED
Immediate Holding Company: E2L LIMITED
Registration no: 03614226 **Date established:** 1998
Turnover: £250,000 - £500,000 **No.of Employees:** 1 - 10
Product Groups: 26, 30, 49, 89

Date of Accounts	Feb 11	Feb 10	Feb 09
Working Capital	-57	-76	-57
Fixed Assets	4	6	8
Current Assets	44	28	16

Grange Marketing
Hillside House Cwmcarvan, Monmouth, NP25 4PL
Tel: 01600-869079 **Fax:** 01600-869079
E-mail: enquiries@gm-uk.com
Website: http://www.grange-marketing.co.uk
Directors: A. Wade-West (Prop)
Date established: 2000 **Turnover:** Up to £250,000
No.of Employees: 1 - 10 **Product Groups:** 40

I K V Tribology Ltd
Bramble Hollow The Narth, Monmouth, NP25 4QJ
Tel: 01600-869120 **Fax:** 01600-869101
E-mail: sales@ikvlubricants.com
Website: http://www.ikvlubricants.com
Directors: M. Arnell (MD)
Immediate Holding Company: IKV TRIBOLOGY LIMITED
Registration no: 05282979 **Date established:** 2004
Turnover: £250,000 - £500,000 **No.of Employees:** 1 - 10
Product Groups: 30, 31

Date of Accounts	Sep 11	Sep 10	Sep 09
Working Capital	54	33	12
Fixed Assets	14	19	N/A
Current Assets	132	127	160

Jewson Ltd
Wonastow Road, Monmouth, NP25 3ZY
Tel: 01600-772636 **Fax:** 01600-772763
Website: http://www.jewson.co.uk
Directors: N. Laurence (MD), P. Hindle (MD)
Managers: D. Lewis (Mgr), J. Harris (District Mgr), J. Mattock (District Mgr)
Immediate Holding Company: JEWSON LIMITED
Registration no: 00348407 **Date established:** 1939 **Turnover:** £2m - £5m
No.of Employees: 1 - 10 **Product Groups:** 66

Security Europe Guarding
Wyastone Leys Ganarew, Monmouth, NP25 3SR
Tel: 01600-891571 **Fax:** 01600-890030
E-mail: info@pauldavissecurity.co.uk
Website: http://www.securityeuropeguarding.co.uk
Directors: D. Jones (MD)
Immediate Holding Company: INSPIRE CONSULTING AND COACHING LIMITED
Registration no: 05644115 **Date established:** 2005 **Turnover:** £1m - £2m
No.of Employees: 1 - 10 **Product Groups:** 36, 52, 67, 84

vertex barrier systems uk Ltd
Wyastone Business Park Wyastone Leys, Monmouth, NP25 3SR
Tel: 01600-891548 **Fax:** 01600-891568
E-mail: info@vbsuk.co.uk
Website: http://www.vbsuk.co.uk
Directors: M. Jones (Dir)
Registration no: 07123875 **Date established:** 1984
No.of Employees: 1 - 10 **Product Groups:** 36

Wyastone Estate Ltd
Wyastone Leys Ganarew, Monmouth, NP25 3SR
Tel: 01600-890007 **Fax:** 01600-891052
E-mail: sales@wyastone.co.uk
Website: http://www.wyastone.co.uk
Directors: A. Smith (Dir)
Immediate Holding Company: WYASTONE ESTATE LIMITED
Registration no: 04307466 **Date established:** 2001
No.of Employees: 11 - 20 **Product Groups:** 28

Date of Accounts	Dec 11	Dec 10	Dec 09
Working Capital	99	55	13
Fixed Assets	2m	2m	2m
Current Assets	421	351	313

Powys

Montgomery

Gareth Pugh Steel Framed Buildings
Agrimont Depot Station Yard, Abermule, Montgomery, SY15 6NH
Tel: 01686-630500 **Fax:** 01686-630441
E-mail: enquiry@garethpugh.co.uk
Website: http://www.garethpugh.co.uk
Directors: G. Pugh (Prop)
Managers: S. Owen (Mgr)
Date established: 1987 **Turnover:** £2m - £5m **No.of Employees:** 21 - 50
Product Groups: 34, 35, 36, 52

Trevor Hamer
Lower Hurdley Farm Church Stoke, Montgomery, SY15 6DY
Tel: 01588-620266
Directors: T. Hamer (Prop)
Date established: 1970 **No.of Employees:** 1 - 10 **Product Groups:** 41

Myrick Training Services
Myrick House Hen-Domen, Montgomery, SY15 6EZ
Tel: 01686-668670 **Fax:** 01686-668771
E-mail: jhowells@myrick.co.uk
Website: http://www.myricktraining.co.uk
Directors: J. Howells (Co Sec), A. Morrison (Pers)
Immediate Holding Company: MID AND NORTH WALES TRAINING GROUP LIMITED
Registration no: 01484530 **Date established:** 1980
Turnover: £250,000 - £500,000 **No.of Employees:** 1 - 10
Product Groups: 86

Date of Accounts	Jul 11	Jul 10	Jul 09
Sales Turnover	384	311	302
Pre Tax Profit/Loss	38	6	5
Working Capital	113	93	79
Fixed Assets	224	205	213
Current Assets	157	122	118
Current Liabilities	21	23	23

Mid-Glamorgan

Mountain Ash

Abtest Ltd
Abercynon, Mountain Ash, CF45 4SF
Tel: 01443-743440 **Fax:** 01443-741033
E-mail: clive.warren@abtest.com
Website: http://www.abtest.com
Directors: A. Breese (MD), R. Mullen (Fin)
Managers: C. Warren, G. Masters (Tech Serv Mgr)
Immediate Holding Company: ABTEST LIMITED
Registration no: 00620992 **Date established:** 1959
Turnover: £500,000 - £1m **No.of Employees:** 1 - 10 **Product Groups:** 38, 48, 85

Date of Accounts	Dec 09	Dec 08	Dec 07
Sales Turnover	781	1m	1m
Pre Tax Profit/Loss	-162	80	188
Working Capital	-83	19	227
Fixed Assets	302	349	146
Current Assets	335	310	401
Current Liabilities	67	91	94

Blore Edwards
Unit 7-8 Pontcynon Industrial Estate, Abercynon, Mountain Ash, CF45 4EP
Tel: 01443-742202 **Fax:** 01443-742192
E-mail: bcxma@aol.com
Website: http://www.blore-ed.com
Bank(s): National Westminster
Directors: A. White (Fin), M. Cryer (MD), B. Cryer (Dir), A. Cyer (MD)
Managers: R. Hopkins (Buyer)
Immediate Holding Company: D.A.B. EDWARDS LIMITED
Registration no: 02464288 **Date established:** 1990
Turnover: £250,000 - £500,000 **No.of Employees:** 11 - 20
Product Groups: 37

Date of Accounts	Mar 08	Mar 07	Mar 06
Working Capital	163	189	210
Fixed Assets	N/A	1	2
Current Assets	176	207	227
Current Liabilities	14	19	16
Total Share Capital	1	1	1

C R Floor Machines
Unit 19 CWM Cynon Business Park, Mountain Ash, CF45 4ER
Tel: 01443-477978 **Fax:** 01443-474024
Website: http://www.crfloormachines.com
Directors: C. Roberts (Prop)
Date established: 1993 **No.of Employees:** 1 - 10 **Product Groups:** 36, 40

Flexicare Medical Ltd
CWM Cynon Business Park, Mountain Ash, CF45 4ER
Tel: 01443-474647 **Fax:** 01443-474222
E-mail: enquiries@flexicare.com
Website: http://www.flexicare.com
Bank(s): HSBC Bank plc
Directors: G. Poormand (MD), G. Davies (Fin), K. Poormand (Develop)
Managers: N. Instone (Purch Mgr), E. Hughes (Personnel)
Ultimate Holding Company: MEDICARE MARKETING S A(PANAMA)
Immediate Holding Company: FLEXICARE MEDICAL LIMITED
Registration no: 02428573 **VAT No.:** GB 520 4204 07
Date established: 1989 **Turnover:** £10m - £20m
No.of Employees: 51 - 100 **Product Groups:** 29, 30, 38, 66

Date of Accounts	Nov 11	Nov 10	Nov 09
Sales Turnover	13m	11m	10m
Pre Tax Profit/Loss	639	685	593
Working Capital	2m	2m	2m
Fixed Assets	2m	2m	2m
Current Assets	7m	5m	4m
Current Liabilities	3m	2m	1m

Good-Buys
2c Oxford Street, Mountain Ash, CF45 3PL
Tel: 01443-475049 **Fax:** 01443-475049
Directors: T. Benny (Prop)
Date established: 1953 **No.of Employees:** 1 - 10 **Product Groups:** 36, 40

Dyfed

Narberth

B P Elkins
Little Redford Farm, Narberth, SA67 8TD
Tel: 01834-860599 **Fax:** 01834-861785
E-mail: brianpelkins@aol.com
Directors: B. Elkins (Prop)
Immediate Holding Company: CELTIC MILKING SYSTEMS LIMITED
Registration no: 04299554 **Date established:** 2009
No.of Employees: 1 - 10 **Product Groups:** 41

Date of Accounts	Oct 10	Oct 09	Oct 08
Working Capital	-45	-75	-87
Fixed Assets	41	50	45
Current Assets	56	31	34

Jellyegg Art Gallery
The Old Town Hall High Street, Narberth, SA67 7AR
Tel: 01834-860061 **Fax:** 01834-860351
E-mail: sales@jellyegg.com
Website: http://www.jellyegg.com
Directors: K. Banister (Prop)
No.of Employees: 1 - 10 **Product Groups:** 22, 24

Jewson Ltd
Unit 1-4 Narberth Bridge Business Park, Narberth, SA67 8RA
Tel: 01834-860770 **Fax:** 01834-869242
Website: http://www.jewson.co.uk
Managers: C. Palmer (District Mgr)
Ultimate Holding Company: COMPAGNIE DE SAINT GOBAIN (FRANCE)
Immediate Holding Company: JEWSON LIMITED
Registration no: 00348407 **Date established:** 1939
Turnover: Over £1,000m **No.of Employees:** 1 - 10 **Product Groups:** 66

Date of Accounts	Dec 11	Dec 10	Dec 09
Sales Turnover	1606m	1547m	1485m
Pre Tax Profit/Loss	18m	100m	45m
Working Capital	-345m	-250m	-349m
Fixed Assets	496m	387m	461m
Current Assets	657m	1005m	1320m
Current Liabilities	66m	120m	64m

Keating Joinery Ltd
Unit 13-14 The Bridge, Narberth, SA67 8QZ
Tel: 01834-861676 **Fax:** 01834-861858
E-mail: keatingjoinery@aol.com
Website: http://www.keatingjoinery.co.uk
Directors: P. Keating (Dir)
Immediate Holding Company: KEATING JOINERY LIMITED
Registration no: 06544644 **Date established:** 2008
No.of Employees: 1 - 10 **Product Groups:** 25, 35

Date of Accounts	Oct 11	Oct 10	Oct 09
Working Capital	-18	-17	-17
Fixed Assets	66	72	80
Current Assets	29	43	28

Narberth Tractors
Station Yard, Narberth, SA67 8TY
Tel: 01834-860805 **Fax:** 01834- 860805
Directors: B. Vaughan (Prop)
Date established: 1976 **No.of Employees:** 1 - 10 **Product Groups:** 41

West Glamorgan

Neath

Blinds 2000
The Blinds Factory Croft Road, Neath, SA11 1RW
Tel: 01639-641589 **Fax:** 0800-068 8876
E-mail: rob@blinds2000.co.uk
Website: http://www.blinds2000.co.uk
Directors: R. Hutchins (Prop)
Turnover: Up to £250,000 **No.of Employees:** 1 - 10 **Product Groups:** 24, 30, 35

Briton Ferry Stevedoring Ltd
Giants Wharf Briton Ferry, Neath, SA11 2LP
Tel: 01639-825700 **Fax:** 01639-822912
E-mail: office@westlandcoal.orangehome.co.uk
Website: http://www.britonferryshipping.co.uk
Directors: D. Forey (Fin)
Immediate Holding Company: BRITON FERRY STEVEDORING LIMITED
Registration no: 04677174 **VAT No.:** GB 558 2684 05
Date established: 2003 **Turnover:** £1m - £2m **No.of Employees:** 1 - 10
Product Groups: 74

Date of Accounts	Aug 11	Aug 10	Aug 09
Working Capital	793	484	611
Current Assets	1m	766	915

Business Connect Neath Port Talbot

Britannic Way Llandarcy, Neath, SA10 6EL
Tel: 01792-817575 **Fax:** 01792-817098
E-mail: admin@bcnpt.co.uk
Website: http://www.bcnpt.co.uk
Directors: G. Kaminaris (MD)
Immediate Holding Company: BUSINESS CONNECT NEATH PORT TALBOT LIMITED
Registration no: 03181914 **Date established:** 1996
Turnover: £250,000 - £500,000 **No.of Employees:** 1 - 10
Product Groups: 80

Date of Accounts	Mar 11	Mar 10	Mar 09
Sales Turnover	365	389	495
Pre Tax Profit/Loss	-72	-93	-154
Working Capital	185	239	329
Fixed Assets	2	20	24
Current Assets	212	265	360
Current Liabilities	15	9	N/A

C S N Precision Engineering

Neath Abbey Road, Neath, SA10 7BR
Tel: 01639-644362 **Fax:** 01639-638596
E-mail: paul@csnprecision.co.uk
Website: http://www.csnprecision.co.uk
Bank(s): National Westminster Bank Plc
Directors: P. Newsham (Co Sec), T. Cloke (Ptnr), P. Newsham (Ptnr), B. Scott (Ptnr), A. Cloke (MD)
Immediate Holding Company: C. S. N. PRECISION ENGINEERING LIMITED
Registration no: 02245327 **VAT No.:** GB 422 7823 57
Date established: 1988 **Turnover:** £500,000 - £1m
No.of Employees: 11 - 20 **Product Groups:** 48

David Abbot Plant

18 Lucy Road, Neath, SA10 6RR
Tel: 07966-901999
E-mail: davidabbotplant@yahoo.co.uk
Website: http://www.DavidAbbotPlant.co.uk
Directors: D. Abbot (Ptnr)
No.of Employees: 1 - 10 **Product Groups:** 45, 67

Equipment Supply Services

Unit 15 Milland Road Industrial Estate, Neath, SA11 1NJ
Tel: 01639-635124 **Fax:** 01639-635124
E-mail: info@agrisprayers.co.uk
Website: http://www.agrisprayers.co.uk
Directors: S. Reilly (MD)
Immediate Holding Company: EQUIPMENT SUPPLY SERVICES LIMITED
Registration no: 04659132 **Date established:** 2003
No.of Employees: 1 - 10 **Product Groups:** 40, 41, 46, 67

European Telecom Solutions

11a Regent Street East, Neath, SA11 2RR
Tel: 08453-309800 **Fax:** 0845-330 8183
E-mail: enquiries@eurotels.info
Website: http://www.europeantelecomsolutions.co.uk
Managers: A. Davies (Ops Mgr)
No.of Employees: 1 - 10 **Product Groups:** 37, 48, 79

Hornbill Engineering Ltd

Unit 6a Darcy Business Park Llandarcy, Neath, SA10 6EJ
Tel: 01792-818111 **Fax:** 01792-321146
E-mail: info@hornbill.co.uk
Website: http://www.hornbill.co.uk
Directors: R. Scaplehorn (Dir), L. Dumayne (Co Sec)
Immediate Holding Company: HORNBILL CONTROLS LIMITED
Registration no: 02685618 **Date established:** 1992 **Turnover:** £2m - £5m
No.of Employees: 11 - 20 **Product Groups:** 38, 40, 84

E G Lewis & Co. Ltd

Tank Farm Road Llandarcy, Neath, SA10 6EN
Tel: 01792-323288 **Fax:** 01792-323255
E-mail: timl@eglewis.com
Website: http://www.eglewis.com
Bank(s): HSBC Bank plc
Directors: E. Lewis (MD)
Managers: J. Williams (Buyer)
Ultimate Holding Company: E. G. LEWIS HOLDINGS LIMITED
Immediate Holding Company: E.G. LEWIS & COMPANY LIMITED
Registration no: 01179246 **VAT No.:** GB 124 3397 80
Date established: 1974 **Turnover:** £2m - £5m **No.of Employees:** 51 - 100
Product Groups: 27, 48, 52

Date of Accounts	Jul 11	Jul 10	Jul 09
Sales Turnover	4m	11m	12m
Pre Tax Profit/Loss	186	321	275
Working Capital	516	1m	1m
Fixed Assets	249	203	288
Current Assets	1m	4m	4m
Current Liabilities	536	1m	2m

Neath Gun Shop

44 Briton Ferry Road, Neath, SA11 1AA
Tel: 01639-632768 **Fax:** 01639-761061
Directors: D. Moses (Prop)
Date established: 1986 **No.of Employees:** 1 - 10 **Product Groups:** 36, 39, 40

Nidum Precision Tooling Ltd

Neath Vale Supplier Park Resolven, Neath, SA11 4SR
Tel: 01639-710086 **Fax:** 01685-813350
E-mail: admin@nidum.co.uk
Website: http://www.nidum.co.uk
Directors: E. Mcconnell (MD)
Immediate Holding Company: NIDUM PRECISION TOOLING LIMITED
Registration no: 00706121 **Date established:** 1961 **Turnover:** £1m - £2m
No.of Employees: 21 - 50 **Product Groups:** 46

Date of Accounts	Aug 11	Aug 10	Aug 09
Working Capital	203	123	225
Fixed Assets	200	208	189
Current Assets	679	757	701

Pipeline Centre

Quay Road, Neath, SA11 1SN
Tel: 01639-636301 **Fax:** 01639-633488
E-mail: neath.k71@wolseley.co.uk
Website: http://www.wolseley.co.uk
Managers: G. Thomas (District Mgr), K. Hartshaw (District Mgr)
Ultimate Holding Company: Wolesely Centers P.L.C.
Turnover: £125m - £250m **No.of Employees:** 11 - 20
Product Groups: 36, 66

Projectworld Ltd

Morvern Works Church Street, Briton Ferry, Neath, SA11 2JP
Tel: 01639-812332 **Fax:** 01639-812496
E-mail: info@projectworld.co.uk
Website: http://www.projectworld.co.uk
Directors: D. Mcdonald (Dir)
Immediate Holding Company: PROJECTWORLD LIMITED
Registration no: 03730338 **VAT No.:** GB 729 0236 41
Date established: 1999 **Turnover:** £500,000 - £1m
No.of Employees: 1 - 10 **Product Groups:** 32, 37, 46

Date of Accounts	Mar 11	Mar 10	Mar 09
Working Capital	25	25	27
Fixed Assets	1	1	1
Current Assets	72	87	100

Safety Letter Box Company Ltd

Unit B Milland Road Industrial Estate, Neath, SA11 1NJ
Tel: 01639-633525 **Fax:** 01639-646359
E-mail: sales@safetyletterbox.com
Website: http://www.safetyletterbox.com
Bank(s): Lloyds TSB Bank plc
Directors: D. Brown (Fin), A. Orrells (MD)
Managers: M. Cook (Comptroller)
Immediate Holding Company: SAFETY LETTER BOX COMPANY LIMITED
Registration no: 01978795 **VAT No.:** GB 438 6751 18
Date established: 1986 **Turnover:** £1m - £2m **No.of Employees:** 21 - 50
Product Groups: 35, 36, 40, 44, 67

Date of Accounts	Apr 12	Apr 11	Apr 10
Working Capital	666	523	603
Fixed Assets	2m	2m	2m
Current Assets	958	749	802

Sandvick Osprey Ltd

Milland Road, Neath, SA11 1NJ
Tel: 01639-634121 **Fax:** 01639-630100
Website: http://www.ospreymetals.co.uk
Bank(s): Barclays
Directors: R. Parker (MD), M. Kearns (Sales)
Managers: P. Williams (Fin Mgr), D. Jackson (Tech Serv Mgr), A. Ogilvy (Mktg Serv Mgr), G. Rudland (Purch Mgr)
Ultimate Holding Company: SANDVIK AB (SWEDEN)
Immediate Holding Company: SANDVIK OSPREY LIMITED
Registration no: 01189998 **VAT No.:** GB 124 6687 56
Date established: 1974 **Turnover:** £20m - £50m
No.of Employees: 51 - 100 **Product Groups:** 32, 34, 48, 66

Date of Accounts	Dec 11	Dec 10	Dec 09
Sales Turnover	21m	15m	10m
Pre Tax Profit/Loss	5m	3m	2m
Working Capital	4m	2m	1m
Fixed Assets	4m	3m	2m
Current Assets	8m	4m	3m
Current Liabilities	3m	1m	970

T R W Steering Systems Ltd

Resolven, Neath, SA11 4HN
Tel: 01639-665000 **Fax:** 01639-665350
E-mail: mark.james@trw.com
Website: http://www.trw.com
Bank(s): Barclays, 54 Lombard St, London
Directors: T. Neudegg (Fin), R. Bull (I.T. Dir), B. Ward (MD), M. James (Dir)
Managers: R. Goodhand (I.T. Exec), P. Emery (Purch Mgr), P. Creutzberg (Personnel), B. Macey, D. Baker, G. Callum, G. Clarke, G. Cullum, J. Walters, P. Tomlinson
Immediate Holding Company: TRW STEERING SYSTEMS LIMITED
Registration no: 00228191 **VAT No.:** GB 196 2343 47
Date established: 1928 **Turnover:** £75m - £125m
No.of Employees: 501 - 1000 **Product Groups:** 35, 39

Thomas Elliot Associates

6 High Street Cwmgwrach, Neath, SA11 5SY
Tel: 0845-500 5682 **Fax:** 05601-508594
E-mail: admin@thomaselliotassociates.co.uk
Website: http://www.thomaselliotassociates.co.uk
Directors: C. Pavett (Fin)
Immediate Holding Company: VALLEY ACCOUNTANTS LIMITED
Registration no: 06382791 **Date established:** 2007
Turnover: £250,000 - £500,000 **No.of Employees:** 1 - 10
Product Groups: 44, 80

Date of Accounts	Mar 11	Sep 09	Sep 08
Working Capital	-24	-12	4
Current Assets	10	6	19

Wernick Buildings Ltd

Nidum Works Neath Abbey Business Park, Neath Abbey, Neath, SA10 7DS
Tel: 01792-321222 **Fax:** 01792-321400
E-mail: eddie.shaw@wernick.co.uk
Website: http://www.wernick.co.uk
Directors: A. King (MD), S. Potter (Fin)
Managers: K. Lewis (Sales Prom Mgr), L. Fennell (Mktg Serv Mgr)
Ultimate Holding Company: WERNICK GROUP (HOLDINGS) LIMITED
Immediate Holding Company: WERNICK BUILDINGS LIMITED
Registration no: 00414489 **Date established:** 1946
Turnover: £10m - £20m **No.of Employees:** 51 - 100 **Product Groups:** 35, 52

Date of Accounts	Dec 11	Dec 10	Dec 09
Sales Turnover	15m	17m	21m
Pre Tax Profit/Loss	504	587	951
Working Capital	5m	5m	5m
Fixed Assets	1m	2m	2m
Current Assets	8m	8m	7m
Current Liabilities	657	1m	1m

Dyfed

Newcastle Emlyn

Celtic Country Wines

Windy Rise Winery Beulah, Newcastle Emlyn, SA38 9QJ
Tel: 01239-858888 **Fax:** 01559-370105
E-mail: nshipp@celticwines.co.uk
Website: http://www.celticwines.co.uk
Directors: N. Shipp (Ptnr)
Date established: 2004 **No.of Employees:** 1 - 10 **Product Groups:** 35

Gwent

Newport

A R Adams & Son Ltd

Pill Bank Works Coomassie Street, Newport, NP20 2US
Tel: 01633-262060 **Fax:** 01633-258295
Directors: M. Beardmore (MD), R. Beere (Fin)
Immediate Holding Company: A.R. ADAMS & SON LIMITED
Registration no: 02659391 **VAT No.:** GB 542 9623 33
Date established: 1991 **Turnover:** £250,000 - £500,000
No.of Employees: 1 - 10 **Product Groups:** 40, 48

Date of Accounts	Mar 11	Mar 10	Mar 09
Working Capital	-7	-20	-19
Fixed Assets	N/A	N/A	1
Current Assets	35	27	27

Advanced Elastomer Systems Ltd

Corporation Road, Newport, NP19 4XF
Tel: 01633-678000 **Fax:** 01633- 282560
E-mail: peta.finch@santoprene.com
Website: http://www.santoprene.com
Bank(s): National Westminster Bank Plc
Directors: A. Clarke (Fin), P. Finch (Dir)
Ultimate Holding Company: SOLUTIA INC (USA)
Immediate Holding Company: ADVANCED ELASTOMER SYSTEMS LIMITED
Registration no: 02512288 **VAT No.:** GB 569 7586 64
Date established: 1990 **Turnover:** £75m - £125m
No.of Employees: 51 - 100 **Product Groups:** 31

Date of Accounts	Dec 11	Dec 10	Dec 09
Sales Turnover	95m	80m	52m
Pre Tax Profit/Loss	16m	19m	6m
Working Capital	38m	36m	22m
Fixed Assets	10m	10m	10m
Current Assets	44m	41m	26m
Current Liabilities	3m	2m	2m

Alcoplan

65 Marlborough Road, Newport, NP19 0BY
Tel: 01633-211764 **Fax:** 01633-843014
E-mail: mike@hwd-alcoplan.co.uk
Website: http://www.hwd-alcoplan.co.uk
Bank(s): Barclays
Directors: A. Daniels (Ch), M. Daniel (MD), E. Dunn (Sales)
Ultimate Holding Company: H.W.D. SHOPFITTERS LIMITED
Immediate Holding Company: ALCOPLAN LIMITED
Registration no: 00962215 **VAT No.:** GB 682 6349 06
Date established: 1969 **Turnover:** £1m - £2m **No.of Employees:** 21 - 50
Product Groups: 35, 36, 49

Alpha Fire Protection

71 Squires Gate Rogerstone, Newport, NP10 0BQ
Tel: 01633-891007 **Fax:** 01633-891441
Directors: W. Evans (Fin), G. Anzani (MD)
Immediate Holding Company: ALPHA FIRE PROTECTION (SOUTH WALES) LIMITED
Registration no: 03408343 **Date established:** 1997
No.of Employees: 1 - 10 **Product Groups:** 38, 42

Date of Accounts	Aug 11	Aug 10	Aug 07
Working Capital	7	11	25
Fixed Assets	14	15	5
Current Assets	121	111	107

Apex Computer Services Wales Ltd

Unit 2 St Michaels Court Church Street, Newport, NP20 2BY
Tel: 01633-215123 **Fax:** 01633-215124
E-mail: support@apexcs.co.uk
Website: http://www.apexcs.co.uk
Directors: M. Green (Dir)
Immediate Holding Company: APEX COMPUTER SERVICES (WALES) LIMITED
Registration no: 02909178 **Date established:** 1994
Turnover: Up to £250,000 **No.of Employees:** 1 - 10 **Product Groups:** 36, 37, 44, 67, 79, 80, 81, 84

Date of Accounts	Aug 11	Aug 10	Aug 09
Working Capital	-10	-8	13
Fixed Assets	144	121	128
Current Assets	78	81	105
Current Liabilities	N/A	73	N/A

Aquascan International Ltd

Aquascan House Hill Street, Newport, NP20 1LZ
Tel: 01633-841117 **Fax:** 01633-254829
E-mail: info@aquascan.co.uk
Website: http://www.aquascan.co.uk
Directors: J. Williams (MD)
Immediate Holding Company: AQUASCAN INTERNATIONAL LIMITED
Registration no: 01670834 **VAT No.:** GB 378 9631 90
Date established: 1982 **Turnover:** £250,000 - £500,000
No.of Employees: 1 - 10 **Product Groups:** 37, 38, 68

Date of Accounts	Nov 11	Nov 10	Nov 09
Working Capital	76	103	59
Fixed Assets	24	34	38
Current Assets	140	135	90

Arch Engineering Ltd

East Side North Dock Alexandra Docks, Newport, NP20 2NP
Tel: 01633-264154 **Fax:** 01633-264154
Directors: K. Casey (Fin)
Ultimate Holding Company: MARINE SHIPPING SERVICES (UK) LIMITED
Immediate Holding Company: ARCH ENGINEERING CO (NEWPORT) LIMITED(THE)
Registration no: 00434945 **VAT No.:** GB 134 6083 81
Date established: 1947 **Turnover:** Up to £250,000
No.of Employees: 1 - 10 **Product Groups:** 48

Date of Accounts	Dec 10	Dec 09	Dec 08
Working Capital	25	26	27
Fixed Assets	16	19	22
Current Assets	57	50	46

Ariel Machine Products Ltd
Yew Tree Lane Caerleon, Newport, NP18 1LL
Tel: 01633-420405 **Fax:** 01633-430072
Directors: S. Thomas (Fin), B. Thomas (MD)
Immediate Holding Company: ARIEL MACHINE PRODUCTS LIMITED
Registration no: 04562589 **VAT No.:** GB 133 4173 96
Date established: 2002 **Turnover:** Up to £250,000
No.of Employees: 1 - 10 **Product Groups:** 48

Date of Accounts	Oct 11	Oct 10	Oct 09
Working Capital	2	-9	-7
Fixed Assets	102	19	28
Current Assets	45	38	53

Asset International Ltd
Stephenson Street, Newport, NP19 4XH
Tel: 01633-273081 **Fax:** 01633-290519
E-mail: sales@assetint.co.uk
Website: http://www.assetint.co.uk
Bank(s): Barclays Bank PLC
Directors: S. Thomas (MD)
Ultimate Holding Company: HILL & SMITH HOLDINGS PLC
Immediate Holding Company: ASSET INTERNATIONAL LIMITED
Registration no: 01983393 **VAT No.:** GB 433 2182 81
Date established: 1986 **Turnover:** £10m - £20m
No.of Employees: 51 - 100 **Product Groups:** 30, 35, 36, 38, 39, 41, 42, 48, 66

Date of Accounts	Dec 11	Dec 10	Dec 09
Sales Turnover	13m	11m	9m
Pre Tax Profit/Loss	1m	503	645
Working Capital	3m	3m	3m
Fixed Assets	1m	1m	2m
Current Assets	8m	6m	5m
Current Liabilities	1m	725	720

Avana Bakeries
Wern Trading Estate Rogerstone, Newport, NP10 9YB
Tel: 01633-644600 **Fax:** 01633-466466
E-mail: avanareception@rhm.com
Website: http://www.avanabakeries.co.uk
Bank(s): Barclays
Directors: S. Wilbraham (Co Sec), J. Blythe (Fin)
Managers: A. Marshall (Mktg Serv Mgr), G. Swanson (Mgr)
Ultimate Holding Company: PREMIER FOODS PLC
Immediate Holding Company: AB OLD CO LIMITED
Registration no: 00815338 **VAT No.:** GB 133 4152 07
Date established: 1964 **Turnover:** £1m - £2m
No.of Employees: 501 - 1000 **Product Groups:** 20

Date of Accounts	Dec 11	Dec 10	Dec 09
Working Capital	7m	7m	7m
Current Assets	7m	7m	7m

Aviza Technology UK Ltd
Ringland Way, Newport, NP18 2TA
Tel: 01633-414000 **Fax:** 01633-414141
E-mail: sales@trikon.com
Website: http://www.avizatechnology.com
Managers: P. O'connor (Comptroller)
Ultimate Holding Company: AVIZA TECHNOLOGY INC (USA)
Immediate Holding Company: TRIKON EQUIPMENTS LIMITED
Registration no: 07037852 **Date established:** 1981
Turnover: £20m - £50m **No.of Employees:** 101 - 250
Product Groups: 40, 47

Date of Accounts	Dec 09
Sales Turnover	4m
Pre Tax Profit/Loss	4m

Bluegg Creative Ltd
Old Custom House 74 Lower Dock Street, Newport, NP20 1EH
Tel: 01633-262670
E-mail: studio@bluegg.co.uk
Website: http://www.bluegg.co.uk
Directors: M. Jordan (Dir)
Immediate Holding Company: BLUEGG CREATIVE LIMITED
Registration no: 05266171 **Date established:** 2004
Turnover: £250,000 - £500,000 **No.of Employees:** 1 - 10
Product Groups: 81

Date of Accounts	Mar 12	Mar 11	Mar 10
Working Capital	-15	-18	-18
Fixed Assets	19	24	29
Current Assets	70	39	54

Blueygreen Ltd
PO Box 2000, Newport, NP19 9ZG
Tel: 08451-297270
E-mail: blueygreen@email.ro
Website: http://www.blueygreen.com
Directors: S. Malpas (Dir)
Managers: A. Hassan (Mgr)
Immediate Holding Company: BLUEYGREEN LIMITED
Registration no: 04445238 **Date established:** 2002
Turnover: Up to £250,000 **No.of Employees:** 1 - 10 **Product Groups:** 44

Border Industrial Services (T/A Border Industrial Services Ltd)
Unit 1 Darren Buildings Prince of Wales Industrial, Abercarn, Newport, NP11 5AR
Tel: 01495-237888 **Fax:** 01495-237900
E-mail: sales@borderbobcat.com
Website: http://www.borderbobcat.com
Directors: C. Cookes (Fin), H. Edwards (Sales)
Immediate Holding Company: BORDER INDUSTRIAL SERVICES LIMITED
Registration no: 02014006 **Date established:** 1986 **Turnover:** £1m - £2m
No.of Employees: 1 - 10 **Product Groups:** 07, 29, 38, 39, 40, 41, 42, 45, 46, 48, 61, 66, 67, 83

Date of Accounts	Sep 11	Sep 10	Sep 09
Working Capital	49	40	77
Fixed Assets	178	204	151
Current Assets	775	453	317

B-SafeUK Ltd
77 Power Street, Newport, NP20 5FS
Tel: 01633-673372
E-mail: inquiry@b-safeuk.co.uk
Website: http://www.b-safeuk.co.uk
Registration no: 04389239 **No.of Employees:** 1 - 10 **Product Groups:** 38, 85

Burt Boulton & Haywood Ltd
Alexandra Docks, Newport, NP20 2WA
Tel: 01633-235800 **Fax:** 01633-235835
E-mail: enquiries@bbhpreservingwood.co.uk
Website: http://www.bbhpreservingwood.co.uk
Bank(s): Merita
Directors: W. Clason (MD)
Managers: C. Watkins (Sales Prom Mgr), D. Clason, L. Perkins (Tech Serv Mgr)
Ultimate Holding Company: METSALIITTO COOPERATIVE (FINLAND)
Immediate Holding Company: BURT BOULTON & HAYWOOD LIMITED
Registration no: 03540326 **Date established:** 1998
Turnover: £10m - £20m **No.of Employees:** 21 - 50 **Product Groups:** 39, 66

Date of Accounts	Dec 11	Dec 10	Dec 09
Sales Turnover	11m	9m	10m
Pre Tax Profit/Loss	485	-195	-146
Working Capital	1m	865	930
Fixed Assets	2m	2m	3m
Current Assets	5m	4m	5m
Current Liabilities	622	431	534

Cambrian Fuelcard Services Ltd
West Market Street, Newport, NP20 2AU
Tel: 01633-677677 **Fax:** 01633-677688
E-mail: sales@fuel-card.co.uk
Website: http://www.fuel-card.co.uk
Directors: D. Stockton (MD)
Immediate Holding Company: CAMBRIAN FUELCARD SERVICES LIMITED
Registration no: 01259685 **Date established:** 1976
Turnover: £250,000 - £500,000 **No.of Employees:** 1 - 10
Product Groups: 30

Date of Accounts	Dec 11	Dec 10	Dec 09
Working Capital	380	359	355
Fixed Assets	133	145	149
Current Assets	1m	1m	1m
Current Liabilities	N/A	16	N/A

Camrasonic Ltd
3 St Michaels Court Church Street, Newport, NP20 2BY
Tel: 01633-267796 **Fax:** 01633-222706
E-mail: mark.ingleson@camrasonic.co.uk
Website: http://www.openviewgroup.com
Directors: P. Whistance (Co Sec), M. Ingleson (Dir), M. Ingleson (MD)
Managers: M. Thomas (Sales Prom Mgr), S. Westacott (Sales Admin)
Ultimate Holding Company: OPENVIEW GROUP LIMITED
Immediate Holding Company: CAMRASONIC LIMITED
Registration no: 01786930 **VAT No.:** GB 394 0001 81
Date established: 1984 **Turnover:** £1m - £2m **No.of Employees:** 1 - 10
Product Groups: 37, 40

Date of Accounts	Jul 11	Jul 10	Jul 09
Sales Turnover	N/A	N/A	1m
Pre Tax Profit/Loss	N/A	N/A	3
Working Capital	290	773	477
Fixed Assets	1	4	6
Current Assets	976	989	842
Current Liabilities	N/A	N/A	86

Celtic Blinds
2 Tynewydd Terrace Newbridge, Newport, NP11 4LU
Tel: 01495-249098 **Fax:** 01495-249098
E-mail: mail@celticblinds.co.uk
Website: http://www.celticblinds.co.uk
Directors: I. Richards (Prop)
Date established: 1994 **No.of Employees:** 1 - 10 **Product Groups:** 24, 63, 66

Celtic Fire Protection Co.
5 Llwynderi Road, Newport, NP20 4LW
Tel: 01633-266207 **Fax:** 01633-266207
Directors: H. Clement (MD)
Immediate Holding Company: CELTIC FIRE PROTECTION LIMITED
Registration no: 01674917 **Date established:** 1982
No.of Employees: 1 - 10 **Product Groups:** 38, 42

Celtic Process Control Ltd
Celtic House Langland Way, Newport, NP19 4PT
Tel: 01633-280482 **Fax:** 01633-282314
E-mail: admin@celticprocesscontrol.co.uk
Website: http://www.celticprocesscontrol.co.uk
Bank(s): Barclays
Directors: D. Morgan (MD)
Managers: B. Sterry (Purch Mgr), C. Harcombe (Fin Mgr)
Immediate Holding Company: CELTIC PROCESS CONTROL LIMITED
Registration no: 01592309 **Date established:** 1981
No.of Employees: 21 - 50 **Product Groups:** 38

Date of Accounts	Mar 11	Mar 10	Mar 09
Working Capital	541	479	412
Fixed Assets	73	85	109
Current Assets	812	1m	820

Color Steels Ltd
Blackvein Industrial Estate Cross Keys, Newport, NP11 7YD
Tel: 01495-279100 **Fax:** 01495-271456
Website: http://www.colorsteels.co.uk
Bank(s): National Westminster Bank Plc
Directors: L. Coates (MD), L. Norman (MD), W. Evans (Dir), R. Rickets (Sales & Mktg), J. Williams (MD), A. Smith (MD), R. Rider (Fin)
Managers: A. James
Ultimate Holding Company: CORUS GROUP LIMITED
Immediate Holding Company: COLOR STEELS LIMITED
Registration no: 00948598 **Date established:** 1969
Turnover: £20m - £50m **No.of Employees:** 101 - 250 **Product Groups:** 34

Colorpro Systems Ltd
Whitehead Estate Docks Way, Newport, NP20 2NW
Tel: 01633-223854 **Fax:** 01633-220175
E-mail: info@colorgroup.co.uk
Website: http://www.colorgroup.co.uk
Bank(s): Lloyds TSB Bank plc
Directors: T. Hosken (Dir), M. Procter (MD), M. Proctor (MD), D. Stanley (Fin)
Managers: A. Downey (Sales Prom Mgr), D. Borston (Sales Prom Mgr), T. Downey (Sales Prom Mgr)
Ultimate Holding Company: AIRBORNE CORPORATION (THE) (BAHAMAS)
Immediate Holding Company: Colorgroup Ltd
Registration no: 02793284 **VAT No.:** GB 615 7772 21
Date established: 1992 **Turnover:** £5m - £10m **No.of Employees:** 21 - 50
Product Groups: 34, 35

Date of Accounts	Sep 09	Sep 08	Mar 08
Sales Turnover	N/A	5m	8m
Pre Tax Profit/Loss	N/A	755	200
Working Capital	4	4	-769
Fixed Assets	N/A	N/A	148
Current Assets	4	4	6m
Current Liabilities	N/A	N/A	3m

Corus U K Ltd
Llanwern Works, Newport, NP19 4QZ
Tel: 01663-290011 **Fax:** 023-8023 3096
E-mail: enquiries@cyrus-engineering.com
Website: http://www.corus-servicecentres.com
Managers: S. McCloy (Chief Mgr)
Ultimate Holding Company: TATA STEEL LIMITED (INDIA)
Immediate Holding Company: CORUS GROUP LIMITED
Registration no: 03811373 **VAT No.:** GB 238 7122 60
Date established: 1999 **No.of Employees:** 1 - 10 **Product Groups:** 34, 48

Cory Bros Shipping Agnecy Ltd
Alexandra Dock, Newport, NP20 2NP
Tel: 01633-266351 **Fax:** 01633-256915
E-mail: corynewport@cory.co.uk
Website: http://www.cory.co.uk
Directors: M. Harrison (MD)
Managers: A. Lewis (Chief Mgr), P. James (Chief Mgr), S. Gibbons (), L. Williams ()
Immediate Holding Company: JP SHIPPING SERVICES LIMITED
Registration no: 05653202 **VAT No.:** GB 244 0497 69
Date established: 1971 **Turnover:** £2m - £5m **No.of Employees:** 1 - 10
Product Groups: 76

Date of Accounts	Mar 11	Mar 10	Mar 09
Sales Turnover	1m	858	2m
Pre Tax Profit/Loss	8	-138	-336
Working Capital	-336	-387	-289
Fixed Assets	440	492	556
Current Assets	598	343	653
Current Liabilities	135	76	152

D B Engineering Ltd
Rock Wharf Mill Parade, Newport, NP20 2JR
Tel: 01633-246018 **Fax:** 01633-259079
E-mail: prichai@aol.com
Website: http://www.dbengltd.com
Directors: B. Pritchard (MD)
Immediate Holding Company: D.B. ENGINEERING LIMITED
Registration no: 01832063 **Date established:** 1984
Turnover: £500,000 - £1m **No.of Employees:** 11 - 20
Product Groups: 35, 48

Date of Accounts	Jun 11	Jun 10	Jun 09
Working Capital	165	156	52
Fixed Assets	23	31	171
Current Assets	354	294	242

D S Smith Celtic Ltd
Rush Drive Pen Y Fan Industrial Estate, Crumlin, Newport, NP11 3EJ
Tel: 01495-248255 **Fax:** 01495-247675
E-mail: head.office@dssp.com
Website: http://www.dssmith-packaging.com
Managers: J. Newton (Sales Prom Mgr), J. Salmon (Mgr)
No.of Employees: 21 - 50 **Product Groups:** 27

Date Electronic Supplies
Lilleshall Street, Newport, NP19 0FB
Tel: 01633-259666 **Fax:** 01633-266939
E-mail: alwyn.treharne@pavecost.com
Website: http://www.dateelectronicsupplies.co.uk
Bank(s): National Westminster Bank Plc
Directors: A. Treharne (Fin)
Immediate Holding Company: PAVECOST LIMITED
Registration no: 01426483 **VAT No.:** GB 302 9068 79
Date established: 1979 **Turnover:** £1m - £2m **No.of Employees:** 21 - 50
Product Groups: 35, 54, 67

Date of Accounts	Oct 11	Oct 10	Oct 09
Working Capital	579	537	516
Fixed Assets	81	83	86
Current Assets	772	614	609

Diesel Injection Systems
Mill Parade, Newport, NP20 2JQ
Tel: 01633-221366 **Fax:** 01633-256783
Directors: R. Thorpe (Prop)
Registration no: 04575405 **Date established:** 2002
No.of Employees: 1 - 10 **Product Groups:** 40

Date of Accounts	Sep 07	Sep 06	Sep 05
Working Capital	-38	-64	-103
Fixed Assets	63	167	285
Current Assets	95	80	94

Dolphin Stairlifts South Wales Ltd
Unit 12 Crawford Trading Estate Crawford Street, Newport, NP19 7AY
Tel: 01633-223121 **Fax:** 01633-221805
E-mail: j.pearce@dolphinlifts.co.uk
Website: http://www.dolphinlifts.com
Directors: J. Pearce (Dir)
Immediate Holding Company: DOLPHIN LIFTS (S WALES) LIMITED
Registration no: 04546621 **Date established:** 2002
No.of Employees: 1 - 10 **Product Groups:** 35, 39, 45

Date of Accounts	Oct 11	Oct 10	Oct 09
Working Capital	112	155	182
Fixed Assets	24	34	24
Current Assets	197	227	277

E T B- Exhausts Tyres & Battery's Worcester Ltd
Frederick Street, Newport, NP20 2XJ
Tel: 01633-266435 **Fax:** 01633-266435
Website: http://www.etbtyres.co.uk
Managers: W. Brown (Mgr)
Immediate Holding Company: ETB LTD
No.of Employees: 1 - 10 **Product Groups:** 29, 68

R Edmunds Sectional Buildings
Lower Malthouse Farm Malthouse Lane, Caerleon, Newport, NP18 3SL
Tel: 01633-420004 **Fax:** 01633-420004
E-mail: enquiries@bobedmunds.co.uk
Website: http://www.comptonbuildings.co.uk

see next page

***R Edmunds Sectional Buildings** - Cont'd*

Directors: B. Edmunds (Prop)
No.of Employees: 1 - 10 **Product Groups:** 25, 33, 35, 66

Eltham Lewis Associates

Phoenix Business Park Telford Street, Newport, NP19 0LW
Tel: 01633-215001 **Fax:** 01633-215001
E-mail: support@scan4u.co.uk
Website: http://www.scan4u.co.uk
Directors: N. Davies (Dir)
Immediate Holding Company: ELTHAM LEWIS ASSOCIATES LIMITED
Registration no: 04461083 **VAT No.:** GB 713 1380 72
Date established: 2002 **Turnover:** £250,000 - £500,000
No.of Employees: 1 - 10 **Product Groups:** 26, 27, 37, 38, 44, 64, 65, 67, 72, 80, 81

Date of Accounts	Aug 11	Aug 10	Aug 09
Working Capital	31	36	39
Fixed Assets	42	61	56
Current Assets	80	117	79

Enersys Ltd

Stephenson Street, Newport, NP19 4XJ
Tel: 01633-590310 **Fax:** 01633-281787
E-mail: lee.wood@uk.enersysinc.com
Website: http://www.enersys.com
Bank(s): Barclays
Managers: H. Leonard (Plant), S. Hopkins (Personnel), M. Maine, J. Gibbon, K. Stockley (Tech Serv Mgr)
Ultimate Holding Company: ENERSYS INC (USA)
Immediate Holding Company: ENERSYS LTD.
Registration no: 00731261 **Date established:** 1962
Turnover: £75m - £125m **No.of Employees:** 251 - 500
Product Groups: 37, 47

Date of Accounts	Mar 12	Mar 11	Mar 10
Sales Turnover	91m	93m	82m
Pre Tax Profit/Loss	5m	4m	4m
Working Capital	54m	51m	53m
Fixed Assets	21m	22m	18m
Current Assets	141m	150m	122m
Current Liabilities	6m	5m	7m

Firequip Firefighting Equipment

1 Sunnybank Bassaleg, Newport, NP10 8JP
Tel: 01633-897383 **Fax:** 01633-894373
Directors: D. Ball (Prop)
Date established: 1998 **No.of Employees:** 1 - 10 **Product Groups:** 38, 42

Freelance Scale Services

Spencer House Alderney Street, Newport, NP20 5NH
Tel: 01633-822022 **Fax:** 01633- 822022
Directors: T. Gibbon (Prop)
Registration no: 05315742 **Date established:** 2004
No.of Employees: 1 - 10 **Product Groups:** 38, 42

Geartrodes South Wales Ltd

Units 1-2 East Bank Road Felnex Industrial Estate, Newport, NP19 4PP
Tel: 01633-283112 **Fax:** 01633-280084
E-mail: sales@geartrodesweldingsupplies.co.uk
Website: http://www.geartrodesweldingsupplies.co.uk
Managers: J. Russell (District Mgr)
Immediate Holding Company: GEAR-TRODES (SOUTH WALES) LIMITED
Registration no: 01402329 **Date established:** 1978
No.of Employees: 1 - 10 **Product Groups:** 46

Date of Accounts	Oct 11	Oct 10	Oct 09
Working Capital	2m	1m	2m
Fixed Assets	413	383	107
Current Assets	2m	2m	2m

Glamair Supplies Ltd

Lewis House Alexandra Docks, Newport, NP20 2NP
Tel: 01633-221300 **Fax:** 01633-221600
E-mail: sales@glamair.co.uk
Website: http://www.glamair.co.uk
Directors: S. Martin (MD)
Immediate Holding Company: GLAMAIR SUPPLIES LIMITED
Registration no: 06781955 **Date established:** 2009
Turnover: £250,000 - £500,000 **No.of Employees:** 1 - 10
Product Groups: 30, 32, 36, 38, 39, 40, 45, 47, 52, 67, 68, 83

Date of Accounts	May 11	Jan 12	Jan 10
Working Capital	50	61	39
Fixed Assets	41	39	45
Current Assets	98	139	106

Gledhill Building Products

Unit 12 Wern Trading Estate Rogerstone, Newport, NP10 9FQ
Tel: 01633-896299 **Fax:** 01633-896300
Website: http://www.gledhill.net
Managers: I. Roe (Mgr)
Immediate Holding Company: GWSL Realisations Ltd
Registration no: 01049873 **Date established:** 1972
No.of Employees: 1 - 10 **Product Groups:** 35, 40, 52

H W D Shopfitters Ltd

65 Marlborough Road, Newport, NP19 0BY
Tel: 01633-211761 **Fax:** 01633-843014
E-mail: mike@alcoplan.co.uk
Website: http://www.hwd-alcoplan.co.uk
Bank(s): Barclays
Directors: M. Daniels (Ch)
Immediate Holding Company: H.W.D. SHOPFITTERS LIMITED
Registration no: 00683226 **Date established:** 1961 **Turnover:** £1m - £2m
No.of Employees: 21 - 50 **Product Groups:** 25, 26

Date of Accounts	Dec 11	Dec 10	Dec 09
Working Capital	87	171	114
Fixed Assets	222	269	347
Current Assets	326	496	230

Industrial Automation & Control Ltd

Meadows Road Queensway Meadows Industrial Estate, Newport, NP19 4SS
Tel: 01633-293000 **Fax:** 01633-293030
E-mail: plewis@iac-ltd.co.uk
Website: http://www.iac-ltd.co.uk
Directors: P. Lewis (MD)
Managers: M. Lewis (Tech Serv Mgr), P. Howell (Sales Prom Mgr), R. Swidenbank (Buyer), K. Lewis (Personnel)
Immediate Holding Company: INDUSTRIAL AUTOMATION AND CONTROL LIMITED
Registration no: 01622878 **Date established:** 1982 **Turnover:** £5m - £10m
No.of Employees: 51 - 100 **Product Groups:** 37, 38, 39, 40, 44, 45

Date of Accounts	Mar 11	Mar 10	Mar 09
Sales Turnover	9m	5m	7m
Pre Tax Profit/Loss	302	-59	1m
Working Capital	3m	3m	3m
Fixed Assets	863	942	501
Current Assets	6m	4m	4m
Current Liabilities	989	342	646

Inner Space Designs

Norfolk Road, Newport, NP19 7SL
Tel: 01633-782505 **Fax:** 01633-782506
E-mail: info@innerspacedesigns.co.uk
Website: http://www.innerspacedesigns.co.uk
Directors: T. Williamson (Prop)
Immediate Holding Company: CHRIS WILLIAMSON CONSULTANCY SERVICES LTD
Registration no: 06902011 **Date established:** 2009
No.of Employees: 1 - 10 **Product Groups:** 24, 37, 52, 63, 66

Intellectual Property Office

Concept House Cardiff Road, Newport, NP10 8QQ
Tel: 01633-814000 **Fax:** 01633-811020
E-mail: information@ipo.gov.uk
Website: http://www.ipo.gov.uk
Directors: J. Cappock (Fin), J. Alty (Grp Chief Exec)
Managers: L. Smyth, R. Wilkinson
Ultimate Holding Company: An Exec Agency of Department of Trade & Industry
No.of Employees: 501 - 1000 **Product Groups:** 80, 87

D J Jenkins

Unit 5 Leeway Court, Leeway Industrial Estate, Newport, NP19 4SJ
Tel: 01633-278007 **Fax:** 01633-277677
E-mail: info@djjpackaging.com
Website: http://www.djjpackaging.com
Directors: D. Jenkins (Ptnr)
Date established: 1980 **No.of Employees:** 1 - 10 **Product Groups:** 38, 42

Jewson Ltd

Bolt Street, Newport, NP20 2TJ
Tel: 01633-264061 **Fax:** 01633-843275
E-mail: gareth.owens@jewson.co.uk
Website: http://www.jewson.co.uk
Managers: G. Owens (Mgr)
Ultimate Holding Company: COMPAGNIE DE SAINT GOBAIN (FRANCE)
Immediate Holding Company: JEWSON LIMITED
Registration no: 00348407 **VAT No.:** GB 394 1212 63
Date established: 1939 **Turnover:** £2m - £5m **No.of Employees:** 1 - 10
Product Groups: 66

Date of Accounts	Dec 11	Dec 10	Dec 09
Sales Turnover	1606m	1547m	1485m
Pre Tax Profit/Loss	18m	100m	45m
Working Capital	-345m	-250m	-349m
Fixed Assets	496m	387m	461m
Current Assets	657m	1005m	1320m
Current Liabilities	66m	120m	64m

Gerry Jones Transport Services Ltd

Unit 25 Darren Drive Prince of Wales Industrial Esta Abercarn, Newport, NP11 5AR
Tel: 01495-240402 **Fax:** 01495-249219
E-mail: gerry@gerryjones.co.uk
Website: http://www.gerryjones.co.uk
Directors: D. Jones (Chief Op Offcr), G. Jones (Prop), M. Jones (Sales & Mktg)
Managers: D. Callow (Fin Mgr)
Immediate Holding Company: GERRY JONES TRANSPORT SERVICES LIMITED
Registration no: 01624405 **Date established:** 1982 **Turnover:** £5m - £10m
No.of Employees: 51 - 100 **Product Groups:** 77

Date of Accounts	Mar 11	Mar 10	Mar 09
Sales Turnover	8m	6m	N/A
Pre Tax Profit/Loss	167	59	246
Working Capital	-120	300	656
Fixed Assets	4m	4m	4m
Current Assets	2m	2m	2m
Current Liabilities	1m	215	332

Kennametal

Lake Road Leeway Industrial Estate, Newport, NP19 4SR
Tel: 01633-636500 **Fax:** 01633-636501
E-mail: newport.info@kennametal.com
Website: http://www.kennametal.com
Bank(s): Barclays
Managers: J. Grainger, R. Oliver, J. Granger (Comptroller), J. Kiff (Buyer)
Immediate Holding Company: KENNAMETAL SINTEC KERAMIK (UK) LIMITED
Registration no: 01316012 **VAT No.:** GB 484 1296 30
Date established: 1977 **Turnover:** £1m - £2m **No.of Employees:** 51 - 100
Product Groups: 31, 40, 48

Date of Accounts	Jun 11	Jun 10	Jun 09
Sales Turnover	N/A	2m	7m
Pre Tax Profit/Loss	27	188	508
Working Capital	6m	6m	4m
Fixed Assets	N/A	N/A	2m
Current Assets	6m	7m	5m
Current Liabilities	1	56	369

Kier Western

Cathedral Chambers Stow Hill, Newport, NP20 4SY
Tel: 01633-244955 **Fax:** 01633-244107
E-mail: info@newport.kier.co.uk
Website: http://www.kier.co.uk
Bank(s): Natwest
Directors: M. Osborne (Dir)
Registration no: 02099533 **Date established:** 1961
No.of Employees: 11 - 20 **Product Groups:** 52

Klockner Pentaplast Ltd

Unit 33-34 Fern Close Pen-Y-Fan Industrial Estate, Crumlin, Newport, NP11 3EH
Tel: 01495-241800 **Fax:** 01495-241811
E-mail: g.peacock@kpfilms.com
Website: http://www.kpfilms.com
Bank(s): Lloyds TSB Bank plc
Directors: G. Peacock (MD)
Managers: D. Bateman (Tech Serv Mgr), J. Davies (Purch Mgr), J. Myers (Fin Mgr)
Ultimate Holding Company: KLEOPATRA LUX 1 SARL (LUXEMBOURG)
Immediate Holding Company: KLOCKNER PENTAPLAST LIMITED
Registration no: 03676460 **Date established:** 1998
Turnover: £20m - £50m **No.of Employees:** 51 - 100 **Product Groups:** 27, 30, 48

Date of Accounts	Sep 11	Sep 10	Sep 09
Sales Turnover	37m	34m	24m
Pre Tax Profit/Loss	11m	4m	27m
Working Capital	143m	135m	133m
Fixed Assets	7m	8m	8m
Current Assets	151m	145m	138m
Current Liabilities	2m	2m	679

L & P Plastics

108 Alexandra Road, Newport, NP20 2JG
Tel: 01633-214654 **Fax:** 01633-214654
Directors: L. Boddy (Prop)
Date established: 1981 **No.of Employees:** 1 - 10 **Product Groups:** 38, 42

John Liscombe Ltd

Mariner Way Felnex Industrial Estate, Newport, NP19 4PQ
Tel: 01633-284100 **Fax:** 01633-284125
E-mail: sales@liscombe.co.uk
Website: http://www.liscombe.co.uk
Directors: R. Morris (Dir)
Immediate Holding Company: JOHN LISCOMBE LIMITED
Registration no: 00144689 **VAT No.:** GB 134 2145 08
Date established: 2016 **Turnover:** £10m - £20m
No.of Employees: 51 - 100 **Product Groups:** 24

Date of Accounts	Dec 11	Dec 10	Dec 09
Sales Turnover	17m	15m	12m
Pre Tax Profit/Loss	235	316	91
Working Capital	3m	3m	3m
Fixed Assets	771	678	661
Current Assets	9m	8m	5m
Current Liabilities	3m	2m	2m

Lithgow Associates

Magor Road Langstone, Newport, NP18 2JX
Tel: 01633-411800 **Fax:** 01633-411810
Website: http://www.lithgow.co.uk
Directors: P. Morgan (Snr Part)
Immediate Holding Company: LITHGOW ASSOCIATES LIMITED
Registration no: 02488420 **Date established:** 1990
Turnover: Up to £250,000 **No.of Employees:** 1 - 10 **Product Groups:** 46, 48

Lloyds Fabrications

Unit 2 Star Trading Estate, Ponthir, Newport, NP18 1PQ
Tel: 01633-430378 **Fax:** 01633-430378
E-mail: sales@lloydsfabrications.co.uk
Website: http://www.lloydsfabrications.co.uk
Directors: S. Pocock (Prop)
No.of Employees: 1 - 10 **Product Groups:** 25, 35, 36, 46, 49, 66

M D M Services Cardiff Ltd

New Quay Road Felnex Industrial Estate, Newport, NP19 4PL
Tel: 01633-277277 **Fax:** 01633-277233
E-mail: mdm@mdmservices.co.uk
Website: http://www.mdmservices.co.uk
Directors: D. Amos (MD)
Immediate Holding Company: MDM SERVICES (CARDIFF) LIMITED
Registration no: 04229272 **Date established:** 2001
No.of Employees: 11 - 20 **Product Groups:** 39, 40, 81

Date of Accounts	Jun 11	Jun 10	Jun 09
Sales Turnover	755	771	841
Pre Tax Profit/Loss	52	-38	77
Working Capital	55	52	135
Fixed Assets	N/A	N/A	1
Current Assets	155	150	210
Current Liabilities	24	21	30

M G Framing

Unit 8 Islwyn Workshops Pontymister Industrial Estate, Risca, Newport, NP11 6NP
Tel: 01633-612034 **Fax:** 01633-612034
E-mail: mgframing@btinternet.com
Website: http://www.mgframing.co.uk
Directors: S. Jones (Prop)
Ultimate Holding Company: ALEXSTEL LIMITED
Immediate Holding Company: RBF COMMS. SERVICES LIMITED
Registration no: 03200457 **Date established:** 1996
No.of Employees: 1 - 10 **Product Groups:** 25, 26, 30

Date of Accounts	Sep 11	Sep 10	Sep 09
Working Capital	377	674	1m
Fixed Assets	318	333	329
Current Assets	831	996	1m

M J K Networks Ltd

The Orion Suite Enterprise Way, Newport, NP20 2DX
Tel: 01633-245965 **Fax:** 01633-245975
E-mail: sales@mjknetworks.com
Website: http://www.mjk-tns.co.uk
Directors: J. King (MD), L. King (Fin)
Managers: M. Payne, V. Edwards
Immediate Holding Company: M J K NETWORKS LIMITED
Registration no: 04686180 **Date established:** 2003
No.of Employees: 1 - 10 **Product Groups:** 26, 35, 37, 38, 40, 44, 48, 52, 67, 79, 83, 84

Date of Accounts	Apr 10	Apr 09	Apr 08
Working Capital	-25	-12	-23
Fixed Assets	27	31	36
Current Assets	36	83	48
Current Liabilities	N/A	80	7

Marlin Industries

Caswell Way Reevesland Industrial Estate, Newport, NP19 4PW
Tel: 01633-290130 **Fax:** 01633-290129
E-mail: bob.menzies@marlinindustries.com
Website: http://www.marlinindustries.com
Managers: R. Menzies (Mgr)
Date established: 2001 **No.of Employees:** 11 - 20 **Product Groups:** 35, 36, 45

Marshalls plc

Eastern Dry Dock Corporation Road, Newport, NP19 4RE
Tel: 01633-284600 **Fax:** 01633-284612
E-mail: sean.clarke@marshalls.co.uk
Website: http://www.marshalls.co.uk
Bank(s): Barclays Corn Street

Managers: S. Clarke (Works Gen Mgr)
Immediate Holding Company: MARSHALLS PLC
Registration no: 05100353 **Date established:** 2004
Turnover: £250m - £500m **No.of Employees:** 51 - 100
Product Groups: 33

Date of Accounts	Dec 11	Dec 10	Dec 09
Sales Turnover	334m	323m	312m
Pre Tax Profit/Loss	14m	9m	-2m
Working Capital	40m	19m	46m
Fixed Assets	246m	237m	257m
Current Assets	129m	114m	123m
Current Liabilities	29m	22m	29m

Metafab
Unit 2 26 Coomassie Street, Newport, NP20 2JP
Tel: 01633-661832 **Fax:** 01633- 661832
E-mail: sales@thegateshop.co.uk
Website: http://www.metafab.co.uk
Directors: R. Brewster (Ptnr)
Date established: 1995 **No.of Employees:** 1 - 10 **Product Groups:** 35

National Roofing (UPVC Distributors Ltd)
Unit 19 Prince of Wales Industrial Estate, Abercarn, Newport, NP11 5AR
Tel: 01495-245066 **Fax:** 01495-248448
E-mail: info@nationalroofing.co.uk
Website: http://www.nationalroofing.co.uk
Managers: M. Locke (Chief Mgr)
Registration no: 03984815 **VAT No.:** GB 770 2124 61
Date established: 2000 **No.of Employees:** 1 - 10 **Product Groups:** 25, 29, 30, 31, 32, 33, 35, 52, 66

Newport Joinery Specialist
Middle Quay Alexandra Dock, Newport, NP20 2NP
Tel: 01633-213186 **Fax:** 01633-213186
E-mail: she.industrial@btinternet.com
Website: http://www.she.ltd.uk
Directors: S. Jenkins (Prop)
Ultimate Holding Company: C H BAILEY PLC
Immediate Holding Company: SPECIALIST HEAVY ENGINEERS LIMITED
Registration no: 00979740 **VAT No.:** GB 531 7060 74
Date established: 1970 **Turnover:** £1m - £2m **No.of Employees:** 1 - 10
Product Groups: 87

Date of Accounts	Mar 09	Mar 08
Sales Turnover	N/A	2m
Pre Tax Profit/Loss	N/A	-18
Working Capital	-848	-848
Current Assets	152	653
Current Liabilities	N/A	158

Novelis UK Ltd
Tregwilym Road Rogerstone, Newport, NP10 9YD
Tel: 01633-202020 **Fax:** 01633-202000
E-mail: marketcentre.uk@novelis.com
Website: http://www.novelis.com
Directors: J. Bunworth (MD), O. Picht (Works), W. Niars (Fin), J. Williams (Pers)
Managers: C. Knight (Mgr), P. Gibbs (Mgr), R. Green (I.T. Exec)
Ultimate Holding Company: HINDALCO INDUSTRIES LTD (INDIA)
Immediate Holding Company: British Alcan Aluminium (UK) Ltd
Registration no: 00279596 **VAT No.:** GB 336 1739 53
Date established: 1933 **Turnover:** £20m - £50m **No.of Employees:** 1 - 10
Product Groups: 34

Oakmain Ltd
Oak House Kendon Road, Crumlin, Newport, NP11 3AP
Tel: 01495-248877 **Fax:** 01495-249854
E-mail: sales@oakmain.co.uk
Website: http://www.oakmain.co.uk
Directors: C. Griffiths (Fin)
Ultimate Holding Company: OAKMAIN PROPERTIES HOLDINGS LIMITED
Immediate Holding Company: OAKMAIN LIMITED
Registration no: 02879991 **Date established:** 1993
No.of Employees: 1 - 10 **Product Groups:** 26, 38, 39, 40, 45, 48, 52, 67, 68, 84, 85

Date of Accounts	Jan 11	Jan 10	Jan 09
Working Capital	500	462	422
Fixed Assets	61	92	77
Current Assets	822	811	785

One 4 Telecoms
11 Grosmont Way Coedkernew, Newport, NP10 8UQ
Tel: 01633-816080 **Fax:** 01633-660147
E-mail: one4.telecoms@ntlworld.com
Website: http://www.one4telecoms.co.uk
Directors: R. Allen (MD)
Product Groups: 37, 79

P C F Secure Document Systems Ltd
Oak House Langstone Business Park, Langstone, Newport, NP18 2LH
Tel: 01633-415570 **Fax:** 01633-415599
E-mail: info@pcf.co.uk
Website: http://www.pcf.co.uk
Directors: I. Hoare (Dir)
Managers: J. Hay (Tech Serv Mgr)
Immediate Holding Company: PCF HOLDINGS LIMITED
Registration no: 06088379 **Date established:** 2007
No.of Employees: 11 - 20 **Product Groups:** 22, 23, 24, 27, 28, 30, 33, 35, 37, 39, 40, 44, 49, 63, 64, 65, 66, 67, 72, 80, 81, 82, 86

Date of Accounts	Sep 11	Sep 10	Sep 09
Working Capital	-1m	-959	-1m
Fixed Assets	2m	2m	2m
Current Assets	16	18	N/A

Panasonic Systems Network
Pencarn Way Duffryn, Newport, NP10 8YE
Tel: 01633-653600 **Fax:** 01633-653989
E-mail: enquiries@kmeuk.co.uk
Website: http://www.kmeuk.co.uk
Directors: N. Mcgrath (MD), C. Jones (Fin)
Managers: A. Heart (Chief Mgr), N. Williams (Purch Mgr), K. Mallorie-davies (Tech Serv Mgr), S. Connolly (Personnel)
Ultimate Holding Company: PANASONIC CORPORATION (JAPAN)
Immediate Holding Company: PANASONIC SYSTEM NETWORKS COMPANY U.K. LIMITED
Registration no: 02030567 **Date established:** 1986
Turnover: £20m - £50m **No.of Employees:** 251 - 500
Product Groups: 37, 44

Date of Accounts	Mar 12	Mar 11	Mar 10
Sales Turnover	33m	38m	35m
Pre Tax Profit/Loss	1m	6m	2m
Working Capital	36m	32m	29m
Fixed Assets	2m	2m	3m
Current Assets	45m	49m	54m
Current Liabilities	3m	7m	8m

The Parts Centre Ltd
Pye Corner House Nash Road, Nash, Newport, NP18 2BW
Tel: 01633-637020 **Fax:** 01633-281011
E-mail: sales@thepartscentre.co.uk
Website: http://www.thepartscentre.co.uk
Directors: J. Dyer (Co Sec)
Immediate Holding Company: THE PARTS CENTRE LIMITED
Registration no: 01702365 **VAT No.:** GB 362 0233 93
Date established: 1983 **Turnover:** £1m - £2m **No.of Employees:** 1 - 10
Product Groups: 40, 66

Date of Accounts	Feb 08	Feb 11	Feb 10
Sales Turnover	495	N/A	N/A
Pre Tax Profit/Loss	83	N/A	N/A
Working Capital	87	64	61
Fixed Assets	12	7	9
Current Assets	173	117	111
Current Liabilities	41	N/A	N/A

Pavecost Manufacturing
Lilleshall Street, Newport, NP19 0FB
Tel: 01633-263986 **Fax:** 01633-266939
E-mail: admin@pavecost.com
Website: http://www.pavecost.com
Bank(s): National Westminster Bank Plc
Directors: A. Treharne (MD)
Immediate Holding Company: PAVECOST MANUFACTURING LIMITED
Registration no: 01984516 **VAT No.:** GB 433 2171 86
Date established: 1986 **Turnover:** £2m - £5m **No.of Employees:** 21 - 50
Product Groups: 37

Date of Accounts	Apr 11	Apr 10	Apr 09
Working Capital	2m	1m	1m
Fixed Assets	342	244	54
Current Assets	3m	2m	2m

Penny & Giles Controls Ltd
Unit 35-36 Nine Mile Point Industrial Estate Cwmfelinfach, Ynysddu, Newport, NP11 7HZ
Tel: 01495-202000 **Fax:** 01495-202006
E-mail: sales@pennyandgiles.com
Website: http://www.pennyandgiles.com
Bank(s): HSBC Bank plc
Directors: J. Watkins (Chief Op Offcr)
Ultimate Holding Company: CURTISS WRIGHT CORPORATION (U.S.A)
Immediate Holding Company: PENNY & GILES CONTROLS LIMITED
Registration no: 00843903 **VAT No.:** GB 682 4436 21
Date established: 1965 **Turnover:** £20m - £50m
No.of Employees: 101 - 250 **Product Groups:** 36, 37, 38, 74

Date of Accounts	Dec 11	Dec 10	Dec 09
Sales Turnover	37m	31m	25m
Pre Tax Profit/Loss	2m	3m	2m
Working Capital	27m	26m	28m
Fixed Assets	2m	1m	1m
Current Assets	34m	31m	31m
Current Liabilities	3m	3m	2m

Precision-Cast Components Holdings Ltd
Usk Way, Newport, NP20 2JY
Tel: 01633-214565 **Fax:** 01633-216204
E-mail: christopher@pcc.eu.com
Website: http://www.precision-cast.co.uk
Directors: C. Isaac (MD)
Immediate Holding Company: PCC.EU LIMITED
Registration no: 04089035 **VAT No.:** GB 483 8025 32
Date established: 2009 **Turnover:** £2m - £5m **No.of Employees:** 1 - 10
Product Groups: 30, 34, 48

Date of Accounts	Dec 07	Dec 06	Dec 05
Working Capital	601	-625	164
Fixed Assets	343	1673	1252
Current Assets	1764	1239	1141
Current Liabilities	1163	1865	977
Total Share Capital	182	182	182

Premier Forest Products Ltd
South Way Alexandra Dock, Newport, NP20 2PQ
Tel: 01633-254422 **Fax:** 01633-254455
E-mail: dhowells@premierforest.co.uk
Website: http://www.premierforestproducts.co.uk
Directors: N. Williams (Dir), P. Morgan (Fin), T. Edgell (Dir), D. Howells (Dir)
Ultimate Holding Company: PREMIER FOREST (HOLDINGS) LIMITED
Immediate Holding Company: PREMIER FOREST PRODUCTS LIMITED
Registration no: 02797766 **Date established:** 1993
Turnover: £50m - £75m **No.of Employees:** 21 - 50 **Product Groups:** 61

Date of Accounts	Apr 12	Apr 11	Apr 10
Sales Turnover	60m	53m	41m
Pre Tax Profit/Loss	2m	801	20
Working Capital	4m	3m	3m
Fixed Assets	438	441	405
Current Assets	23m	20m	15m
Current Liabilities	10m	9m	5m

Priority Industrial Supplies
Unit 15 Abercarn Industrial Estate, Abercarn, Newport, NP11 5AR
Tel: 01495-244940 **Fax:** 01495-243469
E-mail: sales@priorityind.co.uk
Website: http://www.priorityind.co.uk
Managers: M. Evans (Mgr)
VAT No.: GB 535 4705 45 **Turnover:** £500,000 - £1m
No.of Employees: 1 - 10 **Product Groups:** 24, 27, 30, 32, 33, 35, 40, 66

Purcell Jones Associates Ltd
57 Allt-Yr-Yn Close, Newport, NP20 5EE
Tel: 01633-662807
E-mail: admin@purcelljones.com
Website: http://www.purcelljones.com
Directors: M. Purcell Jones (MD)
Immediate Holding Company: PURCELL JONES ASSOCIATES LIMITED
Registration no: 05076211 **Date established:** 2004
Turnover: Up to £250,000 **No.of Employees:** 1 - 10 **Product Groups:** 38, 42

Date of Accounts	Mar 11	Mar 10	Mar 09
Sales Turnover	30	29	51
Working Capital	2	2	1
Fixed Assets	N/A	3	4
Current Assets	4	2	1

Recover Rollers Ltd
Western Industrial Estate Caerleon, Newport, NP18 3NN
Tel: 01633-430814 **Fax:** 01633-430815
E-mail: tony@recoverrollers.co.uk
Website: http://www.recoverrollers.co.uk
Bank(s): Lloyds TSB Bank plc
Directors: A. Thomas (Dir)
Immediate Holding Company: POWER CLEAN (GWENT) LIMITED
Registration no: 05796788 **VAT No.:** GB 535 4575 32
Date established: 1982 **Turnover:** £500,000 - £1m
No.of Employees: 11 - 20 **Product Groups:** 29

Regus Recruitment
24 High Street, Newport, NP20 1FX
Tel: 01633-216666 **Fax:** 01633-216667
E-mail: director@regusrecruitment.co.uk
Website: http://www.regusrecruitment.co.uk
Directors: N. Pilgrim (MD)
Immediate Holding Company: REGUS RECRUITMENT LTD
Registration no: 04434799 **Date established:** 2002
Turnover: Up to £250,000 **No.of Employees:** 1 - 10 **Product Groups:** 80

Date of Accounts	May 12	May 11	May 10
Working Capital	-1	11	6
Fixed Assets	10	10	14
Current Assets	92	86	76

Relats UK Ltd
Suflex Estate Risca, Newport, NP11 7BH
Tel: 01495-271161 **Fax:** 01633-615975
E-mail: relatsuk@relats.com
Website: http://www.relats.com
Bank(s): Banco Sabadell
Directors: P. Relats (Ch), M. Angli (Co Sec)
Managers: H. Ward (Sales Prom Mgr), A. Kirby (Sales Prom)
Ultimate Holding Company: RELATS SA (SPAIN)
Immediate Holding Company: Relats SA (Spain)
Registration no: 02706928 **VAT No.:** 543 0200 03 **Date established:** 1992
Turnover: £1m - £2m **No.of Employees:** 21 - 50 **Product Groups:** 23, 27, 33, 37

Date of Accounts	Dec 07	Dec 06
Sales Turnover	1693	1899
Pre Tax Profit/Loss	4	12
Working Capital	276	291
Fixed Assets	487	547
Current Assets	522	563
Current Liabilities	246	272
Total Share Capital	600	600
ROCE% (Return on Capital Employed)	0.5	1.5
ROT% (Return on Turnover)	0.2	0.6

S & R Spares
64 Allt-Yr-Yn Road, Newport, NP20 5EF
Tel: 01633-259564 **Fax:** 01633-259564
Directors: R. Urrutia (Prop)
Date established: 1992 **No.of Employees:** 1 - 10 **Product Groups:** 36, 40

Safety First Lifting Gear Services Ltd
Unit 17 Estuary Court Queensway Meadows Industrial Estate, Leeway Industrial Estate, Newport, NP19 4SL
Tel: 01633-280444 **Fax:** 0870-134 9816
E-mail: sales@safetyfirstlifting.com
Website: http://www.safetyfirstlifting.com
Directors: S. Marshall (MD)
Immediate Holding Company: SAFETY FIRST LIFTING GEAR SERVICES LIMITED
Registration no: 05374422 **Date established:** 2005
No.of Employees: 1 - 10 **Product Groups:** 22, 23, 35, 40, 45, 52, 66, 83, 84, 85

Date of Accounts	Feb 12	Feb 11	Feb 10
Working Capital	50	41	35
Fixed Assets	12	5	7
Current Assets	104	65	61

Saica Packaging (Factory) UK Central Office
Alexandra Docks, Newport, NP20 2WE
Tel: 01633-776000 **Fax:** 01633-776100
Website: http://www.saicapack.com
Directors: T. Atherton (Dir)
Managers: M. Lucas (Personnel), E. Beuselinck-jones (Cust Serv Mgr), V. Halai (Tech Serv Mgr), R. Snell (I.T. Exec), P. Baldock (Mgr), P. Davies (Fin Mgr), A. Carr (Sales & Mktg Mg), M. Fraser (Personnel)
Date established: 1986 **No.of Employees:** 51 - 100 **Product Groups:** 27

Salty Yacht Productions Ltd
Unit 44 Enterprise Way, Newport, NP20 2AQ
Tel: 01633-250652 **Fax:** 01633-842267
E-mail: sales@saltyyachts.com
Website: http://www.strandek.co.uk
Directors: S. Bowen (Dir)
Immediate Holding Company: SALTY YACHTS (PRODUCTION) LIMITED
Registration no: 01448607 **VAT No.:** GB 356 4970 22
Date established: 1979 **Turnover:** £250,000 - £500,000
No.of Employees: 1 - 10 **Product Groups:** 30

Date of Accounts	Nov 11	Nov 10	Nov 09
Working Capital	-39	-49	-77
Fixed Assets	35	22	348
Current Assets	18	26	22

Santon Switch Gear Ltd
Unit 1 Phoenix Business Park Telford Street, Newport, NP19 0LW
Tel: 01633-252371 **Fax:** 01633-854999
E-mail: sales@santonswitchgear.co.uk
Website: http://www.santonswitchgear.co.uk
Directors: H. Wigmore (MD)
Immediate Holding Company: SANTON SWITCHGEAR LIMITED
Registration no: 03207845 **Date established:** 1996
No.of Employees: 11 - 20 **Product Groups:** 37, 63, 67, 80

Date of Accounts	Dec 11	Dec 10	Dec 09
Working Capital	42	105	142
Fixed Assets	45	3	5
Current Assets	676	495	335

Shine Food Machinery Ltd
New Quay Road Stevenson Street Industrial Estate, Newport, NP19 4PL
Tel: 01633-294800 **Fax:** 01633-294801
E-mail: julian.shine@shine.co.uk
Website: http://www.shine.co.uk

see next page

Shine Food Machinery Ltd - Cont'd

Directors: J. Shine (Dir), P. Reynolds (Fin)
Managers: S. Ryan (Mktg Serv Mgr), L. Carey (Personnel), W. O'Connell (Purch Mgr), C. Hinton (Sales Prom Mgr)
Immediate Holding Company: SHINE FOOD MACHINERY LIMITED
Registration no: 01443265 **Date established:** 1979 **Turnover:** £5m - £10m
No.of Employees: 21 - 50 **Product Groups:** 20, 40, 41

Date of Accounts	Dec 11	Dec 10	Dec 09
Sales Turnover	11m	9m	9m
Pre Tax Profit/Loss	281	285	198
Working Capital	655	667	612
Fixed Assets	894	1m	1m
Current Assets	4m	3m	3m
Current Liabilities	708	734	700

Specialist Steel Wales Ltd

Portland Street, Newport, NP20 2DP
Tel: 01633-216661 **Fax:** 01633-243115
E-mail: kellys@specialiststeels.co.uk
Website: http://www.specialiststeels.co.uk
Directors: N. Barnes (MD)
Immediate Holding Company: MARTIN WATKINS TRANSPORT LIMITED
VAT No.: GB 433 1854 63 **Date established:** 2011
Turnover: £500,000 - £1m **No.of Employees:** 1 - 10 **Product Groups:** 34

Date of Accounts	Sep 11	Sep 10	Sep 09
Working Capital	-43	-9	53
Fixed Assets	396	402	408
Current Assets	335	329	341

Speedy Asset Services Ltd

Kings Parade, Newport, NP20 2DU
Tel: 01633-243244 **Fax:** 01633-243236
E-mail: dillon.owen@speedyservices.com
Website: http://www.speedyservices.com
Managers: D. Owen (District Mgr)
Ultimate Holding Company: SPEEDY HIRE PLC
Immediate Holding Company: SPEEDY ASSET SERVICES LIMITED
Registration no: 06847930 **Date established:** 2009 **Turnover:** £5m - £10m
No.of Employees: 1 - 10 **Product Groups:** 35, 37, 38, 39, 45, 48, 83

Date of Accounts	Mar 12	Mar 11	Mar 10
Sales Turnover	312m	336m	187m
Pre Tax Profit/Loss	24m	-5m	-430
Working Capital	-172m	-194m	-252m
Fixed Assets	210m	198m	268m
Current Assets	101m	144m	120m
Current Liabilities	31m	41m	33m

Stately Albion Ltd

Unit 20 Darren Drive Prince of Wales Industrial Estate, Abercarn, Newport, NP11 5AR
Tel: 01495-244472 **Fax:** 01495-248939
E-mail: sales@stately-albion.co.uk
Website: http://www.stately-albion.co.uk
Bank(s): National Westminster Bank Plc
Directors: C. Golding (Purch), D. Hurd (MD)
Managers: L. Golding, Y. Hurd (Personnel), A. Philips (Sales & Mktg Mg)
Immediate Holding Company: STATELY-ALBION LIMITED
Registration no: 00790270 **Date established:** 1964
Turnover: £20m - £50m **No.of Employees:** 101 - 250
Product Groups: 25, 39

Date of Accounts	Jul 11	Jul 10	Jul 09
Sales Turnover	22m	18m	12m
Pre Tax Profit/Loss	-281	552	-45
Working Capital	5m	6m	6m
Fixed Assets	3m	2m	2m
Current Assets	8m	9m	7m
Current Liabilities	2m	1m	750

Strata Color (Coated Steels) Ltd

Oxwich Road Reevesland Park Industrial Estate, Reevesland Industrial Estate, Newport, NP19 4PU
Tel: 01633-276111 **Fax:** 01633-280044
Bank(s): HSBC Bank plc
Directors: M. Williams (MD), H. Willington (Co Sec), A. Scandrett (Dir)
Managers: I. Soest (Mgr)
Immediate Holding Company: JOJO MAMAN BEBE LTD
Registration no: 02737508 **VAT No.:** GB 379 0460 33
Date established: 1992 **Turnover:** £10m - £20m
No.of Employees: 21 - 50 **Product Groups:** 34

Date of Accounts	Jun 11	Jun 10	Jun 09
Sales Turnover	24m	20m	18m
Pre Tax Profit/Loss	1m	1m	664
Working Capital	3m	496	195
Fixed Assets	3m	3m	3m
Current Assets	6m	4m	3m
Current Liabilities	1m	1m	1m

Superior Heat Treatment

1 Block 5 Broad Quay Road Felnex Indl-Est, Newport, NP19 4PN
Tel: 01633-281629 **Fax:** 01633-290896
Directors: G. Jefferies (Dir)
Immediate Holding Company: FOREST SUPPORT SERVICES LTD
Registration no: 02711607 **Date established:** 2010
No.of Employees: 1 - 10 **Product Groups:** 46, 48

Date of Accounts	Mar 11
Sales Turnover	6m
Pre Tax Profit/Loss	304
Working Capital	626
Fixed Assets	710
Current Assets	4m
Current Liabilities	2m

Survey Supplies Ltd

108 Malpas Road, Newport, NP20 5PL
Tel: 01633-822333 **Fax:** 01633-822444
Website: http://www.surveysupplies.co.uk
Managers: S. Haines (District Mgr)
Ultimate Holding Company: Precise Construction Instruments Limited
Immediate Holding Company: Precise Construction Instruments (U.K.) Ltd
Registration no: 00965862 **Date established:** 1969
Turnover: £10m - £20m **No.of Employees:** 1 - 10 **Product Groups:** 38, 44

Swift Steels Services Ltd

Unit 9 Leeway Industrial Estate Leeway Industrial Estate, Newport, NP19 4SL
Tel: 01633-271188 **Fax:** 01633-278311
E-mail: enquiries@swiftsteel.co.uk
Website: http://www.sherlings.com
Directors: F. Moore (Fin)
Immediate Holding Company: SWIFT STEEL SERVICES LIMITED
Registration no: 02500171 **VAT No.:** GB 535 3318 57
Date established: 1990 **Turnover:** £1m - £2m **No.of Employees:** 1 - 10
Product Groups: 66

Date of Accounts	Feb 08	Feb 11	Feb 10
Working Capital	146	-16	13
Fixed Assets	28	3	9
Current Assets	462	420	310

Symonds UK Ltd

Wern Trading Estate Rogerstone, Newport, NP10 9XX
Tel: 01633-892362 **Fax:** 01633-896618
E-mail: rollandd@symondshydroclean.co.uk
Website: http://www.symondshydroclean.co.uk
Directors: D. Rolland (MD), I. Griffiths (Fin), D. Butters (MD), D. Jeffery (MD)
Managers: K. Lewis (Personnel), K. Lewis (Personnel), D. Bridge (Buyer), D. Butters (Tech Serv Mgr), I. Griffiths (Fin Mgr)
Ultimate Holding Company: WANZL GMBH & CO KG (GERMANY)
Immediate Holding Company: SYMONDS (UK) LIMITED
Registration no: 02774043 **Date established:** 1992 **Turnover:** £5m - £10m
No.of Employees: 51 - 100 **Product Groups:** 29, 39, 40, 43, 45, 48, 49, 52, 67

Date of Accounts	Dec 11	Dec 10	Dec 09
Sales Turnover	24m	22m	20m
Pre Tax Profit/Loss	359	322	153
Working Capital	2m	2m	2m
Fixed Assets	1m	727	855
Current Assets	6m	8m	9m
Current Liabilities	1m	875	1m

Talkmobile Airtime Services Ltd

Clarence House Clarence Place, Newport, NP19 7AA
Tel: 0870-7606692 **Fax:** 0870-7606693
E-mail: info@talkmobiles.com
Website: http://www.talkmobiles.com
Directors: S. Mackie (Dir)
Registration no: 04642060 **Date established:** 2003 **Turnover:** £2m - £5m
No.of Employees: 1 - 10 **Product Groups:** 37, 67

Ted Hopkins

Little Ty Coch St Brides Wentlooge, Newport, NP10 8SR
Tel: 01633-680754 **Fax:** 01633-681491
E-mail: info@tedhopkins.co.uk
Website: http://www.tedhopkins.co.uk
Directors: C. Hopkins (Dir)
Managers: J. Hopkins (Tech Serv Mgr)
Immediate Holding Company: TED HOPKINS LIMITED
Registration no: 02344944 **Date established:** 1989
No.of Employees: 11 - 20 **Product Groups:** 41

Date of Accounts	Dec 11	Dec 10	Dec 09
Working Capital	227	223	224
Fixed Assets	13	7	10
Current Assets	1m	1m	1m

Total Electrical Distributors

T E S Office Crawford Street, Newport, NP19 7AY
Tel: 01633-214348 **Fax:** 01633-254328
E-mail: steve.harris@totalelectrical.co.uk
Website: http://www.totalelectrical.co.uk
Bank(s): Barclays, Blackwood
Managers: S. Harris (Mgr)
Registration no: 03793218 **VAT No.:** GB 542 6873 25
Date established: 1999 **Turnover:** £500,000 - £1m
No.of Employees: 11 - 20 **Product Groups:** 67

Total Print & Promotions

278 Chepstow Road, Newport, NP19 8NN
Tel: 01633-270777
E-mail: sales@jojoprint.com
Website: http://www.jojoprint.com
Directors: N. Troake (Prop), N. Qroake (Prop)
Managers: J. Neal (Ops Mgr)
Immediate Holding Company: NIGEL HARRISON DESIGNS LIMITED
Registration no: 06212051 **Date established:** 2011
No.of Employees: 1 - 10 **Product Groups:** 23

Date of Accounts	Aug 08
Working Capital	-26
Fixed Assets	11
Current Assets	44
Current Liabilities	71

UK Steel Export Ltd

Blackvein Industrial Estate Cross Keys, Newport, NP11 7PX
Tel: 01495-270033 **Fax:** 01495-273190
E-mail: ukstlexp@aol.com
Website: http://www.uksteelexports.co.uk
Directors: B. Hodges (MD)
Immediate Holding Company: U.K. STEEL EXPORTS LIMITED
Registration no: 01968136 **VAT No.:** GB 433 1620 88
Date established: 1985 **No.of Employees:** 1 - 10 **Product Groups:** 61

Date of Accounts	Dec 11	Dec 10	Dec 09
Working Capital	622	316	112
Fixed Assets	8	10	1
Current Assets	3m	901	610

W R C N S F

Unit 30 Fern Close Crumlin, Newport, NP11 3EH
Tel: 01495-236260 **Fax:** 01495-249234
E-mail: info@wrcnsf.com
Website: http://www.wrcnsf.com
Directors: G. Franklin (MD)
Managers: R. Jones, A. Pitson (Personnel), S. Warburton (Ops Mgr)
Ultimate Holding Company: NSF INTERNATIONAL (USA)
Immediate Holding Company: WRC - NSF LIMITED
Registration no: 03754780 **Date established:** 1999 **Turnover:** £2m - £5m
No.of Employees: 21 - 50 **Product Groups:** 54, 85

Date of Accounts	Dec 11	Dec 10	Mar 10
Sales Turnover	2m	2m	2m
Pre Tax Profit/Loss	-4	329	415
Working Capital	1m	954	676
Fixed Assets	391	429	478
Current Assets	2m	2m	1m
Current Liabilities	843	610	368

Newtown

A D Moore & Son Kitchen Installations

Bryn Hafod Aberhafesp, Newtown, SY16 3JJ
Tel: 01686-688967
E-mail: adrianmoore0@lycos.com
Website: http://www.lycos.com
Directors: A. Moore (Prop)
Date established: 1981 **No.of Employees:** 1 - 10 **Product Groups:** 25

Cambrian Containers

Unit 32 Mochdre Industrial Estate Mochdre, Newtown, SY16 4LE
Tel: 01686-611360 **Fax:** 01686-611361
E-mail: sales@cambriancontainers.com
Website: http://www.cambriancontainers.com
Bank(s): HSBC
Directors: M. Simpson (MD)
VAT No.: GB 148 6263 48 **No.of Employees:** 11 - 20 **Product Groups:** 30

Confederate Chemicals Ltd

Mochdre Industrial Estate Mochdre, Newtown, SY16 4LE
Tel: 01686-627158 **Fax:** 01686-627580
E-mail: sales@confederatechemicals.co.uk
Website: http://www.confederatechemicals.co.uk
Directors: R. Stevenson (MD)
Immediate Holding Company: CONFEDERATE CHEMICALS LIMITED
Registration no: 01203074 **VAT No.:** GB 281 6556 39
Date established: 1975 **No.of Employees:** 1 - 10 **Product Groups:** 32, 52

Date of Accounts	Apr 12	Apr 11	Apr 10
Working Capital	226	205	146
Fixed Assets	330	336	340
Current Assets	358	353	249

Contact Attachments Ltd

Unit E Mochdre Industrial Estate, Mochdre, Newtown, SY16 4LE
Tel: 01686-611200 **Fax:** 01686-611201
E-mail: sales@forklift-attachments.co.uk
Website: http://www.forklift-attachments.co.uk
Bank(s): HSBC Bank plc
Directors: E. Cufley (Fin), R. Taylor (MD)
Immediate Holding Company: CONTACT ATTACHMENTS LIMITED
Registration no: 01410701 **VAT No.:** GB 303 8429 72
Date established: 1979 **Turnover:** £1m - £2m **No.of Employees:** 11 - 20
Product Groups: 45

Date of Accounts	Dec 11	Dec 10	Dec 09
Working Capital	88	33	22
Fixed Assets	331	267	255
Current Assets	550	459	421

Control Techniques Ltd

Unit 79 Mochdre Industrial Estate, Mochdre, Newtown, SY16 4LE
Tel: 01686-612300 **Fax:** 01686-612800
E-mail: gareth.d.jones@emerson.com
Website: http://www.controltechniques.com
Directors: I. Jones (Tech Serv), C. Birks (Co Sec)
Managers: K. Sznerc (Personnel), P. Sewell, G. Jones, A. Byles (Mktg Serv Mgr), B. Payton (Purch Mgr)
Ultimate Holding Company: EMERSON ELECTRIC CO INC (USA)
Immediate Holding Company: CONTROL TECHNIQUES DRIVES LIMITED
Registration no: 01384703 **Date established:** 1978
Turnover: £125m - £250m **No.of Employees:** 251 - 500
Product Groups: 38, 44

Date of Accounts	Sep 11	Sep 10	Sep 09
Sales Turnover	126m	97m	69m
Pre Tax Profit/Loss	28m	22m	9m
Working Capital	71m	52m	46m
Fixed Assets	6m	5m	4m
Current Assets	98m	76m	63m
Current Liabilities	7m	5m	3m

Elkay Electrical Manufacturing Co. Ltd A Smiths Group Company

Unit C Mochdre Industrial Estate, Mochdre, Newtown, SY16 4LF
Tel: 01686-611500 **Fax:** 01686-611501
E-mail: info@cm-products.com
Website: http://www.cm-products.com
Bank(s): Lloyds TSB Bank plc
Directors: D. Mckinlay (MD), M. Vitty (Fin)
Ultimate Holding Company: DUNDAS GROUP HOLDINGS LIMITED
Immediate Holding Company: ELKAY ELECTRICAL MANUFACTURING COMPANY LIMITED
Registration no: 00187153 **Date established:** 2023 **Turnover:** £5m - £10m
No.of Employees: 101 - 250 **Product Groups:** 30, 37, 84

Date of Accounts	Jul 08	Jul 07	Jul 06
Working Capital	160	160	2m
Current Assets	160	160	2m

Faber Technology Ltd

Unit 22 Mochdre Industrial Estate Mochdre, Newtown, SY16 4LE
Tel: 01686-621576 **Fax:** 01686-622477
E-mail: info@fabertechnology.co.uk
Website: http://www.fabertechnology.co.uk
Bank(s): HSBC Bank plc
Directors: B. Bancroft (MD), S. Lawrence (Fin)
Immediate Holding Company: FABER TECHNOLOGY LTD
Registration no: 04403613 **VAT No.:** GB 594 0807 21
Date established: 2002 **Turnover:** £500,000 - £1m
No.of Employees: 11 - 20 **Product Groups:** 35, 48

Date of Accounts	Mar 11	Mar 10	Mar 09
Working Capital	206	154	145
Fixed Assets	342	380	440
Current Assets	410	369	297
Current Liabilities	43	N/A	N/A

Hafren Fastners

Mochdre Industrial Estate Mochdre, Newtown, SY16 4LE
Tel: 01686-621300 **Fax:** 01686-621800
Website: http://www.hafrenfasteners.com
Directors: B. Lynes (Ptnr)
Immediate Holding Company: HAFREN FASTENERS
Registration no: 08028610 **Date established:** 2012
No.of Employees: 11 - 20 **Product Groups:** 35

Innova Mill
Unit 83 Mochdre Industrial Estate Mochdre, Newtown, SY16 4LE
Tel: 01686-625100 **Fax:** 01686-620910
E-mail: sales@innovamill.com
Website: http://www.innovamill.com
Bank(s): HSBC, Barnet
Managers: E. Morrish (Sales Prom Mgr)
VAT No.: GB 370 7570 45 **Turnover:** £1m - £2m **No.of Employees:** 11 - 20
Product Groups: 30, 49

Links Electrical Supplies
Unit 35-36 Mochdre Industrial Estate, Mochdre, Newtown, SY16 4LE
Tel: 01686-624555 **Fax:** 01686-623388
Website: http://www.linkselectrical.co.uk
Directors: G. Morgan (Dir)
Immediate Holding Company: LINKS ELECTRICAL SUPPLIES LTD
Registration no: 04113354 **Date established:** 2000
No.of Employees: 11 - 20 **Product Groups:** 36, 40

Date of Accounts	Dec 11	Dec 10	Dec 09
Working Capital	890	839	792
Fixed Assets	604	560	681
Current Assets	2m	2m	2m

Makefast Ltd
Unit 30-31 Mochdre Industrial Estate, Mochdre, Newtown, SY16 4LE
Tel: 01686-629010 **Fax:** 01686-626700
E-mail: sales@makefast.com
Website: http://www.makefast.com
Bank(s): Barclays
Directors: M. Mills (Chief Op Offcr)
Immediate Holding Company: MAKE FAST LIMITED
Registration no: 01165517 **VAT No.:** GB 189 5657 95
Date established: 1974 **Turnover:** £1m - £2m **No.of Employees:** 21 - 50
Product Groups: 35, 39

Date of Accounts	Mar 11	Mar 10	Mar 09
Working Capital	992	971	937
Fixed Assets	1m	1m	1m
Current Assets	2m	1m	1m

Milford Collection
Unit 18 Pool Road, Newtown, SY16 3BD
Tel: 01686-629919 **Fax:** 01686-623918
E-mail: info@milfordcollection.com
Website: http://www.milfordcollection.com
Directors: D. Blower (Ptnr)
Turnover: Up to £250,000 **No.of Employees:** 1 - 10 **Product Groups:** 32, 65

Pamargan Products Ltd (Pamargan Products Ltd)
Unit 47 Mochdre Industrial Estate, Mochdre, Newtown, SY16 4LE
Tel: 01686-625181 **Fax:** 01686-627849
E-mail: sales@pamargan.com
Website: http://www.pamargan.com
Bank(s): Midland
Directors: M. Pace-Bonello (MD)
Managers: C. Halling (Tech Serv Mgr), P. Kenyon (Sales Prom Mgr), R. Evans (Admin Off), R. Pond (Purch Mgr), J. Bennett (Personnel)
Ultimate Holding Company: TOTAL SAFETY INC (USA)
Immediate Holding Company: PAMARGAN PRODUCTS LIMITED
Registration no: 01597523 **VAT No.:** GB 351 7727 46
Date established: 1981 **Turnover:** £10m - £20m
No.of Employees: 51 - 100 **Product Groups:** 29

Date of Accounts	Dec 11	Dec 10	Dec 09
Sales Turnover	11m	9m	5m
Pre Tax Profit/Loss	2m	2m	201
Working Capital	4m	3m	2m
Fixed Assets	708	744	831
Current Assets	5m	4m	3m
Current Liabilities	506	427	212

Precision Protective Coatings Ltd
Units 34-35 Mochdre Industrial Estate, Mochdre, Newtown, SY16 4LE
Tel: 01686-621353 **Fax:** 01686-624678
Directors: E. Hughes (Dir)
Immediate Holding Company: CONTACT ATTACHMENTS LIMITED
Registration no: 01203074 **Date established:** 1979
No.of Employees: 1 - 10 **Product Groups:** 46, 48

Date of Accounts	Dec 11	Dec 10	Dec 09
Working Capital	88	33	22
Fixed Assets	331	267	255
Current Assets	550	459	421

Shermann Audio
Unit 35 Vastre Industrial Estate, Newtown, SY16 1DZ
Tel: 01686-622997 **Fax:** 08456-442251
E-mail: info@shermann.com
Website: http://www.shermann.com
Directors: L. Hughes (Dir)
No.of Employees: 1 - 10 **Product Groups:** 37, 67

Trax
Unit 66 Mochdre Industrial Estate Mochdre, Newtown, SY16 4LE
Tel: 01686-610169 **Fax:** 01938-554597
E-mail: info@traxjh.com
Website: http://www.traxjh.com
Directors: J. Halle (MD), W. Booth (Co Sec), R. Horsley (Co Sec)
Managers: L. Hills (Sales Prom Mgr), N. Morrison (Factory Mgr)
Ultimate Holding Company: T B W LIMITED
Immediate Holding Company: TRAX J H LIMITED
Registration no: 02775943 **Date established:** 1992 **Turnover:** £5m - £10m
No.of Employees: 51 - 100 **Product Groups:** 29, 35, 41

Date of Accounts	Dec 11	Dec 10	Dec 09
Sales Turnover	6m	7m	N/A
Pre Tax Profit/Loss	-320	-189	133
Working Capital	424	434	853
Fixed Assets	1m	1m	882
Current Assets	2m	3m	2m
Current Liabilities	751	983	784

Dyfed

Pembroke

Jewson Ltd
Station Road, Pembroke, SA71 4AH
Tel: 01646-682288 **Fax:** 01646-622660
E-mail: deric.brock@jewson.co.uk
Website: http://www.jewson.co.uk
Managers: D. Brock (District Mgr)
Ultimate Holding Company: COMPAGNIE DE SAINT GOBAIN (FRANCE)
Immediate Holding Company: JEWSON LIMITED
Registration no: 00348407 **Date established:** 1939 **Turnover:** £2m - £5m
No.of Employees: 11 - 20 **Product Groups:** 66

Date of Accounts	Dec 11	Dec 10	Dec 09
Sales Turnover	1606m	1547m	1485m
Pre Tax Profit/Loss	18m	100m	45m
Working Capital	-345m	-250m	-349m
Fixed Assets	496m	387m	461m
Current Assets	657m	1005m	1320m
Current Liabilities	66m	120m	64m

M R C Transmark Ltd
2 Ferry Lane Works Ferry Lane, Pembroke, SA71 4RE
Tel: 01646-622200 **Fax:** 01646-622188
E-mail: mike.omara@mrctransmark.com
Website: http://www.heaton-valves.co.uk
Directors: H. Brown (Fin), M. Omara (MD)
Ultimate Holding Company: QBUSS HOLDING NV (HOLLAND)
Immediate Holding Company: MRC TRANSMARK LIMITED
Registration no: 03471259 **Date established:** 1997 **Turnover:** £2m - £5m
No.of Employees: 1 - 10 **Product Groups:** 63, 66, 67

Date of Accounts	Dec 11	Dec 10	Dec 09
Sales Turnover	36m	35m	48m
Pre Tax Profit/Loss	4m	4m	7m
Working Capital	5m	5m	3m
Fixed Assets	9m	9m	12m
Current Assets	23m	23m	34m
Current Liabilities	2m	2m	3m

Dyfed

Pembroke Dock

Grainger Tubolt Ltd
Unit A - B Meyrick Owen Way, Pembroke Dock, SA72 6WS
Tel: 01646-683584 **Fax:** 01646-621392
E-mail: jwild@graingertubolt.com
Website: http://www.graingertubolt.com
Directors: J. Wild (Dir)
Managers: C. Williams
Immediate Holding Company: GRAINGER TUBOLT LIMITED
Registration no: 01539451 **Date established:** 1981 **Turnover:** £5m - £10m
No.of Employees: 21 - 50 **Product Groups:** 35

Date of Accounts	Oct 11	Oct 10	Oct 09
Working Capital	2m	2m	1m
Fixed Assets	977	1m	1m
Current Assets	3m	2m	2m

Jewson Ltd
4 Meyrick Street, Pembroke Dock, SA72 6UT
Tel: 01646-683212 **Fax:** 01646-621416
Website: http://www.jewson.co.uk
Managers: A. Buckingham (District Mgr), S. Butler (Asst Gen Mgr)
Ultimate Holding Company: Saint-Gobain Ltd
Immediate Holding Company: Saint-Gobain Building Distribution Ltd
Registration no: 00348407 **VAT No.:** GB 497 7184 83
No.of Employees: 1 - 10 **Product Groups:** 66

Ledwood Mechanical Engineering Ltd
Waterloo Industrial Estate Waterloo, Pembroke Dock, SA72 4RR
Tel: 01646-623600 **Fax:** 01646-623699
E-mail: wales@ledwood.co.uk
Website: http://www.ledwood.co.uk
Directors: A. Sangster (Dir)
Ultimate Holding Company: DIAMWNT LIMITED
Immediate Holding Company: LEDWOOD MECHANICAL ENGINEERING LIMITED
Registration no: 04045742 **Date established:** 2000
Turnover: £20m - £50m **No.of Employees:** 101 - 250
Product Groups: 35, 48, 84

Date of Accounts	Dec 11	Aug 10	Aug 09
Sales Turnover	20m	26m	39m
Pre Tax Profit/Loss	5	2m	9m
Working Capital	9m	9m	8m
Fixed Assets	2m	2m	2m
Current Assets	13m	12m	11m
Current Liabilities	2m	1m	2m

Mainport Engineering 1990 Ltd
Glyn Taff Mill London Road, Pembroke Dock, SA72 6DS
Tel: 01646-621563 **Fax:** 01646-621305
E-mail: dave@mpe1990.co.uk
Website: http://www.mpe1990.co.uk
Bank(s): HSBC
Directors: D. Harris (MD)
Managers: L. Schofield (Sales Admin)
Immediate Holding Company: MAINPORT ENGINEERING (1990) LIMITED
Registration no: 02534793 **VAT No.:** GB 485 3630 28
Date established: 1990 **Turnover:** £10m - £20m
No.of Employees: 251 - 500 **Product Groups:** 48

Date of Accounts	Mar 11	Mar 10	Mar 09
Sales Turnover	12m	11m	11m
Pre Tax Profit/Loss	61	540	532
Working Capital	970	952	584
Fixed Assets	392	463	434
Current Assets	2m	3m	2m
Current Liabilities	971	2m	983

Mustang Marine Wales Ltd
The Dock Yard, Pembroke Dock, SA72 6TE
Tel: 01646-681117 **Fax:** 01646-686414
E-mail: lucas@mustangmarine.com
Website: http://www.mustangmarine.com
Bank(s): HSBC
Directors: I. Strugnell (Comm), L. Boissevain (Fin)
Managers: L. Marsden (Buyer), M. Smart (Fin Mgr)
Immediate Holding Company: MUSTANG MARINE (WALES) LIMITED
Registration no: 03086721 **VAT No.:** GB 691 9117 11
Date established: 1995 **Turnover:** £5m - £10m **No.of Employees:** 21 - 50
Product Groups: 39

Date of Accounts	Aug 11	Aug 10	Aug 09
Sales Turnover	6m	3m	5m
Pre Tax Profit/Loss	848	-164	712
Working Capital	536	148	433
Fixed Assets	160	86	79
Current Assets	2m	1m	1m
Current Liabilities	379	432	418

Pembroke Packaging & Print Ltd
Unit 7 Kingswood Trading Estate, Pembroke Dock, SA72 4RS
Tel: 01646-684664 **Fax:** 01646-622226
E-mail: pempack@aol.com
Directors: P. Braddon (MD), S. Braddon (Fin)
Immediate Holding Company: PEMBROKE PACKAGING & PRINT LIMITED
Registration no: 02428834 **Date established:** 1989
No.of Employees: 1 - 10 **Product Groups:** 38, 42

Date of Accounts	Dec 11	Dec 10	Dec 09
Working Capital	89	107	113
Fixed Assets	19	24	30
Current Assets	123	154	157

K Rees
Unit 8a Maritime Industrial Park Criterion Way, Pembroke Dock, SA72 6UL
Tel: 01646-621200 **Fax:** 01646-621200
Directors: K. Rees (Prop)
Immediate Holding Company: PEMBS I.T LLP
Date established: 2012 **No.of Employees:** 1 - 10 **Product Groups:** 26, 35

S D Global Ltd
Unit A5 Maritime Park, Pembroke Dock, SA72 6UL
Tel: 08452-263191 **Fax:** 0845-226 3194
E-mail: info@sdglobal.co.uk
Website: http://www.cctv4u.co.uk
Directors: D. Griffiths (MD)
Immediate Holding Company: SD GLOBAL LIMITED
Registration no: 06236639 **Date established:** 2007 **Turnover:** £2m - £5m
No.of Employees: 1 - 10 **Product Groups:** 37, 38, 40, 67

Date of Accounts	Feb 12	Feb 11	Feb 10
Working Capital	-39	-9	N/A
Fixed Assets	2	1	N/A
Current Assets	29	45	36

South Glamorgan

Penarth

Meter & Instrument Services
Fort Road Lavernock, Penarth, CF64 5UL
Tel: 029-2070 1315 **Fax:** 029-2070 1315
Directors: M. Walsh (Ptnr)
Turnover: Up to £250,000 **No.of Employees:** 1 - 10 **Product Groups:** 38, 49, 85

Metron Wrought Ironwork
2b Station Approach, Penarth, CF64 3EE
Tel: 029-2070 5005
E-mail: metronwroughtiron@btconnect.com
Website: http://www.metron-wrought-ironwork.co.uk
Directors: A. Kirke (Prop)
No.of Employees: 1 - 10 **Product Groups:** 34, 48

Momentive Specialty Chemicals UK Ltd
Sully Moors Road Sully, Penarth, CF64 5YU
Tel: 01446-725500 **Fax:** 08453-109201
E-mail: phil.frampton@momentive.com
Website: http://www.momentive.com
Bank(s): H S B C
Directors: D. Price (Sales), P. Frampton (Purch), R. Healey (Fin)
Managers: L. Jones (Personnel), M. Pugh
Ultimate Holding Company: APOLLO MANAGEMENT LP
Immediate Holding Company: MOMENTIVE SPECIALTY CHEMICALS UK LIMITED
Registration no: 00867053 **VAT No.:** GB 737 2098 22
Date established: 1965 **Turnover:** £75m - £125m
No.of Employees: 51 - 100 **Product Groups:** 30, 31

Date of Accounts	Dec 11	Dec 10	Dec 09
Sales Turnover	106m	89m	73m
Pre Tax Profit/Loss	2m	833	-827
Working Capital	66m	54m	43m
Fixed Assets	16m	18m	20m
Current Assets	86m	72m	62m
Current Liabilities	4m	3m	3m

Printmet Ltd
Sully Moors Road Sully, Penarth, CF64 5RP
Tel: 01446-737417 **Fax:** 01446-748348
E-mail: printmetlimited@btconnect.com
Directors: M. Gibbons (Dir)
Immediate Holding Company: PRINTMET LIMITED
Registration no: 00660831 **VAT No.:** GB 135 2335 94
Date established: 1960 **Turnover:** £500,000 - £1m
No.of Employees: 1 - 10 **Product Groups:** 35, 36, 40, 48

Date of Accounts	May 11	May 10	May 09
Working Capital	2	1	17
Fixed Assets	245	247	249
Current Assets	80	67	89

Silicon Edge
2 Royal Buildings Stanwell Road, Penarth, CF64 3EB
Tel: 029-2019 0109
E-mail: info@siliconedge.co.uk
Website: http://www.siliconedge.co.uk
Directors: J. Dunscombe (Fin), P. Dunscombe (Dir)
Registration no: 06175030 **Date established:** 2007
No.of Employees: 1 - 10 **Product Groups:** 44

Zeon Chemicals Europe Ltd
Sully Moors Road Sully, Penarth, CF64 5ZE
Tel: 01446-725400 **Fax:** 01446-747988
E-mail: debbie.smith@zeon.eu
Website: http://www.zeon.eu
Directors: J. Decostobadie (Sales)
Managers: D. Smith (Personnel)
Ultimate Holding Company: ZEON CORP (JAPAN)
Immediate Holding Company: ZEON CHEMICALS EUROPE LIMITED
Registration no: 02343599 **Date established:** 1989
Turnover: £20m - £50m **No.of Employees:** 101 - 250
Product Groups: 49, 81

Date of Accounts	Dec 11	Dec 10	Dec 09
Sales Turnover	49m	39m	27m
Pre Tax Profit/Loss	2m	1m	959
Working Capital	14m	11m	9m
Fixed Assets	7m	7m	8m
Current Assets	19m	16m	12m
Current Liabilities	957	4m	949

Dyfed

Pencader

Target Direct
Cross Roads Llanllwni, Pencader, SA39 9DY
Tel: 01559-395479
E-mail: sales@target-direct.co.uk
Website: http://www.target-direct.co.uk
Registration no: 03635420 **Date established:** 1998
No.of Employees: 1 - 10 **Product Groups:** 20, 40, 41

Gwynedd

Penmaenmawr

Keimos, IT Training Services
1 Eden Hall Fernbrook Road, Penmaenmawr, LL34 6DE
Tel: 01492-623887
E-mail: info@keimos.co.uk
Website: http://www.keimos.co.uk
Directors: K. Duncan (Ch)
Date established: 2001 **No.of Employees:** 1 - 10 **Product Groups:** 86

Mid-Glamorgan

Pentre

Richardsons Wrought Iron
Workshop Bryn Terrace, Ystrad, Pentre, CF41 7RX
Tel: 01443-435832 **Fax:** 01443-751057
E-mail: maureenhow80@yahoo.co.uk
Directors: H. Richardson (Prop)
Date established: 1985 **No.of Employees:** 1 - 10 **Product Groups:** 26, 35

Mid-Glamorgan

Pontyclun

Allied Aero Systems Ltd
Gwaun Elai Talbot Green, Pontyclun, CF72 8XL
Tel: 01443-234574 **Fax:** 08702-001001
Website: http://www.allied-aerosystems.com
Directors: I. Purnell (MD)
Immediate Holding Company: Allied Aerosystems Ltd
Registration no: 03445123 **Date established:** 1997
Turnover: £500,000 - £1m **No.of Employees:** 21 - 50
Product Groups: 38, 67, 85

D B K Technitherm Ltd
11 Llantrisant Business Park Llantrisant, Pontyclun, CF72 8LF
Tel: 01443-237927 **Fax:** 01443-237867
E-mail: john.weaver@dbk.co.uk
Website: http://www.dbktechnitherm.ltd.uk
Bank(s): Lloyds TSB Bank plc
Directors: J. Webber (Fin)
Managers: T. Jones (Purch Mgr), M. Williams (Sales & Mktg Mg), T. Sommer (Tech Serv Mgr)
Ultimate Holding Company: DAVID AND BAADER GMBH (GERMANY)
Immediate Holding Company: D.B.K.- TECHNITHERM LIMITED
Registration no: 01861693 **VAT No.:** GB 484 0031 71
Date established: 1984 **Turnover:** £5m - £10m
No.of Employees: 51 - 100 **Product Groups:** 37, 40

Date of Accounts	Dec 11	Dec 10	Dec 09
Sales Turnover	10m	9m	6m
Pre Tax Profit/Loss	446	-30	158
Working Capital	2m	2m	2m
Fixed Assets	1m	1m	713
Current Assets	5m	5m	3m
Current Liabilities	442	431	346

Dan Display & Imaging
Harlequwin House Coed Cae Lane, Pontyclun, CF72 9EW
Tel: 01443-225656 **Fax:** 020-8961 6661
E-mail: john@harlequinprintgroup.co.uk
Website: http://www.harlequinprintgroup.co.uk
Bank(s): Barclays Bank PLC
Directors: A. Ingles (Sales), J. Fall (Ch), J. Sall (MD)
Managers: T. Ingles (Sales & Mktg Mg)
Immediate Holding Company: DAN DISPLAY & IMAGING LIMITED
Registration no: 05574268 **VAT No.:** GB 653 3609 36
Date established: 2005 **Turnover:** £2m - £5m **No.of Employees:** 51 - 100
Product Groups: 37, 69, 81, 84

Geesink Norba Ltd
Llantrisant Business Park Llantrisant, Pontyclun, CF72 8XZ
Tel: 01443-222301 **Fax:** 01443-237192
E-mail: geoff.rigg@geesinknorba.com
Website: http://www.geesinknorbagroup.com
Directors: G. Rigg (MD), E. Kalawski (Fin)
Managers: H. Francis (Personnel), K. Peacock (Fin Mgr), R. Phillips (Sales Prom Mgr)
Ultimate Holding Company: OSHKOSH CORPORATION (USA)
Immediate Holding Company: GEESINK NORBA LIMITED
Registration no: 00306452 **VAT No.:** GB 135 0964 73
Date established: 1935 **Turnover:** £20m - £50m
No.of Employees: 21 - 50 **Product Groups:** 39, 42

Date of Accounts	Dec 10	Dec 09	Sep 08
Sales Turnover	30m	38m	21m
Pre Tax Profit/Loss	227	6m	511
Working Capital	8m	8m	3m
Fixed Assets	2m	2m	2m
Current Assets	14m	14m	18m
Current Liabilities	1m	729	2m

Grant Handling Ltd
Unit C2 Coedcae Lane Industrial Estate Talbot Green, Llantrisant, Pontyclun, CF72 9HG
Tel: 01443-223336 **Fax:** 01443-229644
E-mail: southwales@forktrucks.co.uk
Website: http://www.forktrucks.co.uk
Managers: S. Phillips (Mgr)
Immediate Holding Company: GHL Holdings Ltd
Registration no: 01109065 **No.of Employees:** 1 - 10 **Product Groups:** 35, 39, 45

Jell Systems
1 Fairways View Talbot Green, Pontyclun, CF72 8JG
Tel: 07791-909689
E-mail: contact@jell-systems.co.uk
Website: http://www.jell-systems.co.uk
Directors: P. James (Prop)
Turnover: Up to £250,000 **No.of Employees:** 1 - 10 **Product Groups:** 38, 44, 48

Methods Centreline Ltd
Tyla Garw, Pontyclun, CF72 9YN
Tel: 01443-224328 **Fax:** 01443-237662
Website: http://www.mclengineering.com
Directors: B. Smith (Fin)
Immediate Holding Company: METHODS CENTRELINE LIMITED
Registration no: 00886085 **Date established:** 1966
No.of Employees: 21 - 50 **Product Groups:** 46

Date of Accounts	Dec 07	Dec 06	Dec 05
Working Capital	N/A	18	40
Current Assets	5	25	49
Current Liabilities	5	8	9
Total Share Capital	32	32	32

Packstat Ltd
Unit 20 Ely Valley Industrial Estate, Pontyclun, CF72 9DZ
Tel: 01443-223361 **Fax:** 01443-224086
E-mail: enquiries@packstat.co.uk
Website: http://www.packstat.co.uk
Directors: P. Stagg (Co Sec)
Managers: V. Pfleger (Mgr)
Ultimate Holding Company: NEW METALS AND CHEMICALS (HOLDINGS) LIMITED
Immediate Holding Company: PACKSTAT LIMITED
Registration no: 02465609 **Date established:** 1990 **Turnover:** £1m - £2m
No.of Employees: 1 - 10 **Product Groups:** 27, 30, 32

Date of Accounts	May 11	Mar 10	Mar 09
Sales Turnover	1m	1m	N/A
Pre Tax Profit/Loss	68	173	N/A
Working Capital	185	153	112
Fixed Assets	40	70	72
Current Assets	544	439	358
Current Liabilities	117	64	N/A

Purolite International Ltd (Sales Office)
Unit D Llantrisant Business Park, Llantrisant, Pontyclun, CF72 8LF
Tel: 01443-229334 **Fax:** 01443-222336
E-mail: sales@purolite.com
Website: http://www.purolite.com
Bank(s): Barclays, 99 Hatton Gardens, London EC1N 8DN
Directors: A. Wookey (Fin)
Managers: J. Rosie (Sales Prom Mgr), I. Horton (Sales Admin), N. Davies (Tech Serv Mgr), D. Jackson
Ultimate Holding Company: BROTECH CORPORATION (USA)
Immediate Holding Company: PUROLITE INTERNATIONAL LIMITED
Registration no: 01840987 **VAT No.:** GB 666 6508 02
Date established: 1984 **Turnover:** £20m - £50m
No.of Employees: 21 - 50 **Product Groups:** 31, 32, 42, 66, 67

Date of Accounts	Dec 11	Dec 10	Dec 09
Sales Turnover	48m	65m	62m
Pre Tax Profit/Loss	437	309	-540
Working Capital	60m	60m	68m
Fixed Assets	15m	15m	15m
Current Assets	69m	83m	76m
Current Liabilities	920	2m	461

Royal Mint
PO Box 500, Pontyclun, CF72 8YT
Tel: 0845-6088300 **Fax:** 01443-623328
E-mail: b2b@royalmint.com
Website: http://www.royalmint.com
Managers: B. Dyer
Immediate Holding Company: THE ROYAL MINT MUSEUM SERVICES LIMITED
Registration no: 07106468 **Date established:** 2009
Turnover: £75m - £125m **No.of Employees:** 501 - 1000
Product Groups: 49

Salon West
Unit 10 Green Park, Pontyclun, CF72 9GP
Tel: 01443-239139
E-mail: info@salonwest.co.uk
Website: http://www.salonwest.co.uk
Directors: S. Simms (Prop)
Registration no: Partnershi **Date established:** 2005
Turnover: Up to £250,000 **No.of Employees:** 1 - 10 **Product Groups:** 61

Silflex Ltd
Coedcae Lane, Pontyclun, CF72 9HJ
Tel: 01443-238464 **Fax:** 01443-238464
E-mail: orders@silflex.com
Website: http://www.silflex.com
Directors: M. Lloyd (Co Sec)
Managers: L. Jones, A. Lloyd (Chief Mgr), A. Buch
Ultimate Holding Company: CURRIE & WARNER (HOLDINGS) LIMITED
Immediate Holding Company: SILFLEX LIMITED
Registration no: 02569811 **VAT No.:** GB 541 0624 82
Date established: 1990 **Turnover:** £2m - £5m **No.of Employees:** 51 - 100
Product Groups: 29

Date of Accounts	Dec 11	Dec 10	Dec 09
Sales Turnover	5m	4m	3m
Pre Tax Profit/Loss	193	37	-142
Working Capital	2m	2m	2m
Fixed Assets	188	238	274
Current Assets	3m	2m	2m
Current Liabilities	161	123	115

So-Gefi Filtration Ltd
Llantrisant Industrial Estate Llantrisant, Pontyclun, CF72 8YU
Tel: 01443-223000 **Fax:** 01443-225459
E-mail: gareth.havard@sogefifiltration.com
Website: http://www.sogefifiltration.co.uk
Bank(s): Barclays, Cardiff
Directors: A. Clarke (Fin)
Managers: R. Roberts (Purch Mgr), R. Cartlidge (Mktg Serv Mgr), N. Miller (Personnel)
Ultimate Holding Company: CIR SPA (ITALY)
Immediate Holding Company: SOGEFI FILTRATION LIMITED
Registration no: 00693949 **Date established:** 1961
Turnover: £75m - £125m **No.of Employees:** 501 - 1000
Product Groups: 42

Date of Accounts	Dec 11	Dec 10	Dec 09
Sales Turnover	76m	72m	63m
Pre Tax Profit/Loss	-9m	-780	-1m
Working Capital	-3m	3m	5m
Fixed Assets	15m	21m	18m
Current Assets	19m	21m	20m
Current Liabilities	4m	2m	2m

Tarmac Ltd
School Road Miskin, Pontyclun, CF72 8PG
Tel: 01443-227552 **Fax:** 01443-228618
E-mail: a@tarmac.co.uk
Website: http://www.tarmac.co.uk
Directors: B. Browne (Dir)
Ultimate Holding Company: ANGLO AMERICAN PLC
Immediate Holding Company: TARMAC LIMITED
Registration no: 00453791 **Date established:** 1948
Turnover: £20m - £50m **No.of Employees:** 21 - 50 **Product Groups:** 14, 31, 33

Date of Accounts	Dec 11	Dec 10	Dec 09
Sales Turnover	1081m	1069m	1247m
Pre Tax Profit/Loss	-20m	75m	-47m
Working Capital	-86m	-24m	25m
Fixed Assets	1199m	1244m	1391m
Current Assets	329m	321m	431m
Current Liabilities	99m	93m	168m

Gwent

Pontypool

A M C Rollers Ltd
Unit 2 Polo Grounds, New Inn, Pontypool, NP4 0TW
Tel: 01495-769100 **Fax:** 01495-760111
E-mail: tonysmith@amcomponents.co.uk
Website: http://www.amcomponents.co.uk
Directors: A. Smith (Dir), T. Smith (Dir)
Immediate Holding Company: AMC ROLLERS LIMITED
Registration no: 04334328 **Date established:** 2001
Turnover: Up to £250,000 **No.of Employees:** 1 - 10 **Product Groups:** 28, 29, 30, 35, 43, 44, 45, 48, 66

Date of Accounts	Mar 11	Mar 10	Mar 09
Working Capital	112	99	129
Fixed Assets	40	31	45
Current Assets	275	396	305

Biffa Waste Services Ltd
Polo Grounds New Inn, Pontypool, NP4 0TW
Tel: 01495-752135 **Fax:** 01495-763362
E-mail: john.oliver@biffa.co.uk
Website: http://www.biffa.co.uk
Managers: J. Oliver (Mgr)
Immediate Holding Company: BIFFA WASTE SERVICES LIMITED
Registration no: 00946107 **Date established:** 1969
No.of Employees: 21 - 50 **Product Groups:** 32, 54, 84

Date of Accounts	Mar 08	Mar 09	Apr 10
Sales Turnover	555m	574m	492m
Pre Tax Profit/Loss	23m	50m	30m
Working Capital	229m	271m	293m
Fixed Assets	371m	360m	378m
Current Assets	409m	534m	609m
Current Liabilities	50m	100m	115m

Biozyme Holdings Ltd
Trit 6 Gilchrist Thomas Estate Bleanavon, Blaenavon, Pontypool, NP4 9RL
Tel: 01495-790678 **Fax:** 01495-791780
E-mail: info@biozyme.co.uk
Website: http://www.biozyme.com
Bank(s): National Westminster Bank Plc

Directors: J. Chesham (Dir), T. Coombs (Dir), K. Murray (Sales & Mktg)
Managers: A. Williams (Sales Admin), D. Jones (Chief Mgr), J. Bell (Mgr)
Ultimate Holding Company: Bbi Holdings plc
Immediate Holding Company: BIOZYME HOLDINGS LIMITED
Registration no: 02546322 **VAT No.:** GB 208 0543 92
Date established: 1990 **Turnover:** £250,000 - £500,000
No.of Employees: 21 - 50 **Product Groups:** 31, 85

Discount Floor Heating (Wales Distributor for Flexel International)

Studio 24 Gilchrist Thomas Industrial Estate, Blaenavon, Pontypool, NP4 9RL
Tel: 08456-581511 **Fax:** 08716-613557
E-mail: hermitage@discountfloorheating.co.uk
Website: http://www.discountfloorheating.co.uk
Directors: M. Hermitage (MD)
Immediate Holding Company: DISCOUNT FLOOR HEATING LIMITED
Registration no: 05303068 **Date established:** 2004
Turnover: Up to £250,000 **No.of Employees:** 1 - 10 **Product Groups:** 37, 38, 40, 52

Date of Accounts	Mar 11	Mar 09	Mar 08
Sales Turnover	68	117	147
Working Capital	-1	23	32
Current Assets	22	23	33
Current Liabilities	N/A	N/A	1

E M C Ltd

Cwmavon, Pontypool, NP4 8UW
Tel: 01495-772534 **Fax:** 01495-772251
E-mail: sales@capitalvalleyplastics.com
Website: http://www.capitalvalleyplastics.com
Bank(s): Lloyds TSB Bank plc
Directors: R. Phillips (MD)
Ultimate Holding Company: CWMAVON HOLDINGS LIMITED
Immediate Holding Company: EXTRUSION & MOULDING COMPOUNDS LIMITED
Registration no: 00905428 **VAT No.:** GB 134 4792 62
Date established: 1967 **Turnover:** £1m - £2m **No.of Employees:** 21 - 50
Product Groups: 30

Date of Accounts	May 11	May 10	May 09
Working Capital	224	-159	78
Fixed Assets	762	820	877
Current Assets	671	508	472

Ethical Packaging Solutions Ltd

Units 1-2 Gilchrist Thomas Court Gilchrist Thomas, Blaenavon, Pontypool, NP4 9RJ
Tel: 01495-793186
E-mail: tdrake@ethicalpackaging.co.uk
Website: http://www.ethicalpackaging.co.uk
Directors: T. Drake (MD)
Immediate Holding Company: ETHICAL PACKAGING SOLUTIONS LTD
Registration no: 05844836 **Date established:** 2006
No.of Employees: 1 - 10 **Product Groups:** 27, 28, 36

Date of Accounts	Jun 11	Jun 10	Jun 09
Working Capital	5	-19	-48
Fixed Assets	178	117	137
Current Assets	167	100	100

Forest International Gaskets

Unit 1 The Park Business Estate Penperlleni, Pontypool, NP4 0AL
Tel: 01594-810444 **Fax:** 01594-810420
Directors: M. Stuart (Fin)
Managers: M. Stewart (Mgr)
Immediate Holding Company: FOREST INTERNATIONAL GASKETS LTD
Registration no: 04615708 **Date established:** 2002
No.of Employees: 1 - 10 **Product Groups:** 38, 42

Date of Accounts	Apr 11	Apr 10	Apr 09
Working Capital	-85	-79	-69
Fixed Assets	2	2	2
Current Assets	20	51	67

Heathpak Ltd

Unit 3b Torfaen Business Centre Panteg Way, New Inn, Pontypool, NP4 0LS
Tel: 01495-759381 **Fax:** 01495-750632
E-mail: info@heathpak.com
Website: http://www.heathpak.com
Directors: A. Heath (Dir)
Immediate Holding Company: HEATHPAK LTD.
Registration no: 03769734 **Date established:** 1999 **Turnover:** £2m - £5m
No.of Employees: 1 - 10 **Product Groups:** 20, 25, 26, 27, 28, 30, 42, 44, 66, 83, 84, 85

Date of Accounts	May 12	May 11	May 10
Working Capital	86	103	95
Fixed Assets	41	17	22
Current Assets	1m	956	885

I T W Foils

Kays & Kears Industrial Estate Blaenavon, Pontypool, NP4 9AZ
Tel: 01495-796500 **Fax:** 01495-790797
E-mail: info@itwfoils.com
Website: http://www.itwfoils.com
Bank(s): National Westminster Bank Plc
Managers: J. Thomas (Personnel), A. Bannister (Tech Serv Mgr), M. King (Comptroller), J. Dick (Chief Mgr), D. Eccleshire (Comptroller), J. Hyde (Chief Mgr)
Immediate Holding Company: I T W INC (U.S.A.)
Registration no: 00559693 **Turnover:** £10m - £20m
No.of Employees: 51 - 100 **Product Groups:** 34, 44

Maddon Generators

Polo Grounds New Inn, Pontypool, NP4 0TW
Tel: 01495-752450 **Fax:** 01495-752450
E-mail: david@maddongenerators.com
Directors: D. Treharne (Dir)
Immediate Holding Company: SEVERNSIDE CONTINENTAL FREIGHTERS (U.K) LIMITED
Registration no: 01383302 **Date established:** 1978 **Turnover:** £1m - £2m
No.of Employees: 1 - 10 **Product Groups:** 37

Date of Accounts	Mar 11	Mar 10	Mar 09
Working Capital	-98	10	-20
Fixed Assets	307	316	323
Current Assets	388	339	312

Marlin Engineers

Unit 11 Heritage Court Gilchrist Thomas Industrial Estate, Blaenavon, Pontypool, NP4 9RL
Tel: 01495-792202 **Fax:** 01495-792232
E-mail: enquiries@marlinengineers.co.uk
Website: http://www.marlinengineers.co.uk
Directors: M. Talcombe (Ptnr)
Managers: M. Colcombe (Snr Eng)
No.of Employees: 1 - 10 **Product Groups:** 46

Pontypool Rewinds Ltd

Unit 6 Pontnewynydd Industrial Estate Pontnewynydd, Pontypool, NP4 6YW
Tel: 01495-753667 **Fax:** 01495-750174
E-mail: pontypoolrewinds@btconnect.com
Directors: H. Williams (MD)
Immediate Holding Company: PONTYPOOL REWINDS LIMITED
Registration no: 03458015 **Date established:** 1997
No.of Employees: 1 - 10 **Product Groups:** 37, 39, 40, 67

Date of Accounts	Mar 12	Mar 11	Mar 10
Working Capital	25	11	14
Fixed Assets	8	9	11
Current Assets	145	121	125

T C Automation

Unit 10 Panteg Industrial Estate Station Road, Griffithstown, Pontypool, NP4 5LX
Tel: 01495-759011 **Fax:** 01495-757223
Directors: S. Edward (MD)
Date established: 1991 **No.of Employees:** 1 - 10 **Product Groups:** 35, 39, 45

Trico Ltd

Skewfields, Pontypool, NP4 0XZ
Tel: 01495-767700 **Fax:** 01495-767877
E-mail: sales@trico.eu.com
Website: http://www.trico.eu.com
Directors: A. Champion (Fin)
Managers: A. Richards, N. Cole, S. Barlow (Tech Serv Mgr)
Ultimate Holding Company: KTRI HOLDINGS INC (USA)
Immediate Holding Company: TRICO LIMITED
Registration no: 00234268 **Date established:** 2028
Turnover: £10m - £20m **No.of Employees:** 51 - 100 **Product Groups:** 36, 39, 68

Date of Accounts	Dec 11	Jan 10	Jan 09
Sales Turnover	13m	11m	13m
Pre Tax Profit/Loss	375	636	-433
Working Capital	5m	5m	5m
Fixed Assets	397	714	201
Current Assets	7m	7m	7m
Current Liabilities	106	117	117

Wiltan Ltd

Ambassador Buildings Pontnewynydd Industrial Estate, Pontnewynydd, Pontypool, NP4 6YW
Tel: 01495-750711 **Fax:** 01495-753730
E-mail: zou@wilton.co.uk
Website: http://www.wiltan.co.uk
Bank(s): Barclays
Directors: A. Itani (Fin)
Managers: A. Corcoran (Tech Serv Mgr)
Ultimate Holding Company: WILTAN HOLDINGS LIMITED
Immediate Holding Company: WILTAN LIMITED
Registration no: 01892920 **VAT No.:** GB 433 2086 77
Date established: 1985 **Turnover:** £2m - £5m **No.of Employees:** 21 - 50
Product Groups: 37

Date of Accounts	Jun 11	Jun 10	Jun 09
Working Capital	1m	620	217
Fixed Assets	1m	1m	1m
Current Assets	2m	2m	1m

Mid-Glamorgan

Pontypridd

A B Technical Solutions

Riverside Industrial Park Treforest, Pontypridd, CF37 5TG
Tel: 01443-842300 **Fax:** 01443-842300
E-mail: craig@abtechnicalsolutions.com
Website: http://www.abtechnicalsolutions.com
Directors: C. Barrett (Dir)
No.of Employees: 11 - 20 **Product Groups:** 37, 67, 81

Agrisense B C S Ltd

Unit 1 3 Taffs Mead Road, Treforest Industrial Estate, Pontypridd, CF37 5SU
Tel: 01443-841155 **Fax:** 01443-841152
E-mail: sales@agrisense.co.uk
Website: http://www.agrisense.co.uk
Bank(s): HSBC,Pontyclun
Directors: N. Brown (Sales & Mktg), M. Noris (Dir), S. Resnick (Dir), C. Cooper (Co Sec)
Managers: D. Judd (Develop Mgr), D. Padgett (Chief Mgr), N. Bryan (Chief Mgr)
Ultimate Holding Company: ROLL INTERNATIONAL CORP (USA)
Immediate Holding Company: AGRISENSE - BCS LIMITED
Registration no: 01835431 **VAT No.:** GB 402 5287 79
Date established: 1984 **Turnover:** £5m - £10m
No.of Employees: 51 - 100 **Product Groups:** 32, 66, 85

Date of Accounts	Dec 10	Dec 09	Dec 08
Sales Turnover	5m	10m	7m
Pre Tax Profit/Loss	-211	1m	1m
Working Capital	4m	4m	3m
Fixed Assets	781	832	1m
Current Assets	5m	6m	5m
Current Liabilities	484	2m	2m

Albion Workplace Solutions

Unit G Upper Boat Trading Estate, Pontypridd, CF37 5BP
Tel: 01443-842222 **Fax:** 01443-842228
E-mail: sales@albionworkplacesolutions.co.uk
Website: http://www.albionworkplacesolutions.co.uk
Directors: S. Freili (Prop)
Immediate Holding Company: ALBION WORKPLACE SOLUTIONS LIMITED
Registration no: 07028108 **Date established:** 2009
No.of Employees: 1 - 10 **Product Groups:** 35, 42, 45

Date of Accounts	Dec 11	Sep 10
Working Capital	33	1
Fixed Assets	24	N/A
Current Assets	164	1

Andrews Sykes Hire Ltd

Maritime Industrial Estate, Pontypridd, CF37 1PB
Tel: 01443-486789 **Fax:** 01443-403743
E-mail: pontypridd@andrews-sykes.com
Website: http://www.andrews-sykes.com
Managers: J. Smele (Mgr)
Immediate Holding Company: ANDREWS SYKES HIRE LIMITED
Registration no: 02985657 **VAT No.:** GB 100 4295 24
Date established: 1994 **No.of Employees:** 1 - 10 **Product Groups:** 37, 39, 40, 52

Date of Accounts	Dec 11	Dec 10	Dec 09
Sales Turnover	35m	36m	34m
Pre Tax Profit/Loss	10m	10m	8m
Working Capital	8m	6m	2m
Fixed Assets	7m	7m	9m
Current Assets	33m	35m	35m
Current Liabilities	7m	7m	5m

Bush Health Care

20 Taff Street, Pontypridd, CF37 4UA
Tel: 01443-400877
Managers: C. Morgan (Mgr)
No.of Employees: 1 - 10 **Product Groups:** 38, 39, 45

Business In Focus Ltd

Business Development Centre Main Avenue, Treforest Industrial Estate, Pontypridd, CF37 5UR
Tel: 01443-841842 **Fax:** 01443-842925
E-mail: enquiries@businessinfocus.co.uk
Website: http://www.businessinfocus.co.uk
Directors: G. Bray (Grp Chief Exec)
Immediate Holding Company: BUSINESS IN FOCUS LIMITED
Registration no: 02553654 **VAT No.:** GB 540 8347 48
Date established: 1990 **Turnover:** Up to £250,000
No.of Employees: 1 - 10 **Product Groups:** 80, 86

Date of Accounts	Mar 12	Mar 11	Mar 10
Working Capital	-94	-201	-278
Fixed Assets	10m	9m	8m
Current Assets	540	425	329

Clariant

Llantwit Fardre, Pontypridd, CF38 2SN
Tel: 01443-205312 **Fax:** 01443-207746
Website: http://www.clariant.com
Bank(s): Lloyds
Managers: G. Cox (I.T. Exec), D. Bradbury (Personnel), S. Forward (Mgr), L. Payne (Sales & Mktg Mg), N. Wood (Chief Acct)
Ultimate Holding Company: BTP P.L.C.
Registration no: 00353315 **VAT No.:** GB 150 6821 81
No.of Employees: 101 - 250 **Product Groups:** 20, 31, 32, 66

Diamond Auto Repairs

Ynysybwl Road, Pontypridd, CF37 3BL
Tel: 01443-408619
E-mail: johndiamondautos@btconnect.com
Directors: J. Diamond (Prop)
No.of Employees: 1 - 10 **Product Groups:** 40

Graig Environmental Recycling Services Ltd

Unit 2b Maritime Industrial Estate, Pontypridd, CF37 1NY
Tel: 01443-401405 **Fax:** 01443-480829
E-mail: admin@graigrecycling.co.uk
Website: http://www.graigrecycling.co.uk
Directors: N. Selby (MD), G. Selby (Fin)
Immediate Holding Company: GRAIG ENVIRONMENTAL RECYCLING SERVICES LIMITED
Registration no: 03668881 **Date established:** 1998 **Turnover:** £2m - £5m
No.of Employees: 11 - 20 **Product Groups:** 34, 42, 54

Date of Accounts	Nov 11	Nov 10	Nov 09
Working Capital	-10	-20	-66
Fixed Assets	142	98	117
Current Assets	281	168	93

Griffin Mill Garages Ltd

Upper Boat, Pontypridd, CF37 5YE
Tel: 01443-842216 **Fax:** 01443-844799
E-mail: info@griffinmill.co.uk
Website: http://www.griffinmill.co.uk
Bank(s): National Westminster Bank Plc
Directors: M. Pardoe (Sales)
Managers: H. David (Mktg Serv Mgr), A. Gay (Personnel), G. Hopkins (Sales Prom Mgr), P. Jones (Fin Mgr)
Immediate Holding Company: GRIFFIN MILL GARAGES LIMITED
Registration no: 00708095 **VAT No.:** GB 134 6774 54
Date established: 1961 **Turnover:** £20m - £50m
No.of Employees: 51 - 100 **Product Groups:** 39

Date of Accounts	Dec 09	Dec 08	Dec 07
Sales Turnover	21m	20m	19m
Pre Tax Profit/Loss	273	47	59
Working Capital	819	841	1m
Fixed Assets	1m	1m	1m
Current Assets	3m	4m	3m
Current Liabilities	1m	2m	2m

Hi Tec Cathodic Protection Ltd

1 Old Tinplates Works Old Tin Works Road, Pontypridd, CF37 1UD
Tel: 01443-406276 **Fax:** 01443-406276
E-mail: sales@hitec-cathodic.co.uk
Website: http://www.hitec-cathodic.co.uk
Directors: C. Beere (Dir)
Immediate Holding Company: HI-TEC CATHODIC PROTECTION LIMITED
Registration no: 02547135 **Date established:** 1990
No.of Employees: 1 - 10 **Product Groups:** 33, 35, 37, 52, 84

Date of Accounts	Dec 11	Oct 10	Oct 09
Working Capital	-68	-61	-22
Fixed Assets	32	36	41
Current Assets	52	13	51

J J & Son Deliveries Ltd

11 Heol Cawrdaf Beddau, Pontypridd, CF38 2SL
Tel: 01443-218246 **Fax:** 01443-208490
E-mail: pam@jjdeliveries.com
Website: http://www.jjdeliveries.com
Directors: P. Mcguire (Dir)
Immediate Holding Company: JJ & SON DELIVERIES LIMITED
Registration no: 06050993 **Date established:** 2007 **Turnover:** £1m - £2m
No.of Employees: 1 - 10 **Product Groups:** 39, 79

see next page

J J & Son Deliveries Ltd - Cont'd

Date of Accounts	Mar 11	Mar 10	Mar 09
Working Capital	-70	-64	-71
Fixed Assets	112	82	81
Current Assets	32	10	6

Linear Plastics Ltd

Berw Road, Pontypridd, CF37 2AB
Tel: 01443-407500 **Fax:** 01443-480744
E-mail: gareth.bassett@linearplastics.com
Website: http://www.linearplastics.com
Bank(s): Barclays
Directors: R. Farrell (Dir), J. Bassett (Prop), J. Bassett (Dir), P. Powell (I.T. Dir), G. Bassett (MD)
Managers: M. Davis (Sales Admin)
Immediate Holding Company: LINEAR PLASTICS LIMITED
Registration no: 01188570 **VAT No.:** GB 137 0307 00
Date established: 1974 **Turnover:** £500,000 - £1m
No.of Employees: 21 - 50 **Product Groups:** 30

Date of Accounts	Mar 10	Mar 09	Mar 08
Working Capital	2m	2m	2m
Fixed Assets	673	721	770
Current Assets	2m	2m	2m

Melloy Ltd

Unit C10 Treforest Industrial Estate Main Avenue, Treforest Industrial Estate, Pontypridd, CF37 5UD
Tel: 01443-824880 **Fax:** 01443-844797
E-mail: enquiries@melloy.co.uk
Website: http://www.melloy.co.uk
Bank(s): Barclays
Directors: M. Allsop (MD), F. Ryan (Dir)
Managers: A. Ryan, K. Oliver
Immediate Holding Company: MELLOY LIMITED
Registration no: 05162411 **VAT No.:** GB 358 4728 11
Date established: 2004 **Turnover:** £1m - £2m **No.of Employees:** 51 - 100
Product Groups: 34, 66

Date of Accounts	Aug 11	Aug 10	Aug 09
Working Capital	-384	-140	-265
Fixed Assets	2m	2m	2m
Current Assets	1m	1m	1m

Paramount Doors Ltd

Paramount House Taffs Mead Road, Treforest Industrial Estate, Pontypridd, CF37 5TN
Tel: 01443-842100 **Fax:** 01443-842090
Website: http://www.paramountdoors.co.uk
Directors: J. Herbert (Co Sec)
Ultimate Holding Company: CATHGIL HOLDINGS LIMITED
Immediate Holding Company: PARAMOUNT DOORS LIMITED
Registration no: 02463562 **Date established:** 1990
No.of Employees: 21 - 50 **Product Groups:** 26, 35

Date of Accounts	Mar 12	Mar 11	Mar 10
Working Capital	86	169	154
Fixed Assets	8	11	14
Current Assets	214	310	276

P B Gelatins UK

Severn Road Treforest Industrial Estate, Pontypridd, CF37 5SQ
Tel: 01443-849300 **Fax:** 01443-844209
Website: http://www.tessenderlo.com
Bank(s): Fortess Bank, 13/14 Bavaria House, London EC2A 2DP
Managers: L. Doherty (Sales Prom Mgr), W. Gerry (Personnel), R. Jones (Chief Acct), M. Evans (Chief Mgr), B. Davies
Ultimate Holding Company: SNPE SA (FRANCE)
Immediate Holding Company: P B GELATINS U.K. LIMITED
Registration no: 01477674 **VAT No.:** GB 484 2644 28
Date established: 1980 **Turnover:** £20m - £50m
No.of Employees: 51 - 100 **Product Groups:** 32

Date of Accounts	Dec 11	Dec 10	Dec 09
Sales Turnover	30m	26m	23m
Pre Tax Profit/Loss	366	-2m	-452
Working Capital	7m	10m	10m
Fixed Assets	5m	4m	3m
Current Assets	14m	16m	17m
Current Liabilities	2m	994	358

Pontypridd & Llantrisant Observer

10 Market Street, Pontypridd, CF37 2ST
Tel: 01443-665161 **Fax:** 01443-665181
E-mail: wayne.nowaczyk@mediawales.co.uk
Website: http://www.walesonline.co.uk
Bank(s): Royal Bank of Scotland
Directors: W. Nowaczyk (Dir)
Immediate Holding Company: TRINITY HOLDINGS P.L.C.
Registration no: 00046946 **VAT No.:** GB 655 8557 89
Turnover: £2m - £5m **No.of Employees:** 11 - 20 **Product Groups:** 28

The Deritend Group Ltd

Unit C5 Treforest Industrial Estate, Pontypridd, CF37 5UD
Tel: 01443-842777 **Fax:** 01443-844567
E-mail: pontypridd@deritend.co.uk
Website: http://www.deritend.co.uk
Managers: S. Hall (Ops Mgr)
Ultimate Holding Company: DERITEND INDUSTRIES LIMITED
Immediate Holding Company: THE DERITEND GROUP LIMITED
Registration no: 04140677 **Date established:** 2001
No.of Employees: 11 - 20 **Product Groups:** 35, 37, 38, 40, 46, 48, 52, 66, 67, 85

Date of Accounts	Dec 11	Dec 10	Dec 09
Sales Turnover	18m	19m	21m
Pre Tax Profit/Loss	-140	-418	-465
Working Capital	6m	1m	-415
Fixed Assets	N/A	5m	6m
Current Assets	11m	6m	6m
Current Liabilities	884	902	1m

The Marble Warehouse Ltd

Unit 1 Maritime Industrial Estate, Pontypridd, CF37 1NY
Tel: 01443-408548 **Fax:** 01443-480344
E-mail: info@themarblewarehouse.net
Website: http://www.themarblewarehouse.net
Bank(s): Lloyds TSB Bank plc
Directors: L. Lloyd (Dir)
Immediate Holding Company: J.R.J. MANAGEMENT SERVICES LIMITED
Registration no: 01557103 **VAT No.:** GB 438 6383 21
Date established: 1981 **Turnover:** £250,000 - £500,000
No.of Employees: 11 - 20 **Product Groups:** 66

Date of Accounts	Apr 11	Apr 10	Apr 09
Working Capital	321	315	306
Fixed Assets	556	559	565
Current Assets	353	336	318

Wit Systems Ltd

Business Development Centre 7 Main Avenue, Treforest Industrial Estate, Pontypridd, CF37 5UR
Tel: 01443-844565 **Fax:** 01443-842925
E-mail: info@wit-systems.net
Website: http://www.wit-systems.net
Directors: H. Protheroe (MD), H. Prothroe (MD)
Immediate Holding Company: Wit Business Systems Ltd
Registration no: 06030661 **Turnover:** £250,000 - £500,000
No.of Employees: 1 - 10 **Product Groups:** 44

West Glamorgan

Port Talbot

Aberavon Web Design

24 Gordon Crescent, Port Talbot, SA12 7LF
Tel: 07517-896908 **Fax:** 08082-801672
E-mail: info@aberavonwebdesign.co.uk
Website: http://www.aberavonwebdesign.co.uk
Directors: D. Smith (Prop)
Date established: 2008 **Turnover:** Up to £250,000
No.of Employees: 1 - 10 **Product Groups:** 44

Celtic Chemicals Ltd

Unit 25 Kenfig Industrial Estate, Margam, Port Talbot, SA13 2PE
Tel: 01656-749358 **Fax:** 01656-746490
E-mail: ben.donald@celticchemicals.co.uk
Website: http://www.celticchemicals.co.uk
Bank(s): National Westminster Bank
Directors: B. Donald (Dir)
Immediate Holding Company: CELTIC CHEMICALS LIMITED
Registration no: 01438896 **VAT No.:** GB 331 0717 01
Date established: 1979 **Turnover:** £1m - £2m **No.of Employees:** 11 - 20
Product Groups: 31, 32

Date of Accounts	Oct 11	Oct 10	Oct 09
Working Capital	1m	766	589
Fixed Assets	144	147	183
Current Assets	2m	2m	1m

Clean Plastic Mouldings Ltd

Unit 6 Kenfig Industrial Estate, Margam, Port Talbot, SA13 2PE
Tel: 01656-740102 **Fax:** 01656-745354
E-mail: malcolmcpm@btconnect.com
Website: http://www.cpmouldings.com
Bank(s): National Westminster Bank Plc
Directors: G. Ballinger (Co Sec), M. Dennis (Dir), G. Ballinger (Dir), H. Dyer (Dir), M. Dennis (MD)
Immediate Holding Company: CLEAN PLASTIC MOULDINGS LIMITED
Registration no: 00654462 **VAT No.:** GB 587 9615 71
Date established: 1960 **Turnover:** £500,000 - £1m
No.of Employees: 11 - 20 **Product Groups:** 30, 42, 48

Date of Accounts	Dec 11	Dec 10	Dec 09
Working Capital	134	156	176
Fixed Assets	144	166	199
Current Assets	235	265	293

Components Finishers Ltd

15 Aberafon Road Baglan Industrial Park, Port Talbot, SA12 7DJ
Tel: 01639-766800 **Fax:** 01639-766811
Website: http://www.componentprint.fsnet.co.uk
Directors: M. John (MD), J. John (Fin)
Immediate Holding Company: COMPONENT FINISHERS LIMITED
Registration no: 03140610 **Date established:** 1995
No.of Employees: 1 - 10 **Product Groups:** 46, 48

Date of Accounts	Apr 11	Apr 10	Apr 09
Working Capital	6	15	16
Fixed Assets	1	2	3
Current Assets	8	18	28

Cornelius Electronics Ltd

Purcell Avenue, Port Talbot, SA12 7TZ
Tel: 01639-898114 **Fax:** 01639-898111
E-mail: sales@cornelius-electronics.co.uk
Website: http://www.cornelius-electronics.co.uk
Bank(s): Lloyds TSB Bank plc
Directors: D. Cornelius (MD), P. Ward (MD)
Managers: K. Foerunier (Purch Mgr), L. Boxall (Personnel), D. Powell, J. Heren
Immediate Holding Company: CORNELIUS ELECTRONICS LIMITED
Registration no: 01729062 **VAT No.:** GB 380 8523 42
Date established: 1983 **Turnover:** £5m - £10m
No.of Employees: 101 - 250 **Product Groups:** 37

Date of Accounts	Mar 09	Mar 08	Jun 11
Sales Turnover	5m	5m	7m
Pre Tax Profit/Loss	-62	124	162
Working Capital	487	216	607
Fixed Assets	936	1m	840
Current Assets	2m	2m	3m
Current Liabilities	1m	1m	1m

Corus Ltd

Abbey Works Margam, Port Talbot, SA13 2NG
Tel: 01639-871111 **Fax:** 01639-872147
E-mail: enquiries@corusgroup.co.uk
Website: http://www.corusgroup.com
Directors: J. Bryant (Works), M. Carr (MD), P. Dryden (MD), U. Chaturvedi (MD)
Managers: J. Cavanagh (Sales & Mktg Mg)
Immediate Holding Company: CORUS GROUP LIMITED
Registration no: 03811373 **Date established:** 1999
No.of Employees: 51 - 100 **Product Groups:** 33, 34, 36, 40

Gerald Davies Ltd

Kenfig Industrial Estate Margam, Port Talbot, SA13 2PE
Tel: 01656-745525 **Fax:** 01656-746270
E-mail: directors@geralddavies.co.uk
Website: http://www.geralddavies.co.uk
Bank(s): HSBC Bank plc
Directors: H. Davies (Fin), M. Hughes (MD)
Managers: A. Jones (Chief Mgr)
Immediate Holding Company: GERALD DAVIES LIMITED
Registration no: 01959827 **VAT No.:** GB 422 8848 36
Date established: 1985 **Turnover:** £2m - £5m **No.of Employees:** 51 - 100
Product Groups: 51

Date of Accounts	Oct 11	Oct 10	Oct 09
Working Capital	318	228	264
Fixed Assets	294	372	471
Current Assets	1m	795	879

Dragon Pump Services

Frowen Terrace, Port Talbot, SA12 6HF
Tel: 01639-887100 **Fax:** 01639-887519
E-mail: dragonpumps@btconnect.com
Directors: D. Jones (Prop)
Date established: 1990 **No.of Employees:** 1 - 10 **Product Groups:** 40

Durmech International Limited

ECM2 Heol Cefn Gwrgan Margam, Port Talbot, SA13 2EZ
Tel: 01639-864712 **Fax:** 01639-864711
E-mail: info@durmechinternational.com
Website: http://www.durmech.com
Directors: E. Maiden (Sales), J. Hale (Fin), P. Lewis (MD)
Managers: R. Gibbs (Nat Sales Mgr)
Ultimate Holding Company: Compagnie de Fives - Lille (France)
Immediate Holding Company: D J B (Holdings) Ltd
Registration no: 05817583 **VAT No.:** GB 277 0903 45
Date established: 1969 **Turnover:** £2m - £5m **No.of Employees:** 1 - 10
Product Groups: 44, 46

Envases UK Ltd 'c c b

1 Christchurch Road Baglan Industrial Park, Port Talbot, SA12 7BZ
Tel: 01639-814411 **Fax:** 01639-814422
E-mail: joaquin.marquez@envases.co.uk
Website: http://www.envases-group.com
Directors: J. Marquez (MD)
Ultimate Holding Company: ENVASES METALURGICOS DE ALAVA SA (SPAIN)
Immediate Holding Company: ENVASES (UK) LIMITED
Registration no: 02800858 **VAT No.:** GB 615 5170 59
Date established: 1993 **Turnover:** £20m - £50m
No.of Employees: 51 - 100 **Product Groups:** 35

Date of Accounts	Sep 11	Sep 10	Sep 09
Sales Turnover	21m	18m	16m
Pre Tax Profit/Loss	2m	2m	176
Working Capital	2m	4m	3m
Fixed Assets	16m	9m	9m
Current Assets	8m	7m	6m
Current Liabilities	4m	2m	505

Krane Engineering Ltd

Endeavour Close Industrial Estate, Port Talbot, SA12 7PT
Tel: 01639-892893 **Fax:** 01639-886622
E-mail: info@craneengineering.co.uk
Website: http://www.kraneengineering.co.uk
Managers: R. Corish (Mgr), M. Lister (Mgr)
Immediate Holding Company: KRANE ENGINEERING LIMITED
Registration no: 03474113 **Date established:** 1997
No.of Employees: 21 - 50 **Product Groups:** 46, 48

Date of Accounts	Dec 11	Dec 10	Dec 09
Working Capital	94	71	96
Current Assets	196	142	146

Ladders 4 Sale

Unit 10 Mardon Park Central Avenue, Baglan, Port Talbot, SA12 7AX
Tel: 08455-053000 **Fax:** 01639-642522
E-mail: info@ladders4sale.co.uk
Website: http://www.ladders4sale.co.uk
Directors: N. Phillips (Prop)
Immediate Holding Company: ABBEY ACCESS LIMITED
Registration no: 06291230 **Date established:** 2007
No.of Employees: 1 - 10 **Product Groups:** 25, 35, 40, 48, 66, 83, 86

Date of Accounts	Nov 11	Nov 10	Nov 09
Working Capital	-31	-43	37
Fixed Assets	56	59	7
Current Assets	141	86	122

Loxam Access Ltd

Llewellyn Quay, Port Talbot, SA13 1RF
Tel: 01639-888777 **Fax:** 01639-899226
E-mail: awilliams@loxam-access.co.uk
Website: http://www.loxam-access.co.uk
Managers: K. Lewis, A. Williams (Mgr)
Ultimate Holding Company: LOXAM HOLDING (FRANCE)
Immediate Holding Company: LOXAM ACCESS LIMITED
Registration no: 03988789 **VAT No.:** GB 509 4497 23
Date established: 2000 **No.of Employees:** 1 - 10 **Product Groups:** 45

Date of Accounts	Dec 11	Dec 10	Dec 09
Sales Turnover	10m	10m	10m
Pre Tax Profit/Loss	-60	-734	-1m
Working Capital	-6m	-5m	-6m
Fixed Assets	7m	6m	8m
Current Assets	3m	3m	3m
Current Liabilities	612	807	845

Montagne Jeunesse Ltd

Green Barn Astral Court Central Avenue, Baglan, Port Talbot, SA12 7AX
Tel: 01639-861550 **Fax:** 01792-310305
E-mail: cservices@montagnejeunesse.com
Website: http://www.montagnejeunesse.com
Bank(s): Barclays
Directors: K. Rockhill (Sales & Mktg), N. Gossage (Fin), G. Butcher (MD)
Managers: N. Ward (Personnel)
Ultimate Holding Company: MEDICAL EXPRESS (U.K.) LIMITED
Immediate Holding Company: MONTAGNE JEUNESSE INTERNATIONAL LIMITED
Registration no: 04209056 **VAT No.:** GB 644 4321 54
Date established: 2001 **Turnover:** £5m - £10m **No.of Employees:** 21 - 50
Product Groups: 32, 63

Date of Accounts	Dec 11	Dec 10	Dec 09
Sales Turnover	12m	10m	10m
Pre Tax Profit/Loss	2m	954	955
Working Capital	2m	730	83
Fixed Assets	155	178	173
Current Assets	7m	7m	6m
Current Liabilities	786	667	627

Orion Electric UK Co. Ltd
Unit 3 Kenfig Industrial Estate, Margam, Port Talbot, SA13 2PE
Tel: 01656-742400 **Fax:** 01656-744700
E-mail: info@orion-electric.co.uk
Website: http://www.orion-electric.co.uk
Bank(s): Bank of Wales PLC
Managers: T. Yajnik (Mgr)
Immediate Holding Company: ORION ELECTRIC (UK) LIMITED
Registration no: 01991562 **VAT No.:** GB 438 5813 27
Date established: 1986 **Turnover:** £10m - £20m
No.of Employees: 21 - 50 **Product Groups:** 37

Date of Accounts	Mar 11	Mar 10	Mar 09
Sales Turnover	10m	23m	176m
Pre Tax Profit/Loss	943	-2m	-6m
Working Capital	2m	830	-28m
Fixed Assets	1m	1m	22m
Current Assets	7m	24m	77m
Current Liabilities	4m	12m	11m

Quantum Eds
Cefn Gwrgan Road Margam, Port Talbot, SA13 2EZ
Tel: 01639-864646 **Fax:** 01639-864676
E-mail: s.jones@quantumeds.co.uk
Website: http://www.quantumeds.co.uk
Directors: S. Jones (MD)
Managers: A. Bastek (Sales Prom)
Immediate Holding Company: QUANTUM ELECTRONIC DEVELOPMENT SOLUTIONS LIMITED
Registration no: 05552524 **Date established:** 2005
No.of Employees: 11 - 20 **Product Groups:** 84

Date of Accounts	Sep 10	Sep 09	Sep 08
Working Capital	18	19	13
Fixed Assets	2	3	N/A
Current Assets	29	52	36

R P C Tedeco Gizeh UK Ltd
Kenfig Industrial Estate Margam, Port Talbot, SA13 2PE
Tel: 01656-749183 **Fax:** 01656-743074
E-mail: david.lowe@rpc-tedeco-gizeh.com
Website: http://www.rpc-tedeco-gizeh.com
Directors: K. Thomas (Fin)
Managers: R. Phillips (Sales Admin), D. Lowe (Chief Mgr)
Ultimate Holding Company: RPC GROUP PLC
Immediate Holding Company: RPC TEDECO-GIZEH (UK) LIMITED
Registration no: 03289951 **Date established:** 1996
No.of Employees: 51 - 100 **Product Groups:** 30

Date of Accounts	Mar 11	Mar 10	Mar 09
Sales Turnover	16m	15m	17m
Pre Tax Profit/Loss	1m	1m	407
Working Capital	2m	2m	941
Fixed Assets	4m	4m	4m
Current Assets	8m	6m	12m
Current Liabilities	813	429	7m

Renubarth West Wales
31 Baglan Heights, Port Talbot, SA12 8UF
Tel: 01639-812666 **Fax:** 01639-823205
Website: http://www.renubath.co.uk
Directors: P. Brian (Prop), P. Briers (Prop)
Immediate Holding Company: A.P.I. LEGAL CONSULTANCY LTD
Registration no: 06785042 **Date established:** 2009
No.of Employees: 1 - 10 **Product Groups:** 46, 48

Rowecord Engineering
1 Rutherglen Centre Seaway Parade Industrial Estate, Port Talbot, SA12 7BR
Tel: 01639-823125 **Fax:** 01639-821817
E-mail: robert.hornblower@rowecord.com
Website: http://www.rowecord.com
Managers: R. Hornblower (Mgr)
Date established: 2001 **No.of Employees:** 21 - 50 **Product Groups:** 35

Andrew Scott Ltd
The Grange Margam, Port Talbot, SA13 2SP
Tel: 01639-889800 **Fax:** 01639-889829
E-mail: mark.bowen@andrewscott.co.uk
Website: http://www.andrewscott.co.uk
Directors: A. Hoppe (Fin), M. Bowen (MD)
Managers: R. Williams (Buyer)
Ultimate Holding Company: ROWECORD HOLDINGS LIMITED
Immediate Holding Company: ANDREW SCOTT LTD.
Registration no: 00406516 **VAT No.:** GB 484 0552 43
Date established: 1946 **Turnover:** £10m - £20m
No.of Employees: 21 - 50 **Product Groups:** 51

Date of Accounts	Jun 12	Jun 11	Jun 10
Sales Turnover	22m	16m	16m
Pre Tax Profit/Loss	33	-235	-756
Working Capital	3m	3m	3m
Fixed Assets	749	646	764
Current Assets	8m	6m	6m
Current Liabilities	852	421	498

Site Heat Treatment Services Ltd
Unit 2 Henshaw Street, Port Talbot, SA12 6NH
Tel: 01639-899220 **Fax:** 01639-898697
E-mail: a.veysey@shs-group.com
Website: http://www.shs-group.com
Bank(s): Lloyds TSB
Directors: C. Veysey (Fin), A. Veysey (MD)
Immediate Holding Company: SITE HEAT TREATMENT SERVICES LIMITED
Registration no: 01597335 **VAT No.:** GB 359 4673 10
Date established: 1981 **Turnover:** £250,000 - £500,000
No.of Employees: 21 - 50 **Product Groups:** 48

Date of Accounts	Mar 12	Mar 11	Mar 10
Working Capital	183	94	111
Fixed Assets	230	167	182
Current Assets	531	624	328

South Wales Industrial Equipment Ltd
Unit 23 Marden Estate Central Avenue, Baglan, Port Talbot, SA12 7AX
Tel: 01639-823000 **Fax:** 01639-886555
E-mail: kenf@swie.co.uk
Website: http://www.swie.co.uk
Directors: B. Colston (MD), K. Fraser (MD)
Managers: S. Lewis (Fin Mgr), R. Evans (Chief Mgr)
Immediate Holding Company: SOUTH WALES INDUSTRIAL EQUIPMENT LIMITED
Registration no: 04281914 **Date established:** 2001
No.of Employees: 21 - 50 **Product Groups:** 35, 39, 45

Date of Accounts	Aug 11	Aug 10	Aug 09
Working Capital	13	-192	-269
Fixed Assets	1m	1m	1m
Current Assets	1m	777	801

Sparks Fire Protection
89 Llewellyn Street, Port Talbot, SA12 8SG
Tel: 01639-885837
E-mail: kevin@sparksfire.org.uk
Website: http://www.sparksfire.org.uk
Directors: K. Sparks (Prop)
Immediate Holding Company: SPARKS FIRE PROTECTION LIMITED
Registration no: 04460314 **Date established:** 2002
No.of Employees: 11 - 20 **Product Groups:** 38, 42

Date of Accounts	Aug 11	Aug 10	Aug 09
Working Capital	99	57	44
Fixed Assets	39	54	50
Current Assets	167	119	105

Texturing Technology Ltd
PO Box 22, Port Talbot, SA13 2YJ
Tel: 01639-872197 **Fax:** 01639-872196
E-mail: p.burke@texturingtechnology.net
Website: http://www.texturingtechnology.com
Bank(s): Lloyds
Managers: R. Sell (Tech Serv Mgr), J. Williams (Fin Mgr), P. Burke (Chief Mgr)
Immediate Holding Company: TEXTURING TECHNOLOGY LIMITED
Registration no: 02684488 **VAT No.:** GB 557 9904 85
Date established: 1992 **Turnover:** £2m - £5m **No.of Employees:** 21 - 50
Product Groups: 48

Date of Accounts	Mar 08	Mar 09	Apr 10
Sales Turnover	4m	3m	4m
Pre Tax Profit/Loss	-1m	-248	-73
Working Capital	-758	-219	55
Fixed Assets	6m	5m	5m
Current Assets	1m	938	1m
Current Liabilities	1m	941	924

Washerman Rentals
Isaacs Place, Port Talbot, SA12 6NP
Tel: 01639-888637
E-mail: washerman@btconnect.com
Directors: S. Brown (Prop)
Date established: 1987 **No.of Employees:** 1 - 10 **Product Groups:** 43

Date of Accounts	Apr 08	Apr 07	Apr 06
Working Capital	-18	-6	-50
Fixed Assets	126	141	141
Current Assets	32	49	32
Current Liabilities	50	55	82

Western Log Group
Ynys Y Gwas Cwmavon, Port Talbot, SA12 9AB
Tel: 01639-896715 **Fax:** 01639-890993
E-mail: mike@westernloggroup.com
Website: http://www.westernloggroup.com
Directors: D. James (Co Sec), G. James (Dir), M. James (Sales), R. James (MD)
Immediate Holding Company: BURGER MASTER RESTAURANTS LIMITED
Registration no: 06184820 **Date established:** 1992 **Turnover:** £5m - £10m
No.of Employees: 11 - 20 **Product Groups:** 25

Westley Of Cardiff
PO Box 84, Port Talbot, SA13 2ZU
Tel: 01639-875061 **Fax:** 01639-875064
E-mail: rod.mirams@westleygroup.co.uk
Website: http://www.westleygroup.co.uk
Managers: R. Mirams (Ops Mgr)
Immediate Holding Company: WESTLEY LIMITED
Registration no: 02304143 **Date established:** 1988
Turnover: £10m - £20m **No.of Employees:** 1 - 10 **Product Groups:** 34

Mid-Glamorgan

Porth

R A Hulland Group Ltd
235-239 High Street, Porth, CF39 9AD
Tel: 01443-684844 **Fax:** 01443-684847
E-mail: nicola.hulland@homes-to-rent.com
Website: http://www.rahullandgroup.co.uk
Bank(s): Barclays
Directors: A. Hulland (Fin), G. Griffiths (Fin), R. Hulland (MD), N. Hulland (Co Sec), N. Hulland (Dir)
Immediate Holding Company: LIMLYRE LIMITED
Registration no: 01640792 **VAT No.:** GB 134 7217 81
Date established: 1982 **No.of Employees:** 11 - 20 **Product Groups:** 80

Perfect Leather Sales Ltd
Carmel Works Chapel Street, Porth, CF39 0PU
Tel: 01443-757150 **Fax:** 01443-757150
E-mail: petervalek@petervalek.worldonline.co.uk
Website: http://www.leatherwatchstraps.co.uk
Directors: P. Valek (MD), S. Valek (Fin)
Immediate Holding Company: PERFECT LEATHER SALES LIMITED
Registration no: 01492282 **Date established:** 1980
Turnover: Up to £250,000 **No.of Employees:** 1 - 10 **Product Groups:** 49, 65

Date of Accounts	Mar 12	Mar 11	Mar 10
Working Capital	8	7	10
Fixed Assets	10	10	10
Current Assets	34	31	36

Rhonda Mobility Services
43 Francis Street Tonyrefail, Porth, CF39 8DS
Tel: 01443-675043 **Fax:** 01443-673186
Directors: T. Howells (Prop)
No.of Employees: 1 - 10 **Product Groups:** 24, 30, 38

Sign Group
Unit 1 Del Guerra Court Gelligron Industrial Estate, Tonyrefail, Porth, CF39 8ES
Tel: 01443-670300 **Fax:** 01443-670404
Directors: S. Wakely (MD)
No.of Employees: 1 - 10 **Product Groups:** 30, 39, 40

Mid-Glamorgan

Porthcawl

Mark Heating
7 Victoria Avenue, Porthcawl, CF36 3HG
Tel: 07000-781329 **Fax:** 01656-773074
E-mail: p.richards@grehe.com
Website: http://www.grehe.com
Directors: P. Richards (Prop)
Immediate Holding Company: NUTECH LTD
Registration no: 05111234 **Date established:** 2004
No.of Employees: 1 - 10 **Product Groups:** 40

P E Thomas Precision Ltd
Glan Road, Porthcawl, CF36 5DF
Tel: 01656-783555 **Fax:** 01656-783555
E-mail: info@pethomasltd.co.uk
Directors: S. Lloyd (MD), R. Lloyd (Fin)
Immediate Holding Company: P E THOMAS (PRECISION) LIMITED
Registration no: 01802313 **VAT No.:** GB 405 0264 01
Date established: 1984 **Turnover:** £250,000 - £500,000
No.of Employees: 1 - 10 **Product Groups:** 39, 48

Date of Accounts	May 12	May 11	May 10
Working Capital	22	27	18
Fixed Assets	9	10	11
Current Assets	112	91	85
Current Liabilities	34	N/A	N/A

Vale Internet Solutions Ltd
53 Mary Street, Porthcawl, CF36 3YN
Tel: 01656-788862
E-mail: enquiries@valeinternet.co.uk
Website: http://www.valeinternet.co.uk
Directors: R. Diamond (Dir)
Immediate Holding Company: VALE INTERNET SOLUTIONS LIMITED
Registration no: 05051013 **Date established:** 2004
No.of Employees: 1 - 10 **Product Groups:** 44

Date of Accounts	Mar 11	Mar 09	Mar 08
Working Capital	2	5	12
Fixed Assets	8	13	16
Current Assets	12	21	24

Gwynedd

Porthmadog

Ffestiniog Railway
Harbour Station, Porthmadog, LL49 9NF
Tel: 01766-516000 **Fax:** 01766-514576
E-mail: enquiries@festrail.co.uk
Website: http://www.festrail.co.uk
Bank(s): National Westminster
Directors: N. Burbidge (Fin), J. Prideaux (MD)
Managers: C. Britton (Comm)
Immediate Holding Company: FFESTINIOG RAILWAY HOLDINGS LIMITED
Registration no: 02555576 **Date established:** 1990 **Turnover:** £2m - £5m
No.of Employees: 11 - 20 **Product Groups:** 72

Date of Accounts	Dec 11	Dec 10	Dec 09
Sales Turnover	2m	2m	2m
Pre Tax Profit/Loss	70	50	19
Working Capital	203	165	120
Fixed Assets	21	N/A	5
Current Assets	587	487	240
Current Liabilities	384	322	112

Robert Owen Marine Services
The Harbour, Porthmadog, LL49 9AY
Tel: 01766-513435 **Fax:** 01766-512289
Website: http://www.robertowenmarine.co.uk
Managers: R. Owen (Mgr)
Immediate Holding Company: THE FIXINGS STORE LIMITED
Registration no: 05806246 **Date established:** 2006
No.of Employees: 1 - 10 **Product Groups:** 35, 36, 39

Date of Accounts	May 11	May 10	May 09
Working Capital	2	-3	-11
Fixed Assets	13	13	15
Current Assets	85	56	34

Clwyd

Prestatyn

Drain-Medic plumbing
Gwynfa Chapel Road, Prestatyn, LL19 7TH
Tel: 0800-2118301
E-mail: info@drain-medic.com
Website: http://www.drain-medic.com
Directors: M. Simon (Ptnr), P. Ward (Ptnr)
Date established: 2009 **No.of Employees:** 1 - 10 **Product Groups:** 52

Redbows Ltd
24 Bryntirion Drive, Prestatyn, LL19 9NU
Tel: 08458-386368 **Fax:** 0845-838 6369
E-mail: sales@redbows.co.uk
Website: http://www.promotionalgiftsstore.co.uk
Directors: R. Koffler (Fin), D. Koffler (MD)
Immediate Holding Company: REDBOWS LTD
Registration no: 05185125 **Date established:** 2004
Turnover: Up to £250,000 **No.of Employees:** 1 - 10 **Product Groups:** 33, 49, 81

see next page

Redbows Ltd - Cont'd

Date of Accounts	Dec 10	Dec 09	Dec 08
Working Capital	-16	-17	-11
Fixed Assets	18	17	12
Current Assets	85	52	57

REME Industrial Flooring Ltd
79 Victoria Road, Prestatyn, LL19 7SP
Tel: 01745-856572 **Fax:** 01745-856572
E-mail: info@remeflooring.co.uk
Website: http://www.remeflooring.co.uk
Directors: P. Dines (Dir)
Immediate Holding Company: REME INDUSTRIAL FLOORING LIMITED
Registration no: 05290704 **Date established:** 2004
Turnover: Up to £250,000 **No.of Employees:** 1 - 10 **Product Groups:** 52

Date of Accounts	Nov 11	Nov 10	Nov 09
Working Capital	11	16	49
Fixed Assets	14	8	12
Current Assets	142	73	117

Saversoftware.Com
143 High Street, Prestatyn, LL19 9AS
Tel: 08451-235510 **Fax:** 0871-224 7658
E-mail: gareth.sandilands@saversoftware.co.uk
Website: http://www.saversoftware.com
Directors: G. Sandilands (Prop), G. Sandilanes (Prop), G. Sandilands (MD)
Date established: 2000 **Turnover:** £250,000 - £500,000
No.of Employees: 1 - 10 **Product Groups:** 67

Powys

Presteigne

Kaye Presteigne Ltd
Harper Street, Presteigne, LD8 2AL
Tel: 01544-267551 **Fax:** 01544-267032
E-mail: sales@kayepresteigne.co.uk
Website: http://www.kayepresteigne.co.uk
Directors: P. Neagle (MD)
Managers: P. Davidson (Chief Mgr), G. Hayball (Sales Prom Mgr), G. Smith (Fin Mgr), L. Waters (I.T. Exec), S. Lewis (Tech Serv Mgr)
Immediate Holding Company: J.L. French
Registration no: 06783863 **Date established:** 1933 **Turnover:** £2m - £5m
No.of Employees: 51 - 100 **Product Groups:** 34

Mangar International Ltd
Presteigne Industrial Estate, Presteigne, LD8 2UF
Tel: 01544-267674 **Fax:** 01544-260287
E-mail: info@mangar.co.uk
Website: http://www.mangar.co.uk
Directors: F. Garman (Sales & Mktg), R. Morley (Co Sec), C. Arnold (Fin), D. Garman (Ch)
Managers: T. Collis (Tech Serv Mgr)
Ultimate Holding Company: MANGAR INTERNATIONAL (HOLDINGS) LIMITED
Immediate Holding Company: MANGAR INTERNATIONAL LIMITED
Registration no: 01623146 **VAT No.:** GB 359 0957 16
Date established: 1982 **Turnover:** £5m - £10m **No.of Employees:** 21 - 50
Product Groups: 26, 36, 45

Date of Accounts	Jul 11	Jul 10	Jul 09
Sales Turnover	6m	7m	7m
Pre Tax Profit/Loss	79	83	356
Working Capital	3m	3m	3m
Fixed Assets	66	122	192
Current Assets	4m	4m	4m
Current Liabilities	195	272	368

Teledyne Labtech Ltd
Unit 1 Broadaxe Business Park, Presteigne, LD8 2UH
Tel: 01544-260093 **Fax:** 01544-260310
E-mail: j.priday@labtech.ltd.uk
Website: http://www.teledynelabtech.com
Bank(s): Barclays
Managers: J. Priday (Chief Mgr), D. Marshall (Comptroller), E. Latham (Purch Mgr)
Ultimate Holding Company: TELEDYNE TECHNOLOGIES INC (USA)
Immediate Holding Company: TELEDYNE LABTECH LIMITED
Registration no: 01709860 **VAT No.:** GB 393 9216 21
Date established: 1983 **Turnover:** £5m - £10m
No.of Employees: 51 - 100 **Product Groups:** 35, 37, 69

Date of Accounts	Dec 11	Dec 10	Mar 10
Sales Turnover	7m	3m	8m
Pre Tax Profit/Loss	-34	-2m	-385
Working Capital	-638	-672	611
Fixed Assets	2m	2m	2m
Current Assets	4m	3m	3m
Current Liabilities	492	413	450

Gwynedd

Pwllheli

C D S Consultants CDS Industries
Bwlch Tocyn Farm Bwlchtocyn, Pwllheli, LL53 7BN
Tel: 01758-712245 **Fax:** 01758-712014
E-mail: enquiries@cdsconsultants.co.uk
Website: http://www.cdsconsultants.co.uk
Directors: S. Stevenson (MD)
Turnover: £2m - £5m **No.of Employees:** 1 - 10 **Product Groups:** 33, 39, 40, 45, 46, 48

Carl Kammerling International Ltd
C K House Glanydon Industrial Estate, Pwllheli, LL53 5LH
Tel: 01758-704704
E-mail: sales@cki.uk.com
Website: http://www.carlkammerling.com
Bank(s): Barclays
Directors: T. Meyerratken (MD)
Managers: P. Fallon (Mktg Serv Mgr), J. Roberts, J. Hollywood (Tech Serv Mgr), C. Williams (Personnel), I. Walker (Sales Prom Mgr)
Immediate Holding Company: CARL KAMMERLING INTERNATIONAL LIMITED
Registration no: 00764323 **VAT No.:** GB 158 9648 06
Date established: 1963 **Turnover:** £10m - £20m
No.of Employees: 51 - 100 **Product Groups:** 30, 35, 36

Date of Accounts	Dec 11	Dec 10	Dec 09
Sales Turnover	14m	13m	12m
Pre Tax Profit/Loss	657	179	864
Working Capital	7m	6m	6m
Fixed Assets	1m	1m	1m
Current Assets	8m	8m	8m
Current Liabilities	1m	1m	N/A

Gwynedd Gas Supplies Ltd
Bodawen Lane Y Maes, Pwllheli, LL53 5HB
Tel: 01758-614161 **Fax:** 01758-613313
E-mail: sales@gwyneddgas.co.uk
Website: http://www.gwyneddgas.co.uk
Directors: S. Edwards (Dir)
Immediate Holding Company: GWYNEDD GAS SUPPLIES LTD.
Registration no: 03584000 **Date established:** 1998
No.of Employees: 1 - 10 **Product Groups:** 20, 40, 67

Date of Accounts	Jun 11	Jun 10	Jun 09
Working Capital	3	-1	-5
Fixed Assets	5	6	2
Current Assets	10	12	13

Marine Tech
Bodvel Hall Llannor, Pwllheli, LL53 6DW
Tel: 01758-703045
E-mail: marinetech@fsmail.net
Website: http://www.marinetechwales.com
Directors: R. Jones (Prop)
No.of Employees: 1 - 10 **Product Groups:** 35, 37, 39

Clwyd

Rhyl

Cefndy Health Care
Cefndy Road, Rhyl, LL18 2HG
Tel: 01745-343877 **Fax:** 01745-355806
Website: http://www.cefndy.com
Managers: K. Perkins (Purch Mgr), S. Rowlands (Sales & Mktg Mg), D. Holmes-Langstone (Mgr), E. Freeman (Fin Mgr), M. Moore
No.of Employees: 51 - 100 **Product Groups:** 38, 67

Cooper Carriers Ltd
Tir Llwyd Industrial Estate Kinmel Bay, Rhyl, LL18 5JA
Tel: 01745-362800 **Fax:** 01745-362801
Directors: D. McAllister (Fin)
Managers: T. Breton (Mgr)
Ultimate Holding Company: CFG HOLDINGS LIMITED
Immediate Holding Company: COOPER CARRIERS LTD
Registration no: 03133059 **VAT No.:** GB 719 3978 86
Date established: 1995 **Turnover:** £500,000 - £1m
No.of Employees: 51 - 100 **Product Groups:** 45, 72, 74, 75

Davies Bakery Supplies Ltd
Kinmel Park Abergele Road, Bodelwyddan, Rhyl, LL18 5TY
Tel: 01745-583057 **Fax:** 01745-584848
E-mail: cdavies@reynards.com
Website: http://www.reynards.com
Directors: C. Davies (MD)
Immediate Holding Company: DAVIES BAKERY SUPPLIES LTD
Registration no: 01019490 **Date established:** 1971
No.of Employees: 11 - 20 **Product Groups:** 25, 27, 30, 35, 41

Date of Accounts	Mar 12	Mar 11	Mar 10
Working Capital	231	269	402
Fixed Assets	12	16	19
Current Assets	580	619	825

Decantae Mineral Water Ltd
Tir Llwyd Industrial Estate Kinmel Bay, Rhyl, LL18 5JA
Tel: 01745-343504 **Fax:** 01745-331591
E-mail: sales@decantae.co.uk
Website: http://www.decantae.co.uk
Directors: I. Spooner (Dir)
Immediate Holding Company: DECANTAE MINERAL WATER LIMITED
Registration no: 01949922 **VAT No.:** GB 419 9445 18
Date established: 1985 **Turnover:** £1m - £2m **No.of Employees:** 11 - 20
Product Groups: 21

Date of Accounts	Dec 11	Dec 10	Dec 09
Working Capital	-260	-165	-215
Fixed Assets	713	769	846
Current Assets	405	521	453

Ellis Welding
Unit 2 Glan Aber Trading Estate Vale Road, Rhyl, LL18 2PL
Tel: 01745-339400 **Fax:** 01745- 336890
Directors: J. Ellis (Dir)
Date established: 2001 **No.of Employees:** 1 - 10 **Product Groups:** 35

Evadx Ltd
Tir Llwyd Enterprise Park Kinmel Bay, Rhyl, LL18 5JZ
Tel: 01745-336413 **Fax:** 01745-339639
E-mail: sales@evadx.com
Website: http://www.evadx.com
Bank(s): Lloyds TSB Bank plc
Directors: B. Adams (Co Sec)
Managers: B. Adams (Admin Off), A. Jones (Comptroller), J. Glachan (Chief Mgr), S. Adams (Mktg Serv Mgr)
Immediate Holding Company: EVADX LIMITED
Registration no: 01791754 **VAT No.:** GB 419 9317 27
Date established: 1984 **Turnover:** £10m - £20m
No.of Employees: 51 - 100 **Product Groups:** 35

Date of Accounts	Nov 11	Nov 10	Nov 09
Sales Turnover	11m	8m	6m
Pre Tax Profit/Loss	98	-23	-225
Working Capital	600	671	743
Fixed Assets	592	590	588
Current Assets	4m	3m	2m
Current Liabilities	171	196	190

Hive Ltd
P.O.Box 206, Rhyl, LL18 1WY
Tel: 01745-339802
E-mail: sales-marketing@hive-esecurity.com
Website: http://www.hive-esecurity.com
Directors: O. Vigneresse (Prop)
Managers: J. Vigneresse (Consultant)
Registration no: 03937810 **Date established:** 2000
No.of Employees: 21 - 50 **Product Groups:** 44

Industrial Equipment UK Ltd
Green Avenue Kinmel Bay, Rhyl, LL18 5ET
Tel: 01745-337646 **Fax:** 01745-345397
Directors: M. Homer (Prop)
Immediate Holding Company: DOWNEY SERVICES LIMITED
Registration no: 03508067 **VAT No.:** 709 6158 19 **Date established:** 1996
Turnover: £500,000 - £1m **No.of Employees:** 1 - 10 **Product Groups:** 35, 45

Date of Accounts	Dec 10	Dec 09	Dec 08
Working Capital	15	17	10
Fixed Assets	55	55	55
Current Assets	18	20	21

Inwood Cymru Ltd
Unit A1 Cefndy Road Employment Park Cefndy Road, Rhyl, LL18 2HJ
Tel: 01745-362444 **Fax:** 01745-531001
E-mail: enquiries@woodworkersuk.co.uk
Website: http://www.woodworkersuk.co.uk
Directors: J. Culshaw (Dir)
Immediate Holding Company: INWOOD (CYMRU) LIMITED
Registration no: 04792562 **Date established:** 2003
No.of Employees: 1 - 10 **Product Groups:** 25

Date of Accounts	Aug 11	Aug 10	Aug 09
Working Capital	10	18	12
Fixed Assets	5	1	1
Current Assets	38	48	50

N W P Electrical & Mechanical Ltd
Engineers House Tir Llwyd Industrial Estate, Kinmel Bay, Rhyl, LL18 5JA
Tel: 01745-351351
E-mail: info@nwp-ltd.com
Website: http://www.nwp-ltd.com
Directors: S. Cripps (Co Sec), T. Keyes (MD)
Immediate Holding Company: NWP ELECTRICAL & MECHANICAL LIMITED
Registration no: 06115752 **Date established:** 2007
No.of Employees: 21 - 50 **Product Groups:** 37, 52, 84

Date of Accounts	Mar 12	Mar 11	Mar 10
Working Capital	446	301	190
Fixed Assets	185	184	167
Current Assets	3m	2m	870

NWMF
61 Warren Road, Rhyl, LL18 1DR
Tel: 01745-353235 **Fax:** 01745-305700
Directors: S. Jones (Prop)
No.of Employees: 1 - 10 **Product Groups:** 46, 48

Storm Power
13 Pendyffryn Road, Rhyl, LL18 4RU
Tel: 01745-354405 **Fax:** 08701-209724
E-mail: sales@stormpower.co.uk
Website: http://www.stormpower.co.uk
Directors: P. Bate (Prop)
Registration no: 02407796 **VAT No.:** GB 559 8813 81
Date established: 1997 **Turnover:** £250,000 - £500,000
No.of Employees: 1 - 10 **Product Groups:** 37, 38

Trade Frames
Unit 23 H T M Business Park Abergele Road, Rhuddlan, Rhyl, LL18 5UZ
Tel: 01745-590099 **Fax:** 01745-590090
Directors: G. Griffiths (Dir)
No.of Employees: 1 - 10 **Product Groups:** 30, 33, 35

Tyco Electronics UK Ltd
Kinmel Park Bodelwyddan, Rhyl, LL18 5TZ
Tel: 01745-584545 **Fax:** 01745-584780
E-mail: mark.scott@tycoelectronics.com
Website: http://www.te.com
Bank(s): National Westminster
Directors: T. Wilkinson (Fin), S. Vaughn (Fin)
Managers: M. Scott (Personnel), J. Mapson (Purch Mgr), P. Williams (Tech Serv Mgr)
Ultimate Holding Company: TE CONNECTIVITY LTD (SWITZERLAND)
Immediate Holding Company: TYCO ELECTRONICS UK LTD
Registration no: 00550926 **VAT No.:** GB 560 2375 59
Date established: 1955 **Turnover:** £20m - £50m
No.of Employees: 51 - 100 **Product Groups:** 37, 44

Date of Accounts	Sep 11	Sep 10	Sep 09
Sales Turnover	232m	209m	167m
Pre Tax Profit/Loss	22m	15m	-9m
Working Capital	125m	52m	43m
Fixed Assets	221m	261m	284m
Current Assets	323m	330m	327m
Current Liabilities	15m	24m	27m

Vickers & Son Plumbers Merchants Ltd
Greenfield Place, Rhyl, LL18 2BP
Tel: 01745-345300 **Fax:** 01745-344288
E-mail: sales@vickers-rhyl.co.uk
Website: http://www.vickers-rhyl.co.uk
Directors: J. Vickers (Dir)
Managers: E. Hughes (Admin Off)
Immediate Holding Company: VICKERS & SON (PLUMBERS MERCHANTS) LIMITED
Registration no: 00435394 **VAT No.:** GB 158 4311 41
Date established: 1947 **Turnover:** £1m - £2m **No.of Employees:** 21 - 50
Product Groups: 66

Date of Accounts	Dec 11	Dec 10	Dec 09
Working Capital	219	224	229
Fixed Assets	80	88	98
Current Assets	281	309	298

Clwyd

Ruthin

Autoproducts
Lon Parcwr Industrial Estate, Ruthin, LL15 1NJ
Tel: 01824-707555 **Fax:** 01824-707560
E-mail: autoproducts@office-mail.co.uk
Website: http://www.autoproducts.co.uk
Directors: F. Everett (Fin)
Immediate Holding Company: BELLARION LIMITED
Registration no: 01192158 **Date established:** 1974 **Turnover:** £1m - £2m
No.of Employees: 11 - 20 **Product Groups:** 30

Date of Accounts	Dec 11	Dec 10	Dec 09
Working Capital	13	110	146
Fixed Assets	195	196	196
Current Assets	266	263	229

Optical Tools For Industry Ltd
Brickfield Lane Denbigh Road, Ruthin, LL15 2TN
Tel: 01824-704991 **Fax:** 01824-705075
E-mail: john@optical-tools.co.uk
Website: http://www.optical-tools.co.uk
Directors: J. Meelan (Fin)
Immediate Holding Company: OPTICAL TOOLS FOR INDUSTRY LIMITED
Registration no: 05355973 **VAT No.:** 682 0118 55 **Date established:** 2005
No.of Employees: 1 - 10 **Product Groups:** 38

Date of Accounts	Jul 11	Jul 10	Jul 09
Working Capital	28	-6	59
Fixed Assets	124	140	131
Current Assets	122	68	107

Richards Moorehead & Laing Ltd
55 Well Street, Ruthin, LL15 1AF
Tel: 01824-704366 **Fax:** 01824-705450
E-mail: m.richards@rmlconsult.com
Website: http://www.rmlconsult.com
Bank(s): Barclays
Directors: S. Evans (Fin)
Immediate Holding Company: RICHARDS, MOOREHEAD AND LAING LIMITED
Registration no: 01848683 **VAT No.:** GB 401 4243 13
Date established: 1984 **Turnover:** £500,000 - £1m
No.of Employees: 11 - 20 **Product Groups:** 54, 84

Date of Accounts	Dec 11	Dec 10	Dec 09
Working Capital	125	193	207
Fixed Assets	80	70	67
Current Assets	201	251	229

Stillmuchtoofer Ltd
Ysgubor Isa Bontuchel, Ruthin, LL15 2BE
Tel: 01824-710342
E-mail: smto@stillmuchtoofer.co.uk
Website: http://www.stillmuchtoofer.co.uk
Directors: C. May (MD)
Registration no: 06674773 **Date established:** 2009
Turnover: Up to £250,000 **No.of Employees:** 1 - 10 **Product Groups:** 86

Tillwise Cash Registers
10 Mwrog Street, Ruthin, LL15 1LF
Tel: 01824-707361 **Fax:** 01824-707461
E-mail: elfedtillwise@aol.com
Directors: E. Lloyd (Prop)
Date established: 1990 **Turnover:** Up to £250,000
No.of Employees: 1 - 10 **Product Groups:** 44

Valley Arms Co.
Bolero Camp Park Road, Ruthin, LL15 1NB
Tel: 01824-704438 **Fax:** 01824-704438
E-mail: info@valleyarms.co.uk
Website: http://www.valleyarms.co.uk
Directors: R. Davies (Ptnr)
Immediate Holding Company: VALLEY ARMS LIMITED
Registration no: 04970990 **Date established:** 2003
No.of Employees: 1 - 10 **Product Groups:** 36, 39, 40

Date of Accounts	Mar 10	Mar 09	Mar 08
Working Capital	4	30	20
Fixed Assets	N/A	N/A	6
Current Assets	6	43	56

Clwyd

St Asaph

Atkins Consultants Ltd
7 Ffordd Richard Davies St Asaph Business Park, St Asaph, LL17 0LJ
Tel: 01745-585351 **Fax:** 01745-583323
E-mail: lloyd.roberts@atkinsglobal.com
Website: http://www.atkins.com
Directors: L. Roberts (Dir)
Ultimate Holding Company: WS ATKINS PLC
Immediate Holding Company: ATKINS CONSULTANTS LIMITED
Registration no: 00755613 **VAT No.:** GB 209 8612 53
Date established: 1963 **Turnover:** Over £1,000m
No.of Employees: 11 - 20 **Product Groups:** 84

Date of Accounts	Mar 12	Mar 11	Mar 10
Sales Turnover	N/A	N/A	73
Pre Tax Profit/Loss	N/A	-1	-1
Working Capital	248	248	247
Current Assets	285	285	286

Health Care Centre
Alexandra Buildings The Roe, St Asaph, LL17 0NA
Tel: 01745-584818 **Fax:** 01754-584775
E-mail: info@hccwales.com
Website: http://www.hccwales.com
Directors: P. Williams (Prop)
Immediate Holding Company: HCC WALES LIMITED
Registration no: 04911486 **Date established:** 2003
No.of Employees: 11 - 20 **Product Groups:** 38, 67

Date of Accounts	Mar 11	Mar 10	Mar 09
Sales Turnover	N/A	2m	2m
Pre Tax Profit/Loss	N/A	35	27
Working Capital	-49	-49	-83
Fixed Assets	58	72	89
Current Assets	268	322	333
Current Liabilities	N/A	209	159

Optic Glyndwr Technium
Ffordd William Morgan St Asaph Business Park, St Asaph, LL17 0JD
Tel: 01745-535100 **Fax:** 01745-535101
E-mail: p.harris@glyndwr.ac.uk
Website: http://www.optictechnium.com
Directors: P. Harris (MD)
Immediate Holding Company: OPTIC GLYNDWR LTD
Registration no: 06810489 **No.of Employees:** 21 - 50
Product Groups: 40, 69, 80, 86

Technical Support & Supplies Ltd
Llys Edmund Prys St. Asaph Business Park, St Asaph, LL17 0JA
Tel: 01745-582918 **Fax:** 01745-585317
E-mail: sales@tss.com
Website: http://www.tss.com
Directors: R. Mew (Dir)
Registration no: 00954459 **Date established:** 2003
No.of Employees: 1 - 10 **Product Groups:** 36, 40

W R T L Exterior Lighting Ltd
Llys Edmund Prys St Asaph Business Park, St Asaph, LL17 0JA
Tel: 01745-584273
Website: http://www.tss.com
Ultimate Holding Company: INDUSTRIAS DERIVADAS DEL ALUMNIO SL (SPAIN)
Immediate Holding Company: W R T L EXTERIOR LIGHTING LIMITED
Registration no: 03896819 **Date established:** 1999
Turnover: £10m - £20m **No.of Employees:** 1 - 10 **Product Groups:** 37, 67

Date of Accounts	Dec 11	Dec 10	Dec 09
Sales Turnover	29m	24m	19m
Pre Tax Profit/Loss	1m	957	646
Working Capital	5m	4m	3m
Fixed Assets	206	259	229
Current Assets	7m	7m	5m
Current Liabilities	2m	1m	1m

W R T L I-Tunnel
Llys Edmund Prys St Asaph Business Park, St Asaph, LL17 0JA
Tel: 01745-582918 **Fax:** 01745-585317
E-mail: i-tunnel@wrtl.co.uk
Website: http://www.wrtl.co.uk
Managers: S. Ebbrell (Ops Mgr)
Immediate Holding Company: PLANT & ENGINE CLEANING SERVICES (ILFORD) LIMITED
Registration no: 00954459 **VAT No.:** 560 0395 63 **Date established:** 1969
Turnover: £250,000 - £500,000 **No.of Employees:** 1 - 10
Product Groups: 37, 45

Date of Accounts	Mar 12	Mar 11	Mar 10
Working Capital	-117	-86	-78
Fixed Assets	1m	962	956
Current Assets	5	34	27

West Glamorgan

Swansea

A P S Alternative Precision Sheet Metal
Unit 9-10 Prydwen Road, Fforestfach, Swansea, SA5 4HN
Tel: 01792-581032 **Fax:** 01792-587253
E-mail: sales@apsm.co.uk
Website: http://www.apsm.co.uk
Directors: D. Dumbarton (Fin), B. Dumbarton (MD)
Immediate Holding Company: ALTERNATIVE PRECISION SHEET METAL LIMITED
Registration no: 03465595 **Date established:** 1997
Turnover: £500,000 - £1m **No.of Employees:** 11 - 20
Product Groups: 35, 46, 48

Date of Accounts	Dec 11	Dec 10	Dec 09
Working Capital	49	59	121
Fixed Assets	73	93	106
Current Assets	218	219	225

Afon Tinplate Co. Ltd
Afon Works Llangyfelach, Swansea, SA5 7LN
Tel: 01792-312000 **Fax:** 01792-312001
E-mail: sales@afontinplate.co.uk
Website: http://www.afontinplate.co.uk
Bank(s): Barclays, Swansea
Directors: N. Lawley (MD), S. Parsell (Fin)
Managers: K. Peters (Purch Mgr)
Immediate Holding Company: AFON TINPLATE COMPANY LIMITED
Registration no: 00193946 **VAT No.:** GB 121 9634 80
Date established: 2023 **Turnover:** £10m - £20m
No.of Employees: 51 - 100 **Product Groups:** 34

Date of Accounts	Dec 11	Dec 10	Dec 09
Sales Turnover	18m	19m	16m
Pre Tax Profit/Loss	884	1m	1m
Working Capital	5m	5m	4m
Fixed Assets	3m	4m	4m
Current Assets	8m	9m	8m
Current Liabilities	507	639	491

A1K9 Ltd
Cwmdulais House Pontarddulais, Swansea, SA4 8NP
Tel: 01792-883395
E-mail: info@a1k9.co.uk
Website: http://www.a1k9.co.uk
Directors: C. Wall (Dir)
Immediate Holding Company: A1K9 LIMITED
Registration no: 03983104 **Date established:** 2000
No.of Employees: 1 - 10 **Product Groups:** 22, 35, 39, 68

Date of Accounts	Apr 11	Apr 10	Apr 09
Working Capital	29	-7	16
Fixed Assets	113	124	87
Current Assets	118	87	113

Autotorque Engine Reconditioners
Glyncolen Service Station Ynysforgan, Cwmrhydyceirw, Swansea, SA6 6NB
Tel: 01792-793652 **Fax:** 01792-793652
E-mail: info@autotorquesouthwales.co.uk
Website: http://www.autotorquesouthwales.co.uk
Directors: J. O'sullivan (Prop)
No.of Employees: 1 - 10 **Product Groups:** 40, 48

B A W Precision Engineers Ltd
Alloy Industrial Estate Pontardawe, Swansea, SA8 4EZ
Tel: 01792-862141 **Fax:** 01792-865545
E-mail: sales@bawengineering.co.uk
Website: http://www.bawengineering.co.uk
Bank(s): Barclays
Directors: A. Hoseason (Chief Op Offcr), G. Lawrence (Fin), P. Kilbride (MD)
Managers: A. Williams (Works Gen Mgr), L. Thomas (Sales Prom Mgr)
Immediate Holding Company: BAW AUTOMOTIVE LIMITED
Registration no: 04600059 **Date established:** 2002 **Turnover:** £2m - £5m
No.of Employees: 21 - 50 **Product Groups:** 46

H S Bassett & Son Ltd
Unit 13a Coronet Way, Swansea Enterprise Park, Swansea, SA6 8RH
Tel: 01792-790022 **Fax:** 01792-790033
E-mail: info@hsbassett.co.uk
Website: http://www.hsbassett.co.uk
Bank(s): HSBC Bank plc
Directors: N. Bassett (Fin)
Managers: T. Aspland (Chief Acct)
Ultimate Holding Company: H S BASSETT HOLDINGS LIMITED
Immediate Holding Company: H.S.BASSETT & SON LIMITED
Registration no: 00808376 **VAT No.:** GB 122 7142 14
Date established: 1964 **Turnover:** £1m - £2m **No.of Employees:** 21 - 50
Product Groups: 25, 26, 30

Date of Accounts	Oct 11	Oct 10	Oct 09
Sales Turnover	2m	2m	2m
Pre Tax Profit/Loss	94	118	111
Working Capital	161	117	50
Fixed Assets	104	86	110
Current Assets	563	509	462
Current Liabilities	178	193	229

Bellingham Steel & Tinplate Co. Ltd
34 Caswell Road Caswell, Swansea, SA3 4SD
Tel: 01792-360716 **Fax:** 01792-360613
E-mail: info@bellingham-steel.co.uk
Website: http://www.bellingham-steel.co.uk
Directors: A. Bellingham (Dir)
Immediate Holding Company: BELLINGHAM STEEL AND TINPLATE CO. LIMITED
Registration no: 02693154 **VAT No.:** GB 557 9096 90
Date established: 1992 **Turnover:** £250,000 - £500,000
No.of Employees: 1 - 10 **Product Groups:** 34, 35, 66

Date of Accounts	Apr 12	Apr 11	Apr 10
Working Capital	22	22	62
Fixed Assets	9	9	10
Current Assets	295	372	272

Bemis Swansea
Siemens Way Swansea Enterprise Park, Swansea, SA7 9BB
Tel: 01792-784700 **Fax:** 01792-784784
E-mail: info@bemis.com
Website: http://www.bemis.com
Bank(s): National Westminster Bank Plc
Managers: A. Sinclair (Tech Serv Mgr), I. Cole (Comptroller), M. Bird (Plant), J. Mulhern (Personnel)
Ultimate Holding Company: BEMIS CO INC (USA)
Immediate Holding Company: BEMIS SWANSEA LIMITED.
Registration no: 04039373 **Date established:** 2000
Turnover: £20m - £50m **No.of Employees:** 251 - 500
Product Groups: 20, 30

Date of Accounts	Dec 11	Dec 10	Dec 09
Sales Turnover	26m	28m	29m
Pre Tax Profit/Loss	4m	4m	6m
Working Capital	13m	11m	7m
Fixed Assets	14m	13m	14m
Current Assets	16m	15m	12m
Current Liabilities	1m	2m	2m

Biffa Waste Services Ltd
Acorn Court Clarion Close Enterprise Park, Swansea Enterprise Park, Swansea, SA6 8QU
Tel: 01792-791246 **Fax:** 01792-791320
E-mail: mathew.roderick@biffa.co.uk
Website: http://www.biffa.co.uk
Managers: M. Roderick (Mgr)
Immediate Holding Company: BIFFA WASTE SERVICES LIMITED
Registration no: 00946107 **Date established:** 1969
No.of Employees: 21 - 50 **Product Groups:** 32, 54

Date of Accounts	Mar 08	Mar 09	Apr 10
Sales Turnover	555m	574m	492m
Pre Tax Profit/Loss	23m	50m	30m
Working Capital	229m	271m	293m
Fixed Assets	371m	360m	378m
Current Assets	409m	534m	609m
Current Liabilities	50m	100m	115m

Biopharm Leeches
2 Bryngwili Road Pontarddulais, Swansea, SA4 0XT
Tel: 01792-885595 **Fax:** 01792-882440
E-mail: sales@biopharm-leeches.com
Website: http://www.biopharm-leeches.com
Bank(s): Lloyds TSB Bank plc
Directors: L. Sawyer (MD)
Ultimate Holding Company: WISEYARD LIMITED
Immediate Holding Company: BIOPHARM (U.K.) LIMITED
Registration no: 01771079 **VAT No.:** GB 484 2738 19
Date established: 1983 **Turnover:** £250,000 - £500,000
No.of Employees: 11 - 20 **Product Groups:** 67

Date of Accounts	Jul 11	Jul 10	Jul 09
Working Capital	65	43	120
Fixed Assets	51	44	49
Current Assets	104	72	150

B P I Industrial
Clarion Close Swansea Enterprise Park, Swansea, SA6 8QZ
Tel: 01792-772441 **Fax:** 01383-514845
E-mail: sales@bpipoly.com
Website: http://www.bpipoly.com
Bank(s): Clydesdale Bank PLC

see next page

***B P I Industrial** - Cont'd*
Directors: A. Roberts (Sales & Mktg), S. O'hare (Dir), T. Jenkins (MD)
Managers: C. Sinclare (Mgr)
Ultimate Holding Company: BRITISH POLYTHENE INDUSTRIES LTD
Registration no: 00350729 **VAT No.:** GB 268 9911 02
No.of Employees: 51 - 100 **Product Groups:** 30

Brenntag Wales
Nant-Y-Felin Felinfach, Swansea, SA5 4HL
Tel: 01792-561110 **Fax:** 01792-702244
E-mail: gareth.jones@brenntag.co.uk
Website: http://www.brenntag.co.uk
Managers: G. Jones (Chief Mgr)
Immediate Holding Company: HAYS CHEMICALS PLC
Registration no: 00915516 **VAT No.:** GB 556 8495 87
Turnover: £500m - £1,000m **No.of Employees:** 21 - 50
Product Groups: 32

Brookvale Products Ltd
36 Brookvale Road West Cross, Swansea, SA3 5EX
Tel: 01792-518277
Directors: B. Jones (MD)
No.of Employees: 1 - 10 **Product Groups:** 37, 67

Buck & Hickman Ltd
Unit 9 Horizon Park, Swansea Enterprise Park, Swansea, SA6 8RG
Tel: 01792-799988 **Fax:** 01792-700678
E-mail: swansea@buckandhickman.com
Website: http://www.buckandhickman.com
Managers: A. Couch (District Mgr)
Ultimate Holding Company: TRAVIS PERKINS PLC
Immediate Holding Company: BOSTON (2011) LIMITED
Registration no: 06028304 **Date established:** 2006
No.of Employees: 1 - 10 **Product Groups:** 24, 33, 36, 37, 41, 46

Date of Accounts	Dec 10	Mar 10	Mar 09
Working Capital	6m	6m	6m
Current Assets	27m	27m	27m

Bunzl S W S
Unit 2b Abergelly Road, Fforestfach, Swansea, SA5 4DY
Tel: 01792-355600 **Fax:** 01792-355700
E-mail: sales@bunzlsws.com
Website: http://www.bunzlsws.com
Bank(s): Barclays
Managers: L. Day (District Mgr)
Immediate Holding Company: UK Safety Group Ltd
Registration no: 02233168 **Turnover:** Over £1,000m
No.of Employees: 21 - 50 **Product Groups:** 22, 24

Busters Motorcycle Accessories & Lem Distribution Ltd
Unit 6 St. Johns Court Swansea Enterprise Park, Swansea, SA6 8QQ
Tel: 08702-412040 **Fax:** 08702-413041
Website: http://www.busters-accessories.co.uk
Directors: M. Thomas (Dir)
Registration no: 03925333 **Date established:** 2000
Turnover: Up to £250,000 **No.of Employees:** 21 - 50 **Product Groups:** 39, 40

Butterfield Morgan Ltd
Druslyn House De Lane Beche Street, Swansea, SA1 3HJ
Tel: 01792-650381 **Fax:** 01792-468742
E-mail: sarahm@butterfieldmorgan.co.uk
Bank(s): National Westminster Bank Plc
Directors: C. Harry (MD)
Immediate Holding Company: BUTTERFIELD MORGAN LIMITED
Registration no: 04103304 **Date established:** 2000
Turnover: £500,000 - £1m **No.of Employees:** 11 - 20 **Product Groups:** 80

Date of Accounts	Dec 11	Dec 10	Dec 09
Working Capital	5	10	66
Fixed Assets	371	373	373
Current Assets	196	175	169

C E M Day Ltd
Swansea Road Gorseinon, Swansea, SA4 4LL
Tel: 01792-222111 **Fax:** 01792-895459
E-mail: enquiries@days.co.uk
Website: http://www.days.co.uk
Directors: S. Smith (Fin), S. Smith (Fin), M. Grant (Dir)
Managers: D. Phillips (Personnel), F. Berry (Mktg Serv Mgr), N. Wiliams (Tech Serv Mgr)
Immediate Holding Company: C.E.M. DAY LIMITED
Registration no: 00215538 **Date established:** 2026
Turnover: £125m - £250m **No.of Employees:** 251 - 500
Product Groups: 68

Date of Accounts	Dec 11	Dec 10	Dec 09
Sales Turnover	179m	185m	159m
Pre Tax Profit/Loss	5m	5m	4m
Working Capital	6m	-20m	-11m
Fixed Assets	81m	99m	72m
Current Assets	85m	50m	48m
Current Liabilities	12m	10m	8m

C & P Engineering Services Ltd
Gorseinon Road Penllergaer, Swansea, SA4 9GE
Tel: 01792-897002 **Fax:** 01792-895193
E-mail: info@cpengineering.co.uk
Website: http://www.cpengineering.co.uk
Directors: P. Bunyan (MD)
Immediate Holding Company: C. & P. ENGINEERING SERVICES LIMITED
Registration no: 01140574 **Date established:** 1973
No.of Employees: 11 - 20 **Product Groups:** 37, 38, 40, 44, 46, 52, 67, 83

Date of Accounts	Dec 11	Dec 10	Dec 09
Working Capital	209	236	225
Fixed Assets	73	93	78
Current Assets	721	748	848

Caerbont Automotive Instruments Ltd (Sales Office)
Caerbont Abercrave, Swansea, SA9 1SH
Tel: 01639-732200 **Fax:** 01639-732201
E-mail: gavin.roberts@caigauge.com
Website: http://www.caigauge.com
Bank(s): HSBC, Cardiff
Directors: G. Roberts (MD), N. Meakin (Mkt Research), E. Jones (Fin)
Managers: G. Jones (Tech Serv Mgr), A. Enoch (Purch Mgr)
Ultimate Holding Company: CAERBONT HOLDINGS LIMITED
Immediate Holding Company: CAERBONT AUTOMOTIVE INSTRUMENTS LIMITED
Registration no: 02847474 **Date established:** 1993 **Turnover:** £2m - £5m
No.of Employees: 51 - 100 **Product Groups:** 37, 38, 39

Date of Accounts	Dec 11	Dec 10	Dec 09
Working Capital	396	330	315
Fixed Assets	182	188	222
Current Assets	696	706	730

City & County Of Swansea Car Parks
PO Box 588, Swansea, SA1 9GD
Tel: 01792-636411 **Fax:** 01792-637227
E-mail: nigelrichards@swansea.gov.uk
Website: http://www.swansea.gov.uk
Bank(s): HSBC Bank plc
Managers: P. Davies (Mgr), P. Davies (Mgr), S. Sheriff
Turnover: £250m - £500m **No.of Employees:** 11 - 20 **Product Groups:** 87

City Electro Diesel Services
Nantyffin Road South Swansea Enterprise Park, Swansea, SA7 9RG
Tel: 01792-792010 **Fax:** 01792-773190
Website: http://www.cityelectrodiesel.com
Bank(s): National Westminster Bank Plc
Directors: K. Rowland (Prop)
VAT No.: GB 121 9465 77 **Turnover:** £500,000 - £1m
No.of Employees: 11 - 20 **Product Groups:** 39

Class Pools
50 Penderry Road Penlan, Swansea, SA5 7EB
Tel: 07903-591450
E-mail: classpools@ntworld.com
Website: http://www.ntworld.com
Directors: D. Draper (Prop)
No.of Employees: 1 - 10 **Product Groups:** 32, 40, 66, 67

Comcen Computer Supplies Ltd
Bruce Road Fforestfach, Swansea, SA5 4HS
Tel: 01792-515560 **Fax:** 01792-515575
E-mail: info@comcen.co.uk
Website: http://www.comcen.co.uk
Directors: M. Casey (Sales), D. Stroia (Fin), I. Greenhill (Tech Serv)
Managers: L. Bourke (Mktg Serv Mgr)
Ultimate Holding Company: COMCEN TECHNOLOGY LTD
Immediate Holding Company: COMCEN HOLDINGS LIMITED
Registration no: 03709122 **VAT No.:** GB 540 9977 10
Date established: 1999 **Turnover:** £10m - £20m
No.of Employees: 21 - 50 **Product Groups:** 28, 44

Date of Accounts	Dec 11	Dec 10	Dec 09
Pre Tax Profit/Loss	176	98	25
Working Capital	-1m	-1m	-1m
Fixed Assets	2m	2m	2m

Comyn Ching (Solray)
Phoenix Way Gorseinon, Swansea, SA4 9WF
Tel: 01792-892211 **Fax:** 01792-898855
E-mail: sales@solray.co.uk
Website: http://www.solray.co.uk
Bank(s): HSBC Bank plc
Directors: A. Ching (MD)
Managers: R. Chapel (Comptroller)
Immediate Holding Company: COMYN CHING LIMITED
Registration no: 05513031 **VAT No.:** GB 241 7595 52
Date established: 2005 **Turnover:** £2m - £5m **No.of Employees:** 21 - 50
Product Groups: 40, 52

Date of Accounts	Dec 11	Dec 10	Dec 09
Working Capital	-130	-85	-58
Fixed Assets	577	577	577
Current Assets	1m	1m	1m

Conference Services
Singleton Park, Swansea, SA2 8PP
Tel: 01792-295660 **Fax:** 01792-295675
E-mail: conferences@swansea.ac.uk
Website: http://www.swansea.ac.uk/conferences
Managers: L. Black (Mgr), P. Belcher (Mgr)
Ultimate Holding Company: NAVITAS LTD (AUSTRALIA)
Immediate Holding Company: YAMGO LTD
Registration no: 06822392 **Date established:** 1998
Turnover: Up to £250,000 **No.of Employees:** 1 - 10 **Product Groups:** 80

Date of Accounts	Jul 11	Jul 10	Jul 07
Pre Tax Profit/Loss	N/A	N/A	-2
Working Capital	1	1	1
Current Assets	1	1	13
Current Liabilities	N/A	N/A	2

Custom Made Metalwork Ltd
36 Tudor Court Murton, Swansea, SA3 3BB
Tel: 01792-230230
Website: http://www.custommademetalwork.co.uk
Directors: M. Naylor (MD), T. Rees (MD)
Immediate Holding Company: CUSTOM MADE METALWORK LTD
Registration no: 05207068 **Date established:** 2004
No.of Employees: 1 - 10 **Product Groups:** 26, 35

Date of Accounts	Sep 10	Sep 09	Sep 08
Working Capital	8	6	2
Fixed Assets	3	2	2
Current Assets	26	18	16

Cygnet Development Services Ltd
Digital Technium Singleton Park, Swansea, SA2 8PP
Tel: 01792-295622 **Fax:** 01792-295676
E-mail: enquires@cygnetds.co.uk
Website: http://www.cygnetds.co.uk
Directors: J. Orme (MD)
Registration no: 06586742 **Date established:** 2008
No.of Employees: 1 - 10 **Product Groups:** 44

Digitrol Ltd
Coronet Way Swansea Enterprise Park, Swansea, SA6 8RH
Tel: 01792-796000 **Fax:** 01792-701600
E-mail: info@digitrol.com
Website: http://www.digitrol.com
Bank(s): Barclays, Swansea
Directors: P. Rees (Dir)
Immediate Holding Company: DIGITROL LIMITED
Registration no: 00985113 **VAT No.:** GB 558 0520 45
Date established: 1970 **Turnover:** £1m - £2m **No.of Employees:** 11 - 20
Product Groups: 38, 40, 44, 47

Date of Accounts	Oct 11	Oct 10	Oct 09
Working Capital	389	353	694
Fixed Assets	13	21	19
Current Assets	2m	1m	1m
Current Liabilities	N/A	500	N/A

Duo-Fast
Queensway Fforestfach, Swansea, SA5 4AD
Tel: 01792-563540 **Fax:** 01792-587649
Website: http://www.paslode.com
Directors: D. Jordan (Sales)
Managers: K. Hawkes (Comm)
Immediate Holding Company: Illinois Tool Works Inc (ITW)
Registration no: 01843995 **VAT No.:** Gb 322 5556 72
Turnover: £5m - £10m **Product Groups:** 35, 37, 40, 42, 43, 47

EliteXecutive Travel
78 Tal Y Coed Hendy, Pontarddulais, Swansea, SA4 0XR
Tel: 01792-886999
E-mail: enquiries@elitexecutivetravel.co.uk
Website: http://www.elitexecutivetravel.co.uk
Directors: S. Vaughan (MD)
Date established: 2007 **Turnover:** Up to £250,000
No.of Employees: 1 - 10 **Product Groups:** 69

Enterprise Insurance Services Swansea Ltd
22 Tawe Business Village Phoenix Way Enterprise Park, Swansea Enterprise Park, Swansea, SA7 9LA
Tel: 01792-772778 **Fax:** 01792-310130
E-mail: entins1@btconnect.com
Website: http://www.homeenergyinspectorinsurance.co.uk
Directors: K. Davies (MD)
Immediate Holding Company: ENTERPRISE INSURANCE SERVICES (SWANSEA) LIMITED
Registration no: 02490379 **Date established:** 1990
Turnover: £500,000 - £1m **No.of Employees:** 11 - 20 **Product Groups:** 82

Date of Accounts	Jul 11	Jul 10	Jul 09
Working Capital	269	255	260
Fixed Assets	2	2	5
Current Assets	819	814	934

Enterprise Metals
Kemys Way Swansea Enterprise Park, Swansea, SA6 8QF
Tel: 01792-797722 **Fax:** 01792-792974
E-mail: enquiries@ellissteelgroup.co.uk
Website: http://www.ellissteelgroup.co.uk
Bank(s): National Westminster
Directors: A. Lavacall (Sales), R. Ellis (MD), R. Ellis (Prop)
Managers: S. Beniamals (Sales Admin), A. Lavercombe (Sales Prom Mgr)
Immediate Holding Company: ENTERPRISE METALS LIMITED
Registration no: 01575349 **Date established:** 1981 **Turnover:** £2m - £5m
No.of Employees: 21 - 50 **Product Groups:** 34, 36, 66

Date of Accounts	Dec 10	Dec 09	Dec 07
Fixed Assets	5	5	N/A

Eriks (Swansea Electro Mechanical
Normandy Road Landore, Swansea, SA1 2LH
Tel: 01792-653171 **Fax:** 01792-467768
E-mail: swansea.repair@eriks.co.uk
Website: http://www.eriks.co.uk
Bank(s): Lloyds TSB Bank plc
Managers: S. O'leary (Mgr)
VAT No.: GB 277 2632 40 **No.of Employees:** 21 - 50 **Product Groups:** 48

Fan Co
Kemys Way Swansea Enterprise Park, Swansea, SA6 8QF
Tel: 01792-792333 **Fax:** 01792-771713
No.of Employees: 1 - 10 **Product Groups:** 40, 66

Farmers Fabrications & Sheet Metal Works Ltd
Pen Y Vernel Culfor Road, Loughor, Swansea, SA4 6UB
Tel: 01792-899667 **Fax:** 01792-898773
Directors: J. Yates (Prop)
Immediate Holding Company: FARMERS FABRICATION & SHEET METAL WORKS LTD
Registration no: 04245614 **Date established:** 2001
No.of Employees: 1 - 10 **Product Groups:** 35

Fire Protection Services Ltd
19 Brithwen Road Waunarlwydd, Swansea, SA5 4QS
Tel: 01792-874434
E-mail: fpsfire@tiscali.co.uk
Website: http://fpsfire.co.uk
Directors: S. Gwinnett (Dir), J. Gwinnett (Fin)
Immediate Holding Company: FIRE PROTECTION SERVICES LIMITED
Registration no: 05737572 **Date established:** 2006
No.of Employees: 1 - 10 **Product Groups:** 84, 86

Date of Accounts	May 12	May 11	May 10
Working Capital	76	19	30
Fixed Assets	49	44	29
Current Assets	278	200	104

Friulsider UK Ltd
Celtic Trade Park Bruce Road Fforestfach, Swansea, SA5 4EP
Tel: 01792-561911 **Fax:** 01792-578702
E-mail: sales@friulsider.co.uk
Website: http://www.friulsider.com
Directors: J. Scriven (MD), L. Morigi (Dir), R. Lebraut (Dir)
Managers: M. Mason (Accounts)
Ultimate Holding Company: L R ETANCO SA (FRANCE)
Immediate Holding Company: FRIULSIDER UK LIMITED
Registration no: 02389148 **VAT No.:** GB 473 8717 10
Date established: 1989 **Turnover:** £1m - £2m **No.of Employees:** 1 - 10
Product Groups: 30, 32, 35

Date of Accounts	Dec 10	Dec 09	Dec 08
Working Capital	328	311	510
Fixed Assets	205	182	102
Current Assets	619	461	773

Glanmor Disability Equipment
208 High Street, Swansea, SA1 1PE
Tel: 01792-642868 **Fax:** 01792-655804
E-mail: sales@glanmor.co.uk
Website: http://www.glanmor.co.uk
Directors: J. O'brien (Prop)
No.of Employees: 1 - 10 **Product Groups:** 22, 25, 35, 39, 45, 67, 85

Haven Automation Ltd
Measurement House Kingsway, Fforestfach, Swansea, SA5 4EX
Tel: 01792-588722 **Fax:** 01792-582624
E-mail: sales@haven.co.uk
Website: http://www.haven.co.uk
Directors: A. Davies (Co Sec)
Ultimate Holding Company: HAVEN HOLDINGS LIMITED
Immediate Holding Company: HAVEN AUTOMATION LIMITED
Registration no: 00862544 **VAT No.:** GB 541 0442 88
Date established: 1965 **Turnover:** £500,000 - £1m
No.of Employees: 1 - 10 **Product Groups:** 38, 85

Date of Accounts	Dec 11	Dec 10	Dec 09
Working Capital	110	87	138
Current Assets	268	204	226

D G Heath Ltd
Unit 3 Tyn Y Bonau Industrial Estate Tyn Y Bonau Road, Pontarddulais, Swansea, SA4 8SG
Tel: 01792-884828 **Fax:** 01792-884936
E-mail: info@dgheath.co.uk
Website: http://www.dgheath.co.uk
Directors: D. Heath (Dir)
Immediate Holding Company: D.G. HEATH (TIMBER PRODUCTS) LIMITED
Registration no: 01876867 **Date established:** 1985
No.of Employees: 21 - 50 **Product Groups:** 25, 29, 30, 31, 32, 33, 35, 40, 41, 45, 52, 63, 66, 67

Date of Accounts	Dec 11	Dec 10	Dec 09
Working Capital	306	273	226
Fixed Assets	297	277	289
Current Assets	704	693	639

Hydra Technologies ltd
Unit 5 Europa Way, Fforestfach, Swansea, SA5 4AJ
Tel: 01792-586800 **Fax:** 01792-561606
E-mail: salesdept@hydratech.co.uk
Website: http://www.coolflow.co.uk
Directors: S. Hickson (Dir)
Managers: M. Stote (Eng Serv Mgr), J. Roberts (Mktg Serv Mgr)
Registration no: 03651123 **Date established:** 1992 **Turnover:** £1m - £2m
No.of Employees: 11 - 20 **Product Groups:** 31, 32, 66

Imex Group Ltd
Unit 4 Ash Court Viking Way, Winch Wen, Swansea, SA1 7DA
Tel: 01792-704880 **Fax:** 01792-704881
E-mail: print@imex-group.com
Website: http://www.imex-group.com
Directors: G. Jones (Fin), S. Toft (MD)
Ultimate Holding Company: BRIGHTLOOK LIMITED
Immediate Holding Company: IMEX GROUP LIMITED
Registration no: 03925462 **Date established:** 2000
Turnover: Up to £250,000 **No.of Employees:** 21 - 50 **Product Groups:** 81

Date of Accounts	Apr 09	Apr 08	Apr 07
Sales Turnover	140	76	197
Pre Tax Profit/Loss	-80	104	161
Working Capital	-169	-216	-185
Fixed Assets	549	532	535
Current Assets	11	161	88
Current Liabilities	174	372	204

Imex Print Services Ltd
Unit 1 Ash Court Viking Way Winch Wen, Swansea, SA1 7DA
Tel: 01792-719756 **Fax:** 01792-719021
E-mail: info@imex-group.com
Website: http://www.imex-print.co.uk
Directors: S. Toft (Dir)
No.of Employees: 21 - 50 **Product Groups:** 23, 25, 26, 27, 28, 29, 30, 35, 36, 37, 38, 39, 40, 44, 45, 48, 49, 52, 64, 65, 66, 67, 68, 72, 80, 81, 83, 84, 89

Interserve Project Services Ltd
138 Heol Y Gors Cwmbwrla, Swansea, SA5 8LT
Tel: 01792-464001 **Fax:** 01792-467499
E-mail: swansea.office@interserve.com
Website: http://www.interserveprojects.com
Bank(s): HSBC Bank plc
Managers: A. Edmonds (Mgr), T. Bevan, A. Gibbons (Tech Serv Mgr)
Ultimate Holding Company: INTERSERVE PLC
Immediate Holding Company: INTERSERVE PROJECT SERVICES LIMITED
Registration no: 03299588 **Date established:** 1997
Turnover: £250m - £500m **No.of Employees:** 51 - 100
Product Groups: 51, 52

K B Ferguson
95 High Street Gorseinon, Swansea, SA4 4BL
Tel: 01792-894375 **Fax:** 01792-899190
E-mail: enquiries@kbferguson.co.uk
Website: http://www.kbferguson.co.uk
Bank(s): HSBC Bank plc
Directors: T. Jones (Ptnr)
Immediate Holding Company: K B FERGUSON LIMITED
Registration no: 05369324 **VAT No.:** GB 405 0666 78
Date established: 2005 **Turnover:** £500,000 - £1m
No.of Employees: 11 - 20 **Product Groups:** 80

Date of Accounts	May 12	May 11	May 10
Working Capital	49	66	57
Fixed Assets	106	127	147
Current Assets	138	177	137

Kaymac Marine & Civil Engineering
Unit 1 Osprey Business Park Byng Street, Landore, Swansea, SA1 2NR
Tel: 01792-301818 **Fax:** 01792-772373
E-mail: jeff.lippiett@kaymacltd.co.uk
Website: http://www.kaymacmarine.co.uk
Directors: G. Crees (MD)
Managers: C. Williamson (Mktg Serv Mgr)
Immediate Holding Company: KAYMAC MARINE & CIVIL ENGINEERING LIMITED
Registration no: 02975450 **Date established:** 1994
No.of Employees: 21 - 50 **Product Groups:** 45, 51, 52

Date of Accounts	Oct 11	Oct 10	Oct 09
Working Capital	1m	1m	398
Fixed Assets	898	898	917
Current Assets	2m	2m	1m

Knit and Sew (t/a Knitters & Sewers World)
21-22 Park Street, Swansea, SA1 3DJ
Tel: 0845-094 0835 **Fax:** 01792-644535
E-mail: sales@knitandsew.co.uk
Website: http://www.knitandsew.co.uk
Bank(s): HSBC
Directors: P. Boden (MD), R. Casey (Dir), B. Elias (Dir)
Registration no: 01086985 **VAT No.:** GB 122 8970 63
Date established: 1972 **Turnover:** £500,000 - £1m
No.of Employees: 21 - 50 **Product Groups:** 23, 63, 66

Linc-Weld Industrial Supplies Ltd
Unit 10 Tower Court St Davids Road, Swansea Enterprise Park, Swansea, SA6 8RU
Tel: 01792-790990 **Fax:** 01792-794676
E-mail: chris@lincweld.co.uk
Website: http://www.linc-weld.co.uk
Directors: C. Humphries (MD)
Immediate Holding Company: LINC-WELD INDUSTRIAL SUPPLIES LIMITED
Registration no: 04819060 **Date established:** 2003
No.of Employees: 1 - 10 **Product Groups:** 46

Date of Accounts	Dec 11	Dec 10	Dec 09
Working Capital	239	208	201
Fixed Assets	44	59	47
Current Assets	418	483	492

Lyte Industries Wales Ltd
Siemens Way Swansea Enterprise Park, Swansea, SA7 9BB
Tel: 01792-796666 **Fax:** 01792-796796
E-mail: sales@lyteladders.co.uk
Website: http://www.lyteladders.co.uk
Bank(s): Barclays
Directors: J. Greene (MD)
Immediate Holding Company: LYTE INDUSTRIES (WALES) LIMITED
Registration no: 01982317 **VAT No.:** GB 531 7527 52
Date established: 1986 **Turnover:** £5m - £10m
No.of Employees: 51 - 100 **Product Groups:** 35

Date of Accounts	Oct 11	Jun 09	Jun 08
Sales Turnover	8m	6m	7m
Pre Tax Profit/Loss	112	-88	-293
Working Capital	2m	-761	-212
Fixed Assets	4m	1m	1m
Current Assets	6m	3m	3m
Current Liabilities	1m	219	322

Machine Mart Ltd
Unit 7 Samlet Road, Swansea Enterprise Park, Swansea, SA7 9AG
Tel: 01792-792969 **Fax:** 01792-792944
Website: http://www.machinemart.co.uk
Managers: C. Alail (Mgr)
Immediate Holding Company: MACHINE MART LIMITED
Registration no: 01555925 **Date established:** 1981
Turnover: £50m - £75m **No.of Employees:** 1 - 10 **Product Groups:** 40

Date of Accounts	May 11	May 10	May 09
Sales Turnover	67m	64m	56m
Pre Tax Profit/Loss	11m	11m	9m
Working Capital	61m	53m	27m
Fixed Assets	4m	5m	5m
Current Assets	68m	59m	51m
Current Liabilities	3m	3m	21m

T H Martin Ltd
112 Walter Road, Swansea, SA1 5QQ
Tel: 01792-466410 **Fax:** 01792-641887
E-mail: enquiries@thmartin.com
Website: http://www.thmartin.com
Directors: I. Martin (MD)
Ultimate Holding Company: T. H MARTIN INVESTMENT MANAGEMENT LIMITED
Immediate Holding Company: T. H. MARTIN LIMITED
Registration no: 02053846 **Date established:** 1986
Turnover: Up to £250,000 **No.of Employees:** 1 - 10 **Product Groups:** 80, 82

Date of Accounts	Dec 11	Dec 10	Dec 09
Sales Turnover	169	153	196
Pre Tax Profit/Loss	94	88	116
Working Capital	2m	2m	2m
Fixed Assets	409	411	418
Current Assets	2m	2m	2m
Current Liabilities	28	29	31

Metal Masters West Wales Ltd
Unit 16-17 Abertawe House 115 Ystrad Road, Fforestfach, Swansea, SA5 4JB
Tel: 01792-586677 **Fax:** 01792-586677
E-mail: robphil50@aol.com
Directors: P. Pritchard (Dir)
Immediate Holding Company: METAL MASTERS (WEST WALES) LTD
Registration no: 06357863 **Date established:** 2007
No.of Employees: 1 - 10 **Product Groups:** 34, 35, 48, 52

Date of Accounts	Aug 11	Aug 10	Aug 09
Working Capital	-14	-41	-37
Fixed Assets	36	61	71
Current Assets	30	21	33

Morgan Cole
Llys Tawe Kings Road, Swansea, SA1 8PG
Tel: 01792-634634 **Fax:** 01792-634500
E-mail: info@morgan-cole.co.uk
Website: http://www.morgan-cole.co.uk
Directors: P. Jones (Ptnr)
Immediate Holding Company: MORGAN COLE SERVICES LIMITED
Registration no: 03618502 **Date established:** 1998 **Turnover:** £2m - £5m
No.of Employees: 51 - 100 **Product Groups:** 80

Morganite
Upper Fforest Way Swansea Enterprise Park, Swansea, SA6 8PP
Tel: 01792-763000 **Fax:** 01792-702399
Website: http://www.morgancarbon.com
Bank(s): National Westminster Bank Plc
Managers: G. Jones (Tech Serv Mgr), H. Carey (Mktg Serv Mgr), R. Carpenter (Purch Mgr), T. Robbins (Mgr), D. Beavan (Personnel), W. Griffiths (Fin Mgr)
Ultimate Holding Company: MORGAN CRUCIBLE COMPANY PLC(THE)
Immediate Holding Company: MORGANITE SPECIAL CARBONS LIMITED
Registration no: 01034654 **VAT No.:** GB 558 0268 29
Date established: 1971 **Turnover:** £20m - £50m
No.of Employees: 251 - 500 **Product Groups:** 23, 30, 31, 33, 37, 38, 39, 47, 48, 49

Date of Accounts	Jan 09	Jan 10
Working Capital	854	854
Current Assets	854	854

Mumbles Gates
32 Riversdale Road West Cross, Swansea, SA3 5PX
Tel: 01792-542999 **Fax:** 01792-542999
E-mail: a.imlach@ntlworld.com
Website: http://www.mumbleselectricgates.com
Directors: A. Imlach (Prop)
Immediate Holding Company: SOUTH WALES ELECTRIC GATES LTD
Registration no: 04779783 **Date established:** 2011
No.of Employees: 1 - 10 **Product Groups:** 26, 35

Mumbles Shoe Repairs
24 Newton Road Mumbles, Swansea, SA3 4AX
Tel: 01792-369511 **Fax:** 01792-369511
E-mail: mumblescobbler@btinternet.com
Website: http://www.coblers.netfirms.com
Directors: R. Wilkinson (Prop)
No.of Employees: 1 - 10 **Product Groups:** 46, 49, 61

Nationwide Access Ltd
Unit 8 Camffrwd Way Swansea Enterprise Park, Swansea, SA6 8QD
Tel: 01792-781741 **Fax:** 01792- 773782
E-mail: marketing@nationwideaccess.co.uk
Website: http://www.nationwideaccess.co.uk
Managers: G. Morris (Mgr)
Ultimate Holding Company: LAVENDON GROUP PLC
Immediate Holding Company: NATIONWIDE ACCESS LIMITED
Registration no: 04405299 **Date established:** 2002
Turnover: £20m - £50m **No.of Employees:** 1 - 10 **Product Groups:** 45, 83

Oceaneering International Services Ltd
Site 3 Unit 5 Castell Close, Swansea Enterprise Park, Swansea, SA7 9FH
Tel: 01792-700177 **Fax:** 01792-793100
E-mail: jstaff@oceaneering.com
Website: http://www.oceaneering.com
Bank(s): HSBc Bank Plc
Managers: J. Staff (Ops Mgr)
Ultimate Holding Company: OCEANEERING INTERNATIONAL INC (USA)
Immediate Holding Company: OCEANEERING INTERNATIONAL SERVICES LIMITED
Registration no: 01023217 **VAT No.:** GB 377 0558 28
Date established: 1971 **Turnover:** £1m - £2m **No.of Employees:** 21 - 50
Product Groups: 37, 38, 44, 48, 51, 85

Date of Accounts	Dec 11	Dec 10	Dec 09
Sales Turnover	228m	147m	132m
Pre Tax Profit/Loss	29m	12m	17m
Working Capital	12m	-6m	-12m
Fixed Assets	57m	55m	53m
Current Assets	87m	66m	81m
Current Liabilities	19m	21m	11m

On Two Wheels Distribution
Phoenix Way Gorseinon, Swansea, SA4 9WF
Tel: 01792-224470 **Fax:** 08705-703033
E-mail: paul.williams@on2wheels.com
Website: http://www.on2wheels.com
Directors: N. Bassett (Fin), M. Collings (MD)
Managers: L. Burrows (Tech Serv Mgr), S. Rees, S. Maybury (Fin Mgr)
Immediate Holding Company: ON TWO WHEELS DISTRIBUTION LIMITED
Registration no: 05390162 **Date established:** 2005
No.of Employees: 101 - 250 **Product Groups:** 29, 31, 39

Pauline Kotschy Recruitment Lt
Cogent Hous Prydwen Roa, Swansea West Industrial Par, Swansea, SA5 4H
Tel: 01792-472725 **Fax:** 01792-241 12
E-mail: info@paulinek.com
Website: http://www.paulinek.com
Directors: P. Kotschy (Prop)
Registration no: 03865951 **VAT No.:** GB 422 7417 68
Date established: 2001 **No.of Employees:** 1 - 10 **Product Groups:** 80

Penclawdd Forge
Station Square Penclawdd, Swansea, SA4 3XT
Tel: 01792-850124 **Fax:** 01792-416267
E-mail: penclawddforge@aol.com
Directors: J. Richards (Prop)
Date established: 1990 **No.of Employees:** 1 - 10 **Product Groups:** 26, 35

Perma-Soil UK
Phoenix Way Garngoch Industrial Estate, Gorseinon, Swansea, SA4 9WF
Tel: 01792-895906 **Fax:** 01792-899189
E-mail: info@permasoiluk.com
Website: http://www.permasoiluk.com
Managers: W. Roberts (Sales Prom Mgr)
Immediate Holding Company: PERMA-SOIL UK LIMITED
Registration no: 03246543 **Date established:** 1996
No.of Employees: 1 - 10 **Product Groups:** 45, 51, 52

Date of Accounts	Dec 11	Dec 10	Dec 09
Working Capital	46	6	-15
Fixed Assets	108	14	16
Current Assets	116	86	68

L J Perrin Engineering
The Workshop Rear of 85 Bernard Street, Brynmill, Swansea, SA2 0DZ
Tel: 01792-465803
E-mail: lyndon.perrin@ntlworld.com
Directors: J. Perrin (Fin), L. Perrin (MD)
Immediate Holding Company: L. J. PERRIN ENGINEERING LIMITED
Registration no: 04501009 **Date established:** 2002
No.of Employees: 1 - 10 **Product Groups:** 26, 35

Date of Accounts	Aug 11	Aug 10	Aug 08
Working Capital	-23	-18	-21
Fixed Assets	17	18	21
Current Assets	7	6	5

Planeweighs Ltd
Unit 14 Oxwich Court Swansea Enterprise Park, Swansea, SA6 8RA
Tel: 01792-310566 **Fax:** 01792-310584
E-mail: info@planeweighs.com
Website: http://www.planeweighs.com
Directors: D. Dickinson (Dir)
Immediate Holding Company: PLANEWEIGHS LIMITED
Registration no: 01301791 **Date established:** 1977
Turnover: £250,000 - £500,000 **No.of Employees:** 1 - 10
Product Groups: 38, 42

Date of Accounts	Sep 11	Sep 10	Sep 09
Working Capital	189	189	195
Fixed Assets	112	109	120
Current Assets	228	231	253

R J Heale
10 Cambridge Gardens Langland, Swansea, SA3 4PP
Tel: 01792-369328 **Fax:** 01792-369328
E-mail: info@healerjandcompany.co.uk
Website: http://www.welshracking.co.uk
Directors: R. Heale (Prop)
Date established: 2000 **No.of Employees:** 1 - 10 **Product Groups:** 26, 35

Re-Manufacturing Services Ltd
Phoenix Way Garngoch Industrial Estate, Gorseinon, Swansea, SA4 1WF
Tel: 01792-898008 **Fax:** 01792-892224
E-mail: brian@rmsgaseng.com
Website: http://www.rmsgaseng.com
Directors: B. Williams (MD), B. Williams (Fin), P. Roberts (Dir)
Managers: B. Williams (Mgr)
Immediate Holding Company: RE-MANUFACTURING SERVICES LIMITED
Registration no: 02536725 **Date established:** 1990
No.of Employees: 1 - 10 **Product Groups:** 36, 37, 38

Rotafix Ltd
Rotafix House Hennoyadd Road, Abercrave, Swansea, SA9 1UR
Tel: 01639-730481 **Fax:** 01639-730858
E-mail: dave.smedley@rotafix.co.uk
Website: http://www.rotafixltd.co.uk
Directors: D. Smedley (MD)
Immediate Holding Company: ROTAFIX (NORTHERN) LIMITED
Registration no: 01827006 **VAT No.:** GB 405 0433 04
Date established: 1984 **Turnover:** £250,000 - £500,000
No.of Employees: 1 - 10 **Product Groups:** 32

Date of Accounts	Nov 11	Nov 10	Nov 09
Sales Turnover	413	499	410
Pre Tax Profit/Loss	-1	52	41
Working Capital	-25	1	-13
Fixed Assets	144	139	130
Current Assets	112	91	108
Current Liabilities	110	65	98

S E I Interconnect Products Europe Ltd
Axis 10 Axis Court Mallard Way Riverside Business Park, Swansea Vale, Swansea, SA7 0AJ
Tel: 01792-487290 **Fax:** 01792-794357
E-mail: dgillett@sumi-electric.com
Website: http://www.sumi-electric.com
Managers: D. Gillett (Mgr)
Ultimate Holding Company: SUMITOMO ELECTRIC INDUSTRIES LTD (JAPAN)
Immediate Holding Company: SEI INTERCONNECT PRODUCTS (EUROPE) LIMITED
Registration no: 03639819 **VAT No.:** 713 0232 92 **Date established:** 1998
Turnover: £20m - £50m **No.of Employees:** 1 - 10 **Product Groups:** 37

Date of Accounts	Dec 08	Dec 07	Dec 06
Sales Turnover	14m	12m	11m
Pre Tax Profit/Loss	1m	721	-330
Working Capital	-338	216	-75
Fixed Assets	2m	537	539
Current Assets	7m	5m	5m
Current Liabilities	7m	5m	5m
Total Share Capital	4m	4m	4m

S W Industrial Valves Services Ltd
Queensway Swasnsea West Industrial Park, Fforestfach, Swansea, SA5 4DH
Tel: 01792-580260 **Fax:** 01792-579685
E-mail: phil.evans@ivs.co.uk
Website: http://www.ivs.co.uk
Bank(s): Lloyds TSB Bank plc
Managers: B. Hibben (Purch Mgr), P. Evans (Chief Mgr), S. Cooper
Ultimate Holding Company: A.K.HUGHES LIMITED
Immediate Holding Company: SOUTH WALES INDUSTRIAL VALVES SERVICES LIMITED
Registration no: 01582669 **VAT No.:** GB 357 7296 11
Date established: 1981 **Turnover:** £1m - £2m **No.of Employees:** 21 - 50
Product Groups: 29, 30, 31, 33, 34, 35, 36, 37, 38, 39, 40, 41, 45, 46, 48, 49, 66, 67, 68

Date of Accounts	Mar 11	Mar 10	Mar 09
Sales Turnover	2m	2m	2m
Pre Tax Profit/Loss	112	228	132
Working Capital	1m	1m	888
Fixed Assets	177	184	188
Current Assets	1m	2m	1m
Current Liabilities	136	137	124

Selclene Selclene Group
10 Heol Rheolau Abercrave, Swansea, SA9 1TD
Tel: 01639-730205
E-mail: info@selclene.co.uk
Website: http://www.selclene.co.uk
Directors: I. Bloom (Fin), J. Bage (MD)
Managers: M. Ludwig (Mgr)
Ultimate Holding Company: SELCLENE (HOLDINGS) LIMITED
Immediate Holding Company: SELCLENE LIMITED
Registration no: 03120976 **Date established:** 1991 **Turnover:** £2m - £5m
No.of Employees: 1 - 10 **Product Groups:** 23, 40, 52

Date of Accounts	Mar 11	Mar 10	Mar 09
Working Capital	-404	-424	-149
Fixed Assets	2m	2m	2m
Current Assets	227	289	512

Silverwing UK Ltd
Unit 30-31 Cwmdu Industrial Estate Carmarthen Road, Gendros, Swansea, SA5 8JF
Tel: 01792-585533 **Fax:** 01792-586044
E-mail: mfl@silverwinguk.com
Website: http://www.silverwinguk.com
Bank(s): Lloyds Bank P.L.C.
Directors: M. Jones (MD)
Immediate Holding Company: SILVERWING (U.K.) LIMITED
Registration no: 03835805 **VAT No.:** GB 742 2826 38
Date established: 1999 **Turnover:** £500,000 - £1m
No.of Employees: 21 - 50 **Product Groups:** 85

Date of Accounts	Dec 11	Dec 10	Dec 09
Working Capital	541	320	507
Fixed Assets	569	593	206
Current Assets	1m	947	2m

South Wales Chamber Of Commerce
Ethos Project Kings Road Swansea Waterfront, Swansea, SA1 8AS
Tel: 01792-653297 **Fax:** 01792-648345
E-mail: lynn.bray@southwaleschamber.co.uk
Website: http://www.southwaleschamber.co.uk
Managers: L. Bray, A. Jones, A. Jones, L. Harris (Mgr)
Immediate Holding Company: THE WEST WALES CHAMBER OF COMMERCE
Registration no: 00019242 **VAT No.:** GB 647 1888 96
Date established: 1983 **Turnover:** Up to £250,000
No.of Employees: 1 - 10 **Product Groups:** 87

Steel Supply Western Ltd
10 St James Crescent, Swansea, SA1 6DZ
Tel: 01792-472981 **Fax:** 07929-648170
E-mail: arfon@steelsupply.fsnet.co.uk
Directors: I. Jones (Fin)
Ultimate Holding Company: STEEL SUPPLY COMPANY(WESTERN)LIMITED
Immediate Holding Company: STEEL SUPPLY (PROPERTY) LIMITED
Registration no: 02074225 **VAT No.:** GB 540 7073 64
Date established: 1986 **Turnover:** £250,000 - £500,000
No.of Employees: 1 - 10 **Product Groups:** 14, 52

Date of Accounts	Mar 12	Mar 11	Mar 10
Working Capital	-331	-331	-331

Swansea Fasteners
Unit 7-8 Horizon Park Swansea Enterprise Park, Swansea, SA6 8RG
Tel: 01792-310284 **Fax:** 01792-310291
E-mail: sales@swanseafasteners.com
Website: http://www.swanseafasteners.com
Directors: P. Osborne (Fin)
Managers: L. Edwards (Buyer)
Immediate Holding Company: SWANSEA FASTENERS & ENGINEERING SUPPLIES LIMITED
Registration no: 05863368 **VAT No.:** GB 477 6304 21
Date established: 2006 **Turnover:** £500,000 - £1m
No.of Employees: 1 - 10 **Product Groups:** 35, 66

Date of Accounts	Mar 11	Mar 10	Mar 09
Working Capital	357	252	214
Fixed Assets	488	531	578
Current Assets	503	495	447

Swansea Industrial Components Ltd
66-70 Morfa Road, Swansea, SA1 2EF
Tel: 01792-458777 **Fax:** 01792-456252
Bank(s): Barclays, Swansea
Directors: T. Roberts (MD), L. Clayton (Fin)
Managers: S. Ham (Purch Mgr), A. Sheeham (Comm)
Ultimate Holding Company: ALTARVEST LIMITED
Immediate Holding Company: SWANSEA INDUSTRIAL COMPONENTS LIMITED
Registration no: 02707045 **VAT No.:** GB 558 0025 55
Date established: 1992 **Turnover:** £5m - £10m
No.of Employees: 101 - 250 **Product Groups:** 37, 48

Date of Accounts	Jun 11	Jun 10	Jun 09
Sales Turnover	8m	7m	7m
Pre Tax Profit/Loss	402	903	-430
Working Capital	2m	3m	2m
Fixed Assets	170	212	894
Current Assets	4m	5m	3m
Current Liabilities	507	498	348

Swansea Lift Repair & Service Ltd
2 Gilsea Park Mona Close Valley Way, Swansea Enterprise Park, Swansea, SA6 8RJ
Tel: 01792-771118 **Fax:** 01792-772472
E-mail: mail@swansealifts.com
Website: http://www.swansealifts.com
Managers: P. St Claire
Immediate Holding Company: SWANSEA LIFT REPAIR & SERVICE LTD.
Registration no: 04321671 **Date established:** 2001
No.of Employees: 1 - 10 **Product Groups:** 35, 39, 45

Date of Accounts	Dec 11	Dec 10	Dec 09
Working Capital	23	31	88
Fixed Assets	1	27	40
Current Assets	101	109	193

Swansea Precision Engineering Services
Unit 11 Oxwich Court Fendrod Business Park, Swansea Enterprise Park, Swansea, SA6 8RA
Tel: 01792-774817 **Fax:** 01792-412282
Bank(s): Bank of Scotland
Directors: D. Nicholas (Dir), P. Nicholas (Fin)
Immediate Holding Company: SWANSEA PRECISION ENGINEERING SERVICES LIMITED
Registration no: 02365230 **VAT No.:** GB 484 5860 07
Date established: 1989 **Turnover:** Up to £250,000
No.of Employees: 11 - 20 **Product Groups:** 48

Date of Accounts	Mar 11	Mar 10	Mar 09
Working Capital	-28	-11	-22
Fixed Assets	5	15	27
Current Assets	43	59	71

Total Technology Design Partnership Ltd
Unit 2 Tawe Business Village, Swansea Enterprise Park, Swansea, SA7 9LA
Tel: 01792-704460 **Fax:** 01792-701350
E-mail: design@totech.co.uk
Website: http://www.totech.co.uk
Directors: B. Phillips (Dir)
Managers: B. Phillips (Projects)
Immediate Holding Company: TOTAL TECHNOLOGY DESIGN PARTNERSHIP LIMITED
Registration no: 04076413 **Date established:** 2000 **Turnover:** £2m - £5m
No.of Employees: 11 - 20 **Product Groups:** 81

Date of Accounts	Sep 07	Sep 06	Mar 11
Sales Turnover	N/A	521	N/A
Pre Tax Profit/Loss	N/A	197	N/A
Working Capital	534	387	381
Fixed Assets	15	22	347
Current Assets	690	529	552
Current Liabilities	N/A	102	N/A

Tunnel Steels
Prydwen Road Fforestfach, Swansea, SA5 4HN
Tel: 01792-561777 **Fax:** 01792-561444
E-mail: tunnelsteel@btconnect.com
Website: http://www.tunnelsteel.net
Directors: J. Cross (MD)
Immediate Holding Company: TUNNEL STEELS LIMITED
Registration no: 02348957 **Date established:** 1989
Turnover: £500,000 - £1m **No.of Employees:** 1 - 10 **Product Groups:** 30, 34, 36, 39, 45, 48, 51, 66

Date of Accounts	Mar 11	Mar 10	Mar 09
Working Capital	-55	-37	47
Fixed Assets	13	16	13
Current Assets	147	93	219

Tyco Fire & Integrated Solutions
Tyco House Black Horse House Phoenix Way, Swansea Enterprise Park, Swansea, SA7 9EQ
Tel: 01792-465006 **Fax:** 01792-648535
E-mail: fsteel@tycoint.com
Website: http://www.tycofis.co.uk
Bank(s): Barclays
Managers: F. Steel (Chief Mgr)
Ultimate Holding Company: TYCO INTERNATIONAL LIMITED (SWITZERLAND)
Immediate Holding Company: ATLAS FIRE ENGINEERING LIMITED
Registration no: 00121983 **VAT No.:** GB 145 3447 71
Date established: 2012 **Turnover:** £10m - £20m
No.of Employees: 21 - 50 **Product Groups:** 38, 40, 52

W G Davies Landore Ltd
Unit 11 St Davids Road, Swansea Enterprise Park, Swansea, SA6 8QL
Tel: 01792-795705 **Fax:** 01792-797823
E-mail: roger.davies@wgdavies.com
Website: http://www.wgdavies.co.uk
Bank(s): HSBC
Directors: W. Davies (MD), D. Lloyd (Fin)
Managers: M. Jones (Mktg Serv Mgr)
Immediate Holding Company: W.G.DAVIES(LANDORE)LIMITED
Registration no: 00470607 **VAT No.:** GB 121 9159 84
Date established: 1949 **Turnover:** £2m - £5m **No.of Employees:** 21 - 50
Product Groups: 39

Date of Accounts	Dec 11	Dec 10	Dec 09
Working Capital	-702	-737	-857
Fixed Assets	949	751	838
Current Assets	2m	1m	856

Wall Colmonoy Ltd
Alloy Industrial Estate Pontardawe, Swansea, SA8 4HL
Tel: 01792-862287 **Fax:** 01792-830124
E-mail: sales@wallcolmonoy.co.uk
Website: http://www.wallcolmonoy.co.uk
Bank(s): National Westminster
Directors: S. Moran (Co Sec), K. Nolan (MD), P. Allnatt (Sales)
Managers: A. Smith (Personnel), R. John (Tech Serv Mgr)
Ultimate Holding Company: WALL CO INC (USA)
Immediate Holding Company: WALL COLMONOY LIMITED
Registration no: 00788765 **VAT No.:** GB 122 3590 01
Date established: 1964 **Turnover:** £20m - £50m
No.of Employees: 101 - 250 **Product Groups:** 32, 34, 35, 40, 46, 48, 49, 66

Date of Accounts	Dec 11	Dec 10	Dec 09
Sales Turnover	44m	37m	27m
Pre Tax Profit/Loss	4m	4m	2m
Working Capital	9m	8m	7m
Fixed Assets	8m	7m	6m
Current Assets	17m	15m	12m
Current Liabilities	3m	3m	2m

The Wallpaper Shop
Fforest Business Centre Queensway, Fforestfach, Swansea, SA5 4DH
Tel: 01792-578090 **Fax:** 01792-421100
E-mail: divinahill1@hotmail.com
Directors: D. Hill (Prop)
No.of Employees: 1 - 10 **Product Groups:** 27, 32, 66

Waters Creative Ltd
Digital Technium Swansea University, Singleton Park, Swansea, SA2 8PP
Tel: 01792-513773 **Fax:** 0845-6860602
E-mail: info@waters-creative.co.uk
Website: http://www.waters-creative.co.uk
Directors: R. Wheatley (MD), R. Hullin (Ptnr)
Immediate Holding Company: WATERS CREATIVE LIMITED
Registration no: 04825983 **Date established:** 2003
No.of Employees: 1 - 10 **Product Groups:** 49

Weartech International Ltd
Unit 8 Hendy Industrial Estate, Pontarddulais, Swansea, SA4 0XP
Tel: 01792-882650 **Fax:** 01792-882664
E-mail: d.estall@weartecheurope.co.uk
Website: http://www.weartecheurope.co.uk
Bank(s): HSBC Bank plc
Managers: D. Estall (Mgr)
Immediate Holding Company: WEARTECH INTERNATIONAL LIMITED
Registration no: 04118871 **VAT No.:** GB 771 7844 93
Date established: 2000 **Turnover:** £2m - £5m **No.of Employees:** 21 - 50
Product Groups: 34, 35, 40, 48

Date of Accounts	Sep 08	Sep 07	Sep 06
Working Capital	425	241	172
Fixed Assets	458	420	426
Current Assets	1840	1335	859
Current Liabilities	1415	1094	687
Total Share Capital	100	100	100

Wecori Ltd
6 Ynyscedwyn Industrial Estate Trawsffordd Road, Ystradgynlais, Swansea, SA9 1DT
Tel: 01639-842526 **Fax:** 01639-845584
E-mail: wecori@btconnect.com
Website: http://www.wecori.co.uk
Bank(s): Barclays
Directors: R. Gardiner (MD)
Immediate Holding Company: WECORI LIMITED
Registration no: 00436741 **VAT No.:** GB 124 1437 07
Date established: 1947 **Turnover:** £250,000 - £500,000
No.of Employees: 11 - 20 **Product Groups:** 46, 48, 84

Date of Accounts	Jun 12	Jun 11	Jun 10
Working Capital	49	6	3
Fixed Assets	145	166	136
Current Assets	210	183	169

Welsh Boxes & Engineering Co. Ltd
Bruce Road Swansea West Industrial Park, Fforestfach, Swansea, SA5 4HS
Tel: 01792-586527 **Fax:** 01792-585410
E-mail: sales@welshboxes.co.uk
Website: http://www.welshboxes.co.uk
Bank(s): National Westminster Bank Plc
Directors: R. Hinder (MD), N. Pinocci (Sales)
Managers: P. Robinson (Sales Admin)
Immediate Holding Company: WELSH BOXES AND ENGINEERING COMPANY LIMITED
Registration no: 00325158 **VAT No.:** GB 122 6594 75
Date established: 1937 **Turnover:** £2m - £5m **No.of Employees:** 51 - 100
Product Groups: 27, 66

Date of Accounts	Dec 11	Dec 10	Dec 09
Sales Turnover	5m	4m	N/A
Pre Tax Profit/Loss	-40	-97	N/A
Working Capital	-8	-52	58
Fixed Assets	511	591	525
Current Assets	1m	1m	915
Current Liabilities	728	750	N/A

West Wales Galvanising Services
22 Ferryboat Close Enterprise Park, Swansea Enterprise Park, Swansea, SA6 8QN
Tel: 01792-775855 **Fax:** 01792-775855
Managers: M. Fulman (Mgr)
Immediate Holding Company: VISCOSE HOLDINGS LIMITED
Registration no: 03811430 **Date established:** 2011
No.of Employees: 1 - 10 **Product Groups:** 46, 48

Dyfed

Tenby

Argent Architects
1 Montrose Penally, Tenby, SA70 7PU
Tel: 01834-845440 **Fax:** 01834-845440
E-mail: info@argent-architects.co.uk
Website: http://www.argent-architects.co.uk
Directors: M. Argent (MD)
Registration no: 00516011 **Date established:** 1953
Turnover: Up to £250,000 **No.of Employees:** 1 - 10 **Product Groups:** 84

Augusta Golf Products Ltd
16-17 The Salterns, Tenby, SA70 8EQ
Tel: 01834-844972 **Fax:** 01834-843945
E-mail: sales@augustagolf.co.uk
Website: http://www.augustagolf.co.uk
Bank(s): Nat West
Directors: N. Edwards (Tech Serv), R. Turner (MD), D. Durrant (Co Sec)
Immediate Holding Company: AUGUSTA GOLF PRODUCTS LIMITED
Registration no: 01178793 **Date established:** 1974
No.of Employees: 21 - 50 **Product Groups:** 49

Date of Accounts	Nov 11	Nov 10	Nov 09
Working Capital	-294	-285	-310
Fixed Assets	479	466	471
Current Assets	133	142	122

Bartlett Engineering Co.
Sageston, Tenby, SA70 8SH
Tel: 01646-651387 **Fax:** 01646-651385
E-mail: sales@bartlettengineering.co.uk
Website: http://www.bartlettengineering.co.uk
Directors: R. Scourfield (Prop)
Date established: 1972 **Turnover:** £500,000 - £1m
No.of Employees: 1 - 10 **Product Groups:** 35, 48

T-Shirts R'Us
Rumbleway New Hedges, Tenby, SA70 8TN
Tel: 01834-845216 **Fax:** 01834-845216
E-mail: richardlewis@ukonline.co.uk
Website: http://www.teesrus.co.uk
Directors: R. Lewis (Prop)
Immediate Holding Company: TEES-R-US LTD
Date established: 2011 **No.of Employees:** 1 - 10 **Product Groups:** 24, 84

Mid-Glamorgan

Tonypandy

Calpack Ltd
Tonypandy Enterprise Park Llwynypia Road, Tonypandy, CF40 2ET
Tel: 01443-431544 **Fax:** 01443-432447
E-mail: rahul@calpack.co.uk
Website: http://www.calpack.co.uk
Bank(s): Bank of Wales
Managers: C. Campling (Ops Mgr)
Ultimate Holding Company: EAST KENT CARTONS LIMITED
Immediate Holding Company: CALPACK LTD
Registration no: 06812793 **Date established:** 2009 **Turnover:** £2m - £5m
No.of Employees: 11 - 20 **Product Groups:** 27, 28, 30, 48

Date of Accounts	Jan 11	Jan 10
Working Capital	145	128
Fixed Assets	702	63
Current Assets	573	624

M F C Survival Ltd
Naval Yard Tylacelyn Road, Tonypandy, CF40 1JS
Tel: 01443-433075 **Fax:** 01443-437846
E-mail: sales@mfc-survival.com
Website: http://www.mfc-survival.com
Bank(s): Barclays
Directors: A. Barker (MD), R. Morley (Fin)
Managers: R. Marsh
Ultimate Holding Company: MFC SURVIVAL HOLDINGS LIMITED
Immediate Holding Company: M.F.C. SURVIVAL LIMITED
Registration no: 00644778 **VAT No.:** GB 134 2487 77
Date established: 1959 **Turnover:** £1m - £2m **No.of Employees:** 51 - 100
Product Groups: 29, 30, 39

Date of Accounts	Jul 11	Jul 10	Jul 08
Working Capital	669	643	1m
Fixed Assets	585	666	438
Current Assets	2m	2m	2m

N C Ironcraft
350 Brithweunydd Road, Tonypandy, CF40 2NY
Tel: 01443-430219 **Fax:** 01443-430219
Directors: A. Brown (Prop)
Date established: 1987 **No.of Employees:** 1 - 10 **Product Groups:** 26, 35

Gwent

Tredegar

Able Office Furniture
Unit 22 Tafarnaubach Industrial Estate Tafarnaubach Industrial Estate, Tafarnaubach, Tredegar, NP22 3AA
Tel: 01495-726070 **Fax:** 01495-723060
E-mail: sales@ableofficefurniture.com
Website: http://www.ableofficefurniture.com
Directors: P. Jackson (MD)
No.of Employees: 1 - 10 **Product Groups:** 26, 30, 36

Date of Accounts	Aug 07	Aug 06
Working Capital	2	-2
Fixed Assets	9	10
Current Assets	118	64
Current Liabilities	116	66
Total Share Capital	150	110

Beacon Metal Finishers Ltd
Unit 10 Sirhowy Industrial Estate Thomas Ellis Way, Sirhowy, Tredegar, NP22 4QZ
Tel: 01495-711383 **Fax:** 01495-711383
Directors: H. Marchington (MD), M. Marchington (Fin)
Immediate Holding Company: BEACON METAL FINISHERS LIMITED
Registration no: 01779193 **VAT No.:** GB 402 3250 15
Date established: 1983 **Turnover:** £250,000 - £500,000
No.of Employees: 1 - 10 **Product Groups:** 48

Date of Accounts	Dec 10	Dec 09	Dec 07
Working Capital	2	-4	14
Fixed Assets	2	2	1
Current Assets	20	12	40
Current Liabilities	15	15	8

Caparo Tubes
Unit 4 Tafarnaubach Industrial Estate Tafarnaubach, Tredegar, NP22 3AA
Tel: 01495-724333 **Fax:** 01495-717720
E-mail: david.porter@caparotubestredegar.co.uk
Website: http://www.caparo-tubes.co.uk
Bank(s): Barclays
Directors: D. Porter (Dir)
Managers: D. Davies (Tech Serv Mgr)
Immediate Holding Company: RPM VEHICLE LOGISTICS LIMITED
Registration no: 00892463 **VAT No.:** GB 245 2598 47
Date established: 2008 **Turnover:** £20m - £50m
No.of Employees: 51 - 100 **Product Groups:** 34, 36, 45

Date of Accounts	Nov 11	Nov 10	Nov 09
Working Capital	-2	-2	-2
Current Liabilities	2	2	2

Convatec Ltd
Unit 1-2 Heads of The Valley Industrial Estate, Rhymney, Tredegar, NP22 5RL
Tel: 01685-846300 **Fax:** 01685-844068
Website: http://www.convatec.com
Managers: A. Lewis (Mgr), C. Bendall (Mgr), M. Soper (Personnel)
Ultimate Holding Company: CIDRON HEALTHCARE LTD (JERSEY)
Immediate Holding Company: CONVATEC LIMITED
Registration no: 01309639 **Date established:** 1977
No.of Employees: 51 - 100 **Product Groups:** 38, 67

Date of Accounts	Dec 11	Dec 10	Dec 09
Sales Turnover	161m	201m	238m
Pre Tax Profit/Loss	28m	58m	41m
Working Capital	132m	93m	43m
Fixed Assets	100m	101m	117m
Current Assets	156m	137m	136m
Current Liabilities	7m	12m	7m

Excel Industries Ltd
Maerdy Industrial Estate Rhymney, Tredegar, NP22 5PY
Tel: 01685-845200 **Fax:** 01685-844106
E-mail: sales@excelfibre.com
Website: http://www.excelfibre.com
Bank(s): Barclays
Directors: S. Widows (Fin), A. Izod (Dir)
Managers: N. Bosanko, E. Lawrence
Ultimate Holding Company: THOMAS ROBERTS INDUSTRIES LIMITED
Immediate Holding Company: EXCEL INDUSTRIES LIMITED
Registration no: 02072145 **VAT No.:** GB 540 8949 20
Date established: 1986 **Turnover:** £5m - £10m **No.of Employees:** 21 - 50
Product Groups: 23

Date of Accounts	Mar 12	Mar 11	Mar 10
Sales Turnover	8m	8m	9m
Pre Tax Profit/Loss	78	-791	-599
Working Capital	756	-382	-263
Fixed Assets	1m	2m	2m
Current Assets	2m	2m	2m
Current Liabilities	170	244	180

Folkmay Ltd
Old Bullring Dukestown Road, Tredegar, NP22 4QG
Tel: 01495-711075
Managers: R. Edwards (Mgr)
Immediate Holding Company: FOLKMAY LIMITED
Registration no: 01521174 **Date established:** 1980
No.of Employees: 1 - 10 **Product Groups:** 24, 26

Howard Handling
9 The Lawn Rhymney, Tredegar, NP22 5LS
Tel: 01685-843843 **Fax:** 01685-843300
E-mail: info@howardhandling.co.uk
Website: http://www.howardhandling.co.uk
Managers: P. Howard (Mgr)
Date established: 2000 **No.of Employees:** 1 - 10 **Product Groups:** 35, 39, 45

Mountway Ltd
Unit 7-8 Tafarnaubach Industrial Estate Tafarnaubach, Tredegar, NP22 3AA
Tel: 01495-723300 **Fax:** 01495-723360
E-mail: mail@mountway.co.uk
Website: http://www.mountway.com
Managers: M. Hughes (Mktg Serv Mgr), D. Kinsalla (Chief Mgr), R. Llanlois (Buyer)
Immediate Holding Company: MOUNTWAY LIMITED
Registration no: 01594500 **Date established:** 1981 **Turnover:** £5m - £10m
No.of Employees: 21 - 50 **Product Groups:** 26, 36, 48

Date of Accounts	Dec 11	Dec 10	Dec 09
Sales Turnover	4m	5m	6m
Pre Tax Profit/Loss	196	-881	-1m
Working Capital	1m	1m	2m
Fixed Assets	47	565	1m
Current Assets	1m	2m	3m
Current Liabilities	200	230	230

N M C UK Ltd
Unit 5b Tafarnaubach Industrial Estate, Tafarnaubach, Tredegar, NP22 3AA
Tel: 01495-713266 **Fax:** 01495-713277
E-mail: enquiries@nmc-uk.com
Website: http://www.nmc-uk.com
Bank(s): National Westminster Bank Plc
Directors: T. Stone (MD), W. Horton (Fin)
Managers: K. Morgan (Sales & Mktg Mg), W. Churchill (Transport)
Ultimate Holding Company: NMC SA (BELGIUM)
Immediate Holding Company: NMC (UK) LIMITED
Registration no: 01985924 **VAT No.:** GB 441 0592 77
Date established: 1986 **Turnover:** £10m - £20m
No.of Employees: 21 - 50 **Product Groups:** 30

Date of Accounts	Dec 11	Dec 10	Dec 09
Sales Turnover	13m	12m	10m
Pre Tax Profit/Loss	1m	2m	1m
Working Capital	5m	4m	4m
Fixed Assets	993	1m	1m
Current Assets	9m	7m	6m
Current Liabilities	2m	2m	2m

Neuson Ltd
Crown Business Park Dukestown, Tredegar, NP22 4EF
Tel: 01495-723083 **Fax:** 01495-713941
E-mail: ukoffice@neuson.com
Website: http://www.neusonkramer.com
Bank(s): National Westminster Bank Plc
Directors: J. Walmsley (MD)
Managers: M. Warren (Sales Prom Mgr), T. Bishop (I.T. Exec), I. Johnson (Sales Prom Mgr)
Ultimate Holding Company: Neuson Kramer Baumaschinen AG
Immediate Holding Company: Kramer Werke
Registration no: 02903372 **VAT No.:** GB 633 2941 47
Turnover: £10m - £20m **No.of Employees:** 101 - 250
Product Groups: 39, 45, 83

Date of Accounts	Dec 08	Dec 07	Dec 06
Sales Turnover	24230	28412	18357
Pre Tax Profit/Loss	-3958	1930	789
Working Capital	-3832	4215	2788
Fixed Assets	4464	1612	1703
Current Assets	17488	15544	10416
Current Liabilities	21320	11328	7628
Total Share Capital	550	550	550
ROCE% (Return on Capital Employed)	-626.9	33.1	17.6
ROT% (Return on Turnover)	-16.3	6.8	4.3

Pramac UK Ltd
Crown Business Park Dukestown, Tredegar, NP22 4XD
Tel: 01495-713300 **Fax:** 01495-718766
E-mail: info@pramac.com
Website: http://www.pramac.com
Bank(s): Barclays
Directors: W. Steele (MD)
Managers: A. Coughlan (Fin Mgr)
Ultimate Holding Company: PRAMAC INDUSTRIAL SPA (ITALY)
Immediate Holding Company: PRAMAC (UK) LIMITED
Registration no: 01432297 **VAT No.:** GB 337 8309 37
Date established: 1979 **Turnover:** £2m - £5m **No.of Employees:** 11 - 20
Product Groups: 37, 45

Date of Accounts	Dec 11	Dec 10	Dec 09
Sales Turnover	7m	5m	N/A
Pre Tax Profit/Loss	-389	-410	N/A
Working Capital	33	449	900
Fixed Assets	450	475	495
Current Assets	3m	2m	2m
Current Liabilities	378	240	N/A

Prima Care
Unit 26 Heads of The Valley Industrial Estate Rhymney, Tredegar, NP22 5RL
Tel: 01685-845900 **Fax:** 01495-718777
E-mail: info@primacare.co.uk
Website: http://www.primacare.co.uk
Directors: H. Tomlin (Fin), D. Tomlin (MD)
Immediate Holding Company: PRIMACARE LIMITED
Registration no: 05184511 **Date established:** 2004
No.of Employees: 21 - 50 **Product Groups:** 26, 39, 67

Date of Accounts	Jul 11	Jul 10	Jul 09
Working Capital	94	19	167
Fixed Assets	73	77	6
Current Assets	789	517	733

Richards & Appleby Ltd
Unit 3 Heads of The Valley Industrial Estate Rhymney, Tredegar, NP22 5RL
Tel: 01685-843384 **Fax:** 01685-842466
E-mail: enquiries@richardsandappleby.co.uk
Website: http://www.richardsandappleby.co.uk
Bank(s): National Westminster Bank Plc
Directors: M. Field (MD)
Ultimate Holding Company: RICHARDS & APPLEBY HOLDINGS LIMITED
Immediate Holding Company: RICHARDS & APPLEBY LIMITED
Registration no: 00937090 **Date established:** 1968 **Turnover:** £5m - £10m
No.of Employees: 101 - 250 **Product Groups:** 32

see next page

Richards & Appleby Ltd - *Cont'd*

Date of Accounts	Mar 11	Mar 10	Mar 09
Sales Turnover	8m	8m	7m
Pre Tax Profit/Loss	294	270	-347
Working Capital	3m	3m	1m
Fixed Assets	2m	2m	2m
Current Assets	5m	5m	3m
Current Liabilities	733	704	465

Tenneco-Walker UK Ltd
Unit 3 Tafarnaubach Industrial Estate Tafarnaubach, Tredegar, NP22 3AA
Tel: 01495-711211 **Fax:** 01495-723311
E-mail: mlight@taeu.com
Website: http://www.tenneco.com
Bank(s): Barclays
Managers: M. Light (Sales Prom Mgr), D. Higgins, J. Andrews (Personnel), P. Evans (Comptroller), P. Ellis (Comptroller), M. Stanley (Mats Contrlr), G. Jones (I.T. Exec), W. Slate (Tech Serv Mgr), L. Rogers (Personnel), M. Light (Sales Prom Mgr)
Ultimate Holding Company: TENNECO INC
Immediate Holding Company: WALKER UK LTD
Registration no: 00985395 **VAT No.:** GB 290 8447 33
Turnover: £20m - £50m **No.of Employees:** 21 - 50 **Product Groups:** 40

Tredegar Fabrication & Welding
Crown Avenue Dukestown, Tredegar, NP22 4EE
Tel: 01495-717774 **Fax:** 01495-717774
Directors: S. Derick (Prop)
Date established: 2000 **No.of Employees:** 1 - 10 **Product Groups:** 35

Visqueen Building Products South Wales Ltd
Maerdy Industrial Estate Rhymney, Tredegar, NP22 5PY
Tel: 01685-840672 **Fax:** 01685-842580
E-mail: steveharris@visqueenbuilding.co.uk
Website: http://www.visqueenbuilding.co.uk
Bank(s): Barclays
Managers: E. Evans (Personnel), S. Harris (Mgr)
Ultimate Holding Company: THOMAS ROBERTS INDUSTRIES LIMITED
Immediate Holding Company: EXCEL INDUSTRIES LIMITED
Registration no: 02072145 **Date established:** 1986 **Turnover:** £5m - £10m
No.of Employees: 51 - 100 **Product Groups:** 27, 30, 31

Date of Accounts	Mar 12	Mar 11	Mar 10
Sales Turnover	8m	8m	9m
Pre Tax Profit/Loss	78	-791	-599
Working Capital	756	-382	-263
Fixed Assets	1m	2m	2m
Current Assets	2m	2m	2m
Current Liabilities	170	244	180

Williams Medical Supplies
Craiglas House Maerdy Industrial Estate, Rhymney, Tredegar, NP22 5PY
Tel: 01685-844724 **Fax:** 01685-844725
E-mail: kerry.mudd@wms.co.uk
Website: http://www.wms.co.uk
Managers: K. Mudd
Ultimate Holding Company: WILLIAMS MEDICAL HOLDINGS LIMITED
Immediate Holding Company: WILLIAMS MEDICAL SUPPLIES LIMITED
Registration no: 04240054 **Date established:** 2001
Turnover: £50m - £75m **No.of Employees:** 101 - 250
Product Groups: 38, 63

Date of Accounts	Jul 11	Jul 10	Jul 09
Sales Turnover	53m	62m	53m
Pre Tax Profit/Loss	4m	6m	5m
Working Capital	3m	4m	3m
Fixed Assets	6m	6m	6m
Current Assets	14m	15m	15m
Current Liabilities	1m	2m	3m

Mid-Glamorgan

Treharris

G Bridges Welding & Plating
17-19 High Street Nelson, Treharris, CF46 6EU
Tel: 01443-450522
Directors: G. Bridges (Prop)
Date established: 1990 **No.of Employees:** 1 - 10 **Product Groups:** 35

Mid-Glamorgan

Treorchy

Ribbons Ltd
Treorchy Industrial Estate, Treorchy, CF42 6EJ
Tel: 01443-432473 **Fax:** 01443-437413
E-mail: godfreycodrington@ribbons.co.uk
Website: http://www.ribbons.co.uk
Directors: D. Edwards (Fin), G. Codrington (MD)
Managers: P. Hurst (Tech Serv Mgr), T. Spiller (Sales Admin), P. Coburn (Sales Prom Mgr), N. Codrington (Mktg Serv Mgr), M. Porch (Chief Mgr)
Ultimate Holding Company: MANDACO 502 LIMITED
Immediate Holding Company: RIBBONS LIMITED
Registration no: 01905537 **Date established:** 1985 **Turnover:** £2m - £5m
No.of Employees: 51 - 100 **Product Groups:** 23

Date of Accounts	Dec 11	Dec 10	Dec 09
Sales Turnover	4m	3m	3m
Pre Tax Profit/Loss	29	-80	21
Working Capital	753	707	742
Fixed Assets	120	142	171
Current Assets	2m	2m	2m
Current Liabilities	596	103	141

South Wales Metal Finishing Ltd
Caemawr Industrial Estate, Treorchy, CF42 6EJ
Tel: 01443-442992 **Fax:** 01443-442993
Website: http://www.southwalesmetalfinishing.co.uk
Directors: S. Demaid (MD)
Registration no: 04205863 **Date established:** 2001
No.of Employees: 11 - 20 **Product Groups:** 46, 48

Date of Accounts	Apr 10	Apr 09	Apr 08
Working Capital	25	39	49
Fixed Assets	139	191	226
Current Assets	143	142	193

Gwynedd

Tyn-Y-Gongl

Timberwise UK Ltd
65 Breeze Hill Benllech, Tyn-Y-Gongl, LL74 8UB
Tel: 01492-535065 **Fax:** 01492-864004
E-mail: llandudno@timberwise.co.uk
Website: http://www.timberwise.co.uk
Managers: K. Regan (Mgr)
Ultimate Holding Company: TIMBERWISE HOLDINGS LIMITED
Immediate Holding Company: TIMBERWISE (UK) LIMITED
Registration no: 03230356 **Date established:** 1996
No.of Employees: 1 - 10 **Product Groups:** 07, 32, 52

Date of Accounts	Dec 11	Dec 10	Dec 09
Sales Turnover	N/A	N/A	5m
Pre Tax Profit/Loss	N/A	N/A	214
Working Capital	397	343	326
Fixed Assets	265	291	301
Current Assets	1m	1m	1m
Current Liabilities	N/A	N/A	585

Gwynedd

Tywyn

Halo Foods Ltd
Pendre Industrial Estate, Tywyn, LL36 9LW
Tel: 01654-711171 **Fax:** 01654-711744
E-mail: enquiries@halofoods.co.uk
Website: http://www.halofoods.co.uk
Bank(s): HSBC Bank plc
Directors: D. Edwards (Fin), P. Cartwright (Mkt Research), R. Williams (MD), S. Kean (Sales & Mktg)
Managers: G. Wagstaff (Tech Serv Mgr)
Ultimate Holding Company: RAISIO PLC (FINLAND)
Immediate Holding Company: HALO FOODS LIMITED
Registration no: 02411911 **VAT No.:** GB 489 3683 80
Date established: 1989 **Turnover:** £20m - £50m
No.of Employees: 101 - 250 **Product Groups:** 62

Date of Accounts	Dec 11	Dec 10	Jun 09
Sales Turnover	30m	36m	22m
Pre Tax Profit/Loss	12m	1m	-80
Working Capital	7m	192	-2m
Fixed Assets	4m	5m	5m
Current Assets	11m	61m	63m
Current Liabilities	2m	2m	2m

William Hesleton
Quarry Bank Rhoslefain, Tywyn, LL36 9LP
Tel: 01654-710777 **Fax:** 01654-710777
Website: http://www.hesletonrecovery.co.uk
Directors: W. Hesleton (Prop)
Date established: 1980 **No.of Employees:** 1 - 10 **Product Groups:** 41

Hunt Engineering
Unit D Beacon Units, Tywyn, LL36 9RT
Tel: 01654-711577
Directors: L. Hunte (Dir)
Date established: 2006 **No.of Employees:** 1 - 10 **Product Groups:** 35

T T P Precisions Ltd
Bryncrug, Tywyn, LL36 9PT
Tel: 01654-710711 **Fax:** 01654-711899
E-mail: thomas.gardner@ttpltd.com
Website: http://www.ttpltd.com
Directors: D. Gardener (MD), D. Gardner (MD), R. Crawford (Dir), T. Gardner (MD)
Managers: J. Rogers (Quality Control), P. Roberts (Quality Control), T. Hinton (Works Gen Mgr)
Immediate Holding Company: T.T.P. PRECISION LIMITED
Registration no: 00969440 **Date established:** 1970 **Turnover:** £2m - £5m
No.of Employees: 11 - 20 **Product Groups:** 35

Date of Accounts	Apr 08	Apr 07	Apr 06
Sales Turnover	N/A	N/A	2m
Pre Tax Profit/Loss	N/A	N/A	-111
Working Capital	-148	-175	-177
Fixed Assets	680	659	716
Current Assets	454	565	487
Current Liabilities	603	740	664
Total Share Capital	2	2	2

Gwent

Usk

Fast Fuel Ltd
Unit 5 Grange Mill Raglan, Usk, NP15 2BX
Tel: 01291-691402 **Fax:** 01291-691401
E-mail: sales@fast-fuel.co.uk
Website: http://www.fast-fuel.co.uk
Directors: D. Llewellyn (MD)
Immediate Holding Company: FAST FUEL LIMITED
Registration no: 04488820 **Date established:** 2002 **Turnover:** £2m - £5m
No.of Employees: 1 - 10 **Product Groups:** 11, 30, 31, 32, 35, 38, 40, 52, 66, 68

Date of Accounts	Sep 11	Sep 10	Sep 09
Working Capital	-380	-415	-207
Fixed Assets	33	35	43
Current Assets	577	287	441

U S K Refrigeration Service
Davington House Llangeview, Usk, NP15 1EN
Tel: 01291-672565 **Fax:** 01291-673773
Directors: E. Jones (Prop)
No.of Employees: 1 - 10 **Product Groups:** 36, 40

Powys

Welshpool

Boys & Boden Ltd
Mill Lane, Welshpool, SY21 7BL
Tel: 01938-556677 **Fax:** 01938-555773
E-mail: dean@boysandboden.co.uk
Website: http://www.pearstairs.co.uk
Bank(s): HSBC Bank plc
Directors: D. Hammond (MD)
Managers: N. King-sharpe (Personnel), A. Griffiths (Purch Mgr), C. Sharp (Chief Acct), D. Whiteford (Sales Prom Mgr), G. Jones (Tech Serv Mgr)
Immediate Holding Company: BOYS & BODEN, LIMITED
Registration no: 00215444 **Date established:** 2026
Turnover: £10m - £20m **No.of Employees:** 101 - 250
Product Groups: 25, 48, 66

Date of Accounts	Mar 12	Mar 11	Mar 10
Sales Turnover	18m	18m	15m
Pre Tax Profit/Loss	1m	807	657
Working Capital	1m	1m	1m
Fixed Assets	8m	7m	7m
Current Assets	7m	7m	6m
Current Liabilities	2m	1m	1m

Carpenter & Paterson Ltd
Crown Works Henfaes Lane, Welshpool, SY21 7BE
Tel: 01938-552061 **Fax:** 01938-555306
E-mail: info@cp-ltd.co.uk
Website: http://www.cp-ltd.co.uk
Bank(s): Midland
Directors: H. Thomas (Chief Est), J. Lee (MD)
Managers: D. Hardy (Purch Mgr), K. Edwards, M. Williams (Tech Serv Mgr), C. Emberton (Personnel)
Ultimate Holding Company: CARPENTER & PATERSON (HOLDINGS) LIMITED
Immediate Holding Company: CARPENTER & PATERSON (HOLDINGS) LIMITED
Registration no: 02727723 **VAT No.:** GB 158 9478 05
Date established: 1992 **Turnover:** £5m - £10m
No.of Employees: 51 - 100 **Product Groups:** 35, 36, 40

Date of Accounts	Dec 11	Dec 10	Dec 09
Sales Turnover	8m	8m	12m
Pre Tax Profit/Loss	380	-58	1m
Working Capital	3m	3m	4m
Fixed Assets	2m	2m	2m
Current Assets	4m	4m	5m
Current Liabilities	353	196	576

Dixon Turner Wallcoverings Ltd
Henfaes Lane, Welshpool, SY21 7BE
Tel: 01938-552671 **Fax:** 020-7436 0324
E-mail: enquiries@dixon-turner.co.uk
Website: http://www.dixon-turner.co.uk
Directors: T. Morris (MD)
Immediate Holding Company: DIXON TURNER WALLCOVERINGS LIMITED
Registration no: 04131654 **Date established:** 2000 **Turnover:** £2m - £5m
No.of Employees: 1 - 10 **Product Groups:** 27, 30, 65

Richard Downes-Evans Blacksmiths
Oakwood Llangyniew, Welshpool, SY21 0JZ
Tel: 01938-810897
E-mail: richard.downes-evans@virgin.net
Directors: R. Downes-Evans (Prop)
No.of Employees: 1 - 10 **Product Groups:** 37, 40, 48

Eurochem Automotive Chemicals Ltd Splashgroup UK
Dragon Works Henfaes Lane, Welshpool, SY21 7BE
Tel: 01938-553373 **Fax:** 01938-555754
E-mail: support@eurochem.co.uk
Website: http://www.eurochem.co.uk
Directors: T. Hodgson (MD), S. Grimshaw (MD)
Immediate Holding Company: EUROCHEM AUTOMOTIVE CHEMICALS LTD
Registration no: 05973417 **Date established:** 2006 **Turnover:** £2m - £5m
No.of Employees: 11 - 20 **Product Groups:** 32, 39, 66

Date of Accounts	Oct 11	Oct 10	Oct 09
Working Capital	N/A	24	3
Fixed Assets	10	13	11
Current Assets	11	24	21

Ivor Davies Agri
Revel Garage Berriew, Welshpool, SY21 8AJ
Tel: 07967-386151 **Fax:** 01686-640920
E-mail: ivor062@aol.com
Directors: I. Davies (Prop)
Date established: 2000 **No.of Employees:** 1 - 10 **Product Groups:** 41

Motor & Agricultural Engineer
Cefn Coch, Welshpool, SY21 0AX
Tel: 01938-810680 **Fax:** 01938-810680
Directors: D. Isaac (Prop)
Date established: 1976 **No.of Employees:** 1 - 10 **Product Groups:** 41

Newmor Group Ltd
Madoc Works Henfaes Lane, Welshpool, SY21 7BE
Tel: 01938-552671 **Fax:** 01938-554285
E-mail: chris.stephens@newmor.com
Website: http://www.newmor.com
Bank(s): Barclays

Directors: C. Stephens (Fin), T. Morris (MD)
Managers: B. Pritchard, R. Owen (Personnel)
Ultimate Holding Company: JOHN MORRIS HOLDINGS LIMITED
Immediate Holding Company: NEWMOR GROUP LIMITED
Registration no: 00897076 **VAT No.:** GB 326 5982 31
Date established: 1967 **Turnover:** £10m - £20m
No.of Employees: 101 - 250 **Product Groups:** 30

Date of Accounts	Dec 11	Dec 10	Dec 09
Sales Turnover	20m	20m	17m
Pre Tax Profit/Loss	905	774	993
Working Capital	6m	6m	5m
Fixed Assets	4m	3m	4m
Current Assets	9m	9m	8m
Current Liabilities	1m	1m	847

William O'Brien
The Wharf Berriew, Welshpool, SY21 8AN
Tel: 01686-640739
E-mail: willob1@btinternet.com
Website: http://www.sculpturesiniron.co.uk
Directors: W. O'brien (Prop)
Date established: 1995 **No.of Employees:** 1 - 10 **Product Groups:** 26, 35

P T H Tools
Garth Eilun Dolanog, Welshpool, SY21 0LS
Tel: 01938-810557
Directors: W. Gowarth (Prop)
Date established: 1989 **No.of Employees:** 1 - 10 **Product Groups:** 46

Rainbow Recruitment UK Ltd
Park Lane House 7 High Street, Welshpool, SY21 7JP
Tel: 01938-555222 **Fax:** 01938-555800
E-mail: jobs@rainbow-recruitment.co.uk
Website: http://www.rainbow-recruitment.co.uk
Directors: N. Hughes (Fin), A. Mills (MD), H. Collins (MD)
Immediate Holding Company: RAINBOW RECRUITMENT (UK) LIMITED
Registration no: 05385511 **Date established:** 2005
Turnover: £500,000 - £1m **No.of Employees:** 1 - 10 **Product Groups:** 80

Date of Accounts	May 10	May 09	May 08
Working Capital	-133	-137	-189
Fixed Assets	160	189	219
Current Assets	118	71	116

Robert Wyn Jones & Sons
Smithy Buttington, Welshpool, SY21 8SS
Tel: 01938-570452 **Fax:** 01938-570452
Directors: R. Jones (Prop)
Date established: 1975 **No.of Employees:** 1 - 10 **Product Groups:** 35

Technocover Ltd
Unit C Henfaes Lane, Welshpool, SY21 7BE
Tel: 01938-555511 **Fax:** 01938-555527
E-mail: admin@technocover.co.uk
Website: http://www.technocover.co.uk
Bank(s): Barclays
Directors: M. Miles (Dir), P. Webb (Fin)
Managers: J. Lewis (Tech Serv Mgr), P. Ellis, T. Batten (Mktg Serv Mgr), J. Mitten (Personnel)
Immediate Holding Company: TECHNOCOVER LTD.
Registration no: 02845757 **VAT No.:** GB 594 4129 19
Date established: 1993 **Turnover:** £10m - £20m
No.of Employees: 101 - 250 **Product Groups:** 35

Date of Accounts	Aug 10	Aug 09	Aug 08
Sales Turnover	12m	14m	N/A
Pre Tax Profit/Loss	-786	719	17
Working Capital	-270	274	2m
Fixed Assets	4m	6m	4m
Current Assets	3m	4m	5m
Current Liabilities	733	2m	2m

Teme Valley Tractors Welshpool Ltd
Severn Farm Industrial Estate, Welshpool, SY21 7DF
Tel: 01938-552147 **Fax:** 01938-556264
E-mail: martyn@temevalleyw.co.uk
Website: http://www.temevalleyw.co.uk
Directors: M. Hall (Sales)
Immediate Holding Company: TEME VALLEY TRACTORS (WELSHPOOL) LIMITED
Registration no: 02803190 **Date established:** 1993
Turnover: £500,000 - £1m **No.of Employees:** 11 - 20 **Product Groups:** 41

Date of Accounts	Dec 11	Dec 10	Dec 09
Sales Turnover	665	655	577
Pre Tax Profit/Loss	115	131	102
Working Capital	556	474	409
Fixed Assets	143	156	133
Current Assets	2m	2m	2m
Current Liabilities	155	449	96

Trax
Unit 1a Severn Farm Industrial Estate, Welshpool, SY21 7DF
Tel: 01938-554297 **Fax:** 01938-554597
E-mail: n.morrison@traxjh.com
Website: http://www.traxjh.com
Bank(s): HSBC Bank plc
Managers: D. Painton
Ultimate Holding Company: T B W LIMITED
Immediate Holding Company: TRAX J H LIMITED
Registration no: 02775943 **VAT No.:** GB 594 3134 31
Date established: 1992 **Turnover:** £5m - £10m **No.of Employees:** 21 - 50
Product Groups: 35, 39, 41

Date of Accounts	Dec 11	Dec 10	Dec 09
Sales Turnover	6m	7m	N/A
Pre Tax Profit/Loss	-320	-189	133
Working Capital	424	434	853
Fixed Assets	1m	1m	882
Current Assets	2m	3m	2m
Current Liabilities	751	983	784

Wipak UK Ltd
Unit 3 Buttington Cross Enterprise Park Buttington, Welshpool, SY21 8SL
Tel: 01938-555255 **Fax:** 01938-555277
E-mail: info@wipak.com
Website: http://www.wipak.com
Directors: A. Aarnio Wihuri (Ch)
Managers: L. Draper (Comptroller)
Ultimate Holding Company: WIHURI OY (FINLAND)
Immediate Holding Company: WIPAK UK LIMITED
Registration no: 01251293 **Date established:** 1976
Turnover: £10m - £20m **No.of Employees:** 51 - 100 **Product Groups:** 30, 31, 42, 48

Date of Accounts	Dec 11	Dec 10	Dec 09
Sales Turnover	16m	14m	14m
Pre Tax Profit/Loss	942	1m	943
Working Capital	-2m	-200	-466
Fixed Assets	6m	4m	4m
Current Assets	5m	5m	4m
Current Liabilities	781	579	618

Dyfed

Whitland

B & H Fabrications
Unit 7 Spring Gardens Industrial Estate, Whitland, SA34 0HZ
Tel: 01994-241194 **Fax:** 01994-240944
E-mail: info@bhfabrications.co.uk
Website: http://www.bhfabrications.co.uk
Directors: B. Louth (Prop)
Immediate Holding Company: B & H FABRICATIONS (WALES) LIMITED
Registration no: 04523043 **Date established:** 2002
No.of Employees: 1 - 10 **Product Groups:** 20, 40, 41

Date of Accounts	Aug 11	Aug 10	Aug 09
Working Capital	-2	20	-3
Fixed Assets	4	11	19
Current Assets	111	88	74

Magstim Co. Ltd
Spring Gardens, Whitland, SA34 0HR
Tel: 01994-240798 **Fax:** 01994-240061
E-mail: sales@magstim.com
Website: http://www.magstim.com
Bank(s): Lloyds, Carmarthen
Directors: J. Davies-schofield (Fin), R. Lewis (MD)
Managers: A. Nicholas (Personnel), N. Todorov, G. Lloyd (Tech Serv Mgr), J. Scandone (Nat Sales Mgr)
Immediate Holding Company: THE MAGSTIM COMPANY LIMITED
Registration no: 02308367 **VAT No.:** GB 485 2438 25
Date established: 1988 **Turnover:** £5m - £10m
No.of Employees: 51 - 100 **Product Groups:** 38

Date of Accounts	Mar 12	Mar 11	Mar 10
Sales Turnover	8m	9m	9m
Pre Tax Profit/Loss	1m	2m	2m
Working Capital	4m	3m	2m
Fixed Assets	395	431	395
Current Assets	5m	5m	4m
Current Liabilities	927	1m	2m

R-Tech Solutions Ltd
Unit 1 Pinner Parc, Whitland, SA34 0RA
Tel: 01994-240500 **Fax:** 01994-240520
E-mail: sales@r-techsolutions.co.uk
Website: http://www.r-techsolutions.co.uk
Directors: S. Wilson (MD)
Immediate Holding Company: R - TECH SOLUTIONS LTD
Registration no: 03979551 **Date established:** 2000
No.of Employees: 1 - 10 **Product Groups:** 32

Date of Accounts	Apr 11	Apr 10	Apr 09
Working Capital	15	-6	-8
Fixed Assets	35	22	23
Current Assets	181	117	73

Clwyd

Wrexham

A E L Flexaulic Ltd
Llay Hall Industrial Estate Mold Road, Cefn-Y-Bedd, Wrexham, LL12 9YG
Tel: 01978-761848 **Fax:** 01978-762340
E-mail: flexaulic@btconnect.com
Website: http://www.flexaulic.com
Bank(s): Midland, Caergwrle
Directors: J. Roe (MD)
Immediate Holding Company: A. E. L. FLEXAULIC LIMITED
Registration no: 01892851 **VAT No.:** GB 421 9421 73
Date established: 1985 **Turnover:** £250,000 - £500,000
No.of Employees: 21 - 50 **Product Groups:** 38, 46

Date of Accounts	Dec 11	Dec 10	Dec 09
Working Capital	-534	116	115
Fixed Assets	57	62	69
Current Assets	213	203	182

A W Services
Unit 8a Vauxhall Industrial Estate Ruabon, Wrexham, LL14 6HA
Tel: 01978-810055 **Fax:** 01978-821700
E-mail: awservicesltd@aol.com
Directors: A. White (MD)
Immediate Holding Company: A W SERVICES (NORTH WEST) LIMITED
Registration no: 05309674 **Date established:** 2004
No.of Employees: 1 - 10 **Product Groups:** 30, 32, 48, 66

Date of Accounts	Dec 11	Dec 10	Dec 09
Working Capital	-13	-34	-35
Fixed Assets	4	12	13
Current Assets	16	44	15

Adhesive Direct
Cae Brynner House Bowling Bank, Wrexham, LL13 9RL
Tel: 01978-664556 **Fax:** 01978-664557
E-mail: kev.braithwaite@btconnect.com
Website: http://www.adhesives-direct.co.uk
Directors: K. Braithwaite (Dir)
Registration no: 02943163 **VAT No.:** GB 625 3568 33
Date established: 1996 **Turnover:** £250,000 - £500,000
No.of Employees: 1 - 10 **Product Groups:** 32, 42

Aguachem Ltd
Redwither Business Centre Redwither Business Park, Wrexham, LL13 9XR
Tel: 01978-664077 **Fax:** 01352-781871
E-mail: aguachame@fsmail.net
Website: http://www.watertreatmentwaste.co.uk
Directors: J. Holt (Sales)
Immediate Holding Company: AGUACHEM LTD
Registration no: 05316282 **Date established:** 2004
No.of Employees: 1 - 10 **Product Groups:** 32

Date of Accounts	Dec 11	Dec 10	Dec 09
Working Capital	74	14	-1
Fixed Assets	N/A	N/A	1
Current Assets	225	180	210

Allied Fire Alarms & Escapes Co. Ltd (Fire Alarm & Emergency Systems)
Allied House Bryn Lane, Wrexham Industrial Estate, Wrexham, LL13 9UT
Tel: 01978-661874 **Fax:** 01978-661816
E-mail: sales@afaefire.co.uk
Website: http://www.afaefire.co.uk
Directors: J. Westerman (Dir)
Immediate Holding Company: ALLIED FIRE ALARMS AND ESCAPES CO LIMITED
Registration no: 01079718 **VAT No.:** 134 0858 78 **Date established:** 1972
Turnover: £500,000 - £1m **No.of Employees:** 1 - 10 **Product Groups:** 40, 52

Date of Accounts	Nov 11	Nov 10	Nov 09
Working Capital	71	91	103
Fixed Assets	56	58	60
Current Assets	90	115	143

Almetron Ltd
Unit 24 Abenbury Way Wrexham Industrial Estate, Wrexham, LL13 9UZ
Tel: 01978-660297 **Fax:** 01978-661104
E-mail: info@almetron.co.uk
Website: http://www.almetron.co.uk
Bank(s): Barclays
Directors: I. Rogers (MD), P. Tomkins (Fin)
Immediate Holding Company: ALMETRON LIMITED
Registration no: 01744029 **VAT No.:** GB 388 2691 03
Date established: 1983 **Turnover:** £1m - £2m **No.of Employees:** 11 - 20
Product Groups: 32

Date of Accounts	Sep 11	Sep 10	Sep 09
Working Capital	43	707	559
Fixed Assets	153	136	174
Current Assets	932	1m	908

Artificial Limb & Appliance Centre
Croesnewydd Road Wrexham Technology Park, Wrexham, LL13 7TD
Tel: 01978-727524 **Fax:** 01978-727307
Managers: A. Ravenscroft (Mgr)
No.of Employees: 11 - 20 **Product Groups:** 38, 67

AWAYDAYS UK AWAYDAYS
Unit K&L Five Crosses Industrial Estate Minera, Wrexham, LL11 3RD
Tel: 01978-761863 **Fax:** 01978-761863
E-mail: awaydaysuk@hotmail.co.uk
Website: http://www.awaydaysuk.co.uk
Directors: R. Evans (Prop)
No.of Employees: 1 - 10 **Product Groups:** 39, 40, 67, 68

Barloworld Handling Ltd
Unit 104 Coed Aben Road, Wrexham, LL13 9NY
Tel: 01978-661333 **Fax:** 01978- 664234
E-mail: sales@barloworld-handling.co.uk
Website: http://www.barlow.co.uk
Managers: D. Clark (District Mgr)
Ultimate Holding Company: BARLOWORLD LIMITED (SOUTH AFRICA)
Immediate Holding Company: BARLOWORLD HANDLING LIMITED
Registration no: 00564646 **Date established:** 1956
No.of Employees: 21 - 50 **Product Groups:** 35, 39, 45

Date of Accounts	Sep 11	Sep 10	Sep 09
Sales Turnover	106m	96m	96m
Pre Tax Profit/Loss	-3m	-2m	-5m
Working Capital	-20m	10m	-18m
Fixed Assets	37m	55m	46m
Current Assets	33m	55m	23m
Current Liabilities	6m	6m	18m

Bearing Traders Ltd
Unit 101 Coed Aben Road, Wrexham Industrial Estate, Wrexham, LL13 9UH
Tel: 01978-664123 **Fax:** 01978-664122
E-mail: wxsales@bearingtraders.com
Website: http://www.bearingtraders.com
Managers: G. Davies (Mgr)
Immediate Holding Company: BEARING TRADERS LIMITED
Registration no: 01994643 **Date established:** 1986
No.of Employees: 1 - 10 **Product Groups:** 35, 36

Date of Accounts	Apr 11	Apr 10	Apr 09
Sales Turnover	N/A	N/A	4m
Pre Tax Profit/Loss	N/A	N/A	60
Working Capital	-10	-52	-61
Fixed Assets	91	111	115
Current Assets	1m	911	965
Current Liabilities	N/A	N/A	525

Belzona Technosol Ltd
Unit 1 Coppi Industrial Estate Hall Lane, Rhosllanerchrugog, Wrexham, LL14 1TG
Tel: 01978-832932 **Fax:** 01978-844141
E-mail: technosol@technosol.co.uk
Website: http://www.belzona.com
Managers: R. Edwards (Contracts Mgr)
Ultimate Holding Company: ORBEX LTD (BERMUDA)
Immediate Holding Company: BELZONA TECHNOSOL LIMITED
Registration no: 04378958 **Date established:** 2002
No.of Employees: 1 - 10 **Product Groups:** 46, 48

Date of Accounts	Dec 11	Dec 10	Dec 09
Sales Turnover	2m	2m	3m
Pre Tax Profit/Loss	165	-100	102
Working Capital	-64	-191	-113
Fixed Assets	179	194	187
Current Assets	873	433	662
Current Liabilities	79	40	53

Bonaprene Products Ltd
Clywedog Road South Wrexham Industrial Estate, Wrexham, LL13 9XS
Tel: 01978-661478 **Fax:** 01978-661190
E-mail: sales@bonaprene.co.uk
Website: http://www.bonaprene.co.uk
Bank(s): Bank of Scotland
Directors: R. Mills (MD), R. Mills (Fin)
Managers: R. Kinch (Projects), C. Roberts (Personnel), R. Oldfield (Sales Off Mgr)

see next page

Bonaprene Products Ltd - Cont'd

Immediate Holding Company: BONAPRENE PRODUCTS LIMITED
Registration no: 01461678 **VAT No.:** GB 482 5093 36
Date established: 1979 **Turnover:** £1m - £2m **No.of Employees:** 21 - 50
Product Groups: 29, 31

Date of Accounts	Nov 11	Nov 10	Nov 09
Working Capital	293	364	518
Fixed Assets	470	424	482
Current Assets	1m	1m	998

Brake Engineering

Redwither Road Wrexham Industrial Estate, Wrexham, LL13 9RD
Tel: 01978-667800 **Fax:** 01978-667801
E-mail: sales@brake-eng.com
Website: http://www.brake-eng.com
Bank(s): Barclays
Directors: J. Ogara (Sales), S. Willis (Dir), S. Konieczny (Fin), R. Morgan (Purch)
Managers: S. Nesbitt, D. Willis (I.T. Exec), C. McLaren (Tech Serv Mgr)
Immediate Holding Company: PEARSON'S BUILDING AND JOINERY SERVICES LIMITED
Registration no: 05148805 **VAT No.:** GB 289 9534 83
Date established: 2004 **Turnover:** £10m - £20m
No.of Employees: 101 - 250 **Product Groups:** 39, 68

Date of Accounts	Mar 12	Mar 11	Mar 10
Working Capital	-10	-14	-16
Fixed Assets	12	15	14
Current Assets	68	48	67

The British Association For Shooting & Conservatio

Marford Mill Rossett, Wrexham, LL12 0HL
Tel: 01244-573000 **Fax:** 01244-573001
E-mail: sales@basc.org.uk
Website: http://www.basc.org.uk
Bank(s): Natwest
Directors: A. Swift (Prop), P. Bursey (Fin)
Managers: D. Ilsley, J. Harris (Personnel), M. Walker (Tech Serv Mgr)
Ultimate Holding Company: PROMATIC UK LIMITED
Immediate Holding Company: DMQ LIMITED
Registration no: 03449049 **Date established:** 2003
Turnover: Up to £250,000 **No.of Employees:** 51 - 100
Product Groups: 87

Date of Accounts	Dec 10	Dec 09	Dec 08
Sales Turnover	60	64	60
Pre Tax Profit/Loss	-8	-4	5
Working Capital	65	72	74
Fixed Assets	1	3	4
Current Assets	113	88	104
Current Liabilities	1	4	6

Builder Center Ltd

Cambrian Works Station Approach, Wrexham, LL11 2NY
Tel: 01978-354444 **Fax:** 01978-351688
E-mail: s.groom@wolseley.co.uk
Website: http://www.buildcenter.co.uk
Managers: S. Groom (Mgr)
Ultimate Holding Company: WOLSELEY PLC (JERSEY)
Immediate Holding Company: BUILD CENTER LIMITED
Registration no: 00462397 **Date established:** 1948
Turnover: £20m - £50m **No.of Employees:** 11 - 20 **Product Groups:** 66

Date of Accounts	Jul 09
Working Capital	78
Current Assets	78

C L B Valeting

Royal Oak House Stryt Issa Penycae, Wrexham, LL14 2PN
Tel: 01978-846958
E-mail: clbvaleting@tiscali.co.uk
Website: http://www.clbvaleting.com
Immediate Holding Company: CLB VALETING & DETAILING LTD
Registration no: 06598050 **Date established:** 2008
No.of Employees: 1 - 10 **Product Groups:** 32, 39, 68

C M W Controls Ltd

Unit D7 Dutton Road, Redwither Business Park, Wrexham, LL13 9UL
Tel: 01978-661516 **Fax:** 01978-661626
E-mail: geoff.roberts@cmwcontrols.com
Bank(s): HSBC Bank plc
Directors: G. Roberts (Dir)
Immediate Holding Company: C.M.W. CONTROLS LIMITED
Registration no: 03436431 **VAT No.:** GB 310 4278 80
Date established: 1997 **Turnover:** £250,000 - £500,000
No.of Employees: 11 - 20 **Product Groups:** 35, 37

Date of Accounts	Dec 11	Dec 10	Dec 09
Working Capital	511	269	-65
Fixed Assets	303	321	376
Current Assets	2m	1m	769

C P L Petroleum Ltd

Wrexham Depot Bryn Lane, Wrexham Industrial Estate, Wrexham, LL13 9UT
Tel: 01978-661896 **Fax:** 01978-661356
E-mail: david.todd@cplpetroleum.co.uk
Website: http://www.cpldistribution.co.uk
Managers: J. Carnal (Ops Mgr)
Ultimate Holding Company: CPL INDUSTRIES HOLDINGS LIMITED
Immediate Holding Company: CPL PETROLEUM LIMITED
Registration no: 03003860 **VAT No.:** GB 721 5764 39
Date established: 1994 **Turnover:** £500m - £1,000m
No.of Employees: 21 - 50 **Product Groups:** 66

Date of Accounts	Mar 12	Mar 11	Mar 10
Pre Tax Profit/Loss	N/A	878	904
Working Capital	31	30m	30m
Fixed Assets	26	26m	26m
Current Assets	57	56m	56m
Current Liabilities	26	246	253

Charles Owen & Co (Bow) Ltd

Royal Works Croesfoel Industrial Estate, Rhostyllen, Wrexham, LL14 4BJ
Tel: 01978-317777 **Fax:** 01978-317778
E-mail: info@charlesowen.co.uk
Website: http://www.charlesowen.co.uk
Bank(s): HSBC
Directors: R. Burek (Dir)
Managers: R. Storer (Sales Prom Mgr), T. Ellis (Sales Admin)
Immediate Holding Company: Charles Owen & Company (Bow) Ltd
Registration no: 01168237 **VAT No.:** GB 244 8916 35
Date established: 1974 **Turnover:** £2m - £5m **No.of Employees:** 11 - 20
Product Groups: 24, 40

Date of Accounts	Dec 07	Dec 06	Dec 05
Sales Turnover	4934	4589	4189
Pre Tax Profit/Loss	-20	-26	54
Working Capital	1248	646	692
Fixed Assets	303	330	369
Current Assets	3495	2760	2328
Current Liabilities	2247	2114	1636
Total Share Capital	1	1	1
ROCE% (Return on Capital Employed)	-1.3	-2.7	5.1
ROT% (Return on Turnover)	-0.4	-0.6	1.3

Clwyd Compounders Ltd

Gardden Industrial Estate Ruabon, Wrexham, LL14 6RG
Tel: 01978-810551 **Fax:** 01978-810740
E-mail: enquiries@clwydcompounders.com
Website: http://www.clwydcompounders.com
Bank(s): Midland
Directors: K. Watton (Sales), S. Haywood (Dir), K. Wotton (Sales), J. Haywood (Dir)
Managers: C. Simmonds (Sales Admin), D. Lloyd
Immediate Holding Company: CLWYD COMPOUNDERS LIMITED
Registration no: 01378413 **VAT No.:** GB 310 4336 13
Date established: 1978 **Turnover:** £10m - £20m
No.of Employees: 51 - 100 **Product Groups:** 29

Date of Accounts	Nov 11	Nov 10	Nov 09
Sales Turnover	12m	10m	7m
Pre Tax Profit/Loss	1m	724	26
Working Capital	7m	6m	6m
Fixed Assets	1m	890	892
Current Assets	9m	8m	7m
Current Liabilities	1m	800	418

Cytec Engineered Materials Ltd

Abenbury Way Wrexham Industrial Estate, Wrexham, LL13 9UZ
Tel: 01978-665200 **Fax:** 01978-665222
E-mail: info@cytec.com
Website: http://www.cytec.com
Bank(s): HSBC Bank plc
Directors: R. Smith (Dir)
Ultimate Holding Company: CYTEC INDUSTRIES INC (USA)
Immediate Holding Company: CYTEC ENGINEERED MATERIALS LIMITED
Registration no: 02851421 **VAT No.:** GB 625 1689 31
Date established: 1993 **Turnover:** £20m - £50m
No.of Employees: 101 - 250 **Product Groups:** 23, 32, 33, 39, 68

Date of Accounts	Dec 11	Dec 10	Dec 09
Sales Turnover	49m	45m	43m
Pre Tax Profit/Loss	4m	4m	2m
Working Capital	9m	7m	10m
Fixed Assets	8m	7m	5m
Current Assets	17m	18m	16m
Current Liabilities	3m	4m	4m

D S L Mobility Ltd

141 Holt Road, Wrexham, LL13 9DY
Tel: 01978-351926
E-mail: russ.dsl@btconnect.com
Website: http://www.dslmobility.co.uk
Directors: R. Allmand (MD)
Immediate Holding Company: D S L MOBILITY LTD
Registration no: 03734066 **Date established:** 1999
No.of Employees: 11 - 20 **Product Groups:** 35, 39, 45

Date of Accounts	May 12	May 11	May 10
Working Capital	747	726	800
Fixed Assets	196	146	17
Current Assets	852	855	909

Dee Valley Water plc

Pentre Bychan, Wrexham, LL14 4DS
Tel: 01978-846946 **Fax:** 01978-846888
E-mail: contact@deevalleygroup.com
Website: http://www.deevalleywater.co.uk
Bank(s): National Westminster
Directors: D. Guest (Fin), N. Holiday (MD)
Managers: S. Grant (Chief Buyer), H. Jones (Personnel)
Ultimate Holding Company: DEE VALLEY GROUP PLC
Immediate Holding Company: DEE VALLEY SERVICES LIMITED
Registration no: 03022402 **VAT No.:** GB 625 3590 40
Date established: 1995 **Turnover:** £10m - £20m
No.of Employees: 101 - 250 **Product Groups:** 18

Date of Accounts	Mar 12	Mar 11	Mar 10
Working Capital	-138	-138	-138

Dockweiler UK Ltd

2 Dutton Road Redwither Business Park, Wrexham, LL13 9UL
Tel: 01978-660330 **Fax:** 01978-660157
E-mail: sales@dockweiler-uk.com
Website: http://www.dockweiler.co.uk
Directors: J. Klitzke (Co Sec), S. Wilkinson (MD)
Ultimate Holding Company: DOCKWEILIER AG (GERMANY)
Immediate Holding Company: DOCKWEILER U.K. LIMITED
Registration no: 02517146 **Date established:** 1990 **Turnover:** £2m - £5m
No.of Employees: 1 - 10 **Product Groups:** 34, 36, 66

Date of Accounts	Dec 11	Dec 10	Dec 09
Sales Turnover	5m	2m	2m
Pre Tax Profit/Loss	329	74	53
Working Capital	614	426	382
Fixed Assets	145	162	135
Current Assets	1m	908	1m
Current Liabilities	353	193	94

Dragon Field Sports Ltd

8 Egerton Street, Wrexham, LL11 1LW
Tel: 01978-290990 **Fax:** 01978-313799
E-mail: dragonfieldsports@googlemail.com
Website: http://www.dragonfieldsports.co.uk
Directors: I. Okell (Fin), M. Okell (Dir)
Immediate Holding Company: DRAGON FIELD SPORTS LIMITED
Registration no: 04783182 **Date established:** 2003
No.of Employees: 1 - 10 **Product Groups:** 36, 39, 40

Date of Accounts	Jan 11	Jan 10	Jan 09
Working Capital	15	14	13
Fixed Assets	1	2	2
Current Assets	29	35	34

Duracell Wrexham

Unit 11 Ash Road North Wrexham Industrial Estate, Wrexham, LL13 9JT
Tel: 0800-716434 **Fax:** 01978-221001
E-mail: martin-marshall@gillette.co.uk
Website: http://www.duracell.co.uk
Bank(s): National Westminster Bank Plc
Managers: M. Marshall (Mgr)
Ultimate Holding Company: Duracell Batteries Ltd
Registration no: 02242911 **No.of Employees:** 51 - 100
Product Groups: 37

E S I Technology Ltd

Sensor House Wrexham Technology Park, Wrexham, LL13 7YP
Tel: 01978-262255 **Fax:** 01978-262233
E-mail: j.kuehner@esi-tec.com
Website: http://www.esi-tec.com
Bank(s): Barclays
Managers: S. Comer, J. Kuehner (Chief Mgr), J. Gass (Chief Mgr)
Immediate Holding Company: ESI TECHNOLOGY LIMITED
Registration no: 02523392 **Date established:** 1990
Turnover: £500,000 - £1m **No.of Employees:** 21 - 50 **Product Groups:** 37

Date of Accounts	Dec 11	Dec 10	Mar 10
Working Capital	818	796	711
Fixed Assets	660	598	620
Current Assets	1m	1m	1m

Eriks UK (Wrexham Service Centre)

Unit 60 Clywedog Road North, Wrexham Industrial Estate, Wrexham, LL13 9XN
Tel: 01978-661222 **Fax:** 01978-661481
E-mail: wrexham@eriks.co.uk
Website: http://www.eriks.co.uk
Managers: N. Hughes (Mgr)
Turnover: £250m - £500m **No.of Employees:** 1 - 10 **Product Groups:** 66

Evans Maintenance Services Ltd

Derby House 29 Castle Street, Caergwrle, Wrexham, LL12 9AD
Tel: 01978-760000 **Fax:** 01978-761082
E-mail: info@evans-maint.co.uk
Website: http://www.evans-maint.co.uk
Directors: T. Evans (Dir)
Managers: G. Winn (Fin Mgr)
Ultimate Holding Company: SURE MAINTENANCE GROUP LIMITED
Immediate Holding Company: EVANS MECHANICAL SERVICES LIMITED
Registration no: 02523807 **VAT No.:** GB 539 8375 93
Date established: 1990 **Turnover:** £5m - £10m **No.of Employees:** 1 - 10
Product Groups: 52

Date of Accounts	Dec 10	Dec 09	Dec 08
Sales Turnover	7m	5m	N/A
Pre Tax Profit/Loss	-1m	74	N/A
Working Capital	-321	721	692
Fixed Assets	76	106	64
Current Assets	2m	2m	2m
Current Liabilities	599	361	N/A

Exopack Advanced Coatings Ltd

Ash Road North Wrexham Industrial Estate, Wrexham, LL13 9UF
Tel: 01978-660241 **Fax:** 01978-661452
E-mail: peter.morris@exopack.com
Website: http://www.exopackadvancedcoatings.com
Bank(s): Barclays
Directors: P. Morris (Dir)
Managers: G. Foster (Purch Mgr), N. Taylor (Tech Serv Mgr), P. Capstick (Personnel)
Ultimate Holding Company: REXAM PLC
Immediate Holding Company: REXAM CFP LIMITED
Registration no: 00925414 **VAT No.:** GB 793 9294 66
Date established: 1968 **Turnover:** £20m - £50m
No.of Employees: 101 - 250 **Product Groups:** 23, 30, 32, 37, 48

F Bender

Gresford Industrial Park Chester Road, Gresford, Wrexham, LL12 8LX
Tel: 01978-855661 **Fax:** 01978-855101
E-mail: info@benders.co.uk
Website: http://www.benders.co.uk
Directors: D. Lawlor (Dir), M. Woodward (Co Sec)
Ultimate Holding Company: BENDERS UK HOLDINGS LIMITED
Immediate Holding Company: F BENDER LIMITED
Registration no: 01816910 **Date established:** 1984
Turnover: £20m - £50m **No.of Employees:** 251 - 500
Product Groups: 27, 30

Date of Accounts	Dec 11	Dec 10	Dec 09
Sales Turnover	24m	23m	22m
Pre Tax Profit/Loss	-149	284	-2m
Working Capital	-2m	-2m	-3m
Fixed Assets	4m	5m	4m
Current Assets	6m	6m	8m
Current Liabilities	823	822	2m

F W B Cymru Co. Ltd

Five Crosses Industrial Estate Ruthin Road, Minera, Wrexham, LL11 3RD
Tel: 01978-720720 **Fax:** 01978-720721
E-mail: sales@fwb.co.uk
Website: http://www.fwb.co.uk
Bank(s): National Westminster
Managers: N. Peters (Sales Prom Mgr)
Ultimate Holding Company: FWB HOLDINGS LIMITED
Immediate Holding Company: F.W.B. CYMRU LIMITED
Registration no: 00986002 **VAT No.:** GB 278 8080 17
Date established: 1970 **Turnover:** £1m - £2m **No.of Employees:** 21 - 50
Product Groups: 66

Date of Accounts	Dec 11	Dec 10	Dec 09
Working Capital	1	1	1
Current Assets	1	1	1

Fibrax Ltd

Queensway, Wrexham, LL13 8YR
Tel: 01978-356744 **Fax:** 01978-365206
E-mail: info@fibrax.co.uk
Website: http://www.fibrax.co.uk
Bank(s): Barclays
Directors: P. Crawford (Fin), D. Reece (Sales)
Managers: L. Jones (Tech Serv Mgr), S. Baines (Mktg Serv Mgr)
Immediate Holding Company: FIBRAX LIMITED
Registration no: 00117971 **Date established:** 2011
Turnover: £10m - £20m **No.of Employees:** 101 - 250 **Product Groups:** 29

Date of Accounts	Dec 11	Dec 10	Dec 09
Sales Turnover	10m	9m	7m
Pre Tax Profit/Loss	200	209	194
Working Capital	306	412	322
Fixed Assets	2m	2m	3m
Current Assets	4m	3m	3m
Current Liabilities	413	289	534

G S F Promount
Unit 9 Gledrid Industrial Park Gledrid, Chirk, Wrexham, LL14 5DG
Tel: 01691-770303 **Fax:** 01691-776900
E-mail: info@gsfslides.com
Website: http://www.gsf-promounts.com
Managers: C. Roberts (Sales Prom Mgr)
Ultimate Holding Company: CALFIRE GROUP LIMITED
Immediate Holding Company: G.S.F. LTD.
Registration no: 02283017 **VAT No.:** GB 467 9893 65
Date established: 1988 **Turnover:** £2m - £5m **No.of Employees:** 1 - 10
Product Groups: 36

Date of Accounts	Mar 10	Mar 09	Mar 08
Working Capital	200	30	151
Fixed Assets	73	102	105
Current Assets	543	505	557

Genfab Engineering
Unit A6-A7 Bersham Enterprise Centre Plas Grono Road, Rhostyllen, Wrexham, LL14 4EG
Tel: 01978-291437
Website: http://www.genfabengineering.co.uk
Directors: P. Witney (Ptnr)
Date established: 1992 **No.of Employees:** 1 - 10 **Product Groups:** 35

Graphtec GB Ltd
Coed Aben Road Wrexham Industrial Estate, Wrexham, LL13 9UH
Tel: 01978-666700 **Fax:** 01978-666710
E-mail: sales@graphtecgb.com
Website: http://www.graphtecgb.co.uk
Directors: P. Kneale (Dir)
Immediate Holding Company: GRAPHTEC (G.B.) LIMITED
Registration no: 03540001 **Date established:** 1998 **Turnover:** £2m - £5m
No.of Employees: 1 - 10 **Product Groups:** 38

Date of Accounts	Mar 12	Mar 11	Mar 10
Working Capital	320	236	111
Fixed Assets	10	14	38
Current Assets	634	406	395

Hohner Automation Ltd
Unit 14-16 0 Whitegate Road, Wrexham, LL13 8UG
Tel: 01978-363888 **Fax:** 01978-364586
E-mail: info@hohner.com
Website: http://www.hohner.com
Bank(s): National Westminster Bank Plc
Directors: P. Blochle (MD), W. Bloechle (Fin)
Immediate Holding Company: HOHNER AUTOMATION LIMITED
Registration no: 01513353 **VAT No.:** GB 352 0675 68
Date established: 1980 **Turnover:** £2m - £5m **No.of Employees:** 11 - 20
Product Groups: 37, 38

Date of Accounts	Jul 11	Jul 10	Jul 09
Working Capital	794	645	625
Fixed Assets	198	176	185
Current Assets	1m	839	798
Current Liabilities	N/A	103	N/A

Hoya Lens UK Ltd (Holding Company in Japan)
Wrexham Industrial Estate, Wrexham, LL13 9UA
Tel: 01978-663400 **Fax:** 01978-663135
E-mail: enquiries@hoya.co.uk
Website: http://www.hoya.co.uk
Bank(s): Barclays
Directors: L. Cowell (Fin), D. Hewitt (Fin), M. Batho (MD)
Managers: G. Evans (Tech Serv Mgr), K. Roberts (Purch Mgr), F. Hide (Personnel)
Ultimate Holding Company: HOYA CORPORATION (JAPAN)
Immediate Holding Company: HOYA LENS U.K. LIMITED
Registration no: 01484424 **VAT No.:** GB 406 2427 80
Date established: 1980 **Turnover:** £50m - £75m
No.of Employees: 251 - 500 **Product Groups:** 38

Date of Accounts	Mar 12	Mar 11	Mar 10
Sales Turnover	32m	52m	47m
Pre Tax Profit/Loss	2m	4m	2m
Working Capital	6m	5m	-368
Fixed Assets	5m	4m	5m
Current Assets	9m	18m	19m
Current Liabilities	495	3m	2m

Hydro Aluminium Deeside Ltd
Bridge Road South Wrexham Industrial Estate, Wrexham, LL13 9PS
Tel: 01978-660231 **Fax:** 01978-661125
E-mail: d.morear@hydro.com
Website: http://www.hydro.com
Bank(s): National Westminster
Directors: B. Andersen (Dir), D. Morear (Fin)
Managers: C. Clewarth (Personnel), H. Wilkins (Purch Mgr)
Ultimate Holding Company: NORSK HYDRO ASA (NORWAY)
Immediate Holding Company: HYDRO ALUMINIUM DEESIDE LIMITED
Registration no: 01786117 **VAT No.:** GB 406 2820 78
Date established: 1984 **Turnover:** £50m - £75m
No.of Employees: 21 - 50 **Product Groups:** 34

Date of Accounts	Dec 11	Dec 10	Dec 09
Sales Turnover	61m	71m	41m
Pre Tax Profit/Loss	722	1m	1m
Working Capital	13m	10m	9m
Fixed Assets	7m	6m	7m
Current Assets	19m	18m	18m
Current Liabilities	784	958	2m

I M C
Abbey Road Wrexham Industrial Estate, Wrexham, LL13 9RF
Tel: 01978-661155 **Fax:** 01978-729990
E-mail: mail@imco.co.uk
Website: http://www.imco.co.uk
Bank(s): Royal Bank of Scotland, Lincoln
Managers: J. Atherton
Immediate Holding Company: JAMI Q'S LIMITED
Registration no: 00147034 **VAT No.:** GB 336 9587 10
Date established: 2001 **Turnover:** £5m - £10m
No.of Employees: 51 - 100 **Product Groups:** 40, 41

Date of Accounts	May 12	May 11	May 10
Working Capital	-24	-36	-39
Fixed Assets	190	233	251
Current Assets	82	71	102

I P S
Unit 3 Ash Road North Wrexham Industrial Estate, Wrexham, LL13 9JT
Tel: 01978-661671 **Fax:** 01978-661681
E-mail: sales@ips-uk.co.uk
Website: http://www.ips-uk.co.uk
Bank(s): Abbey National
Directors: P. York (Chief Op Offcr)
Immediate Holding Company: INTERACTIVE PACKAGING SOLUTIONS LIMITED
Registration no: 04310062 **VAT No.:** GB 783 3814 06
Date established: 2001 **Turnover:** £500,000 - £1m
No.of Employees: 21 - 50 **Product Groups:** 27, 30

Date of Accounts	Oct 10	Oct 09	Oct 08
Working Capital	-439	-522	-501
Fixed Assets	166	150	170
Current Assets	604	609	636

Independent Twine Manufacturing Co. Ltd
Westbank Road Llay Industrial Estate, Llay, Wrexham, LL12 0PZ
Tel: 01978-854812 **Fax:** 01978-854229
E-mail: robert.macguire@indtwineco.com
Website: http://www.indtwineco.com
Directors: S. Waite (Sales), R. Macguire (MD), R. Macguire (MD)
Immediate Holding Company: INDEPENDENT TWINE MANUFACTURING COMPANY LIMITED
Registration no: 01247981 **Date established:** 1976 **Turnover:** £2m - £5m
No.of Employees: 21 - 50 **Product Groups:** 23

Date of Accounts	Sep 11	Sep 10	Sep 09
Working Capital	356	1m	592
Fixed Assets	2m	2m	2m
Current Assets	1m	2m	2m

Industrial Capacitors Wrexham Ltd
Miners Road Llay Industrial Estate, Llay, Wrexham, LL12 0PJ
Tel: 01978-853805 **Fax:** 01978-853785
E-mail: sales@icwltd.co.uk
Website: http://www.icwltd.co.uk
Bank(s): Barclays, Newcastle upon Tyne
Managers: D. Thomson (Chief Mgr)
Ultimate Holding Company: TECH/OPS SEVCON INC (USA)
Immediate Holding Company: INDUSTRIAL CAPACITORS (WREXHAM) LIMITED
Registration no: 01191459 **VAT No.:** GB 162 7722 59
Date established: 1974 **Turnover:** £1m - £2m **No.of Employees:** 21 - 50
Product Groups: 37

Date of Accounts	Sep 11	Sep 10	Sep 09
Working Capital	369	163	165
Fixed Assets	484	533	384
Current Assets	621	389	400

Inkxperts
13 Yorke Street, Wrexham, LL13 8LW
Tel: 01978-261368 **Fax:** 01978-262735
E-mail: sales@inkxperts.co.uk
Website: http://www.inkxperts.co.uk
Directors: C. Ottley Thistlethwaite (MD)
Immediate Holding Company: 6T'S LIMITED
Registration no: 06566295 **Date established:** 2003
Turnover: Up to £250,000 **No.of Employees:** 1 - 10 **Product Groups:** 30, 44

Date of Accounts	Mar 11	Mar 10	Mar 09
Working Capital	-87	-75	-87
Fixed Assets	12	14	17
Current Assets	8	15	12

Isringhausen GB Ltd
Second Avenue Redwither Industrial Complex, Redwither Business Park, Wrexham, LL13 9XQ
Tel: 01978-666300 **Fax:** 01978-660192
E-mail: sales@isrigb.co.uk
Website: http://www.isri.de
Managers: A. Williams (Tech Serv Mgr), G. Thomas (Ops Mgr), K. Taylor, J. Hemmings
Ultimate Holding Company: ISRINGHAUSEN GMBH & CO KG (GERMANY)
Immediate Holding Company: ISRINGHAUSEN (G.B) LIMITED
Registration no: 01358229 **Date established:** 1978 **Turnover:** £5m - £10m
No.of Employees: 21 - 50 **Product Groups:** 39, 40

Date of Accounts	Dec 11	Dec 10	Dec 09
Sales Turnover	7m	6m	5m
Pre Tax Profit/Loss	509	262	-368
Working Capital	4m	4m	4m
Fixed Assets	2m	2m	2m
Current Assets	5m	5m	4m
Current Liabilities	340	227	166

Graham Jones Crane Hire
Rhosddu Industrial Estate Old Rhosrobin, Rhosrobin, Wrexham, LL11 4YL
Tel: 01978-366458 **Fax:** 01978-310573
E-mail: graham@grahamjonescranes.co.uk
Website: http://www.grahamjonescranes.co.uk
Directors: G. Jones (Prop)
Immediate Holding Company: MATTHEWS CONTROL SOLUTIONS LIMITED
Registration no: 06752771 **Date established:** 1997
No.of Employees: 21 - 50 **Product Groups:** 45, 67, 83

Kronoplus Ltd
Maesgwyn Farm Holyhead Road Chirk, Wrexham, LL14 5NT
Tel: 01691-773361 **Fax:** 01691-773292
E-mail: sales@kronospan.co.uk
Website: http://www.kronospan.co.uk
Directors: C. Ryan (Co Sec), M. Kaindl (MD)
Ultimate Holding Company: KRONOSPAN AG (LICHTENSTEIN)
Immediate Holding Company: Kronospan Holdings Ltd
Registration no: 03425921 **Date established:** 1970
Turnover: £50m - £75m **No.of Employees:** 1 - 10 **Product Groups:** 25, 26, 27, 30

Date of Accounts	Sep 09	Sep 08	Sep 07
Sales Turnover	64m	64m	64m
Pre Tax Profit/Loss	168	186	841
Working Capital	558	558	-194
Fixed Assets	4m	4m	4m
Current Assets	558	558	121
Current Liabilities	N/A	N/A	315

Lloyd Morris Electrical Ltd
Unit 1 Pandy Industrial Estate Plas Acton Road, Wrexham, LL11 2UD
Tel: 01978-291505 **Fax:** 01978-365433
E-mail: sales@lloydmorris.co.uk
Website: http://www.lloydmorris.co.uk
Bank(s): Barclays
Directors: W. Morris (Fin), R. Morris (MD), F. Ciaurro (Dir), F. Caurro (Dir), E. Morris (MD), B. Lewis (Fin)
Managers: S. Merrill (Transport), J. Perrett (Sales Prom Mgr), T. Hopkinson (I.T. Exec), B. Lewis (Personnel), B. Lewis (Comptroller), A. Robertson (I.T. Exec)
Ultimate Holding Company: 02527559
Immediate Holding Company: LLOYD MORRIS ELECTRICAL LIMITED
Registration no: 01185881 **VAT No.:** GB 162 7161 73
Date established: 1974 **Turnover:** £10m - £20m
No.of Employees: 101 - 250 **Product Groups:** 52

Date of Accounts	Oct 07	Oct 06	Oct 05
Pre Tax Profit/Loss	-146	-983	-84
Working Capital	806	792	1763
Fixed Assets	81	107	118
Current Assets	2758	3025	3084
Current Liabilities	1952	2233	1321
Total Share Capital	10	10	10
ROCE% (Return on Capital Employed)	-16.5	-109.4	-4.5

M F D Capacitors 1991 Ltd
Lion Lane Penley, Wrexham, LL13 0LY
Tel: 01978-710551 **Fax:** 01978-710501
E-mail: sales@mfdcapacitors.co.uk
Website: http://www.mfdcapacitors.co.uk
Bank(s): Barclays
Directors: E. Morgan (MD)
Immediate Holding Company: M.F.D. CAPACITORS (1991) LIMITED
Registration no: 02606325 **VAT No.:** GB 595 5394 86
Date established: 1991 **Turnover:** £250,000 - £500,000
No.of Employees: 11 - 20 **Product Groups:** 33, 37, 38, 67

Date of Accounts	Apr 11	Apr 10	Apr 09
Sales Turnover	N/A	360	414
Pre Tax Profit/Loss	N/A	23	64
Working Capital	439	491	522
Fixed Assets	124	131	137
Current Assets	545	587	621
Current Liabilities	N/A	33	72

Magellan Metal Treatments
Miners Road Llay Industrial Estate, Llay, Wrexham, LL12 0PJ
Tel: 01978-852101 **Fax:** 01978-855732
E-mail: john.puttock@magellan.aero
Website: http://www.magellanuk.aero
Directors: E. Shelley (Tech Serv), M. Walker (Pers)
Managers: M. Jones (Comptroller), M. Shorrock (Chief Buyer), J. Puttock (Mgr)
Immediate Holding Company: AT LIMITED
Registration no: 05023853 **Date established:** 2004
No.of Employees: 21 - 50 **Product Groups:** 46, 48

Date of Accounts	Jan 11	Jan 10	Jan 09
Working Capital	-66	-58	-46
Fixed Assets	78	88	84
Current Assets	5	4	3

Manutech Europe Ltd
Unit 20a Vauxhall Industrial Estate, Ruabon, Wrexham, LL14 6HA
Tel: 01978-823990 **Fax:** 01978-810128
E-mail: sales@manutecheurope.com
Website: http://www.manutecheurope.com
Directors: F. Mosnenu (MD)
Immediate Holding Company: MANUTECH EUROPE LIMITED
Registration no: 02008985 **VAT No.:** GB 439 7319 19
Date established: 1986 **Turnover:** £500,000 - £1m
No.of Employees: 1 - 10 **Product Groups:** 33, 34, 37, 38, 67

Date of Accounts	Dec 11	Dec 10	Dec 09
Working Capital	65	224	366
Fixed Assets	261	285	301
Current Assets	365	375	506

Maplin Electronics Ltd
Island Green Retail Park, Wrexham, LL13 7LW
Tel: 08432-277367
E-mail: customercare@maplin.co.uk
Website: http://www.maplin.co.uk
Ultimate Holding Company: MONTAGU PRIVATE EQUITY LLP
Immediate Holding Company: MAPLIN ELECTRONICS LIMITED
Registration no: 01264385 **Date established:** 1976
Turnover: £125m - £250m **No.of Employees:** 1 - 10 **Product Groups:** 37, 61

Date of Accounts	Dec 11	Dec 08	Dec 09
Sales Turnover	205m	204m	204m
Pre Tax Profit/Loss	25m	32m	35m
Working Capital	118m	49m	75m
Fixed Assets	27m	28m	28m
Current Assets	207m	108m	142m
Current Liabilities	78m	51m	59m

Meadowvale Foods
Unit 18-19 Wilkinson Business Park Clywedog Road South, Wrexham Industrial Estate, Wrexham, LL13 9AE
Tel: 01978-666100 **Fax:** 01978-666190
E-mail: sales@meadowvalefoods.co.uk
Website: http://www.meadowvalefoods.co.uk
Bank(s): HSBC
Directors: S. Wantling (MD)
Managers: N. O'Donald (Mgr)
Immediate Holding Company: MEADOWVALE HOLDINGS LTD
Registration no: 02420250 **Turnover:** £20m - £50m
No.of Employees: 21 - 50 **Product Groups:** 20

Meritor HVS Ltd
Rackery Lane Llay, Wrexham, LL12 0PB
Tel: 01978-852141 **Fax:** 01978-856173
E-mail: thomas.hughes@arvinmeritor.com
Website: http://www.arvinmeritor.com
Bank(s): Barclays
Directors: S. Luc (MD), A. Lambe (Fin)
Managers: G. Rowe (Chief Buyer), T. Hughes, T. Johnson (Chief Buyer), R. Garston (), D. Edwards (Sales Prom Mgr), R. Veasey (Sales Prom Mgr), P. Booth (Sales Prom Mgr), R. Rogers
Ultimate Holding Company: FP000091
Immediate Holding Company: MERITOR HEAVY VEHICLE SYSTEMS LIMITED
Registration no: 00379136 **Date established:** 1943
Turnover: £20m - £50m **No.of Employees:** 251 - 500
Product Groups: 25, 29, 37, 39, 40, 45, 46, 68

Metalmin Ltd
Salem Road Coedpoeth, Wrexham, LL11 3SG
Tel: 01978-753469 **Fax:** 01978-758112

see next page

***Metalmin Ltd** - Cont'd*
Directors: M. Johnson (MD), R. Johnson (MD)
Registration no: 01395194 **Turnover:** £5m - £10m
No.of Employees: 1 - 10 **Product Groups:** 31, 34, 66

Morgan Electro Ceramics
Vauxhall Industrial Estate Ruabon, Wrexham, LL14 6HY
Tel: 01978-810456 **Fax:** 01978-824303
E-mail: neil.pritchard@morganplc.com
Website: http://www.morganelectroceramics.com
Managers: P. Slater (Sales Prom Mgr), A. Shaw (Personnel), A. Shaw (Personnel), N. Pritchard (Purch Mgr), Edwards (Chief Mgr)
Ultimate Holding Company: THE MORGAN CRUCIBLE COMPANY P.L.C.
Immediate Holding Company: MORGAN MATROC LTD
Registration no: 00262938 **Turnover:** £20m - £50m
No.of Employees: 101 - 250 **Product Groups:** 33, 37

Multifactor Europe Ltd
Harrison House Rackery Lane, Llay, Wrexham, LL12 0PB
Tel: 01978-855995 **Fax:** 01978-855222
E-mail: enquiries@mfeuk.co.uk
Website: http://www.mfeuk.co.uk
Directors: S. Edwards (Fin)
Managers: M. Beeston (Purch Mgr)
Immediate Holding Company: MULTIFACTOR EUROPE LIMITED
Registration no: 02053333 **Date established:** 1986 **Turnover:** £2m - £5m
No.of Employees: 1 - 10 **Product Groups:** 67

Date of Accounts	Sep 11	Sep 10	Sep 09
Working Capital	349	278	144
Fixed Assets	22	29	35
Current Assets	795	748	490

Nightingale Care Beds
Unit 1 Ash Road South, Wrexham Industrial Estate, Wrexham, LL13 9UG
Tel: 01978-660810 **Fax:** 01978-661705
E-mail: info@nightingalebeds.co.uk
Website: http://www.nightingalebeds.co.uk
Managers: K. Eames (Develop Mgr)
Ultimate Holding Company: NIGHTINGALE CARE BEDS HOLDINGS LIMITED
Immediate Holding Company: NIGHTINGALE CARE BEDS LIMITED
Registration no: 02814128 **Date established:** 1993
Turnover: £500,000 - £1m **No.of Employees:** 11 - 20
Product Groups: 38, 67

Date of Accounts	Apr 11	Apr 10	Apr 09
Sales Turnover	899	940	1m
Pre Tax Profit/Loss	21	41	194
Working Capital	227	165	228
Fixed Assets	38	28	45
Current Assets	395	355	502
Current Liabilities	101	97	96

Omega Technical Supplies Ltd
Unit D5 Dutton Road, Redwither Business Park, Wrexham, LL13 9UL
Tel: 01978-661881 **Fax:** 01978-664643
E-mail: m.griffiths@omegatec.co.uk
Website: http://www.omegatec.co.uk
Directors: M. Griffiths (Sales)
Managers: B. Williams (Mgr)
Immediate Holding Company: OMEGA TECHNICAL SUPPLIES LIMITED
Registration no: 06597283 **Date established:** 2008
No.of Employees: 1 - 10 **Product Groups:** 20, 40, 41

Date of Accounts	May 11	May 10	May 09
Working Capital	-151	4	6
Fixed Assets	7	10	12
Current Assets	165	347	312

Porvair Sciences Ltd (a Division of Porvair Filtration Group Ltd)
Unit 73 Clywedog Road South, Wrexham Industrial Estate, Wrexham, LL13 9XS
Tel: 01978-661144 **Fax:** 01978-664554
E-mail: enquiries@porvair-sciences.com
Website: http://www.porvair-sciences.com
Directors: B. Door (Fin), N. Bright (Chief Op Offcr)
Managers: A. Rowlands (Tech Serv Mgr), R. Rigby (Sales & Mktg Mg)
Ultimate Holding Company: PORVAIR PLC
Immediate Holding Company: PORVAIR FILTRATION GROUP LIMITED
Registration no: 00888596 **VAT No.:** GB 571 6691 16
Date established: 1966 **Turnover:** £20m - £50m **No.of Employees:** 1 - 10
Product Groups: 30, 34, 36, 40, 42

Date of Accounts	Nov 11	Nov 10	Nov 09
Sales Turnover	30m	28m	25m
Pre Tax Profit/Loss	3m	3m	4m
Working Capital	13m	13m	13m
Fixed Assets	16m	17m	18m
Current Assets	23m	22m	20m
Current Liabilities	3m	2m	1m

Price Bros
62 Pen Y Bryn, Wrexham, LL13 7HY
Tel: 01978-351273 **Fax:** 01978-356431
E-mail: info@pricebrothersupholstery.co.uk
Website: http://www.pricebrothersupholstery.co.uk
Directors: R. Price (Prop)
No.of Employees: 1 - 10 **Product Groups:** 29, 63

R C J Precision Ltd
Llay Hall Industrial Estate Mold Road, Cefn-Y-Bedd, Wrexham, LL12 9YG
Tel: 01978-761060 **Fax:** 01978-762337
E-mail: info@rcjprecision.plus.com
Bank(s): HSBC
Directors: A. Smith (MD)
Immediate Holding Company: R.C.J.PRECISION LIMITED
Registration no: 01007459 **VAT No.:** GB 158 9248 22
Date established: 1971 **Turnover:** £500,000 - £1m
No.of Employees: 11 - 20 **Product Groups:** 48

Date of Accounts	Dec 11	Dec 10	Dec 09
Working Capital	101	123	280
Fixed Assets	29	23	25
Current Assets	155	191	332

R S C M
Ash Road North Wrexham Industrial Estate, Wrexham, LL13 9UF
Tel: 01978-661352 **Fax:** 01978-664352
Website: http://www.rscm.co.uk
Directors: S. Ellis (Prop)
Immediate Holding Company: CMS WREXHAM LIMITED
Registration no: 05545902 **VAT No.:** GB 595 5637 86
Date established: 2005 **Turnover:** Up to £250,000
No.of Employees: 1 - 10 **Product Groups:** 48

Date of Accounts	Mar 12	Mar 11	Mar 10
Working Capital	288	260	193
Fixed Assets	199	135	110
Current Assets	365	357	278

Reminis Ltd
Gledrid Industrial Park Gledrid, Chirk, Wrexham, LL14 5DG
Tel: 01691-778899 **Fax:** 01691-773552
E-mail: sales@reminis.co.uk
Website: http://www.reminis.co.uk
Directors: E. Allen (MD), I. Adams (Fin)
Ultimate Holding Company: CALFIRE GROUP LIMITED
Immediate Holding Company: REMINIS LIMITED
Registration no: 04287259 **Date established:** 2001
No.of Employees: 1 - 10 **Product Groups:** 26, 35

Date of Accounts	Mar 11	Mar 10	Mar 09
Working Capital	-241	-219	-194
Current Assets	81	74	64

Sharp Manufacturing Company
Sharp House Davy Way Llay Industrial Estate, Llay, Wrexham, LL12 0PG
Tel: 01978-853939 **Fax:** 01978-857701
Website: http://www.sharp.co.uk
Managers: D. O'Donald (Tech Serv Mgr), N. Igarashi, S. Waring (Purch Mgr), D. Marsden
Immediate Holding Company: MARLIN INDUSTRIES LIMITED
Registration no: 01692323 **Date established:** 1998
No.of Employees: 501 - 1000 **Product Groups:** 36, 40

Date of Accounts	Dec 11	Dec 10	Dec 09
Sales Turnover	9m	8m	7m
Pre Tax Profit/Loss	320	256	392
Working Capital	66	265	382
Fixed Assets	3m	3m	3m
Current Assets	3m	3m	2m
Current Liabilities	1m	488	544

Skanda
Unit 67 Clywedog Road North, Wrexham Industrial Estate, Wrexham, LL13 9XN
Tel: 01978-664255 **Fax:** 01978-661427
E-mail: info@skanda-uk.com
Website: http://www.skanda-uk.com
Directors: A. Carroll (MD)
Immediate Holding Company: SKANDA (UK) LIMITED
Registration no: 03312823 **Date established:** 1997
No.of Employees: 1 - 10 **Product Groups:** 52

Date of Accounts	Mar 11	Mar 10	Mar 09
Working Capital	234	201	213
Fixed Assets	8	15	22
Current Assets	508	683	437

Smith's Solutions
27 Kiln Lane Hope, Wrexham, LL12 9PH
Tel: 01978-769090 **Fax:** 01978-769173
E-mail: info@smiths-solutions.co.uk
Website: http://www.smiths-solutions.co.uk
Directors: M. Smith (MD)
Date established: 2004 **Turnover:** £250,000 - £500,000
No.of Employees: 1 - 10 **Product Groups:** 76

Date of Accounts	Mar 11	Mar 10
Working Capital	-33	-26
Fixed Assets	22	29
Current Assets	22	35

Steni UK Ltd
1-4 Vauxhall Industrial Estate Ruabon, Wrexham, LL14 6HA
Tel: 01978-812111 **Fax:** 01978-810399
E-mail: info@steni.co.uk
Website: http://www.steni.co.uk
Directors: I. Anderson (MD)
Managers: M. Davies (Sales Prom Mgr), S. Osbourne (Prod Mgr), V. Barnard (Mktg Serv Mgr), L. Fishburne
Ultimate Holding Company: STENI HOLDING AS (NORWAY)
Immediate Holding Company: STENI UK LIMITED
Registration no: 06324528 **Date established:** 2007 **Turnover:** £2m - £5m
No.of Employees: 1 - 10 **Product Groups:** 33

Date of Accounts	Dec 11	Dec 10	Dec 09
Sales Turnover	N/A	4m	3m
Pre Tax Profit/Loss	N/A	-53	161
Working Capital	81	613	689
Fixed Assets	2m	2m	2m
Current Assets	833	1m	1m
Current Liabilities	N/A	190	184

Sutures Ltd
New Factory Vauxhall Industrial Estate, Ruabon, Wrexham, LL14 6HA
Tel: 01978-823664 **Fax:** 01978-810669
E-mail: don@sutures.co.uk
Website: http://www.sutures.co.uk
Managers: D. Crump
Immediate Holding Company: SUTURES LIMITED
Registration no: 01015315 **VAT No.:** GB 159 9309 22
Date established: 1971 **Turnover:** £2m - £5m **No.of Employees:** 1 - 10
Product Groups: 38

Date of Accounts	Jun 11	Jun 10	Jun 09
Working Capital	-283	-479	-600
Fixed Assets	479	482	486
Current Assets	1m	1m	2m

T S M Ltd
Sensor House Wrexham Technology Park, Wrexham, LL13 7YP
Tel: 01978-262255 **Fax:** 01978-291888
E-mail: tsm@esi-tec.com
Website: http://www.esi-tec.com
Directors: A. Ellison (MD)
Managers: S. Dixon (Sales Prom Mgr), P. Griffiths (Comm)
Immediate Holding Company: T.S.M. LIMITED
Registration no: 01686094 **VAT No.:** GB 516 9894 96
Date established: 1982 **Turnover:** £1m - £2m **No.of Employees:** 1 - 10
Product Groups: 38

Taylor Engineering Sales
Unit T5 Tower Close Redwither Business Park, Wrexham Industrial Estate, Wrexham, LL13 9WB
Tel: 01978-660303 **Fax:** 01978-660313
E-mail: taylorengsales@4email.net
Website: http://www.taylorengineeringsales.co.uk
Directors: D. Taylor (MD)
VAT No.: GB 482 4410 55 **Date established:** 1988
Turnover: £250,000 - £500,000 **No.of Employees:** 1 - 10
Product Groups: 66

Tenax UK Ltd
Unit 12 Ash Road North Wrexham Industrial Estate, Wrexham, LL13 9JT
Tel: 01978-664667 **Fax:** 01978-664634
E-mail: info@tenax.co.uk
Website: http://www.tenax.co.uk
Directors: M. Abbiati (MD)
Managers: J. Dickson, R. Bence, J. Roberts (Purch Mgr), R. Dickson (Fin Mgr)
Ultimate Holding Company: TENAX INTERNATIONAL BV (NETHERLANDS)
Immediate Holding Company: TENAX UK LIMITED
Registration no: 03446917 **Date established:** 1997 **Turnover:** £5m - £10m
No.of Employees: 21 - 50 **Product Groups:** 63

Date of Accounts	Dec 10	Dec 09	Dec 08
Sales Turnover	7m	8m	9m
Pre Tax Profit/Loss	-617	51	-311
Working Capital	-406	105	270
Fixed Assets	3m	3m	3m
Current Assets	5m	5m	5m
Current Liabilities	263	296	312

Tetra Pak Ltd
Bedwell Road Cross Lanes, Wrexham, LL13 0UT
Tel: 08704-426000 **Fax:** 08704-426001
E-mail: info@tetrapak.com
Website: http://www.cips.org
Directors: A. White (Tech Serv), P. Hollingsworth (Fin), S. Ellis (Comm), U. Brasen (MD), D. Miessen (Fin), J. Rose (Fin), P. Cunutson (MD), P. Knutsson (MD), R. Collin (Fin)
Managers: M. Clemans (I.T. Exec), M. Tydie (Mgr)
Ultimate Holding Company: TETRA LAVAL HOLDINGS BV (NETHERLANDS)
Immediate Holding Company: TETRA PAK LIMITED
Registration no: 00551434 **VAT No.:** GB 215 9159 59
Date established: 1955 **Turnover:** £75m - £125m
No.of Employees: 251 - 500 **Product Groups:** 27, 42

Date of Accounts	Dec 09	Dec 08	Dec 07
Sales Turnover	117m	89m	99m
Pre Tax Profit/Loss	18m	5m	5m
Working Capital	38m	36m	43m
Fixed Assets	2m	2m	2m
Current Assets	68m	60m	68m
Current Liabilities	17m	15m	14m

Toolpak
Rhosddu Industrial Estate Rhosrobin, Wrexham, LL11 4YL
Tel: 01978-291771 **Fax:** 01978-290068
E-mail: orders@toolpak.co.uk
Website: http://www.toolpak.co.uk
Bank(s): Lloyds TSB Bank plc
Directors: C. Howlett (Fin), C. Howlett (MD)
Immediate Holding Company: TOOLPAK PLC
Registration no: 00682792 **VAT No.:** GB 159 2856 28
Date established: 1961 **Turnover:** £2m - £5m **No.of Employees:** 21 - 50
Product Groups: 24, 30, 33, 34, 36, 37, 38, 46

Date of Accounts	Mar 12	Mar 11	Mar 10
Sales Turnover	4m	4m	4m
Pre Tax Profit/Loss	446	162	361
Working Capital	3m	2m	2m
Fixed Assets	1m	1m	1m
Current Assets	3m	3m	3m
Current Liabilities	338	221	293

Tritech Precision Products Ltd
Bridge Road North Wrexham Industrial Estate, Wrexham, LL13 9PS
Tel: 01978-661111 **Fax:** 01978-661392
E-mail: sales@tritechgroup.co.uk
Website: http://www.tritech-precision-products.co.uk
Bank(s): Barclays
Directors: M. Parry (Fin), I. Walker (MD), A. Dustan (Co Sec)
Managers: J. Clark (Purch Mgr), D. Hughes (Eng), A. Cheers (Sales & Mktg Mg), A. Trevor (Personnel)
Ultimate Holding Company: UNI-TRITECH LIMITED
Immediate Holding Company: TRITECH PRECISION PRODUCTS LIMITED
Registration no: 01677427 **VAT No.:** GB 370 5495 43
Date established: 1982 **Turnover:** £10m - £20m
No.of Employees: 101 - 250 **Product Groups:** 34

Date of Accounts	Mar 08	Mar 09	Apr 10
Sales Turnover	14m	15m	14m
Pre Tax Profit/Loss	366	-97	592
Working Capital	4m	4m	5m
Fixed Assets	3m	2m	2m
Current Assets	15m	16m	12m
Current Liabilities	938	2m	5m

Wockhardt
Wrexham Industrial Estate Ash Road North, Wrexham, LL13 9UF
Tel: 01978-661261 **Fax:** 01978-660130
E-mail: mail@wockhardt.co.uk
Website: http://www.wockhardt.co.uk
Bank(s): Lloyds TSB
Managers: B. Parry
Ultimate Holding Company: KHORAKIWALA HOLDINGS AND INVESTMENTS PRIVATE LTD (INDIA

Immediate Holding Company: WOCKHARDT UK LIMITED
Registration no: 05835570 **VAT No.:** GB 625 1298 46
Date established: 2006 **Turnover:** £50m - £75m
No.of Employees: 251 - 500 **Product Groups:** 31

Date of Accounts	Dec 08	Mar 12	Mar 11
Sales Turnover	55m	74m	73m
Pre Tax Profit/Loss	2m	1m	1m
Working Capital	3m	6m	5m
Fixed Assets	81	115	104
Current Assets	26m	52m	42m
Current Liabilities	2m	2m	3m

Wrexham Mineral Cables Ltd

Plot 4 Wynnstay Technology Park Ruabon, Wrexham, LL14 6EN

Tel: 01978-810789 **Fax:** 01978-821502

E-mail: sales@wrexhammineralcable.com

Website: http://www.wrexhammineralcable.com

Bank(s): HSBC

Managers: P. Thomas (Mgr)

Immediate Holding Company: GENERAL CONTRACTING (UK) LTD

Registration no: 00017178 **VAT No.:** GB 585 1661 19
Date established: 1989 **Turnover:** £2m - £5m **No.of Employees:** 21 - 50
Product Groups: 37

SCOTLAND

Aberdeenshire

Aberdeen

2 G Products
Unit 9 Spires Business Units Mugiemoss Road, Bucksburn, Aberdeen, AB21 9NY
Tel: 01224-682682 **Fax:** 01224-682500
E-mail: ron@2gproducts.co.uk
Website: http://www.2gproducts.co.uk
Managers: R. Goodwin (Sales Prom Mgr)
Immediate Holding Company: 2G PRODUCTS LIMITED
Registration no: SC301965 **Date established:** 2006
No.of Employees: 1 - 10 **Product Groups:** 30, 37

Date of Accounts	Oct 11	Oct 10	Oct 09
Working Capital	-63	-105	-89
Fixed Assets	122	166	173
Current Assets	49	57	47

Aalco Aberdeen
Unit 9b Peterseat Drive Peterseat Park, Altens Industrial Estate, Aberdeen, AB12 3HT
Tel: 01224-854810 **Fax:** 01224-871982
E-mail: aberdeen@aalco.co.uk
Website: http://www.aalco.co.uk/locations/aberdeen.aspx
Bank(s): National Westminster Bank Plc
Managers: E. Fulton (Mgr)
Ultimate Holding Company: ROWAN COMPANIES INC (USA)
Immediate Holding Company: ROWAN DRILLING (UK) LIMITED
Registration no: 03551533 **Date established:** 1977
Turnover: £125m - £250m **No.of Employees:** 11 - 20
Product Groups: 34, 35, 36, 66

Aberdeen Drilling Schools & Well Control Training Centre
50 Union Glen, Aberdeen, AB11 6ER
Tel: 01224-572709 **Fax:** 01224-582896
E-mail: info@aberdeen-drilling.com
Website: http://www.aberdeen-drilling.com
Bank(s): Bank of Scotland, 53 Castle Street, Aberdeen
Directors: J. Sutherland (MD)
Immediate Holding Company: ABERDEEN DRILLING SCHOOL LIMITED
Registration no: SC077855 **VAT No.:** GB 376 9554 94
Date established: 1982 **Turnover:** £1m - £2m **No.of Employees:** 11 - 20
Product Groups: 86

Date of Accounts	Dec 11	Dec 10	Dec 09
Working Capital	40	-497	-205
Fixed Assets	200	35	45
Current Assets	705	311	157

Aberdeen Exhibition & Conference Centre
Exhibition Avenue Bridge Of Don, Aberdeen, AB23 8BL
Tel: 01224-824824 **Fax:** 01224-825276
E-mail: egillespie@aecc.co.uk
Website: http://www.aecc.co.uk
Bank(s): Royal Bank Of Scotland
Directors: B. Horspurgh (MD), G. Cumming (Fin)
Managers: S. Corbett, L. Lonie (Sales & Mktg Mg), A. Stott (Tech Serv Mgr)
Immediate Holding Company: ABERDEEN EXHIBITION AND CONFERENCE CENTRE LIMITED
Registration no: 01858349 **Date established:** 1984 **Turnover:** £5m - £10m
No.of Employees: 51 - 100 **Product Groups:** 69, 80

Date of Accounts	Mar 11	Mar 10	Mar 09
Sales Turnover	6m	6m	6m
Pre Tax Profit/Loss	-347	-2m	-1m
Working Capital	13m	13m	13m
Fixed Assets	17m	17m	5m
Current Assets	19m	18m	19m
Current Liabilities	2m	2m	2m

Aberdeen Fluid System Technology
Stoneywood Park Stoneywood Road, Dyce, Aberdeen, AB21 7DZ
Tel: 01224-722468 **Fax:** 01224-723009
E-mail: info@afst.uk.com
Website: http://www.afst.uk.com
Directors: G. Farrel (Dir)
Ultimate Holding Company: DRIL-QUIP INC (USA)
Immediate Holding Company: DRIL-QUIP (EUROPE) LIMITED
Registration no: SC196885 **VAT No.:** GB 456 3223 56
Date established: 1983 **Turnover:** £75m - £125m
No.of Employees: 11 - 20 **Product Groups:** 66

Date of Accounts	Mar 11	Mar 10	Mar 09
Working Capital	2m	2m	2m
Fixed Assets	964	641	644
Current Assets	4m	3m	3m

Aberdeen & Grampian Chamber Of Commerce
The Hub Aberdeen Energy Park, Bridge Of Don, Aberdeen, AB23 8GX
Tel: 01224-343900 **Fax:** 01224-645777
E-mail: info@agcc.co.uk
Website: http://www.agcc.co.uk
Bank(s): Clydesdale Bank PLC
Directors: R. Collier (Grp Chief Exec)
Immediate Holding Company: ABERDEEN AND GRAMPIAN CHAMBER OF COMMERCE
Registration no: SC000791 **Date established:** 1977 **Turnover:** £2m - £5m
No.of Employees: 21 - 50 **Product Groups:** 80

Date of Accounts	Dec 11	Dec 10	Dec 09
Sales Turnover	2m	2m	2m
Pre Tax Profit/Loss	30	30	-50
Working Capital	-4	-29	-51
Fixed Assets	418	415	406
Current Assets	526	397	370
Current Liabilities	457	345	326

AC-CESS Co. UK Ltd
Tyrebagger Works Clinterty, Kinellar, Aberdeen, AB21 0TT
Tel: 01224-790100 **Fax:** 01224-790111
E-mail: info@ac-cess.com
Website: http://www.ac-cess.com
Directors: B. Abel (MD)
Managers: M. Varthese (Mktg Serv Mgr)
Registration no: SC253045 **No.of Employees:** 1 - 10 **Product Groups:** 39, 51, 85

ACI
14 Greenbank Road East Tullos Industrial Estate, Aberdeen, AB12 3BQ
Tel: 01224-515320 **Fax:** 01224-783799
E-mail: jim@acilimited.co.uk
Website: http://www.acilimited.co.uk
Directors: J. Davidson (MD)
Ultimate Holding Company: B J SERVICES COMPANY (USA)
Registration no: SC125585 **Date established:** 1990
Turnover: £75m - £125m **No.of Employees:** 11 - 20 **Product Groups:** 46, 48

ADT Fire & Security plc
Unit 2 The Altec Centre Minto Drive, Altens, Aberdeen, AB12 3LW
Tel: 0800-542 3108 **Fax:** 01224-891888
Website: http://www.adt.co.uk
Managers: A. Wilson (Sales Prom Mgr)
Ultimate Holding Company: TYCO INTERNATIONAL LIMITED (SWITZERLAND)
Immediate Holding Company: ADT FIRE AND SECURITY PLC
Registration no: 01161045 **Date established:** 1974
Turnover: £125m - £250m **No.of Employees:** 21 - 50
Product Groups: 37, 38

Date of Accounts	Sep 11	Sep 08	Sep 09
Sales Turnover	363m	414m	384m
Pre Tax Profit/Loss	18m	4m	10m
Working Capital	450m	618m	561m
Fixed Assets	120m	193m	171m
Current Assets	710m	765m	722m
Current Liabilities	81m	57m	42m

AEL Aberdeen Ltd
Hydropark Tern Place Denmore Road, Bridge Of Don, Aberdeen, AB23 8JX
Tel: 01224-899133 **Fax:** 01224-895550
E-mail: sales@ael-electrical.co.uk
Website: http://www.ael-electrical.co.uk
Directors: G. Mackie (MD), G. McPetrie (Sales)
Immediate Holding Company: A.E.L. (ABERDEEN) LIMITED
Registration no: SC074219 **VAT No.:** GB 361 0387 72
Date established: 1981 **No.of Employees:** 1 - 10 **Product Groups:** 67

Date of Accounts	Sep 11	Sep 10	Sep 09
Working Capital	516	473	378
Fixed Assets	47	29	45
Current Assets	2m	1m	1m

Airpac Bukom Ltd (A VP P.L.C. Division)
Mugiemoss Road Bucksburn, Aberdeen, AB21 9NP
Tel: 01224-715008 **Fax:** 01224-714290
E-mail: david.macmillin@vpplc.com
Website: http://www.airpacbukom.com
Directors: H. Davies (MD), H. Davis (MD)
Ultimate Holding Company: VP PLC
Immediate Holding Company: MECHANICAL ELECTRICAL PRESSFITTINGS LIMITED
Registration no: SC087714 **Date established:** 1989
Turnover: £20m - £50m **No.of Employees:** 21 - 50 **Product Groups:** 29, 40

Date of Accounts	Mar 07	Jan 06	Jan 05
Sales Turnover	2m	N/A	N/A
Pre Tax Profit/Loss	361	N/A	N/A
Working Capital	671	-111	-119
Fixed Assets	43	1m	827
Current Assets	671	758	534

Aker Solutions
Dyce, Aberdeen, AB21 0NA
Tel: 01224-414515 **Fax:** 01224-414400
E-mail: julie.malhan@kvaerner.com
Website: http://www.akersolutions.com
Bank(s): Royal Bank of Scotland
Directors: R. Laycock (Fin)
Managers: D. Harris (Buyer), L. Young (Mktg Serv Mgr), R. Tulloch (Personnel), D. Hoffack (I.T. Exec)
Ultimate Holding Company: DOMINION TECHNOLOGY GASES INVESTMENT LIMITED
Immediate Holding Company: ARGON (ISOTANK) LIMITED
Registration no: 04962691 **Date established:** 2003
Turnover: £75m - £125m **No.of Employees:** 1001 - 1500
Product Groups: 35, 39, 51, 69, 80, 84

Amec Group Ltd
City Gate Altens Farm Road, Nigg, Aberdeen, AB12 3LB
Tel: 01224-892500 **Fax:** 01224-291001
E-mail: frank.stokes@amec.com
Website: http://www.amec.com
Directors: S. Samirpr (Ch), N. Bruce (MD), J. Perason (Jt MD), E. Jones (Mkt Research), C. Bond (Chief Op Offcr)
Managers: V. Yorsten (Mktg Serv Mgr), W. Murray, N. Liberdiss (I.T. Exec), I. Hume (Develop Mgr), G. Mavin (Mgr), A. Norris (I.T. Exec), A. Powell (Purch Mgr), P. Guest (Mgr), J. Field (Sales Prom Mgr)
Ultimate Holding Company: AMEC P L C
Immediate Holding Company: AMEC GROUP LIMITED
Registration no: 04612748 **Date established:** 2002
Turnover: Over £1,000m **No.of Employees:** 1 - 10 **Product Groups:** 39, 51, 84

Date of Accounts	Dec 10	Dec 09	Dec 08
Sales Turnover	720m	675m	941m
Pre Tax Profit/Loss	61m	22m	11m
Working Capital	60m	81m	99m
Fixed Assets	533m	509m	590m
Current Assets	208m	251m	330m
Current Liabilities	73m	88m	94m

Anderson's Packaging Aberdeen Ltd
5 Girdleness Trading Estate Girdleness Road, Aberdeen, AB11 8DG
Tel: 01224-894417 **Fax:** 01224-894291
E-mail: ccb@anderpack.co.uk
Website: http://www.anderpack.co.uk
Bank(s): Bank of Scotland
Directors: C. Brown (MD)
Immediate Holding Company: ANDERSONS PACKAGING (ABERDEEN) LIMITED
Registration no: SC058597 **VAT No.:** GB 267 9491 04
Date established: 1975 **Turnover:** £1m - £2m **No.of Employees:** 11 - 20
Product Groups: 30, 66

Date of Accounts	Mar 12	Mar 11	Mar 10
Working Capital	53	25	6
Fixed Assets	66	80	96
Current Assets	427	499	488

Andersons Guns
201 Hardgate, Aberdeen, AB11 6YB
Tel: 01224-580179 **Fax:** 01224-573952
Directors: N. Anderson (Prop)
Date established: 1976 **No.of Employees:** 1 - 10 **Product Groups:** 36, 39, 40

Andrews Survey
Ocean Spirit House 33 Waterloo Quay, Aberdeen, AB11 5BS
Tel: 01224-256888 **Fax:** 01224-857777
E-mail: enquiries@andrewssurvey.com
Website: http://www.andrewssurvey.com

Directors: P. Hawksley (MD), R. Bridges (Tech Serv), R. Jarman (MD)
Managers: J. Eckert (Trng Mgr)
Registration no: 03571218 **VAT No.:** 491 7484 10 **Date established:** 1996
Turnover: £5m - £10m **No.of Employees:** 1 - 10 **Product Groups:** 51, 84, 85

Arch Henderson LLP (Chartered Civil Engineers)

26 Rubislaw Terrace, Aberdeen, AB10 1XE
Tel: 01224-631122 **Fax:** 01224-632233
E-mail: headoffice@arch-henderson.co.uk
Website: http://www.arch-henderson.co.uk
Bank(s): Bank of Scotland
Directors: G. Alexander (Ptnr)
Immediate Holding Company: ARCH HENDERSON LIMITED LIABILITY PARTNERSHIP
Registration no: SO300202 **VAT No.:** GB 265 4135 63
Date established: 2003 **Turnover:** £1m - £2m **No.of Employees:** 11 - 20
Product Groups: 54, 84

Date of Accounts	Mar 11	Mar 10	Mar 09
Working Capital	1m	902	774
Fixed Assets	319	393	395
Current Assets	2m	2m	2m

Arco Aberdeen Ltd

Blackness Road Altens Industrial Estate, Aberdeen, AB12 3LH
Tel: 01224-249494 **Fax:** 01224-248322
E-mail: enquiries@arco.co.uk
Website: http://www.arco.co.uk
Directors: N. Hildward (Fin)
Managers: D. Lowe (District Mgr), C. Squires (District Mgr), C. Squires (District Mgr)
Ultimate Holding Company: GLOBAL ENERGY (HOLDINGS) LIMITED
Immediate Holding Company: MOUNTWEST ACCLIVITY LIMITED
Registration no: SC163254 **Date established:** 2010
Turnover: £50m - £75m **No.of Employees:** 51 - 100 **Product Groups:** 24, 29, 30, 40

Date of Accounts	Dec 11	Dec 10	Dec 09
Sales Turnover	65m	34m	54m
Pre Tax Profit/Loss	18m	9m	13m
Working Capital	52m	55m	48m
Fixed Assets	17m	7m	9m
Current Assets	75m	69m	59m
Current Liabilities	17m	7m	10m

Ashfield Technology

2 Ashfield Road Cults, Aberdeen, AB15 9NQ
Tel: 07803-015163 **Fax:** 01224-868545
E-mail: ashfield_tec@hotmail.com
Website: http://www.ashfieldtechnology.com
Managers: J. Milne (Mgr)
Registration no: SC105748 **Turnover:** Up to £250,000
No.of Employees: 1 - 10 **Product Groups:** 38

Ashtead Technology Ltd

Unit 3 Kirkton Avenue Dyce, Aberdeen, AB21 0BF
Tel: 01224-771888 **Fax:** 01224-770129
E-mail: info@ashtead-technology.com
Website: http://www.ashtead-technology.com
Bank(s): Lloyds TSB
Directors: P. Simpson (Chief Op Offcr), M. Derry (MD), I. Guthrie (Fin)
Managers: M. Conroy (Buyer), F. Gray (Comptroller), B. Wood, A. Sakapaji (Mktg Serv Mgr)
Ultimate Holding Company: AMAZON GROUP LIMITED
Immediate Holding Company: ASHTEAD TECHNOLOGY LIMITED
Registration no: SC091624 **VAT No.:** GB 209 5687 37
Date established: 1985 **Turnover:** £5m - £10m **No.of Employees:** 21 - 50
Product Groups: 38

Date of Accounts	Apr 11	Apr 10	Apr 09
Sales Turnover	8m	7m	11m
Pre Tax Profit/Loss	2m	2m	3m
Working Capital	6m	5m	2m
Fixed Assets	5m	4m	7m
Current Assets	12m	10m	7m
Current Liabilities	5m	834	2m

W S Atkins Ltd

6 Golden Square, Aberdeen, AB10 1RD
Tel: 01224-620202 **Fax:** 01224-620457
E-mail: ian.anderson@atkinsglobal.com
Website: http://www.atkinsglobal.com
Bank(s): National Westminster
Directors: I. Anderson (Dir), M. Grant (MD)
Managers: S. Duncan (I.T. Exec), D. Lang, R. Fraser
Ultimate Holding Company: WS ATKINS PLC
Immediate Holding Company: ATKINS ABERDEEN LIMITED
Registration no: 00688424 **VAT No.:** GB 209 8612 53
Date established: 2000 **Turnover:** £2m - £5m **No.of Employees:** 51 - 100
Product Groups: 51, 84

Date of Accounts	Dec 11	Dec 10	Dec 09
Sales Turnover	4m	7m	7m
Pre Tax Profit/Loss	-888	-319	466
Working Capital	222	466	734
Fixed Assets	N/A	13	19
Current Assets	1m	2m	2m
Current Liabilities	364	382	433

B E L Valves

Horizons House 81 Waterloo Quay, Aberdeen, AB11 5DE
Tel: 01224-584717
Managers: G. Assleck (Mgr)
Immediate Holding Company: LIVESTOCK MANAGEMENT SYSTEMS LIMITED
Date established: 2005 **No.of Employees:** 1 - 10 **Product Groups:** 36, 37, 38

Date of Accounts	Mar 11	Mar 10	Mar 09
Working Capital	11	5	6
Fixed Assets	6	6	6
Current Assets	27	29	15

B J Services Co UK Ltd

Badentoy Avenue Badentoy Park, Portlethen, Aberdeen, AB12 4YB
Tel: 01224-401401 **Fax:** 01224-401501
E-mail: janderson@bjservices.com
Website: http://www.bjservices.com
Bank(s): The Royal Bank of Scotland
Directors: J. Stewart (Dir), S. Morrison (Fin)
Managers: B. Tony (Purch Mgr), J. Anderson (Mgr), K. Watt (Ops Mgr)
Ultimate Holding Company: BAKER HUGHES INC (USA)
Immediate Holding Company: BJ SERVICES COMPANY LIMITED
Registration no: SC143147 **VAT No.:** GB 605 0202 07
Date established: 1993 **Turnover:** £75m - £125m
No.of Employees: 251 - 500 **Product Groups:** 36, 38, 51, 85

Date of Accounts	Dec 10	Sep 09	Sep 08
Pre Tax Profit/Loss	-1m	-23m	11m
Working Capital	-28m	3m	25m
Fixed Assets	128m	128m	129m
Current Assets	3m	4m	33m

B J Tubular Services

Hareness Circle Altens Industrial Estate, Aberdeen, AB12 3LY
Tel: 01224-249678 **Fax:** 01224-249106
E-mail: kdwatt@bjservices.co.uk
Website: http://www.bjservices.com
Managers: I. Shepherd (Chief Mgr), K. Watt (Chief Mgr), K. Watt (Mgr), S. Barker (Tech Serv Mgr)
Ultimate Holding Company: ADRIA GROUP LIMITED
Immediate Holding Company: DEEDREAM LIMITED
Registration no: SC287070 **VAT No.:** GB 605 0202 07
Date established: 2005 **No.of Employees:** 51 - 100 **Product Groups:** 26, 29, 30, 35, 36, 38, 39, 40, 45, 48, 49

Date of Accounts	Oct 10	Oct 09	Oct 08
Working Capital	-7m	-1m	-153
Fixed Assets	15m	9m	9m
Current Assets	487	194	273

B R T Bearings Ltd

4 Howe Moss Drive Kirkhill Industrial Estate, Dyce, Aberdeen, AB21 0GL
Tel: 01224-772000 **Fax:** 01224-773777
E-mail: faithskeels@brt-bearings.com
Website: http://www.brt-bearings.com
Managers: A. Doak (District Mgr)
Ultimate Holding Company: INSTOCK DISPOSABLES LIMITED
Immediate Holding Company: INSTOCK DISPOSABLES LIMITED
Registration no: 00912230 **Date established:** 1974 **Turnover:** £1m - £2m
No.of Employees: 1 - 10 **Product Groups:** 22, 23, 29, 34, 35, 36, 37

Date of Accounts	Mar 11	Mar 10	Mar 09
Sales Turnover	12m	11m	N/A
Pre Tax Profit/Loss	164	13	5
Working Capital	1m	1m	985
Fixed Assets	406	515	1m
Current Assets	3m	3m	3m
Current Liabilities	579	531	414

B S S (Aberdeen Branch)

5a Greenwell Road East Tullos Industrial Estate, Aberdeen, AB12 3AX
Tel: 01224-292929 **Fax:** 01224-898252
Website: http://www.bssgroup.com
Bank(s): HSBC Bank plc
Managers: J. Mckay (Mgr)
Ultimate Holding Company: JOHN WOOD GROUP P.L.C.
Immediate Holding Company: WOOD GROUP ENGINEERING & OPERATIONS SUPPORT LIMITED
Registration no: 03106393 **Date established:** 1995
No.of Employees: 11 - 20 **Product Groups:** 30, 36, 38, 39, 40, 42

Date of Accounts	Dec 11	Dec 10	Dec 09
Working Capital	-3	-3	-3

Baader UK Ltd

Nautilus House 35 Waterloo Quay, Aberdeen, AB11 5BS
Tel: 01224-597320 **Fax:** 01224-597321
E-mail: sales@baader.co.uk
Website: http://www.baader.com
Managers: K. Buchan (Sales Admin)
Ultimate Holding Company: BAADER BETEILIGUNGS GMBH (GERMANY)
Immediate Holding Company: BAADER (U.K.) LIMITED
Registration no: 01223500 **VAT No.:** GB 598 8597 39
Date established: 1975 **Turnover:** Up to £250,000
No.of Employees: 1 - 10 **Product Groups:** 40, 41

Date of Accounts	Dec 11	Dec 10	Dec 09
Sales Turnover	2m	1m	1m
Pre Tax Profit/Loss	254	104	3
Working Capital	100	102	102
Fixed Assets	8	10	4
Current Assets	578	349	365
Current Liabilities	466	240	241

Baker Hughes

Woodside Road Bridge Of Don Industrial Estate, Aberdeen, AB23 8BW
Tel: 01224-223000 **Fax:** 01224-824015
E-mail: info@bakerhughes.com
Website: http://www.bakerhughes.com
Bank(s): Barclays, 1 Rubislaw Terr, Aberdeen
Directors: P. Enston (Fin), P. Enston (Fin)
Managers: C. Stuart (Purch Mgr), S. Writh (Plant), D. Reid (Personnel), R. Hutchinson (Personnel)
Immediate Holding Company: BAKER OIL TOOLS (UNITED KINGDOM) LIMITED
Registration no: 00855849 **Date established:** 1965
No.of Employees: 251 - 500 **Product Groups:** 45, 51

Baker Hughes

Barclayhill Place Portlethen, Aberdeen, AB12 4PF
Tel: 01224-408000 **Fax:** 01224-408001
E-mail: ian.gellie@bakerhughes.com
Website: http://www.bakerhughes.com
Managers: A. McDonald, I. Gellie (Chief Mgr), J. McCalum (I.T. Exec), R. Gordon (Purch Mgr), B. Berrisford (Personnel)
Turnover: £2m - £5m **No.of Employees:** 101 - 250 **Product Groups:** 48, 51

Balmoral Group

Balmoral Park, Aberdeen, AB12 3GY
Tel: 01224-859200 **Fax:** 01224-859059
E-mail: group@balmoral.co.uk
Website: http://www.balmoral-group.com
Bank(s): Bank of Scotland
Directors: S. Taylor (Dir), W. Main (Fin), J. Milne (Ch), R. Oram (Tech Serv)
Managers: S. Gibb (Mktg Serv Mgr), S. Edmonds (I.T. Exec), J. Forbes (Grp Purch Mgr), A. McIntosh
Immediate Holding Company: BALMORAL GROUP HOLDINGS LIMITED
Registration no: SC277480 **VAT No.:** GB 297 4306 29
Date established: 2004 **Turnover:** £50m - £75m
No.of Employees: 51 - 100 **Product Groups:** 30, 35, 40

Date of Accounts	Mar 11	Mar 10	Mar 09
Sales Turnover	73m	61m	38m
Pre Tax Profit/Loss	14m	11m	2m
Working Capital	10m	9m	-1m
Fixed Assets	23m	21m	19m
Current Assets	22m	23m	19m
Current Liabilities	2m	5m	1m

Balmoral Tanks Ltd

Balmoral Park Wellington Road, Aberdeen, AB12 3GY
Tel: 01224-859 1000 **Fax:** 01224-859123
E-mail: tanks@balmoral.co.uk
Website: http://www.balmoral-group.com
Directors: W. Main (Fin)
Managers: J. Lowden, S. Edmonds (Tech Serv Mgr), J. Hunter (Personnel), S. Cruickshank, S. Gibbs (Mktg Serv Mgr)
Ultimate Holding Company: BALMORAL GROUP HOLDINGS LIMITED
Immediate Holding Company: BALMORAL TANKS LIMITED
Registration no: SC300656 **Date established:** 2006 **Turnover:** £2m - £5m
No.of Employees: 51 - 100 **Product Groups:** 30, 35, 40, 41, 42, 52, 54, 66, 67, 76, 84

Date of Accounts	Mar 11	Mar 10	Mar 09
Sales Turnover	4m	4m	6m
Pre Tax Profit/Loss	-399	4	-586
Working Capital	-2m	-2m	-2m
Fixed Assets	2m	3m	3m
Current Assets	3m	3m	3m
Current Liabilities	145	117	232

Barclay & Mathieson Ltd

Cloverhill Road Bridge of Don, Aberdeen, AB23 8FE
Tel: 01224-702771 **Fax:** 01224-826227
E-mail: aberdeen@bmsteel.co.uk
Website: http://www.bmsteel.co.uk
Bank(s): The Royal Bank of Scotland
Directors: M. Norie (Dir)
Ultimate Holding Company: STEMCOR HOLDINGS LIMITED
Immediate Holding Company: BARCLAY & MATHIESON LIMITED
Registration no: SC030987 **VAT No.:** GB 259 6926 05
Date established: 1955 **Turnover:** £75m - £125m
No.of Employees: 11 - 20 **Product Groups:** 66

Date of Accounts	Dec 11	Dec 10	Dec 09
Sales Turnover	55m	48m	35m
Pre Tax Profit/Loss	2m	2m	-865
Working Capital	11m	13m	13m
Fixed Assets	19m	16m	18m
Current Assets	24m	25m	20m
Current Liabilities	4m	5m	713

Batt Cables plc

Unit 5-6 Forties Industrial Centre Hareness Circle, Altens Industrial Estate, Aberdeen, AB12 3LY
Tel: 01224-897979 **Fax:** 01224-894646
E-mail: j.grey@batt.co.uk
Website: http://www.batt.co.uk
Managers: J. Grey (District Mgr)
Immediate Holding Company: BATT CABLES PLC
Registration no: 01353678 **Date established:** 1978
No.of Employees: 1 - 10 **Product Groups:** 30, 35, 36, 37, 38, 44, 66, 67

Date of Accounts	Mar 12	Mar 11	Mar 10
Sales Turnover	106m	98m	84m
Pre Tax Profit/Loss	8m	9m	5m
Working Capital	41m	36m	31m
Fixed Assets	8m	9m	8m
Current Assets	69m	60m	54m
Current Liabilities	3m	3m	2m

Beautifully Made Hair

Admiral Court Poynernook Road, Aberdeen, AB11 5QX
Tel: 07967-121447
E-mail: sales@beautifullymadehair.com
Website: http://www.beautifullymadehair.com
Directors: E. Ndong (Prop)
Ultimate Holding Company: JOHN LAWRIE (ABERDEEN) LTD.
Registration no: SC087881 **Date established:** 1984 **Turnover:** £2m - £5m
No.of Employees: 1 - 10 **Product Groups:** 32, 49, 67

BI Electronics

Greenmoss Kinellar, Aberdeen, AB21 0SE
Tel: 01224-790615
Managers: B. Inkster (Design Eng)
No.of Employees: 1 - 10 **Product Groups:** 40, 47, 48

S Boyne

Unit 12 50 Cotton Street, Aberdeen, AB11 5EE
Tel: 01224-574716 **Fax:** 01224-593152
Directors: S. Boyne (Prop)
Date established: 1988 **No.of Employees:** 1 - 10 **Product Groups:** 37

Bridon International Ltd

Unit 4 Venue Business Centre Grandholm Crescent, Aberdeen, AB22 8AA
Tel: 01224-702874 **Fax:** 01224-702837
E-mail: aberdeensales@bridon.com
Website: http://www.bridon.com
Bank(s): HSBC Bank plc
Managers: D. Ward (Sales Prom Mgr)
Ultimate Holding Company: FKI P.L.C.
Registration no: 00416671 **VAT No.:** GB 181 4834 56
Date established: 1990 **Turnover:** £20m - £50m
No.of Employees: 21 - 50 **Product Groups:** 23, 30, 35

Briggs Marine

142 Sinclair Road, Aberdeen, AB11 9PR
Tel: 01224-898666 **Fax:** 01224-896950
E-mail: marketing@briggsmarine.co.uk
Website: http://www.briggsmarine.com
Managers: J. Campbell, R. Shum (Sales Prom Mgr), J. Davidson (Sales Admin)
Immediate Holding Company: BRIGGS ENVIRONMENTAL SERVICES LIMITED
Registration no: SC110121 **Date established:** 1988
Turnover: £5m - £10m **No.of Employees:** 1 - 10 **Product Groups:** 38, 40, 54, 84, 85

Date of Accounts	Mar 08	Mar 07	Mar 06
Sales Turnover	4603	4853	3643
Pre Tax Profit/Loss	-717	637	-596

see next page

Briggs Marine - Cont'd

Working Capital	-1992	-1077	-1415
Fixed Assets	3875	3448	2284
Current Assets	1889	3146	1539
Current Liabilities	3881	4223	2955
Total Share Capital	1	1	1
ROCE% (Return on Capital Employed)	-38.1	26.8	-68.6
ROT% (Return on Turnover)	-15.6	13.1	-16.4

Buck & Hickman Ltd

Unit 4 Hareness Park Hareness Circle, Altens Industrial Estate, Aberdeen, AB12 3QY
Tel: 01224-895272 **Fax:** 01224-895248
E-mail: aberdeen@buckandhickman.com
Website: http://www.buckandhickman.com
Managers: G. Leeson (District Mgr)
Ultimate Holding Company: TRAVIS PERKINS PLC
Immediate Holding Company: BOSTON (2011) LIMITED
Registration no: 06028304 **Date established:** 2006
Turnover: £75m - £125m **No.of Employees:** 11 - 20 **Product Groups:** 24, 29, 30, 33, 36, 37, 41, 46

Date of Accounts	Dec 10	Mar 10	Mar 09
Working Capital	6m	6m	6m
Current Assets	27m	27m	27m

C K Weldco

Unit 8 Howe Moss Drive Kirkhill Industrial Estate, Dyce, Aberdeen, AB21 0GL
Tel: 01224-729729 **Fax:** 01224-729730
E-mail: ckw@freightco-group.co.uk
Website: http://www.freightco-group.co.uk
Directors: J. Thornton (MD)
Immediate Holding Company: CK WELD.CO LIMITED
Registration no: SC170872 **Date established:** 1996
No.of Employees: 1 - 10 **Product Groups:** 46

Date of Accounts	Apr 11	Apr 10	Apr 09
Working Capital	143	131	199
Current Assets	894	702	829

Cansco Greig Engineering Ltd

Souter Head Road Altens Industrial Estate, Aberdeen, AB12 3LF
Tel: 01224-898810 **Fax:** 01224-878542
E-mail: mail@cansco.co.uk
Website: http://www.cansco.co.uk
Bank(s): The Royal Bank of Scotland
Directors: A. Sangster (Fin), S. Tough (MD), S. Touth (MD)
Managers: S. Sangster (Purch Mgr)
Ultimate Holding Company: WEATHERFORD INTERNATIONAL LIMITED (BERMUDA)
Immediate Holding Company: CANSCO GREIG ENGINEERING LIMITED
Registration no: SC078562 **VAT No.:** GB 377 0048 51
Date established: 1982 **Turnover:** £5m - £10m
No.of Employees: 51 - 100 **Product Groups:** 30, 35, 40, 42, 45, 48, 67, 84

Date of Accounts	Dec 11	Dec 10	Dec 09
Sales Turnover	10m	8m	8m
Pre Tax Profit/Loss	459	-54	470
Working Capital	-184	-388	13
Fixed Assets	2m	2m	2m
Current Assets	3m	2m	2m
Current Liabilities	499	311	371

Capita Health Solutions

Foresterhill Road, Aberdeen, AB25 2ZP
Tel: 01224-669000 **Fax:** 01224-669030
E-mail: aon.info@aers.co.uk
Website: http://www.capita.co.uk
Directors: R. Jennings (Dir)
Managers: B. Gunnyeon (District Mgr), S. Taylor (Fin Mgr)
Registration no: SC063288 **Turnover:** £2m - £5m
No.of Employees: 51 - 100 **Product Groups:** 84, 88

Cebo UK Ltd

Badentoy Road Portlethen, Aberdeen, AB12 4YA
Tel: 01224-782020 **Fax:** 01224-782340
E-mail: info@cebo-uk.com
Website: http://www.cebo-uk.com
Managers: D. Mackinnon
Immediate Holding Company: CEBO UK LIMITED
Registration no: SC059507 **Date established:** 1976 **Turnover:** £2m - £5m
No.of Employees: 11 - 20 **Product Groups:** 29, 32, 33, 45

Date of Accounts	Dec 11	Dec 10	Dec 09
Sales Turnover	5m	5m	5m
Pre Tax Profit/Loss	266	470	439
Working Capital	1m	2m	2m
Fixed Assets	14	31	55
Current Assets	2m	2m	2m
Current Liabilities	328	275	305

Centrilift (a division of Baker Hughes Ltd)

Howe Moss Place Kirkhill Indl-Est, Dyce, Aberdeen, AB21 0ES
Tel: 01224-772233 **Fax:** 01224-771021
E-mail: william.milne@centrilift.com
Website: http://www.bakerhughes.com
Bank(s): Bank of Scotland
Directors: E. Bespalov (Develop)
Managers: W. Milne (Chief Mgr), W. Milne (District Mgr)
Ultimate Holding Company: USHA MARTIN LIMITED (INDIA)
Immediate Holding Company: EUROPEAN MANAGEMENT & MARINE CORPORATION LIMITED
Registration no: 01388658 **VAT No.:** GB 384 6544 20
Date established: 1996 **Turnover:** £5m - £10m
No.of Employees: 51 - 100 **Product Groups:** 40, 48

Chubb Limited

7 Miller Street, Aberdeen, AB11 5AN
Tel: 01224-590470 **Fax:** 01224-581997
Website: http://www.chubb.co.uk
Managers: H. Scroggie (District Mgr)
Ultimate Holding Company: SCOTOIL GROUP LIMITED
Immediate Holding Company: Bet Security & Communications Ltd
Registration no: 04034666 **Date established:** 2000 **Turnover:** £2m - £5m
No.of Employees: 1 - 10 **Product Groups:** 81

City Sprint UK Ltd

Unit 4 Altens Mini Units Souter Head Road, Altens Industrial Estate, Aberdeen, AB12 3LF
Tel: 01224-898221 **Fax:** 01224-890998
E-mail: aberdeen@citysprint.co.uk
Website: http://www.citysprint.co.uk
Bank(s): Bank of Scotland
Managers: S. Philips
Ultimate Holding Company: CITYSPRINT (UK) GROUP LIMITED
Immediate Holding Company: CITYSPRINT (UK) LIMITED
Registration no: 04327611 **VAT No.:** GB 227 8932 33
Date established: 2001 **No.of Employees:** 11 - 20 **Product Groups:** 79

Date of Accounts	Dec 11	Dec 10	Dec 09
Sales Turnover	74m	61m	47m
Pre Tax Profit/Loss	4m	4m	3m
Working Capital	3m	4m	3m
Fixed Assets	14m	6m	5m
Current Assets	16m	17m	15m
Current Liabilities	6m	5m	4m

Clark & Sutherland Ltd

Smiddy Brae Kingswells, Aberdeen, AB15 8SL
Tel: 01224-740222 **Fax:** 01224-744294
E-mail: clark.sutherland@btconnect.com
Directors: D. Sutherland (Dir), K. Mcdonagh (Dir)
Immediate Holding Company: CLARK & SUTHERLAND LIMITED
Registration no: SC204015 **VAT No.:** GB 265 3032 78
Date established: 2000 **Turnover:** £1m - £2m **No.of Employees:** 1 - 10
Product Groups: 41

Date of Accounts	Mar 12	Mar 11	Mar 10
Working Capital	88	309	423
Fixed Assets	25	68	61
Current Assets	880	688	702

Cmac Electronics Systems

Rashieburn Fintray, Aberdeen, AB21 0YX
Tel: 01651-806888 **Fax:** 01651-806696
E-mail: info@cmac-sys.co.uk
Website: http://www.cmac-sys.co.uk
Directors: C. MacInnon (MD), C. Mackinnon (Prop)
Turnover: £500,000 - £1m **No.of Employees:** 1 - 10 **Product Groups:** 35, 37, 52

Coates Offshore

Unit 6 Dyce Avenue, Dyce, Aberdeen, AB21 0LQ
Tel: 01224-215400 **Fax:** 01224-724616
E-mail: offshore@coatesoffshore.com
Website: http://www.coatesoffshore.com
Bank(s): National Westminster
Directors: A. McLeod (Fin), K. White (Grp Chief Exec)
Managers: N. Pickering, C. Nicholson (Personnel), D. Rennie
Ultimate Holding Company: AMAZON GROUP LIMITED
Immediate Holding Company: ASHTEAD TECHNOLOGY LIMITED
Registration no: 03133771 **VAT No.:** GB 735 4909 13
Date established: 1985 **Turnover:** £1m - £2m **No.of Employees:** 21 - 50
Product Groups: 23, 29, 30, 31, 35, 36, 37, 38, 39, 40, 42, 45, 52, 66, 67, 83

James Cordiner & Son Ltd

Victoria Sawmills Crombie Place, Aberdeen, AB11 9PJ
Tel: 01224-877341 **Fax:** 01224-875510
E-mail: stuart.cordiner@cordiners.com
Website: http://www.cordiners.com
Bank(s): Clydesdale Bank PLC
Directors: J. Cordiner (Co Sec), S. Cordiner (Dir)
Managers: S. Begg (Buyer)
Immediate Holding Company: JAMES CORDINER & SON LIMITED
Registration no: SC019070 **VAT No.:** GB 265 3480 51
Date established: 1936 **Turnover:** £2m - £5m **No.of Employees:** 51 - 100
Product Groups: 45, 66

Date of Accounts	Jun 11	Jun 10	Jun 09
Sales Turnover	N/A	N/A	4m
Pre Tax Profit/Loss	N/A	N/A	227
Working Capital	2m	2m	2m
Fixed Assets	353	373	350
Current Assets	2m	2m	2m
Current Liabilities	N/A	N/A	266

Corex UK

Unit B1-B3 Airport Industrial Park Howe Moss Drive, Dyce, Aberdeen, AB21 0GL
Tel: 01224-770434 **Fax:** 01224-771716
E-mail: santhony@corex.co.uk
Website: http://www.corex.co.uk
Bank(s): Clydesdale Bank PLC
Managers: S. Anthony (Ops Mgr)
Registration no: 02973383 **VAT No.:** GB 651 9722 22
Turnover: £2m - £5m **No.of Employees:** 51 - 100 **Product Groups:** 51, 84, 85

Date of Accounts	Dec 07	Dec 06	Dec 05
Working Capital	1398	1067	768
Fixed Assets	756	578	410
Current Assets	3069	2168	1727
Current Liabilities	1671	1101	959
Total Share Capital	700	700	700

Cormon Aberdeen Ltd

Kirkhill Place Kirkhill Industrial Estate, Dyce, Aberdeen, AB21 0GU
Tel: 01224-723315 **Fax:** 01224-723316
Website: http://www.cormon.com
Managers: K. Barclay (Mgr), I. Grimmer (Mgr)
Registration no: SC249944 **Date established:** 2003
No.of Employees: 1 - 10 **Product Groups:** 46, 48

Date of Accounts	Dec 10	Dec 09	Dec 08
Sales Turnover	N/A	N/A	538
Pre Tax Profit/Loss	N/A	N/A	94
Working Capital	144	71	174
Fixed Assets	5	6	6
Current Assets	181	151	225
Current Liabilities	N/A	23	31

Corporate Software & Asset Management Ltd

Graphix House Wellington Circle, Altens, Aberdeen, AB12 3JG
Tel: 01224-249550 **Fax:** 01244-586866
E-mail: info@c-sam.co.uk
Website: http://www.c-sam.co.uk
Directors: T. Wheeler (MD)
Immediate Holding Company: CORPORATE SOFTWARE AND ASSET MANAGEMENT LTD.
Registration no: SC213890 **Date established:** 2000
No.of Employees: 1 - 10 **Product Groups:** 44

Date of Accounts	Mar 11	Mar 09	Mar 08
Working Capital	230	132	70
Fixed Assets	7	7	7
Current Assets	335	243	182

Corroless Off Shore UK Ltd

2 Lawson Drive Dyce, Aberdeen, AB21 0DR
Tel: 01224-796690 **Fax:** 01224-796691
E-mail: sales@corrolessoffshore.com
Website: http://www.corrolessoffshore.com
Directors: R. Agnew (MD)
Immediate Holding Company: CORROLESS OFFSHORE (UK) LIMITED
Registration no: SC167182 **Date established:** 1996 **Turnover:** £2m - £5m
No.of Employees: 1 - 10 **Product Groups:** 46, 48

Date of Accounts	Jul 11	Jul 10	Jul 09
Working Capital	377	309	42
Fixed Assets	30	31	25
Current Assets	544	601	265

Craig Group Ltd

12 Queens Road, Aberdeen, AB15 4ZT
Tel: 01224-261400 **Fax:** 01224-261401
E-mail: info@craig-group.com
Website: http://www.craig-group.com
Directors: G. Payton (Fin)
Managers: S. Craig (Mktg Serv Mgr), B. Catto (Tech Serv Mgr), K. Stewart, V. Anderson (Personnel)
Immediate Holding Company: CRAIG GROUP LIMITED
Registration no: SC031826 **Date established:** 1956
Turnover: £75m - £125m **No.of Employees:** 21 - 50 **Product Groups:** 61

Date of Accounts	Apr 11	Apr 10	Apr 09
Sales Turnover	112m	92m	105m
Pre Tax Profit/Loss	15m	11m	16m
Working Capital	42m	35m	35m
Fixed Assets	131m	124m	102m
Current Assets	53m	51m	55m
Current Liabilities	6m	6m	8m

Dana Petroleum plc

17 Carden Place, Aberdeen, AB10 1UR
Tel: 01224-652400 **Fax:** 01224-652401
E-mail: john.arnton@dana-petroleum.com
Website: http://www.dana-petroleum.com
Directors: D. Macfarlane (Fin), J. Arnton (Fin)
Managers: M. Richards
Ultimate Holding Company: DANA PETROLEUM PUBLIC LIMITED COMPANY
Immediate Holding Company: DANA PETROLEUM (E&P) LIMITED
Registration no: 02294746 **Date established:** 1988
Turnover: £500m - £1,000m **No.of Employees:** 21 - 50
Product Groups: 31

Date of Accounts	Dec 11	Dec 10	Dec 09
Sales Turnover	505m	293m	234m
Pre Tax Profit/Loss	205m	100m	48m
Working Capital	-246m	-287m	-216m
Fixed Assets	1243m	868m	740m
Current Assets	349m	161m	231m
Current Liabilities	125m	119m	67m

David Morbey Timpani & Percussion

55 Braemar Place, Aberdeen, AB10 6EQ
Tel: 01224-212557 **Fax:** 01224-212557
E-mail: david@timpanisticks.com
Website: http://www.timpanisticks.com
Directors: D. Morbey (Prop)
No.of Employees: 1 - 10 **Product Groups:** 65

Deebridge Electrical Engineers Ltd

Craigshaw Road West Tullos Industrial Estate, Aberdeen, AB12 3AR
Tel: 01224-871548 **Fax:** 01224-899910
E-mail: sales@deebridge.co.uk
Website: http://www.deebridge.co.uk
Directors: B. Mahoney (Fin)
Managers: D. Marr (Mgr)
Ultimate Holding Company: RAINBOW (ABERDEEN) LIMITED
Immediate Holding Company: DEEBRIDGE ELECTRICAL ENGINEERS LIMITED
Registration no: SC044123 **VAT No.:** 265 7076 38 **Date established:** 1966
Turnover: £1m - £2m **No.of Employees:** 11 - 20 **Product Groups:** 37, 48, 67

Date of Accounts	Apr 12	Apr 11	Apr 10
Working Capital	-232	-85	88
Fixed Assets	589	456	315
Current Assets	215	387	447

Digital Applications International Ltd

8 Queens Gardens, Aberdeen, AB15 4YD
Tel: 01224-624422
E-mail: colin.taylor@dai.co.uk
Website: http://www.dai.co.uk
Bank(s): National Westminster Bank Plc
Directors: R. Webber (Dir), D. McLeod (Chief Op Offcr), A. Kishiel (MD)
Managers: F. Richards (Mgr), C. Taylor (Ops Mgr)
Immediate Holding Company: DIGITAL APPLICATIONS INTERNATIONAL LIMITED
Registration no: 01008089 **VAT No.:** GB 238 5973 21
Date established: 1971 **Turnover:** £500,000 - £1m
No.of Employees: 11 - 20 **Product Groups:** 44, 84

Date of Accounts	Nov 10	Nov 09	Nov 08
Sales Turnover	12m	13m	12m
Pre Tax Profit/Loss	2m	2m	2m
Working Capital	6m	8m	6m
Fixed Assets	6m	4m	5m
Current Assets	8m	11m	9m
Current Liabilities	2m	3m	3m

Dowding & Mills Engineeering Services

Unit 3 & 4 Kirkton Avenue Dyce, Aberdeen, AB21 0BF
Tel: 01224-427200 **Fax:** 01224-723560
E-mail: norman.campbell@sulzer.com
Website: http://www.dowdingandmills.com
Directors: N. Campbell (MD)
Managers: A. Crawford
Ultimate Holding Company: AMAZON GROUP LIMITED
Immediate Holding Company: ASHTEAD TECHNOLOGY LIMITED
Registration no: SC028056 **Date established:** 1985
Turnover: £10m - £20m **No.of Employees:** 51 - 100 **Product Groups:** 37

Date of Accounts	Apr 11	Apr 10	Apr 09
Sales Turnover	8m	7m	11m
Pre Tax Profit/Loss	2m	2m	3m
Working Capital	6m	5m	2m
Fixed Assets	5m	4m	7m
Current Assets	12m	10m	7m
Current Liabilities	5m	834	2m

Downhole Products plc
Badentoy Road Badentoy Industrial Estate, Portlethen, Aberdeen, AB12 4YA
Tel: 01224-784411 **Fax:** 01224-785222
E-mail: ian@downhole.co.uk
Website: http://www.downhole.co.uk
Directors: A. Clark (Co Sec), I. Kirk (MD)
Managers: K. Miller
Ultimate Holding Company: ARCAPITA BANK BSC(c) (BAHRAIN)
Immediate Holding Company: DOWNHOLE PRODUCTS LIMITED
Registration no: SC145401 **Date established:** 1993
Turnover: £10m - £20m **No.of Employees:** 21 - 50 **Product Groups:** 40, 45

Date of Accounts	Jul 11	Jul 10	Jul 09
Sales Turnover	17m	10m	9m
Pre Tax Profit/Loss	5m	3m	5m
Working Capital	15m	12m	10m
Fixed Assets	662	645	528
Current Assets	20m	14m	11m
Current Liabilities	2m	114	205

Dresser Rand UK Ltd
Hareness Circle Altens Industrial Estate, Aberdeen, AB12 3LY
Tel: 01224-879445 **Fax:** 01224-894616
E-mail: geoff_king@dresser-rand.com
Website: http://www.dresser-rand.com
Managers: N. Mcglashan (Mgr)
Ultimate Holding Company: DRESSER RAND INC (USA)
Immediate Holding Company: DRESSER -RAND (U.K.) LIMITED
Registration no: 00759945 **Date established:** 1963
Turnover: £20m - £50m **No.of Employees:** 21 - 50 **Product Groups:** 48

Date of Accounts	Dec 11	Dec 10	Dec 09
Sales Turnover	25m	38m	51m
Pre Tax Profit/Loss	5m	6m	11m
Working Capital	24m	22m	19m
Fixed Assets	379	406	446
Current Assets	42m	42m	38m
Current Liabilities	6m	5m	4m

Econosto UK Ltd
Blackness Road Altens Industrial Estate, Aberdeen, AB12 3LH
Tel: 01224-898800 **Fax:** 01224-890882
E-mail: alun.jenkins@econosto.uk.com
Website: http://www.econosto.co.uk
Managers: A. Jenkins (Chief Mgr)
Ultimate Holding Company: SHV HOLDINGS NV (NETHERLANDS)
Immediate Holding Company: ECONOSTO UK LIMITED
Registration no: 01826762 **Date established:** 1984
Turnover: £50m - £75m **No.of Employees:** 1 - 10 **Product Groups:** 36

Date of Accounts	Dec 11	Dec 10	Dec 09
Sales Turnover	11m	11m	14m
Pre Tax Profit/Loss	301	143	1m
Working Capital	2m	2m	2m
Fixed Assets	234	191	141
Current Assets	7m	5m	7m
Current Liabilities	667	407	698

The Emerson Group Ltd
Badentoy Cresent Badentoy Indl-Est, Portlethen, Aberdeen, AB12 4YD
Tel: 01224-783700 **Fax:** 01224-783701
E-mail: john.wellsted@emerson.com
Website: http://www.emerson.co.uk
Bank(s): Bank of Scotland
Directors: J. Masterton (MD), R. Silcock (Dir), A. Milne (Fin), S. Williams (Co Sec)
Managers: F. Ponsonby (Sales & Mktg Mg), J. Wellsted (Reg Sales Mgr), K. Lee (I.T. Exec)
Ultimate Holding Company: EMERSON ELECTRIC CO INC (USA)
Immediate Holding Company: MASTERPOWER ELECTRONICS LIMITED
Registration no: SC129203 **VAT No.:** GB 658 3860 95
Date established: 1991 **Turnover:** £1m - £2m **No.of Employees:** 21 - 50
Product Groups: 52

Date of Accounts	Mar 10	Mar 09	Mar 08
Sales Turnover	2m	11m	8
Pre Tax Profit/Loss	8m	2m	1
Working Capital	11m	3m	1
Fixed Assets	N/A	281	N/A
Current Assets	11m	5m	3
Current Liabilities	124	1m	1

Eriks Industrial Services
Greenwell Road East Tullos Industrial Estate, Aberdeen, AB12 3AX
Tel: 01224-289400 **Fax:** 01224-899627
E-mail: dave.marr@eriks.co.uk
Website: http://www.ERIKS.CO.UK
Bank(s): Bank of Scotland
Managers: D. Marr (Reg Mgr)
Ultimate Holding Company: JOHN WOOD GROUP P.L.C.
Immediate Holding Company: WOOD GROUP ENGINEERING & OPERATIONS SUPPORT LIMITED
Registration no: 03142338 **Date established:** 1995
Turnover: £125m - £250m **No.of Employees:** 21 - 50
Product Groups: 38, 40, 42, 46, 67

Date of Accounts	Dec 11	Dec 10	Dec 09
Working Capital	-3	-3	-3

Eriks UK (MCW Aberdeen)
Greenwell Place East Tullos Industrial Estate, Aberdeen, AB12 3AY
Tel: 01224-898191 **Fax:** 01224-894812
E-mail: aberdeen@eriks.co.uk
Website: http://www.eriks.co.uk
Managers: P. Mcgillivray (Mgr), W. Walker (Sales Prom Mgr), W. Forbes
Ultimate Holding Company: ARYZTA AG (SWITZERLAND)
Immediate Holding Company: UNITED FISH PRODUCTS LIMITED
Registration no: 03142338 **Date established:** 1981 **Turnover:** £1m - £2m
No.of Employees: 21 - 50 **Product Groups:** 83

Exova
Wellheads Way Wellheads Industrial Estate, Aberdeen, AB21 7GD
Tel: 01224-776050 **Fax:** 0121-251 4040
E-mail: europe@exova.com
Website: http://www.exova.com
Directors: J. Williams (Div), A. Burnett (Co Sec), E. Paterson (Develop)
Managers: M. Proctor (Mgr), N. Cartwright (I.T. Exec), N. Griffiths (Consultant)
Immediate Holding Company: LAW LABORATORIES LIMITED
Registration no: 02192582 **Date established:** 2000 **Turnover:** £2m - £5m
No.of Employees: 51 - 100 **Product Groups:** 85

Expro
Kirkhill Place Kirkhill Industrial Estate, Dyce, Aberdeen, AB21 0GU
Tel: 01224-214600 **Fax:** 01224-770295
E-mail: bruce.mackenzie@exprogroup.com
Website: http://www.exprogroup.com
Directors: C. Woodburn (Grp Chief Exec), G. Coupps (MD), G. Watson (Fin), J. Geddes (Pers), K. Drummond (Sales & Mktg), S. Fields (I.T. Dir)
Managers: P. Mccallum (Purch Mgr), L. Roger, L. Dawson
Immediate Holding Company: ABERDEEN SELF STORAGE LTD.
Registration no: SC249944 **Date established:** 2003
Turnover: £125m - £250m **No.of Employees:** 501 - 1000
Product Groups: 51, 85

Eztek Ltd
Eztek House Blackburn Industrial Estate, Kinellar, Aberdeen, AB21 0RX
Tel: 01224-791977 **Fax:** 01224-791399
E-mail: info@eztek.co.uk
Website: http://www.eztek.co.uk
Directors: B. Van Tuijl (MD)
Immediate Holding Company: EZTEK LIMITED
Registration no: SC146531 **Date established:** 1993
Turnover: £250,000 - £500,000 **No.of Employees:** 11 - 20
Product Groups: 37, 38, 44, 45

Date of Accounts	Sep 11	Sep 10	Sep 09
Working Capital	753	545	510
Fixed Assets	174	189	209
Current Assets	1m	725	712

First Point Assessment Ltd
7 Burnbank Business Centre Souter Head Road, Altens Industrial Estate, Aberdeen, AB12 3LF
Tel: 01224-337500 **Fax:** 01224-337522
E-mail: enquiries@fpal.com
Website: http://www.fpal.com
Directors: A. Wilkinson (Fin)
Managers: A. Mackenzie
Immediate Holding Company: FIRST POINT ASSESSMENT LIMITED
Registration no: 03288988 **VAT No.:** GB 678 7952 56
Date established: 1996 **No.of Employees:** 11 - 20 **Product Groups:** 61

Date of Accounts	Apr 04
Sales Turnover	3m
Pre Tax Profit/Loss	-135
Working Capital	-8
Current Assets	1m
Current Liabilities	1m

First Zipper UK Ltd
Orbane House Regent Road, Aberdeen, AB11 5NS
Tel: 01224-576144 **Fax:** 01224-576144
E-mail: billtait@firstzipper.co.uk
Website: http://www.firstzipper.co.uk
Directors: B. Tait (MD), R. Tait (Dir), W. Tait (Dir)
Immediate Holding Company: FIRST ZIPPER (UK) LIMITED
Registration no: SC096397 **Date established:** 1985
Turnover: Up to £250,000 **No.of Employees:** 1 - 10 **Product Groups:** 81

Date of Accounts	Jan 08
Sales Turnover	259
Pre Tax Profit/Loss	4
Working Capital	42
Fixed Assets	26
Current Assets	72
Current Liabilities	29
Total Share Capital	13
ROCE% (Return on Capital Employed)	5.5

A Fleming
19 Laurel Braes Bridge of Don, Aberdeen, AB22 8XY
Tel: 01224-820333
E-mail: info@aflemingcarpetclean.com
Website: http://www.aflemingcarpetclean.com
Directors: A. Fleming (Prop)
Date established: 1987 **No.of Employees:** 1 - 10 **Product Groups:** 23, 32, 52

Flexitallic Ltd
Unit 18d Wellheads Crescent, Wellheads Industrial Estate, Aberdeen, AB21 7GA
Tel: 01224-725241 **Fax:** 01224-722911
E-mail: rmarcella@flexitallic.eu
Website: http://www.flexitallic.eu
Directors: R. Marcella (Dir)
Ultimate Holding Company: OFI PRIVATE EQUITY CAPITAL (FRANCE)
Immediate Holding Company: FLEXITALLIC LTD.
Registration no: 03308289 **VAT No.:** GB 628 8676 84
Date established: 1997 **Turnover:** £20m - £50m **No.of Employees:** 1 - 10
Product Groups: 23, 25, 29, 30, 33, 34, 35, 36, 40, 48

Date of Accounts	Dec 11	Dec 10	Dec 09
Sales Turnover	17m	18m	15m
Pre Tax Profit/Loss	2m	2m	3m
Working Capital	17m	15m	13m
Fixed Assets	4m	4m	4m
Current Assets	21m	23m	21m
Current Liabilities	1m	1m	817

Fugro Survey
Denmore Industrial Estate Denmore Road, Bridge Of Don, Aberdeen, AB23 8JW
Tel: 01224-257500 **Fax:** 01224-853919
E-mail: phil.meaden@fugro.com
Website: http://www.fugro.com
Bank(s): Barclays, London Corporate Banking, PO Box 544, 54 Lombard Street, London, EC3V 9EX
Directors: G. Duncan (Fin), P. Meaden (MD)
Managers: H. Cliffe (Personnel), D. Mason, N. Stewart, S. Black (Contracts Mgr), E. Godding (Mktg Serv Mgr)
Ultimate Holding Company: FUGRO NV (NETHERLANDS)
Immediate Holding Company: FUGRO SURVEY LIMITED
Registration no: SC066833 **VAT No.:** GB 296 9707 89
Date established: 1979 **Turnover:** £50m - £75m
No.of Employees: 101 - 250 **Product Groups:** 39, 51, 84, 85

Date of Accounts	Dec 10	Dec 09	Dec 08
Sales Turnover	64m	50m	55m
Pre Tax Profit/Loss	6m	6m	10m
Working Capital	21m	31m	31m
Fixed Assets	11m	9m	6m
Current Assets	44m	49m	53m
Current Liabilities	8m	8m	10m

G R Fasteners Aberdeen Ltd
Unit 14 Blackhill Industrial Estate Portlethen, Aberdeen, AB12 4RL
Tel: 01224-784449 **Fax:** 01224-784783
E-mail: garyreid@btconnect.com
Directors: G. Reid (Dir)
Immediate Holding Company: G R FASTENERS (ABERDEEN) LIMITED
Registration no: SC393316 **Date established:** 2011
No.of Employees: 1 - 10 **Product Groups:** 35

Grampian Electrodes
44-44a King's Cresent, Aberdeen, AB24 3HL
Tel: 01224-631816 **Fax:** 01224-641107
Website: http://www.grampianelectrodes.co.uk
Directors: M. Macintyre (Prop)
Date established: 1983 **No.of Employees:** 1 - 10 **Product Groups:** 46

Grampian Fastners
Grampian House Pitmedden Road, Dyce, Aberdeen, AB21 0DP
Tel: 01224-772777 **Fax:** 01224-772778
E-mail: sales@grampianfasteners.com
Website: http://www.grampianfasteners.com
Directors: P. Souter (MD)
Managers: D. Barker (Tech Serv Mgr), A. Doyle (Sales Prom Mgr)
No.of Employees: 21 - 50 **Product Groups:** 32, 35, 66

Grampian International Freight Ltd
Mugiemoss Road Bucksburn, Aberdeen, AB21 9NP
Tel: 01224-661000 **Fax:** 01224-661111
E-mail: info@gif.co.uk
Website: http://www.gif.co.uk
Directors: R. Chambers (Dir), G. Tom (MD), N. Wallis (Freight)
Ultimate Holding Company: PANALPINA WORLD TRANSPORT (HOLDING) LTD (SWITZERLAND)
Immediate Holding Company: GRAMPIAN INTERNATIONAL FREIGHT LIMITED
Registration no: SC087714 **Date established:** 1984
Turnover: £20m - £50m **No.of Employees:** 101 - 250 **Product Groups:** 76

Date of Accounts	Dec 11	Dec 10	Dec 09
Working Capital	N/A	N/A	442
Current Assets	N/A	N/A	442

Granite City Events
18 Gairnshiel Avenue, Aberdeen, AB16 5RS
Tel: 07974-397577 **Fax:** 01224-633733
E-mail: info@granitecityevents.com
Website: http://www.granitecityevents.com
Directors: B. Sheriffs (Prop)
No.of Employees: 1 - 10 **Product Groups:** 37, 52, 89

H P F Energy Services
Hareness Road Altens Industrial Estate, Aberdeen, AB12 3LE
Tel: 01224-241640 **Fax:** 01224-241641
E-mail: sales@hpf-energy.com
Website: http://www.hpf-energy.com
Directors: A. Christie (MD)
Immediate Holding Company: COMPASS PRINT HOLDINGS LIMITED
Registration no: SC062202 **Date established:** 2007
Turnover: £20m - £50m **No.of Employees:** 21 - 50 **Product Groups:** 36

Date of Accounts	Jan 12	Jan 11	Jan 10
Working Capital	246	74	11
Fixed Assets	1m	1m	1m
Current Assets	907	669	553

Heath Lambert Group
Denburn House Union Terrace, Aberdeen, AB10 1NN
Tel: 01224-414888 **Fax:** 01224-583933
E-mail: sales@heathlambert.com
Website: http://www.heathlambert.com
Directors: P. Mutch (Dir)
Managers: M. Webster
Ultimate Holding Company: HLG HOLDINGS LIMITED
Immediate Holding Company: HEATH LAMBERT GROUP LIMITED
Registration no: 05347036 **Date established:** 2005
Turnover: £125m - £250m **No.of Employees:** 1 - 10 **Product Groups:** 80, 82

Highland Electroplaters Ltd
Unit 2 Howe Moss Drive Kirkhill Industrial Estate, Dyce, Aberdeen, AB21 0GL
Tel: 01224-725581 **Fax:** 01224-725591
E-mail: norrie@hiplaters.co.uk
Website: http://www.highlandelectroplaters.co.uk
Bank(s): Bank of Scotland
Directors: A. Gray (Fin), N. Jerrard (MD)
Managers: S. Marvin (Tech Serv Mgr)
Ultimate Holding Company: DIESEL MARINE INTERNATIONAL LIMITED
Immediate Holding Company: HIGHLAND ELECTROPLATERS LIMITED
Registration no: SC107064 **VAT No.:** GB 552 9192 27
Date established: 1987 **Turnover:** £1m - £2m **No.of Employees:** 11 - 20
Product Groups: 48

Date of Accounts	Dec 11	Dec 10	Dec 09
Sales Turnover	1m	1m	1m
Pre Tax Profit/Loss	204	179	163
Working Capital	746	685	692
Fixed Assets	26	33	26
Current Assets	999	949	880
Current Liabilities	140	170	132

Hilton Dental Practice
2 Hilton Street, Aberdeen, AB24 4QX
Tel: 01224-486817
E-mail: reception@hiltondentalpractice.co.uk
Website: http://www.hiltondentalpractice.co.uk
Managers: M. Aspey
Date established: 1998 **No.of Employees:** 1 - 10 **Product Groups:** 38, 88

Houlder Ltd
North Point Exploration Drive Aberdeen Science & Energy Park, Bridge Of Don, Aberdeen, AB23 8HZ
Tel: 01224-702200 **Fax:** 01224-703526
E-mail: mike.chew@houlderltd.com
Website: http://www.houlderltd.com
Managers: M. Chew
Ultimate Holding Company: HOULDER BIDCO LIMITED
Immediate Holding Company: HOULDER LIMITED
Registration no: 04400298 **Date established:** 2002
No.of Employees: 11 - 20 **Product Groups:** 84

see next page

***Houlder Ltd** - Cont'd*

Date of Accounts	Dec 11	Dec 10	Dec 09
Sales Turnover	9m	11m	9m
Pre Tax Profit/Loss	249	591	385
Working Capital	1m	2m	2m
Fixed Assets	744	498	97
Current Assets	4m	5m	4m
Current Liabilities	2m	3m	2m

Hydrasun Ltd
Hydrasun House 392 Kings Street, Aberdeen, AB24 3BU
Tel: 01224-618618 **Fax:** 01224-618701
E-mail: info@hydrasun.com
Website: http://www.hydrasun.com
Bank(s): Bank of Scotland
Directors: R. Drummond (MD), B. Drumnlod (Dir), G. Sangster (Sales & Mktg)
Managers: M. Johnson (I.T. Exec), A. Horsburgh (Mktg Serv Mgr)
Immediate Holding Company: HYDRASUN LIMITED
Registration no: SC059688 **VAT No.:** GB 268 0788 20
Date established: 1976 **Turnover:** £50m - £75m
No.of Employees: 101 - 250 **Product Groups:** 30, 36

Hydratight Ltd
Howe Moss Crescent Kirkhill Indl-Est, Dyce, Aberdeen, AB21 0GN
Tel: 01224-215930 **Fax:** 01224-215950
E-mail: aberdeen@hydratight.com
Website: http://www.hydratight.com
Managers: M. Derry (Mgr), S. Clarke (Sales Admin), S. Clark (Mgr)
Ultimate Holding Company: ACTUANT CORP (USA)
Immediate Holding Company: HYDRATIGHT LIMITED
Registration no: 03069889 **Date established:** 1995
No.of Employees: 21 - 50 **Product Groups:** 35, 36, 48, 85

Date of Accounts	Aug 11	Aug 10	Aug 09
Sales Turnover	37m	12m	17m
Pre Tax Profit/Loss	5m	-704	13m
Working Capital	12m	10m	20m
Fixed Assets	9m	3m	3m
Current Assets	52m	20m	28m
Current Liabilities	7m	1m	4m

Hydro Bond Engineering Ltd
Claymore Avenue Bridge Of Don, Aberdeen, AB23 8GW
Tel: 01224-822996 **Fax:** 01224-825142
E-mail: info@hydrohouse.co.uk
Website: http://www.hydrohouse.co.uk
Bank(s): Bank of Scotland
Directors: D. Whyte (Dir), E. Blair (Fin), I. Buxton (Pers)
Managers: D. Reith, N. Smith
Ultimate Holding Company: HYDRO GROUP PLC
Immediate Holding Company: HYDROBOND ENGINEERING LIMITED
Registration no: SC080870 **Date established:** 1982 **Turnover:** £2m - £5m
No.of Employees: 21 - 50 **Product Groups:** 37, 67

Date of Accounts	Mar 12	Mar 11	Mar 10
Sales Turnover	4m	4m	3m
Pre Tax Profit/Loss	108	170	-200
Working Capital	557	399	293
Fixed Assets	549	642	401
Current Assets	2m	2m	1m
Current Liabilities	380	501	599

Hydrocable Systems Ltd
Hydro House Claymore Avenue, Bridge Of Don, Aberdeen, AB23 8GW
Tel: 01224-706611 **Fax:** 01224-706006
E-mail: sales@hydrohouse.co.uk
Website: http://www.hydrohouse.co.uk
Directors: D. Whyte (Dir)
Managers: S. Garden (Mktg Serv Mgr), I. Boxton (Personnel), E. Blair (Comptroller)
Ultimate Holding Company: HYDRO GROUP PLC
Immediate Holding Company: HYDRO-CABLE SYSTEMS LIMITED
Registration no: SC096265 **Date established:** 1985 **Turnover:** £2m - £5m
No.of Employees: 51 - 100 **Product Groups:** 37

Date of Accounts	Mar 12	Mar 11	Mar 10
Sales Turnover	3m	3m	2m
Pre Tax Profit/Loss	24	280	-298
Working Capital	940	838	625
Fixed Assets	489	550	231
Current Assets	1m	2m	1m
Current Liabilities	221	393	367

Iicorr Ltd
1 Minto Place Altens Industrial Estate, Aberdeen, AB12 3SN
Tel: 01224-898282 **Fax:** 01224-898202
E-mail: info@iicorr.com
Website: http://www.iicorr.com
Directors: G. Watson (MD)
Managers: D. Ballantine, D. Morton (Develop Mgr), D. Parr, S. Baston (Ops Mgr), E. Richards (Sales & Mktg Mg), J. Chamberlain
Ultimate Holding Company: Corrision ASA
Immediate Holding Company: IICORR LIMITED
Registration no: SC250015 **Date established:** 2003
Turnover: £10m - £20m **No.of Employees:** 51 - 100 **Product Groups:** 33, 37, 38, 51, 52, 84, 85

Date of Accounts	Dec 07	Dec 06	Dec 05
Sales Turnover	16027	10267	8936
Pre Tax Profit/Loss	927	395	459
Working Capital	3796	2540	1854
Fixed Assets	414	304	343
Current Assets	8543	4903	3784
Current Liabilities	4748	2364	1930
Total Share Capital	100	100	100
ROCE% (Return on Capital Employed)	22.0	13.9	20.9
ROT% (Return on Turnover)	5.8	3.8	5.1

Imes Ltd
Unit C Kettock Lodge Balgownie Drive, Bridge Of Don, Aberdeen, AB22 8GU
Tel: 01224-705777 **Fax:** 01224-824808
E-mail: info@imes-group.com
Website: http://www.imes-group.com
Managers: F. Chatwick
Ultimate Holding Company: IMES GROUP HOLDINGS LIMITED
Immediate Holding Company: BUCHAN INSPECTION LTD.
Registration no: SC091449 **Date established:** 1985 **Turnover:** £2m - £5m
No.of Employees: 11 - 20 **Product Groups:** 38, 84

Date of Accounts	Apr 11	Apr 10	Apr 09
Sales Turnover	N/A	2m	2m
Pre Tax Profit/Loss	-2	-134	161

Working Capital	51	47	153
Fixed Assets	N/A	6	4
Current Assets	68	718	590
Current Liabilities	4	80	107

Independent Corrosion Services Ltd
660 Holburn Street, Aberdeen, AB10 7JQ
Tel: 01224-593366 **Fax:** 01224-319417
E-mail: garry.corbett@btconnect.com
Website: http://www.indcorr.co.uk
Managers: G. Corbett (Mgr)
Immediate Holding Company: INDEPENDENT CORROSION SERVICES LIMITED
Registration no: SC242575 **Date established:** 2003
No.of Employees: 1 - 10 **Product Groups:** 46, 48

Date of Accounts	Mar 12	Mar 11	Mar 10
Working Capital	1	12	11
Fixed Assets	50	46	43
Current Assets	77	97	51

Ingen Ideas Ltd
111 Gallowgate, Aberdeen, AB25 1BU
Tel: 01224-619700 **Fax:** 01224-619749
E-mail: info@ingen-ideas.com
Website: http://www.ingen-ideas.com
Directors: W. Strachan (Comm), A. Robertson (Dir)
Ultimate Holding Company: INGEN HOLDINGS LIMITED
Immediate Holding Company: INGEN-IDEAS LIMITED
Registration no: SC204755 **Date established:** 2000 **Turnover:** £2m - £5m
No.of Employees: 21 - 50 **Product Groups:** 84

Date of Accounts	Mar 11	Mar 10	Mar 09
Working Capital	263	324	195
Fixed Assets	24	41	68
Current Assets	791	1m	1m

Initiative2 Web Site Design
Rosewood Hareburn Road, Bridge of Don, Aberdeen, AB23 8AR
Tel: 01224-820960
E-mail: info@initiative2.com
Website: http://www.initiative2.com
Directors: K. Mackay (Dir)
Turnover: Up to £250,000 **No.of Employees:** 1 - 10 **Product Groups:** 44, 79

Inspectahire Instruments Company Ltd
Unit 11 Whitemyres Business Centre Whitemyres Avenue, Aberdeen, AB16 6HQ
Tel: 01224-789692 **Fax:** 01224-789462
E-mail: enquiries@inspectahire.com
Website: http://www.inspectahire.com
Directors: C. Forrester (MD)
Immediate Holding Company: INSPECTAHIRE INSTRUMENT CO. LTD
Registration no: SC040040 **Date established:** 1999
No.of Employees: 11 - 20 **Product Groups:** 37, 38, 76, 85

Intertech Caleb Brett UK (t/a E M I S)
Unit 19-21 Wellheads Crescent, Wellheads Industrial Estate, Aberdeen, AB21 7GA
Tel: 01224-772540 **Fax:** 01224-772358
E-mail: info@intertech.com
Website: http://www.intertech.com
Bank(s): Royal Bank of Scotland
Managers: J. Petrie
Ultimate Holding Company: INTERTEK GROUP PLC
Immediate Holding Company: R.S. SAFETY SERVICES LIMITED
Registration no: SC176680 **VAT No.:** GB 596 6409 88
Date established: 1993 **Turnover:** £1m - £2m **No.of Employees:** 11 - 20
Product Groups: 85

Date of Accounts	Nov 11	Nov 10	Nov 09
Working Capital	219	55	34
Fixed Assets	932	958	992
Current Assets	519	312	232

Isleburn Ltd
Hareness Road Altens Industrial Estate, Aberdeen, AB12 3LE
Tel: 01224-879700 **Fax:** 01224-879981
E-mail: aberdeen@isleburn.com
Website: http://www.gegroup.com
Directors: D. Masson (Chief Op Offcr)
Ultimate Holding Company: GLOBAL ENERGY (HOLDINGS) LIMITED
Immediate Holding Company: O.I.L. ENGINEERING LIMITED
Registration no: SC072717 **Date established:** 1980 **Turnover:** £2m - £5m
No.of Employees: 101 - 250 **Product Groups:** 42, 84

Date of Accounts	Mar 11	Mar 10	Mar 09
Sales Turnover	5m	10m	14m
Pre Tax Profit/Loss	566	-1m	-757
Working Capital	N/A	-470	494
Fixed Assets	N/A	93	148
Current Assets	N/A	2m	3m
Current Liabilities	N/A	738	1m

J C E Aberdeen Ltd
Blackburn Business Park Woodburn Road, Blackburn, Aberdeen, AB21 0PS
Tel: 01224-798600 **Fax:** 01224-798601
E-mail: info@jcegroup.com
Website: http://www.jcegroup.com
Directors: A. Cox (Fin)
Immediate Holding Company: J C E (ABERDEEN) LIMITED
Registration no: SC095517 **Date established:** 1985
No.of Employees: 21 - 50 **Product Groups:** 35, 37, 40, 48

Date of Accounts	Apr 12	Apr 11	Apr 10
Working Capital	424	418	251
Fixed Assets	597	547	572
Current Assets	3m	2m	2m

J L M Security
43 Rosebank Terrace, Aberdeen, AB11 6LQ
Tel: 01224-594200 **Fax:** 01224-584571
E-mail: jlmlocks@aol.com
Website: http://www.jlmsecurity.com
Directors: J. McComiskie (Prop)
Date established: 1971 **No.of Employees:** 21 - 50 **Product Groups:** 33, 35, 36, 38, 40

Jennifer Jane Stained Glass Ltd
Abbey Studio Fintray, Aberdeen, AB21 0JB
Tel: 01224-791363 **Fax:** 01224-791119
E-mail: jj@jennifer-jane.com
Website: http://www.jennifer-jane.co.uk
Directors: J. Bayliss (Dir)
Immediate Holding Company: JENNIFER-JANE STAINED GLASS LTD
Registration no: SC397758 **Date established:** 2011
No.of Employees: 1 - 10 **Product Groups:** 33

Jewson Ltd
1 Stell Road, Aberdeen, AB11 5QR
Tel: 01224-587399 **Fax:** 01224-583907
E-mail: peter.hindle@jewson.co.uk
Website: http://www.jewson.co.uk
Managers: I. Duncan (District Mgr)
Ultimate Holding Company: COMPAGNIE DE SAINT GOBAIN (FRANCE)
Immediate Holding Company: JEWSON LIMITED
Registration no: 00348407 **Date established:** 1939
Turnover: £500m - £1,000m **No.of Employees:** 21 - 50
Product Groups: 66

Date of Accounts	Dec 11	Dec 10	Dec 09
Sales Turnover	1606m	1547m	1485m
Pre Tax Profit/Loss	18m	100m	45m
Working Capital	-345m	-250m	-349m
Fixed Assets	496m	387m	461m
Current Assets	657m	1005m	1320m
Current Liabilities	66m	120m	64m

John Clark Aberdeen Ltd
Wellington Road West Tullos Industrial Estate, Aberdeen, AB12 3EW
Tel: 01224-335577 **Fax:** 01224-335599
E-mail: ian.henderson@john-clark.co.uk
Website: http://www.johnclarkaberdeenbmw.co.uk
Managers: I. Harrison (Tech Serv Mgr), A. Bishop (Mktg Serv Mgr), J. Stuart (Personnel), G. Dunn (Fin Mgr), I. Henderson (Chief Mgr), K. Simpson
Ultimate Holding Company: JOHN CLARK (HOLDINGS) LIMITED
Immediate Holding Company: JOHN CLARK (ABERDEEN) LIMITED
Registration no: SC063352 **VAT No.:** GB 671 0872 34
Date established: 1977 **Turnover:** £75m - £125m
No.of Employees: 51 - 100 **Product Groups:** 68

Date of Accounts	Dec 10	Dec 09	Dec 08
Sales Turnover	88m	92m	92m
Pre Tax Profit/Loss	1m	1m	-78
Working Capital	137	-725	-666
Fixed Assets	4m	4m	4m
Current Assets	16m	15m	12m
Current Liabilities	8m	7m	6m

John Crane UK Ltd
Grampian House Mugiemoss Road Bucksburn, Aberdeen, AB21 9NP
Tel: 01224-773772 **Fax:** 01224-773900
Website: http://www.johncrane.co.uk
Managers: I. Mcanulty (Reg Sales Mgr)
Ultimate Holding Company: SMITHS GROUP PLC
Immediate Holding Company: JOHN CRANE UK LIMITED
Registration no: 00192121 **Date established:** 2023
Turnover: £50m - £75m **No.of Employees:** 1 - 10 **Product Groups:** 31, 36, 38

Date of Accounts	Jul 11	Jul 10	Jul 09
Sales Turnover	80m	74m	68m
Pre Tax Profit/Loss	15m	17m	4m
Working Capital	77m	62m	49m
Fixed Assets	18m	22m	24m
Current Assets	106m	92m	74m
Current Liabilities	9m	9m	10m

John Smith & Co.
41 Castle Terrace, Aberdeen, AB11 5EA
Tel: 01224-586868 **Fax:** 01224-590768
E-mail: info@johnsmithaberdeen.co.uk
Website: http://www.johnsmithaberdeen.co.uk
Bank(s): Bank of Scotland
Managers: K. Young (Mgr)
Immediate Holding Company: DECCO LTD
Registration no: 00417021 **VAT No.:** GB 431 2745 75
Turnover: £2m - £5m **No.of Employees:** 11 - 20 **Product Groups:** 35, 66

K & L Ross Ltd
303 King Street, Aberdeen, AB24 5AP
Tel: 01224-339800 **Fax:** 01224-339801
E-mail: lucy@klross.com
Website: http://www.klross.com
Directors: L. Stewart (Fin), L. Ross (Fin), L. Ross (Prop), M. Ross (MD)
Managers: A. Milne (Develop Mgr)
Immediate Holding Company: K & L ROSS LIMITED
Registration no: SC227623 **Date established:** 2002
Turnover: £5m - £10m **No.of Employees:** 21 - 50 **Product Groups:** 24, 40, 63, 67

Date of Accounts	Feb 11	Feb 10	Feb 09
Sales Turnover	8m	8m	N/A
Pre Tax Profit/Loss	695	713	684
Working Capital	632	876	666
Fixed Assets	955	980	972
Current Assets	3m	3m	2m
Current Liabilities	895	636	612

Klinger Ltd
Unit 31 Wellheads Crescent, Wellheads Industrial Estate, Aberdeen, AB21 7GA
Tel: 01224-772962 **Fax:** 01224-772953
E-mail: aberdeen@klingeruk.co.uk
Website: http://www.klingeruk.co.uk
Managers: D. Sorrie (Mgr)
Ultimate Holding Company: BETAL NETHERLAND HOLDING BV (NETHERLANDS)
Immediate Holding Company: KLINGER LIMITED
Registration no: 01021936 **Date established:** 1971
No.of Employees: 1 - 10 **Product Groups:** 38, 42

Date of Accounts	Dec 11	Dec 10	Dec 09
Sales Turnover	27m	23m	24m
Pre Tax Profit/Loss	5m	4m	3m
Working Capital	8m	8m	9m
Fixed Assets	2m	1m	2m
Current Assets	11m	11m	12m
Current Liabilities	1m	1m	844

Labtech Services Ltd
Blackness Road Altens Industrial Estate, Aberdeen, AB12 3LH
Tel: 01224-337777 **Fax:** 01224-337770
E-mail: david.soper@labtechmodular.com
Website: http://www.labtechmodular.com
Directors: D. Soper (Dir)
Managers: A. Duguid (Sales Prom Mgr), L. Bruce, G. Charles (Fin Mgr), D. Gordon

Ultimate Holding Company: GLOBAL ENERGY (HOLDINGS) LIMITED
Immediate Holding Company: LABTECH SERVICES LIMITED
Registration no: SC083070 **Date established:** 1983
Turnover: £10m - £20m **No.of Employees:** 101 - 250
Product Groups: 25, 35, 39, 69, 83

Date of Accounts	Mar 12	Mar 11	Mar 10
Sales Turnover	13m	10m	8m
Pre Tax Profit/Loss	1m	385	-291
Working Capital	2m	1m	1m
Fixed Assets	343	324	124
Current Assets	6m	3m	3m
Current Liabilities	2m	670	800

Langstane Press Ltd (Head Office & Office Products Division)

1 Links Place, Aberdeen, AB11 5DY
Tel: 01224-212212 **Fax:** 01224-210066
E-mail: sales@langstane.co.uk
Website: http://www.langstane.co.uk
Directors: J. McWhinnie (Fin), C. Campbell (MD)
Managers: K. McAuley (Personnel), G. Hume (Mktg Serv Mgr), M. Glennie (Tech Serv Mgr), S. Brown (Purch Mgr)
Immediate Holding Company: LANGSTANE PRESS LIMITED
Registration no: SC062202 **VAT No.:** GB 296 5525 18
Date established: 1977 **Turnover:** £20m - £50m
No.of Employees: 101 - 250 **Product Groups:** 64, 66, 67

Date of Accounts	Apr 12	Apr 11	Apr 10
Sales Turnover	22m	20m	21m
Pre Tax Profit/Loss	373	85	-200
Working Capital	1m	1m	949
Fixed Assets	4m	4m	4m
Current Assets	6m	5m	5m
Current Liabilities	571	419	441

Learn It International

St Marys Court 47c Huntly Street, Aberdeen, AB10 1TH
Tel: 01224-793900 **Fax:** 01224-620165
E-mail: neil.harkin@learn-it.net
Website: http://www.learn-it.net
Directors: T. Small (MD), A. Carmicheal (MD), N. Harkin (Comm)
Managers: N. Harkin (Chief Mgr)
Immediate Holding Company: LEARN-IT INTERNATIONAL LIMITED
Registration no: 01632810 **Date established:** 1982 **Turnover:** £1m - £2m
No.of Employees: 1 - 10 **Product Groups:** 44, 80, 86

Date of Accounts	Dec 10	Dec 09	Dec 08
Working Capital	-7	58	145
Fixed Assets	6	18	35
Current Assets	239	230	234

Lloyds Register Integrity Management

25 Denburn House Union Terrace, Aberdeen, AB10 1NN
Tel: 01224-267400 **Fax:** 01224-267401
E-mail: marcus.jones@lr.org
Website: http://www.lr.org
Bank(s): National Westminster
Managers: J. Rose (Tech Serv Mgr), S. Cushmie (Fin Mgr), N. McGilbry (Personnel), K. Anderson (Mktg Serv Mgr), T. Walsh (Chief Mgr), D. Anderson (Personnel), K. Anderson (Mktg Serv Mgr), Z. Davies (Fin Mgr), J. Rose (I.T. Exec)
Registration no: 02275620 **VAT No.:** GB 481 1563 51
Turnover: £250m - £500m **No.of Employees:** 251 - 500
Product Groups: 84, 85

M B Air Systems Ltd

Wellheads Road Farburn Industrial Estate, Dyce, Aberdeen, AB21 7HG
Tel: 01224-723434 **Fax:** 01224-723545
E-mail: sales@mbairsystems.co.uk
Website: http://www.mbairsystems.co.uk
Bank(s): Clydesdale, London
Directors: S. Harkin (Dir)
Immediate Holding Company: MB AIR SYSTEMS LIMITED
Registration no: SC210643 **VAT No.:** GB 556 5568 04
Date established: 2000 **No.of Employees:** 11 - 20 **Product Groups:** 40, 42

Date of Accounts	Dec 11	Dec 10	Dec 09
Sales Turnover	16m	14m	14m
Pre Tax Profit/Loss	604	540	530
Working Capital	965	632	390
Fixed Assets	1m	1m	1m
Current Assets	6m	4m	4m
Current Liabilities	3m	3m	2m

M S I Oilfield Products

Units 5-6 Murcar Industrial Estate Denmore Road, Bridge Of Don, Aberdeen, AB23 8JW
Tel: 01224-708011 **Fax:** 01224-708022
E-mail: bherd@msiproducts.com
Website: http://www.msiproducts.com
Managers: B. Herd (Chief Mgr)
Ultimate Holding Company: BUNZL P.L.C.
Immediate Holding Company: MOSS PLASTIC PARTS LTD
Registration no: 00547495 **Turnover:** £1m - £2m
No.of Employees: 1 - 10 **Product Groups:** 30

Mackay Marine Services Ltd

6 Raik Road, Aberdeen, AB11 5QL
Tel: 01224-575772 **Fax:** 01224-575713
E-mail: sales@mackay-marine.co.uk
Website: http://www.mackay-marine.co.uk
Directors: G. Mackay (MD)
Immediate Holding Company: MACKAY MARINE SERVICES LIMITED
Registration no: SC229170 **Date established:** 2002
No.of Employees: 1 - 10 **Product Groups:** 35, 36, 39

Date of Accounts	Jun 11	Jun 10	Jun 09
Working Capital	865	661	646
Fixed Assets	95	105	109
Current Assets	979	762	783

Maclay Murray & Spens LLP

66 Queens Road, Aberdeen, AB15 4YE
Tel: 01224-356130 **Fax:** 01224-356131
E-mail: lawyer@mms.co.uk
Website: http://www.mms.co.uk
Bank(s): Bank of Scotland
Directors: C. Smylie (Grp Chief Exec)
Ultimate Holding Company: MATTIOLI WOODS PLC
Immediate Holding Company: MACLAY MURRAY & SPENS LLP
Registration no: SO300744 **Date established:** 2005
Turnover: £5m - £10m **No.of Employees:** 21 - 50 **Product Groups:** 80

Date of Accounts	May 11	May 10	May 09
Sales Turnover	47m	52m	55m
Pre Tax Profit/Loss	13m	15m	14m
Working Capital	13m	16m	15m
Fixed Assets	6m	5m	6m
Current Assets	24m	27m	27m
Current Liabilities	8m	9m	8m

Maclean Electrical (t/a Maclean Electrical)

Plot 6 Peterseat Park Peterseat Drive Altens Industrial Estate, Altens Industrial Estate, Aberdeen, AB12 3HT
Tel: 01224-894212 **Fax:** 01224-894214
E-mail: aberdeen@maclean.co.uk
Website: http://www.maclean.co.uk
Managers: A. Freeland (Fin Mgr), C. Innis, J. Hepburn (Sales Prom Mgr), M. Bruce (Mgr)
Ultimate Holding Company: ROWAN COMPANIES INC (USA)
Immediate Holding Company: ROWAN DRILLING (UK) LIMITED
Registration no: SC224908 **VAT No.:** GB 296 9015 21
Date established: 1977 **Turnover:** £20m - £50m
No.of Employees: 51 - 100 **Product Groups:** 30, 31

Maersk Oil GB Ltd

Maersk House Crawpeel Road, Altens Indl-Est, Aberdeen, AB12 3LG
Tel: 01224-242000 **Fax:** 01224-242116
E-mail: nicola.mccloud@maerskoil.com
Website: http://www.maerskoil.com
Directors: B. Hemming (Co Sec), K. Troost (Dir), M. Jensen (MD), V. Rasmusdsen (Fin), N. Mccloud (Fin)
Managers: B. Svejso (I.T. Exec)
Ultimate Holding Company: AP MOLLER MAERSK A/S (DENMARK)
Immediate Holding Company: MAERSK OIL GB LIMITED
Registration no: 03530988 **Date established:** 1998
Turnover: £250m - £500m **No.of Employees:** 251 - 500
Product Groups: 13, 51

Date of Accounts	Dec 07
Pre Tax Profit/Loss	187290
Working Capital	-625560
Fixed Assets	1582m
Current Assets	829250
Current Liabilities	1455m
Total Share Capital	992730
ROCE% (Return on Capital Employed)	19.6

Magic Carpet

12 Abbotswell Drive, Aberdeen, AB12 5QN
Tel: 0800-783 7969
E-mail: info@magic-carpet.net
Website: http://www.magic-carpet.net
Directors: M. Rae (Prop)
Immediate Holding Company: FILIPE RIBEIRO LIMITED
Date established: 2010 **No.of Employees:** 1 - 10 **Product Groups:** 23, 32, 52

Date of Accounts	Apr 11
Working Capital	2
Current Assets	17

Mansell Construction Ltd

Granitehill Road, Aberdeen, AB16 7AW
Tel: 01224-717700 **Fax:** 01224-698262
E-mail: sales@mansell.plc.uk
Website: http://www.constructingcommunities.com
Bank(s): Clydesdale Bank PLC
Directors: G. Hood (MD)
Managers: I. Harrison (Fin Mgr), A. Garvie (I.T. Exec), D. Parkes (Personnel)
Ultimate Holding Company: BALFOUR BEATTY PLC
Immediate Holding Company: MANSELL CONSTRUCTION LTD
Registration no: 03622132 **VAT No.:** GB 265 4020 80
Date established: 1998 **Turnover:** £50m - £75m
No.of Employees: 101 - 250 **Product Groups:** 52, 66

Date of Accounts	Sep 10	Sep 09	Sep 08
Working Capital	55	42	50
Current Assets	97	102	121
Current Liabilities	N/A	60	71

Marinetronix Ltd

Unit 1 Airside Business Park Dyce, Aberdeen, AB21 0GT
Tel: 01224-774423 **Fax:** 01224-724396
E-mail: info@marinetronix.co.uk
Website: http://www.marinetronix.co.uk
Directors: D. Lorimer (Dir)
Immediate Holding Company: MARINETRONIX LIMITED
Registration no: SC293752 **Date established:** 2005
Turnover: £250,000 - £500,000 **No.of Employees:** 1 - 10
Product Groups: 45

Date of Accounts	Mar 12	Mar 11	Mar 10
Working Capital	133	178	75
Fixed Assets	108	77	90
Current Assets	176	247	131

Masterflo Valve Co UK Ltd

Blackness Road Altens Industrial Estate, Aberdeen, AB12 3LH
Tel: 01224-878999 **Fax:** 01224-878989
E-mail: info@masterflo.com
Website: http://www.masterflo.co.uk
Directors: L. Lambert (Co Sec)
Managers: D. Stewart (Ops Mgr), M. Perry (Sales Prom Mgr)
Ultimate Holding Company: STREAM-FLO INDUSTRIES LTD (CANADA)
Immediate Holding Company: MASTER FLO VALVE CO. (UK) LTD.
Registration no: 01907273 **VAT No.:** GB 391 6128 45
Date established: 1985 **Turnover:** £50m - £75m
No.of Employees: 11 - 20 **Product Groups:** 36

Date of Accounts	Mar 12	Mar 11	Mar 10
Sales Turnover	7m	8m	11m
Pre Tax Profit/Loss	584	126	621
Working Capital	2m	2m	3m
Fixed Assets	345	314	343
Current Assets	3m	2m	4m
Current Liabilities	351	313	440

Metrol Technology Ltd

Unit 24 Kirkhill Place Dyce, Aberdeen, AB21 0GU
Tel: 01224-772771 **Fax:** 01224-772660
E-mail: dsmith@metrol.co.uk
Website: http://www.metrol.co.uk
Directors: S. Ross (MD)
Managers: D. Pearson (Fin Mgr), S. Davidson (Purch Mgr), D. Moss (Sales Prom Mgr), M. Lane (Tech Serv Mgr)
Ultimate Holding Company: DUNWILCO (194) LIMITED
Immediate Holding Company: METROL TECHNOLOGY LIMITED
Registration no: SC105658 **Date established:** 1987
Turnover: £20m - £50m **No.of Employees:** 101 - 250
Product Groups: 42, 45

Date of Accounts	Jun 10	Jun 09	Jun 08
Sales Turnover	29m	28m	17m
Pre Tax Profit/Loss	15m	16m	8m
Working Capital	8m	17m	7m
Fixed Assets	6m	5m	3m
Current Assets	19m	29m	17m
Current Liabilities	6m	11m	7m

Charles W Michie Ltd

54 Park Road, Aberdeen, AB24 5PA
Tel: 01224-632281 **Fax:** 01224-649012
E-mail: carolyn@michietransport.co.uk
Website: http://www.michietransport.co.uk
Bank(s): Lloyds TSB, School Road
Directors: C. Michie (MD), F. Michie (Dir), V. Michie (Dir), C. Michie (Dir)
Managers: D. Mattherson (Admin Off)
Immediate Holding Company: CHARLES W. MICHIE LIMITED
Registration no: SC031768 **Date established:** 1956 **Turnover:** £1m - £2m
No.of Employees: 21 - 50 **Product Groups:** 72, 77

Date of Accounts	Mar 08	Mar 07	Mar 06
Working Capital	2423	564	413
Fixed Assets	298	691	764
Current Assets	2788	938	765
Current Liabilities	365	374	353
Total Share Capital	10	10	10

Mondi

Mugiemoss Works Bucksburn, Aberdeen, AB21 9AA
Tel: 01224-712881 **Fax:** 01224-716154
E-mail: alan.stewart@mondigroup.com
Website: http://www.mondigroup.com
Directors: A. Stewart (MD), D. Ellerington (Sales & Mktg)
Managers: A. Craib (Purch Mgr), C. Rothney, S. Milne (Comptroller), G. Retz (Tech Serv Mgr)
Ultimate Holding Company: MONDI PLC
Immediate Holding Company: MONDI ABERDEEN LTD
Registration no: SC261434 **Date established:** 2004
No.of Employees: 51 - 100 **Product Groups:** 38, 42

Ms Services

18 Esk Place, Aberdeen, AB16 6SQ
Tel: 01224-691742 **Fax:** 01224-691742
E-mail: msservices@fsmail.net
Website: http://www.msservices.co.uk
Directors: M. Stewart (Ptnr)
Immediate Holding Company: PDME LTD
Date established: 2010 **No.of Employees:** 1 - 10 **Product Groups:** 36, 48, 52, 66

Date of Accounts	Oct 11
Working Capital	3
Fixed Assets	1
Current Assets	33

N Sys

Balgownie Road Bridge of Don, Aberdeen, AB22 8GT
Tel: 08450-559944 **Fax:** 08450-559945
Website: http://www.nsystems.co.uk
Directors: D. Escott (Mkt Research), J. Keating (MD)
Immediate Holding Company: KONGSBERG INTELLIFIELD LIMITED
Registration no: SC267393 **Date established:** 2006
No.of Employees: 11 - 20 **Product Groups:** 44

Date of Accounts	Sep 07	Sep 06	Sep 05
Sales Turnover	475	844	N/A
Working Capital	-34	-150	-255
Fixed Assets	N/A	138	202
Current Assets	92	81	159
Current Liabilities	126	231	414
Total Share Capital	1	1	1

National Oilwell Varco Mission Products

24 Howe Moss Drive Dyce, Aberdeen, AB21 0GL
Tel: 01224-771877 **Fax:** 01224-771848
E-mail: info@nov.com
Website: http://www.nov.com
Managers: R. Menzies (Sales Prom Mgr)
Ultimate Holding Company: INSTOCK DISPOSABLES LIMITED
Immediate Holding Company: INSTOCK DISPOSABLES LIMITED
Registration no: SC352079 **Date established:** 1974
Turnover: £10m - £20m **No.of Employees:** 1 - 10 **Product Groups:** 45

Date of Accounts	Mar 11	Mar 10	Mar 09
Sales Turnover	12m	11m	N/A
Pre Tax Profit/Loss	164	13	5
Working Capital	1m	1m	985
Fixed Assets	406	515	1m
Current Assets	3m	3m	3m
Current Liabilities	579	531	414

Nationwide Access Ltd

Unit 1Forties Industrial Centre Hareness Circle, Altens Industrial Estate, Aberdeen, AB12 3LY
Tel: 0845-745 0000 **Fax:** 01382-835916
E-mail: dundee@nationwideplatforms.co.uk
Website: http://www.nationwideaccess.co.uk
Directors: H. Cole (MD)
Managers: G. Gurley (Sales Prom Mgr), K. Louch (Mgr)
Ultimate Holding Company: Lavendon Group plc
Immediate Holding Company: Zooom Holdings UK Ltd
Registration no: 04405299 **Turnover:** £20m - £50m
No.of Employees: 1 - 10 **Product Groups:** 45, 83

Nationwide Platforms

Unit 1 Forties Industrial Centre, Hareness Circle, Aberdeen, AB12 3LY
Tel: 0845-7450000 **Fax:** 01382-835916
E-mail: dundee@nationwideplatforms.co.uk
Website: http://www.nationwideplatforms.co.uk
Directors: D. Shipman (MD), H. Walters (Mkt Research), T. Stokes (Reg)
Managers: L. Wyville (District Mgr)
Ultimate Holding Company: Lavendon Group plc
Immediate Holding Company: Panther Platform Rentals Ltd
Registration no: 04405299 **Turnover:** £20m - £50m
No.of Employees: 1 - 10 **Product Groups:** 45, 83

Navigation Engineering Services Ltd
9 Summer Street Woodside, Aberdeen, AB24 4EY
Tel: 01224-276924 **Fax:** 0871-9892090
E-mail: stuart@underwaterinspection.co.uk
Website: http://www.underwaterinspection.co.uk
Directors: S. McCall (Fin)
Registration no: SC283222 **Date established:** 2005
No.of Employees: 1 - 10 **Product Groups:** 39

New Arc Aberdeen Ltd
Unit 4 Howe Moss Drive, Dyce, Aberdeen, AB21 0GL
Tel: 01224-771063 **Fax:** 01224-724536
E-mail: john.fulton@newarc.co.uk
Website: http://www.newarc.co.uk
Managers: J. Fulton (Ops Mgr)
Immediate Holding Company: NEWARC (ABERDEEN) LIMITED
Registration no: 07942630 **Date established:** 2012
No.of Employees: 1 - 10 **Product Groups:** 46

Date of Accounts	Mar 11	Mar 10	Mar 09
Working Capital	374	176	291
Fixed Assets	76	57	50
Current Assets	2m	1m	1m
Current Liabilities	32	219	75

North Offshore Ltd
Saltire House Blackness Avenue, Altens Industrial Estate, Aberdeen, AB12 3PG
Tel: 01224-871906 **Fax:** 01224-878828
E-mail: iancampbell@northgroup.co.uk
Website: http://www.northgroup.co.uk
Bank(s): The Royal Bank of Scotland
Directors: A. Hayes (Fin), I. Campbell (MD), J. Cambell (MD)
Managers: T. Thomson (Personnel)
Ultimate Holding Company: NORTH GROUP LIMITED
Immediate Holding Company: NORTH OFFSHORE LIMITED
Registration no: SC328499 **Date established:** 2007
Turnover: £5m - £10m **No.of Employees:** 51 - 100 **Product Groups:** 48

Date of Accounts	Oct 11	Oct 10	Oct 09
Sales Turnover	10m	8m	10m
Pre Tax Profit/Loss	585	134	265
Working Capital	681	261	146
Fixed Assets	73	63	70
Current Assets	3m	2m	2m
Current Liabilities	2m	978	874

Oceaneering International Services Ltd
Oceaneering House Pitmedden Road, Dyce, Aberdeen, AB21 0DP
Tel: 01224-758500 **Fax:** 01224-758519
E-mail: ghayward@oceaneering.com
Website: http://www.oceaneering.com
Managers: D. Ass (Personnel), G. Hayward, M. McKimmie (Tech Serv Mgr), R. Mitchell (Buyer)
Ultimate Holding Company: AGR GROUP ASA (NORWAY)
Immediate Holding Company: OCEANEERING ASSET INTEGRITY LIMITED
Registration no: SC304564 **Date established:** 2006
Turnover: £500,000 - £1m **No.of Employees:** 251 - 500
Product Groups: 34, 38, 85, 86

Date of Accounts	Dec 11	Dec 10	Dec 09
Sales Turnover	3m	503	679
Pre Tax Profit/Loss	303	-285	-166
Working Capital	-384	-620	-440
Fixed Assets	27	41	66
Current Assets	859	140	69
Current Liabilities	316	28	22

Oil States Industries UK Ltd
Blackness Road Altens Industrial Estate, Aberdeen, AB12 3LH
Tel: 01224-290000 **Fax:** 01224-896199
E-mail: mick.mccafferty@oilstates-uk.com
Website: http://www.oilstates.com
Bank(s): Barclays
Directors: G. Stephen (MD), P. Dalgarno (Fin)
Managers: J. Ramsay (Buyer), B. Mutch (Mktg Serv Mgr), J. Dolson (Tech Serv Mgr), M. Mccafferty (Chief Mgr), N. Gall (Personnel)
Ultimate Holding Company: OIL STATES INTERNATIONAL INC (U.S.A)
Immediate Holding Company: OIL STATES INDUSTRIES (UK) LIMITED
Registration no: SC163254 **VAT No.:** GB 297 2154 36
Date established: 1996 **Turnover:** £20m - £50m
No.of Employees: 101 - 250 **Product Groups:** 36

Date of Accounts	Dec 11	Dec 10	Dec 09
Sales Turnover	65m	34m	54m
Pre Tax Profit/Loss	18m	9m	13m
Working Capital	52m	55m	48m
Fixed Assets	17m	7m	9m
Current Assets	75m	69m	59m
Current Liabilities	17m	7m	10m

P P G Proactive & Marine Coatings Ltd
Unit 4-5 Greenbank Business Centre Greenbank Road, East Tullos Industrial Estate, Aberdeen, AB12 3BN
Tel: 01224-899300 **Fax:** 01224-896323
E-mail: ray.davies@ppg.com
Website: http://www.ppg.com
Managers: R. Davies
Immediate Holding Company: CAMMACH GROUP LIMITED
Date established: 1997 **No.of Employees:** 1 - 10 **Product Groups:** 46, 48

Date of Accounts	Dec 07	Dec 06	Dec 05
Sales Turnover	1809	6990	2932
Pre Tax Profit/Loss	579	404	429
Working Capital	1275	882	428
Fixed Assets	38	55	73
Current Assets	2038	3468	3829
Current Liabilities	763	2587	3402
ROCE% (Return on Capital Employed)	44.1	43.1	85.7
ROT% (Return on Turnover)	32.0	5.8	14.6

Paladon Systems Ltd
Unit 3 House 4 Howe Moss Drive Kirkhill Industrial Estate, Dyce, Aberdeen, AB21 0GL
Tel: 01224-772442 **Fax:** 01224-772868
E-mail: brian.ennever@paladonsystems.com
Website: http://www.paladonsystems.com
Directors: B. Ennever (MD)
Managers: I. Dryburgh (Mgr), J. Grant (Develop Mgr)
Ultimate Holding Company: INSTOCK DISPOSABLES LIMITED
Immediate Holding Company: PALADON SYSTEMS LIMITED
Registration no: 01592919 **Date established:** 1981
No.of Employees: 1 - 10 **Product Groups:** 36, 37, 38

Date of Accounts	Mar 11	Mar 10	Mar 09
Working Capital	-26	-26	-26
Current Liabilities	26	N/A	N/A

Paradigm Geo-Physical UK Ltd
Mackenzie Buildings 168 Skene Street, Aberdeen, AB10 1PE
Tel: 01224-649555 **Fax:** 01224-649496
Website: http://www.paradigmgeo.com
Directors: S. Hunt (MD), E. Jansen (Mkt Research)
Managers: R. Innes (Sales Prom Mgr), M. Rae (Sales Admin)
Immediate Holding Company: Paradigm
Registration no: SC086248 **VAT No.:** GB 415 8917 32
Date established: 1985 **Turnover:** £1m - £2m **No.of Employees:** 11 - 20
Product Groups: 44

Petrasco Services Ltd
Freight House Kirkhill Place Kirkhill Industrial Estate, Dyce, Aberdeen, AB21 0GU
Tel: 01224-337733 **Fax:** 01224-770729
E-mail: enquiries@petrasco.co.uk
Website: http://www.petrasco.co.uk
Managers: L. Bremner (Sales Prom Mgr), J. Cunningham (District Mgr), C. Coombe
Ultimate Holding Company: J. & J. DENHOLM LIMITED
Immediate Holding Company: PETRASCO SERVICES LIMITED
Registration no: SC280844 **Date established:** 2005
No.of Employees: 21 - 50 **Product Groups:** 72, 74

Petrofac
Bridge View 1 North Esplanade West, Aberdeen, AB11 5QF
Tel: 01224-247000 **Fax:** 01224-247001
E-mail: eleanor.bentley@petrofac.com
Website: http://www.petrofac.com
Directors: K. Martin (Fin), E. Bentley (Fin)
Ultimate Holding Company: PETROFAC LTD (JERSEY)
Immediate Holding Company: PETROFAC FACILITIES MANAGEMENT GROUP LIMITED
Registration no: SC109608 **VAT No.:** GB 553 2397 38
Date established: 1988 **Turnover:** £250m - £500m
No.of Employees: 501 - 1000 **Product Groups:** 13, 38, 39, 42, 45, 48, 51, 52, 68, 84

Date of Accounts	Dec 11	Dec 10	Dec 09
Pre Tax Profit/Loss	N/A	3m	6m
Working Capital	16m	16m	-3m
Fixed Assets	4m	4m	4m
Current Assets	19m	19m	83

Pipelines Centre
1 Blackness Industrial Centre Blackness Road, Altens Industrial Estate, Aberdeen, AB12 3LH
Tel: 01224-872990 **Fax:** 01224-890861
E-mail: zo.aberdeen@wolseley.co.uk
Website: http://www.worsley.co.uk
Directors: I. Mills (Div)
Managers: P. Middleton (Sales Prom Mgr), P. Middleton (District Mgr)
Ultimate Holding Company: British Fittings Group P.L.C.
Registration no: 00636455 **Turnover:** Over £1,000m
No.of Employees: 1 - 10 **Product Groups:** 30, 35, 36, 38, 39, 40, 41, 42, 45, 46

Planning & Environmental Services (Aberdeenshire Council)
Woodhill House Westburn Road, Aberdeen, AB16 5GB
Tel: 01224-665510 **Fax:** 01224-664713
E-mail: wendy.thaine@aberdeenshire.gov.uk
Website: http://www.aberdeenshire.gov.uk
Directors: C. Gore (Dir)
Managers: J. Knowles (Mgr)
No.of Employees: 1501 & over **Product Groups:** 80, 82

Quartzelec
51 York Street, Aberdeen, AB11 5DP
Tel: 01224-593008 **Fax:** 01224-592844
E-mail: dave.murray@quartzelec.com
Website: http://www.quartzelec.com
Bank(s): National Westminster Bank Plc
Managers: D. Murray (Mgr)
Immediate Holding Company: QUARTZINVEST LTD
Registration no: 02364716 **VAT No.:** GB 380 8290 39
Date established: 2004 **Turnover:** £20m - £50m
No.of Employees: 21 - 50 **Product Groups:** 48

R B G
Norfolk House Pitmedden Road, Dyce, Aberdeen, AB21 0DP
Tel: 01224-722888 **Fax:** 01224-773568
E-mail: sales@rbgltd.com
Website: http://www.rbgltd.com
Bank(s): Bank of Scotland
Directors: B. Chisholm (Fin)
Ultimate Holding Company: STORK TECHNICAL SERVICES (HOLDINGS) LIMITED
Immediate Holding Company: MACH-TEN OFFSHORE LIMITED
Registration no: SC152300 **VAT No.:** GB 671 0055 66
Date established: 1994 **Turnover:** £250m - £500m
No.of Employees: 251 - 500 **Product Groups:** 84

Date of Accounts	Dec 10	Dec 09	Dec 08
Working Capital	561	561	561
Current Assets	561	561	561

R E D S Services
5 Spires Business Units Mugiemoss Road, Bucksburn, Aberdeen, AB21 9NY
Tel: 01224-693284 **Fax:** 01224-699687
E-mail: info@redsservices.co.uk
Website: http://www.redsservices.co.uk
Directors: D. Higgs (Prop)
Date established: 1996 **No.of Employees:** 1 - 10 **Product Groups:** 38, 42

Ramco Tubular Services Ltd
Badentoy Road Badentoy Park Badentoy Industrial Estate, Portlethen, Aberdeen, AB12 4YA
Tel: 01224-782278 **Fax:** 01224-783001
E-mail: info@ramco-plc.com
Website: http://www.ramcotubular.co.uk
Directors: M. Edward (Co Sec), N. Cumming (MD), R. Taylor (Tech Serv)
Managers: S. Patterson (Comptroller), R. Slater (Sales & Mktg Mg)
Ultimate Holding Company: RAMCO HOLDINGS LIMITED
Immediate Holding Company: RAMCO TUBULAR SERVICES LIMITED
Registration no: SC099251 **VAT No.:** GB 384 7602 27
Date established: 1986 **Turnover:** £5m - £10m
No.of Employees: 51 - 100 **Product Groups:** 54

Date of Accounts	Dec 11	Dec 10	Dec 09
Sales Turnover	9m	8m	8m
Pre Tax Profit/Loss	1m	1m	1m
Working Capital	1m	-106	-1m
Fixed Assets	14m	14m	14m
Current Assets	13m	10m	11m
Current Liabilities	2m	1m	1m

Redstor
Torridon House 73-75 Regent Quay, Aberdeen, AB11 5AR
Tel: 01224-595381
E-mail: paul.esson@redstor.com
Website: http://www.redstor.com
Managers: P. Esson (District Mgr)
No.of Employees: 1 - 10 **Product Groups:** 35, 42, 45

Reed Specialist Recruitment
122a Union Street, Aberdeen, AB10 1JJ
Tel: 01224-643235 **Fax:** 01224-643240
E-mail: enquiries@reedemployment.co.uk
Website: http://www.reed.co.uk
Directors: J. Reed (MD)
Ultimate Holding Company: REED GLOBAL LTD (MALTA)
Immediate Holding Company: REED EMPLOYMENT LIMITED
Registration no: 00669854 **Date established:** 1960
Turnover: £75m - £125m **No.of Employees:** 1 - 10 **Product Groups:** 80

Date of Accounts	Jun 11	Jun 10	Dec 07
Sales Turnover	618	450	287m
Pre Tax Profit/Loss	-2m	310	8m
Working Capital	23m	28m	28m
Fixed Assets	31	36	5m
Current Assets	28m	30m	74m
Current Liabilities	37	29	21m

Refer Scientific
Hareburn House Bridge Of Don, Aberdeen, AB23 8BT
Tel: 01224-825394 **Fax:** 01224-706324
E-mail: info@labsmart.co.uk
Website: http://www.labsmart.co.uk
Directors: K. Ferrier (Ptnr)
VAT No.: GB 361 0190 91 **Date established:** 1981
Turnover: £500,000 - £1m **No.of Employees:** 1 - 10 **Product Groups:** 67

Rider Hunt International Ltd
9 Carden Place, Aberdeen, AB10 1UR
Tel: 01224-650222 **Fax:** 01224-631289
E-mail: elizabeth.robertson@rhi-group.com
Website: http://www.rhi-group.com
Bank(s): National Westminster Bank Plc
Managers: B. Sutherland (Ops Mgr)
Ultimate Holding Company: AMEC P L C
Immediate Holding Company: RIDER HUNT INTERNATIONAL LIMITED
Registration no: 02305615 **VAT No.:** GB 577 4701 13
Date established: 1988 **Turnover:** Up to £250,000
No.of Employees: 21 - 50 **Product Groups:** 51, 80, 84

Date of Accounts	Dec 11	Dec 10	Dec 09
Sales Turnover	8m	9m	10m
Pre Tax Profit/Loss	375	557	313
Working Capital	4m	4m	3m
Fixed Assets	114	110	226
Current Assets	5m	4m	4m
Current Liabilities	564	270	692

Ritson Smith
16 Carden Place, Aberdeen, AB10 1FX
Tel: 01224-643311 **Fax:** 01224-624359
E-mail: admin@ritson-smith.com
Website: http://www.ritson-smith.com
Bank(s): Bank of Scotland
Directors: N. Harper (Snr Part), N. Farquharson (Ptnr)
Managers: E. Alexander, J. Main (Personnel)
Immediate Holding Company: RITSON SMITH LTD
Registration no: SC386525 **VAT No.:** GB 297 4240 33
Date established: 2010 **Turnover:** £2m - £5m **No.of Employees:** 51 - 100
Product Groups: 80, 82

A & J Robertson Granite Ltd
9 Merkland Road East, Aberdeen, AB24 5JT
Tel: 01224-652000 **Fax:** 01224-639572
E-mail: raymond.garden@robertson-granite.co.uk
Website: http://www.robertson-granite.co.uk
Directors: R. Garden (Fin), S. Gibson (Sales)
Immediate Holding Company: A. & J. ROBERTSON (GRANITE) LIMITED
Registration no: SC038450 **VAT No.:** GB 430 1094 04
Date established: 1963 **Turnover:** £5m - £10m **No.of Employees:** 21 - 50
Product Groups: 33

Date of Accounts	Dec 11	Dec 10	Dec 09
Sales Turnover	6m	5m	6m
Pre Tax Profit/Loss	255	-151	79
Working Capital	299	77	205
Fixed Assets	3m	3m	3m
Current Assets	1m	2m	1m
Current Liabilities	761	1m	1m

Rolls Wood Group Repair & Overhauls Ltd
Kirkhill Drive Kirkhill Industrial Estate, Dyce, Aberdeen, AB21 0EU
Tel: 01224-797000 **Fax:** 01224-771552
E-mail: icarmichael@rwgroup.com
Website: http://www.rwgroup.com
Bank(s): HSBC Bank plc
Directors: C. Watson (Fin), I. Carmichael (Grp Chief Exec)
Immediate Holding Company: ROLLS WOOD GROUP (REPAIR & OVERHAULS) LIMITED
Registration no: SC120673 **VAT No.:** GB 552 8827 15
Date established: 1989 **Turnover:** £125m - £250m
No.of Employees: 51 - 100 **Product Groups:** 48

Date of Accounts	Dec 11	Dec 10	Dec 09
Sales Turnover	181m	163m	150m
Pre Tax Profit/Loss	23m	19m	21m
Working Capital	49m	50m	37m
Fixed Assets	24m	14m	14m
Current Assets	104m	95m	77m
Current Liabilities	20m	24m	20m

Ross Off Shore
Unit 12b Peterseat Drive, Altens Industrial Estate, Aberdeen, AB12 3HT
Tel: 01224-877774 **Fax:** 01224-876066
Website: http://www.rossoffshore.com
Directors: T. Ross (Prop)
Immediate Holding Company: ROSS OFFSHORE CONSULTANCY LIMITED

Registration no: SC188687 **Date established:** 1998
No.of Employees: 1 - 10 **Product Groups:** 37, 40, 48

Date of Accounts	Mar 12	Mar 11	Mar 10
Working Capital	511	125	-60
Fixed Assets	53	58	73
Current Assets	1m	502	484

Rotrex Winches
Centurion Court North Esplanade West, Aberdeen, AB11 5QF
Tel: 01224-771818 **Fax:** 01224-770254
E-mail: sales@rotrex.co.uk
Website: http://www.rotrexwinches.co.uk
Managers: S. Constantine (Mgr)
Ultimate Holding Company: L.G.H. GROUP LTD
Immediate Holding Company: ACCRETE PETROLEUM (UK) LTD
Date established: 2009 **Turnover:** £2m - £5m **No.of Employees:** 1 - 10
Product Groups: 35, 37, 38, 39, 45, 48, 83

Date of Accounts	Nov 11	Nov 10
Working Capital	20	N/A
Current Assets	31	N/A

Rubber & Plastic Industries Ltd
Pitmedden Road Dyce, Aberdeen, AB21 0DP
Tel: 01224-729222 **Fax:** 01224-729223
E-mail: sales@rpiscotland.co.uk
Website: http://www.rpiscotland.co.uk
Bank(s): HSBC Bank plc
Directors: D. Mcgill (MD)
Ultimate Holding Company: STORK TECHNICAL SERVICES (HOLDINGS) LIMITED
Immediate Holding Company: NORSE CUTTING & ABANDONMENT LIMITED
Registration no: SC252159 **Date established:** 2006 **Turnover:** £1m - £2m
No.of Employees: 11 - 20 **Product Groups:** 29, 30, 31, 32, 39, 41, 42, 48, 66

Date of Accounts	Dec 11	Dec 10	Dec 09
Sales Turnover	267m	269m	262m
Pre Tax Profit/Loss	4m	10m	5m
Working Capital	38m	5m	-4m
Fixed Assets	23m	26m	29m
Current Assets	87m	80m	64m
Current Liabilities	17m	14m	13m

Ruco Ltd
16 Raeden Park Road, Aberdeen, AB15 5LQ
Tel: 01224-316390 **Fax:** 01224-316397
E-mail: raymond.ruth@ruco.co.uk
Website: http://www.ruco.co.uk
Directors: R. Ruth (Dir)
Immediate Holding Company: RUCO LIMITED
Registration no: SC254098 **Date established:** 2003
No.of Employees: 1 - 10 **Product Groups:** 38

Date of Accounts	Mar 12	Mar 11	Mar 10
Working Capital	173	129	162
Current Assets	336	176	203

Schoeller Bleckmann & Darron
Unit 47 Howe Moss Terrace Kirkhill Industrial Estate, Dyce, Aberdeen, AB21 0GR
Tel: 01224-799600 **Fax:** 01224-770156
E-mail: dfindlay@sbdl.co.uk
Website: http://www.sbdl.co.uk
Directors: D. Findlay (MD), F. Gritsch (Fin)
Managers: N. Sutherland (Fin Mgr)
Ultimate Holding Company: SCHOELLER BLECKMANN OILFIELD EQUIPMENT (AUSTRIA)
Immediate Holding Company: SCHOELLER-BLECKMANN DARRON LIMITED
Registration no: SC145802 **Date established:** 1993
Turnover: £10m - £20m **No.of Employees:** 21 - 50 **Product Groups:** 34, 45, 67, 83, 85

Date of Accounts	Dec 11	Dec 10	Dec 09
Sales Turnover	19m	17m	14m
Pre Tax Profit/Loss	5m	3m	-124
Working Capital	9m	7m	4m
Fixed Assets	4m	3m	4m
Current Assets	12m	14m	13m
Current Liabilities	1m	1m	553

Scotia Instrumentation Ltd
Aberdeen Science & Technology Park Balgownie Road, Bridge of Don, Aberdeen, AB22 8GT
Tel: 01224-222888 **Fax:** 01224-826299
E-mail: info@scotia-computing.com
Website: http://www.scotia-instrumentation.com
Directors: J. Thom (MD)
Managers: M. Irvine (I.T. Exec), K. Anderson (Sales & Mktg Mg)
Immediate Holding Company: SCOTIA INSTRUMENTATION LIMITED
Registration no: SC074997 **Date established:** 1981
Turnover: £5m - £10m **No.of Employees:** 51 - 100 **Product Groups:** 37, 38, 39, 40, 67, 85

Date of Accounts	Dec 11	Dec 10	Dec 09
Sales Turnover	9m	8m	9m
Pre Tax Profit/Loss	1m	1m	238
Working Capital	629	143	674
Fixed Assets	3m	3m	2m
Current Assets	3m	2m	3m
Current Liabilities	1m	857	2m

Scotoil Services Ltd
Miller Street, Aberdeen, AB11 5AN
Tel: 01224-571491 **Fax:** 01224-580861
E-mail: info@scotoil.co.uk
Website: http://www.scotoil.co.uk
Bank(s): Bank of Scotland
Directors: C. Smith (MD)
Managers: L. Miln, R. Davidson (Buyer), A. Shaw (Comm)
Ultimate Holding Company: SCOTOIL REALISATIONS LIMITED
Immediate Holding Company: SCOTOIL SERVICES LIMITED
Registration no: SC077501 **VAT No.:** GB 682 9089 88
Date established: 1982 **Turnover:** £5m - £10m **No.of Employees:** 21 - 50
Product Groups: 84

Date of Accounts	Dec 11	Dec 10	Dec 09
Sales Turnover	6m	6m	5m
Pre Tax Profit/Loss	2m	2m	2m
Working Capital	4m	4m	4m
Fixed Assets	2m	1m	527
Current Assets	5m	5m	4m
Current Liabilities	513	420	379

Severn Unival Ltd
Badentoy Avenue Badentoy Industrial Estate, Portlethen, Aberdeen, AB12 4YB
Tel: 01224-780787 **Fax:** 01224-783501
E-mail: info@severnunival.co.uk
Website: http://www.severnunival.com
Managers: S. Moultrie
Ultimate Holding Company: SEVERN GLOCON GROUP PLC
Immediate Holding Company: SEVERN UNIVAL LIMITED
Registration no: 01564220 **Date established:** 1981
No.of Employees: 21 - 50 **Product Groups:** 36, 37, 38

Date of Accounts	Dec 11	Dec 10	Dec 09
Sales Turnover	18m	16m	18m
Pre Tax Profit/Loss	2m	2m	2m
Working Capital	4m	2m	3m
Fixed Assets	428	446	421
Current Assets	8m	5m	6m
Current Liabilities	2m	849	1m

Shark Group
Howe Moss Drive Kirkhill Industrial Estate, Dyce, Aberdeen, AB21 0GL
Tel: 01224-214444 **Fax:** 01670-761343
E-mail: sales@survival-one.com
Website: http://www.sharkgroup.co.uk
Bank(s): Barclays
Directors: D. Wilman (Fin), J. Nolan (Grp Chief Exec)
Managers: R. Nolan (Comm), D. Casey (Accounts)
Ultimate Holding Company: SGL Ltd
Immediate Holding Company: Survitec Group Ltd
Registration no: 01166443 **VAT No.:** GB 297 9753 76
Date established: 1965 **Turnover:** £1m - £2m **No.of Employees:** 21 - 50
Product Groups: 24, 39, 40, 49

Skene Business Centres
Rubislaw Den House 23 Rubislaw Den North, Aberdeen, AB15 4AL
Tel: 01224-326221 **Fax:** 01224-310037
E-mail: 23rdn@theskenegroup.com
Website: http://www.skene-businesscentres.co.uk
Managers: G. Moncur (Mgr)
Immediate Holding Company: XFOR MANAGEMENT LIMITED
Registration no: SC262865 **Date established:** 2004
Turnover: £5m - £10m **No.of Employees:** 1 - 10 **Product Groups:** 80

Date of Accounts	Mar 09	Mar 08	Mar 07
Working Capital	200	-24	-79
Fixed Assets	185	74	41
Current Assets	669	391	142

Sparrows Baricon Ltd
Denmore Road Bridge of Don, Aberdeen, AB23 8JW
Tel: 01224-704868 **Fax:** 01224-210563
E-mail: sales@sparrowsgroup.com
Website: http://www.sparrowsgroup.com
Bank(s): National Westminster
Directors: D. Sedge (Chief Op Offcr), A. Glen (Fin)
Managers: C. McIntyre
Ultimate Holding Company: CBPE (GENERAL PARTNER) LIMITED
Immediate Holding Company: SPARROWS BARICON LIMITED
Registration no: SC111458 **VAT No.:** 761 7544 15 **Date established:** 1988
Turnover: £2m - £5m **No.of Employees:** 1501 & over
Product Groups: 45, 48, 51, 67

Date of Accounts	Dec 11	Dec 10	Dec 09
Sales Turnover	3m	2m	8m
Pre Tax Profit/Loss	977	-128	1m
Working Capital	5m	4m	4m
Fixed Assets	538	683	563
Current Assets	7m	5m	6m
Current Liabilities	393	222	241

Spencer Coatings Ltd
Froghall Terrace, Aberdeen, AB24 3JN
Tel: 01224-788400 **Fax:** 01355-233847
E-mail: info@spencercoatings.co.uk
Website: http://www.spencercoatings.co.uk
Bank(s): The Royal Bank of Scotland
Directors: P. Buck (MD)
Ultimate Holding Company: SPENCER COATINGS GROUP LIMITED
Immediate Holding Company: SPENCER COATINGS GROUP LIMITED
Registration no: SC123258 **VAT No.:** GB 376 9551 03
Date established: 1990 **Turnover:** £5m - £10m **No.of Employees:** 21 - 50
Product Groups: 23, 30, 32

Date of Accounts	Mar 11	Mar 10	Mar 09
Sales Turnover	6m	6m	N/A
Pre Tax Profit/Loss	456	333	-603
Working Capital	206	141	2m
Fixed Assets	1m	1m	2m
Current Assets	3m	4m	4m
Current Liabilities	1m	1m	3

Stevenson & Kelly Grampian (Gang-Nail Systems Ltd)
Wester Hatton Balmedie, Aberdeen, AB23 8YY
Tel: 01358-743399 **Fax:** 01358-743044
E-mail: t.ralston@btinternet.com
Directors: T. Ralston (Dir)
Registration no: SC273706 **Date established:** 2004
No.of Employees: 1 - 10 **Product Groups:** 35, 66

Date of Accounts	Apr 08
Working Capital	26
Fixed Assets	19
Current Assets	217
Current Liabilities	190

Sub Sea 7 Ltd
Greenwell Base Greenwell Road, East Tullos Industrial Estate, Aberdeen, AB12 3AX
Tel: 01224-292000 **Fax:** 01224-879312
E-mail: jean.cahuzac@subsea7.com
Website: http://www.subsea7.com
Directors: J. Tocher (Fin)
Managers: D. Bloom (Mktg Serv Mgr), G. Mccaw (I.T. Exec), J. Cahuzac
Ultimate Holding Company: SUBSEA 7 S A (LUXEMBOURG)
Immediate Holding Company: SUBSEA 7 LIMITED
Registration no: 04316695 **Date established:** 2001
No.of Employees: 101 - 250 **Product Groups:** 51

Date of Accounts	Dec 11	Dec 10	Dec 09
Sales Turnover	613m	597m	623m
Pre Tax Profit/Loss	10m	71m	120m
Working Capital	85m	47m	-97m
Fixed Assets	754m	752m	680m
Current Assets	314m	173m	143m
Current Liabilities	172m	101m	67m

Swagelok Scotland
Silvertrees Drive
Silvertrees Business Park
Westhill, Aberdeen, AB32 6BH
Tel: 01224-759900 **Fax:** 01224-729495
E-mail: info@scotland.swagelok.com
Website: http://www.swagelok.com/scotland
Directors: P. O'connor (MD)
Managers: J. Wilson (Ops Mgr)
Immediate Holding Company: FLUID SYSTEM TECHNOLOGIES (SCOTLAND) LIMITED
Registration no: SC316064 **Date established:** 2007 **Turnover:** £2m - £5m
No.of Employees: 21 - 50 **Product Groups:** 61

Date of Accounts	Dec 11	Dec 10	Dec 09
Working Capital	1m	1m	710
Fixed Assets	690	585	593
Current Assets	2m	2m	2m

Swire Oilfield Services
Swire House Souter Head Road, Altens Industrial Estate, Aberdeen, AB12 3LF
Tel: 01224-872707 **Fax:** 01224-874516
E-mail: reception@swireos.com
Website: http://www.swireos.com
Directors: G. Anderson (Sales & Mktg), J. Lucas (Sales), R. Burrell (MD)
Managers: P. Fortey (Tech Serv Mgr), T. Garden (Personnel), B. Eitchison (Fin Mgr)
Ultimate Holding Company: WEATHERFORD INTERNATIONAL LIMITED (BERMUDA)
Immediate Holding Company: QUALITY MACHINING SERVICES LIMITED
Registration no: SC055503 **Date established:** 1994
Turnover: Over £1,000m **No.of Employees:** 101 - 250
Product Groups: 23, 35, 39, 45, 76, 77

Date of Accounts	Dec 10	Dec 09	Dec 08
Working Capital	3	3	3
Fixed Assets	372m	372m	372m
Current Assets	3	3	3

The Robert Gordon University
Schoolhill, Aberdeen, AB10 1FR
Tel: 01224-262000 **Fax:** 01224-263803
E-mail: univation@rgu.ac.uk
Website: http://www.rgu.ac.uk
Managers: F. Von-Prondzynski
Immediate Holding Company: UNIVATION LIMITED
Registration no: SC158742 **VAT No.:** GB 658 5634 94
Date established: 1995 **Turnover:** £2m - £5m
No.of Employees: 1001 - 1500 **Product Groups:** 54, 80, 81, 85, 86

Date of Accounts	Jul 08	Jul 07	Jul 06
Sales Turnover	3180	4078	9884
Pre Tax Profit/Loss	73	240	667
Working Capital	305	216	245
Fixed Assets	89	122	149
Current Assets	5904	2091	1873
Current Liabilities	5599	1875	1628
Total Share Capital	100	100	100
ROCE% (Return on Capital Employed)	18.4	71.1	169.0
ROT% (Return on Turnover)	2.3	5.9	6.7

Town & County Service Stations
Greenwell Road East Tullos Indl-Est, Aberdeen, AB12 3AX
Tel: 01224-878879 **Fax:** 01224-870890
E-mail: info@townandcounty.co.uk
Website: http://www.townandcounty.co.uk
Directors: J. Strachan (Jt MD), A. Strachan (Jt MD)
Managers: P. Keith (Chief Mgr)
Ultimate Holding Company: TOWN & COUNTY HOLDINGS LIMITED
Immediate Holding Company: TOWN & COUNTY SERVICE STATIONS LIMITED
Registration no: SC055063 **VAT No.:** GB 604 8797 13
Date established: 1974 **Turnover:** £20m - £50m
No.of Employees: 51 - 100 **Product Groups:** 61, 68

Tricore Ltd
Blackburn Industrial Estate Kinellar, Aberdeen, AB21 0RX
Tel: 01224-790338 **Fax:** 01224-790660
E-mail: info@tricore.co.uk
Website: http://www.tricore.co.uk
Directors: W. Bowie (Fin)
Managers: B. Bowie (Chief Mgr)
Immediate Holding Company: TRICORE LIMITED
Registration no: SC104854 **Date established:** 1987
No.of Employees: 1 - 10 **Product Groups:** 42, 45

Date of Accounts	Sep 11	Sep 10	Sep 09
Working Capital	513	484	438
Fixed Assets	168	195	183
Current Assets	601	554	610

Trojan Crates Ltd
98 Sinclair Road, Aberdeen, AB11 9PP
Tel: 01224-893311 **Fax:** 01224-893322
E-mail: craig@trojancrates.co.uk
Website: http://www.trojancrates.co.uk
Directors: C. Sim (Sales), A. Paterson (MD)
Managers: K. Morrison (Ops Mgr), B. Taylor (Prod Mgr)
Immediate Holding Company: TROJAN CRATES LIMITED
Registration no: SC069827 **Date established:** 1979
Turnover: £250,000 - £500,000 **No.of Employees:** 21 - 50
Product Groups: 20, 25, 30, 35, 45, 48, 66, 67, 76, 84

Date of Accounts	May 11	May 10	May 09
Working Capital	987	884	1m
Fixed Assets	232	201	186
Current Assets	2m	1m	2m

Turner E P S
Unit 1a Dyce Industrial Park Dyce, Aberdeen, AB21 7EZ
Tel: 01224-723925 **Fax:** 01224-723927
E-mail: dave.cox@turner-eps.co.uk
Website: http://www.turner-eps.co.uk
Bank(s): Royal Bank of Scotland
Managers: C. Butchart
Immediate Holding Company: TURNER DIESEL LTD
Registration no: SC359144 **VAT No.:** GB 290 3817 51
Turnover: £1m - £2m **No.of Employees:** 51 - 100 **Product Groups:** 48

see next page

Turner E P S - Cont'd

Date of Accounts	Mar 08	Mar 07
Sales Turnover	18399	24160
Pre Tax Profit/Loss	775	1477
Working Capital	11813	12300
Fixed Assets	840	902
Current Assets	19298	22768
Current Liabilities	7486	10468
Total Share Capital	45	45
ROCE% (Return on Capital Employed)	6.1	11.2
ROT% (Return on Turnover)	4.2	6.1

Tyco Fire & Integrated Solutions

Unit 14-20 Ocean Trade Centre Minto Avenue, Altens Industrial Estate, Aberdeen, AB12 3JZ
Tel: 01224-293500 **Fax:** 01224-895870
E-mail: tfis.marketing.uk@tycoint.com
Website: http://www.tycofis.com
Directors: C. Milling (Chief Op Offcr)
Managers: B. Stewart (District Mgr), G. Langan (Tech Serv Mgr), S. McCarthy (Sales Prom Mgr), D. Petrie (Mktg Serv Mgr)
Ultimate Holding Company: TYCO INTERNATIONAL LIMITED (SWITZERLAND)
Immediate Holding Company: ATLAS FIRE ENGINEERING LIMITED
Registration no: 00121983 **Date established:** 2012
No.of Employees: 101 - 250 **Product Groups:** 38, 40, 54, 84

Tyco Valves & Controls

Wellheads Terrace Wellheads Industrial Estate, Aberdeen, AB21 7GF
Tel: 01224-722562 **Fax:** 01224-771607
E-mail: service_aberdeen@tyco-valves.com
Website: http://www.tyco.com
Managers: D. Watt (Ops Mgr)
Ultimate Holding Company: TYCO INTERNATIONAL LIMITED (SWITZERLAND)
Immediate Holding Company: TYCO VALVES & CONTROLS DISTRIBUTION (UK) LIMITED
Registration no: SC202028 **Date established:** 1999
Turnover: £20m - £50m **No.of Employees:** 21 - 50 **Product Groups:** 36, 38, 40, 48

Date of Accounts	Sep 11	Sep 08	Sep 09
Sales Turnover	39m	60m	81m
Pre Tax Profit/Loss	-2m	-2m	2m
Working Capital	11m	-6m	17m
Fixed Assets	4m	4m	4m
Current Assets	18m	23m	30m
Current Liabilities	2m	3m	3m

United Supplies Ltd

United House 6 Regent Road, Aberdeen, AB11 5NS
Tel: 01224-581321 **Fax:** 01224-573141
E-mail: info@unitedsuppliesltd.co.uk
Website: http://www.unitedsuppliesltd.co.uk
Directors: I. Strachan (Fin)
Managers: J. Strachan (Sales Prom Mgr)
Immediate Holding Company: UNITED SUPPLIES LIMITED
Registration no: SC101434 **Date established:** 1986 **Turnover:** £2m - £5m
No.of Employees: 11 - 20 **Product Groups:** 77

Date of Accounts	Sep 12	Sep 11	Sep 10
Sales Turnover	3m	3m	3m
Pre Tax Profit/Loss	497	384	395
Working Capital	695	456	141
Fixed Assets	274	293	315
Current Assets	1m	908	575
Current Liabilities	140	114	105

Viking Life Saving Equipment

Unit 19 Ocean Trade Centre Minto Avenue, Altens Industrial Estate, Aberdeen, AB12 3JZ
Tel: 01224-898969 **Fax:** 01224-894565
E-mail: viking-uk@viking-life.com
Website: http://www.viking-life.com
Managers: M. Pedersen (District Mgr)
No.of Employees: 1 - 10 **Product Groups:** 20, 23, 24, 29, 32, 36, 37, 38, 39, 40, 42, 45, 67, 74

Vion Food Scotland Ltd - Mcintosh Donald

Meat Factory Cookston Road, Portlethen, Aberdeen, AB12 4QB
Tel: 01224-780381 **Fax:** 01224-782039
Website: http://www.gcfg.com
Bank(s): Bank of Scotland
Directors: A. Mcnaughton (MD), A. McNoughton (MD)
Managers: D. Mitchell (Personnel), K. Naiper (Tech Serv Mgr)
Ultimate Holding Company: VION HOLDING NV (NETHERLANDS)
Immediate Holding Company: MCINTOSH DONALD LIMITED
Registration no: SC030556 **VAT No.:** GB 498 2638 89
Date established: 1955 **Turnover:** £75m - £125m
No.of Employees: 251 - 500 **Product Groups:** 20

Date of Accounts	Dec 11	Dec 10	Dec 09
Sales Turnover	N/A	N/A	112m
Pre Tax Profit/Loss	N/A	12m	3m
Working Capital	16m	15m	10m
Fixed Assets	1	89	6m
Current Assets	16m	15m	19m
Current Liabilities	N/A	N/A	5m

Wallace Whittle & Partners

166 Great Western Road, Aberdeen, AB10 6QE
Tel: 01224-285300 **Fax:** 01224-285301
E-mail: aberdeen@wallacewhittle.com
Website: http://www.wallacewhittle.com
Directors: A. Forbes (Dir)
No.of Employees: 11 - 20 **Product Groups:** 37, 67

Wartsila UK Ltd

11a Peterseat Drive Altens Industrial Estate, Aberdeen, AB12 3HT
Tel: 01224-871166 **Fax:** 01224-871188
E-mail: john.bilton@wartsila.com
Website: http://www.wartsila.com
Directors: F. De Hart (Dir)
Ultimate Holding Company: WARTSILA CORPORATION (FINLAND)
Immediate Holding Company: WARTSILA UK LIMITED
Registration no: 01004816 **Date established:** 1971
Turnover: £20m - £50m **No.of Employees:** 21 - 50 **Product Groups:** 37, 39, 40, 48

Date of Accounts	Dec 11	Dec 10	Dec 09
Sales Turnover	94m	91m	102m
Pre Tax Profit/Loss	7m	8m	8m
Working Capital	-9m	-9m	-13m
Fixed Assets	21m	24m	27m
Current Assets	30m	30m	32m
Current Liabilities	27m	28m	36m

Watt A Dog Grooming

5 Hasman Terrace Cove Bay, Aberdeen, AB12 3GD
Tel: 01224-874841
E-mail: jenifer@watt-a-dog.co.uk
Website: http://www.watt-a-dog.co.uk
Directors: J. Watt (Prop)
No.of Employees: 1 - 10 **Product Groups:** 36, 40, 49, 66

Weatherford UK

Kirkton Drive Pitmedden Industrial Estate Dyce, Dyce, Aberdeen, AB21 0BG
Tel: 01224-767000 **Fax:** 01224-767104
E-mail: gary.fines@eu.weatherford.com
Website: http://www.weatherford.com
Bank(s): The Royal Bank of Scotland
Managers: A. Carter (Reg Mgr), G. Fines (Mgr)
Immediate Holding Company: WEATHERFORD (G.B.) LLP
Registration no: SO300401 **Date established:** 2004
Turnover: £20m - £50m **No.of Employees:** 51 - 100 **Product Groups:** 45, 51

Date of Accounts	Dec 10	Dec 09	Dec 08
Working Capital	3	3	3
Fixed Assets	372m	372m	372m
Current Assets	3	3	3

Weber Shandwick

58 Queens Road, Aberdeen, AB15 4YE
Tel: 01224-806600 **Fax:** 01224-208823
E-mail: jrmacdonald@webershandwick.com
Website: http://www.webershandwick.com
Directors: J. Macdonald (Dir), M. Macdonald (Dir)
Managers: C. Hood (Fin Mgr)
Immediate Holding Company: RNPL OIL & GAS LTD
Registration no: SC368598 **VAT No.:** GB 402 9578 48
Date established: 2011 **Turnover:** £2m - £5m **No.of Employees:** 1 - 10
Product Groups: 81

Weir S P M

S P M House Badentoy CR Badentoy Industrial Estate, Portlethen, Aberdeen, AB12 4YD
Tel: 01224-783666 **Fax:** 01224-784184
E-mail: arobb@weirspm.com
Website: http://www.spmflo.com
Directors: W. Reid (MD), A. Robb (Dir)
Managers: A. Scott, T. Ingram (Personnel), I. Anderson (Chief Mgr), C. McGregor (Comptroller)
Ultimate Holding Company: NATIONAL OILWELL VARCO INC (USA)
Immediate Holding Company: TUBOSCOPE HOLDINGS LIMITED
Registration no: SC002934 **Date established:** 1996
Turnover: £10m - £20m **No.of Employees:** 21 - 50 **Product Groups:** 36, 37, 38

Date of Accounts	Dec 11	Dec 10
Pre Tax Profit/Loss	N/A	-18m
Working Capital	-45m	-13m
Fixed Assets	1034m	1034m
Current Assets	10m	5m
Current Liabilities	18m	N/A

Wellhead Electrical Supplies

Unit 4d Wellheads Crescent Wellheads Industrial Estate, Aberdeen, AB21 7GA
Tel: 01224-723606 **Fax:** 01224-723606
E-mail: sales@wellheads.co.uk
Website: http://www.wellheads.co.uk
Bank(s): Bank of Scotland
Directors: C. Ogg (Fin), R. Rae (MD)
Immediate Holding Company: WELLHEAD ELECTRICAL SUPPLIES LIMITED
Registration no: SC123707 **Date established:** 1990
Turnover: £5m - £10m **No.of Employees:** 11 - 20 **Product Groups:** 36, 37, 40

Date of Accounts	Dec 11	Dec 10	Dec 09
Sales Turnover	8m	7m	6m
Pre Tax Profit/Loss	632	569	500
Working Capital	2m	1m	1m
Fixed Assets	53	54	40
Current Assets	3m	3m	2m
Current Liabilities	349	313	247

Wenaas Ltd

Hareness Circle Altens Industrial Estate, Aberdeen, AB12 3LY
Tel: 01224-894000 **Fax:** 01224-878789
E-mail: richard.wright@wenaas.co.uk
Website: http://www.wenaas.co.uk
Bank(s): Barclays, Hall Quay
Directors: S. Poultney (Sales), R. Wright (MD), B. White (Sales)
Managers: E. Pickin (Tech Serv Mgr), N. Paxton (Mktg Serv Mgr), G. Miller (Comptroller), J. Rimmer
Ultimate Holding Company: KWINTET A/B (SWEDEN)
Immediate Holding Company: WENAAS UK LIMITED
Registration no: SC062062 **VAT No.:** GB 105 3264 10
Date established: 1977 **Turnover:** £10m - £20m
No.of Employees: 21 - 50 **Product Groups:** 22, 24, 40

Date of Accounts	Dec 11	Dec 10	Dec 09
Sales Turnover	13m	15m	16m
Pre Tax Profit/Loss	-2m	-3m	-318
Working Capital	2m	4m	7m
Fixed Assets	2m	2m	2m
Current Assets	9m	8m	11m
Current Liabilities	2m	2m	673

Wesco Sourcing & Procurement Services

Exchange House 24-26 Exchange Street, Aberdeen, AB11 6PH
Tel: 01224-577900 **Fax:** 01224-212186
E-mail: lwatson@wescosps.co.uk
Website: http://www.wescosps.com
Managers: L. Watson
VAT No.: GB 743 0639 41 **Turnover:** Up to £250,000
No.of Employees: 1 - 10 **Product Groups:** 84

William Wilson

Hareness Road Altens Indl-Est, Aberdeen, AB12 3QA
Tel: 01224-877522 **Fax:** 01224-879650
E-mail: contact@williamwilson.co.uk
Website: http://www.williamwilson.co.uk
Bank(s): The Royal Bank of Scotland
Directors: R. Bisset (MD)
Managers: B. Mcallister (Personnel), L. Campbell (Reg Mgr), R. Hill (District Mgr), D. Reid (Mktg Serv Mgr), D. Black (Product), D. Bray (I.T. Exec)
Ultimate Holding Company: WOLSELEY PLC (JERSEY)
Immediate Holding Company: WILLIAM WILSON & COMPANY (GLASGOW) LIMITED
Registration no: SC081737 **Date established:** 1983
Turnover: £125m - £250m **No.of Employees:** 11 - 20
Product Groups: 30, 66, 67

Robert Wiseman Dairies Ltd

Craigshaw Drive West Tullos Industrial Estate, Aberdeen, AB12 3XB
Tel: 01224-896969 **Fax:** 01224-871948
E-mail: grodney@wiseman-dairies.co.uk
Website: http://www.wiseman-dairies.co.uk
Managers: G. Rooney (Site Co-ord)
Immediate Holding Company: ROBERT WISEMAN DAIRIES LIMITED
Registration no: SC146494 **VAT No.:** GB 624 0831 65
Date established: 1993 **Turnover:** £125m - £250m
No.of Employees: 251 - 500 **Product Groups:** 20

Date of Accounts	Jan 12	Apr 09	Apr 10
Sales Turnover	780m	848m	886m
Pre Tax Profit/Loss	8m	31m	49m
Working Capital	-17m	-26m	-41m
Fixed Assets	246m	227m	236m
Current Assets	118m	81m	94m
Current Liabilities	45m	37m	56m

Wood Group Light Industrial Turbines Ltd

Kirkhill Drive Kirkhill Industrial Estate, Dyce, Aberdeen, AB21 0EU
Tel: 01224-413000 **Fax:** 01224-770008
E-mail: sales@wglit.com
Website: http://www.woodgroup.com
Bank(s): Clydesdale
Directors: M. Conway (Mkt Research)
Managers: K. Picken, J. Steed, C. Watson (Comptroller), K. Hart (Fin Mgr), S. Csorba (Personnel), S. Walker
Ultimate Holding Company: JOHN WOOD GROUP P.L.C.
Immediate Holding Company: WOOD GROUP OIL GAS & INDUSTRIAL SERVICES LIMITED
Registration no: 01549768 **VAT No.:** GB 351 9793 23
Date established: 1981 **Turnover:** £10m - £20m
No.of Employees: 21 - 50 **Product Groups:** 48

Date of Accounts	Dec 11	Dec 10	Dec 09
Sales Turnover	18m	15m	16m
Pre Tax Profit/Loss	-588	-4m	-818
Working Capital	9m	9m	13m
Fixed Assets	1m	1m	2m
Current Assets	15m	12m	14m
Current Liabilities	3m	927	793

John Wood Group plc

Greenwell Road East Tullos Industrial Estate, Aberdeen, AB12 3AX
Tel: 01224-851000 **Fax:** 01224-871997
E-mail: allister.langlands@woodgroup.com
Website: http://www.woodgroup.com
Bank(s): Clydesdale Bank PLC
Directors: A. Langlands (Grp Chief Exec), I. Wood (Ch & MD), I. Stirling (MD), A. Semple (Fin)
Immediate Holding Company: JOHN WOOD GROUP P.L.C.
Registration no: SC036219 **Date established:** 1961
Turnover: Over £1,000m **No.of Employees:** 1501 & over
Product Groups: 34, 35, 36, 45, 48

Date of Accounts	Dec 07	Dec 06	Dec 05
Sales Turnover	4433m	3469m	2762m
Pre Tax Profit/Loss	259900	183600	124700
Working Capital	582800	576000	540600
Fixed Assets	903100	677800	582200
Current Assets	1567m	1367m	1131m
Current Liabilities	984600	790900	590000
Total Share Capital	26000	25500	25400
ROCE% (Return on Capital Employed)	17.5	14.6	11.1
ROT% (Return on Turnover)	5.9	5.3	4.5

Woodsons Of Aberdeen Ltd

Goval House Dyce, Aberdeen, AB21 0HT
Tel: 01224-722884 **Fax:** 01224-722859
E-mail: sales@woodsons.co.uk
Website: http://www.woodsons.co.uk
Bank(s): Bank of Scotland
Directors: J. Still (Fin), S. Wood (Dir)
Managers: M. Newman (Tech Serv Mgr)
Immediate Holding Company: WOODSONS OF ABERDEEN LIMITED
Registration no: SC031819 **VAT No.:** GB 266 0627 56
Date established: 1956 **Turnover:** £2m - £5m **No.of Employees:** 21 - 50
Product Groups: 37, 38, 39

Date of Accounts	Nov 11	Nov 10	Nov 09
Working Capital	356	226	156
Fixed Assets	514	359	263
Current Assets	2m	1m	1m

Xodus Group Ltd

Xodus House 50 Huntly Street, Aberdeen, AB10 1RS
Tel: 01224-628300 **Fax:** 01224-628333
E-mail: info@xodusgroup.com
Website: http://www.xodusgroup.com
Managers: R. Sheehan
Immediate Holding Company: XODUS GROUP LIMITED
Registration no: SC286421 **Date established:** 2005
Turnover: £20m - £50m **No.of Employees:** 51 - 100 **Product Groups:** 51

Date of Accounts	Dec 11	Dec 10	Sep 09
Sales Turnover	35m	29m	14m
Pre Tax Profit/Loss	2m	5m	1m
Working Capital	5m	5m	571
Fixed Assets	4m	2m	2m
Current Assets	16m	10m	4m
Current Liabilities	9m	2m	2m

A C Yule & Son Ltd

Craigshaw Road West Tullos Indl-Est, Aberdeen, AB12 3ZG
Tel: 01224-230000 **Fax:** 01224-230011
E-mail: byule@acyule.com
Website: http://www.acyule.co.uk
Bank(s): Bank of Scotland
Directors: M. Yule (Mkt Research), B. Emslie (Co Sec), H. Yule (Dir), B. Yule (MD), E. Yule (Ch)
Managers: S. Ward (I.T. Exec), D. Notman (Sales Prom Mgr)
Immediate Holding Company: A.C. YULE & SON LIMITED
Registration no: SC045388 **Date established:** 1968
Turnover: £20m - £50m **No.of Employees:** 251 - 500 **Product Groups:** 30

Date of Accounts	Jan 10	Jan 09	Jan 08
Sales Turnover	29m	34m	37m
Pre Tax Profit/Loss	-336	547	984
Working Capital	3m	4m	4m
Fixed Assets	5m	5m	6m
Current Assets	8m	11m	12m
Current Liabilities	2m	3m	3m

Banffshire

Aberlour

Highland Distillers Ltd
Macallan Distillery Craigellachie, Aberlour, AB38 9RX
Tel: 01340-871471 **Fax:** 01340-871212
E-mail: info@themacallan.com
Website: http://www.themacallan.com
Bank(s): The Bank of Scotland, Elgin
Managers: R. Anderson (Prod Mgr)
Ultimate Holding Company: THE EDRINGTON GROUP LIMITED
Immediate Holding Company: HIGHLAND DISTILLERS LIMITED
Registration no: SC158731 **VAT No.:** GB 260 9200 83
Date established: 1995 **No.of Employees:** 21 - 50 **Product Groups:** 21

Date of Accounts	Mar 12	Mar 11	Mar 10
Sales Turnover	178m	174m	161m
Pre Tax Profit/Loss	32m	43m	37m
Working Capital	59m	61m	60m
Fixed Assets	34m	37m	37m
Current Assets	263m	231m	242m
Current Liabilities	43m	41m	43m

Walkers Shortbread Ltd
Aberlour House, Aberlour, AB38 9LD
Tel: 01340-871555 **Fax:** 01340-871355
E-mail: enquiries@walkers-shortbread.co.uk
Website: http://www.walkersshortbread.co.uk
Directors: A. Gronbech (Mkt Research), D. Edwards (Fin), J. Walker (MD)
Managers: I. Gibson (Sales Prom Mgr), P. Johnson (Tech Serv Mgr), S. Milne (Personnel), J. Grant (Buyer)
Immediate Holding Company: WALKERS SHORTBREAD LIMITED
Registration no: SC063233 **Date established:** 1977
Turnover: £75m - £125m **No.of Employees:** 1001 - 1500
Product Groups: 20

Date of Accounts	Dec 11	Dec 10	Dec 09
Sales Turnover	119m	106m	100m
Pre Tax Profit/Loss	9m	9m	10m
Working Capital	35m	33m	29m
Fixed Assets	28m	27m	28m
Current Assets	47m	44m	39m
Current Liabilities	8m	8m	8m

Aberdeenshire

Aboyne

Morven Technologies Ltd
Aboyne Industrial Estate Low Road, Aboyne, AB34 5GW
Tel: 01339-887616 **Fax:** 01339-887372
E-mail: morventech@btinternet.com
Website: http://www.morventechnologies.co.uk
Directors: M. Mallett (MD)
Immediate Holding Company: MORVEN TECHNOLOGIES LTD.
Registration no: SC195212 **Date established:** 1999
No.of Employees: 1 - 10 **Product Groups:** 38, 42

Date of Accounts	Mar 12	Mar 11	Mar 10
Working Capital	83	100	90
Fixed Assets	9	14	9
Current Assets	104	114	101

Lanarkshire

Airdrie

Albert Bartlett & Sons Airdrie Ltd
251 Stirling Road Riggend, Airdrie, ML6 7SP
Tel: 01236-762831 **Fax:** 01236-771749
E-mail: ronnie.bartlett@albertbartlett.com
Website: http://www.albertbartlett.com
Directors: R. Bartlett (Prop)
Ultimate Holding Company: BARTLETT INTERNATIONAL HOLDINGS LIMITED
Immediate Holding Company: ALBERT BARTLETT & SONS (AIRDRIE) LIMITED
Registration no: SC037896 **Date established:** 1962
Turnover: £125m - £250m **No.of Employees:** 251 - 500
Product Groups: 02

Date of Accounts	May 11	May 10	May 09
Sales Turnover	130m	136m	182m
Pre Tax Profit/Loss	7m	10m	12m
Working Capital	4m	3m	-15m
Fixed Assets	27m	28m	53m
Current Assets	46m	40m	24m
Current Liabilities	9m	9m	8m

B & B Lifting Equipment Ltd
Unit 8 Stirling Road Industrial Estate, Airdrie, ML6 7UD
Tel: 01236-760765 **Fax:** 01236-748903
E-mail: bill@scottishcrane.co.uk
Website: http://www.scottishcrane.co.uk
Directors: W. Rae (MD), E. Rae (Fin)
Immediate Holding Company: B. & B. LIFTING EQUIPMENT LTD.
Registration no: SC201020 **Date established:** 1999
No.of Employees: 1 - 10 **Product Groups:** 35, 39, 45

Date of Accounts	Apr 12	Apr 11	Apr 10
Working Capital	17	19	59
Fixed Assets	24	29	35
Current Assets	18	34	66

Bestpump
34 Commonhead Street, Airdrie, ML6 6NS
Tel: 08454-672378 **Fax:** 01236-728900
E-mail: john@bestpump.co.uk
Website: http://www.bestpump.co.uk
Directors: J. Best (MD)
Date established: 2000 **Turnover:** £500,000 - £1m
No.of Employees: 1 - 10 **Product Groups:** 67

Date of Accounts	Jan 08
Working Capital	-18
Fixed Assets	27
Current Assets	36
Current Liabilities	54

Caldervale Forge Co. Ltd
Dunrobin Road, Airdrie, ML6 8LS
Tel: 01236-763388 **Fax:** 01236-765259
E-mail: john.ramsay@rockeater.co.uk
Website: http://www.rockeatertools.com
Directors: J. Ramsay (Co Sec), J. Baird-Watson (MD), A. Attala (MD), J. Ramsay (MD)
Managers: R. Wardle (Mgr), M. Tuller (Mktg Serv Mgr), M. Atalla (Mktg Serv Mgr)
Ultimate Holding Company: SC116949
Immediate Holding Company: INDUCTION HEAT TREATMENT SERVICES LIMITED
Registration no: SC044675 **VAT No.:** GB 259 5555 19
Date established: 1967 **Turnover:** £1m - £2m **No.of Employees:** 21 - 50
Product Groups: 36

Date of Accounts	Apr 07	Apr 06
Working Capital	5	118
Fixed Assets	490	369
Current Assets	924	766
Current Liabilities	919	648
Total Share Capital	1	1

Peter Campbell Sales
Unit 27 Block 6 Chapelhall Industrial Estate, Chapelhall, Airdrie, ML6 8QH
Tel: 01236-755003 **Fax:** 01236-755110
E-mail: sales@petercampbellsales.com
Website: http://www.petercampbellsales.com
Directors: A. Jeffrey (MD), P. Campbell (Prop)
Managers: C. Gilmore
Immediate Holding Company: PETER CAMPBELL (SALES) LTD.
Registration no: SC266540 **Date established:** 2004 **Turnover:** £2m - £5m
No.of Employees: 21 - 50 **Product Groups:** 46

Date of Accounts	Mar 11	Mar 10	Mar 09
Sales Turnover	N/A	N/A	4m
Pre Tax Profit/Loss	N/A	N/A	175
Working Capital	857	638	585
Fixed Assets	519	532	541
Current Assets	2m	1m	1m
Current Liabilities	N/A	N/A	149

Darfen Dura Fencing (CRH Fencing Ltd)
Unit 7 Rochsolloch Works Rochsolloch Road, Airdrie, ML6 9BG
Tel: 01236-755001 **Fax:** 01236-747012
E-mail: scotland@darfen.co.uk
Website: http://www.darfen.co.uk
Directors: J. Hughes (Dir)
Registration no: 02840742 **Turnover:** £20m - £50m
No.of Employees: 1 - 10 **Product Groups:** 25, 35, 36, 49, 52, 65, 66

Inver House Distillers Ltd
Moffat Distillery Towers Road, Airdrie, ML6 8PL
Tel: 01236-769377 **Fax:** 01236-769781
E-mail: gstevenson@inverhouse.com
Website: http://www.inverhouse.com
Directors: M. Leask (Sales & Mktg), M. Leask (Sales & Mktg), G. Stevenson (MD), G. Stevenson (MD)
Managers: S. Kirk (Personnel), L. Kerr (Personnel), A. Freel (Tech Serv Mgr), A. Kerr (Purch Mgr)
Ultimate Holding Company: BLAIRMHOR LIMITED
Immediate Holding Company: INVER HOUSE DISTILLERS LIMITED
Registration no: SC040036 **VAT No.:** GB 259 9804 04
Date established: 1964 **Turnover:** £50m - £75m
No.of Employees: 101 - 250 **Product Groups:** 21

Date of Accounts	Dec 11	Dec 10	Dec 09
Sales Turnover	81m	63m	53m
Pre Tax Profit/Loss	15m	10m	10m
Working Capital	58m	57m	50m
Fixed Assets	16m	15m	14m
Current Assets	90m	86m	82m
Current Liabilities	8m	9m	8m

Scottish Crane & Engineering Services
Unit 8 Stirling Road Industrial Estate, Airdrie, ML6 7UD
Tel: 01236-762324 **Fax:** 01236-748903
E-mail: bill@scottishcrane.co.uk
Website: http://www.scottishcrane.co.uk
Directors: W. Rae (Ptnr)
Immediate Holding Company: PAV MANUFACTURING LTD.
Registration no: SC043702 **Date established:** 2005
No.of Employees: 1 - 10 **Product Groups:** 35, 39, 45

Date of Accounts	Aug 11	Aug 10	Aug 09
Working Capital	-40	N/A	N/A
Current Assets	40	55	N/A

R Shanks
143 Greengairs Road Greengairs, Airdrie, ML6 7SY
Tel: 01236-830750 **Fax:** 01236-830736
E-mail: info@shanksgroup.co.uk
Website: http://www.shanksgroup.co.uk
Directors: R. Shanks (Prop), T. Shanks (Prop)
Registration no: SL000972 **Date established:** 1910
No.of Employees: 1 - 10 **Product Groups:** 35

Watts Industrial Tyres plc
Flowerhill Industrial Estate, Airdrie, ML6 6BH
Tel: 01236-769888 **Fax:** 01236-747556
E-mail: andrewkear@watts-group.co.uk
Website: http://www.watts-tyres.co.uk
Managers: D. Murdoch (Mgr), D. Taylor (I.T. Exec), H. Bosshardt (Sales Prom Mgr), I. Bland (Purch Mgr), J. Mitchell (Mktg Serv Mgr)
Ultimate Holding Company: Watts Of Lydney Group Ltd
Immediate Holding Company: Watts Tyres Ltd
Registration no: 01434811 **No.of Employees:** 1 - 10 **Product Groups:** 29, 68

Dunbartonshire

Alexandria

Antartex Village
Lomond Industrial Estate, Alexandria, G83 0TP
Tel: 01389-754263 **Fax:** 01389-750656
E-mail: enquiries@pondenhome.co.uk
Website: http://www.ewm.co.uk
Managers: P. Innes (Chief Mgr)
Immediate Holding Company: LEWIS GORMAN TAXIS LTD.
Registration no: SC262374 **VAT No.:** GB 263 6530 59
Date established: 2004 **Turnover:** £2m - £5m **No.of Employees:** 21 - 50
Product Groups: 22

Date of Accounts	Jan 12	Jan 11	Jan 10
Working Capital	-18	-3	-5
Fixed Assets	11	2	3
Current Assets	N/A	N/A	2

Canopy & Awning People Canopies Awnings & Sign Writers
Unit 12 Lomond Industrial Estate, Alexandria, G83 0TL
Tel: 01389-750033 **Fax:** 01389-750033
E-mail: thecanopypeople@hotmail.com
Website: http://www.thecanopypeople.co.uk
Directors: H. Mossitt (Prop)
Immediate Holding Company: LOCH LOMOND DISTILLERY COMPANY LIMITED
Registration no: SC140039 **Date established:** 1992
Turnover: £10m - £20m **No.of Employees:** 1 - 10 **Product Groups:** 24, 35, 49, 66

Date of Accounts	Mar 11	Mar 10	Mar 09
Sales Turnover	18m	18m	16m
Pre Tax Profit/Loss	296	362	51
Working Capital	-3m	-4m	-8m
Fixed Assets	16m	17m	16m
Current Assets	10m	8m	6m
Current Liabilities	628	375	841

Roscon Services
Main Street Bonhill, Alexandria, G83 9JY
Tel: 01389-602901
E-mail: enquiries@rosconservices.co.uk
Website: http://www.rosconservices.co.uk
Directors: I. Ross (Dir)
Date established: 1999 **Turnover:** Up to £250,000
No.of Employees: 1 - 10 **Product Groups:** 52

United Distillers & Vinters
Dillichip Loan, Alexandria, G83 9HX
Tel: 01389-752784 **Fax:** 01389- 757219
Directors: P. Burns (MD)
Date established: 1966 **No.of Employees:** 1 - 10 **Product Groups:** 35, 36, 45

Web design Glasgow
235 Redburn, Alexandria, G83 9BX
Tel: 01389-605181
E-mail: georgebarr5@yahoo.co.uk
Website: http://www.georgebarr.co.uk
Directors: G. Barr (Prop)
Date established: 2008 **No.of Employees:** 1 - 10 **Product Groups:** 44

Aberdeenshire

Alford

Donside Fire Protection
Keig, Alford, AB33 8BP
Tel: 01975-563841
Directors: K. Lawson (Prop)
Date established: 2000 **No.of Employees:** 1 - 10 **Product Groups:** 38, 42

N G Peters
The Smithy Whitehouse, Alford, AB33 8DQ
Tel: 01975-562556 **Fax:** 01975-562556
Directors: N. Peters (Prop)
Date established: 1999 **No.of Employees:** 1 - 10 **Product Groups:** 41

Clackmannanshire

Alloa

R G Abercrombie
Caledonian Road, Alloa, FK10 1NB
Tel: 01259-222500 **Fax:** 01259-222528
E-mail: info@diageo.com
Bank(s): Clydesdale
Managers: C. King (Ops Mgr)
Ultimate Holding Company: GUINNESS P.L.C.
Immediate Holding Company: UNITED DISTILLERS & VINTNERS
Registration no: SC026675 **Turnover:** £2m - £5m
No.of Employees: 21 - 50 **Product Groups:** 41, 48

Central Metal Craft
11 Devonbank Fishcross, Alloa, FK10 3JE
Tel: 01259-210144
Directors: L. McKinlay (Prop)
Date established: 1998 **No.of Employees:** 1 - 10 **Product Groups:** 26, 35

Energylinx Ltd
The E Centre Cooperage Way, Alloa, FK10 3LP
Tel: 0800-8497077 **Fax:** 0845-225 2890
E-mail: sales@energylinx.co.uk
Website: http://www.energylinx.co.uk
Directors: K. Geddes (Fin), L. Geddes (MD)
Immediate Holding Company: ENERGYLINX LIMITED
Registration no: SC244794 **Date established:** 2003 **Turnover:** £2m - £5m
No.of Employees: 1 - 10 **Product Groups:** 54

G & M Welding Supplies
Unit 2d Castle Street Industrial Estate, Alloa, FK10 1EU
Tel: 01259-211337
Directors: G. Kerr (Prop)
Date established: 1991 **No.of Employees:** 1 - 10 **Product Groups:** 46

Graffters Ltd
Alloa Business Centre The Whins, Alloa, FK10 3SA
Tel: 08456-123111 **Fax:** 0845-612 3112
E-mail: sales@graffterscotland.co.uk
Website: http://www.graffters.co.uk
Managers: M. Espley (Mgr)
Immediate Holding Company: GRAFFTERS SCOTLAND LIMITED
Registration no: SC268644 **Date established:** 2004 **Turnover:** £1m - £2m
No.of Employees: 1 - 10 **Product Groups:** 66, 67

Date of Accounts	Dec 08	Dec 07	Dec 06
Working Capital	-35	44	58
Fixed Assets	56	19	41
Current Assets	536	677	903

J D M Metal Craft
2 Old Russells Yard Clackmannan Road, Alloa, FK10 4DA
Tel: 01259-724278
Directors: D. Guild (Prop)
Date established: 1996 **No.of Employees:** 1 - 10 **Product Groups:** 26, 35

Thermo Box
Unit 1-2 Cooperage Way, Alloa, FK10 3LP
Tel: 01622-872821 **Fax:** 01622-872831
E-mail: info@hygienius.co.uk
Website: http://www.thermo-box.co.uk
Directors: G. Snelgrove (Dir)
No.of Employees: 1 - 10 **Product Groups:** 20, 40, 41

Rossshire

Alness

Portex Technologies Ltd
Merlin House Alness Point Business Park, Alness, IV17 0UP
Tel: 01349-884060 **Fax:** 01349-884076
E-mail: julie.adams@porex.com
Website: http://www.porex.com
Bank(s): The Royal Bank of Scotland
Directors: A. Maclennan (MD)
Immediate Holding Company: PORTEX TECHNOLOGIES LTD
Registration no: 07151922 **VAT No.:** GB 422 5908 59
Date established: 2010 **Turnover:** £1m - £2m **No.of Employees:** 11 - 20
Product Groups: 23, 27, 30, 31, 48

Clackmannanshire

Alva

Scotcrest
Glentana Mill West Stirling Street, Alva, FK12 5EN
Tel: 01259-761827 **Fax:** 01259-769445
E-mail: sales@scotcrest.co.uk
Website: http://www.scotcrest.co.uk
Directors: P. Keers (MD), L. Keers (Fin)
Immediate Holding Company: STAFFHUNT LIMITED
Registration no: SC230351 **Date established:** 2005 **Turnover:** £2m - £5m
No.of Employees: 1 - 10 **Product Groups:** 23

Date of Accounts	Jul 12	Jul 11	Jul 10
Working Capital	16	20	-3
Fixed Assets	4	13	22
Current Assets	100	113	149

Burke Analytical
Alva Industrial Estate, Alva, FK12 5DQ
Tel: 01259-222600 **Fax:** 01259-222619
E-mail: support@speckanalytical.co.uk
Website: http://www.burkeanalytical.co.uk
Directors: M. Speck (MD)
Ultimate Holding Company: SPECK ANALYTICAL LIMITED
Immediate Holding Company: BURKE ELECTRONICS LIMITED
Registration no: SC057125 **Date established:** 1975
Turnover: £250,000 - £500,000 **No.of Employees:** 11 - 20
Product Groups: 38, 67

Date of Accounts	Mar 08	Mar 07
Working Capital	3	3
Current Assets	3	3

Swan-Robes Ltd
Alva Industrial Estate, Alva, FK12 5DQ
Tel: 01259-762669 **Fax:** 01259-760397
E-mail: sr@swanrobes.co.uk
Website: http://www.swanrobes.co.uk
Directors: B. Swan (Dir)
Immediate Holding Company: SWAN-ROBES LIMITED
Registration no: SC240769 **Date established:** 2002
No.of Employees: 11 - 20 **Product Groups:** 35, 42, 45

Date of Accounts	Jun 12	Jun 11	Jun 10
Working Capital	645	623	577
Fixed Assets	145	166	183
Current Assets	861	933	913

Dumfriesshire

Annan

Alpha Solway Ltd
Factory 1 Queensberry Street, Annan, DG12 5BL
Tel: 01461-202452 **Fax:** 01461-202452
E-mail: sales@alphasolway.com
Website: http://www.alphasolway.com
Directors: A. Wright (Fin), M. Gibbons (Sales)
Managers: S. Gracie (Tech Serv Mgr)
Immediate Holding Company: ALPHA SOLWAY LIMITED
Registration no: SC177721 **VAT No.:** GB 680 6850 13
Date established: 1997 **Turnover:** £2m - £5m **No.of Employees:** 51 - 100
Product Groups: 24

Date of Accounts	Dec 11	Dec 10	Dec 09
Working Capital	1m	963	873
Fixed Assets	919	929	943
Current Assets	2m	1m	1m

H & I Engineering Ltd
Annan Road Eastriggs, Annan, DG12 6NJ
Tel: 01461-40500 **Fax:** 01461-40801
E-mail: admin@hi-engineering.co.uk
Website: http://www.hi-engineering.co.uk
Directors: S. Hind (Fin), G. Hind (Dir)
Immediate Holding Company: H & I ENGINEERING LIMITED
Registration no: SC053292 **Date established:** 1973 **Turnover:** £2m - £5m
No.of Employees: 21 - 50 **Product Groups:** 52

Date of Accounts	May 12	May 11	May 10
Working Capital	844	655	705
Fixed Assets	316	320	297
Current Assets	1m	1m	987

J G Trading Co.
Stanfield Works Eastriggs, Annan, DG12 6TF
Tel: 01461-40791 **Fax:** 01461-40978
E-mail: info@jgtradingco.co.uk
Website: http://www.hobbysales.co.uk
Directors: T. Flannigan (Prop)
Date established: 2002 **No.of Employees:** 1 - 10 **Product Groups:** 39, 49, 68

Jewson Ltd
66-68 Port Street, Annan, DG12 6BN
Tel: 01461-202777 **Fax:** 01461-205666
E-mail: richard.wilson@jewson.co.uk
Website: http://www.jewson.co.uk
Managers: R. Wilson (Mgr)
Ultimate Holding Company: COMPAGNIE DE SAINT GOBAIN (FRANCE)
Immediate Holding Company: JEWSON LIMITED
Registration no: 00348407 **VAT No.:** GB 497 7184 83
Date established: 1939 **Turnover:** £1m - £2m **No.of Employees:** 1 - 10
Product Groups: 66

Date of Accounts	Dec 11	Dec 10	Dec 09
Sales Turnover	1606m	1547m	1485m
Pre Tax Profit/Loss	18m	100m	45m
Working Capital	-345m	-250m	-349m
Fixed Assets	496m	387m	461m
Current Assets	657m	1005m	1320m
Current Liabilities	66m	120m	64m

Fife

Anstruther

Metaflake Ltd
Unit 2 Station Road, Anstruther, KY10 3JA
Tel: 01333-313440 **Fax:** 01333-313044
E-mail: enq@metaflake.com
Website: http://www.metaflake.com
Directors: T. Knox (Fin)
Managers: S. Larter (Sales Admin)
Immediate Holding Company: METAFLAKE LIMITED
Registration no: SC165489 **Date established:** 1996
No.of Employees: 1 - 10 **Product Groups:** 32

Date of Accounts	Mar 12	Mar 11	Mar 10
Working Capital	783	503	429
Fixed Assets	376	382	306
Current Assets	1m	740	589

Angus

Arbroath

A G R Automation Ltd
Elliot Industrial Estate, Arbroath, DD11 2NJ
Tel: 01241-872961 **Fax:** 01241-871723
E-mail: craigdickson@agr-automation.com
Website: http://www.agr-automation.com
Bank(s): Lloyds TSB Bank plc
Directors: J. Boardman (Fin)
Managers: P. Mack (Purch Mgr), C. Dickson (Ops Mgr)
Ultimate Holding Company: BLAKELL EUROPLACER LIMITED
Immediate Holding Company: AGR AUTOMATION LIMITED
Registration no: 03994849 **VAT No.:** GB 751 5140 56
Date established: 2000 **Turnover:** £2m - £5m **No.of Employees:** 51 - 100
Product Groups: 37, 42, 45, 46, 47

Date of Accounts	Dec 11	Dec 10	Dec 09
Working Capital	1m	944	842
Fixed Assets	799	772	778
Current Assets	2m	3m	2m
Current Liabilities	573	2m	N/A

Allett Mowers
Baden-Powell Road Kirkton Industrial Estate, Arbroath, DD11 3LS
Tel: 01241-437740 **Fax:** 01241-431715
E-mail: sales@allett.co.uk
Website: http://www.allett.co.uk
Bank(s): Clydesdale Bank PLC
Directors: V. Rogers (Fin)
Ultimate Holding Company: REEKIE ENGINEERING LIMITED
Immediate Holding Company: AMSR LIMITED
Registration no: 01990749 **VAT No.:** GB 330 2901 02
Date established: 1986 **Turnover:** £1m - £2m **No.of Employees:** 11 - 20
Product Groups: 34, 35, 41, 48

Date of Accounts	Mar 11	Mar 10	Mar 09
Working Capital	102	102	105
Current Assets	581	364	618

S G Baker Ltd
Union Street Friockheim, Arbroath, DD11 4TD
Tel: 01241-828681 **Fax:** 01241-828349
E-mail: sales@sgbaker.co.uk
Website: http://www.sgbaker.co.uk
Bank(s): Barclays
Directors: D. Fearon (MD)
Immediate Holding Company: S G BAKER LIMITED
Registration no: 00555739 **VAT No.:** GB 268 6454 19
Date established: 1955 **Turnover:** £5m - £10m **No.of Employees:** 21 - 50
Product Groups: 23, 24

Date of Accounts	Jun 12	Jun 11	Jun 10
Sales Turnover	14m	14m	13m
Pre Tax Profit/Loss	505	555	511
Working Capital	4m	3m	3m
Fixed Assets	413	460	574
Current Assets	5m	4m	4m
Current Liabilities	610	798	805

Geddes Group Ltd
Swirlburn Colliston, Arbroath, DD11 3SH
Tel: 01241-890266 **Fax:** 01241-890445
E-mail: enquiries@geddesgroup.co.uk
Website: http://www.geddesgroup.co.uk
Directors: F. Gedden (MD), F. Geddes (MD), D. Smyth (Dir)
Managers: D. McKerracher, D. Symth (I.T. Exec)
Immediate Holding Company: D. GEDDES (FARMS) LIMITED
Registration no: SC060200 **Date established:** 1957
Turnover: £10m - £20m **No.of Employees:** 101 - 250
Product Groups: 45, 67, 83

John M Henderson & Co. Ltd
Kings Works Sir William Smith Road, Kirkton Industrial Estate, Arbroath, DD11 3RD
Tel: 01241-870774 **Fax:** 01241-875559
E-mail: info@johnmhenderson.com
Website: http://www.johnmhenderson.com
Bank(s): Bank of Scotland
Directors: G. Mccombie (MD), I. Newell (Chief Op Offcr), A. Lauchlan (MD)
Managers: S. Kennedy (Tech Serv Mgr), O. Olaru (Mktg Serv Mgr), N. Millar (Buyer)
Ultimate Holding Company: BELLSHELF (113) LIMITED
Immediate Holding Company: JOHN M. HENDERSON & CO. LIMITED
Registration no: SC013034 **Date established:** 2024
Turnover: £5m - £10m **No.of Employees:** 51 - 100 **Product Groups:** 38, 39, 40, 42, 45, 67, 84

Date of Accounts	Jun 11	Jun 10	Jun 09
Sales Turnover	9m	4m	8m
Pre Tax Profit/Loss	-125	-440	172
Working Capital	3m	3m	3m
Fixed Assets	972	1m	1m
Current Assets	6m	5m	6m
Current Liabilities	2m	968	1m

Ladco
Sir William Smith Road Kirkton Industrial Estate, Arbroath, DD11 3RD
Tel: 01241-434444 **Fax:** 01241-434411
E-mail: enquiries@macintyre.co.uk
Website: http://www.macintyre.co.uk
Directors: I. Robertson (Comm), S. Anderton (MD)
Managers: G. Strachan (Works Gen Mgr), R. Ireland, J. Finley (Mktg Serv Mgr)
Ultimate Holding Company: PITLIVIE HOLDINGS LIMITED
Immediate Holding Company: LADCO ENGINEERING LIMITED
Registration no: SC080904 **VAT No.:** GB 828 4421 24
Date established: 1982 **Turnover:** £5m - £10m
No.of Employees: 51 - 100 **Product Groups:** 35, 39, 48

M Lingard
The Old Bank Gardyne Street, Friockheim, Arbroath, DD11 4SG
Tel: 01241-828649 **Fax:** 01241-828296
E-mail: office@michael-lingard.com
Directors: M. Lingard (Prop)
No.of Employees: 1 - 10 **Product Groups:** 36, 39, 40

MacIntyre Chocolate Systems Ltd (Incl. Petzholdt Heidenauer)
Sir William Smith Rd Kirkton Industrial Estate, Arbroath, DD11 3RD
Tel: 01241-434444 **Fax:** 01241-434411
E-mail: enquiries@macintyre.co.uk
Website: http://www.macintyre.co.uk
Directors: S. Anderson (MD)
Registration no: SC089165 **VAT No.:** GB 828 4421 24
Date established: 1974 **Turnover:** £5m - £10m
No.of Employees: 51 - 100 **Product Groups:** 20, 41, 42, 67

Date of Accounts	Oct 08
Working Capital	11
Current Assets	15
Current Liabilities	5

Mackays Ltd
James Chalmers Road Kirkton Industrial Estate, Arbroath, DD11 3LR
Tel: 01241-432500 **Fax:** 01241-432444
E-mail: info@mackays.com
Website: http://www.mackays.com
Directors: P. Grant (Prop), M. Grant (Comm)
Managers: K. Neave, J. Davidson (Sales Prom Mgr), C. Smith, M. Thomson
Immediate Holding Company: MACKAY'S LTD.
Registration no: SC155016 **VAT No.:** GB 652 0865 39
Date established: 1994 **Turnover:** £10m - £20m
No.of Employees: 51 - 100 **Product Groups:** 20, 62

Date of Accounts	Dec 11	Dec 10	Dec 09
Sales Turnover	12m	11m	10m
Pre Tax Profit/Loss	401	260	-367

Working Capital	-1m	-751	-1m
Fixed Assets	6m	7m	7m
Current Assets	5m	4m	4m
Current Liabilities	327	349	451

Northern Tool & Gear Co. Ltd
John Street West, Arbroath, DD11 1RT
Tel: 01241-872626 **Fax:** 01241-870040
E-mail: general@ntgear.co.uk
Website: http://www.ntgear.co.uk
Bank(s): The Royal Bank of Scotland plc
Directors: G. Strachan (MD)
Managers: F. Henry, C. Richie (Fin Mgr)
Immediate Holding Company: NORTHERN TOOL & GEAR COMPANY LIMITED
Registration no: SC023683 **Date established:** 1945 **Turnover:** £2m - £5m
No.of Employees: 51 - 100 **Product Groups:** 35, 48

Date of Accounts	Jan 12	Jan 11	Jan 10
Sales Turnover	N/A	N/A	3m
Pre Tax Profit/Loss	N/A	N/A	-363
Working Capital	873	554	585
Fixed Assets	2m	2m	2m
Current Assets	1m	983	864
Current Liabilities	N/A	N/A	53

Ramsay Fabrications
Baden-Powell Road Kirkton Industrial Estate, Arbroath, DD11 3LS
Tel: 01241-870314 **Fax:** 01241-870314
Directors: G. Ramsay (Prop)
Immediate Holding Company: ECE CONSTRUCTION LIMITED
Registration no: SC324458 **Date established:** 2007
No.of Employees: 1 - 10 **Product Groups:** 26, 35

Date of Accounts	Mar 11	Mar 10	Mar 09
Working Capital	102	102	105
Current Assets	581	364	618

Turf N Stuff Ltd
Unit 8 Elliot Industrial Estate, Arbroath, DD11 2NJ
Tel: 01241-870415
E-mail: info@turfandstuff.com
Website: http://www.turfnstuff.com
Managers: C. Miller (Chief Mgr)
Immediate Holding Company: TURF 'N' STUFF LIMITED
Registration no: SC278411 **Date established:** 2005
Turnover: £500,000 - £1m **No.of Employees:** 1 - 10 **Product Groups:** 25, 29

Date of Accounts	Jan 12	Jan 11	Jan 10
Working Capital	-3	4	-41
Fixed Assets	25	16	19
Current Assets	86	72	55

Waulkmill Industrial Doors Ltd
Waulkmill House, Arbroath, DD11 4SA
Tel: 01241-830406 **Fax:** 01241-830406
Directors: W. Turner (MD), G. Turner (Fin)
Immediate Holding Company: WAULKMILL INDUSTRIAL DOORS LIMITED
Registration no: SC222241 **Date established:** 2001
No.of Employees: 1 - 10 **Product Groups:** 26, 35

Date of Accounts	Aug 11	Aug 10	Aug 07
Working Capital	10	23	20
Fixed Assets	6	8	8
Current Assets	27	38	31

Ayrshire

Ardrossan

Robertson's Fine Foods (t/a Robertsons Fine Foods)
88 Princes Street, Ardrossan, KA22 8DQ
Tel: 01294-463936 **Fax:** 01294-604060
E-mail: iain@robertsonsfinefoods.eclipse.co.uk
Website: http://www.robertsonsfinefoods.com
Bank(s): Bank of Scotland
Directors: H. Robertson (Sales), A. Brown (Fin), I. Robertson (MD), I. Robertson (MD)
Immediate Holding Company: JOHN ROBERTSON & SONS HAMCURERS LIMITED
Registration no: SC022598 **VAT No.:** GB 263 0667 62
Date established: 1943 **No.of Employees:** 21 - 50 **Product Groups:** 20

Date of Accounts	Mar 11	Mar 08	Apr 09
Sales Turnover	11m	N/A	N/A
Pre Tax Profit/Loss	101	286	-142
Working Capital	2m	2m	2m
Fixed Assets	1m	1m	1m
Current Assets	3m	3m	3m
Current Liabilities	184	294	145

Zebra Signs & Graphics
9 Princes Place, Ardrossan, KA22 8HB
Tel: 01294-608476 **Fax:** 01294-608476
E-mail: nick@zebrasigns.co.uk
Website: http://www.zebrasigns.co.uk
Directors: N. Monir (Prop)
No.of Employees: 1 - 10 **Product Groups:** 30, 39, 40

Perthshire

Auchterarder

Daisy D
West Mains Gleneagles, Auchterarder, PH3 1PJ
Tel: 01764-682202 **Fax:** 01764-682202
E-mail: daisyd@farmersweekly.net
Website: http://www.daisyd.co.uk
Directors: D. Gilcrist (Ptnr)
Immediate Holding Company: DAISY D LIMITED
Registration no: SC077296 **Date established:** 1982
Turnover: Up to £250,000 **No.of Employees:** 1 - 10 **Product Groups:** 07

Date of Accounts	Mar 07
Working Capital	7
Fixed Assets	1
Current Assets	13
Current Liabilities	6
Total Share Capital	4

Rattray A T V
The Workshop Woodend Farm, Auchterarder, PH3 1PF
Tel: 01764-664994 **Fax:** 01764-664997
Website: http://www.rattrayatv.co.uk
Directors: G. Rattray (Prop)
Date established: 1990 **No.of Employees:** 1 - 10 **Product Groups:** 41

Rossshire

Avoch

J L V Industries
Burn Farm Steading Killen, Avoch, IV9 8RQ
Tel: 01463-811355 **Fax:** 01463-811577
Managers: I. Ross (Chief Mgr)
Date established: 1999 **No.of Employees:** 1 - 10 **Product Groups:** 35, 39, 45

Ayrshire

Ayr

Alandola Design
Midton House, Ayr, KA7 4EG
Tel: 01292-442226 **Fax:** 01292-442226
E-mail: adrienne@alandola-design.fsworld.co.uk
Website: http://www.alandola-design.co.uk
Directors: A. Healy (Prop)
No.of Employees: 1 - 10 **Product Groups:** 23, 24, 52, 63

Alex Begg & Co.
17 Viewfield Road, Ayr, KA8 8HJ
Tel: 01292-267615 **Fax:** 01292-269510
E-mail: enquiries@beggscotland.com
Website: http://www.beggscotland.com
Bank(s): HSBC Bank plc
Directors: A. Menzies (Co Sec), I. Laird (Grp MD)
Immediate Holding Company: MOORBROOK HOLDINGS LIMITED
Registration no: SC332250 **Date established:** 2007
Turnover: £5m - £10m **No.of Employees:** 51 - 100 **Product Groups:** 23, 24

Date of Accounts	Dec 11	Dec 10	Dec 09
Pre Tax Profit/Loss	-3	-3	3m
Working Capital	N/A	4	-8m
Fixed Assets	N/A	N/A	9m
Current Assets	N/A	5	8
Current Liabilities	N/A	1	1

Denholm Barwil Ltd
52 North Harbour Street, Ayr, KA8 8AH
Tel: 01292-610451 **Fax:** 01292-610452
Website: http://www.denholm-group.co.uk
Managers: G. Taylor (Mgr)
Immediate Holding Company: DENHOLM BARWIL LIMITED
Registration no: SC032785 **Date established:** 1958 **Turnover:** £1m - £2m
No.of Employees: 1 - 10 **Product Groups:** 72, 74

Electropower Services
82 Macadam Place, Ayr, KA8 0AW
Tel: 01292-287579 **Fax:** 01292-287579
E-mail: wil@xlm.co.uk
Directors: I. Leslie (Prop)
Turnover: Up to £250,000 **No.of Employees:** 1 - 10 **Product Groups:** 37, 67

J H P Training Ltd
3 Killoch Place, Ayr, KA7 2EA
Tel: 01292-288644 **Fax:** 01292-611174
E-mail: ayr.business.centre@jhp-group.com
Website: http://www.jhptraining.com
Directors: I. Dick (Reg), H. Pitman (Ch), S. Williams (MD), I. Dick (Dir)
Managers: J. Bray (Personnel), M. Lohoar (Mgr)
Immediate Holding Company: JHP TRAINING LIMITED
Registration no: 03247918 **Date established:** 1996
No.of Employees: 11 - 20 **Product Groups:** 80, 86

Jewson Ltd
Mccalls Avenue, Ayr, KA8 9AA
Tel: 01292-269318 **Fax:** 01292-611544
Website: http://www.jewson.co.uk
Managers: S. Flynn (District Mgr)
Ultimate Holding Company: COMPAGNIE DE SAINT GOBAIN (FRANCE)
Immediate Holding Company: JEWSON LIMITED
Registration no: 00348407 **VAT No.:** GB 394 1212 63
Date established: 1939 **No.of Employees:** 11 - 20 **Product Groups:** 66

Date of Accounts	Dec 11	Dec 10	Dec 09
Sales Turnover	1606m	1547m	1485m
Pre Tax Profit/Loss	18m	100m	45m
Working Capital	-345m	-250m	-349m
Fixed Assets	496m	387m	461m
Current Assets	657m	1005m	1320m
Current Liabilities	66m	120m	64m

Jewson Ltd
5 Green Street, Ayr, KA8 8AF
Tel: 01292-268712 **Fax:** 01292-611407
Website: http://www.jewson.co.uk
Directors: P. Hindle (MD)
Managers: J. Reid (District Mgr)
Ultimate Holding Company: COMPAGNIE DE SAINT GOBAIN (FRANCE)
Immediate Holding Company: JEWSON LIMITED
Registration no: 00348407 **VAT No.:** GB 497 7184 83
Date established: 1939 **Turnover:** £2m - £5m **No.of Employees:** 11 - 20
Product Groups: 66

Date of Accounts	Dec 11	Dec 10	Dec 09
Sales Turnover	1606m	1547m	1485m
Pre Tax Profit/Loss	18m	100m	45m
Working Capital	-345m	-250m	-349m
Fixed Assets	496m	387m	461m
Current Assets	657m	1005m	1320m
Current Liabilities	66m	120m	64m

Posterplus Digital Ltd
53 Beresford Terrace, Ayr, KA7 2HD
Tel: 08445-678877 **Fax:** 01563-535342
E-mail: info@posterplus.co.uk
Website: http://www.posterplus.co.uk
Directors: G. Hollywood (MD)
Immediate Holding Company: POSTERPLUS DIGITAL LIMITED
Registration no: SC310688 **Date established:** 2006
No.of Employees: 1 - 10 **Product Groups:** 81

Date of Accounts	Oct 11	Oct 10	Oct 09
Working Capital	-123	-190	-219
Fixed Assets	428	492	530
Current Assets	105	146	123

Soil Fertility Dunns Ltd
Carrick Terminal North Harbour, Ayr, KA8 8AH
Tel: 01292-611622 **Fax:** 01292-619990
E-mail: rob.cooper@soilfert.co.uk
Website: http://www.soilfert.co.uk
Bank(s): National Westminster
Directors: S. Mcharg (Comm)
Registration no: 00574511 **VAT No.:** GB 617 4069 41
Turnover: £5m - £10m **No.of Employees:** 11 - 20 **Product Groups:** 66

Date of Accounts	Jul 05
Working Capital	826
Current Assets	826
Total Share Capital	15

Stagecoach Ltd
Bus Station Sandgate, Ayr, KA7 1DD
Tel: 01292-613500 **Fax:** 01292-613501
E-mail: alan.henry@stagecoachbus.com
Website: http://www.stagecoachbus.com
Bank(s): Bank of Scotland
Directors: A. Whitnall (Co Sec)
Managers: A. Henry (Mktg Serv Mgr)
Ultimate Holding Company: STAGECOACH GROUP PLC
Immediate Holding Company: STAGECOACH LIMITED
Registration no: 03092390 **VAT No.:** GB 435 7578 19
Date established: 1995 **Turnover:** £10m - £20m
No.of Employees: 501 - 1000 **Product Groups:** 72

Date of Accounts	Apr 11	Apr 10	Apr 09
Pre Tax Profit/Loss	-251	-240	-531
Working Capital	-13	203	412
Current Assets	2m	2m	2m

Banffshire

Ballindalloch

Precision Rifle Services Ltd
Strathavon Lodge Kirkmichael, Ballindalloch, AB37 9AR
Tel: 01807-580422 **Fax:** 01807-580424
E-mail: info@precisionrifles.com
Website: http://www.precisionrifles.com
Directors: Y. Ferguson (Fin)
Immediate Holding Company: PRECISION RIFLE SERVICES LIMITED
Registration no: SC196657 **Date established:** 1999
No.of Employees: 1 - 10 **Product Groups:** 36, 39, 40

Date of Accounts	Aug 11	Aug 10	Aug 09
Working Capital	109	102	93
Fixed Assets	67	69	76
Current Assets	224	205	193

Kincardineshire

Banchory

Anderson Instruments
East Lodge Drum, Drumoak, Banchory, AB31 5AN
Tel: 01224-733835 **Fax:** 01224-733835
E-mail: ian@anderson-instruments.co.uk
Website: http://www.andersoninstruments.co.uk
Directors: S. Anderson (Prop)
Immediate Holding Company: JDM SAFETY SERVICES LTD.
Registration no: SC280491 **Date established:** 2005
No.of Employees: 1 - 10 **Product Groups:** 38, 42, 67

Skylark Energy Systems Ltd
PO Box 11033, Banchory, AB31 5WS
Tel: 01330-823950 **Fax:** 01330-823966
E-mail: info@skylark.co.uk
Website: http://www.skylark.co.uk
Directors: E. Robertson (Fin), P. Gillan (MD)
Immediate Holding Company: SKYLARK ENERGY SYSTEMS LIMITED
Registration no: SC211220 **Date established:** 2000
Turnover: £250,000 - £500,000 **No.of Employees:** 1 - 10
Product Groups: 37

Date of Accounts	Sep 11	Sep 10	Sep 09
Working Capital	371	396	364
Fixed Assets	3	3	3
Current Assets	496	523	535

Banffshire

Banff

B & M Winton
Itlaw Smithy Alvah, Banff, AB45 3UP
Tel: 01261-821261 **Fax:** 01261-821261
Directors: B. Winton (Prop)
Date established: 1975 **No.of Employees:** 1 - 10 **Product Groups:** 41

Ian Rennie Ltd
Inverboyndie Industrial Estate, Banff, AB45 2JJ
Tel: 01261-818326 **Fax:** 01261-815390
E-mail: ian@ianrennie.co.uk
Website: http://www.ianrennie.co.uk
Directors: E. Rennie (MD)
Immediate Holding Company: IAN RENNIE LTD.
Registration no: SC246663 **Date established:** 2003
No.of Employees: 1 - 10 **Product Groups:** 41

Date of Accounts	May 12	May 11	May 10
Working Capital	215	198	178
Fixed Assets	41	41	17
Current Assets	255	238	223

West Lothian

Bathgate

Caradel Brick Ltd
Lower Bathville Armadale, Bathgate, EH48 2LZ
Tel: 01501-730671 **Fax:** 01501-732991
E-mail: enquiries@caradale.co.uk
Website: http://www.caradel.co.uk
Bank(s): The Royal Bank of Scotland
Directors: J. Turnbull (Sales)
Managers: V. Burgoyne (Chief Mgr)
Registration no: 00001722 **VAT No.:** GB 260 0888 64
Turnover: £2m - £5m **No.of Employees:** 21 - 50 **Product Groups:** 33

Chieftain Forge
Unit 1 Block 4 Whiteside Industrial Estate, Bathgate, EH48 2RX
Tel: 01506-652354 **Fax:** 01506-656017
E-mail: sales@chieftainforge.co.uk
Website: http://www.chieftainforge.co.uk
Directors: W. Chapman (Prop)
VAT No.: GB 703 8451 47 **Turnover:** Up to £250,000
No.of Employees: 1 - 10 **Product Groups:** 41, 45

Computer Training Centre
6 Whitburn Road, Bathgate, EH48 1HH
Tel: 01506-634511 **Fax:** 01506-656688
E-mail: robert@reid-computer-training.co.uk
Managers: R. Wilson (Mgr)
Ultimate Holding Company: ENSERVE GROUP LIMITED
Immediate Holding Company: THISTLE ROAD STONE LIMITED
Registration no: SC309012 **VAT No.:** GB 380 0954 55
Date established: 2012 **Turnover:** £250,000 - £500,000
No.of Employees: 1 - 10 **Product Groups:** 86

Date of Accounts	Apr 11	Apr 10	Apr 09
Working Capital	2m	2m	2m
Current Assets	2m	2m	2m

Dean Plant Hire
Whitburn Road, Bathgate, EH48 2HR
Tel: 01506-630578 **Fax:** 01506-634835
Website: http://www.deanplanthire.co.uk
Directors: E. Maguire (Dir), I. Maguire (Fin)
Ultimate Holding Company: BIRNIEHILL PROPERTIES LIMITED
Immediate Holding Company: DEAN PLANT HIRE LIMITED
Registration no: SC050534 **VAT No.:** GB 502 3385 81
Date established: 1972 **Turnover:** £1m - £2m **No.of Employees:** 21 - 50
Product Groups: 72, 83

Date of Accounts	Dec 11	Dec 10	Dec 09
Working Capital	287	397	165
Fixed Assets	1m	1m	1m
Current Assets	765	775	584

Dacoll Ltd
Gardners Lane, Bathgate, EH48 1TP
Tel: 01506-815000 **Fax:** 01506-656012
E-mail: sales@dacoll.co.uk
Website: http://www.dacoll.co.uk
Bank(s): Clydesdale Bank PLC
Directors: S. Ingledow (MD)
Ultimate Holding Company: DACOLL GROUP LIMITED
Immediate Holding Company: DACOLL LIMITED
Registration no: SC173001 **VAT No.:** GB 268 5327 31
Date established: 1997 **Turnover:** £5m - £10m
No.of Employees: 51 - 100 **Product Groups:** 44

Date of Accounts	Mar 11	Mar 10	Mar 09
Sales Turnover	9m	10m	9m
Pre Tax Profit/Loss	42	-187	161
Working Capital	656	653	861
Fixed Assets	644	639	477
Current Assets	3m	4m	3m
Current Liabilities	2m	2m	2m

Dana Glacier Vandervell
1 Inch Wood Avenue, Bathgate, EH48 2ED
Tel: 01506-635008 **Fax:** 01506-635009
Managers: N. Pittner (Mgr)
No.of Employees: 101 - 250 **Product Groups:** 35, 45

Eagle Envelopes Ltd
Unit 1 Block 1 Whiteside Industrial Estate, Bathgate, EH48 2RX
Tel: 01506-634463 **Fax:** 01506-634366
E-mail: sales@eagle-envelopes.com
Website: http://www.eagle-envelopes.com
Directors: J. Gutteridge (MD), M. Towler (Sales)
Ultimate Holding Company: SMITH ANDERSON GROUP LIMITED
Immediate Holding Company: SMITH ANDERSON ENVELOPES LIMITED
Registration no: SC090157 **Date established:** 1984
Turnover: £10m - £20m **No.of Employees:** 51 - 100 **Product Groups:** 27, 64, 66

Date of Accounts	Sep 09	Sep 08
Pre Tax Profit/Loss	3	-3m
Working Capital	N/A	-3
Current Liabilities	N/A	3

Ewos Ltd
Westfield, Bathgate, EH48 3BP
Tel: 01506-633966 **Fax:** 01506-632730
E-mail: john.christie@ewos.com
Website: http://www.ewos.com
Directors: J. Christie (Fin)
Managers: D. Morrice (Sales & Mktg Mg), N. Burke (Tech Serv Mgr), M. Wilson (Purch Mgr)
Ultimate Holding Company: CERMAQ ASA (NORWAY)
Immediate Holding Company: EWOS LIMITED
Registration no: 01635854 **VAT No.:** GB 368 3775 06
Date established: 1982 **Turnover:** £75m - £125m
No.of Employees: 51 - 100 **Product Groups:** 20, 84

Date of Accounts	Dec 11	Dec 10	Dec 09
Sales Turnover	93m	76m	62m
Pre Tax Profit/Loss	6m	-14m	4m
Working Capital	13m	12m	60m
Fixed Assets	8m	5m	6m
Current Assets	19m	17m	66m
Current Liabilities	1m	2m	962

Glossbrook Engineering Ltd
Westrigg 47 Craig Street, Blackridge, Bathgate, EH48 3AU
Tel: 01501-752995 **Fax:** 01501-751237
E-mail: info@glossbrook.com
Website: http://www.glossbrook.com
Directors: S. Kenny (Fin)
Immediate Holding Company: GLOSSBROOK ENGINEERING LIMITED
Registration no: SC053216 **Date established:** 1973
No.of Employees: 11 - 20 **Product Groups:** 67, 84

Date of Accounts	Aug 11	Feb 08	Feb 10
Working Capital	151	341	217
Fixed Assets	324	439	351
Current Assets	600	517	334

Good Company Discos & Karaoke
7 Burnvale Avenue, Bathgate, EH48 2SY
Tel: 01506-630419 **Fax:** 01506-630419
E-mail: goodcodiscos@hotmail.co.uk
Website: http://www.goodcompanydiscos.co.uk
Directors: A. Watt (Prop)
No.of Employees: 1 - 10 **Product Groups:** 37, 89

Harwoods Cleaning Contractors
Unit 3 Block 13 Whiteside Industrial Estate, Bathgate, EH48 2RX
Tel: 01506-633584 **Fax:** 01506-636868
E-mail: mervin@harwoodscleaning.co.uk
Website: http://www.harwoodscleaningcontractors.co.uk
Directors: M. Guild (Prop)
Immediate Holding Company: HARWOODS CLEANING CONTRACTORS LIMITED
Registration no: SC170708 **Date established:** 1996
No.of Employees: 1 - 10 **Product Groups:** 44, 48, 52, 80, 84

Date of Accounts	Dec 11	Dec 10	Dec 09
Working Capital	23	24	35
Fixed Assets	17	23	26
Current Assets	251	253	225

Highlander Snacks Ltd
Inchcorse Place Whitehill Industrial Estate, Bathgate, EH48 2EE
Tel: 01506-630778 **Fax:** 01506-653781
E-mail: brian.robertson@highlandersnacks.co.uk
Website: http://www.unichips.com
Directors: A. Vitaloni (Co Sec)
Managers: B. Robertson (Factory Mgr), D. Melville (Personnel), E. Drummond (Fin Mgr)
Ultimate Holding Company: UNICHIPS FINANZIARIA (ITALY)
Immediate Holding Company: HIGHLANDER SNACKS LTD
Registration no: SC129809 **Date established:** 1991 **Turnover:** £2m - £5m
No.of Employees: 21 - 50 **Product Groups:** 20

Date of Accounts	Dec 11	Dec 10	Dec 09
Sales Turnover	3m	3m	5m
Pre Tax Profit/Loss	-940	380	-363
Working Capital	-4m	-3m	-2m
Fixed Assets	148	145	153
Current Assets	1m	1m	1m
Current Liabilities	113	193	188

Holemasters Scotland
Unit 2 Block 5 Whiteside Industrial Estate, Bathgate, EH48 2RX
Tel: 01506-653303 **Fax:** 01506-652991
E-mail: jim@holemastersltd.com
Website: http://www.dmhall.co.uk
Directors: J. Mcarthur (MD), J. McArthur (Dir)
Immediate Holding Company: HOLEMASTERS SCOTLAND LIMITED
Registration no: SC144570 **Date established:** 1993
No.of Employees: 21 - 50 **Product Groups:** 51

Date of Accounts	Jun 11	Jun 10	Jun 09
Working Capital	375	537	591
Fixed Assets	369	333	302
Current Assets	729	838	1m

Liebherr GB Ltd
35 Inchmuir Road Whitehill Industrial Estate, Bathgate, EH48 2EP
Tel: 01506-651580 **Fax:** 01506-632637
E-mail: derek.davies@liebherr.com
Website: http://www.liebherr.com
Managers: J. Smith (Depot Mgr)
Immediate Holding Company: LIEBHERR - GREAT BRITAIN LIMITED
Registration no: 00677497 **Date established:** 1960
Turnover: £20m - £50m **No.of Employees:** 11 - 20 **Product Groups:** 45

Date of Accounts	Dec 10	Dec 09	Dec 08
Sales Turnover	130m	100m	162m
Pre Tax Profit/Loss	148	-466	4m
Working Capital	12m	14m	14m
Fixed Assets	17m	16m	20m
Current Assets	43m	45m	50m
Current Liabilities	31m	31m	32m

Lothian Mechanical Handling Ltd
8 Mosshall Industrial Estate Blackburn, Bathgate, EH47 7LY
Tel: 01506-655535 **Fax:** 01506-634799
E-mail: lmh@lothianmechanicalhandling.co.uk
Website: http://www.lothianmechanicalhandling.co.uk
Bank(s): The Royal Bank of Scotland, Cumbernauld
Directors: L. Ferris (MD), C. Ferris (Fin)
Managers: A. Morrison (Sales Prom Mgr)
Immediate Holding Company: LOTHIAN MECHANICAL HANDLING LIMITED
Registration no: SC071394 **VAT No.:** GB 345 3466 51
Date established: 1980 **Turnover:** £1m - £2m **No.of Employees:** 11 - 20
Product Groups: 39, 40, 45, 48, 67

Date of Accounts	Oct 11	Oct 10	Oct 09
Sales Turnover	1m	1m	1m
Pre Tax Profit/Loss	88	129	86
Working Capital	154	157	129
Fixed Assets	448	368	421
Current Assets	458	395	379
Current Liabilities	34	55	60

Lothian Steel Services Ltd
Whitburn Road, Bathgate, EH48 2HR
Tel: 01506-633500 **Fax:** 01506-633648
E-mail: sales@lothiansteels.co.uk
Directors: M. Kerr (Fin)
Ultimate Holding Company: KLS (HOLDINGS) LIMITED
Immediate Holding Company: LOTHIAN STEEL SERVICES LIMITED
Registration no: SC068437 **Date established:** 1979
Turnover: £10m - £20m **No.of Employees:** 11 - 20 **Product Groups:** 35, 66

Date of Accounts	May 11	May 10	May 09
Working Capital	603	551	580
Fixed Assets	176	172	196
Current Assets	1m	1m	1m

Norwood Radiators
Norwood Cottage 25a Longridge Road, Whitburn, Bathgate, EH47 8HB
Tel: 01501-740558 **Fax:** 01501-745793
E-mail: norwood-radiators@ukonline.co.uk
Directors: R. Robertson (Prop)
Immediate Holding Company: TYRES RIMS 'N' TRIMS LIMITED
Date established: 2006 **Turnover:** Up to £250,000
No.of Employees: 1 - 10 **Product Groups:** 40, 42

Date of Accounts	Jul 11	Jul 10	Jul 09
Sales Turnover	N/A	N/A	220
Pre Tax Profit/Loss	N/A	N/A	27
Working Capital	N/A	5	-0
Fixed Assets	12	8	8
Current Assets	63	53	41
Current Liabilities	N/A	N/A	21

Redmill Fabrication Ltd
19 Inchmuir Road Whitehill Industrial Estate, Bathgate, EH48 2EP
Tel: 01506-634333 **Fax:** 01506-634999
E-mail: john@edinburgh-sports-club.co.uk
Website: http://www.edinburgh-sports-club.co.uk
Directors: J. Miller (Fin)
Immediate Holding Company: REDMILL FABRICATION LIMITED
Registration no: SC063324 **VAT No.:** GB 300 5660 00
Date established: 1977 **Turnover:** Up to £250,000
No.of Employees: 1 - 10 **Product Groups:** 35, 48

Date of Accounts	Nov 11	Nov 10	Nov 09
Working Capital	302	282	242
Fixed Assets	123	132	128
Current Assets	424	396	360

Sibcas Ltd
Easton Road, Bathgate, EH48 2SF
Tel: 01506-633122 **Fax:** 01506-634320
E-mail: mail@sibcas.co.uk
Website: http://www.sibcas.co.uk
Bank(s): Royal Bank of Scotland
Directors: E. McLeod (Fin), J. Storrie (MD)
Managers: C. Sine (Purch Mgr), S. Clarke (Mktg Serv Mgr), M. Smith (Tech Serv Mgr)
Ultimate Holding Company: SIBCAS (HOLDINGS) LIMITED
Immediate Holding Company: SIBCAS LIMITED
Registration no: SC052604 **VAT No.:** GB 270 9800 52
Date established: 1973 **Turnover:** £20m - £50m
No.of Employees: 101 - 250 **Product Groups:** 25

Date of Accounts	Mar 11	Mar 10	Mar 09
Sales Turnover	26m	25m	N/A
Pre Tax Profit/Loss	159	155	157
Working Capital	3m	2m	2m
Current Assets	6m	6m	5m
Current Liabilities	2m	2m	1m

Siemens Building Technologies Ltd
Unit 4 Inchcross Industrial Estate Whitburn Road, Bathgate, EH48 2HR
Tel: 01506-633440 **Fax:** 01506-655863
E-mail: dave.houston@siemens.com
Website: http://www.siemens.com
Managers: D. Houston (Projects)
Ultimate Holding Company: OIL STATES INTERNATIONAL INC (U.S.A)
Immediate Holding Company: STEWART MELROSE (BATHGATE) LIMITED
Registration no: 01681983 **Date established:** 1972
Turnover: £10m - £20m **No.of Employees:** 1 - 10 **Product Groups:** 35, 37, 40

Date of Accounts	Oct 11	Oct 10	Oct 09
Working Capital	88	-85	83
Fixed Assets	2m	2m	2m
Current Assets	889	777	759

Think Online Ltd (Design & Development)
Po Box 15489, Bathgate, EH48 2UX
Tel: 0845-6697575
E-mail: info@thinkonline.co.uk
Website: http://www.thinkonline.co.uk
Directors: J. Keenan (Dir)
Registration no: SC291550 **No.of Employees:** 1 - 10 **Product Groups:** 44, 79, 81

Ayrshire

Beith

AEA Technology
Glengarnock Technology Centre Caledonian Road Lochshore Industrial Estate, Glengarnock, Beith, KA14 3DD
Tel: 08701-905150 **Fax:** 08701-905151
Website: http://www.aeat.co.uk
Directors: J. Pitcairn (Dir)
No.of Employees: 11 - 20 **Product Groups:** 37, 44, 80

Anderson Stewart Castings
Block 1 Lochshore Industrial Estate Caledonia Road, Glengarnock, Beith, KA14 3DB
Tel: 01505-683368 **Fax:** 01505-683771
E-mail: brianmcknight@ascast.co.uk
Website: http://www.andersonstewartcastings.co.uk
Bank(s): National Westminster
Directors: L. Train (Fin)
Managers: B. McKnight (Chief Mgr), P. McLaughlin (Tech Serv Mgr)
Immediate Holding Company: CORRIGAN DRYSDALE LIMITED
Registration no: 00577106 **Date established:** 2011 **Turnover:** £1m - £2m
No.of Employees: 21 - 50 **Product Groups:** 34

Orna Metal
Unit 4 Glengarnock Workshops Glengarnock, Beith, KA14 3DA
Tel: 01505-683137 **Fax:** 01505-683137
Website: http://www.ornametal.com
Directors: J. Waldron (Ptnr), J. Waldren (Ptnr)
Date established: 1995 **No.of Employees:** 1 - 10 **Product Groups:** 26, 35

Playline Services Ltd
87 Lomond Crescent, Beith, KA15 2EB
Tel: 01505-502183 **Fax:** 01505-504786
Directors: D. Robertson (MD), P. Robertson (Fin)
Immediate Holding Company: PLAYLINE SERVICES LIMITED
Registration no: SC175642 **Date established:** 1997
Turnover: Up to £250,000 **No.of Employees:** 1 - 10 **Product Groups:** 46, 48

Date of Accounts	Oct 10	Oct 09	Oct 07
Sales Turnover	30	2	3
Pre Tax Profit/Loss	-2	N/A	N/A
Working Capital	1	2	2
Fixed Assets	N/A	1	1
Current Assets	1	2	2

Protective Paint Coatings
East Lugtonridge Farm Lochlibo Road, Burnhouse, Beith, KA15 1LE
Tel: 01560-484151
E-mail: jan@drewery.freeserve.co.uk
Directors: J. Duguid (Prop)
Date established: 2005 **No.of Employees:** 1 - 10 **Product Groups:** 38, 42

Lanarkshire

Bellshill

Anglo Abrasives Ltd
3 Sandpiper Way Strathclyde Business Park, Bellshill, ML4 3NG
Tel: 01698-741020 **Fax:** 01698-741050
E-mail: scotland@angloabrasives.com
Website: http://www.angloabrasives.com
Directors: R. Sneesby (MD)
Managers: R. Watt (Mgr), S. Mcnicol (Sales Prom Mgr)
Ultimate Holding Company: Carbo P.L.C.
Immediate Holding Company: ANGLO ABRASIVES LIMITED
Registration no: 00197881 **Date established:** 1924
Turnover: £250,000 - £500,000 **No.of Employees:** 1 - 10
Product Groups: 33, 47

Ashworth
Marion Street, Bellshill, ML4 1EB
Tel: 01698-742839 **Fax:** 01698-740744
E-mail: sales.bellshill@ashw-fra.co.uk
Website: http://www.ashworth-frazer.co.uk
Bank(s): HSBC Bank plc
Managers: M. Laird (Mgr)
Immediate Holding Company: OLIVER ASHWORTH LTD
Registration no: 00086294 **VAT No.:** GB 617 3765 26
No.of Employees: 11 - 20 **Product Groups:** 30, 32

Beaumont Group
Wren Court Strathclyde Business Park, Bellshill, ML4 3NH
Tel: 01698-845510 **Fax:** 01698- 844819
E-mail: info@esgtechserv.co.uk
Website: http://www.beaumontelectrical.co.uk
Managers: B. Earo (Mgr)
Date established: 1995 **No.of Employees:** 11 - 20 **Product Groups:** 20, 40, 41

Bellshill Metal Works Glasgow Ltd
60-82 Hamilton Road, Bellshill, ML4 1AG
Tel: 01698-747132 **Fax:** 01698-746908
Website: http://www.connectfree.co.uk
Directors: P. Connacher (Co Sec)
Immediate Holding Company: BELLSHILL METAL WORKS (GLASGOW) LIMITED
Registration no: SC026908 **VAT No.:** GB 259 6564 13
Date established: 1949 **Turnover:** £500,000 - £1m
No.of Employees: 1 - 10 **Product Groups:** 36, 48, 66

Date of Accounts	Mar 12	Mar 11	Mar 10
Working Capital	298	262	222
Fixed Assets	60	68	60
Current Assets	379	349	303

Dalziel Ltd
North Industrial Estate Belgowan Street, Bellshill Industrial Estate, Bellshill, ML4 3NS
Tel: 01698-749595 **Fax:** 01698-740503
E-mail: info@dalziel.co.uk
Website: http://www.dalziel.co.uk
Managers: M. Platt (Personnel), T. West (Buyer), R. Clark, D. Darroch (Tech Serv Mgr), R. Clarke (Mgr)
Ultimate Holding Company: J.R. DALZIEL (HOLDINGS) LIMITED
Immediate Holding Company: DALZIEL LIMITED
Registration no: SC063157 **VAT No.:** GB 334 3306 86
Date established: 1977 **Turnover:** £75m - £125m
No.of Employees: 21 - 50 **Product Groups:** 36, 41, 61, 62, 67

Date of Accounts	Sep 11	Sep 08	Oct 09
Sales Turnover	119m	86m	114m
Pre Tax Profit/Loss	8m	4m	7m
Working Capital	3m	3m	3m
Fixed Assets	2m	2m	2m
Current Assets	25m	17m	23m
Current Liabilities	5m	3m	5m

Edmundson Electrical Ltd
10 James Street Righead Industrial Estate, Bellshill, ML4 3LU
Tel: 01698-573970 **Fax:** 01698-573971
E-mail: bellshill.540@eel.co.uk
Website: http://www.edmundson-electrical.co.uk/
Managers: D. Philpott (District Mgr)
Ultimate Holding Company: BLACKFRIARS CORP (USA)
Immediate Holding Company: EDMUNDSON ELECTRICAL LIMITED
Registration no: 02667012 **Date established:** 1991
Turnover: £10m - £20m **No.of Employees:** 1 - 10 **Product Groups:** 37, 67

Date of Accounts	Dec 11	Dec 10	Dec 09
Sales Turnover	1023m	852m	788m
Pre Tax Profit/Loss	57m	53m	45m
Working Capital	256m	225m	184m
Fixed Assets	17m	3m	4m
Current Assets	439m	358m	298m
Current Liabilities	59m	38m	37m

Electricaire Ltd
Unit 2 Darrows Estate 6 John Brannan Way, Bellshill, ML4 3HD
Tel: 01698-844180 **Fax:** 01698-381456
E-mail: info@electricaireltd.co.uk
Website: http://www.electricaireltd.co.uk
Directors: S. Clark (Prop)
Immediate Holding Company: ELECTRICAIRE LIMITED
Registration no: SC301308 **Date established:** 2006 **Turnover:** £2m - £5m
No.of Employees: 11 - 20 **Product Groups:** 40

Date of Accounts	Sep 11	Sep 10	Sep 09
Working Capital	39	54	52
Fixed Assets	42	28	37
Current Assets	188	157	166

Henderson Kerr Ltd
Kirklee Road, Bellshill, ML4 2QW
Tel: 01563-541325 **Fax:** 01563-541325
E-mail: sales@hendersonkerr.com
Website: http://www.hendersonkerr.com
Bank(s): Clydesdale
Directors: K. Nesbitt (Dir), N. Stinson (Co Sec), N. Stinson (Fin), P. Sheppard (Dir)
Immediate Holding Company: HENDERSON KERR LIMITED
Registration no: SC029189 **VAT No.:** GB 259 7901 16
Date established: 1952 **Turnover:** £20m - £50m
No.of Employees: 21 - 50 **Product Groups:** 66

Date of Accounts	Dec 07
Sales Turnover	21520
Pre Tax Profit/Loss	2760
Working Capital	1680
Fixed Assets	2400
Current Assets	3440
Current Liabilities	1760
Total Share Capital	70
ROCE% (Return on Capital Employed)	67.6

Howden Electro Heating
10-12 Belgowan Street Bellshill Industrial Estate, Bellshill, ML4 3NS
Tel: 01698-573100 **Fax:** 01698-573121
E-mail: sales@howden-electric.com
Website: http://www.howden-electric.com
Bank(s): The Bank of Scotland
Directors: I. Siekman (MD), I. Siekman (MD)
Ultimate Holding Company: HUGH HOWDEN HOLDINGS LIMITED
Immediate Holding Company: H.D. HOWDEN, LIMITED
Registration no: SC033215 **VAT No.:** GB 259 5367 20
Date established: 1958 **Turnover:** £1m - £2m **No.of Employees:** 11 - 20
Product Groups: 37, 40, 42, 66, 67

Date of Accounts	Mar 11	Mar 10	Mar 09
Working Capital	323	323	426
Fixed Assets	N/A	16	N/A
Current Assets	710	631	707
Current Liabilities	98	N/A	46

Kaba Door Systems Ltd
Righead Industrial Estate, Bellshill, ML4 3LP
Tel: 01698-835400 **Fax:** 01698-835401
E-mail: kcampbell@kdt.kaba.com
Website: http://www.kabadoorsystems.co.uk
Bank(s): Nat West
Managers: S. Campbell (Admin Off), K. Campbell (Reg Mgr)
Ultimate Holding Company: KABA HOLDING AG (SWITZERLAND)
Immediate Holding Company: KABA LIMITED
Registration no: 03792985 **VAT No.:** GB 736 6734 06
Date established: 1999 **No.of Employees:** 21 - 50 **Product Groups:** 25

Date of Accounts	Jun 11	Jun 10	Jun 09
Sales Turnover	16m	14m	15m
Pre Tax Profit/Loss	371	-283	569
Working Capital	5m	4m	4m
Fixed Assets	2m	2m	2m
Current Assets	7m	6m	7m
Current Liabilities	1m	1m	990

M S A Britain Ltd
Lochard House, Linnet Way,, Strathclyde Business Park,, BELLSHILL, ML4 3RA
Tel: 01698-573357 **Fax:** 01698-740141
E-mail: info@msabritain.co.uk
Website: http://www.msabritain.co.uk
Bank(s): Clydesdale Bank PLC
Directors: F. Mak (Fin), J. Ryan Iii (Dir)
Managers: G. Sweeney (Prod Mgr)
Immediate Holding Company: Mine Safety Appliance Co.
Registration no: 00437745 **VAT No.:** GB 259 5068 30
Turnover: £5m - £10m **No.of Employees:** 11 - 20 **Product Groups:** 38, 40, 45, 84

Date of Accounts	Dec 07	Dec 06	Dec 05
Sales Turnover	7580	7910	6350
Pre Tax Profit/Loss	590	510	500
Working Capital	4560	4680	4120
Fixed Assets	170	170	70
Current Assets	5250	5890	5480
Current Liabilities	690	1210	1360
Total Share Capital	160	160	160
ROCE% (Return on Capital Employed)	12.5	10.5	11.9
ROT% (Return on Turnover)	7.8	6.4	7.9

Morton Mixers & Blenders Ltd
Unit 37 Grovewood Business Centre Wren Court, Strathclyde Business Park, Bellshill, ML4 3NQ
Tel: 08452-770939 **Fax:** 0845-277 0949
E-mail: info@morton-mixers.co.uk
Website: http://www.morton-mixers.co.uk
Directors: B. Walker (MD)
Immediate Holding Company: MORTON MIXERS & BLENDERS LTD
Registration no: SC338320 **VAT No.:** GB 328 7723 83
Date established: 2008 **Turnover:** £2m - £5m **No.of Employees:** 1 - 10
Product Groups: 41, 42, 45, 67

Date of Accounts	Mar 11	Mar 10	Feb 09
Working Capital	14	17	51
Fixed Assets	10	7	7
Current Assets	67	54	215

Multi Metals Ltd
Belgrave Street Bellshill Industrial Estate, Bellshill, ML4 3JA
Tel: 01698-841199 **Fax:** 01698-841812
E-mail: alan.campbell@hillfootmultimetals.com
Website: http://www.hillfootmultimetals.com
Bank(s): Bank of Scotland
Managers: A. Campbell (Develop Mgr)
Ultimate Holding Company: MURRAY INTERNATIONAL HOLDINGS LIMITED
Immediate Holding Company: MULTI METALS LIMITED
Registration no: SC064671 **VAT No.:** GB 446 6789 95
Date established: 1978 **Turnover:** £10m - £20m
No.of Employees: 21 - 50 **Product Groups:** 66

Date of Accounts	Jan 08	Jun 11	Jun 10
Sales Turnover	18m	10m	10m
Pre Tax Profit/Loss	251	82	-432
Working Capital	-928	2m	2m
Fixed Assets	411	286	287
Current Assets	7m	5m	4m
Current Liabilities	516	697	427

Pro-Sealant Solutions
Unit 6 Darrows Estate 13 John Brannan Way, Bellshill, ML4 3HD
Tel: 01698-842995 **Fax:** 01698-842827
E-mail: info@pro-sealant.co.uk
Website: http://www.pro-sealant.co.uk
Registration no: SC336479 **Turnover:** £250,000 - £500,000
No.of Employees: 1 - 10 **Product Groups:** 30, 32, 66

S K F UK Ltd Bellshill Branch
Unit 3 Teal Court Strathclyde Business Park, Bellshill, ML4 3NN
Tel: 01698-740016 **Fax:** 01698-841196
E-mail: bellshill@economos.com
Website: http://www.economos.com
Managers: D. Topping (Mgr)
Ultimate Holding Company: AKTIEBOLAGET SKF (SWEDEN)
Immediate Holding Company: SKF (U.K) LIMITED
Registration no: 00107367 **VAT No.:** GB 532 1465 72
Date established: 2010 **No.of Employees:** 1 - 10 **Product Groups:** 29, 30, 33, 40, 42, 48

Date of Accounts	Dec 11	Dec 10	Dec 09
Sales Turnover	251m	203m	182m
Pre Tax Profit/Loss	54m	35m	21m
Working Capital	83m	64m	76m
Fixed Assets	19m	20m	18m
Current Assets	120m	97m	107m
Current Liabilities	19m	16m	16m

Scotech Welding Supplies Ltd
14 Dunlin Court Strathclyde Business Park, Bellshill, ML4 3NH
Tel: 01698-745400 **Fax:** 01698-746200
E-mail: scotechwelding@tiscali.co.uk
Directors: J. Mcgahn (Dir)
Immediate Holding Company: SCOTECH WELDING SUPPLIES LIMITED
Registration no: SC173249 **Date established:** 1997
No.of Employees: 1 - 10 **Product Groups:** 46

Date of Accounts	Mar 12	Mar 11	Mar 10
Working Capital	71	83	100
Fixed Assets	7	5	6
Current Assets	428	428	380

Tarmac Ltd
Cambusnethan House Linnet Way, Strathclyde Business Park, Bellshill, ML4 3WD
Tel: 01698-575500 **Fax:** 01698-575670
E-mail: john.major@tarmac.co.uk
Website: http://www.tarmac.co.uk
Directors: J. Major (Div), J. Major (Grp Chief Exec), B. Boyd (MD)
Ultimate Holding Company: ANGLO AMERICAN PLC
Immediate Holding Company: TARMAC LIMITED
Registration no: 00453791 **Date established:** 1948
Turnover: £20m - £50m **No.of Employees:** 51 - 100 **Product Groups:** 31, 33, 52, 66

Date of Accounts	Dec 10	Dec 09	Dec 08
Sales Turnover	1069m	1247m	1566m
Pre Tax Profit/Loss	75m	-47m	-29m
Working Capital	-24m	25m	2m
Fixed Assets	1244m	1391m	1434m
Current Assets	321m	431m	447m
Current Liabilities	93m	168m	213m

Lanarkshire

Biggar

Atlas Winch & Hoist Services Ltd
Old Station Yard Station Road, Biggar, ML12 6DQ
Tel: 01899-221577 **Fax:** 01899-221515
E-mail: info@winchhire.com
Website: http://www.winchhire.co.uk
Directors: D. Lavery (Mkt Research), D. Lavery (MD)
Immediate Holding Company: ATLAS WINCH & HOIST SERVICES LTD.
Registration no: SC182734 **Date established:** 1998
No.of Employees: 1 - 10 **Product Groups:** 35, 39, 45, 48, 67, 68, 83

Date of Accounts	Mar 11	Mar 10	Mar 09
Working Capital	300	140	30
Fixed Assets	1m	1m	852
Current Assets	921	702	878

Bedford Opto Technology
1 Biggar Business Park Market Road, Biggar, ML12 6FX
Tel: 01899-221221 **Fax:** 01899-221009
E-mail: enquiries@bot.co.uk
Website: http://www.bot.co.uk
Directors: R. Stott (MD)
Managers: A. Edmund (Tech Serv Mgr), L. Wyllie (Sales Admin)
Immediate Holding Company: BEDFORD OPTO-TECHNOLOGY LIMITED
Registration no: 01583125 **Date established:** 1981
No.of Employees: 11 - 20 **Product Groups:** 37

Date of Accounts	Dec 11	Dec 10	Dec 09
Working Capital	356	243	297
Fixed Assets	836	798	706
Current Assets	480	341	369

James A Cuthbertson Ltd
Station Road, Biggar, ML12 6DQ
Tel: 01899-220020 **Fax:** 01899-220375
E-mail: enquiries@jamescuthbertson.co.uk
Website: http://www.jamescuthbertson.co.uk
Bank(s): The Royal Bank of Scotland
Directors: R. Reid (MD), S. Robertson (Fin)
Immediate Holding Company: JAMES A. CUTHBERTSON, LIMITED
Registration no: SC024322 **VAT No.:** GB 259 8356 10
Date established: 1946 **Turnover:** £500,000 - £1m
No.of Employees: 21 - 50 **Product Groups:** 45

Date of Accounts	Jun 11	Jun 10	Jun 09
Working Capital	1m	909	840
Fixed Assets	178	129	120
Current Assets	1m	1m	935

Lanark Saw Service & Supplies Ltd
Crossridge Cottage Carmichael, Biggar, ML12 6NG
Tel: 01555-880455 **Fax:** 01555-880493
E-mail: lanarksaw@crossridge.fsnet.co.uk
Website: http://www.crossridge.fsnet.co.uk
Directors: R. Nisbet (MD)
Immediate Holding Company: LANARK SAW SERVICES AND SUPPLIES LIMITED
Registration no: SC083872 **Date established:** 1983
No.of Employees: 1 - 10 **Product Groups:** 46, 48

Date of Accounts	Sep 11	Sep 10	Sep 09
Working Capital	-89	-80	-63
Fixed Assets	70	71	73
Current Assets	19	28	44

Renfrewshire

Bishopton

H P Hewlett Packard
Erskine Ferry Road, Bishopton, PA7 5PP
Tel: 08452-704567 **Fax:** 0141-812 7745
E-mail: lesley.rush@hp.com
Website: http://www.hewlettpackard.com
Bank(s): Bank of Scotland
Directors: N. Wilson (MD)
Immediate Holding Company: COMPAQ COMPUTER CORPORATION (U.S.A.)
Registration no: SC103237 **VAT No.:** GB 699 7204 75
No.of Employees: 501 - 1000 **Product Groups:** 44

Perthshire

Blairgowrie

Acrastyle Electrical Engineers
19 Walnut Grove, Blairgowrie, PH10 6TH
Tel: 01250-875687
Website: http://www.acrastyle.co.uk
No.of Employees: 1 - 10 **Product Groups:** 37, 84

Blair Engineering
Balmoral Road Rattray, Blairgowrie, PH10 7AH
Tel: 01250-872244 **Fax:** 01250-872098
E-mail: sales@blairengineering.co.uk
Website: http://www.blairengineering.co.uk
Directors: A. Mcclement (Prop)
Registration no: SC088982 **Date established:** 1984
Turnover: £250,000 - £500,000 **No.of Employees:** 1 - 10
Product Groups: 41, 45

Geomem Ltd
1 Ralston Business Centre Newtyle, Blairgowrie, PH12 8TL
Tel: 01828-650618 **Fax:** 0845-6446290
E-mail: james@geomem.co.uk
Website: http://www.geomem.co.uk
Directors: J. Tweedie (MD), L. Beaton (Fin)
Managers: I. Smith (Admin Off)
Immediate Holding Company: GEOMEM LIMITED
Registration no: SC266547 **VAT No.:** GB 400 9002 16
Date established: 2004 **Turnover:** Up to £250,000
No.of Employees: 1 - 10 **Product Groups:** 38, 41, 44, 61, 84, 85, 86

Date of Accounts	Apr 08	Apr 07	Apr 06
Working Capital	1	5	-6
Fixed Assets	9	12	13
Current Assets	35	35	22
Current Liabilities	34	30	28

N I C C Ltd
West Nevay Farm Cottage Newtyle, Blairgowrie, PH12 8SJ
Tel: 01828-650661 **Fax:** 01828-650551
E-mail: enquiries@armawrap.com
Website: http://www.armawrap.com
Directors: C. McCombe (Fin), D. Stewart (MD)
Immediate Holding Company: N.I.C.C. LIMITED
Registration no: 01560840 **Date established:** 1981
No.of Employees: 1 - 10 **Product Groups:** 46, 48

Date of Accounts	May 11	May 10	May 09
Working Capital	-73	-16	-135
Fixed Assets	190	242	176
Current Assets	114	161	194

Piob Mhor Ltd
39-43 High Street, Blairgowrie, PH10 6DA
Tel: 01250-872131 **Fax:** 01250-873649
E-mail: info@piobmhor-of-scotland.co.uk
Website: http://www.piobmhor-of-scotland.co.uk
Directors: D. Tulloch (MD), A. Tulloch (Fin)
Immediate Holding Company: PIOB MHOR OF SCOTLAND LTD.
Registration no: SC215600 **Date established:** 2001
Turnover: £500,000 - £1m **No.of Employees:** 1 - 10 **Product Groups:** 24

Date of Accounts	Mar 11	Mar 10	Mar 09
Working Capital	98	93	111
Fixed Assets	23	25	28
Current Assets	135	123	139

A Proctor Group Ltd
The Haugh Ashgrove Road, Rattray, Blairgowrie, PH10 7ER
Tel: 01250-872261 **Fax:** 01250-872727
E-mail: sales@proctorgroup.com
Website: http://www.proctorgroup.com
Directors: P. Roy (Fin)
Immediate Holding Company: A. PROCTOR GROUP LIMITED
Registration no: SC105054 **Date established:** 1987
Turnover: £10m - £20m **No.of Employees:** 51 - 100 **Product Groups:** 25, 30, 31, 33, 39

Date of Accounts	Dec 11	Dec 10	Dec 09
Sales Turnover	17m	16m	15m
Pre Tax Profit/Loss	550	573	322
Working Capital	3m	3m	3m
Fixed Assets	2m	1m	1m
Current Assets	6m	6m	5m
Current Liabilities	913	940	558

West Lothian

Boness

Ballantine Engineering Ltd
Links Road, Boness, EH51 9PW
Tel: 01506-822721 **Fax:** 01506-827326
E-mail: ian@ballantineboness.co.uk
Website: http://www.creativeironworks.co.uk
Bank(s): The Royal Bank of Scotland
Directors: A. Sharp (Fin), I. Ballantine (MD)
Ultimate Holding Company: BALLANTINE BONESS IRON CO.LIMITED
Immediate Holding Company: BALLANTINE ENGINEERING LTD.
Registration no: SC104227 **Date established:** 1987
Turnover: £5m - £10m **No.of Employees:** 51 - 100 **Product Groups:** 34, 36

Date of Accounts	Dec 11	Dec 10	Dec 09
Working Capital	-110	-154	-79
Fixed Assets	5	7	10
Current Assets	229	162	108

Blackbourn Geological Services
Carriden House, Boness, EH51 9SN
Tel: 01506-826777 **Fax:** 01506-826888
E-mail: graham@blackbourn.co.uk
Website: http://www.blackbourn.co.uk
Directors: G. Blackbourn (MD), B. Blackbourn (Fin)
Immediate Holding Company: BLACKBOURN GEOLOGICAL SERVICES LIMITED
Registration no: SC250916 **Date established:** 2003
Turnover: £500,000 - £1m **No.of Employees:** 1 - 10 **Product Groups:** 84

Date of Accounts	Jun 11	Jun 10	Jun 09
Working Capital	-27	-60	-72
Fixed Assets	121	125	131
Current Assets	90	31	28

Caledonian Produce Ltd
Carriden Industrial Estate Bridgeness Road, Boness, EH51 9SJ
Tel: 01506-823491 **Fax:** 01506-821206
Website: http://www.bakkavor.co.uk
Bank(s): The Royal Bank of Scotland
Directors: J. Punnett (Co Sec)
Managers: P. Kealy (Chief Mgr), J. Patterson (Personnel), D. Nichol Storie (Personnel), J. Wang, A. Tendell (Purch Mgr), I. Clingan (Chief Mgr)
Ultimate Holding Company: BAKKAVOR HOLDINGS LTD
Immediate Holding Company: BAKKAVOR FOODS LTD
Registration no: SC059986 **VAT No.:** GB 119 7189 44
Date established: 1976 **No.of Employees:** 501 - 1000 **Product Groups:** 20

Donaldson & Mcconnell Ltd
Grangemouth Road, Boness, EH51 0PU
Tel: 01506-828891 **Fax:** 01506-829070
E-mail: samantham@donaldsonandmcconnell.co.uk
Website: http://www.donaldsonandmcconnell.co.uk
Directors: S. Mcconnell (Fin)
Immediate Holding Company: DONALDSON & MCCONNELL HOLDINGS LIMITED
Registration no: 02689909 **Date established:** 1992
Turnover: £10m - £20m **No.of Employees:** 51 - 100 **Product Groups:** 08, 35, 66

Date of Accounts	Apr 10	Apr 09	Apr 08
Sales Turnover	11m	12m	N/A
Pre Tax Profit/Loss	-403	-80	N/A
Working Capital	671	1m	188
Fixed Assets	1m	1m	N/A
Current Assets	5m	5m	188
Current Liabilities	2m	2m	N/A

Walker Timber Ltd
Carriden Sawmills, Boness, EH51 9SN
Tel: 01506-823331 **Fax:** 01506-822590
E-mail: jccampbelln@walkertimber.com
Website: http://www.walkertimber.com
Bank(s): The Royal Bank of Scotland
Directors: D. Fairfoull (Dir), J. Campbell (Fin)
Managers: P. McMichael (I.T. Exec)
Ultimate Holding Company: James Walker (Leith) Ltd
Immediate Holding Company: WALKER TIMBER LIMITED
Registration no: SC046290 **VAT No.:** GB 268 8595 88
Date established: 1969 **Turnover:** £10m - £20m
No.of Employees: 251 - 500 **Product Groups:** 08, 25, 48, 66

Date of Accounts	Mar 08
Sales Turnover	30740
Pre Tax Profit/Loss	1700
Working Capital	7310
Fixed Assets	920
Current Assets	11590
Current Liabilities	4280
ROCE% (Return on Capital Employed)	20.7

Stirlingshire

Bonnybridge

E & O Laboratories Ltd
Burnhouse Farm, Bonnybridge, FK4 2HH
Tel: 01324-840404 **Fax:** 01324-841314
E-mail: info@eolabs.com
Website: http://www.eolabs.com
Directors: V. Lucey (MD)
Managers: P. McKinnon (Buyer), K. Kerr (Personnel), M. Bruce (Tech Serv Mgr), J. Dawkins (Chief Acct)
Immediate Holding Company: E & O LABORATORIES LIMITED
Registration no: SC125360 **Date established:** 1990 **Turnover:** £2m - £5m
No.of Employees: 51 - 100 **Product Groups:** 31, 38

Date of Accounts	May 11	May 10	May 09
Working Capital	898	802	723
Fixed Assets	611	554	572
Current Assets	2m	2m	2m

Logicomms
32 Milnquarter Road, Bonnybridge, FK4 2FG
Tel: 01324-810203
E-mail: ross@loggicomms.com
Website: http://www.loggicomms.com
Managers: R. Bownie (Mgr)
Turnover: Up to £250,000 **No.of Employees:** 1 - 10 **Product Groups:** 37, 38, 52, 79

R H I Refractories UK Ltd
Hillview Road, Bonnybridge, FK4 2EH
Tel: 01324-819400 **Fax:** 01324-814218
Website: http://www.rhi-ag.com
Directors: D. Lawrie (Chief Op Offcr)
Managers: K. Lockhart (I.T. Exec), J. Bauner (Sales & Mktg Mg), M. Stone (Tech Serv Mgr), C. Smith (Comptroller), H. Smith (Personnel)
Ultimate Holding Company: RHI AG (AUSTRIA)
Immediate Holding Company: RHI REFRACTORIES UK LIMITED
Registration no: SC075200 **Date established:** 1981
No.of Employees: 101 - 250 **Product Groups:** 34, 66

Date of Accounts	Dec 11	Dec 10	Dec 09
Sales Turnover	31m	29m	24m
Pre Tax Profit/Loss	819	251	560
Working Capital	10m	7m	9m
Fixed Assets	5m	5m	5m
Current Assets	13m	11m	13m
Current Liabilities	1m	1m	1m

Rollo Engineering Ltd
St Andrews Works, Bonnybridge, FK4 2EJ
Tel: 01324-812469 **Fax:** 01324-814040
E-mail: mail@rolloeng.co.uk
Website: http://www.rollo-ind.co.uk
Bank(s): The Royal Bank of Scotland
Directors: C. McBeath (Dir)
Immediate Holding Company: ROLLO ENGINEERING LIMITED
Registration no: SC242227 **VAT No.:** GB 269 4384 18
Date established: 2003 **Turnover:** Up to £250,000
No.of Employees: 11 - 20 **Product Groups:** 46

Date of Accounts	Mar 11	Mar 10	Mar 09
Working Capital	-17	-8	-15
Fixed Assets	18	18	21
Current Assets	86	129	84
Current Liabilities	N/A	N/A	37

Stewart Electrical Ltd
24-28 High Street, Bonnybridge, FK4 1DA
Tel: 01324-812354 **Fax:** 01324-814075
E-mail: sales@stewartelectrical.co.uk
Website: http://www.stewartelectrical.co.uk
Directors: A. Stewart (MD)
Managers: T. Smith (Chief Acct)
Immediate Holding Company: STEWART ELECTRICAL LIMITED
Registration no: SC167648 **Date established:** 1996
Turnover: £500,000 - £1m **No.of Employees:** 21 - 50 **Product Groups:** 52

Date of Accounts	Jul 11	Jul 10	Jul 09
Working Capital	-214	-171	-51
Fixed Assets	81	95	107
Current Assets	673	674	754

Midlothian

Bonnyrigg

Campbell Control Services
Dalhousie Business Park Carrington Road, Bonnyrigg, EH19 3HY
Tel: 0131-660 4791 **Fax:** 0131-660 6793
E-mail: andy@campbellcontrols.com
Website: http://www.campbellcontrols.com
Directors: A. Graham (Ptnr)
Immediate Holding Company: MJM FLOORING (2000) LTD
Registration no: SC233347 **Date established:** 2008
Turnover: Up to £250,000 **No.of Employees:** 1 - 10 **Product Groups:** 35, 37, 40

Date of Accounts	Jan 12
Working Capital	3
Current Assets	5

Industrial Paint & Powder
7 Burnbrae Loan, Bonnyrigg, EH19 3FR
Tel: 0131-443 8793 **Fax:** 0131-455 7806
E-mail: robin@indpaintandpowder.co.uk
Website: http://www.indpaintandpowder.co.uk
Directors: R. Laing (MD), V. Laing (Co Sec)
Immediate Holding Company: INDUSTRIAL PAINT AND POWDER LIMITED
Registration no: SC035352 **VAT No.:** GB 269 4929 02
Date established: 1960 **Turnover:** £250,000 - £500,000
No.of Employees: 1 - 10 **Product Groups:** 32, 34, 66

Date of Accounts	Aug 11	Aug 10	Aug 09
Working Capital	82	120	-1
Fixed Assets	47	41	215
Current Assets	246	249	150

Q Fabrications
Dalhousie Business Park Carrington Road, Bonnyrigg, EH19 3HY
Tel: 0131-663 6069 **Fax:** 0131-660 5488
Directors: D. Quinn (Snr Part)
Immediate Holding Company: MJM FLOORING (2000) LTD
Registration no: SC233347 **Date established:** 2008
Turnover: Up to £250,000 **No.of Employees:** 1 - 10 **Product Groups:** 35

Date of Accounts	Jan 12
Working Capital	3
Current Assets	5

Sign & Light
Unit 5 Sherwood Industrial Estate, Bonnyrigg, EH19 3LW
Tel: 0131-654 1122 **Fax:** 0131-654 0808
Directors: B. Mack (MD), D. Mcdonald (MD)
Immediate Holding Company: SIGN AND LIGHT LIMITED
Registration no: SC226845 **Date established:** 2002
No.of Employees: 1 - 10 **Product Groups:** 37, 49

Stevenson & Cheyne Ltd
Unit 7 Butlerfield Industrial Estate, Bonnyrigg, EH19 3JQ
Tel: 01875-822822 **Fax:** 01875-823723
E-mail: sales@platerolling.co.uk
Website: http://www.platerolling.net
Directors: T. Smith (MD)
Immediate Holding Company: STEVENSON AND CHEYNE (1983) LIMITED
Registration no: SC083745 **Date established:** 1983
No.of Employees: 1 - 10 **Product Groups:** 35

Date of Accounts	Sep 11	Sep 10	Sep 09
Working Capital	-120	-40	-67
Fixed Assets	347	357	895
Current Assets	66	81	92

Tayco Engineering
Unit 6 Sherwood Industrial Estate, Bonnyrigg, EH19 3LW
Tel: 0131-654 9655 **Fax:** 0131-654 9656
E-mail: graham@tayco.co.uk
Website: http://www.tayco.co.uk
Directors: G. Taylor (Prop), G. Taylor (MD)
VAT No.: GB 577 9635 72 **Date established:** 2001 **Turnover:** £1m - £2m
No.of Employees: 1 - 10 **Product Groups:** 23, 35

Angus

Brechin

A J Allan Brechin Ltd
East Mill Road, Brechin, DD9 7HJ
Tel: 01356-622112 **Fax:** 01356-623020
E-mail: alistair@ajallan.com
Website: http://www.ajallan.com
Managers: A. Melrose (Mgr)
Immediate Holding Company: A.J. ALLAN (BRECHIN) LIMITED
Registration no: SC058078 **Date established:** 1975
Turnover: Up to £250,000 **No.of Employees:** 11 - 20 **Product Groups:** 02

Date of Accounts	Dec 11	Jun 11	Jun 10
Working Capital	121	286	43
Fixed Assets	2m	2m	2m
Current Assets	544	654	404

Angus Horticulture Ltd
Whanland Farnell, Brechin, DD9 6UF
Tel: 01674-674352 **Fax:** 01674-820225
E-mail: admin@angus-horticulture.co.uk
Website: http://www.angus-horticulture.co.uk
Directors: R. Cessford (Fin)
Managers: E. Ramsay (Sales Admin)
Immediate Holding Company: ANGUS HORTICULTURE SERVICES LIMITED
Registration no: SC098785 **Date established:** 1984
No.of Employees: 21 - 50 **Product Groups:** 02, 32

Date of Accounts	Aug 11	Aug 10	Aug 09
Working Capital	2	-17	93
Fixed Assets	307	252	221
Current Assets	776	849	937

Matrix International Ltd
Eastmill Road, Brechin, DD9 7EP
Tel: 01356-602000 **Fax:** 01356-602060
E-mail: info@matrix-international.com
Website: http://www.matrix-international.com
Bank(s): Bank of Scotland
Managers: J. McCabe (Personnel), R. Perry (Chief Mgr), M. Ross (Tech Serv Mgr), M. Perez, D. Robertson (Purch Mgr), I. McGrory (Comptroller)
Ultimate Holding Company: ALTRA HOLDINGS INC (USA)
Immediate Holding Company: MATRIX INTERNATIONAL LIMITED
Registration no: 03690656 **VAT No.:** GB 265 6264 42
Date established: 1998 **Turnover:** £2m - £5m **No.of Employees:** 51 - 100
Product Groups: 35, 43, 46

Date of Accounts	Dec 11	Dec 10	Dec 09
Sales Turnover	11m	8m	7m
Pre Tax Profit/Loss	558	268	-921
Working Capital	5m	4m	4m
Fixed Assets	272	299	591
Current Assets	6m	5m	4m
Current Liabilities	335	396	316

W E Scorgie & Son
Balrownie Menmuir, Brechin, DD9 7RG
Tel: 01356-660229 **Fax:** 01356-660229
Directors: W. Scorgie (Ptnr)
Date established: 1976 **No.of Employees:** 1 - 10 **Product Groups:** 41

Stevens Scotland Ltd
Denburn Way, Brechin, DD9 7DW
Tel: 01356-625111 **Fax:** 01356-623755
E-mail: twalker@stevensscotland.co.uk
Website: http://www.stevenscotland.co.uk
Directors: T. Walker (MD), G. Stevens (MD), R. Stevens (Fin)
Managers: W. Owen (I.T. Exec), R. Elsworth (Sales & Mktg Mg)
Immediate Holding Company: STEVENS (SCOTLAND) LIMITED
Registration no: SC066731 **VAT No.:** GB 296 9664 81
Date established: 1978 **Turnover:** £5m - £10m **No.of Employees:** 1 - 10
Product Groups: 35, 36

Renfrewshire

Bridge Of Weir

Bridge Of Weir Leather Co.
Baltic Works Kilbarchan Road, Bridge Of Weir, PA11 3RH
Tel: 01505-612132 **Fax:** 01505-614964
E-mail: iain.mcfadyen@bowleather.co.uk
Website: http://www.bowleather.co.uk
Bank(s): Clydesdale Bank PLC
Directors: G. Ross (Fin), I. Mcfadyen (MD), J. Lang (Mkt Research), J. Davidson (Sales), V. Morris (Tech Serv)
Managers: S. Keys (Buyer), M. Ross (Personnel)
Ultimate Holding Company: SCOTTISH LEATHER GROUP LIMITED
Immediate Holding Company: BRIDGE OF WEIR LEATHER COMPANY LIMITED
Registration no: SC015274 **Date established:** 2028
Turnover: £50m - £75m **No.of Employees:** 101 - 250 **Product Groups:** 22

Date of Accounts	Mar 11	Mar 10	Mar 09
Sales Turnover	54m	N/A	28m
Pre Tax Profit/Loss	4m	N/A	2m
Working Capital	19m	18m	16m
Fixed Assets	5m	3m	4m
Current Assets	27m	24m	19m
Current Liabilities	1m	1m	940

N C T Leather Ltd
Locher Works Kilbarchan Road, Bridge of Weir, PA11 3RL
Tel: 01505-612182 **Fax:** 01505-612123
E-mail: sales@nctleather.co.uk
Website: http://www.nctleather.co.uk
Bank(s): Clydesdale Bank PLC
Directors: G. Ross (Fin), J. Lang (Mkt Research), W. Riddell (Dir)
Managers: M. Ross (Personnel), S. Keys (Purch Mgr), V. Morris (Tech Serv Mgr)
Ultimate Holding Company: SCOTTISH LEATHER GROUP LIMITED
Immediate Holding Company: NCT LEATHER LIMITED
Registration no: SC019503 **Date established:** 1936
Turnover: £20m - £50m **No.of Employees:** 51 - 100 **Product Groups:** 22

Date of Accounts	Mar 12	Mar 11	Mar 10
Sales Turnover	51m	42m	24m
Pre Tax Profit/Loss	1m	1m	1m
Working Capital	5m	4m	4m
Fixed Assets	3m	3m	3m
Current Assets	8m	11m	7m
Current Liabilities	640	875	1m

West Lothian

Broxburn

Airline Cars & Coaches Edinburgh Ltd
Fernlea Drumshoreland Road, Broxburn, EH52 5PF
Tel: 01506-852473 **Fax:** 01506-857274
E-mail: aircab1@aol.com
Website: http://www.aircabedinburgh.co.uk
Managers: R. Blaikie (Mgr)
Immediate Holding Company: AIRLINE CABS & CARS (EDINBURGH) LTD.
Registration no: SC227048 **Date established:** 2002
No.of Employees: 1 - 10 **Product Groups:** 37, 72, 75

Date of Accounts	Mar 11	Mar 10	Mar 09
Working Capital	-14	-18	-17
Fixed Assets	7	10	13
Current Assets	5	N/A	4

Castlebrae Drainage Services
8 Youngs Road East Mains Industrial Estate, Broxburn, EH52 5LY
Tel: 01506-862286 **Fax:** 01506-858643
E-mail: michelle.ringland@lanesfordrains.co.uk
Website: http://www.castlebraedrainage.co.uk
Managers: B. Murray (Sales Prom Mgr), H. Jay (Personnel), B. Kerr (Sales & Mktg Mg), D. Campbell (Mgr)
No.of Employees: 1 - 10 **Product Groups:** 37, 54, 67, 84

Eriks UK Industrial Services (Broxburn Electro Mechanical)
3 Simpson Road East Mains Industrial Estate, Broxburn, EH52 5NP
Tel: 01506-864710 **Fax:** 01506-858500
E-mail: edinburgh@eriks.co.uk
Website: http://www.eriks.co.uk
Managers: E. Graham (District Mgr), T. Simpson
Immediate Holding Company: Wyko Holdings Ltd
Registration no: 00917112 **No.of Employees:** 21 - 50 **Product Groups:** 66

The Glenmorangie Company Ltd (t/a MacDonald & Muir Ltd)
Macdonald House 18 Westerton Road, East Mains Industrial Estate, Broxburn, EH52 5AQ
Tel: 01506-852929 **Fax:** 01506-855856
E-mail: martha.fleming@glenmorangieplc.co.uk
Website: http://www.glenmorangie.co.uk
Bank(s): Clydesdale Livingston
Directors: M. Fleming (Fin), S. Erilanger (Sales), I. Hamilton (Fin), P. Neap (Grp Chief Exec), P. Neep (MD)
Managers: I. Drysdale (Personnel)
Ultimate Holding Company: LVMH MOET HENNESSY LOUIS VUTTON SA (FRANCE)
Immediate Holding Company: THE GLENMORANGIE COMPANY LIMITED
Registration no: SC026752 **VAT No.:** GB 269 1195 36
Date established: 1948 **Turnover:** £50m - £75m
No.of Employees: 101 - 250 **Product Groups:** 21

Date of Accounts	Dec 07
Sales Turnover	83830
Pre Tax Profit/Loss	10590
Working Capital	80530
Fixed Assets	46670
Current Assets	125510
Current Liabilities	44980
Total Share Capital	1470
ROCE% (Return on Capital Employed)	8.3

Graham
11 Freskyn Place East Mains Industrial Estate, Broxburn, EH52 5NF
Tel: 01506-853498 **Fax:** 01506-854909
E-mail: gordoncree@graham-group.co.uk
Website: http://www.jewson.co.uk
Managers: P. Fairburn (Mgr)
Ultimate Holding Company: SAINT-GOBAIN PLC
Immediate Holding Company: GRAHAM GROUP LTD
Registration no: 00066738 **Date established:** 1987
No.of Employees: 1 - 10 **Product Groups:** 66

Halls Ltd
220 East Main Street, Broxburn, EH52 5AW
Tel: 01506-853300 **Fax:** 01506-857049
E-mail: imcgill@gcfg.com
Website: http://www.hallsofbroxburn.com
Bank(s): Royal Bank of Scotland, Corstorphine Branch, Edinburgh
Directors: R. Fraser (Dir)
Immediate Holding Company: HALLS LIMITED
Registration no: 04465840 **VAT No.:** GB 498 2637 89
Date established: 2002 **Turnover:** £50m - £75m
No.of Employees: 1501 & over **Product Groups:** 20

Date of Accounts	May 11	May 10	May 09
Working Capital	-1	-8	-55
Fixed Assets	148	222	180
Current Assets	81	69	42

John Bean Technology
Simpson Road East Mains Industrial Estate, Broxburn, EH52 5NP
Tel: 01506-857112 **Fax:** 01506-852232
E-mail: sales@double-d.co.uk
Website: http://www.double-d.co.uk
Bank(s): Bank of Scotland
Directors: R. Petrie (MD), I. Wallace (Dir)
Managers: K. Mitchell (Purch Mgr), H. Donnelly (Comptroller)
Immediate Holding Company: LWS 60 LIMITED
Registration no: SC066103 **Date established:** 1978 **Turnover:** £2m - £5m
No.of Employees: 51 - 100 **Product Groups:** 40, 41

Date of Accounts	Sep 11	Sep 10	Sep 09
Sales Turnover	N/A	N/A	3m
Pre Tax Profit/Loss	N/A	N/A	2m
Working Capital	-9	-8	-5
Fixed Assets	42	599	641
Current Assets	3	17	2
Current Liabilities	12	N/A	7

Kwik-Fit GB Ltd
216 East Main Street, Broxburn, EH52 5AS
Tel: 01506-856789 **Fax:** 01506-855912
E-mail: info@kfis.co.uk
Website: http://www.kwik-fit.com
Directors: I. Fraser (Grp Chief Exec)
Managers: B. Criton (Mktg Serv Mgr), J. Rogers (Purch Mgr), J. Nola (Mktg Serv Mgr), A. Corley, C. Mclaren (Mgr)
Ultimate Holding Company: FINANCIERE DAUNOU 2 SA (LUXEMBOURG)
Immediate Holding Company: KWIK-FIT (GB) LIMITED
Registration no: 01009184 **VAT No.:** GB 380 0948 50
Date established: 1971 **Turnover:** £500,000 - £1m
No.of Employees: 1 - 10 **Product Groups:** 39

Date of Accounts	Dec 10	Dec 09	Dec 08
Sales Turnover	527m	495m	449m
Pre Tax Profit/Loss	269m	56m	97m
Working Capital	197m	201m	154m
Fixed Assets	106m	115m	110m
Current Assets	375m	368m	329m
Current Liabilities	36m	36m	38m

MacDonald & Muir Ltd
MacDonald House 18 Westerton Road, Broxburn, EH52 5AQ
Tel: 01506-852929 **Fax:** 01506-855856
E-mail: reception@glenmorangie.co.uk
Website: http://www.glenmorangie.com
Bank(s): Clydesdale Bank PLC
Directors: P. Neep (Grp Chief Exec), I. Drysdale (Dir), S. Erlanger (Dir), I. Hamilton (Dir)

see next page

MacDonald & Muir Ltd - Cont'd
Managers: G. Lindsey (Mktg Serv Mgr), K. McCloud (I.T. Exec)
Registration no: SC010077 **Turnover:** £20m - £50m **Product Groups:** 21, 41

Date of Accounts	Dec 07
Sales Turnover	83830
Pre Tax Profit/Loss	10590
Working Capital	68790
Fixed Assets	46670
Current Assets	125750
Current Liabilities	56960
Total Share Capital	100
ROCE% (Return on Capital Employed)	9.2

Ian Macleod Distillers Ltd
Russell House Dunnet Way, East Mains Industrial Estate, Broxburn, EH52 5BU
Tel: 01506-852205 **Fax:** 01506-856434
E-mail: info@ianmacleod.com
Website: http://www.ianmacleod.com
Bank(s): The Royal Bank of Scotland
Directors: M. Younger (Fin), L. Russell (MD), M. Younger (Fin)
Managers: K. Murdoch (Prod Mgr), I. Weir (Mktg Serv Mgr), I. Weir (Mktg Serv Mgr), G. Cant (Tech Serv Mgr)
Immediate Holding Company: IAN MACLEOD DISTILLERS LIMITED
Registration no: SC032696 **Date established:** 1957
Turnover: £20m - £50m **No.of Employees:** 21 - 50 **Product Groups:** 21

Date of Accounts	Sep 11	Sep 10	Sep 09
Sales Turnover	39m	32m	26m
Pre Tax Profit/Loss	5m	4m	3m
Working Capital	34m	22m	22m
Fixed Assets	15m	7m	6m
Current Assets	45m	35m	30m
Current Liabilities	7m	7m	5m

Mitar & Environmental Services
2a Union Road, Broxburn, EH52 6HR
Tel: 01506-200721 **Fax:** 01506-209058
E-mail: alan@mitar.co.uk
Website: http://www.mitar.co.uk
Managers: A. Russell (Mgr)
No.of Employees: 1 - 10 **Product Groups:** 52

Munro & Miller Fittings Ltd
3 Westerton Road East Mains Industrial Estate, Broxburn, EH52 5AU
Tel: 01506-853531 **Fax:** 01506-856628
E-mail: info@munro-miller.co.uk
Website: http://www.munro-miller.co.uk
Managers: G. Hughes (Mktg Serv Mgr), L. McEwen (Chief Acct), C. Scott-telford, A. Faures (Mgr)
Ultimate Holding Company: GENOYER INTERNATIONAL SA (FRANCE)
Immediate Holding Company: MUNRO & MILLER FITTINGS LIMITED
Registration no: SC148578 **Date established:** 1994
Turnover: £5m - £10m **No.of Employees:** 21 - 50 **Product Groups:** 36, 45, 48

Date of Accounts	Dec 11	Dec 10	Dec 09
Sales Turnover	4m	5m	10m
Pre Tax Profit/Loss	-849	-170	1m
Working Capital	2m	1m	1m
Fixed Assets	3m	816	892
Current Assets	3m	3m	4m
Current Liabilities	502	582	905

Paragon Inks Holdings Ltd
Unit 2 Brocks Way East Mains Industrial Estate, Broxburn, EH52 5NB
Tel: 01506-853535 **Fax:** 01506-853893
Website: http://www.paragoninks.co.uk
Directors: G. Merton (MD)
Immediate Holding Company: Paragon Inks (Holdings) Ltd
Registration no: SC177007 **Date established:** 1997
No.of Employees: 21 - 50 **Product Groups:** 27, 32, 44

Priority Diamond Products Ltd
2 Thistle Industrial Estate 155 East Main Street, Broxburn, EH52 5AS
Tel: 01506-856644 **Fax:** 01506-856644
Directors: D. Cummings (Prop)
Immediate Holding Company: PRIORITY DIAMOND PRODUCTS LIMITED
Registration no: SC291381 **Date established:** 2005
No.of Employees: 1 - 10 **Product Groups:** 37

Date of Accounts	Oct 10	Oct 09	Oct 08
Working Capital	-26	-36	-35
Fixed Assets	35	41	40
Current Assets	150	146	217

Sarco Stopper Ltd
5-7 Brocks Way East Mains Industrial Estate, Broxburn, EH52 5NB
Tel: 01506-855824 **Fax:** 01506-855849
E-mail: mail@sarcostopper.com
Website: http://www.sarcostopper.com
Bank(s): Yorkshire Bank
Directors: B. Menzies (Fin), B. Menzies (MD)
Ultimate Holding Company: AIR BAG STOPPER HOLDINGS LIMITED
Immediate Holding Company: SARCO STOPPER LIMITED
Registration no: 03099903 **VAT No.:** GB 648 5038 20
Date established: 1995 **Turnover:** Up to £250,000
No.of Employees: 11 - 20 **Product Groups:** 29, 36, 48

Date of Accounts	Jul 11	Jul 10	Jul 09
Working Capital	213	180	177
Fixed Assets	8	12	14
Current Assets	427	304	301

Banffshire

Buckie

Buckie Shipyard
Commercial Road, Buckie, AB56 1UR
Tel: 01542-832727 **Fax:** 01542-831825
E-mail: ctaylor@buckieshipyard.com
Website: http://www.buckieshipyard.com
Bank(s): Bank of Scotland
Directors: C. Taylor (Dir)
Managers: A. Matthews (Tech Serv Mgr), J. Grala-wojrezyk, S. Lawson (Fin Mgr), N. McCloy (Personnel)
Immediate Holding Company: BUCKIE SHIPYARD LIMITED
Registration no: SC158728 **Date established:** 1995
No.of Employees: 51 - 100 **Product Groups:** 39

Fife

Burntisland

Esat Electronic Equipment
10 Main Street Aberdour, Burntisland, KY3 0UE
Tel: 01383-860068 **Fax:** 01383-860068
E-mail: info@esat.ltd.uk
Website: http://www.esat.ltd.uk
Directors: G. Lister (Dir), S. Henderson (Fin)
Immediate Holding Company: ESAT LTD
Registration no: SC260289 **Date established:** 2003
Turnover: Up to £250,000 **No.of Employees:** 1 - 10 **Product Groups:** 37

Zeitgeist Design
4 Barclay Road Kinghorn, Burntisland, KY3 9XF
Tel: 01592-890952
E-mail: ritchie@ztgst.com
Website: http://www.ztgst.com
Directors: R. Feenie (Prop)
No.of Employees: 1 - 10 **Product Groups:** 30, 39, 40

Perthshire

Callander

Pisces Engineering
Ballochallan Cambusmore, Callander, FK17 8LJ
Tel: 01877-331117 **Fax:** 01877-331118
E-mail: bob@piscesengineering.co.uk
Website: http://www.piscesengineering.co.uk
Directors: B. Bawden (MD)
Managers: K. Berry (Sales Admin), K. Mckay (Mgr), A. Moore (Mgr)
Immediate Holding Company: PISCES ENGINEERING LTD.
Registration no: SC228052 **Date established:** 2002
No.of Employees: 1 - 10 **Product Groups:** 30, 40

Date of Accounts	Mar 11	Mar 10	Mar 09
Working Capital	-32	-40	-42
Fixed Assets	32	41	51
Current Assets	183	116	103

Argyll

Campbeltown

N Mccormick
5 Witchburn Terrace Dell Road, Campbeltown, PA28 6JG
Tel: 01586-553373 **Fax:** 01586-553373
E-mail: neil.mccormick@tiscali.co.uk
Directors: N. Mccormick (Prop)
Date established: 1986 **No.of Employees:** 1 - 10 **Product Groups:** 26, 35

J & A Mitchell Co. Ltd
Springbank Distillery Well Close, Campbeltown, PA28 6ET
Tel: 01586-552085 **Fax:** 01586-553215
E-mail: stuart@jandamitchell.com
Website: http://www.springbankwhisky.com
Bank(s): Clydesdale Bank PLC
Directors: S. Campbell (Fin)
Managers: L. McCaulay (Personnel), R. Watson (Sales Prom)
Immediate Holding Company: J. & A. MITCHELL AND COMPANY, LIMITED
Registration no: SC003582 **VAT No.:** GB 263 6228 58
Date established: 1997 **Turnover:** £2m - £5m **No.of Employees:** 21 - 50
Product Groups: 21

Date of Accounts	Jul 11	Jul 10	Jul 09
Working Capital	5m	4m	3m
Fixed Assets	1m	1m	1m
Current Assets	6m	5m	5m

Lanarkshire

Carluke

Marmac Services Ltd
124 Lanark Road Braidwood, Carluke, ML8 5PQ
Tel: 01555-759373 **Fax:** 01555-759373
E-mail: enquiries@marmacservices.ltd.uk
Website: http://www.marmacservices.ltd.uk
Directors: T. Mcculloch (MD)
Immediate Holding Company: MARMAC SERVICES LIMITED
Registration no: SC231050 **Date established:** 2002
No.of Employees: 21 - 50 **Product Groups:** 35, 36, 39

Date of Accounts	Nov 11	Nov 10	Nov 09
Working Capital	587	546	483
Fixed Assets	59	62	38
Current Assets	1m	1m	1m

Melton Plastics
Unit 7 Castlehill Industrial Estate, Carluke, ML8 5UF
Tel: 01555-773213 **Fax:** 01555-751567
E-mail: melton.plastics@btopenworld.com
Directors: A. Travis (MD)
Immediate Holding Company: MELTON PLASTICS LIMITED
Registration no: SC070496 **Date established:** 1980
No.of Employees: 1 - 10 **Product Groups:** 30

Mitecon Ltd
28 Cooper Avenue, Carluke, ML8 5US
Tel: 01555-752352 **Fax:** 08707-626223
E-mail: info@mitecon.co.uk
Website: http://www.mitecon.co.uk
Directors: D. Callan (Fin), M. Michorius (MD)
Registration no: SC263920 **Date established:** 2004
Turnover: Up to £250,000 **No.of Employees:** 1 - 10 **Product Groups:** 85

Date of Accounts	Dec 07	Dec 06	Dec 05
Working Capital	-19	-43	-35
Fixed Assets	27	30	23
Current Assets	30	7	6
Current Liabilities	49	49	41

Angus

Carnoustie

Blair Precision Engineering Ltd
15 Philip Street, Carnoustie, DD7 6ED
Tel: 01241-853639 **Fax:** 01241-412511
E-mail: sales@steelmaster.co.uk
Website: http://www.steelmaster.co.uk
Directors: A. Jeans (Dir)
Immediate Holding Company: BLAIR PRECISION ENGINEERING LIMITED
Registration no: SC289345 **Date established:** 2005
Turnover: Up to £250,000 **No.of Employees:** 1 - 10 **Product Groups:** 41

Date of Accounts	Mar 12	Mar 11	Mar 10
Working Capital	-33	-26	-37
Fixed Assets	43	43	43
Current Assets	68	48	32

Kirkcudbrightshire

Castle Douglas

Bean Bags Direct
Eallisaid Corsock, Castle Douglas, DG7 3DW
Tel: 01644-440264
E-mail: bean-bags-direct@epbowery.com
Website: http://www.bean-bags-direct.co.uk
Directors: E. Bowery (Prop)
No.of Employees: 1 - 10 **Product Groups:** 26

Forge Consulting Ltd
Glenswinton Parton, Castle Douglas, DG7 3NL
Tel: 01644-470223 **Fax:** 01644-470227
Directors: P. Jackson (MD), J. Jackson (Fin)
Immediate Holding Company: FORGE CONSULTING LIMITED
Registration no: 01673693 **Date established:** 1982
No.of Employees: 1 - 10 **Product Groups:** 36, 39, 40

Murray Arms Hotel
Gatehouse Of Fleet, Castle Douglas, DG7 2HY
Tel: 01557-814207 **Fax:** 01557-814370
E-mail: info@murrayarmshotel.co.uk
Website: http://www.murrayarmshotel.co.uk
Directors: J. Stewart (Prop)
Immediate Holding Company: MURRAY ARMS HOTEL LIMITED
Registration no: SC031235 **VAT No.:** GB 263 3367 59
Date established: 1955 **Turnover:** £500,000 - £1m
No.of Employees: 1 - 10 **Product Groups:** 69

Date of Accounts	Oct 11	Oct 10	Oct 09
Working Capital	-133	-459	-373
Fixed Assets	N/A	195	198
Current Assets	413	24	26

Picture This Frame That
Easdale High Street, New Galloway, Castle Douglas, DG7 3RN
Tel: 01644-420232
E-mail: andy@picturethisframethat.co.uk
Website: http://www.picturethisframethat.co.uk
Product Groups: 25, 26, 36, 49

Rancher Livestock Equipment
1-2 Carlingwark Street, Castle Douglas, DG7 1DW
Tel: 01556-504888 **Fax:** 01556-504404
E-mail: mail@rancher-equipment.co.uk
Website: http://www.rancher-equipment.co.uk
Directors: J. Robertson (Prop)
No.of Employees: 1 - 10 **Product Groups:** 41

Dunbartonshire

Clydebank

Bodycote plc
4 Bleasdale Court 2 South Avenue, Clydebank Business Park, Clydebank, G81 2LE
Tel: 0141-941 2022 **Fax:** 0141-952 7099
E-mail: info@bodycote.com
Website: http://www.bodycote.com
Directors: A. Hardie (Dir), A. Hardy (MD)
Managers: K. Hepburn (Tech Serv Mgr)
Ultimate Holding Company: Bodycote International PLC
Registration no: 00519057 **VAT No.:** GB 553 5266 38
Turnover: £500,000 - £1m **No.of Employees:** 21 - 50
Product Groups: 54, 85

Clyde Broadcast Products
3 South Avenue Clydebank Business Park, Clydebank, G81 2RX
Tel: 0141-952 7950 **Fax:** 0141-941 1224
E-mail: sales@clydebroadcast.com
Website: http://www.clydebroadcast.com

Directors: B. Rowan (Sales)
Immediate Holding Company: CLYDE BROADCAST PRODUCTS LIMITED
Registration no: SC174692 **VAT No.:** GB 680 5881 07
Date established: 1997 **No.of Employees:** 11 - 20 **Product Groups:** 37, 67

Date of Accounts	May 11	May 10	May 09
Working Capital	14	302	260
Fixed Assets	526	478	368
Current Assets	401	779	663

Corbi Door & Window Furniture
In Shops Sylvania Way South, Clydebank, G81 1RU
Tel: 0141-951 8333
Managers: D. Morton (Mgr)
Date established: 2002 **No.of Employees:** 1 - 10 **Product Groups:** 35, 36

European Circuits Ltd
79 Beardmore Way, Clydebank, G81 4HT
Tel: 0141-941 1388 **Fax:** 0141-951 2084
E-mail: info@european-circuits.co.uk
Website: http://www.european-circuits.co.uk
Directors: M. Briscoe (MD), P. Briscoe (Fin)
Managers: P. Briscoe (Sales Prom Mgr), R. Bradford (Prod Mgr)
Immediate Holding Company: EUROPEAN CIRCUITS LIMITED
Registration no: SC197100 **VAT No.:** GB 435 2943 47
Date established: 1999 **Turnover:** £1m - £2m **No.of Employees:** 21 - 50
Product Groups: 37

Date of Accounts	Jun 11	Jun 10	Jun 09
Working Capital	52	25	92
Fixed Assets	701	675	712
Current Assets	403	473	459

Express Electrical & Engineering Supplies
37 Cable Depot Road, Clydebank, G81 1UY
Tel: 0141-941 3689 **Fax:** 0141-952 8155
E-mail: sales@expresselectrical.co.uk
Website: http://www.expresselectrical.co.uk
Bank(s): Lloyds TSB Bank plc
Directors: R. Perrett (Fin), G. Perrett (Fin)
Managers: G. Perrett (Mgr), D. Perrett (Mgr), N. Buckley (Sales Prom Mgr), R. Perrit (Personnel)
Immediate Holding Company: EXPRESS ELECTRICAL & ENGINEERING SUPPLIES LIMITED
Registration no: SC091868 **VAT No.:** GB 435 2158 66
Date established: 1985 **Turnover:** £2m - £5m **No.of Employees:** 11 - 20
Product Groups: 30, 37

Date of Accounts	Dec 07	Dec 06	Dec 05
Working Capital	978	817	461
Fixed Assets	82	61	590
Current Assets	1428	1297	884
Current Liabilities	450	480	423
Total Share Capital	40	40	40

Foil Ribbon & Impact Printing Scotland Ltd
Unit 4 Rutherford Court 15 North Avenue, Clydebank Business Park, Clydebank, G81 2QP
Tel: 0141-952 5525 **Fax:** 0141-952 5524
E-mail: scotland@frip.co.uk
Website: http://www.frip.co.uk
Directors: J. Gibson (Sales & Mktg), L. Gibson (MD)
Ultimate Holding Company: FOIL RIBBON & IMPACT PRINTING GROUP LIMITED
Immediate Holding Company: FOIL RIBBON & IMPACT PRINTING GROUP LIMITED
Registration no: SC049498 **Date established:** 1971
Turnover: £500,000 - £1m **No.of Employees:** 1 - 10 **Product Groups:** 27, 28, 44

Date of Accounts	Mar 12	Mar 11	Mar 10
Sales Turnover	6m	6m	5m
Pre Tax Profit/Loss	328	154	-345
Working Capital	-180	-571	-699
Fixed Assets	4m	4m	5m
Current Assets	2m	2m	2m
Current Liabilities	1m	2m	2m

Kidde Fire Protection Services Ltd
Bute House Alpha Centre, Clydebank, G81 1PD
Tel: 0141-952 7766 **Fax:** 0141-951 1831
E-mail: markdolan@kiddefps.com
Website: http://www.kiddefps.com
Bank(s): Bank of Scotland
Managers: G. Murchinson (Sales Prom Mgr), M. Dollan (District Mgr)
Immediate Holding Company: KIDDE FIRE PROTECTION SERVICES LIMITED
Registration no: 01054492 **VAT No.:** GB 197 0070 60
Date established: 1972 **Turnover:** £10m - £20m
No.of Employees: 21 - 50 **Product Groups:** 38, 40

Northern Marine Management Ltd
2 Central Avenue Clydebank Business Park, Clydebank, G81 2QR
Tel: 0141-876 3000 **Fax:** 0141-941 2791
E-mail: jacqueline.tierney@stena.com
Website: http://www.nmm-stena.com
Bank(s): Bank of Scotland
Directors: J. Tierney (Fin), H. Ferguson (I.T. Dir)
Managers: B. Caldwell (Tech Serv Mgr), R. Brown (Buyer), I. Macleod (Personnel)
Ultimate Holding Company: STENA AB (PUBL) (SWEDEN)
Immediate Holding Company: NORTHERN MARINE MANAGEMENT LIMITED
Registration no: SC082005 **Date established:** 1983
Turnover: £5m - £10m **No.of Employees:** 101 - 250 **Product Groups:** 84

Date of Accounts	Dec 10	Dec 09	Dec 08
Sales Turnover	10m	10m	8m
Pre Tax Profit/Loss	2m	2m	812
Working Capital	6m	5m	4m
Fixed Assets	4m	5m	5m
Current Assets	9m	9m	7m
Current Liabilities	3m	3m	1m

J C Roxburgh & Co. Ltd
151 Glasgow Road, Clydebank, G81 1LQ
Tel: 0141-952 0371 **Fax:** 0141-952 0255
E-mail: info@jcroxburgh.co.uk
Website: http://www.jcroxburgh.co.uk
Directors: J. Roxburgh (Dir)
Ultimate Holding Company: J.C. ROXBURGH & COMPANY LIMITED
Immediate Holding Company: J.C. ROXBURGH & COMPANY LIMITED
Registration no: SC041244 **Date established:** 1964
Turnover: £250,000 - £500,000 **No.of Employees:** 11 - 20
Product Groups: 82

Date of Accounts	Mar 11	Mar 10	Mar 09
Working Capital	86	130	78
Fixed Assets	947	463	479
Current Assets	352	301	306

S3 Interactive
Unit 1a Dunrobin Court 14 North Avenue, Clydebank Business Park, Clydebank, G81 2QP
Tel: 0141-952 2111 **Fax:** 0141-952 5255
E-mail: enquiries@s3interactive.co.uk
Website: http://www.s3interactive.co.uk
Directors: F. Charleston (Co Sec), P. Johnson (Dir)
Immediate Holding Company: S3 INTERACTIVE LIMITED
Registration no: SC251765 **Date established:** 2003
Turnover: £10m - £20m **No.of Employees:** 51 - 100 **Product Groups:** 48

Date of Accounts	Mar 11	Mar 10	Mar 09
Sales Turnover	14m	15m	8m
Pre Tax Profit/Loss	2m	1m	1m
Working Capital	1m	488	1m
Fixed Assets	167	47	50
Current Assets	3m	3m	3m
Current Liabilities	1m	1m	947

Scottish Enterprise
Spectrum House 1a North Avenue, Clydebank Business Park, Clydebank, G81 2DR
Tel: 0141-951 2121 **Fax:** 0141-951 1907
E-mail: david.anderson@scotent.co.uk
Website: http://www.scottish-enterprise.com/dunbartonshire
Bank(s): Trustees Savings, Glasgow City Branch
Directors: P. Denheen (Pers), D. Anderson (MD)
Managers: G. Cairne (Mktg Serv Mgr), I. Scott (Comptroller)
Immediate Holding Company: SCOTTISH ENTERPRISE DUNBARTONSHIRE
Registration no: SC130793 **Date established:** 1990
Turnover: £10m - £20m **No.of Employees:** 21 - 50 **Product Groups:** 80, 86

Date of Accounts	Mar 08
Sales Turnover	13614
Pre Tax Profit/Loss	-638
Working Capital	285
Fixed Assets	50
Current Assets	671
Current Liabilities	386
ROCE% (Return on Capital Employed)	-190.4

Terasaki
80 Beardmore Way, Clydebank, G81 4HT
Tel: 0141-941 1940 **Fax:** 0141-952 9246
E-mail: liz.ohare@terasaki.co.uk
Website: http://www.terasaki.co.uk
Bank(s): Clydesdale
Directors: L. O'Hare (Pers)
Managers: C. Macdermid (Mats Contrlr), T. Craig (Sales & Mktg Mg), K. Macdougall, A. Morris
Ultimate Holding Company: TERASAKI ELECTRIC CO LTD (JAPAN)
Immediate Holding Company: TERASAKI ELECTRIC (EUROPE) LIMITED
Registration no: SC307759 **VAT No.:** GB 290 3671 47
Date established: 2006 **Turnover:** £10m - £20m
No.of Employees: 51 - 100 **Product Groups:** 37, 38

Date of Accounts	Mar 11	Mar 10	Mar 09
Sales Turnover	19m	15m	16m
Pre Tax Profit/Loss	413	607	1m
Working Capital	6m	5m	5m
Fixed Assets	950	641	856
Current Assets	13m	10m	9m
Current Liabilities	1m	1m	699

Universal Electrical Supplies Ltd
3 South Elgin Place, Clydebank, G81 1XP
Tel: 0141-952 8794 **Fax:** 0141-951 8590
E-mail: universalelectrical@hotmail.com
Directors: S. Mackenzie (Fin), T. Lorimer (MD)
Immediate Holding Company: UNIVERSAL ELECTRICAL SUPPLIES LIMITED
Registration no: SC174238 **Date established:** 1997
No.of Employees: 1 - 10 **Product Groups:** 36, 40

Date of Accounts	May 11	May 10	May 09
Working Capital	114	84	88
Fixed Assets	25	29	34
Current Assets	306	283	333

Lanarkshire

Coatbridge

Affinity Financial Planning Ltd
Kelvin House 87 Calder Street, Coatbridge, ML5 4EY
Tel: 01236-421422
E-mail: info@affinityfp.com
Website: http://www.affinityfp.com
Directors: A. Meehan (MD)
Immediate Holding Company: AFFINITY FINANCIAL PLANNING LIMITED
Registration no: SC222052 **Date established:** 2001
No.of Employees: 1 - 10 **Product Groups:** 80, 82

Date of Accounts	Jun 11	Jun 10	Jun 09
Working Capital	N/A	-3	-24
Fixed Assets	4	4	6
Current Assets	45	45	28

Colvin Smith
Locks Street, Coatbridge, ML5 3RT
Tel: 01236-424333 **Fax:** 01236-440109
E-mail: ray.mccallum@colvinsmith.co.uk
Website: http://www.colvinsmith.co.uk
Bank(s): Cydesdale
Directors: P. Kiel (MD)
Registration no: 00652671 **VAT No.:** GB 176 3765 30
Turnover: £500,000 - £1m **No.of Employees:** 21 - 50
Product Groups: 48, 84

Crane Maintain Ltd
21 Coatbank Street, Coatbridge, ML5 3SP
Tel: 01236-432988 **Fax:** 01236-422388
E-mail: service@cranemaintain.co.uk
Website: http://www.cranemaintain.co.uk
Directors: D. Patterson (MD)
Immediate Holding Company: CRANE MAINTAIN LTD
Registration no: SC317952 **Date established:** 2007
No.of Employees: 1 - 10 **Product Groups:** 35, 39, 45

Date of Accounts	Aug 11	Aug 10	Aug 09
Working Capital	90	40	46
Fixed Assets	54	42	50
Current Assets	223	168	188

C T Engineering Scotland Ltd
Hornock Road, Coatbridge, ML5 2DX
Tel: 01236-433393 **Fax:** 01236-430677
E-mail: jeangraham@ct-eng-scotland.com
Website: http://www.ct-eng-scotland.com
Directors: J. Graham (MD), S. Graham (MD)
Immediate Holding Company: C.T. ENGINEERING (SCOTLAND) LIMITED
Registration no: SC096134 **Date established:** 1985
No.of Employees: 1 - 10 **Product Groups:** 35, 42, 45

Date of Accounts	Mar 11	Mar 10	Mar 09
Working Capital	36	66	67
Fixed Assets	182	198	214
Current Assets	64	119	141

Initial Cleaning Services
Heritage Way, Coatbridge, ML5 1QD
Tel: 01236-433471 **Fax:** 01236-420655
E-mail: initialcleaning@rentokilinitial.com
Website: http://www.initialcleaning.co.uk
Bank(s): HSBC Bank plc
Directors: J. Morris (MD), J. Rooney (Div), L. Burk (Dir)
Ultimate Holding Company: Rentokil Initial plc
Immediate Holding Company: Bet UK Ltd
Registration no: 02329448 **VAT No.:** GB 625 9496 02
Turnover: £250,000 - £500,000 **No.of Employees:** 21 - 50
Product Groups: 52

Lees Of Scotland Ltd
North Caldeen Road, Coatbridge, ML5 4EF
Tel: 01236-441600 **Fax:** 01236-441601
E-mail: sales@leesofscotland.co.uk
Website: http://www.leesofscotland.co.uk
Bank(s): Bank of Scotland
Directors: A. Croll (Sales), C. Miquel (MD), D. Simson (Fin)
Managers: J. Glen (Tech Serv Mgr), J. Leonard (Personnel), S. Purves
Ultimate Holding Company: LEES (SCOTLAND) 2012 LIMITED
Immediate Holding Company: LEES OF SCOTLAND LIMITED
Registration no: SC028236 **VAT No.:** GB 612 3775 53
Date established: 1951 **Turnover:** £10m - £20m
No.of Employees: 101 - 250 **Product Groups:** 20, 62

Date of Accounts	Dec 11	Dec 10	Dec 09
Sales Turnover	17m	15m	15m
Pre Tax Profit/Loss	1m	1m	612
Working Capital	2m	2m	1m
Fixed Assets	3m	3m	3m
Current Assets	8m	7m	6m
Current Liabilities	2m	2m	2m

Opalion Plastics Ltd
9-11 Palacecraig Street, Coatbridge, ML5 4RY
Tel: 01236-420550 **Fax:** 01236-420808
E-mail: sales@opalion.co.uk
Website: http://www.opalion.co.uk
Directors: N. Freeman (Dir)
Managers: C. McChain (Chief Mgr)
Immediate Holding Company: M.S.R. TRANSPORT LIMITED
Registration no: SC358024 **Date established:** 2001
Turnover: Up to £250,000 **No.of Employees:** 1 - 10 **Product Groups:** 38, 42

Reg Vardy Ltd
200 Main Street, Coatbridge, ML5 3RB
Tel: 01236-707500 **Fax:** 01236-707509
Website: http://www.regvardy.co.uk
Directors: J. Mccann (Head), T. Martin (Fin)
Managers: A. Williamson (Chief Acct), J. McGregor (Chief Mgr), P. Macguire (Fin Mgr), P. Smith (Sales Prom Mgr)
Immediate Holding Company: REG VARDY LIMITED
Registration no: 00611190 **Date established:** 1958
Turnover: £500,000 - £1m **No.of Employees:** 51 - 100
Product Groups: 68

Retronix Ltd
North Caldeen Road, Coatbridge, ML5 4EF
Tel: 01236-433345 **Fax:** 01236-433434
E-mail: kathleen.boswell@retronix.co.uk
Website: http://www.retronix.co.uk
Bank(s): Bank of Scotland
Directors: K. Boswell (Fin)
Managers: D. Tinning (Fin Mgr)
Immediate Holding Company: RETRONIX LTD.
Registration no: SC131176 **Date established:** 1991 **Turnover:** £2m - £5m
No.of Employees: 21 - 50 **Product Groups:** 37

Date of Accounts	Aug 11	Aug 10	Aug 09
Working Capital	1m	935	692
Fixed Assets	1m	1m	1m
Current Assets	2m	2m	992

Tannoy Group Ltd
Rosehall Industrial Estate, Coatbridge, ML5 4TF
Tel: 01236-420199 **Fax:** 01236-428230
E-mail: andrzej.sosna@tannoy.co.uk
Website: http://www.tannoy.com
Directors: K. Borup (Fin)
Managers: A. Fisker, T. Lount (Mktg Serv Mgr)
Ultimate Holding Company: T G I P.L.C.
Immediate Holding Company: TANNOY GROUP LTD
Registration no: 01598077 **Date established:** 1926
Turnover: £10m - £20m **No.of Employees:** 51 - 100 **Product Groups:** 37

Date of Accounts	Jun 06	Jun 05
Pre Tax Profit/Loss	3	14
Working Capital	69	66
Fixed Assets	1425	1425
Current Assets	2374	2371
Current Liabilities	2305	2305
Total Share Capital	388	888
ROCE% (Return on Capital Employed)	0.2	0.9

Thistle Packaging Services Ltd

E7 North Caldeen Road, Coatbridge, ML5 4EF
Tel: 01236-437500 **Fax:** 01236-440868
Website: http://www.thistlepackaging.com
Directors: W. Angus (MD), G. Davis (Sales)
Ultimate Holding Company: LEES FOODS PUBLIC LIMITED COMPANY
Immediate Holding Company: THISTLE PACKAGING SERVICES LIMITED
Registration no: SC203420 **Date established:** 2000
Turnover: Up to £250,000 **No.of Employees:** 1 - 10 **Product Groups:** 38, 42

Date of Accounts	May 11	May 10	May 09
Sales Turnover	111	128	131
Pre Tax Profit/Loss	2	8	4
Working Capital	8	-4	10
Fixed Assets	9	20	6
Current Assets	24	7	22

Fife

Cowdenbeath

Beath Enviro Ltd

1 Birnie Ridge Cottage Bridge Street, Cowdenbeath, KY4 8NH
Tel: 01383-611900 **Fax:** 01383-611900
Website: http://www.beathenviro.freeserve.co.uk
Directors: M. Simpson (Fin), J. Simpson (MD)
Immediate Holding Company: BEATH ENVIRO LIMITED
Registration no: SC205876 **Date established:** 2000
Turnover: Up to £250,000 **No.of Employees:** 1 - 10 **Product Groups:** 38, 42

Date of Accounts	Apr 11	Apr 10	Apr 09
Sales Turnover	221	200	172
Pre Tax Profit/Loss	27	28	-6
Working Capital	22	14	6
Fixed Assets	23	20	25
Current Assets	54	36	52
Current Liabilities	27	19	24

Fife Plastics

Fordell, Cowdenbeath, KY4 8EY
Tel: 01383-510256 **Fax:** 01383-510256
Directors: J. Duncan (Prop)
VAT No.: GB 270 4969 37 **Turnover:** Up to £250,000
No.of Employees: 1 - 10 **Product Groups:** 30

MCSHEE SIGN SOLUTIONS

8 Cobden Court Crossgates, Cowdenbeath, KY4 8AU
Tel: 01383-512785
E-mail: jim@mcsheesignsolutions.co.uk
Directors: J. Mcshee (Prop)
No.of Employees: 1 - 10 **Product Groups:** 30, 37, 39, 40, 49, 65, 67, 68

Score Group plc (Specialised Testing)

The Paragon Works Woodend Place, Cowdenbeath, KY4 8EE
Tel: 01383-510510 **Fax:** 01383-514512
E-mail: ian.farrow@score-group.com
Website: http://www.score-group.com
Bank(s): Royal Bank of Scotland
Managers: I. Farrow (Chief Mgr)
Ultimate Holding Company: SCORE GROUP PLC
Immediate Holding Company: SCORE GROUP PLC
Registration no: SC172439 **VAT No.:** GB 498 5817 74
Date established: 1997 **Turnover:** £500,000 - £1m
No.of Employees: 21 - 50 **Product Groups:** 38, 44

Date of Accounts	Sep 10	Sep 11	Oct 08
Sales Turnover	151m	125m	142m
Pre Tax Profit/Loss	6m	9m	8m
Working Capital	25m	27m	24m
Fixed Assets	36m	37m	26m
Current Assets	74m	65m	66m
Current Liabilities	26m	21m	31m

Perthshire

Crieff

Rapid Tyre Services

East Lochlane Farm, Crieff, PH7 4HR
Tel: 07863-335888 **Fax:** 01350-728645
E-mail: mail@rapidtyreservices.co.uk
Website: http://www.rapidtyreservices.co.uk
Directors: G. Halley (Prop)
Turnover: Up to £250,000 **No.of Employees:** 1 - 10 **Product Groups:** 29, 68

Rossshire

Cromarty

Calico UK Ltd

27 High Street, Cromarty, IV11 8YR
Tel: 01381-600580 **Fax:** 01381-600593
E-mail: info@cali.co.uk
Website: http://www.cali.co.uk
Directors: K. Pryer (Dir)
Immediate Holding Company: CALICO 2004 LIMITED
Registration no: SC277431 **Date established:** 2004 **Turnover:** £1m - £2m
No.of Employees: 1 - 10 **Product Groups:** 44

Date of Accounts	Apr 12	Apr 11	Apr 10
Working Capital	-35	-35	-35
Fixed Assets	50	50	50

Ayrshire

Cumnock

Adelphi Engineering & Construction Ltd

Unit 1 Imex Business Centre Lugar, Cumnock, KA18 3JG
Tel: 01290-426677 **Fax:** 01290-425588
Website: http://www.adelphi-engineering.co.uk
Directors: J. Davie (Fin), S. Abercrombie (MD)
Immediate Holding Company: ADELPHI ENGINEERING & CONSTRUCTION LIMITED
Registration no: SC185137 **Date established:** 1998
Turnover: £500,000 - £1m **No.of Employees:** 11 - 20
Product Groups: 34, 66

Date of Accounts	Apr 11	Apr 10	Apr 09
Sales Turnover	N/A	N/A	893
Pre Tax Profit/Loss	N/A	N/A	27
Working Capital	12	47	73
Fixed Assets	76	90	102
Current Assets	228	187	221
Current Liabilities	N/A	N/A	56

Robert W H Brown

Belston Cottage Sinclairston, Ochiltree, Cumnock, KA18 2RT
Tel: 01290-700073
E-mail: enquiries@robertwhbrown.co.uk
Website: http://www.robertwhbrown.co.uk
Directors: R. Brown (Prop)
Immediate Holding Company: RWHB LTD
Registration no: SC344621 **Date established:** 2008
No.of Employees: 1 - 10 **Product Groups:** 35

Pollock Farm Equipment Ltd

Unit 1 Imex Business Centre Lugar, Cumnock, KA18 3JG
Tel: 01290-427000 **Fax:** 01290-427013
E-mail: pollockfarmequip@aol.com
Website: http://www.pollockfarmequip.co.uk
Directors: J. Mcghee (MD)
Immediate Holding Company: POLLOCK FARM EQUIPMENT LIMITED
Registration no: SC181634 **Date established:** 1997
No.of Employees: 11 - 20 **Product Groups:** 41

Date of Accounts	May 11	May 10	May 09
Working Capital	-29	8	48
Fixed Assets	128	141	135
Current Assets	208	220	265

Vycon Products Ltd

57c Main Street Auchinleck, Cumnock, KA18 2AF
Tel: 01290-425463 **Fax:** 01290-420311
E-mail: sales@vycon.co.uk
Website: http://www.vycon.co.uk
Directors: M. Belford (Sales)
Ultimate Holding Company: FERGUSON SCOT LIMITED
Immediate Holding Company: VYCON PRODUCTS LIMITED
Registration no: SC173611 **Date established:** 1997
Turnover: £500,000 - £1m **No.of Employees:** 1 - 10 **Product Groups:** 30

Date of Accounts	Mar 11	Mar 10	Mar 09
Working Capital	98	105	109
Fixed Assets	58	51	61
Current Assets	184	183	188

Fife

Cupar

Brand & Rae

Russell Mills Springfield, Cupar, KY15 5QX
Tel: 01334-652828 **Fax:** 01334-655967
Website: http://www.brandandrae.co.uk
Bank(s): HSBC Bank plc
Directors: A. Morrison (Dir), R. Mcdonald (Co Sec), G. Bell (MD)
Managers: I. MacPherson (Sales Prom Mgr)
Ultimate Holding Company: BREEDON HOLDINGS LIMITED
Immediate Holding Company: BRAND & RAE LIMITED
Registration no: SC251571 **VAT No.:** GB 717 0980 29
Date established: 2003 **Turnover:** £2m - £5m **No.of Employees:** 21 - 50
Product Groups: 33, 66

Date of Accounts	Dec 11	Dec 10	Dec 09
Working Capital	N/A	-767	N/A
Current Liabilities	N/A	767	N/A

Hoggs of Fife Ltd

Eden Valley Business Park, Cupar, KY15 4RB
Tel: 01334-653733 **Fax:** 01334-653553
E-mail: sales@hoggs.co.uk
Website: http://www.hoggs.co.uk
Directors: R. Gibson (MD)
Immediate Holding Company: HOGGS OF FIFE LIMITED
Registration no: SC015281 **Date established:** 2028
Turnover: £5m - £10m **No.of Employees:** 21 - 50 **Product Groups:** 63

Date of Accounts	May 12	May 11	May 10
Sales Turnover	6m	6m	6m
Pre Tax Profit/Loss	504	405	330
Working Capital	3m	3m	3m
Fixed Assets	863	904	939
Current Assets	4m	4m	3m
Current Liabilities	465	354	278

Houston's Of Cupar Ltd

Cupar Muir Industrial Estate Cupar Muir, Cupar, KY15 5RL
Tel: 01334-655331 **Fax:** 01334-656437
E-mail: info@houstonsofcupar.co.uk
Website: http://www.hoc-engineering.co.uk
Bank(s): Royal Bank of Scotland
Directors: A. Curran (MD)
Managers: R. Fernie (Sales Admin)
Immediate Holding Company: HOUSTON'S OF CUPAR LIMITED
Registration no: SC212906 **Date established:** 2000 **Turnover:** £1m - £2m
No.of Employees: 21 - 50 **Product Groups:** 35, 48, 49

Date of Accounts	Apr 11	Apr 10	Apr 09
Working Capital	1	-24	105
Fixed Assets	143	126	90
Current Assets	721	453	515

John White & Son Weighing Machines Ltd

6 Back Dykes Auchtermuchty, Cupar, KY14 7DW
Tel: 01337-827600 **Fax:** 01337-827600
E-mail: enquiries@johnwhiteandson.com
Website: http://www.johnwhiteandson.com
Bank(s): Bank of Scotland
Directors: J. Onuonga (Dir)
Immediate Holding Company: JOHN WHITE & SON (WEIGHING MACHINES) LIMITED
Registration no: SC050045 **Date established:** 1972 **Turnover:** £1m - £2m
No.of Employees: 11 - 20 **Product Groups:** 38, 39, 44, 45, 48, 67, 83, 85

Date of Accounts	Feb 11	Feb 10	Feb 09
Working Capital	48	48	45
Fixed Assets	231	257	227
Current Assets	508	289	230

Monax Glass Ltd

22 Charles Jarvis Court, Cupar, KY15 5EJ
Tel: 01334-657800 **Fax:** 01334-657857
E-mail: monax@sol.co.uk
Website: http://www.monaxglass.com
Directors: I. Grant (MD), M. Osler (Fin)
Immediate Holding Company: MONAX GLASS LIMITED
Registration no: SC184445 **VAT No.:** GB 716 8332 30
Date established: 1998 **Turnover:** £500,000 - £1m
No.of Employees: 1 - 10 **Product Groups:** 33, 38, 48

Date of Accounts	Jul 11	Jul 10	Jul 09
Working Capital	37	44	45
Fixed Assets	16	16	18
Current Assets	168	204	153

G Reekie Group Ltd

Cupar Trading Estate, Cupar, KY15 4SX
Tel: 01334-652445 **Fax:** 01334-653147
E-mail: creekie@reekie.co.uk
Website: http://www.reekie.co.uk
Directors: C. Reekie (MD), S. Mercer (Sales)
Managers: D. Cairns
Immediate Holding Company: G. REEKIE GROUP LIMITED
Registration no: SC041230 **Date established:** 1964
Turnover: £10m - £20m **No.of Employees:** 51 - 100 **Product Groups:** 39, 67

Date of Accounts	Dec 11	Dec 10	Dec 09
Sales Turnover	14m	12m	10m
Pre Tax Profit/Loss	16	38	-25
Working Capital	2m	2m	1m
Fixed Assets	972	955	950
Current Assets	4m	3m	3m
Current Liabilities	685	610	496

Midlothian

Currie

Renishaw plc

Research Park North Riccarton, Currie, EH14 4AP
Tel: 0131-451 1616 **Fax:** 0131-451 1717
E-mail: nick.weston@renishaw.com
Website: http://www.renishaw.com
Managers: N. Weston (Mgr)
Immediate Holding Company: RENISHAW P L C
Registration no: 01106260 **Date established:** 1973
No.of Employees: 21 - 50 **Product Groups:** 36, 37

Date of Accounts	Jun 11	Jun 10	Jun 09
Sales Turnover	289m	182m	171m
Pre Tax Profit/Loss	82m	27m	5m
Working Capital	110m	86m	58m
Fixed Assets	161m	110m	127m
Current Assets	157m	116m	80m
Current Liabilities	33m	19m	21m

Weatherford Edinburgh Petroleum Services Ltd

12 Heriot-Watt Research Park Riccarton, Currie, EH14 4AP
Tel: 0131-449 4536 **Fax:** 0131-449 5123
E-mail: gary.norton@eu.weatherford.com
Website: http://www.e-petroleumservices.com
Directors: W. Fulton (Co Sec)
Managers: F. Macdonald (Admin Off), D. Nicol (Tech Serv Mgr), G. Norton (Mgr)
Ultimate Holding Company: WEATHERFORD INTERNATIONAL LIMITED (BERMUDA)
Immediate Holding Company: EDINBURGH PETROLEUM SERVICES LIMITED
Registration no: SC079517 **VAT No.:** GB 397 9081 91
Date established: 1982 **Turnover:** £5m - £10m **No.of Employees:** 21 - 50
Product Groups: 84

Date of Accounts	Dec 10	Dec 09	Dec 08
Sales Turnover	6m	5m	4m
Pre Tax Profit/Loss	591	1m	964
Working Capital	4m	3m	2m
Fixed Assets	258	169	164
Current Assets	11m	8m	6m
Current Liabilities	431	840	1m

Kirkcudbrightshire

Dalbeattie

Barons Craig Hotel

Rockcliffe, Dalbeattie, DG5 4QF
Tel: 01556-630225 **Fax:** 01556-630328
E-mail: info@baronscraighotel.co.uk
Website: http://www.baronscraighotel.co.uk

Directors: D. Mabbs (Prop)
Date established: 1994 **No.of Employees:** 11 - 20 **Product Groups:** 69

Dalbeattie Finance Co. Ltd
Maxwell Street, Dalbeattie, DG5 4AJ
Tel: 01556-610243 **Fax:** 01556-611717
E-mail: info@dalbeattiefinance.co.uk
Website: http://www.dalbeattiefinance.co.uk
Directors: D. Ireland (Fin)
Immediate Holding Company: DALBEATTIE FINANCE COMPANY LIMITED
Registration no: SC031300 **VAT No.:** GB 262 8117 63
Date established: 1956 **Turnover:** £5m - £10m **No.of Employees:** 1 - 10
Product Groups: 82

Date of Accounts	Mar 12	Mar 11	Mar 10
Pre Tax Profit/Loss	113	130	150
Working Capital	4m	4m	4m
Fixed Assets	90	92	95
Current Assets	6m	6m	6m
Current Liabilities	2m	478	2m

J Paterson & Sons
Bank Square, Dalbeattie, DG5 4HZ
Tel: 01556-610249 **Fax:** 01556-611345
Directors: M. Paterson (Dir)
Immediate Holding Company: SCOTSPEED MOTORCYCLES
No.of Employees: 1 - 10 **Product Groups:** 39

Midlothian

Dalkeith

J Jordan Steel Fabricators Ltd
39 Newbattle Industrial Estate, Dalkeith, EH22 4AD
Tel: 0131-663 7275 **Fax:** 0131-663 7275
E-mail: john.jobin3@sky.com
Bank(s): Bank of Scotland
Directors: J. Jordan (Dir)
Immediate Holding Company: J. JORDAN STEEL FABRICATORS LTD.
Registration no: SC361206 **VAT No.:** GB 345 1197 62
Date established: 2009 **No.of Employees:** 11 - 20 **Product Groups:** 48, 51

Date of Accounts	Jun 11	Jun 10
Working Capital	-7	-7
Fixed Assets	9	9
Current Assets	74	54

K & I Ltd
Hardengreen Coachworks Eskbank, Dalkeith, EH22 3LD
Tel: 0131-663 4545 **Fax:** 0131-654 2373
E-mail: info@k-and-i.co.uk
Website: http://www.k-and-i.co.uk
Directors: S. Kirkness (Dir)
Immediate Holding Company: K. & I. LIMITED
Registration no: SC030680 **VAT No.:** GB 269 8230 25
Date established: 1955 **Turnover:** £1m - £2m **No.of Employees:** 21 - 50
Product Groups: 39

Date of Accounts	Mar 11	Mar 10	Mar 09
Working Capital	-417	-214	64
Fixed Assets	456	508	114
Current Assets	348	354	469

K P Tool Repairs
Newbattle Road Newbattle, Dalkeith, EH22 3LJ
Tel: 0131-663 0572 **Fax:** 0131-663 0572
E-mail: kptoolrepairs@googlemail.com
Directors: K. Perritt (Prop)
Date established: 1999 **No.of Employees:** 1 - 10 **Product Groups:** 37

Charles Letts Group Ltd
Thornybank Industrial Estate, Dalkeith, EH22 2NE
Tel: 0131-663 1971 **Fax:** 0131-660 3225
E-mail: gpresly@letts.co.uk
Website: http://www.letts.co.uk
Bank(s): Hambros
Directors: C. Letts (Sales), G. Presly (Grp Chief Exec), G. Presley (MD), G. Presly (MD), G. Raw (Fin), S. Graham (Pers)
Managers: C. Coughtrie (Mktg Serv Mgr), E. Wheelghan (I.T. Exec)
Immediate Holding Company: CHARLES LETTS & CO LIMITED
Registration no: SC007315 **Date established:** 2009
Turnover: £20m - £50m **No.of Employees:** 251 - 500
Product Groups: 22, 28

Date of Accounts	Jan 08
Pre Tax Profit/Loss	6859
Working Capital	13406
Fixed Assets	4685
Current Assets	13406
Total Share Capital	9535

N S D International Ltd
Mayfield Industrial Estate, Dalkeith, EH22 4AF
Tel: 0131-654 2800 **Fax:** 0131-663 6185
E-mail: e.martin@nsdinternational.co.uk
Website: http://www.nsdinternational.co.uk
Bank(s): Bank of Scotland, Dalkeith
Directors: E. Martin (MD), E. Martin (MD)
Managers: M. Caulder (Cust Serv Mgr), R. Bagnall (Tech Serv Mgr)
Ultimate Holding Company: BEHEERS-EN-EXPLOIT. NEDER. SPECIAAL DRUKKER. BV
Immediate Holding Company: NEDERLAND SPECIAAL DRUKKERIJ
Registration no: 00009731 **Date established:** 1858 **Turnover:** £5m - £10m
No.of Employees: 21 - 50 **Product Groups:** 27, 28, 30, 42, 44

Omega Lift Services Ltd
Unit 1 Hardengreen Industrial Estate Eskbank, Dalkeith, EH22 3NX
Tel: 0131-510 5000 **Fax:** 0131-510 5001
E-mail: info@omegalifts.com
Website: http://www.omegalifts.com
Directors: D. Watt (MD)
Immediate Holding Company: OMEGA LIFT SERVICES LIMITED
Registration no: SC243098 **Date established:** 2003
No.of Employees: 1 - 10 **Product Groups:** 35, 39, 45

Date of Accounts	Mar 12	Mar 11	Mar 10
Working Capital	206	208	126
Fixed Assets	34	27	13
Current Assets	378	416	289

Pentland Tech
Unit 4 Hardengreen Industrial Estate, Dalkeith, EH22 3NX
Tel: 0131-561 9373 **Fax:** 0131-561 9374
E-mail: pentland.tech@virgin.net
Directors: E. Rankin (Prop)
Date established: 2002 **No.of Employees:** 1 - 10 **Product Groups:** 35

Stanley Saw Services
Mayfield Industrial Estate, Dalkeith, EH22 4AD
Tel: 0131-660 1930 **Fax:** 0131-663 2527
E-mail: sales@stanleysawservices.co.uk
Website: http://www.stanleysawservices.co.uk
Directors: E. Stanley (Ptnr)
No.of Employees: 1 - 10 **Product Groups:** 36

Stangard Food Service Equipment Specialists Ltd
Unit 28 28 Hardengreen Industrial Estate, Dalkeith, EH22 3NX
Tel: 0131-660 5000 **Fax:** 0131-660 5001
E-mail: j@stangard.com
Website: http://www.stangard.com
Directors: J. Smith (Dir)
Immediate Holding Company: STANGARD FOOD SERVICE EQUIPMENT SPECIALISTS LIMITED
Registration no: SC213269 **Date established:** 2000 **Turnover:** £1m - £2m
No.of Employees: 1 - 10 **Product Groups:** 67

Date of Accounts	Mar 08	Mar 07	Mar 06
Working Capital	11	24	23
Current Assets	411	353	525

Ayrshire

Dalry

Skyway Helicopters
Mosside Farm, Dalry, KA24 5HJ
Tel: 08456-032955
E-mail: sales@skywayhelicopters.co.uk
Website: http://www.skywayhelicopters.co.uk
Directors: D. Stanners (MD)
Immediate Holding Company: SKYWAY HELICOPTERS LTD.
Registration no: SC311760 **Date established:** 2006
Turnover: Up to £250,000 **No.of Employees:** 1 - 10 **Product Groups:** 75

Date of Accounts	Jan 11	Jan 10	Jan 09
Sales Turnover	N/A	36	58
Pre Tax Profit/Loss	N/A	1	25
Working Capital	27	26	21
Fixed Assets	1	1	2
Current Assets	30	29	34
Current Liabilities	N/A	2	7

Ayrshire

Darvel

John Aird Holdings Ltd
Greenbank Mills East Main Street, Darvel, KA17 0JB
Tel: 01560-323600 **Fax:** 01560-323601
E-mail: johnaird@compuserve.com
Website: http://www.johnaird.co.uk
Directors: M. Winter (Fin)
Immediate Holding Company: JOHN AIRD (HOLDINGS) LIMITED
Registration no: SC155409 **VAT No.:** GB 262 9175 44
Date established: 1995 **Turnover:** £5m - £10m **No.of Employees:** 1 - 10
Product Groups: 23

Date of Accounts	Dec 10	Dec 09	Dec 08
Working Capital	-20	-20	4
Fixed Assets	143	143	143
Current Assets	4	4	4

Stirlingshire

Denny

Exclusive Iron Work
Broadside Filters, Denny, FK6 5JE
Tel: 01324-821111 **Fax:** 01324- 821111
Directors: R. McClung (Prop)
Date established: 2001 **No.of Employees:** 1 - 10 **Product Groups:** 26, 35

Machan Engineering Ltd
103 Broad Street, Denny, FK6 6DX
Tel: 01324-824309 **Fax:** 01324-824890
E-mail: info@machanengineering.fsnet.co.uk
Website: http://www.machanengineering.com
Bank(s): The Royal bank of Scotland
Directors: L. Mcdonald (Fin)
Managers: N. Russell (Admin Off)
Immediate Holding Company: MACHAN ENGINEERING LIMITED
Registration no: SC083928 **VAT No.:** 397 9061 00 **Date established:** 1983
No.of Employees: 21 - 50 **Product Groups:** 26, 39

Date of Accounts	Aug 11	Aug 10	Aug 09
Working Capital	26	-4	7
Fixed Assets	202	215	203
Current Assets	245	245	335

Ian G Mcintyre Maintenance & Repairs
44 Ferguson Drive, Denny, FK6 5AF
Tel: 01324-823260 **Fax:** 01324-823260
Directors: I. Mcintyre (Prop)
Date established: 1993 **No.of Employees:** 1 - 10 **Product Groups:** 46

P C Textiles Wipers Ltd
1 Glasgow Road, Denny, FK6 5DN
Tel: 01324-826993 **Fax:** 01324-826442
E-mail: office@textilewipers.com
Website: http://www.textilewipers.com
Directors: S. Cuthbertson (MD)
Immediate Holding Company: P.C. TEXTILE WIPERS LIMITED
Registration no: SC187271 **Date established:** 1998
No.of Employees: 1 - 10 **Product Groups:** 24, 32, 64

Date of Accounts	Oct 11	Oct 10	Oct 09
Working Capital	214	176	171
Fixed Assets	58	21	21
Current Assets	280	330	328

Paragon Diesel Services
Duncarron Garage Broad Street, Denny, FK6 6DX
Tel: 01324-825523 **Fax:** 01324-825523
Directors: G. Smith (Prop)
Date established: 1982 **No.of Employees:** 1 - 10 **Product Groups:** 40

Simpson Donald & Co.
80 Glasgow Road, Denny, FK6 5DN
Tel: 01324-826622 **Fax:** 01324-826611
E-mail: action@simpsondonald.co.uk
Website: http://www.simpsondonald.co.uk
Directors: A. Donald (Snr Part)
Immediate Holding Company: SIMPSON DONALD & CO LTD
Registration no: SC422944 **Date established:** 2012
Turnover: Up to £250,000 **No.of Employees:** 11 - 20 **Product Groups:** 37

Rossshire

Dingwall

Ian Bisset
Pow Camp Brahan, Maryburgh, Dingwall, IV7 8EE
Tel: 01349-861010
E-mail: ian-bisset@mary-bank.ndo.co.uk
Website: http://www.siromerscotland.co.uk
Directors: I. Bisset (Prop)
Immediate Holding Company: ORMISTON ENTERPRISES LIMITED
Registration no: SC061452 **Date established:** 1977
Turnover: Up to £250,000 **No.of Employees:** 1 - 10 **Product Groups:** 35, 48

Date of Accounts	Jul 11	Jul 10	Jul 09
Working Capital	76	76	277
Current Assets	76	76	302
Current Liabilities	N/A	N/A	26

T C Brown
Ivy Cottage Culbokie, Dingwall, IV7 8JH
Tel: 01349-877292 **Fax:** 01349-877292
Directors: T. Brown (Prop)
Date established: 1988 **No.of Employees:** 1 - 10 **Product Groups:** 35

Shanks Waste Management Ltd
Industrial Estate Evanton, Dingwall, IV16 9XJ
Tel: 01349-830852 **Fax:** 01349-830974
E-mail: g.gunn@shanks.co.uk
Website: http://www.shanks.co.uk
Managers: G. Gunn
Ultimate Holding Company: SHANKS GROUP PLC
Immediate Holding Company: SHANKS WASTE MANAGEMENT LIMITED
Registration no: 02393309 **Date established:** 1989 **Turnover:** £1m - £2m
No.of Employees: 1 - 10 **Product Groups:** 54

Date of Accounts	Mar 11	Mar 10	Mar 09
Sales Turnover	153m	136m	136m
Pre Tax Profit/Loss	-18m	-954	-4m
Working Capital	-16m	16m	-1m
Fixed Assets	59m	61m	64m
Current Assets	67m	75m	48m
Current Liabilities	23m	21m	11m

Thewoodcarver.Co.Uk
Firthview Culbo, Culbokie, Dingwall, IV7 8JX
Tel: 01349-877546
E-mail: info@thewoodcarver.co.uk
Website: http://www.thewoodcarver.co.uk
Directors: S. Horsfall (Prop)
No.of Employees: 1 - 10 **Product Groups:** 25, 30, 41, 67

Clackmannanshire

Dollar

F S G
Gartwhinzean Feus Powmill, Dollar, FK14 7LP
Tel: 01577-840926 **Fax:** 01577-840481
Website: http://www.cambro.com
Directors: C. Hutchinson (Prop)
Date established: 2002 **No.of Employees:** 1 - 10 **Product Groups:** 20, 36, 40, 41

Perthshire

Doune

Harvey Map Services Ltd
12-22 Main Street, Doune, FK16 6BJ
Tel: 01786-841202 **Fax:** 01786-841098
E-mail: sales@harveymaps.co.uk
Website: http://www.harveymaps.co.uk

see next page

Harvey Map Services Ltd - *Cont'd*

Directors: S. Harvey (MD)
Immediate Holding Company: HARVEY MAP SERVICES LIMITED
Registration no: SC063398 **VAT No.:** GB 309 0358 73
Date established: 1977 **Turnover:** £250,000 - £500,000
No.of Employees: 1 - 10 **Product Groups:** 28, 81

Date of Accounts	Oct 11	Oct 10	Oct 09
Working Capital	347	356	292
Fixed Assets	236	218	199
Current Assets	513	529	504

Dunbartonshire

Dumbarton

Aggreko plc

Overburn Avenue Broadmeadow Industrial Estate, Dumbarton, G82 2RL
Tel: 01389-726200 **Fax:** 01389-761577
Website: http://www.aggreko.co.uk
Directors: R. Richardson (MD), R. Soanes (Grp Chief Exec)
Ultimate Holding Company: AGGREKO PLC
Immediate Holding Company: AGGREKO UK LIMITED
Registration no: SC051093 **Date established:** 1972
Turnover: £250m - £500m **No.of Employees:** 21 - 50
Product Groups: 37, 52, 80, 83

Date of Accounts	Dec 11	Dec 10	Dec 09
Sales Turnover	363m	246m	160m
Pre Tax Profit/Loss	31m	31m	34m
Working Capital	23m	11m	15m
Fixed Assets	54m	43m	38m
Current Assets	115m	96m	65m
Current Liabilities	30m	25m	12m

Alchemy I T Ltd

8 Kirkton Road, Dumbarton, G82 4AS
Tel: 07976-262487 **Fax:** 0141-357 4375
E-mail: info@alchemy-it.com
Website: http://www.alchemy-it.com
Directors: J. Mccollum (Dir)
Immediate Holding Company: ALCHEMY IT LIMITED
Registration no: SC255670 **Date established:** 2003
Turnover: Up to £250,000 **No.of Employees:** 1 - 10 **Product Groups:** 44

Date of Accounts	Sep 11	Sep 10	Sep 06
Sales Turnover	N/A	N/A	139
Pre Tax Profit/Loss	N/A	N/A	54
Working Capital	37	54	46
Fixed Assets	N/A	N/A	1
Current Assets	66	89	68
Current Liabilities	N/A	N/A	21

Argyle Metal Services

32 Lime Road Broadmeadow Industrial Estate, Dumbarton, G82 2RP
Tel: 01389-764140 **Fax:** 01389-764140
Directors: D. Cameron (Prop)
Date established: 2005 **No.of Employees:** 1 - 10 **Product Groups:** 35

Diamond Power Specialty Ltd

Block 10 Vale of Leven Industrial Estate, Dumbarton, G82-3AD
Tel: 01389-727900 **Fax:** 01389-757405
E-mail: marketing@diamondpower.co.uk
Website: http://www.diamondpower.co.uk
Bank(s): The Royal Bank of Scotland
Directors: D. Keller (Dir), H. Mattsson (MD), T. Moskal (MD), E. Competti (Dir)
Managers: I. Ritchie (Sales & Mktg Mg)
Ultimate Holding Company: McDermott Inc (USA)
Immediate Holding Company: Diamond Power International Inc.
Registration no: 00127571 **VAT No.:** GB 263 0018 02
Date established: 1913 **Turnover:** £5m - £10m
No.of Employees: 101 - 250 **Product Groups:** 40, 48

Graham Mackinlay & Co.

Strathleven House Vale of Leven Industrial Estate, Dumbarton, G82 3PD
Tel: 01389-751122 **Fax:** 01389-755024
E-mail: enquiries@gmackinlay.com
Website: http://www.gmackinlay.com
Directors: G. Mackinlay (Prop)
Immediate Holding Company: WEST COAST CASES LIMITED
Registration no: SC241846 **Date established:** 2008
No.of Employees: 1 - 10 **Product Groups:** 36, 39, 40

Date of Accounts	Feb 09
Working Capital	1
Current Assets	1

Hutton Engineering Ltd

Carman Works Renton, Dumbarton, G82 4NR
Tel: 01389-756131 **Fax:** 01389-755881
E-mail: huttoneng@aol.com
Bank(s): Bank of Scotland
Directors: G. Hutton (Fin)
Immediate Holding Company: HUTTON ENGINEERING LIMITED
Registration no: SC072227 **VAT No.:** GB 356 8226 33
Date established: 1980 **Turnover:** £2m - £5m **No.of Employees:** 21 - 50
Product Groups: 41

Date of Accounts	Dec 11	Dec 10	Dec 09
Working Capital	-46	-41	26
Fixed Assets	173	186	175
Current Assets	92	174	206

Jewson Ltd

Overburn Avenue Broadmeadow Industrial Estate, Dumbarton, G82 2RL
Tel: 01389-763390 **Fax:** 01389-742448
Website: http://www.jewson.co.uk
Directors: C. Kenward (Fin), P. Hindle (Grp Chief Exec), T. Newman (Sales)
Managers: A. Fraser (District Mgr)
Ultimate Holding Company: COMPAGNIE DE SAINT GOBAIN (FRANCE)
Immediate Holding Company: JEWSON LIMITED
Registration no: 00348407 **VAT No.:** GB 497 7184 83
Date established: 1939 **Turnover:** £500m - £1,000m
No.of Employees: 11 - 20 **Product Groups:** 66

Date of Accounts	Dec 11	Dec 10	Dec 09
Sales Turnover	1606m	1547m	1485m
Pre Tax Profit/Loss	18m	100m	45m
Working Capital	-345m	-250m	-349m
Fixed Assets	496m	387m	461m
Current Assets	657m	1005m	1320m
Current Liabilities	66m	120m	64m

Lennox Motor Factors Ltd

10 Ash Road Broadmeadow Industrial Estate, Dumbarton, G82 2RS
Tel: 01389-761999 **Fax:** 01389-743888
E-mail: lennoxms@tinyworld.com
Website: http://www.tinyworld.com
Directors: C. Lawrie (MD), A. Lawrie (Fin)
Immediate Holding Company: LENNOX MOTOR FACTORS LIMITED
Registration no: SC080087 **Date established:** 1982
Turnover: £250,000 - £500,000 **No.of Employees:** 1 - 10
Product Groups: 39

Date of Accounts	Dec 11	Dec 10	Dec 09
Working Capital	137	116	92
Fixed Assets	21	18	26
Current Assets	201	185	151

Lenwood Conservatories

6 Poplar Road Broadmeadow Industrial Estate, Dumbarton, G82 2RQ
Tel: 01389-761133
Website: http://www.leonardbuilders.co.uk
Directors: J. Leonard (MD)
Managers: A. Lenord (Mgr), A. Leonard (Mktg Serv Mgr)
Ultimate Holding Company: NESTOR PROPERTIES LIMITED
Immediate Holding Company: LEONARD BUILDERS LIMITED
Registration no: SC241954 **Date established:** 1985
No.of Employees: 21 - 50 **Product Groups:** 08, 30

William Whiland

8 Alder Road Broadmeadow Industrial Estate, Dumbarton, G82 2EL
Tel: 01389-730430 **Fax:** 01389-743833
E-mail: sales@whiland.co.uk
Website: http://www.whiland.co.uk
Directors: D. Mazzucco (MD)
Immediate Holding Company: WILLIAM P. WHILAND & SON LIMITED
Registration no: SC067185 **Date established:** 1979
No.of Employees: 11 - 20 **Product Groups:** 35

Date of Accounts	Apr 11	Apr 10	Apr 09
Working Capital	40	34	75
Fixed Assets	310	333	356
Current Assets	167	206	208

Dumfriesshire

Dumfries

Alubrite Ltd

Units 5-9 Huntingdon Road, Dumfries, DG1 1NF
Tel: 01387-251161 **Fax:** 01387-248778
Directors: L. Luebke (Fin)
Immediate Holding Company: ALUBRITE LIMITED
Registration no: SC138243 **Date established:** 1992
Turnover: £250,000 - £500,000 **No.of Employees:** 1 - 10
Product Groups: 46, 48

Date of Accounts	Jul 11	Jul 10	Jul 09
Sales Turnover	N/A	N/A	340
Pre Tax Profit/Loss	N/A	N/A	16
Working Capital	-33	-9	17
Fixed Assets	58	72	77
Current Assets	48	69	106
Current Liabilities	N/A	N/A	48

Currie European Transport Ltd

Edinburgh Road Heathhall, Dumfries, DG1 3NX
Tel: 01387-267333 **Fax:** 01344-77420
E-mail: info@currie-european.com
Website: http://www.currie-european.com
Bank(s): Bank of Scotland
Directors: D. Ross (Comm), S. Turner (Fin), T. Barrie (Co Sec), T. Barry (MD)
Managers: S. Walls (I.T. Exec)
Ultimate Holding Company: Currie International Holdings Ltd
Immediate Holding Company: Currie European Transport Holdings Ltd
Registration no: SC062686 **VAT No.:** GB 724 2836 37
Date established: 1977 **Turnover:** £20m - £50m
No.of Employees: 101 - 250 **Product Groups:** 72

Date of Accounts	Dec 07	Dec 06	Dec 05
Sales Turnover	30771	31031	32833
Pre Tax Profit/Loss	-323	-379	-207
Working Capital	3139	3737	4157
Fixed Assets	5173	5216	4357
Current Assets	13620	14307	13007
Current Liabilities	10481	10570	8850
Total Share Capital	35	35	35
ROCE% (Return on Capital Employed)	-3.9	-4.2	-2.4
ROT% (Return on Turnover)	-1.0	-1.2	-0.6

Goodman Home Improvements

213 Spitfire Road Heathall Industrial Estate, Heathhall, Dumfries, DG1 3PH
Tel: 01387-255544
E-mail: info@goodmanltd.co.uk
Directors: L. Morris (Dir)
Immediate Holding Company: GOODMAN HOME IMPROVEMENTS LIMITED
Registration no: SC272425 **Date established:** 2004
No.of Employees: 1 - 10 **Product Groups:** 30, 52

Date of Accounts	Aug 11	Aug 10	Aug 09
Working Capital	-56	-15	-17
Fixed Assets	50	15	16
Current Assets	128	117	52

Graham Builders Merchants Ltd

Kellwood Road, Dumfries, DG1 2JR
Tel: 01387-254266 **Fax:** 01387-263718
Website: http://www.graham-group.co.uk
Managers: R. Macmillan (Mgr)
Ultimate Holding Company: COMPAGNIE DE SAINT GOBAIN (FRANCE)
Immediate Holding Company: GRAHAM BUILDERS MERCHANTS LIMITED
Registration no: 00066738 **Date established:** 2000
No.of Employees: 11 - 20 **Product Groups:** 66

Date of Accounts	Dec 08
Working Capital	8
Current Assets	8

Homer Burgess Ltd

Burgess House Garroch Business Park Garroch Loaning, Dumfries, DG2 8PN
Tel: 01387-261027 **Fax:** 01387-259070
E-mail: enquiries@homerburgess.com
Website: http://www.homerburgess.com
Directors: S. Burgess (MD), L. Burgess (Fin)
Managers: P. Scott (Tech Serv Mgr)
Immediate Holding Company: HOMER BURGESS LIMITED
Registration no: SC055598 **VAT No.:** GB 293 0350 70
Date established: 1974 **No.of Employees:** 21 - 50 **Product Groups:** 84

Date of Accounts	May 11	May 10	May 09
Working Capital	406	473	308
Fixed Assets	54	79	233
Current Assets	888	835	751

Interfloor Ltd

Edinburgh Road Heathhall, Dumfries, DG1 1QA
Tel: 01387-253111 **Fax:** 01387-268937
Website: http://www.interfloor.com
Directors: D. Kirby (Grp Chief Exec)
Managers: D. Mcquillen (I.T. Exec), G. McQuillen (Personnel), T. Kingstree (Mgr), A. Wilson (Chief Buyer), B. Hayes (Mktg Serv Mgr)
Ultimate Holding Company: INTERFLOOR GROUP LIMITED
Immediate Holding Company: INTERFLOOR LIMITED
Registration no: 00162988 **Date established:** 2020
No.of Employees: 101 - 250 **Product Groups:** 29, 63, 66

Date of Accounts	May 08	May 09	May 10
Sales Turnover	95m	77m	71m
Pre Tax Profit/Loss	11m	2m	3m
Working Capital	6m	8m	11m
Fixed Assets	23m	23m	21m
Current Assets	27m	29m	27m
Current Liabilities	3m	3m	3m

Nelson Removal & Storage

Unit 5 Downs Way Industrial Estate Heathhall, Dumfries, DG1 3RS
Tel: 0800-037 8919 **Fax:** 01387-722321
E-mail: office@nelsonremovals.co.uk
Website: http://www.nelsonremovals.co.uk
Directors: K. Nelson (Ptnr)
Immediate Holding Company: ROBISON & DAVIDSON (HOLDINGS) LIMITED
Registration no: SC307441 **Date established:** 2006
No.of Employees: 1 - 10 **Product Groups:** 30, 35, 45

Penman Engineering Ltd

Heathhall Industrial Estate Heathhall, Dumfries, DG1 3NY
Tel: 01387-252784 **Fax:** 01387-267332
E-mail: info@penman.co.uk
Website: http://www.penman.co.uk
Bank(s): Bank of Scotland
Directors: A. Rodgers (Fin), B. Findlay (MD)
Managers: A. Clark (Tech Sales Eng), D. McCarron
Ultimate Holding Company: PENMAN ENGINEERING HOLDINGS LIMITED
Immediate Holding Company: PENMAN ENGINEERING LIMITED
Registration no: SC084160 **VAT No.:** GB 556 7211 35
Date established: 1983 **Turnover:** £20m - £50m
No.of Employees: 101 - 250 **Product Groups:** 36, 39

Date of Accounts	Mar 11	Mar 10	Mar 09
Sales Turnover	21m	18m	N/A
Pre Tax Profit/Loss	646	646	964
Working Capital	5m	4m	3m
Fixed Assets	70	66	2m
Current Assets	15m	11m	11m
Current Liabilities	6m	5m	5m

Signcraft Signs Ltd

157 Heathhall Industrial Estate Heathhall, Dumfries, DG1 3PH
Tel: 01387-251595 **Fax:** 01387-251820
E-mail: info@signcraft-signs.co.uk
Website: http://www.signcraft-signs.co.uk
Directors: G. Henderson (Prop)
Immediate Holding Company: SIGNCRAFT SIGNS LIMITED
Registration no: SC354879 **Date established:** 2009
No.of Employees: 1 - 10 **Product Groups:** 30, 39, 40

Date of Accounts	Mar 12	Mar 11	Mar 10
Working Capital	57	-51	-135
Fixed Assets	148	167	184
Current Assets	200	183	149

A G Smith

Dykeside Kirkgunzeon, Dumfries, DG2 8LA
Tel: 01387-760666 **Fax:** 01387-760652
Directors: J. Smith (Snr Part)
Date established: 1971 **No.of Employees:** 1 - 10 **Product Groups:** 35, 41

Southern Tractors

Clarence Field Ruthwell, Dumfries, DG1 4NZ
Tel: 01387-870216 **Fax:** 01387-870306
E-mail: accounts@southerntractors.co.uk
Website: http://www.southerntractors.co.uk
Directors: R. Wardhaugh (Prop)
Date established: 1984 **No.of Employees:** 1 - 10 **Product Groups:** 41

Stewart Engineers Ltd

41 Castle Street, Dumfries, DG1 1DU
Tel: 01387-262676
E-mail: david@stewartengineers.co.uk
Website: http://www.stewartengineers.co.uk
Directors: D. Stewart (Prop)
Immediate Holding Company: STEWART ENGINEERS LIMITED
Registration no: SC274592 **Date established:** 2004
No.of Employees: 1 - 10 **Product Groups:** 35, 52, 84

Date of Accounts	Oct 11	Oct 10	Oct 09
Working Capital	-7	-9	-5
Fixed Assets	9	11	9
Current Assets	10	10	19

George Street Design Ltd

40 George Street, Dumfries, DG1 1EH
Tel: 01387-266523
E-mail: edith@georgestdesign.co.uk
Website: http://www.domramos.com

Directors: E. Reyntiens (Dir), S. Dupre (Fin)
Immediate Holding Company: GEORGE STREET DESIGN LIMITED
Registration no: SC285339 **Date established:** 2005
Turnover: Up to £250,000 **No.of Employees:** 1 - 10 **Product Groups:** 26, 49

Date of Accounts	May 09	May 10	May 06
Sales Turnover	7	11	N/A
Pre Tax Profit/Loss	5	-3	N/A
Working Capital	N/A	N/A	-7
Fixed Assets	1	1	N/A
Current Assets	N/A	N/A	5
Current Liabilities	N/A	N/A	12

East Lothian

Dunbar

Belhaven Division
Spott Road Industrial Estate, Dunbar, EH42 1RS
Tel: 01368-862734 **Fax:** 01368-869500
E-mail: ian.herok@belhaven.co.uk
Website: http://www.belhaven.co.uk
Directors: J. Young (Ptnr), E. Bentners (MD)
Managers: S. Fraser (Mktg Serv Mgr), K. Greenan (Tech Serv Mgr), C. Gaffney, D. Lovett (Personnel)
Ultimate Holding Company: GREENE KING PLC
Immediate Holding Company: BELHAVEN BREWERY COMPANY LIMITED
Registration no: SC022860 **Date established:** 1944
Turnover: £20m - £50m **No.of Employees:** 51 - 100 **Product Groups:** 41, 62

Date of Accounts	Apr 12	May 09	May 10
Sales Turnover	26m	26m	30m
Pre Tax Profit/Loss	5m	14m	5m
Working Capital	260m	213m	217m
Current Assets	260m	246m	251m

S & P Blair & Son
Craigcrooke Bayswell Park, Dunbar, EH42 1AE
Tel: 01368-862371 **Fax:** 01368-862051
E-mail: sales@spblair.com
Website: http://www.spblair.com
Directors: M. Blair (Snr Part)
VAT No.: GB 268 3643 31 **Turnover:** £250,000 - £500,000
No.of Employees: 1 - 10 **Product Groups:** 48

Thomas Sherriff & Co. Ltd
West Barns, Dunbar, EH42 1UN
Tel: 01368-862736 **Fax:** 01368-860799
E-mail: jgreenwood@thomassherriff.co.uk
Website: http://www.thomassherriff.co.uk
Directors: J. Greenwood (Fin), J. Winter (MD)
Immediate Holding Company: THOMAS SHERRIFF AND COMPANY LIMITED
Registration no: 00906135 **Date established:** 1967
Turnover: £10m - £20m **No.of Employees:** 11 - 20 **Product Groups:** 41

Date of Accounts	Jan 12	Jan 11	Jan 10
Sales Turnover	24m	17m	19m
Pre Tax Profit/Loss	519	536	562
Working Capital	4m	3m	3m
Fixed Assets	1m	1m	1m
Current Assets	8m	8m	6m
Current Liabilities	239	292	480

Perthshire

Dunblane

Bridgend Financial
9 Stirling Road, Dunblane, FK15 9EP
Tel: 01786-824763 **Fax:** 01786-821853
E-mail: c.duncan@bridgend-financial.co.uk
Website: http://www.bridgend-financial.co.uk
Directors: V. Duncan (Fin)
Managers: C. Duncan (Mgr)
Registration no: SC249899 **Date established:** 2007
Turnover: Up to £250,000 **No.of Employees:** 1 - 10 **Product Groups:** 80, 82

Date of Accounts	Oct 04
Sales Turnover	39
Pre Tax Profit/Loss	12
Working Capital	10
Fixed Assets	2
Current Assets	16
Current Liabilities	6
ROCE% (Return on Capital Employed)	102.3

Little Horseshoe Barn
16 Millhill Drive Greenloaning, Dunblane, FK15 0LS
Tel: 01786-880282
E-mail: info@littlehorseshoebarn.co.uk
Website: http://www.littlehorseshoebarn.co.uk/
Directors: E. Smith (Grp Chief Exec)
Registration no: SC243699 **Date established:** 2003
No.of Employees: 1 - 10 **Product Groups:** 49

Angus

Dundee

Aable Fortress
Unit R Scottway Pearce Avenue Broughty Ferry, Dundee, DD5 3RX
Tel: 01382-736033 **Fax:** 01382-736007
E-mail: info@aablefortress.com
Website: http://www.aablefortress.com
Managers: A. Johnson (Mgr)
Immediate Holding Company: AABLE FORTRESS LLP
Registration no: SO302222 **Date established:** 2009
No.of Employees: 1 - 10 **Product Groups:** 26, 35

Albacom
George Buckman Drive Camperdown Industrial Estate, Dundee, DD2 3SP
Tel: 01382-889311 **Fax:** 01382-810171
E-mail: sales@albacom.co.uk
Website: http://www.albacom.co.uk
Bank(s): Royal Bank of Scotland, Perth
Directors: G. Robertson (Co Sec), K. Henderson (Dir), M. Mackin (Dir)
Immediate Holding Company: ALBACOM LIMITED
Registration no: SC121731 **VAT No.:** GB 561 3587 33
Date established: 1989 **Turnover:** £1m - £2m **No.of Employees:** 11 - 20
Product Groups: 37

Date of Accounts	Mar 12	Mar 11	Mar 10
Sales Turnover	N/A	2m	2m
Pre Tax Profit/Loss	N/A	151	405
Working Capital	928	933	851
Fixed Assets	127	144	171
Current Assets	1m	1m	1m
Current Liabilities	N/A	99	203

Allards International Ltd
Castlecroft Business Centre Tom Johnston Road, Dundee, DD4 8XD
Tel: 01382-770720 **Fax:** 01382-770599
E-mail: email@allards-international.com
Website: http://www.allards-international.com
Managers: C. Wood (Comm)
Immediate Holding Company: ALLARDS INTERNATIONAL LIMITED
Registration no: SC209809 **Date established:** 2000
Turnover: £500,000 - £1m **No.of Employees:** 1 - 10 **Product Groups:** 40

Date of Accounts	Aug 11	Aug 10	Aug 09
Working Capital	300	362	377
Fixed Assets	11	13	11
Current Assets	450	551	505

Axis Shield Ltd
Luna Place Dundee Technology Park, Dundee, DD2 1XA
Tel: 01382-422000 **Fax:** 01382-422088
E-mail: paul.henrickson@axis-shieldux.com
Website: http://www.axis-shieldux.com
Managers: D. Brady, E. Valente (Mktg Serv Mgr), P. Henrickson, P. Whitehead (Tech Serv Mgr), M. Thomson (Personnel)
Ultimate Holding Company: AXIS-SHIELD PUBLIC LIMITED COMPANY
Immediate Holding Company: AXIS-SHIELD DIAGNOSTICS LIMITED
Registration no: SC077359 **VAT No.:** GB 607 6612 43
Date established: 1982 **Turnover:** £20m - £50m **No.of Employees:** 1 - 10
Product Groups: 31

Date of Accounts	Dec 10	Dec 09	Dec 08
Sales Turnover	21m	21m	18m
Pre Tax Profit/Loss	7m	6m	3m
Working Capital	23m	18m	14m
Fixed Assets	4m	3m	4m
Current Assets	28m	22m	19m
Current Liabilities	3m	2m	3m

B D G Ceramics
Ure Street, Dundee, DD1 5JE
Tel: 01382-225985 **Fax:** 01382-229866
E-mail: g.williams@bdf.ltd.uk
Directors: G. Williams (Ptnr)
No.of Employees: 11 - 20 **Product Groups:** 38, 67

Bag Supplies F I B C Ltd
83 Hawick Drive, Dundee, DD4 0JY
Tel: 01382-736334 **Fax:** 01382-732875
E-mail: info@bsfl.biz
Website: http://www.bsfl-bulk-bags.co.uk
Directors: J. Miller (Prop)
Immediate Holding Company: BAG SUPPLIES (FIBC) LTD.
Registration no: SC222749 **Date established:** 2001
Turnover: £250,000 - £500,000 **No.of Employees:** 1 - 10
Product Groups: 23, 24, 30

Date of Accounts	Dec 11	Dec 10	Dec 09
Working Capital	48	31	19
Fixed Assets	25	25	25
Current Assets	76	76	49
Current Liabilities	N/A	2	N/A

Bonar Yarns & Fabrics Ltd
St Salvador Street, Dundee, DD3 7EU
Tel: 01382-227346 **Fax:** 01382-202378
E-mail: info@bonaryarns.com
Website: http://www.bonaryarns.com
Bank(s): Royal Bank of Scotland, Chief Office, 3 High St, Dundee
Directors: R. Danyer (Fin), S. Diderich (Sales), A. Sumner (MD)
Managers: P. Fraser (Mktg Serv Mgr), R. Danyer (Fin Mgr), R. Noppen (Grp Purch Mgr), W. McArthur (Personnel), W. McArthur (Personnel)
Ultimate Holding Company: LOW & BONAR PUBLIC LIMITED COMPANY
Immediate Holding Company: BONAR YARNS & FABRICS LIMITED
Registration no: SC008924 **Date established:** 2014
Turnover: £10m - £20m **No.of Employees:** 101 - 250
Product Groups: 02, 07, 23, 25, 27, 30, 31

Date of Accounts	Nov 11	Nov 10	Nov 09
Sales Turnover	18m	16m	16m
Pre Tax Profit/Loss	-112	-2m	-2m
Working Capital	-4m	-4m	-2m
Fixed Assets	4m	4m	5m
Current Assets	7m	6m	9m
Current Liabilities	235	389	3m

Bruce Douglas Marketing Ltd (t/a Ultratape)
Unit 10-12 Block 22 Kislpindie Road, Dunsinane Industrial Estate, Dundee, DD2 3JP
Tel: 01382-832999 **Fax:** 01382-833422
E-mail: sales@ultratape.com
Website: http://www.ultratape.com
Directors: R. Lamb (Dir), D. Walker (MD), I. Walker (Fin)
Managers: S. Murphy (Buyer), L. Haggert (Tech Serv Mgr)
Immediate Holding Company: RONATREE LIMITED
Registration no: SC098435 **Date established:** 1986
Turnover: £5m - £10m **No.of Employees:** 21 - 50 **Product Groups:** 27

Date of Accounts	Mar 11	Mar 10	Mar 09
Working Capital	73	53	28
Fixed Assets	1m	1m	1m
Current Assets	240	134	106

Bulk Bag Containers Ltd
Old Glamis Road, Dundee, DD3 8JB
Tel: 01382-823824 **Fax:** 01382-823825
E-mail: sales@bulkbag.co.uk
Website: http://www.bulkbag.co.uk
Bank(s): Bank of Scotland
Directors: N. Milne (MD), H. Milne (Dir)
Immediate Holding Company: BULKBAG CONTAINERS LIMITED
Registration no: SC299021 **VAT No.:** GB 561 7378 22
Date established: 2006 **Turnover:** £1m - £2m **No.of Employees:** 21 - 50
Product Groups: 24, 30

Date of Accounts	Jun 12	Jun 11	Jun 10
Working Capital	-117	-152	-205
Fixed Assets	257	196	219
Current Assets	361	318	269

Burns & Harris Retail Ltd
97-99 Commercial Street, Dundee, DD1 2AF
Tel: 01382-322591 **Fax:** 01382-226979
E-mail: shop@burns-harris.co.uk
Website: http://www.burns-harris.co.uk
Directors: R. Burns (Prop), R. Burns (MD)
Managers: D. Scott (District Mgr), R. Craig (Sales Prom Mgr)
Immediate Holding Company: BURNS & HARRIS (RETAIL) LIMITED
Registration no: SC136913 **VAT No.:** GB 607 4172 55
Date established: 1992 **Turnover:** £500,000 - £1m
No.of Employees: 1 - 10 **Product Groups:** 44, 61, 64

Date of Accounts	Feb 08	Feb 11	Feb 10
Sales Turnover	680	N/A	618
Pre Tax Profit/Loss	5	N/A	-6
Working Capital	50	18	37
Fixed Assets	16	8	10
Current Assets	227	161	195
Current Liabilities	28	N/A	23

Cadogan Consultants
Stewart House Kingsway East, Dundee, DD4 7RE
Tel: 0141-270 7060 **Fax:** 01382-451279
E-mail: enquiries@cadogans.com
Website: http://www.cadoganconsultants.co.uk
Managers: A. Brown (Mgr)
Registration no: 109333 **Turnover:** £1m - £2m **No.of Employees:** 1 - 10
Product Groups: 40, 51, 54, 80, 84, 85

Caltech Ltd
Stannergate Road, Dundee, DD1 3NA
Tel: 01382-462810 **Fax:** 01382-454134
E-mail: enquiries@caltechlifts.co.uk
Website: http://www.caltechlifts.co.uk
Directors: H. Renwick (MD), A. Reilly (Fin)
Immediate Holding Company: CALTECH LIMITED
Registration no: SC256589 **VAT No.:** GB 356 3984 16
Date established: 2003 **Turnover:** £1m - £2m **No.of Employees:** 11 - 20
Product Groups: 45, 48

Date of Accounts	Oct 11	Oct 10	Oct 09
Working Capital	37	32	28
Fixed Assets	37	35	25
Current Assets	181	189	115

Canopy Clean Ltd
Unit 4 Peddie Street, Dundee, DD1 5LB
Tel: 01382-646006 **Fax:** 01382-646706
E-mail: canopyclean@btconnect.com
Website: http://www.canopyclean.co.uk
Directors: G. Lees (Prop)
Managers: G. Lees (Chief Acct)
Immediate Holding Company: TAYSIDE HYGIENE SERVICES LIMITED
Registration no: SC253994 **Date established:** 2003
Turnover: Up to £250,000 **No.of Employees:** 1 - 10 **Product Groups:** 52

Date of Accounts	Aug 08	Aug 07	Aug 06
Sales Turnover	104	N/A	N/A
Pre Tax Profit/Loss	12	N/A	N/A
Working Capital	-13	15	3
Fixed Assets	12	8	12
Current Assets	11	40	21
Current Liabilities	21	N/A	N/A

Corrie Service Ltd
Unit 9 Dundonald Street, Dundee, DD3 7PY
Tel: 01382-452552 **Fax:** 01382-453666
E-mail: dundee@iotplc.com
Website: http://www.iotplc.com
Managers: M. Smith (Mgr)
Ultimate Holding Company: CGPENSION LIMITED
Immediate Holding Company: CORRIE SERVICE LIMITED
Registration no: SC111006 **VAT No.:** 464 3948 17 **Date established:** 1988
Turnover: £500,000 - £1m **No.of Employees:** 1 - 10 **Product Groups:** 64, 67

Peter Cox Ltd
Unit 11 Marybank Lane, Dundee, DD2 3DY
Tel: 01382-400242 **Fax:** 01382-400262
E-mail: petercox.dundee@ecolab.com
Website: http://www.petercox.com
Managers: C. Mckinley (District Mgr)
Ultimate Holding Company: GERALDTON SERVICES INC (USA)
Immediate Holding Company: PETER COX LIMITED
Registration no: 02438126 **Date established:** 1989
No.of Employees: 1 - 10 **Product Groups:** 07, 32, 52, 66

Date of Accounts	Dec 11	Dec 10	Dec 09
Sales Turnover	15m	15m	14m
Pre Tax Profit/Loss	645	282	-350
Working Capital	3m	3m	2m
Fixed Assets	459	542	643
Current Assets	6m	5m	4m
Current Liabilities	2m	2m	961

D Copeland Engineering
2 Block 11 Nobel Road, West Gourdie Industrial Estate, Dundee, DD2 4UH
Tel: 01382-624642 **Fax:** 01382-622918
E-mail: jdccopeland@aol.com
Managers: D. Copeland (Mgr)
Registration no: SC169026 **Date established:** 1996
No.of Employees: 11 - 20 **Product Groups:** 35

D P Instrumentation Ltd
2 Ainslie Street West Pitkerro Industrial Estate, Broughty Ferry, Dundee, DD5 3RR
Tel: 01382-731200 **Fax:** 01382-731201
E-mail: sales@dpil.co.uk
Website: http://www.dpil.co.uk
Directors: C. Murphy (Fin), C. Kennedy (MD)
Immediate Holding Company: EOLAS TECHNOLOGY LIMITED
Registration no: SC132095 **Date established:** 1991 **Turnover:** £1m - £2m
No.of Employees: 1 - 10 **Product Groups:** 36, 38

Date of Accounts	Dec 07	Dec 06	Dec 05
Working Capital	32	33	34
Current Assets	224	233	130
Current Liabilities	192	201	96
Total Share Capital	15	15	15

D P & L Group
PO Box 50, Dundee, DD1 9HY
Tel: 01382-203111 **Fax:** 01382-200575
E-mail: abain@dpandl.co.uk
Website: http://www.dpandl.co.uk
Bank(s): Bank of Scotland
Directors: M. Bain (Co Sec)
Ultimate Holding Company: CORTACHY HOLDINGS LIMITED
Immediate Holding Company: DP&L GROUP LIMITED
Registration no: SC030490 **VAT No.:** GB 435 8356 32
Date established: 1954 **Turnover:** £1m - £2m **No.of Employees:** 21 - 50
Product Groups: 74, 76

Date of Accounts	Mar 12	Mar 11	Mar 10
Working Capital	25	-22	12
Fixed Assets	760	795	839
Current Assets	1m	1m	1m

Danaher Tool Group
Kingsway West, Dundee, DD2 3XX
Tel: 01382-591400 **Fax:** 01382-591474
E-mail: sales@dt-europe.com
Website: http://www.dtg-europe.com
Directors: Smith (MD)
Ultimate Holding Company: DANAHER CORP. INC
Immediate Holding Company: DANAHER TOOL GROUP HOLDINGS LTD
Registration no: 00533755 **VAT No.:** GB 268 3195 32
Date established: 1958 **Turnover:** £5m - £10m **No.of Employees:** 1 - 10
Product Groups: 35, 36, 46

Dens Metals Ltd
Constable Works Fowler Road, Broughty Ferry, Dundee, DD5 3RU
Tel: 01382-735801 **Fax:** 01382-735808
Website: http://www.densmetals.co.uk
Directors: N. Cunningham (Ch)
Ultimate Holding Company: MALCOLM, OGILVIE & COMPANY LIMITED
Immediate Holding Company: DENS METALS LIMITED
Registration no: SC212702 **Date established:** 2000 **Turnover:** £2m - £5m
No.of Employees: 51 - 100 **Product Groups:** 34

Date of Accounts	Oct 11	Oct 10	Oct 09
Sales Turnover	N/A	N/A	3m
Pre Tax Profit/Loss	N/A	N/A	-249
Working Capital	845	665	385
Fixed Assets	833	917	1m
Current Assets	4m	3m	2m
Current Liabilities	N/A	N/A	2m

Ductmate (Europe) Ltd
Arrol Road Wesker Gourdie Industrial Estate, Dundee, DD2 4TH
Tel: 01382-622111 **Fax:** 01382-621444
E-mail: enquiries@gallowaygroup.co.uk
Website: http://www.ductmate.co.uk
Directors: C. Hutchison (Dir)
Managers: F. George (Admin Off), J. Cunningham (Sales Admin)
Ultimate Holding Company: Galloway Group Ltd
Registration no: 00078814 **Turnover:** £2m - £5m
No.of Employees: 21 - 50 **Product Groups:** 36

Dundee Plant Co. Ltd
Longtown Street, Dundee, DD4 8LF
Tel: 01382-507506 **Fax:** 01382-507550
E-mail: brian@dpcl.demon.co.uk
Website: http://www.dpcl.demon.co.uk
Bank(s): Bank of Scotland
Directors: B. Hassan (MD)
Immediate Holding Company: DUNDEE PLANT COMPANY LIMITED
Registration no: SC151550 **VAT No.:** GB 651 9032 47
Date established: 1994 **Turnover:** £5m - £10m
No.of Employees: 51 - 100 **Product Groups:** 51, 52

Date of Accounts	Dec 11	Dec 10	Dec 09
Sales Turnover	8m	7m	7m
Pre Tax Profit/Loss	-234	-49	-399
Working Capital	2m	2m	1m
Fixed Assets	734	2m	2m
Current Assets	4m	3m	3m
Current Liabilities	659	721	609

Electric Co.
190 Main Street Invergowrie, Dundee, DD2 5BD
Tel: 0774-060 9881
E-mail: bob@theelectriccompany.co.uk
Website: http://www.theelectriccompany.co.uk
Directors: B. Lamb (Dir)
Date established: 1998 **No.of Employees:** 1 - 10 **Product Groups:** 83

Elm Bank
22 Claypotts Road Broughty Ferry, Dundee, DD5 1BW
Tel: 01382-477782 **Fax:** 01382-477782
E-mail: mail@elmbanktowing.co.uk
Website: http://www.elmbanktowing.co.uk
Directors: S. Nutt (Prop)
Turnover: Up to £250,000 **No.of Employees:** 1 - 10 **Product Groups:** 40, 68

Encon Insulations Ltd
Block 9 Myrekirk Road, Dundee, DD2 4SH
Tel: 01382-610040 **Fax:** 01382-610036
E-mail: info@encon.co.uk
Website: http://www.encon.co.uk
Directors: A. Clift (Dir)
Ultimate Holding Company: WOLSELEY PLC (JERSEY)
Immediate Holding Company: ENCON INSULATION LIMITED
Registration no: 01377342 **Date established:** 1978 **Turnover:** £5m - £10m
No.of Employees: 11 - 20 **Product Groups:** 33

Forman Construction Ltd
6 Donalds Lane, Dundee, DD2 4PF
Tel: 01382-610612 **Fax:** 01382-400464
E-mail: stewart.pringle@formanconstruction.co.uk
Website: http://www.formanconstruction.co.uk
Bank(s): The Royal Bank of Scotland
Directors: A. Cowan (Dir), C. Connaghan (MD), S. Pringle (Dir), S. Pringle (Fin)
Managers: D. Bell (Buyer), A. Rodgers (Admin Off)
Immediate Holding Company: FORMAN CONSTRUCTION LIMITED
Registration no: SC051319 **VAT No.:** GB 268 3435 38
Date established: 1972 **Turnover:** £5m - £10m
No.of Employees: 51 - 100 **Product Groups:** 52

Date of Accounts	Aug 07	Aug 06
Sales Turnover	12962	17111
Pre Tax Profit/Loss	317	175
Working Capital	994	725
Fixed Assets	438	454
Current Assets	4221	5443
Current Liabilities	3227	4718
Total Share Capital	30	30
ROCE% (Return on Capital Employed)	22.1	14.8
ROT% (Return on Turnover)	2.4	1.0

Frazer
Mid Craigie Road, Dundee, DD4 7RN
Tel: 01382-458989 **Fax:** 01382-458998
E-mail: callum.hynes@frazereu.com
Website: http://www.ashworth-frazer.co.uk
Managers: C. Hynes (District Mgr)
Ultimate Holding Company: SAINT GUBAIN
Immediate Holding Company: OLIVER ASHWORTH GROUP
Registration no: 00003645 **Date established:** 2004
Turnover: £10m - £20m **No.of Employees:** 1 - 10 **Product Groups:** 33, 34, 35

G A Engineering Ltd
Fowler Road West Pitkerro Industrial Estate, Broughty Ferry, Dundee, DD5 3RU
Tel: 01382-480888 **Fax:** 01382-480999
E-mail: sales@gaengineering.net
Website: http://www.gaengineering.net
Directors: G. McDonald (Co Sec), J. Mcdonald (Co Sec), A. McCafferty (Fin)
Ultimate Holding Company: DEANSTON HOLDINGS LIMITED
Immediate Holding Company: BONSPIEL ENGINEERING LIMITED
Registration no: SC119379 **Date established:** 1989
No.of Employees: 21 - 50 **Product Groups:** 35, 48

Date of Accounts	Mar 12	Mar 11	Mar 10
Working Capital	-513	-1m	-716
Fixed Assets	2m	2m	1m
Current Assets	919	883	88

Galloway Group Ltd
Arrol Road West Gourdie Industrial Estate, Dundee, DD2 4TH
Tel: 01382-611444 **Fax:** 01382-621444
E-mail: sales@gallowaygroup.co.uk
Website: http://www.gallowaygroup.co.uk
Bank(s): HSBC Bank plc
Directors: J. Mathieson (MD)
Managers: M. Higgins (Tech Serv Mgr), N. Dimarco (Mktg Serv Mgr), T. Paterson (Purch Mgr), F. Milne
Ultimate Holding Company: GALLOWAY (HOLDINGS) LIMITED
Immediate Holding Company: GALLOWAY GROUP LTD.
Registration no: SC036181 **Date established:** 1961
Turnover: £10m - £20m **No.of Employees:** 101 - 250
Product Groups: 30, 34, 36, 40, 51, 54

Date of Accounts	Feb 08	Feb 11	Feb 10
Sales Turnover	20m	17m	19m
Pre Tax Profit/Loss	2m	432	671
Working Capital	2m	2m	2m
Fixed Assets	4m	4m	4m
Current Assets	6m	6m	6m
Current Liabilities	1m	953	899

Hilti GT Britain Ltd
Unit 1 Dunsinane Avenue Dunsinane Indl-Est, Dundee, DD2 3QN
Tel: 0800-886100 **Fax:** 0800-886200
Website: http://www.hilti.co.uk
Managers: R. Mitchell (Mgr)
Ultimate Holding Company: HILTI AG (LIECHTENSTEIN)
Immediate Holding Company: HILTI (GT.BRITAIN) LIMITED
Registration no: 00479786 **Date established:** 1950
Turnover: £75m - £125m **No.of Employees:** 1 - 10 **Product Groups:** 35, 37, 48

Date of Accounts	Dec 10	Dec 09	Dec 08
Sales Turnover	65m	66m	79m
Pre Tax Profit/Loss	766	-379	-48
Working Capital	12m	15m	12m
Fixed Assets	5m	5m	6m
Current Assets	33m	25m	23m
Current Liabilities	6m	4m	5m

I C S 2 Ltd
Unit 1-3 Pearce Avenue, Broughty Ferry, Dundee, DD5 3RX
Tel: 01382-772743 **Fax:** 01382-772742
E-mail: sales@ics-2.co.uk
Website: http://www.ics-2.co.uk
Directors: P. Munroe (MD)
Immediate Holding Company: ICS2 LIMITED
Registration no: SC228233 **Date established:** 2002 **Turnover:** £1m - £2m
No.of Employees: 11 - 20 **Product Groups:** 37

Date of Accounts	Jul 11	Jul 10	Jul 09
Working Capital	-163	-137	-411
Fixed Assets	540	490	569
Current Assets	418	371	177
Current Liabilities	N/A	N/A	29

I R T Surveys Ltd
28 Greenmarket, Dundee, DD1 4QB
Tel: 01382-228700 **Fax:** 01382-201 680
E-mail: enquiries@irtsurveys.co.uk
Website: http://www.irtsurveys.com
Managers: J. Kydd (Sales Admin)
Immediate Holding Company: IRT SURVEYS LIMITED
Registration no: SC227199 **Date established:** 2002
No.of Employees: 1 - 10 **Product Groups:** 85

Date of Accounts	Dec 11	Dec 10	Dec 09
Working Capital	-8	-48	-74
Fixed Assets	144	115	111
Current Assets	270	164	208

J T Inglis & Sons Ltd
Riverside Works Carolina Port Stannergate Road, Dundee, DD1 3LU
Tel: 01382-462131 **Fax:** 01382-462846
E-mail: enquiries@jtinglis.com
Website: http://www.jtinglis.com
Bank(s): Royal Bank of Scotland
Managers: J. Coulter (Chief Mgr)
Ultimate Holding Company: RENEWAL ENTERPRISES LIMITED
Immediate Holding Company: JTI REALISATIONS LIMITED
Registration no: SC009831 **VAT No.:** GB 268 6200 50
Date established: 2017 **Turnover:** £2m - £5m **No.of Employees:** 51 - 100
Product Groups: 23

Date of Accounts	Apr 05	Apr 04	Apr 03
Sales Turnover	4m	5m	5m
Pre Tax Profit/Loss	71	328	437
Working Capital	726	936	1m
Fixed Assets	2m	1m	1m
Current Assets	3m	3m	2m
Current Liabilities	346	471	319

Jackson Steel Structures Ltd
Densfield Works Tannadice Street, Dundee, DD3 7QP
Tel: 01382-858439 **Fax:** 01382-833964
E-mail: sales@jacksonsteel.co.uk
Website: http://www.jacksonsteel.co.uk
Directors: M. D'arcy (Fin), S. McArthur (MD)
Immediate Holding Company: JACKSON STEEL STRUCTURES LIMITED
Registration no: SC047786 **Date established:** 1970 **Turnover:** £1m - £2m
No.of Employees: 11 - 20 **Product Groups:** 84

Date of Accounts	Dec 11	Dec 10	Dec 09
Working Capital	1m	1m	878
Fixed Assets	229	211	583
Current Assets	1m	1m	1m

Johnston Oils Ltd
11 Andersons Lane, Dundee, DD2 2RD
Tel: 01382-611164 **Fax:** 01382-612995
E-mail: sales@johnston-oils.co.uk
Website: http://www.joil.co.uk
Directors: S. Johnston (Dir)
Ultimate Holding Company: JOHNSTON FUELS LIMITED
Immediate Holding Company: JOHNSTON OILS LIMITED
Registration no: SC097681 **VAT No.:** GB 270 7674 41
Date established: 1986 **Turnover:** £20m - £50m **No.of Employees:** 1 - 10
Product Groups: 66

Date of Accounts	Dec 11	Dec 10	Dec 09
Sales Turnover	130m	92m	74m
Pre Tax Profit/Loss	320	1m	11
Working Capital	-728	-446	-1m
Fixed Assets	5m	4m	4m
Current Assets	13m	12m	8m
Current Liabilities	433	783	254

Kinnes Shipping Ltd
Fish Dock Road, Dundee, DD1 3LZ
Tel: 01382-462858 **Fax:** 01382-462870
E-mail: agency@kinnes-shipping.co.uk
Website: http://www.kinnes-shipping.co.uk
Directors: M. Ross (Dir)
Immediate Holding Company: KINNES SHIPPING LIMITED
Registration no: SC043351 **VAT No.:** GB 268 9418 08
Date established: 1966 **Turnover:** £2m - £5m **No.of Employees:** 1 - 10
Product Groups: 76

Date of Accounts	Dec 11	Dec 10	Dec 09
Working Capital	54	92	79
Fixed Assets	38	32	41
Current Assets	1m	1m	1m

Langlands & Mcainsh (Packaging) Ltd
133 Seagate, Dundee, DD1 2HP
Tel: 01382-224657 **Fax:** 01382-201969
Bank(s): The Royal Bank of Scotland
Directors: A. Jardine (Sales), M. Jardine (Fin)
Immediate Holding Company: LANGLANDS & MCAINSH LIMITED
Registration no: SC083212 **Date established:** 1983
Turnover: £250,000 - £500,000 **No.of Employees:** 11 - 20
Product Groups: 25, 27

Date of Accounts	May 11	May 10	May 09
Sales Turnover	N/A	375	563
Pre Tax Profit/Loss	N/A	42	143
Working Capital	-556	-599	885
Fixed Assets	657	693	712
Current Assets	463	780	972
Current Liabilities	N/A	1m	80

M G M Timber Scotland Ltd
37 Hospital Street, Dundee, DD3 8DJ
Tel: 01382-817738 **Fax:** 01382-832394
E-mail: frank.fagen@mgmtimber.com
Website: http://www.mgmtimber.co.uk
Managers: F. Fagen (Mgr)
Ultimate Holding Company: JAMES DONALDSON & SONS LIMITED
Immediate Holding Company: MGM TIMBER (SCOTLAND) LIMITED
Registration no: SC129921 **Date established:** 1991
No.of Employees: 11 - 20 **Product Groups:** 08, 25, 66

Date of Accounts	Mar 12	Mar 11	Mar 10
Sales Turnover	36m	33m	29m
Pre Tax Profit/Loss	1m	1m	721
Working Capital	3m	2m	1m
Fixed Assets	785	952	957
Current Assets	11m	9m	8m
Current Liabilities	1m	1m	811

George Martin Builders Ltd
5-9 Fairfield Road, Dundee, DD3 8HR
Tel: 01382-815415 **Fax:** 01382-825199
E-mail: enquiries@geomartinbld.co.uk
Website: http://www.geomartinbld.co.uk
Directors: D. Maxwell (MD), N. Boyle (Fin)
Immediate Holding Company: GEORGE MARTIN (BUILDERS) LIMITED
Registration no: SC028729 **Date established:** 1952 **Turnover:** £1m - £2m
No.of Employees: 11 - 20 **Product Groups:** 45, 61, 81

Date of Accounts	Jan 12	Jan 11	Jan 10
Working Capital	603	570	550
Fixed Assets	447	463	511
Current Assets	2m	2m	2m

Mcgill Security
Harrison Road, Dundee, DD2 3SN
Tel: 01382-833999 **Fax:** 01382-828777
E-mail: info@mcgill.co.uk
Website: http://www.mcgill-electrical.co.uk
Bank(s): Bank of Scotland
Managers: R. Murray (Mgr)
Immediate Holding Company: MCGILL ELECTRICAL LIMITED
Registration no: SC074785 **VAT No.:** GB 356 0119 74
Date established: 1981 **Turnover:** £20m - £50m
No.of Employees: 11 - 20 **Product Groups:** 52

Date of Accounts	Mar 11	Mar 10	Mar 09
Sales Turnover	24m	22m	28m
Pre Tax Profit/Loss	301	805	1m
Working Capital	1m	1m	1m
Fixed Assets	1m	1m	1m
Current Assets	6m	6m	7m
Current Liabilities	2m	2m	2m

N C R Ltd
Discovery Centre 3 Fulton Road, Dundee, DD2 4SW
Tel: 01382-611511 **Fax:** 01382-622722
E-mail: adam.crighton@ncr.com
Website: http://www.ncr.com
Bank(s): Bank of Scotland
Directors: D. Lynch (Fin)
Managers: A. Crighton, M. Nicol (Fin Mgr), N. Macdonald (Tech Serv Mgr), R. Todd (Personnel)
Ultimate Holding Company: NCR CORP (USA)
Immediate Holding Company: NCR LIMITED
Registration no: 00045916 **Date established:** 1995
Turnover: Over £1,000m **No.of Employees:** 251 - 500
Product Groups: 44

Date of Accounts	Dec 11	Dec 10	Dec 09
Sales Turnover	165m	188m	155m
Pre Tax Profit/Loss	-4m	2m	6m
Working Capital	120m	126m	105m
Fixed Assets	41m	41m	41m
Current Assets	199m	222m	177m
Current Liabilities	19m	30m	13m

Nicoll & Jack Ltd
Locarno Works Brown Street, Dundee, DD1 5EE
Tel: 01382-228071 **Fax:** 01382-228591
E-mail: scot.elec.grp@btconnect.com
Directors: G. Lannen (Dir)
Immediate Holding Company: NICOLL & JACK LIMITED
Registration no: SC111052 **Date established:** 1988
No.of Employees: 1 - 10 **Product Groups:** 35, 39, 45

Date of Accounts	May 08	May 07	May 06
Working Capital	-45	-69	-78
Current Assets	161	163	157
Current Liabilities	206	232	235
Total Share Capital	20	20	20

North Engineering Works Ltd
Block 24 Kilspindie Road Dunsinane Industrial Estate, Dundee, DD2 3QH
Tel: 01382-889693 **Fax:** 01382-889808
E-mail: peter.cochrane@northeng.com
Website: http://www.northengineering.com
Directors: P. Cochrane (MD), E. Paterson (Fin)
Immediate Holding Company: NORTH ENGINEERING WORKS LIMITED
Registration no: SC084215 **VAT No.:** GB 269 2795 07
Date established: 1983 **Turnover:** £500,000 - £1m
No.of Employees: 1 - 10 **Product Groups:** 46

Date of Accounts	Aug 11	Aug 10	Aug 09
Working Capital	351	338	521
Fixed Assets	503	510	561
Current Assets	685	573	1m

Nynas UK Ab
East Camperdown Street, Dundee, DD1 3LG
Tel: 01382-462211 **Fax:** 01382-456846
E-mail: steven.lockhart@nynas.com
Website: http://www.nynas.com
Bank(s): Midland Bank
Managers: B. Riley, S. Lockheart (Site Co-ord), S. Godfrey (Tech Serv Mgr)
Immediate Holding Company: NYNAS A.B. PETROLEUM (SWEDEN)
Registration no: 05564315 **VAT No.:** GB 607 4069 48
Turnover: £75m - £125m **No.of Employees:** 21 - 50 **Product Groups:** 17, 31

Pacson Valves Ltd
Unit F Claverhouse Industrial Park Claverhouse Industrial Park, Dundee, DD4 9UA
Tel: 01382-513655 **Fax:** 01382-513656
E-mail: info@pacson.co.uk
Website: http://www.pacson.co.uk
Directors: K. Crawford (MD)
Managers: G. Rew, W. Ferrie, C. Mansi
Ultimate Holding Company: EVOTEK LIMITED
Immediate Holding Company: PACSON LIMITED
Registration no: SC114098 **Date established:** 1988 **Turnover:** £2m - £5m
No.of Employees: 101 - 250 **Product Groups:** 36, 37, 38

Date of Accounts	Sep 11	Sep 08	Oct 09
Pre Tax Profit/Loss	116	281	667
Working Capital	3m	2m	2m
Fixed Assets	462	642	543
Current Assets	6m	4m	4m
Current Liabilities	502	689	651

Plastics W Graham Ltd
114 Cowgate, Dundee, DD1 2JU
Tel: 01382-223734 **Fax:** 01382-201799
E-mail: sales@pwgsigns.com
Website: http://www.pwgsigns.com
Bank(s): The Royal Bank of Scotland
Directors: E. North (MD)
Ultimate Holding Company: I.C.L. PLASTICS LIMITED
Immediate Holding Company: PLASTICS W. GRAHAM LIMITED
Registration no: SC056960 **VAT No.:** GB 262 5689 33
Date established: 1975 **Turnover:** £500,000 - £1m
No.of Employees: 11 - 20 **Product Groups:** 27, 30, 35, 40, 49, 84

Date of Accounts	Nov 11	Nov 10	Nov 09
Working Capital	513	476	465
Fixed Assets	7	9	8
Current Assets	626	585	588

Protective Supplies & Services Ltd
Castlecroft Business Centre Tom Johnston Road, Dundee, DD4 8XD
Tel: 01382-731073 **Fax:** 01224-890030
E-mail: sales@protectivesupplies.com
Website: http://www.protectivesupplies.com
Directors: J. Hill (Dir)
Immediate Holding Company: PROTECTIVE SUPPLIES & SERVICES LIMITED
Registration no: SC164946 **Date established:** 1996
Turnover: £250,000 - £500,000 **No.of Employees:** 1 - 10
Product Groups: 61

Date of Accounts	Sep 10	Sep 09	Sep 08
Sales Turnover	564	402	N/A
Pre Tax Profit/Loss	-21	16	N/A
Working Capital	28	28	12
Fixed Assets	4	4	5
Current Assets	48	48	68
Current Liabilities	20	4	N/A

Rautomead Ltd
Nobel Road West Gourdie Industrial Estate, Dundee, DD2 4UH
Tel: 01382-622341 **Fax:** 01382-622941
E-mail: michaelnairn@rautomead.co.uk
Website: http://www.rautomead.co.uk
Directors: M. Nairn (Ch), G. Wood (Co Sec), B. Frame (MD)
Managers: S. Tocher, M. Cooper (Ops Mgr), G. Henderson (Sales Prom Mgr)
Ultimate Holding Company: RAUTOMEAD HOLDINGS LIMITED
Immediate Holding Company: RAUTOMEAD LIMITED
Registration no: SC152367 **Date established:** 1994
Turnover: £5m - £10m **No.of Employees:** 21 - 50 **Product Groups:** 67

Date of Accounts	Jun 11	Jun 10	Jun 09
Sales Turnover	8m	8m	5m
Pre Tax Profit/Loss	755	953	12
Working Capital	1m	190	-539
Fixed Assets	568	560	368
Current Assets	4m	4m	2m
Current Liabilities	964	2m	1m

S P Technology Ltd
Unit3 Camperdown Industrial Park George Buckman Drive, Dundee, DD2 3SP
Tel: 01382-880088 **Fax:** 01382-880099
E-mail: info@sptechnology.co.uk
Website: http://www.sptechnology.co.uk
Directors: R. Chisholm (Dir)
Immediate Holding Company: S P TECHNOLOGY LIMITED
Registration no: SC087192 **Date established:** 1984 **Turnover:** £2m - £5m
No.of Employees: 21 - 50 **Product Groups:** 37, 42, 45, 46, 47, 84

Date of Accounts	Dec 11	Dec 10	Dec 09
Working Capital	338	444	349
Fixed Assets	28	36	48
Current Assets	2m	1m	550

Safehouse Habitats
Unit 2-3 Bowbridge Works Thistle Street, Dundee, DD3 7RF
Tel: 01382-814122 **Fax:** 01382-489952
E-mail: mike@safehouseltd.com
Website: http://www.safehousehabitats.com
Bank(s): Clydesdale
Directors: M. Garty (MD)
Immediate Holding Company: SAFEHOUSE HABITATS (SCOTLAND) LIMITED
Registration no: SC261216 **VAT No.:** GB 838 8315 93
Date established: 2003 **Turnover:** £1m - £2m **No.of Employees:** 51 - 100
Product Groups: 35, 37, 38, 40, 46

Date of Accounts	May 11	May 10	May 09
Working Capital	2m	-746	1m
Fixed Assets	1m	824	662
Current Assets	4m	2m	2m

Safety Training Courses
5E Tulloch Court, Dundee, DD3 6LG
Tel: 08452-693805 **Fax:** 0845-370 0206
E-mail: info@uksafetytrainingcourses.co.uk
Website: http://www.safetytrainingcourses.health.officelive.com
Directors: J. Horseurgh (Prop)
Managers: P. Horsburgh (Admin Off)
Date established: 2008 **Turnover:** Up to £250,000
No.of Employees: 1 - 10 **Product Groups:** 86

Scotherbs
Longforgan, Dundee, DD2 5HU
Tel: 01382-360642 **Fax:** 01382-360637
E-mail: sales@scotherbs.co.uk
Website: http://www.scotherbs.co.uk
Directors: F. Lamotte (MD), S. Gillie (Fin)
Managers: K. Ozetelska (Personnel), L. Chre (Sales Prom Mgr), M. Edmiston
Turnover: Up to £250,000 **No.of Employees:** 101 - 250
Product Groups: 20

Skinner Motorcycles
Unit 1 Block B Smeaton Road, West Gourdie Industrial Estate, Dundee, DD2 4UT
Tel: 01382-611500 **Fax:** 01382-612500
Website: http://www.skinnermotorcycles.co.uk
Directors: M. Skinnner (Prop)
No.of Employees: 1 - 10 **Product Groups:** 39, 40, 68

Karl Storz Endoscopy UK Ltd
Thomas Wise Place, Dundee, DD2 1UB
Tel: 01382-647500 **Fax:** 01382-644999
E-mail: customerservice@karlstorz-uk.com
Website: http://www.karlstorz.com
Directors: D. Mcarthur (Fin)
Ultimate Holding Company: KARL STORZ VERTRIEBS GMBH (GERMANY)
Immediate Holding Company: KARL STORZ ENDOSCOPY (UK) LIMITED
Registration no: SC151965 **Date established:** 1994
Turnover: £20m - £50m **No.of Employees:** 11 - 20 **Product Groups:** 38, 48, 67

Date of Accounts	Dec 11	Dec 10	Dec 09
Sales Turnover	33m	35m	39m
Pre Tax Profit/Loss	4m	3m	4m
Working Capital	12m	13m	12m
Fixed Assets	2m	654	716
Current Assets	22m	23m	21m
Current Liabilities	7m	7m	6m

Tayside Automatic Doors
Unit N Scottway Pearce Avenue, Broughty Ferry, Dundee, DD5 3RX
Tel: 01382-731965 **Fax:** 01382-731967
Website: http://www.taysidedoors.co.uk
Directors: R. Wilson (Dir)
Immediate Holding Company: TAYSIDE AUTOMATIC DOORS LIMITED
Registration no: SC273869 **Date established:** 2004
No.of Employees: 1 - 10 **Product Groups:** 26, 35

Date of Accounts	Mar 11	Mar 10	Mar 09
Working Capital	-44	-12	-20
Fixed Assets	509	313	276

Tayside Cash Registers
68 Logie Street, Dundee, DD2 2QE
Tel: 07711-625274 **Fax:** 01382-566335
Directors: A. Douglas (Prop)
Immediate Holding Company: TAYSIDE CASH REGISTERS
Registration no: 00185702 **Date established:** 1981
Turnover: Up to £250,000 **No.of Employees:** 1 - 10 **Product Groups:** 44

Tayside Diesel Engineering Ltd
Fowler Road Broughty Ferry, Dundee, DD5 3RU
Tel: 01382-735960 **Fax:** 01382-735969
E-mail: info@tdedundee.co.uk
Website: http://www.tdedundee.co.uk
Bank(s): Clydesdale
Directors: E. Kydd (MD), J. Docherty (Fin)
Immediate Holding Company: TAYSIDE DIESEL ENGINEERING LIMITED
Registration no: SC140399 **VAT No.:** GB 607 5137 52
Date established: 1992 **Turnover:** £1m - £2m **No.of Employees:** 11 - 20
Product Groups: 68, 84

Date of Accounts	Jan 12	Jan 11	Jan 10
Working Capital	626	460	421
Fixed Assets	266	266	260
Current Assets	988	841	618

Tayside Laser Services
7 Westgreen Wynd Liff, Dundee, DD2 5RQ
Tel: 01382-581646 **Fax:** 01382-581646
E-mail: ian@taysidelaser.co.uk
Directors: I. Thackeray (Prop)
No.of Employees: 1 - 10 **Product Groups:** 37, 38, 44, 48

Tayside Plumbing & Building Supplies Ltd
1 Dens Road, Dundee, DD3 7SR
Tel: 01382-229401 **Fax:** 01382-202447
E-mail: sales@tayside-plumbing.co.uk
Website: http://www.tayside-plumbing.co.uk
Bank(s): The Royal Bank of Scotland
Directors: D. Crawford (MD), G. Raitt (Fin)
Managers: M. Robertson (Chief Mgr)
Immediate Holding Company: TAYSIDE PLUMBING AND BUILDING SUPPLIES LIMITED
Registration no: SC056782 **VAT No.:** GB 271 4714 64
Date established: 1974 **Turnover:** £2m - £5m **No.of Employees:** 21 - 50
Product Groups: 66

Date of Accounts	Dec 11	Dec 10	Dec 09
Working Capital	694	800	849
Fixed Assets	251	270	288
Current Assets	1m	1m	1m

Tayside Precision Tools
9 Coldside Road, Dundee, DD3 8DF
Tel: 01382-812888 **Fax:** 01382-812881
Directors: J. Forrester (Prop)
No.of Employees: 1 - 10 **Product Groups:** 36

Tayside Ventilation Ltd
6 Milton Street, Dundee, DD3 6QQ
Tel: 01382-828822 **Fax:** 01382-828833
E-mail: vent@taysidesheetmetal.freeserve.co.uk
Website: http://www.taysidesheetmetal.freeserve.co.uk
Directors: R. Rourke (Dir)
Immediate Holding Company: TAYSIDE SHEET METAL LIMITED
Registration no: SC216153 **Date established:** 2001
No.of Employees: 1 - 10 **Product Groups:** 48

Date of Accounts	Jan 09	Jan 08	Jan 07
Working Capital	8	7	23
Fixed Assets	11	13	16
Current Assets	106	76	89

D C Thomson & Co. Ltd
Albert Square, Dundee, DD1 9QJ
Tel: 01382-223131 **Fax:** 01382-225778
E-mail: idouglas@dcthomson.co.uk
Website: http://www.dcthomson.co.uk
Directors: I. Douglas (Fin)
Immediate Holding Company: D.C. THOMSON & COMPANY. LIMITED
Registration no: SC005830 **VAT No.:** GB 415 3404 86
Date established: 2005 **Turnover:** £250m - £500m
No.of Employees: 1 - 10 **Product Groups:** 28

Date of Accounts	Mar 11	Mar 10	Mar 09
Sales Turnover	285m	276m	272m
Pre Tax Profit/Loss	29m	27m	32m
Working Capital	154m	145m	174m
Fixed Assets	1024m	1021m	866m
Current Assets	211m	204m	236m
Current Liabilities	40m	39m	23m

Tubular Inspection Products
Unit 13 Barlow Park West Pitkerro Industrial Estate, Broughty Ferry, Dundee, DD5 3UB
Tel: 01382-778259 **Fax:** 01382-779987
E-mail: martin@tubularproducts.co.uk
Website: http://www.tubularproducts.co.uk
Directors: M. Devlin (MD), C. Devlin (Fin)
Immediate Holding Company: TUBULAR INSPECTION PRODUCTS LTD.
Registration no: SC316897 **Date established:** 2007
No.of Employees: 1 - 10 **Product Groups:** 38, 85

Date of Accounts	Mar 11	Mar 10	Mar 09
Working Capital	68	45	53
Fixed Assets	25	31	3
Current Assets	254	108	226

Umicore Coarting Services Ltd

Kinnoull Street Dunsinane Industrial Estate, Dundee, DD2 3ED
Tel: 01382-833022 **Fax:** 01382-833824
E-mail: kenny.rogers@umicore.com
Website: http://www.coatingservices.umicore.com
Bank(s): Clydesdale
Directors: J. Franks (MD), K. Rogers (Dir)
Managers: B. Bullions (Chief Acct)
Ultimate Holding Company: UMICORE SA (BELGIUM)
Immediate Holding Company: UMICORE COATING SERVICES LIMITED
Registration no: SC118425 **VAT No.:** GB 503 0068 05
Date established: 1989 **Turnover:** £2m - £5m **No.of Employees:** 21 - 50
Product Groups: 48

Date of Accounts	Dec 11	Dec 10	Dec 09
Sales Turnover	2m	2m	2m
Pre Tax Profit/Loss	186	157	159
Working Capital	625	597	775
Fixed Assets	713	751	539
Current Assets	866	774	1m
Current Liabilities	135	85	131

W T Stud Welding Scotland Ltd

Unit 4 Marybank Lane, Dundee, DD2 3DY
Tel: 01382-400405 **Fax:** 01382-400406
E-mail: william.tosh@wtstudwelding.co.uk
Website: http://www.wtstudwelding.co.uk
Directors: W. Tosh (Dir)
Immediate Holding Company: W.T. STUD WELDING SCOTLAND LIMITED
Registration no: SC132578 **VAT No.:** GB 561 6884 12
Date established: 1991 **No.of Employees:** 1 - 10 **Product Groups:** 35, 46, 48

Date of Accounts	Aug 11	Aug 10	Aug 09
Working Capital	219	186	149
Fixed Assets	122	123	120
Current Assets	306	279	186

Wemyss Weavecraft Ltd

Unit 7a Nobel Road, West Gourdie Industrial Estate, Dundee, DD2 4UH
Tel: 01382-908300 **Fax:** 01382-908308
E-mail: wemyss@wemyss-fabrics.co.uk
Website: http://www.wemyssfabric.com
Bank(s): Bank of Scotland
Directors: M. Moir (MD), M. Wigglesworth (Dir)
Managers: P. Scott (Mgr), I. Worf (Sales Prom Mgr)
Ultimate Holding Company: SC072907
Immediate Holding Company: WEMYSS WEAVECRAFT LIMITED
Registration no: SC025062 **Date established:** 1947 **Turnover:** £1m - £2m
No.of Employees: 11 - 20 **Product Groups:** 23, 63

Date of Accounts	Nov 07	Nov 06	Nov 05
Sales Turnover	N/A	1649	1526
Pre Tax Profit/Loss	N/A	-22	100
Working Capital	-13	1215	1261
Fixed Assets	29	33	1
Current Assets	1771	1851	1696
Current Liabilities	1784	636	435
Total Share Capital	5	5	5
ROCE% (Return on Capital Employed)		-1.8	7.9
ROT% (Return on Turnover)		-1.3	6.6

Wright Dental Group

Block 11a Dunsinane Avenue, Dunsinane Industrial Estate, Dundee, DD2 3QT
Tel: 01382-833866 **Fax:** 01382-811042
E-mail: sales@wright-cottrell.co.uk
Website: http://www.wright-cottrell.co.uk
Bank(s): The Royal Bank of Scotland
Directors: K. Souter (Fin)
Managers: S. Hendrie, I. Kennedy (Chief Mgr)
Ultimate Holding Company: WRIGHT HEALTH GROUP LIMITED
Immediate Holding Company: WRIGHT DENTAL SALES (GLASGOW) LIMITED
Registration no: SC014980 **Date established:** 2028
Turnover: £50m - £75m **No.of Employees:** 21 - 50 **Product Groups:** 30, 31, 32, 38

XM Services (Michelin Group)

Baldovie Road, Dundee, DD4 8UQ
Tel: 01382-734567 **Fax:** 01382-734489
E-mail: sales@xmservices.co.uk
Website: http://www.xmservices.co.uk
Directors: B. Bennett (MD)
Managers: B. De Vauguerin, P. Edwards, A. Duffy (Eng Serv Mgr), S. Goring (Consultant)
Ultimate Holding Company: COMPAGNIE GENERALE DES ETABLISSEMENTS MICHELIN (FR
Immediate Holding Company: MICHELIN TYRE PUBLIC LIMITED COMPANY
Registration no: SC149205 **Date established:** 1994 **Turnover:** £2m - £5m
No.of Employees: 101 - 250 **Product Groups:** 85, 86

Date of Accounts	Dec 07	Dec 06	Dec 05
Sales Turnover	4311	4838	5315
Pre Tax Profit/Loss	-647	-633	-106
Working Capital	-907	-560	73
Current Assets	1929	2038	2304
Current Liabilities	2836	2598	2230
ROCE% (Return on Capital Employed)	71.3	113.1	-143.8
ROT% (Return on Turnover)	-15.0	-13.1	-2.0

Fife

Dunfermline

A and C Audio Visual Ltd

1A Dickson Court Elgin Street Industrial Estate, Dunfermline, KY12 7SG
Tel: 01383-726072 **Fax:** 01383-732971
E-mail: sales@aandcaudio.co.uk
Website: http://www.aandcaudio.co.uk
Directors: A. Borthwick (Ptnr)
Registration no: SC259661 **Date established:** 1991
No.of Employees: 1 - 10 **Product Groups:** 37, 38, 40, 44, 63, 65, 67

Amatek Precision Instruments UK Ltd (AMETEK Precision Instruments (UK) Ltd)

21 Ridge Way Hillend, Dunfermline, KY11 9JN
Tel: 01383-825630 **Fax:** 01383-825715
E-mail: steve.faulis@amatek.com
Website: http://www.amatekpower.com
Managers: D. Thomson (Serv Eng)
Ultimate Holding Company: AMETEK INC
Immediate Holding Company: AMERTEK INC
Registration no: 00684869 **VAT No.:** GB 747 8845 71
Turnover: £1m - £2m **No.of Employees:** 1 - 10 **Product Groups:** 40

Axon Cable Ltd

Admiralty Park Rosyth, Dunfermline, KY11 2YW
Tel: 01383-421500 **Fax:** 01383-821080
E-mail: info@axon-cable.co.uk
Website: http://www.axon-cable.co.uk
Bank(s): The Royal Bank of Scotland
Directors: J. Weir (MD)
Managers: G. Allan (Buyer), L. Callan
Ultimate Holding Company: AXON CABLE SAS (FRANCE)
Immediate Holding Company: AXON CABLE LIMITED
Registration no: SC122228 **Date established:** 1990
Turnover: £5m - £10m **No.of Employees:** 21 - 50 **Product Groups:** 37

Date of Accounts	Dec 11	Dec 10	Dec 09
Sales Turnover	6m	8m	6m
Pre Tax Profit/Loss	87	261	23
Working Capital	116	44	-791
Fixed Assets	2m	2m	2m
Current Assets	2m	2m	1m
Current Liabilities	935	386	521

Barr R & T Electrical Ltd

142-158 Pittencrieff Street, Dunfermline, KY12 8AN
Tel: 01383-722096 **Fax:** 01383-739226
E-mail: rtbarr@hotmail.co.uk
Bank(s): Barclays
Directors: T. Barr (Dir)
Immediate Holding Company: R. & T. BARR (ELECTRICAL) DUNFERMLINE LTD.
Registration no: SC164683 **VAT No.:** GB 694 0309 29
Date established: 1996 **Turnover:** £1m - £2m **No.of Employees:** 11 - 20
Product Groups: 48, 52

Date of Accounts	Dec 11	Dec 10	Dec 09
Working Capital	-178	-160	-143
Fixed Assets	5	6	7
Current Assets	32	40	39

C R Smith Glaziers Dunfermline Ltd

27 Gardeners Street, Dunfermline, KY12 0RN
Tel: 0800-200444 **Fax:** 01383-739095
E-mail: sales@crsmith.co.uk
Website: http://www.crsmith.co.uk
Directors: G. Eadie (Ch), I. McFarnam (MD), A. Gardner (Mkt Research), G. Eadie (MD), M. Orwin (Sales)
Managers: F. Dickson, D. Salt (Grp Purch Mgr), A. French (Mgr), G. McCluskey, G. Mccluskey ()
Ultimate Holding Company: CAIRNSMILL LIMITED
Immediate Holding Company: C R SMITH GLAZIERS (DUNFERMLINE) LIMITED
Registration no: SC051530 **VAT No.:** GB 561 6629 28
Date established: 1972 **Turnover:** £20m - £50m
No.of Employees: 11 - 20 **Product Groups:** 25, 33, 52

Date of Accounts	Mar 11	Mar 10	Mar 09
Sales Turnover	16m	N/A	N/A
Pre Tax Profit/Loss	8	109	584
Working Capital	172	58	230
Fixed Assets	1m	1m	1m
Current Assets	6m	6m	6m
Current Liabilities	4m	4m	4m

Cadenergy Ltd

Unit 6 Pitreavie Court Pitreavie Business Park, Dunfermline, KY11 8UU
Tel: 08450-204302 **Fax:** 01383-627430
E-mail: gary@cadenergy.com
Website: http://www.cadenergy.com
Directors: G. Baird (Dir)
Immediate Holding Company: CADENERGY LTD.
Registration no: SC255178 **Date established:** 2003
No.of Employees: 1 - 10 **Product Groups:** 37, 44, 81, 84

Date of Accounts	Mar 11	Mar 10	Nov 08
Working Capital	3	5	32
Fixed Assets	N/A	1	2
Current Assets	69	62	76

Cashmaster International

Fairykirk Road Rosyth, Dunfermline, KY11 2QQ
Tel: 01383-416098 **Fax:** 01383-414731
E-mail: info@cashmaster.com
Website: http://www.cashmaster.com
Directors: D. Reid (Eng Serv), M. Hunter (Sales & Mktg)
Managers: D. Welsh (Tech Serv Mgr), D. Ross (Comptroller), N. Hunter
Immediate Holding Company: CASHMASTER INTERNATIONAL LIMITED
Registration no: SC139775 **Date established:** 1992 **Turnover:** £2m - £5m
No.of Employees: 51 - 100 **Product Groups:** 38

Date of Accounts	Aug 12	Aug 11	Aug 10
Working Capital	2m	915	438
Fixed Assets	115	171	244
Current Assets	2m	1m	2m

City Plumbing Supplies Ltd

26-42 Gardeners Street, Dunfermline, KY12 0RN
Tel: 01383-735585 **Fax:** 01383-732987
E-mail: colin.hughes@cityplumbing.co.uk
Website: http://www.cityplumbing.co.uk
Managers: C. Hughes (District Mgr)
Immediate Holding Company: CITY PLUMBING SUPPLIES LIMITED
Registration no: 01617423 **Date established:** 1982
Turnover: £20m - £50m **No.of Employees:** 1 - 10 **Product Groups:** 66

Date of Accounts	Dec 10	Dec 09	Dec 07
Working Capital	101	101	101
Current Assets	192	192	192
Current Liabilities	91	N/A	N/A

Claude Systems Ltd

4 Bellman Way Donibristle Industrial Park, Hillend, Dunfermline, KY11 9JW
Tel: 01383-820011 **Fax:** 01383-820093
E-mail: kimrose@claudesystems.com
Website: http://www.claudesystems.com
Directors: M. Gorill (Dir), D. Gorrill (MD), J. Doby (MD), A. Macklin (Co Sec), K. Rose (Grp Chief Exec)
Managers: A. Machlin (Sales Prom Mgr), K. Rose
Immediate Holding Company: CLAUDE SYSTEMS LIMITED
Registration no: SC144490 **Date established:** 1993
Turnover: £500,000 - £1m **No.of Employees:** 1 - 10 **Product Groups:** 37, 40

Date of Accounts	Jan 11	Jan 10	Jan 09
Working Capital	70	55	93
Fixed Assets	10	10	11
Current Assets	132	141	138

Craig & Rose Ltd

Unit 8 Halbeath Industrial Estate, Dunfermline, KY11 7EG
Tel: 01383-740011 **Fax:** 01383-740010
E-mail: customerservice@craigandrose.com
Website: http://www.craigandrose.com
Directors: S. Percy-Robb (MD)
Managers: B. Robertson (Purch Mgr), C. Godfrey (Mktg Serv Mgr), R. Smith (Sales Prom Mgr)
Registration no: SC004650 **VAT No.:** GB 268 6455 17
Turnover: £2m - £5m **No.of Employees:** 1 - 10 **Product Groups:** 31, 32

Dedicated Mortgage Solutions Ltd

Dunfermline Business Centre Izatt Avenue, Dunfermline, KY11 3BZ
Tel: 0845-602 5541 **Fax:** 01383-626450
E-mail: enquiries@dedicatedmortgages.co.uk
Website: http://www.dedicatedmortgages.co.uk
Directors: M. Mchardy (Dir)
Managers: E. Davey (Mgr)
Registration no: SC325564 **Date established:** 2007
No.of Employees: 1 - 10 **Product Groups:** 36, 37, 38

Date of Accounts	Nov 08
Working Capital	-2
Fixed Assets	2
Current Assets	5
Current Liabilities	7

Dunfermline Building Society

Carnegie Avenue, Dunfermline, KY11 8PE
Tel: 01383-622678 **Fax:** 01383-627800
E-mail: comments@dunfermline-bs.com
Website: http://www.dunfermline-bs.co.uk
Directors: G. Dalziel (Grp Chief Exec)
Managers: B. Morton (Sales & Mktg Mg)
Registration no: SC113201 **Date established:** 1988
No.of Employees: 1 - 10 **Product Groups:** 82

Dunfermline Press

Pitreavie Business Park Queensferry Road, Dunfermline, KY11 8QS
Tel: 01383-728201 **Fax:** 01383-737040
E-mail: editorial@dunfermlinepress.co.uk
Website: http://www.dunfermlinepress.com
Bank(s): Bank of Scotland
Directors: D. Romanes (MD)
Immediate Holding Company: DUNFERMLINE PRESS LIMITED,THE
Registration no: SC083620 **VAT No.:** GB 270 1389 70
Date established: 1983 **Turnover:** £20m - £50m
No.of Employees: 11 - 20 **Product Groups:** 27, 28, 81

Date of Accounts	Mar 07	Mar 08	Mar 09
Sales Turnover	22m	30m	25m
Pre Tax Profit/Loss	4m	-1m	160
Working Capital	-5m	-3m	-4m
Fixed Assets	45m	48m	46m
Current Assets	3m	6m	4m
Current Liabilities	5m	5m	4m

Esa Mcintosh Ltd

West Way Hillend Industrial Park, Hillend, Dunfermline, KY11 9HE
Tel: 01592-656200 **Fax:** 01592-656299
E-mail: bill.mccoll@esamcintosh.co.uk
Website: http://www.esamcintosh.co.uk
Bank(s): Bank of Scotland
Directors: A. McMenzie (Reg), D. Blackford (Ptnr), E. Prescot (Grp Chief Exec), G. Findlay (Fin), R. McDonald (Sales), R. Wallace (Procurement)
Managers: G. Carruthers (Tech Serv Mgr)
Ultimate Holding Company: HAVELOCK EUROPA PLC
Immediate Holding Company: E.S.A. MCINTOSH LIMITED
Registration no: SC090149 **VAT No.:** GB 415 3814 67
Date established: 1984 **Turnover:** £10m - £20m
No.of Employees: 101 - 250 **Product Groups:** 26

Date of Accounts	Dec 10	Dec 09	Dec 08
Sales Turnover	N/A	10m	40m
Pre Tax Profit/Loss	N/A	-2m	1m
Working Capital	4m	4m	3m
Fixed Assets	N/A	N/A	4m
Current Assets	4m	4m	17m
Current Liabilities	N/A	N/A	604

F M C Technologies Ltd

Pitreavie Business Park Queensferry Road, Dunfermline, KY11 8UD
Tel: 01383-731531 **Fax:** 01383-731297
Website: http://www.fmctechnologies.com
Directors: P. Lucas (Pers), M. Langaas (Fin), I. Wishert (Co Sec)
Managers: J. Tait (Reg Sales Mgr), B. Blanshan (Comptroller), P. Lucas (Personnel), J. Tate (Sales & Mktg Mg), F. Flemming, A. Atkin (I.T. Exec), A. Atkin (Tech Serv Mgr)
Ultimate Holding Company: FMC TECHNOLOGIES INC. (USA)
Immediate Holding Company: FMC TECHNOLOGIES LIMITED
Registration no: 00259569 **Date established:** 1931
No.of Employees: 501 - 1000 **Product Groups:** 45, 48

Date of Accounts	Dec 11	Dec 10	Dec 09
Sales Turnover	206m	199m	239m
Pre Tax Profit/Loss	-7m	29m	41m
Working Capital	30m	39m	60m
Fixed Assets	43m	33m	30m
Current Assets	196m	155m	139m
Current Liabilities	36m	33m	32m

Flear & Thomson Ltd

128-140 Pittencrieff Street, Dunfermline, KY12 8AN
Tel: 01383-722565 **Fax:** 01383-733927
E-mail: sales@flearandthomson.co.uk
Website: http://www.flearandthomson.co.uk
Bank(s): Bank of Scotland
Directors: P. Buchannon (Head)
Managers: T. McCann (Sales Prom Mgr), M. Greasley (Chief Acct)
Immediate Holding Company: FLEAR & THOMSON LIMITED
Registration no: SC028660 **VAT No.:** GB 356 1757 37
Date established: 1951 **Turnover:** £20m - £50m
No.of Employees: 21 - 50 **Product Groups:** 68, 82

Date of Accounts	Mar 12	Mar 11	Mar 10
Working Capital	110	45	-81
Fixed Assets	849	820	828
Current Assets	1m	1m	1m

Graham
Pitreavie Business Park, Dunfermline, KY11 8UH
Tel: 01383-738728 **Fax:** 01383-622560
Website: http://www.graham-group.co.uk
Managers: A. Thomson (Mgr)
Immediate Holding Company: JAMIESON CONTRACTING (HOLDINGS) LIMITED
Registration no: 00066738 **Date established:** 2003
No.of Employees: 1 - 10 **Product Groups:** 66

Havelock Europa plc
Moss Way Hillend Industrial Park, Hillend, Dunfermline, KY11 9JS
Tel: 01383-820044 **Fax:** 01383-820064
E-mail: richard.lowery@havelockeuropa.com
Website: http://www.havelockeuropa.com
Directors: G. Finlay (Fin), R. Wallis (Procurement), R. Lowery (Dir), M. Hilton (Sales & Mktg), G. Findlay (Co Sec), A. McMenzie (Sales & Mktg), P. Gascoigne (Pers)
Managers: G. Carruthers (Tech Serv Mgr), G. Carruthers
Ultimate Holding Company: HAVELOCK EUROPA PLC
Immediate Holding Company: HAVELOCK EUROPA PLC
Registration no: 00782546 **Date established:** 1963
Turnover: £75m - £125m **No.of Employees:** 251 - 500
Product Groups: 52

Date of Accounts	Dec 11	Dec 10	Dec 09
Sales Turnover	99m	99m	108m
Pre Tax Profit/Loss	-5m	-5m	-6m
Working Capital	4m	17m	15m
Fixed Assets	17m	25m	28m
Current Assets	41m	42m	41m
Current Liabilities	9m	8m	8m

Heil Europe Ltd
Taxi Way Hillend Industrial Park, Hillend, Dunfermline, KY11 9ES
Tel: 01383-823625 **Fax:** 01383-824062
E-mail: michael.jobe@heil-europe.co.uk
Website: http://www.heileuro.com
Bank(s): Bank of Scotland
Directors: M. Jobe (Pres), J. Law (Pers)
Managers: K. Reed, P. Parkyn (Chief Buyer), B. Armour, C. Backhouse
Ultimate Holding Company: DOVER CORPORATION (U.S.A.)
Immediate Holding Company: HEIL-EUROPE LIMITED
Registration no: SC053003 **Date established:** 1993
Turnover: £10m - £20m **No.of Employees:** 101 - 250 **Product Groups:** 39

Date of Accounts	Dec 11	Dec 10	Dec 09
Sales Turnover	18m	18m	21m
Pre Tax Profit/Loss	322	140	697
Working Capital	9m	9m	9m
Fixed Assets	411	606	348
Current Assets	13m	12m	12m
Current Liabilities	2m	1m	928

Ingenico Ltd
Ridge Way Hillend, Dunfermline, KY11 9JU
Tel: 0131-459 8800 **Fax:** 0131-479 8321
E-mail: reception@ingenico.com
Website: http://www.ingenico.com
Directors: J. Graham (Pers), P. McCourt (Fin), C. Doyle (MD), D. O'Mara (Sales & Mktg)
Managers: R. Glennon (Purch Mgr), P. Juan (Tech Serv Mgr)
Ultimate Holding Company: INGENICO SA (FRANCE)
Immediate Holding Company: INGENICO (UK) LIMITED
Registration no: 02135540 **VAT No.:** GB 238 9404 40
Date established: 1987 **Turnover:** £50m - £75m
No.of Employees: 251 - 500 **Product Groups:** 37, 44, 67

Date of Accounts	Dec 11	Dec 10	Dec 09
Sales Turnover	73m	51m	48m
Pre Tax Profit/Loss	13m	519	584
Working Capital	19m	11m	7m
Fixed Assets	2m	2m	6m
Current Assets	35m	29m	22m
Current Liabilities	11m	10m	8m

Invictus Locks & Security
10c Carnock Road, Dunfermline, KY12 9AX
Tel: 07726-012000
E-mail: invictuslocks@tiscali.co.uk
Website: http://www.invictuslocks.co.uk
Directors: A. Morrison (Prop)
Date established: 2005 **Turnover:** Up to £250,000
No.of Employees: 1 - 10 **Product Groups:** 36

Isle Burn
Pitreavie Business Park Queensferry Road, Dunfermline, KY11 8UE
Tel: 01383-732266 **Fax:** 01383-734094
E-mail: norrie.bishop@isleburn.com
Website: http://www.isleburn.com
Directors: J. Murrey (MD), J. Murray (MD), R. Forsyth (Ch)
Managers: N. Bishop, W. Bishop (Buyer), D. Cant (Projects), S. McNaughton (Sales Admin), S. McNorton (Mktg Serv Mgr)
Immediate Holding Company: Sovereign Oilfield Group plc
Registration no: SC106415 **VAT No.:** GB 398 2521 21
Turnover: £10m - £20m **No.of Employees:** 51 - 100 **Product Groups:** 48

Lojigma International Ltd
Block 19 Ridge Way, Hillend, Dunfermline, KY11 9JN
Tel: 01383-822003 **Fax:** 01383-822007
E-mail: admin@lojigma.com
Website: http://www.lojigma.com
Directors: J. Duncan (MD)
Immediate Holding Company: LOJIGMA INTERNATIONAL LIMITED
Registration no: SC096228 **VAT No.:** GB 400 8782 66
Date established: 1985 **Turnover:** £500,000 - £1m
No.of Employees: 1 - 10 **Product Groups:** 24

Date of Accounts	Dec 11	Dec 10	Dec 09
Working Capital	657	720	760
Fixed Assets	3	5	4
Current Assets	725	776	867

M V P European
4 Castle Court Carnegie Campus, Dunfermline, KY11 8PB
Tel: 01383-629960 **Fax:** 01383-629979
E-mail: ntomlinson@visionpro.com
Website: http://www.visionpro.com
Managers: N. Tomlinson
Immediate Holding Company: RADIO SITE SERVICES LIMITED
Registration no: SC178374 **Date established:** 2004
No.of Employees: 1 - 10 **Product Groups:** 37, 38

Date of Accounts	Sep 11	Sep 08	Sep 06
Pre Tax Profit/Loss	N/A	12	-4
Working Capital	N/A	N/A	-13

Marlaw Pallets Services Ltd (t/a Tripack Solutions Ltd)
Scott Group Halbeath Interchange Business Park Kingseat Road, Halbeath, Dunfermline, KY11 8RY
Tel: 01759-319 519 **Fax:** 01698-712801
E-mail: andrea@marlaw.co.uk
Website: http://www.marlaw.co.uk
Directors: M. Lawlar (MD)
Managers: S. Kyle (Sales Prom Mgr)
Registration no: SC110919 **No.of Employees:** 21 - 50
Product Groups: 25, 45, 66

Multi Valve Technology Ltd
M V T House 85 New Row, Dunfermline, KY12 7DZ
Tel: 01383-733380 **Fax:** 01383-733383
E-mail: multivalve@aol.com
Website: http://www.multivalve.com
Directors: A. Pennycook (Fin), R. Weymes (MD)
Immediate Holding Company: MULTI-VALVE TECHNOLOGY LIMITED
Registration no: SC174086 **Date established:** 1997 **Turnover:** £2m - £5m
No.of Employees: 1 - 10 **Product Groups:** 36, 37, 38

Date of Accounts	Dec 11	Dec 10	Dec 09
Working Capital	331	478	639
Fixed Assets	35	37	40
Current Assets	1m	971	799

Narvida Ltd
Taxi Way Hillend Industrial Park, Hillend, Dunfermline, KY11 9JT
Tel: 01383-823417 **Fax:** 01383-823148
E-mail: info@narvida.co.uk
Website: http://www.narvida.co.uk
Bank(s): Royal Bank of Scotland
Directors: D. Caton (MD), C. Caton (Fin)
Managers: A. Miller
Immediate Holding Company: NARVIDA LIMITED
Registration no: SC025940 **VAT No.:** GB 269 2972 11
Date established: 1947 **Turnover:** £1m - £2m **No.of Employees:** 21 - 50
Product Groups: 40, 48

Date of Accounts	Dec 11	Dec 10	Dec 09
Working Capital	202	173	276
Fixed Assets	482	472	468
Current Assets	515	410	458

Oceaneering Umbilical Solutions
Dundas Road Rosyth, Dunfermline, KY11 2XS
Tel: 01383-643400 **Fax:** 01383-643590
E-mail: enquiry@oceaneering.com
Website: http://www.oceaneering.com
Directors: J. Birkett (Co Sec)
Managers: N. Turner (Tech Serv Mgr), Y. Valentine (Purch Mgr), N. Turner (I.T. Exec), M. Smith (Chief Mgr), A. Stevenson (Sales Prom Mgr), A. Stevenson (Sales Prom Mgr), D. Portius (Fin Mgr)
Ultimate Holding Company: OCEANEERING INTERNATIONAL INC. HOUSTON, TEXAS
Immediate Holding Company: OCEANEERING INTERNATIONAL SERVICES LTD
Registration no: 01023217 **Date established:** 1975
Turnover: £10m - £20m **No.of Employees:** 101 - 250
Product Groups: 30, 37, 45

Polyscot Polystyrene
4 Craigluscar Road, Dunfermline, KY12 9JA
Tel: 01383-732296 **Fax:** 01383-620365
E-mail: eps@polyscot.co.uk
Website: http://www.polyscot.co.uk
Directors: G. Helm (Prop)
Immediate Holding Company: POLYSCOT POLYSTYRENE LTD.
Registration no: SC316867 **Date established:** 2007
Turnover: £500,000 - £1m **No.of Employees:** 1 - 10 **Product Groups:** 30

Date of Accounts	Feb 10	Feb 09
Working Capital	1	1
Current Assets	1	1

Retail Websites Limited
Unit 24 - Business Centre Izatt Avenue, Dunfermline, KY11 3BZ
Tel: 0845-313 4747
E-mail: sales@retail-websites.com
Website: http://www.quicksafe.co.uk
Directors: M. Rowan (Prop)
Registration no: SC303118 **Product Groups:** 07, 35, 37, 38, 40, 67, 81

Rolls Royce plc
Taxi Way Hillend Industrial Park, Hillend, Dunfermline, KY11 9JT
Tel: 01383-823188 **Fax:** 01383-824038
E-mail: andrew.carnegie@rolls-royce.com
Website: http://www.rolls-royce.com
Bank(s): Bank of Scotland
Directors: A. Carnegie (MD)
Ultimate Holding Company: ROLLS-ROYCE HOLDINGS PLC
Immediate Holding Company: ROLLS-ROYCE PLC
Registration no: 01003142 **VAT No.:** GB 271 4998 24
Date established: 1971 **Turnover:** £1m - £2m
No.of Employees: 101 - 250 **Product Groups:** 39, 48, 84

Date of Accounts	Dec 11	Dec 10	Dec 09
Sales Turnover	11124m	11085m	10414m
Pre Tax Profit/Loss	1106m	703m	2957m
Working Capital	1558m	2484m	3144m
Fixed Assets	8108m	6410m	6048m
Current Assets	8510m	9823m	9443m
Current Liabilities	5864m	6189m	5430m

S Q M C Training Services
Carnegie Conference Centre Halbeath, Dunfermline, KY11 8DY
Tel: 01383-725000 **Fax:** 01383-725571
E-mail: admin@sqmc.co.uk
Website: http://www.sqmc.co.uk
Directors: I. Hannah (Dir), J. Hannah (Fin)
Immediate Holding Company: CARNEGIE CONFERENCE CENTRE LIMITED
Registration no: SC187145 **Date established:** 2007
No.of Employees: 1 - 10 **Product Groups:** 80, 86

Shering Weighing Ltd
Pitreavie Business Park Queensferry Road, Dunfermline, KY11 8UL
Tel: 01383-621505 **Fax:** 01383-620262
E-mail: sales@shering.com
Website: http://www.shering.com
Directors: D. Rowe (Co Sec), D. Shering (MD), R. Maclaren (Fin)
Managers: B. Watt
Immediate Holding Company: SHERING WEIGHING LIMITED
Registration no: SC095802 **VAT No.:** GB 502 7670 62
Date established: 1985 **Turnover:** £5m - £10m **No.of Employees:** 11 - 20
Product Groups: 38

Date of Accounts	Sep 11	Sep 10	Sep 09
Working Capital	117	310	185
Fixed Assets	58	61	44
Current Assets	972	968	1m

Simclar International Ltd
Queensferry Road, Dunfermline, KY11 8UN
Tel: 01383-727272 **Fax:** 01383-739986
E-mail: ian.durie@simclar.com
Website: http://www.simclar.com
Bank(s): Bank of Scotland
Directors: J. Durie (Fin)
Managers: I. Kennedy (Mgr)
Ultimate Holding Company: SIMCLAR GROUP LIMITED
Immediate Holding Company: SIMCLAR INTERNATIONAL LIMITED
Registration no: SC059937 **VAT No.:** GB 272 0771 66
Date established: 1976 **Turnover:** £5m - £10m
No.of Employees: 101 - 250 **Product Groups:** 37, 48

Date of Accounts	Dec 09	Dec 08	Dec 06
Sales Turnover	7m	8m	15m
Pre Tax Profit/Loss	-462	-1m	-1m
Working Capital	8m	8m	8m
Fixed Assets	10m	11m	13m
Current Assets	14m	16m	13m
Current Liabilities	484	464	515

Speedy Hire Centre
Inglis Lane, Dunfermline, KY12 9DP
Tel: 01383-620406 **Fax:** 01383-624106
Website: http://www.speedyhire.co.uk
Managers: R. Maule (Mgr)
Immediate Holding Company: SPEEDY HIRE CENTRES LIMITED
Registration no: 06207105 **Date established:** 2007
Turnover: £20m - £50m **No.of Employees:** 1 - 10 **Product Groups:** 35, 37, 38, 39, 45, 48, 83

Date of Accounts	Mar 08	Mar 07	Apr 06
Sales Turnover	6313	20629	16194
Pre Tax Profit/Loss	394	978	757
Working Capital	2931	1399	463
Fixed Assets	218	1645	3565
Current Assets	4765	7333	5777
Current Liabilities	1834	5934	5314
Total Share Capital	100	100	100
ROCE% (Return on Capital Employed)	12.5	32.1	18.8
ROT% (Return on Turnover)	6.2	4.7	4.7

Static Scotland Ltd
16 Cromarty Campus Rosyth, Dunfermline, KY11 2WX
Tel: 01383-419833 **Fax:** 01383-413028
E-mail: staticscotland@aol.com
Website: http://www.staticscotland.co.uk
Directors: S. Veitch (Dir)
Managers: A. Raleigh (I.T. Exec)
Registration no: SC247586 **Date established:** 2003
Turnover: £250,000 - £500,000 **No.of Employees:** 1 - 10
Product Groups: 76

Toolcom Supplies
Pitreavie Business Park, Dunfermline, KY11 8UQ
Tel: 01383-728970 **Fax:** 01383-620079
E-mail: sales@toolcom.co.uk
Website: http://www.toolcom.co.uk
Directors: G. Doherty (MD), P. Delhez (Co Sec)
Ultimate Holding Company: BARNES GROUP INC (USA)
Immediate Holding Company: BARNES GROUP (SCOTLAND) LIMITED
Registration no: SC063330 **VAT No.:** GB 327 3619 54
Date established: 1977 **Turnover:** £5m - £10m **No.of Employees:** 11 - 20
Product Groups: 35, 66

Date of Accounts	May 11	May 10	May 09
Pre Tax Profit/Loss	123	123	401
Working Capital	10m	10m	10m
Current Assets	10m	10m	10m

Perthshire

Dunkeld

Burhouse 2 0
Inver Sawmill Inver, Dunkeld, PH8 0JR
Tel: 01350-727723 **Fax:** 01350-727261
E-mail: enquiries@jeanburhouse.com
Website: http://www.burhouse.co.uk
Directors: C. Anderson (Ptnr)
Registration no: 02970222 **Date established:** 1986
No.of Employees: 1 - 10 **Product Groups:** 23, 32, 65, 66

Maclean
Upper Woodinch Dalguise, Dunkeld, PH8 0JU
Tel: 01350-727535 **Fax:** 01350-727535
Website: http://www.constructionplus.net
Directors: J. Maclean (Prop)
Date established: 2002 **No.of Employees:** 1 - 10 **Product Groups:** 35

Argyll

Dunoon

Murray Cormack Associates
Old Bank House Innellan, Dunoon, PA23 7TP
Tel: 01369-830210 **Fax:** 01369-830790
E-mail: admin@murraycormack.com
Website: http://www.murraycormack.com
Directors: M. Murray (Ptnr)
VAT No.: GB 264 5539 40 **Turnover:** Up to £250,000
No.of Employees: 1 - 10 **Product Groups:** 84

Midlothian

Edinburgh

1st Class Media
32/6 Hardengreen Business Park Eskbank, Edinburgh, EH22 3NX
Tel: 0131-510 5105 **Fax:** 0131-516 8121
E-mail: design@1stclassmedia.co.uk
Website: http://www.1stclassmedia.co.uk
Directors: M. Lawson (Develop)
No.of Employees: 1 - 10 **Product Groups:** 44

A & A Studios Ltd
8-10 Tanfield, Edinburgh, EH3 5HF
Tel: 0131-556 7057 **Fax:** 0131-556 3223
E-mail: sales@aastudios.co.uk
Website: http://www.aastudios.co.uk
Bank(s): The Royal Bank of Scotland
Directors: G. Theurer (Dir)
Immediate Holding Company: A & A STUDIOS LIMITED
Registration no: SC025492 **VAT No.:** GB 268 3701 43
Date established: 1947 **Turnover:** £500,000 - £1m
No.of Employees: 11 - 20 **Product Groups:** 32, 49

Date of Accounts	Mar 11	Mar 10	Mar 09
Working Capital	576	540	395
Fixed Assets	265	247	245
Current Assets	704	716	743

A B Welding & Fabrication
Boghall Farm Biggar Road, Edinburgh, EH10 7DX
Tel: 0131-445 3834
Directors: A. Breen (Prop)
Immediate Holding Company: VIVA ONE LTD
Registration no: SC376288 **Date established:** 2012
No.of Employees: 1 - 10 **Product Groups:** 35

A W G Property Ltd
47 Melville Street, Edinburgh, EH3 7HL
Tel: 0131-260 5260 **Fax:** 0131-343 3355
Website: http://www.awgproperty.co.uk
Directors: D. Tony (MD), G. Shepheard (Co Sec), J. Hope (Fin), T. Donnerley (MD)
Managers: I. Flynn (Chief Buyer), G. Joyner (Personnel)
Ultimate Holding Company: Awg UK Holdings Ltd
Immediate Holding Company: Awg Shelf 11 Ltd
Registration no: SC067190 **Turnover:** £75m - £125m
No.of Employees: 21 - 50 **Product Groups:** 80

Aberdeen Asset Management
40 Princes Street, Edinburgh, EH2 2BY
Tel: 0131-528 4000 **Fax:** 0131-528 4400
Website: http://www.aberdeen-asset.com
Directors: G. Marshall (Sales & Mktg), M. Gilbert (Grp Chief Exec), A. Richards (MD)
Managers: G. Steward (Sales Admin)
Immediate Holding Company: SHIRES SMALLER COMPANIES PLC
Registration no: SC143266 **Date established:** 1996
Turnover: £250,000 - £500,000 **No.of Employees:** 51 - 100
Product Groups: 82

Aberforth Partners
14 Melville Street, Edinburgh, EH3 7NS
Tel: 0131-220 0733 **Fax:** 0131-220 0735
E-mail: enquiries@aberforth.co.uk
Website: http://www.aberforth.co.uk
Directors: A. Waite (Ptnr)
Ultimate Holding Company: ABERFORTH PARTNERS LLP
Immediate Holding Company: ABERFORTH LGP IB LIMITED
Registration no: SC215035 **VAT No.:** GB 553 5584 24
Date established: 2001 **No.of Employees:** 11 - 20 **Product Groups:** 82

Date of Accounts	Apr 12	Apr 11	Apr 10
Pre Tax Profit/Loss	N/A	-0	-0
Working Capital	2	2	2
Current Assets	2	2	2

Aegon Scottish Equitable plc
Scottish Equitable House 1 Lochside Crescent, Edinburgh, EH12 9SE
Tel: 08702-426789 **Fax:** 0131-339 3147
E-mail: enquiries@aegon.co.uk
Website: http://www.scottishequitable.co.uk
Directors: I. Young (Co Sec)
Managers: A. Grace, L. Connelly, K. Grady (Personnel), A. Marchant (Mktg Serv Mgr), P. Chong (Tech Serv Mgr), D. Jarrett (Sales Prom Mgr)
Ultimate Holding Company: AEGON NV (NETHERLANDS)
Immediate Holding Company: SCOTTISH EQUITABLE PLC
Registration no: SC144517 **Date established:** 1993
Turnover: £50m - £75m **No.of Employees:** 1501 & over
Product Groups: 82

Date of Accounts	Dec 11	Dec 10	Dec 09
Pre Tax Profit/Loss	-51m	112m	129m
Fixed Assets	55647m	52662m	45598m
Current Assets	1720m	4374m	4918m
Current Liabilities	53266m	53361m	47754m

Alba Beverage Co. Ltd
4 Sauchiebank, Edinburgh, EH11 2NN
Tel: 0131-539 2755 **Fax:** 0131-346 8008
E-mail: info@albabeverage.co.uk
Website: http://www.albabeverage.co.uk
Directors: P. Jones (Ptnr)
Immediate Holding Company: ALBA BEVERAGE COMPANY LTD.
Registration no: SC186883 **Date established:** 1998
Turnover: £500,000 - £1m **No.of Employees:** 1 - 10 **Product Groups:** 20, 21, 40, 49, 62, 65, 66

Date of Accounts	Jan 12	Dec 10	Dec 09
Working Capital	23	7	-1
Fixed Assets	115	118	112
Current Assets	111	95	91

American Express Europe Ltd
69 George Street, Edinburgh, EH2 2JG
Tel: 0131-718 2505 **Fax:** 0131-225 6116
E-mail: edinburgh@amexfranchise.co.uk
Website: http://www.amercianexpress.co.uk
Managers: K. Mattherson (Mgr), F. Binnie
Immediate Holding Company: AMERICAN EXPRESS EUROPE LIMITED
Registration no: FC011790 **VAT No.:** GB 190 1985 48
Date established: 1983 **No.of Employees:** 1 - 10 **Product Groups:** 69

Aon Ltd
40 Torphichen Street, Edinburgh, EH3 8JB
Tel: 0131-456 3000 **Fax:** 0131-456 3045
Website: http://www.aon.co.uk
Managers: S. Brown (Mgr)
Ultimate Holding Company: AON CORPORATION INC (USA)
Immediate Holding Company: A1 VENTURES LIMITED
Registration no: 04578543 **Date established:** 2002 **Turnover:** £2m - £5m
No.of Employees: 51 - 100 **Product Groups:** 82

Date of Accounts	Feb 12	Feb 11	Feb 10
Sales Turnover	6m	5m	N/A
Pre Tax Profit/Loss	5m	4m	4m
Working Capital	-10m	-16m	-6m
Fixed Assets	321m	328m	203m
Current Assets	2m	2m	1m
Current Liabilities	4m	4m	1m

B M G Office Equipment
151 Dalry Road, Edinburgh, EH11 2EA
Tel: 0131-346 1494 **Fax:** 0131-346 4193
E-mail: charlie@bmgoffice.co.uk
Website: http://www.bmgoffice.co.uk
Directors: C. Mcginlay (Prop)
No.of Employees: 1 - 10 **Product Groups:** 44

Backtracks Music & Games Shop
17 Brougham Street, Edinburgh, EH3 9JS
Tel: 0131-228 4898
E-mail: tommy@backtracksmusic.co.uk
Website: http://www.backtracksmusic.co.uk
Directors: T. Robertson (Prop)
No.of Employees: 1 - 10 **Product Groups:** 37, 89

Balfour Beatty Construction Ltd
Dean House 24 Ravelston Terrace, Edinburgh, EH4 3TP
Tel: 0131-332 9411 **Fax:** 0131-332 5937
E-mail: admin@bbcl.co.uk
Website: http://www.balfourbeattyconstruction.co.uk
Bank(s): The Royal Bank of Scotland
Directors: B. Clark (MD), G. Taylor (Fin), J. Quick (Mkt Research)
Managers: J. Colraine (Personnel)
Ultimate Holding Company: BALFOUR BEATTY PLC
Immediate Holding Company: BALFOUR BEATTY CONSTRUCTION LIMITED
Registration no: SC106247 **VAT No.:** GB 217 9672 35
Date established: 1987 **Turnover:** £250m - £500m
No.of Employees: 101 - 250 **Product Groups:** 18, 35, 51, 52, 84

Balfour & Manson LLP
54-66 Frederick Street, Edinburgh, EH2 1LS
Tel: 0131-200 1200 **Fax:** 0131-200 1300
E-mail: enquiry@balfour-manson.co.uk
Website: http://www.balfour-manson.co.uk
Bank(s): Bank of Scotland
Directors: S. Majithia-jaswal (Mkt Research), A. Tyler (Ch)
Managers: M. Peet (Personnel), H. Pringle (Tech Serv Mgr), D. Hestie (Chief Acct), D. Hastie (Comptroller)
Immediate Holding Company: BALFOUR + MANSON LLP
Registration no: SO301386 **Date established:** 2007
Turnover: £5m - £10m **No.of Employees:** 101 - 250 **Product Groups:** 80

Date of Accounts	Oct 11	Oct 10	Oct 09
Sales Turnover	8m	8m	7m
Pre Tax Profit/Loss	3m	3m	3m
Working Capital	3m	5m	6m
Fixed Assets	779	812	790
Current Assets	6m	6m	7m
Current Liabilities	714	478	1m

Basil Paterson College
66 Queen Street, Edinburgh, EH2 4NA
Tel: 0131-225 3802 **Fax:** 0131-226 6701
E-mail: info@basilpaterson.co.uk
Website: http://www.basilpaterson.co.uk
Bank(s): The Royal Bank of Scotland
Directors: M. Sleter (Head), M. Slater (Head)
Ultimate Holding Company: OISE HOLDINGS LIMITED
Immediate Holding Company: BASIL PATERSON LIMITED
Registration no: SC206283 **VAT No.:** GB 271 8483 37
Date established: 2000 **Turnover:** £500,000 - £1m
No.of Employees: 51 - 100 **Product Groups:** 86

Belinda Robertson Retail Ltd
13a Dundas Street, Edinburgh, EH3 6QG
Tel: 0131-557 8118 **Fax:** 0131-226 2148
E-mail: mj@belindarobertson.co.uk
Website: http://www.belindarobertson.com
Directors: B. Robertson (Dir), J. Grove White (Co Sec)
Immediate Holding Company: BELINDA ROBERTSON RETAIL LIMITED
Registration no: SC234891 **Date established:** 2002
No.of Employees: 1 - 10 **Product Groups:** 24

Date of Accounts	Dec 11	Dec 10	Dec 09
Working Capital	-250	-232	-173
Fixed Assets	4	6	N/A
Current Assets	43	35	50

Bell Donaldson Steele
17 Westfield Street, Edinburgh, EH11 2QQ
Tel: 0131-337 6303 **Fax:** 0131-313 5328
E-mail: edinburgh.049@decco.co.uk
Website: http://www.belldonaldsonsteele.com
Bank(s): National Westminster Bank Plc
Managers: A. Frazer (Mgr)
Ultimate Holding Company: GALATEA LIMITED
Immediate Holding Company: DECCO LIMITED
Registration no: 00417021 **VAT No.:** GB 431 2745 75
Turnover: £1m - £2m **No.of Employees:** 11 - 20 **Product Groups:** 35, 66

Berlitz Language Centre
14 Frederick Street, Edinburgh, EH2 2HB
Tel: 0131-226 7198 **Fax:** 0131-225 2918
E-mail: edinburgh@languagecentres.com
Website: http://www.berlitzedinburgh.co.uk
Directors: S. Penmen (Dir)
Registration no: 00072162 **Date established:** 1979
No.of Employees: 1 - 10 **Product Groups:** 80, 86

James Blake & Co Engineers Ltd
30-32 South Fort Street, Edinburgh, EH6 5NU
Tel: 0131-554 1646 **Fax:** 0131-553 4128
E-mail: info@blakegroup.co.uk
Website: http://www.blakegroup.co.uk
Bank(s): Bank of Scotland
Directors: R. Blake (Prop), R. Hamill (Fin)
Managers: E. Blake (Mktg Serv Mgr), J. Blake (Tech Serv Mgr)
Immediate Holding Company: JAMES BLAKE & CO (ENGINEERS) LIMITED
Registration no: SC036390 **VAT No.:** GB 268 5255 30
Date established: 1961 **Turnover:** £2m - £5m **No.of Employees:** 51 - 100
Product Groups: 26, 35, 48

Date of Accounts	Mar 11	Mar 10	Mar 09
Working Capital	287	382	380
Fixed Assets	180	190	222
Current Assets	868	811	897

Blueparrot Production & Events Ltd
Unit 5 Forth Industrial Centre, Sealcarr Street, Edinburgh, EH5 1RF
Tel: 0131-510 3333 **Fax:** 0131-510 3334
E-mail: info@blueparrotevents.com
Website: http://www.blueparrotproduction.com
Managers: J. Clough (Chief Acct)
Registration no: 03896657 **Date established:** 2000
Turnover: Up to £250,000 **No.of Employees:** 1 - 10 **Product Groups:** 83

George Brown & Sons
5-6 Shore, Edinburgh, EH6 6QS
Tel: 0131-554 5436 **Fax:** 0131-554 5443
E-mail: george.brown@georgebrown.co.uk
Website: http://www.georgebrown.co.uk
Bank(s): Bank of Scotland
Directors: G. Brown (MD), R. Humphries (Fin)
Immediate Holding Company: GEORGE BROWN & SONS, ENGINEERS (LEITH) LIMITED
Registration no: SC022512 **VAT No.:** GB 268 3259 32
Date established: 1943 **Turnover:** £1m - £2m **No.of Employees:** 21 - 50
Product Groups: 35, 36, 45

Date of Accounts	Dec 11	Dec 10	Dec 09
Working Capital	740	622	590
Fixed Assets	132	103	125
Current Assets	1m	907	792

Builder Center Ltd
72-74 Eyre Place, Edinburgh, EH3 5EL
Tel: 0131-557 1717 **Fax:** 0131-557 5310
Website: http://www.buildcenter.co.uk
Managers: P. Chambers (District Mgr), P. Mullen (District Mgr), D. McLaren (District Mgr)
Ultimate Holding Company: WOLSELEY PLC (JERSEY)
Immediate Holding Company: BUILD CENTER LIMITED
Registration no: 00462397 **VAT No.:** GB 362 0233 93
Date established: 1948 **Turnover:** £500m - £1,000m
No.of Employees: 1 - 10 **Product Groups:** 25, 66

Date of Accounts	Jul 11	Jul 10	Jul 09
Working Capital	N/A	N/A	78
Current Assets	N/A	N/A	78

Butterworths Lenses
85 Peffer Place, Edinburgh, EH16 4BB
Tel: 0131-661 4555 **Fax:** 0131-661 8555
Website: http://www.butterworthsaccountants.co.uk
Managers: T. Martin (Mgr)
Immediate Holding Company: BUTTERWORTHS LENSES LIMITED
Registration no: SC225522 **Date established:** 2001
Turnover: £250,000 - £500,000 **No.of Employees:** 11 - 20
Product Groups: 45

Date of Accounts	Oct 11	Oct 10	Oct 09
Working Capital	-80	-52	-105
Fixed Assets	45	45	51
Current Assets	93	95	112

C A L A Group
Adam House 5 Mid New Cultins, Edinburgh, EH11 4DU
Tel: 0131-535 5200 **Fax:** 0131-535 5200
E-mail: info@cala.co.uk
Website: http://www.cala.co.uk
Bank(s): Clydesdale Bank PLC
Directors: C. Turnbull (Pers), A. Murray (Tech Serv), M. Sibbald (Co Sec), A. Brown (Grp Chief Exec)
Managers: J. Reid, C. Hart (Sales & Mktg Mg)
Ultimate Holding Company: CALA GROUP LIMITED
Immediate Holding Company: CALA 1999 LIMITED
Registration no: SC194813 **VAT No.:** GB 356 0493 50
Date established: 1999 **Turnover:** £125m - £250m
No.of Employees: 51 - 100 **Product Groups:** 52, 80

Date of Accounts	Jun 12	Jun 11	Jun 10
Pre Tax Profit/Loss	-500	-250	135m
Working Capital	32m	32m	32m
Fixed Assets	151m	151m	151m
Current Assets	32m	32m	32m

C A Magazine (The Institute of Chartered Accountants of Scotland)
C A House 21 Haymarket Yards, Edinburgh, EH12 5BH
Tel: 0131-343 7500 **Fax:** 0131-343 7505
E-mail: i.marion@icas.org.uk
Website: http://www.icas.org.uk
Directors: I. Marion (Grp Chief Exec)
Immediate Holding Company: THE FOUNDATION FOR ACCOUNTANCY AND FINANCIAL MANAGEMENT
Registration no: SC145100 **Date established:** 1993
No.of Employees: 11 - 20 **Product Groups:** 28

Caiyside Imaging Ltd
Suite 2 7 Washington Lane, Edinburgh, EH11 2HA
Tel: 0131-337 9996 **Fax:** 0870-051 7085
E-mail: info@caiysideimaging.co.uk
Website: http://www.caiysideimaging.co.uk
Directors: R. Mciver (MD)
Immediate Holding Company: CAIYSIDE IMAGING LTD.
Registration no: SC330907 **Date established:** 2007
Turnover: Up to £250,000 **No.of Employees:** 1 - 10 **Product Groups:** 37

Date of Accounts	Sep 11	Sep 10	Sep 09
Working Capital	52	44	48
Fixed Assets	6	6	7
Current Assets	72	54	58

Christie
17 Salamander Yards, Edinburgh, EH6 7HB
Tel: 0131-554 6116 **Fax:** 0131-553 7914
E-mail: sales@gchristies.co.uk
Website: http://www.gchristies.co.uk
Directors: B. Christie (Ptnr)
Ultimate Holding Company: GEORGE CHRISTIE & SONS (LEITH) LIMITED
Immediate Holding Company: GEORGE CHRISTIE & SONS (LEITH) LIMITED
Registration no: SC031856 **VAT No.:** GB 268 3502 49
Date established: 1956 **Turnover:** £500,000 - £1m
No.of Employees: 1 - 10 **Product Groups:** 35, 36, 48

Date of Accounts	Mar 11	Mar 10	Mar 09
Working Capital	283	257	221
Fixed Assets	519	532	536
Current Assets	382	345	348

Chubb Security Ltd
38 South Gyle Crescent, Edinburgh, EH12 9EB
Tel: 0131-317 4800 **Fax:** 0131-317 4829
E-mail: edinburgh.security@chubb.co.uk
Website: http://www.chubbsecurity.co.uk
Bank(s): National Westminster Bank Plc
Managers: N. Blythe (Mgr), J. Stewart (District Mgr), H. Wilson (District Mgr)
Immediate Holding Company: INITIAL ELECTRONIC SECURITY SYSTEMS LTD
Registration no: 00715168 **VAT No.:** GB 174 6053 62
Turnover: £20m - £50m **No.of Employees:** 11 - 20 **Product Groups:** 40

Circlit International Ltd
83 Princes Street, Edinburgh, EH2 2ER
Tel: 08702-406303
Managers: B. Steven (Mgr)
Immediate Holding Company: CORPORATE CAR CLUB LIMITED
Date established: 2011 **No.of Employees:** 1 - 10 **Product Groups:** 37, 67

Date of Accounts	May 12	May 11
Working Capital	1	N/A
Fixed Assets	N/A	1
Current Assets	19	8

City Sprint
Unit 11c West Craigs Industrial Estate Turnhouse Road, Edinburgh, EH12 0BD
Tel: 0131-453 1800 **Fax:** 0131-339 7942
E-mail: edinburgh@citysprint.co.uk
Website: http://www.citysprint.co.uk
Managers: K. Angus (Mgr)
Immediate Holding Company: CITYSPRINT (UK) LIMITED
Registration no: 04327611 **Date established:** 2001
No.of Employees: 1 - 10 **Product Groups:** 79

Clustan Ltd
16 Kingsburgh Road, Edinburgh, EH12 6DZ
Tel: 0131-337 1448
E-mail: sales@clustan.com
Website: http://www.clustan.com
Directors: D. Wishart (Fin), D. Wishart (MD)
Immediate Holding Company: CLUSTAN LIMITED
Registration no: SC080676 **Date established:** 1982
Turnover: Up to £250,000 **No.of Employees:** 1 - 10 **Product Groups:** 44

Date of Accounts	Dec 11	Dec 10	Dec 09
Working Capital	-11	50	59
Fixed Assets	417	266	268
Current Assets	17	67	63

Companies House
37 Castle Terrace, Edinburgh, EH1 2EB
Tel: 08703-333636 **Fax:** 0131-535 5820
E-mail: sales@companieshouse.gov.uk
Website: http://www.companieshouse.gov.uk
Managers: C. Clancy (Mgr), J. Henderson
Registration no: SC292432 **Date established:** 2005
No.of Employees: 1 - 10 **Product Groups:** 81, 82

Cookerclean Cleaning Services
82 Bughtlin Park, Edinburgh, EH12 8UT
Tel: 0800-061 2727
E-mail: enquiries@cookerclean.co.uk
Website: http://www.cookerclean.co.uk
Directors: B. Donnelly (Prop)
Immediate Holding Company: COOKER CLEAN LTD
Registration no: SC213739 **Date established:** 2000
No.of Employees: 1 - 10 **Product Groups:** 40, 42, 48, 67

Cooper-Walker Microelectronics Ltd
3 Arthur Street Lane, Edinburgh, EH6 5DR
Tel: 0131-555 0801 **Fax:** 01546-606173
E-mail: sales@cwmicro.com
Website: http://www.cwmicro.com
Directors: D. Murray (Fin), J. Walker (MD)
Immediate Holding Company: COOPER-WALKER MICROELECTRONICS LIMITED
Registration no: SC079033 **Date established:** 1982
No.of Employees: 1 - 10 **Product Groups:** 35, 38, 46

Date of Accounts	Oct 11	Oct 10	Oct 09
Working Capital	1	-0	2
Fixed Assets	3	3	4
Current Assets	2	2	3

The Coverdale Organisation Ltd
Westpoint 4 Redheughs Rigg, Edinburgh, EH12 9DQ
Tel: 0131-338 6126 **Fax:** 0131-338 6700
E-mail: info@coverdale.co.uk
Website: http://www.coverdale.com
Directors: M. De Luca (MD)
Managers: P. North (I.T. Exec), J. Grey (Mktg Serv Mgr)
Registration no: 00927686 **VAT No.:** GB 238 7005 64
Turnover: £2m - £5m **No.of Employees:** 1 - 10 **Product Groups:** 80, 86

Date of Accounts	Sep 08	Sep 07	Sep 06
Sales Turnover	1445	1042	1107
Pre Tax Profit/Loss	260	-47	122
Working Capital	720	602	728
Fixed Assets	64	45	215
Current Assets	941	732	932
Current Liabilities	221	131	204
Total Share Capital	272	272	272
ROCE% (Return on Capital Employed)	33.1	-7.2	13.0
ROT% (Return on Turnover)	18.0	-4.5	11.1

D F Wishart Holdings Ltd
PO Box 208 St Clair Street, Edinburgh, EH6 8LJ
Tel: 0131-554 4393 **Fax:** 0131-553 7242
E-mail: info@wishart.co.uk
Website: http://www.wishart.co.uk
Directors: N. Wishart (Dir), B. Wishart (Ch), R. Law (Co Sec), K. Patterson-Brown (MD), G. Wishart (MD)
Managers: T. Miller (Purch Mgr), I. Tunniclisse (I.T. Exec), G. Gardner (Mktg Serv Mgr)
Immediate Holding Company: D.F. WISHART (HOLDINGS) LIMITED
Registration no: SC015030 **Date established:** 1928
Turnover: £5m - £10m **No.of Employees:** 1 - 10 **Product Groups:** 35, 66

Date of Accounts	Dec 07	Dec 06
Pre Tax Profit/Loss	1159	251
Working Capital	3600	2558
Fixed Assets	393	341
Current Assets	4924	4266
Current Liabilities	1323	1708
ROCE% (Return on Capital Employed)	29.0	8.6

D W F Biggart Baillie
96 Fountainbridge, Edinburgh, EH3 9QA
Tel: 0131-226 5541 **Fax:** 0131-226 2278
E-mail: sales@biggartbaillie.co.uk
Website: http://www.dwf.co.uk
Bank(s): Royal Bank of Scotland, Edinburgh
Directors: A. Davidson (Fin), A. Peacock (Snr Part), A. Wilson (Pers)
Managers: A. Mackenzie (Tech Serv Mgr), R. McInally (Develop Mgr), S. Findlay (Personnel)
Immediate Holding Company: THE VIRTUAL HAMILTON PALACE TRUST
Registration no: SO301366 **Date established:** 2003
Turnover: £5m - £10m **No.of Employees:** 51 - 100 **Product Groups:** 80

Date of Accounts	Jul 11	Jul 10	Jul 09
Sales Turnover	3	3	4
Pre Tax Profit/Loss	-1	1	-2
Working Capital	1	2	1
Current Assets	1	2	1
Current Liabilities	N/A	N/A	1

Daisy Hygiene Supplies Ltd
9 King's Haugh Peffermill Road, Edinburgh, EH16 5UY
Tel: 0800-056 3636 **Fax:** 0800-073 1333
E-mail: info@daisydirect.co.uk
Website: http://www.daisyhygienesupplies.co.uk
Directors: R. Green (Dir)
Ultimate Holding Company: SPOTLESS COMMERCIAL CLEANING LIMITED
Immediate Holding Company: DAISY HYGIENE SUPPLIES LIMITED
Registration no: SC289455 **Date established:** 2005
No.of Employees: 11 - 20 **Product Groups:** 66

Date of Accounts	Sep 11	Sep 10	Sep 09
Working Capital	-120	-5	N/A
Fixed Assets	16	25	25
Current Assets	359	247	238

Stephen G Dalton
52-66 Salamander Street Leith, Edinburgh, EH6 7LA
Tel: 0131-555 4111 **Fax:** 0131-555 3900
E-mail: daltonforscrap@aoll.com
Website: http://www.daltonsforscrap.co.uk
Directors: D. Walters (Fin), S. Dalton (Dir)
Immediate Holding Company: DALTON GROUP LIMITED
Registration no: SC088385 **Date established:** 1984
Turnover: £5m - £10m **No.of Employees:** 1 - 10 **Product Groups:** 51, 66, 72

Diageo Distilling Ltd
5 Lochside Way, Edinburgh, EH12 9DT
Tel: 0131-519 2000 **Fax:** 01631-572006
Website: http://www.diageo.com
Bank(s): Bank of America
Directors: S. Loramier (Fin), B. Donaughy (MD)
Ultimate Holding Company: DIAGEO PLC
Immediate Holding Company: DIAGEO DISTILLING LIMITED
Registration no: SC009211 **VAT No.:** GB 217 1127 03
Date established: 2014 **Turnover:** £500m - £1,000m
No.of Employees: 101 - 250 **Product Groups:** 21

Date of Accounts	Jun 11	Jun 10	Jun 09
Sales Turnover	256m	260m	277m
Pre Tax Profit/Loss	-36m	-21m	18m
Working Capital	454m	119m	137m
Fixed Assets	N/A	387m	386m
Current Assets	454m	240m	190m
Current Liabilities	N/A	14m	5m

Diamond Gleam
45 Frederick Street, Edinburgh, EH2 1EP
Tel: 0131-337 2680 **Fax:** 0131-225 3402
E-mail: diamondgleam@btinternet.com
Website: http://www.diamondgleam.co.uk
Directors: R. Dodds (Prop)
Ultimate Holding Company: N BROWN GROUP PLC
Immediate Holding Company: HEATHER VALLEY (WOOLLENS) LIMITED
Registration no: SC051344 **Date established:** 1961
Turnover: Up to £250,000 **No.of Employees:** 1 - 10 **Product Groups:** 46, 48

Date of Accounts	Mar 11	Mar 10	Mar 09
Sales Turnover	59	59	N/A
Pre Tax Profit/Loss	25	31	N/A
Working Capital	-965	-995	-10
Fixed Assets	980	984	991
Current Assets	3	33	30
Current Liabilities	8	3	N/A

Dla Piper UK Llp
Rutland Building Rutland Square, Edinburgh, EH1 2AA
Tel: 08700-111111 **Fax:** 0131-242 5555
E-mail: info@dlapiper.com
Website: http://www.dlapiper.com
Managers: D. Muir, M. Fitzgerald (Sales & Mktg Mg), T. Stewart (Personnel), D. Bradley
Ultimate Holding Company: DLA PIPER INTERNATIONAL LLP
Immediate Holding Company: DLA PIPER UK MANAGEMENT SERVICES LIMITED
Registration no: 02894382 **Date established:** 1994
Turnover: £75m - £125m **No.of Employees:** 101 - 250
Product Groups: 80

Date of Accounts	Apr 11	Apr 10	Apr 09
Sales Turnover	108m	107m	121m
Pre Tax Profit/Loss	14	19	15
Working Capital	13	33	69
Current Assets	8m	9m	10m
Current Liabilities	8m	9m	9m

Dolphin Lifts Scotland
4 Damhead Lothianburn, Edinburgh, EH10 7DZ
Tel: 0131-445 5574 **Fax:** 0131-445 5644
E-mail: ianherdis@dolphinliftsscotland.wandaoo.co.uk
Directors: I. Herdis (Prop)
Date established: 1998 **No.of Employees:** 1 - 10 **Product Groups:** 35, 39, 45

Dorval Lighting Ltd
36-36c Newhaven Road Elizafield, Edinburgh, EH6 5PY
Tel: 0131-554 8950 **Fax:** 0131-553 7417
E-mail: enquiries@dorvallighting.co.uk
Directors: V. Green (Dir)
Immediate Holding Company: DORVAL LIGHTING LIMITED
Registration no: SC062953 **Date established:** 1977
No.of Employees: 1 - 10 **Product Groups:** 37, 67

Date of Accounts	Dec 11	Dec 10	Dec 09
Working Capital	76	74	52
Fixed Assets	37	4	12
Current Assets	168	156	119

Dunedin Capital Partners Ltd
Saltire Court 20 Castle Terrace, Edinburgh, EH1 2EN
Tel: 0131-225 6699 **Fax:** 0131-718 2300
E-mail: info@dunedin.com
Website: http://www.dunedin.com
Directors: R. Marshall (Grp Chief Exec)
Managers: K. Sanders (Sales Admin), C. McCorquodale (Sales & Mktg Mg)
Ultimate Holding Company: DUNEDIN CAPITAL GROUP LIMITED
Immediate Holding Company: DUNEDIN CAPITAL PARTNERS LIMITED
Registration no: SC082727 **Date established:** 1983
Turnover: £5m - £10m **No.of Employees:** 11 - 20 **Product Groups:** 82

Date of Accounts	Feb 08	Feb 11	Feb 10
Sales Turnover	9m	8m	7m
Pre Tax Profit/Loss	2m	725	1m
Working Capital	2m	2m	2m
Fixed Assets	114	218	84
Current Assets	6m	5m	4m
Current Liabilities	4m	3m	2m

Dunira Strategy Ltd
33 West Preston Street, Edinburgh, EH8 9PY
Tel: 08453-708076 **Fax:** 0845-370 8188
E-mail: info@dunira.com
Website: http://www.dunira.com
Directors: B. Carey (MD)
Immediate Holding Company: DUNIRA LIMITED
Registration no: SC229031 **Date established:** 2002
Turnover: Up to £250,000 **No.of Employees:** 1 - 10 **Product Groups:** 61, 80, 81, 84, 85, 86

Date of Accounts	Mar 11	Mar 10	Mar 09
Working Capital	-19	-2	-6
Fixed Assets	2	2	2
Current Assets	34	45	29

Edinburgh University Press Ltd
22 George Square, Edinburgh, EH8 9LF
Tel: 0131-650 4218 **Fax:** 0131-662 0053
E-mail: marketing@eup.ed.ac.uk
Website: http://www.euppublishing.com
Bank(s): The Royal Bank of Scotland
Directors: T. Wright (MD)
Managers: M. McElligott (Mgr)
Immediate Holding Company: EDINBURGH UNIVERSITY PRESS LIMITED
Registration no: SC139240 **VAT No.:** GB 593 0701 43
Date established: 1992 **Turnover:** £1m - £2m **No.of Employees:** 21 - 50
Product Groups: 28

Date of Accounts	Jul 08	Jul 07	Jul 06
Sales Turnover	50	2118	1922
Pre Tax Profit/Loss	10	7	-3
Working Capital	696	723	770
Fixed Assets	33	23	19
Current Assets	1364	1485	1557
Current Liabilities	668	762	788
ROCE% (Return on Capital Employed)	1.3	1.0	-0.4
ROT% (Return on Turnover)	19.4	0.4	-0.2

Edmundson Electrical Ltd
6 Cutlins Road, Edinburgh, EH11 4DG
Tel: 0131-453 2311 **Fax:** 0131-442 1590
E-mail: edinburgh.o72@eel.co.uk
Website: http://www.edmundson-electrical.co.uk/

see next page

Edmundson Electrical Ltd - Cont'd

Managers: B. Baxter (District Mgr)
Ultimate Holding Company: BLACKFRIARS CORP (USA)
Immediate Holding Company: EDMUNDSON ELECTRICAL LIMITED
Registration no: 02667012 **Date established:** 1991
No.of Employees: 11 - 20 **Product Groups:** 77

Date of Accounts	Dec 11	Dec 10	Dec 09
Sales Turnover	1023m	852m	788m
Pre Tax Profit/Loss	57m	53m	45m
Working Capital	256m	225m	184m
Fixed Assets	17m	3m	4m
Current Assets	439m	358m	298m
Current Liabilities	59m	38m	37m

Elsevier Limited

20-22 East London Street, Edinburgh, EH7 4BQ
Tel: 0131-524 1700 **Fax:** 0131-524 1800
Website: http://www.elsevier.com
Bank(s): National Westminster Bank Plc
Directors: A. Stevenson (MD)
Ultimate Holding Company: Reed Elsevier
Registration no: 01982084 **VAT No.:** GB 278 5371 21
Turnover: £10m - £20m **No.of Employees:** 51 - 100 **Product Groups:** 28

Evans Halshaw Edinburgh

25 Baileyfield Road, Edinburgh, EH15 1BT
Tel: 0131-669 6261 **Fax:** 0131-669 7018
Website: http://www.evanshalshaw.com
Managers: D. Gibb
Ultimate Holding Company: PENDRAGON PLC
Immediate Holding Company: PENDRAGON MOTOR GROUP LTD
Registration no: 01359849 **VAT No.:** GB 635 0104 83
Turnover: £2m - £5m **No.of Employees:** 21 - 50 **Product Groups:** 68

Event Video Services

84 The Loan Loanhead, Edinburgh, EH20 9AQ
Tel: 0131-440 3454
E-mail: mail@eventvideoservices.tv
Website: http://www.eventvideoservices.tv
Registration no: SC341932 **Date established:** 2007
No.of Employees: 1 - 10 **Product Groups:** 44, 79, 89

F & C Asset Management plc

80 George Street, Edinburgh, EH2 3BU
Tel: 0131-718 1000 **Fax:** 0131-225 2375
Website: http://www.fandc.com
Directors: S. Smith (Pers), M. Tomkin (Co Sec), D. Logan (Fin)
Managers: D. O'Niell, J. Whyte (Tech Serv Mgr)
Ultimate Holding Company: F&C ASSET MANAGEMENT PLC
Immediate Holding Company: F&C ASSET MANAGEMENT PLC
Registration no: SC073508 **Date established:** 1980
Turnover: £250m - £500m **No.of Employees:** 51 - 100
Product Groups: 82

Date of Accounts	Dec 11	Dec 10	Dec 09
Sales Turnover	283m	260m	242m
Pre Tax Profit/Loss	-2m	-19m	9m
Working Capital	166m	171m	188m
Fixed Assets	786m	839m	856m
Current Assets	769m	919m	951m
Current Liabilities	600m	744m	759m

Farnbeck Ltd

32 Swanfield, Edinburgh, EH6 5RX
Tel: 0131-553 5353 **Fax:** 0131-553 3979
E-mail: dm001@post.almac.co.uk
Website: http://www.almac.co.uk/farnbeck
Bank(s): Clydesdale Bank PLC
Directors: D. Main (MD)
Immediate Holding Company: FARNBECK LIMITED
Registration no: SC230635 **VAT No.:** GB 356 3204 68
Date established: 2002 **Turnover:** £1m - £2m **No.of Employees:** 11 - 20
Product Groups: 28, 29, 44

Date of Accounts	Sep 11	Sep 10	Sep 09
Working Capital	434	442	470
Fixed Assets	149	164	180
Current Assets	883	845	878

Ferrier Pumps Ltd

15 Burlington Street, Edinburgh, EH6 5JL
Tel: 0131-553 4001 **Fax:** 0131-553 1272
E-mail: edinburgh@ferrierpumps.co.uk
Website: http://www.ferrierpumps.co.uk
Directors: B. Ferrier (MD), D. Calendar (Fin)
Ultimate Holding Company: BRIAN FERRIER (HOLDINGS) LIMITED
Immediate Holding Company: FERRIER PUMPS LIMITED
Registration no: SC097840 **VAT No.:** GB 345 4857 31
Date established: 1986 **Turnover:** £5m - £10m **No.of Employees:** 21 - 50
Product Groups: 67, 83

Date of Accounts	Apr 11	Apr 10	Apr 09
Working Capital	1m	1m	931
Fixed Assets	108	83	120
Current Assets	2m	2m	2m

First State Investments

23 St Andrew Square, Edinburgh, EH2 1BB
Tel: 0131-473 2200 **Fax:** 0131-473 2516
E-mail: enquiries@firststate.co.uk
Website: http://www.firststate.co.uk
Directors: C. Crawford (Mkt Research), G. Withers (Grp Chief Exec)
Managers: G. Ferguson, J. Breyley, H. Wells (Personnel), S. Dunne (Mktg Serv Mgr)
Ultimate Holding Company: SI HOLDINGS LIMITED
Immediate Holding Company: FIRST STATE INVESTMENTS INTERNATIONAL LIMITED
Registration no: SC079063 **Date established:** 1982
Turnover: £20m - £50m **No.of Employees:** 101 - 250 **Product Groups:** 82

Date of Accounts	Jun 12	Jun 11	Jun 10
Sales Turnover	40m	36m	27m
Pre Tax Profit/Loss	10m	8m	10m
Working Capital	24m	21m	18m
Current Assets	35m	37m	24m
Current Liabilities	3m	2m	3m

Forth Ports plc (Leith & Granton Office Dock)

1 Prince of Wales Dock Leith Docks, Edinburgh, EH6 7DX
Tel: 0131-555 8700 **Fax:** 0131-553 7462
E-mail: charles.hammond@forthports.co.uk
Website: http://www.forthports.co.uk
Bank(s): Bank of Scotland
Directors: M. McNeill (Co Sec), C. Hammond (Grp Chief Exec), T. Smith (Property), W. Murray (Fin)
Managers: B. Devlin (I.T. Exec), C. Miller (Mktg Serv Mgr), L. Marshall (Personnel), C. Hammond
Immediate Holding Company: FORTH PORTS LIMITED
Registration no: SC134741 **VAT No.:** GB 592 9785 69
Date established: 1991 **Turnover:** £125m - £250m
No.of Employees: 21 - 50 **Product Groups:** 71

Franklin Templeton Investments

5 Morrison Street, Edinburgh, EH3 8BH
Tel: 0131-242 4000 **Fax:** 0131-242 4533
Website: http://www.franklintempleton.co.uk
Directors: D. Smart (Reg MD)
Managers: C. Everett (Tech Serv Mgr), J. White (Sales Admin), K. Cooy (Personnel)
Immediate Holding Company: TEMPLETON EMERGING MARKETS INVESTMENT TRUST PUBLIC LIMITED COMPANY
Registration no: SC118022 **Date established:** 1989
No.of Employees: 251 - 500 **Product Groups:** 82

Date of Accounts	Mar 12	Mar 11	Mar 10
Sales Turnover	58m	N/A	30m
Pre Tax Profit/Loss	31m	24m	11m
Working Capital	11m	14m	12m
Fixed Assets	2088m	2355m	2034m
Current Assets	13m	17m	15m
Current Liabilities	2m	3m	3m

Fushi

34 St. Andrew Square, Edinburgh, EH2 2AD
Tel: 0131-524 8335
Website: http://www.fushi.co.uk
Managers: D. Campbell (Mgr)
No.of Employees: 1 - 10 **Product Groups:** 32, 63

Graham

96 Temple Park Crescent, Edinburgh, EH11 1HZ
Tel: 0131-228 2345 **Fax:** 0131-228 5405
E-mail: mikedick@graham-group.co.uk
Website: http://www.graham-group.co.uk
Managers: G. Smith (Mgr)
Ultimate Holding Company: SAINT GOBAIN
Registration no: 00348407 **VAT No.:** GB 497 7184 83
Turnover: £2m - £5m **No.of Employees:** 1 - 10 **Product Groups:** 37, 52

James Gray & Son Ltd

19 West Bowling Green Street, Edinburgh, EH6 5PQ
Tel: 0131-554 1573 **Fax:** 0131-220 4210
E-mail: mail@graysofedinburgh.co.uk
Website: http://www.graysofedinburgh.co.uk
Directors: B. Smellie (MD), J. Smellie (Fin)
Managers: L. Leask (Accounts)
Immediate Holding Company: JAMES GRAY (HOLDINGS) LIMITED
Registration no: SC110372 **VAT No.:** GB 268 6531 27
Date established: 1988 **Turnover:** £1m - £2m **No.of Employees:** 11 - 20
Product Groups: 52

Date of Accounts	Jan 08
Sales Turnover	1743
Pre Tax Profit/Loss	-72
Working Capital	180
Fixed Assets	185
Current Assets	409
Current Liabilities	229
Total Share Capital	50
ROCE% (Return on Capital Employed)	-19.6

Guardian Financial Services

Edinburgh Park 1 Lochside Crescent, Edinburgh, EH12 9SE
Tel: 01253-733151 **Fax:** 08706-090669
E-mail: otto.thoresen@gre-group.e-mail.com
Website: http://www.aegon.co.uk
Bank(s): Barclays
Directors: O. Thoresen (Grp Chief Exec)
Managers: A. Marchant (Mktg Serv Mgr), P. Chong (Tech Serv Mgr), R. McEwan (Fin Mgr), G. Scott (Personnel)
Ultimate Holding Company: AEGON NV (NETHERLANDS)
Immediate Holding Company: GUARDIAN PENSIONS MANAGEMENT LIMITED
Registration no: 00985480 **Date established:** 1970
Turnover: £10m - £20m **No.of Employees:** 501 - 1000
Product Groups: 82

Date of Accounts	Dec 09	Dec 08	Dec 07
Sales Turnover	18m	27m	N/A
Pre Tax Profit/Loss	7m	12m	11m
Working Capital	-257m	-260m	N/A
Fixed Assets	364m	356m	87m
Current Assets	21m	12m	388m
Current Liabilities	259m	249m	39m

Hanson Premix (Hanson Aggregates)

14 West Shore Road, Edinburgh, EH5 1QG
Tel: 01786-450200 **Fax:** 0845-4510772
Website: http://www.hanson.biz
Directors: P. O'shea (Dir)
Managers: M. Colligan (Chief Mgr)
Ultimate Holding Company: Pioneer International Ltd
Immediate Holding Company: Pioneer Concrete
Registration no: SC329402 **Date established:** 2007
Turnover: £500,000 - £1m **No.of Employees:** 1 - 10 **Product Groups:** 33, 52

Haskoning UK Ltd

10 Bernard Street, Edinburgh, EH6 6PP
Tel: 0131-561 2270 **Fax:** 0131-555 0502
E-mail: j.freer@royalhaskoning.com
Website: http://www.royalhaskoning.com
Directors: J. Freer (Dir)
Ultimate Holding Company: KONINKLIJKE HASKONING GROEP BV (NETHERLANDS)
Immediate Holding Company: HASKONING UK LIMITED
Registration no: 01336844 **Date established:** 1977 **Turnover:** £1m - £2m
No.of Employees: 21 - 50 **Product Groups:** 84

Date of Accounts	Dec 11	Dec 10	Dec 09
Sales Turnover	65m	66m	68m
Pre Tax Profit/Loss	5m	2m	2m
Working Capital	14m	11m	10m
Fixed Assets	1m	1m	1m
Current Assets	23m	24m	22m
Current Liabilities	4m	8m	5m

Hastie & Co. Ltd

31 Assembly Street, Edinburgh, EH6 7BQ
Tel: 0131-554 6550 **Fax:** 0131- 5550051
E-mail: sales@hastie.co.uk
Website: http://www.hastie.co.uk
Directors: S. Hastie (MD), C. Swan (Fin)
Ultimate Holding Company: E (EDINBURGH) LTD
Immediate Holding Company: ASLAR GUEST HOUSE LTD
Registration no: SC079345 **VAT No.:** 268 6456 15
Turnover: £500,000 - £1m **No.of Employees:** 1 - 10 **Product Groups:** 48

Date of Accounts	Jun 08	Jun 07	Jun 06
Sales Turnover	N/A	160	336
Pre Tax Profit/Loss	N/A	44	59
Working Capital	-144	-739	4
Fixed Assets	809	999	307
Current Assets	2	22	76
Current Liabilities	146	761	72
Total Share Capital	5	5	5
ROCE% (Return on Capital Employed)		17.0	18.8
ROT% (Return on Turnover)		27.6	17.4

Charles Henshaw & Sons Ltd

Russell Road, Edinburgh, EH11 2LS
Tel: 0131-337 4204 **Fax:** 0131-346 2441
E-mail: tlamb@charles-henshaw.co.uk
Website: http://www.charles-henshaw.com
Bank(s): The Royal Bank of Scotland
Directors: W. Ramage (Fin), K. Ramage (Fin), G. Chung (Sales), T. Lamb (MD)
Managers: W. Oakes (Tech Serv Mgr)
Ultimate Holding Company: MAJOR'S PLACE INDUSTRIES LIMITED
Immediate Holding Company: CHARLES HENSHAW & SONS LIMITED
Registration no: SC021330 **Date established:** 1940
Turnover: £10m - £20m **No.of Employees:** 51 - 100 **Product Groups:** 33, 40

Date of Accounts	Jan 12	Jan 11	Jan 10
Sales Turnover	12m	10m	18m
Pre Tax Profit/Loss	52	509	910
Working Capital	3m	3m	2m
Fixed Assets	2m	1m	1m
Current Assets	5m	4m	6m
Current Liabilities	542	556	2m

Hyder Consulting UK Ltd

9-10 St Andrew Square, Edinburgh, EH2 2AF
Tel: 0131-226 4638 **Fax:** 0131-226 3645
E-mail: john.robertson@hyderconsulting.com
Website: http://www.hyderconsulting.com
Directors: J. Robertson (Tech Serv)
Ultimate Holding Company: HYDER CONSULTING PLC
Immediate Holding Company: HYDER CONSULTING (UK) LIMITED
Registration no: 02212959 **Date established:** 1988
Turnover: £125m - £250m **No.of Employees:** 1 - 10 **Product Groups:** 54, 84

Date of Accounts	Mar 12	Mar 11	Mar 10
Sales Turnover	70m	88m	96m
Pre Tax Profit/Loss	2m	5m	2m
Working Capital	24m	25m	23m
Fixed Assets	7m	8m	10m
Current Assets	41m	49m	45m
Current Liabilities	9m	11m	13m

Ideal Studios

11 Maritime Street, Edinburgh, EH6 6SB
Tel: 0131-2026209
E-mail: info@ideal-studios.co.uk
Website: http://www.ideal-studios.co.uk
Managers: A. Lebik (Mktg Serv Mgr)
Date established: 2010 **Turnover:** **No.of Employees:** 1 - 10
Product Groups: 23, 28, 38, 44, 81

J T Projects Ltd

32 Bellevue Terrace, Edinburgh, EH7 4DS
Tel: 07980-750040
E-mail: info@jtprojects.com
Website: http://www.jtprojects.com
Directors: S. Smith (Fin), J. Taylor (MD)
Immediate Holding Company: JT PROJECTS LIMITED
Registration no: SC251051 **Date established:** 2003
Turnover: Up to £250,000 **No.of Employees:** 1 - 10 **Product Groups:** 44

Date of Accounts	Jun 11	Jun 10	Jun 09
Working Capital	21	37	62
Fixed Assets	1	1	1
Current Assets	36	52	79

Jewson Ltd

153 Slateford Road, Edinburgh, EH14 1NZ
Tel: 0131-443 0122 **Fax:** 0131-455 7726
Website: http://www.jewson.co.uk
Managers: K. Forbes
Ultimate Holding Company: COMPAGNIE DE SAINT GOBAIN (FRANCE)
Immediate Holding Company: JEWSON LIMITED
Registration no: 00348407 **VAT No.:** GB 394 1212 63
Date established: 1939 **Turnover:** £500m - £1,000m
No.of Employees: 1 - 10 **Product Groups:** 25, 66

Date of Accounts	Dec 11	Dec 10	Dec 09
Sales Turnover	1606m	1547m	1485m
Pre Tax Profit/Loss	18m	100m	45m
Working Capital	-345m	-250m	-349m
Fixed Assets	496m	387m	461m
Current Assets	657m	1005m	1320m
Current Liabilities	66m	120m	64m

John Martin Group

23 Seafield Road East, Edinburgh, EH15 1ED
Tel: 0131-468 7326 **Fax:** 0131-442 3636
E-mail: postmaster@jmgroup.co.uk
Website: http://www.dealer.citroen.co.uk
Directors: P. Sweeney (Co Sec), V. Martin (Dir)
Ultimate Holding Company: JOHN MARTIN HOLDINGS LIMITED
Immediate Holding Company: JOHN MARTIN GROUP LIMITED
Registration no: SC033069 **VAT No.:** GB 271 8205 65
Date established: 1958 **Turnover:** £75m - £125m
No.of Employees: 501 - 1000 **Product Groups:** 68

Date of Accounts	Dec 11	Dec 10	Dec 09
Sales Turnover	65m	124m	147m
Pre Tax Profit/Loss	-408	654	-728

Working Capital	-6m	1m	-194
Fixed Assets	3m	1m	1m
Current Assets	14m	16m	27m
Current Liabilities	3m	3m	4m

Johnston Press

108 Holyrood Road, Edinburgh, EH8 8AS
Tel: 0131-225 3361 **Fax:** 0131-225 4580
E-mail: enquiries@johnstonpress.co.uk
Website: http://www.johnstonpress.co.uk
Bank(s): The Royal Bank of Scotland
Directors: P. Mccall (Co Sec), P. Cooper (Co Sec), R. Davies (Tech Serv), G. Murray (Fin), M. Vickers (Pers)
Managers: M. Knight (Purch Mgr)
Immediate Holding Company: JOHNSTON PRESS PLC
Registration no: SC015382 **Date established:** 2028
Turnover: £250m - £500m **No.of Employees:** 251 - 500
Product Groups: 28

Date of Accounts	Dec 11	Dec 08	Jan 10
Sales Turnover	374m	532m	428m
Pre Tax Profit/Loss	-144m	-429m	-114m
Working Capital	-341m	8m	-41m
Fixed Assets	915m	1358m	1160m
Current Assets	82m	176m	104m
Current Liabilities	37m	111m	99m

Jones Lang Lasalle

1-7 Conference Square, Edinburgh, EH3 8LL
Tel: 0131-225 8344 **Fax:** 0131-225 2147
E-mail: alastair.humphery@eu.jll.com
Website: http://www.joneslanglasalle.com
Managers: A. Humphery
Ultimate Holding Company: WARWICK STREET (KSI) LLP
Immediate Holding Company: WARWICK STREET (KS) LLP
Registration no: OC311501 **Date established:** 2005
Turnover: £50m - £75m **No.of Employees:** 51 - 100 **Product Groups:** 80, 82

Date of Accounts	Dec 07	Dec 06	Dec 05
Sales Turnover	162070	134910	109950
Pre Tax Profit/Loss	13130	-2910	-1910
Working Capital	-59660	-51120	-51550
Fixed Assets	291910	239670	222060
Current Assets	146420	140430	131420
Current Liabilities	206080	191550	182970
Total Share Capital	121090	121090	121090
ROCE% (Return on Capital Employed)	5.7	-1.5	-1.1
ROT% (Return on Turnover)	8.1	-2.2	-1.7

K S L D

4 Baltic Street, Edinburgh, EH6 7BW
Tel: 0131-555 5553 **Fax:** 0131-555 5559
E-mail: office@ksld.com
Website: http://www.ksld.com
Directors: K. Shaw (MD)
Immediate Holding Company: ELUCIDATION (2000) LIMITED
Registration no: SC213106 **Date established:** 2000
No.of Employees: 1 - 10 **Product Groups:** 37, 52, 84

Date of Accounts	Jan 12	Jan 11	Jan 10
Working Capital	-1	10	38
Fixed Assets	3	5	5
Current Assets	53	76	118

Knowledge Partnership

Catchpell House Business Centre 5 Carpet Lane, Edinburgh, EH6 6SS
Tel: 0131-553 9376 **Fax:** 0131-467 0099
E-mail: alan@kpartners.co.uk
Website: http://www.kpartners.co.uk
Directors: A. Kennedy (MD)
Turnover: Up to £250,000 **No.of Employees:** 1 - 10 **Product Groups:** 80

Lambert Smith Hampton

912 George Street, Edinburgh, EH2 3ES
Tel: 0131-226 0333 **Fax:** 0131-226 0321
Website: http://www.lsh.co.uk
Directors: D. Smith (Dir)
Ultimate Holding Company: LAMBERT SMITH HAMPTON HOLDINGS LTD
Immediate Holding Company: LAMBERT SMITH HAMPTON
Registration no: NF002871 **Date established:** 1990
Turnover: £250,000 - £500,000 **No.of Employees:** 1 - 10
Product Groups: 80, 82

Len Lothian U Store

11 Bankhead Broadway, Edinburgh, EH11 4DB
Tel: 0131-538 8200 **Fax:** 0131-538 8210
E-mail: info@lenlothain.com
Website: http://www.lenlothian.com
Managers: G. Cameron (Mgr)
Immediate Holding Company: NETWORK DESIGN & SUPPORT LIMITED
Registration no: SC270713 **Date established:** 2004 **Turnover:** £1m - £2m
No.of Employees: 1 - 10 **Product Groups:** 77

Date of Accounts	Oct 11	Oct 10	Oct 09
Working Capital	155	143	108
Fixed Assets	14	13	10
Current Assets	576	832	318

Live Systems

6 North Leith Sands, Edinburgh, EH6 4ER
Tel: 0131-555 5200 **Fax:** 08704-580615
E-mail: hire@livesystems.co.uk
Website: http://www.livesystems.co.uk
Directors: S. Robb (Prop)
Immediate Holding Company: LIVE SYSTEMS LTD.
Registration no: SC208647 **Date established:** 2000
No.of Employees: 1 - 10 **Product Groups:** 37, 83

Date of Accounts	Jun 11	Jun 10	Jun 09
Working Capital	-26	-27	-53
Fixed Assets	128	121	124
Current Assets	31	45	13

Lothian Appliances

1 Brunton Terrace, Edinburgh, EH7 5EH
Tel: 0131-652 2576
Directors: S. Rushbury (Prop)
Date established: 1994 **No.of Employees:** 1 - 10 **Product Groups:** 36, 40

Lothian Buses plc

55 Annandale Street, Edinburgh, EH7 4AZ
Tel: 0131-554 4494 **Fax:** 0131-554 3942
E-mail: mail@lothianbuses.co.uk
Website: http://www.lothianbuses.co.uk
Directors: I. Craig (MD), N. Strachan (Fin)
Immediate Holding Company: LOTHIAN BUSES PLC
Registration no: SC096849 **VAT No.:** GB 446 3555 38
Date established: 1986 **Turnover:** £75m - £125m
No.of Employees: 1501 & over **Product Groups:** 72

Date of Accounts	Dec 11	Dec 10	Dec 09
Sales Turnover	117m	113m	112m
Pre Tax Profit/Loss	10m	30m	8m
Working Capital	-9m	-6m	-12m
Fixed Assets	91m	80m	84m
Current Assets	12m	15m	10m
Current Liabilities	13m	14m	14m

LVR business to business Ltd

111 George Street, Edinburgh, EH2 4JN
Tel: 0131-208 1651
E-mail: enquiries@lvr-uk.com
Website: http://www.lvr-uk.com
Directors: L. van Rhyn (Dir)
Registration no: SC366592 **Date established:** 2005
No.of Employees: 1 - 10 **Product Groups:** 61, 81

The M A D Virtual Assistant

23 Corstorphine Hill Road, Edinburgh, EH12 6LQ
Tel: 0131-629 5117
E-mail: twmacgregor@yahoo.co.uk
Website: http://www.themadvirtualassistant.co.uk
Directors: T. Macgregor (Prop)
Date established: 2011 **Turnover:** **No.of Employees:** 1 - 10
Product Groups: 80

M & S Fabrication

1 Corunna Place, Edinburgh, EH6 5JG
Tel: 0131-553 7134 **Fax:** 0131-554 4171
Directors: M. Buchanan (Prop)
Date established: 2004 **No.of Employees:** 1 - 10 **Product Groups:** 35

Macfarlan Smith Ltd

Wheatfield Road, Edinburgh, EH11 2QA
Tel: 0131-337 2434 **Fax:** 0131-337 9813
E-mail: simon@macsmith.com
Website: http://www.macsmith.com
Bank(s): Bank of Scotland
Directors: D. Armstrong (Fin), R. Scullion (Sales), S. Farrant (Co Sec)
Managers: D. Boni (Personnel), A. Mcleod (I.T. Exec)
Ultimate Holding Company: JOHNSON MATTHEY PLC
Immediate Holding Company: MACFARLAN SMITH LIMITED
Registration no: SC035640 **VAT No.:** GB 553 5888 04
Date established: 1960 **Turnover:** £75m - £125m
No.of Employees: 251 - 500 **Product Groups:** 31, 42, 61

Date of Accounts	Mar 12	Mar 11	Mar 10
Sales Turnover	98m	96m	88m
Pre Tax Profit/Loss	15m	15m	14m
Working Capital	-79m	-93m	-88m
Fixed Assets	111m	115m	118m
Current Assets	97m	81m	64m
Current Liabilities	4m	15m	10m

Mackenzie Leather Goods

23a Dundas Street, Edinburgh, EH3 6QQ
Tel: 0131-557 6444 **Fax:** 0131-220 0089
E-mail: andrew@mackenziebags.co.uk
Website: http://www.mackenziebags.co.uk
Directors: A. Leggatt (Prop), A. MacKenzie (Dir)
Date established: 1993 **Turnover:** Up to £250,000
No.of Employees: 1 - 10 **Product Groups:** 22, 63

Duncan Mclaren's

29 Bread Street, Edinburgh, EH3 9AL
Tel: 0131-229 7802 **Fax:** 0131-228 8155
Directors: P. Manson (Ptnr)
Date established: 1902 **No.of Employees:** 11 - 20 **Product Groups:** 35, 36

Macroberts Solicitors

30 Semple Street, Edinburgh, EH3 8BL
Tel: 0131-229 5046 **Fax:** 0131-229 0849
E-mail: info@macroberts.co.uk
Website: http://www.macroberts.com
Bank(s): Royal Bank of Scotland
Directors: N. Patterson (Snr Part), C. Turnbull (Snr Part)
Immediate Holding Company: MACROBERTS LLP
Registration no: SO301699 **Date established:** 2008
Turnover: £10m - £20m **No.of Employees:** 51 - 100 **Product Groups:** 80, 82

Date of Accounts	Apr 11	Apr 10	Apr 09
Sales Turnover	18m	20m	20m
Pre Tax Profit/Loss	6m	7m	7m
Working Capital	5m	7m	6m
Fixed Assets	4m	4m	2m
Current Assets	8m	10m	8m
Current Liabilities	2m	2m	1m

Maplin Electronics Ltd

118-126 Dalry Road, Edinburgh, EH11 2EZ
Tel: 08432-277393 **Fax:** 0131-313 1811
E-mail: customercare@maplin.co.uk
Website: http://www.maplin.co.uk
Managers: J. Rigby (Mgr)
Ultimate Holding Company: MONTAGU PRIVATE EQUITY LLP
Immediate Holding Company: MAPLIN ELECTRONICS LIMITED
Registration no: 01264385 **Date established:** 1976
Turnover: £125m - £250m **No.of Employees:** 1 - 10 **Product Groups:** 37, 61

Date of Accounts	Dec 11	Dec 08	Dec 09
Sales Turnover	205m	204m	204m
Pre Tax Profit/Loss	25m	32m	35m
Working Capital	118m	49m	75m
Fixed Assets	27m	28m	28m
Current Assets	207m	108m	142m
Current Liabilities	78m	51m	59m

Martin Currie Investment Management Ltd

Saltire Court 20 Castle Terrace, Edinburgh, EH1 2ES
Tel: 0131-229 5252 **Fax:** 0131-228 5959
E-mail: enquiries@martincurrie.com
Website: http://www.martincurrie.com
Bank(s): Royal Bank of Scotland
Managers: W. Watt
Ultimate Holding Company: MARTIN CURRIE (HOLDINGS) LTD
Immediate Holding Company: SECURITIES TRUST OF SCOTLAND PLC
Registration no: SC283272 **VAT No.:** GB 429 3989 01
Date established: 2005 **Turnover:** £5m - £10m
No.of Employees: 101 - 250 **Product Groups:** 82

Date of Accounts	Mar 12	Mar 11	Mar 10
Sales Turnover	6m	5m	N/A
Pre Tax Profit/Loss	6m	4m	5m
Working Capital	-11m	-14m	-13m
Fixed Assets	131m	131m	124m
Current Assets	718	1m	3m
Current Liabilities	242	848	2m

Matchpoint

16 Walker Street, Edinburgh, EH3 7LP
Tel: 0131-477 7755 **Fax:** 0131-477 7766
E-mail: neil.cunningham@matchpoint.co.uk
Website: http://www.matchpoint.co.uk
Directors: J. Cunningham (Prop)
Ultimate Holding Company: MATCH POINT (HOSPITALITY) LIMITED
Immediate Holding Company: MATCH POINT LIMITED
Registration no: SC153357 **VAT No.:** GB 651 9752 13
Date established: 1994 **Turnover:** £2m - £5m **No.of Employees:** 1 - 10
Product Groups: 81, 87

Date of Accounts	Dec 11	Dec 10	Dec 09
Working Capital	80	21	446
Fixed Assets	N/A	N/A	385
Current Assets	97	572	1m

Maxam

14 Cultins Road, Edinburgh, EH11 4DZ
Tel: 0131-442 4343 **Fax:** 0131-477 2112
E-mail: info@maxam.co.uk
Website: http://www.maxam.co.uk
Directors: J. Edwards (Ptnr)
VAT No.: GB 271 2161 89 **Date established:** 1995
Turnover: £500,000 - £1m **No.of Employees:** 1 - 10 **Product Groups:** 66

Mayburn International Ltd

117 Piersfield Terrace, Edinburgh, EH8 7BS
Tel: 0131-661 0590 **Fax:** 0131-652 1603
Website: http://www.waitrose.com
Directors: J. Walmsley (MD)
Immediate Holding Company: MAYBURN DESIGN LIMITED
Registration no: SC061121 **VAT No.:** GB 272 2080 83
Date established: 1976 **Turnover:** £1m - £2m **No.of Employees:** 1 - 10
Product Groups: 80

Date of Accounts	Dec 11	Dec 10
Working Capital	-26	-38
Fixed Assets	1	N/A
Current Assets	5	7

MDC Learning Systems

Waterside House 46 The Shore, Edinburgh, EH6 6QU
Tel: 0131-553 1126 **Fax:** 0131-553 1223
E-mail: info@mdconline.co.uk
Website: http://www.rigzone.com
Directors: S. Walters (Fin), C. Blaydon (MD)
Immediate Holding Company: Learnpro Ltd
Registration no: SC191241 **No.of Employees:** 1 - 10 **Product Groups:** 81

John Menzies plc

108 Princes Street, Edinburgh, EH2 3AA
Tel: 0131-225 8555 **Fax:** 0131-459 1150
E-mail: paul.dollman@johnmenziesplc.com
Website: http://www.menziesgroup.com
Bank(s): Bank of Scotland, National Westminster,
Directors: P. Dollman (Fin)
Ultimate Holding Company: CHELSEA STORES HOLDINGS LIMITED
Immediate Holding Company: JOHN MENZIES PLC
Registration no: SC034970 **Date established:** 1960
Turnover: Over £1,000m **No.of Employees:** 1501 & over
Product Groups: 64

Date of Accounts	Dec 11	Dec 10	Dec 09
Sales Turnover	1900m	1838m	1726m
Pre Tax Profit/Loss	49m	38m	22m
Working Capital	-21m	-78m	-21m
Fixed Assets	275m	281m	303m
Current Assets	211m	207m	206m
Current Liabilities	119m	167m	100m

Charlie Miller Hairdressing

13 Stafford Street, Edinburgh, EH3 7BR
Tel: 0131-226 5551 **Fax:** 0131-225 4949
Website: http://www.charliemiller.co.uk
Directors: C. Millar (Ptnr)
Immediate Holding Company: CHARLIE MILLER HAIRDRESSING LIMITED
Registration no: SC252444 **Date established:** 2003
No.of Employees: 21 - 50 **Product Groups:** 61

Date of Accounts	Dec 11	Dec 10	Dec 09
Working Capital	-237	-331	-447
Fixed Assets	712	784	850
Current Assets	273	165	296

Minerva Business Systems Ltd

12a South East Cumberland Street Lane, Edinburgh, EH3 6RU
Tel: 08452-450008 **Fax:** 0844-412 8804
E-mail: info@minervabs.net
Website: http://www.minervabs.net
Managers: B. Maxwell
Immediate Holding Company: MINERVA BUSINESS SYSTEMS LTD.
Registration no: SC243836 **Date established:** 2003
No.of Employees: 1 - 10 **Product Groups:** 44

Date of Accounts	Mar 12	Mar 11	Mar 10
Working Capital	45	-1	16
Current Assets	65	17	29

J P Morgan Ltd

3 Lochside View, Edinburgh, EH12 9DH
Tel: 0131-270 4300 **Fax:** 0131-270 4301
Website: http://www.jpmorganchase.com

see next page

J P Morgan Ltd - *Cont'd*

Directors: G. Butcher (Dir)
Ultimate Holding Company: JP MORGAN CHASE & CO (USA)
Immediate Holding Company: JPMORGAN FUNDS LIMITED
Registration no: SC019438 **Date established:** 1936
Turnover: £75m - £125m **No.of Employees:** 251 - 500
Product Groups: 82

Date of Accounts	Dec 11	Dec 10	Dec 09
Sales Turnover	124m	119m	94m
Pre Tax Profit/Loss	9m	12m	4m
Working Capital	35m	28m	55m
Current Assets	79m	84m	90m
Current Liabilities	17m	27m	23m

Morgan Mcdonnell

Belgrave Mews, Edinburgh, EH4 3AX
Tel: 0131-332 4200 **Fax:** 0131-332 6300
E-mail: anthony@morganmcdonnell.co.uk
Website: http://www.morganmcdonnell.co.uk
Directors: A. Mcdonnell (Dir)
Immediate Holding Company: MORGAN MCDONNELL ARCHITECTURE LIMITED
Registration no: SC235151 **Date established:** 2002
No.of Employees: 1 - 10 **Product Groups:** 84

Date of Accounts	Oct 11	Oct 10	Oct 09
Working Capital	166	179	-99
Fixed Assets	232	235	427
Current Assets	268	287	10

Morton Fraser Partnership

15-19 York Place, Edinburgh, EH1 3EB
Tel: 0131-550 1000 **Fax:** 0131-550 1002
E-mail: mfhq@aol.com
Managers: L. Urquhart, J. Urquhart, J. Rust (Consultant), P. Braid, R. Girdwood, R. Wood, H. Allan, A. Davidson, H. Bowman, S. Rae, C. Harte, H. Henderson, A. Bell, D. Hossack, D. Kellas (Consultant), D. McNeil, D. Stewart, G. Clark, G. Kerr (Consultant), G. Mair
Immediate Holding Company: CALTON HILL LIMITED
Registration no: SC355615 **Date established:** 2002 **Turnover:** £2m - £5m
No.of Employees: 11 - 20 **Product Groups:** 80, 82

D Narro

35 Argyle Place, Edinburgh, EH9 1JT
Tel: 0131-229 5193 **Fax:** 0131-229 5090
E-mail: info@davidnarro.co.uk
Website: http://www.davidnarro.co.uk
Directors: D. Narro (MD)
Immediate Holding Company: DAVID NARRO ASSOCIATES LIMITED
Registration no: SC237904 **Date established:** 2002
No.of Employees: 11 - 20 **Product Groups:** 35

Date of Accounts	Dec 11	Dec 10	Dec 09
Working Capital	211	245	209
Fixed Assets	103	89	105
Current Assets	362	366	320

Negotiate Ltd

5 Kilmaurs Road, Edinburgh, EH16 5DA
Tel: 0131-667 7127
E-mail: florence@negweb.com
Website: http://www.negotiate.co.uk
Directors: P. Kennedy (Fin), F. Kennedy (Dir)
Immediate Holding Company: NEGOTIATE LIMITED
Registration no: SC099484 **VAT No.:** GB 592 8130 26
Date established: 1986 **No.of Employees:** 1 - 10 **Product Groups:** 80

Date of Accounts	Aug 11	Aug 10	Aug 09
Working Capital	25	33	15
Fixed Assets	N/A	1	N/A
Current Assets	34	45	27

Net Resources Ltd

22 Palmerston Place, Edinburgh, EH12 5AL
Tel: 0131-477 7127 **Fax:** 0131- 4777126
E-mail: sara@netresources.co.uk
Website: http://www.netresources.co.uk
Directors: S. Dodd (MD), P. Dodd (Fin)
Immediate Holding Company: NET RESOURCES LIMITED
Registration no: SC176830 **Date established:** 1997
No.of Employees: 1 - 10 **Product Groups:** 44, 79

Date of Accounts	Mar 11	Mar 10	Mar 09
Working Capital	90	29	26
Fixed Assets	5	3	3
Current Assets	102	37	53

North British Distillery Co. Ltd

9 Wheatfield Road, Edinburgh, EH11 2PX
Tel: 0131-337 3363 **Fax:** 0131-346 7488
E-mail: info@northbritish.co.uk
Website: http://www.northbritish.co.uk
Directors: D. Rae (MD), F. Macdonald (Co Sec)
Managers: G. Cave (Personnel), G. Donaldson (Tech Serv Mgr)
Ultimate Holding Company: LOTHIAN DISTILLERS LIMITED
Immediate Holding Company: NORTH BRITISH DISTILLERY COMPANY LIMITED
Registration no: SC001491 **Date established:** 1985
Turnover: £50m - £75m **No.of Employees:** 101 - 250 **Product Groups:** 21

Date of Accounts	Dec 11	Dec 10	Dec 09
Sales Turnover	72m	55m	58m
Pre Tax Profit/Loss	9m	7m	8m
Working Capital	23m	23m	23m
Fixed Assets	32m	31m	31m
Current Assets	31m	30m	28m
Current Liabilities	3m	4m	3m

Northern Light Ltd (t/a Northern Light)

39-41 Assembly Street, Edinburgh, EH6 7RG
Tel: 0131-622 9100 **Fax:** 0131-553 3296
E-mail: info@northernlight.co.uk
Website: http://www.northernlight.co.uk
Directors: C. Cope (Fin), C. Cuthbert (MD), D. Webster (Tech Serv)
Managers: R. Ball, P. Brown, L. Ferguson (Mktg Serv Mgr)
Ultimate Holding Company: PERFORMING ARTS TECHNOLOGY LIMITED
Immediate Holding Company: NORTHERN LIGHT STAGE AND TECHNICAL SERVICES LIMITED
Registration no: SC181667 **Date established:** 1997
Turnover: £10m - £20m **No.of Employees:** 51 - 100 **Product Groups:** 24, 37, 83

Date of Accounts	Mar 12	Mar 11	Mar 10
Sales Turnover	10m	9m	8m
Pre Tax Profit/Loss	287	258	148
Working Capital	565	349	304
Fixed Assets	900	859	776
Current Assets	3m	2m	2m
Current Liabilities	673	495	527

One Stop Office Supplies Ltd

20 West Gorgie Parks, Edinburgh, EH14 1UT
Tel: 0131-443 2211 **Fax:** 0131-443 2212
E-mail: sales@onestopos.co.uk
Website: http://www.onestopos.co.uk
Directors: J. Smith (Dir)
Immediate Holding Company: ONE STOP OFFICE SUPPLIES LTD.
Registration no: SC270394 **Date established:** 2004
No.of Employees: 1 - 10 **Product Groups:** 61

Date of Accounts	Jul 11	Jul 10	Jul 09
Working Capital	-11	-13	-19
Fixed Assets	13	1	6
Current Assets	56	61	51

Orchard Independent

12 Dalziel Place, Edinburgh, EH7 5TR
Tel: 0131-620 6202 **Fax:** 0131-620 6203
E-mail: info@orchardindependent.co.uk
Website: http://www.orchardindependent.co.uk
Directors: L. Cumming (Dir)
Immediate Holding Company: ORCHARD INDEPENDENT LIMITED
Registration no: SC355263 **Date established:** 2009
No.of Employees: 1 - 10 **Product Groups:** 80, 82

Date of Accounts	Jun 11	Jun 10
Working Capital	-92	-153
Fixed Assets	176	185
Current Assets	112	51

P H P R Ltd

Communications House 3 Lower Joppa, Edinburgh, EH15 2ER
Tel: 0131-669 5190
E-mail: info@phpr.co.uk
Website: http://www.phpr.co.uk
Directors: P. Haywood (MD)
Immediate Holding Company: PHPR LIMITED
Registration no: SC201117 **Date established:** 1999
Turnover: Up to £250,000 **No.of Employees:** 1 - 10 **Product Groups:** 81

Date of Accounts	Mar 11	Mar 10	Mar 05
Sales Turnover	15	N/A	23
Pre Tax Profit/Loss	N/A	N/A	-3
Working Capital	3	6	-8
Fixed Assets	N/A	1	2
Current Assets	12	14	3
Current Liabilities	N/A	N/A	2

Paramount Printers Ltd

199 Causewayside, Edinburgh, EH9 1PH
Tel: 0131-667 4441 **Fax:** 0131-662 0659
E-mail: sales@paramountprinters.co.uk
Website: http://www.paramountprinters.co.uk
Bank(s): Bank of Scotland
Directors: P. Hepburn (MD), G. Hunter (Sales)
Immediate Holding Company: PARAMOUNT PRINTERS LIMITED
Registration no: SC042075 **VAT No.:** GB 270 0456 86
Date established: 1965 **Turnover:** £1m - £2m **No.of Employees:** 21 - 50
Product Groups: 28, 81

Date of Accounts	Mar 12	Mar 11	Mar 10
Working Capital	-52	-57	-90
Fixed Assets	1m	1m	1m
Current Assets	199	208	382

Pentlands Component Parts

23 Bankhead Drive, Edinburgh, EH11 4DW
Tel: 0131-538 7920 **Fax:** 0131-538 7919
E-mail: a.small@pentlandcomponents.com
Website: http://www.pentlandcomponents.com
Managers: A. Small (Mgr)
No.of Employees: 21 - 50 **Product Groups:** 33, 37, 39

Peoples

1 Cultins Road, Edinburgh, EH11 4DF
Tel: 0131-453 0200 **Fax:** 0131-453 0222
E-mail: info@peoples-cars.com
Website: http://www.peoplescars.co.uk
Directors: B. Gilda (Ch)
Registration no: SC080359 **Turnover:** £75m - £125m
No.of Employees: 51 - 100 **Product Groups:** 68

Pinpoint Scotland Ltd

9 Gayfield Square, Edinburgh, EH1 3NT
Tel: 0131-557 4184 **Fax:** 0131-557 4701
E-mail: justin@pinpoint-scotland.com
Website: http://www.pinpoint-scotland.com
Bank(s): Bank of Scotland
Directors: J. Chater (MD)
Immediate Holding Company: PINPOINT SCOTLAND LIMITED
Registration no: SC068684 **VAT No.:** GB 345 2276 61
Date established: 1979 **Turnover:** £1m - £2m **No.of Employees:** 11 - 20
Product Groups: 28, 81

Date of Accounts	Jun 11	Jun 10	Jun 09
Working Capital	394	424	382
Fixed Assets	602	647	653
Current Assets	554	545	507

Property Log Book Company Ltd

5 New Mart Place, Edinburgh, EH14 1RW
Tel: 08456-120205 **Fax:** 08456-120206
E-mail: enquiries@propertylogbook.co.uk
Website: http://www.propertylogbook.co
Managers: D. Cumming (Mgr)
Immediate Holding Company: I7 INNOVATIONS LIMITED
Registration no: sc270734 **Date established:** 2010
Turnover: Up to £250,000 **No.of Employees:** 1 - 10 **Product Groups:** 44

Date of Accounts	Aug 11
Current Assets	3

Reception Business Centre

21 Lansdowne Crescent, Edinburgh, EH12 5EH
Tel: 0131-535 1045 **Fax:** 0131-535 1065
E-mail: info@receptionedinburgh.co.uk
Website: http://www.receptionedinburgh.co.uk
Directors: I. Ali (Prop)
Managers: M. Williamson
Ultimate Holding Company: EGLINTON MANAGEMENT CENTRE HOLDINGS LIMITED
Immediate Holding Company: EGLINTON MANAGEMENT CENTRE LIMITED
Registration no: SC198632 **VAT No.:** GB 345 3783 39
Date established: 1993 **Turnover:** £250,000 - £500,000
No.of Employees: 1 - 10 **Product Groups:** 79, 80

Date of Accounts	Jan 11	Jan 10	Jan 08
Working Capital	-0	-1	N/A
Fixed Assets	1	1	2
Current Assets	2	3	8

Reed Accountancy

40 Ardmore House George Street, Edinburgh, EH2 2LE
Tel: 0131-226 3686 **Fax:** 0131-225 5817
E-mail: mike.harrison@reedglobal.com
Website: http://www.reed.co.uk
Managers: M. Harrison (Mgr)
Immediate Holding Company: REED PERSONNEL SERVICES LTD
Registration no: 00973629 **Turnover:** £125m - £250m
No.of Employees: 1 - 10 **Product Groups:** 80

Reed Hospitality

Ardmore House 40 George Street, Edinburgh, EH2 2LE
Tel: 0131-240 8820 **Fax:** 0131-240 8829
E-mail: i.moffat@reed.co.uk
Website: http://www.reed.co.uk
Managers: I. Moffat (District Mgr)
Registration no: SC141711 **Date established:** 1992 **Turnover:** £1m - £2m
No.of Employees: 1 - 10 **Product Groups:** 80

R M J M Ltd

10 Bells Brae, Edinburgh, EH4 3BJ
Tel: 0131-225 2532 **Fax:** 0131-226 5117
E-mail: edinburgh@rmjm.com
Website: http://www.rmjm.com
Bank(s): Bank of Scotland
Directors: D. Thompson (Fin), J. Doyle (Tech Serv), P. Rodgers (Head)
Managers: A. Wilson, D. Suckling (Personnel), S. Watt (Mktg Serv Mgr)
Ultimate Holding Company: RMJM GROUP LIMITED
Immediate Holding Company: LAVA NATION LIMITED
Registration no: SC142495 **VAT No.:** GB 502 4272 89
Date established: 1993 **Turnover:** £10m - £20m
No.of Employees: 51 - 100 **Product Groups:** 84

Rose Street Quartet

1 56 Temple Park Crescent, Edinburgh, EH11 1HX
Tel: 07719-702 265
E-mail: enquiries@rosestreetquartet.co.uk
Website: http://www.RoseStreetQuartet.co.uk
Directors: P. Harvey (Ptnr), P. Harvie (Ptnr)
Date established: 1997 **Turnover:** Up to £250,000
No.of Employees: 1 - 10 **Product Groups:** 49

Royal Incorporation Of Architects In Scotland

15 Rutland Square, Edinburgh, EH1 2BE
Tel: 0131-229 7545 **Fax:** 0131-228 2188
E-mail: nbaxter@rias.org.uk
Website: http://www.rias.org.uk
Managers: N. Baxter
Immediate Holding Company: SCOTTISH BUILDING CONTRACT COMMITTEE LIMITED
Registration no: SC002753 **VAT No.:** GB 416 0345 85
Date established: 2003 **Turnover:** £5m - £10m **No.of Employees:** 11 - 20
Product Groups: 84

Date of Accounts	Apr 11	Apr 10	Apr 09
Working Capital	66	69	65
Fixed Assets	2	3	4
Current Assets	96	99	97

Ryden

46 North Castle Street, Edinburgh, EH2 3BN
Tel: 0131-225 6612 **Fax:** 0131-225 5766
E-mail: fiona.drennan@ryden.co.uk
Website: http://www.ryden.co.uk
Bank(s): Clydesdale Bank PLC
Directors: F. Morton (MD), F. Drennan (Mkt Research)
Managers: S. Scott, T. Doig (Tech Serv Mgr), L. Rookyard, L. Rookyard
Ultimate Holding Company: RYDEN LLP
Immediate Holding Company: RYDEN LLP
Registration no: SO300405 **Date established:** 2004
Turnover: £10m - £20m **No.of Employees:** 51 - 100 **Product Groups:** 52, 80, 82, 84

Date of Accounts	Apr 11	Apr 10	Apr 09
Sales Turnover	10m	11m	10m
Pre Tax Profit/Loss	2m	4m	3m
Working Capital	4m	4m	4m
Fixed Assets	598	611	700
Current Assets	6m	6m	6m
Current Liabilities	2m	2m	900

S I A S Ltd

37 Manor Place, Edinburgh, EH3 7EB
Tel: 0131-225 7900 **Fax:** 0131-225 9229
E-mail: admin@sias.com
Website: http://www.sias.com
Directors: S. Muirhead (Dir)
Immediate Holding Company: SIAS LIMITED
Registration no: SC112949 **Turnover:** £1m - £2m
No.of Employees: 21 - 50 **Product Groups:** 84

Date of Accounts	Dec 07	Dec 06	Dec 05
Working Capital	924	750	607
Fixed Assets	49	49	65
Current Assets	1752	1326	1135
Current Liabilities	828	576	528
Total Share Capital	50	50	50

S T Microelectronics

33 Pinkhill, Edinburgh, EH12 7BF
Tel: 0131-336 6000 **Fax:** 0131-336 6001
E-mail: steve.east@st.com
Website: http://www.st.com
Bank(s): Bank of Scotland
Managers: S. East (Site Co-ord), J. Wood (I.T. Exec)
Immediate Holding Company: ST MICROELECTRONICS
Registration no: SC123534 **VAT No.:** 553 5163 48 **Date established:** 1990
Turnover: £10m - £20m **No.of Employees:** 101 - 250 **Product Groups:** 37

Saw & Tooling Service
50a Sighthill Crescent, Edinburgh, EH11 4QB
Tel: 0131-458 3886 **Fax:** 0131-458 3887
E-mail: andy@sawandtooling.co.uk
Website: http://www.sawandtooling.co.uk
Directors: A. Mcilwaine (Ptnr)
Date established: 1987 **No.of Employees:** 1 - 10 **Product Groups:** 36

Scotia UK
4 Castle Terrace, Edinburgh, EH1 2DP
Tel: 0131-228 2295 **Fax:** 0131-228 3823
E-mail: sales@scotiauk.com
Website: http://www.scotiauk.com
Bank(s): Royal Bank of Scotland
Directors: M. Forbes (Fin), S. Mackay (Dir), G. McLoughlin (MD), G. Turner (Dir), J. McLoughlin (MD), S. McLoughlin (MD), S. McKay (Dir), S. Mackay (Mkt Research)
Managers: K. Williamson (Sales Prom Mgr), A. Adams (Sales Admin)
Immediate Holding Company: SCOTIA UK PLC
Registration no: SC039144 **VAT No.:** GB 268 7663 05
Date established: 1963 **Turnover:** £2m - £5m **No.of Employees:** 21 - 50
Product Groups: 37

Date of Accounts	Apr 08
Sales Turnover	4778
Pre Tax Profit/Loss	71
Working Capital	574
Fixed Assets	301
Current Assets	1310
Current Liabilities	735
Total Share Capital	56
ROCE% (Return on Capital Employed)	8.2

Scotlands Personal Hotels
58 Whitehouse Road, Edinburgh, EH4 6PH
Tel: 0131-476 1590 **Fax:** 0131-476 1968
E-mail: mark@scotland-hotels.com
Website: http://www.scotland-hotels.com
Directors: M. Linklater (Prop)
Immediate Holding Company: LINKLATERSCA LTD
Registration no: SC046653 **Date established:** 2005
Turnover: £500,000 - £1m **No.of Employees:** 1 - 10 **Product Groups:** 69

Date of Accounts	Nov 11	Nov 10	Nov 09
Working Capital	13	13	8
Fixed Assets	41	51	61
Current Assets	39	39	29

Scottish Bakers
4 Torphichen Street, Edinburgh, EH3 8JQ
Tel: 0131-229 1401 **Fax:** 0131-229 8239
E-mail: master.bakers@samb.co.uk
Website: http://www.samb.co.uk
Directors: A. Clarke (Grp Chief Exec)
Immediate Holding Company: SCOTTISH BAKERS LTD
Registration no: SC372276 **VAT No.:** GB 703 8226 54
Date established: 2010 **Turnover:** £250,000 - £500,000
No.of Employees: 1 - 10 **Product Groups:** 87

Scottish Council For Development & Industry
23 Chester Street, Edinburgh, EH3 7ET
Tel: 0131-225 7911 **Fax:** 0131-220 2116
E-mail: iain.mclaren@scdi.org.uk
Website: http://www.scdi.org.uk
Bank(s): Clydesdale Bank PLC
Directors: A. Wilson (Grp Chief Exec), I. Mclaren (Fin), S. Macpherfon (Ch)
Managers: I. Mctaggart (Chief Mgr)
Immediate Holding Company: THE SCOTTISH COUNCIL FOR DEVELOPMENT AND INDUSTRY
Registration no: SC024724 **VAT No.:** GB 271 5135 75
Date established: 1946 **Turnover:** £1m - £2m **No.of Employees:** 21 - 50
Product Groups: 80, 81

Scottish Daily Newspaper Society
48 Palmerston Place, Edinburgh, EH12 5DE
Tel: 0131-220 4353 **Fax:** 0131-220 4344
E-mail: info@spef.org.uk
Website: http://www.spef.org.uk
Directors: J. Raeburn (Dir), S. Fairclough (Dir)
Registration no: SC279250 **VAT No.:** GB 664 0611 51
Date established: 2005 **Turnover:** £1m - £2m **No.of Employees:** 1 - 10
Product Groups: 87

Scottish & Newcastle Pub Co.
2-4 Broadway Park South Gyle Broadway, Edinburgh, EH12 9JZ
Tel: 08459-009074 **Fax:** 0131-314 3273
E-mail: enquiries@s-npubcompany.co.uk
Website: http://www.snpubs.co.uk
Bank(s): Bank of Scotland, Edinburgh; Lloyds, Newcastle
Directors: W. Crawshay (MD)
Ultimate Holding Company: HEINEKEN NV (NETHERLANDS)
Immediate Holding Company: HEINEKEN UK LIMITED
Registration no: SC065527 **VAT No.:** GB 268 6449 12
Date established: 1978 **Turnover:** Over £1,000m
No.of Employees: 51 - 100 **Product Groups:** 62

Date of Accounts	Dec 11	Dec 10	Dec 09
Sales Turnover	1596m	1663m	1693m
Pre Tax Profit/Loss	351m	731m	-202m
Working Capital	-1514m	-2304m	-2963m
Fixed Assets	2727m	3236m	3295m
Current Assets	4419m	4109m	5612m
Current Liabilities	258m	260m	245m

Shepherd & Wedderburn
1-7 Conference Square, Edinburgh, EH3 8UL
Tel: 0131-228 9900 **Fax:** 0131-228 1222
E-mail: info@shepwedd.co.uk
Website: http://www.shepwedd.co.uk
Bank(s): Bank of Scotland
Directors: K. Wilson (Fin), S. Gibb (Grp Chief Exec)
Managers: J. Watson, C. Ritchie (Personnel), S. Chaudhry
Immediate Holding Company: SHEPHERD AND WEDDERBURN LLP
Registration no: SO300895 **Date established:** 2006
Turnover: £20m - £50m **No.of Employees:** 251 - 500 **Product Groups:** 80

Date of Accounts	Apr 11	Apr 10	Apr 09
Sales Turnover	37m	35m	39m
Pre Tax Profit/Loss	N/A	11m	11m
Working Capital	13m	11m	12m
Fixed Assets	4m	4m	5m
Current Assets	21m	19m	17m
Current Liabilities	6m	6m	4m

W M Sinclair & Son
1 Madeira Street Leith, Edinburgh, EH6 4AJ
Tel: 0131-554 3489
E-mail: enquiries@sinclair-bagpipes.co.uk
Website: http://www.sinclair-bagpipes.co.uk
Directors: A. Sinclar (Ptnr)
VAT No.: GB 269 9597 73 **Date established:** 1933
Turnover: Up to £250,000 **No.of Employees:** 1 - 10 **Product Groups:** 49

Solas Computer Services
181 Dalry Road, Edinburgh, EH11 2EB
Tel: 0131-337 8206 **Fax:** 0131-337 8206
Website: http://www.ed-solas.co.uk
Directors: S. Brockbank (Prop)
No.of Employees: 1 - 10 **Product Groups:** 37, 67

Sopra Group
Queensway House 1 Queensferry Terrace, Edinburgh, EH4 3ER
Tel: 0131-332 3311 **Fax:** 0131-332 5938
E-mail: info@uk.sopragroup.com
Website: http://www.sopragroup.com
Bank(s): National Westminster Bank Plc
Directors: M. Everest (Fin)
Managers: C. Redmond (Personnel), D. Binard, L. Mieszek (Tech Serv Mgr)
Ultimate Holding Company: SOPRA SA
Immediate Holding Company: NEWELL & BUDGE LIMITED
Registration no: NF004230 **VAT No.:** GB 429 3771 28
Date established: 1985 **Turnover:** £20m - £50m
No.of Employees: 101 - 250 **Product Groups:** 44, 80

Specialised Catering Services
3 Wolseley Cresent, Edinburgh, EH8 7DF
Tel: 0131-539 0863 **Fax:** 0131-539 0863
E-mail: gordon@scsinstallations.co.uk
Directors: G. Angell (MD), J. Angell (Fin)
Immediate Holding Company: SPECIALISED CATERING SERVICES LIMITED
Registration no: SC145964 **Date established:** 1993
No.of Employees: 1 - 10 **Product Groups:** 20, 40, 41

Date of Accounts	Aug 10	Aug 09	Aug 08
Working Capital	19	17	-4
Fixed Assets	5	7	9
Current Assets	51	76	24
Current Liabilities	N/A	N/A	28

Speedy Hire Centres Northern Ltd
220-222 Sir Harry Lauder Road, Edinburgh, EH15 2QA
Tel: 0131-657 1555 **Fax:** 0131-657 1222
Website: http://www.speedyhire.co.uk
Directors: J. Commings (Dir)
Managers: C. Cumine (Mgr), S. Wright (Mgr)
Immediate Holding Company: SPEEDY HIRE CENTRES (NORTHERN) LTD
Registration no: 00245380 **Date established:** 1930
No.of Employees: 1 - 10 **Product Groups:** 35, 39, 45

Standard Life plc
Standard Life House 30 Lothian Road, Edinburgh, EH1 2DH
Tel: 0131-225 2552 **Fax:** 0131-245 8390
E-mail: gerry_grimstone@standardlife.com
Website: http://www.standardlife.com
Bank(s): Bank of Scotland
Directors: G. Grimstone (Ch), S. Begbie (Tech Serv)
Managers: J. Hunt, C. Black, K. O'Shaughnessy
Immediate Holding Company: STANDARD LIFE PLC
Registration no: SC286832 **VAT No.:** GB 207 3474 69
Date established: 2005 **No.of Employees:** 1501 & over
Product Groups: 82

Date of Accounts	Dec 11	Dec 10	Dec 09
Pre Tax Profit/Loss	595m	971m	419m
Fixed Assets	14622m	14221m	118159m
Current Assets	38683m	39895m	28454m
Current Liabilities	118136m	147755m	140923m

Standard Life Investments Corporate Funds Ltd
Investment House 1 George Street, Edinburgh, EH2 2LL
Tel: 0131-245 3535 **Fax:** 0131-245 6105
E-mail: keith_skeoch@standardlife.com
Website: http://www.standardlife.com
Directors: K. Skeoch (Fin), C. Walklin (Fin)
Managers: G. Teasdale (Personnel), N. Walsh (Mktg Serv Mgr)
Ultimate Holding Company: STANDARD LIFE PLC
Immediate Holding Company: STANDARD LIFE INVESTMENTS (CORPORATE FUNDS) LIMITED
Registration no: SC111488 **Date established:** 1988
Turnover: £10m - £20m **No.of Employees:** 1501 & over
Product Groups: 82

Date of Accounts	Dec 11	Dec 10	Dec 09
Sales Turnover	14m	13m	13m
Pre Tax Profit/Loss	630	-23	-24
Working Capital	6m	6m	6m
Current Assets	8m	8m	8m
Current Liabilities	N/A	222	542

Stevenson Reeves Ltd
40 Oxgangs Bank, Edinburgh, EH13 9LH
Tel: 0131-445 7151 **Fax:** 0131-445 7323
E-mail: renton@stevenson-reeves.co.uk
Website: http://www.stevenson-reeves.co.uk
Directors: R. Mein (MD)
Immediate Holding Company: STEVENSON REEVES LTD.
Registration no: SC011787 **VAT No.:** GB 269 7321 27
Date established: 2021 **Turnover:** £250,000 - £500,000
No.of Employees: 1 - 10 **Product Groups:** 38, 41

Date of Accounts	Jan 12	Jan 11	Jan 10
Working Capital	108	41	23
Fixed Assets	416	430	466
Current Assets	174	160	147

Stoneyport Associates
130 Leith Walk, Edinburgh, EH6 5DT
Tel: 0131-554 2614 **Fax:** 0870-051 0557
E-mail: jb@stoneyport.demon.co.uk
Website: http://www.stoneyport.co.uk
Managers: J. Barrow
Immediate Holding Company: GOLDLION TAKEAWAY LIMITED
Date established: 2012 **Turnover:** Up to £250,000
No.of Employees: 1 - 10 **Product Groups:** 89

Sykes Global Service
Calder House Pentland Gait 599 Calder Road, Edinburgh, EH11 4GA
Tel: 0131-458 6500 **Fax:** 0131-458 6565
E-mail: marco.kelly@sykes.com
Website: http://www.sykes.com
Directors: J. Goldie (Procurement), W. Bell (Pers), C. Bowick (Mkt Research), M. Kelly (Chief Op Offcr), S. Gush (Tech Serv)
Managers: J. Chapman (Fin Mgr)
Ultimate Holding Company: SYKES ENTERPRISES INC
Turnover: £250m - £500m **No.of Employees:** 501 - 1000
Product Groups: 44, 84

Date of Accounts	Dec 08	Dec 07	Dec 06
Sales Turnover	24925	25211	22423
Pre Tax Profit/Loss	3876	896	984
Working Capital	13025	10767	10848
Fixed Assets	3111	2638	2679
Current Assets	17386	14140	13295
Current Liabilities	4361	3373	2447
Total Share Capital	22	22	22
ROCE% (Return on Capital Employed)	24.0	6.7	7.3
ROT% (Return on Turnover)	15.5	3.6	4.4

T Ward Shipping Ltd
3 Johns Place Leith, Edinburgh, EH6 7EL
Tel: 0131-554 1231 **Fax:** 0131-553 3631
E-mail: shipping@tward.co.uk
Website: http://www.tward.co.uk
Directors: N. Souter (Dir)
Immediate Holding Company: T. WARD SHIPPING LIMITED
Registration no: SC162121 **Date established:** 1995
No.of Employees: 1 - 10 **Product Groups:** 07, 11, 14, 17, 18, 20, 21, 25, 27, 30, 31, 32, 33, 34, 35, 36, 37, 39, 40, 41, 42, 45, 47, 48, 54, 61, 66, 67, 68, 71, 72, 74, 76, 77, 80, 81, 82, 84, 87

Date of Accounts	Dec 11	Dec 10	Dec 09
Working Capital	49	-23	-33
Fixed Assets	4	2	1
Current Assets	531	318	156

Tayburn
15 Kittle Yards, Edinburgh, EH9 1PJ
Tel: 0131-662 0662 **Fax:** 0131-662 0606
E-mail: bill.davidson@tayburn.co.uk
Website: http://www.tayburn.co.uk
Bank(s): The Royal Bank of Scotland
Directors: W. Davidson (Chief Op Offcr)
Managers: I. Davidson (Tech Serv Mgr)
Ultimate Holding Company: TAYBURN HOLDINGS LIMITED
Immediate Holding Company: TAYBURN HOLDINGS LIMITED
Registration no: SC112753 **Date established:** 1988
Turnover: £5m - £10m **No.of Employees:** 21 - 50 **Product Groups:** 81

Date of Accounts	Mar 11	Mar 10	Mar 09
Working Capital	23	-19	-12
Fixed Assets	903	903	903
Current Assets	181	168	178

Techs in the City
21 Hill Street, Edinburgh, EH2 3JP
Tel: 0845-6210852 **Fax:** 0845-6210852
E-mail: info@techsinthecity.co.uk
Website: http://www.techsinthecity.co.uk
Directors: S. Shinnie (MD)
Registration no: SC306651 **Date established:** 2006
No.of Employees: 1 - 10 **Product Groups:** 44

The Edinburgh Woollen Mill
139 Princes Street, Edinburgh, EH2 4BL
Tel: 0131-226 3840
Website: http://www.ewm.co.uk
Managers: J. Rowley (Mgr)
Ultimate Holding Company: THE EDINBURGH WOOLLEN MILL (GROUP) LIMITED
Immediate Holding Company: FABIANO LTD.
Registration no: SC024081 **Date established:** 2008
Turnover: £125m - £250m **No.of Employees:** 1 - 10 **Product Groups:** 23, 24

Date of Accounts	Feb 09	Feb 10	Feb 11
Sales Turnover	158m	157m	160m
Pre Tax Profit/Loss	23m	22m	21m
Working Capital	138m	149m	155m
Fixed Assets	19m	19m	19m
Current Assets	159m	168m	180m
Current Liabilities	14m	13m	15m

The North Minch Fish Selling Company Ltd
12 Timberbush, Edinburgh, EH6 6QH
Tel: 0131-554 9340 **Fax:** 0131-554 9447
E-mail: info@denholm-seafoods.co.uk
Website: http://www.denholm-seafoods.co.uk
Directors: G. Hanson (MD), J. Denholm (Fin)
Ultimate Holding Company: J & J DENHOLM LTD
Immediate Holding Company: J. & J. DENHOLM LTD
Registration no: SC036711 **VAT No.:** GB 268 1572 38
Date established: 1961 **Turnover:** £5m - £10m **No.of Employees:** 1 - 10
Product Groups: 62

T N S (The Media Monitoring Service)
19 Atholl CR, Edinburgh, EH3 8HQ
Tel: 0131-656 4000 **Fax:** 0131-656 4078
E-mail: scotland.enquiries@tns-global.com
Website: http://www.tns-global.co.uk
Directors: C. Eynon (MD), M. Whyte (Dir)
Managers: G. Cowcher (District Mgr), R. Wood (Accounts)
Ultimate Holding Company: PUBLIC ATTITUDE SURVEYS LIMITED
Immediate Holding Company: Public Attitude Surveys Ltd
Registration no: SC081084 **Date established:** 1982
Turnover: £250,000 - £500,000 **No.of Employees:** 21 - 50
Product Groups: 79

United Wire
Granton Park Avenue, Edinburgh, EH5 1HT
Tel: 0131-552 6241 **Fax:** 0131-552 8462
E-mail: pjohnson@unitedwire.com
Website: http://www.unitedwire.com
Bank(s): National Westminster Bank Plc
Directors: I. Thomson (MD)
Managers: P. Johnston (Prod Mgr), P. Johnson (Sales Prom Mgr), A. Hughes (Tech Serv Mgr), D. Thomson (Purch Mgr)
Ultimate Holding Company: MI LLC
Registration no: SC001878 **VAT No.:** GB 842 8433 19
Date established: 1825 **Turnover:** £20m - £50m
No.of Employees: 51 - 100 **Product Groups:** 35, 45

Date of Accounts	Dec 07
Sales Turnover	23970
Pre Tax Profit/Loss	10690
Working Capital	13340
Fixed Assets	2820
Current Assets	19330
Current Liabilities	5990
Total Share Capital	120
ROCE% (Return on Capital Employed)	66.2

Wade
15 Great Stuart Street, Edinburgh, EH3 7TP
Tel: 0131-625 3333 **Fax:** 0131-625 3334
E-mail: mbrown@fce.com
Website: http://www.localpower.org
Directors: M. Brown (Dir)
Immediate Holding Company: DELTA ENERGY & ENVIRONMENT LIMITED
Date established: 2003 **No.of Employees:** 1 - 10 **Product Groups:** 37, 40, 67

Walker Woodstock (t/a Walker Woodstock)
48-50 Iona Street, Edinburgh, EH6 8SW
Tel: 0131-554 9414 **Fax:** 0131-553 3893
E-mail: robertadams@walkertimber.com
Bank(s): The Royal Bank of Scotland
Managers: R. Adams (Mgr)
Registration no: SC046290 **VAT No.:** GB 268 8595 88
Turnover: £500,000 - £1m **No.of Employees:** 11 - 20
Product Groups: 08, 25, 48, 66

Walker Woodstock (t/a Walker Woodstock)
483 Gorgie Road, Edinburgh, EH11 3AD
Tel: 0131-443 8803 **Fax:** 0131-444 1241
Managers: J. Valente (Mgr)
Immediate Holding Company: WALKER TIMBER LTD
Registration no: SC046290 **Turnover:** £5m - £10m
No.of Employees: 1 - 10 **Product Groups:** 08, 25

Waterless Valeting Company Edinburgh
1a Landsdowne Crescent, Edinburgh, EH12 5LQ
Tel: 0131-225 3220
E-mail: brian.anderson22@btopenworld.com
Website: http://www.car-valeting-edinburgh.co.uk
Directors: B. Anderson (Prop)
Ultimate Holding Company: NEWMILLS HOLDINGS LIMITED
Registration no: SC160330 **Date established:** 1995
Turnover: Up to £250,000 **No.of Employees:** 1 - 10 **Product Groups:** 32, 39, 68

William Waugh Edinburgh Ltd
West Harbour Road, Edinburgh, EH5 1PH
Tel: 0131-552 5559 **Fax:** 0131-552 7758
E-mail: recycle@williamwaugh.co.uk
Website: http://www.williamwaugh.co.uk
Directors: A. Waugh (MD)
Ultimate Holding Company: NIKKORD LIMITED
Immediate Holding Company: WILLIAM WAUGH (EDINBURGH) LIMITED
Registration no: SC075659 **VAT No.:** GB 694 0728 09
Date established: 1981 **Turnover:** £2m - £5m **No.of Employees:** 11 - 20
Product Groups: 66

Date of Accounts	Aug 11	Aug 10	Aug 09
Sales Turnover	7m	N/A	4m
Pre Tax Profit/Loss	472	N/A	42
Working Capital	1m	1m	2m
Fixed Assets	2m	2m	1m
Current Assets	3m	2m	2m
Current Liabilities	1m	N/A	457

Western Automobile Co.
116 Colinton Road, Edinburgh, EH14 1BY
Tel: 0131-443 6091 **Fax:** 0131- 4557383
E-mail: mbreception@easternholdings.co.uk
Website: http://www.easternholdings.co.uk
Managers: T. Oaks (Mgr)
Ultimate Holding Company: EASTERN HOLDINGS LIMITED
Immediate Holding Company: WESTERN AUTOMOBILE COMPANY LIMITED
Registration no: SC148914 **Date established:** 1994
Turnover: £75m - £125m **No.of Employees:** 251 - 500
Product Groups: 39, 82

Date of Accounts	Dec 11	Dec 10	Dec 09
Sales Turnover	107m	101m	91m
Pre Tax Profit/Loss	571	1m	451
Working Capital	1m	747	15
Fixed Assets	2m	2m	2m
Current Assets	21m	18m	18m
Current Liabilities	10m	8m	18m

Grant Westfield Ltd
3 Westfield Avenue, Edinburgh, EH11 2QH
Tel: 0131-337 6262 **Fax:** 0131-337 2859
E-mail: sales@grantwestfield.co.uk
Website: http://www.grantwestfield.co.uk
Bank(s): The Royal Bank of Scotland
Directors: E. Sturgeon (Fin), R. Macdonald (Dir)
Managers: I. Stewart (Buyer), M. McGimley (Tech Serv Mgr), M. Dobson (Mktg Serv Mgr), S. Dobson (Sales Prom Mgr)
Ultimate Holding Company: GRANFIT HOLDINGS LIMITED
Immediate Holding Company: GRANT WESTFIELD LIMITED
Registration no: SC043553 **VAT No.:** GB 269 2146 44
Date established: 1966 **Turnover:** £10m - £20m
No.of Employees: 101 - 250 **Product Groups:** 26, 42

Date of Accounts	Dec 11	Dec 10	Dec 09
Sales Turnover	19m	17m	17m
Pre Tax Profit/Loss	2m	1m	1m
Working Capital	4m	4m	3m
Fixed Assets	848	834	599
Current Assets	7m	6m	6m
Current Liabilities	1m	1m	800

Wolfson Microelectronics Ltd
Westfield House 26 Westfield Road, Edinburgh, EH11 2QB
Tel: 0131-272 7000 **Fax:** 0131-272 7001
E-mail: europe@wolfsonmicro.com
Website: http://www.wolfsonmicro.com
Bank(s): Bank of Scotland
Managers: A. Ralston (Tech Serv Mgr), D. Milne (Mktg Serv Mgr), M. Cubitt (Comptroller), M. Hickey, J. Suttie (Personnel), S. Docherty (Buyer)
Immediate Holding Company: WOLFSON MICROELECTRONICS PLC
Registration no: SC089839 **VAT No.:** GB 667 4737 17
Date established: 1984 **Turnover:** £125m - £250m
No.of Employees: 251 - 500 **Product Groups:** 37, 44, 67, 84

Date of Accounts	Jan 10
Sales Turnover	121m
Pre Tax Profit/Loss	-15m
Working Capital	111m
Fixed Assets	68m
Current Assets	129m
Current Liabilities	8m

Wolseley UK Ltd
20 Hawkhill Avenue Hawkhill Industrial Estate, Drain Center, Edinburgh, EH7 6BU
Tel: 0131-652 1670 **Fax:** 0131-661 7685
E-mail: info@wolseley.co.uk
Website: http://www.wolseley.co.uk
Bank(s): Bank of Scotland
Managers: A. Thompson (Mgr), B. Gray (Sales Prom)
Immediate Holding Company: Fife Indmar P.L.C.
Registration no: 00636445 **VAT No.:** GB 269 6253 23
Turnover: £1m - £2m **No.of Employees:** 11 - 20 **Product Groups:** 48, 66, 83

The World Markets Company Public Limited Company
525 Ferry Road, Edinburgh, EH5 2AW
Tel: 0131-315 5515 **Fax:** 0131-315 2999
E-mail: wmreuters.sales@wmcompany.com
Website: http://www.wmcompany.com
Directors: M. Walsh (MD)
Managers: S. Dixon (Personnel), M. Morrison (I.T. Exec)
Registration no: SC088378 **VAT No.:** GB 402 8923 62
Turnover: £20m - £50m **No.of Employees:** 501 - 1000
Product Groups: 80

Morayshire

Elgin

AC Yule & Son Ltd
1 Pinefield Parade, Elgin, IV30 6AG
Tel: 01343-545222 **Fax:** 01343-542246
E-mail: info@pinefieldglass.com
Website: http://www.acyule.com
Bank(s): The Royal Bank of Scotland
Directors: B. Yule (Prop), E. Yule (Ch), B. Emslie (Fin)
Managers: L. Flint (Personnel), J. Archibald (Div Mgr), S. Ward (I.T. Exec)
Immediate Holding Company: A.C. YULE & SON LIMITED
Registration no: SC045388 **VAT No.:** GB 265 3943 37
Date established: 1968 **No.of Employees:** 11 - 20 **Product Groups:** 30, 33, 35, 48

Date of Accounts	Jan 10	Jan 09	Jan 08
Sales Turnover	29m	34m	37m
Pre Tax Profit/Loss	-336	547	984
Working Capital	3m	4m	4m
Fixed Assets	5m	5m	6m
Current Assets	8m	11m	12m
Current Liabilities	2m	3m	3m

Bibacity Drinks
7 Linkwood Place, Elgin, IV30 1HZ
Tel: 01343-556499 **Fax:** 01343-552083
E-mail: admin@bibacity.co.uk
Website: http://www.bibacity.co.uk
Directors: D. Bremner (MD)
Date established: 1998 **Turnover:** Up to £250,000
No.of Employees: 1 - 10 **Product Groups:** 62

C S Controls Ltd
Parade Spur South, Elgin, IV30 6AJ
Tel: 01343-555055
Website: http://www.cscontrolsltd.com
Immediate Holding Company: C&S CONTROLS LIMITED
Registration no: 07084313 **Date established:** 2009
No.of Employees: 1 - 10 **Product Groups:** 37, 67

Date of Accounts	Dec 11	Dec 10
Working Capital	88	191
Fixed Assets	168	118
Current Assets	328	378

Celtic
Wester Alves Farm Alves, Elgin, IV30 8XB
Tel: 01343-850008 **Fax:** 01343-850005
E-mail: celticfood1@aol.com
Directors: I. Smith (Prop)
Immediate Holding Company: CELTIC FOOD MACHINERY LIMITED
Registration no: SC262302 **Date established:** 2004
No.of Employees: 1 - 10 **Product Groups:** 20, 40, 41

Date of Accounts	Dec 11	Dec 10	Dec 09
Working Capital	137	147	132
Fixed Assets	14	7	9
Current Assets	214	260	245

Gordon & Macphail
58 South Street, Elgin, IV30 1JX
Tel: 01343-545110 **Fax:** 01343-540155
E-mail: info@gordonandmacphail.com
Website: http://www.gordonandmacphail.com
Bank(s): Clydesdale Bank PLC
Managers: M. Angus (Mgr)
Immediate Holding Company: SPEYMALT WHISKEY DISTRIBUTORS LTD
Registration no: SC037522 **VAT No.:** GB 266 0705 62
Turnover: £500,000 - £1m **No.of Employees:** 11 - 20
Product Groups: 21, 62

Date of Accounts	Feb 08	Feb 07
Sales Turnover	16505	15491
Pre Tax Profit/Loss	1350	1326
Working Capital	12669	11679
Fixed Assets	3887	3643
Current Assets	15091	14715
Current Liabilities	2422	3036
Total Share Capital	190	190
ROCE% (Return on Capital Employed)	8.2	8.7
ROT% (Return on Turnover)	8.2	8.6

Highland Industrial Supplies Ltd
2 Pinefield Parade, Elgin, IV30 6AG
Tel: 01343-547561 **Fax:** 01343-540549
E-mail: sales@hisltd.co.uk
Website: http://www.hisltd.co.uk
Directors: E. Mcintosh (MD)
Immediate Holding Company: HIGHLAND INDUSTRIAL SUPPLIES LIMITED
Registration no: SC088770 **Date established:** 1984
No.of Employees: 11 - 20 **Product Groups:** 37, 41, 66, 67

Date of Accounts	Jan 11	Jan 10	Jan 09
Sales Turnover	31m	28m	N/A
Pre Tax Profit/Loss	271	334	411
Working Capital	2m	2m	2m
Fixed Assets	1m	1m	1m
Current Assets	9m	8m	8m
Current Liabilities	812	779	870

Peter Mitchell & Son
Longmorn, Elgin, IV30 8SL
Tel: 01343-860257 **Fax:** 01343-860478
E-mail: enquiries@petermitchellandson.co.uk
Directors: I. Mitchell (Ptnr)
Date established: 1954 **No.of Employees:** 11 - 20 **Product Groups:** 20, 40, 41

TechnoWord Ltd
Burgie Cottage Duffus, Elgin, IV30 5QZ
Tel: 01343-815901
E-mail: twl@technoword.co.uk
Website: http://www.technoword.co.uk
Directors: B. Moir (Tech Serv), A. Moir (MD)
Registration no: SC179206 **Date established:** 1987
Turnover: Up to £250,000 **No.of Employees:** 1 - 10 **Product Groups:** 80

Date of Accounts	Nov 06	Nov 05
Working Capital	N/A	3
Fixed Assets	9	8
Current Assets	10	8
Current Liabilities	10	5

Trap & Field Supplies
North Darkland, Elgin, IV30 8LB
Tel: 01343-842216
E-mail: kaystevenson@hartsllp.com
Directors: J. Silvestri (Prop)
Date established: 1984 **No.of Employees:** 1 - 10 **Product Groups:** 36, 39, 40

Aberdeenshire

Ellon

Advanced Refrigeration Ltd
Prop View Monteach Road, Methlick, Ellon, AB41 7JT
Tel: 01651-806211 **Fax:** 08452-805554
E-mail: jodi@advanced-refrigeration.co.uk
Website: http://www.advanced-refrigeration.co.uk
Directors: J. Thomson (Fin)
Immediate Holding Company: ADVANCED REFRIGERATION LTD.
Registration no: SC339321 **Date established:** 2008
Turnover: Up to £250,000 **No.of Employees:** 1 - 10 **Product Groups:** 40, 52

Date of Accounts	Mar 11	Mar 10	Mar 09
Working Capital	-7	-51	-33
Fixed Assets	18	25	21
Current Assets	115	149	101

City Financial Aberdeen Ltd
21 Bridge Street, Ellon, AB41 9AA
Tel: 01358-721000 **Fax:** 01358-726205
E-mail: info@city-financial.co.uk
Website: http://www.city-financial.co.uk
Directors: A. Bain (Dir)
Ultimate Holding Company: SCOTIA HOMES LIMITED
Immediate Holding Company: CITY FINANCIAL (ABERDEEN) LIMITED
Registration no: SC181194 **Date established:** 1997 **Turnover:** £1m - £2m
No.of Employees: 11 - 20 **Product Groups:** 82

Date of Accounts	Apr 11	Apr 10	Apr 09
Working Capital	755	679	616
Fixed Assets	38	14	35
Current Assets	1m	931	854

Continental Freight Forwarding Ltd
PO Box 11438, Ellon, AB41 9WZ
Tel: 01358-723418 **Fax:** 01358-723613
E-mail: fgb@continental-freight.co.uk
Directors: F. Bristo (MD), O. Bristo (Fin)
Immediate Holding Company: CONTINENTAL FREIGHT FORWARDING LIMITED
Registration no: SC081650 **Date established:** 1983
Turnover: £500,000 - £1m **No.of Employees:** 1 - 10 **Product Groups:** 76

Date of Accounts	Jul 11	Jul 10	Jul 09
Working Capital	103	106	113
Fixed Assets	1	1	2
Current Assets	149	154	166

G F M Agriculture
Greenacres, Ellon, AB41 8QY
Tel: 01358-720843 **Fax:** 01358-720273
E-mail: gfmagriculture@hotmail.com
Directors: G. Gray (MD)
Immediate Holding Company: GFM AGRICULTURE LTD.
Registration no: SC207772 **Date established:** 2000
No.of Employees: 1 - 10 **Product Groups:** 41

Date of Accounts	Jun 11	Jun 09	Jun 08
Working Capital	167	93	64
Fixed Assets	53	24	13
Current Assets	222	248	158

J Hendry
Upper Crichie Smithy Auchnagatt, Ellon, AB41 8UN
Tel: 01771-623103
Directors: J. Hendry (Prop)
Date established: 1983 **No.of Employees:** 1 - 10 **Product Groups:** 41

Marrs Of Methlick
Schoolbrae Garage Methlick, Ellon, AB41 7DS
Tel: 01651-806910 **Fax:** 01651-806911
E-mail: marrsofmethlick@btconnect.com
Website: http://www.marrsofmethlick.com
Directors: G. Cameron (MD)
Date established: 1999 **No.of Employees:** 1 - 10 **Product Groups:** 41

Murray Machinery Ltd
Dinneswood Tarves, Ellon, AB41 7LR
Tel: 01651-851636 **Fax:** 01651-851880
E-mail: sales@murraymachinery.com
Website: http://www.murraymachinery.com
Directors: P. Murray (MD), S. Murray (Fin)
Immediate Holding Company: MURRAY MACHINERY LTD
Registration no: SC218070 **Date established:** 2001
No.of Employees: 1 - 10 **Product Groups:** 41

Date of Accounts	Apr 11	Apr 10	Apr 09
Working Capital	417	376	523
Fixed Assets	129	177	23
Current Assets	603	518	625

Ornamental Garden Products
Windy Neuk Gight, Ellon, AB41 7HX
Tel: 01651-806340
Directors: G. Dennison (Prop)
No.of Employees: 1 - 10 **Product Groups:** 30, 36, 51

R & R Corrosion
Unit 5d Broomiesburn Road, Ellon, AB41 9RD
Tel: 01358-729644 **Fax:** 01358-729655
E-mail: info@rrcorrosion.com
Website: http://www.rrcorrosion.com
Directors: J. Rae (Dir), J. Rae (Fin)
Immediate Holding Company: R & R CORROSION LIMITED
Registration no: SC235930 **Date established:** 2002
No.of Employees: 1 - 10 **Product Groups:** 46, 48

Date of Accounts	Sep 11	Sep 10	Sep 09
Working Capital	58	83	60
Fixed Assets	63	79	99
Current Assets	162	172	139

Searchwise Ltd
6 Broomiesburn Road, Ellon, AB41 9RD
Tel: 01358-722990 **Fax:** 01358-722933
E-mail: sales@searchwise.co.uk
Website: http://www.searchwise.co.uk
Bank(s): Bank of Scotland
Directors: H. Kelsall (Prop)
Immediate Holding Company: SEARCHWISE LIMITED
Registration no: SC140987 **VAT No.:** 604 9855 20 **Date established:** 1992
No.of Employees: 11 - 20 **Product Groups:** 24, 39, 40, 49

Date of Accounts	Oct 11	Oct 10	Oct 09
Working Capital	184	103	109
Fixed Assets	70	86	64
Current Assets	483	447	443

Sulzer Wood
Castle Street Castlepark Industrial Estate, Ellon, AB41 9RF
Tel: 01358-721068 **Fax:** 01358-724176
E-mail: enquiries@sulzerwood.co.uk
Website: http://www.sulzerwood.co.uk
Directors: B. Asher (Fin), I. Johnson (Co Sec)
Managers: G. Glen (Chief Mgr)
Ultimate Holding Company: SULZER AG (SWITZERLAND)
Immediate Holding Company: SULZER WOOD LIMITED
Registration no: SC147952 **Date established:** 1993
Turnover: £20m - £50m **No.of Employees:** 51 - 100 **Product Groups:** 48

Date of Accounts	Dec 11	Dec 10	Dec 09
Sales Turnover	26m	23m	22m
Pre Tax Profit/Loss	5m	3m	3m
Working Capital	4m	3m	4m
Fixed Assets	490	549	464
Current Assets	10m	9m	9m
Current Liabilities	3m	4m	2m

J Watson Smith
38 Craigpark Place, Ellon, AB41 9FG
Tel: 01358-720916 **Fax:** 01358-720916
Website: http://www.jwatson-smith.co.uk
Directors: J. Smith (MD)
Immediate Holding Company: J WATSON SMITH LIMITED
Registration no: SC263732 **Date established:** 2004
No.of Employees: 1 - 10 **Product Groups:** 26, 35

Date of Accounts	Mar 11	Mar 10	Mar 08
Working Capital	1	10	9
Fixed Assets	5	6	10
Current Assets	30	38	55

Stirlingshire

Falkirk

A L Gordon Engineering Ltd
Bankside Industrial Estate Abbots Road, Falkirk, FK2 7XJ
Tel: 01324-622055 **Fax:** 01324-613383
E-mail: ttuplin@al-gordon.co.uk
Website: http://www.al-gordon.co.uk
Bank(s): The Royal Bank of Scotland
Directors: T. Tuplin (Prop)
Immediate Holding Company: A L GORDON ENGINEERING LTD.
Registration no: SC272630 **VAT No.:** GB 502 9632 60
Date established: 2004 **Turnover:** £500,000 - £1m
No.of Employees: 21 - 50 **Product Groups:** 39, 48

Date of Accounts	Dec 11	Dec 10	Dec 09
Working Capital	-12	25	50
Fixed Assets	570	568	587
Current Assets	620	350	668

Adlington Welding Supplies
14 Castle Road Bankside Industrial Estate, Falkirk, FK2 7UY
Tel: 01324-636376 **Fax:** 01324-622874
Website: http://www.adweld.co.uk
Directors: H. Turner (Prop)
Date established: 2002 **No.of Employees:** 1 - 10 **Product Groups:** 46

Birrell Tarpaulins
102 Thornhill Road, Falkirk, FK2 7AA
Tel: 01324-623311 **Fax:** 01324-623311
E-mail: birrelltarpaulin@btconnect.com
Directors: G. Campbell (Prop)
Turnover: £250,000 - £500,000 **No.of Employees:** 1 - 10
Product Groups: 23, 24, 63

C Jenkins Windows Ltd
Scotia Place, Falkirk, FK2 7AJ
Tel: 01324-631357 **Fax:** 01324-629339
Bank(s): Bank of Scotland
Directors: A. Jenkins (MD)
Immediate Holding Company: C. JENKINS WINDOWS LIMITED
Registration no: SC106699 **VAT No.:** GB 345 3284 57
Date established: 1987 **Turnover:** £500,000 - £1m
No.of Employees: 11 - 20 **Product Groups:** 52

Date of Accounts	Apr 12	Apr 11	Apr 10
Working Capital	739	703	715
Fixed Assets	26	32	38
Current Assets	850	791	839

Carron Phoenix
West Carron Works Stenhouse Road, Carron, Falkirk, FK2 8DR
Tel: 01324-638321 **Fax:** 01324-620978
E-mail: sales@carron.com
Website: http://www.carron.com
Bank(s): The Royal Bank of Scotland
Directors: S. Cotton (MD), I. King (Co Sec)
Managers: D. Young, A. McKinlay (Purch Mgr), N. Clark (Sales & Mktg Mg)
Ultimate Holding Company: FRANKE HOLDING AG (SWITZERLAND)
Immediate Holding Company: CARRON PHOENIX LIMITED
Registration no: SC108168 **VAT No.:** GB 502 6594 57
Date established: 1987 **Turnover:** £20m - £50m
No.of Employees: 251 - 500 **Product Groups:** 36, 66

Date of Accounts	Dec 11	Dec 10	Dec 09
Sales Turnover	31m	35m	32m
Pre Tax Profit/Loss	-2m	-48	-414
Working Capital	4m	4m	2m
Fixed Assets	10m	12m	14m
Current Assets	8m	9m	7m
Current Liabilities	2m	2m	2m

Alexander Dennis Ltd
91 Glasgow Road Camelon, Falkirk, FK1 4JB
Tel: 01324-621672 **Fax:** 01324-632469
E-mail: helen.webster@alexander-dennis.com
Website: http://www.alexander-dennis.com
Bank(s): National Westminster
Directors: B. McFie (Fin), M. Barr (Dir)
Managers: C. Hester (Tech Serv Mgr), M. McMenamin (Purch Mgr), T. McKeown (Personnel)
Immediate Holding Company: ALEXANDER DENNIS LIMITED
Registration no: SC268016 **Date established:** 2004
Turnover: £50m - £75m **No.of Employees:** 501 - 1000
Product Groups: 39, 68

Date of Accounts	Dec 11	Dec 10	Dec 09
Sales Turnover	357m	283m	290m
Pre Tax Profit/Loss	15m	5m	3m
Working Capital	36m	41m	414
Fixed Assets	39m	40m	46m
Current Assets	140m	98m	84m
Current Liabilities	45m	27m	17m

F B S Engineering & Sanitary Supplies Ltd
Cockburn Works Gowan Avenue, Falkirk, FK2 7HJ
Tel: 01324-628431 **Fax:** 01324-611175
E-mail: info@fbsplumbing.co.uk
Website: http://www.fbsplumbing.co.uk
Bank(s): The Royal Bank of Scotland, Glasgow
Directors: A. Sime (MD)
Immediate Holding Company: F B S ENGINEERING AND SANITARY SUPPLIES LIMITED
Registration no: SC073411 **Date established:** 1980 **Turnover:** £1m - £2m
No.of Employees: 11 - 20 **Product Groups:** 30, 34

Date of Accounts	Jan 12	Jan 11	Jan 10
Working Capital	441	395	364
Fixed Assets	294	303	329
Current Assets	642	628	616

Ferguson Engineering
6 Middlefield Road, Falkirk, FK2 9AG
Tel: 01324-888000 **Fax:** 01324-633672
E-mail: enquiries@smith-electrical.co.uk
Website: http://www.scsbuildingservices.co.uk
Directors: A. Smith (Prop)
Managers: G. Callan, G. Callan (Admin Off)
Immediate Holding Company: SCS BUILDING SERVICES (SCOTLAND) LIMITED
Registration no: SC372040 **VAT No.:** GB 272 1979 43
Date established: 2010 **Turnover:** £20m - £50m **No.of Employees:** 1 - 10
Product Groups: 39

Date of Accounts	Dec 10	Dec 09	Dec 08
Sales Turnover	21m	17m	22m
Pre Tax Profit/Loss	-1m	742	1m
Working Capital	549	2m	1m
Fixed Assets	197	234	348
Current Assets	6m	4m	5m
Current Liabilities	322	640	1m

G M S Music
Kinneil House Kirk Entry Boness Road, Polmont, Falkirk, FK2 0QS
Tel: 01324-711011 **Fax:** 01324-711533
E-mail: info@gmsmusic.com
Website: http://www.gmsmusic.com
Directors: F. Mcrae (MD)
Immediate Holding Company: G.M.S.(RECORDINGS)LIMITED
Registration no: SC059883 **Date established:** 1976
Turnover: £250,000 - £500,000 **No.of Employees:** 1 - 10
Product Groups: 37, 79

Date of Accounts	Sep 11	Sep 10	Sep 09
Working Capital	-286	-312	-454
Fixed Assets	525	530	509
Current Assets	136	184	179

M J Gleeson Group plc
Unit 7-9 Callendar Business Park Callendar Road, Falkirk, FK1 1XR
Tel: 01324-678460 **Fax:** 01324-623741
Website: http://www.mjgleeson.com
Directors: J. Harrison (MD), M. Ramsay (MD)
Managers: A. Fairweather (Comm)
Immediate Holding Company: M J GLEESON GROUP PUBLIC LIMITED COMPANY
Registration no: 00479529 **VAT No.:** GB 216 2716 82
Date established: 1950 **Turnover:** £1m - £2m **No.of Employees:** 11 - 20
Product Groups: 51, 52

Date of Accounts	Dec 11	Dec 10	Dec 09
Sales Turnover	962m	828m	737m
Pre Tax Profit/Loss	39m	33m	9m
Working Capital	149m	121m	120m
Fixed Assets	154m	155m	157m
Current Assets	451m	380m	351m
Current Liabilities	29m	26m	24m

Gray Precision Engineering Ltd
Unit 3 Castle Court Bankside Industrial Estate, Falkirk, FK2 7UU
Tel: 01324-612679 **Fax:** 01324-612209
E-mail: stuart.gray@btconnect.com
Directors: S. Gray (MD)
Immediate Holding Company: GRAY PRECISION ENGINEERING LIMITED
Registration no: SC231828 **VAT No.:** GB 400 7973 64
Date established: 2002 **Turnover:** £250,000 - £500,000
No.of Employees: 1 - 10 **Product Groups:** 46, 48

Date of Accounts	May 11	May 10	May 09
Working Capital	62	29	39
Fixed Assets	31	38	48
Current Assets	104	68	102

Horizon Reinforcing & Crane Hire Ltd
Dollar Industrial Estate, Falkirk, FK2 7YS
Tel: 01324-623977 **Fax:** 01324-612613
E-mail: info@horizonreinforcing.co.uk
Website: http://www.horizonreinforcing.co.uk
Directors: S. Dougall (Ptnr), M. Dougall (Fin)
Immediate Holding Company: HORIZON (REINFORCING & CRANE HIRE) COMPANY LIMITED
Registration no: SC053010 **Date established:** 1973
No.of Employees: 11 - 20 **Product Groups:** 35

Date of Accounts	Mar 12	Mar 11	Mar 10
Working Capital	-760	-975	-893
Fixed Assets	3m	3m	2m
Current Assets	364	319	354

Ironworks
Unit E Bryson Street, Falkirk, FK2 7BT
Tel: 01324-611133 **Fax:** 01324-872158
Directors: J. Mcateer (Prop)
No.of Employees: 1 - 10 **Product Groups:** 26, 35

J E M Engines
23 Polmont Road Laurieston, Falkirk, FK2 9QQ
Tel: 01324-633266 **Fax:** 01324-633870
E-mail: info@jemengines.co.uk
Website: http://www.jemengines.co.uk
Directors: J. Lipski (MD)
Immediate Holding Company: JEM ENGINES LTD
Registration no: SC187580 **Date established:** 1998
No.of Employees: 11 - 20 **Product Groups:** 35, 36, 39

Laird Security
18 Burnbank Road, Falkirk, FK2 7PE
Tel: 01324-633889 **Fax:** 01324-633767
E-mail: sales@lairdsecurity.co.uk
Website: http://www.furnex.co.uk
Managers: A. Browne (Mgr)
No.of Employees: 1 - 10 **Product Groups:** 30, 35, 36

Metal Creations Falkirk
11a Smith Street, Falkirk, FK2 7NB
Tel: 01324-632255
Directors: D. Murphy (Prop)
Date established: 2003 **No.of Employees:** 1 - 10 **Product Groups:** 35

Mossley Scotland Ltd
Mount Pleasant Binniehill Road, Slamannan, Falkirk, FK1 3BE
Tel: 01324-861100 **Fax:** 01324-861100
E-mail: mossleyscotland@yahoo.co.uk
Website: http://www.mossleyscotlandltd.co.uk
Directors: A. Tetlow (MD)
Immediate Holding Company: MOSSLEY (SCOTLAND) LTD.
Registration no: SC221111 **Date established:** 2001
Turnover: £250,000 - £500,000 **No.of Employees:** 1 - 10
Product Groups: 52

Date of Accounts	Jun 11	Jun 10	Jun 09
Sales Turnover	N/A	N/A	315
Pre Tax Profit/Loss	N/A	N/A	18

see next page

Mossley Scotland Ltd - Cont'd

Working Capital	-10	-5	-4
Fixed Assets	13	15	17
Current Assets	37	32	47
Current Liabilities	N/A	N/A	42

Original Sandwich Board Ltd
32 Pender Gardens Rumford, Falkirk, FK2 0BJ
Tel: 01324-411158
E-mail: sales@originalsandwichboard.co.uk
Website: http://www.originalsandwichboard.co.uk
Directors: J. Willoughby (MD), M. Beer (Fin)
Immediate Holding Company: PIN IN IT LIMITED
Registration no: 04741818 **Date established:** 2010
Turnover: Up to £250,000 **No.of Employees:** 1 - 10 **Product Groups:** 81

Photogold Web Design
40 Dunvegan Place Polmont, Falkirk, FK2 0NX
Tel: 01324-883305
E-mail: sales@photogoldecommerce.com
Website: http://www.photogoldecommerce.com
Directors: D. Rankin (Prop)
Date established: 2000 **Turnover:** Up to £250,000
No.of Employees: 1 - 10 **Product Groups:** 44

Polmont Metal Craft
20 Randolph Cresent Brightons, Falkirk, FK2 0HA
Tel: 01324-882544
Directors: N. Laird (Prop)
Date established: 1990 **No.of Employees:** 1 - 10 **Product Groups:** 26, 35

Process & Instrumentation Valves Ltd
Stewart House Stewart Road, Falkirk, FK2 7AS
Tel: 01324-630030 **Fax:** 01324-629112
E-mail: sales@piv-online.com
Website: http://www.piv-online.com
Directors: B. Thomson (MD)
Ultimate Holding Company: JOHN BELL PIPELINE EQUIPMENT COMPANY LIMITED
Immediate Holding Company: PROCESS AND INSTRUMENTATION VALVES LIMITED
Registration no: SC154857 **Date established:** 1994
No.of Employees: 1 - 10 **Product Groups:** 36, 37, 38

Date of Accounts	Mar 11	Mar 10	Mar 09
Working Capital	218	180	182
Fixed Assets	60	46	38
Current Assets	472	421	345

Protrol Instrumentation Ltd
Calibration Centre Bankside Industrial Estate, Falkirk, FK2 7XY
Tel: 01324-611506 **Fax:** 01324-611506
E-mail: info@protrol.co.uk
Website: http://www.protrol.co.uk
Directors: A. Ralston (MD)
Immediate Holding Company: PROTROL INSTRUMENTATION LTD.
Registration no: SC161889 **Date established:** 1995
No.of Employees: 1 - 10 **Product Groups:** 38, 48, 85

Date of Accounts	Dec 11	Dec 10	Dec 09
Working Capital	65	28	89
Fixed Assets	8	9	10
Current Assets	128	97	113

James Scott & Sons Kitchen Equipment Ltd
Glenfuir Works Portdownie, Falkirk, FK1 4QY
Tel: 01324-629416 **Fax:** 01324-612161
E-mail: office@jsske.co.uk
Website: http://www.jsske.co.uk
Bank(s): Toyal Bank of Scotland
Directors: J. Scott (Dir), M. Scott (Dir), S. Scott (Dir)
Managers: D. Barclay (Sales Admin)
Immediate Holding Company: JAMES SCOTT & SONS (KITCHEN EQUIPMENT) LIMITED
Registration no: SC049875 **VAT No.:** GB 269 4895 90
Date established: 1972 **Turnover:** £5m - £10m
No.of Employees: 51 - 100 **Product Groups:** 36, 40, 67, 69

Date of Accounts	Apr 11	Apr 10	Apr 09
Sales Turnover	N/A	8m	N/A
Pre Tax Profit/Loss	N/A	223	N/A
Working Capital	503	501	367
Fixed Assets	519	402	427
Current Assets	2m	2m	2m
Current Liabilities	N/A	370	N/A

The Sign Factory
Burnbank Road Bainsford, Falkirk, FK2 7PE
Tel: 01324-501950 **Fax:** 01324-501950
E-mail: info@thesignfactory-falkirk.co.uk
Website: http://www.thesignfactory-falkirk.co.uk
Bank(s): Clydesdale Bank PLC
Managers: S. Murphy (Sales Prom Mgr)
Immediate Holding Company: SOVEREIGN DEVELOPMENTS LIMITED
Registration no: SC298201 **VAT No.:** GB 663 8965 79
Date established: 1984 **No.of Employees:** 21 - 50 **Product Groups:** 28, 39, 40, 45, 49

Source
Castlelaurie Industrial Estate, Falkirk, FK2 7XE
Tel: 01324-670128 **Fax:** 01324-634636
E-mail: sales@sourcepromo.co.uk
Website: http://www.sourcepromo.co.uk
Directors: G. Halliday (Prop), K. Johnson (Sales)
Immediate Holding Company: APPLIED SWEEPERS INTERNATIONAL LIMITED
Registration no: SC045871 **Date established:** 1989
No.of Employees: 1 - 10 **Product Groups:** 24

Tofco
9 Forbes Court Middlefield Industrial Estate, Falkirk, FK2 9HQ
Tel: 01324-630621 **Fax:** 01324-633832
Website: http://www.tofco.co.uk
No.of Employees: 1 - 10 **Product Groups:** 37, 67

Unico Ltd
North Main Street Carronshore, Falkirk, FK2 8HT
Tel: 01324-573410 **Fax:** 01324-573401
E-mail: sales@unicodirect.com
Website: http://www.unicodirect.com
Bank(s): Clydesdale, Larbert
Directors: D. Ross (Ch), T. Slater (Fin)
Managers: L. Gibbs (Purch Mgr), M. O'Donnell (Mktg Serv Mgr), P. Smith (Tech Serv Mgr), H. Forgie (Personnel)
Ultimate Holding Company: ALEXANDER ROSS HOLDINGS LIMITED
Immediate Holding Company: UNICO LIMITED
Registration no: 00861294 **VAT No.:** 268 3355 36 **Date established:** 1965
Turnover: £5m - £10m **No.of Employees:** 21 - 50 **Product Groups:** 32, 63, 66

Date of Accounts	Dec 11	Dec 10	Dec 09
Sales Turnover	N/A	8m	8m
Pre Tax Profit/Loss	N/A	295	172
Working Capital	904	830	1m
Fixed Assets	214	156	127
Current Assets	3m	3m	4m
Current Liabilities	N/A	412	1m

Viking Stainless Products
Unit 9 Castlelaurie Industrial Estate, Falkirk, FK2 7XF
Tel: 01324-636298 **Fax:** 01324-634818
E-mail: hgsvsp@gmail.com
Directors: H. Sneddon (Prop)
Immediate Holding Company: VIKING STAINLESS PRODUCTS LTD.
Registration no: SC217627 **Date established:** 2001
No.of Employees: 1 - 10 **Product Groups:** 20, 40, 41

Date of Accounts	Apr 11	Apr 10	Apr 09
Working Capital	26	26	37
Fixed Assets	11	15	20
Current Assets	41	39	52
Current Liabilities	9	N/A	N/A

Morayshire

Fochabers

Baxters Food Group Ltd
Northern Preserve Works, Fochabers, IV32 7LD
Tel: 01343-820393 **Fax:** 01343-821790
E-mail: bill.king@baxters.co.uk
Website: http://www.baxters.co.uk
Bank(s): Bank of Scotland
Directors: N. Soutar (MD), A. Baxter (Dir), A. Field (Sales & Mktg), B. King (Grp Chief Exec)
Managers: S. Duncan (Chief Mgr), G. Carol (I.T. Exec)
Immediate Holding Company: BAXTERS FOOD GROUP LIMITED
Registration no: SC023572 **Date established:** 1945
Turnover: £125m - £250m **No.of Employees:** 501 - 1000
Product Groups: 02, 20

Date of Accounts	May 08
Sales Turnover	116360
Pre Tax Profit/Loss	240
Working Capital	17550
Fixed Assets	72980
Current Assets	43110
Current Liabilities	25560
Total Share Capital	640
ROCE% (Return on Capital Employed)	0.3

Tata Steel
6 Mosstodloch Industrial Estate Mosstodloch, Fochabers, IV32 7LH
Tel: 01343-820606 **Fax:** 01343-821295
Website: http://www.tatasteel.com
Managers: I. Prince (Chief Mgr)
Ultimate Holding Company: TATA STEEL LIMITED (INDIA)
Immediate Holding Company: CORUS GROUP LIMITED
Registration no: 03811373 **VAT No.:** GB 238 7122 60
Date established: 1999 **Turnover:** £500,000 - £1m
No.of Employees: 1 - 10 **Product Groups:** 61, 66

Angus

Forfar

Agrico UK Ltd
Castleton of Eassie Eassie, Forfar, DD8 1SJ
Tel: 01307-840551 **Fax:** 01307-840245
E-mail: archiegibson@agrico.co.uk
Website: http://www.agrico.co.uk
Directors: A. Gibson (Dir)
Managers: M. Oughtred (Mktg Serv Mgr), L. Carr (Comptroller)
Immediate Holding Company: AGRICO UK LIMITED
Registration no: SC183233 **Date established:** 1998
Turnover: £5m - £10m **No.of Employees:** 21 - 50 **Product Groups:** 02

Date of Accounts	Jul 12	Jul 11	Jul 10
Working Capital	751	1m	1m
Fixed Assets	532	543	569
Current Assets	1m	1m	2m

David Ritchie Implements Ltd (David Ritchie (Implements) Ltd)
Carseview Road, Forfar, DD8 3BT
Tel: 01307-462271 **Fax:** 01307-464081
E-mail: info@ritchie-uk.com
Website: http://www.ritchie-uk.com
Bank(s): The Royal Bank of Scotland
Directors: D. Ritchie (Fin)
Managers: B. Ritchie (Sales Prom Mgr), S. Young
Immediate Holding Company: DAVID RITCHIE (IMPLEMENTS) LIMITED
Registration no: SC029454 **Date established:** 1953
Turnover: £10m - £20m **No.of Employees:** 101 - 250
Product Groups: 26, 30, 33, 35, 36, 38, 41, 42, 44, 45, 67, 81

Date of Accounts	May 11	May 10	May 09
Sales Turnover	12m	9m	12m
Pre Tax Profit/Loss	307	-176	364
Working Capital	3m	2m	2m
Fixed Assets	2m	2m	2m
Current Assets	5m	4m	4m
Current Liabilities	813	667	756

Don & Low
Broad Cross Depot 15 St James Road, Forfar, DD8 1LE
Tel: 01307-452249 **Fax:** 01307-452201
E-mail: info@donlow.co.uk
Website: http://www.donlow.co.uk
Managers: J. Johnston
Ultimate Holding Company: THRACE PLASTICS SA (GREECE)
Immediate Holding Company: DON & LOW (HOLDINGS) LIMITED
Registration no: SC026425 **VAT No.:** GB 296 2120 62
Date established: 1948 **Turnover:** £50m - £75m **No.of Employees:** 1 - 10
Product Groups: 23, 30, 85

Date of Accounts	Dec 11	Dec 10	Dec 09
Working Capital	50	50	50
Current Assets	50	50	50

Flo-Steel Ltd
East Den Brae Letham, Forfar, DD8 2PJ
Tel: 01307-818843 **Fax:** 01307-818935
E-mail: mail@flosteel.plus.com
Website: http://www.flosteel.co.uk
Directors: K. Florence (MD)
Ultimate Holding Company: DONEGAL CREAMERIES PUBLIC LIMITED COMPANY
Immediate Holding Company: FLOSTEEL LIMITED
Registration no: SC273440 **Date established:** 2004
No.of Employees: 1 - 10 **Product Groups:** 35

Date of Accounts	Mar 12	Mar 11	Mar 10
Working Capital	749	657	896
Fixed Assets	301	305	131
Current Assets	909	803	1m

G L F Services
Cherryfield House Kingsmuir, Forfar, DD8 2LH
Tel: 01307-460352 **Fax:** 01307-460352
Directors: G. Fleming (Prop)
Registration no: SC144590 **Date established:** 1993
No.of Employees: 1 - 10 **Product Groups:** 35, 39, 45

Ian Frasier Machinery
Traquair 31 Arbroath Road, Forfar, DD8 2JJ
Tel: 01307-462095 **Fax:** 01307-466093
Directors: P. Frasier (Prop), I. Fraser (Prop)
Date established: 1989 **No.of Employees:** 1 - 10 **Product Groups:** 43

Laird Bros Forfar Ltd
Old Brechin Road Lunanhead, Forfar, DD8 3NQ
Tel: 01307-466577 **Fax:** 01307-468642
E-mail: enquiries@lairdbros.co.uk
Website: http://www.lairdbros.co.uk
Directors: J. Laird (Dir)
Managers: A. Laird (Sales Admin)
Immediate Holding Company: LAIRD BROTHERS (FORFAR) LIMITED
Registration no: SC036052 **Date established:** 1961
No.of Employees: 21 - 50 **Product Groups:** 31, 51, 66

Date of Accounts	Mar 12	Mar 11	Mar 10
Working Capital	950	575	191
Fixed Assets	3m	3m	4m
Current Assets	2m	2m	1m
Current Liabilities	N/A	114	261

Nutscene
Breahead Works, Forfar, DD8 2NS
Tel: 01307-468589 **Fax:** 01307-467051
E-mail: sales@nutscene.com
Website: http://www.nutscene.com
Directors: S. Leslie (Co Sec), S. Young (MD), L. Clarke (Chief Op Offcr)
Immediate Holding Company: NUTSCENE LIMITED
Registration no: SC233771 **VAT No.:** GB 607 6951 21
Date established: 2002 **Turnover:** £500,000 - £1m
No.of Employees: 1 - 10 **Product Groups:** 23, 27

Date of Accounts	Sep 07	Sep 06	Sep 05
Working Capital	-139	-67	16
Fixed Assets	378	394	68
Current Assets	282	299	307
Current Liabilities	421	367	291
Total Share Capital	46	46	15

Ramsay Ladders Ltd (t/a Ramsay Ladders)
61 West High Street, Forfar, DD8 1BG
Tel: 01307-462255 **Fax:** 01307-466956
E-mail: enquiries@ramsayladders.co.uk
Website: http://www.ramsayladders.co.uk
Directors: G. Lowson (Dir)
Immediate Holding Company: RAMSAY & SONS (FORFAR) LIMITED
Registration no: SC024001 **Date established:** 1946
No.of Employees: 21 - 50 **Product Groups:** 35

Date of Accounts	Dec 11	Dec 10	Dec 09
Sales Turnover	3m	3m	3m
Pre Tax Profit/Loss	296	94	324
Working Capital	2m	2m	2m
Fixed Assets	2m	2m	2m
Current Assets	2m	2m	3m
Current Liabilities	218	162	144

Strathmore Woollen Co. Ltd
Station Works North Street, Forfar, DD8 3BN
Tel: 01307-462135 **Fax:** 01307-468603
E-mail: info@tartanbystrathmore.co.uk
Website: http://www.tartanbystrathmore.co.uk
Directors: D. Cowley (MD)
Immediate Holding Company: STRATHMORE WOOLLEN COMPANY LIMITED
Registration no: SC083127 **VAT No.:** GB 397 9430 92
Date established: 1983 **Turnover:** £1m - £2m **No.of Employees:** 1 - 10
Product Groups: 23

Date of Accounts	Dec 11	Dec 10	Dec 09
Working Capital	-7	-12	-12
Fixed Assets	112	119	119
Current Assets	203	196	196

Superfine Manufacturing Ltd
Orchardbank Industrial Estate, Forfar, DD8 1TD
Tel: 01307-463538 **Fax:** 01307-468505
E-mail: sales@superfine.co.uk
Website: http://www.superfine.co.uk
Directors: G. Archer (MD)
Immediate Holding Company: SUPERFINE MANUFACTURING LIMITED
Registration no: SC038321 **Date established:** 1963
No.of Employees: 11 - 20 **Product Groups:** 32

Date of Accounts	Dec 11	Dec 10	Dec 09
Working Capital	2m	2m	2m
Fixed Assets	512	466	432
Current Assets	2m	2m	2m

Morayshire

Forres

Scotland Electronics
28 West Road Greshop Industrial Estate, Forres, IV36 2GW
Tel: 01309-671339 **Fax:** 01309-678909
E-mail: diane.middleton@scotlandelectronics.co.uk
Website: http://www.scotlandelectronics.co.uk
Bank(s): Lloyds, TSB
Directors: D. Middleton (Fin)
Immediate Holding Company: SCOTLAND ELECTRONICS LIMITED
Registration no: SC169046 **VAT No.:** GB 553 1985 26
Date established: 1996 **Turnover:** £2m - £5m **No.of Employees:** 21 - 50
Product Groups: 37, 44, 84

Date of Accounts	Oct 11	Oct 10	Oct 09
Working Capital	-4	-4	-4
Fixed Assets	8	8	8
Current Liabilities	N/A	N/A	4

SIGNed Graphics
Mundole, Forres, IV36 2TA
Tel: 01309-671345
E-mail: info@signed-graphics.com
Website: http://www.signed-graphics.com
Directors: J. Gillespie (Prop)
Immediate Holding Company: KERRBRO LTD.
Date established: 2007 **Turnover:** Up to £250,000
No.of Employees: 1 - 10 **Product Groups:** 30, 39, 40

Date of Accounts	Sep 10	Sep 09	Sep 08
Working Capital	-7	-6	-6
Fixed Assets	N/A	3	6
Current Assets	1	1	2

W Thomson Saw Service Ltd
Waterford Way, Forres, IV36 3EE
Tel: 01309-672461 **Fax:** 01309-676833
E-mail: thomson.sawservice@gmail.com
Directors: J. Cummock (Prop)
Immediate Holding Company: W THOMSON SAW SERVICE LTD
Registration no: SC412713 **Date established:** 2011
No.of Employees: 1 - 10 **Product Groups:** 36

Wheelchair Care Ltd
Unit 2 Greshop Industrial Estate, Forres, IV36 2GW
Tel: 01309-676677 **Fax:** 01309-674479
E-mail: orders@wheelchaircare.co.uk
Website: http://www.wheelchaircare.co.uk
Directors: E. Mackintosh (Fin), J. Maccorkell (MD)
Registration no: SC235224 **Date established:** 2002
No.of Employees: 1 - 10 **Product Groups:** 38, 67

Invernesshire

Fort William

Sundolitt Packaging Supplies
Unit 9 Annat Point Industrial Estate Corpach, Fort William, PH33 7NA
Tel: 01397-772929 **Fax:** 01397-772930
E-mail: john.docherty@sundolitt.co.uk
Website: http://www.sundolitt.co.uk
Managers: J. Docherty (District Mgr)
Date established: 1994 **No.of Employees:** 11 - 20 **Product Groups:** 38, 42

Travis Perkins plc
Unit 1 Ben Nevis Estate Ben Nevis Industrial Estate, Fort William, PH33 6RU
Tel: 01397-705195 **Fax:** 01397-705282
E-mail: richard.shaw@travisperkins.co.uk
Website: http://www.travisperkins.co.uk
Bank(s): Royal Bank of Scotland
Managers: R. Shaw (Mgr)
Immediate Holding Company: TRAVIS PERKINS PLC
Registration no: 00824821 **VAT No.:** GB 408 5567 37
Date established: 1964 **Turnover:** £2m - £5m **No.of Employees:** 11 - 20
Product Groups: 25, 66

Date of Accounts	Dec 11	Dec 10	Dec 09
Sales Turnover	4779m	3153m	2931m
Pre Tax Profit/Loss	270m	197m	213m
Working Capital	133m	159m	248m
Fixed Assets	2771m	2749m	2108m
Current Assets	1421m	1329m	1035m
Current Liabilities	473m	412m	109m

Aberdeenshire

Fraserburgh

Ardlaw Country Stores
Ardlaw, Fraserburgh, AB43 7DA
Tel: 01346-541497 **Fax:** 01346-541497
Website: http://www.ardlawcountrystore.co.uk
Managers: H. Partridge (Mgr)
Date established: 2003 **No.of Employees:** 1 - 10 **Product Groups:** 36, 39, 40

The Caledonian Stone Company
Caledonian House Lonmay, Fraserburgh, AB43 8RN
Tel: 01346-532747 **Fax:** 01346-532547
E-mail: admin@caledonianstone.com
Website: http://www.caledonianstone.com
Directors: P. Rabey (Snr Part)
Immediate Holding Company: CALEDONIAN STONE COMPANY LLP
Registration no: SO303768 **Date established:** 2012
No.of Employees: 11 - 20 **Product Groups:** 49

Charles Tait Marine Engineers
Harbour Road, Fraserburgh, AB43 9BR
Tel: 01346-517681 **Fax:** 01346-514724
E-mail: charles_tait@btconnect.com
Directors: C. Tait (Prop)
Immediate Holding Company: GRAMPIAN INDUSTRIAL SERVICES LTD.
Registration no: SC166311 **VAT No.:** GB 296 5234 29
Date established: 2002 **Turnover:** £1m - £2m **No.of Employees:** 1 - 10
Product Groups: 37, 39, 40, 45, 68

Cooper Printers
43 Manse Street, Fraserburgh, AB43 9JB
Tel: 01346-518831 **Fax:** 01346-511311
E-mail: cooper.printers@virgin.net
Directors: S. Boylan (MD), S. Boylan (Prop)
Managers: S. Sutherland (Chief Mgr)
Turnover: Up to £250,000 **No.of Employees:** 1 - 10 **Product Groups:** 28

Darg Engineering Ltd
South Harbour Road, Fraserburgh, AB43 9TA
Tel: 01346-513068 **Fax:** 01346-518118
E-mail: sales@darg.co.uk
Website: http://www.darg.co.uk
Directors: D. Duthie (MD), W. Bruce (Fin)
Immediate Holding Company: PETER DUTHIE (C-SHELLS) LTD.
Registration no: SC072894 **VAT No.:** GB 297 4776 89
Date established: 1997 **Turnover:** £1m - £2m **No.of Employees:** 1 - 10
Product Groups: 30, 33

Date of Accounts	Jun 07	Jun 06	Jun 05
Working Capital	-20	-21	-21
Fixed Assets	145	144	146
Current Assets	221	235	228

Gray & Adams Holdings Ltd
South Road, Fraserburgh, AB43 9HU
Tel: 01346-518001 **Fax:** 01346-519175
E-mail: sales@gray-adams.com
Website: http://www.gray-adams.com
Directors: J. Watt (Co Sec)
Ultimate Holding Company: GRAY & ADAMS HOLDINGS LIMITED
Immediate Holding Company: GRAY & ADAMS GROUP LIMITED
Registration no: SC230241 **VAT No.:** GB 265 3874 30
Date established: 2002 **Turnover:** £75m - £125m
No.of Employees: 501 - 1000 **Product Groups:** 39

Date of Accounts	Apr 11	Apr 10	Apr 09
Sales Turnover	109m	86m	98m
Pre Tax Profit/Loss	4m	1m	3m
Working Capital	15m	13m	14m
Fixed Assets	11m	10m	10m
Current Assets	38m	29m	29m
Current Liabilities	5m	3m	6m

Macduff Shipyards Ltd Fraserburgh
Reclaimed Ground, Fraserburgh, AB43 9TD
Tel: 01346-519163 **Fax:** 01346-510548
Website: http://www.macduffshipyards.com
Managers: J. Watt (Mgr), C. Mckessick (Mgr)
No.of Employees: 11 - 20 **Product Groups:** 39, 40, 83

Date of Accounts	Feb 12	Feb 11	Feb 10
Sales Turnover	15m	12m	15m
Pre Tax Profit/Loss	1m	639	533
Working Capital	4m	3m	3m
Fixed Assets	3m	3m	3m
Current Assets	7m	6m	6m
Current Liabilities	1m	1m	960

Pneuropower Scotland Ltd
South Harbour Road, Fraserburgh, AB43 9TA
Tel: 01346-511345 **Fax:** 01346-518118
E-mail: sales@pneuropower.co.uk
Website: http://www.pneuropower.co.uk
Directors: D. Duthie (MD)
Immediate Holding Company: PNEUROPOWER (SCOTLAND) LIMITED
Registration no: SC147814 **Date established:** 1993
Turnover: Up to £250,000 **No.of Employees:** 1 - 10 **Product Groups:** 37

Date of Accounts	Jan 11	Jan 10	Jan 07
Working Capital	4	8	-9
Current Assets	65	63	48

Power Jacks Ltd
South Harbour Road, Fraserburgh, AB43 9BZ
Tel: 01346-513131 **Fax:** 01346-519737
E-mail: charlesb@powerjacks.co.uk
Website: http://www.powerjacks.com
Bank(s): The Royal Bank of Scotland
Directors: B. Bultitude (MD), P. White (Fab), G. King (Sales), A. Horne (Fin), A. Greig (Tech Serv), C. Bultitude (MD)
Managers: W. Hamper
Immediate Holding Company: POWER JACKS LIMITED
Registration no: SC103849 **VAT No.:** GB 470 9558 17
Date established: 1987 **Turnover:** £5m - £10m
No.of Employees: 51 - 100 **Product Groups:** 35, 37, 38, 39, 40, 41, 42, 44, 45, 46, 47, 48

Date of Accounts	Mar 11	Mar 10	Mar 09
Sales Turnover	5m	10m	11m
Pre Tax Profit/Loss	-216	1m	3m
Working Capital	2m	4m	4m
Fixed Assets	5m	2m	2m
Current Assets	3m	5m	7m
Current Liabilities	269	975	1m

Selkirkshire

Galashiels

A E Robb & Associates Ltd
1 Wilderhaugh, Galashiels, TD1 1QJ
Tel: 01896-664955 **Fax:** 01896-664956
E-mail: aerobb.borders@btconnect.com
Website: http://www.aerobb.co.uk
Directors: J. Stephenson (MD), L. Dart (Dir)
Immediate Holding Company: A.E. ROBB & ASSOCIATES LIMITED
Registration no: 01309169 **VAT No.:** GB 297 5907 95
Date established: 1977 **Turnover:** £1m - £2m **No.of Employees:** 1 - 10
Product Groups: 84

A G Lees Garage
Huddersfield Street, Galashiels, TD1 3AX
Tel: 01896-754298 **Fax:** 01896-759288
Website: http://www.aglees-cars.com
Directors: A. Lees (Prop)
Turnover: £2m - £5m **No.of Employees:** 1 - 10 **Product Groups:** 39, 68

The Ceramic Experience
Unit 4 Wheatlands Mill, Galashiels, TD1 2HQ
Tel: 01896-668666
E-mail: info@theceramicexperience.com
Website: http://www.theceramicexperience.com
Directors: R. Kennard (Prop)
No.of Employees: 1 - 10 **Product Groups:** 32, 33, 44, 63

Creagaran Scotland Ltd
Unit 9 Huddersfield Street Workshop Huddersfield Street, Galashiels, TD1 3BF
Tel: 01896-754711 **Fax:** 01896-755487
E-mail: creagaran1@btconnect.com
Directors: T. Casey (MD), P. Casey (Fin)
Immediate Holding Company: CREAGARAN SCOTLAND LIMITED
Registration no: SC212382 **Date established:** 2000
No.of Employees: 1 - 10 **Product Groups:** 35, 43

Date of Accounts	Mar 11	Mar 10	Mar 09
Working Capital	9	33	-27
Fixed Assets	13	15	27
Current Assets	90	152	-27

Graham
71 Island Street, Galashiels, TD1 1PA
Tel: 01896-757713 **Fax:** 01896-758800
E-mail: michelormiston@graham-group.co.uk
Website: http://www.jewson.co.uk
Managers: M. Ormsden (Mgr)
Ultimate Holding Company: SAINT-GOBAIN PLC
Immediate Holding Company: GRAHAM GROUP LTD
Registration no: 00066738 **No.of Employees:** 21 - 50
Product Groups: 52, 66

Jewson Ltd
71 Island Street, Galashiels, TD1 1PA
Tel: 01896-758871 **Fax:** 01896-759220
Website: http://www.jewson.co.uk
Directors: T. Newman (Sales), I. MacKay (MD)
Managers: G. Noble (District Mgr)
Ultimate Holding Company: COMPAGNIE DE SAINT GOBAIN (FRANCE)
Immediate Holding Company: JEWSON LIMITED
Registration no: 00348407 **VAT No.:** GB 497 7184 83
Date established: 1939 **Turnover:** £500m - £1,000m
No.of Employees: 1 - 10 **Product Groups:** 66

Date of Accounts	Dec 11	Dec 10	Dec 09
Sales Turnover	1606m	1547m	1485m
Pre Tax Profit/Loss	18m	100m	45m
Working Capital	-345m	-250m	-349m
Fixed Assets	496m	387m	461m
Current Assets	657m	1005m	1320m
Current Liabilities	66m	120m	64m

Schofield Dyers & Finishers
Gala Mill Huddersfield Street, Galashiels, TD1 3AY
Tel: 01896-754848 **Fax:** 01896-754417
E-mail: douglas.ormeston@schofield.df.co.uk
Website: http://www.schofield-df.co.uk
Bank(s): Barclays
Directors: E. Queen (Prop)
Managers: D. Ormiston (Chief Mgr)
Immediate Holding Company: LAGNHOLM DYEING CO.
Registration no: 00190166 **VAT No.:** GB 663 9928 80
Date established: 1983 **Turnover:** £1m - £2m **No.of Employees:** 21 - 50
Product Groups: 23

Scottish Enterprise Borders
3 Bridge Street, Galashiels, TD1 1SW
Tel: 01896-758991 **Fax:** 01896-758625
E-mail: alistair.mckinnon@scotent.co.uk
Website: http://www.scottish-enterprise.com
Directors: A. Mckinnon (MD), C. Mackie (Fin)
Managers: L. Birse (Mktg Serv Mgr)
Immediate Holding Company: SCOTTISH ENTERPRISE BORDERS
Registration no: SC126506 **Date established:** 1990
Turnover: Up to £250,000 **No.of Employees:** 21 - 50 **Product Groups:** 87

Date of Accounts	Mar 11	Mar 10	Mar 09
Pre Tax Profit/Loss	-4	-3	22
Working Capital	-37	-33	-30
Current Assets	45	48	57
Current Liabilities	N/A	N/A	87

Thomas Sherriff & Co. Ltd
150-162 Galashiels Road Stow, Galashiels, TD1 2RA
Tel: 01578-730282 **Fax:** 01578-730284
E-mail: donaldj@thomassherriff.co.uk
Website: http://www.thomassherriff.co.uk
Managers: D. Jack (District Mgr)
Immediate Holding Company: THOMAS SHERRIFF AND COMPANY LIMITED
Registration no: 00906135 **Date established:** 1967
No.of Employees: 1 - 10 **Product Groups:** 41

Date of Accounts	Jan 12	Jan 11	Jan 10
Sales Turnover	24m	17m	19m
Pre Tax Profit/Loss	519	536	562
Working Capital	4m	3m	3m
Fixed Assets	1m	1m	1m
Current Assets	8m	8m	6m
Current Liabilities	239	292	480

Ayrshire

Galston

Mathiesons
Ayr Road, Galston, KA4 8LE
Tel: 01563-820505 **Fax:** 01563-820015
E-mail: darren@mathiesonweld.co.uk
Website: http://www.jmco.freeseve.co.uk
Directors: D. Mathieson (Ptnr)
No.of Employees: 1 - 10 **Product Groups:** 46

Raewinds Ltd
Maxwood Road, Galston, KA4 8JN
Tel: 01563-821076 **Fax:** 01563-821192
E-mail: raewinds@aol.com
Website: http://www.raewinds.co.uk
Directors: J. Mcnamara (MD)
Immediate Holding Company: RAEWINDS LIMITED
Registration no: SC211108 **VAT No.:** GB 653 0938 32
Date established: 2000 **Turnover:** Up to £250,000
No.of Employees: 1 - 10 **Product Groups:** 48

Date of Accounts	May 11	May 09	May 08
Working Capital	-4	-13	70
Fixed Assets	36	48	55
Current Assets	155	95	70

Ayrshire

Girvan

Carrick Cooperage
Grangestone Industrial Estate Ladywell Avenue, Girvan, KA26 9PL
Tel: 01465-710001 **Fax:** 01465-713743
E-mail: carrickcooperage@aol.com
Website: http://www.carrickcooperage.co.uk
Directors: R. Hubbard (Fin), S. Law (Prop)
Immediate Holding Company: CARRICK COOPERAGE AND GARDEN SUPPLIES LIMITED
Registration no: SC236970 **Date established:** 2002
No.of Employees: 1 - 10 **Product Groups:** 35, 36, 45

Date of Accounts	Oct 11	Oct 10	Oct 09
Working Capital	-6	9	-1
Fixed Assets	31	39	48
Current Assets	59	80	74

F M C Biopolymer UK Ltd
Ladyburn Works Dipple, Girvan, KA26 9JN
Tel: 01655-333000 **Fax:** 01655-333100
E-mail: peter.byth@fmc.com
Website: http://www.fmc.com
Managers: C. McGuian (Fin Mgr), M. Miller (Ops Mgr), S. McRonald (Purch Mgr), L. Plunkett (Personnel), S. Hamilton
Ultimate Holding Company: FMC CORPORATION (USA)
Immediate Holding Company: FMC BIOPOLYMER UK LIMITED
Registration no: 03823108 **Date established:** 1999 **Turnover:** £5m - £10m
No.of Employees: 51 - 100 **Product Groups:** 20, 31, 32

Date of Accounts	Dec 11	Dec 10	Dec 09
Sales Turnover	6m	6m	12m
Pre Tax Profit/Loss	-637	-3m	-12m
Working Capital	11m	-7m	-2m
Fixed Assets	6m	6m	5m
Current Assets	15m	2m	3m
Current Liabilities	253	198	4m

Gentech International Ltd
10 Grangestone Industrial Estate Ladywell Avenue, Girvan, KA26 9PS
Tel: 01465-713581 **Fax:** 01465-714974
E-mail: sales@gentechsensors.com
Website: http://www.gentechsensors.com
Bank(s): The Royal Bank of Scotland
Directors: I. Hood (I.T. Dir), A. Simkins (MD)
Ultimate Holding Company: RUBICON PARTNERS INDUSTRIES LLP
Immediate Holding Company: GENTECH INTERNATIONAL LIMITED
Registration no: SC050236 **VAT No.:** GB 751 1757 35
Date established: 1972 **Turnover:** £5m - £10m
No.of Employees: 51 - 100 **Product Groups:** 37, 38, 40, 45, 68, 84

Date of Accounts	Dec 10	Dec 09	Dec 08
Sales Turnover	5m	3m	3m
Pre Tax Profit/Loss	-96	-104	163
Working Capital	1m	1m	1m
Fixed Assets	181	203	166
Current Assets	2m	2m	2m
Current Liabilities	291	155	249

Grangestone Engineering Co.
Grangestone Industrial Estate 30 Ladywell Avenue, Girvan, KA26 9PL
Tel: 01465-712505 **Fax:** 01465-712505
Directors: A. Muir (Ptnr)
Immediate Holding Company: GRANGESTONE COMMERCIALS LIMITED
Registration no: SC298329 **VAT No.:** GB 264 9510 44
Date established: 2006 **Turnover:** Up to £250,000
No.of Employees: 1 - 10 **Product Groups:** 46, 48

Lanarkshire

Glasgow

A & D Cartwright
7 Robert Drive, Glasgow, G51 3HE
Tel: 0141-445 2000 **Fax:** 0141-445 0002
E-mail: glasgow.484@eel.co.uk
Website: http://www.edmundson-electrical.co.uk/
Managers: J. O'neil (District Mgr)
VAT No.: GB 265 2794 33 **Turnover:** £2m - £5m **No.of Employees:** 1 - 10
Product Groups: 67, 77

A G B Steel Products Ltd
146 Crownpoint Road, Glasgow, G40 2AE
Tel: 0141-556 7551 **Fax:** 0141-556 1516
E-mail: info@agbsteelproducts.co.uk
Website: http://www.agbsteelproducts.co.uk
Bank(s): The Royal Bank of Scotland
Directors: B. Garvey (Ch)
Managers: G. Reiff (Comm)
Immediate Holding Company: AGB STEEL PRODUCTS LIMITED
Registration no: SC282790 **VAT No.:** GB 259 7000 54
Date established: 2005 **No.of Employees:** 11 - 20 **Product Groups:** 36

Date of Accounts	Apr 11	Apr 10	Apr 09
Working Capital	229	120	133
Fixed Assets	173	202	169
Current Assets	3m	3m	2m

A G Barr plc
Westfield House 4 Mollins Road, Cumbernauld, Glasgow, G68 9HD
Tel: 01236-852400 **Fax:** 01236-852477
E-mail: info@agbarr.co.uk
Website: http://www.agbarr.co.uk
Bank(s): Bank of Scotland
Directors: A. Short (Fin)
Managers: A. Memmott (Mgr), A. Flynn (Personnel), G. Irving, J. McAlaney
Immediate Holding Company: A&R GLASGOW LIMITED
Registration no: SC083923 **VAT No.:** GB 259 9805 02
Date established: 1983 **Turnover:** £500,000 - £1m
No.of Employees: 51 - 100 **Product Groups:** 20, 21

Date of Accounts	Mar 84	Feb 85
Sales Turnover	114	518
Pre Tax Profit/Loss	12	42
Fixed Assets	69	115
Current Assets	16	111

A K Waugh Ltd
14 Loanbank Quadrant, Glasgow, G51 3HZ
Tel: 0141-440 5775
E-mail: sales@akwaugh.com
Website: http://www.akwaugh.com
Directors: A. Waugh (Dir)
Immediate Holding Company: A K WAUGH LIMITED
Registration no: SC049830 **Date established:** 1972
No.of Employees: 1 - 10 **Product Groups:** 37, 40, 52

Date of Accounts	Jun 11	Jun 10	Jun 09
Working Capital	34	6	5
Fixed Assets	7	8	10
Current Assets	99	84	63

A K Waugh Ltd
49 Dalsetter Avenue, Glasgow, G15 8TE
Tel: 0141-944 3303 **Fax:** 0141-944 4750
E-mail: sales@akwaugh.com
Website: http://www.processheaters.co.uk
Directors: A. Waugh (MD), A. Waugh (Fin), M. Waugh (Dir)
Immediate Holding Company: A K WAUGH LIMITED
Registration no: SC049830 **VAT No.:** GB 262 5897 26
Date established: 1972 **Turnover:** Up to £250,000
No.of Employees: 1 - 10 **Product Groups:** 37, 40, 66

Date of Accounts	Jun 11	Jun 10	Jun 09
Working Capital	34	6	5
Fixed Assets	7	8	10
Current Assets	99	84	63

A T A Grinding Processes Ltd
37 Dalsetter Avenue Drumchapel, Glasgow, G15 8TE
Tel: 0141-940 4720 **Fax:** 0141-940 4721
E-mail: ata@atagrinding.co.uk
Website: http://www.atagrinding.co.uk
Bank(s): Bank of Scotland
Directors: S. Messenger (I.T. Dir), B. Lemond (MD)
Managers: D. Harrison (Sales Prom Mgr)
Ultimate Holding Company: PCT Group PLC
Registration no: 00751205 **VAT No.:** GB 435 2785 39
Turnover: £2m - £5m **No.of Employees:** 51 - 100 **Product Groups:** 33, 36, 40, 46

A T Blacksmiths
Bridgeton Business Centre 277 Abercromby Street, Glasgow, G40 2DD
Tel: 0141-554 2224
Directors: T. Taylor (Prop)
Registration no: SC296048 **Date established:** 2006
No.of Employees: 1 - 10 **Product Groups:** 26, 35

A & T Industrial Supplies Ltd
Seath Road Rutherglen, Glasgow, G73 1RW
Tel: 0141-647 6001 **Fax:** 0141-647 6788
E-mail: domains@onthespot.co.uk
Website: http://www.a-and-t.net
Directors: A. Houston (MD), I. Houston (Fin)
Immediate Holding Company: A & T INDUSTRIAL SUPPLIES LIMITED
Registration no: SC132175 **VAT No.:** GB 334 2727 67
Date established: 1991 **Turnover:** £1m - £2m **No.of Employees:** 1 - 10
Product Groups: 24

Date of Accounts	May 11	May 10	May 09
Working Capital	19	48	79
Fixed Assets	14	19	24
Current Assets	78	123	168

Aalco
117 Clydesmill Place Clydesmill Industrial Estate, Glasgow, G32 8RF
Tel: 0141-646 3200 **Fax:** 0141-646 3260
E-mail: glasgow@aalco.co.uk
Website: http://www.aalco.co.uk
Bank(s): National Westminster Bank Plc
Managers: D. Adams (Mgr)
Ultimate Holding Company: U K STEELSTOCK LTD
Immediate Holding Company: AMARI METALS LTD
Registration no: 03551533 **Date established:** 1997
Turnover: £125m - £250m **No.of Employees:** 21 - 50
Product Groups: 34, 35, 36, 66

Aardee Security Shutters Ltd
5 Dalsholm Avenue, Glasgow, G20 0TS
Tel: 0141-810 3444 **Fax:** 0141-810 3777
E-mail: sales@aardee.co.uk
Website: http://www.aardee.co.uk
Directors: M. Meikle (Dir), M. Meikle (Dir), R. Dunbar (Dir)
Immediate Holding Company: AARDEE SECURITY SHUTTERS LIMITED
Registration no: SC131633 **VAT No.:** GB 742 9999 69
Date established: 1991 **Turnover:** £2m - £5m **No.of Employees:** 11 - 20
Product Groups: 36, 52

Date of Accounts	Dec 11	Dec 10	Dec 09
Working Capital	120	55	169
Fixed Assets	25	30	17
Current Assets	321	304	399

Abacus
359 Nuneaton Street, Glasgow, G40 3JU
Tel: 0141-554 8115 **Fax:** 0141-556 0104
E-mail: chiltern@abacus.co.uk
Website: http://www.abacus.co.uk
Directors: S. Harvey (Prop)
Turnover: Up to £250,000 **No.of Employees:** 1 - 10 **Product Groups:** 52

Henry Abram & Sons Ltd
17 Sandyford Place, Glasgow, G3 7NB
Tel: 0141-221 3075 **Fax:** 0141-226 5501
E-mail: info@henryabram.co.uk
Website: http://www.henryabram.co.uk
Bank(s): Clydesdale Bank PLC
Directors: S. Abram (Dir)
Managers: H. Ewart (Fin Mgr)
Immediate Holding Company: HENRY ABRAM & SONS LIMITED
Registration no: SC128293 **VAT No.:** GB 596 5216 07
Date established: 1990 **Turnover:** £10m - £20m
No.of Employees: 21 - 50 **Product Groups:** 72, 74, 76, 82

Date of Accounts	Sep 11	Sep 10	Sep 09
Sales Turnover	14m	13m	7m
Pre Tax Profit/Loss	4m	1m	1m
Working Capital	2m	-519	-3m
Fixed Assets	2m	2m	3m
Current Assets	8m	3m	2m
Current Liabilities	3m	3m	1m

Active Energy Solutions
33-41 Kelvin Avenue Hillington Industrial Estate, Hillington Park, Glasgow, G52 4LT
Tel: 0141-892669
E-mail: j.mcburnie@activeenergysolutions.com
Website: http://www.aessolutions.co.uk
Directors: J. Mcburnie (Dir)
Immediate Holding Company: ACTIVE ENERGY SOLUTIONS LTD.
Registration no: SC230311 **Date established:** 2002
No.of Employees: 1 - 10 **Product Groups:** 40, 66

Date of Accounts	Jul 11	Jul 10	Jul 09
Working Capital	186	114	113
Fixed Assets	92	164	163
Current Assets	640	815	762

John R Adam & Sons Ltd
Riverside Berth King George V Dock, Glasgow, G51 4SD
Tel: 0141-440 0424 **Fax:** 0141-440 0874
E-mail: johnadams@jradams.co.uk
Website: http://www.jradam.co.uk
Bank(s): Bank of Scotland
Directors: D. McWatt (Fin), D. Walker (Dir), J. Adam (MD)
Ultimate Holding Company: JOHN R ADAM & SONS (HOLDINGS) LIMITED
Immediate Holding Company: JOHN R ADAM & SONS (HOLDINGS) LIMITED
Registration no: SC271214 **VAT No.:** GB 476 9758 70
Date established: 2004 **Turnover:** £75m - £125m
No.of Employees: 51 - 100 **Product Groups:** 42, 66

Date of Accounts	Dec 11	Dec 10	Dec 09
Sales Turnover	84m	70m	48m
Pre Tax Profit/Loss	3m	3m	3m
Working Capital	9m	7m	4m
Fixed Assets	4m	5m	5m
Current Assets	19m	17m	13m
Current Liabilities	7m	8m	6m

Adam Millar and Sons Ltd
22 Muriel Street Barrhead, Glasgow, G78 1QB
Tel: 0141-881 6000 **Fax:** 0141-881 6060
E-mail: info@adammillar.com
Website: http://www.adammillar.com
Directors: A. Millar (Prop), L. Millar (Fin)
Immediate Holding Company: Adam Millar & Sons Ltd
Registration no: SC245027 **VAT No.:** GB 343 2998 35
Date established: 2003 **Turnover:** Up to £250,000
No.of Employees: 1 - 10 **Product Groups:** 48

Adline Personalised Products
Sterling House 20 Renfield Street, Glasgow, G2 5AP
Tel: 0141-221 1491 **Fax:** 0141-248 4411
E-mail: sales@adlinepersonalised.com
Website: http://www.adlinepersonalised.com
Directors: D. Calder (Ptnr)
Ultimate Holding Company: BARWELL PLC
Immediate Holding Company: OPTOSWIM TECHNOLOGIES LTD
Registration no: SO302242 **VAT No.:** GB 376 5156 29
Date established: 2007 **Turnover:** £2m - £5m **No.of Employees:** 1 - 10
Product Groups: 49, 81

Date of Accounts	Sep 11	Sep 10	Sep 09
Sales Turnover	252	311	238
Pre Tax Profit/Loss	-55	-35	-94
Working Capital	72	79	63
Fixed Assets	12	19	26
Current Assets	111	110	84
Current Liabilities	17	15	13

Advanced Data Services
77 Dunn Street, Glasgow, G40 3PA
Tel: 0141-550 3408 **Fax:** 0141-550 3409
E-mail: rprior@ads.uk.com
Website: http://www.ads.uk.com
Directors: R. Prior (MD)
Managers: C. McCoombes (Personnel), G. Hunter (Fin Mgr), J. Nolan (Mgr)
Immediate Holding Company: ADVANCED DATA SERVICES LTD.
Registration no: SC176453 **Date established:** 1997
No.of Employees: 21 - 50 **Product Groups:** 44

Date of Accounts	Dec 09	Dec 08	Dec 07
Working Capital	47	121	228
Fixed Assets	510	546	517
Current Assets	276	606	596

Aeron Automation Ltd
46-48 Wilson Place East Kilbride, Glasgow, G74 4QD
Tel: 01355-226022 **Fax:** 01355-235077
E-mail: info@aeron.co.uk
Website: http://www.aeron.co.uk
Directors: A. Rae (MD)
Immediate Holding Company: AERON AUTOMATION LIMITED
Registration no: SC087533 **VAT No.:** GB 383 0591 47
Date established: 1984 **Turnover:** £500,000 - £1m
No.of Employees: 1 - 10 **Product Groups:** 48

Date of Accounts	Mar 12	Mar 11	Mar 10
Working Capital	140	83	82
Fixed Assets	88	14	64
Current Assets	285	232	148

Agripa Solutions
43 Colquhoun Avenue Hillington Park, Glasgow, G52 4BN
Tel: 0141-810 8780 **Fax:** 08700-859001
E-mail: info@agripa.com
Website: http://www.agripa.com
Directors: A. Shearer (Dir), J. Pitt (MD)
Managers: D. Gibson (Nat Sales Mgr), M. Hendry (Publicity)
Immediate Holding Company: AGRIPA SOLUTIONS LIMITED
Registration no: SC345011 **Date established:** 2008
Turnover: Over £1,000m **No.of Employees:** 21 - 50 **Product Groups:** 28, 30

Date of Accounts	Feb 11	Feb 10	Feb 09
Working Capital	-6	-125	32
Fixed Assets	276	143	N/A
Current Assets	752	746	88

Air Power & Hydraulics Ltd
13-15 Watt Road, Glasgow, G52 4PQ
Tel: 0141-810 4511 **Fax:** 0141-883 3825
E-mail: hydraulics@aph.co.uk
Website: http://www.aph.co.uk
Directors: I. Paterson (MD), K. Bookman (Dir), E. Bookman (Fin)
Managers: R. Sim (Comm), H. McQueen (Project Eng)
Immediate Holding Company: AIR POWER AND HYDRAULICS LIMITED
Registration no: SC041287 **Date established:** 1964 **Turnover:** £1m - £2m
No.of Employees: 21 - 50 **Product Groups:** 38, 40, 45, 46, 48, 67, 84

Date of Accounts	Dec 11	Dec 10	Dec 09
Sales Turnover	9m	N/A	N/A
Pre Tax Profit/Loss	661	N/A	N/A
Working Capital	2m	2m	1m
Fixed Assets	526	545	512
Current Assets	4m	6m	3m
Current Liabilities	2m	N/A	N/A

Alarm Supply Direct
Lorimer Crescent East Kilbride, Glasgow, G75 9AZ
Tel: 01355-574667
Directors: R. Stewart (Prop)
No.of Employees: 1 - 10 **Product Groups:** 40, 52, 67

Alba Forklift Training
6 Lenziemill Road Cumbernauld, Glasgow, G67 2RL
Tel: 01236-630300 **Fax:** 01236-630300
E-mail: andy@albatraining.co.uk
Website: http://www.albatraining.co.uk
Directors: A. Westbury (Dir)
Immediate Holding Company: ALBA FORKLIFT TRAINING LIMITED
Registration no: SC348473 **Date established:** 2008
Turnover: Up to £250,000 **No.of Employees:** 1 - 10 **Product Groups:** 86

Date of Accounts	Sep 11	Sep 10	Sep 09
Working Capital	5	7	-0
Fixed Assets	2	4	1
Current Assets	17	15	7

Albion Automotive Ltd
1187 South Street, Glasgow, G14 0DT
Tel: 0141-434 2400 **Fax:** 0141-959 6362
E-mail: garry.mcfarlane@aam.com
Website: http://www.aam.com
Directors: B. Haswell (Pers), G. McFarlane (Fin), P. Lancaster (Co Sec)
Managers: T. McKinlay (Purch Mgr), B. Macleod (Mgr), N. McCall
Ultimate Holding Company: AMERICAN AXLE AND MANUFACTURING INC (USA)
Immediate Holding Company: ALBION AUTOMOTIVE (HOLDINGS) LIMITED
Registration no: SC159013 **Date established:** 1995
Turnover: £20m - £50m **No.of Employees:** 101 - 250 **Product Groups:** 39

Date of Accounts	Dec 11	Dec 10	Dec 09
Pre Tax Profit/Loss	-25	-27	-1m
Working Capital	3m	3m	3m
Current Assets	3m	3m	3m

Matthew Algie & Co. Ltd
16 Lawmoor Road, Glasgow, G5 0UL
Tel: 0141-429 2817 **Fax:** 0141-429 3389
E-mail: garynicol@matthewalgie.com
Website: http://www.matthewalgie.com
Directors: C. Moxham (Sales & Mktg), G. Nicol (Fin)
Managers: B. Corkindale (Tech Serv Mgr), C. McTavish (Personnel), G. McCready (Comptroller), G. Muir (Mktg Serv Mgr), N. King (Purch Mgr)
Immediate Holding Company: MATTHEW ALGIE & COMPANY LIMITED
Registration no: SC028433 **Date established:** 1951
Turnover: £20m - £50m **No.of Employees:** 101 - 250
Product Groups: 40, 62, 67, 86

Date of Accounts	Dec 11	Dec 10	Dec 09
Sales Turnover	33m	33m	29m
Pre Tax Profit/Loss	2m	2m	1m
Working Capital	8m	7m	5m
Fixed Assets	5m	5m	6m
Current Assets	12m	11m	9m
Current Liabilities	2m	2m	1m

Allan Interiors Ltd
27 Lister Road, Glasgow, G52 4BH
Tel: 0141-882 5761 **Fax:** 0141-810 5026
E-mail: office@allaninteriors.com
Website: http://www.allaninteriors.com
Directors: B. Allan (MD)
Immediate Holding Company: ALLAN COMMERCIAL AND INDUSTRIAL INTERIORS LIMITED
Registration no: SC239838 **Date established:** 2002
No.of Employees: 1 - 10 **Product Groups:** 25, 35

Date of Accounts	Dec 11	Dec 10	Dec 09
Sales Turnover	792	N/A	N/A
Pre Tax Profit/Loss	54	N/A	N/A
Working Capital	-45	-45	-62
Fixed Assets	8	7	14
Current Assets	99	67	63
Current Liabilities	N/A	48	32

Allmet Surface Coatings Ltd
48 Lochburn Road, Glasgow, G20 9AE
Tel: 0141-945 4790 **Fax:** 0141-946 6656
E-mail: allmetcoatings@aol.com
Website: http://www.hometown.aol.co.uk/allmetcoatings/myhomepage/business.html
Directors: A. Meechan (MD)
Immediate Holding Company: ALLMET SURFACE COATINGS LTD.
Registration no: SC192738 **Date established:** 1999
Turnover: £250,000 - £500,000 **No.of Employees:** 1 - 10
Product Groups: 37, 48

Date of Accounts	Jan 12	Jan 11	Jan 10
Working Capital	-9	-0	-6
Fixed Assets	14	19	21
Current Assets	67	73	50

Almet Doors
1a Blairlinn Road Cumbernauld, Glasgow, G67 2TF
Tel: 01236-730303 **Fax:** 01236-739937
E-mail: adeas@almetdoors.co.uk
Website: http://www.almetdoors.co.uk
Directors: A. Deas (Prop)
Date established: 2000 **No.of Employees:** 11 - 20 **Product Groups:** 26, 35

American Express Travel (Branch Office, Travel Division)
115 Hope Street, Glasgow, G2 6LL
Tel: 08706-001060 **Fax:** 0141-204 2685
E-mail: sales@americanexpress.co.uk
Website: http://www.americanexpress.co.uk
Managers: B. Dillon (Mgr)
Immediate Holding Company: AMERICAN EXPRESS EUROPE LIMITED
Registration no: FC011790 **VAT No.:** GB 190 1985 48
Date established: 1983 **No.of Employees:** 1 - 10 **Product Groups:** 69

Anderside Tools Ltd
19-25 Colvilles Place Kelvin Industrial Estate, East Kilbride, Glasgow, G75 0PZ
Tel: 01355-245455 **Fax:** 01355-245054
E-mail: admin@andersidetools.com
Website: http://www.andersidetools.com
Bank(s): Clydesdale
Directors: H. Mckinnon (MD)
Managers: G. McKinnon (Tech Serv Mgr)
Immediate Holding Company: ANDERSIDE TOOLS LIMITED
Registration no: SC082501 **VAT No.:** GB 376 6821 15
Date established: 1983 **Turnover:** £2m - £5m **No.of Employees:** 21 - 50
Product Groups: 48

Date of Accounts	Aug 11	Aug 10	Aug 09
Working Capital	-230	-304	-298
Fixed Assets	417	365	317
Current Assets	565	415	162

Aon Ltd
131 St Vincent Street, Glasgow, G2 5JF
Tel: 0141-222 7000 **Fax:** 0141-222 7100
E-mail: james.grant@aon.co.uk
Website: http://www.aon.com
Bank(s): The Royal Bank of Scotland
Directors: J. Grant (Dir)
Ultimate Holding Company: AON PLC
Immediate Holding Company: A1 VENTURES LIMITED
Registration no: 04578543 **Date established:** 2002
Turnover: £500,000 - £1m **No.of Employees:** 101 - 250
Product Groups: 86

Date of Accounts	Dec 11	Dec 10	Dec 09
Sales Turnover	486	540	600
Pre Tax Profit/Loss	636	10m	748
Working Capital	21m	21m	11m
Fixed Assets	4	4	4
Current Assets	21m	21m	11m
Current Liabilities	84	33	97

Aon Ltd
103-105 Waterloo Street, Glasgow, G2 7BW
Tel: 0141-248 5070 **Fax:** 0141-222 3345
E-mail: morris.mcewan@ars.aon.co.uk
Website: http://www.aon.co.uk
Bank(s): National Westminster Bank Plc
Directors: M. Cromar (Div)
Immediate Holding Company: A1 VENTURES LIMITED
Registration no: 04578543 **VAT No.:** GB 508 9239 26
Date established: 2002 **Turnover:** £20m - £50m
No.of Employees: 11 - 20 **Product Groups:** 82

Date of Accounts	Dec 11	Dec 10	Dec 09
Sales Turnover	669m	640m	646m
Pre Tax Profit/Loss	140m	100m	28m
Working Capital	537m	591m	540m
Fixed Assets	141m	148m	156m
Current Assets	5145m	5612m	5565m
Current Liabilities	4455m	4790m	4866m

Apollo Distribution Solutions Ltd
Anderston Centre Blythswood Court, Glasgow, G2 7PH
Tel: 0141-221 5577 **Fax:** 0141-221 0044
E-mail: glasgow@apollods.co.uk
Website: http://www.apollods.co.uk
Directors: D. Grant (MD)
Immediate Holding Company: APOLLO DISTRIBUTION SOLUTIONS LTD
Registration no: 04352970 **Date established:** 2002
No.of Employees: 1 - 10 **Product Groups:** 79

Date of Accounts	Mar 12	Mar 11	Mar 10
Working Capital	45	37	58
Fixed Assets	21	13	10
Current Assets	45	59	78

Arc Force
35 Tollpark Place Wardpark East, Cumbernauld, Glasgow, G68 0LN
Tel: 01236-451199 **Fax:** 01236-780305
Website: http://www.arcforce.co.uk
Directors: J. Shirkie (Fin)
Immediate Holding Company: ARC FORCE WELDING EQUIPMENT SERVICES LIMITED
Registration no: SC258358 **Date established:** 2003
No.of Employees: 1 - 10 **Product Groups:** 46

Date of Accounts	Sep 11	Sep 10	Sep 09
Working Capital	30	32	25
Current Assets	101	98	91

Arnold Clark Automobiles Ltd
134 Nithsdale Drive, Glasgow, G41 2PP
Tel: 0141-422 2700 **Fax:** 0141-422 2784
E-mail: glasgow.fiat@arnoldclark.co.uk
Website: http://www.arnoldclark.co.uk
Directors: W. Gall (Dir), P. Clark (Dir), K. Mclean (MD), J. Clark (Dir)
Managers: K. Whyte (Parts Mgr), C. Phillips, C. Philips (Chief Mgr), S. Kinnaird (Sales Prom Mgr)
Ultimate Holding Company: ARNOLD CLARK AUTOMOBILES LIMITED
Immediate Holding Company: ARNOLD CLARK FINANCE LIMITED.
Registration no: SC039597 **VAT No.:** GB 334 3318 79
Date established: 1963 **Turnover:** £125m - £250m
No.of Employees: 1 - 10 **Product Groups:** 68

Date of Accounts	Dec 11	Dec 10	Dec 09
Sales Turnover	161m	155m	142m
Pre Tax Profit/Loss	9m	8m	7m
Working Capital	-160m	-158m	-167m
Fixed Assets	383m	375m	364m
Current Assets	52m	58m	63m
Current Liabilities	47m	49m	42m

Arnold Clark Automobiles
163 St Georges Road, Glasgow, G3 6LB
Tel: 0141-352 5252 **Fax:** 0141-352 5253
E-mail: acf@arnoldclark.co.uk
Website: http://www.arnoldclarkfinance.co.uk
Bank(s): The Royal Bank of Scotland
Managers: S. Longridge (Chief Mgr)
Immediate Holding Company: ARNOLD CLARK AUTOMOBILES LIMITED
Registration no: SC036386 **Date established:** 1961
Turnover: £500m - £1,000m **No.of Employees:** 51 - 100
Product Groups: 72

Artstore Ltd
94 Queen Street, Glasgow, G1 3AQ
Tel: 0141-221 1101 **Fax:** 0141-204 2902
E-mail: customerservices@artstore.co.uk
Website: http://www.artstore.co.uk
Bank(s): Bank of Scotland
Directors: M. Kilmurry (MD)
Immediate Holding Company: ARTSTORE LIMITED
Registration no: SC153095 **VAT No.:** GB 290 3109 78
Date established: 1994 **Turnover:** £1m - £2m **No.of Employees:** 11 - 20
Product Groups: 25, 36, 49, 64

Date of Accounts	Mar 11	Mar 10	Mar 09
Working Capital	135	-347	-441
Fixed Assets	309	348	398
Current Assets	378	330	290

Asco Extinguishers Company Ltd
Unit 1.1 9 Brand Place, Glasgow, G51 1DR
Tel: 0141-427 1144 **Fax:** 0141-427 6644
E-mail: sales@asco.uk.com
Website: http://www.asco.uk.com
Managers: H. Hyman (Mgr)
Ultimate Holding Company: EOI FIRE SARL (LUXEMBOURG)
Immediate Holding Company: ASCO EXTINGUISHERS COMPANY LIMITED
Registration no: SC049134 **VAT No.:** GB 259 6570 18
Date established: 1971 **Turnover:** £1m - £2m **No.of Employees:** 21 - 50
Product Groups: 40, 52, 86

Date of Accounts	Dec 11	Dec 10	Dec 09
Sales Turnover	2m	2m	2m
Pre Tax Profit/Loss	244	218	508
Working Capital	2m	1m	3m
Fixed Assets	143	241	437
Current Assets	2m	2m	3m
Current Liabilities	217	238	327

Aviat Networks
2 Bell Drive Hamilton International Technology Park, Blantyre, Glasgow, G72 0FB
Tel: 01698-717200 **Fax:** 01698-717204
E-mail: martin_broomfield@stratexnet.com
Website: http://www.aviatnetworks.com
Directors: M. Broomfield (Dir)
Immediate Holding Company: THE KILBRYDE HOSPICE
Registration no: SC224366 **Date established:** 2001
Turnover: £250,000 - £500,000 **No.of Employees:** 21 - 50
Product Groups: 37, 38

Date of Accounts	Mar 11	Mar 10	Mar 09
Sales Turnover	385	371	343
Pre Tax Profit/Loss	124	163	229
Working Capital	2m	2m	2m
Fixed Assets	5	6	7
Current Assets	2m	2m	2m
Current Liabilities	26	23	25

B G S Productions Ltd
Newtown Street Kilsyth, Glasgow, G65 0LY
Tel: 01236-821081 **Fax:** 01236-826900
E-mail: info@scotdisc.co.uk
Website: http://www.scotdisc.co.uk
Directors: D. Stevenson (Fin)
Managers: J. Mackintosh (Cust Serv Mgr)
Immediate Holding Company: B.G.S.Productions Ltd
Registration no: SC060598 **VAT No.:** GB 262 7640 53
Date established: 1976 **Turnover:** £500,000 - £1m
No.of Employees: 1 - 10 **Product Groups:** 61

Date of Accounts	Apr 08	Apr 07
Working Capital	-88	-104
Fixed Assets	98	140
Current Assets	589	680
Current Liabilities	677	783
Total Share Capital	1	1

B S S Group
Unit A Vermont Street, Glasgow, G41 1LU
Tel: 0141-418 4444 **Fax:** 0141-429 2638
E-mail: 1540.sales@bssgroup.com
Website: http://www.bssgroup.com
Bank(s): HSBC Bank plc

see next page

B S S Group - Cont'd
Managers: T. Stewart (District Mgr)
Ultimate Holding Company: TRAVIS PERKINS PLC
Immediate Holding Company: RG BESPOKE JOINERY LIMITED
Registration no: 00060987 **Date established:** 2006
Turnover: £10m - £20m **No.of Employees:** 21 - 50 **Product Groups:** 35, 84

Date of Accounts	Nov 08	Nov 07
Working Capital	-144	-83
Fixed Assets	30	41
Current Assets	14	34

Ted Baker plc
The Glasshouse Princes Square 48 Buchanan Street, Glasgow, G1 3JN
Tel: 0141-221 9664 **Fax:** 0141-221 3544
Website: http://www.tedbaker.com
Managers: M. Bentley (Mgr)
Immediate Holding Company: TED BAKER PLC
Registration no: 03393836 **Date established:** 1997
No.of Employees: 11 - 20 **Product Groups:** 24, 63

Date of Accounts	Jan 09	Jan 10	Jan 11
Sales Turnover	153m	164m	188m
Pre Tax Profit/Loss	18m	20m	24m
Working Capital	31m	39m	45m
Fixed Assets	31m	29m	33m
Current Assets	65m	67m	84m
Current Liabilities	17m	18m	20m

Banlaw Systems Europe Ltd
Unit 1-3 Rosendale Way Blantyre, Glasgow, G72 0NJ
Tel: 01698-824431 **Fax:** 01698-826725
E-mail: info@banlawsystems.com
Website: http://www.banlawsystems.com
Managers: A. McAteer (Mgr)
Immediate Holding Company: BANLAW (EUROPE) LIMITED
Registration no: SC126306 **Date established:** 1990
No.of Employees: 1 - 10 **Product Groups:** 30, 84, 87

Date of Accounts	Apr 11	Apr 10	Apr 09
Working Capital	48	46	48
Current Assets	292	261	287
Current Liabilities	117	117	N/A

Barclay & Mathieson Ltd
180 Hardgate Road, Glasgow, G51 4TB
Tel: 0141-445 2591 **Fax:** 0141-445 6964
E-mail: admin@bmsteel.co.uk
Website: http://www.bmsteel.co.uk
Bank(s): Bank of Scotland
Directors: J. Walker (MD), M. Norrie (Dir), N. Watson (MD), P. Bradburn (Fin), A. Dykes (Dir)
Managers: A. Miller (Purch Mgr), P. Mckendrick (Sales Prom Mgr), A. MacKay (Accounts)
Ultimate Holding Company: STEMCOR HOLDINGS LIMITED
Immediate Holding Company: BARCLAY & MATHIESON LIMITED
Registration no: SC030987 **VAT No.:** GB 723 9322 39
Date established: 1955 **Turnover:** £20m - £50m
No.of Employees: 21 - 50 **Product Groups:** 34, 35, 48, 66

Date of Accounts	Dec 11	Dec 10	Dec 09
Sales Turnover	55m	48m	35m
Pre Tax Profit/Loss	2m	2m	-865
Working Capital	11m	13m	13m
Fixed Assets	19m	16m	18m
Current Assets	24m	25m	20m
Current Liabilities	4m	5m	713

Bardyke Chemicals Ltd
Hamilton Road Cambuslang, Glasgow, G72 7XL
Tel: 01698-823361 **Fax:** 01698-820535
E-mail: sales@bardyke.com
Website: http://www.bardyke.com
Bank(s): Bank of Scotland, East Kilbridge
Managers: D. Wightman (Comm)
Immediate Holding Company: BARDYKE CHEMICALS LIMITED
Registration no: SC045492 **VAT No.:** GB 259 7411 33
Date established: 1968 **Turnover:** £5m - £10m **No.of Employees:** 11 - 20
Product Groups: 31

Date of Accounts	Dec 11	Dec 10	Dec 09
Sales Turnover	6m	6m	4m
Pre Tax Profit/Loss	476	750	541
Working Capital	2m	2m	1m
Fixed Assets	687	625	636
Current Assets	3m	3m	2m
Current Liabilities	521	419	464

Barr Wray Ltd
324 Drumoyne Road, Glasgow, G51 4DY
Tel: 0141-882 5757 **Fax:** 0141-882 3690
E-mail: sales@barrandwray.com
Website: http://www.barrandwray.com
Bank(s): Clydesdale Bank PLC
Directors: A. Macdonald (Fin)
Ultimate Holding Company: BARR + WRAY GROUP LIMITED
Immediate Holding Company: BARR + WRAY LIMITED
Registration no: SC040952 **VAT No.:** GB 680 6451 27
Date established: 1964 **Turnover:** £10m - £20m
No.of Employees: 51 - 100 **Product Groups:** 33, 38, 42

Date of Accounts	Sep 11	Sep 10	Sep 09
Sales Turnover	14m	12m	12m
Pre Tax Profit/Loss	1m	843	777
Working Capital	2m	1m	888
Fixed Assets	2m	2m	2m
Current Assets	10m	7m	6m
Current Liabilities	6m	4m	4m

Begg Cousland & Co. Ltd
Building 5 Studio 3 Templeton Business Centre 62 Templeton Street, Glasgow, G40 1DA
Tel: 0141-556 5288 **Fax:** 0141-554 7447
E-mail: sales@beggcousland.com
Website: http://www.beggcousland.com
Directors: I. Ross (Fin)
Ultimate Holding Company: BEGG, COUSLAND HOLDINGS LIMITED
Immediate Holding Company: BEGG.COUSLAND & COMPANY LIMITED
Registration no: SC013244 **VAT No.:** GB 552 2727 49
Date established: 2024 **Turnover:** £2m - £5m **No.of Employees:** 1 - 10
Product Groups: 40, 42

Date of Accounts	Mar 11	Mar 10	Mar 09
Working Capital	-2m	-2m	-1m
Fixed Assets	2	2	2
Current Assets	942	1m	2m

Bell & Bain Ltd
303 Burnfield Road Thornliebank, Glasgow, G46 7UQ
Tel: 0141-649 5697 **Fax:** 0141-632 8733
E-mail: info@bell-bain.co.uk
Website: http://www.bell-bain.com
Bank(s): Clydesdale Bank PLC
Directors: D. Stewart (Sales), I. Walker (MD), S. Docherty (Dir)
Ultimate Holding Company: BELL & BAIN (2009) LIMITED
Immediate Holding Company: BELL & BAIN LIMITED
Registration no: SC002168 **VAT No.:** GB 259 5286 20
Date established: 1991 **Turnover:** £5m - £10m
No.of Employees: 51 - 100 **Product Groups:** 28, 44

Date of Accounts	Dec 11	Dec 10	Dec 09
Sales Turnover	8m	8m	8m
Pre Tax Profit/Loss	598	525	305
Working Capital	579	1m	1m
Fixed Assets	4m	4m	4m
Current Assets	5m	5m	5m
Current Liabilities	1m	1m	349

Biffa Waste Services Ltd
Clydesmill Industrial Estate, Glasgow, G32 8RG
Tel: 0141-646 3700 **Fax:** 0141-646 1745
E-mail: hugh.hamilton@biffa.co.uk
Website: http://www.biffa.co.uk
Managers: H. Hamilton (Mgr)
Immediate Holding Company: BIFFA WASTE SERVICES LIMITED
Registration no: 00946107 **Date established:** 1969
No.of Employees: 21 - 50 **Product Groups:** 32, 54

Date of Accounts	Mar 08	Mar 09	Apr 10
Sales Turnover	555m	574m	492m
Pre Tax Profit/Loss	23m	50m	30m
Working Capital	229m	271m	293m
Fixed Assets	371m	360m	378m
Current Assets	409m	534m	609m
Current Liabilities	50m	100m	115m

Biggars Music Shops Ltd
273 Sauchiehall Street, Glasgow, G2 3HQ
Tel: 0141-332 8676 **Fax:** 0141-572 6963
E-mail: david@biggars.co.uk
Website: http://www.biggars.co.uk
Directors: G. Hutchison (Dir), D. Hutchison (MD), D. Hutchison (Dir)
Immediate Holding Company: BEARSDEN BUSINESS SERVICES LIMITED
Registration no: SC226520 **Date established:** 2012
No.of Employees: 1 - 10 **Product Groups:** 49

Biggart Baillie
Dalmore House 310 St Vincent Street, Glasgow, G2 5QR
Tel: 0141-228 8000 **Fax:** 0141-228 8310
E-mail: info@biggartbaillie.co.uk
Website: http://www.biggartbaillie.co.uk
Bank(s): Clydesdale Bank PLC & The Royal Bank of Scotland
Directors: A. Davidson (Fin), A. McKenzie (Tech Serv), R. McNially (Mkt Research)
Managers: A. Peacock (Mgr), D. Lindsay (Personnel)
Immediate Holding Company: BIGGART BAILLIE LLP
Registration no: SO301366 **Date established:** 2007
Turnover: £10m - £20m **No.of Employees:** 101 - 250 **Product Groups:** 80

Date of Accounts	Jun 11	Jun 10	Jun 09
Sales Turnover	16m	16m	17m
Pre Tax Profit/Loss	6m	5m	4m
Working Capital	5m	6m	6m
Fixed Assets	2m	2m	2m
Current Assets	9m	8m	8m
Current Liabilities	2m	2m	2m

Biochannel Partners Ltd
81 Clouston Street North Kelvinside, Glasgow, G20 8QW
Tel: 0141-945 0228 **Fax:** 0141-626 3403
E-mail: info@biochannelpartners.com
Website: http://www.biochannelpartners.com
Directors: A. Corber (MD)
Immediate Holding Company: BIOCHANNEL PARTNERS LIMITED
Registration no: SC243337 **Date established:** 2003
No.of Employees: 1 - 10 **Product Groups:** 30, 31, 38

Date of Accounts	Feb 08	Feb 11	Feb 10
Working Capital	-1	-18	-4
Current Assets	4	4	4

Walter Black Foods Ltd
3 Drumhead Road Cambusland Investment Park, Glasgow East Investment Park, Glasgow, G32 8EX
Tel: 0141-641 0000 **Fax:** 0141-641 0133
E-mail: sales@walterblack.co.uk
Website: http://www.walterblack.co.uk
Bank(s): Bank of Scotland
Directors: S. Black (Fin), W. Black (MD), W. Black (MD)
Managers: E. Foster (Personnel), C. Macaleer (Buyer)
Ultimate Holding Company: WALTER BLACK (HOLDINGS) LIMITED
Immediate Holding Company: WALTER BLACK FOODS LIMITED
Registration no: SC037050 **VAT No.:** GB 259 5157 31
Date established: 1961 **Turnover:** £10m - £20m
No.of Employees: 21 - 50 **Product Groups:** 20

Date of Accounts	Sep 09	Sep 08	Sep 07
Sales Turnover	7m	N/A	N/A
Pre Tax Profit/Loss	181	105	-0
Working Capital	2m	2m	2m
Fixed Assets	370	356	335
Current Assets	4m	3m	2m
Current Liabilities	300	157	130

Blockstopper Greasetraps
Unit 6 Priestfield Industrial Estate Blantyre, Glasgow, G72 0DN
Tel: 01698-828131
E-mail: info@blockstopper.co.uk
Website: http://www.blockstopper.co.uk
Managers: J. Yoker (Mgr)
No.of Employees: 1 - 10 **Product Groups:** 32, 40, 48, 84

Botterills
Block 9 South Avenue, Blantyre, Glasgow, G72 0XB
Tel: 01698-824311 **Fax:** 01698-824231
E-mail: allan.craig@botterills.net
Website: http://www.botterills.net
Bank(s): Clydesdale Bank PLC
Directors: A. Craig (Fin), B. Straiton (Dir), T. Gibson (I.T. Dir), I. Lane (Dir), L. Craig (MD)
Managers: D. Boyle (Sales Admin)
Immediate Holding Company: BOTTERILLS CONVENIENCE STORES LIMITED
Registration no: SC150446 **VAT No.:** GB 259 6291 22
Date established: 1994 **Turnover:** £75m - £125m
No.of Employees: 501 - 1000 **Product Groups:** 49, 61

Braid Logistics UK Ltd
Maritime House 143 Woodville Street, Glasgow, G51 2RQ
Tel: 0141-445 2525 **Fax:** 0141-440 1238
E-mail: ngray@braidco.com
Website: http://www.braidco.com
Bank(s): The Royal Bank of Scotland
Directors: S. Penson (Co Sec), A. Haldane (Fin)
Managers: N. Gray, G. Watson (Sales Prom Mgr)
Ultimate Holding Company: BRAID GROUP (HOLDINGS) LIMITED
Immediate Holding Company: BRAID LOGISTICS (UK) LIMITED
Registration no: SC048793 **VAT No.:** GB 552 3767 32
Date established: 1971 **Turnover:** £20m - £50m
No.of Employees: 51 - 100 **Product Groups:** 76

Date of Accounts	Jun 11	Jun 10	Jun 09
Sales Turnover	42m	44m	46m
Pre Tax Profit/Loss	1m	2m	2m
Working Capital	2m	3m	4m
Fixed Assets	4m	4m	4m
Current Assets	9m	13m	13m
Current Liabilities	4m	6m	5m

Brighthouse Ltd
404 Dumbarton Road, Glasgow, G11 6BY
Tel: 0141-357 6434 **Fax:** 0141-357 6488
E-mail: customer.relations@brighthouse.co.uk
Website: http://www.brighthouse.co.uk
Managers: S. Hunter (Mgr)
Ultimate Holding Company: VISION CAPITAL PARTNERS VI B LP
Immediate Holding Company: BRIGHTHOUSE LIMITED
Registration no: 06073794 **Date established:** 2007
No.of Employees: 1 - 10 **Product Groups:** 36, 40

Date of Accounts	Mar 12	Mar 11	Mar 10
Sales Turnover	266m	228m	197m
Pre Tax Profit/Loss	29m	25m	20m
Working Capital	57m	49m	68m
Fixed Assets	171m	161m	123m
Current Assets	97m	87m	98m
Current Liabilities	29m	26m	22m

British Heat Treatments
40 Milton Road East Kilbride, Glasgow, G74 5BU
Tel: 01355-225288 **Fax:** 01355-265845
E-mail: jbridges@ajt-engineering.co.uk
Website: http://www.bmt-eastkilbride.co.uk
Managers: J. Bridges (Chief Mgr)
Immediate Holding Company: BRITISH METAL TREATMENTS LTD
Turnover: £500,000 - £1m **No.of Employees:** 1 - 10 **Product Groups:** 48, 84, 85

Brodie Label Services Ltd
4 Dunnwoods Road Cumbernauld, Glasgow, G67 3EN
Tel: 01236-736984 **Fax:** 01236-731953
E-mail: info@brodielabels.co.uk
Website: http://www.brodielabels.co.uk
Directors: T. Brodie (MD), M. Brodie (Dir)
Immediate Holding Company: BRODIE LABEL SERVICES LIMITED
Registration no: SC158023 **VAT No.:** GB 624 4074 59
Date established: 1995 **Turnover:** £500,000 - £1m
No.of Employees: 1 - 10 **Product Groups:** 27, 28, 30, 42

Date of Accounts	Feb 12	Feb 11	Feb 10
Working Capital	-116	-94	-97
Fixed Assets	160	170	196
Current Assets	135	103	129

Brown Son & Ferguson Ltd
4-10 Darnley Street, Glasgow, G41 2SD
Tel: 0141-429 1234 **Fax:** 0141-420 1694
E-mail: richard@skipper.co.uk
Website: http://www.skipper.co.uk
Directors: N. Brown (Fin), R. Brown (Dir)
Immediate Holding Company: BROWN SON AND FERGUSON, LIMITED
Registration no: SC011878 **VAT No.:** GB 259 5244 36
Date established: 2021 **Turnover:** £500,000 - £1m
No.of Employees: 1 - 10 **Product Groups:** 28, 64

Date of Accounts	Dec 11	Dec 10	Dec 09
Working Capital	800	758	713
Fixed Assets	40	53	57
Current Assets	1m	1m	1m

Buck & Hickman
70 Lancefield Street, Glasgow, G3 8JD
Tel: 0141-221 7174 **Fax:** 0141-221 8877
E-mail: glasgow@buckandhickman.com
Website: http://www.buckandhickman.com
Managers: L. Johnson (Mgr)
Ultimate Holding Company: TRAVIS PERKINS PLC
Immediate Holding Company: BOSTON (2011) LIMITED
Registration no: 06028304 **Date established:** 2006
No.of Employees: 1 - 10 **Product Groups:** 24, 29, 30, 33, 36, 37, 41, 46

Date of Accounts	Dec 10	Mar 10	Mar 09
Working Capital	6m	6m	6m
Current Assets	27m	27m	27m

Business Cost Consultants
Pavilion 3 Business Park Minerva Way, Glasgow, G3 8AU
Tel: 0141-226 8525 **Fax:** 0141-226 8526
E-mail: info@businesscostconsultants.co.uk
Website: http://www.businesscostconsultants.co.uk
Directors: D. Maclean (MD)
Immediate Holding Company: BUSINESS COST CONSULTANTS LIMITED
Registration no: SC294893 **Date established:** 2005
No.of Employees: 11 - 20 **Product Groups:** 80

Date of Accounts	Mar 11	Mar 10	Mar 09
Working Capital	125	49	11
Fixed Assets	51	64	69
Current Assets	265	179	128

C A F Designs Ltd
53 Calderglen Avenue Blantyre, Glasgow, G72 9UP
Tel: 01698-825660 **Fax:** 01698-825660
E-mail: info@cafdesigns.co.uk
Website: http://www.cafdesigns.co.uk

Directors: C. Fullerton (MD)
Immediate Holding Company: CAF DESIGNS LIMITED
Registration no: 06162536 **Date established:** 2007
No.of Employees: 1 - 10 **Product Groups:** 84

Date of Accounts	Mar 11	Mar 10	Mar 09
Working Capital	-1	N/A	4
Fixed Assets	2	N/A	N/A
Current Assets	9	10	8

C G L Systems

2 Young Place East Kilbride, Glasgow, G75 0TD
Tel: 01355-235561 **Fax:** 01355-247189
E-mail: sales@cglsystems.co.uk
Website: http://www.cglsystems.co.uk
Bank(s): Bank of Scotland, Prince Mall, East Kilbride
Directors: B. Mcintyre (MD), C. Macbride (Sales)
Managers: A. Keenan (Fin Mgr), J. Chaney, P. Bissett (Tech Serv Mgr), D. Traynor
Ultimate Holding Company: CGL SYSTEMS (HOLDINGS) LIMITED
Immediate Holding Company: CGL SYSTEMS LIMITED
Registration no: SC024587 **VAT No.:** GB 376 5549 10
Date established: 1946 **Turnover:** £5m - £10m
No.of Employees: 51 - 100 **Product Groups:** 52, 84

Date of Accounts	Mar 12	Mar 11	Mar 10
Sales Turnover	7m	5m	6m
Pre Tax Profit/Loss	244	-47	-8
Working Capital	562	-367	-381
Fixed Assets	2m	2m	2m
Current Assets	3m	1m	2m
Current Liabilities	472	210	342

C P L Petroleum

22 Hawbank Road East Kilbride, Glasgow, G74 5HA
Tel: 01355-249077 **Fax:** 01355-264043
E-mail: eastkilbride@cplpetroleum.co.uk
Website: http://www.cplpetroleum.co.uk
Managers: L. Wright (Mgr)
Ultimate Holding Company: CPL INDUSTRIES HOLDINGS LIMITED
Immediate Holding Company: CPL PETROLEUM LIMITED
Registration no: 03003860 **VAT No.:** GB 721 5764 39
Date established: 1994 **Turnover:** £2m - £5m **No.of Employees:** 1 - 10
Product Groups: 66

Date of Accounts	Mar 12	Mar 11	Mar 10
Pre Tax Profit/Loss	N/A	878	904
Working Capital	31	30m	30m
Fixed Assets	26	26m	26m
Current Assets	57	56m	56m
Current Liabilities	26	246	253

C T S Corporation

Block 6 Fourth Road Blantyre, Glasgow, G72 0XA
Tel: 01698-505050 **Fax:** 01698-506050
E-mail: allan.white@ctscorp.com
Website: http://www.ctscorp.com
Directors: K. Hall (Fin), A. White (MD), D. Kerr (Dir)
Managers: S. Martin (Mktg Serv Mgr), M. Macgregor (I.T. Exec), G. Lusk (Personnel), A. Murphy (Personnel), R. Milligan, G. Macgregor (Tech Serv Mgr), S. Hughes (Sales Prom Mgr)
Ultimate Holding Company: CTS CORPORATION INC. (USA)
Immediate Holding Company: CTS CORPORATION U.K. LIMITED
Registration no: SC090209 **Date established:** 1984
Turnover: £20m - £50m **No.of Employees:** 101 - 250
Product Groups: 48, 49

Date of Accounts	Dec 11	Dec 10	Dec 09
Sales Turnover	29m	27m	22m
Pre Tax Profit/Loss	5m	865	-3m
Working Capital	34m	31m	30m
Fixed Assets	5m	3m	4m
Current Assets	41m	37m	35m
Current Liabilities	2m	1m	2m

Cadogan Consultants Ltd

39 Cadogan Street, Glasgow, G2 7AB
Tel: 0141-270 7060 **Fax:** 0141-270 7061
E-mail: d.mcintyre@cadoganconsultants.co.uk
Website: http://www.cadoganconsultants.co.uk
Directors: D. Jackson (Co Sec), D. McIntyre (Dir)
Immediate Holding Company: CADOGAN CONSULT LIMITED
Registration no: SC267537 **Date established:** 2004 **Turnover:** £1m - £2m
No.of Employees: 1 - 10 **Product Groups:** 13, 25, 31, 32, 38, 40, 42, 45, 46, 48, 52, 54, 80, 81, 82, 84

Date of Accounts	May 11	May 10	May 08
Working Capital	10	10	18
Current Assets	357	99	22
Current Liabilities	310	44	N/A

Caledonian Care Systems

Unit H Taywood Enterprise Centre Duchess Place, Rutherglen, Glasgow, G73 1DR
Tel: 0141-647 8654 **Fax:** 0141-647 8263
E-mail: sales@caledoniancaresystems.co.uk
Website: http://www.disabilityequipment.com
Directors: D. Cheal (Co Sec), I. Dyer (Dir)
Immediate Holding Company: CALEDONIAN CARE SYSTEMS LIMITED
Registration no: SC262312 **Date established:** 2004
No.of Employees: 1 - 10 **Product Groups:** 35, 39, 45

Date of Accounts	Dec 11	Dec 10	Dec 09
Working Capital	117	120	118
Fixed Assets	58	34	23
Current Assets	270	243	228

Caledonian Industries Ltd

5 Atholl Avenue, Glasgow, G52 4UA
Tel: 0141-882 4691 **Fax:** 0141-810 3402
E-mail: alan@caledonian-group.co.uk
Website: http://www.caledonian-group.co.uk
Bank(s): Bank of Scotland
Directors: A. Thornton (MD), G. Fleming (Fin)
Ultimate Holding Company: MATERIALS CONSULTING LIMITED
Immediate Holding Company: CALEDONIAN INDUSTRIES LIMITED
Registration no: SC216439 **VAT No.:** GB 743 1207 65
Date established: 2001 **Turnover:** £5m - £10m **No.of Employees:** 21 - 50
Product Groups: 23, 25, 27, 29, 30, 31, 39, 76

Date of Accounts	Mar 11	Mar 10	Mar 09
Working Capital	1m	1m	925
Fixed Assets	180	242	311
Current Assets	2m	2m	2m

Camelot Catering Services Ltd

72 Coltness Street, Glasgow, G33 4JD
Tel: 0141-774 6666 **Fax:** 0141-774 6633
E-mail: camelotcatering@btconnect.com
Website: http://www.bt-internet.com
Directors: J. Ballantyne (MD), J. Ballantyne (Dir)
Immediate Holding Company: CAMELOT CATERING SERVICES LTD.
Registration no: SC226409 **Date established:** 2001
No.of Employees: 1 - 10 **Product Groups:** 20, 40, 41

Date of Accounts	Dec 11	Dec 10	Dec 09
Working Capital	149	213	253
Fixed Assets	11	22	33
Current Assets	213	274	320

Cameron Interiors Ltd

458-462 Crow Road, Glasgow, G11 7DR
Tel: 0141-334 9532 **Fax:** 0141-357 3869
E-mail: sales@cameroninteriors.co.uk
Website: http://www.cameroninteriors.co.uk
Directors: K. Robeson (Dir)
Immediate Holding Company: CAMERON INTERIORS LIMITED
Registration no: SC069523 **VAT No.:** GB 596 6798 51
Date established: 1979 **Turnover:** £500,000 - £1m
No.of Employees: 1 - 10 **Product Groups:** 25, 26, 33, 63, 66

Date of Accounts	Dec 11	Dec 10	Dec 09
Working Capital	-100	-152	-18
Fixed Assets	206	240	209
Current Assets	353	85	103

Cameron Presentations Ltd

Burnfield Road Giffnock, Glasgow, G46 7TH
Tel: 0141-637 0368 **Fax:** 0141-637 3559
E-mail: chris@cameronpres.co.uk
Website: http://www.cameronpres.co.uk
Directors: C. Cameron (Dir), E. Cameron (Fin)
Immediate Holding Company: CAMERON PRESENTATIONS LIMITED
Registration no: SC092410 **Date established:** 1985
Turnover: £500,000 - £1m **No.of Employees:** 11 - 20
Product Groups: 38, 44

Date of Accounts	Dec 11	Dec 10	Dec 09
Working Capital	525	612	726
Fixed Assets	211	247	296
Current Assets	923	931	1m

Campbell Miller Tools Ltd

20 Jordanvale Avenue, Glasgow, G14 0QU
Tel: 0141-954 9557 **Fax:** 0141-954 9979
E-mail: sales@cmtl.co.uk
Website: http://www.cmtl.co.uk
Managers: R. Cohn (Mgr)
Immediate Holding Company: CAMPBELL MILLER (TOOLS) LIMITED
Registration no: SC034278 **VAT No.:** GB 259 6495 06
Date established: 1959 **Turnover:** £1m - £2m **No.of Employees:** 11 - 20
Product Groups: 37, 41

Date of Accounts	Dec 11	Dec 10	Dec 09
Working Capital	288	313	364
Fixed Assets	12	10	12
Current Assets	1m	1m	1m

Cap Gemini

Regent Court 70 West Regent Street, Glasgow, G2 2QZ
Tel: 0141-331 0414 **Fax:** 0141- 3535858
Website: http://www.uk.capgemini.com
Directors: D. Meades (Fin), P. Spence (Grp Chief Exec), C. Williams (Grp Chief Exec)
Ultimate Holding Company: CAP GEMINI SA (FRANCE)
Immediate Holding Company: GEHELLISON FOODS LTD
Registration no: 00943935 **Date established:** 2010
Turnover: £125m - £250m **No.of Employees:** 1 - 10 **Product Groups:** 44, 84, 86

Date of Accounts	Aug 11
Working Capital	-0

Cardowan Creameries Ltd

49 Holywell Street, Glasgow, G31 4BT
Tel: 0141-554 1137 **Fax:** 0141-551 0619
E-mail: sales@cardowan.co.uk
Website: http://www.cardowan.co.uk
Bank(s): The Royal Bank of Scotland, Parkhead
Directors: J. Kyle (MD), L. McGhee (Fin)
Immediate Holding Company: CARDOWAN CREAMERIES LIMITED
Registration no: SC016247 **VAT No.:** GB 259 6999 75
Date established: 1930 **Turnover:** £10m - £20m
No.of Employees: 21 - 50 **Product Groups:** 20

Date of Accounts	Mar 12	Mar 11	Mar 10
Sales Turnover	18m	14m	11m
Pre Tax Profit/Loss	618	487	301
Working Capital	2m	2m	1m
Fixed Assets	311	379	454
Current Assets	4m	3m	2m
Current Liabilities	642	497	247

Careers Scotland

150 Broomielaw Atlantic Quay, Glasgow, G2 8LU
Tel: 0141-248 2700 **Fax:** 0141-221 5129
E-mail: investment@scotint.co.uk
Website: http://www.careers-scotland.org.uk
Directors: M. Togneri (MD)
Immediate Holding Company: Careers Trust Scotland Ltd
Registration no: SC194328 **Date established:** 1999
Turnover: £500,000 - £1m **No.of Employees:** 11 - 20 **Product Groups:** 87

Carlac

Unit 6-7 Block 3 356 Nuneaton Street, Glasgow, G40 3JU
Tel: 0141-554 1393 **Fax:** 0141-556 4862
Managers: A. Sim (Mgr), A. Simm (District Mgr), A. Sim (District Mgr)
Date established: 1986 **No.of Employees:** 1 - 10 **Product Groups:** 38, 42

Date of Accounts	Dec 10	Dec 09	Dec 08
Working Capital	N/A	N/A	-3m

James G Carrick & Co. Ltd

450 Petershill Road, Glasgow, G21 4PB
Tel: 0141-558 6008 **Fax:** 0141-557 0318
E-mail: sales@jamesgcarrick.com
Website: http://www.jamesgcarrick.com
Bank(s): Clydesdale
Directors: G. Carrick (MD)
Managers: R. Phillips (Sales Prom Mgr), E. Thomas (Sales Admin)
Ultimate Holding Company: CARRICK HOLDINGS LIMITED
Immediate Holding Company: JAMES G CARRICK & COMPANY LIMITED
Registration no: SC115023 **VAT No.:** GB 259 8244 33
Date established: 1988 **Turnover:** £5m - £10m
No.of Employees: 51 - 100 **Product Groups:** 30, 35, 36

Date of Accounts	Dec 11	Dec 10	Dec 09
Working Capital	2m	2m	1m
Fixed Assets	638	656	745
Current Assets	3m	3m	2m

Castle Precision Engineering Glasgow Ltd

241 Drakemire Drive, Glasgow, G45 9SZ
Tel: 0141-634 1377 **Fax:** 0141-634 3678
E-mail: sales@castleprecision.com
Website: http://www.castleprecision.com
Bank(s): Bank of Scotland, Glasgow
Directors: M. Tiefenbrun (MD)
Managers: A. Furniss, S. Docherty (Buyer), D. Lindsay (Tech Serv Mgr), J. Forrest (Fin Mgr), J. Hughes
Immediate Holding Company: CASTLE PRECISION ENGINEERING (GLASGOW) LIMITED
Registration no: SC039355 **Date established:** 1963
Turnover: £10m - £20m **No.of Employees:** 101 - 250
Product Groups: 48, 84

Date of Accounts	Jul 11	Jul 10	Jul 09
Sales Turnover	14m	13m	14m
Pre Tax Profit/Loss	-188	261	1m
Working Capital	2m	3m	3m
Fixed Assets	8m	8m	7m
Current Assets	5m	5m	5m
Current Liabilities	736	637	501

Caurnie Soap Co.

The Organic Herb Garden Canal Lane, Kirkintilloch, Glasgow, G66 1QZ
Tel: 0141-776 1218 **Fax:** 0141-776 1218
E-mail: jim@caurnie.com
Website: http://www.caurnie.com
Managers: J. Little (Mgr)
VAT No.: GB 334 3001 11 **Turnover:** Up to £250,000
No.of Employees: 1 - 10 **Product Groups:** 32, 63

Celtic Art Ltd

1 Hawbank Road East Kilbride, Glasgow, G74 5EG
Tel: 01355-244493 **Fax:** 01355-232541
E-mail: info@celtic-art.ltd.uk
Website: http://www.celtic-art-ltd.com
Bank(s): Bank Of Scotland, East Kilbride
Directors: J. Robson (Fin)
Immediate Holding Company: CELTIC ART LIMITED
Registration no: SC071837 **VAT No.:** GB 343 2448 70
Date established: 1980 **Turnover:** £500,000 - £1m
No.of Employees: 11 - 20 **Product Groups:** 49

Date of Accounts	Mar 12	Mar 11	Mar 10
Working Capital	80	90	79
Fixed Assets	165	171	162
Current Assets	166	219	158

Centri-Force Engineering Co. Ltd

1-7 Montrose Avenue Hillington Park, Glasgow, G52 4LA
Tel: 0141-882 3351 **Fax:** 0141-882 9965
E-mail: enquiries@centri-force.co.uk
Website: http://www.centri-force.co.uk
Directors: R. Montanaro (MD)
Managers: F. Conn (Buyer), J. Wilson (Project Eng), B. Johnston (Chief Acct)
Immediate Holding Company: CENTRI-FORCE ENG. CO., LIMITED
Registration no: SC070659 **Date established:** 1980
Turnover: £250,000 - £500,000 **No.of Employees:** 21 - 50
Product Groups: 38, 41, 42

Date of Accounts	Dec 11	Dec 10	Dec 09
Working Capital	279	282	105
Fixed Assets	103	110	93
Current Assets	832	839	901

Centurion Signs UK Ltd (t/a Centurion Signs)

38 Carron Place East Kilbride, Glasgow, G75 0TS
Tel: 01355-265222 **Fax:** 01355-230331
E-mail: sales@centurionsigns.co.uk
Website: http://www.centurionsigns.co.uk
Directors: C. Westland (Sales)
Managers: L. Queen (Fin Mgr)
Immediate Holding Company: CENTURION SIGNS (U.K.) LIMITED
Registration no: SC048487 **VAT No.:** GB 316 2261 89
Date established: 1971 **Turnover:** £250,000 - £500,000
No.of Employees: 21 - 50 **Product Groups:** 30

Date of Accounts	Mar 12	Mar 11	Mar 10
Working Capital	128	12	93
Fixed Assets	204	128	67
Current Assets	577	497	402

Chalmit Lighting

388 Hillington Road Hillington Park, Glasgow, G52 4BL
Tel: 0141-882 5555 **Fax:** 0141-883 3704
E-mail: info@hubbell-scotland.com
Website: http://www.chalmit.com
Bank(s): Barclays
Directors: J. McKie (Fin)
Managers: A. Ferguson (Tech Serv Mgr), C. Postlethwaite, S. Davidson, S. Winkle
Immediate Holding Company: HUBBELL LIGHTING LTD
Registration no: 00669157 **VAT No.:** GB 723 8252 39
Date established: 1984 **No.of Employees:** 101 - 250 **Product Groups:** 37, 39

Charles Tennant & Co. Ltd

Craighead Whistleberry Road Blantyre, Glasgow, G72 0TH
Tel: 01698-717900 **Fax:** 01698-717890
E-mail: tennants.scot@dial.pipex.com
Website: http://www.tennantsdistribution.com
Bank(s): Bank of Scotland
Directors: C. Tennant (MD)
Ultimate Holding Company: TENNANTS CONSOLIDATED LIMITED
Immediate Holding Company: CHARLES TENNANT & COMPANY, LIMITED

see next page

Charles Tennant & Co. Ltd - *Cont'd*

Registration no: SC008811 **Date established:** 2013
Turnover: £10m - £20m **No.of Employees:** 11 - 20 **Product Groups:** 30, 63, 66

Date of Accounts	Dec 11	Dec 10	Dec 09
Sales Turnover	15m	14m	15m
Pre Tax Profit/Loss	712	621	581
Working Capital	5m	4m	4m
Fixed Assets	597	623	662
Current Assets	7m	6m	6m
Current Liabilities	596	639	495

Chiltern Invadex Ltd

Unit 16 Evans Business Centre 68-74 Queen Elizabeth Avenue, Hillington Park, Glasgow, G52 4NQ
Tel: 0141-880 9986 **Fax:** 0141-880 9990
Website: http://www.chilterninvadex.co.uk
Managers: G. Deuchars (Mgr)
Immediate Holding Company: CHILTERN INVADEX LIMITED
Registration no: 06050608 **Date established:** 2007
No.of Employees: 1 - 10 **Product Groups:** 26, 38, 39

Date of Accounts	Feb 08
Pre Tax Profit/Loss	87
Working Capital	-1m
Fixed Assets	2m
Current Assets	3m
Current Liabilities	2m

Chubb Electronic Security Ltd (Regional Office)

186 Garscube Road, Glasgow, G4 9RQ
Tel: 0141-332 3230 **Fax:** 0141-332 6128
E-mail: george.lynch@chubb.co.uk
Website: http://www.chubb.co.uk
Directors: Patchette (Pers), J. Turnball (I.T. Dir)
Managers: G. Lynch (Chief Mgr)
Immediate Holding Company: CHUBB GROUP SECURITY LTD
Registration no: 00524469 **VAT No.:** GB 439 4758 08
No.of Employees: 101 - 250 **Product Groups:** 40

Chubb Security Personnel

186 Garscube Road, Glasgow, G4 9RQ
Tel: 0141-352 7033 **Fax:** 0141- 3531148
Website: http://www.chubb.co.uk
Managers: H. Scroggie (Comm)
Immediate Holding Company: CHUBB GROUP SECURITY LTD
Registration no: 01062876 **Date established:** 1981
No.of Employees: 1 - 10 **Product Groups:** 52, 81

City Refrigeration Holdings UK Ltd

Caledonia House Lawmoor Street, Glasgow, G5 0US
Tel: 0141-418 9000 **Fax:** 0141-647 7184
E-mail: enquiries@city-holdings.co.uk
Website: http://www.city-holdings.co.uk
Directors: W. Haughey (Dir)
Ultimate Holding Company: CITY REFRIGERATION HOLDINGS (UK) LIMITED
Immediate Holding Company: CITY REFRIGERATION (UK) LIMITED
Registration no: SC161511 **Date established:** 1995 **Turnover:** £2m - £5m
No.of Employees: 251 - 500 **Product Groups:** 63, 66

Date of Accounts	Dec 11	Dec 10	Dec 09
Sales Turnover	4m	3m	4m
Pre Tax Profit/Loss	17	52	-3
Working Capital	50	37	-0
Fixed Assets	4	7	10
Current Assets	1m	1m	1m
Current Liabilities	305	363	328

Citywide Estate Agents

1016 Cathcart Road, Glasgow, G42 9XL
Tel: 0141-649 8899 **Fax:** 0141-636 0045
E-mail: john@citywide.cc
Website: http://www.citywide.cc
Directors: J. Guidi (MD)
Immediate Holding Company: CITYWIDE GLASGOW LIMITED
Registration no: SC330299 **Date established:** 2007
Turnover: £500,000 - £1m **No.of Employees:** 1 - 10 **Product Groups:** 80

Arnold Clark Automobiles Ltd

459 Crow Road, Glasgow, G11 7DN
Tel: 0141-954 1577 **Fax:** 0141-950 1388
E-mail: malcolm.campbell@arnoldclark.co.uk
Website: http://www.arnoldclark.co.uk
Directors: J. Clark (Mkt Research), K. Maclane (Fin)
Managers: S. Brown (Chief Mgr)
Immediate Holding Company: ARNOLD CLARK AUTOMOBILES LIMITED
Registration no: SC036386 **Date established:** 1961
No.of Employees: 51 - 100 **Product Groups:** 68

Date of Accounts	Dec 11	Dec 10	Dec 09
Sales Turnover	2253m	2271m	2139m
Pre Tax Profit/Loss	52m	51m	74m
Working Capital	-86m	-97m	-80m
Fixed Assets	764m	740m	676m
Current Assets	413m	368m	386m
Current Liabilities	234m	197m	173m

Arnold Clark Automobiles Ltd

320 Peat Road, Glasgow, G53 6SB
Tel: 0141-880 5353 **Fax:** 0141-880 5279
E-mail: alistair.lobben@arnoldclark.co.uk
Website: http://www.arnoldclark.co.uk
Bank(s): The Royal Bank of Scotland
Managers: A. Lobban (Chief Mgr)
Immediate Holding Company: ARNOLD CLARK AUTOMOBILES LIMITED
Registration no: SC036386 **VAT No.:** GB 334 3318 79
Date established: 1961 **Turnover:** £250m - £500m
No.of Employees: 21 - 50 **Product Groups:** 39

Date of Accounts	Dec 11	Dec 10	Dec 09
Sales Turnover	2253m	2271m	2139m
Pre Tax Profit/Loss	52m	51m	74m
Working Capital	-86m	-97m	-80m
Fixed Assets	764m	740m	676m
Current Assets	413m	368m	386m
Current Liabilities	234m	197m	173m

Classic Lifts

1 Buchanan Court Buchanan Business Park Cumbernauld Road, Stepps, Glasgow, G33 6HZ
Tel: 0141-578 0330 **Fax:** 0141-578 0331
E-mail: helpdesk@liftengineers.co.uk
Website: http://www.liftengineers.co.uk
Directors: D. Mccoll (MD)
Immediate Holding Company: CLASSIC LIFTS (SCOTLAND) LIMITED
Registration no: 03571736 **Date established:** 1998
No.of Employees: 11 - 20 **Product Groups:** 35, 39, 45

Date of Accounts	Mar 12	Mar 11	Mar 10
Working Capital	117	90	154
Fixed Assets	81	88	104
Current Assets	641	507	476

Clow Group Ltd

185 Broad Street, Glasgow, G40 2QR
Tel: 0141-554 6272 **Fax:** 0141-551 9087
E-mail: enquiries@clowgroup.co.uk
Website: http://www.clowgroup.co.uk
Bank(s): Clydesdale Bank PLC
Directors: A. Keates (Sales), C. Clow (MD), J. McKechnie (Co Sec), J. Gardiner (Dir)
Managers: J. Mountford (Prod Mgr)
Ultimate Holding Company: W.J. CLOW & COMPANY LIMITED
Immediate Holding Company: CLOW GROUP LTD.
Registration no: SC051941 **VAT No.:** GB 680 4059 37
Date established: 1972 **Turnover:** £5m - £10m **No.of Employees:** 21 - 50
Product Groups: 35

Clyde Bergmann Ltd

47 Broad Street, Glasgow, G40 2QR
Tel: 0141-550 5400 **Fax:** 0141-551 5402
E-mail: info@clydebergemann.co.uk
Website: http://www.clydebergemann.co.uk
Bank(s): Bank of Scotland
Managers: V. Frasier (Personnel), L. Monaghan (Sales Prom Mgr), M. Peoples (Chief Mgr), P. Wilson (Tech Serv Mgr), K. Forbes (Chief Acct)
Ultimate Holding Company: CLYDE BERGEMANN POWER GROUP INC (USA)
Immediate Holding Company: CLYDE BERGEMANN LIMITED
Registration no: SC139238 **Date established:** 1992
Turnover: £5m - £10m **No.of Employees:** 51 - 100 **Product Groups:** 40

Date of Accounts	Feb 12	Feb 11	Feb 10
Sales Turnover	8m	9m	7m
Pre Tax Profit/Loss	1m	2m	1m
Working Capital	4m	3m	3m
Fixed Assets	58	60	77
Current Assets	6m	6m	5m
Current Liabilities	980	2m	1m

Clyde Building Group

161-181 Whitefield Road, Glasgow, G51 2SD
Tel: 0141-445 1242 **Fax:** 0141-440 5375
E-mail: tracymccolgan@tiscali.co.uk
Website: http://www.cbc.uk.com
Directors: T. McColgan (Fin)
Immediate Holding Company: CLYDE BUILDING GROUP LIMITED
Registration no: SC322053 **Date established:** 2007 **Turnover:** £1m - £2m
No.of Employees: 1 - 10 **Product Groups:** 52

Date of Accounts	Mar 12	Mar 11	Mar 10
Working Capital	-75	529	2m
Fixed Assets	40	41	41
Current Assets	444	1m	2m

Clyde Fasteners Ltd (Head Office & Works)

5 Hawbank Road East Kilbride, Glasgow, G74 5ET
Tel: 01355-225451 **Fax:** 01355-263191
E-mail: info@clydefasteners.com
Website: http://www.clydefasteners.com
Bank(s): The Royal Bank of Scotland, London
Directors: I. Boyd (Fin), J. Boyd (Comm)
Managers: L. Dundes (Sales Prom Mgr)
Ultimate Holding Company: CLYDE FASTENERS (HOLDINGS) LIMITED
Immediate Holding Company: CLYDE FASTENERS LIMITED
Registration no: SC042783 **VAT No.:** GB 259 8304 29
Date established: 1965 **Turnover:** £2m - £5m **No.of Employees:** 21 - 50
Product Groups: 35

Date of Accounts	Dec 11	Dec 10	Dec 09
Working Capital	565	498	467
Fixed Assets	143	147	168
Current Assets	1m	994	719

Clyde Leather Co. (Props: Bevan Harris Ltd)

Broadlie Works Neilston, Glasgow, G78 3AB
Tel: 0141-881 4558 **Fax:** 0141-881 0522
E-mail: richard@bevanharris.co.uk
Website: http://www.clydemarineleather.co.uk
Bank(s): Barclays, Glasgow
Directors: E. Harris (Co Sec), R. Harris (Dir)
Managers: G. Peacock (Sales Admin)
Immediate Holding Company: BKC HOLDINGS LIMITED
Registration no: SC020608 **VAT No.:** GB 262 8743 38
Date established: 1938 **No.of Employees:** 11 - 20 **Product Groups:** 22

Date of Accounts	Aug 07
Sales Turnover	802
Pre Tax Profit/Loss	52
Working Capital	497
Fixed Assets	538
Current Assets	634
Current Liabilities	137
Total Share Capital	40
ROCE% (Return on Capital Employed)	5.0

Clyde Space Ltd

Kelvin Campus Maryhill Road, Glasgow, G20 0SP
Tel: 0141-946 4440 **Fax:** 0141-945 1591
E-mail: enquiries@clyde-space.com
Website: http://www.clyde-space.com
Directors: C. Clark (Dir)
Immediate Holding Company: CLYDE SPACE LIMITED
Registration no: SC285287 **Date established:** 2005
No.of Employees: 11 - 20 **Product Groups:** 37

Date of Accounts	Apr 12	Apr 11	Apr 10
Working Capital	-142	143	-94
Fixed Assets	68	85	24
Current Assets	332	608	280
Current Liabilities	N/A	58	N/A

Clyde Valley Lifts Ltd

Unit 16 120 Stepps Road, Glasgow, G33 3NQ
Tel: 0141-774 0786 **Fax:** 0141-774 3867
E-mail: info@clydevalleylifts.co.uk
Website: http://www.clydevalleylift.co.uk
Directors: F. Mckenna (Fin)
Immediate Holding Company: CLYDE VALLEY LIFTS LIMITED
Registration no: SC183498 **Date established:** 1998
No.of Employees: 21 - 50 **Product Groups:** 35, 39, 45

Date of Accounts	Mar 12	Mar 11	Mar 10
Sales Turnover	N/A	N/A	1m
Pre Tax Profit/Loss	N/A	N/A	151
Working Capital	39	42	51
Fixed Assets	35	35	24
Current Assets	722	606	527
Current Liabilities	N/A	N/A	196

Clydesdale Bank plc

14 Bothwell Street, Glasgow, G2 6QY
Tel: 08447-362616 **Fax:** 0141-204 3704
Website: http://www.clydesdalebank.co.uk
Managers: M. O'Donnell (Mgr)
Immediate Holding Company: CLYDESDALE BANK PLC
Registration no: SC001111 **Date established:** 1982
No.of Employees: 1 - 10 **Product Groups:** 80, 82

Date of Accounts	Sep 11	Sep 10	Sep 09
Pre Tax Profit/Loss	21m	49m	48m
Fixed Assets	7348m	8788m	9465m
Current Assets	39904m	34872m	32905m
Current Liabilities	44233m	41043m	40056m

Clydeside Galvanizers Ltd

96 Eastvale Place, Glasgow, G3 8QG
Tel: 0141-334 9678 **Fax:** 0141-337 1830
E-mail: ross@clydegalv.co.uk
Website: http://www.clydegalv.co.uk
Bank(s): Lloyds TSB Bank plc
Directors: R. Mccrosson (MD)
Immediate Holding Company: CLYDESIDE GALVANIZERS LIMITED
Registration no: NI034322 **VAT No.:** GB 316 3748 56
Date established: 1998 **Turnover:** £1m - £2m **No.of Employees:** 11 - 20
Product Groups: 48

Date of Accounts	Aug 11	Aug 10	Aug 09
Working Capital	-615	-528	-450
Fixed Assets	746	780	806
Current Assets	494	433	450

Clydeside Steel Fabrications Ltd

180 Hardgate Road, Glasgow, G51 4TB
Tel: 0141-445 2898 **Fax:** 0141-445 6964
E-mail: colin.salisbury@clydesidesteelfabrications.co.uk
Website: http://www.bmsteel.co.uk
Directors: P. Bradburn (Fin)
Managers: J. Graham (Mgr)
Ultimate Holding Company: STEMCOR HOLDINGS LIMITED
Immediate Holding Company: CLYDESIDE STEEL FABRICATIONS LIMITED
Registration no: SC034675 **VAT No.:** GB 259 6927 03
Date established: 1959 **Turnover:** £500,000 - £1m
No.of Employees: 1 - 10 **Product Groups:** 26, 30, 34, 35, 36, 40, 45, 48

Date of Accounts	Dec 11	Dec 10	Dec 09
Sales Turnover	557	708	868
Pre Tax Profit/Loss	48	-60	-155
Working Capital	57	21	72
Fixed Assets	3	4	13
Current Assets	266	214	198
Current Liabilities	85	44	34

J E Cockayne Ltd

The Exchange Scottish Enterprise Technology Park James Watt Avenue, East Kilbride, Glasgow, G75 0QD
Tel: 01355-272305 **Fax:** 01355-272306
E-mail: ian.cockayne@cockayne.co.uk
Website: http://www.cockayne.co.uk
Directors: I. Cockayne (MD)
Immediate Holding Company: J E COCKAYNE LIMITED
Registration no: SC042488 **VAT No.:** GB 259 5921 20
Date established: 1965 **Turnover:** £2m - £5m **No.of Employees:** 11 - 20
Product Groups: 38

Date of Accounts	Mar 12	Mar 11	Mar 10
Working Capital	192	171	223
Fixed Assets	34	50	67
Current Assets	498	396	458

Coilcraft Europe Ltd

21 Napier Place Wardpark North, Cumbernauld, Glasgow, G68 0LL
Tel: 01236-730595 **Fax:** 01236-730627
E-mail: caroleh@coilcraft-europe.com
Website: http://www.coilcraft.com
Managers: R. Kidd (Personnel), C. Holden (Cust Serv Mgr), C. Holburn (Mgr), D. McLaughlin (Fin Mgr)
Ultimate Holding Company: COILCRAFT INC (USA)
Immediate Holding Company: COILCRAFT EUROPE LIMITED
Registration no: SC209057 **VAT No.:** GB 481 4294 37
Date established: 2000 **Turnover:** £20m - £50m
No.of Employees: 21 - 50 **Product Groups:** 37

Date of Accounts	Dec 11	Dec 10	Dec 09
Sales Turnover	29m	28m	18m
Pre Tax Profit/Loss	6m	6m	3m
Working Capital	7m	6m	4m
Fixed Assets	430	450	495
Current Assets	10m	11m	7m
Current Liabilities	2m	1m	1m

Coley Instruments Ltd (Stewarts Group)

7 Garrel Road Burnside Industrial Estate, Kilsyth, Glasgow, G65 9JX
Tel: 01236-821533 **Fax:** 01236-824090
E-mail: sales@stewarts-group.com
Website: http://www.stewarts-group.com
Directors: L. Kelman (Fin), F. Phair (MD), J. O'Neill (Sales & Mktg)
Managers: R. Baird (I.T. Exec), M. Bryson (Sales Admin), J. Hamilton (Personnel)
Immediate Holding Company: Stewart Buchanan Gauges Ltd
Registration no: SC021724 **VAT No.:** GB 552 5461 46
Date established: 1933 **Turnover:** £2m - £5m
No.of Employees: 101 - 250 **Product Groups:** 36, 38, 40

Comtec Cable Accessories
20 Couper Street, Glasgow, G4 0DL
Tel: 0141-564 1234 **Fax:** 0141-564 4644
E-mail: sales@tait-components.com
Website: http://www.tait-components.com
Directors: M. Tait (Dir)
Immediate Holding Company: TAIT COMPONENTS LIMITED
Registration no: SC066552 **VAT No.:** GB 316 3648 60
Date established: 1978 **Turnover:** £500,000 - £1m
No.of Employees: 1 - 10 **Product Groups:** 35, 37, 44, 67

Date of Accounts	Jan 09	Jan 08	Jan 07
Working Capital	449	465	441
Fixed Assets	65	92	98
Current Assets	935	961	823

Connect Ad
Block 59 Unit 4 Hillington Park, Glasgow, G52 4LT
Tel: 0141-880 9797 **Fax:** 0141-880 2818
E-mail: info@connectad.co.uk
Website: http://www.connectad.co.uk
Directors: P. Tritschler (Dir)
Immediate Holding Company: CONNECT A.D. LIMITED
Registration no: SC218166 **VAT No.:** GB 456 5552 27
Date established: 2001 **No.of Employees:** 11 - 20 **Product Groups:** 33, 35, 66

Cookson Electronics
Unit 1h International House Stanley Boulevard Hamilton Intnl Technology Park, Blantyre, Glasgow, G72 0BN
Tel: 01355-276500 **Fax:** 01355-264770
E-mail: dcorlett@cooksonelectronics.com
Website: http://www.alphametals.com
Managers: D. Corlett (District Mgr), D. Corlett (Mgr)
Ultimate Holding Company: ENERGETICS NETWORKED ENERGY LTD.
Immediate Holding Company: ENERGETICS ELECTRICITY LIMITED
Date established: 2002 **No.of Employees:** 1 - 10 **Product Groups:** 36, 37

Corporate Insignia Ltd
1-5 Duncan Mcintosh Road Wardpark North, Cumbernauld, Glasgow, G68 0HH
Tel: 01236-738520 **Fax:** 01236-786149
E-mail: sales@corporate-insignia.com
Website: http://www.corporate-insignia.com
Bank(s): The Royal Bank of Scotland
Directors: J. Kent (Dir)
Immediate Holding Company: CORPORATE INSIGNIA LIMITED
Registration no: SC242080 **VAT No.:** GB 671 6059 28
Date established: 2003 **Turnover:** £1m - £2m **No.of Employees:** 21 - 50
Product Groups: 49

Date of Accounts	Feb 12	Feb 11	Feb 10
Working Capital	1m	899	900
Fixed Assets	332	336	136
Current Assets	1m	1m	1m

Corston Sinclair Ltd
36 Glenburn Road East Kilbride, Glasgow, G74 5BA
Tel: 01355-222273 **Fax:** 01355-263682
E-mail: sales@corstonsinclair.com
Website: http://www.corstonsinclair.com
Directors: A. McIlwham (MD), D. Schofield (Sales), E. Schofield (Fin)
Managers: A. Cruickshank (Purch Mgr), S. Mcilwham (Purch Mgr), Z. Mcilwham (Mktg Serv Mgr)
Immediate Holding Company: CORSTON SINCLAIR LIMITED
Registration no: SC045987 **VAT No.:** GB 259 7398 96
Date established: 1968 **Turnover:** £2m - £5m **No.of Employees:** 11 - 20
Product Groups: 22, 24, 40

Date of Accounts	Jan 11	Jan 10	Jan 09
Working Capital	-41	-61	24
Fixed Assets	160	167	167
Current Assets	364	381	382

Coughtrie International Ltd
Montrose Avenue Hillington, Glasgow, G52 4LZ
Tel: 0141-810 4516 **Fax:** 0141-882 0191
E-mail: info@coughtrie.com
Website: http://www.coughtrie.com
Bank(s): The Royal Bank of Scotland
Directors: N. Layton (MD)
Managers: L. Shukur (Buyer)
Immediate Holding Company: J. & G. COUGHTRIE LIMITED
Registration no: SC021634 **Date established:** 1941 **Turnover:** £2m - £5m
No.of Employees: 11 - 20 **Product Groups:** 37

Date of Accounts	Mar 06	Mar 05	Mar 04
Pre Tax Profit/Loss	-94	-61	-127
Working Capital	65	165	59
Fixed Assets	2m	2m	3m
Current Assets	2m	2m	2m
Current Liabilities	1m	1m	226

Craigton Industries Ltd
Craigton Works Milngavie, Glasgow, G62 7HF
Tel: 0141-956 6585 **Fax:** 0141-956 3757
E-mail: info@craigtonindustries.co.uk
Website: http://www.craigtonindustries.co.uk
Directors: I. McCormick (Sales), S. Mccann (Dir)
Immediate Holding Company: CRAIGTON INDUSTRIES (SALES) LIMITED
Registration no: SC046807 **Date established:** 1969
No.of Employees: 1 - 10 **Product Groups:** 30, 33, 51

Date of Accounts	Jan 12	Jan 11	Jan 10
Working Capital	112	94	77
Fixed Assets	210	226	228
Current Assets	353	299	249

Creative Promotions Ltd
79 West Regent Street, Glasgow, G2 2AW
Tel: 0141-332 7471 **Fax:** 0141-331 2801
E-mail: enquiries@creativepromotions.co.uk
Website: http://www.creativepromotions.co.uk
Directors: L. Sibbald (Fin), A. Sibbald (MD)
Immediate Holding Company: CREATIVE PROMOTIONS LIMITED
Registration no: SC048464 **VAT No.:** GB 261 5381 67
Date established: 1971 **No.of Employees:** 1 - 10 **Product Groups:** 22, 23, 29, 30, 49

Date of Accounts	Aug 11	Aug 10	Aug 09
Working Capital	-13	-17	5
Fixed Assets	20	23	28
Current Assets	73	64	102

Crittall Windows Ltd
The Claremont Centre 39 Durham Street, Glasgow, G41 1BS
Tel: 0141-427 4931 **Fax:** 0141-427 1463
E-mail: hq@crittall-windows.co.uk
Website: http://www.crittall-windows.com
Directors: J. Pyatt (MD)
Ultimate Holding Company: CRITTALL HOLDINGS LIMITED
Immediate Holding Company: CRITTALL WINDOWS LIMITED
Registration no: 00200794 **VAT No.:** GB 665 7740 96
Date established: 2024 **Turnover:** £10m - £20m **No.of Employees:** 1 - 10
Product Groups: 25, 35

Date of Accounts	Dec 11	Dec 10	Dec 09
Sales Turnover	10m	11m	13m
Pre Tax Profit/Loss	-186	63	404
Working Capital	334	198	-166
Fixed Assets	596	675	744
Current Assets	3m	3m	3m
Current Liabilities	841	1m	1m

Crolla Ice Cream Co. Ltd
48 Jessie Street, Glasgow, G42 0PG
Tel: 0141-423 1161 **Fax:** 0141-423 2596
E-mail: sales@crollaicecream.co.uk
Website: http://www.crollaicecream.co.uk
Bank(s): The Royal Bank of Scotland
Directors: P. Crolla (MD), E. Lennox (Fin)
Immediate Holding Company: CROLLA ICE CREAM COMPANY LTD. (THE)
Registration no: SC033156 **VAT No.:** GB 259 6929 96
Date established: 1958 **Turnover:** £2m - £5m **No.of Employees:** 11 - 20
Product Groups: 20, 62

Date of Accounts	Dec 11	Dec 10	Dec 09
Working Capital	338	354	411
Fixed Assets	794	762	713
Current Assets	619	573	635

Cummins UK
16 Dunnswood Road Wardpark South, Cumbernauld, Glasgow, G67 3EW
Tel: 01236-505800 **Fax:** 01236-725082
E-mail: william.logan@cummins.com
Website: http://www.cummins-uk.com
Managers: C. Smith
No.of Employees: 21 - 50 **Product Groups:** 35, 36, 39

David Auld Valves Ltd
Finlas Street Cowlairs Industrial Estate, Glasgow, G22 5DQ
Tel: 0141-557 0515 **Fax:** 0141-558 1059
E-mail: sales@auldvalves.com
Website: http://www.auldvalves.com
Bank(s): Bank of Scotland
Directors: A. Pearson (MD)
Ultimate Holding Company: ORD ENGINEERING LIMITED
Immediate Holding Company: AULD VALVES LIMITED
Registration no: SC007754 **Date established:** 2010 **Turnover:** £1m - £2m
No.of Employees: 11 - 20 **Product Groups:** 36, 40

Date of Accounts	Dec 11	Dec 10	Dec 09
Working Capital	241	114	104
Fixed Assets	18	17	26
Current Assets	613	529	462

Davies Turner
7 Grayshill Road Cumbernauld, Glasgow, G68 9HQ
Tel: 01236-725985 **Fax:** 01236-726983
E-mail: sales@daviesturner.com
Website: http://www.daviesturner.co.uk
Managers: D. McGlockan (District Mgr), D. Mclaughlan (District Mgr)
Ultimate Holding Company: DAVIES TURNER HOLDINGS PLC
Immediate Holding Company: DAVIES TURNER & CO. LIMITED
Registration no: 04345197 **VAT No.:** GB 235 6746 45
Date established: 2001 **Turnover:** £5m - £10m **No.of Employees:** 11 - 20
Product Groups: 72, 74, 76

Denco
Unit 19 Langlands Avenue Kelvin South Business Park, East Kilbride, Glasgow, G75 0YG
Tel: 01355-271020 **Fax:** 01355-271039
E-mail: alex.ritchie@denco.co.uk
Website: http://www.denco.co.uk
Directors: A. Richie (Dir), A. Richie (MD)
Managers: J. McCloskey (Personnel), R. Troke (Tech Serv Mgr), S. Moss (Buyer)
Turnover: Up to £250,000 **No.of Employees:** 21 - 50 **Product Groups:** 40, 52, 66

Denholm Group Ltd
18 Woodside Crescent, Glasgow, G3 7UL
Tel: 0141-353 2090 **Fax:** 0141-353 2190
E-mail: enquiries@denholm-group.co.uk
Website: http://www.denholm-group.co.uk
Directors: D. Harris (Dir), J. Denholm (Dir)
Managers: C. McHugh (Personnel), T. Brown (Tech Serv Mgr), A. Nicholson (Mktg Serv Mgr)
Ultimate Holding Company: J. & J. DENHOLM LIMITED
Immediate Holding Company: DENHOLM LOGISTICS LIMITED
Registration no: SC244269 **Date established:** 2003
No.of Employees: 21 - 50 **Product Groups:** 72, 74

Date of Accounts	Dec 11	Dec 10	Dec 09
Pre Tax Profit/Loss	1m	922	961
Working Capital	9m	7m	3m
Fixed Assets	12m	11m	11m
Current Assets	9m	8m	4m
Current Liabilities	127	1m	1m

Designer Cakes By Paige & Barracks
203-205 Maryhill Road, Glasgow, G20 7XJ
Tel: 0141-332 7730
E-mail: buyacake@cakeawish.co.uk
Website: http://www.designercakesbypaige.com
Directors: L. Ross (Prop)
No.of Employees: 1 - 10 **Product Groups:** 20, 62

Devro plc
Moodiesburn Chryston, Glasgow, G69 0JE
Tel: 01236-872261 **Fax:** 01236-872557
E-mail: information@devro.com
Website: http://www.devro.plc.uk
Bank(s): Clydesdale Bank PLC
Directors: A. Kilpatrick (MD), J. Meredith (Co Sec)
Ultimate Holding Company: DEVRO PLC
Immediate Holding Company: DEVRO (SCOTLAND) LIMITED
Registration no: SC129787 **Date established:** 1991
Turnover: £50m - £75m **No.of Employees:** 251 - 500 **Product Groups:** 20

Date of Accounts	Dec 11	Dec 10	Dec 09
Sales Turnover	59m	55m	79m
Pre Tax Profit/Loss	11m	26m	3m
Working Capital	4m	6m	7m
Fixed Assets	44m	36m	31m
Current Assets	15m	14m	19m
Current Liabilities	9m	7m	6m

The Diageo
Dundas House 99 Borron Street, Glasgow, G4 9XF
Tel: 0141-332 3323 **Fax:** 0141-333 2121
E-mail: donald.a.dempsey@diageo.com
Website: http://www.diageo.com
Directors: D. Dempsey (Dir)
Managers: J. Reekie (I.T. Exec), L. McNeil (Personnel), M. McMillan (Comptroller)
No.of Employees: 101 - 250 **Product Groups:** 21

J & H M Dickson Ltd
Seath Road Rutherglen, Glasgow, G73 1RW
Tel: 0141-643 0244 **Fax:** 0141-643 0219
E-mail: info@sackmaker.com
Website: http://www.sackmaker.com
Directors: A. Dickson (MD), B. Dickson (Co Sec)
Immediate Holding Company: J. & H.M. DICKSON LIMITED
Registration no: SC028536 **Date established:** 1951
No.of Employees: 11 - 20 **Product Groups:** 23, 24, 30

Date of Accounts	Sep 11	Sep 10	Sep 09
Working Capital	-90	-144	-155
Fixed Assets	519	540	559
Current Assets	617	893	585

Directional Data Systems Ltd
5 Dalsholm Avenue, Glasgow, G20 0TS
Tel: 0141-945 4243 **Fax:** 0141-945 4238
E-mail: ronald.dunbar@directionaldata.co.uk
Website: http://www.directionaldata.co.uk
Directors: R. Dunbar (Dir)
Immediate Holding Company: DIRECTIONAL DATA SYSTEMS LIMITED
Registration no: SC118459 **Date established:** 1989 **Turnover:** £1m - £2m
No.of Employees: 1 - 10 **Product Groups:** 49

Date of Accounts	Sep 11	Sep 10	Sep 09
Working Capital	47	122	163
Fixed Assets	465	478	484
Current Assets	358	343	336
Current Liabilities	N/A	N/A	74

Doig & Smith Ltd
6 Lynedoch Place, Glasgow, G3 6AQ
Tel: 0141-332 8907 **Fax:** 0141-332 4967
E-mail: glasgow@doigandsmith.co.uk
Website: http://www.doigandsmith.co.uk
Bank(s): Bank of Scotland
Directors: G. McLintock (Fin), L. Shaw (Dir)
Managers: A. Conner (Mktg Serv Mgr), L. Jean-shaw (Comm)
Immediate Holding Company: DOIG & SMITH PROPERTY COMPANY LIMITED
Registration no: SC047058 **Date established:** 1969 **Turnover:** £2m - £5m
No.of Employees: 21 - 50 **Product Groups:** 80, 84

Date of Accounts	Mar 12	Mar 11	Mar 10
Working Capital	-7	-6	-5
Fixed Assets	625	625	625

Dolphin Enterprises
4 Eddington Drive Newton Mearns, Glasgow, G77 5AX
Tel: 0141-639 4551 **Fax:** 0141-639 4551
E-mail: dolphinenterprizes@btconnect.com
Directors: J. Munn (Prop)
Turnover: Up to £250,000 **No.of Employees:** 1 - 10 **Product Groups:** 40, 41, 42, 54, 67

Dow Group Ltd (Wm Dow Holdings Ltd)
23 Lenziemill Road Cumbernauld, Glasgow, G67 2RL
Tel: 01236-730730 **Fax:** 01236-730555
E-mail: sales@wmdow.com
Website: http://www.wmdow.com
Directors: S. Dow (Grp Chief Exec)
No.of Employees: 21 - 50 **Product Groups:** 72, 83

Drain Centre a division of Wolseley UK
115 Clydesmill Place Clydesmill Industrial Estate, Glasgow, G32 8RF
Tel: 0141-646 1646 **Fax:** 0141-646 2145
E-mail: william.connolly@wolseley.co.uk
Website: http://www.draincentre.co.uk
Managers: W. Connolly (District Mgr)
Immediate Holding Company: ETEX P.L.C.
Turnover: £2m - £5m **No.of Employees:** 1 - 10 **Product Groups:** 30, 36, 39, 40, 42, 48, 66

DSSR
9 Crown Terrace, Glasgow, G12 9EY
Tel: 0141-334 6161 **Fax:** 0141-357 1993
E-mail: glasgow@dssr.co.uk
Website: http://www.dssr.co.uk
Directors: H. Currie (Snr Part)
Turnover: £5m - £10m **No.of Employees:** 51 - 100 **Product Groups:** 84, 85

Dundas & Wilson
191 West George Street, Glasgow, G2 2LD
Tel: 0141-222 2200 **Fax:** 0141-222 2201
E-mail: donald.shaw@dundas-wilson.com
Website: http://www.dundas-wilson.com
Directors: T. Stanley (Pers), L. Adams (Pers), J. Middleton (Fin), Middleton (Fin), W. Kirkwood (I.T. Dir), D. Shaw (Snr Part), A. Henderson (Develop)
Managers: J. Cambell (Tech Serv Mgr), L. Coultas (Mktg Serv Mgr)
Ultimate Holding Company: TORONTO-DOMINION BANK (THE)
Immediate Holding Company: ECOVISION SCOTLAND LIMITED
Registration no: SC374364 **VAT No.:** GB 328 7096 34
Date established: 2009 **No.of Employees:** 101 - 250 **Product Groups:** 80

Dustacco Engineering Ltd
83 Carron Place Kelvin Indl-Est, East Kilbride, Glasgow, G75 0YL
Tel: 01355-229191
Website: http://www.dustacco.com
Directors: A. Mckay (Dir), A. Summerville (MD)
Immediate Holding Company: DUSTACCO ENGINEERING LIMITED
Registration no: SC042982 **Date established:** 1966
No.of Employees: 1 - 10 **Product Groups:** 34, 66

Date of Accounts	Dec 10	Dec 09	Dec 08
Working Capital	1m	1m	985
Fixed Assets	146	177	337
Current Assets	2m	2m	2m

E C I S Scotland Ltd
40 Moness Drive, Glasgow, G52 1ER
Tel: 0141-882 8448 **Fax:** 0141-880 9953
E-mail: ecis100@hotmail.com
Directors: E. Coffee (Dir)
Immediate Holding Company: ECIS (SCOTLAND) LTD.
Registration no: SC222636 **Date established:** 2001
Turnover: Up to £250,000 **No.of Employees:** 1 - 10 **Product Groups:** 46

Date of Accounts	Aug 11	Aug 10	Aug 09
Sales Turnover	N/A	N/A	124
Pre Tax Profit/Loss	N/A	N/A	-11
Working Capital	1	-12	-8
Fixed Assets	9	15	16
Current Assets	32	25	27
Current Liabilities	N/A	32	7

E M Mackenzie & Co. Ltd
37 Meiklewood Road, Glasgow, G51 4GB
Tel: 0141-334 6262 **Fax:** 0141-334 9117
E-mail: emmackenzie@compuserve.com
Website: http://www.emmackenzie.co.uk
Directors: F. Mackenzie (Co Sec), K. Mackenzie (MD)
Immediate Holding Company: E.M. MACKENZIE & CO. LIMITED
Registration no: SC035301 **Date established:** 1960
No.of Employees: 51 - 100 **Product Groups:** 52

Date of Accounts	Mar 11	Mar 10	Mar 09
Working Capital	516	600	474
Fixed Assets	132	161	199
Current Assets	869	995	1m

E S Alternators
7 Eastside Industrial Estate Kilsyth Road, Kirkintilloch, Glasgow, G66 1QG
Tel: 0141-776 3689 **Fax:** 0141-776 1115
E-mail: injectionelectronics@fsmail.net
Website: http://www.esalternators.co.uk
Directors: B. Sinclair (Prop)
Date established: 1982 **Turnover:** Up to £250,000
No.of Employees: 1 - 10 **Product Groups:** 39

R M Easdale
67 Washington Street, Glasgow, G3 8BB
Tel: 0141-221 2708 **Fax:** 0141-204 3159
E-mail: robert.easdale@rmeasdale.com
Website: http://www.rmeasdale.com
Bank(s): The Royal Bank of Scotland, Clydesdale
Directors: R. Easdale (Prop)
Immediate Holding Company: R.M. EASDALE & COMPANY LIMITED
Registration no: SC035960 **VAT No.:** GB 259 9780 89
Date established: 1960 **Turnover:** £50m - £75m
No.of Employees: 21 - 50 **Product Groups:** 34, 66

Date of Accounts	Dec 11	Dec 10	Dec 09
Sales Turnover	63m	54m	37m
Pre Tax Profit/Loss	920	1m	309
Working Capital	3m	1m	901
Fixed Assets	1m	2m	2m
Current Assets	10m	7m	6m
Current Liabilities	2m	2m	2m

Easy Debt Solutions
135 Buchanan Street, Glasgow, G1 2JA
Tel: 0800-377 7549
E-mail: davidnelson@easydebtsolutions.com
Website: http://www.easydebtsolutions.com
Managers: D. Nelson
Immediate Holding Company: EASYDEBTSOLUTIONS LTD.
Registration no: SC307864 **Date established:** 2006
No.of Employees: 11 - 20 **Product Groups:** 82

The Edrington Group Limited
2500 Great Western Road, Glasgow, G15 6RW
Tel: 0141-940 4000 **Fax:** 0141-940 4040
Website: http://www.edringtongroup.com
Directors: B. Farrer (MD)
Managers: G. Macwilame (Chief Mgr)
Ultimate Holding Company: THE EDRINGTON GROUP LIMITED
Immediate Holding Company: THE MACALLAN DISTILLERY LIMITED
Registration no: SC036374 **Date established:** 1984 **Turnover:** £2m - £5m
No.of Employees: 21 - 50 **Product Groups:** 21

Elite Bedding Co. Ltd
135 Moffat Street, Glasgow, G5 0NG
Tel: 0141-429 1124 **Fax:** 0141-429 1599
E-mail: info@simplyelite.co.uk
Website: http://www.simplyelite.co.uk
Bank(s): Bank of Scotland
Directors: B. Winston (MD)
Immediate Holding Company: ELITE BEDDING COMPANY LIMITED
Registration no: SC030076 **VAT No.:** GB 659 0893 89
Date established: 1954 **Turnover:** £2m - £5m **No.of Employees:** 11 - 20
Product Groups: 26, 52

Date of Accounts	Jan 10	Jan 09	Jan 08
Working Capital	92	151	181
Fixed Assets	224	275	325
Current Assets	470	699	920

Elyo Services
10 Couper Street, Glasgow, G4 0DL
Tel: 0141-552 6031 **Fax:** 0141-552 2535
Managers: B. Flemming (Mgr)
No.of Employees: 11 - 20 **Product Groups:** 40, 66

Emergency Power Systems
Suite 16 Enterprise House Strathkelvin Place, Kirkintilloch, Glasgow, G66 1XQ
Tel: 0141-775 1815 **Fax:** 0141-775 1609
E-mail: bob.thomson@emergencypowersystems.co.uk
Website: http://www.emergencypowersystems.com
Managers: B. Thomson (Sales Prom Mgr)
Registration no: 02752248 **Turnover:** £2m - £5m
No.of Employees: 1 - 10 **Product Groups:** 37

Date of Accounts	Sep 08	Sep 07
Sales Turnover	7431	5748
Pre Tax Profit/Loss	309	142
Working Capital	516	381
Fixed Assets	1548	1636
Current Assets	3506	3163
Current Liabilities	2990	2782
Total Share Capital	50	50
ROCE% (Return on Capital Employed)	15.0	7.0
ROT% (Return on Turnover)	4.2	2.5

Emreco International Ltd
69 Springkell Avenue, Glasgow, G41 4NU
Tel: 0141-424 1914 **Fax:** 0141-423 2997
E-mail: info@emreco.co.uk
Website: http://www.emreco.co.uk
Bank(s): The Royal Bank of Scotland
Directors: A. Carduff (Fin), R. Reinhold (MD)
Managers: C. Carmichael (Mktg Serv Mgr), M. Simpson (Tech Serv Mgr)
Ultimate Holding Company: EMRECO HOLDINGS LIMITED
Immediate Holding Company: EMRECO INTERNATIONAL LIMITED
Registration no: SC014066 **VAT No.:** GB 260 0993 67
Date established: 2026 **Turnover:** £2m - £5m **No.of Employees:** 11 - 20
Product Groups: 24

Date of Accounts	Mar 11	Mar 10	Mar 09
Sales Turnover	N/A	5m	N/A
Pre Tax Profit/Loss	N/A	201	-250
Working Capital	4m	4m	4m
Fixed Assets	76	83	112
Current Assets	4m	4m	4m
Current Liabilities	N/A	337	268

Encon Insulation Scotland Ltd
80 Cambuslang Road, Glasgow, G32 8NB
Tel: 0141-641 0011 **Fax:** 0141-641 5170
E-mail: glasgow@encon.co.uk
Website: http://www.encon.co.uk
Directors: D. Crawford (Dir)
Managers: P. Caroll
Ultimate Holding Company: WOLSELEY PLC (JERSEY)
Immediate Holding Company: Refracpac Ltd
Date established: 1976 **No.of Employees:** 21 - 50 **Product Groups:** 33, 66

Date of Accounts	Jul 11
Working Capital	-5

Enterprise Control Engineers Ltd
Barclay Curle House 739 South Street, Glasgow, G14 0BX
Tel: 0141-959 2277 **Fax:** 0141-959 4157
E-mail: admin@enterprisecontrols.co.uk
Website: http://www.enterprisecontrol.co.uk
Directors: A. Alexander (MD), C. Armstrong (Dir)
Managers: A. Heron, D. Walker (Tech Serv Mgr)
Immediate Holding Company: ENTERPRISE CONTROL ENGINEERS LIMITED
Registration no: SC136901 **VAT No.:** GB 596 6321 05
Date established: 1992 **No.of Employees:** 21 - 50 **Product Groups:** 38

Date of Accounts	Apr 12	Apr 11	Apr 10
Working Capital	115	360	566
Fixed Assets	19	28	33
Current Assets	1m	2m	2m

Eriks UK (Glasgow Electrical Mechanical)
Unit 1-2 Ballochmill Road, Rutherglen, Glasgow, G73 1PT
Tel: 0141-419 0112 **Fax:** 0141-419 0444
E-mail: glasgow@eriks.co.uk
Website: http://www.eriks.co.uk
Directors: S. Asking (MD)
Managers: K. McCombie (District Mgr), J. Cunningham (District Mgr), D. Marr (Reg Mgr)
Registration no: 03142338 **Turnover:** £1m - £2m
No.of Employees: 1 - 10 **Product Groups:** 35

Ernst & Young Ltd
George House 50 George Square, Glasgow, G2 1RR
Tel: 0141-626 5000 **Fax:** 0141-626 5001
E-mail: jniven@uk.ey.com
Website: http://www.ey.com
Directors: B. Hawkins (Sales), D. Nisbet (Snr Part), J. Nisbet (Ptnr)
Managers: T. Brown (I.T. Exec), F. Dixon (Mktg Serv Mgr)
Ultimate Holding Company: INVENSYS PLC
Immediate Holding Company: ERNST & YOUNG LIMITED
Registration no: 05458987 **VAT No.:** GB 524 1472 70
Date established: 2005 **Turnover:** £5m - £10m
No.of Employees: 101 - 250 **Product Groups:** 80, 82

Euro PC Ltd
90 Fifty Pitches Road, Glasgow, G51 4EB
Tel: 0800-073 3800
E-mail: sales@europc.co.uk
Website: http://www.europc.co.uk
Directors: G. Cockburn (Purch), J. Mackie (Dir), G. Grieve (Sales)
Immediate Holding Company: EUROPC LIMITED
Registration no: SC158752 **Date established:** 1995
Turnover: £5m - £10m **No.of Employees:** 21 - 50 **Product Groups:** 44

Date of Accounts	May 09	May 08	Jan 11
Sales Turnover	9m	11m	8m
Pre Tax Profit/Loss	85	351	138
Working Capital	650	726	608
Fixed Assets	3m	2m	3m
Current Assets	2m	2m	2m
Current Liabilities	246	330	262

European Metals Recycling Ltd
739 South Street, Glasgow, G14 0BX
Tel: 0141-954 9371 **Fax:** 0141-958 0266
E-mail: richard.muldoon@emrltd.com
Website: http://www.emrltd.com
Managers: R. Muldoon (Mgr)
Immediate Holding Company: EUROPEAN METAL RECYCLING LIMITED
Registration no: 02954623 **Date established:** 1994
Turnover: £10m - £20m **No.of Employees:** 11 - 20 **Product Groups:** 42, 66

Date of Accounts	Dec 11	Dec 10	Dec 09
Sales Turnover	3032m	2431m	1843m
Pre Tax Profit/Loss	116m	155m	91m
Working Capital	414m	371m	167m
Fixed Assets	518m	483m	480m
Current Assets	1027m	717m	557m
Current Liabilities	124m	118m	185m

Expotel Hotel Reservations Ltd
Albert Chambers 13 Bath Street, Glasgow, G2 1HY
Tel: 0141-331 1771 **Fax:** 0141-331 1117
E-mail: sbelfour@expotel.com
Website: http://www.expotel.co.uk
Managers: S. Belfour (Mgr), L. Kinving (Mktg Serv Mgr), S. Balfour (Chief Mgr)
Ultimate Holding Company: 06631240
Immediate Holding Company: EXPOTEL HOTEL RESERVATIONS LIMITED
Registration no: 02643040 **Date established:** 1991
Turnover: Up to £250,000 **No.of Employees:** 11 - 20 **Product Groups:** 69, 81

F E P Heat Care Ltd
194 Cumbernauld Road Chryston, Glasgow, G69 9NB
Tel: 0141-779 2215 **Fax:** 0141-779 9191
E-mail: fepheatcare@hotmail.co.uk
Website: http://www.fepheatcare.com
Directors: A. Bonnyman (MD)
Immediate Holding Company: F.E.P. HEATCARE LIMITED
Registration no: SC091564 **Date established:** 1985
No.of Employees: 11 - 20 **Product Groups:** 52

Date of Accounts	Mar 08	Mar 07	Mar 06
Working Capital	315	339	392
Fixed Assets	197	184	211
Current Assets	533	542	624
Current Liabilities	219	203	232

Ferguson & Menzies Ltd
312 Broomloan Road, Glasgow, G51 2JW
Tel: 0141-445 3555 **Fax:** 0141-425 1079
E-mail: joyce.duthie@fergusonmenzies.co.uk
Website: http://www.fergusonmenzies.co.uk
Bank(s): Clydesdale Bank PLC
Directors: B. Duthie (Co Sec)
Immediate Holding Company: FERGUSON & MENZIES LIMITED
Registration no: SC034282 **VAT No.:** GB 259 7858 88
Date established: 1959 **Turnover:** £1m - £2m **No.of Employees:** 11 - 20
Product Groups: 61

Date of Accounts	Mar 12	Mar 11	Mar 10
Working Capital	364	352	338
Fixed Assets	467	487	453
Current Assets	2m	2m	2m

Ferrari Packaging Ltd
26 Peel Park Place East Kilbride, Glasgow, G74 5LW
Tel: 01355-233527 **Fax:** 01355-234743
Directors: T. Ferrari (Dir)
Immediate Holding Company: FERRARI PACKAGING LTD.
Registration no: SC228545 **Date established:** 2002
No.of Employees: 11 - 20 **Product Groups:** 38, 42

Date of Accounts	Dec 11	Dec 10	Dec 09
Working Capital	48	-51	-82
Fixed Assets	119	154	219
Current Assets	3m	2m	2m

J W Filshill Ltd
Ainslie Avenue, Glasgow, G52 4HE
Tel: 0141-883 7071 **Fax:** 0141-883 2224
E-mail: sales@filshill.co.uk
Website: http://www.filshill.co.uk
Bank(s): Bank of Scotland, Paisley
Directors: F. Harrison (Fin), I. McDonald (Sales)
Managers: A. Allison (Tech Serv Mgr), J. Monaghan, J. Brown (Personnel)
Immediate Holding Company: J.W. FILSHILL LIMITED
Registration no: SC019246 **VAT No.:** GB 262 8672 13
Date established: 1936 **Turnover:** £125m - £250m
No.of Employees: 251 - 500 **Product Groups:** 20, 62

Date of Accounts	Jan 11	Jan 10	Jan 09
Sales Turnover	169m	172m	163m
Pre Tax Profit/Loss	1m	2m	2m
Working Capital	7m	6m	5m
Fixed Assets	6m	6m	6m
Current Assets	30m	29m	27m
Current Liabilities	837	867	1m

First Group Ltd
197 Victoria Road, Glasgow, G42 7AD
Tel: 0141-423 6600 **Fax:** 0141-636 3111
E-mail: sales@firstgroup.co.uk
Website: http://www.firstgroup.com
Directors: M. Lochhead (Dir)
Ultimate Holding Company: FIRSTGROUP PLC
Immediate Holding Company: FIRST GLASGOW (NO.1) LIMITED
Registration no: SC097299 **Date established:** 1986
Turnover: £20m - £50m **No.of Employees:** 501 - 1000
Product Groups: 71, 72

Date of Accounts	Mar 08	Mar 09	Mar 10
Sales Turnover	88m	95m	92m
Pre Tax Profit/Loss	11m	12m	8m
Working Capital	-33m	-28m	-20m
Fixed Assets	69m	62m	55m
Current Assets	57m	55m	43m
Current Liabilities	17m	16m	15m

Fleming Buildings Ltd
23 Auchinloch Road Lenzie, Kirkintilloch, Glasgow, G66 5ET
Tel: 0141-776 1181 **Fax:** 0141-775 1394
E-mail: office@fleming-buildings.co.uk
Website: http://www.fleming-buildings.co.uk
Bank(s): The Royal Bank of Scotland
Directors: M. Burrows (MD), R. Burrows (Co Sec)
Managers: K. Noel (Buyer)
Immediate Holding Company: FLEMING BUILDINGS LIMITED
Registration no: SC049540 **VAT No.:** GB 259 6822 17
Date established: 1971 **Turnover:** £5m - £10m
No.of Employees: 51 - 100 **Product Groups:** 52

Date of Accounts	Nov 11	Nov 10	Nov 09
Sales Turnover	7m	7m	14m
Pre Tax Profit/Loss	59	48	95

Working Capital	1m	1m	1m
Fixed Assets	163	149	185
Current Assets	4m	4m	4m
Current Liabilities	223	239	439

Flexible Ducting Ltd
Cloberfield Industrial Estate Milngavie, Glasgow, G62 7LW
Tel: 0141-956 4551 **Fax:** 0141-956 4847
E-mail: sales@flexibleducting.co.uk
Website: http://www.flexibleducting.co.uk
Bank(s): Barclays
Directors: T. Smith (Dir)
Managers: C. Maclean (Sales Prom Mgr), D. Gibson (Tech Serv Mgr), J. Park (Purch Mgr), A. McIntyre, C. Cubbage (Factory Mgr), A. Wood (Export Sales Mg), E. Robinson, A. McEwan, L. Thomson (Comptroller)
Immediate Holding Company: Smiths Group PLC
Registration no: SC029203 **Date established:** 1952
Turnover: £10m - £20m **No.of Employees:** 101 - 250
Product Groups: 29, 30, 36, 40, 66

Date of Accounts	Jul 08	Jul 07
Working Capital	45	45
Current Assets	45	45
Total Share Capital	45	45

Food Service Equipment Marketing Ltd
10 Carron Place Kelvin Industrial Estate, East Kilbride, Glasgow, G75 0YL
Tel: 01355-244111 **Fax:** 01355-241471
E-mail: sales@fem.co.uk
Website: http://www.fem.co.uk
Directors: J. Doherty (Dir), H. Hogan (MD)
Managers: J. Henderson (Comptroller)
Immediate Holding Company: FOODSERVICE EQUIPMENT MARKETING LIMITED
Registration no: SC145354 **Date established:** 1993
Turnover: £5m - £10m **No.of Employees:** 11 - 20 **Product Groups:** 40

Date of Accounts	Dec 11	Dec 10	Dec 09
Sales Turnover	9m	N/A	N/A
Pre Tax Profit/Loss	1m	N/A	N/A
Working Capital	3m	1m	446
Fixed Assets	110	430	687
Current Assets	4m	3m	2m
Current Liabilities	1m	N/A	N/A

Force Measurement Systems Ltd
3-5 Lister Road, Glasgow, G52 4BH
Tel: 0141-882 8858 **Fax:** 0141-810 3434
E-mail: archie@forcemeasurement.co.uk
Website: http://www.forcemeasurement.co.uk
Directors: A. Paterson (MD)
Immediate Holding Company: FORCE MEASUREMENT SYSTEMS LIMITED
Registration no: SC070056 **VAT No.:** GB 338 8278 16
Date established: 1979 **Turnover:** £500,000 - £1m
No.of Employees: 1 - 10 **Product Groups:** 37, 38, 48

Date of Accounts	Nov 11	Nov 10	Nov 09
Working Capital	59	40	56
Fixed Assets	2	N/A	N/A
Current Assets	104	72	82

Fosroc Ltd
28 Nurseries Road Baillieston, Glasgow, G69 6UL
Tel: 0141-781 1878 **Fax:** 0141-781 0785
E-mail: audrey.reid@fosroc.com
Website: http://www.fosroc.com
Directors: J. Revillin (Fin), J. Hayes (Prop), G. Kennett (Co Sec)
Managers: D. Jones (Sales Prom Mgr), A. Reid (Mgr)
Ultimate Holding Company: JMH FZCO (UNITED ARAB EMIRATES)
Immediate Holding Company: FOSROC LIMITED
Registration no: 04589343 **Date established:** 2002 **Turnover:** £2m - £5m
No.of Employees: 1 - 10 **Product Groups:** 25, 31, 32, 33

Date of Accounts	Dec 10	Dec 09	Dec 08
Sales Turnover	17m	18m	21m
Pre Tax Profit/Loss	-803	-163	950
Working Capital	4m	6m	6m
Fixed Assets	405	409	347
Current Assets	7m	8m	9m
Current Liabilities	1m	1m	1m

Foster Wheeler Energy
Foley House 5 Seaward Place, Glasgow, G41 1HH
Tel: 0141-420 3414 **Fax:** 0141-420 3416
E-mail: frazer_mackay@fwuk.fwe.co.uk
Website: http://www.fwc.com
Bank(s): Bank of Scotland, 63 Waterloo St, Glasgow G2 7BP
Directors: F. Mackay (MD)
Ultimate Holding Company: FOSTER WHEELER CORPORATION (U.S.A.)
Immediate Holding Company: FOSTER WHEELER LTD
Registration no: 00163609 **Turnover:** £20m - £50m
No.of Employees: 101 - 250 **Product Groups:** 84

4c Design
Unit 13 Rankine House 100 Borron Street, Port Dundas Business Park, Glasgow, G4 9XG
Tel: 0141-353 5490 **Fax:** 0141-353 5491
E-mail: info@4cdesign.co.uk
Website: http://www.4cdesign.co.uk
Directors: W. Mitchell (MD)
Immediate Holding Company: 4C DESIGN LIMITED
Registration no: SC228254 **VAT No.:** GB 789 4919 48
Date established: 2002 **Turnover:** Up to £250,000
No.of Employees: 1 - 10 **Product Groups:** 44, 47, 80, 81, 84, 85

Date of Accounts	Dec 11	Dec 10	Dec 09
Working Capital	79	-4	14
Fixed Assets	20	21	18
Current Assets	127	69	109

Fraser & Macdonald Electric Motors Ltd
176 Woodville Street, Glasgow, G51 2RN
Tel: 0141-445 3874 **Fax:** 0141-425 1135
E-mail: graeme.macdonald@fraser-macdonald.com
Website: http://www.fraser-macdonald.com
Directors: G. Macdonald (MD)
Immediate Holding Company: FRASER & MACDONALD (ELECTRIC MOTORS) LIMITED
Registration no: SC046742 **VAT No.:** GB 260 1546 87
Date established: 1969 **Turnover:** £1m - £2m **No.of Employees:** 11 - 20
Product Groups: 37, 52

Date of Accounts	May 11	May 10	May 09
Working Capital	2m	2m	2m
Fixed Assets	432	438	443
Current Assets	2m	2m	2m

Freshlink Foods
17 Old Shettleston Road, Glasgow, G32 7ES
Tel: 0141-778 9123 **Fax:** 0141-778 1736
E-mail: reception@freshlinkfoods.co.uk
Website: http://www.freshlinkfoods.co.uk
Bank(s): Barclays
Managers: D. O'neill (Chief Mgr)
Ultimate Holding Company: ANGLO BEEF PROCESSORS HOLDINGS
Immediate Holding Company: FRESHLINK FOODS
Registration no: 05186763 **VAT No.:** GB 474 7222 36
Date established: 2004 **Turnover:** £20m - £50m
No.of Employees: 101 - 250 **Product Groups:** 62

Fugro Structural Monitoring
1 Queenslie Court Somerlee Street, Glasgow, G33 4DB
Tel: 0141-774 8828 **Fax:** 0141-774 6112
E-mail: a.dougan@geos.com
Website: http://www.geos.com
Bank(s): Barclays
Managers: A. Dougan (Mgr)
Ultimate Holding Company: FUGRO NV (NETHERLANDS)
Immediate Holding Company: FUGRO SCOTLAND LIMITED
Registration no: SC070939 **Date established:** 1980
Turnover: £10m - £20m **No.of Employees:** 21 - 50 **Product Groups:** 44, 85

Date of Accounts	Dec 10	Dec 09	Dec 08
Sales Turnover	19m	20m	17m
Pre Tax Profit/Loss	5m	6m	5m
Working Capital	5m	5m	4m
Fixed Assets	2m	2m	2m
Current Assets	8m	9m	10m
Current Liabilities	2m	2m	4m

G A P Group Ltd
Carrick House 40 Carrick Street, Glasgow, G2 8DA
Tel: 0141-225 4600 **Fax:** 0141-243 2540
E-mail: info@gap-group.co.uk
Website: http://www.gap-group.co.uk
Bank(s): Clydesdale Bank PLC
Directors: A. Stewart (Fin)
Managers: C. Dunning (Personnel), F. McGrory (Tech Serv Mgr), J. Stewart (Mktg Serv Mgr), K. Stewart (Purch Mgr)
Ultimate Holding Company: GAP HOLDINGS LIMITED
Immediate Holding Company: GAP GROUP LIMITED
Registration no: 00198823 **VAT No.:** GB 259 7931 07
Date established: 2024 **Turnover:** £50m - £75m
No.of Employees: 51 - 100 **Product Groups:** 72, 83

Date of Accounts	Mar 12	Mar 11	Mar 10
Sales Turnover	85m	74m	68m
Pre Tax Profit/Loss	6m	2m	-776
Working Capital	-19m	-18m	-16m
Fixed Assets	80m	71m	68m
Current Assets	25m	20m	19m
Current Liabilities	25m	11m	11m

G E M Lift Services Ltd
7 Laundry Lane Stepps, Glasgow, G33 6LT
Tel: 0141-779 3353 **Fax:** 07970-463658
E-mail: alice.wallace@gemlifts.com
Website: http://www.gemlifts.com
Directors: A. Wallace (Fin)
Immediate Holding Company: G.E.M. LIFT SERVICES LIMITED
Registration no: SC109290 **Date established:** 1988
No.of Employees: 1 - 10 **Product Groups:** 35, 39, 45

Date of Accounts	Apr 11	Apr 10	Apr 09
Working Capital	-28	24	8
Fixed Assets	13	7	9
Current Assets	57	90	54

Garring Ltd
Unit 24 Clyde Workshops Fullarton Road, Glasgow East Investment Park, Glasgow, G32 8YL
Tel: 0141-641 7816 **Fax:** 0141-641 7816
E-mail: garring@scottishnet.co.uk
Website: http://www.garring.co.uk
Directors: A. Gardiner (MD), I. Gardiner (Fin)
Immediate Holding Company: GARRING LIMITED
Registration no: SC068079 **VAT No.:** GB 328 6536 37
Date established: 1979 **Turnover:** £250,000 - £500,000
No.of Employees: 1 - 10 **Product Groups:** 52

Date of Accounts	Dec 10	Dec 09	Dec 08
Sales Turnover	385	261	N/A
Pre Tax Profit/Loss	98	31	N/A
Working Capital	166	87	54
Fixed Assets	12	14	8
Current Assets	200	149	107

Gillett & Sibert Ltd
Kirktonfield Road Neilston, Glasgow, G78 3PL
Tel: 0141-881 5825 **Fax:** 0141-881 5825
E-mail: mail@elcomatic.co.uk
Website: http://www.elcomatic.co.uk
Directors: W. Jardine (Fin), J. Jardine (MD)
Managers: H. Cambell (Quality Control), B. McKee (Prod Eng), R. Colquhoun (I.T. Exec)
Ultimate Holding Company: Elcomatic Holdings Ltd
Immediate Holding Company: Elcomatic Ltd
Registration no: SC056229 **VAT No.:** GB 406 6154 69
Turnover: £2m - £5m **No.of Employees:** 21 - 50 **Product Groups:** 38, 84

Gilmour Ecometal
245 Govan Road, Glasgow, G51 2SQ
Tel: 0141-427 1264 **Fax:** 0141-427 2205
E-mail: info@gilmour-ecometal.co.uk
Website: http://www.gilmour-ecometal.co.uk
Bank(s): Bank of Scotland
Directors: J. Gilmour (Dir)
Managers: S. Gilmour
Date established: 1969 **Turnover:** £5m - £10m
No.of Employees: 51 - 100 **Product Groups:** 30, 32, 46, 48

Glascord Co. Ltd
14 Knapdale Street, Glasgow, G22 6PN
Tel: 0141-336 7061 **Fax:** 0141-347 0525
Directors: I. Kerr (Works)
Immediate Holding Company: GLASCORD COMPANY LTD (THE)
Registration no: SC048409 **Date established:** 1971
No.of Employees: 1 - 10 **Product Groups:** 23, 33

Date of Accounts	Nov 11	Nov 10	Nov 09
Working Capital	667	587	593
Fixed Assets	892	1m	1m
Current Assets	777	587	646

Glasgow Chamber Of Commerce
30 George Square, Glasgow, G2 1EQ
Tel: 0141-204 2121 **Fax:** 0141-221 2336
E-mail: chamber@glasgowchamber.org
Website: http://www.glasgowchamber.org
Bank(s): Bank of Scotland
Directors: S. Patrick (Grp Chief Exec)
Immediate Holding Company: SCOTTISH CHAMBERS OF COMMERCE LIMITED
Registration no: SC313336 **Date established:** 2006 **Turnover:** £1m - £2m
No.of Employees: 11 - 20 **Product Groups:** 87

Date of Accounts	Dec 11	Dec 10	Dec 09
Working Capital	290	277	234
Fixed Assets	3	5	7
Current Assets	549	543	487

Glasgow Disabled Aid Specialists
Blantyre Ferme Road Uddingston, Glasgow, G71 7RN
Tel: 0141-641 3656 **Fax:** 0141-641 3656
Directors: G. Prow (Ptnr)
No.of Employees: 11 - 20 **Product Groups:** 38, 67

Glasgow Steel Nail Co. Ltd
Unit 3 Lancaster Road Bishopbriggs, Glasgow, G64 2HX
Tel: 0141-762 3355 **Fax:** 0141-762 0914
E-mail: glasgowsteelnail@compuserve.com
Website: http://www.glasgowsteelnail.com
Directors: A. Richmond (MD)
Immediate Holding Company: GLASGOW STEEL NAIL COMPANY LIMITED
Registration no: SC047541 **VAT No.:** GB 260 0303 21
Date established: 1970 **No.of Employees:** 1 - 10 **Product Groups:** 35, 39

Date of Accounts	Jun 11	Jun 10	Jun 09
Working Capital	188	215	232
Fixed Assets	80	82	86
Current Assets	249	290	289

Glasgow Studio Electronics
224 West Regent Street, Glasgow, G2 4DQ
Tel: 0141-204 0111
E-mail: info@glse.co.uk
Website: http://www.glse.co.uk
Directors: I. Mcclean (Prop)
Turnover: Up to £250,000 **No.of Employees:** 1 - 10 **Product Groups:** 37, 48

Glasgow Trailer Centre Indespension Scotland Ltd
4-6 Riverside Milngavie, Glasgow, G62 6PS
Tel: 0141-956 3055 **Fax:** 0141-956 2385
E-mail: enquiries@indespension.co.uk
Website: http://www.indespension.co.uk
Managers: P. Bonar (District Mgr)
Registration no: 01358221 **Turnover:** £1m - £2m
No.of Employees: 1 - 10 **Product Groups:** 39

Glitterati Dresswear Hire
99 King Street, Glasgow, G1 5RB
Tel: 0141-552 3567 **Fax:** 0141-552 3567
Directors: W. Withers (MD), M. Withers (Fin)
Immediate Holding Company: GLITTERATI LIMITED
Registration no: SC126250 **Date established:** 1990
Turnover: Up to £250,000 **No.of Employees:** 1 - 10 **Product Groups:** 24

Date of Accounts	Jul 11	Jul 10	Jul 09
Working Capital	-84	-85	-72
Fixed Assets	2	2	3
Current Assets	63	60	70

H P F Energy Services Ltd
3 Buccleuch Avenue Hillington Park, Glasgow, G52 4NR
Tel: 0141-882 4611 **Fax:** 0141-883 0826
E-mail: graham.bradley@hpf-energy.com
Website: http://www.hpf-energy.com
Directors: G. Bradley (MD)
Ultimate Holding Company: MARLA TUBE FITTINGS LIMITED
Immediate Holding Company: PROMAT BD LIMITED
Registration no: SC084811 **Date established:** 2000
No.of Employees: 11 - 20 **Product Groups:** 36

Date of Accounts	Oct 11	Oct 10	Oct 09
Sales Turnover	10m	N/A	N/A
Pre Tax Profit/Loss	1m	N/A	N/A
Working Capital	524	107	126
Fixed Assets	1m	1m	2m
Current Assets	6m	3m	2m
Current Liabilities	374	N/A	N/A

H T E Controls
17 Bessemer Drive Kelvin Industrial Estate, East Kilbride, Glasgow, G75 0QX
Tel: 01355-238641 **Fax:** 01355-231335
E-mail: steve.mcguire@uk-electric.net
Website: http://www.ukelectric.net
Bank(s): HSBC Bank plc
Directors: D. MacKillenan (MD)
Managers: H. Barr (District Mgr), S. Maguire (District Mgr), S. Mcguire (District Mgr), L. McSorley (Gen Contact)
Ultimate Holding Company: ARLEN P.L.C.
Immediate Holding Company: HIGHLAND ELECTRONICS
Registration no: SC036539 **VAT No.:** GB 260 4517 79
Turnover: £2m - £5m **No.of Employees:** 11 - 20 **Product Groups:** 87

P W Hall Ltd
Woodilee Industrial Estate Lenzie, Kirkintilloch, Glasgow, G66 3UR
Tel: 0141-776 2384 **Fax:** 0141-776 2382
E-mail: gordon.mccallum@pwhall.co.uk
Website: http://www.pwhall.co.uk
Bank(s): Bank of Scotland
Directors: B. Syme (Fin), G. McCallum (MD)
Managers: A. Matheson (Chief Acct), R. Jackson (Tech Serv Mgr), I. Miller (Purch Mgr)
Immediate Holding Company: P.W. HALL LIMITED
Registration no: SC170917 **VAT No.:** GB 259 6874 95
Date established: 1996 **Turnover:** £10m - £20m
No.of Employees: 51 - 100 **Product Groups:** 30, 31, 32

see next page

***P W Hall Ltd** - Cont'd*

Date of Accounts	Dec 11	Dec 10	Dec 09
Sales Turnover	11m	10m	9m
Pre Tax Profit/Loss	352	407	247
Working Capital	1m	1m	1m
Fixed Assets	2m	2m	2m
Current Assets	3m	3m	2m
Current Liabilities	288	472	297

Hamble Distribution Ltd

15 Ashley Street, Glasgow, G3 6DR
Tel: 0141-332 3232 **Fax:** 0141-332 6335
E-mail: david@blackspur.com
Website: http://www.blackspur.com
Directors: D. Robertson (MD)
Immediate Holding Company: HAMBLE DISTRIBUTION LIMITED
Registration no: SC076058 **Date established:** 1981
Turnover: £10m - £20m **No.of Employees:** 1 - 10 **Product Groups:** 30, 35, 66, 67

Date of Accounts	Dec 11	Dec 10	Dec 09
Sales Turnover	19m	18m	17m
Pre Tax Profit/Loss	1m	1m	77
Working Capital	6m	5m	5m
Fixed Assets	1m	2m	2m
Current Assets	8m	8m	7m
Current Liabilities	1m	977	442

Hay Group

Clydeway Skypark 8 Elliot Place, Glasgow, G3 8EP
Tel: 0141-226 5855 **Fax:** 0141-204 5021
E-mail: linda_power@haygroup.com
Website: http://www.haygroup.co.uk
Managers: J. Douglas (Mgr)
Immediate Holding Company: MUIR KAY LIMITED
Registration no: SC066959 **Date established:** 1947
No.of Employees: 1 - 10 **Product Groups:** 80

Hayward Tyler Fluid Handling

41-43 Glenburn Road East Kilbride, Glasgow, G74 5BJ
Tel: 01355-225461 **Fax:** 01355-263496
E-mail: pauln@haywardtyler.com
Website: http://www.haywardtyler.com
Bank(s): Lloyds TSB Bank plc
Directors: P. Noble (MD)
Immediate Holding Company: HAYWARD TYLER FLUID HANDLING LTD
Registration no: 06625350 **VAT No.:** GB 510 0529 06
Date established: 2008 **Turnover:** £2m - £5m **No.of Employees:** 11 - 20
Product Groups: 40, 41

Henry Technologies Ltd

Mossland Road Hillington Park, Glasgow, G52 4XZ
Tel: 0141-882 4621 **Fax:** 0141-882 4624
E-mail: sales@henrytech.co.uk
Website: http://www.henrytech.co.uk
Bank(s): The Royal Bank of Scotland
Directors: A. Macdonald (MD), L. Leslie (Fin)
Managers: F. Fuggle, I. Armstrong, K. Duffy (Purch Mgr)
Ultimate Holding Company: HENDRICKS HOLDING COMPANY INC (USA)
Immediate Holding Company: HENRY TECHNOLOGIES LIMITED
Registration no: SC069447 **VAT No.:** GB 328 7954 14
Date established: 1979 **Turnover:** £5m - £10m
No.of Employees: 51 - 100 **Product Groups:** 36, 40

Date of Accounts	Dec 11	Dec 10	Dec 09
Sales Turnover	8m	7m	6m
Pre Tax Profit/Loss	724	721	652
Working Capital	3m	2m	2m
Fixed Assets	1m	869	817
Current Assets	3m	3m	3m
Current Liabilities	436	398	557

Hilti GT Britain Ltd

Unit 1-2 Farm Castle Indl-Est Duchess Place, Rutherglen, Glasgow, G73 1DR
Tel: 0800-886100 **Fax:** 0800-886200
Website: http://www.hilti.co.uk
Directors: F. Dannheim (Fin), R. Hudspeth (Sales), J. Lo'piccolo (MD), J. Rood (MD)
Ultimate Holding Company: HILTI AG (LIECHTENSTEIN)
Immediate Holding Company: HILTI (GT.BRITAIN) LIMITED
Registration no: 00479786 **Date established:** 1950
No.of Employees: 1 - 10 **Product Groups:** 30, 35, 36, 37, 40

Date of Accounts	Dec 10	Dec 09	Dec 08
Sales Turnover	65m	66m	79m
Pre Tax Profit/Loss	766	-379	-48
Working Capital	12m	15m	12m
Fixed Assets	5m	5m	6m
Current Assets	33m	25m	23m
Current Liabilities	6m	4m	5m

Holland House Electrical Co. Ltd

120 Scotland Street, Glasgow, G5 8NX
Tel: 0141-429 5681 **Fax:** 0141-420 1065
E-mail: hhousegla@aol.com
Website: http://www.hh-electrical.co.uk
Bank(s): The Royal Bank of Scotland
Directors: I. Smith (Fin), L. Dunnitt (MD), A. Dunnet (MD), A. Dunnitt (Dir)
Managers: T. Sherry (Mgr), J. Smith (Chief Mgr)
Immediate Holding Company: HOLLAND HOUSE ELECTRICAL COMPANY, LIMITED
Registration no: SC006246 **VAT No.:** GB 259 6222 41
Date established: 2006 **Turnover:** £10m - £20m
No.of Employees: 21 - 50 **Product Groups:** 77

Date of Accounts	Feb 08	Feb 11	Feb 10
Sales Turnover	18m	17m	15m
Pre Tax Profit/Loss	1m	83	-99
Working Capital	7m	7m	7m
Fixed Assets	3m	4m	3m
Current Assets	9m	9m	9m
Current Liabilities	977	553	545

Robert Horne Group plc

1 Deerdykes Court South Cumbernauld, Glasgow, G68 9HW
Tel: 01236-617777 **Fax:** 01236-735463
E-mail: rh.scotland@roberthorne.co.uk
Website: http://www.roberthornepaper.co.uk
Bank(s): National Westminster Bank Plc
Managers: R. Ferguson (Mgr), A. Fagen
Ultimate Holding Company: PAPERLINX LIMITED (AUSTRALIA)
Immediate Holding Company: ROBERT HORNE GROUP LIMITED
Registration no: 00584756 **VAT No.:** GB 235 7221 76
Date established: 1957 **Turnover:** £10m - £20m
No.of Employees: 21 - 50 **Product Groups:** 25, 27, 30

Date of Accounts	Jun 11	Jun 10	Jun 09
Sales Turnover	303m	303m	301m
Pre Tax Profit/Loss	222	-6m	-313
Working Capital	61m	66m	71m
Fixed Assets	22m	23m	22m
Current Assets	126m	129m	137m
Current Liabilities	8m	5m	5m

Howden Compressors Ltd

133 Barfillan Drive, Glasgow, G52 1BE
Tel: 0141-882 3346 **Fax:** 0141-882 8648
E-mail: robert.cleland@howdencompressors.com
Website: http://www.howdencompressors.co.uk
Bank(s): Clydesdale Bank PLC
Directors: F. Maclean (Co Sec), J. Shipley (Tech Serv), R. Cleland (Grp Chief Exec)
Managers: I. Macdougall (Purch Mgr), S. Griffin (Mktg Serv Mgr)
Ultimate Holding Company: CHARTER INTERNATIONAL PLC (JERSEY)
Immediate Holding Company: HOWDEN COMPRESSORS LIMITED
Registration no: SC053832 **VAT No.:** GB 261 9302 69
Date established: 1973 **Turnover:** £10m - £20m
No.of Employees: 101 - 250 **Product Groups:** 40

Date of Accounts	Dec 11	Dec 10	Dec 09
Sales Turnover	30m	19m	17m
Pre Tax Profit/Loss	6m	3m	4m
Working Capital	10m	8m	7m
Fixed Assets	8m	7m	6m
Current Assets	18m	16m	12m
Current Liabilities	4m	5m	4m

Hurry Bros Ltd

2117 London Road, Glasgow, G32 8XQ
Tel: 0141-778 5591 **Fax:** 0141-778 2110
E-mail: enquiries@hurrybros.co.uk
Website: http://www.hurrybros.co.uk
Directors: B. Borland (Dir)
Ultimate Holding Company: A. BORLAND & CO. (GLAZIERS) LIMITED
Immediate Holding Company: HURRY BROTHERS LIMITED
Registration no: SC102043 **Date established:** 1985 **Turnover:** £2m - £5m
No.of Employees: 21 - 50 **Product Groups:** 52

Date of Accounts	Sep 11	Sep 10	Sep 09
Sales Turnover	2m	N/A	N/A
Pre Tax Profit/Loss	-270	N/A	N/A
Working Capital	-213	39	297
Fixed Assets	1m	1m	1m
Current Assets	644	785	1m
Current Liabilities	167	N/A	N/A

Hussmann Refrigeration Ltd

Clydeway Skypark 8 Elliot Place, Glasgow, G3 8EP
Tel: 0141-285 8500 **Fax:** 0141-227 2734
Website: http://www.hussmann.com
Bank(s): HSBC Bank plc
Directors: M. Duffey (MD), D. O' Gorman (Chief Op Offcr), D. O'Gorman (MD), J. McQuillan (MD), K. Doak (Fin), S. Cox (Sales), E. Mcauley (Dir)
Managers: B. Copland (I.T. Exec), B. Rankin (Purch Mgr), P. Mullholland (Personnel)
Ultimate Holding Company: THE CAPITA GROUP PLC
Immediate Holding Company: HUSSMANN HOLDINGS LIMITED
Registration no: 02510891 **VAT No.:** GB 239 0924 53
Date established: 1990 **Turnover:** £20m - £50m
No.of Employees: 251 - 500 **Product Groups:** 40

Hydrasun Ltd

Unit 1-2 Block 20 85-87 Clydesmill Place, Clydesmill Industrial Estate, Glasgow, G32 8RF
Tel: 0141-641 5188 **Fax:** 0141-641 9467
E-mail: sales@hydrasun.com
Website: http://www.hydrasun.com
Bank(s): Clydesdale Bank PLC
Managers: R. Lundie
Ultimate Holding Company: HYDRASUN HOLDINGS LIMITED
Immediate Holding Company: HYDRASUN LIMITED
Registration no: SC059688 **Date established:** 1976
Turnover: £20m - £50m **No.of Employees:** 21 - 50 **Product Groups:** 30, 36

Date of Accounts	Mar 11	Mar 10	Mar 09
Sales Turnover	65m	58m	60m
Pre Tax Profit/Loss	7m	7m	8m
Working Capital	35m	31m	25m
Fixed Assets	3m	3m	2m
Current Assets	51m	40m	37m
Current Liabilities	6m	2m	2m

Ibstock Scottish Brick Ltd

Tannochside Factory Old Edinburgh Road, Uddingston, Glasgow, G71 6HL
Tel: 01698-810686 **Fax:** 01698-812364
E-mail: enquiries@ibstock.co.uk
Website: http://www.ibstock.co.uk
Bank(s): Clydesdale Bank PLC
Directors: S. Hardy (Fin)
Managers: S. Williamson (Reg Sales Mgr), J. Benny
Ultimate Holding Company: CRH PUBLIC LIMITED COMPANY
Immediate Holding Company: IBSTOCK SCOTTISH BRICK LIMITED
Registration no: SC063714 **Date established:** 1977 **Turnover:** £2m - £5m
No.of Employees: 51 - 100 **Product Groups:** 33

Date of Accounts	Dec 08
Working Capital	2m
Current Assets	2m

Ignis Asset Management Ltd

50 Bothwell Street, Glasgow, G2 6HR
Tel: 0141-222 8000 **Fax:** 0141-222 8300
E-mail: sales@britannicasset.com
Website: http://www.ignisasset.com
Directors: S. Griffin (Co Sec)
Managers: G. Jackson (Cust Serv Mgr), W. Steel, G. Hotson, M. Straub (Personnel)
Ultimate Holding Company: PHOENIX GROUP HOLDINGS (CAYMAN ISLANDS)
Immediate Holding Company: IGNIS ASSET MANAGEMENT LIMITED
Registration no: SC200801 **Date established:** 1999
Turnover: £10m - £20m **No.of Employees:** 251 - 500 **Product Groups:** 82

Date of Accounts	Dec 11	Dec 10	Dec 09
Sales Turnover	19m	43m	13m
Pre Tax Profit/Loss	19m	21m	13m
Working Capital	-543	-291	305
Fixed Assets	232m	232m	203m
Current Assets	42	66	537
Current Liabilities	N/A	N/A	232

Ikon Test Solutions

Unit 27A Evans Business Centre, Queen Elizabeth Avenue, Glasgow, G52 4NQ
Tel: 0141-416 0928
E-mail: enquiries@ikontestsolutions.com
Website: http://www.ikontestsolutions.com/
Managers: S. Shearer (Develop Mgr)
Registration no: 06627387 **Date established:** 2008
No.of Employees: 1 - 10 **Product Groups:** 38

In House Gas Manufacturing Ltd

Baptiston House Killearn, Glasgow, G63 9LE
Tel: 01360-551600 **Fax:** 01360-551555
E-mail: info@inhousegas.com
Website: http://www.inhousegas.com
Directors: G. Sinclair (MD), A. Patrick (Dir)
Managers: M. Kerr (Eng), A. Patrick (Sales Admin)
Immediate Holding Company: IN HOUSE GAS (MANUFACTURING) LIMITED
Registration no: SC274327 **Date established:** 2004
No.of Employees: 1 - 10 **Product Groups:** 31

Date of Accounts	Dec 10	Dec 09	Dec 08
Working Capital	-67	-70	-23
Fixed Assets	40	49	3
Current Assets	109	109	107
Current Liabilities	112	80	N/A

Inca UK Ltd

Gleniffer Road Uplawmoor, Glasgow, G78 4BE
Tel: 01505-850625
E-mail: sales@incaukltd.co.uk
Website: http://www.incaukltd.co.uk
Directors: S. Ford (Prop)
Immediate Holding Company: INCA (UK) LTD.
Registration no: SC343916 **Date established:** 2008
Turnover: Up to £250,000 **No.of Employees:** 1 - 10 **Product Groups:** 25, 40

Date of Accounts	Jun 11	Jun 10	Jun 09
Working Capital	39	23	-6
Fixed Assets	4	4	3
Current Assets	62	47	5

Indupart Door Manufacturers

Queensleigh Industrial Estste 1 Coltness Lane, Glasgow, G33 4DR
Tel: 0141-774 8314 **Fax:** 0141-774 8354
E-mail: james@indupart.co.uk
Website: http://www.indupart.co.uk
Managers: J. Currie (Mgr)
Date established: 2001 **No.of Employees:** 1 - 10 **Product Groups:** 26, 35

Alex Inglis & Co Blantyre Ltd

Main Street Blantyre, Glasgow, G72 0XG
Tel: 01698-823213 **Fax:** 01698-829129
E-mail: admin@alexinglis.co.uk
Website: http://www.alexinglis.co.uk
Bank(s): Clydesdale Bank PLC
Directors: S. Paxton (Co Sec), H. Seki (Dir)
Ultimate Holding Company: NOBLET MUNICIPAL SERVICES LIMITED
Immediate Holding Company: ALEX. INGLIS & COMPANY (BLANTYRE) LIMITED
Registration no: SC029452 **VAT No.:** GB 260 0843 86
Date established: 1953 **Turnover:** £2m - £5m **No.of Employees:** 11 - 20
Product Groups: 48

Date of Accounts	Dec 11	Dec 10	Dec 09
Sales Turnover	2m	2m	3m
Pre Tax Profit/Loss	54	85	-214
Working Capital	976	716	285
Fixed Assets	196	452	827
Current Assets	1m	1m	974
Current Liabilities	142	169	179

J Inglis Engineering Sales

2 Clairmont Gardens, Glasgow, G3 7LW
Tel: 0141-353 6225 **Fax:** 0141-353 6229
Website: http://www.jinglis.co.uk
Directors: J. Inglis (Prop)
Immediate Holding Company: FXW LIMITED
Registration no: SC327495 **Date established:** 2007
No.of Employees: 1 - 10 **Product Groups:** 35, 39, 45

Institute Of Marine Engineering Science & Technology

36 Greystone Avenue Rutherglen, Glasgow, G73 3SL
Tel: 0141-647 7225 **Fax:** 0141-647 7225
E-mail: imarestscot@tiscali.co.uk
Managers: L. Wylie
Registration no: FP007155 **Date established:** 1962
No.of Employees: 1 - 10 **Product Groups:** 35, 36, 39

Instrument Transformers Ltd

8 Lithgow Place East Kilbride, Glasgow, G74 1PW
Tel: 01355-236057 **Fax:** 01355-239259
E-mail: sales@itl-uk.com
Website: http://www.itl-uk.com
Bank(s): The Royal Bank of Scotland
Directors: R. Porrelli (Tech Serv)
Ultimate Holding Company: WESTMINSTER (SCOTLAND) LIMITED
Immediate Holding Company: INSTRUMENT TRANSFORMERS LIMITED
Registration no: SC054448 **VAT No.:** GB 261 9187 43
Date established: 1973 **Turnover:** £2m - £5m **No.of Employees:** 21 - 50
Product Groups: 37, 40

Date of Accounts	Jun 11	Jun 10	Jun 09
Working Capital	1m	1m	902
Fixed Assets	373	364	319
Current Assets	2m	2m	1m

International Doors & Windows

9 Tollpark Road Wardpark East, Cumbernauld, Glasgow, G68 0LW
Tel: 01236-724839 **Fax:** 01236-726997
E-mail: info@idaw.co.uk
Website: http://www.idaw.co.uk

Directors: G. Davidson (MD)
Ultimate Holding Company: GROUP TOPEK HOLDINGS LIMITED
Immediate Holding Company: TOPEK ROOFING LIMITED
Registration no: SC065560 **Date established:** 1978 **Turnover:** £2m - £5m
No.of Employees: 11 - 20 **Product Groups:** 25, 33, 35, 66

Date of Accounts	Aug 92	Aug 91	Aug 90
Sales Turnover	4m	5m	6m
Pre Tax Profit/Loss	88	100	227
Fixed Assets	94	91	133
Current Assets	3m	3m	2m

Richard Irvin
28 Earl Haig Road Hillington Park, Glasgow, G52 4JU
Tel: 0141-892 2222 **Fax:** 0141-892 2211
E-mail: admin@richard-irvin.co.uk
Website: http://www.richard-irvin.co.uk
Bank(s): Royal Bank of Scotland
Managers: B. Irvin (Mgr)
Immediate Holding Company: RICHARD IRVIN & SONS
Registration no: 00096281 **VAT No.:** GB 553 1132 79
Date established: 1900 **Turnover:** £5m - £10m **No.of Employees:** 11 - 20
Product Groups: 48, 52

J V C Manufacturing UK Ltd
2 Glenburn Road East Kilbride, Glasgow, G74 5BA
Tel: 01355-241166 **Fax:** 01355-265231
E-mail: enquiries@jvc.co.uk
Website: http://www.jvc.co.uk
Directors: T. Knowles (MD)
Managers: H. Totten, K. Honda (Comptroller)
Ultimate Holding Company: VICTOR COMPANY OF JAPAN LTD (JAPAN)
Immediate Holding Company: JVC MANUFACTURING U.K. LIMITED
Registration no: SC106646 **Date established:** 1987
Turnover: £125m - £250m **No.of Employees:** 1 - 10 **Product Groups:** 37

Date of Accounts	Mar 08	Mar 07	Mar 06
Sales Turnover	187m	266m	248m
Pre Tax Profit/Loss	-6m	-11m	-10m
Working Capital	-9m	-4m	-2m
Fixed Assets	N/A	N/A	12m
Current Assets	62m	60m	96m
Current Liabilities	3m	12m	5m

J Wilson & Co.
96 David Street, Glasgow, G40 2UH
Tel: 0141-551 0268 **Fax:** 0141-554 4620
E-mail: info@jwilsongroup.co.uk
Website: http://www.jwilsongroup.co.uk
Directors: J. Lambert (Dir)
Registration no: SC061483 **VAT No.:** GB 290 3616 61
No.of Employees: 11 - 20 **Product Groups:** 37

Jacobs Engineering UK Ltd
95 Bothwell Street, Glasgow, G2 7HX
Tel: 0141-243 8000 **Fax:** 0141-226 3109
E-mail: david.biggott@jacobs.com
Website: http://www.jacobs.com
Bank(s): Bank of Scotland, Glasgow Head Office, 110 St. Vincent St
Directors: D. Biggott (Fin)
Managers: A. Donald (Mgr)
Ultimate Holding Company: JACOBS ENGINEERING GROUP INC USA
Immediate Holding Company: JACOBS ENGINEERING U.K. LIMITED
Registration no: 08111269 **VAT No.:** GB 624 2989 20
Date established: 2012 **Turnover:** Up to £250,000
No.of Employees: 501 - 1000 **Product Groups:** 34, 42, 51, 54, 80, 81, 84, 85

Date of Accounts	Sep 11	Sep 10	Sep 09
Pre Tax Profit/Loss	-0	N/A	-2
Working Capital	899	899	899
Current Assets	934	934	934
Current Liabilities	N/A	14	15

Jacobs & Turner Ltd
Vermont House 149 Vermont Street, Glasgow, G41 1LU
Tel: 0141-568 8000 **Fax:** 0141-568 8080
E-mail: grahamh@trespass.co.uk
Website: http://www.trespass.co.uk
Managers: S. Melvil, M. Macdonald, G. Hancock (Chief Acct)
Immediate Holding Company: JACOBS & TURNER LIMITED
Registration no: SC047678 **VAT No.:** GB 260 3705 83
Date established: 1970 **Turnover:** £50m - £75m
No.of Employees: 51 - 100 **Product Groups:** 24

Date of Accounts	Jun 10	Jun 09	Jun 08
Sales Turnover	53m	47m	40m
Pre Tax Profit/Loss	2m	2m	2m
Working Capital	19m	18m	16m
Fixed Assets	22m	22m	23m
Current Assets	28m	29m	26m
Current Liabilities	3m	3m	4m

James Laird Gold Beaters Ltd (Office)
18 Craig Road, Glasgow, G44 3DR
Tel: 0141-637 8288 **Fax:** 0141-637 8288
E-mail: goldleaf@jameslaird.fsnet.co.uk
Website: http://www.jameslaird.com
Directors: S. Mitchell (Fin), K. Laird (MD)
Immediate Holding Company: JAMES LAIRD (GOLD BEATERS) LIMITED
Registration no: SC028711 **VAT No.:** GB 260 6112 95
Date established: 1952 **Turnover:** £500,000 - £1m
No.of Employees: 1 - 10 **Product Groups:** 34

Date of Accounts	Dec 11	Dec 10	Dec 09
Working Capital	69	73	57
Fixed Assets	410	411	412
Current Assets	83	99	97

J G Jarvie & Sons
110 Carntynehall Road, Glasgow, G32 6AS
Tel: 0141-763 2142
Directors: S. Jarvie (Prop)
Date established: 1986 **No.of Employees:** 1 - 10 **Product Groups:** 26, 35

Jewson Ltd
300 Bearsden Road, Glasgow, G13 1EP
Tel: 0141-954 8021 **Fax:** 0141-950 1692
E-mail: sales@jewson.co.uk
Website: http://www.jewson.co.uk
Managers: P. Menzies (Mgr)
Ultimate Holding Company: COMPAGNIE DE SAINT GOBAIN (FRANCE)
Immediate Holding Company: JEWSON LIMITED
Registration no: 00348407 **VAT No.:** GB 497 7184 83
Date established: 1939 **No.of Employees:** 11 - 20 **Product Groups:** 66

Date of Accounts	Dec 11	Dec 10	Dec 09
Sales Turnover	1606m	1547m	1485m
Pre Tax Profit/Loss	18m	100m	45m
Working Capital	-345m	-250m	-349m
Fixed Assets	496m	387m	461m
Current Assets	657m	1005m	1320m
Current Liabilities	66m	120m	64m

Jewson Ltd
Glasgow Road Rutherglen, Glasgow, G73 1SG
Tel: 0141-647 9621 **Fax:** 0141-643 0646
E-mail: kenny.hughes@jewson.co.uk
Website: http://www.jewson.co.uk
Managers: K. Hughes (District Mgr)
Ultimate Holding Company: COMPAGNIE DE SAINT GOBAIN (FRANCE)
Immediate Holding Company: JEWSON LIMITED
Registration no: 00348407 **VAT No.:** GB 394 1212 63
Date established: 1939 **Turnover:** £2m - £5m **No.of Employees:** 1 - 10
Product Groups: 66

Date of Accounts	Dec 11	Dec 10	Dec 09
Sales Turnover	1606m	1547m	1485m
Pre Tax Profit/Loss	18m	100m	45m
Working Capital	-345m	-250m	-349m
Fixed Assets	496m	387m	461m
Current Assets	657m	1005m	1320m
Current Liabilities	66m	120m	64m

Jewson Ltd
127 Craighall Road, Glasgow, G4 9TP
Tel: 0141-331 1287 **Fax:** 0141-331 1432
Website: http://www.jewson.co.uk
Directors: P. Hindall (MD)
Ultimate Holding Company: COMPAGNIE DE SAINT GOBAIN (FRANCE)
Immediate Holding Company: JEWSON LIMITED
Registration no: 00348407 **Date established:** 1939
No.of Employees: 1 - 10 **Product Groups:** 66

Date of Accounts	Dec 11	Dec 10	Dec 09
Sales Turnover	1606m	1547m	1485m
Pre Tax Profit/Loss	18m	100m	45m
Working Capital	-345m	-250m	-349m
Fixed Assets	496m	387m	461m
Current Assets	657m	1005m	1320m
Current Liabilities	66m	120m	64m

Jewson Ltd
99 Harmony Row, Glasgow, G51 3NZ
Tel: 0141-425 2200 **Fax:** 0141-445 8471
Website: http://www.jewson.co.uk
Bank(s): Barclays
Directors: C. Kenward (Fin), P. Hindle (MD), T. Newman (Sales)
Managers: D. Kennedy (District Mgr), J. Flemming (District Mgr)
Ultimate Holding Company: COMPAGNIE DE SAINT GOBAIN (FRANCE)
Immediate Holding Company: JEWSON LIMITED
Registration no: 00348407 **Date established:** 1939
Turnover: £500m - £1,000m **No.of Employees:** 51 - 100
Product Groups: 66

Date of Accounts	Dec 11	Dec 10	Dec 09
Sales Turnover	1606m	1547m	1485m
Pre Tax Profit/Loss	18m	100m	45m
Working Capital	-345m	-250m	-349m
Fixed Assets	496m	387m	461m
Current Assets	657m	1005m	1320m
Current Liabilities	66m	120m	64m

Jewson Ltd
2347-2349 London Road, Glasgow, G32 8YS
Tel: 0141-778 8341 **Fax:** 0141-778 6857
E-mail: tommy.stevenson@jewson.co.uk
Website: http://www.jewson.co.uk
Managers: T. Stevenson (Mgr)
Ultimate Holding Company: COMPAGNIE DE SAINT GOBAIN (FRANCE)
Immediate Holding Company: JEWSON LIMITED
Registration no: 00348407 **VAT No.:** GB 497 7184 83
Date established: 1939 **Turnover:** £500m - £1,000m
No.of Employees: 11 - 20 **Product Groups:** 66

Date of Accounts	Dec 11	Dec 10	Dec 09
Sales Turnover	1606m	1547m	1485m
Pre Tax Profit/Loss	18m	100m	45m
Working Capital	-345m	-250m	-349m
Fixed Assets	496m	387m	461m
Current Assets	657m	1005m	1320m
Current Liabilities	66m	120m	64m

John Dickie Homes Humbie2007
Burnfield Avenue Thornliebank, Glasgow, G46 7TT
Tel: 0141-633 1234
E-mail: morgan.hogarth@dickiegroup.com
Website: http://www.dickiegroup.com
Directors: M. Hogarth (Fin)
Immediate Holding Company: THOMSONS COFFEE COMPANY LIMITED
Registration no: SC324804 **Date established:** 2001
No.of Employees: 1 - 10 **Product Groups:** 52

Date of Accounts	Jul 11	Jul 10	Jul 09
Working Capital	-50	-58	-74
Fixed Assets	35	38	35
Current Assets	67	32	18

John Simpson Junior Glasgow Ltd
28 Coxhill Street, Glasgow, G21 1HN
Tel: 0141-332 3231 **Fax:** 0141-332 7325
E-mail: sales@simpsonsteel.co.uk
Website: http://www.simpsonsteel.co.uk
Directors: J. Paterson (MD)
Immediate Holding Company: JSJR 2012 LIMITED
Registration no: SC014594 **VAT No.:** GB 260 0041 25
Date established: 2027 **Turnover:** £1m - £2m **No.of Employees:** 1 - 10
Product Groups: 66

William Johnston & Company Ltd
9 Spiersbridge Terrace Thornliebank Industrial Estate, Glasgow, G46 8JH
Tel: 0141-620 1666 **Fax:** 0141-620 1888
E-mail: sales@williamjohnston.co.uk
Website: http://www.williamjohnston.co.uk
Bank(s): Bank of Scotland
Directors: T. McKnight (MD)
Managers: A. Cochrane (Works Gen Mgr), M. Murchie (Accounts)
Registration no: SC045228 **VAT No.:** GB 260 0736 87
No.of Employees: 21 - 50 **Product Groups:** 36

Date of Accounts	Apr 07	Dec 05
Working Capital	10	27
Fixed Assets	12	5

Current Assets	40	34
Current Liabilities	30	7

Jones Lang Lasalle
150 St Vincent Street, Glasgow, G2 5ND
Tel: 0141-248 6040 **Fax:** 0141-221 9032
Website: http://www.joneslanglasalle.com
Directors: N. Cockburn (MD)
Ultimate Holding Company: JONES LANG LASALLE INC (USA)
Immediate Holding Company: JONES LANG LASALLE (SCOTLAND) LIMITED
Registration no: SC188350 **Date established:** 1998
Turnover: £5m - £10m **No.of Employees:** 51 - 100 **Product Groups:** 80

Date of Accounts	Dec 11	Dec 10	Dec 09
Sales Turnover	7m	9m	8m
Pre Tax Profit/Loss	-306	555	197
Working Capital	3m	4m	3m
Fixed Assets	31	31	31
Current Assets	3m	27m	24m
Current Liabilities	N/A	178	44

K B Refrigeration Ltd
31-33 Colquhoun Avenue Hillington Park, Glasgow, G52 4BN
Tel: 0141-810 5577 **Fax:** 01463-713264
E-mail: enquiries@kb-services.co.uk
Website: http://www.kb-services.co.uk
Directors: B. Feeney (MD)
Ultimate Holding Company: LONGDON ESTATES LIMITED
Immediate Holding Company: K B REFRIGERATION LIMITED
Registration no: SC102356 **Date established:** 1986
Turnover: £10m - £20m **No.of Employees:** 1 - 10 **Product Groups:** 40, 68

Date of Accounts	Dec 11	Dec 10	Dec 09
Sales Turnover	13m	16m	11m
Pre Tax Profit/Loss	255	310	58
Working Capital	2m	2m	2m
Fixed Assets	718	685	458
Current Assets	4m	5m	4m
Current Liabilities	828	532	381

K R L
PO Box 5577, Glasgow, G77 9BH
Tel: 0141-616 0900 **Fax:** 0141-883 3686
E-mail: krl@krl.co.uk
Website: http://www.krl.co.uk
Managers: I. Waugh (Mgr)
Registration no: 04765124 **VAT No.:** GB 309 1985 41
Date established: 1978 **Turnover:** £1m - £2m **No.of Employees:** 1 - 10
Product Groups: 28, 89

Kelly Rail Ltd
15 Nurseries Road Baillieston, Glasgow, G69 6UL
Tel: 0141-773 1750 **Fax:** 0141-773 1573
E-mail: robert.burnside@kelly.co.uk
Website: http://www.kelly.co.uk
Directors: J. Bradley (Fin)
Managers: R. Burnside (Mgr)
Immediate Holding Company: KELLY INTEGRATED TRANSPORT SERVICES LTD
Registration no: 04411283 **Date established:** 2002
Turnover: £20m - £50m **No.of Employees:** 51 - 100 **Product Groups:** 37, 52, 80

Kelvin Conference Centre
The West of Scotland Science Park, Glasgow, G20 0TH
Tel: 0141-330 3939 **Fax:** 0141-330 2828
E-mail: kenny.gough@glasgow.ac.uk
Website: http://www.gla.ac.uk
Bank(s): The Clydesdale Bank
Managers: K. Gough
Immediate Holding Company: UNIVERSITY OF GLASGOW
VAT No.: GB 671 7980 93 **Turnover:** £250,000 - £500,000
No.of Employees: 21 - 50 **Product Groups:** 69

Kelvin Diesels British Polar Engines Ltd
133 Helen Street Govan, Glasgow, G51 3HD
Tel: 0141-445 2455 **Fax:** 0141-445 2185
E-mail: stewart.davis@britishpolarengines.co.uk
Website: http://www.BritishPolarEngines.co.uk
Bank(s): The Royal Bank of Scotland Ltd, Govan West Branch
Directors: S. Davis (MD)
Managers: J. Duncan (Eng Serv Mgr), M. Flemming (Prod Mgr), R. McTrustery (Purch Mgr), E. McMillan
Ultimate Holding Company: ASSOCIATED BRITISH ENGINEERING PLC
Immediate Holding Company: BRITISH POLAR ENGINES LIMITED
Registration no: SC014560 **VAT No.:** GB 259 6394 12
Date established: 2027 **Turnover:** £2m - £5m **No.of Employees:** 21 - 50
Product Groups: 37, 39, 40, 48

Date of Accounts	Mar 12	Mar 11	Mar 10
Sales Turnover	3m	4m	3m
Pre Tax Profit/Loss	564	916	556
Working Capital	3m	3m	2m
Fixed Assets	67	83	90
Current Assets	5m	6m	4m
Current Liabilities	309	577	248

Kelvin Steels Ltd
Spiersbridge Lane Thornliebank Industrial Estate, Thornliebank, Glasgow, G46 8JT
Tel: 0141-638 7988 **Fax:** 0141-638 1097
E-mail: info@kelvinsteels.com
Website: http://www.kelvinsteels.com
Directors: H. Nugent (MD)
Ultimate Holding Company: WESTSTRAND LIMITED
Immediate Holding Company: KELVIN STEELS LIMITED
Registration no: SC205181 **VAT No.:** GB 361 2634 56
Date established: 2000 **Turnover:** £5m - £10m **No.of Employees:** 21 - 50
Product Groups: 34, 66

Date of Accounts	Nov 11	Nov 10	Nov 09
Sales Turnover	N/A	N/A	5m
Pre Tax Profit/Loss	N/A	N/A	231
Working Capital	2m	1m	2m
Fixed Assets	161	170	185
Current Assets	3m	3m	2m
Current Liabilities	N/A	N/A	289

Kelvin Valley Properties
23 Main Street Kilsyth, Glasgow, G65 0AH
Tel: 01236-826661 **Fax:** 01236-826661
E-mail: jrafferty@kelvinvalleyproperties.co.uk
Website: http://www.kvps.co.uk

see next page

***Kelvin Valley Properties** - Cont'd*

Directors: S. Rafferty (Co Sec), J. Rafferty (Ptnr)
Immediate Holding Company: KELVIN VALLEY PROPERTIES LIMITED
Registration no: SC237631 **Date established:** 2002
Turnover: £250,000 - £500,000 **No.of Employees:** 1 - 10
Product Groups: 80

Kelvinside Electronics Ltd

2 Gavell Road Kilsyth, Glasgow, G65 9BS
Tel: 01236-824433 **Fax:** 01236-826333
E-mail: ianf@kelvinside.co.uk
Website: http://www.kelvinside.co.uk
Directors: I. Ferguey (Dir)
Managers: G. Brownlee, S. Macmillan (Mktg Serv Mgr), A. Burns (Personnel)
Immediate Holding Company: KELVINSIDE ELECTRONICS LIMITED
Registration no: SC105407 **VAT No.:** GB 456 6347 23
Date established: 1987 **Turnover:** £5m - £10m
No.of Employees: 51 - 100 **Product Groups:** 84

Date of Accounts	Nov 10	Nov 09	Nov 08
Sales Turnover	6m	6m	N/A
Pre Tax Profit/Loss	562	36	24
Working Capital	55	-319	384
Fixed Assets	3m	3m	2m
Current Assets	4m	4m	4m
Current Liabilities	474	737	149

Keith Kendal

Block 8 Unit 2 New Albion Industrial Estate Halley Street, Glasgow, G13 4DJ
Tel: 0141-952 8801 **Fax:** 0141-952 8804
Directors: K. Kendal (Prop)
Date established: 1998 **No.of Employees:** 1 - 10 **Product Groups:** 35

Kendlebell

Carron House Suite 6 Carron Way, Cumbernauld, Glasgow, G67 1ER
Tel: 01236-868400 **Fax:** 0870-067 3120
E-mail: info@kbvo.co.uk
Website: http://www.kbvo.co.uk
Directors: C. Munro (MD), A. Munro (Ptnr)
Managers: C. Monro (Mgr)
Immediate Holding Company: WEATHERSEALED EXTERIORS LTD
Registration no: 03356950 **Date established:** 2012
No.of Employees: 11 - 20 **Product Groups:** 79

Date of Accounts	Sep 08
Working Capital	-342
Fixed Assets	329
Current Assets	105
Current Liabilities	447
Total Share Capital	16

Kestral Controls Ltd

3 Garrell Road Kilsyth, Glasgow, G65 9JX
Tel: 01236-821564 **Fax:** 01236-825676
E-mail: sales@kestralcontrols.co.uk
Website: http://www.kestralcontrols.co.uk
Bank(s): Royal Bank of Scotland, Stirling
Directors: J. Fullerton (MD)
Immediate Holding Company: KESTRAL CONTROLS LIMITED
Registration no: SC044824 **VAT No.:** GB 260 5706 71
Date established: 1967 **Turnover:** £1m - £2m **No.of Employees:** 11 - 20
Product Groups: 37

Date of Accounts	Jul 11	Jul 10	Jul 09
Working Capital	354	360	443
Fixed Assets	76	59	80
Current Assets	601	523	625

Keypoint Technologies Keypoint Technologies

1 Ainslie Road Hillington Industrial Estate, Hillington Park, Glasgow, G52 4RU
Tel: 0141-585 6492
E-mail: info@keypoint-tech.com
Website: http://www.adaptexlive.com/
Managers: A. Howat (Fin Mgr)
Immediate Holding Company: KEYPOINT TECHNOLOGIES (UK) LIMITED
Registration no: SC269107 **Date established:** 2004
Turnover: £250,000 - £500,000 **No.of Employees:** 21 - 50
Product Groups: 44

Date of Accounts	Jun 11	Jun 10	Jun 09
Working Capital	-1m	-1m	-490
Fixed Assets	2m	1m	872
Current Assets	976	1m	1m

Kilts-4-U

2 Erskine Square, Glasgow, G42 4BJ
Tel: 0141-571 2282
E-mail: sales@kilts-4-u.com
Website: http://www.kilts-4-u.com
Directors: S. Cerlton (Prop)
Immediate Holding Company: KILTS 4 U LTD.
Registration no: SC372083 **Date established:** 2010
No.of Employees: 1 - 10 **Product Groups:** 24

Date of Accounts	Mar 11
Working Capital	-1
Fixed Assets	7
Current Assets	12

Klinge Chemicals Ltd

1 Bessemer Drive Kelvin Industrial Estate, East Kilbride, Glasgow, G75 0QX
Tel: 01355-238464 **Fax:** 01355-264328
E-mail: enquiries@klinge-chemicals.co.uk
Website: http://www.klinge-chemicals.co.uk
Directors: M. Klinge (MD), R. Templeton (Co Sec)
Managers: C. Klinge (Sales & Mktg Mg), S. Lockie (Ops Mgr)
Immediate Holding Company: KLINGE CHEMICALS LIMITED
Registration no: 01291684 **Date established:** 1976
No.of Employees: 21 - 50 **Product Groups:** 17

Date of Accounts	Dec 11	Dec 10	Dec 09
Working Capital	262	206	81
Fixed Assets	1m	1m	1m
Current Assets	3m	4m	3m

Konecranes UK Ltd (Industrial Crane Division)

Peel Park Place East Kilbride, Glasgow, G74 5LR
Tel: 01355-220591 **Fax:** 01355-263654
E-mail: gordon.adie@konecranes.com
Website: http://www.konecranes.com
Bank(s): Nordea Bank, London
Directors: G. Adie (MD), D. Roberton (Fin), G. Adie (MD)
Managers: D. Evans (Purch Mgr)
Ultimate Holding Company: KONECRANES PLC (FINLAND)
Immediate Holding Company: J.H. CARRUTHERS LIMITED
Registration no: SC075148 **Date established:** 1981
Turnover: £10m - £20m **No.of Employees:** 51 - 100 **Product Groups:** 39, 45, 46, 67

Date of Accounts	Dec 11	Dec 10	Dec 09
Sales Turnover	N/A	N/A	17m
Pre Tax Profit/Loss	N/A	N/A	298
Working Capital	3m	3m	3m
Current Assets	3m	3m	3m
Current Liabilities	N/A	N/A	2

Kooltech Ltd

433-437 Hillington Road Hillington Park, Glasgow, G52 4BL
Tel: 0141-883 0447 **Fax:** 0141-883 5642
E-mail: murray.sharp@kooltech.co.uk
Website: http://www.kooltech.co.uk
Directors: J. Gray (Fin), M. Sharp (MD)
Managers: K. McMahon (Tech Serv Mgr)
Ultimate Holding Company: KOOLTECH LIMITED
Immediate Holding Company: KOOLTECH MARKETING LIMITED
Registration no: SC069448 **Date established:** 1979
Turnover: £20m - £50m **No.of Employees:** 51 - 100 **Product Groups:** 29, 38, 39, 40

Date of Accounts	Oct 11	Oct 10	Oct 09
Working Capital	50	50	50
Current Assets	50	50	50

KPMG UK Ltd

191 West George Street, Glasgow, G2 2LJ
Tel: 0141-226 5511 **Fax:** 0141-204 1584
Website: http://www.kpmg.co.uk
Directors: C. Anderson (Snr Part)
Ultimate Holding Company: KPMG EUROPE LLP
Immediate Holding Company: KPMG UK LIMITED
Registration no: 03580549 **Date established:** 1998 **Turnover:** £2m - £5m
No.of Employees: 251 - 500 **Product Groups:** 80

Date of Accounts	Sep 11	Sep 10	Sep 09
Sales Turnover	698m	632m	624m
Pre Tax Profit/Loss	655	593	584
Working Capital	1m	847	419
Current Assets	23m	21m	25m
Current Liabilities	22m	20m	20m

Kuka Studios

201 Mosspark Drive, Glasgow, G52 1LH
Tel: 07900-923289
E-mail: enquiry@kukastudios.com
Website: http://www.kukastudios.com
Directors: H. Glenn (Prop), H. Glen (Ptnr)
Managers: H. Glen (Consultant)
Immediate Holding Company: KUKA STUDIOS LIMITED
Registration no: SC352558 **Date established:** 2008
No.of Employees: 1 - 10 **Product Groups:** 44

Date of Accounts	Dec 10	Dec 09
Working Capital	-3	-2
Current Assets	N/A	1
Current Liabilities	3	3

Laidlaw Solutions

171 Woodville Street, Glasgow, G51 2RQ
Tel: 0141-445 8892 **Fax:** 0141-445 8871
E-mail: infoglasgow@laidlaw.net
Website: http://www.laidlaw.net
Managers: I. Walker (Reg Sales Mgr), I. Walker (Mgr), L. Cress (Ops Mgr)
Ultimate Holding Company: LAIDLAW (UK) LIMITED
Immediate Holding Company: INGERSOLL RAND
Registration no: SC054128 **VAT No.:** GB 110 6214 33
No.of Employees: 1 - 10 **Product Groups:** 36, 40, 66

Lamptech Special Purpose Lamps

265 Cambuslang Road Cambuslang, Glasgow, G72 7DB
Tel: 0141-641 5175 **Fax:** 0141-643 3917
E-mail: mail@lamptechglasgow.com
Website: http://www.lamptechglasgow.com
Directors: I. Paynter (Prop)
No.of Employees: 1 - 10 **Product Groups:** 33, 37, 67

M B Langmuir & Hay

60 Kelvingrove Street, Glasgow, G3 7SA
Tel: 0141-332 6266 **Fax:** 0141-332 6267
E-mail: mail@langmuirandhay.com
Website: http://www.langmuirandhay.com
Directors: M. Langmuir (Ptnr), M. Langmuir (Snr Part)
Immediate Holding Company: M.B. LANGMUIR & HAY LLP
Registration no: SO300400 **VAT No.:** GB 260 3144 00
Date established: 2004 **Turnover:** £250,000 - £500,000
No.of Employees: 1 - 10 **Product Groups:** 80

Date of Accounts	Mar 11	Mar 10	Mar 09
Sales Turnover	442	N/A	N/A
Pre Tax Profit/Loss	260	N/A	N/A
Working Capital	35	194	153
Fixed Assets	8	11	37
Current Assets	215	328	305
Current Liabilities	179	N/A	N/A

Learning & Teaching Scotland (Scottish Council for Educational Technology)

58 Robertson Street, Glasgow, G2 8DU
Tel: 0141-282 5000 **Fax:** 01382-443645
E-mail: b.mcleary@ltscotland.org.uk
Website: http://www.ltscotland.org.uk
Bank(s): The Royal Bank of Scotland
Managers: B. Mcleary
Immediate Holding Company: LEARNING AND TEACHING SCOTLAND
Registration no: SC200241 **Date established:** 1999 **Turnover:** £2m - £5m
No.of Employees: 51 - 100 **Product Groups:** 86

Date of Accounts	Mar 11	Mar 10	Mar 09
Sales Turnover	2m	2m	3m
Pre Tax Profit/Loss	-20m	-23m	-18m
Working Capital	5m	5m	5m
Fixed Assets	2m	2m	2m
Current Assets	9m	10m	10m
Current Liabilities	4m	4m	3m

Lesmac Fasteners Ltd

73 Dykehead Street, Glasgow, G33 4AQ
Tel: 0141-774 0004 **Fax:** 0141-774 2229
E-mail: sales@lesmac.co.uk
Website: http://www.lesmac.co.uk
Bank(s): Royal Bank of Scotland
Directors: L. Wood (Fin), E. Kneale (MD)
Immediate Holding Company: LESMAC (FASTENERS) LIMITED
Registration no: SC048774 **Date established:** 1971 **Turnover:** £1m - £2m
No.of Employees: 11 - 20 **Product Groups:** 66

Date of Accounts	May 11	May 10	May 09
Working Capital	199	434	432
Fixed Assets	317	41	53
Current Assets	791	909	1m

Linde Material Handling Scotland Ltd

3 Milton Road East Kilbride, Glasgow, G74 5BU
Tel: 01355-233601 **Fax:** 01355-235833
E-mail: stan.harris@linde-mh-scotland.co.uk
Website: http://www.linde-mh-scotland.co.uk
Bank(s): Barclays Bank PLC
Directors: S. Harris (MD)
Ultimate Holding Company: SUPERLIFT HOLDINGS SARL (LUXEMBOURG)
Immediate Holding Company: LINDE MATERIAL HANDLING SCOTLAND LIMITED
Registration no: 03446986 **Date established:** 1997
No.of Employees: 11 - 20 **Product Groups:** 45

Date of Accounts	Dec 11	Dec 10	Dec 09
Sales Turnover	14m	14m	13m
Pre Tax Profit/Loss	1m	1m	967
Working Capital	3m	1m	-557
Fixed Assets	3m	3m	4m
Current Assets	6m	5m	3m
Current Liabilities	2m	2m	2m

Lismor Recordings

PO Box 7264, Glasgow, G46 6AL
Tel: 0141-637 6010 **Fax:** 0141-637 6010
E-mail: lismor@lismor.com
Website: http://www.allcelticmusic.com
Directors: C. Kenna (Co Sec)
Managers: R. Simpson (Mgr)
Immediate Holding Company: LISMOR RECORDINGS LIMITED
Registration no: SC142256 **VAT No.:** GB 343 2758 55
Date established: 1993 **Turnover:** £500,000 - £1m
No.of Employees: 1 - 10 **Product Groups:** 37

Date of Accounts	Mar 08	Mar 07	Mar 06
Working Capital	-65	-46	-49
Fixed Assets	106	2	3
Current Assets	174	162	134
Current Liabilities	239	208	182
Total Share Capital	1	1	1

L'Occitane

46 Buchanan Street, Glasgow, G1 3JX
Tel: 0141-248 7940 **Fax:** 0141-847 0335
Website: http://www.loccitane.co.uk
Managers: T. Graham (Mgr)
Ultimate Holding Company: L'Occitane International SA (Luxembourg)
Immediate Holding Company: L OCCITANE LIMITED
Registration no: 03278335 **Date established:** 1996
Turnover: £10m - £20m **No.of Employees:** 1 - 10 **Product Groups:** 32, 63

Date of Accounts	Mar 11	Mar 10	Mar 09
Sales Turnover	33m	27m	22m
Pre Tax Profit/Loss	748	122	-54
Working Capital	-949	-654	-35
Fixed Assets	4m	3m	3m
Current Assets	11m	9m	8m
Current Liabilities	4m	3m	2m

Logitech Ltd

Erskine Ferry Road Old Kilpatrick, Glasgow, G60 5EU
Tel: 01389-875444 **Fax:** 01389-879042
E-mail: sales@logitech.uk.com
Website: http://www.logitech.uk.com
Directors: A. McWilliam (Fin), D. Humphries (MD)
Managers: R. Owens (Tech Serv Mgr), A. Howie
Ultimate Holding Company: ROPER INDUSTRIES INC (USA)
Immediate Holding Company: LOGITECH LIMITED
Registration no: SC042330 **Date established:** 1965
Turnover: £5m - £10m **No.of Employees:** 21 - 50 **Product Groups:** 33, 42, 45, 46, 48, 61, 67

Date of Accounts	Dec 11	Dec 10	Dec 09
Sales Turnover	7m	6m	4m
Pre Tax Profit/Loss	2m	2m	940
Working Capital	5m	4m	3m
Fixed Assets	269	269	321
Current Assets	6m	5m	3m
Current Liabilities	781	754	454

Logowear

77 Torrisdale Street, Glasgow, G42 8PW
Tel: 0141-423 2001 **Fax:** 0141-423 2010
E-mail: jsweeney@logowearimages.co.uk
Website: http://www.logowearimages.co.uk
Directors: J. Sweeney (Dir)
Immediate Holding Company: PROCLEAN GLASGOW LIMITED
Registration no: SC224048 **Date established:** 2010
Turnover: Up to £250,000 **No.of Employees:** 1 - 10 **Product Groups:** 23

Date of Accounts	Mar 08	Mar 07	Mar 06
Working Capital	-42	-47	-46
Fixed Assets	6	7	8
Current Assets	79	70	64
Current Liabilities	122	116	109

Lomo Industries Ltd

11 10 Paladin Avenue, Glasgow, G13 3HP
Tel: 0141-954 6511 **Fax:** 0141-954 6511
E-mail: admin@ewetsuits.com
Website: http://www.ewetsuits.com
Directors: B. Morrison (MD), M. Lowery (Fin)
Immediate Holding Company: LOMO INDUSTRIES LTD.
Registration no: SC203510 **Date established:** 2000
No.of Employees: 1 - 10 **Product Groups:** 24, 65

Date of Accounts	Feb 11	Feb 10	Feb 09
Working Capital	131	99	55
Fixed Assets	4	5	7
Current Assets	215	188	124

Len Lothian Ltd
31-35 Maclellan Street, Glasgow, G41 1RR
Tel: 0141-419 1100 **Fax:** 0141-419 1120
E-mail: info@lenlothian.com
Website: http://www.lenlothian.com
Directors: A. Lothian (MD)
Immediate Holding Company: LEN LOTHIAN LIMITED
Registration no: SC042919 **VAT No.:** GB 271 0126 04
Date established: 1965 **Turnover:** £250,000 - £500,000
No.of Employees: 1 - 10 **Product Groups:** 07, 24, 26, 72, 76, 77, 80, 84

Date of Accounts	Dec 11	Dec 10	Dec 09
Working Capital	-394	-576	-701
Fixed Assets	6m	6m	6m
Current Assets	505	449	473

M R H Marine Ltd
3 Crofthead Mill Lochlibo Road, Neilston, Glasgow, G78 3NE
Tel: 0141-880 6939
E-mail: info@mrhmarine.com
Website: http://www.mrhmarine.com
Directors: A. Higginbotham (MD)
Immediate Holding Company: MRH MARINE LIMITED
Registration no: SC181695 **Date established:** 1997
No.of Employees: 1 - 10 **Product Groups:** 45, 52

Date of Accounts	Jun 12	Jun 11	Jun 10
Working Capital	242	26	71
Fixed Assets	25	32	41
Current Assets	531	489	576

M S P Scotland Ltd
1-9 Telford Road Cumbernauld, Glasgow, G67 2AX
Tel: 01236-729591 **Fax:** 01236-721859
E-mail: johnallan@mspscot.co.uk
Website: http://www.mspscot.co.uk
Directors: J. Allan (Dir), W. Lagan (Dir), G. Ross (Co Sec), G. Thomson (Fin)
Immediate Holding Company: M.S.P. (SCOTLAND) LIMITED
Registration no: SC141564 **VAT No.:** GB 624 2527 58
Date established: 1992 **Turnover:** £2m - £5m **No.of Employees:** 21 - 50
Product Groups: 30, 31, 35

Date of Accounts	Dec 11	Dec 10	Dec 09
Working Capital	-90	-120	-100
Fixed Assets	1m	1m	1m
Current Assets	1m	1m	1m
Current Liabilities	40	35	19

M Suleman & Co.
32-36 Stromness Street, Glasgow, G5 8HS
Tel: 0141-429 3017 **Fax:** 0141-429 3473
E-mail: margaret@msulemangroup.com
Website: http://www.msulemangroup.com
Bank(s): Bank of Scotland
Directors: A. Suleman (Prop)
Managers: A. Sulerman (Buyer), K. Suleman (Buyer), M. Leard
Ultimate Holding Company: M SULEMAN GROUP LIMITED
Immediate Holding Company: M SULEMAN AND COMPANY LIMITED
Registration no: SC351210 **VAT No.:** GB 229 2253 22
Date established: 2008 **Turnover:** £10m - £20m
No.of Employees: 51 - 100 **Product Groups:** 61

Date of Accounts	Dec 11	Dec 10	Dec 09
Sales Turnover	11m	11m	8m
Pre Tax Profit/Loss	257	339	577
Working Capital	1m	467	-2m
Fixed Assets	1m	2m	2m
Current Assets	5m	5m	5m
Current Liabilities	711	490	325

Macandrews Glasgow
Festival House 177 West George Street, Glasgow, G2 2LB
Tel: 0141-221 9971 **Fax:** 0141-221 9977
Website: http://www.macandrews.com
Managers: G. Myers (Mgr)
Ultimate Holding Company: CMA CGM SA (FRANCE)
Immediate Holding Company: MACANDREWS & COMPANY LIMITED
Registration no: 00334790 **VAT No.:** GB 242 2925 70
Date established: 1937 **Turnover:** £75m - £125m
No.of Employees: 1 - 10 **Product Groups:** 74

Date of Accounts	Dec 10	Dec 09	Dec 08
Sales Turnover	111m	89m	91m
Pre Tax Profit/Loss	7m	10m	-7m
Working Capital	21m	14m	3m
Fixed Assets	5m	5m	6m
Current Assets	47m	41m	24m
Current Liabilities	11m	17m	15m

Mccormick John & Co. Ltd
46 Darnley Street, Glasgow, G41 2TY
Tel: 0141-429 4222 **Fax:** 0141-429 6777
E-mail: david.mccormick@jmccormick.co.uk
Website: http://www.jmccormick.co.uk
Bank(s): Clydesdale Bank PLC
Directors: A. Dempster (Fin), C. Mccormick (Sales & Mktg), C. McCormick (Dir), D. McCormick (Dir), D. McCormick (MD)
Managers: R. Dickson, R. Dickson (Personnel), P. Rees ()
Ultimate Holding Company: S. GRAHAM & COMPANY LIMITED
Immediate Holding Company: JOHN MCCORMICK & COMPANY LIMITED
Registration no: SC030498 **Date established:** 1954 **Turnover:** £2m - £5m
No.of Employees: 11 - 20 **Product Groups:** 23, 27, 28, 30, 33, 35, 44, 49

Date of Accounts	Dec 09	Dec 08	Dec 07
Sales Turnover	N/A	N/A	2m
Pre Tax Profit/Loss	N/A	N/A	9
Working Capital	53	254	508
Fixed Assets	838	970	713
Current Assets	621	848	985
Current Liabilities	N/A	N/A	120

Macdonald Kinnaird
5 Blythswood Square, Glasgow, G2 4AD
Tel: 0141-204 2070 **Fax:** 0141-248 8833
E-mail: enquiries@macdonaldkinnaird.com
Website: http://www.macdonaldkinnaird.com
Managers: D. Kinnaird (Mgr)
Immediate Holding Company: THE INTERIM MANAGEMENT EXCHANGE LIMITED
Registration no: SC284190 **Date established:** 2005
No.of Employees: 1 - 10 **Product Groups:** 80

Macfarlane Group UK Ltd
21 Newton Place, Glasgow, G3 7PY
Tel: 0141-333 9666 **Fax:** 0141-333 1988
E-mail: pdatkinson@macfarlanegroup.net
Website: http://www.macfarlanegroup.net
Directors: P. Atkinson (Dir), A. Cotton (Co Sec)
Ultimate Holding Company: MACFARLANE GROUP PLC
Immediate Holding Company: MACFARLANE GROUP PLC
Registration no: SC004221 **Date established:** 1999
Turnover: £125m - £250m **No.of Employees:** 1 - 10 **Product Groups:** 27, 30, 35, 66

Date of Accounts	Dec 11	Dec 10	Dec 09
Sales Turnover	145m	135m	124m
Pre Tax Profit/Loss	4m	4m	2m
Working Capital	3m	4m	5m
Fixed Assets	42m	40m	42m
Current Assets	45m	44m	40m
Current Liabilities	16m	7m	5m

John Mcgavigan Ltd
111 Westerhill Road Bishopbriggs, Glasgow, G64 2QR
Tel: 0141-302 0000 **Fax:** 0141-302 0290
E-mail: david.taylor@mcgavigan.com
Website: http://www.advanceddecorative.com
Bank(s): Bank of Scotland, Queen Street Branch, 110 Queen St, Glasgow
Directors: D. Taylor (MD)
Managers: I. Murrey (Sales Prom Mgr), A. McKeown (Purch Mgr), B. Hendry (Quality Control)
Ultimate Holding Company: RIVERLAKE PARTNERS LLC USA
Immediate Holding Company: JOHN MCGAVIGAN LIMITED
Registration no: SC144766 **VAT No.:** GB 596 6945 64
Date established: 1993 **Turnover:** £5m - £10m
No.of Employees: 101 - 250 **Product Groups:** 84

Date of Accounts	Dec 10	Dec 08	Dec 07
Sales Turnover	10m	N/A	N/A
Pre Tax Profit/Loss	2m	N/A	N/A
Working Capital	795	-136	-136
Fixed Assets	932	N/A	N/A
Current Assets	3m	N/A	N/A
Current Liabilities	1m	N/A	N/A

James Mcgowan Engineering Ltd
Dechmont Works Hamilton Road, Cambuslang, Glasgow, G72 7XS
Tel: 0141-641 3648 **Fax:** 0141-641 5147
E-mail: info@mcgowaneng.co.uk
Website: http://www.mcgowaneng.co.uk
Directors: E. McGowan (Co Sec), D. Macbain (Dir), J. Ritchie (Fin)
Ultimate Holding Company: MMNR LIMITED
Immediate Holding Company: JAMES MCGOWAN ENGINEERING LIMITED
Registration no: SC057956 **VAT No.:** GB 262 4065 76
Date established: 1975 **Turnover:** £1m - £2m **No.of Employees:** 21 - 50
Product Groups: 45

Date of Accounts	May 12	May 11	May 10
Working Capital	409	546	135
Fixed Assets	688	701	297
Current Assets	1m	1m	590

MacGregor & Moir
Unit 4 95 Westburn Drive, Cambuslang, Glasgow, G72 7NA
Tel: 0141-643 3636 **Fax:** 0141-641 8505
E-mail: terry.c@macgregorandmoir.com
Website: http://www.macgregorandmoir.com
Managers: K. Brennan (Chief Mgr), S. Haldane (Sales Prom Mgr), T. Campbell (Purch Mgr), T. Campbell (Mgr)
Ultimate Holding Company: SIG PLC
Immediate Holding Company: MACGREGOR & MOIR LIMITED
Registration no: SC314081 **Date established:** 2007 **Turnover:** £2m - £5m
No.of Employees: 1 - 10 **Product Groups:** 33, 40, 46, 66

Date of Accounts	Dec 10	Dec 09	Dec 08
Working Capital	578	578	578
Current Assets	578	578	578

Mcgrigors
Pacific House 70 Wellington Street, Glasgow, G2 6SB
Tel: 0141-248 6677 **Fax:** 0141-204 1351
E-mail: enquiries@mcgrigors.com
Website: http://www.mcgrigors.com
Directors: K. Murdock (Snr Part), C. Gray (Snr Part), K. Murdoch (Dir)
Managers: J. Barnes (I.T. Exec), D. Bright (Mktg Serv Mgr)
Immediate Holding Company: Mcgrigor Donald Ltd
Registration no: SC097693 **Date established:** 1986
Turnover: £20m - £50m **No.of Employees:** 101 - 250 **Product Groups:** 80

Machine Control Engineers Ltd
Unit A1 Block 9a South Avenue Blantyre Industrial Estate, Blantyre, Glasgow, G72 0XB
Tel: 01698-829566 **Fax:** 01698-821608
E-mail: sales@mce.uk.com
Website: http://www.mce.uk.com
Bank(s): Bank of Scotland
Directors: J. Murphy (MD), S. Sinclair (Co Sec)
Managers: A. Strokosch (Sales Prom Mgr), T. Patterson (Mktg Serv Mgr), K. Share (Sales Admin)
Immediate Holding Company: KRG Industries Ltd
Registration no: SC079865 **VAT No.:** GB 423 9878 16
No.of Employees: 21 - 50 **Product Groups:** 67

Mckay Flooring Ltd
123 Harmony Row, Glasgow, G51 3NB
Tel: 0141-440 1586 **Fax:** 0141-425 1020
E-mail: enquiries@mckayflooring.co.uk
Website: http://www.mckayflooring.co.uk
Directors: R. Mckay (MD)
Immediate Holding Company: MCKAY FLOORING LIMITED
Registration no: SC195254 **Date established:** 1999 **Turnover:** £2m - £5m
No.of Employees: 11 - 20 **Product Groups:** 25

Date of Accounts	Aug 11	Aug 10	Aug 09
Working Capital	39	-575	-589
Fixed Assets	870	886	1m
Current Assets	799	901	1m

Ritchie MacKenzie & Co. Ltd
Broomhill Industrial Estate Kirkintilloch, Glasgow, G66 1TQ
Tel: 0141-776 6274 **Fax:** 0141-776 0285
E-mail: sales@ritmac.co.uk
Website: http://www.ritmac.co.uk
Bank(s): Bank of Scotland
Directors: P. Mitchell (Sales)
Managers: T. Stevenson
Immediate Holding Company: RITCHIE, MACKENZIE & COMPANY LIMITED
Registration no: SC037717 **VAT No.:** GB 260 1156 03
Date established: 1962 **Turnover:** £250,000 - £500,000
No.of Employees: 21 - 50 **Product Groups:** 35, 38, 39, 40, 41, 45, 46, 48

Date of Accounts	Sep 11	Sep 10	Sep 09
Working Capital	586	636	617
Fixed Assets	611	613	634
Current Assets	1m	1m	1m

John Mackie
95-99 Causewayside Street, Glasgow, G32 8LT
Tel: 0141-778 4545 **Fax:** 0141-778 4476
E-mail: info@mackie-transmission.com
Website: http://www.johnmackie.co.uk
Directors: J. Mackie (Prop)
Immediate Holding Company: JOHN MACKIE AUTOMATIC TRANSMISSIONS LIMITED
Registration no: SC160655 **Date established:** 1995
No.of Employees: 11 - 20 **Product Groups:** 35, 45

Date of Accounts	Jun 11	Jun 10	Jun 09
Working Capital	-134	-108	-100
Fixed Assets	178	176	166
Current Assets	212	272	319

Maclay Murray & Spens LLP
1 George Square, Glasgow, G2 1AL
Tel: 0141-248 5011 **Fax:** 0141-248 5819
E-mail: chris.smylie@mms.co.uk
Website: http://www.mms.co.uk
Bank(s): Bank of Scotland
Directors: C. Higgins (Co Sec), D. Sanders (Mkt Research), A. Mackenzie (I.T. Dir), C. Smylie (Grp Chief Exec)
Managers: C. Burgess
Immediate Holding Company: MACLAY MURRAY & SPENS
Registration no: SC103363 **Date established:** 1987
Turnover: Up to £250,000 **No.of Employees:** 101 - 250
Product Groups: 80

John Mcnicol & Co Electrical Engineers Ltd
123 Elliot Street, Glasgow, G3 8EY
Tel: 0141-221 0725 **Fax:** 0141-248 4569
E-mail: info@johnmcnicol.co.uk
Website: http://johnmcnicol.co.uk
Directors: N. Mcnicol (Dir)
Ultimate Holding Company: JOHN MCNICOL & CO. (HOLDINGS) LIMITED
Immediate Holding Company: JOHN MCNICOL & CO. (1938) LIMITED
Registration no: SC020722 **VAT No.:** GB 260 6651 65
Date established: 1938 **Turnover:** £1m - £2m **No.of Employees:** 1 - 10
Product Groups: 52, 84

Macroberts LLP
Capella 60 York Street, Glasgow, G2 8JX
Tel: 0141-303 1100 **Fax:** 0141-332 8886
E-mail: maildesk@macroberts.com
Website: http://www.macroberts.com
Bank(s): Royal Bank of Scotland
Directors: R. Crichton (Tech Serv)
Managers: M. Graham (Fin Mgr), L. Wright, A. McIntosh (Mktg Serv Mgr), A. McAdam (Personnel)
Immediate Holding Company: MACROBERTS TRUSTEES LIMITED
Registration no: SC241503 **Date established:** 2002
Turnover: £5m - £10m **No.of Employees:** 101 - 250 **Product Groups:** 80

Mcvities
Victoria Biscuit Works 35 Clydeford Drive, Glasgow, G32 8YW
Tel: 0141-550 6800 **Fax:** 0141-554 8601
E-mail: peter_senior@unitedbiscuits.com
Website: http://www.unitedbiscuits.com
Bank(s): Royal Bank of Scotland
Managers: J. Simpson (Personnel), A. Colwell (Fin Mgr), M. Grant (Personnel), B. Gretis (Fin Mgr), B. Bebbington (Buyer), P. Senior (Chief Mgr)
Ultimate Holding Company: UNITED BISCUITS HOLDINGS P.L.C.
Registration no: 02506007 **VAT No.:** GB 225 4766 56
Turnover: £75m - £125m **No.of Employees:** 501 - 1000
Product Groups: 20

Mac-Welding Supplies
22 Maxwell Road, Glasgow, G41 1QE
Tel: 0141-423 7688 **Fax:** 0141-429 3698
Website: http://www.themacgroup.co.uk
Directors: P. Mccourt (Dir)
Date established: 1973 **No.of Employees:** 1 - 10 **Product Groups:** 46

Maersk Line (UK) Ltd
58 Robertson Street, Glasgow, G2 8DU
Tel: 028-9030 5450 **Fax:** 0141-248 3496
E-mail: glamng@mearsk.co.uk
Website: http://www.maerskline.com
Directors: M. Woods (MD)
Managers: R. Willock (Personnel), J. Waters (Sales & Mktg Mg), I. Burns (Mgr)
Immediate Holding Company: Maersk Line (Copenhagen)
Registration no: 00857789 **No.of Employees:** 11 - 20
Product Groups: 74, 76

Malin Marine Consultants
17 Sandyford Place, Glasgow, G3 7NB
Tel: 0141-243 2242 **Fax:** 0141-226 5501
E-mail: info@malinmarine.com
Website: http://www.malinmarine.com
Directors: J. Macsween (MD)
Immediate Holding Company: MALIN MARINE CONSULTANTS LIMITED
Registration no: SC228212 **Date established:** 2002
No.of Employees: 1 - 10 **Product Groups:** 35, 36, 39

Date of Accounts	Sep 11	Sep 10	Sep 09
Working Capital	1m	2m	-288
Fixed Assets	928	1m	564
Current Assets	2m	4m	1m

Maplin Electronics Ltd

264-266 Great Western Road, Glasgow, G4 9EJ
Tel: 08432-277404 **Fax:** 0141-353 1838
E-mail: customercare@maplin.co.uk
Website: http://www.maplin.co.uk
Managers: C. Crawford
Ultimate Holding Company: MONTAGU PRIVATE EQUITY LLP
Immediate Holding Company: MAPLIN ELECTRONICS LIMITED
Registration no: 01264385 **Date established:** 1976
Turnover: £125m - £250m **No.of Employees:** 1 - 10 **Product Groups:** 37, 61

Date of Accounts	Dec 11	Dec 08	Dec 09
Sales Turnover	205m	204m	204m
Pre Tax Profit/Loss	25m	32m	35m
Working Capital	118m	49m	75m
Fixed Assets	27m	28m	28m
Current Assets	207m	108m	142m
Current Liabilities	78m	51m	59m

Marks & Clark

120 Bothwell Street, Glasgow, G2 7JS
Tel: 0141-221 5767 **Fax:** 0141-221 7739
E-mail: edinburgh@marks-clerk.com
Website: http://www.marks-clerk.com
Managers: D. Mooreland (Mgr)
Ultimate Holding Company: AGGREKO PLC
Immediate Holding Company: AGGREKO HOLDINGS LIMITED
Registration no: OC343273 **Date established:** 1981
No.of Employees: 21 - 50 **Product Groups:** 80

Date of Accounts	Dec 10	Dec 09	Dec 08
Pre Tax Profit/Loss	92m	203m	77m
Working Capital	-127m	-131m	-132m
Fixed Assets	291m	289m	294m
Current Assets	45m	49m	71m

Marpet Fabrications 1997 Ltd

Unit 04 Clyde Workshops Fullarton Road, Glasgow East Investment Park, Glasgow, G32 8YL
Tel: 0141-641 1778 **Fax:** 0141-641 7118
E-mail: info@marpet.co.uk
Website: http://www.marpet.co.uk
Directors: J. Chisholm (Co Sec), W. Chisholm (MD)
Immediate Holding Company: MARPET FABRICATIONS (1997) LTD.
Registration no: SC172812 **Date established:** 1997
Turnover: £500,000 - £1m **No.of Employees:** 1 - 10 **Product Groups:** 48

Date of Accounts	Aug 11	Aug 10	Aug 09
Working Capital	51	71	96
Fixed Assets	29	5	19
Current Assets	278	270	244

Martec Engineering Group Ltd

Block 7 20 Clydesmill Drive Cambuslang Investment Park, Clydesmill Industrial Estate, Glasgow, G32 8RG
Tel: 0141-646 5220 **Fax:** 0141-646 1056
E-mail: info@martecengineering.co.uk
Website: http://www.martecengineering.co.uk
Bank(s): Bank Of Scotland
Directors: M. Mchugh (Dir)
Immediate Holding Company: MARTEC ENGINEERING GROUP LIMITED
Registration no: SC165315 **Date established:** 1996 **Turnover:** £1m - £2m
No.of Employees: 51 - 100 **Product Groups:** 35, 40

Date of Accounts	Dec 11	Dec 10	Dec 09
Working Capital	-123	-108	-462
Fixed Assets	1m	1m	1m
Current Assets	1m	995	1m

Maven Capital Partners UK LLP

Sutherland House 149 St. Vincent Street, Glasgow, G2 5NW
Tel: 0141-306 7400 **Fax:** 0141-306 7401
E-mail: andrew.craig@mavencp.com
Website: http://www.mavencp.com
Directors: M. Hoffman (Ch)
Registration no: 07505438 **No.of Employees:** 11 - 20 **Product Groups:** 82

Date of Accounts	Feb 08	Feb 07	Feb 06
Sales Turnover	477	N/A	N/A
Pre Tax Profit/Loss	150	-281	-211
Working Capital	-1318	-1415	1345
Fixed Assets	14908	14855	19260
Current Assets	284	323	1549
Current Liabilities	1602	1738	204
Total Share Capital	2714	2714	2764
ROCE% (Return on Capital Employed)	1.1	-2.1	-1.0
ROT% (Return on Turnover)	31.4		

Maxim Power Tools Ltd

Unit 5 40 Couper Street, Glasgow, G4 0DL
Tel: 0141-552 5591 **Fax:** 0141-552 5064
E-mail: enquiries@maximpower.co.uk
Website: http://www.maximpower.co.uk
Directors: A. Kelly (Dir)
Ultimate Holding Company: KILPATRICK FRASER (HOLDINGS) LIMITED
Immediate Holding Company: MAXIM POWER TOOLS (SCOTLAND) LIMITED
Registration no: SC080609 **VAT No.:** GB 596 9831 62
Date established: 1982 **Turnover:** £2m - £5m **No.of Employees:** 1 - 10
Product Groups: 37

Date of Accounts	Dec 11	Dec 10	Dec 09
Working Capital	1m	994	933
Fixed Assets	56	66	26
Current Assets	2m	1m	1m

Mbs Int'L Limited

Olympic House 142 Queen Street, Glasgow, G1 3BU
Tel: 0141-221 3298 **Fax:** 0141-221 3409
E-mail: sales@mbs-int-marketing.com
Website: http://www.mbs-int-marketing.com
Directors: P. McMahon (Ptnr), R. Wilson (Grp Chief Exec), S. Burns (Ptnr)
Registration no: 07581536 **VAT No.:** GB 481 6852 19
Date established: 2005 **Turnover:** £1m - £2m **No.of Employees:** 1 - 10
Product Groups: 81

Mcalpine & Company Ltd

45 Kelvin Avenue Hillington Park, Glasgow, G52 4LF
Tel: 0141-882 3213 **Fax:** 0141-891 5065
E-mail: kennethg.mcalpine@mcalpine.demon.co.uk
Website: http://www.mcalpineplumbing.com
Bank(s): Bank of Scotland, Ibrox
Directors: G. McAlpine (MD), K. Mcalpine (Dir)
Immediate Holding Company: MCALPINE & COMPANY. LIMITED
Registration no: SC006445 **VAT No.:** GB 260 5251 86
Date established: 2007 **Turnover:** £20m - £50m
No.of Employees: 501 - 1000 **Product Groups:** 30, 36

Date of Accounts	Dec 11	Dec 10	Dec 09
Sales Turnover	39m	38m	36m
Pre Tax Profit/Loss	2m	2m	408
Working Capital	19m	18m	17m
Fixed Assets	6m	6m	6m
Current Assets	24m	23m	22m
Current Liabilities	4m	4m	4m

Mclelland Cheese Packing Ltd

New Cheese Market Townhead, Glasgow, G4 0EF
Tel: 0141-552 2962 **Fax:** 0141-552 1215
E-mail: admin@mclelland.co.uk
Website: http://www.mclelland.co.uk
Directors: A. Smith (Dir), D. Jaouen (Dir), J. Mcgregor (Sales)
Managers: B. Skessington (Purch Mgr)
Immediate Holding Company: MCLELLAND CHEESE PACKING LIMITED
Registration no: SC240059 **Date established:** 2002
Turnover: £75m - £125m **No.of Employees:** 101 - 250
Product Groups: 48

Mcphee Bros Servicing Ltd

58 John Street Blantyre, Glasgow, G72 0JF
Tel: 01698-823422 **Fax:** 01698-823853
E-mail: info@mcpheemixers.co.uk
Website: http://www.mcpheemixers.co.uk
Directors: B. McFarlane (MD), L. Mcfarlane (Dir)
Immediate Holding Company: MCPHEE BROS (BLANTYRE) LIMITED
Registration no: SC085303 **VAT No.:** GB 382 9844 05
Date established: 1983 **No.of Employees:** 1 - 10 **Product Groups:** 45

Date of Accounts	Dec 11	Dec 10	Dec 09
Working Capital	-24	-5	134
Fixed Assets	1m	1m	1m
Current Assets	781	565	609

Mechdoors

69 Kelvin Avenue Hillington Park, Glasgow, G52 4LT
Tel: 0141-882 1671
E-mail: paul@mechdoors.co.uk
Website: http://www.mechdoors.co.uk
Directors: P. Tritschler (Dir)
Immediate Holding Company: MECHDOORS LIMITED
Registration no: SC218167 **Date established:** 2001
No.of Employees: 11 - 20 **Product Groups:** 26, 35

Memex Technology Ltd

2 Redwood Court East Kilbride, Glasgow, G74 5PF
Tel: 01355-233804 **Fax:** 01355-239676
E-mail: info@memex.com
Website: http://www.memex.com
Managers: D. Carrick, P. Anderson (Tech Serv Mgr), W. Scott (Comptroller), A. Walker (Personnel), L. Marshall (Mktg Serv Mgr)
Ultimate Holding Company: S A S INSTITUTE INC (USA)
Immediate Holding Company: MEMEX TECHNOLOGY LIMITED
Registration no: SC108095 **Date established:** 1987
Turnover: £5m - £10m **No.of Employees:** 51 - 100 **Product Groups:** 44

Date of Accounts	Dec 11	Dec 10	Dec 09
Sales Turnover	5m	6m	5m
Pre Tax Profit/Loss	5m	-2m	100
Working Capital	5m	2m	4m
Fixed Assets	234	100	46
Current Assets	8m	4m	7m
Current Liabilities	4m	2m	2m

Mentholatum Co. Ltd

1 Redwood Avenue East Kilbride, Glasgow, G74 5PE
Tel: 01355-848484 **Fax:** 01355-263387
E-mail: a.tasker@mentholatum.co.uk
Website: http://www.mentholatum.co.uk
Bank(s): National Westminster
Directors: B. Simpson (Mkt Research), D. Smart (Fin), A. Tasker (MD)
Managers: S. Hill (Buyer), J. Tannahill (Personnel)
Ultimate Holding Company: ROHTO PHARMACEUTICAL CO LTD (JAPAN)
Immediate Holding Company: MENTHOLATUM COMPANY LIMITED(THE)
Registration no: 00197071 **VAT No.:** GB 208 3100 14
Date established: 2024 **Turnover:** £20m - £50m
No.of Employees: 51 - 100 **Product Groups:** 31, 32, 63

Date of Accounts	Feb 12	Feb 11	Feb 10
Sales Turnover	33m	32m	30m
Pre Tax Profit/Loss	1m	3m	3m
Working Capital	8m	8m	7m
Fixed Assets	9m	9m	9m
Current Assets	15m	15m	13m
Current Liabilities	3m	2m	2m

Mercer

26 Blythswood Square, Glasgow, G2 4BP
Tel: 0141-248 4222 **Fax:** 0141-221 4615
E-mail: stuart.robinson@mercer.com
Website: http://www.mercer.com
Managers: S. Robinson (Mgr)
Ultimate Holding Company: MARSH & MCLENNAN COMPANIES INC (U.S.A)
Immediate Holding Company: MERCER LIMITED
Registration no: 00984275 **Date established:** 1970
No.of Employees: 101 - 250 **Product Groups:** 28

Date of Accounts	Dec 11	Dec 10	Dec 09
Sales Turnover	331m	319m	329m
Pre Tax Profit/Loss	77m	73m	73m
Working Capital	424m	370m	331m
Fixed Assets	15m	43m	20m
Current Assets	487m	426m	389m
Current Liabilities	51m	48m	46m

Microcom Training Ltd

Cambridge House Cambridge Street, Glasgow, G2 3DZ
Tel: 0141-353 0100 **Fax:** 0141-353 0200
E-mail: sales@microcomtraining.ltd.uk
Website: http://www.microcomtraining.ltd.uk
Bank(s): Royal Bank of Scotland
Directors: F. Watson (Dir)
Immediate Holding Company: MICROCOM TRAINING LIMITED
Registration no: SC126684 **VAT No.:** GB 552 4729 35
Date established: 1990 **Turnover:** £2m - £5m **No.of Employees:** 21 - 50
Product Groups: 86

Date of Accounts	Mar 11	Mar 10	Mar 09
Working Capital	2m	1m	901
Fixed Assets	56	66	544
Current Assets	2m	2m	2m

Midland Filtration Ltd

28-30 Carron Place East Kilbride, Glasgow, G75 0YL
Tel: 01355-267730 **Fax:** 01355-267811
E-mail: scotland@midfilters.co.uk
Website: http://www.midfilters.co.uk
Managers: P. Holmes (District Mgr)
Immediate Holding Company: MIDLAND FILTRATION LIMITED
Registration no: 01936235 **Date established:** 1985 **Turnover:** £1m - £2m
No.of Employees: 1 - 10 **Product Groups:** 23, 24, 33, 34, 35, 39, 40, 42, 45, 48

Date of Accounts	May 11	May 10	May 09
Working Capital	81	66	62
Fixed Assets	73	81	86
Current Assets	673	680	599

Midnight Storm

2 Trees Park Gardens Barrhead, Glasgow, G78 1AH
Tel: 07884-333777 **Fax:** 0141-951 1600
E-mail: sales@midnight-storm.com
Website: http://www.midnight-storm.com
Directors: C. Mcnair (Prop)
Turnover: Up to £250,000 **No.of Employees:** 11 - 20 **Product Groups:** 32, 81, 89

Millers Oils Ltd

6 Carlyle Avenue Hillington Park, Glasgow, G52 4XX
Tel: 0141-882 3216 **Fax:** 01224-248335
E-mail: info@millersoils.co.uk
Website: http://www.millersoils.co.uk
Managers: P. Woodward (Tech Serv Mgr), J. Flannery (Depot Mgr)
Ultimate Holding Company: MILLERS OILS LIMITED
Immediate Holding Company: MILLERS OILS (ABERDEEN) LIMITED
Registration no: SC107687 **VAT No.:** GB 183 5337 52
Date established: 1987 **No.of Employees:** 1 - 10 **Product Groups:** 31, 36, 42

Date of Accounts	Mar 09
Working Capital	-27

Mirror Doors Direct

Canal Street Kirkintilloch, Glasgow, G66 1QW
Tel: 0141-777 6123 **Fax:** 0141-775 0108
Website: http://www.mirrordoorsdirectltd.co.uk
Directors: L. McDonald (Dir)
Managers: L. McDonald (Mgr)
Immediate Holding Company: WEBSTER BUILDING SUPPLIES LIMITED
Date established: 2000 **No.of Employees:** 11 - 20 **Product Groups:** 26, 35

Andrew Mitchell & Co. Ltd

15 Dunivaig Road, Glasgow, G33 4TT
Tel: 0141-773 5454 **Fax:** 0141-773 5455
E-mail: kmoodie@mitco.co.uk
Website: http://www.mitco.co.uk
Bank(s): Royal Bank of Scotland, Cathcart Street, Greenock
Directors: B. McGown (Pers), K. Moodie (Co Sec), A. Moodie (MD)
Managers: K. Archer (Fin Mgr), W. Pollock (Tech Serv Mgr)
Immediate Holding Company: ANDREW MITCHELL & COMPANY LIMITED
Registration no: SC003736 **VAT No.:** GB 383 0428 58
Date established: 1998 **Turnover:** £2m - £5m **No.of Employees:** 51 - 100
Product Groups: 23, 24, 35

Date of Accounts	Dec 11	Dec 10	Dec 09
Sales Turnover	N/A	2m	2m
Pre Tax Profit/Loss	N/A	168	-47
Working Capital	1m	1m	1m
Fixed Assets	69	86	102
Current Assets	2m	2m	1m
Current Liabilities	N/A	179	90

The Mitchell Library

North Street, Glasgow, G3 7DN
Tel: 0141-287 2999 **Fax:** 0141-287 2815
E-mail: libraries@glasgowlife.org.uk
Website: http://www.glasgowlife.org.uk
Managers: K. Cunningham (Mgr)
Date established: 2009 **Turnover:** **No.of Employees:** 51 - 100
Product Groups: 80

Mitchell Thomson Ltd

Robslee Drive Giffnock, Glasgow, G46 7TY
Tel: 0141-638 0906 **Fax:** 0141-638 9014
E-mail: simondrew@btconnect.com
Directors: S. Drew (Prop)
Immediate Holding Company: MITCHELL THOMSON LIMITED
Registration no: SC028501 **Date established:** 1951
Turnover: Up to £250,000 **No.of Employees:** 1 - 10 **Product Groups:** 54

Date of Accounts	Aug 11	Aug 10	Aug 09
Working Capital	126	157	110
Fixed Assets	74	89	109
Current Assets	222	235	215

Mobrey

Unit P Taywood Enterprise Centre Duchess Place, Rutherglen, Glasgow, G73 1DR
Tel: 0141-613 1441 **Fax:** 0141-613 2093
E-mail: iain.robertson@emerson.com
Website: http://www.mobrey.com
Managers: I. Robertson (District Mgr)
Ultimate Holding Company: SOLAR TRON MOBREY LTD
Immediate Holding Company: ROXBURGH P.L.C.
VAT No.: GB 285 1163 59 **Turnover:** £5m - £10m **No.of Employees:** 1 - 10
Product Groups: 38, 48, 52

Morison & Miller Engineering Ltd

249 Glasgow Road Rutherglen, Glasgow, G73 1SU
Tel: 0141-647 0825 **Fax:** 0141-647 3133
E-mail: sales@morisonandmiller.co.uk
Website: http://www.morisonandmiller.co.uk
Bank(s): The Royal Bank of Scotland
Directors: D. Morison (Dir), S. Gunn (Mkt Research)
Immediate Holding Company: MORISON AND MILLER ENGINEERING LIMITED
Registration no: SC038869 **VAT No.:** GB 260 5257 74
Date established: 1963 **Turnover:** £2m - £5m **No.of Employees:** 11 - 20
Product Groups: 40

Date of Accounts	Mar 11	Mar 10	Mar 09
Working Capital	586	581	578
Fixed Assets	76	87	89
Current Assets	881	1m	1m

H. Morris & Co. Ltd
89 Southcroft Road, Glasgow, G73 1UG
Tel: 0141-300 7200 **Fax:** 0141-300 7240
E-mail: enquiries@morrisfurniture.co.uk
Website: http://www.morrisfurniture.co.uk
Bank(s): Clydesdale Bank PLC
Directors: G. McGraw (Jt MD), I. McEwan (Grp Chief Exec), R. Morris (MD), R. Morris (Jt MD)
Managers: G. Douglas (Mktg Serv Mgr), C. Dolan (Buyer), L. King, S. Wheeler (I.T. Exec), V. Day (Personnel)
Ultimate Holding Company: Neidpath Invest Co. Ltd
Registration no: 00133248 **VAT No.:** GB 659 1932 03
Turnover: £20m - £50m **Product Groups:** 26

Morris & Spottiswood Ltd
54 Helen Street, Glasgow, G51 3HQ
Tel: 0141-425 1133 **Fax:** 0141-425 1155
E-mail: georgem@morrisandspottiswood.co.uk
Website: http://www.morrisandspottiswood.co.uk
Directors: G. Morris (MD)
Ultimate Holding Company: MORRIS & SPOTTISWOOD LIMITED
Immediate Holding Company: ASSAB LIMITED
Registration no: SC099747 **VAT No.:** GB 261 4722 72
Date established: 1986 **Turnover:** £75m - £125m
No.of Employees: 1 - 10 **Product Groups:** 52

Date of Accounts	Dec 11	Dec 10	Dec 09
Sales Turnover	85m	85m	100m
Pre Tax Profit/Loss	332	310	315
Working Capital	633	604	2m
Fixed Assets	5m	5m	6m
Current Assets	26m	25m	24m
Current Liabilities	17m	16m	13m

Morrison Bowmore Distillers Ltd
Springburn Bond Carlisle Street, Glasgow, G21 1EQ
Tel: 0141-558 9011 **Fax:** 0141-558 9010
E-mail: info@morrisonbowmore.co.uk
Website: http://www.morrisonbowmore.com
Bank(s): Royal Bank of Scotland, Gordon Street
Directors: J. Brown (Co Sec), D. Crawford (Fin), S. Nagata (Dir)
Managers: I. Hamilton (Buyer), R. Hanson (Tech Serv Mgr)
Ultimate Holding Company: SUNTORY HOLDINGS LIMITED (JAPAN)
Immediate Holding Company: MORRISON BOWMORE DISTILLERS LIMITED
Registration no: SC119227 **Date established:** 1989
Turnover: £20m - £50m **No.of Employees:** 101 - 250 **Product Groups:** 21

Date of Accounts	Dec 11	Dec 10	Dec 09
Sales Turnover	45m	42m	39m
Pre Tax Profit/Loss	6m	3m	4m
Working Capital	38m	35m	32m
Fixed Assets	26m	24m	25m
Current Assets	78m	69m	65m
Current Liabilities	9m	8m	4m

Moulded Foams
1 Wardpark Road Wardpark South, Cumbernauld, Glasgow, G67 3EX
Tel: 01236-781733
E-mail: th@mouldedfoams.com
Website: http://www.mouldedfoams.com
Managers: D. Christie (Plant)
Ultimate Holding Company: MOULDED FOAMS (SCOTLAND) LTD
Immediate Holding Company: MOULDED FOAMS LIMITED
Registration no: SC146277 **Date established:** 1993
Turnover: £5m - £10m **No.of Employees:** 21 - 50 **Product Groups:** 30, 52

Date of Accounts	Dec 11	Dec 10	Dec 09
Sales Turnover	11m	10m	9m
Pre Tax Profit/Loss	190	618	154
Working Capital	362	778	20
Fixed Assets	4m	3m	3m
Current Assets	3m	3m	3m
Current Liabilities	1m	487	612

Andrew Muirhead & Son Ltd
Dalmarnock Leather Works 273-289 Dunn Street, Glasgow, G40 3EA
Tel: 0141-554 3724 **Fax:** 01282-420209
E-mail: sales@muirhead.co.uk
Website: http://www.muirhead.co.uk
Bank(s): Clydesdale Bank PLC
Directors: A. Browning (Sales), J. Ferguson (Comm)
Ultimate Holding Company: SCOTTISH LEATHER GROUP LIMITED
Immediate Holding Company: ANDREW MUIRHEAD & SON LIMITED
Registration no: SC047567 **Date established:** 1970
Turnover: £10m - £20m **No.of Employees:** 21 - 50 **Product Groups:** 22

Date of Accounts	Mar 12	Mar 11	Mar 10
Sales Turnover	14m	12m	10m
Pre Tax Profit/Loss	669	235	879
Working Capital	7m	6m	8m
Fixed Assets	1m	1m	688
Current Assets	8m	8m	9m
Current Liabilities	398	339	574

Murgitroyd & Co. Ltd Incorporating Fitzpatricks
Scotland House 165-169 Scotland Street, Glasgow, G5 8PL
Tel: 0141-307 8400 **Fax:** 0141-307 8401
E-mail: mail@murgitroyd.com
Website: http://www.murgitroyd.com
Directors: G. Edwards (Fin), I. Murgitroyd (MD)
Managers: F. Mason, M. Quinn, P. McBride (Tech Serv Mgr), F. McKenzie (Sales & Mktg Mg), K. Young
Ultimate Holding Company: MURGITROYD GROUP PLC
Immediate Holding Company: MURGITROYD GROUP PLC
Registration no: SC221766 **Date established:** 2001
Turnover: £20m - £50m **No.of Employees:** 101 - 250 **Product Groups:** 80

Date of Accounts	May 11	May 10	May 09
Sales Turnover	33m	29m	29m
Pre Tax Profit/Loss	4m	4m	3m
Working Capital	6m	5m	4m
Fixed Assets	17m	17m	17m
Current Assets	15m	13m	13m
Current Liabilities	2m	3m	2m

N I F E S Consulting Group (Regional Office)
8 Woodside Terrace, Glasgow, G3 7UY
Tel: 0141-332 2453 **Fax:** 0141-333 0402
E-mail: glasgow@nifes.co.uk
Website: http://www.nifes.co.uk
Bank(s): Barclays
Directors: A. Hannah (Comm)
Immediate Holding Company: Phoenix Holdings
Registration no: 06115895 **VAT No.:** GB 437 8684 03
Turnover: £500,000 - £1m **No.of Employees:** 21 - 50
Product Groups: 54, 80, 84

National Sign Co. Ltd
Alleysbank Road Rutherglen, Glasgow, G73 1LX
Tel: 0141-647 4348 **Fax:** 0141-613 1309
E-mail: info@nationalsign.co.uk
Website: http://www.nationalsign.co.uk
Bank(s): Bank of Scotland
Directors: K. Montgomerrie (Dir), W. Mcintosh (MD), W. Mackintosh (MD)
Managers: S. Mackintosh, C. Sherwood (Works Gen Mgr)
Ultimate Holding Company: PYSOCAL (HOLDINGS) LIMITED
Immediate Holding Company: PYSOCAL (HOLDINGS) LIMITED
Registration no: SC058767 **VAT No.:** GB 299 2615 14
Date established: 1987 **Turnover:** Up to £250,000
No.of Employees: 21 - 50 **Product Groups:** 37, 49

Date of Accounts	Dec 09	Dec 08	Dec 07
Working Capital	-270	-271	-210
Fixed Assets	281	288	296
Current Assets	135	302	143

James Neilson's Engineering Ltd
Nasmyth Avenue East Kilbride, Glasgow, G75 0QR
Tel: 01355-248830
Directors: C. Mcclory (Prop)
Immediate Holding Company: JAMES NEILSON (ENGINEERING) LIMITED
Registration no: SC136936 **Date established:** 1992
No.of Employees: 1 - 10 **Product Groups:** 35

Date of Accounts	Jun 11	Jun 10	Jun 09
Working Capital	-19	-10	-16
Fixed Assets	24	13	25
Current Assets	77	49	49

Neptune Fabrications Ltd
5 Ibrox Industrial Estate Carmichael Street, Glasgow, G51 2QU
Tel: 0141-427 1415 **Fax:** 0141-427 3703
E-mail: nepfab@btconnect.com
Website: http://www.neptunefabrications.co.uk
Bank(s): Clydesdale Bank PLC
Directors: J. Donald (Fin)
Immediate Holding Company: NEPTUNE FABRICATIONS (HOLDINGS) LIMITED
Registration no: SC214471 **Date established:** 2001
Turnover: £250,000 - £500,000 **No.of Employees:** 11 - 20
Product Groups: 48

Date of Accounts	May 11	May 10	May 09
Working Capital	242	242	242
Current Assets	243	244	244

Newsquest Group
200 Renfield Street, Glasgow, G2 3QB
Tel: 0141-302 7000 **Fax:** 0141-302 7799
E-mail: tim.blott@glasgow.newsquest.co.uk
Website: http://www.glasgow.newsquest.co.uk
Bank(s): Clydesdale Bank PLC
Directors: J. Tames (Co Sec), M. Hogg (MD), N. Carpenter (Dir), T. Blott (Dir), E. Partyka (Dir)
Managers: B. Jackson (Sales Prom Mgr)
Immediate Holding Company: STV PRODUCTIONS LIMITED
Registration no: SC139254 **Date established:** 1992
Turnover: £10m - £20m **No.of Employees:** 21 - 50 **Product Groups:** 28

Nextwave It Ltd
Flat 2/2 268 Berryknowes Road, Glasgow, G52 2DA
Tel: 07806-197987
E-mail: enquiry@nextwaveit.biz
Website: http://www.nextwaveit.biz
Directors: M. Bower (Dir)
Immediate Holding Company: Nextwave.It Ltd
Registration no: SC177797 **Date established:** 1997
Turnover: Up to £250,000 **No.of Employees:** 1 - 10 **Product Groups:** 44

Date of Accounts	Oct 07	Oct 06	Oct 05
Sales Turnover	5	7	4
Working Capital	-1	-1	-1
Fixed Assets	6	6	6
Current Liabilities	1	1	1

Norit UK Ltd
Clydesmill Place Cambuslang Industrial Estate, Clydesmill Industrial Estate, Glasgow, G32 8RF
Tel: 0141-641 8841 **Fax:** 0141-641 8411
E-mail: sales@norit.com
Website: http://www.norit.com
Bank(s): The Royal Bank of Scotland
Directors: J. Vesterre (Co Sec)
Managers: G. Barrack (Plant), L. Thern
Ultimate Holding Company: NORIT NV (THE NETHERLANDS)
Immediate Holding Company: NORIT (UK) LIMITED
Registration no: SC010502 **VAT No.:** GB 260 2065 01
Date established: 2019 **Turnover:** £10m - £20m
No.of Employees: 21 - 50 **Product Groups:** 23, 31, 32, 33, 37, 40, 42

Date of Accounts	Dec 11	Dec 10	Dec 09
Sales Turnover	20m	18m	17m
Pre Tax Profit/Loss	3m	3m	1m
Working Capital	2m	-358	-3m
Fixed Assets	8m	8m	8m
Current Assets	16m	12m	9m
Current Liabilities	2m	1m	879

Northgate Management Solutions
20 Sandyford Place, Glasgow, G3 7NG
Tel: 0141-248 2767 **Fax:** 0141-221 9994
E-mail: stephany.dolan@northgate-is.com
Website: http://www.northgate-is.com
Managers: J. Turnbull (Mgr)
Ultimate Holding Company: NORTHGATE INFORMATION SOLUTIONS HOLDINGS LTD
Immediate Holding Company: NORTHGATE MANAGED SERVICES LTD
Registration no: SC066117 **Turnover:** £5m - £10m
No.of Employees: 21 - 50 **Product Groups:** 44

North Lanarkshire Council (Department of Planning & Environment)
PO Box 14, Glasgow, G67 1AA
Tel: 01236-723966 **Fax:** 01236-618099
E-mail: econdev@northlan.gov.uk
Website: http://www.northlan.gov.uk
Directors: D. Porch (Dir)
Managers: L. Milne
Immediate Holding Company: North Lanarkshire Women's Aid Ltd
Registration no: SC134961 **VAT No.:** GB 659 2820 09
Date established: 1991 **Turnover:** Up to £250,000
No.of Employees: 1 - 10 **Product Groups:** 54, 80, 84, 87

Northern Lifts
4 Somerset Place, Glasgow, G3 7JT
Tel: 0141-332 9444
E-mail: info@northernlifts.com
Website: http://www.northernlifts.com
Directors: R. Milligan (Fin)
Managers: J. Thompson (Sales Prom Mgr), M. McReadie (Sales Admin)
Immediate Holding Company: NORTHERN LIFTS LIMITED
Registration no: SC224410 **Date established:** 2001
No.of Employees: 1 - 10 **Product Groups:** 45, 48, 84

Date of Accounts	Oct 09	Oct 08	Oct 07
Working Capital	28	172	163
Fixed Assets	15	15	8
Current Assets	153	319	232

Northern Recruitment Group
Culzean House 36 Renfield Street, Glasgow, G2 1LU
Tel: 0141-572 2222 **Fax:** 0141-572 2020
E-mail: glasgow@nrgplc.co.uk
Website: http://www.nrgplc.co.uk
Bank(s): The Royal Bank of Scotland
Directors: Liddle (MD), L. Moran (Grp Chief Exec)
Immediate Holding Company: NORTHERN RECRUITMENT GROUP LIMITED
Registration no: 01756216 **Date established:** 1983 **Turnover:** £1m - £2m
No.of Employees: 21 - 50 **Product Groups:** 80

Date of Accounts	Dec 10	Dec 09	Jun 08
Sales Turnover	20m	30m	20m
Pre Tax Profit/Loss	680	1m	1m
Working Capital	4m	4m	5m
Fixed Assets	246	250	383
Current Assets	7m	6m	8m
Current Liabilities	2m	2m	2m

Nova Ltd
20 Dixon Place East Kilbride, Glasgow, G74 5JF
Tel: 01355-234443 **Fax:** 01355-247301
E-mail: info@nova.uk.com
Website: http://www.novaelectrical.co.uk
Directors: D. Tinney (MD)
Immediate Holding Company: NOVA LIMITED
Registration no: SC355117 **Date established:** 2009
No.of Employees: 11 - 20 **Product Groups:** 30, 33, 36, 37, 38, 45, 49

Date of Accounts	Mar 12	Mar 11	Mar 10
Working Capital	124	532	-28
Fixed Assets	77	83	90
Current Assets	547	532	444

O K I UK Ltd
1 Oki Way Wardpark North, Cumbernauld, Glasgow, G68 0FQ
Tel: 01236-502502 **Fax:** 01236-502528
E-mail: niall.macdonald@okieurope.com
Website: http://www.okidirect.co.uk
Directors: D. Gunn (Co Sec), N. Macdonald (MD)
Ultimate Holding Company: OKI ELECTRIC INDUSTRY CO., LTD.
Immediate Holding Company: OKI (UK) LIMITED
Registration no: SC105284 **Date established:** 1987
Turnover: £50m - £75m **No.of Employees:** 251 - 500 **Product Groups:** 44

Date of Accounts	Mar 12	Mar 11	Mar 10
Sales Turnover	69m	92m	106m
Pre Tax Profit/Loss	2m	299	4m
Working Capital	13m	13m	13m
Fixed Assets	3m	4m	5m
Current Assets	31m	34m	34m
Current Liabilities	3m	3m	4m

O'Briens Sandwich Bars UK
The Isokon Building 98 Holm Street, Glasgow, G2 6SY
Tel: 0141-222 2600 **Fax:** 0141-222 2700
E-mail: obriens.scotland@btconnect.com
Website: http://www.obriensonline.com
Directors: P. Patel (Prop)
Immediate Holding Company: O'BRIENS SANDWICH BAR (HEMEL HEMPSTEAD) LTD
Registration no: 04507429 **Date established:** 2002
No.of Employees: 1 - 10 **Product Groups:** 67

Date of Accounts	Aug 10	Aug 09	Aug 08
Working Capital	-13	-13	-28
Fixed Assets	5	5	29
Current Assets	10	18	60

P S Auto Grinding
17 Deerdykes View Cumbernauld, Glasgow, G68 9HN
Tel: 01236-724215 **Fax:** 01698-849346
E-mail: info@psautogrinding.co.uk
Website: http://www.psautogrinding.com
Directors: P. Smith (Prop)
Registration no: SC214767 **Date established:** 2002
No.of Employees: 11 - 20 **Product Groups:** 46

Glen Pack Ltd
36 Kelvinhaugh Street, Glasgow, G3 8PB
Tel: 0141-221 5012 **Fax:** 0141-248 2555
E-mail: glenpack@lineone.net
Directors: I. Nimmo (Fin), R. Howden (MD)
Immediate Holding Company: GLEN PACK LIMITED
Registration no: SC053732 **Date established:** 1973
Turnover: £500,000 - £1m **No.of Employees:** 11 - 20
Product Groups: 27, 28

Date of Accounts	Jul 11	Jul 10	Jul 09
Working Capital	203	194	289
Fixed Assets	102	67	74

see next page

***Glen Pack Ltd** - Cont'd*

Current Assets	363	338	402

Panalux Ltd

110 Lancefield Street, Glasgow, G3 8JD
Tel: 0141-221 5175 **Fax:** 0141-248 2751
E-mail: info@panalux.biz
Website: http://www.panalux.biz
Directors: M. Ritchie (Reg)
Managers: A. Hendry (Chief Mgr)
Ultimate Holding Company: PANAVISION INC (USA)
Immediate Holding Company: PANALUX LIMITED
Registration no: 04197837 **Date established:** 2001
No.of Employees: 1 - 10 **Product Groups:** 37

Date of Accounts	Dec 11	Dec 10	Dec 09
Sales Turnover	32m	34m	29m
Pre Tax Profit/Loss	3m	4m	2m
Working Capital	7m	3m	2m
Fixed Assets	13m	13m	12m
Current Assets	17m	15m	13m
Current Liabilities	8m	3m	2m

The Paper Company Ltd

217 Maclellen Street Kinning Park, Glasgow, G41 1RR
Tel: 0141-427 9900 **Fax:** 0141-427 9911
E-mail: sales@donaldmurray.co.uk
Website: http://www.paperco.co.uk
Directors: A. MacDonald (Mkt Research), I. Mackintosh (MD), R. Ide (Mkt Research), S. King (Dir), C. Sigley (Co Sec)
Immediate Holding Company: Paperlinx Investments (Europe) Ltd
Registration no: 01995271 **Date established:** 2009
Turnover: £250m - £500m **No.of Employees:** 501 - 1000
Product Groups: 64, 66

Paper Pulp Solutions Ltd

Pulp Mill House Banton Mill Mill Road, Kilsyth, Glasgow, G65 0RD
Tel: 08707-708883 **Fax:** 0870-770 8884
E-mail: sales@pulp-tec.com
Website: http://www.pulp-tec.com
Directors: G. Shaw (MD)
Date established: 2004 **Turnover:** £1m - £2m **No.of Employees:** 1 - 10
Product Groups: 27

Date of Accounts	Mar 08	Mar 07	Mar 06
Working Capital	-4	-8	43
Fixed Assets	49	42	2
Current Assets	79	56	80
Current Liabilities	84	64	37
Total Share Capital	30	30	30

Parks Of Hamilton Coach Hire

Blantyre, Glasgow, G72 0JL
Tel: 01698-281222 **Fax:** 01698-303901
E-mail: info@parks.uk.com
Website: http://www.parks.uk.com
Managers: P. France (Mktg Serv Mgr)
Ultimate Holding Company: PARK'S OF HAMILTON (HOLDINGS) LIMITED
Immediate Holding Company: PARKS OF HAMILTON (COACH HIRERS) LIMITED
Registration no: SC066568 **VAT No.:** GB 316 3597 51
Date established: 1979 **Turnover:** £250m - £500m
No.of Employees: 1 - 10 **Product Groups:** 68, 72

Date of Accounts	Mar 08	Mar 07	Mar 06
Working Capital	-52	-52	-52
Current Liabilities	52	52	52

Parmley Graham Ltd

6 Flakefield East Kilbride, Glasgow, G74 1PF
Tel: 01355-264000 **Fax:** 01355-247661
E-mail: glasgow@parmley-graham.co.uk
Website: http://www.parmley-graham.co.uk
Managers: M. Drummond (District Mgr)
Immediate Holding Company: PARMLEY GRAHAM LIMITED
Registration no: 00172842 **VAT No.:** GB 176 7006 54
Date established: 2021 **Turnover:** Up to £250,000
No.of Employees: 1 - 10 **Product Groups:** 37, 39

Date of Accounts	Dec 11	Dec 10	Dec 09
Sales Turnover	34m	33m	26m
Pre Tax Profit/Loss	1m	910	353
Working Capital	4m	4m	3m
Fixed Assets	1m	1m	1m
Current Assets	10m	9m	7m
Current Liabilities	1m	900	415

Pascoe Engineering Ltd

127 Nitshill Road, Glasgow, G53 7TD
Tel: 0141-880 6444 **Fax:** 0141-881 4832
E-mail: info@pascoelimited.com
Website: http://www.pascoelimited.com
Directors: F. Patterson (Fin), R. Smith (MD)
Immediate Holding Company: PASCOE ENGINEERING (BARRHEAD) LIMITED
Registration no: SC089522 **VAT No.:** GB 406 6700 68
Date established: 1984 **Turnover:** £1m - £2m **No.of Employees:** 21 - 50
Product Groups: 30, 48

Date of Accounts	Oct 11	Oct 10	Oct 09
Working Capital	499	492	462
Fixed Assets	1m	1m	1m
Current Assets	535	534	485

Paterson Safety Anchors Ltd

18 Muriel Street Barrhead, Glasgow, G78 1QB
Tel: 0141-881 9261 **Fax:** 0141-880 7986
Website: http://www.patersonsafetyanchors.co.uk
Directors: R. Paterson (MD), V. Paterson (Fin)
Immediate Holding Company: PATERSON SAFETY ANCHORS LIMITED
Registration no: SC162825 **Date established:** 1996
Turnover: £250,000 - £500,000 **No.of Employees:** 1 - 10
Product Groups: 40

Date of Accounts	Jun 11	Jun 10	Jun 09
Working Capital	-110	-78	-135
Fixed Assets	142	146	149
Current Assets	78	76	65

Paul Darroch & Co.

272 Bath Street, Glasgow, G2 4JR
Tel: 0141-353 9516 **Fax:** 0141-353 9517
E-mail: advice@darroch-hearing.co.uk
Website: http://www.pauldarroch.co.uk
Managers: P. Darroch (Mgr)
Immediate Holding Company: CACTUS CREATIVE CONSULTANTS LIMITED
Registration no: SC349760 **Date established:** 1996
No.of Employees: 1 - 10 **Product Groups:** 37, 40, 54, 63

Date of Accounts	Sep 11	Sep 10	Sep 09
Working Capital	10	32	7
Fixed Assets	1	N/A	1
Current Assets	135	46	23

Perfect Glazing Scotland Ltd

15 Caledonia Avenue, Glasgow, G5 0EX
Tel: 0141-429 6661
E-mail: perfectscotland@hotmail.co.uk
Website: http://www.perfectglazingscotland.com
Directors: G. Singh (MD), R. Kaur (Fin)
Immediate Holding Company: PERFECT GLAZING (GLASGOW) LTD.
Registration no: SC231662 **Date established:** 2002 **Turnover:** £1m - £2m
No.of Employees: 1 - 10 **Product Groups:** 25, 30, 35

Date of Accounts	May 10	May 09	May 08
Sales Turnover	N/A	2m	2m
Pre Tax Profit/Loss	N/A	254	248
Working Capital	18	172	-33
Fixed Assets	1m	776	780
Current Assets	269	322	272
Current Liabilities	N/A	74	110

Peter Cox Ltd

St Andrews House 385 Hillington Road, Hillington Park, Glasgow, G52 4BL
Tel: 0141-810 9100 **Fax:** 01786-448614
Website: http://www.petercox.com
Managers: P. Ross (Mgr)
Immediate Holding Company: PETER COX LIMITED
Registration no: 02438126 **Date established:** 1989
No.of Employees: 1 - 10 **Product Groups:** 07, 32, 52, 66

Pickerings Europe Ltd

9 Glasgow Road Baillieston, Glasgow, G69 6JT
Tel: 0141-771 7575 **Fax:** 0141-771 8585
E-mail: info@pickerings.co.uk
Website: http://www.pickerings.co.uk
Managers: L. Robertson (Mgr)
Ultimate Holding Company: KIPLUN LIMITED
Immediate Holding Company: PICKERINGS EUROPE LIMITED
Registration no: 03217853 **Date established:** 1996
Turnover: £250,000 - £500,000 **No.of Employees:** 1 - 10
Product Groups: 45

Date of Accounts	Dec 11	Dec 10	Dec 09
Sales Turnover	22m	20m	23m
Pre Tax Profit/Loss	3m	35m	5m
Working Capital	25m	25m	19m
Fixed Assets	11m	9m	9m
Current Assets	31m	30m	24m
Current Liabilities	4m	4m	3m

Picturelinks Ltd

Unit 12-14 Clydesmill Grove, Clydesmill Industrial Estate, Glasgow, G32 8NL
Tel: 0141-646 1231 **Fax:** 0141-646 2323
E-mail: sales@picturelinks.co.uk
Website: http://www.picturelinks.co.uk
Directors: D. Links (MD)
Immediate Holding Company: PICTURELINKS LIMITED
Registration no: SC176887 **VAT No.:** GB 370 5365 56
Date established: 1997 **Turnover:** £250,000 - £500,000
No.of Employees: 1 - 10 **Product Groups:** 25, 65

Date of Accounts	Oct 10	Oct 09	Oct 08
Working Capital	59	50	25
Fixed Assets	42	47	53
Current Assets	226	214	221

Plenty Mirrlees Pumps

8 Earl Haig Road Hillington Industrial Estate, Glasgow, G52 4JN
Tel: 0141-883 0314 **Fax:** 0141-882 2752
E-mail: plentypumps@spx.com
Website: http://www.spxft.com
Directors: R. Wilkinson (Prop)
Turnover: £5m - £10m **No.of Employees:** 1 - 10 **Product Groups:** 40

Pointer Ltd

65 North Wallace Street, Glasgow, G4 0DT
Tel: 0141-564 2500 **Fax:** 0141-552 3368
E-mail: enquiries@pointer.co.uk
Website: http://www.pointer.co.uk
Bank(s): Bank of Scotland
Directors: A. Urquhart (Co Sec)
Managers: A. Kirby (Mktg Serv Mgr), M. Rafiq (Tech Serv Mgr), C. Harkins (Personnel)
Immediate Holding Company: POINTER LIMITED
Registration no: SC047359 **VAT No.:** GB 552 1804 62
Date established: 1970 **Turnover:** £10m - £20m
No.of Employees: 101 - 250 **Product Groups:** 38, 40

Date of Accounts	Mar 11	Mar 10	Mar 09
Sales Turnover	16m	15m	14m
Pre Tax Profit/Loss	-111	16	319
Working Capital	-509	-326	310
Fixed Assets	1m	1m	938
Current Assets	5m	5m	4m
Current Liabilities	2m	2m	2m

Polytech Food Systems Ltd

2 Block E 50 Glenwood Place, Glasgow, G45 9UH
Tel: 0141-630 0655 **Fax:** 0141-630 0650
Directors: E. Grant (Fin), J. Grant (MD)
Immediate Holding Company: POLYTECH FOOD SYSTEMS LIMITED
Registration no: SC130182 **Date established:** 1991
No.of Employees: 1 - 10 **Product Groups:** 20, 40, 41

Date of Accounts	Apr 12	Apr 11	Apr 10
Working Capital	232	219	190
Fixed Assets	11	15	19
Current Assets	292	316	260

Porcelain Plus

3-5 Lenziemill Road Cumbernauld, Glasgow, G67 2RL
Tel: 01236-728436
Website: http://www.porcelainplus.co.uk
Directors: K. Pollock (Prop)
Immediate Holding Company: PORCELAIN PLUS LIMITED
Registration no: SC269984 **Date established:** 2004
No.of Employees: 1 - 10 **Product Groups:** 35, 52

Date of Accounts	Sep 11	Sep 10	Sep 09
Working Capital	17	31	33
Fixed Assets	31	41	34
Current Assets	274	204	169

Portman Travel Ltd

215 West Campbell Street, Glasgow, G2 4TT
Tel: 0141-225 3700 **Fax:** 0141-204 1125
E-mail: dcarey@portmantravel.com
Website: http://www.portmantravel.com
Directors: M. Hare (MD)
Ultimate Holding Company: SUPER SELECTOR SARL
Immediate Holding Company: PORTMAN TRAVEL LIMITED
Registration no: 00620104 **VAT No.:** GB 680 4034 53
Date established: 1959 **Turnover:** £75m - £125m
No.of Employees: 11 - 20 **Product Groups:** 69

Date of Accounts	Dec 11	Dec 10	Dec 09
Sales Turnover	260m	257m	239m
Pre Tax Profit/Loss	4m	4m	2m
Working Capital	14m	13m	15m
Fixed Assets	6m	5m	4m
Current Assets	27m	30m	29m
Current Liabilities	2m	3m	2m

Possilpark Shotblasting Co. Ltd

73 Dunn Street, Glasgow, G40 3PE
Tel: 0141-556 6221 **Fax:** 0141-551 0714
E-mail: admin@possilpark.co.uk
Website: http://www.possilpark.co.uk
Bank(s): Clydesdale
Directors: A. Lapsley (MD)
Managers: S. Forsyth
Immediate Holding Company: POSSILPARK SHOTBLASTING COMPANY LIMITED
Registration no: SC045833 **VAT No.:** GB 261 2951 67
Date established: 1968 **Turnover:** £1m - £2m **No.of Employees:** 21 - 50
Product Groups: 48

Date of Accounts	Jul 11	Jul 10	Jul 09
Working Capital	385	367	369
Fixed Assets	21	40	47
Current Assets	608	613	685

Powershield Doors Ltd

Burnfield House 4 Burnfield Avenue, Thornliebank, Glasgow, G46 7TL
Tel: 0141-633 5300 **Fax:** 0141-637 1111
E-mail: e.brown@powershield.co.uk
Website: http://www.burnfieldhouse.com
Directors: E. Brown (Dir)
Ultimate Holding Company: ASSA ABLOY AB (PUBL) (SWEDEN)
Immediate Holding Company: POWERSHIELD DOORS LTD
Registration no: NI026027 **Date established:** 1991
No.of Employees: 1 - 10 **Product Groups:** 26, 35

Date of Accounts	Dec 08	Jun 11	Jun 10
Sales Turnover	6m	N/A	11m
Pre Tax Profit/Loss	638	N/A	115
Working Capital	3m	4m	4m
Fixed Assets	821	N/A	N/A
Current Assets	5m	4m	4m
Current Liabilities	1m	N/A	N/A

Powervac Ltd

111 Lightburn Road Cambuslang, Glasgow, G72 8XN
Tel: 0141-641 6611 **Fax:** 0141-641 9988
E-mail: info@powervac.co.uk
Website: http://www.powervac-hesco.co.uk
Directors: E. McGowan (Co Sec), D. Macbain (Dir)
Ultimate Holding Company: MMNR LIMITED
Immediate Holding Company: POWERVAC LIMITED
Registration no: SC071522 **VAT No.:** GB 334 3891 49
Date established: 1980 **Turnover:** £500,000 - £1m
No.of Employees: 1 - 10 **Product Groups:** 41, 45

Date of Accounts	May 12	May 11	May 10
Working Capital	147	175	96
Fixed Assets	1	1	2
Current Assets	191	233	125

Powwow Ltd

15-17 Earl Haig Road Hillington Park, Glasgow, G52 4JU
Tel: 0141-880 9801 **Fax:** 08456- 072725
Directors: I. Deschamps (Co Sec)
Ultimate Holding Company: NESTLE SA (SWITZERLAND)
Immediate Holding Company: NESTL++ WATERS UK LIMITED
Registration no: 02334804 **Date established:** 1989
Turnover: £50m - £75m **No.of Employees:** 501 - 1000
Product Groups: 40, 66

Date of Accounts	Dec 11	Dec 10	Dec 09
Sales Turnover	67m	62m	55m
Pre Tax Profit/Loss	2m	2m	-8m
Working Capital	-38m	-15m	-13m
Fixed Assets	39m	15m	14m
Current Assets	22m	24m	29m
Current Liabilities	6m	10m	10m

Precision Identification Ltd

Redwood CR East Kilbride, Glasgow, G74 5PA
Tel: 01355-840021 **Fax:** 01355-230875
E-mail: scotlandinfo@donprint.com
Website: http://www.worldmark.com
Directors: J. Dargon (Grp Chief Exec)
Ultimate Holding Company: WORLDMARK INTERNATIONAL HOLDINGS LIMITED
Immediate Holding Company: PRECISION ID PRODUCTS LIMITED
Registration no: SC146892 **Date established:** 1993
No.of Employees: 11 - 20 **Product Groups:** 38, 42

Precision Supply Co.

5 Thornliebank Industrial Estate Thornliebank, Glasgow, G46 8JR
Tel: 0141-638 9060 **Fax:** 0141-638 9848
E-mail: sales@scottishtools.co.uk
Website: http://www.scottishtools.co.uk
Directors: K. Hargreaves (Prop)
Immediate Holding Company: PRECISION SUPPLY COMPANY LIMITED
Registration no: SC255172 **VAT No.:** GB 261 1160 06
Date established: 2003 **Turnover:** Up to £250,000
No.of Employees: 1 - 10 **Product Groups:** 48

Date of Accounts	Dec 10	Dec 09	Dec 07
Working Capital	N/A	13	28
Current Assets	N/A	14	42

Premier Bonding Co.
87 Carron Place Kelvin Industrial Estate, East Kilbride, Glasgow, G75 0YL
Tel: 01355-268643 **Fax:** 01355-268645
E-mail: premier.bonding@btconnect.com
Directors: D. Killin (Dir)
Date established: 2000 **No.of Employees:** 11 - 20 **Product Groups:** 38, 42

Premier Housewares LLP
55 Jordanvale Avenue, Glasgow, G14 0QP
Tel: 0141-579 2000 **Fax:** 0141-579 2005
E-mail: info@premierhousewares.co.uk
Website: http://www.premierhousewares.co.uk
Bank(s): Clydesdale
Directors: S. Mobarik (MD), S. Yusif (Fin), N. Rashid (Fin)
Managers: W. Hand (Personnel), L. Jaimeson (Mktg Serv Mgr), C. Ewen, H. Cutherbertson (Tech Serv Mgr)
Immediate Holding Company: PREMIER HOUSEWARES (SCOTLAND) LLP
Registration no: SO300290 **VAT No.:** GB 481 4582 32
Date established: 2003 **Turnover:** £10m - £20m
No.of Employees: 51 - 100 **Product Groups:** 61

Date of Accounts	Dec 08	Dec 07	Mar 11
Sales Turnover	N/A	N/A	11m
Pre Tax Profit/Loss	-255	-262	-680
Working Capital	-6m	-6m	-6m
Fixed Assets	3m	3m	3m
Current Assets	4m	4m	3m
Current Liabilities	210	240	115

Premier Welding Services Scotland Ltd
Unit 5 28 Queen Elizabeth Avenue, Hillington Park, Glasgow, G52 4NQ
Tel: 0141-882 4514 **Fax:** 0141-810 4659
E-mail: ronnie@premierwelding.com
Website: http://www.premierwelding.co.uk
Directors: A. Young (Dir)
Immediate Holding Company: PREMIER WELDING SERVICES (SCOT.) LTD.
Registration no: SC058575 **Date established:** 1975
Turnover: £250,000 - £500,000 **No.of Employees:** 1 - 10
Product Groups: 48, 83

Date of Accounts	May 12	May 11	May 10
Working Capital	375	320	453
Fixed Assets	243	243	241
Current Assets	682	528	850

Professional H R Services
25 Borden Road, Glasgow, G13 1RB
Tel: 0141-959 6871 **Fax:** 0141-959 6871
E-mail: enquiries@professionalhrservices.co.uk
Website: http://www.betterjobscotland.co.uk
Directors: A. Mcfarlane (Prop)
No.of Employees: 1 - 10 **Product Groups:** 80

Protektor UK Ltd
10 Carlyle Avenue, Glasgow, G52 4JJ
Tel: 0141-810 4411 **Fax:** 0141-810 4414
E-mail: sales@protektor.co.uk
Website: http://www.protektor.co.uk
Directors: J. Lamont (MD)
Ultimate Holding Company: PROTEKTORWERK FLORENZ MAISCH GMBH & CO KG (GERMANY)
Immediate Holding Company: PROTEKTOR UK LIMITED
Registration no: SC086301 **VAT No.:** GB 671 4443 37
Date established: 1984 **No.of Employees:** 1 - 10 **Product Groups:** 33, 34, 35

Date of Accounts	Dec 11	Dec 10	Dec 09
Working Capital	187	646	274
Fixed Assets	33	43	268
Current Assets	2m	2m	356

Purton Carbons Ltd
Clydesmill Place Cambuslang Industrial Place, Clydesmill Industrial Estate, Glasgow, G32 8RF
Tel: 0141-641 8841 **Fax:** 0141-641 7042
Directors: J. Vesterre (Fin), M. Knuttel (MD)
Ultimate Holding Company: NORIT NV (THE NETHERLANDS)
Immediate Holding Company: PURTON CARBONS LIMITED
Registration no: SC141139 **VAT No.:** 624 0169 68 **Date established:** 1992
Turnover: £2m - £5m **No.of Employees:** 1 - 10 **Product Groups:** 32

Date of Accounts	Dec 11	Dec 10	Dec 09
Sales Turnover	3m	2m	2m
Pre Tax Profit/Loss	303	346	-11
Working Capital	2m	1m	682
Fixed Assets	1m	1m	2m
Current Assets	4m	3m	1m
Current Liabilities	137	212	221

R A Young & Abercairn Of Scotland Ltd
1145 Cathcart Road, Glasgow, G42 9HD
Tel: 0141-632 5950 **Fax:** 0141-636 1656
E-mail: abercairn@abercairn.co.uk
Website: http://www.abercairn.co.uk
Directors: S. Anson (MD)
Immediate Holding Company: ABERCAIRN OF SCOTLAND LTD.
Registration no: SC054571 **VAT No.:** GB 261 9786 21
Date established: 1973 **Turnover:** £250,000 - £500,000
No.of Employees: 1 - 10 **Product Groups:** 24

Date of Accounts	Jan 12	Jan 11	Jan 10
Working Capital	-20	-33	-39
Fixed Assets	151	158	167
Current Assets	39	38	30

R S Components Ltd
38 Baird Street, Glasgow, G4 0ED
Tel: 0141-552 4446 **Fax:** 0141-552 4448
E-mail: rsint@rs-components.com
Website: http://www.rs.com
Managers: J. Blake (Mgr)
Immediate Holding Company: RS COMPONENTS LIMITED
Registration no: 01002091 **Date established:** 1971
Turnover: £250m - £500m **No.of Employees:** 1 - 10 **Product Groups:** 67

R W Greeff E & E Ltd
Baillieston Trading Estate Baillieston, Glasgow, G69 6UL
Tel: 0141-773 2223 **Fax:** 0141-771 5559
Website: http://www.univarsc.com
Directors: M. Hughes (MD), P. Munn (Dir)
Managers: D. Drakeley (Mktg Serv Mgr), M. Keenan (Depot Mgr), P. Munn (Mgr)
Turnover: £250,000 - £500,000 **No.of Employees:** 11 - 20
Product Groups: 32, 33, 66

Rapid Export Packing Services Ltd
Maritime House 143 Woodville Street, Glasgow, G51 2RQ
Tel: 0141-440 2899 **Fax:** 0141-440 2877
E-mail: sales-gl@stadium-packing.co.uk
Website: http://www.rapid-eps.co.uk
Directors: C. Knox (MD)
Ultimate Holding Company: BRAID GROUP (HOLDINGS) LIMITED
Immediate Holding Company: RAPID EXPORT PACKING SERVICES LTD.
Registration no: SC297595 **Date established:** 2006
Turnover: £75m - £125m **No.of Employees:** 11 - 20 **Product Groups:** 25, 35, 76

Date of Accounts	Feb 08	Feb 11	Feb 10
Working Capital	57	61	68
Fixed Assets	22	29	38
Current Assets	261	194	206
Current Liabilities	59	N/A	N/A

Rawlplug Ltd
Skibo Drive Thornliebank Industrial Estate, Thornliebank, Glasgow, G46 8JR
Tel: 0141-638 7961 **Fax:** 0141-638 7397
E-mail: sales@rawlplug.co.uk
Website: http://www.artexrawlplug.co.uk
Bank(s): National Westminster
Directors: S. Tecza (MD), J. Grove (Fin)
Managers: K. Murphy (Purch Mgr), P. Whelan (Sales & Mktg Mg), E. Scott (Personnel)
Immediate Holding Company: RAWLPLUG LIMITED
Registration no: 05497750 **Date established:** 2005
No.of Employees: 21 - 50 **Product Groups:** 30, 35, 36, 66

Date of Accounts	Dec 11	Dec 10	Dec 09
Sales Turnover	9m	12m	13m
Pre Tax Profit/Loss	7m	-1m	-3m
Working Capital	12m	-4m	-2m
Fixed Assets	2m	11m	11m
Current Assets	15m	6m	6m
Current Liabilities	392	811	944

Raytel Security Systems Ltd
Unit 3 Block 5 Oakbank Industrial Estate Garscube Road, Glasgow, G20 7LU
Tel: 0141-332 4232 **Fax:** 0141-332 6952
E-mail: sales@raytelsecurity.co.uk
Website: http://www.raytelsecurity.co.uk
Managers: I. Blackwood (District Mgr)
Immediate Holding Company: RAYTEL SECURITY SYSTEMS LIMITED
Registration no: 01280393 **Date established:** 1976
No.of Employees: 1 - 10 **Product Groups:** 37, 40

Date of Accounts	Jun 11	Jun 10	Jun 09
Working Capital	269	254	246
Fixed Assets	N/A	1	4
Current Assets	744	660	846

Recycle Inc
67 Mill Street, Glasgow, G40 1HZ
Tel: 0141-556 5937 **Fax:** 0141-556 5937
Website: http://www.recycleinc.com
Directors: B. Williamson (MD)
No.of Employees: 1 - 10 **Product Groups:** 37, 54, 80

Recycled Packaging Ltd
Units 10-21 Shanks Park Shanks Way, Barrhead, Glasgow, G78 1SP
Tel: 0141-881 6622 **Fax:** 0141-881 6633
E-mail: recycled.packaging@googlemail.com
Website: http://www.recycledpackagingltd.co.uk
Directors: P. Frazher (MD)
Immediate Holding Company: RECYCLED PACKAGING LTD.
Registration no: SC304939 **Date established:** 2006
Turnover: Up to £250,000 **No.of Employees:** 1 - 10 **Product Groups:** 27

Date of Accounts	Jul 11	Jul 10	Jul 09
Sales Turnover	450	375	167
Pre Tax Profit/Loss	2	50	6
Working Capital	32	46	27
Fixed Assets	72	56	41
Current Assets	75	85	48
Current Liabilities	25	25	11

Red Mosquito Ltd
27 Blairtummock Place, Glasgow, G33 4EN
Tel: 08719-181984 **Fax:** 0871-918 1984
E-mail: andy@redmosquito.co.uk
Website: http://www.redmosquito.co.uk
Directors: A. Stark (Dir)
Immediate Holding Company: RED MOSQUITO LIMITED
Registration no: SC258294 **Date established:** 2003 **Turnover:** £1m - £2m
No.of Employees: 11 - 20 **Product Groups:** 44

Date of Accounts	Dec 11	Dec 10	Dec 09
Working Capital	28	-3	19
Fixed Assets	21	21	8
Current Assets	209	135	134

Reid Furniture Ltd
Mavor Avenue East Kilbride, Glasgow, G74 4QX
Tel: 01355-270890
Website: http://www.reidfurniture.co.uk
Managers: P. McIntosh (Mgr)
Immediate Holding Company: FURNITURE PROPERTY NO 1 LIMITED
Registration no: SC192579 **Date established:** 1999
Turnover: £75m - £125m **No.of Employees:** 1 - 10 **Product Groups:** 26, 40

Date of Accounts	Dec 05	Jun 07	Jun 08
Sales Turnover	75m	115m	79m
Pre Tax Profit/Loss	1m	-1m	-347
Working Capital	-5m	-8m	-9m
Fixed Assets	9m	10m	10m
Current Assets	12m	14m	12m
Current Liabilities	8m	10m	10m

Reid Printers
79-109 Glasgow Road Blantyre, Glasgow, G72 0LY
Tel: 01698-826000 **Fax:** 01698-824944
E-mail: sales@reidprinters.com
Website: http://www.reid-print-group.co.uk
Bank(s): Clydesdale Bank PLC
Directors: C. Lindsay (Develop), I. Johnson (Ch), S. Cumming (Fin), T. Brown (MD)
Managers: F. Donald (Personnel)
Ultimate Holding Company: THE GT4 GROUP LIMITED
Immediate Holding Company: REID PRINTERS LIMITED
Registration no: SC051794 **VAT No.:** GB 262 1177 80
Date established: 1972 **Turnover:** £2m - £5m **No.of Employees:** 21 - 50
Product Groups: 22, 27, 28, 30, 44, 49, 64, 81

Date of Accounts	Apr 11	Apr 10	Apr 08
Working Capital	34	31	-158
Fixed Assets	N/A	N/A	2m
Current Assets	35	34	737

Reid Wire Ltd
162 Glenpark Street, Glasgow, G31 1PG
Tel: 0141-554 7081 **Fax:** 0141-556 4483
E-mail: sales@reidwire.com
Website: http://www.reidwire.com
Managers: S. Reid (Ops Mgr)
Immediate Holding Company: REID WIRE LIMITED
Registration no: SC089462 **VAT No.:** GB 388 9728 68
Date established: 1984 **Turnover:** £1m - £2m **No.of Employees:** 1 - 10
Product Groups: 35

Date of Accounts	Jun 11	Jun 10	Jun 09
Working Capital	71	60	120
Fixed Assets	96	113	134
Current Assets	262	277	292

Reliance Security Group Limited
Unit 10, 1st Floor, Platinum House 23 Eagle Street, Craighall Business Park, Glasgow, G4 9XA
Tel: 0870-6068999 **Fax:** 0141-353 2050
E-mail: info@reliancesecurity.co.uk
Website: http://www.reliancesecurity.co.uk
Directors: K. Allison (Ch), R. Ban (Fin)
Managers: K. Murray (Mgr)
Immediate Holding Company: Reliance Security Group Ltd
Registration no: 01473721 **Date established:** 1988
Turnover: £10m - £20m **No.of Employees:** 1 - 10 **Product Groups:** 81

Renew All
3e Manse Court Barrhead, Glasgow, G78 2RJ
Tel: 0141-880 8933 **Fax:** 0141-880 8959
E-mail: renewall@btconnect.com
Website: http://www.renewall.co.uk
Directors: B. Pattison (Prop)
Date established: 1994 **No.of Employees:** 1 - 10 **Product Groups:** 46, 48

Retropet Ltd
F1-2, 47 Wilton Street, Glasgow, G20 6RT
Tel: 07973-816270 **Fax:** 0141-945 2701
E-mail: mail@retropet.biz
Website: http://www.retropet.biz
Directors: R. Wherrett (MD)
Registration no: 04075174 **Turnover:** Up to £250,000
No.of Employees: 1 - 10 **Product Groups:** 80

Richard Austin Alloys Scotland Ltd
31 Dunivaig Road, Glasgow, G33 4TP
Tel: 0141-771 8391 **Fax:** 0141-771 9454
E-mail: sales@raaltd.com
Website: http://www.raaltd.com
Directors: J. Johnston (Sales), J. Murdoch (Fin)
Ultimate Holding Company: RICHARD AUSTIN ALLOYS LIMITED
Immediate Holding Company: RICHARD AUSTIN ALLOYS (NORTH WEST) LIMITED
Registration no: SC149020 **VAT No.:** GB 481 4047 54
Date established: 1994 **Turnover:** £10m - £20m
No.of Employees: 21 - 50 **Product Groups:** 34, 66

Date of Accounts	Mar 12	Mar 11	Mar 10
Sales Turnover	21m	19m	13m
Pre Tax Profit/Loss	602	667	261
Working Capital	3m	3m	2m
Fixed Assets	1m	1m	1m
Current Assets	9m	10m	7m
Current Liabilities	714	526	355

Richard Lees Steel Decking
Buchanan Business Park Buchanan Business Park Cumbe Rnauld Road, Stepps, Glasgow, G33 6FB
Tel: 0141-779 3795 **Fax:** 0141-779 5971
Managers: W. Pringle (Mgr)
No.of Employees: 1 - 10 **Product Groups:** 35

Righton Ltd
120 Cambuslang Road, Glasgow, G32 8NB
Tel: 0141-646 3730 **Fax:** 0141-959 3467
E-mail: kenny.lamont@righton.co.uk
Website: http://www.righton.co.uk
Bank(s): Royal Bank of Scotland
Directors: K. Lamont (Reg)
Ultimate Holding Company: HENLEY MANAGEMENT COMPANY (USA)
Immediate Holding Company: RIGHTON LIMITED
Registration no: 00143411 **VAT No.:** GB 655 1301 62
Date established: 2016 **Turnover:** £20m - £50m
No.of Employees: 11 - 20 **Product Groups:** 34

Date of Accounts	Dec 11	Dec 10	Dec 09
Sales Turnover	71m	74m	50m
Pre Tax Profit/Loss	943	1m	-632
Working Capital	11m	7m	6m
Fixed Assets	1m	2m	2m
Current Assets	31m	30m	27m
Current Liabilities	2m	4m	2m

Robert Wiseman Dairies
159 Glasgow Road Nerston, East Kilbride, Glasgow, G74 4PA
Tel: 01355-244261 **Fax:** 01355-230352
E-mail: sales@wiseman-dairies.co.uk
Website: http://www.wiseman-dairies.co.uk
Directors: A. Wiseman (Ch), A. Wilkie (Sales & Mktg), D. Clemenson (Tech Serv), G. Wiseman (Purch), G. Sweeney (Fin), I. McLean (Pers)
Immediate Holding Company: ROBERT WISEMAN DAIRIES LIMITED
Registration no: SC146494 **VAT No.:** GB 625 0831 65
Date established: 1993 **Turnover:** £500m - £1,000m
No.of Employees: 101 - 250 **Product Groups:** 62

Date of Accounts	Jan 12	Apr 09	Apr 10
Sales Turnover	780m	848m	886m
Pre Tax Profit/Loss	8m	31m	49m
Working Capital	-17m	-26m	-41m
Fixed Assets	246m	227m	236m
Current Assets	118m	81m	94m
Current Liabilities	45m	37m	56m

Roevin Management Services Limited
Thomson House 8 Minerva Way, Glasgow, G3 8AU
Tel: 0845-643 0514 **Fax:** 0141-221 5768
E-mail: glasgow@roevin.co.uk
Website: http://www.roevin.co.uk
Managers: G. Comnene (Sales Prom Mgr), G. Neechan (District Mgr)
Ultimate Holding Company: WPP GROUP PLC
Immediate Holding Company: WPP Investments Ltd
Registration no: 02436481 **VAT No.:** GB 262 7756 34
Date established: 1974 **Turnover:** £1m - £2m **No.of Employees:** 1 - 10
Product Groups: 80

Ross Storage Equipment Co.
2 Abbotsford Bishopbriggs, Glasgow, G64 1ED
Tel: 0141-772 2453 **Fax:** 0141-772 2453
Directors: S. Ross (Ptnr)
Date established: 1985 **No.of Employees:** 1 - 10 **Product Groups:** 35, 42, 45

Rowebb Ltd
33-53 Charles Street, Glasgow, G21 2PR
Tel: 0141-548 6010 **Fax:** 0141-553 1039
E-mail: rowebbltd@aol.com
Website: http://www.rowebb.com
Bank(s): Bank of Scotland
Directors: B. Balloch (MD)
Immediate Holding Company: ROWEBB LIMITED
Registration no: SC173218 **VAT No.:** GB 680 5182 33
Date established: 1997 **Turnover:** £1m - £2m **No.of Employees:** 11 - 20
Product Groups: 14, 33, 66

Date of Accounts	Mar 12	Mar 11	Mar 10
Working Capital	61	106	167
Fixed Assets	2m	2m	2m
Current Assets	1m	1m	1m

Roy Easton & Co.
14 Carmyle Avenue, Glasgow, G32 8HJ
Tel: 0141-778 5491 **Fax:** 0141-763 2032
E-mail: enquiries@royeaston.co.uk
Website: http://www.royeaston.co.uk
Directors: D. Bailey (Prop)
Ultimate Holding Company: AB VENTILATION GROUP LIMITED
Immediate Holding Company: AB AIRSUPPORT LIMITED
Date established: 2009 **Turnover:** Up to £250,000
No.of Employees: 1 - 10 **Product Groups:** 84

Date of Accounts	Mar 11	Mar 10	Mar 09
Working Capital	-37	-75	-127
Fixed Assets	66	99	133
Current Assets	407	335	409

Rude Goose Design
Balfron, Glasgow, G63 0LF
Tel: 020-8144 8427
E-mail: info@rudegoose.com
Website: http://www.rudegoose.com
Directors: Z. Tucker (MD)
Registration no: SC280048 **Date established:** 2005
No.of Employees: 1 - 10 **Product Groups:** 44

S C A Packaging
166 Riverford Road, Glasgow, G43 1PT
Tel: 0141-632 0999 **Fax:** 0141-632 8111
E-mail: info@sca.com
Website: http://www.sca.com
Bank(s): National Westminster
Directors: P. Cook (Fin)
Managers: A. Forbes (Purch Mgr), J. Jackson (Plant), K. Gold (Sales Prom Mgr), C. Morrison (Personnel)
Ultimate Holding Company: SVENSKA CELLULOSA AB (SWEDEN)
Immediate Holding Company: ALEX. COWAN & SONS LIMITED
Registration no: NF002827 **VAT No.:** 703 1225 91 **Date established:** 1989
Turnover: £20m - £50m **No.of Employees:** 101 - 250
Product Groups: 27, 28, 30, 49

S D C Industries Ltd
18 Colvilles Place Kelvin Industrial Estate, East Kilbride, Glasgow, G75 0PZ
Tel: 01355-265959 **Fax:** 01355-265484
E-mail: info@sdcindustries.co.uk
Website: http://www.sdcindustries.co.uk
Bank(s): Bank of Scotland
Directors: S. Coomes (MD)
Immediate Holding Company: SDC INDUSTRIES LIMITED
Registration no: SC092940 **VAT No.:** GB 476 8370 04
Date established: 1985 **No.of Employees:** 21 - 50 **Product Groups:** 37, 52

Date of Accounts	Mar 11	Mar 10	Mar 09
Working Capital	2m	2m	1m
Fixed Assets	154	171	185
Current Assets	3m	3m	2m

S L T Handling Services Ltd
4 Napier Way Wardpark North, Cumbernauld, Glasgow, G68 0EH
Tel: 01236-725552 **Fax:** 01236-723005
E-mail: sales@slt-handling.co.uk
Website: http://www.slt-handling.co.uk
Directors: A. Maclean (MD), G. Maclean (Fin)
Immediate Holding Company: SLT HANDLING SERVICES LIMITED
Registration no: SC137331 **Date established:** 1992
Turnover: £500,000 - £1m **No.of Employees:** 1 - 10 **Product Groups:** 35, 39, 45

Date of Accounts	Mar 11	Mar 10	Mar 09
Working Capital	153	152	183
Fixed Assets	185	143	154
Current Assets	436	429	450

S P Filtration
3 Wellside Drive Cambuslang, Glasgow, G72 8TA
Tel: 0141-641 1168 **Fax:** 0141-641 6903
E-mail: matt@spfiltration.co.uk
Website: http://www.spfiltration.co.uk
Directors: M. Mcdermott (Prop)
Date established: 1976 **No.of Employees:** 1 - 10 **Product Groups:** 38, 42

S P M Wolverine Proctor Ltd
3 Langlands Avenue East Kilbride, Glasgow, G75 0YG
Tel: 01355-575350 **Fax:** 01355-575351
E-mail: sscouller@wolverineproctor.co.uk
Website: http://www.cpmwolverineproctor.co.uk
Bank(s): Clydesdale Bank PLC
Directors: A. Nguyen (Fin), S. Scouller (MD)
Managers: A. Morrison (Comptroller), B. Fee (Sales & Mktg Mg), G. Coulter (Tech Serv Mgr), J. Kaprot (Buyer), T. Watson (Personnel)
Ultimate Holding Company: WOLVERINE PROCTOR & SCHWARTZ INC USA
Registration no: 02423408 **VAT No.:** GB 703 6856 31
Date established: 1927 **Turnover:** £1m - £2m **No.of Employees:** 21 - 50
Product Groups: 40, 41, 42, 43, 45, 67

Saint-Gobain Weber Ltd
Unit 1 Spiersbridge Business Park Spiersbridge Avenue, Thornliebank, Glasgow, G46 8NL
Tel: 0141-621 2510 **Fax:** 0141-445 0122
E-mail: idris.crumlish@netweber.co.uk
Website: http://www.netweber.co.uk
Managers: I. Crumlish
Ultimate Holding Company: COMPAGNIE DE SAINT GOBAIN (FRANCE)
Immediate Holding Company: SAINT-GOBAIN WEBER LIMITED
Registration no: 02544294 **Date established:** 1990
No.of Employees: 1 - 10 **Product Groups:** 33

Date of Accounts	Dec 11	Dec 10	Dec 09
Sales Turnover	38m	35m	36m
Pre Tax Profit/Loss	1m	-690	-1m
Working Capital	-3m	-3m	2m
Fixed Assets	25m	26m	27m
Current Assets	12m	12m	11m
Current Liabilities	6m	7m	6m

Sales Recruitment Network Ltd
The Retreat Wardend Road, Torrance, Glasgow, G64 4DG
Tel: 01360-620061 **Fax:** 01360-620065
E-mail: paulcrilley@aol.com
Website: http://www.tsrn.co.uk
Directors: P. Crilley (Dir)
No.of Employees: 1 - 10 **Product Groups:** 80

Salon Services Hair & Beauty Supplies Ltd
Unit 7 Evanton Drive Thornliebank Industrial Estate, Glasgow, G46 8HZ
Tel: 0141-621 3600 **Fax:** 0141-621 3660
E-mail: enquiries@salon-services.com
Website: http://www.salon-services.com
Directors: M. Connolly (MD)
Managers: J. Morrison (Mktg Serv Mgr)
Ultimate Holding Company: Salon Services (Holdings) Ltd
Immediate Holding Company: SALON SERVICES (HAIR AND BEAUTY SUPPLIES) LTD.
Registration no: SC049239 **VAT No.:** GB 369 1181 39
Date established: 1971 **Turnover:** £50m - £75m **No.of Employees:** 1 - 10
Product Groups: 63

Frank Sammeroff Ltd
131 Woodhead Road, Glasgow, G53 7NN
Tel: 0141-881 5701 **Fax:** 0141-881 4919
E-mail: elaine.morrison@sammeroff.co.uk
Website: http://www.sammeroff.co.uk
Bank(s): Bank of Scotland
Directors: L. Sammeroff (MD)
Managers: P. Rodgers (Sales Prom Mgr)
Immediate Holding Company: FRANK S REALISATIONS LIMITED
Registration no: SC023217 **VAT No.:** GB 259 5741 22
Date established: 1945 **Turnover:** £2m - £5m **No.of Employees:** 21 - 50
Product Groups: 24

Date of Accounts	Mar 08	Mar 07	Mar 06
Working Capital	773	814	583
Fixed Assets	473	508	538
Current Assets	1573	1827	1402
Current Liabilities	800	1013	819
Total Share Capital	1	1	1

Samtec Europe Ltd
117 Deerdykes View Cumbernauld, Glasgow, G68 9HN
Tel: 01236-739292 **Fax:** 01236-727113
E-mail: info@samtec.com
Website: http://www.samtec.com
Bank(s): Royal Bank of Scotland, Village Branch, Cumbernauld
Directors: J. Shine (MD)
Ultimate Holding Company: SAMTEC INC (USA)
Immediate Holding Company: SAMTEC (EUROPE) LIMITED
Registration no: SC096674 **Date established:** 1985
Turnover: £10m - £20m **No.of Employees:** 11 - 20 **Product Groups:** 37, 67

Date of Accounts	Dec 11	Dec 10	Dec 09
Sales Turnover	12m	10m	7m
Pre Tax Profit/Loss	715	6m	4m
Working Capital	5m	4m	3m
Fixed Assets	107	100	84
Current Assets	5m	6m	4m
Current Liabilities	229	1m	859

Save & Invest Financial Planning
100 West Regent Street, Glasgow, G2 2QD
Tel: 0141-332 8088 **Fax:** 01738-441315
E-mail: jdeans@saveandinvest.co.uk
Website: http://www.saveandinvest.co.uk
Bank(s): HSBC
Directors: J. Deans (MD)
Ultimate Holding Company: SAVE & INVEST GROUP LIMITED
Immediate Holding Company: SAVE & INVEST (FINANCIAL PLANNING) LIMITED
Registration no: SC113651 **Date established:** 1988 **Turnover:** £1m - £2m
No.of Employees: 21 - 50 **Product Groups:** 82

Date of Accounts	Jun 11	Jun 10	Jun 09
Working Capital	976	704	639
Fixed Assets	39	82	65
Current Assets	1m	1m	876

Saw Centre Ltd
650 Eglinton Street, Glasgow, G5 9RP
Tel: 08707-280222 **Fax:** 0141-429 5609
E-mail: sales@thesawcentre.co.uk
Website: http://www.thesawcentre.co.uk
Directors: T. Galbraith (MD), D. Stevenson (Dir)
Immediate Holding Company: SAW CENTRE LIMITED THE
Registration no: SC053377 **VAT No.:** GB 259 9693 84
Date established: 1973 **Turnover:** £2m - £5m **No.of Employees:** 21 - 50
Product Groups: 36, 37, 46

Date of Accounts	May 11	May 10	May 09
Working Capital	-2	3	22
Fixed Assets	36	30	5
Current Assets	5	4	25

Scale Direct Scotland Ltd
Unit 1 Strathclyde Business Centre 391 Langmuir Road Bargeddie, Baillieston, Glasgow, G69 7TU
Tel: 01236-872810
E-mail: sales@scaledirect.co.uk
Website: http://www.scaledirect.co.uk
Managers: A. Armstrong
Immediate Holding Company: SCALE DIRECT (SCOTLAND) LTD.
Registration no: SC232612 **Date established:** 2002
No.of Employees: 1 - 10 **Product Groups:** 38, 87

Date of Accounts	Jun 12	Jun 11	Jun 10
Working Capital	15	18	17
Fixed Assets	N/A	N/A	1
Current Assets	41	82	80

The Scobie & Junor Group Ltd
1 Singer Road Kelvin Industrial Estate, East Kilbride, Glasgow, G75 0XS
Tel: 01355-237041 **Fax:** 01355-263585
E-mail: info@scobiesdirect.com
Website: http://www.scobie-junor.co.uk
Directors: A. Wicklow (Fin), T. Lawn (Dir)
Managers: V. McLean (Personnel), D. Frew (Tech Serv Mgr)
Immediate Holding Company: SCOBIE & JUNOR (HOLDINGS) LTD
Registration no: SC010710 **VAT No.:** GB 659 1432 23
Turnover: £2m - £5m **No.of Employees:** 21 - 50 **Product Groups:** 20, 41

Sco-Fro Group Ltd
229 St Vincent Street, Glasgow, G2 5QY
Tel: 0141-223 7707 **Fax:** 0141-221 4701
E-mail: stewart.macliver@scofro.com
Website: http://www.scofro.com
Managers: C. Liddell, S. Bader
Ultimate Holding Company: INTERLOCK INVESTMENTS LIMITED
Immediate Holding Company: NEIDPATH INVESTMENT COMPANY LIMITED
Registration no: SC034854 **Date established:** 1960
Turnover: £20m - £50m **No.of Employees:** 11 - 20 **Product Groups:** 09, 20, 62

Date of Accounts	Jan 12	Jan 11	Jan 10
Sales Turnover	18m	22m	42m
Pre Tax Profit/Loss	-11	344	354
Working Capital	6m	7m	13m
Fixed Assets	16m	16m	17m
Current Assets	10m	15m	17m
Current Liabilities	3m	7m	2m

Scotbeef Ltd
27 Glenburn Road East Kilbride, Glasgow, G74 5BA
Tel: 01355-225381 **Fax:** 01355-264327
E-mail: longleys@scotbeef.com
Website: http://www.scotbeef.com
Bank(s): Clydesdale
Directors: A. Hill (Co Sec), I. Galloway (Ch)
Ultimate Holding Company: J.W. GALLOWAY LIMITED
Immediate Holding Company: SCOTBEEF LIMITED
Registration no: SC039434 **VAT No.:** GB 260 1373 92
Date established: 1963 **Turnover:** £125m - £250m
No.of Employees: 51 - 100 **Product Groups:** 20

Date of Accounts	Feb 10	Feb 11	Feb 08
Sales Turnover	167m	189m	119m
Pre Tax Profit/Loss	5m	6m	1m
Working Capital	13m	20m	3m
Fixed Assets	24m	23m	26m
Current Assets	30m	30m	14m
Current Liabilities	3m	3m	2m

Scotec Lifts
Unit 1 Block 14 Clydesmill Drive, Clydesmill Industrial Estate, Glasgow, G32 8RG
Tel: 0141-646 0900 **Fax:** 0141-646 0909
E-mail: enquiries@scoteclifts.co.uk
Website: http://www.scoteclifts.co.uk
Directors: D. Plunkett (Prop)
Immediate Holding Company: SCOTEC LIFTS LTD.
Registration no: SC227713 **Date established:** 2002
No.of Employees: 1 - 10 **Product Groups:** 35, 39, 45

Date of Accounts	Mar 11	Mar 10	Mar 09
Working Capital	131	176	210
Fixed Assets	39	16	15
Current Assets	288	290	317

The Scotia Fencing Company Ltd
Howe Road Kilsyth, Glasgow, G65 0TA
Tel: 01236-823339 **Fax:** 01236-826434
Directors: C. Mcclean (MD), J. McClean (Fin)
Immediate Holding Company: THE SCOTIA FENCING COMPANY LTD.
Registration no: SC030555 **Date established:** 1955
Turnover: £250,000 - £500,000 **No.of Employees:** 1 - 10
Product Groups: 25

Date of Accounts	Dec 11	Dec 10	Dec 09
Working Capital	80	57	25
Fixed Assets	66	69	73
Current Assets	127	134	59

Scotia Radio Services Ltd
33 Townsend Street, Glasgow, G4 0LA
Tel: 0141-341 3390 **Fax:** 0141-341 3399
E-mail: admin@scotia-radio.co.uk
Website: http://www.scotia-radio.co.uk
Directors: E. Gibson (MD)
Immediate Holding Company: SCOTIA RADIO SERVICES LIMITED
Registration no: SC198359 **Date established:** 1999
No.of Employees: 1 - 10 **Product Groups:** 37, 39, 48

Date of Accounts	Aug 11	Aug 10	Aug 09
Working Capital	-62	-10	61
Fixed Assets	84	74	75
Current Assets	98	138	174

Scottish Enterprise
Atrium Court 50 Waterloo Street, Glasgow, G2 6HQ
Tel: 0141-204 1111 **Fax:** 0141-248 1600
E-mail: enquiries@scotent.co.uk
Website: http://www.scottish-enterprise.com
Bank(s): The Royal Bank of Scotland
Managers: J. Crawford, P. Martin (Buyer), C. Stewart (Personnel)
Immediate Holding Company: SCOTTISH ENTERPRISE GLASGOW
Registration no: SC126249 **Date established:** 1990
Turnover: £50m - £75m **No.of Employees:** 101 - 250 **Product Groups:** 80

Date of Accounts	Mar 11	Mar 10	Mar 09
Pre Tax Profit/Loss	1	2	24
Working Capital	2m	2m	2m
Fixed Assets	7m	N/A	N/A
Current Assets	2m	2m	8m
Current Liabilities	2	2	9

Scottish Exhibition & Conference Centre Ticket Office

1 Exhibition Way, Glasgow, G3 8YW
Tel: 0844-3954000 **Fax:** 0141-226 3423
E-mail: info@secc.co.uk
Website: http://www.ticketsoup.com
Directors: J. Sharkey (Grp Chief Exec), J. Sharky (Fin), M. Close (Chief Op Offcr), M. Closier (Grp Chief Exec), R. Eynon (Mkt Research), P. Duthie (Co Sec), P. Duthie (Fin)
Managers: M. Lawson, E. McAusland (Catering)
Immediate Holding Company: SCOTTISH EXHIBITION CENTRE LIMITED
Registration no: SC082081 **Date established:** 1983
Turnover: £5m - £10m **No.of Employees:** 1 - 10 **Product Groups:** 69, 81

Date of Accounts	Mar 08	Mar 07
Sales Turnover	4083	4813
Pre Tax Profit/Loss	228	70
Working Capital	4052	3926
Fixed Assets	105	62
Current Assets	4172	3993
Current Liabilities	120	68
ROCE% (Return on Capital Employed)	5.5	1.8
ROT% (Return on Turnover)	5.6	1.5

Scottish Galvanizers Ltd

Maclellan Street, Glasgow, G41 1RR
Tel: 0141-427 3041 **Fax:** 0141-427 4981
E-mail: scottish@wedge-galv.co.uk
Website: http://www.wedge-galv.co.uk
Managers: P. Cameron (Chief Mgr)
Ultimate Holding Company: B.E. WEDGE HOLDINGS LIMITED
Immediate Holding Company: SCOTTISH GALVANIZERS LIMITED
Registration no: SC027121 **Date established:** 1949
No.of Employees: 21 - 50 **Product Groups:** 46, 48

Date of Accounts	Mar 11	Mar 10	Mar 09
Pre Tax Profit/Loss	12	12	12
Working Capital	100	100	100
Current Assets	103	103	102
Current Liabilities	3	3	2

Scottish Health Innovations

206 St Vincent Street, Glasgow, G2 5SG
Tel: 0141-248 7334 **Fax:** 0141-248 6454
E-mail: gillian.taylor@shil.co.uk
Website: http://www.shil.co.uk
Directors: F. McCulloch (Co Sec), G. Taylor (Dir)
Managers: A. Whiteside (Research & Deve)
Immediate Holding Company: SCOTTISH HEALTH INNOVATIONS LIMITED
Registration no: SC236303 **Date established:** 2002 **Turnover:**
No.of Employees: 11 - 20 **Product Groups:** 38, 85

Scottish Quest

49 Castle Gate Uddingston, Glasgow, G71 7HU
Tel: 01698-816100 **Fax:** 01698-814846
E-mail: info@scottishquest.com
Website: http://www.scottishquest.com
Directors: L. Cadenhead (Prop)
Immediate Holding Company: QUEST GAMES LIMITED
Registration no: SC 259611 **Date established:** 2011
Turnover: Up to £250,000 **No.of Employees:** 1 - 10 **Product Groups:** 49

Scottoilers Scotland Ltd

2 Riverside Milngavie, Glasgow, G62 6PL
Tel: 0141-955 1100 **Fax:** 0141-956 5896
E-mail: sales@scottoiler.com
Website: http://www.scottoiler.com
Directors: D. Thomson (Co Sec), F. Thomson (Dir)
Immediate Holding Company: SCOTTOILER HOLDINGS LTD.
Registration no: SC342913 **Date established:** 2008
No.of Employees: 11 - 20 **Product Groups:** 38, 42

Date of Accounts	Oct 11	Oct 10	Oct 09
Working Capital	68	69	70
Fixed Assets	25	25	25
Current Assets	70	75	70

Scotwood Interiors Ltd

48 Milton Road East Kilbride, Glasgow, G74 5BU
Tel: 01355-241727 **Fax:** 01355-241601
E-mail: jim@scotwood.com
Website: http://www.scotwood.com
Bank(s): Clydesdale, Glasgow
Directors: D. Kerr (Fin), J. Scott (MD)
Managers: G. Scott (Buyer)
Immediate Holding Company: SCOTWOOD INTERIORS LTD.
Registration no: SC100704 **VAT No.:** GB 424 0335 93
Date established: 1986 **Turnover:** £2m - £5m **No.of Employees:** 21 - 50
Product Groups: 26, 35, 52, 84

Date of Accounts	Jan 12	Jan 11	Jan 10
Working Capital	510	555	553
Fixed Assets	81	74	248
Current Assets	1m	1m	1m

Service Point UK Ltd

539-543 Sauchiehall Street, Glasgow, G3 7PG
Tel: 0141-275 2424 **Fax:** 0141-204 3801
E-mail: glasgow@servicepointuk.com
Website: http://www.servicepointuk.com
Bank(s): Royal Bank of Scotland
Managers: P. Bellard (District Mgr)
Ultimate Holding Company: GRUPO PICKING PACK SA (SPAIN)
Immediate Holding Company: SIME MALLOCH LIMITED
Registration no: SC036475 **Date established:** 1961
Turnover: £20m - £50m **No.of Employees:** 21 - 50 **Product Groups:** 64, 80

Shannon Games Limited

2 Orchard Place Kirkintilloch, Glasgow, G66 3JE
Tel: 0141-578 9324 **Fax:** 0141-776 3331
E-mail: sales@shannonboardgames.net
Website: http://www.shannongames.com
Directors: E. Shannon (Dir)
Registration no: SC299141 **Date established:** 2003
No.of Employees: 1 - 10 **Product Groups:** 48, 49

Signature Industries Ltd

Unit 19 Atlas Industrial Estate Foundry Street, Glasgow, G21 4PR
Tel: 0141-558 2121 **Fax:** 0141-558 9696
E-mail: info@sigcom.co.uk
Website: http://www.signatureindustries.com
Bank(s): National Westminster Bank
Managers: J. Grant (Mgr)
Ultimate Holding Company: DIGITAL ANGEL CORPORATION (USA)
Immediate Holding Company: SIGNATURE INDUSTRIES LIMITED
Registration no: 02800561 **VAT No.:** GB 626 3127 57
Date established: 1993 **Turnover:** £500,000 - £1m
No.of Employees: 11 - 20 **Product Groups:** 37

Date of Accounts	Dec 11	Dec 10	Dec 09
Sales Turnover	3m	6m	21m
Pre Tax Profit/Loss	-5m	-2m	3m
Working Capital	-2m	2m	3m
Fixed Assets	63	653	1m
Current Assets	3m	6m	9m
Current Liabilities	1m	2m	3m

Simpac

311 Burnfield Road Thornliebank, Glasgow, G46 7UF
Tel: 0141-571 0220 **Fax:** 0141-571 0260
E-mail: enquiries@simpac.co.uk
Website: http://www.simpac.co.uk
Bank(s): Bank of Scotland
Directors: G. Barnes (MD), S. Bole (Sales & Mktg), T. Clarke (Dir), C. Dell (Fin)
Managers: A. Mccusker (Personnel), R. Harridane (Purch Mgr)
Ultimate Holding Company: SIMPAC (HOLDINGS) LIMITED
Immediate Holding Company: SIMPAC LIMITED
Registration no: SC178973 **VAT No.:** GB 316 3110 08
Date established: 1997 **No.of Employees:** 51 - 100 **Product Groups:** 27, 30

Skylight International Ltd

75 Birkmyre Road Govan, Glasgow, G51 3JH
Tel: 0141-445 4219 **Fax:** 0141-425 1511
E-mail: john@skylight.co.uk
Website: http://www.skylight.co.uk
Directors: J. Mccloughlin (Prop)
Immediate Holding Company: SKYLIGHT INTERNATIONAL LIMITED
Registration no: SC109466 **Date established:** 1988
No.of Employees: 1 - 10 **Product Groups:** 26, 35

Date of Accounts	Mar 12	Mar 11	Mar 10
Working Capital	87	3	29
Fixed Assets	300	317	324
Current Assets	401	209	251

Skytec Aviation Ltd

Unit 23 Langlands Avenue Kelvin South Business Park, East Kilbride, Glasgow, G75 0YG
Tel: 01355-279633 **Fax:** 01355-279634
E-mail: skytecaviation@btconnect.com
Website: http://www.skytecaviationltd.co.uk
Managers: C. Dow (Sales Admin)
Immediate Holding Company: SKYTEC AVIATION LTD.
Registration no: SC147731 **VAT No.:** GB 653 0911 52
Date established: 1993 **Turnover:** £500,000 - £1m
No.of Employees: 1 - 10 **Product Groups:** 38, 48

Date of Accounts	Sep 11	Sep 10	Sep 09
Working Capital	713	590	573
Fixed Assets	5	5	5
Current Assets	885	894	888

Slaters

165 Howard Street, Glasgow, G1 4HF
Tel: 0141-552 7171 **Fax:** 0141-553 1720
E-mail: paulslater@slatermenswear.com
Website: http://www.slatermenswear.com
Directors: C. McKenna (Sales), P. Rose (Fin), P. Slater (MD)
Managers: W. Mould (Tech Serv Mgr)
Immediate Holding Company: SLATER MENSWEAR
Registration no: SC052746 **Date established:** 1973
Turnover: £20m - £50m **No.of Employees:** 251 - 500 **Product Groups:** 24

Date of Accounts	May 92	May 93	May 90
Sales Turnover	25m	26m	19m
Pre Tax Profit/Loss	3m	3m	2m
Fixed Assets	2m	3m	719
Current Assets	9m	11m	6m

Smail Engineers Glasgow Ltd

30 Napier Road Hillington Park, Glasgow, G52 4DR
Tel: 0141-882 4882 **Fax:** 0141-810 5460
E-mail: smail@compserve.com
Directors: R. Fletcher (Dir)
Immediate Holding Company: SMAIL ENGINEERS (GLASGOW) LIMITED
Registration no: SC148360 **VAT No.:** GB 617 3481 40
Date established: 1994 **Turnover:** £1m - £2m **No.of Employees:** 1 - 10
Product Groups: 40, 45, 46, 65

Date of Accounts	May 12	May 11	May 10
Working Capital	45	-0	4
Fixed Assets	72	59	68
Current Assets	345	301	239

Smart Control

Unit 2 21 Clydebrae Street, Glasgow, G51 2AJ
Tel: 0141-445 5377
E-mail: user@smartcontrols.co.uk
Website: http://www.smcontrol.co.uk
Directors: R. Burke (Fin)
Immediate Holding Company: Smart Control Ltd
Registration no: SC279959 **Date established:** 2005
No.of Employees: 1 - 10 **Product Groups:** 38, 48, 84

Smith Medical Ltd

52 Grayshill Road Cumbernauld, Glasgow, G68 9HQ
Tel: 01236-737138 **Fax:** 01236-738503
E-mail: lynn.jardine@smiths-medical.com
Website: http://www.smiths-medical.com
Bank(s): Barclays
Directors: L. Jardine (Dir)
Immediate Holding Company: SMITH MEDICAL LIMITED
Registration no: 07204174 **Date established:** 2010
No.of Employees: 51 - 100 **Product Groups:** 24

Date of Accounts	Jun 11
Working Capital	1
Fixed Assets	1
Current Assets	19

Smith & Roger Ltd

34 Elliott Street, Glasgow, G3 8EA
Tel: 0141-248 6341 **Fax:** 0141-248 6475
E-mail: i.mcaslan@smithandrodger.co.uk
Website: http://www.frenchpolishes.com
Directors: I. Mcaslan (Dir)
Immediate Holding Company: SMITH AND RODGER, LIMITED
Registration no: SC011502 **VAT No.:** GB 259 5924 14
Date established: 2020 **Turnover:** £500,000 - £1m
No.of Employees: 1 - 10 **Product Groups:** 32

Date of Accounts	Dec 11	Dec 10	Dec 09
Working Capital	182	171	159
Fixed Assets	119	122	126
Current Assets	225	196	189

Thomas Smith Fasteners

14 Forrest Street Blantyre, Glasgow, G72 0JP
Tel: 01698-826464 **Fax:** 01698-826585
Website: http://www.thomassmithfasteners.com
Managers: C. Maclachlen (Mgr)
Date established: 2002 **No.of Employees:** 1 - 10 **Product Groups:** 35

Snapco Ltd

15 Kelvin Avenue Hillington Park, Glasgow, G52 4LT
Tel: 0141-883 0331 **Fax:** 0141-882 2717
E-mail: sales@snapco.org
Website: http://www.snapco.org
Directors: S. Mcfarlane (Dir)
Immediate Holding Company: SNAPCO LIMITED
Registration no: SC096274 **Date established:** 1985
No.of Employees: 11 - 20 **Product Groups:** 38, 42

Date of Accounts	Dec 11	Dec 10	Dec 09
Working Capital	259	371	334
Fixed Assets	131	10	32
Current Assets	877	745	745

Spaceright Europe Ltd

38 Tollpark Road Wardpark East, Cumbernauld, Glasgow, G68 0LW
Tel: 01236-853120 **Fax:** 01923-237546
E-mail: sales@spacerighteurope.com
Website: http://www.spacerighteurope.com
Bank(s): Royal Bank of Scotland, Market Street
Directors: A. Syman (MD)
Managers: S. Love (Purch Mgr), J. Evans (Fin Mgr), N. Scott (Mktg Serv Mgr)
Immediate Holding Company: SPACERIGHT EUROPE LIMITED
Registration no: SC344257 **VAT No.:** GB 260 8068 62
Date established: 2008 **Turnover:** £5m - £10m
No.of Employees: 51 - 100 **Product Groups:** 26

Date of Accounts	Oct 11	Oct 10	Oct 09
Working Capital	789	888	1m
Fixed Assets	90	114	71
Current Assets	2m	2m	2m

Spark Erosion Centre

Unit 13-14 Block 4 Third Road Blantyre Industrial Estate, Blantyre, Glasgow, G72 0UP
Tel: 01698-823486 **Fax:** 01698-825466
E-mail: sales@sparkerosioncentre.co.uk
Website: http://www.sparkerosioncentre.co.uk
Directors: W. Brynes (MD)
Immediate Holding Company: THE SPARK EROSION CENTRE LTD
Registration no: SC048839 **Date established:** 1971
Turnover: £50m - £75m **No.of Employees:** 11 - 20 **Product Groups:** 46

Date of Accounts	Mar 08	Mar 07	Mar 06
Working Capital	N/A	N/A	-64
Fixed Assets	600	600	600
Current Liabilities	N/A	N/A	65

Spectrex Inc

6 Applecross Road Kirkintilloch, Glasgow, G66 3TJ
Tel: 0141-578 0693 **Fax:** 0141-578 9689
E-mail: ian@spectrex-inc.com
Website: http://www.spectrex-inc.com
Managers: I. Buchanan
Turnover: £5m - £10m **No.of Employees:** 101 - 250 **Product Groups:** 38, 54, 67

SPEED Laboratory

University Of Glasgow Oakfield Avenue, Glasgow, G12 8LT
Tel: 0141-330 3157 **Fax:** 0141-330 3158
Website: http://www.gla.ac.uk/speed
Directors: T. Miller (Dir)
No.of Employees: 1 - 10 **Product Groups:** 37, 44, 67

Spiraflex UK

Unit 28 New Albion Indl-Est Halley Street, Glasgow, G13 4DJ
Tel: 0141-951 4023 **Fax:** 0141-951 4024
E-mail: info@spiraflex.co.uk
Website: http://www.spiraflex.co.uk
Directors: M. Thomas (Fin), S. Hawthorn (MD)
Managers: S. Hawthorn (Ops Mgr)
Immediate Holding Company: SPIRAFLEX LTD
Registration no: SC140986 **VAT No.:** GB 435 1394 59
Date established: 1992 **Turnover:** £500,000 - £1m
No.of Employees: 1 - 10 **Product Groups:** 29, 40

Springstop (UK) Ltd

95 Boden Street, Glasgow, G40 3QF
Tel: 0141-554 4424 **Fax:** 0141-554 4423
E-mail: info@spring-stop.com
Website: http://www.spring-stop.com
Directors: M. Campbell (Fin), T. Woods (Dir), M. Woods (Dir)
Managers: A. McGregor (Mktg Serv Mgr), L. Feely (Sales Prom Mgr), N. Dochard (Purch Mgr)
Registration no: SC277024 **VAT No.:** GB 735 0549 37
Date established: 1999 **Turnover:** £500,000 - £1m
No.of Employees: 1 - 10 **Product Groups:** 34, 35, 36, 38, 39, 40, 43, 49, 66, 68, 85

Date of Accounts	Dec 07
Working Capital	-314
Fixed Assets	97

see next page

Springstop (UK) Ltd - *Cont'd*

Current Assets	1701
Current Liabilities	2014
Total Share Capital	633

Star Refrigeration Ltd
Thornliebank Industrial Estate Thornliebank, Glasgow, G46 8JW
Tel: 0141-638 7916 **Fax:** 0141-638 8111
E-mail: star@star-ref.co.uk
Website: http://www.star-ref.co.uk
Directors: S. Pearson (Dir)
Managers: D. Bolster, N. Silva (Personnel), J. Dixon (Buyer), A. Walkinshaw (Sales Prom Mgr), C. Wright (Tech Serv Mgr)
Immediate Holding Company: STAR REFRIGERATION LIMITED
Registration no: SC048005 **Date established:** 1970
Turnover: £20m - £50m **No.of Employees:** 251 - 500 **Product Groups:** 52

Date of Accounts	Dec 11	Dec 10	Dec 09
Sales Turnover	38m	44m	38m
Pre Tax Profit/Loss	-488	1m	825
Working Capital	3m	4m	3m
Fixed Assets	2m	2m	2m
Current Assets	12m	11m	11m
Current Liabilities	4m	4m	5m

Stevenson Aluminium Systems Ltd
Block 14 West Avenue Blantyre Industrial Estate, Blantyre, Glasgow, G72 0XE
Tel: 01698-823366 **Fax:** 01698-823946
Directors: J. Stevenson (Dir), I. Stevenson (Co Sec)
Ultimate Holding Company: ALEXANDER GATEY & CO LIMITED
Immediate Holding Company: STEVENSON ALUMINIUM SYSTEMS LIMITED
Registration no: SC096593 **Date established:** 1985
No.of Employees: 1 - 10 **Product Groups:** 26, 35

Date of Accounts	Jun 11	Jun 10	Jun 09
Working Capital	172	202	232
Fixed Assets	3	4	6
Current Assets	305	318	387

Stewart Plant Sales Ltd
Townmill Road, Glasgow, G31 3AR
Tel: 0141-554 6881 **Fax:** 0141-550 2358
E-mail: enquiries@scot-jcb.co.uk
Website: http://www.scot-jcb.co.uk
Bank(s): Barclays
Directors: D. Park (Sales), S. Barker (Fin)
Managers: R. Cameron (Personnel), E. Meachan (Buyer)
Ultimate Holding Company: SCOT JCB (HOLDINGS) LIMITED
Immediate Holding Company: STEWART PLANT SALES LIMITED
Registration no: SC034905 **VAT No.:** GB 260 6296 59
Date established: 1960 **Turnover:** £10m - £20m
No.of Employees: 21 - 50 **Product Groups:** 40, 45

Date of Accounts	Dec 11	Dec 10	Dec 09
Sales Turnover	10m	7m	6m
Pre Tax Profit/Loss	464	436	145
Working Capital	4m	3m	3m
Fixed Assets	13	19	29
Current Assets	6m	5m	4m
Current Liabilities	224	223	149

Stewart-Buchanan Gauges Ltd
Burnside Industrial Estate 7 Garrell Road Kilsyth, Glasgow, G65 9JX
Tel: 01236-821533 **Fax:** 01236-824090
E-mail: sales@stewarts-group.com
Website: http://www.stewarts-group.com
Bank(s): Clydesdale
Directors: L. Kelman (Fin), L. Kelman (Fin)
Managers: J. O'Donnell (Sales Prom Mgr), R. Baird (Tech Serv Mgr), E. Weldon (Purch Mgr)
Immediate Holding Company: STEWART-BUCHANAN GAUGES LIMITED
Registration no: SC021724 **VAT No.:** GB 552 5461 46
Date established: 1941 **Turnover:** £5m - £10m
No.of Employees: 101 - 250 **Product Groups:** 38, 40

Date of Accounts	Dec 11	Dec 10	Dec 09
Sales Turnover	7m	7m	7m
Pre Tax Profit/Loss	371	214	339
Working Capital	2m	3m	2m
Fixed Assets	2m	2m	2m
Current Assets	3m	3m	3m
Current Liabilities	612	344	489

Stirling Park LLP
24 St Enoch Square, Glasgow, G1 4DB
Tel: 0141-565 5765 **Fax:** 01463-250921
E-mail: info@stirlingpark.co.uk
Website: http://www.stirlingpark.co.uk
Managers: S. Ross (Mgr)
Immediate Holding Company: STIRLING PARK LLP
Registration no: SO300097 **Date established:** 2002 **Turnover:** £2m - £5m
No.of Employees: 1 - 10 **Product Groups:** 82

Date of Accounts	Dec 11	Dec 10	Dec 09
Sales Turnover	N/A	5m	5m
Pre Tax Profit/Loss	N/A	1m	757
Working Capital	1m	1m	997
Fixed Assets	81	97	155
Current Assets	3m	3m	2m
Current Liabilities	N/A	1m	1m

Stockline Plastics Ltd
Grovepark Mills Hopehill Road, Glasgow, G20 7NF
Tel: 0141-332 9077 **Fax:** 0141-332 9079
E-mail: sales@stockline-plastics.co.uk
Website: http://www.stockline-plastics.co.uk
Managers: S. O'brien (Sales Prom Mgr)
Ultimate Holding Company: I.C.L. PLASTICS LIMITED
Immediate Holding Company: STOCKLINE PLASTICS LIMITED
Registration no: SC054597 **Date established:** 1973
No.of Employees: 1 - 10 **Product Groups:** 30

Date of Accounts	Nov 11	Nov 10	Nov 09
Working Capital	541	508	484
Fixed Assets	N/A	1	3
Current Assets	843	817	797

Street Works Qualifications Register
Optima Building 58 Robertson Street, Glasgow, G2 8DQ
Tel: 08452-702720 **Fax:** 0141-242 2244
E-mail: customer@sqa.org.uk
Website: http://www.swqr.org.uk
Managers: L. Toher
Immediate Holding Company: SQA SOLAS LIMITED
Date established: 2011 **No.of Employees:** 21 - 50 **Product Groups:** 87

Sunvic Controls Ltd
Bellshill Road Uddingston, Glasgow, G71 6NP
Tel: 01698-812944 **Fax:** 01698-813637
E-mail: info@sunvic.co.uk
Website: http://www.sunvic.co.uk
Bank(s): Midland, Darlston
Directors: P. Samborek (Sales & Mktg), G. Laing (MD), G. Moultrie (Fin), D. Watkinson (Fin), A. Williams (Fab), D. Paulin (MD), A. Burgess (Tech Serv)
Ultimate Holding Company: TAYCLYDE LTD
Immediate Holding Company: SUNVIC CONTROLS LIMITED
Registration no: 00786405 **Date established:** 1964 **Turnover:** £5m - £10m
No.of Employees: 51 - 100 **Product Groups:** 36, 38, 49

Date of Accounts	May 11	May 10	May 09
Sales Turnover	4m	N/A	6m
Pre Tax Profit/Loss	187	N/A	30
Working Capital	555	422	354
Fixed Assets	78	70	83
Current Assets	2m	2m	2m
Current Liabilities	829	N/A	1m

Super Nova Events & Weddings
14 Fairlie Park Drive, Glasgow, G11 7SR
Tel: 0845-269 2189
E-mail: enquires@supernovaevents.co.uk
Website: http://www.supernovaevents.co.uk
Directors: R. Marshall (Prop)
Date established: 2002 **No.of Employees:** 1 - 10 **Product Groups:** 81

Date of Accounts	Dec 06	Dec 05
Sales Turnover	N/A	98
Pre Tax Profit/Loss	N/A	9
Working Capital	-8	-9
Fixed Assets	348	35
Current Assets	2	9
Current Liabilities	9	18
ROCE% (Return on Capital Employed)		35.7
ROT% (Return on Turnover)		9.4

Surface Technology plc
15-17 Colvilles Place Kelvin Industrial Estate, East Kilbride, Glasgow, G75 0PZ
Tel: 01355-248223 **Fax:** 01355-237141
E-mail: ronnie.ross@surfacetechnology.co.uk
Website: http://www.surfacetechnology.co.uk
Directors: R. Ross (MD)
Ultimate Holding Company: NORMAN HAY PLC
Immediate Holding Company: SURFACE TECHNOLOGY PLC
Registration no: 04021109 **Date established:** 2000
No.of Employees: 21 - 50 **Product Groups:** 48

Date of Accounts	Dec 11	Dec 10	Dec 09
Sales Turnover	23m	19m	15m
Pre Tax Profit/Loss	2m	1m	1m
Working Capital	7m	6m	6m
Fixed Assets	3m	3m	3m
Current Assets	17m	13m	13m
Current Liabilities	5m	3m	4m

T P L Labels Ltd
18 Singer Road Kelvin Industrial Estate, East Kilbride, Glasgow, G75 0XS
Tel: 01355-900900 **Fax:** 01355-900600
E-mail: amt@tpl-labels.com
Website: http://www.tpl-labels.com
Bank(s): Clydesdale Bank PLC
Directors: R. Taylor (Ch)
Immediate Holding Company: TPL LABELS LIMITED
Registration no: SC118695 **VAT No.:** GB 445 5483 12
Date established: 1989 **Turnover:** £2m - £5m **No.of Employees:** 21 - 50
Product Groups: 27, 28, 30, 32, 35, 37, 42, 44, 49, 67, 81

Date of Accounts	Mar 11	Mar 10	Mar 09
Working Capital	1m	1m	894
Fixed Assets	358	398	435
Current Assets	2m	1m	1m

T P S Engineering Ltd
84 Dykehead Street, Glasgow, G33 4AQ
Tel: 0141-774 6675 **Fax:** 0141-774 6677
E-mail: allan@tps-engineering.co.uk
Website: http://www.tps-engineering.co.uk
Directors: A. Manuel (MD)
Immediate Holding Company: T.P.S. ENGINEERING LIMITED
Registration no: SC214219 **Date established:** 2000
No.of Employees: 1 - 10 **Product Groups:** 35, 39, 45

Date of Accounts	Feb 11	Feb 10	Feb 09
Working Capital	-66	-103	-140
Fixed Assets	85	99	113
Current Assets	159	154	123

Tarak Manufacturing Co. Ltd
61 Hydepark Street, Glasgow, G3 8BW
Tel: 0141-569 1544 **Fax:** 0141-569 1545
E-mail: info@kidsclothing.co.uk
Website: http://www.kidsclothing.co.uk
Directors: S. Ramzan (Fin), T. Ramsan (MD)
Managers: K. Ramzan (Sales Prom Mgr), P. Wynne (Admin Off)
Immediate Holding Company: TARAK MANUFACTURING COMPANY LIMITED
Registration no: SC051132 **VAT No.:** GB 388 9934 65
Date established: 1972 **Turnover:** Up to £250,000
No.of Employees: 51 - 100 **Product Groups:** 63

Date of Accounts	Mar 11	Mar 10	Nov 08
Working Capital	158	182	251
Fixed Assets	3m	3m	2m
Current Assets	285	289	525

Taylor Clarke Partnership Ltd
4 Fitzroy Place, Glasgow, G3 7RH
Tel: 0141-221 1707 **Fax:** 0141-221 6266
E-mail: info@taylorclarke.co.uk
Website: http://www.taylorclarke.co.uk
Bank(s): Royal Bank of Scotland
Directors: L. Clarke (MD)
Immediate Holding Company: THE TAYLOR CLARKE PARTNERSHIP LIMITED
Registration no: SC135704 **Date established:** 1991 **Turnover:** £1m - £2m
No.of Employees: 11 - 20 **Product Groups:** 80

Date of Accounts	Dec 11	Dec 10	Dec 09
Sales Turnover	N/A	N/A	2m
Pre Tax Profit/Loss	N/A	N/A	29
Working Capital	392	406	419
Fixed Assets	41	51	56
Current Assets	541	590	654
Current Liabilities	N/A	N/A	139

Taylor H M G Ltd
19 Elm Road Rutherglen, Glasgow, G73 4JR
Tel: 0141-634 7080 **Fax:** 0141-631 3861
Directors: D. Taylor (Fin)
Immediate Holding Company: TAYLOR HMG SCOTLAND LIMITED
Registration no: SC080376 **Date established:** 1982
No.of Employees: 1 - 10 **Product Groups:** 46, 48

Date of Accounts	Dec 11	Dec 10	Dec 09
Working Capital	20	19	16
Fixed Assets	1	1	1
Current Assets	176	133	88

R D Taylor & Co. Ltd
240 Edmiston Drive, Glasgow, G51 2YU
Tel: 0141-427 5103 **Fax:** 0141-427 1881
E-mail: sales@rdtaylor.co.uk
Website: http://www.rdtaylor.co.uk
Bank(s): Barclays Bank PLC
Directors: A. Drummond (MD), D. Callaghan (Dir)
Managers: C. Wilson (Purch Mgr)
Ultimate Holding Company: UMECO LIMITED
Immediate Holding Company: R.D. TAYLOR & COMPANY LIMITED
Registration no: SC050238 **Date established:** 1972
Turnover: £5m - £10m **No.of Employees:** 21 - 50 **Product Groups:** 31, 32, 36, 42

Date of Accounts	Dec 11	Dec 10	Dec 09
Sales Turnover	9m	9m	10m
Pre Tax Profit/Loss	1m	335	621
Working Capital	4m	3m	2m
Fixed Assets	112	169	225
Current Assets	5m	5m	5m
Current Liabilities	471	607	522

Taylor Scotland Ltd
14 Westgarth Place East Kilbride, Glasgow, G74 5NT
Tel: 01355-236422 **Fax:** 01355-264790
E-mail: taylorscotland@inbox.com
Website: http://www.taylor-company.co.uk
Managers: G. Hughes (Chief Mgr)
Immediate Holding Company: TAYLOR SCOTLAND LIMITED
Registration no: SC420202 **Date established:** 2012
No.of Employees: 1 - 10 **Product Groups:** 41

Teledyne Control
9-13 Napier Road Wardpark North, Cumbernauld, Glasgow, G68 0EF
Tel: 01236-458555 **Fax:** 01236-780651
E-mail: hbarnshaw@teledyne.com
Website: http://www.teledyne.com
Managers: H. Barnshaw (Mgr)
No.of Employees: 21 - 50 **Product Groups:** 37, 38

Tennent Caledonian Breweries Ltd
Wellpark Brewery 161 Duke Street, Glasgow, G31 1JD
Tel: 0141-552 6552 **Fax:** 0141-559 2366
Website: http://www.tennents.com
Bank(s): Royal Bank of Scotland
Directors: J. Hayrman (Prop)
Immediate Holding Company: TENNENT CALEDONIAN BREWERIES UK LIMITED
Registration no: SC362352 **VAT No.:** GB 232 1538 95
Date established: 2009 **No.of Employees:** 101 - 250 **Product Groups:** 21

Date of Accounts	Feb 11	Feb 10
Sales Turnover	171m	97m
Pre Tax Profit/Loss	3m	1m
Working Capital	32m	33m
Fixed Assets	75m	74m
Current Assets	71m	78m
Current Liabilities	25m	45m

The Grinding Centre Ltd
8 Erskine Square Hillington Park, Glasgow, G52 4BJ
Tel: 0141-564 8888 **Fax:** 0141-564 1084
E-mail: sales@grindingcentre.co.uk
Website: http://www.grindingcentre.co.uk
Directors: C. Caldwell (MD)
Immediate Holding Company: THE GRINDING CENTRE LIMITED
Registration no: SC352272 **Date established:** 2008
Turnover: £250,000 - £500,000 **No.of Employees:** 1 - 10
Product Groups: 33

Date of Accounts	Dec 09	Mar 11
Sales Turnover	326	N/A
Pre Tax Profit/Loss	31	N/A
Working Capital	-136	-150
Fixed Assets	160	167
Current Assets	149	182
Current Liabilities	18	N/A

Thistle Bearings & Engineering Products Ltd
38 Singer Road Kelvin Industrial Estate, East Kilbride, Glasgow, G75 0XS
Tel: 01355-225491 **Fax:** 01355-242502
E-mail: George@thistlebearings.co.uk
Website: http://www.thistlebearings.com
Directors: G. Foggo (Dir)
Immediate Holding Company: THISTLE BEARINGS AND ENGINEERING PRODUCTS LIMITED
Registration no: SC075852 **VAT No.:** GB 361 3165 75
Date established: 1981 **Turnover:** £500,000 - £1m
No.of Employees: 1 - 10 **Product Groups:** 35, 66

Date of Accounts	Aug 11	Aug 10	Aug 09
Working Capital	23	28	33
Fixed Assets	94	98	69
Current Assets	240	206	197

Thistle Generators Ltd
Faraday House Coalburn Road Fallside, Bothwell, Glasgow, G71 8DA
Tel: 01698-814888 **Fax:** 01698-802592
E-mail: mailroom@thistlegenerators.com
Website: http://www.thistlegenerators.com
Directors: K. Berrie (Tech Serv), N. Feeney (Sales), P. Moore (Sales), D. Feeney (MD)
Immediate Holding Company: TG REALISATIONS LIMITED
Registration no: SC045557 **VAT No.:** GB 260 2957 61
Date established: 1968 **Turnover:** £5m - £10m **No.of Employees:** 21 - 50
Product Groups: 37, 52

Date of Accounts	Dec 07	Dec 06	Dec 05
Working Capital	183	37	311
Fixed Assets	249	327	288
Current Assets	2639	1720	1561
Current Liabilities	2455	1683	1250
Total Share Capital	45	45	45

Tri Pac Logistics

Unit 7 Block C Nurseries Road, Baillieston, Glasgow, G69 6UL
Tel: 0141-773 2942 **Fax:** 0141-773 2507
E-mail: enquiries@tripaclogistics.co.uk
Website: http://www.tripaclogistics.co.uk
Directors: D. Sullivan (Dir), J. Mckellar (Dir), J. McKellor (MD)
Managers: D. Sutherland (Sales Admin)
Date established: 2002 **Turnover:** £250,000 - £500,000
No.of Employees: 1 - 10 **Product Groups:** 27, 30, 35, 66

Trimite Scotland Ltd

38 Welbeck Road, Glasgow, G53 7RG
Tel: 0141-881 9595 **Fax:** 0141-881 9333
E-mail: sales@tslpaints.com
Website: http://www.trimite.co.uk
Managers: D. Robotham (Mgr)
Immediate Holding Company: TRIMITE SCOTLAND LIMITED
Registration no: SC114154 **VAT No.:** GB 222 5827 75
Date established: 1988 **No.of Employees:** 1 - 10 **Product Groups:** 31, 32

Date of Accounts	Oct 11	Oct 10	Oct 09
Working Capital	120	46	25
Fixed Assets	69	61	61
Current Assets	289	237	299
Current Liabilities	13	N/A	N/A

Triogen Ltd

117 Barfillan Drive, Glasgow, G52 1BD
Tel: 0141-810 4861 **Fax:** 0141-810 5561
E-mail: sales@triogen.com
Website: http://www.triogen.com
Directors: A. Arafa (Sales & Mktg), J. Wheatley (MD)
Managers: A. Crawford (Export Sales Mg), P. Castle (Product), T. Kelly (Prod Mgr)
Ultimate Holding Company: SUEZ SA (FRANCE)
Immediate Holding Company: TRIOGEN LIMITED
Registration no: SC120472 **Date established:** 1989 **Turnover:** £2m - £5m
No.of Employees: 21 - 50 **Product Groups:** 31, 32, 37, 38, 39, 41, 42, 67, 89

Tripack Solutions Ltd

37 Block 5 Third Road Blantyre Industrial Estate, Blantyre, Glasgow, G72 0UP
Tel: 01698-712800 **Fax:** 01698-712801
E-mail: enquiries@tripackscotland.co.uk
Website: http://www.pallet.co.uk
Bank(s): Clydesdale Bank PLC
Directors: D. McCallister (MD), M. Lawlor (Dir), M. Robson (Sales), N. Scott (Co Sec), N. Scott (Fin)
Managers: D. McAllister (Chief Mgr), N. Lawlor (I.T. Exec)
Ultimate Holding Company: Lochford Ltd
Immediate Holding Company: TRIPACK SOLUTIONS LIMITED
Registration no: SC215872 **VAT No.:** GB 263 3702 71
Date established: 2001 **Turnover:** £2m - £5m **No.of Employees:** 51 - 100
Product Groups: 25, 27

Date of Accounts	Mar 08	Mar 07	Mar 06
Sales Turnover	4371	4601	N/A
Pre Tax Profit/Loss	126	88	N/A
Working Capital	616	528	446
Fixed Assets	57	63	99
Current Assets	2223	1562	1160
Current Liabilities	1607	1034	714
Total Share Capital	30	30	30
ROCE% (Return on Capital Employed)	18.8	15.0	
ROT% (Return on Turnover)	2.9	1.9	

Tube Development

Queenzieburn Industrial Estate Kilsyth, Glasgow, G65 9BN
Tel: 01236-823551 **Fax:** 01236-825660
E-mail: info@tubedev.com
Website: http://www.tubedev.com
Bank(s): Bank of Scotland
Directors: I. Fraser (MD), D. Kay (Fin)
Managers: C. Donelly (Purch Mgr), G. Ure (Tech Serv Mgr)
Immediate Holding Company: TUBE DEVELOPMENTS LIMITED
Registration no: SC042597 **VAT No.:** GB 260 6356 67
Date established: 1965 **Turnover:** £20m - £50m
No.of Employees: 21 - 50 **Product Groups:** 34, 35, 36

Date of Accounts	Sep 11	Sep 10	Sep 09
Sales Turnover	27m	20m	29m
Pre Tax Profit/Loss	3m	3m	3m
Working Capital	21m	18m	16m
Fixed Assets	3m	3m	3m
Current Assets	31m	25m	23m
Current Liabilities	1m	2m	2m

Tubular Scaffolding Ltd

1081 Duke Street, Glasgow, G31 5NX
Tel: 0141-554 3801 **Fax:** 0141-554 3801
Directors: B. Cole-Hamilton (MD), B. Cole Hamilton (Co Sec), B. Cole-Hamilton (Dir), N. Scargill (Dir), R. Booth (MD)
Immediate Holding Company: TUBULAR SCAFFOLDING LIMITED
Registration no: SC017003 **VAT No.:** GB 260 3032 11
Date established: 1932 **Turnover:** £500,000 - £1m
No.of Employees: 1 - 10 **Product Groups:** 52

Date of Accounts	Nov 08	Oct 07	Oct 06
Working Capital	-12	87	80
Fixed Assets	34	51	65
Current Assets	71	143	137
Current Liabilities	83	57	58
Total Share Capital	38	38	38

Tufnol Composites Ltd (Machining and Stockholding)

3 James Watt Place East Kilbride, Glasgow, G74 5HQ
Tel: 01355-233876 **Fax:** 01355-264573
E-mail: info@tufnol.co.uk
Website: http://www.tufnol.co.uk
Managers: L. Hunter (Mgr)
Immediate Holding Company: TUFNOL COMPOSITES LIMITED
Registration no: 05261357 **Date established:** 2004
Turnover: £500,000 - £1m **No.of Employees:** 1 - 10 **Product Groups:** 23, 27, 30, 31, 33, 35, 37

Date of Accounts	Oct 11	Oct 10	Oct 09
Working Capital	137	69	337
Fixed Assets	473	321	146
Current Assets	2m	2m	2m

Thomas Tunnocks Ltd

34 Old Mill Road Uddingston, Glasgow, G71 7HH
Tel: 01698-813551 **Fax:** 01698-815691
E-mail: sales@tunnock.co.uk
Website: http://www.tunnock.co.uk
Bank(s): Bank of Scotland
Directors: B. Reidford (Co Sec), K. Loudon (Pers)
Managers: W. Henderson (Tech Serv Mgr)
Immediate Holding Company: THOMAS TUNNOCK LIMITED
Registration no: SC028747 **Date established:** 1952
Turnover: £20m - £50m **No.of Employees:** 501 - 1000
Product Groups: 20

Date of Accounts	Feb 11	Feb 10	Feb 09
Sales Turnover	33m	35m	36m
Pre Tax Profit/Loss	3m	1m	1m
Working Capital	12m	11m	14m
Fixed Assets	16m	15m	12m
Current Assets	17m	14m	17m
Current Liabilities	3m	2m	2m

Turner Aviation Ltd

Spiersbridge Terrace Thornliebank, Glasgow, G46 8JQ
Tel: 0141-638 2265 **Fax:** 0141-638 9694
E-mail: info@turner-aviation.co.uk
Website: http://www.turner-aviation.co.uk
Bank(s): The Royal Bank of Scotland
Directors: I. Brown (Fin), G. Turner (MD)
Managers: D. Underwood (Sales Prom Mgr)
Ultimate Holding Company: TURNER & CO. (GLASGOW) LIMITED.
Immediate Holding Company: TURNER AVIATION LIMITED
Registration no: SC044355 **VAT No.:** GB 261 0269 86
Date established: 1967 **Turnover:** £5m - £10m
No.of Employees: 51 - 100 **Product Groups:** 39

Date of Accounts	Mar 08	Mar 09	Mar 10
Sales Turnover	6m	7m	7m
Pre Tax Profit/Loss	173	1m	846
Working Capital	3m	4m	4m
Fixed Assets	421	326	237
Current Assets	4m	6m	6m
Current Liabilities	381	869	655

Turner Hire Drive Ltd

65 Craigton Road, Glasgow, G51 3EQ
Tel: 0141-440 1900 **Fax:** 0141-307 1213
E-mail: glasgow@turner-hiredrive.co.uk
Website: http://www.turner-hiredrive.co.uk
Directors: M. Park (Fin), M. Clark (Fin)
Managers: M. Millard (Mktg Serv Mgr)
Ultimate Holding Company: TURNER & CO. (GLASGOW) LIMITED.
Immediate Holding Company: TURNER HIRE DRIVE LIMITED
Registration no: SC092995 **Date established:** 1985
Turnover: £5m - £10m **No.of Employees:** 51 - 100 **Product Groups:** 52, 72, 82

Date of Accounts	Mar 08	Mar 09	Mar 10
Sales Turnover	11m	10m	8m
Pre Tax Profit/Loss	769	-66	-183
Working Capital	-5m	4m	2m
Fixed Assets	16m	14m	11m
Current Assets	5m	6m	3m
Current Liabilities	563	662	229

UK Recon

3 Salkeld Street, Glasgow, G5 8HE
Tel: 0141-429 7338 **Fax:** 0141-429 7338
E-mail: info@cylinderheadsglasgow.co.uk
Website: http://www.cylinderheadsglasgow.co.uk
Directors: D. Brown (Prop)
No.of Employees: 1 - 10 **Product Groups:** 39, 40, 48, 68

U P V C Door Company

Unit 2 Block 1 Rosendale Way Blantyre, Glasgow, G72 0NJ
Tel: 08701-121652 **Fax:** 01698-826125
E-mail: finance@upvccompany.co.uk
Website: http://www.upvcdoorcompany.co.uk
Directors: J. Mcgill (Prop)
Immediate Holding Company: SCOT INDUSTRIAL PRODUCTS LIMITED
Registration no: SC347665 **Date established:** 2002
No.of Employees: 1 - 10 **Product Groups:** 26, 35

Date of Accounts	Mar 11	Mar 10	Mar 09
Working Capital	-55	-30	-21
Fixed Assets	286	61	55
Current Assets	377	272	358

UBC Central Ltd

Gainsborough House 151 West George Street, Glasgow, G2 2JJ
Tel: 0141-228 6307 **Fax:** 0141-228 6001
Website: http://www.ubcltd.co.uk
Directors: P. Lightfoot (Chief Op Offcr), P. Orvis (Dir), T. Carlisle (MD)
Managers: A. Prescott (Mktg Serv Mgr)
Immediate Holding Company: Interbulk Group plc
Registration no: SC336170 **VAT No.:** GB 551 7194 39
Date established: 1982 **Turnover:** £75m - £125m
No.of Employees: 101 - 250 **Product Groups:** 30, 45

Date of Accounts	Mar 09	Mar 08	Mar 07
Working Capital	N/A	20	N/A
Current Assets	N/A	20	N/A

UK Cables Ltd

Unit 2 Buchanan Business Park 138 Cumbernauld Road, Stepps, Glasgow, G33 6HZ
Tel: 0141-779 7804 **Fax:** 0141-779 7801
E-mail: glasgow.610@ukcables.co.uk
Website: http://www.ukcables.co.uk
Managers: B. Corner (Mgr)
Ultimate Holding Company: NEWBURY INVESTMENTS BV (NETHERLANDS)
Immediate Holding Company: UK CABLES LIMITED
Registration no: 02832874 **VAT No.:** GB 614 8056 48
Date established: 1993 **No.of Employees:** 1 - 10 **Product Groups:** 67

Date of Accounts	Dec 11	Dec 10	Dec 09
Sales Turnover	55m	47m	33m
Pre Tax Profit/Loss	2m	3m	-384
Working Capital	11m	9m	7m
Fixed Assets	288	412	449
Current Assets	29m	22m	16m
Current Liabilities	2m	2m	1m

UK Safety Signs

2318 Dumbarton Road, Glasgow, G14 ONL
Tel: 0141-954 2307 **Fax:** 0141-954 5365
E-mail: office@doubleimage.co.uk
Website: http://www.doubleimage.co.uk/safetysi.html
Directors: G. Hanlon (Dir)
Managers: S. Brown (Consultant)
Registration no: 00304762 **Date established:** 1984
Turnover: £500,000 - £1m **No.of Employees:** 1 - 10 **Product Groups:** 28, 40

United Wholesale Grocers Ltd

246 Flemington Street, Glasgow, G21 4BY
Tel: 0141-557 2255 **Fax:** 0141-557 2220
E-mail: info@uwgl.co.uk
Website: http://www.uwgl.co.uk
Bank(s): Natwest
Directors: M. Ramzan (MD), N. Ramzan (Dir), K. Javed (Co Sec)
Managers: P. Collins (Mgr), W. Badar
Ultimate Holding Company: UNITED HOLDINGS UK LTD.
Immediate Holding Company: UNITED WHOLESALE GROCERS LIMITED
Registration no: SC080027 **VAT No.:** GB 309 0406 88
Date established: 1982 **Turnover:** £75m - £125m
No.of Employees: 101 - 250 **Product Groups:** 61

Date of Accounts	Dec 11	Dec 10	Dec 09
Sales Turnover	125m	113m	95m
Pre Tax Profit/Loss	1m	1m	702
Working Capital	2m	2m	846
Fixed Assets	5m	5m	5m
Current Assets	19m	16m	15m
Current Liabilities	1m	829	435

Valmar Sideloaders Ltd

17 Springburn Place East Kilbride, Glasgow, G74 5NU
Tel: 01355-264333 **Fax:** 01355-263587
E-mail: sales@valmarhandling.co.uk
Website: http://www.valmarhandling.co.uk
Directors: A. Park (Fin)
Managers: C. Park (Develop Mgr)
Ultimate Holding Company: VALMAR HANDLING HOLDINGS LIMITED
Immediate Holding Company: VALMAR SIDELOADERS LIMITED
Registration no: SC335849 **Date established:** 2008
No.of Employees: 11 - 20 **Product Groups:** 35, 39, 45

Date of Accounts	Mar 11	Mar 10	Jan 09
Working Capital	29	-49	N/A
Fixed Assets	208	85	N/A
Current Assets	332	25	N/A

Valve Components Ltd

Block 1 5 Kelvin Park South, East Kilbride, Glasgow, G75 0RH
Tel: 01355-263884 **Fax:** 01355-245146
E-mail: info@vcl.uk.com
Website: http://www.vcl.uk.com
Bank(s): Bank of Scotland
Directors: R. Whitecross (Tech Serv), D. Church (Fin)
Managers: S. Moffatt (Sales & Mktg Mg), M. Diciecce (Personnel), B. Linskey (Tech Serv Mgr)
Ultimate Holding Company: GLENALMOND GROUP LIMITED
Immediate Holding Company: VALVE COMPONENTS LIMITED
Registration no: SC102241 **VAT No.:** GB 481 4484 32
Date established: 1986 **Turnover:** £20m - £50m
No.of Employees: 101 - 250 **Product Groups:** 38

Date of Accounts	Mar 11	Mar 10	Mar 09
Sales Turnover	22m	18m	23m
Pre Tax Profit/Loss	2m	963	2m
Working Capital	5m	4m	3m
Fixed Assets	3m	3m	3m
Current Assets	13m	10m	11m
Current Liabilities	1m	1m	2m

Ventrac Sheet Metal Ltd

20 Nimmo Drive, Glasgow, G51 3SX
Tel: 0141-445 3040 **Fax:** 0141-425 1550
E-mail: john@ventrac.co.uk
Website: http://www.ventrac.co.uk
Directors: A. McCartney (MD)
Managers: S. Dick (Fin Mgr)
Immediate Holding Company: VENTRAC SHEET METAL LIMITED
Registration no: SC073161 **VAT No.:** GB 261 2486 68
Date established: 1980 **Turnover:** £500,000 - £1m
No.of Employees: 11 - 20 **Product Groups:** 36, 40

Date of Accounts	Mar 12	Mar 11	Mar 10
Working Capital	89	108	49
Fixed Assets	227	208	229
Current Assets	508	736	556

Verve Ltd

29 Dalmarnock Road Rutherglen, Glasgow, G73 1BL
Tel: 0141-647 0511 **Fax:** 0141-613 1712
E-mail: enquiries@verveltd.net
Website: http://www.arnoldclark.com
Directors: A. Colthart (Fin)
Managers: K. Scott (Mktg Serv Mgr), F. Dixon (Sales Prom Mgr), D. Ewart (Chief Mgr), P. McKeown (Tech Serv Mgr)
Ultimate Holding Company: THE VERVE LIMITED
Immediate Holding Company: VERVE FLEET MANAGEMENT LIMITED
Registration no: 03509308 **VAT No.:** GB 717 2635 36
Date established: 2004 **Turnover:** £75m - £125m
No.of Employees: 51 - 100 **Product Groups:** 39, 68

Vicarey Davidson & Company

30a Cumberland Street, Glasgow, G5 9QJ
Tel: 0141-420 1778 **Fax:** 0141-429 3273
E-mail: sales@vicareydavidson.com
Website: http://www.vicareydavidson.com
Directors: G. Livingstone (Prop)
Turnover: £500,000 - £1m **No.of Employees:** 1 - 10 **Product Groups:** 24, 27, 29, 30, 31, 32, 33, 36, 38, 49, 67

Vipond Fire Protection Ltd

10 Glenfield Road Kelvin Industrial Estate, East Kilbride, Glasgow, G75 0RA
Tel: 01355-237525 **Fax:** 01355-263399
E-mail: christine.taylor@vipondltd.co.uk
Website: http://www.vipondfire.co.uk
Bank(s): Midland Bank, Glasgow

see next page

***Vipond Fire Protection Ltd** - Cont'd*

Directors: W. Beadie (Co Sec), C. Taylor (Co Sec)
Managers: R. Macdonald (Purch Mgr)
Ultimate Holding Company: API GROUP INC (USA)
Immediate Holding Company: VIPOND FIRE PROTECTION LIMITED
Registration no: SC057058 **VAT No.:** 262 3264 75 **Date established:** 1975
Turnover: £5m - £10m **No.of Employees:** 51 - 100 **Product Groups:** 40, 52

Date of Accounts	Dec 11	Dec 10	Dec 09
Sales Turnover	9m	8m	8m
Pre Tax Profit/Loss	-116	92	465
Working Capital	2m	2m	2m
Fixed Assets	510	379	367
Current Assets	3m	3m	3m
Current Liabilities	488	383	707

W B Alloy Welding Products

37 Dalsetter Avenue, Glasgow, G15 8TE
Tel: 0141-940 4730 **Fax:** 0141-944 9000
E-mail: gerry-lipton@pctgroup.co.uk
Website: http://www.wballoys.co.uk
Directors: N. Ward (Sales)
Managers: P. Houston
Ultimate Holding Company: OAKENASH GROUP LIMITED
Immediate Holding Company: WB ALLOY WELDING PRODUCTS LIMITED
Registration no: SC184781 **Date established:** 1998 **Turnover:** £2m - £5m
No.of Employees: 11 - 20 **Product Groups:** 34, 35, 38

Date of Accounts	Dec 10	Dec 09	Dec 08
Sales Turnover	4m	3m	3m
Pre Tax Profit/Loss	157	27	21
Working Capital	795	694	559
Fixed Assets	27	15	13
Current Assets	3m	2m	2m
Current Liabilities	226	269	192

W S Diesel

Glenhead Road Kirkintilloch, Glasgow, G66 5EX
Tel: 0141-775 0613 **Fax:** 0141-777 8558
E-mail: info@wsdiesel.com
Website: http://www.wsdiesel.com
Directors: W. Sim (Prop)
Immediate Holding Company: W.S.DIESEL LIMITED
Registration no: SC064069 **Date established:** 1978
No.of Employees: 11 - 20 **Product Groups:** 35, 36, 39

Date of Accounts	Jan 11	Jan 10	Jan 09
Working Capital	61	87	129
Fixed Assets	24	33	43
Current Assets	120	148	186

Walker Woodstock

16 Albert Drive, Glasgow, G41 2PE
Tel: 0141-422 1500 **Fax:** 0141-423 0035
E-mail: stephenburt@walkerwoodstock.co.uk
Website: http://www.walkertimber.com
Bank(s): Royal Bank of Scotland
Managers: S. Burt (Mgr)
Registration no: SC046290 **VAT No.:** GB 268 8595 88
Turnover: £1m - £2m **No.of Employees:** 11 - 20 **Product Groups:** 66, 76

Waterline Ltd

Jenna House 6 Mollins Court, Cumbernauld, Glasgow, G68 9HP
Tel: 0870-556 1560 **Fax:** 01236- 453868
E-mail: lyn.beveridge@waterline.co.uk
Website: http://www.waterline.co.uk
Managers: L. Beveridge (Mgr)
Ultimate Holding Company: WATERLINE GROUP PLC
Immediate Holding Company: WATERLINE LIMITED
Registration no: 00428931 **VAT No.:** GB 229 8275 31
Date established: 1947 **Turnover:** £1m - £2m **No.of Employees:** 1 - 10
Product Groups: 26

Date of Accounts	Mar 11	Mar 10	Mar 09
Sales Turnover	46m	38m	47m
Pre Tax Profit/Loss	896	-1m	-3m
Working Capital	-4m	-5m	-5m
Fixed Assets	9m	11m	12m
Current Assets	14m	12m	10m
Current Liabilities	5m	6m	7m

Gavin Watson Ltd

79-109 Glasgow Road, Blantyre, Glasgow, G72 0LY
Tel: 01698-826000 **Fax:** 0141-336 3698
E-mail: sales@gavinwatson.co.uk
Website: http://www.gavinwatson.co.uk
Directors: S. Cumming (Fin), C. Lindsay (Develop), I. Johnstone (Dir)
Managers: F. Donald (Personnel), G. Grimason (Purch Mgr)
Ultimate Holding Company: THE GT4 GROUP LIMITED
Immediate Holding Company: GAVIN WATSON LIMITED
Registration no: SC023460 **VAT No.:** GB 260 3054 01
Date established: 1945 **Turnover:** £2m - £5m **No.of Employees:** 21 - 50
Product Groups: 28

Date of Accounts	Apr 11	Apr 10	Apr 08
Working Capital	-205	-350	63
Fixed Assets	3m	3m	1m
Current Assets	3m	2m	1m

Watts Group plc

176 Bath Street, Glasgow, G2 4HG
Tel: 0141-353 2211 **Fax:** 0141-353 2277
E-mail: glasgow@watts-int.com
Website: http://www.watts.co.uk
Directors: A. Gear (Dir)
Immediate Holding Company: WATTS GROUP PLC
Registration no: 05728557 **VAT No.:** GB 205 9609 61
Date established: 2006 **Turnover:** £250,000 - £500,000
No.of Employees: 1 - 10 **Product Groups:** 80, 84

Date of Accounts	Apr 11	Apr 10	Apr 12
Sales Turnover	14m	15m	13m
Pre Tax Profit/Loss	-581	-2m	967
Working Capital	-440	9	87
Fixed Assets	268	375	204
Current Assets	5m	6m	4m
Current Liabilities	2m	2m	2m

Waverley Bakery Ltd

Drumhead Road Glasgow East Investment Park, Glasgow, G32 8EX
Tel: 0141-641 0203 **Fax:** 0141-641 0608
E-mail: info@waverleybakery.co.uk
Website: http://www.leesofscotland.co.uk
Directors: N. Miller (MD), D. Simson (Fin), R. Murray (Fin)
Ultimate Holding Company: LEES FOODS LIMITED
Immediate Holding Company: THE WAVERLEY BAKERY LIMITED
Registration no: SC195092 **Date established:** 1999 **Turnover:** £2m - £5m
No.of Employees: 51 - 100 **Product Groups:** 20, 40, 41

Date of Accounts	Dec 11	Dec 10	Dec 09
Sales Turnover	4m	3m	3m
Pre Tax Profit/Loss	71	131	96
Working Capital	105	91	46
Fixed Assets	302	338	330
Current Assets	2m	2m	1m
Current Liabilities	120	149	152

Weatherproofing Advisors Ltd

Advisor House Block 13 West Avenue Blantyre, Glasgow, G72 0UZ
Tel: 01698-826928 **Fax:** 01698-824616
E-mail: john.kelly@weatherproofing.co.uk
Website: http://www.weatherproofing.co.uk
Directors: J. Kelly (Ch)
Managers: C. Henderson (Chief Acct)
Immediate Holding Company: WEATHERPROOFING ADVISORS LIMITED
Registration no: SC103301 **Date established:** 1987
Turnover: £5m - £10m **No.of Employees:** 21 - 50 **Product Groups:** 52

Date of Accounts	Mar 12	Mar 11	Mar 10
Sales Turnover	9m	8m	11m
Pre Tax Profit/Loss	-200	-282	610
Working Capital	2m	2m	2m
Fixed Assets	330	310	395
Current Assets	3m	3m	4m
Current Liabilities	462	415	771

Weber Shandwick Design

9 Lynedoch Crescent, Glasgow, G3 6EQ
Tel: 0141-333 0445 **Fax:** 0141-333 9909
E-mail: glasgow@webershandwick.co.uk
Website: http://www.shandwickdesign.com
Directors: K. Greene (Fin)
Managers: T. Jones
Ultimate Holding Company: INTERPUBLIC GROUP OF COMPANIES INC (USA)
Immediate Holding Company: CMGRP UK LIMITED
Registration no: SC088389 **VAT No.:** GB 402 95678 48
Date established: 1984 **Turnover:** £2m - £5m **No.of Employees:** 1 - 10
Product Groups: 81

Date of Accounts	Dec 04	Dec 03
Working Capital	950	950
Current Assets	950	950
Total Share Capital	5	5

Weir Group Senior Executives Pension Trust Ltd

Clydesdale Bank Exchange Building 20 Waterloo Street, Glasgow, G2 6DB
Tel: 0141-637 7111 **Fax:** 0141-221 9789
E-mail: pr@weir.co.uk
Website: http://www.weir.co.uk
Directors: M. Dearden (Dir), M. Salway (Grp Chief Exec), O. Turner (MD), A. Mitchelson (Dir)
Immediate Holding Company: WEIR GROUP SENIOR EXECUTIVES PENSION TRUST LIMITED (THE)
Registration no: SC060549 **VAT No.:** GB 259 6944 03
Date established: 1976 **Turnover:** Over £1,000m **No.of Employees:** 1 - 10
Product Groups: 40, 42, 45, 48, 67, 85

Weld-Tec Industrial Services Ltd

Unit 1 Block 2 Tollcross Industrial Estate, Glasgow, G32 8LT
Tel: 0141-763 1211
E-mail: welding-tec@btconnect.com
Website: http://www.weld-tec.co.uk
Directors: S. Hay (MD)
Immediate Holding Company: WELD-TEC INDUSTRIAL SERVICES LIMITED
Registration no: SC164741 **Date established:** 1996
No.of Employees: 1 - 10 **Product Groups:** 46

Date of Accounts	Mar 11	Mar 10	Mar 09
Working Capital	44	38	61
Fixed Assets	1	2	3
Current Assets	235	197	236

West Coast Controls Ltd

10-14 Crossveggate Milngavie, Glasgow, G62 6RA
Tel: 0141-956 4327 **Fax:** 0141-956 6639
E-mail: wccn@btconnect.com
Website: http://www.westcoastcontrols.co.uk
Bank(s): The Royal Bank of Scotland
Directors: G. Mccomb (Dir)
Immediate Holding Company: WEST COAST CONTROLS LIMITED
Registration no: SC120849 **VAT No.:** GB 552 2551 60
Date established: 1989 **Turnover:** £2m - £5m **No.of Employees:** 21 - 50
Product Groups: 37, 38

Date of Accounts	May 11	May 10	May 09
Working Capital	1m	1m	806
Fixed Assets	99	103	141
Current Assets	2m	2m	2m

Westfield Caledonian Ltd

4 Mollins Court Cumbernauld, Glasgow, G68 9HP
Tel: 01236-786300 **Fax:** 01236-786301
E-mail: johnbryson@west-cal.co.uk
Website: http://www.west-cal.co.uk
Bank(s): Royal Bank Scotland
Directors: J. Bryson (MD)
Immediate Holding Company: WESTFIELD CALEDONIAN LIMITED
Registration no: SC199151 **Date established:** 1999
Turnover: £250,000 - £500,000 **No.of Employees:** 11 - 20
Product Groups: 80

Date of Accounts	Mar 11	Mar 10	Mar 09
Working Capital	-7	-34	-29
Fixed Assets	88	56	47
Current Assets	175	152	117

William Bain Fencing Ltd

Lochrin Works 7 Limekilns Road, Cumbernauld, Glasgow, G67 2RN
Tel: 01236-457333 **Fax:** 01236-451166
E-mail: ikerr@lochrin-bain.co.uk
Website: http://www.lochrin-bain.co.uk
Bank(s): Bank of Scotland
Directors: I. Kerr (MD), S. Kerr (Fin)
Managers: A. McLean (Sales Prom)
Ultimate Holding Company: HW MARTIN HOLDINGS LIMITED
Immediate Holding Company: WILLIAM BAIN FENCING LIMITED
Registration no: SC181830 **VAT No.:** GB 556 5342 30
Date established: 1997 **Turnover:** £2m - £5m **No.of Employees:** 11 - 20
Product Groups: 35, 49

Date of Accounts	Oct 09	Oct 08	Jul 11
Sales Turnover	N/A	N/A	2m
Pre Tax Profit/Loss	N/A	N/A	50
Working Capital	258	153	-58
Fixed Assets	584	617	516
Current Assets	786	913	2m
Current Liabilities	N/A	N/A	37

William Walker & Co.

4-12 Rockbank Street, Glasgow, G40 2UY
Tel: 0141-554 7011 **Fax:** 0141-554 9273
E-mail: dtwalker@williamwalker.co.uk
Website: http://www.williamwalker.co.uk
Directors: D. Walker (Prop)
No.of Employees: 1 - 10 **Product Groups:** 46, 48

Wise Property Care

8 Muriel Street Barrhead, Glasgow, G78 1QB
Tel: 0141-848 9922 **Fax:** 0141-876 0301
E-mail: andy.ferguson@wisepropertycare.com
Website: http://www.wisepropertycare.com
Managers: A. Ferguson (Mktg Serv Mgr), P. Ross (Mgr)
Immediate Holding Company: WISE PROPERTY CARE LTD.
Registration no: SC168153 **Date established:** 1996 **Turnover:** £2m - £5m
No.of Employees: 21 - 50 **Product Groups:** 32

Date of Accounts	Sep 11	Sep 10	Sep 09
Sales Turnover	5m	5m	N/A
Pre Tax Profit/Loss	423	723	N/A
Working Capital	2m	2m	1m
Fixed Assets	233	215	256
Current Assets	3m	3m	2m
Current Liabilities	439	568	N/A

Wood Group Hit Field Services

6 Grayshill Road Cumbernauld, Glasgow, G68 9HQ
Tel: 01236-868180 **Fax:** 01236-458872
E-mail: recruitmenthit@woodgroup.com
Website: http://www.wghit.com
Managers: R. Bradley (Parts Mgr), J. Marmion, G. Nepier (Personnel), B. Gibson (Fin Mgr)
Registration no: 00149291 **No.of Employees:** 51 - 100
Product Groups: 35, 36, 39

Woolgar Hunter

100 West Regent Street, Glasgow, G2 2QD
Tel: 0141-332 0471 **Fax:** 0141-332 6246
E-mail: info@woolgarhunter.com
Website: http://www.woolgarhunter.com
Bank(s): Bank of Scotland
Directors: W. Neilson (MD), M. Skimming (Fin)
Managers: M. Campbell (I.T. Exec), L. Cameron (Sales & Mktg Mg), M. Skimming (Fin Mgr)
Ultimate Holding Company: WOOLGAR HUNTER LIMITED
Immediate Holding Company: WOOLGAR HUNTER LIMITED
Registration no: SC142064 **VAT No.:** GB 624 0009 09
Date established: 1993 **Turnover:** £2m - £5m **No.of Employees:** 21 - 50
Product Groups: 35, 54, 81, 84, 85

Date of Accounts	Oct 11	Oct 10	Oct 09
Working Capital	517	572	637
Fixed Assets	79	72	88
Current Assets	1m	1m	1m

X C L Framing Solutions

76 Queen Elizabeth Avenue Hillington Park, Glasgow, G52 4NQ
Tel: 0141-882 4195 **Fax:** 0141-883 6860
E-mail: reception@xclfs.com
Website: http://www.xclfs.com
Directors: P. Smith (MD)
Immediate Holding Company: XCL FRAMING SOLUTIONS LTD.
Registration no: SC322059 **Date established:** 2007
No.of Employees: 11 - 20 **Product Groups:** 35

Date of Accounts	Apr 11	Apr 10	Apr 09
Working Capital	-1	-1	-1
Current Liabilities	1	N/A	N/A

Archibald Young Ltd

Milton Road Kirkintilloch, Glasgow, G66 1SY
Tel: 0141-776 7701 **Fax:** 0141-775 1743
E-mail: enquiries@archibaldyoung.co.uk
Website: http://www.archibaldyoung.co.uk
Directors: I. Young (MD), A. Young (MD)
Immediate Holding Company: ARCHIBALD YOUNG LIMITED
Registration no: SC034469 **Date established:** 1959
No.of Employees: 21 - 50 **Product Groups:** 34

Date of Accounts	Oct 11	Oct 10	Oct 09
Working Capital	863	714	691
Fixed Assets	339	343	397
Current Assets	1m	962	884

Younique Products

South Avenue Blantyre Industrial Estate, Blantyre, Glasgow, G72 0XB
Tel: 01698-723330 **Fax:** 01698-327066
Website: http://www.prommtcontrols.com
Immediate Holding Company: MACHINE TOOL ENGINEERS (E.K.) LIMITED
Registration no: SC048839 **Date established:** 1971
No.of Employees: 1 - 10 **Product Groups:** 36, 37

Fife

Glenrothes

Advision Professional Services

111 Huntly Drive, Glenrothes, KY6 2HT
Tel: 01592-758746 **Fax:** 01592-566318
E-mail: sales@advisionweb.com
Website: http://www.fifeserve.com

Directors: A. Donaldson (Prop)
Date established: 2000 **No.of Employees:** 21 - 50 **Product Groups:** 44

Ardmel Group Ltd

52 Nasmyth Road, Glenrothes, KY6 2SD
Tel: 01592-777000 **Fax:** 01592-771071
E-mail: ardmel@ardmel-group.co.uk
Website: http://www.ardmel-group.co.uk
Bank(s): Royal Bank of Scotland
Directors: R. Anderson (Fin), S. Fernando (Dir), R. Anderson (Dir), R. Barr (Fin), R. Fernando (Dir), R. Barr (Co Sec)
Managers: A. Kidd (Mktg Serv Mgr), R. Anderson (Prod Mgr)
Immediate Holding Company: ARDMEL AUTOMATION LIMITED
Registration no: SC071946 **VAT No.:** GB 607 3838 32
Date established: 1980 **Turnover:** £5m - £10m **No.of Employees:** 21 - 50
Product Groups: 43

Date of Accounts	Jun 11	Jun 10	Jun 09
Working Capital	1m	1m	1m
Fixed Assets	597	619	557
Current Assets	3m	2m	2m

BI Technologies Ltd

Telford Road Eastfield Industrial Park, Glenrothes, KY7 4NX
Tel: 01592-662200 **Fax:** 01592-662299
E-mail: sales@bitechnologies.co.uk
Website: http://www.bitechnologies.com
Bank(s): HSBC, Weybridge
Directors: J. MacKay (MD), J. Makay (MD), R. Fletcher (Dir), W. Sharp (Co Sec)
Managers: P. Core (I.T. Exec), J. White (Export Sales Mg)
Ultimate Holding Company: TT Electronics plc
Immediate Holding Company: Crystalate Holdings Ltd
Registration no: 02368235 **VAT No.:** GB 398 2646 01
Date established: 1998 **Turnover:** £5m - £10m
No.of Employees: 51 - 100 **Product Groups:** 37

Date of Accounts	Dec 07	Dec 06
Sales Turnover	10974	8155
Pre Tax Profit/Loss	39	2959
Working Capital	4113	4013
Fixed Assets	1204	1304
Current Assets	6702	6344
Current Liabilities	2589	2331
Total Share Capital	1	1
ROCE% (Return on Capital Employed)	0.7	55.7
ROT% (Return on Turnover)	0.4	36.3

Blackwater Manufacturing Ltd

2 Faraday Road, Glenrothes, KY6 2RU
Tel: 01592-774637 **Fax:** 01592-775160
E-mail: sales@blackwatermfg.co.uk
Website: http://www.blackwatermfg.co.uk
Directors: A. Douglas (Fin), J. Douglas (MD)
Immediate Holding Company: BLACKWATER MANUFACTURING LIMITED
Registration no: SC107568 **VAT No.:** GB 502 6241 90
Date established: 1987 **No.of Employees:** 1 - 10 **Product Groups:** 36

Date of Accounts	Jan 12	Jan 11	Jan 10
Working Capital	40	-161	-236
Fixed Assets	227	236	250
Current Assets	286	289	312

Brand Rex Ltd

Viewfield Industrial Estate, Glenrothes, KY6 2RS
Tel: 01592-772124 **Fax:** 01592-775314
E-mail: loswald@brand-rex.com
Website: http://www.brand-rex.co.uk
Bank(s): Bank of Scotland
Directors: H. Stewart (Fin), D. Hills (Fin), D. Jones (Chief Op Offcr), P. Lines (MD), D. Malone (Pers)
Managers: B. Hunter (Quality Control), B. Wilson, G. Martin, I. Ballingall, J. Tinson, R. Bennett, R. O'Malley (Comm), S. Kujawa, T. Chapman (Cust Serv Mgr), K. Baker
Ultimate Holding Company: Murray International Holdings Ltd
Immediate Holding Company: Brand-Rex Holdings Ltd
Registration no: 02340157 **VAT No.:** GB 232 5797 51
Turnover: £50m - £75m **No.of Employees:** 251 - 500
Product Groups: 34, 35, 37, 39, 44, 45, 46, 67

Date of Accounts	Dec 07
Sales Turnover	71330
Pre Tax Profit/Loss	-3450
Working Capital	-18640
Fixed Assets	8700
Current Assets	28150
Current Liabilities	46790
Total Share Capital	32000
ROCE% (Return on Capital Employed)	34.7

Classic Iron Design

Unit 7 Strathenry Mill Leslie, Glenrothes, KY6 3HU
Tel: 01592-749600
Directors: R. Thomas (Prop)
No.of Employees: 1 - 10 **Product Groups:** 26, 35

Compugraphics International Ltd

Unit F Newark Road North, Glenrothes, KY7 4NT
Tel: 01592-772557 **Fax:** 01592-775359
E-mail: brian.young@cgi.co.uk
Website: http://www.cgi.co.uk
Bank(s): National Westminster Bank Plc
Directors: B. Young (MD)
Managers: P. Livingston (Comptroller), L. Forrest (Tech Serv Mgr), I. McMenamin (Mktg Serv Mgr), B. Gibson (Prod Mgr)
Ultimate Holding Company: OM GROUP INC (UNITED STATES)
Immediate Holding Company: COMPUGRAPHICS INTERNATIONAL LIMITED
Registration no: 00895170 **VAT No.:** GB 400 8967 54
Date established: 1967 **Turnover:** £10m - £20m
No.of Employees: 51 - 100 **Product Groups:** 37, 47

Date of Accounts	Dec 11	Dec 10	Dec 09
Sales Turnover	10m	11m	11m
Pre Tax Profit/Loss	-356	-862	-2m
Working Capital	4m	6m	4m
Fixed Assets	2m	4m	6m
Current Assets	6m	7m	6m
Current Liabilities	731	416	609

D D L Patternshop Ltd

31 Rutherford Road, Glenrothes, KY6 2RT
Tel: 01592-775551 **Fax:** 01592-775420
E-mail: patternshop@ftvproclad.co.uk
Website: http://www.patternshop.co.uk
Managers: W. Duncan (Mgr)
Turnover: Up to £250,000 **No.of Employees:** 11 - 20 **Product Groups:** 27, 30, 48

Dawson Downie Lamont Ltd (Thom Lamont Ltd)

13 Faraday Road, Glenrothes, KY6 2RU
Tel: 01592-775577 **Fax:** 01592-775517
E-mail: sales@ddl-ltd.com
Website: http://www.ddl-ltd.com
Managers: I. Bickett (Chief Mgr)
Ultimate Holding Company: FTV Proclad (UK) Ltd
Immediate Holding Company: DAWSON DOWNIE LAMONT LIMITED
Registration no: SC294845 **Date established:** 2005 **Turnover:** £2m - £5m
No.of Employees: 11 - 20 **Product Groups:** 39, 40, 42

D G Installations

70 Malcolm Road, Glenrothes, KY7 4JX
Tel: 0774-911 9630
E-mail: info@dginstallations.com
Website: http://www.dginstallations.com
Directors: D. Greig (Prop)
Date established: 2007 **Turnover:** Up to £250,000
No.of Employees: 1 - 10 **Product Groups:** 40

Direct Marketing Scotland Ltd

8 Pentland Court, Glenrothes, KY6 2DA
Tel: 01592-630063 **Fax:** 01592-631163
E-mail: info@directmarketingscotland.co.uk
Website: http://www.directmarketingscotland.co.uk
Directors: E. McLean (Fin), J. Mclean (MD)
Managers: E. McLean (Publicity)
Immediate Holding Company: DIRECT MARKETING (SCOTLAND) LIMITED
Registration no: SC210976 **Date established:** 2000
No.of Employees: 1 - 10 **Product Groups:** 24, 49

Date of Accounts	Sep 08	Sep 07	Feb 11
Working Capital	-34	11	-18
Fixed Assets	9	41	N/A
Current Assets	109	132	N/A

Ductform Ventilation UK Ltd

17 Faraday Road Southfield Industrial Estate, Glenrothes, KY6 2RU
Tel: 01592-778330 **Fax:** 01592-778357
E-mail: sales@ductform.com
Website: http://www.ductform.com
Bank(s): Royal Bank of Scotland, Hillend
Directors: A. Mathieson (Sales), R. Ferry (Chief Op Offcr), S. Spence (MD)
Managers: W. Dunn (Buyer), L. Wade (Personnel)
Immediate Holding Company: DUCTFORM VENTILATION (U.K.) LTD.
Registration no: SC061780 **Date established:** 1977
Turnover: £5m - £10m **No.of Employees:** 51 - 100 **Product Groups:** 40, 46, 52, 54

Date of Accounts	Apr 11	Apr 10	Apr 09
Working Capital	428	369	418
Fixed Assets	772	772	775
Current Assets	2m	1m	2m

Eurocastors Ltd

Dalton Road, Glenrothes, KY6 2SS
Tel: 01592-774770 **Fax:** 01592-772736
E-mail: sales@eurocastors.co.uk
Website: http://www.eurocastors.co.uk
Directors: S. Butchart (Fin)
Ultimate Holding Company: CORSIE INDUSTRIAL HOLDINGS LIMITED
Immediate Holding Company: EUROCASTORS LIMITED
Registration no: SC045570 **VAT No.:** GB 268 9693 83
Date established: 1968 **Turnover:** £1m - £2m **No.of Employees:** 1 - 10
Product Groups: 39

Date of Accounts	Mar 12	Mar 11	Mar 10
Working Capital	475	463	N/A
Fixed Assets	262	270	N/A
Current Assets	534	538	N/A

F T V Proclad International Ltd

Viewfield, Glenrothes, KY6 2RD
Tel: 01592-772568 **Fax:** 01592-631252
E-mail: darbon@ftvproclad.co.uk
Website: http://www.procladgroup.com
Bank(s): Bank of Scotland
Directors: M. Penman (Fin), D. Arbon (MD)
Managers: H. Byers (Personnel), S. Anwar (Tech Serv Mgr), D. Shephard (Sales Prom Mgr), C. Robertson (Purch Mgr)
Ultimate Holding Company: NATIONAL INDUSTRIES GROUP (HOLDING) SAK (KUWAIT)
Immediate Holding Company: FTV PROCLAD (U.K.) LIMITED
Registration no: SC271316 **Date established:** 2004 **Turnover:** £2m - £5m
No.of Employees: 101 - 250 **Product Groups:** 48, 84

Date of Accounts	Dec 10	Dec 09	Dec 08
Sales Turnover	4m	4m	5m
Pre Tax Profit/Loss	932	602	734
Working Capital	2m	1m	1m
Fixed Assets	2m	2m	3m
Current Assets	3m	2m	2m
Current Liabilities	396	158	521

Fife Fabrications Ltd

29 Rutherford Road, Glenrothes, KY6 2RT
Tel: 01592-776700 **Fax:** 01592-772101
E-mail: johnp@fifab.co.uk
Website: http://www.fifab.co.uk
Bank(s): The Royal Bank of Scotland, Glenrothes
Directors: S. Koronka (Dir), J. Penman (Sales)
Managers: R. McArthur (Tech Serv Mgr)
Immediate Holding Company: FIFE FABRICATIONS LIMITED
Registration no: SC051054 **Date established:** 1972
Turnover: £5m - £10m **No.of Employees:** 51 - 100 **Product Groups:** 48

Date of Accounts	Sep 11	Sep 10	Sep 09
Sales Turnover	7m	5m	6m
Pre Tax Profit/Loss	188	-86	2
Working Capital	550	469	682
Fixed Assets	2m	2m	2m
Current Assets	2m	2m	2m
Current Liabilities	470	355	384

Flexcon Europe Ltd

Whitworth Road, Glenrothes, KY6 2TF
Tel: 01592-663200 **Fax:** 01592-663201
E-mail: drosen@flexcon.com
Website: http://www.flexcon.com
Directors: M. Hubble (Fin), D. Rosen (MD)
Managers: L. Macnamara (Mktg Serv Mgr), J. Brown (Personnel), T. Orr
Ultimate Holding Company: FLEXCON COMPANY INC (USA)
Immediate Holding Company: FLEXCON EUROPE LIMITED
Registration no: SC170245 **Date established:** 1996
Turnover: £20m - £50m **No.of Employees:** 101 - 250 **Product Groups:** 30

Date of Accounts	Sep 11	Sep 10	Sep 09
Sales Turnover	26m	26m	20m
Pre Tax Profit/Loss	2m	1m	-582
Working Capital	9m	7m	6m
Fixed Assets	1m	1m	2m
Current Assets	12m	13m	12m
Current Liabilities	1m	2m	1m

Flexel International Ltd

Flemington Road, Glenrothes, KY7 5QF
Tel: 01592-757313 **Fax:** 01592-754535
E-mail: george.graham@flexel.co.uk
Website: http://www.flexel.co.uk
Bank(s): Bank of Scotland, Glenrothes
Directors: A. Neilson (Fin), G. Graham (MD)
Managers: A. Faulkner, R. Graham (Tech Serv Mgr)
Immediate Holding Company: FLEXEL INTERNATIONAL LIMITED
Registration no: SC145068 **VAT No.:** GB 121 5582 93
Date established: 1993 **Turnover:** £5m - £10m **No.of Employees:** 21 - 50
Product Groups: 37, 40, 41, 49

Date of Accounts	Dec 11	Dec 10	Dec 09
Working Capital	1m	1m	1m
Fixed Assets	775	430	404
Current Assets	2m	2m	2m

Glendale Plastics Ltd

Unit D Glover Road, Glenrothes, KY7 4AD
Tel: 01592-774888 **Fax:** 01592-771680
E-mail: sales@glendaleplastics.co.uk
Website: http://www.glendaleplastics.co.uk
Bank(s): Royal Bank of Scotland, Glenrothes.
Directors: B. Galloway (MD)
Managers: S. Payne, F. Healy (Sales Admin)
Immediate Holding Company: GLENDALE PLASTICS LIMITED
Registration no: SC070131 **Date established:** 1979
Turnover: £5m - £10m **No.of Employees:** 51 - 100 **Product Groups:** 30, 48, 66

Date of Accounts	Dec 11	Dec 10	Dec 09
Sales Turnover	7m	7m	N/A
Pre Tax Profit/Loss	157	489	N/A
Working Capital	640	719	101
Fixed Assets	1m	1m	1m
Current Assets	3m	3m	2m
Current Liabilities	1m	1m	N/A

Glenhire Express Ltd

2 Osprey Road Fife Airport Industrial Estate, Glenrothes, KY6 2SZ
Tel: 01592-882222 **Fax:** 01592-882444
E-mail: glenhire@aol.com
Website: http://www.palletforce.com
Directors: B. Johnston (MD), U. Johnston (Fin)
Immediate Holding Company: GLENHIRE EXPRESS LIMITED
Registration no: SC221896 **Date established:** 2001
No.of Employees: 11 - 20 **Product Groups:** 77

Date of Accounts	Dec 11	Dec 10	Dec 09
Working Capital	106	220	350
Fixed Assets	7	17	40
Current Assets	230	325	479

H C S Control Systems Ltd

Unit V2 Viewfield, Glenrothes, KY6 2QX
Tel: 01592-770786 **Fax:** 01592-775737
E-mail: sales@hcscsl.com
Website: http://www.hcscsl.com
Directors: I. Reid (MD)
Ultimate Holding Company: HCS CONTROL SYSTEMS (HOLDINGS) LIMITED
Immediate Holding Company: HCS CONTROL SYSTEMS LIMITED
Registration no: SC185931 **Date established:** 1998
Turnover: £500,000 - £1m **No.of Employees:** 51 - 100
Product Groups: 38, 40, 67

Date of Accounts	Dec 11	Dec 10	Dec 09
Sales Turnover	11m	9m	9m
Pre Tax Profit/Loss	510	907	785
Working Capital	1m	968	461
Fixed Assets	303	381	443
Current Assets	4m	4m	4m
Current Liabilities	1m	1m	2m

Haldane UK Ltd

7 Blackwood Way Bankhead Industrial Estate, Glenrothes, KY7 6JF
Tel: 01592-775656 **Fax:** 01592-775757
E-mail: sales@haldaneuk.com
Website: http://www.haldaneuk.com
Bank(s): Bank of Scotland
Directors: E. Adam (Fin), F. Adam (MD)
Ultimate Holding Company: FEARN LIMITED
Immediate Holding Company: HALDANE (UK) LIMITED
Registration no: SC058135 **VAT No.:** GB 217 8523 51
Date established: 1975 **Turnover:** £1m - £2m **No.of Employees:** 21 - 50
Product Groups: 25

Date of Accounts	Jun 12	Jun 11	Jun 10
Working Capital	263	542	431
Fixed Assets	632	676	712
Current Assets	618	952	795

I T W

1 Wheatstone Place, Glenrothes, KY6 2SW
Tel: 01842-755530 **Fax:** 01842-755588
E-mail: b.meacher@cullen-bp.com
Website: http://www.cullen-bp.com
Managers: H. Sherry (Mgr)
Ultimate Holding Company: ILLINOIS TOOL WORKS INC (USA)
Immediate Holding Company: CULLEN BUILDING PRODUCTS LIMITED
Registration no: SC063162 **VAT No.:** GB 300 5817 96
Date established: 1977 **Turnover:** £5m - £10m **No.of Employees:** 1 - 10
Product Groups: 66

Date of Accounts	Nov 10	Nov 09	Nov 08
Sales Turnover	N/A	6m	9m
Pre Tax Profit/Loss	3m	-284	71
Working Capital	5m	1m	1m
Fixed Assets	N/A	1m	1m
Current Assets	5m	3m	4m
Current Liabilities	336	492	501

Ilasco Ltd
52-53 Nasmyth Road Southfield Industrial Estate, Glenrothes, KY6 2SD
Tel: 01592-771241 **Fax:** 01592-771071
E-mail: sales@ardmel-group.co.uk
Website: http://www.ardmel-group.co.uk
Directors: R. Anderson (Dir), R. Fernando (Dir)
Ultimate Holding Company: ARDMEL AUTOMATION LIMITED
Immediate Holding Company: ILASCO LIMITED
Registration no: SC071900 **VAT No.:** GB 607 3838 32
Date established: 1980 **Turnover:** £1m - £2m **No.of Employees:** 1 - 10
Product Groups: 24

Date of Accounts	Jun 11	Jun 10	Jun 09
Working Capital	318	265	210
Fixed Assets	16	19	23
Current Assets	1m	833	1m

K C C Electrical & Home Automation
8 New Law House Pentland Court, Glenrothes, KY6 2DA
Tel: 01592-631898
E-mail: admin@kccelectrical.co.uk
Website: http://www.kccelectrical.co.uk
Directors: F. Kumesu (Dir)
Immediate Holding Company: FAGLITES LIMITED
Date established: 2012 **Turnover:** Up to £250,000
No.of Employees: 1 - 10 **Product Groups:** 44, 52, 84

Kingdom Blinds
189 Rannoch Road Balfarg, Glenrothes, KY7 6XR
Tel: 01592-787715
E-mail: infokingdomblinds@yahoo.co.uk
Website: http://www.kingdomblinds.co.uk
Managers: A. Steele (District Mgr)
Date established: 2008 **Turnover:** Up to £250,000
No.of Employees: 1 - 10 **Product Groups:** 23, 24, 25, 30, 66

McDonald's Restaurants Ltd
Flemington Road, Glenrothes, KY7 5QF
Tel: 01592-754191 **Fax:** 01592-759305
E-mail: bill@mcdonald-engineers.com
Website: http://www.mcdonalds.co.uk
Bank(s): Royal Bank of Scotland, Kirkcaldy
Managers: B. Ewen (Chief Mgr)
Ultimate Holding Company: MCDONALDS CORPORATION (USA)
Immediate Holding Company: MCDONALD'S RESTAURANTS LIMITED
Registration no: 01002769 **Date established:** 1971 **Turnover:** £1m - £2m
No.of Employees: 51 - 100 **Product Groups:** 35, 40, 48

Date of Accounts	Dec 11	Dec 10	Dec 09
Sales Turnover	1249m	1184m	1130m
Pre Tax Profit/Loss	177m	157m	114m
Working Capital	-229m	-288m	-365m
Fixed Assets	759m	719m	704m
Current Assets	140m	61m	64m
Current Liabilities	134m	122m	102m

Mongoose Plastics Ltd
57-58 Nasmyth Road, Glenrothes, KY6 2SD
Tel: 01592-774800 **Fax:** 01592-775032
E-mail: jean@mongoose-plastics.co.uk
Website: http://www.mongoose-plastics.co.uk
Bank(s): The Royal Bank of Scotland, Newburgh
Directors: J. Cameron (Dir)
Immediate Holding Company: MONGOOSE PLASTICS LIMITED
Registration no: SC081787 **VAT No.:** GB 380 0778 49
Date established: 1983 **Turnover:** £500,000 - £1m
No.of Employees: 11 - 20 **Product Groups:** 26, 30, 48, 49, 66

Date of Accounts	Sep 11	Sep 10	Sep 09
Working Capital	2	7	-3
Fixed Assets	4	7	10
Current Assets	263	323	356

Peddinghaus Corporation
Greenwell Park, Glenrothes, KY6 3QH
Tel: 01592-742842
Website: http://www.peddinghaus.com
Directors: I. Maxwell (Prop)
No.of Employees: 1 - 10 **Product Groups:** 45

Phoenix Precision Ltd
Crompton Road, Glenrothes, KY6 2SF
Tel: 01592-772077 **Fax:** 01592-773535
E-mail: ian@phoenixprecision.com
Website: http://www.phoenixprecision.com
Bank(s): Bank of Scotland
Directors: A. Russell (Sales), I. Moffat (MD), J. Drury (Fab), L. Smith (Fin)
Managers: N. Smith (Purch Mgr)
Immediate Holding Company: PHOENIX PRECISION LIMITED
Registration no: SC098188 **Date established:** 1985 **Turnover:** £2m - £5m
No.of Employees: 21 - 50 **Product Groups:** 48

Date of Accounts	Dec 11	Dec 10	Dec 09
Working Capital	-14	-25	-156
Fixed Assets	1m	735	805
Current Assets	974	979	866

Pipemore
3 Crompton Road, Glenrothes, KY6 2SF
Tel: 01592-630633 **Fax:** 01592-630623
E-mail: sales@pipemorescotland.co.uk
Website: http://www.pipemorescotland.co.uk
Directors: R. Smedley (MD)
Registration no: SC114831 **Date established:** 1988
Turnover: £500,000 - £1m **No.of Employees:** 1 - 10 **Product Groups:** 36, 38

Premier Purchasing Group
The Old Manse Milton Of Balgonie, Glenrothes, KY7 6QD
Tel: 08451-000250 **Fax:** 0845-080 0451
E-mail: info@ppg-uk.co.uk
Website: http://www.ppg-uk.co.uk
Managers: I. Ladd (Mgr)
No.of Employees: 1 - 10 **Product Groups:** 80

Production Glassfibre
2 Whitworth Road, Glenrothes, KY6 2TF
Tel: 01592-774910 **Fax:** 01592-652444
E-mail: robert@productionglassfibre.co.uk
Website: http://www.productionglassfibre.co.uk

Managers: R. Drybrugh (Chief Mgr)
Immediate Holding Company: SPECTROGON U.K. LIMITED
Registration no: SC352070 **VAT No.:** GB 561 4238 53
Date established: 2004 **Turnover:** £2m - £5m **No.of Employees:** 21 - 50
Product Groups: 30

Date of Accounts	Dec 11	Dec 10	Dec 09
Working Capital	169	123	78
Current Assets	197	186	120

Raytheon UK
Fullerton Road Queensway Industrial Estate, Glenrothes, KY7 5PY
Tel: 01592-754311 **Fax:** 01592-759775
E-mail: jim.trail@raytheon.co.uk
Website: http://www.raytheon.co.uk
Bank(s): Bank of Scotland, Glenrothes, Fife, Scotland
Directors: J. Reilly (Co Sec)
Managers: J. Trail (Chief Mgr)
Ultimate Holding Company: RAYTHEON COMPANY (USA)
Immediate Holding Company: RAYTHEON SYSTEMS LIMITED
Registration no: 00406809 **VAT No.:** GB 268 8397 92
Date established: 1946 **Turnover:** £250m - £500m
No.of Employees: 501 - 1000 **Product Groups:** 37

Date of Accounts	Dec 11	Dec 10	Dec 09
Sales Turnover	300m	268m	212m
Pre Tax Profit/Loss	332m	-105m	-190m
Working Capital	305m	76m	4m
Fixed Assets	213m	21m	18m
Current Assets	401m	199m	205m
Current Liabilities	22m	37m	42m

Reel Service Ltd
55-56 Nasmyth Road, Glenrothes, KY6 2SD
Tel: 01592-773208 **Fax:** 01592-774696
E-mail: marketing@reelserviceltd.com
Website: http://www.reelservice.com
Bank(s): Bank of Scotland
Directors: J. Simpson (MD), J. Miller (Co Sec)
Managers: G. Birrell (Tech Serv Mgr), V. Bern (Personnel), B. Melrose (Purch Mgr)
Ultimate Holding Company: ASTI HOLDINGS LTD (SINGAPORE)
Immediate Holding Company: REEL SERVICE LIMITED
Registration no: SC101979 **VAT No.:** 435 7169 36 **Date established:** 1986
Turnover: £2m - £5m **No.of Employees:** 51 - 100 **Product Groups:** 37, 47

Date of Accounts	Dec 11	Dec 10	Dec 09
Sales Turnover	3m	2m	2m
Pre Tax Profit/Loss	487	189	-216
Working Capital	378	-80	-410
Fixed Assets	601	714	876
Current Assets	912	1m	832
Current Liabilities	196	143	98

Scotia Heating
451 Blair Avenue, Glenrothes, KY7 4RD
Tel: 0845-224 0451 **Fax:** 0845-224 0452
E-mail: info@scotiaheating.co.uk
Website: http://www.scotiaheating.co.uk
Directors: A. Browne (Fin), S. Findlay (Dir)
Registration no: SC315905 **Turnover:** Up to £250,000
No.of Employees: 1 - 10 **Product Groups:** 40, 52, 67

Semefab Ltd
Newark Road South Eastfield Industrial Estate, Glenrothes, KY7 4NS
Tel: 01592-630630 **Fax:** 01592-775265
E-mail: reception@semefab.com
Website: http://www.semefab.com
Bank(s): Barclays
Managers: A. Vandeck, I. McNought (Mktg Serv Mgr), P. Gorniak (I.T. Exec), C. Cooper, G. Fisher (Fin Mgr), J. Cushnie, G. Beswick (Buyer), P. Martin (Personnel)
Ultimate Holding Company: HICKS (1) LIMITED
Immediate Holding Company: SEMEFAB LIMITED
Registration no: SC100193 **Date established:** 1985
Turnover: £5m - £10m **No.of Employees:** 51 - 100 **Product Groups:** 37, 38

Date of Accounts	Oct 11	Oct 10	Oct 09
Sales Turnover	9m	8m	6m
Pre Tax Profit/Loss	254	264	317
Working Capital	2m	2m	1m
Fixed Assets	12m	12m	10m
Current Assets	4m	4m	3m
Current Liabilities	488	848	888

Venture Oilfield Services
Viewfield Road, Glenrothes, KY6 2RD
Tel: 01592-772176 **Fax:** 01592-775455
E-mail: mail@ventureoil.com
Website: http://www.ventureoil.com
Bank(s): The Royal Bank of Scotland
Directors: W. Mccartney (MD)
Immediate Holding Company: VENTURE OILFIELD SERVICES LIMITED
Registration no: SC081796 **VAT No.:** GB 380 8005 07
Date established: 1983 **Turnover:** £1m - £2m **No.of Employees:** 11 - 20
Product Groups: 39, 45, 48, 85

Date of Accounts	Mar 12	Mar 11	Mar 10
Working Capital	-59	-42	-38
Fixed Assets	398	145	156
Current Assets	468	306	275
Current Liabilities	N/A	25	N/A

Walter Watson Ltd
2 Edison House Fullerton Road, Glenrothes, KY7 5QR
Tel: 01592-612500 **Fax:** 01592-612900
E-mail: info@walter-watson.co.uk
Website: http://www.walter-watson.co.uk
Managers: P. Hopcroft (Mgr)
Immediate Holding Company: WALTER WATSON LIMITED
Registration no: NI010745 **Date established:** 1975
No.of Employees: 1 - 10 **Product Groups:** 35

Date of Accounts	Dec 11	Dec 10	Dec 09
Sales Turnover	36m	30m	29m
Pre Tax Profit/Loss	307	417	-380
Working Capital	2m	2m	3m
Fixed Assets	7m	7m	5m
Current Assets	14m	12m	13m
Current Liabilities	2m	2m	620

Woodstock Neckwear Ltd
Telford Road, Glenrothes, KY7 4NX
Tel: 01592-771777 **Fax:** 01592-631717
Website: http://www.randa.net
Bank(s): R B S

Directors: B. Kovaly (Dir)
Managers: A. Peebles (Fin Mgr)
Ultimate Holding Company: RANDA CORP INC (USA)
Immediate Holding Company: RANDA ACCESSORIES UK LIMITED
Registration no: 02840222 **Date established:** 1993 **Turnover:** £5m - £10m
No.of Employees: 21 - 50 **Product Groups:** 22, 24

Date of Accounts	Dec 11	Dec 10	Dec 09
Sales Turnover	6m	7m	7m
Pre Tax Profit/Loss	337	690	685
Working Capital	9m	9m	8m
Fixed Assets	374	410	478
Current Assets	11m	11m	11m
Current Liabilities	2m	2m	2m

Midlothian

Gorebridge

Thomas Andrew Brannan
3 Millstone Brow, Gorebridge, EH23 4PD
Tel: 01875-820591 **Fax:** 01875-833204
Managers: T. Brannan (Mgr)
Date established: 1969 **No.of Employees:** 1 - 10 **Product Groups:** 46, 48

C P S Mailing Systems UK Ltd
Suite 7 Stuart House Eskmills Park, Gorebridge, EH23 7PH
Tel: 0131-273 4328 **Fax:** 0131-476 2935
Directors: K. Davies (Fin), J. Nisbet (MD)
Date established: 2002 **No.of Employees:** 1 - 10 **Product Groups:** 44

Renfrewshire

Gourock

Caledonian Macbrayne Ltd
The Pier Station Road, Gourock, PA19 1QP
Tel: 01475-650100 **Fax:** 01475-637607
E-mail: marketing@calmac.co.uk
Website: http://www.calmac.co.uk
Bank(s): Royal Bank of Scotland, Glasgow
Directors: R. Drummond (Fin), K. Macleod (Grp Chief Exec), J. Pettigrew (Co Sec), W. Allardes (Pers)
Managers: M. Markie (Purch Mgr), S. Paterson (Mktg Serv Mgr), D. Macdonald (Tech Serv Mgr)
Ultimate Holding Company: DAVID MACBRAYNE LIMITED
Immediate Holding Company: CALEDONIAN MARITIME ASSETS LIMITED
Registration no: SC001854 **VAT No.:** GB 554 3476 31
Date established: 1989 **Turnover:** £10m - £20m
No.of Employees: 101 - 250 **Product Groups:** 76

Date of Accounts	Mar 11	Mar 10	Mar 09
Sales Turnover	16m	16m	14m
Pre Tax Profit/Loss	-4m	-4m	4m
Working Capital	11m	11m	9m
Fixed Assets	199m	122m	116m
Current Assets	28m	19m	17m
Current Liabilities	16m	7m	7m

Stirlingshire

Grangemouth

Andrews Sykes Hire Ltd
Westmains Industrial Estate, Grangemouth, FK3 8YE
Tel: 01324-474550 **Fax:** 01324-665020
E-mail: depot.gra@andrews-sykes.com
Website: http://www.andrews-sykes.com
Directors: R. Simpson (Dir)
Ultimate Holding Company: EOI EUROPEAN & OVERSEAS INVESTMENTS SARL (LUXEMBOURG)
Immediate Holding Company: ANDREWS SYKES HIRE LIMITED
Registration no: 02985657 **VAT No.:** GB 100 4295 24
Date established: 1994 **Turnover:** £10m - £20m
No.of Employees: 11 - 20 **Product Groups:** 83

Date of Accounts	Dec 11	Dec 10	Dec 09
Sales Turnover	35m	36m	34m
Pre Tax Profit/Loss	10m	10m	8m
Working Capital	8m	6m	2m
Fixed Assets	7m	7m	9m
Current Assets	33m	35m	35m
Current Liabilities	7m	7m	5m

Bilanco Blinds Ltd
Unit 3-4 Powdrake Road, Grangemouth, FK3 9UT
Tel: 01324-473707 **Fax:** 01324-471926
E-mail: sales@bilancoblinds.co.uk
Website: http://bilancoblinds.co.uk
Directors: A. Quigley (MD)
No.of Employees: 11 - 20 **Product Groups:** 24, 63, 66

Build Centre
Earls Road, Grangemouth, FK3 8DJ
Tel: 01324-483574 **Fax:** 01324-665442
E-mail: sales@buildcentre.co.uk
Website: http://www.wolseley.co.uk
Bank(s): Bank of Scotland
Managers: A. Strathern (District Mgr), A. Strathearn (Mgr), S. Gibson (Sales Prom Mgr)
Ultimate Holding Company: WOLSELEY PLC
Immediate Holding Company: BUILD CENTER LIMITED
Registration no: 00462397 **VAT No.:** GB 269 6253 23
Date established: 1948 **Turnover:** £20m - £50m
No.of Employees: 11 - 20 **Product Groups:** 37

Business Directions & Development
1 Lennox Terrace, Grangemouth, FK3 0BY
Tel: 01324-482741
E-mail: alastair@businessdirections.co.uk
Website: http://www.businessdirections.co.uk
Directors: A. Wood (Ptnr), A. Wood (MD)
Registration no: SC246499 **No.of Employees:** 1 - 10 **Product Groups:** 80

C P L Petroleum
Forth Line House The Docks, Grangemouth, FK3 8UB
Tel: 01324-482795 **Fax:** 01324-665712
E-mail: grangemouth@cplpetroleum.co.uk
Website: http://www.cplpetroleum.co.uk
Bank(s): Natwest
Managers: G. Burnes (District Mgr)
Ultimate Holding Company: CPL INDUSTRIES HOLDINGS LIMITED
Immediate Holding Company: CPL PETROLEUM LIMITED
Registration no: 03003860 **VAT No.:** GB 721 5764 39
Date established: 1994 **Turnover:** £500m - £1,000m
No.of Employees: 11 - 20 **Product Groups:** 66

Date of Accounts	Mar 12	Mar 11	Mar 10
Pre Tax Profit/Loss	N/A	878	904
Working Capital	31	30m	30m
Fixed Assets	26	26m	26m
Current Assets	57	56m	56m
Current Liabilities	26	246	253

Denholm Barwil Ltd
Epoch House Falkirk Road, Grangemouth, FK3 8WW
Tel: 01324-482201 **Fax:** 0131-555 5588
E-mail: agency.forth@denholm-barwil.com
Website: http://www.denholm-barwil.com
Directors: J. Watt (Dir)
Immediate Holding Company: D BARCLAY ENGINEERING & INSPECTION LTD
Registration no: SC032785 **Date established:** 2007
No.of Employees: 11 - 20 **Product Groups:** 72, 74

Duncan Adams Ltd
The Docks, Grangemouth, FK3 8UB
Tel: 01324-484951 **Fax:** 0191-496 7536
E-mail: admin@duncanadams.co.uk
Website: http://www.duncanadams.co.uk
Directors: C. Adams (Dir)
Immediate Holding Company: DUNCAN ADAMS LIMITED
Registration no: SC138033 **Date established:** 1992
Turnover: £10m - £20m **No.of Employees:** 51 - 100 **Product Groups:** 35, 44, 45, 48, 61, 67, 72, 74, 75, 76, 77, 82, 84

Date of Accounts	Oct 11	Oct 10	Oct 09
Sales Turnover	15m	14m	14m
Pre Tax Profit/Loss	-34	-65	7
Working Capital	-150	-58	-28
Fixed Assets	2m	2m	2m
Current Assets	4m	3m	3m
Current Liabilities	2m	1m	1m

Ferelco UK Ltd
6 The Docks, Grangemouth, FK3 8UB
Tel: 01324-665455 **Fax:** 01324-474754
Website: http://www.feralco.com
Bank(s): Barclays
Managers: A. Campbell (Plant)
Immediate Holding Company: JW TANK SERVICES LTD.
Registration no: SC027101 **VAT No.:** GB 196 6494 06
Date established: 2002 **Turnover:** £1m - £2m **No.of Employees:** 11 - 20
Product Groups: 31, 32

Date of Accounts	Jun 12	Jun 11	Jun 10
Working Capital	17	31	-14
Fixed Assets	255	198	218
Current Assets	204	168	92

Finn Forest UK Ltd
PO Box 9, Grangemouth, FK3 8XF
Tel: 01324-502300 **Fax:** 01324-665448
E-mail: rod.allen@finnforest.com
Website: http://www.finnforest.co.uk
Directors: R. Ellan (Prop), R. Allen (MD), R. Ellan (Fab)
Managers: R. Kay (Sales Prom Mgr)
Ultimate Holding Company: METSALIITTO OSUUSKUNTA (FINLAND)
Immediate Holding Company: FINNFOREST UK LIMITED
Registration no: 03071064 **Date established:** 1995
Turnover: £50m - £75m **No.of Employees:** 51 - 100 **Product Groups:** 08, 25

Forth Ports Ltd
Port Office Grangemouth Docks, Grangemouth, FK3 8UE
Tel: 01324-482591 **Fax:** 01324-665106
E-mail: reception@forthports.co.uk
Website: http://www.forthports.co.uk
Bank(s): Bank of Scotland
Directors: S. Patterson (Fin)
Managers: N. Scott-grqy, J. Anderson (Personnel), D. Knox, D. McNeish, B. Devlin
Immediate Holding Company: FORTH PORTS LIMITED
Registration no: SC134741 **VAT No.:** GB 592 9785 69
Date established: 1991 **No.of Employees:** 101 - 250 **Product Groups:** 71, 74, 77

Date of Accounts	Dec 11	Dec 10	Dec 09
Sales Turnover	184m	182m	174m
Pre Tax Profit/Loss	16m	56m	36m
Working Capital	289m	41m	30m
Fixed Assets	568m	578m	563m
Current Assets	339m	83m	68m
Current Liabilities	43m	36m	32m

Forth Yacht Marina Ltd
4-6 South Lumley Street, Grangemouth, FK3 8BT
Tel: 01324-665071 **Fax:** 01324-483635
E-mail: keith@fym.co.uk
Website: http://www.fym.co.uk
Directors: C. Greggs (Dir), K. Stewart (MD), R. Muir (Dir), P. Stewart (Co Sec)
Immediate Holding Company: FORTH YACHT MARINA LIMITED
Registration no: SC045536 **Date established:** 1968 **Turnover:** £2m - £5m
No.of Employees: 1 - 10 **Product Groups:** 39

Date of Accounts	Oct 08	Oct 07	Oct 06
Working Capital	340	382	417
Fixed Assets	143	159	166
Current Assets	630	1096	624
Current Liabilities	291	714	207
Total Share Capital	200	200	200

Klinger UK Ltd
Unit 2a Westmains Industrial Estate, Grangemouth, FK3 8YE
Tel: 01324-472231 **Fax:** 01324-482111
E-mail: sales@acornseals.com
Website: http://www.klingeruk.co.uk
Managers: D. Brealey (District Mgr)
Immediate Holding Company: KLINGER LIMITED
Registration no: 01021936 **Date established:** 1971
No.of Employees: 11 - 20 **Product Groups:** 38, 42

Leengate Industrial Welding Supplies
8-9 Abbotsinch Court, Grangemouth, FK3 9UN
Tel: 01324-664433 **Fax:** 01324-664422
Website: http://www.leengate.com
Directors: G. Gill (MD)
No.of Employees: 1 - 10 **Product Groups:** 46

Midland Electrical Winding & Contracting Scotland Ltd
12 Inchyra Road, Grangemouth, FK3 9XB
Tel: 01324-484444 **Fax:** 01324-474834
E-mail: sales@midlandgroup.co.uk
Website: http://www.midland-electrical.com
Bank(s): Clydesdale
Directors: S. Girvan (Dir)
Ultimate Holding Company: MIDLAND ELECTRICAL HOLDINGS LIMITED
Immediate Holding Company: MIDLAND ELECTRICAL WINDING & CONTRACTING (SCOTLAND) LIMITED
Registration no: SC229372 **VAT No.:** GB 272 0203 06
Date established: 2002 **Turnover:** £1m - £2m **No.of Employees:** 11 - 20
Product Groups: 48

Date of Accounts	Jan 12	Jan 11	Jan 10
Working Capital	41	46	142
Fixed Assets	76	93	117
Current Assets	194	248	286

Murray Power Tools & Abrasives
14 Primrose Avenue, Grangemouth, FK3 8YG
Tel: 01324-666185 **Fax:** 01324-666184
E-mail: sales@murraypowertools.co.uk
Website: http://www.murraypowertools.co.uk
Directors: M. Clark (Prop)
Date established: 1991 **No.of Employees:** 1 - 10 **Product Groups:** 37

Ondeo Industrial Solutions Ltd
SUEZ ENVIRONNEMENT House Bo ness Road, Grangemouth, FK3 9XD
Tel: 0870-2416643 **Fax:** 0870-2416645
E-mail: enquiries_uk@ondeo-is.com
Website: http://www.ondeo-is.com
Managers: M. Jordan (Sales Prom Mgr)
Registration no: 02528695 **Date established:** 2002
No.of Employees: 101 - 250 **Product Groups:** 18

Polimeri Europa UK Ltd
Bo'Ness Road, Grangemouth, FK3 9XE
Tel: 01324-692200 **Fax:** 01324-473915
E-mail: andrew.tomb@polimerieuropa.com
Website: http://www.polimerieuropa.it
Managers: A. Woodger, A. Tomb (Mgr)
Ultimate Holding Company: ENI SPA (ITALY)
Immediate Holding Company: POLIMERI EUROPA UK LIMITED
Registration no: 00557780 **Date established:** 1955
No.of Employees: 101 - 250 **Product Groups:** 29, 63, 66

Date of Accounts	Dec 11	Dec 10	Dec 09
Sales Turnover	270m	218m	163m
Pre Tax Profit/Loss	21m	13m	-2m
Working Capital	19m	12m	6m
Fixed Assets	19m	17m	19m
Current Assets	108m	72m	72m
Current Liabilities	5m	34m	961

S A I C A Pack
Westmains Industrial Estate, Grangemouth, FK3 8YE
Tel: 01324-665501 **Fax:** 01324-665502
E-mail: ronnie.mckinlay@saica.com
Website: http://www.sca.com
Managers: R. Mckinlay (Mgr)
Ultimate Holding Company: EOI EUROPEAN & OVERSEAS INVESTMENTS SARL (LUXEMBOURG)
Immediate Holding Company: HEAT FOR HIRE (SCOTLAND) LIMITED
Registration no: 00053913 **Date established:** 1977
No.of Employees: 11 - 20 **Product Groups:** 27, 28, 30, 49

Samskip Multimodal Container Logistics
6 Primrose Avenue, Grangemouth, FK3 8YG
Tel: 01324-664409 **Fax:** 01324-664413
E-mail: grangemouth@samskip.com
Website: http://www.samskip.com
Managers: A. Wilson (Mgr)
No.of Employees: 1 - 10 **Product Groups:** 76

Scott Direct Ltd
2 Caledon Green, Grangemouth, FK3 8TR
Tel: 01324-667500 **Fax:** 01324-667516
E-mail: sales@scott-direct.com
Website: http://www.scott-direct.com
Bank(s): The Royal Bank of Scotland
Directors: A. Cheatham (Fin), C. Quinn (Dir)
Managers: E. Marshall, K. Kelly (Purch Mgr), M. Spaven (Personnel), D. Candalsh (I.T. Exec), D. Holmes (Tech Serv Mgr)
Ultimate Holding Company: SCOTT GROUP LIMITED
Immediate Holding Company: SCOTT DIRECT INSURANCE SERVICES LIMITED
Registration no: SC383723 **VAT No.:** GB 327 4331 71
Date established: 2010 **Turnover:** £2m - £5m **No.of Employees:** 51 - 100
Product Groups: 35, 36, 66

Signs Express Ltd
Unit 2e West Mains Industrial Estate, Grangemouth, FK3 8YE
Tel: 01324-666966 **Fax:** 01324-666969
E-mail: falkirk@signsexpress.co.uk
Website: http://www.signsexpress.co.uk
Directors: S. Mcmurray (Dir)
Immediate Holding Company: SIGNS EXPRESS LIMITED
Registration no: 02375913 **Date established:** 1989
No.of Employees: 1 - 10 **Product Groups:** 28, 30, 37, 40

Date of Accounts	May 11	May 10	May 09
Working Capital	2m	1m	988
Fixed Assets	112	87	105
Current Assets	2m	2m	1m

Morayshire

Grantown On Spey

My Web Partners N.England & Scotland
Lodge of Finlarig Dulnain Bridge, Grantown On Spey, PH26 3NU
Tel: 0870-3502550
E-mail: ib@mywebpartners.co.uk
Website: http://www.mywebpartners.co.uk
Directors: D. Manfield (Comm)
Managers: N. Lukyanova, J. Bruce (Mgr)
Date established: 2003 **No.of Employees:** 1 - 10 **Product Groups:** 44

Ritchies
41-45 High Street, Grantown On Spey, PH26 3EG
Tel: 01479-872183 **Fax:** 01479-873489
E-mail: info@ritchies.co.uk
Website: http://www.ritchies.co.uk
Directors: J. Ritchie (Prop)
Date established: 1988 **No.of Employees:** 1 - 10 **Product Groups:** 36, 39, 40

Renfrewshire

Greenock

Thomas Auld & Sons Ltd
5-9 Brisbane Street, Greenock, PA16 8LS
Tel: 01475-725288 **Fax:** 01475-725191
E-mail: enquiries@aulds.co.uk
Website: http://www.aulds.co.uk
Directors: A. Marr (MD), B. Drummond (Dir), F. Marr (Dir)
Ultimate Holding Company: AULDS HOLDINGS LIMITED
Immediate Holding Company: THOMAS AULD & SONS LIMITED
Registration no: SC018677 **Date established:** 1935
Turnover: £5m - £10m **No.of Employees:** 1 - 10 **Product Groups:** 20

Date of Accounts	Mar 11	Mar 10	Mar 09
Sales Turnover	9m	9m	N/A
Pre Tax Profit/Loss	-80	-220	6
Working Capital	327	348	658
Fixed Assets	510	524	385
Current Assets	1m	2m	2m
Current Liabilities	419	365	430

Boat Electric & Electronics Ltd
Inverkip Marina Inverkip, Greenock, PA16 0AS
Tel: 01475-522268 **Fax:** 01475-522716
E-mail: sales@boatelectrics.com
Website: http://www.boatelectrics.com
Directors: S. Coleman (Dir)
Immediate Holding Company: BOAT ELECTRICS & ELECTRONICS LIMITED
Registration no: SC066331 **Date established:** 1978
Turnover: £5m - £10m **No.of Employees:** 11 - 20 **Product Groups:** 35, 36, 39

Date of Accounts	Sep 11	Sep 10	Sep 09
Working Capital	234	189	180
Fixed Assets	42	34	20
Current Assets	801	496	328

Brimac Environmental Services Ltd
21 Dellingburn Street, Greenock, PA15 4TP
Tel: 01475-720273 **Fax:** 01475-720016
E-mail: info@brimacservices.com
Website: http://www.brimacservices.com
Bank(s): Bank of Scotland
Managers: M. Thomas (Sales Admin), D. McEwen (Comptroller)
Immediate Holding Company: HA1 NATURAL LIMITED
Registration no: 04031593 **VAT No.:** GB 751 5242 48
Date established: 2000 **Turnover:** £5m - £10m **No.of Employees:** 21 - 50
Product Groups: 31, 32, 33, 36, 37, 41, 42, 49, 52, 54, 66, 85

Date of Accounts	Mar 11	Mar 10	Mar 09
Working Capital	-176	-270	-326
Fixed Assets	2m	2m	2m
Current Assets	2m	2m	2m

British Polythene Industries plc
96 Port Glasgow Road, Greenock, PA15 2UL
Tel: 01475-501100 **Fax:** 01475-743143
E-mail: carolanderson@bpipoly.com
Website: http://www.bpipoly.co.uk
Directors: H. Grossart (Dir), C. McLatchie (Ch), A. Green (MD), E. Hagman (Fin)
Managers: J. Chamberlain (Sales Prom Mgr)
Ultimate Holding Company: BRITISH POLYTHENE INDUSTRIES PLC
Immediate Holding Company: BRITISH POLYTHENE INDUSTRIES PLC
Registration no: 00108191 **VAT No.:** GB 268 9911 02
Date established: 2010 **Turnover:** £250m - £500m
No.of Employees: 1 - 10 **Product Groups:** 30, 45

Date of Accounts	Dec 10	Dec 09	Dec 08
Sales Turnover	478m	425m	481m
Pre Tax Profit/Loss	17m	12m	4m
Working Capital	40m	38m	32m
Fixed Assets	104m	106m	100m
Current Assets	122m	112m	124m
Current Liabilities	18m	17m	14m

Denholm Shipping Company Ltd
Greenock Ocean Terminal Patrick Street, Greenock, PA16 8UU
Tel: 01475-722276 **Fax:** 01475-781658
Website: http://www.denholm-shipping.co.uk

see next page

Denholm Shipping Company Ltd - *Cont'd*
Managers: G. Taylor
Ultimate Holding Company: J. & J. DENHOLM LIMITED
Immediate Holding Company: DENHOLM SHIPPING COMPANY LIMITED
Registration no: 00709942 **Date established:** 1961
No.of Employees: 1 - 10 **Product Groups:** 72, 74

Date of Accounts	Dec 11	Dec 10	Dec 09
Sales Turnover	7m	8m	9m
Pre Tax Profit/Loss	283	372	406
Working Capital	72	-6	-176
Fixed Assets	312	399	613
Current Assets	6m	7m	5m
Current Liabilities	1m	2m	2m

Devol Engineering Ltd
13 Clarence Street, Greenock, PA15 1LR
Tel: 01475-720934 **Fax:** 01475-787873
E-mail: sales@devol.com
Website: http://www.devol.com
Directors: A. Erskine (Fin)
Ultimate Holding Company: JAMES WALKER GROUP LIMITED
Immediate Holding Company: DEVOL ENGINEERING LIMITED
Registration no: SC043459 **Date established:** 1966
Turnover: £5m - £10m **No.of Employees:** 101 - 250 **Product Groups:** 30, 35

Date of Accounts	Mar 12	Mar 11	Mar 10
Sales Turnover	9m	7m	6m
Pre Tax Profit/Loss	1m	67	-447
Working Capital	142	-874	-1m
Fixed Assets	2m	2m	2m
Current Assets	4m	3m	2m
Current Liabilities	444	328	199

Greenock Telegraph Ltd
2 Crawford Street, Greenock, PA15 1LH
Tel: 01475-726511 **Fax:** 01475-783734
E-mail: gmorrison@cfpress.co.uk
Website: http://www.greenocktelegraph.co.uk
Bank(s): Royal Bank of Scotland
Directors: G. Morrison (Chief Op Offcr)
Managers: N. McAlister (Personnel), R. Bruce (Tech Serv Mgr), G. Faulds, S. Povey (Sales Prom Mgr)
Ultimate Holding Company: Clyde & Forth Press Ltd
Immediate Holding Company: Orr Pollock & Co. Ltd
Registration no: SC132609 **Turnover:** £5m - £10m
No.of Employees: 51 - 100 **Product Groups:** 28

Halliday Electrical Ltd
31 Lynedoch Industrial Estate, Greenock, PA15 4AX
Tel: 01475-888440 **Fax:** 01475-888220
E-mail: info@hallidayelectrical.co.uk
Directors: F. Nixon (Co Sec), J. Banks (MD)
Immediate Holding Company: CONTRACT RESOURCES LTD
Registration no: 00160342 **Date established:** 2009 **Turnover:** £1m - £2m
No.of Employees: 1 - 10 **Product Groups:** 52

Jewson Ltd
East Hamilton Street Cappielow Industrial Estate, Greenock, PA15 2TQ
Tel: 01475-725095 **Fax:** 01475-722466
E-mail: gary.anderson@jewson.co.uk
Website: http://www.jewson.co.uk
Managers: G. Anderson (Mgr)
Ultimate Holding Company: COMPAGNIE DE SAINT GOBAIN (FRANCE)
Immediate Holding Company: JEWSON LIMITED
Registration no: 00348407 **VAT No.:** GB 394 1212 63
Date established: 1939 **Turnover:** £500m - £1,000m
No.of Employees: 1 - 10 **Product Groups:** 66

Date of Accounts	Dec 11	Dec 10	Dec 09
Sales Turnover	1606m	1547m	1485m
Pre Tax Profit/Loss	18m	100m	45m
Working Capital	-345m	-250m	-349m
Fixed Assets	496m	387m	461m
Current Assets	657m	1005m	1320m
Current Liabilities	66m	120m	64m

Mackenzie Jewellers
29 West Stewart Street, Greenock, PA15 1SH
Tel: 01475-721408 **Fax:** 01475-721408
E-mail: info@mackenziejewellers.co.uk
Website: http://www.mackenziejewellers.co.uk
Directors: H. Mackenzie (Prop)
Immediate Holding Company: FINANCIAL FITNESS RESOURCE TEAM
Registration no: SC033998 **Date established:** 2003
No.of Employees: 1 - 10 **Product Groups:** 22, 33, 49

Date of Accounts	Mar 12	Mar 11	Mar 10
Sales Turnover	229	275	337
Pre Tax Profit/Loss	-40	4	23
Working Capital	50	90	87
Current Assets	69	97	94
Current Liabilities	19	6	7

Dumfriesshire

Gretna

Direct Strike
18 Canberra Road, Gretna, DG16 5DP
Tel: 01461-337951
E-mail: enquiries@directstrike.co.uk
Website: http://www.directstrike.co.uk
Directors: K. Ireland (Prop)
Immediate Holding Company: DIRECT STRIKE LIMITED
Registration no: SC400284 **Date established:** 2011
No.of Employees: 1 - 10 **Product Groups:** 37, 84

Hunter Wilson Ltd
The Sawmill Rigg, Gretna, DG16 5JL
Tel: 01461-338454 **Fax:** 01461-338468
E-mail: sales@hunterwilson.co.uk
Website: http://www.hunterwilson.co.uk
Directors: A. Jones (Dir)
Ultimate Holding Company: CLIFFORD JONES TIMBER LIMITED
Immediate Holding Company: HUNTER WILSON LIMITED
Registration no: SC049247 **Date established:** 1971
Turnover: £500,000 - £1m **No.of Employees:** 11 - 20
Product Groups: 25, 26, 66

Date of Accounts	Dec 11	Dec 10	Dec 09
Working Capital	599	439	383
Fixed Assets	1m	888	913
Current Assets	1m	967	875

East Lothian

Haddington

Henderson Grass Machinery Ltd
Bye-Pass Road, Haddington, EH41 3PQ
Tel: 01620-823171 **Fax:** 01620-826696
E-mail: info@hendersongm.co.uk
Website: http://www.hendersongm.co.uk
Bank(s): The Royal Bank of Scotland
Directors: A. Henderson (Fin), G. Henderson (MD)
Managers: P. McArthur (Parts Mgr), R. Connell (Tech Serv Mgr)
Immediate Holding Company: HENDERSON GRASS MACHINERY LIMITED
Registration no: SC215348 **VAT No.:** GB 268 5769 96
Date established: 2001 **Turnover:** £5m - £10m **No.of Employees:** 21 - 50
Product Groups: 07, 35

Date of Accounts	Oct 11	Oct 10	Oct 09
Sales Turnover	9m	7m	7m
Pre Tax Profit/Loss	140	-77	41
Working Capital	1m	1m	2m
Fixed Assets	667	679	639
Current Assets	4m	3m	4m
Current Liabilities	537	341	425

Hunter & Foulis
Unit 3 Gateside Commerce Park, Haddington, EH41 3ST
Tel: 01620-826379 **Fax:** 01620-829485
E-mail: info@hunterfoulis.co.uk
Website: http://www.hunterfoulis.co.uk
Bank(s): Bank of Scotland
Directors: A. Montgomery (MD)
Registration no: SC023484 **Turnover:** £5m - £10m
No.of Employees: 51 - 100 **Product Groups:** 28

Lothian Electrics
Hospital Road, Haddington, EH41 3PD
Tel: 01620-828700 **Fax:** 01620-828730
E-mail: info@lemac.com
Website: http://www.lemac.com
Directors: L. Blunsun (MD), L. Blunsum (MD)
Managers: K. Hampshire (Sales Admin)
Immediate Holding Company: LOTHIAN ELECTRIC MACHINES LIMITED
Registration no: SC036737 **Date established:** 1961
No.of Employees: 251 - 500 **Product Groups:** 35, 37

Date of Accounts	Jul 11	Jul 10	Jan 09
Sales Turnover	26m	31m	N/A
Pre Tax Profit/Loss	649	-371	225
Working Capital	550	-543	957
Fixed Assets	2m	2m	1m
Current Assets	6m	6m	9m
Current Liabilities	2m	618	361

Alexander Pollock Ltd
Hospital Road, Haddington, EH41 3PD
Tel: 01620-823344 **Fax:** 01620-824252
E-mail: brussell@alexander-pollock.co.uk
Website: http://www.alexander-pollock.co.uk
Directors: J. Stewart (MD), J. Kennedy (Fin), Z. Garvey (Co Sec), B. Russell (MD)
Managers: B. Russell (Mgr), A. Hampshire (Prod Mgr), D. Hampshire (Prod Mgr)
Immediate Holding Company: ALEXANDER POLLOCK LIMITED
Registration no: SC047145 **Date established:** 1969
Turnover: £500,000 - £1m **No.of Employees:** 1 - 10 **Product Groups:** 34, 35, 36, 48, 49

Date of Accounts	Mar 08	Sep 10	Sep 09
Working Capital	130	208	180
Fixed Assets	16	4	10
Current Assets	203	279	232

Pure Malt Products Ltd
Victoria Bridge, Haddington, EH41 4BD
Tel: 01620-824696 **Fax:** 01620-822018
E-mail: bruce.turner@puremalt.com
Website: http://www.puremalt.com
Bank(s): Bank of Scotland
Directors: B. Turner (MD), J. Ralph (Fin), J. Ralph (Fin), T. Thomson (Mkt Research)
Managers: M. Kelly
Immediate Holding Company: PURE MALT PRODUCTS LIMITED
Registration no: SC039605 **VAT No.:** 300 5441 18 **Date established:** 1963
Turnover: £10m - £20m **No.of Employees:** 51 - 100 **Product Groups:** 20

Date of Accounts	Mar 11	Mar 10	Mar 09
Sales Turnover	12m	11m	10m
Pre Tax Profit/Loss	1m	1m	974
Working Capital	1m	535	68
Fixed Assets	4m	4m	4m
Current Assets	4m	4m	3m
Current Liabilities	780	1m	1m

Thomas Sherriff & Company Ltd
Mill Wynd, Haddington, EH41 4DB
Tel: 01620-823132 **Fax:** 01620-822858
E-mail: rlyall@thomassherriff.co.uk
Website: http://www.thomassherriff.co.uk
Managers: R. Lyall (District Mgr)
Immediate Holding Company: THOMAS SHERRIFF AND COMPANY LIMITED
Registration no: 00906135 **Date established:** 1967
No.of Employees: 11 - 20 **Product Groups:** 41

Date of Accounts	Jan 12	Jan 11	Jan 10
Sales Turnover	24m	17m	19m
Pre Tax Profit/Loss	519	536	562
Working Capital	4m	3m	3m
Fixed Assets	1m	1m	1m
Current Assets	8m	8m	6m
Current Liabilities	239	292	480

Lanarkshire

Hamilton

Axis Scotland Ltd
Axis House 12 Auchingramont Road, Hamilton, ML3 6JT
Tel: 01698-785000 **Fax:** 01698-785111
E-mail: ken.mackay@acis.gb.com
Website: http://www.axisscotlandlimitedhamilton.co.uk
Bank(s): Bank of Scotland
Directors: K. McKay (MD), K. Mackay (MD)
Managers: T. Dryberer (I.T. Exec)
Immediate Holding Company: AXIS SCOTLAND LTD.
Registration no: SC268880 **Date established:** 2004
Turnover: £5m - £10m **No.of Employees:** 11 - 20 **Product Groups:** 26

Date of Accounts	Sep 11	Sep 10	Sep 09
Working Capital	220	114	69
Fixed Assets	1m	1m	1m
Current Assets	1m	985	745

Barnshaw Steel Benders
89 Bothwell Road, Hamilton, ML3 0DW
Tel: 01698-421010 **Fax:** 01698-421177
E-mail: barbara.powell@barnshaws.com
Website: http://www.barnshaw.com
Managers: B. Powell (Mgr)
Turnover: £1m - £2m **No.of Employees:** 11 - 20 **Product Groups:** 35, 43, 45, 46, 48

Bernafon UK Ltd
Cadzow Industrial Estate Off Low Waters Road, Hamilton, ML3 7QE
Tel: 01698-285968 **Fax:** 01698-421456
Website: http://www.bernafon.co.uk
Directors: A. Tait (Co Sec), E. Spahr (MD), P. Sydserff (MD)
Registration no: 02434295 **Date established:** 2008
No.of Employees: 1 - 10 **Product Groups:** 38, 44, 67

Bothwell Chauffeur Drive Ltd
69 Bothwell Road, Hamilton, ML3 0DW
Tel: 01698-285920 **Fax:** 01698-307076
E-mail: info@bothwellbridalcars.co.uk
Website: http://www.bothwellbridecars.co.uk
Directors: J. Duffy (Dir)
Immediate Holding Company: EDENBRAE INVESTMENTS LIMITED
Registration no: SC362705 **Date established:** 2007
No.of Employees: 1 - 10 **Product Groups:** 39, 72

Cakes By Ann
6 Carron Court, Hamilton, ML3 8TD
Tel: 01698-336448
E-mail: fpeter@blueyonder.co.uk
Website: http://www.cakesbyann.co.uk
Directors: P. Fletcher (Prop)
Date established: 2003 **Turnover:** Up to £250,000
No.of Employees: 1 - 10 **Product Groups:** 20

Cuthbertson Laird Group
Parkburn Court Parkburn Industrial Estate, Hamilton, ML3 0QQ
Tel: 01698-829711 **Fax:** 01698-828363
E-mail: hamilton@cuthbertsonlaird.co.uk
Website: http://www.cuthbertsonlaird.co.uk
Directors: P. Greenshields (MD)
Immediate Holding Company: CUTHBERTSON & LAIRD INSTRUMENTS LIMITED
Registration no: SC070763 **Date established:** 1980 **Turnover:** £2m - £5m
No.of Employees: 11 - 20 **Product Groups:** 37, 38

Date of Accounts	Aug 11	Aug 10	Aug 09
Working Capital	402	265	174
Fixed Assets	283	277	314
Current Assets	2m	1m	992
Current Liabilities	355	N/A	N/A

Graham
Block 1 Cadzow Industrial Estate, Hamilton, ML3 7QU
Tel: 01698-422522 **Fax:** 01698-423284
E-mail: sales@grahamgroup.com
Website: http://www.graham-group.co.uk
Managers: P. McGinley (District Mgr)
Immediate Holding Company: MACGREGOR FLOORING COMPANY LIMITED
Registration no: 00066738 **Date established:** 1985 **Turnover:** £1m - £2m
No.of Employees: 1 - 10 **Product Groups:** 66

Date of Accounts	Aug 11	Aug 10	Aug 09
Working Capital	572	643	651
Fixed Assets	49	36	38
Current Assets	1m	2m	2m

H O B Ltd
17 Douglas Street, Hamilton, ML3 0BZ
Tel: 01698-281520 **Fax:** 01698-891508
E-mail: john@hobltd.co.uk
Bank(s): Clydesdale Bank PLC
Directors: J. Bayne (MD), A. Shand (Dir)
Managers: G. Foster
Immediate Holding Company: H.O.B. LIMITED
Registration no: SC101065 **VAT No.:** GB 424 0710 93
Date established: 1986 **Turnover:** £1m - £2m **No.of Employees:** 21 - 50
Product Groups: 38, 48

Date of Accounts	Nov 11	Nov 10	Nov 09
Working Capital	346	320	308
Fixed Assets	500	415	471
Current Assets	723	617	497

Ireland Alloys Ltd
Whistleberry Road, Hamilton, ML3 0HP
Tel: 01698-822461 **Fax:** 01698-825166
E-mail: trader@ireland-alloys.co.uk
Website: http://www.ireland-alloys.co.uk
Bank(s): Bank of Scotland
Directors: K. Granderson (MD)
Ultimate Holding Company: MURRAY INTERNATIONAL HOLDINGS LIMITED
Immediate Holding Company: IRELAND ALLOYS LIMITED
Registration no: SC040892 **Date established:** 1964
Turnover: £20m - £50m **No.of Employees:** 21 - 50 **Product Groups:** 34

Date of Accounts	Jan 08	Jun 11	Jun 10
Sales Turnover	30m	24m	19m
Pre Tax Profit/Loss	1m	-110	13
Working Capital	4m	5m	5m
Fixed Assets	2m	2m	2m
Current Assets	8m	8m	8m
Current Liabilities	428	244	558

North Aluminium
31 Argyle Crescent Hillhouse Industrial Estate, Hamilton, ML3 9BQ
Tel: 01698-284088 **Fax:** 01698-891825
E-mail: sales@northaluminium.com
Website: http://www.northaluminium.com
Directors: M. North (Dir)
Managers: L. Gaughan (Sales Prom Mgr)
Date established: 1997 **No.of Employees:** 11 - 20 **Product Groups:** 26, 35, 36

Smith For Stairlifts
4 Woodhall Avenue, Hamilton, ML3 9BT
Tel: 01698-424433 **Fax:** 01698-424433
Directors: E. Smith (Fin), J. Smith (Sales)
Immediate Holding Company: SMITH FOR STAIRLIFTS LTD.
Registration no: SC253906 **Date established:** 2003
Turnover: Up to £250,000 **No.of Employees:** 1 - 10 **Product Groups:** 35, 39, 45

Date of Accounts	Mar 09	Mar 08	Sep 11
Sales Turnover	N/A	20	N/A
Pre Tax Profit/Loss	N/A	-1	N/A
Working Capital	-2	-0	-7
Current Assets	N/A	2	N/A
Current Liabilities	N/A	1	N/A

E G Steele & Co. Ltd
25 Dalziel Street, Hamilton, ML3 9AU
Tel: 01698-283765 **Fax:** 01698-891550
E-mail: info@egsteele.com
Website: http://www.egsteele.com
Bank(s): The Royal Bank of Scotland
Directors: D. Steele (MD), A. Steele (Fin)
Ultimate Holding Company: E.G. STEELE HOLDINGS LIMITED
Immediate Holding Company: E.G. STEELE & COMPANY LIMITED
Registration no: SC024956 **VAT No.:** GB 260 8010 93
Date established: 1947 **Turnover:** £2m - £5m **No.of Employees:** 11 - 20
Product Groups: 39, 51

Date of Accounts	Apr 12	Apr 11	Apr 10
Working Capital	397	504	545
Fixed Assets	66	59	225
Current Assets	761	837	848

Templeton Tools & Machinery Ltd
Unit 6-7 Parkburn Industrial Estate, Hamilton, ML3 0QQ
Tel: 01698-821111 **Fax:** 01698-825454
E-mail: sales@engineeringsupplies.co.uk
Website: http://www.engineeringsupplies.co.uk
Directors: S. Thompson (Dir)
Immediate Holding Company: TEMPLETON TOOLS & MACHINERY LIMITED
Registration no: SC077414 **Date established:** 1982
No.of Employees: 1 - 10 **Product Groups:** 46

Date of Accounts	Mar 12	Mar 11	Mar 10
Working Capital	479	342	303
Fixed Assets	41	31	21
Current Assets	581	542	365

Vacua Therm Sales Ltd
5 Parkburn Court Parkburn Industrial Estate, Hamilton, ML3 0QQ
Tel: 01698-825169 **Fax:** 01698-824265
E-mail: callum@vacuathermsales.co.uk
Website: http://www.vacuathermsales.co.uk
Directors: C. Dick (MD)
Ultimate Holding Company: VACUA-THERM DESIGN LIMITED
Immediate Holding Company: VACUA-THERM SALES LIMITED
Registration no: SC096460 **Date established:** 1985
No.of Employees: 1 - 10 **Product Groups:** 40, 42, 46

Date of Accounts	May 11	May 10	May 09
Working Capital	108	84	100
Fixed Assets	125	122	118
Current Assets	212	155	160

Roxburghshire

Hawick

Barrie Knitwear
Burnfoot Industrial Estate, Hawick, TD9 8RJ
Tel: 01450-365500 **Fax:** 01450-365501
E-mail: enquiries@barrie.co.uk
Website: http://www.barrie.co.uk
Bank(s): Bank of Scotland, H.O., Edinburgh
Directors: C. Brown (Sales), J. Carrie (MD)
Managers: M. Tirtwood (I.T. Exec), M. Kirkwood (Tech Serv Mgr), C. Sulley (Ops Mgr)
Ultimate Holding Company: DAWSON INTERNATIONAL PUBLIC LIMITED COMPANY
Immediate Holding Company: BARRIE KNITWEAR LIMITED
Registration no: SC028892 **VAT No.:** GB 592 9908 79
Date established: 1952 **Turnover:** £5m - £10m
No.of Employees: 101 - 250 **Product Groups:** 24

Date of Accounts	Dec 06
Working Capital	2m
Current Assets	2m

Michael Brandon Ltd
15-17 Oliver Cresent, Hawick, TD9 9BJ
Tel: 01450-373333 **Fax:** 01450-375252
E-mail: sales@brandonltd.co.uk
Website: http://www.brandonltd.co.uk
Directors: H. Brandon (Fin), M. Brandon (MD)
Immediate Holding Company: MICHAEL BRANDON LIMITED
Registration no: 00978704 **VAT No.:** GB 269 9485 84
Date established: 1970 **No.of Employees:** 11 - 20 **Product Groups:** 39

Date of Accounts	Dec 11	Dec 10	Dec 09
Working Capital	-324	-288	-150
Fixed Assets	814	819	820

Current Assets	536	417	521

Clan Douglas
PO Box 13331, Hawick, TD9 0WX
Tel: 01450-363140 **Fax:** 01450-363111
E-mail: sales@clan-douglas.com
Website: http://www.clan-douglas.com
Directors: B. Hartop (MD), J. Gutteridge (Dir)
Managers: B. Hartop (Mgr)
Ultimate Holding Company: TOYOBOSHI KOGYO CO. LTD (JAPAN)
VAT No.: GB 848 0452 19 **No.of Employees:** 101 - 250
Product Groups: 24

Commercial Electric Heat Ltd
20 Commercial Road, Hawick, TD9 7AQ
Tel: 01937-844994 **Fax:** 01937-844123
E-mail: sales@cehltd.co.uk
Website: http://www.cehltd.co.uk
Directors: A. Abbot (Fin), N. Blunt (Dir)
Registration no: 02838593 **Date established:** 1993
Turnover: £250,000 - £500,000 **No.of Employees:** 1 - 10
Product Groups: 40, 66

Date of Accounts	Aug 09	Aug 08	Aug 07
Working Capital	54	50	31
Fixed Assets	6	12	21
Current Assets	158	168	189

Dawson International plc
Burnfoot Industrial Estate, Hawick, TD9 8RJ
Tel: 01577-867000 **Fax:** 01577-867010
E-mail: enquiries@dawson-international.co.uk
Website: http://www.dawson-international.co.uk
Directors: P. Munn (Grp Chief Exec), A. Bartmess (Grp Chief Exec), M. Hartley (Ch)
Managers: S. Balfour (I.T. Exec)
Ultimate Holding Company: DAWSON INTERNATIONAL PUBLIC LIMITED COMPANY
Immediate Holding Company: DAWSON INTERNATIONAL TRADING LIMITED
Registration no: SC162162 **VAT No.:** GB 271 3271 77
Date established: 1995 **Turnover:** £75m - £125m
No.of Employees: 1 - 10 **Product Groups:** 23, 63

Date of Accounts	Dec 07	Jan 09	Apr 11
Sales Turnover	26m	29m	9m
Pre Tax Profit/Loss	-4m	N/A	-6m
Working Capital	14m	15m	5m
Fixed Assets	3m	2m	1m
Current Assets	60m	58m	17m
Current Liabilities	7m	5m	2m

Emtelle UK Ltd
Haughhead, Hawick, TD9 8LF
Tel: 01450-364000 **Fax:** 01450-364001
E-mail: info@emtelle.com
Website: http://www.emtelle.com
Bank(s): Midland
Directors: R. Langdon (Fin), D. Stockton (I.T. Dir), S. King (MD)
Managers: G. Campbell (Tech Serv Mgr), J. Whisker (Comptroller)
Ultimate Holding Company: MAUNA INTERNATIONAL SARL (LUXEMBOURG)
Immediate Holding Company: EMTELLE UK LIMITED
Registration no: SC079486 **Date established:** 1982
Turnover: £50m - £75m **No.of Employees:** 101 - 250 **Product Groups:** 66

Date of Accounts	Dec 11	Dec 10	Dec 09
Sales Turnover	65m	56m	44m
Pre Tax Profit/Loss	4m	4m	2m
Working Capital	10m	7m	6m
Fixed Assets	7m	8m	8m
Current Assets	18m	17m	14m
Current Liabilities	2m	1m	2m

John D Falla & Son
Bonchester Bridge, Hawick, TD9 8JN
Tel: 01450-860218 **Fax:** 01450-860345
E-mail: jfalla@johndfalla.co.uk
Directors: J. Falla (Prop)
Date established: 1908 **No.of Employees:** 1 - 10 **Product Groups:** 41

Forever Scotland IT Consultancy
22 Leishman Place, Hawick, TD9 8EZ
Tel: 01450-377071
E-mail: labourparty@foreverscotland.co.uk
Website: http://www.foreverscotland.co.uk
Directors: M. Grieve (Ch)
Date established: 2008 **No.of Employees:** 1 - 10 **Product Groups:** 44

Gloverall PLC T/A Peter Scotts
11 Buccleuch Street, Hawick, TD9 0HJ
Tel: 01450-372311 **Fax:** 01450-374610
E-mail: sales@peterscott.co.uk
Website: http://www.peterscott.co.uk
Bank(s): The Royal Bank of Scotland
Directors: D. Kim (MD)
Managers: A. De Luca
Immediate Holding Company: PETER SCOTT & COMPANY, LTD
Registration no: SC004892 **VAT No.:** GB 268 8069 12
Date established: 2001 **No.of Employees:** 51 - 100 **Product Groups:** 63

Date of Accounts	Dec 07	Dec 06
Pre Tax Profit/Loss	-820	-255
Working Capital	1141	1936
Fixed Assets	892	944
Current Assets	2609	2888
Current Liabilities	1468	953
Total Share Capital	360	360
ROCE% (Return on Capital Employed)	-40.4	-8.9

Jewson Ltd
Burnfoot Industrial Estate, Hawick, TD9 8SL
Tel: 01450-377766 **Fax:** 01450-377741
E-mail: colin.mcheugh@jewson.co.uk
Website: http://www.jewson.co.uk
Managers: C. McHeugh (Mgr)
Ultimate Holding Company: COMPAGNIE DE SAINT GOBAIN (FRANCE)
Immediate Holding Company: JEWSON LIMITED
Registration no: 00348407 **VAT No.:** GB 497 7184 83
Date established: 1939 **Turnover:** £2m - £5m **No.of Employees:** 1 - 10
Product Groups: 66

Date of Accounts	Dec 11	Dec 10	Dec 09
Sales Turnover	1606m	1547m	1485m
Pre Tax Profit/Loss	18m	100m	45m

Working Capital	-345m	-250m	-349m
Fixed Assets	496m	387m	461m
Current Assets	657m	1005m	1320m
Current Liabilities	66m	120m	64m

John C Laurie Textile Engineers Ltd
15 Teviot Crescent, Hawick, TD9 9RQ
Tel: 01450-373149 **Fax:** 01450-373091
E-mail: keith.johnson@johnclaurie.com
Website: http://www.johnclaurie.com
Directors: J. Douglas (Fin), K. Johnson (MD)
Immediate Holding Company: JOHN C. LAURIE (HAWICK) LIMITED
Registration no: SC030397 **Date established:** 1954
Turnover: £250,000 - £500,000 **No.of Employees:** 1 - 10
Product Groups: 43

Date of Accounts	Mar 11	Mar 10	Mar 09
Working Capital	-2	4	19
Fixed Assets	16	17	19
Current Assets	23	23	39

William Lockie & Co. Ltd
27-28 Drumlanrig Square, Hawick, TD9 0AW
Tel: 01450-372645 **Fax:** 01450-373846
E-mail: info@williamlockie.com
Website: http://www.williamlockie.com
Bank(s): Royal Bank of Scotland
Directors: H. Graham (Co Sec), R. Nuttall (Fab), D. Nuttall (MD)
Managers: I. McRobert (Sales Admin), A. Gilcrist (Mktg Serv Mgr)
Immediate Holding Company: WILLIAM LOCKIE & COMPANY LIMITED
Registration no: SC023788 **VAT No.:** GB 269 6331 29
Date established: 1946 **Turnover:** £5m - £10m
No.of Employees: 101 - 250 **Product Groups:** 24

Date of Accounts	Feb 12	Feb 11	Feb 10
Sales Turnover	6m	6m	4m
Pre Tax Profit/Loss	820	571	320
Working Capital	4m	4m	4m
Fixed Assets	315	336	345
Current Assets	5m	5m	4m
Current Liabilities	495	454	397

Northern Environmental Services Ltd
Burnfoot Workshops Burnfoot Road, Hawick, TD9 8EL
Tel: 01450-370277 **Fax:** 01450-371134
E-mail: info@nesltduk.co.uk
Website: http://www.northernenvironmentalservices.co.uk
Directors: C. White (MD)
Immediate Holding Company: NORTHERN ENVIRONMENTAL SERVICES LIMITED
Registration no: SC126764 **Date established:** 1990
No.of Employees: 11 - 20 **Product Groups:** 38, 42

Date of Accounts	Mar 12	Mar 11	Mar 10
Working Capital	320	290	302
Fixed Assets	141	155	161
Current Assets	525	864	818

N Peal
Victoria Road, Hawick, TD9 7AH
Tel: 020-7493 9220 **Fax:** 01450-377581
E-mail: d@npeal.co.uk
Website: http://www.npeal.co.uk
Bank(s): National Westminster
Directors: D. Hartop (MD), R. Ranken (Sales)
Managers: M. Marshall (Sales Admin)
Immediate Holding Company: BORDER AUTOCARE & TYRE SERVICES LIMITED
Registration no: SC217592 **VAT No.:** GB 671 2065 53
Date established: 2001 **Turnover:** £2m - £5m **No.of Employees:** 21 - 50
Product Groups: 24

Date of Accounts	May 11	May 10	May 09
Working Capital	-0	23	22
Fixed Assets	23	26	24
Current Assets	52	89	70

Premier Braking Ltd
15-17 Oliver Crescent, Hawick, TD9 9BJ
Tel: 01450-373333 **Fax:** 01450-375252
E-mail: sales@premierbraking.com
Directors: A. Freeman (MD), M. Brandon (Fin)
Immediate Holding Company: PREMIER BRAKING LIMITED
Registration no: SC133975 **Date established:** 1991
No.of Employees: 1 - 10 **Product Groups:** 33, 34

Date of Accounts	Dec 10	Dec 08	Dec 07
Working Capital	310	1m	869
Fixed Assets	N/A	1	1
Current Assets	370	1m	886

Scottish Borders Housing Association
West Port, Hawick, TD9 0BG
Tel: 01450-360650 **Fax:** 01450-360651
E-mail: enquiries@sbha.org.uk
Website: http://www.sbha.org.uk
Directors: J. Mulloy (Grp Chief Exec)
Immediate Holding Company: SCOTTISH BORDERS CHAMBER OF COMMERCE
Registration no: SC270371 **VAT No.:** GB 663 7265 15
Date established: 2004 **Turnover:** Up to £250,000
No.of Employees: 11 - 20 **Product Groups:** 87

Date of Accounts	Jul 09	Mar 12	Mar 11
Sales Turnover	N/A	28	32
Pre Tax Profit/Loss	N/A	1	-11
Working Capital	19	-3	-4
Current Assets	29	3	8
Current Liabilities	N/A	4	9

Turnbull & Scott Engineers Ltd
Unit 1a Burnfoot Industrial Estate, Hawick, TD9 8RW
Tel: 01450-372053 **Fax:** 01450-377800
E-mail: info@turnbull-scott.co.uk
Website: http://www.turnbull-scott.co.uk
Bank(s): HSBC
Directors: H. Marshall (Co Sec), P. Murphy (MD)
Managers: S. Carruthers (Sales Admin)
Ultimate Holding Company: SEACLIFF DEVELOPMENTS LIMITED
Immediate Holding Company: SILVERSWIFT DEVELOPMENTS LIMITED
Registration no: SC029804 **VAT No.:** GB 928 9645 56
Date established: 1954 **Turnover:** £1m - £2m **No.of Employees:** 21 - 50
Product Groups: 30, 35, 36, 37, 40, 42, 46, 48, 52, 54, 66, 84

Date of Accounts	Dec 10	Dec 09	Dec 08
Working Capital	14	19	20
Fixed Assets	600	600	600

see next page

Turnbull & Scott Engineers Ltd - *Cont'd*

Current Assets	116	92	69

Vision Dental Laboratory

25 North Bridge Street, Hawick, TD9 9BD
Tel: 01450-363665
E-mail: wayne@visiondentalab.com
Website: http://www.visiondentalab.com
Directors: W. Flack (Ptnr)
No.of Employees: 1 - 10 **Product Groups:** 38, 88

Charles N Whillans Partnership

Teviotdale Mill Commercial Road, Hawick, TD9 7AQ
Tel: 01450-373311 **Fax:** 01450-376082
E-mail: chasnwhillans@ip3.co.uk
Directors: A. Whillans (Ptnr), D. Whillans (Ptnr), I. Whillans (Ptnr)
VAT No.: GB 300 7830 94 **Turnover:** £2m - £5m **No.of Employees:** 1 - 10
Product Groups: 61

Dunbartonshire

Helensburgh

Caledonian Marine Ltd

Rhu Marina Pier Road, Rhu, Helensburgh, G84 8LH
Tel: 01436-821184 **Fax:** 01436-820645
E-mail: caledonianmarine@btconnect.com
Website: http://www.caledonianmarine.co.uk
Directors: R. Ferguson (Co Sec), S. Lindsay (MD)
Immediate Holding Company: CALEDONIAN MARINE LIMITED
Registration no: SC206423 **Date established:** 2000
No.of Employees: 1 - 10 **Product Groups:** 35, 36, 39

Date of Accounts	Mar 07	Mar 06
Working Capital	-10	-14
Fixed Assets	12	15
Current Assets	82	65
Current Liabilities	92	79

Macinnes Tooling Ltd

Thistle House 29 Adelaide Street, Helensburgh, G84 7DL
Tel: 01436-676913 **Fax:** 01436-678877
E-mail: sales@macinnes.co.uk
Website: http://www.macinnes.co.uk
Directors: J. Boyle (Dir)
Immediate Holding Company: MACINNES TOOLING LIMITED
Registration no: 02742082 **VAT No.:** GB 263 6216 65
Date established: 1992 **Turnover:** £2m - £5m **No.of Employees:** 1 - 10
Product Groups: 36, 46

Date of Accounts	Aug 11	Aug 10	Aug 09
Working Capital	77	68	19
Fixed Assets	184	186	184
Current Assets	157	164	125

Aberdeenshire

Huntly

Black Gold Oil Tools Ltd

Steven Road, Huntly, AB54 8SX
Tel: 01466-793457 **Fax:** 01466-793095
Directors: C. Grant (Dir), T. Flynn (Sales)
Managers: C. Grant (Mgr)
Immediate Holding Company: BLACK GOLD OIL TOOLS LIMITED
Registration no: SC055675 **Date established:** 1974
No.of Employees: 1 - 10 **Product Groups:** 42, 45

Keith Rose Engineering Ltd

Workshop Rose Newton Clatt, Huntly, AB54 4PH
Tel: 01464-831297 **Fax:** 01464-831641
E-mail: keith@keith-rose.co.uk
Website: http://www.keith-rose.co.uk
Directors: K. Rose (MD)
Immediate Holding Company: KEITH ROSE LIMITED
Registration no: SC246493 **Date established:** 2003
No.of Employees: 1 - 10 **Product Groups:** 41

Long Technology Ltd

1 Richmond Lane, Huntly, AB54 8FJ
Tel: 01466-794646 **Fax:** 01466-794111
E-mail: sales@longtechnology.com
Website: http://www.longtechnology.com
Directors: B. Long (MD)
Immediate Holding Company: LONG TECHNOLOGY LIMITED
Registration no: SC105350 **Date established:** 1987
Turnover: £500,000 - £1m **No.of Employees:** 1 - 10 **Product Groups:** 35, 39, 66

Date of Accounts	Nov 11	Nov 10	Nov 09
Working Capital	267	331	176
Fixed Assets	38	39	39
Current Assets	408	586	293

Aberdeenshire

Insch

Aardvark Clear Mine Ltd

Shevock Estate, Insch, AB52 6XQ
Tel: 01464-820122 **Fax:** 01464-820985
E-mail: office@aardvarkclearmine.com
Website: http://www.aardvarkclearmine.com
Managers: M. Padgett (Site Co-ord)
Ultimate Holding Company: PENMAN ENGINEERING HOLDINGS LIMITED
Immediate Holding Company: AARDVARK CLEAR MINE LIMITED
Registration no: SC080167 **VAT No.:** GB 384 5442 33
Date established: 1982 **Turnover:** £250,000 - £500,000
No.of Employees: 1 - 10 **Product Groups:** 51

Date of Accounts	Mar 11	Mar 10	Mar 09
Sales Turnover	839	2m	6m
Pre Tax Profit/Loss	-79	350	634
Working Capital	2m	2m	2m
Fixed Assets	2	5	50
Current Assets	3m	4m	5m
Current Liabilities	442	748	3m

Gordon C Smith

Edinvale Colpy, Insch, AB52 6XD
Tel: 01464-841308
Directors: G. Smith (Prop)
Date established: 1993 **No.of Employees:** 1 - 10 **Product Groups:** 36, 39, 40

A G Stuart Holdings Ltd

Old Rayne, Insch, AB52 6RX
Tel: 01464-851208 **Fax:** 01464-851202
E-mail: sales@slyvanstuart.com
Website: http://www.sylvanstuart.com
Directors: B. Stuart (MD)
Immediate Holding Company: A.G. STUART HOLDINGS LIMITED
Registration no: SC144258 **Date established:** 1993
Turnover: £500,000 - £1m **No.of Employees:** 1 - 10 **Product Groups:** 25

Date of Accounts	Apr 11	Apr 10	Apr 09
Working Capital	-78	-84	-82
Fixed Assets	400	400	430
Current Assets	N/A	1	N/A

Rossshire

Invergordon

Cromarty Firth Port Authority

Port Office Shore Road, Invergordon, IV18 0HD
Tel: 01349-852308 **Fax:** 01349-854172
E-mail: ken@cfpa.co.uk
Website: http://www.cfpa.co.uk
Bank(s): The Royal Bank of Scotland
Managers: V. Smith (Sales & Mktg Mg), R. Fea (Fin Mgr), K. Gray
Immediate Holding Company: CRUISE HIGHLANDS LIMITED
Registration no: SC361707 **Date established:** 2003 **Turnover:** £2m - £5m
No.of Employees: 21 - 50 **Product Groups:** 39, 77

Date of Accounts	Dec 11	Dec 10	Dec 09
Working Capital	101	65	80
Current Assets	290	230	191

Services Supplies Ltd

131-133 High Street, Invergordon, IV18 0AJ
Tel: 01349-854050 **Fax:** 01349-853960
E-mail: info@sersupplies.co.uk
Website: http://www.sersupplies.co.uk
Directors: S. Ruck (MD), J. Ruck (Dir)
Immediate Holding Company: SVS SUPPLIES LIMITED
Registration no: 06357001 **Date established:** 2007
No.of Employees: 1 - 10 **Product Groups:** 46

Date of Accounts	Oct 11	Oct 10	Oct 09
Working Capital	156	170	204
Fixed Assets	219	227	238
Current Assets	409	439	399

Fife

Inverkeithing

Caledonian Industrial Solutions Ltd

58 Whinny Hill Crest, Inverkeithing, KY11 1BD
Tel: 07854-457676 **Fax:** 01383-412943
E-mail: caledonianindustrialsolutions@googlemail.com
Website: http://glovesuk.co.uk
Registration no: SC335792 **Date established:** 2008
No.of Employees: 1 - 10 **Product Groups:** 24, 47, 63

E S C

Ferryhill Road, Inverkeithing, KY11 1HD
Tel: 01383-418610 **Fax:** 01383-417244
E-mail: sales@eosc.co.uk
Website: http://www.eosc.co.uk
Directors: A. Bankier (Ptnr)
No.of Employees: 1 - 10 **Product Groups:** 27, 30

Muir Group Ltd

Muir House Bellknowes Industrial Estate, Inverkeithing, KY11 1HY
Tel: 01383-416191 **Fax:** 01383-410193
E-mail: muir@muir-group.co.uk
Website: http://www.muirgroup.co.uk
Directors: R. Muir (Dir), I. Muir (Dir), J. Muir (Ch), A. Muir (Develop), J. McHarding (Fin), C. Muir (Dir)
Managers: J. McCardae (I.T. Exec)
Registration no: SC058738 **VAT No.:** GB 401 0063 35
Turnover: £20m - £50m **No.of Employees:** 101 - 250 **Product Groups:** 52

Date of Accounts	Feb 08	Feb 07
Sales Turnover	92433	92558
Pre Tax Profit/Loss	10359	9603
Working Capital	55877	51614
Fixed Assets	8849	6337
Current Assets	80690	77592
Current Liabilities	24813	25978
Total Share Capital	50	50
ROCE% (Return on Capital Employed)	16.0	16.6
ROT% (Return on Turnover)	11.2	10.4

Tarmac Ltd

Upper Cruiks, Inverkeithing, KY11 1HH
Tel: 01383-413241 **Fax:** 01383-413244
Website: http://www.tarmac.co.uk
Managers: D. Simmons (Mgr)
Ultimate Holding Company: ANGLO AMERICAN PLC
Immediate Holding Company: TARMAC LIMITED
Registration no: 00453791 **Date established:** 1948
No.of Employees: 11 - 20 **Product Groups:** 14, 31, 33, 66

Date of Accounts	Dec 11	Dec 10	Dec 09
Sales Turnover	1081m	1069m	1247m
Pre Tax Profit/Loss	-20m	75m	-47m
Working Capital	-86m	-24m	25m
Fixed Assets	1199m	1244m	1391m
Current Assets	329m	321m	431m
Current Liabilities	99m	93m	168m

Invernesshire

Inverness

Alba Traffic Management

24 Longman Drive, Inverness, IV1 1SU
Tel: 01463-259195
E-mail: info@albatraffic.co.uk
Website: http://www.albatraffic.co.uk
Managers: I. Bruce (Mgr)
Immediate Holding Company: EDINBURGH PUBS AND INNS LIMITED
Date established: 2010 **No.of Employees:** 11 - 20 **Product Groups:** 40, 51

Atlantic Focus Limited

17 Leachkin Avenue, Inverness, IV3 8LH
Tel: 07786-704420 **Fax:** 0560-1310827
E-mail: sales@atlanticfocus.com
Website: http://www.atlanticfocus.com
Directors: D. Forrester (MD)
Registration no: 04411831 **Product Groups:** 29, 39, 68

C P L Petroleum Ltd

33 Harbour Road, Inverness, IV1 1UA
Tel: 01463-238989 **Fax:** 01463-712352
E-mail: sales@cplpetroleum.co.uk
Website: http://www.cplpetroleum.co.uk
Managers: D. Mackey (Mgr), M. Daley (Mgr)
Ultimate Holding Company: CPL Industries Holdings Ltd
Immediate Holding Company: CPL Industries Ltd
Registration no: 03003860 **VAT No.:** GB 721 5764 39
Turnover: £1m - £2m **No.of Employees:** 1 - 10 **Product Groups:** 66

City Mobility

46a Seafield Road, Inverness, IV1 1SG
Tel: 01463-250850 **Fax:** 01463-250950
E-mail: info@citymobility.co.uk
Website: http://www.citymobility.co.uk
Directors: S. Hendry (Fin)
Immediate Holding Company: GALAXY MARKETING SCOTLAND LTD
Registration no: SC236798 **Date established:** 2002
No.of Employees: 1 - 10 **Product Groups:** 24, 30, 38

Date of Accounts	Sep 11	Sep 10	Sep 09
Working Capital	-10	-30	-37
Fixed Assets	28	19	20
Current Assets	83	63	46

City Plumbing Supplies Ltd

City Heating Spares 1214 Harbour Road Longman Estate, Inverness, IV1 1SY
Tel: 01463-716166 **Fax:** 01463-716164
Website: http://www.cityplumbing.co.uk
Directors: A. Pike (Co Sec)
Managers: G. Wright (District Mgr)
Immediate Holding Company: CITY PLUMBING SUPPLIES LIMITED
Registration no: 01617423 **VAT No.:** GB 497 7184 83
Date established: 1982 **Turnover:** £250m - £500m
No.of Employees: 1001 - 1500 **Product Groups:** 52, 66

Date of Accounts	Dec 10	Dec 09	Dec 07
Working Capital	101	101	101
Current Assets	192	192	192
Current Liabilities	91	N/A	N/A

Comcat Engineering

3a3 Unit Smithton Industrial Estate, Smithton, Inverness, IV2 7WL
Tel: 01463-796060 **Fax:** 01463-796061
E-mail: comcat@fsmail.net
Website: http://www.comcatltd.co.uk
Directors: J. McKenzie (Dir)
Immediate Holding Company: COMCAT ENGINEERING LTD.
Registration no: SC173105 **Date established:** 1997
No.of Employees: 11 - 20 **Product Groups:** 20, 40, 41

Date of Accounts	Aug 11	Aug 10	Aug 09
Working Capital	82	41	34
Fixed Assets	57	62	63
Current Assets	330	257	194

CPL Petroleum Ltd

33 Harbour Road, Inverness, IV1 1UA
Tel: 01463-238989 **Fax:** 01463-712352
E-mail: sales@cplpetroleum.co.uk
Website: http://www.cplpetroleum.co.uk
Managers: I. Glasper (District Mgr), P. Docherty (Mgr)
Ultimate Holding Company: CPL Industries Holdings Ltd
Immediate Holding Company: CPL Industries Ltd
Registration no: 03003860 **Date established:** 2008
No.of Employees: 1 - 10 **Product Groups:** 66

Gael Force Marine Ltd

Anderson Street, Inverness, IV3 8DH
Tel: 01463-229400 **Fax:** 01463-229421
E-mail: sales@gaelforce.net
Website: http://www.gaelforce.net
Bank(s): The Royal Bank of Scotland
Directors: S. Graham (MD)
Immediate Holding Company: GAEL FORCE (HOLDINGS) LTD.
Registration no: SC229244 **VAT No.:** GB 430 4597 80
Date established: 2002 **Turnover:** £10m - £20m
No.of Employees: 51 - 100 **Product Groups:** 23, 35, 39, 74

Date of Accounts	Dec 11	Dec 10	Dec 09
Working Capital	92	290	16
Fixed Assets	N/A	N/A	52
Current Assets	92	290	16

Highland Fork Lifts
15 Culloden Park Culloden, Inverness, IV2 7AY
Tel: 01463-793105 **Fax:** 01463-793105
E-mail: veronicadent@yahoo.co.uk
Directors: V. Dent (Ptnr)
Date established: 1998 **No.of Employees:** 1 - 10 **Product Groups:** 35, 39, 45

Highland Fuels Ltd
Affric House Beechwood Business Park, Inverness, IV2 3BW
Tel: 0800-224224 **Fax:** 01463-710899
E-mail: sales@highlandfuels.co.uk
Website: http://www.highlandfuels.co.uk
Bank(s): National Westminster Bank Plc
Directors: P. Maclean (Sales)
Managers: T. Donoghue (Sales Prom Mgr)
Ultimate Holding Company: HIGHLAND FUELS (INVESTMENTS) LIMITED
Immediate Holding Company: HIGHLAND FUELS HOLDINGS LIMITED
Registration no: SC215790 **VAT No.:** GB 693 9889 43
Date established: 2001 **Turnover:** £125m - £250m
No.of Employees: 21 - 50 **Product Groups:** 31

Date of Accounts	Dec 11	Dec 10	Dec 09
Sales Turnover	N/A	174m	132m
Pre Tax Profit/Loss	50	3m	2m
Working Capital	-3m	4m	2m
Fixed Assets	4m	6m	7m
Current Assets	N/A	26m	19m
Current Liabilities	N/A	2m	2m

Highland Motor Parts Ltd
21 Henderson Road, Inverness, IV1 1SN
Tel: 01463-223700 **Fax:** 01463-711351
E-mail: christine@highlandmotorparts.co.uk
Website: http://www.highlandmotorparts.co.uk
Bank(s): Clydesdale Bank PLC
Directors: D. Maclellan (MD), C. Milton (Co Sec)
Managers: R. Maclellan (Sales Admin)
Immediate Holding Company: HIGHLAND MOTOR PARTS LIMITED
Registration no: SC228871 **VAT No.:** GB 589 2301 20
Date established: 2002 **Turnover:** £2m - £5m **No.of Employees:** 21 - 50
Product Groups: 68

Date of Accounts	Jun 11	Jun 10	Jun 09
Working Capital	701	526	612
Fixed Assets	171	166	188
Current Assets	2m	2m	1m

Highland News Group
New Century House Stadium Road, Inverness, IV1 1FG
Tel: 01463-732222 **Fax:** 01463-221251
E-mail: smg@spp-group.com
Website: http://www.highland-news.co.uk
Bank(s): Royal Bank of Scotland, Inverness
Directors: R. Dudley (Fin)
Managers: J. Currie (Tech Serv Mgr), K. Brown (Tech Serv Mgr), S. Grant
Ultimate Holding Company: PETER PRESS LIMITED
Immediate Holding Company: THE HIGHLAND PRINTING & PUBLISHING GROUP LIMITED
Registration no: SC120730 **Date established:** 1989
Turnover: £10m - £20m **No.of Employees:** 51 - 100 **Product Groups:** 28

Date of Accounts	Sep 11	Sep 10	Sep 09
Working Capital	N/A	5m	5m
Current Assets	N/A	5m	5m

Highlands & Islands Airports Ltd
Inverness Airport Dalcross, Inverness, IV2 7JB
Tel: 01667-462445 **Fax:** 01667-464216
E-mail: info@hial.co.uk
Website: http://www.hial.co.uk
Bank(s): The Royal Bank of Scotland
Managers: A. Pearce (Tech Serv Mgr), G. Haston (Personnel), E. Linn, N. Ross (Comptroller), C. Williams (Develop Mgr)
Immediate Holding Company: HIGHLANDS AND ISLANDS AIRPORTS LIMITED
Registration no: SC097647 **VAT No.:** GB 652 4396 28
Date established: 1985 **Turnover:** £10m - £20m
No.of Employees: 51 - 100 **Product Groups:** 71

Date of Accounts	Mar 11	Mar 10	Mar 09
Sales Turnover	17m	16m	17m
Pre Tax Profit/Loss	-2m	283	-319
Working Capital	13m	12m	11m
Fixed Assets	84m	87m	92m
Current Assets	18m	19m	16m
Current Liabilities	5m	6m	3m

Highlands & Islands Enterprise
Cowan House Highlander Way, Inverness Business & Retail Park, Inverness, IV2 7GF
Tel: 01463-234171 **Fax:** 01463-244469
E-mail: info@hient.co.uk
Website: http://www.hie.co.uk
Directors: F. Duthie (Fin)
Managers: S. Myles (Personnel), C. Roberts, W. Tunicliffe (Sales Admin), D. Scott (Personnel)
Immediate Holding Company: HIGHLANDS AND ISLANDS AIRPORTS LIMITED
Registration no: SC097647 **Date established:** 1985
Turnover: £10m - £20m **No.of Employees:** 51 - 100 **Product Groups:** 08, 80, 81, 84, 87

Date of Accounts	Jun 11	Jun 10	Jun 09
Sales Turnover	32	54	50
Pre Tax Profit/Loss	-6	-5	-29
Working Capital	19	25	30
Current Assets	21	28	33
Current Liabilities	2	3	2

Highlands & Islands Fire Safety
36 Millerton Avenue, Inverness, IV3 8RY
Tel: 01463-223117 **Fax:** 01463-223117
Directors: F. Ogston (Prop)
Date established: 2000 **No.of Employees:** 1 - 10 **Product Groups:** 38, 42

J B T Distribution Ltd
Unit 1 Dalcross Industrial Estate, Inverness, IV2 7XB
Tel: 01667-462999 **Fax:** 01667-462788
E-mail: enquiries@jbt.co.uk
Website: http://www.jbt.co.uk
Bank(s): The Royal Bank of Scotland
Directors: I. Wilson (Fin), M. Beverage (MD)
Managers: P. Fleming, A. Robertson (Comptroller)
Ultimate Holding Company: INCHMUIR LIMITED
Immediate Holding Company: JBT DISTRIBUTION LIMITED
Registration no: SC146191 **Date established:** 1993
Turnover: £5m - £10m **No.of Employees:** 21 - 50 **Product Groups:** 72, 77

Date of Accounts	Dec 07	Mar 11	Mar 10
Sales Turnover	N/A	16m	15m
Pre Tax Profit/Loss	334	-804	62
Working Capital	-741	-1m	-394
Fixed Assets	2m	2m	991
Current Assets	3m	4m	3m
Current Liabilities	2m	3m	2m

William Johnston & Co. Ltd
44b Seafield Road, Inverness, IV1 1SG
Tel: 01463-238673 **Fax:** 01463-236941
E-mail: john@williamjohnston.co.uk
Website: http://www.williamjohnston.co.uk
Directors: J. Johnston (Fin)
Managers: J. Love (Mgr)
Immediate Holding Company: WILLIAM JOHNSTON ENGLAND LTD
Registration no: 04625647 **Date established:** 1902
No.of Employees: 1 - 10 **Product Groups:** 35

Lifescan Scotland
Beechwood Park North, Inverness, IV2 3ED
Tel: 01463-721000 **Fax:** 01463-722000
Website: http://www.lifescan.com
Directors: L. Fraser (Fin), L. Lawton (Pers), W. Printie (MD)
Managers: D. Footitt, S. Dingwell
Ultimate Holding Company: JOHNSON & JOHNSON (USA)
Immediate Holding Company: LIFESCAN SCOTLAND LIMITED
Registration no: SC154012 **Date established:** 1994
Turnover: £250,000 - £500,000 **No.of Employees:** 1001 - 1500
Product Groups: 38, 67

Date of Accounts	Dec 08	Jan 10	Jan 11
Sales Turnover	171m	165m	168m
Pre Tax Profit/Loss	66m	61m	85m
Working Capital	98m	145m	149m
Fixed Assets	55m	52m	58m
Current Assets	142m	193m	182m
Current Liabilities	14m	13m	16m

Macrae & Dick
59 Harbour Road, Inverness, IV1 1UF
Tel: 01463-713713 **Fax:** 01463-668990
E-mail: sales015@macraeanddick.co.uk
Website: http://www.macraeanddick.com
Managers: S. Mackenzie (Chief Mgr)
Immediate Holding Company: MACRAE & DICK, LIMITED
Registration no: SC012270 **Date established:** 2022
Turnover: £125m - £250m **No.of Employees:** 21 - 50 **Product Groups:** 68

Date of Accounts	Dec 11	Dec 10	Dec 09
Sales Turnover	128m	135m	129m
Pre Tax Profit/Loss	2m	2m	2m
Working Capital	4m	5m	3m
Fixed Assets	16m	16m	16m
Current Assets	27m	34m	31m
Current Liabilities	2m	4m	4m

Maybrook Supplies
Greneford Main Street, North Kessock, Inverness, IV1 3XN
Tel: 01463-731063 **Fax:** 0871-2421259
E-mail: enquiries@maybrook-supplies.co.uk
Website: http://www.maybrook-supplies.co.uk
Directors: M. Brooker (Prop)
No.of Employees: 1 - 10 **Product Groups:** 27, 30, 44, 49, 67

Norbord
Morayhill Dalcross Dalcross, Inverness, IV2 7JQ
Tel: 01463-795100 **Fax:** 01463-791764
E-mail: cameron.lewis@norbord.net
Website: http://www.norbord.com
Managers: L. Clark (Personnel), G. Mackenzie, C. Lewis (Mgr)
Ultimate Holding Company: NORBORD INVESTMENTS UK LTD
Immediate Holding Company: NORBORD LIMITED
Registration no: 00357722 **Date established:** 1939
No.of Employees: 101 - 250 **Product Groups:** 25, 27, 31, 63, 66

P D G Helicopters
The Heliport Dalcross Industrial Estate, Inverness, IV2 7XB
Tel: 01667-462740 **Fax:** 01667-462376
E-mail: reception@pdghelicopters.com
Website: http://www.pdghelicopters.com
Directors: J. Francis (Grp Chief Exec)
Managers: J. Davies (Tech Serv Mgr), S. Kempley, R. Hill
Immediate Holding Company: ASSOCIATED ASIAN FOODS LIMITED
Registration no: SC269815 **Date established:** 2004
Turnover: £10m - £20m **No.of Employees:** 51 - 100 **Product Groups:** 39, 75

Date of Accounts	Jun 05
Working Capital	-44
Fixed Assets	83
Current Assets	595

Precision Engine Services Inverness (Inverness)
Units 1-4 48 Seafield Road, Inverness, IV1 1SG
Tel: 01463-235537 **Fax:** 01463-712634
E-mail: info@precisionengineservices.co.uk
Website: http://www.precisionengineservices.co.uk
Directors: A. Horne (Prop)
Immediate Holding Company: ANDERSON BUILDING & CONSTRUCTION LIMITED
Date established: 2007 **No.of Employees:** 1 - 10 **Product Groups:** 35, 36, 39

Precision Relays Ltd
3 Seafield Road, Inverness, IV1 1SG
Tel: 01463-233929 **Fax:** 01463-712514
E-mail: admin@precisionrelays.co.uk
Website: http://www.precisionrelays.co.uk
Directors: H. Mackay-Ross (MD)
Ultimate Holding Company: JOHN MACKAY (PLANT) LIMITED
Immediate Holding Company: PRECISION RELAYS LIMITED
Registration no: SC046810 **Date established:** 1969
Turnover: Up to £250,000 **No.of Employees:** 1 - 10 **Product Groups:** 37

Date of Accounts	Mar 11	Mar 10	Sep 08
Sales Turnover	228	316	278
Pre Tax Profit/Loss	63	31	-5
Working Capital	712	681	940
Fixed Assets	294	303	17
Current Assets	779	701	968
Current Liabilities	21	16	20

James Pringle Weavers
Holm Woollen Mills, Inverness, IV2 4RB
Tel: 01463-223311 **Fax:** 01463-231042
E-mail: nsouter@hotmail.com
Website: http://www.foreverscotland.com
Managers: N. Souter (Mgr)
Ultimate Holding Company: EDINBURGH WOOLLEN MILLS
VAT No.: GB 263 6530 59 **No.of Employees:** 11 - 20 **Product Groups:** 24, 43

Rewarding Dogs
Alburn Drummond Road, Inverness, IV2 4NA
Tel: 01463-230757
E-mail: info@rewardingdogs.com
Website: http://www.rewardingdogs.com
Directors: M. Grantham (Prop)
Date established: 1999 **No.of Employees:** 1 - 10 **Product Groups:** 01

Scott Burke Mbathh Mwfhyp Msto
3 Gordon Terrace, Inverness, IV2 3HD
Tel: 01463-250854
E-mail: scottburke@scottburke.com
Website: http://www.scottburke.com
Directors: S. Burke (Prop)
Immediate Holding Company: HEBRIDES.NET LIMITED
Date established: 2009 **Turnover:** Up to £250,000
No.of Employees: 1 - 10 **Product Groups:** 89

Date of Accounts	Jun 10	Jun 09	Jun 08
Working Capital	16	2	-10
Fixed Assets	18	2	13
Current Assets	172	114	103

The Tomatin Distillery Co. Ltd
Tomatin, Inverness, IV13 7YT
Tel: 01463-248144 **Fax:** 01808-511373
E-mail: info@tomatin.com
Website: http://www.tomatin.com
Bank(s): The Royal Bank of Scotland
Directors: R. Anderson (MD)
Managers: S. Smith (Site Co-ord), M. Macleod
Ultimate Holding Company: TAKARA HOLDINGS INC (JAPAN)
Immediate Holding Company: THE TOMATIN DISTILLERY PENSION TRUSTEES LIMITED
Registration no: SC336558 **VAT No.:** GB 664 0955 19
Date established: 2008 **Turnover:** £5m - £10m **No.of Employees:** 21 - 50
Product Groups: 21

Top Tier Sugarcraft
10 Meadow Road Balloch, Inverness, IV2 7JR
Tel: 01463-790456
E-mail: toptier@btconnect.com
Website: http://www.toptiersugarcraft.co.uk
Directors: D. Turner (Prop), D. Turner (MD)
Turnover: Up to £250,000 **No.of Employees:** 1 - 10 **Product Groups:** 20

Travis Perkins plc (t/a Builders and Plumbers Merchant)
Shore Street, Inverness, IV1 1NT
Tel: 01463-231171 **Fax:** 01463-710315
Website: http://www.travisperkins.co.uk
Managers: J. Kelman (Reg Mgr), R. Forbes (District Mgr)
Immediate Holding Company: TRAVIS PERKINS PLC
Registration no: 00824821 **Date established:** 1964
No.of Employees: 11 - 20 **Product Groups:** 66

Date of Accounts	Dec 11	Dec 10	Dec 09
Sales Turnover	4779m	3153m	2931m
Pre Tax Profit/Loss	270m	197m	213m
Working Capital	133m	159m	248m
Fixed Assets	2771m	2749m	2108m
Current Assets	1421m	1329m	1035m
Current Liabilities	473m	412m	109m

Whites Electronics Ltd
35j Harbour Road, Inverness, IV1 1UA
Tel: 01463-223456 **Fax:** 01463-224048
E-mail: sales@whites.co.uk
Website: http://www.whites.co.uk
Bank(s): Clydesdale
Managers: A. Wilson (Chief Mgr)
Ultimate Holding Company: WHITES ELECTRONICS INC (USA)
Immediate Holding Company: WHITE'S ELECTRONICS (UK) LIMITED
Registration no: SC074107 **VAT No.:** GB 361 0229 90
Date established: 1981 **Turnover:** £1m - £2m **No.of Employees:** 11 - 20
Product Groups: 38

Date of Accounts	Dec 11	Dec 10	Dec 09
Working Capital	937	914	1m
Fixed Assets	417	413	426
Current Assets	1m	1m	1m

Aberdeenshire

Inverurie

Aberdeen PAT Test Services
Office 10Thainstone Business Centre Thainstone, Inverurie, AB51 5TB
Tel: 01467-681376
E-mail: info@aberdeenpattestservices.com
Website: http://www.aberdeen-pat-testing.com
Directors: M. Jaffray (Prop)
Registration no: SC260441 **Date established:** 2008
Turnover: Up to £250,000 **No.of Employees:** 1 - 10 **Product Groups:** 67, 85

R M Archibald
Unit 2 Cairnhall Industrial Estate Kintore, Inverurie, AB51 0YQ
Tel: 01467-633400 **Fax:** 01467-633555
Directors: R. Archibald (Prop)
Immediate Holding Company: R M ARCHIBALD LTD
Registration no: SC342532 **Date established:** 2008
No.of Employees: 1 - 10 **Product Groups:** 46

B S Joinery Services
2 Harlaw Business Centre Harlaw Road, Inverurie, AB51 4FR
Tel: 01467-625300 **Fax:** 01467-625643
E-mail: bsjoinery@bsjoinery.com
Website: http://www.dogkennels.co.uk
Directors: D. Stewart (Prop)
No.of Employees: 1 - 10 **Product Groups:** 25, 35, 41, 66

Cable Solutions
Craigearn Business Park Morrison Way, Kintore, Inverurie, AB51 0TH
Tel: 01467-633790 **Fax:** 01224-725360
E-mail: info@1st4cables.com
Website: http://www.1st4cables.com
Directors: C. Fraser (MD)
Immediate Holding Company: CABLE SOLUTIONS (WORLDWIDE) LIMITED
Registration no: SC259846 **Date established:** 2003
No.of Employees: 1 - 10 **Product Groups:** 35, 37, 45

Date of Accounts	Mar 12	Mar 11	Mar 10
Working Capital	615	517	261
Fixed Assets	22	26	32
Current Assets	2m	1m	2m

Ferguson Group Ltd
Harlaw Drive Harlaw Road Industrial Estate, Inverurie, AB51 4SF
Tel: 01467-626500 **Fax:** 01467-626559
E-mail: info@fergusonmodular.com
Website: http://www.fergusonmodular.com
Bank(s): The Royal Bank of Scotland
Directors: S. Ferguson (MD)
Ultimate Holding Company: ARDEN HOLDINGS LIMITED
Immediate Holding Company: FERGUSON GROUP LIMITED
Registration no: SC309083 **Date established:** 2006
Turnover: £5m - £10m **No.of Employees:** 51 - 100 **Product Groups:** 35, 39, 45, 51, 69, 76, 82

Date of Accounts	Dec 11	Dec 10	Dec 09
Sales Turnover	52m	39m	36m
Pre Tax Profit/Loss	16m	15m	14m
Working Capital	2m	16m	6m
Fixed Assets	104m	73m	66m
Current Assets	37m	44m	29m
Current Liabilities	4m	5m	5m

First Ebusiness Solutions
Burghmuir Way, Inverurie, AB51 4FT
Tel: 01467-623900 **Fax:** 01467-624120
E-mail: info@firstebusiness.co.uk
Website: http://www.firstebusiness.co.uk
Directors: B. Booker (Dir)
Managers: P. Findlay (Mktg Serv Mgr), M. Gray, J. Johnston (Fin Mgr), L. Charles, M. Stephen
Ultimate Holding Company: TEARSHEET LIMITED
Immediate Holding Company: FIRST EBUSINESS SOLUTIONS LIMITED
Registration no: SC127126 **VAT No.:** GB 671 1572 41
Date established: 1990 **Turnover:** £1m - £2m **No.of Employees:** 21 - 50
Product Groups: 44, 84

Date of Accounts	Mar 11	Mar 10	Mar 09
Working Capital	633	605	536
Fixed Assets	44	29	67
Current Assets	1m	1m	1m

Fisher Offshore
North Meadows Oldmeldrum, Inverurie, AB51 0GQ
Tel: 01651-873932 **Fax:** 01651-873939
E-mail: info@fisheroffshore.com
Website: http://www.fisher.co.uk
Directors: C. Winward (Fin), I. Diack (MD)
Ultimate Holding Company: JAMES FISHER AND SONS PUBLIC LIMITED COMPANY
Immediate Holding Company: MONYANA ENGINEERING SERVICES LIMITED
Registration no: SC289788 **Date established:** 2005
Turnover: £5m - £10m **No.of Employees:** 51 - 100 **Product Groups:** 40, 45

Date of Accounts	Dec 11	Dec 10	Dec 09
Working Capital	-19	-19	-19

Grampian Steel Services Ltd
Greenford Oldmeldrum, Inverurie, AB51 0BH
Tel: 01651-872040 **Fax:** 01651-872069
E-mail: sales@grampian-steel.co.uk
Website: http://www.grampian-steel.co.uk
Directors: A. Dunbar (MD)
Immediate Holding Company: GRAMPIAN STEEL SERVICES LIMITED
Registration no: SC088118 **VAT No.:** GB 415 7160 68
Date established: 1984 **Turnover:** £1m - £2m **No.of Employees:** 1 - 10
Product Groups: 35, 66

Date of Accounts	May 11	May 10	May 09
Working Capital	167	232	207
Fixed Assets	968	818	769
Current Assets	2m	1m	1m

H B Rentals Ltd
Kirkwood Business Park Sauchen, Inverurie, AB51 7LE
Tel: 01224-772304 **Fax:** 01224-772641
E-mail: norman.porter@hbrental.com
Website: http://www.hbrental.com
Bank(s): HSBC
Directors: N. Porter (Dir)
Managers: M. Bradley (Sales Prom Mgr), T. Minty (Personnel), K. Knowells (Fin Mgr)
Ultimate Holding Company: SUPERIOR ENERGY SERVICES INC (USA)
Immediate Holding Company: HB RENTALS LIMITED
Registration no: 03650140 **Date established:** 1998
No.of Employees: 21 - 50 **Product Groups:** 37, 51, 67, 69

Date of Accounts	Dec 11	Dec 10	Dec 09
Sales Turnover	5m	6m	9m
Pre Tax Profit/Loss	-1m	241	3m
Working Capital	3m	5m	4m
Fixed Assets	20m	20m	20m
Current Assets	7m	8m	7m
Current Liabilities	248	202	271

International Paper Equipment Finance LP
Inverurie Mills, Inverurie, AB51 5NR
Tel: 01467-627000 **Fax:** 01467-627102
E-mail: bill.conn@ipaper.com
Website: http://www.ipaper.com
Directors: D. Steel (MD), W. Oldham (Jt MD), K. Lennox (Fin), D. Steele (Jt MD)
Ultimate Holding Company: INTERNATIONAL PAPER INC (USA)
Immediate Holding Company: INTERNATIONAL PAPER (UK) LIMITED
Registration no: SC004787 **VAT No.:** GB 265 6054 53
Date established: 2001 **Turnover:** £125m - £250m
No.of Employees: 1 - 10 **Product Groups:** 66

Date of Accounts	Dec 06	Dec 05
Pre Tax Profit/Loss	10	10
Working Capital	7730	7720
Current Assets	8670	7720
Current Liabilities	940	N/A
Total Share Capital	25280	25280
ROCE% (Return on Capital Employed)	0.1	

John Bell Pipeline Ltd
3-4 Camiestone Road Thainstone Business Park, Inverurie, AB51 5GT
Tel: 01224-714514 **Fax:** 01224-716079
E-mail: sales@jbpipeline.co.uk
Website: http://www.jbpipeline.co.uk
Bank(s): Clydesdale
Managers: R. Legingham (Ops Mgr)
Ultimate Holding Company: JOHN BELL PIPELINE EQUIPMENT COMPANY LIMITED
Immediate Holding Company: THE EUROPEAN PIPELINE CO. LTD.
Registration no: SC145795 **Date established:** 1993
Turnover: £20m - £50m **No.of Employees:** 21 - 50 **Product Groups:** 36, 66

Date of Accounts	Mar 11	Mar 10	Mar 09
Working Capital	226	201	251
Fixed Assets	13	17	21
Current Assets	342	301	295

Brian Middleton Garden Machinery
5 Keith-Hall Road, Inverurie, AB51 3UA
Tel: 01467-623658
Directors: B. Middleton (Prop)
Date established: 1995 **No.of Employees:** 1 - 10 **Product Groups:** 41

Poseidon Engineering
Colpy Way Colpy Road Industrial Estate, Oldmeldrum, Inverurie, AB51 0BZ
Tel: 01651-872999 **Fax:** 01651-873888
E-mail: info@poseidonengineering.com
Website: http://www.poseidonengineering.com
Managers: M. Crichton (Mgr)
Immediate Holding Company: POSEIDON ENGINEERING LIMITED
Registration no: SC269184 **Date established:** 2004
Turnover: Up to £250,000 **No.of Employees:** 1 - 10 **Product Groups:** 42, 45

Date of Accounts	Nov 11	Nov 10	Nov 09
Working Capital	232	139	22
Fixed Assets	145	177	206
Current Assets	377	293	107
Current Liabilities	N/A	138	N/A

Premier Plates UK
Highthorn House Daviot, Inverurie, AB51 0JJ
Tel: 0845-6523040 **Fax:** 01467-671036
E-mail: info@premierplates.co.uk
Website: http://www.premierplates.co.uk
Directors: C. Kaye (Sales), T. Kaye (MD)
No.of Employees: 1 - 10 **Product Groups:** 39

Red Rooster Industrial UK Ltd
The Meadows Meldrum Meg Way Oldmeldrum, Inverurie, AB51 0EZ
Tel: 01651-872101 **Fax:** 01651-871405
E-mail: info@rriuk.com
Website: http://www.rriuk.com
Managers: L. Fraser
Immediate Holding Company: RED ROOSTER INDUSTRIAL (UK) LIMITED
Registration no: SC113779 **VAT No.:** GB 498 3903 91
Date established: 1988 **Turnover:** £2m - £5m **No.of Employees:** 21 - 50
Product Groups: 38, 39, 45, 67, 68, 83

Date of Accounts	Mar 12	Mar 11	Mar 10
Working Capital	1m	946	1m
Fixed Assets	1m	1m	1m
Current Assets	2m	2m	2m

Safelift Offshore Ltd
Forties Business Centre School Road, Kintore, Inverurie, AB51 0UX
Tel: 01224-775774 **Fax:** 01224-775779
E-mail: info@safelift.co.uk
Website: http://www.safelift.co.uk
Directors: P. Innes (MD)
Immediate Holding Company: SAFELIFT OFFSHORE LIMITED
Registration no: SC152357 **Date established:** 1994
No.of Employees: 21 - 50 **Product Groups:** 35, 39, 45

Date of Accounts	Oct 11	Oct 10	Oct 09
Working Capital	287	172	37
Fixed Assets	175	196	153
Current Assets	1m	841	636

Scotch Premier Meat Ltd
North Street, Inverurie, AB51 4TL
Tel: 01467-620631 **Fax:** 01467-624653
E-mail: raymond@scotchpremier.co.uk
Website: http://www.goann.co.uk
Bank(s): Clydesdale
Directors: M. Hetherintton (MD), M. Rafferty (Fin), R. White (MD), R. Wight (Sales)
Managers: B. Noble (Sales Prom Mgr), G. Bethan (Personnel), N. Cumming (Purch Mgr)
Ultimate Holding Company: ANM GROUP LTD
Immediate Holding Company: SCOTCH PREMIER MEAT LIMITED
Registration no: SC122991 **VAT No.:** 265 9486 09 **Date established:** 1990
Turnover: £50m - £75m **No.of Employees:** 101 - 250
Product Groups: 20, 62

Date of Accounts	Dec 11	Dec 10	Dec 09
Sales Turnover	63m	55m	53m
Pre Tax Profit/Loss	-2m	-74	-1m
Working Capital	-1m	758	1m
Fixed Assets	4m	4m	3m
Current Assets	7m	8m	7m
Current Liabilities	552	566	600

Stewart Agricultural Ltd
Broadward Daviot, Inverurie, AB51 0JL
Tel: 01467-681418 **Fax:** 01467-681285
E-mail: sales@stewart-trailers.co.uk
Website: http://www.stewart-trailers.co.uk
Directors: M. Stewart (Dir)
Immediate Holding Company: STEWART AGRICULTURAL LIMITED
Registration no: SC165316 **Date established:** 1996
No.of Employees: 21 - 50 **Product Groups:** 41

Date of Accounts	Aug 11	Aug 10	Aug 09
Working Capital	1m	1m	1m
Fixed Assets	306	272	333
Current Assets	2m	2m	2m

Ayrshire

Irvine

Albann Ltd
Unit 69 Third Avenue Heatherhouse Industrial Estate, Irvine, KA12 8HN
Tel: 01294-272311 **Fax:** 01294-276677
E-mail: sales@albann.co.uk
Website: http://www.albann.co.uk
Directors: I. Mcdonald (MD)
Ultimate Holding Company: ALBANN LIMITED
Immediate Holding Company: ALBANN IRVINE LIMITED
Registration no: SC205801 **Date established:** 2000
Turnover: £5m - £10m **No.of Employees:** 11 - 20 **Product Groups:** 35, 52

Date of Accounts	Sep 10	Sep 09	Sep 08
Sales Turnover	N/A	5m	N/A
Pre Tax Profit/Loss	N/A	438	695
Working Capital	2m	2m	2m
Fixed Assets	345	323	404
Current Assets	3m	3m	3m
Current Liabilities	N/A	427	530

Arco West Scotland
PO Box 6, Irvine, KA12 8LG
Tel: 01294-315900 **Fax:** 01294-271335
E-mail: arco.westscotland@arco.co.uk
Website: http://www.arco.co.uk
Managers: A. Little (Mgr)
Ultimate Holding Company: ARCO LIMITED
Immediate Holding Company: W. WALKER & SONS-SAFETY-LIMITED
Registration no: SC023714 **Date established:** 1946 **Turnover:** £1m - £2m
No.of Employees: 1 - 10 **Product Groups:** 24, 29, 30, 40

Date of Accounts	Jun 11	Jun 10	Jun 06
Working Capital	2	2	2
Current Assets	2	2	2

Ardagh Glass Ltd
Portland Road Irvine Industrial Estate, Irvine, KA12 8JA
Tel: 01294-278641 **Fax:** 01294-272754
E-mail: ray.blackwell@ardaghglass.com
Website: http://www.ardaghgroup.com
Directors: L. Mantell (Purch), R. Blackwell (Dir)
Managers: M. Green (Tech Serv Mgr)
Ultimate Holding Company: ARDAGH GLASS GROUP SA (LUXEMBOURG)
Immediate Holding Company: ARDAGH GLASS LIMITED
Registration no: 00567801 **Date established:** 1956
No.of Employees: 101 - 250 **Product Groups:** 33

Date of Accounts	Dec 11	Dec 10	Dec 09
Sales Turnover	297m	288m	283m
Pre Tax Profit/Loss	29m	46m	24m
Working Capital	326m	313m	153m
Fixed Assets	114m	124m	132m
Current Assets	406m	378m	224m
Current Liabilities	27m	27m	9m

Ayrshire Saw Centre
Unit 13 West Bowhouse Workshops West Bowhouse Gardens, Girdle Toll, Irvine, KA11 1PR
Tel: 01294-217000 **Fax:** 01560-483600
E-mail: bandsaw@btinternet.com
Directors: R. Aitchison (Prop)
Date established: 2001 **No.of Employees:** 1 - 10 **Product Groups:** 36

Corsehill Packaging Ltd
Ailsa Road Irvine Industrial Estate, Irvine, KA12 8NG
Tel: 01294-275133 **Fax:** 01294-312300
E-mail: sales@gmccorsehill.co.uk
Website: http://www.gmccorsehill.co.uk
Directors: M. Mather (Fin)
Immediate Holding Company: CORSEHILL PACKAGING LIMITED
Registration no: SC111181 **Date established:** 1988
No.of Employees: 11 - 20 **Product Groups:** 30, 32, 49, 62, 63

Date of Accounts	Jun 08	Jun 07
Working Capital	16	16
Current Assets	16	16
Total Share Capital	59	59

G M C Corsehill
Ailsa Road Irvine Industrial Estate, Irvine, KA12 8NG
Tel: 01294-322807 **Fax:** 01294-312300
E-mail: sales@gmccorsehill.co.uk
Website: http://www.corsehill.co.uk
Managers: M. Mether (Mgr)
Immediate Holding Company: CORSEHILL PACKAGING LIMITED
Registration no: SC111181 **Date established:** 1988
No.of Employees: 11 - 20 **Product Groups:** 30, 32, 49, 62, 63

Jewson Ltd
Gottries Road, Irvine, KA12 8QE
Tel: 01294-273892 **Fax:** 01294-271006
Website: http://www.jewson.co.uk
Bank(s): The Royal Bank of Scotland
Directors: P. Hindle (MD)
Managers: B. Sargenson (District Mgr)
Ultimate Holding Company: COMPAGNIE DE SAINT GOBAIN (FRANCE)
Immediate Holding Company: JEWSON LIMITED
Registration no: 00348407 **VAT No.:** GB 497 7184 83
Date established: 1939 **Turnover:** Up to £250,000
No.of Employees: 11 - 20 **Product Groups:** 66

Date of Accounts	Dec 11	Dec 10	Dec 09
Sales Turnover	1606m	1547m	1485m
Pre Tax Profit/Loss	18m	100m	45m
Working Capital	-345m	-250m	-349m
Fixed Assets	496m	387m	461m
Current Assets	657m	1005m	1320m
Current Liabilities	66m	120m	64m

Maxi Haulage Ltd

Elliot House Redburn Industrial Estate Kilwinning Road, Irvine, KA12 8TG
Tel: 01294-272531 **Fax:** 01294-275916
E-mail: gerald.atkinson@maxihaulage.co.uk
Website: http://www.maxihaulage.co.uk
Bank(s): Clydesdale
Directors: A. Miles (MD), G. Atkinson (Grp Chief Exec), G. Atkinson (Ch), J. Actions (MD), C. Logan (Fin)
Managers: J. McGomory (I.T. Exec), R. Atkinson (Sales & Mktg Mg)
Immediate Holding Company: MAXI HAULAGE LIMITED
Registration no: SC054932 **VAT No.:** GB 271 4619 58
Date established: 1974 **Turnover:** £20m - £50m
No.of Employees: 101 - 250 **Product Groups:** 72, 77

Nacco Materials Handling Scotland Ltd

Centenary Road 11 Riverside Way Riverside Business Park, Irvine, KA11 5DP
Tel: 01294-315600 **Fax:** 01294-315800
E-mail: john.short@nmhg.com
Website: http://www.nacco.com
Bank(s): Royal bank of scotland
Directors: J. Short (Pers), R. Mock (MD), J. English (Fab)
Managers: J. Short (Mgr), T. Alexander (Comptroller), D. Rowell (Nat Sales Mgr), I. Robertson (Buyer)
Ultimate Holding Company: Hyster Yale Materials Inc (USA)
Immediate Holding Company: Hyster Co (USA)
Registration no: 01020654 **Turnover:** £5m - £10m
No.of Employees: 101 - 250 **Product Groups:** 67

Plastic Mouldings Ltd

4 Ailsa Road, Irvine, KA12 8LP
Tel: 01294-278091 **Fax:** 01294-311655
E-mail: info@plasticmouldings.com
Website: http://www.plasticmouldings.com
Bank(s): National Westminster Bank Plc
Directors: W. Houston (Ch), N. Ballintyne (Fin)
Managers: P. Aitken
Ultimate Holding Company: PLASTICS INDUSTRIES LIMITED
Immediate Holding Company: PLASTIC MOULDINGS LIMITED
Registration no: 00772753 **VAT No.:** GB 428 1012 88
Date established: 1963 **Turnover:** £2m - £5m **No.of Employees:** 21 - 50
Product Groups: 29, 30

Date of Accounts	Dec 11	Dec 10	Dec 09
Working Capital	216	138	-111
Fixed Assets	469	478	526
Current Assets	535	717	579

Vanity Case

26 Blairdenon Way Bourtreehill South, Irvine, KA11 1EN
Tel: 01294-211000
E-mail: vanity-case@hotmail.co.uk
Directors: A. Hasty (Prop)
Date established: 2005 **No.of Employees:** 1 - 10 **Product Groups:** 61

Isle of Arran

Isle of Arran

S Macalister

Shedock Farm Shiskine, Isle of Arran, KA27 8EW
Tel: 01770-860261 **Fax:** 01770-860462
E-mail: andy@shedockfarm.fsnet.co.uk
Directors: S. Macalister (Prop)
VAT No.: GB 444 2721 64 **Date established:** 1984 **Turnover:** £1m - £2m
No.of Employees: 1 - 10 **Product Groups:** 09

Isle of Bute

Isle Of Bute

Bute Fabrics

4 Barone Road Rothesay, Isle Of Bute, PA20 0DP
Tel: 01700-503734 **Fax:** 01700-504545
E-mail: sales@butefabrics.com
Website: http://www.butefabrics.com
Bank(s): Clydesdale Bank PLC
Directors: J. Sprint (MD), J. Black (Fin)
Managers: F. Hardie (Sales & Mktg Mg), E. Plank (Purch Mgr)
Ultimate Holding Company: CUMBRAE PROPERTIES (1963) LIMITED
Immediate Holding Company: BUTE FABRICS LIMITED
Registration no: SC062040 **VAT No.:** GB 292 9471 19
Date established: 1977 **Turnover:** £2m - £5m **No.of Employees:** 21 - 50
Product Groups: 23

Date of Accounts	Dec 11	Dec 10	Dec 09
Working Capital	4	103	362
Fixed Assets	91	77	98
Current Assets	799	762	677

Flexible Technology Ltd

Townhead Rothesay, Isle of Bute, PA20 9JH
Tel: 01700-504515 **Fax:** 01700-502232
E-mail: peter.timms@flexibletechnology.org
Website: http://www.flexibletechnology.com
Bank(s): The Royal Bank of Scotland
Directors: P. Timms (MD)
Managers: C. White (Chief Acct), B. Banfield (Sales & Mktg Mg), S. Elliott (Buyer), S. Timms (Tech Serv Mgr)
Immediate Holding Company: FLEXIBLE TECHNOLOGY LIMITED
Registration no: SC138019 **VAT No.:** GB 554 7932 11
Date established: 1992 **Turnover:** £2m - £5m **No.of Employees:** 21 - 50
Product Groups: 37

Date of Accounts	Jul 11	Jul 10	Jul 09
Working Capital	553	482	430
Fixed Assets	373	365	421
Current Assets	985	1m	963

Orissor Trust Ltd

14 Craigmore Road Rothesay, Isle Of Bute, PA20 9LB
Tel: 01700-503540 **Fax:** 01700-505394
E-mail: admin@orissor.net
Website: http://www.orissor.com
Bank(s): Royal Bank of Scotland, 37 Victoria St, Rothesay, Bute, PA20 0AN
Directors: B. Dawson (MD)
Immediate Holding Company: ORISSOR TRUST LTD.
Registration no: SC337786 **Date established:** 2008
No.of Employees: 11 - 20 **Product Groups:** 80

Date of Accounts	Dec 11	Dec 10	Dec 09
Working Capital	-165	-163	-220
Fixed Assets	328	336	343
Current Assets	20	61	22
Current Liabilities	151	N/A	N/A

Isle of Harris

Isle of Harris

Sea Harris

East Tarbert, Isle of Harris, HS3 3DB
Tel: 01859-502007 **Fax:** 07760-216555
E-mail: seumas@seaharris.co.uk
Website: http://www.seaharris.co.uk
Directors: S. Morrison (Grp Chief Exec)
Date established: 2008 **No.of Employees:** 1 - 10 **Product Groups:** 69, 74

Isle of Islay

Isle of Islay

Clear Water Marine

Unit 4 The Business Park Port Ellen, Isle of Islay, PA42 7BU
Tel: 01496-300301 **Fax:** 01496-300302
E-mail: clearwatermarine@tiscali.co.uk
Directors: P. Pardington (Prop), T. Pardington (Prop)
Date established: 2003 **No.of Employees:** 1 - 10 **Product Groups:** 35, 36, 39

Isle of Lewis

Isle Of Lewis

Builder Center Ltd

Parkend Industrial Estate Sandwick, Isle Of Lewis, HS2 0AN
Tel: 01851-705151 **Fax:** 01851-705347
Website: http://www.buildcenter.co.uk
Managers: C. Mckenzie (Mgr)
Ultimate Holding Company: WOLSELEY PLC (JERSEY)
Immediate Holding Company: BUILD CENTER LIMITED
Registration no: 00462397 **VAT No.:** GB 363 0233 93
Date established: 1948 **Turnover:** £2m - £5m **No.of Employees:** 1 - 10
Product Groups: 25, 66

Date of Accounts	Jul 09
Working Capital	78
Current Assets	78

Butt of Lewis Textiles

9b Knockaird Knockaird, Isle of Lewis, HS2 0XF
Tel: 01851-810600 **Fax:** 01851-810600
E-mail: callum9b@hotmail.com
Date established: 2008 **No.of Employees:** 1 - 10 **Product Groups:** 23

Isle of Mull

Isle Of Mull

Mull Building Supplies

Craignure, Isle Of Mull, PA65 6AY
Tel: 01680-812488 **Fax:** 01680-812385
E-mail: keithrobbie@btconnect.com
Website: http://www.mullbuildingsupplies.co.uk
Directors: K. Robbie (Ptnr), I. Robbie (Ptnr)
Ultimate Holding Company: T.S.L. CONTRACTORS LTD.
Immediate Holding Company: MULL DEVELOPMENTS LTD
Registration no: SC067094 **VAT No.:** GB 659 3069 06
Date established: 1980 **Turnover:** £5m - £10m **No.of Employees:** 1 - 10
Product Groups: 08, 25, 66, 72

Date of Accounts	Jul 09	Jul 08	Jul 05
Pre Tax Profit/Loss	-0	-0	N/A
Working Capital	-11	-11	-11
Current Liabilities	11	11	N/A

Isle of Skye

Isle of Skye

Gaeltec Devices Ltd

Glendale Road Dunvegan, Isle of Skye, IV55 8GU
Tel: 01470-521385 **Fax:** 01470-521369
E-mail: sales@gaeltec.com
Website: http://www.gaeltec.com
Directors: J. Smale (MD)
Ultimate Holding Company: DIGITIMER LIMITED
Immediate Holding Company: GAELTEC DEVICES LIMITED
Registration no: SC373428 **VAT No.:** GB 266 6666 16
Date established: 2010 **Turnover:** £500,000 - £1m
No.of Employees: 1 - 10 **Product Groups:** 37, 38

Date of Accounts	Oct 11	Oct 10
Working Capital	16	3
Fixed Assets	12	16
Current Assets	125	99

Roxburghshire

Jedburgh

Adding Value Solutions

Unit 2 Friars, Jedburgh, TD8 6BN
Tel: 01835-864527
E-mail: info@addingvaluesolutions.co.uk
Website: http://www.addingvaluesolutions.co.uk
Directors: S. Heather (Prop)
Registration no: 04204176 **No.of Employees:** 1 - 10 **Product Groups:** 81

W M Dodds

Old Bongate Mill, Jedburgh, TD8 6DR
Tel: 01835-863381 **Fax:** 01835-863119
E-mail: admin@wmdodds.co.uk
Website: http://www.wmdodds.co.uk
Directors: J. Laing (Prop)
Immediate Holding Company: W.M. DODDS LIMITED
Registration no: SC376287 **Date established:** 2010
No.of Employees: 11 - 20 **Product Groups:** 41

Date of Accounts	Mar 11
Working Capital	-221
Fixed Assets	447
Current Assets	1m

Footeprint

Edinburgh Road, Jedburgh, TD8 6EA
Tel: 01835-862667 **Fax:** 01835-862042
E-mail: info@footeprint.co.uk
Website: http://www.footeprint.co.uk
Directors: J. Hewitt (MD)
No.of Employees: 1 - 10 **Product Groups:** 28

L S Starrett Co. Ltd

Oxnam Road, Jedburgh, TD8 6LR
Tel: 01835-863501 **Fax:** 01835-863018
E-mail: ggill@starrett.co.uk
Website: http://www.starrett.co.uk
Managers: J. Peters (Tech Serv Mgr), C. Watters (Personnel), J. Cole (Sales & Mktg Mg), G. Gill, D. Peggie (Purch Mgr)
Ultimate Holding Company: L S STARRETT CO, THE (USA)
Immediate Holding Company: L.S. STARRETT COMPANY LTD. (THE)
Registration no: SC032886 **Date established:** 1958
Turnover: £10m - £20m **No.of Employees:** 101 - 250
Product Groups: 36, 37, 38, 46, 47, 48

Date of Accounts	May 10	May 09	Jun 12
Sales Turnover	14m	17m	14m
Pre Tax Profit/Loss	470	1m	354
Working Capital	16m	15m	16m
Fixed Assets	2m	2m	2m
Current Assets	19m	17m	18m
Current Liabilities	1m	878	632

Mainetti UK Ltd

Oxnam Road, Jedburgh, TD8 6NN
Tel: 01835-865000 **Fax:** 01835-863879
E-mail: sales.uk@mainetti.com
Website: http://www.mainetti.com
Bank(s): Midland
Directors: J. Hutchison (Fin)
Managers: A. Parsons
Ultimate Holding Company: MAUNA NV (NETHERLANDS ANTILLES)
Immediate Holding Company: MAINETTI (UK) LIMITED
Registration no: SC170666 **VAT No.:** GB 682 8656 84
Date established: 1996 **Turnover:** £20m - £50m
No.of Employees: 251 - 500 **Product Groups:** 30

Date of Accounts	Dec 11	Dec 10	Dec 09
Sales Turnover	25m	26m	23m
Pre Tax Profit/Loss	181	385	-323
Working Capital	3m	3m	1m
Fixed Assets	7m	7m	8m
Current Assets	14m	15m	15m
Current Liabilities	3m	3m	4m

Renfrewshire

Johnstone

Hardmet Grinding Company

18 The Meadows Houston, Johnstone, PA6 7DJ
Tel: 01505-615066 **Fax:** 01505-615066
Directors: J. Smyth (Prop)
VAT No.: GB 293 4479 22 **Turnover:** £250,000 - £500,000
No.of Employees: 1 - 10 **Product Groups:** 34, 36, 37, 46

Horne Engineering Ltd
PO Box 7, Johnstone, PA5 8BD
Tel: 01505-321455 **Fax:** 01505-336287
E-mail: sales@horne.co.uk
Website: http://www.horne.co.uk
Bank(s): The Royal Bank of Scotland
Directors: D. Gillies (Fin), J. Horne (Sales), A. Horne (MD)
Immediate Holding Company: HORNE ENGINEERING LIMITED
Registration no: SC016062 **Date established:** 1930
No.of Employees: 11 - 20 **Product Groups:** 36

Date of Accounts	Dec 11	Dec 10	Dec 09
Working Capital	3m	3m	2m
Fixed Assets	435	404	438
Current Assets	3m	3m	3m

Paisley & Johnstone Training Group Ltd
Laighcartside Street, Johnstone, PA5 8DB
Tel: 01505-323026 **Fax:** 01505-336063
E-mail: learn@pjtraining.com
Website: http://www.pjtraining.co.uk
Bank(s): The Royal Bank of Scotland
Managers: H. Murray (Chief Mgr)
Immediate Holding Company: PAISLEY AND JOHNSTONE TRAINING GROUP LIMITED
Registration no: SC043685 **Date established:** 1966
Turnover: £500,000 - £1m **No.of Employees:** 11 - 20 **Product Groups:** 86

Date of Accounts	Dec 11	Dec 10	Dec 09
Sales Turnover	457	615	569
Pre Tax Profit/Loss	-90	16	22
Working Capital	150	227	238
Fixed Assets	113	125	98
Current Assets	181	254	264
Current Liabilities	24	23	22

Smith & McLaurin Ltd
Cartside Mill Kilbarchan Road Kilbarchan Road, Kilbarchan, Johnstone, PA10 2AF
Tel: 01505-707700 **Fax:** 01505-704992
E-mail: info@smcl.co.uk
Website: http://www.smcl.co.uk
Bank(s): The Royal Bank of Scotland plc The Royal Bank of Scotland plc The Royal Bank of Scotland plc
Directors: B. Murphy (Fin), C. Galt (MD), J. Radford (Sales)
Managers: C. Gray, A. Chopde (Mktg Serv Mgr)
Ultimate Holding Company: SMITH & MCLAURIN GROUP LIMITED
Immediate Holding Company: SMITH & MCLAURIN LIMITED
Registration no: SC229817 **Date established:** 2002
Turnover: £10m - £20m **No.of Employees:** 51 - 100 **Product Groups:** 27, 30, 40, 42, 66

Date of Accounts	Jul 11	Jul 10	Jul 09
Sales Turnover	25m	23m	21m
Pre Tax Profit/Loss	1m	1m	620
Working Capital	190	-187	-371
Fixed Assets	3m	3m	3m
Current Assets	8m	7m	7m
Current Liabilities	1m	1m	841

Roxburghshire

Kelso

Border Precision Ltd
Pinnaclehill Industrial Estate, Kelso, TD5 8DW
Tel: 01573-224941 **Fax:** 01573-225220
E-mail: sales@borderprecision.com
Website: http://www.borderprecision.com
Bank(s): The Royal Bank of Scotland, Jedburgh
Directors: G. Ballantyne (Dir), W. Valentine (MD), P. Sanderson (Fin), G. Young (Sales)
Managers: J. McKechnie (Personnel), T. Chapman (Tech Serv Mgr)
Immediate Holding Company: BORDER PRECISION LIMITED
Registration no: SC049389 **VAT No.:** GB 268 4206 48
Date established: 1971 **Turnover:** £5m - £10m
No.of Employees: 101 - 250 **Product Groups:** 45, 48

Date of Accounts	Oct 11	Oct 10	Oct 09
Sales Turnover	7m	7m	6m
Pre Tax Profit/Loss	-645	-171	-412
Working Capital	69	386	618
Fixed Assets	4m	3m	3m
Current Assets	3m	2m	2m
Current Liabilities	2m	249	189

D M I Mechanical Engineers
Pinnaclehill Industrial Estate, Kelso, TD5 8DW
Tel: 01573-226255 **Fax:** 01573-228255
E-mail: enquiries@dmi.gb.net
Website: http://www.dmi.gb.net
Directors: G. Brown (Ptnr)
Immediate Holding Company: D.M.I. MECHANICAL ENGINEERS LIMITED
Registration no: SC245295 **Date established:** 2003
Turnover: £500,000 - £1m **No.of Employees:** 11 - 20 **Product Groups:** 41

Date of Accounts	Jan 11	Jan 10	Jan 09
Working Capital	-14	-3	-3
Fixed Assets	33	55	70
Current Assets	172	193	156

Plexus Corp UK Ltd
Pinnaclehill Industrial Estate, Kelso, TD5 8XX
Tel: 01573-223601 **Fax:** 01573-223600
E-mail: willie.mackinnon@plexus.com
Website: http://www.plexus.com
Bank(s): The Royal Bank of Scotland
Directors: L. Middlemass (Co Sec), D. Kerr (Fin)
Managers: W. Mackinnon, L. Christie, G. Purdie (Personnel), R. Millingan, J. Seibart (Sales Prom Mgr), C. McKintee (Tech Serv Mgr)
Ultimate Holding Company: PLEXUS CORP INC (USA)
Immediate Holding Company: PLEXUS CORP. LIMITED
Registration no: SC207257 **VAT No.:** GB 634 8175 26
Date established: 2000 **Turnover:** £20m - £50m
No.of Employees: 251 - 500 **Product Groups:** 37, 38, 44, 48, 79, 84

Date of Accounts	Sep 08	Oct 09	Oct 10
Sales Turnover	35m	N/A	N/A
Pre Tax Profit/Loss	888	-1m	-581
Working Capital	35m	-2m	-1m
Fixed Assets	13m	35m	35m
Current Assets	44m	22	181
Current Liabilities	2m	N/A	N/A

Ayrshire

Kilbirnie

W.& J. Knox Ltd
PO Box 1, Kilbirnie, KA25 7GY
Tel: 01505-682511 **Fax:** 01505-682980
E-mail: nets@wjknox.co.uk
Website: http://www.wjknox.co.uk
Bank(s): Clydesdale Bank PLC
Directors: J. Traynor (MD), R. Dehany (Dir & Gen Mgr), J. Templeton (Fab), J. Dehany (Sales)
Registration no: 00473980 **VAT No.:** GB 455 4353 44 006
Date established: 1778 **Turnover:** £5m - £10m
No.of Employees: 101 - 250 **Product Groups:** 23, 39, 41

Date of Accounts	Dec 11	Dec 10	Dec 09
Sales Turnover	10m	9m	7m
Pre Tax Profit/Loss	521	300	143
Working Capital	599	480	412
Fixed Assets	2m	2m	2m
Current Assets	2m	2m	2m
Current Liabilities	1m	2m	1m

Ayrshire

Kilmarnock

A E S Jeros
Crossbush Cottage, Kilmarnock, KA1 5LN
Tel: 01563-551122 **Fax:** 01563-573103
E-mail: mcrawford10@gmail.com
Website: http://www.aes-labs.co.uk
Directors: M. Crawford (Prop)
Date established: 1989 **No.of Employees:** 1 - 10 **Product Groups:** 20, 40, 41

A & J Menswear Retail Ltd
Marathon House Olympic Business Park Drybridge Road, Dundonald, Kilmarnock, KA2 9AE
Tel: 01563-852200 **Fax:** 01563-851127
Website: http://www.d2jeans.com
Directors: A. Kinney (Dir), H. Templeton (Fin)
Managers: S. McBreatry (Personnel), J. Doig
Ultimate Holding Company: THE GARDEN CENTRE GROUP LIMITED
Immediate Holding Company: A & J MENSWEAR (RETAIL) LIMITED
Registration no: SC186063 **Date established:** 1998
Turnover: Up to £250,000 **No.of Employees:** 21 - 50 **Product Groups:** 61

Date of Accounts	Jul 08	Jul 07	Jan 10
Working Capital	25	25	-681
Fixed Assets	N/A	N/A	2m
Current Assets	25	25	2m

Aird Walker & Ralston
12 Lawson Street, Kilmarnock, KA1 3JP
Tel: 01563-522236 **Fax:** 01563-521304
E-mail: sales@airdwalker.co.uk
Website: http://www.airdwalker.co.uk
Directors: A. Jay (MD)
Managers: M. Farrell (Fin Mgr), M. Lacey, B. Kiltie, M. Morris (Personnel), G. Christie (Sales Prom Mgr)
Ultimate Holding Company: PRESTWICK INVESTMENT TRUST P.L.C.
Immediate Holding Company: PRESTWICK INVESTMENT TRUST PLC
Registration no: SC020812 **VAT No.:** GB 262 8439 41
Turnover: £2m - £5m **No.of Employees:** 21 - 50 **Product Groups:** 37, 52

A-Plant Ltd
Holmquarry Road, Kilmarnock, KA1 4DA
Tel: 01563-528721 **Fax:** 01563-570135
E-mail: enquiries@aplant.com
Website: http://www.aplant.com
Bank(s): Lloyds TSB Bank plc
Managers: B. Gault (Chief Mgr)
Immediate Holding Company: A.PLANT LIMITED
Registration no: 05407712 **VAT No.:** GB 205 5687 37
Date established: 2005 **Turnover:** Up to £250,000
No.of Employees: 11 - 20 **Product Groups:** 83

Date of Accounts	Mar 07	Mar 06
Working Capital	12	-3
Fixed Assets	9	12
Current Assets	35	8

Brian O'Neill Associates
4 Howard Street, Kilmarnock, KA1 2BP
Tel: 01563-520344 **Fax:** 01563-536754
Directors: B. O'neill (Prop)
Immediate Holding Company: WELDING AND POSITIONING INTERNATIONAL LIMITED
Registration no: SC207876 **Date established:** 2000
No.of Employees: 11 - 20 **Product Groups:** 46

Checker Leather Ltd
Unit 2 Western Industrial Estate Crathie Road, Kilmarnock, KA3 1LU
Tel: 01563-541709 **Fax:** 01563-537819
E-mail: sales@checkerleather.com
Website: http://www.checkerleather.com
Directors: P. Pattison (Fin)
Immediate Holding Company: CHECKER LEATHER LIMITED
Registration no: SC069706 **VAT No.:** GB 406 6860 46
Date established: 1979 **No.of Employees:** 1 - 10 **Product Groups:** 22, 49, 66

Date of Accounts	Dec 11	Dec 10	Dec 09
Working Capital	281	283	300
Fixed Assets	26	31	39
Current Assets	1m	956	1m

Connect Water Cooler Scotland
Unit 1 Block 14 Smiddy Court, Glencairn Industrial Estate, Kilmarnock, KA1 4BY
Tel: 01563-525233 **Fax:** 01563-541380
E-mail: martinr@connectpurewater.co.uk
Website: http://www.connectpurewater.co.uk
Directors: M. Ross (Dir)
Registration no: SC333107 **Date established:** 2007
No.of Employees: 1 - 10 **Product Groups:** 40, 66

Deanston Electrical Wholesalers Ltd
27 Munro Place, Kilmarnock, KA1 2NP
Tel: 01563-533921 **Fax:** 01563-536409
E-mail: helen@deanston-electrical.co.uk
Website: http://www.deanston-electrical.co.uk
Directors: H. Forsythe (Fin), G. Duffy (Sales)
Immediate Holding Company: DEANSTON ELECTRICAL WHOLESALERS LIMITED
Registration no: SC137486 **VAT No.:** GB 264 1886 39
Date established: 1992 **Turnover:** £2m - £5m **No.of Employees:** 1 - 10
Product Groups: 33, 35, 40, 67, 77

Date of Accounts	Jan 12	Jan 11	Jan 10
Working Capital	94	84	129
Fixed Assets	436	456	473
Current Assets	494	378	401

Detection Instruments Northern Ltd
Unit 2a Crookedholm Commercial Centre 81 Main Road, Crookedholm, Kilmarnock, KA3 6JU
Tel: 01563-525525 **Fax:** 01563-542350
E-mail: alan@di-northern.com
Website: http://www.di-northern.com
Directors: M. Savery (Dir), A. Broad (MD), A. Stroad (MD), K. Mactaggart (Fin)
Managers: B. McLaren (), C. Young (Sales Prom Mgr), A. Broad (Tech Serv Mgr), L. Howie (Sales Admin)
Immediate Holding Company: DETECTION INSTRUMENTS (NORTHERN) LIMITED
Registration no: SC096066 **Date established:** 1985 **Turnover:** £1m - £2m
No.of Employees: 1 - 10 **Product Groups:** 38, 40, 42, 47

Eriks UK
Block 3-4 Bonnyton Industrial Estate Munro Place, Kilmarnock, KA1 2NP
Tel: 01563-533553 **Fax:** 01563-571226
E-mail: fpt.kilmarnock@wyko.co.uk
Website: http://www.eriks.co.uk
Managers: D. Dalton (District Mgr)
Registration no: 03142339 **Turnover:** £250m - £500m
No.of Employees: 1 - 10 **Product Groups:** 30

Gibson Wight Ltd
14-18 East Shaw Street, Kilmarnock, KA1 4AN
Tel: 01563-523633 **Fax:** 01563-536472
E-mail: charles.gibson@gibsonwight.co.uk
Website: http://www.gibsonwight.co.uk
Bank(s): Bank of Scotland
Directors: C. Gibson (MD)
Immediate Holding Company: GIBSON-WIGHT LIMITED
Registration no: SC021955 **VAT No.:** GB 263 1011 11
Date established: 1942 **Turnover:** £2m - £5m **No.of Employees:** 21 - 50
Product Groups: 52

Date of Accounts	Mar 12	Mar 11	Mar 10
Working Capital	316	318	295
Fixed Assets	351	362	340
Current Assets	1m	1m	1m

Glenfield Valves Ltd
Glenfield Works Queens Drive, Kilmarnock, KA1 3XF
Tel: 01563-521150 **Fax:** 01563-541013
E-mail: enquiries@glenfield.co.uk
Website: http://www.glenfieldvalves.co.uk
Bank(s): Bank of Scotland
Directors: P. Hubbard (Ch)
Managers: A. McNivan, L. Kudsk (Comptroller), C. Drummond (Personnel), J. McAllister (Purch Mgr), E. Stewart (Fin Mgr)
Ultimate Holding Company: ASX 14,145 APS (DENMARK)
Immediate Holding Company: GLENFIELD VALVES LIMITED
Registration no: SC220455 **VAT No.:** GB 389 0608 20
Date established: 2001 **Turnover:** £2m - £5m **No.of Employees:** 51 - 100
Product Groups: 36

Date of Accounts	Sep 11	Sep 10	Sep 09
Sales Turnover	4m	7m	6m
Pre Tax Profit/Loss	-1m	48	-792
Working Capital	-2m	-929	-771
Fixed Assets	1m	1m	1m
Current Assets	3m	5m	4m
Current Liabilities	133	238	260

Jewson Ltd
Southhook Road, Kilmarnock, KA1 2NN
Tel: 01563-529115 **Fax:** 01563-571072
Website: http://www.jewson.co.uk
Directors: P. Hindle (MD), C. Kenward (Fin)
Managers: C. Johnstone (District Mgr)
Ultimate Holding Company: COMPAGNIE DE SAINT GOBAIN (FRANCE)
Immediate Holding Company: JEWSON LIMITED
Registration no: 00348407 **Date established:** 1939
Turnover: £500m - £1,000m **No.of Employees:** 1 - 10
Product Groups: 66

Date of Accounts	Dec 11	Dec 10	Dec 09
Sales Turnover	1606m	1547m	1485m
Pre Tax Profit/Loss	18m	100m	45m
Working Capital	-345m	-250m	-349m
Fixed Assets	496m	387m	461m
Current Assets	657m	1005m	1320m
Current Liabilities	66m	120m	64m

Lennox Design Architectural Services
6 Cromdale Road, Kilmarnock, KA1 3RJ
Tel: 01563-534455
E-mail: l_d_e@btinternet.com
Website: http://www.lennoxdesignarchitectural.co.uk
Directors: B. Lennox (Prop)
Date established: 2006 **No.of Employees:** 1 - 10 **Product Groups:** 84

Mahle Engine Systems
New Street Kirkstyle, Kilmarnock, KA1 3NA
Tel: 01563-521190 **Fax:** 01563-539730
Website: http://www.mahle.com
Bank(s): National Westminster

Directors: P. Mathieson (Fin)
Managers: M. Hutchison (Tech Serv Mgr), B. Hamill (Personnel), J. English (Plant), D. Muir (Buyer), D. Ohare (Personnel), D. Chalis (Mktg Serv Mgr)
Immediate Holding Company: GLACIER METAL CO. LTD
VAT No.: GB 119 1676 79 **Turnover:** £125m - £250m
No.of Employees: 251 - 500 **Product Groups:** 34, 35, 48

Proven Engineering Products Ltd

Wardhead Park Stewarton, Kilmarnock, KA3 5LH
Tel: 01560-485570
E-mail: info@provenenergy.com
Website: http://www.provenenergy.com
Directors: S. Proven (Fin), G. Proven (MD)
Immediate Holding Company: PROVEN ENGINEERING PRODUCTS LIMITED
Registration no: SC275229 **Date established:** 2004
No.of Employees: 51 - 100 **Product Groups:** 35, 36, 39

Strathvac

65 Old Rome Drive Springhill Meadows, Kilmarnock, KA1 2RU
Tel: 01563-555881
E-mail: info@strathvac.co.uk
Website: http://www.strathvac.co.uk
Directors: J. Graham (MD)
Date established: 2008 **Turnover:** Up to £250,000
No.of Employees: 1 - 10 **Product Groups:** 40

T P S Fronius Ltd

5 Simonsburn Road, Kilmarnock, KA1 5LE
Tel: 01563-529435 **Fax:** 01563-523510
E-mail: tomp@tps-fronius.co.uk
Website: http://www.tps-fronius.co.uk
Directors: M. Palmer (Fin), T. Palmer (MD)
Managers: J. Muir (Chief Mgr), M. Leiper (Purch Mgr), J. Stevenson (Research & Deve), B. Divers (Mktg Serv Mgr)
Immediate Holding Company: TPS-FRONIUS LTD.
Registration no: SC053928 **Date established:** 1973 **Turnover:**
No.of Employees: 51 - 100 **Product Groups:** 37

Date of Accounts	Dec 10	Dec 09	Dec 08
Sales Turnover	N/A	N/A	8m
Pre Tax Profit/Loss	N/A	N/A	581
Working Capital	1m	773	669
Fixed Assets	1m	2m	2m
Current Assets	2m	2m	3m
Current Liabilities	N/A	N/A	521

Tannock Fixings Scotland Ltd

1a Tannock Street, Kilmarnock, KA1 4DN
Tel: 01563-574832 **Fax:** 01563- 524605
Directors: D. Murphy (Prop)
Managers: D. Murphy (Mgr)
Date established: 2002 **No.of Employees:** 1 - 10 **Product Groups:** 37

William Tracey Group

Dunniflats Depot Lugton, Kilmarnock, KA3 4EA
Tel: 0141-889 3207 **Fax:** 01505-850102
E-mail: dunniflats@wmtracey.co.uk
Website: http://www.williamtraceygroup.com
Directors: G. McDonald (Dir)
Managers: M. Cunningham (Sales Admin), M. Mcpherson (Sales Admin)
Registration no: sc057052 **No.of Employees:** 21 - 50
Product Groups: 31, 54, 66

Twist & Design Metalcraft

37 Treeswoodhead Road, Kilmarnock, KA1 4NB
Tel: 01563-529915
Directors: G. Rattray (Ptnr)
No.of Employees: 1 - 10 **Product Groups:** 26, 35

Vacuum Lifting

Rowallan, Kilmarnock, KA3 2LW
Tel: 01563-540400 **Fax:** 01563-520139
E-mail: sales@vacuumliftinguk.co.uk
Website: http://www.vacuumliftinguk.co.uk
Directors: P. Watson (MD)
No.of Employees: 1 - 10 **Product Groups:** 35, 39, 45

Date of Accounts	Aug 07	Aug 06
Working Capital	-5	N/A
Fixed Assets	6	6
Current Assets	95	108
Current Liabilities	100	108

Ayrshire

Kilwinning

G M Instruments Ltd

6 Ashgrove Workshops, Kilwinning, KA13 6PU
Tel: 01294-554664 **Fax:** 01294-551154
E-mail: gminstruments@aol.com
Website: http://www.gm-instruments.com
Directors: E. Greig (MD)
Immediate Holding Company: GM INSTRUMENTS LIMITED
Registration no: SC135969 **VAT No.:** GB 554 7463 20
Date established: 1992 **Turnover:** Up to £250,000
No.of Employees: 1 - 10 **Product Groups:** 37, 38

Date of Accounts	Dec 11	Dec 10	Dec 09
Working Capital	138	138	137
Fixed Assets	1	2	2
Current Assets	234	248	245
Current Liabilities	74	69	79

Perthshire

Kinross

Blue Chip Hospitlity

40 South Street Milnathort, Kinross, KY13 9XA
Tel: 08702-340201 **Fax:** 08702-340202
E-mail: info@bluechiphospitality.com
Website: http://www.bluechiphospitality.com
Directors: A. Green (Dir), A. Greene (Grp Chief Exec), A. Green (Grp Chief Exec)
Immediate Holding Company: BLUE CHIP HOSPITALITY LIMITED
Registration no: SC284267 **Date established:** 2005
Turnover: £250,000 - £500,000 **No.of Employees:** 1 - 10
Product Groups: 89

Date of Accounts	Jun 11	Jun 10	Jun 09
Sales Turnover	855	550	449
Pre Tax Profit/Loss	9	-2	11
Working Capital	-15	-23	-22
Current Assets	304	249	197
Current Liabilities	319	273	217

George Colliar Ltd

Middle Balado Farm Balado, Kinross, KY13 0NH
Tel: 01577-863173 **Fax:** 01577-864768
E-mail: colliar@harleys.co.uk
Website: http://www.georgecollier.com
Directors: W. Sneddon (Dir)
Ultimate Holding Company: ALEXANDER HARLEY SEEDS LIMITED
Immediate Holding Company: GEORGE COLLIAR LTD
Registration no: SC068901 **Date established:** 1979
No.of Employees: 1 - 10 **Product Groups:** 07, 41, 45, 48

Date of Accounts	May 11	May 10	May 09
Working Capital	103	41	175
Fixed Assets	420	381	337
Current Assets	2m	1m	1m
Current Liabilities	N/A	4	N/A

Fife Computers

113 High Street, Kinross, KY13 8AQ
Tel: 01577-861878 **Fax:** 01577-864801
E-mail: info@fifecomputers.com
Website: http://www.fifecomputers.co.uk
Managers: K. Celentolo (Mgr)
Turnover: £250,000 - £500,000 **No.of Employees:** 1 - 10
Product Groups: 44, 67

Date of Accounts	Mar 08	Mar 07	Mar 06
Working Capital	10	13	17
Fixed Assets	N/A	1	3
Current Assets	26	25	31
Current Liabilities	16	12	14

John Moncrieff Ltd

Unit 5 Clashburn Road Bridgend Industrial Estate, Kinross, KY13 8GB
Tel: 01577-864870 **Fax:** 01577-861060
E-mail: enquiries@jmoncrieff.co.uk
Website: http://www.jmoncrieff.co.uk
Bank(s): Royal Bank of Scotland
Directors: S. Gilmore (Dir)
Managers: D. Lloyd (Sales Prom Mgr), K. Veale (Fin Mgr)
Registration no: 00209212 **Date established:** 1865 **Turnover:** £1m - £2m
No.of Employees: 21 - 50 **Product Groups:** 33, 37, 38

Todd & Duncan Ltd

Lochleven Mills, Kinross, KY13 8DH
Tel: 01577-863521 **Fax:** 01577-864533
E-mail: enq@todd-duncan.com
Website: http://www.todd-duncan.com
Bank(s): The Bank of Scotland, Edinburgh
Directors: G. Ferrier (Fin), I. Cormack (Fin), R. Binch (Pers), C. Bordini (Sales & Mktg)
Managers: S. Belfour (Tech Serv Mgr), H. Devany
Immediate Holding Company: TODD & DUNCAN LIMITED
Registration no: SC355840 **VAT No.:** 671 2525 45 **Date established:** 2009
Turnover: £20m - £50m **No.of Employees:** 101 - 250 **Product Groups:** 23

Date of Accounts	Dec 11	Dec 10	Jun 09
Sales Turnover	24m	22m	N/A
Pre Tax Profit/Loss	402	2m	N/A
Working Capital	7m	3m	N/A
Fixed Assets	5m	5m	N/A
Current Assets	21m	16m	N/A
Current Liabilities	578	2m	N/A

Fife

Kirkcaldy

A K F Blacksmiths Services

17 Brodick Road, Kirkcaldy, KY2 6EZ
Tel: 01592-569712 **Fax:** 01592-596867
Website: http://www.akfblacksmith.co.uk
Directors: A. Crawford (Prop)
Immediate Holding Company: AKF BLACKSMITH SERVICES LTD
Registration no: SC274500 **Date established:** 2004
No.of Employees: 1 - 10 **Product Groups:** 26, 35

Date of Accounts	Oct 11	Oct 10	Oct 09
Working Capital	5	4	4
Fixed Assets	3	3	3
Current Assets	7	5	5

Carrs Flower Hutchinson Ltd

East Bridge, Kirkcaldy, KY1 2SR
Tel: 01592-267191 **Fax:** 01592-641805
E-mail: sales@roberthutchison.co.uk
Website: http://www.roberthutchison.co.uk
Bank(s): Bank of Scotland
Directors: G. Wishart (Fin), J. Duncan (Sales), R. Wood (Fin), T. Hall (Chief Op Offcr)
Ultimate Holding Company: CARR'S MILLING INDUSTRIES PUBLIC LIMITED COMPANY
Immediate Holding Company: ROBERT HUTCHISON LIMITED
Registration no: 03446518 **VAT No.:** GB 700 2872 71
Date established: 1997 **Turnover:** Up to £250,000
No.of Employees: 51 - 100 **Product Groups:** 20

Concrete Products Kirkcaldy Ltd

Hayfield Place Hayfield Industrial Estate, Kirkcaldy, KY2 5DH
Tel: 01592-261326 **Fax:** 01592-200498
E-mail: johnsmart@concrete-products.co.uk
Bank(s): The Royal Bank of Scotland
Directors: J. Smart (MD), A. McClure (Fin)
Ultimate Holding Company: J SMART & CO (CONTRACTORS) P L C
Immediate Holding Company: CONCRETE PRODUCTS (KIRKCALDY) LIMITED
Registration no: SC031013 **VAT No.:** GB 268 3862 19
Date established: 1955 **Turnover:** £1m - £2m **No.of Employees:** 11 - 20
Product Groups: 33

Date of Accounts	Jul 11	Jul 10	Jul 09
Sales Turnover	2m	2m	2m
Pre Tax Profit/Loss	-211	-85	-47
Working Capital	235	333	370
Fixed Assets	326	387	416
Current Assets	623	650	652
Current Liabilities	150	144	114

C F Cruickshenk

12 Hayfield Road, Kirkcaldy, KY2 5DG
Tel: 01592-590006 **Fax:** 01592-590006
Managers: C. Cruikshent (Mgr)
Date established: 1990 **No.of Employees:** 1 - 10 **Product Groups:** 35

Fermentation Stop

122 Commercial Street, Kirkcaldy, KY1 2NX
Tel: 01592-204660
Directors: D. Laine (Prop)
Date established: 1988 **No.of Employees:** 1 - 10 **Product Groups:** 20, 40, 41

Fife Fire Engineers

Unit 5 Waverley Road, Mitchelston Industrial Estate, Kirkcaldy, KY1 3NH
Tel: 01592-653661 **Fax:** 01592-653990
Directors: R. Hutcheson (MD), R. Hutchison (Fin), C. McKenzie (Chief Op Offcr)
Managers: I. Macdonald
Ultimate Holding Company: CALEDONIA FIRE AND SECURITY LIMITED
Immediate Holding Company: FIFE FIRE ENGINEERS AND CONSULTANTS LIMITED
Registration no: SC059150 **Date established:** 1975
No.of Employees: 21 - 50 **Product Groups:** 37, 40, 52, 67

Date of Accounts	Dec 11	Dec 10	Dec 09
Working Capital	215	1m	1m
Fixed Assets	71	83	74
Current Assets	497	1m	1m

Forbo

PO Box 1, Kirkcaldy, KY1 2SB
Tel: 01592-643111 **Fax:** 01772-627361
E-mail: headoffice@forbo.com
Website: http://www.forbo.com
Bank(s): Barclays, National Westminster, Bank of Scotland
Directors: A. Fotheringham (MD), C. Woodford (Co Sec), E. Speed (Fin)
Managers: D. Bowden, J. Lowe (Mktg Serv Mgr), L. Binns (Personnel), L. Bins (Personnel)
Ultimate Holding Company: FORBO HOLDING AG/SA (SWITZERLAND)
Immediate Holding Company: FORBO FLOORING UK LIMITED
Registration no: SC041400 **VAT No.:** GB **Date established:** 1964
Turnover: £20m - £50m **No.of Employees:** 51 - 100 **Product Groups:** 23, 30

Glass Bullet Productions

Suite 19 The Round House, Kirkcaldy, KY1 2QT
Tel: 01592-223889
E-mail: mail@glassbullet.co.uk
Website: http://www.glassbullet.co.uk
Directors: L. Binnie (Dir), G. Campbell (Fin)
Immediate Holding Company: GLASS BULLET PRODUCTIONS LIMITED
Registration no: SC331056 **Date established:** 2007
No.of Employees: 1 - 10 **Product Groups:** 89

Date of Accounts	Mar 11	Mar 10	Mar 09
Working Capital	-1	-1	-2
Fixed Assets	5	N/A	1
Current Assets	-0	1	-2

Good to Go Safety Ltd

Waverley Road Mitchelston Industrial Estate, Kirkcaldy, KY1 3NH
Tel: 01592-655646 **Fax:** 01592-655330
E-mail: enquiries@goodtogosafety.co.uk
Website: http://www.goodtogosafety.co.uk
Managers: G. Halliday (Product)
Registration no: SC354697 **Date established:** 1989
No.of Employees: 21 - 50 **Product Groups:** 45, 84

Hettich International

Adam Smith Court, Kirkcaldy, KY1 1SW
Tel: 01592-644805 **Fax:** 01592-644805
E-mail: sales@hettich.uk.com
Website: http://www.hettich.uk.com
Managers: D. Browne (Mgr)
Date established: 1989 **No.of Employees:** 1 - 10 **Product Groups:** 35, 36

Legge Steel Fabrications Ltd

Hayfield Place, Kirkcaldy, KY2 5DJ
Tel: 01592-205320 **Fax:** 01592-651617
E-mail: paul@leggesteel.co.uk
Website: http://www.leggesteel.co.uk
Bank(s): The Royal Bank of Scotland
Managers: P. Witcombe (Mgr)
Ultimate Holding Company: BARCLAY DOUGALL (HOLDINGS) LIMITED
Immediate Holding Company: LEGGE STEEL (FABRICATIONS) LIMITED
Registration no: SC088016 **Date established:** 1984
Turnover: £5m - £10m **No.of Employees:** 11 - 20 **Product Groups:** 35, 48, 49

Date of Accounts	Mar 11	Mar 10	Mar 09
Working Capital	257	288	246
Fixed Assets	60	54	95
Current Assets	449	505	562

Lindab Building Systems
Evans Business Centre Mitchelston Drive, Mitchelston Industrial Estate, Kirkcaldy, KY1 3NB
Tel: 01592-652300 **Fax:** 01592-653135
E-mail: info@astron.biz
Website: http://www.lindabbuildings.com
Managers: A. Small (Mgr)
Immediate Holding Company: LINDAB
Registration no: SC333496 **VAT No.:** GB 735 1008 66
Date established: 2007 **Turnover:** Up to £250,000
No.of Employees: 1 - 10 **Product Groups:** 25, 35

Mirrey Mcgregor Electrical Ltd
Unit 2 Carberry Place, Mitchelston Industrial Estate, Kirkcaldy, KY1 3NQ
Tel: 01592-654155 **Fax:** 01592-655222
E-mail: enquiries@merymcgrefsnet.co.uk
Directors: C. Mirrey (Dir), J. McGregor (MD), J. Stevenson (Fin)
Immediate Holding Company: MIRREY MCGREGOR ELECTRICAL LIMITED
Registration no: SC151307 **VAT No.:** GB 415 4891 44
Date established: 1994 **Turnover:** £500,000 - £1m
No.of Employees: 1 - 10 **Product Groups:** 52

Date of Accounts	Jul 08	Jul 07	Jul 06
Working Capital	13	2	-16
Fixed Assets	106	101	104
Current Assets	207	184	171
Current Liabilities	194	182	187
Total Share Capital	69	69	69

Ornamental Metals
2-24 Mill Street, Kirkcaldy, KY1 1SD
Tel: 01592-206335 **Fax:** 01592-641507
Directors: A. Harrow (Prop)
Date established: 1987 **No.of Employees:** 1 - 10 **Product Groups:** 26, 35

Peter Greig & Co.
Victoria Linen Works 147-151 St Clair Street, Kirkcaldy, KY1 2BU
Tel: 01592-651901 **Fax:** 01592-655596
E-mail: rosie@petergreig.co.uk
Website: http://www.petergreig.co.uk
Bank(s): The Royal Bank of Scotland
Directors: H. Nicoll (Dir)
Managers: R. Nicoll (Chief Acct)
Ultimate Holding Company: PETER GREIG & COMPANY (HOLDINGS) LIMITED
Immediate Holding Company: PETER GREIG & COMPANY LIMITED
Registration no: SC013173 **VAT No.:** GB 723 8344 34
Date established: 2024 **Turnover:** £2m - £5m **No.of Employees:** 21 - 50
Product Groups: 23, 63

Date of Accounts	Nov 10	Nov 11	Nov 08
Working Capital	589	677	460
Fixed Assets	298	271	368
Current Assets	1m	1m	856

R & M Distribution Ltd
Unit 1 Carwhinney Mitchelston Industrial Estate, Kirkcaldy, KY1 3LS
Tel: 01592-655565 **Fax:** 01592-655542
E-mail: enquiries@rmdist.com
Website: http://www.rmdist.com
Bank(s): Bank of Scotland
Directors: M. Brown (Fin)
Immediate Holding Company: R. & M. DISTRIBUTION LIMITED
Registration no: SC099757 **VAT No.:** GB 400 9624 79
Date established: 1986 **Turnover:** £2m - £5m **No.of Employees:** 11 - 20
Product Groups: 63, 66

Date of Accounts	Feb 12	Feb 11	Feb 10
Working Capital	463	438	779
Fixed Assets	58	48	48
Current Assets	910	914	1m
Current Liabilities	N/A	100	N/A

Raith Rovers Football Club
Starks Park Pratt Street, Kirkcaldy, KY1 1SA
Tel: 01592-263514 **Fax:** 01592-642833
E-mail: eric.drysdale@raithroversfc.com
Website: http://www.raithroversfc.com
Directors: E. Drysdale (Fin)
Managers: C. Lumsden (Mktg Serv Mgr), B. Mullen (Chief Mgr)
Immediate Holding Company: RAITH ROVERS FOOTBALL CLUB LIMITED
Registration no: SC026287 **Date established:** 1948 **Turnover:** £1m - £2m
No.of Employees: 21 - 50 **Product Groups:** 87

Date of Accounts	Jun 11	Jun 10	Jun 09
Sales Turnover	1m	N/A	N/A
Pre Tax Profit/Loss	-162	N/A	N/A
Working Capital	-310	-282	-252
Fixed Assets	N/A	1	1
Current Assets	158	123	46
Current Liabilities	323	N/A	N/A

Scotfire Protection Ltd
Unit 5 Waverley Road, Mitchelston Industrial Estate, Kirkcaldy, KY1 3NH
Tel: 01592-653661 **Fax:** 01224-739777
E-mail: s.bell@ffec.co.uk
Directors: R. Hutcheson (Fin)
Managers: B. Hutcheson
Immediate Holding Company: SCOTFIRE PROTECTION LIMITED
Registration no: SC189882 **Date established:** 1998
Turnover: Up to £250,000 **No.of Employees:** 21 - 50 **Product Groups:** 38, 42

Strachan & Livingston
23-25 Kirk Wynd, Kirkcaldy, KY1 1EP
Tel: 01592-261451 **Fax:** 01592-204180
Website: http://www.fifetoday.co.uk
Bank(s): The Royal Bank of Scotland
Directors: R. Bell (Dir), S. Henderson (Dir), K. McCallum (Co Sec)
Managers: J. Mackay (Publicity), A. Arnott (Sec), K. McCallan (Sec)
Immediate Holding Company: STRACHAN AND LIVINGSTON, LIMITED
Registration no: SC011226 **VAT No.:** 551 0827 61 **Date established:** 1920
Turnover: £1m - £2m **No.of Employees:** 11 - 20 **Product Groups:** 28

Date of Accounts	Dec 07
Sales Turnover	1674
Working Capital	1283
Current Assets	1283
Total Share Capital	50

The Wemyss Development Co. Ltd
Mains House East Wemyss, Kirkcaldy, KY1 4GE
Tel: 01592-651316 **Fax:** 01592-653233
E-mail: wde-lm@bosinternet.com
Directors: W. Wemyss (Dir)
No.of Employees: 1 - 10 **Product Groups:** 80

Kirkcudbrightshire

Kirkcudbright

Galloway Boats & Mouldings Ltd
Culdoach Road Tongland, Kirkcudbright, DG6 4LU
Tel: 01557-331973 **Fax:** 01557-331978
E-mail: i.carson.gbm@btconnect.com
Bank(s): The Royal Bank of Scotland
Directors: I. Carson (MD)
Managers: B. Spears, M. Green (Sales Prom Mgr)
Immediate Holding Company: GALLOWAY BOATS & MOULDINGS LIMITED
Registration no: SC141422 **VAT No.:** GB 612 4281 73
Date established: 1992 **Turnover:** £500,000 - £1m
No.of Employees: 51 - 100 **Product Groups:** 48

Date of Accounts	Nov 11	Nov 10	Nov 09
Working Capital	1m	1m	970
Fixed Assets	201	189	211
Current Assets	2m	1m	1m

Galloway Eggs Ltd
Kempleton Mill Twynholm, Kirkcudbright, DG6 4NJ
Tel: 01557-860268 **Fax:** 01557-860257
E-mail: info@gallowayglassfibremoulds.co.uk
Website: http://www.gallowayglassfibremoulds.co.uk
Directors: D. Shamash (Dir)
Immediate Holding Company: GALLOWAY EGGS LIMITED
Registration no: SC064455 **Date established:** 1978
Turnover: Up to £250,000 **No.of Employees:** 1 - 10 **Product Groups:** 48

Date of Accounts	May 11	May 10	May 09
Working Capital	151	110	112
Fixed Assets	818	823	868
Current Assets	242	163	178

Twynholm Smithy
2 Arden Road Twynholm, Kirkcudbright, DG6 4PB
Tel: 01557-860273 **Fax:** 01557-860273
E-mail: d.bone777@btinternet.com
Directors: D. Bone (Prop)
Date established: 1986 **No.of Employees:** 1 - 10 **Product Groups:** 41

West Lothian

Kirkliston

Flexistore
Royal Elizabeth Yard, Kirkliston, EH29 9EN
Tel: 0131-331 1500 **Fax:** 0131-331 1599
E-mail: edinburgh@flexistore.co.uk
Website: http://www.flexistore.co.uk
Directors: K. Grant (Dir), J. Brown (Co Sec)
Immediate Holding Company: FLEXISTORE LTD.
Registration no: SC261971 **Date established:** 2004
No.of Employees: 1 - 10 **Product Groups:** 72

Nationwide Access Ltd
Unit 11, Royal Elizabeth Yard, Kirkliston, EH29 9AN
Tel: 0845-7450000 **Fax:** 01382-835916
E-mail: dundee@nationwideplatforms.co.uk
Website: http://www.nationwideaccess.co.uk
Directors: C. Cavings (MD), H. Cole (Ch), H. Walters (Mkt Research)
Managers: C. McCauley (Sales Prom Mgr)
Ultimate Holding Company: Lavendon Group plc
Immediate Holding Company: Zooom Holdings UK Ltd
Registration no: 04405299 **Turnover:** £20m - £50m
No.of Employees: 1 - 10 **Product Groups:** 45, 83

Midlothian

Kirknewton

Marriott Dalmahoy Hotel & Country Club
Kirknewton, Kirknewton, EH27 8EB
Tel: 0131-333 1845 **Fax:** 0131-333 1433
E-mail: alistair.kinchin@marriotthotels.com
Website: http://www.marriott.co.uk
Bank(s): Girobank
Directors: A. Kinchin (MD)
Managers: A. Stanton (Ops Mgr), A. Kichin (District Mgr), A. Kinchin (Chief Mgr)
Immediate Holding Company: Whitbread Hotel Company
Registration no: 00000000 **Date established:** 1990 **Turnover:** £5m - £10m
No.of Employees: 101 - 250 **Product Groups:** 69

Orkney Isles

Kirkwall

Confetti Dreams
Costies Pavilion Main Street, Kirkwall, KW15 1BU
Tel: 01856-876066 **Fax:** 0871-242 5406
E-mail: confetti.dreams@yahoo.co.uk
Website: http://www.confetti-dreams.co.uk
Directors: S. Charmers (Ptnr)
Registration no: 07354895 **Date established:** 2006
No.of Employees: 1 - 10 **Product Groups:** 28, 49

Ortak Jewellery Ltd
Hatston Hatston Industrial Estate, Kirkwall, KW15 1RH
Tel: 01856-872224 **Fax:** 01856-875165
E-mail: alistair@ortak.co.uk
Website: http://www.ortak.co.uk
Directors: Y. Carr (Dir), A. Gray (Dir)
Managers: B. Corsie (Tech Serv Mgr)
Immediate Holding Company: ORTAK JEWELLERY LIMITED
Registration no: SC065690 **VAT No.:** GB 296 8827 84
Date established: 1978 **Turnover:** £5m - £10m
No.of Employees: 101 - 250 **Product Groups:** 65

Date of Accounts	Jan 11	Jan 10	Jan 09
Sales Turnover	7m	8m	7m
Pre Tax Profit/Loss	111	215	-229
Working Capital	3m	2m	1m
Fixed Assets	781	854	1m
Current Assets	4m	4m	4m
Current Liabilities	508	632	573

Robertsons
8 Crowness Road Hatston, Kirkwall, KW15 1RG
Tel: 01856-876068 **Fax:** 01856-876288
E-mail: sales@robertsons-orkney.co.uk
Website: http://www.robertsons-orkney.co.uk
Directors: E. Stout (Dir), K. Stout (Fin)
Immediate Holding Company: ROBERTSONS-ORKNEY LIMITED
Registration no: SC280095 **Date established:** 2005
No.of Employees: 1 - 10 **Product Groups:** 41

Date of Accounts	Nov 11	Nov 10	Nov 09
Working Capital	220	225	219
Fixed Assets	122	140	169
Current Assets	2m	1m	1m

Angus

Kirriemuir

J & D Wilkie Ltd
Marywell Brae, Kirriemuir, DD8 4BJ
Tel: 01575-572502 **Fax:** 01575-574564
E-mail: sales@jdwilkie.co.uk
Website: http://www.jdwilkie.co.uk
Bank(s): Bank of Scotland
Directors: S. Liddell (Sales)
Ultimate Holding Company: J. & D. WILKIE (HOLDING COMPANY) LIMITED
Immediate Holding Company: CFTNR LIMITED
Registration no: SC277995 **Date established:** 2005
Turnover: £5m - £10m **No.of Employees:** 101 - 250 **Product Groups:** 23, 49, 63

Date of Accounts	Jun 11	Jun 10	Jun 09
Working Capital	-2m	-2m	-1m
Fixed Assets	N/A	187	200
Current Assets	430	261	224

Lanarkshire

Lanark

Clydewide Taxis
99 High Street, Lanark, ML11 7LN
Tel: 01555-663813 **Fax:** 01555-678937
E-mail: ron@clydewidetaxis.co.uk
Website: http://www.taxislanark.co.uk
Directors: R. Jenkins (Prop)
Date established: 2002 **Turnover:** £250,000 - £500,000
No.of Employees: 11 - 20 **Product Groups:** 23, 30, 38

Glenmuir Ltd
Delves Road, Lanark, ML11 9DX
Tel: 01555-662244 **Fax:** 01555-665734
E-mail: customerservice@glenmuir.com
Website: http://www.glenmuir.com
Bank(s): The Royal Bank of Scotland
Directors: C. Mee (MD), G. Hayward (Sales), B. Mair (Mkt Research)
Managers: C. Mackay (Tech Serv Mgr), A. Miller (Purch Mgr), F. Barclay (Comptroller)
Immediate Holding Company: GLENMUIR LIMITED
Registration no: 04533812 **VAT No.:** GB 743 0747 38
Date established: 2002 **Turnover:** £5m - £10m
No.of Employees: 51 - 100 **Product Groups:** 24

Date of Accounts	Dec 11	Dec 10	Dec 09
Sales Turnover	10m	12m	9m
Pre Tax Profit/Loss	679	804	329
Working Capital	3m	3m	2m
Fixed Assets	949	935	1m
Current Assets	5m	5m	3m
Current Liabilities	1m	865	537

Graham

Unit 1 Block 3 Caldwellside Industrial Estate, Lanark, ML11 7SR
Tel: 01555-661708 **Fax:** 01555-666697
E-mail: kenny.simpson@graham-group.co.uk
Website: http://www.graham-group.co.uk
Managers: B. Gray (Mgr)
Ultimate Holding Company: SAINT-GOBAIN PLC
Immediate Holding Company: GRAHAM GROUP LTD
Registration no: 00066738 **No.of Employees:** 1 - 10 **Product Groups:** 66

Incamet Holdings Ltd

Incamet Foundry Springhill Industrial Estate, Douglas, Lanark, ML11 0RE
Tel: 01555-851280 **Fax:** 01555-851127
E-mail: info@incametltd.co.uk
Website: http://www.incametltd.co.uk
Directors: R. Wright (MD), W. Ramage (Co Sec)
Managers: I. Smith (Sales Admin)
Immediate Holding Company: ANGUS TERRACE LTD
Registration no: SC059232 **VAT No.:** GB 268 6448 14
Date established: 2007 **Turnover:** £2m - £5m **No.of Employees:** 1 - 10
Product Groups: 34

Date of Accounts	Jan 08	Jan 07	Jan 06
Working Capital	282	432	463
Fixed Assets	N/A	319	331
Current Assets	421	682	725
Current Liabilities	138	250	262
Total Share Capital	15	15	15

Nicholson Plastics Ltd

Riverside Road Kirkfieldbank, Lanark, ML11 9JS
Tel: 01555-664316 **Fax:** 01555-663056
E-mail: info@nicholsonplastics.co.uk
Website: http://www.nicholsonplastics.co.uk
Bank(s): HSBC Bank plc
Directors: D. Nicholson (Co Sec), S. Dempster (MD)
Managers: R. Keltie (Sales Prom Mgr)
Ultimate Holding Company: ACSTK HOLDINGS
Immediate Holding Company: NICHOLSON PLASTICS LIMITED.
Registration no: SC045599 **Date established:** 1968 **Turnover:** £2m - £5m
No.of Employees: 21 - 50 **Product Groups:** 30

Date of Accounts	Dec 11	Dec 10	Dec 09
Working Capital	671	836	853
Fixed Assets	569	390	360
Current Assets	2m	1m	1m

Wailes Dove Northern Ltd

Norwood House Auchenheath, Lanark, ML11 9UT
Tel: 01555-893333 **Fax:** 01555-895774
Directors: J. Wilson (MD), M. Wilson (Fin)
Immediate Holding Company: WD TANK INSTALLATIONS LIMITED
Registration no: SC133020 **Date established:** 2005
Turnover: Up to £250,000 **No.of Employees:** 1 - 10 **Product Groups:** 46, 48

Date of Accounts	Jul 11	Jul 09	Jul 08
Sales Turnover	120	129	109
Pre Tax Profit/Loss	16	46	12
Working Capital	36	1	2
Fixed Assets	23	10	13
Current Assets	41	8	14
Current Liabilities	5	5	7

William Withers & Co

186 Hyndford Road, Lanark, ML11 9BG
Tel: 01555-665878 **Fax:** 01555-665878
E-mail: sales@withers.co.uk
Website: http://www.withers.co.uk
Directors: A. Gracie (Prop)
Immediate Holding Company: COUNTRY CARPETS (SCOTLAND) LTD.
Registration no: SC359501 **Date established:** 2009
No.of Employees: 1 - 10 **Product Groups:** 41

Dumfriesshire

Langholm

Chas Paisley & Sons

2 Caroline Street, Langholm, DG13 0AF
Tel: 01387-380308 **Fax:** 01387-381048
Website: http://www.pittards.com
Directors: R. Paisley (Prop)
Immediate Holding Company: PITTARDS P.L.C.
Date established: 1997 **Turnover:** £10m - £20m **No.of Employees:** 1 - 10
Product Groups: 22

Reid & Taylor Ltd

Williams Street Langholm Woollen Mills, Langholm, DG13 0BN
Tel: 01387-380311 **Fax:** 01387-380720
E-mail: office@reidandtaylor.com
Website: http://www.reidandtaylor.co.uk
Bank(s): Barclays
Directors: D. Ogilvie (MD), S. Tait (Co Sec), P. Sharp (Sales)
Managers: A. Charlton (Chief Acct)
Ultimate Holding Company: REID & TAYLOR (HOLDINGS) LTD (BVI)
Immediate Holding Company: REID & TAYLOR LIMITED
Registration no: 03320402 **VAT No.:** GB 711 1154 93
Date established: 1997 **Turnover:** £500,000 - £1m
No.of Employees: 21 - 50 **Product Groups:** 23

Date of Accounts	Sep 11	Sep 10	Sep 09
Working Capital	548	-64	-355
Fixed Assets	70	68	116
Current Assets	1m	918	953

Stirlingshire

Larbert

Catering Supplies & Repair Co. Ltd

122 Muirhall Road, Larbert, FK5 4AP
Tel: 01324-552601 **Fax:** 01324-563329
E-mail: allan.pinkerton@csr-ltd.co.uk
Website: http://www.csr-ltd.co.uk
Bank(s): The Royal Bank of Scotland
Directors: A. Pinkerton (MD), G. Pinkerton (Fin)
Managers: L. Stewart (Sales Admin)
Immediate Holding Company: CATERING SUPPLIES & REPAIRS COMPANY LIMITED
Registration no: SC158570 **VAT No.:** GB 658 5102 30
Date established: 1995 **No.of Employees:** 21 - 50 **Product Groups:** 48, 67

Date of Accounts	Jun 11	Jun 10	Jun 09
Working Capital	144	142	337
Fixed Assets	194	197	203
Current Assets	467	416	625

Drysdale Brothers Larbert Ltd

340 Main Street Stenhousemuir, Larbert, FK5 3BG
Tel: 01324-562447 **Fax:** 01324-556726
E-mail: enquiries@drysdalebrothers.com
Website: http://www.drysdalebrothers.com
Bank(s): Bank of Scotland
Directors: A. Drysdale (Dir)
Immediate Holding Company: DRYSDALE BROTHERS (LARBERT) LIMITED
Registration no: SC015465 **VAT No.:** GB 268 3160 51
Date established: 2029 **Turnover:** £2m - £5m **No.of Employees:** 21 - 50
Product Groups: 34, 48

Date of Accounts	Dec 11	Dec 10	Dec 09
Working Capital	609	570	323
Fixed Assets	2m	2m	2m
Current Assets	2m	1m	1m

James Jones & Sons Ltd

Broomage Avenue, Larbert, FK5 4NQ
Tel: 01324-562241 **Fax:** 01324-558755
E-mail: sales@jamesjones.co.uk
Website: http://www.jamesjones.co.uk
Directors: J. Armstrong (Dir)
Immediate Holding Company: JAMES JONES & SONS LIMITED
Registration no: SC005832 **VAT No.:** GB 268 7001 51
Date established: 2005 **Turnover:** £75m - £125m
No.of Employees: 501 - 1000 **Product Groups:** 25

Date of Accounts	Dec 11	Dec 10	Dec 09
Sales Turnover	106m	94m	73m
Pre Tax Profit/Loss	25m	20m	10m
Working Capital	20m	19m	5m
Fixed Assets	94m	85m	79m
Current Assets	39m	36m	25m
Current Liabilities	6m	5m	3m

Lightways Contractors Ltd

Lochlands Industrial Estate, Larbert, FK5 3NS
Tel: 01324-553025 **Fax:** 01324-557870
E-mail: john.mclauchlan@lightways.co.uk
Website: http://www.lightways.co.uk
Bank(s): Bank of Scotland
Directors: J. Mclauchlan (Dir), D. Hornall (Pers), J. Hornall (MD)
Managers: K. Cassells (Buyer)
Immediate Holding Company: LIGHTWAYS (CONTRACTORS) LIMITED
Registration no: SC064413 **VAT No.:** GB 300 6843 90
Date established: 1978 **Turnover:** £10m - £20m
No.of Employees: 51 - 100 **Product Groups:** 51, 52

Date of Accounts	Dec 11	Dec 10	Dec 09
Sales Turnover	11m	11m	10m
Pre Tax Profit/Loss	-201	195	155
Working Capital	27	82	298
Fixed Assets	972	1m	621
Current Assets	2m	2m	2m
Current Liabilities	687	488	545

Logan Vent

Logans House Lochlands Industrial Estate, Larbert, FK5 3NS
Tel: 01324-579900 **Fax:** 01324-579901
Directors: A. Wilson (Dir)
No.of Employees: 1 - 10 **Product Groups:** 40, 66

Overland Leisure & Caravans

263 Main Street, Larbert, FK5 4PX
Tel: 01324-554131 **Fax:** 01324-563165
E-mail: graeme@overlandcaravans.co.uk
Website: http://www.overlandcaravans.co.uk
Bank(s): Bank of Scotland
Directors: G. Patterson (Ptnr)
Immediate Holding Company: OVERLAND LEISURE LIMITED
Registration no: SC299866 **VAT No.:** GB 356 2911 48
Date established: 2006 **Turnover:** £2m - £5m **No.of Employees:** 11 - 20
Product Groups: 39

Scottish Fuels

Glenbervie Business Park, Larbert, FK5 4RB
Tel: 08453-008844 **Fax:** 01324-408109
Website: http://www.scottishfuels.co.uk
Directors: T. Stewart (Sales)
Ultimate Holding Company: BROGAN HOLDINGS LIMITED
Immediate Holding Company: BROGAN DEVELOPMENTS LIMITED
Registration no: 04130805 **Date established:** 2008
Turnover: £10m - £20m **No.of Employees:** 1 - 10 **Product Groups:** 66

Smith Packaging Services

Lochlands Industrial Estate, Larbert, FK5 3NS
Tel: 01324-555521 **Fax:** 01324-555988
E-mail: smith.packaging@btinternet.com
Website: http://www.smith-packaging.com
Bank(s): Clydesdale
Directors: A. Ray (Prop)
Managers: M. Ray (Comptroller)
Immediate Holding Company: SMITH PACKAGING SERVICES LIMITED
Registration no: SC344603 **VAT No.:** 502 3562 85 **Date established:** 2008
Turnover: £500,000 - £1m **No.of Employees:** 11 - 20
Product Groups: 25, 45

Ayrshire

Largs

Amarok Multimedia Ltd

3 Anthony Court, Largs, KA30 8TA
Tel: 01475-689096 **Fax:** 01475-689096
E-mail: mail@amarok.uk.com
Website: http://www.amarok.uk.com
Directors: E. Letton (MD), E. Letton (Fin), P. Letton (MD)
Immediate Holding Company: AMAROK MULTIMEDIA LTD.
Registration no: SC206961 **Date established:** 2000
Turnover: £250,000 - £500,000 **No.of Employees:** 1 - 10
Product Groups: 44

Kelvin Top-Set Ltd

55a Main Road Fairlie, Largs, KA29 0AA
Tel: 01475-560007 **Fax:** 01475-569011
E-mail: sales@kelvin.org
Website: http://www.kelvintopset.com
Directors: D. Ramsay (MD), L. Ramsay (Fin)
Ultimate Holding Company: THE KELVIN CONSULTANTS LIMITED
Immediate Holding Company: KELVIN TOP-SET LIMITED
Registration no: SC342121 **VAT No.:** GB 456 5059 33
Date established: 2008 **No.of Employees:** 1 - 10 **Product Groups:** 54, 80, 84, 86

Date of Accounts	Dec 11	Dec 10	Dec 09
Working Capital	514	414	117
Fixed Assets	41	19	12
Current Assets	1m	1m	648

North Western Automarine

Largs Yacht Haven Irvine Road, Largs, KA30 8EZ
Tel: 01475-687139 **Fax:** 01475-687139
Directors: G. Humphreys (Ptnr)
Immediate Holding Company: MARITIME CRAFT SERVICES (CLYDE) LIMITED
Registration no: SC223121 **Date established:** 1977
Turnover: £250,000 - £500,000 **No.of Employees:** 1 - 10
Product Groups: 35, 36, 39

Date of Accounts	Oct 09	Oct 08
Sales Turnover	6m	N/A
Pre Tax Profit/Loss	4m	4m
Working Capital	-267	-2m
Fixed Assets	19m	18m
Current Assets	2m	1m
Current Liabilities	502	492

Lanarkshire

Larkhall

Ashgill Electronics Ltd

Block 6 Industrial Estate, Larkhall, ML9 2PA
Tel: 01698-883226 **Fax:** 01698-887615
E-mail: andy@ashgill.com
Website: http://www.ashgill.com
Directors: J. Corbett (Fin), A. Corbett (MD)
Managers: P. Corbett (Comptroller)
Immediate Holding Company: ASHGILL ELECTRONICS LIMITED
Registration no: SC069440 **VAT No.:** GB 261 0393 85
Date established: 1979 **Turnover:** £5m - £10m **No.of Employees:** 1 - 10
Product Groups: 35, 37

Date of Accounts	Dec 11	Dec 10	Dec 09
Sales Turnover	4m	4m	N/A
Pre Tax Profit/Loss	262	166	N/A
Working Capital	2m	1m	1m
Fixed Assets	714	794	857
Current Assets	2m	2m	2m
Current Liabilities	225	141	N/A

Gilmour Tools Ltd

Baird Avenue Strutherhill Industrial Estate, Larkhall, ML9 2PJ
Tel: 01698-884856 **Fax:** 01698-886634
E-mail: info@gilmourtools.co.uk
Website: http://www.gilmourtools.co.uk
Bank(s): Bank of Scotland
Directors: L. Gilmour (Fin), G. Gilmour (MD)
Ultimate Holding Company: GILMOUR TOOLS (HOLDINGS) LIMITED
Immediate Holding Company: GILMOUR TOOLS LIMITED
Registration no: SC092332 **VAT No.:** GB 262 5128 73
Date established: 1985 **Turnover:** £1m - £2m **No.of Employees:** 21 - 50
Product Groups: 36, 46

Date of Accounts	Mar 12	Mar 11	Mar 10
Working Capital	2m	1m	1m
Fixed Assets	405	344	395
Current Assets	2m	2m	2m

Melvin Brothers Ltd

Unit 3 Baird Avenue Strutherhill Industrial Estate, Larkhall, ML9 2PJ
Tel: 01698-887605 **Fax:** 01698-884871
E-mail: andrewmelvin1953@googlemail.com
Website: http://www.melvin-brothers-limited.co.uk
Bank(s): Royal Bank of Scotland, Stonehouse
Directors: A. Melvin (Ptnr)
Managers: E. Melvin (Admin Off)
Immediate Holding Company: MELVIN BROTHERS LIMITED
Registration no: SC274845 **VAT No.:** GB 416 0194 80
Date established: 2004 **Turnover:** £1m - £2m **No.of Employees:** 21 - 50
Product Groups: 48

Date of Accounts	Mar 11	Mar 10	Mar 09
Sales Turnover	N/A	2m	2m
Pre Tax Profit/Loss	N/A	121	172

see next page

Melvin Brothers Ltd - *Cont'd*

Working Capital	-37	27	36
Fixed Assets	95	108	73
Current Assets	664	817	805
Current Liabilities	N/A	360	400

Permag Ltd
Baird Avenue Block Unit 2 Strutherhill Industrial Estate, Larkhall, ML9 2PJ
Tel: 01698-884823 **Fax:** 01698-884823
E-mail: sales@permag.freeuk.com
Website: http://www.permag.net
Directors: U. Laing (Co Sec)
Immediate Holding Company: PERMAG LIMITED
Registration no: SC077253 **VAT No.:** GB 361 3826 57
Date established: 1982 **Turnover:** £500,000 - £1m
No.of Employees: 11 - 20 **Product Groups:** 37

Date of Accounts	May 12	May 11	May 10
Working Capital	711	783	766
Fixed Assets	81	80	85
Current Assets	796	862	886

Rosti UK Ltd
Baird Avenue Strutherhill Industrial Estate, Larkhall, ML9 2PJ
Tel: 01698-552200 **Fax:** 01698-888389
E-mail: bco@rosti.com
Website: http://www.rosti.com
Directors: B. Coughlan (MD)
Managers: D. Walker (Buyer), J. Fagan (Sales & Mktg Mg), M. McCorry, L. He (Fin Mgr), P. Loudan (Personnel)
Ultimate Holding Company: NORDSTJERNAN AB (SWEDEN)
Immediate Holding Company: ROSTI UK LTD
Registration no: 02501256 **Date established:** 1990
Turnover: £20m - £50m **No.of Employees:** 101 - 250
Product Groups: 30, 48

Date of Accounts	Dec 11	Dec 10	Dec 09
Sales Turnover	16m	15m	14m
Pre Tax Profit/Loss	224	40	322
Working Capital	-1m	-1m	-2m
Fixed Assets	4m	4m	5m
Current Assets	5m	5m	5m
Current Liabilities	967	861	530

Smurfit Kappa GB Limited
Carlisle Road, Larkhall, ML9 3PN
Tel: 01698-885848 **Fax:** 01698-882421
E-mail: sales@larkhallmondipackaging.com
Website: http://www.mondigroup.com
Directors: G. McArthur (Div), R. Mcbride (MD)
Registration no: 00531292 **No.of Employees:** 51 - 100
Product Groups: 27, 28, 38, 49, 85

Solar Fans Ltd
Unit 4 Block 1 Industrial Estate, Larkhall, ML9 2PA
Tel: 01698-889829 **Fax:** 01698-886769
E-mail: info@solarfans.com
Website: http://www.solarfans.com
Directors: D. Ross (MD)
Immediate Holding Company: SOLAR FANS (SCOTLAND) LIMITED
Registration no: SC236108 **VAT No.:** GB 259 7844 02
Date established: 2002 **Turnover:** £1m - £2m **No.of Employees:** 1 - 10
Product Groups: 40, 48

Date of Accounts	Aug 11	Aug 10	Aug 09
Working Capital	507	491	388
Fixed Assets	205	206	219
Current Assets	629	606	481

Taymore Ltd
Unit 8 Block 4a Industrial Estate, Larkhall, ML9 2PA
Tel: 01698-884000 **Fax:** 01698-886888
E-mail: sales@taymore.co.uk
Website: http://www.taymore.co.uk
Directors: J. Dunsmore (MD)
Ultimate Holding Company: SDRM LIMITED
Immediate Holding Company: TAYMORE LIMITED
Registration no: SC125104 **Date established:** 1990
No.of Employees: 1 - 10 **Product Groups:** 35, 36

Date of Accounts	May 11	May 10	May 09
Working Capital	1m	852	606
Fixed Assets	52	52	49
Current Assets	2m	1m	1m

Midlothian

Lasswade

Dobbie's Gardern World
Melville Nurseries, Lasswade, EH18 1AZ
Tel: 0131-663 1941 **Fax:** 0131-654 2548
E-mail: postmaster@dobbies.com
Website: http://www.dobbies.com
Directors: S. Brown (Fin)
Managers: B. Mackie (Tech Serv Mgr), S. Macdonald (Buyer), S. Martin (Mgr)
Ultimate Holding Company: TESCO PLC
Immediate Holding Company: DOBBIES GARDEN CENTRES LIMITED
Registration no: SC010975 **Date established:** 2020
Turnover: £75m - £125m **No.of Employees:** 21 - 50 **Product Groups:** 02

Date of Accounts	Feb 12	Feb 11	Feb 10
Sales Turnover	136m	112m	104m
Pre Tax Profit/Loss	10m	10m	10m
Working Capital	8m	-3m	4m
Fixed Assets	259m	222m	182m
Current Assets	33m	25m	19m
Current Liabilities	14m	18m	8m

Secure Telecom UK Ltd
Unit 7 Poltonhall Industrial Estate, Lasswade, EH18 1BW
Tel: 08707-776670 **Fax:** 0870-777 6672
E-mail: info@securetelecom.co.uk
Website: http://www.securetelecom.co.uk
Directors: A. Hussain (Dir)
Immediate Holding Company: SECURE TELECOM UK LIMITED
Registration no: SC287150 **Date established:** 2005
No.of Employees: 1 - 10 **Product Groups:** 37, 44

Date of Accounts	Dec 11	Dec 10	Dec 09
Working Capital	478	130	88
Fixed Assets	38	13	16
Current Assets	1m	345	296

Kincardineshire

Laurencekirk

Scroll Products
31a Blackiemuir Avenue, Laurencekirk, AB30 1DX
Tel: 01561-377798 **Fax:** 01561-377798
E-mail: info@scrollproducts.co.uk
Website: http://www.scrollproducts.co.uk
Directors: E. Petrie (Prop)
Date established: 1981 **No.of Employees:** 1 - 10 **Product Groups:** 26, 35

Thistle Special Beltings
Bridge of Mondynes Fordoun, Laurencekirk, AB30 1LD
Tel: 01569-740204 **Fax:** 01569-740322
E-mail: mail@thistle.uk.com
Website: http://www.thistle.uk.com
Directors: S. Powada (Fin)
Managers: F. Powada (Ops Mgr)
Immediate Holding Company: THISTLE POLYMER COMPOSITES LIMITED
Registration no: SC245376 **VAT No.:** GB 327 2368 58
Date established: 2003 **No.of Employees:** 1 - 10 **Product Groups:** 30

Date of Accounts	Mar 11	Mar 10	Mar 09
Working Capital	62	53	46
Fixed Assets	6	3	29
Current Assets	105	79	65

Fife

Leven

Box Yellow Consultancy
37 Toll Court Lundin Links, Leven, KY8 6HH
Tel: 01333-329358 **Fax:** 01333-329358
E-mail: info@boxyellow.co.uk
Website: http://www.boxyellow.co.uk
Directors: J. Lockhart (MD)
Immediate Holding Company: Box Yellow Consultancy Ltd
Registration no: SC242723 **Date established:** 2003
No.of Employees: 1 - 10 **Product Groups:** 80, 82

Diageo Global Supply
Banbeath Industrial Estate, Leven, KY8 5HD
Tel: 01333-424000 **Fax:** 01333-425037
E-mail: john.paterson@diageo.com
Website: http://www.diageo.com
Directors: J. Patterson (Dir)
Managers: M. Simpkinson (Fin Mgr), M. Doherty (Tech Serv Mgr)
Immediate Holding Company: DIAGEO PLC
Registration no: 00023307 **Date established:** 1986
Turnover: £250m - £500m **No.of Employees:** 251 - 500
Product Groups: 21

Fife Welding & Safety Services Ltd
An Sealladh Baintown, Leven, KY8 5SJ
Tel: 01333-350101 **Fax:** 01333-352693
Directors: J. Gillon (Co Sec), Gillan (Prop), P. Gillan (Prop)
Immediate Holding Company: FIFE WELDING & SAFETY SERVICES LIMITED
Registration no: SC146555 **Date established:** 1993
No.of Employees: 1 - 10 **Product Groups:** 46

Date of Accounts	May 11	Nov 09	Nov 08
Working Capital	31	16	30
Fixed Assets	N/A	7	8
Current Assets	57	35	59

Hydraulic & Pneumatic Power Services Ltd
Methilhaven Road Methil, Leven, KY8 3LA
Tel: 01333-429690 **Fax:** 01333-422952
E-mail: info@fcegroup.com
Website: http://www.fcegroup.com
Bank(s): T.S.B.
Directors: J. Rintoul (MD)
Managers: J. Rintoul (Chief Mgr), L. Mackenna (Sales Admin)
Immediate Holding Company: FCE HYDRAULIC POWER SERVICES LIMITED
Registration no: SC191289 **VAT No.:** GB 502 6928 54
Date established: 1998 **Turnover:** £500,000 - £1m
No.of Employees: 21 - 50 **Product Groups:** 48

Date of Accounts	Nov 11	Nov 10	Nov 09
Working Capital	279	194	46
Fixed Assets	203	221	242
Current Assets	521	358	227

Ravenscroft Associates
56 Leven Road Lundin Links, Leven, KY8 6AH
Tel: 01333-329525 **Fax:** 01333-329525
E-mail: e.j.ravenscroft@talk21.com
Directors: E. Ravenscroft (Prop)
Date established: 1992 **No.of Employees:** 1 - 10 **Product Groups:** 35

Silberline Ltd
Unit 2 Banbeath Industrial Estate, Leven, KY8 5HD
Tel: 01333-424734 **Fax:** 01333-421369
E-mail: info@silberline.com
Website: http://www.silberline.com
Managers: K. Woodward (Personnel), P. Pearley (Plant), R. Robertson (Buyer), S. Blair (Comptroller)
Ultimate Holding Company: SILBERLINE MANUFACTURING CO INC (USA)
Immediate Holding Company: SILBERLINE LIMITED
Registration no: SC055281 **VAT No.:** GB 271 5685 40
Date established: 1974 **Turnover:** £20m - £50m
No.of Employees: 101 - 250 **Product Groups:** 32, 34

Date of Accounts	Dec 11	Dec 10	Dec 09
Sales Turnover	26m	28m	23m
Pre Tax Profit/Loss	1m	2m	2m
Working Capital	10m	8m	11m
Fixed Assets	9m	10m	9m
Current Assets	12m	12m	14m
Current Liabilities	916	1m	1m

West Lothian

Linlithgow

A R C O East Scotland
Avon Mill Industrial Estate Mill Road, Linlithgow Bridge, Linlithgow, EH49 7QY
Tel: 01506-844661 **Fax:** 01506-847816
E-mail: arco.eastscotland@arco.co.uk
Website: http://www.arco.co.uk
Managers: S. Beats (District Mgr), S. Brennan (Sales Prom Mgr)
Immediate Holding Company: ARCO GROUP LTD
Registration no: 00486220 **Turnover:** £1m - £2m
No.of Employees: 51 - 100 **Product Groups:** 24, 29, 30, 40

Cape Industrial Services Ltd
Mill Road Industrial Estate Linlithgow Bridge, Linlithgow, EH49 7SF
Tel: 01506-670200 **Fax:** 01506-670190
Website: http://www.cisgl.com
Bank(s): National Westminster Bank Plc
Managers: S. Atterton (Chief Mgr)
Ultimate Holding Company: CAPE PLC
Immediate Holding Company: CAPE INDUSTRIAL SERVICES LIMITED
Registration no: 03337119 **Date established:** 1997
Turnover: £50m - £75m **No.of Employees:** 11 - 20 **Product Groups:** 52, 54

Date of Accounts	Dec 11	Dec 10	Dec 09
Sales Turnover	311m	284m	326m
Pre Tax Profit/Loss	29m	25m	-44m
Working Capital	92m	96m	80m
Fixed Assets	28m	22m	24m
Current Assets	151m	142m	136m
Current Liabilities	46m	35m	43m

Juice Direct UK
Mill Road Industrial Estate Linlithgow Bridge, Linlithgow, EH49 7SF
Tel: 01506-632994
E-mail: enquiries@juicedirectuk.com
Website: http://www.juicedirectuk.com/
Directors: J. Watson (Dir)
Managers: J. Watson (Mgr)
Immediate Holding Company: MCKAY (HOLDINGS) LTD.
Registration no: SC310821 **Date established:** 2008
No.of Employees: 1 - 10 **Product Groups:** 40, 41

R G K UK Ltd
Champfleurie House, Linlithgow, EH49 6NB
Tel: 01506-847999 **Fax:** 01506-847174
E-mail: sales@rgk.co.uk
Website: http://www.rgk.co.uk
Directors: R. Kerr (MD)
Immediate Holding Company: R G K (UK) LIMITED
Registration no: SC077454 **Date established:** 1982
Turnover: £250,000 - £500,000 **No.of Employees:** 1 - 10
Product Groups: 33, 36, 37, 38, 40, 46, 52, 63, 66, 67

Date of Accounts	Feb 12	Feb 11	Feb 10
Working Capital	26	21	33
Fixed Assets	47	55	38
Current Assets	138	121	110

West Lothian

Livingston

A P I Foils Ltd
Firth Road Houstoun Industrial Estate, Livingston, EH54 5DJ
Tel: 01506-438611 **Fax:** 01506-438262
E-mail: tony.stephens@api-foils.co.uk
Website: http://www.apigroup.com
Bank(s): Royal Bank of Scotland, Livingston, Barclays
Directors: A. Turner (Grp Chief Exec), C. Hyndman (Fin)
Ultimate Holding Company: API GROUP PLC
Immediate Holding Company: API FOILS LIMITED
Registration no: 00202034 **VAT No.:** GB 345 1022 00
Date established: 2024 **Turnover:** £20m - £50m
No.of Employees: 101 - 250 **Product Groups:** 34

Date of Accounts	Mar 12	Mar 11	Mar 10
Sales Turnover	23m	22m	21m
Pre Tax Profit/Loss	-2m	-1m	182
Working Capital	657	2m	3m
Fixed Assets	2m	2m	3m
Current Assets	9m	10m	9m
Current Liabilities	657	556	668

Bruce Anchor Ltd
Royston Road Deans Industrial Estate, Deans, Livingston, EH54 8AH
Tel: 01506-415454 **Fax:** 01506-461202
E-mail: info@bruceanchor.myzen.co.uk
Website: http://www.lineone.net
Directors: E. Bruce (Dir)
Ultimate Holding Company: BRUHOLD LTD (ISLE OF MAN)
Immediate Holding Company: BRUCE ANCHOR (SCOTLAND) LIMITED
Registration no: SC050598 **VAT No.:** GB 269 6151 37
Date established: 1972 **Turnover:** £250,000 - £500,000
No.of Employees: 1 - 10 **Product Groups:** 39

Date of Accounts	Dec 11	Dec 10	Dec 09
Working Capital	181	188	195
Fixed Assets	1	1	2
Current Assets	202	206	216

Antalis Mcnaughton Paper Merchants Ltd
Gateway House Royston Road Deans, Livingston, EH54 8AL
Tel: 08706-073108 **Fax:** 01698-815181
E-mail: admin@antalis.co.uk
Website: http://www.jmcpaper.com
Bank(s): HSBC Bank plc
Managers: J. McKenzie (Mgr)
Immediate Holding Company: ANTALIS LIMITED
Registration no: NF003153 **Date established:** 1994
Turnover: £20m - £50m **No.of Employees:** 11 - 20 **Product Groups:** 64, 66

Date of Accounts	Dec 11	Dec 10	Dec 09
Sales Turnover	451m	393m	256m
Pre Tax Profit/Loss	-1m	-6m	-11m
Working Capital	40m	44m	-21m
Fixed Assets	525	8m	37m
Current Assets	140m	161m	121m
Current Liabilities	14m	11m	43m

B C F Technology Ltd
Unit 3 Tailend Court, Livingston, EH54 8TE
Tel: 01506-460023 **Fax:** 01506-460045
E-mail: office@bcftech.demon.co.uk
Website: http://www.bcftechnology.com
Bank(s): Bank of Scotland
Directors: A. Picken (MD), G. Mitchell (Sales)
Ultimate Holding Company: BCF HOLDINGS LIMITED
Immediate Holding Company: BCF TECHNOLOGY LIMITED
Registration no: SC085981 **VAT No.:** GB 734 8038 28
Date established: 1983 **Turnover:** £5m - £10m
No.of Employees: 51 - 100 **Product Groups:** 37, 38, 47

Date of Accounts	Dec 11	Dec 10	Dec 09
Sales Turnover	9m	8m	N/A
Pre Tax Profit/Loss	569	382	N/A
Working Capital	4m	3m	3m
Fixed Assets	187	257	312
Current Assets	5m	5m	4m
Current Liabilities	689	601	N/A

Batt Cables plc
1 Chalmers Square Deans, Livingston, EH54 8RJ
Tel: 01506-401540 **Fax:** 01506-401541
E-mail: craig.bruce@batt.co.uk
Website: http://www.batt.co.uk
Managers: D. Sutter (District Mgr)
Immediate Holding Company: BATT CABLES PLC
Registration no: 01353688 **Date established:** 1978
No.of Employees: 1 - 10 **Product Groups:** 30, 35, 36, 37, 38, 44, 66, 67

Date of Accounts	Mar 12	Mar 11	Mar 10
Sales Turnover	106m	98m	84m
Pre Tax Profit/Loss	8m	9m	5m
Working Capital	41m	36m	31m
Fixed Assets	8m	9m	8m
Current Assets	69m	60m	54m
Current Liabilities	3m	3m	2m

Carillion Plant Maintenance
Unit 2 Oakbank Park Way Mid Calder, Livingston, EH53 0TH
Tel: 01506-449350 **Fax:** 01506-449351
E-mail: angela.gray@carillionplc.com
Website: http://www.carillionplc.com
Directors: M. Clarke (Dir)
Managers: D. Cope (Sales Prom), A. Clixby (Sales Prom), D. Rogers (Sales Prom)
Immediate Holding Company: SCOT-PETSHOP LTD
Registration no: 1686252 **Date established:** 2010 **Turnover:** £20m - £50m
No.of Employees: 21 - 50 **Product Groups:** 30, 33, 45, 52, 66, 84

Date of Accounts	Dec 10	Dec 09	Dec 08
Sales Turnover	7m	7m	5m
Pre Tax Profit/Loss	-2m	-294	57
Working Capital	1m	866	993
Fixed Assets	2m	2m	2m
Current Assets	3m	4m	2m
Current Liabilities	772	2m	724

D & D Stainless Ltd
16 Nettlehill Road Houstoun Industrial Estate, Livingston, EH54 5DL
Tel: 01506-434325 **Fax:** 01506-435345
E-mail: sales@danddstainless.co.uk
Website: http://www.danddstainless.co.uk
Directors: D. Hamilton (Dir)
Immediate Holding Company: D. & D. STAINLESS LIMITED
Registration no: SC127533 **VAT No.:** GB 553 6348 31
Date established: 1990 **No.of Employees:** 11 - 20 **Product Groups:** 66

Date of Accounts	Oct 11	Oct 10	Oct 09
Working Capital	132	124	151
Fixed Assets	77	81	86
Current Assets	925	916	847

Diagnostic Sonar Ltd
Baird Road Kirkton Campus, Livingston, EH54 7BX
Tel: 01506-411877 **Fax:** 01506-412410
E-mail: vivien@diagnosticsonar.com
Website: http://www.diagnosticsonar.com
Bank(s): Bank of Scotland
Directors: H. Gassert (MD), H. Gassert (MD)
Immediate Holding Company: DIAGNOSTIC SONAR LIMITED
Registration no: SC058829 **VAT No.:** GB 271 8540 51
Date established: 1975 **No.of Employees:** 11 - 20 **Product Groups:** 38

Date of Accounts	Apr 11	Apr 10	Apr 09
Working Capital	44	50	82
Fixed Assets	20	33	45
Current Assets	540	706	589

Edinburgh Sensors Ltd
2 Bain Square, Livingston, EH54 7DQ
Tel: 01506-425300 **Fax:** 01506-425320
E-mail: sales@edinst.com
Website: http://www.edinst.com
Bank(s): Bank of Scotland
Directors: G. Gilligan (Co Sec), D. McCarlie (Fin)
Managers: J. Brown (Tech Serv Mgr), S. Macconnachie, R. Thomas (Sales Prom Mgr), A. Faichney, R. Joshi (Mktg Serv Mgr)
Immediate Holding Company: EDINBURGH INSTRUMENTS LIMITED
Registration no: 00962331 **VAT No.:** 271 7379 37 **Date established:** 1969
Turnover: £5m - £10m **No.of Employees:** 51 - 100 **Product Groups:** 27, 37, 38

Date of Accounts	Mar 12	Mar 11	Mar 10
Sales Turnover	8m	N/A	N/A
Pre Tax Profit/Loss	438	N/A	N/A

Working Capital	2m	2m	2m
Fixed Assets	235	198	201
Current Assets	4m	3m	3m
Current Liabilities	735	N/A	N/A

Effective Cosmetics
Mcarthur Glen Almondvale Avenue, Livingston, EH54 6QX
Tel: 01506-463344 **Fax:** 01506-463282
Website: http://www.virginvieathome.com
Managers: L. Swanston (District Mgr)
Ultimate Holding Company: Virgin Group Holdings Ltd (BVI)
Immediate Holding Company: Victory Corporation Ltd
Registration no: 03177571 **Date established:** 1996
Turnover: £20m - £50m **No.of Employees:** 1 - 10 **Product Groups:** 32, 63

Empteezy Ltd
4 Muir Road Houstoun Industrial Estate, Livingston, EH54 5DR
Tel: 01506-430309 **Fax:** 01506-441466
E-mail: sales@empteezy.co.uk
Website: http://www.empteezy.co.uk
Bank(s): National Westminster Bank Plc
Directors: B. Wishart (MD), D. Mitchell (Co Sec)
Managers: K. Carr (Chief Mgr), A. Lawrence (Mktg Serv Mgr), I. Forrest (Buyer)
Immediate Holding Company: EMPTEEZY LIMITED
Registration no: SC100049 **VAT No.:** GB 446 4044 58
Date established: 1986 **Turnover:** £20m - £50m
No.of Employees: 21 - 50 **Product Groups:** 26, 45, 67

Date of Accounts	Oct 11	Oct 10	Oct 09
Sales Turnover	21m	22m	22m
Pre Tax Profit/Loss	451	1m	493
Working Capital	5m	5m	5m
Fixed Assets	6m	5m	5m
Current Assets	10m	11m	10m
Current Liabilities	2m	2m	2m

Flexible Surface Technology Ltd
Nairn Road Deans, Livingston, EH54 8AY
Tel: 01506-460515 **Fax:** 01506-460510
E-mail: garycummings@fstltd.co.uk
Website: http://www.fstltd.co.uk
Directors: J. Jamieson (Dir)
Ultimate Holding Company: THE FLEXIBLE MANUFACTURING GROUP LIMITED
Immediate Holding Company: FLEXIBLE SURFACE TECHNOLOGY LTD.
Registration no: SC126581 **Date established:** 1990 **Turnover:** £1m - £2m
No.of Employees: 21 - 50 **Product Groups:** 48

Date of Accounts	May 12	May 11	May 10
Working Capital	3m	2m	2m
Fixed Assets	654	616	654
Current Assets	3m	3m	3m

Formold Thermo Plastic
5b Grange Road Houstoun Industrial Estate Houstoun Industrial Estate, Livingston, EH54 5DE
Tel: 01506-430902 **Fax:** 01506-436148
E-mail: reception@formold.co.uk
Website: http://www.hpp.co.uk
Directors: A. Barnes (Dir)
Immediate Holding Company: WAVE IMAGES LIMITED
Registration no: 04276908 **Date established:** 2009 **Turnover:** £2m - £5m
No.of Employees: 1 - 10 **Product Groups:** 30

W L Gore & Associates UK Ltd
Simpson Parkway Kirkton Campus, Livingston, EH54 7BH
Tel: 01506-460123 **Fax:** 01506-420004
Website: http://www.wlgore.com
Bank(s): The Royal Bank of Scotland, Dunfermline
Directors: J. Kings (Fin)
Ultimate Holding Company: W L GORE & ASSOCIATES INC (USA)
Immediate Holding Company: W.L. GORE AND ASSOCIATES (U.K.) LIMITED
Registration no: 00856254 **VAT No.:** GB 268 6378 09
Date established: 1965 **Turnover:** £75m - £125m
No.of Employees: 101 - 250 **Product Groups:** 23, 30, 38, 42

Date of Accounts	Mar 12	Mar 11	Mar 10
Sales Turnover	N/A	118m	102m
Pre Tax Profit/Loss	N/A	23m	10m
Working Capital	72	54m	38m
Fixed Assets	16	12m	13m
Current Assets	94	76m	56m
Current Liabilities	N/A	8m	6m

J Hewit & Sons Ltd
12 Nettlehill Road Houstoun Industrial Estate, Livingston, EH54 5DL
Tel: 01506-444160 **Fax:** 0131-451 5081
E-mail: sales@hewit.com
Website: http://www.hewit.com
Bank(s): Royal Bank of Scotland, Edinburgh
Directors: D. Lanning (Fin), R. Barlee (MD)
Immediate Holding Company: J. HEWIT & SONS LIMITED
Registration no: SC016424 **VAT No.:** GB 268 6272 25
Date established: 1931 **Turnover:** £1m - £2m **No.of Employees:** 11 - 20
Product Groups: 22, 23, 27, 35, 67

Date of Accounts	Mar 09	Mar 08	Feb 11
Working Capital	487	475	529
Fixed Assets	206	215	829
Current Assets	541	546	616

Highlander Scotland Ltd
Todd Square Houstoun Industrial Estate Houstoun Industrial Estate, Livingston, EH54 5EF
Tel: 01506-438438 **Fax:** 01506-438443
E-mail: info@highlander-outdoor.com
Website: http://www.highlander-outdoor.com
Directors: R. Golzari (Dir)
Immediate Holding Company: HIGHLANDER (SCOTLAND) LIMITED
Registration no: SC162378 **Date established:** 1995
Turnover: Up to £250,000 **No.of Employees:** 21 - 50 **Product Groups:** 22, 24, 29, 37, 40, 49, 65

Date of Accounts	Feb 11	Feb 10	Feb 09
Working Capital	3m	2m	3m
Fixed Assets	2m	2m	2m
Current Assets	4m	3m	3m

Interserve Construction
2 Almondview Business Park Almondview, Livingston, EH54 6SF
Tel: 01506-447660 **Fax:** 01506-440700
E-mail: brian.reid@interserve.com
Website: http://www.interserve.com
Bank(s): HSBC Bank plc
Directors: B. Reid (Div), D. Ewing (Comm)
Managers: K. Hamilton (Buyer), P. Brannock
Ultimate Holding Company: INTERSERVE PLC
Immediate Holding Company: INTERSERVE PROJECT SERVICES LIMITED
Registration no: 00303359 **Date established:** 1935
Turnover: £500m - £1,000m **No.of Employees:** 21 - 50
Product Groups: 51, 52

J C Welding & Fabrication
1 Arrol Square Deans Industrial Estate, Deans, Livingston, EH54 8QZ
Tel: 01506-461925 **Fax:** 01506-461925
E-mail: info@jcwelding.co.uk
Website: http://www.jcwelding.co.uk
Directors: J. Charles (Prop)
Immediate Holding Company: J C WELDING & FABRICATION LTD
Registration no: SC393545 **Date established:** 2011
No.of Employees: 1 - 10 **Product Groups:** 25, 35, 48, 49

Johnson & Johnson Medical
Simpson Parkway Kirkton Campus, Livingston, EH54 7AT
Tel: 01506-594500 **Fax:** 01506-460714
Website: http://www.jandjgateway.com
Directors: B. Collings (Dir), C. Morgan (MD)
Ultimate Holding Company: JOHNSON & JOHNSON (USA)
Immediate Holding Company: JOHNSON & JOHNSON MEDICAL LIMITED
Registration no: SC132162 **Date established:** 1991
Turnover: £250m - £500m **No.of Employees:** 251 - 500
Product Groups: 38

Date of Accounts	Dec 08	Jan 10	Jan 11
Sales Turnover	469m	449m	395m
Pre Tax Profit/Loss	308m	53m	77m
Working Capital	188m	37m	31m
Fixed Assets	165m	165m	162m
Current Assets	408m	129m	632m
Current Liabilities	97m	21m	35m

Knightsridge Engineering Services
10 Nettlehill Road Houstoun Industrial Estate, Livingston, EH54 5DL
Tel: 01506-430605 **Fax:** 01506-440380
E-mail: kesl@btconnect.com
Website: http://www.knightsridgeengineering.co.uk
Directors: P. Forster (Prop)
Ultimate Holding Company: CDF HOLDINGS LIMITED
Immediate Holding Company: KNIGHTSRIDGE ENGINEERING SERVICES LIMITED
Registration no: SC078665 **VAT No.:** GB 397 9295 72
Date established: 1982 **Turnover:** £250,000 - £500,000
No.of Employees: 1 - 10 **Product Groups:** 35, 46, 48

Date of Accounts	Mar 11	Mar 10	Mar 09
Working Capital	225	239	232
Fixed Assets	150	146	166
Current Assets	309	265	306

Litho Supplies Scotland Ltd
12 Brewster Square Brucefield Industrial Estate, Livingston, EH54 9BJ
Tel: 01506-462555 **Fax:** 01506-465678
E-mail: gordon.low@litho.co.uk
Website: http://www.litho.co.uk
Managers: G. Low (Mgr)
Immediate Holding Company: LITHO SUPPLIES (UK) LTD
VAT No.: GB 567 5624 07 **Turnover:** £75m - £125m
No.of Employees: 1 - 10 **Product Groups:** 32, 44

M V Commerical Ltd
1 Muir Road Houstoun Industrial Estate, Livingston, EH54 5DR
Tel: 01506-440042
E-mail: info@mvcommercial.co.uk
Website: http://www.mvcommercial.co.uk
Directors: S. Cairns (Chief Op Offcr)
Immediate Holding Company: MV COMMERCIAL LIMITED
Registration no: SC134714 **Date established:** 1991
Turnover: £10m - £20m **No.of Employees:** 11 - 20 **Product Groups:** 72

Date of Accounts	Jun 11	Jun 10	Jun 09
Sales Turnover	13m	11m	11m
Pre Tax Profit/Loss	840	217	-573
Working Capital	-3m	-2m	-2m
Fixed Assets	13m	7m	9m
Current Assets	2m	3m	2m
Current Liabilities	906	990	1m

Mark McVey Sports Surfaces
116 Nelson Avenue, Livingston, EH54 6LA
Tel: 01506-493913 **Fax:** 01506-493913
E-mail: sales@mcveysportssurfaces.co.uk
Website: http://www.mcveysportssurfaces.co.uk
Directors: M. Mcvey (Prop)
Date established: 1989 **No.of Employees:** 1 - 10 **Product Groups:** 52

Norville Optical Co. Ltd
8 Grange Road Houstoun Industrial Estate, Livingston, EH54 5DE
Tel: 01506-434261 **Fax:** 01506-431851
E-mail: livingston@norville.co.uk
Website: http://www.norville.co.uk
Managers: N. McClean (District Mgr)
Immediate Holding Company: NORVILLE OPTICAL (SCOTLAND) LIMITED
Registration no: SC062626 **Date established:** 1977
No.of Employees: 11 - 20 **Product Groups:** 37, 38, 65

Optocap Ltd
5 Bain Square, Livingston, EH54 7DQ
Tel: 01506-403550 **Fax:** 01506-403551
E-mail: info@optocap.com
Website: http://www.optocap.com
Directors: D. Ruxton (Co Sec), S. Duffy (Dir)
Managers: G. White (Tech Serv Mgr)
Immediate Holding Company: OPTOCAP LIMITED
Registration no: SC244596 **Date established:** 2003 **Turnover:** £1m - £2m
No.of Employees: 21 - 50 **Product Groups:** 37, 48

Date of Accounts	Mar 12	Mar 11	Mar 10
Sales Turnover	2m	1m	1m
Pre Tax Profit/Loss	154	54	15
Working Capital	279	127	14
Fixed Assets	184	182	241
Current Assets	870	500	300
Current Liabilities	416	235	N/A

Paterson Arran The Royal Burgh Bakery Ltd
Nettlehill Road Houstoun Industrial Estate, Livingston, EH54 5DN
Tel: 01506-431031 **Fax:** 01506-432800
E-mail: enquiries@paterson-arran.com
Website: http://www.paterson-arran.com
Bank(s): Bank of Scotland, Glasgow
Directors: A. Miller (Sales), J. Appleton (Fin)
Managers: J. Driver (Tech Serv Mgr), M. Devine, E. Gallagher (Personnel), D. Connacher (Mktg Serv Mgr)
Ultimate Holding Company: HOUSTON (HOLDINGS) LIMITED
Immediate Holding Company: PATERSON ARRAN LIMITED
Registration no: SC160041 **Date established:** 1995
Turnover: £20m - £50m **No.of Employees:** 101 - 250
Product Groups: 20, 62

Date of Accounts	Dec 11	Dec 10	Dec 09
Sales Turnover	17m	22m	17m
Pre Tax Profit/Loss	366	1m	1m
Working Capital	7m	7m	6m
Fixed Assets	3m	3m	3m
Current Assets	10m	11m	9m
Current Liabilities	990	1m	1m

Pool Installers
18 Easter Bankton, Livingston, EH54 9BD
Tel: 07772-736120
E-mail: info@poolinstallers.co.uk
Website: http://www.poolinstallers.co.uk
Directors: M. Sutherland (Ptnr)
Date established: 2006 **Turnover:** Up to £250,000
No.of Employees: 1 - 10 **Product Groups:** 30, 32, 35, 40, 42, 52, 66

Proclad International Forging Ltd
Nettlehill Road Telford Square Houstoun Industrial Estate, Livingston, EH54 5DL
Tel: 01506-607500 **Fax:** 01506-607501
E-mail: jgordon@procladint.com
Website: http://www.procladforging.com
Bank(s): National Westminster Bank Plc
Directors: M. Penman (Fin)
Managers: J. Colquhoun
Ultimate Holding Company: NATIONAL INDUSTRIES GROUP (HOLDING) SAK (KUWAIT)
Immediate Holding Company: PROCLAD INTERNATIONAL FORGING LIMITED
Registration no: SC085645 **VAT No.:** GB 402 7706 75
Date established: 1983 **Turnover:** £5m - £10m **No.of Employees:** 21 - 50
Product Groups: 48, 85

Date of Accounts	Dec 10	Dec 09	Dec 08
Sales Turnover	5m	6m	8m
Pre Tax Profit/Loss	3m	828	2m
Working Capital	4m	4m	3m
Fixed Assets	1m	1m	1m
Current Assets	5m	4m	4m
Current Liabilities	354	326	399

Pumpmasters Ltd
14a Nasmyth Court Houstoun Industrial Estate, Livingston, EH54 5EG
Tel: 01506-668740 **Fax:** 01506-668741
E-mail: sales@pumpmasters.co.uk
Website: http://www.pumpmasters.co.uk
Directors: M. Brown (Dir)
Immediate Holding Company: PUMPMASTERS LIMITED
Registration no: SC100605 **Date established:** 1986
Turnover: £500,000 - £1m **No.of Employees:** 1 - 10 **Product Groups:** 48

Date of Accounts	Dec 11	Dec 10	Dec 09
Working Capital	30	24	19
Fixed Assets	12	4	6
Current Assets	94	94	72

Rittal Ltd
7 Dunlop Square Deans Industrial Estate, Deans, Livingston, EH54 8SB
Tel: 0844-8006004 **Fax:** 01506-461499
E-mail: amcphee@rittal.co.uk
Website: http://www.rittal.co.uk
Managers: A. Mcphee (Mgr)
Immediate Holding Company: RITTAL LIMITED
Registration no: 01389120 **Date established:** 1978
Turnover: £75m - £125m **No.of Employees:** 1 - 10 **Product Groups:** 26, 37, 44

S E H Europe Ltd
Wilson Road, Livingston, EH54 7DA
Tel: 01506-415555 **Fax:** 01506-417171
E-mail: sumisato_hirose@sehe.com
Website: http://www.sehe.com
Directors: S. Hirose (MD)
Managers: M. Murray (Purch Mgr), M. Longman, J. Wallace (Sales & Mktg Mg), S. Hirose (Mgr), M. Longman (Personnel), D. Bird (Fin Mgr)
Date established: 1984 **No.of Employees:** 251 - 500 **Product Groups:** 36, 37, 48

S K F UK Ltd
2 Michaelson Square Kirkton Campus, Livingston, EH54 7DP
Tel: 01506-470011 **Fax:** 01506-470012
E-mail: john.mcglone@skf.com
Website: http://www.skf.com
Directors: J. Mcglone (MD)
Managers: C. Hannah
Ultimate Holding Company: AKTIEBOLAGET SKF (SWEDEN)
Immediate Holding Company: SKF (U.K) LIMITED
Registration no: 00107367 **Date established:** 2010 **Turnover:** £5m - £10m
No.of Employees: 21 - 50 **Product Groups:** 38

Date of Accounts	Dec 11	Dec 10	Dec 09
Sales Turnover	251m	203m	182m
Pre Tax Profit/Loss	54m	35m	21m
Working Capital	83m	64m	76m
Fixed Assets	19m	20m	18m
Current Assets	120m	97m	107m
Current Liabilities	19m	16m	16m

Schuh Ltd
1 Neilson Square Deans Industrial Estate, Deans, Livingston, EH54 8RQ
Tel: 01506-460250 **Fax:** 01506-460251
E-mail: colin@schuh.co.uk
Website: http://www.schuh.co.uk
Directors: C. Temple (MD), K. Ball (Tech Serv), M. Crutchley (Fin)
Managers: D. Reid (Fin Mgr), D. Spencer (Product), N. Blackburn (Mktg Serv Mgr)
Ultimate Holding Company: SCHUH GROUP LIMITED
Immediate Holding Company: SCHUH LIMITED
Registration no: SC125327 **VAT No.:** GB 553 6113 58
Date established: 1990 **Turnover:** £125m - £250m
No.of Employees: 251 - 500 **Product Groups:** 63

Date of Accounts	Mar 08	Mar 09	Mar 10
Sales Turnover	119m	135m	146m
Pre Tax Profit/Loss	8m	11m	14m
Working Capital	20m	26m	33m
Fixed Assets	14m	14m	15m
Current Assets	33m	41m	50m
Current Liabilities	7m	8m	8m

Scomac Catering Equipment Ltd
1 Bell Square Brucefield Industrial Estate, Livingston, EH54 9BY
Tel: 01506-426200 **Fax:** 01506-426279
E-mail: info@scomaccateringequipment.com
Website: http://www.scomaccateringequipment.com
Bank(s): Bank of Scotland
Directors: I. Munro (Dir), M. Street (Fin), S. Shepherd (Chief Op Offcr), W. Adams (Co Sec)
Ultimate Holding Company: UNITECH INDUSTRIES LIMITED
Immediate Holding Company: SCOMAC CATERING EQUIPMENT LIMITED
Registration no: 02841935 **VAT No.:** 664 0076 47 **Date established:** 1993
Turnover: £10m - £20m **No.of Employees:** 51 - 100 **Product Groups:** 29, 30, 35, 36, 40

Date of Accounts	Dec 11	Dec 10	Dec 09
Sales Turnover	15m	11m	8m
Pre Tax Profit/Loss	535	343	484
Working Capital	697	484	304
Fixed Assets	412	427	314
Current Assets	5m	4m	2m
Current Liabilities	1m	1m	633

Steward Ltd
5 Cochrane Square Brucefield Industry Park, Livingston, EH54 9DR
Tel: 01506-414200 **Fax:** 01506-410694
E-mail: europe@steward.com
Website: http://www.stewards.com
Directors: A. Downie (Co Sec), B. Tilly (MD), K. Eischeid (Pres)
Ultimate Holding Company: Steward Inc.
Registration no: SC168406 **VAT No.:** GB 671 2849 19
Date established: 1996 **Turnover:** £5m - £10m **No.of Employees:** 1 - 10
Product Groups: 34, 37, 38, 44, 67, 85

Date of Accounts	Dec 06	Sep 06	Sep 05
Sales Turnover	N/A	N/A	1597
Pre Tax Profit/Loss	N/A	N/A	-294
Working Capital	561	565	297
Fixed Assets	N/A	3	7
Current Assets	675	662	700
Current Liabilities	113	97	404
Total Share Capital	5	5	5
ROCE% (Return on Capital Employed)			-96.6
ROT% (Return on Turnover)			-18.4

Stylerite Blinds
Unit 10 Abbotsford Rise Dedridge East Industrail Estate, Livingston, EH54 6QD
Tel: 01506-461721 **Fax:** 01506-462547
E-mail: enquiries@styleriteliving.co.uk
Website: http://www.styleriteliving.co.uk
Directors: E. Mitchell (Prop)
Registration no: 296617 **Date established:** 2006
Turnover: Up to £250,000 **No.of Employees:** 1 - 10 **Product Groups:** 24, 25

Syngro Ltd
Alba Innovation Centre Alba Campus, Livingston, EH54 7GA
Tel: 01506-592224 **Fax:** 01506-592225
E-mail: info@syngro.com
Website: http://www.syngro.com
Directors: K. Schorah (Dir), N. Martin (Mkt Research), T. Wild (Chief Op Offcr)
Immediate Holding Company: SYNGRO LIMITED
Registration no: SC266066 **Date established:** 2004
Turnover: Up to £250,000 **No.of Employees:** 11 - 20 **Product Groups:** 81

Date of Accounts	Mar 11	Mar 10	Mar 09
Working Capital	835	536	262
Fixed Assets	10	4	5
Current Assets	1m	854	460

Trion Anti Graffiti Systems UK
Unit 2, Kelvin Square Houstoun Industrial Estate, Livingston, EH54 8JA
Tel: 01506-433119 **Fax:** 01506-433900
E-mail: admin@tags.co.uk
Website: http://www.tags.co.uk
Product Groups: 30, 32

Vion Food Group
7 Bain Square, Livingston, EH54 7DQ
Tel: 01506-400400 **Fax:** 01506-400444
E-mail: info@vionfood.com
Website: http://www.vionfood.com
Bank(s): Bank of Scotland
Managers: R. Oconnor, A. Cox, M. Steven (Comptroller)
Ultimate Holding Company: VION HOLDING NV (NETHERLANDS)
Immediate Holding Company: VION FOOD UK LIMITED
Registration no: SC220000 **Date established:** 2001
Turnover: Over £1,000m **No.of Employees:** 21 - 50 **Product Groups:** 20

Date of Accounts	Dec 11	Dec 10	Dec 09
Sales Turnover	1173m	1211m	562m
Pre Tax Profit/Loss	-47m	-20m	-20m
Working Capital	-28m	6m	-26m
Fixed Assets	165m	129m	89m
Current Assets	169m	143m	67m
Current Liabilities	33m	34m	21m

Loanhead

Aquaid Lothian
Unit 4 42 Dryden Road, Loanhead, EH20 9LZ
Tel: 0131-448 0680 **Fax:** 0131-448 0980
E-mail: aquaidlothian@fish.co.uk
Website: http://www.aquaid.co.uk
Directors: G. Sandilands (Prop)
No.of Employees: 1 - 10 **Product Groups:** 40, 66

Bishops Move Edinburgh
Bishop House Pentland Industrial Estate, Loanhead, EH20 9QH
Tel: 0131-556 6666 **Fax:** 0131-440 3444
E-mail: edinburgh@bishopsmove.com
Website: http://www.bishopsmove.com
Bank(s): Royal Bank of Scotland, London
Managers: A. Nisbet, D. Mills-Pearce (Chief Mgr), A. Nisbet
Ultimate Holding Company: BISHOP & SONS DEPOSITORIES LIMITED
Immediate Holding Company: JMW MEDICAL LIMITED
Registration no: 00318120 **Date established:** 1994 **Turnover:** £1m - £2m
No.of Employees: 21 - 50 **Product Groups:** 72, 76, 77

Date of Accounts	Sep 11	Sep 10	Sep 09
Working Capital	30	30	30
Current Assets	32	37	35

Bryant & Cairns (Bryant Windows Ltd)
Borthwick View Pentland Industrial Estate, Loanhead, EH20 9QH
Tel: 0131-440 2855 **Fax:** 0131-448 2096
E-mail: sales@bryantandcairns.co.uk
Website: http://www.bryantandcairns.co.uk
Directors: G. Bell (Sales)
Immediate Holding Company: JMW MEDICAL LIMITED
Registration no: SC151297 **Date established:** 1994
No.of Employees: 21 - 50 **Product Groups:** 08, 30

Date of Accounts	Sep 11	Sep 10	Sep 09
Working Capital	30	30	30
Current Assets	32	37	35

Canongate Technology Ltd
17 Edgefield Road Industrial Estate, Loanhead, EH20 9TB
Tel: 0131-448 0786 **Fax:** 0131-440 1739
E-mail: sales@canongatetechnology.co.uk
Website: http://www.canongatetechnology.co.uk
Bank(s): Bank of Scotland, Sighthill, Edinburgh
Directors: B. Taylor (Sales & Mktg), B. Taylor (MD), R. Cuthbertson (MD)
Managers: T. Moug (Systems Mgr)
Immediate Holding Company: CANONGATE TECHNOLOGY LIMITED
Registration no: SC167138 **VAT No.:** GB 671 2695 20
Date established: 1996 **Turnover:** £5m - £10m **No.of Employees:** 11 - 20
Product Groups: 38, 41

Date of Accounts	Sep 07	Sep 08	Sep 09
Working Capital	-20	-18	214
Fixed Assets	127	138	135
Current Assets	1m	1m	1m

Harveys UK Ltd
Edgefield Road Industrial Estate, Loanhead, EH20 9SX
Tel: 0131-440 0074 **Fax:** 0131-440 3478
E-mail: sales@harveys.ltd.uk
Website: http://www.notjustbinders.com
Bank(s): Royal Bank of Scotland, Edinburgh
Directors: P. McCraw (MD), T. Dalgeish (MD), T. Dalgleish (MD)
Immediate Holding Company: HARVEYS LIMITED
Registration no: SC008235 **VAT No.:** GB 268 7619 08
Date established: 2012 **Turnover:** £2m - £5m **No.of Employees:** 21 - 50
Product Groups: 23, 28, 30

Date of Accounts	Mar 11	Mar 10	Mar 09
Sales Turnover	2m	2m	N/A
Pre Tax Profit/Loss	-335	-489	N/A
Working Capital	15	160	802
Fixed Assets	511	702	550
Current Assets	766	710	1m
Current Liabilities	248	215	N/A

Icarus GB Ltd
5 Engine Road, Loanhead, EH20 9RF
Tel: 0131-440 4450 **Fax:** 0131-440 4780
E-mail: aquafire@talk21.com
Website: http://www.aquafire.co.uk
Directors: N. King (Dir)
Immediate Holding Company: ICARUS GB LTD
Registration no: SC293791 **Date established:** 2005
No.of Employees: 1 - 10 **Product Groups:** 25, 32

Date of Accounts	Mar 12	Mar 11	Mar 10
Working Capital	23	64	65
Fixed Assets	21	28	38
Current Assets	42	88	95

International Metrology Systems Ltd
Unit 2 Dryden Place Bilston Glen Industrial Estate, Loanhead, EH20 9HP
Tel: 0131-440 7500 **Fax:** 0131-440 7501
E-mail: info@ims-cmm.com
Website: http://www.ims-cmm.com
Managers: K. Dearden (Eng Serv Mgr)
Ultimate Holding Company: IMS LIMITED (SOUTH KOREA)
Immediate Holding Company: INTERNATIONAL METROLOGY SYSTEMS LIMITED
Registration no: SC138045 **Date established:** 1992 **Turnover:** £1m - £2m
No.of Employees: 1 - 10 **Product Groups:** 38, 45

Date of Accounts	Dec 10	Dec 09	Dec 08
Sales Turnover	962	1m	1m
Pre Tax Profit/Loss	-130	178	-1m
Working Capital	-7m	-6m	-7m
Fixed Assets	6	13	22
Current Assets	1m	908	524
Current Liabilities	1m	841	869

Lothian Daf
Pentland Industrial Estate, Loanhead, EH20 9QH
Tel: 0131-440 4100 **Fax:** 0131-448 2070
E-mail: jhastey@lothiandaf.co.uk
Website: http://www.lothiandaf.co.uk

Managers: J. Hastie
Registration no: 04292964 **Turnover:** £5m - £10m
No.of Employees: 21 - 50 **Product Groups:** 68

McLaren Plastics Ltd
Pentland Industrial Estate, Loanhead, EH20 9QH
Tel: 0131-448 2200 **Fax:** 0131-448 2221
E-mail: sales@mclaren-plastics.co.uk
Website: http://www.mclaren-plastics.co.uk
Bank(s): Bank of Scotland, Edinburgh
Directors: C. McLaren (MD), I. Stedman (Co Sec)
Immediate Holding Company: MCLAREN PLASTICS LIMITED
Registration no: SC035460 **VAT No.:** GB 269 9850 87
Date established: 1960 **Turnover:** £1m - £2m **No.of Employees:** 21 - 50
Product Groups: 30, 36

Date of Accounts	Dec 11	Dec 10	Dec 09
Working Capital	460	338	373
Fixed Assets	599	604	539
Current Assets	842	567	590

Mclennan Garage
1b Park Avenue, Loanhead, EH20 9AZ
Tel: 0131-440 0597 **Fax:** 0131-440 0295
E-mail: mclennansgarage@btconnect.com
Website: http://www.mclennansgarage.co.uk
Directors: S. Mclennan (Prop)
No.of Employees: 1 - 10 **Product Groups:** 39

Macscott Bond Ltd
PO Box 1, Loanhead, EH20 9SP
Tel: 0131-448 2950 **Fax:** 0131-448 2941
E-mail: msb@macscott.com
Website: http://www.macscottbond.co.uk
Directors: R. Prenter (Co Sec)
Managers: R. Henderson (Admin Off)
Ultimate Holding Company: MACTAGGART SCOTT (HOLDINGS) LIMITED
Immediate Holding Company: MACSCOTT BOND LIMITED
Registration no: SC054745 **Date established:** 1973 **Turnover:** £2m - £5m
No.of Employees: 1 - 10 **Product Groups:** 38, 40

Date of Accounts	Apr 11	Apr 10	Apr 09
Sales Turnover	N/A	N/A	3m
Pre Tax Profit/Loss	N/A	N/A	702
Working Capital	903	759	644
Fixed Assets	753	676	534
Current Assets	2m	1m	1m
Current Liabilities	N/A	N/A	443

Mactaggart Scott & Co. Ltd
PO Box 1, Loanhead, EH20 9SP
Tel: 0131-440 0311 **Fax:** 0131-440 4493
E-mail: bill_marsh@mactag.com
Website: http://www.mactag.com
Bank(s): Bank of Scotland
Directors: G. Booton (Fin), R. Prenter (MD)
Managers: L. Fisher (Personnel), M. Mitchell-henry (Tech Serv Mgr), P. Gray (Purch Mgr)
Ultimate Holding Company: MACTAGGART SCOTT (HOLDINGS) LIMITED
Immediate Holding Company: MACTAGGART, SCOTT & COMPANY LIMITED
Registration no: SC055532 **Date established:** 1974
Turnover: £20m - £50m **No.of Employees:** 251 - 500
Product Groups: 39, 40, 45

Date of Accounts	Apr 11	Apr 10	Apr 09
Sales Turnover	31m	33m	27m
Pre Tax Profit/Loss	4m	4m	4m
Working Capital	10m	9m	8m
Fixed Assets	4m	5m	4m
Current Assets	28m	26m	28m
Current Liabilities	15m	14m	18m

Ross Heat Exchangers Ltd
Dryden Park, Loanhead, EH20 9HS
Tel: 0131-440 0066 **Fax:** 0131-440 4188
E-mail: nmarshal@rossheat.co.uk
Website: http://www.ross-heatexchangers.co.uk
Directors: T. Dalgleish (MD)
Immediate Holding Company: ROSS HEAT EXCHANGERS LIMITED
Registration no: SC113075 **Date established:** 1988
No.of Employees: 1 - 10 **Product Groups:** 30, 35, 36, 39, 40, 42

Date of Accounts	Mar 11	Mar 10	Mar 09
Working Capital	30	36	39
Fixed Assets	3	4	9
Current Assets	42	44	50

Thistle Design M M C Ltd
Borthwick View Pentland Industrial Estate, Loanhead, EH20 9QH
Tel: 0131-440 3747 **Fax:** 0131-440 3949
E-mail: r.logan@thistledesign.com
Website: http://www.thistledesign.com
Directors: R. Frew (Fin), R. Logan (Eng Serv)
Immediate Holding Company: THISTLE DESIGN (M M C) LIMITED
Registration no: SC166769 **VAT No.:** GB 593 1436 31
Date established: 1996 **Turnover:** £250,000 - £500,000
No.of Employees: 1 - 10 **Product Groups:** 37, 38

Date of Accounts	Dec 11	Dec 10	Dec 09
Working Capital	253	269	370
Fixed Assets	34	37	13
Current Assets	286	302	414

Fife

Lochgelly

Adtec
Unit 9 Avenue Industrial Estate, Lochgelly, KY5 9HQ
Tel: 01592-782155 **Fax:** 01592-783191
E-mail: matt@adtech.co.uk
Website: http://www.adtec.co.uk
Managers: V. Mcgregor (Prod Mgr)
Turnover: £500,000 - £1m **No.of Employees:** 1 - 10 **Product Groups:** 30

Andrew Ltd
The Avenue, Lochgelly, KY5 9HG
Tel: 01592-780561 **Fax:** 01592-782380
E-mail: paul.bell@commscope.com
Website: http://www.commscope.com
Directors: S. Davie (Co Sec), P. Bell (MD), N. Shankand (Fin)
Managers: K. McCracken (Buyer), H. Reid (Personnel), M. Carter (Personnel), G. Moffat, G. Jack (I.T. Exec)
Ultimate Holding Company: ANDREW CORPORATION (USA)
Immediate Holding Company: ANDREW ANTENNAS LIMITED
Registration no: SC059745 **VAT No.:** GB 268 3280 41
Date established: 1976 **Turnover:** £10m - £20m
No.of Employees: 101 - 250 **Product Groups:** 37

Bed & Pine Centre
20 Wallsgreen Road Cardenden, Lochgelly, KY5 0JF
Tel: 01592-720373 **Fax:** 01592-721665
E-mail: g.simpson@bedsandpine.co.uk
Website: http://www.itsbedsandpine.co.uk
Directors: D. Mackenzie (Dir), G. Simpson (Ptnr)
Date established: 1987 **Turnover:** Up to £250,000
No.of Employees: 1 - 10 **Product Groups:** 26, 63

Brae Scotland
41-44 Main Street Crosshill Business Centre Crosshill, Lochgelly, KY5 8BJ
Tel: 01592-862309 **Fax:** 01592-862310
E-mail: info@braescotland.com
Website: http://www.braescotland.com
Managers: J. Johnson (Comm)
Date established: 2006 **Turnover:** £500,000 - £1m
No.of Employees: 1 - 10 **Product Groups:** 80

Foxrect
21 Main Street Kinglassie, Lochgelly, KY5 0XA
Tel: 01592-882601 **Fax:** 01592-882601
E-mail: info@foxrect.com
Website: http://foxrect.com
Directors: A. Fox (Dir)
Immediate Holding Company: FOXRECT LIMITED
Registration no: SC224339 **Date established:** 2001
No.of Employees: 1 - 10 **Product Groups:** 35

Date of Accounts	Mar 11	Mar 10	Mar 09
Working Capital	-23	-32	-7
Fixed Assets	2	3	11
Current Assets	24	33	66

Regal Rubber Co. Ltd
Cartmore Industrial Estate, Lochgelly, KY5 8LL
Tel: 01592-780632 **Fax:** 01592-782888
E-mail: graeme@regalrubber.co.uk
Website: http://www.regalrubber.co.uk
Directors: G. Noble (Ptnr)
Immediate Holding Company: REGAL RUBBER COMPANY LIMITED
Registration no: SC092739 **VAT No.:** GB 397 9329 81
Date established: 1985 **Turnover:** Up to £250,000
No.of Employees: 11 - 20 **Product Groups:** 29

Date of Accounts	Mar 11	Mar 10	Mar 09
Working Capital	93	174	119
Fixed Assets	280	280	280
Current Assets	137	243	164
Current Liabilities	N/A	70	46

Thistle Structures Ltd
Thistle House Cartmore Industrial Estate, Lochgelly, KY5 8LL
Tel: 01592-780202 **Fax:** 01592-781908
E-mail: iain.letham@purvisgroup.co.uk
Website: http://www.thistlestructures.co.uk
Directors: J. Thomson (MD), J. Hepburn (Fin)
Managers: I. Letham (Chief Mgr)
Immediate Holding Company: THISTLE STRUCTURES LIMITED
Registration no: SC184674 **Date established:** 1998
Turnover: £250,000 - £500,000 **No.of Employees:** 11 - 20
Product Groups: 35

Date of Accounts	Mar 11	Mar 10	Mar 09
Working Capital	-287	-240	98
Fixed Assets	2	3	44
Current Assets	201	223	639

Argyll

Lochgilphead

Argyll P C Rescue
St Clair Way Ardrishaig, Lochgilphead, PA30 8FB
Tel: 01546-600269
E-mail: info@argyll-pcrescue.co.uk
Website: http://www.argyll-pcrescue.co.uk
Directors: G. Johnson (Prop)
No.of Employees: 1 - 10 **Product Groups:** 37, 44

Jewson Ltd
Bishopton Road, Lochgilphead, PA31 8PY
Tel: 01546-602821 **Fax:** 01546-602634
Website: http://www.jewson.co.uk
Managers: G. Kidd (Mgr)
Ultimate Holding Company: COMPAGNIE DE SAINT GOBAIN (FRANCE)
Immediate Holding Company: JEWSON LIMITED
Registration no: 00348407 **Date established:** 1939
Turnover: £500m - £1,000m **No.of Employees:** 11 - 20
Product Groups: 66

Date of Accounts	Dec 11	Dec 10	Dec 09
Sales Turnover	1606m	1547m	1485m
Pre Tax Profit/Loss	18m	100m	45m
Working Capital	-345m	-250m	-349m
Fixed Assets	496m	387m	461m
Current Assets	657m	1005m	1320m
Current Liabilities	66m	120m	64m

Keyline Builders Merchants
Kilmory Industrial Estate Kilmory, Lochgilphead, PA31 8RR
Tel: 01546-602071 **Fax:** 01546-603192
E-mail: wmalo@keyline.co.uk
Website: http://www.keyline.co.uk

Managers: J. Vallis (Mgr)
Immediate Holding Company: DIRECT BUILDING SUPPLIES TRURO LIMITED
Registration no: 02711617 **VAT No.:** GB 456 5069 30
Date established: 1992 **Turnover:** £500,000 - £1m
No.of Employees: 1 - 10 **Product Groups:** 25, 66

Dumfriesshire

Lockerbie

R Beeton
The Workshop Broomhill Farm, Lockerbie, DG11 1LT
Tel: 01387-810878
Directors: R. Beeton (Prop)
Date established: 1987 **No.of Employees:** 1 - 10 **Product Groups:** 41

Border Frames Ltd
Dumfries Road Lochmaben, Lockerbie, DG11 1RF
Tel: 01387-810455 **Fax:** 01387-810693
E-mail: info@borderframes.com
Website: http://www.borderframes.com
Bank(s): Royal Bank of Scotland, Lochmaben
Directors: A. Sloan (MD)
Immediate Holding Company: BORDER FRAMES LIMITED
Registration no: SC068448 **Date established:** 1979 **Turnover:** £1m - £2m
No.of Employees: 11 - 20 **Product Groups:** 25, 26, 27, 36

Date of Accounts	Dec 11	Dec 10	Dec 09
Working Capital	123	168	150
Fixed Assets	199	198	205
Current Assets	219	233	273

D S Smith Speciality Packaging Ltd Packaging Ltd
King Edward Park, Lockerbie, DG11 2BL
Tel: 01576-203111 **Fax:** 01576-203436
E-mail: simon.hamer@dssp.com
Website: http://www.dssmith-packaging.com
Directors: A. Platts (Sales), A. Platts (Sales), D. Gallagher (Pers), I. Piersosn (I.T. Dir), S. Hamer (MD), S. Pickernill (Fin)
Managers: S. Laurie (Tech Serv Mgr), S. Carmichael (Personnel)
Immediate Holding Company: DAVID S. SMITH PACKAGING GROUP
Registration no: 00630681 **VAT No.:** GB 556 5514 27
Turnover: £75m - £125m **No.of Employees:** 101 - 250
Product Groups: 27

R C Dalgliesh
Glassel Field, Lockerbie, DG11 1BL
Tel: 01576-202422 **Fax:** 01576-204100
E-mail: info@rcdalgliesh.com
Website: http://www.rcdalgliesh.com
Directors: R. Dalgliesh (Prop)
Date established: 1983 **No.of Employees:** 11 - 20 **Product Groups:** 41

Grange Quarry Ltd
Grange Quarry Tundergarth, Lockerbie, DG11 2QG
Tel: 01576-710288 **Fax:** 01576-710288
E-mail: admin@grangeornamentalstone.co.uk
Website: http://www.grangeQUARRY.CO.UK
Directors: S. Dodd (Dir)
Immediate Holding Company: GRANGE QUARRY LIMITED
Registration no: SC203651 **Date established:** 2000
No.of Employees: 11 - 20 **Product Groups:** 33

Date of Accounts	Mar 11	Mar 10	Mar 09
Working Capital	-142	890	593
Fixed Assets	3m	2m	2m
Current Assets	649	1m	2m

Mcpherson Forklifts Ltd
Lamoie Tunergarth, Tundergarth, Lockerbie, DG11 2PT
Tel: 01576-203180 **Fax:** 01576-202580
E-mail: mcpherson.engineering@virgin.net
Directors: A. McPherson (Fin), N. Mcpherson (MD)
Immediate Holding Company: MCPHERSON FORKLIFTS LIMITED
Registration no: SC244000 **Date established:** 2003
No.of Employees: 1 - 10 **Product Groups:** 35, 39, 45

Date of Accounts	Oct 11	Oct 10	Oct 07
Working Capital	241	210	75
Current Assets	309	271	89

Nordic Tyres UK Ltd
Unit 2 Sydney Place, Lockerbie, DG11 2JA
Tel: 01576-203020 **Fax:** 01576-203029
E-mail: lindsay@nordic-tyres.demon.co.uk
Website: http://www.nordictyres.com
Directors: A. Lindsay (MD)
Immediate Holding Company: NORDIC TYRES (UK) LIMITED
Registration no: SC197337 **Date established:** 1999 **Turnover:** £2m - £5m
No.of Employees: 1 - 10 **Product Groups:** 29, 37, 39, 41, 68

Date of Accounts	Sep 11	Sep 10	Sep 09
Working Capital	690	519	308
Fixed Assets	53	23	266
Current Assets	2m	1m	967

Alex Thomson & Son
16 Mains Street, Lockerbie, DG11 2DQ
Tel: 01576-202653 **Fax:** 01576-202453
Directors: A. Thomson (Ptnr)
Date established: 1925 **No.of Employees:** 1 - 10 **Product Groups:** 35

East Lothian

Longniddry

Infinite Apps Ltd
6 Tranter Road Aberlady, Longniddry, EH32 0UE
Tel: 07740-433961
E-mail: info@infiniteapps.com
Website: http://www.infiniteapps.com
Directors: H. Donnelly (Chief Op Offcr)
Immediate Holding Company: INFINITE APPS LIMITED
Registration no: SC262602 **Date established:** 2004
No.of Employees: 1 - 10 **Product Groups:** 44

Date of Accounts	Jan 11	Jan 10	Jan 07
Working Capital	11	19	9
Fixed Assets	3	3	1
Current Assets	74	67	28

Morayshire

Lossiemouth

Optom Shop Ltd
81 Clifton Road, Lossiemouth, IV31 6DP
Tel: 07515-789661 **Fax:** 0870-838 1365
E-mail: info@optomshop.co.uk
Website: http://www.optomshop.co.uk
Directors: W. Mohammed (Dir), N. Mohammed (Fin)
Immediate Holding Company: OPTOM SHOP LTD
Registration no: SC311743 **Date established:** 2006
No.of Employees: 1 - 10 **Product Groups:** 38, 47, 61, 67

Date of Accounts	Nov 11	Nov 10	Nov 09
Sales Turnover	N/A	118	142
Pre Tax Profit/Loss	N/A	56	65
Working Capital	-45	-55	35
Fixed Assets	165	165	N/A
Current Assets	N/A	2	180
Current Liabilities	15	12	13

Paterson & Campbell
Shore Street, Lossiemouth, IV31 6PB
Tel: 01343-813113 **Fax:** 01343-813113
E-mail: stevenalawson@sky.com
Directors: S. Lawson (Prop)
Immediate Holding Company: RUGS 123 LTD
Registration no: SC327674 **Date established:** 2010
No.of Employees: 1 - 10 **Product Groups:** 35

Date of Accounts	Jul 11	Jul 10	Jul 09
Working Capital	-1	3	-0
Fixed Assets	710	710	644
Current Assets	6	11	5

Ayrshire

Mauchline

Craftsman Cladding
Unit 1-4 Station Industrial Estate Station Road, Mauchline, KA5 5EU
Tel: 01290-551055 **Fax:** 01290-551958
E-mail: sales@craftsmancladding.co.uk
Website: http://www.craftsmancladding.co.uk
Directors: P. Keegan (Prop)
Immediate Holding Company: CRAFTSMAN CLADDING LTD
Registration no: SC296583 **Date established:** 2006
No.of Employees: 1 - 10 **Product Groups:** 30, 31, 66

Date of Accounts	Jan 11	Jan 10	Jan 09
Working Capital	7	68	101
Fixed Assets	67	86	98
Current Assets	174	185	317

Miller Steel 2000 Ltd
Unit 33 Station Industrial Estate Station Road, Mauchline, KA5 5EU
Tel: 01290-550230 **Fax:** 01290-550330
E-mail: sales@millersteel.co.uk
Website: http://www.millersteel.co.uk
Directors: S. Miller (Dir), L. Ross (Fin)
Immediate Holding Company: MILLER STEELS 2000 LIMITED
Registration no: SC204118 **Date established:** 2000
No.of Employees: 11 - 20 **Product Groups:** 26, 35

Date of Accounts	Mar 11	Mar 10	Mar 09
Working Capital	219	284	241
Fixed Assets	61	83	106
Current Assets	471	520	561

Ramsay & Jackson Ltd
Knowehead Works, Mauchline, KA5 6EY
Tel: 01290-550329 **Fax:** 01290-552508
E-mail: service@ramjack.co.uk
Website: http://www.ramjack.co.uk
Directors: W. Ramsay (Dir), N. Ramsay (Fin)
Immediate Holding Company: RAMSAY & JACKSON LIMITED
Registration no: SC298598 **Date established:** 2006
No.of Employees: 11 - 20 **Product Groups:** 41

Date of Accounts	Mar 11	Mar 10	Mar 09
Working Capital	1m	1m	893
Fixed Assets	251	204	211
Current Assets	3m	2m	2m

Water Of Ayr
Dalmore Stair, Mauchline, KA5 5PA
Tel: 01292-591204
Directors: K. Montgomerie (MD)
Managers: K. Montgomerie (Mgr)
Immediate Holding Company: THE WATER OF AYR AND TAM O'SHANTER HONE WORKS LIMITED
Registration no: SC004634 **VAT No.:** GB 338 9877 86
Date established: 2000 **Turnover:** Up to £250,000
No.of Employees: 1 - 10 **Product Groups:** 33, 49

Ayrshire

Maybole

A Dewar Rattray Ltd
Whitefaulds Farm Culzean Road, Maybole, KA19 8AH
Tel: 01655-883531 **Fax:** 01655-882281
E-mail: info@dewarrattray.com
Website: http://www.adrattray.com
Directors: N. White (Co Sec), S. Morrison (Prop), T. Morrison (MD), F. Dupuy (Dir)
Managers: S. Webster (Sales Prom Mgr)
Immediate Holding Company: A. DEWAR RATTRAY LIMITED
Registration no: SC021038 **Date established:** 1939
Turnover: £500,000 - £1m **No.of Employees:** 1 - 10 **Product Groups:** 21

Date of Accounts	Mar 11	Mar 10	Mar 09
Working Capital	350	304	252
Fixed Assets	18	15	8
Current Assets	629	580	519

Crawford Henderson Ltd
3 Welltrees Street, Maybole, KA19 7AW
Tel: 01655-883193 **Fax:** 01655-889526
E-mail: info@crhltd.com
Website: http://www.crhltd.com
Directors: A. Henderson (MD), S. Henderson (Fin)
Immediate Holding Company: CRAWFORD HENDERSON LIMITED
Registration no: SC049520 **VAT No.:** GB 444 2142 80
Date established: 1971 **Turnover:** £250,000 - £500,000
No.of Employees: 1 - 10 **Product Groups:** 22, 49

Date of Accounts	Dec 11	Dec 10	Dec 09
Working Capital	76	56	52
Fixed Assets	57	8	9
Current Assets	187	145	148

Gab Audio Engineers
Barbrethan Kirkmichael, Maybole, KA19 7PS
Tel: 01655-740330 **Fax:** 01655-740524
E-mail: jimbryan@gab-audio.co.uk
Website: http://www.gab-audio.co.uk
Directors: J. Bryan (Prop)
Turnover: £500,000 - £1m **No.of Employees:** 1 - 10 **Product Groups:** 37, 67, 83

International Packaging Corporation
14 Redbrae, Maybole, KA19 7HJ
Tel: 01655-882381 **Fax:** 01655-883789
E-mail: sales@interpak.co.uk
Website: http://www.interpak.co.uk
Bank(s): The Royal Bank of Scotland
Directors: T. Potter (Dir), A. Garry (Fin)
Ultimate Holding Company: INTERNATIONAL PACKAGING CORP INC (USA)
Immediate Holding Company: INTERNATIONAL PACKAGING CORPORATION (U.K.) LIMITED
Registration no: SC053678 **Date established:** 1973 **Turnover:** £2m - £5m
No.of Employees: 21 - 50 **Product Groups:** 22, 25, 27, 30, 35, 49, 65

Date of Accounts	Dec 11	Dec 10	Dec 09
Pre Tax Profit/Loss	N/A	-68	-189
Working Capital	3m	3m	3m
Fixed Assets	163	208	313
Current Assets	3m	3m	4m
Current Liabilities	N/A	189	78

Roxburghshire

Melrose

Astral Hygiene Ltd
Charlesfield Industrial Estate St Boswells, Melrose, TD6 0HH
Tel: 01835-824342 **Fax:** 01835-824343
E-mail: sales@astralhygiene.co.uk
Website: http://www.astralhygiene.co.uk
Directors: Y. Armstrong (Dir)
Immediate Holding Company: ASTRAL HYGIENE LIMITED
Registration no: SC394265 **Date established:** 2011
Turnover: Over £1,000m **No.of Employees:** 11 - 20 **Product Groups:** 27, 32

enquiries@purvesca.co.uk
St. Dunstans House High Street, Melrose, TD6 9RU
Tel: 01896-823506 **Fax:** 01896-823009
E-mail: enquiries@purvesca.co.uk
Website: http://www.andypurves.co.uk
Directors: A. Purves (MD)
Registration no: SC254901 **No.of Employees:** 1 - 10 **Product Groups:** 80

Aberdeenshire

Milltimber

Esslemont Marquees
The Rock Westfield Contlaw Road, Milltimber, AB13 0EX
Tel: 01224-739188 **Fax:** 01224-739888
E-mail: dan@esslemontmarquees.co.uk
Website: http://www.esslemontmarquees.co.uk
Directors: D. Whyiteford (Prop)
Immediate Holding Company: D.S. MONTGOMERY LIMITED
Registration no: SC152618 **Date established:** 1994
Turnover: Up to £250,000 **No.of Employees:** 1 - 10 **Product Groups:** 83

Date of Accounts	Sep 11	Sep 10	Sep 09
Sales Turnover	N/A	N/A	145
Pre Tax Profit/Loss	N/A	N/A	124

Working Capital	-11	-3	2
Current Assets	15	24	31
Current Liabilities	N/A	N/A	29

Angus

Montrose

Gemini Corrosion Services Ltd
Brent Avenue Forties Road, Montrose, DD10 9PB
Tel: 01674-672678 **Fax:** 01674-671111
E-mail: enquiries@geminicorrosion.com
Website: http://www.gemini-corrosion.co.uk
Directors: J. Mcsporran (MD)
Immediate Holding Company: GEMINI CORROSION SERVICES LIMITED
Registration no: SC101799 **Date established:** 1986
No.of Employees: 21 - 50 **Product Groups:** 46, 48

Date of Accounts	Dec 11	Dec 10	Dec 09
Working Capital	-22	-1m	-790
Fixed Assets	2m	2m	2m
Current Assets	2m	770	971

I M T Marine Consultants Ltd
South Quay Ferryden, Montrose, DD10 9SL
Tel: 01674-678999 **Fax:** 01674-678982
E-mail: info@imtmarine.com
Website: http://www.imtmarine.co.uk
Directors: A. Richards (Tech Serv), B. Johanesson (Dir), B. Johannesson (Dir), J. Mountford (Fin), N. Patterson (MD), R. Dow (Fin)
Managers: E. Bryson (I.T. Exec), I. Johnson, K. Stead (Sales Admin)
Immediate Holding Company: HITECH CAD SERVICES LTD
Registration no: SC298023 **Date established:** 2006 **Turnover:** £2m - £5m
No.of Employees: 1 - 10 **Product Groups:** 84

Date of Accounts	Dec 07	Dec 06	Sep 05
Working Capital	N/A	N/A	349
Fixed Assets	N/A	N/A	117
Current Assets	N/A	N/A	975
Current Liabilities	N/A	N/A	626
Total Share Capital	26	26	126

John Lawrie Aberdeen Ltd
Forties Road, Montrose, DD10 9ET
Tel: 01674-672005 **Fax:** 01674-677911
E-mail: info@johnlawrie.com
Website: http://www.johnlawrie.com
Directors: I. Rodger (Comm)
Ultimate Holding Company: MONTROSE SCOTA LTD.
Immediate Holding Company: JOHN LAWRIE (ABERDEEN) LTD.
Registration no: SC036725 **Date established:** 1961
Turnover: £20m - £50m **No.of Employees:** 11 - 20 **Product Groups:** 66

Date of Accounts	Dec 11	Dec 10	Dec 09
Sales Turnover	109m	85m	66m
Pre Tax Profit/Loss	11m	4m	2m
Working Capital	20m	12m	14m
Fixed Assets	16m	15m	10m
Current Assets	41m	32m	32m
Current Liabilities	7m	5m	2m

Marine & Engineering Supply Co.
51 Invergarry Park St Cyrus, Montrose, DD10 0BU
Tel: 01674-850250 **Fax:** 01674-850020
Directors: E. Weir (Fin), W. Weir (MD)
Immediate Holding Company: MARINE & ENGINEERING SUPPLY CO. LIMITED
Registration no: SC242346 **Date established:** 2003
No.of Employees: 1 - 10 **Product Groups:** 35, 36, 39

Date of Accounts	Dec 11	Dec 10	Dec 08
Working Capital	35	46	40
Fixed Assets	6	2	4
Current Assets	60	69	94

Oil Technics Ltd
Linton Road Gourdon, Montrose, DD10 0NH
Tel: 01561-361515 **Fax:** 01785-225519
E-mail: info@oiltechnics.co.uk
Website: http://www.oiltechnics.co.uk
Directors: D. Evans (Dir)
Ultimate Holding Company: OIL TECHNICS HOLDINGS LIMITED
Immediate Holding Company: OIL TECHNICS LIMITED
Registration no: 02119389 **Date established:** 1987
No.of Employees: 21 - 50 **Product Groups:** 32, 36

Date of Accounts	Apr 11	Apr 10	Apr 09
Working Capital	-33	-97	-162
Fixed Assets	659	695	727
Current Assets	727	731	486

Steel Design
21-23 King Street Inverbervie, Montrose, DD10 0RQ
Tel: 01561-360036 **Fax:** 01224- 899171
E-mail: pat@steeldesign.co.uk
Website: http://www.steeldesign.co.uk
Directors: P. Veal (Ptnr)
Date established: 1999 **No.of Employees:** 1 - 10 **Product Groups:** 26, 35

Wartsila UK Ltd
Harbour Office South Quay, Ferryden, Montrose, DD10 9SL
Tel: 01674-678429 **Fax:** 01674-678447
E-mail: info@epeuk.com
Website: http://www.wartsila.com
Managers: G. Pithie, R. Bell (Chief Mgr)
Ultimate Holding Company: WARTSILA CORPORATION (FINLAND)
Immediate Holding Company: WARTSILA UK LIMITED
Registration no: 01004816 **Date established:** 1971
Turnover: £10m - £20m **No.of Employees:** 11 - 20 **Product Groups:** 84, 85

Date of Accounts	Dec 11	Dec 10	Dec 09
Sales Turnover	94m	91m	102m
Pre Tax Profit/Loss	7m	8m	8m
Working Capital	-9m	-9m	-13m
Fixed Assets	21m	24m	27m
Current Assets	30m	30m	32m
Current Liabilities	27m	28m	36m

Lanarkshire

Motherwell

B R C Ltd
Block 14 Newhouse Industrial Estate, Motherwell, ML1 5SE
Tel: 01698-732343 **Fax:** 01698-833894
E-mail: bob.allan@brc.ltd.uk
Website: http://www.brc.com
Directors: R. Hislop (Fin)
Managers: B. Allan (Sales Prom Mgr), H. Cree (Personnel)
Immediate Holding Company: BRC LIMITED
Registration no: 06662824 **Date established:** 2008
No.of Employees: 21 - 50 **Product Groups:** 25, 29, 30, 31, 32, 33, 34, 35, 36, 45, 66

Date of Accounts	Dec 11	Dec 10	Dec 09
Sales Turnover	124m	105m	79m
Pre Tax Profit/Loss	689	1m	515
Working Capital	19m	11m	-2m
Fixed Assets	22m	23m	25m
Current Assets	40m	26m	18m
Current Liabilities	917	3m	4m

Calcarb Ltd
11 Woodside Eurocentral, Holytown, Motherwell, ML1 4XL
Tel: 01698-838710 **Fax:** 01698-838711
E-mail: sales@calcarb.com
Website: http://www.mersen.com
Bank(s): The Royal Bank of Scotland
Directors: G. MacKay (Fin), J. Morgan (MD)
Managers: D. Robertson (Sales & Mktg Mg), J. Gregory (I.T. Exec)
Ultimate Holding Company: Inductotherm Industries Inc. (USA)
Immediate Holding Company: Calgraphite Holding Ltd
Registration no: 07545299 **VAT No.:** GB 383 0080 72
Date established: 1983 **Turnover:** £1m - £2m
No.of Employees: 101 - 250 **Product Groups:** 33

Date of Accounts	Dec 08	Dec 07	Dec 06
Sales Turnover	13787	9064	8183
Pre Tax Profit/Loss	1386	858	2215
Working Capital	-4011	-2841	3113
Fixed Assets	17138	9810	2938
Current Assets	4230	4320	4362
Current Liabilities	8241	7161	1250
Total Share Capital	2459	1709	1709
ROCE% (Return on Capital Employed)	10.6	12.3	36.6
ROT% (Return on Turnover)	10.1	9.5	27.1

Caledonian Lift Services Ltd
Units 1-8 Regency Way Coronation Road Industrial Estate, Motherwell, ML1 4HR
Tel: 08448-007808 **Fax:** 01698-735368
E-mail: admin@caledonianlifts.net
Website: http://www.caledonianlifts.net
Directors: J. Mcguire (Dir)
Immediate Holding Company: CALEDONIAN LIFT SERVICES LIMITED
Registration no: SC202262 **Date established:** 1999
No.of Employees: 11 - 20 **Product Groups:** 35, 39, 45

Date of Accounts	Dec 11	Dec 10	Dec 09
Working Capital	94	93	87
Fixed Assets	18	19	21
Current Assets	288	265	238

W Hamilton & Son
37 Bellside Road Cleland, Motherwell, ML1 5NP
Tel: 01698-860692 **Fax:** 01698-860692
Directors: E. Hamilton (Prop)
Date established: 1993 **No.of Employees:** 1 - 10 **Product Groups:** 46, 48

William Hook Ltd
Unit 35 Flemington Industrial Estate Craigneuk Street, Motherwell, ML1 2NT
Tel: 01698-269982 **Fax:** 01698-275152
E-mail: mail@williamhook.com
Website: http://www.williamhook.com
Directors: M. Smith (Fin), K. Smith (MD)
Immediate Holding Company: WILLIAM HOOK LIMITED
Registration no: SC150908 **Date established:** 1994
Turnover: Up to £250,000 **No.of Employees:** 1 - 10 **Product Groups:** 45, 48, 85

Date of Accounts	May 11	May 10	May 09
Working Capital	30	20	-49
Fixed Assets	90	58	63
Current Assets	230	211	222

JHP group Limited
Dalziel Building 7 Scott Street, Motherwell, ML1 1PN
Tel: 01698-327824 **Fax:** 01698-327825
E-mail: motherwell@jhptraining.com
Website: http://www.jhptraining.com
Directors: S. Williams (MD)
Managers: S. Martin (Mgr)
Immediate Holding Company: JHP Group Ltd
Registration no: 03247918 **Date established:** 2005
No.of Employees: 1 - 10 **Product Groups:** 86

Nub Engineering Ltd
Newhouse Industrial Estate Newhouse, Motherwell, ML1 5RX
Tel: 01698-833873 **Fax:** 01698-734322
E-mail: sales@nubeng.com
Website: http://www.nubeng.com
Bank(s): The Royal Bank of Scotland
Directors: P. Jantz (Dir)
Managers: S. Clements (Mgr), E. Campbell (Mgr)
Ultimate Holding Company: PPD ENTERPRISES LIMITED
Immediate Holding Company: N.U.B. ENGINEERING LIMITED
Registration no: SC071921 **VAT No.:** GB 343 2641 76
Date established: 1980 **Turnover:** £2m - £5m **No.of Employees:** 21 - 50
Product Groups: 40, 45

Date of Accounts	Mar 11	Mar 10	Mar 09
Sales Turnover	N/A	3m	N/A
Pre Tax Profit/Loss	N/A	97	N/A
Working Capital	867	948	394
Fixed Assets	165	188	226
Current Assets	2m	2m	2m
Current Liabilities	N/A	143	N/A

Olgelin Ltd
Block 17 Unit 155 Newhouse Industrial Estate, Newhouse, Motherwell, ML1 5RX
Tel: 01698-832343 **Fax:** 01698-732106
E-mail: plaslant@aol.com
Bank(s): Bank of Scotland
Directors: J. Tooth (Fin), G. Tooth (MD)
Immediate Holding Company: OLGELIN LIMITED
Registration no: 01317420 **VAT No.:** GB 299 2261 23
Date established: 1977 **Turnover:** £2m - £5m **No.of Employees:** 11 - 20
Product Groups: 30

Date of Accounts	Jun 11	Jun 10	Jun 05
Working Capital	36	21	24
Fixed Assets	2	3	26
Current Assets	102	70	59

Park Draughting
32 The Loaning, Motherwell, ML1 3HE
Tel: 01698-263756 **Fax:** 01698-263756
E-mail: jpark8@btinternet.com
Website: http://www.3d-cad-steelwork.com
Directors: J. Park (Prop)
Turnover: Up to £250,000 **No.of Employees:** 1 - 10 **Product Groups:** 44, 81

Plaslant Ltd
Unit 154-156 Block 17 Newhouse Industrial Estate, Newhouse, Motherwell, ML1 5RX
Tel: 01698-732009 **Fax:** 01698-732106
E-mail: plaslant@aol.com
Website: http://www.plaslant.com
Directors: J. Tooth (Fin), G. Tooth (MD)
Immediate Holding Company: PLASLANT LIMITED
Registration no: 00846255 **VAT No.:** GB 261 9106 69
Date established: 1965 **Turnover:** £250,000 - £500,000
No.of Employees: 1 - 10 **Product Groups:** 30, 48

Date of Accounts	Jun 11	Jun 10	Jun 09
Working Capital	72	42	79
Fixed Assets	178	188	145
Current Assets	235	195	168

Leslie Plummer
267 Brandon Street, Motherwell, ML1 1RS
Tel: 01698-253414 **Fax:** 01698-276526
Directors: S. Alexander (Prop)
Date established: 1995 **No.of Employees:** 1 - 10 **Product Groups:** 35

Precision Windows & Doors Ltd
Block 3 Unit 19a Carfin Industrial Estate, Motherwell, ML1 4UZ
Tel: 01698-730800
Directors: K. Macdonald (Fin), J. Cassidy (MD)
Immediate Holding Company: PRECISION WINDOWS & DOORS LTD.
Registration no: SC270061 **Date established:** 2004
No.of Employees: 21 - 50 **Product Groups:** 33, 35, 36

Date of Accounts	Jul 11	Jul 10	Jul 09
Working Capital	-66	-50	-43
Fixed Assets	111	111	116
Current Assets	132	159	94

Sam Anderson Newhouse Ltd
Wilsons Road Newhouse, Motherwell, ML1 5NB
Tel: 01698-870274 **Fax:** 01698-870279
Directors: P. Brooks (Fin), J. Anderson (MD)
Ultimate Holding Company: S.A.H. LIMITED
Immediate Holding Company: SAM ANDERSON (NEWHOUSE) LIMITED
Registration no: SC032304 **Date established:** 1957
Turnover: £5m - £10m **No.of Employees:** 51 - 100 **Product Groups:** 72

Date of Accounts	Dec 11	Dec 10	Dec 09
Sales Turnover	9m	7m	7m
Pre Tax Profit/Loss	335	467	392
Working Capital	947	720	1m
Fixed Assets	6m	6m	6m
Current Assets	2m	2m	2m
Current Liabilities	504	507	548

Scott Grant Ltd
98 Hamilton Road, Motherwell, ML1 3DG
Tel: 01698-269698 **Fax:** 01698-259680
E-mail: info@scott-grant.co.uk
Website: http://www.scott-grant.co.uk
Directors: J. Brennan (Chief Op Offcr)
Immediate Holding Company: SCOTT-GRANT LIMITED
Registration no: 05214287 **Date established:** 2004
Turnover: £500,000 - £1m **No.of Employees:** 1 - 10 **Product Groups:** 80, 86

Date of Accounts	Dec 11	Dec 10	Dec 09
Working Capital	5	-29	-49
Fixed Assets	68	41	53
Current Assets	529	470	408
Current Liabilities	260	6	192

Technical Metal Finishes Scotland Ltd
Park Road Carfin Industrial Estate, Motherwell, ML1 4UZ
Tel: 01698-732777 **Fax:** 01698-834666
Directors: E. Robertson (Fin)
Immediate Holding Company: TECHNICAL METAL FINISHES (SCOTLAND) LIMITED
Registration no: SC046847 **Date established:** 1969
Turnover: Up to £250,000 **No.of Employees:** 1 - 10 **Product Groups:** 46, 48

Date of Accounts	Sep 11	Sep 10	Sep 09
Working Capital	-50	-58	-64
Fixed Assets	1	2	2
Current Assets	32	29	31

Terex Equipment Ltd
Newhouse Industrial Estate, Motherwell, ML1 5RY
Tel: 01698-732121 **Fax:** 01698-734046
E-mail: paul.douglas@terex.com
Website: http://www.terex.co.uk
Bank(s): Barclays
Directors: E. Cohen (Fin), K. O'Donald (Fin)
Managers: P. Douglas (Chief Mgr)
Ultimate Holding Company: TEREX CORP (USA)
Immediate Holding Company: TEREX EQUIPMENT LIMITED
Registration no: SC086323 **Date established:** 1984
Turnover: £75m - £125m **No.of Employees:** 251 - 500
Product Groups: 39, 45

Date of Accounts	Dec 10	Dec 09	Dec 08
Sales Turnover	114m	88m	183m
Pre Tax Profit/Loss	-3m	-12m	-17m
Working Capital	23m	26m	41m
Fixed Assets	18m	18m	18m
Current Assets	87m	77m	101m
Current Liabilities	3m	3m	6m

Valve Spares Ltd
Ravenshill Drive Cleland, Motherwell, ML1 5QW
Tel: 01698-860738 **Fax:** 01698-861739
E-mail: valvesspares@btconnect.com
Directors: M. Walker (MD)
Ultimate Holding Company: WALKER ENGINEERING (CLELAND) LTD
Registration no: 06054236 **Turnover:** Up to £250,000
No.of Employees: 1 - 10 **Product Groups:** 66

Date of Accounts	May 03	May 02
Working Capital	3	25
Current Assets	27	56
Current Liabilities	24	31

Workability Ltd
Dalziel Building 7 Scott Street, Motherwell, ML1 1PN
Tel: 01698-253724 **Fax:** 01698-304533
E-mail: info@workability.ltd.uk
Website: http://www.workability.ltd.uk
Directors: W. Thom (MD)
Managers: A. Watson (Ops Mgr), A. Ledgerwood (I.T. Exec)
Immediate Holding Company: WORKABILITY LTD.
Registration no: SC207405 **Date established:** 2000
No.of Employees: 1 - 10 **Product Groups:** 82, 88

Date of Accounts	May 08	May 07
Working Capital	53	41
Fixed Assets	1	1
Current Assets	72	63
Current Liabilities	19	23

X L Steel Ltd
Unit 104 Block 11 Newhouse Industrial Estate, Newhouse, Motherwell, ML1 5RX
Tel: 01698-834777 **Fax:** 01698-834999
E-mail: sales@xlsteel.co.uk
Managers: J. Cullion (Mgr)
Immediate Holding Company: X L STEEL LTD
Registration no: SC093323 **VAT No.:** GB 402 9898 30
Turnover: £2m - £5m **No.of Employees:** 1 - 10 **Product Groups:** 66

X-Met
Unit 106-107 Newhouse Industrial Estate, Newhouse, Motherwell, ML1 5RX
Tel: 01698-733533 **Fax:** 01698-734617
E-mail: sean@x-met.com
Website: http://www.x-met.com
Directors: C. McClymont (Fin), S. Neville (Snr Part)
Managers: C. Byrne (Purch Mgr)
Immediate Holding Company: X-MET FABRICATION & FINISHING LIMITED
Registration no: SC238499 **Date established:** 2002
No.of Employees: 51 - 100 **Product Groups:** 35

Date of Accounts	Dec 11	Dec 10	Dec 09
Working Capital	271	171	266
Fixed Assets	401	468	556
Current Assets	1m	1m	1m
Current Liabilities	407	397	N/A

Rossshire

Muir Of Ord

Craigton Fabs Ltd
Unit 4 Muir of Ord Industrial Estate Great North Road, Muir Of Ord, IV6 7UA
Tel: 01463-871264 **Fax:** 01463-871238
E-mail: sales@craigtonfabs.com
Website: http://www.craigtonfabs.com
Directors: I. Mackintosh (Fin), P. Logan (MD)
Immediate Holding Company: CRAIGTON FABS LIMITED
Registration no: SC173086 **Date established:** 1997
No.of Employees: 1 - 10 **Product Groups:** 45

Date of Accounts	Feb 12	Feb 11	Feb 10
Working Capital	-164	-91	-87
Fixed Assets	266	251	269
Current Assets	96	140	107

Midlothian

Musselburgh

Bruntons Aero Products Ltd
Unit 1-3 Block 1 Inveresk Industrial Estate, Musselburgh, EH21 7PA
Tel: 0131-665 3888 **Fax:** 0131-653 2236
E-mail: info@bruntons.co.uk
Website: http://www.bruntons.co.uk
Directors: I. Williamson (Dir), E. Cook (Fin)
Managers: M. Drummond (Sales Prom Mgr), B. Wylie (Purch Mgr), I. Weston
Ultimate Holding Company: CARCLO PLC
Immediate Holding Company: BRUNTONS AERO PRODUCTS LIMITED
Registration no: 00045894 **Date established:** 1995 **Turnover:** £2m - £5m
No.of Employees: 21 - 50 **Product Groups:** 35, 39, 48, 84

Date of Accounts	Mar 11	Mar 10	Mar 09
Sales Turnover	3m	3m	4m
Pre Tax Profit/Loss	226	57	656
Working Capital	553	536	469
Fixed Assets	1m	1m	1m
Current Assets	1m	1m	1m
Current Liabilities	234	195	408

Graham Plumbers Merchants
Plot 1a Newhailes Industrial Estate Newhailes Road, Musselburgh, EH21 6SY
Tel: 0131-665 6250 **Fax:** 0131-653 6457
Website: http://www.graham-group.co.uk
Managers: C. Reed (District Mgr), C. Reid (Mgr), G. Mean (Mgr)
Immediate Holding Company: PUCCINO'S WORLDWIDE LIMITED
Registration no: SC201577 **Date established:** 2009
Turnover: £20m - £50m **No.of Employees:** 1 - 10 **Product Groups:** 66

Industrial Spraying Systems Ltd
Unit 21 Fisherroe Industrial Estate, Musselburgh, EH21 6RU
Tel: 0131-665 2777 **Fax:** 0131-665 2888
Website: http://www.industrialsprayingsystems.com
Directors: M. Macdonald (MD)
Immediate Holding Company: INDUSTRIAL SPRAYING SYSTEMS LIMITED
Registration no: SC164406 **Date established:** 1996
No.of Employees: 1 - 10 **Product Groups:** 38, 42

Date of Accounts	Mar 11	Mar 10	Mar 07
Working Capital	78	94	90
Fixed Assets	N/A	5	19
Current Assets	129	158	134

Paragon Products UK Ltd
8 Newhailes Industrial Estate Newhailes Road, Musselburgh, EH21 6SY
Tel: 0131-653 2222 **Fax:** 0131-653 2272
E-mail: sales@paragononline.co.uk
Website: http://www.paragononline.co.uk
Directors: I. Urquhart (MD), P. Urquhart (Dir), A. Urquhart (Fin)
Managers: D. Ingham (Tech Serv Mgr)
Immediate Holding Company: PARAGON PRODUCTS (UK) LIMITED
Registration no: SC112318 **Date established:** 1988
No.of Employees: 11 - 20 **Product Groups:** 27, 32, 33, 36, 40, 41, 42

Date of Accounts	Jan 11	Jan 10	Jan 09
Working Capital	-109	-84	-82
Fixed Assets	570	565	560
Current Assets	203	206	206

Sunrite Blinds Ltd
Newhailes Industrial Estate Newhailes Road, Musselburgh, EH21 6SY
Tel: 0131-665 9933 **Fax:** 0131-665 7711
E-mail: info@sunrite.co.uk
Website: http://www.sunrite.co.uk
Directors: T. Colliander (Prop)
Immediate Holding Company: SUNRITE LIMITED
Registration no: SC348843 **VAT No.:** GB 271 0262 93
Date established: 2008 **No.of Employees:** 21 - 50 **Product Groups:** 24, 35, 63

Zot Engineering Ltd
Inveresk Mills Industrial Park, Musselburgh, EH21 7UQ
Tel: 0131-653 6834 **Fax:** 0131-653 6025
E-mail: info@zot.co.uk
Website: http://www.zot.co.uk
Directors: C. Antonelli (Fin), A. Millar (MD)
Managers: M. Wilson, E. McGow (Personnel)
Immediate Holding Company: ZOT ENGINEERING LIMITED
Registration no: SC057167 **VAT No.:** GB 271 6008 77
Date established: 1975 **Turnover:** £10m - £20m
No.of Employees: 101 - 250 **Product Groups:** 37, 48

Date of Accounts	Feb 08	Feb 11	Feb 10
Sales Turnover	13m	14m	13m
Pre Tax Profit/Loss	548	530	560
Working Capital	2m	2m	2m
Fixed Assets	5m	5m	4m
Current Assets	5m	5m	5m
Current Liabilities	1m	1m	1m

Nairnshire

Nairn

Claymore Dairies Ltd
Head Office Balmakeith Industrial Estate, Nairn, IV12 5QW
Tel: 01667-453344 **Fax:** 01667-454678
E-mail: sales@expressdairies.co.uk
Website: http://www.claymoredairies.co.uk
Bank(s): Bank of Scotland
Managers: M. Farquher (Sales Prom Mgr)
Ultimate Holding Company: ARLA FOODS AMBA (DENMARK)
Immediate Holding Company: ARLA FOODS NAIRN LIMITED
Registration no: SC188780 **Date established:** 1998 **Turnover:** £1m - £2m
No.of Employees: 51 - 100 **Product Groups:** 20

Date of Accounts	Dec 11	Dec 10	Dec 09
Sales Turnover	N/A	1m	17m
Pre Tax Profit/Loss	N/A	-486	-1m
Working Capital	N/A	-5m	497
Current Assets	N/A	N/A	1m
Current Liabilities	N/A	N/A	585

Midlothian

Newbridge

Aviagen
Lockhend Road Ratho Station, Newbridge, EH28 8SZ
Tel: 0131-333 1056 **Fax:** 0131-333 3296
E-mail: info@aviagen.com
Website: http://www.aviagen.com
Bank(s): Barclays
Directors: G. Hogarth (Dir)
Immediate Holding Company: AVIAGEN PENSION TRUSTEES LIMITED
Registration no: SC257501 **VAT No.:** GB 723 8563 22
Date established: 2003 **Turnover:** £10m - £20m
No.of Employees: 51 - 100 **Product Groups:** 01

Bodycoat Materials Testing Ltd
Lochend Industrial Estate Queen Anne Drive, Newbridge, EH28 8PL
Tel: 0131-333 4360 **Fax:** 0131-333 5135
E-mail: sales-uk@bodycote-mt.com
Website: http://www.bodycoat-mt.com
Directors: A. Burnett (Fin), D. Sleight (Ch), G. Higgins (MD), S. Bulloch (I.T. Dir), L. Riddell (Pers)
Managers: J. Clark (Ops Mgr), S. Martin (Purch Mgr), L. Riddle (Personnel)
Immediate Holding Company: Bodycote International P.L.C.
Registration no: SC 70429 **VAT No.:** GB 553 5266 38
Turnover: £20m - £50m **No.of Employees:** 1 - 10 **Product Groups:** 39, 51, 54, 85

Date of Accounts	Dec 07	Dec 06	Dec 05
Sales Turnover	57078	38463	24581
Pre Tax Profit/Loss	9458	5561	5794
Working Capital	-6081	-8724	5704
Fixed Assets	16364	13280	8479
Current Assets	25348	17183	13776
Current Liabilities	31429	25907	8072
Total Share Capital	10	10	10
ROCE% (Return on Capital Employed)	92.0	122.1	40.9
ROT% (Return on Turnover)	16.6	14.5	23.6

Guardall Ltd
Lochend Industrial Estate Queen Anne Drive, Newbridge, EH28 8PL
Tel: 0131-333 2900 **Fax:** 0131-333 4919
E-mail: clive.garlick@guardall.co.uk
Website: http://www.guardall.com
Bank(s): Bank of Scotland
Directors: D. Johnson (Co Sec), C. Garlic (Fin), C. Garlick (Dir), C. Garlick (Fin), G. Fenwick (Purch), J. Dary (Sales), P. Eldridge (MD)
Managers: S. Dunn (Personnel), T. Pinder (Product), R. Cockburn (I.T. Exec)
Immediate Holding Company: GUARDALL LIMITED
Registration no: SC069196 **VAT No.:** GB 402 7891 54
Date established: 1979 **Turnover:** £5m - £10m **No.of Employees:** 21 - 50
Product Groups: 35, 37, 40

Date of Accounts	Dec 07	Dec 06	Dec 05
Sales Turnover	7821	7284	7995
Pre Tax Profit/Loss	-2071	-1184	-167
Working Capital	-2181	-251	782
Fixed Assets	1669	1694	1906
Current Assets	4423	4579	4564
Current Liabilities	6604	4830	3781
Total Share Capital	1	1	1
ROCE% (Return on Capital Employed)	404.8	-82.1	-6.2
ROT% (Return on Turnover)	-26.5	-16.3	-2.1

Premier Hytemp Ltd
Newbridge Industrial Estate, Newbridge, EH28 8PJ
Tel: 0131-333 4140 **Fax:** 0131-333 4727
E-mail: contactus@premierhytemp.com
Website: http://www.premierhytemp.com
Bank(s): Bank of Scotland, Edinburgh
Directors: D. Wilson (MD), W. Gold (Fin), G. Grassick (Fin)
Managers: M. Holme (Sales Prom Mgr), N. Quiggley (Sales Admin)
Ultimate Holding Company: MURRAY INTERNATIONAL HOLDINGS LIMITED
Immediate Holding Company: PREMIER HYTEMP LIMITED
Registration no: SC093051 **VAT No.:** GB 446 6789 95
Date established: 1985 **Turnover:** £10m - £20m
No.of Employees: 51 - 100 **Product Groups:** 34

Date of Accounts	Jan 08	Jun 11	Jun 10
Sales Turnover	16m	19m	18m
Pre Tax Profit/Loss	2m	-373	-4m
Working Capital	3m	9m	9m
Fixed Assets	3m	11m	12m
Current Assets	7m	15m	12m
Current Liabilities	296	368	337

Russell Play Ltd
Newbridge Industrial Estate, Newbridge, EH28 8PJ
Tel: 0131-335 5400 **Fax:** 0131-335 5401
E-mail: sales@russell-play.com
Website: http://www.russell-play.com
Directors: T. Wellwood (Dir), R. Auld (Sales)
Managers: S. Deans (Tech Serv Mgr), A. Burgess (Fin Mgr)
Immediate Holding Company: RUSSELL LEISURE LIMITED
Registration no: SC162280 **VAT No.:** 398 1255 21 **Date established:** 1995
Turnover: £2m - £5m **No.of Employees:** 11 - 20 **Product Groups:** 26, 49

Date of Accounts	Dec 11	Dec 10	Dec 09
Sales Turnover	4m	4m	N/A
Pre Tax Profit/Loss	51	105	N/A
Working Capital	304	264	191
Fixed Assets	33	48	49
Current Assets	916	1m	1m
Current Liabilities	161	259	N/A

V T S Royalite
Cliftonhall Road, Newbridge, EH28 8PW
Tel: 0131-333 2819 **Fax:** 0131-333 5161
E-mail: sales@vtsroyalite.co.uk
Website: http://www.vitasheetgroup.com
Bank(s): National Westminster
Directors: T. Harkins (Fin)
Managers: A. Blair, R. Lewis (Sales & Mktg Mg), S. Hall (I.T. Exec), G. Shaw (Mgr), P. Murray (Tech Serv Mgr)
Ultimate Holding Company: ROLLAND HOLDINGS LIMITED
Immediate Holding Company: ROLLAND PROPERTIES LIMITED
Registration no: SC097825 **VAT No.:** GB 593 0075 42
Date established: 1992 **Turnover:** £10m - £20m
No.of Employees: 21 - 50 **Product Groups:** 30

Date of Accounts	Dec 06	Dec 05	Dec 04
Sales Turnover	N/A	66	47
Pre Tax Profit/Loss	N/A	1	6
Working Capital	-190	-122	-91
Fixed Assets	2m	2m	1m
Current Assets	N/A	N/A	3
Current Liabilities	N/A	N/A	1

Ayrshire

Newmilns

Dustacco Engineering Ltd
Tower Works 4-8 Stoneygate Road, Newmilns, KA16 9AJ
Tel: 01560-321394 **Fax:** 01560-323093
E-mail: sales@dustacco.com
Website: http://www.dustacco.com
Bank(s): Clydesdale Bank PLC
Directors: A. Somerville (Dir)
Managers: A. Woodhead (Comptroller), J. Paterson (Buyer)
Immediate Holding Company: DUSTACCO ENGINEERING LIMITED
Registration no: SC042982 **VAT No.:** GB 260 2140 13
Date established: 1966 **Turnover:** £1m - £2m **No.of Employees:** 21 - 50
Product Groups: 35, 36, 66

Date of Accounts	Dec 11	Dec 10	Dec 09
Working Capital	1m	1m	1m
Fixed Assets	128	146	177
Current Assets	2m	2m	2m

Morton Young & Borland Ltd
Stoneygate Road, Newmilns, KA16 9AL
Tel: 01560-321210 **Fax:** 01560-323153
E-mail: info@mybtextiles.com
Website: http://www.mybtextiles.com
Bank(s): The Royal Bank of Scotland
Directors: J. Mansell (Fin), S. Davidson (MD)
Ultimate Holding Company: MORTON YOUNG & BORLAND (SCOTLAND) LTD.
Immediate Holding Company: MORTON YOUNG & BORLAND LIMITED
Registration no: SC084953 **Date established:** 1983
Turnover: £250,000 - £500,000 **No.of Employees:** 51 - 100
Product Groups: 23

Date of Accounts	Jan 12	Jan 11	Jan 10
Working Capital	67	8	-27
Fixed Assets	803	625	658
Current Assets	1m	1m	1m

Smith & Archibald Ltd
14 Stoneygate Road, Newmilns, KA16 9AL
Tel: 01560-320240 **Fax:** 01560-323024
E-mail: enquiries@sandalace.co.uk
Website: http://www.sandalace.co.uk
Bank(s): Clydesdale Bank PLC
Directors: J. Weppenaar (Dir), B. Hill (Dir)
Ultimate Holding Company: MORTON YOUNG & BORLAND (SCOTLAND) LTD.
Immediate Holding Company: SMITH & ARCHIBALD LIMITED
Registration no: SC090031 **VAT No.:** GB 263 0252 91
Date established: 1984 **Turnover:** £500,000 - £1m
No.of Employees: 11 - 20 **Product Groups:** 23

Date of Accounts	Mar 11	Mar 10	Mar 09
Working Capital	1m	951	822
Fixed Assets	109	118	123
Current Assets	1m	1m	961

Vesuvius UK Ltd
Irvinebank Factory Brown Street, Newmilns, KA16 9AG
Tel: 01560-320861 **Fax:** 01560-321592
E-mail: info@vesuvius.com
Website: http://www.vesuvius.com
Bank(s): HSBC
Directors: R. Sykes (Fin), S. Howard (Dir)
Managers: D. Moore, G. Platt (Sales & Mktg Mg)
Ultimate Holding Company: COOKSON GROUP PLC
Immediate Holding Company: VESUVIUS ZYALONS HOLDINGS LIMITED
Registration no: SC090543 **VAT No.:** 172 3242 86 **Date established:** 1984
Turnover: £20m - £50m **No.of Employees:** 251 - 500 **Product Groups:** 33

Date of Accounts	Dec 98	Dec 10	Dec 09
Working Capital	5m	5m	5m
Current Assets	5m	5m	5m

Watermiser Ltd
Tower Works 4-8 Stoneygate Road, Newmilns, KA16 9AJ
Tel: 01560-320762 **Fax:** 01560-323093
E-mail: alison@watermiser.co.uk
Website: http://www.watermiser.co.uk
Bank(s): Clydesdale Bank PLC
Directors: S. McAughlin (Fin)
Managers: J. Paterson (Buyer), R. Samson (Mgr)
Immediate Holding Company: WATERMISER LIMITED
Registration no: SC047271 **VAT No.:** GB 264 5734 42
Date established: 1970 **Turnover:** £500,000 - £1m
No.of Employees: 21 - 50 **Product Groups:** 40, 48, 84

Date of Accounts	Dec 11	Dec 10	Dec 09
Working Capital	872	876	776
Fixed Assets	45	56	72
Current Assets	974	1m	964

Wigtownshire

Newton Stewart

Galloway Granite Works
Sorbie, Newton Stewart, DG8 8EW
Tel: 01988-850350 **Fax:** 01988-850340
E-mail: info@gallowaygranite.co.uk
Website: http://www.gallowaygranite.co.uk
Bank(s): Bank of Scotland
Directors: R. MacKenzie (MD)
Managers: J. Service (Sec), G. Christison (Accounts)
VAT No.: GB 263 1256 78 **Turnover:** £500,000 - £1m
No.of Employees: 11 - 20 **Product Groups:** 66

East Lothian

North Berwick

Gilmerton Land Services
Gilmerton House, North Berwick, EH39 5LQ
Tel: 01620-880207 **Fax:** 01620-880276
E-mail: reception@gilmertonhouse.com
Website: http://www.gilmertonlandservices.com
Directors: D. Kinross (Prop)
Date established: 1969 **No.of Employees:** 1 - 10 **Product Groups:** 37, 51, 52, 67

Argyll

Oban

Boat Electrics & Electronics Ltd
Tradewinds North Connel, Oban, PA37 1RA
Tel: 01631-710852 **Fax:** 08704-460145
E-mail: sales@boatelectrics.com
Website: http://www.boatelectrics.com
Directors: J. Coleman (Dir)
Immediate Holding Company: BOAT ELECTRICS & ELECTRONICS LIMITED
Registration no: SC066331 **Date established:** 1978
No.of Employees: 1 - 10 **Product Groups:** 35, 36, 39

Date of Accounts	Sep 11	Sep 10	Sep 09
Working Capital	234	189	180
Fixed Assets	42	34	20
Current Assets	801	496	328

Falls of Lora Hotel
Connel, Oban, PA37 1PB
Tel: 01631-710483 **Fax:** 01631-710694
E-mail: info@fallsoflora.com
Website: http://www.fallsoflora.com
Bank(s): Royal Bank of Scotland, Oban
Directors: C. Webster (Prop)
VAT No.: GB 356 9632 17 **Turnover:** £500,000 - £1m
No.of Employees: 11 - 20 **Product Groups:** 69

Jewson Ltd
Sinclair Drive, Oban, PA34 4DR
Tel: 01631-562208 **Fax:** 01631-566612
Website: http://www.jewson.co.uk
Managers: C. McPherson (Mgr)
Ultimate Holding Company: COMPAGNIE DE SAINT GOBAIN (FRANCE)
Immediate Holding Company: JEWSON LIMITED
Registration no: 00348407 **VAT No.:** GB 497 7184 83
Date established: 1939 **Turnover:** £2m - £5m **No.of Employees:** 1 - 10
Product Groups: 66

Date of Accounts	Dec 11	Dec 10	Dec 09
Sales Turnover	1606m	1547m	1485m
Pre Tax Profit/Loss	18m	100m	45m
Working Capital	-345m	-250m	-349m
Fixed Assets	496m	387m	461m
Current Assets	657m	1005m	1320m
Current Liabilities	66m	120m	64m

Eddie Murphy Builders
Ariogan Farm House Soroba, Oban, PA34 4SD
Tel: 01631-564338 **Fax:** 01631-564338
E-mail: eddie@builder130.fsnet.co.uk
Directors: E. Murphy (Prop)
Date established: 1980 **No.of Employees:** 1 - 10 **Product Groups:** 52

Orkney Isles

Orkney

Frotoft
Rousay, Orkney, KW17 2PT
Tel: 01856-821476 **Fax:** 01856-821476
Directors: D. Hall (Ptnr)
Immediate Holding Company: J. & R. MARWICK LIMITED
Registration no: SC261966 **Date established:** 2004
No.of Employees: 1 - 10 **Product Groups:** 35

Date of Accounts	Jan 11	Jan 10	Jan 08
Working Capital	462	426	317
Fixed Assets	62	67	33
Current Assets	482	477	360

Renfrewshire

Paisley

Abbey Gates
115 Neilston Road, Paisley, PA2 6ER
Tel: 0800-0728043 **Fax:** 0141-884 4826
E-mail: enquiries@abbeygates.co.uk
Website: http://www.abbeygates.co.uk
Directors: J. McLean (Prop), L. Twells (Prop)
Date established: 2002 **No.of Employees:** 1 - 10 **Product Groups:** 26, 35

Acupaq
108 St James Business Centre Junction 29 Linwood Road, Linwood, Paisley, PA3 3AT
Tel: 0141-950 6643 **Fax:** 07092-185928
E-mail: stuart.craig@acupaq.com
Website: http://www.acupaq.com
Directors: S. Craig (MD)
Immediate Holding Company: ACUPAQ LTD.
Registration no: SC290380 **Date established:** 2005
No.of Employees: 1 - 10 **Product Groups:** 30, 84

Date of Accounts	Dec 08	Dec 07	Dec 06
Working Capital	-128	-138	68
Fixed Assets	122	99	3
Current Assets	140	149	157

Allbright Signs Ltd
80 Glasgow Road, Paisley, PA1 3PN
Tel: 0141-840 4049
Directors: D. McMahon (Ptnr)
Registration no: SC309920 **No.of Employees:** 1 - 10 **Product Groups:** 30, 40, 84

Alpress Hydraulic Engineers
65 Back Sneddon Street, Paisley, PA3 2DD
Tel: 0141-848 7175 **Fax:** 0141-889 5280
E-mail: al-press@btconnect.com
Website: http://www.alpress.co.uk
Directors: A. Young (Snr Part), A. Young (Prop)
Immediate Holding Company: ALPRESS HYDRAULIC SERVICES LTD.
Registration no: SC389888 **Date established:** 2010
Turnover: £500,000 - £1m **No.of Employees:** 1 - 10 **Product Groups:** 40, 41, 42, 43, 44, 46, 47, 48, 54

Aqua Energy
St James Business Centre Junction 29 Linwood Road, Linwood, Paisley, PA3 3AT
Tel: 0141-849 6888 **Fax:** 0141-848 5777
E-mail: sales@aquaenergy.com
Website: http://www.aquaenergy.com
Directors: D. Lafferty (MD)
Immediate Holding Company: AQUA ENERGY (UK) LTD.
Registration no: SC360274 **Date established:** 2009
No.of Employees: 1 - 10 **Product Groups:** 40, 42, 45, 46, 47, 48

Campbell Medical Supplies
2 Victoria Estate Violet Street, Paisley, PA1 1PA
Tel: 0141-889 3500 **Fax:** 0141-848 7139
E-mail: campbellmedical@ukonline.co.uk
Directors: J. Campbell (MD)
VAT No.: GB 265 2132 79 **Turnover:** £250,000 - £500,000
No.of Employees: 1 - 10 **Product Groups:** 61

Carlton Die Castings Ltd
88 Greenhill Road, Paisley, PA3 1RD
Tel: 0141-887 8355 **Fax:** 0141-848 1157
E-mail: gilwilson@carltondie.com
Website: http://www.carltondie.com
Bank(s): The Royal Bank of Scotland
Directors: G. Wilson (MD), E. Wilson (Purch), J. Purvis (Fin), G. Wilson (Sales)
Managers: N. Forbes, R. Keane (Sales Admin)
Ultimate Holding Company: KENYART LIMITED
Immediate Holding Company: CARLTON DIECASTINGS LIMITED
Registration no: SC083494 **Date established:** 1983 **Turnover:** £2m - £5m
No.of Employees: 21 - 50 **Product Groups:** 30, 32, 34, 36, 38, 48, 66

Date of Accounts	Mar 11	Mar 10	Mar 09
Working Capital	232	37	322
Fixed Assets	330	368	344
Current Assets	1m	997	1m

Excel Solutions
10 Jennys Well Road, Paisley, PA2 7HF
Tel: 0141-887 8781 **Fax:** 0141-887 8781
E-mail: info@xcelsolutions.co.uk
Website: http://www.excelsolutions.co.uk
Directors: F. Graham (Prop)
Date established: 2002 **No.of Employees:** 1 - 10 **Product Groups:** 44

F H G Guides Ltd
Abbey Mill Business Centre Seedhill, Paisley, PA1 1TJ
Tel: 0141-887 0428 **Fax:** 0141-889 7204
E-mail: admin@fhguides.co.uk
Website: http://www.holidayguides.com
Directors: G. Pratt (Publishing)
Immediate Holding Company: FHG GUIDES LIMITED
Registration no: 05248105 **Date established:** 2004
No.of Employees: 11 - 20 **Product Groups:** 28

Date of Accounts	Dec 11	Dec 10	Dec 09
Working Capital	-105	-93	-85
Fixed Assets	175	186	191
Current Assets	86	160	165

Fibreglass Fabrications Ltd
33 Abercorn Street, Paisley, PA3 4AL
Tel: 0141-889 8723 **Fax:** 0141-561 7163
E-mail: shannonking70@aol.com
Website: http://www.fibreglassfabrications.com
Directors: S. King (MD)
Immediate Holding Company: FIBREGLASS FABRICATIONS LTD.
Registration no: SC217628 **Date established:** 2001
Turnover: Up to £250,000 **No.of Employees:** 1 - 10 **Product Groups:** 30

Date of Accounts	Mar 12	Mar 11	Mar 10
Working Capital	110	162	216
Fixed Assets	105	109	94
Current Assets	189	251	316

Glenbar Electrical Ltd
2-4 North Croft Street, Paisley, PA3 4AD
Tel: 0141-887 4040 **Fax:** 0141-889 6789
Directors: G. Wade (MD), J. Hall (Fin)
Immediate Holding Company: GLENBAR ELECTRICAL SERVICES LTD.
Registration no: SC308246 **VAT No.:** GB 265 1896 30
Date established: 2006 **Turnover:** Up to £250,000
No.of Employees: 1 - 10 **Product Groups:** 39

Date of Accounts	Sep 11	Sep 10	Sep 09
Working Capital	32	17	10
Fixed Assets	5	6	7
Current Assets	42	27	25

Hub L E Bas (a division of Caparo Precision Tubes Ltd)
Studio 200 Embroidery Mill Abbey Mill Business Centre, Paisley, PA1 1TJ
Tel: 0141-848 6767 **Fax:** 0141-848 6991
E-mail: scotsales@hublebas.co.uk
Website: http://www.hublebas.co.uk
Managers: B. Sutherland (Chief Acct)
Ultimate Holding Company: TYCO INTERNATIONAL LTD
Immediate Holding Company: TYCO EUROPEAN TUBING LTD
No.of Employees: 1 - 10 **Product Groups:** 36

Ingram Bros Ltd
15 East Lane, Paisley, PA1 1QA
Tel: 0141-840 5870
E-mail: sales@ingrambrothers.com
Website: http://www.ingrambrothers.com
Bank(s): Bank of Scotland
Managers: M. Young (Sales Prom Mgr)
Ultimate Holding Company: GEORGE INGRAM (GLASGOW) LIMITED
Immediate Holding Company: GEORGE INGRAM (GLASGOW) LIMITED
Registration no: SC046731 **VAT No.:** GB 259 9470 07
Date established: 1969 **Turnover:** £5m - £10m **No.of Employees:** 21 - 50
Product Groups: 20

Date of Accounts	Dec 11	Dec 10	Dec 09
Working Capital	16	16	34
Fixed Assets	122	122	122
Current Assets	16	16	35

Jewson Ltd
10-12 Greenhill Road, Paisley, PA3 1RN
Tel: 0141-889 1725 **Fax:** 0141-840 1600
E-mail: michael.patterson@jewson.co.uk
Website: http://www.jewson.co.uk
Bank(s): Barclays
Directors: P. Hindle (Ch), T. Newman (Sales), C. Kenward (Fin)
Managers: M. Patterson (Site Co-ord)
Ultimate Holding Company: COMPAGNIE DE SAINT GOBAIN (FRANCE)
Immediate Holding Company: JEWSON LIMITED
Registration no: 00348407 **Date established:** 1939
Turnover: £500m - £1,000m **No.of Employees:** 21 - 50
Product Groups: 66

Date of Accounts	Dec 11	Dec 10	Dec 09
Sales Turnover	1606m	1547m	1485m
Pre Tax Profit/Loss	18m	100m	45m
Working Capital	-345m	-250m	-349m
Fixed Assets	496m	387m	461m
Current Assets	657m	1005m	1320m
Current Liabilities	66m	120m	64m

Joseph Beattie & Son Ltd Beattie Glass
2-4 Abercorn Street, Paisley, PA3 4AB
Tel: 0141-561 7567 **Fax:** 0141-561 4140
E-mail: joebeattie@beattie-glass.co.uk
Website: http://www.beattieglass.com
Directors: J. Beattie (MD), J. Beatty (MD)
Immediate Holding Company: JOSEPH BEATTIE & SON, LIMITED
Registration no: SC028383 **Date established:** 1951
No.of Employees: 21 - 50 **Product Groups:** 26, 34, 36

Korec UK
Unit 12 Greenhill Business Park Greenhill Road, Paisley, PA3 1RQ
Tel: 0141-887 4800 **Fax:** 0141-887 2884
Website: http://www.korecgroup.com
Managers: S. Noble (Mgr)
Ultimate Holding Company: PRECISE CONSTRUCTION INSTRUMENTS LIMITED
Immediate Holding Company: PRECISE CONSTRUCTION INSTRUMENTS (U.K.) LTD
Registration no: 00965862 **Date established:** 1969
Turnover: £10m - £20m **No.of Employees:** 1 - 10 **Product Groups:** 38, 44

Kuehne & Nagel
Unit C Abbotsinch, Paisley, PA3 2SJ
Tel: 0141-842 3900 **Fax:** 0141-842 3901
E-mail: leigh.baldwin@kuehne-nagel.com
Website: http://www.kuehne-nagel.com
Bank(s): Lloyds TSB Bank plc
Managers: L. Baldwin (District Mgr), S. Mallon (Fin Mgr)
Immediate Holding Company: LION UK HOLDINGS LTD
Registration no: 01722216 **No.of Employees:** 21 - 50 **Product Groups:** 76

Loganair Ltd
Glasgow Airport Abbotsinch, Paisley, PA3 2TG
Tel: 08714-321338 **Fax:** 0141-887 6020
E-mail: davidharrison@loganair.co.uk
Website: http://www.loganair.co.uk
Bank(s): The Royal Bank of Scotland
Directors: D. Harrison (Fin)
Immediate Holding Company: LOGANAIR LIMITED
Registration no: SC170072 **Date established:** 1996
Turnover: £50m - £75m **No.of Employees:** 251 - 500 **Product Groups:** 75

Date of Accounts	Mar 12	Mar 11	Mar 10
Sales Turnover	73m	60m	59m
Pre Tax Profit/Loss	4m	3m	3m
Working Capital	5m	4m	2m
Fixed Assets	11m	10m	11m
Current Assets	16m	14m	11m
Current Liabilities	7m	7m	6m

James Mcdowall & Son
191 George Street, Paisley, PA1 2UN
Tel: 0141-889 2606
E-mail: j.h.mcdowall@btinternet.com
Directors: J. McDowall (Ptnr)
Turnover: Up to £250,000 **No.of Employees:** 1 - 10 **Product Groups:** 20

Mackays Stores Group Ltd
Caledonia House 25-33 Caledonia Street, Paisley, PA3 2JG
Tel: 0141-889 8783 **Fax:** 0141-887 8069
Website: http://www.mackaysstores.co.uk
Directors: C. Willilamson (Mkt Research), I. McSkimmim (Dir)
Immediate Holding Company: MACKAYS STORES GROUP LIMITED
Registration no: SC223864 **Date established:** 2001
Turnover: £125m - £250m **No.of Employees:** 51 - 100
Product Groups: 61

Date of Accounts	Feb 10	Feb 11	Feb 08
Sales Turnover	182m	187m	171m
Pre Tax Profit/Loss	10m	11m	9m
Working Capital	15m	12m	-9m
Fixed Assets	122m	120m	137m
Current Assets	36m	30m	34m
Current Liabilities	13m	12m	10m

Colin Mackenzie Engineering Ltd

3 Murray Street, Paisley, PA3 1QG
Tel: 0141-889 3031 **Fax:** 0141-889 3031
Directors: H. Mackenzie (Fin), C. Mackenzie (MD)
Immediate Holding Company: COLIN MACKENZIE ENGINEERING LIMITED
Registration no: SC104016 **VAT No.:** GB 464 0532 63
Date established: 1987 **Turnover:** Up to £250,000
No.of Employees: 1 - 10 **Product Groups:** 48

Date of Accounts	Jun 12	Jun 11	Jun 10
Working Capital	2	2	1
Fixed Assets	1	1	2
Current Assets	60	58	70

Macom Technologies Ltd

17 Glasgow Road, Paisley, PA1 3QS
Tel: 0141-849 6287 **Fax:** 0141-849 6497
E-mail: info@macomtech.net
Website: http://www.macomtech.net
Directors: A. Abdelharim (MD), I. Youseff (Dir)
Immediate Holding Company: Macom Technologies UK Ltd
Registration no: SC199769 **Date established:** 1999
Turnover: Up to £250,000 **No.of Employees:** 1 - 10 **Product Groups:** 38, 48, 67, 84, 85

Magi Films Ltd

14 Oakwood Avenue Corsebar, Paisley, PA2 9NG
Tel: 0141-884 1110 **Fax:** 0141-884 1110
E-mail: info@magifilms.co.uk
Website: http://www.magifilms.co.uk
Directors: C. Cumming (MD), P. Hannay (Fin)
Immediate Holding Company: MAGI FILMS LIMITED
Registration no: SC241145 **Date established:** 2002
No.of Employees: 1 - 10 **Product Groups:** 89

Date of Accounts	Dec 11	Dec 10	Dec 09
Working Capital	3	2	3
Fixed Assets	1	1	1
Current Assets	9	8	12

Mcpherson Document Solutions Ltd

14-16 Macdowall Street, Paisley, PA3 2NB
Tel: 0141-887 4379 **Fax:** 0141-887 7847
E-mail: sales@trmcpherson.co.uk
Website: http://www.trmcpherson.co.uk
Bank(s): Clydesdale
Directors: G. Mcpherson (MD)
Immediate Holding Company: MCPHERSON DOCUMENT SOLUTIONS LIMITED
Registration no: SC240071 **VAT No.:** GB 263 9715 32
Date established: 2002 **Turnover:** £500,000 - £1m
No.of Employees: 11 - 20 **Product Groups:** 38, 44

P T M Security Solutions Ltd (Total Encapsulation & Protection Solutions Ltd)

Unit 16 Abercorn Street, Paisley, PA3 4AY
Tel: 0141-849 1425 **Fax:** 0141-849 1426
E-mail: admin@ptmservices.co.uk
Website: http://www.ptmservices.com
Directors: P. Mcgill (MD), L. McGill (Fin)
Immediate Holding Company: PTM SECURITY SOLUTIONS LTD
Registration no: SC212934 **VAT No.:** GB 890 6449 88
Date established: 2000 **No.of Employees:** 1 - 10 **Product Groups:** 30, 31, 52

Date of Accounts	Feb 11	Feb 10	Feb 09
Working Capital	104	62	109
Fixed Assets	5	11	11
Current Assets	167	128	191

Russell Ferguson Marketing Ltd

21 Forbes Place, Paisley, PA1 1UT
Tel: 0141-226 2400 **Fax:** 0141-226 3322
E-mail: courses@rfm.co.uk
Website: http://www.rfm.co.uk
Directors: J. Coulter (Fin), R. Ferguson (MD)
Immediate Holding Company: RUSSELL FERGUSON MARKETING LIMITED
Registration no: SC291730 **Date established:** 2005
Turnover: £500,000 - £1m **No.of Employees:** 1 - 10 **Product Groups:** 80, 81, 86

Date of Accounts	Sep 11	Sep 10	Sep 09
Working Capital	80	19	49
Fixed Assets	41	49	58
Current Assets	157	104	126

Scot Test Ltd

12 Thomas Street, Paisley, PA1 2RE
Tel: 0141-887 7925 **Fax:** 0141-889 0665
E-mail: scot-testltd@btconnect.com
Website: http://www.scot-test-ltd.sol.co.uk
Directors: D. Smith (MD), J. Taggart (Fin)
Immediate Holding Company: SCOT-TEST LIMITED
Registration no: SC052584 **Date established:** 1973
Turnover: £500,000 - £1m **No.of Employees:** 1 - 10 **Product Groups:** 85

Date of Accounts	Sep 11	Sep 10	Sep 09
Working Capital	-7	32	62
Fixed Assets	147	116	88
Current Assets	250	131	227

Scottish Enterprise Renfrewshire

27 Causeyside Street, Paisley, PA1 1UL
Tel: 0141-848 0101 **Fax:** 0141-848 6930
E-mail: enquiries@scotent.co.uk
Website: http://www.scotent.co.uk
Bank(s): TSB, Clyesdale
Directors: C. Stewart (Co Sec)
Managers: J. Biggam (Sales Admin)
Immediate Holding Company: SCOTTISH ENTERPRISE RENFREWSHIRE
Registration no: SC130490 **Date established:** 1991
Turnover: Up to £250,000 **No.of Employees:** 51 - 100
Product Groups: 86

Date of Accounts	Mar 11	Mar 10	Mar 09
Sales Turnover	N/A	N/A	3
Pre Tax Profit/Loss	322	2	33
Working Capital	943	675	674
Current Assets	975	678	691
Current Liabilities	N/A	1	17

Seadrec Ltd

Unit 21 Sir James Clark Building Abbey Mill Business Centre, Paisley, PA1 1TJ
Tel: 0141-887 4131 **Fax:** 0141-887 6437
E-mail: info@lobnitz.com
Website: http://www.lobnitz.com
Bank(s): The Royal Bank of Scotland
Directors: B. Mckinney (MD)
Managers: C. Caufield
Immediate Holding Company: SEADREC LIMITED
Registration no: SC046928 **VAT No.:** GB 659 1105 38
Date established: 1969 **Turnover:** £500,000 - £1m
No.of Employees: 21 - 50 **Product Groups:** 39, 40

Date of Accounts	Mar 12	Mar 11	Mar 10
Working Capital	2m	969	782
Fixed Assets	N/A	1	1
Current Assets	2m	2m	903

Set School Wear

10 Broomlands Street, Paisley, PA1 2LR
Tel: 0141-889 0467 **Fax:** 0141-887 4035
E-mail: sales@setschoolwear.co.uk
Website: http://www.schoolwearscotland.com
Directors: A. Ahmed (Prop)
Date established: 1996 **No.of Employees:** 1 - 10 **Product Groups:** 22, 24

Spanish Life Properties

251 Embroide Mill Abbeymill Business Centre Seedhill Road, Paisley, PA1 1JS
Tel: 0141-889 6264
E-mail: graeme@spanishlifeproperties.co.uk
Website: http://www.spanishlifeproperties.co.uk
Directors: H. Glenn (Grp Chief Exec), G. Elder (MD)
Managers: H. Glen (Mktg Serv Mgr)
Immediate Holding Company: INTELLEMETRICS GLOBAL LIMITED
Registration no: SC272957 **Date established:** 2010
No.of Employees: 1 - 10 **Product Groups:** 61, 80

Spirax Sarco Ltd

Room 7 St James Business Centre Linwood Road, Linwood, Paisley, PA3 3AT
Tel: 0141-849 0006 **Fax:** 0141-849 1647
E-mail: williamshearer@spiraxsarco.com
Website: http://www.spiraxsarco.com
Managers: W. Shearer (Sales Prom Mgr)
Immediate Holding Company: SPIRAX-SARCO LIMITED
Registration no: 00509018 **Date established:** 1952
Turnover: £75m - £125m **No.of Employees:** 1 - 10 **Product Groups:** 38, 48, 84

Supply Technologies Ltd

West Brookfield House 2 Burnbrae Drive, Linwood, Paisley, PA3 3BU
Tel: 01505-333880 **Fax:** 01505-333480
E-mail: farquhar.mckinnon@supplytechnologies.com
Website: http://www.supplytechnologies.com
Directors: F. Mckinnon (MD)
Ultimate Holding Company: THE MALCOLM GROUP LIMITED
Immediate Holding Company: SUPPLY TECHNOLOGIES LIMITED
Registration no: SC201587 **Date established:** 1999
Turnover: £250m - £500m **No.of Employees:** 21 - 50
Product Groups: 27, 30, 34, 35, 39, 48

Taylor & Fraser Ltd

117 Abercorn Street, Paisley, PA3 4DH
Tel: 0141-887 6151 **Fax:** 0141-889 0696
E-mail: info@taylorandfraser.com
Website: http://www.taylor-and-fraser.co.uk
Bank(s): Lloyds TSB Bank plc
Directors: E. Kennedy (Co Sec), A. Fortune (Fin)
Ultimate Holding Company: BARNAIGH GROUP LIMITED
Immediate Holding Company: TAYLOR & FRASER LIMITED
Registration no: SC155035 **VAT No.:** GB 652 4767 19
Date established: 1994 **Turnover:** £20m - £50m
No.of Employees: 51 - 100 **Product Groups:** 52, 84

Date of Accounts	Jun 11	Jun 10	Jun 09
Sales Turnover	20m	21m	26m
Pre Tax Profit/Loss	833	1m	1m
Working Capital	3m	4m	3m
Fixed Assets	189	241	267
Current Assets	9m	10m	12m
Current Liabilities	5m	6m	8m

Tercet Precision

Millarston Industrial Estate, Paisley, PA1 2XR
Tel: 0141-887 4153 **Fax:** 0141-887 4586
E-mail: sales@tercet.co.uk
Website: http://www.tercet.co.uk
Bank(s): The Royal Bank of Scotland
Directors: V. Docherty (Fin), A. Burns (MD), R. Gordon (Fin)
Managers: G. Coyle (Personnel), J. Davis (Buyer), D. Adams
Immediate Holding Company: TERCET PRECISION LIMITED
Registration no: SC186797 **VAT No.:** GB 680 4917 17
Date established: 1998 **Turnover:** £2m - £5m **No.of Employees:** 51 - 100
Product Groups: 66

Date of Accounts	Mar 11	Mar 10	Mar 09
Sales Turnover	N/A	N/A	3m
Pre Tax Profit/Loss	N/A	N/A	111
Working Capital	786	645	52
Fixed Assets	2m	2m	2m
Current Assets	2m	2m	967
Current Liabilities	N/A	N/A	249

Thomas Reid Holdings Ltd

Napier Street Linwood, Paisley, PA3 3AN
Tel: 01505-321591 **Fax:** 01505-321645
E-mail: contact@reidgear.com
Website: http://www.reidgear.com
Directors: T. Reid (MD)
Immediate Holding Company: THOMAS REID (HOLDINGS) LIMITED
Registration no: SC318074 **VAT No.:** GB 263 4931 51
Date established: 2007 **Turnover:** £1m - £2m **No.of Employees:** 1 - 10
Product Groups: 39, 45

Date of Accounts	Mar 11	Mar 10	Mar 09
Working Capital	10	-277	358
Fixed Assets	360	485	172
Current Assets	14	515	363

Turbine Services Ltd

Phoenix Business Park, Paisley, PA1 2BH
Tel: 0141-849 6123 **Fax:** 0141-849 7023
E-mail: snicol@tsltd.uk.com
Website: http://www.turbineserviceslimited.com
Directors: S. Winton (Dir)
Managers: S. Nicol (Chief Mgr)
Ultimate Holding Company: SEQUA CORPORATION (USA)
Immediate Holding Company: TURBINE SERVICES LIMITED
Registration no: 01536507 **Date established:** 1980
No.of Employees: 51 - 100 **Product Groups:** 35, 36, 39

Date of Accounts	Dec 07	Dec 06	Dec 05
Sales Turnover	42732	42708	35971
Pre Tax Profit/Loss	6134	4155	4500
Working Capital	27140	22586	19728
Fixed Assets	6269	6448	6439
Current Assets	31404	30295	27296
Current Liabilities	4263	7709	7568
Total Share Capital	16064	16064	16064
ROCE% (Return on Capital Employed)	18.4	14.3	17.2
ROT% (Return on Turnover)	14.4	9.7	12.5

W J W Lang Ltd

White Cart Workshops 1 Seedhill, Paisley, PA1 1JL
Tel: 0141-889 3134 **Fax:** 0141-889 3182
E-mail: sales@langwetblue.co.uk
Website: http://www.langwetblue.co.uk
Bank(s): Clydesdale Bank PLC
Directors: G. Ross (Co Sec), J. Lang (Dir)
Ultimate Holding Company: SCOTTISH LEATHER GROUP LIMITED
Immediate Holding Company: W.J. & W. LANG LIMITED
Registration no: SC025996 **Date established:** 1947
Turnover: £20m - £50m **No.of Employees:** 51 - 100 **Product Groups:** 22

Date of Accounts	Mar 12	Mar 11	Mar 10
Sales Turnover	28m	27m	17m
Pre Tax Profit/Loss	3m	2m	2m
Working Capital	8m	7m	6m
Fixed Assets	2m	1m	1m
Current Assets	10m	10m	9m
Current Liabilities	965	1m	955

W Oswald Wholesale Ironmonger

1-3 Greenhill Road, Paisley, PA3 1RJ
Tel: 0141-889 0528 **Fax:** 0141-887 3615
E-mail: info@w-oswald.co.uk
Website: http://www.w-oswald.co.uk
Directors: W. Oswald (Prop)
Date established: 1978 **No.of Employees:** 1 - 10 **Product Groups:** 35, 36, 66

Peebleshire

Peebles

Auto Security Systems

St Ronans Venlaw High Road, Peebles, EH45 8RL
Tel: 0800-387897
E-mail: info@autosecuritysystems.co.uk
Website: http://www.autosecuritysystems.co.uk
Directors: R. Campbell (Prop)
No.of Employees: 1 - 10 **Product Groups:** 37, 39

Holland & Sherry

PO Box 1, Peebles, EH45 8RN
Tel: 01721-720101 **Fax:** 01721-722309
E-mail: enquiries@hollandandsherry.co.uk
Website: http://www.hollandandsherry.co.uk
Directors: L. Taylor (Sales), C. Stewart (Grp Chief Exec), F. O'Riley (Fin)
Managers: D. Murray (Personnel)
Ultimate Holding Company: HANSON REAL ESTATE LIMITED
Immediate Holding Company: SCOTTISH CROFTER-WEAVERS LIMITED
Registration no: 00194697 **VAT No.:** GB 268 3587 15
Date established: 1955 **Turnover:** £250,000 - £500,000
No.of Employees: 51 - 100 **Product Groups:** 63, 82

Robert Noble

March Street, Peebles, EH45 8ER
Tel: 01721-720146 **Fax:** 01721-721893
E-mail: enquiries@robert-noble.co.uk
Website: http://www.robert-noble.co.uk
Bank(s): HSBC, Huddersfield
Directors: E. Martin (Fin), I. Taylor (Sales & Mktg), D. Barr (Fin), A. McDeed (Mkt Research), A. McDeed (Mkt Research), I. Laird (MD)
Managers: D. McGill (Tech Serv Mgr)
Ultimate Holding Company: YORKLYDE LIMITED
Immediate Holding Company: PREMIER FABRICS LIMITED
Registration no: SC023533 **VAT No.:** GB 333 4477 60
Date established: 1945 **No.of Employees:** 51 - 100 **Product Groups:** 23

Replin Fabrics

March Street Mills March Street, Peebles, EH45 8ER
Tel: 01721-724310 **Fax:** 01721-721893
E-mail: enquiries@replin-fabrics.co.uk
Website: http://www.robert-noble.co.uk
Bank(s): HSBC
Directors: I. Taylor (Sales & Mktg), D. Breckenridge (MD), E. Martin (Fin)
Ultimate Holding Company: YORKLYDE LIMITED
Immediate Holding Company: PREMIER FABRICS LIMITED
Registration no: SC023533 **VAT No.:** GB 333 4477 60
Date established: 1945 **Turnover:** £5m - £10m
No.of Employees: 51 - 100 **Product Groups:** 23

Midlothian

Penicuik

Findlay Irvine
42-44 Bog Road, Penicuik, EH26 9BU
Tel: 01968-671200 **Fax:** 01968-671237
E-mail: sales@findlayirvine.com
Website: http://www.findlayirvine.com
Bank(s): Bank of Scotland, London
Directors: C. Irvine (MD), A. Scougall (Co Sec)
Managers: A. Thomson (Tech Serv Mgr), K. Hanratty (Prod Mgr)
Immediate Holding Company: FINDLAY, IRVINE LIMITED
Registration no: SC035193 **VAT No.:** GB 268 7657 00
Date established: 1960 **Turnover:** £2m - £5m **No.of Employees:** 21 - 50
Product Groups: 37, 84

Date of Accounts	May 11	May 10	May 09
Working Capital	1m	895	853
Fixed Assets	301	272	279
Current Assets	2m	1m	1m

Hycor Biomedical Ltd
Douglas House Pentland Science Park Bush Loan, Penicuik, EH26 0PL
Tel: 0131-445 7111 **Fax:** 0131-445 7112
E-mail: jweston@hycorbiomedical.com
Website: http://www.hycorbiomedical.com
Bank(s): Clydesdale
Directors: R. Simpson (Co Sec)
Managers: J. Western (Mgr)
Ultimate Holding Company: AGILENT TECHNOLOGIES INC (USA)
Immediate Holding Company: HYCOR BIOMEDICAL LIMITED
Registration no: SC122739 **VAT No.:** 553 6006 59 **Date established:** 1990
Turnover: £2m - £5m **No.of Employees:** 11 - 20 **Product Groups:** 31

Date of Accounts	Oct 11	Oct 10	Oct 09
Sales Turnover	3m	1m	1m
Pre Tax Profit/Loss	184	-63	-151
Working Capital	995	1m	-1m
Fixed Assets	49	123	45
Current Assets	1m	1m	2m
Current Liabilities	38	58	38

Select
The Walled Garden Bush Estate, Penicuik, EH26 0SB
Tel: 0131-445 5577 **Fax:** 0131-445 5548
E-mail: admin@select.org.uk
Website: http://www.select.org.uk
Directors: J. McGhee (Co Sec), N. Mcguiness (Dir)
Managers: D. Wright, C. Boyd, C. Shaw (Projects)
Ultimate Holding Company: SELECT (RETAIL HOLDINGS) LIMITED
Immediate Holding Company: SELECT (RETAIL) LIMITED
Registration no: 01769250 **Date established:** 1983
Turnover: Up to £250,000 **No.of Employees:** 21 - 50 **Product Groups:** 87

Date of Accounts	Jan 05	Jan 06	Jan 03
Sales Turnover	66m	73m	61m
Pre Tax Profit/Loss	-166	2m	724
Working Capital	-2m	-3m	-2m
Fixed Assets	7m	8m	6m
Current Assets	9m	10m	7m
Current Liabilities	2m	4m	3m

Perthshire

Perth

Cellular Devices
Ardoch Hatton Road, Perth, PH2 7DB
Tel: 01738-638299 **Fax:** 01738-580409
Directors: E. Adam (MD)
Immediate Holding Company: INVERALMOND HOLDINGS LIMITED
Registration no: SC047913 **Date established:** 1970
No.of Employees: 1 - 10 **Product Groups:** 36, 37

Clive Refrigeration
18 Daleally Cresent Errol, Perth, PH2 7QA
Tel: 01821-642709
Directors: N. Shedlock (Prop)
Date established: 1993 **No.of Employees:** 1 - 10 **Product Groups:** 36, 40

C S C Crop Protection Ltd
Glenearn Road, Perth, PH2 0NL
Tel: 01738-623201 **Fax:** 01738-630360
E-mail: sales@csccrop.co.uk
Website: http://www.csccrop.co.uk
Bank(s): Bank of Scotland
Directors: A. Watt (Ch), S. Drake (Co Sec), J. Watt (Non Exec)
Managers: M. Officer (), M. Officer
Ultimate Holding Company: ARYZTA AG (SWITZERLAND)
Immediate Holding Company: CSC CROP PROTECTION LIMITED
Registration no: SC153036 **VAT No.:** GB 268 7804 13
Date established: 1994 **Turnover:** £20m - £50m
No.of Employees: 101 - 250 **Product Groups:** 30, 32

Date of Accounts	Jun 08	Jun 07	Jun 06
Sales Turnover	35081	27908	22351
Pre Tax Profit/Loss	2482	1105	738
Working Capital	2586	1387	959
Fixed Assets	2539	2481	2119
Current Assets	20305	14227	12178
Current Liabilities	17718	12840	11219
Total Share Capital	307	307	307
ROCE% (Return on Capital Employed)	48.4	28.6	24.0
ROT% (Return on Turnover)	7.1	4.0	3.3

Diatech Scotland
Target House Ruthvenfield Road, Inveralmond Industrial Estate, Perth, PH1 3EE
Tel: 01738-444606 **Fax:** 01738-621155
E-mail: sales@diatechscotland.co.uk
Website: http://www.diatechscotland.co.uk
Managers: R. Burgess
Immediate Holding Company: DIATECH SCOTLAND
Registration no: SC355888 **Date established:** 2009
No.of Employees: 1 - 10 **Product Groups:** 33, 36

Edrington Group
West Kinfauns Kinfauns, Perth, PH2 7XZ
Tel: 01738-440000 **Fax:** 01738-493838
E-mail: group@edrington.co.uk
Website: http://www.edringtongroup.com
Directors: B. Farrer (MD), K. Grier (Mkt Research)
Ultimate Holding Company: THE EDRINGTON GROUP LIMITED
Immediate Holding Company: JAMES GRANT & COMPANY (HIGHLAND PARK DISTILLERY) LIMITED
Registration no: SC357426 **Date established:** 1936
No.of Employees: 51 - 100 **Product Groups:** 21, 62

Date of Accounts	Mar 12	Mar 11	Mar 10
Pre Tax Profit/Loss	4m	-90	1m
Working Capital	-6m	-8m	-10m
Fixed Assets	11m	9m	11m
Current Assets	14	4	51
Current Liabilities	3	4	1

Edwards Engineering Perth Ltd
Glenearn Road, Perth, PH2 0NJ
Tel: 01738-627101 **Fax:** 01738-630769
E-mail: mail@edwardsengineering.co.uk
Website: http://www.edwardsengineering.co.uk
Directors: D. Campbell (MD), D. Campbell (MD), A. Kirk (Sales)
Managers: R. Robertson (Buyer), S. Kirk (Mktg Serv Mgr)
Immediate Holding Company: EDWARDS ENGINEERING (PERTH) LIMITED
Registration no: SC046562 **VAT No.:** GB 269 8070 21
Date established: 1969 **Turnover:** £2m - £5m **No.of Employees:** 51 - 100
Product Groups: 52

Date of Accounts	Jan 12	Jan 11	Jan 10
Sales Turnover	4m	5m	7m
Pre Tax Profit/Loss	-189	576	575
Working Capital	1m	1m	1m
Fixed Assets	784	753	824
Current Assets	2m	3m	3m
Current Liabilities	697	866	1m

Farquhar & Son Ltd
St Andrew Street, Perth, PH2 8HY
Tel: 01738-624173 **Fax:** 01738-630838
E-mail: alistair.mcwilliam@farquhars.net
Website: http://www.farquhars.net
Bank(s): Bank of Scotland
Directors: A. Mcwilliam (Dir)
Immediate Holding Company: FARQUHAR & SON LIMITED
Registration no: SC022380 **Date established:** 1943
Turnover: £500,000 - £1m **No.of Employees:** 11 - 20
Product Groups: 27, 28, 81

Date of Accounts	Mar 12	Mar 11	Mar 10
Working Capital	117	120	134
Fixed Assets	277	317	327
Current Assets	200	248	255

Firesafe Consultancy Ltd
80 Spoutwells Drive Scone, Perth, PH2 6PQ
Tel: 01738-551106 **Fax:** 01738-551106
E-mail: mark@firesafe-consultancy.co.uk
Website: http://www.firesafe-consultancy.co.uk
Directors: P. Ross (Fin), M. Ross (MD)
Immediate Holding Company: FIRESAFE CONSULTANCY LIMITED
Registration no: SC247276 **Date established:** 2003
No.of Employees: 1 - 10 **Product Groups:** 38, 42

Date of Accounts	Jun 11	Jun 09	Jun 08
Working Capital	3	5	22
Fixed Assets	20	9	12
Current Assets	22	21	30

Gillies & Mackay
East Inchmichael Farm Errol, Perth, PH2 7SP
Tel: 01821-642713 **Fax:** 01821-642996
E-mail: grant@gilliesandmackay.com
Website: http://www.gilliesandmackay.com
Directors: G. Gillies (Ptnr)
No.of Employees: 11 - 20 **Product Groups:** 25, 35, 41, 66

Graham
Arran Road, Perth, PH1 3DZ
Tel: 01738-629231 **Fax:** 01738-441568
E-mail: kevin.mcgregor@graham-group.co.uk
Website: http://www.graham-group.co.uk
Directors: K. McGregor (Dir)
Ultimate Holding Company: NORTHERN PRODUCTS (SCOTLAND) LIMITED
Immediate Holding Company: ARRAN ESTATES LIMITED
Registration no: 04076768 **Date established:** 1985
No.of Employees: 1 - 10 **Product Groups:** 66

Date of Accounts	Aug 11	Aug 10	Aug 09
Working Capital	-14	-19	-18
Fixed Assets	12	13	14
Current Assets	62	48	39

Hydro Static Extrusions Ltd
Arran Road North Muirton Industrial Estate, Perth, PH1 3DX
Tel: 01738-494500 **Fax:** 01738-633933
E-mail: sales@hydrostatic.co.uk
Website: http://www.hydrostatic.co.uk
Directors: D. Wheeler (Dir)
Ultimate Holding Company: BRUKER CORPORATION (USA)
Immediate Holding Company: HYDROSTATIC EXTRUSIONS LIMITED
Registration no: 02667044 **Date established:** 1991 **Turnover:** £1m - £2m
No.of Employees: 11 - 20 **Product Groups:** 34, 35, 37, 46, 48, 67

Date of Accounts	Dec 11	Dec 10	Dec 09
Sales Turnover	3m	2m	1m
Pre Tax Profit/Loss	229	34	-241
Working Capital	1m	-242	-289
Fixed Assets	71	66	86
Current Assets	1m	1m	899
Current Liabilities	156	84	23

I & H Brown Ltd
PO Box 51, Perth, PH1 3YD
Tel: 01738-637171 **Fax:** 01738-637175
E-mail: enquiries@ihbrown.com
Website: http://www.ihbrown.com
Bank(s): The Royal Bank of Scotland
Directors: S. Brown (MD), L. Campbell (Fin)
Managers: R. Douglas (Tech Serv Mgr), I. Munro (Est)
Immediate Holding Company: I. & H. BROWN LIMITED
Registration no: SC040891 **VAT No.:** GB 268 3196 30
Date established: 1964 **Turnover:** £20m - £50m
No.of Employees: 51 - 100 **Product Groups:** 51, 72

Date of Accounts	Aug 08	Aug 09	Aug 10
Sales Turnover	38m	29m	36m
Pre Tax Profit/Loss	2m	1m	313
Working Capital	10m	14m	13m
Fixed Assets	17m	16m	16m
Current Assets	26m	30m	32m
Current Liabilities	9m	10m	10m

Jewson Ltd
Glenearn Road, Perth, PH2 0NJ
Tel: 01738-635386 **Fax:** 01738-639834
E-mail: perth445sales@jewson.co.uk
Website: http://www.jewson.co.uk
Directors: P. Hindle (MD)
Managers: A. Patterson (District Mgr)
Ultimate Holding Company: COMPAGNIE DE SAINT GOBAIN (FRANCE)
Immediate Holding Company: JEWSON LIMITED
Registration no: 00348407 **VAT No.:** GB 394 1212 63
Date established: 1939 **Turnover:** £2m - £5m **No.of Employees:** 1 - 10
Product Groups: 66

Date of Accounts	Dec 11	Dec 10	Dec 09
Sales Turnover	1606m	1547m	1485m
Pre Tax Profit/Loss	18m	100m	45m
Working Capital	-345m	-250m	-349m
Fixed Assets	496m	387m	461m
Current Assets	657m	1005m	1320m
Current Liabilities	66m	120m	64m

Johnson Apparelmaster
1 Ruthvenfield Road, Perth, PH1 3SW
Tel: 01738-623456 **Fax:** 01738-635160
E-mail: janicespence@johnsonplc.com
Website: http://www.apparelmaster.co.uk
Bank(s): Clydesdale Bank PLC
Managers: A. Smith, J. Spence (Sales Admin)
Ultimate Holding Company: JOHNSON SERVICE GROUP PLC
Immediate Holding Company: JOHNSON WORKPLACE MANAGEMENT SCOTLAND LIMITED
Registration no: SC153070 **Date established:** 1994 **Turnover:** £2m - £5m
No.of Employees: 101 - 250 **Product Groups:** 23

Date of Accounts	Dec 04
Working Capital	1m
Current Assets	1m

Kerr Compressor Engineers
Unit 15c Riverview Business Park Friarton Road, Perth, PH2 8DF
Tel: 01738-631427 **Fax:** 01738-630136
E-mail: roy@kerrcompressors.co.uk
Website: http://www.kerrcompressors.co.uk
Directors: R. Coull (Sales)
Immediate Holding Company: GREENER TIMES PUBLISHING LTD
Date established: 2011 **No.of Employees:** 21 - 50 **Product Groups:** 28, 40, 83

Date of Accounts	Mar 09	Mar 08	Jun 11
Working Capital	-111	-115	-108
Fixed Assets	115	115	115
Current Assets	4	N/A	7

Logsnstuff
3a moncreiffe terrace craigie, Perth, PH2 0DB
Tel: 01738-626053 **Fax:** 01738-626053
E-mail: steven@logsnstuff.com
Website: http://www.logsnstuff.com
Directors: S. Laing (Prop)
Date established: 2006 **Turnover:** Up to £250,000
No.of Employees: 1 - 10 **Product Groups:** 25, 66

Margaret Morrison
Unit 7 Ruthvenfield Grove, Perth, PH1 3GL
Tel: 01738-630103 **Fax:** 01738-63105
E-mail: sales@morrison-sporrans.co.uk
Website: http://www.morrison-sporrans.co.uk
Directors: G. Whyte (Dir)
Immediate Holding Company: UNDERFLOOR HEATING MERCHANTS LIMITED
Registration no: SC251857 **Date established:** 2005
No.of Employees: 1 - 10 **Product Groups:** 23, 30, 35, 63

Date of Accounts	Apr 12	Apr 11	Apr 10
Working Capital	252	196	198
Fixed Assets	18	15	14
Current Assets	648	515	364

Mcewens Of Perth
56 St John Street, Perth, PH1 5SN
Tel: 01738-623444 **Fax:** 01738-620564
E-mail: mail@mcewensofperth.co.uk
Website: http://www.mcewensofperth.com
Bank(s): Royal Bank of Scotland
Directors: J. Bullough (MD), J. Bullocgh (Fin), G. Gilfillan (Fin)
Managers: V. Harden (Buyer), G. Bullough (Mktg Serv Mgr), J. Cleisham (Personnel)
Ultimate Holding Company: MCEWENS DIRECT LIMITED
Immediate Holding Company: MCEWENS OF PERTH LIMITED
Registration no: SC046297 **Date established:** 1969
Turnover: £5m - £10m **No.of Employees:** 101 - 250 **Product Groups:** 32, 63

Date of Accounts	Jan 09	Jan 10	Jan 11
Working Capital	172	172	172
Current Assets	172	172	172

Ontop Tractors
Balgowan Tibbermore, Perth, PH1 1QP
Tel: 01738-730341 **Fax:** 01738-730258
E-mail: ontop@fwi.co.uk
Website: http://www.ontoptractors.co.uk
Directors: I. Gillon (Dir)
Immediate Holding Company: ONTOP TRACTORS LIMITED
Registration no: SC059965 **Date established:** 1976
Turnover: £250,000 - £500,000 **No.of Employees:** 1 - 10
Product Groups: 41

Date of Accounts	Nov 11	Nov 10	Nov 09
Working Capital	-61	-65	-57
Fixed Assets	47	47	48

see next page

Ontop Tractors - Cont'd

Current Assets	40	70	62
Current Liabilities	18	N/A	18

W & D Peddie Ltd
284 High Street, Perth, PH1 5QS
Tel: 01738-621449 **Fax:** 01738-629232
E-mail: sales@peddies.co.uk
Directors: A. Borthwick (MD)
Immediate Holding Company: W & D PEDDIE LIMITED
Registration no: SC046791 **VAT No.:** GB 268 7052 34
Date established: 1969 **Turnover:** £1m - £2m **No.of Employees:** 11 - 20
Product Groups: 66

Date of Accounts	Dec 11	Dec 10	Dec 09
Working Capital	357	382	393
Fixed Assets	76	78	82
Current Assets	436	454	455

G Reekie Group Ltd
Ruthvenfield Road Inveralmond Industrial Estate, Perth, PH1 3EE
Tel: 01738-622471 **Fax:** 01738-639613
E-mail: info@reekiegroup.wannadoo.co.uk
Website: http://www.reekie.co.uk
Directors: S. Mercer (Sales)
Immediate Holding Company: G. REEKIE GROUP LIMITED
Registration no: SC041230 **Date established:** 1964
Turnover: £10m - £20m **No.of Employees:** 11 - 20 **Product Groups:** 45

Date of Accounts	Dec 11	Dec 10	Dec 09
Sales Turnover	14m	12m	10m
Pre Tax Profit/Loss	16	38	-25
Working Capital	2m	2m	1m
Fixed Assets	972	955	950
Current Assets	4m	3m	3m
Current Liabilities	685	610	496

Ritchie Engineering
Fairfield Guildtown, Perth, PH2 6AE
Tel: 01738-550005
E-mail: info@fairfieldtechnologies.co.uk
Website: http://www.yellowjacket.com
Managers: N. Stuart (Mgr)
No.of Employees: 1 - 10 **Product Groups:** 40, 46, 67

Sandvik
Ruthvenfield Road Inveralmond Industrial Estate, Perth, PH1 3ED
Tel: 01738-493300 **Fax:** 01738-493301
E-mail: harry.furuberg@kanthal.se
Website: http://www.kanthal.com
Bank(s): Clydesdale Bank PLC
Directors: M. McIver (Co Sec), M. Mciber (MD)
Managers: K. Harpering (Sales Prom), L. Bell (Purch Mgr), G. Peden (Personnel), R. Jackson (Comptroller), D. Whyte
Ultimate Holding Company: SANDVIK AB (SWEDEN)
Immediate Holding Company: SANDVIK MATERIALS TECHNOLOGY UK LIMITED
Registration no: SC032614 **VAT No.:** GB 263 3005 93
Date established: 1957 **Turnover:** £20m - £50m
No.of Employees: 101 - 250 **Product Groups:** 33, 37, 40

Date of Accounts	Dec 11	Dec 10	Dec 09
Sales Turnover	39m	36m	31m
Pre Tax Profit/Loss	2m	4m	3m
Working Capital	11m	7m	4m
Fixed Assets	3m	4m	4m
Current Assets	26m	22m	18m
Current Liabilities	4m	4m	4m

Scottish Salmon Producers Organisation Ltd
Durn Isla Road, Perth, PH2 7HG
Tel: 01738-587000 **Fax:** 01738-621454
E-mail: enquiries@scottishsalmon.co.uk
Website: http://www.scottishsalmon.co.uk
Managers: L. Drane (Sales Admin)
Immediate Holding Company: SCOTTISH SALMON PRODUCERS ORGANISATION LIMITED
Registration no: SC152347 **Date established:** 1994
Turnover: Up to £250,000 **No.of Employees:** 1 - 10 **Product Groups:** 09, 20, 62, 84, 85, 87

Date of Accounts	Dec 11	Dec 10	Dec 09
Working Capital	73	74	73
Fixed Assets	26	19	19
Current Assets	517	389	598

Scottish & Southern Energy P.L.C. Energy Sales
Inveralmond House 200 Dunkeld Road, Perth, PH1 3AQ
Tel: 01738-456000 **Fax:** 01256-304269
E-mail: marketing.enquiries@sse.com
Website: http://www.sse.com
Bank(s): National Westminster Bank Plc
Directors: G. Alexander (Fin), I. Marchant (Grp Chief Exec), R. Smith (Ch)
Managers: A. Phillips-Davies, C. Hood
Registration no: SC117119 **VAT No.:** GB 527 1558 42
Turnover: Over £1,000m **No.of Employees:** 1501 & over
Product Groups: 13, 18, 37

Scottish & Southern Energy plc
Inveralmond House 200 Dunkeld Road, Perth, PH1 3AQ
Tel: 0800-0727282 **Fax:** 01738-456520
E-mail: info@scottish-southern.co.uk
Website: http://www.sse.com
Bank(s): National Westminster
Directors: H. Casley (Non Exec), I. Marchant (Grp Chief Exec), T. Keeling (I.T. Dir), R. Smith (Ch)
Managers: N. Bibby (Mktg Serv Mgr)
Registration no: SC117119 **VAT No.:** GB 553 7696 03
Date established: 1989 **Turnover:** Over £1,000m
No.of Employees: 1501 & over **Product Groups:** 18

Date of Accounts	Mar 08	Mar 07	Mar 06
Sales Turnover	15256m	11867m	10145m
Pre Tax Profit/Loss	1084m	1132m	896900
Working Capital	-1555m	-206800	-445300
Fixed Assets	8622m	6303m	6145m
Current Assets	5354m	2762m	2035m
Current Liabilities	6909m	2969m	2480m
Total Share Capital	435100	431000	430200
ROCE% (Return on Capital Employed)	15.3	18.6	15.7
ROT% (Return on Turnover)	7.1	9.5	8.8

Stagecoach Bus
10 Dunkeld Road, Perth, PH1 5TW
Tel: 01738-442111 **Fax:** 01738-643648
E-mail: info@stagecoachgroup.com
Website: http://www.stagecoachgroup.com
Bank(s): Bank of Scotland
Directors: A. Whitnall (Co Sec), A. Smith (Tech Serv)
Managers: M. Griffiths
Ultimate Holding Company: STAGECOACH GROUP PLC
Immediate Holding Company: STAGECOACH HOLDINGS LIMITED
Registration no: SC212093 **VAT No.:** GB 435 7578 19
Date established: 2000 **Turnover:** £10m - £20m
No.of Employees: 251 - 500 **Product Groups:** 72

Date of Accounts	Apr 12	Apr 11	Apr 10
Sales Turnover	21m	18m	20m
Pre Tax Profit/Loss	-6m	-4m	-5m
Working Capital	5m	10m	-9m
Fixed Assets	2m	N/A	N/A
Current Assets	21m	21m	14m

Strathmore
Arran Road, Perth, PH1 3DZ
Tel: 01738-622156 **Fax:** 01738-621010
E-mail: sales@strathmoreonline.co.uk
Website: http://www.strathmoreonline.co.uk
Bank(s): Royal Bank of Scotland
Directors: D. Cameron (Dir), J. Cameron (Fin), N. Leishman (Sales)
Ultimate Holding Company: IAN H. CAMERON LIMITED
Immediate Holding Company: STRATHMORE MOTORS LIMITED
Registration no: SC163407 **VAT No.:** GB 269 5556 10
Date established: 1996 **No.of Employees:** 21 - 50 **Product Groups:** 68

Tayside Contracts
Collace Quarry Collace, Perth, PH2 6JB
Tel: 01821-650222 **Fax:** 01821-650440
E-mail: john.mccormick@tayside-contracts.co.uk
Website: http://www.tayside-contracts.co.uk
Managers: J. Mccormick
Immediate Holding Company: D AND M CONTRACTORS (PERTHSHIRE) LIMITED
Registration no: SC078458 **Date established:** 1982
No.of Employees: 11 - 20 **Product Groups:** 31, 33, 66

Date of Accounts	Mar 11	Mar 10	Mar 09
Working Capital	26	76	67
Fixed Assets	17	22	15
Current Assets	73	106	129

Wilks Bros
Murthly, Perth, PH1 4HG
Tel: 01738-710381 **Fax:** 01738-710581
Directors: W. Wilks (Ptnr)
Date established: 1929 **No.of Employees:** 1 - 10 **Product Groups:** 41

Aberdeenshire

Peterhead

Ashgrove Trading
Dales Industrial Estate, Peterhead, AB42 3JF
Tel: 01779-470606
E-mail: info@ashgrovetrading.com
Website: http://www.ashgrovetrading.com
Directors: G. Smith (Prop)
No.of Employees: 1 - 10 **Product Groups:** 28, 32

Metal Art Co.
Cadgerhill Glendaveny, Peterhead, AB42 3DY
Tel: 01779-838888 **Fax:** 01779-838333
Directors: R. Cowie (Ptnr)
Date established: 1998 **No.of Employees:** 1 - 10 **Product Groups:** 26, 35

Smiths Of Peter Head
Buchan Blaes Boddam, Peterhead, AB42 3AR
Tel: 01779-871400 **Fax:** 01779-478989
E-mail: marian@smithsofpeterhead.com
Website: http://www.smithsofpeterhead.com
Bank(s): Clydesdale
Directors: C. Rodland (Sales & Mktg), M. Shildrick (MD)
Immediate Holding Company: SMITHS OF PETERHEAD LIMITED
Registration no: SC279416 **VAT No.:** 266 6710 39 **Date established:** 2005
Turnover: £5m - £10m **No.of Employees:** 21 - 50 **Product Groups:** 66

Date of Accounts	Jul 08	Mar 08	Mar 07
Working Capital	150	178	237
Fixed Assets	490	440	425
Current Assets	1430	1370	1399
Current Liabilities	1280	1192	1162
Total Share Capital	120	120	120

Transmission Engineering
Unit 1 Albert Street, Peterhead, AB42 1ZW
Tel: 01779-480481 **Fax:** 01779-480481
E-mail: info@tesl-phd.com
Website: http://www.tesl-phd.com
Directors: E. Finnie (Dir)
Immediate Holding Company: TRANSMISSION ENGINEERING (SCOTLAND) LTD
Registration no: SC270341 **Date established:** 2004
No.of Employees: 1 - 10 **Product Groups:** 48

Date of Accounts	Jun 10	Jun 09	Jun 08
Working Capital	-5	-4	-3
Fixed Assets	22	24	11
Current Assets	51	65	30

Ugie Salmon
The Fish House Golf Road, Peterhead, AB42 1LS
Tel: 01779-476209 **Fax:** 01779-471475
E-mail: sales@ugie-salmon.co.uk
Website: http://www.ugie-salmon.co.uk
Managers: J. Yule (Mgr)
Registration no: SC352849 **Date established:** 2008
No.of Employees: 1 - 10 **Product Groups:** 20

Perthshire

Pitlochry

Gelplane International Ltd
5 Sawmill Yard Blair Atholl, Pitlochry, PH18 5TL
Tel: 01796-482104 **Fax:** 01796-482111
E-mail: sales@gelplane.co.uk
Website: http://www.gelplane.co.uk
Directors: C. Coruthers (MD)
Managers: E. Philips (Mgr)
No.of Employees: 1 - 10 **Product Groups:** 40, 41, 67

Rannoch Smokery
Kinloch Rannoch, Pitlochry, PH16 5QD
Tel: 01796-472194 **Fax:** 08701-601558
E-mail: enquiries@rannochsmokery.co.uk
Website: http://www.rannochsmokery.co.uk
Directors: R. Barclay (Prop)
Turnover: £500,000 - £1m **No.of Employees:** 11 - 20 **Product Groups:** 20

Simply Control Ltd
Saw Mill Yard Blair Atholl, Pitlochry, PH18 5TL
Tel: 01796-482128
E-mail: info@simplycontrol.com
Website: http://www.simplycontrol.com
Directors: A. Carruthers (MD)
Date established: 1989 **No.of Employees:** 1 - 10 **Product Groups:** 36

Renfrewshire

Port Glasgow

British Metal Treatments Ltd
Block 9 Scottish Industrial Estate, Port Glasgow, PA14 5XR
Tel: 01475-741023 **Fax:** 01475-741241
E-mail: bkenny@ajt-engineering.co.uk
Website: http://www.bmt-fescol-portglasgow.co.uk
Bank(s): Natwest, Maidstone Branch, Kent
Managers: B. Kenny (Mgr)
Ultimate Holding Company: CAMELLIA PUBLIC LIMITED COMPANY
Immediate Holding Company: BRITISH METAL TREATMENTS LIMITED
Registration no: 00616411 **VAT No.:** GB 554 6824 19
Date established: 1958 **Turnover:** £2m - £5m **No.of Employees:** 11 - 20
Product Groups: 34, 46, 48

Date of Accounts	Dec 11	Dec 10	Dec 09
Sales Turnover	1m	1m	1m
Pre Tax Profit/Loss	-16	65	87
Working Capital	1m	1m	1m
Fixed Assets	2m	2m	2m
Current Assets	1m	1m	2m
Current Liabilities	85	99	97

Interlok Packaging Ltd
Block 16 Gareloch Industrial Estate Dubbs Road, Port Glasgow, PA14 5UG
Tel: 01475-707669 **Fax:** 01475-706392
E-mail: david@interlokpackaging.co.uk
Website: http://www.interlokpackaging.co.uk
Directors: D. Shearer (Prop)
Immediate Holding Company: INTERLOK PACKAGING LTD.
Registration no: SC307293 **Date established:** 2006
No.of Employees: 51 - 100 **Product Groups:** 66

Date of Accounts	Jun 11	Jun 10	Jun 09
Working Capital	-106	-185	-199
Fixed Assets	238	280	303
Current Assets	855	725	768

Lithgow Ltd
Langbank, Port Glasgow, PA14 6YG
Tel: 01475-540692 **Fax:** 01475-540558
E-mail: enquiries@lithgows.co.uk
Website: http://www.lithgows.co.uk
Bank(s): Bank of Scotland
Directors: A. Wishart (Fin)
Immediate Holding Company: LITHGOWS LIMITED
Registration no: SC010170 **Date established:** 2018
Turnover: £5m - £10m **No.of Employees:** 101 - 250 **Product Groups:** 09, 35, 84

Date of Accounts	Dec 11	Dec 10	Dec 09
Sales Turnover	6m	8m	8m
Pre Tax Profit/Loss	295	-3m	478
Working Capital	4m	7m	12m
Fixed Assets	6m	5m	10m
Current Assets	6m	12m	16m
Current Liabilities	2m	4m	3m

Mclaren Packaging Ltd
Block 4 Gareloch Road Industrial Estate Gareloch Road, Port Glasgow, PA14 5XH
Tel: 01475-745246 **Fax:** 01475-744446
E-mail: sales@mclarenpackaging.com
Website: http://www.mclarenpackaging.com
Directors: J. Mclaren (MD)
Managers: E. Sheard (Personnel), C. Hazel
Immediate Holding Company: MCLAREN PACKAGING LIMITED
Registration no: SC068174 **Date established:** 1979
Turnover: £5m - £10m **No.of Employees:** 21 - 50 **Product Groups:** 27

Date of Accounts	Feb 11	Feb 10	Feb 09
Sales Turnover	10m	8m	8m
Pre Tax Profit/Loss	1m	801	691
Working Capital	481	261	-136
Fixed Assets	9m	9m	8m
Current Assets	3m	3m	3m
Current Liabilities	2m	1m	1m

Playtex Ltd
Unit D Park Industrial Estate Gareloch Road, Port Glasgow, PA14 5XH
Tel: 01475-741631 **Fax:** 01475-743119
E-mail: dougie.bratt@dbaeu.com
Website: http://www.playtex.co.uk
Bank(s): Clydesdale

Directors: D. Bratt (Co Sec), T. Wood (Fin), S. Holbrook (Mkt Research), M. Hooper (Sales), E. Clyne (Sales), Wood (Fin), M. Daly (Pers)
Managers: G. Milby (Tech Serv Mgr), J. Nolan (Mktg Serv Mgr), A. Douglas (Personnel), G. Milby (I.T. Exec)
Ultimate Holding Company: TRAVEL CORPORATION LIMITED (BRITISH VIRGIN ISLANDS)
Immediate Holding Company: INSIGHT INTERNATIONAL TOURS LIMITED
Registration no: 00552438 **VAT No.:** 428 2608 50 **Date established:** 1978
Turnover: £20m - £50m **No.of Employees:** 251 - 500 **Product Groups:** 24

Date of Accounts	Dec 10	Dec 09	Dec 08
Sales Turnover	N/A	4m	6m
Pre Tax Profit/Loss	-26	56	331
Working Capital	916	1m	1m
Fixed Assets	N/A	3	4
Current Assets	986	1m	3m
Current Liabilities	8	175	2m

Sangamo Ltd
Auchenfoil Road, Port Glasgow, PA14 5XG
Tel: 01475-745131 **Fax:** 01475-744567
E-mail: enquiries@sangamo.co.uk
Website: http://www.sangamo.co.uk
Bank(s): Bank of Scotland
Directors: M. Robinson (MD), J. Murdoch (Co Sec)
Managers: D. McGhee, K. Miller (Develop Mgr)
Immediate Holding Company: SANGAMO LIMITED
Registration no: 04494864 **Date established:** 2002 **Turnover:** £2m - £5m
No.of Employees: 11 - 20 **Product Groups:** 37, 38, 39, 40, 49, 65, 67

Date of Accounts	Dec 11	Dec 10	Dec 09
Working Capital	1m	1m	1m
Fixed Assets	62	117	226
Current Assets	2m	2m	2m

Isle of Skye

Portree

Castle Keep
1 Creag An Iolaire, Portree, IV51 9HN
Tel: 01478-612114
Directors: R. Miller (Prop)
Date established: 1991 **No.of Employees:** 1 - 10 **Product Groups:** 36, 40

Jewson Ltd
Dunvegan Road, Portree, IV51 9HQ
Tel: 01478-613222 **Fax:** 01478-613266
Website: http://www.jewson.co.uk
Directors: B. Dunlop (MD)
Managers: H. Corrigall (District Mgr), W. Burge (Mgr)
Ultimate Holding Company: COMPAGNIE DE SAINT GOBAIN (FRANCE)
Immediate Holding Company: JEWSON LIMITED
Registration no: 00348407 **Date established:** 1939
Turnover: Up to £250,000 **No.of Employees:** 1 - 10 **Product Groups:** 66

Date of Accounts	Dec 11	Dec 10	Dec 09
Sales Turnover	1606m	1547m	1485m
Pre Tax Profit/Loss	18m	100m	45m
Working Capital	-345m	-250m	-349m
Fixed Assets	496m	387m	461m
Current Assets	657m	1005m	1320m
Current Liabilities	66m	120m	64m

Vacman Specialist Cleaning
Budmhor, Portree, IV51 9DJ
Tel: 01478-613111 **Fax:** 01478-613321
E-mail: info@vacman.co.uk
Website: http://www.vacman.co.uk
Directors: N. Montgomery (MD)
Immediate Holding Company: Vacman Cleaning Ltd
Registration no: SC249555 **Date established:** 2003
Turnover: £500,000 - £1m **No.of Employees:** 101 - 250
Product Groups: 23, 30, 32, 39, 40, 44, 46, 48, 51, 52, 54, 71, 74

Ayrshire

Prestwick

G E Caledonian Ltd
Shawfarm Industrial Estate Monument Cresent, Prestwick, KA9 2RX
Tel: 01292-673000 **Fax:** 01292-673001
E-mail: d.crews@ae.ge.com
Website: http://www.ge.com
Directors: S. Henderson (Dir), B. McAlister (Co Sec)
Ultimate Holding Company: GENERAL ELECTRIC COMPANY (USA)
Immediate Holding Company: GE CALEDONIAN LIMITED
Registration no: SC064580 **Date established:** 1978
Turnover: £500m - £1,000m **No.of Employees:** 501 - 1000
Product Groups: 39

Date of Accounts	Dec 06
Sales Turnover	730750
Pre Tax Profit/Loss	32200
Working Capital	220550
Fixed Assets	36040
Current Assets	347160
Current Liabilities	126610
Total Share Capital	28560
ROCE% (Return on Capital Employed)	12.5

Gavin Lawrie Surfacing Ltd
207 Main Street, Prestwick, KA9 1LH
Tel: 01292-479226 **Fax:** 01292-474801
Website: http://www.gavinlawrie.com
Bank(s): The Royal Bank of Scotland
Directors: E. Mckellar (MD)
Immediate Holding Company: GAVIN LAWRIE (SURFACING) LIMITED
Registration no: SC050824 **VAT No.:** 262 8396 33 **Date established:** 1972
Turnover: £1m - £2m **No.of Employees:** 11 - 20 **Product Groups:** 14, 52

Date of Accounts	Sep 11	Sep 10	Sep 09
Working Capital	384	362	392
Fixed Assets	135	166	214
Current Assets	665	562	619

Glasgow Prestwick Airport Parking
Aviation House Glasgow Prestwick Intnl Airport, Prestwick, KA9 2PL
Tel: 08701-181844 **Fax:** 01292-511120
E-mail: sales@upia.co.uk
Website: http://www.glasgowprestwick.com
Managers: A. Fleming (Mgr)
Ultimate Holding Company: INFRATIL LTD (NEW ZEALAND)
Immediate Holding Company: GLASGOW PRESTWICK AIRPORT LIMITED
Registration no: SC135362 **Date established:** 1991
Turnover: £10m - £20m **No.of Employees:** 1 - 10 **Product Groups:** 71

Date of Accounts	Mar 11	Mar 10	Mar 09
Sales Turnover	13m	14m	18m
Pre Tax Profit/Loss	-7m	-4m	-6m
Working Capital	-20m	-15m	-12m
Fixed Assets	4m	6m	8m
Current Assets	24m	19m	39m
Current Liabilities	3m	3m	3m

Rainbow Glass Studios
14 Shaw Road, Prestwick, KA9 2LN
Tel: 01292-474279 **Fax:** 01292-471426
E-mail: info@rainbowglass.biz
Website: http://www.rainbowglass.biz
Directors: M. Malcolm (Prop)
Immediate Holding Company: RAINBOW GLASS STUDIO LIMITED
Registration no: SC257693 **Date established:** 2003
No.of Employees: 1 - 10 **Product Groups:** 40, 45, 46

Date of Accounts	Nov 11	Nov 10	Nov 09
Working Capital	-21	29	22
Fixed Assets	246	32	34
Current Assets	175	203	93

Tool-Care UK Ltd
Muirhouse Building Kilmarnock Road, Monkton, Prestwick, KA9 2RJ
Tel: 01292-474557 **Fax:** 01292-474040
E-mail: sales@tool-care.com
Website: http://www.tool-care.com
Directors: J. Derwent (MD)
Immediate Holding Company: TOOL-CARE (UK) LTD
Registration no: SC400945 **Date established:** 2011
No.of Employees: 1 - 10 **Product Groups:** 36

Renfrewshire

Renfrew

Bray Controls UK Ltd
16-18 Fountain Crescent Inchinnan, Renfrew, PA4 9RE
Tel: 0141-812 5199 **Fax:** 0141-812 6199
E-mail: george.crooks@bray.com
Website: http://www.bray.com
Directors: G. Crooks (Dir), C. Brown (Fin)
Managers: J. Mallon (Mktg Serv Mgr), V. Taylor (Tech Serv Mgr), P. Gallagher (Comptroller), D. Dearie (Buyer)
Ultimate Holding Company: BRAY INTERNATIONAL INC (USA)
Immediate Holding Company: BRAY CONTROLS (UK) LIMITED
Registration no: SC163206 **Date established:** 1996
Turnover: £10m - £20m **No.of Employees:** 21 - 50 **Product Groups:** 36, 38

Date of Accounts	Dec 11	Dec 10	Dec 09
Sales Turnover	11m	9m	8m
Pre Tax Profit/Loss	417	374	592
Working Capital	3m	3m	4m
Fixed Assets	2m	2m	2m
Current Assets	6m	5m	5m
Current Liabilities	326	247	269

Brown Street Coachbuilders
Unit 3-4 Brown Street, Renfrew, PA4 8HW
Tel: 0141-885 1818 **Fax:** 0141-885 1818
Directors: M. Wilson (Prop)
Date established: 1982 **Turnover:** Up to £250,000
No.of Employees: 1 - 10 **Product Groups:** 39

Eclipse Blind Systems
10 Fountain Crescent Inchinnan Business Park, Inchinnan, Renfrew, PA4 9RE
Tel: 0141-812 3322 **Fax:** 0141-812 5253
E-mail: info@eclipse-blinds.co.uk
Website: http://www.eclipse-blinds.co.uk
Bank(s): The Royal Bank of Scotland
Directors: M. Dempsey (Fin)
Managers: L. Hamilton, D. Orr (Mktg Serv Mgr), R. Calvert (Buyer), J. Jeffery (I.T. Exec), M. Sloan (Personnel)
Registration no: SC047712 **No.of Employees:** 101 - 250
Product Groups: 24, 35, 36

Gormac Coachworks
5 Thomson Street, Renfrew, PA4 8HQ
Tel: 0141-886 4072 **Fax:** 0141-885 2821
E-mail: bodyshop@gormaccoachworks.com
Website: http://www.gormaccoachworks.com
Bank(s): The Royal Bank of Scotland
Directors: G. Mcintyre (Dir), M. McIntyre (Fin)
Immediate Holding Company: GORMAC COACHWORKS LTD.
Registration no: SC246029 **VAT No.:** GB 264 0294 69
Date established: 2003 **Turnover:** Up to £250,000
No.of Employees: 11 - 20 **Product Groups:** 39

Date of Accounts	Apr 11	Apr 10	Apr 09
Working Capital	5	19	-48
Fixed Assets	269	304	324
Current Assets	128	186	132

MML Ltd
30 Fountain Crescent Inchinnan Business Park, Inchinnan, Renfrew, PA4 9RE
Tel: 0141-814 6550 **Fax:** 0141-814 6554
E-mail: sales@m-m-l.com
Website: http://www.mmlmarine.com
Managers: S. Gray (Sales Prom Mgr)
Registration no: 04303020 **Date established:** 1987 **Turnover:** £2m - £5m
No.of Employees: 51 - 100 **Product Groups:** 35, 69

Reekie Machining Ltd (David Reekie & Son)
Inchinnan Business Park South Street, Inchinnan, Renfrew, PA4 9RL
Tel: 0141-812 0411 **Fax:** 0141-812 0137
E-mail: info@reekiemachining.co.uk
Website: http://www.reekiemachining.co.uk
Bank(s): Clydesdale Bank PLC
Directors: L. Reekie (Fin), J. Reekie (Dir), C. Reekie (MD)
Managers: A. Blakey (Tech Serv Mgr), C. McIlroy (Ops Mgr)
Immediate Holding Company: REEKIE MACHINING LIMITED
Registration no: SC145110 **Date established:** 1993 **Turnover:** £2m - £5m
No.of Employees: 21 - 50 **Product Groups:** 34, 36, 37, 38, 39, 44, 45, 46, 47, 48, 54, 67, 84

Renfrew Motor Engineers
Unit 2 Brown Street, Renfrew, PA4 8HW
Tel: 0141-886 6667 **Fax:** 0141-561 1019
Managers: A. Ayr (Mgr)
VAT No.: GB 498 6162 92 **No.of Employees:** 1 - 10 **Product Groups:** 39

Skandiaverken Ltd
PO Box 31, Renfrew, PA4 9RW
Tel: 0141-812 8121 **Fax:** 0141-812 8124
E-mail: spares@skvuk.com
Website: http://www.skandiaverken.com
Bank(s): Barclays
Directors: S. Bannerman (Fin)
Managers: F. Hellweag (Sales Prom Mgr), F. Hellweg (Sales Prom Mgr), F. Crawford (Purch Mgr), A. Watt (Personnel)
Ultimate Holding Company: NEW SKV LLC (DELAWARE)
Immediate Holding Company: SKANDIAVERKEN LTD.
Registration no: SC201669 **VAT No.:** GB 414 3515 83
Date established: 1999 **Turnover:** £5m - £10m **No.of Employees:** 11 - 20
Product Groups: 40

Date of Accounts	Dec 11	Dec 10	Dec 09
Sales Turnover	5m	3m	4m
Pre Tax Profit/Loss	3m	-991	603
Working Capital	3m	3m	4m
Fixed Assets	2m	2m	49
Current Assets	5m	5m	4m
Current Liabilities	259	219	256

Sword Ciboodle
India of Inchinnan Greenock Road Inchinnan, Renfrew, PA4 9LH
Tel: 0141-533 4000 **Fax:** 0141-533 4199
E-mail: info@sword-ciboodle.com
Website: http://www.swordciboodle.com
Directors: M. Hughes (MD)
Ultimate Holding Company: SWORD GROUP SA (FRANCE)
Immediate Holding Company: CIBOODLE LIMITED
Registration no: SC143434 **Date established:** 1993
Turnover: £5m - £10m **No.of Employees:** 101 - 250 **Product Groups:** 44

Date of Accounts	Dec 10	Dec 09	Dec 08
Sales Turnover	10m	16m	12m
Pre Tax Profit/Loss	779	5m	2m
Working Capital	9m	9m	7m
Fixed Assets	2m	1m	900
Current Assets	12m	13m	15m
Current Liabilities	954	3m	4m

Teknek Ltd
River Drive Inchinnan, Renfrew, PA4 9RT
Tel: 0141-568 8100 **Fax:** 0141-568 8101
E-mail: jenniw@teknek.co.uk
Website: http://www.teknek.co.uk
Bank(s): Bank of Scotland
Directors: C. Mackillop (Fin)
Managers: J. Hamill (Purch Mgr), T. Brown (Personnel), A. Pitman (Tech Serv Mgr)
Ultimate Holding Company: ILLINOIS TOOL WORKS INC (USA)
Immediate Holding Company: TEKNEK LIMITED
Registration no: SC102874 **VAT No.:** GB 406 5792 42
Date established: 1987 **Turnover:** £5m - £10m
No.of Employees: 101 - 250 **Product Groups:** 32, 40

Date of Accounts	Dec 11	May 11	May 10
Sales Turnover	7m	12m	8m
Pre Tax Profit/Loss	1m	2m	513
Working Capital	886	-116	1m
Fixed Assets	701	749	185
Current Assets	4m	2m	3m
Current Liabilities	1m	1m	592

V F Intimates Ltd
Block L Westways Business Park Porterfield Road, Renfrew, PA4 8DJ
Tel: 0141-885 4730 **Fax:** 0141-885 4731
E-mail: robert_latter@eu.vfblp.com
Bank(s): Royal Bank of Scotland
Directors: R. Latter (MD)
Immediate Holding Company: ELECTROMAGNETIC COMPATIBILITY CENTRE (PAISLEY) LTD.
Registration no: SC271587 **VAT No.:** GB 259 6463 19
Date established: 2004 **No.of Employees:** 11 - 20 **Product Groups:** 24

Date of Accounts	Aug 11	Aug 10	Aug 09
Working Capital	-48	-43	-38
Fixed Assets	1	1	1
Current Assets	4	25	10

Ayrshire

Saltcoats

C M P
Ardrossan Road, Saltcoats, KA21 5BP
Tel: 01294-603050 **Fax:** 01294-603050
Directors: J. Lindsay (Prop)
Date established: 2003 **No.of Employees:** 1 - 10 **Product Groups:** 46, 48

Lite Systems UK Ltd
58 Dalry Road, Saltcoats, KA21 6LB
Tel: 01475-689138
Directors: C. Cracknell (MD)
Registration no: SC202525 **No.of Employees:** 1 - 10 **Product Groups:** 37, 67

Ro Tech Marine Services Ltd
3 Adair Avenue, Saltcoats, KA21 5QS
Tel: 01294-602521 **Fax:** 01294-602521
Directors: J. Holmes (MD), J. Holmes (Co Sec)
Immediate Holding Company: RO-TECH MARINE SERVICES LIMITED
Registration no: SC202902 **Date established:** 2000
Turnover: Up to £250,000 **No.of Employees:** 1 - 10 **Product Groups:** 35, 39, 45

Date of Accounts	Feb 09	Feb 08	Feb 06
Sales Turnover	N/A	N/A	188
Pre Tax Profit/Loss	N/A	N/A	31
Working Capital	2	1	1
Fixed Assets	1	1	1
Current Assets	49	41	36
Current Liabilities	N/A	N/A	10

Dumfriesshire

Sanquhar

Educational & Municipal Equipment Scotland Ltd
Blackaddie Road, Sanquhar, DG4 6DE
Tel: 01659-50404 **Fax:** 01659-50107
E-mail: info@emefurniture.co.uk
Website: http://www.emefurniture.co.uk
Bank(s): Lloyds TSB Bank plc
Managers: N. Maceachran (Ops Mgr), J. Hutson (Fin Mgr)
Ultimate Holding Company: A & F HOWLAND (WYCOMBE) LTD
VAT No.: GB 208 1730 88 **No.of Employees:** 21 - 50 **Product Groups:** 26

Selkirkshire

Selkirk

R P Adam Ltd
Arpal Works Riverside Road, Selkirk, TD7 5DU
Tel: 01750-21586 **Fax:** 01750-21506
E-mail: salesinfo@rpadam.co.uk
Website: http://www.rpadam.co.uk
Bank(s): Clydesdale
Directors: M. Adam (Mkt Research), G. Adam (Ch)
Managers: P. Chalmers (Buyer), J. Taylor (Comptroller)
Ultimate Holding Company: ADAM INVESTMENT COMPANY LIMITED
Immediate Holding Company: R P ADAM LIMITED
Registration no: SC148256 **VAT No.:** 651 9610 33 **Date established:** 1994
Turnover: £5m - £10m **No.of Employees:** 51 - 100 **Product Groups:** 37, 40, 63, 66

Date of Accounts	Jun 11	Jun 10	Jun 09
Sales Turnover	7m	8m	8m
Pre Tax Profit/Loss	962	2m	-8
Working Capital	227	-401	-665
Fixed Assets	5m	5m	5m
Current Assets	3m	2m	2m
Current Liabilities	1m	1m	1m

Cademuir Toolmaking Ltd
8 Weavers Court Forest Mill, Selkirk, TD7 5NY
Tel: 01750-21050 **Fax:** 01750-22520
E-mail: cademuir@scottishborders.co.uk
Directors: C. Mcmillan (Dir)
Immediate Holding Company: CADEMUIR TOOLMAKING LIMITED
Registration no: SC069993 **Date established:** 1979
Turnover: £500,000 - £1m **No.of Employees:** 21 - 50
Product Groups: 30, 42, 48

Date of Accounts	Dec 11	Dec 10	Dec 09
Working Capital	-45	-25	15
Fixed Assets	663	624	443
Current Assets	587	569	405

Gardiner Of Selkirk Ltd
Riverside Mills Dunsdalehaugh, Selkirk, TD7 5EF
Tel: 01750-20283 **Fax:** 01750-22525
E-mail: sales@gardiner.yarns.co.uk
Directors: S. Henry (Sales), S. Hendry (Sales)
Managers: S. Hendry (Sales Prom Mgr)
Ultimate Holding Company: WORTHINGTON GROUP PLC
Immediate Holding Company: GARDINER OF SELKIRK LIMITED
Registration no: SC007472 **VAT No.:** GB 179 6420 31
Date established: 2010 **Turnover:** £500,000 - £1m
No.of Employees: 1 - 10 **Product Groups:** 23

Date of Accounts	Mar 06	Mar 05	Mar 04
Working Capital	N/A	827	868
Current Assets	N/A	827	868

Shetland Isles

Shetland

Anderson & Co.
The Shetland Warehouse Commercial Street, Lerwick, Shetland, ZE1 0BD
Tel: 01595-693714 **Fax:** 01595-694811
E-mail: info@shetlandknitwear.com
Website: http://www.shetlandknitwear.com
Directors: E. Leask (Ptnr)
VAT No.: GB 265 3208 67 **Date established:** 1873
Turnover: £250,000 - £500,000 **No.of Employees:** 1 - 10
Product Groups: 24, 26, 63

Arch Henderson LLP (Branch Office)
Stuart Building Esplanade, Lerwick, Shetland, ZE1 0LL
Tel: 01595-695512 **Fax:** 01595-694401
E-mail: lerwick@arch-henderson.co.uk
Website: http://www.arch-henderson.co.uk
Managers: A. Sanderson (Mgr)
Immediate Holding Company: ARCH HENDERSON LIMITED LIABILITY PARTNERSHIP
Registration no: SO300202 **VAT No.:** GB 265 4135 63
Date established: 2003 **Turnover:** Up to £250,000
No.of Employees: 1 - 10 **Product Groups:** 84

Date of Accounts	Mar 11	Mar 10	Mar 09
Working Capital	1m	902	774
Fixed Assets	319	393	395
Current Assets	2m	2m	2m

H N P Engineers Ltd
Commercial Road Lerwick, Shetland, ZE1 0NJ
Tel: 01595-692493 **Fax:** 01595-695258
E-mail: hnpengineers@btconnect.com
Directors: I. Walterson (MD)
Immediate Holding Company: H.N.P. ENGINEERS (LERWICK) LIMITED
Registration no: SC056090 **Date established:** 1974
No.of Employees: 11 - 20 **Product Groups:** 35, 36, 39

Date of Accounts	Nov 11	Nov 10	Nov 09
Working Capital	435	362	419
Fixed Assets	66	72	68
Current Assets	520	425	501

Ian Irvine Engineering
Strath Haven Symbister, Whalsay, Shetland, ZE2 9AE
Tel: 01806-566 627 **Fax:** 01806-566220
E-mail: info@iieng.co.uk
Website: http://www.iieng.co.uk
Directors: I. Irvine (Prop)
Date established: 1996 **No.of Employees:** 1 - 10 **Product Groups:** 35, 36, 39

Laurence Odie Knitwear
Hoswick Sandwick, Shetland, ZE2 9HR
Tel: 01950-431215 **Fax:** 01950-431202
E-mail: laurence@odie-knitwear.co.uk
Bank(s): Bank of Scotland
Directors: L. Odie (Prop)
Immediate Holding Company: LAURENCE ODIE (KNITWEAR) LIMITED
Registration no: SC263281 **VAT No.:** GB 260 2091 61
Date established: 2004 **Turnover:** £1m - £2m **No.of Employees:** 11 - 20
Product Groups: 24, 63

Date of Accounts	Jan 12	Jan 11	Jan 10
Working Capital	150	127	85
Fixed Assets	30	35	24
Current Assets	274	233	171
Current Liabilities	24	27	N/A

Malakoff Ltd
North Ness Lerwick, Shetland, ZE1 0LZ
Tel: 01595-695544 **Fax:** 01595-695720
E-mail: enquiries@malakofflimited.co.uk
Website: http://www.malakoff.co.uk
Bank(s): Bank of Scotland
Directors: D. Stevenson (Dir), A. Gould (Dir)
Managers: C. Duncan (Chief Acct), V. Clark (Personnel)
Immediate Holding Company: MALAKOFF LIMITED
Registration no: SC242516 **VAT No.:** 299 2938 87 **Date established:** 2003
Turnover: £2m - £5m **No.of Employees:** 51 - 100 **Product Groups:** 39

Date of Accounts	Dec 11	Dec 10	Dec 09
Working Capital	388	325	273
Fixed Assets	661	690	687
Current Assets	2m	2m	2m
Current Liabilities	78	72	67

Shetland Seafish Ltd
Symbister Whalsay, Shetland, ZE2 9AA
Tel: 01595-696949 **Fax:** 01595-696929
E-mail: info@shetland-seafish.co.uk
Website: http://www.shetlandseafish.co.uk
Directors: J. Tate (MD), V. Leask (Fin), F. Johnson (Prop), V. Leask (Co Sec)
Immediate Holding Company: SHETLAND SEAFISH LTD.
Registration no: SC200595 **Date established:** 1999
Turnover: £5m - £10m **No.of Employees:** 21 - 50 **Product Groups:** 62

Lanarkshire

Shotts

Chocolate Paradise
122 Station Road, Shotts, ML7 4BQ
Tel: 01501-821958
E-mail: bookings@chocolate-paradise.co.uk
Website: http://www.chocolate-paradise.co.uk
Managers: S. Wallace (Chief Acct)
Registration no: 06715111 **Date established:** 2006
No.of Employees: 1 - 10 **Product Groups:** 20

Stove Experience
3 Main Street, Shotts, ML7 5EE
Tel: 01501-823006 **Fax:** 01501-829703
E-mail: eoin@stove-experience.co.uk
Website: http://www.stove-experience.co.uk
Directors: A. Gill (Prop)
No.of Employees: 1 - 10 **Product Groups:** 40, 63, 66, 67

West Lothian

South Queensferry

Advantage Technical Resourcing
Westcott 4 Ferrymuir, South Queensferry, EH30 9QZ
Tel: 0131-331 3030 **Fax:** 0131-331 2518
E-mail: sqf@sgstps.co.uk
Website: http://www.sgstps.co.uk
Directors: J. Forbes (Dir), M. Doubleday (MD), R. Cox (Fin), L. Valence-Bull (Dir), L. Valence Bull (Dir)
Managers: P. Ainsworth (Develop Mgr)
Immediate Holding Company: Societe Generale de Surveillance Holding S.A.
Registration no: 01162072 **VAT No.:** GB 394 6262 23
Turnover: £20m - £50m **No.of Employees:** 1 - 10 **Product Groups:** 80

Arup
Scotstoun House, South Queensferry, EH30 9SE
Tel: 0131-331 1999 **Fax:** 0131-331 3730
E-mail: alan.richmond@arup.com
Website: http://www.arup.com
Directors: A. Richmond (Dir), D. Anderson (Pers), A. Coventry (I.T. Dir)
Ultimate Holding Company: ARUP GROUP LIMITED
Immediate Holding Company: OVE ARUP & PARTNERS SCOTLAND LIMITED
Registration no: SC062237 **Date established:** 1977
No.of Employees: 51 - 100 **Product Groups:** 80

Fife

St Andrews

The Royal & Ancient Golf Club Of St Andrews
Golf Place, St Andrews, KY16 9JD
Tel: 01334-460000 **Fax:** 01334-460001
E-mail: thesecretary@randagc.org
Website: http://www.randa.org
Directors: P. Dawson (Grp Chief Exec)
Immediate Holding Company: THE ROYAL & ANCIENT GOLF CLUB OF ST. ANDREWS TRUST
Registration no: SC102624 **Date established:** 1986
Turnover: £250,000 - £500,000 **No.of Employees:** 51 - 100
Product Groups: 89

Date of Accounts	Dec 11	Dec 10	Dec 09
Sales Turnover	576	645	741
Pre Tax Profit/Loss	34	197	215
Working Capital	620	593	548
Fixed Assets	3m	3m	3m
Current Assets	712	660	649
Current Liabilities	64	46	71

St Andrews Link Trust
Pilmour House, St Andrews, KY16 9SF
Tel: 01334-466666 **Fax:** 01334-479555
E-mail: alanmcgregor@standrews.org.uk
Website: http://www.standrews.org.uk
Directors: E. Macgregor (Fin)
Managers: A. McGregor (Chief Mgr), A. Mcgreger (Chief Mgr), C. Nurse (Commun Mgr)
Immediate Holding Company: ST. ANDREWS LINKS LIMITED
Registration no: SC141590 **Date established:** 1992
Turnover: £5m - £10m **No.of Employees:** 101 - 250 **Product Groups:** 69, 89

Date of Accounts	Dec 10	Dec 09	Dec 08
Working Capital	-355	-53	-44
Fixed Assets	439	96	45
Current Assets	159	74	63

Ayrshire

Stevenston

Mcevoy Engineering Ltd
53 Stevenston Industrial Estate, Stevenston, KA20 3LR
Tel: 01294-467677 **Fax:** 01294-467677
E-mail: alison@mcevoyengineering.co.uk
Website: http://www.mcevoyengineering.co.uk
Directors: P. McEvoy (Fin)
Managers: A. Mcevoy (Mgr)
Immediate Holding Company: MCEVOY ENGINEERING LTD.
Registration no: SC120681 **Date established:** 1989
No.of Employees: 1 - 10 **Product Groups:** 35

Date of Accounts	Jan 12	Jan 11	Jan 10
Working Capital	176	147	146
Fixed Assets	179	184	184
Current Assets	393	307	372

Stirlingshire

Stirling

A A Components
Airthrey Mill Blairforkie Drive, Bridge Of Allan, Stirling, FK9 4PE
Tel: 01786-834040 **Fax:** 01786-833336
E-mail: nwa@aa-components.com
Website: http://www.aa-components.com
Directors: N. Ainsley (MD), N. Ainslie (MD), M. Ainsley (Ptnr)
Registration no: SC390193 **Date established:** 1962
No.of Employees: 1 - 10 **Product Groups:** 46

Advanced Perimeter Systems Ltd
16 Cunningham Road, Stirling, FK7 7TP
Tel: 01786-479862 **Fax:** 01786-470331
E-mail: admin@apsltd.net
Website: http://www.apsltd.net
Directors: E. Rogerson (Fin)
Immediate Holding Company: ADVANCED PERIMETER SYSTEMS LIMITED
Registration no: SC164963 **Date established:** 1996
No.of Employees: 1 - 10 **Product Groups:** 35, 36, 37, 38, 40, 52, 67, 80, 81

Date of Accounts	Mar 12	Mar 11	Mar 10
Working Capital	438	243	176
Fixed Assets	393	393	407

Current Assets	535	331	270

Alexander Stirling & Co.
Meadowforth Road, Stirling, FK7 5SA
Tel: 01786-473333 **Fax:** 01786-450408
E-mail: sales@alexanderstirling.co.uk
Website: http://www.alexanderstirling.co.uk
Bank(s): Bank of Scotland
Directors: G. Martin (Fin)
Managers: S. Sharp (Chief Mgr), E. Miller (Sales Admin)
Immediate Holding Company: ALEXANDER (STIRLING) & CO.
Registration no: SC238504 **Date established:** 2002
Turnover: £500,000 - £1m **No.of Employees:** 21 - 50 **Product Groups:** 66

Bett Homes
Argyll Court The Castle Business Park, Stirling, FK9 4TT
Tel: 01786-477777 **Fax:** 01383-734576
E-mail: admin@betthomes.com
Website: http://www.gladedale.com
Bank(s): Bank of Scotland, Edinburgh
Directors: J. Kirkpatrick (MD), K. Douglas (Fin), N. Yardley (MD), R. Hanna (Grp Chief Exec), S. Anderson (MD), K. Davidson (Sales), G. Suiter (I.T. Dir), L. Celland (Sales), K. Davidson (Sales & Mktg), D. Ghandi (Dir), G. Coster (MD), I. Bett (Ch), I. Townsend (Dir)
Managers: E. Wallace (Buyer), E. Mason (Personnel), D. Gordon (I.T. Exec)
Ultimate Holding Company: GLADEDALE GROUP HOLDINGS LIMITED
Immediate Holding Company: ASSOCIATION OF SCOTLAND'S COLLEGES
Registration no: SC121949 **VAT No.:** GB 502 7871 52
Date established: 1993 **Turnover:** £10m - £20m
No.of Employees: 51 - 100 **Product Groups:** 52, 80

Date of Accounts	Jul 11	Jul 10	Jul 09
Sales Turnover	594	843	731
Pre Tax Profit/Loss	149	175	100
Working Capital	743	624	449
Fixed Assets	453	N/A	N/A
Current Assets	783	664	966
Current Liabilities	34	21	507

Bushwear
7 Glen Tye Road, Stirling, FK7 7LH
Tel: 01786-450404 **Fax:** 08452-269329
E-mail: sales@bushwear.co.uk
Website: http://www.bushwear.co.uk
Directors: A. Troup (Dir)
Turnover: £250,000 - £500,000 **No.of Employees:** 1 - 10
Product Groups: 22, 24, 49, 63

Cable Pressure Systems Ltd
Borrowmeadow Road Springkerse Industrial Estate, Stirling, FK7 7UW
Tel: 01786-449292 **Fax:** 01786-449393
E-mail: dferguson@fernan.com
Website: http://www.cablepressure.co.uk
Directors: D. Ferguson (MD)
Immediate Holding Company: CABLE PRESSURE SYSTEMS LIMITED
Registration no: SC151137 **Date established:** 1994
No.of Employees: 1 - 10 **Product Groups:** 37, 39, 47

Date of Accounts	Dec 11	Dec 10	Dec 09
Working Capital	14	47	5
Fixed Assets	1	1	1
Current Assets	51	64	58

Castle View International Holdings Limited
Steuart Road Bridge of Allan, Stirling, FK9 4JX
Tel: 01786-834060 **Fax:** 01786-832658
E-mail: enquiries@castleview.co.uk
Website: http://www.castleview.co.uk
Bank(s): Bank of Scotland
Directors: F. Bell (Prop), M. Bell (MD), B. Copland (Grp Mktg)
Managers: A. Gordon (Purch Mgr), L. Skinner (), S. Hughes (Personnel)
Immediate Holding Company: Castle View International Holdings Ltd
Registration no: SC129442 **VAT No.:** GB 652 0224 77
Date established: 1991 **Turnover:** £20m - £50m
No.of Employees: 11 - 20 **Product Groups:** 69

Central Convertors
Unit 3 Bandeath Industrial Estate Throsk, Stirling, FK7 7NP
Tel: 01786-814033 **Fax:** 01786-817477
E-mail: convertors@superglass.co.uk
Website: http://www.superglass.co.uk
Bank(s): Bank of Scotland, Newcastle
Directors: R. Paterson (MD), R. Patterson (MD)
Managers: H. Young (Sales Prom Mgr)
Immediate Holding Company: ENCON INSULATION
Registration no: 02160591 **VAT No.:** GB 561 6705 38
Turnover: £1m - £2m **No.of Employees:** 21 - 50 **Product Groups:** 33

Crown U C P plc
1 Stuart Road Bridge Of Allan, Stirling, FK9 4JG
Tel: 01786-833613
E-mail: mark.gewhurst@gcs.com
Website: http://www.gcs.com
Directors: S. Edwards (Dir)
Ultimate Holding Company: FINANCIERE DAUNOU 5 SARL (LUXEMBOURG)
Immediate Holding Company: UNITED CLOSURES AND PLASTICS LIMITED
Registration no: SC119026 **Date established:** 1989
Turnover: £75m - £125m **No.of Employees:** 101 - 250
Product Groups: 35, 45

Daniel Europe Ltd
Logie Court Stirling University Innovation Park, Stirling, FK9 4NF
Tel: 01786-433400 **Fax:** 01786-433401
E-mail: mark.dutton@emerson.com
Website: http://www.daniel.co.uk
Bank(s): The Royal Bank of Scotland
Directors: M. Meston (Fin), M. Dutton (MD)
Managers: D. Kipps (Tech Serv Mgr), L. Reynolds (Buyer), R. Gillespie (Personnel)
Ultimate Holding Company: EMERSON ELECTRIC CO INC (USA)
Immediate Holding Company: DANIEL EUROPE LIMITED
Registration no: 00971554 **Date established:** 1970
Turnover: £20m - £50m **No.of Employees:** 51 - 100 **Product Groups:** 36, 38

Date of Accounts	Sep 11	Sep 10	Sep 09
Pre Tax Profit/Loss	-85	-111	-10
Working Capital	-12m	-12m	-12m
Fixed Assets	1m	1m	1m
Current Assets	959	959	959

R L Dolby & Co. Ltd
Monitor House Kerse Road, Stirling, FK7 7RZ
Tel: 01786-446640 **Fax:** 01733-446630
E-mail: andy.allen@dolbymedical.com
Website: http://www.dolby-ltd.co.uk
Bank(s): The Royal Bank of Scotland
Directors: A. Allen (Dir), H. Ferguson (Sales)
Managers: J. O'Neill (Mktg Serv Mgr), R. Hennessey (Personnel), S. Howison (Comm), A. Dick
Ultimate Holding Company: DOLBY HEALTHCARE LIMITED
Immediate Holding Company: DOLBY MEDICAL HOME RESPIRATORY CARE LIMITED
Registration no: SC063902 **VAT No.:** GB 309 0813 75
Date established: 1978 **Turnover:** £2m - £5m **No.of Employees:** 51 - 100
Product Groups: 31, 37

Date of Accounts	Dec 11	Dec 10	Dec 09
Sales Turnover	4m	8m	10m
Pre Tax Profit/Loss	187	1m	948
Working Capital	-407	4m	3m
Fixed Assets	6m	845	984
Current Assets	5m	5m	5m
Current Liabilities	3m	635	1m

Dron & Dickson Ltd
Whitehouse Road, Stirling, FK7 7SS
Tel: 01786-449444 **Fax:** 01786-448118
E-mail: info@drondickson.com
Website: http://www.drondickson.com
Bank(s): The Royal Bank of Scotland
Directors: C. Rowley (MD), G. Lafferty (Fin)
Managers: A. Nichol (Personnel), M. Sands (Buyer), P. Smith (Mktg Serv Mgr), C. Noble (Tech Serv Mgr)
Ultimate Holding Company: DRON & DICKSON GROUP LIMITED
Immediate Holding Company: DRON & DICKSON LIMITED
Registration no: 00221355 **VAT No.:** GB 260 2324 03
Date established: 2027 **Turnover:** £20m - £50m
No.of Employees: 11 - 20 **Product Groups:** 37, 40

Date of Accounts	May 11	May 10	May 09
Sales Turnover	28m	24m	28m
Pre Tax Profit/Loss	953	519	972
Working Capital	2m	2m	1m
Fixed Assets	758	941	978
Current Assets	9m	6m	7m
Current Liabilities	5m	3m	4m

Robert Dykes & Son
Burnside Works Westend, Thornhill, Stirling, FK8 3PS
Tel: 01786-850242 **Fax:** 01786-850740
Directors: G. Dykes (Ptnr)
Date established: 1947 **No.of Employees:** 1 - 10 **Product Groups:** 41

Fernan Trading Ltd
4 Borrowmeadow Road Springkerse Industrial Estate, Stirling, FK7 7UW
Tel: 01786-450900 **Fax:** 01786-450049
E-mail: sales@fernan.com
Website: http://www.fernan.com
Managers: D. Ferguson (Mgr)
Immediate Holding Company: FERNAN TRADING LIMITED
Registration no: SC339877 **Date established:** 2008
Turnover: Up to £250,000 **No.of Employees:** 11 - 20 **Product Groups:** 63

Date of Accounts	Dec 10	Dec 09	Dec 08
Working Capital	86	150	138
Fixed Assets	10	19	34
Current Assets	437	424	369

Kilronan House
15 Kenilworth Road Bridge of Allan, Stirling, FK9 4DU
Tel: 01786-831054
E-mail: info@kilronan.co.uk
Website: http://www.kilronan.co.uk
Managers: C. George (Mgr)
No.of Employees: 1 - 10 **Product Groups:** 69

Linnet Technology Ltd
Unit 90-91 Stirling Enterprise Park, Stirling, FK7 7RP
Tel: 01786-450433 **Fax:** 01786-446278
E-mail: sales@linnet-tec.co.uk
Website: http://www.linnet-tec.co.uk
Directors: J. Loughlin (MD)
Ultimate Holding Company: LINNET HOLDINGS LIMITED
Immediate Holding Company: LINNET TECHNOLOGY LIMITED
Registration no: SC168688 **Date established:** 1996 **Turnover:** £1m - £2m
No.of Employees: 1 - 10 **Product Groups:** 37, 48, 51

Date of Accounts	Oct 11	Oct 10	Oct 09
Working Capital	768	627	570
Fixed Assets	91	140	146
Current Assets	1m	1m	1m

C & R Munro Ltd
Unit 7e Bandeath Industrial Estate Throsk, Stirling, FK7 7NP
Tel: 01786-813618 **Fax:** 01786-815113
E-mail: sales@cmmpools.com
Directors: G. Ried (Ptnr)
Immediate Holding Company: C.M.M. POOLS LTD.
Registration no: SC257791 **VAT No.:** GB 262 7742 45
Date established: 2003 **No.of Employees:** 1 - 10 **Product Groups:** 48, 52

Date of Accounts	Jan 12	Jan 11	Jan 10
Working Capital	-31	-33	-34
Fixed Assets	51	52	53
Current Assets	152	134	136

Norbord
Station Road Cowie, Stirling, FK7 7BQ
Tel: 01786-812921 **Fax:** 01786-815622
E-mail: info@norbord.com
Website: http://www.norbord.com
Directors: A. McMeekin (Fin), K. Morris (MD)
Managers: G. Campbell (Purch Mgr), M. Buick (Mktg Serv Mgr), T. Hastie (Tech Serv Mgr), D. Dick
Immediate Holding Company: NORBORD (UK) LTD
Registration no: SC407126 **Date established:** 2011
Turnover: £20m - £50m **No.of Employees:** 101 - 250 **Product Groups:** 25

Redland Roofing Systems Ltd Monier Ltd
Stirling Works Station Road, Cowie, Stirling, FK7 7BP
Tel: 08705-601000 **Fax:** 08705-642742
Website: http://www.redland.co.uk
Directors: C. Morgan (MD)
Managers: K. Dosanjh (I.T. Exec), M. Selsby (Personnel), K. Barrett (Admin Off), L. Tyas (Purch Mgr), C. Hitchcock (Mktg Serv Mgr)
Immediate Holding Company: LAFARGE ROOFING LIMITED
Registration no: NF003570 **Date established:** 2001
Turnover: £500,000 - £1m **No.of Employees:** 21 - 50
Product Groups: 14, 24, 33, 37, 40, 66

S E W Eurodrive Ltd
Unit 37 Enterprise House Springkerse Business Park, Stirling, FK7 7UF
Tel: 01786-478730 **Fax:** 01786-450223
Website: http://www.sew-eurodrive.co.uk
Managers: M. Macfarlane (Mgr)
Ultimate Holding Company: BV BETEILGUNG GMBH & CO KG
Immediate Holding Company: SEW-EURODRIVE LIMITED
Registration no: 00947360 **Date established:** 1969
No.of Employees: 1 - 10 **Product Groups:** 35, 37, 39

Date of Accounts	Feb 08	Feb 11	Feb 10
Sales Turnover	25m	27m	22m
Pre Tax Profit/Loss	5m	5m	2m
Working Capital	11m	11m	9m
Fixed Assets	2m	8m	6m
Current Assets	14m	16m	14m
Current Liabilities	1m	2m	367

Scientific & Analytical Services Ltd
Unit 64-65 John Player Building Stirling Enterprise Park, Stirling, FK7 7RP
Tel: 01786-460355 **Fax:** 01786-460377
E-mail: service@scianal.co.uk
Website: http://www.scianal.co.uk
Directors: P. Currie (Dir)
Immediate Holding Company: SCIENTIFIC & ANALYTICAL SERVICES LIMITED
Registration no: SC092624 **Date established:** 1985
Turnover: £250,000 - £500,000 **No.of Employees:** 1 - 10
Product Groups: 48

Date of Accounts	Oct 11	Oct 10	Oct 09
Working Capital	72	69	55
Fixed Assets	10	13	18
Current Assets	79	77	72

Scotmaz
Glen Tye Road, Stirling, FK7 7LH
Tel: 01786-450235 **Fax:** 01786-450237
E-mail: sales@scotmaz.com
Website: http://www.scotmaz.com
Directors: S. Hunter (MD)
Ultimate Holding Company: MCDOWELL ENGINEERING LIMITED
Immediate Holding Company: SCOTMAZ MACHINE TOOLS LIMITED
Registration no: SC081932 **Date established:** 1983
No.of Employees: 11 - 20 **Product Groups:** 46

Date of Accounts	Dec 11	Dec 10	Dec 09
Working Capital	395	362	223
Fixed Assets	77	60	108
Current Assets	1m	1m	2m

Scottish Enterprise
Laurel House Laurelhill Business Park, Stirling, FK7 9JQ
Tel: 01786-451919 **Fax:** 01786-452140
E-mail: forthvalley@scotent.co.uk
Website: http://www.scottish-enterprise.com
Bank(s): Royal Bank of Scotland
Directors: L. Wilson (Dir)
Immediate Holding Company: KERRERA FISHERIES LIMITED
Registration no: SC125232 **VAT No.:** GB 561 4240 66
Date established: 1982 **Turnover:** £10m - £20m
No.of Employees: 51 - 100 **Product Groups:** 80, 87

Date of Accounts	Dec 09	Dec 08
Sales Turnover	N/A	12m
Pre Tax Profit/Loss	N/A	3m
Working Capital	427	427
Current Assets	427	427

Scottish Youth Hostel
7 Glebe Crescent, Stirling, FK8 2JA
Tel: 01786-891400 **Fax:** 01786-891333
E-mail: syha@syha.org.uk
Website: http://www.hostellingscotland.com
Managers: A. Wellens
Immediate Holding Company: SCOTTISH YOUTH HOSTELS ASSOCIATION
Registration no: SC310841 **Date established:** 2006
Turnover: £5m - £10m **No.of Employees:** 1 - 10 **Product Groups:** 80

Date of Accounts	Jan 12	Jan 11	Jan 10
Sales Turnover	8m	9m	9m
Pre Tax Profit/Loss	-479	204	335
Working Capital	-328	1m	1m
Fixed Assets	16m	15m	16m
Current Assets	2m	3m	3m
Current Liabilities	2m	1m	2m

Sterling Precast Ltd
Springkerse Industrial Estate, Stirling, FK7 7SX
Tel: 01786-472191 **Fax:** 01786-451284
E-mail: general@sterlingprecast.com
Website: http://www.sterlingprecast.com
Bank(s): Bank of Scotland
Directors: A. Walker (MD), J. Gillespie (MD), M. Ross (Fin), N. McGregor (Co Sec)
Ultimate Holding Company: PLEAN PRECAST LIMITED
Immediate Holding Company: STERLING PRECAST LIMITED
Registration no: SC066160 **Date established:** 1978 **Turnover:** £2m - £5m
No.of Employees: 21 - 50 **Product Groups:** 33

Date of Accounts	Jun 11	Jun 10	Jun 09
Sales Turnover	3m	2m	2m
Pre Tax Profit/Loss	371	-371	-154
Working Capital	6m	6m	6m
Fixed Assets	71	89	113
Current Assets	7m	6m	7m
Current Liabilities	193	118	69

Storage Products SPS Ltd
3-5 Borrowmeadow Road Springkerse Indl-Est, Stirling, FK7 7UW
Tel: 01786-447716 **Fax:** 01786-449321
E-mail: archive@spslimited.com
Website: http://www.spslimited.com
Directors: J. Steel (MD), J. Steel (Develop)
Immediate Holding Company: STORAGE PRODUCTS ENGINEERING LIMITED
Registration no: SC183603 **Date established:** 1998
No.of Employees: 1 - 10 **Product Groups:** 80

see next page

Storage Products SPS Ltd - Cont'd

Date of Accounts	Jun 11	Jun 10	Jun 09
Working Capital	72	359	58
Fixed Assets	43	36	N/A
Current Assets	177	367	67

Sundolitt Ltd
Stirling Agricultural Centre, Stirling, FK9 4RN
Tel: 01786-471586 **Fax:** 01786-464825
E-mail: enquiries@sundolitt.com
Website: http://www.sundolitt.com
Bank(s): Royal Bank of Scotland, Glasgow
Managers: C. Brunton (Fin Mgr), P. Cheshire (Chief Mgr)
Immediate Holding Company: SUNDOLITT LIMITED
Registration no: SC211936 **VAT No.:** GB 751 6907 17
Date established: 2000 **Turnover:** £10m - £20m
No.of Employees: 51 - 100 **Product Groups:** 23, 30

Date of Accounts	Dec 11	Dec 10	Dec 09
Sales Turnover	10m	8m	7m
Pre Tax Profit/Loss	839	96	-404
Working Capital	856	800	694
Fixed Assets	2m	2m	3m
Current Assets	2m	2m	2m
Current Liabilities	1m	1m	798

Sungerlitt Ltd
Suite A2 Stirling Agriculture Centre, Stirling, FK9 4RN
Tel: 01786-471 586 **Fax:** 01786-464 825
E-mail: enquiries@sundolitt.com
Website: http://www.sundolitt.co.uk
Managers: C. Brunton (Fin Mgr)
Immediate Holding Company: James Crean P.L.C.
Registration no: SC095898 **Date established:** 2000
Turnover: £5m - £10m **No.of Employees:** 1 - 10 **Product Groups:** 31

Super Glass Insulation Ltd
Thistle Industrial Estate Kerse Road, Stirling, FK7 7QQ
Tel: 01786-451170 **Fax:** 01786-451245
E-mail: info@superglass.co.uk
Website: http://www.superglass.co.uk
Directors: A. Clow (Fin)
Managers: A. Mcleod, G. Williamson (Tech Serv Mgr), I. Leith (Purch Mgr), T. Gordon (Sales Prom Mgr)
Ultimate Holding Company: SUPERGLASS HOLDINGS PLC
Immediate Holding Company: SUPERGLASS INSULATION LIMITED
Registration no: 02160591 **VAT No.:** GB 561 6705 38
Date established: 1987 **Turnover:** £20m - £50m
No.of Employees: 101 - 250 **Product Groups:** 33, 66

Date of Accounts	Aug 11	Aug 10	Aug 09
Sales Turnover	33m	32m	39m
Pre Tax Profit/Loss	-13m	4m	7m
Working Capital	-5m	8m	5m
Fixed Assets	15m	15m	15m
Current Assets	11m	22m	18m
Current Liabilities	3m	3m	3m

Toshiba Medical Systems Ltd (Scottish Office)
Hillside House Laurelhill Business Park, Stirling, FK7 9JQ
Tel: 01786-449447 **Fax:** 01786-449443
E-mail: sjackson@tmse.nl
Website: http://www.toshiba-medical.co.uk
Managers: B. Mcnally
Ultimate Holding Company: TOSHIBA CORPORATION (JAPAN)
Immediate Holding Company: TOSHIBA MEDICAL SYSTEMS LIMITED
Registration no: 00983579 **Date established:** 1970
No.of Employees: 1 - 10 **Product Groups:** 37, 44

Date of Accounts	Mar 11	Mar 10	Mar 09
Sales Turnover	50m	46m	44m
Pre Tax Profit/Loss	2m	2m	1m
Working Capital	6m	6m	5m
Fixed Assets	3m	3m	3m
Current Assets	19m	25m	20m
Current Liabilities	10m	9m	7m

Travelcare Uk Ltd
68-70 Henderson Street Bridge of Allan, Stirling, FK9 4HS
Tel: 01786-833685 **Fax:** 01786-834340
Website: http://www.belltravel.co.uk
Directors: J. Chalmers (MD)
Managers: J. Chalmers (Mgr)
Ultimate Holding Company: RADCLIFFES TRUSTEE CO. S.A. GENEVA
Registration no: 04337708 **VAT No.:** GB 259 8031 38
Date established: 1975 **Turnover:** £10m - £20m **No.of Employees:** 1 - 10
Product Groups: 69

Date of Accounts	Mar 06
Working Capital	146
Fixed Assets	84
Current Assets	265
Current Liabilities	120

United Closures & Plastics Ltd
1 Stuart Road Bridge Of Allan, Stirling, FK9 4JG
Tel: 01786-833613 **Fax:** 01786-834233
E-mail: ucp@gcs.com
Website: http://www.ucplimited.com
Managers: S. Rundle, D. Jones (Tech Serv Mgr), A. Thomson
Ultimate Holding Company: FINANCIERE DAUNOU 5 SARL (LUXEMBOURG)
Immediate Holding Company: UNITED CLOSURES AND PLASTICS LIMITED
Registration no: SC119026 **VAT No.:** GB 274 7764 16
Date established: 1989 **Turnover:** £75m - £125m
No.of Employees: 251 - 500 **Product Groups:** 66

Date of Accounts	Dec 11	Dec 10	Dec 09
Sales Turnover	93m	86m	77m
Pre Tax Profit/Loss	6m	5m	2m
Working Capital	-2m	-2m	-6m
Fixed Assets	21m	22m	21m
Current Assets	32m	30m	27m
Current Liabilities	6m	4m	3m

Up To Five
Stratherick Callander Road, Thornhill, Stirling, FK8 3PR
Tel: 01786-850249 **Fax:** 01786-850249
E-mail: sales@uptofive.co.uk
Website: http://www.uptofive.co.uk
Directors: H. Mchardy (Prop)
No.of Employees: 1 - 10 **Product Groups:** 24, 26, 61, 63

Kincardineshire

Stonehaven

James Macgregor & Associates
3 Mill of Uras, Stonehaven, AB39 2TQ
Tel: 01569-750623 **Fax:** 01569-750624
Directors: J. Macgregor (Fin), D. Macgregor (MD)
Immediate Holding Company: JAMES MACGREGOR AND ASSOCIATES LIMITED
Registration no: SC218499 **Date established:** 2001
No.of Employees: 1 - 10 **Product Groups:** 35, 36, 39

Macphie of Glenbervie Ltd
Glenbervie, Stonehaven, AB39 3YG
Tel: 01569-740641 **Fax:** 01569-740677
E-mail: cservice@macphie.com
Website: http://www.macphie.com
Bank(s): Royal Bank of Scotland, Glasgow
Directors: A. Underwood (Sales & Mktg), R. Howitt (Fin)
Managers: A. Macphie, A. Smith (Tech Serv Mgr), G. Bernett (Personnel), R. White (Purch Mgr)
Ultimate Holding Company: MACPHIE OF GLENBERVIE LIMITED
Immediate Holding Company: MACPHIE OF GLENBERVIE LIMITED
Registration no: SC031780 **VAT No.:** GB 552 9806 18
Date established: 1956 **Turnover:** £20m - £50m
No.of Employees: 101 - 250 **Product Groups:** 20

Date of Accounts	Mar 11	Mar 10	Mar 09
Sales Turnover	45m	42m	41m
Pre Tax Profit/Loss	333	958	1m
Working Capital	5m	4m	3m
Fixed Assets	10m	11m	12m
Current Assets	14m	12m	12m
Current Liabilities	2m	2m	3m

Stonehaven Engineering Ltd
Spurryhillock Industrial Estate Broomhill Road, Stonehaven, AB39 2NH
Tel: 01569-766700 **Fax:** 01569-766147
E-mail: info@stonehaven-eng.com
Website: http://www.stonehaven-eng.com
Bank(s): Bank of Scotland
Directors: A. Dow (Tech Serv)
Immediate Holding Company: STONEHAVEN ENGINEERING LTD.
Registration no: SC125606 **VAT No.:** GB 561 4392 43
Date established: 1990 **Turnover:** Up to £250,000
No.of Employees: 11 - 20 **Product Groups:** 40, 45, 84

Date of Accounts	Oct 11	Oct 10	Oct 09
Working Capital	210	246	259
Fixed Assets	1	2	2
Current Assets	237	472	936

Isle of Lewis

Stornoway

Macgregor Industrial Supplies Ltd
Unit 2 Clintons Yard Rigs Road, Stornoway, HS1 2RF
Tel: 01851-706799 **Fax:** 01851-706289
E-mail: sales@macgregorsupplies.co.uk
Website: http://www.macgregorsupplies.co.uk
Managers: C. Macmillan (Mgr)
Immediate Holding Company: MACGREGOR INDUSTRIAL SUPPLIES LIMITED
Registration no: SC173566 **Date established:** 1997
No.of Employees: 1 - 10 **Product Groups:** 22, 37, 45

Date of Accounts	Mar 11	Mar 10	Mar 09
Sales Turnover	19m	16m	N/A
Pre Tax Profit/Loss	613	429	847
Working Capital	5m	4m	4m
Fixed Assets	1m	2m	1m
Current Assets	8m	7m	7m
Current Liabilities	926	699	955

Wigtownshire

Stranraer

Border Cars
Fountain Way, Stranraer, DG9 7BZ
Tel: 01776-702478 **Fax:** 01776-706521
E-mail: tommydownie@gk-group.co.uk
Website: http://www.border-cars.co.uk
Bank(s): Royal Bank of Scotland
Managers: A. Kenning (Mktg Serv Mgr), C. Watson, J. Mcculloch, L. Sternan (Tech Serv Mgr), T. Downey (Chief Mgr)
Immediate Holding Company: G K GROUP LIMITED
Registration no: 02086705 **VAT No.:** GB 263 1362 79
Date established: 1987 **Turnover:** £2m - £5m **No.of Employees:** 21 - 50
Product Groups: 68

Caledonia Matting International Ltd
Thistle Business Park Station Street, Stranraer, DG9 7HJ
Tel: 01776-889000
E-mail: sales@entrance-mats.com
Website: http://www.entrance-mats.com
Directors: S. Burns (Dir)
Immediate Holding Company: CALEDONIA MATTING LIMITED
Registration no: SC274104 **Date established:** 2004
No.of Employees: 1 - 10 **Product Groups:** 30, 33, 37

Date of Accounts	Oct 09	Oct 08
Working Capital	1	1
Current Assets	1	1

Lanarkshire

Strathaven

I 2 I Television Ltd
Bankhead Farm Road Glassford, Strathaven, ML10 6TR
Tel: 01698-794100
E-mail: crews@i2itv.com
Website: http://www.i2itv.com
Directors: A. Ross (Fin), G. Ross (MD)
Immediate Holding Company: I2I TELEVISION LIMITED
Registration no: 07443070 **Date established:** 2010
No.of Employees: 1 - 10 **Product Groups:** 37, 89

Date of Accounts	Nov 11
Working Capital	-128
Fixed Assets	143
Current Assets	36

Rossshire

Strathcarron

Lochcarron Metalwork
Doneve Croft Road, Lochcarron, Strathcarron, IV54 8YA
Tel: 01520-722560
Managers: D. Mackay (Mgr)
Immediate Holding Company: LOCHCARRON METAL WORK LTD
Registration no: SC383278 **Date established:** 2010
No.of Employees: 1 - 10 **Product Groups:** 35

Date of Accounts	Aug 11
Working Capital	-28
Fixed Assets	107
Current Assets	182

Rossshire

Strome Ferry

Lighthouse Diving Ltd
Dunbeag, Strome Ferry, IV53 8UJ
Tel: 01599-577277 **Fax:** 01599-577277
Website: http://www.lighthousediving.co.uk
Directors: E. Bird (MD)
Immediate Holding Company: LIGHTHOUSE DIVING LIMITED
Registration no: 03411154 **Date established:** 1997
No.of Employees: 1 - 10 **Product Groups:** 37, 49

Rossshire

Tain

Robertsons Of Tain Ltd
Shore Road, Tain, IV19 1HY
Tel: 01862-892276 **Fax:** 01862-894244
E-mail: sales@robertsonsoftain.co.uk
Website: http://www.robertsonsoftain.co.uk
Directors: R. Robertson (MD)
Immediate Holding Company: ROBERTSONS OF TAIN LIMITED
Registration no: SC041420 **Date established:** 1964
No.of Employees: 1 - 10 **Product Groups:** 41

Date of Accounts	Jun 11	Jun 10	Jun 09
Working Capital	244	269	267
Fixed Assets	274	290	299
Current Assets	440	395	473

Argyll

Tarbert

N Robertson
1 Lochgair Place, Tarbert, PA29 6XH
Tel: 01880-820445 **Fax:** 01880-820445
Directors: N. Robertson (Prop)
Date established: 1991 **No.of Employees:** 1 - 10 **Product Groups:** 35, 36

Fife

Tayport

Prove Systems Ltd
1 Mill Court Mill Lane, Tayport, DD6 9EL
Tel: 01382-552085 **Fax:** 01382-550291
Directors: P. Hubert (Dir)
Immediate Holding Company: P.R.O.V.E. SYSTEMS LIMITED
Registration no: SC114256 **Date established:** 1988
No.of Employees: 1 - 10 **Product Groups:** 35, 36, 39

Date of Accounts	Oct 11	Oct 10	Oct 09
Working Capital	65	58	36
Fixed Assets	2	3	4
Current Assets	88	83	60

Scott & Fyfe Ltd
Tayport Works Links Road, Tayport, DD6 9EE
Tel: 01382-554000 **Fax:** 01382-552170
E-mail: solutions@scott-fyfe.com
Website: http://www.scott-fyfe.com
Bank(s): Clydesdale Bank PLC
Directors: I. Lamb (Sales), J. Lupton (Grp Chief Exec), C. Cameron (Fin)
Managers: R. Pap (Purch Mgr)
Immediate Holding Company: SCOTT & FYFE LIMITED
Registration no: SC017244 **VAT No.:** GB 269 3142 47
Date established: 1933 **Turnover:** £10m - £20m
No.of Employees: 51 - 100 **Product Groups:** 23, 27, 63, 66

Date of Accounts	Dec 11	Dec 10	Dec 09
Sales Turnover	12m	16m	13m
Pre Tax Profit/Loss	-71	-323	-4m
Working Capital	10m	11m	12m
Fixed Assets	3m	4m	4m
Current Assets	12m	14m	13m
Current Liabilities	977	1m	795

Dumfriesshire

Thornhill

Adventure Baby
Stratherick Callander Road, Thornhill, FK8 3PR
Tel: 01786-850249
E-mail: sales@adventurebaby.co.uk
Website: http://www.adventurebaby.co.uk
Directors: P. McHardy (Co Sec)
Date established: 2003 **Turnover:** £1m - £2m **No.of Employees:** 1 - 10
Product Groups: 22

Caithness

Thurso

Arch Henderson LLP (Branch Office)
12 Princes Street, Thurso, KW14 7BQ
Tel: 01847-896896 **Fax:** 01847-893009
E-mail: thurso@arch-henderson.co.uk
Website: http://www.archhenderson.co.uk
Directors: J. Simpson (Ptnr)
Immediate Holding Company: ARCH HENDERSON LIMITED LIABILITY PARTNERSHIP
Registration no: SO300202 **VAT No.:** GB 265 4135 63
Date established: 2003 **Turnover:** £2m - £5m **No.of Employees:** 1 - 10
Product Groups: 84

Clackmannanshire

Tillicoultry

Daiglen
27 Stirling Street, Tillicoultry, FK13 6EA
Tel: 01259-750440 **Fax:** 01259-752212
E-mail: daiglen@macall.co.uk
Website: http://www.mccalls.co.uk
Directors: I. Hawthorn (MD)
Managers: M. Kidson (Mgr), M. Kitson (Mgr), E. White (Sales Prom Mgr)
Registration no: SC154982 **No.of Employees:** 1 - 10 **Product Groups:** 24

East Lothian

Tranent

Bairds Malt Ltd
Pencaitland, Tranent, EH34 5DQ
Tel: 01875-340381 **Fax:** 01875-340633
Website: http://www.bairds-malt.co.uk
Directors: P. Wright (Fin)
Managers: M. Laidlaw (Plant)
Ultimate Holding Company: UNITED MALT HOLDINGS INC (USA)
Immediate Holding Company: BAIRDS MALT LIMITED
Registration no: 03580592 **VAT No.:** GB 524 8509 38
Date established: 1998 **Turnover:** Up to £250,000
No.of Employees: 11 - 20 **Product Groups:** 20

Date of Accounts	Dec 08	Sep 11	Sep 10
Sales Turnover	195m	208m	139m
Pre Tax Profit/Loss	10m	2m	2m
Working Capital	11m	44m	40m
Fixed Assets	50m	73m	76m
Current Assets	48m	90m	75m
Current Liabilities	23m	10m	7m

Charles River
Elpinstone Research Centre, Tranent, EH33 2NE
Tel: 01875-614545 **Fax:** 01875-614555
Website: http://www.criver.com
Bank(s): Bank of Scotland
Directors: W. Nimmo (Grp Chief Exec)
Ultimate Holding Company: CHARLES RIVER LABORATORIES INTERNATIONAL INC (USA)
Immediate Holding Company: CHARLES RIVER LABORATORIES GROUP
Registration no: SC198206 **VAT No.:** GB 300 5422 22
Date established: 1999 **Turnover:** £75m - £125m
No.of Employees: 501 - 1000 **Product Groups:** 38, 84, 85, 88

Date of Accounts	Dec 04	Dec 03	Dec 02
Sales Turnover	112m	165m	157m
Pre Tax Profit/Loss	-2m	30m	3m
Working Capital	7m	36m	-8m
Fixed Assets	111m	112m	138m
Current Assets	56m	73m	55m
Current Liabilities	25m	28m	40m

R S Fire
51 Kemps End, Tranent, EH33 2GZ
Tel: 01875-616674 **Fax:** 0131-476 1375
Directors: R. Stahl (Ptnr)
Date established: 2005 **No.of Employees:** 1 - 10 **Product Groups:** 38, 42

Ralph Plastics
Unit 12b Macmerry Industrial Estate, Tranent, EH33 1RD
Tel: 01875-615247 **Fax:** 01875-615247
E-mail: trishralph@aol.com
Directors: J. Ralph (Prop)
VAT No.: GB 398 1645 08 **Turnover:** Up to £250,000
No.of Employees: 1 - 10 **Product Groups:** 30

W N Lindsay Ltd
Gladsmuir Granary Gladsmuir, Tranent, EH33 1EJ
Tel: 01875-852151 **Fax:** 01875-852926
E-mail: enquiries@wnlindsay.com
Website: http://www.wnlindsay.com
Bank(s): Bank of Scotland, Haddington
Directors: A. Lindsay (Dir)
Ultimate Holding Company: W.N. LINDSAY LIMITED
Immediate Holding Company: W.N. LINDSAY LIMITED
Registration no: SC015288 **VAT No.:** GB 276 4122 95
Date established: 2028 **Turnover:** £75m - £125m
No.of Employees: 11 - 20 **Product Groups:** 62

Date of Accounts	May 11	May 10	May 09
Sales Turnover	82m	64m	76m
Pre Tax Profit/Loss	2m	2m	2m
Working Capital	3m	3m	2m
Fixed Assets	7m	6m	6m
Current Assets	14m	9m	10m
Current Liabilities	1m	956	872

Weber Marking Systems
Macmerry Industrial Estate, Tranent, EH33 1HD
Tel: 01875-611111 **Fax:** 01875-613310
E-mail: sales@weber.co.uk
Website: http://www.weber.co.uk
Bank(s): The Royal Bank of Scotland
Managers: P. Hughes (Mgr), S. Ferguson, M. Swan (Tech Serv Mgr)
Ultimate Holding Company: WEBER MARKING SYSTEMS INC (USA)
Immediate Holding Company: WEBER MARKING LIMITED
Registration no: SC169985 **Date established:** 1996
Turnover: £5m - £10m **No.of Employees:** 51 - 100 **Product Groups:** 27, 28, 29, 30, 42, 44, 48, 49, 87

Date of Accounts	Dec 11	Dec 10	Dec 09
Sales Turnover	6m	6m	6m
Pre Tax Profit/Loss	-265	-317	-318
Working Capital	1m	1m	2m
Fixed Assets	1m	2m	2m
Current Assets	3m	3m	3m
Current Liabilities	367	513	500

Ayrshire

Troon

Hook Marine
PO Box 8578, Troon, KA10 6WQ
Tel: 01292-679500 **Fax:** 01292-679501
E-mail: mail@hookmarine.com
Website: http://www.hookmarine.com
Directors: K. Smith (Dir)
No.of Employees: 1 - 10 **Product Groups:** 45

Date of Accounts	May 08	May 07	May 06
Working Capital	-77	-60	-57
Fixed Assets	1	2	2
Current Assets	14	9	-2
Current Liabilities	91	69	55
Total Share Capital	37	37	37

Troon Marine Services Ltd
Harbour Road, Troon, KA10 6DJ
Tel: 01292-316180 **Fax:** 01292-316180
Website: http://www.troonmarine.co.uk
Directors: A. Wood (Dir), J. Wood (MD)
Immediate Holding Company: TROON MARINE SERVICES LIMITED
Registration no: SC068446 **Date established:** 1979
No.of Employees: 1 - 10 **Product Groups:** 35, 36, 39

Date of Accounts	Jan 08	Jan 07	Jan 06
Working Capital	24	15	11
Fixed Assets	3	7	8
Current Assets	52	51	52
Current Liabilities	28	37	41
Total Share Capital	20	20	20

Ultraclean Systems UK Ltd
11 Gillies Street, Troon, KA10 6QH
Tel: 01292-679348 **Fax:** 01292-679585
E-mail: sales@ultraclean-systems.com
Website: http://www.ultraclean-systems.com
Directors: P. Weidig (MD)
Immediate Holding Company: ULTRACLEAN SYSTEMS (UK) LIMITED
Registration no: SC331334 **Date established:** 2007
Turnover: Up to £250,000 **No.of Employees:** 1 - 10 **Product Groups:** 24, 30, 38

Date of Accounts	Mar 12	Mar 11	Mar 10
Working Capital	38	36	32
Fixed Assets	7	5	6
Current Assets	66	53	60

Aberdeenshire

Turriff

Harbro Ltd
Markethill Industrial Estate Markethill Road, Turriff, AB53 4PA
Tel: 01888-545200 **Fax:** 01888-563939
E-mail: info@harbro.co.uk
Website: http://www.harbro.co.uk
Directors: G. Baxter (MD), I. Mennie (Tech Serv), R. Baxter (Fin)
Managers: G. Badenoch (Personnel), R. Ingam (Mktg Serv Mgr)
Ultimate Holding Company: THE HARBRO GROUP LTD.
Immediate Holding Company: HARBRO LIMITED
Registration no: SC230773 **Date established:** 2002
Turnover: £50m - £75m **No.of Employees:** 21 - 50 **Product Groups:** 20

Date of Accounts	Jun 11	Jun 10	Jun 09
Sales Turnover	71m	63m	60m
Pre Tax Profit/Loss	2m	1m	407
Working Capital	6m	5m	5m
Fixed Assets	6m	6m	6m
Current Assets	15m	14m	12m
Current Liabilities	2m	964	790

B Sinclair
Kirkton Cottage Auchterless, Turriff, AB53 8BA
Tel: 01888-511406 **Fax:** 01888- 511406
Directors: B. Sinclair (Prop)
Immediate Holding Company: BOB SINCLAIR MARINE ENGINEERING LIMITED
Registration no: SC237729 **Date established:** 2002
Turnover: Up to £250,000 **No.of Employees:** 1 - 10 **Product Groups:** 39

Date of Accounts	Sep 11	Sep 10	Sep 09
Working Capital	117	134	121
Fixed Assets	31	10	12
Current Assets	173	179	165

West Lothian

West Calder

BRANDMOO (LONDON)
4 Cuthill Brae Willow Wood Park, West Calder, EH55 8QE
Tel: 01501-762082
E-mail: molly@brandmoo.com
Website: http://www.brandmoo.com
Managers: C. Linn (Sales Prom Mgr)
Date established: 2001 **Turnover:** Up to £250,000
No.of Employees: 1 - 10 **Product Groups:** 24

Home Ideas
Unit A Young Street, West Calder, EH55 8AG
Tel: 01506-872221 **Fax:** 01506-872705
Directors: S. McKenzie (Dir), J. Dickson (Co Sec)
Immediate Holding Company: KNIGHT SHADES BLINDS SYSTEMS LTD.
Registration no: SC355937 **Date established:** 2010
No.of Employees: 1 - 10 **Product Groups:** 25, 30

Date of Accounts	Apr 11
Working Capital	-7
Fixed Assets	2
Current Assets	10

M G K Scotland Ltd
Polbeth Industrial Estate Polbeth, West Calder, EH55 8TJ
Tel: 01506-871757 **Fax:** 01506-873400
E-mail: sales@mgkscot.com
Website: http://www.mgkscot.com
Bank(s): Lloyds TSB Bank plc
Directors: S. Johnston (MD)
Immediate Holding Company: M G K (SCOTLAND) LIMITED
Registration no: SC079685 **VAT No.:** GB 356 3515 51
Date established: 1982 **Turnover:** £1m - £2m **No.of Employees:** 11 - 20
Product Groups: 26, 36

Date of Accounts	Oct 11	Oct 10	Oct 09
Working Capital	39	4	57
Fixed Assets	4	6	6
Current Assets	76	68	106

Scotbench Ltd
Polbeth Industrial Estate Polbeth, West Calder, EH55 8TJ
Tel: 01506-871757 **Fax:** 01506-873400
E-mail: sales@scotbench.com
Website: http://www.scotbench.com
Directors: S. Johnson (MD)
Managers: M. Stewart (Mktg Serv Mgr), S. Johnston (Gen Contact)
Registration no: 00079685 **No.of Employees:** 11 - 20
Product Groups: 35, 36, 42, 48

T J C Central Heating
14a Mungle Street, West Calder, EH55 8BX
Tel: 01506-872891
Website: http://www.tjcscotland.co.uk
Directors: W. Crookston (Ptnr)
No.of Employees: 1 - 10 **Product Groups:** 37, 48, 85

Aberdeenshire

Westhill

A S E P Elmar
Enterprise Drive Westhill Indl-Est, Westhill, AB32 6TQ
Tel: 01224-740261 **Fax:** 01224-743138
E-mail: sales@elmar.co.uk
Website: http://www.nov.com
Directors: J. Swansey (Sales & Mktg), F. Crear (Pers), D. Crouch (I.T. Dir), D. Brebner (Fin)

see next page

A S E P Elmar - Cont'd
Managers: J. Burnett (Mats Contrlr), D. Burnett (), L. Wheelan (Mgr), M. Nicholson (Accounts), M. Nicholson, S. John (Sales Prom Mgr), D. Burnett, F. Crear, A. Douglas (Chief Mgr), N. Hendrey (), G. Duthie (Chief Buyer)
Immediate Holding Company: WESTHILL CARS LIMITED
Registration no: SC075821 **Date established:** 2003
Turnover: £20m - £50m **No.of Employees:** 251 - 500 **Product Groups:** 84

W J Brown Agricultural Services Ltd
Rowdenbrae Terryvale Dunecht, Westhill, AB32 7BS
Tel: 01330-860870 **Fax:** 01330-860870
Directors: W. Brown (MD)
Immediate Holding Company: W.J. BROWN AGRICULTURAL SERVICES LIMITED
Registration no: SC133395 **Date established:** 1991
No.of Employees: 1 - 10 **Product Groups:** 41

Date of Accounts	Dec 11	Dec 10	Dec 09
Working Capital	-11	-15	-26
Fixed Assets	24	27	26
Current Assets	49	66	38

Chap Construction Aberdeen Ltd
Head Office Westhill Industrial Estate Westhill Industrial Estate, Westhill, AB32 6TQ
Tel: 01224-748500 **Fax:** 01224-748501
E-mail: mail@chap.co.uk
Website: http://www.chap.co.uk
Bank(s): Clydesdale Bank PLC
Managers: M. Mchardy (Mgr)
Ultimate Holding Company: CHAP (HOLDINGS) LIMITED
Immediate Holding Company: CHAP CONSTRUCTION (ABERDEEN) LIMITED
Registration no: SC086917 **VAT No.:** GB 430 2832 86
Date established: 1984 **Turnover:** £20m - £50m
No.of Employees: 101 - 250 **Product Groups:** 51, 52

Date of Accounts	Mar 11	Mar 10	Mar 09
Sales Turnover	23m	18m	39m
Pre Tax Profit/Loss	387	2m	2m
Working Capital	7m	7m	5m
Fixed Assets	410	430	526
Current Assets	11m	10m	10m
Current Liabilities	497	660	1m

Divex
Enterprise Drive Westhill Industrial Estate, Westhill, AB32 6TQ
Tel: 01224-740145 **Fax:** 01224-740172
E-mail: info@divexglobal.com
Website: http://www.divex.co.uk
Directors: D. Godsman (Dir), D. Godsman (Fin)
Managers: J. Donnelly (Personnel), J. Shirran (Tech Serv Mgr), I. Fraser (Purch Mgr), G. Clark, D. Allen (Mktg Serv Mgr)
Immediate Holding Company: DIVEX LIMITED
Registration no: SC123684 **Date established:** 1990
Turnover: £20m - £50m **No.of Employees:** 101 - 250
Product Groups: 24, 29, 30, 35, 36, 37, 38, 39, 40, 45, 48, 49, 67, 68, 74

Date of Accounts	Nov 11	Nov 10	Nov 09
Sales Turnover	34m	41m	79m
Pre Tax Profit/Loss	3m	4m	3m
Working Capital	9m	8m	8m
Fixed Assets	1m	1m	3m
Current Assets	16m	19m	29m
Current Liabilities	4m	5m	12m

Nessco Group Ltd
Discovery Drive Arnhall Business Park, Westhill, AB32 6FG
Tel: 01224-428400 **Fax:** 01224-722707
E-mail: enquiries@nesscogroup.com
Website: http://www.nesscogroup.com
Bank(s): Bank of Scotland
Managers: I. Mcpherson (Chief Mgr)
Ultimate Holding Company: NESSCO GROUP HOLDINGS LIMITED
Immediate Holding Company: NESSCOINVSAT LIMITED
Registration no: 03673679 **VAT No.:** GB 297 0902 33
Date established: 1998 **Turnover:** £10m - £20m
No.of Employees: 101 - 250 **Product Groups:** 37, 38, 79, 84

Date of Accounts	Mar 12	Mar 11	Mar 10
Sales Turnover	33m	17m	13m
Pre Tax Profit/Loss	3m	2m	1m
Working Capital	9m	7m	5m
Fixed Assets	4m	4m	4m
Current Assets	22m	11m	8m
Current Liabilities	9m	536	159

Sub-Drill Supply Ltd
Endeavour Drive Arnhall Business Park, Westhill, AB32 6UF
Tel: 01224-724600 **Fax:** 01224-772300
E-mail: sales@subdrill.co.uk
Website: http://www.subdrill.com
Directors: A. Paton (MD), L. Paton (Fin)
Ultimate Holding Company: OIL WELL LIMITED
Immediate Holding Company: SUB-DRILL SUPPLY LIMITED
Registration no: SC137517 **Date established:** 1992
No.of Employees: 11 - 20 **Product Groups:** 38, 42

Date of Accounts	May 11	May 10	May 09
Working Capital	2m	3m	2m
Fixed Assets	2m	190	103
Current Assets	3m	4m	3m

Technip UK Ltd
Enterprise Drive Westhill Industrial Estate, Westhill, AB32 6TQ
Tel: 01224-271000 **Fax:** 01224-271271
E-mail: enquiries@technip-coflexip.com
Website: http://www.technip.com
Directors: B. Morrice (MD), Y. Cookson (MD)
Managers: A. Macpherson
Ultimate Holding Company: TECHNIP S A (FRANCE)
Immediate Holding Company: TECHNIP UK LIMITED
Registration no: 00200086 **Date established:** 2024
Turnover: £50m - £75m **No.of Employees:** 501 - 1000
Product Groups: 36, 39, 51, 84, 85

Date of Accounts	Dec 10	Dec 09	Dec 08
Sales Turnover	930m	860m	743m
Pre Tax Profit/Loss	48m	16m	60m
Working Capital	6m	20m	-22m
Fixed Assets	254m	231m	230m
Current Assets	405m	461m	442m
Current Liabilities	341m	355m	386m

Vallourec Mannesmann Oil & Gas UK Ltd
4 Prospect Place, Westhill, AB32 6SY
Tel: 01224-279340 **Fax:** 01224-279341
E-mail: info@vmog.co.uk
Website: http://www.vmog.co.uk
Directors: D. Dauron (MD)
Managers: A. Clark (Sales Prom Mgr)
Ultimate Holding Company: VALLOUREC SA (FRANCE)
Immediate Holding Company: VALLOUREC MANNESMANN OIL & GAS UK LTD.
Registration no: SC147386 **Date established:** 1993
No.of Employees: 21 - 50 **Product Groups:** 36, 45

Date of Accounts	Dec 11	Dec 10	Dec 09
Sales Turnover	126m	109m	148m
Pre Tax Profit/Loss	12m	6m	17m
Working Capital	28m	26m	27m
Fixed Assets	11m	11m	11m
Current Assets	59m	48m	45m
Current Liabilities	6m	5m	6m

Caithness

Wick

K P Technology Ltd
Burn Street, Wick, KW1 5EH
Tel: 01955-602777 **Fax:** 01955-605122
E-mail: iain@kptechnology.ltd.uk
Website: http://www.kelvinprobe.com
Directors: I. Baikie (Dir)
Immediate Holding Company: KP TECHNOLOGY LTD.
Registration no: SC207302 **Date established:** 2000
No.of Employees: 11 - 20 **Product Groups:** 38, 85

Date of Accounts	Mar 12	Mar 11	Mar 10
Working Capital	764	602	390
Fixed Assets	147	144	144
Current Assets	874	667	414

Maclean Electricals (t/a Maclean Electrical)
16d Airport Industrial Estate Wick Airport, Wick, KW1 4QS
Tel: 01955-606611 **Fax:** 01955-606636
E-mail: wick@maclean.co.uk
Website: http://www.maclean.co.uk
Managers: N. Fraser (District Mgr)
Registration no: SC069126 **VAT No.:** GB 296 9015 21
No.of Employees: 1 - 10 **Product Groups:** 67

North Of Scotland Newspapers
42 Union Street, Wick, KW1 5ED
Tel: 01955-602424 **Fax:** 01955-604822
E-mail: advertising@nosn.co.uk
Website: http://www.johnogroat-journal.co.uk
Bank(s): The Royal Bank of Scotland
Managers: S. Campbell
Immediate Holding Company: SCOTTISH PROVINCIAL PRESS
Registration no: SC120732 **VAT No.:** GB 552 4388 35
Date established: 1894 **Turnover:** £1m - £2m **No.of Employees:** 11 - 20
Product Groups: 28

Robertsons Of Tain Ltd
Harbour Place, Wick, KW1 5EZ
Tel: 01955-602296 **Fax:** 01955-603401
E-mail: kenmackenziewick@btconnect.com
Managers: K. Mackenzie (Mgr)
Immediate Holding Company: ROBERTSONS OF TAIN LIMITED
Registration no: SC041420 **Date established:** 1964
No.of Employees: 1 - 10 **Product Groups:** 41

Date of Accounts	Dec 10	Dec 09	Dec 08
Working Capital	31	34	44
Fixed Assets	13	14	7
Current Assets	78	85	69

Lanarkshire

Wishaw

Astute Electronics
2 Canyon Road Netherton Industrial Estate, Wishaw, ML2 0EG
Tel: 01698-377450 **Fax:** 01698-375860
E-mail: sales@astute.co.uk
Website: http://www.astute.co.uk
Managers: J. Docherty (Mgr)
No.of Employees: 21 - 50 **Product Groups:** 36, 37

Bone Steel Ltd
PO Box 9300, Wishaw, ML2 0YA
Tel: 01698-375000 **Fax:** 01698-372727
E-mail: admin@bonesteel.co.uk
Website: http://www.bonesteel.co.uk
Directors: M. Magunnigle (Co Sec)
Immediate Holding Company: Bone Group Ltd
Registration no: SC168428 **Date established:** 1996
No.of Employees: 101 - 250 **Product Groups:** 35, 52, 84

C J Electronics
Netherton Road, Wishaw, ML2 0EQ
Tel: 01698-375684 **Fax:** 01698-372763
Directors: R. Cuthbertson (MD)
VAT No.: GB 261 7864 37 **No.of Employees:** 1 - 10 **Product Groups:** 38

Caring 4 U
232 Main Street Wishaww, Wishaw, ML2 7ND
Tel: 01698-375058 **Fax:** 01698- 375058
Directors: C. Clarke (Prop)
No.of Employees: 1 - 10 **Product Groups:** 38

Daiwa Sports Ltd
Netherton Industrial Estate, Wishaw, ML2 0EY
Tel: 01698-355723 **Fax:** 01698-372505
E-mail: info@daiwasports.co.uk
Website: http://www.daiwasports.co.uk
Bank(s): Barclays, Glasgow
Directors: R. Morikawa (MD)
Managers: C. Seagrave (Fin Mgr), S. McCaveny (Mktg Serv Mgr), R. Morley (Mktg Serv Mgr), D. Peele (Sales Prom Mgr), J. Dixon (Personnel), P. Seyner (Tech Serv Mgr)
Ultimate Holding Company: GLOBERIDE INC (JAPAN)
Immediate Holding Company: DAIWA SPORTS LIMITED
Registration no: 01295286 **Date established:** 1977
Turnover: £10m - £20m **No.of Employees:** 101 - 250 **Product Groups:** 49

Date of Accounts	Dec 11	Dec 10	Dec 09
Sales Turnover	17m	15m	14m
Pre Tax Profit/Loss	985	575	194
Working Capital	6m	4m	3m
Fixed Assets	1m	1m	1m
Current Assets	10m	8m	7m
Current Liabilities	540	430	411

Danskin
1 Pickering Works Netherton Road, Wishaw, ML2 0EQ
Tel: 01698-356000 **Fax:** 01698-372222
Website: http://www.danskin.co.uk
Managers: G. Wilson (Chief Mgr)
Immediate Holding Company: BONE GROUP LIMITED
Registration no: SC225633 **Date established:** 2001
No.of Employees: 11 - 20 **Product Groups:** 36, 40

Electrical Catering Services Ltd
11 Russell Street, Wishaw, ML2 7AL
Tel: 01698-374394 **Fax:** 01698-327467
Directors: G. Gallacher (MD)
Immediate Holding Company: ELECTRICAL CATERING SERVICES LIMITED
Registration no: SC149565 **Date established:** 1994
No.of Employees: 1 - 10 **Product Groups:** 36, 40

Date of Accounts	Mar 11	Mar 10	Mar 09
Working Capital	27	30	14
Fixed Assets	3	7	9
Current Assets	49	93	85

Emcom
11 hoey drive Overtown, Wishaw, ML2 0RZ
Tel: 01698-358796
E-mail: jim.mccann@emcom.co.uk
Website: http://www.emcom.co.uk
Directors: J. Mccann (Head)
Date established: 2001 **Turnover:** Up to £250,000
No.of Employees: 1 - 10 **Product Groups:** 44

Jewson Ltd
Excelsior Street, Wishaw, ML2 7SS
Tel: 01698-355831 **Fax:** 01698-350353
Website: http://www.jewson.co.uk
Bank(s): R O B S
Managers: A. Frame (Sales Prom Mgr), J. Allison (Mgr)
Ultimate Holding Company: COMPAGNIE DE SAINT GOBAIN (FRANCE)
Immediate Holding Company: JEWSON LIMITED
Registration no: 00348407 **VAT No.:** GB 497 7184 83
Date established: 1939 **No.of Employees:** 11 - 20 **Product Groups:** 66

Date of Accounts	Dec 11	Dec 10	Dec 09
Sales Turnover	1606m	1547m	1485m
Pre Tax Profit/Loss	18m	100m	45m
Working Capital	-345m	-250m	-349m
Fixed Assets	496m	387m	461m
Current Assets	657m	1005m	1320m
Current Liabilities	66m	120m	64m

Lanarkshire Welding Co. Ltd
John Street, Wishaw, ML2 7TQ
Tel: 01698-264271 **Fax:** 01698-265711
E-mail: enquiries@lanarkshirewelding.co.uk
Website: http://www.lanarkshirewelding.co.uk
Bank(s): Royal Bank of Scotland
Directors: J. Hett (Fin)
Immediate Holding Company: LANARKSHIRE WELDING COMPANY LIMITED
Registration no: SC023232 **VAT No.:** GB 260 2331 06
Date established: 1945 **Turnover:** £5m - £10m **No.of Employees:** 21 - 50
Product Groups: 30, 34, 35

Date of Accounts	Feb 08	Feb 11	Feb 10
Sales Turnover	10m	N/A	N/A
Pre Tax Profit/Loss	-1	N/A	N/A
Working Capital	229	326	226
Fixed Assets	1m	930	1m
Current Assets	3m	2m	1m
Current Liabilities	2m	N/A	N/A

Powerwall Space Frame Systems Ltd
4 Netherton Road, Wishaw, ML2 0EQ
Tel: 01698-373305 **Fax:** 01698-374503
E-mail: sales@powerwall.co.uk
Website: http://www.powerwall.co.uk
Directors: H. Forsyth (Co Sec), D. Tedesco (Dir)
Ultimate Holding Company: CBI INVESTMENTS LIMITED
Immediate Holding Company: POWERWALL SYSTEMS LIMITED
Registration no: SC136183 **VAT No.:** GB 612 3961 56
Date established: 1992 **Turnover:** £1m - £2m **No.of Employees:** 51 - 100
Product Groups: 29, 30, 31, 42

Date of Accounts	Jun 08	Jun 07	Jun 06
Pre Tax Profit/Loss	224	446	-2m
Working Capital	-2m	-2m	-2m
Fixed Assets	3m	3m	2m
Current Assets	2m	2m	3m
Current Liabilities	2m	2m	2m

Record UK Ltd
Garrion Business Park, Wishaw, ML2 0RY
Tel: 01698-376411 **Fax:** 01698-376422
E-mail: info@recorduk.co.uk
Website: http://www.recorduk.co.uk
Bank(s): National Westminster
Directors: H. Plaut (MD), D. Miller (Mkt Research), E. Hume (Pers), M. Barrie (Co Sec)

Managers: P. Campbell (Tech Serv Mgr), S. Frew (Fin Mgr)
Ultimate Holding Company: AGTA RECORD AG (SWITZERLAND)
Immediate Holding Company: RECORD U.K. LIMITED
Registration no: SC124392 **VAT No.:** GB 586 9396 63
Date established: 1990 **Turnover:** £10m - £20m
No.of Employees: 51 - 100 **Product Groups:** 26, 35

Date of Accounts	Dec 11	Dec 10	Dec 09
Sales Turnover	15m	15m	16m
Pre Tax Profit/Loss	-1m	-951	-966
Working Capital	796	1m	2m
Fixed Assets	5m	6m	6m
Current Assets	9m	9m	9m
Current Liabilities	7m	7m	6m

Rhinowash Ltd

149a Glasgow Road, Wishaw, ML2 7QJ
Tel: 08708-600600 **Fax:** 01698-356697
E-mail: info@rhinowash.com
Website: http://www.rhinowash.com
Bank(s): The Royal Bank of Scotland
Directors: M. Burns (Dir)
Immediate Holding Company: RHINOWASH LIMITED
Registration no: SC272881 **Date established:** 2004
No.of Employees: 11 - 20 **Product Groups:** 39

Date of Accounts	Sep 11	Sep 10	Sep 09
Working Capital	39	68	92
Fixed Assets	89	75	90
Current Assets	232	193	234

Swissmatic Ltd

19-21 Canyon Road Netherton Industrial Estate, Wishaw, ML2 0EG
Tel: 01698-374548 **Fax:** 01698-359454
E-mail: info@swissmatic.co.uk
Website: http://www.swissmatic.co.uk
Bank(s): Clydesdale Bank PLC
Directors: J. Corbally (MD)
Immediate Holding Company: SWISSMATIC LIMITED
Registration no: SC070065 **Date established:** 1979 **Turnover:** £2m - £5m
No.of Employees: 11 - 20 **Product Groups:** 35, 48

Date of Accounts	Feb 08	Feb 11	Feb 10
Working Capital	423	612	530
Fixed Assets	1m	1m	953
Current Assets	907	1m	939

T F C Cable Assemblies Ltd

Excelsior Park Netherton Industrial Estate, Wishaw, ML2 0ER
Tel: 01698-355017 **Fax:** 01698-350559
E-mail: info@tfcasm.co.uk
Website: http://www.ncmail.com
Directors: J. Nelson (MD), F. Ferris (Grp Chief Exec), M. Barker (Dir), F. Gayne (Dir)
Managers: G. Wands (Sales Prom Mgr)
Immediate Holding Company: TFC CABLE ASSEMBLIES LIMITED
Registration no: SC049305 **Date established:** 1971
Turnover: £5m - £10m **No.of Employees:** 1 - 10 **Product Groups:** 26, 30, 35, 37, 39, 47, 48, 67, 68, 84, 85

Date of Accounts	Dec 11	Dec 10	Dec 09
Working Capital	347	699	621
Fixed Assets	1m	1m	1m
Current Assets	2m	2m	2m

William Waddell Ltd

30 Russell Street, Wishaw, ML2 7AN
Tel: 01698-355034 **Fax:** 01698-374970
Directors: M. Stevenson (MD), E. Cameron (Fin)
Immediate Holding Company: WILLIAM WADDELL, LIMITED
Registration no: SC021126 **VAT No.:** GB 260 6074 77
Date established: 1939 **Turnover:** £250,000 - £500,000
No.of Employees: 1 - 10 **Product Groups:** 48

Date of Accounts	Jun 11	Jun 10	Jun 09
Working Capital	133	131	156
Fixed Assets	21	24	20
Current Assets	190	167	241

NORTHERN IRELAND

Co. Antrim

Antrim

Allen & Partners
22 Market Square, Antrim, BT41 4DT
Tel: 028-9446 3129 **Fax:** 028-9446 5654
Directors: R. Balmer (Ptnr), R. Balemer (Dir), P. Nichol (Prop)
Immediate Holding Company: NICHOL ALLEN LTD
Registration no: NI050428 **VAT No.:** GB 311 1001 53
Date established: 2011 **Turnover:** Up to £250,000
No.of Employees: 1 - 10 **Product Groups:** 80

Antrim Aluminium & Glass
5 Plasketts Close, Antrim, BT41 4LY
Tel: 028-9446 6887 **Fax:** 028-9446 8802
E-mail: reception@boxite.co.uk
Directors: B. Martin (Ch), J. Martin (MD)
Registration no: NI069222 **Date established:** 2008
No.of Employees: 11 - 20 **Product Groups:** 26, 35

Antrim Borough Council
Antrim Civic Centre 50 Stiles Way, Antrim, BT41 2UB
Tel: 028-9446 3113 **Fax:** 028-9448 1334
E-mail: info@antrim.gov.uk
Website: http://www.antrim.gov.uk
Managers: D. Mccammick
Immediate Holding Company: RURAL ECONOMIC ACTION PARTNERSHIP (REAP) SOUTH ANTRIM
Registration no: NI035394 **Date established:** 2002
No.of Employees: 101 - 250 **Product Groups:** 87

Date of Accounts	Mar 11	Mar 10	Mar 09
Working Capital	2	2	16
Current Assets	2	2	18

Antrim Builder Centre
Springfarm Industrial Estate, Antrim, BT41 4NT
Tel: 028-9446 5921 **Fax:** 028-9446 1844
E-mail: johnmcmurry@macblair.com
Bank(s): Bank of Ireland
Managers: F. Goodall (Mgr), D. Perrin
Immediate Holding Company: MCCOMBE BROTHERS (NI) LIMITED
Registration no: NI024423 **VAT No.:** GB 251 7859 37
Date established: 1990 **Turnover:** £10m - £20m
No.of Employees: 21 - 50 **Product Groups:** 35, 66

Date of Accounts	Feb 08	Feb 11	Feb 10
Sales Turnover	19m	3m	3m
Pre Tax Profit/Loss	-1m	-56	-1m
Working Capital	-2m	-2m	-2m
Fixed Assets	8m	2m	3m
Current Assets	7m	160	177
Current Liabilities	4m	429	292

Antrim Physio
Unit 4 Springfarm Industrial Estate, Antrim, BT41 4NT
Tel: 028-9446 9672 **Fax:** 028-9446 5921
Website: http://www.antrimphysio.co.uk
Directors: W. Colhoun (Prop)
Ultimate Holding Company: MCCOMBE BROTHERS (NI) LIMITED
Immediate Holding Company: MBA REALISATIONS LIMITED
Registration no: NI006740 **VAT No.:** GB 432 7701 64
Date established: 1966 **Turnover:** £5m - £10m **No.of Employees:** 1 - 10
Product Groups: 45, 83

Date of Accounts	Feb 08	Feb 10	Feb 09
Sales Turnover	16m	8m	9m
Pre Tax Profit/Loss	-2m	-250	-257
Working Capital	-2m	-2m	-2m
Fixed Assets	3m	2m	2m
Current Assets	7m	4m	6m
Current Liabilities	3m	2m	2m

Antrim Printers
Steeple Road Industrial Estate, Antrim, BT41 1AB
Tel: 028-9442 8053 **Fax:** 028-9442 8052
E-mail: rodney@antrimprinters.co.uk
Website: http://www.antrimprinters.co.uk
Directors: R. Mccullough (Ptnr)
Immediate Holding Company: Q BUS HOLDINGS LIMITED
Registration no: NI065448 **VAT No.:** GB 311 1431 28
Date established: 2007 **Turnover:** £500,000 - £1m
No.of Employees: 11 - 20 **Product Groups:** 28

Date of Accounts	Dec 10	Dec 09	Dec 08
Pre Tax Profit/Loss	N/A	320	N/A
Working Capital	-2m	-2m	-2m
Fixed Assets	3m	3m	3m
Current Assets	14	10	6
Current Liabilities	N/A	4	N/A

Antrim Transformers Ltd
25 Enkalon Industrial Estate Randalstown Road, Antrim, BT41 4LD
Tel: 028-9442 8734 **Fax:** 028-9446 8745
E-mail: technical@antrimtransformers.com
Website: http://www.antrimtransformers.com
Bank(s): Bank of Ireland
Directors: R. Turkington (MD)
Managers: T. Monaghan (Tech Sales Eng)
Registration no: NI032857 **VAT No.:** GB 432 7478 41
Date established: 1997 **Turnover:** £1m - £2m **No.of Employees:** 21 - 50
Product Groups: 37

Black Box Network Services
Unit 11-13 Antrim Enterprise Agency Park 58 Greystone Road, Antrim, BT41 1JZ
Tel: 028-9442 8325 **Fax:** 028-9446 3250
E-mail: damien.lynch@blackbox.co.uk
Website: http://www.blackbox.co.uk
Bank(s): Ulster
Directors: D. Lynch (MD)
Managers: N. Bogle
Ultimate Holding Company: BLACK BOX CORPORATION (USA)
Immediate Holding Company: BLACK BOX NETWORK SERVICES (NORTHERN IRELAND) LIMITED
Registration no: NI038509 **VAT No.:** GB 432 6871 44
Date established: 2000 **Turnover:** £1m - £2m **No.of Employees:** 11 - 20
Product Groups: 44, 52, 67

Date of Accounts	Mar 11	Mar 10	Mar 09
Fixed Assets	1m	1m	1m

Blackbourne Ltd (a division of Karl Holdings)
Springfarm Indl-Est, Antrim, BT41 4NZ
Tel: 028-9448 0104 **Fax:** 028-9446 7109
E-mail: info@blackbourne.co.uk
Website: http://www.blackbourne.co.uk
Bank(s): First Trust
Directors: D. Thompson (MD), M. Cairns (Comm), T. McAllister (Dir)
Ultimate Holding Company: JERAS LIMITED
Immediate Holding Company: BLACKBOURNE LIMITED
Registration no: NI007963 **Date established:** 1970
Turnover: £10m - £20m **No.of Employees:** 101 - 250
Product Groups: 25, 52, 84

Date of Accounts	Mar 11	Mar 10	Mar 09
Sales Turnover	16m	17m	N/A
Pre Tax Profit/Loss	678	318	211
Working Capital	2m	2m	1m
Fixed Assets	424	372	227
Current Assets	6m	5m	5m
Current Liabilities	1m	692	379

Thomas Brownen
46 Blackpark Road Toomebridge, Antrim, BT41 3SL
Tel: 028-7965 0704 **Fax:** 028-7965 0817
Directors: T. Brownen (Prop)
Date established: 1978 **No.of Employees:** 1 - 10 **Product Groups:** 35

Browntex Ltd
Unit 9 Steeple Road Industrial Estate, Antrim, BT41 1AB
Tel: 028-9446 2475 **Fax:** 028-9446 2475
E-mail: basil.brown@ukgateway.net
Directors: B. Brown (MD)
Immediate Holding Company: BROWNTEX LIMITED
Registration no: NI006034 **VAT No.:** GB 253 9211 67
Date established: 1964 **No.of Employees:** 1 - 10 **Product Groups:** 24

Date of Accounts	Apr 11	Apr 10	Apr 09
Working Capital	124	110	118
Fixed Assets	70	78	65
Current Assets	150	133	137
Current Liabilities	N/A	N/A	2

Butlers
14 Shanes Street Randalstown, Antrim, BT41 2AD
Tel: 028-9447 3996 **Fax:** 028-9447 3996
E-mail: bmsystems@fsmail.net
Website: http://www.butlersmobilesystems.co.uk
Directors: P. Butler (Prop)
VAT No.: GB 349 9680 05 **Date established:** 1993
No.of Employees: 1 - 10 **Product Groups:** 40, 72, 83

Castle Homes N I Ltd
6 Springfarm Industrial Estate, Antrim, BT41 4NZ
Tel: 028-9446 0070 **Fax:** 028-9446 8222
Directors: J. Mcneill (Dir)
Immediate Holding Company: CASTLE HOMES (N.I.) LIMITED
Registration no: NI019304 **VAT No.:** GB 432 6210 88
Date established: 1986 **Turnover:** £500,000 - £1m
No.of Employees: 1 - 10 **Product Groups:** 25, 26, 35

Date of Accounts	Apr 11	Apr 10	Apr 09
Working Capital	-146	-148	-131
Fixed Assets	189	203	217
Current Assets	138	117	147

Contact Marketing
29 Magherabeg Road Randalstown, Antrim, BT41 2PL
Tel: 028-9447 3840 **Fax:** 028-9447 2104
E-mail: info@favour.co.uk
Website: http://www.contactmarketing.co.uk
Bank(s): Ulster Bank
Directors: N. Mcgarry (MD)
Immediate Holding Company: Contact Marketing (NI) Limited
Registration no: NI047646 **VAT No.:** GB 349 7399 93
Date established: 2003 **Turnover:** £1m - £2m **No.of Employees:** 11 - 20
Product Groups: 20

Date of Accounts	Sep 11	Sep 10	Sep 09
Working Capital	244	179	116
Fixed Assets	679	703	757
Current Assets	789	693	718

Creagh Concrete Products Ltd
Blackpark Road Toomebridge, Antrim, BT41 3SL
Tel: 028-7965 0500 **Fax:** 028-7965 9596
E-mail: smckeague@creaghconcrete.com
Website: http://www.creaghconcrete.com
Bank(s): First Trust
Directors: S. Mckeague (MD)
Ultimate Holding Company: CREAGH CONCRETE PRODUCTS LIMITED
Immediate Holding Company: CREAGH CONCRETE PRODUCTS LIMITED
Registration no: NI010644 **VAT No.:** GB 286 3131 56
Date established: 1975 **Turnover:** £50m - £75m
No.of Employees: 251 - 500 **Product Groups:** 33, 66

Date of Accounts	Mar 11	Mar 10	Mar 09
Sales Turnover	51m	39m	54m
Pre Tax Profit/Loss	499	59	655
Working Capital	-1m	-2m	-4m
Fixed Assets	15m	16m	19m
Current Assets	14m	14m	11m
Current Liabilities	4m	4m	5m

Digital Wiring Ltd
41 Clady Road Dunadry, Antrim, BT41 4QR
Tel: 028-9443 2080 **Fax:** 028-9443 2992
E-mail: info@digitalwiring.co.uk
Website: http://www.digitalwiring.co.uk
Directors: D. Camlin (Dir)
Immediate Holding Company: DIGITAL WIRING LTD
Registration no: NI032795 **VAT No.:** GB 432 6803 61
Date established: 1997 **Turnover:** £500,000 - £1m
No.of Employees: 1 - 10 **Product Groups:** 52

Date of Accounts	Jul 11	Jul 10	Jul 09
Working Capital	818	840	824
Fixed Assets	9	14	19
Current Assets	872	947	892

Envelope Print & Design Co.
Rathenraw Industrial Estate, Antrim, BT41 2SJ
Tel: 028-9446 9446 **Fax:** 028-9446 6500
E-mail: sales@envelopesireland.com
Website: http://www.envelopesofgreatbritain.co.uk
Directors: B. Glass (Ptnr)
Immediate Holding Company: Solar Screening Protection Ltd
Registration no: NI069084 **VAT No.:** GB 617 7445 24
Date established: 2008 **Turnover:** £2m - £5m **No.of Employees:** 1 - 10
Product Groups: 27

Date of Accounts	Feb 11
Working Capital	140
Fixed Assets	17
Current Assets	357

Fast Engineering Ltd
5 Windmill Court, Antrim, BT41 2TX
Tel: 028-9442 8686 **Fax:** 028-9442 9929
E-mail: info@fastank.com
Website: http://www.fastank.com
Bank(s): Bank of Ireland
Managers: C. Mulholland (Chief Mgr)
Immediate Holding Company: FAST ENGINEERING LIMITED
Registration no: NI015098 **VAT No.:** GB 353 0243 91
Date established: 1981 **Turnover:** £1m - £2m **No.of Employees:** 11 - 20
Product Groups: 35

Date of Accounts	Sep 11	Sep 10	Sep 09
Working Capital	2m	2m	2m
Fixed Assets	683	678	704
Current Assets	2m	2m	2m

Framing Fantastic
149 Seven Mile Straight Muckamore, Antrim, BT41 4QT
Tel: 028-9443 9287 **Fax:** 028-9443 9287
E-mail: sales@framingfantastic.co.uk
Website: http://www.framingfantastic.co.uk
Directors: S. Noble (Prop)
No.of Employees: 1 - 10 **Product Groups:** 25, 26, 27, 36, 38, 49, 64

Fujitsu Telecommunications Ireland
10 Technology Park Belfast Road, Muckamore, Antrim, BT41 1QS
Tel: 028-9442 8394 **Fax:** 028-9442 8395
E-mail: ftel@ftel.co.uk
Website: http://www.ftel.co.uk
Managers: P. Bowman (Chief Mgr), P. Stanley (Purch Mgr), W. Moore, T. Lees (Personnel)
Immediate Holding Company: FUJITSU TELECOMMUNICATIONS EUROPE LTD
Registration no: NF003223 **Date established:** 1995
Turnover: £500,000 - £1m **No.of Employees:** 51 - 100
Product Groups: 44, 48

G E Mclarnon & Sons Ltd
126 Moneynick Road Randalstown, Antrim, BT41 3HU
Tel: 028-7965 0321 **Fax:** 028-7965 0905
E-mail: info@gemclarnon.co.uk
Website: http://www.mclarnonfeeds.com
Bank(s): Ulster Bank
Managers: W. Mackey (Mgr)
Immediate Holding Company: G.E. MCLARNON & SONS LIMITED
Registration no: NI015263 **VAT No.:** GB 331 8066 73
Date established: 1981 **No.of Employees:** 51 - 100 **Product Groups:** 20, 62

Geoff Rodgers Catering Equipment
Unit 2 211 Castle Road Randalstown, Antrim, BT41 2EB
Tel: 028-9447 3992 **Fax:** 028-9447 8310
E-mail: info@sweetequipmentdeals.co.uk
Website: http://www.sweetequipmentdeals.co.uk
Directors: G. Rodgers (Prop)
Date established: 1998 **No.of Employees:** 1 - 10 **Product Groups:** 20, 40, 41

Glenwood Of Antrim
6 Springfarm Industrial Estate, Antrim, BT41 4NZ
Tel: 028-9446 7828 **Fax:** 028-9446 8222
E-mail: sales@glenwoodofantrim.com
Website: http://www.glenwoodofantrim.com
Directors: J. Mcneill (Prop)
VAT No.: GB 432 6210 88 **No.of Employees:** 1 - 10 **Product Groups:** 26

I F S Global Logistics
I F S Logistics Park Seven Mile Straight, Muckamore, Antrim, BT41 4QE
Tel: 028-9446 4211 **Fax:** 028-9446 7723
E-mail: sales@antrim.ifsgroup.com
Website: http://www.ifsgroup.com
Bank(s): Ulster Bank
Directors: S. Fleck (Fin)
Managers: M. Duke (Sales Prom Mgr), G. McBroom (Tech Serv Mgr), S. Copeland
Immediate Holding Company: IFS Global Logistics Ltd
Registration no: NI008228 **VAT No.:** 222553001 **Date established:** 1971
Turnover: £10m - £20m **No.of Employees:** 51 - 100 **Product Groups:** 75, 76

Date of Accounts	Dec 11	Dec 10	Dec 09
Sales Turnover	12m	17m	12m
Pre Tax Profit/Loss	1m	2m	798
Working Capital	3m	3m	2m
Fixed Assets	144	201	243
Current Assets	7m	8m	5m
Current Liabilities	880	2m	295

Irish Organ Co. Ltd
Steeple Road Industrial Estate, Antrim, BT41 1AB
Tel: 028-9446 7954 **Fax:** 028-9446 7954
Website: http://www.irishorgan.co.uk
Directors: R. Davidson (MD)
Immediate Holding Company: IRISH ORGAN COMPANY LIMITED
Registration no: R0000285 **VAT No.:** GB 252 5464 64
Date established: 1998 **Turnover:** £500,000 - £1m
No.of Employees: 1 - 10 **Product Groups:** 49

Date of Accounts	Jan 11	Jan 10	Jan 09
Working Capital	4	8	7
Fixed Assets	20	20	20
Current Assets	14	24	29
Current Liabilities	3	7	6

Islandbawn Stores Ltd
128 Belfast Road, Antrim, BT41 2BA
Tel: 028-9446 4512 **Fax:** 028-9442 9459
Bank(s): Northern Bank
Directors: R. Kirkpatrick (Prop), S. Kirkpatrick (Dir)
Managers: D. Douglas (Admin Off)
Immediate Holding Company: ISLANDBAWN STORES LIMITED
Registration no: NI020133 **VAT No.:** GB 349 7076 20
Date established: 1987 **Turnover:** Up to £250,000
No.of Employees: 11 - 20 **Product Groups:** 62, 66

Date of Accounts	Apr 11	Apr 10	Apr 09
Working Capital	63	218	377
Fixed Assets	2m	1m	1m
Current Assets	785	856	1m

Laboratory Supplies & Instruments Ltd
Unit 13b-13d Rathenraw Industrial Estate, Antrim, BT41 2SJ
Tel: 028-9446 3070 **Fax:** 028-9446 8642
E-mail: info@labsuppliesltd.co.uk
Website: http://www.labsuppliesltd.co.uk
Directors: C. Mclean (Dir)
Immediate Holding Company: LABORATORY SUPPLIES AND INSTRUMENTS LIMITED
Registration no: NI004169 **VAT No.:** GB 254 9914 27
Date established: 1958 **No.of Employees:** 1 - 10 **Product Groups:** 67

Date of Accounts	Oct 11	Oct 10	Oct 09
Working Capital	224	251	269
Fixed Assets	8	11	13
Current Assets	349	362	396

M & M
204 Staffordstown Road Toomebridge, Antrim, BT41 3NY
Tel: 028-7965 0023 **Fax:** 028-7965 9178
E-mail: martinamclernon@aol.com
Website: http://www.gatesni.com
Directors: M. Mclernon (Prop)
Immediate Holding Company: GATE COMPONENTS LIMITED
Registration no: NI068090 **Date established:** 2008
No.of Employees: 1 - 10 **Product Groups:** 26, 35

M & T Industrial Switchgear Ltd
Unit E 1 A Enkalon Industrial Estate Randalstown Road, Antrim, BT41 4LJ
Tel: 028-946 5900 **Fax:** 028-9442 8008
Website: http://www.grantselectrical.co.uk
Directors: R. Mcgill (Dir)
Managers: R. Cregg (Mgr)
Immediate Holding Company: M & T INDUSTRIAL SWITCHGEAR LIMITED
Registration no: NI028835 **VAT No.:** GB 432 6714 60
Date established: 1994 **No.of Employees:** 1 - 10 **Product Groups:** 37, 67

Mccloy D Gunsmith
21 Hillhead Road Toomebridge, Antrim, BT41 3SF
Tel: 028-7965 0641 **Fax:** 028-7965 9033
E-mail: donalmccloy@mccloys.com
Website: http://www.mccloyguns.com
Directors: D. Mccloy (Snr Part)
Immediate Holding Company: COPPER INDUSTRIES (IRELAND) LIMITED
Registration no: NI041404 **Date established:** 1997
No.of Employees: 1 - 10 **Product Groups:** 36, 39, 40

Date of Accounts	Mar 12	Mar 11	Mar 10
Working Capital	302	208	278
Fixed Assets	219	243	191
Current Assets	791	540	533
Current Liabilities	N/A	32	N/A

Mccomb N I Ltd
Unit 10 Springfarm Industrial Estate, Antrim, BT41 4NT
Tel: 028-9446 2611 **Fax:** 028-9446 2794
E-mail: myles@mccobebros.co.uk
Website: http://www.mccombebros.co.uk
Managers: M. Carville (Fin Mgr)
Ultimate Holding Company: MCCOMBE BROTHERS (NI) LIMITED
Immediate Holding Company: MBA REALISATIONS LIMITED
Registration no: NI006740 **VAT No.:** GB 251 9367 48
Date established: 1966 **Turnover:** £5m - £10m **No.of Employees:** 11 - 20
Product Groups: 52

Date of Accounts	Feb 08	Feb 10	Feb 09
Sales Turnover	16m	8m	9m
Pre Tax Profit/Loss	-2m	-250	-257
Working Capital	-2m	-2m	-2m
Fixed Assets	3m	2m	2m
Current Assets	7m	4m	6m
Current Liabilities	3m	2m	2m

Mivan Ltd
Newpark Greystone Road, Antrim, BT41 2QN
Tel: 028-9448 1000 **Fax:** 028-9448 1015
E-mail: hq@mivan.com
Website: http://www.mivan.com
Bank(s): Northern Bank
Directors: J. Winter (Fin)
Managers: G. Cowan (Purch Mgr), L. Campbell (Mktg Serv Mgr)
Ultimate Holding Company: MIVAN (UK) LIMITED
Immediate Holding Company: MIVAN LIMITED
Registration no: NI019876 **VAT No.:** GB 353 1676 55
Date established: 1986 **Turnover:** £75m - £125m
No.of Employees: 251 - 500 **Product Groups:** 52, 84

Date of Accounts	Dec 09	Dec 08	Dec 07
Sales Turnover	66m	68m	56m
Pre Tax Profit/Loss	-26m	6m	2m
Working Capital	-6m	5m	2m
Fixed Assets	19m	39m	80m
Current Assets	37m	61m	40m
Current Liabilities	5m	18m	6m

Nanabelle's Gift Shops
24b Railway Street, Antrim, BT41 4AE
Tel: 028-9448 7787 **Fax:** 028-9448 7787
E-mail: info@nanabellesgifts.com
Website: http://www.nanabellesgifts.com
Directors: K. McCurdy (Prop)
Turnover: Up to £250,000 **No.of Employees:** 1 - 10 **Product Groups:** 32, 36, 49, 65

Old Mill Business Park
Seven Mile Straight Muckamore, Antrim, BT41 4QE
Tel: 028-9446 2204 **Fax:** 028-9446 0905
Directors: I. McCullough (Prop)
Ultimate Holding Company: IRELAND FREIGHT SERVICES (U.K.) LIMITED
Immediate Holding Company: IRELAND FREIGHT (FORWARDING) SERVICES LTD.
Registration no: NI031698 **VAT No.:** GB 255 6386 35
Date established: 2009 **Turnover:** £20m - £50m
No.of Employees: 21 - 50 **Product Groups:** 52, 66

Date of Accounts	Dec 10	Dec 09	Dec 08
Sales Turnover	27m	17m	N/A
Pre Tax Profit/Loss	3m	898	2m
Working Capital	5m	3m	4m
Fixed Assets	925	1m	1m
Current Assets	12m	7m	9m
Current Liabilities	3m	633	576

P I L Ltd
5 Caulside Drive, Antrim, BT41 2DU
Tel: 028-9448 1800 **Fax:** 028-9448 1801
E-mail: raymond@pneutrol.com
Website: http://www.pneutral.com
Directors: E. McPherson (MD)
Managers: A. McPherson (Tech Serv Mgr)
Ultimate Holding Company: CHASE PHARMACY LIMITED
Immediate Holding Company: PNEUTROL INTERNATIONAL LIMITED
Registration no: 04231998 **Date established:** 1976
No.of Employees: 21 - 50 **Product Groups:** 38, 42

Date of Accounts	May 12	May 11	May 10
Working Capital	806	864	918
Fixed Assets	837	784	857
Current Assets	1m	1m	1m

Personnel Hygiene Services Washrooms Ltd
Unit 5 Ankalon Indl-Est, Antrim, BT41 4LT
Tel: 028-9448 8485 **Fax:** 028-9446 5580
E-mail: antrim@phs.co.uk
Website: http://www.phs.co.uk
Bank(s): Northern Bank
Directors: R. McAullugh (MD), P. Cohen (Grp Chief Exec)
Managers: K. McDermott (Asst Gen Mgr), R. McCulloch (Mgr)
VAT No.: GB 432 7252 67 **Turnover:** £10m - £20m
No.of Employees: 11 - 20 **Product Groups:** 54, 63

John H Place Steels Ltd
44 Black Park Road Toomebridge, Antrim, BT41 3SL
Tel: 028-7965 0481 **Fax:** 028-7965 0175
E-mail: johnhplace@btconnect.com
Website: http://www.johnhplace.com
Directors: D. Gribbin (MD)
Immediate Holding Company: John H. Place (Steels) Limited
Registration no: NI052160 **VAT No.:** GB 252 3275 77
Date established: 2004 **Turnover:** Up to £250,000
No.of Employees: 1 - 10 **Product Groups:** 61, 66

Date of Accounts	Mar 12	Mar 11	Mar 10
Working Capital	515	424	361
Fixed Assets	268	272	271
Current Assets	883	625	621

Pneutrol International Ltd
5 Caulside Drive, Antrim, BT41 2DU
Tel: 028-9448 1800 **Fax:** 028-9448 1801
E-mail: info@pneutrol.com
Website: http://www.pneutrol.com
Bank(s): Ulster Bank
Directors: G. Mcpherson (MD)
Immediate Holding Company: PNEUTROL INTERNATIONAL LIMITED
Registration no: NI011109 **VAT No.:** 283128067 **Date established:** 1976
Turnover: £2m - £5m **No.of Employees:** 21 - 50 **Product Groups:** 37, 38

Date of Accounts	May 12	May 11	May 10
Working Capital	806	864	918
Fixed Assets	837	784	857
Current Assets	1m	1m	1m

Project Design Engineers Ltd
Enkalon Business Centre 25 Randalstown Road, Antrim, BT41 4LJ
Tel: 028-9448 3000 **Fax:** 028-9448 3010
E-mail: bob.pearson@pde.co.uk
Website: http://www.pde.co.uk
Bank(s): First Trust Bank
Directors: S. Murray (Dir), C. Younge (Dir)
Managers: M. Pye (Personnel), B. McMaster (Tech Serv Mgr), E. Black (Fin Mgr)
Immediate Holding Company: PROJECT DESIGN ENGINEERS LIMITED
Registration no: NI023197 **VAT No.:** GB 516 6583 31
Date established: 1989 **Turnover:** £2m - £5m **No.of Employees:** 21 - 50
Product Groups: 84

Date of Accounts	Mar 11	Mar 10	Mar 09
Working Capital	2m	2m	2m
Fixed Assets	67	39	41
Current Assets	3m	3m	2m

R & D Laboratories Ltd
Unit U Enkalon Industrial Estate Randalstown Road, Antrim, BT41 4LJ
Tel: 028-9446 5753 **Fax:** 028-9446 0754
E-mail: agnes.mcfarlane@rdlabs.co.uk
Website: http://www.mistralni.com
Managers: A. Mcfarlane (Admin Off)
Immediate Holding Company: R & D LABORATORIES LIMITED
Registration no: NI029750 **Date established:** 1995
Turnover: £500,000 - £1m **No.of Employees:** 11 - 20
Product Groups: 32, 68

Date of Accounts	Sep 11	Sep 10	Sep 09
Working Capital	176	162	202
Fixed Assets	20	27	18
Current Assets	366	412	412

Racking & Shelving Ltd
10 Fergusons Way Kilbegs Road, Antrim, BT41 4LZ
Tel: 028-9442 9037 **Fax:** 028-9442 9036
E-mail: info@rslni.com
Website: http://www.rslni.com
Managers: E. Scott (Comptroller)
Immediate Holding Company: RACKING & SHELVING LIMITED
Registration no: NI043858 **Date established:** 2002
No.of Employees: 11 - 20 **Product Groups:** 26, 67

Date of Accounts	Dec 11	Dec 10	Dec 09
Working Capital	300	295	285
Fixed Assets	44	63	94
Current Assets	581	619	579

Roof Clad Profiles
Unit 11a Rathenraw Industrial Estate, Antrim, BT41 2SJ
Tel: 028-9446 9665 **Fax:** 028-9446 6088
E-mail: roofclad@btconnect.com
Directors: S. Nelson (Prop)
Immediate Holding Company: Roofclad Profiles Limited
Registration no: NI066247 **Date established:** 2007
No.of Employees: 1 - 10 **Product Groups:** 35

Date of Accounts	Sep 11	Sep 10	Sep 09
Working Capital	108	143	113
Fixed Assets	78	92	107
Current Assets	342	413	513

Russell Simpson Construction Ltd
12 Market Square, Antrim, BT41 4AW
Tel: 028-9446 4844 **Fax:** 028-9446 4142
E-mail: info@russell-simpson.com
Website: http://www.russell-simpson.com
Bank(s): First Trust
Directors: G. Hannah (Sales & Mktg), S. Harris (Fin), R. Simpson (Dir)
Managers: A. Docherty (Sales Admin)
Ultimate Holding Company: MAY ESTATES LTD
Immediate Holding Company: RUSSELL SIMPSON CONSTRUCTION COMPANY LIMITED
Registration no: NI013560 **VAT No.:** GB 331 8560 65
Date established: 1979 **Turnover:** £5m - £10m **No.of Employees:** 11 - 20
Product Groups: 52

Date of Accounts	Apr 11	Apr 10	Apr 09
Sales Turnover	8m	11m	10m
Pre Tax Profit/Loss	21	-171	623
Working Capital	792	718	844
Fixed Assets	715	802	795
Current Assets	3m	4m	3m
Current Liabilities	138	193	252

S D C Trailers
116 Deer Park Road Toomebridge, Antrim, BT41 3SS
Tel: 028-7965 0765 **Fax:** 028-7965 0142
E-mail: robertstanley@sdctrailers.com
Website: http://www.sdctrailers.com
Bank(s): Northern Bank
Directors: C. McCauley (Fin)
Managers: C. Reid (Buyer), R. Patton, R. Stanley (Sales Prom Mgr), J. Millar (Personnel)
Ultimate Holding Company: RETLAN MANUFACTURING LTD
Immediate Holding Company: SDC TRAILERS LIMITED
Registration no: NI015713 **VAT No.:** GB 349 7219 24
Date established: 1982 **Turnover:** £75m - £125m
No.of Employees: 251 - 500 **Product Groups:** 39

Date of Accounts	Mar 12	Mar 11	Mar 09
Sales Turnover	89m	81m	75m
Pre Tax Profit/Loss	2m	1m	2m
Working Capital	17m	15m	13m
Fixed Assets	20m	21m	22m
Current Assets	60m	61m	45m
Current Liabilities	5m	4m	5m

Schrader Electronics Ltd
11 Technology Park Belfast Road, Muckamore, Antrim, BT41 1QS
Tel: 028-9446 1300 **Fax:** 028-9446 8440
E-mail: info@schrader.co.uk
Website: http://www.schrader.co.uk
Directors: G. Thompson (Fin)
Ultimate Holding Company: TOMKINS LIMITED
Immediate Holding Company: SCHRADER ELECTRONICS LIMITED
Registration no: NI025720 **VAT No.:** GB 574 5255 23
Date established: 1991 **Turnover:** £125m - £250m
No.of Employees: 501 - 1000 **Product Groups:** 39

Date of Accounts	Dec 11	Dec 10	Jan 09
Sales Turnover	170m	147m	109m
Pre Tax Profit/Loss	15m	8m	7m
Working Capital	16m	16m	21m
Fixed Assets	14m	17m	23m
Current Assets	48m	40m	35m
Current Liabilities	5m	6m	3m

Shanes Castle Estates Co. Ltd
Shanes Castle Park, Antrim, BT41 4NE
Tel: 028-9442 8216 **Fax:** 028-9446 8457
E-mail: shanescastle@nireland.com
Managers: S. O'neill (Mgr)
Immediate Holding Company: SHANES CASTLE ESTATES COMPANY LIMITED
Registration no: NI015648 **VAT No.:** GB 254 6557 40
Date established: 1982 **No.of Employees:** 11 - 20 **Product Groups:** 69, 89

Date of Accounts	Mar 11	Mar 10	Mar 09
Working Capital	129	650	261
Fixed Assets	6m	5m	4m
Current Assets	671	1m	734

Springfarm Architectural Mouldings Ltd
Newpark Industrial Estate Greystone Road, Antrim, BT41 2RU
Tel: 028-9442 8288 **Fax:** 028-9442 8244
E-mail: samm@sammouldings.co.uk
Website: http://www.sammouldings.co.uk
Bank(s): First Trust
Directors: G. Wilson (Sales)
Managers: S. Mccrea, T. Patton, S. Shaw (Fin Mgr), G. McClean (Personnel)
Immediate Holding Company: SPRINGFARM ARCHITECTURAL MOULDINGS LIMITED
Registration no: NI024953 **Date established:** 1990
Turnover: £10m - £20m **No.of Employees:** 51 - 100 **Product Groups:** 30

Date of Accounts	Feb 08	Feb 11	Feb 10
Sales Turnover	N/A	10m	10m
Pre Tax Profit/Loss	118	-117	-2m
Working Capital	-427	-149	-453
Fixed Assets	6m	5m	5m
Current Assets	6m	4m	3m
Current Liabilities	1m	2m	1m

Target Transport Ltd
112 Staffordstown Road Randalstown, Antrim, BT41 3LH
Tel: 028-9447 2062 **Fax:** 028-9447 3853
E-mail: mark.tait@targettransport.co.uk
Website: http://www.targettransport.co.uk
Directors: M. Tait (Prop)
Immediate Holding Company: TARGET TRANSPORT LIMITED
Registration no: NI030534 **VAT No.:** GB 432 6355 62
Date established: 1996 **No.of Employees:** 1 - 10 **Product Groups:** 72, 76

Date of Accounts	Apr 12	Apr 11	Apr 10
Working Capital	-15	-6	-8
Fixed Assets	16	11	9
Current Assets	257	241	170

Ulster Fire Extinguishers Service Ltd
Unit 9 Antrim Enterprise Park 58 Greystone Road, Antrim, BT41 1JZ
Tel: 028-9446 1524 **Fax:** 028-9442 9515
E-mail: sid.ufe@btinternet.com
Directors: S. Armstrong (Dir)
Immediate Holding Company: ULSTER FIRE EXTINGUISHERS SERVICE DIVISION LIMITED
Registration no: NI019560 **Date established:** 1986
No.of Employees: 1 - 10 **Product Groups:** 38, 42

Date of Accounts	Dec 11	Dec 10	Dec 09
Working Capital	42	54	76
Fixed Assets	6	N/A	1
Current Assets	69	85	108

Ulster Wool Group Ltd
20 Tirgracy Road Muckamore, Antrim, BT41 4PS
Tel: 028-9446 2131 **Fax:** 028-9446 0723
E-mail: sales@ulsterwool-farmsupplies.co.uk
Managers: J. Wilson (Mgr)
Immediate Holding Company: ULSTER WOOL GROUP LIMITED
Registration no: NI014871 **VAT No.:** GB 516 9442 32
Date established: 1981 **Turnover:** £500,000 - £1m
No.of Employees: 1 - 10 **Product Groups:** 23, 66

Date of Accounts	Apr 12	Apr 11	Apr 10
Working Capital	310	282	224
Fixed Assets	159	158	174
Current Assets	382	355	510

W H Rea Engineering
290 Lisnevenagh Road Lisnevenagh Raod, Antrim, BT41 2JL
Tel: 028-9446 2193 **Fax:** 028-9446 0716
E-mail: info@whrea.com
Website: http://www.whrea.com
Directors: G. Rea (Prop)
Turnover: Up to £250,000 **No.of Employees:** 1 - 10 **Product Groups:** 07, 41

Co. Armagh

Armagh

A & N Shilliday & Co.
Ballynahonemore Road, Armagh, BT60 1ED
Tel: 028-3752 3591 **Fax:** 028-3752 2150
E-mail: sales@shillidayref.com
Website: http://www.shillidayref.com
Bank(s): Bank of Ireland
Directors: A. Shilliday (Prop)
Immediate Holding Company: A & N SHILLIDAY & CO. LIMITED
Registration no: NI012137 **Date established:** 1977
No.of Employees: 21 - 50 **Product Groups:** 52

Date of Accounts	Mar 11	Mar 10	Mar 09
Working Capital	140	148	118
Fixed Assets	148	143	161
Current Assets	940	725	760

Armagh Construction Ltd
14 Ennislare Road, Armagh, BT60 2AX
Tel: 028-3752 3047 **Fax:** 028-3752 3166
E-mail: acl_scc@ireland.com
Directors: S. Griven (Gen Sec), T. Mckeown (Dir), N. Campbell (Dir), J. Gribben (MD)
Managers: T. McKeonn (Mktg Serv Mgr), A. Mone (Fin Mgr)
Immediate Holding Company: ARMAGH CONSTRUCTION LIMITED
Registration no: NI009240 **VAT No.:** GB 252 0676 74
Date established: 1973 **Turnover:** £250,000 - £500,000
No.of Employees: 1 - 10 **Product Groups:** 52

Date of Accounts	Feb 11	Feb 10	Feb 09
Working Capital	59	80	84
Fixed Assets	51	60	71
Current Assets	82	93	109

Armatile Tile Stockists
Station Road, Armagh, BT61 7NP
Tel: 028-3752 7007 **Fax:** 028-3752 6944
E-mail: enquiry@armatile.com
Website: http://www.armatile.com
Directors: J. Mccann (Prop), P. Quinn (MD)
Managers: F. Smith (Tech Serv Mgr), C. Moore (Chief Acct)
Immediate Holding Company: SHABRA RECYCLING (NORTHERN IRELAND) LIMITED
Registration no: NI602216 **VAT No.:** GB 286 5583 11
Date established: 1998 **Turnover:** £2m - £5m **No.of Employees:** 21 - 50
Product Groups: 33

Avolon Window Blinds & Awnings
Unit 52 Armagh Business Centre Lough Gall Road, Armagh, BT61 7NH
Tel: 028-3752 7874 **Fax:** 028-3752 7468
E-mail: info@avolonblinds.com
Website: http://www.avolonblinds.com
Managers: P. Corrigan (Mgr)
Immediate Holding Company: HIGH SPEC PRODUCTS LTD
Date established: 1997 **No.of Employees:** 1 - 10 **Product Groups:** 25, 35

Brookwood Kitchens & Bedrooms
42 Cladymilltown Road Mowhan, Armagh, BT60 2EF
Tel: 028-3750 7417 **Fax:** 028-3750 7417
E-mail: info@brookwoodkitchens.co.uk
Website: http://www.brookwoodkitchens.co.uk
Directors: R. Duggan (Dir)
Immediate Holding Company: BROOKWOOD KITCHENS LTD
Registration no: NI610424 **VAT No.:** GB 517 7925 18
Date established: 2011 **No.of Employees:** 1 - 10 **Product Groups:** 26

Bunzl Catering Supplies
30 Loughgall Road, Armagh, BT61 7NX
Tel: 028-3751 5152 **Fax:** 028-9127 5872
E-mail: info@bunzl.co.uk
Managers: M. Donnelly
Ultimate Holding Company: BUNZL PUBLIC LIMITED COMPANY
Immediate Holding Company: CENTRAL CATERING SUPPLIES LIMITED
Registration no: 03888254 **VAT No.:** GB 392 5049 40
Date established: 1999 **No.of Employees:** 11 - 20 **Product Groups:** 52

Cootes' Concrete Ltd
Redrock Road Collone, Armagh, BT60 2BL
Tel: 028-3755 1126 **Fax:** 028-3755 1207
E-mail: cootes@tiscali.co.uk
Directors: D. Cootes (MD)
Immediate Holding Company: COOTES (CONCRETE PRODUCTS) LIMITED
Registration no: NI013081 **VAT No.:** GB 253 0342 00
Date established: 1978 **No.of Employees:** 1 - 10 **Product Groups:** 14, 33

Date of Accounts	Dec 11	Dec 10	Dec 09
Working Capital	169	144	146
Fixed Assets	4m	4m	4m
Current Assets	1m	992	1m

Electric Motor Rewinds
19 Castleblayney Road Keady, Armagh, BT60 3QP
Tel: 028-3753 1526 **Fax:** 028-3753 1526
Directors: J. Kinsella (Prop)
VAT No.: GB 283 1174 66 **Turnover:** Up to £250,000
No.of Employees: 1 - 10 **Product Groups:** 48

Fairline Sales & Marketing Ltd
35 Legacorry Road Richhill, Armagh, BT61 9LA
Tel: 028-3887 1779 **Fax:** 028-3887 0642
E-mail: fairlinesales@btconnect.com
Website: http://www.fairlinekitchens.com
Directors: A. Tedford (Prop)
Immediate Holding Company: FAIRLINE SALES & MARKETING LIMITED
Registration no: NI025949 **VAT No.:** GB 517 5469 28
Date established: 1991 **No.of Employees:** 1 - 10 **Product Groups:** 26

Date of Accounts	Dec 11	Dec 10	Dec 09
Working Capital	63	96	148
Fixed Assets	139	143	149
Current Assets	177	231	271

Fane Valley
Alexander Road, Armagh, BT61 7JJ
Tel: 028-3752 2344 **Fax:** 028-3751 0511
E-mail: contact@fanevalley.co.uk
Website: http://www.fanevalley.com
Bank(s): Ulster Bank
Directors: M. Gowdy (Mkt Research), T. Lockhart (Grp Chief Exec)
Managers: W. McConnell, G. Pelan (Tech Serv Mgr), S. Milligan (Comptroller), T. Enderby (Personnel)
Immediate Holding Company: FANE VALLEY STORES LIMITED
Registration no: NI032151 **VAT No.:** GB 252 0423 06
Date established: 1997 **Turnover:** £75m - £125m
No.of Employees: 21 - 50 **Product Groups:** 62

Date of Accounts	Sep 11	Sep 10	Sep 09
Sales Turnover	N/A	4m	3m
Pre Tax Profit/Loss	N/A	130	158
Working Capital	180	766	733
Fixed Assets	360	89	27
Current Assets	7m	2m	1m
Current Liabilities	N/A	160	54

R J Farrell
100 Mowhan Road Markethill, Armagh, BT60 1RQ
Tel: 028-3755 1519 **Fax:** 028-3755 1494
E-mail: info@rjfarrelljoinery.com
Website: http://www.rjfarrelljoinery.com
Directors: R. Farrell (Prop)
VAT No.: GB 286 5869 90 **Date established:** 1974
Turnover: Up to £250,000 **No.of Employees:** 1 - 10 **Product Groups:** 25

J Flanigan & Son Ltd
14 Irish Street Richhill, Armagh, BT61 9PS
Tel: 028-3887 1208 **Fax:** 028-3887 0808
E-mail: mail@flaniganfurniture.com
Website: http://www.flaniganfurniture.com
Directors: A. Flanigan (Dir)
VAT No.: GB 252 2357 80 **Turnover:** £250,000 - £500,000
No.of Employees: 11 - 20 **Product Groups:** 26

Hewitt Meats
Lisheffield House Loughgall, Armagh, BT61 8QB
Tel: 028-3889 1522 **Fax:** 028-3889 1211
E-mail: james@hewittmeats.co.uk
Website: http://www.hewittmeats.co.uk
Directors: J. Hewitt (Dir)
Managers: J. Annett (Factory Mgr)
Immediate Holding Company: HEWITT MEATS
Registration no: NI045689 **VAT No.:** GB 283 0420 82
Date established: 2003 **Turnover:** £2m - £5m **No.of Employees:** 1 - 10
Product Groups: 62

James Zwecker Transport & Storage Ltd
40 Cormeen Road Killylea, Armagh, BT60 4ND
Tel: 028-3752 2143 **Fax:** 028-3752 7640
E-mail: info@zweckertransport.co.uk
Website: http://www.zweckertransport.co.uk
Directors: N. Zwecker (Prop), J. Zwecker (Fin)
Managers: J. Zwecker, I. Anderson (Mktg Serv Mgr), P. Bradshaw (Personnel)
Immediate Holding Company: NOEL ZWECKER INTERNATIONAL TRANSPORT LIMITED
Registration no: NI020378 **VAT No.:** GB 253 3928 52
Date established: 1987 **Turnover:** £5m - £10m
No.of Employees: 51 - 100 **Product Groups:** 72

Date of Accounts	May 10	May 09	May 08
Sales Turnover	7m	7m	N/A
Pre Tax Profit/Loss	-244	14	-93
Working Capital	-455	-344	-342
Fixed Assets	1m	2m	2m
Current Assets	1m	2m	2m
Current Liabilities	425	632	571

John Woods L Ltd
190 Monaghan Road, Armagh, BT60 4EZ
Tel: 028-3756 8477 **Fax:** 028-3756 8865
E-mail: info@linwoods.co.uk
Website: http://www.linwoods.co.uk
Directors: J. Woods (MD)
Managers: A. Gillespie (Sales Prom Mgr), J. Robinson (Tech Serv Mgr), P. Lappin (Fin Mgr), B. Beattie (Mktg Serv Mgr), O. Moore (Personnel)
Immediate Holding Company: JOHN WOODS (LISGLYN) LIMITED
Registration no: NI006498 **VAT No.:** GB 252 7669 36
Date established: 1965 **Turnover:** £20m - £50m
No.of Employees: 251 - 500 **Product Groups:** 61

Date of Accounts	Jul 11	Jul 10	Jul 09
Sales Turnover	34m	31m	29m
Pre Tax Profit/Loss	375	-272	1m
Working Capital	-104	-510	332
Fixed Assets	10m	11m	10m
Current Assets	7m	6m	5m
Current Liabilities	607	773	838

Johnstons Of Mountnorris
48 Lower Lisdrumchor Road Glenanne, Armagh, BT60 2HT
Tel: 028-3750 7281 **Fax:** 028-3750 7333
E-mail: jam.johnston@btconnect.com
Website: http://www.johnstonspoultry.co.uk
Bank(s): Ulster
Directors: W. Johnston (Snr Part)
VAT No.: GB 254 1685 56 **Date established:** 1960 **Turnover:** £1m - £2m
No.of Employees: 11 - 20 **Product Groups:** 67

Killeen Hardware
1 Killycapple Road, Armagh, BT60 2AG
Tel: 028-3752 2317 **Fax:** 028-3752 8411
E-mail: sales@killeenhardware.com
Website: http://www.killeenhardware.com
Directors: K. Hughes (Ptnr)
Immediate Holding Company: Killeen Hardware inc Hillocks
Registration no: NI060352 **VAT No.:** GB 390 7477 21
Date established: 2006 **Turnover:** Up to £250,000
No.of Employees: 11 - 20 **Product Groups:** 66

Mcardle Peat
90 Ballygassoon Road, Armagh, BT61 8DT
Tel: 028-3889 1506 **Fax:** 028-3889 1529
E-mail: sales@mcardle-mushrooms.com
Website: http://www.mcardle-mushrooms.com
Directors: J. Mcardle (MD)
Immediate Holding Company: McArdle Peat Limited
Registration no: NI043531 **Date established:** 2002
No.of Employees: 1 - 10 **Product Groups:** 02, 11, 62, 81

Date of Accounts	Dec 11	Dec 10	Dec 09
Working Capital	-112	-115	-111
Fixed Assets	311	314	310
Current Assets	45	49	61
Current Liabilities	N/A	64	69

F Mccone & Sons Ltd
84 Coolmillish Road Markethill, Armagh, BT60 1SH
Tel: 028-3755 1363 **Fax:** 028-3755 2041
E-mail: fmccone@hotmail.com
Website: http://www.f/mccone.co.uk
Directors: P. Mccone (MD)
Immediate Holding Company: FRANCIS MCCONE & SONS LIMITED
Registration no: NI006382 **VAT No.:** GB 254 5964 32
Date established: 1965 **No.of Employees:** 1 - 10 **Product Groups:** 45

Date of Accounts	Dec 11	Dec 10	Dec 09
Working Capital	13	19	1
Fixed Assets	109	121	174
Current Assets	54	87	155

J F Mckenna Ltd
66 Cathedral Road, Armagh, BT61 8AE
Tel: 028-3752 4800 **Fax:** 028-3752 2227
E-mail: jfm@jfmckenna.com
Website: http://www.jfmckenna.com
Bank(s): Ulster Bank
Directors: N. Vanderveen (Fin), B. Mckenna (MD)
Managers: J. Dunleavy (Tech Serv Mgr), L. McVeighty (Personnel), E. Kelly
Immediate Holding Company: J.F. MCKENNA LIMITED
Registration no: NI015435 **Date established:** 1982 **Turnover:** £5m - £10m
No.of Employees: 51 - 100 **Product Groups:** 27, 30

Date of Accounts	Jun 11	Jun 10	Jun 09
Sales Turnover	9m	8m	8m
Pre Tax Profit/Loss	163	139	157
Working Capital	1m	1m	478
Fixed Assets	2m	2m	2m
Current Assets	3m	3m	3m
Current Liabilities	345	343	385

Mcelmeel Mobility Services Ltd
15 Ballyscandal Road, Armagh, BT61 8BL
Tel: 028-3752 5333 **Fax:** 028-3752 7740
E-mail: info@mobility-services.com
Website: http://www.mobility-services.com
Directors: E. McElmeel (Gen Sec), M. Mcelmeel (MD), N. Hughes (Co Sec)
Managers: P. Donley (Fin Mgr)
Immediate Holding Company: MCELMEEL MOBILITY SERVICES LIMITED
Registration no: NI031911 **Date established:** 1997
No.of Employees: 11 - 20 **Product Groups:** 38, 67

Date of Accounts	Jan 12	Jan 11	Jan 10
Working Capital	704	579	502
Fixed Assets	121	134	150
Current Assets	917	748	632

N C Engineering Hamiltonsbawn Ltd
2 Killyruddan Road Hamiltonsbawn, Armagh, BT61 9SF
Tel: 028-3887 1970 **Fax:** 028-3887 0362
E-mail: info@nc-engineering.com
Website: http://www.nc-engineering.com
Directors: N. Nicholl (Dir), N. Nicholl (MD), W. Carson (Dir)
Managers: A. Mcroberts (Purch Mgr)
Immediate Holding Company: NC Engineering (Hamiltonsbawn) Limited
Registration no: NI015976 **Date established:** 1982
Turnover: £10m - £20m **No.of Employees:** 51 - 100 **Product Groups:** 41

Date of Accounts	Aug 11	Aug 10	Aug 09
Sales Turnover	11m	N/A	N/A
Pre Tax Profit/Loss	4	43	186
Working Capital	1m	1m	1m
Fixed Assets	2m	2m	3m
Current Assets	4m	3m	4m
Current Liabilities	243	317	355

Nederman Ltd
Unit 9-10 Market Hill Business Centre Fairgreen Road, Markethill, Armagh, BT60 1PW
Tel: 028-3755 1529 **Fax:** 028-3755 1608
E-mail: info@nederman.com
Website: http://www.nederman.com
Directors: C. Wilkinson (Dir)
Ultimate Holding Company: NEDERMAN HOLDINGS AB (SWEDEN)
Immediate Holding Company: NEDERMAN LIMITED
Registration no: 01393492 **VAT No.:** GB 434 2044 87
Date established: 1978 **No.of Employees:** 11 - 20 **Product Groups:** 40, 54

Date of Accounts	Dec 11	Dec 10	Dec 09
Sales Turnover	13m	10m	N/A
Pre Tax Profit/Loss	446	545	-477
Working Capital	57	2m	2m
Fixed Assets	3m	739	816
Current Assets	6m	4m	3m
Current Liabilities	2m	652	599

Nugent & Gibney
149 Loughgall Road, Armagh, BT61 8EP
Tel: 028-3752 3927 **Fax:** 028-3752 8105
E-mail: p.nugent@btconnect.com
Website: http://www.nugentandgibney.com
Bank(s): Northern Bank
Directors: V. Nugent (Ptnr)
Immediate Holding Company: NUGENT & GIBNEY LIMITED
Registration no: NI011715 **VAT No.:** GB 286 7263 19
Date established: 1976 **Turnover:** Up to £250,000
No.of Employees: 21 - 50 **Product Groups:** 26

Date of Accounts	Jan 12	Jan 11	Jan 10
Working Capital	633	668	695
Fixed Assets	334	336	374
Current Assets	830	850	872

Red Rhino Interactive Ltd
Maranatha House 55 Legacorry Road, Richhill, Armagh, BT61 9LF
Tel: 028-3887 9909
E-mail: marketing@redrhino.co.uk
Website: http://www.redrhino.co.uk
Directors: R. Kenny (MD)
Immediate Holding Company: RED RHINO INTERACTIVE LTD
Registration no: NI043777 **Date established:** 2002
Turnover: Up to £250,000 **No.of Employees:** 1 - 10 **Product Groups:** 44

Date of Accounts	Jun 11	Jun 10	Jun 09
Working Capital	8	14	15
Fixed Assets	32	2	3
Current Assets	37	49	55

Redrock Machinery Ltd
77 Redrock Road Collone, Armagh, BT60 2BL
Tel: 028-3755 2390 **Fax:** 028-3755 2399
E-mail: info@redrockmachinery.com
Website: http://www.redrockmachinery.com
Bank(s): Northern Bank
Directors: F. Flynn (MD)
Managers: A. Smyth (Tech Serv Mgr), M. Linden (Sales Prom Mgr)
Immediate Holding Company: REDROCK MACHINERY LIMITED
Registration no: NI602382 **VAT No.:** GB 286 8635 03
Date established: 2010 **No.of Employees:** 21 - 50 **Product Groups:** 41

Date of Accounts	Mar 11
Working Capital	755
Fixed Assets	1m
Current Assets	2m

Reen Compost Ltd
19 Mullanary Road Middletown, Armagh, BT60 4HW
Tel: 028-3756 8746 **Fax:** 028-3756 8708
E-mail: reencompost@hotmail.com
Directors: J. Mcardle (Dir)
Immediate Holding Company: REEN COMPOST LIMITED
Registration no: NI022440 **VAT No.:** GB 331 2992 66
Date established: 1989 **No.of Employees:** 11 - 20 **Product Groups:** 32, 41

Date of Accounts	Mar 11	Mar 10	Mar 09
Working Capital	-185	-141	-236
Fixed Assets	194	218	237
Current Assets	363	327	363

Rosco Engineering N I Ltd
Fruitfield Factory 10 Crewcatt Road, Richhill, Armagh, BT61 8QN
Tel: 028-3887 1979 **Fax:** 028-3887 0657
E-mail: info@roscoeng.co.uk
Website: http://www.roscoeng.co.uk
Bank(s): First Trust
Directors: R. Scott (MD)
Immediate Holding Company: ROSCO ENGINEERING (NI) LIMITED
Registration no: NI037574 **VAT No.:** GB 287 2695 09
Date established: 1999 **Turnover:** £2m - £5m **No.of Employees:** 11 - 20
Product Groups: 35

Date of Accounts	Mar 12	Mar 11	Mar 10
Working Capital	154	162	108
Fixed Assets	561	501	511
Current Assets	570	524	341

R Thompson & Son Armagh Ltd
58a Hamiltonsbawn Road, Armagh, BT60 1HW
Tel: 028-3752 2707 **Fax:** 028-3752 7987
E-mail: accounts@farmlayeggs.co.uk
Website: http://www.farmlayeggs.co.uk
Directors: D. Thompson (Prop)
Managers: J. Thompson (Comm)
Immediate Holding Company: R. THOMPSON & SON (ARMAGH) LIMITED
Registration no: NI007069 **VAT No.:** GB 253 4046 81
Date established: 1967 **Turnover:** £10m - £20m
No.of Employees: 21 - 50 **Product Groups:** 01

Date of Accounts	Dec 11	Dec 10	Dec 09
Sales Turnover	11m	10m	10m
Pre Tax Profit/Loss	155	353	528
Working Capital	2m	2m	2m
Fixed Assets	946	993	1m
Current Assets	4m	4m	3m
Current Liabilities	136	170	253

Tretzo
18 Ballynahonemore Road, Armagh, BT60 1ED
Tel: 028-3752 3735 **Fax:** 028-3752 5349
E-mail: info@tretzo.com
Website: http://www.tretzo.com
Directors: G. Clarke (MD)
Immediate Holding Company: C. AND R. FURNITURE (ARMAGH) LIMITED
Registration no: NI009243 **Date established:** 1973
No.of Employees: 11 - 20 **Product Groups:** 26, 63

Date of Accounts	Jul 12	Jul 11	Jul 10
Working Capital	8	-5	-301
Fixed Assets	446	478	515
Current Assets	198	202	155

Trimprint Ltd
36 Upper English Street, Armagh, BT61 7BE
Tel: 028-3752 2063 **Fax:** 028-3752 5618
E-mail: admin@trimprint.com
Website: http://www.trimprint.com
Directors: T. Trimble (Dir)
Immediate Holding Company: TRIMPRINT LIMITED
Registration no: NI009852 **Date established:** 1973
No.of Employees: 11 - 20 **Product Groups:** 27, 28

Date of Accounts	Mar 11	Mar 10	Mar 09
Working Capital	265	272	250
Fixed Assets	146	158	163
Current Assets	326	340	329

Ulster Builder Providers Ltd
Annvale Industrial Estate 8 Annvale Road, Keady, Armagh, BT60 2RP
Tel: 028-3753 1756 **Fax:** 028-3753 8244
E-mail: dominic@ulsterbuildersproviders.co.uk
Website: http://www.ulsterbuildersproviders.co.uk
Directors: D. Rice (Dir)
Immediate Holding Company: ULSTER BUILDERS PROVIDERS LIMITED
Registration no: NI011666 **VAT No.:** GB 286 5890 02
Date established: 1976 **Turnover:** £250,000 - £500,000
No.of Employees: 11 - 20 **Product Groups:** 66

Date of Accounts	Sep 11	Sep 10	Sep 09
Working Capital	174	243	139
Fixed Assets	3m	3m	3m
Current Assets	1m	995	1m
Current Liabilities	N/A	25	50

The Ulster Gazette
56 Scotch Street, Armagh, BT61 7DQ
Tel: 028-3752 2639 **Fax:** 028-3752 7029
E-mail: personnel@alphanewspapers.co.uk
Website: http://www.ulsternet-ni.co.uk
Managers: J. Taylor
Ultimate Holding Company: TONTINE ROOMS HOLDING COMPANY LIMITED - THE
Immediate Holding Company: SOVEREIGN PROPERTIES (NI) LIMITED
Registration no: NI022271 **VAT No.:** GB 517 5686 20
Date established: 1988 **No.of Employees:** 1 - 10 **Product Groups:** 28

Date of Accounts	Dec 11	Dec 10	Dec 09
Working Capital	-846	-1m	-748
Fixed Assets	6m	6m	6m
Current Assets	2m	2m	2m

Co. Tyrone

Augher

Augher Co-Operative Agricultural & Dairy Society Ltd
9 Crossowen Road, Augher, BT77 0BA
Tel: 028-8554 8214 **Fax:** 028-8554 8651
Managers: I. Rutherford (Mgr)
Immediate Holding Company: AMK FOODS LIMITED
Registration no: NI021873 **VAT No.:** GB 253 4944 49
Date established: 1988 **No.of Employees:** 21 - 50 **Product Groups:** 20, 61

Co. Tyrone

Aughnacloy

Window Fix
27 Rehaghy Road, Aughnacloy, BT69 6EW
Tel: 0774-087 7132 **Fax:** 028-8555 7965
Directors: S. O'donnell (Prop)
No.of Employees: 1 - 10 **Product Groups:** 30, 35, 36

Co. Antrim

Ballycastle

Duncan Plant & Construction
54 Glenshesk Road, Ballycastle, BT54 6PY
Tel: 028-2076 3828 **Fax:** 028-2076 8645
E-mail: info@duncanplant.com
Website: http://www.duncanplant.com
Managers: G. Doran (Chief Mgr)
Date established: 1992 **No.of Employees:** 1 - 10 **Product Groups:** 35, 36, 39

Moyle District Council
Sheskburn House 7 Mary Street, Ballycastle, BT54 6QH
Tel: 028-2076 2225 **Fax:** 028-2076 2515
E-mail: rlewis@moyle-council.org
Website: http://www.moyle-council.org
Directors: J. Lewis (Grp Chief Exec), R. Lewis (Grp Chief Exec)
Managers: S. Kelly (Personnel)
Immediate Holding Company: MOYLE LOCAL STRATEGY PARTNERSHIP LTD
Registration no: NI042603 **Date established:** 2002
No.of Employees: 21 - 50 **Product Groups:** 87

Co. Antrim

Ballyclare

Antrim Hills Spring Water Co. Ltd
100 Irish Hill Road, Ballyclare, BT39 9NL
Tel: 028-9332 2325
E-mail: sales@antrimhills.com
Website: http://www.antrimhills.com
Directors: S. Geary (MD)
Immediate Holding Company: ANTRIM HILLS SPRING WATER COMPANY LIMITED
Registration no: NI023146 **VAT No.:** GB 517 1734 55
Date established: 1989 **No.of Employees:** 11 - 20 **Product Groups:** 21

see next page

Antrim Hills Spring Water Co. Ltd - Cont'd

Date of Accounts	Jan 12	Jan 11	Jan 10
Working Capital	-881	-872	-880
Fixed Assets	821	880	1m
Current Assets	246	206	174

Ballyclare Forklift Training
1 Hawthorn Way, Ballyclare, BT39 9EH
Tel: 028-9332 3960 **Fax:** 028-9332 3960
Directors: T. Brown (Prop)
Date established: 2000 **No.of Employees:** 1 - 10 **Product Groups:** 35, 39, 45

Ballyclare Motor Auctions
Unit 31 Dennison Industrial Estate Avondale Drive, Ballyclare, BT39 9EB
Tel: 028-9332 3819 **Fax:** 028-9334 2890
E-mail: sales@kingscarhire.com
Website: http://www.kingscarhire.com
Directors: I. King (Prop)
Immediate Holding Company: BALLYCLARE CAR HIRE LTD
Registration no: NI026619 **Date established:** 1992
No.of Employees: 1 - 10 **Product Groups:** 68

Bandsaw Services
137b Mill Road, Ballyclare, BT39 9DZ
Tel: 028-9334 4077 **Fax:** 028-9334 4077
E-mail: alanburrows01@btinternet.com
Directors: A. Burrows (Prop)
Date established: 2002 **No.of Employees:** 1 - 10 **Product Groups:** 36

Beechwood Laboratories Ltd
120 Ballymena Road Doagh, Ballyclare, BT39 0TL
Tel: 028-9335 2691 **Fax:** 028-9335 2702
E-mail: accounts@beechwood-laboratories.com
Website: http://www.beechwood-laboratories.com
Bank(s): Northern Bank
Directors: J. Fletcher (Dir)
Immediate Holding Company: Beechwood Laboratories Limited
Registration no: NI046017 **VAT No.:** GB 392 5804 30
Date established: 2003 **Turnover:** £500,000 - £1m
No.of Employees: 11 - 20 **Product Groups:** 85

Date of Accounts	Mar 11	Mar 10	Mar 09
Working Capital	110	110	112
Fixed Assets	12	16	22
Current Assets	181	164	160

C G Automation
19a Lismenary Road Ballynure, Ballyclare, BT39 9UE
Tel: 028-9334 1689 **Fax:** 028-9334 1689
Directors: C. Gillilard (Prop)
Date established: 1998 **No.of Employees:** 1 - 10 **Product Groups:** 26, 35

Colemans Garden Centre
6 Old Ballyclare Road Templepatrick, Ballyclare, BT39 0BJ
Tel: 028-9443 2513 **Fax:** 028-9443 2151
E-mail: richard@colemansgardencentre.co.uk
Website: http://www.colemansgardencentre.co.uk
Directors: R. Fry (Prop)
Date established: 1978 **Turnover:** £500,000 - £1m
No.of Employees: 1 - 10 **Product Groups:** 27, 84

D H L
Unit 13 Dennisons Industrial Estate, Ballyclare, BT39 9EB
Tel: 028-9335 2151 **Fax:** 028-9334 3960
E-mail: lindsay.mclaughlin@dhl.com
Website: http://www.exel.co.uk
Managers: L. Mclaughlin (Chief Mgr), A. Hanna (Admin Off), L. Mclaughlin (Depot Mgr), L. Mclaughlin (Ops Mgr)
No.of Employees: 11 - 20 **Product Groups:** 72

Fleck Brothers Coachworks Ltd
85 Templepatrick Road, Ballyclare, BT39 9RQ
Tel: 028-9332 3866 **Fax:** 028-9335 2830
Directors: S. Fleck (MD)
Immediate Holding Company: FLECK BROTHERS (COACH WORKS) LIMITED
Registration no: NI014972 **VAT No.:** GB 252 9271 55
Date established: 1981 **Turnover:** £1m - £2m **No.of Employees:** 1 - 10
Product Groups: 39

Date of Accounts	Oct 11	Oct 10	Oct 09
Working Capital	-88	-59	-15
Fixed Assets	502	520	907
Current Assets	50	89	115

Glengormley Metal Fabrications
A 1 Manse Road Templepatrick, Ballyclare, BT39 0DA
Tel: 028-9443 3778
Directors: D. Mcglinchey (Prop)
No.of Employees: 1 - 10 **Product Groups:** 26, 35

Hagans Leisure
184 Templepatrick Road Doagh, Ballyclare, BT39 0RA
Tel: 028-9334 0200 **Fax:** 028-9334 2457
E-mail: enquiries@hagansleisure.co.uk
Website: http://www.hagansleisure.co.uk
Bank(s): Ulster Bank
Directors: S. Hagans (Prop)
Managers: J. Morrison (Chief Acct), L. Callaghan (Sales Prom Mgr)
Immediate Holding Company: HAGANS LEISURE LTD
Registration no: NI015602 **VAT No.:** GB 254 5243 68
Date established: 1982 **No.of Employees:** 21 - 50 **Product Groups:** 39, 69, 72

Date of Accounts	Sep 11	Sep 10	Sep 09
Working Capital	353	310	2m
Fixed Assets	2m	2m	2m
Current Assets	2m	2m	4m

Hilton Templepatrick
Paradise Walk Castle Upton Estate, Templepatrick, Ballyclare, BT39 0DD
Tel: 028-9443 5500 **Fax:** 028-9443 5511
E-mail: mark.walker@hilton.com
Website: http://www.hilton.com/templepatrick
Managers: D. Mongan (Tech Serv Mgr), T. Campbell (Mktg Serv Mgr), T. Philips (Personnel), G. Docherty (Sales Prom Mgr), P. Collins (Chief Mgr)
Registration no: 00022163 **Turnover:** £250m - £500m
No.of Employees: 101 - 250 **Product Groups:** 69, 84

J A Mcclelland Sons Auctioneers Ltd
2 Doagh Road, Ballyclare, BT39 9BH
Tel: 028-9335 2727 **Fax:** 028-9334 2447
E-mail: sales@jamcclelland.com
Website: http://www.jamcclelland.com
Managers: S. Irvine (Mgr).
Immediate Holding Company: J. A. MCCLELLAND & SONS (AUCTIONEERS) LIMITED
Registration no: NI003530 **VAT No.:** GB 252 3507 82
Date established: 1955 **Turnover:** £2m - £5m **No.of Employees:** 1 - 10
Product Groups: 80

Date of Accounts	Apr 11	Apr 10	Apr 09
Working Capital	-514	-470	-824
Fixed Assets	5m	5m	5m
Current Assets	3m	3m	2m

Macneill Consultancy
8 Old Coach Mews Templepatrick, Ballyclare, BT39 0JS
Tel: 028-9443 9129
E-mail: info@macneillconsultancy.com
Website: http://www.macneillconsultancy.com
Directors: B. Macneill (Prop)
Turnover: Up to £250,000 **No.of Employees:** 1 - 10 **Product Groups:** 81

N G Engineering Ltd
29 Church Road Ballynure, Ballyclare, BT39 9UF
Tel: 028-9334 2427 **Fax:** 028-9334 0135
E-mail: michelle_mcalister@btconnect.com
Website: http://www.ng-engineering.co.uk
Directors: M. Mcalister (MD)
Immediate Holding Company: N.G. ENGINEERING LIMITED
Registration no: NI035048 **Date established:** 1998
No.of Employees: 1 - 10 **Product Groups:** 37, 68, 79

Date of Accounts	Oct 11	Oct 10	Oct 09
Working Capital	-5	9	18
Fixed Assets	77	85	95
Current Assets	154	156	155

S Rice Market Research
62 Ballygowan Road Ournook, Ballyclare, BT39 9UR
Tel: 028-9334 4559 **Fax:** 028-9334 4552
E-mail: lvmovers@aol.com
Directors: S. Rice (Prop)
Date established: 1984 **Turnover:** Up to £250,000
No.of Employees: 1 - 10 **Product Groups:** 81

Fred C Robinson Ltd
40 Hillhead Road, Ballyclare, BT39 9DS
Tel: 028-9334 0455 **Fax:** 028-9335 2393
E-mail: info@fcrobinson.co.uk
Website: http://www.fcrobinson.co.uk
Directors: R. Hamill (Fin), D. Hamill (MD)
Managers: A. Vonaghy (Sales Prom Mgr), P. Adamson (Purch Mgr), I. Louden (Tech Serv Mgr)
Immediate Holding Company: FRED C.ROBINSON LIMITED
Registration no: NI000908 **Date established:** 1934
Turnover: £10m - £20m **No.of Employees:** 51 - 100 **Product Groups:** 20

Date of Accounts	Sep 11	Sep 10	Sep 09
Sales Turnover	12m	11m	11m
Pre Tax Profit/Loss	59	268	2
Working Capital	2m	2m	2m
Fixed Assets	2m	2m	2m
Current Assets	4m	3m	3m
Current Liabilities	283	242	208

Saint Gobain Weber Ltd
Unit 15 Dennison Industrial Estate, Ballyclare, BT39 9EB
Tel: 028-9335 2999 **Fax:** 028-9332 3232
Website: http://www.netweber.co.uk
Bank(s): Clyesdale Bank
Managers: L. Campbell (Prod Mgr)
Ultimate Holding Company: COMPAGNIE DE SAINT GOBAIN (FRANCE)
Immediate Holding Company: SAINT-GOBAIN WEBER LIMITED
Registration no: 02544294 **VAT No.:** GB 422 2312 10
Date established: 1990 **No.of Employees:** 21 - 50 **Product Groups:** 32, 33

Date of Accounts	Dec 11	Dec 10	Dec 09
Sales Turnover	38m	35m	36m
Pre Tax Profit/Loss	1m	-690	-1m
Working Capital	-3m	-3m	2m
Fixed Assets	25m	26m	27m
Current Assets	12m	12m	11m
Current Liabilities	6m	7m	6m

Springvale Insulation Ltd
75 Springvale Road Doagh, Ballyclare, BT39 0SS
Tel: 028-9334 0203 **Fax:** 01457-869 269
E-mail: plong@springvale.com
Website: http://www.springvale.com
Bank(s): Northern Bank
Managers: P. Mccabe (Mgr)
Ultimate Holding Company: CRH PUBLIC LIMITED COMPANY
Immediate Holding Company: SPRINGVALE BUSINESSES LIMITED
Registration no: NI031781 **VAT No.:** GB 422 2426 92
Date established: 1996 **Turnover:** £10m - £20m
No.of Employees: 21 - 50 **Product Groups:** 30, 33, 84, 85

Date of Accounts	Dec 10	Dec 09	Dec 08
Working Capital	92	91	89
Fixed Assets	3	3	3
Current Assets	97	102	110

Vita Liberata
181a Templepatrick Road Doagh, Ballyclare, BT39 0RA
Tel: 028-9334 4411
E-mail: enquiries@vitaliberata.com
Website: http://www.vitaliberata.com
Managers: A. Hogg (Mgr)
Immediate Holding Company: VITA LIBERATA LIMITED
Registration no: NI046592 **Date established:** 2003
No.of Employees: 1 - 10 **Product Groups:** 32, 63

Date of Accounts	Dec 11	Aug 10	Aug 09
Working Capital	-374	-72	-126
Fixed Assets	72	54	83
Current Assets	426	496	257

Wilson Food Systems
98 Templepatrick Road, Ballyclare, BT39 9RQ
Tel: 028-9335 2569 **Fax:** 028-9335 2641
E-mail: clnwilson@aol.com
Directors: C. Wilson (Prop)
Date established: 1981 **No.of Employees:** 1 - 10 **Product Groups:** 20, 40, 41

Wishart Group
Mile Water House 10a Mill Road, Ballyclare, BT39 9DY
Tel: 028-9334 0889 **Fax:** 028-9334 0760
E-mail: sales@wishartgroup.co.uk
Website: http://www.wishartgroup.co.uk
Bank(s): Northern Bank
Directors: R. Wishart (MD)
VAT No.: 422 1574 82 **Date established:** 1985 **No.of Employees:** 11 - 20
Product Groups: 67

Co. Antrim

Ballymena

Ace Fixings Ltd
Omco Industrial Estate Woodside Road, Ballymena, BT42 4HX
Tel: 028-2564 9323 **Fax:** 028-2565 9334
E-mail: sales@acefixings.com
Website: http://www.acefixings.com
Directors: A. McGillian (MD)
Managers: D. Clarke (Buyer), E. McStarvick (Tech Serv Mgr), D. Atkinson (Personnel)
Immediate Holding Company: ACE FIXINGS LTD
Registration no: NI055683 **VAT No.:** GB 331 8642 63
Date established: 2005 **Turnover:** £2m - £5m **No.of Employees:** 21 - 50
Product Groups: 66

Date of Accounts	Jul 11	Jul 10	Jul 09
Sales Turnover	N/A	5m	6m
Pre Tax Profit/Loss	N/A	22	94
Working Capital	2m	2m	2m
Fixed Assets	338	391	500
Current Assets	3m	3m	4m
Current Liabilities	N/A	133	564

Alexander Bonar & Co. Ltd Ltd
Pennybridge Industrial Estate, Ballymena, BT42 3HB
Tel: 028-2565 2449 **Fax:** 028-2564 1838
E-mail: info@alexanderbonar.com
Website: http://www.alexanderbonar.com
Bank(s): Ulster Bank
Directors: A. Mcauley (MD)
Immediate Holding Company: ALEXANDER BONAR & CO. LIMITED
Registration no: NI011417 **VAT No.:** GB 286 4964 04
Date established: 1976 **Turnover:** £500,000 - £1m
No.of Employees: 21 - 50 **Product Groups:** 52

Date of Accounts	Jul 11	Jul 10	Jul 09
Working Capital	513	453	359
Fixed Assets	79	76	88
Current Assets	826	732	538

Aquasun
Unit 17 Pennybridge Industrial Estate, Ballymena, BT42 3HB
Tel: 028-2565 9123 **Fax:** 028-2565 9096
E-mail: patricia@aquasun.co.uk
Website: http://www.aquasun.co.uk
Directors: K. Storey (Prop), P. Storey (Ptnr)
Managers: K. Storey (Mgr)
Turnover: £500,000 - £1m **No.of Employees:** 1 - 10 **Product Groups:** 37

Date of Accounts	Mar 11	Mar 10	Mar 09
Working Capital	16	49	98
Fixed Assets	115	141	152
Current Assets	607	514	579

Arcon Engineering
75 Old Portglenone Road Ahoghill, Ballymena, BT42 1LQ
Tel: 028-2587 8729 **Fax:** 028-2587 9023
E-mail: info@arconeng.com
Website: http://www.arconeng.com
Directors: P. Mcloughlin (MD)
No.of Employees: 11 - 20 **Product Groups:** 48

Auto Tune
Uni 22a Pennybridge Industrial Estate, Ballymena, BT42 3HB
Tel: 07759-366244
E-mail: info@auto-tune.co.uk
Website: http://www.auto-tune.co.uk
Directors: R. Clarke (Prop)
No.of Employees: 1 - 10 **Product Groups:** 38, 39

Ballymena Borough Council
Ardeevin 80 Galgorm Road, Ballymena, BT42 1AB
Tel: 028-2566 0300 **Fax:** 028-2566 0400
E-mail: mervyn.rankin@ballymena.gov.uk
Website: http://www.ballymena.gov.uk
Managers: R. Mcknight, S. Faulkner, S. Moore (Tech Serv Mgr), S. Cole (Fin Mgr)
Turnover: £500,000 - £1m **No.of Employees:** 51 - 100
Product Groups: 87

Ballymena Fire Extinguishers
36 Tobar Park Cullybackey, Ballymena, BT42 1NL
Tel: 028-2588 0882 **Fax:** 028-2588 0675
Directors: M. Arbuthnot (Prop)
Date established: 2001 **No.of Employees:** 1 - 10 **Product Groups:** 38, 42

Ballymena Guardian (a division of Northern Newspaper Groups)
83-85 Wellington Street, Ballymena, BT43 6AD
Tel: 028-2564 1221 **Fax:** 028-2565 3920
E-mail: editor@ballymenaguardian.co.uk
Website: http://www.ballymenaguardian.co.uk
Managers: J. Flanagan
VAT No.: GB 393 5977 90 **Date established:** 1981
No.of Employees: 11 - 20 **Product Groups:** 28

Ballymena Meats
Pennybridge Industrial Estate, Ballymena, BT42 3HB
Tel: 028-2565 3710 **Fax:** 028-2564 7593
E-mail: ballymena.meats@nireland.com
Website: http://www.nireland.com

Bank(s): Ulster Bank
Directors: B. Kerney (Ptnr)
Immediate Holding Company: Fyfes Vehicle and Engineering Supplies Ltd
Registration no: NI039006 **VAT No.:** GB 252 6592 50
Date established: 2000 **Turnover:** £250m - £500m
No.of Employees: 51 - 100 **Product Groups:** 62

Date of Accounts	Feb 08	Feb 11	Feb 10
Sales Turnover	N/A	14m	13m
Pre Tax Profit/Loss	559	2m	1m
Working Capital	2m	3m	3m
Fixed Assets	626	712	748
Current Assets	4m	5m	5m
Current Liabilities	236	761	555

Ballymena Times
22-24 Ballymoney Street, Ballymena, BT43 6AL
Tel: 028-2565 3300 **Fax:** 028-2564 1517
E-mail: d-blackadder@ballymenanews.com
Website: http://www.ballymenatimes.com
Managers: D. Blackadder
VAT No.: GB 076 2326 161 **Turnover:** £250,000 - £500,000
No.of Employees: 21 - 50 **Product Groups:** 28

Braid Electrical Services Ltd
2 Braid River Business Park Railway Street, Ballymena, BT42 2AF
Tel: 028-2564 3238 **Fax:** 028-2564 0973
E-mail: george.kernohan@braidelectrical.co.uk
Website: http://www.jbelectrical.co.uk
Directors: G. Kernohan (MD)
Immediate Holding Company: BRAID ELECTRICAL SERVICES LTD
Registration no: NI004755 **VAT No.:** GB 331 9461 62
Date established: 1960 **No.of Employees:** 21 - 50 **Product Groups:** 52

Date of Accounts	Apr 11	Apr 10	Apr 09
Working Capital	650	620	589
Fixed Assets	126	128	142
Current Assets	912	955	1m

Clady Plumbing Supplies Ltd
37 Glenone Road Portglenone, Ballymena, BT44 8LD
Tel: 028-2582 1448 **Fax:** 028-2582 2363
E-mail: info@cladyplumbing.com
Website: http://www.cladyplumbing.com
Bank(s): Northern Bank
Directors: S. Mackle (Dir)
Immediate Holding Company: CLADY PLUMBING SUPPLIES LIMITED
Registration no: NI006968 **VAT No.:** GB 251 7009 84
Date established: 1967 **Turnover:** £1m - £2m **No.of Employees:** 11 - 20
Product Groups: 52, 66, 83

Date of Accounts	Jul 11	Jul 10	Jul 09
Working Capital	1m	1m	2m
Fixed Assets	29	27	37
Current Assets	3m	2m	3m

Clarke Contracts
89 Bann Road Rasharkin, Ballymena, BT44 8SZ
Tel: 028-2954 0191 **Fax:** 028-2954 0401
E-mail: info@clarkecontracts.com
Website: http://www.clarkecontracts.com
Directors: B. Clarke (Prop)
Immediate Holding Company: CLARKE CONTRACTS (PLASTERING & FLOORING) LTD
Registration no: NI602032 **VAT No.:** GB 349 7887 80
Date established: 2010 **Turnover:** £2m - £5m **No.of Employees:** 11 - 20
Product Groups: 29, 30, 33, 52

Contact Security Systems
30 Ballymoney Road, Ballymena, BT43 5BY
Tel: 028-2564 4386 **Fax:** 028-2564 4386
E-mail: contact.security@btconnect.com
Directors: G. White (Prop)
Turnover: £250,000 - £500,000 **No.of Employees:** 11 - 20
Product Groups: 52, 67

Robert Craig & Sons
39 Parkfield Road Ahoghill, Ballymena, BT42 1LY
Tel: 028-2587 1344 **Fax:** 028-2587 1156
E-mail: robertcraigsons@aol.com
Directors: K. Craig (Prop)
Immediate Holding Company: ROBERT CRAIG & SONS (MERCHANTS) LIMITED
Registration no: NI003340 **VAT No.:** GB 251 9291 51
Date established: 1954 **Turnover:** £2m - £5m **No.of Employees:** 1 - 10
Product Groups: 01

Date of Accounts	Mar 12	Mar 11	Mar 10
Working Capital	587	670	781
Fixed Assets	1m	2m	2m
Current Assets	662	765	882

Dale Farm Ltd
75 Dunminning Road Cullybackey, Ballymena, BT42 1PE
Tel: 028-2588 0253 **Fax:** 028-2588 0097
E-mail: sales@uniteddairyfarmers.com
Website: http://www.dalefarm.co.uk
Managers: J. Dickey (Mgr)
Ultimate Holding Company: UNITED DAIRY FARMERS LTD (IRELAND)
Immediate Holding Company: Dale Farm Limited
Registration no: NI025356 **VAT No.:** GB 617 7466 16
Date established: 1991 **No.of Employees:** 21 - 50 **Product Groups:** 20

Date of Accounts	Mar 11	Mar 10	Mar 09
Sales Turnover	192m	171m	176m
Pre Tax Profit/Loss	1m	2m	4m
Working Capital	3m	5m	4m
Fixed Assets	43m	41m	38m
Current Assets	47m	39m	44m
Current Liabilities	4m	4m	12m

Dale Farms
Everton Building Pennybridge Industrial Estate, Ballymena, BT42 3ER
Tel: 028-2566 1572 **Fax:** 028-2564 1320
E-mail: davidmccracken@dalefarm.co.uk
Website: http://www.dalefarm.co.uk
Managers: R. Wilson (Sales Prom Mgr)
Immediate Holding Company: FYFES VEHICLE AND ENGINEERING SUPPLIES LTD
Registration no: NI039006 **VAT No.:** GB 283 1086 63
Date established: 2000 **No.of Employees:** 1 - 10 **Product Groups:** 20, 41, 61

Date of Accounts	Feb 08	Feb 11	Feb 10
Sales Turnover	N/A	14m	13m
Pre Tax Profit/Loss	559	2m	1m
Working Capital	2m	3m	3m
Fixed Assets	626	712	748
Current Assets	4m	5m	5m
Current Liabilities	236	761	555

Design 3
15 Kilmandil Road Dunloy, Ballymena, BT44 9BH
Tel: 028-2763 8653 **Fax:** 028-2763 8653
E-mail: info@design-3.co.uk
Website: http://www.design-3.co.uk
Directors: K. Casey (Prop)
Immediate Holding Company: PINEWOOD FURNITURE LIMITED
Registration no: NI022905 **Date established:** 1989
Turnover: Up to £250,000 **No.of Employees:** 1 - 10 **Product Groups:** 26, 63

Date of Accounts	Mar 11	Mar 10	Mar 09
Sales Turnover	96	117	101
Pre Tax Profit/Loss	16	19	-17
Working Capital	-13	-33	-57
Fixed Assets	17	21	26
Current Assets	13	21	24
Current Liabilities	N/A	2	3

Francis Dinsmore Ltd
25 Greenfield Road Kells, Ballymena, BT42 3JL
Tel: 028-2589 1203 **Fax:** 028-2589 2295
E-mail: info@dinsmore.co.uk
Website: http://www.dinsmore.co.uk
Directors: B. Corrigan (MD), K. Wilson (Fin)
Immediate Holding Company: FRANCIS DINSMORE LIMITED
Registration no: NI002413 **VAT No.:** GB 251 7169 62
Date established: 1947 **Turnover:** £2m - £5m **No.of Employees:** 21 - 50
Product Groups: 23, 61

Date of Accounts	Dec 11	Dec 10	Dec 09
Sales Turnover	N/A	5m	4m
Pre Tax Profit/Loss	N/A	199	-156
Working Capital	1m	1m	959
Fixed Assets	1m	1m	1m
Current Assets	3m	4m	4m
Current Liabilities	N/A	835	537

P Dougan Electrical
5 Church Street Ahoghill, Ballymena, BT42 2PA
Tel: 028-2587 1224 **Fax:** 028-2587 8084
E-mail: info@pcdcontracts.com
Website: http://www.pdougan-eletrical.freesreve.co.uk
Directors: P. Dougan (Prop), P. Dougan (MD)
Managers: E. Dougan (Mktg Serv Mgr), K. Trainer (Accounts)
VAT No.: GB 311 1866 90 **Date established:** 1978
No.of Employees: 21 - 50 **Product Groups:** 52

Dunbia
146 Fenaghy Road Cullybackey, Ballymena, BT42 1EA
Tel: 028-2588 1180 **Fax:** 028-2588 1368
E-mail: cquigg@dunbia.com
Website: http://www.dunbia.com
Managers: K. Johnston (Chief Acct), S. Looby (Sales Prom Mgr), C. Quigg (Mgr)
Immediate Holding Company: STEVENSON AND COMPANY
Registration no: NI012594 **VAT No.:** GB 311 1349 13
Date established: 1978 **No.of Employees:** 101 - 250 **Product Groups:** 20

G & A Frames
The Brade Gallery Railway Street, Ballymena, BT42 2AF
Tel: 028-2564 1265 **Fax:** 028-2564 1265
Website: http://www.gaframes.com
Directors: G. Elkin (Prop)
VAT No.: GB 283 1922 53 **Date established:** 1992
No.of Employees: 1 - 10 **Product Groups:** 25, 26, 30, 33, 49, 65

Galgorm Group
7 Corbally Road Galgorm, Ballymena, BT42 1JQ
Tel: 028-2564 3211 **Fax:** 028-2564 7614
E-mail: michael.scullion@galgormgroup.com
Website: http://www.galgormgroup.com
Directors: M. Scullion (Fin)
Immediate Holding Company: BELFAST BOTTLE COMPANY LIMITED
VAT No.: GB 252 7379 45 **Date established:** 1978
No.of Employees: 1 - 10 **Product Groups:** 67

Garage Door Systems
Unit G3 Wakehurst Industrial Estate, Ballymena, BT42 3AZ
Tel: 028-2565 5555 **Fax:** 028-2564 4030
E-mail: info@gdsdoors.eu
Website: http://www.gdsdoors.eu
Directors: P. McAdoo (Sales & Mktg)
Managers: P. McWilliams (Comptroller)
Immediate Holding Company: GARAGE DOOR SYSTEMS LIMITED
Registration no: NI028130 **VAT No.:** GB 574 5787 87
Date established: 1994 **No.of Employees:** 21 - 50 **Product Groups:** 35

Date of Accounts	Apr 11	Apr 10	Apr 09
Working Capital	792	734	839
Fixed Assets	304	403	393
Current Assets	1m	1m	1m
Current Liabilities	N/A	N/A	79

Gault Engineering
187 Largy Road Ahoghill, Ballymena, BT42 2RH
Tel: 028-7965 1909 **Fax:** 028-7965 1908
Directors: D. Gault (Prop)
Immediate Holding Company: ROBERT GAULT LIMITED
Date established: 2004 **No.of Employees:** 1 - 10 **Product Groups:** 35, 48

Gillen Machine Tools Ltd
Railway Yard Railway Street, Ballymena, BT42 2AF
Tel: 028-2564 3705 **Fax:** 028-2564 2711
E-mail: philip@gillenmachines.com
Website: http://www.gillenmachines.com
Directors: P. Gillen (Prop)
Immediate Holding Company: GILLEN MACHINE TOOLS LIMITED
Registration no: NI024776 **VAT No.:** GB 432 7617 53
Date established: 1990 **Turnover:** £1m - £2m **No.of Employees:** 1 - 10
Product Groups: 67

Date of Accounts	Apr 12	Apr 11	Apr 10
Working Capital	647	684	754
Fixed Assets	1	11	15
Current Assets	730	780	941

Glens Of Antrim Potatoes
118 Middlepark Road Cushendall, Ballymena, BT44 0SH
Tel: 028-2177 1396 **Fax:** 028-2177 1193
E-mail: info@goapotatoes.co.uk
Website: http://www.goapotatoes.co.uk
Directors: C. Mckillop (Prop)
Immediate Holding Company: GLENS OF ANTRIM POTATOES LIMITED
Registration no: NI030390 **VAT No.:** GB 255 2830 62
Date established: 1996 **No.of Employees:** 51 - 100 **Product Groups:** 62

Grants Electrical Services Ni Ltd
Pennybridge Industrial Estate, Ballymena, BT42 3HB
Tel: 028-2565 6406 **Fax:** 028-2565 2738
E-mail: sales@grantselectrical.co.uk
Website: http://www.grantselectrical.co.uk
Directors: T. Grant (MD)
Managers: C. Mitchell, E. Boyd
Immediate Holding Company: GRANT'S ELECTRICAL SERVICES (N.I.) LIMITED
Registration no: NI012273 **Date established:** 1977
No.of Employees: 51 - 100 **Product Groups:** 48, 52, 67

Date of Accounts	Sep 11	Sep 10	Sep 09
Working Capital	11	-67	-137
Fixed Assets	606	627	640
Current Assets	2m	2m	2m

Gun Shop
51b Main Street Portglenone, Ballymena, BT44 8HP
Tel: 028-2582 1935 **Fax:** 028-2582 1935
E-mail: noelgunshop@aol.com
Directors: N. Stewart (Prop)
Date established: 1995 **No.of Employees:** 1 - 10 **Product Groups:** 36, 39, 40

William Hamill & Sons
Duke Street, Ballymena, BT43 6BN
Tel: 028-2565 2751 **Fax:** 028-2564 7188
E-mail: williamhamill@ukf.net.co.uk
Directors: W. Hamill (Prop), B. Hamill (Prop), W. Hamill (Ptnr)
VAT No.: 05252313887 **Turnover:** Up to £250,000
No.of Employees: 1 - 10 **Product Groups:** 62

John Hanna Ltd
Kildrum Dyeworks Kells, Ballymena, BT42 3DL
Tel: 028-2589 1206 **Fax:** 028-2589 1423
E-mail: clifford.barr@birdmcnutt.com
Website: http://www.bairdmcnutt.com
Managers: C. Barr (Chief Mgr), J. Smith (Admin Off), S. Barr (Chief Acct)
Ultimate Holding Company: ELECTROEDIT BELFAST LIMITED
Immediate Holding Company: JOHN HANNA LIMITED
Registration no: NI000168 **Date established:** 2024 **Turnover:** £2m - £5m
No.of Employees: 21 - 50 **Product Groups:** 23

Date of Accounts	Apr 11	Apr 10	Apr 09
Sales Turnover	4m	5m	3m
Pre Tax Profit/Loss	-2m	-78	395
Working Capital	5m	6m	6m
Fixed Assets	277	345	463
Current Assets	8m	10m	10m
Current Liabilities	1m	1m	1m

Herbison Concrete Products
179 Carniny Road, Ballymena, BT43 5NJ
Tel: 028-2565 3989 **Fax:** 028-2565 3989
E-mail: herbison8@talktalk.net
Directors: B. Herbison (Dir)
VAT No.: GB 286 3666 17 **Date established:** 1969
Turnover: Up to £250,000 **No.of Employees:** 1 - 10 **Product Groups:** 33

High Tech Scales
Unit 22a-6 Pennybridge Industrial Estate Lyon Road, Ballymena, BT42 3HB
Tel: 028-2563 0041
E-mail: bill@hitecscales.co.uk
Directors: R. Clark (Prop)
Registration no: NI031577 **Date established:** 1996
No.of Employees: 1 - 10 **Product Groups:** 38, 42

Robert Hoy Engineering
68a Cardonaghy Road Ahoghill, Ballymena, BT42 1JE
Tel: 028-2587 1207 **Fax:** 028-2587 8011
Directors: Y. Hoy (Ptnr)
VAT No.: GB 516 6210 70 **Turnover:** Up to £250,000
No.of Employees: 1 - 10 **Product Groups:** 39, 48

Huston Engineering
52 Kilmandil Road Dunloy, Ballymena, BT44 9BH
Tel: 028-2763 8513 **Fax:** 028-2765 7217
E-mail: perry@hustoneng.co.uk
Website: http://www.genie.co.uk
Directors: P. Huston (Prop)
Date established: 1996 **No.of Employees:** 1 - 10 **Product Groups:** 41

Impress Business Gifts Ltd
21 Liminary Road, Ballymena, BT42 3HL
Tel: 028-2564 5196 **Fax:** 028-2564 2821
E-mail: promotions@impressuk.com
Website: http://www.impressuk.com
Directors: S. O'neill (Prop)
Immediate Holding Company: IMPRESS BUSINESS GIFTS LIMITED
Registration no: NI041595 **VAT No.:** GB 349 7504 25
Date established: 2001 **No.of Employees:** 1 - 10 **Product Groups:** 64, 65, 81

Date of Accounts	Dec 11	Dec 10	Dec 09
Working Capital	4	-119	955
Fixed Assets	1m	1m	325
Current Assets	594	655	2m

J B E Building Services
Lamont House 105 Railway Street, Ballymena, BT42 2AF
Tel: 028-2565 8522 **Fax:** 028-2564 0898
E-mail: info@jbebuildingservices.com
Website: http://www.jbebuildingservices.com
Directors: J. Blair (MD)
Managers: M. Murphy (I.T. Exec)
Immediate Holding Company: J.B. ELECTRICAL LIMITED
Registration no: 02323925 **VAT No.:** GB 393 5512 37
Date established: 1988 **No.of Employees:** 101 - 250 **Product Groups:** 52

see next page

J B E Building Services - Cont'd

Date of Accounts	Dec 10	Dec 09	Dec 08
Working Capital	-91	-74	13
Fixed Assets	N/A	1	1
Current Assets	61	24	116

Londonderry Arms Hotel
20 Harbour Road Carnlough, Ballymena, BT44 0EU
Tel: 028-2888 5255 **Fax:** 028-2888 5263
E-mail: lda@glensofantrim.com
Website: http://www.glensofantrim.com
Directors: D. O'neil (Prop)
No.of Employees: 11 - 20 **Product Groups:** 69

Mcburney Transport
205 Moorfields Road, Ballymena, BT42 3EG
Tel: 028-2589 1419 **Fax:** 028-2589 1719
E-mail: carolyn@mcburneytransport.com
Website: http://www.mcburneytransport.com
Directors: P. McRae (Fin)
Managers: I. McKewon (Transport), L. Forde (Purch Mgr), S. Hamil Junior (Tech Serv Mgr), C. Mcburney (Mgr)
Immediate Holding Company: McBURNEY TRANSPORT
Registration no: NI043332 **VAT No.:** GB 252 8336 58
Date established: 2002 **Turnover:** £10m - £20m
No.of Employees: 21 - 50 **Product Groups:** 72

Mccutcheon & Wilkinson
18 Linenhall Street, Ballymena, BT43 5AL
Tel: 028-2564 9525 **Fax:** 028-2564 5791
E-mail: mccw@btconnect.com
Bank(s): Northern Bank
Directors: I. Robinson (Ptnr), R. Bigger (Ptnr)
VAT No.: GB 252 3207 94 **Date established:** 1946
No.of Employees: 11 - 20 **Product Groups:** 84

A A Mcguckian Ltd
29 Drumbare Road Cloughmills, Ballymena, BT44 9LA
Tel: 028-2763 8677 **Fax:** 028-2763 8243
Directors: L. Mcguckian (Dir)
Immediate Holding Company: A.A. MCGUCKIAN LIMITED
Registration no: NI001045 **VAT No.:** GB 253 0049 95
Date established: 1936 **No.of Employees:** 11 - 20 **Product Groups:** 01, 62

Date of Accounts	Dec 11	Dec 10	Dec 09
Working Capital	754	657	493
Fixed Assets	827	738	755
Current Assets	1m	1m	1m

Mckillen's Ballymena Ltd
78-90 Church Street, Ballymena, BT43 6DF
Tel: 028-2565 6169 **Fax:** 028-2564 1103
E-mail: thomas.mckillens@btconnect.com
Bank(s): Northern Bank
Directors: T. Mckillens (Dir), T. McKillen (Dir)
Managers: J. Caldwell (Buyer)
Immediate Holding Company: MCKILLENS (BALLYMENA) LIMITED
Registration no: NI009761 **VAT No.:** GB 331 9180 70
Date established: 1973 **Turnover:** £2m - £5m **No.of Employees:** 51 - 100
Product Groups: 61, 63, 65

Date of Accounts	Jan 12	Jan 11	Jan 10
Sales Turnover	3m	3m	3m
Pre Tax Profit/Loss	14	-24	72
Working Capital	330	285	278
Fixed Assets	3m	3m	3m
Current Assets	674	607	582
Current Liabilities	151	124	113

D Mcmillan
3 Mckeestown Lane Shankbridge, Ballymena, BT42 2LU
Tel: 028-2589 1546 **Fax:** 028-2589 2846
Website: http://www.kings-estate-agents.co.uk
Directors: R. Mcmillan (Prop)
Date established: 1981 **No.of Employees:** 1 - 10 **Product Groups:** 48

Maine Microwave Services
51 Killyless Road Cullybackey, Ballymena, BT42 1HD
Tel: 028-2588 1088 **Fax:** 028-2588 2667
Directors: W. Mckibbin (Prop)
No.of Employees: 1 - 10 **Product Groups:** 36, 40

Martin Engineering Supplies Ltd The Martin Group of Companies
Unit 37 Ballymena Business Development Centre Fenaghy Road Galgorm, Ballymena, BT42 1FL
Tel: 028-2563 0022 **Fax:** 028-2563 0044
E-mail: mes-ltd@btconnect.com
Website: http://www.mes-ltd.net
Directors: C. Martin (Dir)
Immediate Holding Company: MARTIN ENGINEERING SUPPLIES LIMITED
Registration no: NI055296 **Date established:** 2005
No.of Employees: 1 - 10 **Product Groups:** 35, 66

Date of Accounts	May 11	May 10	May 09
Working Capital	-2	-8	5
Fixed Assets	19	21	25
Current Assets	58	31	53

Maxwell Packaging
86f Railway Street, Ballymena, BT42 2AF
Tel: 028-2564 4769 **Fax:** 028-2563 0505
E-mail: maxwellpackaging@btconnect.com
Directors: J. Maxwell (Prop)
Registration no: NI024776 **VAT No.:** GB 393 6110 52
Date established: 1990 **Turnover:** £250,000 - £500,000
No.of Employees: 1 - 10 **Product Groups:** 66

Metal Imagineers
7 Tullynahinnion Road Portglenone, Ballymena, BT44 8ET
Tel: 028-2582 1891 **Fax:** 028-2582 1891
Website: http://www.metalimagineers.co.uk
Directors: W. Mccaughern (Prop)
Date established: 1995 **No.of Employees:** 1 - 10 **Product Groups:** 26, 35

Mid Antrim Signs
Unit 5 Pennybridge Industrial Estate, Ballymena, BT42 3HB
Tel: 028-2565 2205 **Fax:** 028-2564 3459
E-mail: office@midantrimsigns.com
Website: http://www.midantrimsigns.com
Directors: J. Stevenson (Prop)
VAT No.: GB 516 9012 59 **Date established:** 1972
Turnover: Up to £250,000 **No.of Employees:** 11 - 20 **Product Groups:** 37, 39, 49

Montrose Garden Supplies
Unit 4 11-17 Paradise Avenue, Ballymena, BT42 3AE
Tel: 028-2565 3796 **Fax:** 028-2564 8642
Website: http://www.montrosegardensupply.com
Directors: C. Montgomery (Prop)
No.of Employees: 1 - 10 **Product Groups:** 26, 35

Moy Park Ltd
117 Raceview Road, Ballymena, BT42 4HY
Tel: 028-2586 1445 **Fax:** 028-2586 2179
E-mail: des.okane@okanepoultry.com
Website: http://www.okanepoultry.com
Bank(s): Ulster Bank
Directors: D. O'Kane (Dir)
Managers: S. Davison (Mgr), W. Patton
Ultimate Holding Company: O'KANE GROUP LTD
Immediate Holding Company: O'KANE HATCHERIES LIMITED
Registration no: NI006514 **VAT No.:** GB 252 3825 68
Date established: 1965 **No.of Employees:** 21 - 50 **Product Groups:** 01

Date of Accounts	May 09	May 10
Working Capital	20	20
Current Assets	20	20

North Stone Ltd
Craitado Road Moorfields, Ballymena, BT42 4RB
Tel: 028-2589 1353 **Fax:** 028-2589 1508
Website: http://www.rjmaxwell.com
Managers: C. Mcilroy
Immediate Holding Company: NORTHSTONE LIMITED
Registration no: 03862752 **Date established:** 1999
No.of Employees: 1 - 10 **Product Groups:** 45, 52, 67

Date of Accounts	Nov 11	Nov 10	Nov 09
Working Capital	-21	-10	4
Fixed Assets	10	14	8
Current Assets	186	181	166

Northern Salmon
8 Castle Demesne, Ballymena, BT44 0BD
Tel: 028-2884 1691 **Fax:** 028-2884 1637
E-mail: northern.salmon@btclick.com
Managers: J. Russell (Mgr)
Immediate Holding Company: NORTHERN SALMON COMPANY LIMITED
Registration no: NI020944 **VAT No.:** GB 497 1425 20
Date established: 1987 **Turnover:** £500,000 - £1m
No.of Employees: 1 - 10 **Product Groups:** 09

Date of Accounts	Jul 08	Mar 11	Mar 10
Working Capital	118	2m	1m
Fixed Assets	143	71	49
Current Assets	445	2m	1m

O'Kane Poultry Ltd
170 Larne Road, Ballymena, BT42 3HA
Tel: 028-2564 1111 **Fax:** 028-2566 0680
E-mail: reception@okanepoultry.com
Website: http://www.okanepoultry.com
Bank(s): Ulster Bank
Directors: T. O'neill (Fin)
Managers: A. Gibson (Sales Prom Mgr), J. McCook (Purch Mgr), S. Fletcher, N. Donaldson (Personnel)
Ultimate Holding Company: MARFRIG ALIMENTOS SA (BRAZIL)
Immediate Holding Company: O'KANE POULTRY LIMITED
Registration no: NI005917 **VAT No.:** GB 256 1646 54
Date established: 1964 **Turnover:** £50m - £75m
No.of Employees: 1001 - 1500 **Product Groups:** 20

Date of Accounts	Dec 11	Dec 10	Jul 10
Sales Turnover	144m	62m	161m
Pre Tax Profit/Loss	-4m	1m	-1m
Working Capital	3m	5m	6m
Fixed Assets	20m	19m	15m
Current Assets	35m	45m	29m
Current Liabilities	3m	8m	7m

Omya UK
Demesne Quarry 17 Munie Road, Glenarm, Ballymena, BT44 0BG
Tel: 028-2884 1333 **Fax:** 028-2884 1687
E-mail: marvethblack@omya.co.uk
Website: http://www.omya.co.uk
Bank(s): Northern Bank
Managers: M. Foster (Sales Prom Mgr)
Immediate Holding Company: PLUSS-STAUFER LTD
Registration no: 00436591 **VAT No.:** GB 252 5851 57
Turnover: £2m - £5m **No.of Employees:** 11 - 20 **Product Groups:** 14

Plumb Center Ltd
Subunit 6a Unit 23 Pennybridge Trade Centre, Ballymena, BT42 3HB
Tel: 028-2564 1222 **Fax:** 028-2564 1777
Website: http://www.plumbcenter.co.uk
Managers: A. Pierce (Mgr)
Ultimate Holding Company: WOLSELEY PLC (JERSEY)
Immediate Holding Company: PLUMB-CENTER LIMITED
Registration no: 00581770 **Date established:** 1957
No.of Employees: 21 - 50 **Product Groups:** 36, 37

Portglenone Refrigeration Services
53 Main Street Portglenone, Ballymena, BT44 8HP
Tel: 028-2582 1818 **Fax:** 028-2582 2295
E-mail: info@fridgeservices.com
Website: http://www.fridgeservices.com
Managers: T. Mcdonnell (Projects)
Immediate Holding Company: Portglenone Refrigeration Services Ltd
Registration no: NI040931 **VAT No.:** GB 516 6348 41
Date established: 2001 **Turnover:** £1m - £2m **No.of Employees:** 11 - 20
Product Groups: 66

Date of Accounts	Aug 11	Aug 10	Aug 09
Working Capital	876	810	731
Fixed Assets	48	47	61
Current Assets	1m	1m	1m
Current Liabilities	90	75	49

Richard Reade Cabinet Maker
40 Carnlough Road Broughshane, Ballymena, BT43 7HF
Tel: 028-2586 1030
E-mail: sales@richardreade.co.uk
Website: http://www.richardreade.co.uk
Directors: R. Reade (Prop)
Date established: 1985 **Turnover:** Up to £250,000
No.of Employees: 1 - 10 **Product Groups:** 26

Red Bay Boats Ltd
Coast Road Cushendall, Ballymena, BT44 0QW
Tel: 028-2177 1331 **Fax:** 028-2177 1474
E-mail: info@redbayboats.com
Website: http://www.redbayboats.com
Bank(s): Northern Bank
Directors: T. McLaughlin (Dir)
Immediate Holding Company: RED BAY BOATS LIMITED
Registration no: NI007565 **VAT No.:** 331 8135 80 **Date established:** 1969
Turnover: £250,000 - £500,000 **No.of Employees:** 11 - 20
Product Groups: 39

Date of Accounts	Apr 11	Apr 10	Apr 09
Working Capital	1m	1m	1m
Fixed Assets	577	589	330
Current Assets	2m	2m	2m

Robinson Quarry Masters Ltd
32 Glenhead Road Glenwherry, Ballymena, BT42 4RE
Tel: 028-2583 1245 **Fax:** 028-2583 1470
E-mail: sales@robinsonquarry.co.uk
Website: http://www.robinsonquarry.co.uk
Directors: S. Robinson (Dir)
Immediate Holding Company: ROBINSON QUARRY MASTERS LIMITED
Registration no: NI009269 **VAT No.:** GB 253 8276 44
Date established: 1973 **No.of Employees:** 21 - 50 **Product Groups:** 33, 51

Date of Accounts	Dec 11	Dec 10	Dec 09
Working Capital	4m	4m	4m
Fixed Assets	3m	3m	4m
Current Assets	5m	4m	5m

Ross Park Hotel
20 Doagh Road Kells, Ballymena, BT42 3LZ
Tel: 028-2589 1663 **Fax:** 028-2589 1477
E-mail: info@rosspark.com
Website: http://www.rosspark.com
Managers: R. Gilchrist, W. Rae (Chief Mgr), A. McGuaghy, C. Sloan (Mktg Serv Mgr)
VAT No.: GB 516 7635 33 **Turnover:** £2m - £5m **No.of Employees:** 21 - 50
Product Groups: 69

S Dooey & Co. Ltd
7 Presbytery Lane Dunloy, Ballymena, BT44 9DZ
Tel: 028-2765 7221 **Fax:** 028-2765 7464
E-mail: accounts@sdooey.com
Website: http://www.sdooey.com
Bank(s): First Trust
Directors: J. Dooey (MD)
Managers: J. Stewart (Sales Prom Mgr), J. Doherty (Buyer), M. Molloy (Personnel)
Immediate Holding Company: S DOOEY & CO LIMITED
Registration no: NI036519 **Date established:** 1999
No.of Employees: 21 - 50 **Product Groups:** 30, 66

Date of Accounts	Mar 11	Mar 10	Mar 09
Working Capital	273	251	314
Fixed Assets	572	614	673
Current Assets	547	515	698

Signs Plus
14 Liscoom Road, Ballymena, BT42 1AR
Tel: 028-2565 2325 **Fax:** 028-2564 4637
Directors: R. Fleming (Prop)
VAT No.: GB 254 1268 72 **Date established:** 1969
No.of Employees: 1 - 10 **Product Groups:** 37, 52

Stephens Catering Equipment Co. Ltd
205 Carnalbanagh Road Broughshane, Ballymena, BT42 4NY
Tel: 028-2586 1711 **Fax:** 028-2586 2006
E-mail: pcaves@stephens-catering.com
Website: http://www.stephens-catering.com
Bank(s): Ulster
Directors: P. Caves (MD), P. McLean (Fin)
Managers: G. Long (Mktg Serv Mgr)
Immediate Holding Company: STEPHENS CATERING EQUIPMENT COMPANY LIMITED
Registration no: NI011092 **VAT No.:** GB 286 2047 45
Date established: 1975 **Turnover:** £10m - £20m
No.of Employees: 51 - 100 **Product Groups:** 67

Date of Accounts	Apr 11	Apr 10	Apr 09
Sales Turnover	12m	14m	N/A
Pre Tax Profit/Loss	121	195	196
Working Capital	2m	2m	2m
Fixed Assets	1m	1m	1m
Current Assets	5m	5m	5m
Current Liabilities	820	822	748

James Stevenson Quarries Ltd
215 Doury Road, Ballymena, BT43 6SS
Tel: 028-2565 6114 **Fax:** 028-2564 6495
E-mail: robert.stevenson@virgin.net
Directors: R. Stevenson (Dir), J. Stevenson (MD)
Immediate Holding Company: JAMES STEVENSON (QUARRIES) LIMITED
Registration no: NI026102 **VAT No.:** GB 255 3058 67
Date established: 1991 **Turnover:** £1m - £2m **No.of Employees:** 21 - 50
Product Groups: 51

Date of Accounts	Mar 12	Mar 11	Mar 10
Working Capital	746	603	520
Fixed Assets	3m	3m	3m
Current Assets	2m	2m	2m
Current Liabilities	N/A	N/A	7

Stevenson & Wilson Chartered Accountants
22 Broadway Avenue, Ballymena, BT43 7AA
Tel: 028-2564 7712 **Fax:** 028-2564 5035
E-mail: info@stevensonandwilson.co.uk
Website: http://www.stevensonandwilson.co.uk
Directors: E. Mcdowell (Ptnr)
Immediate Holding Company: STEVENSON & WILSON LIMITED
Registration no: NI018079 **VAT No.:** GB 393 6090 32
Date established: 1984 **Turnover:** Up to £250,000
No.of Employees: 21 - 50 **Product Groups:** 80

Date of Accounts	Dec 10	Dec 09	Dec 08
Working Capital	3	3	2
Fixed Assets	99	99	99

Current Assets	10	10	10

William Telford & Son
99 Broughshane Street, Ballymena, BT43 6ED
Tel: 028-2565 3880 **Fax:** 028- 25656956
E-mail: telford_plumbing@talk21.com
Directors: W. Telford (Prop)
VAT No.: GB 311 0868 91 **Date established:** 1972
No.of Employees: 1 - 10 **Product Groups:** 52

Viewpoint Windows
26 Brookvale Broughshane, Ballymena, BT43 7JQ
Tel: 028-2586 2619
E-mail: se.submissions@iomartinternet.com
Website: http://www.talktalk.net
Directors: K. Cross (MD), K. Cross (Prop)
No.of Employees: 1 - 10 **Product Groups:** 30, 35

Wilkinsons Plaster Mouldings Ltd
154 Fenaghy Road Cullybackey, Ballymena, BT42 1EA
Tel: 028-2588 0714 **Fax:** 028-2588 0714
E-mail: david@wilkinsonsplastermouldings.com
Website: http://www.wilkinsonsplastermouldings.com
Directors: D. Manson (Dir)
Immediate Holding Company: WILKINSON PLASTERMOULD LIMITED
Registration no: NI019936 **VAT No.:** GB 393 6771 08
Date established: 1986 **No.of Employees:** 1 - 10 **Product Groups:** 33

Date of Accounts	Dec 11	Dec 10	Dec 09
Working Capital	-69	-41	-33
Fixed Assets	151	158	167
Current Assets	8	16	18

Woolf Engineering Ltd
Pennybridge Industrial Estate, Ballymena, BT42 3HB
Tel: 028-2564 7938 **Fax:** 028-2564 5102
E-mail: info@woolfengineering.com
Bank(s): Bank Of Ireland
Directors: I. Duff (MD)
Immediate Holding Company: Woolf Engineering Ltd
Registration no: NI060935 **VAT No.:** GB 252 6215 80
Date established: 2006 **Turnover:** £1m - £2m **No.of Employees:** 11 - 20
Product Groups: 35, 39, 48, 67

Date of Accounts	Sep 07	Apr 11	Apr 10
Working Capital	N/A	-284	-107
Fixed Assets	N/A	298	318
Current Assets	N/A	134	179

T Wright
Railway Yard Railway Street, Ballymena, BT42 2AF
Tel: 028-2563 9400
Directors: T. Wright (Prop)
Immediate Holding Company: GILLEN MACHINE TOOLS LIMITED
Registration no: NI024776 **Date established:** 1990
No.of Employees: 1 - 10 **Product Groups:** 40

Date of Accounts	Apr 11	Apr 10	Apr 09
Working Capital	684	754	783
Fixed Assets	11	15	12
Current Assets	780	941	940

Wrightbus Ltd
Galgorm Industrial Estate Fenaghy Road, Galgorm, Ballymena, BT42 1PY
Tel: 028-2564 1212 **Fax:** 028-2564 9703
E-mail: mnodder@wright-bus.com
Website: http://www.wright-bus.com
Bank(s): Barclays
Directors: M. Johnston (Fin), D. Steirn (Sales), M. Nodder (Grp MD)
Managers: M. Graham (Tech Serv Mgr), C. Coulter (Mktg Serv Mgr), R. Cromie (Personnel), T. Lee
Ultimate Holding Company: WRIGHTS GROUP LIMITED
Immediate Holding Company: Wrightbus Limited
Registration no: NI006119 **VAT No.:** GB 254 2580 65
Date established: 1964 **Turnover:** £125m - £250m
No.of Employees: 1001 - 1500 **Product Groups:** 39

Date of Accounts	Sep 11	Sep 10	Sep 09
Sales Turnover	133m	117m	134m
Pre Tax Profit/Loss	1m	-2m	4m
Working Capital	9m	7m	9m
Fixed Assets	10m	11m	11m
Current Assets	44m	37m	40m
Current Liabilities	7m	5m	7m

Co. Antrim

Ballymoney

Acorn The Business Centre
2 Riada Avenue, Ballymoney, BT53 7LH
Tel: 028-2766 6133 **Fax:** 028-2766 5019
E-mail: enquiries@acornbusiness.co.uk
Website: http://www.acornbusiness.co.uk
Managers: F. Ashe (Mgr)
Immediate Holding Company: ACORN THE BUSINESS CENTRE LTD
Registration no: NI029665 **VAT No.:** GB 516 6073 54
Date established: 1995 **Turnover:** Up to £250,000
No.of Employees: 1 - 10 **Product Groups:** 80

Date of Accounts	Dec 11	Dec 10	Dec 09
Working Capital	-46	-87	-140
Fixed Assets	2m	2m	2m
Current Assets	25	14	59

Countrywide Garage Doors
89 Hillside Road Armoy, Ballymoney, BT53 8RX
Tel: 028-2075 1660 **Fax:** 028-2075 1272
Directors: K. McErlain (Prop)
Date established: 2007 **No.of Employees:** 1 - 10 **Product Groups:** 66

Darraghs Coaches
22 Lisheegan Road, Ballymoney, BT53 7JY
Tel: 028-2954 0684 **Fax:** 028-2954 0785
E-mail: kdarragh@hotmail.co.uk
Directors: R. Darryl (Prop)
VAT No.: GB 311 0797 88 **Turnover:** £250,000 - £500,000
No.of Employees: 1 - 10 **Product Groups:** 72

George Peden Ltd
19 Tummock Road, Ballymoney, BT53 8LP
Tel: 028-2766 2048 **Fax:** 028-2766 3298
Directors: G. Peden (MD)
Immediate Holding Company: GEORGE PEDEN LIMITED
Registration no: NI010676 **VAT No.:** GB 286 4124 48
Date established: 1975 **No.of Employees:** 1 - 10 **Product Groups:** 51

Date of Accounts	Dec 11	Dec 10	Dec 09
Working Capital	-1m	-1m	-1m
Fixed Assets	195	207	281
Current Assets	15	72	255

Glover Site Investigations Ltd
8 Drumahiskey Road Bendooragh, Ballymoney, BT53 7QL
Tel: 028-2766 2083 **Fax:** 028-2766 4875
E-mail: pauld@glover-si.com
Website: http://www.glover-si.com
Directors: P. Rainey (Grp Chief Exec), P. Dunlop (MD)
Managers: J. Sterling (Sales Admin), D. Cameron (Mgr), P. Rainy (I.T. Exec), P. Rainey
Immediate Holding Company: GLOVER SITE INVESTIGATIONS LIMITED
Registration no: NI006240 **VAT No.:** GB 252 0535 92
Date established: 1965 **Turnover:** £5m - £10m
No.of Employees: 51 - 100 **Product Groups:** 51, 85

Date of Accounts	Dec 09	Dec 08	Dec 07
Sales Turnover	9m	11m	N/A
Pre Tax Profit/Loss	-1m	426	2m
Working Capital	-624	529	341
Fixed Assets	4m	4m	4m
Current Assets	3m	4m	4m
Current Liabilities	559	1m	2m

Groundsman Industries Ltd
30 Ballybrakes Road, Ballymoney, BT53 6LG
Tel: 028-2766 7049 **Fax:** 028-2766 6855
E-mail: bwarke@groundsmanindustries.com
Website: http://www.groundsmanindustries.com
Directors: W. Warke (Dir)
Immediate Holding Company: GROUNDSMAN INDUSTRIES LIMITED
Registration no: NI025895 **Date established:** 1991
Turnover: Up to £250,000 **No.of Employees:** 1 - 10 **Product Groups:** 41, 42

The Haslett Group
86 Bendooragh Road Killymaddy, Ballymoney, BT53 7NJ
Tel: 028-2766 7333 **Fax:** 028-2766 7333
E-mail: haslett.group@talk21.com
Website: http://www.haslettgroup.co.uk
Directors: B. Haslett (Prop)
No.of Employees: 1 - 10 **Product Groups:** 33

Health Care UK Ltd
20 Garryduff Road, Ballymoney, BT53 7AP
Tel: 028-2766 3234 **Fax:** 028-2766 4799
Website: http://www.tycohealthcare.com
Directors: A. Mills (MD)
Managers: E. O'Neil (Mgr), R. Dos-Santos (Plant), S. Watt (Chief Mgr), J. Irwin (Purch Mgr)
Ultimate Holding Company: Tyco International
Immediate Holding Company: Healthcare UK Ltd
Registration no: 04123617 **VAT No.:** 143 7168 67 **Date established:** 1967
No.of Employees: 101 - 250 **Product Groups:** 27, 30

Date of Accounts	Jan 08	Jan 07	Jan 06
Working Capital	55	106	108
Fixed Assets	1	1	1
Current Assets	82	142	121
Current Liabilities	26	35	13

J H Office Supplies
18-20 Charles Street, Ballymoney, BT53 6DY
Tel: 028-2766 4523 **Fax:** 028-2766 5689
E-mail: info@jhos.com
Website: http://www.jhos.com
Managers: T. Mckendry (Mgr)
VAT No.: GB 251 7051 85 **Date established:** 1983
No.of Employees: 1 - 10 **Product Groups:** 64

J M C Q Huston & Son
24a Meeting House Street, Ballymoney, BT53 6JN
Tel: 028-2766 2195 **Fax:** 028-2766 5056
E-mail: jmcqhuston@gmail.com
Directors: J. Huston (Prop)
VAT No.: GB 283 1315 74 **Date established:** 1945
No.of Employees: 1 - 10 **Product Groups:** 24

J M F Metal Fabrications
69 Frosses Road, Ballymoney, BT53 7HN
Tel: 028-2766 5817 **Fax:** 028-2766 5887
E-mail: sales@jmf-ltd.co.uk
Website: http://www.jmf-ltd.co.uk
Directors: J. Murray (MD), R. Nixon (Fin)
Managers: S. McIlwrath (Personnel), P. Donaghy (Buyer)
Immediate Holding Company: J.M.F. LTD.
Registration no: NI024927 **Date established:** 1990
Turnover: £10m - £20m **No.of Employees:** 101 - 250 **Product Groups:** 35

Date of Accounts	Oct 11	Oct 10	Oct 09
Sales Turnover	16m	11m	N/A
Pre Tax Profit/Loss	166	-484	-1m
Working Capital	-2m	-2m	-2m
Fixed Assets	5m	5m	5m
Current Assets	7m	5m	3m
Current Liabilities	450	421	295

Mcauley Kitchens Ltd
1 Market Street, Ballymoney, BT53 6EA
Tel: 028-2766 4944 **Fax:** 028- 27666529
E-mail: ballymoney@mcauleyskitchens.co.uk
Website: http://www.mcauleykitchens.com
Bank(s): The Bank of Ireland
Directors: W. McCauley (MD)
Immediate Holding Company: McAULEY KITCHENS LIMITED
Registration no: NI044921 **VAT No.:** GB 802 8636 33
Date established: 2002 **Turnover:** £500,000 - £1m
No.of Employees: 11 - 20 **Product Groups:** 52, 63

Date of Accounts	Dec 09	Dec 08	Dec 07
Working Capital	368	83	-9
Fixed Assets	813	892	744
Current Assets	2m	2m	2m

Moore Unidrill Ltd
33 Kirk Road, Ballymoney, BT53 6PP
Tel: 028-2766 4444 **Fax:** 028-2766 5696
E-mail: info@moore-unidrill.com
Website: http://www.moore-unidrill.com
Directors: S. Moore (MD)
Immediate Holding Company: MOORE (UNIDRILL) LIMITED
Registration no: NI010383 **Date established:** 1974
No.of Employees: 1 - 10 **Product Groups:** 41

Date of Accounts	Apr 11	Apr 10	Apr 09
Working Capital	2m	2m	2m
Fixed Assets	209	185	132
Current Assets	3m	3m	2m

Nature Nook
14 Church Street, Ballymoney, BT53 6DL
Tel: 028-2766 4178 **Fax:** 028-2766 4178
Website: http://www.timmcilveen.talktalk.net
Directors: P. McIlveem (Prop)
No.of Employees: 1 - 10 **Product Groups:** 31, 32

North Antrim Pallets
Ballybrakes Industrial Estate Ballybrakes Road, Ballymoney, BT53 6LW
Tel: 028-2766 4333 **Fax:** 028-2766 7704
Directors: V. Gilmore (Prop)
Date established: 1994 **Turnover:** Up to £250,000
No.of Employees: 1 - 10 **Product Groups:** 25, 45, 48

Northern Fork Lifts
22 Ballybrakes Road, Ballymoney, BT53 6LQ
Tel: 028-2766 3030 **Fax:** 028-2766 9191
E-mail: sales@northernforklifts.com
Directors: S. Parry (Prop)
Immediate Holding Company: NORTHERN MATERIALS HANDLING (IRELAND) LIMITED
Registration no: NI048838 **Date established:** 2003
No.of Employees: 21 - 50 **Product Groups:** 35, 39, 45

Date of Accounts	Dec 11	Dec 10	Dec 09
Working Capital	72	15	65
Fixed Assets	469	517	371
Current Assets	718	1m	731

James Pollock & Son
53-61 Castle Street, Ballymoney, BT53 6JZ
Tel: 028-2766 3333 **Fax:** 028-2766 5951
Directors: G. Pollock (Ptnr)
VAT No.: GB 252 3281 82 **No.of Employees:** 1 - 10 **Product Groups:** 30, 66

R Robinson & Sons
Albany Villas 59 High Street, Ballymoney, BT53 6BG
Tel: 028-2766 2127 **Fax:** 028-2766 6027
E-mail: generaloffice@rrandsltd.com
Website: http://www.robinsonandsonsarchitects.co.uk
Directors: N. Robinson (Dir), R. Hunter (Dir)
Immediate Holding Company: R. ROBINSON & SONS (CHARTERED ARCHITECTS & CIVIL ENGINEERS) LTD
Registration no: NI051045 **Date established:** 2004
No.of Employees: 21 - 50 **Product Groups:** 84

Date of Accounts	Jun 11	Jun 10	Jun 09
Working Capital	619	684	606
Fixed Assets	149	194	235
Current Assets	957	1m	1m

Smak Beverages
35 Ballymena Road, Ballymoney, BT53 7EX
Tel: 028-2766 2594 **Fax:** 028-2766 6112
E-mail: bruce@mainesoftdrinksltd.co.uk
Website: http://www.mainesoftdrinksltd.co.uk
Bank(s): Ulster Bank
Directors: B. Harkness (Prop)
Managers: A. Hallam (Admin Off), J. Harkness (I.T. Exec), J. Harkness (Tech Serv Mgr)
Immediate Holding Company: MAINE SOFT DRINKS LIMITED
Registration no: NI020377 **VAT No.:** GB 252 6414 74
Date established: 1987 **Turnover:** £1m - £2m **No.of Employees:** 51 - 100
Product Groups: 21

Date of Accounts	Mar 11	Mar 10	Mar 09
Working Capital	-165	837	40
Fixed Assets	975	1m	1m
Current Assets	909	837	1m

Taggart & Company Ltd
38-44 Main Street, Ballymoney, BT53 6AP
Tel: 028-2766 2130 **Fax:** 028-2766 6129
E-mail: info@taggartandco.co.uk
Managers: D. McIntyre (Mgr)
Immediate Holding Company: TAGGART & COMPANY LIMITED
Registration no: NI002086 **VAT No.:** GB 252 5201 96
Date established: 1946 **No.of Employees:** 1 - 10 **Product Groups:** 66

Date of Accounts	Mar 11	Mar 10	Mar 09
Working Capital	249	249	250
Fixed Assets	90	93	96
Current Assets	289	325	306

Hugh Taggart & Sons Ltd
18 Meeting House Street, Ballymoney, BT53 6JP
Tel: 028-2766 3048 **Fax:** 028-2766 6129
E-mail: info@hughtaggart.com
Website: http://www.hughtaggart.com
Bank(s): Northern Bank
Directors: C. Taggart (Dir)
Immediate Holding Company: HUGH TAGGART & SONS LIMITED
Registration no: NI002087 **Date established:** 1946 **Turnover:** £1m - £2m
No.of Employees: 11 - 20 **Product Groups:** 52, 84

Date of Accounts	Mar 11	Mar 10	Mar 09
Working Capital	426	526	843
Fixed Assets	40	68	92
Current Assets	766	1m	2m

Transmission Services
10 Riada Avenue, Ballymoney, BT53 7LH
Tel: 028-2766 4455 **Fax:** 028-2766 9444
Directors: P. Mcmullan (Prop)
Immediate Holding Company: J.M.F. LTD.
Registration no: NI024927 **Date established:** 1990
No.of Employees: 1 - 10 **Product Groups:** 35, 66

Co. Down

Ballynahinch

A Total Security Service
10 Millbrook Drive, Ballynahinch, BT24 8HQ
Tel: 07793-982004
E-mail: office@totsec.co.uk
Website: http://www.totsec.co.uk
Directors: T. Ritchie (Dir)
No.of Employees: 1 - 10 **Product Groups:** 37, 39, 40, 67

Ballykine Structural Engineers Ltd
51 Lisburn Road, Ballynahinch, BT24 8TT
Tel: 028-9756 2560 **Fax:** 028-9756 2751
E-mail: info@ballykine.com
Website: http://www.ballykine.com
Bank(s): AIB Group
Directors: J. Thackray (Fin), I. Care (MD), I. Kerr (MD)
Managers: G. McQuaid (Mktg Serv Mgr)
Ultimate Holding Company: BALLYKINE STEEL CONSTRUCTION LIMITED
Immediate Holding Company: BALLYKINE STRUCTURAL ENGINEERS LIMITED
Registration no: NI032665 **VAT No.:** GB 331 7037 85
Date established: 1997 **Turnover:** £2m - £5m **No.of Employees:** 21 - 50
Product Groups: 35, 51

Date of Accounts	Sep 11	Sep 10	Sep 09
Working Capital	1m	2m	2m
Current Assets	2m	2m	2m

Central Business Systems
Windmill Business Park Windmill Road, Saintfield, Ballynahinch, BT24 7DX
Tel: 028-9751 0991 **Fax:** 028-9751 1465
E-mail: sales@cbsni.co.uk
Website: http://www.cbsni.co.uk
Directors: M. Mckeag (MD)
VAT No.: GB 255 2192 68 **Turnover:** £500,000 - £1m
No.of Employees: 1 - 10 **Product Groups:** 64, 67

R F Clarke Ltd
31 Windmill Road Saintfield, Ballynahinch, BT24 7DX
Tel: 028-9751 2920 **Fax:** 028-9751 2929
E-mail: joe@rfclarke.com
Website: http://www.rfclarke.com
Directors: R. Darnley (MD)
Managers: J. Mercer (Admin Off)
Immediate Holding Company: R. F. CLARKE LTD
Registration no: NI003680 **VAT No.:** GB 251 8535 58
Date established: 1956 **Turnover:** £500,000 - £1m
No.of Employees: 1 - 10 **Product Groups:** 23, 29, 38, 45, 63, 66

Date of Accounts	Mar 12	Mar 11	Mar 10
Working Capital	306	348	299
Fixed Assets	376	274	285
Current Assets	549	544	417

Enva N I Ltd
The Old Mill Drumaness, Ballynahinch, BT24 8LS
Tel: 028-9756 1574 **Fax:** 028-9756 1576
E-mail: sales@envani.com
Website: http://www.envani.com
Managers: G. Healy (Chief Acct), E. Merrifield (Tech Serv Mgr), G. Phillips (Sales & Mktg Mg), B. Johnson (Chief Mgr)
Registration no: NI017996 **No.of Employees:** 21 - 50
Product Groups: 32, 66

Garden Show Ireland
Montalto Estate Spa Road, Ballynahinch, BT24 8PT
Tel: 028-9756 1993 **Fax:** 028-9756 5073
E-mail: info@gardenshowireland.com
Website: http://www.gardenshowireland.com
Managers: C. Faulkner (Mgr)
VAT No.: GB 454 5140 62 **Turnover:** Up to £250,000
No.of Employees: 1 - 10 **Product Groups:** 81

Glas Seal N I Ltd
80 Belfast Road, Ballynahinch, BT24 8EB
Tel: 028-9756 2932 **Fax:** 028-9756 1096
E-mail: michael@glasseal.co.uk
Website: http://www.glasseal.co.uk
Managers: M. Moore (Sales & Mktg Mg), M. Ravey (Chief Mgr), J. Neill (Ops Mgr), I. Stewart (Personnel), C. Clements, S. Shaw (Chief Acct)
Ultimate Holding Company: JOHN FRACKELTON & SON, LIMITED,
Immediate Holding Company: GLAS-SEAL (NI) LIMITED
Registration no: NI009272 **Date established:** 1973 **Turnover:** £2m - £5m
No.of Employees: 21 - 50 **Product Groups:** 33

Date of Accounts	Dec 11	Dec 10	Dec 09
Sales Turnover	5m	5m	5m
Pre Tax Profit/Loss	-298	17	-173
Working Capital	-1m	-765	-762
Fixed Assets	3m	3m	4m
Current Assets	2m	2m	2m
Current Liabilities	2m	1m	1m

Gordons Electrical Supplies
49 Windmill Street, Ballynahinch, BT24 8HB
Tel: 028-9756 3901 **Fax:** 028-9756 1048
E-mail: info@gordonselectricalsupplies.co.uk
Website: http://www.gordonselectricalsupplies.co.uk
Bank(s): Northern Bank
Directors: B. Quigley (Fin)
Managers: T. Woods (Mgr)
Immediate Holding Company: EASTOWER (N.I.) LTD
Registration no: NI018750 **VAT No.:** GB 454 5137 51
Date established: 1985 **Turnover:** £1m - £2m **No.of Employees:** 21 - 50
Product Groups: 67

Date of Accounts	Feb 11	Feb 10	Feb 09
Sales Turnover	N/A	N/A	1m
Pre Tax Profit/Loss	N/A	N/A	376
Working Capital	783	890	1m
Fixed Assets	196	238	223
Current Assets	2m	3m	3m
Current Liabilities	N/A	N/A	190

Macspec Engineering
86 Moss Road, Ballynahinch, BT24 8XZ
Tel: 028-9756 2591 **Fax:** 028-9756 1055
E-mail: info@macspec.co.uk
Website: http://www.macspec.co.uk
Directors: J. McCormick (Prop)
Immediate Holding Company: MACSPEC ENGINEERING LTD
Registration no: NI042683 **Date established:** 2002
No.of Employees: 11 - 20 **Product Groups:** 35

Date of Accounts	Mar 12	Mar 11	Mar 10
Working Capital	-97	-152	-184
Fixed Assets	405	428	459
Current Assets	279	350	264

The National Trust
Rowallane House Saintfield, Ballynahinch, BT24 7JA
Tel: 028-9751 0721 **Fax:** 028-9751 1242
E-mail: sales@ntni.org.uk
Website: http://www.nationaltrust.org.uk
Managers: L. Mcknight
Registration no: 09000351 **No.of Employees:** 21 - 50 **Product Groups:** 87

Nitronica
4 Antrim Road, Ballynahinch, BT24 8AN
Tel: 028-9756 6200 **Fax:** 028-9756 6256
E-mail: info@nitronica.com
Website: http://www.nitronica.com
Directors: J. Mellon (MD), J. Melon (MD)
Managers: L. Fegan (Personnel), R. Bradford (Tech Serv Mgr), N. Harvey (Mktg Serv Mgr), G. Kennedy (Sales Prom Mgr), J. Tarr (Purch Mgr)
Immediate Holding Company: NITRONICA LIMITED
Registration no: NI044632 **Date established:** 2002 **Turnover:** £5m - £10m
No.of Employees: 51 - 100 **Product Groups:** 37, 44

Date of Accounts	Dec 11	Dec 10	Dec 09
Working Capital	1m	616	594
Fixed Assets	133	185	186
Current Assets	4m	2m	3m
Current Liabilities	N/A	N/A	90

Pinewick Ltd
10a Magheraknock Road, Ballynahinch, BT24 8TJ
Tel: 028-9756 1708 **Fax:** 028-9756 3943
E-mail: pinewick1@aol.com
Website: http://www.pinewick.co.uk
Directors: T. Pollock (Dir)
Managers: C. Smart (Sales Prom Mgr), M. Lucas (Mgr)
Immediate Holding Company: PINEWICK LIMITED
Registration no: NI010973 **VAT No.:** GB 353 0726 71
Date established: 1975 **No.of Employees:** 1 - 10 **Product Groups:** 26, 63

Spa Security Solutions
8 Spa Road, Ballynahinch, BT24 8LU
Tel: 028-9756 1065 **Fax:** 028-9756 1065
E-mail: sales@spacctv.com
Website: http://www.spacctv.com
Directors: S. Maguire (MD)
No.of Employees: 1 - 10 **Product Groups:** 37, 40, 52, 67

Stanley Patterson Agricultural Machinery
3 Blacks Lane, Ballynahinch, BT24 8UT
Tel: 028-9756 3141
E-mail: info@stanleypatterson.co.uk
Website: http://www.stanleypatterson.co.uk
Directors: S. Patterson (Prop)
No.of Employees: 1 - 10 **Product Groups:** 41

Maurice Walsh & Co. Ltd
Drumaness Industrial Estate Old Park Road, Drumaness, Ballynahinch, BT24 8SE
Tel: 028-9756 2842 **Fax:** 028-9756 2592
E-mail: info@mauricewalsh.com
Website: http://www.mauricewalsh.com
Bank(s): Ulster
Directors: B. Walsh (Dir)
Immediate Holding Company: MAURICE WALSH & COMPANY LIMITED
Registration no: NI012771 **VAT No.:** GB 331 7261 80
Date established: 1978 **Turnover:** £500,000 - £1m
No.of Employees: 11 - 20 **Product Groups:** 35

Date of Accounts	Sep 11	Sep 10	Sep 09
Working Capital	925	666	1m
Fixed Assets	52	60	71
Current Assets	1m	927	1m

Co. Down

Banbridge

Artistic Impressions Advertising
PO Box 93, Banbridge, BT32 5PQ
Tel: 028-4067 1100 **Fax:** 028-4067 1122
E-mail: info@pensplus.eu
Website: http://www.pensplus.eu
Directors: D. Kelly (Prop)
VAT No.: GB 617 6569 11 **Date established:** 2002
Turnover: Up to £250,000 **No.of Employees:** 1 - 10 **Product Groups:** 28, 49

Ballykelly Group
22 Ballykelly Road, Banbridge, BT32 4PS
Tel: 028-4062 5639 **Fax:** 028-4062 8211
E-mail: info@baljomar.co.uk
Website: http://www.ballykellygroup.co.uk
Directors: S. Mcanerney (Dir), M. McAnerney (MD)
Immediate Holding Company: THE BALLYKELLY GROUP LTD
Registration no: NI068580 **VAT No.:** GB 331 2667 77
Date established: 2008 **No.of Employees:** 11 - 20 **Product Groups:** 25, 52

Date of Accounts	Aug 11	Aug 10	Aug 09
Working Capital	-527	-539	-801
Fixed Assets	389	435	769
Current Assets	326	358	486

Banbridge Chronicle Press Ltd
16 Downshire Place, Banbridge, BT32 3DF
Tel: 028-4066 2322 **Fax:** 028-4062 4397
E-mail: news@thebanbridgechronicle.com
Website: http://www.thebanbridgechronicle.com
Directors: J. Hodgett (Dir)
Immediate Holding Company: BANBRIDGE CHRONICLE PRESS LIMITED
Registration no: NI002964 **VAT No.:** GB 254 1536 73
Date established: 1951 **Turnover:** £500,000 - £1m
No.of Employees: 1 - 10 **Product Groups:** 28

Date of Accounts	Jan 12	Jan 11	Jan 10
Working Capital	15	75	165
Fixed Assets	542	498	521
Current Assets	494	463	436

Belmont Hotel
Rathfriland Road, Banbridge, BT32 3LH
Tel: 028-4066 2517 **Fax:** 028-4062 9770
E-mail: hotelbelmont@btconnect.com
Website: http://www.belmont-hotel.com
Managers: E. O'Connor (Tech Serv Mgr), I. Curran (Mgr), K. McGiven (Mgr)
Immediate Holding Company: BELMONT HOTEL (BANBRIDGE) LIMITED
Registration no: NI036118 **VAT No.:** GB 390 8568 13
Date established: 1999 **No.of Employees:** 101 - 250 **Product Groups:** 69

Date of Accounts	Apr 12	Apr 11	Apr 10
Working Capital	-339	-308	-178
Fixed Assets	2m	2m	3m
Current Assets	78	88	82

Bowman Windows
1 Scarva Road Industrial Estate Scarva Road, Banbridge, BT32 3QD
Tel: 028-4066 2000 **Fax:** 028-4062 2661
E-mail: info@bowman-windows.co.uk
Website: http://www.bowman-windows.co.uk
Directors: V. Bowman (Ptnr)
Managers: R. Brown (Sales & Mktg Mg), A. Graham (Tech Serv Mgr), A. Bowman, D. Waddell
VAT No.: GB 251 8916 46 **Date established:** 1970
No.of Employees: 51 - 100 **Product Groups:** 33, 52

Chain Care Lifting Services Ltd
3a Hill Road Ballinaskeagh, Banbridge, BT32 5EH
Tel: 028-4065 1522 **Fax:** 028-4065 1211
E-mail: john@chaincare.com
Website: http://www.chaincare.com
Managers: J. Reid (Mgr)
Immediate Holding Company: Chain Care Lifting Services Limited
Registration no: NI059902 **Date established:** 2006
No.of Employees: 1 - 10 **Product Groups:** 35, 39, 45

Date of Accounts	Sep 11	Sep 10	Sep 09
Working Capital	40	6	10
Fixed Assets	39	54	63
Current Assets	214	266	227

Craftstone 2000
17 Skeltons Road, Banbridge, BT32 4HL
Tel: 028-9269 9777 **Fax:** 028-9269 9577
E-mail: info@craftstone.co.uk
Website: http://www.craftstone.co.uk
Directors: R. Campbell (Grp Chief Exec)
Managers: V. McKelvey (Sales & Mktg Mg)
Immediate Holding Company: CRAFTSTONE 2000 LIMITED
Registration no: NI031174 **Date established:** 1996
Turnover: £250,000 - £500,000 **No.of Employees:** 11 - 20
Product Groups: 33

Date of Accounts	Jun 11	Jun 10	Jun 09
Working Capital	3	-8	-54
Fixed Assets	95	111	130
Current Assets	170	165	152

Dask Timber Products Ltd
80 Moss Road, Banbridge, BT32 3NZ
Tel: 028-3831 8696 **Fax:** 028-3831 8698
E-mail: info@dasktimber.co.uk
Website: http://www.dasktimber.co.uk
Directors: D. Clarke (MD)
Immediate Holding Company: DASK TIMBER PRODUCTS LIMITED
Registration no: NI009563 **VAT No.:** GB 255 5955 27
Date established: 1973 **No.of Employees:** 11 - 20 **Product Groups:** 25

Date of Accounts	Dec 11	Dec 10	Dec 09
Working Capital	-128	-1	144
Fixed Assets	457	506	550
Current Assets	562	646	726

Ef Engineering
59 Blue Road, Banbridge, BT32 3QH
Tel: 028-4066 2064 **Fax:** 028-4062 9505
E-mail: e.fullerton@hotmail.co.uk
Directors: E. Fullerton (Prop)
No.of Employees: 1 - 10 **Product Groups:** 35

Thomas Ferguson & Co. Ltd
54 Scarva Road, Banbridge, BT32 3AU
Tel: 028-4062 3491 **Fax:** 028-4062 2453
E-mail: info@fergusonsirishlinen.com
Website: http://www.fergusonsirishlinen.com
Bank(s): HSBC
Directors: D. Neilly (MD), M. Lenehan (Co Sec)
Managers: S. Lennon (Purch Mgr), E. Quinn (Prod Mgr), A. Quinn (Purch Mgr), K. Perry (Admin Off), C. Bower (I.T. Exec)
Ultimate Holding Company: FRANKLINS INTERNATIONAL LTD
Immediate Holding Company: THOMAS FERGUSON & COMPANY, LIMITED
Registration no: R0000713 **VAT No.:** GB 251 7854 47
Date established: 1984 **No.of Employees:** 21 - 50 **Product Groups:** 23, 24

Date of Accounts	Dec 11	Dec 10	Dec 09
Working Capital	778	654	815
Fixed Assets	36	28	46
Current Assets	874	756	932

Gibson Brothers Ltd
1 Kilmacrew Road, Banbridge, BT32 4ES
Tel: 028-4066 2771 **Fax:** 028-4062 6704
E-mail: liam@gibbros.freeserve.co.uk
Directors: J. Gibson (Dir)
Managers: L. Murtagh (Chief Mgr)
Immediate Holding Company: GIBSON BROS LIMITED
Registration no: NI019852 **VAT No.:** GB 252 0898 56
Date established: 1986 **Turnover:** £10m - £20m
No.of Employees: 51 - 100 **Product Groups:** 14, 51

Date of Accounts	Oct 11	Oct 10	Oct 09
Sales Turnover	10m	7m	9m
Pre Tax Profit/Loss	1m	1m	1m
Working Capital	11m	10m	9m
Fixed Assets	1m	2m	2m
Current Assets	14m	12m	12m
Current Liabilities	444	575	2m

Glazing Design Systems Ltd

Huntly Road, Banbridge, BT32 3UR
Tel: 028-4062 3866 **Fax:** 028-4062 3844
E-mail: admin@glazingdesign.co.uk
Website: http://www.glazingdesign.co.uk
Directors: D. Macauley (MD)
Immediate Holding Company: GLAZING DESIGN SYSTEMS LIMITED
Registration no: NI027342 **VAT No.:** GB 617 6330 46
Date established: 1993 **Turnover:** £1m - £2m **No.of Employees:** 1 - 10
Product Groups: 35

Date of Accounts	Jul 11	Jul 10	Jul 09
Working Capital	187	267	261
Fixed Assets	19	39	62
Current Assets	338	337	399

James Coburn & Sons Ltd

32 Scarva Street, Banbridge, BT32 3DD
Tel: 028-4066 2207 **Fax:** 028-4062 7250
E-mail: sales@coburns.co.uk
Website: http://www.coburns.co.uk
Directors: B. Bell (MD)
Ultimate Holding Company: GERMINAL HOLDINGS LIMITED
Immediate Holding Company: JAMES COBURN & SON LIMITED
Registration no: NI002983 **VAT No.:** GB 287 1105 60
Date established: 1951 **Turnover:** £1m - £2m **No.of Employees:** 1 - 10
Product Groups: 02, 62, 66

Date of Accounts	Jun 11	Jun 10	Jun 09
Working Capital	307	240	204
Fixed Assets	23	44	44
Current Assets	738	832	967

Jones Peters

6 Church Street, Banbridge, BT32 4AA
Tel: 028-4062 5427 **Fax:** 028-4062 5102
E-mail: business.advise@jonespeters.co.uk
Website: http://www.jonespeters.co.uk
Directors: K. Jones (Snr Part), P. Cummings (Ptnr)
Managers: J. Houston (Mgr)
Immediate Holding Company: JONES PETERS CONSULTANCY SERVICES LIMITED
Registration no: NI016814 **VAT No.:** GB 366 3077 42
Date established: 1983 **Turnover:** £500,000 - £1m
No.of Employees: 21 - 50 **Product Groups:** 80

Mckinstry Plant Painting

5 Glen Road Ballinaskeagh, Banbridge, BT32 5DY
Tel: 028-4065 1506 **Fax:** 028-4065 1485
E-mail: wallace@plantpainting.co.uk
Directors: W. Mckinstry (Prop)
No.of Employees: 1 - 10 **Product Groups:** 42, 45

Mcdermott Readymix Concrete

76a Ballymoney Road, Banbridge, BT32 4DX
Tel: 028-4062 2204 **Fax:** 028-4062 2419
Directors: E. McDermott (Dir)
VAT No.: GB 255 0229 81 **Date established:** 2005
Turnover: £250,000 - £500,000 **No.of Employees:** 1 - 10
Product Groups: 33

Joseph Morton Ltd

Commercial Road, Banbridge, BT32 3ES
Tel: 028-4066 2521 **Fax:** 028-4066 2036
E-mail: ray.morrison@josephmorton.co.uk
Website: http://www.mortonseeds.com
Directors: R. Morrison (Dir)
Ultimate Holding Company: GERMINAL HOLDINGS LIMITED
Immediate Holding Company: JOSEPH MORTON LIMITED
Registration no: NI000051 **VAT No.:** GB 287 1105 60
Date established: 2022 **Turnover:** £1m - £2m **No.of Employees:** 11 - 20
Product Groups: 62

Date of Accounts	Jun 11	Jun 10	Jun 09
Working Capital	294	189	192
Fixed Assets	87	121	52
Current Assets	3m	3m	3m

Kevin Murphy Engineering Ltd

4 Waringsford Road, Banbridge, BT32 4EH
Tel: 028-4066 2547 **Fax:** 028-4066 2822
E-mail: info@kme-steelworks.co.uk
Website: http://www.kme-steelworks.co.uk
Directors: J. Quinn (MD)
Managers: J. Quinn (Admin Off)
Immediate Holding Company: Murphy Hitchfork Ltd
Registration no: NI045987 **VAT No.:** GB 255 5964 26
Date established: 2003 **No.of Employees:** 11 - 20 **Product Groups:** 46, 48

Radius Plastics

Scarva Road, Banbridge, BT32 3QD
Tel: 028-4066 9999 **Fax:** 028-4066 9996
E-mail: gd@radius-systems.com
Website: http://www.radius-systems.com
Bank(s): Northern Bank
Directors: G. Devine (MD), J. Doherty (Fin)
Ultimate Holding Company: INHOCO 3443 LIMITED
Immediate Holding Company: RADIUS PLASTICS LIMITED
Registration no: NI013308 **VAT No.:** GB 496 9282 79
Date established: 1979 **Turnover:** £20m - £50m
No.of Employees: 51 - 100 **Product Groups:** 30

Date of Accounts	Dec 10	Dec 09	Dec 08
Sales Turnover	26m	26m	29m
Pre Tax Profit/Loss	-14m	1m	836
Working Capital	-14m	-11m	-3m
Fixed Assets	7m	17m	14m
Current Assets	17m	15m	15m
Current Liabilities	3m	2m	2m

Stewart Systems

21 Lisnaward Hill, Banbridge, BT32 4HG
Tel: 028-9269 9315
E-mail: stewart.systems@tiscali.co.uk
Directors: W. Stewart (Prop)
No.of Employees: 1 - 10 **Product Groups:** 35

Super Spares Ltd

Brookfield Industrial Estate Peggys Loaning, Banbridge, BT32 3AP
Tel: 028-4066 2166 **Fax:** 028-4062 6642
E-mail: brian@super-spares.com
Website: http://www.super-spares.com
Directors: S. Oneill (MD)
Immediate Holding Company: SUPER SPARES (PARTS) LIMITED
Registration no: NI011612 **VAT No.:** GB 390 7024 58
Date established: 1976 **Turnover:** £1m - £2m **No.of Employees:** 1 - 10
Product Groups: 66, 67

Date of Accounts	Feb 12	Feb 11	Feb 10
Working Capital	150	218	213
Fixed Assets	14	22	23
Current Assets	506	518	533

Tullyraine Quarries Ltd

122 Dromore Road, Banbridge, BT32 4EG
Tel: 028-4066 2481 **Fax:** 028-4066 2748
E-mail: enquiries@tullyrainequarries.co.uk
Website: http://www.tullyrainequarries.co.uk
Bank(s): Northern bank
Managers: J. Mccartan (Mgr)
Immediate Holding Company: TULLYRAINE QUARRIES LIMITED
Registration no: NI004047 **VAT No.:** GB 254 1963 54
Date established: 1958 **Turnover:** £2m - £5m **No.of Employees:** 21 - 50
Product Groups: 51

Date of Accounts	Dec 11	Dec 10	Dec 09
Working Capital	95	-98	-135
Fixed Assets	2m	3m	3m
Current Assets	2m	1m	2m

Ulster Weavers Apparel Ltd

245 Castlewellan Road, Banbridge, BT32 3SG
Tel: 028-4062 4490 **Fax:** 028-4062 1100
E-mail: sales@ulsterweavers.com
Website: http://www.ulsterweavers.com
Bank(s): Northern Bank
Directors: A. Webb (MD)
Ultimate Holding Company: JOHN HOGG & CO. LIMITED
Immediate Holding Company: ULSTER WEAVERS APPAREL LIMITED
Registration no: R0000460 **VAT No.:** GB 311 2152 27
Date established: 2020 **Turnover:** £2m - £5m **No.of Employees:** 11 - 20
Product Groups: 24

Date of Accounts	Apr 12	Apr 11	Apr 10
Sales Turnover	N/A	N/A	2m
Pre Tax Profit/Loss	N/A	N/A	314
Working Capital	4m	4m	4m
Fixed Assets	27	27	52
Current Assets	4m	4m	5m
Current Liabilities	N/A	N/A	90

Co. Down

Bangor

A M Control Systems

Unit 27 2 Innotec Drive, Bangor, BT19 7PD
Tel: 028-9145 1313 **Fax:** 028-9145 2200
E-mail: amcontrols@yahoo.co.uk
Directors: R. Caddell (Prop)
Registration no: NI047431 **VAT No.:** GB 5171 1615 63
Date established: 2003 **No.of Employees:** 1 - 10 **Product Groups:** 37, 38, 40, 52

D E Alexander & Sons Ltd

91 Main Street, Bangor, BT20 4AF
Tel: 028-9127 0270 **Fax:** 028-9127 1544
E-mail: advertiising@spectatornewspapers.co.uk
Website: http://www.spectatornewspapers.co.uk
Directors: D. Alexander Jnr (MD)
Managers: G. Leacock (Tech Serv Mgr), N. Evans (Sales Prom Mgr)
Immediate Holding Company: D. E. ALEXANDER & SONS LIMITED
Registration no: NI001942 **VAT No.:** GB 252 0120 24
Date established: 1945 **No.of Employees:** 21 - 50 **Product Groups:** 28

Date of Accounts	Aug 11	Aug 10	Aug 09
Working Capital	4m	4m	4m
Fixed Assets	1m	1m	904
Current Assets	4m	4m	5m

Anderson Manning Associates

Ama Communication Centre 2 Enterprise Road, Bangor, BT19 7TA
Tel: 028-9147 2525 **Fax:** 028-9147 2797
E-mail: kevin.houston@andersonmanning.com
Website: http://www.andersonmanning.com
Directors: K. Houston (MD), S. Anderson (Ptnr), J. Manning (Ptnr)
Managers: S. Grey (Accounts)
Immediate Holding Company: ANDERSON MANNING ASSOCIATES LTD
Registration no: NI033516 **VAT No.:** GB 617 7582 04
Date established: 1998 **No.of Employees:** 101 - 250 **Product Groups:** 81

Balloo Hire Centre Ltd

21 Balloo Drive, Bangor, BT19 7QY
Tel: 028-9145 4457 **Fax:** 028-9127 1239
E-mail: dan@balloohire.com
Website: http://www.balloohire.com
Directors: P. Avery (MD)
Managers: M. Grundy (Sales Prom Mgr)
Immediate Holding Company: BALLOO HIRE CENTRE LIMITED
Registration no: NI020540 **VAT No.:** GB 454 6234 48
Date established: 1987 **Turnover:** £5m - £10m **No.of Employees:** 21 - 50
Product Groups: 83

Date of Accounts	Mar 11	Mar 10	Mar 09
Sales Turnover	5m	5m	N/A
Pre Tax Profit/Loss	162	-340	-28
Working Capital	-2m	-2m	-2m
Fixed Assets	6m	5m	6m
Current Assets	2m	1m	1m
Current Liabilities	285	467	400

Ballyrobert Cars Ltd

402 Belfast Road, Bangor, BT19 1UE
Tel: 028-9185 2262 **Fax:** 028-9185 2707
E-mail: ballyrobert@yahoo.co.uk
Website: http://www.ballyrobert.co.uk
Directors: R. Lyle (MD), J. Lyle (MD)
Managers: R. Martin (Serv Mgr), S. Roy (Sales Prom Mgr)
Ultimate Holding Company: BALLYROBERT SERVICE STATION LIMITED
Immediate Holding Company: BALLYROBERT LIMITED
Registration no: NI041276 **VAT No.:** GB 252 6371 48
Date established: 2001 **Turnover:** £10m - £20m
No.of Employees: 21 - 50 **Product Groups:** 68

Date of Accounts	Dec 10	Dec 09	Dec 08
Sales Turnover	24m	27m	29m
Pre Tax Profit/Loss	-179	337	215
Working Capital	933	1m	746
Fixed Assets	985	1m	1m
Current Assets	8m	8m	6m
Current Liabilities	639	1m	477

Bigger & Johnston Ltd

20 Balloo Avenue, Bangor, BT19 7QT
Tel: 028-9127 1255 **Fax:** 028-9127 0365
Directors: H. Bigger (Dir)
Immediate Holding Company: BIGGER & JOHNSTON LIMITED
Registration no: NI011234 **VAT No.:** GB 286 3899 91
Date established: 1976 **Turnover:** £250,000 - £500,000
No.of Employees: 1 - 10 **Product Groups:** 41

Date of Accounts	Mar 09	Mar 08	Apr 11
Working Capital	11	42	52
Fixed Assets	53	56	N/A
Current Assets	43	61	53

Boland Reilly Homes Ltd

1 Ballycrochan Crescent, Bangor, BT19 7LG
Tel: 028-9127 0835 **Fax:** 028-9145 8940
E-mail: admin@bolandreillyhomes.com
Website: http://www.bolandreillyhomes.com
Directors: B. Alcorn (MD)
Ultimate Holding Company: BOLAND HOLDINGS LIMITED
Immediate Holding Company: BOLAND REILLY HOMES LIMITED
Registration no: NI032132 **VAT No.:** GB 286 3919 14
Date established: 1997 **Turnover:** £2m - £5m **No.of Employees:** 1 - 10
Product Groups: 52

Date of Accounts	Dec 11	Dec 10	Dec 09
Sales Turnover	2m	3m	6m
Pre Tax Profit/Loss	-7m	-336	10
Working Capital	1m	14m	11m
Fixed Assets	877	997	575
Current Assets	11m	18m	19m
Current Liabilities	98	125	141

C T Finishing

Unit 7 2-4 Balloo Road, Bangor, BT19 7PG
Tel: 07711-286553
Directors: C. Todd (Prop)
No.of Employees: 1 - 10 **Product Groups:** 26

Celtic Bride

73 Belfast Road, Bangor, BT20 3PW
Tel: 028-9146 0222 **Fax:** 0870-284 0851
E-mail: donna@celticbride.com
Website: http://www.celticbride.com
Directors: D. Kernan (MD), D. Kerlan (Prop)
Date established: 2002 **No.of Employees:** 1 - 10 **Product Groups:** 49

City Electrical Factors Ltd

1a Balloo Way, Bangor, BT19 7QZ
Tel: 028-9145 6880 **Fax:** 028-9145 6024
E-mail: a.long@cef.co.uk
Website: http://www.cef.co.uk
Managers: A. Long (District Mgr)
Ultimate Holding Company: CEF HOLDINGS LIMITED
Immediate Holding Company: CITY ELECTRICAL FACTORS LIMITED
Registration no: 00336408 **VAT No.:** GB 273 5927 30
Date established: 1938 **No.of Employees:** 1 - 10 **Product Groups:** 67

Date of Accounts	Apr 11	Apr 10	Apr 09
Sales Turnover	439m	406m	444m
Pre Tax Profit/Loss	22m	26m	34m
Working Capital	53m	172m	164m
Fixed Assets	13m	17m	18m
Current Assets	179m	250m	227m
Current Liabilities	53m	23m	20m

Coates Engineering

56a Balloo Road, Bangor, BT19 7PG
Tel: 028-9127 5001 **Fax:** 028-9147 0652
Website: http://www.power.coates-engineering.co.uk
Managers: D. Coates
Date established: 1990 **No.of Employees:** 11 - 20 **Product Groups:** 35

Corporate Wardrobe

Enterprise House Balloo Avenue, Bangor, BT19 7QT
Tel: 028-9127 0718 **Fax:** 028-9127 4763
E-mail: harrym@corporate-wardrobe.co.uk
Website: http://www.corporate-wardrobe.com
Directors: H. McLeese (MD)
Managers: C. Spin (I.T. Exec), C. McCann (Personnel), C. Spence (I.T. Exec), A. Heron (Sales Prom Mgr)
Immediate Holding Company: CORPORATE WARDROBE LIMITED-THE
Registration no: NI029653 **VAT No.:** GB 375 8206 31
Date established: 1995 **No.of Employees:** 11 - 20 **Product Groups:** 24

Denman International Ltd

Clandeboye Road, Bangor, BT20 3JH
Tel: 028-9146 2141 **Fax:** 028-9145 1654
E-mail: info@denmanpro.com
Website: http://www.denmanpro.com
Bank(s): Northern, Bangor
Directors: J. Rainey (MD), J. King (Co Sec), W. Kirkpatrick (Fin), F. Rainey (Ch)
Managers: E. Taylor (Tech Sales Mgr), B. Robinson (Nat Sales Mgr), F. Tomkins
Immediate Holding Company: Denroy Group Ltd
Registration no: NI008800 **Date established:** 1972 **Turnover:** £5m - £10m
No.of Employees: 101 - 250 **Product Groups:** 30, 40, 49

Emos-Infineer Ltd
Balloo Avenue, Bangor, BT19 7QT
Tel: 028-9147 6000 **Fax:** 028-9147 6001
E-mail: phunter@infineer.com
Website: http://www.infineer.com
Bank(s): Northern, Belfast
Managers: P. Hunter (Chief Mgr)
Ultimate Holding Company: PUBLICARD INC (USA)
Immediate Holding Company: Infineer Ltd
Registration no: NI008086 **Date established:** 1970 **Turnover:** £1m - £2m
No.of Employees: 11 - 20 **Product Groups:** 28, 30, 37, 44, 49, 82

Date of Accounts	Dec 07	Dec 06	Dec 05
Sales Turnover	2m	2m	2m
Pre Tax Profit/Loss	42	-110	-189
Working Capital	-2m	-2m	-1m
Fixed Assets	1	3	13
Current Assets	397	437	565
Current Liabilities	2m	2m	1m

Higher Profile Advertising
74 Ballycrochan Road, Bangor, BT19 6NF
Tel: 028-9127 1016 **Fax:** 028-9127 1016
E-mail: mcquistonjohn@aol.co.uk
Directors: J. Mcquiston (Prop)
Date established: 1988 **Turnover:** Up to £250,000
No.of Employees: 1 - 10 **Product Groups:** 81

John Kelly & Sons Glass Ltd
96 Abbey Street, Bangor, BT20 4JB
Tel: 028-9127 1339 **Fax:** 028-9146 3839
E-mail: info@jkglass.co.uk
Website: http://www.jkglass.co.uk
Directors: J. Flesby (MD), R. Holdson (MD), S. Flesby (MD)
Managers: S. McMillan (Chief Acct)
Immediate Holding Company: JOHN KELLY & SON (GLASS) LIMITED
Registration no: NI031094 **VAT No.:** GB 252 4300 02
Date established: 1996 **No.of Employees:** 1 - 10 **Product Groups:** 30, 35, 48, 52

Kingsbury Packaging
Unit 68 Enterprise House 2-4 Balloo Avenue, Bangor, BT19 7QT
Tel: 028-9147 1515
Managers: N. Skehin (Mgr)
Date established: 1999 **No.of Employees:** 1 - 10 **Product Groups:** 38, 42

Knox & Markwell
14 Donaghadee Road, Bangor, BT20 5RU
Tel: 028-9145 6677 **Fax:** 028-9127 1261
E-mail: design@akm.org.uk
Website: http://www.akm.org.uk
Directors: B. Knox (Ptnr)
Immediate Holding Company: ARCHITECTS KNOX AND MARKWELL LIMITED
Registration no: NI608169 **VAT No.:** GB 286 4579 07
Date established: 2011 **Turnover:** £500,000 - £1m
No.of Employees: 1 - 10 **Product Groups:** 84

Legal & Trade Collections Ltd
2-4 Balloo Avenue, Bangor, BT19 7QT
Tel: 028-9146 1465 **Fax:** 028-9147 1124
E-mail: brian.snowden@legalandtrade.fsnet.co.uk
Managers: B. Snowdon (Mgr)
Ultimate Holding Company: IRMC HOLDINGS INC (USA)
Immediate Holding Company: LEGAL & TRADE COLLECTIONS LIMITED
Registration no: 00165247 **VAT No.:** GB 483 0271 57
Date established: 2020 **No.of Employees:** 1 - 10 **Product Groups:** 82

Date of Accounts	Dec 11	Dec 10	Dec 09
Working Capital	-424	-424	-424

Lindsay Ford
3 Balloo Park, Bangor, BT19 7PP
Tel: 028-9147 4700 **Fax:** 028-9147 1658
E-mail: reception.binder@lindsays.co.uk
Website: http://www.lindsayford.co.uk
Managers: J. Tyson (District Mgr)
Immediate Holding Company: LINDSAY CARS LIMITED
Registration no: NI005514 **VAT No.:** GB 255 9502 44
Date established: 1963 **No.of Employees:** 21 - 50 **Product Groups:** 68

Date of Accounts	Dec 11	Dec 10	Dec 09
Sales Turnover	104m	115m	114m
Pre Tax Profit/Loss	-1m	825	1m
Working Capital	1m	2m	1m
Fixed Assets	8m	9m	12m
Current Assets	33m	32m	43m
Current Liabilities	29m	5m	9m

M M Group Ireland
Clandeboye Retail Park West Circular Road, Bangor, BT19 1AR
Tel: 028-9147 4000 **Fax:** 028-9147 4505
E-mail: info@mmgroup.co.uk
Website: http://www.teleperformance.com
Directors: A. Ashdon (Fin), J. Smith (MD)
Ultimate Holding Company: TELEPERFORMANCE SA (FRANCE)
Immediate Holding Company: MM Group Ireland Limited
Registration no: NI032342 **Date established:** 1997
Turnover: £10m - £20m **No.of Employees:** 251 - 500 **Product Groups:** 81

Date of Accounts	Dec 10	Dec 09	Dec 08
Working Capital	N/A	50	50
Current Assets	N/A	50	50

Mcwhinneys Sausages
10 Balloo Way Balloo Industrial Estate, Bangor, BT19 7QZ
Tel: 028-9127 1811 **Fax:** 028-9127 1795
E-mail: info@mcwhinneys.com
Website: http://www.mcwhinneys.com
Bank(s): Northern Bank
Managers: A. Gibson (Sales Admin)
Immediate Holding Company: MCWHINNEY'S SAUSAGES LIMITED
Registration no: NI602478 **VAT No.:** GB 253 1950 69
Date established: 2010 **No.of Employees:** 11 - 20 **Product Groups:** 20

Date of Accounts	Mar 11
Working Capital	74
Fixed Assets	602
Current Assets	391

Marine Court Hotel
18-20 Quay Street, Bangor, BT20 5ED
Tel: 028-9145 1100 **Fax:** 028-9145 1200
E-mail: sales@marinecourthotel.net
Website: http://www.marinecourthotel.net
Directors: A. Henderson (Fin), E. Diamond (Prop)
Managers: A. Macauley, B. McCann (Chief Mgr)
Date established: 1996 **No.of Employees:** 51 - 100 **Product Groups:** 69

Munster Simms Engineering Ltd
Old Belfast Road, Bangor, BT19 1LT
Tel: 028-9127 0531 **Fax:** 028-9146 6421
E-mail: info@whalepumps.com
Website: http://www.whalepumps.com
Bank(s): Bank of Ireland
Directors: P. Hurst (Dir)
Managers: A. Bell (Tech Serv Mgr), P. Roberts, W. Hanson, K. Roberts (Personnel)
Ultimate Holding Company: PSW (NI) Limited
Immediate Holding Company: MUNSTER SIMMS ENGINEERING LIMITED
Registration no: NI006278 **Date established:** 1965
Turnover: £10m - £20m **No.of Employees:** 101 - 250
Product Groups: 36, 39, 40, 45

Date of Accounts	Dec 11	Dec 10	Dec 09
Sales Turnover	14m	13m	10m
Pre Tax Profit/Loss	1m	2m	837
Working Capital	13m	12m	12m
Fixed Assets	4m	4m	4m
Current Assets	17m	16m	15m
Current Liabilities	778	1m	892

N I I B Group Ltd
26-32 Central Avenue, Bangor, BT20 3AS
Tel: 028-9146 9415 **Fax:** 028-9147 4455
E-mail: support@boiuk.co.uk
Website: http://www.niibfinance.com
Bank(s): Bank of Ireland
Directors: M. Andrews (MD)
Managers: G. Mcgempsey (Sec), L. Lagan (Mktg Serv Mgr), J. McGee (Sales Prom Mgr), F. Johnston (I.T. Exec), G. McGempsey
Ultimate Holding Company: GOVERNOR AND COMPANY OF THE BANK OF IRELAND
Immediate Holding Company: N.I.I.B. GROUP LIMITED
Registration no: NI003721 **VAT No.:** GB 168 1961 35
Date established: 1956 **Turnover:** £500,000 - £1m
No.of Employees: 21 - 50 **Product Groups:** 82

Date of Accounts	Dec 10	Mar 10	Mar 09
Sales Turnover	2m	797	N/A
Pre Tax Profit/Loss	13m	20m	10m
Working Capital	17m	24m	78m
Fixed Assets	2m	2m	4m
Current Assets	1012m	1141m	1345m
Current Liabilities	N/A	8m	1268m

North Down Developments Ltd
1a Brookvale Avenue, Bangor, BT19 7ZP
Tel: 028-9127 1525 **Fax:** 028-9127 0080
E-mail: mail@nddo.co.uk
Website: http://www.nddo.co.uk
Directors: L. Vance (Grp Chief Exec)
Managers: S. Quinn, H. McAuley, E. Pearson, H. McCauley (Fin Mgr)
Immediate Holding Company: North Down Developments Ltd
Registration no: NI049446 **VAT No.:** GB 392 6953 08
Date established: 2004 **No.of Employees:** 1 - 10 **Product Groups:** 80

Robin Gray Computers
Enterprise House 2-4 Balloo Avenue, Bangor, BT19 7QT
Tel: 028-9145 9845 **Fax:** 028-9147 0868
E-mail: info@robingray.co.uk
Website: http://www.robingray.co.uk
Directors: R. Gray (Prop)
Registration no: NI060737 **Date established:** 2001
No.of Employees: 1 - 10 **Product Groups:** 44

Robinson Goldsmiths
38 Prospect Road, Bangor, BT20 5DF
Tel: 028-9127 0766 **Fax:** 028-9146 9509
E-mail: enquiries@robinsongoldsmiths.com
Website: http://www.robinsongoldsmiths.com
Directors: R. Robinson (Prop)
Date established: 1983 **No.of Employees:** 1 - 10 **Product Groups:** 49

Royal Hotel
26 Quay Street, Bangor, BT20 5ED
Tel: 028-9127 1866 **Fax:** 028-9146 7810
E-mail: theroyalhotel@aol.com
Website: http://www.royalhotelbangor.com
Bank(s): First Trust
Directors: P. Donegan (Prop)
Managers: A. Graham (Comptroller)
Immediate Holding Company: ROYAL HOTEL (BANGOR)
Registration no: NI019013 **VAT No.:** GB 253 0841 79
Date established: 1985 **No.of Employees:** 21 - 50 **Product Groups:** 69

Date of Accounts	Dec 01	Dec 00	Jan 00
Pre Tax Profit/Loss	187	-165	N/A
Working Capital	-597	-640	-283
Fixed Assets	3m	3m	2m
Current Assets	261	256	N/A
Current Liabilities	207	250	N/A

Safety Advice Centre
Unit 73-74 1 Balloo Link, Bangor, BT19 7HJ
Tel: 028-9127 1640 **Fax:** 028-9146 6291
E-mail: safety.advice@btconnect.com
Website: http://www.safetyadvicecentre.com
Directors: B. Mcallister (MD)
Registration no: 42210152 **VAT No.:** GB 422 1015 21
Turnover: £500,000 - £1m **No.of Employees:** 1 - 10 **Product Groups:** 54, 84

Sealing Devices
71 Deanfield, Bangor, BT19 6NX
Tel: 028-9145 7148 **Fax:** 028-9127 1001
Directors: C. Davis (Prop)
VAT No.: GB 353 1839 53 **Date established:** 1984
Turnover: Up to £250,000 **No.of Employees:** 1 - 10 **Product Groups:** 29, 63

The Signature Works
Unit 11-14 Dunlop Industrial Units, Bangor, BT19 7QY
Tel: 028-9127 1131 **Fax:** 028-9127 0799
E-mail: reception@thesignatureworks.co.uk
Website: http://www.thesignatureworks.co.uk
Directors: M. Ditty (MD)
Managers: P. McConvey (Mgr)
Immediate Holding Company: THE SIGNATURE WORKS LIMITED
Registration no: NI008426 **VAT No.:** 251 9376 47 **Date established:** 1971
No.of Employees: 21 - 50 **Product Groups:** 23, 24, 84

Date of Accounts	Oct 11	Oct 10	Oct 09
Working Capital	346	367	433
Fixed Assets	17	55	127
Current Assets	680	769	741

Spectator Newspapers (t/a De Alexander & Sons Ltd)
91 Main Street, Bangor, BT20 4AF
Tel: 028-9127 0270 **Fax:** 028-9127 1544
E-mail: editor@spectatornewspapers.co.uk
Website: http://www.spectatornewspapers.co.uk
Bank(s): Northern Bank
Directors: D. Alexander (Prop), D. Alexander (Prop)
Managers: G. Leacock (Tech Serv Mgr)
Immediate Holding Company: D. E. ALEXANDER & SONS LIMITED
Registration no: NI001942 **VAT No.:** GB 252 0120 24
Date established: 1945 **No.of Employees:** 21 - 50 **Product Groups:** 28

Date of Accounts	Aug 11	Aug 10	Aug 09
Working Capital	4m	4m	4m
Fixed Assets	1m	1m	904
Current Assets	4m	4m	5m

Thermomax Ltd
Balloo Industrial Estate Balloo Crescent, Bangor, BT19 7UP
Tel: 028-9127 0411 **Fax:** 028-9127 0572
E-mail: sales@thermomax.com
Website: http://www.thermomax.com
Directors: S. Sabba (Comm)
Managers: C. Houston (Comptroller), T. Irwin (Tech Serv Mgr)
Registration no: 01537121 **VAT No.:** GB 336 3236 69
Date established: 1981 **No.of Employees:** 101 - 250 **Product Groups:** 37

Date of Accounts	Sep 05
Pre Tax Profit/Loss	-158
Working Capital	2896
Fixed Assets	2166
Current Assets	6407
Current Liabilities	3511
Total Share Capital	552
ROCE% (Return on Capital Employed)	-3.1

3m Industrial Tapes Ltd
5-7 Balloo Drive, Bangor, BT19 7PB
Tel: 028-9127 8200 **Fax:** 028-9145 1072
Website: http://www.3m.co.uk
Bank(s): Lloyds TSB Bank plc
Managers: A. Millar (Chief Buyer), J. Ramsay, M. Little (Tech Serv Mgr), L. Owens (Mgr)
Ultimate Holding Company: 3M INC (USA)
Immediate Holding Company: 3M INDUSTRIAL TAPES LIMITED
Registration no: FC005839 **Date established:** 1966 **Turnover:** £2m - £5m
No.of Employees: 51 - 100 **Product Groups:** 27

Date of Accounts	Dec 99	Dec 98	Dec 96
Working Capital	40	40	40
Current Assets	40	40	40

Valpar Industrial Ltd
13 Balloo Drive, Bangor, BT19 7QY
Tel: 028-9145 4544 **Fax:** 028-9145 7512
E-mail: info@valpar.co.uk
Website: http://www.valpar.co.uk
Bank(s): Ulster Bank
Directors: J. O'neill (MD), L. Rafferty (Fin)
Managers: B. Nelson (Tech Serv Mgr), C. Barnett (Buyer), S. Perry (Personnel)
Ultimate Holding Company: BALLYLIFFAN LIMITED
Immediate Holding Company: VALPAR INDUSTRIAL LIMITED
Registration no: NI019417 **VAT No.:** GB 375 7857 92
Date established: 1986 **Turnover:** £5m - £10m
No.of Employees: 51 - 100 **Product Groups:** 40

Date of Accounts	Jul 11	Jul 10	Jul 09
Sales Turnover	9m	8m	8m
Pre Tax Profit/Loss	960	910	834
Working Capital	4m	6m	5m
Fixed Assets	276	345	357
Current Assets	5m	7m	6m
Current Liabilities	521	470	661

Co. Antrim

Belfast

A B Equipment
Unit 13a Owen O'Cork Mills 288 Beersbridge Road, Belfast, BT5 5DX
Tel: 028-9045 5520 **Fax:** 028-9045 5520
E-mail: ab_equipment@yahoo.co.uk
Directors: B. Finlay (Prop)
VAT No.: GB 454 5949 12 **Turnover:** £250,000 - £500,000
No.of Employees: 1 - 10 **Product Groups:** 67, 83

A C Electric Ltd
219 City Business Park Dunmurry, Belfast, BT17 9HY
Tel: 028-9068 1551 **Fax:** 028-9066 3096
E-mail: admin@ac-electric.co.uk
Website: http://www.ac-electric.co.uk
Directors: P. Mcevoy (Dir)
Immediate Holding Company: A.& C. ELECTRIC LIMITED
Registration no: NI003127 **VAT No.:** GB 253 3290 75
Date established: 1952 **Turnover:** Up to £250,000
No.of Employees: 1 - 10 **Product Groups:** 81

Date of Accounts	Mar 04	Jun 11	Jun 10
Working Capital	395	227	251
Fixed Assets	58	96	129
Current Assets	525	246	251

A G Crawford & Co.
Alpha House 2nd Floor 3 Rosemary Street, Belfast, BT1 1QA
Tel: 028-9024 0286 **Fax:** 028-9033 3236
E-mail: info@agcrawford.co.uk
Website: http://www.agcrawford.co.uk
Directors: D. Rea (Prop)
Immediate Holding Company: INCLUDE YOUTH
Registration no: NI038084 **VAT No.:** GB 251 7902 62
Date established: 2000 **Turnover:** £1m - £2m **No.of Employees:** 1 - 10
Product Groups: 80, 84

Date of Accounts	Mar 11	Mar 10	Mar 09
Sales Turnover	2m	1m	1m
Pre Tax Profit/Loss	89	33	240
Working Capital	496	378	343
Fixed Assets	47	76	78
Current Assets	692	747	374
Current Liabilities	196	369	31

A G M Equipment Ltd
40 Ravenhill Road, Belfast, BT6 8EB
Tel: 028-9045 2613 **Fax:** 028-9045 0023
E-mail: sales@agmequipment.co.uk
Directors: A. Armstrong (Dir)
Immediate Holding Company: AGM EQUIPMENT LIMITED
Registration no: NI007725 **VAT No.:** GB 253 8183 57
Date established: 1969 **Turnover:** £1m - £2m **No.of Employees:** 1 - 10
Product Groups: 63, 66

Date of Accounts	Aug 11	Aug 10	Aug 09
Working Capital	59	82	171
Fixed Assets	132	136	139
Current Assets	119	140	244

A J Stuart & Co. Ltd
161 Dargan Crescent, Belfast, BT3 9JP
Tel: 028-9077 6808 **Fax:** 028-9077 6802
E-mail: sales@ajstuart.co.uk
Website: http://www.ajstuart.co.uk
Directors: D. Dunwoody (Dir)
Immediate Holding Company: A.J. STUART & CO LIMITED
Registration no: NI002190 **VAT No.:** GB 252 9206 66
Date established: 1946 **No.of Employees:** 1 - 10 **Product Groups:** 67

Date of Accounts	Jan 12	Jan 11	Jan 10
Working Capital	337	344	389
Fixed Assets	502	514	535
Current Assets	468	429	464

A1
94 University Avenue, Belfast, BT7 1GY
Tel: 028-9024 4909 **Fax:** 028-9023 0136
E-mail: a1businessservicecentre@hotmail.com
Directors: L. Connerley (MD)
Managers: L. Connolly (Mgr)
Immediate Holding Company: SMITH IMPORTS LIMITED
Registration no: NI046910 **Date established:** 2003
No.of Employees: 1 - 10 **Product Groups:** 28, 79, 81

A V Browne
46 Bedford Street, Belfast, BT2 7GH
Tel: 028-9032 0663 **Fax:** 028-9024 4279
E-mail: info@avb.co.uk
Website: http://www.avb.co.uk
Directors: D. Wilson (Fin), S. Conway (MD)
Managers: S. McClune (Tech Serv Mgr), S. Core
Immediate Holding Company: A.V BROWNE ADVERTISING LIMITED
Registration no: NI016796 **Date established:** 1983 **Turnover:** £5m - £10m
No.of Employees: 51 - 100 **Product Groups:** 81

Date of Accounts	Aug 11	Aug 10	Aug 09
Sales Turnover	10m	10m	13m
Pre Tax Profit/Loss	-205	43	112
Working Capital	99	230	127
Fixed Assets	447	506	590
Current Assets	3m	3m	3m
Current Liabilities	246	356	751

G R Adair & Sons
17 Beit Street, Belfast, BT12 5QF
Tel: 028-9032 8878
Managers: G. Adair (Mgr)
No.of Employees: 1 - 10 **Product Groups:** 35

Adair & Milliken Ltd
1 Parkside Gardens, Belfast, BT15 3AW
Tel: 028-9074 8271 **Fax:** 028-9075 1064
E-mail: info@adairandmilliken.co.uk
Bank(s): Ulster Bank
Directors: M. Hilliant (MD), M. Hilliant (MD)
Immediate Holding Company: ADAIR AND MILLIKEN LIMITED
Registration no: NI006102 **VAT No.:** GB 251 9454 53
Date established: 1964 **Turnover:** £1m - £2m **No.of Employees:** 11 - 20
Product Groups: 52

Date of Accounts	Jan 12	Jan 11	Jan 10
Working Capital	2m	2m	2m
Fixed Assets	957	967	980
Current Assets	2m	2m	2m

J M Adams
2 Tamar Commercial Centre Tamar Street, Belfast, BT4 1HS
Tel: 028-9045 5954 **Fax:** 028-9073 1060
Directors: J. Adams (Prop)
No.of Employees: 1 - 10 **Product Groups:** 36, 40

Adamsez NI Ltd
766 Upper Newtownards Road Dundonald, Belfast, BT16 1TQ
Tel: 028-9048 0465 **Fax:** 028-9048 0485
E-mail: info@adamsez.com
Website: http://www.adamsez.com
Bank(s): First Trust
Directors: L. Dunlop (Ch), R. Brown (Sales), R. Dunlop (MD)
Managers: S. Downs (Purch Mgr), J. Henderson (Sales Prom Mgr), H. Joy-Crawford (Mktg Serv Mgr), K. Graham (I.T. Exec)
Immediate Holding Company: ADAMSEZ (N.I.) LIMITED
Registration no: NI021068 **VAT No.:** GB 452 6867 09
Date established: 1987 **Turnover:** £250,000 - £500,000
No.of Employees: 21 - 50 **Product Groups:** 30, 33, 36, 39, 40, 46, 63, 66, 67, 68

Date of Accounts	Jun 10	Jun 09	Jun 08
Pre Tax Profit/Loss	N/A	-345	-168
Working Capital	-472	-250	56
Fixed Assets	3m	3m	3m
Current Assets	910	1m	2m
Current Liabilities	538	607	735

AGB Scientific Apparatus Ltd
A10 Harbour Court 7 Heron Road, Sydenham Business Par, Belfast, BT3 9HB
Tel: 028-9058 5800 **Fax:** 028-9080 7812
E-mail: INFO@AGBscientific.co.uk
Website: http://ie.vwr.com
Directors: J. Campbell (MD)
Managers: J. Hughes (Sales Admin), J. Burgess (Sales Prom), W. Jardine (Sales Prom), N. Boyle (Sales Prom)
Ultimate Holding Company: VWR INTERNATIONAL LIMITED
Immediate Holding Company: VWR International Ltd
Registration no: NI014511 **VAT No.:** GB 375 7008 40
Date established: 1980 **No.of Employees:** 1 - 10 **Product Groups:** 24, 27, 28, 29, 30, 31, 32, 33, 35, 37, 38, 40, 41, 42, 44, 49, 67

Albion Chemicals Ltd
46-50 Sydney Street West, Belfast, BT13 3GX
Tel: 028-9078 7450 **Fax:** 028-9075 2500
E-mail: sales@albionchemicals.co.uk
Website: http://www.brenntag.co.uk
Bank(s): Lloyds TSB Bank plc
Directors: A. McGill (MD)
Managers: N. McCallum (Ops Mgr), J. McCartney (Chief Mgr)
Immediate Holding Company: Woodland 2 Ltd
Registration no: NF004134 **VAT No.:** GB 556 8495 87
Turnover: £500,000 - £1m **No.of Employees:** 11 - 20
Product Groups: 62, 66

Alfred J Hurst Ltd
Unit 10 Graham Industrial Park Dargan Crescent, Belfast, BT3 9LP
Tel: 028-9077 0037 **Fax:** 028-9077 9749
E-mail: admin@ajhurst.com
Website: http://www.ajhurst.com
Directors: M. Goldsbrough (Dir)
Immediate Holding Company: ALFRED J HURST LIMITED
Registration no: NI001047 **Date established:** 1936 **Turnover:** £2m - £5m
No.of Employees: 11 - 20 **Product Groups:** 18, 37, 47, 67

Date of Accounts	Dec 11	Dec 10	Dec 09
Working Capital	123	69	150
Fixed Assets	218	253	141
Current Assets	2m	2m	2m

A B Allen Engineering
20 Duncrue Cresent, Belfast, BT3 9BW
Tel: 028-9037 0269 **Fax:** 028-9077 7817
E-mail: sales@allenengineering.co.uk
Website: http://www.allenengineering.co.uk
Bank(s): Ulster Bank
Managers: G. Simpson, I. Shannon (Mgr)
Immediate Holding Company: A.B. ALLEN ENGINEERING LIMITED
Registration no: NI011841 **VAT No.:** GB 311 2088 10
Date established: 1977 **Turnover:** £2m - £5m **No.of Employees:** 21 - 50
Product Groups: 25, 26, 30, 35, 36, 40, 45, 52, 66, 67, 84

Date of Accounts	Dec 11	Dec 10	Dec 09
Working Capital	-161	-153	-125
Fixed Assets	4	6	8
Current Assets	273	270	186

Alliance & Leicester plc
63 Royal Avenue, Belfast, BT1 1FT
Tel: 028-9024 1957 **Fax:** 028-9031 4366
E-mail: info@allianceandleicester.co.uk
Website: http://www.alliance-leicester.co.uk
Managers: G. Beattie (District Mgr), H. Gorman (District Mgr), H. Tufts (Sec)
Immediate Holding Company: ALLIANCE & LEICESTER PUBLIC LIMITED COMPANY
Registration no: 03263713 **Date established:** 1996
Turnover: £75m - £125m **No.of Employees:** 1 - 10 **Product Groups:** 80

Allied Bakeries Ireland
2-12 Orby Link, Belfast, BT5 5HW
Tel: 08434-877007 **Fax:** 028-9079 3411
E-mail: info@allliedbakeries.co.uk
Website: http://www.alliedbakeries.co.uk
Managers: C. Stevenson (Nat Sales Mgr), I. Bell (Fin Mgr), R. Blair (Mktg Serv Mgr), P. Logue (Personnel)
Immediate Holding Company: ALLIED BAKERIES (N.I.) LIMITED
Registration no: NI002656 **Date established:** 1949
Turnover: Up to £250,000 **No.of Employees:** 251 - 500
Product Groups: 20, 41, 62

All-Route Shipping N I Ltd
14-16 West Bank Road Belfast Harbour Estate, Belfast, BT3 9JL
Tel: 028-9077 9088 **Fax:** 028-9037 1104
E-mail: shipping@allroute.com
Website: http://www.allroute.com
Bank(s): Northern Bank
Directors: C. McMullan (Dir), C. Mcnullan (MD)
Managers: I. Dickie (Mktg Serv Mgr)
Immediate Holding Company: ALL-ROUTE SHIPPING (N.I.) LIMITED
Registration no: NI010667 **VAT No.:** GB 282 9148 33
Date established: 1975 **Turnover:** £500,000 - £1m
No.of Employees: 21 - 50 **Product Groups:** 72, 76

Date of Accounts	Mar 11	Apr 10	Apr 09
Working Capital	1m	1m	1m
Fixed Assets	389	408	421
Current Assets	3m	2m	2m

Allways Couriers
Unit 12a Lowes Indl-Est 31 Ballynahinch Road, Carryduff, Belfast, BT8 8EH
Tel: 028-9081 7496 **Fax:** 028- 90815694
E-mail: info@allwayscouriers.com
Website: http://www.allwayscouriers.com
Directors: P. Bryson (Prop)
Managers: B. Dalzell (Chief Acct), G. Campbell (Chief Acct)
Registration no: NI040734 **Date established:** 2001
Turnover: £500,000 - £1m **No.of Employees:** 1 - 10 **Product Groups:** 79

Alpha Precision
Seymour Hill Industrial Estate Dunmurry, Belfast, BT17 9PH
Tel: 028-9030 1929 **Fax:** 028-9061 0379
E-mail: alpha_precision@btconnect.com
Directors: K. Doland (MD), K. Dolan (Prop)
Immediate Holding Company: ALPHA PRECISION LTD
Registration no: NI026669 **VAT No.:** GB 331 3706 88
Date established: 1992 **No.of Employees:** 1 - 10 **Product Groups:** 48

Alphagraphic Inks Ltd
Unit 3 Beechill Industrial Park 96 Beechill Road, Belfast, BT8 7QN
Tel: 028-9049 2249 **Fax:** 028-9049 3300
E-mail: info@alpha-prepress.co.uk
Directors: W. Moody (MD)
Immediate Holding Company: ALPHAGRAPHIC INKS LIMITED
Registration no: NI021053 **VAT No.:** GB **Date established:** 1987
Turnover: Up to £250,000 **No.of Employees:** 1 - 10 **Product Groups:** 66, 67

Date of Accounts	Feb 11	Feb 10	Feb 09
Working Capital	677	663	837
Fixed Assets	139	160	175
Current Assets	956	938	1m

Amphora Non-Destructive Testing Ltd
David Keir Building Stranmillis Road, Belfast, BT9 5AG
Tel: 028-9066 4964 **Fax:** 028-9068 7492
E-mail: enquiries@amphorandt.com
Website: http://www.amphorandt.com
Directors: M. Basheer (MD), N. Harman (Dir)
Registration no: NI043380 **No.of Employees:** 1 - 10 **Product Groups:** 38, 84, 85

Anchor Data Systems Ltd
Unit 36 North City Business Centre 2 Duncairn Gardens, Belfast, BT15 2GG
Tel: 028-9074 0315 **Fax:** 028-9035 1531
E-mail: davidwalker@anchordata.co.uk
Website: http://www.anchordata.co.uk
Directors: D. Walker (Serv)
Immediate Holding Company: ANCHOR DATA SYSTEMS (N.I.) LIMITED
Registration no: NI030115 **VAT No.:** GB 316 3096 81
Date established: 1995 **Turnover:** £250,000 - £500,000
No.of Employees: 1 - 10 **Product Groups:** 44, 67

Date of Accounts	Oct 11	Oct 10	Oct 09
Working Capital	3	-9	-1
Fixed Assets	3	N/A	1
Current Assets	55	49	48

Anderson Haulage Ltd
85 Channing Street, Belfast, BT5 5GP
Tel: 028-9045 1771 **Fax:** 028-9073 9047
E-mail: info@andersonhaulage.co.uk
Website: http://www.andersonhaulage.co.uk
Bank(s): Northern Bank
Directors: T. Anderson (MD)
Managers: S. Wyle (Fin Mgr)
Immediate Holding Company: ANDERSON HAULAGE LIMITED
Registration no: NI009447 **VAT No.:** GB 252 3949 50
Date established: 1973 **Turnover:** £500,000 - £1m
No.of Employees: 21 - 50 **Product Groups:** 72

Date of Accounts	Apr 12	Apr 11	Apr 10
Working Capital	749	791	743
Fixed Assets	741	752	844
Current Assets	1m	1m	1m

Anderson Spratt Group
Anderson House Holywood Road, Belfast, BT4 2GU
Tel: 028-9080 2000 **Fax:** 028-9080 2001
E-mail: info@asgireland.com
Website: http://www.asgireland.com
Directors: C. Anderson (MD), P. Spratt (Ptnr), R. Ross (Sales & Mktg)
Registration no: NI026707 **Turnover:** £2m - £5m
No.of Employees: 21 - 50 **Product Groups:** 81

Anderson Spratt Group Holdings
Anderson House 409 Holywood Road, Belfast, BT4 2GU
Tel: 028-9080 2000 **Fax:** 028-9080 2021
E-mail: smckenna@asgireland.com
Website: http://www.asgireland.com
Directors: C. Anderson (Ch), P. Spratt (Grp MD), R. Douglas (Dir), S. McKenna (MD)
Managers: A. Rooney (Mgr), L. Gillen (Purch Mgr), P. Currie (Tech Serv Mgr), S. McKenna
Immediate Holding Company: ANDERSON SPRATT GROUP HOLDINGS LIMITED
Registration no: NI015945 **VAT No.:** GB 375 7679 90
Date established: 1982 **Turnover:** £5m - £10m **No.of Employees:** 21 - 50
Product Groups: 80, 81

Anderson Williamson Ltd
Citylink Business Park Albert Street, Belfast, BT12 4HQ
Tel: 028-9027 9810 **Fax:** 028-9024 3442
E-mail: reception@andersonwilliamson.com
Website: http://www.andersonwilliamson.com
Directors: V. Prior (Dir)
Ultimate Holding Company: HEDDERMAN STANLEY & ASSOCIATES LIMITED
Immediate Holding Company: ANDERSON WILLIAMSON LIMITED
Registration no: NI050163 **VAT No.:** GB 252 7748 40
Date established: 2004 **No.of Employees:** 1 - 10 **Product Groups:** 80

Date of Accounts	Dec 10	Dec 09	Dec 08
Working Capital	-870	-892	104
Fixed Assets	11	12	59
Current Assets	156	69	316

Andor Technology Ltd
9 Millennium Way, Belfast, BT12 7AL
Tel: 028-9023 7126 **Fax:** 028-9031 0792
E-mail: sales@andor-tech.com
Website: http://www.andor-tech.com
Bank(s): Bank of Ireland
Directors: S. Quinn (Fin)
Managers: P. Bannan, S. Murray (Tech Serv Mgr), S. Semington (Personnel), V. Gold (Mktg Serv Mgr)
Immediate Holding Company: ANDOR TECHNOLOGY PLC
Registration no: NI022466 **VAT No.:** GB 517 1829 44
Date established: 1989 **Turnover:** £50m - £75m
No.of Employees: 101 - 250 **Product Groups:** 37, 38, 44, 67

Date of Accounts	Sep 11	Sep 10	Sep 09
Sales Turnover	57m	43m	33m
Pre Tax Profit/Loss	9m	6m	3m
Working Capital	20m	13m	15m
Fixed Assets	26m	23m	6m
Current Assets	30m	23m	21m
Current Liabilities	6m	8m	4m

Ansell Sales & Distribution Ltd
Unit 2 M2 Business Park Duncrue Street, Belfast, BT3 9AQ
Tel: 028-9077 3750 **Fax:** 028-9077 3783
E-mail: sales@anselluk.com
Website: http://www.anselluk.com
Directors: A. Nappin (MD), B. Carson (Fin)
Immediate Holding Company: ANSELL (SALES & DISTRIBUTION) LIMITED
Registration no: 01638648 **VAT No.:** GB 375 7665 04
Date established: 1982 **Turnover:** £2m - £5m **No.of Employees:** 11 - 20
Product Groups: 67

Date of Accounts	Apr 11	Apr 10	Apr 09
Working Capital	868	865	839
Fixed Assets	2m	2m	2m
Current Assets	2m	2m	2m

Anti Friction Components Ltd
24 Duncrue Road Duncrue Industrial Estate, Belfast, BT3 9BP
Tel: 028-9077 8399 **Fax:** 028-9037 0497
E-mail: darren.potter@afc-uk.com
Website: http://www.afc-uk.com
Managers: D. Potter (Reg Mgr)
Ultimate Holding Company: KOWLOON INVESTMENTS LIMITED (MAURITIUS)
Immediate Holding Company: ANTI-FRICTION COMPONENTS LIMITED
Registration no: 01275175 **VAT No.:** GB 488 5105 19
Date established: 1976 **Turnover:** £2m - £5m **No.of Employees:** 1 - 10
Product Groups: 66, 68

Date of Accounts	Sep 11	Sep 10	Sep 09
Sales Turnover	12m	11m	9m
Pre Tax Profit/Loss	427	231	93
Working Capital	592	357	275
Fixed Assets	206	17	28
Current Assets	4m	4m	3m
Current Liabilities	1m	1m	1m

Antrim Contract Carpets Ltd
Kennedy Way Industrial Estate, Belfast, BT11 9DT
Tel: 028-9062 3888 **Fax:** 028-9061 6710
E-mail: info@antrimcarpets.com
Website: http://www.antrimcarpets.com
Bank(s): Bank of Ireland
Managers: R. Taylor (Contracts Mgr)
Immediate Holding Company: ANTRIM CONTRACT CARPETS LTD
Registration no: NI022245 **VAT No.:** GB 517 6483 29
Date established: 1988 **No.of Employees:** 11 - 20 **Product Groups:** 23

Date of Accounts	Sep 11	Sep 10	Sep 09
Working Capital	43	5	216
Fixed Assets	275	315	376
Current Assets	633	663	955
Current Liabilities	590	658	739

Any Old Iron
Unit 34 Bloomfield Commercial Centre 5 Factory Street, Belfast, BT5 5AW
Tel: 028-9020 7060
Directors: S. Davis (Prop)
Date established: 1998 **No.of Employees:** 1 - 10 **Product Groups:** 26, 35

Appian Fasteners Ltd
40 The Cutts Dunmurry, Belfast, BT17 9HS
Tel: 028-9030 1979 **Fax:** 028-9062 2794
E-mail: sales@appianfasteners.com
Website: http://www.appianfasteners.com
Directors: D. Broderick (Grp Chief Exec)
Immediate Holding Company: APPIAN FASTENERS LIMITED
Registration no: 06246685 **VAT No.:** GB 366 3514 46
Date established: 2007 **Turnover:** £1m - £2m **No.of Employees:** 1 - 10
Product Groups: 66

Date of Accounts	Dec 11	Dec 10	Dec 09
Sales Turnover	2m	2m	2m
Pre Tax Profit/Loss	-21	5	38
Working Capital	1m	1m	1m
Fixed Assets	32	19	32
Current Assets	1m	2m	2m
Current Liabilities	19	208	355

Apple Recruitment Services
Causeway Tower James Street South, Belfast, BT2 8DN
Tel: 028-9024 9747 **Fax:** 028-9024 2203
E-mail: mail@applerecruitment.com
Website: http://www.applerecruitment.com
Directors: K. Houston (Prop)
Immediate Holding Company: BUILDING CONCEPTS LIMITED
Registration no: NI053115 **VAT No.:** GB 454 6300 61
Date established: 1996 **Turnover:** £500,000 - £1m
No.of Employees: 1 - 10 **Product Groups:** 80

Date of Accounts	Dec 09	Dec 08	Dec 07
Working Capital	-356	-342	18
Fixed Assets	1m	945	707
Current Assets	264	278	110

Arabesque Braids
103 Wandsworth Road, Belfast, BT4 3LU
Tel: 028-9065 5141
E-mail: info@arabesquebraids.co.uk
Website: http://www.arabesquebraids.co.uk
Directors: F. Robinson (Prop)
Turnover: Up to £250,000 **No.of Employees:** 1 - 10 **Product Groups:** 23

Architectural Salvage
2a Millar Street, Belfast, BT6 8JZ
Tel: 028-9035 1475 **Fax:** 028-9077 6457
E-mail: consultants@handr.co.uk
Website: http://www.handr.co.uk
Directors: D. Hunter (Prop)
Registration no: NI046666 **VAT No.:** 454699304 **Date established:** 2003
No.of Employees: 1 - 10 **Product Groups:** 52, 84

Arnotts Fruit Ltd
16-20 Dunbar Street, Belfast, BT1 2LH
Tel: 028-9032 4236 **Fax:** 028-9024 5316
E-mail: info@arnottsfruit.com
Website: http://www.arnottsfruit.com
Directors: W. Orr (MD), S. Lawson (Fin)
Managers: S. Docherty (Mktg Serv Mgr), E. Reid (Buyer)
Ultimate Holding Company: GUNDAGAI
Immediate Holding Company: ARNOTTS (FRUIT) LIMITED
Registration no: NI034859 **VAT No.:** GB 251 9386 44
Date established: 1998 **Turnover:** £5m - £10m **No.of Employees:** 21 - 50
Product Groups: 62

Date of Accounts	Nov 09	Nov 10	Nov 11
Working Capital	675	729	788
Fixed Assets	185	201	144
Current Assets	2m	2m	2m

Arqiva
Unit 1-2 Adelaide Busines Centre Apollo Road, Belfast, BT12 6HP
Tel: 028-9094 2120 **Fax:** 028-9066 6839
E-mail: andrew.mcclean@arqiva.com
Website: http://www.arqiva.com
Managers: A. Mcclean (Mgr)
Immediate Holding Company: ELITE HAND CAR WASH LTD
Registration no: SC075177 **Date established:** 2011
No.of Employees: 1 - 10 **Product Groups:** 67

Arup Ltd
Linenhall 8th Floor 32-38 Linenhall Street, Belfast, BT2 8BG
Tel: 028-9089 0900
E-mail: belfast@arup.com
Website: http://www.arup.com
Managers: P. Johnston
Immediate Holding Company: ARUP LIMITED
Registration no: 02461313 **Date established:** 1990
No.of Employees: 21 - 50 **Product Groups:** 44

Date of Accounts	Mar 11	Mar 10	Mar 09
Sales Turnover	3m	2m	N/A
Pre Tax Profit/Loss	582	416	N/A
Working Capital	819	-153	73
Fixed Assets	15m	16m	N/A
Current Assets	3m	497	73
Current Liabilities	538	610	N/A

Ashdale Engineering Ltd
39a York Park, Belfast, BT15 3PX
Tel: 028-9078 3000 **Fax:** 028-9037 0003
E-mail: info@ashdale.co.uk
Website: http://www.ashdale.co.uk
Directors: C. Berry (Fin), P. Ford (Tech Serv)
Managers: P. Ford (Tech Serv Mgr), R. Sweeney (Purch Mgr)
Immediate Holding Company: ASHDALE ENGINEERING LIMITED
Registration no: NI013950 **Date established:** 1979 **Turnover:** £2m - £5m
No.of Employees: 21 - 50 **Product Groups:** 77

Date of Accounts	Aug 11	Aug 10	Aug 09
Sales Turnover	3m	3m	3m
Pre Tax Profit/Loss	74	66	67
Working Capital	743	679	614
Fixed Assets	106	112	127
Current Assets	1m	1m	1m
Current Liabilities	282	236	167

Ashworth & Thompson Ltd
22 Duncrue Cresent, Belfast, BT3 9BW
Tel: 028-9077 0292 **Fax:** 028-9037 1054
E-mail: sclarke@ashworthandthompson.co.uk
Website: http://www.ashworthandthompson.co.uk
Directors: M. Checkley (Fin), P. Thompson (MD)
Immediate Holding Company: ASHWORTH & THOMPSON LIMITED
Registration no: 01405716 **Date established:** 1978 **Turnover:** £2m - £5m
No.of Employees: 1 - 10 **Product Groups:** 25, 26

Date of Accounts	Dec 11	Dec 10	Dec 09
Working Capital	246	250	234
Fixed Assets	647	673	707
Current Assets	856	900	958

Atlantic Container Agencies
Premier Business Centre 20 Adelaide Street, Belfast, BT2 8GD
Tel: 028-9051 7029 **Fax:** 028-9077 6134
E-mail: pwallace@aclcargo.com
Website: http://www.aclcargo.com
Directors: P. Wallace (Dir)
Immediate Holding Company: RECRUITMENT DIRECT LIMITED
Registration no: NF003620 **Date established:** 1999 **Turnover:** £2m - £5m
No.of Employees: 1 - 10 **Product Groups:** 76

Date of Accounts	Jul 11	Jul 10	Jul 09
Working Capital	-17	-2	13
Fixed Assets	25	28	32
Current Assets	32	36	52

Audio Processing Technology Ltd
729 Springfield Road, Belfast, BT12 7FP
Tel: 028-9067 7200 **Fax:** 028-9067 7201
E-mail: woodside@worldcastsystems.com
Website: http://www.aptcodex.com
Bank(s): Northern Bank
Directors: K. Campbell (Sales)
Managers: W. Woodside (Ops Mgr)
Immediate Holding Company: AUDIO PROCESSING TECHNOLOGY LIMITED
Registration no: NI022049 **VAT No.:** GB 517 0363 69
Date established: 1988 **Turnover:** £5m - £10m **No.of Employees:** 21 - 50
Product Groups: 44

Date of Accounts	Dec 11	Dec 10	Dec 09
Working Capital	204	475	439
Fixed Assets	130	182	204
Current Assets	502	995	1m

Automation Controls Ltd
Musgrave Park Industrial Estate Stockmans Way, Belfast, BT9 7JU
Tel: 028-9068 1391 **Fax:** 028-9066 3533
E-mail: info@automationcontrolsltd.co.uk
Website: http://www.automationcontrolsltd.co.uk
Managers: T. Mcgoran (Mgr)
Immediate Holding Company: AUTOMATION CONTROLS (BELFAST) LIMITED
Registration no: NI013117 **VAT No.:** GB 287 2177 31
Date established: 1978 **Turnover:** £500,000 - £1m
No.of Employees: 1 - 10 **Product Groups:** 37

Date of Accounts	Oct 11	Oct 10	Oct 09
Working Capital	306	289	263
Fixed Assets	43	45	46
Current Assets	478	447	446
Current Liabilities	98	81	69

Avenue Recycling
208 Tate's Avenue, Belfast, BT12 6ND
Tel: 028-9032 6391 **Fax:** 028-9032 6391
Directors: E. Nesbitt (Dir)
Immediate Holding Company: AVENUE RECYCLING LIMITED
Registration no: NI050132 **VAT No.:** GB 255 4494 42
Date established: 2004 **No.of Employees:** 1 - 10 **Product Groups:** 35, 42, 54, 66, 85

Date of Accounts	Mar 12	Mar 11	Mar 10
Working Capital	397	241	172
Fixed Assets	650	723	779
Current Assets	672	505	637

Avis Rent A Car Ltd
Belfast Int Airport, Belfast, BT29 4AA
Tel: 08445-446012 **Fax:** 028-9442 3378
E-mail: belfast-international-airport@avis.co.uk
Website: http://www.avis.co.uk
Managers: A. Murphy (Mgr)
Ultimate Holding Company: SA D'IETEREN NV (BELGIUM)
Immediate Holding Company: AVIS RENT A CAR LIMITED
Registration no: 00802486 **VAT No.:** GB 222 6271 91
Date established: 1964 **Turnover:** £2m - £5m **No.of Employees:** 1 - 10
Product Groups: 72, 82

Date of Accounts	Dec 10	Dec 09	Dec 08
Sales Turnover	134m	124m	125m
Pre Tax Profit/Loss	-12m	-16m	-21m
Working Capital	-160m	-84m	-117m
Fixed Assets	172m	110m	159m
Current Assets	62m	54m	64m
Current Liabilities	29m	29m	25m

Henry R Ayton Ltd
40 The Cutts Dunmurry, Belfast, BT17 9HS
Tel: 028-9061 8511 **Fax:** 028-9060 2436
E-mail: sales@hrayton.com
Website: http://www.hrayton.com
Bank(s): Bank of Ireland
Directors: J. Mccord (Fin)
Immediate Holding Company: HENRY R. AYTON LIMITED
Registration no: NI001046 **VAT No.:** GB 390 8264 33
Date established: 1936 **No.of Employees:** 11 - 20 **Product Groups:** 66

Date of Accounts	Mar 11	Mar 10	Mar 09
Working Capital	139	210	260
Fixed Assets	442	463	495
Current Assets	1m	1m	1m

B C D Partnership
3-5 Dalton Street, Belfast, BT5 4BA
Tel: 028-9045 9898 **Fax:** 028-9045 9798
E-mail: gc@bcdpartnership.co.uk
Website: http://www.bcdpartnership.co.uk
Directors: G. Cunningham (Dir), J. Douglas (Ptnr)
Immediate Holding Company: B C D Partnership Limited
Registration no: NI047882 **VAT No.:** GB 422 2571 83
Date established: 2003 **Turnover:** Up to £250,000
No.of Employees: 1 - 10 **Product Groups:** 52, 84

B S Design Consultants
31 Ravenhill Park, Belfast, BT6 0DG
Tel: 028-9049 3777 **Fax:** 028-9049 3888
E-mail: info@bsdesignconsultants.com
Website: http://www.bsdesignconsultants.com
Directors: T. Burns (Ptnr)
VAT No.: GB 375 7699 84 **Date established:** 1997
No.of Employees: 1 - 10 **Product Groups:** 52

B & S Labels
Units 2-3 23 Sunwich Street, Belfast, BT6 8JT
Tel: 028-9073 8200 **Fax:** 028-9073 8931
E-mail: neilbarrett@bandslabels.com
Website: http://www.bandslabels.co.uk
Directors: N. Barrett (Prop)
VAT No.: GB 353 1089 70 **Date established:** 1977
Turnover: £500,000 - £1m **No.of Employees:** 1 - 10 **Product Groups:** 23, 27, 28

B S S
36-38 Duncrue Road, Belfast, BT3 9BP
Tel: 028-9078 4000 **Fax:** 028-9078 4010
E-mail: c.young@bssgroup.com
Website: http://www.bssuk.co.uk
Bank(s): HSBC Bank plc
Managers: C. Young (District Mgr)
Immediate Holding Company: BUSINESS SUPPORT SERVICES UK LTD
Registration no: 03106393 **VAT No.:** GB 361 0004 22
No.of Employees: 11 - 20 **Product Groups:** 38, 66

Balmoral Textiles Ltd
17a Station View Dunmurry, Belfast, BT17 0AE
Tel: 028-9061 7431 **Fax:** 028-9061 1696
E-mail: sales@balmoraltextiles.co.uk
Website: http://www.balmoraltextiles.com
Bank(s): Ulster Bank
Directors: T. Moffett (Dir)
Managers: C. Moffett (Mgr)
Ultimate Holding Company: TEL PROPERTIES LIMITED
Immediate Holding Company: BALMORAL TEXTILES LIMITED
Registration no: NI033916 **VAT No.:** GB 366 3150 58
Date established: 1998 **No.of Employees:** 11 - 20 **Product Groups:** 26

Date of Accounts	Mar 12	Mar 11	Mar 10
Working Capital	167	168	152
Fixed Assets	69	89	98
Current Assets	954	972	853

Baltor Systems Ltd
19 Kennedy Enterprise Centre Kennedy Way Industrial Estate, Belfast, BT11 9DT
Tel: 028-9060 3232 **Fax:** 028-9060 3452
E-mail: sales@baltor.co.uk
Website: http://www.baltor.co.uk
Directors: P. Walker (MD)
Immediate Holding Company: BALTOR SYSTEMS LIMITED
Registration no: NI024416 **VAT No.:** GB 517 7308 42
Date established: 1990 **Turnover:** £1m - £2m **No.of Employees:** 1 - 10
Product Groups: 38, 41

Date of Accounts	Mar 12	Mar 11	Mar 10
Working Capital	890	818	828
Fixed Assets	33	43	59
Current Assets	972	919	930

Bank Of Scotland Ireland Ltd
10-15 Doegall Square North, Belfast, BT1 5GB
Tel: 028-9043 4565 **Fax:** 028-9023 9843
Website: http://www.bankofscotland.co.uk

Managers: H. Hugh-Donnally (District Mgr)
Immediate Holding Company: BANK OF SCOTLAND (IRELAND) LIMITED
Registration no: NF003236 **Date established:** 1995
Turnover: Over £1,000m **No.of Employees:** 1 - 10 **Product Groups:** 82

Bannons
71 North Street, Belfast, BT1 1NB
Tel: 028-9032 9335 **Fax:** 028-9023 5152
E-mail: tony.bannons@ukgateway.net
Website: http://www.bannons.com
Bank(s): Ulster Bank
Directors: T. Bannon (Prop), E. Bannon (MD), L. Bannon (Ch), T. Bannon (Dir & Co Sec)
Managers: J. McAllister (Purch Mgr), T. McCabe (Sales Prom Mgr)
Ultimate Holding Company: Bannons Group Limited
Immediate Holding Company: BANNONS LIMITED
Registration no: NI002929 **Date established:** 1951 **Turnover:** £2m - £5m
No.of Employees: 51 - 100 **Product Groups:** 61, 82

Date of Accounts	Jan 08	Jan 09	Jan 10
Sales Turnover	N/A	N/A	4m
Pre Tax Profit/Loss	719	500	478
Working Capital	3m	3m	3m
Fixed Assets	4m	392	348
Current Assets	3m	3m	4m
Current Liabilities	554	530	435

Barclays Mercantile Business Finance Ltd
Imperial House 4-10 Donegall Square East, Belfast, BT1 5HD
Tel: 028-9032 3822 **Fax:** 028-9024 6462
Website: http://www.barclays.co.uk
Managers: R. Cartwright (Mgr), N. Norris (Mgr)
Ultimate Holding Company: BARCLAYS PLC
Immediate Holding Company: BARCLAYS MERCANTILE BUSINESS FINANCE LIMITED
Registration no: 00898129 **Date established:** 1967
No.of Employees: 1 - 10 **Product Groups:** 82

Date of Accounts	Dec 10	Dec 09	Dec 08
Sales Turnover	118m	182m	269m
Pre Tax Profit/Loss	63m	24m	-131m
Working Capital	-1072m	-1633m	-2059m
Fixed Assets	1372m	1876m	2342m
Current Assets	2926m	4001m	5080m
Current Liabilities	1737m	2183m	86m

Barnes Mccrum Patnership
Unit 21 Somerton Industrial Park Dargan Crescent, Belfast, BT3 9JB
Tel: 028-9078 1889 **Fax:** 028- 90781874
E-mail: barnes@btconnect.com
Directors: S. Whyatt (Ptnr)
Turnover: £500,000 - £1m **No.of Employees:** 1 - 10 **Product Groups:** 84

Basement Textile Merchandisers
51 Osborne Park, Belfast, BT9 6JP
Tel: 028-9050 8222 **Fax:** 028-9050 8221
E-mail: swbasement@yahoo.ie
Website: http://www.yahoo.ie
Directors: S. Whittley (Prop)
Registration no: 00172074 **Turnover:** £1m - £2m
No.of Employees: 1 - 10 **Product Groups:** 49, 81

Bavarian Garages
2 Boucher Crescent, Belfast, BT12 6HU
Tel: 028-9038 1311 **Fax:** 028-9038 5898
E-mail: joe.rogers@agnews.co.uk
Website: http://www.bavarianbmw.co.uk
Bank(s): Northern Bank
Managers: J. Rogers
Immediate Holding Company: BAVARIAN GARAGES (N.I) LIMITED
Registration no: NI013932 **VAT No.:** GB 251 8906 49
Date established: 1979 **Turnover:** £75m - £125m
No.of Employees: 51 - 100 **Product Groups:** 68

Beck & Scott Ltd
Unit 1 Ravenhill Business Park, Belfast, BT6 8AW
Tel: 028-9073 4444 **Fax:** 028-9073 4440
E-mail: stephenbruce@beckandscott.com
Website: http://www.beckandscott.com
Directors: S. Brann (MD)
Immediate Holding Company: BECK & SCOTT LIMITED
Registration no: NI000153 **VAT No.:** GB 251 8674 44
Date established: 2024 **Turnover:** £2m - £5m **No.of Employees:** 11 - 20
Product Groups: 20, 21, 62, 82

Date of Accounts	Feb 11	Feb 10	Feb 09
Working Capital	283	266	276
Fixed Assets	20	21	23
Current Assets	464	458	409

Beggs & Partners
Great Patrick Street, Belfast, BT1 2NX
Tel: 028-9023 5791 **Fax:** 028-9023 3273
E-mail: info@beggsandpartners.com
Website: http://www.beggsandpartners.com
Bank(s): Bank of Ireland
Directors: G. Meldrum (Grp MD)
Immediate Holding Company: BEGGS & PARTNERS
Registration no: NI004593 **VAT No.:** GB 251 7184 66
Date established: 1960 **No.of Employees:** 21 - 50 **Product Groups:** 63, 66, 67

Bel-Air Services Ltd
Unit 12 Westbank Business Park 2 West Bank Road, Belfast, BT3 9JL
Tel: 028-9077 8031 **Fax:** 028-9077 5496
E-mail: markm@bel-air.uk.com
Website: http://www.bel-air.uk.com
Bank(s): Ulster Bank
Managers: G. Carson (Chief Acct), M. Montgomery, H. Hurley
Immediate Holding Company: BA COLLECT OUT LIMITED
Registration no: NI016990 **VAT No.:** GB 282 9947 03
Date established: 1983 **Turnover:** £5m - £10m
No.of Employees: 51 - 100 **Product Groups:** 52

Date of Accounts	Oct 10	Oct 09	Oct 08
Sales Turnover	6m	6m	N/A
Pre Tax Profit/Loss	88	200	424
Working Capital	935	1m	2m
Fixed Assets	129	162	176
Current Assets	2m	2m	3m
Current Liabilities	492	420	512

Belfast Brake Specialists Ltd
Unit 2-3 Agnes Street Industrial Estate Agnes Street, Belfast, BT13 1GB
Tel: 028-9074 6436 **Fax:** 028-9074 6437
E-mail: belfastbrakes@btconnect.com
Website: http://www.belfastbrakespecialist.co.uk
Directors: G. Begs (Dir), R. Beggs (Dir)
Immediate Holding Company: Belfast Brake Specialists Ltd
Registration no: NI064499 **VAT No.:** GB 454 5774 27
Date established: 2007 **Turnover:** £500,000 - £1m
No.of Employees: 1 - 10 **Product Groups:** 39

Date of Accounts	May 11	May 10	May 09
Working Capital	-75	-53	-31
Fixed Assets	75	53	40
Current Assets	30	46	84

Belfast Castle
Antrim Road, Belfast, BT15 5GR
Tel: 028-9077 6925 **Fax:** 028-9037 0228
E-mail: cf@belfastcastle.co.uk
Website: http://www.belfastcastle.co.uk
Managers: B. Toland
No.of Employees: 21 - 50 **Product Groups:** 65, 69

Belfast Central Library
Central Library Royal Avenue, Belfast, BT1 1EA
Tel: 028-9050 9150 **Fax:** 028-9033 2819
E-mail: info.belb@ni-libraries.net
Website: http://www.librariesni.org.uk
Managers: M. Bryson (Mgr)
VAT No.: GD081 **No.of Employees:** 51 - 100 **Product Groups:** 80, 89

Belfast City Airport Ltd
Sydenham Bypass, Belfast, BT3 9JH
Tel: 028-9093 9093 **Fax:** 028-9093 9094
E-mail: info@belfastcityairport.com
Website: http://www.belfastcityairport.com
Bank(s): Ulster Bank
Directors: B. Ambrose (Grp Chief Exec)
Managers: M. Hatfield (Personnel), N. Henderson, R. McNair (Fin Mgr), K. Best
Ultimate Holding Company: EISER INFRASTRUCTURE LIMITED
Immediate Holding Company: BELFAST CITY AIRPORT LIMITED
Registration no: NI016363 **Date established:** 1983
Turnover: £10m - £20m **No.of Employees:** 251 - 500 **Product Groups:** 71

Date of Accounts	Dec 11	Dec 10	Dec 09
Sales Turnover	18m	17m	17m
Pre Tax Profit/Loss	863	15	433
Working Capital	-764	-3m	-6m
Fixed Assets	37m	36m	37m
Current Assets	15m	12m	8m
Current Liabilities	3m	3m	2m

Belfast City Council
City Hall, Belfast, BT1 5GS
Tel: 028-9032 0202 **Fax:** 028-9043 8075
E-mail: mcnaneyp@belfastcity.gov.uk
Website: http://www.belfastcity.gov.uk
Directors: R. Cregan (Fin)
Managers: V. Cupples (Purch Mgr), P. Gribben (Tech Serv Mgr), A. Deeny, J. Minne (Personnel)
Turnover: £250m - £500m **No.of Employees:** 11 - 20 **Product Groups:** 87

Belfast Co-Operative Chemists Ltd
70 Ballygomartin Road, Belfast, BT13 3NE
Tel: 028-9039 1068 **Fax:** 028-9039 1068
Website: http://www.co-operative.coop/pharmacy
Managers: R. Wright (Mgr)
Turnover: £250,000 - £500,000 **No.of Employees:** 1 - 10
Product Groups: 61, 63

Belfast Crystal Ltd
2 Factory Kennedy Way, Belfast, BT11 9DT
Tel: 028-9062 2051 **Fax:** 028-9062 2051
Website: http://www.belfastcrystal.com
Directors: T. Abbate (Dir)
Immediate Holding Company: BELFAST CRYSTAL LIMITED
Registration no: NI013156 **VAT No.:** GB 287 0473 37
Date established: 1978 **Turnover:** £1m - £2m **No.of Employees:** 1 - 10
Product Groups: 33

Date of Accounts	Sep 11	Sep 10	Sep 09
Working Capital	95	94	88
Fixed Assets	26	27	27
Current Assets	125	121	111

Belfast Education & Library Board
40 Academy Street, Belfast, BT1 2NQ
Tel: 028-9056 4112 **Fax:** 028-9033 1714
E-mail: david.cargo@belb.co.uk
Website: http://www.belb.org.uk
Bank(s): Ulster Bank
Directors: D. Cargo (Grp Chief Exec)
Managers: D. Megaughin (Fin Mgr), G. Jackson (Tech Serv Mgr), J. Martin (Press Officer), C. Burnett, L. McGowan (Personnel)
No.of Employees: 251 - 500 **Product Groups:** 86, 87, 89

Belfast International Airport
Belfast International Airport, Belfast, BT29 4AB
Tel: 028-9448 4848 **Fax:** 028-9445 2096
Website: http://www.belfastairport.com
Bank(s): Ulster Bank
Directors: D. McKnight (Fin), A. Harrison (MD), J. Doran (MD)
Managers: D. Brown (I.T. Exec), E. Uhohouy (Mktg Serv Mgr)
Immediate Holding Company: BELFAST INTERNATIONAL AIRPORT LIMITED
Registration no: NI027630 **VAT No.:** GB 251 8194 58
Date established: 1993 **Turnover:** £20m - £50m
No.of Employees: 1501 & over **Product Groups:** 71

Belfast Sign Conmpany
93-95 Ravenhill Road, Belfast, BT6 8DQ
Tel: 028-9073 2220 **Fax:** 028-9020 7131
E-mail: belsignco@yahoo.co.uk
Directors: G. Wilson (Prop)
VAT No.: GB 353 0499 56 **Turnover:** Up to £250,000
No.of Employees: 1 - 10 **Product Groups:** 28, 49

Belfast Theatrical Linens Ltd
Portside Business Park Airport Road West, Belfast, BT3 9ED
Tel: 028-9073 6990 **Fax:** 028-9045 8889
E-mail: info@johnengland.com
Website: http://www.johnengland.com
Directors: R. Saunders (Dir)
Immediate Holding Company: Belfast Theatrical Linens Limited
Registration no: NI058112 **Date established:** 2006
Turnover: £250,000 - £500,000 **No.of Employees:** 1 - 10
Product Groups: 24, 89

Date of Accounts	Aug 11	Feb 10	Feb 09
Working Capital	37	30	20
Fixed Assets	N/A	2	5
Current Assets	45	52	30

BHS Ltd
24-26 Castle Place, Belfast, BT1 1GB
Tel: 028-9024 3068 **Fax:** 028-9031 1602
Website: http://www.bhs.co.uk
Managers: N. Furguson, L. Lavery (Mgr)
Ultimate Holding Company: TAVETA INVESTMENTS LIMITED
Immediate Holding Company: BHS LIMITED
Registration no: 00229606 **VAT No.:** GB 440 6445 66
Date established: 2028 **Turnover:** £1m - £2m **No.of Employees:** 21 - 50
Product Groups: 61

Date of Accounts	Aug 09	Mar 08	Aug 10
Sales Turnover	1121m	850m	795m
Pre Tax Profit/Loss	-62m	21m	-7m
Working Capital	-88m	-41m	-96m
Fixed Assets	282m	315m	269m
Current Assets	129m	117m	102m
Current Liabilities	65m	61m	59m

Bio Search N I Ltd
Dufferin Road, Belfast, BT3 9AA
Tel: 028-9035 2066 **Fax:** 028-9035 2161
E-mail: karen@biosearch.co.uk
Website: http://www.biosearch.co.uk
Managers: K. Topping (Mgr)
Ultimate Holding Company: W.& R. BARNETT LIMITED
Immediate Holding Company: BIO SEARCH (N.I.) LIMITED
Registration no: NI023096 **VAT No.:** GB 517 1709 54
Date established: 1989 **Turnover:** £500,000 - £1m
No.of Employees: 1 - 10 **Product Groups:** 85

Date of Accounts	Jul 11	Jul 10	Mar 10
Working Capital	179	154	143
Fixed Assets	199	231	249
Current Assets	341	269	313

Blackstaff Press
4c Heron Wharf Heron Road, Belfast, BT3 9LE
Tel: 028-9045 5006 **Fax:** 028-9046 6237
E-mail: info@blackstaffpress.com
Website: http://www.blackstaffpress.com
Directors: P. Horton (Dir)
VAT No.: GB 252 0302 18 **Turnover:** £500,000 - £1m
No.of Employees: 1 - 10 **Product Groups:** 28

Blamphin & Associates
80 Malone Avenue, Belfast, BT9 6ES
Tel: 028-9066 7918 **Fax:** 028-9068 2016
Website: http://www.blamphin.com
Directors: P. Blamphin (Ptnr)
Turnover: Up to £250,000 **No.of Employees:** 1 - 10 **Product Groups:** 80, 81, 84

Blueprint Specialist Appointments
The Boat 49 Queens Square, Belfast, BT1 3FG
Tel: 028-9032 3333 **Fax:** 028-9032 3338
E-mail: info@blueprintappointments.com
Website: http://www.blueprintappointments.com
Managers: A. Mckee (Chief Mgr)
Turnover: £2m - £5m **No.of Employees:** 11 - 20 **Product Groups:** 80

Boc Gas
Prince Regent Road, Belfast, BT5 6RW
Tel: 028-9040 5136 **Fax:** 028-9040 1379
Website: http://www.bocindustrial.co.uk
Managers: N. Thompson (Mgr)
Ultimate Holding Company: LINDE UK HOLDINGS LTD
Immediate Holding Company: BOC NETHERLANDS HOLDINGS LTD
Registration no: 00337663 **Date established:** 1969
No.of Employees: 1 - 10 **Product Groups:** 31

Bow Homes Ltd
27 Colinglen Road Dunmurry, Belfast, BT17 0LR
Tel: 028-9030 1785 **Fax:** 028-9060 3030
E-mail: jim@bowhomes.com
Website: http://www.bowhomes.com
Directors: J. Ferguson (Dir), P. Ferguson (Dir)
Managers: C. Malloy (Sales Admin)
Immediate Holding Company: BOW HOMES LIMITED
Registration no: NI016743 **Date established:** 1983 **Turnover:** £5m - £10m
No.of Employees: 21 - 50 **Product Groups:** 84

Boyd Partnership
1 Rivers Edge 13 Ravenhill Road, Belfast, BT6 8DN
Tel: 028-9046 1414 **Fax:** 028-9046 1616
E-mail: info@boydpartnership.co.uk
Website: http://www.boydpartnership.co.uk
Directors: A. Acheson (Ptnr)
Immediate Holding Company: THE BOYD PARTNERSHIP CHARTERED ARCHITECTS LLP
Registration no: NC000165 **VAT No.:** GB 251 8498 38
Date established: 2006 **Turnover:** £250,000 - £500,000
No.of Employees: 1 - 10 **Product Groups:** 84

Date of Accounts	Mar 12	Mar 11	Mar 10
Working Capital	214	327	375
Fixed Assets	5	8	13
Current Assets	290	439	458

Bracken Equestrian
87 Ballycoan Road, Belfast, BT8 8LP
Tel: 028-9081 7412 **Fax:** 028-9081 7413
E-mail: brackcjack@aol.com
Directors: C. Jackson (Prop)
VAT No.: GB 434 2567 55 **Date established:** 1985
Turnover: £500,000 - £1m **No.of Employees:** 1 - 10 **Product Groups:** 22

Bracken Window Blinds
Unit 4 Edgar Road, Carryduff, Belfast, BT8 8NB
Tel: 028-9081 2424 **Fax:** 028-9081 4741
E-mail: ronnie@bracken-interiors.co.uk
Website: http://www.bracken-interiors.co.uk
Directors: R. Mclean (Prop)
Immediate Holding Company: R.K. TRUCKS CENTRE LIMITED
Registration no: NI015281 **VAT No.:** GB 331 2161 12
Date established: 1981 **No.of Employees:** 1 - 10 **Product Groups:** 24, 35

Date of Accounts	Dec 11	Dec 10	Dec 09
Working Capital	2m	2m	2m
Fixed Assets	1m	1m	1m
Current Assets	2m	3m	2m

Bradbury Surgical
2 Marshalls Road, Belfast, BT5 6SR
Tel: 028-9040 1111 **Fax:** 028-9040 1958
E-mail: alison.mcbride@sangers.co.uk
Website: http://www.united-drug.ie
Directors: P. Surgenor (MD)
Managers: S. Loney (Sales Prom Mgr), A. Ward (I.T. Exec), D. Jackson (Mktg Serv Mgr)
Immediate Holding Company: J. BRADBURY (SURGICAL) LIMITED
Registration no: NI035736 **Date established:** 1999
No.of Employees: 101 - 250 **Product Groups:** 61, 67

British Telecom Ltd
Sydenham Business Park 201 Airport Road West, Belfast, BT3 9ED
Tel: 028-9055 0161 **Fax:** 028-9056 0056
E-mail: info@bicsystems.com
Website: http://www.bicsystems.com
Bank(s): Bank of Ireland
Directors: E. Vernon (MD), C. Murphy (Sales)
Immediate Holding Company: BI&C LTD
Registration no: 06438701 **VAT No.:** 392612839 **Date established:** 1984
Turnover: £10m - £20m **No.of Employees:** 11 - 20 **Product Groups:** 44, 67, 86

Britvic N I plc
468-472 Castlereagh Road, Belfast, BT5 6RG
Tel: 028-9079 9335 **Fax:** 028-9079 8143
E-mail: brian.magennis@britvic.com
Website: http://www.britvic.ie
Bank(s): Bank of Ireland
Managers: B. Magennis (Comm)
Immediate Holding Company: AQUAPORTE LIMITED
Registration no: NF000009 **VAT No.:** GB 251 7334 73
Date established: 1997 **No.of Employees:** 21 - 50 **Product Groups:** 62

Bronze Craft
3 Knockbreda Gardens, Belfast, BT6 0HH
Tel: 028-9064 7839 **Fax:** 028-9064 7839
E-mail: fitzpatrick@babyshoebronzing.net
Website: http://www.babyshoebronzing.net
Directors: D. Fitzpatrick (Prop)
Date established: 1985 **No.of Employees:** 1 - 10 **Product Groups:** 46, 48

Brook Design Hardware Ltd
City Business Park Dunmurry, Belfast, BT17 9GW
Tel: 028-9061 6505 **Fax:** 028-9061 6518
E-mail: info@brookvent.co.uk
Website: http://www.brookvent.co.uk
Bank(s): First Trust
Directors: D. Gormley (Dir)
Managers: M. McLaughlin (Tech Serv Mgr), R. McCandless (Personnel), D. Duffey (Mktg Serv Mgr), D. McBrien (Fin Mgr), B. Logue (Eng Serv Mgr), P. Russell (Buyer)
Immediate Holding Company: BROOK DESIGN HARDWARE LIMITED
Registration no: NI019735 **VAT No.:** GB 390 8747 13
Date established: 1986 **Turnover:** £2m - £5m **No.of Employees:** 21 - 50
Product Groups: 40, 48

Date of Accounts	Oct 11	Oct 10	Oct 09
Sales Turnover	N/A	N/A	3m
Pre Tax Profit/Loss	N/A	N/A	134
Working Capital	3m	4m	4m
Fixed Assets	1m	1m	1m
Current Assets	5m	5m	5m
Current Liabilities	N/A	N/A	720

Brookfield Business Centre Ltd
333 Crumlin Road, Belfast, BT14 7EA
Tel: 028-9074 5241 **Fax:** 028-9074 8025
E-mail: bob.mcneill@brookfieldcampus.com
Website: http://www.flaxtrust.com
Directors: J. Patterson (Grp Chief Exec)
Immediate Holding Company: BROOKFIELD BUSINESS CENTRE LTD
Registration no: NI019579 **Date established:** 1986
Turnover: Up to £250,000 **No.of Employees:** 1 - 10 **Product Groups:** 86

Date of Accounts	Mar 11	Mar 10	Mar 09
Sales Turnover	21	18	54
Pre Tax Profit/Loss	-108	-123	-120
Working Capital	625	733	856
Current Assets	639	753	888
Current Liabilities	14	19	30

Brooks Group U K Ltd
27 Duncrue Street, Belfast, BT3 9AR
Tel: 028-9074 4201 **Fax:** 028-9074 8952
E-mail: brooks.belfast@brooksgroup.ie
Website: http://www.brooksgroup.co.uk
Bank(s): Ulster Bank
Directors: G. Cousten (MD), M. Brook (Dir)
Ultimate Holding Company: Wolseley PLC
Immediate Holding Company: Wolseley Ireland Holdings Limited
Registration no: NI030859 **VAT No.:** GB 232 2186 95
Date established: 1996 **Turnover:** £20m - £50m
No.of Employees: 21 - 50 **Product Groups:** 66

Browns Removals
35-41 Gawn Street, Belfast, BT4 1GE
Tel: 028-9045 9243 **Fax:** 028- 90731686
E-mail: sales@brownsremovals.com
Website: http://www.brownsremovals.com
Directors: A. Brown (Prop)
Immediate Holding Company: BROWNS REMOVALS & STORAGE LTD
Registration no: NI021364 **VAT No.:** GB 497 1304 32
Date established: 1988 **No.of Employees:** 1 - 10 **Product Groups:** 72, 77

Bruce-Shaw Partnership
1-9 Linfield Road, Belfast, BT12 5DR
Tel: 028-9032 1056 **Fax:** 028-9023 8084
E-mail: john.mcilwaine@bruceshaw.com
Website: http://www.bruceshaw.com
Bank(s): Ulster Bank
Directors: J. Mcilwaine (Snr Part), J. McIlwrine (MD)
Managers: A. Elliott (Personnel)
Immediate Holding Company: Bruce Shaw Management Services (NI) Limited
Registration no: NI065840 **VAT No.:** GB 256 0854 52
Date established: 2007 **No.of Employees:** 21 - 50 **Product Groups:** 80, 84

Bryson Architects
Lynden Gate 50 Knockbreda Road, Belfast, BT6 0JB
Tel: 028-9064 8111 **Fax:** 028-9064 8444
E-mail: info@bryson-architects.net
Website: http://www.bryson-architects.co.uk
Directors: P. Gillespie (Dir)
Immediate Holding Company: Bryson Architects Ltd
Registration no: NI055688 **Date established:** 2005
Turnover: Up to £250,000 **No.of Employees:** 1 - 10 **Product Groups:** 84

Date of Accounts	Jun 11	Jun 10	Jun 09
Working Capital	-9	59	133
Fixed Assets	399	418	442
Current Assets	31	108	264

Bryson Charitable Group
Bryson House 28 Bedford Street, Belfast, BT2 7FE
Tel: 028-9032 5835 **Fax:** 028-9043 9156
E-mail: jo.marley@dnet.co.uk
Website: http://www.brysongroup.org
Bank(s): First Trust
Directors: J. Mcmullan (Grp Chief Exec)
Immediate Holding Company: BRYSON CHARITABLE GROUP
Registration no: NI001319 **VAT No.:** GB 392 5887 00
Date established: 1939 **Turnover:** £20m - £50m
No.of Employees: 101 - 250 **Product Groups:** 88

Date of Accounts	Mar 11	Mar 10	Mar 09
Sales Turnover	31m	25m	20m
Pre Tax Profit/Loss	1m	2m	-374
Working Capital	3m	2m	1m
Fixed Assets	10m	10m	10m
Current Assets	6m	5m	4m
Current Liabilities	846	1m	1m

Burke Office
Unit 28 Ormeau Business Park 8 Cromac Avenue, Belfast, BT7 2JA
Tel: 028-9087 6020 **Fax:** 028-9087 6677
E-mail: enquiries@burke-office.co.uk
Website: http://www.burke-office.co.uk
Directors: M. Burke (Prop)
VAT No.: GB 256 1910 63 **Turnover:** £2m - £5m **No.of Employees:** 1 - 10
Product Groups: 26, 27, 44, 49, 61

Burns Owens & Co. Ltd
3 Duncrue Crescent, Belfast, BT3 9BW
Tel: 028-9077 9342 **Fax:** 028-9078 1210
E-mail: burns.owens@btconnect.com
Directors: G. O'kane (MD)
Immediate Holding Company: BURNS OWENS & COMPANY (AGENCIES) LIMITED
Registration no: NI008158 **VAT No.:** GB 255 2005 93
Date established: 1971 **Turnover:** £500,000 - £1m
No.of Employees: 1 - 10 **Product Groups:** 66

Date of Accounts	Feb 12	Feb 11	Feb 10
Working Capital	151	230	255
Fixed Assets	16	21	28
Current Assets	282	352	419

Business & Scientific Services
Unit 2 Falcon Way, Belfast, BT12 6SQ
Tel: 028-9022 6000 **Fax:** 028-9022 6100
E-mail: sales@bss-ltd.com
Website: http://www.bss-ltd.com
Directors: W. Mckee (Prop)
Managers: D. McCartney (Purch Mgr)
Immediate Holding Company: BUSINESS AND SCIENTIFIC SERVICES LTD
Registration no: NI018033 **VAT No.:** GB 252 4149 77
Date established: 1984 **Turnover:** £10m - £20m
No.of Employees: 21 - 50 **Product Groups:** 44

Date of Accounts	Dec 11	Dec 10	Dec 09
Sales Turnover	16m	15m	16m
Pre Tax Profit/Loss	-312	-349	-132
Working Capital	365	504	759
Fixed Assets	137	193	257
Current Assets	6m	4m	3m
Current Liabilities	1m	743	644

C A S Engineering
6-16 Duncrue Crescent, Belfast, BT3 9BW
Tel: 028-9078 1155
E-mail: casengineering@hotmail.co.uk
Directors: S. Ohare (Prop)
Immediate Holding Company: C.A.S. ENGINEERING (NI) LIMITED
Registration no: NI058189 **Date established:** 2006
No.of Employees: 1 - 10 **Product Groups:** 35

Date of Accounts	Feb 11	Feb 10	Feb 09
Working Capital	151	120	109
Fixed Assets	100	108	125
Current Assets	228	210	264

C B Richard Ellis
Imperial House 4-10 Donegall Square East, Belfast, BT1 5HD
Tel: 028-9043 8555 **Fax:** 028-9043 9444
E-mail: brian.lavery@cbreg.ie
Website: http://www.cbregunne.com
Bank(s): Bank of Ireland
Directors: B. Lavery (Dir)
Ultimate Holding Company: CB RICHARD ELLIS GROUP INC (USA)
Immediate Holding Company: CBRE N.I. LIMITED
Registration no: NI032803 **VAT No.:** GB 701 8680 44
Date established: 1997 **Turnover:** £1m - £2m **No.of Employees:** 21 - 50
Product Groups: 80

Date of Accounts	Dec 11	Dec 10	Dec 09
Sales Turnover	2m	1m	445
Pre Tax Profit/Loss	163	101	N/A

Working Capital	451	265	183
Fixed Assets	104	127	109
Current Assets	796	759	486
Current Liabilities	288	323	49

C E F S Ltd
Unit 1 Farm Business Centre Blackstaff Road, Belfast, BT11 9DT
Tel: 028-9061 0040 **Fax:** 028-9061 4913
E-mail: info@cefs-ni.com
Website: http://www.cefs-ni.com
Directors: L. Ali (Prop)
Immediate Holding Company: CEFS Limited
Registration no: NI054503 **Date established:** 2005
No.of Employees: 1 - 10 **Product Groups:** 20, 40, 41

Date of Accounts	Apr 12	Apr 11	Apr 10
Sales Turnover	271	N/A	N/A
Working Capital	-123	-93	60
Fixed Assets	2	3	9
Current Assets	108	99	130

C & H Electrical Co.
85a Imperial Street, Belfast, BT6 8JP
Tel: 028-9045 9123 **Fax:** 028-9073 8062
E-mail: chelecco@aol.com
Directors: A. Hall (Prop)
VAT No.: GB 252 2699 52 **Turnover:** £250,000 - £500,000
No.of Employees: 1 - 10 **Product Groups:** 48

C P D plc
6 Balmoral Road, Belfast, BT12 6QA
Tel: 028-9038 0060 **Fax:** 028-9038 5099
E-mail: stephen_maginn@cpdplc-ni.co.uk
Website: http://www.cpdplc.co.uk
Managers: S. Magill (District Mgr)
Registration no: 04451765 **Turnover:** £10m - £20m
No.of Employees: 11 - 20 **Product Groups:** 52, 66

Calvert Office Equipment Ltd
20 Orby Link, Belfast, BT5 5HU
Tel: 028-9040 1360 **Fax:** 028-9040 1236
E-mail: info@calvert-office.co.uk
Website: http://www.calvert-office.co.uk
Directors: K. Houston (Dir), D. Calvert (MD), R. Calvert (MD)
Managers: T. Craig
Immediate Holding Company: CALVERT OFFICE EQUIPMENT LIMITED
Registration no: NI006103 **VAT No.:** GB 252 3220 05
Date established: 1964 **Turnover:** £5m - £10m **No.of Employees:** 21 - 50
Product Groups: 48, 67

Date of Accounts	Aug 11	Aug 10	Aug 09
Sales Turnover	7m	7m	N/A
Pre Tax Profit/Loss	1m	1m	2m
Working Capital	3m	2m	1m
Fixed Assets	2m	2m	2m
Current Assets	5m	4m	2m
Current Liabilities	800	785	658

Campbell & Campbell
100 University Street, Belfast, BT7 1HE
Tel: 028-9023 4541 **Fax:** 028-9023 2860
E-mail: office@candcaccountants.co.uk
Website: http://www.candcaccountants.co.uk
Directors: L. Campbell (Prop)
Immediate Holding Company: JSR Homes Ltd
Registration no: NI009762 **VAT No.:** GB 375 8988 72
Date established: 2007 **No.of Employees:** 1 - 10 **Product Groups:** 80

Date of Accounts	Oct 11	Oct 10	Oct 09
Working Capital	10	-34	-42
Fixed Assets	41	50	59
Current Assets	72	44	71

Campbell Mccleave & Co. Ltd
35-39 Middlepath Street, Belfast, BT5 4BG
Tel: 028-9045 8558 **Fax:** 028-9045 8588
E-mail: info@cmcfreight.co.uk
Website: http://www.cmcfreight.co.uk
Bank(s): Ulster Bank
Directors: R. Peoples (MD), B. Peoples (Fin)
Managers: P. Carrol (I.T. Exec), P. Carrol (Tech Serv Mgr), M. Harte (Sales Prom Mgr), D. O'Connor
Immediate Holding Company: CAMPBELL MCCLEAVE & COMPANY LIMITED
Registration no: NI017231 **VAT No.:** GB 392 5202 58
Date established: 1984 **Turnover:** £5m - £10m **No.of Employees:** 21 - 50
Product Groups: 72, 74, 75, 76, 77

Date of Accounts	Mar 12	Mar 11	Mar 10
Sales Turnover	9m	10m	7m
Pre Tax Profit/Loss	204	118	-38
Working Capital	747	598	515
Fixed Assets	22	29	42
Current Assets	3m	3m	3m
Current Liabilities	327	330	364

Campbells Caterers Ltd
11 Arthur Street, Belfast, BT1 4GA
Tel: 028-9032 2658 **Fax:** 028-9031 4999
Directors: E. Mcpeak (MD)
Immediate Holding Company: CAMPBELLS (CATERERS) LIMITED
Registration no: NI001769 **Date established:** 1944
No.of Employees: 1 - 10 **Product Groups:** 20

Canon Business Solutions
1 Cromac Quay, Belfast, BT7 2JD
Tel: 028-9072 7500 **Fax:** 028-9072 7555
E-mail: janette_thompson@cuk.canon.co.uk
Website: http://www.canon.co.uk
Managers: P. Brady
Turnover: £2m - £5m **No.of Employees:** 21 - 50 **Product Groups:** 67

Cardiac Services Ltd
6 Wildflower Way Northern Ireland, Belfast, BT12 6TA
Tel: 028-9066 9000 **Fax:** 028-9068 7100
E-mail: sales@cardiac-services.com
Website: http://www.cardiac-services.com
Bank(s): Bank of Ireland
Directors: M. Reid (Dir)
Ultimate Holding Company: SICON LIMITED
Immediate Holding Company: SISK HEALTHCARE (UK) LIMITED
Registration no: NI018037 **VAT No.:** GB 252 4149 77
Date established: 1984 **Turnover:** £20m - £50m
No.of Employees: 21 - 50 **Product Groups:** 67

Date of Accounts	Dec 11	Dec 10	Jun 09
Sales Turnover	17m	29m	24m
Pre Tax Profit/Loss	126	1m	614
Working Capital	7m	15m	15m
Fixed Assets	1m	2m	2m
Current Assets	12m	23m	21m
Current Liabilities	1m	2m	1m

Cards Galore Ltd
Unit 9 D C Enterprise Centre Kennedy Way, Belfast, BT11 9AP
Tel: 028-9062 2030 **Fax:** 028-9030 1354
E-mail: email@cardsgalore-ni.co.uk
Website: http://www.cardsgalore.co.uk
Directors: G. Crawford (Prop)
Immediate Holding Company: CARDS GALORE LIMITED
Registration no: 04581832 **VAT No.:** GB 366 3023 28
Date established: 2002 **No.of Employees:** 1 - 10 **Product Groups:** 64

Date of Accounts	Mar 10	Mar 09	Mar 08
Sales Turnover	53	53	52
Pre Tax Profit/Loss	14	18	18
Working Capital	2	2	4
Current Assets	6	7	9
Current Liabilities	4	6	5

Cardwell Boiler Services
36 Abbey Park, Belfast, BT5 7HQ
Tel: 028-9048 1148 **Fax:** 028-9048 1148
Directors: R. Cardwell (Prop)
Date established: 1983 **No.of Employees:** 1 - 10 **Product Groups:** 48, 52

Cargo Forwarding
Transit 1 West Bank Way, Belfast, BT3 9LB
Tel: 028-9037 3700 **Fax:** 028-9037 3736
E-mail: info@cargo-forwarding.co.uk
Website: http://www.trlogistics.co.uk
Bank(s): Bank of Ireland
Managers: P. Mckeown (Fin Mgr)
Ultimate Holding Company: MUS LIMITED
Immediate Holding Company: CARGO FORWARDING LIMITED
Registration no: NI024601 **VAT No.:** GB 517 2977 24
Date established: 1990 **Turnover:** £5m - £10m
No.of Employees: 51 - 100 **Product Groups:** 76

Date of Accounts	Sep 11	Sep 10	Sep 09
Sales Turnover	10m	8m	8m
Pre Tax Profit/Loss	518	114	-138
Working Capital	813	268	169
Fixed Assets	58	92	127
Current Assets	5m	4m	4m
Current Liabilities	953	627	376

Carrier Air Conditioning
Unit 4 Carrowreagh Business Park Carrowreagh Road, Dundonald, Belfast, BT16 1QQ
Tel: 028-9048 3671 **Fax:** 028-9046 6418
E-mail: billy.miskelly@carrier.utc.com
Managers: B. Miskelly (Reg Mgr)
No.of Employees: 1 - 10 **Product Groups:** 52

Carson Mcdowell
Murray House 4 Murray Street, Belfast, BT1 6DN
Tel: 028-9024 4951 **Fax:** 028-9024 5768
E-mail: law@carson-mcdowell.com
Website: http://www.carson-mcdowell.com
Directors: M. Johnston (Snr Part)
Managers: R. Mullan (Systems Mgr), K. Doran (Mktg Serv Mgr), M. McKeown (Sales Admin)
Ultimate Holding Company: BERENDSEN PLC
Immediate Holding Company: CARSON MCDOWELL LLP
Registration no: NC000908 **VAT No.:** GB 251 7099 57
Date established: 2012 **No.of Employees:** 51 - 100 **Product Groups:** 80

Cartridge World Ltd
543 Lisburn Road, Belfast, BT9 7GQ
Tel: 028-9068 1254 **Fax:** 028-9068 1242
Website: http://www.belfast.cartridgeworld.co.uk
Immediate Holding Company: CARTRIDGE WORLD LIMITED
Registration no: 04124067 **Date established:** 2000 **Turnover:** £5m - £10m
No.of Employees: 51 - 100 **Product Groups:** 28, 30, 44, 64

Date of Accounts	Dec 11	Dec 10	Dec 09
Sales Turnover	6m	7m	8m
Pre Tax Profit/Loss	373	164	210
Working Capital	1m	967	878
Fixed Assets	403	455	524
Current Assets	7m	7m	6m
Current Liabilities	4m	1m	2m

Carvill Group Ltd
Unit 75 Vico House Dunmurry Industrial Estate, Dunmurry, Belfast, BT17 9HU
Tel: 028-9061 5624 **Fax:** 028-9062 4200
E-mail: sales@carvill-group.com
Website: http://www.carvill-group.com
Directors: M. Carvill (Dir), C. Carvill (MD)
Managers: C. Foy (Chief Acct)
Immediate Holding Company: CARVILL GROUP LIMITED
Registration no: NI013947 **VAT No.:** GB 287 2329 34
Date established: 1979 **Turnover:** £10m - £20m
No.of Employees: 11 - 20 **Product Groups:** 52, 80

Date of Accounts	Aug 09	Aug 08	Aug 07
Sales Turnover	19m	36m	37m
Pre Tax Profit/Loss	-6m	2m	4m
Working Capital	88m	83m	68m
Fixed Assets	4m	5m	5m
Current Assets	135m	119m	109m
Current Liabilities	35m	29m	35m

Carville Engineering
Unit 11 Seymour Hill Industrial Estate Dunmurry, Belfast, BT17 9PH
Tel: 028-9062 6999 **Fax:** 028-9062 7300
E-mail: carvilleeng@btconnect.com
Managers: D. Carroll (Mgr)
Registration no: 00926788 **VAT No.:** GB 375 7515 23
Date established: 1982 **Turnover:** £500,000 - £1m
No.of Employees: 1 - 10 **Product Groups:** 83

Castormart Ltd
102 University Avenue, Belfast, BT7 1GY
Tel: 028-9032 3263 **Fax:** 028-9024 9784
E-mail: belfast@castormart.com
Website: http://www.castormart.com
Managers: S. Dean (Mgr)
Immediate Holding Company: CASTORMART LIMITED
Registration no: NI013085 **VAT No.:** GB 287 0145 54
Date established: 1978 **Turnover:** £250,000 - £500,000
No.of Employees: 1 - 10 **Product Groups:** 29, 35, 39, 66

Date of Accounts	Dec 10	Dec 09	Dec 08
Working Capital	273	277	300
Fixed Assets	76	77	79
Current Assets	300	301	326
Current Liabilities	N/A	16	9

CBI
6th Floor Scottish Amicable Building, 11 Donegall Square South, Belfast, BT1 5JE
Tel: 028-9010 1100 **Fax:** 028-90 0 1119
E-mail: sarah.smart@cbi.org.uk
Website: http://www.cbi.org.uk
Directors: M. Smyth (Dir), N. Smyth (Reg), W. Poole (Develop), D. Stewart (Asst MD)
Registration no: NF002815 **VAT No.:** GB 238 7864 16
Date established: 2005 **No.of Employees:** 1 - 10 **Product Groups:** 87

Central Translations Ni Ltd
23-31 Warings Street, Belfast, BT1 2DX
Tel: 028-9043 6659 **Fax:** 028-9043 6699
E-mail: cen.tran@btinternet.com
Website: http://www.central-translations.co.uk
Directors: M. Verner (MD)
Immediate Holding Company: CENTRAL TRANSLATIONS (NI) LIMITED
Registration no: NI036143 **Date established:** 1999
No.of Employees: 1 - 10 **Product Groups:** 80

Date of Accounts	Jun 12	Jun 11	Jun 10
Working Capital	19	57	72
Fixed Assets	1	2	2
Current Assets	51	98	115

Century Electrical Wholesale Ltd
City Business Park Dunmurry, Belfast, BT17 9HY
Tel: 028-9061 8666 **Fax:** 028-9038 6722
Website: http://www.centuryelectrical.co.uk
Managers: G. Doogan (Chief Acct)
Ultimate Holding Company: THE COLLINS FAMILY PARTNERSHIP (ISLE OF MAN)
Immediate Holding Company: CENTURY ELECTRICAL WHOLESALE LTD
Registration no: NI053328 **Date established:** 2004 **Turnover:** £5m - £10m
No.of Employees: 11 - 20 **Product Groups:** 36, 40

Date of Accounts	Mar 12	Mar 11	Mar 10
Sales Turnover	7m	5m	4m
Pre Tax Profit/Loss	78	39	101
Working Capital	2m	2m	966
Fixed Assets	204	181	169
Current Assets	4m	2m	2m
Current Liabilities	753	352	359

Charles Hurst Group
62 Boucher Road, Belfast, BT12 6LR
Tel: 028-9038 1721 **Fax:** 028-9038 3585
E-mail: ken.surgenor@toyota.co.uk
Website: http://www.charleshurstgroup.co.uk
Directors: K. Surgenor (Ch), P. Gordon (Dir), F. Mcguire (Ch), K. Surgenor (MD)
Managers: G. Rooney (Chief Mgr), T. Robinson (I.T. Exec), G. Jack (Sales Prom Mgr)
Ultimate Holding Company: LOOKERS PUBLIC LIMITED COMPANY
Immediate Holding Company: CHARLES HURST HOLDINGS LIMITED
Registration no: R0000134 **Date established:** 2011
Turnover: £500,000 - £1m **No.of Employees:** 501 - 1000
Product Groups: 68, 82

Date of Accounts	Dec 10	Dec 09	Dec 08
Sales Turnover	527	2m	1m
Pre Tax Profit/Loss	2m	1m	4
Working Capital	-79	-116	-181
Fixed Assets	1m	1m	1m
Current Assets	2m	3m	3m
Current Liabilities	213	1m	374

Chem Vite Ltd
6 Northern Road, Belfast, BT3 9AL
Tel: 028-9074 9176 **Fax:** 028-9075 4937
E-mail: info@chemvite.co.uk
Website: http://www.chem-vite.co.uk
Directors: A. Wilson (Dir)
Immediate Holding Company: CHEM-VITE LIMITED
Registration no: NI007724 **Date established:** 1969 **Turnover:** £2m - £5m
No.of Employees: 1 - 10 **Product Groups:** 32, 33

Date of Accounts	Aug 11	Jan 11	Jan 10
Working Capital	230	223	190
Fixed Assets	183	205	238
Current Assets	541	540	465

Chemical Treatment Services Ltd
19 Harbour Court 9 Heron Road, Belfast, BT3 9HB
Tel: 028-9092 1212 **Fax:** 028-9092 1211
E-mail: info@ctsltd.com
Website: http://www.ctsltd.com
Managers: R. Fergusson (Mgr)
Immediate Holding Company: CHEMICAL TREATMENT SERVICES (IRELAND) LIMITED
Registration no: NI017799 **VAT No.:** GB 412 5185 80
Date established: 1984 **No.of Employees:** 11 - 20 **Product Groups:** 32, 51, 52

Date of Accounts	Apr 11	Apr 10	Apr 09
Working Capital	572	568	534
Fixed Assets	9	17	25
Current Assets	722	755	702

Choice Apollo Blinds
338 Cregagh Road, Belfast, BT6 9EX
Tel: 028-9079 6974 **Fax:** 028-9045 7261
Website: http://www.apolloblindswatford.co.uk
Directors: E. Paul (Prop)
VAT No.: 311214818 **No.of Employees:** 1 - 10 **Product Groups:** 25, 35

Church Of Ireland Young Men's Society
91 Circular Road, Belfast, BT4 2GD
Tel: 028-9076 0120 **Fax:** 028-9067 2126
E-mail: aceventures@btconnect.com
Website: http://www.ciyms.org
Managers: R. Barnes (Mgr)
Registration no: NI055719 **Date established:** 2005
Turnover: Up to £250,000 **No.of Employees:** 1 - 10 **Product Groups:** 86

City Air Express Ni Ltd
West Bank Drive, Belfast, BT3 9LA
Tel: 028-9078 1878 **Fax:** 028-9078 1788
E-mail: jknapper@cityairexpress.com
Website: http://www.cityairexpress.com
Directors: J. Knapper (Dir), S. Wallace (MD)
Ultimate Holding Company: CITY TRANSPORT HOLDINGS LIMITED
Immediate Holding Company: CITY AIR EXPRESS (N.I.) LTD.
Registration no: 02504413 **VAT No.:** GB 517 3533 55
Date established: 1990 **Turnover:** £1m - £2m **No.of Employees:** 21 - 50
Product Groups: 75, 76, 79

Date of Accounts	Dec 11	Dec 10	Dec 09
Working Capital	170	128	112
Fixed Assets	7	10	14
Current Assets	462	336	353

City TV
Castle Lane, Belfast, BT1 5DA
Tel: 028-9032 5564 **Fax:** 028-9024 3523
E-mail: sales@citytvbelfast.com
Website: http://www.citytvbelfast.com
Directors: A. Cryton (Dir), L. Creighton (MD), A. Creighton (Prop)
Registration no: 00017226 **VAT No.:** 392569803 **Date established:** 2002
No.of Employees: 1 - 10 **Product Groups:** 81

Cleaver Fulton Rankin
50 Bedford Street, Belfast, BT2 7FW
Tel: 028-9024 3141 **Fax:** 028-9024 9096
E-mail: k.blair@cfrlaw.co.uk
Website: http://www.cfrlaw.co.uk
Directors: K. Blair (Snr Part), S. Kennedy (Dir)
Managers: E. Lewis (Sales Admin), K. Collie (Fin Mgr), K. Leckie (Mktg Serv Mgr)
Immediate Holding Company: CLEAVER FULTON RANKIN LIMITED
Registration no: NI031078 **Date established:** 1996
No.of Employees: 51 - 100 **Product Groups:** 80

Coachfinish Northern Ireland Ltd
180-190 Donegall Avenue, Belfast, BT12 6LY
Tel: 028-9032 0541 **Fax:** 028-9024 5750
E-mail: sales@coachfinish.com
Website: http://www.coachfinish.com
Bank(s): Northern Bank
Managers: G. Kidd (Mgr)
Immediate Holding Company: COACHFINISH (NI) LTD
Registration no: NI010205 **VAT No.:** GB 251 7585 48
Date established: 1974 **Turnover:** £250,000 - £500,000
No.of Employees: 11 - 20 **Product Groups:** 32

Date of Accounts	Mar 11	Mar 10	Mar 09
Working Capital	713	623	666
Fixed Assets	101	113	101
Current Assets	1m	1m	1m

Coey Advertising
Victoria Lodge 158 Upper Newtownards Road, Belfast, BT4 3EQ
Tel: 028-9047 1221 **Fax:** 028-9047 1509
E-mail: info@coeyadvertising.co.uk
Website: http://www.coeyadvertising.co.uk
Directors: I. Coey (Prop), M. Johnston (Fin)
Immediate Holding Company: COEY ADVERTISING COMPANY LIMITED - THE
Registration no: NI029679 **VAT No.:** GB 454 5794 15
Date established: 1995 **Turnover:** £2m - £5m **No.of Employees:** 1 - 10
Product Groups: 38, 81

Date of Accounts	Mar 11	Mar 10	Mar 09
Working Capital	119	340	487
Fixed Assets	21	38	55
Current Assets	323	420	626

Collins Electrical Co.
2a Deramore Avenue, Belfast, BT7 3ER
Tel: 028-9064 2001 **Fax:** 028-9064 0998
E-mail: info@belfastelectricians.com
Website: http://www.collinselectric.co.uk
Directors: M. Collins (Prop)
Immediate Holding Company: K F COLLINS ELECTRIC LIMITED
Registration no: NI016259 **VAT No.:** GB 286 4914 19
Date established: 1982 **No.of Employees:** 1 - 10 **Product Groups:** 52

Date of Accounts	Dec 11	Dec 10	Dec 09
Working Capital	-16	-11	6
Fixed Assets	2	3	4
Current Assets	44	50	93

Comco Plastics Ltd
Musgrave Park Industrial Estate Stockmans Way, Belfast, BT9 7ET
Tel: 028-9066 8358 **Fax:** 028-9066 0623
E-mail: michael.oneil@camcoplastics.co.uk
Website: http://www.comcoplastics.co.uk
Directors: L. Woods (Dir)
Ultimate Holding Company: COPPERFIELDS PROPERTY LIMITED
Immediate Holding Company: CFR 23 LIMITED
Registration no: NI048874 **Date established:** 2003
No.of Employees: 11 - 20 **Product Groups:** 30, 66

Community Telegraph
124-144 Royal Avenue, Belfast, BT1 1DN
Tel: 028-9026 4396 **Fax:** 028-9055 4585
E-mail: vsloss@belfasttelegraph.co.uk
Website: http://www.thect.co.uk
Directors: M. Gower (MD)
Managers: V. Sloss (Publishing), G. McWilliams, G. Mcwilliams (Publishing)
Registration no: NI761000 **VAT No.:** GB 233 3986 52
Turnover: £500,000 - £1m **No.of Employees:** 1 - 10 **Product Groups:** 28

The Company Shop
79 Chichester Street, Belfast, BT1 4JE
Tel: 028-9055 9955 **Fax:** 028-9055 0078
E-mail: formations@thecompanyshop.co.uk
Website: http://www.thecompanyshop.co.uk
Directors: K. Redpath (MD)
Immediate Holding Company: THE COMPANY SHOP (NI) LIMITED
Registration no: NI061439 **Date established:** 2006
Turnover: Up to £250,000 **No.of Employees:** 1 - 10 **Product Groups:** 80

Compass Group UK Ltd
Suite 1 Boucher Plaza 4-6 Boucher Road, Belfast, BT12 6HR
Tel: 028-9033 2639 **Fax:** 028-9066 2806
Website: http://www.Compass-Group.co.uk
Bank(s): Bank of Ireland
Directors: M. Campbell (MD)
Managers: C. Murray (Sales Prom Mgr), M. Campbell
Immediate Holding Company: COMPASS GROUP (UK) LIMITED
Registration no: 06942046 **VAT No.:** GB 466 4777 01
Date established: 2009 **Turnover:** £1m - £2m **No.of Employees:** 11 - 20
Product Groups: 52, 69

Construction Employers Federation Ltd
143 Malone Road, Belfast, BT9 6SX
Tel: 028-9066 3535 **Fax:** 028-9087 7155
E-mail: mail@cefni.co.uk
Website: http://www.cef.eunet.co.uk
Directors: J. Armstrong (MD)
Managers: N. Lucas (Sec), C. Murray (Sales Admin), E. Dobbin (Admin Off)
Immediate Holding Company: CONSTRUCTION EMPLOYERS FEDERATION LIMITED
Registration no: NI001944 **Date established:** 1945
Turnover: £500,000 - £1m **No.of Employees:** 11 - 20 **Product Groups:** 87

Date of Accounts	Dec 11	Dec 10	Dec 09
Sales Turnover	526	515	571
Pre Tax Profit/Loss	-24	3	28
Working Capital	148	87	8
Fixed Assets	536	626	687
Current Assets	333	451	189
Current Liabilities	175	347	164

Conveyor Co Ireland Ltd
Unit 33a Bloomfield Commercial Centre 5 Factory Street, Belfast, BT5 5AW
Tel: 028-9045 0609 **Fax:** 028-9045 1575
E-mail: cciltd@utvinternet.com
Website: http://www.utvinternet.com
Managers: S. Mitchell (Mgr)
Immediate Holding Company: CONVEYOR COMPANY OF IRELAND LIMITED-THE
Registration no: NI027260 **VAT No.:** GB 311 3998 73
Date established: 1993 **No.of Employees:** 1 - 10 **Product Groups:** 45

Date of Accounts	Dec 11	Dec 10	Dec 09
Working Capital	-9	13	2
Fixed Assets	12	13	14
Current Assets	106	149	131

Cooke & Kettyle
72 University Street, Belfast, BT7 1HB
Tel: 028-9032 4200 **Fax:** 028-9032 0275
E-mail: admin@cookeandkettyle.co.uk
Website: http://www.ck.onyxnet.co.uk
Directors: R. Cooke (Ptnr)
Immediate Holding Company: COOKE & KETTYLE LLP
Registration no: NC000471 **Date established:** 2008
No.of Employees: 11 - 20 **Product Groups:** 84

Date of Accounts	Dec 11	Dec 10	Dec 09
Working Capital	348	420	266
Fixed Assets	17	23	30
Current Assets	437	508	331

Copeland Linens Ltd
59 Boundary Street, Belfast, BT13 2EJ
Tel: 028-9032 1065 **Fax:** 028-9032 2786
E-mail: copeland.linens@btclick.com
Website: http://www.copelandlinens.com
Directors: P. Smyth (MD)
Immediate Holding Company: COPELAND LINENS LIMITED
Registration no: NI003837 **Date established:** 1957 **Turnover:** £2m - £5m
No.of Employees: 1 - 10 **Product Groups:** 23, 44

Date of Accounts	Feb 12	Feb 11	Feb 10
Working Capital	-27	-19	-28
Fixed Assets	18	19	20
Current Assets	14	20	23

Corps Security
12 Cromac Place, Belfast, BT7 2JB
Tel: 028-9023 0031 **Fax:** 028-9023 6547
E-mail: info@corpssecurity.co.uk
Website: http://www.corpssecurity.co.uk
Managers: R. Whittle
Immediate Holding Company: MILBREEN LIMITED
Registration no: 01107779 **VAT No.:** GB 241 6328 80
Date established: 2001 **No.of Employees:** 1 - 10 **Product Groups:** 80

Date of Accounts	Mar 08	Mar 07	Mar 06
Sales Turnover	65147	56794	55438
Pre Tax Profit/Loss	654	442	531
Working Capital	2225	1606	1682
Fixed Assets	4161	4086	3012
Current Assets	10934	7250	6203
Current Liabilities	8709	5644	4521
ROCE% (Return on Capital Employed)	10.2	7.8	11.3
ROT% (Return on Turnover)	1.0	0.8	1.0

Crane Communications Ltd
B5 Heron Road, Belfast, BT3 9LE
Tel: 028-9045 6071 **Fax:** 028-9045 4961
E-mail: david@cranecommunication.co.uk
Website: http://www.cranecommunications.co.uk
Bank(s): Ulster Bank
Directors: D. Mcconkey (MD)
Ultimate Holding Company: HANSA ENTERPRISES LTD
Immediate Holding Company: CRANE COMMUNICATIONS LIMITED
Registration no: NI014794 **VAT No.:** GB 286 4776 05
Date established: 1981 **Turnover:** £1m - £2m **No.of Employees:** 11 - 20
Product Groups: 37, 40, 52, 63, 67, 83

Date of Accounts	Jun 11	Jun 10	Jun 09
Working Capital	213	132	72
Fixed Assets	7	12	28
Current Assets	1m	1m	929

Crane Stockham Valve Ltd
Alexander Road, Belfast, BT6 9HJ
Tel: 028-9070 4222 **Fax:** 028-9040 1582
E-mail: sales@cranebelfast.com
Website: http://www.crane-energy.com
Bank(s): Barclays, 54 Lombard St, London EC3V 9EX
Directors: E. Fast (Dir)
Managers: C. Ross, E. Rafferty (Tech Serv Mgr), J. McIlroy (Sales Prom Mgr), M. Campbell (Personnel), S. Wynne (Comptroller)
Ultimate Holding Company: CRANE CO. (USA)
Immediate Holding Company: CRANE STOCKHAM VALVE LIMITED
Registration no: 00549383 **Date established:** 1955
Turnover: £10m - £20m **No.of Employees:** 51 - 100 **Product Groups:** 36, 39

Date of Accounts	Dec 11	Dec 10	Dec 09
Sales Turnover	15m	12m	12m
Pre Tax Profit/Loss	950	1m	2m
Working Capital	6m	6m	5m
Fixed Assets	1m	1m	1m
Current Assets	11m	9m	8m
Current Liabilities	1m	1m	1m

Crescent Townhouse
13 Lower Cresent, Belfast, BT7 1NR
Tel: 028-9032 3349 **Fax:** 028-9032 0646
E-mail: admin@crescenttownhouse.co.uk
Website: http://www.crescenttownhouse.com
Managers: J. Duff (Mgr)
Turnover: £1m - £2m **No.of Employees:** 21 - 50 **Product Groups:** 69

Cunningham Coates Stockbrokers
19 Donegall Street, Belfast, BT1 2HA
Tel: 028-9032 3456 **Fax:** 028-9032 1479
E-mail: randal.herron@ccstockbrokers.com
Website: http://www.ccstockbrokers.com
Bank(s): Ulster Bank
Directors: J. Cunningham (Grp Chief Exec), J. Cunningham (MD)
Managers: L. Yeaman (Mktg Serv Mgr)
Immediate Holding Company: CUNNINGHAM COATES LIMITED
Registration no: NI024478 **VAT No.:** GB 251 7317 73
Date established: 1990 **Turnover:** £2m - £5m **No.of Employees:** 21 - 50
Product Groups: 82

Cutting Industries
Units 12-13 Dunmurry Industrial Estate Dunmurry, Belfast, BT17 9HU
Tel: 028-9060 5550 **Fax:** 028-9060 5535
E-mail: mark@cuttingindustries.co.uk
Website: http://www.cuttingindustries.com
Directors: M. Smiley (MD)
Ultimate Holding Company: VITA FIVE FIVE (ROI)
Registration no: NI007032 **Date established:** 1967
No.of Employees: 1 - 10 **Product Groups:** 46

D B Mclarnon Fire Protection Agency
Unit 44 Work West Enterprise Centre 301 Glen Road, Andersonstown, Belfast, BT11 8BU
Tel: 028-9030 1752 **Fax:** 028-9030 2838
Website: http://www.mclarnonfire.co.uk
Directors: D. Mclarnon (Ptnr), D. McLarnon (Prop)
Immediate Holding Company: CLONTARA LIMITED
Registration no: NI600978 **Date established:** 2010
No.of Employees: 1 - 10 **Product Groups:** 38, 42

Date of Accounts	Mar 11
Working Capital	-634
Fixed Assets	1m
Current Assets	82

D T Z Pieda Consulting
Scottish Providence Buildings 7 Donegall Square West, Belfast, BT1 6AA
Tel: 028-9024 7623 **Fax:** 028-9024 7632
E-mail: dtzpc@dtz.com
Website: http://www.dtzpiedaconsulting.com
Directors: E. Harvey (Dir)
Managers: N. Bonnor (Sales Admin)
Ultimate Holding Company: DTZ Holdings plc
Immediate Holding Company: Cranfield Grange (Rubane) Management Co. Limited
Registration no: NI058445 **Date established:** 2006 **Turnover:** £2m - £5m
No.of Employees: 11 - 20 **Product Groups:** 54, 80, 84

Dale Farm Ltd
15 Dargan Road, Belfast, BT3 9LS
Tel: 028-9037 2000 **Fax:** 028-9037 2211
E-mail: info@dalefarm.co.uk
Website: http://www.dalefarm.co.uk
Bank(s): First Trust
Directors: D. Dobbin (MD)
Ultimate Holding Company: UNITED DAIRY FARMERS LTD (IRELAND)
Immediate Holding Company: Dale Farm Limited
Registration no: NI025356 **VAT No.:** GB 252 1841 80
Date established: 1991 **Turnover:** £125m - £250m
No.of Employees: 51 - 100 **Product Groups:** 20

Date of Accounts	Mar 11	Mar 10	Mar 09
Sales Turnover	192m	171m	176m
Pre Tax Profit/Loss	1m	2m	4m
Working Capital	3m	5m	4m
Fixed Assets	43m	41m	38m
Current Assets	47m	39m	44m
Current Liabilities	4m	4m	12m

Danlor Services
48b Duncairn Gardens, Belfast, BT15 2GG
Tel: 028-9027 9970 **Fax:** 028-9027 9727
E-mail: davina@danlor.co.uk
Website: http://www.danlor.co.uk
Directors: B. Loughran (Prop)
Immediate Holding Company: BRANDON CONSTRUCTION LIMITED
Registration no: NI000454 **Date established:** 2027
No.of Employees: 11 - 20 **Product Groups:** 32, 40, 52, 66

Date of Accounts	Mar 11	Mar 10	Mar 09
Working Capital	69	70	70
Current Assets	69	70	70

David Mccullough & Co.
33 Garnerville Gardens, Belfast, BT4 2PA
Tel: 028-9076 3576
Directors: G. McCullough (Ptnr)
Date established: 1982 **No.of Employees:** 1 - 10 **Product Groups:** 38, 42

David Murphy Ltd
182 Belfast Road Carryduff, Belfast, BT8 8AS
Tel: 028-9081 2439 **Fax:** 028-9081 4536
Directors: D. Murphy (Prop)
Immediate Holding Company: DAVID MURPHY TOWING BRACKETS LIMITED
Registration no: NI013924 **VAT No.:** GB 287 2534 33
Date established: 1979 **No.of Employees:** 1 - 10 **Product Groups:** 39

Date of Accounts	Oct 11	Oct 10	Oct 09
Working Capital	702	693	620
Fixed Assets	69	61	61
Current Assets	828	803	793

Davidson & Hardy Lab Supplies Ltd
453-459 Antrim Road, Belfast, BT15 3BL
Tel: 028-9077 3376 **Fax:** 028-9077 2801
E-mail: info@dhlab.com
Website: http://www.dhlab.com
Bank(s): First Trust
Directors: M. Burton (Fin)
Managers: A. Johnstone (Purch Mgr)
Immediate Holding Company: DAVIDSON & HARDY LIMITED
Registration no: NI016125 **VAT No.:** GB 375 8694 89
Date established: 1982 **Turnover:** £2m - £5m **No.of Employees:** 21 - 50
Product Groups: 67, 85

Date of Accounts	Dec 08
Working Capital	20
Current Assets	20

Dawson & Company Ltd
171 University Street, Belfast, BT7 1HR
Tel: 028-9024 5217 **Fax:** 028-9182 0202
E-mail: mail@dawsonaccountants.co.uk
Website: http://www.dawsonaccountants.co.uk
Directors: M. Dawson (Dir)
Immediate Holding Company: MICHAEL GRIFFITH AGENCIES LIMITED
Registration no: 03083185 **VAT No.:** GB 454 6100 69
Date established: 2010 **Turnover:** £250,000 - £500,000
No.of Employees: 1 - 10 **Product Groups:** 80

Date of Accounts	Oct 11	Oct 10	Oct 09
Working Capital	-3	-7	-9
Fixed Assets	4	7	10
Current Assets	18	18	19

Dean & Wood Ltd
54 Boucher Place, Belfast, BT12 6HT
Tel: 028-9066 4935 **Fax:** 028-9068 3175
E-mail: sales@dean-wood.co.uk
Website: http://www.dean-wood.co.uk
Managers: C. Mcaleese (Comm)
Ultimate Holding Company: G & L BEIJER AB (SWEDEN)
Immediate Holding Company: DEAN & WOOD LIMITED
Registration no: 00467637 **Date established:** 1949
No.of Employees: 1 - 10 **Product Groups:** 66

Date of Accounts	Dec 11	Dec 10	Dec 09
Sales Turnover	44m	43m	33m
Pre Tax Profit/Loss	1m	1m	233
Working Capital	5m	5m	5m
Fixed Assets	2m	2m	2m
Current Assets	20m	20m	15m
Current Liabilities	3m	3m	2m

Decco Ltd
Prince Regent Road, Belfast, BT5 6RQ
Tel: 028-9079 8444 **Fax:** 028-9070 5000
E-mail: belfast.066@decco.co.uk
Bank(s): Ulster Bank
Managers: K. McElroy (Mgr)
Ultimate Holding Company: NEWBURY INVESTMENTS BV (NETHERLANDS)
Immediate Holding Company: DECCO LIMITED
Registration no: 00417021 **VAT No.:** GB 431 2745 75
Date established: 1946 **No.of Employees:** 11 - 20 **Product Groups:** 30, 63

Date of Accounts	Dec 11	Dec 10	Dec 09
Sales Turnover	94m	90m	88m
Pre Tax Profit/Loss	-485	5m	4m
Working Capital	21m	17m	14m
Fixed Assets	1m	3m	2m
Current Assets	34m	32m	30m
Current Liabilities	4m	5m	4m

Deloitte LLP
19 Bedford Street, Belfast, BT2 7EJ
Tel: 028-9032 2861 **Fax:** 028-9023 4786
E-mail: kferris@deloitte.co.uk
Website: http://www.deloitte.co.uk
Directors: G. Roberts (Snr Part)
Immediate Holding Company: DELOITTE LLP
Registration no: OC303675 **VAT No.:** GB 243 8771 41
Date established: 2003 **No.of Employees:** 101 - 250 **Product Groups:** 80

Date of Accounts	May 12	May 11	May 10
Sales Turnover	2329m	2098m	1953m
Pre Tax Profit/Loss	560m	510m	543m
Working Capital	221m	263m	365m
Fixed Assets	233m	242m	251m
Current Assets	713m	623m	623m
Current Liabilities	330m	300m	239m

Delta Communications
6 Knockbreda Park, Belfast, BT6 0HB
Tel: 028-9049 1212 **Fax:** 028-9049 1833
E-mail: marketing@deltacommunication.co.uk
Directors: R. Boyce (Prop)
Date established: 1971 **Turnover:** Up to £250,000
No.of Employees: 1 - 10 **Product Groups:** 35, 36, 37, 40, 48, 52, 67

Delta Print & Packaging
Factory 10 Blackstaff Road, Belfast, BT11 9DT
Tel: 028-9062 8626 **Fax:** 028-9061 3535
E-mail: info@deltapack.com
Website: http://www.deltapack.com
Bank(s): Bank of Ireland
Directors: C. Bradley (MD)
Managers: P. McGibben (Fin Mgr)
Ultimate Holding Company: DELTA PRINT & PACKAGING (PROPERTIES) LIMITED
Immediate Holding Company: DELTA PRINT AND PACKAGING LIMITED
Registration no: NI018004 **VAT No.:** GB 353 0621 85
Date established: 1984 **Turnover:** £20m - £50m
No.of Employees: 101 - 250 **Product Groups:** 27, 28, 48, 84

Date of Accounts	Jun 11	Jun 10	Jun 09
Sales Turnover	27m	24m	21m
Pre Tax Profit/Loss	430	2m	525
Working Capital	4m	3m	2m
Fixed Assets	6m	9m	7m
Current Assets	11m	10m	8m
Current Liabilities	2m	3m	1m

The Department For Employment & Learning

Adelaide House 39-49 Adelaide Street, Belfast, BT2 8FD
Tel: 028-9025 7777 **Fax:** 028-9025 7778
E-mail: derek.black.tea@nics.gov.uk
Website: http://www.delni.gov.uk
Directors: J. Smith (Fin), A. Shammon (Fin)
Managers: A. Armstrong, G. McConbille (Tech Serv Mgr), B. Harrison (Personnel), G. Trehern (Mktg Serv Mgr), D. Connor (Personnel), Gamble (I.T. Exec), A. Shannon
Immediate Holding Company: DEPARTMENT FOR EMPLOYMENT & LEARNING
Turnover: £500,000 - £1m **No.of Employees:** 251 - 500
Product Groups: 80

Dessian Products Ltd

9 Apollo Road, Belfast, BT12 6HP
Tel: 028-9038 1118 **Fax:** 028-9066 0741
E-mail: nbothwell@dessian.co.uk
Website: http://www.dessian.co.uk
Bank(s): Bank of Ireland
Directors: N. Bothwell (MD)
Managers: S. Drysdale (Mktg Serv Mgr), I. Knight (Tech Serv Mgr), S. Thurley (Prod Mgr), G. Cousins (Chief Acct), P. Barber (Personnel), A. Swift (Nat Sales Mgr)
Ultimate Holding Company: Gaffer (NI) Limited
Immediate Holding Company: DESSIAN PRODUCTS LIMITED
Registration no: NI019016 **VAT No.:** GB 422 2542 90
Date established: 1985 **Turnover:** £5m - £10m
No.of Employees: 51 - 100 **Product Groups:** 30

Date of Accounts	Dec 11	Dec 10	Dec 09
Sales Turnover	8m	8m	8m
Pre Tax Profit/Loss	105	60	48
Working Capital	714	663	581
Fixed Assets	1m	1m	1m
Current Assets	2m	2m	2m
Current Liabilities	383	370	585

John Devlin

557 Donegall Road, Belfast, BT12 6DX
Tel: 028-9032 1906 **Fax:** 028-9032 1906
Directors: T. Devlin (Prop)
Date established: 1975 **Turnover:** Up to £250,000
No.of Employees: 1 - 10 **Product Groups:** 28

Diageo

Gilbey House 58 Boucher Road, Belfast, BT12 6HR
Tel: 028-9068 2021 **Fax:** 028- 90660767
Website: http://www.diageo.com
Directors: C. Vandini (Mkt Research), J. Bell (Fin), J. Bell (Fin)
Managers: J. Gilmore (Mgr)
Ultimate Holding Company: DIAGEO PLC
Immediate Holding Company: Diageo Global Supply N.I. Logistics Limited
Registration no: NI021315 **Date established:** 1988
Turnover: £125m - £250m **No.of Employees:** 51 - 100
Product Groups: 62

Date of Accounts	Jun 11	Jun 10	Jun 09
Sales Turnover	167m	180m	178m
Pre Tax Profit/Loss	-19m	-9m	20m
Working Capital	52m	51m	59m
Fixed Assets	32m	55m	67m
Current Assets	96m	89m	94m
Current Liabilities	16m	15m	12m

Docherty Architescts

6 Kinnaird Street, Belfast, BT14 6BE
Tel: 028-9074 6386 **Fax:** 028-9035 1481
E-mail: info@doharch.com
Website: http://www.doharch.com
Directors: L. Docherty (Ptnr)
Immediate Holding Company: DOHERTY ARCHITECTS LIMITED
Registration no: NI613645 **VAT No.:** GB 253 0566 75
Date established: 2012 **No.of Employees:** 1 - 10 **Product Groups:** 84

Dolphin Plant Hire

Owen O'Cork Mill 288 Beersbridge Road, Belfast, BT5 5DX
Tel: 028-9058 0200 **Fax:** 028-9058 0400
E-mail: dolphinhire@aol.com
Website: http://www.dolphinplanthire.co.uk
Managers: K. Mcguire (District Mgr)
Immediate Holding Company: Dolphin Plant Hire Limited
Registration no: NI035308 **VAT No.:** GB 255 0663 65
Date established: 1998 **No.of Employees:** 1 - 10 **Product Groups:** 83

Date of Accounts	Dec 11	Dec 10	Dec 09
Working Capital	3	-2	-27
Fixed Assets	3	7	10
Current Assets	25	22	35

Dorman & Sons Ltd

Unit 2-2a Boucher Business Centre Apollo Road, Belfast, BT12 6HP
Tel: 028-9066 6700 **Fax:** 028-9066 1881
E-mail: info@dormans-print.co.uk
Website: http://www.dormans-print.co.uk
Bank(s): Northern Bank
Directors: P. Dorman (Dir), P. Dorman (Dir)
Immediate Holding Company: DORMAN & SONS LIMITED
Registration no: NI002328 **VAT No.:** GB 253 0867 61
Date established: 1947 **No.of Employees:** 11 - 20 **Product Groups:** 28, 80

Date of Accounts	Dec 11	Dec 10	Dec 09
Working Capital	96	94	78
Fixed Assets	1m	1m	1m
Current Assets	493	539	502

Dowds Kitchens & Bedrooms

2 Dargan Industrial Estate Dargan Cresent, Belfast, BT3 9JP
Tel: 028-9077 3333 **Fax:** 028-9077 3333
E-mail: dowdskitchens@btconnect.com
Directors: B. Dowds (Prop)
Date established: 1984 **Turnover:** Up to £250,000
No.of Employees: 1 - 10 **Product Groups:** 26, 63

Downhill Enterprises Ltd

62 Skegoneill Avenue, Belfast, BT15 3JQ
Tel: 028-9037 0165 **Fax:** 028-9037 0204
Bank(s): First Trust
Directors: H. Robinson (Prop), J. McDonald (Head), R. Orchard (MD)
Managers: H. Robinson (Transport), L. McKibben ()
Immediate Holding Company: DOWNHILL ENTERPRISES LIMITED
Registration no: NI018808 **VAT No.:** GB 422 2288 78
Date established: 1985 **No.of Employees:** 21 - 50 **Product Groups:** 52

Date of Accounts	Dec 10	Dec 09	Dec 08
Working Capital	11	53	71
Fixed Assets	263	280	298
Current Assets	310	361	458

John J Doyle Ltd

100 Great Patrick Street, Belfast, BT1 2LU
Tel: 028-9024 7864 **Fax:** 028-9032 7370
E-mail: sales@johnjdoyle.com
Website: http://www.johnjdoyle.com
Directors: J. Doyle (MD)
Immediate Holding Company: JOHN J. DOYLE LIMITED
Registration no: NI005866 **VAT No.:** GB 251 8378 48
Date established: 1964 **No.of Employees:** 11 - 20 **Product Groups:** 33, 52, 84

Date of Accounts	Mar 12	Mar 11	Mar 10
Working Capital	76	192	154
Fixed Assets	662	611	604
Current Assets	1m	1m	637

Dukes Hotel

65-67 University Street, Belfast, BT7 1FY
Tel: 028-9023 6666 **Fax:** 028-9023 7177
E-mail: info@dukesatqueens.com
Website: http://www.dukesatqueens.com
Managers: C. Mcnamara (Chief Mgr)
VAT No.: GB 255 3339 59 **Date established:** 1990
No.of Employees: 21 - 50 **Product Groups:** 69

Dunmurry Glass & Glazing Company

1 Glebe Road Dunmurry, Belfast, BT17 0PN
Tel: 028-9061 7682 **Fax:** 028-9061 7682
E-mail: dunmurryglass@email.com
Directors: A. Todd (Prop)
Date established: 1984 **No.of Employees:** 1 - 10 **Product Groups:** 30, 33, 35

Eason & Son N I Ltd

Unit 5a Meadows Retail Park Boucher Place, Belfast, BT12 6HT
Tel: 028-9038 1200 **Fax:** 028- 90682544
E-mail: ihunter@easons.com
Website: http://www.eason.ie
Bank(s): Northern Bank
Directors: A. Tinsley (MD), K. Brabazon (Ch), J. McKelvey (Dir), J. Cuddlipp (Sales & Mktg), I. Hunter (Dir), I. Hunter (Co Sec), M. Ryder (Dir)
Managers: T. Duggan (Personnel), R. Gourley (Buyer), G. Murray (Buyer), J. Dudley (I.T. Exec), S. Carter (Personnel), M. Mcnulty (Systems Mgr), T. Duggan, G. McKlown (Mktg Serv Mgr)
Ultimate Holding Company: EASON & SON LIMITED (EIRE)
Immediate Holding Company: EASON & SON (N.I.) LIMITED
Registration no: NF001324 **VAT No.:** GB 422 2966 60
Date established: 1965 **Turnover:** £20m - £50m
No.of Employees: 251 - 500 **Product Groups:** 64, 72

Date of Accounts	Jan 10	Jan 09	Jan 11
Sales Turnover	24m	25m	22m
Pre Tax Profit/Loss	1m	6m	-1m
Working Capital	21m	29m	2m
Fixed Assets	43m	33m	39m
Current Assets	24m	32m	10m
Current Liabilities	1m	1m	795

Ecom Software Ltd

Innovation Centre Queens Road, Belfast, BT3 9DT
Tel: 028-9073 7891 **Fax:** 028-9051 1201
E-mail: solutions@ecomsoftware.com
Website: http://www.ecomsoftware.com
Directors: R. Martin (MD)
Immediate Holding Company: ECOM SOFTWARE LIMITED
Registration no: NI037779 **Date established:** 2000
No.of Employees: 1 - 10 **Product Groups:** 44

Date of Accounts	Mar 12	Mar 11	Mar 10
Working Capital	185	181	137
Fixed Assets	9	3	4
Current Assets	347	242	185

Edm Ceco Holdings Ltd

1 Carryduff Business Park Comber Road, Carryduff, Belfast, BT8 8AN
Tel: 028-9081 5303 **Fax:** 028-9081 5449
E-mail: reception@spanwall.com
Website: http://www.edmspanwall.com
Bank(s): Northern Bank
Directors: K. Toner (MD)
Managers: A. Hannah (Chief Acct)
Immediate Holding Company: EDM-CECO LIMITED
Registration no: NI041059 **VAT No.:** GB 331 3026 13
Date established: 2001 **Turnover:** £2m - £5m **No.of Employees:** 21 - 50
Product Groups: 25, 33, 35

Date of Accounts	Jun 11	Jun 10	Jun 09
Working Capital	-12	-25	-13
Fixed Assets	2m	2m	2m
Current Assets	354	379	407

Eilis Og Hand Knits

11 Stewartstown Avenue, Belfast, BT11 9GE
Tel: 028-9062 3763 **Fax:** 028-9062 3763
E-mail: elizabeth@eilisog.com
Website: http://www.eilisog.com
Directors: E. Savage (Prop)
Turnover: Up to £250,000 **No.of Employees:** 1 - 10 **Product Groups:** 24, 61, 63

The Electrical Equipment Company (Edmondson Electrical Ltd)

58 Boucher Place, Belfast, BT12 6HT
Tel: 028-9066 1177 **Fax:** 028-9038 1502
Website: http://www.edmundson-electrical.co.uk/
Bank(s): National Westminster Bank Plc
Managers: R. Magill (District Mgr)
VAT No.: GB 338 2468 41 **Turnover:** £250,000 - £500,000
No.of Employees: 11 - 20 **Product Groups:** 66, 67

Elite Car Products

62b-62c Raby Street, Belfast, BT7 2GY
Tel: 028-9049 1292 **Fax:** 028-9049 1292
Website: http://www.elitecarcareproducts.co.uk
Managers: R. Nelson (Mgr)
Date established: 1969 **No.of Employees:** 1 - 10 **Product Groups:** 32

Elite Training Services

4th Floor Thomas House 14-16 James Street South, Belfast, BT2 7GA
Tel: 028-9031 6840 **Fax:** 028-9031 6841
E-mail: swalsh@elitetraining.com
Website: http://www.elitetraining.com
Bank(s): Northern Bank
Directors: S. Walsh (Prop), K. McKinley (MD)
Managers: M. Short (Mktg Serv Mgr)
Immediate Holding Company: ELITE TRAINING AND CONSULTANCY SERVICES LTD
Registration no: NI028063 **VAT No.:** GB 617 7288 14
Date established: 1994 **No.of Employees:** 11 - 20 **Product Groups:** 44, 86

Elliott Duffy Garrett

Royston House 34 Upper Queen Street, Belfast, BT1 6FD
Tel: 028-9024 5034 **Fax:** 028-9024 1337
E-mail: edg@edgsolicitors.co.uk
Website: http://www.edglegal.com
Directors: G. Wylie (Co Sec), M. Wilson (Snr Part)
Managers: A. Kerr, A. Dolaghan (Buyer)
Ultimate Holding Company: MACDONALD DETTWILER & ASSOCIATES LTD (CANADA)
Immediate Holding Company: BALLYLOAN LIMITED
Registration no: NI033648 **Date established:** 2005 **Turnover:** £2m - £5m
No.of Employees: 21 - 50 **Product Groups:** 80

Date of Accounts	Dec 10	Dec 09	Dec 08
Working Capital	396	396	396
Current Assets	396	396	396

Emo

Airport Road West, Belfast, BT3 9ED
Tel: 028-9045 4555 **Fax:** 028-9045 7371
E-mail: enquiries@emooil.com
Website: http://www.emooil.com
Bank(s): Ulster Bank
Directors: P. O'neill (MD)
Ultimate Holding Company: DCC PUBLIC LIMITED COMPANY
Immediate Holding Company: KANE FUELS LIMITED
Registration no: NI029148 **VAT No.:** GB 390 8133 48
Date established: 1995 **Turnover:** £125m - £250m
No.of Employees: 11 - 20 **Product Groups:** 31, 66

Date of Accounts	Mar 09
Working Capital	-192

Engine & Truck N I Ltd

Unit 4 M2 Trade Centre Duncrue Crescent, Belfast, BT3 9BW
Tel: 028-9077 1411 **Fax:** 028-9077 5085
E-mail: trevor.ets@btconnect.com
Website: http://www.enginetruck.co.uk
Directors: T. Buchanan (MD)
Immediate Holding Company: ENGINE & TRUCK (N.I.) LIMITED
Registration no: NI044225 **VAT No.:** GB 617 6679 04
Date established: 2002 **No.of Employees:** 11 - 20 **Product Groups:** 68

Date of Accounts	Sep 11	Sep 10	Sep 09
Working Capital	179	211	206
Fixed Assets	8	11	9
Current Assets	405	446	429

Engineering Distributors Ltd

13 Sydenham Road, Belfast, BT3 9DH
Tel: 028-9073 2111 **Fax:** 028-9073 2382
E-mail: peter.clarke@edlni.co.uk
Website: http://www.ceccltd.co.uk
Bank(s): Ulster Bank
Directors: P. Clarke (MD)
Managers: B. Mcclure (Sales Prom Mgr), D. Woods (Sales Prom Mgr), D. Boyd
Immediate Holding Company: ENGINEERING DISTRIBUTORS LIMITED
Registration no: NI009577 **Date established:** 1973 **Turnover:** £5m - £10m
No.of Employees: 11 - 20 **Product Groups:** 37, 66, 67

Date of Accounts	Dec 11	Dec 10	Dec 09
Sales Turnover	N/A	7m	6m
Pre Tax Profit/Loss	N/A	-15	29
Working Capital	2m	2m	2m
Fixed Assets	209	170	77
Current Assets	3m	3m	3m
Current Liabilities	N/A	187	83

Engineering Employers Federation

7 Heron Road, Belfast, BT3 9LE
Tel: 028-9059 5050 **Fax:** 028-9059 5059
E-mail: lbusby@eef-fed.org.uk
Website: http://www.eef.org.uk
Directors: P. Block (Dir)
Immediate Holding Company: IMAGE ZOO LIMITED
Registration no: NI049292 **Date established:** 2004
No.of Employees: 1 - 10 **Product Groups:** 87

Engineering Equipment Company N I Ltd

Unit 17 Kennedy Way Industrial Estate, Belfast, BT11 9DT
Tel: 028-9062 6621 **Fax:** 028-9061 6327
E-mail: info@eecni.com
Website: http://www.eecni.com
Managers: B. Bonner (Mgr)
Immediate Holding Company: ENGINEERING EQUIPMENT COMPANY (NORTHERN IRELAND) LIMITED
Registration no: NI010794 **VAT No.:** GB 283 0260 57
Date established: 1975 **Turnover:** £500,000 - £1m
No.of Employees: 1 - 10 **Product Groups:** 66, 67

Date of Accounts	Jul 11	Jul 10	Jul 09
Working Capital	608	407	453
Fixed Assets	157	167	176
Current Assets	608	519	574
Current Liabilities	N/A	112	122

John England Textiles Ltd

Portside Business Park Airport Road West, Belfast, BT3 9ED
Tel: 028-9073 6990 **Fax:** 028-9073 6989
E-mail: info@johnengland.com
Website: http://www.johnengland.com

see next page

John England Textiles Ltd - Cont'd

Directors: R. Saunders (Prop)
Immediate Holding Company: JOHN ENGLAND (TEXTILES) LIMITED
Registration no: NI006438 **VAT No.:** GB 251 9878 23
Date established: 1965 **No.of Employees:** 1 - 10 **Product Groups:** 63

Date of Accounts	Sep 11	Sep 10	Sep 09
Working Capital	395	380	378
Fixed Assets	798	816	837
Current Assets	540	613	542

Enterprise Equity Ltd

78a Dublin Road, Belfast, BT2 7HP
Tel: 028-9024 2500 **Fax:** 028-9024 2487
E-mail: info@eeni.com
Website: http://www.eeni.com
Directors: A. Langan (Grp Chief Exec)
Immediate Holding Company: ENTERPRISE EQUITY MANAGERS GP LIMITED
Registration no: NI063482 **VAT No.:** GB 517 0516 70
Date established: 2007 **Turnover:** Up to £250,000
No.of Employees: 1 - 10 **Product Groups:** 82

Date of Accounts	Mar 09
Working Capital	1
Current Assets	1

Ernst & Young Ltd

Bedford House 16-22 Bedford Street, Belfast, BT2 7DT
Tel: 028-9044 3500 **Fax:** 028-9044 3501
E-mail: mfinlay@uk.ey.com
Website: http://www.ey.com
Directors: M. Hall (Snr Part)
Ultimate Holding Company: ERNST & YOUNG EUROPE LLP
Immediate Holding Company: ERNST & YOUNG LIMITED
Registration no: 05458987 **VAT No.:** GB 524 1472 70
Date established: 2005 **Turnover:** £2m - £5m
No.of Employees: 101 - 250 **Product Groups:** 80

Date of Accounts	Jun 08	Jul 09	Jul 10
Sales Turnover	217	2m	4m
Pre Tax Profit/Loss	N/A	529	649
Working Capital	N/A	155	303
Fixed Assets	N/A	N/A	21
Current Assets	500	2m	2m
Current Liabilities	500	902	679

Errigle Inn

312-320 Ormeau Road, Belfast, BT7 2GE
Tel: 028-9064 1410 **Fax:** 028-9064 0772
E-mail: info@errigle.com
Website: http://www.errigleinn.com
Bank(s): Northern Bank
Directors: P. Mcgurran (Prop)
Registration no: NI006497 **VAT No.:** GB 252 4414 84
No.of Employees: 51 - 100 **Product Groups:** 62, 89

Eurocables Belfast Ltd

1 West Bank Road, Belfast, BT3 9JL
Tel: 028-9077 7771 **Fax:** 028-9077 0912
E-mail: sales@eurocables.co.uk
Website: http://www.eurocables.co.uk
Managers: G. Thompson (Chief Mgr), J. Watson (Comptroller)
Immediate Holding Company: EUROCABLES (BELFAST) LIMITED
Registration no: NI031739 **VAT No.:** GB 517 3565 42
Date established: 1996 **No.of Employees:** 21 - 50 **Product Groups:** 67

Date of Accounts	Dec 11	Dec 10	Dec 09
Working Capital	3m	3m	3m
Fixed Assets	191	179	159
Current Assets	3m	3m	3m

Europa Hotel

Great Victoria Street, Belfast, BT2 7AP
Tel: 028-9027 1066 **Fax:** 028-9032 7800
E-mail: res@eur.hastingshotels.com
Website: http://www.hastingshotels.com
Directors: F. Trevor (Pers), R. Stewart (I.T. Dir)
Managers: L. Carroll, R. Nagra (Personnel), O. Johnston, J. McGinn (Chief Mgr), M. Doyle
Immediate Holding Company: BELFCARD LIMITED
Registration no: NF003737 **Date established:** 2004 **Turnover:** £2m - £5m
No.of Employees: 101 - 250 **Product Groups:** 69

Executive Development Systems

89 The Park Millar Forge, Dundonald, Belfast, BT16 1QP
Tel: 028-9048 4565 **Fax:** 028-9048 2642
E-mail: michelle.eds@dnet.co.uk
Directors: M. Toner (Dir)
Immediate Holding Company: BALANCED LIFE SYSTEMS LTD
Registration no: NI047530 **Date established:** 2003
No.of Employees: 1 - 10 **Product Groups:** 86

Holiday Inn Ltd

106a University Street, Belfast, BT7 1HP
Tel: 028-9031 1909 **Fax:** 028-9031 1910
E-mail: mail@exhi-belfast.com
Website: http://www.ichotelsgroup.com/redirect?path=hd&hotelCode=bfsex
Managers: L. Madden (Mgr)
Immediate Holding Company: HOLIDAY INN LIMITED
Registration no: 05479356 **Date established:** 2005 **Turnover:** £5m - £10m
No.of Employees: 21 - 50 **Product Groups:** 69

F Mccready & Co. Ltd

123 Corporation Street, Belfast, BT1 3EJ
Tel: 028-9023 2842 **Fax:** 028-9023 6187
Directors: H. Elliott (Dir)
Immediate Holding Company: J. MCCREADY & COMPANY LIMITED
Registration no: NI001577 **Date established:** 1942 **Turnover:** £1m - £2m
No.of Employees: 1 - 10 **Product Groups:** 24, 74

Date of Accounts	Sep 11	Sep 10	Sep 09
Working Capital	394	520	632
Fixed Assets	1	2	2
Current Assets	681	695	722

F W Consulting

Unit 2 Bellsbridge Office Park 100 Ladas Drive, Belfast, BT6 9FH
Tel: 028-9046 9669 **Fax:** 028-9045 6308
Website: http://www.fwconsulting.co.uk
Directors: C. Malseed (MD)
VAT No.: GB 392 5990 07 **No.of Employees:** 1 - 10 **Product Groups:** 80, 81, 84

Farmlea Foods Ltd

SHS House 199 Airport Road West, Belfast, BT3 9ED
Tel: 028-9073 1777 **Fax:** 028-9042 7538
E-mail: sales@shs-group.co.uk
Website: http://www.shs-group.co.uk
Directors: J. Sloan (Ch), A. Richmond (Fin)
Managers: L. Gibson (Sec)
Ultimate Holding Company: SHS GROUP LIMITED
Immediate Holding Company: FARMLEA FOODS LTD
Registration no: NI016607 **VAT No.:** GB 311 2598 84
Date established: 1983 **Turnover:** £250m - £500m
No.of Employees: 101 - 250 **Product Groups:** 20, 62

Date of Accounts	Dec 10	Dec 11	Jan 09
Sales Turnover	262m	317m	287m
Pre Tax Profit/Loss	3m	4m	3m
Working Capital	8m	11m	6m
Fixed Assets	2m	122	2m
Current Assets	107m	95m	116m
Current Liabilities	10m	9m	15m

Farrans Construction Ltd

99 Kingsway Dunmurry, Belfast, BT17 9NU
Tel: 020-8055 1200 **Fax:** 028-9055 1309
E-mail: mail@whbeckett.com
Website: http://www.whbeckett.com
Directors: E. Sweeney (MD)
Managers: J. Jones (Chief Mgr), G. Moore (Chief Mgr)
Immediate Holding Company: FARRANS (CONSTRUCTION) LIMITED
Registration no: NI001654 **VAT No.:** GB 252 2574 72
Date established: 1943 **No.of Employees:** 251 - 500 **Product Groups:** 52

Date of Accounts	Dec 10	Dec 09	Dec 08
Working Capital	55	55	55
Current Assets	55	55	55

Fenix Solutions

Unit 3 Alexander House 478 Castlereagh Road, Belfast, BT5 6BQ
Tel: 028-9040 0400 **Fax:** 028-9400 4040
E-mail: service@fenixsolutions.co.uk
Website: http://www.fenixsolutions.co.uk
Directors: K. Mcguire (MD)
Immediate Holding Company: Fenix Solutions Ltd
Registration no: NI055759 **VAT No.:** GB 252 1606 90
Date established: 2005 **No.of Employees:** 11 - 20 **Product Groups:** 37, 38, 44, 48, 52, 67, 79, 80, 81, 84, 86

Date of Accounts	Mar 11	Mar 10	Mar 09
Working Capital	51	73	16
Fixed Assets	40	50	54
Current Assets	232	309	214

Finchmere Office Equipment Ltd

128 Lisburn Road, Belfast, BT9 6AH
Tel: 028-9048 5549 **Fax:** 028-9066 6107
E-mail: sales@finchmere.com
Website: http://www.finchmere.com
Directors: M. McCready (MD)
Managers: E. McIlwaine (Sales Prom Mgr), J. Bell, A. Preshaw (Comptroller)
Immediate Holding Company: FINCHMERE OFFICE EQUIPMENT LTD
Registration no: NI030405 **VAT No.:** GB 422 1558 80
Date established: 1996 **No.of Employees:** 1 - 10 **Product Groups:** 67

Date of Accounts	Mar 11	Mar 10	Mar 09
Working Capital	35	77	205
Fixed Assets	60	70	33
Current Assets	156	197	275

Fireplaces NI

Unit 30 Bloomfield Commercial Centre Connswater Shopping Centre(Just Behind Laser), Belfast, BT5 5DL
Tel: 028-9045 9482 **Fax:** 028-9045 2342
E-mail: fireplacesni@gmail.com
Website: http://www.castlestonefireplaces.co.uk
Directors: R. Speers (Prop), R. Spiers (Prop)
VAT No.: 286414540 **Turnover:** £250,000 - £500,000
No.of Employees: 1 - 10 **Product Groups:** 33

First Trust Bank plc

92 Ann Street, Belfast, BT1 3HH
Tel: 028-9024 2423 **Fax:** 028-9024 7712
E-mail: lorna.j.hill@aib.ie
Website: http://www.firsttrustbank.co.uk
Directors: J. Magee (Dir), T. Mcdaid (MD), J. McGuckan (Dir), R. Toland (Dir)
Managers: L. Hill, J. McKnight (Mgr)
Immediate Holding Company: FIRST TRUST LEASING (NO.4) N.I. LIMITED
Registration no: NI022444 **Date established:** 1989 **Turnover:** £2m - £5m
No.of Employees: 1 - 10 **Product Groups:** 82

Date of Accounts	Dec 11	Dec 10	Dec 09
Sales Turnover	2m	3m	4m
Pre Tax Profit/Loss	-613	-819	-141
Working Capital	3m	4m	4m
Fixed Assets	236	37	33
Current Assets	4m	4m	5m
Current Liabilities	3	2	1m

Fitch Chartered Accountants

Gordon Street Mews 27-29 Gordon Street, Belfast, BT1 2LG
Tel: 028-9032 4271 **Fax:** 028-9032 3798
E-mail: office@fitch.tv
Website: http://www.fitch.tv
Directors: M. Fitch (Prop)
Immediate Holding Company: FITCH CONSULTING LTD
Registration no: NI043515 **VAT No.:** GB 254 1494 63
Date established: 2002 **Turnover:** £500,000 - £1m
No.of Employees: 11 - 20 **Product Groups:** 80

Flexform Ltd

Unit 1 34 Montgomery Road, Belfast, BT6 9HL
Tel: 028-9079 2155 **Fax:** 028-9079 9031
E-mail: info@cablespecialists.co.uk
Website: http://www.cablespecialists.co.uk
Directors: N. Harper (MD)
Ultimate Holding Company: E.J. HARPER & CO. LIMITED
Immediate Holding Company: FLEXFORM LTD
Registration no: NI031339 **Date established:** 1996
No.of Employees: 1 - 10 **Product Groups:** 37, 44, 67

Date of Accounts	Apr 11	Apr 10	Apr 09
Working Capital	183	150	123
Fixed Assets	21	28	36
Current Assets	305	300	251

Flogas

Airport Road West Sydenham, Belfast, BT3 9ED
Tel: 028-9073 2611 **Fax:** 028-9073 2020
E-mail: info@flogasni.com
Website: http://www.flogasni.com
Bank(s): Ulster Bank
Directors: R. Martin (MD)
Ultimate Holding Company: DCC PUBLIC LIMITED COMPANY
Immediate Holding Company: FLOGAS UK LIMITED
Registration no: 00993638 **VAT No.:** GB 286 8120 36
Date established: 1970 **No.of Employees:** 101 - 250 **Product Groups:** 66

Date of Accounts	Mar 12	Mar 11	Mar 10
Sales Turnover	171m	176m	145m
Pre Tax Profit/Loss	3m	10m	9m
Working Capital	-15m	-45m	-45m
Fixed Assets	82m	79m	80m
Current Assets	42m	44m	43m
Current Liabilities	6m	6m	6m

Fone Zone Telecommunications

Grove House 145-149 Donegall Passage, Belfast, BT7 1DT
Tel: 028-9096 0366 **Fax:** 028-9023 2679
E-mail: info@barclaycomms.com
Website: http://www.barclaycomms.com
Directors: A. Mccourt (Dir), J. Stweart (Mkt Research)
Managers: C. Blayney, J. McCreary, J. Campbell (Personnel)
Immediate Holding Company: Barclay Communications Ltd
Registration no: NI053702 **Date established:** 2005
No.of Employees: 51 - 100 **Product Groups:** 37, 44, 79

Francis Hanna & Co.

32-36 May Street, Belfast, BT1 4NZ
Tel: 028-9024 3901 **Fax:** 028-9024 4215
E-mail: gdaly@fhanna.co.uk
Website: http://www.fhanna.co.uk
Bank(s): Bank of Ireland
Directors: G. Daly (Ptnr), L. Johnston (Snr Part)
Ultimate Holding Company: SAVILLS COMMERCIAL (IRELAND) LIMITED
Immediate Holding Company: COMERTON & HILL LLP
Date established: 2011 **No.of Employees:** 21 - 50 **Product Groups:** 80

Date of Accounts	Dec 10	Dec 09	Dec 08
Sales Turnover	296	364	912
Pre Tax Profit/Loss	-44	3	417
Working Capital	573	607	591
Fixed Assets	18	28	41
Current Assets	594	621	681
Current Liabilities	16	13	89

Fredrick Jones Ltd

17 Napier Street, Belfast, BT12 5FE
Tel: 028-9032 4467 **Fax:** 028-9032 5252
E-mail: tony.jones@fjones.com
Website: http://www.fjones.com
Bank(s): Ulster Bank
Directors: T. Jones (MD)
Immediate Holding Company: F P & T PROPERTY COMPANY LIMITED
Registration no: NI014485 **VAT No.:** GB 251 9944 36
Date established: 1980 **Turnover:** £5m - £10m **No.of Employees:** 21 - 50
Product Groups: 27, 45, 66

Date of Accounts	Jul 09	Jul 08
Working Capital	289	289
Current Assets	289	289

Fridge Spares N I Ltd

Wildflower Way, Belfast, BT12 6TA
Tel: 028-9066 5999 **Fax:** 028-9066 5888
E-mail: don@fridge-spares.com
Website: http://www.fridge-spares.com
Directors: D. Munn (Dir)
Ultimate Holding Company: FRIDGE SPARES WHOLESALE LTD
Immediate Holding Company: FRIDGE SPARES (N.I.) LIMITED
Registration no: NI034841 **Date established:** 1998
No.of Employees: 1 - 10 **Product Groups:** 40, 66

Date of Accounts	Dec 11	Dec 10	Dec 09
Working Capital	1m	1m	1m
Fixed Assets	N/A	N/A	28
Current Assets	1m	1m	2m

Albert Fry Associates

125 Ormeau Road, Belfast, BT7 1SH
Tel: 028-9032 2025 **Fax:** 028-9032 2057
E-mail: office@albertfryassociates.com
Website: http://www.albertfryassociates.com
Directors: J. Kerr (MD)
Immediate Holding Company: ALBERT FRY ASSOCIATES LTD
Registration no: NI020489 **Date established:** 1987
No.of Employees: 1 - 10 **Product Groups:** 35

Date of Accounts	Nov 11	Nov 10	Nov 09
Working Capital	239	296	345
Fixed Assets	115	124	145
Current Assets	350	487	525

Fujitsu Technology Solutions

110-112 Holywood Road, Belfast, BT4 1NU
Tel: 08433-544200 **Fax:** 028-9068 2168
E-mail: maurice.wright@uk.fujitsu.com
Website: http://www.fujitsu.com
Bank(s): Bank of Ireland
Directors: W. Mckenna (Chief Op Offcr), A. Goss (Fin)
Managers: B. Robertson, L. Murray (Personnel)
Ultimate Holding Company: SIEMENS AG (GERMANY)
Immediate Holding Company: ATOS IT SOLUTIONS AND SERVICES LIMITED
Registration no: 01203466 **VAT No.:** GB 576 9836 68
Date established: 1975 **Turnover:** £250m - £500m
No.of Employees: 11 - 20 **Product Groups:** 44

Date of Accounts	Dec 11	Sep 10	Sep 09
Sales Turnover	612m	434m	540m
Pre Tax Profit/Loss	159m	-3m	-14m
Working Capital	-84m	-36m	-106m
Fixed Assets	215m	168m	192m
Current Assets	159m	212m	227m
Current Liabilities	110m	72m	86m

G A Smythe Business Machines Ltd

Unit 6 Harbour Court Heron Road, Belfast, BT3 9HB
Tel: 028-9020 7000 **Fax:** 028-9020 7001
E-mail: sbm@ukonline.co.uk
Website: http://www.sbmonline.co.uk

Directors: G. Bell (MD)
Immediate Holding Company: G.A. SMYTHE (BUSINESS MACHINES) LIMITED
Registration no: NI007988 **VAT No.:** GB 252 6739 43
Date established: 1970 **Turnover:** Up to £250,000
No.of Employees: 1 - 10 **Product Groups:** 44, 67

Date of Accounts	Jul 11	Jul 10	Jul 09
Working Capital	62	101	76
Fixed Assets	121	115	125
Current Assets	153	178	169

G M K Graphics
57 Cromwell Road, Belfast, BT7 1JY
Tel: 028-9032 7905 **Fax:** 028-9043 8893
E-mail: gerry.gmk@btconnect.com
Website: http://www.gmkgraphics.com
Directors: G. Mckervey (Prop)
VAT No.: GB 282 9589 03 **Date established:** 1975
No.of Employees: 1 - 10 **Product Groups:** 23, 28, 30

G & O Services
Upper Dunmurry Lane Kilwee Business Park, Dunmurry, Belfast, BT17 0HD
Tel: 028-9030 1121 **Fax:** 028-9062 3077
Directors: G. McGivern (Prop)
VAT No.: GB 286 9801 07 **No.of Employees:** 11 - 20 **Product Groups:** 48

G P S Colour Graphics Ltd
Alexander Road, Belfast, BT6 9HP
Tel: 028-9070 2020 **Fax:** 028-9079 8463
E-mail: sales@gpscolour.co.uk
Website: http://www.gpscolour.co.uk
Bank(s): Bank of Ireland
Directors: L. Bell (Sales & Mktg), I. Mccurry (MD)
Managers: G. Taylor (Personnel), J. Burrows (Purch Mgr), M. Miskelly (Chief Acct)
Immediate Holding Company: G.P.S. COLOUR GRAPHICS LIMITED
Registration no: R0000524 **VAT No.:** GB 251 9131 77
Date established: 2012 **Turnover:** £1m - £2m **No.of Employees:** 21 - 50
Product Groups: 28

Date of Accounts	Jan 12	Jan 11	Jan 10
Sales Turnover	6m	N/A	N/A
Pre Tax Profit/Loss	298	N/A	N/A
Working Capital	-258	-365	181
Fixed Assets	5m	5m	3m
Current Assets	2m	2m	1m
Current Liabilities	557	N/A	N/A

Gabbey Business Machines 1979 Ltd
Unit 34 East Belfast Enterprise Park 308 Albertbridge Road, Belfast, BT5 4GX
Tel: 028-9045 1517 **Fax:** 028-9045 9516
Website: http://www.gabbeybusiness.co.uk
Directors: A. Irvine (Dir)
Immediate Holding Company: GABBEY BUSINESS MACHINES (1979) LIMITED
Registration no: NI013926 **Date established:** 1979
No.of Employees: 1 - 10 **Product Groups:** 64, 67

Date of Accounts	Dec 11	Dec 10	Dec 09
Working Capital	41	39	27
Fixed Assets	10	13	18
Current Assets	170	160	171

Gardiner Security Ltd
6 Enterprise House Boucher Place, Belfast, BT12 6HT
Tel: 028-9068 2994 **Fax:** 028-9066 9932
Website: http://www.gardinersecurity.co.uk
Managers: J. Lanyon (Mgr)
Immediate Holding Company: GARDINER SECURITY LIMITED
Registration no: 04124719 **Date established:** 2000
No.of Employees: 1 - 10 **Product Groups:** 37, 40

William Gardiner & Sons Ltd
Unit 14 Alanbrooke Park Industrial Estate Alanbrooke Road, Belfast, BT6 9HB
Tel: 028-9079 7360 **Fax:** 028-9079 0586
E-mail: peter@wgardiner-sons.co.uk
Website: http://www.wgardiner-sons.co.uk
Directors: P. Gardiner (Dir)
Immediate Holding Company: WILLIAM GARDINER & SONS LIMITED
Registration no: NI004133 **Date established:** 1958
No.of Employees: 1 - 10 **Product Groups:** 20, 40, 41

Date of Accounts	Apr 12	Apr 11	Apr 10
Working Capital	38	59	110
Fixed Assets	N/A	12	19
Current Assets	63	84	217

General Consumer Council For N I
116 Holywood Road, Belfast, BT4 1NY
Tel: 028-9067 2488 **Fax:** 028-9067 5501
E-mail: info@consumercouncil.org.uk
Website: http://www.consumercouncil.org.uk
Directors: A. Mckeown (Grp Chief Exec)
Managers: J. Donnelly, D. Magee (Personnel)
No.of Employees: 21 - 50 **Product Groups:** 81, 85

Geodelft Environmental
Unit 1c-1d Castlereagh Business Park 478 Castlereagh Road, Belfast, BT5 6BQ
Tel: 028-9040 2000 **Fax:** 028-9181 6634
E-mail: info@geodelft-ire.co.uk
Website: http://www.geodelft-ire.co.uk
Directors: P. Papafio (MD)
Managers: D. Colter (Chief Mgr), P. Papasio (Mgr)
Immediate Holding Company: CULLAMORE LIMITED
Registration no: NI045872 **Date established:** 2006
No.of Employees: 1 - 10 **Product Groups:** 54

Gilbarco Veeder Root plc
Unit 7 18 West Bank Road, Belfast, BT3 9JL
Tel: 028-9078 2782 **Fax:** 028-9077 1108
E-mail: jim.anderson@gilbarco.com
Website: http://gilbarco.com
Managers: J. Anderson (Mgr)
VAT No.: GB 239 1370 65 **Turnover:** £1m - £2m **No.of Employees:** 1 - 10
Product Groups: 39, 42, 68

Gilchrist & Company
90 Donegall Pass, Belfast, BT7 1BX
Tel: 028-9023 2453 **Fax:** 028-9032 6700
E-mail: gilchristsigns@ukonline.co.uk
Managers: T. Curry (Mgr)
VAT No.: GB 287 0602 52 **Date established:** 1994
No.of Employees: 1 - 10 **Product Groups:** 36, 49

Gilligan & Partners Ltd
Suite B 174-184 Ormeau Road, Belfast, BT7 2ED
Tel: 028-9023 2841 **Fax:** 028-9024 7104
E-mail: post@gilligans.co.uk
Website: http://www.gilligan.co.uk
Directors: G. Coulter (MD), D. Whyte (Fin)
Immediate Holding Company: GILLIGAN & PARTNERS LIMITED
Registration no: NI048755 **VAT No.:** GB 252 0183 00
Date established: 2003 **No.of Employees:** 1 - 10 **Product Groups:** 84

Date of Accounts	Mar 11	Mar 10	Mar 09
Working Capital	189	307	286
Fixed Assets	29	40	56
Current Assets	314	363	379

Gilmore Signs Ltd
41 Middlepath Street, Belfast, BT5 4BG
Tel: 028-9045 5419 **Fax:** 028-9045 8451
E-mail: sales@gilmoresigns.com
Website: http://www.gilmoresigns.com
Directors: M. Connolly (MD)
Managers: A. Gibson (Fin Mgr)
Ultimate Holding Company: ACADEMY LITHOPLATES LIMITED
Immediate Holding Company: GILMORE SIGNS LIMITED
Registration no: NI030992 **VAT No.:** GB 254 5185 56
Date established: 1996 **No.of Employees:** 1 - 10 **Product Groups:** 23, 28, 30, 37

Date of Accounts	Mar 11	Mar 10	Mar 09
Working Capital	103	115	114
Fixed Assets	101	126	160
Current Assets	179	222	206

Glenhill Merchants
Musgrave Park Industrial Estate Stockmans Way, Belfast, BT9 7ET
Tel: 028-9066 9444 **Fax:** 028-9066 3217
E-mail: enquiries@glenhill.co.uk
Website: http://www.glenhill.co.uk
Directors: B. Farnan (Dir)
Managers: A. McCrory, K. Toland (Sales & Mktg Mg), M. O'Reilly (Buyer)
Ultimate Holding Company: Glenhill Merchants Limited
Immediate Holding Company: JUNIPER MERCHANTS LIMITED
Registration no: NI017277 **VAT No.:** GB 390 7644 28
Date established: 1984 **No.of Employees:** 21 - 50 **Product Groups:** 63

Date of Accounts	Dec 11	Dec 10	Dec 09
Working Capital	734	734	734
Current Assets	734	734	734

Grafton Recuitment
49 Queens Square, Belfast, BT1 3FG
Tel: 028-9032 9032 **Fax:** 028-9032 6032
E-mail: hq@grafton-group.com
Website: http://www.graftonrecruitment.com
Bank(s): First Trust Bank plc
Directors: A. Mizzoni (MD), J. Kilbarne (Grp Ch), M. Glenfield (Dir), K. Belshaw (Co Sec), J. Nelson (Fin), C. Hamill (Sales), K. Belshaw (Grp MD)
Managers: J. Scates (Mgr)
Immediate Holding Company: GRAFTON RECRUITMENT LIMITED
Registration no: NF002589 **Date established:** 1985
Turnover: £50m - £75m **No.of Employees:** 51 - 100 **Product Groups:** 80, 81, 87

Grant Thornton Ltd
Waters Edge Clarendon Dock, Belfast, BT1 3BH
Tel: 028-9031 5500 **Fax:** 028-9031 4036
E-mail: webmaster@grant-thornton.co.uk
Website: http://www.grantthornton.co.uk
Directors: M. Allen (Ptnr)
Ultimate Holding Company: GRANT THORNTON UK LLP
Immediate Holding Company: GRANT THORNTON LIMITED
Registration no: 02917818 **Date established:** 1994
No.of Employees: 101 - 250 **Product Groups:** 80

Guinness Northern Ireland Ltd
Adelaide Industrial Estate Boucher Road, Belfast, BT12 6HR
Tel: 028-9068 2021 **Fax:** 028-9066 0767
Website: http://www.guinness.com
Bank(s): Ulster Bank
Directors: M. McCan (MD), R. Patterson (Pers)
Managers: B. Clenhehan, D. Stewart (Fin Mgr)
Ultimate Holding Company: DIAGEO PLC
Immediate Holding Company: JOHN MENZIES (G.B.) LIMITED
Registration no: NI003755 **VAT No.:** GB 217 1127 03
Date established: 1990 **Turnover:** £125m - £250m
No.of Employees: 51 - 100 **Product Groups:** 62

Gull Leisure Wear
246c Newtownards Road, Belfast, BT4 1HB
Tel: 028-9045 8112 **Fax:** 028-9045 8112
Directors: G. Killough (Prop)
VAT No.: GB 497 1318 21 **Date established:** 1985 **Turnover:** £1m - £2m
No.of Employees: 1 - 10 **Product Groups:** 24

H Downey & Co.
65 Eglantine Avenue, Belfast, BT9 6EW
Tel: 028-9258 4022 **Fax:** 028-9095 0693
E-mail: accountants@ntlworld.com
Website: http://www.accountants.co.nr
Directors: L. Downey (Prop)
Immediate Holding Company: LARKFIELD DEVELOPMENTS LIMITED
Registration no: NI052154 **VAT No.:** GB 283 0674 51
Date established: 1986 **Turnover:** Up to £250,000
No.of Employees: 1 - 10 **Product Groups:** 80

Date of Accounts	Jan 11	Jan 10	Jan 09
Working Capital	-2	-2	-5
Current Assets	3	5	8

H M G Powder Coatings Ltd
Dill Road Castlereagh Industrial Estate, Belfast, BT6 9HU
Tel: 028-9079 4930 **Fax:** 028-9040 1187
E-mail: sales@hmgpowdercoatings.co.uk
Website: http://www.hmgpowdercoatings.co.uk
Directors: D. Corry (Dir), N. Corry (Fin)
Managers: R. McIlorum (Mktg Serv Mgr)
Immediate Holding Company: H.M.G. POWDER COATINGS LIMITED
Registration no: NI021911 **VAT No.:** GB 517 0509 67
Date established: 1988 **Turnover:** £500,000 - £1m
No.of Employees: 21 - 50 **Product Groups:** 32

Date of Accounts	Dec 11	Dec 10	Dec 09
Working Capital	1m	1m	918
Fixed Assets	383	287	288
Current Assets	2m	2m	1m

Hall Black Douglas
152 Albertbridge Road, Belfast, BT5 4GS
Tel: 028-9045 0681 **Fax:** 028-9073 8117
E-mail: info@hallblackdouglas.co.uk
Website: http://www.hallblackdouglas.co.uk
Directors: R. Hall (Dir)
Immediate Holding Company: Hall Black Douglas Limited
Registration no: NI064121 **VAT No.:** GB 422 2572 61
Date established: 2007 **No.of Employees:** 11 - 20 **Product Groups:** 52, 84

Date of Accounts	Aug 11	Aug 10	Aug 09
Working Capital	-64	-7	-271
Fixed Assets	1m	1m	1m
Current Assets	341	382	438

Hamilton Process Engineering
Unit B2 Dundonald Enterprise Park Carrowreagh Road, Dundonald, Belfast, BT16 1QT
Tel: 028-9057 0010 **Fax:** 028-9057 0009
E-mail: hamilton.engineering@dnet.co.uk
Website: http://www.dnet.co.uk
Directors: J. Hamilton (Ptnr)
Immediate Holding Company: NDM AGENCIES LTD
Registration no: NI051507 **Date established:** 1998
No.of Employees: 1 - 10 **Product Groups:** 20, 40, 41

Date of Accounts	Oct 11	Oct 10	Oct 09
Working Capital	47	26	6
Fixed Assets	N/A	3	6
Current Assets	67	58	34
Current Liabilities	16	20	5

Hamiltons Shipping
210 Clarendon Road, Belfast, BT1 3BG
Tel: 028-9035 7000 **Fax:** 028-9053 3222
E-mail: containers@hamiltonshipping.com
Website: http://www.hamiltonshipping.com
Directors: G. Hamilton (Dir), G. Jess (Comm)
Managers: K. Craig (Mgr), T. Newman (Sales Prom Mgr), J. Silcock (Mgr)
Immediate Holding Company: ALEX M HAMILTON & CO (TRAVEL) LIMITED
Registration no: NI024294 **VAT No.:** GB 375 8663 03
Date established: 1982 **Turnover:** £10m - £20m
No.of Employees: 11 - 20 **Product Groups:** 76

Handel Export Consulting
17 Malone Road, Belfast, BT9 6RT
Tel: 028-9092 3378 **Fax:** 028-9092 3334
E-mail: suzanne@handelexport.com
Website: http://www.handelexport.com
Directors: S. Hill (Dir)
Ultimate Holding Company: MAGMA PRODUCTIONS LIMITED
Immediate Holding Company: ULYSSES FILMS NORTHERN IRELAND LIMITED
Registration no: NI055920 **Date established:** 2005
No.of Employees: 1 - 10 **Product Groups:** 80

Harland & Wolfe Heavy Industries Ltd
Queens Island, Belfast, BT3 9DU
Tel: 028-9045 8456 **Fax:** 028-9045 8515
E-mail: sales@harland-wolff.com
Website: http://www.harland-wolff.com
Bank(s): Bank of Ireland
Directors: C. O'Neill (Fin)
Managers: H. McIlvenny (Personnel), R. McIlwaine (Tech Serv Mgr), R. Cooper, D. McVeigh (Sales Prom Mgr), D. Calder
Ultimate Holding Company: FRED OLSEN ENERGY ASA (NORWAY)
Immediate Holding Company: HARLAND AND WOLFF HEAVY INDUSTRIES LIMITED
Registration no: NI038867 **Date established:** 2000
Turnover: £20m - £50m **No.of Employees:** 101 - 250 **Product Groups:** 39

Date of Accounts	Dec 11	Dec 10	Dec 09
Sales Turnover	25m	6m	21m
Pre Tax Profit/Loss	2m	-4m	5m
Working Capital	12m	10m	15m
Fixed Assets	5m	5m	5m
Current Assets	19m	16m	20m
Current Liabilities	3m	4m	3m

R Harris Systems Ltd
89 University Street, Belfast, BT7 1HP
Tel: 028-9032 6802 **Fax:** 028-9032 5269
E-mail: pframe@harrissystems.co.uk
Website: http://www.harrissystems.co.uk
Directors: P. Frame (MD)
Immediate Holding Company: R. HARRIS (SYSTEMS) LIMITED
Registration no: NI007614 **Date established:** 1969
No.of Employees: 11 - 20 **Product Groups:** 80

Date of Accounts	Jul 11	Jul 10	Jul 09
Working Capital	141	144	150
Fixed Assets	132	144	164
Current Assets	265	276	237

Hastings Hotels Group Ltd
Upper Newtownards Road, Belfast, BT4 3LP
Tel: 028-9075 1066 **Fax:** 028-9048 0240
E-mail: info@hastinghotels.com
Website: http://www.hastingshotels.com
Bank(s): Bank of Ireland
Directors: H. Hastings (MD), J. Maguire (Grp Mktg), A. Martin (Sales), J. Toner (Dir)
Managers: J. Harvey (Grp Mktg Mgr), S. Hamill (Grp Purch Mgr), J. Shields (Chief Acct)
Registration no: NI008164 **VAT No.:** GB 251 9940 44
Date established: 1971 **Turnover:** £20m - £50m
No.of Employees: 501 - 1000 **Product Groups:** 69

Hawaiian Tropic
Grosvenor Road, Belfast, BT12 5AP
Tel: 028-9031 2518
Website: http://www.hotspottravelzone.com
No.of Employees: 21 - 50 **Product Groups:** 32, 63

Heartsine Medical Equipment Mnfrs
Queens Island, Belfast, BT3 9DU
Tel: 028-9053 4210 **Fax:** 028- 90534211
Website: http://www.heartsine.com
Managers: L. McCullough (Mgr)
Ultimate Holding Company: FRED OLSEN ENERGY ASA (NORWAY)
Immediate Holding Company: HARLAND AND WOLFF VLCC LIMITED
Registration no: NI047575 **Date established:** 2001
No.of Employees: 21 - 50 **Product Groups:** 38, 67

Date of Accounts	Dec 11	Dec 10	Dec 09
Sales Turnover	25m	6m	21m
Pre Tax Profit/Loss	2m	-4m	5m
Working Capital	12m	10m	15m
Fixed Assets	5m	5m	5m
Current Assets	19m	16m	20m
Current Liabilities	3m	4m	3m

Heat Ltd
27-29 Sydenham Road, Belfast, BT3 9DH
Tel: 028-9046 9000 **Fax:** 028-9046 9799
E-mail: info@heat.co.uk
Website: http://www.heat.co.uk
Directors: R. Rodgers (Dir), R. Coleman (Grp Mktg), M. Emery (Sales), J. Morgan (Pers)
Managers: K. Adams (Comm), D. Vennard (Fin Mgr), A. Mathers (Tech Serv Mgr)
Ultimate Holding Company: EAGA NI LIMITED
Immediate Holding Company: N.I. HEATING COMPANY LIMITED - THE
Registration no: NI038213 **Date established:** 2000
Turnover: £20m - £50m **No.of Employees:** 251 - 500 **Product Groups:** 37

Helm Housing Association
38-52 Lisburn Road, Belfast, BT9 6AA
Tel: 028-9032 0485 **Fax:** 028-9033 0402
E-mail: office@helmhousing.org
Website: http://www.helmhousing.org
Managers: P. Morgan, P. Balmer (Tech Serv Mgr), A. Harris (Mgr), R. Mullholland (Personnel)
Registration no: NP000163 **Date established:** 1986
No.of Employees: 1 - 10 **Product Groups:** 80, 84

Heyn Forktrucks Solutions
Unit 1-2 Duncrue Street, Belfast, BT3 9AQ
Tel: 028-9074 1000 **Fax:** 028-9074 1010
E-mail: boss.trucks@heyn.co.uk
Website: http://niforklifts.co.uk
Bank(s): Northern Bank
Managers: T. Mulholland (Chief Mgr)
Ultimate Holding Company: HEYN HANDLING SOLUTIONS LTD
Immediate Holding Company: HEYN ENGINEERING (NI) LIMITED
Registration no: NI038423 **VAT No.:** GB 255 2089 61
Date established: 2000 **No.of Employees:** 11 - 20 **Product Groups:** 67, 68

Date of Accounts	Sep 11	Sep 10	Sep 09
Working Capital	1m	1m	1m
Fixed Assets	157	112	140
Current Assets	3m	3m	2m

G Heyn & Sons Ltd
1 Corry Place, Belfast, BT3 9AH
Tel: 028-9035 0000 **Fax:** 028-9035 0011
E-mail: davidc@heyn.co.uk
Website: http://www.heyn.co.uk
Directors: D. Clarke (Ch), D. Duncan (Sales & Mktg), D. Clarke (MD), A. Toland (Tech Serv)
Ultimate Holding Company: NI050301
Immediate Holding Company: G. HEYN & SONS LIMITED
Registration no: NI001996 **VAT No.:** GB 252 4493 36
Date established: 1946 **Turnover:** £500,000 - £1m
No.of Employees: 21 - 50 **Product Groups:** 72, 74, 76

Hill Bellacott
22 Great Victoria Street, Belfast, BT2 7BA
Tel: 028-9044 2000 **Fax:** 028-9044 2050
E-mail: mail@hillvellacott.com
Website: http://www.hillvellacott.com
Directors: D. Wilkinson (Ptnr)
Immediate Holding Company: HILL VELLACOTT LLP
Registration no: NC000515 **VAT No.:** GB 311 3258 06
Date established: 2009 **Turnover:** £250,000 - £500,000
No.of Employees: 1 - 10 **Product Groups:** 80

Hillside Textiles
11 Falcon Road, Belfast, BT12 6RD
Tel: 028-9066 6122 **Fax:** 028-9066 1633
E-mail: richard@hillside-textiles.com
Website: http://www.nireland.com
Directors: P. Mills (Snr Part)
Immediate Holding Company: BELFAST TILE COMPANY LIMITED - THE
Registration no: NI028411 **VAT No.:** GB 256 1640 66
Date established: 1994 **Turnover:** Up to £250,000
No.of Employees: 1 - 10 **Product Groups:** 23, 24

Date of Accounts	Dec 08	Dec 07	Dec 04
Working Capital	300	366	174
Fixed Assets	32	29	71
Current Assets	393	497	363

Hilti GT Britain Ltd
Woodstock Link, Belfast, BT6 8AE
Tel: 08448-156254 **Fax:** 0800-886200
Website: http://www.hilti.co.uk
Ultimate Holding Company: HILTI AG (LIECHTENSTEIN)
Immediate Holding Company: HILTI (GT.BRITAIN) LIMITED
Registration no: 00479786 **Date established:** 1950
Turnover: £75m - £125m **No.of Employees:** 11 - 20 **Product Groups:** 35, 37, 48

Date of Accounts	Dec 11	Dec 10	Dec 09
Sales Turnover	87m	65m	66m
Pre Tax Profit/Loss	838	766	-379
Working Capital	12m	12m	15m
Fixed Assets	6m	5m	5m
Current Assets	45m	33m	25m
Current Liabilities	10m	6m	4m

Hood Mcgowan Kirk
Boucher Centre Boucher Road, Belfast, BT12 6HR
Tel: 028-9066 7932 **Fax:** 028-9066 5810
E-mail: info@hmkni.com
Website: http://www.hmkni.com
Bank(s): First Trust
Directors: A. Murton (Ptnr)
Immediate Holding Company: HOUSEWORKS (NI) LIMITED
Registration no: NF002877 **VAT No.:** GB 252 5371 97
Date established: 2005 **No.of Employees:** 11 - 20 **Product Groups:** 80, 84

Hospital Services Ltd
2 Wildflower Way, Belfast, BT12 6TA
Tel: 028-9038 1481 **Fax:** 028-9066 2476
E-mail: sales@hsl.ie
Website: http://www.hsl.ie
Directors: M. Elliot (Dir)
Managers: J. Anderson (Sales Prom Mgr), T. Remenyik (I.T. Exec)
Immediate Holding Company: HOSPITAL SERVICES LIMITED
Registration no: NI005155 **VAT No.:** GB 252 4984 43
Date established: 1962 **Turnover:** £5m - £10m **No.of Employees:** 11 - 20
Product Groups: 67

Date of Accounts	Mar 11	Mar 10	Mar 09
Sales Turnover	7m	9m	N/A
Pre Tax Profit/Loss	1m	782	226
Working Capital	4m	3m	3m
Fixed Assets	2m	2m	3m
Current Assets	5m	5m	5m
Current Liabilities	1m	1m	884

Howden UK Ltd
Channel Commercial Park Queens Road, Belfast, BT3 9DT
Tel: 028-9045 7251 **Fax:** 028-9073 2980
E-mail: reception@howden.com
Website: http://www.howden.com
Directors: W. Thomson (MD)
Ultimate Holding Company: CHARTER INTERNATIONAL PLC (JERSEY)
Immediate Holding Company: HOWDEN UK LIMITED
Registration no: R0000173 **VAT No.:** GB 254 5764 40
Date established: 1998 **Turnover:** £20m - £50m
No.of Employees: 51 - 100 **Product Groups:** 40, 48

Date of Accounts	Dec 11	Dec 10	Dec 09
Sales Turnover	54m	50m	74m
Pre Tax Profit/Loss	10m	7m	6m
Working Capital	79m	70m	65m
Fixed Assets	4m	5m	5m
Current Assets	101m	97m	90m
Current Liabilities	11m	18m	14m

Hyder Consulting (UK) Limited
The Mount 2 Woodstock Link, Belfast, BT6 8DD
Tel: 028-9073 0182 **Fax:** 028-9073 0186
E-mail: joe.mcclintock@hyderconsulting.com
Website: http://www.hyderconsulting.com
Directors: A. Proctor (Dir)
Ultimate Holding Company: Hyder P.L.C.
Immediate Holding Company: Hyder Infrastructure Developments Ltd
Registration no: 02212959 **Turnover:** £125m - £250m
No.of Employees: 101 - 250 **Product Groups:** 54, 84

Hynds Architectural Systems Ltd
69-73 Glenmachan Street, Belfast, BT12 6JB
Tel: 028-9082 3700 **Fax:** 028-9082 3701
E-mail: michaelb@hynds.com
Website: http://www.hynds.com
Directors: M. Bryne (MD), M. Brown (Dir), D. Hynds (Pers)
Immediate Holding Company: HYNDS ARCHITECTURAL SYSTEMS LIMITED
Registration no: NI018556 **VAT No.:** GB 353 1898 37
Date established: 1985 **No.of Employees:** 21 - 50 **Product Groups:** 30

I B M UK Ltd
4 Bruce Street, Belfast, BT2 7JA
Tel: 028-9051 2500 **Fax:** 028-9051 2501
E-mail: uk_crc@uk.ibm.com
Website: http://www.ibm.com/uk
Directors: P. Clarke (Prop)
Ultimate Holding Company: INTERNATIONAL BUSINESS MACHINES CORP (USA)
Immediate Holding Company: IBM UNITED KINGDOM LIMITED
Registration no: 00741598 **Date established:** 1962
Turnover: £75m - £125m **No.of Employees:** 1 - 10 **Product Groups:** 44

Date of Accounts	Dec 11	Dec 10	Dec 09
Sales Turnover	3974m	3846m	3717m
Pre Tax Profit/Loss	328m	299m	170m
Working Capital	1121m	980m	729m
Fixed Assets	917m	915m	754m
Current Assets	2722m	2427m	2121m
Current Liabilities	1412m	1447m	817m

I C A Motor Products
146 University Street, Belfast, BT7 1HH
Tel: 028-9024 2191 **Fax:** 028-9033 3866
Managers: P. Doran (Mgr)
Immediate Holding Company: Braketech Ireland Ltd
Registration no: NI047081 **VAT No.:** GB 375 8248 15
Date established: 2003 **Turnover:** £250,000 - £500,000
No.of Employees: 1 - 10 **Product Groups:** 33, 35, 68

Date of Accounts	Aug 11	Aug 10	Aug 09
Working Capital	-35	-35	-35

I C C Computers & Support N I Ltd
236 Upper Newtownards Road, Belfast, BT4 3EU
Tel: 028-9065 5788 **Fax:** 028-9067 3433
E-mail: alex@marketsolutionsni.co.uk
Website: http://www.iccsupport.co.uk
Directors: A. Adams (Dir)
Immediate Holding Company: ICC (Computers & Support) NI Ltd
Registration no: NI041568 **Date established:** 2001
No.of Employees: 1 - 10 **Product Groups:** 44

Date of Accounts	Dec 10	Dec 09	Dec 08
Working Capital	-25	-24	-25
Fixed Assets	1	1	1
Current Assets	10	10	9

I C C Information Ltd
Wellington Park, Belfast, BT9 6DJ
Tel: 028-9055 9559 **Fax:** 028-9055 0072
E-mail: jane@iccinformationni.com
Website: http://www.iccinformationni.com
Managers: J. Sweeney (Mgr)
Immediate Holding Company: ICC INFORMATION LIMITED
Registration no: NF003592 **VAT No.:** GB 392 5699 01
Date established: 2001 **Turnover:** £500,000 - £1m
No.of Employees: 1 - 10 **Product Groups:** 81, 82

I C S Computing Ltd
205 Airport Road West, Belfast, BT3 9ED
Tel: 028-9045 4166 **Fax:** 028-9045 2651
E-mail: sales@icscomputing.co.uk
Website: http://www.icscomputing.co.uk
Directors: D. Mawhinney (Sales), G. Jordan (Co Sec), M. Erskine (Dir)
Managers: S. Wilson (Purch Mgr), P. McCorkell (Tech Serv Mgr), C. Covin (Personnel), J. Kelly (Fin Mgr)
Ultimate Holding Company: W.& R. BARNETT LIMITED
Immediate Holding Company: ICS COMPUTING LIMITED
Registration no: FC022318 **Date established:** 2000
Turnover: £10m - £20m **No.of Employees:** 101 - 250 **Product Groups:** 44

Date of Accounts	Mar 08	Mar 07	Mar 06
Pre Tax Profit/Loss	2m	807	365
Working Capital	610	2m	2m
Fixed Assets	4m	4m	4m
Current Assets	4m	5m	4m
Current Liabilities	2m	2m	2m

Impact Training
16 Lanark Way, Belfast, BT13 3BH
Tel: 028-9033 9910 **Fax:** 028-9024 2777
E-mail: florence@impactraining.com
Website: http://www.impacttraining.com
Managers: F. Irvine (Mgr)
Immediate Holding Company: IMPACT ENTERPRISES (NORTHERN IRELAND) LIMITED
Registration no: NI047574 **Date established:** 2003
No.of Employees: 21 - 50 **Product Groups:** 86

Date of Accounts	Mar 12	Mar 11	Mar 10
Working Capital	-42	-42	-46
Fixed Assets	357	365	373
Current Assets	42	42	33

Impro Printing
Dargan Road, Belfast, BT3 9JU
Tel: 028-9077 7795 **Fax:** 028-9077 9099
E-mail: accounts@impro.co.uk
Website: http://www.impro.co.uk
Directors: C. Irvin (Ptnr), E. Culley (Snr Part)
Managers: K. Patton
Registration no: 00009002 **VAT No.:** GB 517 6981 13
Date established: 1974 **No.of Employees:** 21 - 50 **Product Groups:** 28, 81

Independent News & Media (NI) Ltd
Independent News & Media (Northern Ireland)
124-144 Royal Avenue, Belfast, BT1 1EB
Tel: 028-9026 4000 **Fax:** 028-9055 4506
E-mail: writeback@belfasttelegraph.co.uk
Website: http://www.belfasttelegraph.co.uk
Bank(s): First Trust Bank, Belfast
Directors: K. Simpson (Fin), M. Brophey (MD), M. Reid (Tech Serv), R. McClean (Mkt Research), S. Mann (Adv), T. Foster (Chief Op Offcr)
Managers: E. Curran, M. Lindsay, R. Lyttle, D. McGrogan (Personnel)
Ultimate Holding Company: Independent News & Media Plc
Immediate Holding Company: Independent News & Media Ltd
Registration no: 03899652 **VAT No.:** GB 248 1845 43
Date established: 1870 **Turnover:** £50m - £75m
No.of Employees: 501 - 1000 **Product Groups:** 28

Industrial Floorcare Machines
Unit 31-33 North City Business Centre 2 Duncairn Gardens, Belfast, BT15 2GG
Tel: 028-9074 9669 **Fax:** 028-9074 9667
E-mail: sales@cleanireland.com
Website: http://www.cleanireland.com
Directors: G. Cullen (Dir)
Immediate Holding Company: INDUSTRIAL FLOORCARE MACHINES LTD
Registration no: NI607250 **Date established:** 2011
Turnover: £250,000 - £500,000 **No.of Employees:** 11 - 20
Product Groups: 36, 40

Inform Communications N I
13 University Street, Belfast, BT7 1FY
Tel: 028-9023 3550 **Fax:** 028-9033 1017
E-mail: info@informcommunications.com
Website: http://www.informcommunications.com
Directors: L. Beers (MD)
Immediate Holding Company: INFORM COMMUNICATIONS PLC
Registration no: 02644647 **VAT No.:** GB 454 5065 50
Date established: 1991 **Turnover:** £500,000 - £1m
No.of Employees: 1 - 10 **Product Groups:** 81

Date of Accounts	Sep 11	Sep 10	Sep 09
Sales Turnover	790	1m	1m
Pre Tax Profit/Loss	-190	105	86
Working Capital	-223	18	-51
Fixed Assets	61	26	17
Current Assets	236	385	227
Current Liabilities	98	175	52

Initial Electronic Security Systems Ltd
213 Castlereagh Road, Belfast, BT5 5FH
Tel: 028-9045 9441 **Fax:** 028-9073 8677
E-mail: belfast@ies.uk.com
Website: http://www.ies.uk.com
Managers: A. Wetherall (Mgr), C. McClinton (District Mgr), R. Woods (District Mgr), T. Cullen (Sales Prom Mgr), S. Dempster
Ultimate Holding Company: Rentokil Initial Plc
Immediate Holding Company: SHORROCK LIMITED
Registration no: 00715168 **Date established:** 1994
Turnover: £20m - £50m **No.of Employees:** 21 - 50 **Product Groups:** 52

Irish Feeds Ltd (Divison of British Salt)
Sinclair Wharf, Belfast, BT3 9AA
Tel: 028-9074 4915 **Fax:** 028-9074 8607
E-mail: pshields@irishfeeds.com
Website: http://www.irishfeeds.com

Managers: P. Shields (Mgr)
Ultimate Holding Company: CHESHIRE SALT HOLDINGS LIMITED
Immediate Holding Company: IRISH FEEDS LIMITED
Registration no: NI010146 **VAT No.:** GB 255 9521 40
Date established: 1974 **Turnover:** £2m - £5m **No.of Employees:** 1 - 10
Product Groups: 17, 62, 77

Date of Accounts	Dec 10	Dec 09	Dec 08
Sales Turnover	3m	3m	2m
Pre Tax Profit/Loss	124	87	48
Working Capital	445	351	256
Fixed Assets	10	16	25
Current Assets	947	1m	819
Current Liabilities	70	60	83

Irish Waste Services Ltd

94-96 Hillsborough Road Carryduff, Belfast, BT8 8HT
Tel: 028-9081 0000 **Fax:** 028-9081 0001
E-mail: info@irishwaste.net
Website: http://www.irishwaste.net
Bank(s): First Trust
Directors: N. McGarth (Co Sec)
Managers: W. Devine (Ops Mgr), R. Mulgrew (Personnel)
Immediate Holding Company: IRISH WASTE SERVICES LIMITED
Registration no: NI008172 **VAT No.:** GB 251 8848 37
Date established: 1971 **Turnover:** £2m - £5m **No.of Employees:** 21 - 50
Product Groups: 54

Date of Accounts	Nov 11	Nov 10	Nov 09
Sales Turnover	8m	6m	6m
Pre Tax Profit/Loss	135	350	613
Working Capital	1m	981	1m
Fixed Assets	3m	4m	4m
Current Assets	3m	3m	3m
Current Liabilities	971	916	868

Isherwood & Ellis

15 Malone Road, Belfast, BT9 6RT
Tel: 028-9066 3291 **Fax:** 028-9068 2727
E-mail: architects@isherwood-ellis.com
Website: http://www.isherwood-ellis.com
Directors: K. Fleming (Ptnr)
Immediate Holding Company: ISHERWOOD + ELLIS LLP
Registration no: NC000076 **VAT No.:** GB 255 9355 31
Date established: 2005 **Turnover:** Up to £250,000
No.of Employees: 11 - 20 **Product Groups:** 80, 84

Island Fork Lifts Ltd

Unit D Dargan Court Dargan Crescent, Belfast, BT3 9JP
Tel: 028-9077 0937 **Fax:** 028-9077 0812
E-mail: info@islandforklifts.co.uk
Website: http://www.islandforklifts.co.uk
Managers: N. Mckee (Mgr)
Immediate Holding Company: ISLAND FORKLIFTS LIMITED
Registration no: NI016670 **Date established:** 1983
No.of Employees: 1 - 10 **Product Groups:** 35, 39, 45

Date of Accounts	May 11	May 10	May 09
Working Capital	112	204	144
Fixed Assets	610	683	800
Current Assets	502	544	450

J C P Consulting Ltd

Lomond House 85-87 Holywood Road, Belfast, BT4 3BD
Tel: 028-9022 1100 **Fax:** 028-9022 1101
E-mail: consult@jcpconsulting.co.uk
Website: http://www.jcpconsulting.co.uk
Bank(s): Northern Bank
Directors: J. Kingsmore (MD), W. Carson (Fin)
Managers: P. Hanna (Tech Serv Mgr)
Immediate Holding Company: JCP CONSULTING LIMITED
Registration no: NI042055 **VAT No.:** GB 252 0339 92
Date established: 2001 **Turnover:** Up to £250,000
No.of Employees: 21 - 50 **Product Groups:** 80, 84

Date of Accounts	May 11	May 10	May 09
Working Capital	1m	1m	1m
Fixed Assets	246	352	437
Current Assets	2m	2m	2m

J H C Hardware Ltd

145-151 Dargan Crescent, Belfast, BT3 9JP
Tel: 028-9077 7912 **Fax:** 028-9077 5463
E-mail: info@jhchardware.com
Website: http://www.jhchardware.com
Bank(s): First Trust
Directors: A. Campbell (MD), D. McMullan (Fin)
Managers: D. Watson (Buyer), E. McNeill (Tech Serv Mgr), B. Lynch (Personnel)
Immediate Holding Company: J.H.C.HARDWARE LIMITED
Registration no: NI007231 **VAT No.:** GB 252 6234 76
Date established: 1968 **Turnover:** £5m - £10m **No.of Employees:** 21 - 50
Product Groups: 66

Date of Accounts	Dec 11	Dec 10	Dec 09
Sales Turnover	8m	9m	10m
Pre Tax Profit/Loss	345	374	243
Working Capital	4m	4m	4m
Fixed Assets	4m	4m	4m
Current Assets	6m	6m	6m
Current Liabilities	633	937	1m

J P R

Sylvan House 232-240 Belmont Road, Belfast, BT4 2AW
Tel: 028-9076 0066 **Fax:** 028-9076 0011
E-mail: mail@jprni.com
Website: http://www.jprni.com
Directors: J. Wells (MD)
Immediate Holding Company: JPR ni Ltd
Registration no: NI040714 **Date established:** 2001 **Turnover:** £1m - £2m
No.of Employees: 1 - 10 **Product Groups:** 81

Date of Accounts	Apr 12	Apr 11	Apr 10
Working Capital	61	68	47
Fixed Assets	26	17	23
Current Assets	284	242	196

J Tohill & Co.

799b Lisburn Road, Belfast, BT9 7GX
Tel: 028-9038 1898 **Fax:** 028-9038 1897
E-mail: j.tohill@ntlworld.com
Directors: J. Tohill (Prop)
Date established: 1987 **No.of Employees:** 1 - 10 **Product Groups:** 35

James Grant & Co. Ltd

6 Windsor Business Park Boucher Place, Belfast, BT12 6HT
Tel: 028-9068 6959 **Fax:** 028-9066 1107
E-mail: info@jamesgrantltd.co.uk
Website: http://www.bluewaterspas.co.uk
Directors: P. Grant (Dir)
Immediate Holding Company: James Grant & Co. (Belfast) Ltd
Registration no: NI005187 **VAT No.:** GB 252 0256 96
Date established: 1962 **No.of Employees:** 1 - 10 **Product Groups:** 66

James H Givan Ltd

Unit 5 Prince Regent Commercial Centre 8 Prince Regent Road, Belfast, BT5 6QT
Tel: 028-9040 1626 **Fax:** 028-9040 1509
Website: http://www.givan.com
Directors: J. Givan (Dir)
Immediate Holding Company: JAMES H. GIVAN LIMITED
Registration no: NI013592 **VAT No.:** GB 331 6731 74
Date established: 1979 **No.of Employees:** 1 - 10 **Product Groups:** 20

Date of Accounts	Mar 11	Mar 10	Mar 09
Working Capital	-70	-212	-294
Fixed Assets	483	487	515
Current Assets	258	269	243

Jamison & Green Ltd

102-108 Ann Street, Belfast, BT1 3HU
Tel: 028-9032 2444 **Fax:** 028-9033 0491
E-mail: sales@jamisonandgreen.co.uk
Website: http://www.jamisonandgreen.co.uk
Bank(s): Bank of Ireland
Directors: G. Mayne (Fin), K. Mayne (Fin), P. Hirst (MD)
Managers: D. Anderson (Mktg Serv Mgr)
Immediate Holding Company: JAMISON & GREEN, LIMITED
Registration no: R0000395 **VAT No.:** GB 251 8484 49
Date established: 2016 **Turnover:** £2m - £5m **No.of Employees:** 21 - 50
Product Groups: 63, 66, 74

Date of Accounts	Dec 11	Dec 10	Dec 09
Working Capital	226	-47	78
Fixed Assets	253	116	126
Current Assets	545	598	698

C & H Jefferson

Norwich Union House 7 Fountain Street, Belfast, BT1 5EA
Tel: 028-9032 9545 **Fax:** 028-9024 4644
E-mail: law@chjefferson.co.uk
Website: http://www.chjefferson.co.uk
Directors: G. Jones (Snr Part)
Managers: T. Aiken (Personnel)
Immediate Holding Company: C & H Jefferson Secretarial Services Limited
Registration no: NI053812 **Date established:** 2005
No.of Employees: 51 - 100 **Product Groups:** 80

Jim Morrison Architects

31 Cricklewood Park, Belfast, BT9 5GW
Tel: 028-9066 0017 **Fax:** 028-9020 1710
E-mail: jim.morrison4@ntlworld.com
Website: http://www.jimmorrisonarchitects.com
Directors: J. Morrison (Prop)
No.of Employees: 1 - 10 **Product Groups:** 84

John Morgan & Sons Ltd

30 Island Street, Belfast, BT4 1DH
Tel: 028-9073 2333 **Fax:** 028-9045 7402
E-mail: ops@morgandocumentsecurity.com
Website: http://www.morgandocumentsecurity.com
Bank(s): Ulster Bank
Directors: W. Morgan (MD)
Ultimate Holding Company: JOHN MORGAN HOLDINGS LIMITED
Immediate Holding Company: JOHN MORGAN & SONS LIMITED
Registration no: NI003479 **VAT No.:** GB 251 9934 39
Date established: 1955 **No.of Employees:** 11 - 20 **Product Groups:** 72

Date of Accounts	Mar 11	Mar 10	Mar 09
Working Capital	2m	2m	2m
Fixed Assets	536	487	535
Current Assets	3m	4m	3m

John Thompson & Sons Ltd

35-39 York Road, Belfast, BT15 3GW
Tel: 028-9035 1321 **Fax:** 028-9267 7202
E-mail: info@thompson.co.uk
Website: http://www.thompson.co.uk
Directors: D. Billington (Dir), P. Magee (Fin)
Ultimate Holding Company: BHH LIMITED
Immediate Holding Company: JOHN THOMPSON & SONS, LIMITED
Registration no: R0000447 **VAT No.:** GB 336 3983 32
Date established: 2006 **No.of Employees:** 101 - 250 **Product Groups:** 20, 62

Date of Accounts	Jul 11	Jul 10	Jul 09
Sales Turnover	212m	177m	186m
Pre Tax Profit/Loss	5m	5m	5m
Working Capital	8m	7m	6m
Fixed Assets	10m	10m	12m
Current Assets	44m	35m	28m
Current Liabilities	7m	6m	4m

Johns Elliot Solicitors

40 Linenhall Street, Belfast, BT2 8BA
Tel: 028-9032 6881 **Fax:** 028-9024 8236
E-mail: vera.woods@johnselliot.com
Website: http://www.johnselliot.co.uk
Bank(s): Northern Bank
Directors: V. Woods (Ptnr), G. Ord (Ptnr)
Immediate Holding Company: SIR M MACDONALD ASSOCIATES
Registration no: NI073901 **VAT No.:** GB 251 8935 42
Date established: 1984 **Turnover:** £250,000 - £500,000
No.of Employees: 11 - 20 **Product Groups:** 80

Date of Accounts	Dec 11	Dec 10
Working Capital	73	612
Fixed Assets	2m	397
Current Assets	514	911

Johnstone's Paints Ltd

Unit 7 Boucher Cresent, Belfast, BT12 6HU
Tel: 028-9066 4772 **Fax:** 028-9066 4783
Website: http://www.johnstontrade.com
Managers: N. Bradshaw (Mgr)
Ultimate Holding Company: P P G INDUSTRIES INC (USA)
Immediate Holding Company: JOHNSTONE'S PAINTS LIMITED
Registration no: 00513910 **Date established:** 1952
Turnover: £500,000 - £1m **No.of Employees:** 1 - 10 **Product Groups:** 42, 66

Date of Accounts	Dec 11	Dec 10	Dec 09
Working Capital	41m	41m	41m
Fixed Assets	1m	1m	1m
Current Assets	42m	42m	42m
Current Liabilities	N/A	9	9

Jurys Inn

Great Victoria Street, Belfast, BT2 7AP
Tel: 028-9053 3500 **Fax:** 028-9053 3511
E-mail: ryan_foster@jurysinns.com
Website: http://www.jurysdoyle.com
Managers: R. Foster (Mgr), D. McCormack (Personnel)
Immediate Holding Company: BELFCARD LIMITED
Registration no: 06063534 **Date established:** 2004
No.of Employees: 51 - 100 **Product Groups:** 69

Kainos Software Ltd

4-6 Upper Crescent, Belfast, BT7 1NT
Tel: 028-9057 1100 **Fax:** 028-9023 6935
E-mail: info@kainos.com
Website: http://www.kainos.com
Bank(s): Bank of Ireland
Directors: B. Mooney (MD)
Immediate Holding Company: KAINOS SOFTWARE LIMITED
Registration no: NI019370 **VAT No.:** GB 454 5988 02
Date established: 1986 **Turnover:** £10m - £20m
No.of Employees: 101 - 250 **Product Groups:** 44

Date of Accounts	Mar 11	Mar 10	Mar 09
Sales Turnover	17m	16m	21m
Pre Tax Profit/Loss	111	13	2m
Working Capital	6m	6m	5m
Fixed Assets	2m	2m	2m
Current Assets	13m	8m	10m
Current Liabilities	5m	2m	4m

Keeble N I Ltd

Unit 13 Derriaghy Industrial Estate, Dunmurry, Belfast, BT17 9HU
Tel: 028-9030 6888 **Fax:** 028-9060 3905
E-mail: info@keebleni.com
Website: http://www.keebleni.com
Directors: N. Mcnally (MD)
Immediate Holding Company: KEEBLE (N.I.) LIMITED
Registration no: NI021246 **VAT No.:** GB 517 9783 17
Date established: 1988 **No.of Employees:** 1 - 10 **Product Groups:** 28

Date of Accounts	Dec 11	Dec 10	Dec 09
Working Capital	19	-9	-35
Fixed Assets	163	186	195
Current Assets	231	204	183

Graham Kells

71 Greystown Avenue, Belfast, BT9 6UH
Tel: 028-9061 3195
Directors: G. Kells (Prop)
No.of Employees: 1 - 10 **Product Groups:** 20, 40, 41

Kennedy Fitzgerald & Associates

3 Eglantine Place, Belfast, BT9 6EY
Tel: 028-9066 1632 **Fax:** 028-9066 4532
E-mail: info@kfani.com
Website: http://www.kfani.com
Directors: J. Sempey (Ptnr), P. Acheson (Ptnr)
Immediate Holding Company: KENNEDY FITZGERALD ARCHITECTS LLP
Registration no: NC000425 **VAT No.:** GB 252 8420 69
Date established: 2008 **No.of Employees:** 21 - 50 **Product Groups:** 84

Date of Accounts	Mar 12	Mar 11	Mar 10
Working Capital	824	745	662
Fixed Assets	52	63	80
Current Assets	1m	948	1m

Kennedy Recruitment Ltd

31-May Street, Belfast, BT1 4NG
Tel: 028-9033 0555 **Fax:** 028-9033 2878
E-mail: info@kennedyrecruitment.co.uk
Website: http://www.kennedyrecruitment.co.uk
Bank(s): First Trust
Directors: E. Kennedy (Dir)
Managers: C. Wallace (Mgr)
Immediate Holding Company: KENNEDY RECRUITMENT LTD
Registration no: NI032852 **Date established:** 1997
No.of Employees: 11 - 20 **Product Groups:** 80

The King's Hall Complex

Balmoral, Belfast, BT9 6GW
Tel: 028-9066 5225 **Fax:** 028-9066 1264
E-mail: info@kingshall.co.uk
Website: http://www.kingshall.co.uk
Directors: C. Mcdonald (Grp Chief Exec), M. Guest (MD)
Immediate Holding Company: King's Hall Exhibition & Conference Centre Ltd - The
Registration no: NI033140 **No.of Employees:** 21 - 50 **Product Groups:** 69

Kingsberry Fuels Ltd

Herdman Channel Road, Belfast, BT3 9BL
Tel: 028-9035 1444 **Fax:** 028-9075 1706
E-mail: kwilson@kingsberryfuels.com
Website: http://www.kingsberryfuels.com
Directors: K. Wilson (Dir), E. Rebbeck (Dir), K. Wilson (MD)
Managers: A. Grant (Mgr)
Ultimate Holding Company: W.& R. BARNETT LIMITED
Immediate Holding Company: BIO SEARCH (N.I.) LIMITED
Registration no: NI030035 **Date established:** 1989 **Turnover:** £1m - £2m
No.of Employees: 21 - 50 **Product Groups:** 66

Kingsway Decorators

91a Stockmans Lane, Belfast, BT9 7JD
Tel: 028-9038 1427 **Fax:** 028-9038 1795
E-mail: admin@kingswaycontractors.com
Website: http://www.nireland.com
Bank(s): First Trust
Managers: S. Cunningham (Fin Mgr), C. Murphy (Mgr), C. Murphy (Mgr), M. McCormick (Char Surv)

see next page

Kingsway Decorators - Cont'd
Immediate Holding Company: KINGSWAY PAINTING & CONTRACTING CO. LIMITED
Registration no: NI020242 **VAT No.:** GB 253 4229 73
Date established: 1987 **Turnover:** Up to £250,000
No.of Employees: 21 - 50 **Product Groups:** 52

Kitchen Master Ni Ltd

11 Comber Road Carryduff, Belfast, BT8 8AN
Tel: 028-9081 4777 **Fax:** 028-9081 2881
E-mail: brian@kitchenmaster-ni.com
Website: http://www.kitchenmaster-ni.com
Bank(s): Northern Bank
Directors: B. O'kane (MD)
Ultimate Holding Company: Kitchenmaster (Holdings) Limited
Immediate Holding Company: KITCHENMASTER (N.I.) LIMITED
Registration no: NI018324 **VAT No.:** GB 392 6948 01
Date established: 1985 **No.of Employees:** 11 - 20 **Product Groups:** 32

Date of Accounts	Aug 11	Aug 10	Aug 09
Working Capital	1m	979	844
Fixed Assets	94	104	111
Current Assets	2m	1m	1m

Kone Lifts

31 Clarendon Road, Belfast, BT1 3DD
Tel: 028-9031 2099 **Fax:** 028-9024 6604
E-mail: info@kone.com
Website: http://www.kone.com
Directors: J. Graham (Mkt Research), S. Adair (MD)
Registration no: NI003522 **VAT No.:** GB 251 9949 26
Turnover: £10m - £20m **No.of Employees:** 1 - 10 **Product Groups:** 45

KPMG UK Ltd

Stokes House 17 College Square East, Belfast, BT1 6DH
Tel: 028-9024 3377 **Fax:** 028-9089 3893
E-mail: jon.darcy@kpmg.ie
Website: http://www.kpmg.ie
Directors: J. Darcy (Snr Part)
Ultimate Holding Company: KPMG EUROPE LLP
Immediate Holding Company: KPMG UK LIMITED
Registration no: 03580549 **VAT No.:** 256136366 **Date established:** 1998
No.of Employees: 51 - 100 **Product Groups:** 80, 84

Date of Accounts	Sep 11	Sep 10	Sep 09
Sales Turnover	698m	632m	624m
Pre Tax Profit/Loss	655	593	584
Working Capital	1m	847	419
Current Assets	23m	21m	25m
Current Liabilities	22m	20m	20m

L R G Sound & Vision Ltd

171-175 Albertbridge Road, Belfast, BT5 4PS
Tel: 028-9045 1381 **Fax:** 028-9073 1478
E-mail: info@lrgsoundandvision.com
Website: http://www.lrgsoundandvision.com
Directors: R. Marsh (MD)
Managers: J. Anderson (Sales Prom Mgr)
Immediate Holding Company: L.R.G. SOUND & VISION LIMITED
Registration no: NI012527 **VAT No.:** GB 311 2747 93
Date established: 1978 **No.of Employees:** 1 - 10 **Product Groups:** 61, 83

Date of Accounts	Jan 11	Jan 10	Jan 09
Working Capital	-181	-157	-67
Fixed Assets	4	5	5
Current Assets	74	93	163

Labour Relations Agency

2-16 Gordon Street Belfast, Belfast, BT1 2LG
Tel: 028-9032 1442 **Fax:** 028-9033 0827
E-mail: info@lra.org.uk
Website: http://www.lra.org.uk
Directors: W. Patterson (Grp Chief Exec)
Managers: A. Peake (Sales Admin), F. Davey, H. Grove (Personnel), Y. Belle
No.of Employees: 51 - 100 **Product Groups:** 81

Lagan Cement Group Ltd

19 Clarendon Road, Belfast, BT1 3BG
Tel: 028-9026 1000 **Fax:** 028-9026 1010
E-mail: finance@lagan-group.com
Website: http://www.lagan-group.com
Directors: D. Canavan (Dir), F. Montgomery (Tech Serv), S. McCann (Fin)
Managers: R. Acheson (Personnel)
Immediate Holding Company: Lagan Holdings Limited
Registration no: NI049714 **Date established:** 2004 **Turnover:** £5m - £10m
No.of Employees: 21 - 50 **Product Groups:** 14, 17, 33

Date of Accounts	Mar 11	Mar 10	Mar 09
Sales Turnover	5m	328m	321m
Pre Tax Profit/Loss	16m	-4m	15m
Working Capital	11m	63m	61m
Fixed Assets	3m	77m	101m
Current Assets	36m	121m	150m
Current Liabilities	14m	33m	40m

Lagan Construction

21-23 Sydenham Road, Belfast, BT3 9HA
Tel: 028-9045 5531 **Fax:** 028-9045 8940
E-mail: colin.loughran@laganconstruction.com
Website: http://www.laganconstruction.com
Bank(s): Ulster
Directors: A. Hanna (Tech Serv), C. Loughran (Comm), S. Martin (Fin)
Managers: J. Sennel (I.T. Exec), P. Gillon (Personnel)
Ultimate Holding Company: Lagan Holdings Limited
Immediate Holding Company: CHARLES BRAND LIMITED
Registration no: NI013689 **VAT No.:** GB 517 1601 74
Date established: 1979 **Turnover:** £75m - £125m
No.of Employees: 51 - 100 **Product Groups:** 51

Date of Accounts	Mar 09	Mar 08	Mar 07
Working Capital	969	969	969
Current Assets	969	969	969

Langston Trade Frames

Unit 16 Alanbrooke Park Industrial Estate Alanbrooke Road, Belfast, BT6 9HB
Tel: 028-9079 2929 **Fax:** 028-9079 4765
Website: http://www.langstontradeframes.co.uk
Directors: A. Langston (Prop)
No.of Employees: 1 - 10 **Product Groups:** 30

Larsen Building Products

4 West Bank Road, Belfast, BT3 9JL
Tel: 028-9077 4000 **Fax:** 028-9077 6945
E-mail: peter.mcgill@larson-building.co.uk
Website: http://www.larsenbuildingproducts.com
Bank(s): Bank of Ireland
Directors: P. Mcgill (MD)
Managers: E. Mazariae (Comptroller)
Ultimate Holding Company: LARSEN NEWCO 3 LIMITED
Immediate Holding Company: LARSEN BUILDING PRODUCTS LTD
Registration no: NI027912 **VAT No.:** GB 393 5687 02
Date established: 1993 **No.of Employees:** 21 - 50 **Product Groups:** 31, 32

Date of Accounts	Nov 08
Working Capital	541
Current Assets	2m

Law Society Of Northern Ireland

Law Society House 96 Victoria Street, Belfast, BT1 3GN
Tel: 028-9023 1614 **Fax:** 028-9023 2606
E-mail: alan.hunter@lawsoc-ni.org
Website: http://www.lawsoc-ni.org
Bank(s): Barclays
Directors: A. Hunter (Grp Chief Exec)
Immediate Holding Company: LAW SOCIETY OF NORTHERN IRELAND (FINANCIAL SERVICES) LIMITED
Registration no: NI021806 **Date established:** 1988
No.of Employees: 21 - 50 **Product Groups:** 87

Date of Accounts	Dec 09	Dec 08

James Leckey Design

Upper Dunmurry Lane Kilwee Business Park, Dunmurry, Belfast, BT17 0HD
Tel: 028-9060 2277 **Fax:** 028-9060 0795
E-mail: info@leckey.com
Website: http://www.leckey.com
Directors: I. Hendry (Sales), J. Leckey (Prop), R. Plunkett (Fin)
Managers: G. Parker (Mktg Serv Mgr), M. McKnight (Buyer)
Immediate Holding Company: JAMES LECKEY DESIGN LIMITED
Registration no: NI023037 **VAT No.:** GB 366 4071 49
Date established: 1989 **Turnover:** £5m - £10m
No.of Employees: 51 - 100 **Product Groups:** 38, 67

Date of Accounts	Jun 11	Jun 10	Jun 09
Sales Turnover	10m	8m	9m
Pre Tax Profit/Loss	1m	349	994
Working Capital	2m	1m	1m
Fixed Assets	583	479	487
Current Assets	4m	2m	3m
Current Liabilities	824	453	820

Lilliput Dunmurry Ltd

Unit 9 City Business Park The Cutts, Dunmurry, Belfast, BT17 9GX
Tel: 028-9061 8555 **Fax:** 028-9060 1922
E-mail: david@lilliputservices.com
Bank(s): Ulster Bank
Directors: D. Griffith (MD)
Immediate Holding Company: LILLIPUT (DUNMURRY) LIMITED
Registration no: NI001375 **VAT No.:** GB 251 7015 89
Date established: 1939 **No.of Employees:** 101 - 250 **Product Groups:** 23, 83

Date of Accounts	Dec 11	Dec 10	Dec 09
Working Capital	-798	-532	-655
Fixed Assets	2m	2m	2m
Current Assets	1m	997	1m

Lindsay Ford Belfast

391-397 Upper Newtownards Road, Belfast, BT4 3LG
Tel: 028-9065 4687 **Fax:** 028-9067 1054
E-mail: barry.mcmillan@lindsay-cars.co.uk
Website: http://www.lindsay-ford.co.uk
Managers: S. Roy (Mgr), B. McMillan (Sales Prom Mgr)
Immediate Holding Company: LINDSAY CARS LIMITED
Registration no: NI005514 **VAT No.:** GB 253 3313 89
Date established: 1963 **Turnover:** £500,000 - £1m
No.of Employees: 21 - 50 **Product Groups:** 68

Lisney LLP

Montgomery House 29-31 Montgomery Street, Belfast, BT1 4NX
Tel: 028-9050 1501 **Fax:** 028-9050 1505
E-mail: property@lisney-belfast.com
Website: http://www.lisney.com
Directors: D. Flynn (MD), D. Spurles (Fin)
Managers: K. Kent (Mktg Serv Mgr), C. Dixon (Sales Admin), G. Laing (Comptroller)
Immediate Holding Company: LISNEY BELFAST LIMITED
Registration no: NI028854 **VAT No.:** GB 653 4848 13
Date established: 1994 **Turnover:** £2m - £5m **No.of Employees:** 21 - 50
Product Groups: 80

Date of Accounts	Mar 12	Mar 11	Mar 10
Working Capital	125	14	14
Fixed Assets	33	33	33
Current Assets	278	78	78

Lister Machine Tools Ni Ltd

Unit 4b 37a Upper Dunmurry Lane, Dunmurry, Belfast, BT17 0AA
Tel: 028-9066 3804 **Fax:** 028-9066 3801
E-mail: sales@listermachinetools.com
Website: http://www.listermachinetools.com
Directors: T. McCann (Dir)
Ultimate Holding Company: LANTEC TRADING LIMITED
Immediate Holding Company: LISTER MACHINE TOOLS (N.I.) LIMITED
Registration no: NI010580 **VAT No.:** GB 434 2579 48
Date established: 1975 **No.of Employees:** 1 - 10 **Product Groups:** 66, 67

Date of Accounts	Sep 11	Sep 10	Sep 09
Working Capital	441	315	269
Fixed Assets	365	357	359
Current Assets	2m	670	636

Lobill Water Conservation Ltd

Unit 16 East Belfast Enterprise Park, Belfast, BT5 4GX
Tel: 028-9046 1755 **Fax:** 028-9046 1776
E-mail: sales@lobillwc.co.uk
Website: http://www.lobillwc.co.uk
Directors: M. Gilmore (MD)
Immediate Holding Company: LOBILL WATER CONSERVATION LIMITED
Registration no: NI026764 **VAT No.:** GB 617 5453 35
Date established: 1992 **Turnover:** £1m - £2m **No.of Employees:** 1 - 10
Product Groups: 67

Date of Accounts	Jul 11	Jul 10	Jul 09
Working Capital	64	47	25
Fixed Assets	13	21	27
Current Assets	306	199	234

Lockton Ltd

40 Linenhall Street, Belfast, BT2 8BA
Tel: 028-9024 8989 **Fax:** 028-9023 3902
Website: http://www.lockton.com
Directors: G. Ennis (MD)
Immediate Holding Company: SIR M MACDONALD ASSOCIATES
Registration no: NI070392 **Date established:** 1984 **Turnover:** £5m - £10m
No.of Employees: 21 - 50 **Product Groups:** 82

Date of Accounts	Dec 11	Dec 10
Working Capital	73	612
Fixed Assets	2m	397
Current Assets	514	911

Lylebailie International Ltd

31 Bruce Street, Belfast, BT2 7JD
Tel: 028-9033 1044 **Fax:** 028-9033 1622
E-mail: directors@lylebailie.com
Website: http://www.lylebailie.com
Bank(s): Ulster Bank
Directors: D. Lyle (MD)
Managers: R. Lyle (Mktg Serv Mgr), W. Mcwilliams, M. Carroll (Chief Acct)
Immediate Holding Company: Lyle Bailie International Limited
Registration no: NI019463 **VAT No.:** GB 466 2488 18
Date established: 1986 **No.of Employees:** 11 - 20 **Product Groups:** 81

Date of Accounts	Dec 11	Dec 10	Dec 09
Working Capital	287	214	290
Fixed Assets	24	42	65
Current Assets	1m	2m	2m

Lynn Recruitment

Ground Floor Lesley Studios 32-36 May Street, Belfast, BT1 4NZ
Tel: 028-9023 4324 **Fax:** 028-9023 4383
E-mail: maureen.lynn@lynnrecruitment.co.uk
Website: http://www.lynnrecruitment.co.uk
Bank(s): First Trust
Directors: M. Lynn (MD)
Immediate Holding Company: LYNN RECRUITMENT LTD
Registration no: NI036999 **VAT No.:** GB 517 2477 44
Date established: 1999 **No.of Employees:** 11 - 20 **Product Groups:** 80

M D S Pharma Services

22-24 Lisburn Road, Belfast, BT9 6AD
Tel: 028-9055 4055 **Fax:** 028-9055 4141
E-mail: fionamcneilly@mdsps.com
Website: http://www.mdsharris.com
Bank(s): Bank of Ireland
Directors: F. McNeilly (Dir)
Registration no: 00023061 **VAT No.:** GB 517 2356 56
Turnover: £500,000 - £1m **No.of Employees:** 101 - 250
Product Groups: 85, 88

M R C B Paints Ltd

4 Balmoral Road, Belfast, BT12 6QR
Tel: 028-9068 2605 **Fax:** 028-9038 2662
E-mail: steven.whyte@macblair.com
Website: http://macblair.com
Managers: S. Whyte (Chief Mgr)
Immediate Holding Company: MRCB PAINTS LIMITED
Registration no: NI025504 **VAT No.:** GB 517 4689 19
Date established: 1991 **No.of Employees:** 1 - 10 **Product Groups:** 66

Date of Accounts	Dec 08	Dec 07
Working Capital	-65	-65

M S L Search & Selection

Horwath House 20 Rosemary Street, Belfast, BT1 1QD
Tel: 028-9023 4444 **Fax:** 028-9024 9333
E-mail: ireiney@msl-ni.com
Website: http://www.msl-ni.com
Directors: I. Rainey (Prop)
Immediate Holding Company: MSL SEARCH AND SELECTION LIMITED
Registration no: NI055493 **VAT No.:** GB 517 2666 41
Date established: 2005 **Turnover:** £5m - £10m **No.of Employees:** 1 - 10
Product Groups: 80

Date of Accounts	Apr 12	Apr 11	Apr 10
Working Capital	-212	-265	-296
Fixed Assets	214	268	314
Current Assets	21	12	23

M S O Cleland

399 Castlereagh Road, Belfast, BT5 6QP
Tel: 028-9040 0200 **Fax:** 028-9070 5446
E-mail: toni.mcdonagh@mso.co.uk
Website: http://www.msocleland.co.uk
Bank(s): Bank of Ireland
Managers: T. McDonagh, T. Mcdonaheh
Ultimate Holding Company: PRINTCAST LIMITED
Immediate Holding Company: MSO CLELAND LIMITED
Registration no: NI015669 **VAT No.:** GB 393 5490 21
Date established: 1982 **Turnover:** £20m - £50m
No.of Employees: 101 - 250 **Product Groups:** 27, 28, 30, 66

Date of Accounts	Dec 10	Dec 09	Dec 08
Sales Turnover	21m	20m	N/A
Pre Tax Profit/Loss	-4m	71	489
Working Capital	-2m	2m	3m
Fixed Assets	7m	6m	4m
Current Assets	10m	12m	15m
Current Liabilities	890	1m	1m

Mcauley & Browne

250 Ravenhill Road, Belfast, BT6 8GJ
Tel: 028-9046 6199 **Fax:** 028-9046 6509
E-mail: info@mcauleyandbrowne.co.uk
Website: http://www.mcauleyandbrowne.co.uk
Directors: G. Browne (Dir)
Immediate Holding Company: McAuley and Browne Limited
Registration no: NI056079 **VAT No.:** GB 252 9877 19
Date established: 2005 **No.of Employees:** 1 - 10 **Product Groups:** 84

Date of Accounts	Jul 11	Jul 10	Jul 09
Working Capital	18	28	-16
Fixed Assets	10	15	42
Current Assets	91	119	77

Mccaig Collim

92-94 Dargan Cresent, Belfast, BT3 9JP
Tel: 028-9077 7788 **Fax:** 028-9077 6865
E-mail: sales@mccaig-collim.co.uk
Website: http://www.mccaig-collim.co.uk

Directors: N. Collim (Dir)
Managers: M. Pervis (Tech Serv Mgr)
Immediate Holding Company: MCCAIG COLLIM
Registration no: NI007965 **VAT No.:** GB 254 0855 62
Date established: 1970 **No.of Employees:** 21 - 50 **Product Groups:** 66

Brian Mccance Steel Ltd

1 Dargan Road, Belfast, BT3 9JU
Tel: 028-9077 2326 **Fax:** 028-9077 9698
E-mail: neil@mccancesteel.com
Website: http://www.mccancesteel-belfast.co.uk
Bank(s): Northern Bank
Directors: N. Mccance (MD)
Immediate Holding Company: BRIAN MCCANCE (STEEL) LIMITED
Registration no: NI011457 **VAT No.:** GB 286 4695 05
Date established: 1976 **Turnover:** £5m - £10m **No.of Employees:** 11 - 20
Product Groups: 61

Date of Accounts	Sep 11	Sep 10	Sep 09
Sales Turnover	N/A	N/A	5m
Pre Tax Profit/Loss	N/A	N/A	-3
Working Capital	1m	1m	1m
Fixed Assets	77	30	74
Current Assets	3m	3m	2m
Current Liabilities	N/A	N/A	103

Mcdevitt Electrical Engineers (V H McDevitt & Son Ltd)

212-218 Upper Newtownards Road, Belfast, BT4 3ET
Tel: 028-9047 2626 **Fax:** 028-9047 3636
E-mail: robertlally@vhmcdevitt.co.uk
Website: http://www.vhmcdevitt.co.uk
Directors: M. Bridges (MD), R. Lally (MD)
Registration no: NI010638 **VAT No.:** GB 286 6597 92
Turnover: £2m - £5m **No.of Employees:** 1 - 10 **Product Groups:** 52

Mcdowell Service Dental Laboratory

Unit 4c Dargan Court Dargan Crescent, Belfast, BT3 9JP
Tel: 028-9037 0708 **Fax:** 028-9077 2647
E-mail: enquiries@mcdowell-service.com
Website: http://www.mcdowell-service.com
Bank(s): Bank of Ireland
Directors: J. Cochrane (Dir)
Immediate Holding Company: McDowell & Service Dental Laboratory Limited
Registration no: NI038047 **Date established:** 2000
No.of Employees: 21 - 50 **Product Groups:** 38, 67

Date of Accounts	Mar 12	Mar 11	Mar 10
Working Capital	307	380	194
Fixed Assets	495	573	658
Current Assets	422	537	532

J D Mcgeown Ltd

Windsor Business Park 16-18 Lower Windsor Avenue, Belfast, BT9 7DW
Tel: 028-9068 1176 **Fax:** 028-9030 1712
E-mail: info@jdmcg.co.uk
Website: http://www.jdmcg.co.uk
Directors: M. McCusker (Contracts), J. McGeown (MD)
Managers: J. Fegan (Tech Serv Mgr), I. Fiddis (Personnel), F. Kennedy (Comptroller)
Immediate Holding Company: J.D. MCGEOWN LIMITED
Registration no: NI014309 **VAT No.:** GB 252 8425 59
Date established: 1980 **Turnover:** £5m - £10m
No.of Employees: 51 - 100 **Product Groups:** 52

Date of Accounts	Mar 11	Mar 10	Mar 09
Sales Turnover	6m	7m	N/A
Pre Tax Profit/Loss	495	597	317
Working Capital	7m	7m	7m
Fixed Assets	539	520	547
Current Assets	9m	9m	9m
Current Liabilities	371	1m	685

Mcgregor & Manning

32 Montgomery Road, Belfast, BT6 9HL
Tel: 028-9079 6050 **Fax:** 028- 90401883
E-mail: sales@mcgm.co.uk
Website: http://www.mcgm.co.uk
Directors: G. Harrison (Jt MD), N. Massey (Jt MD), H. Scott (Jt MD)
Ultimate Holding Company: Mascott Harrison Limited
Immediate Holding Company: McGREGOR & MANNING LIMITED
Registration no: NI028000 **VAT No.:** GB 286 4050 51
Date established: 1993 **No.of Employees:** 1 - 10 **Product Groups:** 66

Date of Accounts	Dec 10	Dec 09	Dec 08
Working Capital	1m	955	855
Fixed Assets	127	179	193
Current Assets	2m	3m	3m

Mac's Quality Foods

Dunmurry Industrial Estate Dunmurry, Belfast, BT17 9HU
Tel: 028-9062 2725 **Fax:** 028-9062 2842
E-mail: info@macsqualityfoods.co.uk
Website: http://www.macsqualityfoods.co.uk
Bank(s): Ulster Bank
Directors: D. Mcilroy (Prop)
VAT No.: GB 353 1707 72 **Date established:** 1981
Turnover: £500,000 - £1m **No.of Employees:** 11 - 20 **Product Groups:** 20

Mail Matters Direct

Unit A4 Portview Trade Centre 310 Newtownards Road, Belfast, BT4 1HE
Tel: 028-9045 3345 **Fax:** 028-9045 0143
E-mail: john.hughes@mailmatters.co.uk
Website: http://www.postalgroup.com
Bank(s): Northern Bank
Managers: T. Hughes (Mgr)
Immediate Holding Company: MAIL MATTERS DIRECT LIMITED
Registration no: NI024517 **VAT No.:** GB 617 5710 41
Date established: 1990 **Turnover:** £1m - £2m **No.of Employees:** 21 - 50
Product Groups: 28, 80, 81

Date of Accounts	Sep 11	Sep 10	Sep 09
Working Capital	-101	-105	-100
Fixed Assets	150	164	195
Current Assets	855	622	566

Makro Self Service Wholesalers Ltd

97 Kingsway Dunmurry, Belfast, BT17 9NS
Tel: 08444-457445 **Fax:** 028-9060 9010
E-mail: david.wilson@makro.co.uk
Website: http://www.makro.co.uk
Managers: D. Wilson (Mgr)
Ultimate Holding Company: METRO AG (GERMANY)
Immediate Holding Company: MAKRO SELF SERVICE WHOLESALERS LIMITED
Registration no: 00973269 **Date established:** 1970
No.of Employees: 1501 & over **Product Groups:** 61

Date of Accounts	Dec 11	Dec 10	Dec 09
Sales Turnover	766m	797m	868m
Pre Tax Profit/Loss	-62m	-20m	-45m
Working Capital	-132m	-58m	-163m
Fixed Assets	101m	101m	92m
Current Assets	105m	165m	152m
Current Liabilities	20m	16m	89m

Maplin Electronics Ltd

55 Boucher Road, Belfast, BT12 6HR
Tel: 028-9068 3929 **Fax:** 028-9068 3867
E-mail: belfast@maplin.co.uk
Website: http://www.maplin.co.uk
Managers: W. Watt (Mgr)
Ultimate Holding Company: MONTAGU PRIVATE EQUITY LLP
Immediate Holding Company: MAPLIN ELECTRONICS LIMITED
Registration no: 01264385 **Date established:** 1976
Turnover: £125m - £250m **No.of Employees:** 11 - 20
Product Groups: 37, 61

Date of Accounts	Dec 11	Dec 08	Dec 09
Sales Turnover	205m	204m	204m
Pre Tax Profit/Loss	25m	32m	35m
Working Capital	118m	49m	75m
Fixed Assets	27m	28m	28m
Current Assets	207m	108m	142m
Current Liabilities	78m	51m	59m

Marenco Ltd

Adelaide Business Centre Apollo Road, Belfast, BT12 6HP
Tel: 028-9068 2275 **Fax:** 028-9066 4939
E-mail: paul.mccardal@marenco.co.uk
Website: http://www.marenco.co.uk
Directors: P. Mcardal (MD)
Immediate Holding Company: MARENCO LIMITED
Registration no: NI020095 **VAT No.:** GB 454 5718 31
Date established: 1987 **Turnover:** £500,000 - £1m
No.of Employees: 1 - 10 **Product Groups:** 54, 85

Date of Accounts	Dec 11	Dec 10	Dec 09
Working Capital	88	85	68
Fixed Assets	2	4	5
Current Assets	97	94	104

F R Mark & Associates

155 Bloomfield Avenue, Belfast, BT5 5AB
Tel: 028-9045 7210 **Fax:** 028-9045 7220
E-mail: info@frmark.com
Website: http://www.frmark.com
Directors: S. Hetherington (Snr Part)
Turnover: Up to £250,000 **No.of Employees:** 1 - 10 **Product Groups:** 54, 85

Market Research Northern Ireland Ltd

44-46 Elmwood Avenue, Belfast, BT9 6AZ
Tel: 028-9066 1037 **Fax:** 028-9068 2007
E-mail: info@mrni.co.uk
Website: http://www.mrni.co.uk
Managers: S. Dowling
Immediate Holding Company: MRNI Research Ltd
Registration no: NI019182 **Date established:** 1986
Turnover: £250,000 - £500,000 **No.of Employees:** 1 - 10
Product Groups: 80, 81

Date of Accounts	Jun 11	Jun 10	Jun 09
Working Capital	48	44	47
Fixed Assets	4	6	10
Current Assets	119	158	93

Market Solutions Ni

236 Upper Newtownards Road, Belfast, BT4 3EU
Tel: 028-9067 1333 **Fax:** 028-9067 3433
E-mail: mail@marketsolutionsni.co.uk
Website: http://www.marketsolutionsni.co.uk
Directors: G. Gaston (Ptnr)
Immediate Holding Company: ICC (Computers & Support) NI Ltd
Registration no: NI041568 **VAT No.:** GB 517 2077 60
Date established: 2001 **Turnover:** £2m - £5m **No.of Employees:** 1 - 10
Product Groups: 81

Date of Accounts	Dec 10	Dec 09	Dec 08
Working Capital	-25	-24	-25
Fixed Assets	1	1	1
Current Assets	10	10	9

Martin Foods Ltd

22-23north City Business Centre 2 Duncairn Gardens, Belfast, BT15 2GG
Tel: 028-9035 1673 **Fax:** 028-9075 1673
E-mail: kvernon@martinfoods.co.uk
Website: http://www.martinfoods.co.uk
Directors: K. Vernon (MD)
Managers: L. Mccrory (Chief Mgr)
Immediate Holding Company: MARTIN FOODS LIMITED
Registration no: NI612547 **VAT No.:** GB 251 8371 62
Date established: 2012 **Turnover:** £1m - £2m **No.of Employees:** 1 - 10
Product Groups: 20, 62

Date of Accounts	Mar 11	Mar 10	Mar 09
Sales Turnover	N/A	393	381
Pre Tax Profit/Loss	N/A	-18	-45
Working Capital	196	217	225
Fixed Assets	612	611	621
Current Assets	213	236	244
Current Liabilities	N/A	13	9

Masonry Fixings

83 Sydenham Road, Belfast, BT3 9DJ
Tel: 028-9050 7500 **Fax:** 028-9050 7501
E-mail: belfastpc@masonryfixings.ie
Website: http://www.masonryfixings.ie
Managers: R. Blundell (Mgr)
Immediate Holding Company: MASONRY FIXING SERVICES LIMITED
Registration no: NI027872 **VAT No.:** GB 575 5726 04
Date established: 1993 **No.of Employees:** 1 - 10 **Product Groups:** 66

Date of Accounts	May 11	May 10	May 09
Working Capital	67	37	59
Fixed Assets	9	10	17
Current Assets	168	195	208
Current Liabilities	54	108	115

Mater Hospital

Crumlin Road, Belfast, BT14 6AB
Tel: 028-9074 1211 **Fax:** 028-9074 1342
Website: http://www.mater.n-i.nhs.uk
Managers: A. Perry
Turnover: £500,000 - £1m **No.of Employees:** 501 - 1000
Product Groups: 88

Mcallister Armstrong & Partners

Carroll House 463 Ormeau Road, Belfast, BT7 3GR
Tel: 028-9050 4504 **Fax:** 028-9050 4514
E-mail: info@map_architects.com
Website: http://www.map-architects.com
Bank(s): Northern Bank
Directors: J. Quinn (Dir)
Immediate Holding Company: McALISTER ARMSTRONG & PARTNERS LTD
Registration no: NI033603 **VAT No.:** GB 253 0177 36
Date established: 1998 **No.of Employees:** 11 - 20 **Product Groups:** 52, 84

Date of Accounts	Mar 12	Mar 11	Mar 10
Working Capital	217	221	627
Fixed Assets	31	37	42
Current Assets	296	266	716

Mcconnell Chartered Surveyors Ltd

11 Rosemary Street, Belfast, BT1 1QF
Tel: 028-9020 5900 **Fax:** 028-9031 3705
E-mail: info@mcconnellproperty.com
Website: http://www.mcconnellproperty.com
Bank(s): First Trust
Directors: R. Mcconnel (Dir)
Immediate Holding Company: MCCONNELL CHARTERED SURVEYORS LIMITED
Registration no: NI602539 **VAT No.:** GB 667 9449 68
Date established: 2010 **No.of Employees:** 21 - 50 **Product Groups:** 80

Date of Accounts	Jun 11
Working Capital	226
Fixed Assets	145
Current Assets	3m

Mckay Newtownardsltd

Westminster Avenue North, Belfast, BT4 1QQ
Tel: 028-9065 9900 **Fax:** 028-9047 1785
E-mail: westavenue@mckaypharmacy.com
Website: http://www.mckaypharmacy.com
Directors: J. McKay (MD)
Immediate Holding Company: MCKAY (NEWTOWNARDS) LIMITED
Registration no: NI011586 **VAT No.:** GB 617 5741 30
Date established: 1976 **No.of Employees:** 1 - 10 **Product Groups:** 63

Date of Accounts	Mar 11	Mar 10	Mar 09
Pre Tax Profit/Loss	445	704	189
Working Capital	1m	2m	1m
Fixed Assets	2m	2m	2m
Current Assets	3m	3m	2m
Current Liabilities	235	314	165

Mckinty & Wright Solicitors

5-7 Upper Queen Street, Belfast, BT1 6FS
Tel: 028-9024 6751 **Fax:** 028-9023 1432
E-mail: post@mckinty-wright.co.uk
Website: http://www.mckinty-wright.co.uk
Directors: P. Johnston (Snr Part)
Registration no: NI025723 **VAT No.:** 252 2580 74 **Date established:** 1991
Turnover: £20m - £50m **No.of Employees:** 51 - 100 **Product Groups:** 80

Mcneill & Thriftway Travel

421 Lisburn Road, Belfast, BT9 6AA
Tel: 028-9038 1010 **Fax:** 028-9038 1122
E-mail: mukesh.sharma@thriftway.co.uk
Website: http://www.thriftway.co.uk
Directors: M. Sharma (MD)
Immediate Holding Company: MCNEILL RIGBY TRAVEL LIMITED
Registration no: NI010853 **VAT No.:** GB 251 7268 60
Date established: 1975 **No.of Employees:** 21 - 50 **Product Groups:** 69

Date of Accounts	Oct 11	Oct 10	Jun 09
Working Capital	1m	988	538
Fixed Assets	24	45	26
Current Assets	3m	4m	901

Mcquoids

432-434 Ormeau Road, Belfast, BT7 3HY
Tel: 028-9064 0018 **Fax:** 028-9064 1452
E-mail: office@mcquoids.co.uk
Website: http://www.mcquoids.co.uk
Directors: B. Mcquoid (Ptnr)
Immediate Holding Company: KNOCKBURN PROPERTIES LIMITED
Registration no: NI049365 **VAT No.:** GB 252 2122 10
Date established: 2004 **No.of Employees:** 1 - 10 **Product Groups:** 80

Date of Accounts	Apr 09	Apr 08
Working Capital	25	25
Current Assets	442	442

Mercado Floor Sales Ltd

101b Airport Road West, Belfast, BT3 9ED
Tel: 028-9046 7680 **Fax:** 028-9046 7699
E-mail: sales@merbelfast.co.uk
Website: http://www.merbelfast.co.uk
Bank(s): Bank of Ireland
Directors: P. Edgar (Dir)
Managers: D. Adair (Chief Acct)
Registration no: 02674152 **VAT No.:** GB 450 0405 04
Turnover: £500m - £1,000m **No.of Employees:** 11 - 20
Product Groups: 63

Mercer

Clarendon House 23 Clarendon Road, Belfast, BT1 3BG
Tel: 028-9032 7891 **Fax:** 028-9033 2809
E-mail: sarah.kerr@mercer.com
Website: http://www.mercer.com
Managers: P. Mccarron, S. Kerr (District Mgr)
Ultimate Holding Company: MARSH & MCLENNAN COMPANIES INC (U.S.A)
Immediate Holding Company: MERCER LIMITED
Registration no: 00984275 **VAT No.:** GB 244 3537 68
Date established: 1970 **No.of Employees:** 51 - 100 **Product Groups:** 82

Date of Accounts	Jul 11	Jul 10	Mar 10
Sales Turnover	351m	43m	139m
Pre Tax Profit/Loss	18m	4m	24m

see next page

***Mercer** - Cont'd*

Working Capital	77m	68m	66m
Fixed Assets	92m	69m	70m
Current Assets	135m	78m	74m
Current Liabilities	39m	6m	7m

Mercer Walter S & Son
Unit 11-12 Duncrue Industrial Estate Duncrue Crescent, Belfast, BT3 9BW
Tel: 028-9037 1888 **Fax:** 028-9037 1471
E-mail: belfast.386@eel.co.uk
Website: http://www.eel.co.uk
Bank(s): National Westminster Bank Plc
Managers: J. Boyd (Mgr)
Immediate Holding Company: RUMENCO LIMITED
Registration no: 00008370 **Date established:** 1985
No.of Employees: 11 - 20 **Product Groups:** 67

Merex Construction Ltd
Old Channel Road, Belfast, BT3 9DE
Tel: 028-9045 9021 **Fax:** 028-9045 7531
E-mail: merek@nireland.com
Website: http://www.merexconstructionltd.co.uk
Directors: M. Gillfillan (MD)
Immediate Holding Company: MEREX CONSTRUCTION LIMITED
Registration no: NI014683 **VAT No.:** GB 353 1157 79
Date established: 1981 **No.of Employees:** 1 - 10 **Product Groups:** 52

Date of Accounts	May 11	May 10	May 09
Working Capital	-64	92	358
Fixed Assets	227	706	751
Current Assets	423	383	861

Metal Tech Engineering
Unit 21 City Business Park Dunmurry, Belfast, BT17 9HY
Tel: 028-9062 5364 **Fax:** 028-9030 0366
E-mail: info@metaltech-ni.com
Directors: N. Stewart (MD)
Immediate Holding Company: METAL TECH ENGINEERING LTD
Registration no: NI037496 **Date established:** 1999
No.of Employees: 11 - 20 **Product Groups:** 35

Date of Accounts	Dec 11	Dec 10	Dec 09
Working Capital	-31	-80	-8
Fixed Assets	363	380	403
Current Assets	534	313	433

Michael Ferguson Flowers
18 Wellington Place, Belfast, BT1 6GE
Tel: 028-9024 0111 **Fax:** 028-9023 5706
E-mail: flowers@fergusonflowers.co.uk
Website: http://www.fergusonflowers.co.uk
Directors: M. Ferguson (Prop)
Immediate Holding Company: LOWOOD DEVELOPMENTS LIMITED
Registration no: NI020091 **Date established:** 2006
No.of Employees: 1 - 10 **Product Groups:** 62

Modern Plant Components Ltd
30 Ravenhill Road, Belfast, BT6 8EA
Tel: 028-9045 3941 **Fax:** 028-9045 3748
E-mail: sales@modernplant.ie
Website: http://www.modernplant.ie
Directors: B. Bolger (Dir)
Managers: P. Kinkaid (Mgr), R. Glynn (Admin Off)
Immediate Holding Company: MODERN PLANT COMPONENTS LIMITED
Registration no: NI014736 **VAT No.:** GB 353 0593 64
Date established: 1981 **No.of Employees:** 1 - 10 **Product Groups:** 33

Moffett Thallon & Co. Ltd
143 Northumberland Street, Belfast, BT13 2JF
Tel: 028-9032 2802 **Fax:** 028-9024 1428
E-mail: info@moffett-thallon.co.uk
Website: http://www.doorways.co.uk
Bank(s): Bank of Ireland
Managers: K. Mcguckin (Mgr)
Ultimate Holding Company: GRAFTON GROUP PUBLIC LIMITED COMPANY
Immediate Holding Company: Moffett Thallon & Company Limited
Registration no: NI039308 **VAT No.:** GB 517 1630 67
Date established: 2000 **Turnover:** £2m - £5m **No.of Employees:** 21 - 50
Product Groups: 66

Date of Accounts	Dec 10	Dec 09	Apr 09
Working Capital	2m	2m	2m
Current Assets	2m	2m	2m

Molton Brown Emporium
16 Donegall Square North, Belfast, BT1 5GB
Tel: 028-9024 6674
Website: http://www.moltonbrown.co.uk
Managers: M. Mccomb (Mgr)
Ultimate Holding Company: KAO CORPORATION (JAPAN)
Immediate Holding Company: MOLTON BROWN LIMITED
Registration no: 02414997 **Date established:** 1989
No.of Employees: 1 - 10 **Product Groups:** 32, 63

Date of Accounts	Dec 11	Dec 10	Dec 09
Sales Turnover	57m	57m	58m
Pre Tax Profit/Loss	2m	6m	4m
Working Capital	42m	40m	36m
Fixed Assets	6m	6m	7m
Current Assets	53m	54m	49m
Current Liabilities	5m	5m	6m

Montgomery Refrigeration Ltd
5 Falcon Road Adelaide Industrial Estate, Belfast, BT12 6RD
Tel: 028-9066 2111 **Fax:** 028-9068 1130
E-mail: sales@montgomery-ltd.co.uk
Website: http://www.montgomery-ltd.co.uk
Bank(s): Ulster Bank
Directors: M. Montgomery (MD), M. Montgomery (MD)
Managers: A. Riley (Sales Admin), A. Shanks (Personnel), J. Cowan (Chief Acct), T. Macdonald (Tech Serv Mgr)
Ultimate Holding Company: DENIS MONTGOMERY LIMITED
Immediate Holding Company: MONTGOMERY REFRIGERATION LIMITED
Registration no: NI013088 **VAT No.:** GB 375 7247 22
Date established: 1978 **Turnover:** £20m - £50m
No.of Employees: 101 - 250 **Product Groups:** 40, 52, 66, 84

Date of Accounts	Sep 11	Sep 10	Sep 09
Sales Turnover	22m	21m	22m
Pre Tax Profit/Loss	1m	243	527
Working Capital	2m	2m	2m
Fixed Assets	244	288	326
Current Assets	9m	7m	8m
Current Liabilities	3m	1m	4m

Montupet UK Ltd
The Cutts Dunmurry, Belfast, BT17 9HN
Tel: 028-9030 1049 **Fax:** 028-9030 3030
E-mail: montupet@montupet.co.uk
Website: http://www.montupet.com
Directors: S. Magnan (Ch), P. Bonnel (MD)
Managers: I. Moore (I.T. Exec)
Ultimate Holding Company: MONTUPET SA (FRANCE)
Immediate Holding Company: MONTUPET (U.K.) LIMITED
Registration no: NI022131 **Date established:** 1988
Turnover: £50m - £75m **No.of Employees:** 251 - 500
Product Groups: 39, 40

Date of Accounts	Dec 11	Dec 10	Dec 09
Sales Turnover	71m	62m	48m
Pre Tax Profit/Loss	9m	6m	-582
Working Capital	18m	10m	6m
Fixed Assets	21m	21m	21m
Current Assets	33m	24m	24m
Current Liabilities	5m	5m	4m

Moore Stephens Chartered Accountants
Donegall House 7 Donegall Square North, Belfast, BT1 5GB
Tel: 028-9032 9481 **Fax:** 028-9043 9185
E-mail: dmclean@msca.co.uk
Website: http://www.msca.co.uk
Bank(s): Northern
Directors: D. McClean (Snr Part)
Immediate Holding Company: VLS CATERING LTD
Registration no: OC313071 **VAT No.:** GB 251 7971 43
Date established: 2002 **Turnover:** £2m - £5m **No.of Employees:** 21 - 50
Product Groups: 80

Date of Accounts	Mar 11	Mar 10	Mar 09
Working Capital	-81	-84	-106
Fixed Assets	180	199	197
Current Assets	454	417	418

Mulholland & Bailie Ltd
183 Ravenhill Avenue, Belfast, BT6 8LE
Tel: 028-9045 0654 **Fax:** 028-9045 0673
E-mail: mulhollandbailie@hotmail.com
Website: http://www.mulhollandandbailie.com
Bank(s): Bank of Ireland
Directors: D. Mulholland (MD)
Immediate Holding Company: MULHOLLAND & BAILIE LIMITED
Registration no: NI008486 **VAT No.:** GB 252 4976 42
Date established: 1971 **Turnover:** £500,000 - £1m
No.of Employees: 11 - 20 **Product Groups:** 49

Date of Accounts	Feb 11	Feb 10	Feb 09
Working Capital	68	70	116
Fixed Assets	2	3	5
Current Assets	124	111	166

Murphy & O'Rawe
4th Floor Scottish Provident Building 7 Donegall Square West, Belfast, BT1 6JH
Tel: 028-9032 6636 **Fax:** 028-9024 3777
E-mail: pateastwood@murphy-orawe.com
Website: http://www.murphy-orawe.com
Directors: P. Eastwood (Snr Part)
Managers: P. Conlon
Immediate Holding Company: CRANFIELD GRANGE (RUBANE) MANAGEMENT CO. LIMITED
Registration no: NI058445 **Date established:** 2006
Turnover: Up to £250,000 **No.of Employees:** 21 - 50 **Product Groups:** 80

N C S North
Unit A1 19 Heron Road, Belfast, BT3 9LE
Tel: 028-9073 5555 **Fax:** 028-9073 5556
E-mail: info@ncsnorth.com
Website: http://www.ncsnorth.com
Bank(s): Northern Bank
Managers: D. Allen (Mgr)
Ultimate Holding Company: NCS GROUP LIMITED
Immediate Holding Company: NCS (North) Limited
Registration no: NI040447 **VAT No.:** GB 282 9550 30
Date established: 2001 **Turnover:** £2m - £5m **No.of Employees:** 21 - 50
Product Groups: 48, 64, 67

Date of Accounts	Feb 08	Feb 11	Feb 10
Sales Turnover	3m	3m	3m
Pre Tax Profit/Loss	49	30	28
Working Capital	476	586	549
Fixed Assets	12	22	40
Current Assets	1m	1m	1m
Current Liabilities	523	441	192

N I A V A C Ltd
Conlavon House 5 Prince Regent Road, Belfast, BT5 6QR
Tel: 028-9079 3000 **Fax:** 028-9049 1285
E-mail: james@niavac.com
Website: http://www.niavac.com
Directors: J. Conlon (Dir)
Immediate Holding Company: NIAVAC LTD
Registration no: NI018608 **VAT No.:** GB 287 0636 35
Date established: 1985 **Turnover:** £500,000 - £1m
No.of Employees: 11 - 20 **Product Groups:** 28

Date of Accounts	Oct 11	Oct 10	Oct 09
Working Capital	668	290	379
Fixed Assets	2m	2m	2m
Current Assets	891	672	694

N X P Semiconductors Ltd
75-77 Malone Road, Belfast, BT9 6SB
Tel: 028-9050 4000 **Fax:** 028-9050 4001
E-mail: stephen.farson@nxp.com
Website: http://www.nxp.com
Managers: C. McGowan (Tech Serv Mgr), C. Dodds (Admin Off), S. Farson
Immediate Holding Company: AMPHION SEMICONDUCTOR
Registration no: NI024395 **Turnover:** £2m - £5m
No.of Employees: 21 - 50 **Product Groups:** 37, 44, 67

Napier Tanks Group & Co
5 Agnes Street Indl-Est Agnes Street, Belfast, BT13 1GB
Tel: 028-9075 4002
E-mail: garybingham@napiertanks.fsnet.co.uk
Directors: G. Bingham (Prop)
Date established: 1994 **No.of Employees:** 1 - 10 **Product Groups:** 35, 42, 45

National Air Traffic Services Ltd
C T B Belfast International Airport, Belfast, BT29 4AA
Tel: 028-9448 4267 **Fax:** 028-9442 2643
E-mail: bill.henry@nats.co.uk
Bank(s): National Westminster
Managers: M. Ruddy (Chief Mgr)
Ultimate Holding Company: NATS HOLDINGS LIMITED
Immediate Holding Company: NATIONAL AIR TRAFFIC SERVICES LIMITED
Registration no: 05685495 **Date established:** 2006 **Turnover:** £2m - £5m
No.of Employees: 21 - 50 **Product Groups:** 84

National Car Parks Ltd
Montgomery Street, Belfast, BT1 4NX
Tel: 028-9024 4751 **Fax:** 028-9024 3944
E-mail: james.clarke@ncp.co.uk
Website: http://www.ncp.co.uk
Managers: B. Crilly (Mgr)
Ultimate Holding Company: MACQUARIE EUROPEAN INFRASTRUCTURE FUND II (GUERNSEY)
Immediate Holding Company: NATIONAL CAR PARKS LIMITED
Registration no: 00253240 **VAT No.:** GB 239 0546 59
Date established: 1931 **No.of Employees:** 1 - 10 **Product Groups:** 80

Date of Accounts	Mar 12	Mar 09	Mar 10
Sales Turnover	203m	225m	229m
Pre Tax Profit/Loss	-7m	8m	11m
Working Capital	136m	95m	106m
Fixed Assets	51m	82m	76m
Current Assets	686m	651m	666m
Current Liabilities	51m	81m	70m

Navigator Blue Ltd
The Baths 18 Ormeau Avenue, Belfast, BT2 8HS
Tel: 028-9024 6722 **Fax:** 028-9023 1607
E-mail: m.dalm@navigatorblue.com
Website: http://www.navigatorblue.com
Directors: A. Dalm (MD)
Managers: G. Plant (Fin Mgr), T. Axon
Immediate Holding Company: NAVIGATOR BLUE LIMITED
Registration no: NI024464 **VAT No.:** GB 517 2962 37
Date established: 1990 **No.of Employees:** 21 - 50 **Product Groups:** 81

Date of Accounts	Dec 11	Dec 10	Dec 09
Working Capital	31	31	31
Fixed Assets	82	58	47
Current Assets	832	1m	939

Nichem Ltd
286 Ballydowns Road, Unit 3D Maryland Industrial Estate, Belfast, BT23 6BL
Tel: 028-9044 9989 **Fax:** 028-9044 9939
E-mail: info@nichem.co.uk
Website: http://www.nichem.co.uk
Directors: A. McKinley (Comm), C. Stewart (MD), J. Hodges (MD)
Registration no: NI026155 **Date established:** 1991 **Turnover:** £1m - £2m
No.of Employees: 1 - 10 **Product Groups:** 31, 32, 52, 66

Nilfix Ltd
Unit 9 48 Duncrue Street, Belfast, BT3 9AR
Tel: 028-9074 1444 **Fax:** 028-9075 4555
E-mail: sales@nilfix.co.uk
Website: http://www.nilfix.co.uk
Directors: L. Muir (Ptnr)
Registration no: NI040247 **No.of Employees:** 1 - 10 **Product Groups:** 30, 33, 40, 42

Nisoft UK Ltd
Nisoft House Ravenhill Business Park, Belfast, BT6 8AW
Tel: 028-9050 7555 **Fax:** 028-9050 7556
E-mail: cead@nisoft.com
Website: http://www.nisoft.com
Managers: A. McIvor (Sales Prom Mgr), C. Ead (Systems Mgr)
Immediate Holding Company: NiSoft (UK) Limited
Registration no: NI033201 **VAT No.:** GB 517 4306 61
Date established: 1997 **Turnover:** £500,000 - £1m
No.of Employees: 21 - 50 **Product Groups:** 44

Date of Accounts	Mar 11	Mar 10	Mar 09
Working Capital	439	125	-173
Fixed Assets	1m	1m	2m
Current Assets	1m	1m	501

Noel Grimley
450 Donegall Road, Belfast, BT12 6HS
Tel: 028-9031 1522
Directors: N. Grimley (Dir)
Date established: 1998 **No.of Employees:** 1 - 10 **Product Groups:** 36, 40

Date of Accounts	Mar 11	Mar 10	Mar 09
Working Capital	384	354	386
Fixed Assets	901	930	960
Current Assets	795	760	778

North Down Marquees Ltd
39 Ballynahinch Road Carryduff, Belfast, BT8 8DL
Tel: 028-9081 5535 **Fax:** 028-9081 2344
E-mail: info@northdownmarquees.co.uk
Website: http://www.northdownmarquees.co.uk
Bank(s): Ulster Bank
Managers: A. Mcilveen (Chief Mgr)
Immediate Holding Company: NORTH DOWN MARQUEES LIMITED
Registration no: NI017378 **VAT No.:** GB 422 1696 68
Date established: 1984 **Turnover:** £500,000 - £1m
No.of Employees: 11 - 20 **Product Groups:** 83

Date of Accounts	Dec 11	Dec 10	Dec 09
Working Capital	-146	-55	-285
Fixed Assets	592	703	869
Current Assets	180	286	275

Northair Ltd
39 Malone Road, Belfast, BT9 6RX
Tel: 028-9038 1350 **Fax:** 028-9066 4330
Directors: A. Mckeown (MD)
Immediate Holding Company: NORTHAIR LIMITED
Registration no: NI027138 **VAT No.:** GB 617 5850 25
Date established: 1993 **Turnover:** £250,000 - £500,000
No.of Employees: 1 - 10 **Product Groups:** 52

Date of Accounts	Dec 11	Dec 10	Dec 09
Sales Turnover	450	291	433
Pre Tax Profit/Loss	-9	-23	1

Working Capital	156	165	187
Current Assets	245	211	216
Current Liabilities	15	24	12

Northern Bank Ltd

Donegall Square West, Belfast, BT1 6JS
Tel: 028-9004 6100 **Fax:** 028-9032 0010
Website: http://www.northernbank.co.uk
Managers: S. Calley (District Mgr), R. Houston (Reg Sales Mgr)
Ultimate Holding Company: FC011846
Immediate Holding Company: NORTHERN BANK LIMITED
Registration no: R0000568 **VAT No.:** GB 261 3007 66
Date established: 1983 **Turnover:** £500,000 - £1m
No.of Employees: 1 - 10 **Product Groups:** 82

Date of Accounts	Dec 10	Dec 09	Dec 08
Pre Tax Profit/Loss	-100m	-113m	7m
Fixed Assets	149m	114m	285m
Current Assets	6933m	6820m	6287m
Current Liabilities	6201m	6168m	4062m

Northern Ireland Electricity

120 Malone Road, Belfast, BT9 5HT
Tel: 028-9066 1100 **Fax:** 028-9073 5660
E-mail: harry.mccracken@nie.co.uk
Website: http://www.nie.co.uk
Directors: J. Omahony (MD), J. Omomaghy (Grp Chief Exec), C. Bothwell (Fin)
Managers: G. Parkes (Tech Serv Mgr), S. Holland
Immediate Holding Company: NORTHERN IRELAND ELECTRICITY LIMITED
Registration no: NI026041 **Date established:** 1991
Turnover: £125m - £250m **No.of Employees:** 1 - 10 **Product Groups:** 18

Date of Accounts	Mar 11	Mar 10	Mar 09
Pre Tax Profit/Loss	141m	99m	94m
Working Capital	274m	320m	276m
Fixed Assets	189m	734m	735m
Current Assets	678m	861m	831m
Current Liabilities	20m	9m	537m

Northern Ireland Public Service Alliance

Harkin House 54-56 Wellington Park, Belfast, BT9 6DP
Tel: 028-9066 1831 **Fax:** 028-9066 5847
E-mail: info@nipsa.org.uk
Website: http://www.nipsa.org.uk
Managers: R. McClelland (Personnel), B. Campfield (Mgr), J. Thompson (Tech Serv Mgr), M. Murphy (Fin Mgr)
Immediate Holding Company: NORTHERN IRELAND WOMEN'S EUROPEAN PLATFORM
Registration no: NI035910 **Date established:** 2001
No.of Employees: 51 - 100 **Product Groups:** 87

Date of Accounts	Mar 11	Mar 10	Mar 09
Sales Turnover	N/A	N/A	20
Pre Tax Profit/Loss	N/A	N/A	-17
Working Capital	12	6	15
Current Assets	12	6	16
Current Liabilities	N/A	N/A	1

Northern Ireland Tourist Board

St Annes Court 59 North Street, Belfast, BT1 1NB
Tel: 028-9023 1221 **Fax:** 028-9024 0960
E-mail: info@nitb.com
Website: http://www.nitb.com
Directors: A. Clarke (Grp Chief Exec)
Registration no: NI027173 **Date established:** 1993
No.of Employees: 101 - 250 **Product Groups:** 81

Northern Whig Ltd

107 Limestone Road, Belfast, BT15 3AH
Tel: 028-9035 2233 **Fax:** 028-9035 2181
E-mail: trevor@thewhig.co.uk
Website: http://www.thewhig.co.uk
Bank(s): Northern Bank
Directors: W. Marrow (MD), W. Morrow (Dir)
Managers: S. Cordner, M. Erwin (Cr Control), S. Cordner (Sales Prom Mgr)
Immediate Holding Company: NORTHERN WHIG, LIMITED
Registration no: R0000571 **VAT No.:** GB 252 0216 11
Date established: 2002 **Turnover:** £250,000 - £500,000
No.of Employees: 21 - 50 **Product Groups:** 28

Date of Accounts	Jun 10	Jun 09	Jun 08
Working Capital	105	-33	25
Fixed Assets	940	1m	1m
Current Assets	956	940	835

Northway Fire Security Services Ltd

Unit 19 Farset Enterprise Park 638 Springfield Road, Belfast, BT12 7DY
Tel: 028-9024 1700 **Fax:** 028-9024 1901
Website: http://www.northwayfire.com
Directors: J. Mcilroy (Prop)
Immediate Holding Company: NORTHWAY FIRE SECURITY SERVICES LIMITED
Registration no: NI601618 **Date established:** 2009
No.of Employees: 1 - 10 **Product Groups:** 38, 42

Date of Accounts	Dec 10
Working Capital	14
Fixed Assets	2
Current Assets	51

Norwich Union Life Services Ltd

5 Donegall Square South, Belfast, BT1 5AN
Tel: 028-9032 2232 **Fax:** 028-9023 8731
Website: http://www.norwich-union.co.uk
Directors: A. Berisford (Div)
Managers: E. Thorne (Mgr)
Immediate Holding Company: NORWICH UNION LIFE SERVICES LIMITED
Registration no: NF003083 **Date established:** 1993
No.of Employees: 1501 & over **Product Groups:** 82

Nu Life Engineering

Unit 73a Dunmurry Industrial Estate Dunmurry, Belfast, BT17 9HU
Tel: 028-9062 3196 **Fax:** 028-9060 2884
E-mail: info@nulifeengineering.com
Website: http://www.nulifeengineering.com
Directors: N. Haslem (Dir)
Date established: 1986 **No.of Employees:** 11 - 20 **Product Groups:** 35

Nu Star Ltd

Airport Road, Belfast, BT3 9DY
Tel: 028-9045 5321 **Fax:** 028-9045 7792
Directors: A. Bann (MD)
Immediate Holding Company: NUSTAR LTD
Registration no: 05135406 **Date established:** 2004
Turnover: Up to £250,000 **No.of Employees:** 11 - 20 **Product Groups:** 77

Date of Accounts	Mar 12	Mar 11	Mar 09
Working Capital	-1	-3	1
Fixed Assets	1	1	N/A
Current Assets	7	5	10

O C F Support Services Ni Ltd

Unit 18-21 Bloomfield Commercial Centre Factory Street, Belfast, BT5 5AW
Tel: 028-9045 8510 **Fax:** 028-9073 2022
E-mail: sales@ocf.co.uk
Website: http://www.ocf.co.uk
Directors: M. Forysth (MD)
Managers: P. Mccormax (Mgr)
Registration no: 00012904 **VAT No.:** GB 238 0343 79
No.of Employees: 1 - 10 **Product Groups:** 52

Office Monkey Ni Ltd

42 Somerton Inustrial Estate Dargan Crescent, Belfast, BT3 9JP
Tel: 028-9037 3910
E-mail: sales@officemonkeyni.com
Website: http://www.officemonkeyni.com
Directors: B. Carson (Dir)
Immediate Holding Company: Office Monkey (NI) Ltd
Registration no: NI060348 **Date established:** 2006
No.of Employees: 1 - 10 **Product Groups:** 26, 30, 44

Date of Accounts	Aug 11	Aug 10	Aug 09
Working Capital	-98	31	65
Fixed Assets	111	4	13
Current Assets	173	196	220

The Open University

110 Victoria Street, Belfast, BT1 3GN
Tel: 028-9024 5025 **Fax:** 028-9023 0565
E-mail: ireland@open.ac.uk
Website: http://www.open.ac.uk/ireland
Directors: J. Darcy (Reg)
Immediate Holding Company: OPEN UNIVERSITY WORLDWIDE LIMITED
Registration no: 01260275 **Date established:** 1976
Turnover: £250,000 - £500,000 **No.of Employees:** 51 - 100
Product Groups: 86

Date of Accounts	Jul 11	Jul 10	Jul 09
Sales Turnover	10m	10m	10m
Pre Tax Profit/Loss	2m	953	2m
Working Capital	3m	3m	3m
Current Assets	9m	8m	8m
Current Liabilities	1m	967	1m

Osborne King

6-9 Donegall Square West, Belfast, BT1 6JA
Tel: 028-9027 0000 **Fax:** 028-9027 0011
E-mail: property@osborneking.com
Website: http://www.osborneking.com
Directors: P. Henry (Fin)
Managers: L. Anderson, P. Greaves, P. Greeves
Immediate Holding Company: OSBORNE KING LIMITED
Registration no: NI041268 **Date established:** 2001
No.of Employees: 21 - 50 **Product Groups:** 80

P Kane Metals Ltd

31-43 Shiels Street, Belfast, BT12 7LQ
Tel: 028-9032 4191 **Fax:** 028-9033 0435
E-mail: p.kane@btconnect.com
Website: http://www.pkanemetals.com
Directors: H. Kane (Prop)
Immediate Holding Company: P KANE METALS LTD
Registration no: NI068267 **Date established:** 2008
Turnover: Up to £250,000 **No.of Employees:** 1 - 10 **Product Groups:** 66

Date of Accounts	Mar 12	Mar 11	Mar 10
Working Capital	603	431	190
Fixed Assets	29	35	35
Current Assets	1m	967	656

P W C

Waterfront Plaza 8 Laganbank Road, Belfast, BT1 3LR
Tel: 028-9024 5454 **Fax:** 028-9041 5600
E-mail: pwc.ni@uk.com
Website: http://www.pwc.co.uk/ni
Bank(s): Bank of Ireland
Directors: H. Quigg (Pers), P. Terrington (Snr Part)
Managers: L. McCullagh (Fin Mgr), J. Rankin (Tech Serv Mgr)
Immediate Holding Company: PRICEWATERHOUSECOOPERS ASSOCIATES (N.I.) LIMITED
Registration no: NI009326 **VAT No.:** GB 524 9340 47
Date established: 1973 **No.of Employees:** 501 - 1000 **Product Groups:** 80

Palmer Agencies Ltd

Unit 1 Beechill Business Park 96 Beechill Road, Belfast, BT8 7QN
Tel: 028-9064 7119 **Fax:** 028-9064 5655
E-mail: brent@palmeragencies.com
Website: http://www.palmeragencies.com
Directors: B. Palmer (MD)
Immediate Holding Company: PALMER AGENCIES LIMITED
Registration no: NI007156 **VAT No.:** GB 517 0693 48
Date established: 1968 **Turnover:** £250,000 - £500,000
No.of Employees: 1 - 10 **Product Groups:** 49

Date of Accounts	Dec 11	Dec 10	Dec 09
Working Capital	946	992	893
Fixed Assets	253	275	306
Current Assets	1m	1m	1m

Parfix Equipment Company Ltd

Unit 4 Locksley Business Park Montgomery Road, Belfast, BT6 9UP
Tel: 028-9070 6800 **Fax:** 028-9070 6801
E-mail: mrutherford@parfixwholesaledirect.com
Website: http://www.parfix.ie
Directors: M. Rutherford (MD)
Ultimate Holding Company: LOCKSLEY PROPERTIES LIMITED
Immediate Holding Company: PARFIX EQUIPMENT COMPANY LIMITED
Registration no: NI021336 **Date established:** 1988
No.of Employees: 11 - 20 **Product Groups:** 66

Date of Accounts	Mar 11	Mar 10	Mar 09
Working Capital	711	829	860
Fixed Assets	102	60	96
Current Assets	1m	1m	2m

Park Avenue Hotel

158 Holywood Road, Belfast, BT4 1PB
Tel: 028-9065 6520 **Fax:** 028-9047 1417
E-mail: frontdesk@parkavenuehotel.co.uk
Website: http://www.parkavenuehotel.co.uk
Bank(s): Norlan
Directors: M. Martin (MD)
Immediate Holding Company: PARK AVENUE HOTEL LIMITED
Registration no: NI006459 **Date established:** 1965 **Turnover:** £2m - £5m
No.of Employees: 101 - 250 **Product Groups:** 69

Date of Accounts	Mar 11	Mar 10	Mar 09
Sales Turnover	3m	3m	N/A
Pre Tax Profit/Loss	94	12	-1m
Working Capital	-840	-788	-547
Fixed Assets	3m	9m	9m
Current Assets	119	85	85
Current Liabilities	191	142	138

Park Electrical Services

84 Dargan Road, Belfast, BT3 9JU
Tel: 028-9077 0799 **Fax:** 028-9077 9853
E-mail: jim@parkelect.co.uk
Website: http://www.parkelect.co.uk
Bank(s): Northern Bank
Directors: J. Mcconaghie (MD)
Managers: T. McConnell (Mgr)
Immediate Holding Company: PARKELECT LIMITED
Registration no: NI026999 **VAT No.:** GB 255 6967 15
Date established: 1992 **Turnover:** £10m - £20m
No.of Employees: 21 - 50 **Product Groups:** 38, 67

Parker Butler Ltd

Prince Regent Road, Belfast, BT5 6QR
Tel: 028-9070 5678 **Fax:** 028-9079 4567
E-mail: valerie@parkerbutler.co.uk
Website: http://www.parkerbutler.co.uk
Directors: V. Butler (Ptnr), V. Butler (Dir), C. Parker (Ptnr)
Managers: N. Watson (Admin Off)
Immediate Holding Company: PARKER BUTLER LIMITED
Registration no: NI027840 **VAT No.:** GB 617 7193 25
Date established: 1993 **No.of Employees:** 1 - 10 **Product Groups:** 52, 89

Date of Accounts	May 09
Working Capital	36
Fixed Assets	6
Current Assets	217

Patterson Electronics Ltd

12 Falcon Road, Belfast, BT12 6RD
Tel: 028-9038 1387 **Fax:** 028-9038 1741
E-mail: info@patterson-electronics.com
Website: http://www.patterson-electronics.com
Bank(s): Northern Bank
Directors: I. Culbert (Sales)
Immediate Holding Company: PATTERSON ELECTRONICS LIMITED
Registration no: NI028633 **VAT No.:** GB 743 7445 19
Date established: 1994 **No.of Employees:** 21 - 50 **Product Groups:** 67

Date of Accounts	Mar 11	Mar 10	Mar 09
Working Capital	81	129	103
Fixed Assets	86	86	106
Current Assets	419	417	390

Patterson Protective Coatings Ltd

347b Albertbridge Road, Belfast, BT5 4PY
Tel: 028-9073 1333 **Fax:** 028-9046 6569
E-mail: info@ppcoatings.co.uk
Website: http://www.ppcoatings.co.uk
Directors: W. Patterson (Dir)
Immediate Holding Company: PATTERSON PROTECTIVE COATINGS LTD
Registration no: NI035851 **Date established:** 1999
No.of Employees: 1 - 10 **Product Groups:** 46, 48

Date of Accounts	Mar 12	Mar 11	Mar 10
Working Capital	122	136	147
Fixed Assets	199	197	126
Current Assets	243	323	331

Pension & Financial Consultants Ltd

PFC House Quayside Office Park 14 Dargan Crescent, Belfast, BT3 9JP
Tel: 028-9078 3030 **Fax:** 028-9078 3031
E-mail: mail@pfc.co.uk
Website: http://www.pfc.co.uk
Bank(s): Northern Bank
Directors: S. Warke (MD)
Managers: H. Patterson (Mgr)
Ultimate Holding Company: PFC Industries Limited
Immediate Holding Company: PENSION & FINANCIAL CONSULTANTS LIMITED
Registration no: NI028952 **Date established:** 1994 **Turnover:** £2m - £5m
No.of Employees: 21 - 50 **Product Groups:** 80, 82

Date of Accounts	Dec 11	Dec 10	Dec 09
Sales Turnover	3m	3m	3m
Pre Tax Profit/Loss	213	202	146
Working Capital	2m	2m	1m
Fixed Assets	25	53	97
Current Assets	3m	2m	2m
Current Liabilities	771	761	715

Pierce Group Ltd

17 Dargan Crescent, Belfast, BT3 9RP
Tel: 028-9037 1010 **Fax:** 028-9037 2501
E-mail: rpierce@pierce-group.com
Website: http://www.pierce-group.com
Bank(s): Northern Bank
Directors: R. Pierce (MD)
Managers: K. Hannah (Tech Serv Mgr), A. Brownlee (Chief Acct)
Ultimate Holding Company: SENTRY ENTERPRISES LIMITED
Immediate Holding Company: RW PIERCE SECURITY PRINT SOLUTIONS LTD
Registration no: NI029923 **VAT No.:** GB 286 5846 05
Date established: 1995 **Turnover:** £2m - £5m **No.of Employees:** 51 - 100
Product Groups: 27, 28

Date of Accounts	Aug 11	Aug 10	Aug 09
Working Capital	302	359	455
Fixed Assets	254	180	182
Current Assets	430	635	693

Platinum Expo Ltd
Saintfield Road Carryduff, Belfast, BT8 8ES
Tel: 028-9081 7555 **Fax:** 028-9081 7666
E-mail: info@platinumexpo.com
Website: http://www.platinumexpo.com
Directors: A. Mcloughlin (MD)
Immediate Holding Company: Platinum Expo Limited
Registration no: NI045859 **Date established:** 2003
No.of Employees: 11 - 20 **Product Groups:** 26, 35, 49, 67, 81

Date of Accounts	Jun 11	Jun 10	Jun 09
Working Capital	-45	-13	-12
Fixed Assets	72	87	102
Current Assets	317	325	376

Plumb Center Ltd
Unit 11 Montgomery Business Park 3 Montgomery Road, Belfast, BT6 9JD
Tel: 028-9079 8222 **Fax:** 028-9079 0051
E-mail: david.frew@wolseley.co.uk
Website: http://www.plumbcenter.co.uk
Managers: D. Fiew (District Mgr)
Ultimate Holding Company: WOLSELEY PLC (JERSEY)
Immediate Holding Company: PLUMB-CENTER LIMITED
Registration no: 00581770 **VAT No.:** GB 311 2556 03
Date established: 1957 **Turnover:** £250,000 - £500,000
No.of Employees: 1 - 10 **Product Groups:** 66

Potter Cowan & Co Belfast Ltd
Phoenix House 20 Duncrue Cresent, Belfast, BT3 9BW
Tel: 028-9037 0050 **Fax:** 028-9077 7333
E-mail: sales@pottercowan.com
Website: http://www.pottercowan.com
Directors: A. Allen (Dir), A. Lyon (Sales)
Immediate Holding Company: POTTER COWAN & COMPANY (BELFAST) LIMITED
Registration no: NI002438 **Date established:** 1947 **Turnover:** £2m - £5m
No.of Employees: 21 - 50 **Product Groups:** 26

Date of Accounts	Dec 11	Dec 10	Dec 09
Working Capital	243	167	220
Fixed Assets	3m	3m	3m
Current Assets	1m	1m	1m

Povall Worthington
5 Pilots View Heron Road, Belfast, BT3 9LE
Tel: 028-9045 0105 **Fax:** 028-9045 0104
E-mail: johnl@pwmail.co.uk
Website: http://www.povallworthington.com
Directors: J. Lee (MD)
Immediate Holding Company: POVALL WORTHINGTON LTD
Registration no: 04095761 **VAT No.:** GB 618 7577 01
Turnover: £250,000 - £500,000 **No.of Employees:** 1 - 10
Product Groups: 84

Date of Accounts	Aug 07	Aug 06
Working Capital	73	50
Fixed Assets	284	298
Current Assets	697	676
Current Liabilities	624	626
Total Share Capital	97	97

Pressure Test Services
Musgrave Park Industrial Estate Stockmans Way, Belfast, BT9 7JU
Tel: 028-9066 9837 **Fax:** 028-9066 4496
E-mail: george.sproule@calorgas.ie
Bank(s): Ulster Bank
Managers: G. Sproule (Mgr)
Ultimate Holding Company: SHV HOLDINGS NV (NETHERLANDS)
Immediate Holding Company: PRESSURE TEST SERVICES LIMITED
Registration no: NI003380 **VAT No.:** GB 251 7679 39
Date established: 1954 **No.of Employees:** 11 - 20 **Product Groups:** 35, 48

Date of Accounts	Dec 11	Dec 10	Dec 09
Working Capital	587	587	587
Current Assets	587	587	587

Prestige Metal Craft
Unit 42 Work West Centre 301-331 Glen Road, Andersonstown, Belfast, BT11 8BU
Tel: 028-9062 9706 **Fax:** 028- 90622001
Directors: A. Denny (Prop)
Date established: 1989 **No.of Employees:** 1 - 10 **Product Groups:** 26

Profast Ni Ltd
26-30 Rydalmere Street, Belfast, BT12 6GF
Tel: 028-9024 3215 **Fax:** 028-9033 3301
E-mail: sales@profast.co.uk
Website: http://www.profast.co.uk
Bank(s): Ulster Bank
Directors: P. Grant (Fin)
Managers: A. Kelson, A. Johnston (Sales Prom Mgr)
Ultimate Holding Company: PROFAST HOLDINGS LIMITED
Immediate Holding Company: PROFAST (NI) LIMITED
Registration no: NI003765 **VAT No.:** GB 689 7265 62
Date established: 1956 **Turnover:** £2m - £5m **No.of Employees:** 21 - 50
Product Groups: 66

Date of Accounts	Dec 11	Dec 10	Dec 09
Sales Turnover	4m	4m	4m
Pre Tax Profit/Loss	30	44	102
Working Capital	389	357	313
Fixed Assets	347	358	372
Current Assets	2m	2m	2m
Current Liabilities	413	467	439

Progressive Building Society
Progressive House 33-37 Wellington Place, Belfast, BT1 6HH
Tel: 028-9024 4926 **Fax:** 028-9033 0431
E-mail: darmstrong@theprogressive.com
Website: http://www.theprogressive.com
Bank(s): Ireland
Directors: D. Armstrong (Fin), D. Armstrong (Grp Chief Exec)
Managers: D. Huey (Purch Mgr), P. Martin (Personnel), T. O'Neill (Tech Serv Mgr), S. Towe (Mktg Serv Mgr)
No.of Employees: 51 - 100 **Product Groups:** 82

Progressive Unionists Party
299 Newtownards Road, Belfast, BT4 1AG
Tel: 028-9022 5040 **Fax:** 028-9022 5041
Website: http://www.prog-pakphonix.co.uk
Directors: E. Hamilton (MD)
Managers: M. Wilson (Mgr)
Date established: 1973 **No.of Employees:** 1 - 10 **Product Groups:** 38, 42

Pumps & Fuel Installions
729 Springfield Road, Belfast, BT12 7FP
Tel: 028-9024 2421 **Fax:** 028-9024 2425
E-mail: info@pumpsandfuel.com
Website: http://www.pumpsandfuel.com
Managers: P. Wright
Immediate Holding Company: PUMPS & FUEL INSTALLATIONS LIMITED
Registration no: NI025803 **Date established:** 1991 **Turnover:** £2m - £5m
No.of Employees: 21 - 50 **Product Groups:** 38, 48, 67

Date of Accounts	Dec 11	Dec 10	Dec 09
Working Capital	39	103	4
Fixed Assets	676	720	746
Current Assets	1m	1m	745

Punjana Ltd
2 Carnforth Street, Belfast, BT5 4QA
Tel: 028-9045 0631 **Fax:** 028-9045 3261
E-mail: info@punjana.com
Website: http://www.punjana.com
Bank(s): Northern Bank
Directors: L. Skinner (Mkt Research), D. Thompson (Jt MD), J. Thompson (Jt MD)
Managers: Thompson (), G. Kane (Comptroller)
Immediate Holding Company: PUNJANA LIMITED
Registration no: NI003724 **VAT No.:** GB 251 7483 56
Date established: 1956 **Turnover:** £10m - £20m
No.of Employees: 21 - 50 **Product Groups:** 20, 62

Date of Accounts	Aug 11	Aug 10	Aug 09
Sales Turnover	11m	9m	9m
Pre Tax Profit/Loss	951	522	589
Working Capital	396	1	-168
Fixed Assets	4m	4m	5m
Current Assets	4m	3m	3m
Current Liabilities	865	584	558

Pyeroy Ltd
Queens Island, Belfast, BT3 9DU
Tel: 028-9045 9523 **Fax:** 028-9045 2232
E-mail: info@pyeroy.co.uk
Website: http://www.pyeroy.co.uk
Bank(s): Bank of Ireland
Directors: D. Spence (Co Sec), R. Thompson (MD)
Managers: J. Bowmaker (District Mgr)
Ultimate Holding Company: PYEROY GROUP LIMITED
Immediate Holding Company: PYEROY LIMITED
Registration no: 01126224 **VAT No.:** 392588993 **Date established:** 1973
No.of Employees: 21 - 50 **Product Groups:** 48, 52

Date of Accounts	Dec 11	Dec 10	Dec 09
Sales Turnover	68m	60m	58m
Pre Tax Profit/Loss	3m	4m	3m
Working Capital	11m	10m	11m
Fixed Assets	6m	6m	4m
Current Assets	25m	21m	20m
Current Liabilities	8m	6m	5m

Q Electrical
385 Holywood Road, Belfast, BT4 2LS
Tel: 028-9047 1727 **Fax:** 028-9047 1153
E-mail: sales@edwardsandedwards.co.uk
Website: http://www.qelectrical.co.uk
Managers: D. Adgey (Mgr)
Ultimate Holding Company: MANET INVESTMENTS LIMITED
Immediate Holding Company: NADIE LIMITED
Registration no: NI000483 **VAT No.:** GB 375 8932 02
Date established: 2028 **No.of Employees:** 11 - 20 **Product Groups:** 67

Date of Accounts	May 11	May 10	May 09
Working Capital	184	184	237
Current Assets	209	205	266

Quay Marine Cargo & Transit Surveyors & Adjusters
PO Box 1164, Belfast, BT1 9HN
Tel: 07824-636512 **Fax:** 028-90796357
E-mail: contact@quaymarine.eu
Website: http://www.quaymarine.eu
Directors: R. Eddy (Prop)
Date established: 2008 **No.of Employees:** 1 - 10 **Product Groups:** 82

Queen's University Belfast
University Road, Belfast, BT7 1NN
Tel: 028-9024 5133 **Fax:** 028-9024 7895
E-mail: k.neeson@qub.ac.uk
Website: http://www.qub.ac.uk
Bank(s): Northern Bank Ltd
Directors: W. Galbraites (Fin), S. McGuickin (Pers)
Managers: I. Jennings, P. Massey, J. Gormley, K. Neeson
Immediate Holding Company: QUEEN'S UNIVERSITY OF BELFAST FOUNDATION -THE
Registration no: NI034280 **Date established:** 1998 **Turnover:** £2m - £5m
No.of Employees: 1501 & over **Product Groups:** 86

Date of Accounts	Jul 11	Jul 10	Jul 09
Sales Turnover	4m	4m	5m
Pre Tax Profit/Loss	2m	-382	-4m
Working Capital	3m	1m	2m
Current Assets	3m	2m	3m
Current Liabilities	267	667	1m

R F D Beaufort Ltd
Kingsway Dunmurry, Belfast, BT17 9AF
Tel: 028-9030 1531 **Fax:** 028-9062 1765
E-mail: dbaxter@rfdbeaufort.com
Website: http://www.rfdbeaufort.com
Bank(s): Ulster Bank
Directors: D. Keown (Tech Serv), D. Wilman (Co Sec), D. Baxter (Grp Chief Exec), W. McChesney (MD)
Managers: C. Neill (Mktg Serv Mgr), C. Thompson (I.T. Exec)
Ultimate Holding Company: SGL LIMITED
Immediate Holding Company: RFD LIMITED
Registration no: 00488183 **VAT No.:** NI1 5965 96 **Date established:** 1950
Turnover: £2m - £5m **No.of Employees:** 101 - 250 **Product Groups:** 39, 40

Date of Accounts	Mar 11	Mar 10	Mar 09
Working Capital	2m	2m	2m
Current Assets	2m	2m	2m

Radication Ltd
157 Glenburn Road Dunmurry, Belfast, BT17 9BB
Tel: 028-9061 8343 **Fax:** 028-9061 1233
E-mail: info@radication.co.uk
Website: http://www.radication.co.uk
Directors: J. Curry (MD)
Immediate Holding Company: RADICATION LIMITED
Registration no: NI007035 **VAT No.:** GB 253 1130 10
Date established: 1967 **No.of Employees:** 11 - 20 **Product Groups:** 32

Date of Accounts	Mar 11	Mar 10	Mar 09
Sales Turnover	391	N/A	N/A
Pre Tax Profit/Loss	185	N/A	N/A
Working Capital	119	74	53
Fixed Assets	50	49	16
Current Assets	126	104	107
Current Liabilities	5	N/A	N/A

Radiocontact Ltd
37 Castlereagh Industrial Estate Montgomery Road, Belfast, BT6 9HL
Tel: 028-9040 1742 **Fax:** 028-9040 1746
E-mail: info@radcon.com
Website: http://www.radcon.co.uk
Directors: J. Glenn (Dir)
Managers: P. Hagan (Purch Mgr), T. Kearney (Fin Mgr)
Immediate Holding Company: RADIOCONTACT LIMITED
Registration no: NI009841 **VAT No.:** GB 255 7813 37
Date established: 1973 **Turnover:** £5m - £10m **No.of Employees:** 21 - 50
Product Groups: 37, 85

Date of Accounts	Sep 11	Sep 10	Sep 09
Working Capital	-1	-96	-288
Fixed Assets	839	790	852
Current Assets	1m	985	753

Rainey & Best
64 Donegall Pass, Belfast, BT7 1BU
Tel: 028-9023 9499 **Fax:** 028-9023 9599
E-mail: mail@raineybest.com
Website: http://www.raineybest.com
Directors: E. Mccullagh (Ptnr)
Immediate Holding Company: RAINEY & BEST LLP
Registration no: NC000190 **Date established:** 2007
No.of Employees: 1 - 10 **Product Groups:** 84

Date of Accounts	Apr 11	Apr 10	Apr 09
Working Capital	80	173	177
Fixed Assets	76	66	79
Current Assets	859	806	690
Current Liabilities	207	203	259

J C Ramsay & Son Ltd
4 Prince Regent Road, Belfast, BT5 6QR
Tel: 028-9079 0088 **Fax:** 028-9070 2225
E-mail: enquiries@ramsay-joinery.co.uk
Website: http://www.ramsay-joinery.co.uk
Directors: H. Ramsay (Dir)
Managers: T. Brown (Chief Mgr), A. Ramsey (Mgr)
Immediate Holding Company: J.C.RAMSAY & SON LIMITED
Registration no: NI013385 **VAT No.:** GB 331 7160 86
Date established: 1979 **Turnover:** Up to £250,000
No.of Employees: 21 - 50 **Product Groups:** 25, 26

Date of Accounts	Mar 11	Mar 10	Mar 09
Working Capital	-499	-681	-620
Fixed Assets	909	963	1m
Current Assets	360	62	343

Relay Software Ltd
The Gas Office 12 Cromac Quay, Belfast, BT7 2JD
Tel: 028-9092 1500 **Fax:** 028-9092 1900
E-mail: info@relay.ie
Website: http://www.relay.ie
Bank(s): First Trust
Directors: G. Mackenzie (Fin), A. Bell (MD)
Managers: L. Fearon, Y. Bell (Sales & Mktg Mg), C. Stevenson (Personnel), N. Kellett (Sales Admin)
Immediate Holding Company: RELAY BUSINESS SOFTWARE LIMITED
Registration no: NI018376 **VAT No.:** GB 422 1293 90
Date established: 1985 **Turnover:** £500,000 - £1m
No.of Employees: 51 - 100 **Product Groups:** 44, 86

Date of Accounts	Jan 07	Jan 06	Jan 05
Working Capital	-127	-140	100
Fixed Assets	1m	1m	1m
Current Assets	824	670	833

Rensburg Sheppards Investment Management
5th Floor Centrepoint 58-60 Bedford Street, Belfast, BT2 7DR
Tel: 028-9032 1002 **Fax:** 028-9024 4852
E-mail: samuel.brown@rsim.co.uk
Website: http://www.rensburgsheppards.co.uk
Directors: S. Brown (Dir)
Immediate Holding Company: RENSBURG SHEPPARDS INVESTMENT MANAGEMENT LTD
Registration no: NF004080 **VAT No.:** GB 482 7533 24
Date established: 2006 **No.of Employees:** 11 - 20 **Product Groups:** 80, 82

Date of Accounts	Mar 11	Mar 10	Mar 09
Sales Turnover	109m	100m	100m
Pre Tax Profit/Loss	28m	31m	34m
Working Capital	49m	68m	59m
Fixed Assets	9m	9m	10m
Current Assets	204m	204m	179m
Current Liabilities	32m	22m	21m

Rentokil Initial
133 Albertbridge Road, Belfast, BT5 4PS
Tel: 028-9046 0080 **Fax:** 028-9046 0090
E-mail: belfast@ri-facilities.com
Website: http://www.initialcleaning.co.uk
Managers: D. Mcdonald (Purch Mgr), R. McGee (Sales Prom), T. Frost (I.T. Exec), A. Browne (Mgr), G. McKenzie (Personnel)
Immediate Holding Company: INITIAL CONTRACT SERVICES LIMITED
Registration no: NF002225 **VAT No.:** GB 625 9496 02
Date established: 1978 **Turnover:** £75m - £125m
No.of Employees: 1 - 10 **Product Groups:** 52

Ridgeway Plant Company Ltd
103 Airport Road West, Belfast, BT3 9ED
Tel: 028-9045 4599 **Fax:** 028-9045 4596
E-mail: info@ridgeway-online.com
Website: http://www.ridgeway-online.com
Bank(s): Northern Bank
Directors: D. Toner (Fin), D. Kelly (Fab), S. Kane (MD)
Immediate Holding Company: RIDGEWAY PLANT CO LIMITED
Registration no: NI007818 **VAT No.:** GB 253 1722 82
Date established: 1970 **Turnover:** £5m - £10m **No.of Employees:** 21 - 50
Product Groups: 66, 67, 83

Date of Accounts	Dec 11	Dec 10	Dec 09
Sales Turnover	N/A	N/A	6m
Pre Tax Profit/Loss	N/A	N/A	93
Working Capital	2m	2m	2m
Fixed Assets	2m	2m	2m
Current Assets	3m	3m	3m
Current Liabilities	N/A	N/A	346

Ritchie Hart
18 Cyprus Avenue, Belfast, BT5 5NT
Tel: 028-9065 4594 **Fax:** 028-9065 6196
E-mail: raymond@ritchiehart.co.uk
Website: http://www.ritchiehart.co.uk
Directors: R. Harvey (Dir)
Immediate Holding Company: RITCHIE HART & CO. (1986) LIMITED
Registration no: NI022442 **Date established:** 1989
No.of Employees: 11 - 20 **Product Groups:** 35, 39, 45

Date of Accounts	Jun 11	Jun 10	Jun 09
Working Capital	104	106	98
Fixed Assets	22	35	24
Current Assets	353	388	386

Rla
90 Lisburn Road, Belfast, BT9 6AG
Tel: 028-9066 4444 **Fax:** 028-9066 3548
E-mail: info@rlagroup.co.uk
Website: http://www.rlaireland.co.uk
Directors: I. Erwin (MD)
Immediate Holding Company: HAPPY CHILDREN CHARITABLE FOUNDATION
Registration no: NI035033 **Date established:** 2010
Turnover: £500,000 - £1m **No.of Employees:** 21 - 50 **Product Groups:** 81

Robinson Interiors Ltd
10 Boucher Way, Belfast, BT12 6RE
Tel: 028-9068 3838 **Fax:** 028-9066 6643
E-mail: design@robinsoninteriors.com
Website: http://www.robinsoninteriors.com
Directors: M. Robinson (MD)
No.of Employees: 11 - 20 **Product Groups:** 52

Robinson & Mcilwaine
84-94 Great Patrick Street, Belfast, BT1 2LU
Tel: 028-9024 8922 **Fax:** 028-9024 2688
E-mail: admin@rmi.uk.com
Website: http://www.rmi.uk.com
Directors: J. Reid (Ptnr)
Immediate Holding Company: ROBINSON MCILWAINE LLP
Registration no: NC000606 **VAT No.:** GB 253 8301 77
Date established: 2010 **No.of Employees:** 11 - 20 **Product Groups:** 84

Date of Accounts	Mar 12	Mar 11
Working Capital	25	60
Fixed Assets	113	98
Current Assets	233	235

Robinson & Mornin Bookbinders Ltd
Belfast Industrial Complex Louden Street, Belfast, BT13 2EZ
Tel: 028-9024 0942 **Fax:** 028-9033 0687
E-mail: rmbbinders@btconnect.com
Website: http://www.rmbookbinders.com
Directors: T. Robinson (Dir)
Immediate Holding Company: RMB ROBINSON & MORNIN BOOKBINDERS LIMITED
Registration no: NI046033 **VAT No.:** GB 331 6899 36
Date established: 2003 **No.of Employees:** 11 - 20 **Product Groups:** 28

Date of Accounts	Apr 11	Apr 10	Apr 09
Working Capital	-11	-49	30
Fixed Assets	557	681	862
Current Assets	281	325	474

Robinson Patterson
Clarence Gallery Linenhall Street, Belfast, BT2 8BG
Tel: 028-9024 5777 **Fax:** 028-9024 6864
E-mail: info@rpparchitects.com
Website: http://www.rpparchitects.com
Directors: A. Sheild (MD), A. Shields (Dir), G. Robinson (MD), J. Patterson (Dir), P. McGirr (Dir)
Registration no: NI017333 **Date established:** 1984 **Turnover:** £1m - £2m
No.of Employees: 21 - 50 **Product Groups:** 80, 84

W T Robson Ltd
1-5 The Cutts Dunmurry, Belfast, BT17 9HN
Tel: 028-9061 0117 **Fax:** 028-9060 2196
E-mail: sales@wtrobson.co.uk
Website: http://www.wtrobson.co.uk
Directors: J. McClure (MD)
Ultimate Holding Company: WT Robson Holdings Limited
Immediate Holding Company: W. T. ROBSON LIMITED
Registration no: NI007407 **VAT No.:** GB 252 5594 51
Date established: 1968 **No.of Employees:** 11 - 20 **Product Groups:** 30

Date of Accounts	Dec 11	Dec 10	Dec 09
Working Capital	780	665	569
Fixed Assets	147	156	178
Current Assets	1m	1m	1m

Rotary Bearing & Transmission Co. Ltd
Unit 11 Forty 8 North 48 Duncrue Street, Belfast, BT3 9BJ
Tel: 028-9074 9377 **Fax:** 028-9035 2949
E-mail: sales@rotarybearings-ni.com
Website: http://www.rotarybearings.co.uk
Directors: D. Mcclumb (MD)
Immediate Holding Company: ROTARY BEARING AND TRANSMISSION CO. LIMITED
Registration no: NI019822 **Date established:** 1986
Turnover: £500,000 - £1m **No.of Employees:** 1 - 10 **Product Groups:** 67, 68

Date of Accounts	Aug 11	Aug 10	Aug 09
Working Capital	-21	-31	-30
Fixed Assets	157	163	177
Current Assets	114	142	123

Royal & Sun Alliance Insurance Company
42 Queen Street, Belfast, BT1 6HL
Tel: 028-9024 4433 **Fax:** 028-9026 2357
E-mail: sales@royalsunalliance.com
Website: http://www.royalsunalliance.com
Managers: L. Anderson, M. Mclean (Mgr)
Immediate Holding Company: ROYAL & SUN ALLIANCE INSURANCE PLC
Registration no: NF003488 **Date established:** 1999
No.of Employees: 51 - 100 **Product Groups:** 82

Royal Ulster Agricultural Society General Office
Lisburn Road Kings Hall, Belfast, BT9 6GW
Tel: 028-9066 5225 **Fax:** 028-9066 1264
E-mail: info@kingshall.co.uk
Website: http://kingshall.co.uk
Bank(s): Northern Bank
Directors: R. Geary (Chief Op Offcr), T. Morrissey (Comm)
VAT No.: GB 53 8840 41 **Turnover:** Up to £250,000
No.of Employees: 21 - 50 **Product Groups:** 81

Rubber & Plastics
30-38 Duncrue Place, Belfast, BT3 9BU
Tel: 028-9050 1050 **Fax:** 028-9050 1021
E-mail: sales@rpgrouponline.com
Website: http://www.rpgrouponline.com
Bank(s): Ulster Bank
Directors: S. Gillham (Dir)
Immediate Holding Company: RP Group (Holdings) Ltd
Registration no: NI024851 **VAT No.:** GB 251 9639 41
Date established: 2002 **Turnover:** £2m - £5m **No.of Employees:** 21 - 50
Product Groups: 29, 30, 36, 66

S C M
B T 3 Business Centre Dargan Crescent, Belfast, BT3 9JP
Tel: 028-9037 0327 **Fax:** 028-9077 6906
E-mail: gs@scmni.fsbusiness.co.uk
Directors: G. Simpson (Prop)
Immediate Holding Company: COMPU B LIMITED
Registration no: NF003345 **Date established:** 1997
Turnover: Up to £250,000 **No.of Employees:** 1 - 10 **Product Groups:** 81

S D Carbons Ltd
Unit 8 Tamar Street, Belfast, BT4 1HS
Tel: 028-9045 9990 **Fax:** 028-9046 1601
E-mail: sdcarbons@aol.com
Website: http://www.carbonbrushes.co.uk
Directors: D. Hughes (MD)
Immediate Holding Company: S.D. CARBONS LTD
Registration no: NI029709 **Date established:** 1995
Turnover: Up to £250,000 **No.of Employees:** 1 - 10 **Product Groups:** 33

Date of Accounts	Aug 11	Aug 10	Aug 09
Working Capital	37	46	42
Fixed Assets	14	15	16
Current Assets	54	74	68

S M S Services Ltd
8-11 Louden Street Belfast Industrial Complex, Belfast, BT13 2EZ
Tel: 028-9032 2948 **Fax:** 028-9024 8677
E-mail: paul.mann@steelmetalsupplies.com
Website: http://www.steelmetalsupplies.com
Directors: P. Mann (Dir)
Immediate Holding Company: SMS SERVICES LIMITED
Registration no: 06942694 **VAT No.:** GB 375 7353 23
Date established: 2009 **No.of Employees:** 1 - 10 **Product Groups:** 67

S & R Electric Ltd
56 Holywood Road, Belfast, BT4 1NT
Tel: 028-9065 5929 **Fax:** 028-9065 8846
E-mail: service@samdrelectric.co.uk
Website: http://www.samsyerman.co.uk
Directors: V. Duff (Sales), J. Brown (Adv), J. Anders (Jt MD), S. Duff (Jt MD), B. Reid (Fin)
Managers: G. Haddock (Mgr), T. Harper (Serv Mgr)
Immediate Holding Company: S. & R. ELECTRIC LIMITED
Registration no: NI017617 **VAT No.:** GB 253 0653 80
Date established: 1984 **Turnover:** £5m - £10m **No.of Employees:** 21 - 50
Product Groups: 61

Date of Accounts	Jun 11	Jun 10	Jun 09
Sales Turnover	N/A	6m	8m
Pre Tax Profit/Loss	N/A	-415	75
Working Capital	-950	-765	-744
Fixed Assets	3m	3m	3m
Current Assets	995	2m	2m
Current Liabilities	N/A	201	485

Sanderson Multi Channel Systems Ltd
Unit 3a Heron Wharf Heron Road, Belfast, BT3 9LE
Tel: 028-9073 4600 **Fax:** 028-9073 1440
E-mail: marketing@sanderson.com
Website: http://www.sanderson.com
Bank(s): Northern Bank, Belfast
Directors: M. Beatty (Dir)
Ultimate Holding Company: ULSTER TUBULAR FURNITURE LIMITED
Immediate Holding Company: CO-TEM-CO LIMITED
Registration no: NI011975 **Date established:** 1977 **Turnover:** £1m - £2m
No.of Employees: 21 - 50 **Product Groups:** 44

Date of Accounts	Jul 99	Jul 98	Jul 97
Working Capital	422	324	291
Fixed Assets	271	288	363
Current Assets	724	855	642
Current Liabilities	N/A	N/A	247

Sangers N I Ltd
2 Marshalls Road, Belfast, BT5 6SR
Tel: 028-9070 2220 **Fax:** 028-9070 5623
E-mail: peter.surgenor@sangers.co.uk
Website: http://www.united-drug.com
Bank(s): First Trust
Directors: D. Jackson (MD), P. Surgenor (MD)
Managers: J. Gwynne (Personnel), P. McForley (Sales Prom Mgr), A. Ward (Tech Serv Mgr)
Ultimate Holding Company: UNITED DRUG PUBLIC LIMITED COMPANY
Immediate Holding Company: SANGERS (NORTHERN IRELAND) LIMITED
Registration no: NI018941 **VAT No.:** GB 574 9030 27
Date established: 1985 **Turnover:** £2m - £5m
No.of Employees: 101 - 250 **Product Groups:** 63, 67, 84

Date of Accounts	Sep 11	Sep 10	Sep 09
Sales Turnover	215m	214m	200m
Pre Tax Profit/Loss	6m	5m	4m
Working Capital	3m	2m	7
Fixed Assets	9m	9m	9m
Current Assets	76m	72m	68m
Current Liabilities	42m	44m	41m

Saville Audio Visual
11 Duncrue Crescent, Belfast, BT3 9BW
Tel: 028-9077 2772 **Fax:** 028-9078 1154
E-mail: peter.balloch@saville-av.com
Website: http://www.saville.co.uk
Managers: P. Balloch (Mgr)
Ultimate Holding Company: SEA HOLDINGS LIMITED
Immediate Holding Company: THE SAVILLE GROUP LIMITED
Registration no: 02170847 **VAT No.:** GB 517 2579 36
Date established: 1987 **Turnover:** £5m - £10m **No.of Employees:** 1 - 10
Product Groups: 28, 37, 38, 48, 61, 63, 83

Date of Accounts	Dec 11	Dec 10	Dec 09
Sales Turnover	26m	25m	25m
Pre Tax Profit/Loss	3	84	88
Working Capital	1m	1m	684
Fixed Assets	1m	1m	1m
Current Assets	6m	7m	6m
Current Liabilities	3m	3m	2m

Selecta Ltd
28 Duncrue Road, Belfast, BT3 9BP
Tel: 028-9077 1177 **Fax:** 028-9037 0051
E-mail: sales@uk.selecta.com
Website: http://www.selecta.com
Bank(s): Northern Bank
Directors: J. Lancaster (Dir)
Managers: B. Wallace
Immediate Holding Company: SELECTA LIMITED
Registration no: NI027017 **VAT No.:** GB 244 5228 71
Date established: 1992 **Turnover:** £1m - £2m **No.of Employees:** 21 - 50
Product Groups: 49, 61

Sepha Pharmaceuticals Ltd
Unit 25 Carrowreagh Business Park Carrowreagh Road, Dundonald, Belfast, BT16 1QQ
Tel: 028-9048 4848 **Fax:** 028-9048 0890
E-mail: enquiries@sepha.com
Website: http://www.sepha.com
Bank(s): Northern Bank
Managers: P. Kelly (Mktg Serv Mgr)
Ultimate Holding Company: SEPHA HOLDINGS LIMITED
Immediate Holding Company: Sepha Limited
Registration no: NI014142 **Date established:** 1980
No.of Employees: 11 - 20 **Product Groups:** 42, 48

Date of Accounts	Sep 11	Sep 10	Sep 09
Working Capital	450	395	345
Fixed Assets	608	635	726
Current Assets	1m	809	920

Sere Ltd
7-13 Boucher Road, Belfast, BT12 6HR
Tel: 028-9020 5100 **Fax:** 028-9020 5865
E-mail: sales@seremotors.com
Website: http://www.seremotors.com
Directors: S. Edgar (MD)
Immediate Holding Company: S.E.R.E. HOLDINGS LTD
Registration no: NI040095 **VAT No.:** GB 353 0698 51
Date established: 2001 **Turnover:** £20m - £50m
No.of Employees: 21 - 50 **Product Groups:** 68

Date of Accounts	Dec 11	Dec 10	Dec 09
Sales Turnover	31m	31m	35m
Pre Tax Profit/Loss	-80	211	221
Working Capital	-2m	-857	-752
Fixed Assets	4m	2m	2m
Current Assets	7m	6m	6m
Current Liabilities	6m	5m	5m

Servoll Lubricants Ni Ltd
22 Heron Road, Belfast, BT3 9LE
Tel: 028-9045 9999 **Fax:** 028-9073 2015
E-mail: gary.robb@servoll.com
Website: http://www.servoll.com
Directors: G. Robb (MD), G. Robb (Dir)
Immediate Holding Company: SERVOLL LUBRICANTS (N.I) LIMITED
Registration no: NI010201 **Date established:** 1974
No.of Employees: 1 - 10 **Product Groups:** 66

Date of Accounts	Apr 11	Apr 10	Apr 09
Working Capital	43	126	35
Fixed Assets	68	98	154
Current Assets	976	977	1m

Shanway Press
1-3 Eia Street, Belfast, BT14 6BT
Tel: 028-9022 2070 **Fax:** 028-9022 2077
E-mail: info@shanway.com
Website: http://www.shanway.com
Directors: M. Mckerman (Prop)
VAT No.: GB 353 1148 80 **Date established:** 2003
No.of Employees: 1 - 10 **Product Groups:** 28

Sharpe Mechanical Services
57 Sydenham Road, Belfast, BT3 9DJ
Tel: 028-9045 8185 **Fax:** 028-9073 1034
E-mail: info@sharpegroup.com
Website: http://www.sharpegroup.com
Bank(s): First Trust
Managers: E. Mcmaster (Mgr)
Immediate Holding Company: SHARPE MECHANICAL SERVICES
Registration no: NI011704 **VAT No.:** GB 286 7670 06
Date established: 1976 **Turnover:** £5m - £10m
No.of Employees: 51 - 100 **Product Groups:** 39, 40

Date of Accounts	Sep 11	Sep 10	Sep 09
Sales Turnover	8m	11m	12m
Pre Tax Profit/Loss	140	459	630
Working Capital	827	1m	1m
Fixed Assets	2m	2m	2m
Current Assets	5m	6m	5m
Current Liabilities	270	502	501

Sherwood Systems Ltd Sherwood Systems Ireland
Ash Grove Wildflower Way, Belfast, BT12 6TA
Tel: 028-9066 8585 **Fax:** 028-9066 5547
E-mail: info@sherwoodsys.com
Website: http://www.sherwoodsys.com

see next page

Sherwood Systems Ltd Sherwood Systems Ireland - Cont'd

Directors: J. Howard (MD), H. Coulder (Tech Serv)
Managers: P. Crozier (Sales & Mktg Mg)
Immediate Holding Company: Sherwood Direct Ltd
Registration no: NI016625 **VAT No.:** GB 375 8324 25
Date established: 1983 **No.of Employees:** 21 - 50 **Product Groups:** 67

Date of Accounts	Dec 08
Working Capital	622
Fixed Assets	20
Current Assets	1m

Shopacheck Financial Services

3 Fort William Business Park Dargan Road, Belfast, BT3 9LZ
Tel: 028-9077 4791 **Fax:** 028-9077 1950
Website: http://www.cattles.co.uk
Managers: C. McManus (District Mgr), C. McManus (Mgr), J. Moores (District Mgr)
Ultimate Holding Company: BOVESS HOLDING LIMITED
Immediate Holding Company: SHOPACHECK FINANCIAL SERVICES LIMITED
Registration no: 07067456 **VAT No.:** GB 254 9018 55
Date established: 2009 **No.of Employees:** 1 - 10 **Product Groups:** 82

Date of Accounts	Dec 10
Pre Tax Profit/Loss	-0

Signage Ltd

Units 31-32 Bloomfield Commercial Centre 5 Factory Street, Belfast, BT5 5AW
Tel: 028-9045 0145 **Fax:** 028-9073 2533
E-mail: signageltd@btconnect.com
Website: http://www.signage.co.uk
Managers: M. Busby (Mgr)
Immediate Holding Company: SIGNAGE LIMITED
Registration no: NI021184 **VAT No.:** 454 6760 27 **Date established:** 1987
Turnover: £250,000 - £500,000 **No.of Employees:** 1 - 10
Product Groups: 24, 37, 49, 81

Silver Lining Industries Ireland Ltd

Unit 6c Castleton Centre, Belfast, BT15 3HE
Tel: 028-9074 6352 **Fax:** 0113-385 4323
E-mail: admin@itwaste.com
Website: http://www.silverlining.co.uk
Directors: P. Hunt (MD)
Managers: A. Cook (Mktg Serv Mgr), S. West (Depot Mgr)
Immediate Holding Company: SILVER LINING INDUSTRIES (IRELAND) LIMITED
Registration no: NF003160 **VAT No.:** GB 653 8898 75
Date established: 1994 **No.of Employees:** 1 - 10 **Product Groups:** 34, 54

Sita UK Ltd

110 Duncrue Street, Belfast, BT3 9AR
Tel: 028-9074 7341 **Fax:** 028-9074 0533
E-mail: alan.sproule@sita.co.uk
Website: http://www.sita.co.uk
Bank(s): Barclays Bank
Managers: A. Sproule (Chief Mgr)
Ultimate Holding Company: GDF SUEZ SA (FRANCE)
Immediate Holding Company: WILSON WASTE MANAGEMENT LIMITED
Registration no: NI038799 **VAT No.:** GB 352 1129 90
Date established: 2000 **No.of Employees:** 21 - 50 **Product Groups:** 54

Date of Accounts	Dec 11	Dec 10	Dec 09
Working Capital	398	398	398
Current Assets	398	398	400

Specialist Computer Centre

Unit 1-2 Nella House 96 Dargan Crescent, Belfast, BT3 9JP
Tel: 028-9037 0160 **Fax:** 028-9037 0195
E-mail: belfast.sales@scc.com
Website: http://www.scc.com
Managers: D. Gault
Registration no: 14831017 **VAT No.:** GB 643 1847 37
Turnover: Over £1,000m **No.of Employees:** 1 - 10 **Product Groups:** 44

Stanley Motor Works

19 Boucher Cresent, Belfast, BT12 6HU
Tel: 028-9068 6000 **Fax:** 028-9068 6001
E-mail: brian.gribben@agnews.co.uk
Website: http://www.agnewcars.co.uk
Directors: M. Wood (Sales)
Managers: B. Gribben (), B. McGeown (Comptroller), B. Gribben (Sales Prom Mgr), D. Craig (Sales Admin), Y. Magee (Chief Mgr)
Ultimate Holding Company: ISAAC AGNEW (HOLDINGS) LIMITED
Immediate Holding Company: STANLEY MOTOR WORKS (1932) LIMITED
Registration no: NI000727 **VAT No.:** GB 251 8906 49
Date established: 1932 **Turnover:** £20m - £50m
No.of Employees: 21 - 50 **Product Groups:** 39, 68

Star Instruments Ltd

Dunmurry Industrial Estate Dunmurry, Belfast, BT17 9HU
Tel: 028-9061 8221 **Fax:** 028-9060 1803
E-mail: sales@star-instruments.co.uk
Website: http://www.star-instruments.co.uk
Bank(s): Ulster Bank
Directors: S. Donnelly (MD)
Managers: T. Smyth (Admin Off), J. Spears (Fin Mgr), S. Boniface (Sales Prom Mgr)
Immediate Holding Company: Star Instruments Limited
Registration no: NI047049 **VAT No.:** GB 251 7688 38
Date established: 2003 **Turnover:** £2m - £5m **No.of Employees:** 21 - 50
Product Groups: 38, 85

Date of Accounts	Jul 12	Jul 11	Jul 10
Working Capital	1m	1m	1m
Fixed Assets	135	98	99
Current Assets	2m	2m	2m

Steel Structures N I Ltd

24 Barbour Gardens Dunmurry, Belfast, BT17 9AB
Tel: 028-9030 1308 **Fax:** 028-9062 3989
E-mail: info@steelstructuresni.com
Website: http://www.steelstructuresni.com
Directors: D. Milligan (Dir), D. Milligan (Dir)
Immediate Holding Company: STEEL STRUCTURES (N.I.) LTD
Registration no: NI029255 **Date established:** 1995
No.of Employees: 11 - 20 **Product Groups:** 35

Date of Accounts	Nov 11	Nov 10	Nov 09
Working Capital	-34	-42	46
Fixed Assets	118	151	192
Current Assets	327	164	427

Stena Line Holidays Ltd

Ballast Quay Corry Road, Belfast, BT3 9SS
Tel: 028-9074 7747 **Fax:** 028-9088 4091
E-mail: sales@stenaline.ie
Website: http://www.stenaline.co.uk
Managers: B. McMonagle (Reg Mgr), W. Weeks (Mgr), P. Grant (Sales & Mktg Mg)
Immediate Holding Company: STENA LINE HOLIDAYS LIMITED
Registration no: NF002606 **Date established:** 1985
No.of Employees: 1 - 10 **Product Groups:** 74

Date of Accounts	Dec 06	Dec 05	Dec 04
Sales Turnover	1220	1000	3100
Pre Tax Profit/Loss	70	70	350
Working Capital	8630	8580	8570
Current Assets	8680	8800	8800
Current Liabilities	50	220	230
Total Share Capital	2000	2000	2000
ROCE% (Return on Capital Employed)	0.8	0.8	4.1
ROT% (Return on Turnover)	5.7	7.0	11.3

Stevenson Munn

Greenwood House, Belfast, BT9 5NF
Tel: 028-9066 9537 **Fax:** 028-9066 0309
E-mail: john_taggart@stevensonmunn.com
Website: http://www.stevensonmunn.com
Directors: J. Taggart (Snr Part), J. Taggart (Ptnr), R. Telford (Ptnr)
Immediate Holding Company: NEWFORGE LIMITED
Registration no: NI020047 **VAT No.:** GB 252 5020 03
Date established: 1986 **Turnover:** £1m - £2m **No.of Employees:** 1 - 10
Product Groups: 84

Stiona Software Ltd

91-97 Ormeau Road, Belfast, BT7 1SH
Tel: 028-9032 2011
E-mail: info@stiona.com
Website: http://www.stiona.com
Managers: C. Okane
Immediate Holding Company: STIONA SOFTWARE LIMITED
Registration no: 03299479 **Date established:** 1997
Turnover: £250,000 - £500,000 **No.of Employees:** 1 - 10
Product Groups: 44

Date of Accounts	Aug 11	Aug 10	Feb 09
Working Capital	218	-95	-115
Fixed Assets	8	374	372
Current Assets	297	162	190
Current Liabilities	40	62	N/A

Stirling Film & Television Productions Ltd

137 University Street, Belfast, BT7 1HP
Tel: 028-9033 3848 **Fax:** 028-9043 8644
E-mail: anne.stirling@stirlingtelevision.co.uk
Website: http://www.stirlingtelevision.co.uk
Bank(s): Olster
Directors: A. Stirling (MD)
Managers: A. Auld (Chief Acct), J. Healy (Prod Mgr)
Immediate Holding Company: STIRLING FILM AND TELEVISION PRODUCTIONS LIMITED
Registration no: NI028684 **Date established:** 1994
No.of Employees: 21 - 50 **Product Groups:** 89

Date of Accounts	Oct 11	Oct 10	Oct 09
Working Capital	-130	-119	-137
Fixed Assets	243	214	202
Current Assets	436	514	281

Stormont Hotel

587 Upper Newtownards Road, Belfast, BT4 3LP
Tel: 028-9065 1066 **Fax:** 028-9048 0240
E-mail: gm@stor.hastingshotels.com
Website: http://www.hastingshotels.com
Managers: G. Carty (Chief Mgr), P. McKeown (Personnel), P. McIntosh
Immediate Holding Company: HASTINGS HOTELS GROUP LIMITED
Registration no: NI008164 **Date established:** 1971
Turnover: £20m - £50m **No.of Employees:** 51 - 100 **Product Groups:** 69

Date of Accounts	Oct 11	Oct 10	Oct 09
Sales Turnover	28m	30m	33m
Pre Tax Profit/Loss	742	2m	3m
Working Capital	-13m	-16m	-18m
Fixed Assets	47m	49m	51m
Current Assets	6m	6m	5m
Current Liabilities	4m	3m	3m

Stothers M & E Ltd

Radiant Works 23 Sunwich Street, Belfast, BT6 8HR
Tel: 028-9045 0821 **Fax:** 028-9045 8342
E-mail: enquiry@stothersm-e.co.uk
Website: http://www.stothersm-e.co.uk
Directors: C. Cherry (MD)
Managers: D. Collon (Chief Acct)
Ultimate Holding Company: JEH LIMITED
Immediate Holding Company: STOTHERS (M. & E.) LIMITED
Registration no: NI024313 **Date established:** 1990
Turnover: £10m - £20m **No.of Employees:** 51 - 100 **Product Groups:** 52

Date of Accounts	Jun 11	Jun 10	Jun 09
Pre Tax Profit/Loss	1m	2m	268
Working Capital	4m	3m	1m
Fixed Assets	106	107	182
Current Assets	7m	7m	10m
Current Liabilities	942	1m	5m

Sureskills

Callender House 58-60 Upper Arthur Street, Belfast, BT1 4GJ
Tel: 028-9093 5555 **Fax:** 028-9093 5566
E-mail: info@sureskills.com
Website: http://www.sureskills.com
Managers: G. Morgan (Sales Prom Mgr)
Ultimate Holding Company: SURESKILLS LTD (REGISTERED IN DUBLIN)
Date established: 1993 **Turnover:** £5m - £10m **No.of Employees:** 1 - 10
Product Groups: 44, 80, 86

Swift Screw Products

Dunmore Alexandra Park Avenue, Belfast, BT15 3GD
Tel: 028-9077 0721 **Fax:** 028-9037 0914
E-mail: sales@swiftscrewproducts.co.uk
Website: http://www.swiftscrewproducts.co.uk
Managers: G. Scullion (Mgr)
Ultimate Holding Company: FERGAL HOLDING COMPANY LIMITED
Immediate Holding Company: SWIFT SCREW PRODUCTS LIMITED
Registration no: NI010837 **Date established:** 1975 **Turnover:** £1m - £2m
No.of Employees: 1 - 10 **Product Groups:** 66

Date of Accounts	Oct 11	Oct 10	May 09
Working Capital	833	788	815
Fixed Assets	89	106	1m
Current Assets	942	944	1m

T R Shipping Services

Victoria Terminal 3, Belfast, BT3 9JL
Tel: 028-9037 3200 **Fax:** 028-9077 4299
E-mail: moreinfo@trshipping.co.uk
Website: http://www.trshipping.co.uk
Managers: M. Telford (Mgr)
Ultimate Holding Company: TOKENHOUSE LIMITED (ISLE OF MAN)
Immediate Holding Company: COASTAL CONTAINER LINE LIMITED
Registration no: NI013153 **VAT No.:** GB 331 7664 58
Date established: 1978 **Turnover:** £10m - £20m **No.of Employees:** 1 - 10
Product Groups: 76, 77

Date of Accounts	Mar 11	Mar 10	Mar 09
Sales Turnover	16m	16m	24m
Pre Tax Profit/Loss	-1m	-2m	-2m
Working Capital	-5m	-4m	-5m
Fixed Assets	5m	5m	5m
Current Assets	6m	7m	8m
Current Liabilities	1m	1m	2m

Target Dry Ltd

7 Alanbrooke Park Industrial Estate Alanbrooke Road, Belfast, BT6 9HB
Tel: 028-9079 0588 **Fax:** 028-9079 2164
E-mail: sales@targetdry.co.uk
Website: http://www.targetdry.co.uk
Directors: J. Breen (MD), N. Mcaneary (Dir)
Immediate Holding Company: TARGET DRY LIMITED
Registration no: NI034940 **Date established:** 1998
Turnover: £500,000 - £1m **No.of Employees:** 21 - 50 **Product Groups:** 61

Date of Accounts	Dec 11	Mar 11	Mar 10
Working Capital	1m	1m	1m
Fixed Assets	88	74	46
Current Assets	1m	2m	2m

Taylor & Boyd

107 Malone Avenue, Belfast, BT9 6EQ
Tel: 028-9066 7951 **Fax:** 028-9066 4961
E-mail: paul.taylor@taylor-boyd.co.uk
Website: http://www.taylor-boyd.co.uk
Bank(s): Northern Bank
Directors: P. Taylor (Snr Part)
Managers: M. Linberg (Sales & Mktg Mg), M. Buckley (Fin Mgr), P. Lockwood
Immediate Holding Company: TAYLOR AND BOYD LLP
Registration no: NC000025 **VAT No.:** GB 253 0226 02
Date established: 2005 **Turnover:** Over £1,000m
No.of Employees: 21 - 50 **Product Groups:** 84

Date of Accounts	Apr 12	Apr 11	Apr 10
Working Capital	484	440	361
Fixed Assets	39	24	11
Current Assets	673	647	670

Technisource Ltd

65 Sydenham Road, Belfast, BT3 9DJ
Tel: 028-9045 5644 **Fax:** 028-9045 5030
E-mail: source@kct-group.com
Website: http://www.technicut.ltd.uk
Managers: J. Mcconaghie (Sales Admin)
Ultimate Holding Company: KCT HOLDINGS LIMITED
Immediate Holding Company: TECHNISOURCE LIMITED
Registration no: NI040590 **VAT No.:** GB 286 5426 27
Date established: 2001 **Turnover:** £500,000 - £1m
No.of Employees: 1 - 10 **Product Groups:** 66

Date of Accounts	Apr 11	Apr 10	Apr 09
Sales Turnover	N/A	810	3m
Pre Tax Profit/Loss	N/A	-184	-181
Working Capital	573	555	738
Fixed Assets	3	3	4
Current Assets	897	943	2m
Current Liabilities	N/A	37	36

Tenants Bitumen

9 Airport Road West, Belfast, BT3 9ED
Tel: 028-9045 5135 **Fax:** 028-9046 0077
E-mail: info@ctni.co.uk
Website: http://www.ctni.co.uk
Bank(s): Ulster Bank
Directors: R. Peden (MD)
Ultimate Holding Company: TENNANTS CONSOLIDATED LIMITED
Immediate Holding Company: TENNANTS TAR DISTILLERS AND ENGINEERING SUPPLIES LIMITED
Registration no: NI001972 **VAT No.:** GB 253 3547 64
Date established: 1945 **No.of Employees:** 11 - 20 **Product Groups:** 31

Date of Accounts	Dec 11	Dec 10	Dec 09
Working Capital	N/A	2m	2m
Fixed Assets	2m	N/A	N/A
Current Assets	N/A	2m	2m

Charles Tennant

8 Herdman Channel Road, Belfast, BT3 9LG
Tel: 028-9074 0002 **Fax:** 028-9075 3142
E-mail: georges@ctni.co.uk
Website: http://www.ctni.co.uk
Managers: G. Smith (Mgr)
Ultimate Holding Company: TENNANTS CONSOLIDATED LIMITED
Immediate Holding Company: CHARLES TENNANT AND COMPANY (NORTHERN IRELAND) LIMITED
Registration no: NI001969 **VAT No.:** GB 252 0054 11
Date established: 1945 **Turnover:** £20m - £50m **No.of Employees:** 1 - 10
Product Groups: 29, 30, 33, 62, 66

Date of Accounts	Dec 10	Dec 09	Dec 08
Sales Turnover	34m	35m	42m
Pre Tax Profit/Loss	567	914	1m
Working Capital	10m	10m	11m
Fixed Assets	2m	2m	2m
Current Assets	17m	18m	18m
Current Liabilities	1m	968	1m

Tilos Ltd
North City Business Centre 2 Duncairn Gardens, Belfast, BT15 2GG
Tel: 028-9074 8222 **Fax:** 028-9074 8100
E-mail: sales@tilosltd.co.uk
Website: http://www.tilosltd.co.uk
Directors: B. Simms (Fin)
Immediate Holding Company: TILOS LIMITED
Registration no: NI025083 **VAT No.:** GB 574 9170 11
Date established: 1990 **Turnover:** Up to £250,000
No.of Employees: 1 - 10 **Product Groups:** 48

Date of Accounts	Jun 11	Jun 10	Jun 09
Working Capital	34	44	42
Fixed Assets	63	9	19
Current Assets	213	166	174

Tk-Ecc Ltd
770 Upper Newtownards Road Dundonald, Belfast, BT16 1UL
Tel: 028-9055 7200 **Fax:** 028-9055 7400
E-mail: glynis.thompson@tk-ecc.com
Bank(s): Northern Bank, Bank of Ireland
Directors: B. Doyle (Fin), L. Boyd (MD)
Managers: N. Jenkinson (Sales & Mktg Mg)
Immediate Holding Company: TK-ECC LIMITED
Registration no: NF003105 **VAT No.:** 617 6105 53 **Date established:** 1993
No.of Employees: 501 - 1000 **Product Groups:** 39

Todd Architects Ltd
4143 Hill Street, Belfast, BT1 2PB
Tel: 028-9024 5587 **Fax:** 028-9023 3363
E-mail: paul.crowe@toddarch.co.uk
Website: http://www.toddarch.com
Directors: M. McKeown (Fin)
Managers: T. Geary, S. Kelly (Mktg Serv Mgr), S. Irwin (Personnel)
Ultimate Holding Company: TODD (HOLDINGS) LIMITED
Immediate Holding Company: TODD ARCHITECTS LTD
Registration no: NI021213 **VAT No.:** GB 454 6967 05
Date established: 1988 **Turnover:** £2m - £5m **No.of Employees:** 21 - 50
Product Groups: 84

Date of Accounts	Jun 11	Jun 10	Jun 09
Sales Turnover	N/A	4m	6m
Pre Tax Profit/Loss	N/A	327	2m
Working Capital	4m	4m	4m
Fixed Assets	19	18	49
Current Assets	4m	5m	6m
Current Liabilities	N/A	696	1m

Topaz Energy
5 Airport Road, Belfast, BT3 9EU
Tel: 0800-460046 **Fax:** 028-9055 3855
E-mail: roz@shell-direct.com
Website: http://www.topazoildirect.co.uk
Managers: M. Strain (Chief Mgr)
Ultimate Holding Company: TOPAZ ENERGY GROUP LIMITED
Immediate Holding Company: TOPAZ ENERGY LIMITED
Registration no: NI012629 **VAT No.:** GB 235 7632 55
Date established: 1978 **Turnover:** £125m - £250m
No.of Employees: 1 - 10 **Product Groups:** 31, 32, 66

Date of Accounts	Mar 11	Mar 10	Mar 09
Sales Turnover	135m	147m	272m
Pre Tax Profit/Loss	-299	5m	-2m
Working Capital	4m	4m	-247
Fixed Assets	482	235	206
Current Assets	18m	28m	141m
Current Liabilities	656	3m	775

Total Cargo Services Ni Ltd
Victoria House 28 West Bank Road, Belfast, BT3 9JL
Tel: 028-9053 0053 **Fax:** 028-9053 0054
E-mail: gmaxwell@totalcargoservices.co.uk
Website: http://www.total-group.com
Bank(s): First Trust
Directors: G. Maxwell (MD)
Immediate Holding Company: TOTAL CARGO SERVICES (N.I.) LIMITED
Registration no: NI023228 **VAT No.:** GB 517 1836 47
Date established: 1989 **Turnover:** £2m - £5m **No.of Employees:** 11 - 20
Product Groups: 74, 76

Date of Accounts	Sep 11	Sep 10	Sep 09
Working Capital	275	206	225
Fixed Assets	1m	914	954
Current Assets	2m	1m	1m

Townsend Enterprise Park Ltd
28 Townsend Street, Belfast, BT13 2ES
Tel: 028-9043 5778 **Fax:** 028-9031 2328
E-mail: clare.savage@townsend.co.uk
Website: http://www.townsend.co.uk
Directors: C. Savage (MD)
Immediate Holding Company: TOWNSEND ENTERPRISE PARK LIMITED
Registration no: NI020329 **VAT No.:** GB 577 1794 37
Date established: 1987 **Turnover:** £250,000 - £500,000
No.of Employees: 1 - 10 **Product Groups:** 80

Date of Accounts	Mar 11	Mar 10	Mar 09
Sales Turnover	294	304	N/A
Pre Tax Profit/Loss	-13	35	N/A
Working Capital	2	17	3
Fixed Assets	994	1m	1m
Current Assets	92	102	84
Current Liabilities	61	66	N/A

Translink Ltd
Milewater Road, Belfast, BT3 9BG
Tel: 028-9035 1201
E-mail: stephen.armstrong@translink.co.uk
Website: http://www.translink.co.uk
Bank(s): Bank of Ireland
Directors: A. Mercer (Pers), S. Armstrong (Fin), S. Armstrong (Dir), P. O'Neill (MD)
Managers: C. Rogan (Mktg Serv Mgr), D. Laird (I.T. Exec)
Immediate Holding Company: TRANSLINK (NI) LIMITED
Registration no: NI006673 **Date established:** 1966
No.of Employees: 101 - 250 **Product Groups:** 72

Travelodge Hotels Ltd
15 Brunswick Street, Belfast, BT2 7GE
Tel: 08719-846188 **Fax:** 028-9023 2999
E-mail: belfast@travellodge.ie
Website: http://www.travelodge.co.uk
Managers: L. Bell (Mgr)
Ultimate Holding Company: DUBAI INTERNATIONAL CAPITAL LLP (UAE)
Immediate Holding Company: TRAVELODGE HOTELS LIMITED
Registration no: 00769170 **Date established:** 1963
No.of Employees: 21 - 50 **Product Groups:** 67, 69

Date of Accounts	Dec 10	Dec 09	Dec 08
Sales Turnover	332m	294m	287m
Pre Tax Profit/Loss	15m	67m	9m
Working Capital	377m	335m	275m
Fixed Assets	558m	571m	566m
Current Assets	566m	508m	411m
Current Liabilities	70m	30m	65m

Triplicate Design
Floor 5 22 Adelaide Street, Belfast, BT2 8GD
Tel: 028-9023 3296 **Fax:** 028-9024 9252
E-mail: studio@triplicatedesign.com
Website: http://www.triplicatedesign.com
Directors: C. Hume (MD)
Immediate Holding Company: TRIPLICATE DESIGN LIMITED
Registration no: NI021883 **Date established:** 1988
Turnover: £500,000 - £1m **No.of Employees:** 11 - 20
Product Groups: 80, 81, 84

Date of Accounts	Dec 11	Dec 10	Dec 09
Working Capital	166	250	184
Fixed Assets	681	711	755
Current Assets	396	535	410

Trouw Nutrition
36 Ship Street, Belfast, BT15 1JL
Tel: 028-9074 8233 **Fax:** 028-9035 2767
E-mail: karen.montgomery@nutreco.com
Website: http://www.nutreco.com
Managers: J. Arneill (Chief Mgr), K. Montgomery (Mgr), K. Smith (Comptroller)
Immediate Holding Company: TROUW NUTRITION (NORTHERN IRELAND) LIMITED
Registration no: NI006605 **VAT No.:** GB 616 1702 66
Date established: 1966 **No.of Employees:** 21 - 50 **Product Groups:** 20

Date of Accounts	Dec 09	Dec 07
Working Capital	10	10
Current Assets	10	10

Tudor Journals Ltd
97 Botanic Avenue, Belfast, BT7 1JN
Tel: 028-9032 0088 **Fax:** 028-9032 3163
E-mail: sales@tudorjournals.com
Website: http://www.tudorjournals.com
Bank(s): Northern Bank
Directors: W. Campbell (MD)
Managers: P. Pavis (Sales Admin)
Immediate Holding Company: TUDOR JOURNALS LIMITED
Registration no: NI021185 **VAT No.:** GB 286 9022 31
Date established: 1987 **Turnover:** £250,000 - £500,000
No.of Employees: 11 - 20 **Product Groups:** 28

Tughans
Marlborough House 28-32 Victoria Street, Belfast, BT1 3GG
Tel: 028-9055 3300 **Fax:** 028-9055 0096
E-mail: law@tughans.com
Website: http://www.tughans.com
Directors: I. Coulter (Snr Part)
Immediate Holding Company: TUGHANS NOMINEE LIMITED
Registration no: NI613443 **VAT No.:** GB 252 0251 09
Date established: 2012 **Turnover:** £2m - £5m
No.of Employees: 101 - 250 **Product Groups:** 80

U T V Internet
Havelock House Ormeau Road, Belfast, BT7 1EB
Tel: 028-9020 1555 **Fax:** 028-9033 0039
E-mail: sales@thewave.co.uk
Website: http://www.u.tv
Directors: P. Hutchinson (Sales)
Managers: T. Jordan (Sales Prom Mgr), D. Gibson (Sales Prom Mgr), E. Kent ()
Ultimate Holding Company: UTV Media plc
Immediate Holding Company: UTV Internet Limited
Registration no: NI032652 **Date established:** 1997 **Turnover:** £5m - £10m
No.of Employees: 21 - 50 **Product Groups:** 81

Date of Accounts	Dec 11	Dec 10	Dec 09
Sales Turnover	7m	8m	9m
Pre Tax Profit/Loss	-601	91	133
Working Capital	-445	-224	144
Fixed Assets	154	355	494
Current Assets	2m	2m	2m
Current Liabilities	1m	1m	1m

Ulster Bank Group (Head Office)
11-16 Donegall Square East, Belfast, BT1 5UB
Tel: 028-9027 6000 **Fax:** 028-9027 5507
E-mail: cormac.mccarthy@ulsterbank.com
Website: http://www.ulsterbank.co.uk
Bank(s): Ulster Bank
Directors: P. McMahon (Dir), R. McNulty (Dir), S. Daniels (Pers), P. Halliday-McKie (Dir), W. O'Kane (Jnr) (Dir), A. Gillesby (Ch), T. Reid (Dir), M. Rafferty (Dir), C. Mccarthy (Grp Chief Exec), J. McNally (Dep Chief Exec), M. McCarthy (Grp Chief Exec), H. Gray (Dir)
Managers: W. Caldwell, O. Lynas (Mgr), P. O'Neill, R. Price, D. McArdle, N. Fitzpatrick (Mgr), B. Robertson (Ops Mgr), D. Peacock (Sec), D. O'Neill, G. Caldwell (Mgr), G. Simms, I. Laird (Comptroller), J. West, K. Gallen
Ultimate Holding Company: THE ROYAL BANK OF SCOTLAND GROUP PUBLIC LIMITED COMPANY
Immediate Holding Company: ULSTER BANK, LIMITED
Registration no: R0000733 **Date established:** 1967
No.of Employees: 501 - 1000 **Product Groups:** 82

Date of Accounts	Dec 10	Dec 09	Dec 08
Pre Tax Profit/Loss	-3233m	-1368m	-694m
Fixed Assets	1588m	1872m	507m
Current Assets	52559m	59879m	69178m
Current Liabilities	47662m	55805m	65346m

Ulster Factors
7 North Street, Belfast, BT1 1NA
Tel: 028-9032 4522 **Fax:** 028-9023 0336
E-mail: wjm@ulsterfactors.com
Website: http://www.ulsterfactors.com
Directors: W. Murray (MD)
Immediate Holding Company: ANTLER ESTATES LIMITED
Registration no: NI030738 **VAT No.:** GB 353 0684 61
Date established: 1962 **Turnover:** £1m - £2m **No.of Employees:** 1 - 10
Product Groups: 82

Ulster Farmers Union
Head Office 475 Antrim Road, Belfast, BT15 3DA
Tel: 028-9037 0222 **Fax:** 028-9037 1231
E-mail: acuthbert@ufuhq.com
Website: http://www.ufuni.org
Bank(s): Northern Bank
Directors: A. Cuthbert (MD)
Immediate Holding Company: FARMERS JOURNAL LIMITED -THE
Registration no: NI002715 **Date established:** 1949
No.of Employees: 11 - 20 **Product Groups:** 87

Date of Accounts	Dec 08
Working Capital	1
Current Assets	1

Ulster Independent Clinic
245 Stranmillis Road, Belfast, BT9 5JH
Tel: 028-9066 1212 **Fax:** 028-9063 8174
E-mail: secretary@uic.org.uk
Website: http://www.ulsterindependentclinic.co.uk
Bank(s): Northern Bank
Managers: D. Graham
Immediate Holding Company: ULSTER INDEPENDENT CLINIC LIMITED
Registration no: NI012066 **VAT No.:** 749 3944 82 **Date established:** 1977
Turnover: £20m - £50m **No.of Employees:** 251 - 500 **Product Groups:** 88

Date of Accounts	Apr 11	Apr 10	Apr 09
Sales Turnover	23m	22m	22m
Pre Tax Profit/Loss	2m	2m	2m
Working Capital	7m	5m	3m
Fixed Assets	23m	25m	26m
Current Assets	10m	7m	7m
Current Liabilities	845	1m	2m

Ulster Tatler
39 Boucher Road, Belfast, BT12 6UT
Tel: 028-9066 3311 **Fax:** 028-9038 1915
E-mail: edit@ulstertatler.com
Website: http://www.ulstertatler.com
Managers: C. Sherry
VAT No.: GB 254 0786 55 **Date established:** 1961
No.of Employees: 21 - 50 **Product Groups:** 28

United Dairy Farmers
15 Dargan Road, Belfast, BT3 9LS
Tel: 028-9037 2237 **Fax:** 028-9037 2222
E-mail: info@utdni.co.uk
Website: http://www.utdni.co.uk
Directors: D. Brown (I.T. Dir), D. Dobbin (Grp Chief Exec), M. Mullen (Pers)
Managers: B. Burdock (Personnel), J. Anderson (Purch Mgr), J. Hempton (Sales Prom Mgr), E. Hunter (Mktg Serv Mgr)
Ultimate Holding Company: PARITY GROUP PUBLIC LIMITED COMPANY
Immediate Holding Company: PARITY SOLUTIONS (IRELAND) LIMITED
Registration no: NI019418 **VAT No.:** GB 617 7465 18
Date established: 1986 **Turnover:** Up to £250,000
No.of Employees: 1 - 10 **Product Groups:** 62, 87

United Feeds Ltd
8 Northern Road, Belfast, BT3 9AL
Tel: 028-9075 9000 **Fax:** 028-9075 1170
E-mail: sales@ufeed.com
Website: http://www.ufeed.com
Managers: D. Stewart
Immediate Holding Company: United Feeds Limited
Registration no: NI038000 **VAT No.:** GB 251 7274 65
Date established: 2000 **Turnover:** £20m - £50m **No.of Employees:** 1 - 10
Product Groups: 20, 32

Date of Accounts	Mar 11	Mar 10	Sep 09
Sales Turnover	33m	16m	30m
Pre Tax Profit/Loss	995	364	776
Working Capital	920	1m	1m
Fixed Assets	1m	2m	2m
Current Assets	7m	6m	4m
Current Liabilities	629	786	794

United Paper Merchants Ltd
15 Linfield Industrial Estate Linfield Road, Belfast, BT12 5LA
Tel: 028-9032 7303 **Fax:** 028-9043 8702
E-mail: sales@united-paper.com
Website: http://www.united-paper.com
Bank(s): Bank of Ireland
Directors: E. Mccullough (MD)
Immediate Holding Company: UNITED PAPER MERCHANTS LIMITED
Registration no: NI023245 **VAT No.:** GB 252 2372 84
Date established: 1989 **Turnover:** £2m - £5m **No.of Employees:** 11 - 20
Product Groups: 66

Date of Accounts	Dec 11	Dec 10	Dec 09
Working Capital	1m	904	905
Fixed Assets	82	78	32
Current Assets	2m	2m	1m

Universal Industrial Spraying
10 Kilwee Business Park Upper Dunmurry Lane, Dunmurry, Belfast, BT17 0HD
Tel: 028-9030 1094 **Fax:** 028-9060 0030
E-mail: gerry.dodds@btconnect.com
Directors: M. Nesbitt (MD)
Date established: 1985 **No.of Employees:** 1 - 10 **Product Groups:** 46, 48

Viridian Group Ltd
PO Box 2, Belfast, BT9 5HT
Tel: 028-9066 8416 **Fax:** 028-9068 9117
E-mail: harry.mccracken@viridiangroup.co.uk
Website: http://www.viridiangroup.co.uk
Bank(s): Bank of Ireland
Directors: H. Mccracken (MD), I. Thom (Co Sec), L. McKenzie (MD), P. Bourke (Grp Chief Exec)
Ultimate Holding Company: ARCAPITA BANK BSC(C) (BAHRAIN)
Immediate Holding Company: VIRIDIAN GROUP LIMITED
Registration no: NI033250 **Date established:** 1997
Turnover: Over £1,000m **No.of Employees:** 1501 & over
Product Groups: 18

see next page

Viridian Group Ltd - Cont'd

Date of Accounts	Mar 11	Mar 10	Mar 09
Pre Tax Profit/Loss	141m	99m	94m
Working Capital	274m	320m	276m
Fixed Assets	189m	734m	735m
Current Assets	678m	861m	831m
Current Liabilities	20m	9m	537m

W D Engineering

54 Tamar Street, Belfast, BT4 1HS
Tel: 028-9045 9739 **Fax:** 028-9073 1318
E-mail: mail@wdengineering.co.uk
Directors: W. Dawson (Prop)
Immediate Holding Company: W.D. MATERIALS HANDLING LTD
Registration no: NI038311 **Date established:** 2000
No.of Employees: 1 - 10 **Product Groups:** 35, 39, 45

Date of Accounts	Aug 10	Aug 09	Aug 08
Working Capital	322	214	206
Fixed Assets	1	1	1
Current Assets	707	292	365
Current Liabilities	45	10	51

W H Mcavoy

7 Wellington Park, Belfast, BT9 6DJ
Tel: 028-9066 9541 **Fax:** 028-9066 6363
E-mail: whmcevoybelfast@btconnect.com
Directors: M. McAvoy (MD)
Immediate Holding Company: W.H. MCEVOY LIMITED
Registration no: NI018908 **Date established:** 1985
No.of Employees: 1 - 10 **Product Groups:** 84

Date of Accounts	Oct 09	Oct 08	Oct 07
Working Capital	-179	-83	-11
Fixed Assets	18	26	34
Current Assets	120	127	201

W H Stephens

63 Malone Road, Belfast, BT9 6SA
Tel: 028-9066 3123 **Fax:** 028-9066 4973
E-mail: info@whstephens.com
Website: http://www.whstephens.com
Bank(s): Northern Bank
Directors: M. Scullion (Snr Part)
VAT No.: GB 252 8087 53 **Turnover:** £250,000 - £500,000
No.of Employees: 21 - 50 **Product Groups:** 80, 84

W J Miscampbell & Co.

6 Annadale Avenue, Belfast, BT7 3JH
Tel: 028-9049 1711 **Fax:** 028-9069 2938
E-mail: office@miscampbell.co.uk
Website: http://www.miscampbell.co.uk
Bank(s): Northern Bank
Directors: B. Miscampbell (Prop)
Immediate Holding Company: CHILDREN'S SUNSHINE TRUST LTD
Registration no: NI018839 **VAT No.:** GB 251 7574 53
Date established: 2009 **Turnover:** £1m - £2m **No.of Employees:** 11 - 20
Product Groups: 80

Date of Accounts	Jun 11	Jun 10	Jun 09
Working Capital	4m	4m	4m
Fixed Assets	55	30	40
Current Assets	4m	4m	4m

W M B Stainless

Block B1 Channel Commercial Park Queens Road, Belfast, BT3 9DT
Tel: 028-9045 0464 **Fax:** 0870-732 1304
E-mail: d.whaley@wmbstainless.co.uk
Website: http://www.wmbstainless.co.uk
Directors: D. Whaley (MD)
Managers: S. Johnson (Chief Mgr)
Immediate Holding Company: W.M.B. STAINLESS LIMITED
Registration no: NI015209 **Date established:** 1981
No.of Employees: 21 - 50 **Product Groups:** 35

Date of Accounts	Oct 08	Oct 07	Oct 06
Working Capital	675	480	148
Fixed Assets	215	178	139
Current Assets	2m	2m	2m

W N R Engineering

20 Ballykeel Road South Carryduff, Belfast, BT8 8AL
Tel: 028-9081 3501 **Fax:** 028-9081 4807
Website: http://www.nitd.com
Directors: W. Rodger (Prop)
Date established: 1981 **No.of Employees:** 1 - 10 **Product Groups:** 38, 42

W Y G

Unit 1 Locksley Business Park Montgomery Road, Belfast, BT6 9UP
Tel: 028-9070 6000 **Fax:** 028-9070 6050
E-mail: belfast@wyg.com
Website: http://www.wyg.com
Directors: H. Brett (Reg)
Immediate Holding Company: WHITE YOUNG GREEN CONSULTING LIMITED
Registration no: NF003673 **VAT No.:** GB 454 5936 21
Date established: 2002 **Turnover:** £2m - £5m
No.of Employees: 101 - 250 **Product Groups:** 54, 84

Waterfront Hall Conference & Concert Centre

Lanyon Place, Belfast, BT1 3WH
Tel: 028-9033 4400 **Fax:** 028-9024 9862
E-mail: enquiries@waterfront.co.uk
Website: http://www.waterfront.co.uk
Managers: N. Sadlier, J. Patterson, P. Mulholland, T. Husbands (Chief Mgr)
Turnover: £2m - £5m **No.of Employees:** 21 - 50 **Product Groups:** 69, 83, 89

Watts Group plc

Forsythe House Cromac Square, Belfast, BT2 8LA
Tel: 028-9024 8222 **Fax:** 028-9024 8007
E-mail: harry.dowey@watts-ing.com
Website: http://www.watts-international.com
Directors: H. Dowey (Dir)
Immediate Holding Company: WATTS GROUP PLC
Registration no: 05728557 **VAT No.:** GB 205 9609 61
Date established: 2006 **Turnover:** £10m - £20m **No.of Employees:** 1 - 10
Product Groups: 80, 84

Date of Accounts	Apr 11	Apr 10	Apr 12
Sales Turnover	14m	15m	13m
Pre Tax Profit/Loss	-581	-2m	967
Working Capital	-440	9	87
Fixed Assets	268	375	204
Current Assets	5m	6m	4m
Current Liabilities	2m	2m	2m

Watts Industrial Tyres plc

Unit 14 Somerton Park Dargan Cresent, Belfast, BT3 9JP
Tel: 028-9077 3443 **Fax:** 028-9077 0095
E-mail: belfast@watts-tyres.co.uk
Website: http://www.industrialtyre.com
Directors: J. Mindermann (MD), J. Thurstan (Ch)
Managers: T. Hinton (District Mgr), J. Pick (Mktg Serv Mgr), R. Minett (Personnel)
Immediate Holding Company: WATTS INDUSTRIAL TYRES LIMITED
Registration no: 01434811 **Date established:** 1979
No.of Employees: 1 - 10 **Product Groups:** 29, 68

We Find It Press Clippings

40 Galwally Avenue, Belfast, BT8 7AJ
Tel: 028-9064 6008 **Fax:** 028-9064 6008
E-mail: avrilwefindit@hotmail.com
Directors: A. Forsyth (Prop), A. Forsythe (Prop)
VAT No.: GB 517 2749 37 **Date established:** 1986
Turnover: Up to £250,000 **No.of Employees:** 1 - 10 **Product Groups:** 81

Weber Shandwick

32-38 Linenhall Street, Belfast, BT2 8BG
Tel: 028-9076 1007 **Fax:** 028-9076 1012
E-mail: info@shandwickdesign.com
Website: http://www.webershandwick.co.uk
Directors: S. Cassidy (MD), R. Williamson (MD)
Immediate Holding Company: GILMONT DEVELOPMENTS LIMITED
Registration no: NI018738 **VAT No.:** 517448143 **Date established:** 2007
Turnover: £5m - £10m **No.of Employees:** 1 - 10 **Product Groups:** 44, 81

Date of Accounts	Apr 12	Apr 11	Apr 10
Working Capital	562	653	2
Fixed Assets	N/A	2	N/A
Current Assets	562	653	3
Current Liabilities	N/A	N/A	1

Wellington Computer Systems Ltd

91 Wellington Park, Belfast, BT9 6DP
Tel: 028-9068 1531 **Fax:** 028-9066 0181
E-mail: info@w-c-s.co.uk
Website: http://www.wellingtoncomputers.com
Directors: K. Taylor (Dir)
Managers: N. Burns, P. Knight (Sales & Mktg Mg), P. Mahood (Sales Admin)
Immediate Holding Company: WELLINGTON COMPUTER SYSTEMS LIMITED
Registration no: NI016424 **VAT No.:** GB 375 8418 16
Date established: 1983 **No.of Employees:** 21 - 50 **Product Groups:** 44, 84, 86

Date of Accounts	Sep 11	Sep 10	Sep 09
Working Capital	1m	1m	1m
Fixed Assets	56	80	41
Current Assets	2m	2m	2m
Current Liabilities	N/A	327	352

William Clements Chemicals

Witham Street, Belfast, BT4 1HP
Tel: 028-9073 8395 **Fax:** 028-9045 0532
E-mail: info@clementschemicals.com
Website: http://www.clementschemicals.com
Bank(s): Northern Bank
Directors: R. Farley (Prop)
Immediate Holding Company: WILLIAM CLEMENTS (CHEMICALS) LTD
Registration no: NI022376 **VAT No.:** GB 517 0975 38
Date established: 1989 **Turnover:** £1m - £2m **No.of Employees:** 11 - 20
Product Groups: 32, 66, 68

Date of Accounts	Mar 12	Mar 11	Mar 10
Working Capital	366	312	242
Fixed Assets	631	715	848
Current Assets	789	791	779
Current Liabilities	N/A	N/A	500

Williams & Shaw Ltd

Agar House 31 Ballynahinch Road, Carryduff, Belfast, BT8 8EH
Tel: 028-9081 3075 **Fax:** 028-9081 4135
E-mail: info@williams-shaw.co.uk
Website: http://www.williamsandshaw.co.uk
Bank(s): Ulster Bank
Directors: S. Cupples (MD)
Immediate Holding Company: WILLIAMS & SHAW LIMITED
Registration no: NI036380 **VAT No.:** GB 286 7722 13
Date established: 1999 **No.of Employees:** 11 - 20 **Product Groups:** 84

Date of Accounts	Jun 11	Jun 10	Jun 09
Working Capital	127	148	175
Fixed Assets	85	113	141
Current Assets	413	487	473

Willis Ltd

24 Ormeau Avenue, Belfast, BT2 8HS
Tel: 028-9024 2131 **Fax:** 028-9032 1087
Website: http://www.willis.com
Bank(s): Northern Bank
Directors: C. Stanley (Fin), D. Workman (MD)
Managers: T. Nichol (Personnel)
Ultimate Holding Company: WILLIS GROUP HOLDINGS LIMITED (BERMUDA)
Immediate Holding Company: WILLIS HARRIS MARRIAN LIMITED
Registration no: NI006228 **VAT No.:** GB 334 1289 70
Date established: 1965 **Turnover:** £2m - £5m **No.of Employees:** 21 - 50
Product Groups: 80, 82

Date of Accounts	Dec 09	Dec 08
Working Capital	20	20
Current Assets	20	20

Willis Heating & Plumbing Co. Ltd

Unit 28-29 Dargan Crescent, Belfast, BT3 9JB
Tel: 028-9078 1236 **Fax:** 028-9077 4877
E-mail: mail@willis-renewables.com
Website: http://www.willis-heating.com
Bank(s): First Trust
Directors: S. Collins (Dir)
Managers: J. Willis (Comm)
Immediate Holding Company: WILLIS HEATING AND PLUMBING CO LTD
Registration no: NI024071 **VAT No.:** GB 253 0099 80
Date established: 1990 **Turnover:** £500,000 - £1m
No.of Employees: 11 - 20 **Product Groups:** 52

Date of Accounts	Apr 11	Apr 10	Apr 09
Working Capital	302	304	295
Fixed Assets	10	9	16
Current Assets	723	652	539

Wilmor & Co. Ltd

Morton House 10 Lorne Street, Belfast, BT9 7EB
Tel: 028-9068 6600 **Fax:** 028-9066 8961
Directors: C. Greer (Prop)
Managers: M. Ruthers (Mktg Serv Mgr)
Ultimate Holding Company: LORNE HOLDINGS LIMITED
Immediate Holding Company: WILMOR & CO. LIMITED
Registration no: NI021600 **VAT No.:** GB 287 0446 40
Date established: 1988 **Turnover:** £5m - £10m **No.of Employees:** 11 - 20
Product Groups: 63

Date of Accounts	Jun 11	Jun 10	Jun 09
Sales Turnover	8m	11m	11m
Pre Tax Profit/Loss	-181	148	320
Working Capital	2m	2m	2m
Current Assets	3m	4m	4m
Current Liabilities	67	137	248

Windsor Photoprints

130 Eglantine Avenue, Belfast, BT9 6EU
Tel: 028-9066 8831 **Fax:** 028-9066 5431
E-mail: accounts@windsorphotoprints.co.uk
Website: http://www.windsorphotoprints.co.uk
Bank(s): First Trust
Directors: M. Mooney (Prop)
Immediate Holding Company: WINDSOR PHOTOPRINTS LTD
Registration no: NI021703 **VAT No.:** GB 517 3790 35
Date established: 1988 **Turnover:** £500,000 - £1m
No.of Employees: 11 - 20 **Product Groups:** 80

Woodtox Dampcheck Ltd

100 Sydenham Avenue, Belfast, BT4 2DT
Tel: 028-9065 1750 **Fax:** 028-9065 0090
Directors: D. Browne (MD), D. Brown (MD)
Date established: 1947 **Turnover:** Up to £250,000
No.of Employees: 1 - 10 **Product Groups:** 52

Xtra Vision

Rose House First Floor 2a Derryvolgie Avenue, Belfast, BT9 6FL
Tel: 028-9066 0304 **Fax:** 028-9066 3714
E-mail: sales@etravision.co.uk
Website: http://www.xtravision.co.uk
Directors: A. Frel (Pers)
Immediate Holding Company: XTRA-VISION LIMITED
Registration no: NF004355 **VAT No.:** GB 617 5627 28
Date established: 2009 **No.of Employees:** 1 - 10 **Product Groups:** 83

03 Solutions Ltd

Centre House 79 Chichester St, Belfast, BT1 4JE
Tel: 028-9065 6552
E-mail: mail@o3solutions.com
Website: http://www.o3solutions.com
Directors: R. O'Hare (Dir)
Registration no: NI049766 **Date established:** 2004
Turnover: Up to £250,000 **No.of Employees:** 1 - 10 **Product Groups:** 30, 32, 36, 37, 38, 40, 41, 49, 61, 63, 66, 83

Co. Antrim

Bushmills

J C Halliday & Sons

206 Straid Road, Bushmills, BT57 8XJ
Tel: 028-2073 1452 **Fax:** 028-2073 2290
E-mail: sales@citroenireland.com
Website: http://www.citroenireland.com
Directors: L. Halliday (Prop)
Managers: A. Brogan (Sales Prom Mgr), G. McBride (Comptroller)
Immediate Holding Company: J.C. HALLIDAY & SONS LIMITED
Registration no: NI061832 **VAT No.:** GB 311 1429 15
Date established: 2006 **No.of Employees:** 11 - 20 **Product Groups:** 68

Old Bushmills Distillery Co. Ltd

The Distillery, Bushmills, BT57 8XH
Tel: 028-2073 1521 **Fax:** 028-2073 1339
E-mail: gordon.donoghue@diageo.com
Website: http://www.bushmills.com
Bank(s): Northern Bank
Directors: G. Donoghue (MD), L. McConaghie (Fin)
Ultimate Holding Company: DIAGEO PLC
Immediate Holding Company: OLD BUSHMILLS DISTILLERY COMPANY - THE LIMITED
Registration no: NI000601 **VAT No.:** GB 252 5097 65
Date established: 1930 **Turnover:** £20m - £50m
No.of Employees: 101 - 250 **Product Groups:** 21

Date of Accounts	Jun 11	Jun 10	Jun 09
Sales Turnover	40m	35m	27m
Pre Tax Profit/Loss	14m	8m	3m
Working Capital	43m	32m	31m
Fixed Assets	43m	40m	34m
Current Assets	75m	69m	68m
Current Liabilities	2m	2m	4m

Co. Tyrone

Caledon

Caledon Precision Engineering

110 Derrycourtney Road, Caledon, BT68 4XP
Tel: 028-3756 8550 **Fax:** 028-3756 9911
E-mail: info@caledonengineering.com
Website: http://www.caledonengineering.com
Directors: B. Marshall (Prop), T. Knox (Dir)
Immediate Holding Company: Caledon Precision Engineering Ltd
Registration no: NI068450 **VAT No.:** GB 286 9230 24
Date established: 2008 **No.of Employees:** 11 - 20 **Product Groups:** 45

Date of Accounts	Mar 11	Mar 10	Mar 09
Working Capital	-435	-592	-413
Fixed Assets	938	979	1m
Current Assets	612	461	291

Co. Antrim

Carrickfergus

A Engineering
45 Broadlands Park, Carrickfergus, BT38 7DB
Tel: 028-9336 6516 **Fax:** 028-9336 6516
E-mail: info@aplusengineering.co.uk
Website: http://www.aplusengineering.co.uk
Directors: N. Anthony (Prop)
No.of Employees: 1 - 10 **Product Groups:** 40, 42, 45, 67

B Crowe & Sons Ltd
22 Marshallstown Road, Carrickfergus, BT38 9DE
Tel: 028-9336 3686 **Fax:** 028-9336 2452
E-mail: info@homesbycrowe.co.uk
Website: http://www.homesbycrowe.co.uk
Directors: R. Crowe (Dir), S. Crowe (Dir)
Immediate Holding Company: MILEBUSH JOINERY & SUPPLY CO. LIMITED
Registration no: NI030675 **VAT No.:** GB 251 8334 68
Date established: 1996 **No.of Employees:** 1 - 10 **Product Groups:** 52

Date of Accounts	Apr 11	Apr 10	Apr 09
Working Capital	408	860	982
Fixed Assets	132	159	184
Current Assets	10m	11m	11m

Carrickfergus Advertiser & East Antrim Gazette
6 Market Place, Carrickfergus, BT38 7AW
Tel: 028-9336 3651 **Fax:** 028-9336 3092
E-mail: editor@carrickadvertiser.co.uk
Website: http://www.carrickfergusadvertiser.co.uk
Managers: D. Hall
Immediate Holding Company: CARRICKFERGUS ADVERTISER LIMITED
Registration no: NI027016 **VAT No.:** GB 517 5517 43
Date established: 1992 **No.of Employees:** 1 - 10 **Product Groups:** 28

Date of Accounts	Dec 10	Dec 09	Dec 08
Working Capital	-1	-1m	-1m
Fixed Assets	N/A	6	6
Current Assets	1	367	318

Castle Signs
75 Carrickfergus Industrial Centre Belfast Road, Carrickfergus, BT38 8PH
Tel: 028-9335 1182 **Fax:** 028-9336 3562
E-mail: castlesigns@aol.com
Website: http://www.castlesigns.co.uk
Managers: N. Hall (Mgr)
Ultimate Holding Company: ELECTRACTION LIMITED
Immediate Holding Company: INDUSTRIAL SALES AGENCIES (N.I.) LTD
Registration no: NI025863 **VAT No.:** GB 255 6587 25
Date established: 1987 **No.of Employees:** 1 - 10 **Product Groups:** 30, 49

Date of Accounts	Jan 09
Working Capital	-31
Current Assets	10

Classique Fireplaces
Unit 5 Kilroot Park, Carrickfergus, BT38 7PR
Tel: 028-9336 6050 **Fax:** 028-9336 6050
E-mail: sales@classiquefireplaces.co.uk
Website: http://www.classiquefireplaces.com
Directors: E. Fyfe (Prop)
No.of Employees: 1 - 10 **Product Groups:** 33, 40

Coast Road Hotel
28 Scotch Quarter, Carrickfergus, BT38 7DP
Tel: 028-9335 1021 **Fax:** 028-9336 2254
E-mail: info@coastroadhotel.co.uk
Website: http://www.coastroadhotel.co.uk
Directors: R. Bailie (Prop), R. Bailey (Head)
Immediate Holding Company: BAILIE HOTELS LTD
Registration no: NI039118 **VAT No.:** GB 375 8814 08
Date established: 2000 **No.of Employees:** 21 - 50 **Product Groups:** 69

David Graham Structures
Unit 4a Kilroot Park, Carrickfergus, BT38 7PR
Tel: 028-9336 7774 **Fax:** 028-9336 7779
E-mail: david@dgstructures.co.uk
Directors: D. Graham (Prop)
Date established: 2006 **No.of Employees:** 1 - 10 **Product Groups:** 35

Dobbins Inn Hotel
6-8 High Street, Carrickfergus, BT38 7AF
Tel: 028-9335 1905 **Fax:** 028-9335 1905
E-mail: bookingdobbins@btconnect.com
Website: http://www.dobbinsinnhotel.co.uk
Directors: D. Fallis (Prop), M. Fallis (Prop)
VAT No.: GB 311 3033 30 **No.of Employees:** 11 - 20 **Product Groups:** 69, 84

East Antrim Mini Mix
64 Larne Road Whitehead, Carrickfergus, BT38 9TF
Tel: 028-9336 7771 **Fax:** 028-9336 6949
E-mail: ronnie@eastantrimminimix.co.uk
Website: http://www.eastantrimminimix.co.uk
Directors: R. Mcilroy (Prop)
Date established: 1987 **Turnover:** Up to £250,000
No.of Employees: 1 - 10 **Product Groups:** 32, 33

Electraction N I Ltd
75 Carrickfergus Industrial Centre Belfast Road, Carrickfergus, BT38 8PH
Tel: 028-9336 4454 **Fax:** 028-9336 4455
E-mail: sales@electraction.co.uk
Directors: N. Craigy (MD)
Ultimate Holding Company: ELECTRACTION LIMITED
Immediate Holding Company: ELECTRACTION (N.I.) LIMITED
Registration no: FC022405 **Date established:** 2000 **Turnover:** £2m - £5m
No.of Employees: 1 - 10 **Product Groups:** 37

Date of Accounts	Dec 01	Dec 00
Sales Turnover	2m	974
Pre Tax Profit/Loss	-88	89
Working Capital	286	413
Fixed Assets	32	37
Current Assets	711	479
Current Liabilities	135	43

Geoff Castles Boiler Services Ltd
97a Belfast Road, Carrickfergus, BT38 8BX
Tel: 028-9336 8949 **Fax:** 028-9336 3378
E-mail: info@geoffcastles.co.uk
Website: http://www.geoffcastles.co.uk
Bank(s): First Trust
Directors: G. Castles (Dir)
Managers: J. McKinney
Immediate Holding Company: GEOFF CASTLES BOILER SERVICES (N.I.) LIMITED
Registration no: NI029781 **VAT No.:** GB 375 7027 36
Date established: 1995 **Turnover:** Up to £250,000
No.of Employees: 21 - 50 **Product Groups:** 48, 52, 83

Date of Accounts	Dec 11	Dec 10	Dec 09
Working Capital	729	693	610
Fixed Assets	111	117	172
Current Assets	1m	1m	1m

Hilton Meat Products Ltd
21a Kilroot Park, Carrickfergus, BT38 7PR
Tel: 028-9336 3155 **Fax:** 028-9335 1027
E-mail: info@hiltonmeats.com
Website: http://www.hiltonmeats.com
Bank(s): Ulster Bank
Managers: J. Richardson (Chief Acct), M. Beggs (Chief Mgr), M. Betts (Chief Mgr)
Immediate Holding Company: HILTON MEAT PRODUCTS LIMITED
Registration no: NI018068 **VAT No.:** GB 422 1227 06
Date established: 1984 **Turnover:** £5m - £10m **No.of Employees:** 21 - 50
Product Groups: 20

Date of Accounts	Sep 11	Sep 10	Sep 09
Sales Turnover	5m	6m	7m
Pre Tax Profit/Loss	341	824	1m
Working Capital	1m	813	3m
Fixed Assets	172	168	143
Current Assets	2m	2m	4m
Current Liabilities	567	682	643

Homestart Carrickfergus
8 Meadowbank Road, Carrickfergus, BT38 8YF
Tel: 028-9332 8875 **Fax:** 028-9336 9979
E-mail: info@ceal.co.uk
Website: http://www.ceal.co.uk
Managers: H. Gault
Immediate Holding Company: SOL R HUB LTD
Registration no: NI015089 **VAT No.:** GB 617 7309 32
Date established: 2011 **Turnover:** Up to £250,000
No.of Employees: 1 - 10 **Product Groups:** 87

Date of Accounts	Dec 11
Working Capital	-4
Fixed Assets	1
Current Assets	87

L D Units Ltd
7 Sloefield Park, Carrickfergus, BT38 8GR
Tel: 028-9336 9297 **Fax:** 028-9335 9173
E-mail: info@ldunits.co.uk
Website: http://www.ldunits.co.uk
Managers: A. Mcormick (Mgr)
Immediate Holding Company: L.D. UNITS LIMITED
Registration no: NI029783 **VAT No.:** GB 422 2788 58
Date established: 1995 **No.of Employees:** 11 - 20 **Product Groups:** 26

Date of Accounts	Oct 11	Oct 10	Oct 09
Working Capital	70	94	118
Fixed Assets	168	166	163
Current Assets	253	258	346

David Martin & Son Ltd
Carrickfergus Industrial Centre Belfast Road, Carrickfergus, BT38 8PH
Tel: 028-9335 1294 **Fax:** 028-9335 1763
E-mail: info@davidmartinandson.co.uk
Website: http://www.davidmartinandson.co.uk
Directors: P. Martin (Dir)
Ultimate Holding Company: ELECTRACTION LIMITED
Immediate Holding Company: David Martin and Son Limited
Registration no: NI068481 **VAT No.:** GB 375 8775 89
Date established: 2008 **No.of Employees:** 1 - 10 **Product Groups:** 28, 30, 66

Date of Accounts	Mar 12	Mar 11	Mar 10
Working Capital	422	475	472
Fixed Assets	99	99	99
Current Assets	554	585	605

N K Fencing
40 Trailcock Road, Carrickfergus, BT38 7NU
Tel: 028-9335 1172 **Fax:** 028-9084 0618
E-mail: mail@nkfencing.com
Website: http://www.nkfencing.com
Directors: P. McCoy (Fin)
Managers: A. McAlistair (Purch Mgr), F. Maginn (Tech Serv Mgr), S. Ferguson (Personnel)
Ultimate Holding Company: N.K. HOLDINGS LIMITED
Immediate Holding Company: N.K. FENCING LIMITED
Registration no: NI014866 **VAT No.:** GB 353 1307 86
Date established: 1981 **Turnover:** £5m - £10m **No.of Employees:** 21 - 50
Product Groups: 35, 52

Date of Accounts	Apr 11	Apr 10	Apr 09
Sales Turnover	6m	8m	10m
Pre Tax Profit/Loss	-76	-151	266
Working Capital	1m	2m	2m
Fixed Assets	312	462	551
Current Assets	3m	4m	4m
Current Liabilities	343	451	767

Northern Ireland Railways Co. Ltd
Victoria Street, Carrickfergus, BT38 8AQ
Tel: 028-9336 1582 **Fax:** 028-9336 2772
E-mail: frank.moore@translink.co.uk
Website: http://www.co-op.co.uk
Bank(s): Co-op Bank
Managers: F. Moore
Ultimate Holding Company: NORTHERN IRELAND TRANSPORT HOLDING COMPANY (NORTHERN IR
Immediate Holding Company: NORTHERN IRELAND RAILWAYS COMPANY LIMITED
Registration no: NI006929 **VAT No.:** GB 145 1242 02
Date established: 1967 **No.of Employees:** 11 - 20 **Product Groups:** 61

Date of Accounts	Mar 10	Mar 09	Mar 11
Sales Turnover	52m	51m	54m
Pre Tax Profit/Loss	21m	-4m	-1m
Working Capital	52m	17m	24m
Fixed Assets	183m	184m	235m
Current Assets	62m	65m	56m
Current Liabilities	10m	9m	19m

Old Mill Saddlery
110 Larne Road Ballycarry, Carrickfergus, BT38 9JN
Tel: 028-9335 3268 **Fax:** 028-9335 3111
E-mail: robert@saddlery.biz
Website: http://www.saddlery.biz
Directors: R. Pattern (Prop)
No.of Employees: 11 - 20 **Product Groups:** 22, 35, 43

Pollock Lifts Ltd
Unit 1 Sloefield Drive, Carrickfergus, BT38 8GX
Tel: 028-9336 8167 **Fax:** 028-9336 7846
E-mail: info@pollocklifts.co.uk
Website: http://www.pollocklifts.co.uk
Directors: S. Graham (Dir), G. McCahon (Fin)
Managers: G. McConcille (Mktg Serv Mgr), M. Lednicka
Ultimate Holding Company: JOHN POLLOCK DESIGNS FOR DISABLED LIMITED
Immediate Holding Company: POLLOCK LIFTS LIMITED
Registration no: NI018971 **VAT No.:** GB 422 2892 63
Date established: 1985 **Turnover:** £5m - £10m
No.of Employees: 51 - 100 **Product Groups:** 45

Date of Accounts	Jun 11	Jun 10	Jun 09
Sales Turnover	8m	8m	8m
Pre Tax Profit/Loss	194	311	269
Working Capital	972	780	688
Fixed Assets	1m	1m	495
Current Assets	4m	4m	4m
Current Liabilities	644	699	1m

Ryobi Aluminium Casting UK Ltd
5 Meadowbank Road, Carrickfergus, BT38 8YF
Tel: 028-9335 1043 **Fax:** 028-9336 5644
E-mail: info@ryobi.co.uk
Website: http://www.ryobi.co.uk
Directors: V. Manson (Fin), J. Hughes (MD), D. Martin (Pers)
Managers: S. Bell (Sales & Mktg Mg), S. McCullough (Purch Mgr), P. Osullivan (Tech Serv Mgr)
Ultimate Holding Company: RYOBI LTD (JAPAN)
Immediate Holding Company: RYOBI ALUMINIUM CASTING (UK) LIMITED
Registration no: NI024284 **VAT No.:** GB 517 3735 43
Date established: 1990 **Turnover:** £20m - £50m
No.of Employees: 101 - 250 **Product Groups:** 34

Date of Accounts	Dec 11	Dec 10	Dec 09
Sales Turnover	41m	25m	18m
Pre Tax Profit/Loss	120	-3m	-2m
Working Capital	2m	-161	2m
Fixed Assets	23m	25m	27m
Current Assets	16m	10m	7m
Current Liabilities	7m	5m	2m

Sound Acoustic Management
3 Donegall Park Whitehead, Carrickfergus, BT38 9ND
Tel: 028-9337 2547 **Fax:** 028-9337 2547
E-mail: sam@noise1.co.uk
Website: http://www.noise1.co.uk
Directors: S. Bell (Prop)
Turnover: Up to £250,000 **No.of Employees:** 1 - 10 **Product Groups:** 54

Thermal Consultancy Ltd
PO Box 79, Carrickfergus, BT38 0AL
Tel: 07748-988467
E-mail: aaron@thermalconsultancy.com
Website: http://www.thermalconsultancy.com
Registration no: NI059479 **Product Groups:** 38, 85

Ulster Industrial Explosives Ltd
PO Box 100, Carrickfergus, BT38 0BN
Tel: 028-9335 1444 **Fax:** 028-9335 1474
E-mail: info@uielimited.com
Website: http://www.uielimited.com
Managers: R. Tweed (Site Co-ord)
Ultimate Holding Company: KEMEK LIMITED
Immediate Holding Company: ULSTER INDUSTRIAL EXPLOSIVES LIMITED
Registration no: NI009832 **Date established:** 1973
No.of Employees: 1 - 10 **Product Groups:** 32

Date of Accounts	Dec 11	Dec 10	Dec 09
Working Capital	771	995	868
Fixed Assets	431	611	766
Current Assets	1m	1m	1m

Woodburn Engineering Ltd
Rosganna Works Trailcock Road, Carrickfergus, BT38 7NU
Tel: 028-9336 6404 **Fax:** 028-9336 7539
E-mail: info@woodburnengineeringltd.co.uk
Website: http://www.woodburnengineeringltd.co.uk
Managers: M. McAleer (Chief Buyer), T. Cowan (Mgr), S. Stephenson (Chief Acct)
Immediate Holding Company: WOODBURN ENGINEERING (CONTRACTS) LIMITED
Registration no: NI020157 **Date established:** 1987
No.of Employees: 21 - 50 **Product Groups:** 35

Date of Accounts	Sep 11	Sep 10	Sep 09
Working Capital	312	305	369
Fixed Assets	67	84	104
Current Assets	657	802	994
Current Liabilities	203	254	264

Co. Tyrone

Castlederg

Linian Knitwear
13a Mill Avenue Spamount, Castlederg, BT81 7NB
Tel: 028-8167 1181 **Fax:** 028-8167 0492
E-mail: ian@liniandesign.com
Directors: L. Gillespie (Ptnr)
Immediate Holding Company: LINIAN KNITWEAR LIMITED
Registration no: NI013116 **VAT No.:** GB 287 0894 13
Date established: 1978 **Turnover:** £1m - £2m **No.of Employees:** 1 - 10
Product Groups: 24

Date of Accounts	Nov 99	Nov 98	Nov 97
Working Capital	214	210	202
Fixed Assets	189	212	191
Current Assets	386	384	452
Current Liabilities	59	74	N/A

R Loughlin Electrical Services
10 Grove Road, Castlederg, BT81 7JJ
Tel: 028-8167 0065 **Fax:** 028-8167 0065
E-mail: rloughlin@freenet.co.uk
Directors: R. Loughlin (Ptnr)
No.of Employees: 11 - 20 **Product Groups:** 37

William J Mcguckin
59a Main Street, Castlederg, BT81 7AN
Tel: 028-8167 1247 **Fax:** 028-8167 9863
E-mail: sales@caterfreeze.com
Website: http://www.caterfreeze.com
Directors: W. McGuckin (Prop)
Date established: 1991 **No.of Employees:** 1 - 10 **Product Groups:** 20, 40, 41

C J Mcsorley
25 Laghel Road Killen, Castlederg, BT81 7SX
Tel: 028-8167 9383 **Fax:** 028-8167 9383
Directors: C. Mcsorley (Prop)
Date established: 1995 **No.of Employees:** 1 - 10 **Product Groups:** 35

North West Ducting
7 Ashburn Park, Castlederg, BT81 7BA
Tel: 028-8167 9323
Directors: L. Cassady (Ptnr)
Immediate Holding Company: NORTH WEST CABLE & DUCTING CONTRACTORS LIMITED
Registration no: NF003245 **Date established:** 1996
No.of Employees: 1 - 10 **Product Groups:** 37, 40, 48

Co. Down

Castlewellan

Feedwell Animal Foods
Annsborough, Castlewellan, BT31 9NH
Tel: 028-4377 8765 **Fax:** 028-4377 1420
E-mail: info@feedwell.com
Website: http://www.feedwell.com
Directors: R. Clegg (MD), S. Clegg (Fin)
Immediate Holding Company: FEEDWELL ANIMAL FOODS LIMITED
Registration no: 01233131 **VAT No.:** GB 286 3361 39
Date established: 1975 **Turnover:** £1m - £2m **No.of Employees:** 11 - 20
Product Groups: 20

Date of Accounts	Jul 11	Jul 10	Jul 09
Working Capital	155	146	142
Fixed Assets	74	100	104
Current Assets	311	268	275

F S Herron
4 Backaderry Road Ballyward, Castlewellan, BT31 9SL
Tel: 028-4065 0236 **Fax:** 028-4065 0754
Directors: D. Aiken (Prop)
Immediate Holding Company: F S Herron Limited
Registration no: NI071694 **VAT No.:** GB 2541 129 86
Date established: 2009 **No.of Employees:** 11 - 20 **Product Groups:** 62

Date of Accounts	Sep 11	Sep 10	Sep 09
Working Capital	-460	-543	N/A
Fixed Assets	699	656	N/A
Current Assets	771	694	N/A

Legmore Concrete Ltd
14 Clonvaraghan Road, Castlewellan, BT31 9JT
Tel: 028-4377 8465 **Fax:** 028-4377 8891
E-mail: legmoreconctrete@aol.com
Directors: B. Murphy (MD)
Immediate Holding Company: LEGMORE CONCRETE LIMITED
Registration no: NI011838 **VAT No.:** GB 286 7027 31
Date established: 1977 **No.of Employees:** 1 - 10 **Product Groups:** 14, 33, 66

Date of Accounts	Aug 11	Aug 10	Aug 09
Working Capital	-51	-35	24
Fixed Assets	284	271	291
Current Assets	305	259	285

T S Foods
40 Mary Street, Castlewellan, BT31 9DU
Tel: 028-4377 8227 **Fax:** 028-4377 1498
E-mail: info@tsfoods.co.uk
Website: http://www.tsfoods.co.uk
Bank(s): First Trust
Directors: J. Molloy (Dir), B. Still (Sales)
Managers: M. Burns (Fin Mgr), P. O'Hara (Chief Acct), J. McBride (Buyer), J. Burns (Sales Prom Mgr), D. Steele (Mktg Serv Mgr)
Immediate Holding Company: T.S. FOODS LIMITED
Registration no: NI014115 **VAT No.:** GB 331 2753 84
Date established: 1980 **Turnover:** £2m - £5m **No.of Employees:** 21 - 50
Product Groups: 09, 20, 62

Date of Accounts	May 11	May 10	May 09
Working Capital	1m	840	649
Fixed Assets	1m	1m	1m
Current Assets	2m	2m	2m

Walter Watson Ltd
124 Ballylough Road, Castlewellan, BT31 9JQ
Tel: 028-4377 8711 **Fax:** 028-4377 1008
E-mail: info@walter-watson.co.uk
Website: http://www.walter-watson.co.uk
Bank(s): Northern Bank
Directors: W. Watson (MD)
Immediate Holding Company: WALTER WATSON LIMITED
Registration no: NI010745 **VAT No.:** GB 283 0307 78
Date established: 1975 **Turnover:** £20m - £50m
No.of Employees: 101 - 250 **Product Groups:** 51, 66

Date of Accounts	Dec 11	Dec 10	Dec 09
Sales Turnover	36m	30m	29m
Pre Tax Profit/Loss	307	417	-380
Working Capital	2m	2m	3m
Fixed Assets	7m	7m	5m
Current Assets	14m	12m	13m
Current Liabilities	2m	2m	620

William Kirkwood & Sons
5 Newcastle Road, Castlewellan, BT31 9DP
Tel: 028-4377 8276 **Fax:** 028-4377 1770
E-mail: wkirkwoodandsons@btconnect.com
Website: http://wkirkwoodandsons.co.uk
Directors: W. Kirkwood (Prop)
VAT No.: GB 253 9657 27 **Date established:** 1905 **Turnover:** £1m - £2m
No.of Employees: 1 - 10 **Product Groups:** 25

Co. Tyrone

Clogher

L E Haslett & Co.
21 Ballagh Road, Clogher, BT76 0JY
Tel: 028-8554 8285 **Fax:** 028-8554 8683
E-mail: info@lehaslett.com
Website: http://www.lehaslett.com
Managers: W. Primrose (Mgr)
VAT No.: GB 252 0184 95 **Date established:** 1949
Turnover: Up to £250,000 **No.of Employees:** 11 - 20 **Product Groups:** 66

Co. Londonderry

Coleraine

Armstrong Medical Services Ltd
Wattstown Business Park Newbridge Road, Coleraine, BT52 1BS
Tel: 028-7035 6029 **Fax:** 028-7035 6875
E-mail: info@armstrongmedical.net
Website: http://www.armstrongmedical.net
Directors: J. Armstrong (MD)
Managers: P. Doherty (Purch Mgr), K. Smith (Personnel), J. Cathcart (Mktg Serv Mgr), W. White (Tech Serv Mgr), D. Campbell (Sales Prom Mgr), D. Hart (Fin Mgr)
Immediate Holding Company: LANGHOLM OPERATIONS LIMITED
Registration no: NI033316 **VAT No.:** GB 432 5789 34
Date established: 1997 **Turnover:** £10m - £20m
No.of Employees: 51 - 100 **Product Groups:** 30, 38, 40

B K S Surveys Ltd
47 Ballycairn Road, Coleraine, BT51 3HZ
Tel: 028-7035 2311 **Fax:** 028-7035 7637
E-mail: sales@bks.co.uk
Website: http://www.bks.co.uk
Bank(s): Barclays Bank
Directors: N. O'Hagen (Sales), R. Blackwood (I.T. Dir), L. Neil (MD)
Managers: Y. Moore (Sec), R. Madden (Estimating), R. Curry (I.T. Exec), J. McNally (Sales Prom Mgr), A. Campbell (Prod Mgr), J. Lennox (Sales Admin), P. Garland
Ultimate Holding Company: FUGRO NV (NETHERLANDS)
Immediate Holding Company: Fugro-BKS Limited
Registration no: NI005303 **VAT No.:** GB 251 8897 24
Date established: 1962 **Turnover:** £2m - £5m **No.of Employees:** 51 - 100
Product Groups: 44, 54, 75, 80, 81, 84

Date of Accounts	Dec 10	Dec 09	Dec 08
Sales Turnover	4m	6m	6m
Pre Tax Profit/Loss	-696	119	155
Working Capital	1m	2m	1m
Fixed Assets	293	419	539
Current Assets	2m	3m	2m
Current Liabilities	338	508	473

Ballyrashane Creamery
18 Creamery Road Cloyfin, Coleraine, BT52 2NE
Tel: 028-7034 3265 **Fax:** 028-7035 1653
E-mail: reception@ballyrashanecoop.com
Directors: N. Kemps (Grp Chief Exec)
Managers: E. Birrell (Personnel), E. Birrell (Personnel), D. Faulkner (Comptroller), V. McCook (Sales & Mktg Mg)
Immediate Holding Company: BALLYRASHANE FOODS LIMITED
Registration no: NI019806 **VAT No.:** GB 251 7923 54
Date established: 1986 **Turnover:** £2m - £5m
No.of Employees: 101 - 250 **Product Groups:** 61

Date of Accounts	Dec 03	Dec 02	Dec 01
Working Capital	155	132	125
Fixed Assets	N/A	15	18
Current Assets	456	1m	1m
Current Liabilities	300	N/A	N/A

H & T Bellas Ltd
12-14 Mountsandel Road, Coleraine, BT52 1JD
Tel: 028-7034 2205 **Fax:** 028-7035 2413
E-mail: info@bellas.co.uk
Website: http://www.bellas.co.uk
Directors: K. Hydman (Dir), M. Henry (MD)
Immediate Holding Company: H. & T. BELLAS LIMITED
Registration no: NI001380 **VAT No.:** GB 251 7447 60
Date established: 1939 **Turnover:** £5m - £10m **No.of Employees:** 11 - 20
Product Groups: 66

Date of Accounts	Dec 11	Dec 10	Dec 09
Working Capital	2m	2m	2m
Fixed Assets	1m	6m	6m
Current Assets	3m	2m	3m

Patrick Bradley Ltd
Craigall Quarry Cullyrammer Road, Garvagh, Coleraine, BT51 5YF
Tel: 028-2954 0965 **Fax:** 028-2954 1059
E-mail: johnshannon@patrickbradley.co.uk
Website: http://www.patrickbradley.co.uk
Directors: J. Shannon (MD)
Managers: K. McKinley (Personnel), K. McDonald (Fin Mgr)
Immediate Holding Company: PATRICK BRADLEY LIMITED
Registration no: NI001586 **VAT No.:** GB 252 8022 81
Date established: 1942 **Turnover:** £20m - £50m
No.of Employees: 51 - 100 **Product Groups:** 14, 33, 51

Date of Accounts	Dec 11	Dec 10	Dec 09
Pre Tax Profit/Loss	166	52	-175
Working Capital	-663	-810	-868
Fixed Assets	4m	4m	4m
Current Assets	7m	6m	6m
Current Liabilities	581	638	535

Buildings & Tanks
11 Wattstown Business Park Newbridge Road, Coleraine, BT52 1BS
Tel: 028-7035 6001 **Fax:** 028-7035 6633
E-mail: buildingsandtanks@btinternet.com
Website: http://www.buildingsandtanks.co.uk
Directors: B. Thompson (Dir)
No.of Employees: 11 - 20 **Product Groups:** 35, 42, 45

The Bush Training Centre
57 Ballylagan Road, Coleraine, BT52 2PQ
Tel: 028-7035 2653
E-mail: belinda@bushtraining.fsnet.co.uk
Directors: R. Gault (Prop)
No.of Employees: 1 - 10 **Product Groups:** 72

C A Hutchinson Ltd
Loguestown Industrial Estate, Coleraine, BT52 2NS
Tel: 028-7035 8888 **Fax:** 028-7035 7477
E-mail: info@hutchinsontiles.co.uk
Website: http://www.hutchinsontiles.co.uk
Directors: A. Hutchinson (MD)
Immediate Holding Company: A. HUTCHINSON (FLOOR AND WALL SUPPLIES) LIMITED
Registration no: NI011746 **VAT No.:** GB 311 1239 20
Date established: 1977 **No.of Employees:** 11 - 20 **Product Groups:** 27, 30, 63

Date of Accounts	Mar 12	Mar 11	Mar 10
Working Capital	234	247	248
Fixed Assets	48	57	70
Current Assets	427	390	360

C P Hire
102 Bushmills Road, Coleraine, BT52 2BT
Tel: 028-7034 4313 **Fax:** 028-7035 1982
E-mail: hire@cphire.com
Website: http://www.cphire.com
Directors: A. Hutchingson (Prop), A. Hutchinson (Prop)
Immediate Holding Company: C. P. HIRE LIMITED
Registration no: NI011306 **VAT No.:** GB 286 4052 47
Date established: 1976 **Turnover:** £5m - £10m
No.of Employees: 51 - 100 **Product Groups:** 83

Date of Accounts	May 12	May 11	May 10
Sales Turnover	7m	6m	6m
Pre Tax Profit/Loss	505	72	-544
Working Capital	-1m	-1m	-2m
Fixed Assets	7m	8m	9m
Current Assets	2m	2m	2m
Current Liabilities	1m	992	1m

Brian Canavan Associates Chartered Quantity Surveyors
22 Lodge Road, Coleraine, BT52 1NB
Tel: 028-7035 8484 **Fax:** 028-7034 4238
E-mail: george@canavans-qs.com
Website: http://www.canavans-qs.com
Directors: G. Williamson (Ptnr)
Immediate Holding Company: G.M. DESIGN ASSOCIATES LIMITED
Registration no: NI042733 **VAT No.:** GB 432 6554 56
Date established: 1999 **Turnover:** £2m - £5m **No.of Employees:** 1 - 10
Product Groups: 80, 84

Date of Accounts	Nov 11	Nov 10	Nov 09
Working Capital	-334	-334	-324
Current Assets	1m	1m	1m

Castleroe Pre-Cast Concrete Ltd
130a Castleroe Road, Coleraine, BT51 3RW
Tel: 028-7035 2839 **Fax:** 028-7035 4115
E-mail: castleroeconcrete@btopenworld.com
Website: http://www.castleroeprecastconcrete.co.uk
Directors: R. Hall (Dir)
Immediate Holding Company: CASTLEROE PRE-CAST CONCRETE LIMITED
Registration no: NI044855 **VAT No.:** GB 255 6991 18
Date established: 2002 **No.of Employees:** 1 - 10 **Product Groups:** 33

Date of Accounts	Jun 11	Jun 10	Jun 09
Working Capital	100	82	36
Fixed Assets	569	580	603
Current Assets	601	651	645

Cogan & Shackleton
35 Railway Road, Coleraine, BT52 1PE
Tel: 028-7034 4036 **Fax:** 028-7035 7028
E-mail: admin@coshack.co.uk
Website: http://www.coshack.co.uk
Bank(s): Northern Bank
Directors: J. Mcreynolds (Prop)
VAT No.: GB 251 8817 48 **Date established:** 1967
Turnover: £500,000 - £1m **No.of Employees:** 11 - 20 **Product Groups:** 84

Coleraine Chronicle Company Ltd
20 Railway Road, Coleraine, BT52 1PD
Tel: 028-7034 3344 **Fax:** 028-2766 7682
E-mail: editor@colerainechronicle.com
Website: http://www.ulsternet.co.uk
Directors: R. Baker (Dir)
Managers: A. Mussen (Tech Serv Mgr), S. McNichol (Personnel), R. Stratten, E. Butterwick
Ultimate Holding Company: TONTINE ROOMS HOLDING COMPANY LIMITED - THE
Immediate Holding Company: Coleraine Chronicle Company Limited - The
Registration no: NI045153 **Date established:** 2003
No.of Employees: 1 - 10 **Product Groups:** 28

Date of Accounts	Dec 11	Dec 10	Dec 09
Working Capital	2m	2m	2m
Fixed Assets	743	767	782
Current Assets	2m	2m	2m

Coleraine Fireplaces
New Mills Road Lower, Coleraine, BT52 2JR
Tel: 028-7035 6850 **Fax:** 028-7035 6858
E-mail: colerainefireplaces@yahoo.com
Directors: J. Duddy (Prop)
Immediate Holding Company: COLERAINE FIREPLACES LIMITED
Registration no: NI045927 **VAT No.:** GB 393 5189 18
Date established: 2003 **No.of Employees:** 11 - 20 **Product Groups:** 30, 33, 35, 40

Date of Accounts	Dec 10	Dec 09	Dec 08
Working Capital	-313	-286	-327
Fixed Assets	317	349	393
Current Assets	210	234	209

Coleraine Harbour Commissioners
4 Riversdale Road, Coleraine, BT52 1XA
Tel: 028-7034 2012 **Fax:** 028-7035 2000
Website: http://www.coleraineharbour.f9.co.uk
Managers: P. Mckeegan
VAT No.: GB 254 2190 78 **Date established:** 1879
No.of Employees: 1 - 10 **Product Groups:** 71

Coleraine Printing Co.
117 Ballycastle Road, Coleraine, BT52 2DZ
Tel: 028-7035 4873 **Fax:** 028-7034 2069
E-mail: info@coleraineprinting.com
Managers: R. Smith (Prod Mgr)
VAT No.: GB 331 9165 66 **Turnover:** £500,000 - £1m
No.of Employees: 1 - 10 **Product Groups:** 27, 28, 49

Coleraine Registration Of Births Deaths Marriages Civil P'Ships
66 Portstewart Road, Coleraine, BT52 1EY
Tel: 028-7034 7034 **Fax:** 028-7034 7026
E-mail: gwyneth.kerr@colerainebc.gov.uk
Website: http://www.colerainebc.gov.uk
Managers: G. Kerr
Immediate Holding Company: TRIANGLE SKATEPARK LTD
Registration no: NI045105 **Date established:** 2003
No.of Employees: 1 - 10 **Product Groups:** 87

Computer Accounting Bureau
2 Beresford Road, Coleraine, BT52 1GE
Tel: 028-7034 4666 **Fax:** 028-7035 2761
E-mail: enquiries@stocktaking.com
Website: http://www.stocktaking.com
Managers: M. Dinsmore (Mgr)
VAT No.: GB 286 3315 46 **Date established:** 1984
Turnover: £250,000 - £500,000 **No.of Employees:** 1 - 10
Product Groups: 80

D & C Forklifts
32 Drumimerick Road Kilrea, Coleraine, BT51 5SY
Tel: 028-2954 0817 **Fax:** 028-2954 0818
Directors: C. Carruthers (Ptnr)
Date established: 1982 **No.of Employees:** 1 - 10 **Product Groups:** 35, 39, 45

Dairy Produce Packers Ltd
Millburn Road, Coleraine, BT52 1QZ
Tel: 028-7032 5500 **Fax:** 028-7035 6412
E-mail: garnette.faulkner@kerry.ie
Website: http://www.kerrygroup.com
Bank(s): First Trust Bank
Managers: B. Mehigan (Comptroller)
Ultimate Holding Company: KERRY GROUP PUBLIC LIMITED COMPANY
Immediate Holding Company: DAIRY PRODUCE PACKERS LIMITED
Registration no: NI022009 **VAT No.:** GB 517 1036 79
Date established: 1988 **Turnover:** £125m - £250m
No.of Employees: 251 - 500 **Product Groups:** 20

Date of Accounts	Dec 11	Dec 10	Dec 09
Sales Turnover	139m	136m	132m
Pre Tax Profit/Loss	1m	6m	14m
Working Capital	56m	27m	20m
Fixed Assets	18m	27m	30m
Current Assets	67m	39m	33m
Current Liabilities	541	3m	7m

Dalzell & Campbell
1a Pates Lane, Coleraine, BT51 3DE
Tel: 028-7034 3366 **Fax:** 028-7035 2174
Website: http://www.dalzellandcampbell.co.uk
Directors: G. Mccook (Head)
Registration no: 00052411 **VAT No.:** GB 251 8718 50
Turnover: £500,000 - £1m **No.of Employees:** 1 - 10 **Product Groups:** 84

De Zeeuw
2 Abbey Street, Coleraine, BT52 1DS
Tel: 028-7035 8489 **Fax:** 028-7035 8490
E-mail: rdez@qsservices.freeserve.co.uk
Directors: I. Mcgeehan (Ptnr)
VAT No.: GB 432 6782 43 **Date established:** 2007
No.of Employees: 1 - 10 **Product Groups:** 80, 84

A Diamond & Son Timber Ltd
35 New Mills Road, Coleraine, BT52 2JB
Tel: 028-7034 3452 **Fax:** 028-7034 3279
E-mail: sales@adiamondandson.co.uk
Website: http://www.adiamondandson.co.uk
Bank(s): Bank of Ireland
Directors: L. Diamond (Dir), A. McCulley (Dir)
Immediate Holding Company: A. DIAMOND & SON (TIMBER) LIMITED
Registration no: NI008235 **VAT No.:** GB 251 9705 54
Date established: 1971 **Turnover:** £1m - £2m **No.of Employees:** 51 - 100
Product Groups: 66

Date of Accounts	Apr 12	Apr 11	Apr 10
Pre Tax Profit/Loss	N/A	234	4
Working Capital	188	120	124
Fixed Assets	4m	4m	4m
Current Assets	1m	1m	1m
Current Liabilities	N/A	235	154

E & M Associates
42a & 44a New Row, Coleraine, BT52 1AF
Tel: 028-7034 2164 **Fax:** 028-7035 1160
E-mail: emassociates@bizonline.co.uk
Managers: E. Mchugh (Mgr)
Immediate Holding Company: C MCSORLEY LTD
Registration no: NI038070 **Date established:** 2011
No.of Employees: 1 - 10 **Product Groups:** 80

E S L Engineering Ltd
11 Farrenlester Road, Coleraine, BT51 3QR
Tel: 028-7035 6145 **Fax:** 028-7035 4606
E-mail: sales@eslengineering.co.uk
Website: http://www.eslengineering.com
Bank(s): Ulster Bank
Directors: S. Elliott (MD), J. Nichols (Fin)
Immediate Holding Company: E.S.L. ENGINEERING LIMITED
Registration no: NI038277 **VAT No.:** GB 349 7458 06
Date established: 2000 **Turnover:** £1m - £2m **No.of Employees:** 11 - 20
Product Groups: 87

Date of Accounts	Mar 12	Mar 11	Mar 10
Working Capital	571	575	430
Fixed Assets	148	249	274
Current Assets	954	922	697

Errigal Trophies
Mayboy View Garvagh, Coleraine, BT51 5HJ
Tel: 028-2955 8186 **Fax:** 028-2955 8186
E-mail: errigaltrophies@gmail.com
Directors: T. Mcgahon (Prop)
Date established: 1977 **Turnover:** Up to £250,000
No.of Employees: 1 - 10 **Product Groups:** 33, 49

A Farlow
39 Ballynameen Road Garvagh, Coleraine, BT51 5PN
Tel: 028-2955 8330 **Fax:** 028-2955 7081
E-mail: info@farlow-engineering.co.uk
Website: http://www.farlow-engineering.co.uk
Bank(s): Northern Bank
Directors: A. Farlow (MD), J. Farlow (Dir)
Immediate Holding Company: A. FARLOW (ENGINEERING) LTD
Registration no: NI042808 **VAT No.:** GB 331 8333 76
Date established: 2002 **Turnover:** £500,000 - £1m
No.of Employees: 11 - 20 **Product Groups:** 45

Date of Accounts	Mar 12	Mar 11	Mar 10
Working Capital	606	447	898
Fixed Assets	651	654	439
Current Assets	1m	1m	1m

Gardiner Engineering Design Services
115 Moneygran Road Kilrea, Coleraine, BT51 5SL
Tel: 028-2954 0951 **Fax:** 028-2954 0951
E-mail: gardinerengineering@ic24.net
Directors: K. Gardiner (Prop)
VAT No.: GB 516 5741 44 **Turnover:** Up to £250,000
No.of Employees: 1 - 10 **Product Groups:** 84

W & M Given
2 Beresford Road, Coleraine, BT52 1GE
Tel: 028-7035 1111 **Fax:** 028-7035 1115
E-mail: info@wmgivenarchitects.co.uk
Website: http://www.wmgivenarchitects.co.uk
Directors: M. Lennox (Snr Part)
VAT No.: GB 251 8449 51 **Date established:** 1888
Turnover: Up to £250,000 **No.of Employees:** 1 - 10 **Product Groups:** 84

Haire Bros Advanced Roofing Ltd
48 Cloyfin Road, Coleraine, BT52 2NY
Tel: 028-7034 2696 **Fax:** 028-7034 2387
E-mail: office@hairebros.co.uk
Website: http://www.hairebros.co.uk
Directors: R. Murphy (Dir)
Immediate Holding Company: HAIRE BROS. (ADVANCED ROOFING) LIMITED
Registration no: NI013961 **VAT No.:** GB 331 8883 41
Date established: 1979 **No.of Employees:** 1 - 10 **Product Groups:** 30, 31, 52

Date of Accounts	Sep 11	Sep 10	Sep 09
Working Capital	-3	27	47
Fixed Assets	54	36	26
Current Assets	207	231	297

Harte & Eakin Contractors N I Ltd
48 Cloyfin Road, Coleraine, BT52 2NY
Tel: 028-7035 1575 **Fax:** 028-7035 8270
E-mail: enquiries@harteandeakin.com
Website: http://www.harteandeakin.com
Directors: D. Harte (MD), W. Harte (Dir)
Managers: S. Buick
Immediate Holding Company: HARTE & EAKIN (CONTRACTORS) NI LIMITED
Registration no: NI029527 **VAT No.:** GB 331 9412 75
Date established: 1995 **No.of Employees:** 1 - 10 **Product Groups:** 52

Date of Accounts	Mar 11	Mar 10	Mar 09
Working Capital	314	318	353
Fixed Assets	482	517	527
Current Assets	970	945	1m

Hidden Hearing Ltd
51 New Row, Coleraine, BT52 1EJ
Tel: 028-7032 0301 **Fax:** 028-7035 8210
E-mail: timfletcher@hiddenhearing.ie
Website: http://hiddenhearing.ie
Managers: T. Fletcher (Chief Acct)
Ultimate Holding Company: WILLIAM DEMANT HOLDING A/S (DENMARK)
Immediate Holding Company: HIDDEN HEARING LIMITED
Registration no: 01990227 **Date established:** 1986
Turnover: £500,000 - £1m **No.of Employees:** 1 - 10 **Product Groups:** 37, 38, 49

Date of Accounts	Dec 11	Dec 10	Dec 09
Sales Turnover	34m	30m	38m
Pre Tax Profit/Loss	-1m	-4m	-2m
Working Capital	-1m	181	-2m
Fixed Assets	7m	6m	7m
Current Assets	5m	5m	6m
Current Liabilities	4m	4m	3m

J K C Specialist Cars
1-9 Millburn Road, Coleraine, BT52 1QS
Tel: 028-7035 5222 **Fax:** 028-7035 7341
E-mail: mail@jkcbmw.co.uk
Website: http://www.jkcbmw.co.uk
Directors: J. Cassidy (Prop), M. Cassidy (Fin)
Managers: B. Monaghan (Mktg Serv Mgr), J. Doherty (Sales Prom Mgr), J. Kearney (Sales Admin), N. McFlynn (Chief Mgr), E. Mcguinness (Sales Prom Mgr), D. Docherty (Mktg Serv Mgr), D. Docherty (Develop Mgr), J. Humprhy (Comm)
Ultimate Holding Company: J. K. C. GARAGES (COLERAINE) LIMITED
Immediate Holding Company: J.K.C.SPECIALIST CARS LIMITED
Registration no: NI013216 **Date established:** 1978
Turnover: £20m - £50m **No.of Employees:** 21 - 50 **Product Groups:** 68

Date of Accounts	Dec 10	Dec 09	Dec 08
Sales Turnover	28m	28m	N/A
Pre Tax Profit/Loss	269	595	-343
Working Capital	1m	1m	693
Fixed Assets	2m	2m	2m
Current Assets	6m	5m	4m
Current Liabilities	173	508	110

Johnston Printing Ltd
Mill Road Kilrea, Coleraine, BT51 5RJ
Tel: 028-2954 0312 **Fax:** 028-2954 1070
E-mail: service@johnston-printing.co.uk
Website: http://www.johnston-printing.co.uk
Directors: G. Craig (MD)
Immediate Holding Company: JOHNSTON PRINTING LIMITED
Registration no: NI003987 **VAT No.:** GB 252 1729 74
Date established: 1957 **Turnover:** £500,000 - £1m
No.of Employees: 21 - 50 **Product Groups:** 28

Date of Accounts	Dec 11	Dec 10	Dec 09
Working Capital	-35	-91	-83
Fixed Assets	84	120	166
Current Assets	162	214	186

G E Kee
17 Bridge Street, Coleraine, BT52 1DR
Tel: 028-7034 3525 **Fax:** 028-7035 2857
E-mail: shop@kee-arts.demon.co.uk
Website: http://www.kee-arts.demon.co.uk
Directors: I. Kee (Prop)
Turnover: Up to £250,000 **No.of Employees:** 21 - 50 **Product Groups:** 25, 36, 64

Kennedy Concrete Products Ltd
1 Letterloan Road Macosquin, Coleraine, BT51 4PP
Tel: 028-7035 1421 **Fax:** 028-7035 1610
E-mail: sales@kennedyconcrete.co.uk
Website: http://www.kennedygroup.co.uk
Directors: M. Baudina (MD)
Managers: M. Budina (Mgr), R. Kennedy (Asst Gen Mgr), G. Taylor (Admin Off)
Ultimate Holding Company: Kennedy Group Holdings Ltd
Immediate Holding Company: KENNEDY CONCRETE PRODUCTS LIMITED
Registration no: NI011211 **VAT No.:** GB 286 3163 43
Date established: 1976 **No.of Employees:** 11 - 20 **Product Groups:** 33

Lamont Fireplaces & Stone
1 Wattstown Business Park Newbridge Road, Coleraine, BT52 1BS
Tel: 028-7032 8882 **Fax:** 028-7032 8884
E-mail: mail@lamontstone.com
Website: http://www.lamontstone.com
Directors: M. Lamont (Prop)
Immediate Holding Company: LAMONT FIREPLACES LTD
Registration no: NI031454 **VAT No.:** GB 311 1731 16
Date established: 1996 **No.of Employees:** 21 - 50 **Product Groups:** 33

Date of Accounts	Dec 11	Dec 10	Dec 09
Working Capital	2m	2m	2m
Fixed Assets	3m	3m	3m
Current Assets	2m	2m	3m

Lee Property Sales
26 New Row, Coleraine, BT52 1AF
Tel: 028-7035 1122 **Fax:** 028-7035 1123
E-mail: leeproperty@talk21.com
Website: http://www.propertynews.com
Directors: J. Lee (Prop)
No.of Employees: 1 - 10 **Product Groups:** 80

Alan Leighton
4 Park Street, Coleraine, BT52 1BD
Tel: 028-7035 6752 **Fax:** 028-7035 6752
E-mail: alan.leighton@btconnect.com
Directors: A. Leighton (Prop)
Date established: 1985 **Turnover:** Up to £250,000
No.of Employees: 1 - 10 **Product Groups:** 81

R B Lyttle
60 Station Road Garvagh, Coleraine, BT51 5LA
Tel: 028-2955 8264 **Fax:** 028-2955 7043
Directors: R. Little (Prop)
Date established: 1985 **No.of Employees:** 1 - 10 **Product Groups:** 41

David L Mccollum
136 Curragh Road Aghadowey, Coleraine, BT51 4BT
Tel: 07860-618424 **Fax:** 08717- 335376
E-mail: davidmccollum@btopenworld.com
Website: http://www.rhaa-lane.freeserve.co.uk
Directors: D. Mccollum (Prop)
Date established: 1995 **No.of Employees:** 1 - 10 **Product Groups:** 38, 42

E Mcintyre & Sons Ltd

14 Drumagarner Road Kilrea, Coleraine, BT51 5TB
Tel: 028-2954 0300 **Fax:** 028-2954 1069
E-mail: sales@emcintyre.com
Website: http://www.emcintyre.com
Managers: L. Mcgonigle (Mktg Serv Mgr)
Immediate Holding Company: E. McINTYRE & SONS LIMITED
Registration no: NI038690 **VAT No.:** GB 253 4673 54
Date established: 2000 **Turnover:** £1m - £2m **No.of Employees:** 21 - 50
Product Groups: 67

Date of Accounts	Oct 11	Oct 10	Oct 09
Working Capital	2m	1m	1m
Fixed Assets	32	45	46
Current Assets	3m	2m	2m

Micro Flexitronics Ltd

Unit 7 12 Spittal Hill, Coleraine, BT52 2BY
Tel: 028-7035 2541 **Fax:** 028-7035 2543
E-mail: sean@mflstraingauges.com
Website: http://www.mflstraingauges.com
Directors: S. Dovbans (Prop)
Immediate Holding Company: MICRO-FLEXITRONICS LIMITED
Registration no: NF004170 **VAT No.:** GB 642 1295 56
Date established: 2007 **Turnover:** £500,000 - £1m
No.of Employees: 1 - 10 **Product Groups:** 37, 38, 85

Date of Accounts	Aug 07	Aug 06
Working Capital	48	46
Fixed Assets	18	20
Current Assets	58	64
Current Liabilities	11	18
Total Share Capital	45	45

Moneycarrie Engineering Ltd

43 Moneycarrie Road Garvagh, Coleraine, BT51 4EG
Tel: 028-2955 8329 **Fax:** 028-2955 7210
Directors: D. Torrens (Dir)
Immediate Holding Company: MONEYCARRIE ENGINEERING LIMITED
Registration no: NI013891 **VAT No.:** GB 331 8816 56
Date established: 1979 **Turnover:** £250,000 - £500,000
No.of Employees: 1 - 10 **Product Groups:** 07

Date of Accounts	Dec 11	Dec 10	Dec 09
Working Capital	454	445	446
Fixed Assets	105	93	91
Current Assets	531	500	485

R H Burke & Sons

72-74 Long Commons, Coleraine, BT52 1LH
Tel: 028-7034 2804 **Fax:** 028-7034 2804
E-mail: info@countrysportswarehouse.com
Website: http://www.countrysportswarehouse.com
Directors: H. Burke (Prop)
Date established: 1908 **No.of Employees:** 1 - 10 **Product Groups:** 36, 39, 40

Reid Machinery Sales Ltd

101 Carrowreagh Road Garvagh, Coleraine, BT51 5LH
Tel: 028-2955 8474 **Fax:** 028-2955 8804
E-mail: info@reidmachinerysales.com
Website: http://www.reidmachinerysales.com
Directors: C. Reid (Dir)
Immediate Holding Company: REID MACHINERY SALES LIMITED
Registration no: NI013749 **VAT No.:** GB 331 8585 49
Date established: 1979 **No.of Employees:** 1 - 10 **Product Groups:** 66

Date of Accounts	Jan 12	Jan 11	Jan 10
Working Capital	198	174	152
Fixed Assets	6	8	12
Current Assets	443	440	442

Right Price Carpets & Furniture Ltd

Bushmills Road, Coleraine, BT52 2BN
Tel: 028-7034 4482 **Fax:** 028-7034 3021
E-mail: info@rightprice.co.uk
Website: http://www.rightprice.co.uk
Directors: R. Pollock (MD)
Immediate Holding Company: RIGHT PRICE CARPETS AND FURNITURE LIMITED
Registration no: NI013092 **Date established:** 1978
Turnover: £10m - £20m **No.of Employees:** 21 - 50 **Product Groups:** 63

Date of Accounts	Feb 12	Feb 11	Feb 10
Working Capital	12	61	147
Fixed Assets	1m	1m	2m
Current Assets	533	596	689

S R K Equipment Co.

31 Ardreagh Road, Coleraine, BT51 4DN
Tel: 028-7086 8305 **Fax:** 028-7086 8777
E-mail: info@srkequipment.com
Website: http://www.srkequipment.com
Directors: S. Kennedy (MD)
Managers: S. Archibald (District Mgr)
VAT No.: GB 252 0342 06 **Date established:** 1969
Turnover: Up to £250,000 **No.of Employees:** 1 - 10 **Product Groups:** 63, 67

Skyline Windows

Unit 4b Loughanhill Industrial Estate, Coleraine, BT52 2NJ
Tel: 028-7035 7520 **Fax:** 028-7035 5520
E-mail: lynneill69@aol.com
Website: http://www.skylinewindows.4t.com
Directors: L. Neill (Prop)
Immediate Holding Company: SKYLINE WINDOWS LTD
Registration no: NI071307 **VAT No.:** GB 255 8427 37
Date established: 2008 **No.of Employees:** 11 - 20 **Product Groups:** 25, 26, 33, 35

Date of Accounts	Nov 10	Nov 09
Working Capital	-33	49
Fixed Assets	34	42
Current Assets	231	213

Smyth Steel Ltd

15 Gorran Road Garvagh, Coleraine, BT51 4HA
Tel: 028-7086 8544 **Fax:** 028-7086 8102
E-mail: mail@smyth-steel.co.uk
Website: http://www.smyth-steel.co.uk
Bank(s): Northern Bank
Directors: D. Kerr (Fin), J. Smyth (MD)
Managers: H. Scott
Immediate Holding Company: SMYTH STEEL LIMITED
Registration no: NI014105 **VAT No.:** GB 255 6939 20
Date established: 1980 **Turnover:** £2m - £5m **No.of Employees:** 21 - 50
Product Groups: 35, 52

Date of Accounts	Apr 11	Apr 10	Apr 09
Sales Turnover	3m	4m	8m
Pre Tax Profit/Loss	128	-400	350
Working Capital	2m	1m	1m
Fixed Assets	915	1m	1m
Current Assets	2m	2m	2m
Current Liabilities	183	121	317

Spa-Jet Ltd

17 Hawthorne Terrace, Coleraine, BT52 2BW
Tel: 028-7035 7103 **Fax:** 028-7032 9549
E-mail: spajetltd@btconnect.com
Website: http://www.spajet.co.uk
Directors: E. Mckay (MD)
Immediate Holding Company: SPA-JET LIMITED
Registration no: NI036381 **Date established:** 1999
No.of Employees: 11 - 20 **Product Groups:** 30, 32, 36, 67

Date of Accounts	Jun 11	Jun 10	Jun 09
Working Capital	523	601	1m
Fixed Assets	733	750	154
Current Assets	692	877	1m

Spanboard Products Ltd

10 Curragh Road, Coleraine, BT51 3RY
Tel: 028-7035 5111 **Fax:** 028-7034 5700
E-mail: postmaster@spanboard.co.uk
Website: http://www.sonae.co.uk
Directors: N. Graham (MD), A. Knox (Co Sec)
Managers: R. Loughrey (Mgr), L. Eakins (Plant), L. Eakin (Mgr)
Ultimate Holding Company: EFANOR INVESTIMENTOS SGPS SA (PORTUGAL)
Immediate Holding Company: SPANBOARD PRODUCTS LIMITED
Registration no: NI022500 **VAT No.:** GB 573 4025 51
Date established: 1989 **Turnover:** £5m - £10m **No.of Employees:** 21 - 50
Product Groups: 25

Date of Accounts	Dec 10	Dec 09	Dec 08
Sales Turnover	8m	10m	15m
Pre Tax Profit/Loss	-157	-2m	-1m
Working Capital	500	-560	1m
Fixed Assets	727	742	704
Current Assets	2m	3m	5m
Current Liabilities	2m	2m	3m

T B F Thompson Garvagh Ltd

6-10 Killyvally Road Garvagh, Coleraine, BT51 5JZ
Tel: 028-2955 8353 **Fax:** 028-9083 3155
E-mail: sales@tbfthompson.co.uk
Website: http://www.tbfthompson.com
Directors: A. Magowan (MD), R. Crilly (Fin)
Managers: R. McBride
Ultimate Holding Company: Killyvally Holdings Limited
Immediate Holding Company: T B F Thompson (Engineering) Limited
Registration no: NI036300 **VAT No.:** GB 252 2574 72
Date established: 1999 **Turnover:** £20m - £50m
No.of Employees: 51 - 100 **Product Groups:** 67

Date of Accounts	Dec 09	Dec 08

Triangle Engineering Co. Ltd

Hillmans Fancy, Coleraine, BT52 2DX
Tel: 028-7034 2798 **Fax:** 028-7035 5917
E-mail: ivan@triangleeng.co.uk
Website: http://www.triangleeng.co.uk
Directors: I. Mcgrotty (Dir)
Immediate Holding Company: TRIANGLE ENGINEERING COMPANY LIMITED
Registration no: NI010746 **VAT No.:** GB 283 1977 28
Date established: 1975 **No.of Employees:** 11 - 20 **Product Groups:** 26, 35, 36, 49

Date of Accounts	Sep 11	Sep 10	Sep 09
Working Capital	121	206	246
Fixed Assets	157	135	144
Current Assets	268	317	398

Ulster Electro Finishes Ltd

78 Ballyrashane Road, Coleraine, BT52 2LJ
Tel: 028-7034 3022 **Fax:** 028-7035 5985
E-mail: uefltd@aol.com
Directors: S. Millar (MD)
Immediate Holding Company: ULSTER ELECTRO FINISHES LIMITED
Registration no: NI006937 **VAT No.:** GB 253 1346 84
Date established: 1967 **Turnover:** Up to £250,000
No.of Employees: 1 - 10 **Product Groups:** 32

Date of Accounts	Mar 12	Mar 11	Mar 10
Working Capital	13	17	18
Fixed Assets	176	181	185
Current Assets	28	39	36

University Of Ulster Accommodation Department

Cromore Road, Coleraine, BT52 1SA
Tel: 028-7012 4664 **Fax:** 028-7032 4931
E-mail: c.scott@ulster.ac.uk
Website: http://www.ulster.ac.uk
Managers: C. Scott
Ultimate Holding Company: UNIVERSITY OF ULSTER (UK)
Immediate Holding Company: UNIVERSITY OF ULSTER FOUNDATION
Registration no: NI031544 **Date established:** 1996
Turnover: £500,000 - £1m **No.of Employees:** 1 - 10 **Product Groups:** 69, 86

Date of Accounts	Jul 11	Jul 10	Jul 09
Sales Turnover	629	685	528
Pre Tax Profit/Loss	-6	-47	-8
Working Capital	42	49	95
Current Assets	59	100	107
Current Liabilities	5	5	12

W Oliver Exorna Ltd

Hillmans Way, Coleraine, BT52 2EB
Tel: 028-7035 6501 **Fax:** 028-7035 3674
E-mail: sales@oliverexorna.co.uk
Website: http://www.oliverexorna.co.uk
Bank(s): First Trust
Directors: W. Oliver (MD)
Managers: A. Oliver (Transport)
Immediate Holding Company: W. OLIVER (EXORNA) LIMITED
Registration no: NI016697 **VAT No.:** GB 393 5968 91
Date established: 1983 **No.of Employees:** 21 - 50 **Product Groups:** 26

Date of Accounts	Mar 11	Mar 10	Mar 09
Working Capital	243	254	228
Fixed Assets	1m	1m	1m
Current Assets	1m	1m	909

Weldtec Industrial Supplies Ltd

232 Drumcroon Road, Coleraine, BT51 3SQ
Tel: 028-7032 9523 **Fax:** 028-7032 9295
Website: http://www.parts4tools.co.uk
Directors: J. Hutchinson (Prop)
Immediate Holding Company: WELDTEC INDUSTRIAL SUPPLIES LIMITED
Registration no: NI033570 **Date established:** 1998
No.of Employees: 1 - 10 **Product Groups:** 46

Date of Accounts	Feb 10	Feb 09	Feb 08
Working Capital	-120	-115	-119
Fixed Assets	240	250	267
Current Assets	43	78	92

Zing Design & Print

Loughanhill Industrial Estate Gateside Road, Coleraine, BT52 2NR
Tel: 028-7034 2472 **Fax:** 028-7034 4152
E-mail: info@zingdp.com
Website: http://www.zingdp.com
Managers: R. Yates (Mgr)
Immediate Holding Company: Lynas Foods Limited
Registration no: NI061153 **VAT No.:** GB 252 3358 73
Date established: 2004 **Turnover:** £5m - £10m **No.of Employees:** 11 - 20
Product Groups: 28, 80, 81

Date of Accounts	Oct 11	Oct 10	Oct 09
Working Capital	1	1	1
Fixed Assets	21m	21m	21m
Current Assets	1	1	1

Co. Tyrone

Cookstown

D Acheson Ltd

Sweep Road, Cookstown, BT80 8JW
Tel: 028-8676 3219 **Fax:** 028-8676 5502
Directors: J. Acheson (MD)
Managers: A. Wilson
Immediate Holding Company: D. ACHESON (LIMEWORKS) LIMITED
Registration no: NI012614 **VAT No.:** GB 516 6834 32
Date established: 1978 **No.of Employees:** 1 - 10 **Product Groups:** 33

Date of Accounts	Jun 11	Jun 10	Jun 09
Working Capital	-108	-30	30
Fixed Assets	2m	2m	3m
Current Assets	320	314	383

AES Installation Services Ltd

Unit A 4 Annagh Road, Cookstown, BT80 9AS
Tel: 028-8676 7878 **Fax:** 028-8676 0085
E-mail: sales@aes-ni.co.uk
Website: http://www.aes-ni.co.uk
Managers: M. Creighton (Mgr)
Immediate Holding Company: AES Installation Services Ltd
Registration no: NI072786 **Date established:** 2009
No.of Employees: 1 - 10 **Product Groups:** 36, 37, 67

Date of Accounts	May 11	May 10
Working Capital	-41	-18
Fixed Assets	8	11
Current Assets	24	49

Allens Cookstown

26 James Street, Cookstown, BT80 8LW
Tel: 028-8676 3628 **Fax:** 028-8676 2764
E-mail: info@allens-property.com
Website: http://www.allens-property.com
Managers: D. Allen (Mgr)
Immediate Holding Company: Allens Cookstown Ltd
Registration no: NI065577 **VAT No.:** GB 252 1359 81
Date established: 2007 **Turnover:** £250,000 - £500,000
No.of Employees: 1 - 10 **Product Groups:** 80

Date of Accounts	Mar 11	Mar 10	Mar 09
Working Capital	48	49	58
Current Assets	154	123	478
Current Liabilities	N/A	29	358

Allied Metal Products

1 Derryloran Industrial Estate Sandholes Road, Cookstown, BT80 9LU
Tel: 028-8676 5366 **Fax:** 028-8676 2713
E-mail: tony@alliedmetalproducts.com
Website: http://www.alliedmetalproducts.co.uk
Directors: T. McCan (Dir)
Immediate Holding Company: ALLIED METAL PRODUCTS LIMITED
Registration no: NI037794 **Date established:** 2000
No.of Employees: 11 - 20 **Product Groups:** 26, 35

Date of Accounts	Dec 10	Dec 09	Dec 08
Working Capital	73	-141	-115
Fixed Assets	144	192	205
Current Assets	228	180	245

B A Components

Derryloran Industrial Estate Sandholes Road, Cookstown, BT80 9LU
Tel: 028-8676 4600 **Fax:** 028-8676 4404
E-mail: sales@bacomponents.co.uk
Website: http://www.bacomponents.co.uk
Directors: B. Macracken (MD)
Managers: P. Corrigan (Chief Acct)
Immediate Holding Company: SYNCHRON LIMITED
Registration no: NI020880 **VAT No.:** GB 516 6768 19
Date established: 2002 **No.of Employees:** 21 - 50 **Product Groups:** 25

Date of Accounts	Mar 11	Mar 10	Mar 09
Working Capital	42	38	25
Fixed Assets	46	35	26
Current Assets	105	85	51

C & C Engineering
51a Castle Road, Cookstown, BT80 8TN
Tel: 028-8676 4464 **Fax:** 028-8676 4464
E-mail: donaldthompson@btconnect.com
Directors: D. Thompson (Prop)
VAT No.: GB 331 9676 41 **Date established:** 1993
Turnover: Up to £250,000 **No.of Employees:** 1 - 10 **Product Groups:** 48

Calendar Sales
192 Oritor Road, Cookstown, BT80 9RF
Tel: 028-8676 3377 **Fax:** 028-8676 3706
E-mail: info@calendarsales.co.uk
Managers: W. Mcado (Mgr), W. McAdoo (Sales Prom Mgr), J. Boyd (Sales Prom Mgr)
VAT No.: GB 251 7191 69 **Turnover:** £250,000 - £500,000
No.of Employees: 11 - 20 **Product Groups:** 28

Central Laundries Ltd
14 Tullylagan Road, Cookstown, BT80 9AY
Tel: 028-8676 4040 **Fax:** 028-8676 6660
E-mail: info@centrallaundries.com
Managers: P. Ferguson (I.T. Exec), L. Brown (Chief Acct), O. Hamilton (Chief Mgr), P. Ferguson (Tech Serv Mgr), W. Adam
Ultimate Holding Company: BERENDSEN PLC
Immediate Holding Company: CENTRAL LAUNDRIES LIMITED
Registration no: NI047803 **Date established:** 2003
No.of Employees: 51 - 100 **Product Groups:** 23

Date of Accounts	Dec 11	Dec 10	Dec 09
Sales Turnover	5m	5m	5m
Pre Tax Profit/Loss	1m	1m	1m
Working Capital	2m	883	968
Fixed Assets	3m	3m	3m
Current Assets	3m	2m	3m
Current Liabilities	771	850	1m

Cookstown Office Supplies
1-3 Limekiln Lane, Cookstown, BT80 8NL
Tel: 028-8676 3696 **Fax:** 028-8676 5050
E-mail: info@cos-ni.co.uk
Website: http://www.cos-ni.co.uk
Managers: N. Mcgirr (Mgr)
Immediate Holding Company: COOKSTOWN OFFICE SUPPLIES LIMITED
Registration no: NI022786 **VAT No.:** GB 283 1540 67
Date established: 1989 **Turnover:** Up to £250,000
No.of Employees: 1 - 10 **Product Groups:** 48, 67

Date of Accounts	Mar 10	Mar 09	Mar 08
Working Capital	23	51	75
Fixed Assets	11	11	13
Current Assets	127	148	157

Cookstown Rewinds
Derryloran Industrial Estate Sandholes Road, Cookstown, BT80 9LU
Tel: 028-8676 1070
Directors: M. Scullion (MD), M. Scullion (Prop)
Immediate Holding Company: Cookstown Enterprise Centre Ltd
Registration no: NI035820 **Date established:** 1999
No.of Employees: 1 - 10 **Product Groups:** 37, 67

F J Dingley
53 Annaghone Road, Cookstown, BT80 8SW
Tel: 028-8676 2956 **Fax:** 028-8676 2956
Directors: F. Dingley (Prop), F. Dingley (Prop)
Turnover: Up to £250,000 **No.of Employees:** 1 - 10 **Product Groups:** 25

R J Donaghy & Sons
71b Lissan Road, Cookstown, BT80 8QX
Tel: 028-8676 3202 **Fax:** 028-8676 2835
Directors: L. Donaghy (Prop)
VAT No.: GB 252 0055 09 **Turnover:** £500,000 - £1m
No.of Employees: 1 - 10 **Product Groups:** 14, 33

Euroscroll
90 Tulnacross Road, Cookstown, BT80 9NP
Tel: 028-8675 1926 **Fax:** 028-8675 1926
E-mail: sales@euroscroll.com
Website: http://www.euroscroll.com
Directors: U. Mccormack (Dir)
Turnover: Up to £250,000 **No.of Employees:** 1 - 10 **Product Groups:** 35, 36, 37, 48, 49, 66

F S L (Displays Division)
Sandholes Road, Cookstown, BT80 9AR
Tel: 028-8676 6131 **Fax:** 028-8676 2414
E-mail: info@fslelectronics.com
Website: http://www.fslelectronics.com
Directors: J. Meenan (MD)
Immediate Holding Company: FSL COMPUTER SYSTEMS LTD
Registration no: NI031406 **VAT No.:** GB 515 5008 70
Date established: 1996 **Turnover:** £2m - £5m **No.of Employees:** 11 - 20
Product Groups: 84

Date of Accounts	Oct 97	May 99	May 98
Working Capital	-65	-49	-41
Fixed Assets	128	159	140
Current Assets	192	119	165

Hilton Meats Cookstown Ltd
Derryloran Indl-Est Sandholes Road, Cookstown, BT80 9LU
Tel: 028-8676 2106 **Fax:** 028-8676 2327
E-mail: info@foylefoodgroup.com
Website: http://www.foylefoodgroup.com
Directors: R. Woodson (MD), T. Atkinson (Dir)
Immediate Holding Company: HILTON MEATS (COOKSTOWN) LIMITED
Registration no: NI017248 **VAT No.:** GB 432 6812 60
Date established: 1984 **Turnover:** £20m - £50m
No.of Employees: 51 - 100 **Product Groups:** 20

Date of Accounts	Dec 10	Dec 09	Dec 08
Sales Turnover	25m	25m	21m
Pre Tax Profit/Loss	716	616	-56
Working Capital	929	350	334
Fixed Assets	962	1m	1m
Current Assets	3m	2m	2m
Current Liabilities	2m	2m	2m

H S Engineering
Unit 19 Derryloran Industrial Estate Sandholes Road, Cookstown, BT80 9LU
Tel: 028-8676 1194 **Fax:** 028-8676 1887
Directors: H. Swaile (Prop)
Date established: 1994 **No.of Employees:** 1 - 10 **Product Groups:** 41

Hutchinson Feeds
4 Ballygillen Road, Cookstown, BT80 0AL
Tel: 028-8673 7209 **Fax:** 028-8673 6421
Directors: I. Hutchinson (Prop)
Immediate Holding Company: THOMAS HUTCHINSON AND SONS LIMITED
Registration no: NI003804 **VAT No.:** GB 252 2053 03
Date established: 1956 **Turnover:** Up to £250,000
No.of Employees: 21 - 50 **Product Groups:** 20

Date of Accounts	Mar 11	Mar 10	Mar 09
Working Capital	1m	914	949
Fixed Assets	767	730	727
Current Assets	2m	1m	1m

Hydraulic Pumps N I
4 Derrycrin Road, Cookstown, BT80 0HJ
Tel: 028-8673 6711 **Fax:** 028-8673 6891
E-mail: info@hydraulicpumpsni.com
Website: http://www.hydraulicpumpsni.com
Directors: C. Mcivor (Prop)
Immediate Holding Company: MODULAR BUILD SYSTEMS (NI) LIMITED
Registration no: NI053814 **Date established:** 2010
No.of Employees: 1 - 10 **Product Groups:** 35, 39, 68, 84

J J Loughran
155 Drum Road, Cookstown, BT80 9DW
Tel: 028-8676 2295 **Fax:** 028-8676 4980
E-mail: sales@jjloughran.com
Website: http://www.jjloughran.com
Directors: J. Loughran (Prop)
VAT No.: GB 254 2843 59 **Turnover:** Up to £250,000
No.of Employees: 21 - 50 **Product Groups:** 67

Mcaleer & Rushe Ltd
24 Dungannon Road, Cookstown, BT80 8TL
Tel: 028-8676 3741 **Fax:** 028-8676 5265
E-mail: info@mcaleer-rushe.co.uk
Website: http://www.mcaleer-rushe.co.uk
Bank(s): Ulster Bank
Directors: E. Higgins (Fin), E. Higgins (Fin)
Managers: M. Kelly (Buyer), P. Gormley (Tech Serv Mgr), M. Connolly
Ultimate Holding Company: MCALEER AND RUSHE (CONSTRUCTION) LIMITED
Immediate Holding Company: MCALEER & RUSHE LIMITED
Registration no: NI010410 **VAT No.:** GB 256 1385 56
Date established: 1974 **Turnover:** £75m - £125m
No.of Employees: 101 - 250 **Product Groups:** 52, 84

Date of Accounts	Mar 11	Mar 10	Mar 09
Sales Turnover	88m	55m	91m
Pre Tax Profit/Loss	998	800	3m
Working Capital	52m	48m	56m
Fixed Assets	1m	4m	4m
Current Assets	87m	80m	94m
Current Liabilities	2m	2m	4m

Mallon Technology
Union House Union Place, Cookstown, BT80 8NP
Tel: 028-8676 1800 **Fax:** 028-8676 6489
E-mail: info@mallontechnology.com
Website: http://www.mallontechnology.com
Directors: C. McQuillan (MD)
Ultimate Holding Company: MALLON TECHNOLOGY LIMITED
Immediate Holding Company: MALLON TECHNOLOGY (NORTHERN IRELAND) LIMITED
Registration no: NI037657 **VAT No.:** GB 516 5907 36
Date established: 2000 **Turnover:** £250,000 - £500,000
No.of Employees: 51 - 100 **Product Groups:** 44

Date of Accounts	Mar 11	Mar 10	Mar 09
Working Capital	-31	-7	61
Fixed Assets	76	81	72
Current Assets	310	35	168

Meteor Electrical Ltd
7 Corchoney Road, Cookstown, BT80 9HU
Tel: 028-8675 1515 **Fax:** 028-8672 8961
E-mail: enquiries@meteorelectrical.com
Website: http://www.meteorelectrical.com
Directors: E. Conway (Dir)
Immediate Holding Company: METEOR ELECTRICAL LIMITED
Registration no: NI073275 **VAT No.:** GB 432 5537 61
Date established: 2009 **Turnover:** £2m - £5m **No.of Employees:** 1 - 10
Product Groups: 38, 49, 65, 66, 67

Date of Accounts	Dec 11	Dec 10
Working Capital	32	97
Fixed Assets	41	37
Current Assets	385	319

Mid Ulster Reproductions
Sandholes Road, Cookstown, BT80 9AR
Tel: 028-8676 4488 **Fax:** 028-8676 6655
E-mail: info@midulsterreproductions.com
Website: http://www.midulsterreproductions.com
Directors: M. O'neill (Prop)
Ultimate Holding Company: DRUMBEARN LIMITED
Immediate Holding Company: Mid-Ulster Reproductions Limited
Registration no: NI050094 **VAT No.:** GB 516 9735 19
Date established: 2004 **Turnover:** Up to £250,000
No.of Employees: 11 - 20 **Product Groups:** 25

Date of Accounts	Sep 11	Sep 10	Sep 09
Working Capital	119	138	223
Fixed Assets	289	281	621
Current Assets	294	317	383

Newpark Security Ltd
Unit A15 Kilcronagh Business Park, Cookstown, BT80 9HJ
Tel: 08448-793319 **Fax:** 028-8676 9338
E-mail: info@newparksecurity.com
Website: http://www.newparksecurity.com
Managers: C. Mainwaring (Mgr)
Immediate Holding Company: Newpark Security Ltd
Registration no: NI061344 **Date established:** 2006
Turnover: £250,000 - £500,000 **No.of Employees:** 1 - 10
Product Groups: 39

Date of Accounts	Feb 11	Feb 10	Feb 09
Working Capital	-167	195	64
Fixed Assets	658	575	354
Current Assets	146	283	189

Northern Mouldings Ltd
69 Drum Road, Cookstown, BT80 8QS
Tel: 028-8676 6831 **Fax:** 028-8676 3701
E-mail: info@northernmouldings.com
Website: http://www.northernmouldings.com
Managers: C. O'Neil (Admin Off), J. Hogg (Mgr), P. McDaid (Chief Mgr)
Immediate Holding Company: NORTHERN MOULDINGS LIMITED
Registration no: NI031984 **Date established:** 1997 **Turnover:** £1m - £2m
No.of Employees: 11 - 20 **Product Groups:** 25

Date of Accounts	May 11	May 10	May 09
Working Capital	2m	2m	2m
Fixed Assets	77	157	180
Current Assets	2m	2m	3m

S K E Solutions Ltd
3 Derryloran Business Centre Sandholes Road, Cookstown, BT80 9LU
Tel: 028-8676 9600 **Fax:** 028-8676 0033
E-mail: info@skesolutions.com
Website: http://www.skesolutions.com
Directors: S. Kerlin (MD)
Immediate Holding Company: SKE Solutions Ltd
Registration no: NI042833 **Date established:** 2002
No.of Employees: 1 - 10 **Product Groups:** 35, 39, 45

Date of Accounts	Dec 11	Dec 10	Dec 09
Working Capital	10	65	77
Fixed Assets	16	20	25
Current Assets	186	273	388

Scott Contracts Ltd
20 Sandholes Road, Cookstown, BT80 9AR
Tel: 028-8675 8655 **Fax:** 028-8675 8677
Website: http://www.scottcontracts.com
Directors: D. Scott (MD)
Immediate Holding Company: SCOTT CONTRACTS LIMITED
Registration no: NI042103 **Date established:** 2001
No.of Employees: 1 - 10 **Product Groups:** 36, 40

Date of Accounts	Feb 08	Feb 11	Feb 10
Working Capital	52	-27	-36
Fixed Assets	66	38	45
Current Assets	304	207	439

Steelweld Fabrications Ltd
3 Sandholes Road, Cookstown, BT80 9AP
Tel: 028-8676 6495 **Fax:** 028-8676 6496
E-mail: sales@steelweld.co.uk
Website: http://www.steelweld.co.uk
Managers: A. O'Connor, D. Crilley (Mgr), D. Crilly (Mgr), S. McAleer (Personnel), P. McKernan (Fin Mgr)
Immediate Holding Company: STEELWELD FABRICATIONS LIMITED
Registration no: NI025337 **Date established:** 1991
No.of Employees: 51 - 100 **Product Groups:** 35

Date of Accounts	Aug 11	Aug 10	Aug 09
Sales Turnover	N/A	5m	3m
Pre Tax Profit/Loss	N/A	207	-779
Working Capital	-175	461	479
Fixed Assets	3m	2m	2m
Current Assets	2m	2m	2m
Current Liabilities	N/A	104	187

Trade Mouldings Ltd
Cookstown Business Park Sandholes Road, Cookstown, BT80 9AR
Tel: 028-8676 2993 **Fax:** 028-8676 5684
E-mail: damien@trademouldings.com
Website: http://www.trademoulding.co.uk
Directors: D. Connolly (MD)
Managers: J. Campton (Sales Admin), J. Kavanagh (Fin Mgr)
Immediate Holding Company: TRADE MOULDINGS LIMITED
Registration no: NI015596 **VAT No.:** GB 349 6452 23
Date established: 1982 **Turnover:** £5m - £10m **No.of Employees:** 21 - 50
Product Groups: 30, 63

Date of Accounts	Mar 11	Mar 10	Mar 09
Pre Tax Profit/Loss	2m	2m	611
Working Capital	3m	2m	2m
Fixed Assets	3m	3m	4m
Current Assets	5m	5m	5m
Current Liabilities	1m	1m	1m

Tyre Safety Centre
2-4 Dungannon Road, Cookstown, BT80 8TL
Tel: 028-8676 2528 **Fax:** 028-8676 6634
E-mail: info@alloywheelsni.com
Website: http://www.alloywheelsni.com
Directors: M. Simpson (Dir)
Immediate Holding Company: TYRE SAFETY CENTRE (CO.TYRONE) LIMITED
Registration no: NI008504 **VAT No.:** GB 253 2874 54
Date established: 1971 **Turnover:** £2m - £5m **No.of Employees:** 11 - 20
Product Groups: 40, 68

Date of Accounts	Dec 11	Dec 10	Dec 09
Working Capital	66	235	267
Fixed Assets	630	483	514
Current Assets	360	541	701

Co. Armagh

Craigavon

A J Electrical Engineering Ltd
123-125 Market Street Tandragee, Craigavon, BT62 2BS
Tel: 028-3884 0037 **Fax:** 028-3884 1893
E-mail: mail@ajelectrical.co.uk
Website: http://www.ajelectrical.co.uk
Directors: J. Scott (Fin)
Immediate Holding Company: A.J. ELECTRICAL ENGINEERING LIMITED
Registration no: NI022845 **VAT No.:** GB 286 8376 01
Date established: 1989 **Turnover:** £250,000 - £500,000
No.of Employees: 1 - 10 **Product Groups:** 52

Date of Accounts	Aug 11	Aug 10	Aug 09
Working Capital	121	135	152
Fixed Assets	84	73	84
Current Assets	497	295	353
Current Liabilities	N/A	N/A	4

A1 Rewinds
Unit 14 Cido Business Complex Carn Drive, Portadown, Craigavon, BT63 5WH
Tel: 028-3833 2280 **Fax:** 028-3833 2280
E-mail: morrisross@hotmail.co.uk
Directors: M. Ross (Prop)
VAT No.: GB 517 6155 46 **Date established:** 1989
Turnover: £500,000 - £1m **No.of Employees:** 1 - 10 **Product Groups:** 67

Abbicoil Springs
21 Carn Road Portadown, Craigavon, BT63 5WG
Tel: 028-3833 3245 **Fax:** 028-3833 5997
E-mail: sales@abbicoil.co.uk
Website: http://www.abbicoil.co.uk
Bank(s): First Trust, (Lurgon)
Managers: C. Jordan (Tech Sales Mgr), A. Carlisle (Comptroller)
Ultimate Holding Company: TECHNICAL METALS LIMITED
Immediate Holding Company: ABBICOIL SPRINGS LIMITED
Registration no: NI003956 **VAT No.:** GB 251 8352 66
Date established: 1957 **Turnover:** £500,000 - £1m
No.of Employees: 21 - 50 **Product Groups:** 30, 35

Date of Accounts	Aug 11	Aug 10	Aug 09
Working Capital	-13	-46	-102
Fixed Assets	99	127	160
Current Assets	2m	345	89

Adco Distributors NI Ltd
Unit 16 Seagoe Industrial Area Portadown, Craigavon, BT63 5QD
Tel: 028-3835 3121 **Fax:** 028-3833 8291
E-mail: info@adcoltd.com
Website: http://www.adcoltd.com
Managers: G. Leathem (Sales Prom Mgr)
Immediate Holding Company: ALMAC (NO.2) LIMITED
Registration no: NI003735 **Date established:** 1956
Turnover: £500,000 - £1m **No.of Employees:** 1 - 10 **Product Groups:** 29

Date of Accounts	Sep 10	Sep 09	Sep 08
Working Capital	142	128	108
Fixed Assets	57	58	54
Current Assets	305	261	189

Agrihealth
9 Silverwood Industrial Area Silverwood Road, Lurgan, Craigavon, BT66 6LN
Tel: 028-3831 4570 **Fax:** 01630-658280
E-mail: info@agrihealth.co.uk
Website: http://www.agrihealth.co.uk
Directors: J. Murphy (MD)
Managers: W. Hurst (Sales Prom Mgr), S. Thompson (Sales Admin)
Ultimate Holding Company: AGRI HEALTH LIMITED
Immediate Holding Company: EDDIE PALIN DISTRIBUTION LIMITED
Registration no: 02325511 **VAT No.:** GB 488 8648 63
Date established: 1988 **Turnover:** £500,000 - £1m
No.of Employees: 21 - 50 **Product Groups:** 20, 35, 41

Date of Accounts	Dec 10	Dec 09	Dec 08
Working Capital	214	227	270
Fixed Assets	53	64	68
Current Assets	548	852	916
Current Liabilities	334	N/A	N/A

J N Aldred
33 Derryhale Lane Portadown, Craigavon, BT62 4HL
Tel: 028-3833 3320 **Fax:** 028-3833 3320
Directors: J. Aldred (Prop)
Date established: 1966 **No.of Employees:** 1 - 10 **Product Groups:** 30

Anfield Transport
18 Esky Drive Portadown, Craigavon, BT63 5WD
Tel: 028-3833 3553 **Fax:** 028-3833 6564
E-mail: anfieldtransport@btconnect.com
Directors: T. Cambell (Dir)
Immediate Holding Company: ANFIELD TRANSPORT LIMITED
Registration no: NI063167 **VAT No.:** GB 287 1455 34
Date established: 2007 **Turnover:** £2m - £5m **No.of Employees:** 21 - 50
Product Groups: 72

Date of Accounts	Mar 12	Mar 11	Mar 10
Working Capital	178	126	1
Fixed Assets	245	160	219
Current Assets	667	527	459

Apex Blinds Ltd
Unit 19 46-48 Avenue Road Lurgan, Craigavon, BT66 7BD
Tel: 028-3834 2525 **Fax:** 028-3832 7835
E-mail: apexblinds@btopenworld.co.uk
Website: http://www.apexblinds.co.uk
Directors: K. Walker (MD)
Immediate Holding Company: APEX BLINDS LIMITED
Registration no: NI027694 **VAT No.:** GB 575 5513 21
Date established: 1993 **No.of Employees:** 1 - 10 **Product Groups:** 30, 35, 66

Date of Accounts	Aug 11	Aug 10	Aug 09
Sales Turnover	N/A	258	N/A
Pre Tax Profit/Loss	N/A	39	N/A
Working Capital	-32	-46	-48
Fixed Assets	45	47	48
Current Assets	42	38	47

Ardmac Performance Contracting Ltd
Annesborough Industrial Area 15 Annesborough Road, Lurgan, Craigavon, BT67 9JD
Tel: 028-3834 7093 **Fax:** 028-3834 1604
E-mail: info@ardmac.com
Website: http://www.ardmac.com
Managers: R. Miller (Mgr)
Ultimate Holding Company: ARDMAC GROUP LIMITED
Immediate Holding Company: ARDMAC PERFORMANCE CONTRACTING LIMITED
Registration no: 01880651 **Date established:** 1985
Turnover: £20m - £50m **No.of Employees:** 21 - 50 **Product Groups:** 25, 35, 52

Date of Accounts	Dec 11	Dec 10	Dec 09
Pre Tax Profit/Loss	226	248	165
Working Capital	769	615	400
Fixed Assets	10	16	49
Current Assets	5m	4m	4m
Current Liabilities	1m	1m	835

Avondale Foods Craigavon Ltd
15 Dukestown Lane Lurgan, Craigavon, BT66 8TB
Tel: 028-3834 1619 **Fax:** 028-3834 3779
E-mail: info@avondale-foods.co.uk
Website: http://www.avondale-foods.co.uk
Directors: G. Senninger (Fin)
Managers: N. Copeland (Tech Serv Mgr), P. Conway (Sales & Mktg Mg), G. Geddis (Fin Mgr), M. McKeown (Personnel), J. McBennett (Purch Mgr)
Immediate Holding Company: AVONDALE FOODS (CRAIGAVON) LIMITED
Registration no: NI015099 **VAT No.:** GB 331 3123 15
Date established: 1981 **Turnover:** £20m - £50m
No.of Employees: 251 - 500 **Product Groups:** 20

Date of Accounts	Mar 11	Mar 10	Mar 09
Sales Turnover	40m	37m	31m
Pre Tax Profit/Loss	3m	5m	-182
Working Capital	7m	5m	3m
Fixed Assets	11m	11m	10m
Current Assets	13m	13m	10m
Current Liabilities	2m	3m	5m

B D G Conservatories
5 Wenlock Road Lurgan, Craigavon, BT66 8QR
Tel: 028-3832 7741 **Fax:** 028-3832 4358
E-mail: ben.robinson@bdg.co.uk
Website: http://www.bdg.co.uk
Managers: W. Osbourne (Chief Mgr)
Ultimate Holding Company: MANDERLEY FOOD GROUP LIMITED
Immediate Holding Company: BDG GROUP LIMITED
Registration no: NI014086 **VAT No.:** GB 496 9797 46
Date established: 1980 **Turnover:** £2m - £5m **No.of Employees:** 51 - 100
Product Groups: 30, 35, 52, 66

Date of Accounts	Jul 08	Jul 09	Jul 10
Sales Turnover	5m	3m	4m
Pre Tax Profit/Loss	-202	-546	-371
Working Capital	-434	-936	-1m
Fixed Assets	194	143	105
Current Assets	2m	1m	850
Current Liabilities	598	1m	155

B H Technical Services
35 Monree Hill Donaghcloney, Craigavon, BT66 7GY
Tel: 028-3882 0733
E-mail: sales@bhtservices.co.uk
Website: http://www.bhtservices.co.uk
Directors: B. Wilson (Prop)
Registration no: 984064300 **Date established:** 2009 **Turnover:**
No.of Employees: 1 - 10 **Product Groups:** 27, 28, 42, 44

Ballydougan Pottery
171 Plantation Road Portadown, Craigavon, BT63 5NN
Tel: 028-3834 2201 **Fax:** 028-3834 2201
E-mail: info@ballydouganpottery.co.uk
Website: http://www.ballydouganpottery.co.uk
Directors: S. Odowd (Prop)
Immediate Holding Company: BALLYDOUGAN POTTERY LIMITED
Registration no: NI053645 **Date established:** 2005
Turnover: £500,000 - £1m **No.of Employees:** 1 - 10 **Product Groups:** 33

Date of Accounts	Jun 11	Jun 10	Jun 09
Working Capital	-595	-622	-643
Fixed Assets	789	785	773
Current Assets	108	99	91

Bedeck Ltd
189 Lurgan Road Magheralin, Craigavon, BT67 0QS
Tel: 028-3832 5836 **Fax:** 028-3831 3001
E-mail: customerservices@bedeck.co.uk
Website: http://www.bedeckhome.com
Bank(s): Northern Bank
Directors: B. Monroe (Fin), G. Irwin (MD), P. Donegan (Sales)
Managers: T. Johnson (Mktg Serv Mgr), G. Marcer (Personnel), M. Sergant (Tech Serv Mgr)
Ultimate Holding Company: BEDECK HOLDINGS LIMITED
Immediate Holding Company: Bedeck Holdings Limited
Registration no: NI062739 **VAT No.:** GB 517 7059 37
Date established: 2007 **Turnover:** £20m - £50m
No.of Employees: 101 - 250 **Product Groups:** 23, 24, 61, 63

Date of Accounts	Sep 11	Sep 10	Sep 09
Sales Turnover	26m	24m	23m
Pre Tax Profit/Loss	1m	943	706
Working Capital	1m	-69	-253
Fixed Assets	2m	2m	2m
Current Assets	9m	8m	8m
Current Liabilities	5m	5m	5m

Beechmount Ironcraft
23 Moygannon Lane Donaghcloney, Craigavon, BT66 7ND
Tel: 028-3888 1162 **Fax:** 028-3888 1162
Directors: P. Brooker (Prop)
VAT No.: GB 496 9032 06 **No.of Employees:** 1 - 10 **Product Groups:** 26, 35

Beverage Plastics Ltd (Bottles & Containers Division)
70 Silverwood Road Lurgan, Craigavon, BT66 6LN
Tel: 028-3832 2221 **Fax:** 028-3832 1888
E-mail: enquiries@bevplas.com
Website: http://www.bevplas.com
Directors: I. Beecroft (Dir), L. Daulton (Fin)
Managers: D. Horn (Sales Prom Mgr), S. Dew (Tech Serv Mgr)
Ultimate Holding Company: BEVERAGE PLASTICS (HOLDINGS) LIMITED
Immediate Holding Company: BEVERAGE PLASTICS LIMITED
Registration no: NI017684 **VAT No.:** GB 517 5438 39
Date established: 1984 **Turnover:** £20m - £50m
No.of Employees: 51 - 100 **Product Groups:** 28, 30, 66

Date of Accounts	Dec 11	Dec 10	Dec 08
Sales Turnover	25m	21m	24m
Pre Tax Profit/Loss	-621	-57	396
Working Capital	8m	9m	8m
Fixed Assets	4m	3m	3m
Current Assets	18m	18m	14m
Current Liabilities	4m	4m	6m

Alfred Briggs Alwood Ltd
Alfred Briggs Lurgan Limited Shaerf Drive, Lurgan, Craigavon, BT66 8DD
Tel: 028-3832 3296 **Fax:** 028-3832 4256
E-mail: mail@alwood.co.uk
Website: http://www.alwoodkitchens.com
Directors: W. Briggs (MD)
Managers: A. Briggs (Mgr), I. Edgar (Personnel), E. Pyper (Chief Mgr)
Immediate Holding Company: ALFRED BRIGGS (ALWOOD) LTD
Registration no: NI048198 **VAT No.:** GB 251 7945 44
Date established: 2003 **No.of Employees:** 1 - 10 **Product Groups:** 26

Date of Accounts	Dec 11	Dec 10	Dec 09
Working Capital	194	216	233
Fixed Assets	329	335	313
Current Assets	480	897	612
Current Liabilities	75	N/A	N/A

Brownlow Heat Transfer Services
1 Wenlock Road Lurgan, Craigavon, BT66 8QR
Tel: 028-3832 4382 **Fax:** 028-3832 3626
E-mail: sales@brownlowradiators.com
Website: http://www.brownlowheattransfer.com
Directors: C. Nash (Dir)
Immediate Holding Company: BROWNLOW HEAT TRANSFER LIMITED
Registration no: NI041271 **VAT No.:** GB 287 2198 23
Date established: 2001 **No.of Employees:** 1 - 10 **Product Groups:** 39, 48

Date of Accounts	Sep 11	Sep 10	Sep 09
Working Capital	454	436	408
Fixed Assets	154	165	35
Current Assets	664	685	667

C J Radiator & Welding
Craigavon Enterprise Centre Carn Industrial Area, Portadown, Craigavon, BT63 5RH
Tel: 028-3835 0036 **Fax:** 028-3835 0036
E-mail: sales@jjservices.co.uk
Managers: C. Mcsherry (Mgr)
VAT No.: GB 517 9668 12 **Turnover:** £500,000 - £1m
No.of Employees: 1 - 10 **Product Groups:** 48

C M Machinery
25 Charlestown Avenue Portadown, Craigavon, BT63 5ZF
Tel: 028-3833 3341 **Fax:** 028-3833 0915
E-mail: info@cmmachinery.co.uk
Website: http://www.cmmachinery.co.uk
Bank(s): Northern, Portadown
Directors: R. Mcallen (Dir)
Immediate Holding Company: CMMT LTD
Registration no: NI053487 **Date established:** 2005
Turnover: £500,000 - £1m **No.of Employees:** 11 - 20
Product Groups: 42, 43, 44, 46

Date of Accounts	Dec 11	Dec 10	Dec 09
Working Capital	81	-120	422
Fixed Assets	1m	1m	484
Current Assets	1m	489	963

Carpet Tiles Sales N I Ltd
56 Clonmakate Road Portadown, Craigavon, BT62 1TZ
Tel: 028-3885 1991 **Fax:** 028-3885 1991
Managers: H. Abraham (Mgr)
Immediate Holding Company: CARPET TILE SALES (N.I.) LIMITED
Registration no: NI020843 **VAT No.:** GB 434 1788 44
Date established: 1987 **Turnover:** Up to £250,000
No.of Employees: 1 - 10 **Product Groups:** 23, 29, 30, 63

Date of Accounts	Dec 11	Dec 10	Dec 09
Working Capital	87	124	131
Fixed Assets	60	20	22
Current Assets	170	151	157

Cirrus Plastics
2 Esky Drive Carn Industrial Area, Portadown, Craigavon, BT63 5YY
Tel: 028-3835 0001 **Fax:** 028-3835 0002
E-mail: sales@cirrusplastics.com
Website: http://www.cirrusplastics.com
Bank(s): Ulster
Directors: A. Doak (MD)
Immediate Holding Company: CIRRUS LIMITED
Registration no: NI020574 **VAT No.:** GB 434 2834 58
Date established: 1987 **Turnover:** £5m - £10m **No.of Employees:** 21 - 50
Product Groups: 30

Date of Accounts	Nov 11	Nov 10	Nov 09
Sales Turnover	9m	7m	6m
Pre Tax Profit/Loss	312	225	291
Working Capital	404	334	654
Fixed Assets	2m	1m	840
Current Assets	3m	3m	2m
Current Liabilities	2m	1m	780

Clarehill Plastics Ltd
New Building 21 Clarehill Road, Moira, Craigavon, BT67 0PB
Tel: 028-9261 1077 **Fax:** 028-9261 2672
E-mail: nicola@clarehill.com
Website: http://www.harlequinplastics.co.uk
Directors: N. Coey (Tech Serv), M. Kinder (Fin)
Managers: J. Switzer (Mktg Serv Mgr), J. Kerr (Personnel), L. Coey (Buyer)
Immediate Holding Company: CLAREHILL PLASTICS LIMITED
Registration no: NI015227 **VAT No.:** GB 366 3255 44
Date established: 1981 **Turnover:** £10m - £20m
No.of Employees: 51 - 100 **Product Groups:** 30, 33, 35, 36, 42

Date of Accounts	Dec 10	Dec 09	Dec 08
Sales Turnover	11m	8m	N/A
Pre Tax Profit/Loss	658	290	310
Working Capital	137	216	-34
Fixed Assets	3m	2m	2m
Current Assets	4m	2m	3m
Current Liabilities	759	281	305

Classic Career Clothing
84a Plantation Road Portadown, Craigavon, BT63 5NN
Tel: 028-3883 0838 **Fax:** 028-3883 0833
E-mail: info@classiccareerclothing.com
Website: http://www.classiccareerclothing.com
Bank(s): Bank of Ireland
Directors: B. Reilly (Dir)
Immediate Holding Company: CLASSIC CAREER CLOTHING LTD
Registration no: NI037754 **VAT No.:** GB 575 4651 14
Date established: 2000 **Turnover:** £250,000 - £500,000
No.of Employees: 11 - 20 **Product Groups:** 24

Date of Accounts	Mar 11	Mar 10	Mar 09
Working Capital	-57	-46	-31
Fixed Assets	151	165	162
Current Assets	123	175	229

Clearway Ltd
41 Dobbin Road Portadown, Craigavon, BT62 4EY
Tel: 028-3833 7333 **Fax:** 028-3833 6716
E-mail: info@clearwaypordesign.ffs.uk
Managers: J. Cullen (Buyer), K. McCuskar (Comptroller), K. Mccusker (Comptroller)

Ultimate Holding Company: Clearway Holdings Limited
Immediate Holding Company: CLEARWAY DISPOSALS LIMITED
Registration no: NI014852 **VAT No.:** GB 255 4084 61
Date established: 1981 **Turnover:** £75m - £125m
No.of Employees: 51 - 100 **Product Groups:** 34, 54

Date of Accounts	Dec 11	Dec 10	Dec 09
Sales Turnover	153m	119m	83m
Pre Tax Profit/Loss	10m	11m	10m
Working Capital	38m	41m	33m
Fixed Assets	23m	25m	26m
Current Assets	46m	50m	41m
Current Liabilities	3m	4m	4m

Comiskey Engineering Works

Mahon Industrial Area Mahon Road, Portadown, Craigavon, BT62 3EH
Tel: 028-3833 2040 **Fax:** 028-3833 0383
E-mail: comiskey3@btinternet.com
Website: http://www.comiskeyengineeringworks.com
Directors: J. Comiskey (Sales)
Immediate Holding Company: REFA LIMITED
Registration no: NI011696 **VAT No.:** GB 253 0019 07
Date established: 1976 **No.of Employees:** 1 - 10 **Product Groups:** 40, 48

Craigavon Borough Council

PO Box 66, Craigavon, BT64 1AL
Tel: 028-3831 2400 **Fax:** 028-3831 2444
E-mail: info@craigavon.gov.uk
Website: http://www.craigavon.gov.uk
Directors: T. Donaldson (Grp Chief Exec)
No.of Employees: 251 - 500 **Product Groups:** 87

Craigavon Cornicing

Unit 4 Annesborough Industrial Estate Annesborough Road, Lurgan, Craigavon, BT67 9JD
Tel: 028-3834 2222 **Fax:** 028-3834 2222
E-mail: craigavoncornicing@hotmail.com
Website: http://www.craigavoncornicing.com
Directors: J. Hawkin (Prop)
Date established: 1985 **Turnover:** Up to £250,000
No.of Employees: 1 - 10 **Product Groups:** 33

Craigavon Industrial Development Organisation

Charlestown Road Industrial Estate Charlestown Road, Portadown, Craigavon, BT63 5PP
Tel: 028-3839 6520 **Fax:** 028-3835 0390
E-mail: info@cido.co.uk
Website: http://www.cido.co.uk
Directors: J. Smith (Grp Chief Exec)
Immediate Holding Company: CRAIGAVON INDUSTRIAL DEVELOPMENT ORGANISATION
Registration no: NI017745 **Date established:** 1984
Turnover: £500,000 - £1m **No.of Employees:** 1 - 10 **Product Groups:** 80, 82, 86

Date of Accounts	Mar 11	Mar 10	Mar 09
Sales Turnover	986	777	587
Pre Tax Profit/Loss	126	-9	-102
Working Capital	198	-87	-194
Fixed Assets	3m	3m	3m
Current Assets	435	182	158
Current Liabilities	106	126	137

Craigavon Marble Products

Unit 9 Ulster Street Industrial Area Lurgan, Craigavon, BT67 9AN
Tel: 028-3832 6736 **Fax:** 028-3832 7764
E-mail: craigavonmarble@btconnect.com
Website: http://www.craigavonmarble.co.uk
Directors: M. Mcilduff (Dir)
Immediate Holding Company: CRAIGAVON MARBLE PRODUCTS LTD
Registration no: NI045085 **VAT No.:** GB 287 2552 31
Date established: 2003 **Turnover:** £250,000 - £500,000
No.of Employees: 1 - 10 **Product Groups:** 33, 52

Date of Accounts	Feb 12	Feb 11	Feb 10
Working Capital	227	208	282
Fixed Assets	43	44	48
Current Assets	257	223	301

Crossbows Optical Ltd

Unit 1 Halfpenny Valley Industrial Estate Lurgan, Craigavon, BT66 8TP
Tel: 028-3832 2301 **Fax:** 028-3832 8923
E-mail: general@crossbowsoptical.com
Website: http://www.crossbowsoptical.com
Bank(s): Bank of Ireland
Directors: M. McCrey (MD), M. McCrea (MD)
Managers: D. McClure (Maint)
Ultimate Holding Company: ESSILOR INTERNATIONAL SA (FRANCE)
Immediate Holding Company: CROSSBOWS OPTICAL LIMITED
Registration no: NI020335 **VAT No.:** GB 434 2816 60
Date established: 1987 **Turnover:** £1m - £2m **No.of Employees:** 21 - 50
Product Groups: 38, 45, 65

Date of Accounts	Dec 11	Dec 10	Dec 09
Sales Turnover	3m	2m	2m
Pre Tax Profit/Loss	1m	562	2m
Working Capital	1m	2m	4m
Fixed Assets	2m	2m	2m
Current Assets	2m	2m	4m
Current Liabilities	230	200	150

D & D Kitchens

Monree Road Donaghcloney, Craigavon, BT66 7LZ
Tel: 028-3888 2201 **Fax:** 028-3888 2201
Directors: D. Graham (Ptnr)
VAT No.: GB 517 7236 41 **Date established:** 1986
No.of Employees: 1 - 10 **Product Groups:** 26

D & J Group Ltd

5 Hanover Street Portadown, Craigavon, BT62 3ER
Tel: 028-3833 9624 **Fax:** 028-3833 5599
E-mail: info@drfhouse.com
Website: http://www.drfhouse.com
Directors: J. Fogarty (Dir)
Immediate Holding Company: The D & J Group Ltd
Registration no: NI043174 **Date established:** 1992
Turnover: Up to £250,000 **No.of Employees:** 1 - 10 **Product Groups:** 80

Dairy Fresh Foods Ltd

Unit 65 Craigavon Enterprise Centre Carn Industrial Area, Portadown, Craigavon, BT63 5RH
Tel: 028-3833 2359 **Fax:** 028-3836 3003
E-mail: info@dairyfreshfoods.co.uk
Website: http://www.dairyfreshfoods.co.uk
Directors: T. Mccullough (Dir)
Immediate Holding Company: DAIRY FRESH FOODS LIMITED
Registration no: NI015777 **VAT No.:** GB 496 9939 52
Date established: 1982 **Turnover:** Up to £250,000
No.of Employees: 1 - 10 **Product Groups:** 20, 62

Date of Accounts	Jun 11	Jun 10	Jun 09
Working Capital	-4	11	41
Fixed Assets	4	10	13
Current Assets	145	147	165

Datos Professional Solutions Ltd

16 Armagh Road Portadown, Craigavon, BT62 3DP
Tel: 028-3836 2002 **Fax:** 028-3833 4485
E-mail: info@datos.co.uk
Website: http://www.datos.co.uk
Directors: D. Mckane (MD)
Immediate Holding Company: DATOS PROFESSIONAL SOLUTIONS LTD.
Registration no: NI024049 **Date established:** 1990
Turnover: £500,000 - £1m **No.of Employees:** 11 - 20 **Product Groups:** 44

Date of Accounts	Feb 11	Feb 10	Feb 09
Working Capital	80	56	48
Fixed Assets	175	174	177
Current Assets	128	93	108

Datum Monitoring Ireland

36 Lurganville Road Moira, Craigavon, BT67 0PL
Tel: 028-9261 6800 **Fax:** 028-9261 0524
E-mail: info@lloydacoustics.co.uk
Website: http://www.datumireland.com
Directors: N. Dillan (MD)
Immediate Holding Company: DATUM MONITORING IRELAND LIMITED
Registration no: NI055284 **Date established:** 2005
Turnover: £500,000 - £1m **No.of Employees:** 1 - 10 **Product Groups:** 85

Date of Accounts	Apr 11	Apr 10	Apr 09
Working Capital	74	104	104
Fixed Assets	36	63	122
Current Assets	148	181	224

De Luxe Arts Ltd

2 Mahon Industrial Area Mahon Road, Portadown, Craigavon, BT62 3EH
Tel: 028-3833 0468 **Fax:** 028-3835 0915
E-mail: info@deluxefx.com
Website: http://www.deluxefx.com
Directors: C. O'farrell (MD)
Managers: S. Uprichard (Chief Acct), C. Hawthorn (Develop Mgr)
Immediate Holding Company: DELUXE ART & THEME LIMITED
Registration no: NI042943 **VAT No.:** GB 287 0073 53
Date established: 2002 **No.of Employees:** 21 - 50 **Product Groups:** 52, 66

Date of Accounts	Sep 11	Sep 10	Sep 09
Working Capital	185	69	847
Fixed Assets	341	184	216
Current Assets	2m	1m	2m

Colin Deane Partners

16 Market Street Lurgan, Craigavon, BT66 6AQ
Tel: 028-3832 2346 **Fax:** 028- 38349014
Directors: I. Mitchell (Snr Part)
Date established: 1974 **No.of Employees:** 1 - 10 **Product Groups:** 84

Derrys Ltd

85 Teagy Road Portadown, Craigavon, BT62 1LX
Tel: 028-3885 1509 **Fax:** 028-3885 2202
E-mail: sales@derrys.com
Website: http://www.derrys.com
Directors: G. Derry (MD), G. Derry (MD), D. O'Hagan (Sales)
Managers: P. Mallon (Chief Acct)
Immediate Holding Company: DERRYS LIMITED
Registration no: NI020031 **VAT No.:** GB 331 2162 10
Date established: 1986 **No.of Employees:** 21 - 50 **Product Groups:** 26

Date of Accounts	Dec 11	Dec 10	Dec 09
Working Capital	2m	2m	2m
Fixed Assets	420	546	644
Current Assets	2m	2m	2m

Dunlop Engineering

93 Loughgall Road Portadown, Craigavon, BT62 4EG
Tel: 028-3833 3683 **Fax:** 028-3833 3683
E-mail: dunlopengineering@btinternet.com
Website: http://www.DUNLOPENGINEERING.CO.UK
Directors: J. Dunlop (Ptnr)
No.of Employees: 1 - 10 **Product Groups:** 26, 35

James N Emerson

15 Cannagola Road Portadown, Craigavon, BT62 1RG
Tel: 028-3885 1491 **Fax:** 028-3885 2671
E-mail: info@forecourtinstallations.co.uk
Website: http://www.forecourtinstallations.co.uk
Directors: J. Emerson (Prop)
Date established: 1960 **No.of Employees:** 1 - 10 **Product Groups:** 40

Stanley Emerson & Sons Ltd

39 Banbridge Road Lurgan, Craigavon, BT66 7HG
Tel: 028-3832 3487 **Fax:** 028-3832 5717
Directors: W. Emerson (Prop)
Immediate Holding Company: STANLEY EMERSON & SONS LIMITED
Registration no: NI013897 **VAT No.:** GB 287 2711 37
Date established: 1979 **Turnover:** £250,000 - £500,000
No.of Employees: 1 - 10 **Product Groups:** 14, 66, 83

Date of Accounts	Dec 11	Dec 10	Dec 09
Working Capital	2m	2m	2m
Fixed Assets	589	692	805
Current Assets	3m	2m	2m

Enterprise Stationery Ltd

Unit7 Silverwood Industrial Area Silverwo Od Road Lurgan, Craigavon, BT66 6LN
Tel: 028-3832 6718 **Fax:** 028-3832 1047
E-mail: info@enterprisestationery.com
Website: http://www.enterprisestationery.com
Managers: P. Mccann (Comm)
Ultimate Holding Company: PLUMBRIDGE LIMITED
Immediate Holding Company: ENTERPRISE STATIONERY LIMITED
Registration no: NI016089 **Date established:** 1982
Turnover: £500,000 - £1m **No.of Employees:** 51 - 100
Product Groups: 27, 28

Date of Accounts	Oct 11	Oct 10	Oct 09
Working Capital	2m	2m	2m
Fixed Assets	100	192	200
Current Assets	3m	3m	3m

Euro Stock Foods Ni Ltd

67 Crowhill Road Lurgan, Craigavon, BT66 7AT
Tel: 028-3834 4224 **Fax:** 028-3026 6120
E-mail: info@eurostockfoods.com
Website: http://www.eurostockfoods.com
Directors: M. White (Ch)
Ultimate Holding Company: EUROSTOCK FOOD GROUP LTD
Immediate Holding Company: EUROSTOCK FOODS NI LTD
Registration no: NI017910 **VAT No.:** GB 412 5454 79
Date established: 1984 **No.of Employees:** 51 - 100 **Product Groups:** 20

Date of Accounts	Jan 11	Jan 10	Jan 09
Sales Turnover	28m	22m	N/A
Pre Tax Profit/Loss	301	290	-411
Working Capital	-2m	-2m	-775
Fixed Assets	8m	8m	8m
Current Assets	8m	6m	8m
Current Liabilities	253	353	337

Evron Foods Ltd

Carn Industrial Estate Portadown, Craigavon, BT63 5WD
Tel: 028-3833 7170 **Fax:** 028-3833 1334
E-mail: p.moore@evronfoods.co.uk
Website: http://www.evronfoods.co.uk
Directors: R. McKeadney (Fin), P. Morre (Fin)
Managers: D. Downey, C. Morton, R. Paisley (Personnel)
Immediate Holding Company: EVRON FOODS LIMITED
Registration no: NI016912 **VAT No.:** GB 390 8074 38
Date established: 1983 **No.of Employees:** 101 - 250 **Product Groups:** 20

Date of Accounts	Aug 11	Aug 10	Aug 09
Sales Turnover	27m	27m	24m
Pre Tax Profit/Loss	377	468	468
Working Capital	-2m	-2m	-422
Fixed Assets	12m	13m	13m
Current Assets	7m	7m	7m
Current Liabilities	856	584	2m

F D Metal Craft

19 Derryvar Road Portadown, Craigavon, BT62 1XD
Tel: 028-3885 1159 **Fax:** 028-3885 1159
E-mail: f.devlin878@btinternet.com
Directors: F. Devlin (Prop)
Turnover: Up to £250,000 **No.of Employees:** 1 - 10 **Product Groups:** 36, 48

James A S Finlay Holdings Ltd

29 Maghaberry Road Moira, Craigavon, BT67 0JG
Tel: 028-9261 1300 **Fax:** 028-9261 1971
E-mail: sales@finlayfoods.com
Website: http://www.finlayfoods.com
Directors: D. Anthony (Sales), M. Finlay (Dir), B. Chambers (Co Sec), J. Finlay (Ch), S. Finlay (MD)
Managers: K. Dunleavy (Purch Mgr)
Immediate Holding Company: JAMES A. S. FINLAY (HOLDINGS) LIMITED
Registration no: NI012625 **VAT No.:** GB 287 1402 55
Date established: 1978 **Turnover:** £10m - £20m **No.of Employees:** 1 - 10
Product Groups: 02, 20, 62

Date of Accounts	Aug 11	Aug 10	Aug 09
Sales Turnover	13m	12m	12m
Pre Tax Profit/Loss	237	238	247
Working Capital	1m	985	867
Fixed Assets	2m	2m	2m
Current Assets	4m	4m	4m
Current Liabilities	980	1m	897

Fuel Tank Renu

1 Wenlock Road Portadown Road, Lurgan, Craigavon, BT66 8QR
Tel: 028-3831 6661 **Fax:** 028-3832 3626
E-mail: charlene@brownlowradiators.com
Website: http://www.brownlowradiators.com
Directors: C. Nash (MD)
Immediate Holding Company: BROWNLOW HEAT TRANSFER LIMITED
Registration no: NI041271 **Date established:** 2001
No.of Employees: 1 - 10 **Product Groups:** 39, 40

Date of Accounts	Sep 11	Sep 10	Sep 09
Working Capital	454	436	408
Fixed Assets	154	165	35
Current Assets	664	685	667

Galen (PDMS Division)

22 Seagoe Industrial Area Portadown, Craigavon, BT63 5YY
Tel: 028-3833 4974 **Fax:** 028-3835 0206
E-mail: info@almacgroup.com
Website: http://www.almacgroup.com
Bank(s): Bank of Ireland
Directors: M. Scutton (MD)
Immediate Holding Company: Galen Limited
Registration no: NI056542 **VAT No.:** GB 575 4885 86
Date established: 2005 **Turnover:** £20m - £50m
No.of Employees: 21 - 50 **Product Groups:** 31

Date of Accounts	Sep 11	Sep 10	Sep 09
Sales Turnover	38m	31m	27m
Pre Tax Profit/Loss	4m	-1m	-3m
Working Capital	-14m	-19m	-21m
Fixed Assets	28m	27m	30m
Current Assets	15m	12m	9m
Current Liabilities	9m	10m	7m

Gilliland

4 Main Street Donaghcloney, Craigavon, BT66 7NL
Tel: 028-3888 1328 **Fax:** 028-3882 0505
Managers: T. Massey (Mgr)
Immediate Holding Company: MGR CRUSHING LIMITED
Date established: 2003 **No.of Employees:** 1 - 10 **Product Groups:** 35

Date of Accounts	Dec 10	Dec 09	Dec 08
Working Capital	-4	-65	-25
Fixed Assets	19	261	157
Current Assets	20	32	152

Glanbia Cheese Ltd
35 Steps Road Magheralin, Craigavon, BT67 0QY
Tel: 028-9261 1274 **Fax:** 028-9261 2464
E-mail: info@glanbiacheese.co.uk
Website: http://www.glanbiacheese.co.uk
Directors: P. Vernon (Grp Chief Exec), G. Fedrigoni (Dir), S. Lombardini (Dir), J. Kylie (Fin)
Managers: P. Mccrea (Plant), T. Mackin (Accounts), A. Rogers (Sales & Mktg Mg)
Immediate Holding Company: GLANBIA CHEESE LIMITED
Registration no: NF003539 **VAT No.:** GB 575 4327 23
Date established: 2000 **No.of Employees:** 101 - 250 **Product Groups:** 20

Haldane Fisher
Castle Street Portadown, Craigavon, BT62 1BD
Tel: 028-3833 7321 **Fax:** 028-3833 0896
E-mail: a.culley@haldane-fisher.com
Website: http://www.haldane-fisher.com
Managers: A. Culley (Chief Mgr), D. White (Sales Prom Mgr), I. Poots (Purch Mgr)
Ultimate Holding Company: HALDANE SHIELLS AND COMPANY LIMITED
Immediate Holding Company: HALDANE FISHER LIMITED
Registration no: NI024075 **VAT No.:** GB 253 8272 52
Date established: 1990 **No.of Employees:** 21 - 50 **Product Groups:** 66

Date of Accounts	Dec 11	Dec 10	Dec 09
Sales Turnover	45m	48m	50m
Pre Tax Profit/Loss	202	18	1m
Working Capital	8m	7m	7m
Fixed Assets	2m	2m	2m
Current Assets	17m	16m	17m
Current Liabilities	1m	1m	2m

Harrisons Printers
Irwin House 18 Bridge Street, Portadown, Craigavon, BT62 1JD
Tel: 028-3833 0252 **Fax:** 028-3833 0252
E-mail: sales@harrisonprint.com
Website: http://www.harrisonprint.com
Directors: B. Harrison (Prop)
VAT No.: GB 412 6464 71 **Date established:** 1985
No.of Employees: 1 - 10 **Product Groups:** 81

Hobart UK
Carn Drive Portadown, Craigavon, BT63 5WH
Tel: 08448-887777
E-mail: sales@hobartuk.com
Website: http://www.hobartuk.com
Managers: E. Paterson (Mgr)
Registration no: NI055879 **Date established:** 2005
No.of Employees: 1 - 10 **Product Groups:** 20, 40, 41

Huhtamaki Packaging Supplies
Inn Road Dollingstown, Craigavon, BT66 7JW
Tel: 028-3832 7711 **Fax:** 028-3832 1782
E-mail: philip.woolsey@gb.huhtamaki.com
Website: http://www.huhtamaki.com
Managers: C. McNally (Tech Serv Mgr), P. Horne (Sales & Mktg Mg), P. Woolsey (Mgr), R. McShane (Purch Mgr), S. Porter (Fin Mgr), J. Curry (Personnel)
Ultimate Holding Company: HUHTAMAKI VAN LEER OYJ (FINLAND)
Immediate Holding Company: Huhtamaki (Lurgan) Limited
Registration no: NI001006 **Date established:** 1935
Turnover: £20m - £50m **No.of Employees:** 101 - 250
Product Groups: 38, 42

Date of Accounts	Dec 11	Dec 10	Dec 09
Sales Turnover	27m	26m	26m
Pre Tax Profit/Loss	3m	3m	3m
Working Capital	2m	6m	4m
Fixed Assets	8m	9m	8m
Current Assets	9m	13m	11m
Current Liabilities	1m	4m	3m

W R Hunter
51 Loughbrickland Road Gilgord, Gilford, Craigavon, BT63 6BN
Tel: 028-3883 1340 **Fax:** 028-3883 1362
Managers: W. Hunter (Mgr)
No.of Employees: 1 - 10 **Product Groups:** 41

R A Irwin & Co. Ltd
Bannside Industrial Estate Goban Street, Portadown, Craigavon, BT63 5AG
Tel: 028-3833 6215 **Fax:** 028-3835 0310
E-mail: h.wick@ra-irwin.co.uk
Website: http://www.ra-irwin.co.uk
Bank(s): Northern Bank
Managers: H. Wick (Chief Mgr)
Immediate Holding Company: R.A. IRWIN & COMPANY LIMITED
Registration no: NI013665 **VAT No.:** GB 252 4929 51
Date established: 1979 **Turnover:** £5m - £10m
No.of Employees: 101 - 250 **Product Groups:** 23

Date of Accounts	Sep 11	Sep 10	Sep 09
Sales Turnover	7m	7m	7m
Pre Tax Profit/Loss	58	245	178
Working Capital	5m	5m	5m
Fixed Assets	5m	5m	5m
Current Assets	6m	6m	6m
Current Liabilities	512	593	518

Irwin's Bakery (W.D. Irwin & Sons (1985) Ltd)
The Food Park Carne Industrial Estate, Portadown, Craigavon, BT63 5WE
Tel: 028-3833 2421 **Fax:** 028-3833 3918
E-mail: info@irwinsbakery.com
Website: http://www.irwinsbakery.com
Bank(s): Ulster Bank, Portadown
Directors: B. Irwin (MD)
Managers: L. Mckinney (I.T. Exec), J. Hopkins (Sales Prom Mgr), M. Murphy (Mktg Serv Mgr), S. Tottom (Personnel)
Registration no: NI007236 **VAT No.:** GB 252 2577 66
Turnover: £20m - £50m **Product Groups:** 20

Izz Design
26 Tarsan Lane Portadown, Craigavon, BT63 5RT
Tel: 028-3833 7043 **Fax:** 028-3833 0809
Website: http://www.amserve.co.uk
Directors: J. Davison (Prop), L. Ferguson (Prop)
Date established: 1984 **No.of Employees:** 1 - 10 **Product Groups:** 52, 84

David Johnston Design Ltd
100 Main Street Moira, Craigavon, BT67 0LH
Tel: 028-9261 9999 **Fax:** 028-9261 9999
E-mail: jdavidjohnston@live.co.uk
Website: http://www.davidjohnstondesign.co.uk
Directors: D. Johnston (MD)
Immediate Holding Company: DAVID JOHNSTON DESIGN LIMITED
Registration no: NI016723 **Date established:** 1983
No.of Employees: 1 - 10 **Product Groups:** 26

Date of Accounts	May 11	May 10	May 09
Working Capital	-33	-64	-15
Fixed Assets	9	19	32
Current Assets	87	98	124

Knox Cash & Carry
William Street Lurgan, Craigavon, BT66 6JD
Tel: 028-3832 2771 **Fax:** 028-3832 9846
E-mail: lurgan@haslett.co.uk
Bank(s): Northern Bank
Directors: T. Knox (Dir), R. Knox (MD)
Managers: C. O'hare (Mgr), B. Simpson (Mgr), C. O'Share (Mgr)
Registration no: 00006172 **VAT No.:** 252662953 **Date established:** 1989
No.of Employees: 11 - 20 **Product Groups:** 61

Date of Accounts	Dec 10	Dec 09	Dec 08
Working Capital	1m	1m	1m
Current Assets	1m	1m	1m

Lamont
Victoria Street Lurgan, Craigavon, BT67 9DA
Tel: 028-3831 1980 **Fax:** 028-3834 3095
Website: http://www.samuellamont.co.uk
Directors: D. Lamont (MD)
Immediate Holding Company: SAMUEL LAMONT (HOLDINGS) LIMITED
Registration no: NI004020 **Date established:** 1958
No.of Employees: 21 - 50 **Product Groups:** 23, 24

Date of Accounts	Dec 10	Dec 09	Dec 08
Sales Turnover	29	N/A	N/A
Pre Tax Profit/Loss	-71	N/A	N/A
Working Capital	542	614	685
Fixed Assets	542	550	562
Current Assets	1m	919	985
Current Liabilities	10	N/A	N/A

Lindsay Ford
2 Highfield Park, Craigavon, BT64 3AF
Tel: 028-3834 2424 **Fax:** 028-3834 2440
E-mail: billy.purvis@lindsay-cars.co.uk
Website: http://www.lindsayford.co.uk
Managers: B. Purvis (Mgr)
Immediate Holding Company: LINDSAY CARS LIMITED
Registration no: NI005514 **Date established:** 1963 **Turnover:** £1m - £2m
No.of Employees: 21 - 50 **Product Groups:** 68

Date of Accounts	Dec 11	Dec 10	Dec 09
Sales Turnover	104m	115m	114m
Pre Tax Profit/Loss	-1m	825	1m
Working Capital	1m	2m	1m
Fixed Assets	8m	9m	12m
Current Assets	33m	32m	43m
Current Liabilities	29m	5m	9m

Alan Little Ltd
30-32 Queens Place Lurgan, Craigavon, BT66 8BY
Tel: 028-3832 2322 **Fax:** 028-3832 1248
E-mail: ian@littleelectrical.com
Website: http://www.littleelectrical.com
Directors: I. Little (Prop)
Managers: J. Daley (Mgr)
Immediate Holding Company: ALAN LITTLE LIMITED
Registration no: NI010565 **VAT No.:** GB 256 1783 44
Date established: 1975 **No.of Employees:** 21 - 50 **Product Groups:** 48, 52

Date of Accounts	Oct 08	Oct 07	Mar 11
Working Capital	976	938	1m
Fixed Assets	86	81	60
Current Assets	2m	2m	2m

Lurgan Metal Works
Site 7 Ulster Street Lurgan, Craigavon, BT67 9AN
Tel: 028-3834 3727
Directors: P. Coleman (Prop)
Date established: 1977 **No.of Employees:** 1 - 10 **Product Groups:** 26, 35

M L Tools
Goban Street Portadown, Craigavon, BT63 5AG
Tel: 028-3833 7316 **Fax:** 028-3833 3375
Directors: M. Murray (Prop)
Date established: 1996 **No.of Employees:** 1 - 10 **Product Groups:** 37

J Mcareavey
2a Glen Road Moira, Craigavon, BT67 0JH
Tel: 028-9262 1557 **Fax:** 028-9262 2189
Managers: I. Purdey (Mgr)
Immediate Holding Company: McAREAVEY PROPERTIES LIMITED
Registration no: NI052347 **VAT No.:** GB 253 6922 49
Date established: 2004 **Turnover:** £250,000 - £500,000
No.of Employees: 11 - 20 **Product Groups:** 25

Date of Accounts	Mar 11	Mar 10	Mar 09
Working Capital	145	173	294
Current Assets	310	310	310

Mcconville Bros
55-57 Kilvergan Road Lurgan, Craigavon, BT66 6LJ
Tel: 028-3834 1452 **Fax:** 028-3834 8892
Directors: S. Mcconville (Prop)
Immediate Holding Company: MCCONVILLE BROS. LIMITED
Registration no: NI002182 **VAT No.:** GB 254 7261 56
Date established: 1946 **No.of Employees:** 1 - 10 **Product Groups:** 24

Date of Accounts	May 11	May 10	May 09
Working Capital	293	136	106
Fixed Assets	108	116	34
Current Assets	398	204	148

Mcmullen Architectural Systems Ltd
66 Lurgan Road Moira, Craigavon, BT67 0LX
Tel: 028-9261 9688 **Fax:** 028-9261 9711
E-mail: info@mcmullenarchitectural.com
Website: http://www.mcmullenarchitectural.com
Bank(s): Northern Bank
Directors: J. Pentland (Fin), T. Mcmullen (MD)
Managers: O. Rafferty (Personnel), D. Casey (Purch Mgr), F. O'Hare (Tech Serv Mgr), D. Millar (Sales & Mktg Mg)
Ultimate Holding Company: McMullen Group Holdings Limited
Immediate Holding Company: MCMULLEN ARCHITECTURAL SYSTEMS LIMITED
Registration no: NI016891 **VAT No.:** GB 254 6480 49
Date established: 1983 **Turnover:** £10m - £20m
No.of Employees: 101 - 250 **Product Groups:** 35, 52

Date of Accounts	Jan 11	Jan 10	Jan 09
Sales Turnover	17m	36m	N/A
Pre Tax Profit/Loss	-624	3m	3m
Working Capital	5m	6m	5m
Fixed Assets	912	1m	1m
Current Assets	11m	11m	11m
Current Liabilities	646	3m	1m

Macneice Fruit Ltd
Ardress Road Portadown, Craigavon, BT62 1SQ
Tel: 028-3885 1381 **Fax:** 028-3885 2224
E-mail: admin@macneicefruit.com
Website: http://www.macneicefruit.com
Directors: G. Macneice (MD)
Immediate Holding Company: MacNeice Fruit Limited
Registration no: NI058704 **VAT No.:** GB 254 2081 83
Date established: 2006 **No.of Employees:** 11 - 20 **Product Groups:** 20

Date of Accounts	Apr 12	Apr 11	Apr 10
Working Capital	120	89	65
Fixed Assets	839	845	852
Current Assets	525	539	515

J S Massey
17b Maghaberry Road Moira, Craigavon, BT67 0JE
Tel: 028-9261 9009 **Fax:** 028- 92611998
E-mail: gillian@masseycatering.co.uk
Website: http://www.masseycatering.co.uk
Directors: J. Massey (Prop)
Date established: 1994 **No.of Employees:** 11 - 20 **Product Groups:** 20, 40, 41

Edwin May Ltd
128 Bridge Street Portadown, Craigavon, BT63 5AP
Tel: 028-3833 2238 **Fax:** 028-3835 0181
E-mail: ian.hutchinson@edwinmay.co.uk
Website: http://www.edwinmay.co.uk
Directors: I. Hutchinson (Dir)
Managers: G. Crooks (Sales Prom Mgr)
Ultimate Holding Company: ROADSIDE MOTORS LIMITED
Immediate Holding Company: EDWIN MAYLIMITED
Registration no: NI003528 **VAT No.:** GB 252 3428 78
Date established: 1955 **Turnover:** £20m - £50m
No.of Employees: 21 - 50 **Product Groups:** 68, 84

Date of Accounts	Sep 11	Sep 10	Sep 09
Sales Turnover	21m	23m	21m
Pre Tax Profit/Loss	188	284	288
Working Capital	1m	1m	856
Fixed Assets	110	109	128
Current Assets	5m	3m	4m
Current Liabilities	381	430	318

Mccaw Allan Ltd
Victoria Street Lurgan, Craigavon, BT67 9DU
Tel: 028-3834 1412 **Fax:** 028-3832 4867
E-mail: mail@samuellamont.co.uk
Website: http://www.mccaw-allan.com
Bank(s): Ulster
Directors: D. Lamont (Dir)
Managers: E. Hadden, P. Convery (Chief Acct)
Immediate Holding Company: MCCAW ALLAN & CO LIMITED
Registration no: NI001294 **VAT No.:** GB 251 7361 70
Date established: 1938 **No.of Employees:** 21 - 50 **Product Groups:** 23, 24

Date of Accounts	Apr 99	Apr 00
Working Capital	547	527
Fixed Assets	34	25
Current Assets	780	782

Mid-Ulster Granite & Stone Co. Ltd
67 Queen Street Lurgan, Craigavon, BT66 8BP
Tel: 028-3832 2251 **Fax:** 028-3832 1802
Directors: K. Rowe (MD), E. Rowe (Co Sec)
Managers: T. McCauley (Mgr)
Immediate Holding Company: MID-ULSTER GRANITE & STONE CO. LIMITED
Registration no: NI006159 **VAT No.:** GB 251 8772 38
Date established: 1964 **Turnover:** £1m - £2m **No.of Employees:** 1 - 10
Product Groups: 14, 33, 66

Date of Accounts	Dec 11	Dec 10	Dec 09
Working Capital	340	390	407
Fixed Assets	325	372	420
Current Assets	916	1m	1m

Molloy Engineering
49 Kilvergan Road Lurgan, Craigavon, BT66 6LF
Tel: 028-3832 4662 **Fax:** 028-3834 9123
E-mail: info@molloy-eng.co.uk
Website: http://www.molloy-eng.co.uk
Directors: T. Molloy (Prop)
Immediate Holding Company: MOLLOY ENGINEERING LIMITED
Registration no: NI056757 **Date established:** 2005
No.of Employees: 1 - 10 **Product Groups:** 37, 40, 48

Date of Accounts	Apr 11	Apr 10	Apr 09
Working Capital	-165	-153	-177
Fixed Assets	218	226	243
Current Assets	109	66	81

Montgomery Refridgerated
11 Vicarage Road Portadown, Craigavon, BT62 4HF
Tel: 028-3833 5544 **Fax:** 028-3835 0777
E-mail: mark.snowden@montgomerytransportgroup.com
Website: http://www.montgomerytransportgroup.com
Bank(s): Northern Bank
Directors: W. Duke (Dir)
Managers: T. Kerr (Mktg Serv Mgr), M. Snowden (Chief Mgr), G. Clements (I.T. Exec)
Ultimate Holding Company: BALLYVESEY HOLDINGS LIMITED
Immediate Holding Company: MONTGOMERY REFRIGERATED LIMITED
Registration no: NI046407 **VAT No.:** GB 252 3783 58
Date established: 2003 **Turnover:** £10m - £20m
No.of Employees: 11 - 20 **Product Groups:** 72

Date of Accounts	Sep 10	Sep 09	Sep 08
Pre Tax Profit/Loss	857	944	817
Working Capital	3m	3m	2m
Fixed Assets	571	75	60
Current Assets	5m	5m	4m
Current Liabilities	740	1m	878

Morton Newspapers Ltd

2 Esky Drive Carn Industrial Area, Portadown, Craigavon, BT63 5YY
Tel: 028-3839 3939 **Fax:** 028-3839 3940
E-mail: jean.long@jpress.co.uk
Website: http://www.jpress.co.uk
Bank(s): Bank of Ireland
Directors: D. Long (MD), J. Long (MD), B. McConveille (Fin)
Ultimate Holding Company: JOHNSTON PRESS PLC
Immediate Holding Company: MORTON NEWSPAPERS LIMITED
Registration no: NI002197 **VAT No.:** GB 252 7975 29
Date established: 1946 **Turnover:** £5m - £10m
No.of Employees: 251 - 500 **Product Groups:** 28

Date of Accounts	Dec 08	Dec 07	Jan 10
Sales Turnover	9m	8m	9m
Pre Tax Profit/Loss	-115	N/A	N/A
Working Capital	5m	5m	5m
Fixed Assets	191	306	191
Current Assets	5m	5m	5m

Moy Park Ltd

Food Park 39 Seagoe Industrial Area, Portadown, Craigavon, BT63 5QE
Tel: 028-3835 2233 **Fax:** 028-3836 8011
E-mail: enquiries@moypark.com
Website: http://www.moypark.com
Directors: K. Baird (Tech Serv), T. Campbell (MD), J. O'Toole (Sales & Mktg), E. Reid (Fab)
Ultimate Holding Company: MARFRIG ALIMENTOS SA (BRAZIL)
Immediate Holding Company: MOY PARK LIMITED
Registration no: NI004842 **VAT No.:** GB 496 9761 67
Date established: 1961 **Turnover:** £500m - £1,000m
No.of Employees: 1001 - 1500 **Product Groups:** 20, 77

Date of Accounts	Dec 11	Dec 10	Dec 09
Sales Turnover	1072m	921m	781m
Pre Tax Profit/Loss	5m	28m	18m
Working Capital	7m	2m	9m
Fixed Assets	179m	171m	131m
Current Assets	208m	207m	142m
Current Liabilities	28m	50m	23m

New Quay Construction Ltd

68 Armagh Road Tandragee, Craigavon, BT62 2HS
Tel: 028-3884 0444 **Fax:** 028-3884 1811
E-mail: info@newquayconstruction.com
Website: http://www.newquayconstruction.com
Directors: B. Quinn (MD)
Ultimate Holding Company: KLASS HOLDINGS (NI) LIMITED
Immediate Holding Company: NEW QUAY DEVELOPMENTS LIMITED
Registration no: NI023195 **VAT No.:** GB 617 5382 32
Date established: 1989 **Turnover:** £5m - £10m **No.of Employees:** 1 - 10
Product Groups: 52

Date of Accounts	Jun 11	Jun 10	Jun 09
Sales Turnover	7m	7m	12m
Pre Tax Profit/Loss	-178	88	-935
Working Capital	587	221	-798
Fixed Assets	107	251	465
Current Assets	6m	9m	8m
Current Liabilities	476	478	636

Norman Emerson Group

118 Ardmore Road Derryadd, Craigavon, BT66 6QP
Tel: 028-3834 0222 **Fax:** 028-3834 0011
E-mail: info@normanemerson.com
Website: http://www.normanemerson.com
Bank(s): Northern Bank
Directors: C. Jordan (I.T. Dir), G. Emerson (MD)
Immediate Holding Company: Norman Emerson Group Limited
Registration no: NI007919 **VAT No.:** GB 252 0369 83
Date established: 1970 **Turnover:** £5m - £10m
No.of Employees: 101 - 250 **Product Groups:** 14, 33

Date of Accounts	Jan 11	Jan 10	Jan 09
Sales Turnover	8m	10m	13m
Pre Tax Profit/Loss	323	-546	-1m
Working Capital	-730	-2m	-3m
Fixed Assets	3m	4m	5m
Current Assets	2m	3m	4m
Current Liabilities	2m	2m	3m

Orby Engineering Ltd

26 Seagoe Industrial Area Portadown, Craigavon, BT63 5QD
Tel: 028-3833 9145 **Fax:** 028-3835 0540
E-mail: orbyengineering@btconnect.com
Website: http://home.btconnect.com/orby-engineering
Directors: O. Brown (MD)
Immediate Holding Company: ORBY ENGINEERING LIMITED
Registration no: NI002471 **VAT No.:** GB 251 8403 75
Date established: 1948 **No.of Employees:** 1 - 10 **Product Groups:** 41

Date of Accounts	Mar 11	Mar 10	Mar 09
Working Capital	483	508	508
Fixed Assets	69	46	54
Current Assets	595	626	662

J J Pierson & Sons

113 Dobbin Road Portadown, Craigavon, BT62 4EZ
Tel: 028-3887 1618 **Fax:** 028-3887 0697
E-mail: john.pierson@btconnect.com
Website: http://www.jjpierson.co.uk
Directors: J. Pierson (Ptnr)
Immediate Holding Company: J.J. Pierson Ltd
Registration no: NI054571 **VAT No.:** GB 254 0649 65
Date established: 2005 **Turnover:** £500,000 - £1m
No.of Employees: 1 - 10 **Product Groups:** 26

R 4 Ltd

16 Seagoe Industrial Area Portadown, Craigavon, BT63 5QD
Tel: 028-3835 3121 **Fax:** 028-3835 3121
E-mail: lynn@rfour.net
Website: http://www.greentyre.net
Directors: L. Kerr (MD)
Immediate Holding Company: Advert NI Limited
Registration no: NI044059 **Date established:** 2002
Turnover: £250,000 - £500,000 **No.of Employees:** 1 - 10
Product Groups: 44, 79

Date of Accounts	Mar 11	Sep 09	Sep 08
Working Capital	2	3	7
Current Assets	5	7	11

Rainbow Vacuum

36 Derrylettiff Road Portadown, Craigavon, BT62 1QU
Tel: 028-3833 8070
E-mail: sales@rainbowireland.com
Website: http://www.rainbowireland.com
Directors: N. Mcclelland (Prop)
No.of Employees: 1 - 10 **Product Groups:** 38, 42

Rapid International Ltd

96 Mullavilly Road Tandragee, Craigavon, BT62 2LX
Tel: 028-3884 0671 **Fax:** 028-3884 0880
E-mail: info@rapidinternational.com
Website: http://www.rapidinternational.com
Bank(s): Northern Bank
Directors: B. Compton (Fin), J. Gilmore (Mkt Research)
Managers: G. Pollock (Purch Mgr)
Immediate Holding Company: RAPID INTERNATIONAL LIMITED
Registration no: NI013822 **VAT No.:** GB 252 1475 79
Date established: 1979 **Turnover:** £2m - £5m **No.of Employees:** 21 - 50
Product Groups: 35, 45

Date of Accounts	Aug 11	Aug 10	Aug 09
Sales Turnover	N/A	N/A	5m
Pre Tax Profit/Loss	N/A	N/A	183
Working Capital	2m	1m	2m
Fixed Assets	904	929	1m
Current Assets	3m	3m	3m
Current Liabilities	N/A	N/A	519

Regal Processors Ltd

2 Silverwood Industrial Area Silverwood Road, Lurgan, Craigavon, BT66 6LN
Tel: 028-3834 1422 **Fax:** 028-3834 5008
E-mail: george@regals.co.uk
Website: http://www.regals.co.uk
Managers: R. Kernaghan, G. Jordan (Chief Mgr)
Immediate Holding Company: REGAL PROCESSORS LIMITED
Registration no: NI029485 **VAT No.:** GB 656 9389 73
Date established: 1995 **Turnover:** £2m - £5m **No.of Employees:** 21 - 50
Product Groups: 31

Date of Accounts	Dec 11	Dec 10	Dec 09
Working Capital	1m	408	-410
Fixed Assets	3m	2m	2m
Current Assets	4m	3m	2m

Clive Richardson Ltd

54 Derrycoose Road Portadown, Craigavon, BT62 1LY
Tel: 028-3885 3200 **Fax:** 028-3885 3201
E-mail: priscilla@cliverichardsonltd.co.uk
Website: http://www.cliverichardsonltd.co.uk
Bank(s): Northern Bank
Directors: P. McFarland (MD)
Managers: P. McFarland (Chief Mgr), C. Richardson (Contracts Mgr)
Ultimate Holding Company: Richardson Holdings Limited
Immediate Holding Company: Clive Richardson Limited
Registration no: NI011758 **Date established:** 1977
Turnover: £10m - £20m **No.of Employees:** 101 - 250 **Product Groups:** 52

Date of Accounts	Dec 10	Dec 09	Dec 08
Sales Turnover	12m	10m	N/A
Pre Tax Profit/Loss	193	148	562
Working Capital	1m	1m	3m
Fixed Assets	2m	3m	3m
Current Assets	4m	4m	5m
Current Liabilities	376	240	498

Russell Bros & Co Builders Ltd

63a Kilvergan Road Lurgan, Craigavon, BT66 6LJ
Tel: 028-3834 2011 **Fax:** 028-3834 1855
E-mail: enquiries@russellbrothersbuilders.com
Website: http://www.russellbrothersbuilders.com
Directors: D. Fraser (Dir)
Immediate Holding Company: RUSSELL BROTHERS AND CO (BUILDERS) LIMITED
Registration no: NI007392 **VAT No.:** GB 252 1459 77
Date established: 1968 **Turnover:** £1m - £2m **No.of Employees:** 1 - 10
Product Groups: 52

Date of Accounts	Dec 11	Dec 10	Dec 09
Working Capital	-69	-74	8
Fixed Assets	230	264	261
Current Assets	1m	1m	2m

S C A Packaging Ltd

16 Robert Street Lurgan, Craigavon, BT66 8BE
Tel: 028-3832 4222 **Fax:** 028-3832 1788
E-mail: info@sca.com
Website: http://www.sca.com
Bank(s): Northern Bank
Managers: A. Pedlow (Chief Mgr)
Ultimate Holding Company: SVENSKA CELLULOSA AB (SWEDEN)
Immediate Holding Company: DS SMITH CORRUGATED PACKAGING LIMITED
Registration no: 00053913 **VAT No.:** GB 252 1113 16
Date established: 1997 **Turnover:** £1m - £2m **No.of Employees:** 11 - 20
Product Groups: 27, 28, 30, 49

Date of Accounts	Dec 10	Dec 09	Dec 08
Sales Turnover	125m	129m	332m
Pre Tax Profit/Loss	8m	-15m	-62m
Working Capital	269m	277m	290m
Fixed Assets	51m	54m	75m
Current Assets	297m	297m	411m
Current Liabilities	6m	5m	22m

Salters Powerwashers

40a Derrylettiff Road Portadown, Craigavon, BT62 1QU
Tel: 028-3833 8355 **Fax:** 028-3833 5774
E-mail: salterstm@aol.com
Website: http://www.salter28.fsnet.co.uk
Directors: S. Salter (Snr Part)
VAT No.: GB 434 2474 62 **Turnover:** £250,000 - £500,000
No.of Employees: 1 - 10 **Product Groups:** 46, 48, 52

Seagoe Hotel

22 Upper Church Lane Portadown, Craigavon, BT63 5JE
Tel: 028-3833 3076 **Fax:** 028-3835 0210
E-mail: reservations@seagoe.com
Website: http://www.seagoehotel.com
Directors: B. Scullion (Dir)
Managers: E. Fitzpatrick (Fin Mgr), M. Scullion (Chief Mgr)
Immediate Holding Company: SEAGOE HOTEL 2007 LLP
Registration no: NC000266 **VAT No.:** GB 287 2419 33
Date established: 2007 **Turnover:** £500,000 - £1m
No.of Employees: 21 - 50 **Product Groups:** 69

Date of Accounts	Jun 11	Jun 10	Jun 09
Working Capital	-8m	-7m	-8m
Fixed Assets	7m	7m	8m
Current Assets	483	595	49

Sensor Systems

180 Gilford Road Portadown, Craigavon, BT63 5LE
Tel: 028-3836 4411 **Fax:** 028-3836 4412
E-mail: sales@sensor-systems.com
Website: http://www.sensor-systems.com
Bank(s): Northern
Directors: B. Finnigan (MD), C. Adamson (Dir), C. Gough (Fin)
Managers: A. Telfurd (I.T. Exec), T. Clark (Mktg Serv Mgr)
Registration no: NI014093 **Date established:** 1996
No.of Employees: 21 - 50 **Product Groups:** 37, 38

Sergeants Portable Buildings

26a Vicarage Road Portadown, Craigavon, BT62 4HF
Tel: 028-3833 9547 **Fax:** 028-3839 4411
E-mail: sales@sergeantportablebuildings.co.uk
Website: http://www.sergeantsportablebuildings.co.uk
Directors: W. Sergeant (Prop)
VAT No.: GB 390 8241 45 **Turnover:** £250,000 - £500,000
No.of Employees: 1 - 10 **Product Groups:** 25, 35

Serious P R

First Floor Davidson House Glenavy Road Business Park, Moira, Craigavon, BT67 0LT
Tel: 028-9261 6840 **Fax:** 028-9019 0310
Website: http://www.seriouspr.com
Directors: D. Mccavery (MD)
Immediate Holding Company: Serious P R Limited
Registration no: NI066754 **Date established:** 2007
No.of Employees: 1 - 10 **Product Groups:** 81

Date of Accounts	Oct 08	Apr 12	Apr 11
Working Capital	-26	-35	-45
Fixed Assets	34	41	48
Current Assets	79	100	108

Signode Ireland

Sido Innovation Centre 73 Charlestown Road Portadown, Craigavon, BT63 5PP
Tel: 028-3833 3527 **Fax:** 028-3835 0309
E-mail: email@signode-ireland.co.uk
Website: http://www.signode-ireland.co.uk
Managers: M. Mcdonald
Immediate Holding Company: VENTURE TECHNOLOGY ACCELERATOR LIMITED
Registration no: 03012987 **VAT No.:** GB 650 1837 51
Date established: 2006 **Turnover:** £500,000 - £1m
No.of Employees: 1 - 10 **Product Groups:** 42

Sonoco-Alcore Ltd

4 Portadown Road Lurgan, Craigavon, BT66 8QW
Tel: 028-3832 3501 **Fax:** 028-3832 3781
E-mail: tim.colbeck@sonoco.com
Website: http://www.sonoco.com
Managers: G. Burgess (Factory Mgr), T. Colbeck (Factory Mgr)
Immediate Holding Company: JAMES DAVIDSON & SONS LIMITED
Registration no: SC174220 **VAT No.:** GB 562 7977 91
Date established: 1997 **Turnover:** £2m - £5m **No.of Employees:** 21 - 50
Product Groups: 27

Sound Support

PO Box 12, Craigavon, BT62 3EG
Tel: 028-3833 0231 **Fax:** 028-3833 8721
E-mail: sales@springco.co.uk
Directors: R. Callaghan (Prop)
Registration no: 00003360 **VAT No.:** GB 252 9117 65
Date established: 1993 **Turnover:** Up to £250,000
No.of Employees: 1 - 10 **Product Groups:** 37, 40

Spence Bryson Ltd

Unit 14a Seagoe Industrial Area Portadown, Craigavon, BT63 5QD
Tel: 028-3833 2521 **Fax:** 028-3835 1043
E-mail: sales@spencebryson.co.uk
Website: http://www.spencebryson.co.uk
Directors: N. Gray (MD)
Immediate Holding Company: SPENCE BRYSON LIMITED
Registration no: NI042468 **VAT No.:** GB 788 6624 63
Date established: 2002 **Turnover:** £1m - £2m **No.of Employees:** 1 - 10
Product Groups: 24

Date of Accounts	Mar 12	Mar 11	Mar 10
Working Capital	938	868	816
Fixed Assets	1	9	20
Current Assets	1m	1m	1m

Springco N I Ltd

21 Carn Road Portadown, Craigavon, BT63 5WG
Tel: 028-3833 3482 **Fax:** 028-3833 8721
E-mail: sales@springco.co.uk
Website: http://www.springco.co.uk
Bank(s): Ulster Bank
Directors: A. Calaghan (MD)
Managers: U. McGeown (Fin Mgr), A. Carlisle (Comptroller)
Ultimate Holding Company: TECHNICAL METALS LIMITED
Immediate Holding Company: SPRINGCO (N.I.) LIMITED
Registration no: NI003360 **VAT No.:** GB 252 9117 65
Date established: 1954 **Turnover:** £1m - £2m **No.of Employees:** 11 - 20
Product Groups: 35

Date of Accounts	Aug 11	Aug 10	Aug 09
Working Capital	1m	1m	918
Fixed Assets	55	73	90
Current Assets	3m	1m	1m

Springhill Springs

63 Springhill Road Magheralin, Craigavon, BT67 0RW
Tel: 028-3832 5656 **Fax:** 028-3832 6394
Directors: L. Robinson (Snr Part)
Date established: 1986 **No.of Employees:** 1 - 10 **Product Groups:** 35

William Sprott Ltd
Edward Street Portadown, Craigavon, BT62 3NB
Tel: 028-3833 2157 **Fax:** 028-3833 2652
E-mail: williamsprott@aol.com
Website: http://www.williamsprott.com
Directors: G. Forbes (MD), A. Forbes (MD)
Managers: D. Preston, B. Hunter (Chief Mgr)
Immediate Holding Company: WILLIAM SPROTT (PORTADOWN) LIMITED
Registration no: NI002045 **VAT No.:** GB 252 6091 72
Date established: 1946 **No.of Employees:** 21 - 50 **Product Groups:** 20

Date of Accounts	Dec 11	Dec 10	Dec 09
Working Capital	853	901	894
Fixed Assets	675	698	703
Current Assets	1m	1m	1m

Maurice Stevenson Ltd
Unit 32 Annesborough Industrial Estate Annesborough Road, Lurgan, Craigavon, BT67 9JD
Tel: 028-3832 7636 **Fax:** 028-3832 4311
E-mail: mech@mauricestevenson.co.uk
Website: http://www.mauricestevenson.co.uk
Directors: D. Hamilton (Chief Op Offcr), D. Stevenson (Dir)
Managers: J. Thompson (Chief Acct), M. Kitchen
Immediate Holding Company: MAURICE STEVENSON LIMITED
Registration no: NI006329 **VAT No.:** GB 253 1478 67
Date established: 1965 **No.of Employees:** 21 - 50 **Product Groups:** 52

Date of Accounts	Mar 12	Mar 11	Mar 10
Working Capital	577	492	480
Fixed Assets	408	423	498
Current Assets	3m	3m	3m

Tayto Group Ltd
Tandragee Castle Tandragee, Craigavon, BT62 2AB
Tel: 028-3884 0249 **Fax:** 028-3884 0085
E-mail: info@tayto.com
Website: http://www.tayto.com
Bank(s): Northern Bank
Directors: J. McQuaid (Sales), C. Sterritt (Pers), E. Hunter (Mkt Research)
Managers: J. Cross (Tech Serv Mgr), P. Allen
Ultimate Holding Company: MANDERLEY FOOD GROUP LIMITED
Immediate Holding Company: TAYTO (N.I.) LIMITED
Registration no: NI003670 **VAT No.:** GB 575 4909 01
Date established: 1956 **Turnover:** £10m - £20m
No.of Employees: 251 - 500 **Product Groups:** 20

Date of Accounts	Jul 08	Jul 09	Jul 10
Sales Turnover	26m	18m	18m
Pre Tax Profit/Loss	371	-1m	-848
Working Capital	4m	44m	42m
Fixed Assets	15m	13m	12m
Current Assets	18m	48m	42m
Current Liabilities	6m	3m	77

Tennelly Products
69 Greenisland Road Portadown, Craigavon, BT62 1XB
Tel: 028-3885 1214
E-mail: sdonnlett@aol.com
Directors: S. Donnelly (Snr Part)
Immediate Holding Company: DERRYLARD NURSERIES LIMITED
Registration no: NI053825 **Date established:** 2005
No.of Employees: 1 - 10 **Product Groups:** 26, 35

Date of Accounts	Mar 11	Mar 10	Mar 09
Working Capital	113	98	110
Fixed Assets	559	640	644
Current Assets	252	284	233

Tidyware Products
4a Derryhubbert Road Birches, Portadown, Craigavon, BT62 1TH
Tel: 028-3885 2773 **Fax:** 028-3885 2773
E-mail: tidyware@btinternet.com
Directors: T. Ramsey (Dir)
Immediate Holding Company: TidyWare Products Limited
Registration no: NI050060 **VAT No.:** GB 517 7919 13
Date established: 2004 **No.of Employees:** 1 - 10 **Product Groups:** 23, 26, 30, 49

Date of Accounts	Mar 11	Mar 10	Mar 09
Working Capital	-58	-65	-75
Fixed Assets	30	22	27
Current Assets	14	20	13

Turkington Windows & Conservatories
James Park Mahon Road, Portadown, Craigavon, BT62 3EH
Tel: 028-3833 2807 **Fax:** 028-3835 0276
E-mail: ballymena@turkington-windows.com
Website: http://www.turkington-construction.com
Directors: J. McKegg (MD)
Managers: J. Clegg (Transport), P. Lynes (Purch Mgr), C. Hindman (Sales & Mktg Mg), C. Smith (I.T. Exec), N. O'Leary (Mktg Serv Mgr)
Immediate Holding Company: Turkington Holdings Limited
Registration no: NI036179 **VAT No.:** GB 253 1940 72
Date established: 1999 **Turnover:** £10m - £20m
No.of Employees: 51 - 100 **Product Groups:** 52

Date of Accounts	Jul 10	Jul 09	Jul 08
Sales Turnover	23m	41m	29m
Pre Tax Profit/Loss	-813	-3m	-1m
Working Capital	-9m	9m	-10m
Fixed Assets	65m	61m	73m
Current Assets	41m	43m	51m
Current Liabilities	8m	6m	8m

Ulster Carpet Mills Ltd
Castleisland Factory Garvaghy Road, Portadown, Craigavon, BT62 1EE
Tel: 028-3833 4433 **Fax:** 028-3833 3142
E-mail: marketing@ulstercarpets.com
Website: http://www.ulstercarpets.com
Bank(s): Northern Bank and Bank of Ireland
Directors: D. Acheson (Fin), N. Coburn (MD)
Managers: R. McKeown (Purch Mgr)
Ultimate Holding Company: ULSTER CARPET MILLS (HOLDINGS) LIMITED
Immediate Holding Company: ULSTER CARPET MILLS LIMITED
Registration no: NI022358 **VAT No.:** 251 7683 48 **Date established:** 1989
Turnover: £50m - £75m **No.of Employees:** 251 - 500 **Product Groups:** 23

Date of Accounts	Mar 12	Mar 11	Mar 10
Working Capital	-358	-358	-358
Fixed Assets	165	165	165

Universal Meat Co.
17a Derrycoose Road Portadown, Craigavon, BT62 1LY
Tel: 028-3885 2772 **Fax:** 028-3882 2662
E-mail: osmond@universalmeat.co.uk
Website: http://www.universalmeats.com
Directors: O. Gurgam (Prop)
Immediate Holding Company: UNIVERSAL MEAT COMPANY
Registration no: NI018527 **VAT No.:** GB 366 4555 27
Date established: 1985 **No.of Employees:** 1 - 10 **Product Groups:** 20

Whites Speedicook Ltd
Scarva Road Tandragee, Craigavon, BT62 2BZ
Tel: 028-3884 0592 **Fax:** 028-3884 1895
E-mail: info@whitesoats.com
Website: http://www.whitesoats.co.uk
Directors: T. Lockhart (MD)
Ultimate Holding Company: FANE VALLEY CO-OPERATIVE SOCIETY LIMITED
Immediate Holding Company: WHITES SPEEDICOOK LIMITED
Registration no: NI016825 **VAT No.:** GB 390 7562 30
Date established: 1983 **Turnover:** £2m - £5m **No.of Employees:** 21 - 50
Product Groups: 20

Date of Accounts	Sep 11	Sep 10	Sep 09
Sales Turnover	N/A	4m	4m
Pre Tax Profit/Loss	N/A	-258	-148
Working Capital	-651	41	189
Fixed Assets	2m	2m	2m
Current Assets	2m	2m	1m
Current Liabilities	N/A	60	93

Woodcraft Systems
26a Moygannon Road Donaghcloney, Craigavon, BT66 7NB
Tel: 028-3888 2929 **Fax:** 028-3888 2928
E-mail: j.lyons@woodcraftsystems.co.uk
Website: http://www.woodcraftsystems.co.uk
Directors: J. Lyons (Prop)
Date established: 1992 **No.of Employees:** 1 - 10 **Product Groups:** 35, 36

R E Woolsey & Sons Ltd
72 Ahorey Road Portadown, Craigavon, BT62 3ST
Tel: 028-3887 1334 **Fax:** 028-3887 0532
Website: http://www.woolsey-concrete.co.uk
Directors: R. Woolsey (Prop)
Ultimate Holding Company: Woolsey Concrete Limited
Immediate Holding Company: RE WOOLSEY & SONS LIMITED
Registration no: NI020505 **VAT No.:** GB 575 6197 00
Date established: 1987 **Turnover:** £250,000 - £500,000
No.of Employees: 11 - 20 **Product Groups:** 33

Date of Accounts	Dec 11	Dec 10	Dec 09
Working Capital	879	584	337
Fixed Assets	141	176	227
Current Assets	2m	1m	1m
Current Liabilities	N/A	N/A	361

XPRESS LIFTS
96 Avenue Road Lurgan, Craigavon, BT66 7BH
Tel: 028-3832 3603 **Fax:** 028-3832 3603
E-mail: sales@xpresslifts.co.uk
Website: http://www.xpresslifts.co.uk
Directors: J. Mcfeeters (Prop)
Immediate Holding Company: XPRESS LIFTS LTD
Registration no: NI065953 **Date established:** 2007
No.of Employees: 1 - 10 **Product Groups:** 45

Co. Antrim

Crumlin

Access Control Management Solutions (ACMS)
87 Crewe Road Glenavy, Crumlin, BT29 4NH
Tel: 028-9445 4944
E-mail: accesscms@aol.com
Website: http://www.acms.me.uk
Directors: M. Greenberg (Prop)
Turnover: Up to £250,000 **No.of Employees:** 1 - 10 **Product Groups:** 26, 35

K 2 Industrial Cutting Tools
29 Ballyhill Lane Nutts Corner, Crumlin, BT29 4YP
Tel: 028-9082 5921 **Fax:** 028-9082 4000
E-mail: enquiries@k2industrialcuttingtools.co.uk
Directors: A. Dickson (Prop)
Date established: 1993 **No.of Employees:** 1 - 10 **Product Groups:** 46, 48

L J Electrical Services
66 Nutts Corner Road Nutts Corner, Crumlin, BT29 4SJ
Tel: 028-9082 5342 **Fax:** 028-9082 5633
E-mail: d-jackson@ljelectrical.com
Website: http://www.ljelectricalservices.com
Directors: J. Jackson (Prop)
Immediate Holding Company: J.L.J ELECTRICAL SERVICES LLP
Registration no: NC000695 **Date established:** 2010
No.of Employees: 1 - 10 **Product Groups:** 52

Park Plaza Belfast
197 Ballyrobin Road Aldergrove, Crumlin, BT29 4ZY
Tel: 028-9445 7000 **Fax:** 028-9442 3500
E-mail: reception@parkplazabelfast.com
Website: http://www.parkplazabelfast.com
Managers: R. Baker (Chief Mgr)
No.of Employees: 21 - 50 **Product Groups:** 69

Randox Laboratories Ltd
30 Cherryvalley Road, Crumlin, BT29 4QN
Tel: 028-9442 2413 **Fax:** 028-9442 5912
E-mail: reception@randox.com
Website: http://www.randox.com
Managers: A. Dougan (Mgr)
Immediate Holding Company: RANDOX LABORATORIES LIMITED
Registration no: NI015738 **Date established:** 1982
Turnover: £50m - £75m **No.of Employees:** 501 - 1000
Product Groups: 31, 41, 85

Date of Accounts	Dec 11	Dec 10	Dec 09
Sales Turnover	69m	60m	63m
Pre Tax Profit/Loss	2m	3m	3m
Working Capital	14m	13m	17m
Fixed Assets	24m	20m	16m
Current Assets	44m	36m	33m
Current Liabilities	4m	6m	5m

Rea Saw Mills
26 Crosshill Road, Crumlin, BT29 4BQ
Tel: 028-9442 3293 **Fax:** 028-9442 3288
E-mail: sales@rea-sawmills.co.uk
Website: http://www.rea-sawmills.co.uk
Directors: B. Rea (Prop)
VAT No.: GB 254 5619 49 **Date established:** 1961
Turnover: £500,000 - £1m **No.of Employees:** 11 - 20
Product Groups: 25, 45

Transport Training Services Ltd
15 Dundrod Road Nutts Corner, Crumlin, BT29 4SS
Tel: 028-9082 5653 **Fax:** 028-9082 5689
E-mail: mail@transport-training.co.uk
Website: http://www.transport-training.co.uk
Bank(s): Ulster Bank
Directors: S. Mccullagh (Grp Chief Exec)
Immediate Holding Company: TRANSPORT TRAINING SERVICES LIMITED
Registration no: NI026072 **VAT No.:** GB 517 4366 43
Date established: 1991 **Turnover:** £500,000 - £1m
No.of Employees: 11 - 20 **Product Groups:** 72, 86

Date of Accounts	Dec 11	Dec 10	Dec 09
Sales Turnover	614	622	581
Pre Tax Profit/Loss	-23	-24	-97
Working Capital	85	111	150
Fixed Assets	118	167	190
Current Assets	326	319	361
Current Liabilities	193	158	183

Ulster Farm By-Products Ltd
29 Ballyvannon Road Glenavy, Crumlin, BT29 4QL
Tel: 028-9442 2401 **Fax:** 028-9442 2697
E-mail: info@ulsterfarm.co.uk
Website: http://www.ulsterfarm.co.uk
Bank(s): Ulster Bank
Directors: G. Miller (MD)
Managers: P. Mccarroll (Mgr), L. Finni (Purch Mgr), K. Law (Chief Acct)
Ultimate Holding Company: GLENFARM HOLDINGS LIMITED
Immediate Holding Company: ULSTER FARM BY-PRODUCTS LIMITED
Registration no: NI028004 **VAT No.:** GB 253 8155 77
Date established: 1993 **Turnover:** £5m - £10m **No.of Employees:** 11 - 20
Product Groups: 20, 31

Date of Accounts	Dec 10	Dec 09	Dec 08
Sales Turnover	7m	9m	11m
Pre Tax Profit/Loss	-2m	365	1m
Working Capital	351	2m	1m
Fixed Assets	6m	6m	7m
Current Assets	2m	3m	2m
Current Liabilities	383	410	492

Co. Down

Donaghadee

Hugh Drennan & Sons Cabinet Makers
278 Killaughey Road, Donaghadee, BT21 0LY
Tel: 028-9182 0892 **Fax:** 028-9181 0363
E-mail: hughdrennanandsons@fsmail.net
Website: http://www.handmadekitchensireland.co.uk
Directors: H. Drennan (Ptnr)
Turnover: Up to £250,000 **No.of Employees:** 1 - 10 **Product Groups:** 26

Gordons Chemists
23 New Street, Donaghadee, BT21 0AG
Tel: 028-9188 2546 **Fax:** 028-9188 8372
E-mail: info@gordons-chemists.com
Website: http://www.gordons-chemists.com
Managers: M. Caughers (Mgr)
Immediate Holding Company: DOWN PERFUMERY LIMITED
Registration no: NI020394 **VAT No.:** GB 331 7803 70
Date established: 1987 **Turnover:** £1m - £2m **No.of Employees:** 1 - 10
Product Groups: 63

Date of Accounts	Jan 99	Jan 98	Jan 97
Working Capital	259	236	115
Fixed Assets	137	140	133
Current Assets	354	318	306

Metaltec Metal Products
278 Killaughey Road, Donaghadee, BT21 0LY
Tel: 028-9182 1800 **Fax:** 028-9182 1800
Managers: M. Miller (Mgr)
No.of Employees: 1 - 10 **Product Groups:** 35

Northern Ireland Belting Co.
Mosside Business Park 295 Killaughey Road, Donaghadee, BT21 0LY
Tel: 028-9182 1110 **Fax:** 028-9182 1110
E-mail: sales@nibelting.com
Website: http://www.nibelting.com
Directors: M. Gallaher (Ptnr)
Turnover: Up to £250,000 **No.of Employees:** 1 - 10 **Product Groups:** 29, 30, 33, 35, 45

Co. Down

Downpatrick

B P F Distributors & Pumps Ltd
Cloonagh Road, Downpatrick, BT30 6LJ
Tel: 028-4461 5777 **Fax:** 028-4461 4250
E-mail: marketing@bpf-ltd.com
Website: http://www.bpf-ltd.com

Managers: N. Fitzsimons (Sales Prom Mgr), O. Vaughan (Mktg Serv Mgr)
Immediate Holding Company: BPF DISTRIBUTORS AND PUMPS LIMITED
Registration no: NI015588 **VAT No.:** GB 375 7358 13
Date established: 1982 **Turnover:** £500,000 - £1m
No.of Employees: 11 - 20 **Product Groups:** 40, 42, 48, 51, 67

Date of Accounts	Apr 11	Apr 10	Apr 09
Working Capital	92	71	169
Fixed Assets	200	201	192
Current Assets	369	280	298

Bells Motorworks Ltd
1 Downpatrick Road Crossgar, Downpatrick, BT30 9EQ
Tel: 028-4483 3233 **Fax:** 028-4483 1122
E-mail: sales@bellscrossgar.com
Website: http://www.bellscrossgar.com
Directors: C. Bell (MD)
Ultimate Holding Company: BELLS CROSSGAR LIMITED
Immediate Holding Company: BELLS MOTOR WORKS LIMITED
Registration no: NI027445 **VAT No.:** GB 252 3659 59
Date established: 1993 **Turnover:** £10m - £20m
No.of Employees: 51 - 100 **Product Groups:** 68

Date of Accounts	Dec 11	Dec 10	Dec 09
Sales Turnover	11m	16m	13m
Pre Tax Profit/Loss	-99	66	92
Working Capital	864	. 937	887
Fixed Assets	497	597	677
Current Assets	3m	3m	3m
Current Liabilities	237	349	207

L K Brennan
24 Shanes Road Killyleagh, Downpatrick, BT30 9SA
Tel: 028-4482 8088 **Fax:** 028-4482 8369
Bank(s): Bank of Ireland
Directors: L. Brennan (Prop)
Immediate Holding Company: LKB Developments Limited
Registration no: NI045810 **VAT No.:** GB 283 1195 68
Date established: 2003 **Turnover:** £250,000 - £500,000
No.of Employees: 11 - 20 **Product Groups:** 26, 51, 52, 66

Date of Accounts	Nov 11	Nov 10	Nov 09
Sales Turnover	N/A	4	N/A
Pre Tax Profit/Loss	N/A	-106	N/A
Working Capital	533	7m	748
Current Assets	7m	7m	7m
Current Liabilities	N/A	36	N/A

Brooks Downpatrick
20-22 Church Street, Downpatrick, BT30 6ER
Tel: 028-4461 6325 **Fax:** 028-4461 5353
Website: http://www.brooksgroup.co.uk
Directors: G. Custon (Ch)
Managers: J. Ward (Mgr), K. Murray (Sales Prom Mgr), M. Higgins (District Mgr)
VAT No.: GB 232 2186 95 **No.of Employees:** 1 - 10 **Product Groups:** 66

C M Precison Components Ltd
3 Brannish Road, Downpatrick, BT30 6LL
Tel: 028-4461 9920 **Fax:** 028-4461 4733
E-mail: keiran@cmprecision.co.uk
Website: http://www.cmprecisioncomponents.co.uk
Bank(s): Northern, Downpatrick
Directors: K. Cooper (MD)
Immediate Holding Company: CM PRECISION COMPONENTS LTD
Registration no: NI062344 **VAT No.:** GB 251 7520 76
Date established: 2006 **No.of Employees:** 11 - 20 **Product Groups:** 48

Date of Accounts	May 11	May 10	May 09
Working Capital	-120	7	-75
Fixed Assets	301	N/A	N/A
Current Assets	269	289	134

C & O Milligan N I Ltd
Downpatrick Road Ardglass, Downpatrick, BT30 7SF
Tel: 028-4484 1098 **Fax:** 028-4484 1896
E-mail: milligan@globalnet.co.uk
Directors: O. Milligan (MD)
Immediate Holding Company: C & O MILLIGAN (N.I.) LIMITED
Registration no: NI034232 **VAT No.:** GB 252 7410 77
Date established: 1998 **Turnover:** £1m - £2m **No.of Employees:** 1 - 10
Product Groups: 20

Date of Accounts	Jan 12	Jan 11	Jan 10
Working Capital	2m	2m	1m
Fixed Assets	552	717	726
Current Assets	4m	4m	2m

Cool Heat Refrigeration
10 Downpatrick Business Centre Brannish Road, Downpatrick, BT30 6LL
Tel: 07881-807788 **Fax:** 028-4484 2228
E-mail: coolheatrefrig@aol.com
Directors: H. Hart (Prop)
No.of Employees: 1 - 10 **Product Groups:** 38, 40, 63

Crossgar Food Service
11 Kilmore Road Crossgar, Downpatrick, BT30 9HJ
Tel: 028-4483 0301 **Fax:** 028-4483 2301
E-mail: enquiries@crossgar.ie
Website: http://www.crossgar.ie
Bank(s): Northern Bank
Directors: C. Bell (Ptnr), G. Bell (Grp Chief Exec), P. Bell (MD)
Managers: M. Morrissey (Chief Acct)
Immediate Holding Company: CROSSGAR FOODSERVICE LTD
Registration no: NI020409 **VAT No.:** GB 454 5906 30
Date established: 1987 **Turnover:** £20m - £50m
No.of Employees: 101 - 250 **Product Groups:** 20

D Cunningham Landscapes
5 Church Road, Downpatrick, BT30 9BQ
Tel: 028-4461 2965 **Fax:** 028-4461 4449
E-mail: dc@duffycunningham.com
Website: http://www.cunninghamlandscapes.com
Directors: D. Cunningham (Dir)
Immediate Holding Company: T&T (NI) LTD
VAT No.: GB 256 1048 74 **Date established:** 2011
No.of Employees: 1 - 10 **Product Groups:** 84

D J Dickson Ltd
127 Derryboy Road Crossgar, Downpatrick, BT30 9DH
Tel: 028-4483 0434 **Fax:** 028-4483 1492
E-mail: dickson.david@btconnect.com
Directors: K. Dickson (Dir)
Immediate Holding Company: D.J. DICKSON LIMITED
Registration no: NI011881 **VAT No.:** GB 286 7233 28
Date established: 1977 **Turnover:** £500,000 - £1m
No.of Employees: 11 - 20 **Product Groups:** 52

Date of Accounts	May 11	May 10	May 09
Working Capital	76	32	86
Fixed Assets	70	93	133
Current Assets	252	262	249

Down District Council
24 Strangford Road, Downpatrick, BT30 6SR
Tel: 028-4461 0800 **Fax:** 028-4461 0801
E-mail: council@downdc.gov.uk
Website: http://www.downdc.gov.uk
Directors: J. Dumigan (Grp Chief Exec)
Immediate Holding Company: DOWN CLUBMARK SPORTS ASSOCIATION
Registration no: NI047153 **Date established:** 2003
Turnover: Up to £250,000 **No.of Employees:** 101 - 250
Product Groups: 87

Date of Accounts	Jun 11	Jun 10	Jun 09
Sales Turnover	N/A	N/A	41
Pre Tax Profit/Loss	N/A	N/A	9
Working Capital	22	13	18
Fixed Assets	1	1	1
Current Assets	23	14	19
Current Liabilities	N/A	1	1

Electrical & Electronic Services
5 St Josephs Park, Downpatrick, BT30 7EN
Tel: 028-4484 1631
E-mail: info@testni.co.uk
Website: http://www.testni.co.uk
Directors: A. Moore (Prop)
Date established: 1982 **Turnover:** Up to £250,000
No.of Employees: 1 - 10 **Product Groups:** 38, 85

George Milligan & Son
North Quay Ardglass, Downpatrick, BT30 7SD
Tel: 028-4484 1254 **Fax:** 028-4484 2078
E-mail: john@georgemilliganfish.com
Website: http://www.georgemilliganfish.com
Directors: J. Milligan (Dir)
Managers: O. Strain (Admin Off)
Immediate Holding Company: GEORGE MILLIGAN & SONS (FISH MERCHANTS) LIMITED
Registration no: NI011889 **VAT No.:** GB 286 7785 86
Date established: 1977 **Turnover:** £2m - £5m **No.of Employees:** 21 - 50
Product Groups: 62

Date of Accounts	Feb 11	Feb 10	Feb 09
Sales Turnover	N/A	4m	N/A
Pre Tax Profit/Loss	N/A	433	N/A
Working Capital	883	622	259
Fixed Assets	630	693	742
Current Assets	2m	1m	1m
Current Liabilities	N/A	105	N/A

Get Noticed Signs
65 Abbeyview Road Crossgar, Downpatrick, BT30 9JD
Tel: 028-4483 1469
E-mail: info@getnoticedsigns.co.uk
Website: http://www.getnoticedsigns.co.uk
Managers: P. Houston (Mgr)
No.of Employees: 1 - 10 **Product Groups:** 26, 30, 49, 81

International Net & Twine Ltd
19 Cuttyshane Road Killyleagh, Downpatrick, BT30 9SL
Tel: 07767-272044 **Fax:** 028-9263 8027
E-mail: alan@i-n-t.net
Website: http://www.i-n-t.net
Directors: A. Boyd (Prop)
Immediate Holding Company: INTERNATIONAL NET & TWINE LIMITED
Registration no: NI027959 **VAT No.:** GB 575 5909 93
Date established: 1993 **Turnover:** £500,000 - £1m
No.of Employees: 1 - 10 **Product Groups:** 22, 23, 24, 29, 30, 33, 35, 37, 38, 39, 40, 41, 43, 45, 49, 63, 66

Date of Accounts	Dec 11	Dec 10	Dec 09
Working Capital	71	56	41
Current Assets	203	227	171
Current Liabilities	111	111	111

J P Corry
Ballydugan Industrial Estate 8-10 Ballydugan Road, Downpatrick, BT30 6TE
Tel: 028-4461 2011 **Fax:** 028-4461 5635
Website: http://www.jpcorry.com
Managers: N. Mcgrattan (District Mgr)
VAT No.: GB 454 5875 15 **No.of Employees:** 11 - 20 **Product Groups:** 61, 66

J & W Mccall Supplies Ltd
10 Dundrum Road Clough, Downpatrick, BT30 8SH
Tel: 028-4481 1685 **Fax:** 028-4481 1774
E-mail: info@jwmccall.com
Website: http://www.jwmccall.com
Directors: W. McCall (Dir), O Neil (Fin), M. McCall (Dir), J. McCall (MD), R. McCall (Dir)
Managers: D. Harmon (Sales Prom Mgr), D. Scott (I.T. Exec), T. Burtney (Mktg Serv Mgr)
Immediate Holding Company: J. & W. MCCALL SUPPLIES (N.I.) LIMITED
Registration no: NI012888 **VAT No.:** GB 311 3327 13
Date established: 1978 **Turnover:** £5m - £10m **No.of Employees:** 1 - 10
Product Groups: 25, 66

Date of Accounts	Dec 10	Dec 09	Dec 08
Sales Turnover	7m	8m	N/A
Pre Tax Profit/Loss	2	2	-143
Working Capital	994	1m	1m
Fixed Assets	622	705	781
Current Assets	4m	4m	4m
Current Liabilities	1m	1m	349

Loughview Guns
45 St Patricks Road, Downpatrick, BT30 7JQ
Tel: 028-4461 5656 **Fax:** 028-4461 5364
E-mail: loughviewguns@btconnect.com
Directors: J. Higgins (Prop)
Date established: 1977 **No.of Employees:** 1 - 10 **Product Groups:** 36, 39, 40

M K L Meats
45a Saul Road, Downpatrick, BT30 6PA
Tel: 028-4461 2123 **Fax:** 028-4461 7009
E-mail: mklmeat@btconnect.com
Website: http://www.mklmeats.com
Managers: M. Ward (Mgr)
VAT No.: GB 255 7262 48 **No.of Employees:** 1 - 10 **Product Groups:** 20

Macnabb Brothers Waste Management Ltd
23 Downpatrick Road Killough, Downpatrick, BT30 7QB
Tel: 028-4484 2248 **Fax:** 028-4484 2248
E-mail: vincent@macnabbbros.co.uk
Website: http://www.macnabbbros.co.uk
Bank(s): Northern Bank Ltd
Directors: V. Macnabb (Dir)
Immediate Holding Company: MACNABB BROS (WASTE MANAGEMENT) LTD
Registration no: NI027206 **VAT No.:** GB 252 8107 73
Date established: 1993 **No.of Employees:** 21 - 50 **Product Groups:** 54, 83

Date of Accounts	Apr 11	Apr 10	Apr 09
Working Capital	826	853	675
Fixed Assets	946	959	1m
Current Assets	1m	1m	1m

S & P Milligan
20 Downpatrick Road Ardglass, Downpatrick, BT30 7SF
Tel: 028-4484 1595 **Fax:** 028-4484 2145
E-mail: sales@sp-milligan.co.uk
Website: http://www.sp-milligan.co.uk
Bank(s): Bank of Ireland
Directors: S. Milligan (Snr Part)
Immediate Holding Company: COASTAL SEA PRODUCTS LIMITED
Registration no: NI026946 **VAT No.:** GB 286 5100 57
Date established: 1992 **Turnover:** £1m - £2m **No.of Employees:** 11 - 20
Product Groups: 62

Northern Ireland Plastics Ltd
39 Shrigley Road Killyleagh, Downpatrick, BT30 9SR
Tel: 028-4482 8753 **Fax:** 028-4482 8809
E-mail: sales@nip-ltd.co.uk
Website: http://www.niplastics.com
Bank(s): Bank of Ireland
Directors: D. Simpson (Ch)
Managers: F. Heaney (Site Co-ord), K. Glover (Sales Prom Mgr)
Ultimate Holding Company: PACIFIC SHELF 1218 LIMITED
Immediate Holding Company: NORTHERN IRELAND PLASTICS LIMITED
Registration no: NI013346 **VAT No.:** GB 617 8281 23
Date established: 1979 **Turnover:** £250,000 - £500,000
No.of Employees: 51 - 100 **Product Groups:** 30

Date of Accounts	Sep 11	Sep 10	Sep 09
Pre Tax Profit/Loss	151	-284	480
Working Capital	-409	-554	-462
Fixed Assets	962	991	1m
Current Assets	2m	2m	2m
Current Liabilities	834	1m	1m

Ollard Westcombe
Cameo Works Bridge Street, Downpatrick, BT30 6HD
Tel: 028-4461 7557 **Fax:** 028-4461 3580
E-mail: admin@cameoequestrian.co.uk
Website: http://www.cameoequestrian.co.uk
Directors: R. Thomason (MD)
Immediate Holding Company: OLLARD WESTCOMBE (2000) LIMITED
Registration no: NI037318 **VAT No.:** GB 252 2575 70
Date established: 1999 **Turnover:** Up to £250,000
No.of Employees: 1 - 10 **Product Groups:** 23, 63

Date of Accounts	Dec 11	Dec 10	Dec 09
Working Capital	80	81	81
Fixed Assets	4	2	2
Current Assets	107	122	111

Teletronics
117 Manse Road Crossgar, Downpatrick, BT30 9LZ
Tel: 028-9751 1303 **Fax:** 028-9751 1586
Directors: J. Gallagher (Prop)
VAT No.: GB 286 4921 22 **Date established:** 1989
Turnover: Up to £250,000 **No.of Employees:** 1 - 10 **Product Groups:** 48

Brian Ward Ornimental Metal Craft
44 Manse Road Crossgar, Downpatrick, BT30 9LZ
Tel: 028-4483 0428 **Fax:** 028-4483 0267
Directors: B. Ward (MD)
Immediate Holding Company: Brian Ward Ornamental Metalcraft Ltd
Registration no: NI062970 **Date established:** 2007
No.of Employees: 1 - 10 **Product Groups:** 35

Date of Accounts	Dec 10	Dec 09	Dec 08
Working Capital	2	-1	-13
Fixed Assets	16	19	22
Current Assets	46	40	55

Co. Down

Dromore

B G Sales & Hydraulics
30 Katesbridge Road Dromara, Dromore, BT25 2PN
Tel: 028-9753 2144 **Fax:** 028-9753 2144
Directors: G. Dickins (Prop), G. Dickson (Prop)
Date established: 1986 **Turnover:** £500,000 - £1m
No.of Employees: 1 - 10 **Product Groups:** 30, 36, 67

B K Window Systems
72 Finnis Road Dromara, Dromore, BT25 2DB
Tel: 028-9753 3059 **Fax:** 028-9753 3004
Directors: B. Kelly (Prop)
VAT No.: GB 412 6711 80 **Turnover:** Up to £250,000
No.of Employees: 1 - 10 **Product Groups:** 30, 52

Control Zone Security
12 Bridge Street, Dromore, BT25 1AN
Tel: 028-9269 9999
Website: http://www.controlzonesecurity.co.uk

see next page

Control Zone Security - Cont'd
Directors: G. Ingrim (Prop)
No.of Employees: 1 - 10 **Product Groups:** 37, 40, 52

Leader Newspaper
30a Market Square, Dromore, BT25 1AW
Tel: 028-9269 2217 **Fax:** 028-9269 9260
E-mail: paul.wilkinson@dromoreleader.co.uk
Website: http://www.dromoreleader.co.uk
Directors: J. Morton (Dir), H. Hannah (MD)
Managers: P. Wilkinson (District Mgr), T. McCann (Mgr)
Immediate Holding Company: Scottish Radio Holdings
Date established: 1996 **No.of Employees:** 1 - 10 **Product Groups:** 28

Lisnasure Interiors
43 Lisnasure Road, Dromore, BT25 1JH
Tel: 028-3888 1628 **Fax:** 028-3888 2253
E-mail: lyttle@btconnect.com
Website: http://www.hanna-browne.com
Directors: D. Little (Ptnr), H. Lyttle (Ptnr)
Immediate Holding Company: SUN RENEWABLES LIMITED
Registration no: NI061306 **VAT No.:** GB 283 0772 51
Date established: 2006 **Turnover:** £500,000 - £1m
No.of Employees: 21 - 50 **Product Groups:** 63

M C N Automation
29 Mullafernaghan Road, Dromore, BT25 1JZ
Tel: 028-9269 3495 **Fax:** 028-9269 9554
E-mail: gem@mcnautomation.com
Website: http://www.mcnautomation.com
Directors: R. Mcnaugher (Prop)
Immediate Holding Company: McN Automation Ltd
Registration no: NI044984 **VAT No.:** GB 287 2836 17
Date established: 2002 **No.of Employees:** 11 - 20 **Product Groups:** 48

Date of Accounts	Dec 11	Dec 10	Dec 09
Working Capital	882	899	918
Fixed Assets	102	150	193
Current Assets	1m	1m	1m

Steve Orr Ltd
1 Quillyburn Business Park Banbridge Road, Dromore, BT25 1BY
Tel: 028-9269 9020 **Fax:** 028-9269 9029
E-mail: info@steve-orr.com
Website: http://www.steve-orr.com
Directors: B. Doyle (Fin), P. Orr (MD)
Managers: T. Foran, S. Beggs (Personnel)
Immediate Holding Company: STEVE ORR LIMITED
Registration no: NI012419 **Date established:** 1977
Turnover: £10m - £20m **No.of Employees:** 21 - 50 **Product Groups:** 23

Date of Accounts	Sep 11	Sep 10	Sep 09
Sales Turnover	18m	17m	18m
Pre Tax Profit/Loss	2m	3m	3m
Working Capital	5m	3m	2m
Fixed Assets	8m	8m	9m
Current Assets	10m	10m	8m
Current Liabilities	684	1m	1m

Turner Grain Engineering Ireland Ltd
31 Ballysallagh Road, Dromore, BT25 1PD
Tel: 028-9269 9590 **Fax:** 028-9269 9992
Directors: B. Beggs (MD)
Immediate Holding Company: Turner Grain Engineering (Ireland) Limited
Registration no: NI053811 **Date established:** 2005
No.of Employees: 1 - 10 **Product Groups:** 41

Date of Accounts	Mar 12	Mar 11	Mar 10
Working Capital	16	22	24
Fixed Assets	2	3	3
Current Assets	58	62	74

Co. Tyrone

Dungannon

3d Steel Works
2a Washingbay Road Coalisland, Dungannon, BT71 4ND
Tel: 028-8774 8873
E-mail: shane@3dsteelwork.com
Website: http://www.3dsteelwork.co.uk
Directors: S. O'neill (MD)
Managers: B. O'Neil (Sales Prom Mgr), U. McVeigh (Fin Mgr)
Immediate Holding Company: 3D Steelwork Ltd
Registration no: NI049231 **Date established:** 2004
No.of Employees: 51 - 100 **Product Groups:** 35

Date of Accounts	Dec 11	Jan 11	Jan 10
Working Capital	255	49	19
Fixed Assets	375	167	146
Current Assets	2m	936	256

Acheson & Glover Ltd
64 Old Moy Road, Dungannon, BT71 6PU
Tel: 028-8778 4208 **Fax:** 028-8778 4805
E-mail: solutions@acheson-glover.com
Website: http://www.acheson-glover.com
Directors: S. Acheson (MD)
Ultimate Holding Company: Acheson & Glover Group Limited
Immediate Holding Company: ACHESON & GLOVER LIMITED
Registration no: NI004475 **Date established:** 1960
Turnover: £75m - £125m **No.of Employees:** 21 - 50 **Product Groups:** 33, 51, 52, 66

Date of Accounts	Mar 12	Feb 11	Feb 10
Sales Turnover	21m	22m	25m
Pre Tax Profit/Loss	790	-6m	-4m
Working Capital	14m	-17m	-18m
Fixed Assets	21m	22m	35m
Current Assets	21m	9m	13m
Current Liabilities	1m	N/A	904

Armstrong Structural Ltd
153 Benburb Road, Dungannon, BT71 7QA
Tel: 028-3754 8048
Directors: R. Armstrong (MD)
Immediate Holding Company: ARMSTRONG STRUCTURAL LIMITED
Registration no: NI058648 **Date established:** 2006
No.of Employees: 1 - 10 **Product Groups:** 33, 35

Date of Accounts	Jun 11	Jun 10	Jun 09
Working Capital	214	193	260
Fixed Assets	90	108	113
Current Assets	452	446	525

The Art Centre
Beechvalley, Dungannon, BT71 7BN
Tel: 028-8772 4298 **Fax:** 028-8772 6470
E-mail: jamespcullen@aol.com
Directors: J. Cullen (Prop)
VAT No.: GB 282 9638 16 **No.of Employees:** 1 - 10 **Product Groups:** 25, 26

Autogen Technologies Ltd
Annaghmore Road Coalisland, Dungannon, BT71 4QZ
Tel: 028-8774 7500 **Fax:** 028-8774 9868
E-mail: reception@autogen-technologies.com
Website: http://www.autogen-generators.com
Directors: D. Mccabe (MD), J. O'Neill (Fin)
Managers: W. Anderson (Mktg Serv Mgr), P. Coney (Buyer), E. McCabe (Personnel)
Immediate Holding Company: SILENT SOLUTIONS LTD
Registration no: NI073034 **VAT No.:** GB 412 6989 35
Date established: 2009 **Turnover:** £1m - £2m **No.of Employees:** 21 - 50
Product Groups: 37, 48

Joseph Barrett & Sons Ltd
128 Eglish Road, Dungannon, BT70 1LB
Tel: 028-3754 8646 **Fax:** 028-3754 8863
Directors: M. Barrett (MD)
Immediate Holding Company: JOSEPH BARRETT & SONS LIMITED
Registration no: NI021951 **VAT No.:** GB 253 1962 51
Date established: 1988 **Turnover:** £2m - £5m **No.of Employees:** 1 - 10
Product Groups: 14, 33, 52

Date of Accounts	Jul 11	Jul 10	Jul 09
Sales Turnover	3m	3m	5m
Pre Tax Profit/Loss	-406	-653	-2m
Working Capital	-4m	-3m	-2m
Fixed Assets	12m	12m	12m
Current Assets	2m	3m	3m
Current Liabilities	672	3m	5m

T J Booth & Sons Ltd
39 Ballynany Road Ballygawley, Dungannon, BT70 2LZ
Tel: 028-8556 8229 **Fax:** 028-8556 8229
Website: http://www.swiftsoft.net
Bank(s): Ulster
Directors: A. Booth (Dir)
Immediate Holding Company: T.J. BOOTH & SONS LIMITED
Registration no: NI014628 **VAT No.:** 251 8195 56 **Date established:** 1980
Turnover: £10m - £20m **No.of Employees:** 11 - 20 **Product Groups:** 20

Date of Accounts	May 11	May 10	May 09
Sales Turnover	15m	13m	14m
Pre Tax Profit/Loss	1m	750	664
Working Capital	3m	3m	2m
Fixed Assets	520	649	705
Current Assets	5m	4m	3m
Current Liabilities	421	327	374

C R Print
Stangmore Park Far Circular Road, Dungannon, BT71 6LW
Tel: 028-8772 4291 **Fax:** 028-8775 3261
E-mail: info@crprint.freeserve.co.uk
Website: http://www.cr-print.co.uk
Managers: G. Leonard (Sales Admin)
VAT No.: GB 287 1211 62 **Date established:** 1977 **Turnover:** £1m - £2m
No.of Employees: 1 - 10 **Product Groups:** 28

Capper Trading Ltd
124 Tamnamore Road, Dungannon, BT71 6HW
Tel: 028-8772 3736 **Fax:** 028-8772 7276
E-mail: michele.clements@cappertrading.com
Website: http://www.cappertrading.com
Directors: M. Clements (Dir)
Managers: C. Flannigan (Personnel), R. Capper
Immediate Holding Company: CAPPER TRADING LIMITED
Registration no: NI020754 **Date established:** 1987
Turnover: £10m - £20m **No.of Employees:** 21 - 50 **Product Groups:** 20, 72

Date of Accounts	Jun 11	Jun 10	Apr 09
Sales Turnover	18m	22m	18m
Pre Tax Profit/Loss	-50	-7	987
Working Capital	2m	2m	2m
Fixed Assets	7m	6m	6m
Current Assets	5m	4m	5m
Current Liabilities	455	371	647

Classic Marble Showers Ltd
185 Omagh Road, Dungannon, BT70 2AL
Tel: 028-8556 8081 **Fax:** 028-8556 8082
E-mail: info@classic-marble.com
Website: http://www.classic-marble.com
Directors: D. Harte (MD)
Immediate Holding Company: CLASSIC MARBLE (SHOWERS) LIMITED
Registration no: NI027517 **VAT No.:** GB 390 7981 10
Date established: 1993 **Turnover:** £2m - £5m **No.of Employees:** 1 - 10
Product Groups: 30

Date of Accounts	Sep 11	Sep 10	Sep 09
Working Capital	94	142	153
Fixed Assets	87	86	100
Current Assets	487	379	367

Coalisland Fireplace Co. Ltd
66 Brackaville Road Coalisland, Dungannon, BT71 4NJ
Tel: 028-8774 0327 **Fax:** 028-8774 6313
E-mail: sales@coalislandfireplace.co.uk
Website: http://www.coalislandfireplace.co.uk
Directors: E. Treanor (Prop)
Immediate Holding Company: COALISLAND FIREPLACE COMPANY LIMITED
Registration no: NI010312 **VAT No.:** GB 283 1422 73
Date established: 1974 **No.of Employees:** 1 - 10 **Product Groups:** 33, 40

Date of Accounts	Dec 11	Dec 10	Dec 09
Working Capital	16	6	13
Fixed Assets	30	33	37
Current Assets	87	75	79

Concrete Flooring Systems Ltd
Gortgonis Road Coalisland, Dungannon, BT71 4QF
Tel: 028-8774 0326 **Fax:** 028-8774 7193
E-mail: ccorr@concreteflooringsystems.co.uk
Website: http://www.concreteflooringsystems.co.uk
Bank(s): Bank of Ireland
Directors: C. Corr (Sales), P. O'Hanlon (Ch), J. Corr (Sales)
Managers: S. Cassidy (Prod Mgr), D. O'Hanlon (Mktg Serv Mgr)
Immediate Holding Company: CONCRETE FLOORING SYSTEMS LIMITED
Registration no: NI016539 **VAT No.:** GB 575 4090 28
Date established: 1983 **Turnover:** £2m - £5m **No.of Employees:** 21 - 50
Product Groups: 33

Date of Accounts	Aug 09	Aug 08	Aug 07
Working Capital	-1m	-1m	-95
Fixed Assets	4m	4m	3m
Current Assets	1m	2m	2m

Connolly & Fee Ltd
144 Annagher Road Coalisland, Dungannon, BT71 4NF
Tel: 028-8774 0515 **Fax:** 028-8774 7439
E-mail: info@connolly-fee.com
Website: http://www.connolly-fee.com
Directors: M. Connolly (Ptnr)
Immediate Holding Company: CONNOLLY & FEE LIMITED
Registration no: NI007874 **VAT No.:** GB 251 7474 57
Date established: 1970 **Turnover:** £2m - £5m **No.of Employees:** 1 - 10
Product Groups: 52

Date of Accounts	Nov 11	Nov 10	Nov 09
Sales Turnover	3m	3m	N/A
Pre Tax Profit/Loss	54	74	N/A
Working Capital	92	68	43
Fixed Assets	88	114	120
Current Assets	1m	1m	449
Current Liabilities	270	359	N/A

Coote Engineering Ltd
12 Lisdoart Road Ballygawley, Dungannon, BT70 2NG
Tel: 028-8556 8123 **Fax:** 028-8556 8974
E-mail: office@coote.co.uk
Website: http://www.coote.co.uk
Directors: P. Coote (Dir), R. Coote (Dir)
Managers: L. Coote
Immediate Holding Company: COOTE ENGINEERING LIMITED
Registration no: NI020910 **VAT No.:** GB 286 8713 09
Date established: 1987 **Turnover:** £2m - £5m **No.of Employees:** 21 - 50
Product Groups: 45, 46

Date of Accounts	Dec 11	Dec 10	Dec 09
Working Capital	699	922	739
Fixed Assets	85	115	171
Current Assets	2m	2m	1m

Demedne Electrical Sales Ni Ltd
14 Ballygawley Road, Dungannon, BT71 7DF
Tel: 028-8772 5033 **Fax:** 028-8772 7618
E-mail: chris.mckenna@demesne.ie
Website: http://www.domain.ie
Directors: C. McKenna (Dir), N. McLoughlin (MD)
Managers: C. McLoughlin (Chief Mgr), C. McKenna (Mgr), K. Quinn (Sales Prom Mgr), M. Devins (Comptroller)
Registration no: 00029315 **VAT No.:** GB 707 0465 52
No.of Employees: 1 - 10 **Product Groups:** 27, 30, 35, 37, 38, 40, 46, 49, 67

Derryvale Furniture Ltd
102 Derryvale Road, Dungannon, BT71 4DY
Tel: 028-8774 8685 **Fax:** 028-8774 6099
Website: http://www.derryvalefurniture.co.uk
Directors: J. O'rouke (MD)
Registration no: NI016460 **VAT No.:** GB 496 9606 79
Date established: 1983 **No.of Employees:** 1 - 10 **Product Groups:** 26

Donaghmore Construction Ltd
3 William Street, Dungannon, BT70 1DX
Tel: 028-8772 6500 **Fax:** 028-8772 4138
E-mail: info@donaghmoreconstruction.com
Website: http://www.donaghmoreconstruction.com
Directors: M. Currie (MD)
Immediate Holding Company: DONAGHMORE CONSTRUCTION LIMITED
Registration no: NI021609 **VAT No.:** GB 286 8152 23
Date established: 1988 **No.of Employees:** 1 - 10 **Product Groups:** 52

Date of Accounts	Jul 11	Jul 10	Jul 09
Working Capital	136	151	86
Fixed Assets	71	77	78
Current Assets	648	878	799
Current Liabilities	N/A	N/A	34

Donnelly Group
57-59 Moy Road, Dungannon, BT71 7DT
Tel: 028-8772 2887 **Fax:** 028-8772 6999
E-mail: info@donnellygroup.co.uk
Website: http://www.donnellygroup.co.uk
Bank(s): First Trust
Directors: T. Donnelly (Dir), R. Fitzpatrick (Pers), M. Hopper (Tech Serv), D. Martin (Fin)
Managers: R. Donnelley (Mktg Serv Mgr)
Ultimate Holding Company: DONNELLY BROS. GARAGES (DUNGANNON) LIMITED
Immediate Holding Company: DONNELLY BROS (HONDA) LTD
Registration no: NI070608 **VAT No.:** GB 366 3030 68
Date established: 2008 **No.of Employees:** 501 - 1000 **Product Groups:** 68

Date of Accounts	May 11	May 10	May 09
Working Capital	347	81	-118
Fixed Assets	175	242	310
Current Assets	3m	2m	2m

Dungannon Window Co.
Viewfort, Dungannon, BT71 6LP
Tel: 028-8772 5016 **Fax:** 028-8772 7232
E-mail: sales@dungannonwindows.co.uk
Website: http://www.dungannonwindows.co.uk
Directors: T. Givans (Prop)
Immediate Holding Company: DUNGANNON WINDOW COMPANY LIMITED
Registration no: NI046056 **Date established:** 2003
Turnover: £500,000 - £1m **No.of Employees:** 11 - 20
Product Groups: 35, 52

Date of Accounts	Apr 12	Apr 11	Apr 10
Working Capital	2m	2m	2m
Fixed Assets	446	384	224

Current Assets	3m	3m	2m

Enhance Sliding Wardrobes (a divsion of Trade Robes Ltd)
Unit 56 Dungannon Enterprise Centre 2 Coalisland Road, Dungannon, BT71 6JT
Tel: 028-8775 3055 **Fax:** 028-8775 3070
E-mail: info@enhanceslidingwardrobes.com
Website: http://www.enhanceslidingwardrobes.com
Directors: A. Reid (MD)
Registration no: NI032884 **Date established:** 1997
No.of Employees: 1 - 10 **Product Groups:** 26

Forbes Furniture
137 Mullanahoe Road, Dungannon, BT71 5AX
Tel: 028-8673 7348 **Fax:** 028-8673 6348
E-mail: p.forbes@forbescontracts.fsnet.co.uk
Website: http://www.forbesfurnituregroup.com
Bank(s): Northern Bank
Directors: P. Forbes (MD)
Managers: C. Collin (I.T. Exec), M. Bell (Sales Admin), M. Kelly (Accounts)
Registration no: 00006923 **VAT No.:** GB 252 0544 91
Turnover: £1m - £2m **No.of Employees:** 21 - 50 **Product Groups:** 26

Gormleys Engineering Works Ltd
81 Omagh Road Seskilgreen, Dungannon, BT70 2BQ
Tel: 028-8556 8220 **Fax:** 028-8556 8916
E-mail: patsy@gormleyseng.com
Managers: P. Turbitt (Sales Admin)
Immediate Holding Company: GORMLEYS ENGINEERING WORKS LIMITED
Registration no: NI013295 **VAT No.:** GB 287 1342 47
Date established: 1979 **Turnover:** £500,000 - £1m
No.of Employees: 11 - 20 **Product Groups:** 41

Date of Accounts	Aug 11	Aug 10	Aug 09
Working Capital	846	719	707
Fixed Assets	96	91	97
Current Assets	1m	1m	986

Harpscreen
Unit 3 Granville Industrial Estate, Dungannon, BT70 1NJ
Tel: 028-8772 7273 **Fax:** 028-8772 4287
E-mail: sales@harpscreen.com
Website: http://www.harpscreen.com
Managers: M. McCabe, S. Kevan (Sales Prom Mgr), J. Robins (Mgr)
Immediate Holding Company: QUARRYTECH LIMITED
Registration no: NI029428 **VAT No.:** GB 517 5453 53
Date established: 1995 **Turnover:** £5m - £10m **No.of Employees:** 21 - 50
Product Groups: 35, 45, 48

Date of Accounts	Dec 11	Dec 10	Dec 09
Sales Turnover	7m	5m	N/A
Pre Tax Profit/Loss	773	641	N/A
Working Capital	2m	2m	466
Fixed Assets	6m	6m	6m
Current Assets	5m	4m	2m
Current Liabilities	881	2m	N/A

J P M Trailers
60b Killyharry Road, Dungannon, BT70 3BG
Tel: 028-8776 7337 **Fax:** 028-8776 7949
E-mail: sales@jpmtrailers.com
Website: http://www.jpmtrailers.com
Directors: P. O'neill (Prop)
Managers: C. Herson, L. Abertnethy (Personnel)
Immediate Holding Company: JPM TRAILERS LTD
Registration no: NI064002 **Date established:** 2007
No.of Employees: 21 - 50 **Product Groups:** 39, 45, 67, 68

Date of Accounts	Apr 12	Apr 11	Apr 10
Working Capital	52	-46	-111
Fixed Assets	224	238	253
Current Assets	837	726	641

S Jordan Engineering Ltd
224 Rehaghy Road, Dungannon, BT70 1LH
Tel: 028-3754 8377 **Fax:** 028-3754 8836
E-mail: info@seanjordanengineering.com
Website: http://www.seanjordanengineering.com
Directors: S. Jordan (Prop)
Registration no: NI025436 **VAT No.:** GB 282 9706 25
No.of Employees: 1 - 10 **Product Groups:** 35, 45

Lewis & Robinson
6 Findrum Road Ballygawley, Dungannon, BT70 2JL
Tel: 028-8556 8639 **Fax:** 028-8556 7921
E-mail: sales@roblew.com
Website: http://www.roblew.co.uk
Directors: D. Robinson (Ptnr)
Date established: 1980 **No.of Employees:** 1 - 10 **Product Groups:** 41

Linden Foods
Granville Industrial Estate Granville Road, Dungannon, BT70 1NJ
Tel: 028-8772 4777 **Fax:** 028-8772 4714
E-mail: richardm@lindenfoods.com
Website: http://www.lindenfoods.com
Bank(s): Northern Bank
Directors: J. Lyttle (Co Sec), R. Morre (MD), N. Sweeney (Sales & Mktg), J. Mguire (MD), G. Maguire (MD), J. Maquire (MD)
Managers: R. Wilson (I.T. Exec)
Ultimate Holding Company: 09000530
Immediate Holding Company: LINDEN FOODS LIMITED
Registration no: NI014930 **VAT No.:** GB 366 3156 46
Date established: 1981 **Turnover:** £125m - £250m
No.of Employees: 251 - 500 **Product Groups:** 20

J F Little
68 Mullaghmore Road, Dungannon, BT70 1RB
Tel: 028-8772 7011 **Fax:** 028- 87727299
E-mail: jflittleelctrical@btconnect.com
Directors: S. Little (Prop)
Immediate Holding Company: LITTLE DEVELOPMENTS LIMITED
Registration no: NI026870 **Date established:** 1992
No.of Employees: 1 - 10 **Product Groups:** 48, 52

N Mckane
81 Aghnagar Road Galbally, Dungannon, BT70 2PN
Tel: 028-8556 8389 **Fax:** 028-8556 8389
Directors: N. Mckane (Prop)
Date established: 1960 **No.of Employees:** 1 - 10 **Product Groups:** 41

P Mckenna Engineering
79a Drumflugh Road, Dungannon, BT71 7QF
Tel: 028-3754 9944 **Fax:** 028-3754 9679
Directors: P. Mckenna (Prop)
Registration no: NI045746 **Date established:** 2003
No.of Employees: 1 - 10 **Product Groups:** 35

T J Mckenna & Son Ltd
54 Reclain Road, Dungannon, BT70 3BS
Tel: 028-8775 8600 **Fax:** 028-8775 8981
E-mail: tjmckennasonltd@hotmail.com
Directors: S. Mccartan (MD)
Immediate Holding Company: T.J.MCKENNA AND SON LIMITED
Registration no: NI012706 **Date established:** 1978
No.of Employees: 11 - 20 **Product Groups:** 41

Date of Accounts	Jun 10	Jun 09	Jun 08
Working Capital	642	614	602
Fixed Assets	185	208	223
Current Assets	2m	2m	2m

Mcmullan & O'Donnell
101 Drumflugh Road, Dungannon, BT71 7LF
Tel: 028-3754 8791 **Fax:** 028-3754 8543
E-mail: info@mcmullanodonnell.com
Website: http://www.mcmullanodonnell.com
Directors: P. McMullan (MD)
Managers: F. O'Donnell (Transport), B. O'Donnell (Tech Serv Mgr)
Immediate Holding Company: McMULLAN & O'DONNELL LIMITED
Registration no: NI031571 **VAT No.:** GB 366 3392 34
Date established: 1996 **Turnover:** £5m - £10m
No.of Employees: 51 - 100 **Product Groups:** 30, 35

Date of Accounts	Dec 11	Dec 10	Dec 09
Sales Turnover	6m	7m	6m
Pre Tax Profit/Loss	-42	224	N/A
Working Capital	1m	1m	1m
Fixed Assets	3m	3m	2m
Current Assets	2m	2m	2m
Current Liabilities	26	29	32

Mcquaid Engineering
84 Cookstown Road, Dungannon, BT71 4BS
Tel: 028-8774 9869 **Fax:** 028-8774 9698
E-mail: paul@mcquaidengineering.com
Website: http://www.mcquaidengineering.com
Directors: P. Mcquaid (Dir)
Managers: A. Cardwell (Tech Serv Mgr), J. McQuaid (Fin Mgr)
Immediate Holding Company: McQuaid Engineering Ltd
Registration no: NI059712 **Date established:** 2006
No.of Employees: 21 - 50 **Product Groups:** 45

Date of Accounts	Oct 11	Oct 10	Oct 09
Working Capital	74	25	-26
Fixed Assets	208	186	197
Current Assets	616	544	374

Mcavoy Group Ltd
76 Ballynakilly Road, Dungannon, BT71 6HD
Tel: 028-8774 0372 **Fax:** 028-8774 7345
E-mail: peterbrowne@mcavoygroup.co.uk
Website: http://www.mcavoygroup.com
Bank(s): Allied Irish Bank
Directors: P. Browne (Sales), L. Tumilty (Fin), O. Corr (Mkt Research)
Managers: A. Walsh, P. Coulter (Purch Mgr), A. Watson (Personnel)
Ultimate Holding Company: McAVOY GROUP LIMITED - THE
Immediate Holding Company: ROANCABIN BUILDING SYSTEMS LIMITED
Registration no: NI013372 **VAT No.:** GB 253 6600 71
Date established: 1979 **Turnover:** £10m - £20m
No.of Employees: 21 - 50 **Product Groups:** 25, 35

Date of Accounts	Dec 09	Dec 08
Fixed Assets	50	50

Metso Minerals Cappagh Ltd
55 Cappagh Road Galbally, Dungannon, BT70 2PD
Tel: 028-8775 8396 **Fax:** 028-8775 8557
E-mail: paul.ward@metso.com
Website: http://www.metsominerals.com
Bank(s): Ulster Bank
Directors: P. Mcneil (Co Sec)
Managers: P. Ward (Purch Mgr), G. Donnelly (Comptroller), P. McMeel (Mgr)
Ultimate Holding Company: METSO OY (FINLAND)
Immediate Holding Company: METSO MINERALS (CAPPAGH) LIMITED
Registration no: NI011870 **VAT No.:** GB 286 7849 86
Date established: 1977 **Turnover:** £20m - £50m
No.of Employees: 51 - 100 **Product Groups:** 35, 45

Date of Accounts	Dec 08	Dec 07	Dec 06
Sales Turnover	21m	15m	14m
Pre Tax Profit/Loss	2m	401	2m
Working Capital	872	933	1m
Fixed Assets	993	856	916
Current Assets	10m	7m	7m
Current Liabilities	1m	873	674

Mid Ulster Diesel Services
20 North Street Stewartstown, Dungannon, BT71 5JF
Tel: 028-8773 8328
E-mail: roger.doey@btconnect.com
Directors: R. Doey (Ptnr)
No.of Employees: 1 - 10 **Product Groups:** 40

Moore & Faloon
Castlecaulfield Road, Dungannon, BT70 3HF
Tel: 028-8776 7200 **Fax:** 028-8776 7025
E-mail: moore_faloon@btconnect.com
Directors: M. Faloon (Ptnr)
VAT No.: 252741861 **Date established:** 1970 **No.of Employees:** 1 - 10
Product Groups: 52

Muldoon Transport Systems Ltd
181 Clonmore Road, Dungannon, BT71 6HX
Tel: 028-3885 1873 **Fax:** 028-3885 2203
E-mail: info@muldoon.com
Website: http://www.muldoon.com
Directors: T. Muldoon (Dir)
Immediate Holding Company: MULDOON TRANSPORT SYSTEMS LIMITED
Registration no: NI033944 **VAT No.:** GB 287 2132 83
Date established: 1998 **No.of Employees:** 21 - 50 **Product Groups:** 39, 68

Date of Accounts	Mar 11	Mar 10	Mar 09
Working Capital	467	204	122
Fixed Assets	418	412	431
Current Assets	2m	1m	1m

Northern Ireland TV & Video Distributors Ltd
117 Eglish Road, Dungannon, BT70 1LB
Tel: 028-3754 9580 **Fax:** 028-8772 3666
E-mail: sales@nitd.co.uk
Website: http://www.nitd.co.uk
Directors: B. Lughran (Dir)
Immediate Holding Company: N.I. TV & VIDEO DISTRIBUTORS LTD
Registration no: NI039591 **Date established:** 2000
No.of Employees: 1 - 10 **Product Groups:** 36, 40

Date of Accounts	Oct 11	Oct 10	Oct 09
Working Capital	19	25	33
Fixed Assets	25	25	14
Current Assets	332	282	388
Current Liabilities	89	72	63

Nugent Trailers
15 Aghnagar Road Ballygawley, Dungannon, BT70 2HP
Tel: 028-8775 9400 **Fax:** 028-8775 8956
E-mail: info@nugentengineering.com
Website: http://www.nugenttrailers.com
Bank(s): Ulster Bank
Directors: S. Nugent (MD)
Immediate Holding Company: NUGENT TRAILERS LIMITED
Registration no: NI053585 **VAT No.:** GB 412 5885 52
Date established: 2005 **Turnover:** £2m - £5m **No.of Employees:** 21 - 50
Product Groups: 35, 41

Date of Accounts	Mar 12	Mar 11	Mar 10
Working Capital	-48	-68	-11
Fixed Assets	53	57	64
Current Assets	784	594	554

Plantec Furniture Systems
54a Mousetown Road Coalisland, Dungannon, BT71 4PJ
Tel: 028-8774 0108 **Fax:** 028-8774 6112
E-mail: info@plantec.ie
Website: http://www.plantec.ie
Directors: O. O'Neill (Ptnr)
Immediate Holding Company: Plantec Furniture Systems Ltd
Registration no: NI061199 **VAT No.:** GB 517 8891 04
Date established: 2006 **No.of Employees:** 11 - 20 **Product Groups:** 26

Date of Accounts	Dec 11	Dec 10	Dec 09
Working Capital	-22	-22	-25
Fixed Assets	5	6	8
Current Assets	77	87	89

Powertech
8 Torrent Valley Business Park Donaghmore, Dungannon, BT70 3BF
Tel: 028-8776 9200 **Fax:** 028-8776 1776
Website: http://www.powertech-industrial.co.uk
Directors: D. Fox (Dir)
Date established: 2001 **No.of Employees:** 1 - 10 **Product Groups:** 35, 37, 39, 45

R K Trucks Ltd
126 Tamnamore Road, Dungannon, BT71 6HW
Tel: 028-8772 2111 **Fax:** 028-8773 7393
E-mail: lambsales@erf.com
Website: http://www.rktrucks.com
Bank(s): Ulster Bank
Directors: D. Rice (MD)
Immediate Holding Company: LAMIX LIMITED
Registration no: NI012892 **VAT No.:** GB 286 9769 74
Date established: 1978 **No.of Employees:** 11 - 20 **Product Groups:** 68

Date of Accounts	Oct 11	Oct 10	Oct 09
Working Capital	99	548	83
Fixed Assets	899	459	919
Current Assets	204	643	183

Sandvik
Aghnagar Road Ballygawley, Dungannon, BT70 2HW
Tel: 028-8556 7799 **Fax:** 028-8556 7007
E-mail: mobilecs.smcuk@sandvik.com
Website: http://www.mc.sandvik.com
Bank(s): Ulster Bank
Directors: P. Colton (MD)
Managers: R. Galbraith (Personnel), A. McBride (Fin Mgr), C. Leaper (Tech Serv Mgr), L. Donaghy (Purch Mgr)
Registration no: 02387945 **VAT No.:** GB 517 7122 56
Turnover: £1m - £2m **No.of Employees:** 101 - 250 **Product Groups:** 45

Southern Cross Dental Laboratory Ltd
28 Dungannon Street Moy, Dungannon, BT71 7SH
Tel: 028-8778 9919 **Fax:** 028-8778 4876
E-mail: ireland@scdlab.com
Website: http://www.scdlab.com
Directors: D. Reaney (Dir)
Immediate Holding Company: Southern Cross Dental Laboratories Ltd
Registration no: NI045484 **Date established:** 2003
No.of Employees: 1 - 10 **Product Groups:** 38, 88

Date of Accounts	Mar 11	Mar 10	Mar 09
Working Capital	906	570	381
Fixed Assets	9	12	7
Current Assets	1m	777	537

Spec-Drum Engineering
24 Farlough Road, Dungannon, BT71 4DT
Tel: 028-8774 1122 **Fax:** 028-8774 1133
E-mail: pm@nm.tm
Website: http://www.specdrum.co.uk
Directors: D. Mccabe (MD)
Immediate Holding Company: Spec-Drum Engineering
Registration no: NI048459 **Date established:** 2003
No.of Employees: 51 - 100 **Product Groups:** 30, 45

Topline Cabins
127 Tandragee Road Pomeroy, Dungannon, BT70 3ED
Tel: 028-8775 8873
E-mail: margret.r.cunninham@btinternet.com
Directors: S. Cunningham (Ptnr)
Turnover: Up to £250,000 **No.of Employees:** 1 - 10 **Product Groups:** 35

Trade Robes

Unit 56 Dungannon Enterprise Centre 2 Coalisland Road, Dungannon, BT71 6JT
Tel: 028-8775 3070 **Fax:** 028-8775 3055
E-mail: sales@traderobes.com
Website: http://www.traderobes.com
Directors: A. Reid (Prop)
Immediate Holding Company: Trade Robes Limited
Registration no: NI046044 **Date established:** 2003
Turnover: £500,000 - £1m **No.of Employees:** 1 - 10 **Product Groups:** 25, 26, 33, 35, 36

Tullyleek Precast Concrete

41 Pomeroy Road, Dungannon, BT70 3AZ
Tel: 028-8776 1313 **Fax:** 028-8776 1155
E-mail: tulleyleek@btconnect.com
Website: http://www.tullyleek.co.uk
Directors: J. Dobson (Ptnr)
Immediate Holding Company: TULLYLEEK PRECAST CONCRETE LIMITED
Registration no: NI053787 **VAT No.:** GB 253 6320 77
Date established: 2005 **No.of Employees:** 1 - 10 **Product Groups:** 33

Date of Accounts	Apr 12	Apr 11	Apr 10
Working Capital	361	211	187
Fixed Assets	202	263	327
Current Assets	428	265	229

Western Building Systems

11 Mountjoy Road Coalisland, Dungannon, BT71 5DQ
Tel: 028-8774 0740 **Fax:** 028-8774 7697
E-mail: contact@westernbuild.com
Website: http://www.westernbuild.com
Managers: D. McCloskey (Chief Mgr), L. Hughes (Purch Mgr), M. Mccloskey (Mgr), M. Canavan (Comptroller)
Immediate Holding Company: WESTERN BUILDING SYSTEMS LTD
Registration no: NI025833 **VAT No.:** GB 390 7628 26
Date established: 1991 **Turnover:** £10m - £20m
No.of Employees: 51 - 100 **Product Groups:** 25, 30, 52

Date of Accounts	Apr 11	Apr 10	Apr 09
Sales Turnover	11m	12m	27m
Pre Tax Profit/Loss	702	2m	6m
Working Capital	10m	9m	7m
Fixed Assets	1m	2m	2m
Current Assets	14m	12m	11m
Current Liabilities	986	746	2m

Wylie Engineering Ltd

Moy Road, Dungannon, BT71 7DX
Tel: 028-8778 4420 **Fax:** 028-8778 4761
E-mail: info@wylieengineering.com
Website: http://www.wylieengineering.com
Directors: S. Wylie (MD)
Immediate Holding Company: WYLIE ENGINEERING LIMITED
Registration no: NI043447 **VAT No.:** GB 286 8864 85
Date established: 2002 **No.of Employees:** 1 - 10 **Product Groups:** 41, 45

Date of Accounts	Apr 11	Apr 10	Apr 09
Working Capital	-43	-45	-63
Fixed Assets	72	97	113
Current Assets	150	220	175

Co. Fermanagh

Enniskillen

J F Andrews Engineering Ltd

23 Killivilly Road Killyvilly, Enniskillen, BT74 4DS
Tel: 028-6632 4884 **Fax:** 028-6632 4932
E-mail: info@jfaengineering.com
Website: http://www.jfaengineering.com
Directors: R. Hampsey (MD), H. Andrews (Fin)
Immediate Holding Company: ANDREWS ENGINEERING LTD
Registration no: 03390894 **VAT No.:** GB 256 0851 58
Date established: 1997 **No.of Employees:** 1 - 10 **Product Groups:** 67, 83

Date of Accounts	Mar 11	Mar 09	Mar 08
Working Capital	1m	865	672
Fixed Assets	26	21	35
Current Assets	1m	1m	827

Belleek Pottery

Main Street Rathmore, Belleek, Enniskillen, BT93 3FY
Tel: 028-6865 8501 **Fax:** 028-6865 8625
E-mail: info@belleek.ie
Website: http://www.belleek.ie
Directors: M. Sharkey (Fin), J. Maguire (MD)
Managers: R. Wallis (Purch Mgr), C. Flaherty (Sales & Mktg Mg)
Ultimate Holding Company: FOSSGATE LIMITED (ISLE OF MAN)
Immediate Holding Company: BELLEEK POTTERY, LIMITED - THE
Registration no: R0000099 **VAT No.:** GB 251 9354 57
Date established: 2020 **Turnover:** £5m - £10m
No.of Employees: 101 - 250 **Product Groups:** 33, 65

Date of Accounts	Mar 12	Mar 11	Mar 10
Sales Turnover	8m	7m	8m
Pre Tax Profit/Loss	-49	-50	-116
Working Capital	17m	16m	16m
Fixed Assets	4m	4m	4m
Current Assets	17m	17m	17m
Current Liabilities	67	129	72

Belmore Court Motel

Tempo Road Wickham Drive, Enniskillen, BT74 6HX
Tel: 028-6632 6633 **Fax:** 028-6632 6362
E-mail: info@motel.co.uk
Website: http://www.motel.co.uk
Directors: T. Mccartney (Prop)
Date established: 1990 **No.of Employees:** 11 - 20 **Product Groups:** 69

Campbell Solutions Ltd

Enniskillen Road Ballinamallard, Enniskillen, BT94 2ER
Tel: 028-6638 8496 **Fax:** 028-6638 8332
E-mail: info@campbelljoinerysolutions.com
Website: http://www.campbelljoinerysolutions.com
Directors: W. Campbell (MD)
Immediate Holding Company: CAMPBELL SOLUTIONS LIMITED
Registration no: NI609839 **VAT No.:** GB 253 4914 58
Date established: 2011 **Turnover:** Up to £250,000
No.of Employees: 11 - 20 **Product Groups:** 25, 30

Date of Accounts	Mar 07	Sep 10	Sep 09
Working Capital	33	495	638
Fixed Assets	2m	963	1m
Current Assets	230	618	753

F R Cathcart Ltd

Breandrum Tempo Road, Enniskillen, BT74 6HR
Tel: 028-6632 3551 **Fax:** 028-6632 4705
E-mail: christine.little@frcathcartltd.com
Website: http://www.frcathcartltd.com
Managers: C. Little
Immediate Holding Company: F.R. CATHCART LIMITED
Registration no: NI009221 **VAT No.:** GB 252 4991 46
Date established: 1973 **Turnover:** £5m - £10m **No.of Employees:** 11 - 20
Product Groups: 66

Date of Accounts	Dec 11	Dec 10	Dec 09
Working Capital	493	515	636
Fixed Assets	3m	3m	3m
Current Assets	2m	2m	2m

John K Cathcart Ltd

Trory Ballinamallard, Enniskillen, BT94 2FH
Tel: 028-6632 4325 **Fax:** 028-6632 5939
E-mail: general@cathcart.co.uk
Website: http://www.cathcart.co.uk
Directors: A. Cathcart (MD)
Immediate Holding Company: JOHN K. CATHCART LIMITED
Registration no: NI018970 **VAT No.:** GB 252 5978 33
Date established: 1985 **Turnover:** £250,000 - £500,000
No.of Employees: 11 - 20 **Product Groups:** 48

Date of Accounts	Dec 11	Dec 10	Dec 09
Working Capital	740	756	730
Fixed Assets	115	129	149
Current Assets	1m	2m	2m

T Chambers & Sons Enniskillen Ltd

58 Tempo Road, Enniskillen, BT74 6HR
Tel: 028-6632 2447 **Fax:** 028-6632 3882
E-mail: t.chambers@swiftsoft.net
Website: http://www.swiftsoft.net
Directors: V. Chambers (Dir)
Immediate Holding Company: T.CHAMBERS & SONS (ENNISKILLEN) LIMITED
Registration no: NI010831 **VAT No.:** GB 283 1015 86
Date established: 1975 **Turnover:** £1m - £2m **No.of Employees:** 1 - 10
Product Groups: 52

Date of Accounts	Aug 11	Aug 10	Aug 09
Working Capital	2m	3m	2m
Fixed Assets	39	77	157
Current Assets	3m	3m	3m

Cleaning Doctor Ltd

8 Boho Road Moyglass, Enniskillen, BT74 8DL
Tel: 028-6634 1288 **Fax:** 028-6634 1690
E-mail: info@cleaningdoctor.net
Website: http://www.cleaningdoctor.net
Directors: W. Little (MD)
Immediate Holding Company: CLEANING DOCTOR LIMITED
Registration no: NI034179 **Date established:** 1998
No.of Employees: 1 - 10 **Product Groups:** 23, 52

Date of Accounts	Jun 11	Jun 10	Jun 09
Working Capital	769	661	570
Fixed Assets	204	203	207
Current Assets	836	707	625

R T D Crawford Ltd

34 Inishmore Road Lisbellaw, Enniskillen, BT94 5DX
Tel: 028-6638 7315 **Fax:** 028-6638 7227
E-mail: info@rtdcrawford.com
Website: http://www.rtdcrawford.com
Managers: R. Allen (Chief Mgr)
Immediate Holding Company: R.T.D. CRAWFORD LIMITED
Registration no: NI013709 **VAT No.:** GB 287 1181 45
Date established: 1979 **Turnover:** £10m - £20m
No.of Employees: 21 - 50 **Product Groups:** 25

Date of Accounts	Dec 11	Dec 10	Dec 09
Sales Turnover	12m	12m	14m
Pre Tax Profit/Loss	428	533	1m
Working Capital	11m	10m	10m
Fixed Assets	6m	7m	7m
Current Assets	11m	11m	11m
Current Liabilities	182	247	418

Deane Public Works Ltd

Dallas Buninubber Irvinestown, Enniskillen, BT94 1NZ
Tel: 028-6862 1555 **Fax:** 028-6862 8523
E-mail: info@deanepublicworks.com
Website: http://www.deanepublicworks.com
Directors: G. Deane (MD)
Managers: M. Kerringan (Personnel), M. Kerringan (Comptroller)
Immediate Holding Company: DEANE PUBLIC WORKS LIMITED
Registration no: NI020009 **VAT No.:** GB 496 9518 76
Date established: 1986 **Turnover:** £5m - £10m **No.of Employees:** 21 - 50
Product Groups: 51

Date of Accounts	Feb 08	Feb 11	Feb 10
Sales Turnover	N/A	7m	9m
Pre Tax Profit/Loss	-1m	-86	935
Working Capital	5m	5m	5m
Fixed Assets	1m	624	696
Current Assets	12m	8m	10m
Current Liabilities	2m	477	1m

Robert Dickie & Sons Ltd

7 Down Street, Enniskillen, BT74 7DL
Tel: 028-6632 6191 **Fax:** 028-6632 2558
E-mail: robertdickie@btconnect.com
Directors: L. Dickie (Dir)
Immediate Holding Company: ROBERT DICKIE AND SONS LIMITED
Registration no: NI002905 **VAT No.:** GB 252 3486 64
Date established: 1950 **Turnover:** £250,000 - £500,000
No.of Employees: 1 - 10 **Product Groups:** 66

Date of Accounts	Jan 12	Jan 11	Jan 10
Working Capital	715	677	634
Fixed Assets	236	238	259
Current Assets	929	906	802

Dunlop Kitchens

47 Drumgoon Road Maguiresbridge, Enniskillen, BT94 4QX
Tel: 028-6772 1919 **Fax:** 028-6772 3743
E-mail: sales@dunlopkitchens.co.uk
Website: http://www.dunlopkitchens.co.uk
Directors: W. Dunlop (Prop)
VAT No.: GB 496 9138 86 **Date established:** 1987
No.of Employees: 1 - 10 **Product Groups:** 26

Erne Diesel Services

Link Road Irvinestown, Enniskillen, BT94 1GR
Tel: 028-6862 8111 **Fax:** 028-6862 8111
Directors: M. Mcgarrity (Prop)
Immediate Holding Company: IRVINESTOWN TRUSTEE ENTERPRISE COMPANY LIMITED
Registration no: NI026819 **Date established:** 1992
No.of Employees: 1 - 10 **Product Groups:** 40

Date of Accounts	Mar 11	Mar 10	Mar 09
Working Capital	81	91	70
Fixed Assets	977	1m	1m
Current Assets	85	150	116

Erne Eggs Ltd

Dp1 Milltate Lisnaskea, Enniskillen, BT92 0BN
Tel: 028-6772 1345 **Fax:** 028-6772 1655
E-mail: info@erne-eggs.com
Directors: C. Crawford (MD), D. Charters (Dir)
Immediate Holding Company: ERNE EGGS LIMITED
Registration no: NI015561 **VAT No.:** GB 286 8451 13
Date established: 1982 **Turnover:** £5m - £10m
No.of Employees: 51 - 100 **Product Groups:** 01

F Dowler Ltd

Main Street Lisnaskea, Enniskillen, BT92 0JH
Tel: 028-6772 1308 **Fax:** 028-6772 2111
E-mail: drew@dowler.co.uk
Website: http://www.dowler.co.uk
Bank(s): Ulster Bank
Directors: D. McMullen (Dir), D. Wigham (Dir), S. Graham (Dir)
Managers: T. Elliot (Chief Acct)
Immediate Holding Company: F.Dowler Ltd
Registration no: NI000912 **VAT No.:** GB 251 8884 33
Date established: 1934 **Turnover:** £2m - £5m **No.of Employees:** 21 - 50
Product Groups: 62, 65, 66, 88

Fermanagh District Council

Townhall Townhall Street, Enniskillen, BT74 7BA
Tel: 028-6632 5050 **Fax:** 028-6632 2024
E-mail: brendan.hegarty@fermanagh.gov.uk
Website: http://www.fermanagh.gov.uk
Directors: B. Hegarty (Grp Chief Exec), P. Thompson (Mkt Research)
Managers: T. McCabe
VAT No.: GB 255 7089 36 **No.of Employees:** 251 - 500
Product Groups: 87

Fermanagh Enterprises Ltd

Lackaghboy Industrial Estate Lackaghboy, Enniskillen, BT74 4RL
Tel: 028-6632 3117 **Fax:** 028-6632 7878
E-mail: info@fermanaghenterprise.com
Website: http://www.fermanaghenterprise.com
Directors: J. Treacy (MD)
Immediate Holding Company: FERMANAGH ENTERPRISE LIMITED
Registration no: NI018464 **VAT No.:** GB 517 5489 22
Date established: 1985 **No.of Employees:** 11 - 20 **Product Groups:** 80

Date of Accounts	Mar 12	Mar 11	Mar 10
Sales Turnover	450	490	N/A
Pre Tax Profit/Loss	84	83	N/A
Working Capital	444	322	201
Fixed Assets	2m	2m	2m
Current Assets	494	375	378
Current Liabilities	50	53	N/A

The Fermanagh Herald

30 Belmore Street, Enniskillen, BT74 6AA
Tel: 028-6632 2066 **Fax:** 028-6632 5521
E-mail: editor@fermanaghherald.com
Website: http://www.fermanaghherald.com
Managers: M. Kennedy
Date established: 1951 **No.of Employees:** 1 - 10 **Product Groups:** 28

Fisher Engineering Ltd

Main Street Ballinamallard, Enniskillen, BT94 2FY
Tel: 028-6638 8521 **Fax:** 028-6638 8706
E-mail: wesley@fisher-engineering.co.uk
Website: http://www.sfrplc.com
Directors: W. Knox (Fin)
Managers: G. Culbert (Chief Buyer)
Ultimate Holding Company: SEVERFIELD-ROWEN PLC
Immediate Holding Company: FISHER ENGINEERING LIMITED
Registration no: NI010328 **Date established:** 1974
Turnover: £20m - £50m **No.of Employees:** 251 - 500 **Product Groups:** 84

Date of Accounts	Dec 11	Dec 10	Dec 09
Sales Turnover	60m	45m	57m
Pre Tax Profit/Loss	6m	5m	14m
Working Capital	26m	22m	26m
Fixed Assets	5m	5m	5m
Current Assets	61m	55m	56m
Current Liabilities	3m	5m	5m

Killyhevlin Hotel

Dublin Road, Enniskillen, BT74 6RW
Tel: 028-6632 3481 **Fax:** 028-6632 4726
E-mail: info@killyhevlin.com
Website: http://www.killyhevlin.com
Managers: P. Kavanagh, L. Watson (Personnel), J. Gallagher (Sales & Mktg Mg), D. Morrison (Chief Mgr)
Immediate Holding Company: KILLYHEVLIN HOTEL LIMITED
Registration no: NI005182 **Date established:** 1962 **Turnover:** £5m - £10m
No.of Employees: 101 - 250 **Product Groups:** 69

Date of Accounts	Sep 11	Sep 10	Sep 09
Sales Turnover	6m	6m	6m
Pre Tax Profit/Loss	402	715	867
Working Capital	-2	-15	-372
Fixed Assets	8m	8m	8m
Current Assets	1m	2m	1m
Current Liabilities	693	958	1m

Lakeland Engine Spares
209 Clabby Road Imeroo Tempo, Enniskillen, BT94 3LA
Tel: 028-8954 1409 **Fax:** 028-8954 1409
Directors: D. Armstrong (Prop)
VAT No.: GB 366 4259 31 **Date established:** 1982
Turnover: Up to £250,000 **No.of Employees:** 1 - 10 **Product Groups:** 39, 40

B Mccaffrey & Sons Ltd
Derrylin, Enniskillen, BT92 9JT
Tel: 028-6774 8666 **Fax:** 028-6774 8365
E-mail: info@mccaffreyquarries.com
Managers: P. Mccaffrey (Mgr)
Immediate Holding Company: B.MCCAFFREY & SONS LIMITED
Registration no: NI007251 **VAT No.:** GB 253 1942 68
Date established: 1968 **Turnover:** £2m - £5m **No.of Employees:** 21 - 50
Product Groups: 51

Date of Accounts	Apr 12	Apr 11	Apr 10
Sales Turnover	N/A	N/A	3m
Pre Tax Profit/Loss	89	235	-219
Working Capital	326	253	108
Fixed Assets	4m	4m	4m
Current Assets	2m	2m	1m
Current Liabilities	N/A	2m	212

Macneary Rasdale & Co.
30 Darling Street, Enniskillen, BT74 7EW
Tel: 028-6632 2235 **Fax:** 028-6632 5625
E-mail: macneary@trfs.freeserve.co.uk
Bank(s): HSBC
Directors: K. Daly (MD)
Immediate Holding Company: MACNEARY RASDALE & CO. LTD
Registration no: NI058698 **VAT No.:** GB 254 8559 26
Date established: 2006 **Turnover:** £2m - £5m **No.of Employees:** 11 - 20
Product Groups: 80

Date of Accounts	Mar 12	Mar 11	Mar 10
Working Capital	350	259	306
Fixed Assets	257	260	256
Current Assets	350	385	407

R J Mitten & Sons
Rockfield Quarry Rockfield, Lisnaskea, Enniskillen, BT92 5EA
Tel: 028-6772 1668 **Fax:** 028-6772 2789
E-mail: info@rjmittens.co.uk
Directors: R. Mitten (Prop)
VAT No.: GB 286 9895 69 **Date established:** 1980
No.of Employees: 21 - 50 **Product Groups:** 51

Modern Tyre Service
56 Tempo Road, Enniskillen, BT74 6HR
Tel: 028-6632 2299 **Fax:** 028-6634 4715
E-mail: sales@moderntyres.com
Website: http://www.moderntyres.com
Directors: C. Byrne (Snr Part)
Managers: J. McKee (Comptroller), S. Shaw (Mktg Serv Mgr)
Immediate Holding Company: ARDS TYRE SERVICE LIMITED
Registration no: NI031242 **VAT No.:** GB 331 2082 08
Date established: 1996 **No.of Employees:** 11 - 20 **Product Groups:** 68

Date of Accounts	Dec 11	Dec 10	Dec 09
Sales Turnover	9m	9m	9m
Pre Tax Profit/Loss	1m	925	749
Working Capital	3m	2m	1m
Fixed Assets	4m	4m	4m
Current Assets	5m	4m	4m
Current Liabilities	864	426	753

Petal Postforming Ltd
Dromore Road Irvinestown, Enniskillen, BT94 1ET
Tel: 028-6862 1766 **Fax:** 028-6862 1004
E-mail: sales@petalgroup.com
Website: http://www.petalgroup.com
Bank(s): Bank of Ireland
Directors: P. Monaghan (MD)
Managers: B. Boylan (Sales Prom Mgr), K. Farrell
Immediate Holding Company: PETAL POSTFORMING LIMITED
Registration no: NI014306 **VAT No.:** GB 331 3290 93
Date established: 1980 **No.of Employees:** 21 - 50 **Product Groups:** 30, 35, 36

Date of Accounts	Mar 11	Mar 10	Mar 09
Working Capital	974	2m	2m
Fixed Assets	703	785	387
Current Assets	2m	2m	3m

Prunty Contracts
Lettergreen Newtownbutler, Enniskillen, BT92 8DF
Tel: 028-6773 8266 **Fax:** 028-6773 8005
E-mail: pruntypitches@btconnect.com
Website: http://www.pruntypitches.com
Directors: J. Prunty (MD)
Immediate Holding Company: PRUNTY CONTRACTS LIMITED
Registration no: NI009630 **VAT No.:** GB 255 8391 32
Date established: 1973 **No.of Employees:** 21 - 50 **Product Groups:** 51

Date of Accounts	Nov 11	Nov 10	Nov 09
Working Capital	-25	-155	-209
Fixed Assets	387	514	604
Current Assets	746	758	1m

Quinn Building Products
Derrylin Road Derrylin, Enniskillen, BT92 9AU
Tel: 028-6774 8866 **Fax:** 028-6774 8800
E-mail: info@quinn-group.com
Website: http://www.quinn-group.com
Bank(s): Northern Bank
Directors: M. Heaney (Mkt Research), D. Oreilly (Fin), S. McMahon (Sales & Mktg), P. O'brien (MD), P. Dixon (Fin)
Managers: C. McCaffrey (Personnel), M. McGrath (Purch Mgr), C. McCaffrey (Personnel), J. Fitzpatrick (I.T. Exec), J. Malloy (Tech Serv Mgr)
Immediate Holding Company: QUINN GROUP LIMITED
Registration no: NI041532 **VAT No.:** GB 331 2640 00
Date established: 2001 **Turnover:** Over £1,000m
No.of Employees: 1501 & over **Product Groups:** 14, 33, 45

Date of Accounts	Dec 08	Dec 07
Sales Turnover	2234m	1881m
Pre Tax Profit/Loss	83m	-425m
Working Capital	247m	392m
Fixed Assets	1849m	3752m
Current Assets	504m	633m
Current Liabilities	118m	93m

John Sheridan & Sons
72 Old Rossorry Road, Enniskillen, BT74 7LF
Tel: 028-6632 2510 **Fax:** 028-6632 3895
E-mail: seansheridan@email.com
Directors: S. Sheridan (MD)
Immediate Holding Company: JOHN SHERIDAN & SONS LIMITED
Registration no: NI013903 **VAT No.:** GB 287 2216 47
Date established: 1979 **No.of Employees:** 11 - 20 **Product Groups:** 26, 49

Date of Accounts	Mar 11	Mar 10	Mar 09
Working Capital	64	167	654
Fixed Assets	508	537	573
Current Assets	311	296	837

Steel Solutions
Derrylin Enterprse Park Derrylin, Enniskillen, BT92 9LA
Tel: 028-6774 8499
E-mail: info@steelsolutions.ie
Website: http://www.steelsolutions.ie
Directors: J. Rooney (Prop)
Managers: N. Woods (Comptroller)
Immediate Holding Company: STEEL SOLUTIONS (N.I.) LIMITED
Registration no: NI035112 **Date established:** 1998
No.of Employees: 11 - 20 **Product Groups:** 35

Date of Accounts	Dec 07	Jun 11	Jun 10
Working Capital	570	876	45
Fixed Assets	345	928	1m
Current Assets	2m	2m	2m

Steelcraft Engineering
Killyhelvin Industrial Estate Killyhevlin, Enniskillen, BT74 4EJ
Tel: 028-6632 9980 **Fax:** 028-6632 9981
E-mail: tonygreen@freenet.co.uk
Website: http://www.freenet.co.uk
Directors: T. Green (Ptnr)
VAT No.: GB 517 5651 39 **Date established:** 1989
Turnover: £500,000 - £1m **No.of Employees:** 1 - 10 **Product Groups:** 48

Swiftsoft Computer Systems N I Ltd
Ferney Business Park Ferney, Ballinamallard, Enniskillen, BT94 2HH
Tel: 028-6638 8833 **Fax:** 028-6638 8709
E-mail: sales@swiftsoft.com
Website: http://www.swiftsoft.com
Directors: K. Darragh (MD)
Immediate Holding Company: SWIFTSOFT COMPUTER SYSTEMS (NORTHERN IRELAND) LIMITED
Registration no: NI011531 **VAT No.:** GB 412 5389 64
Date established: 1976 **Turnover:** £250,000 - £500,000
No.of Employees: 1 - 10 **Product Groups:** 67

Date of Accounts	Mar 11	Mar 10	Mar 09
Working Capital	453	389	382
Fixed Assets	86	112	127
Current Assets	522	450	442

T P Topping Ltd
12 Dublin Road, Enniskillen, BT74 6HL
Tel: 028-6632 3475 **Fax:** 028-6632 3477
E-mail: info@tptopping.com
Website: http://www.tptopping.com
Bank(s): Northern Bank
Directors: P. Little (Prop)
Managers: H. Logan (Sales & Mktg Mg)
Immediate Holding Company: T.P. TOPPING & COMPANY LIMITED
Registration no: NI002996 **VAT No.:** GB 253 5227 72
Date established: 1951 **Turnover:** £5m - £10m **No.of Employees:** 21 - 50
Product Groups: 68

Date of Accounts	Nov 11	Nov 10	Nov 09
Working Capital	377	310	316
Fixed Assets	305	371	400
Current Assets	2m	2m	2m

Thomas Hanna & Co.
74 Main Street Brookeborough, Enniskillen, BT94 4FA
Tel: 028-8953 1373 **Fax:** 028-8953 1363
E-mail: info@thomashanna.co.uk
Website: http://www.thomashanna.co.uk
Directors: M. Hanna (Ptnr)
Immediate Holding Company: THOMAS HANNA & CO. LTD
Registration no: NI045650 **VAT No.:** 253 7707 48 **Date established:** 2003
Turnover: £1m - £2m **No.of Employees:** 1 - 10 **Product Groups:** 52

Date of Accounts	Mar 12	Mar 11	Mar 10
Working Capital	675	786	894
Fixed Assets	243	272	291
Current Assets	936	1m	1m

S Timoney & Sons
Mullanaskea, Enniskillen, BT74 4JQ
Tel: 028-6638 7394 **Fax:** 028-6632 4262
E-mail: enquiries@timoneywindows.com
Website: http://www.timoneywindows.com
Bank(s): First Trust
Directors: R. Timoney (Prop)
Turnover: £500,000 - £1m **No.of Employees:** 51 - 100
Product Groups: 30, 35, 49

Tracey Bros
Drumlyon House Drumlyon, Enniskillen, BT74 5TB
Tel: 028-6632 3471 **Fax:** 028-6632 3843
E-mail: info@traceyconcrete.com
Website: http://www.traceybrothers.com
Directors: J. Tracey (MD), P. McBrien (Fin)
Managers: M. Breen, R. Tracey (Tech Serv Mgr)
Immediate Holding Company: TRACEY BROTHERS LIMITED
Registration no: NI035032 **VAT No.:** GB 253 8370 58
Date established: 1998 **Turnover:** £10m - £20m
No.of Employees: 51 - 100 **Product Groups:** 52

Date of Accounts	Mar 11	Mar 10	Mar 09
Sales Turnover	19m	22m	30m
Pre Tax Profit/Loss	2m	1m	1m
Working Capital	8m	6m	6m
Fixed Assets	770	826	1m
Current Assets	16m	15m	16m
Current Liabilities	7m	7m	9m

Tracey Concrete Ltd
Old Rossory Road, Enniskillen, BT74 7LF
Tel: 028-6632 6437 **Fax:** 028-6632 4908
E-mail: headoffice@traceyconcrete.com
Website: http://www.traceyconcrete.com
Bank(s): First Trust
Directors: P. Tracey (MD)
Managers: C. Gallagher (Fin Mgr), M. Conlan (Sales Admin)
Immediate Holding Company: TRACEY CONCRETE LIMITED
Registration no: NI013514 **VAT No.:** GB 287 0897 07
Date established: 1979 **Turnover:** £5m - £10m
No.of Employees: 51 - 100 **Product Groups:** 33

Date of Accounts	Mar 11	Mar 10	Mar 09
Sales Turnover	7m	9m	N/A
Pre Tax Profit/Loss	-154	634	1m
Working Capital	6m	6m	6m
Fixed Assets	4m	4m	5m
Current Assets	7m	8m	8m
Current Liabilities	175	319	234

Ulster Farmers Mart Co. Ltd
The Agricultural Centre Lackaghboy, Enniskillen, BT74 4RL
Tel: 028-6632 2218 **Fax:** 028-6632 3606
E-mail: stuartjohnston41@yahoo.co.uk
Managers: S. Johnston (Mgr)
Immediate Holding Company: ULSTER FARMER'S MART COMPANY LIMITED
Registration no: NI002330 **Date established:** 1947
No.of Employees: 1 - 10 **Product Groups:** 07

Date of Accounts	Jun 11	Jun 10	Jun 09
Working Capital	-1m	-2m	-1m
Fixed Assets	12m	12m	4m
Current Assets	1m	935	956

Webtech Ni Ltd
Killyhevlin Industrial Estate Killyhevlin, Enniskillen, BT74 4EJ
Tel: 028-6632 5757 **Fax:** 028-6632 6231
E-mail: admin@webtechni.com
Website: http://www.webtechni.com
Directors: M. Harkness (Sales), N. Mcforley (MD)
Managers: R. Fox (Chief Acct), L. Murray (Mktg Serv Mgr), W. McKeown
Ultimate Holding Company: MARCHMONT PACKAGING EXPORTS LIMITED
Immediate Holding Company: WEBTECH (N.I.) LIMITED
Registration no: NI024109 **Date established:** 1990
No.of Employees: 101 - 250 **Product Groups:** 30

Date of Accounts	Dec 10	Dec 09	Dec 08
Pre Tax Profit/Loss	2m	1m	542
Working Capital	4m	3m	2m
Fixed Assets	4m	4m	5m
Current Assets	8m	6m	5m
Current Liabilities	1m	1m	895

Co. Tyrone

Fivemiletown

Cooneen Textiles Ltd
23 Cooneen Road, Fivemiletown, BT75 0NE
Tel: 028-8952 1401 **Fax:** 028-8952 1488
E-mail: info@cooneen.com
Website: http://www.cooneen.com
Directors: K. McMerhan (Fin), M. Coles (Sales & Mktg)
Managers: N. McGrath (Tech Serv Mgr), N. Mcilwrath (I.T. Exec), S. Gaynor (Personnel)
Ultimate Holding Company: COONEEN TEXTILES LIMITED
Immediate Holding Company: COONEEN TEXTILES LIMITED
Registration no: NI006648 **Date established:** 1966
Turnover: £75m - £125m **No.of Employees:** 51 - 100 **Product Groups:** 24

Date of Accounts	Nov 08	Nov 09	Nov 10
Sales Turnover	42m	41m	41m
Pre Tax Profit/Loss	4m	3m	4m
Working Capital	10m	12m	14m
Fixed Assets	1m	1m	1m
Current Assets	13m	15m	20m
Current Liabilities	458	2m	2m

Co. Down

Hillsborough

Advance Fasteners
Old Coach Road, Hillsborough, BT26 6PB
Tel: 028-9268 3578 **Fax:** 028-9268 3596
E-mail: advancefasteners@btconnect.com
Directors: H. Williamson (Dir)
Ultimate Holding Company: B.C. PLANT LIMITED
Immediate Holding Company: IRISH PLANT & HYDRAULICS LIMITED
Registration no: NI030961 **VAT No.:** GB 349 6216 35
Date established: 1970 **Turnover:** Up to £250,000
No.of Employees: 1 - 10 **Product Groups:** 39, 66

Andrew Ingredients Ltd
141 Dromore Road, Hillsborough, BT26 6JA
Tel: 028-9268 3030 **Fax:** 028-9268 3798
E-mail: timandrew@andrewingredients.co.uk
Website: http://www.andrewingredients.co.uk
Directors: T. Andrew (MD)
Managers: A. Harris (Sales Admin)
Immediate Holding Company: ANDREW INGREDIENTS LTD
Registration no: NI007639 **Date established:** 1969
No.of Employees: 21 - 50 **Product Groups:** 62

Armstrong Taylor
10 Lisburn Street, Hillsborough, BT26 6AB
Tel: 028-9268 0600 **Fax:** 028-9268 0601
E-mail: info@armstrongtaylor.co.uk
Website: http://www.armstrongtaylor.co.uk
Directors: R. Armstrong (Dir)
Date established: 1999 **No.of Employees:** 1 - 10 **Product Groups:** 35

B C Plant Ltd
Old Coach Road, Hillsborough, BT26 6PB
Tel: 028-9268 2573 **Fax:** 028-9268 2929
E-mail: alan.wiley@bcplantjcb.com
Website: http://www.bcpjcb.com

see next page

B C Plant Ltd - Cont'd

Managers: A. Wylie (Chief Acct)
Immediate Holding Company: B.C. PLANT LIMITED
Registration no: NI008439 **Date established:** 1971
Turnover: £10m - £20m **No.of Employees:** 51 - 100 **Product Groups:** 67

Date of Accounts	Oct 11	Oct 10	Oct 09
Sales Turnover	10m	9m	9m
Pre Tax Profit/Loss	-55	-232	-697
Working Capital	1m	1m	2m
Fixed Assets	122	149	197
Current Assets	4m	4m	4m
Current Liabilities	193	143	395

D J V Insulations Ltd

Dromore Road, Hillsborough, BT26 6HU
Tel: 028-9268 8686 **Fax:** 028-9268 8687
E-mail: inquiries@djvinsulations.com
Website: http://www.djvinsulations.com
Directors: D. Osborne (Dir)
Immediate Holding Company: DJV INSULATIONS LIMITED
Registration no: NI602834 **Date established:** 2010
No.of Employees: 21 - 50 **Product Groups:** 54

Date of Accounts	Apr 11
Working Capital	68
Fixed Assets	784
Current Assets	481

Industrial Packaging Services

26 Harrys Road, Hillsborough, BT26 6HJ
Tel: 028-9268 9755 **Fax:** 028-9268 9749
E-mail: ips@utvinternet.com
Website: http://www.utvinternet.com
Directors: J. Mckee (Prop)
Immediate Holding Company: WEBRO ENGINEERING LIMITED
Registration no: NI018446 **Date established:** 1985
No.of Employees: 1 - 10 **Product Groups:** 38, 42

Jacobs Ltd

3, Hillsborough, BT26 6JU
Tel: 028-9268 2644 **Fax:** 028-9266 3804
E-mail: info@ibni.freeserve.co.uk
Website: http://www.jacobsbiscuits.com
Directors: B. Maloret (MD), B. Taylor (MD), M. Taylor (MD)
Managers: B. Smith (Mktg Serv Mgr)
Immediate Holding Company: JACOBS U.K. LTD
Registration no: SC062616 **VAT No.:** GB 286 8082 18
No.of Employees: 21 - 50 **Product Groups:** 62

Lagan Valley Steel Ltd

10 Aghnatrisk Road, Hillsborough, BT26 6JJ
Tel: 028-9268 0900 **Fax:** 028-9268 9993
E-mail: tommya@lvsteels.com
Website: http://www.lvsteels.com
Directors: T. Anderson (MD), T. Anderson (MD)
Immediate Holding Company: LAGAN VALLEY STEELS LIMITED
Registration no: NI011660 **VAT No.:** GB 412 6801 79
Date established: 1976 **Turnover:** £10m - £20m
No.of Employees: 21 - 50 **Product Groups:** 34, 36, 66

Date of Accounts	Mar 11	Mar 10	Mar 09
Sales Turnover	11m	8m	N/A
Pre Tax Profit/Loss	455	329	356
Working Capital	3m	3m	4m
Fixed Assets	2m	2m	853
Current Assets	7m	6m	6m
Current Liabilities	205	104	332

Lilburn Contracts

103 Culcavy Road, Hillsborough, BT26 6HH
Tel: 028-9268 3283 **Fax:** 028-9268 9785
E-mail: info@lilburncontracts.com
Website: http://www.lilburncontracts.com
Bank(s): Bank of Ireland
Directors: T. Lilburn (MD), A. Lilburn (Ptnr), D. Currie (Ptnr)
Immediate Holding Company: LEWIS TOWER CRANE SERVICES LTD
VAT No.: 252 9892 23 **Date established:** 2010 **Turnover:** £1m - £2m
No.of Employees: 11 - 20 **Product Groups:** 52

N I Food Equipment Co.

Old Coach Road, Hillsborough, BT26 6PB
Tel: 028-9268 9590 **Fax:** 028-9268 9525
E-mail: mifoodequipment@btconnect.com
Directors: N. Boyd (Prop)
Ultimate Holding Company: B.C. PLANT LIMITED
Immediate Holding Company: IRISH PLANT & HYDRAULICS LIMITED
Registration no: NI030961 **Date established:** 1970
No.of Employees: 1 - 10 **Product Groups:** 20, 40, 41

R J R Crop Driers

40 Ballygowan Road, Hillsborough, BT26 6EJ
Tel: 028-9268 9004 **Fax:** 028-9268 2968
Directors: R. Robinson (Prop)
Date established: 1988 **No.of Employees:** 1 - 10 **Product Groups:** 41

Rainbow Signs & Maintenance

8 Ballykeel Road, Hillsborough, BT26 6NW
Tel: 028-9263 8653 **Fax:** 028-9263 9129
E-mail: leont@rainbow-signs.co.uk
Website: http://www.rainbowsigns.co.uk
Directors: I. Greer (Prop)
VAT No.: GB 331 3346 92 **Date established:** 1986 **Turnover:** £1m - £2m
No.of Employees: 11 - 20 **Product Groups:** 37, 49

Snoddons Construction Ltd

10 Ballynahinch Street, Hillsborough, BT26 6AW
Tel: 028-9268 2866 **Fax:** 028-9268 3496
E-mail: sales@snoddonsconstructionltd.co.uk
Website: http://www.snoddonsconstructionltd.co.uk
Directors: S. Harris (Dir)
Immediate Holding Company: SNODDONS CONSTRUCTION LIMITED
Registration no: NI008584 **VAT No.:** GB 253 1539 73
Date established: 1972 **Turnover:** £5m - £10m **No.of Employees:** 1 - 10
Product Groups: 52

Date of Accounts	Mar 11	Mar 10	Mar 09
Working Capital	2m	12m	12m
Fixed Assets	189	193	201
Current Assets	2m	12m	15m

Sound Control

32 Culcavy Road, Hillsborough, BT26 6JD
Tel: 028-9268 8060 **Fax:** 028-9268 9279
E-mail: info@soundcon.co.uk
Website: http://www.soundcon.com
Directors: J. Connelly (Prop)
Immediate Holding Company: SOUND CONTROL HOLDINGS LTD
Registration no: SC242214 **Turnover:** £1m - £2m
No.of Employees: 1 - 10 **Product Groups:** 54

Spence Engineering Ltd

67 Tullynore Road, Hillsborough, BT26 6QE
Tel: 028-9268 2435 **Fax:** 028-9268 9045
E-mail: paul@spenceengineering.co.uk
Website: http://www.spenceengineering.co.uk
Directors: P. Spence (Dir)
Immediate Holding Company: SPENCE ENGINEERING LIMITED
Registration no: NI011833 **VAT No.:** GB 286 8651 05
Date established: 1977 **No.of Employees:** 1 - 10 **Product Groups:** 45

Date of Accounts	Mar 12	Mar 11	Mar 10
Working Capital	265	231	204
Fixed Assets	493	458	455
Current Assets	354	303	280

Co. Down

Holywood

Ardmore Advertising & Marketing

Ardmore House Kinnegar Drive, Holywood, BT18 9JQ
Tel: 028-9042 5344 **Fax:** 028-9042 4823
E-mail: john.keane@ardmore.co.uk
Website: http://www.ardmore.co.uk
Directors: J. Keane (MD), T. Craig (Fin)
Managers: N. Dornan
Immediate Holding Company: ARDMORE ADVERTISING & MARKETING LIMITED
Registration no: NI022062 **Date established:** 1988
Turnover: Up to £250,000 **No.of Employees:** 21 - 50 **Product Groups:** 81

Date of Accounts	Oct 11	Oct 10	Oct 09
Working Capital	104	13	32
Fixed Assets	197	187	196
Current Assets	3m	3m	2m

Business Micro Systems

3 Carlston Avenue, Holywood, BT18 0NF
Tel: 028-9042 4366 **Fax:** 028-9042 5031
E-mail: chris@businessmicrosystems.co.uk
Website: http://www.businessmicrosystems.co.uk
Directors: C. Boyd (Prop)
VAT No.: GB 311 3858 79 **Turnover:** Up to £250,000
No.of Employees: 1 - 10 **Product Groups:** 44

Denis Lavelle & Associates Ltd

29 Shore Road, Holywood, BT18 9HX
Tel: 028-9042 5114 **Fax:** 028-9042 3068
Directors: D. Lavelle (Dir), D. Lavelle (MD)
Managers: N. McGuinness (Sec)
Registration no: NI026876 **VAT No.:** GB 255 5426 54
Date established: 1992 **Turnover:** Up to £250,000
No.of Employees: 1 - 10 **Product Groups:** 84

Dingles Builders Ltd

14 Downshire Road, Holywood, BT18 9LX
Tel: 028-9042 4252 **Fax:** 028-9042 8329
E-mail: info@dinglesbuilders.co.uk
Website: http://www.dinglesbuilders.co.uk
Directors: D. Clulow (Comm)
Ultimate Holding Company: KATHLEEN AND MICHAEL CONNOLLY FOUNDATION (UK) LIMITED
Immediate Holding Company: DINGLES BUILDERS (N.I.) LIMITED
Registration no: NI010800 **VAT No.:** GB 286 6207 34
Date established: 1975 **Turnover:** £2m - £5m **No.of Employees:** 1 - 10
Product Groups: 52, 80

Date of Accounts	May 11	May 10	May 09
Sales Turnover	4m	7m	6m
Pre Tax Profit/Loss	16	347	-833
Working Capital	5m	5m	4m
Fixed Assets	31	854	850
Current Assets	11m	11m	14m
Current Liabilities	706	817	987

Grainger Building Services Ltd

163 Church Road, Holywood, BT18 9BZ
Tel: 028-9042 2555 **Fax:** 028-9042 5428
E-mail: info@grainger-uk.com
Website: http://www.grainger-uk.com
Bank(s): Northern Bank
Directors: C. Pegg (MD), D. Wylde (Comm), N. Jackson (Fin)
Ultimate Holding Company: BALLYKEEL DEVELOPMENTS LIMITED
Immediate Holding Company: GRAINGER BUILDING SERVICES LIMITED
Registration no: NI010297 **VAT No.:** GB 256 0316 80
Date established: 1974 **Turnover:** £10m - £20m
No.of Employees: 21 - 50 **Product Groups:** 52

Date of Accounts	Dec 11	Dec 10	Dec 09
Sales Turnover	17m	13m	14m
Pre Tax Profit/Loss	-3m	-798	118
Working Capital	780	1m	2m
Fixed Assets	25	81	113
Current Assets	2m	3m	4m
Current Liabilities	512	416	575

Hobart Heron Architects

140 High Street, Holywood, BT18 9HS
Tel: 028-9042 3333 **Fax:** 028-9042 6161
Website: http://www.hobartheron.com
Directors: B. Gorden (Ptnr), A. Hull (Ptnr)
Managers: B. Hobart (Consultant)
Registration no: NI044176 **VAT No.:** GB 251 4941 47
Date established: 1890 **No.of Employees:** 11 - 20 **Product Groups:** 84

Internet Business Ltd

Holywood House 1 Innis Court, Holywood, BT18 9HF
Tel: 028-9042 4190 **Fax:** 028-9042 4709
E-mail: info@tibus.com
Website: http://www.tibus.net
Directors: G. Dunlop (Dir)
Ultimate Holding Company: NI065086
Immediate Holding Company: INTERNET BUSINESS LIMITED-THE
Registration no: NI031235 **Date established:** 1996 **Turnover:** £2m - £5m
No.of Employees: 21 - 50 **Product Groups:** 44, 79, 81

Mccready's Sailboats Ltd

2 Priory Park, Holywood, BT18 0LG
Tel: 028-9042 1821 **Fax:** 028-9042 2998
E-mail: w.mccready@mccreadysailboats.co.uk
Website: http://www.mccreadysailboats.co.uk
Directors: W. Mccready (Dir)
Immediate Holding Company: MCCREADY SAILBOATS LIMITED
Registration no: NI005834 **VAT No.:** GB 252 7996 21
Date established: 1964 **Turnover:** £500,000 - £1m
No.of Employees: 1 - 10 **Product Groups:** 63, 74

Date of Accounts	Sep 11	Sep 10	Sep 09
Working Capital	173	156	190
Fixed Assets	83	90	37
Current Assets	223	227	257

Moore Macdonald & Partners

2 High Street, Holywood, BT18 9AZ
Tel: 028-9042 7178 **Fax:** 028-9042 2889
E-mail: bqs@surveyorsmooremcd.co.uk
Website: http://www.surveyorsmooremcd.co.uk
Directors: D. Murray (Dir)
Date established: 1966 **Turnover:** Up to £250,000
No.of Employees: 1 - 10 **Product Groups:** 80

Morrow Communications Ltd

Hanwood House Kinnegar Drive, Holywood, BT18 9JQ
Tel: 028-9039 3837 **Fax:** 028-9039 3830
E-mail: mail@morrowcommunications.com
Website: http://www.morrowcommunications.com
Bank(s): Northern Bank
Directors: P. Morrow (MD)
Managers: A. Alexander
Immediate Holding Company: MORROW COMMUNICATIONS LIMITED
Registration no: NI018741 **VAT No.:** GB 422 2462 88
Date established: 1985 **Turnover:** £500,000 - £1m
No.of Employees: 11 - 20 **Product Groups:** 81

Date of Accounts	Mar 11	Mar 10	Mar 09
Working Capital	76	104	159
Fixed Assets	636	650	665
Current Assets	425	553	747

Mouchel

Shorefield House Kinnegar Drive, Holywood, BT18 9JQ
Tel: 028-9042 4117 **Fax:** 028-9042 7039
E-mail: info@mouchel.com
Website: http://www.mouchel.com
Directors: M. Carlisle (Dir)
Immediate Holding Company: Mouchel Parkman (NI) Limited
Registration no: NI021928 **VAT No.:** GB 166 0999 27
Date established: 1988 **No.of Employees:** 51 - 100 **Product Groups:** 84

Steria

Pavillions Office Park Kinnegar Drive, Holywood, BT18 9JQ
Tel: 028-9039 3700 **Fax:** 028-9039 3729
E-mail: info@steria.co.uk
Website: http://www.steria.co.uk
Directors: J. Torrie (Grp Chief Exec)
Immediate Holding Company: STERIA LIMITED
Registration no: NF004262 **VAT No.:** GB 453 0499 48
Date established: 2008 **Turnover:** £2m - £5m **No.of Employees:** 1 - 10
Product Groups: 44, 67

Ulster Folk & Transport Museum

153 Bangor Road, Holywood, BT18 0EU
Tel: 028-9042 8428 **Fax:** 028-9042 8728
E-mail: tim.cooke@magni.org.uk
Website: http://www.nmni.com
Directors: J. Helliker (Pers)
Managers: G. Kenloch (Tech Serv Mgr), T. Cooke, G. McLean, J. Sloan
Turnover: £500,000 - £1m **No.of Employees:** 101 - 250
Product Groups: 69

Ulster Weavers Home Fashions

Unit 1-6 St Helens Business Park, Holywood, BT18 9HQ
Tel: 028-9032 9494 **Fax:** 028-9032 6612
E-mail: sales@ulsterweavers.com
Website: http://www.ulsterweavers.com
Directors: M. Reid (Fin), M. Mullen (Tech Serv), P. Kirkwood (Chief Op Offcr), W. Hamilton (Sales), M. Mullen (Fin)
Managers: G. Bleakley (Transport), A. Laird (Personnel)
Ultimate Holding Company: JOHN HOGG & CO. LIMITED
Immediate Holding Company: ULSTER WEAVERS HOME FASHIONS LIMITED
Registration no: R0000751 **VAT No.:** GB 311 2152 27
Date established: 1998 **Turnover:** £2m - £5m **No.of Employees:** 21 - 50
Product Groups: 23, 24, 30

Date of Accounts	Apr 12	Apr 11	Apr 10
Sales Turnover	N/A	2m	7m
Pre Tax Profit/Loss	N/A	191	408
Working Capital	3m	3m	2m
Fixed Assets	25	25	97
Current Assets	3m	3m	4m
Current Liabilities	N/A	56	324

Co. Antrim

Larne

A C J Trading

49 Low Road Islandmagee, Larne, BT40 3RD
Tel: 07854-892147
Website: http://www.acjwindturbines.co.uk

Directors: A. Marsden (Prop)
No.of Employees: 1 - 10 **Product Groups:** 36

Abbey Insulation Ltd
Unit 5 Redlands Coastguard Road, Larne, BT40 1AX
Tel: 028-2827 0319 **Fax:** 028-9042 7641
E-mail: sales@warmfill.com
Website: http://www.abbeyinsulation.co.uk
Directors: B. Mccrea (MD)
Managers: T. Knocker (Sales Prom Mgr)
Immediate Holding Company: ABBEY INSULATION LTD
Registration no: NI026088 **VAT No.:** GB 617 7380 26
Date established: 1991 **No.of Employees:** 11 - 20 **Product Groups:** 30, 52, 84

Date of Accounts	Oct 11	Oct 10	Oct 09
Working Capital	218	209	149
Fixed Assets	14	11	90
Current Assets	443	914	1m

Anvil Engineering
48 Ballyrickard Road, Larne, BT40 3EQ
Tel: 028-2827 7350 **Fax:** 028-2827 7350
E-mail: a-prop@utvinternet.com
Directors: J. Anderson (Prop)
VAT No.: GB 432 6542 63 **Date established:** 1983
Turnover: Up to £250,000 **No.of Employees:** 1 - 10 **Product Groups:** 39, 48

Ballyloran Trailer Repairs Ltd
Ballyboley Road, Larne, BT40 2SY
Tel: 028-2826 0264 **Fax:** 028-2826 0018
E-mail: ballyloran@btconnect.com
Bank(s): Bank of Ireland
Directors: J. Craig (Dir)
Immediate Holding Company: BALLYLORAN TRAILER REPAIRS LIMITED
Registration no: NI021032 **VAT No.:** GB 432 7816 47
Date established: 1987 **Turnover:** £500,000 - £1m
No.of Employees: 11 - 20 **Product Groups:** 39

Date of Accounts	Jun 11	Jun 10	Jun 09
Working Capital	367	365	463
Fixed Assets	500	513	446
Current Assets	667	803	785

John Craig Haulage
Ballyboley Road, Larne, BT40 2SY
Tel: 028-2826 0264 **Fax:** 028-2826 0018
E-mail: ballyloran@btconnect.com
Bank(s): Bank of Ireland
Directors: J. Craig (Dir)
Managers: P. Divine (Fin Mgr)
Immediate Holding Company: BALLYLORAN TRAILER REPAIRS LIMITED
Registration no: NI021032 **VAT No.:** GB 254 2445 71
Date established: 1987 **Turnover:** Up to £250,000
No.of Employees: 11 - 20 **Product Groups:** 72

Date of Accounts	Jun 11	Jun 10	Jun 09
Working Capital	367	365	463
Fixed Assets	500	513	446
Current Assets	667	803	785

Ivex Pharmaceuticals
Old Belfast Road Millbrook, Larne, BT40 2SH
Tel: 028-2827 3631 **Fax:** 028-2827 3719
E-mail: info@ivex.co.uk
Website: http://www.ivex.co.uk
Bank(s): Bank of Ireland
Directors: S. Brunt (Fin), J. Mckelvey (MD)
Managers: J. Armstrong, Y. Irvine (Personnel), C. Oslahergy (Tech Serv Mgr), J. Beggs (Sales & Mktg Mg)
Ultimate Holding Company: WARNER CHILCOTT HOLDINGS COMPANY LIMITED (BERMUDA)
Immediate Holding Company: WARNER CHILCOTT UK LIMITED
Registration no: NI023272 **VAT No.:** GB 575 4885 86
Date established: 1989 **Turnover:** £5m - £10m
No.of Employees: 101 - 250 **Product Groups:** 63

Date of Accounts	Dec 11	Dec 10	Dec 09
Sales Turnover	61m	65m	15m
Pre Tax Profit/Loss	3m	5m	2m
Working Capital	16m	13m	3m
Fixed Assets	45m	45m	44m
Current Assets	36m	47m	7m
Current Liabilities	5m	9m	3m

J Iong & Son
10A Upper Cairncastle Road, Larne, BT40 2DT
Tel: 028-2827 5980 **Fax:** 028-2827 5980
E-mail: info@jlongandson.com
Website: http://www.jlongandson.com
Directors: J. Iong (Dir)
Registration no: NI071661 **Date established:** 2009
Turnover: £500,000 - £1m **No.of Employees:** 1 - 10 **Product Groups:** 14, 33

R J F Jennings Bakery
52-55 Curran Road, Larne, BT40 1BU
Tel: 028-2826 0508 **Fax:** 028-2827 9776
E-mail: djenni7710@aol.com
Website: http://www.butterflybuns.co.uk
Bank(s): Ulster Bank
Directors: S. Jennings (Prop)
Managers: J. Hughes (Chief Mgr)
Immediate Holding Company: RJF JENNINGS BAKERY LIMITED
Registration no: NI042869 **VAT No.:** GB 432 5301 90
Date established: 2002 **Turnover:** £1m - £2m **No.of Employees:** 21 - 50
Product Groups: 20

Date of Accounts	Jul 12	Jul 11	Jul 10
Working Capital	343	420	397
Fixed Assets	431	453	490
Current Assets	703	679	737

Kilwaughter Chemical Co. Ltd
Kilwaughter Lime Works 9 Starbog Road, Kilwaughter, Larne, BT40 2TJ
Tel: 028-2826 0766 **Fax:** 028-2826 0136
E-mail: sales@kilwaughter.com
Website: http://www.kilwaughter.com
Bank(s): Ulster Bank
Directors: S. Mcdowell (MD)
Managers: G. Cumberland (Sales Prom Mgr), G. Evans (Personnel), J. Bonugli (Tech Serv Mgr), F. Moorcroft (Chief Acct), L. Blair (Mktg Serv Mgr)
Immediate Holding Company: KILWAUGHTER CHEMICAL COMPANY LIMITED
Registration no: NI001351 **VAT No.:** GB 255 7995 23
Date established: 1939 **Turnover:** £10m - £20m
No.of Employees: 101 - 250 **Product Groups:** 14, 33, 45

Date of Accounts	Apr 11	Apr 10	Apr 09
Sales Turnover	18m	17m	22m
Pre Tax Profit/Loss	4m	4m	1m
Working Capital	13m	10m	8m
Fixed Assets	22m	22m	23m
Current Assets	16m	13m	14m
Current Liabilities	2m	2m	4m

Lambda Technical Services Ltd
65 Ballylumford Road Islandmagee, Larne, BT40 3RN
Tel: 028-9338 2777
E-mail: sales@lambdats.co.uk
Website: http://www.lambdats.co.uk
Directors: B. Garner (MD)
Immediate Holding Company: LAMBDA TECHNICAL SERVICES LIMITED
Registration no: NI053599 **Date established:** 2005
Turnover: Up to £250,000 **No.of Employees:** 1 - 10 **Product Groups:** 27, 44

Date of Accounts	Dec 09	Dec 08	Mar 11
Working Capital	9	3	9
Fixed Assets	2	2	2
Current Assets	15	10	21

Larne Borough Council
Smiley Buildings Victoria Road, Larne, BT40 1RU
Tel: 028-2827 2313 **Fax:** 028-2826 0660
E-mail: mcgaheyg@larne.gov.uk
Website: http://www.larne.gov.uk
Directors: G. Mcgahey (Grp Chief Exec)
No.of Employees: 21 - 50 **Product Groups:** 87

Longmore Electronics
97 Old Glenarm Road, Larne, BT40 1NQ
Tel: 028-2827 0707 **Fax:** 028-2827 7278
E-mail: michael@longmoreelectronics.com
Website: http://www.longmoreelectronics.com
Directors: M. Longmore (MD)
Immediate Holding Company: LONGMORE ELECTRONICS LIMITED
Registration no: NI028310 **VAT No.:** GB 349 7427 17
Date established: 1994 **Turnover:** Up to £250,000
No.of Employees: 1 - 10 **Product Groups:** 48, 52

Date of Accounts	Mar 11	Mar 10	Mar 09
Working Capital	229	229	78
Fixed Assets	1	63	127
Current Assets	367	432	373

John Mcloughlin & Son Shipping Ltd
North End Larne Harbour, Larne, BT40 1AJ
Tel: 028-2827 3785 **Fax:** 028-2826 0382
E-mail: j@johnmcloughlinshipping.co.uk
Website: http://www.johnmcloughlinshipping.co.uk
Directors: J. Mcloughlin (MD), D. Lavery (Fin)
Managers: A. Tasker (Mktg Serv Mgr), D. Beck (Personnel)
Immediate Holding Company: JOHN MCLOUGHLIN & SON (SHIPPING) LIMITED
Registration no: NI013603 **Date established:** 1979 **Turnover:** £1m - £2m
No.of Employees: 21 - 50 **Product Groups:** 74

Date of Accounts	Mar 12	Mar 11	Mar 10
Working Capital	-190	-407	-501
Fixed Assets	1m	1m	1m
Current Assets	577	227	224

P & O Ferrymasters Ltd
2a Redlands Estate Port Business Park, Larne, BT40 1FF
Tel: 028-2887 1500 **Fax:** 028-2887 1516
E-mail: harry.mcveigh@pofm.com
Website: http://www.poferrymasters.com
Bank(s): Northern Bank
Managers: H. Mcveigh (Chief Mgr)
Ultimate Holding Company: DUBAI WORLD CORPORATION (DUBAI)
Immediate Holding Company: P&O FERRYMASTERS LIMITED
Registration no: NI004115 **Date established:** 1958
Turnover: £250m - £500m **No.of Employees:** 11 - 20 **Product Groups:** 72

Date of Accounts	Dec 11	Dec 10	Dec 09
Sales Turnover	434m	425m	410m
Pre Tax Profit/Loss	430	-2m	-1m
Working Capital	9m	9m	7m
Fixed Assets	5m	5m	7m
Current Assets	85m	90m	86m
Current Liabilities	5m	6m	6m

Polysorb Art
Unit 2 Curran Point Coastguard Road, Larne, BT40 1AU
Tel: 0333-7001881 **Fax:** 028-2827 5105
E-mail: polysorb@btconnect.com
Website: http://www.polysorb.net
Directors: W. Brines (Ptnr)
Managers: A. Brines (Mgr)
VAT No.: GB 516 7386 28 **Date established:** 1990
Turnover: £250,000 - £500,000 **No.of Employees:** 1 - 10
Product Groups: 29, 32, 38

Safety Service Agency
Unit 52 Ledcom Industrial Estate Bank Road, Larne, BT40 3AW
Tel: 028-2827 6609 **Fax:** 028-2826 0648
E-mail: sales@ssani.co.uk
Website: http://www.ssani.co.uk
Directors: J. Robinson (MD)
VAT No.: GB 432 6777 36 **Date established:** 1980
Turnover: Up to £250,000 **No.of Employees:** 1 - 10 **Product Groups:** 67

Slate N I
1 Carson Street, Larne, BT40 1SF
Tel: 028-2827 2200 **Fax:** 028-28 273900
E-mail: sales@slateni.com
Website: http://www.slateni.com
Directors: P. Mccullough (Prop)
No.of Employees: 1 - 10 **Product Groups:** 14, 33, 35, 52, 66

M G Stitt Marine Services
195 Gobbins Road Islandmagee, Larne, BT40 3TX
Tel: 028-9338 2278 **Fax:** 028-9338 2666
E-mail: martin@stittmarine.com
Website: http://www.stittmarine.com
Directors: M. Stitt (Ptnr)
VAT No.: GB 393 6088 19 **Date established:** 1981
No.of Employees: 1 - 10 **Product Groups:** 48, 68

Topping Meats
15 Old Belfast Road Millbrook, Larne, BT40 2SH
Tel: 028-2827 9217 **Fax:** 028-2826 0296
E-mail: atopping20@hotmail.com
Bank(s): Ulster Bank
Directors: T. Topping (Prop)
VAT No.: GB 311 2675 92 **Date established:** 1980
No.of Employees: 11 - 20 **Product Groups:** 20

F G Wilson Engineering Ltd
Old Glenarm Road, Larne, BT40 1EJ
Tel: 028-2826 1000 **Fax:** 028-2826 1111
E-mail: marksweeney@fgwilson.co.uk
Website: http://www.fgwilson.com
Directors: N. Jones (Pers), M. Sweeney (MD)
Managers: B. Sonnemaker (Tech Serv Mgr)
Ultimate Holding Company: CATERPILLAR INC (USA)
Immediate Holding Company: FG Wilson (Engineering) Limited
Registration no: NI006692 **Date established:** 1966
Turnover: £500m - £1,000m **No.of Employees:** 1001 - 1500
Product Groups: 37, 38, 44, 52, 83

Date of Accounts	Dec 11	Dec 10	Dec 09
Sales Turnover	771m	654m	555m
Pre Tax Profit/Loss	-5m	8m	4m
Working Capital	59m	57m	52m
Fixed Assets	84m	91m	85m
Current Assets	203m	206m	142m
Current Liabilities	28m	23m	9m

Co. Londonderry

Limavady

Arbarr Electronics
Unit 3 Aghanloo Industrial Estate Aghanloo Road, Limavady, BT49 0HE
Tel: 028-7776 6611 **Fax:** 028-9442 6178
E-mail: johnpaul@arbarr.co.uk
Website: http://www.arbarr.co.uk
Directors: J. McCawley (MD), J. Mccorley (MD)
Managers: M. McCollum, C. McNichol
Immediate Holding Company: L M GLAZING LIMITED
Registration no: NI025382 **Date established:** 2002
No.of Employees: 11 - 20 **Product Groups:** 37, 67, 84

Date of Accounts	Mar 11	Mar 10	Mar 09
Working Capital	11	15	-21
Fixed Assets	91	79	75
Current Assets	268	153	84

Canning Properties
6-8 Ballyclose Street, Limavady, BT49 0BN
Tel: 028-7776 2442 **Fax:** 028-7772 2414
Directors: J. Canning (Prop)
Turnover: Up to £250,000 **No.of Employees:** 1 - 10 **Product Groups:** 80

Country Stoves
Ardnargle, Limavady, BT49 9DW
Tel: 028-7776 2105 **Fax:** 028-7776 3321
Directors: H. Boyle (Prop)
No.of Employees: 1 - 10 **Product Groups:** 40

Drenagh Sawmills Ltd
89 Dowland Road, Limavady, BT49 0HR
Tel: 028-7776 5611 **Fax:** 028-7776 5984
E-mail: m@drenagh.co.uk
Website: http://www.drenagh.co.uk
Directors: M. Mckeever (MD), E. O'Connor (Fin)
Managers: L. Hamilton (Personnel), P. Higgins (Sales Prom Mgr)
Immediate Holding Company: DRENAGH SAWMILLS LIMITED
Registration no: NI010241 **VAT No.:** GB 282 9446 25
Date established: 1974 **Turnover:** £5m - £10m **No.of Employees:** 21 - 50
Product Groups: 25, 66

Date of Accounts	Mar 11	Mar 10	Mar 09
Sales Turnover	N/A	7m	6m
Pre Tax Profit/Loss	N/A	468	460
Working Capital	2m	3m	1m
Fixed Assets	5m	7m	5m
Current Assets	6m	5m	5m
Current Liabilities	N/A	800	498

Fire-Care Ltd
72 Tartnakilly Road, Limavady, BT49 9NA
Tel: 028-7776 4002 **Fax:** 028-7176 4002
Website: http://www.fire-care.co.uk
Directors: C. Toner (MD)
Immediate Holding Company: FIRECARE LIMITED
Registration no: NI032461 **Date established:** 1997
No.of Employees: 1 - 10 **Product Groups:** 67

Date of Accounts	Mar 11	Mar 10	Mar 09
Working Capital	-2	2	7
Fixed Assets	8	10	11
Current Assets	11	14	17

D A Forgie
16 Seacoast Road, Limavady, BT49 9DW
Tel: 028-7772 2375 **Fax:** 028-7776 6540
E-mail: d.forgie@forgie.com
Website: http://www.forgie.com
Directors: D. Forgie (Prop)
Immediate Holding Company: D.A. Forgie Ltd
Registration no: NI043932 **VAT No.:** GB 256 1782 46
Date established: 2002 **No.of Employees:** 1 - 10 **Product Groups:** 67

Huco Lightronic Ni Ltd
Limavady Industrial Park 89 Dowland Road, Limavady, BT49 0HR
Tel: 028-7776 8567 **Fax:** 028-7776 8515
E-mail: n.hunter@bagelectronics.com
Website: http://www.huco.co.uk
Directors: N. Hunter (Dir), W. Donaghy (MD)
Managers: E. McGregor (Mgr), L. Pyne (Tech Sales Mgr), R. Wallace (I.T. Exec)

see next page

***Huco Lightronic Ni Ltd** - Cont'd*

Immediate Holding Company: HUCO LIGHTRONIC N.I. LIMITED
Registration no: NI022167 **VAT No.:** GB 516 6320 63
Date established: 1988 **Turnover:** £5m - £10m **No.of Employees:** 1 - 10
Product Groups: 37

Limavady Printing Company Ltd

22 Windyhill Road, Limavady, BT49 0JW
Tel: 028-7776 2051 **Fax:** 028-7776 2132
E-mail: sales@limprint.com
Website: http://www.limprint.com
Directors: J. O'Brien (MD), P. O'brien (Dir), S. Rogers (MD)
Managers: J. Wilson (Chief Acct), Y. Love (Personnel)
Immediate Holding Company: LIMAVADY PRINTING COMPANY LIMITED
Registration no: NI010217 **VAT No.:** GB 311 1251 30
Date established: 1974 **Turnover:** £2m - £5m **No.of Employees:** 51 - 100
Product Groups: 28

Date of Accounts	Mar 11	Mar 10	Mar 09
Sales Turnover	4m	4m	N/A
Pre Tax Profit/Loss	-341	41	178
Working Capital	-2m	-1m	-1m
Fixed Assets	2m	3m	3m
Current Assets	934	933	948
Current Liabilities	188	189	686

Mccloskey & O'Kane Building Co. Ltd

16 Windyhill Road, Limavady, BT49 0RA
Tel: 028-7772 2711 **Fax:** 028-7776 8505
E-mail: info@mcok.co.uk
Website: http://www.mccloskeyandokane.com
Bank(s): Northern Bank
Directors: N. Brown (MD), S. Mccloskey (Dir), S. McCluskey (MD)
Managers: F. Busby (Fin Mgr)
Ultimate Holding Company: McC & O'K Group Limited
Immediate Holding Company: MCCLOSKEY AND O'KANE BUILDING COMPANY LIMITED
Registration no: NI010142 **VAT No.:** 256 1058 71 **Date established:** 1974
Turnover: £5m - £10m **No.of Employees:** 21 - 50 **Product Groups:** 52

Date of Accounts	Dec 11	Dec 10	Dec 09
Pre Tax Profit/Loss	N/A	N/A	-575
Working Capital	45m	48m	48m
Fixed Assets	737	797	712
Current Assets	48m	50m	49m
Current Liabilities	N/A	N/A	816

North West Independant Hospital

Churchill House Main Street Ballykelly, Limavady, BT49 9HS
Tel: 028-7776 3090 **Fax:** 028-7776 8306
E-mail: info@nwih.co.uk
Website: http://www.nwih.co.uk
Bank(s): Northern Bank
Managers: P. Dallas
Registration no: NI012508 **Date established:** 1989
No.of Employees: 51 - 100 **Product Groups:** 88

Northern Ceramics Ltd

58 Drumsurn Road, Limavady, BT49 0PD
Tel: 028-7776 2839 **Fax:** 028-7776 2839
Directors: B. McClusky (Prop)
No.of Employees: 1 - 10 **Product Groups:** 25, 33, 35

Paragon Tiles Ltd

90 Tartnakilly Road, Limavady, BT49 9NA
Tel: 028-7776 6248 **Fax:** 028-7776 3007
E-mail: sales@paragontiles.com
Website: http://www.paragontiles.com
Directors: J. Tracey (Dir)
Immediate Holding Company: PARAGON TILES LIMITED
Registration no: NI017448 **VAT No.:** GB 393 5880 08
Date established: 1984 **Turnover:** £1m - £2m **No.of Employees:** 1 - 10
Product Groups: 33

Date of Accounts	Mar 11	Mar 10	Mar 09
Working Capital	217	285	418
Fixed Assets	128	143	153
Current Assets	368	450	564

St John's Foundry Limavady Ltd

17 Drumsurn Road Drummond, Limavady, BT49 0PD
Tel: 028-7776 2710 **Fax:** 028-7776 6990
Directors: M. Forest (Dir), J. Scott (MD)
Managers: J. Kriscadden (Sales Admin)
Immediate Holding Company: ST JOHN'S FOUNDRY (LIMAVADY) LIMITED
Registration no: NI017542 **VAT No.:** GB 393 6413 34
Date established: 1984 **No.of Employees:** 1 - 10 **Product Groups:** 35, 36, 45

Date of Accounts	Feb 11	Feb 10	Feb 09
Working Capital	-15	18	22
Fixed Assets	34	35	38
Current Assets	52	94	111

Co. Antrim

Lisburn

A B B

Unit 24 Blaris Industrial Estate Altona Road, Lisburn, BT27 5QB
Tel: 028-9260 3500 **Fax:** 028-9260 3484
Website: http://www.abb.com
Managers: W. Davidson (Mgr)
No.of Employees: 1 - 10 **Product Groups:** 37, 38

Date of Accounts	Dec 11	Dec 10	Dec 09
Sales Turnover	540m	499m	476m
Pre Tax Profit/Loss	39m	16m	13m
Working Capital	78m	139m	104m
Fixed Assets	76m	63m	62m
Current Assets	286m	342m	276m
Current Liabilities	151m	148m	122m

A & B Pneumatics

117 Halftown Road, Lisburn, BT27 5RF
Tel: 028-9268 3440 **Fax:** 028-9268 3440
E-mail: peter@abpneumatics.com
Website: http://www.abpneumatics.com
Directors: P. Blair (Dir)
Ultimate Holding Company: DONUT LTD
Immediate Holding Company: A & B PNEUMATICS LIMITED
Registration no: NI055332 **VAT No.:** GB 390 7756 17
Date established: 2005 **Turnover:** £500,000 - £1m
No.of Employees: 1 - 10 **Product Groups:** 29, 35, 40, 43

Date of Accounts	Dec 11	Dec 10	Dec 09
Working Capital	70	33	-24
Fixed Assets	26	23	42
Current Assets	196	107	93

A S A Marketing Co UK

8 Flush Park, Lisburn, BT28 2DX
Tel: 028-9266 7866 **Fax:** 028-9266 7001
E-mail: sales@asamarketing.ie
Website: http://www.asamarketing.co.uk
Managers: C. Bourke (Mgr)
Ultimate Holding Company: ASA MARKETING GROUP
Registration no: 00009676 **VAT No.:** GB 255 7166 44
Date established: 1999 **Turnover:** £1m - £2m **No.of Employees:** 1 - 10
Product Groups: 81

The Alexander Group Handling & Storage Equipment Company Ltd

20 Blaris Industrial Estate Altona Road, Lisburn, BT27 5QB
Tel: 028-9266 1010 **Fax:** 028-9266 7711
E-mail: enquiries@avgs.co.uk
Website: http://www.avgs.co.uk
Directors: G. Warke (Fin), M. Alexander (MD), R. Logan (Sales)
Ultimate Holding Company: A.V.G.S. HOLDINGS LIMITED
Immediate Holding Company: HANDLING AND STORAGE EQUIPMENT COMPANY LIMITED
Registration no: NI007122 **VAT No.:** GB 286 9124 23
Date established: 1967 **No.of Employees:** 21 - 50 **Product Groups:** 45, 48, 83

Date of Accounts	Mar 12	Mar 11	Mar 10
Working Capital	330	335	301
Fixed Assets	57	59	57
Current Assets	932	2m	1m
Current Liabilities	N/A	196	75

Architectural Engineering & Manufacturing Design Co. Ltd

17 Ballinderry Road, Lisburn, BT28 2SA
Tel: 028-9260 2211 **Fax:** 028-9266 1119
Directors: S. Hall (MD)
Managers: J. Mckay (Chief Mgr)
Immediate Holding Company: ARCHITECTURAL ENGINEERING & MANUFACTURING DESIGN COMPANY LIMITED
Registration no: NI017747 **VAT No.:** GB 412 5890 59
Date established: 1984 **Turnover:** £2m - £5m **No.of Employees:** 11 - 20
Product Groups: 84

Date of Accounts	Apr 11	Apr 10	Apr 09
Working Capital	3m	3m	3m
Fixed Assets	2m	1m	2m
Current Assets	3m	3m	3m

Armstrong Heating & Plumbing

113 Saintfield Road, Lisburn, BT27 5PA
Tel: 028-9267 6875 **Fax:** 028-9266 5543
E-mail: tom@armstrongheating.co.uk
Website: http://www.armstrongheating.co.uk
Directors: T. Armstrong (Prop)
VAT No.: GB 390 7696 09 **Turnover:** £2m - £5m **No.of Employees:** 1 - 10
Product Groups: 52

Asdon Group

Systems House Enterprise Crescent, Lisburn, BT28 2BH
Tel: 028-9267 5114 **Fax:** 028-9266 0256
E-mail: sales@asdongroup.com
Website: http://www.asdongroup.com
Bank(s): First Trust
Directors: W. Shaw (Co Sec), L. Jackson (Mkt Research), B. Marshall (Dir), R. Hill (Dir)
Immediate Holding Company: A.& S. DONALDSON (NORTHERN IRELAND) LIMITED
Registration no: NI009814 **VAT No.:** GB 412 5148 86
Date established: 1973 **No.of Employees:** 21 - 50 **Product Groups:** 64, 67

Date of Accounts	Sep 11	Sep 10	Sep 09
Working Capital	281	320	418
Fixed Assets	59	75	61
Current Assets	955	1m	1m

B M Agencies

14 Craig Crescent, Lisburn, BT28 1HB
Tel: 028-9267 7354 **Fax:** 028-9267 7354
E-mail: bm.agencies@virgin.net
Website: http://www.ryko.com
Directors: W. Morrow (MD)
Date established: 1983 **No.of Employees:** 1 - 10 **Product Groups:** 43, 49

Bodel Distributors Ltd

9 Hulls Lane, Lisburn, BT28 2SR
Tel: 028-9267 2412 **Fax:** 028-9267 1873
E-mail: sales@bodel.com
Website: http://www.bodel.com
Bank(s): Northern Bank
Directors: G. Featherstone (MD), G. Fetherston (MD), L. Hansen (Fin), G. Featherston (Prop)
Ultimate Holding Company: BODEL HOLDINGS LIMITED
Immediate Holding Company: BODEL DISTRIBUTORS LIMITED
Registration no: NI011262 **VAT No.:** GB 286 4238 33
Date established: 1976 **Turnover:** £5m - £10m **No.of Employees:** 21 - 50
Product Groups: 63, 66

Date of Accounts	Aug 11	Aug 10	Aug 09
Working Capital	1m	1m	1m
Fixed Assets	278	287	297
Current Assets	2m	1m	1m

Boilerhouse Services Ltd

Unit 50 Ballinderry Industrial Estate Ballinderry Road, Lisburn, BT28 2SA
Tel: 028-9267 2321 **Fax:** 028-9260 1555
E-mail: philip@bhsgroup.co.uk
Website: http://www.bhsgroup.co.uk
Bank(s): Northern Bank
Directors: A. Walker (Dir)
Immediate Holding Company: BOILERHOUSE SERVICES LIMITED
Registration no: NI012357 **VAT No.:** GB 286 9876 73
Date established: 1977 **Turnover:** £1m - £2m **No.of Employees:** 11 - 20
Product Groups: 48, 66

Date of Accounts	Dec 11	Dec 10	Dec 09
Working Capital	1m	1m	954
Fixed Assets	672	710	739
Current Assets	2m	1m	1m

Boomer Industries Ltd

Knockmore Hill Industrial Estate 6 Ferguson Road, Lisburn, BT28 2FW
Tel: 028-9266 2881 **Fax:** 028-9266 1119
E-mail: orders@boomer.co.uk
Website: http://www.boomer.co.uk
Bank(s): Ulster
Directors: J. Irwin (Mkt Research), A. Robinson (MD)
Managers: A. Wallace (Fin Mgr), J. Stewart (Purch Mgr), J. Little (Personnel)
Ultimate Holding Company: Boomer Industries Ltd
Immediate Holding Company: BOOMER INDUSTRIES LIMITED
Registration no: NI008036 **VAT No.:** GB 251 7066 72
Date established: 1970 **Turnover:** £2m - £5m **No.of Employees:** 21 - 50
Product Groups: 30, 35

Date of Accounts	Dec 11	Dec 10	Dec 09
Sales Turnover	4m	N/A	N/A
Pre Tax Profit/Loss	216	N/A	N/A
Working Capital	-165	-305	-150
Fixed Assets	1m	1m	2m
Current Assets	1m	1m	1m
Current Liabilities	211	N/A	N/A

Alexander Boyd Displays Ltd

Lambeg Mills Ballyskeagh Road, Lisburn, BT27 5SX
Tel: 028-9030 1115 **Fax:** 028-9030 1305
E-mail: alexboyd@eircom.net
Website: http://www.alexanderboyd.com
Bank(s): Northern Bank
Directors: S. Boyd (MD)
Managers: N. Smith (Sales Admin)
Immediate Holding Company: ALEXANDER BOYD DISPLAYS LIMITED
Registration no: NI005035 **VAT No.:** GB 251 8672 48
Date established: 1961 **Turnover:** £1m - £2m **No.of Employees:** 21 - 50
Product Groups: 28, 81

Date of Accounts	Sep 11	Sep 10	Sep 09
Working Capital	32	92	252
Fixed Assets	1m	589	979
Current Assets	3m	3m	3m
Current Liabilities	N/A	2m	N/A

Brookmount Building Supplies Ltd

3 Brookmount Road, Lisburn, BT28 2TD
Tel: 028-9262 1559 **Fax:** 028-9262 1182
Website: http://www.macblair.com
Managers: J. O'hare (Mgr)
Ultimate Holding Company: KAMAR HOLDINGS LIMITED
Immediate Holding Company: BROOKMOUNT BUILDING SUPPLIES LIMITED
Registration no: NI014333 **VAT No.:** 331273096 **Date established:** 1980
No.of Employees: 1 - 10 **Product Groups:** 66

Date of Accounts	Dec 08	Dec 07	Dec 01
Working Capital	185	185	131
Fixed Assets	N/A	N/A	110
Current Assets	185	185	235

Brookvale Kitchens

14 Bresagh Road, Lisburn, BT27 6TU
Tel: 028-9263 8461 **Fax:** 028-9263 8953
E-mail: info@brookvalekitchens.co.uk
Website: http://www.brookvalekitchens.co.uk
Directors: J. Robinson (Prop)
Registration no: NI064165 **VAT No.:** GB 434 2444 71
Date established: 2007 **Turnover:** £250,000 - £500,000
No.of Employees: 1 - 10 **Product Groups:** 26

Broomhedge Joinery

25c Lurganure Road, Lisburn, BT28 2TS
Tel: 028-9262 1288 **Fax:** 028-9262 1288
E-mail: broomhedgejoinery@btconnect.com
Directors: M. Anderson (Prop)
VAT No.: GB 434 1114 00 **Turnover:** £500,000 - £1m
No.of Employees: 1 - 10 **Product Groups:** 25

C H C Aerial Supplies

Unit 24e Blaris Industrial Estate Altona Road, Lisburn, BT27 5QB
Tel: 028-9266 4771 **Fax:** 028-9266 0830
E-mail: mail@chcni.co.uk
Website: http://www.chcni.co.uk
Directors: J. Cromie (Ptnr)
VAT No.: GB 286 7370 18 **Date established:** 1977
Turnover: Up to £250,000 **No.of Employees:** 1 - 10 **Product Groups:** 67

C W S Design

Unit C2 9 Ferguson Drive, Lisburn, BT28 2EX
Tel: 028-9267 0364 **Fax:** 028-9260 2842
E-mail: colin@cwsdesign.co.uk
Website: http://www.cwsdesign.co.uk
Directors: C. Suckling (Prop)
Immediate Holding Company: CWS DESIGN LIMITED
Registration no: NI053885 **VAT No.:** GB 283 1978 26
Date established: 2005 **Turnover:** £1m - £2m **No.of Employees:** 1 - 10
Product Groups: 33

Date of Accounts	Jan 11	Jan 10	Jan 09
Working Capital	37	-49	-73
Fixed Assets	119	138	159
Current Assets	122	93	96

Central Security Systems

37a Bachelors Walk, Lisburn, BT28 1XN
Tel: 028-9266 0066 **Fax:** 028-9266 1662
E-mail: info@centralsecuritysystems.co.uk
Website: http://www.centralsecuritysystems.co.uk
Directors: B. Hunter (Prop)
VAT No.: GB 412 6809 63 **Turnover:** £500,000 - £1m
No.of Employees: 1 - 10 **Product Groups:** 52, 67

Charles Hurst Vauxhall

70 Belfast Road, Lisburn, BT27 4AU
Tel: 028-9266 5270 **Fax:** 028-9266 2127
E-mail: garypickering@charleshurstgroup.co.uk
Website: http://www.charleshurstgroup.co.uk

Managers: G. Pickering, W. Hamilton (Sales Admin)
Ultimate Holding Company: LOOKERS PUBLIC LIMITED COMPANY
Immediate Holding Company: CHARLES HURST HOLDINGS LIMITED
Registration no: R0000134 **VAT No.:** GB 530 9442 56
Date established: 2011 **Turnover:** £250m - £500m
No.of Employees: 101 - 250 **Product Groups:** 39, 68

Date of Accounts	Dec 11	Dec 10	Dec 09
Sales Turnover	428	527	2m
Pre Tax Profit/Loss	625	2m	1m
Working Capital	-70	-79	-116
Fixed Assets	1m	1m	1m
Current Assets	2m	2m	3m
Current Liabilities	23	213	1m

Clarion Hotel

75 Belfast Road, Lisburn, BT28 8BX
Tel: 028-9336 4556 **Fax:** 028-9335 1620
E-mail: info@qualitycarrick.co.uk
Website: http://www.clarioncarrick.com
Managers: Gillespin (Mgr), F. Barbour (Chief Mgr), T. Boyd (Mgr), J. McKnight (Develop Mgr)
Registration no: 01796064 **VAT No.:** GB 353 1408 80
No.of Employees: 1 - 10 **Product Groups:** 69

Comada N I Ltd

50 Ballinderry Road, Lisburn, BT28 2SA
Tel: 028-9260 5568 **Fax:** 028-9260 5962
E-mail: info@comada.co.uk
Website: http://www.comada.co.uk
Directors: W. Baxter (MD)
Immediate Holding Company: COMADA (N.I.) LIMITED
Registration no: NI024046 **VAT No.:** GB 517 2342 67
Date established: 1990 **Turnover:** £500,000 - £1m
No.of Employees: 1 - 10 **Product Groups:** 85

Date of Accounts	Dec 11	Dec 10	Dec 09
Working Capital	171	165	165
Fixed Assets	37	26	34
Current Assets	219	210	207

Communisis

5 Blaris Industrial Estate Altona Road, Lisburn, BT27 5QB
Tel: 028-9260 6800 **Fax:** 028-9260 6801
E-mail: joe.mallon@communisis.com
Website: http://www.communisis.com
Bank(s): First Trust
Managers: J. Mallon (Chief Mgr)
Immediate Holding Company: communisis ni ltd
Registration no: R0000396 **Date established:** 2012 **Turnover:** £2m - £5m
No.of Employees: 21 - 50 **Product Groups:** 28

Date of Accounts	Dec 08
Working Capital	44
Current Assets	44

Comtrol Electronic Engineers

25 Lambeg Road, Lisburn, BT27 4QA
Tel: 028-9260 2277 **Fax:** 028-9260 1118
E-mail: jd@btconnect.com
Directors: J. Dickson (Prop)
VAT No.: GB 496 9014 07 **Date established:** 1987
Turnover: £250,000 - £500,000 **No.of Employees:** 1 - 10
Product Groups: 48, 67

Corus

216a Moira Road, Lisburn, BT28 2SN
Tel: 028-9266 0747 **Fax:** 028-9266 0748
Website: http://www.corusgroup.com
Directors: G. Lucas (MD)
Managers: G. Lucas (Grp Mgr), M. McHolme (Sales Prom Mgr)
Immediate Holding Company: CORUS GROUP LIMITED
Registration no: 03811373 **Date established:** 1999
No.of Employees: 51 - 100 **Product Groups:** 66, 77

Robert Craig & Sons Ltd

Unit 10 Knock Moore Hill Industrial Estate Ferguson Drive, Lisburn, BT28 2EX
Tel: 028-9266 8500 **Fax:** 028-9266 8550
E-mail: info@craigs-products.co.uk
Website: http://www.craigs.ie
Directors: D. Craig (Prop)
Immediate Holding Company: ROBERT CRAIG & SONS LIMITED
Registration no: NI063921 **VAT No.:** GB 252 0313 13
Date established: 2007 **Turnover:** £2m - £5m **No.of Employees:** 11 - 20
Product Groups: 66, 74

Date of Accounts	Dec 11	Dec 10	Dec 09
Working Capital	149	110	73
Fixed Assets	215	259	269
Current Assets	564	624	640

Creative Composites Ltd

1 Ferguson Road, Lisburn, BT28 2FW
Tel: 028-9267 3312 **Fax:** 028-9260 7381
E-mail: enquiries@creativecomposites.co.uk
Website: http://www.creativecomposites.co.uk
Bank(s): Northern Bank
Managers: J. Graham (Sales Prom Mgr), N. Hanna, R. Telford (Mktg Serv Mgr), T. Morgan (Purch Mgr), A. Adamson (Chief Acct), C. Kelly (Personnel)
Immediate Holding Company: CREATIVE COMPOSITES LIMITED
Registration no: NI038590 **VAT No.:** GB 760 6486 14
Date established: 2000 **Turnover:** £5m - £10m
No.of Employees: 101 - 250 **Product Groups:** 30, 49

Date of Accounts	Dec 11	Dec 10	Dec 09
Sales Turnover	9m	6m	N/A
Pre Tax Profit/Loss	692	501	-141
Working Capital	930	1m	665
Fixed Assets	5m	4m	4m
Current Assets	3m	3m	2m
Current Liabilities	693	625	528

M E Crowe Ltd

41a Quarterlands Road, Lisburn, BT27 5TN
Tel: 028-9082 6596 **Fax:** 028-9082 6595
E-mail: info@mecrowe.co.uk
Website: http://www.mecrowe.co.uk
Directors: M. Crowe (MD)
Immediate Holding Company: M E Crowe Limited
Registration no: NI064487 **VAT No.:** 331 3204 15 **Date established:** 2007
No.of Employees: 1 - 10 **Product Groups:** 25, 52

Date of Accounts	Jun 11	Jun 10
Working Capital	-69	-84
Fixed Assets	153	180
Current Assets	417	353

D Macweld Ltd

223 Moira Road, Lisburn, BT28 2ST
Tel: 028-9262 1851 **Fax:** 028-9262 1553
E-mail: dmacweld223@yahoo.com
Directors: D. Mcpherson (Dir)
Immediate Holding Company: DMACWELD LIMITED
Registration no: NI011737 **VAT No.:** GB 286 6520 30
Date established: 1977 **Turnover:** Up to £250,000
No.of Employees: 1 - 10 **Product Groups:** 35, 49

Date of Accounts	May 12	May 11	May 10
Working Capital	59	65	58
Fixed Assets	18	25	29
Current Assets	88	89	80

Dalkia

Unit 7 Lissue Industrial Estate Moira Road, Lisburn, BT28 2SN
Tel: 028-9262 2332 **Fax:** 028-9262 2312
E-mail: sarah.brown@dalkia.ie
Website: http://www.dalkia.ie
Managers: T. Docherty (Mgr)
Immediate Holding Company: Dalkia Energy and Utility Services Limited
Registration no: NI073352 **VAT No.:** GB 188 5824 11
Date established: 2009 **Turnover:** £250,000 - £500,000
No.of Employees: 1 - 10 **Product Groups:** 67

Date of Accounts	Dec 11	Dec 10	Dec 09
Sales Turnover	4m	4m	379
Pre Tax Profit/Loss	455	375	47
Working Capital	-126	-691	-1m
Fixed Assets	948	1m	2m
Current Assets	1m	2m	1m
Current Liabilities	653	691	405

De La Rue Ni Ltd Security Printers

Lissue Indl-Est East, Lisburn, BT28 2RB
Tel: 028-9262 2999 **Fax:** 028-9262 2600
Website: http://www.dlrs.group.com
Managers: K. Irwin (District Mgr), P. Thomas (Chief Mgr), T. O'Mahomy (Chief Mgr)
No.of Employees: 21 - 50 **Product Groups:** 28

Dentaquip Ltd

1 Altona Road, Lisburn, BT27 5QB
Tel: 028-9260 1000 **Fax:** 028-9267 6550
E-mail: tom.kennedy@dentaquip.co.uk
Website: http://www.dentaquip.co.uk
Managers: T. Kennedy (Chief Mgr)
Immediate Holding Company: DENTAQUIP LIMITED
Registration no: NI045016 **VAT No.:** GB 255 6877 16
Date established: 2002 **Turnover:** £1m - £2m **No.of Employees:** 11 - 20
Product Groups: 67

Date of Accounts	Dec 11	Dec 10	Dec 09
Working Capital	227	231	36
Fixed Assets	3	16	34
Current Assets	828	839	937

Donite Plastics

Prima Business Park 280 Comber Road, Lisburn, BT27 6TA
Tel: 028-9263 9995 **Fax:** 028-9263 9996
E-mail: ricky@donite.com
Website: http://www.donite.com
Managers: R. Knight (Prod Mgr)
Immediate Holding Company: Donite Plastics Ltd
Registration no: NI064142 **VAT No.:** GB 353 0792 58
Date established: 2007 **Turnover:** £250,000 - £500,000
No.of Employees: 1 - 10 **Product Groups:** 48

Date of Accounts	Sep 11	Sep 10	Sep 09
Working Capital	-3	-23	-94
Fixed Assets	90	109	128
Current Assets	83	97	80

Dreams

Riverside Centre Young Street, Lisburn, BT27 5EA
Tel: 028-9267 7000 **Fax:** 028-9267 7800
Website: http://www.dreams.co.uk
Managers: K. Longridge (Mgr)
Ultimate Holding Company: EXPONENT PRIVATE EQUITY LLP
Immediate Holding Company: DREAMS PLC
Registration no: 02189427 **Date established:** 1987
Turnover: £125m - £250m **No.of Employees:** 1 - 10 **Product Groups:** 24, 26

Date of Accounts	Dec 10	Dec 09	Dec 08
Sales Turnover	256m	244m	194m
Pre Tax Profit/Loss	4m	18m	-3m
Working Capital	25m	9m	-4m
Fixed Assets	34m	43m	40m
Current Assets	71m	48m	33m
Current Liabilities	20m	17m	13m

Earney Contracts Ltd

221 Comber Road, Lisburn, BT27 6XY
Tel: 028-9263 8269 **Fax:** 028-9263 9009
E-mail: info@earneycontracts.co.uk
Website: http://www.earneycontracts.co.uk
Bank(s): Northern Bank
Directors: T. Earney (MD)
Managers: S. Earney (Mgr)
Immediate Holding Company: EARNEY CONTRACTS LIMITED
Registration no: NI011627 **VAT No.:** GB 287 0402 60
Date established: 1976 **Turnover:** £2m - £5m **No.of Employees:** 21 - 50
Product Groups: 51

Date of Accounts	Nov 07	Apr 11	Apr 10
Working Capital	2m	-0	-48
Fixed Assets	260	92	113
Current Assets	3m	1m	989

Ecoat Ireland Ltd

Unit 13 Blaris Industrial Estate, Lisburn, BT27 5QB
Tel: 028-9260 4798 **Fax:** 028-9260 4798
E-mail: info@ecoat.co.uk
Website: http://www.ecoatireland.com
Bank(s): Bank of Ireland
Directors: T. Bradley (Dir)
Immediate Holding Company: Ecoat Ireland Limited
Registration no: NI020517 **Date established:** 1987
Turnover: £500,000 - £1m **No.of Employees:** 21 - 50 **Product Groups:** 48

Date of Accounts	Mar 11	Mar 10	Mar 09
Working Capital	201	180	380
Fixed Assets	106	112	127
Current Assets	298	232	439

Fisher Metal Ni Ltd

1 Hallstown Road Ballinderry Upper, Lisburn, BT28 2NE
Tel: 028-9262 2650 **Fax:** 028-9262 2651
E-mail: info@fishermetal.co.uk
Website: http://www.fishermetal.co.uk
Directors: R. Fisher (MD)
Managers: D. Irwin (Mgr), M. Ogilby
Immediate Holding Company: FISHER METAL (NI) LIMITED
Registration no: NI603614 **Date established:** 2010
No.of Employees: 21 - 50 **Product Groups:** 35

G E Energy Ltd

Lissue Industrial Estate, Lisburn, BT28 2RE
Tel: 028-9262 2915 **Fax:** 028-9262 2202
Website: http://www.kelman.co.uk
Managers: M. Borzecki (Tech Serv Mgr), P. Fearon (Mktg Serv Mgr), R. Ormsby (Fin Mgr), R. Weir (Sales Prom Mgr), L. Caskey (Personnel), P. Gelston
Immediate Holding Company: PRM Logistics Ltd
Registration no: NI027892 **Date established:** 2005
Turnover: £10m - £20m **No.of Employees:** 101 - 250
Product Groups: 37, 39

Date of Accounts	Dec 11	Dec 10	Dec 09
Working Capital	-2m	-2m	-1m
Fixed Assets	5m	5m	4m
Current Assets	45	265	536

Green's Food Fare

23-25 Bow Street, Lisburn, BT28 1BJ
Tel: 028-9266 2124 **Fax:** 028-9267 0579
E-mail: orders@greensfoodfare.com
Website: http://www.greensfoodfare.com
Directors: G. Browne (Fin), R. Black (MD)
Managers: D. Thompson, G. McKinstry (Personnel)
Immediate Holding Company: GREENS FOODFARE LIMITED
Registration no: NI021642 **VAT No.:** GB 253 9348 40
Date established: 1988 **No.of Employees:** 51 - 100 **Product Groups:** 61

Haldane Fisher

Enterprise Crescent, Lisburn, BT28 2BP
Tel: 028-9267 6161 **Fax:** 028-9266 0541
E-mail: martin.mcnair@haldanefisher.com
Website: http://www.haldanefisher.com
Managers: M. Mcnair (Chief Mgr)
Ultimate Holding Company: HALDANE SHIELLS AND COMPANY LIMITED
Immediate Holding Company: HALDANE FISHER LIMITED
Registration no: NI024075 **VAT No.:** GB 286 7513 22
Date established: 1990 **No.of Employees:** 1 - 10 **Product Groups:** 66

Date of Accounts	Dec 11	Dec 10	Dec 09
Sales Turnover	45m	48m	50m
Pre Tax Profit/Loss	202	18	1m
Working Capital	8m	7m	7m
Fixed Assets	2m	2m	2m
Current Assets	17m	16m	17m
Current Liabilities	1m	1m	2m

Hanna Thompson Chartered Accountants

Century House Enterprise Crescent, Lisburn, BT28 2BP
Tel: 028-9260 7355 **Fax:** 028-9260 1656
E-mail: accounts@hannathompson.com
Website: http://www.hannathompson.com
Managers: S. Houston
Immediate Holding Company: Hanna Thompson Limited
Registration no: NI059660 **VAT No.:** GB 412 5688 54
Date established: 2006 **No.of Employees:** 21 - 50 **Product Groups:** 80

Date of Accounts	Jun 08	Apr 11	Apr 10
Working Capital	N/A	8	-451
Fixed Assets	N/A	1m	1m
Current Assets	N/A	757	703

H R Holfeld Belfast Ltd

Altona Road, Lisburn, BT27 5RU
Tel: 028-9267 7523 **Fax:** 028-9266 0263
E-mail: pumps@holfeld.com
Website: http://www.holfeldni.com
Directors: L. Colughan (MD)
Managers: T. Withers (Sales Prom Mgr)
Immediate Holding Company: H.R. HOLFELD (BELFAST) LIMITED
Registration no: NI006412 **VAT No.:** GB 251 7104 90
Date established: 1965 **No.of Employees:** 1 - 10 **Product Groups:** 42

Date of Accounts	Dec 09	Dec 08	Dec 07
Working Capital	-104	-129	-179
Fixed Assets	461	329	341
Current Assets	141	184	131

Howell House Bakery

3e Drumalig Road, Lisburn, BT27 6UD
Tel: 028-9751 1324 **Fax:** 028-9751 1724
E-mail: kstewart@howellhouse.co.uk
Managers: J. Read (Mgr)
Immediate Holding Company: HOWELL HOUSE BAKERY LIMITED
Registration no: NI027902 **VAT No.:** GB 454 5265 42
Date established: 1993 **No.of Employees:** 21 - 50 **Product Groups:** 20

Huhpamaki Lisburn Ltd

66 Ravarnet Road, Lisburn, BT27 5NB
Tel: 028-9267 2116 **Fax:** 028-9266 0538
E-mail: ian.thompson@gb.huhtamaki.com
Website: http://www.huhtamaki.com
Directors: A. Jones (Dir)
VAT No.: GB 254 9267 34 **No.of Employees:** 1 - 10 **Product Groups:** 27, 80

Hydrodynamics Power Engineering

Knockmore Industrial Estate Moira Road, Lisburn, BT28 2EJ
Tel: 028-9266 2781 **Fax:** 028-9266 0554
E-mail: info@nelsonhydraulics.com
Website: http://www.nelsonhydraulics.com
Directors: M. Nelson (Prop)
Immediate Holding Company: HYDRODYNAMICS POWER ENGINEERING LIMITED
Registration no: NI014225 **VAT No.:** GB 252 8283 53
Date established: 1980 **Turnover:** £500,000 - £1m
No.of Employees: 21 - 50 **Product Groups:** 30, 36, 40

see next page

Hydrodynamics Power Engineering - Cont'd

Date of Accounts	Sep 11	Sep 10	Sep 09
Working Capital	863	854	769
Fixed Assets	180	180	310
Current Assets	1m	1m	1m

Integrated Process Control & Engineering Ltd

Unit 509 512 Lisburn Enterprise Centre Enterprise CR, Lisburn, BT28 2BP
Tel: 028-9262 8040 **Fax:** 028-9264 1523
E-mail: ipce.mk@btinternet.com
Website: http://www.ipce.co.uk
Directors: M. Kearney (MD)
Immediate Holding Company: IPCE LIMITED
Registration no: NI015418 **VAT No.:** GB 375 7887 83
Date established: 1982 **Turnover:** £250,000 - £500,000
No.of Employees: 11 - 20 **Product Groups:** 38

Date of Accounts	Feb 11	Feb 10	Feb 09
Working Capital	26	29	35
Fixed Assets	49	29	31
Current Assets	123	123	147

J & T Enterprises Ltd

Knockmore Industrial Estate Moira Road, Lisburn, BT28 2EJ
Tel: 028-9266 4648 **Fax:** 028-9260 4555
E-mail: jtenterprises@btclick.com
Directors: R. Conlin (Dir)
Immediate Holding Company: J. & T. ENTERPRISES LIMITED
Registration no: NI012637 **VAT No.:** GB 287 0179 37
Date established: 1978 **Turnover:** Up to £250,000
No.of Employees: 1 - 10 **Product Groups:** 20

Date of Accounts	Dec 11	Dec 10	Dec 09
Working Capital	180	169	177
Fixed Assets	108	110	118
Current Assets	471	463	475

Jesse Blinds & Shutters Ltd

64b Stoneyford Road, Lisburn, BT28 3SR
Tel: 028-9264 8471 **Fax:** 028-9264 8472
E-mail: info@jesseblinds.co.uk
Website: http://www.jesseblinds.co.uk
Directors: J. Scott (MD)
Immediate Holding Company: JESSE BLINDS & SHUTTERS LTD
Registration no: NI029306 **VAT No.:** GB 331 3387 78
Date established: 1995 **Turnover:** £250,000 - £500,000
No.of Employees: 1 - 10 **Product Groups:** 24, 35, 36, 66

Date of Accounts	Mar 11	Mar 10	Mar 09
Working Capital	111	108	122
Fixed Assets	4	5	1
Current Assets	161	177	198

J & G Hamilton Ltd

2 Rathdown Road Lissue Industrial Estate, Lisburn, BT28 2RE
Tel: 028-9262 1982 **Fax:** 028-9262 1956
E-mail: info@jghamilton.co.uk
Website: http://www.jghamilton.co.uk
Directors: P. Holland (MD)
Immediate Holding Company: J & G HAMILTON LIMITED
Registration no: NI056785 **VAT No.:** GB 255 6815 38
Date established: 2005 **Turnover:** Up to £250,000
No.of Employees: 1 - 10 **Product Groups:** 35, 52, 66

Date of Accounts	Oct 11	Oct 10	Oct 09
Working Capital	136	143	143
Fixed Assets	80	84	91
Current Assets	373	336	320

Jordan Concrete Ltd

10 Sheepwalk Road, Lisburn, BT28 3RD
Tel: 028-9264 8648 **Fax:** 028-9264 8775
E-mail: trevor.jordan@jordanconcrete.co.uk
Website: http://www.jordanconcrete.co.uk
Bank(s): Northern Bank
Directors: T. Jordan (MD)
Immediate Holding Company: JORDAN CONCRETE LTD
Registration no: NI009560 **VAT No.:** GB 255 6483 37
Date established: 1973 **No.of Employees:** 21 - 50 **Product Groups:** 33, 66

Date of Accounts	Sep 11	Sep 10	Sep 09
Working Capital	462	571	628
Fixed Assets	434	531	622
Current Assets	642	727	819

Lathgo Threading Tools

6 Hillsborough Old Road, Lisburn, BT27 5EW
Tel: 028-9266 5422 **Fax:** 028- 92665848
E-mail: sales@5ssupplyltd.co.uk
Directors: I. Bothwell (Prop), L. Bothwell (Prop)
VAT No.: GB 286 4978 90 **Date established:** 1973
Turnover: Up to £250,000 **No.of Employees:** 1 - 10 **Product Groups:** 66

Lester Engineering Ltd

Rathdown Road Lissue Industrial Estate, Lisburn, BT28 2RE
Tel: 028-9262 1681 **Fax:** 028-9262 1681
E-mail: info@alloywheelslisburn.com
Website: http://www.alloywheelslisburn.com
Directors: B. Lester (Dir)
Immediate Holding Company: LESTER ENGINEERING LTD
Registration no: 06483942 **Date established:** 2008
No.of Employees: 1 - 10 **Product Groups:** 33

Date of Accounts	Mar 11	Jan 10	Jan 09
Working Capital	74	53	35
Fixed Assets	4	N/A	N/A
Current Assets	98	74	97

P Lewis Engineering

3 Hammonds Road Ballinderry Upper, Lisburn, BT28 2NG
Tel: 028-9261 1364 **Fax:** 028-9261 3987
Website: http://www.plewisengineering.co.uk
Directors: P. Lewis (Prop)
Immediate Holding Company: P. LEWIS & SON (FARM) LIMITED
Registration no: NI024894 **Date established:** 1990
No.of Employees: 1 - 10 **Product Groups:** 26, 35

Lindsay Cars Ltd (t/a Lindsay Ford & Lindsay Mazda)

Unit C, Lisburn, BT28 2EJ
Tel: 028-9267 3121 **Fax:** 028-9260 6208
E-mail: laura.cochrane@lindsay-cars.co.uk
Website: http://www.lindsayford.co.uk
Managers: L. Cochrane (Mktg Serv Mgr)
Ultimate Holding Company: FORD MOTOR COMPANY (USA)
Immediate Holding Company: LINDSAY CARS LIMITED
Registration no: NI005514 **Date established:** 1963
Turnover: £75m - £125m **No.of Employees:** 21 - 50 **Product Groups:** 68

Date of Accounts	Dec 11	Dec 10	Dec 09
Sales Turnover	104m	115m	114m
Pre Tax Profit/Loss	-1m	825	1m
Working Capital	1m	2m	1m
Fixed Assets	8m	9m	12m
Current Assets	33m	32m	43m
Current Liabilities	29m	5m	9m

Lisburn Glass Ltd

Altona Road, Lisburn, BT27 5PU
Tel: 028-9267 4111 **Fax:** 028-9267 1552
Website: http://www.lisburnglass.co.uk
Directors: M. Alexander (Ptnr)
Managers: H. Moody (Buyer), A. Mee, A. Lewis
Immediate Holding Company: LISBURN GLASS (HOLDINGS) LIMITED
Registration no: NI016900 **VAT No.:** GB 254 6019 68
Date established: 1983 **No.of Employees:** 21 - 50 **Product Groups:** 66

Date of Accounts	Mar 09	Mar 08
Working Capital	-0	-0

Lisburn Proteins Animal By-Products

211 Moira Road, Lisburn, BT28 2SN
Tel: 028-9262 1441 **Fax:** 028-9262 1960
E-mail: tony@ulsterfarm.co.uk
Website: http://www.proteins.co.uk
Bank(s): Bank of Ireland
Directors: S. Spence (Co Sec), C. Thompson (Dir)
Managers: T. Addis (Chief Mgr), T. Addis (Mgr)
Immediate Holding Company: LISBURN PROTEINS
Registration no: NI032198 **VAT No.:** GB 390 7211 59
Date established: 1997 **Turnover:** £2m - £5m **No.of Employees:** 11 - 20
Product Groups: 20, 31

Litton Group Ltd

38 Young Street, Lisburn, BT27 5EB
Tel: 028-9267 2325 **Fax:** 028-9260 7473
E-mail: graham.green@ukcities.co.uk
Website: http://www.litton.co.uk
Bank(s): Northern Bank
Directors: P. Keenan (Fin), G. Green (MD)
Managers: J. Forbes
Ultimate Holding Company: LITTON ESTATES LTD
Immediate Holding Company: LITTON GROUP LTD
Registration no: NI019140 **VAT No.:** GB 517 8268 23
Date established: 1986 **Turnover:** £5m - £10m
No.of Employees: 51 - 100 **Product Groups:** 52

Date of Accounts	Oct 11	Oct 10	Oct 09
Sales Turnover	7m	4m	5m
Pre Tax Profit/Loss	522	-203	322
Working Capital	593	189	570
Fixed Assets	23	46	83
Current Assets	3m	2m	2m
Current Liabilities	355	228	317

Lowe Refrigeration Co.

Unit J Knockmore Industrial Estate Moira Road, Lisburn, BT28 2EJ
Tel: 028-9260 4619 **Fax:** 028-9081 2608
E-mail: mail@loweref.co.uk
Website: http://www.loweref.co.uk
Bank(s): Northern Bank
Directors: R. Lowry (Dir)
Ultimate Holding Company: LOWE REFRIGERATION SOLUTIONS LIMITED
Immediate Holding Company: Lowe Refrigeration Limited
Registration no: NI058627 **VAT No.:** GB 286 8140 30
Date established: 2006 **No.of Employees:** 11 - 20 **Product Groups:** 63

Date of Accounts	Aug 11	Aug 10	Aug 09
Working Capital	-2m	-2m	-2m
Fixed Assets	3m	3m	3m
Current Assets	2m	2m	1m

Mccormick Macnaughton Ni Ltd

Blaris Industrial Estate Altona Road, Lisburn, BT27 5QB
Tel: 028-9266 1221 **Fax:** 028-9266 1355
E-mail: sales@mccormickmacnaughton.com
Website: http://www.mccormickmacnaughton.com
Bank(s): First Trust
Directors: H. Goode (Fin), W. Stewart (Sales), M. MacNaughton (MD)
Managers: C. Hunter (Serv Mgr), A. Stevens (I.T. Exec), E. Heath (Sales Prom Mgr), S. Harper (Sales Prom Mgr), J. Geoghagam (Personnel)
Ultimate Holding Company: BALLYMANA HOLDINGS LIMITED
Immediate Holding Company: MCCORMICK MACNAUGHTON (N.I.) LIMITED
Registration no: NI002990 **VAT No.:** GB 254 1347 76
Date established: 1951 **Turnover:** £20m - £50m
No.of Employees: 51 - 100 **Product Groups:** 66, 67

R A Mcmullen

3a Ballyvannon Road Ballinderry Upper, Lisburn, BT28 2LD
Tel: 028-9442 3133 **Fax:** 028-9445 2830
Directors: R. McMullan (Prop)
Date established: 1976 **No.of Employees:** 1 - 10 **Product Groups:** 41

Mcquillan Civil Engineers

11 Ballinderry Road, Lisburn, BT28 2SA
Tel: 028-9266 8831 **Fax:** 028-9266 8832
E-mail: contracts@johnmcquillan.com
Website: http://www.mcquillancompanies.com
Bank(s): Ulster Bank
Directors: C. Ryan (Fin), J. Mcquillan (MD)
Ultimate Holding Company: JOHN MCQUILLAN (CONTRACTS) LIMITED
Immediate Holding Company: MCQUILLAN DEVELOPMENTS LIMITED
Registration no: NI014012 **VAT No.:** GB 252 5353 73
Date established: 1979 **Turnover:** £250,000 - £500,000
No.of Employees: 11 - 20 **Product Groups:** 51, 52

Date of Accounts	Mar 12	Mar 11	Mar 10
Working Capital	117	-46	79
Fixed Assets	945	903	941
Current Assets	1m	1m	953

Modern Machinery Supplies

Unit 3-4 Building 5 Rathdown Road Lissue Industrial Estate West, Lisburn, BT28 2RE
Tel: 028-9262 2011 **Fax:** 028-9262 2181
E-mail: sales@modernmachinerysupplies.co.uk
Website: http://www.modernmachinerysupplies.co.uk
Managers: E. Miecinski (Sales Admin)
Immediate Holding Company: MODERN MACHINERY SUPPLIES LIMITED
Registration no: NI006595 **VAT No.:** GB 252 1971 67
Date established: 1966 **No.of Employees:** 1 - 10 **Product Groups:** 66

Date of Accounts	Dec 11	Dec 10	Dec 09
Working Capital	700	676	641
Fixed Assets	561	563	570
Current Assets	1m	1m	1m

Mourne Rosettes

67 Carnbane Road, Lisburn, BT27 5NG
Tel: 028-9268 8049 **Fax:** 028-9268 8049
Directors: V. Stewart (Prop)
Date established: 1983 **Turnover:** Up to £250,000
No.of Employees: 1 - 10 **Product Groups:** 23

N M Forktrucks Ltd

Unit 7 Rathdown Road Lissue Industrial Estate, Lisburn, BT28 2RE
Tel: 028-9262 1922 **Fax:** 028-9262 1108
Website: http://www.nmforktrucks.com
Directors: N. Morrow (MD)
Immediate Holding Company: N.M. FORKTRUCKS LIMITED
Registration no: NI020731 **Date established:** 1987
No.of Employees: 11 - 20 **Product Groups:** 35, 39, 45

Date of Accounts	Aug 10	Aug 09	Aug 08
Working Capital	131	119	156
Fixed Assets	522	509	387
Current Assets	921	920	716

Nationwide Access Ltd

115 Halftown Road, Lisburn, BT27 5RF
Tel: 028-9268 9336 **Fax:** 028-9268 9337
E-mail: mail@nationwideaccess.co.uk
Website: http://www.nationwideaccess.co.uk
Directors: H. Walters (Mkt Research), K. Molbs (Dir)
Managers: N. Mckonn (District Mgr)
Ultimate Holding Company: Lavendon Group plc
Immediate Holding Company: NATIONWIDE ACCESS LIMITED
Registration no: 04405299 **Date established:** 2002
Turnover: £20m - £50m **No.of Employees:** 1 - 10 **Product Groups:** 45, 83

Nuaire Ltd

10 Enterprise Crescent, Lisburn, BT28 2BP
Tel: 028-9267 0363 **Fax:** 028-9267 2980
E-mail: michael.kane@nuaire.co.uk
Website: http://www.nuaire.co.uk
Directors: C. Hunter (MD)
Managers: M. Kane (Mgr)
Ultimate Holding Company: NU-OVAL ACQUISITIONS 1 LIMITED
Immediate Holding Company: NUAIRE LIMITED
Registration no: 00877308 **Date established:** 1966
No.of Employees: 11 - 20 **Product Groups:** 40, 66

Date of Accounts	Sep 11	Sep 10	Sep 09
Sales Turnover	52m	45m	47m
Pre Tax Profit/Loss	7m	7m	8m
Working Capital	52m	44m	37m
Fixed Assets	10m	11m	11m
Current Assets	64m	53m	46m
Current Liabilities	4m	2m	2m

O-Kane Food Services Ltd

221 Hillhall Road, Lisburn, BT27 5JQ
Tel: 028-9266 4231 **Fax:** 028-9266 1089
E-mail: sales@okfs.co.uk
Website: http://www.okfs.co.uk
Bank(s): Northern Bank
Directors: R. Bester (Fin)
Managers: M. Douglas (Buyer), E. Bohill (Personnel), G. Hopkins (Mktg Serv Mgr), A. Bird (Tech Serv Mgr), A. Waite
Ultimate Holding Company: CUCINA (BC) LUXCO SARL(LUXEMBOURG)
Immediate Holding Company: O'Kane Food Service Limited
Registration no: NI066355 **Date established:** 2007
Turnover: £50m - £75m **No.of Employees:** 101 - 250 **Product Groups:** 62

Date of Accounts	Dec 11	Dec 10	Dec 09
Sales Turnover	62m	41m	43m
Pre Tax Profit/Loss	-745	691	102
Working Capital	-4m	-3m	-4m
Fixed Assets	5m	6m	4m
Current Assets	17m	14m	13m
Current Liabilities	212	574	516

Olympic Lifts Ltd

Olympic House Rathdown Close Lissue Industrial Estate East, Lisburn, BT28 2RB
Tel: 028-9262 2331 **Fax:** 028-9262 2339
E-mail: info@olympiclifts.co.uk
Website: http://www.olympiclifts.co.uk
Bank(s): Northern Bank
Directors: E. Patterson (Fin)
Managers: W. Halliday, M. Forsyth (Sales Prom Mgr), J. Patterson (Chief Mgr)
Ultimate Holding Company: ROSEPARK HOLDINGS LTD
Immediate Holding Company: OLYMPIC LIFTS LIMITED
Registration no: NI018449 **VAT No.:** GB 422 1496 76
Date established: 1985 **No.of Employees:** 21 - 50 **Product Groups:** 45

Date of Accounts	Dec 11	Dec 10	Dec 09
Working Capital	717	682	597
Fixed Assets	531	588	723
Current Assets	2m	2m	2m

P D W Replacements Ltd

Sans Souci Gardens, Lisburn, BT28 3AF
Tel: 028-9267 1863 **Fax:** 028-9266 0273
Directors: P. Walker (MD)
Immediate Holding Company: P.D.W. REPLACEMENTS LIMITED
Registration no: NI022618 **VAT No.:** GB 331 2177 94
Date established: 1989 **Turnover:** £500,000 - £1m
No.of Employees: 1 - 10 **Product Groups:** 30

Date of Accounts	Mar 11	Mar 10	Mar 09
Working Capital	-36	-1	41
Fixed Assets	89	91	93
Current Assets	34	49	114

Pentland Ltd

5 Station Road Ballinderry Upper, Lisburn, BT28 2LW
Tel: 0844-3578825 **Fax:** 020-8457 5021
E-mail: info@pentland.com
Website: http://www.pentlands.com

Directors: A. Rubin (Grp Chief Exec), K. Grenyer (MD)
Registration no: 04257636 **Turnover:** £2m - £5m
No.of Employees: 251 - 500 **Product Groups:** 24, 81

Robert Phillips & Sons

3e White Mountain Road, Lisburn, BT28 3QY
Tel: 028-9266 4721 **Fax:** 028-9267 6896
Website: http://www.phillipsfireplaces.com
Directors: A. Phillips (Ptnr)
VAT No.: GB 517 9324 34 **Date established:** 1964
Turnover: £250,000 - £500,000 **No.of Employees:** 1 - 10
Product Groups: 14, 25, 33

Powerair Ltd

Unit 20b Blaris Industrial Estate Altona Road, Lisburn, BT27 5QB
Tel: 028-9262 8885 **Fax:** 028-9262 8898
E-mail: johnny@powerair.co.uk
Website: http://www.powerair.co.uk
Bank(s): Ulster Bank
Directors: J. Camblin (MD)
Immediate Holding Company: Powerair Limited
Registration no: NI049676 **VAT No.:** GB 286 9124 23
Date established: 2004 **Turnover:** £1m - £2m **No.of Employees:** 11 - 20
Product Groups: 67

Date of Accounts	Nov 11	Nov 10	Nov 09
Sales Turnover	1m	1m	913
Pre Tax Profit/Loss	-25	83	-74
Working Capital	92	104	13
Fixed Assets	23	26	43
Current Assets	361	467	257
Current Liabilities	51	97	102

Powershield Doors Ltd

21 Ferguson Drive Knockmore Hill Industrial Park, Lisburn, BT28 2EX
Tel: 028-9266 2200 **Fax:** 028-9260 3600
E-mail: sales@powershield.co.uk
Website: http://www.powershield.co.uk
Bank(s): Northern Bank
Directors: G. Crymble (MD), M. Best (Dir)
Managers: B. Softley (Sales Prom Mgr), J. Clayton (I.T. Exec)
Ultimate Holding Company: ASSA ABLOY AB (PUBL) (SWEDEN)
Registration no: NI026027 **VAT No.:** GB 343 2628 61
Date established: 1991 **Turnover:** £5m - £10m
No.of Employees: 51 - 100 **Product Groups:** 66

Pressford Shutters

Unit E 280 Comber Road, Lisburn, BT27 6TA
Tel: 028-9263 9277 **Fax:** 028-9263 9288
E-mail: info@pressfordshutters.com
Website: http://www.pressfordshutters.com
Directors: D. Press (MD)
Date established: 1987 **No.of Employees:** 1 - 10 **Product Groups:** 26, 35

John Preston & Co Belfast Ltd

Unit 7a Blaris Industrial Estate Altona Road, Lisburn, BT27 5QB
Tel: 028-9267 7077 **Fax:** 028-9267 7099
E-mail: info@johnpreston.co.uk
Website: http://www.johnpreston.co.uk
Bank(s): Northern Bank
Directors: N. Cooke (Comm)
Immediate Holding Company: JOHN PRESTON & CO. (BELFAST) LIMITED
Registration no: NI005891 **Date established:** 1964 **Turnover:** £1m - £2m
No.of Employees: 11 - 20 **Product Groups:** 24, 63, 67

Date of Accounts	Dec 11	Dec 10	Dec 09
Working Capital	715	591	515
Fixed Assets	123	55	58
Current Assets	1m	1m	1m

Roadside Motors Lisburn

22 Market Place, Lisburn, BT28 1AN
Tel: 028-9267 7412 **Fax:** 028-9267 2815
E-mail: jeff.mcilroy@roadsidemotors.com
Website: http://www.peugeotmail.co.uk
Directors: J. Mcilroy (Dir)
Immediate Holding Company: DORNAN'S SERVICE STATION (LISBURN)LIMITED
Registration no: NI011237 **VAT No.:** GB 286 3934 18
Date established: 1976 **Turnover:** £5m - £10m **No.of Employees:** 11 - 20
Product Groups: 39, 68, 72, 85

Roberts Robert Ltd (Edwards Food Products)

Flush Park, Lisburn, BT28 2DX
Tel: 028-9267 3316 **Fax:** 028-9266 1131
E-mail: savoury@easynet.co.uk
Website: http://www.robt-roberts.co.uk
Bank(s): Bank of Ireland
Directors: G. Bradley (MD)
Ultimate Holding Company: DCC PUBLIC LIMITED COMPANY
Immediate Holding Company: Robert Roberts (NI) Limited
Registration no: NI044270 **VAT No.:** GB 283 7681 49
Date established: 2002 **Turnover:** £10m - £20m
No.of Employees: 21 - 50 **Product Groups:** 62

Date of Accounts	Mar 11	Mar 10	Mar 09
Sales Turnover	7m	6m	13m
Pre Tax Profit/Loss	-414	-498	-337
Working Capital	2m	701	897
Fixed Assets	2m	129	302
Current Assets	3m	1m	3m
Current Liabilities	551	458	523

Scales Equipment

51 Lambeg Road, Lisburn, BT27 4QA
Tel: 028-9267 1800 **Fax:** 028-9267 3639
E-mail: secmatt.trimble@yahoo.co.uk
Website: http://www.scales-ireland.com
Managers: M. Trimble (Chief Mgr)
Immediate Holding Company: CATERING KITCHENS LTD
Registration no: NI045989 **Date established:** 2003
No.of Employees: 11 - 20 **Product Groups:** 38, 42

Scott Medical Ltd

Saintfield Park, Lisburn, BT27 5BG
Tel: 028-9266 5482 **Fax:** 028-9264 0986
E-mail: sales@scottmedical.co.uk
Website: http://www.scottmedical.co.uk
Directors: S. Tollerton (Dir)
Immediate Holding Company: Scott Medical Limited
Registration no: NI065193 **Date established:** 2007
No.of Employees: 1 - 10 **Product Groups:** 24, 30, 38, 67

Date of Accounts	Jul 11	Jul 10	Jul 09
Working Capital	104	106	69
Fixed Assets	242	279	301
Current Assets	237	241	220

Silverwood Doors

17 Ferguson Drive, Lisburn, BT28 2EX
Tel: 028-9267 7333 **Fax:** 028-9267 7334
E-mail: info@silverwood-doors.co.uk
Website: http://www.silverwood-doors.co.uk
Directors: B. Guthrie (MD), B. Guthrie (MD)
Managers: J. Gregory (Sales Prom Mgr)
Immediate Holding Company: W.C. GUTHRIE LIMITED
Registration no: NI013065 **Date established:** 1972
No.of Employees: 21 - 50 **Product Groups:** 25

Date of Accounts	Dec 11	Dec 10	Dec 09
Working Capital	-104	-186	184
Fixed Assets	3m	3m	3m
Current Assets	962	953	1m

Smiley Monroe

Ferguson Drive, Lisburn, BT28 2EX
Tel: 028-9267 3777 **Fax:** 028-9266 3666
E-mail: sales@smileymonroe.com
Website: http://www.smileymonroe.com
Directors: V. Monroe (MD)
Managers: A. Marais (Tech Serv Mgr), D. Mcgrady (Ops Mgr), T. Munroe (Mktg Serv Mgr)
Ultimate Holding Company: SMILEY MONROE HOLDINGS LIMITED
Immediate Holding Company: SMILEY MONROE HOLDINGS LIMITED
Registration no: NI042483 **VAT No.:** GB 287 1797 06
Date established: 2002 **Turnover:** £10m - £20m
No.of Employees: 51 - 100 **Product Groups:** 48, 84

Date of Accounts	Dec 11	Dec 10	Dec 09
Sales Turnover	14m	11m	6m
Pre Tax Profit/Loss	688	411	-401
Working Capital	918	7	-283
Fixed Assets	3m	3m	3m
Current Assets	6m	5m	3m
Current Liabilities	2m	2m	1m

Stoneyford Engineers Ltd

17 White Mountain Road, Lisburn, BT28 3QZ
Tel: 028-9264 8822 **Fax:** 028-9276 4882
E-mail: declan.phillips@stoneyfordeng.com
Directors: D. Phillips (MD)
Immediate Holding Company: STONEYFORD ENGINEERING LTD
Registration no: NI064616 **Date established:** 2007
No.of Employees: 1 - 10 **Product Groups:** 37, 40, 48

Date of Accounts	Mar 11	Mar 09
Working Capital	-146	N/A
Fixed Assets	194	N/A
Current Assets	203	N/A

Structural Design & Detailing

Unit 34 Crescent Business Park, Lisburn, BT28 2GN
Tel: 028-9266 6860 **Fax:** 028-9266 6898
E-mail: office@sdd-ltd.com
Directors: J. Mccarter (Co Sec)
Immediate Holding Company: Structural Design & Detailing Limited
Registration no: NI066890 **Date established:** 2007
No.of Employees: 1 - 10 **Product Groups:** 35

Date of Accounts	Dec 11	Dec 10	Dec 09
Working Capital	-152	-177	-197
Fixed Assets	156	182	207
Current Assets	126	151	132

T A L Ltd

Tal House Lissue Industrial Estate East, Lisburn, BT28 2RB
Tel: 028-9262 2345 **Fax:** 028-9262 0950
E-mail: construct@tal.ltd.uk
Website: http://www.tal.ltd.uk
Directors: T. Hughes (MD)
Immediate Holding Company: TAL Civil Engineering Limited
Registration no: NI015017 **Date established:** 1981
Turnover: £20m - £50m **No.of Employees:** 51 - 100 **Product Groups:** 51, 52

Date of Accounts	Mar 11	Mar 10	Mar 09
Pre Tax Profit/Loss	N/A	N/A	176
Working Capital	720	687	602
Fixed Assets	14	44	97
Current Assets	3m	2m	3m
Current Liabilities	N/A	N/A	2m

Taylor Signs Ltd

Unit 22 Blaris Industrial Estate Altona Road, Lisburn, BT27 5QB
Tel: 028-9267 1383 **Fax:** 028-9266 6054
E-mail: taylorsigns@btconnect.com
Website: http://www.taylorsigns.com
Directors: P. Mcnamee (MD)
Ultimate Holding Company: BLACKWOOD TRADING LIMITED
Immediate Holding Company: TAYLOR SIGNS LIMITED
Registration no: NI024751 **VAT No.:** GB 517 8246 33
Date established: 1990 **No.of Employees:** 1 - 10 **Product Groups:** 30, 37, 39, 49

Date of Accounts	Jul 11	Jul 10	Jul 09
Working Capital	22	62	59
Fixed Assets	40	6	6
Current Assets	241	176	113

Tech Europe

15 Ballinderry Road Ballinderry Industrial Estate, Lisburn, BT28 2SA
Tel: 028-9266 5721 **Fax:** 028-9260 1611
E-mail: hwrightturner@euratyrerepair.com
Bank(s): Ulster Bank
Directors: M. Noble (MD)
Managers: C. McAneney (Purch Mgr)
Immediate Holding Company: PRIME PAINTS LIMITED
Registration no: NI024200 **VAT No.:** 9B517955613 **Date established:** 1990
Turnover: £5m - £10m **No.of Employees:** 21 - 50 **Product Groups:** 29, 39

Ulster PVC Ltd

2b Glenavy Road Ballinderry Upper, Lisburn, BT28 2EU
Tel: 028-9265 1007 **Fax:** 028-9265 2019
E-mail: info@terapin.com
Website: http://www.terapin.com
Directors: I. Mcclelland (Dir)
Immediate Holding Company: ULSTER P.V.C. LIMITED
Registration no: NI008338 **Date established:** 1971
Turnover: £500,000 - £1m **No.of Employees:** 1 - 10 **Product Groups:** 24

Date of Accounts	Apr 12	Apr 11	Apr 10
Working Capital	126	73	101
Fixed Assets	109	124	138
Current Assets	222	182	188
Current Liabilities	96	N/A	88

Uni Trunk Ltd

4 Altona Road, Lisburn, BT27 5QB
Tel: 028-9262 5100 **Fax:** 028-9262 5101
E-mail: david.morrow@unitrunk.co.uk
Website: http://www.unitrunk.co.uk
Bank(s): Northern Bank
Directors: W. Loughnan (Co Sec), M. Morrow (MD), M. Clarke (Fin)
Managers: N. Hopkins (Tech Serv Mgr), D. Pritchard (Sales Prom Mgr), D. Morrow (Chief Mgr), H. Jess (Personnel)
Ultimate Holding Company: UNI-TRUNK HOLDINGS LIMITED
Immediate Holding Company: UNI-TRUNK LIMITED
Registration no: FC018247 **VAT No.:** GB 251 8123 81
Date established: 1994 **Turnover:** £10m - £20m
No.of Employees: 21 - 50 **Product Groups:** 37

Date of Accounts	Dec 99	Dec 02	Dec 01
Sales Turnover	N/A	14m	N/A
Pre Tax Profit/Loss	322	577	623
Working Capital	2m	4m	2m
Fixed Assets	2m	5m	4m
Current Assets	5m	8m	5m
Current Liabilities	306	769	633

Unicorn Hygienics

5 Ferguson Drive, Lisburn, BT28 2EX
Tel: 028-9264 0827 **Fax:** 028-9262 5616
E-mail: info@unicorn-hygienics.com
Website: http://www.unicorn-hygienics.com
Bank(s): Bank of Ireland
Directors: S. Greeves (Fin), R. Pannell (MD)
Managers: B. Taylor, B. James (Sales & Mktg Mg), K. Diver
Ultimate Holding Company: FHS GROUP LIMITED
Immediate Holding Company: UNICORN CONTAINERS LIMITED
Registration no: NI029839 **VAT No.:** GB 663 1041 67
Date established: 1995 **Turnover:** £2m - £5m **No.of Employees:** 11 - 20
Product Groups: 30

Date of Accounts	Sep 11	Sep 10	Sep 09
Working Capital	1m	951	1m
Fixed Assets	299	295	294
Current Assets	4m	2m	2m

Universal Facades Ltd

64 Antrim Street, Lisburn, BT28 1AU
Tel: 028-9260 3777 **Fax:** 028-9260 3777
E-mail: paul@universalfacades.com
Website: http://www.universalfacades.com
Directors: P. O'Neill (Prop), P. O'neill (MD), G. O'neill (Fin)
Immediate Holding Company: UNIVERSAL FACADES LIMITED
Registration no: NI041891 **Date established:** 2001
No.of Employees: 21 - 50 **Product Groups:** 26, 35

Date of Accounts	Oct 10	Oct 09	Oct 08
Working Capital	-2m	-1m	-916
Fixed Assets	10	16	58
Current Assets	2m	2m	2m

W J Law Group Ltd

Rosevale House 171 Moira Road, Lisburn, BT28 1RW
Tel: 028-9267 7317 **Fax:** 028-9266 1733
E-mail: info@wjlaw.co.uk
Website: http://www.wjlaw.co.uk
Directors: D. Law (MD)
Immediate Holding Company: W.J. LAW GROUP LTD
Registration no: NI008590 **Date established:** 1972
No.of Employees: 11 - 20 **Product Groups:** 52, 72

Date of Accounts	Mar 12	Mar 11	Mar 10
Working Capital	2m	2m	3m
Fixed Assets	8	8	8
Current Assets	2m	2m	3m

W J Macnab & Co Sales Ltd

45 Waterloo Road, Lisburn, BT27 5NJ
Tel: 028-9267 8423 **Fax:** 028-9267 5210
E-mail: info@wjmacnab.co.uk
Website: http://www.wjmacnab.co.uk
Directors: M. Whittaker (Dir)
Immediate Holding Company: WM. J. MACNAB & CO. (SALES) LIMITED
Registration no: NI006165 **VAT No.:** GB 251 7293 61
Date established: 1964 **Turnover:** £250,000 - £500,000
No.of Employees: 1 - 10 **Product Groups:** 66

Date of Accounts	Dec 11	Dec 10	Dec 09
Working Capital	283	217	179
Fixed Assets	559	571	626
Current Assets	716	558	531

Robert Walsh

2 Haddockstown Road Ballinderry Upper, Lisburn, BT28 2JJ
Tel: 028-9265 1410 **Fax:** 028-9265 1409
Directors: R. Walsh (Prop)
Date established: 1967 **No.of Employees:** 1 - 10 **Product Groups:** 20, 40, 41

Warmflow Engineering

Rathdown Walk Lissue Industrial Estate, Lisburn, BT28 2RF
Tel: 028-9262 0980 **Fax:** 028-9262 0987
E-mail: reception@warmflow.co.uk
Website: http://www.warmflow.co.uk
Bank(s): Northern
Directors: P. Martin (Dir)
Ultimate Holding Company: Warmflow Holdings Limited
Immediate Holding Company: WARMFLOW ENGINEERING CO.LIMITED
Registration no: NI016292 **VAT No.:** GB 390 7355 35
Date established: 1982 **Turnover:** £10m - £20m
No.of Employees: 51 - 100 **Product Groups:** 40

Date of Accounts	Jun 11	Jun 10	Jun 09
Sales Turnover	16m	17m	17m
Pre Tax Profit/Loss	365	476	32
Working Capital	7m	6m	6m
Fixed Assets	645	769	1m
Current Assets	9m	10m	8m
Current Liabilities	874	1m	1m

Wells Kennedy Partnership
85-87 Gregg Street, Lisburn, BT27 5AW
Tel: 028-9266 4257 **Fax:** 028-9260 3722
E-mail: dmcelderry@btconnect.com
Website: http://www.wk.dnet.co.uk
Directors: D. Mcelderry (Prop)
Immediate Holding Company: WELLS KENNEDY PARTNERSHIP LIMITED
Registration no: NI013649 **VAT No.:** GB 287 2020 64
Date established: 1979 **No.of Employees:** 1 - 10 **Product Groups:** 49

White Mountain Tyre & Battery Co
11 Sheepwalk Road, Lisburn, BT28 3RD
Tel: 028-9264 8251 **Fax:** 028-9250 1100
E-mail: mark.kelly@lagen-group.com
Directors: B. McNamara (Dir), M. Kelly (MD)
Managers: L. Mcdonald (Comptroller)
Registration no: NI055953 **VAT No.:** 392 6858 02 **Date established:** 2005
Turnover: £10m - £20m **No.of Employees:** 1 - 10 **Product Groups:** 51

Whitemountain Quarries
26 Ballycarngannon Road, Lisburn, BT27 6YA
Tel: 028-9263 9750 **Fax:** 028-9263 9751
E-mail: info@lagan-group.com
Website: http://www.lagan-group.com
Bank(s): H S B C
Directors: C. Jenkins (Co Sec), M. Lagam (MD), M. Lagan (MD)
Managers: A. Devlin (Sales Admin), B. King (Sales Admin)
Immediate Holding Company: Whitemountain Quarries Ltd
Registration no: NI018140 **VAT No.:** GB 617 7162 36
Date established: 1985 **Turnover:** £1m - £2m **No.of Employees:** 21 - 50
Product Groups: 51

www.grit-bins.com Unicorn Containers Group Sites
Unicorn 5 Ferguson Drive, Knockmore Hill Industrial Park, Lisburn, BT28 2EX
Tel: 0845-247 7264
E-mail: contactus@grit-bins.com
Website: http://www.grit-bins.com
Turnover: Up to £250,000 **No.of Employees:** 51 - 100
Product Groups: 17, 40, 45, 47, 67

Zenith Hygiene Systems Ltd
Blaris Industrial Estate Altona Road, Lisburn, BT27 5QB
Tel: 028-9267 3331 **Fax:** 028-9267 3939
E-mail: david.mcilroy@zhgplc.com
Website: http://www.zhgplc.com
Directors: D. Mcilroy (Chief Op Offcr)
Managers: A. McCutcheon (Personnel), T. Mackin (Fin Mgr), M. Perry (Sales Prom Mgr), G. Quinn (Purch Mgr)
Ultimate Holding Company: ZENITH HYGIENE GROUP PLC
Immediate Holding Company: S.B. CHEMICALS LIMITED
Registration no: NI015925 **VAT No.:** GB 366 4125 52
Date established: 1982 **Turnover:** £5m - £10m
No.of Employees: 51 - 100 **Product Groups:** 32

Date of Accounts	Feb 12	Feb 11	Feb 10
Sales Turnover	N/A	N/A	8m
Pre Tax Profit/Loss	N/A	N/A	2m
Working Capital	4m	4m	4m
Fixed Assets	N/A	N/A	569
Current Assets	4m	4m	12m
Current Liabilities	N/A	N/A	298

Co. Londonderry

Londonderry

A E Mccandless & Company Ltd
23 Bishop Street, Londonderry, BT48 6PR
Tel: 028-7136 2071 **Fax:** 028-7126 8996
E-mail: sportprinters@aol.com
Bank(s): Ulster Bank
Directors: R. McCandless (MD)
Ultimate Holding Company: A.E. McCandless (Shirt Makers) Limited
Immediate Holding Company: A. E. MCCANDLESS & CO. LIMITED
Registration no: NI001349 **VAT No.:** GB 252 5029 82
Date established: 1939 **No.of Employees:** 21 - 50 **Product Groups:** 24

Date of Accounts	Apr 11	Apr 10	Apr 09
Working Capital	278	297	292
Fixed Assets	749	750	760
Current Assets	334	342	337

Albert Fry Associates
69 Clarendon Street, Londonderry, BT48 7ER
Tel: 028-7137 1881 **Fax:** 028-7126 6656
E-mail: info@afaderry.com
Website: http://www.albertfryassociates.com
Directors: S. Sands (MD)
Immediate Holding Company: ALBERT FRY ASSOCIATES (DERRY) LTD
Registration no: NI025519 **VAT No.:** GB 516 8370 38
Date established: 1991 **Turnover:** £2m - £5m **No.of Employees:** 1 - 10
Product Groups: 84

Date of Accounts	Nov 11	Nov 10	Nov 09
Working Capital	166	179	197
Fixed Assets	34	39	43
Current Assets	187	213	262

Ardmore Precast Concrete Ltd
25 Ballybogie Road Ardmore, Londonderry, BT47 3RE
Tel: 028-7134 9566 **Fax:** 028-7131 1100
E-mail: info@ardmoreprecast.co.uk
Website: http://www.ardmoreprecast.co.uk
Managers: W. Mclaughlin (Prod Mgr)
Immediate Holding Company: ARDMORE (CO.DERRY) PRE-CAST CONCRETE LIMITED
Registration no: NI011632 **VAT No.:** GB 311 1234 30
Date established: 1976 **Turnover:** £500,000 - £1m
No.of Employees: 1 - 10 **Product Groups:** 33

Date of Accounts	Dec 11	Dec 10	Dec 09
Working Capital	-386	-387	-280
Fixed Assets	376	442	505
Current Assets	130	145	170

Arntz Belting Co. Ltd
Pennyburn Passage, Londonderry, BT48 0AE
Tel: 028-7126 1221 **Fax:** 028-7126 3386
E-mail: abc@optibelt.com
Website: http://www.optibelt.com
Directors: T. Smith (Fin), R. Moore (MD)
Managers: E. Grant (Personnel), R. Burrows (Purch Mgr)
Ultimate Holding Company: ARNTZ BETEILLGUNGS GMBH & CO KG (GERMANY)
Immediate Holding Company: ARNTZ BELTING COMPANY LIMITED
Registration no: NI007315 **VAT No.:** GB 251 7475 55
Date established: 1968 **Turnover:** £2m - £5m **No.of Employees:** 1 - 10
Product Groups: 35

Date of Accounts	Dec 10	Dec 09	Dec 08
Sales Turnover	4m	10m	14m
Pre Tax Profit/Loss	-1m	-922	930
Working Capital	634	1m	2m
Fixed Assets	387	851	1m
Current Assets	747	2m	3m
Current Liabilities	51	144	207

Besam Automatic Doors
Unit 43 Eurocentre West Pennyburn Industrial Estate, Londonderry, BT48 0LU
Tel: 028-7126 8011 **Fax:** 028-7127 1115
E-mail: sales@besam.com
Website: http://www.besam.com
Managers: P. Mcarty (Mgr)
Ultimate Holding Company: ATLANTIC HARVEST LIMITED
Registration no: NI008448 **Date established:** 1971
No.of Employees: 1 - 10 **Product Groups:** 26, 35

B-Fast Parcels
8c Ballougry Road, Londonderry, BT48 9XJ
Tel: 028-7126 6117 **Fax:** 028-7126 6635
E-mail: info@courierireland.com
Website: http://www.courierireland.com
Directors: T. Quigley (Prop)
No.of Employees: 21 - 50 **Product Groups:** 79

C P C Office Supplies Ltd
Carrakeel Drive Maydown, Londonderry, BT47 6UQ
Tel: 028-7186 1000 **Fax:** 028-7186 1010
E-mail: sales@cpcofficesupplies.com
Website: http://www.cpcofficesupplies.com
Directors: I. Crowe (MD)
Immediate Holding Company: CPC OFFICE SUPPLIES LIMITED
Registration no: NI017588 **VAT No.:** GB 393 6099 14
Date established: 1984 **Turnover:** £1m - £2m **No.of Employees:** 1 - 10
Product Groups: 64, 67

Date of Accounts	Sep 11	Sep 10	Sep 09
Working Capital	225	236	251
Fixed Assets	304	305	319
Current Assets	353	410	402

Carella Laminate Systems Ltd
11 Campsie Business Park Mclean Road, Eglinton, Londonderry, BT47 3XX
Tel: 028-7181 0330 **Fax:** 028-7181 1604
E-mail: info@carella.com
Website: http://www.carella.com
Directors: S. Heron (MD)
Managers: J. Patton (Sales Prom Mgr), P. Villa (Chief Mgr), S. Flanagan, S. Mullan (Chief Acct)
Immediate Holding Company: CARELLA LAMINATE SYSTEMS LTD.
Registration no: NI022972 **VAT No.:** GB 311 1165 23
Date established: 1989 **Turnover:** £500,000 - £1m
No.of Employees: 21 - 50 **Product Groups:** 26, 49

Date of Accounts	Jul 11	Jul 10	Jul 09
Working Capital	411	633	726
Fixed Assets	2m	2m	2m
Current Assets	1m	2m	2m

City Industrial Waste Ltd
60 Mobuoy Road, Londonderry, BT47 3JQ
Tel: 028-7136 5544 **Fax:** 028-7186 1881
E-mail: mail@cityindustrialwaste.com
Website: http://www.cityindustrialwaste.com
Directors: G. Farmer (Dir)
Immediate Holding Company: CITY INDUSTRIAL WASTE LIMITED
Registration no: NI048959 **Date established:** 2003 **Turnover:** £1m - £2m
No.of Employees: 51 - 100 **Product Groups:** 51, 83

Date of Accounts	Feb 11	Feb 10	Feb 09
Sales Turnover	447	N/A	N/A
Pre Tax Profit/Loss	-1m	-2m	-894
Working Capital	1m	2m	N/A
Fixed Assets	12m	12m	10m
Current Assets	3m	2m	841
Current Liabilities	2m	N/A	N/A

City Roofing & Asphalt Services Ltd
3a Pennyburn Business Park Pennyburn Industrial Estate, Londonderry, BT48 0LU
Tel: 028-7126 9648 **Fax:** 028-7136 7016
E-mail: info@cityroofing.eu
Website: http://www.cityroofing.eu
Managers: T. O'Hare (Sales Admin)
Immediate Holding Company: CITY ROOFING AND ASPHALT SERVICES LIMITED
Registration no: NI016504 **VAT No.:** GB 331 8286 59
Date established: 1983 **No.of Employees:** 11 - 20 **Product Groups:** 31, 52

Date of Accounts	May 11	May 10	May 09
Working Capital	263	266	274
Fixed Assets	106	120	139
Current Assets	525	497	490

F M Corr & Associates
1 Bayview Terrace, Londonderry, BT48 7EE
Tel: 028-7126 1331 **Fax:** 028-7137 1985
E-mail: info@fmcorrarchitects.com
Website: http://www.fmcorrarchitects.com
Directors: P. Gallagher (Ptnr)
VAT No.: GB 331 8739 48 **Date established:** 1968
No.of Employees: 1 - 10 **Product Groups:** 84

Cottage Conservatories
12 Clooney Road, Londonderry, BT47 6TB
Tel: 028-7134 5571 **Fax:** 028-7134 9400
Directors: P. Wallace (Prop)
Registration no: NI018739 **Date established:** 1985
No.of Employees: 21 - 50 **Product Groups:** 08, 25, 35

J J Coyle
416 Ballyquin Road Dungiven, Londonderry, BT47 4NQ
Tel: 028-7774 1311 **Fax:** 028-7774 2344
Directors: N. Coyle (Prop)
Immediate Holding Company: JJ COYLE LIMITED
Registration no: NI047291 **VAT No.:** GB 252 7140 80
Date established: 2003 **No.of Employees:** 11 - 20 **Product Groups:** 66

Date of Accounts	Dec 11	Dec 10	Dec 09
Working Capital	154	287	511
Fixed Assets	1m	1m	1m
Current Assets	465	589	925

D & M Farm Services
36 Carmoney Road Eglinton, Londonderry, BT47 3JJ
Tel: 028-7181 1134 **Fax:** 028-7181 1600
E-mail: dandmfarmservice@btconnect.com
Website: http://www.dandmfarmservices.com
Directors: J. Dinsmore (Dir)
Immediate Holding Company: D & M FARM SERVICES LIMITED
Registration no: NI058420 **VAT No.:** GB 432 6809 49
Date established: 2006 **Turnover:** Up to £250,000
No.of Employees: 1 - 10 **Product Groups:** 48, 67

Date of Accounts	Mar 12	Mar 11	Mar 10
Working Capital	213	190	173
Fixed Assets	82	96	114
Current Assets	921	543	563

Derry City Council
98 Strand Road, Londonderry, BT48 7NN
Tel: 028-7136 5151 **Fax:** 028-7126 4858
E-mail: info@derrycity.gov.uk
Website: http://www.derrycity.gov.uk
Directors: J. Campbell (Fin), W. Tabbett (Tech Serv), S. McNicholl (Pers)
Managers: F. Haggerty (Personnel), T. Monaghan (Mgr), J. Campbell (Fin Mgr), U. Harvey (I.T. Exec)
Immediate Holding Company: DERRY INVESTMENT INITIATIVE LIMITED
Registration no: NI034536 **Date established:** 1998
No.of Employees: 11 - 20 **Product Groups:** 87

Diamond Corrugated Cases Ltd
14 Campsie Industrial Estate Mclean Road, Eglinton, Londonderry, BT47 3XX
Tel: 028-7126 2957 **Fax:** 028-7126 7094
E-mail: mail@diamondcorr.com
Website: http://www.diamondcorr.com
Bank(s): Bank of Ireland
Directors: S. Mckeegan (Prop), T. Houston (Fin)
Immediate Holding Company: DIAMOND CORRUGATED CASES LIMITED
Registration no: NI009409 **VAT No.:** GB 253 3663 62
Date established: 1973 **Turnover:** £10m - £20m
No.of Employees: 21 - 50 **Product Groups:** 27, 28, 30, 33, 34, 35, 36, 37, 38, 41, 44, 66, 85

Date of Accounts	Mar 10	Mar 09	Mar 08
Sales Turnover	10m	N/A	N/A
Pre Tax Profit/Loss	144	N/A	N/A
Working Capital	611	700	698
Fixed Assets	4m	4m	4m
Current Assets	3m	3m	2m
Current Liabilities	216	N/A	N/A

James Doherty Meats Ltd
7 Pennyburn Industrial Estate, Londonderry, BT48 0LU
Tel: 028-7126 7884 **Fax:** 028-7136 1091
E-mail: mail@jdm.co.uk
Website: http://www.jdm.co.uk
Directors: S. Doherty (Dir), I. Doherty (Sales & Mktg), J. Doherty (Fin)
Immediate Holding Company: JAMES DOHERTY (MEATS) LIMITED
Registration no: NI020410 **VAT No.:** GB 252 0258 92
Date established: 1987 **Turnover:** £2m - £5m **No.of Employees:** 21 - 50
Product Groups: 20

Date of Accounts	Sep 11	Sep 10	Sep 09
Working Capital	14	-54	-238
Fixed Assets	1m	1m	2m
Current Assets	667	552	695

W Donnell
Benbow Industrial Estate 15 Killylane Road, Eglinton, Londonderry, BT47 3DW
Tel: 028-7181 0609 **Fax:** 028-7181 1167
Directors: W. Donnell (Prop)
Date established: 1989 **No.of Employees:** 1 - 10 **Product Groups:** 20, 40, 41

E R M Mechanical Services Ltd
Unit 10 Northland Road Industrial Estate, Londonderry, BT48 0LD
Tel: 028-7130 8446 **Fax:** 028-7137 7232
E-mail: admin@ermmechanical.com
Website: http://www.ermmechanical.com
Directors: A. Mcclean (MD)
Immediate Holding Company: E.R.M. MECHANICAL SERVICES LIMITED
Registration no: NI028540 **Date established:** 1994
No.of Employees: 11 - 20 **Product Groups:** 35

Eakin Bros Ltd
48 Main Street Claudy, Londonderry, BT47 4HR
Tel: 028-7133 8641 **Fax:** 028-7133 8890
E-mail: p.eakin@eakinbros.com
Directors: P. Eakin (Dir)
Immediate Holding Company: EAKIN BROTHERS LIMITED
Registration no: NI004445 **VAT No.:** GB 251 7749 44
Date established: 1959 **Turnover:** £10m - £20m
No.of Employees: 11 - 20 **Product Groups:** 68

Date of Accounts	Dec 11	Dec 10	Dec 09
Sales Turnover	12m	12m	11m
Pre Tax Profit/Loss	-150	-69	-9
Working Capital	2m	2m	2m
Fixed Assets	663	721	757
Current Assets	3m	3m	3m
Current Liabilities	59	139	145

Ever Rest Bedding
Unit 4 Springtown Business Park Industrial Estate Springtown Road, Londonderry, BT48 0LY
Tel: 028-7137 1925 **Fax:** 028-7136 0016
Managers: J. Doherty (Mgr)
Immediate Holding Company: MERLIN ENVIRONMENTAL TECHNOLOGIES LIMITED
Registration no: NI059182 **Date established:** 2011
Turnover: £500,000 - £1m **No.of Employees:** 1 - 10 **Product Groups:** 61

Evergreen Lawns
12 Foyle Avenue Greysteel, Londonderry, BT47 3EB
Tel: 028-7181 0225 **Fax:** 028-7181 2521
E-mail: john@evergreenlawns.co.uk
Website: http://www.evergreenlawns.co.uk
Managers: J. Jameson (Sales Admin)
Immediate Holding Company: EVERGREEN LAWNS LIMITED
Registration no: NI044633 **Date established:** 2002
Turnover: Up to £250,000 **No.of Employees:** 1 - 10 **Product Groups:** 07

Date of Accounts	Apr 11	Apr 10	Apr 09
Working Capital	-32	-19	29
Fixed Assets	339	405	375
Current Assets	268	298	353

Feeney Electrical
Unit 7b 15 Killylane Road, Eglinton, Londonderry, BT47 3DW
Tel: 028-7181 1085 **Fax:** 028-7181 2471
E-mail: info@feeneyelectrical.com
Website: http://www.feeneyelectrical.com
Directors: L. Feeney (Prop)
Immediate Holding Company: FEENEY ELECTRICAL LIMITED
Registration no: NI028779 **VAT No.:** GB 393 5485 14
Date established: 1994 **No.of Employees:** 1 - 10 **Product Groups:** 84

Date of Accounts	Sep 11	Sep 10	Sep 09
Working Capital	-79	-101	-48
Fixed Assets	39	42	47
Current Assets	121	64	53

Fleming Agri Products Ltd
New Buildings Industrial Estate Victoria Road, Newbuildings, Londonderry, BT47 2SX
Tel: 028-7134 2637 **Fax:** 028-7134 4735
E-mail: info@fleming-agri.co.uk
Website: http://www.fleming-agri.co.uk
Directors: G. Fleming (MD), J. Lecky (Fab)
Managers: A. Hunter (Personnel), R. Brattan (Comptroller), B. Hunter (Sales Prom Mgr)
Immediate Holding Company: FLEMING AGRI-PRODUCTS LIMITED
Registration no: NI016347 **Date established:** 1983
Turnover: £500,000 - £1m **No.of Employees:** 51 - 100
Product Groups: 67

Date of Accounts	Mar 11	Mar 10	Mar 09
Sales Turnover	7m	6m	N/A
Pre Tax Profit/Loss	596	730	694
Working Capital	3m	3m	2m
Fixed Assets	2m	1m	1m
Current Assets	5m	4m	4m
Current Liabilities	378	404	343

Foyle Meats
Temple Road Strathfoyle, Londonderry, BT47 6TJ
Tel: 028-7186 0691 **Fax:** 028-7186 0700
E-mail: info@foylemeats.com
Website: http://www.foylefoodgroup.com
Directors: T. Acheson (MD), N. McIlwaine (Fin)
Managers: J. Newell (Personnel), R. Wallace (Tech Serv Mgr), S. McAdam (Grp Sales Mgr)
Ultimate Holding Company: FAUGHAN LIMITED
Immediate Holding Company: FOYLE MEATS
Registration no: NI011193 **VAT No.:** GB 286 6290 21
Date established: 1976 **Turnover:** £20m - £50m
No.of Employees: 101 - 250 **Product Groups:** 20

Date of Accounts	Dec 10	Dec 09	Dec 08
Working Capital	19	19	3m
Fixed Assets	5m	5m	5m
Current Assets	19	19	3m

GB Engineering
Unit 3d Maydown Industrial Estate 15a Carrakeel Drive, Maydown, Londonderry, BT47 6UQ
Tel: 028-7186 1111 **Fax:** 028-7186 1100
E-mail: info@gb-engineering.co.uk
Website: http://www.gb-engineering.co.uk
Managers: C. Graham (Mgr)
Immediate Holding Company: MAYDOWN PRECISION ENGINEERING LIMITED
Registration no: NI017934 **Date established:** 1984 **Turnover:** £2m - £5m
No.of Employees: 11 - 20 **Product Groups:** 26, 35, 39, 45, 46

Date of Accounts	Mar 11	Mar 10	Mar 09
Sales Turnover	5m	5m	N/A
Pre Tax Profit/Loss	-38	32	288
Working Capital	246	383	343
Fixed Assets	2m	3m	3m
Current Assets	1m	1m	2m
Current Liabilities	501	313	414

Garvan O'Doherty
7 Northland Road, Londonderry, BT48 7HY
Tel: 028-7126 4876 **Fax:** 028-7137 4508
E-mail: info@god-group.com
Website: http://www.god-group.com
Directors: G. O'doherty (Prop)
Immediate Holding Company: OMERTA INVESTMENTS LIMITED
Registration no: NI029968 **VAT No.:** GB 393 6750 16
Date established: 1995 **Turnover:** £1m - £2m **No.of Employees:** 1 - 10
Product Groups: 69

Date of Accounts	Dec 11	Dec 10	Dec 09
Working Capital	1m	209	480
Fixed Assets	4m	4m	4m
Current Assets	2m	549	540

Glen Park Environmental Services Ltd
33 Campsie Industrial Estate Mclean Road, Eglinton, Londonderry, BT47 3XX
Tel: 028-7181 1183 **Fax:** 028-7181 1431
E-mail: enquiries@glenpark.co.uk
Website: http://www.glenpark.co.uk
Bank(s): Ulster Bank
Directors: M. O'kane (MD)
Immediate Holding Company: GLENPARK ENVIRONMENTAL SERVICES LTD
Registration no: NI019574 **VAT No.:** GB 432 6112 88
Date established: 1986 **Turnover:** £500,000 - £1m
No.of Employees: 11 - 20 **Product Groups:** 26, 34, 35, 36, 40, 84

Date of Accounts	May 11	May 10	May 09
Working Capital	-135	-31	40
Fixed Assets	315	458	468
Current Assets	223	128	184

Guildhall
Shipquay Place, Londonderry, BT48 6DQ
Tel: 028-7137 7335 **Fax:** 028-7136 8536
Website: http://www.derrycitycouncil.gov.uk
Managers: C. Sharp (Chief Mgr)
No.of Employees: 1 - 10 **Product Groups:** 69

Haslett Monumental Sculptors
8 Church Brae Altnagelvin, Londonderry, BT47 2LS
Tel: 028-7134 5333 **Fax:** 028-7134 5333
E-mail: haslett.group@talk21.com
Website: http://www.haslettgroup.co.uk
Directors: B. Haslett (Prop)
Date established: 2002 **No.of Employees:** 1 - 10 **Product Groups:** 33

H M D Architects Ltd
13 Queen Street, Londonderry, BT48 7EG
Tel: 028-7126 7143 **Fax:** 028-7126 5995
E-mail: info@hmdarchitects.com
Website: http://www.hmbarchitects.com
Directors: M. O'kane (Dir)
Immediate Holding Company: HMD ARCHITECTS LTD
Registration no: NI041000 **VAT No.:** GB 286 5459 12
Date established: 2001 **Turnover:** £500,000 - £1m
No.of Employees: 1 - 10 **Product Groups:** 80, 84

Date of Accounts	Dec 11	Dec 10	Dec 09
Working Capital	214	215	247
Fixed Assets	228	262	298
Current Assets	490	571	868

I A W S Ltd
4a Mclean Road Eglinton, Londonderry, BT47 3PF
Tel: 028-7181 0340 **Fax:** 028-7181 0062
Website: http://www.iaws.ie
Managers: M. Mcinctok (Mgr), M. Owens (Mgr)
Ultimate Holding Company: ARYZTA AG (SWITZERLAND)
Immediate Holding Company: IAWS UK HOLDINGS LIMITED
Registration no: NI006802 **VAT No.:** GB 254 8360 49
Date established: 1966 **No.of Employees:** 1 - 10 **Product Groups:** 20, 23, 27, 32, 62

K Mcduff & Co. Ltd
177 Strand Road, Londonderry, BT48 7PU
Tel: 028-7136 6800 **Fax:** 028-7126 5490
Website: http://www.yell.com/buildersmerchants
Directors: A. Tollant (Ch), K. McDuff (MD), P. Macduff (Dir), P. McDuff (Dir)
Managers: T. McDuff (Mktg Serv Mgr)
Immediate Holding Company: K.MCDUFF & COMPANY LIMITED
Registration no: NI013268 **VAT No.:** GB 311 1770 06
Date established: 1978 **Turnover:** £2m - £5m **No.of Employees:** 21 - 50
Product Groups: 66

L M Fabrications
Unit 16 Blighs Lane, Londonderry, BT48 0LZ
Tel: 028-7126 0126 **Fax:** 028-7137 1743
E-mail: robert@lmfni.com
Website: http://www.lmfni.com
Bank(s): Bank of Ireland
Directors: R. Irwin (Ch), R. Irwin (MD)
Registration no: 00028768 **VAT No.:** GB 432 7463 54
Date established: 1987 **Turnover:** £500,000 - £1m
No.of Employees: 11 - 20 **Product Groups:** 52

Long's Supermarkets Ltd
Carrakeel Drive Maydown, Londonderry, BT47 6UQ
Tel: 028-7186 0004 **Fax:** 028-7186 0604
E-mail: brian.long@mrlong.co.uk
Directors: B. Long (MD)
Managers: M. Donnnell (Personnel), J. Finlay
Immediate Holding Company: LONG'S SUPERMARKETS LIMITED
Registration no: NI014135 **VAT No.:** GB 331 9500 78
Date established: 1980 **Turnover:** £10m - £20m
No.of Employees: 251 - 500 **Product Groups:** 61

Date of Accounts	Jan 11	Jan 10	Jan 09
Sales Turnover	18m	19m	N/A
Pre Tax Profit/Loss	14	315	162
Working Capital	-682	-918	-818
Fixed Assets	13m	13m	7m
Current Assets	3m	3m	3m
Current Liabilities	254	227	213

J Mccauley
45 Clarendon Street, Londonderry, BT48 7ER
Tel: 028-7126 5635 **Fax:** 028-7126 3146
E-mail: info@mccauleyqs.co.uk
Website: http://www.mccauleyqs.co.uk
Directors: P. Deeny (Prop)
VAT No.: GB 393 6265 23 **Turnover:** £250,000 - £500,000
No.of Employees: 1 - 10 **Product Groups:** 84

Mcguckin & Scott
17a Groarty Road, Londonderry, BT48 0JX
Tel: 028-7126 8415 **Fax:** 028-7137 1773
E-mail: scotthomes17a@hotmail.com
Directors: R. Scott (Ptnr)
Date established: 1978 **No.of Employees:** 1 - 10 **Product Groups:** 52

Mcgurk & Moore
Springtown Road, Londonderry, BT48 0LY
Tel: 028-7126 2960 **Fax:** 028-7137 1838
E-mail: info@mcgurk-moore.co.uk
Website: http://www.mcgurk-moore.co.uk
Managers: P. Mcgurk (Mgr)
Immediate Holding Company: MCGURK & MOORE LIMITED
Registration no: NI606766 **Date established:** 2011 **Turnover:** £2m - £5m
No.of Employees: 1 - 10 **Product Groups:** 52

Mcivor Plastics Ltd
161-171 Strand Road, Londonderry, BT48 7PT
Tel: 028-7126 7535 **Fax:** 028-7126 9313
E-mail: info@mcivor.co.uk
Website: http://www.mcivor.co.uk
Directors: P. Mcivor (MD)
Immediate Holding Company: MCIVOR PLASTICS LIMITED
Registration no: NI019282 **VAT No.:** GB 253 2542 79
Date established: 1986 **No.of Employees:** 11 - 20 **Product Groups:** 22, 30

Date of Accounts	Dec 11	Dec 10	Dec 09
Working Capital	330	327	368
Fixed Assets	328	347	362
Current Assets	397	381	425

Marc Five Ltd
3 Carrakeel Drive Maydown, Londonderry, BT47 6UQ
Tel: 028-7186 1288 **Fax:** 028-7186 1285
E-mail: info@marcfivejoinery.com
Website: http://www.marcfivejoinery.com
Bank(s): Ulster Bank
Directors: L. Rosborough (Dir)
Immediate Holding Company: MARC-FIVE LIMITED
Registration no: NI005655 **VAT No.:** GB 311 0063 36
Date established: 1963 **Turnover:** £250,000 - £500,000
No.of Employees: 11 - 20 **Product Groups:** 25

Date of Accounts	Dec 11	Dec 10	Dec 09
Working Capital	-232	-211	-177
Fixed Assets	981	1m	1m
Current Assets	204	180	121

Mona Units
56 Monadore Road Claudy, Londonderry, BT47 4DP
Tel: 028-7778 1600 **Fax:** 028-7778 1500
E-mail: enquiries@monaunits.com
Website: http://www.monaunits.com
Directors: J. Mcgaughey (Prop)
Immediate Holding Company: MONA UNITS LIMITED
Registration no: NI058256 **VAT No.:** GB 349 7876 55
Date established: 2006 **Turnover:** £250,000 - £500,000
No.of Employees: 1 - 10 **Product Groups:** 26

Date of Accounts	Mar 11	Mar 10	Mar 08
Working Capital	-548	-561	-478
Fixed Assets	258	307	762
Current Assets	197	257	569

Mulheron Partnership
18-20 Bishop Street, Londonderry, BT48 6PW
Tel: 028-7126 8539 **Fax:** 028-7127 1246
E-mail: info@mulheron.com
Website: http://www.mulheron.com
Directors: J. Mulheron (Prop)
Registration no: 00048581 **VAT No.:** GB 735 6557 08
Date established: 1979 **Turnover:** £500,000 - £1m
No.of Employees: 1 - 10 **Product Groups:** 84

Niche Drinks Co.
10 Rossdowney Road, Londonderry, BT47 6NS
Tel: 028-7134 3434 **Fax:** 028-7134 2723
E-mail: info@nichedrinks.com
Website: http://www.nichedrinks.com
Directors: C. Mulgrew (MD), R. Young (Fin)
Managers: F. Miller (Sales & Mktg Mg), K. Fulson
Ultimate Holding Company: KERRY GROUP PUBLIC LIMITED COMPANY
Immediate Holding Company: ST. BRENDANS IRISH CREAM LIQUEUR COMPANY LIMITED
Registration no: NI016383 **VAT No.:** GB 635 8381 17
Date established: 1983 **Turnover:** £10m - £20m
No.of Employees: 21 - 50 **Product Groups:** 21, 62

Date of Accounts	Dec 11	Dec 10	Dec 09
Pre Tax Profit/Loss	N/A	N/A	17
Working Capital	21m	21m	21m
Current Assets	21m	21m	21m

Nicholl Fuel Oils
Clooney Road Greysteel, Londonderry, BT47 3DY
Tel: 08458-505050 **Fax:** 028-7181 1057
E-mail: info@nicholoils.com
Website: http://www.nichollois.com
Directors: C. Nicholl (Dir), G. Nicholl (Dir), H. Nicholl (MD), L. Nicholl (Dir & Co Sec), L. Nicholls (Dir)
Immediate Holding Company: NICHOLLS'(FUEL OILS) LIMITED
Registration no: NI005816 **VAT No.:** GB 253 5505 70
Date established: 1964 **No.of Employees:** 1 - 10 **Product Groups:** 66

Date of Accounts	May 11	May 10	May 09
Sales Turnover	287m	288m	281m
Pre Tax Profit/Loss	5m	5m	6m
Working Capital	13m	12m	11m
Fixed Assets	22m	19m	17m
Current Assets	45m	41m	39m
Current Liabilities	215	398	765

Nor-Den Electrical
Unit 3 Springtown Industrial Estate Springtown Road, Londonderry, BT48 0LY
Tel: 028-7137 7210 **Fax:** 028-7127 1671
E-mail: norden@norden.co.uk
Website: http://www.nor-den.co.uk
Directors: K. Louden (D-G), M. Lowden (Grp Chief Exec), J. Louden (Grp Chief Exec)
Managers: M. Louden (Fin Mgr)
Immediate Holding Company: NOR-DEN ELECTRICAL
Registration no: NI025413 **VAT No.:** GB 331 9208 74
Date established: 1991 **No.of Employees:** 1 - 10 **Product Groups:** 52

North West Catering Equipment
Unit 19 The Vale Centre Clooney Road, Greysteel, Londonderry, BT47 3GE
Tel: 028-7181 0000 **Fax:** 028-7181 1100
Website: http://www.northwestcatering.co.uk
Managers: S. Mcgilloway (Mgr)
Immediate Holding Company: North West Catering Equipment Ltd
Registration no: NI050139 **Date established:** 2004
No.of Employees: 1 - 10 **Product Groups:** 20, 40, 41

Date of Accounts	Apr 11	Apr 10	Apr 09
Working Capital	17	14	9
Fixed Assets	3	7	12
Current Assets	67	103	112

North West Fencing
45 Curragh Road Dungiven, Londonderry, BT47 4SE
Tel: 028-7774 2220 **Fax:** 028-7774 2220
Directors: G. O'neil (Prop)
VAT No.: GB 516 8145 45 **No.of Employees:** 1 - 10 **Product Groups:** 26, 41

North & West Housing Ltd
18 Magazine Street, Londonderry, BT48 6HH
Tel: 028-7126 3819 **Fax:** 028-7126 3362
E-mail: info@nwh-group.com
Website: http://www.nwh-group.com

see next page

North & West Housing Ltd - Cont'd

Directors: G. Kelly (Grp Chief Exec), K. Ciarney (Dir)
Immediate Holding Company: North & West Properties Ltd
Registration no: NI040719 **Date established:** 2001
Turnover: £250,000 - £500,000 **No.of Employees:** 1 - 10
Product Groups: 88

T O'Connell & Sons

2 New Street Dungiven, Londonderry, BT47 4LJ
Tel: 028-7774 1370 **Fax:** 028-7774 1073
E-mail: info@toconnells.com
Bank(s): Northern Bank
Directors: G. O'connell (Ptnr), T. O'Connell (MD)
Immediate Holding Company: T O'CONNELL (UTILITIES) LIMITED
Registration no: NI607565 **VAT No.:** GB 252 3948 52
Date established: 2011 **No.of Employees:** 21 - 50 **Product Groups:** 33, 52, 66

O'Kane Bros Woodworking Ltd (Gang-Nail Systems Ltd)

13 Hass Road Dungiven, Londonderry, BT47 4QH
Tel: 028-7774 1705 **Fax:** 028-7774 2343
E-mail: okanebros@aol.com
Website: http://www.compasswd.com
Bank(s): Bank of Ireland
Directors: F. O'Kane (MD)
Managers: S. McCluskey (Personnel), L. McCarney (Chief Mgr)
Registration no: ni016389 **No.of Employees:** 21 - 50 **Product Groups:** 25, 30

The Old Oak Forge Eglinton

15 Killylane Road Eglinton, Londonderry, BT47 3DW
Tel: 028-7181 2742 **Fax:** 028-7181 2742
Directors: S. Greer (Prop)
Date established: 2006 **No.of Employees:** 1 - 10 **Product Groups:** 26, 35

O'Neill Bros

18 Pennyburn Industrial Estate, Londonderry, BT48 0LU
Tel: 028-7126 2701 **Fax:** 028-7126 3215
E-mail: info@oneillbros.com
Website: http://www.oneillbros.com
Directors: J. O'neill (MD)
Immediate Holding Company: O'NEILL BROS. MASTER JOINERS LTD
Registration no: NI609597 **VAT No.:** GB 253 1463 80
Date established: 2011 **No.of Employees:** 11 - 20 **Product Groups:** 52

P B Forklifts

Unit 24b Pennyburn Industrial Estate, Londonderry, BT48 0LU
Tel: 028-7136 0950 **Fax:** 028-7137 3434
E-mail: paul@apb4u.com
Website: http://www.apb4u.com
Directors: P. Sheerin (Ptnr)
Immediate Holding Company: ELMORETON LIMITED
Registration no: NI027101 **Date established:** 1993
No.of Employees: 1 - 10 **Product Groups:** 35, 39, 45

Date of Accounts	Dec 10	Dec 09	Dec 08
Working Capital	-630	-338	-350
Fixed Assets	915	687	687
Current Assets	12	9	9

P & L Fork Lifts

Unit 19b Campsie Industrial Estate Mclean Road, Eglinton, Londonderry, BT47 3PF
Tel: 028-7181 1307 **Fax:** 028-7181 1434
Directors: C. Strawbridge (Prop)
Ultimate Holding Company: ARYZTA AG (SWITZERLAND)
Immediate Holding Company: R & H Hall Trading Limited
Registration no: NI012184 **Date established:** 2006
No.of Employees: 1 - 10 **Product Groups:** 35, 39, 45

Date of Accounts	Jul 11	Jul 10	Jul 09
Sales Turnover	90m	83m	91m
Pre Tax Profit/Loss	2m	1m	2m
Working Capital	8m	6m	5m
Fixed Assets	86	72	55
Current Assets	21m	17m	16m
Current Liabilities	3m	3m	4m

Partridge Pear Tree Promotions Ltd

Partridge Peartree House Carrowkeel Drive, Maydown, Londonderry, BT47 6UQ
Tel: 028-7186 0090 **Fax:** 028-7186 0092
E-mail: sales@partridge-peartree.com
Website: http://www.partridge-peartree.com
Directors: C. Desmond (MD)
Immediate Holding Company: PARTRIDGE PEARTREE PROMOTIONS LIMITED
Registration no: NI021865 **VAT No.:** GB 516 5092 55
Date established: 1988 **No.of Employees:** 1 - 10 **Product Groups:** 23, 49

Date of Accounts	Dec 11	Dec 10	Dec 09
Working Capital	189	213	246
Fixed Assets	27	23	13
Current Assets	451	391	399

Peninsula Construction Ltd

38 Buncrana Road, Londonderry, BT48 8LB
Tel: 028-7126 3865 **Fax:** 028-7127 1294
E-mail: info@peninsulaconstruction.co.uk
Website: http://www.ulsterscienceparK.com
Directors: P. Shortall (MD)
Immediate Holding Company: PENINSULA CONSTRUCTION LIMITED
Registration no: NI014664 **Date established:** 1980
No.of Employees: 21 - 50 **Product Groups:** 52, 80

Date of Accounts	Sep 11	Sep 10	Sep 09
Working Capital	9m	9m	8m
Fixed Assets	77	102	130
Current Assets	10m	10m	9m

Precision Industrial Services Ltd

28 Campsie Industrial Estate Mclean Road, Eglinton, Londonderry, BT47 3XX
Tel: 028-7186 0135 **Fax:** 028-7186 0942
E-mail: sales@precisiongroup.co.uk
Website: http://www.precisiongroup.co.uk
Bank(s): Ulster Bank
Directors: J. Mcfadden (Dir), K. Williams (Fin), C. McFadden (Dir)
Immediate Holding Company: PRECISION INDUSTRIAL SERVICES LIMITED
Registration no: NI035996 **VAT No.:** GB 349 7570 12
Date established: 1999 **Turnover:** £5m - £10m
No.of Employees: 101 - 250 **Product Groups:** 52, 54

Date of Accounts	Dec 11	Dec 10	Dec 09
Sales Turnover	9m	7m	4m
Pre Tax Profit/Loss	419	163	14
Working Capital	747	514	127
Fixed Assets	2m	2m	2m
Current Assets	3m	3m	1m
Current Liabilities	751	836	547

Precision Processing Services Ltd

60 Clooney Road, Londonderry, BT47 6TR
Tel: 028-7186 1600 **Fax:** 028-7186 1211
E-mail: info@precisiongroup.co.uk
Website: http://www.pps1.co.uk
Directors: J. Mcfadden (Dir)
Immediate Holding Company: PRECISION PROCESSING SERVICES LIMITED
Registration no: NI037013 **Date established:** 1999
No.of Employees: 11 - 20 **Product Groups:** 38, 42

Date of Accounts	Dec 11	Dec 10	Dec 09
Working Capital	268	196	157
Fixed Assets	49	67	40
Current Assets	504	338	348

Premiair Refrigeration Ltd

Balliniska Business Park Balliniska Road, Londonderry, BT48 0NA
Tel: 028-7128 0711 **Fax:** 028-7128 1737
Directors: D. Harkin (Dir)
Immediate Holding Company: PREMIAIR REFRIGERATION & AIR CONDITIONING LIMITED
Registration no: NI057476 **Date established:** 2005
No.of Employees: 1 - 10 **Product Groups:** 40, 66

Date of Accounts	Dec 11	Dec 10	Dec 09
Working Capital	189	121	110
Fixed Assets	172	175	190
Current Assets	681	460	490

Rubbertec International Ltd

Carrakeel Drive Maydown, Londonderry, BT47 6UQ
Tel: 028-7186 0005 **Fax:** 028-7186 1411
E-mail: info@rubbertecinternational.com
Website: http://www.duramould.com
Bank(s): First Trust
Directors: H. Sharkey (Dir), C. Grant (Dir), H. Sharkey (MD)
Immediate Holding Company: RUBBERTEC INTERNATIONAL LIMITED
Registration no: NI062292 **Date established:** 2006 **Turnover:** £1m - £2m
No.of Employees: 11 - 20 **Product Groups:** 29

Date of Accounts	May 09	May 08
Working Capital	-65	-3
Fixed Assets	193	214
Current Assets	337	284

Sammon Chartered Surveyors

35 Clarendon Street, Londonderry, BT48 7ER
Tel: 028-7127 1323 **Fax:** 028-7136 4144
E-mail: james@iol.ie
Website: http://www.sammon.eu
Directors: J. Sammon (MD)
Ultimate Holding Company: JAMES SAMMON & COMPANY (IRELAND) LIMITED
Immediate Holding Company: JAMES SAMMON & CO LTD
Registration no: NI024864 **VAT No.:** GB 516 7805 34
Date established: 1990 **Turnover:** £500,000 - £1m
No.of Employees: 1 - 10 **Product Groups:** 80

Date of Accounts	Sep 10	Sep 09	Sep 08
Working Capital	244	306	425
Fixed Assets	708	737	614
Current Assets	533	526	614

Schlotter Ireland

15 Brockagh Road Eglinton, Londonderry, BT47 3AT
Tel: 028-7181 2818 **Fax:** 028-7181 2518
Website: http://www.schlotter.ie
Immediate Holding Company: GSL (Ireland) Limited
Date established: 2007 **No.of Employees:** 1 - 10 **Product Groups:** 32, 48, 66

Seagate Technology Ltd

1 Disc Drive, Londonderry, BT48 0BF
Tel: 028-7127 4000 **Fax:** 028-7127 4202
E-mail: ian-oleary@seagate.com
Website: http://www.seagate.com
Directors: B. McLaughlin (Tech Serv), B. Burns (MD), K. Colwell (Pers)
Managers: D. McHugh (Fin Mgr)
Date established: 1993 **No.of Employees:** 1001 - 1500
Product Groups: 44

Search Workshop Supplies

Altnagelvin Industrial Estate Trench Road, Londonderry, BT47 2ED
Tel: 028-7131 2225 **Fax:** 028-7131 8811
E-mail: sales@swsni.com
Website: http://www.swsni.com
Directors: S. Glass (Ptnr)
Immediate Holding Company: NEWSPREAD LTD
Registration no: NI009233 **Date established:** 2008
No.of Employees: 1 - 10 **Product Groups:** 26, 36

Signs Express

Unit 6 Diamond Park Pennyburn Industrial Estate, Londonderry, BT48 0LU
Tel: 028-7126 5577 **Fax:** 028-7126 5588
E-mail: derry@signsexpress.co.uk
Website: http://www.signsexpress.co.uk
Directors: R. Mcgoningle (Prop)
Immediate Holding Company: SIGNS EXPRESS LIMITED
Registration no: 02375913 **Date established:** 1989
No.of Employees: 1 - 10 **Product Groups:** 28, 30, 37, 40

Singularity Ltd

100 Patrick Street, Londonderry, BT48 7EL
Tel: 028-7126 7767 **Fax:** 028-7126 8085
E-mail: sharon.devine@singularitylive.com
Website: http://www.singularitylive.com
Directors: S. Devine (Co Sec)
Managers: P. Canavan, S. Madden (Personnel)
Immediate Holding Company: KOFAX NORTHERN IRELAND LIMITED
Registration no: NI031519 **Date established:** 1996
Turnover: £10m - £20m **No.of Employees:** 51 - 100 **Product Groups:** 44

Date of Accounts	Sep 11	Sep 10	Sep 09
Sales Turnover	10m	10m	13m
Pre Tax Profit/Loss	639	104	2m
Working Capital	8m	8m	7m
Fixed Assets	497	226	173
Current Assets	11m	10m	10m
Current Liabilities	3m	2m	3m

Robert Smith & Co Derry Ltd

76 Glenshane Road, Londonderry, BT47 3SF
Tel: 028-7130 1411 **Fax:** 028-7130 1126
E-mail: rdsdrum@aol.com
Website: http://www.united-drug.ie
Directors: R. Smith (MD)
Managers: D. Cairns (Sales Admin)
Ultimate Holding Company: United Drug P.L.C.
Immediate Holding Company: Alchem P.L.C.
Registration no: NI002884 **VAT No.:** GB 251 7032 89
Date established: 1875 **Turnover:** £10m - £20m
No.of Employees: 21 - 50 **Product Groups:** 63

Stewart & Mcconnell Derry Ltd

Unit 30 Springtown Industrial Estate, Londonderry, BT48 0LU
Tel: 028-7126 9372 **Fax:** 028-7126 9372
E-mail: info@stewart-and-mcconnell.com
Website: http://www.stewart-and-mcconnell.com
Managers: P. Deighan (Mgr)
Immediate Holding Company: ULSTER SYSTEMS LIMITED
Registration no: NI013921 **VAT No.:** GB 331 8869 35
Date established: 1971 **No.of Employees:** 1 - 10 **Product Groups:** 51, 52

Date of Accounts	Dec 11	Dec 10	Dec 09
Working Capital	190	119	431
Fixed Assets	319	444	447
Current Assets	199	135	538

Total Engineering & Design Ltd

Waterville House Balliniska Road, Londonderry, BT48 0NA
Tel: 028-7128 2930 **Fax:** 028-7128 3848
E-mail: paulh@total-engineering.com
Website: http://www.total.demon.co.uk
Directors: P. Hyndman (MD)
Immediate Holding Company: Total Engineering and Design Limited
Registration no: NI044940 **VAT No.:** GB 516 8435 36
Date established: 2002 **Turnover:** Up to £250,000
No.of Employees: 11 - 20 **Product Groups:** 80

Date of Accounts	Dec 11	Dec 10	Dec 09
Working Capital	203	81	184
Fixed Assets	31	29	24
Current Assets	286	188	262

Vital Services Ltd

16 Thistlewood Park, Londonderry, BT48 0NW
Tel: 028-7126 0071
E-mail: kiaran.baker@btopenworld.com
Managers: C. Baker (Sales Admin)
Immediate Holding Company: VITAL SERVICES LIMITED
Registration no: NI028055 **VAT No.:** GB 574 6131 36
Date established: 1993 **Turnover:** Up to £250,000
No.of Employees: 1 - 10 **Product Groups:** 48

Date of Accounts	Mar 11	Mar 10	Mar 09
Working Capital	N/A	-1	-1
Fixed Assets	1	1	1
Current Assets	9	9	7

Western Connect Ltd

25d Bishop Street Derry, Londonderry, BT48 6PR
Tel: 028-7137 9100 **Fax:** 028-7137 4726
E-mail: info@westernconnect.com
Website: http://www.westernconnect.com
Bank(s): Bank of Ireland
Directors: A. Slavin (MD), A. Slavean (Ch)
Managers: D. Vincent (Chief Mgr), M. Brown (Sales Prom Mgr)
Registration no: NI027340 **VAT No.:** GB 574 5123 40
Date established: 1993 **No.of Employees:** 11 - 20 **Product Groups:** 80

J Young & Son

90 Duke Street, Londonderry, BT47 6DQ
Tel: 028-7134 3409 **Fax:** 028-7131 1075
E-mail: jys@globalnet.co.uk
Website: http://www.globalnet.co.uk
Directors: I. Young (MD)
Immediate Holding Company: J. YOUNG & SONS LIMITED
Registration no: NI030674 **VAT No.:** GB 254 6740 49
Date established: 1996 **Turnover:** £500,000 - £1m
No.of Employees: 1 - 10 **Product Groups:** 52

Co. Londonderry

Maghera

Crawford Sports

34 Main Street, Maghera, BT46 5AE
Tel: 028-7964 2672 **Fax:** 028-7964 4275
Directors: G. Crawford (Prop)
Date established: 1988 **No.of Employees:** 1 - 10 **Product Groups:** 36, 39, 40

Crossland Tankers

114 Grove Road, Maghera, BT46 5QZ
Tel: 028-7940 1555
E-mail: sales@crosslandtankers.com
Website: http://www.crosslandtankers.com
Immediate Holding Company: CROSSLAND TANKERS LIMITED
Registration no: NI018916 **Date established:** 1985
No.of Employees: 21 - 50 **Product Groups:** 35

Date of Accounts	Sep 11	Sep 10	Sep 09
Pre Tax Profit/Loss	N/A	N/A	352
Working Capital	1m	1m	1m
Fixed Assets	100	120	126
Current Assets	3m	3m	3m
Current Liabilities	N/A	N/A	441

Drennan Transport
24 Lisgorgan Lane Upperlands, Maghera, BT46 5TE
Tel: 028-7964 2116 **Fax:** 028-7964 3570
E-mail: will@drennan-transport.co.uk
Website: http://www.drennan-transport.co.uk
Directors: W. Drennan (MD), S. Thompson (Fin)
Immediate Holding Company: DRENNAN TRANSPORT LIMITED
Registration no: NI018389 **VAT No.:** GB 349 6243 32
Date established: 1985 **Turnover:** £2m - £5m **No.of Employees:** 1 - 10
Product Groups: 72

Date of Accounts	Mar 11	Mar 10	Mar 09
Working Capital	-1m	-1m	-1m
Fixed Assets	2m	2m	2m
Current Assets	376	403	316

H M Electrics
95 Glen Road, Maghera, BT46 5JG
Tel: 028-7964 2112 **Fax:** 028-7964 3945
E-mail: hugh@hmelectrics.com
Website: http://www.hmelectrics.com
Directors: H. Mcalary (MD)
Managers: D. McAlary (Mgr)
Immediate Holding Company: H.M. ELECTRICS LIMITED
Registration no: NI012055 **VAT No.:** GB 311 0094 25
Date established: 1977 **No.of Employees:** 21 - 50 **Product Groups:** 84

Date of Accounts	Dec 11	Dec 10	Dec 09
Working Capital	4m	4m	4m
Fixed Assets	1m	1m	1m
Current Assets	4m	4m	4m

B P Mckeefry Ltd
114 Grove Road, Maghera, BT46 5QZ
Tel: 028-7940 1333 **Fax:** 028-7940 1297
E-mail: peter@bpmckeefry.com
Website: http://www.bpmckeefry.com
Directors: P. Esler (MD)
Ultimate Holding Company: B.P. MCKEEFRY HOLDINGS LIMITED
Immediate Holding Company: B.P. McKeefry Holdings Limited
Registration no: NI064820 **VAT No.:** GB 252 9353 53
Date established: 2007 **No.of Employees:** 51 - 100 **Product Groups:** 72, 76

Date of Accounts	Sep 11	Sep 09	Sep 08
Working Capital	-0	-0	-0
Fixed Assets	500	500	500
Current Assets	439	N/A	N/A

Mckees
11 Fairhill, Maghera, BT46 5AY
Tel: 028-7964 2559 **Fax:** 028-7964 5727
E-mail: mckeespies@btopenworld.com
Website: http://www.mckeespies.com
Bank(s): Ulster
Directors: W. Mckee (Prop), W. McKee (MD)
VAT No.: GB 252 4411 90 **No.of Employees:** 21 - 50 **Product Groups:** 20

Northern Countys Co-Operative Ltd
Garvagh Road Swatragh, Maghera, BT46 5QE
Tel: 028-7940 1246 **Fax:** 028-7940 1533
E-mail: info@carnfasteners.com
Website: http://www.carnfasteners.com
Bank(s): Northern Bank
Directors: F. Hughes (MD)
Immediate Holding Company: NORTHERN COUNTIES DEVELOPMENT ASSOCIATION
Registration no: 00009090 **VAT No.:** GB 253 1848 60
Date established: 1999 **Turnover:** Up to £250,000
No.of Employees: 11 - 20 **Product Groups:** 67

Date of Accounts	Dec 10	Dec 09	Dec 08
Working Capital	27	24	19
Fixed Assets	122	130	138
Current Assets	30	27	21

Road Safety Contracts Ltd
102 Glen Road, Maghera, BT46 5JG
Tel: 028-7964 3038 **Fax:** 028-7964 4569
Website: http://www.roadsafetycontracts.com
Directors: C. McGuinness (Co Sec), P. Henry (Co Sec), E. McHugh (Ptnr), J. Mchugh (Dir)
Immediate Holding Company: ROAD SAFETY CONTRACTS LIMITED
Registration no: NI024282 **VAT No.:** GB 349 7794 87
Date established: 1990 **Turnover:** £250,000 - £500,000
No.of Employees: 51 - 100 **Product Groups:** 51, 54

Alexander Scott & Son Ltd
2-4 Main Street, Maghera, BT46 5AD
Tel: 028-7964 2212 **Fax:** 028-7964 4431
Managers: C. Neely (Sales Admin)
Immediate Holding Company: ALEXANDER SCOTT & SON LIMITED
Registration no: NI002358 **VAT No.:** GB 253 8042 69
Date established: 1947 **Turnover:** £1m - £2m **No.of Employees:** 11 - 20
Product Groups: 62, 66

Date of Accounts	Dec 11	Dec 10	Dec 09
Working Capital	-320	-270	-275
Fixed Assets	197	178	199
Current Assets	830	890	919

Ulster Ceramics
29 Garvagh Road Swatragh, Maghera, BT46 5QE
Tel: 028-7940 1260 **Fax:** 028-7940 1739
E-mail: potterysupplies@btconnect.com
Website: http://www.ulsterceramicspotterysupplies.co.uk
Directors: F. Hughes (Prop)
Ultimate Holding Company: NORTHERN COUNTIES CO-OPERATIVE ENTERPRISES LTD (N.IRELA
Immediate Holding Company: ULSTER CERAMICS LIMITED
Registration no: NI006873 **VAT No.:** GB 253 2916 64
Date established: 1967 **No.of Employees:** 1 - 10 **Product Groups:** 33

Date of Accounts	Dec 11	Dec 10	Dec 09
Working Capital	1m	1m	1m
Fixed Assets	13	17	10
Current Assets	1m	1m	1m

William Clark & Sons Ltd
72 Upperlands, Maghera, BT46 5RZ
Tel: 028-7954 7200 **Fax:** 028-7954 7207
E-mail: sales@wmclark.co.uk
Website: http://www.wmclark.co.uk
Managers: A. Woods (Ops Mgr)
Immediate Holding Company: WILLIAM CLARK & SONS HOLDINGS LIMITED
Registration no: R0000796 **VAT No.:** GB 251 8509 59
Date established: 2024 **Turnover:** £1m - £2m **No.of Employees:** 21 - 50
Product Groups: 23

Date of Accounts	May 12	May 11	May 10
Working Capital	2m	3m	3m
Current Assets	2m	3m	3m

Co. Londonderry

Magherafelt

J R Bedi & Sons
Fairhill Road, Magherafelt, BT45 6BL
Tel: 028-7963 2188 **Fax:** 028-7963 4077
E-mail: info@kkschoolwear.com
Website: http://www.kkschoolwear.com
Directors: V. Bedi (Ptnr), M. Houston (Ptnr)
VAT No.: GB 251 8439 54 **Turnover:** £250,000 - £500,000
No.of Employees: 11 - 20 **Product Groups:** 24

B M K Steel Ltd
59 Magherafelt Road Draperstown, Magherafelt, BT45 7JT
Tel: 028-7962 8664 **Fax:** 028-7962 7031
E-mail: info@bmksteel.co.uk
Directors: B. Mckenna (Dir)
Immediate Holding Company: B.M.K. Steel Ltd
Registration no: NI037864 **Date established:** 2000
No.of Employees: 1 - 10 **Product Groups:** 35

Date of Accounts	Mar 11	Mar 10	Mar 09
Working Capital	374	384	410
Fixed Assets	46	46	53
Current Assets	486	509	512

Business Success Strategies Ltd
14 Maghera Road Tobermore, Magherafelt, BT45 5QB
Tel: 028-7964 2333 **Fax:** 028-7964 5222
E-mail: hugh.bradley@bradleyproducts.co.uk
Website: http://www.swirlweb.co.uk
Directors: J. Bradley (MD)
Immediate Holding Company: BUSINESS SUCCESS STRATEGIES LTD
Registration no: NI027409 **VAT No.:** GB 574 4895 89
Date established: 1993 **No.of Employees:** 1 - 10 **Product Groups:** 38

Date of Accounts	Apr 11	Apr 10	Apr 09
Working Capital	-265	48	-252
Current Assets	3	2	3

F P Mccann Ltd
Quarry 3 Drumard Road, Knockloughrim, Magherafelt, BT45 8QA
Tel: 028-7964 2558 **Fax:** 01530-240015
E-mail: info@fpmccann.co.uk
Website: http://www.fpmccann.co.uk
Directors: D. Mulholland (Fin), E. Mccann (MD)
Managers: B. Low (Tech Serv Mgr), B. Greer-sayer (Personnel), J. McCollam, D. McGuckin (Mktg Serv Mgr)
Immediate Holding Company: F.P. MCCANN LIMITED
Registration no: NI013563 **Date established:** 1979
Turnover: £75m - £125m **No.of Employees:** 51 - 100 **Product Groups:** 51

Date of Accounts	Jan 12	Jan 11	Jan 10
Sales Turnover	78m	70m	57m
Pre Tax Profit/Loss	3m	3m	2m
Working Capital	984	771	949
Fixed Assets	52m	53m	55m
Current Assets	16m	15m	13m
Current Liabilities	7m	5m	5m

Farrell Products
1a Aughrim Road, Magherafelt, BT45 6AY
Tel: 028-7963 2245 **Fax:** 028-7963 1702
E-mail: sales@farrellproducts.com
Website: http://www.farrellproducts.com
Directors: A. Murray (MD)
Immediate Holding Company: Farrell Products Ltd
Registration no: NI049085 **VAT No.:** GB 286 4288 18
Date established: 2003 **No.of Employees:** 1 - 10 **Product Groups:** 30, 66

Date of Accounts	Jan 11	Jan 10	Jan 09
Working Capital	76	59	160
Fixed Assets	14	16	15
Current Assets	241	237	338

Four Dee Ni Ltd
Unit 10 Station Road Industrial Estate Station Road, Magherafelt, BT45 5EY
Tel: 028-7930 0815 **Fax:** 028-7930 0816
Website: http://www.4d-ni.co.uk
Directors: A. Donnelly (Dir)
Immediate Holding Company: FOUR DEE (NI) LIMITED
Registration no: NI030696 **Date established:** 1996
No.of Employees: 21 - 50 **Product Groups:** 35, 39, 48

Date of Accounts	Mar 11	Mar 10	Mar 09
Working Capital	130	-149	157
Fixed Assets	2m	2m	2m
Current Assets	2m	823	715

H C Paul
7 Carricknakielt Lane Knockloughrim, Magherafelt, BT45 8PX
Tel: 028-7964 2504 **Fax:** 028-7964 2504
Directors: H. Paul (Prop)
Date established: 1988 **No.of Employees:** 1 - 10 **Product Groups:** 41

Henderson Fireplaces
27a Moneyhaw Road Moneymore, Magherafelt, BT45 7XL
Tel: 028-8674 8536 **Fax:** 028-8674 8808
E-mail: derekhenderson27@btinternet.com
Directors: D. Henderson (Prop)
VAT No.: GB 283 0099 59 **Turnover:** £1m - £2m **No.of Employees:** 1 - 10
Product Groups: 26, 33

Henry Brothers Magherafelt Ltd
108-114 Moneymore Road, Magherafelt, BT45 6HJ
Tel: 028-7963 1631 **Fax:** 028-7963 3967
E-mail: info@henrybrothers.co.uk
Website: http://www.henrybrothers.co.uk
Directors: D. Henry (MD), D. Carson (Fin), J. Brown (Dir)
Managers: J. McDevitt, T. Murray (Tech Serv Mgr)
Ultimate Holding Company: HENRY GROUP (NI) LIMITED
Immediate Holding Company: HENRY BROTHERS (MAGHERAFELT) LIMITED
Registration no: NI011711 **VAT No.:** GB 422 1321 14
Date established: 1976 **Turnover:** £20m - £50m
No.of Employees: 251 - 500 **Product Groups:** 51, 52

Date of Accounts	Mar 12	Mar 11	Mar 10
Sales Turnover	48m	28m	54m
Pre Tax Profit/Loss	997	580	1m
Working Capital	3m	3m	2m
Fixed Assets	11m	12m	13m
Current Assets	22m	23m	27m
Current Liabilities	6m	7m	9m

Heron Bros Ltd
2 St Patricks Street Draperstown, Magherafelt, BT45 7AL
Tel: 028-7962 8505 **Fax:** 028-7962 7028
E-mail: info@heronbros.com
Website: http://www.heronbros.com
Directors: D. Heron (MD), P. McTaggart (Fin)
Managers: G. O'Kane (Personnel)
Immediate Holding Company: HERON BROS. LIMITED
Registration no: NI016051 **Date established:** 1982
Turnover: £20m - £50m **No.of Employees:** 51 - 100 **Product Groups:** 14, 25, 66, 80, 84

Date of Accounts	Feb 11	Feb 10	Feb 09
Sales Turnover	43m	33m	44m
Pre Tax Profit/Loss	1m	1m	1m
Working Capital	17m	16m	15m
Fixed Assets	3m	3m	3m
Current Assets	39m	33m	33m
Current Liabilities	1m	611	2m

John J Higgins Ltd
Unit 4 Station Road Industrial Estate Station Road, Magherafelt, BT45 5EY
Tel: 028-7963 2369 **Fax:** 028-7963 1790
E-mail: info@johnjhiggins.com
Website: http://www.johnjhiggins.com
Bank(s): Bank of Ireland
Managers: L. Mallon, C. Mcmurray (Sales Admin)
Immediate Holding Company: JOHN J. HIGGINS (MAGHERAFELT) LIMITED
Registration no: NI006913 **VAT No.:** GB 252 5054 83
Date established: 1967 **No.of Employees:** 11 - 20 **Product Groups:** 25, 52

Date of Accounts	Mar 12	Mar 11	Mar 10
Working Capital	85	38	162
Fixed Assets	181	213	251
Current Assets	577	409	453

J P Corry A R D S Timber
15 Moyola Road Castledawson, Magherafelt, BT45 8BH
Tel: 028-7946 8622 **Fax:** 028-7946 8948
E-mail: info@ardstimber.com
Website: http://www.jpcorry.co.uk
Managers: C. Collins (Mgr)
Immediate Holding Company: Coolhaven Developments Ltd
Registration no: NI011606 **VAT No.:** GB 286 5546 17
Date established: 1976 **Turnover:** £2m - £5m **No.of Employees:** 11 - 20
Product Groups: 66

Date of Accounts	Dec 11	Dec 10	Dec 09
Working Capital	4m	4m	2m
Fixed Assets	72	75	1m
Current Assets	4m	4m	3m

K Kerr
High Street Draperstown, Magherafelt, BT45 7AA
Tel: 028-7962 8441 **Fax:** 028-7962 8748
Directors: K. Kerr (Prop)
Date established: 1974 **No.of Employees:** 1 - 10 **Product Groups:** 35

Mcerlains Bakery
31 Aughrim Road, Magherafelt, BT45 6BB
Tel: 028-7963 2465 **Fax:** 028-7963 4207
E-mail: brian.mcerlain@genesisbreads.com
Website: http://www.genesisbreads.com
Bank(s): Northern Bank
Directors: B. Maclane (MD), B. Mcerlain (MD), B. Mcerlaine (MD)
Immediate Holding Company: MCERLAIN'S BAKERY (MAGHERAFELT) LIMITED
Registration no: NI030432 **VAT No.:** GB 252 3130 06
Date established: 1996 **Turnover:** £20m - £50m
No.of Employees: 51 - 100 **Product Groups:** 20

Date of Accounts	Oct 11	Oct 10	Oct 09
Sales Turnover	22m	13m	11m
Pre Tax Profit/Loss	955	518	299
Working Capital	791	317	117
Fixed Assets	1m	1m	2m
Current Assets	3m	2m	2m
Current Liabilities	807	562	417

Minstrel Metalcraft Co
300a Hillhead Road Knockloughrim, Magherafelt, BT45 8QT
Tel: 028-7964 4454 **Fax:** 028-7964 4453
Directors: P. Mckenna (Prop)
Immediate Holding Company: Minstrel Engineering Ltd
Registration no: NI064960 **Date established:** 2007
No.of Employees: 1 - 10 **Product Groups:** 26, 35

Moyola Building Services N I Ltd
90 Oldtown Road Castledawson, Magherafelt, BT45 8BZ
Tel: 028-7946 9686 **Fax:** 028-7946 8371
E-mail: ruthkalgore@moyolabuildingservices.com
Website: http://www.moyolabuildingservices.com
Directors: K. Williams (Fin), R. Kilgore (Dir)
Managers: C. McFadden (Personnel), I. Gillespie (Mgr)
Immediate Holding Company: MOYOLA BUILDING SERVICES LTD
Registration no: NI014166 **VAT No.:** GB 422 1321 14
Date established: 1980 **Turnover:** Up to £250,000
No.of Employees: 21 - 50 **Product Groups:** 52

Date of Accounts	Jun 11	Jun 10	Jun 09
Working Capital	546	568	483
Fixed Assets	N/A	N/A	181
Current Assets	808	912	1m

Moyola Mattress Company Ltd
14 Bells Hill Castledawson, Magherafelt, BT45 8HG
Tel: 028-7946 8192 **Fax:** 028-7946 8945
E-mail: jcraig@hotmail.com
Bank(s): Northern Bank
Directors: J. Craig (Dir)
Immediate Holding Company: MOYOLA MATTRESS COMPANY LIMITED
Registration no: NI010309 **VAT No.:** GB 286 3237 40
Date established: 1974 **No.of Employees:** 11 - 20 **Product Groups:** 26

Date of Accounts	Sep 11	Sep 10	Sep 09
Working Capital	-141	25	13
Fixed Assets	30	36	43
Current Assets	283	334	475

Peden Power Ltd
Unit 11 Station Road Industrial Estate Station Road, Magherafelt, BT45 5EY
Tel: 028-7963 2609 **Fax:** 028-7963 3707
E-mail: des@pedenpower.co.uk
Website: http://www.pedenpower.co.uk
Directors: D. Peden (Prop)
Managers: D. McFadden
Immediate Holding Company: Peden Power Limited
Registration no: NI040988 **Date established:** 2001
No.of Employees: 21 - 50 **Product Groups:** 41

Date of Accounts	Sep 11	Sep 10	Sep 09
Working Capital	2m	2m	2m
Fixed Assets	43	34	44
Current Assets	3m	3m	3m

Progress Joinery
28 Tamnadeese Road Castledawson, Magherafelt, BT45 8DW
Tel: 028-7946 8456 **Fax:** 028-7946 8456
E-mail: info@progressjoinery.com
Website: http://www.progressjoinery.com
Directors: E. Strathern (Ptnr)
VAT No.: GB 286 5783 03 **Date established:** 1976
No.of Employees: 1 - 10 **Product Groups:** 25

Regan Tile Design
56 Glenshane Road Knockloughrim, Magherafelt, BT45 8RE
Tel: 028-7964 5144 **Fax:** 028-7964 5141
E-mail: info@regantiledesign.co.uk
Website: http://www.regantiledesign.com
Directors: G. Madden (Dir)
Managers: G. Madden (Mgr)
Immediate Holding Company: REGAN TILE DESIGN LIMITED
Registration no: NI035054 **VAT No.:** GB 722 5813 46
Date established: 1998 **No.of Employees:** 1 - 10 **Product Groups:** 52, 63

Sperrin Bakery
7 Tobermore Road Draperstown, Magherafelt, BT45 7AG
Tel: 028-7962 8895 **Fax:** 028-7962 8895
Directors: E. Burke (Prop)
Immediate Holding Company: SPERRIN BAKERY LIMITED
Registration no: NI611261 **VAT No.:** 432 5112 93 **Date established:** 2012
No.of Employees: 1 - 10 **Product Groups:** 20

Sperrin Metal Products Ltd
Cahore Road Draperstown, Magherafelt, BT45 7AP
Tel: 028-7962 8362 **Fax:** 028-7962 8972
E-mail: info@sperrin-metal.com
Website: http://www.sperrin-metal.com
Bank(s): Northern
Directors: P. Gormley (MD), P. Gormley (Sales)
Managers: P. Gormley (Purch Mgr), G. Scullion (Tech Serv Mgr), P. McAllister (Fin Mgr)
Ultimate Holding Company: SPERRIN HOLDINGS LIMITED
Immediate Holding Company: SPERRIN METAL PRODUCTS LIMITED
Registration no: NI005683 **VAT No.:** GB 252 6649 47
Date established: 1963 **Turnover:** £10m - £20m
No.of Employees: 51 - 100 **Product Groups:** 26

Date of Accounts	Dec 11	Dec 10	Dec 09
Sales Turnover	13m	12m	10m
Pre Tax Profit/Loss	216	127	293
Working Capital	3m	3m	3m
Fixed Assets	2m	2m	2m
Current Assets	6m	5m	5m
Current Liabilities	723	507	566

Strain Engineering & Co. Ltd
6 New Ferry Road Bellaghy, Magherafelt, BT45 8ND
Tel: 028-7938 6848 **Fax:** 028-7938 6150
E-mail: info@strainengineering.com
Website: http://www.strainengineering.co.uk
Directors: A. Mulholland (Prop)
Immediate Holding Company: STRAIN ENGINEERING (NI) LIMITED
Registration no: NI602286 **Date established:** 2010
No.of Employees: 11 - 20 **Product Groups:** 45

The Workspace Group
Business Centre Tobermore Road, Draperstown, Magherafelt, BT45 7AG
Tel: 028-7962 8113 **Fax:** 028-7962 8975
E-mail: info@theworkspacegroup.org
Website: http://www.workspace.org.uk
Directors: B. Murray (Grp Chief Exec)
Immediate Holding Company: WORKSPACE (DRAPERSTOWN) LIMITED
Registration no: NI018240 **VAT No.:** 393697002 **Date established:** 1985
No.of Employees: 11 - 20 **Product Groups:** 24

Date of Accounts	Mar 10	Mar 08	Mar 07
Working Capital	-646	-502	-979
Fixed Assets	7m	5m	4m
Current Assets	1m	1m	846
Current Liabilities	N/A	306	N/A

Tobermore Concrete Products Ltd
2 Lisnamuck Road Tobermore, Magherafelt, BT45 5QF
Tel: 028-7964 2411 **Fax:** 028-7964 4145
E-mail: info@tobermore.co.uk
Website: http://www.tobermore.co.uk
Directors: K. Fields (Mkt Research)
Managers: G. Robinson (Chief Mgr)
Ultimate Holding Company: TOBERMORE CONCRETE PRODUCTS LIMITED
Immediate Holding Company: TOBERMORE CONCRETE PRODUCTS LIMITED
Registration no: NI011280 **VAT No.:** GB 252 3777 53
Date established: 1976 **Turnover:** £20m - £50m
No.of Employees: 101 - 250 **Product Groups:** 33

Date of Accounts	Apr 11	Apr 10	Apr 09
Sales Turnover	21m	23m	33m
Pre Tax Profit/Loss	406	2m	4m
Working Capital	7m	18m	16m
Fixed Assets	36m	25m	25m
Current Assets	10m	21m	21m
Current Liabilities	1m	2m	2m

Top Frame Engineering
72 Glenshane Road Castledawson, Magherafelt, BT45 8DQ
Tel: 028-7946 9959 **Fax:** 028-7946 9077
Directors: S. Connery (Prop)
Date established: 1999 **No.of Employees:** 1 - 10 **Product Groups:** 35

Wright Engineering
8 Ballyriff Road, Magherafelt, BT45 6NL
Tel: 028-7941 8656
Directors: R. Wright (Prop)
No.of Employees: 1 - 10 **Product Groups:** 41

Yardmaster International
Cahore Road Draperstown, Magherafelt, BT45 7AP
Tel: 028-7962 8270 **Fax:** 028-7962 8670
E-mail: info@yardmaster.co.uk
Website: http://www.yardmaster.co.uk
Directors: W. McKewan (MD)
Managers: M. Keyes (Tech Serv Mgr), C. Craig
Date established: 1985 **No.of Employees:** 51 - 100 **Product Groups:** 26, 35

Co. Down

Newcastle

Coastline Kitchens
75 Ballagh Road, Newcastle, BT33 0LA
Tel: 028-4372 4616 **Fax:** 028-4372 4616
Directors: K. Sloan (Prop)
VAT No.: GB 517 8263 33 **Date established:** 1987
No.of Employees: 1 - 10 **Product Groups:** 26

Joseph Mcclune & Son Ltd
205 Main Street Dundrum, Newcastle, BT33 0LY
Tel: 028-4375 1223 **Fax:** 028-4375 1556
Website: http://www.jmccluneandsonltd.co.uk
Directors: D. Mcclune (Prop)
Immediate Holding Company: Joseph McClune & Son Limited
Registration no: NI034835 **VAT No.:** GB 254 0166 85
Date established: 1998 **Turnover:** Up to £250,000
No.of Employees: 11 - 20 **Product Groups:** 25, 52

Date of Accounts	May 11	May 10	May 09
Working Capital	874	936	929
Fixed Assets	106	124	156
Current Assets	1m	1m	1m

William Keown Trust
3 Church View Dundrum, Newcastle, BT33 0NA
Tel: 028-4375 1243 **Fax:** 028-4375 1444
E-mail: wkeowntrust@btconnect.com
Website: http://www.wkeowntrust.co.uk
Directors: B. Keown (Grp Chief Exec)
Immediate Holding Company: WILLIAM KEOWN TRUST - THE
Registration no: NI037314 **Date established:** 1999
Turnover: Up to £250,000 **No.of Employees:** 1 - 10 **Product Groups:** 80

Date of Accounts	Dec 11	Dec 10	Dec 09
Sales Turnover	82	80	87
Pre Tax Profit/Loss	-1	-1	10
Working Capital	34	35	35
Fixed Assets	2	3	4
Current Assets	62	60	55
Current Liabilities	28	24	20

Co. Down

Newry

A C T
8 Milltown Industrial Estate Greenan Road, Warrenpoint, Newry, BT34 3FN
Tel: 028-4175 2255 **Fax:** 028-4175 3336
E-mail: charliefagan@btconnect.com
Directors: C. Fegan (Prop)
No.of Employees: 1 - 10 **Product Groups:** 35

A G-Con Products Ltd
45 Newtown Road Rostrevor, Newry, BT34 3BZ
Tel: 028-4173 8963 **Fax:** 028-4173 8971
E-mail: sales@agconproducts.com
Website: http://www.agconproducts.com
Managers: B. Colwell (Mgr)
Immediate Holding Company: AG-CON PRODUCTS LIMITED
Registration no: NI041689 **VAT No.:** GB 497 0010 54
Date established: 2001 **No.of Employees:** 1 - 10 **Product Groups:** 35

Date of Accounts	Feb 12	Feb 11	Feb 10
Working Capital	195	114	523
Fixed Assets	600	650	219
Current Assets	1m	1m	1m

A J Plumbing Supplies
Warrenpoint Road, Newry, BT34 2PF
Tel: 028-3026 3348 **Fax:** 028-3026 3263
E-mail: info@ajplumbing.co.uk
Website: http://www.ajplumbing.co.uk
Directors: J. O'brien (Dir), J. Obrien (MD)
Immediate Holding Company: A.J. PLUMBING SUPPLIES LIMITED
Registration no: NI020515 **Date established:** 1987
Turnover: £10m - £20m **No.of Employees:** 21 - 50 **Product Groups:** 66

Date of Accounts	Jan 12	Jan 11	Jan 10
Sales Turnover	12m	12m	13m
Pre Tax Profit/Loss	-127	386	617
Working Capital	4m	3m	3m
Fixed Assets	3m	4m	3m
Current Assets	6m	6m	5m
Current Liabilities	648	529	763

Astrak
52 Chancellors Road, Newry, BT35 8PX
Tel: 028-3083 4888 **Fax:** 028-3083 3663
Directors: D. Brennan (Ptnr)
Date established: 2000 **No.of Employees:** 1 - 10 **Product Groups:** 45, 48, 84

Bank Of Ireland
12 Trevor Hill, Newry, BT34 1DN
Tel: 028-3026 5137 **Fax:** 028-3026 3125
Website: http://www.bankofireland.com
Managers: C. Marley (District Mgr), E. O'Neill (Mgr)
Immediate Holding Company: BANK OF IRELAND UK HOLDINGS PLC
Registration no: NI006941 **Date established:** 1967
No.of Employees: 1 - 10 **Product Groups:** 80, 82

Benagh Engineering
35 Benagh Road Mayobridge, Newry, BT34 2JE
Tel: 028-3085 1328 **Fax:** 028-3085 1328
E-mail: info@benaghengineering.co.uk
Website: http://www.benaghengineering.co.uk
Directors: E. Dornan (Prop)
Immediate Holding Company: BENAGH ENGINEERING & MOTOR WORKS LTD
Registration no: NI048670 **Date established:** 2003
No.of Employees: 1 - 10 **Product Groups:** 38, 42

Date of Accounts	Nov 11	Nov 10	Nov 09
Working Capital	-22	4	-23
Fixed Assets	64	47	41
Current Assets	31	29	28

Bizsalesni
K2 WIN Business Park, Newry, BT35 6BP
Tel: 028-3025 4713 **Fax:** 0845-6382731
E-mail: info@bizsalesni.com
Website: http://www.BizSalesNI.com
Directors: M. Crilley (Prop)
Managers: S. Johnson (Sales Admin)
Registration no: NI063125 **Date established:** 2006
Turnover: Over £1,000m **No.of Employees:** 21 - 50 **Product Groups:** 80

Brown Bros
11 Rathfriland Road Hilltown, Newry, BT34 5TA
Tel: 028-4063 0258 **Fax:** 028-4063 0889
E-mail: sales@brownbrothers.com
Website: http://www.brownbrothers.net
Directors: A. Brown (Snr Part), A. Brown (Ptnr)
Managers: V. Brown (Sales Admin)
Immediate Holding Company: Brown Brothers Development Limited
Registration no: NI043463 **VAT No.:** GB 254 3368 58
Date established: 2002 **Turnover:** £250,000 - £500,000
No.of Employees: 21 - 50 **Product Groups:** 52

Burns Plaster Mouldings
Unit C1 Win Business Park, Newry, BT35 6PH
Tel: 028-3026 8629 **Fax:** 028-3026 1316
Directors: V. Callaghan (MD)
Registration no: NI028374 **Date established:** 1994
Turnover: Up to £250,000 **No.of Employees:** 1 - 10 **Product Groups:** 33

C B C Distributors
Greenbank, Newry, BT34 2JP
Tel: 028-3026 5216 **Fax:** 028-3026 3927
E-mail: sales@cbcdistributors.co.uk
Website: http://www.cbcdistributors.co.uk
Directors: D. Woods (Prop)
Managers: C. Malloy (Chief Acct)
Immediate Holding Company: C.B.C. (DISTRIBUTORS)
Registration no: NI002842 **Date established:** 1950
No.of Employees: 21 - 50 **Product Groups:** 49, 64, 65

C H Marine N I Ltd (t/a K T S Sea Safety)
The Harbour Kilkeel, Newry, BT34 4AX
Tel: 028-4176 2655 **Fax:** 028-4176 4502
E-mail: sales@chmarine.co.uk
Website: http://www.chmarine.com
Directors: K. Mcilroy (MD)
Immediate Holding Company: CH Marine (NI) Limited
Registration no: NI043379 **VAT No.:** GB 517 8049 35
Date established: 2002 **Turnover:** £500,000 - £1m
No.of Employees: 1 - 10 **Product Groups:** 39

Date of Accounts	Oct 11	Oct 10	Oct 09
Working Capital	99	-63	-43
Fixed Assets	36	44	52
Current Assets	326	423	420

Care4yourskin.com
Tan City 7-9 Railway Avenue, Newry, BT35 6BA
Tel: 028-3025 0707
E-mail: vicki@care4yourskin.com
Website: http://www.care4yourskin.com
Product Groups: 32, 65, 66

Carton Die Co. Ltd
Rampart Road Greenbank Industrial Estate, Newry, BT34 2QU
Tel: 028-3026 5972 **Fax:** 028-3026 6662
E-mail: info@cartondie.co.uk
Website: http://www.cartondie.co.uk
Directors: M. Shields (MD)
Immediate Holding Company: CARTON DIE COMPANY (NORTHERN IRELAND) LTD
Registration no: NI026235 **VAT No.:** GB 286 6027 36
Date established: 1992 **Turnover:** £1m - £2m **No.of Employees:** 1 - 10
Product Groups: 27, 44

Date of Accounts	Feb 99	Feb 98	Feb 97
Working Capital	-313	-203	-192
Fixed Assets	558	373	414
Current Assets	172	234	216

CDI Security Solutions Ltd
70a Chancellors Road, Newry, BT35 8QB
Tel: 028-3026 0034 **Fax:** 028-3026 0034
E-mail: cdisecuritysolutions@googlemail.com
Website: http://www.cdisecure.net

Directors: G. O'Hare (Prop), K. O'Hare (Prop)
Managers: K. O'hare (Sales Prom Mgr)
Immediate Holding Company: CDI SECURE LIMITED
Registration no: NI601074 **VAT No.:** GB 434 1946 52
Date established: 2009 **Turnover:** Up to £250,000
No.of Employees: 11 - 20 **Product Groups:** 81

City Plant Services Ltd
12 Craigmore Road, Newry, BT35 6PL
Tel: 028-3082 5522 **Fax:** 02830-825533
E-mail: sales@cpsnewry.com
Website: http://www.cpsnewry.com
Directors: J. Kellie (Prop), S. Kelly (Prop)
Registration no: NI047953 **Date established:** 2007
No.of Employees: 1 - 10 **Product Groups:** 45, 48

Clanrye Electrical Supplies Ltd
11 Upper Edward Street, Newry, BT35 6AX
Tel: 028-3026 4090 **Fax:** 028-3025 3611
E-mail: bronagh@shinnx.plus.com
Website: http://www.clanryelighting.com
Directors: B. Sheppard (Co Sec)
Immediate Holding Company: CLANRYE ELECTRICAL SUPPLIES LIMITED
Registration no: NI022183 **VAT No.:** GB 517 5808 82
Date established: 1988 **No.of Employees:** 1 - 10 **Product Groups:** 35, 37, 67

Date of Accounts	Feb 12	Feb 11	Feb 10
Working Capital	621	655	437
Fixed Assets	69	73	378
Current Assets	806	897	722

Clanrye Press Ltd
Unit 18 Greenbank Industrial Estate Rampart Road, Newry, BT34 2QU
Tel: 028-3026 2570 **Fax:** 028-3026 0451
E-mail: info@clanryepress.com
Website: http://www.clanryepress.com
Directors: C. Hare (Prop)
Immediate Holding Company: CLANRYE PRESS LIMITED
Registration no: NI048282 **VAT No.:** GB 255 5455 47
Date established: 2003 **Turnover:** Up to £250,000
No.of Employees: 1 - 10 **Product Groups:** 28

Date of Accounts	Oct 11	Oct 10	Oct 09
Working Capital	-166	-147	-154
Fixed Assets	262	289	320
Current Assets	77	81	87

Cloughana Contracts
14 Villa Grove Warrenpoint, Newry, BT34 3PQ
Tel: 028-4177 2171 **Fax:** 028-4177 2171
Directors: F. O'Hare (Prop)
Managers: N. O'Hare (Sales Admin), F. Ohare (Mgr)
Date established: 1980 **No.of Employees:** 1 - 10 **Product Groups:** 52

Codico Distributors N I Ltd
Unit B3-B4 Win Business Park Canal Quay, Newry, BT35 6PH
Tel: 028-3026 1066 **Fax:** 028-3026 6614
Website: http://www.codico-distributors.com
Managers: N. Cooney
Ultimate Holding Company: CODICO DISTRIBUTORS LIMITED
Immediate Holding Company: CODICO DISTRIBUTORS (N.I.) LIMITED
Registration no: NI025628 **Date established:** 1991
Turnover: £500,000 - £1m **No.of Employees:** 1 - 10 **Product Groups:** 37

Date of Accounts	Mar 11	Mar 10	Mar 09
Working Capital	651	686	685
Fixed Assets	58	33	47
Current Assets	767	734	772
Current Liabilities	22	N/A	20

David Cooper & Associates
44 Victoria Square Rostrevor, Newry, BT34 3EU
Tel: 028-4173 9406 **Fax:** 028-4173 8456
E-mail: d.cooper@cooper-engineering.com
Website: http://www.cooper-engineering.com
Directors: D. Cooper (Prop)
Immediate Holding Company: ORFIN DEVELOPMENTS LIMITED
VAT No.: GB 696 7176 72 **Date established:** 2006 **Turnover:** £2m - £5m
No.of Employees: 1 - 10 **Product Groups:** 44, 86

Date of Accounts	Dec 11	Dec 10	Dec 09
Working Capital	-290	-278	-250
Fixed Assets	802	795	782
Current Assets	36	34	34

John Crilly Transport
4 Milltown Industrial Estate Greenan Road, Warrenpoint, Newry, BT34 3FN
Tel: 028-4177 3347 **Fax:** 028-4177 3978
Directors: J. Crilly (Dir)
Immediate Holding Company: JOHN CRILLY TRANSPORT LIMITED
Registration no: NI030395 **VAT No.:** GB 286 7990 79
Date established: 1996 **Turnover:** Up to £250,000
No.of Employees: 1 - 10 **Product Groups:** 72, 76, 77

Date of Accounts	Apr 11	Apr 10	Apr 09
Working Capital	-35	-27	-24
Fixed Assets	22	28	28
Current Assets	29	30	38

P Crilly
49 Carrickrovaddy Road Cullyhanna, Newry, BT35 0QN
Tel: 028-3087 8304
Directors: P. Crilly (Prop)
Date established: 1994 **No.of Employees:** 1 - 10 **Product Groups:** 35

Dunnes Stores (Bangor) Ltd
28 Hill Street, Newry, BT34 1AR
Tel: 028-3026 1907 **Fax:** 028-3026 8119
Website: http://www.dunnesstores.co.uk
Managers: J. Nugent (Comptroller), M. Wood (I.T. Exec)
Immediate Holding Company: DUNNES STORES (BANGOR) LIMITED
Registration no: NI007608 **VAT No.:** GB 434 1649 58
Date established: 1969 **Turnover:** £125m - £250m
No.of Employees: 1501 & over **Product Groups:** 61

Date of Accounts	Jan 09	Jan 10	Jan 11
Sales Turnover	188m	195m	178m
Pre Tax Profit/Loss	28m	28m	26m
Working Capital	187m	166m	180m
Fixed Assets	126m	121m	115m
Current Assets	298m	371m	203m
Current Liabilities	6m	10m	11m

F M Environmental Ltd
Ballinacraig Way Greenbank Industrial Estate, Newry, BT34 2QX
Tel: 028-3026 6616 **Fax:** 028-3026 3233
E-mail: sales@fmenvironmental.com
Website: http://www.fmenvironmental.com
Directors: K. Fitzpatrick (MD), M. Farrugia (Tech Serv), P. Kane (Fin)
Ultimate Holding Company: FITZPATRICK SYSTEMS LIMITED
Immediate Holding Company: F M Environmental Limited
Registration no: NI021657 **VAT No.:** GB 517 9723 20
Date established: 1988 **Turnover:** £5m - £10m **No.of Employees:** 21 - 50
Product Groups: 18, 38, 40, 42, 48, 51

Date of Accounts	Mar 12	Mar 11	Mar 10
Working Capital	1m	1m	-723
Fixed Assets	1m	1m	1m
Current Assets	2m	3m	2m
Current Liabilities	N/A	N/A	1m

F P M
Dromalane Mill The Quays Complex, Newry, BT35 8AL
Tel: 028-3026 1010 **Fax:** 028-3026 2345
E-mail: info@fpmca.co.uk
Website: http://www.fpmca.com
Bank(s): Bank of Ireland
Directors: F. McCormack (Snr Part), F. Mccormack (MD), P. Harty (Ptnr)
Managers: C. Mcferran (Sec)
Immediate Holding Company: FPM ACCOUNTANTS LTD
VAT No.: GB 517 8082 37 **Date established:** 1989 **Turnover:** £10m - £20m
No.of Employees: 21 - 50 **Product Groups:** 80

Fane Valley Co-Operative Ltd
Clanrye Mills 10 New Street, Newry, BT35 6JD
Tel: 028-3026 2305 **Fax:** 028-3026 8730
E-mail: robin.irvine@fanevalley.co.uk
Website: http://www.fanevalley.co.uk
Directors: R. Irvine (MD)
Immediate Holding Company: MCNAMEE MCDONNELL DUFFY SOLICITORS LLP
VAT No.: GB 251 7362 68 **Date established:** 2009
No.of Employees: 11 - 20 **Product Groups:** 20

Date of Accounts	Mar 11	Mar 10
Sales Turnover	N/A	52
Pre Tax Profit/Loss	N/A	-67
Working Capital	71	52
Current Assets	742	108
Current Liabilities	N/A	55

Fearon Bros
41 Foughilletra Road Jonesborough, Newry, BT35 8JE
Tel: 028-3084 8693 **Fax:** 028-3084 8393
E-mail: info@fearonbros.co.uk
Website: http://www.fearonbros.co.uk
Managers: D. Fearon (Mgr)
Immediate Holding Company: DECLAN FEARON T/A FEARON BROS LTD
Registration no: NI052067 **VAT No.:** GB 366 4544 32
Date established: 2004 **Turnover:** £500,000 - £1m
No.of Employees: 11 - 20 **Product Groups:** 26

Date of Accounts	Mar 11	Mar 10	Mar 09
Working Capital	-49	6	9
Fixed Assets	97	32	40
Current Assets	106	7	42

Fibreglass Sales UK Ltd
Unit 10-11 Milltown Industrial Estate Greenan Road, Warrenpoint, Newry, BT34 3FN
Tel: 028-4175 3738 **Fax:** 028-4175 4131
E-mail: sales@fibreglasssales.com
Website: http://www.fibreglasssales.com
Directors: J. Jones (Dir)
Ultimate Holding Company: ACSTK HOLDINGS
Immediate Holding Company: FIBRE GLASS SALES (U.K.) LIMITED
Registration no: NI031814 **Date established:** 1997
Turnover: £250,000 - £500,000 **No.of Employees:** 1 - 10
Product Groups: 31, 32, 63

Date of Accounts	Dec 11	Dec 10	Dec 09
Working Capital	869	858	821
Fixed Assets	7	8	13
Current Assets	1m	1m	1m

First 4 Skills
16 Canal Quay, Newry, BT35 6BP
Tel: 028-3026 4440 **Fax:** 028-3026 5941
E-mail: jacquelinedevlin@first4skills.com
Website: http://www.first4skills.com
Managers: J. Devlin (Mgr)
Ultimate Holding Company: PROTOCOL ASSOCIATES NV (BELGIUM)
Immediate Holding Company: PROTOCOL TRAINING LIMITED
Registration no: 03826857 **Date established:** 1999
No.of Employees: 1 - 10 **Product Groups:** 82

Date of Accounts	Jun 06	Jun 05
Working Capital	68	23
Fixed Assets	167	95
Current Assets	1m	280

Freeza Meats Ltd
Unit 10 Ballinacraig Way Greenbank Industrial Estate, Newry, BT34 2QX
Tel: 028-3026 6023 **Fax:** 028-3026 5944
E-mail: sales@freezameats.co.uk
Website: http://www.freezameats.co.uk
Directors: I. Mackile (MD)
Managers: J. Furburn (Mgr)
Immediate Holding Company: FREEZA MEATS LIMITED
Registration no: NI010257 **VAT No.:** GB 162 7582 49
Date established: 1974 **No.of Employees:** 21 - 50 **Product Groups:** 20

Date of Accounts	Aug 11	Aug 10	Aug 09
Working Capital	282	252	91
Fixed Assets	3m	2m	2m
Current Assets	2m	2m	2m

Garrivan & O'Rourke
19 Burren Hill Warrenpoint, Newry, BT34 3RF
Tel: 028-4177 3063 **Fax:** 028-4177 2089
E-mail: info@garrivanorourke.co.uk
Website: http://www.garrivanorourke.co.uk
Managers: L. Evoy (Mgr)
Immediate Holding Company: GARRIVAN & O'ROURKE LTD
Registration no: NI025754 **VAT No.:** GB 517 9267 20
Date established: 1991 **No.of Employees:** 11 - 20 **Product Groups:** 52

Date of Accounts	Apr 11	Apr 10	Apr 09
Working Capital	2m	2m	2m
Fixed Assets	514	554	617
Current Assets	7m	7m	5m

Genersys Ireland Ltd
Unit 14 Warrenpoint Enterprise Centre Newry Road, Warrenpoint, Newry, BT34 3LA
Tel: 028-4173 7777 **Fax:** 028-4173 8456
E-mail: info@genersys-ireland.com
Website: http://www.genersys-ireland.com
Directors: D. Cooper (Prop)
Immediate Holding Company: Genersys Ireland Ltd
Registration no: NI051912 **Date established:** 2004
No.of Employees: 1 - 10 **Product Groups:** 37

Date of Accounts	Sep 11	Sep 10	Sep 09
Working Capital	-114	-90	90
Fixed Assets	2	2	5
Current Assets	60	67	269

Glen Electric Ltd
Greenbank Industrial Estate Rampart Road, Newry, BT34 2QU
Tel: 028-3026 4621 **Fax:** 028-3026 6122
E-mail: neil.collins@glendimplex.com
Website: http://www.glendimplex.com
Managers: M. Dawson (Personnel), N. Collins (Chief Mgr), W. Anderson
Immediate Holding Company: GLEN ELECTRIC LIMITED
Registration no: NI009677 **VAT No.:** GB 287 1315 50
Date established: 1973 **Turnover:** £500m - £1,000m
No.of Employees: 101 - 250 **Product Groups:** 40

Date of Accounts	Mar 11	Mar 10	Mar 09
Sales Turnover	839m	823m	881m
Pre Tax Profit/Loss	74m	66m	59m
Working Capital	289m	249m	192m
Fixed Assets	152m	157m	165m
Current Assets	543m	519m	473m
Current Liabilities	110m	126m	106m

Isaac Hamilton & Sons Ltd
25 Glassdrumman Road Annalong, Newry, BT34 4QJ
Tel: 028-4376 8206 **Fax:** 028-4376 8873
E-mail: clive@isaachamilton.co.uk
Website: http://www.isaachamilton.co.uk
Directors: C. Russell (MD)
Immediate Holding Company: ISAAC HAMILTON & SONS LIMITED
Registration no: NI002581 **VAT No.:** GB 252 0944 75
Date established: 1948 **Turnover:** £500,000 - £1m
No.of Employees: 1 - 10 **Product Groups:** 33

Date of Accounts	Sep 11	Sep 10	Sep 09
Working Capital	246	344	416
Fixed Assets	781	813	846
Current Assets	424	531	613

Harvard Manufacturing Ltd
Newry Road Warrenpoint, Newry, BT34 3LA
Tel: 028-4175 4004 **Fax:** 028-4175 4005
E-mail: harvard@dnet.co.uk
Website: http://www.skmprod.com
Managers: G. Morgan (Mgr)
Immediate Holding Company: HARVARD MANUFACTURING LTD
Registration no: NI025272 **VAT No.:** GB 574 9060 18
Date established: 1991 **Turnover:** Up to £250,000
No.of Employees: 1 - 10 **Product Groups:** 44, 48

Date of Accounts	Mar 11	Mar 10	Mar 09
Working Capital	88	77	77
Fixed Assets	3	4	1
Current Assets	131	114	119

J Graham & Sons Ltd
40 Greencastle Street Kilkeel, Newry, BT34 4BH
Tel: 028-4176 2777 **Fax:** 028-4176 4783
E-mail: j.grahamsons@yahoo.co.uk
Directors: R. Quinn (Co Sec)
Immediate Holding Company: J. GRAHAM & SONS (KILKEEL) LIMITED
Registration no: NI006333 **VAT No.:** GB 252 4367 67
Date established: 1965 **No.of Employees:** 1 - 10 **Product Groups:** 52

Date of Accounts	Mar 11	Mar 10	Mar 09
Working Capital	14	-48	-61
Fixed Assets	227	218	234
Current Assets	436	697	774

J K Fabrications Ltd
Unit 5 Carnbane Business Park, Newry, BT35 6QH
Tel: 028-3025 2142
E-mail: info@jkfab.com
Website: http://www.jkfab.com
Directors: J. King (Dir)
Immediate Holding Company: J.K. FABRICATIONS LIMITED
Registration no: NI035239 **Date established:** 1998
No.of Employees: 11 - 20 **Product Groups:** 35

Date of Accounts	Apr 11	Apr 10	Apr 09
Working Capital	-351	-209	-243
Fixed Assets	2m	2m	2m
Current Assets	325	368	462

John A Shannon Ltd
14-16 Newry Street Kilkeel, Newry, BT34 4DN
Tel: 028-4176 2315 **Fax:** 028-4176 4407
E-mail: robert@johnashannon.co.uk
Website: http://www.johnashannon.co.uk
Directors: R. Shannon (Dir)
Immediate Holding Company: JOHN A SHANNON LTD.
Registration no: NI603391 **VAT No.:** GB 252 9085 52
Date established: 2010 **No.of Employees:** 11 - 20 **Product Groups:** 52, 63

Date of Accounts	Jan 12	Jan 11
Working Capital	-384	-412
Fixed Assets	485	516
Current Assets	452	440

John L O'Hagan & Co. Ltd
The Masters House Abbey Yard, Newry, BT34 2EG
Tel: 028-3026 2828 **Fax:** 028-3026 3344
E-mail: info@jlohagan.co.uk
Directors: G. O'hagan (MD)
Immediate Holding Company: A.D.L. Horizons Limited
Registration no: NI048215 **VAT No.:** GB 252 0015 21
Date established: 2002 **Turnover:** Up to £250,000
No.of Employees: 1 - 10 **Product Groups:** 84

see next page

John L O'Hagan & Co. Ltd - Cont'd

Date of Accounts	Dec 10	Dec 09	Dec 08
Working Capital	-64	-129	-178
Fixed Assets	58	117	177
Current Assets	99	75	280

John Kearney Ltd

36-40 Main Street Annalong, Newry, BT34 4QH
Tel: 028-4376 8234 **Fax:** 028-4376 8616
Directors: J. Kearney (Dir)
Immediate Holding Company: JOHN KEARNEY LIMITED
Registration no: NI010162 **VAT No.:** GB 282 9988 86
Date established: 1974 **No.of Employees:** 1 - 10 **Product Groups:** 39

Date of Accounts	Dec 11	Dec 10	Dec 09
Working Capital	134	114	102
Fixed Assets	31	36	41
Current Assets	262	244	218

Kilkeel Concrete Co.

Newcastle Street Kilkeel, Newry, BT34 4AQ
Tel: 028-4176 3593 **Fax:** 028-4176 4783
Directors: J. Grahan (MD)
VAT No.: GB 287 0859 15 **Date established:** 1979
No.of Employees: 1 - 10 **Product Groups:** 33

Kilkeel Fish Selling Company

The Harbour Kilkeel, Newry, BT34 4AX
Tel: 028-4176 3896 **Fax:** 028-4176 4664
E-mail: kilkeelfishselling@btopenworld.com
Website: http://www.kilkeelfishselling.com
Directors: M. McCready (Fin)
Managers: J. Mcdowell (Chief Mgr)
Immediate Holding Company: KILKEEL FISH SELLING COMPANY LIMITED
Registration no: FC015061 **VAT No.:** GB 831 3993 59
Date established: 1989 **Turnover:** £5m - £10m **No.of Employees:** 1 - 10
Product Groups: 62

Date of Accounts	Sep 05	Sep 04	Sep 03
Sales Turnover	5m	6m	6m
Pre Tax Profit/Loss	5	30	75
Working Capital	193	179	170
Fixed Assets	194	204	219
Current Assets	301	437	622
Current Liabilities	21	80	N/A

Kilkeel Joinery Works

39 Greencastle Road Kilkeel, Newry, BT34 4DE
Tel: 028-4176 3084 **Fax:** 028-4176 3119
E-mail: keith.kjw@tiscali.co.uk
Managers: S. Graham (Mgr)
VAT No.: GB 255 6758 24 **No.of Employees:** 1 - 10 **Product Groups:** 25

M & M Steel Fabrications Ltd

Unit 5 Carnbane East Industrial Estate, Newry, BT35 6PQ
Tel: 028-3026 7089 **Fax:** 028-3025 1931
E-mail: info@mmsteelfab.plus.com
Directors: M. Maguire (Dir)
Immediate Holding Company: M. & M. (STEEL FABRICATIONS) LIMITED
Registration no: NI018192 **Date established:** 1985
No.of Employees: 11 - 20 **Product Groups:** 35

Date of Accounts	Mar 11	Mar 10	Mar 09
Working Capital	76	85	34
Fixed Assets	728	712	738
Current Assets	254	232	178

M P M Fabrications Ltd

Unit 5 Cowans Yard 39 Newtown Road, Camlough, Newry, BT35 7JJ
Tel: 028-3083 7479 **Fax:** 028-3083 7479
Directors: P. Mcgivern (MD)
Date established: 2001 **No.of Employees:** 1 - 10 **Product Groups:** 35

Terence Mccormack Ltd

17 Camlough Road, Newry, BT35 6JS
Tel: 028-3026 7369 **Fax:** 028-3026 8177
E-mail: pj@mccormacksteel.com
Website: http://www.mccormacksteel.com
Directors: T. McCormack (Dir), R. McCormack (Chief Op Offcr), D. McComack (Grp Chief Exec), D. McCormack (MD), P. Burns (MD), K. Farrell (Co Sec)
Managers: B. Collis (I.T. Exec)
Immediate Holding Company: TERENCE MCCORMACK LIMITED
Registration no: NI006356 **VAT No.:** GB 253 9494 40
Date established: 1965 **No.of Employees:** 21 - 50 **Product Groups:** 51

Macwaste Ltd

Unit 6 Milltown Industrial Estate Greenan Road, Warrenpoint, Newry, BT34 3FN
Tel: 028-4177 3100 **Fax:** 028-4177 3150
E-mail: macwasteltd@btconnect.com
Website: http://www.macwaste.com
Bank(s): First Trust
Directors: B. Mccoy (Dir)
Immediate Holding Company: MACWASTE LTD
Registration no: NI026203 **VAT No.:** GB 575 5114 35
Date established: 1992 **Turnover:** £250,000 - £500,000
No.of Employees: 11 - 20 **Product Groups:** 54

Date of Accounts	Mar 11	Mar 10	Mar 09
Working Capital	374	354	264
Fixed Assets	716	748	715
Current Assets	665	587	414

Magill Henshaw Ltd

Unit 16 Ashtree Enterprise Park Rathfriland Road, Newry, BT34 1BY
Tel: 028-3026 1311 **Fax:** 028-3026 2930
E-mail: nuala@magillhenshaw.com
Website: http://www.magillhenshaw.com
Directors: N. Magill Henshaw (MD)
Immediate Holding Company: MAGILL HENSHAW (NI) LIMITED
Registration no: NI045805 **VAT No.:** GB 255 7359 33
Date established: 2003 **Turnover:** £1m - £2m **No.of Employees:** 1 - 10
Product Groups: 63

Date of Accounts	Mar 11	Mar 10	Mar 09
Working Capital	72	68	71
Fixed Assets	59	78	45
Current Assets	504	465	415

Masters Choice Ltd

4 Carrive Road Silverbridge, Newry, BT35 9LJ
Tel: 028-3086 1032 **Fax:** 028-3086 1693
E-mail: chenjian80515@163.com
Website: http://www.masterschoice.co.uk
Managers: R. Mcelery (Chief Mgr)
Immediate Holding Company: MASTERS CHOICE LIMITED
Registration no: NI049036 **Date established:** 2003
Turnover: £500,000 - £1m **No.of Employees:** 11 - 20 **Product Groups:** 25

Date of Accounts	Dec 10	Dec 09	Dec 08
Working Capital	-294	-364	-401
Fixed Assets	528	538	548
Current Assets	209	190	211

Meadowbrook Kitchen Centre

110c Armagh Road, Newry, BT35 6PU
Tel: 028-3026 8401 **Fax:** 028-3026 8401
E-mail: david@meadowbrookkitchens.co.uk
Website: http://www.meadowbrookkitchens.co.uk
Directors: D. Brown (Prop)
Immediate Holding Company: RM AUTOPARTS LTD
Registration no: NI025772 **VAT No.:** GB 412 5285 76
Date established: 1991 **No.of Employees:** 1 - 10 **Product Groups:** 26

Date of Accounts	Aug 11	Aug 10	Aug 09
Working Capital	29	31	44
Fixed Assets	11	14	12
Current Assets	170	168	152

Mentor

Win Business Park Canal Quay, Newry, BT35 6PH
Tel: 028-3026 1229 **Fax:** 028-3026 8233
E-mail: frank.dolaghan@btclick.com
Website: http://www.mentorconsultants.com
Directors: F. Dolaghan (MD)
Immediate Holding Company: MENTOR TRAINING LIMITED
Registration no: NI029904 **VAT No.:** GB 575 4097 14
Date established: 1995 **No.of Employees:** 1 - 10 **Product Groups:** 80

Date of Accounts	Nov 11	Nov 10	Nov 09
Working Capital	162	104	85
Fixed Assets	6	1	2
Current Assets	270	157	116

Metaflex Ltd

Milltown Industrial Estate Greenan Road, Warrenpoint, Newry, BT34 3FN
Tel: 028-4177 3604 **Fax:** 028-4177 3266
E-mail: timsgibbons@hotmail.com
Website: http://www.metaflex.co.uk
Directors: T. Gibbons (Dir)
Immediate Holding Company: METAFLEX LIMITED
Registration no: NI006633 **VAT No.:** GB 252 4238 78
Date established: 1966 **Turnover:** Up to £250,000
No.of Employees: 1 - 10 **Product Groups:** 35

Date of Accounts	Dec 11	Dec 10	Dec 09
Working Capital	-107	-160	-106
Fixed Assets	381	1m	1m
Current Assets	71	97	147

Met-Art

10b Church Street Poyntzpass, Newry, BT35 6SW
Tel: 028-3831 8535
Directors: G. Hudson (Prop)
Date established: 1985 **No.of Employees:** 1 - 10 **Product Groups:** 35

Middleton Seafoods

3 The Harbour Kilkeel, Newry, BT34 4AX
Tel: 028-4176 2649 **Fax:** 028-4176 3464
E-mail: info@wmiddleton.co.uk
Website: http://www.dnet.co.uk
Bank(s): Ulster Bank
Directors: J. Cowden (MD), S. Wormald (Fin)
Immediate Holding Company: TOUGHGLASS HOLDINGS LIMITED
Registration no: NI015705 **VAT No.:** GB 375 8071 28
Date established: 1982 **No.of Employees:** 51 - 100 **Product Groups:** 20

Modern Fireplace Company & Monumental Works

Cecil Street, Newry, BT35 6AU
Tel: 028-3026 4185 **Fax:** 028-3026 7901
E-mail: info@modernfireplaces.co.uk
Website: http://www.granartstone.com
Directors: P. Keenan (Prop)
Immediate Holding Company: GRAN-ART STONE LIMITED
Registration no: NI033404 **VAT No.:** GB 331 3040 19
Date established: 1997 **Turnover:** £500,000 - £1m
No.of Employees: 1 - 10 **Product Groups:** 33

J Morgan & Sons Mayobridge Ltd

49 Leode Road Hilltown, Newry, BT34 5TJ
Tel: 028-3085 1277 **Fax:** 028-3085 1772
Managers: C. Morgan (Mgr)
Immediate Holding Company: J.MORGAN & SONS (MAYOBRIDGE) LIMITED
Registration no: NI006785 **VAT No.:** GB 252 3115 02
Date established: 1966 **No.of Employees:** 11 - 20 **Product Groups:** 14, 52

Date of Accounts	Mar 11	Mar 10	Mar 09
Working Capital	243	341	426
Fixed Assets	246	235	210
Current Assets	421	507	543

Mourne Fine Foods

24a Rampart Road Greenbank Industrial Estate, Newry, BT34 2QU
Tel: 028-3026 4968 **Fax:** 028-3026 0189
E-mail: brian@mournecountry.com
Website: http://www.mournecountry.com
Directors: B. Powell (MD), L. Powell (MD)
Managers: M. Powell (Sales Prom Mgr)
Immediate Holding Company: MOURNE COUNTRY MEATS LIMITED
Registration no: NI017064 **VAT No.:** GB 517 7168 32
Date established: 1983 **Turnover:** £5m - £10m
No.of Employees: 51 - 100 **Product Groups:** 20

Date of Accounts	Nov 09	Nov 08	Nov 07
Sales Turnover	8m	8m	N/A
Pre Tax Profit/Loss	-191	53	-108
Working Capital	-179	-271	-589
Fixed Assets	2m	2m	2m
Current Assets	3m	3m	2m
Current Liabilities	394	266	414

Murdock Hardwood Industries Ltd

51 Rathfriland Road, Newry, BT34 1LD
Tel: 028-3026 1011 **Fax:** 028-3026 6929
E-mail: info@murdockhardwood.com
Website: http://www.murdockhardwood.com
Directors: S. Murdock (Dir), A. Murdock (Fin), C. Murdock (Mkt Research)
Immediate Holding Company: MURDOCK HARDWOOD INDUSTRIES LIMITED
Registration no: NI015426 **VAT No.:** GB 517 5994 09
Date established: 1982 **Turnover:** £5m - £10m **No.of Employees:** 21 - 50
Product Groups: 25

Date of Accounts	Mar 11	Mar 10	Mar 09
Sales Turnover	9m	10m	N/A
Pre Tax Profit/Loss	339	776	1m
Working Capital	5m	5m	4m
Fixed Assets	1m	1m	940
Current Assets	6m	6m	6m
Current Liabilities	638	877	952

Newry & Mourne Enterprise Agency

W I N Industrial Estate Canal Quay, Newry, BT35 6BP
Tel: 028-3026 7011 **Fax:** 028-3026 1316
E-mail: info@nmea.net
Website: http://www.nmea.net
Directors: C. Patterson (Grp Chief Exec)
Immediate Holding Company: MOBIPAYPOINT UK LTD
Registration no: NI020058 **VAT No.:** GB 366 4302 56
Date established: 2011 **Turnover:** £1m - £2m **No.of Employees:** 11 - 20
Product Groups: 80, 86

Date of Accounts	Apr 99	Apr 98	Apr 97
Working Capital	33	26	5
Fixed Assets	29	25	18
Current Assets	314	177	121
Current Liabilities	N/A	N/A	53

Norbrook Research

Camlough Road, Newry, BT35 6JP
Tel: 028-3026 4435 **Fax:** 028-3025 1141
E-mail: enquiries@norbrook.co.uk
Website: http://www.norbrook.co.uk
Bank(s): Bank of Ireland
Directors: M. Murdock (Co Sec)
Immediate Holding Company: NORBROOK LABORATORIES LIMITED
Registration no: FC021326 **VAT No.:** GB 252 3648 64
Date established: 1998 **Turnover:** £75m - £125m
No.of Employees: 501 - 1000 **Product Groups:** 31

Date of Accounts	Jul 05	Jul 06	Aug 07
Sales Turnover	90m	93m	103m
Pre Tax Profit/Loss	8m	3m	965
Working Capital	4m	4m	4m
Fixed Assets	66m	74m	90m
Current Assets	57m	66m	69m
Current Liabilities	15m	14m	12m

Norlect Engineering Ltd

Caulfield House Caulfield Place, Newry, BT35 6AS
Tel: 028-3026 3890 **Fax:** 028-3026 2843
E-mail: norlect.eng@btinternet.com
Directors: S. Sheppard (Dir)
Immediate Holding Company: NORLECT ENGINEERING (UK) LTD
Registration no: NI028752 **VAT No.:** GB 434 2062 85
Date established: 1994 **No.of Employees:** 21 - 50 **Product Groups:** 52

Date of Accounts	Aug 11	Aug 10	Aug 09
Working Capital	741	799	791
Fixed Assets	277	285	298
Current Assets	1m	1m	1m

Northern Candles

10 Carrickrovaddy Road, Newry, BT34 1SN
Tel: 028-3082 1424 **Fax:** 028-3082 1735
E-mail: brendanreavey@hotmail.com
Directors: B. Reavey (Prop)
Immediate Holding Company: NORTHERN CANDLES LIMITED
Registration no: NI015405 **VAT No.:** GB 366 3264 43
Date established: 1982 **Turnover:** Up to £250,000
No.of Employees: 1 - 10 **Product Groups:** 32

Date of Accounts	Nov 11	Nov 10	Nov 09
Working Capital	151	151	150
Fixed Assets	184	196	206
Current Assets	181	186	185

O'Hare & Mcgovern

Carnbane House Shepherds Waycarnbane Indestate, Carnbane Industrial Estate, Newry, BT35 6EE
Tel: 028-3026 4662 **Fax:** 028-3026 2747
E-mail: carnbanehouse@ohareandmcgovern.com
Website: http://www.ohmg.com
Directors: P. Duffy (Fin), P. Duffy (Fin), T. Mcvicker (Purch), E. O'hare (MD)
Managers: N. McKee (Mktg Serv Mgr), T. McVicker (Chief Buyer)
Ultimate Holding Company: CARNBANE HOUSE LIMITED
Immediate Holding Company: O'HARE & MCGOVERN LIMITED
Registration no: NI011033 **VAT No.:** GB 283 1687 37
Date established: 1975 **Turnover:** £50m - £75m
No.of Employees: 21 - 50 **Product Groups:** 51, 52

Date of Accounts	Dec 11	Dec 10	Dec 09
Sales Turnover	41m	67m	62m
Pre Tax Profit/Loss	3m	6m	3m
Working Capital	20m	16m	10m
Fixed Assets	3m	3m	3m
Current Assets	46m	43m	35m
Current Liabilities	17m	19m	N/A

O'Hanlon & Farrell

Units 7a-7e Springhill Road, Carnbane Industrial Estate, Newry, BT35 6EF
Tel: 028-3026 9213 **Fax:** 028-3026 9015
E-mail: info@ohanlonfarrell.com
Website: http://www.ohanlonfarrell.com
Bank(s): AIB Group
Directors: C. Farrell (Dir), B. Crawford (MD), J. O'Hanlon (Dir)
Managers: C. Fagin (Buyer)
Immediate Holding Company: O'Hanlon & Farrell Holdings Limited
Registration no: NI066224 **VAT No.:** GB 286 8207 24
Date established: 2007 **Turnover:** £20m - £50m
No.of Employees: 11 - 20 **Product Groups:** 52

Date of Accounts	Nov 11	Nov 10	Nov 09
Pre Tax Profit/Loss	-46	357	250
Working Capital	-356	512	2m
Fixed Assets	5m	3m	5m
Current Assets	N/A	4m	5m
Current Liabilities	2	561	1m

Felix O'Hare & Co. Ltd

88 Chancellors Road Cloughoge, Newry, BT35 8NG
Tel: 028-3026 1134 **Fax:** 028-3026 1397
E-mail: admin@felixohare.co.uk
Website: http://www.felixohareandco.co.uk
Bank(s): First Trust
Directors: D. Gill (Dir), G. Gray (MD), M. Marcusflannagan (Mkt Research)
Managers: M. Flanagan (Chief Acct), M. Flannagan (Chief Acct)
Immediate Holding Company: FELIX O'HARE & COMPANY LIMITED
Registration no: NI001808 **VAT No.:** GB 251 9323 68
Date established: 1944 **Turnover:** £20m - £50m
No.of Employees: 51 - 100 **Product Groups:** 25, 52

Date of Accounts	Mar 12	Mar 11	Mar 10
Sales Turnover	24m	24m	23m
Pre Tax Profit/Loss	679	139	799
Working Capital	1m	729	510
Fixed Assets	5m	5m	5m
Current Assets	7m	6m	5m
Current Liabilities	756	435	547

O'Hare Steel

115 Newry Road Mayobridge, Newry, BT34 2JF
Tel: 028-3085 1637 **Fax:** 028-3085 1637
Directors: P. O'hare (Prop)
Immediate Holding Company: O'HARE STEEL LIMITED
Registration no: NI602093 **Date established:** 2010
No.of Employees: 1 - 10 **Product Groups:** 35

Date of Accounts	Mar 11
Working Capital	-137
Fixed Assets	193
Current Assets	426

Outlook Press

20 Castle Street Rathfriland, Newry, BT34 5QR
Tel: 028-4063 0781 **Fax:** 028-4063 1022
E-mail: news@outlooknews.co.uk
Website: http://www.outlookpress.com
Managers: S. Linton (Sales Admin)
Registration no: 02427896 **VAT No.:** GB 283 0896 33
No.of Employees: 1 - 10 **Product Groups:** 28

P & R Motors

6-7 Merchants Quay, Newry, BT35 6AL
Tel: 028-3026 7722 **Fax:** 028-3026 5025
E-mail: sales@prmotors.net
Website: http://www.volkswagen.co.uk
Directors: D. Goss (Dir)
Immediate Holding Company: AUTOBAHN MOTORS (N.I.) LIMITED
Registration no: NI017461 **VAT No.:** GB 252 2138 92
Date established: 1984 **Turnover:** £1m - £2m **No.of Employees:** 11 - 20
Product Groups: 68

Date of Accounts	Jun 11	Jun 10	Jun 09
Working Capital	1m	797	916
Fixed Assets	449	468	504
Current Assets	1m	1m	1m

P W S Ireland Ltd

Ballinacraig Way Greenbank Industrial Estate, Newry, BT34 2PB
Tel: 028-3026 4511 **Fax:** 028-3026 9633
E-mail: info@pwssigns.com
Website: http://www.pwssigns.com
Bank(s): Ulster Bank
Directors: J. Macateer (MD)
Immediate Holding Company: P W S IRELAND LIMITED
Registration no: NI003761 **VAT No.:** GB 254 0838 62
Date established: 1956 **Turnover:** £1m - £2m **No.of Employees:** 21 - 50
Product Groups: 33, 39, 45

Date of Accounts	Dec 11	Dec 10	Dec 09
Working Capital	603	720	840
Fixed Assets	1m	1m	1m
Current Assets	1m	1m	1m

Peter Fitzpatrick Asphalt Ltd

Leod Road Hilltown, Newry, BT34 5TJ
Tel: 028-4063 0690 **Fax:** 028-4063 1079
E-mail: damian@pfitzpatrick.com
Website: http://www.pfitzpatrick.com
Bank(s): Bank of Ireland
Directors: D. Fitzpatrick (Dir), S. Fitzpatrick (MD)
Managers: P. Fitzpatrick (Ops Mgr)
Immediate Holding Company: PETER FITZPATRICK LIMITED
Registration no: NI016868 **VAT No.:** GB 252 7550 61
Date established: 1983 **Turnover:** £1m - £2m **No.of Employees:** 21 - 50
Product Groups: 14, 32, 51

Date of Accounts	Mar 11	Mar 10	Mar 09
Working Capital	480	-73	-241
Fixed Assets	2m	2m	3m
Current Assets	2m	2m	2m

Phoenix Insulated Door Panels

15 Glenmore Road Mullaghbawn, Newry, BT35 9YE
Tel: 028-3088 8000 **Fax:** 028-3088 8674
Directors: M. Mcceresh (Ptnr)
Immediate Holding Company: FRANCIS STREET FUELS LTD.
Date established: 2011 **No.of Employees:** 1 - 10 **Product Groups:** 26, 35

Phoenix Merchants Ltd

16 Canal Quay, Newry, BT35 6BP
Tel: 028-3026 0911 **Fax:** 028-3026 0935
E-mail: info@phoenixmerchants.ltd.uk
Website: http://www.phoenixmerchants.ltd.uk
Bank(s): Ulster Bank
Directors: K. Brown (Dir), R. Sterritt (Dir)
Immediate Holding Company: PHOENIX MERCHANTS LIMITED
Registration no: NI024196 **VAT No.:** GB 517 7701 40
Date established: 1990 **Turnover:** £250,000 - £500,000
No.of Employees: 11 - 20 **Product Groups:** 66

Date of Accounts	Jan 11	Jan 10	Jan 09
Working Capital	287	373	497
Fixed Assets	44	85	114
Current Assets	1m	1m	2m

Rafferty Hospitality Products Ltd

Unit 1 Shepherds Drive Carnbane Industrial Estate, Newry, BT35 6JQ
Tel: 028-3025 2205 **Fax:** 028-3025 2206
E-mail: sales@raffertyhospitality.com
Website: http://www.raffertyhospitality.com
Directors: A. Blaney (MD)
Ultimate Holding Company: BUNZL PUBLIC LIMITED COMPANY
Immediate Holding Company: RAFFERTY HOSPITALITY PRODUCTS LIMITED
Registration no: NI032114 **VAT No.:** GB 412 5549 68
Date established: 1997 **Turnover:** £2m - £5m **No.of Employees:** 21 - 50
Product Groups: 28, 48, 81

Date of Accounts	Dec 11	Dec 10	Dec 09
Sales Turnover	N/A	5m	5m
Pre Tax Profit/Loss	N/A	146	87
Working Capital	5m	5m	4m
Fixed Assets	N/A	70	147
Current Assets	5m	6m	7m
Current Liabilities	N/A	146	592

Rockall Seafoods Ltd

The Harbour Kilkeel, Newry, BT34 4AX
Tel: 028-4176 2809 **Fax:** 028-4176 2022
E-mail: prawns@easynet.co.uk
Website: http://www.niseafood.co.uk
Directors: W. Newell (MD)
Managers: N. Newell (Sec), S. Warmold (Fin Mgr)
Ultimate Holding Company: WHITBY SEAFOODS LIMITED
Immediate Holding Company: ROCKALL SEAFOODS LIMITED
Registration no: NI019652 **VAT No.:** GB 434 2503 81
Date established: 1986 **Turnover:** £2m - £5m **No.of Employees:** 51 - 100
Product Groups: 20

Date of Accounts	Dec 11	Apr 11	Apr 10
Sales Turnover	4m	4m	4m
Pre Tax Profit/Loss	-192	130	142
Working Capital	2m	2m	2m
Fixed Assets	2	470	582
Current Assets	3m	3m	3m
Current Liabilities	83	183	301

S G Fabrication

Brackenagh West Road Ballymartin, Newry, BT34 4PP
Tel: 028-4376 7599 **Fax:** 028-4376 7599
Directors: S. Gann (Prop)
Date established: 2003 **No.of Employees:** 1 - 10 **Product Groups:** 35

Sands & Toner

50 Rathfriland Road, Newry, BT34 1LD
Tel: 028-3026 7821 **Fax:** 028-3026 5562
Directors: D. Toner (Ptnr)
Immediate Holding Company: SANDS & TONER (NEWRY) LIMITED
Registration no: NI010226 **VAT No.:** GB 255 8467 25
Date established: 1974 **Turnover:** £2m - £5m **No.of Employees:** 1 - 10
Product Groups: 52

Date of Accounts	Jun 08	Jun 07	Jun 06
Working Capital	-240	109	71
Fixed Assets	16	20	24
Current Assets	478	725	749

Sea Ice

2 Meadowlands Avenue Kilkeel, Newry, BT34 4YA
Tel: 028-4176 3082 **Fax:** 028-4176 3802
Website: http://www.seaice.co.uk
Directors: J. White (Prop)
Immediate Holding Company: SEA ICE LIMITED
Registration no: NI025156 **Date established:** 1990
No.of Employees: 1 - 10 **Product Groups:** 20, 40, 41

Smith Concrete

Ballinacraig Way Greenbank Industrial Estate, Newry, BT34 2QX
Tel: 028-3026 5745 **Fax:** 028-3022 5229
E-mail: info@smithconcrete.co.uk
Website: http://www.smithconcrete.co.uk
Directors: J. Smith (Prop)
Registration no: NI074059 **VAT No.:** GB 412 5020 15
Date established: 2009 **Turnover:** £500,000 - £1m
No.of Employees: 21 - 50 **Product Groups:** 33

Specialist Plating & Engineering

Carnbane Industrial Estate Tandragee Road, Newry, BT35 6QJ
Tel: 028-3025 6052 **Fax:** 028- 30834736
Directors: A. McGibbon (Dir)
Immediate Holding Company: SPECIALIST PLATING & ENGINEERING LIMITED
Registration no: NI038526 **Date established:** 2000
No.of Employees: 1 - 10 **Product Groups:** 46, 48

Date of Accounts	May 01	Apr 04	Apr 03
Working Capital	16	-131	-231
Fixed Assets	17	209	186
Current Assets	39	9	34

Spectrim Building Products Ltd

Greenbank Industrial Estate Rampart Road, Newry, BT34 2QU
Tel: 028-3025 0477 **Fax:** 028-3025 0223
E-mail: sales@spectrum.co.uk
Website: http://www.spectrim.co.uk
Directors: N. Mcmannus (Dir), C. Murdock (MD)
Managers: M. McGill (Sales Prom Mgr), D. Robinson (I.T. Exec)
Immediate Holding Company: UNILIN DISTRIBUTION LIMITED
Registration no: NI025830 **Date established:** 1991
Turnover: £20m - £50m **No.of Employees:** 51 - 100 **Product Groups:** 66

T C Diesel

1 Chequer Hill, Newry, BT35 6DY
Tel: 028-3025 7797 **Fax:** 028-3025 7059
Directors: T. Mcardle (Prop)
Registration no: NI029263 **Date established:** 1995
No.of Employees: 1 - 10 **Product Groups:** 40

Thornford Ltd

2 Abbey Yard, Newry, BT34 2EG
Tel: 028-3026 1061 **Fax:** 028-3026 1061
Directors: B. McConville (MD)
Immediate Holding Company: THORNFORD LIMITED
Registration no: NI023153 **VAT No.:** GB 517 7092 39
Date established: 1989 **No.of Employees:** 1 - 10 **Product Groups:** 52

Timber & Tile Products Ltd

Springhill Road Carnbane Industrial Estate, Newry, BT35 6EF
Tel: 028-3026 2609 **Fax:** 028-3026 4400
E-mail: ejpurdy@timberandtilesproducts.com
Bank(s): Ulster Bank
Directors: A. Mateer (MD)
Immediate Holding Company: TIMBER & TILE PRODUCTS LIMITED
Registration no: NI006004 **VAT No.:** GB 251 8951 44
Date established: 1964 **Turnover:** £1m - £2m **No.of Employees:** 11 - 20
Product Groups: 23, 25, 33, 35

Date of Accounts	May 09	May 07	May 06
Working Capital	4m	3m	3m
Fixed Assets	3m	4m	3m
Current Assets	5m	4m	4m

John Tinnelly & Sons

46 Forkhill Road Cloughoge, Newry, BT35 8LZ
Tel: 028-3026 5331 **Fax:** 028-3026 8491
E-mail: patricktinnelly@tinnelly.com
Website: http://www.tinnelly.com
Directors: R. Franklin (Fin), P. Tinnelly (Prop)
Managers: J. Campbell
Immediate Holding Company: JOHN TINNELLY & SONS LIMITED
Registration no: NI008644 **VAT No.:** GB 253 4783 47
Date established: 1972 **Turnover:** £5m - £10m
No.of Employees: 51 - 100 **Product Groups:** 30, 51, 54, 66

Date of Accounts	Jan 12	Jan 11	Jan 10
Sales Turnover	8m	7m	5m
Pre Tax Profit/Loss	71	-64	-357
Working Capital	3m	3m	3m
Fixed Assets	3m	3m	4m
Current Assets	4m	4m	4m
Current Liabilities	179	260	206

Typerite Ltd

Milltown East Industrial Estate Upper Dromore Road, Warrenpoint, Newry, BT34 3PN
Tel: 028-4177 2111 **Fax:** 028-4175 2022
E-mail: info@typerite.com
Website: http://www.typerite.com
Directors: M. Barlow (Dir)
Immediate Holding Company: TYPE-RITE LIMITED
Registration no: NI017995 **VAT No.:** GB 412 6585 59
Date established: 1984 **Turnover:** £5m - £10m **No.of Employees:** 11 - 20
Product Groups: 23

Ulster Bullion Embroidery Co. Ltd

Unit 5 Cornmill Quay Marine Park, Annalong, Newry, BT34 4QJ
Tel: 028-4376 8270 **Fax:** 028-4376 8270
E-mail: enquiries@handembroidery.com
Website: http://www.ulsterbullion.co.uk
Directors: A. Macleod (Ch)
Registration no: 00003950 **VAT No.:** 232 2536 94 **Date established:** 1953
Turnover: £250,000 - £500,000 **No.of Employees:** 1 - 10
Product Groups: 23, 84

Urban Forest Ltd

Unit 2 Derryboy Road Carnbane Business Park, Newry, BT35 6QH
Tel: 028-3025 3630 **Fax:** 028-3025 1350
E-mail: sales@allbed.ie
Website: http://www.allbed.ie
Managers: D. Quale, L. Foley (Personnel)
Immediate Holding Company: URBAN FOREST LIMITED
Registration no: NI053454 **Date established:** 2005
No.of Employees: 21 - 50 **Product Groups:** 40, 47

Date of Accounts	Jun 11	Jun 10	Jun 09
Working Capital	-327	-386	-2m
Fixed Assets	3m	3m	3m
Current Assets	272	390	476

Vanstar Meats Ltd

Millvale Road Bessbrook, Newry, BT35 7NH
Tel: 028-3026 6033 **Fax:** 028-3026 5550
E-mail: sales@vanstarmeats.com
Website: http://www.vanstarmeats.com
Directors: J. Murray (Dir), C. Gilpin (Dir)
Immediate Holding Company: VANSTAR MEATS LIMITED
Registration no: NI023215 **VAT No.:** GB 517 7715 29
Date established: 1989 **Turnover:** £10m - £20m
No.of Employees: 21 - 50 **Product Groups:** 20

Vitafresh Wholesale Fruit & Vegetable

8 Upper Edward Street, Newry, BT35 6AX
Tel: 028-3026 5225 **Fax:** 028-3026 8516
Directors: M. Hughes (Prop)
Registration no: NI187160 **VAT No.:** GB 252 7542 60
Date established: 1997 **Turnover:** £500,000 - £1m
No.of Employees: 1 - 10 **Product Groups:** 62

Warrenpoint Harbour Authority

The Docks Warrenpoint, Newry, BT34 3JR
Tel: 028-4177 3381 **Fax:** 028-4177 3962
E-mail: info@warrenpointharbour.co.uk
Website: http://www.warrenpointharbour.co.uk
Bank(s): Ulster Bank
Directors: K. Grant (Fin)
Managers: P. Conway (Mgr)
Immediate Holding Company: Warrenpoint Harbour Authority Marina Limited
Registration no: NI066227 **Date established:** 2007
No.of Employees: 51 - 100 **Product Groups:** 71

Co. Antrim

Newtownabbey

A G Air & Co.

Building 10 Unit 6b Central Park Mallusk, Newtownabbey, BT36 4FS
Tel: 028-9083 6008 **Fax:** 028-9083 6098
E-mail: a.gibson@agair.co.uk
Website: http://www.agair.co.uk
Directors: A. Gibson (Prop)
Date established: 1990 **Turnover:** £250,000 - £500,000
No.of Employees: 1 - 10 **Product Groups:** 40, 68

A I Services Ni Ltd Ltd
Ballycraigy A I Centre 671 Antrim Road, Newtownabbey, BT36 4RL
Tel: 028-9083 3123 **Fax:** 028-9084 2640
E-mail: info@ai-services.co.uk
Website: http://www.ai-services.co.uk
Directors: W. Campbell (Grp Chief Exec)
Managers: L. Peoples, B. Cully (Chief Acct), M. Hill
Immediate Holding Company: AI SERVICES (NORTHERN IRELAND) LIMITED
Registration no: NI021745 **VAT No.:** GB 517 0111 96
Date established: 1988 **Turnover:** £2m - £5m **No.of Employees:** 21 - 50
Product Groups: 38

Date of Accounts	Sep 11	Sep 10	Sep 09
Working Capital	2m	1m	1m
Fixed Assets	642	639	685
Current Assets	2m	2m	2m

Aalco
The Belfast Metal Centre 20 Mckinney Road, Newtownabbey, BT36 4PE
Tel: 028-9083 8838 **Fax:** 028-9083 7837
E-mail: belfast@aalco.co.uk
Website: http://www.aalco.co.uk/belfast
Managers: B. Watson (Chief Mgr)
Immediate Holding Company: AMARI METALS LTD
Registration no: NI022616 **Date established:** 1989
Turnover: £125m - £250m **No.of Employees:** 11 - 20
Product Groups: 34, 35, 36, 66

Abbey Kitchens & Bathrooms Ltd
46b Old Carrick Road, Newtownabbey, BT37 0UE
Tel: 028-9085 3277 **Fax:** 028-9086 7952
E-mail: s.barnett@abbeykitchensandbathrooms.co.uk
Website: http://www.abbeykitchensandbathrooms.co.uk
Directors: S. Barnett (MD)
Immediate Holding Company: ABBEY KITCHENS & BATHROOMS LIMITED
Registration no: NI029404 **VAT No.:** GB 331 6308 85
Date established: 1995 **No.of Employees:** 21 - 50 **Product Groups:** 25, 26

Date of Accounts	Dec 11	Dec 10	Dec 09
Working Capital	648	674	703
Fixed Assets	49	73	103
Current Assets	878	864	903

Abbey Upholsterers Ltd
8 Abbeyville Place, Newtownabbey, BT37 0AQ
Tel: 028-9336 7073 **Fax:** 028-9036 5034
E-mail: info@abbeyupholsterers.com
Website: http://www.abbeyupholsterers.com
Bank(s): Ulster Bank
Managers: G. Devlin (Admin Off), V. Kelly, K. McDonald (I.T. Exec)
Registration no: NI010849 **VAT No.:** GB 286 3206 51
Date established: 1975 **No.of Employees:** 21 - 50 **Product Groups:** 26

Acksen Ltd
28 Station Road, Newtownabbey, BT37 0AW
Tel: 08702-251790 **Fax:** 028-9020 1060
E-mail: sales@acksen.com
Website: http://www.acksen.com
Directors: K. Stafford (MD)
Immediate Holding Company: ACKSEN LTD
Registration no: NI019167 **VAT No.:** GB 617 8156 26
Date established: 1986 **Turnover:** £250,000 - £500,000
No.of Employees: 1 - 10 **Product Groups:** 37, 38

Date of Accounts	Jul 12	Jul 11	Jul 10
Sales Turnover	N/A	N/A	410
Pre Tax Profit/Loss	N/A	N/A	78
Working Capital	198	183	150
Fixed Assets	17	7	7
Current Assets	219	212	184
Current Liabilities	9	12	5

Agnew Corporate Ltd
45 Mallusk Road, Newtownabbey, BT36 4PS
Tel: 028-9080 4408 **Fax:** 028-9034 1083
Website: http://www.agnewcorporate.com
Directors: N. Mckibben (Ch)
Ultimate Holding Company: PAMD LIMITED
Immediate Holding Company: AGNEW CORPORATE LTD
Registration no: NI011916 **Date established:** 1977
Turnover: £20m - £50m **No.of Employees:** 11 - 20 **Product Groups:** 68

Date of Accounts	Dec 11	Dec 10	Dec 09
Sales Turnover	31m	29m	22m
Pre Tax Profit/Loss	993	971	262
Working Capital	440	877	189
Fixed Assets	3m	1m	840
Current Assets	3m	4m	2m
Current Liabilities	1m	1m	837

Anchor Fixings
Cottonmount House Sealstown Road, Newtownabbey, BT36 4QU
Tel: 028-9084 2373 **Fax:** 028-9084 4311
E-mail: sales@a1anchor.com
Website: http://www.a1anchor.com
Managers: T. Mcmullen (Mgr)
No.of Employees: 1 - 10 **Product Groups:** 35

Anderson Plastics Ltd
Sanda Road, Newtownabbey, BT37 9UD
Tel: 028-9086 8738 **Fax:** 028-9036 5158
E-mail: andersonplastics@dnet.co.uk
Website: http://www.andersonplastics.co.uk
Directors: P. Lismore (MD)
Ultimate Holding Company: LEPTUS LTD
Immediate Holding Company: Anderson Plastics (NI) Ltd
Registration no: NI048652 **VAT No.:** GB 311 2864 89
Date established: 2003 **No.of Employees:** 1 - 10 **Product Groups:** 30

Date of Accounts	Dec 11	Dec 10	Dec 09
Working Capital	27	40	35
Current Assets	62	81	71

Aquaforce 09 Ltd
32 Boghill Road, Newtownabbey, BT36 4QS
Tel: 028-9084 2202 **Fax:** 028-9083 9997
E-mail: info@aquaforce.org.uk
Website: http://www.aquaforce.org.uk
Directors: B. Stewart (Dir)
Immediate Holding Company: AQUAFORCE LIMITED
Registration no: NI027150 **Date established:** 1993
Turnover: £500,000 - £1m **No.of Employees:** 1 - 10 **Product Groups:** 52

Ashcroft Trailer Hire Ltd
11 Ormonde Avenue, Newtownabbey, BT36 5AT
Tel: 028-9083 2641 **Fax:** 028-9084 0291
E-mail: sales@ashcrofttrailer.co.uk
Website: http://www.ashcrofttrailer.co.uk
Directors: R. Ashcroft (Prop)
Immediate Holding Company: ASHCROFT TRAILER HIRE LIMITED
Registration no: NI019000 **VAT No.:** GB 331 7702 76
Date established: 1985 **Turnover:** Up to £250,000
No.of Employees: 1 - 10 **Product Groups:** 72

Date of Accounts	Mar 12	Mar 11	Mar 10
Working Capital	176	75	10
Fixed Assets	3m	3m	976
Current Assets	339	351	202

Ballyrobert (t/a Dencourt Motors)
1 Mallusk Road, Newtownabbey, BT36 4XS
Tel: 028-9034 2221 **Fax:** 028-9083 6126
E-mail: sales@ballyrobert.co.uk
Website: http://www.ballyrobert.co.uk
Managers: B. Paterson (Comm), J. Lisle, J. Lyle, N. Wylie (Sales Prom Mgr)
VAT No.: 28312077 **No.of Employees:** 21 - 50 **Product Groups:** 68

Barloworld Handling C M S Lift Trucks Ltd
9 Michelin Road, Newtownabbey, BT36 4PT
Tel: 028-9084 2537 **Fax:** 028-9084 2947
E-mail: info@handling.barloworld.co.uk
Website: http://www.barloworld.co.uk
Bank(s): Bank of Ireland
Managers: A. Neill (Chief Mgr), P. Smith (Buyer), J. Conlon (Chief Acct), C. McNeely (Sales Prom Mgr)
Ultimate Holding Company: BARLOWORLD LIMITED (SOUTH AFRICA)
Immediate Holding Company: CMS LIFT TRUCKS LIMITED
Registration no: NI016407 **VAT No.:** GB 375 8340 27
Date established: 1983 **Turnover:** £2m - £5m **No.of Employees:** 21 - 50
Product Groups: 48, 67, 83

Date of Accounts	Sep 11	Sep 10	Sep 09
Sales Turnover	4m	4m	4m
Pre Tax Profit/Loss	355	327	538
Working Capital	3m	3m	3m
Fixed Assets	2m	3m	3m
Current Assets	4m	4m	4m
Current Liabilities	518	557	658

Belfast Grinding Services
51 Mallusk Road, Newtownabbey, BT36 4PU
Tel: 028-9083 6524 **Fax:** 028-9083 9827
Directors: G. Mcmullan (Prop)
Immediate Holding Company: ZKJ LIMITED
Date established: 2009 **No.of Employees:** 1 - 10 **Product Groups:** 46

Boxpak Ltd
65 Church Road, Newtownabbey, BT36 7LR
Tel: 028-9036 5421 **Fax:** 028-9086 6731
E-mail: mmaitland@boxpak.co.uk
Website: http://www.boxpak.co.uk
Bank(s): Northern Bank
Directors: J. Wallace (Fin)
Managers: M. Maitland (Sales Prom Mgr)
Immediate Holding Company: BOXPAK LIMITED
Registration no: NI002891 **VAT No.:** GB 252 5909 52
Date established: 1950 **Turnover:** £5m - £10m
No.of Employees: 51 - 100 **Product Groups:** 27, 35

Date of Accounts	Mar 12	Mar 11	Mar 10
Sales Turnover	9m	8m	7m
Pre Tax Profit/Loss	280	169	-619
Working Capital	2m	1m	1m
Fixed Assets	1m	1m	2m
Current Assets	4m	4m	3m
Current Liabilities	238	249	224

J G Burns Ltd
63 Church Road, Newtownabbey, BT36 7LQ
Tel: 028-9085 3045 **Fax:** 028-9036 5787
E-mail: jim.smith@jgburns.co.uk
Website: http://www.jgburns.com
Managers: J. Smith (Mgr)
Ultimate Holding Company: SHS GROUP LIMITED
Immediate Holding Company: J.G. BURNS LIMITED
Registration no: NI013146 **VAT No.:** GB 311 3767 82
Date established: 1978 **Turnover:** £500,000 - £1m
No.of Employees: 1 - 10 **Product Groups:** 46, 67

Date of Accounts	Dec 10	Dec 11	Jan 09
Sales Turnover	925	1m	N/A
Pre Tax Profit/Loss	1	13	N/A
Working Capital	157	156	178
Fixed Assets	N/A	11	N/A
Current Assets	295	371	355
Current Liabilities	32	26	N/A

C B Services
Unit 5 Building 14 Central Park Mallusk, Newtownabbey, BT36 4FS
Tel: 028-9083 7738 **Fax:** 028-9083 2093
E-mail: info@cb-services.com
Website: http://www.cb-services.com
Directors: I. Collins (MD)
VAT No.: GB 375 7107 38 **Turnover:** £2m - £5m **No.of Employees:** 11 - 20
Product Groups: 68

C G P Enterprises
B27 Valley Business Centre Church Road, Newtownabbey, BT36 7LS
Tel: 028-9055 1610 **Fax:** 028- 90551666
Directors: C. White (Ptnr)
Ultimate Holding Company: WTB HOLDINGS LIMITED
Immediate Holding Company: HALESWORTH INVESTMENTS (UK) LIMITED
Registration no: NI033966 **Date established:** 1990
No.of Employees: 1 - 10 **Product Groups:** 38, 42

Date of Accounts	Dec 01	Jun 10	Jun 09
Working Capital	357	N/A	357
Current Assets	357	N/A	357

Cahill Motor Engineering Ltd
10 Quay Road, Newtownabbey, BT37 9TE
Tel: 028-9036 5652 **Fax:** 028-9036 5606
E-mail: warranty@cahillmotorengineering.co.uk
Website: http://www.cahillmotorengineering.co.uk
Bank(s): Northern Bank
Directors: J. Cahill (Dir)
Immediate Holding Company: CAHILL MOTOR ENGINEERING (N.I.) LIMITED
Registration no: NI009153 **VAT No.:** GB 253 4287 59
Date established: 1972 **No.of Employees:** 11 - 20 **Product Groups:** 39

Date of Accounts	Dec 11	Dec 10	Dec 09
Working Capital	472	469	525
Fixed Assets	977	1m	1m
Current Assets	1m	1m	1m

Campbell Engineering & Design Ltd
Valley Business Centre 67 Church Road, Newtownabbey, BT36 7LS
Tel: 028-9055 1611 **Fax:** 028-9055 1666
E-mail: info@cednet.co.uk
Website: http://www.cednet.co.uk
Directors: B. Campbell (Dir)
Immediate Holding Company: Campbell Engineering & Design Limited
Registration no: NI067096 **VAT No.:** GB 286 9608 01
Date established: 2007 **Turnover:** £1m - £2m **No.of Employees:** 1 - 10
Product Groups: 84

Date of Accounts	Oct 11	Oct 10	Oct 09
Working Capital	21	17	22
Fixed Assets	14	16	15
Current Assets	126	111	87

Canyon Europe Ltd Canyon Corporation Japan
4 Mallusk Road, Newtownabbey, BT36 4PR
Tel: 028-9084 1917 **Fax:** 028-9084 4528
E-mail: sales@canyoneurope.com
Website: http://www.canyoneurope.com
Directors: R. Kane (Fin), H. Ross (MD)
Managers: S. Cooke (Personnel), E. Looby (Develop Mgr), M. Johnson (Tech Serv Mgr), J. Paffey
Ultimate Holding Company: CANYON CORPORATION (JAPAN)
Immediate Holding Company: CANYON EUROPE LIMITED
Registration no: NI019880 **VAT No.:** GB 454 6024 59
Date established: 1986 **Turnover:** £10m - £20m
No.of Employees: 101 - 250 **Product Groups:** 30, 32, 37, 38, 40, 41

Date of Accounts	Dec 11	Dec 10	Dec 09
Sales Turnover	12m	13m	11m
Pre Tax Profit/Loss	366	115	2m
Working Capital	-187	-2m	-3m
Fixed Assets	6m	7m	9m
Current Assets	4m	4m	4m
Current Liabilities	584	568	595

Catchy Signs
10 Sanda Road, Newtownabbey, BT37 9UB
Tel: 028-9086 0349 **Fax:** 028-9086 0349
E-mail: sales@catchysigns.co.uk
Website: http://www.catchysigns.co.uk
Directors: P. Averell (Prop)
Immediate Holding Company: KILLETER LIMITED
Date established: 1986 **Turnover:** £500,000 - £1m
No.of Employees: 1 - 10 **Product Groups:** 28, 30, 37, 39, 40

Date of Accounts	Feb 08	Feb 11	Feb 10
Working Capital	70	241	96
Fixed Assets	1m	769	900
Current Assets	252	435	591

Civil & Structural Computer Services
1 Circular Road, Newtownabbey, BT37 0RA
Tel: 028-9036 5950 **Fax:** 028-9036 5102
E-mail: help@masterseries.co.uk
Website: http://www.masterseries.co.uk
Managers: T. White (Snr Eng)
Immediate Holding Company: CIVIL AND STRUCTURAL COMPUTER SERVICES LIMITED
Registration no: NI019163 **VAT No.:** GB 422 2750 83
Date established: 1986 **No.of Employees:** 1 - 10 **Product Groups:** 44, 86

Date of Accounts	Sep 11	Sep 10	Sep 09
Working Capital	147	93	149
Fixed Assets	26	31	39
Current Assets	336	344	573

Cleancare Services Ireland
Patrick House Commercial Way, Newtownabbey, BT36 4UE
Tel: 028-9084 8595 **Fax:** 028-9084 8506
Directors: W. Jones (Prop)
VAT No.: GB 283 1301 85 **Turnover:** Up to £250,000
No.of Employees: 1 - 10 **Product Groups:** 52

Commercial & Industrial Flooring
10 Sanda Road, Newtownabbey, BT37 9UB
Tel: 028-9085 1421 **Fax:** 028-9036 5687
E-mail: jim@comindflo.co.uk
Directors: J. Weir (Prop)
Immediate Holding Company: KILLETER LIMITED
VAT No.: GB 422 2658 71 **Date established:** 1986
No.of Employees: 1 - 10 **Product Groups:** 23, 25, 29, 30, 33, 49, 52, 66

Date of Accounts	Feb 08	Feb 11	Feb 10
Working Capital	70	241	96
Fixed Assets	1m	769	900
Current Assets	252	435	591

Component Distributors
Blackwater Road, Newtownabbey, BT36 4UA
Tel: 028-9034 1900 **Fax:** 028-9034 1977
E-mail: info@cd-group.com
Website: http://www.cd-group.com
Bank(s): Northern Bank
Managers: T. Taggart (Mgr)
Ultimate Holding Company: COMPONENT DISTRIBUTORS GROUP LIMITED
Immediate Holding Company: OLYMPIC TYRE & AUTO LIMITED
Registration no: NI005518 **VAT No.:** GB 251 7290 67
Date established: 1974 **No.of Employees:** 51 - 100 **Product Groups:** 68

Countrywide Freights
Mallusk Way, Newtownabbey, BT36 4AA
Tel: 028-9080 0800 **Fax:** 028-9080 0844
E-mail: julie.westray@countrywide-freight.co.uk
Website: http://www.countrywide-freight.co.uk
Bank(s): Northern Bank
Directors: D. Macallister (Dir)
Managers: B. McQuinn (Comptroller), K. Brier (I.T. Exec), R. Beatty (Personnel)

Ultimate Holding Company: CFG HOLDINGS LIMITED
Immediate Holding Company: COUNTRYWIDE EXPRESS LIMITED
Registration no: NI019251 **VAT No.:** GB 283 0992 37
Date established: 1986 **Turnover:** £20m - £50m
No.of Employees: 51 - 100 **Product Groups:** 44, 72, 76, 79, 84

Date of Accounts	Dec 09	Dec 08
Working Capital	254	254
Current Assets	254	254

D Engineering Ltd
22 Mckinney Road, Newtownabbey, BT36 4PE
Tel: 028-9083 0483 **Fax:** 028-9083 0638
E-mail: info@d-eng.com
Website: http://www.d-eng.com
Directors: B. Duffin (MD)
Immediate Holding Company: D Engineering Limited
Registration no: NI015582 **Date established:** 1982
No.of Employees: 11 - 20 **Product Groups:** 46

Date of Accounts	Sep 11	Sep 10	Sep 09
Working Capital	-79	-204	-153
Fixed Assets	803	862	939
Current Assets	536	456	457

D S V Air & Sea
World Cargo Centre 605 Antrim Road, Newtownabbey, BT36 4RF
Tel: 028-9084 9000 **Fax:** 028-9083 5777
E-mail: marshall.boyd@uk.dsv.com
Website: http://www.dsv.com
Managers: J. Rainey (Mgr), M. Boyd (Mgr)
Immediate Holding Company: CAMPBELL FREIGHT AGENCIES LIMITED
Registration no: NI013519 **Date established:** 1979
Turnover: £10m - £20m **No.of Employees:** 11 - 20 **Product Groups:** 75, 76, 77

Date of Accounts	Dec 10	Dec 09	Dec 08
Sales Turnover	N/A	10m	11m
Pre Tax Profit/Loss	2m	759	498
Working Capital	4m	1m	1m
Fixed Assets	N/A	693	799
Current Assets	4m	3m	4m
Current Liabilities	16	324	369

Decor Ireland
58 Trench Road, Newtownabbey, BT36 4TY
Tel: 028-9083 4910 **Fax:** 028-9083 4919
E-mail: info@decorireland.com
Directors: S. Hughes (Ptnr), P. Hamilton (Ptnr), L. Hamilton (Ptnr)
VAT No.: GB 256 0232 86 **Date established:** 1976
No.of Employees: 1 - 10 **Product Groups:** 87

Diskshred
Unit 2 Mallusk View, Newtownabbey, BT36 4FR
Tel: 028-9084 4400
E-mail: info@amiltd.ie
Website: http://www.amiltd.ie
Directors: P. Mcmichael (Chief Op Offcr)
Registration no: NI071752 **Date established:** 2008
No.of Employees: 21 - 50 **Product Groups:** 80

Eagle Electro Plating Company
7 Ormonde Avenue, Newtownabbey, BT36 5AT
Tel: 028-9084 1733 **Fax:** 028-9084 4724
Directors: D. Morton (Prop)
Date established: 1991 **No.of Employees:** 1 - 10 **Product Groups:** 46, 48

Eglantine Timber Products
145-147 Glenville Road, Newtownabbey, BT37 0DP
Tel: 028-9036 5146 **Fax:** 028-9086 2968
E-mail: whiteabbey@eglantine-timber.co.uk
Website: http://www.eglantinetimber.com
Managers: A. McReavie (Sales Prom Mgr), M. Richardson (Chief Mgr), B. Savage (Fin Mgr)
Immediate Holding Company: EGLANTINE TIMBER PRODUCTS LIMITED
Registration no: NI015069 **VAT No.:** GB 353 1438 71
Date established: 1981 **Turnover:** Up to £250,000
No.of Employees: 11 - 20 **Product Groups:** 25

Date of Accounts	Sep 11	Sep 10	Sep 09
Working Capital	-356	-514	-828
Fixed Assets	1m	1m	1m
Current Assets	603	721	810
Current Liabilities	N/A	101	718

Exel Europe Ltd
McKinney Industrial Estate Mallusk, Newtownabbey, BT36 8YZ
Tel: 028-9084 3481 **Fax:** 028-9083 3153
E-mail: pam.millar@dhl.co.uk
Website: http://www.exel.com
Directors: P. Miller (Co Sec)
Managers: C. Cassidy (Sales Admin), I. Hawthorne (Chief Mgr), J. Hughes (Site Co-ord), K. Ruddock (I.T. Exec)
Registration no: 00528867 **Turnover:** £500,000 - £1m
No.of Employees: 21 - 50 **Product Groups:** 72, 84

F B Smyth & Co. Ltd
Unit 56 Mallusk Enterprise Park Mallusk Drive, Newtownabbey, BT36 4GN
Tel: 028-9084 2229 **Fax:** 028-9084 1119
E-mail: fbsmyth@aol.com
Directors: K. Smyth (MD)
Immediate Holding Company: F. B. Smyth & Co Limited
Registration no: NI045764 **VAT No.:** GB 617 5887 02
Date established: 2003 **Turnover:** Up to £250,000
No.of Employees: 1 - 10 **Product Groups:** 66

Date of Accounts	Mar 11	Mar 10	Mar 09
Working Capital	179	161	136
Fixed Assets	124	120	132
Current Assets	301	278	234

Fortress Doors Ni Ltd
6 Trench Road, Newtownabbey, BT36 4TY
Tel: 028-9034 2655 **Fax:** 028-9034 2651
E-mail: info@fortaxa.com
Website: http://www.fortaxa.com
Bank(s): Northern
Directors: F. Gambale (Tech Serv)
Managers: L. Smith (Sales Admin)
Immediate Holding Company: FORTRESS INDUSTRIES LIMITED
Registration no: NI007885 **VAT No.:** GB 254 6345 55
Date established: 1970 **Turnover:** £2m - £5m **No.of Employees:** 21 - 50
Product Groups: 35, 36, 66

Date of Accounts	Dec 10	Dec 09	Dec 08
Working Capital	635	624	612
Fixed Assets	1m	1m	1m
Current Assets	1m	1m	1m

Gray & Adams Ireland
Houstons Corner Doagh Road, Newtownabbey, BT36 4TP
Tel: 028-9034 2160 **Fax:** 028-9084 8933
E-mail: enquiries@gray-adams.com
Website: http://www.gray-adams.com
Directors: B. Dougan (MD)
Managers: S. Kerr, J. Robinson (Chief Acct), J. Robinson (Chief Acct)
Ultimate Holding Company: GRAY & ADAMS HOLDINGS LIMITED
Immediate Holding Company: GRAY & ADAMS (IRELAND) LIMITED
Registration no: NI015858 **VAT No.:** GB 375 7568 02
Date established: 1982 **Turnover:** £5m - £10m **No.of Employees:** 21 - 50
Product Groups: 45

Date of Accounts	Apr 11	Apr 10	Apr 09
Sales Turnover	11m	8m	10m
Pre Tax Profit/Loss	176	7	15
Working Capital	426	456	593
Fixed Assets	780	633	489
Current Assets	2m	2m	3m
Current Liabilities	572	243	398

W Hall Ltd
Hydepark Industrial Estate Cloughmore Road, Newtownabbey, BT36 4WW
Tel: 028-9084 1444 **Fax:** 028-9034 2466
E-mail: info@whall.co.uk
Website: http://www.whall.co.uk
Directors: W. Hall (Fin)
Managers: C. Hall
Ultimate Holding Company: FIRST FORKLIFTS LIMITED
Immediate Holding Company: W. HALL LIMITED
Registration no: NI012158 **Date established:** 1977
No.of Employees: 11 - 20 **Product Groups:** 35, 39, 45

Date of Accounts	Jul 11	Jul 10	Jul 09
Working Capital	2m	2m	2m
Fixed Assets	428	379	340
Current Assets	2m	2m	2m

Robert Hart Memorials
65 O'Neill Road, Newtownabbey, BT36 6UN
Tel: 028-9085 4121 **Fax:** 028-9036 5549
Directors: G. Mckernan (Prop)
Immediate Holding Company: ROBERT HART MEMORIALS LIMITED
Registration no: NI021688 **VAT No.:** GB 392 5203 56
Date established: 1988 **No.of Employees:** 1 - 10 **Product Groups:** 33, 52

Harvey Group plc
14 Glenwell Road, Newtownabbey, BT36 7RF
Tel: 028-9034 2444 **Fax:** 028-9034 2924
E-mail: reception@harveygroup.co.uk
Website: http://www.harveygroup.co.uk
Bank(s): Northern Bank
Directors: B. Harvey (Dir)
Managers: T. Brown (Tech Serv Mgr)
Immediate Holding Company: HARVEY GROUP PLC
Registration no: NI013009 **VAT No.:** GB 517 4340 61
Date established: 1978 **Turnover:** £10m - £20m
No.of Employees: 51 - 100 **Product Groups:** 52

Date of Accounts	Aug 11	Aug 10	Aug 09
Sales Turnover	19m	27m	17m
Pre Tax Profit/Loss	453	409	305
Working Capital	4m	4m	3m
Fixed Assets	758	1m	1m
Current Assets	11m	11m	9m
Current Liabilities	622	727	595

Henderson Group Ltd
9 Hightown Avenue, Newtownabbey, BT36 4RT
Tel: 028-9034 2733 **Fax:** 028-9034 2484
E-mail: info@henderson-group.com
Website: http://www.henderson-group.com
Bank(s): Northern Bank
Directors: J. Agnew (Ch), R. Whitten (Fin)
Managers: G. Somerville (Personnel), A. Fitzsimmins, B. Luke, D. Hutchinson (Tech Serv Mgr)
Ultimate Holding Company: ARDBARRON TRUST LIMITED
Immediate Holding Company: JOHN HENDERSON (HOLDINGS) LIMITED
Registration no: NI010588 **VAT No.:** GB 251 9143 70
Date established: 1975 **Turnover:** £500m - £1,000m
No.of Employees: 501 - 1000 **Product Groups:** 62

Date of Accounts	Dec 11	Dec 10	Dec 09
Sales Turnover	583m	532m	507m
Pre Tax Profit/Loss	14m	14m	16m
Working Capital	-7m	-6m	824
Fixed Assets	127m	123m	114m
Current Assets	77m	78m	76m
Current Liabilities	27m	26m	23m

Holemasters Ni Ltd
Canon House 57-59 Manse Road, Newtownabbey, BT36 6RR
Tel: 028-9034 2235 **Fax:** 028-9034 2053
E-mail: holemast@indigo.ie
Website: http://www.holemasters.co.uk
Managers: B. Twaite-Warren (Mgr), D. O'Connor (Mgr), D. O'Neill (Mgr), D. Turner (Mgr), J. Sweeney (Mgr), P. Brooks (Mgr), T. Williamson (Chief Mgr), M. O'Neill (Sec), D. Baine (Mgr)
Immediate Holding Company: HOLEMASTERS (N.I.) LIMITED
Registration no: NI025918 **Date established:** 1991
No.of Employees: 1 - 10 **Product Groups:** 51

Houston Thornton & Company Ltd
70 Doagh Road, Newtownabbey, BT37 9NY
Tel: 028-9036 5803 **Fax:** 028-9036 5875
Website: http://www.houstonthornton.co.uk
Directors: G. Houston (MD)
Ultimate Holding Company: Prestige Insurance Holdings Limited
Immediate Holding Company: HOUSTON THORNTON & CO LIMITED
Registration no: NI604220 **VAT No.:** GB 286 4682 14
Date established: 2010 **Turnover:** £250,000 - £500,000
No.of Employees: 1 - 10 **Product Groups:** 52

Date of Accounts	Mar 11
Sales Turnover	445
Pre Tax Profit/Loss	43
Working Capital	25
Fixed Assets	9
Current Assets	248
Current Liabilities	60

Jennings Ltd
Unit 3 Sentry Lane, Newtownabbey, BT36 4XX
Tel: 028-9083 7799 **Fax:** 028-9083 7762
Directors: G. Jennings (MD)
Immediate Holding Company: JENNINGS LIMITED
Registration no: NI024090 **VAT No.:** GB 517 3197 45
Date established: 1990 **Turnover:** Up to £250,000
No.of Employees: 1 - 10 **Product Groups:** 68

Date of Accounts	Oct 11	Oct 10	Oct 09
Working Capital	-9	95	118
Fixed Assets	5	7	8
Current Assets	103	183	425

T & A Kernoghan Ltd
5 Blackwater Road, Newtownabbey, BT36 4TZ
Tel: 028-9084 2311 **Fax:** 028-9084 3107
E-mail: info@t-agroup.com
Website: http://www.t-akernoghan.co.uk
Bank(s): Ulster Bank
Directors: M. Thompson (MD)
Ultimate Holding Company: T & A Kernoghan (Holdings) Limited
Immediate Holding Company: T & A Kernoghan Limited
Registration no: NI063712 **VAT No.:** GB 617 5265 36
Date established: 2007 **Turnover:** £20m - £50m
No.of Employees: 51 - 100 **Product Groups:** 52

Date of Accounts	Dec 09	Dec 08	Dec 07
Sales Turnover	22m	24m	12m
Pre Tax Profit/Loss	459	1m	461
Working Capital	178	667	197
Fixed Assets	260	195	136
Current Assets	5m	8m	6m
Current Liabilities	265	608	395

Lamp Source
4 Nicholson Drive, Newtownabbey, BT36 4FH
Tel: 028-9083 6565
E-mail: sales@lampsourceirl.com
Website: http://www.lampsourceirl.com
Directors: W. Robb (Dir)
Date established: 2003 **No.of Employees:** 1 - 10 **Product Groups:** 33, 37

M A N Engineering
64 Mallusk Enterprise Park Mallusk Drive, Newtownabbey, BT36 4GN
Tel: 028-9084 2573 **Fax:** 028-9084 2573
E-mail: info@manengineering.co.uk
Website: http://www.manengineering.co.uk
Directors: S. Mackay (Prop)
Date established: 1979 **No.of Employees:** 1 - 10 **Product Groups:** 35

M E T Steel Ltd
51 Mallusk Road, Newtownabbey, BT36 4PX
Tel: 028-9083 7311 **Fax:** 028-9084 3548
E-mail: sales@metsteel.com
Website: http://www.metsteel.co.uk
Bank(s): First Trust
Directors: T. Marshall (Dir)
Managers: H. Marron (Purch Mgr)
Ultimate Holding Company: MET STEEL GROUP LTD
Immediate Holding Company: M.E.T. STEEL LIMITED
Registration no: NI011767 **VAT No.:** GB 735 9103 32
Date established: 1977 **Turnover:** £10m - £20m
No.of Employees: 51 - 100 **Product Groups:** 66

Date of Accounts	Aug 11	Aug 10	Aug 09
Sales Turnover	17m	8m	13m
Pre Tax Profit/Loss	501	75	-388
Working Capital	2m	481	-198
Fixed Assets	4m	4m	3m
Current Assets	11m	6m	7m
Current Liabilities	188	369	217

M M K Express
4 Sentry Lane, Newtownabbey, BT36 4XX
Tel: 028-9083 8388 **Fax:** 028-9084 8822
E-mail: sales@mmkexpress.co.uk
Website: http://www.mmkexpress.co.uk
Bank(s): Ulster Bank
Directors: W. Marley (Dir), M. Marley (Dir)
Managers: T. Ballentine (Fin Mgr)
Immediate Holding Company: M.M.K. EXPRESS LIMITED
Registration no: NI015607 **VAT No.:** GB 454 5568 24
Date established: 1982 **Turnover:** £2m - £5m **No.of Employees:** 11 - 20
Product Groups: 72, 76, 79

Date of Accounts	Jan 11	Jan 10	Jan 09
Working Capital	766	552	442
Fixed Assets	389	433	461
Current Assets	2m	2m	2m

Brett Martin Ltd
24 Roughfort Road, Newtownabbey, BT36 4RB
Tel: 028-9084 9999 **Fax:** 028-9083 6666
E-mail: mail@brettmartin.com
Website: http://www.brettmartin.com
Bank(s): Barclays
Directors: L. Martin (MD)
Ultimate Holding Company: BRETT MARTIN HOLDINGS LTD
Immediate Holding Company: BRETT MARTIN LIMITED
Registration no: NI008627 **VAT No.:** GB 353 0990 54
Date established: 1972 **Turnover:** £75m - £125m
No.of Employees: 251 - 500 **Product Groups:** 30, 66

Date of Accounts	Dec 11	Dec 10	Dec 09
Sales Turnover	101m	99m	82m
Pre Tax Profit/Loss	1m	2m	3m
Working Capital	20m	21m	21m
Fixed Assets	16m	13m	13m
Current Assets	60m	60m	51m
Current Liabilities	24m	24m	17m

Montgomery Tank Services Ltd
607 Antrim Road Glengormley, Newtownabbey, BT36 4RF
Tel: 028-9084 3723 **Fax:** 028-9084 9111
E-mail: sales@montgomerytankservices.co.uk
Website: http://www.montgomerytankservices.co.uk
Bank(s): Northern Bank
Directors: P. Jackson (MD), M. Lane (Fin)
Ultimate Holding Company: BALLYVESEY HOLDINGS LIMITED
Immediate Holding Company: MONTGOMERY TANK SERVICES LIMITED
Registration no: NI014185 **VAT No.:** 653872803 **Date established:** 1980
No.of Employees: 51 - 100 **Product Groups:** 72, 76

see next page

Montgomery Tank Services Ltd - Cont'd

Date of Accounts	Sep 11	Sep 10	Sep 09
Pre Tax Profit/Loss	427	719	463
Working Capital	2m	2m	1m
Fixed Assets	2m	2m	2m
Current Assets	5m	4m	4m
Current Liabilities	745	896	878

Donald Murray Paper Ltd
9 Michelin Road, Newtownabbey, BT36 4PT
Tel: 028-9084 3161 **Fax:** 028-9084 0119
E-mail: sales@donaldmurraypaper.com
Website: http://www.paperco.co.uk
Managers: S. Vante (Mgr)
Ultimate Holding Company: BARLOWORLD LIMITED (SOUTH AFRICA)
Immediate Holding Company: DONALD MURRAY (PAPER) LIMITED
Registration no: NF002726 **VAT No.:** GB 286 7096 12
Date established: 1987 **Turnover:** £250,000 - £500,000
No.of Employees: 1 - 10 **Product Groups:** 28, 44, 66

N K Coatings Ltd
4 Michelin Road, Newtownabbey, BT36 4PT
Tel: 028-9083 3725 **Fax:** 028-9083 7433
E-mail: mail@nkcoatings.com
Website: http://www.nkcoatings.com
Managers: P. Harvey (Chief Mgr)
Ultimate Holding Company: N.K. HOLDINGS LIMITED
Immediate Holding Company: N.K. COATINGS LTD
Registration no: NI007111 **VAT No.:** GB 252 0445 93
Date established: 1967 **Turnover:** £2m - £5m **No.of Employees:** 21 - 50
Product Groups: 48

Date of Accounts	Apr 11	Apr 10	Apr 09
Sales Turnover	4m	4m	6m
Pre Tax Profit/Loss	-246	-48	360
Working Capital	1m	1m	1m
Fixed Assets	1m	1m	2m
Current Assets	2m	2m	3m
Current Liabilities	159	172	708

Nicholson & Bass Ltd
3 Nicholson Drive, Newtownabbey, BT36 4FB
Tel: 028-9034 2433 **Fax:** 028-9034 2066
E-mail: rsouth@nicholsonbass.com
Website: http://www.nicholsonbass.com
Bank(s): Northern Bank
Directors: R. South (Sales), H. Montgomery (Fin), B. Gillespie (Chief Op Offcr)
Managers: D. Hawthorn (Mgr), N. Hannah (Buyer)
Immediate Holding Company: NICHOLSON & BASS LIMITED
Registration no: NI003800 **VAT No.:** GB 252 2409 87
Date established: 1956 **Turnover:** £2m - £5m **No.of Employees:** 21 - 50
Product Groups: 28

Date of Accounts	Dec 11	Dec 10	Dec 09
Working Capital	1m	2m	2m
Fixed Assets	2m	2m	2m
Current Assets	2m	3m	3m

Northern Lift & Escalators Ltd
Unit 1 Enterprise Way, Newtownabbey, BT36 4EW
Tel: 028-9084 1358 **Fax:** 028-9077 2123
E-mail: info@nleltd.co.uk
Website: http://www.nleltd.co.uk
Directors: S. Garland (MD)
Ultimate Holding Company: MID-WESTERN LIFTS LIMITED
Registration no: NI046959 **Date established:** 2003
No.of Employees: 11 - 20 **Product Groups:** 35, 39, 45

Northgate Managed Services Ltd
61 Church Road The Linen Green, Newtownabbey, BT36 7LQ
Tel: 028-9085 9085 **Fax:** 028-9085 9086
E-mail: sales@northgate-is.com
Website: http://www.northgate-is.com
Bank(s): Bank of Ireland
Directors: A. Ross (Grp Chief Exec), J. Phipps (Fin), E. Lee (Mkt Research)
Managers: S. McCann (Personnel), S. Jackson (Tech Serv Mgr), D. McCullough (Buyer)
Ultimate Holding Company: NIS HOLDINGS SARL (LUXEMBOURG)
Immediate Holding Company: Northgate Managed Services Limited
Registration no: NI032979 **Date established:** 1997
Turnover: £125m - £250m **No.of Employees:** 251 - 500
Product Groups: 44, 67, 80, 86

Date of Accounts	Apr 11	Apr 10	Apr 09
Sales Turnover	129m	114m	125m
Pre Tax Profit/Loss	5m	671	4m
Working Capital	57m	50m	49m
Fixed Assets	18m	28m	34m
Current Assets	119m	123m	109m
Current Liabilities	40m	36m	26m

Palmer & Harvey Mclane Ltd
1 Trench Road, Newtownabbey, BT36 4TY
Tel: 028-9084 3535 **Fax:** 028-9083 7455
E-mail: belfast@palmerharvey.co.uk
Directors: J. Davis (Ptnr)
Ultimate Holding Company: PALMER & HARVEY (HOLDINGS) PLC
Immediate Holding Company: PALMER & HARVEY MCLANE LIMITED
Registration no: 01874153 **VAT No.:** GB 232 1690 89
Date established: 1984 **Turnover:** £250,000 - £500,000
No.of Employees: 21 - 50 **Product Groups:** 61

Date of Accounts	Apr 12	Apr 09	Apr 10
Sales Turnover	4166m	4081m	4179m
Pre Tax Profit/Loss	23m	28m	19m
Working Capital	111m	50m	62m
Fixed Assets	55m	67m	69m
Current Assets	938m	832m	976m
Current Liabilities	17m	16m	12m

Pauley Equipment Solutions
625 Shore Road, Newtownabbey, BT37 0ST
Tel: 028-9086 5186 **Fax:** 08712-641552
E-mail: info@pauleyequipment.co.uk
Website: http://www.pauleyequipment.co.uk
Directors: M. Pauley (Prop)
Date established: 2006 **Turnover:** Up to £250,000
No.of Employees: 1 - 10 **Product Groups:** 38

Power Plant & Drives
Hydepark Industrial Estate McKinney Road, Newtownabbey, BT36 4PX
Tel: 0845-6256256 **Fax:** 028-9002 0424
E-mail: sales@wpmurray.com
Website: http://www.wpmurray.com
Directors: B. Murray (Prop)
VAT No.: 617 8206 45 **Date established:** 1994
Turnover: £250,000 - £500,000 **No.of Employees:** 1 - 10
Product Groups: 67

Prestige Enterprises
PO Box 1160, Newtownabbey, BT36 5YP
Tel: 028-9084 7000 **Fax:** 0845-230 3819
E-mail: sales@prestigeenterprises.com
Website: http://www.prestigeenterprises.com
Managers: B. Mcardle (Mktg Serv Mgr)
VAT No.: GB 331 6616 74 **Turnover:** £1m - £2m **No.of Employees:** 1 - 10
Product Groups: 24, 35, 38, 49

Richard Atkinson
10 Nicholson Drive, Newtownabbey, BT36 4FD
Tel: 028-9084 3323 **Fax:** 020-8908 4850
E-mail: info@atkinsons-irishpoplin-ties.com
Website: http://www.atkinsonsties.com
Directors: P. Nicholson (MD)
Immediate Holding Company: RICHARD ATKINSON AND COMPANY LIMITED
Registration no: NI003485 **VAT No.:** 251707767 **Date established:** 1955
Turnover: £1m - £2m **No.of Employees:** 1 - 10 **Product Groups:** 24

Date of Accounts	Dec 11	Dec 10	Dec 09
Working Capital	411	352	244
Fixed Assets	497	497	539
Current Assets	500	460	381

Scan Alarms & Security Systems UK Ltd
52 Trench Road, Newtownabbey, BT36 4TY
Tel: 028-9034 2233 **Fax:** 028-9083 0444
E-mail: sales@scanalarms.co.uk
Website: http://www.scanalarms.co.uk
Directors: D. Allen (MD)
Managers: H. McGregor (Sales Admin), L. Allen (Fin Mgr)
Immediate Holding Company: SCAN ALARMS AND SECURITY SYSTEMS (U.K.) LIMITED
Registration no: NI015649 **Date established:** 1982
No.of Employees: 21 - 50 **Product Groups:** 40, 52

Date of Accounts	Mar 11	Mar 10	Mar 09
Working Capital	361	317	304
Fixed Assets	89	94	111
Current Assets	984	971	936

Spencer Coating Ltd
36 Trench Road, Newtownabbey, BT36 4TY
Tel: 028-9084 3300 **Fax:** 028-9084 4990
E-mail: spbelfast@aol.com
Website: http://www.spencercoatings.co.uk
Managers: G. Hughes (Mgr)
VAT No.: GB 376 9551 03 **Turnover:** Up to £250,000
No.of Employees: 1 - 10 **Product Groups:** 66

Stevenson & Reid
Sanda Road, Newtownabbey, BT37 9UD
Tel: 028-9085 2212 **Fax:** 028-9036 5139
E-mail: sam@stevensonandreid.co.uk
Website: http://www.stevensonandreid.co.uk
Directors: W. Stevenson (MD)
Immediate Holding Company: STEVENSON AND REID
Registration no: NI013942 **VAT No.:** GB 331 7106 92
Date established: 1979 **No.of Employees:** 11 - 20 **Product Groups:** 66

Carl Stuart Ltd
33 Valley Business Centre Church Road, Newtownabbey, BT36 7LS
Tel: 028-9055 1705 **Fax:** 028-9055 1706
E-mail: info@carlstuart.com
Website: http://www.carlstuart.co.uk
Directors: S. Smith (Dir), D. Smith (Dir)
Managers: G. Smith (Comptroller), P. Byrne (Sales Admin)
Immediate Holding Company: CARL STUART (N.I.) LIMITED
Registration no: NI022429 **Date established:** 1989
No.of Employees: 1 - 10 **Product Groups:** 67

Date of Accounts	Dec 11	Dec 10	Dec 09
Working Capital	32	37	15
Fixed Assets	22	22	22
Current Assets	42	44	16
Current Liabilities	1	5	2

Transbus International Ltd
Hydepark Indl-Est Mallusk, Newtownabbey, BT36 8NP
Tel: 028-9034 2006 **Fax:** 028-9034 2678
E-mail: m.craig@transbus.co.uk
Directors: G. Cardwell (MD)
Managers: W. McMullan (Personnel)
Ultimate Holding Company: THE MAYFLOWER CORPORATION PLC
Immediate Holding Company: TRANSBUS INTERNATIONAL LIMITED
Registration no: 00970239 **VAT No.:** 251 7128 76 **Date established:** 1970
No.of Employees: 1 - 10 **Product Groups:** 39

Date of Accounts	Dec 99	Dec 02	Dec 01
Sales Turnover	200m	153m	104m
Pre Tax Profit/Loss	15m	14m	9m
Working Capital	13m	4m	3m
Fixed Assets	17m	61m	8m
Current Assets	117m	71m	92m
Current Liabilities	14m	7m	31m

University Of Ulster
Shore Road, Newtownabbey, BT37 0QB
Tel: 028-7012 3456 **Fax:** 028-9036 6821
E-mail: careers@ulster.ac.uk
Website: http://www.ulster.ac.uk
Managers: D. McGibbon (Mgr), R. Barnett (Print Purch Mgr), A. Tate, U. Donnelly (Mgr)
Immediate Holding Company: YOUNG ENTERPRISE
Registration no: RC000726 **Date established:** 1995
No.of Employees: 1 - 10 **Product Groups:** 86

Vaughan Engineering Group Ltd
Aercon Works 556 Antrim Road, Newtownabbey, BT36 4RF
Tel: 028-9083 7441 **Fax:** 028-9034 2469
E-mail: info@vaughan-group.co.uk
Website: http://www.vaughan-group.co.uk
Bank(s): Northern Bank
Directors: M. Vaughan (Chief Op Offcr)
Managers: G. Vaughan, J. Brown (Tech Serv Mgr)
Ultimate Holding Company: RATHMORE ESTATES LIMITED
Immediate Holding Company: VAUGHAN ENGINEERING GROUP LIMITED
Registration no: NI008727 **VAT No.:** GB 253 3655 66
Date established: 1972 **Turnover:** £20m - £50m
No.of Employees: 251 - 500 **Product Groups:** 52

Date of Accounts	Mar 12	Mar 11	Mar 10
Sales Turnover	49m	40m	42m
Pre Tax Profit/Loss	475	408	-47
Working Capital	3m	3m	3m
Fixed Assets	5m	5m	5m
Current Assets	18m	15m	11m
Current Liabilities	3m	4m	2m

E Wilson & Co Steeplejacks Ltd
Longlands Avenue, Newtownabbey, BT36 7NE
Tel: 028-9085 1455 **Fax:** 028-9085 3535
E-mail: ewilson.steeplejacks@virgin.net
Website: http://www.ewilsonsteeplejacks.co.uk
Directors: K. Wilson (MD)
Immediate Holding Company: EDWARD WILSON & CO (STEEPLEJACKS) LIMITED
Registration no: NI011079 **VAT No.:** GB 286 7356 12
Date established: 1975 **Turnover:** £250,000 - £500,000
No.of Employees: 1 - 10 **Product Groups:** 37, 52

Date of Accounts	Mar 12	Mar 11	Mar 10
Working Capital	18	66	67
Fixed Assets	24	31	39
Current Assets	60	122	138

Window Fixing & Maintenance
10 Trench Road, Newtownabbey, BT36 4TY
Tel: 028-9084 2280 **Fax:** 028-9084 0062
E-mail: info@wfm.org.uk
Website: http://www.wfm.org.uk
Directors: C. Mccarthy (MD)
Immediate Holding Company: WINDOW FIXING AND MAINTENANCE LIMITED
Registration no: NI008146 **VAT No.:** GB 253 4898 30
Date established: 1971 **No.of Employees:** 11 - 20 **Product Groups:** 30, 35, 52

Date of Accounts	Jun 11	Jun 10	Jun 09
Working Capital	-64	16	77
Fixed Assets	155	203	220
Current Assets	552	546	602
Current Liabilities	62	23	N/A

Co. Down

Newtownards

Abbey Labels & Packaging Ltd
36 Ballyrogan Road, Newtownards, BT23 4ST
Tel: 028-9181 0000 **Fax:** 028-9181 3121
E-mail: g.mann@abbeylabels.co.uk
Directors: G. Mann (MD)
Immediate Holding Company: ABBEY LABELS & PACKAGING LIMITED
Registration no: NI029217 **Date established:** 1995
Turnover: Up to £250,000 **No.of Employees:** 1 - 10 **Product Groups:** 27, 30

Date of Accounts	Dec 11	Dec 10	Dec 09
Working Capital	-45	-58	-90
Fixed Assets	153	156	152
Current Assets	94	69	74

Action Coach
3 The Square Greyabbey, Newtownards, BT22 2QA
Tel: 028-4278 8460 **Fax:** 028-4278 8844
E-mail: info@hayburycoaching.com
Website: http://www.actioncoach.com/tonyhayes
Managers: T. Hayes (Mgr)
Immediate Holding Company: HAYBURY BUSINESS COACHING LIMITED
Registration no: NI049872 **Date established:** 2004
No.of Employees: 1 - 10 **Product Groups:** 80

Date of Accounts	Feb 11	Feb 10	Feb 09
Working Capital	-129	-129	-134
Fixed Assets	114	116	119
Current Assets	1	9	5

George Adams Engineering
Unit 24 Irish Tapestry Buildings South Street, Newtownards, BT23 4JU
Tel: 028-9181 5457 **Fax:** 028-9182 0738
E-mail: gaengineering@aol.com
Directors: G. Adams (Prop)
Registration no: NI013561 **VAT No.:** GB 375 7243 30
Date established: 1979 **Turnover:** Up to £250,000
No.of Employees: 1 - 10 **Product Groups:** 48, 67

Advance Vacuum & Lift
4 Beverley Avenue, Newtownards, BT23 7UE
Tel: 028-9181 8095 **Fax:** 028-9182 7523
E-mail: sales@avlift.com
Website: http://www.avlift.com
Directors: M. Lilburn (Prop)
No.of Employees: 1 - 10 **Product Groups:** 42, 45, 67

F S Andrews Car Electrics
71-73 Court Street, Newtownards, BT23 7NX
Tel: 028-9181 2509
E-mail: auto12v@yahoo.com
Website: http://www.andrewscarelectrics.com
Directors: I. Martin (Prop)
No.of Employees: 1 - 10 **Product Groups:** 36, 40

Ards Business Centre
Jubilee Road Comber Road, Newtownards, BT23 4YH
Tel: 028-9181 2365 **Fax:** 028-9182 0625
E-mail: postbox@ardsbusiness.com
Website: http://www.ardsbusiness.com

Directors: L. Ross (Grp Chief Exec)
Managers: I. Stevenson (Sales Admin), K. Lindsay (Comm)
Immediate Holding Company: ARDS BUSINESS CENTRE LTD
Registration no: NI021680 **VAT No.:** GB 517 1951 47
Date established: 1988 **Turnover:** £250,000 - £500,000
No.of Employees: 1 - 10 **Product Groups:** 69, 80

Date of Accounts	Mar 12	Mar 11	Mar 10
Sales Turnover	461	N/A	N/A
Pre Tax Profit/Loss	-140	N/A	N/A
Working Capital	-180	-64	-73
Fixed Assets	4m	4m	4m
Current Assets	92	108	62
Current Liabilities	67	N/A	N/A

Ards Slings & Ropes
20 Jubilee Road, Newtownards, BT23 4YH
Tel: 028-9182 1001 **Fax:** 028-9182 1002
Directors: W. Blakeley (Prop), W. Blakely (Prop)
Managers: W. Bleakley (Mgr)
Immediate Holding Company: TILT-A-DOR LIMITED
Registration no: NI056638 **Date established:** 1987
No.of Employees: 1 - 10 **Product Groups:** 35, 39, 45

Aura Jewellery
5 Ardvanagh Court Conlig, Newtownards, BT23 7XR
Tel: 07921-994695
E-mail: info@aurajewellery.com
Website: http://www.aurajewellery.com
Directors: J. Richie (Prop)
No.of Employees: 1 - 10 **Product Groups:** 24, 49, 65

Avalon Guitar Co. Ltd
8 Glenford Way, Newtownards, BT23 4BX
Tel: 028-9182 0542 **Fax:** 028-9182 0650
E-mail: info@avalonguitars.com
Website: http://www.avalonguitars.com
Directors: S. Mcilwrath (MD), S. Mcilwrath (Dir)
Ultimate Holding Company: FOURMACS LIMITED
Immediate Holding Company: AVALON GUITARS LIMITED
Registration no: NI022341 **VAT No.:** GB 517 0621 73
Date established: 1989 **Turnover:** £1m - £2m **No.of Employees:** 1 - 10
Product Groups: 49

Date of Accounts	Sep 11	Sep 10	Sep 09
Working Capital	91	152	176
Fixed Assets	43	41	45
Current Assets	194	199	201

B G Interiors
6 Quarry Heights, Newtownards, BT23 7SZ
Tel: 028-9181 3881 **Fax:** 028-9181 3881
Website: http://www.bginteriors.co.uk
Directors: B. Barr (Ptnr)
VAT No.: GB 497 1229 20 **Date established:** 1986
Turnover: Up to £250,000 **No.of Employees:** 1 - 10 **Product Groups:** 26, 52, 63

B M Heat Services Ltd
Unit 1 Scrabo Business Park 14 Jubilee Road, Newtownards, BT23 4YH
Tel: 028-9181 3460 **Fax:** 028-9181 9909
E-mail: info@bmheat.com
Website: http://www.bmheat.com
Managers: T. Whittle (Chief Mgr)
Immediate Holding Company: BM HEAT SERVICES LIMITED
Registration no: NI055557 **VAT No.:** GB 617 5579 13
Date established: 2005 **Turnover:** £500,000 - £1m
No.of Employees: 1 - 10 **Product Groups:** 40

Date of Accounts	Oct 11	Oct 10	Oct 09
Working Capital	-189	-194	-186
Fixed Assets	185	229	282
Current Assets	251	261	464

N G Bell & Son Ltd
30 Greyabbey Road Ballywalter, Newtownards, BT22 2NY
Tel: 028-4275 8243 **Fax:** 028-4275 8192
E-mail: norman@ngbell.com
Website: http://www.ngbell.com
Directors: G. Bell (MD)
Immediate Holding Company: N.G. BELL & SON LIMITED
Registration no: NI013320 **VAT No.:** GB 331 6242 89
Date established: 1979 **No.of Employees:** 1 - 10 **Product Groups:** 66

Date of Accounts	Dec 11	Dec 10	Dec 09
Working Capital	327	382	443
Fixed Assets	416	487	527
Current Assets	908	965	1m

C C P Gransden
17 Moss Road Ballygowan, Newtownards, BT23 6JQ
Tel: 028-9752 8501 **Fax:** 028-9752 1024
E-mail: info@ccp-gransden.com
Website: http://www.ccp-gransden.com
Bank(s): Ulster Bank
Directors: J. Erskin (MD)
Immediate Holding Company: CCP Gransden Ltd
Registration no: NI010592 **VAT No.:** GB 286 6841 10
Date established: 1975 **No.of Employees:** 11 - 20 **Product Groups:** 30, 35, 40, 48, 66

Date of Accounts	Apr 11	Apr 10	Apr 09
Working Capital	364	359	338
Fixed Assets	85	58	51
Current Assets	833	662	701

C N C Pressings
276 Ballygowan Road Moneyrea, Newtownards, BT23 6BL
Tel: 028-9044 8569 **Fax:** 028-9044 8221
E-mail: harry@crossenengineering.co.uk
Website: http://www.rapidial.co.uk
Directors: D. Crossen (Prop)
Immediate Holding Company: CNC Pressings Limited
Registration no: NI063213 **VAT No.:** GB 617 7433 31
Date established: 2007 **Turnover:** £500,000 - £1m
No.of Employees: 1 - 10 **Product Groups:** 30, 46

Date of Accounts	Mar 11	Mar 10	Mar 09
Working Capital	-6	-67	-103
Fixed Assets	141	150	176
Current Assets	421	273	229

Consumable Products Ltd
180 Belfast Road, Newtownards, BT23 4TA
Tel: 028-9181 4818 **Fax:** 028-9181 9677
E-mail: sales@consumable-products.co.uk
Website: http://www.consumable-products.co.uk
Directors: N. Mcgowan (MD)
Immediate Holding Company: CONSUMABLE PRODUCTS LIMITED
Registration no: NI002425 **VAT No.:** GB 251 7655 53
Date established: 1947 **Turnover:** £2m - £5m **No.of Employees:** 21 - 50
Product Groups: 63, 64

Date of Accounts	Jun 11	Jun 10	Jun 09
Working Capital	1m	1m	936
Fixed Assets	795	729	637
Current Assets	1m	1m	1m

Corries Meats Ltd
Crossnamuckley Road, Newtownards, BT22 2AA
Tel: 028-9181 2297 **Fax:** 028-9181 4531
E-mail: will@corriesmeats.co.uk
Website: http://www.corriesonthefarm.co.uk
Directors: W. Corrie (MD)
Immediate Holding Company: CORRIE'S MEATS LIMITED
Registration no: NI015090 **VAT No.:** GB 252 7723 56
Date established: 1981 **No.of Employees:** 11 - 20 **Product Groups:** 20

Date of Accounts	Mar 12	Mar 11	Mar 10
Working Capital	212	139	78
Fixed Assets	186	215	248
Current Assets	590	428	416

Court Contract Upholstery
Unit 3 Quarry Heights, Newtownards, BT23 7SZ
Tel: 028-9181 8574 **Fax:** 028-9182 2666
E-mail: desi.orwin@btopenworld.com
Directors: D. Orwin (Prop)
Immediate Holding Company: Stephen Leyland Limited
Date established: 2007 **Turnover:** Up to £250,000
No.of Employees: 1 - 10 **Product Groups:** 26

Date of Accounts	Mar 11	Mar 10	Mar 09
Working Capital	-126	-127	-143
Fixed Assets	184	216	248
Current Assets	904	914	732

Cuan Sea Fisheries Ltd
Sketrick Island Killinchy, Newtownards, BT23 6QH
Tel: 028-9754 1461 **Fax:** 028-9754 1787
E-mail: info@cuanoysters.com
Website: http://www.cuanoysters.com
Directors: J. McElreavey (MD)
Immediate Holding Company: CUAN SEA FISHERIES LIMITED
Registration no: NI011364 **VAT No.:** GB 517 4569 29
Date established: 1976 **Turnover:** £500,000 - £1m
No.of Employees: 1 - 10 **Product Groups:** 41

Date of Accounts	Dec 11	Dec 10	Dec 09
Working Capital	-254	-95	-95
Fixed Assets	500	682	695
Current Assets	29	138	165

David Johnstone Environmental Services
1 Ballyalloly Road Comber, Newtownards, BT23 5PU
Tel: 028-9044 9944 **Fax:** 028-9044 9900
E-mail: ajefni@aol.com
Directors: D. Johnstone (Prop)
Immediate Holding Company: DAVID JOHNSTON ENVIRONMENTAL SERVICES LIMITED
Registration no: NI039714 **VAT No.:** GB 517 3706 50
Date established: 2000 **No.of Employees:** 1 - 10 **Product Groups:** 83

Down Fabrication & Garage Equipment Services Ltd
109a Moneyreagh Road Moneyrea, Newtownards, BT23 6BH
Tel: 028-9044 8184 **Fax:** 028-9044 9090
Directors: J. Davison (Ptnr)
Managers: A. Davison (Sales Prom Mgr), C. Murray (Sales Admin)
Immediate Holding Company: DOWN FABRICATION AND GARAGE EQUIPMENT SERVICES LTD
Registration no: NI041221 **VAT No.:** GB 375 8037 28
Date established: 2001 **Turnover:** Up to £250,000
No.of Employees: 1 - 10 **Product Groups:** 48

Downtown Radiocool FM Ltd
Kiltonga Industrial Estate, Newtownards, BT23 4ES
Tel: 028-9181 5555 **Fax:** 028-9181 5252
E-mail: info@downtown.co.uk
Website: http://www.downtown.co.uk
Directors: A. McDowell (Mkt Research), G. Crothers (Fin), M. Mahaffy (MD)
Managers: R. Collett (I.T. Exec), R. Hoey (Tech Serv Mgr), S. Mann (Mktg Serv Mgr)
Ultimate Holding Company: HEINRICH BAUER VERLAG KG (GERMANY)
Immediate Holding Company: COMMUNITY RADIO SERVICES LIMITED
Registration no: NI023353 **VAT No.:** GB 282 9258 26
Date established: 1989 **Turnover:** £5m - £10m
No.of Employees: 51 - 100 **Product Groups:** 79

Drilling & Pumping Supplies Ltd
29 Jubilee Road, Newtownards, BT23 4YJ
Tel: 028-9181 8347 **Fax:** 028-9181 3837
E-mail: sales@dps-ni.com
Website: http://www.dps-ni.com
Bank(s): First Trust
Directors: A. Wilson (MD)
Immediate Holding Company: DRILLING AND PUMPING SUPPLIES LIMITED
Registration no: NI025876 **VAT No.:** GB 375 8764 94
Date established: 1991 **Turnover:** £1m - £2m **No.of Employees:** 21 - 50
Product Groups: 18, 51

Date of Accounts	Sep 11	Sep 10	Sep 09
Working Capital	13	58	14
Fixed Assets	85	112	115
Current Assets	928	925	813

Greer Engineering
49 Quarry Road Comber, Newtownards, BT23 6ED
Tel: 028-9754 1072 **Fax:** 028-9754 2242
E-mail: sales@greer-engineering.co.uk
Website: http://www.greer-engineering.co.uk
Directors: A. Greer (Prop)
VAT No.: GB 375 8146 20 **Turnover:** £250,000 - £500,000
No.of Employees: 1 - 10 **Product Groups:** 37

Hughes Insurance
Strangford House 4 Jubilee Road, Newtownards, BT23 4WN
Tel: 028-9181 7375 **Fax:** 028-2564 7077
E-mail: carquoteonline@hughesinsurance.co.uk
Website: http://www.hughesandcompany.co.uk
Directors: L. Hughes (Prop), L. Hughes (Ch)
Managers: S. Martin (I.T. Exec), M. Fealty (Sales Prom Mgr), B. Moore (Comptroller)
Immediate Holding Company: HUGHES & CO (FINANCIAL SERVICES) LIMITED
Registration no: NI020279 **Date established:** 1987
No.of Employees: 101 - 250 **Product Groups:** 82

Date of Accounts	Mar 11	Mar 10	Mar 09
Working Capital	53	53	45
Current Assets	54	55	53
Current Liabilities	N/A	N/A	7

J I M Hydraulic Services
Unit C5 Ards Business Centre Jubilee Road, Newtownards, BT23 4YH
Tel: 028-9182 0064 **Fax:** 028-9182 0064
E-mail: jim-hydraulic@utvinternet.com
Directors: J. Morrison (Prop)
Managers: D. Morrison (Accounts), G. Morrison (Tech Serv Mgr)
Immediate Holding Company: IAN'S TRAINING SOLUTIONS LIMITED
Registration no: NI049787 **VAT No.:** GB 375 7336 23
Date established: 2011 **No.of Employees:** 1 - 10 **Product Groups:** 38, 40, 48

R J S Kennedy
40 Drumfad Road Millisle, Newtownards, BT22 2JA
Tel: 028-9186 2000 **Fax:** 028-9186 2077
Directors: R. Kennedy (Prop)
Date established: 1970 **No.of Employees:** 1 - 10 **Product Groups:** 46

Ian A Kernohan NI Ltd
Fir Trees Greenway, Conlig, Newtownards, BT23 7SU
Tel: 028-9127 0233 **Fax:** 028-9127 0597
E-mail: v.stanex@iakonline.com
Website: http://www.iakonline.com
Directors: V. Stanex (MD), T. Black (Fin)
Managers: C. Miller (Mktg Serv Mgr)
Immediate Holding Company: IAN A KERNOHAN (NI) LIMITED
Registration no: NI019120 **VAT No.:** GB 283 0685 46
Date established: 1986 **Turnover:** £5m - £10m **No.of Employees:** 21 - 50
Product Groups: 63, 66

Date of Accounts	May 11	May 10	May 09
Sales Turnover	8m	10m	10m
Pre Tax Profit/Loss	148	134	255
Working Capital	1m	1m	1m
Fixed Assets	850	893	880
Current Assets	3m	3m	4m
Current Liabilities	471	532	856

H Mccullough & Sons
29 Rowreagh Road Kircubbin, Newtownards, BT22 1AS
Tel: 028-4273 8307 **Fax:** 028-4273 8708
E-mail: hdmcculloch@btinternet.com
Directors: B. Mccullough (Snr Part)
Immediate Holding Company: HUGH D. MCCULLOUGH & SONS LIMITED
Registration no: NI013661 **VAT No.:** GB 353 0659 60
Date established: 1979 **Turnover:** £500,000 - £1m
No.of Employees: 1 - 10 **Product Groups:** 51

Date of Accounts	Dec 11	Dec 10	Dec 09
Working Capital	-34	-24	14
Fixed Assets	62	83	94
Current Assets	315	368	413

N P Mcgowan
29 Whiterock Road Killinchy, Newtownards, BT23 6PT
Tel: 028-9754 1549 **Fax:** 028-9754 1658
E-mail: office@npmcgowan.com
Website: http://www.npmcgowan.com
Directors: N. Mcgowan (Prop)
Immediate Holding Company: NP McGOWAN LIMITED
Registration no: NI064127 **VAT No.:** GB 331 7104 96
Date established: 2007 **Turnover:** £500,000 - £1m
No.of Employees: 1 - 10 **Product Groups:** 26

Date of Accounts	Aug 11	Aug 10	Aug 09
Working Capital	-47	-38	-70
Fixed Assets	93	116	139
Current Assets	22	58	13

Maintech Solutions
30 Mountstewart Road, Newtownards, BT22 2AL
Tel: 028-4278 8011
Directors: R. Cusack (Prop)
Date established: 1996 **No.of Employees:** 1 - 10 **Product Groups:** 38, 42

Marine Mechanical Services
5 Ballybryan Road Greyabbey, Newtownards, BT22 2RB
Tel: 07713-081793 **Fax:** 0870-706 5677
E-mail: garry@mmsni.co.uk
Website: http://www.mmsni.co.uk
Directors: G. Brown (Prop)
No.of Employees: 1 - 10 **Product Groups:** 68

Maryland Country Sports
Merryland Industrial Estate 286 Ballygowan Road, Moneyrea, Newtownards, BT23 6BL
Tel: 028-9044 8598 **Fax:** 028-9044 8961
Website: http://www.marylandcountrysports.co.uk
Directors: W. Stringer (Prop)
Immediate Holding Company: R & R ELECTRICAL ENGINEERING LIMITED
Date established: 1994 **No.of Employees:** 1 - 10 **Product Groups:** 36, 39, 40

Date of Accounts	Sep 11	Sep 10	Sep 09
Working Capital	6	6	6
Current Assets	6	6	6

Matik Ltd
Unit C2 Ards Business Centre, Jubliee Road, Newtownards, BT23 4YH
Tel: 028-9146 4847 **Fax:** 028-9182 8844
E-mail: matik@nireland.com
Website: http://www.matik-ni.co.uk

see next page

Matik Ltd - Cont'd

Directors: E. Burns (Ch & MD)
Managers: K. Kennedy (Accounts)
Immediate Holding Company: Pneumatic Equipment Services Ltd
Registration no: NI032802 **VAT No.:** GB 454 6939 10
Date established: 1992 **No.of Employees:** 1 - 10 **Product Groups:** 48

Met Work Technology

10 North Side Park, Newtownards, BT23 7EY
Tel: 028-9180 0500 **Fax:** 028-9180 0501
Directors: R. Ringland (MD)
Date established: 2001 **No.of Employees:** 1 - 10 **Product Groups:** 46

Micwall Developments Ltd

12 Prospect Road Ballygowan, Newtownards, BT23 6LS
Tel: 028-9752 8373 **Fax:** 028-9752 8907
E-mail: info@micwall.co.uk
Website: http://www.micwall.co.uk
Directors: B. Walls (MD), B. McCreight (Fin)
Managers: D. Walls (Mktg Serv Mgr)
Immediate Holding Company: MICWALL DEVELOPMENTS LIMITED
Registration no: NI007064 **VAT No.:** GB 253 8837 30
Date established: 1967 **Turnover:** £1m - £2m **No.of Employees:** 1 - 10
Product Groups: 52

Date of Accounts	Jan 10	Jan 09	Jan 08
Pre Tax Profit/Loss	N/A	-2m	-1m
Working Capital	-10m	-4m	-588
Fixed Assets	1m	3m	2m
Current Assets	18m	26m	25m
Current Liabilities	N/A	2m	1m

G W Monson & Sons Ltd

Unit 4 Block B Scrabo Business Park Jubilee Road, Newtownards, BT23 4YH
Tel: 028-9181 2350 **Fax:** 028-9181 8559
E-mail: info@gwmonson.com
Website: http://www.gwmonson.com
Directors: R. Monson (MD)
Managers: E. Lennox (Chief Acct)
Immediate Holding Company: G.W. MONSON AND SONS LIMITED
Registration no: NI011905 **VAT No.:** GB 331 6118 90
Date established: 1977 **Turnover:** £500,000 - £1m
No.of Employees: 1 - 10 **Product Groups:** 48

Date of Accounts	Mar 11	Mar 10	Mar 09
Working Capital	174	189	258
Fixed Assets	45	60	44
Current Assets	334	341	368

Newtownards Chronicle Ltd

25 Frances Street, Newtownards, BT23 7DT
Tel: 028-9181 3333 **Fax:** 028-9182 0087
E-mail: news@ardschronicle.co.uk
Website: http://www.newtownardschronicle.co.uk
Bank(s): Northern Bank
Directors: I. Alexander (MD)
Immediate Holding Company: NEWTOWNARDS CHRONICLE LIMITED
Registration no: NI002567 **VAT No.:** GB 252 5717 61
Date established: 1948 **Turnover:** £1m - £2m **No.of Employees:** 11 - 20
Product Groups: 28

Date of Accounts	Aug 11	Aug 10	Aug 09
Working Capital	2m	2m	2m
Fixed Assets	882	984	688
Current Assets	2m	2m	3m

Newtownards & District Shooting Club

251 Abbey Road Millisle, Newtownards, BT22 2JG
Tel: 028-9186 1171
Directors: R. Furguson (Ch)
Immediate Holding Company: NEWTOWNARDS & DISTRICT SHOOTING CLUB LTD
Date established: 2012 **No.of Employees:** 1 - 10 **Product Groups:** 36, 39, 40

North Down Diesel Engineering

30b Green Road Conlig, Newtownards, BT23 7PZ
Tel: 028-9127 5501
E-mail: richard.ndd@sky.com
Directors: R. Dickson (Prop)
Date established: 2001 **No.of Employees:** 1 - 10 **Product Groups:** 40

Park Gate Foods Ltd

7-9 Princess Anne Road Portavogie, Newtownards, BT22 1DT
Tel: 028-4277 1947 **Fax:** 028-4277 1241
E-mail: parkgatefoods@compuserve.com
Website: http://www.parkgatefoods.co.uk
Managers: M. Beckett, W. Green (Fin Mgr)
Immediate Holding Company: PARK GATE FOODS LIMITED
Registration no: NI017043 **VAT No.:** GB 392 5884 06
Date established: 1983 **Turnover:** £2m - £5m **No.of Employees:** 21 - 50
Product Groups: 20

Date of Accounts	Dec 09	Dec 08	Dec 07
Sales Turnover	N/A	2m	N/A
Pre Tax Profit/Loss	N/A	-260	N/A
Working Capital	388	601	814
Fixed Assets	237	267	313
Current Assets	611	926	1m
Current Liabilities	N/A	122	N/A

Pritchitts

46 Belfast Road, Newtownards, BT23 4TU
Tel: 028-9182 4800 **Fax:** 028-9181 3538
E-mail: info@pritchitt.com
Website: http://www.pritchitt.com
Directors: T. Acheson (Dir)
Managers: B. Smith (I.T. Exec), B. Smith (Tech Serv Mgr), I. McGuinness (Chief Acct), I. McGuinness (Chief Acct), M. Ferguson (Buyer), H. Bunting (Personnel), H. Bunting (Personnel), L. Kyria (Mktg Serv Mgr)
Immediate Holding Company: Belcav Limited
Registration no: NI028855 **Date established:** 1994
Turnover: Up to £250,000 **No.of Employees:** 101 - 250
Product Groups: 20, 27

R Brown & Co.

20 Portaferry Road, Newtownards, BT23 8NN
Tel: 028-9181 2115 **Fax:** 028-9181 2115
Directors: R. Brown (Prop)
VAT No.: GB 251 7451 69 **Date established:** 1886
Turnover: Up to £250,000 **No.of Employees:** 1 - 10 **Product Groups:** 33, 36

S Clarke & Son Building Maintenance & Glazing

1 Kennel Lane, Newtownards, BT23 7HR
Tel: 028-9182 0333 **Fax:** 028-9182 0333
E-mail: stephen@sclarkeglazing.co.uk
Directors: S. Clarke (Prop)
VAT No.: GB 311 3038 20 **Turnover:** Up to £250,000
No.of Employees: 1 - 10 **Product Groups:** 52, 66

Signs Of The Times Ltd

66 Hillsborough Road Moneyrea, Newtownards, BT23 6AY
Tel: 028-9044 8471 **Fax:** 028-9044 8837
E-mail: info@signsni.com
Website: http://www.signsni.com
Directors: D. Cleland (MD)
Immediate Holding Company: SIGNS OF THE TIMES IRELAND LTD
Registration no: NI062514 **VAT No.:** GB 392 6842 17
Date established: 2007 **Turnover:** Up to £250,000
No.of Employees: 1 - 10 **Product Groups:** 28, 37

Date of Accounts	Apr 11	Apr 10	Apr 09
Working Capital	-29	-69	-119
Fixed Assets	221	231	246
Current Assets	144	137	129

The Skip

12 Ann Street, Newtownards, BT23 7AB
Tel: 028-9181 7955 **Fax:** 028-9181 3020
Bank(s): Forward Trust
Directors: K. Halliwell (Prop)
VAT No.: GB 331 4732 79 **No.of Employees:** 11 - 20 **Product Groups:** 24

Fred Storey Ltd

Old Crow Building 2 Glen Road, Comber, Newtownards, BT23 5EL
Tel: 028-9187 0033 **Fax:** 028-9187 0090
E-mail: info@fredstorey.com
Website: http://www.fredstorey.com
Directors: L. Murphy (MD)
Immediate Holding Company: FRED STOREY BELFAST LIMITED
Registration no: NI012067 **VAT No.:** GB 353 0576 64
Date established: 1977 **No.of Employees:** 11 - 20 **Product Groups:** 67

Date of Accounts	Oct 11	Oct 10	Oct 09
Working Capital	286	418	447
Fixed Assets	116	72	76
Current Assets	418	495	605

Strangfor Arms Hotel

92 Church Street, Newtownards, BT23 4AL
Tel: 028-9181 4141 **Fax:** 028-9181 1010
E-mail: info@strangfordhotel.com
Website: http://www.strangfordhotel.co.uk
Bank(s): Northern
Directors: G. Metcalfe (Ptnr)
Managers: M. Nugent (Chief Mgr), M. Newgent (Chief Mgr)
VAT No.: GB 253 0561 85 **Date established:** 2000
Turnover: Up to £250,000 **No.of Employees:** 21 - 50 **Product Groups:** 69

Swiss Windows & Conservatoris

8 Carsons Lane Ballygowan, Newtownards, BT23 5GE
Tel: 028-9752 1352 **Fax:** 028-9752 8568
E-mail: info@windows-conservatories.com
Website: http://www.windows-conservatories.com
Directors: R. Greer (Prop)
Date established: 1999 **No.of Employees:** 1 - 10 **Product Groups:** 35

T I Electrical Mechanical Services

Unit 9 Merryland Industrial Estate Ballygowan Road, Moneyrea, Newtownards, BT23 6BL
Tel: 028-9044 8882 **Fax:** 028-9044 8882
E-mail: info@timachinerysales.com
Website: http://www.timachinerysales.com
Directors: T. Henry (Ptnr)
VAT No.: GB 517 2131 80 **Turnover:** £250,000 - £500,000
No.of Employees: 1 - 10 **Product Groups:** 42, 48

Tarmac Northern Ltd

73 Holywood Road, Newtownards, BT23 4TQ
Tel: 028-9042 3251 **Fax:** 028-9042 1177
E-mail: info@tarmac-northern.co.uk
Website: http://www.tarmac.co.uk
Managers: S. Horner
Immediate Holding Company: TARMAC NORTHERN LIMITED
Registration no: NF003614 **VAT No.:** GB 532 3679 43
Date established: 2001 **No.of Employees:** 1 - 10 **Product Groups:** 14, 31

Technical Metals

Unit 3 Kiltonga Industrial Estate Belfast Road, Newtownards, BT23 4TJ
Tel: 028-9181 1212 **Fax:** 028-9182 0112
E-mail: gareth.reilly@techmetals.co.uk
Website: http://www.techmetals.co.uk
Directors: D. Sales (Chief Op Offcr)
Managers: A. Carlisle (Comptroller)
Immediate Holding Company: TECHNICAL METALS LIMITED
Registration no: NI029892 **Date established:** 1995
No.of Employees: 11 - 20 **Product Groups:** 46, 48

Date of Accounts	Aug 11	Aug 10	Aug 09
Working Capital	-726	-515	-561
Fixed Assets	2m	1m	1m
Current Assets	2m	1m	451

Thyssenkrupp Ltd

Kiltonga Industrial Estate Belfast Road, Newtownards, BT23 4TJ
Tel: 028-9184 4100 **Fax:** 028-9184 4199
E-mail: stephen.emerson@alcoe.com
Website: http://www.alcoa.co.uk
Managers: S. Emerson (Sales Prom Mgr), T. McCloskey (Personnel)
Immediate Holding Company: T.J. KIRKPATRICK & SON LIMITED
Registration no: NI014479 **VAT No.:** GB 336 7395 53
Date established: 1987 **Turnover:** £2m - £5m **No.of Employees:** 21 - 50
Product Groups: 66

Date of Accounts	Jul 99	Jul 98	Jul 97
Working Capital	31	-6	1
Fixed Assets	3	5	13
Current Assets	95	49	61

Transparent Film Products Ltd

6 Greenway Industrial Estate Conlig, Newtownards, BT23 7SU
Tel: 028-9127 0578 **Fax:** 028-9145 0688
E-mail: info@transparentfilm.co.uk
Website: http://www.transparentfilm.co.uk
Directors: J. Jordan (MD)
Immediate Holding Company: TRANSPARENT FILM PRODUCTS LIMITED
Registration no: NI012294 **VAT No.:** GB 311 2593 94
Date established: 1977 **No.of Employees:** 1 - 10 **Product Groups:** 30

Date of Accounts	Jan 11	Jan 10	Jan 09
Working Capital	1	47	92
Fixed Assets	525	570	620
Current Assets	278	254	407

Ulster Anaesthetics Ltd

Maryland Industrial Estate Moneyrea, Newtownards, BT23 6BL
Tel: 028-9044 8800 **Fax:** 028-9044 9400
E-mail: info@ua-ltd.co.uk
Directors: C. Campbell (MD)
Immediate Holding Company: ULSTER ANAESTHETICS LIMITED
Registration no: NI006959 **Date established:** 1967
Turnover: £10m - £20m **No.of Employees:** 21 - 50 **Product Groups:** 67

Date of Accounts	Sep 11	Sep 10	Sep 09
Sales Turnover	11m	8m	7m
Pre Tax Profit/Loss	606	451	492
Working Capital	350	-94	847
Fixed Assets	214	206	220
Current Assets	6m	5m	8m
Current Liabilities	1m	434	426

Unit Design

9d Portaferry Road, Newtownards, BT23 8NN
Tel: 028-9181 7160 **Fax:** 028-9181 3172
E-mail: info@unitdesign-ni.co.uk
Website: http://www.unitdesign-ni.co.uk
Directors: J. Armstrong (Prop)
VAT No.: GB 311 2385 04 **No.of Employees:** 1 - 10 **Product Groups:** 26

Warden Bros Newtownards Ltd

45-47 High Street, Newtownards, BT23 7HS
Tel: 028-9181 2147 **Fax:** 028-9182 0226
E-mail: enquiries@wardenbros.com
Website: http://www.wardenbros.com
Managers: G. Skelton (Mgr), J. Reynolds (Fin Mgr), D. McCann (Mktg Serv Mgr)
Immediate Holding Company: WARDEN BROTHERS (NEWTOWNARDS) LIMITED
Registration no: NI003087 **VAT No.:** GB 252 5249 68
Date established: 1952 **Turnover:** £2m - £5m **No.of Employees:** 51 - 100
Product Groups: 61, 63

Date of Accounts	Jan 12	Jan 11	Jan 10
Sales Turnover	3m	4m	N/A
Pre Tax Profit/Loss	-282	204	177
Working Capital	3m	3m	3m
Fixed Assets	488	604	615
Current Assets	3m	3m	3m
Current Liabilities	263	303	315

Website Direction Ltd

17 Philip Way Comber, Newtownards, BT23 5BE
Tel: 028-9187 0611
E-mail: info@websitedirection.com
Website: http://www.websitedirection.com
Directors: A. Pollock (Dir)
Immediate Holding Company: BOSPEAK LTD
Registration no: NI051090 **Date established:** 2004
No.of Employees: 1 - 10 **Product Groups:** 44

Williamson Johnston Partnership

71 Frances Street, Newtownards, BT23 7DX
Tel: 028-9181 3354 **Fax:** 028-9181 0527
E-mail: wjpsurveyors@fsbdial.co.uk
Directors: J. Kelly (Ptnr)
Date established: 1976 **Turnover:** Up to £250,000
No.of Employees: 1 - 10 **Product Groups:** 84

Willowbrook Foods

50a Whiterock Road Killinchy, Newtownards, BT23 6PT
Tel: 028-9754 1603 **Fax:** 028-9754 2420
E-mail: jmccann@willowbrookfoods.co.uk
Website: http://www.willowbrookfoods.co.uk
Directors: J. Mccann (MD), B. O'Prey (Fin)
Managers: P. Somerton (Factory Mgr)
Immediate Holding Company: WILLOWBROOK FOODS LIMITED
Registration no: NI037757 **Date established:** 2000
Turnover: £10m - £20m **No.of Employees:** 101 - 250 **Product Groups:** 20

Date of Accounts	Jan 12	Jan 11	Jan 10
Sales Turnover	20m	19m	15m
Pre Tax Profit/Loss	-279	1m	677
Working Capital	-1m	758	1m
Fixed Assets	8m	6m	5m
Current Assets	5m	5m	4m
Current Liabilities	1m	1m	1m

Co. Tyrone

Omagh

A & B Fire Equipment

12 Campsie Road, Omagh, BT79 0AG
Tel: 028-8224 3910
E-mail: sales@abfireequipment.com
Website: http://www.abfireequipment.com
Directors: T. Burns (Prop)
Immediate Holding Company: A & B FIRE EQUIPMENT LTD
Registration no: NI609470 **Date established:** 2011
No.of Employees: 1 - 10 **Product Groups:** 38, 42

Active Packaging Ltd

Omagh Business Complex Gortrush Industrial Estate Great Northern Road, Omagh, BT78 5LU
Tel: 028-8224 1616 **Fax:** 028-8224 9393
E-mail: sales@active-pkg.com
Website: http://www.active-pkg.com

Managers: M. Kelly
Immediate Holding Company: ACTIVE PACKAGING LIMITED
Registration no: NI045581 **Date established:** 2003
No.of Employees: 1 - 10 **Product Groups:** 38, 42

Date of Accounts	Mar 12	Mar 11	Mar 10
Working Capital	540	347	195
Fixed Assets	12	23	18
Current Assets	1m	717	471

Arch-Aid Design

37 Dublin Road, Omagh, BT78 1HE
Tel: 028-8225 0071 **Fax:** 028-8224 1131
E-mail: info@arch-aid.net
Directors: J. Lafferty (Fin)
Immediate Holding Company: Arch Aid Design Limited
Registration no: NI070504 **Date established:** 2008
Turnover: Up to £250,000 **No.of Employees:** 1 - 10 **Product Groups:** 52, 84

Date of Accounts	Dec 10	Dec 09
Working Capital	-124	-79
Fixed Assets	119	158
Current Assets	57	95

Barrett Electrical Contracts Ltd

Unit 29 Gortrush Industrial Estate, Omagh, BT78 5EJ
Tel: 028-8224 9111 **Fax:** 028-8224 6815
E-mail: alan@barrettelectrical.com
Website: http://www.barrettelectrical.com
Directors: A. Leeper (Dir)
Immediate Holding Company: BARRETT ELECTRICAL CONTRACTS LIMITED
Registration no: NI011162 **VAT No.:** GB 286 3708 27
Date established: 1976 **Turnover:** £250,000 - £500,000
No.of Employees: 11 - 20 **Product Groups:** 52

Date of Accounts	Sep 11	Sep 10	Sep 09
Working Capital	-244	-247	166
Fixed Assets	712	1m	1m
Current Assets	384	670	885

Baxters Joinery

Unit 20 Gortrush Industrial Estate, Omagh, BT78 5EJ
Tel: 028-8224 3645 **Fax:** 028-8224 3645
Directors: D. Baxter (Prop)
VAT No.: GB 432 6446 59 **Turnover:** Up to £250,000
No.of Employees: 1 - 10 **Product Groups:** 25

Bradley Construction

25 Main Street Mountfield, Omagh, BT79 7PY
Tel: 028-8077 1245 **Fax:** 028-8077 1304
E-mail: kbradley.construction@btopenworld.com
Website: http://www.bradleyconstruction.eu.com
Directors: K. Mooham (Ptnr)
Immediate Holding Company: BRADLEY CONSTRUCTION (IRE) LIMITED
Registration no: NI608179 **VAT No.:** GB 331 3392 85
Date established: 2011 **Turnover:** £500,000 - £1m
No.of Employees: 11 - 20 **Product Groups:** 52

Campbell & Slevin Electrical Contractors Ltd

33 Tattykeel Road, Omagh, BT78 5DA
Tel: 028-8224 1166 **Fax:** 028-8224 1244
E-mail: office@campbellandslevin.com
Website: http://www.campbellandslevin.com
Directors: A. Denver (Dir)
Immediate Holding Company: CAMPBELL & SLEVIN LIMITED
Registration no: NI025591 **VAT No.:** GB 393 6979 81
Date established: 1991 **Turnover:** £2m - £5m **No.of Employees:** 1 - 10
Product Groups: 52

Date of Accounts	Dec 08	Jul 11	Jul 10
Pre Tax Profit/Loss	-147	N/A	N/A
Working Capital	12m	10m	11m
Fixed Assets	3m	1m	2m
Current Assets	13m	11m	12m
Current Liabilities	88	N/A	N/A

Compressor Sales

24 Merchantstown Road Loughmacrory, Omagh, BT79 9PW
Tel: 028-8077 1286
Directors: P. Mcaleer (Prop)
No.of Employees: 1 - 10 **Product Groups:** 36

Corey Joinery Works

151 Cavan Road Dromore, Omagh, BT78 3EU
Tel: 028-8289 8365 **Fax:** 028-8289 8999
E-mail: corys@tiscali.co.uk
Directors: B. Corey (MD), B. Corey (Ptnr)
VAT No.: GB 287 1938 14 **Turnover:** £500,000 - £1m
No.of Employees: 1 - 10 **Product Groups:** 25, 52

Diesel Services

83 Dromore Road, Omagh, BT78 5JH
Tel: 028-8224 9560 **Fax:** 028-8224 2390
E-mail: dieselservicesomagh@gmail.com
Directors: J. Mcgrenaghan (Prop)
Date established: 1996 **No.of Employees:** 1 - 10 **Product Groups:** 40

J J Donnelly & Sons

164 Ecclesville Road Fintona, Omagh, BT78 2EQ
Tel: 028-8284 1588 **Fax:** 028-8284 0144
E-mail: jjdandsons@yahoo.co.uk
Directors: J. Donnelly (Prop)
VAT No.: GB 252 8042 75 **Turnover:** £1m - £2m **No.of Employees:** 1 - 10
Product Groups: 66, 67

F & H Engineering

7 Bankmore Way East, Omagh, BT79 0NZ
Tel: 028-8225 1200 **Fax:** 028-8224 7200
E-mail: fh.engineering@btconnect.com
Website: http://www.fandhengineering.com
Directors: I. Hunter (Dir)
Date established: 1996 **No.of Employees:** 11 - 20 **Product Groups:** 35

Fane Valley Feeds Ltd

Bankmore Way, Omagh, BT79 0NW
Tel: 028-8224 3221 **Fax:** 028-8224 5992
E-mail: info@fanevalleyfeeds.com
Website: http://www.scottsfeeds.com
Bank(s): AIB Group
Directors: D. Garrett (Dir), P. Gibbons (Purch), S. Kelly (Fin), A. Mcausauld (I.T. Dir)
Managers: G. Phelan (Tech Serv Mgr), A. Miller
Ultimate Holding Company: W. & C. SCOTT, LIMITED
Immediate Holding Company: FANE VALLEY FEEDS LIMITED
Registration no: NI025752 **VAT No.:** GB 516 8837 16
Date established: 1991 **Turnover:** £20m - £50m
No.of Employees: 21 - 50 **Product Groups:** 20, 62

Date of Accounts	Sep 11	Sep 10	Sep 09
Sales Turnover	42m	30m	28m
Pre Tax Profit/Loss	-513	511	840
Working Capital	5m	-10m	-6m
Fixed Assets	20m	21m	12m
Current Assets	11m	8m	6m
Current Liabilities	356	813	345

General Trading Services Ltd

4 Moyle Road Newtownstewart, Omagh, BT78 4JS
Tel: 028-8166 1242 **Fax:** 028-8166 1591
E-mail: info@gtstrading.co.uk
Website: http://www.gtstrading.co.uk
Directors: J. Davis (MD)
Immediate Holding Company: GENERAL TRADING SERVICES LIMITED
Registration no: NI001845 **Date established:** 1945
No.of Employees: 1 - 10 **Product Groups:** 72

Date of Accounts	Jul 11	Jul 10	Jul 09
Working Capital	146	111	32
Fixed Assets	2m	1m	1m
Current Assets	914	824	841

Graham & Sons Printers

51 Gortin Road, Omagh, BT79 7HZ
Tel: 028-8224 9222 **Fax:** 028-8224 9886
E-mail: sales@thepostcardcompany.com
Website: http://www.thepostcardcompany.com
Directors: R. Villiers (MD)
Immediate Holding Company: POSTCARD COMPANY LIMITED - THE
Registration no: NI009179 **VAT No.:** GB 251 8983 31
Date established: 1996 **Turnover:** £500,000 - £1m
No.of Employees: 11 - 20 **Product Groups:** 28

Date of Accounts	Mar 11	Mar 10	Mar 09
Working Capital	289	292	339
Fixed Assets	108	123	137
Current Assets	489	475	506

Herbst Machinery Ltd

120 Drumnakilly Road, Omagh, BT79 0JT
Tel: 028-8077 1568 **Fax:** 028-8077 1569
E-mail: sales@herbst.co.uk
Website: http://www.herbstmachinery.co.uk
Bank(s): Ulster Bank
Directors: N. Good (MD)
Immediate Holding Company: HERBST MACHINERY LTD
Registration no: NI051422 **VAT No.:** GB 390 8600 43
Date established: 2004 **Turnover:** Up to £250,000
No.of Employees: 11 - 20 **Product Groups:** 41, 45

Date of Accounts	Jan 12	Jan 11	Jan 10
Working Capital	920	873	711
Fixed Assets	112	120	127
Current Assets	1m	1m	1m

Interventus Business Psychologists

12 Church Street, Omagh, BT78 1DG
Tel: 028-8224 3100
E-mail: info@interventus.net
Website: http://www.interventus.net
Directors: D. Mccanny (Prop)
Date established: 1998 **Turnover:** **No.of Employees:** 1 - 10
Product Groups: 80

Irwin & White Construction Co. Ltd

141 Curr Road Beragh, Sixmilecross, Omagh, BT79 0RD
Tel: 028-8556 8357 **Fax:** 028-8556 8132
Directors: W. White (MD)
Immediate Holding Company: IRWIN & WHITE CONSTRUCTION CO. LIMITED
Registration no: NI011837 **VAT No.:** GB 286 8262 16
Date established: 1977 **Turnover:** £500,000 - £1m
No.of Employees: 1 - 10 **Product Groups:** 66

Date of Accounts	Feb 12	Feb 11	Feb 10
Working Capital	805	845	845
Fixed Assets	22	27	36
Current Assets	926	1m	1m

Johnston Bros

6 Carnalea Road Fintona, Omagh, BT78 2BY
Tel: 028-8284 1365 **Fax:** 028-8284 1299
E-mail: vajohnston2009@yahoo.co.uk
Website: http://www.johnstonbros.com
Directors: V. Johnston (Prop)
Date established: 1964 **No.of Employees:** 1 - 10 **Product Groups:** 41

Kerry Foods

19 Tamlaght Road, Omagh, BT78 5AW
Tel: 028-8224 6146 **Fax:** 028-8224 1434
Website: http://www.kerrygroup.com
Bank(s): Ulster Bank
Managers: O. Gahan (Mgr)
Immediate Holding Company: LECKPATRICK DAIRIES LIMITED
Registration no: NI022542 **VAT No.:** GB 516 8307 45
Date established: 1989 **No.of Employees:** 51 - 100 **Product Groups:** 20

Mcaleer & Teague

22 Camderry Road Dromore, Omagh, BT78 3AU
Tel: 028-8289 8535 **Fax:** 028-8289 8244
E-mail: info@mcatni.co.uk
Website: http://www.mcatni.co.uk
Bank(s): Allied Irish Bank
Directors: T. Teague (Snr Part)
Immediate Holding Company: TEAGUE BROS LTD
Registration no: NI062617 **VAT No.:** GB 251 7640 66
Date established: 2007 **No.of Employees:** 21 - 50 **Product Groups:** 52

Date of Accounts	Jan 11	Jan 10	Jan 09
Working Capital	-43	-41	-40
Fixed Assets	6	8	9
Current Assets	240	240	240

Mcgurk Screening Systems Ltd

52 Fingrean Road Loughmacrory, Omagh, BT79 9LR
Tel: 028-8077 1079
Website: http://www.mcgurkscreenings.com
Immediate Holding Company: MCGURK SCREENING SYSTEMS LIMITED
Registration no: NI036721 **Date established:** 1999
No.of Employees: 1 - 10 **Product Groups:** 42, 45

Mccaul Group

3 Bankmore Business Park, Omagh, BT79 0BE
Tel: 028-8225 1155 **Fax:** 028-8225 1250
E-mail: info@pmccaul.com
Website: http://www.pmccaul.com
Directors: P. McCaul (Prop)
Immediate Holding Company: Patrick McCaul Environmental Consulting Engineers Limited
Registration no: NI067836 **Date established:** 2008
Turnover: £500,000 - £1m **No.of Employees:** 1 - 10 **Product Groups:** 84

Morris Polythene Greenhouses

53a Lenagh Road, Omagh, BT79 7RG
Tel: 028-8164 8205
E-mail: info@morrispolytunnels.co.uk
Website: http://www.morrispolytunnels.co.uk
Directors: J. Morris (Prop)
Immediate Holding Company: MORRIS POLYTHENE GREENHOUSES LTD
Registration no: NI032255 **Date established:** 1997
No.of Employees: 1 - 10 **Product Groups:** 26, 35

Date of Accounts	Oct 11	Oct 10	Oct 09
Working Capital	31	27	29
Fixed Assets	6	7	8
Current Assets	50	44	53

Naturelle Consumer Products Ltd

Unit 5 Bankmore Way East, Omagh, BT79 0NZ
Tel: 028-8224 9396 **Fax:** 028-8224 7793
E-mail: info@naturelle.iol.ie
Website: http://www.naturelle.ie
Bank(s): AIB Group
Directors: K. Low (Ptnr)
Ultimate Holding Company: SILVERBUSH DEVELOPMENTS LIMITED
Immediate Holding Company: NATURELLE CONSUMER PRODUCTS LIMITED
Registration no: NI020533 **VAT No.:** GB 432 7727 46
Date established: 1987 **Turnover:** £2m - £5m **No.of Employees:** 21 - 50
Product Groups: 24

Date of Accounts	Sep 11	Sep 10	Sep 09
Working Capital	3m	3m	3m
Fixed Assets	2m	2m	2m
Current Assets	5m	5m	5m

Omagh Aluminium Systems Ltd

Unit 1 Gortrush Industrial Estate, Omagh, BT78 5EJ
Tel: 028-8224 6871 **Fax:** 028-8224 6874
E-mail: info@oasltd.net
Website: http://www.oasltd.net
Directors: E. Loughran (Prop)
Immediate Holding Company: Omagh Aluminium Systems Ltd
Registration no: NI046751 **Date established:** 2003
No.of Employees: 11 - 20 **Product Groups:** 35, 48

Date of Accounts	Dec 09	Dec 11	Dec 10
Working Capital	143	43	81
Fixed Assets	349	275	327
Current Assets	826	1m	843

Omagh District Council

The Grange Mountjoy Road, Omagh, BT79 7BL
Tel: 028-8224 5321 **Fax:** 028-8224 3888
E-mail: info@omagh.gov.uk
Website: http://www.omagh.gov.uk
Directors: D. Mcsorley (Grp Chief Exec)
Turnover: £2m - £5m **No.of Employees:** 251 - 500 **Product Groups:** 87

Omagh Meats Ltd

52 Doogary Road, Omagh, BT79 0BQ
Tel: 028-8224 3201 **Fax:** 028-8224 3013
E-mail: info@omaghmeats.com
Website: http://www.foylefoodgroup.com
Managers: D. Campbell (Sales Prom Mgr), C. Graham (Chief Acct), J. McGuinness (Tech Serv Mgr), A. Richardson (Personnel)
Immediate Holding Company: OMATRADE
Registration no: NI025364 **VAT No.:** GB 286 6290 21
Date established: 1992 **Turnover:** £50m - £75m
No.of Employees: 101 - 250 **Product Groups:** 20, 62

Date of Accounts	Dec 10	Dec 09
Current Assets	5	5
Current Liabilities	3	3

Outsource Ireland Ltd

30 Market Street, Omagh, BT78 1EH
Tel: 07590-367207
E-mail: sales@outsourceireland.co.uk
Website: http://www.outsourceireland.co.uk
Directors: J. Brown (Dir)
Registration no: NI071371 **Date established:** 2008
Turnover: Up to £250,000 **No.of Employees:** 1 - 10 **Product Groups:** 80

Provita

21 Bankmore Road, Omagh, BT79 0EU
Tel: 028-8225 2352 **Fax:** 028-8224 1734
E-mail: info@provita.co.uk
Website: http://www.provita.co.uk
Directors: M. Kerr (MD)
Immediate Holding Company: PROVITA EUROTECH LTD
Registration no: NI024160 **Date established:** 1990 **Turnover:** £1m - £2m
No.of Employees: 11 - 20 **Product Groups:** 20, 31, 62, 84, 85

Date of Accounts	Dec 11	Dec 10	Dec 09
Working Capital	449	319	227
Fixed Assets	26	37	37
Current Assets	841	652	533

Rankin Carmichael Mechanical Services Ltd

7 Doogary Avenue, Omagh, BT79 0BL
Tel: 028-8224 2201 **Fax:** 028-8224 9171
E-mail: rankin-carmichael@hotmail.co.uk

see next page

Rankin Carmichael Mechanical Services Ltd - Cont'd

Directors: L. Carmichael (MD)
Immediate Holding Company: RANKIN CARMICHAEL MECHANICAL SERVICES LIMITED
Registration no: NI044773 **Date established:** 2002
No.of Employees: 1 - 10 **Product Groups:** 35

Date of Accounts	Nov 11	Nov 10	Nov 09
Working Capital	99	91	92
Fixed Assets	2	2	3
Current Assets	197	124	123

Rushe Signs & Displays

Unit 11 Gortrush Industrial Estate, Omagh, BT78 5EJ
Tel: 028-8224 4288 **Fax:** 028-8224 0634
Website: http://www.rushesigns.com
Directors: H. Bradley (Prop)
Managers: R. Bradley (I.T. Exec)
Immediate Holding Company: RUSHE SIGNS LIMITED
Registration no: NI028397 **VAT No.:** TB7 7402 93 **Date established:** 1994
Turnover: Up to £250,000 **No.of Employees:** 1 - 10 **Product Groups:** 49

Scotts Fuels (t/a Scotts Fuels)

51 Curr Road Sixmilecross, Omagh, BT79 0UW
Tel: 028-6632 3228 **Fax:** 028-8225 2250
E-mail: sales@scottsfuels.com
Website: http://www.scottsfuels.com
Directors: R. Scott (Prop)
Immediate Holding Company: T.W. SCOTT & SONS (FUELS) LIMITED
Registration no: NI017420 **Date established:** 1984
Turnover: £50m - £75m **No.of Employees:** 1 - 10 **Product Groups:** 66

Date of Accounts	Dec 11	Dec 10	Dec 09
Sales Turnover	59m	47m	32m
Pre Tax Profit/Loss	-96	239	323
Working Capital	1m	1m	1m
Fixed Assets	642	528	601
Current Assets	6m	5m	4m
Current Liabilities	62	143	152

Signal Signs

10 Abbey Street, Omagh, BT78 1BZ
Tel: 028-8224 0504 **Fax:** 028-8225 0707
Website: http://www.signalsigns.co.uk
Directors: C. Mccallion (Prop)
Immediate Holding Company: SIGNAL SIGNS LIMITED
Registration no: NI052069 **Date established:** 2004
No.of Employees: 1 - 10 **Product Groups:** 28, 37, 40

Date of Accounts	Oct 11	Oct 10	Oct 09
Working Capital	-30	-24	-12
Fixed Assets	130	138	153
Current Assets	246	231	267

Silverbirch Hotel

Gortin Road, Omagh, BT79 7DH
Tel: 028-8224 2520 **Fax:** 028-8224 9061
E-mail: info@silverbirchhotel.com
Website: http://www.silverbirchhotel.com
Directors: J. Duncan (MD)
Managers: J. Ferguson (Personnel), H. Fleming, A. Duncan (Chief Mgr)
VAT No.: GB 286 8797 74 **No.of Employees:** 101 - 250
Product Groups: 69

Taggart Jack

1 Carnkenny Road Newtownstewart, Omagh, BT78 4LN
Tel: 028-8166 1271 **Fax:** 028-8166 2194
E-mail: info@taggartjack.co.uk
Website: http://www.taggartjack.co.uk
Directors: C. Jack (Prop)
VAT No.: GB 251 9148 60 **No.of Employees:** 11 - 20 **Product Groups:** 32, 62

Terex Finlay

Gillygooly Road, Omagh, BT78 5PN
Tel: 028-8241 8700 **Fax:** 028-8224 4294
E-mail: sales@terexfinlay.com
Website: http://www.terexfinlay.com
Bank(s): Northern Bank
Managers: P. O'donnell (Chief Mgr)
Ultimate Holding Company: TEREX CORP (USA)
Immediate Holding Company: FINLAY HYDRASCREENS (OMAGH) LIMITED
Registration no: NI014047 **VAT No.:** GB 517 7124 52
Date established: 1980 **Turnover:** £10m - £20m
No.of Employees: 501 - 1000 **Product Groups:** 45, 67

Date of Accounts	Dec 10	Dec 09	Dec 08
Sales Turnover	13m	43m	108m
Pre Tax Profit/Loss	2m	-5m	21m
Working Capital	56m	54m	57m
Fixed Assets	N/A	5m	6m
Current Assets	57m	90m	86m
Current Liabilities	N/A	1m	2m

Tyrone Constitution

25-27 High Street, Omagh, BT78 1BD
Tel: 028-8224 2721 **Fax:** 028-8224 3549
E-mail: news@tyronecon.co.uk
Website: http://www.tyronecon.co.uk
Directors: M. Taylor (MD)
Managers: F. Gallagher (Works Gen Mgr), S. Gallagher (I.T. Exec), W. Atchison (Publishing), P. Scott (Publicity)
Ultimate Holding Company: TONTINE ROOMS HOLDING COMPANY LIMITED - THE
Registration no: R0000730 **VAT No.:** GB 254 3721 68
Date established: 1903 **No.of Employees:** 1 - 10 **Product Groups:** 28

Ulster American Folk Park

2 Mellon Road Castletown, Omagh, BT78 5QU
Tel: 028-8224 3292 **Fax:** 028-8224 2241
E-mail: sales@folkpark.com
Website: http://www.folkpark.com
Bank(s): HSBC
Managers: L. Edwards (Mgr), P. Donnelly (Mktg Serv Mgr)
Immediate Holding Company: M A G N I
VAT No.: GB 286 4245 36 **Date established:** 1978
No.of Employees: 51 - 100 **Product Groups:** 69

Ulster Herald

14 John Street, Omagh, BT78 1DT
Tel: 028-8224 3444 **Fax:** 028-8225 5953
E-mail: editor@ulsterherald.com
Website: http://www.ulsterherald.com
Managers: D. Farnan (Mktg Serv Mgr), D. Clemence (Chief Mgr), D. Mcclements (Chief Mgr), A. Mooney (Sales Prom Mgr), J. Hetherington (Personnel), L. Fenton (Tech Serv Mgr), S. Kelly (Fin Mgr)
No.of Employees: 51 - 100 **Product Groups:** 28

Ultra Building Products Ltd

Deerpark Industrial Estate Baronscourt Road, Newtownstewart, Omagh, BT78 4EX
Tel: 028-8166 1316 **Fax:** 028-8166 1815
E-mail: sales@ultrabuilding.com
Website: http://www.ultrabuilding.com
Directors: S. Mcguigan (Dir)
Immediate Holding Company: ULTRA BUILDING PRODUCTS LIMITED
Registration no: NI019194 **Date established:** 1986 **Turnover:** £5m - £10m
No.of Employees: 51 - 100 **Product Groups:** 25, 26, 30, 31, 35, 40, 48

Date of Accounts	Apr 11	Apr 10	Apr 09
Sales Turnover	5m	5m	7m
Pre Tax Profit/Loss	341	437	1m
Working Capital	4m	4m	4m
Fixed Assets	2m	1m	1m
Current Assets	5m	5m	5m
Current Liabilities	236	285	706

Co. Antrim

Portrush

B & E Security Systems

10 Oakland Avenue, Portrush, BT56 8JP
Tel: 028-7082 4001 **Fax:** 028-7082 3757
E-mail: info@besecuritysystems.com
Website: http://www.besecuritysystems.com
Bank(s): Ulster Bank
Directors: B. Mcintyre (Dir)
Immediate Holding Company: B & E SECURITY SYSTEMS LIMITED
Registration no: NI036454 **VAT No.:** 393550240 **Date established:** 1999
Turnover: Up to £250,000 **No.of Employees:** 21 - 50 **Product Groups:** 52

Date of Accounts	Aug 11	Aug 10	Aug 09
Working Capital	289	288	276
Fixed Assets	131	118	127
Current Assets	374	386	375

Cemex UK Ltd

45 Craighulliar Road, Portrush, BT56 8NN
Tel: 028-7082 3374 **Fax:** 028-7082 2682
Website: http://www.cemex.co.uk
Managers: P. Wilson (Mgr)
Ultimate Holding Company: CEMEX S A B DE CV (MEXICO)
Immediate Holding Company: CEMEX UK
Registration no: 05196131 **VAT No.:** GB 222 8284 72
Date established: 2004 **No.of Employees:** 1 - 10 **Product Groups:** 33

Date of Accounts	Dec 10	Dec 09	Dec 08
Pre Tax Profit/Loss	-64m	612m	-101m
Working Capital	-2m	-3m	-452m
Fixed Assets	2432m	2432m	1721m
Current Assets	N/A	218	11m
Current Liabilities	2m	3m	10m

Hampton Conservatories Ltd

218 Ballybogey Road, Portrush, BT56 8NE
Tel: 028-7082 4100 **Fax:** 028-7082 4492
E-mail: info@hc-online.co.uk
Website: http://www.hamptonconservatories.co.uk
Directors: K. Montgomery (Fin), M. Montgomery (MD)
Managers: M. Hastings (Sales & Mktg Mg), T. Gilmore (Buyer)
Immediate Holding Company: Hampton Conservatories Limited
Registration no: NI051114 **VAT No.:** GB 393 5792 05
Date established: 2004 **Turnover:** £1m - £2m **No.of Employees:** 21 - 50
Product Groups: 25

Date of Accounts	Dec 11	Dec 10	Dec 09
Working Capital	-784	-762	-772
Fixed Assets	2m	2m	2m
Current Assets	216	199	247

Magherabuoy House Hotel Ltd

41 Magheraboy Road, Portrush, BT56 8NX
Tel: 028-7082 3507 **Fax:** 028-7082 4687
E-mail: reservations@magherabuoy.co.uk
Website: http://www.magherabuoy.co.uk
Managers: Y. McClean (Comptroller), T. Clarke (Chief Mgr), T. Clarke (Chief Mgr)
Immediate Holding Company: HILLGROVE HOTEL LIMITED
Registration no: NI018204 **VAT No.:** GB 432 5710 75
Date established: 1985 **Turnover:** £2m - £5m **No.of Employees:** 21 - 50
Product Groups: 69

Date of Accounts	Feb 12	Feb 11	Feb 10
Working Capital	-483	-397	-395
Fixed Assets	4m	4m	4m
Current Assets	48	48	61

Ramada Portrush

73 Main Street, Portrush, BT56 8BN
Tel: 028-7082 6100 **Fax:** 028-7082 6160
E-mail: info@ramadaportrush.com
Website: http://www.ramadaportrush.com
Managers: M. O'Neill (Mktg Serv Mgr), A. Donaghy (Mgr)
Immediate Holding Company: EUROLANTIC LEISURE LIMITED
Registration no: 04329157 **Date established:** 2001
No.of Employees: 21 - 50 **Product Groups:** 69

Co. Tyrone

Strabane

A S Ballantine Ltd

214 Lisnaragh Road Dunamanagh, Strabane, BT82 0SB
Tel: 028-7139 8276 **Fax:** 028-7139 8189
E-mail: asballantine@btconnect.com
Website: http://www.asballantine.co.uk
Directors: W. Ballantine (Prop)
Immediate Holding Company: A. S. BALLANTINE LIMITED
Registration no: NI011897 **Date established:** 1977
No.of Employees: 21 - 50 **Product Groups:** 31, 33, 52, 83

Date of Accounts	Dec 11	Dec 10	Dec 09
Working Capital	131	246	615
Fixed Assets	2m	2m	2m
Current Assets	470	582	965

Boran Mopack Ltd

Ballycolman Estate, Strabane, BT82 9AQ
Tel: 028-7188 4095 **Fax:** 028-7138 2758
E-mail: boran@boran.ie
Website: http://www.boranmopack.com
Directors: M. Boran (MD)
Managers: D. McNulty (Tech Serv Mgr), S. Coy (Sales Prom Mgr), C. Blee (Purch Mgr)
Immediate Holding Company: Boran-Mopack Limited
Registration no: NI046138 **VAT No.:** GB 331 9571 55
Date established: 2003 **No.of Employees:** 51 - 100 **Product Groups:** 31

Date of Accounts	Dec 11	Dec 10	Dec 09
Sales Turnover	11m	10m	N/A
Pre Tax Profit/Loss	176	240	309
Working Capital	2m	2m	2m
Fixed Assets	2m	1m	1m
Current Assets	4m	4m	3m
Current Liabilities	314	374	376

C K S Catering Ltd

23a Towncastle Road, Strabane, BT82 0AH
Tel: 028-7188 6414 **Fax:** 028-7188 2141
E-mail: andrew.cks@gmail.com
Website: http://www.cks-ni.co.uk
Directors: A. Casey (MD)
Immediate Holding Company: CKS CATERING LTD
Registration no: NI069173 **Date established:** 2008
No.of Employees: 1 - 10 **Product Groups:** 20, 40, 41

Date of Accounts	May 11	May 10	May 09
Working Capital	-79	-15	-20
Fixed Assets	50	15	20
Current Assets	-43	55	67

C O'Doherty & Sons

29-31 Railway Street, Strabane, BT82 8EG
Tel: 028-7188 3361 **Fax:** 028-7188 5438
E-mail: info@coffinsireland.com
Website: http://www.coffinsireland.com
Directors: C. O'doherty (Dir)
Immediate Holding Company: CHARLES O'DOHERTY & SONS LIMITED
Registration no: NI003294 **Date established:** 1953
Turnover: £250,000 - £500,000 **No.of Employees:** 1 - 10
Product Groups: 49

Devine Sand & Gravel Ltd

65 Moorlough Road Artigarvan, Strabane, BT82 0ER
Tel: 028-7139 8208 **Fax:** 028-7139 8208
E-mail: devinesandgravel@btconnect.com
Bank(s): Ulster Bank
Directors: S. Devine (Prop)
Immediate Holding Company: DEVINE SAND & GRAVEL LIMITED
Registration no: NI029533 **VAT No.:** GB 252 1883 64
Date established: 1995 **Turnover:** £250,000 - £500,000
No.of Employees: 11 - 20 **Product Groups:** 14

Date of Accounts	Dec 11	Dec 10	Dec 09
Working Capital	498	718	737
Fixed Assets	258	341	438
Current Assets	540	747	759

Infotronic Electronic Display Systems

6 Beech Park Sion Mills, Strabane, BT82 9PZ
Tel: 028-8165 9522 **Fax:** 028- 81659909
E-mail: infotronic@excite.com
Website: http://www.infotronic.co.uk
Directors: J. Boyle (Prop)
VAT No.: GB 392 5491 25 **Turnover:** £250,000 - £500,000
No.of Employees: 1 - 10 **Product Groups:** 37, 81, 84

John A Gamble & Co.

38 Park Road, Strabane, BT82 8LH
Tel: 028-7138 2385 **Fax:** 028-7138 2182
E-mail: info@jagamble.co.uk
Directors: G. King (MD), R. Gamble (Dir)
Immediate Holding Company: J.A. GAMBLE & CO. LTD
Registration no: NI017756 **VAT No.:** GB 252 0901 93
Date established: 1984 **Turnover:** £250,000 - £500,000
No.of Employees: 21 - 50 **Product Groups:** 52

L J Millar & Sons

25 Seein Road Sion Mills, Strabane, BT82 9NH
Tel: 028-8165 8503 **Fax:** 028-8165 9555
Directors: S. Millar (Prop)
Date established: 1972 **No.of Employees:** 1 - 10 **Product Groups:** 52

Linton Robinson

Abercorn Square, Strabane, BT82 8DH
Tel: 028-7138 4920 **Fax:** 028-7138 4921
E-mail: info@linton-robinson.co.uk
Website: http://www.linton-robinson.co.uk
Directors: T. Linton (MD)
Managers: A. Smyth (Mktg Serv Mgr), N. Coyle (Personnel)
Immediate Holding Company: LINTON & ROBINSON LIMITED
Registration no: NI009915 **VAT No.:** GB 282 9106 49
Date established: 1973 **Turnover:** £5m - £10m **No.of Employees:** 21 - 50
Product Groups: 49

Date of Accounts	Jan 11	Jan 10	Jan 09
Sales Turnover	N/A	N/A	9m
Pre Tax Profit/Loss	N/A	N/A	197
Working Capital	293	114	1m
Fixed Assets	2m	2m	2m
Current Assets	2m	2m	3m
Current Liabilities	211	84	96

Mccolgans

New Factory Dublin Road, Strabane, BT82 9EA
Tel: 028-7138 2797 **Fax:** 028-7138 3490
E-mail: brian@mccolgans.ie
Website: http://www.mccqf.co.uk
Bank(s): Bank of Ireland
Directors: B. McColgan (Prop), P. Cullen (Fin)
Managers: B. Brolley (Tech Serv Mgr), C. Farrell (Purch Mgr), A. McColgan (Personnel), A. McManaman (Sales Prom Mgr)
Immediate Holding Company: McCOLGANS QUALITY FOODS LIMITED
Registration no: NI012744 **VAT No.:** GB 349 6078 21
Date established: 1978 **Turnover:** £10m - £20m
No.of Employees: 101 - 250 **Product Groups:** 20

Date of Accounts	Mar 11	Mar 10	Mar 09
Sales Turnover	11m	9m	N/A
Pre Tax Profit/Loss	329	791	316
Working Capital	-190	284	1m
Fixed Assets	6m	5m	3m
Current Assets	3m	2m	2m
Current Liabilities	1m	1m	N/A

O'Neills Irish International Sports Company Ltd

Unit 1 Dublin Road Industrial Estate, Strabane, BT82 9EA
Tel: 028-7188 2320 **Fax:** 028-7188 2902
E-mail: info@oneills.com
Website: http://www.oneills.com
Directors: W. McChrystal (Fin), K. Kennedy (MD)
Managers: P. Cairns (Personnel), R. McSorley (Tech Serv Mgr)
Immediate Holding Company: O'NEILLS IRISH INTERNATIONAL SPORTS COMPANY LIMITED
Registration no: NI010400 **VAT No.:** GB 283 0428 66
Date established: 1974 **No.of Employees:** 251 - 500 **Product Groups:** 24, 61

Date of Accounts	Dec 11	Dec 10	Dec 09
Pre Tax Profit/Loss	404	523	560
Working Capital	-175	-365	-306
Fixed Assets	7m	7m	7m
Current Assets	2m	2m	3m
Current Liabilities	566	541	2m

Pedro Pet Foods Ltd

51a Brocklis Road Sion Mills, Strabane, BT82 9LZ
Tel: 028-8165 8808 **Fax:** 028-8165 9903
E-mail: info@pedropetfoods.com
Website: http://www.pedropetfoods.com
Managers: E. Kelly
Immediate Holding Company: Pedro Pet Foods Limited
Registration no: NI045902 **Date established:** 2003
No.of Employees: 1 - 10 **Product Groups:** 20, 62

Date of Accounts	Apr 11	Apr 10	Apr 09
Working Capital	93	149	90
Fixed Assets	171	176	235
Current Assets	436	496	402

Polycolor Industrial Coatings

92 Orchard Road, Strabane, BT82 9QU
Tel: 028-8165 8976 **Fax:** 028-8165 8976
Directors: P. Henry (MD)
Immediate Holding Company: MOYLE HILL PROPERTIES LIMITED
Registration no: NI031086 **VAT No.:** GB 432 8268 47
Date established: 1996 **Turnover:** £500,000 - £1m
No.of Employees: 1 - 10 **Product Groups:** 32

Date of Accounts	Jul 10	Jul 09	Jul 08
Working Capital	-1m	-665	-476
Fixed Assets	930	1m	1m
Current Assets	3m	4m	4m

Quantum Hosiery

9 Derry Road, Strabane, BT82 8DT
Tel: 028-7138 2568 **Fax:** 028-7138 2910
E-mail: gerry.mccolgan@quantumclothing.com
Website: http://www.quantumclothing.com
Directors: G. Mccolgan (Dir)
Ultimate Holding Company: BRAMHOPE GROUP HOLDINGS LIMITED
Immediate Holding Company: QUANTUM HOSIERY LIMITED
Registration no: NI005074 **VAT No.:** GB 116 2604 04
Date established: 1961 **Turnover:** £20m - £50m
No.of Employees: 11 - 20 **Product Groups:** 24

Date of Accounts	Apr 08	Apr 09	Apr 10
Sales Turnover	18m	18m	20m
Pre Tax Profit/Loss	-634	-287	710
Working Capital	-7m	-7m	-3m
Fixed Assets	48	37	22
Current Assets	4m	4m	8m
Current Liabilities	572	2m	2m

Strabane District Council

47 Derry Road, Strabane, BT82 8DY
Tel: 028-7138 2204 **Fax:** 028-7138 1348
E-mail: info@strabanedc.com
Website: http://www.strabanedc.com
Managers: D. Sorley (Mgr)
Immediate Holding Company: STRABANE 2000
Registration no: NI040977 **Date established:** 2001
Turnover: £500,000 - £1m **No.of Employees:** 101 - 250
Product Groups: 87

Date of Accounts	Mar 11	Mar 10	Mar 09
Sales Turnover	N/A	6	N/A
Pre Tax Profit/Loss	N/A	1	N/A
Working Capital	-0	1	5
Current Assets	N/A	2	5